19th EDITION

CARDIFF
CAERDYDD

THE
GOOD
SCHOOLS
GUIDE

LUCAS
PUBLICATIONS

www.goodschoolsguide.co.uk

Nineteenth Edition published 2014 by Lucas Publishing Ltd

Address 3 Craven Mews, London SW11 5PW

Website www.goodschoolsguide.co.uk

ISBN 978-0-9552821-9-5

Copyright (c) 2014, Lucas Publications Ltd

Typeset by Theresa Hare, Optima Information Design

Printed by Beam Reach

Writers:

Ali Hutchinson
Alison Cooper
Amanda Lyath
Anna Colclough
Anne Hadley
Anne Prendergast
Ashley Cavers
Bernadette Henniker
Bernadette John
Bethan Hutton
Beth Noakes
Carolyn Murphy
Carolyn Thomas
Catriona Prest
Charles Cowling
Charlotte Obolensky
Charlotte Phillips
Christine Jefferson
Deirdre Shields
Denise Roberts
Emma Jones
Emma Lee-Potter
Emma Vickers
Faye Monserrat
Godfrey Bishop
Grace Moody-Stuart
Harriet Plyler
Hazel Davis
Jackie Lixenburg
Janet Breeze
Janette Wallis

Janita Clamp
Jill Kastner
Judith French
Juliet Austin
Kalantha Brewis
Kate Symington
Lisa Freedman
Liz Coatman
Liz Moody-Stuart
Lucy Heywood
Mary-Ann Smillie
Mary Langford
Mary Pegler
Melanie Bloxham
Melanie Sanderson
Nicky Adams
Patrea More-Nesbitt
Paul Grahamslaw
Ralph Lucas
Reena Shaughnessy
Richard Field
Rosemary Taylor
Sally Walker
Sandra Hutchinson
Sara Freakley
Sophie Irwin
Stewart Binns
Sue Fieldman
Susan Bailes
Susan Hamlyn
Suzanne Everest

Design: David Preston, Harriet Plyler

Editorial review by Beth Noakes and team: Janita Clamp, Emma Lee-Potter, Nicky Adams, Charlotte Phillips, Kathryn Berger, Lindsey Noakes, Amanda Perkins, Sandra Hutchinson, Fiona Boult

Advertising sales by Charlotte Hollingshead and team: Jo Dodds, Peter Thompson and Hugh Sutton

Website: Sandra Hutchinson, Anthony Back

Project management: Ruth Baker and Bill Visick

Everything organised and kept ticking over by Brilliant Administrator: Shari Lord

Acknowledgements

We should also like to thank the countless friends, pupils, parents, staff, moles – they know who they are but we're not telling – who contribute invaluably and to whom we are deeply indebted. Please keep the information coming.

Each one an epic adventure.

What will *your* daughter's story be?

+44 (0)1923 725354
www.royalmasonic.herts.sch.uk

**The Royal Masonic School for Girls
Rickmansworth Hertfordshire WD3 4HF**

Registered Charity No. 276784

Est. 1788

THE ROYAL MASONIC SCHOOL

FOR GIRLS

AT RICKMANSWORTH PARK SINCE 1934

Contents

Queen Ethelburga's

The best year ever...

The North's leading independent school is celebrating being ranked second place in the country's top independent co-educational day and boarding schools, by the Daily Telegraph thanks to its record-breaking A-Level results.

Queen Ethelburga's
Thorpe Underwood
York, YO26 9SS

01423 333 330
www.qe.org

Not only did the College repeat its 100% overall pass rate for its Year 13 pupils, but its average university admissions (UCAS) points score increased to 495 – the equivalent to over 4 A grades at A-Level. The percentage of grades at A* and A was 80% and A* to B was 97%. 72% of all A-Level students in the College achieved at least 3 A grades.

The Faculty of Queen Ethelburga's, which offers both A-Level and BTEC qualifications, saw a similarly impressive 100% pass rate and students gained an average UCAS points score of 469. The percentage of grades at A* and A was 68% and A* to B was 96%. 91% of BTECs were awarded a Distinction* or Distinction grade – equivalent to A* and

A grades at A-Level. In the Daily Telegraph league tables the Faculty is placed 6.

The Principal of Queen Ethelburga's, Steven Jandrell, is delighted with the rankings of both schools: "Without a doubt we can now comfortably say we are on a world-class level. Not only have our A-Level results put us head and shoulders above our local competitors but we have beaten some of the best educational establishments in the country."

"It is so satisfying to know that the success of our schools is down to the fact that we assess each student individually so that we can find something at which he or she really excels. Our teachers work very closely with our pupils from the moment they arrive to make sure they support them with their subject choices, university applications and career aspirations," he added.

"And that work has paid off with not only our best ever A-Level results but our best ever rankings as well!" said Mr Jandrell.

Why not come and see for yourself what makes us so special. **Call Pat on 01423 333 330 to arrange a visit.**

Introduction

Welcome to the The Good Schools Guide, now in its 28th year. Updating The Guide is always an educative process (rightly so) and as we process the information received from schools – principally public examination results but also leavers' destinations and significant changes – trends emerge.

This year we note that GCSE and A level grades have deflated with many schools reporting a reduction in papers awarded A*-C. We have also observed a small but significant reduction in the number of schools offering the IB in addition to A levels – presumably down to economics since running two curricula must be a bursar's nightmare. On the other hand, a few schools have gone the other way and abandoned A levels entirely in favour of the IB – probably for similar fiscal reasons.

Independent senior schools seem to be riding out the economic squeeze, indeed many report significant building projects – presumably to keep up with St Jones' next door. This is good news all round since in many areas of the country a big school can be one of the major local employers, and the effects of any closure are felt way beyond staff and pupils.

One indicator of our uncertain economic times is the surge in demand for grammar school places. This year there has been a 20 per cent increase in applications to top-performing selective state grammars with up to 20 children competing for each place. A consequence of this means it's boom time for private tutors, some of whom reportedly charge up to £100 an hour. A tutor to help your state primary school child with grammar school entrance tests seems like a reasonable investment, but they are equally sought after in the private school sector. Heads tell us that 4 and 5 year olds are being primed for entrance tests and that many parents employ tutors in addition to paying private school fees.

What better time, then, to launch our Scholarships and Bursaries Advice Service? It used to be the case that only the most determined (or desperate) parent could navigate the labyrinthine complexities of charitable trusts, ancient bequests and quixotic criteria that might lead to financial assistance. Schools tend not to shout about the help they are able to give, and nowhere was this precious information to be found under one roof. Until now. The Good Schools Guide Scholarships and Bursaries Service, part of our advisory wing, provides the only such resource in the UK. Parents can specify the type of help they need, the type of school they prefer and the location(s)

and we can tell them what the schools seem so reluctant to divulge! For more information see page 4.

Whether you use this book or subscribe to The Guide's online services, we hope you find our reviews and advice as frank and independent as ever. We can't visit every school, especially small local primaries, but strive to include as many as possible. As schools' marketing hype becomes ever slicker and prospectuses ever more air brushed, we hope that our reviewers' candid opinions, written from the parents' point of view, will help you find the school that is is not just good, but good for your child.

GSG Charter

For over 25 years The Good Schools Guide has been the leading independent reviewer of schools in the UK. Our national team of reviewers are honest, opinionated and fearless. No school can pay to be included in (or choose to be excluded from) The Good Schools Guide and schools are not charged for reviews.

In recent years we have helped to defray our costs by selling advertising space and licensing schools to reprint their own reviews for a fee. These offers are only made to schools that are already in The Guide on merit. Schools that advertise have no influence on the contents of their reviews and their decision on whether or not to advertise has no bearing on their inclusion in The Guide. If a school has not been selected, by us, for coverage in The Guide, we do not allow them to advertise.

From time to time we publish other books in addition to The Good Schools Guide which may be partly sponsored by some of the organisations included. When these feature schools, they will always be selected from those already in The Guide: participation is voluntary and gives them no editorial control.

The Good Schools Guide Advice Service is a fee paying, personal consultancy service for parents. The Guide and our website also offer other advice on a vast range of educational matters, which is free to subscribers. We receive no commission or any other payment from any school for these services.

We provide information on tutor companies on our website as an additional service to parents. We do charge tutor companies for carrying out the review but they are only included after careful vetting.

We take our independence very seriously and the separation of commercial and editorial content is absolute. If you have any questions or concerns about our commercial policy, please write in the first instance to editor@goodschoolsguide.co.uk.

The Good Schools Guide Advice Service

www.gsgexpertschoolsconsultants.co.uk.

The Good Schools Guide Advice Service (GSGAS) is a personal service for individual families covering every aspect of schools and education. Our advisors are our most experienced and knowledgeable writers. They have visited countless schools, quizzed innumerable parents, children, headteachers and moles. This vast experience, coupled with the data, inside information and expertise of the entire team, is available to any parents who need assistance with their child's education.

Typically, our advisors help parents find the right school for their child, whether state, independent, junior, senior, day or boarding, but they deal on a daily basis with a wide range of other educational quandaries. Many GSGAS clients are relocating, some have children who are unhappy in their present school, others have a child with special needs. Increasingly, our clients have babies yet unborn or very new but are planning ahead.

Why Us?

As a Good Schools Guide reader, you will know that we take no commission from schools and no school can pay to get into The Good Schools Guide. The Good Schools Guide selects its schools on the basis of parental recommendation first and then on our own experience when we research and visit them — nothing else. Therefore, the advice that our advisors give you is completely independent and based exclusively on what matters to you. No other UK organisation has resources, experience and knowledge that begin to compare with The Good Schools Guide Advice Service. Above all, all our advisors are deeply committed to the best education for all. Many become friends with their clients as they work toward the common goal – a happy, stimulated child, at the right school.

How can we help?

Because The Good Schools Guide Advice Service is a personal service, run on a one-to-one basis, we can help you in whatever way you need us to. You tell us what you need and we tell you how we can help. And then we do!

For example?

Your child is in primary school and doing well but you're not happy with the senior schools in your area. Should you move house to be in the catchment area for a grammar school? Or should you take the plunge and aim for the independent sector? And what can you do to prepare your child? We can untangle it all for you.

Or...

You are living overseas but you want to send your child to board in the UK. He is dead keen on sailing and will need to keep up his Arabic. Oh, and the school must be near an airport. Can we help? Of course! You will tell your advisor exactly what you need and she will help you find it, guiding you every step of the way.

Or...

We hope it doesn't happen but your daughter has been badly bullied and her school is not dealing with it properly. You need to move her — fast. Call us. We will find you a sympathetic, knowledgeable and effective advisor who will be on the case at once.

Or...

You're moving overseas and need to know whether the schools in eg Singapore are good enough to take your children along. Perhaps your posting is in America and you need advice on how to make the transition from British to American education and, possibly, in a few years, back to British. Fortunately, our partners, GSG International, have the answers. See: www.gsgi.co.uk .

Is that it?

It might be. But The Good Schools Guide Advice Service can offer you far more. We have built up relationships with the best experts in fields such as special educational needs, educational psychology, tutoring, English language preparation for school entrance and many others. Just tell us what you need. We will find an expert schools and education advisor to work with you.

And we advise on more than just schools. Our expertise extends to tutor agencies, sixth form colleges and even university applications. We can offer you advisors in several different languages. And – perhaps most importantly – we understand how hard it can be to be a parent. We are sympathetic and will help in whatever way we can to set you and your child on the right track.

So what should I do?

Visit our website and see just how much we offer. You can also see details about all our advisors and how they can help you. Phone us on +44 (0)203 286 6824 or send us a brief email to advice@ goodschoolsguide.co.uk outlining what you need. Tell us the age of your child and whereabouts in the country you are considering, plus your contact details. We will contact you within 48 hours of your initial phone call or email and make sure that we match you with the right education advisor. Consultations are mainly conducted over the phone and by email, however, our advisors are happy to meet you, depending on where you are. Urgent enquiries are dealt with urgently. We can find an advisor to speak with you within the hour if necessary.

Our services

Introductory Service:
A 30 minute personal advice session to help with queries and dilemmas of limited scope eg deciding between two schools, understanding basic facts about UK education.

Classic Service:
No set format — this service provides whatever individual parents need. We begin with a consultation to establish exactly what is required. Then the advisor does what has been agreed with the client eg schools research leading to a list of schools which meet your requirements, advice on place availability, interviews or entrance exams, weighing up merits of comparable schools, post-visit discussion. This involves up to seven and a half hours dedicated work for you and the resources of the entire Good Schools Guide Advice Service team as required.

Premier Service:
All that is included in the Classic Service, plus help with all paperwork, academic assessment, liaison with schools etc. This service is best for those on a tight time scale, with several children, with a complex relocation project etc and involves up to two days dedicated work for you and the resources of the entire Good Schools Guide Advice Service team as required.

Global Premier Service:
This is for international families. If you relocate frequently or are based abroad and want to send your children to board in the UK, this service will help you with every aspect of finding the best school(s). All the Premier Service offers plus a completely flexible support system to assist with eg assessment, English language help, guidance on UK education provision and how to achieve the best possible education from arrival to university.

State School Service
This service guides parents who are only interested in state schools. It is a unique service — you tell us what you want to know and we will work with you to give you all the information you need. This is our busiest service and as reasonably priced as we possibly can make it.

SEN Service
We have five expert specialist advisors who between them can assist with every kind of SEN. We are only too aware of the stresses on a family with a 'special' child — whether he is mildly dyslexic, or deals with complex mobility difficulties, or outstandingly gifted. Call us and you will find a sympathetic, knowledgeable and understanding advisor will help you achieve whatever it is you know your child needs and deserves.

Scholarships and Bursaries Service
Our unique database of scholarships and bursaries covers more than 400 schools and is the only place in the UK which can provide you with information on what financial assistance might be available to you and at which schools.

Data Service:
A service for clients who are principally interested in state schools and who want data and statistics rather than advice. This is priced on an individual basis.

Bespoke Service
Individually tailored service which will meet your precise individual requirements, whatever they may be. Fees by negotiation.

International Service:
Our GSG international advisers can give you the inside information on schools, education, expat survival and networks in their host cities.

The GSG University Advice Service

www.uu.goodschoolsguide.co.uk

These days, many look overseas for their university education – especially to the US. Our university educational consultants have been in this business for years and will expertly walk your son or daughter through the labyrinthine application process, whether US or UCAS. They'll help develop a list of universities that meet your child's needs and match his or her dreams, and plan strategies to optimise chances of admission.

How much?

We provide one of the most competitively priced tailor-made advice services in the UK. Check our website, and email advice@goodschoolsguide.co.uk or call +44(0)203 286 6824 to find out our current fees and discuss how we can help you.

NB Charges for consultations and advisory services involving more than mild SEN are arranged on an individual basis. Accompanied school visits or visits on behalf of clients are also priced on an individual basis.

The Good Schools Guide Promise
All information is treated in the strictest confidence. We will refund your fee if you are not entirely satisfied with the results.

BROMLEY HIGH
SCHOOL

INDEPENDENT EDUCATION FOR GIRLS AGED 4-18 YEARS

4+, 7+, 11+, 13+ & 16+

Fees assistance & Scholarships available in the Senior School

With **Us** *she will* *Thrive*

Tel: 020 8781 7000

admissions@bro.gdst.net **www.bromleyhigh.gdst.net**

gdst Girls' Day School Trust

From sport to music.
And everything in between.

The Good Schools Guide on the Web

www.goodschoolsguide.co.uk

There is so much more to The Good Schools Guide than we can fit in this book; we'd need a tome the size of a trunk! Fortunately The Good Schools Guide website captures all things educational, makes it personal and is constantly updated.

Online subscribers will find:

- all the school reviews that appear in The Good Schools Guide and some that don't;
- a wealth of advice for your education journey from nursery to university;
- English state school catchment area maps;
- in-depth examination of results (including university courses and destinations) and a facility to compare schools;
- a directory of ALL schools in the UK, with data from us, comments from schools and from you;
- extensive special educational needs information including an invaluable SEN search links to inspection reports, schools and others;
- The Good Schools Guide Community and so much more!

Use www.goodschoolsguide.co.uk to answer your questions.

Finding a school

Whether your criteria are simple or complex, our 'Find a School' search is unsurpassed.

My child has special educational needs — help!

We have a wealth of expertly written articles, offering advice on all aspects of SEN and we've number-crunched, so you can see how well English state schools serve children with special needs. Plus, thousands of schools have completed our detailed, searchable SEN survey. In our dedicated SEN section, we detail different types of special needs, help and support to be found in and outside of school and the classroom; the law, specialist help and school choices. Plus, we review the best specialist schools for children with a range of needs.

My child is gifted/talented — do you cover this?

As well as giving advice, we identify grammar and selective school provision; feature scholarship and specialist schools' information; show (for senior schools) how many pupils go to which top universities, and include gifted/talented feedback in our SEN survey.

Can I find results by subject?

Our online schools pages detail subject results by gender and popularity. Alternatively, use 'Six of the Best': choose a subject and level and see which schools made the grade and who should do better!

How do I know if a school is good for my child?

We offer advice on what to consider when choosing a school and our value-added data, for English state schools, show how well a school does for all children — bright, average or struggling.

What about catchment areas?

We've got admissions covered. See where children at an English state school come from or use our unique, interactive catchment maps to see the schools you are in catchment for.

Where can I study A level archaeology and physics?

Use our search to help locate subject combinations and compile a list of schools. You can even compare them using MySchools to find the best for you; a school may be great for one subject but not so hot for others.

Finding a tutor

For some children a tutor is essential as they are off school with a long-term health problem. Occasionally, families who are travelling for an extended period take a tutor with them to keep junior's brain ticking over. Others need someone to maintain schoolwork during a difficult period – an exclusion or a family break-up – or to help in the run up to exams.

We feature a variety of the larger tutoring agencies on the Good Schools Guide website. These are ones of which we have had good reports from both parents and tutors. The best tutors can make an immense difference to children's academic confidence and enjoyment as well as grades.

Subscribe

We add to and constantly update our website. Some information is free but ALL this is yours if you subscribe to The Good Schools Guide online, for a year — or just for a month.

The Good Schools Guide International

www.gsgi.co.uk

The Good Schools Guide International does for international schools what The Good Schools Guide does for the UK ... finds, visits and reviews the best ones for children 3-18, state or independent, wherever they are.

Like The Good Schools Guide, the GSGI is completely independent, forthright, and doesn't shy away from judgement calls. All school reviews are unsolicited — selected and paid for by The Guide, not the school. That means complete editorial freedom, so we pull no punches. Its crisp, clear advice will give you the inside scoop on schools, headmasters, sports, school runs and local traffic, and life on the ground for expats.

All GSGI editors are expat parents themselves and know which schools in their host cities should make the cut. Schools are in (or out) whether they like it or not.

Aimed at English-speaking expatriates, the GSGI:

- reviews top British, American, IB and international schools in over 55 cities worldwide
- offers brisk, personal expat and educational overviews for each city including real-time updates, red alerts (coups d'état, evacuations, closures etc)

Over 280 articles explain and decode:

- curricula and exams (GCSEs, SATs, IB, AP etc)
- special educational needs
- transitions (between curricula, systems, hemispheres, countries)
- accreditations and inspections (the real vs the bogus)

Purchasers of The Good Schools Guide are entitled to a 50 per cent discount. Go to: www.GSGI.co.uk. Enter the reference code GSG412P and answer the question about The Good Schools Guide.

There's even a Good Schools Guide International Advisory Service. GSGI advisors can give you (by phone, email or face to face):

- insider info on top (or not) local schools
- pros and cons for your own child
- overviews of local education
- advice for expat survival in their host cities
- a network to other parents and expats
- schooling and entertainment suggestions, even for small children.

Call the Good Schools Guide office on +44(0) 203 286 6824 to discuss how we can help (or alternatively email advice@ goodschoolsguide.co.uk and we will contact you).

Want to help spread the word? If you help us successfully contact and secure a new corporate subscriber who then becomes a GSGI customer, we will pay you 10 per cent of our net receipts from them, for a period of five years. To read more about this offer, and for terms and conditions in full, go to www.gsgi.co.uk/articles/want-to-work-for-us/ finders¬fee-for-new-corporate-subscriptions.

Know someone living in a distant corner of the world who might be qualified to work for us? Go to www.gsgi.co.uk/ articles/want-to-work-for-us.

Uni in the USA

The British students' guide to great universities in the USA from Harvard to Hopkins

Tells you how to choose, how to apply and how to pay

£17.99 for the book, eBook or 12-month subscription
visit **www.uniintheusa.com**

Expert advice on applying to university abroad or in the UK

Call The Good Schools Guide University Advice Service
on **0203 286 6824** or email **advice@uniintheusa.com**

Uni in the USA...and Beyond

www.UniintheUSA.com

The definitive UK guide to universities abroad

How many Harvard students does it take to change a light bulb?

One — he holds the bulb and the world revolves around him.

Written by funny, sharp-eyed British students, with expert input from Anthony Nemecek, former Director of the Fulbright US Education Service, our entertaining and popular British students' guide to US universities is now available as a paperback, an ebook and online. The new and expanded version has three times more US unis, and the electronic editions now include — for the first time — selected universities in Europe, China, Canada and Australia.

The down-to-earth, often hilarious, reviews of selected American colleges and international universities could only have been written by real students interviewing real students.

In particular, one Cambridge student who crisscrossed the US by Greyhound bus writing spot-on reviews based on hundreds of interviews, then legged it across Europe to review the first universities for the globally expanded ...And Beyond section.

Still more intrepid souls — all students — took on universities in Asia, Australia and Canada. All told, they reviewed 96 universities in 12 countries, with insider info on getting in, money matters, fellow students, life on campus and life outside. In short, what it's really like to be there.

A must-read for anyone...before you think of applying. Remember — the world is your oyster — find your university pearl!

To subscribe online or buy the ebook or new paperback edition, or ask questions on our uni community forum, go to our website: www.uniintheusa.com for full details. And follow us on Twitter @uniintheusa.

To contact the GSG University Advice Service, email advice@ goodschoolsguide.co.uk or call us on +44(0) 203 286 6824 to speak to one of our educational experts and to discuss how we can help.

The System

Starting school

You may need to book a place soon after birth in the private sector; for the best state schools you have three or four years to move into the catchment area. If you are after a religious school, take a careful note of its admissions arrangements, and of the admissions arrangements of the religious secondary school too (you can miss out on some Catholic schools because you did not baptise your child within six months of birth); at the very least you are likely to have to go to church every week.

The main choice is between state and private education and nowadays you can definitely mix and match. Although, how you do it will very much depend on where you live (are there good local primaries, excellent comprehensives, grammar schools?); the sex of your child (in general pay for boys before girls, they need all the help they can get); the religion you practise (convert to Catholicism and go straight to education heaven); and, of course, upon your child's personality and ability.

State education

The advantages are that it's usually close by and part of the community; a school bus operates in some country areas (often but by no means always avoiding the need to become full-time driver); a broad social mix; no school fees; often greater understanding of the wide world at the end of it. State schools in England come in two old flavours (grammar and comprehensive) and four new ones (academies, free schools, studio schools and university technical colleges). See Coalition education policy (page 15)

Private education

Advantages of the private system are usually a greater chance of doing well in public exams, especially for an average child (although there are many exceptions); often better academic (as opposed to pastoral) care; a wider range of extras and often at a higher standard; smaller classes; the opportunity to study subjects such as Ancient Greek and start modern languages earlier; the opportunity to board.

Alternatives

Montessori education
Pioneered by Maria Montessori to educate the poor in Italy, this method is a hot favourite in many middle-class enclaves. The Montessori method concentrates on personal development and progress; homework, testing and exams are seldom found. Mostly confined to early years education in the UK.

To the uninitiated, Montessori methods may seem like a free-for-all. However, the reality is carefully thought out and planned learning aims, objectives and outcomes. What isn't prescriptive is the route a child will take to get there; creativity, exploration and problem-solving are encouraged, children move freely around the classroom and are wholly involved with and absorbed in their learning, they work at their own pace and are assisted or prompted to solutions only as necessary. Older children join forces with younger, they become instructors and befrienders, revising and reinforcing their own knowledge by working with and helping younger ones. The apparent lack of structure can be a problem for some youngsters; others relish the freedom to explore.

Steiner-Waldorf Education
Designed by Rudolf Steiner, with a strong emphasis on creativity, Steiner education aims to develop the whole child. Steiner believed in fulfilling potential but not in pushing towards adult goals. Like Montessori, underpinning Steiner education is a belief that children should be enthusiastic about and enjoy learning for its own sake, not to pass exams, so enquiry and exploration are encouraged. Play, storytelling, drawing, and nature are fundamentals for younger children, with the three Rs reserved principally for the post-7 brigade, yet foreign languages are taught from an early age. Children are often immersed in a subject over a prolonged period. Steiner schools (several are featured in this Guide), have a 'college of teachers' rather than a headteacher and the usual hierarchy. Often seen as a helpful alternative for children who don't 'fit the box', but not totally alternative: Steiner education still offers a route to GCSEs and A levels (though generally in limited numbers). However, ensure that you are happy with Steiner's philosophy of Anthroposophy and theories on child development.

Other alternatives
Schools that depart in varying degrees from the traditional UK system generally have in common no uniform and first name terms for pupils and teachers. These include Sands School, in Devon, which has a strong democratic core; lessons are not compulsory (as at its better known counterpart, Summerhill) and pupils help with the physical day-to-day running of the school. Brockwood Park in Hampshire follows the teachings of spiritual philosopher Krishnamurti. While students do take exams, these are not the main thrust of school life.

Coalition Education Policy

Since May 2010 it has been hard to keep up with the stream of innovations emanating from the Department for Education. Away went the cheerful rainbow logo of Labour's Department for Children, Schools and Families, in came Michael Gove's more traditional and sober heraldic one.

In July 2010 the guillotine fell on the Building Schools for the Future programme and by December the £3,290 cap on university fees had been raised to £9,000. Against a background of cuts, the Pupil Premium gave looked after children and those on free school meals an extra £488 per head in 2011, rising to £623 in 2012 and £900 in 2013. The Coalition abolished the Education Maintenance Allowance (EMA), which had given sixth formers from poor families some £30 a week to help them continue studying, replacing it with a much more limited bursary scheme.

Academies

Arguably the coalition's most radical policy is the plan to make academies rather than community schools the norm in state education. There are now 3049 academies, accounting for slightly over half of all secondary schools and six per cent of primaries. This number includes 83 per cent of the remaining maintained grammars and a few independent schools that have ceased to charge fees and use selection. Academies began under Labour as a way to replace failing comprehensives in deprived areas, with schools benefiting from external sponsors and extra funding, often with lavish new buildings, new heads, uniforms and strict discipline policies, plus plenty of support and monitoring.

The majority of the new wave of Gove-style converter academies have good or outstanding Ofsteds and are often located in professional middle class areas. The attraction for schools has more been control over funding that would otherwise go on purchasing services from the local authorities. Academies also have the freedom to control the length of terms and days, plus teachers' pay and conditions, and to opt out of the national curriculum – though only within limits, as they are still subject to Ofsted inspections and national targets. They are even, very controversially, allowed to employ unqualified teachers.

All new maintained schools have to be academies or free schools. Some belong to chains, eg Harris, Ark, which may be large – 10 or more academies; others have ambitions extending to 20 to 40 schools, whilst the largest, the Academies Enterprise Trust, runs over 70. In March the DfE announced that it was barring AET from taking over more schools because of concerns that its rapid expansion was hitting standards. The chain has also been criticised for paying nearly £500,000 into the private business interests of its trustees and executives.

Only six per cent of primaries have converted so far, though there are more in the pipeline — the maths usually only works for them if they are part of groups or federations, as on their own they tend to get overwhelmed by the extra admin. Despite this, the Coalition is now threatening hundreds of the least successful primaries with enforced academy status (and several, despite, parental protests, are faced with being 'given' to one of the education chains).

While academies are their own admissions authorities, they still have to conform to the statutory admissions and appeals codes and parents need to use the local authority's common application form. However, there is evidence that some academies have manipulated the process to raise their results, eg limiting the number of children with special needs and those on free school meals, using 'equivalent' qualifications that are not valued by universities. Instances of financial mismanagement and extravagance indicate a need for tighter accountability.

The government claims that academies have higher exam success, but the evidence is not clear cut, and many doubt that the Department for Education will be able to spot sinking schools without the monitoring eye of local authorities, especially now the academy numbers are so high. Their growth is also making it harder for local authorities to regulate the provision of all the school places needed. There is a consensus amongst educationalists that the critical factors determining children's attainment are the quality of teaching and learning in a school and the ability and backgrounds of the children; the head plays an important role, too. Mr Gove, however, appears convinced that simply increasing the quantity of academies will solve all problems, and is not prepared to wait for more supporting evidence before radically altering the landscape of the education system in a way that will be very difficult to undo.

Free schools

Inspired by the example of Swedish free and American Charter schools, these are set up by parents, teachers, charities, businesses, universities, existing schools, community, educational and faith groups (the last can select up to 50 per cent of pupils on the basis of religion). They enjoy the same freedoms as academies, also being independent of local authorities. Eighty-one have opened and a further 211 approved. They include primaries, secondaries, all through, special, alternative provision, post-16 and 14-19 schools.

Despite the lack of achievement data in the case of completely new schools, the majority are oversubscribed (the average is 3:1); the West London Free School that is particularly associated with journalist Toby Young received over 500 applications for 120 places in its first year and 1178 in 2012 (10:1). There is an exciting variety of specialisms – a bilingual Chinese-English primary in Manchester; a school for teenagers keen to work in the music industry in east London; two schools for exceptionally able mathematicians supported by King's College London and Exeter University. Two sixth form colleges, one in east London, established by a group of prominent independent schools, and another in east Manchester, established by Altrincham Girls' Grammar and partnered by Manchester City FC, aim to improve the chances of students from deprived areas progressing to the best universities.

However, the free schools programme has been criticised for a lack of transparency about costs and how successful bids are chosen; there has been a large-scale waste of money when projected schools have failed to open. Some have opened in areas with a surplus of places in existing schools, at a time when there is a critical shortage of primary school places nationally; others have opened despite being under-subscribed by up to 50 per cent. Overall they are failing to take their fair share of the poorest children and some have breached the Schools Admissions Code.

Studio schools

Not aimed at aspiring film directors, these schools, usually around 300 pupils, provide a bridge between education and work for 14-19 year olds, who study a mix of vocational and academic qualifications taught in practical and project-based ways. Initially, pupils also work for four hours a week at local and national partner employers; this rises to two days a week, with pay, when they are 16. Sixteen have opened and 28 more been approved across the country from Devon (linked to the NHS), Southampton (marine and cruise industries) and London (backed by Fulham FC, the BBC and Age UK) to Stevenage (the Da Vinci School of Science and Engineering, backed by Glaxo), Birmingham (catering and hospitality, in conjunction with Hilton Hotels, National Express and Aston Villa FC) to Liverpool (games development and digital futures, backed by Sony and several universities).

University technology colleges

These are academies for 14-19 year olds, funded under the free schools programme, specialising in demanding technical subjects such as advanced engineering, digital technologies and biomedical sciences. Almost 200 major national and local employers have been involved in developing the curriculum, including JCB, Heathrow, BA, Jaguar Landrover, Sony and The Lowry Arts Centre; they will also provide work experience or training. All UTCs are sponsored by universities. Many will be run on business hours rather than the standard school day. Five have opened, 27 are preparing to do so and 13 more have been approved. The Baker-Dearing Educational Trust is aiming to establish a national network.

Primary school places

A soaring birth rate is putting huge pressure on schools and many are exceeding the statutory 30 pupils limit for infant classes and converting playground space, music rooms and libraries into classrooms. Concerns have been raised as to whether the Department for Education has allocated sufficient funding to create all the places that will be needed in the coming years. Local authorities are responsible for providing places but have no influence on where new free schools open.

Back to the future

The English education system is now the most diverse on earth, and it requires a considerable exercise of imagination to see how the Department for Education will be able to steer it, let alone control it. The above — plus many changes to the national curriculum (see Exams Update, page 23) — looks like more of this mixture, with an added flavour of back to the future as well as a highly stressful time for teachers having to adapt to it all. The introduction of the English Baccalaureate shows one lever still works: league tables. Sir Michael Wilshaw's crispening-up of Ofsted's systems for dealing with failing schools demonstrates another. More needs to be done to ensure that a diverse, free system of schools does not lead to children being disadvantaged by glitches in local provision, and that central initiatives such as fair admissions codes and inspired ideas on improving school dinners can still be effective when academies and free schools are not forced to adhere to them.

WELLINGTON
COLLEGE

One child: eight aptitudes.

wellingtoncollege.org.uk | +44 (0)1344 444013

Wellington College. The intelligent choice for the best in coeducation.

INSPIRE | ENCOURAGE | EMPOWER

SURBITON

HIGH SCHOOL

Education Chains

Cognita – controversy continues

Educators come in all shades of opinion, from finely nuanced to highly colourful. Few, however, can match Sir Chris Woodhead, former chief inspector of schools, who has courted (and apparently relished) controversy in just about every post he has held. No surprises, then, that Cognita, the for-profit schools group he founded in 2004, now owned by investment trust Bregal Capital, who sold a substantial share of the business to private equity firm KKR earlier this year, still garners more than its fair share of attention.

Rumbling along in the background, meanwhile, is the discontent at Southbank International School in central London, which just won't go away. Cognita's (alleged) lack of investment in the school was given a thorough airing in the media, which seized gleefully on the row as a way of highlighting just what goes wrong when you attempt to introduce a profit motive into education.

The school's parents, while happy with the academic results — in 2013 the best ever — forcefully expressed their dissatisfaction with just about everything else. Sir Chris is rumoured to be unconverted, if word on the corridors is to be believed, to the International Baccalaureate curriculum — which is used all the way through the school, a rarity in the UK, though the norm in international schools elsewhere. There are fears that the school might bring in a more conventional curriculum, with only the IB Diploma surviving and recast in a more British framework.

The school, however, serves what one insider describes as a transient community including diplomats and journalists, whose children were often academically able but had only a smattering of English, and for whom the school was a wonderful comfort zone. 'The changes suggest that the constituency is no longer one that owners value,' thought an insider.

So concerned are parents that one group has set up its own school, Halcyon London International School, which has accreditation as an IB world school.

None of this should detract from Cognita's achievements. Its 43 UK schools, some acquired from the Asquith Court group, walk the walk academically, and official inspections and on-line comments by parents record many sunny hours, with few brickbats.

Alpha Plus – lower profile but ambitious

That's also the case with Alpha Plus, Cognita's nearest rival, at least in terms of its scale of operations. Owned by ... yes, another investment group (Delancey, this time) the group has its roots in the 1970s when, as Davies, Lang and Dick, it started collecting pre-preps and preps. Its portfolio of schools tends, as with Cognita's, to be skewed largely to the 'right' areas of London and the home countries where the richest pickings in terms of pupil numbers are to be found.

A less flamboyant management style has led, predictably, to an altogether more subdued public profile. Don't be deceived, however, as it is every bit as ambitious, recently raising £50 million by issuing a retail bond and announcing plans to build a new accommodation block in central London for pupils at Abbey and DLD colleges.

Also similar is its founding philosophy — a focus on taking away all that time and cost-consuming admin from individual schools, thus leaving heads and teachers free to concentrate on delivering academic excellence. Schools in need of capital investment can pitch for a share of the available funding.

GEMS – UK restructuring

Then there are the GEMS schools. Though the firm is a rapidly growing worldwide operator — it plans, according to one of its many upbeat announcements, to create 50 new schools in India alone by 2018 — its profile in the UK has somewhat diminished, following the sale of five schools in Yorkshire and Lancashire to tiny group Alpha Schools (not to be confused with Alpha Plus). This leaves the GEMs with a few well-run establishments in the wealthier south and, it says, no plans to bail out of the UK completely.

GEMS is a family firm, founded in Dubai in 1959 by Mr and Mrs Varkey and now run by their son Sunny, whose lifestyle on and off the pitch, as a quick internet search will reveal, is a vibrant one. With patrons including Prince Michael of Kent and a charitable trust which operates a buy one, get 10 free system, educating 100 deprived children for every 10 fee payers.

The company is good at reeling in heavyweight names, including Dr Martin Stephen, a former St Paul's high master and, current catch of the day, Audrey Peverelli, snapped up from headship of the International School of Paris. It's not always quite so good at hanging on to them, however. Zenna Atkins, former chair of Ofsted, lasted just seven weeks at GEMs as 'chief executive, UK, Europe and Africa' before departing — reason unspecified.

Quieter players

It's worth pointing out that other educational chains such as the Priory Group (of celebrity detox fame) and Cambian have also been hard at work, with far less fanfare, developing sizeable networks of generally very well regarded special schools for children with often complex learning difficulties.

The state sector – a glittering prize

To date, the smart money has headed for independent schools – and it's proved relatively fruitful. But the serious operators have their eyes fixed on the state sector. Already something of a hot date when it comes to the investment community's interest levels, education is set to become an even more attractive proposition with Michael Gove's apparent willingness to allow with-profits firms an increased presence when it comes to running academies and, more controversially, free schools, too.

International English Schools UK, the offshoot of Swedish educational firm Internationella Engelska Skolan (IES) has secured what could amount to the very first of the state-hatched golden eggs – the first government contract for a for profit company to run a free school, IES Breckland, which opened in September 2012.

As with healthcare, feelings tend to run high when there's any whiff of a money-making culture associated with state schools. Lack of accountability, sheer greed and the potential for making an almighty hash of things are the main factors cited, though it's fair to say that other independents, most run as charities, haven't been universally in favour of chains either – one head of the HMC was quoted in the FT about the risks of prioritising the profit motive.

The industry doesn't always help itself. The chosen image for one, well-attended education investment conference was a jolly-looking teddy bear helping itself to coins spilling out of a vast treasure chest, while the spectacular implosion of private equity firm Delauncey Day in a welter of management shortcomings shortly after they had acquired the Asquith Nursery group did little to present investors as the good guys.

When it comes to academies and, increasingly, free schools, assorted clashes between public sentiment, political will and parent power could tip the scales either way. What's clear, though, is that things are unlikely to stay the same.

The bottom line for parents?

Check to see if you're signing up to a lean, mean, educational machine or one that's being fattened for market (investment firms are known for sweating their assets). When you talk to the head, are you hearing an authentic voice or are s/he and the staff lip-syncing to a corporate script?

Find out who owns the school you're interested in. If it's recently been acquired by a private firm and staff turnover is high, is this a praiseworthy attempt to shift dead wood, or a series of protest resignations? Don't rule it out on that account, especially if the place meets all your requirements.

"If everyone is thinking alike, then no one is thinking."

Benjamin Franklin

At Frensham Heights, we are proud to think differently. Founded on values of tolerance, respect and creativity, we treat every child as an individual and ensure that everyone truly flourishes.

Our unique approach to learning begins in our vibrant nursery and extends to our thriving sixth form. Situated in 120 acres of beautiful Surrey countryside and less than an hour from London, we provide unrivalled opportunities to both day and boarding students.

Visit www.frensham.org or call 01252 792561 to find out more.

Frensham Heights | Think, Create, Explore

Frensham Heights, Rowledge, Farnham, Surrey GU10 4EA . Tel. 01252 792561 Charity No. 312052

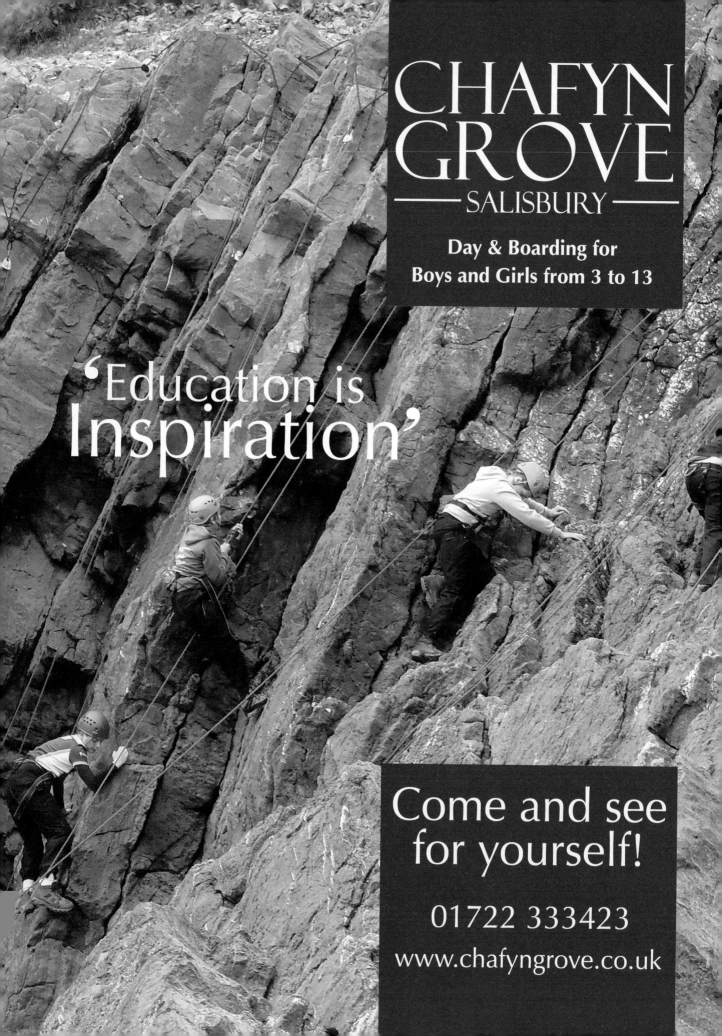

Exams Update

Testing times: early assessments

Sign up to any nursery or reception class and your 2, 3, 4 or 5 year old will be under levels of observation formerly reserved for maximum security prisoners. Their significant doings will be noted, photographed, even filmed, and checked off against a comprehensive list of development criteria – all in the name of the Early Years Foundation Stage.

In primary schools the synthetic phonics approach is now firmly established, with a diagnostic reading test for 6-year-olds containing made-up words that has teachers protesting confident readers may fail the test because they try to translate the made-up words into real ones, and unconvinced the results reveal any more than their own regular assessments. Year 6s now take a discrete grammar and spelling test (replacing extended writing) whose educational value has also been questioned. From 2014, it has been proposed that children will be ranked nationally according to 10 per cent ability bands rather than given a level 4 or 5. We wonder how it can be a good idea to tell a child on the verge of starting their secondary education that they belong to the bottom 10/20 per cent of children in the country. Reception children may be given baseline tests when they start school for measuring later progress, instead of using key stage 1 tests.

The revised primary national curriculum is due to start in 2014. The proposals for English involve more focus on spelling, punctuation and grammar, including mastery of the subjunctive and semi-colons, plus the ability to spell 200 complex words such as *controversy, environment, conscience* and *mischievous,* by the end of key stage 2. They also include the use of formal spoken English, to be developed through, eg, poetry reciting – St Michael of Gove slays the 1960s progressive dragon.

Maths is to be made more demanding (fractions at age 5, the 12 times table at age 9, algebra and long division at age 11), in the hope of matching the Pacific Rim PISA super stars. Facts, facts, facts in science, history (mainly British and mostly up to 1066) and geography, leavened by practical work in the first. Computing (programming, the internet and using digital devices) replaces ICT. Foreign languages, ancient and modern, are to be compulsory at key stage 2. Design and (cutting edge) technology includes using mechanical and electronic systems (there has been talk of 3-D printers) and learning about good food and how to cook it – cordon and sacré bleu!

There is much disquiet amongst educationalists about the focus on memorising and regurgitating facts, with less space for developing skills and wider understanding — particularly as much of the English and maths content is seen as too demanding for the expected ages, and no attention seems to have been paid to the situation of the less able and special needs children. The most puzzling question is why academies and free schools should be allowed to choose the extent to which they enter this brave new world.

Common entrance – all change?

Some 250 senior independents administer the test created and set by the Independent Schools Examination Boards (which derives around £70,000 from the entrances fees) consisting of three core subjects plus a range of add-ons. Many others, Eton amongst them, run their own. All schools mark their own prospective candidates' papers and set grade boundaries. Grades or the percentage marks they represent aren't just unequal but tend to mean, in best Humpty Dumpty style, just what schools choose them to mean. 'Grade boundaries go up and down like the FTSE depending on how many applicants there are,' says one head.

In the case of over-subscribed schools, merely sitting the exam at 13+ is something of an achievement as it's increasingly preceded by qualifying rounds in years 5, 6 or 7 which eliminate no-hopers and allow senior schools first dibs on the best and brightest, often pocketing a large deposit in the process.

Its detractors argue that CE in its current form has had its day. A venerable beast, introduced in 1904, it's fact-heavy, light on creativity, reins in the imagination and requires the last two years to be devoted to teaching to the test, say critics (though others reckon that inspired teaching can add a little sparkle to most prescriptive syllabus). Objections have been partially countered through the introduction of coursework in subjects like geography: great, say some, though others wonder just how many well-motivated and ambitious parents refrain from stamping their own personality on the project.

Others want root and branch reform. September 2013 saw the launch of an alternative, the Prep School Baccalaureate (PSB). Six schools, the Beacon School in Amersham, Taunton Preparatory School, Yateley Manor in Hampshire, Moorlands School in Leeds, Old Buckenham Hall in Suffolk and Edenhurst in Yorkshire are teaching the full monty, while a further 12 are likely to sign up as partner schools when a taster version is launched in September 2014.

Broadly based on national curriculum levels (3 to 6 for those in year 7, and 5 to 7 in year 8), the PSB has developed its own 10 point scale with lots of on-going tests and teacher assessments and is designed to develop a passion for learning rather than teaching to the test. (Parroting the capitals of the world is singled out for particular ire by CE opponents, though remaining a good party trick in later life.) Schools have the freedom to develop their own curricula and while subject-based achievement accounts for 70 per cent of the PSB marks, pupils acquire the remainder by demonstrating a range of learning skills such as teamwork, leadership and communications.

MERCHISTON STORY
IN THE MAKING

Listen to some of our pupils talk about their
Merchiston journey www.merchiston.co.uk
A Boarding and Day School for Boys aged 8-18

Applications for means-tested financial assistance welcome

Merchiston Castle School, Colinton Road,
Edinburgh, EH13 0PU, Scotland
Tel. 0131 312 2200.
Recognised by the Inland Revenue as a Charity,
number SC016580

www.merchiston.co.uk

MERCHISTON
EDINBURGH | Boys first

It's up there with the latest in educational thinking, 'how' as well as 'what' you learn being an on-going preoccupation. So far, the PSB has gained the stamp of approval from 12 senior school associates, including Marlborough, Wellington, Radley and Charterhouse. Acceptance of the PSB as a lock, stock and barrel replacement for the CE is the long-term goal. Some schools are keen. Others are asking pupils to sit additional maths, English and ability exams. All in all, though currently a small scale development, it's one worth watching.

GCSEs – the exams that wouldn't die

Wellington College suggested replacing them. Eton wanted them done away with altogether. Reports of their demise seem to have been exaggerated, however, and it looks as if GCSEs are here to stay. For a while, they seemed doomed as Michael Gove flirted with some attractive new initials. Was it going to be RIP GCSEs and hello EBCs, (English Baccalaureate Certificates) which, despite sounding like a wonky alphabet rhyme, were to be the saviour of the 16 plus exam system? After a brief flowering, however, they withered and died under the merciless glare of all-round criticism, and now Mr Gove has opted for a Frankenstein meets Robocop-inspired makeover for GCSEs.

No longer the soft underbelly of the exams system, GCSEs are imbued with so much extra rigour you can almost smell it, with content refurbishment underway for completion in September 2016, most key subjects ready a year earlier, paint still drying on the title pages.

It's in with a once a year June sittings for first timers and retakers alike (November resits in English and maths are the only exceptions) marking the end of the modular approach which allowed candidates to collect GCSEs in instalments, like football cards, with plenty of opportunities for grade swapsies en route if they weren't happy with what they got first time round.

Out, too, go tiered exams, (foundation for the flounderers, higher for the top grade chasers) with a one exam fits all replacement, thanks to a levels 1 to 8 marking system that incorporates plenty of growing room – from 9 to infinity and beyond – should an explosion in academic achievement require it.

Though GCSEs are likely to remain the default choice for the majority of schools, their cousins, IGCSEs (variously described by the press – sometimes in the same newspaper – as much harder or much easier than GCSEs) are doing exceptionally well. Since receiving clearance for use in state schools (and shedding their black sheep league table status), UK entries shot up, more than doubling between 2012 and 2013 to 115,000. Admittedly, this is still a tiny figure compared with the 5.9 million GCCSs taken in 2012, but growth like this hints at fairly substantial pent-up demand.

IB or not IB?

So far, the third mainstream option, the middle years IB programme, remains small scale, currently offered, international schools aside, by just three others. Two, Dartford Grammar and Havelock Academy (the latter a formerly failing comprehensive, now on the up) are in the state sector. Probably its strongest (and certainly most vocal) advocate is Wellington College, which since 2009 has let year 9 pupils choose between GCSEs and the IB (though everyone does IGCSEs or GCSEs in English lit, lang and maths). Teacher-designed courses pack in as much fun and stimulation as required (within an approved framework) and it comes with the blessing of top universities.

Wellington's website features a ringing endorsement from Cambridge's head of admissions, no less.

Bespoke alternatives

But they're far from being the dernier cri in custom-designed education. Bedales, which has a reputation as something of a free spirit to maintain, runs its very own exams, the BACs (Bedales Assessed Courses). UCAS-endorsed and coursework heavy, they're proving a hit not just with pupils, who mix and match with GCSEs, but Oxbridge, too, says the school, which reports healthy numbers of offers.

Others, too, are joining in. The Steiner-inspired Acorn School in Gloucestershire (second branch on the way in London) has ditched public exams altogether, instead opting for a multi-subject curriculum and continuous assessment. Universities have bought in, it says, and pupils often receive unconditional offers. Tempted? Prospective Acorn parents must also share the head's way of thinking on matters beyond public examinations, which doesn't admit many shades of grey. They include robust views on everything from food — 'We are slowly poisoning our children by filling their bodies with sugars and red meat' – to technology (banned at home and school until pupils reach 14).

So far, and perhaps surprisingly in these branding-conscious days (St Custard's Prix D'Excellence, Raffia work, anyone?) they remain, like the middle years IB (in the UK at least) a niche educational development.

A new standard in Scotland

It's all change in Scotland too: Standard grades are being abandoned and replaced by new national qualifications. Some of the country's more academic schools ditched them a while back, opting for Intermediate I or II. The state system, however, prefers National 4 or 5. The syllabus, as a result, has been substantially changed. State schools, at the time of writing, were calling for extra government funding to pay for the new materials required, a plea, some felt, that would fall on deaf ears.

EBac, Best 8 and more rigour throughout

The result, to the relief of many, seems to be the end of the grade inflation that has bedeviled GCSEs' value as a truly objective test of attainment (for many, the UK's slide down the world educational rankings, as monitored by the OECD but now questioned in various quarters, paints a black, but more accurate picture).

There's no let up in monitoring schools' attainment, however. Down south, the EBac, or English Baccalaureate (not to be confused with the EBC), awarded to candidates achieving A*/C grades in big hitter subjects — English, maths, science, a language and humanities – will stay, helping to reverse what had seemed like a terminal decline in physics, chemistry, French and German amongst others in recent years.

It's likely to take a Bac seat, however, as a new measure, popularly known as the Best 8 which measures average scores across a range of subjects, takes precedence. To the delight of those who felt the EBac gave schools little incentive to focus on unlisted subjects such as performing and visual arts, the Best 8

Boarding at Whitgift.

One of Britain's finest independent day and boarding schools for boys

excellent academic results
more than 200 Oxbridge entrants in the past ten years

unrivalled sporting success
over 75 national titles in the past two years

professional creative connections
partnership with the Royal Philharmonic Orchestra

unsurpassed curriculum
IB, Bilingual IB, A Level or BTEC

exciting range of co-curricular activities
80 diverse clubs and societies, from astronomy to wakeboarding

superb location
close to central London yet situated in beautiful parkland

Whitgift. An outstanding education.

WHITGIFT

For further details,
please contact the
Admissions Office at
admissions@whitgift.co.uk
tel: +44 (0)20 8688 9222

Whitgift School
Haling Park
South Croydon
CR2 6YT
United Kingdom

www.whitgift.co.uk

can include any three subjects that pupils are good at, making it worth schools' while to hone pupils' all-round strengths.

New, more rigorous and demanding GCSEs are scheduled for 2015/16, with, for example, the reading of a whole Shakespeare play, Romantic poetry and a heavyweight Victorian novel in English Literature. They will mostly be assessed solely by terminal exams (modules ended in 2012) and graded on a scale of 1-8 instead of G-A*, presumably to mark their superior quality. Parents may not regret the passing of coursework – to which many made significant contributions – but there will be an educational loss when children no longer have a chance to produce a polished piece of extended writing.

The speaking and listening component of English no longer counts towards the final grade, which means it will play only a very minor role in the course. It is true that some teachers have not been able to resist the temptation to use it to inflate grades, but it seems short sighted when so many employers bemoan the lack of communication skills of school leavers. New accountability measures may produce some league table surprises for education aficianados; parents, though, may find them overly complex.

A radical culling of vocational qualifications followed the Wolf Review, which demanded that all such qualifications should support progress to further and higher education. Subjects involving extended writing now have marks allocated for accurate spelling, punctuation and grammar. Add a focus on a 'knowledge based' national curriculum (news for anyone who thought that was at least one of the main reasons for going to school) and marks in writing-heavy subjects allocated to correct spelling, punctuation and grammar, and hopes are rising that GCSEs can regain the credibility of the O level and become, if not loved by candidates, something they can at least take pride in passing.

16-18: Back to the Bacc

Look at the current crop of sixth form courses and you'd be forgiven for thinking that the future's not so much orange as laureate-shaped. AQA do one: three A levels, a semi in critical thinking and an extended project (incorporating original research), as do the Welsh (three handy sizes to fit 16 and 17 as well as 18 year olds).

Sixth form colleges have also got in on the act with their own baccalaureate, currently being piloted in 11 mainly state establishments. Offering at least a nod in the direction of inclusiveness, it recognises not just A level and BTec – 'breadth as well as depth of study taken into account,' says one college – and offers 'a kite-mark of curriculum quality rather than a qualification in its own right' – which may come as news to the students it honours.

Most recent of all, however, is the TechBacc, unveiled in 2013 and intended as the vocational equivalent of A levels, helping 16-19 year olds acquire a quiverful of employer-pleasing maths, practical and research-based skills.

The daddy of them all, however, is the IB or International Baccalaureate, whose Geneva-based founders presumably are presumably basking in their 'onlie begetter' status, though possibly kicking themselves for not filing a patent on the name.

Originally designed to provide a credible, transferable education for country-hopping families – and with the laudable aim of shaping model world citizens into the bargain – the IB has gained a loyal (if still petite) following for its

consistency and rigour (grade inflation is an unknown concept). Its offering, a smorgasbord of required achievements, isn't for the fainthearted, consisting of six subjects and must-do add-ons including a lengthy essay, theory of knowledge module and 150 hours of creative, sports and community-based work.

As you'd expect, it's no picnic for participating schools, either. While the IB parent organisation is quick to scotch rumours that costs put it at the Harrods end of the exam system – there's even a 'mythbusters' secton on its website – it does admit that 'the difficulty comes in actually offering the course, with the need to recruit more and better teachers, teacher training, extra staff, etc.' Quite, especially that 'etc'.

As government enthusiasm and sixth form funding appear to have waned, state schools seem to be rethinking the advisability of offering dual systems, especially as university offers consistently, if anecdotally, appear to be set higher for IB candidates. Independents, too, are finding the going tough. 'When the IB originally came in, it was given quite a generous scaling. Now that has been scaled back, so a lot of schools are thinking that in a cost/benefit analysis, it's better to stick with the A level,' felt one head. Scan through the IB figures, and the impact is already being felt. Though the popularity of the IB is increasing worldwide, UK entries have dropped, though very slightly, from 5,114 in 2011 to 5,000 in 2012. At the time of writing, the IB communications team had not yet let us know whether they saw this as a one-off or the start of a longer-term trend.

Pre-U

Of course, you can avoid the B-word altogether by opting for exam specialists Cambridge International, whose Pre-U, in some eyes a nostalgic revisiting of old fashioned A levels, comes with a three-subject and research based diploma, together (gasp) with courses that challenge and exams that reward candidates who think for themselves. Its finely shaded grading system goes beyond the A*, making it easier to identify the very brightest pupils. Introduced by Cambridge International in 2008 with Winchester College and Charterhouse among the early adopters, it is now offered by over 150 UK schools – static since last year, though entries have risen – with an almost 50/50 state and independent split. Instead of a baccalaureate, there's the diploma: three subjects (either all Pre-Us or a mix and match with A levels) plus a global perspectives 'portfolio'.

The future looks...deflated and a bit tougher

All this change is down to what was, until 2012, the inexorable rise and rise in top A level grades. In 2010 alone, 45,000 candidates achieved three straight As. Stripped of grade inflation in both 2012 and 2013, A levels are now shedding modules in favour of linear courses with exams at the end of the second year only, while content is also under review. One thing's for sure. They won't be getting any easier.

As governments (as with GCSEs) prefer to extol the growing brilliance of pupils and teachers alike (easy) rather than opt for tougher marking (hard), would-be undergraduates have had to accomplish ever more inside and outside the classroom to stand out. For very competitive courses, applications have acquired the edge and effort of an extreme sport. Would-be doctors aren't yet asked to develop a cure for cancer or donate a kidney to a friend as proof of dedication, but some parents wouldn't bat an eyelid if they were, so quixotic are the requirements. 'One asked my son for grade 8 music, presumably so he could hone his bedside skills by singing lullabies to the patients,' snarls a disillusioned mother.

As A levels become, once again, a respected way of distinguishing between the merely bright and the outstanding, it remains to be seen whether laureates and their ilk stay the course or are discarded as fripperies and furbelows that are no longer needed on the educational voyage.

Best of Both Worlds? Mixing State and Independent

All those scary newspaper statistics about the long-term costs of keeping your child in nappies and birthday presents pale into insignificance when set beside the £150,000+ you'll need to educate a child privately from nursery to university.

But paying for a private education from finger painting to Freshers' Week is not an option for most families. More people than ever before are opting for the independent sector, but those without private means or surplus wealth often choose to pay selectively.

However you choose to play the education game, be reassured that no decision is final. If something is not working out for you or your child at any point, it's almost always possible to change, and often much easier to do at a stage when not everyone else is making the same decision.

Move at year 3, age 7/8

State primary school works particularly well if you have an able child who finds little difficulty with the three Rs. At the other extreme, those with serious learning difficulties, particularly if they are 'statemented' (officially recognised as needing support) will be given one-to-one help at no charge to you (though you will probably need to fight hard for this).

Those in the middle may be the ones who thrive least well in a busy primary school — as much psychologically as academically. A hard-pressed teacher with a mixed-ability class of 30 children often simply doesn't have the energy to focus on this unexciting middle group, and a parent with an under-confident, just-getting-by child may decide it's worth pinching pennies for the extra attention that a private school can provide.

If you want to check how a primary school matches up to the private sector, one of the best indicators is the percentage of year 6 children (10-11-year-olds) who achieve level 5 in their key stage 2 Sats — the level that would be expected from the great majority of children in a good prep school. These figures are now included in performance tables and you will find them on our website. However, bear in mind that this probably shows as much about the intake as the quality of teaching.

Some parents choose to use the state system for the early years only, changing to a prep school at 7 or 8. However, some over-subscribed London prep schools make little allowance for a child who cannot read and write as fluently as candidates from more results-driven pre-preps so you may want to consider coaching at home. Country preps and less pressured schools, on the other hand, may delight in taking youngsters who need their small-class nurturing to bring them along fast.

Move at year 7, age 11

State to private

Many independent schools too, ever mindful of those A level league tables, are increasingly keen to attract the brightest and the best, so much of the emphasis of the 11 plus entrance test is now put on raw IQ, which is generally gauged by verbal and non-verbal reasoning tests (English and maths are also on the menu at many schools though fewer every year). The high-flying City of London School for Boys, for example — which has always had a broad intake in terms of means and social class — takes two-thirds of its 11 plus entrants from the state sector and adjusts its marking according to the provenance of the candidates, giving leeway to those from state primary schools. Even academically and socially elite public schools such as Westminster and Eton are now eager to attract the ablest 11-year-olds from the state sector, and are prepared to educate them in the years between 11 and 13 at their own or allied prep schools. Harrow now provides free prep school education to the brightest boys aged 11-13 from particular London boroughs.

IQ alone, however, is not the only factor. Parents keen to make the transition at this point may wish to hire a tutor (or tutor them themselves) from the middle of year 5 (year 6 is too late!) to solidify their child's literacy and numeracy and prepare their child for the unfamiliar and idiosyncratic verbal and non-verbal reasoning tests. Alternatively, many prep schools welcome pupils aged 10 or 11 to train them up for senior school entrance at 13 — although this mostly applies to boys' or co-ed schools and is complicated by senior schools' increasing tendency to pre-test in year 6 or 7.

Private to state

If you live in an area such as Kent or Buckinghamshire, still primarily served by grammar or selective state schools, the approach is often to concentrate expenditure at primary level. However, if you feel your child doesn't have the raw material to compete in these immensely cut-throat exams, be prepared to go private all the way. It is hard for some parents to accept that their child's expensive prep school preparation will not help them through grammar school entrance tests which are increasingly just reasoning papers — and increasingly done online. And the state schools don't, mostly, interview.

Move at year 12, age 16/17

At odds with the long-standing myth that children from state schools are given preference over similarly-qualified private school applicants by the top universities, recent studies have shown that private school Oxford applicants with three A* grades at A level are significantly more likely to gain a place than those with the same grades from state schools. Of course, offers are mostly made before the exams are taken, but this does suggest that public school polish can tip the balance at interviews. Independent school sixth forms often have scholarships for those with talent in music, art, sports or academics, so transferring to the private sector at this stage can make financial as well as scholastic sense.

However, there are reasons for going the other way too. Many move to state sixth forms for a greater range of A level options and a greater social mix of friends. Sometimes a move after GCSE is an opportunity for a pupil to make a fresh start and can revitalise interest in academic work; a move from single sex to co-ed can also be a source of motivation (though sometimes a mixed blessing). Catchment areas become more flexible at this level, as do religious schools' requirements of church attendance and so on.

What the League Tables Don't Tell You

League tables have caused a lot of agony and misunderstanding. As raw statistics, they are more or less meaningless. You will observe, for a start, that results swing wildly according to which newspaper you happen to look at. Among other things they don't tell you:

- The pupils' IQs: Two Ds for some pupils is a triumph of wonderful teaching.

- The pupils' backgrounds: How much help/support are they getting at home?

- The school's background: Is it academically selective or mixed ability?

- The school's policy towards A levels: Does it allow pupils to 'have a go' or to take an extra A level (for stretching/breadth), or does it operate a policy of dissuading borderline candidates from taking a subject? We are hearing some disturbing stories these days of schools chucking out pupils who have not done well enough at AS level, to keep them from polluting the school's A level results.

- The school's policy at sixth form: Is it pinching, for example, bright girls from neighbouring schools? Or is it turfing out the less able pupils? Does it insist on very high (A* grade) GCSEs in proposed A level subjects for those entering the school at sixth form?

- Good years and bad years: Is this a blip, a one-off? There may be exceptional circumstances, such as the death of a teacher six months before the exam.

- What examinations are taken? The top score in the International Baccalaureate is rated in the tables as worth more than five A* grade A levels — a considerable overestimate, so IB schools appear higher up than they perhaps deserve.

- What subjects are taken? Some, eg business studies and classical civilisation, are considered easier than others (and are marked down by Oxbridge as a result). The league tables do not tell you which schools are taking general studies at A level: A level general studies can push league table ratings up no end.

- The spread of subjects at A level: Which are popular? Which neglected? Does that profile fit your child? Does it reflect the relative quality of teaching, or just the spirit of the school?

- Whether a large enough number of children are doing really well, especially in subjects that you are interested in. A cohort of excellence will give leadership and confidence to the rest of the school. Are sufficiently few pupils failing, to avoid the reverse effect?

- The quality of education overall: Depth, breadth, all-round, music, debating... things that help pupils learn to think for themselves. By sheer swotting, exams can be successfully passed — but at the expense of what?

- The reliability of the figures: The more pupils there are, the more statistically significant the results are.

- Watch out for Scottish schools lurking within the newspaper league tables: Many Scottish schools offer two systems — Scottish Highers (usually for the weaker brethren) and A levels. Only the A levels show up in the league tables.

- And while we are on the subject of statistics, treat class size figures with care too. How you teach, what you teach and to whom all govern the size that a class can be before performance deteriorates. The only certain thing about small class sizes is that they mean large bills.

Interpreting results (as best you can)

This is what you need to ask the schools you are interested in:

1. Have they anything to declare — any special circumstances? Did they take in several pupils with little English a year or two before public exams? Did the geography teacher fall ill? Understanding the school is the key to understanding its statistics.

2. Next study the extensive analyses of examination results that are available on the schools' pages on our website. They incorporate the most recent three years' published results, and you can use them to get deep under the skin of the schools' league table positions.

3. Look to see where the weaknesses and strengths are to be found. Which subjects are most popular when compared to similar schools? This can be an indication of the quality of teaching, or of the spirit of the school ('only girls do art'), or both. In which subjects do pupils do best, relative to the same pupils' performance in other subjects? Mostly this is due to teaching quality. Is one subject pulling the overall results up? Or down? Or is a 100 per cent A* grade pass in Norwegian translated as one pupil (with a Norwegian mother)? Is it pure coincidence that the best two subjects at A level are Chinese and mathematics? Look at our analysis of university destinations. This will show you something of the level of ambition that the school has instilled in its students and indications of the directions in life which it has encouraged them to take. NB Some children opt for universities near home for religious or social reasons.

4. How many pupils are taking exams over all? A school with a sixth form of 40 (three children doing each subject) should find it considerably easier to come high on the league tables than a larger school. The more taking any

one subject, the more commendable when the results are strong, and the wider the scope for failure.

5. For state schools, look at the analyses of pupil performance on our website. You can see how selective a school is from the profiles of pupil attainment at key stage 1 (for primary schools) and key stage 2 (for senior schools). You can see how well they do by bright children, and children with SEN, and how good their value added is overall.

6. For independent schools ask for the ALIS/MIDYIS/ YELLIS (systems covering the A level, middle and primary years respectively, managed by the University of Durham) or other value-added data, which should show how good the results really are, allowing for the quality of individual pupils. There are several competing systems — all good in their ways — so a school that has none is (by modern standards) not taking as close an interest in its pupils' performance as it might. This will give you quite a good idea of what is going on, and where the weak teaching might be.

7. Now you are in a position to ask the head to explain those appalling geography results, and to tell you what is being done about the situation. Listen carefully, because all schools have weaknesses, and the important thing is what is being done to remedy them.

8. All schools, even the highest achieving, have some less-than-stellar teachers. Their influence may be masked by stars in the same department. Ask pupils when you go round the school or, less directly, ask what systems are used to monitor pupils' and teachers performance, and how they are linked to remedial action — if the school is well run and up-to-date they should happily tell stories of lost sheep found.

Inspection Reports From Ofsted and Others

Ofsted — www.ofsted.gov.uk
ISI — www.isi.net (for independent schools)
HMIe — www.hmie.gov.uk (for Scottish schools)
ETI — www.etini.gov.uk/index/inspection-reports.htm
Estyn — www.estyn.gov.uk (for the Welsh)

As with most reports, there's a code to decipher and a few questions to ask. The local school gets a glowing report, yet you know half the population are banned from the shopping centre. Puzzling?

So just what do inspection reports tell us and have they any value? The answers are lots, and yes, if you know how to read them. Each section is headed and graded:

1 means Outstanding (and we've seen several of these), 4 Inadequate, with Good and Requires Improvement in between. Helpful comments are made about what the school should do to improve.

The overall effectiveness grade is supplemented by four more in the new, slimmed down version introduced in 2012. Achievement covers progress and attainment. This includes test/exam results, how well learners with disabilities or learning difficulties progress and the extent to which the gap is narrowing between the progress and attainment of the poorer pupils and the rest of the school. It also assesses how well pupils are prepared for the next stage of their education, training or employment.

The second grade is for the quality of teaching, which now receives more focus — schools can no longer be judged outstanding unless this aspect is too, which has led to the downgrading of a large number of previously outstanding schools. Teachers are expected to meet the needs of all abilities (teaching to the middle no longer an option), to engage and have high expectations of all pupils.

The third judgement is on the behaviour and safety of pupils; the fourth on the quality of leadership and management, again with a focus on the promotion of high quality teaching. Governors can expect to be grilled and, at times, criticised in the report (and they don't even get paid for the privilege of doing their job!). Comments on spiritual, moral, social and cultural development occur within the overall and separate categories, but in less detail than before. At present there is no reference to healthy lifestyles, but it has been announced that inspectors are to include evaluation of school food and the lunch environment.

Parents are consulted via an online questionnaire, but the numerical data is no longer included with the report – a pity, as it was very informative, and knowing the percentage of parents that had responded was also revealing.

Use your imagination and read reports with care – inspectors have seen too many schools and tend to think everyone knows what's meant by, eg, 'low-level disruption'. Nothing much then? No! They actually mean the most annoying kind, the sort that's much worse for other pupils than the occasional, spectacular blow-out followed by a quick expulsion.

On the whole, despite the obvious improvements, we have our doubts about the current system. Mechanistic (relying on statistical analysis), not getting under the skin of a school and unsupportive are some of the complaints we've heard. Is a two-day visit really enough to make an accurate judgement of a school? Are 20-30 minutes' observation really enough to make an accurate judgement of a teacher?

In England, the most outstanding schools will be named as such, with the consistently great assigned to The Ofsted Hall of Fame — complete with framed certificate. At the other end of the scale, just under one in 10 are either given a 'significant improvement judgement' (formerly a notice to improve) or are placed in special measures, pressure to convert to an academy, like it or not, now being a probable consequence.

Ofsted has also taken over the 'care' inspection of boarding schools, to check they meet national minimum standards. The safety aspect is taken very seriously, and though we have yet to see a disastrous report (boarding schools are much better than they used to be), you may gain some insights from reading it.

FINE
ARTS
COLLEGE

WE OFFER A WIDE RANGE OF SUBJECTS
AT A LEVEL AND GCSE

INDEPENDENT
SCHOOLS
ASSOCIATION

Accredited Member

Centre Studios
41–43 Englands Lane
London NW3 4YD

020 7586 0312

www.hampsteadfinearts.com

Ofsted
Outstanding
2012

Money Matters

Schools in the UK are mostly funded by the state — that is, they're paid for by the government and local authorities from taxes. A small proportion are independent, funded mostly from fees paid by parents and investments but also, indirectly, by the state, given that most independent schools enjoy charitable status. Approximately seven per cent of children in UK education are at fee-paying schools. Fees range from under £1,000 to £8,000 and above per term for a day pupil, with wide variations depending on the age of the child, the staff/pupil ratio, school facilities and so on — and up to £12,000 and over per term for boarding.

Help with school fees

Your very reasonable question may well be: 'Where can I find out about scholarships and bursaries? Tell me how to find a central resource where all the information is collected and I can search for something in the right area for which my child – and we as a family – might qualify.'

The short, and disgraceful answer has been, until now, 'There isn't one!' We tried everything to get the various bodies that represent the independent schools to collaborate with us to provide a resource for parents in which they could see what might be available to them in the way of scholarships and bursaries but collaboration was not forthcoming and they clearly weren't — despite piety about 'outreach' and wanting to reach the most deserving — going to do it themselves. So, we wrote to all the independent schools in The Guide, received replies from over 400 of them and now have a unique database of information on scholarships and bursaries available to parents.

It's been an immense amount of work and we will be keeping it constantly updated so we have to make a charge for searching if you tell us what you need and where you need it to be. The fee is likely to be £100-200 depending on how extensive a search you require. But — the potential rewards are amazing. A 100 per cent bursary at a boarding school for seven years could save you £210,000.

It could be you.....

Consult us here: www.gsgexpertschoolsconsultants.co.uk , phone 0203 286 6824 or email advice@goodschoolsguide.co.uk .

Help with school fees – which may otherwise be quite beyond the reach of most – is now plentiful and there for the taking if you know where it is and how to grab it. All good independent schools want the brightest and most talented pupils and they will stretch their finances to offer bursarial help to those who deserve it and who will bring them glory in future years. If you are broke but your child is talented, you may well be able to give him or her an education that your own parents could never have afforded for you.

Scholarships

In recent years, many schools have directed their discretionary funds into means-tested bursaries rather than academic scholarships — see below — leaving scholarships as mere shells, with all the honour but little of the cash. Some scholarships are designed to attract those with specific talents eg art, music, science, sports, all-round. Getting your child up to a distinction at grade 5 in an instrument by age 11 can be a profitable investment. Girls' schools, alas, can offer fewer and less valuable scholarships. In general, the old famous foundations are the richest: they may well disclaim this but all is relative. Scholarships awarded by HMC and GSA (the top schools' trade organisations) schools now vary widely. Few are now as much as 50 per cent of the full fees and most are capped at around 10-15 per cent, but almost all schools offer to top up your scholarship with a means-tested bursary if they want your child and you are deserving. If you have a bright, talented child and no money, you could find his or her education is pretty much all found by the school. Some schools (eg Eton, Westminster, St Paul's, City of London) also have a statutory number of full scholarships to offer — and from them 'full' may even include the cost of uniforms and travel to school.

Look out for esoteric scholarships for, for example, sons and daughters of clergy, medics, single mothers, fallen members of the armed forces. Licensed Victuallers' in Ascot gives discounts to children of parents working in the licensed drinks trade (from bar staff to brewers). If your name is West and you live in the parish of Twickenham there could be a bursary waiting for you (at Christ's Hospital). Scholarships to choir schools are worth thinking about but they will not cover full fees and the children work incredibly hard for them (and it is worth asking what happens when their voices break). But this could well be the beginning of a music scholarship into public school. If you are after a musical scholarship then the publication Music Awards at Independent Schools from the Music Masters' and Mistresses' Association, by David Bunkell, may be just what you need.

Keep your eyes open for internal scholarships which run at various stages, sixth form especially. Of course, there are also increasing numbers of schools luring pupils in at sixth form with generous scholarships: might be worth moving schools for.

Useless scholarships — don't fall for them. It is a false economy to be flattered into going to the wrong school for £200 off the bill. You may be better off with a school that charges slightly lower fees to start with but no scholarship on offer. Many schools now offer discounted fees for more than one sibling and, in any case, it is well worth lobbying for 10 per cent off or even more in this climate — if you have three or more children you should be able to negotiate a job lot. Talk to the bursar. Most schools – especially country boarding schools – are often happy to negotiate these days. Scholarships can also be combined with bursaries to make the fees affordable.

Bursaries

A bursary is help with school fees – academic and/or boarding – offered by schools to attract bright or talented pupils from homes in which the parental income would not otherwise be enough to afford fees. Bursaries are means-tested – and reviewed annually. Your family circumstances – home, income, commitments, number of dependants etc – will need to be disclosed and you may well be visited by a member of the school staff to check that your disclosures are true.

There is no agreed level of income below which you may be eligible for a bursary. Each family – each application – will be considered on its individual merits and may well be influenced by how much the school wants your child as a pupil, how many other deserving applicants it has, how many other calls eg family emergency it has on its resources so, frustrating though it is, do not expect any school to give you a hard and fast rule of thumb on this.

Bursaries can be well worth considering if your family income fluctuates eg you live on short term contracts or on individual commissions. Actors and musicians often fall into this category. Schools should be flexible and understand that whereas one year your earnings may enable you to take a world cruise, the following year may see you going cap-in-hand from the in-laws to the bursar's office.

Assume that any school with charitable status, and many without, will offer bursaries. You will need to prove genuine need — no school should wish to risk falling foul of the Charities Commission – and you should not even consider being less than scrupulously honest in your application. Never be afraid to visit the bursar and discuss possibilities. That's what bursars are for. Never see a bursarial place as a stigma – rather as an honour – and the teaching staff will neither know nor care who is on a bursary or who owns half a county.

Charitable trusts

Charitable grant-making trusts can help in cases of genuine need. ISCias (the Independent Schools Council information and advice service) warns parents considering this route: 'Do not apply for an education grant for your child unless the circumstances are exceptional. The grant-giving trust will reject applications unless their requirements are satisfied.' The genuine needs recognised by the grant-making trusts are:

- boarding need, where the home environment is unsuitable because of the disability or illness of the parents or of siblings

- unforeseen family disaster, such as the sudden death of the breadwinner when a child is already at school

- need for continuity when a pupil is in the middle of a GCSE or A level course and a change in parental circumstances threatens withdrawal from school

- need for special education where there is a genuine recognised barrier to learning which cannot be catered for at a state school.

If you want to explore this, see Educational Grants Advice Service): +44 (0)1932 865619 www.educational-grants.org; or The Guide to Educational Grants by Sarah Johnston (specifically directed at funding for schoolchildren and students in need); or The Guide to the Major Trusts : Part 1 by Tom Traynor, Jude Doherty and Lucy Lernelius-Tonks; or The Directory of Grant Making Trusts by Tom Traynor or the Charities Digest.

Most come out annually with a year suffix to the title, and you should be able to find one or more in your local library.

Bargain hunting and help

Certain schools are relatively cheap. The Livery Companies, such as Haberdashers and Mercers, fund various schools, eg Haberdasher's Monmouth, Gresham's. Such schools are usually excellent value — not only cheap(er), but with good facilities.

Also offering value for money are the Girls' Day Schools Trust (GDST) schools – long-time providers of top quality academic and cultural education but less pricy than many of their competitors.

It may well be worth considering sending your child as a day pupil to a big strong boarding school. This way you will reap the benefits at a lesser price (although sometimes the day fees are unconscionably disproportionate). A new organisation – Springboard Bursary Foundation, headed by the former head of Blundell's School, Mr Ian Davenport – was launched in 2012, and says it aims to fund some 2,000 places for disadvantaged children at leading private and state boarding schools within a decade. This admirable sounding venture has yet to get up steam, but we watch with hope and enthusiasm and exhort parents to do the same.

Fees

Take care when you compare fees at different schools. Some quote an all-in fee, others seem cheaper but bolt on a load of compulsory 'extras' that can add an extra 25 per cent to the bill. We have noticed an increasing tendency to pop in items with a footnote (inertia selling) saying that 'unless you notify the school and deduct the amounts mentioned, it will automatically be charged to you'. For example, the Old Boys/Girls Society; the ISIS membership, your 'contribution' to charities. Do not be shy about deducting these sums from your cheque.

Insurance needs particular care. Often policies are taken out automatically unless you say otherwise — and we know of sickness policies on offer, for example, that only pay up once the child has been ill for at least eight days, but don't pay up for illnesses lasting longer than a term.

Bills may include:

- Lunches. Many day schools charge for these on top.

- Uniform. Many schools have a flourishing secondhand shop — Eton has several.

- Books. An extra in some schools.

- Trips. At some schools almost all included (bar holiday expeditions); at others you will pay even for ones that are part of the curriculum. The greater likelihood, though, is that trips that are nominally optional will be socially compulsory.

- Transport on school buses can be very steep at some day schools.
- Capital levy. Usually a large, one-off impost, supposedly to pay for new buildings.
- Special needs support such as one-to-one aid in classroom, dyslexia support or tutoring or EFL.
- Insurance.
- Unusual subjects eg languages, where there are fewer than, say, four in a class.
- Seriously hefty deposit on a firm offer of a place (£2,000 and rising in London) to try to stop well-off parents keeping their options open.
- Keeping up with the Joneses. In a money or status-conscious school, all sorts of possessions or expenditure may be required for a child to remain one of the in-crowd.

It may be wise to ask beady-eyed questions before you sign your first cheque.

Paying the fees

There are any number of wizard wheezes on the market. The schools that offer 'composition fees', which means, in a nutshell, you put a sum of money down one year and get a sum of money back later. The 'school fee specialists' that offer endowment-backed, mortgage-backed schemes and so on which, in effect, do the same thing. Either way, you are stepping into deep waters. Unless you totally understand what you are doing and all the implications — how the money is being invested, what the returns are, how it compares with any other investment, what the charges are, hidden and otherwise — we think it might be safest to avoid such schemes.

This does not mean you should not save and invest. The earlier you start, the better — obviously enough. We have commissioned a survey of the options: see Finance for Fees on our website.

Getting in and out of financial difficulties

If you do get into financial difficulties, you will not be alone, and schools are very used to this. Their attitude to bill-paying and money varies hugely. The best schools are wonderful and increasingly flexible over payment, allowing arrangements such as monthly instalments. Bursars are expecting this request — no shame attached. Indeed the bursar has changed from the enemy to being the father/mother confessor (with some notable exceptions — best description received: 'the bursar is a most evil toad').

A lot will depend on how well funded the school is: it is worth investigating this before you go any further. A few well-funded, rich schools will pick up the tab until further notice if you fall on hard times and your child is a good egg. Most will do their very best to see you through exam periods, but most poor schools simply cannot afford to do this for long, however much they may wish to.

Don't assume that because they are called 'charities' that they will be charitable to you. Some may send out the debt collectors. They will hold you to the small print — one term's payment or one term's notice to quit really means it. They may well threaten to take you to court — although of course it will be an extremely different matter if your child is especially bright.

In these cold times, it is a wise school that reciprocates the loyalty of its parents by allowing them to postpone payment, knowing that they will honour the debt when they can. Of course the school has to have the financial strength to afford this — and the parent has to have shown the loyalty.

Action

1. Speak to the head. Mothers (and sometimes fathers) may burst into tears at this point.

2. The head will immediately direct you to the bursar.

3. Explain your position — as optimistically, positively and realistically as possible.

4. Hope for flexible arrangements: monthly payments or deferred payment.

5. Have all the scholarships gone? Is there a spare bursary?

6. Assess the situation. How vital is it to keep your child in this school? Will the world fall apart if he/she leaves now?

7. If you really feel it is vital the child stays put, try touching a relation for a loan/gift. Grandparents are still the number one source of school fees. Investigate the possibility of an extra mortgage.

8. And if it is not vital, start looking for state alternatives. See Entrance – State Sector (page 52).

Come and see us at
The Unicorn School
for the Dyslexic Child

The Unicorn School

A unique school offering dyslexic children every opportunity to gain confidence and develop skills to enable them to reach their full potential.

- Daily individual 1:1 lessons.
- Speech Therapy.
- Occupational Therapy.
- Sporting activities including team sports and sailing.

The children and staff at the Unicorn School would like to extend a warm welcome to all who come and visit us.

The Unicorn School,
20 Marcham Road, Abingdon,
Oxon OX14 AA

Tel: 01235 530222
E-mail: info@unicorndyslexia.co.uk
www.unicorndyslexia.co.uk

A Special Educational Need or a Passing Phase?

Special educational needs (SEN) affect all social classes and intellects. Children do not outgrow SEN but, with help, learn to cope. Some children with special needs are readily identified, others develop coping strategies — children can use common sense, quick-wittedness, intelligence and other virtues (or vices) to disguise the effects of an SEN. Later, particularly when public exams loom and youngsters are openly 'measured' against their peers, they may lack self-esteem and become increasingly anxious. We have come across cases where severe dyslexia has been diagnosed in mid A level when the adaptability finally ran out.

Bright but undiagnosed severe dyslexics have even made it to Oxbridge. The list of talented people with a special educational need is a long one but includes such well-known personalities as: Richard Branson, Cher, Leonardo Da Vinci, Albert Einstein, Bill Gates, Keira Knightley, Michael Phelps, Steve Redgrave, Stephen Spielberg and Virginia Woolf.

Signs of special educational needs in school-age children

Most children will experience some of the symptoms listed to a lesser or greater extent but, if you can count off more than three or four and have concerns, it may be time to consider enlisting extra help. These are all characteristics of normal childhood too, which is why some SENs are difficult to spot. Importantly, don't wait for teachers to flag up difficulties; parents, with their holistic knowledge of their child are often the first to spot difficulties. Unless a school tests every child (and some now screen all children on entry — worries about future litigation abound), some children will be missed.

Look out for the child who:

- Is easily distracted.
- Generates distraction or is considered the class clown.
- Engages in disruptive or aggressive behaviour.
- Gets angry with themselves, often over seemingly trivial issues. May be a perfectionist and/or have demonstrably low self-esteem.
- Does not enjoy school.
- Becomes stressed when starting tasks or when asked to work on their own.
- Is reluctant to do homework, especially unaided.
- Makes little or no progress at school (some children may even regress).
- Avoids reading or takes no pleasure from it.
- Can read but reads slowly.
- Has good eyesight but is monosyllabic when reading aloud (or may refuse to read out loud). May struggle to scan text.
- Declares they 'hate maths' when in reality 'they don't get it'.
- Is disorganised — late settling to work, last to finish packing up and leaving the classroom. 'Forgets' to do homework or revise for tests.
- Forgets what the task is; has trouble remembering more than two or three instructions at once.
- Has spider hand-writing; presentation of work is messy and paintings indecipherable.
- Is articulate but can't or won't put pen to paper.
- Has an awkward pencil grip. May have difficulty remembering where to start writing and/or struggle to copy accurately from the board.
- Bumps into things, is clumsy and has poor spatial awareness. May have difficulty hopping, jumping or catching a ball and will literally trip over own feet.
- Hears but frequently mis-hears what is said.
- May be able to repeat sentences verbatim but not comprehend meaning or grasp nuance.
- Finds making and sustaining friendships problematic, even avoiding social contact altogether.
- May be shy and withdrawn and/or avoid eye-contact altogether.
- Has difficulty with change: can find even pleasant surprises upsetting.
- Has parents with these symptoms!

When should I ask for my child to be helped?

You don't have to have a formal diagnosis to request help for your child. If you suspect your child has a 'learning difference' or difficulty, or you're just worried about them, seek advice; your child's class teacher, the school SENCo, GP or health-visitor are good starting points. Depending on the type of need and your circumstances, help may be available before your child starts school.

A Lesson in **Education**

Independent
Show
SCHOOLS
LONDON 2014

the **essential event** for all parents

Battersea Evolution
Battersea Park London
Saturday 8th November 10:00 - 17:00
Sunday 9th November 10:30 - 16:30

*" Thank you very much! I had to drag
a reluctant hubby along in the pouring rain, so was
not in the most positive frame of mind for attending,
but both of us got so much out of the show.
We feel far more positive about the future of our children. "*

ISS Visitor 2013

simply register online at **www.schoolsshow.com**
and claim your **free** tickets

Meeting over **190** top independent schools
is just a walk in the park

What can I expect?

Teachers and others working with children are becoming notably more alert to SEN, and supportive of formal assessment. Many schools now routinely screen for specific learning difficulties and a good classroom teacher will be alert to special needs. However, formal assessment for SEN is not something a classroom teacher can do; they have neither the time nor the training. It is carried out by educational psychologists (EP). Don't be put off by the title: the good ones are friendly, helpful and accommodating. If you have any reason to suspect your child has special or additional needs, consider getting a formal assessment. A good EP will administer a battery of well-proven tests in a way that your child will find interesting, even fun, rather than frightening. They will produce a detailed written report that describes your child's educational characteristics and the reasons for them and clearly explains any terminology used as well as the impact of their findings. Generally, that's it — no further analysis or treatment, though you may want a progress report after a few years. An EP's report (especially one from an EP known to the school) can be a most marvellous lever in your dealings with a school: 'He did this, because you did that — as you should have expected, because it says so here'. Closest thing in this world to the Elder Wand.

Helping the child who is struggling at school

The type of school and provision that you should look for will depend very much on your child's abilities and on the extent to which their disability affects their learning. Consider the extent to which your child's disability is affecting their progress: you want a school that happily talks of successes with pupils who face similar challenges and is at least as interested in your child's ability, talents and interests as they are in their difficulties or differences.

Typically SEN children will need additional or special assistance or consideration to put them on a level playing field with their peers. For some, equality can be achieved by relatively simple measures: having a scribe or being given extra time in exams; for others, even specialist equipment and many-to-one teaching will not make life equable.

The Good Schools Guide online www.goodschoolsguide.co.uk features schools for children with a range of special needs; in this guide we include a number of dyslexia specialist schools as well as many mainstream schools that offer good provision for children with mild to moderate SEN, dyslexia and related specific learning difficulties. On the whole, these schools subscribe to the view that the needs of the learner take centre stage.

They are likely to:

- Teach a child one thing 20 ways (if required), not 20 things one way.
- Understand the learning processes and work diagnostically, closely monitoring, recording and reviewing progress and using that as a catalyst for further learning.
- Use multi-sensory learning and teaching styles.
- Understand that when a child's needs are not being met and seek to address those shortcomings.
- Actively assist with access arrangements.

- Work with parents/carers to agree suitable strategies for the child.
- Have some specialist help on hand.
- Listen to parents and act on their concerns.

Choosing a school

Choose your school with care: don't assume any school with a good special needs department will be perfect. A sympathetic special needs coordinator (SENCo) is a great starting point, but the head's attitude to special needs will have a pervasive influence on the school; if the head is cautious you should be wary. Timely (and possibly individual) intervention is great, but will only be really effective if set against a backdrop of understanding across all teaching and support staff. A child doesn't abandon their difficulties when they leave the learning support department. A dyslexic child may well have a very high verbal and/or non-verbal IQ yet struggle to read, scan, write or spell. If a child has poor memory or processing difficulties these will, if left unattended, impact on their overall progress and subsequent self-esteem. Dyslexia may be mainly associated with reading and writing, but it affects more than just English lessons: the writing and sequencing demands of history can be a problem; similarly, the multi-tasking of many sports can create difficulties for the dyslexic and/or the dyspraxic child if the coaching style is not empathetic. A child with Asperger's may be desperate to join in activities and to mix with others but require support and reassurance to do so — not just in the classroom but on the sports pitch, in the playground and beyond.

Which school?

There are many other schools in this guide whose SEN provision may suit your particular child. If a school appears perfect, get in touch and find out how they would be prepared to help – you may be surprised by the response. Schools offer a range of provision from fairly minimal intervention to tailor-made curricula; read the reviews with care and check online too www.goodschoolsguide.co.uk to view the school's response to our online SEN survey.

If you're choosing a mainstream school for a child with a relatively mild/moderate SEN, request a copy of the school's special educational needs policy and (if the school is independent) ask how much extra you will have to pay for the support that you want.

A good school will:

- Test /screen all children, for SEN, on entry or at the first sign of any difficulties.
- Likely have other pupils in the school with special needs supported by qualified specialist teachers.
- Ensure special needs support is an integral part of the school, with a two-way flow of information between specialists and subject teachers. Schools where SEN support is an 'add on', are really only suitable for very mild cases.
- Give careful consideration to what a pupil will miss out on to receive extra help.
- Have a supportive head. If the head is not enthusiastic about helping SEN children staff may not be as supportive or understanding as they should be.

- Seek to build self-esteem — to find something your child is good at and encourage your child's areas of strength.

- Use multi-sensory learning and teaching methods with lessons in relatively short sections.

- Have full regard to the SEN code of practice and make use of concessions for exams, such as providing a laptop, or an amanuensis and train children in the use of these. For public examination concessions you will need an up-to-date educational psychologist's report.

Never ask 'Is this the best you can do?' For some children with SENs pastoral care can be as important as specialist understanding of a particular disability.

When you visit, talk to some pupils with the same diagnosis as your child — are they bubbling with pride and confidence?

Boarding Schools

Traditionally, heartless British parents sent their little darlings off to school at seven or eight and didn't give them another thought until it was time for university. Tom Brown's schooldays? Go to the bottom of the class. Cold showers, initiation ceremonies and enforced runs are more or less a thing of the past.

So why board? It depends on where you live. If you happily live near a seriously good state or independent day school, and that is the most rewarding solution either morally or financially, then don't even think about it. If you live in the depths of the country or overseas, or both work long hours, then boarding may be your answer.

But beware, boarding schools are not a universal panacea. Putting your child in boarding school implies partnership and trust between school and parent. It is no use sending your utterly revolting child away to school and assuming you will get an angel back at half-term: boarding schools can, and will, expel your child for a variety of reasons (drugs, serious bad behaviour, bullying etc) and you will probably have no recourse. So think carefully before you embark on what can be a seriously expensive process. This can often be ameliorated by scholarships, bursaries, state boarding schools, kindly grandparents, employment benefits or Forces' Continuity of Education allowance. In the case of the last you can't just chop and change schools at will but must stick with the one you first thought of.

Do not be taken in by charming heads or their marketing genies entertaining you with PowerPoint presentations and handing out DVDs (always taken on sunny days and always displaying the best of everything). Again, give some thought to what sort of character you want your child to turn out to be. Boarding schools, because they enfold your child for so much of the year, will make a substantial contribution to their character, and different boarding schools mould character in very different ways. You will never pick this up from the school's marketing material: they all want to appear blandly wonderful.

The Good Schools Guide does its best to capture the character of a school, and you should be able to get a taste of it when you visit. Have a clear view, too, of where you want your child to go on to next. It is easier to get a guide to whether a school is the right place for this ambition: all schools publish lists of where their pupils go on to, and if the education that they provide and the spirit that they inculcate is capable of taking your child where you want them to go, then other children will have gone that way before, probably in some numbers.

Meet matron

When looking for potential schools, be sure to meet your child's likely houseparents and the matron as well as the head. These three are the ones who really make a difference to the day-to-day happiness of a boarder. And if your child is to have a tutor who stays with them throughout their time at school, meet them too. Get the home phone number of whoever has charge of your child's welfare, and ask if you can call at any time.

Ask how parent and child communicate. Weekly letter? A phone for each 50 pupils? Or nightly emails and a mobile phone? This is definitely something to talk to pupils about when you visit.

Be relentlessly questioning about any requirements which are particular to you. If your child has special educational needs (and there are many boarding schools in the UK which make superb provision for these) you will need to know exactly what is on offer, and how the school proposes to make you part of the decision-making process on such questions as whether to include or exclude your child from particular lessons. How good are the EFL lessons, and how much extra do they cost? What provision do they make for your faith? Don't just take this on trust, talk to a co-religionist who is already at the school and find out what really happens. If you live overseas, see Applying to a British School from Abroad (page 45).

Some problems that are easily tackled by local parents become much harder to deal with when a parent is distant. Discover whether matron will replenish (and mend) school (and home) clothes and if she can do it out of the secondhand shop. At the very same time you can be sussing out whether matron, and the under matrons, are cuddly, or moustachioed dragons who grump. Find out if boarders are allowed into town at weekends. How does the school control what they get up to? How can parents ditto? It helps a lot if a child has a bolt hole in town where they can go rather than be dragged into some den of iniquity by their friends because they have no alternative. Do you have a friend or relative who is willing to let them have a key?

The same problem of distance applies to bullying. Being able to recharge courage and self-confidence at home makes a child much more resilient in the face of low-level bullying than a child who has no such resort. Don't be satisfied with the mere absence of stories about bullying; look for stories (particularly from gentler pupils) about how well bullying is dealt with.

If you leave boarding until your child has done his/her GCSEs or equivalent they'll have developed a reasonable degree of maturity and independence. Many schools now have expanded sixth forms and happily take children either from the UK (state or other independent schools) or from further afield for a two-year sixth form course leading to A levels or an IB and university entrance globally. Take care to suit the school to the student: the range of styles is particularly broad at this age, from the disciplinarian academic to the 'almost university'.

State boarding

State boarding schools are a well-kept secret. They charge for board and lodging, but not tuition, so are vastly cheaper than their private counterparts – usually between £10,000 and £15,000 a year. Some have only a small number of boarding places, in some around half the school boards; some are academically selective, some not; many have facilities to rival the independent sector. For more information, take at look at http://www.sbsa.org.uk/index.php.

Remember that not all boarding schools are in the UK. Most European countries have one or two. Switzerland has some which follow the English academic syllabus (although many 'Swiss boarding schools' no longer live up to their almost mythical reputation for academic excellence), and so do many of the Middle and Far Eastern countries. Some follow the traditional British A level syllabus and some the IB. Ditto Australia and New Zealand (which have several really great boarding schools). There's less boarding in the Americas, though Canada and especially the US have a surprising number of very good ones, and there are a few in South America — particularly in former British colonies. And then there's Africa. There are schools in South Africa that appear to be so British the only real difference is the minuscule fees (but caveat emptor ... as is true anywhere, there are still cultural differences beneath the surface).

NB Some of the above schools have made the cut in our sister publication, The Good Schools Guide International, and some have not.

Our writers have experienced boarding schools as expats and as locals, as members of families who have used boarding schools for generations and as parents who are tackling boarding for the first time. All of them confirm that, in the words of one editor, 'boarding schools can be brilliant, children make friends for life, share the experiences and cultures, and learn tolerance for their fellow man'. That said, there are still many children who end up miserable: you need to take care to match the child to the school, and to watch how things develop thereafter. It should be totally obvious if things are going well.

Applying to a British School From Abroad

Most UK schools are now genuinely thrilled to welcome foreign students, and no longer regard a cosmopolitan mix as a matter for shame (that they cannot fill the school with home-grown products). Foreign students are perceived to add breadth, excitement, new horizons, not to mention fantastic exam results in exotic languages (Turkish, Norwegian, Polish, Mandarin, Japanese, Gujerati, Urdu among the most common), high intelligence (often), motivation and — last but not least — cash.

The best schools in this country are outstanding by any standards. Beware, though, of being fobbed off with second-rate places.

A few thoughts for parents looking to send their children to a British boarding school:

1. Look for a school that is popular with the British, as well as with foreigners. Read the reviews in this book to get a feel for that and, better still, talk to personal contacts if possible.

2. Do not assume a school is good simply because it is famous: an obvious point, but you would be surprised how many people believe famous equals good.

3. Do not be over-reliant on exam result league tables. Many overseas parents come see us waving newspaper league tables and considering only the schools in the highest echelons. A school's high placement on league tables may owe more to its selective intake than to the quality of the education. See What the League Tables Don't Tell You on page 31

4. Beware educational agencies that will 'place' your child in a British school for you for free. Such agents are usually paid fat commissions by the schools they recommend, and may be reluctant to mention those schools that do not pay them a commission (this includes many of the best ones). Equally, you should not need to pay many thousands of pounds for a 'guaranteed place'.

5. Always go and see a school you are interested in yourself, and bring your child if possible.

6. If a school says it has got 'provision' for teaching English as a Foreign Language (EFL) ask exactly what that provision consists of, and whether it will cost extra. EFL teachers need to have a proper teaching degree/ diploma AND an EFL qualification: the latter alone means very little. However quick at learning your child is, he/she will certainly struggle at public exam level without a sound knowledge of English — the pressure of work is just too high.

7. If your child is genuinely outstanding academically, musically, sports-wise or in some other way, make sure to tell the school, providing evidence if possible. When we say outstanding we mean the very best in his or her or current class or in an even larger pool. En passant, be prepared to 'sell' yourself a bit to the school too if you eg have a fascinating line of work (think Russian cosmonaut!).

8. Be on guard against worthless scholarships. We have seen several schools offering 'scholarships' with zero, or miniscule, financial value to overseas pupils. If you like the school, fine, but don't let the 'scholarship' sway you.

9. You will usually be asked to appoint a UK guardian for your child — someone with whom the school can deal on day-to-day matters, and whom your child can turn to for help, outings and so on. Don't try to get by without – we get stories every year of a child who has surreptitiously taken himself off to a London bed and breakfast each school holiday. Handy grandparents, godparents, cousins make logistical sense but you may well opt for paid guardians. Read Finding a Guardian on page 47.

10. Take care with your timing. The best ages to come into a British independent school from abroad are anytime up to age 11, and the ages 13 and 16. 14 can work well, but only at schools that didn't fill up at 11 and 13. Do not try to get a child into school mid-GCSE (aged 15) or mid-A level (aged 17).

11. Check out how full the 'full boarding' is. There is an increasing tendency in the UK towards 'weekly' and 'flexi' boarding where pupils can go home any weekend they want and even mid-week. If you live overseas, this can be bad news. It's best, if you can, to opt for a 'full' boarding school, which has a proper programme of activities at weekends. A few schools have flexible exeats so that the school is never closed during term time, except at half-term. But check how many children of your child's age consistently stay at school at weekends.

12. Ask prospective schools how many pupils from your country will be in your child's year – fewer means more opportunities to learn English; more means an easier landing.

13. 'International Study Centres' offer pre-boarding school programmes for non-English speakers and there are now loads of them attached to existing boarding schools. Pupils learn English while studying a slimmed down range of subjects like maths and science. Typically they spend a year at the school before moving on to a mainstream boarding school. These can work well for the child who arrives with no English, but they are a pricey option. Make sure to ask for a full list of their leavers' destinations.

14. Don't over-commit yourself too much on the school fees front that you can't - if need be - fly over in an emergency.

15. Try to accompany your child for the first day at a new school. It helps to know the layout, meet the matron, the housemaster and tutor. Explore the school together; it makes communication that much easier in the future.

Brockhurst and Marlston House Preparatory Schools

Boys and Girls 3 – 13 years. Day and Boarding

We offer a unique education with small single-sex classes and shared extra-curricular activities at the centre of which is a magnificent Jacobean style mansion set in stunning Berkshire countryside yet only forty minutes from Heathrow Airport.

At Brockhurst (boys) and Marlston House (girls) Schools our dedicated and experienced staff will be at the heart of your child's education offering a range of learning experiences to include the gifted and talented on extended learning programmes, EAL taught in very small groups, and support for pupils with learning difficulties thus meeting the specific needs of each child, all combined in the newly opened Learning Development Centre.

We pride ourselves on
- Happy, well mannered children within a family atmosphere for the 3-13 age range
- Preparing children for entry to leading independent schools
- Pupils regularly gain academic, art, music and all-rounder scholarships.

We have outstanding facilities with 21 acres of games fields within a 500 acre site
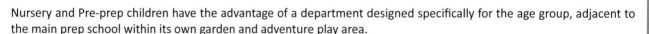
- A sports hall, indoor 25m Swimming Pool, Tennis Courts
- Art and Design Studios,
- ICT suite
- Learning Development Centre (2011) and a superb Equestrian School.

- 18th-century chateau in SW France where our pupils practise their French.
- Full/ flexi and weekly boarding

Nursery and Pre-prep children have the advantage of a department designed specifically for the age group, adjacent to the main prep school within its own garden and adventure play area.

NEW MUSIC SCHOOL AND PERFORMING ARTS CENTRE OPENING 2014

Marlston Road, Hermitage, Berkshire RG18 9UL
t: 01635 200293   e: registrar@brockmarl.org.uk
www.brockmarl.org.uk

Finding a Guardian

British boarding schools will not admit an overseas pupil under the age of 18 unless he or she has a local guardian. It can seem an unnecessary annoyance, especially for older children, but most schools have had enough grim experiences (such as children left unclaimed on day one of the Christmas holidays) that they have learned to demand it.

Guardians perform several roles. They provide a place for your child to stay during the — sometimes numerous — school holidays (and many schools also have compulsory exeats and half-term breaks when all pupils have to vamoose). Guardians may also need to serve as your representatives, making some decisions for your child, signing forms, attending parents' evenings and being available in an emergency — for instance, if your child falls ill or is temporarily or permanently excluded from school (it happens more often than you think). Guardians may need to assist with transport to and from school or from airports etc. In addition, guardians are sometimes required to act as a sort of bank, doling out pocket money, funds for school trips etc. In general, the younger the pupil, the more comprehensive the service will need to be.

How do you find a guardian? Start by asking friends in your own country who have used one. If they had a good experience with a firm, there is a good chance you will too.

If you don't know anyone who has used a guardian, then ask the school your child will be attending. Most schools will be reluctant to recommend one guardianship firm — they don't want to be responsible if you end up with a duff one — but if you ask them to name a few companies that have supplied guardians for their pupils in the past, schools will often give you good leads. Schools have a lot of experience with guardians and will be likely to know of the smaller, more local (and perhaps less expensive) firms that may be just what you need. Be on guard, however, if a school is tied to one particular firm. There may be a financial relationship between the two that can lead to a conflict of interest — do you really want your guardian in cahoots with the school when Johnny and his housemaster have a conflict that you would like the guardian to help resolve?

Many schools will point you towards one of two accredited associations of guardians. The largest of these is the Association for the Education and Guardianship of International Students (Aegis) (www.aegisuk.net, email secretary@aegisuk.net). Aegis members include such giants in the field as Gabbitas and Sutherland Education. Members of this organisation are vetted and insured and all their host families are carefully checked.

There are, of course, alternatives to using a professional guardianship agency. The first choice for most expat Brits, and for many foreign families, is to house children with British relatives. The benefits are that it is cheap and the guardian is likely to have a genuine interest in the welfare of the child. On the downside, relatives may be working people who will find a long journey to fetch their cousin's wife's niece a bind, not to mention looking after her for a week or more, or even between terms. Financial arrangements with relatives can also become a strain, as they will need to pay out in advance for your child's travel expenses, entertainment, clothes etc. Occasionally, schools will not accept relatives as guardians if they live very far away from the school.

Language schools and tutorial colleges will sometimes have families on their books who can take in older teenagers, thereby sidestepping guardianship firms. You will need to find out how carefully the families have been checked and whether there is any back-up from the school if the family can no longer fulfil its role. You should also ask for references on the families (ideally from pupils who have previously lodged with them) and check them rigorously.

Some parents try to dispense with formal guardians all together, looking to house their child with the local exile community in exchange for some light work. Parents of older teenagers often ask if they can billet their youngsters in a bed and breakfast during school holidays rather than fuss with the expense of guardians. While we admire their ingenuity, these parents are leaving themselves open to trouble if anything goes wrong. And you would be amazed how things can go wrong. Schools sometimes find themselves on the phone to guardianship agencies at the last minute asking for help with a student whose guardian has proved to be non-existent.

Ideally you will want to meet the family your child will be staying with. If that is impossible, you can cover a lot of ground on the telephone or via email.

Questions for guardianship firms:

1. What exactly will I be paying for? Go through this with a fine-toothed comb. You do not want to pay for more than you will need, nor do you want to be caught short.

2. Will my child be able to stay with the same family throughout the time they are educated in the UK?

3. Can my child move to a different host family if things don't work out?

4. Do you offer 24-hour cover in case of an emergency?

5. Are you fully insured?

6. Who will be the legal guardian — the host family or the director of the guardianship firm? Who should my child contact if he or she is having a problem? It is key that you establish this because in many firms the appointed guardian is actually the director of the firm, not the host family.

7. How do you choose and inspect your guardians? Are they CRB (now DBS – Disclosure and Barring Service) checked?

8. Will my child's host family have other overseas pupils staying with them? Will the others speak my child's language (there are pros and cons)?

Questions for the host family:

1. Do you have children of your own? What ages?

2. Have you been a guardian before?

3. What are your rules on television viewing, homework, going out with friends, use of telephone and computer, drinking (for older teenagers) etc?

4. What will the arrangements be for pocket money and my child's other financial needs?

Emergencies can arise when you least expect them – travel problems, perhaps, or sudden infectious illness – that need someone who is on hand 24 hours a day to sort them out. And, as one pupil said, 'guardians are the people who make a different country like home.'

What to Look for on a School Visit

You may be one of hundreds of parents on a school open day, or meet the head as part of a select group. Either way, you can glean a lot about how the school is likely to suit your child and your family.

- What do you want for your child? Make a list of what matters to your family and the kind of education you think would suit your son or daughter. Much depends on parents' own educational experience and this can raise strong emotions – old school days are not always fondly remembered. And don't forget to ask your child what he or she wants…

- Is it looking good? A school should appear at its best at the start of a new academic year. This doesn't mean everything should be new, but if the fabric is already looking shabby or dilapidated (ditto the staff) that could tell you something about resources or morale.

- Make sure you attend the head's talk – does she fire you with enthusiasm? Did he make you nod off? This is a head's big moment and if you leave feeling uninspired it might be time for a rethink.

- What's it really like? Take a tour with pupils – it might start out polite and formal but if you're friendly and ask enough questions you'll learn plenty 'off message'. Are they obviously proud of their school?

- If you're there during a school day, do lessons seem lively but under control? Are you likely to be trampled to death whilst crossing the playground? Are there huddled groups smoking in corners? Could you see your child happily settled here?

- If the atmosphere seems relaxed, is your child likely to flourish or run riot? If it is tightly controlled, will she welcome the structure or kick against the pricks?

- Top marks? Parents consistently put academic performance at the top of their checklist, but league tables don't tell the whole story. Great exam results may be the desired destination, but what of the journey? School websites usually publish past years' results so look at these for trends. Don't just focus on the subjects offered at GCSE or A level, you should also consider what isn't on offer (see What the League Tables Don't Tell you, page 31).

- A selective school that creams off the brightest students will always perform well, but what about value added? This is the differential between the attainment levels of pupils when they enter and leave; if your child isn't a high flyer you need to be sure that the school can support and enable him or her to achieve their potential.

- Check out loos, litter and lunches if you can. Little things can make a big difference to a child's feeling of wellbeing and, by extension, their ability to learn.

- Sport for all? Prospectus designers love actions shots – rugby, tennis, hockey, polo even – but check out the fixtures. Is it only the A teams that get matches and specialist coaching? In a co-ed school, do the girls get equal opportunities and kudos?

- Check out the noticeboards. Are they full of fixtures and photos, messages about upcoming events, clubs and outings? Not everything promised in the prospectus necessarily materialises.

- What do the neighbours say? It's worth checking out a school's local reputation, especially if you are new to the area. Ask taxi drivers or nearby shopkeepers, buttonhole people with children of a similar age to yours.

Careers Departments and How to Judge Them

The careers department, too often that neglected airless cubicle occupied by uninspiring books and a sidelined teacher, could (if it is any good) make a big difference to the value your child gets out of his or her years of education (and perhaps a good deal of your money too). No school can now command places for its students at the best universities, so what they teach their pupils ought to be aimed as much at the lives which will follow university as at those dreaded examinations — and the careers department ought to be a strong part of that focus. Undergraduates who started the career decision-making process at school will be likely to make better, more focused, use of their time at university, and do much better at the gladiatorial pre-graduation milk round than their unprepared counterparts.

The Coalition has more-or-less abolished the Connexions system that paid careers professionals to give face-to-face advice to pupils – it now mostly exists only online. Schools are now expected to provide their own careers advice but are not given any extra funding for this, and evidence suggests that it is patchy at best.

Some schools seem to bundle the assistance that they give to pupils in choosing university courses in with 'careers advice', and lump the two subjects together as 'careers and further education'. There is some logic in this for those few professions where particular subjects and degree courses are required, but for the vast majority of pupils the choice of degree will have little consequence for what they do afterwards.

A school which has begun to wake up to the benefits of good careers advice will have appointed an impressive (is your child going to follow advice from someone who is not?) 'head of careers', sometimes supported by a small team of helpers. Some will go to the trouble of arranging the school's annual (or, worse, bi-annual) careers fair, rounding up recent alumni and parents to talk to the pupils (not that this guarantees coverage of the best options, or depth of wisdom). If they are doing better than this, then you are in luck.

Here are some questions for the head of careers or headteacher (or a sixth former); just pick a few that appeal to you.

1. How do you make your pupils interesting to future employers? Have those who study sciences read a novel or learnt a language? Are your arts students numerate? How do you advise your pupils to present themselves in all respects ranging from the sartorial to the written word (letters and emails) and body language? Do you provide advice and training on CV writing and successful interview technique — after all, the job interview process normally has a significant subjective element and those candidates who have a polished CV and are skilled at interview technique will normally do better than those candidates who arrive at the interview unprepared.

2. How do you make pupils aware of their various career options? Have they been exposed to people who understand what particular careers are really about? How large is the careers team and what are their roles? Are they employed full-time or part-time? This should help you determine whether the school defines 'filling in university application forms' as 'careers advice'.

3. Does the school actively seek work experience opportunities for its senior pupils? If so, what is the process? How much time is spent with pupils one-to-one helping them to think about their career options? Do they programme sessions or do they sit back and 'provide a service' to which pupils can go to if they are sufficiently interested? Is advice offered to them about leadership qualities and the attractiveness of this trait to future employers?

4. Does the school contact university careers departments to bridge the work that they (the school) have been doing, in order that the university careers department can continue to advise? What advice is given to pupils on the best use of their gap year for adding to their attractiveness to future employers?

5. Now find a sixth former or two. Do their experiences with the careers department bear any resemblance to what you have just been told? What sort of advice have they been offered on choosing a course, perhaps one that they haven't studied at school eg anthropology? Have they had good advice on writing their personal statements? Have Oxbridge/medical candidates had practice interviews and entrance exams? Have they been encouraged to aim high or to aim safe? Some of the highest ranking schools offer surprisingly little help.

A Quiet Word About Child Protection

With reports of schools refusing to let parents attend sports days or take photos of their children in nativity plays, it can be easy to assume to child protection policies can over-rule common sense. However, recent highly-publicised cases of child abuse in schools (some music schools and faith schools seem to be particularly prone) are a stark reminder that those very people who smilingly welcome our children into their care at school might be the last people to whom we would entrust them, did we know all.

It can be hard to keep a sense of proportion faced with the emotional battering from media and pressure groups. Things were much worse in the past; prisons would have been full of school staff, and older pupils, had current rules applied 40 years ago. Schools, and society generally, have improved out of all recognition. Successive governments have legislated to protect children and the abuses of the past are now far less likely to happen. Indeed it may seem that the pendulum has swung too far, with the demand that more-or-less any volunteer must get a CRB — now called DBS — check.

We take the view that parents should trust schools, but should nonetheless be on their guard. The effects of abuse can be horrid and life-long. Children tend to keep their miseries to themselves. The film Chosen — www.chosen. org.uk — is an uncomfortably well-made documentary of suffering that was once commonplace.

Parents do well to warn their children — gently but seriously — of the dangers, however remote these may be, so they feel that it is easy to speak to you should they meet them. It is worth pointing out that abuse can come from anyone — even a teacher or an adult they know well.

It is also worth thinking about raising your own antennae at any school you may be considering. Most prospective parents feel awkward enough asking head teachers about exam results or careers advice without the almost unbearable discomfort of probing them on how they protect pupils from teachers and other adults. Which is why parents almost never bring it up.

Keep your questions neutral and matter-of-fact. As always, much can be gleaned from the head's attitude — and eyes — when questions about child protection are asked. Is he or she ill at ease? Dismissive? Or are they happy to engage, and proud of the steps their school has taken?

Openness is what you're looking for. Do not rule out a school because a case of abuse has been brought to light there. Tabloid coverage can be the price the school has to pay for handling a case of abuse or bullying honourably and openly.

After You've Chosen a School

You've been and looked at your shortlist and made a decision about where you want your child to go. What next? The path is different in the state and independent sectors but get armed with all the information as soon as you can, the process of entrance can be long and convoluted.

If, once your child is in a school, he or she tells you about being miserable/homesick/bullied — believe them. Act at once by telephoning the school and explaining the problem. If the problem persists, consider taking your child out of the school and finding another, more compatible one. Better a temporary disruption to your child's schooling than permanent damage.

Entrance — state sector

State schools in England

Start looking early — you may need to move house. Get the admissions booklets from your Local Authority, and any neighbouring Local Authority whose schools you might consider — they should give you a good idea of what you will have to do to get in. Apply for your chosen schools a good year before the likely date of entry if they are not part of a 'co-ordinated admissions policy' (see below).

Geographical location is one of the key factors in admission criteria. This can be defined many different ways — distance as the crow flies, distance by a safe route, catchment area, previous school attended etc — and liable to change each year as applications vary. Parents have been known to rent houses within the requisite area of the school in order to establish residence there, or 'borrow' an address, or invent one. Heads of schools particularly affected have resorted to peeking through letterboxes to see if there's someone really living there, or asking to see electricity bills — '£10 for the quarter and you say you were living there ...'

Getting into the nursery class at a primary school does not guarantee admission to the main school and, vice versa, you do not usually have a lesser chance of getting into the main school if you choose another nursery school.

For all England, there is a system of co-ordinated admissions arrangements, and applications are all (or almost all) made through the local authority. You will be faced with arrangements that require you to state your preferences in order of priority. You put the schools that you like (up to three, usually, but six in some places) in order of preference; the Local Authority passes your application on to the schools concerned but does not tell them what position they are on your list. NB If you are applying to a faith school, you will almost certainly have to fill in a supplementary form (generally available from the school) detailing your adherence to the particular faith.

Each school then assesses its applicants against its admissions criteria and tells the Local Authority who it will accept. The Local Authority looks to see what acceptances you have received, and passes on to you the acceptance that you gave the highest priority to — let's say that it is number 2 on your list — and that is where, barring appeals, you go. Or is it? Because schools will have had some of their acceptances disregarded by the Local Authority (because parents have put another acceptance higher up their list) they will have some unfilled places, for which they will issue acceptances to children who just missed the cut on the first round. If your child gets offered a place by your number 1 choice in this way, then you can choose to go there and rescind your place at number 2. Up to a dozen rounds may be required to sort everyone out. Complicated for the Local Authority? Certainly. Uncertain for schools? Indeed so. But wonderful for parents and something to be grateful to the last government for.

Take care, though, that you have a rock-solid case for getting into at least one of the schools you are aiming at or you're liable to land up in a dump if none of your long-shots hit.

If you get what appears to be a 'no' on any count you have the right of appeal, stating to an appeal committee why you think little Edna should go to Grunts and not St Dumps. One of the most successful reasons seems to be health: if you can get a doctor's letter stating that your ewe lamb gets asthma and will only flourish in the pure air of Grunts, you are half-way there. Like any other appeal you need to lobby like mad — the head, the governors, the doctor, the local authority, your MP, the lollipop man — whoever seems good to you. The admissions section of the Department for Education website www.education.gov.uk has hitherto been a good place to bone up on appeals procedures. However, up-to-date guidance from your Local Authority is the best reliable source of help. Don't get your hopes up too high — 70 per cent of appeals fail. Some small businesses and other organisations offer help with appeals, and claim that they double your chances — we don't endorse any, but you can find names on our website.

You must study the current version of the particular (and often peculiar) admissions criteria of each school that interests you — and do take a look at the catchment area maps on our website. Key factors are usually:

A 'banding' system to ensure that their intake is a fair reflection of the ability spectrum of their applicants or neighbourhood — this inevitably leads to different geographical limits for each ability band — you may need a local tutor to help your child do badly. Some schools set bands according to national averages, others according to applications made to the school (so loads of applications from on-the-ball parents will push up the percentage of their children in the school).

Sibling policies are a real pain if you're trying to get your first-born into a school — geographical boundaries can fluctuate wildly year by year, depending on the percentage of places taken up in this way. Thereafter, of course, they are a real blessing. It is noticeable in our catchment area maps how many families, having secured the first place, move out to nicer — and cheaper — houses.

Ballots are starting to appear in popular city schools. If there's an over-subscription, places will be allocated by random ballot. No known way of working this system to your advantage, and when lots of schools in an area ballot for entry it can lead to parents having no effective influence on where their child goes. Works best when it's only the occasional school in an area, or for out-of-catchment pupils only.

Religion. Some of the best UK schools have a religious foundation, and are more or less devoted to educating children of that religion. You need to start attending church weekly at least a year before conception to have a chance at some schools. Make sure that you have thoroughly studied the admission requirements of the schools that interest you. Do it now. As a result of pressure from all sides, the boundaries are moving on this. The Church of England's policy for its schools is now that they should offer 25 per cent of their places without religious requirements, and the more socially selective entrance policies such as attendance at Sunday school are being whittled away. The good Catholic schools will remain 100 per cent Catholic, however — and they are a vital component of the state school scene in areas such as Central London. Many will insist that your child has been baptised in the first sixth months after birth; some are being rapped on the knuckles by the Schools Adjudicator for policies that give brownie points to organised (usually middle class) parents who have arranged flowers in the local church or helped with Sunday school for four years or more.

Attainments. There are still almost 200 academically selective schools in England, and others that have special admissions arrangements for particular talents — they may specialise in languages, science or sports, or they may admit a few talented musicians. Understand how the criteria work, and consider some targeted coaching. Ask those whose children succeeded last year and who have no younger children — they have nothing to lose by letting you in on their secrets. NB Grammar schools must now carry out entrance tests early in the autumn term of the year before entry, and give out preliminary results before you put in your applications to the local authority, so you know whether or not to include the grammar school on your list. This means you may well have to register in the summer term of year 5.

SEN or medical grounds. If this might apply to your child (even cleaner air for an asthmatic), get your case documented — it can be an overriding criterion.

State schools in Scotland

The system in Scotland is pretty much catchment area based, though with a right for a parent to ask for another school. As the government website says: 'If you have a child who is due to start primary school or who will be transferring to secondary school soon, you have a right to express a preference for a particular school. Your Council will probably suggest that you should use the local school designated by them, and of course you may be happy to do so, but the Council must also tell you of your right to choose a different school, and give you an address where you can get help in making up your mind.' Some councils are more helpful than others.

State schools in Wales

You have a right to attend your local school but can apply for another. Your choice will be respected if (as far as we can see) the school and the Local Authority feel so inclined.

Entrance — independent sector

As a rule of thumb this is what you do:

1. Register your child's name at the school(s) you have chosen. Telephone the school and it will send you an application/ registration form. If your child is still in the cradle, and the schools you have your eye on are very over-subscribed, you may decide to register before visiting.

2. Filling in the form has to be done at the right moment or the 'list' may be 'full'. Embryos are acceptable at some schools; the lists for many successful schools will close several years before the date of entry — Radley closes shortly after birth. However, in the current financial climate it's always worth phoning up later on to see if anyone has dropped out. It will usually cost a registration fee (most are non-returnable) ranging from £25 to £200 or more.

3. The school will then contact you and your child's current school or nursery about the next stage (it doesn't hurt to telephone and check, though, if you think it may have forgotten you — and don't forget to tell the school if you change your address). They will usually get a report from the head of your child's current school and attention is paid to that.

4. Your child is usually, though not always, put through their paces, which might (at a young age) mean an exam, a test or two, 'meaningful play' or whatever. (NB You might also — openly or surreptitiously — be put through your paces as well: Are you a good parent? Is there discipline in the home? Are you educated? Are you a complainer or a worrier? Have you some wonderful attribute the school might be able to use? Will you fit in with the school's image of itself?) For entry to senior schools there may be a scholarship/entrance exam or common entrance — a standard exam, but marked by the school of first choice.

5. All being well, the school will then offer a firm place. You must write and confirm acceptance of this place or it may be offered to someone else. NB You will probably be asked for a large non-returnable deposit at this stage, which can be many hundreds of pounds — many, many hundreds of pounds in London (especially the lower ranked schools, which offer places earlier in a bid to catch the nervous parents of bright pupils) or in schools that offer places years in advance of entry dates (see below).

6. Pay school fees — in advance of the term is normal practice, alas.

7. Read any contract you have to sign carefully: if in any doubt — such as what do they mean by 'a term's notice'? — a little legal advice at this stage can save you a lot of agony later.

There are variations on this theme. For example, some may accept entries up to the last minute, though there will be an official date for closing the 'list', from about three weeks to three terms before the entrance exam.

One exceptionally tiresome and damaging/convenient and helpful (delete according to circumstances and prejudices) current trend is for senior schools to 'pre-test' – putting 10-year-olds through the mill to see if they're likely to pass at 13. Eton has an excuse for this, as it frees up parents to look carefully at other good schools while there's still room, but now all and sundry feel the need for an early test or interview to prove that they too have overflowing waiting lists. Opponents of this development — and that includes most of us at The Good Schools Guide — point out that many 10/11-year-old boys will by no means have come into academic flower yet, and face stress and rejection as a result. Advocates say that rejection frees the parents to look at other good schools while there is still time. If you're determined on a pre-testing senior school, choose a prep school that trains children for it. If you are considering senior schools that do not pre-test, you'll have the luxury of choosing a prep that spends its time educating rather than coaching your child.

The pre-test is now virtually uncoachable for, dependent as it largely is on a computerised reasoning test which, the schools who have paid mega-bucks for it claim, is a better determiner of final achievement than the trad English/maths exercises are. Get junior to build up speed on VR and non-VR tests and don't be conned by anyone who tells you they can tutor for the real thing. Not yet they can't.

TIP: All things being equal, always have a go at the school you think is right for your child. Even those schools you have been told are jam-packed may have a place. Don't restrict yourself to trying at the 'normal' entry periods. Dare to try mid-term, and mid-academic year, or even the day before term starts. If you get a no, don't be afraid to try again. NB Some schools simply refuse to consider non-standard entries. Play the rules as far as you can.

Interviews

'I'll always be grateful to Gordon Brown. Not because of his macro-management of the economy, but because his name was the correct answer to my son's 11 plus interview question: 'Who is the Chancellor of the Exchequer?' It was the possession of this crucial piece of information that, in my view, tipped the balance in his search for a secondary school place.

While state schools are prohibited from interviewing any but potential sixth form students, the interview is an integral part of nearly every private school admissions process, and tends to send the applicant's parents, rather than the actual applicant, into a spin. Parents feel considerably more responsible for their child's social presentation than for his or her ability to do long division or conjugate French verbs. And, while a school may breezily describe the interview as 'just a chance to get to know the child better', this hardly quells fears about sending young Daniel or Daniella into the lion's den.

The London prep or senior day-school interview is perhaps the most straightforward. Over-subscribed at every point, the selective urban independent tends to concentrate on the academic. The majority usually only meet the child after a written exam (generally used as a first edit), and the interview itself will contain a significant component of maths, comprehension or reasoning. The aim here is to probe intellectual strengths and weaknesses in order to select from the central bulk of candidates or to pick scholarship material. Finding out a little about a child's character is only of secondary importance.

Even the most academic schools, however, are not necessarily just looking for those guaranteed to deliver a stream of A*s. Some use interviews as an opportunity to create as balanced a community as possible:

'I didn't want all extroverts or all eggheads,' said one ex-junior school head. 'Most children who sat our exam scored between 40 and 65 per cent in the written paper, so I was looking for an individual spark. At the age of 7, particularly, the interview is a crucial counter-balance to the exam. Those born between September and December always scored higher marks in the written paper. At interview we would go back to the list and bring in some younger children.'

Parents, relax

Concerned parents often do their best to control the outcome of the interview, but professional preparation is seen as a waste of time, both by those who interview and by teachers. 'I always tell parents if they're paying to coach 3-year-olds, they might as well burn £20 notes,' says Jo Newman, headmistress of North London Collegiate Junior School, who has the daunting task of selecting 40 4-year-olds from 200 applicants in a two-tier interview. 'The only useful preparation is to talk to them, play with them and read them stories.'

Further up the system, the advice is equally non-prescriptive. The head of a west London pre-prep does her best to relax the 7-year-olds she sends to prep school interviews by providing them with as much factual information as she can beforehand. 'I try to prepare them for what they'll find. I usually describe the head — because I'm a smallish woman they might expect all heads to be like me — and I'll tell them what the school looks like. Beyond that I just say, "Look them in the eye, answer carefully and be honest." Children sell themselves.'

Some pre-preps and prep schools provide mock interviews, some will carefully guide children on what books or hobbies that might show to best advantage, but most interviewers say they always know when a child has been coached, and honesty — at least in theory — is the quality they're looking for. 'I tell children,' says one private tutor who prepares children for 11 plus, 'to say what's in their heart, not what their teacher told them to say.'

Personality, of course, will always be the most variable aspect of any interview and all interviewers have a personal bias. They may hate boastful children, or those who say their favourite leisure activity is computer games; they may prefer Arsenal fans to Tottenham supporters; but some schools do make a strenuous attempt to counteract the sense of one adult sitting in judgement on one child. City of London School, for example, sees candidates individually before sending them off to a lesson where they can be observed by another teacher as they work in a group. At Rugby, every child is interviewed by at least two people.

The best interviewers can and do overcome the limitations both of the written examination and of the child. 'Children, even very shy ones, like to talk about themselves, their friends, their families and their pets. I get them to describe what they did on Sunday, or I turn my back and ask them to describe something in the room. Sometimes I even get a child to sing or dance. I am looking for sparkly eyes and interest. If a child just sits there like a pudding, you usually don't take them.'

Some schools get over the 'what to talk about' dilemma by asking children to bring along a favourite object. Rugby sensibly provides a questionnaire about hobbies and interests to fill in in advance, which not only provides a talking point, but also allows parents to feel they've done what they can. If, however, the child pitches up with a copy of Proust or boasts a collection of Roman ceramics, parents shouldn't be surprised if the interviewer is somewhat sceptical.

The truth will out

Although a number of leading boarding schools — Marlborough, for example — still rely solely on the prep school report and common entrance papers, most now feel that the interview can identify serious pastoral concerns. 'We sometimes discover that a child really doesn't want to come to boarding school,' said the registrar of Rugby. 'The interview is also very helpful in establishing the academic level the prep school is working at. We ask children to bring in their exercise books. Some London prep schools are so geared up at that point that all the child is doing is practice papers. Country prep schools tend to be more relaxed.'

Although most heads are honest in their report about a child — after all, their reputation depends on it — the interview can also benefit them. 'Occasionally, a prep-school head knows perfectly well that a child is not suited to our school, but the parents just won't listen. Coming from us it doesn't sour the relationship with the school.'

Parents in the spotlight

Boarding schools, of course, tend to have another layer to their selection process and interview when they match boys and girls to an appropriate house. Here the parent, even more than the child, can be in the spotlight. Dr Andrew Gailey, now Eton vice provost but formerly housemaster of Manor House, Prince William's house at Eton, always tries to strike a balance of the sporty and industrious, the musical and the generally decent in his annual selection of 10 boys but, for him, the parental part of the equation plays an even greater role. 'The boy is going to change, but you have shared management of the child's adolescence with the parents and you have to have some common bond for that to work.'

That's a common theme for those interviews where parents appear — notably in London pre-preps. Most of the time the school is really interviewing you, and it's you who need the preparation while your child can happily be him or herself. A balance between steady, respectful (schools are ever keen to avoid the parent from hell) and interesting (but nor do they like dull ones) is best.

Tutors and Tutoring — Can You Afford not To?

The fact that you are reading this suggests that you are a thoughtful, caring and intelligent parent. It also suggests that you might be interested in engaging a tutor for your child. But — Why? Who? Where from? How? How much? For how long? Who do you ask and whom can you trust?

Do you need a tutor?

Do you need a tutor? Apart from children who have missed school through illness or some other crisis, the majority of tutoring either helps prepare candidates for 11+ or 13+ entry to academically selective senior schools or helps them with the GCSE/A level subjects they are finding difficult. This is good, sensible, necessary and, in the main, worthwhile, tutoring. Unnecessary tutoring is the tutoring of children of 2, 3 and 4 years old. This is nonsense, oppressive and driven by anxiety. People who purport to tutor this age group are charlatans. Unnecessary tutoring is tutoring of children at sound and successful preps whose pupils are tutored because their friends are tutored. This, again, is driven only by parental panic and anxiety and is foolish. It enrages the schools and achieves nothing.

The press veers from reports that everyone who doesn't employ a tutor for their children is clearly a hopeless parent, whose children will fail at everything and curse them to the end of their days, to the line that that modern children are pressurised, we are all tiger parents or helicopter parents and what children really need is time to stick pasta on sugar paper, dam streams and watch butterflies.

The fact is that a good tutor can be a godsend. Your child may have missed school, be struggling with a particular subject, have a poor or over-stretched teacher, be competing for a place at an academically selective school against children primed at the local prep — there could be numerous reasons why a little one-to-one in skilled hands could make all the difference. A teacher sitting quietly with your child, concentrating solely on his areas of confusion or his gaps can build confidence and up results in no time. Confidence is all and a shy child with a friendly teacher to himself can ask questions, sort confusions, be supported socially in a way that can make an immense difference to how he feels about himself and his achievement at school.

Where to look?

Where to look? It hugely depends on where you are. If you are in central London you may well be familiar with many of the tutor companies we appraise in the Good Schools Guide Tutor Companies Review. You may also have tucked away the names of one or two precious local tutors whose waiting lists are gold dust and whose techniques and results are legendary. These people don't advertise and they may well be turning away a dozen would-be tutees each week. If you are in a rural area or even in one of the smaller cities, it is probably very different. There may be no reputable local tutor companies and the local website listings may look suspiciously like recruiting grounds for local paedos – stoked by media stories of predatory teachers and 'grooming' seemingly aimed to make one wary of any poor young man who genuinely wants to teach the young.

Only a tiny percentage of tutoring is via a tutor company. However, there can be advantages to engaging one of these to help you. You should have a choice of tutor, you should know they are trained, assessed and monitored by the company and there should be redress if you are not happy. Tutor companies range from the upmarket ones charging an unconscionable £100 an hour, whose tutors are bright young Oxbridge graduates who could inspire a clod of earth, to online listing companies who know nothing of the people they list and don't care. There are plenty of sound and sensible tutor companies — especially in London. The Good Schools Guide website reviews cover most of the best and give you sensible advice about how to deal with them. Interview your tutor; make sure he/she knows exactly what they are there to teach; speak to their previous clients; check that your child likes them and is happy; sit in on lessons if you like to — the first one at least — and if they interest you and make you want to stay, you've probably found the right tutor.

Best, though, is to ask around. All settled neighbourhoods will have local tutors who've coached generations of children, who are tried, tested, trusted and treasured. Mostly parents only pass on their names once they no longer need them themselves but someone will tell you. Ask early, be charming when you call, explain how they are really the only person who is right for your child and that you are prepared to wait. They will soften and fit you in, if they can and you'll thank your diplomatic skills for ever. They will probably expect you to come to them, whereas tutor company tutors will come to you but — it's your choice.

There are moves afoot — largely driven by the central London tutor companies — to 'professionalise' the 'industry' — to form a professional association with 'benefits' and to encourage tutors to sign up, be accredited, regulated, monitored etc. The rationale behind this is, purportedly, to up the profile and the standards of the profession, to protect children from predators calling themselves tutors, to subject tutors to some sort of scrutiny and appraisal so that parents can be sure what they are getting. Part of this would be to ensure that accredited tutors have CRB (now known as DBS) checks. Sadly, there are occasional cases of 'tutors' abusing their privileged positions and molesting children. If you don't recall reading about these in the press it is usually because the child is protected from the publicity. And the truth is that, however you safeguard, warn and protect children, a determined child molester will find a way of molesting. Current rules mean that no self-employed tutor can apply on her own behalf for a DBS check. So where does this leave the 95 per cent of tutors who currently work at home, untroubled by such interference? We are profoundly sceptical that attempts to 'professionalise' what has been, till now, a successful and self-regulating cottage industry will be any safer or more 'professional' via this means.. We have seen no convincing arguments for forming an association of tutors and fear that it will simply bully good, popular and successful local tutors out of the market.

The fact, as we said at the outset, that you are reading this suggests that you are a thoughtful, caring and intelligent parent. So — trust yourself and trust your child. Ask around if and when you need a tutor. Take someone who has been recommended by someone you know and trust. Don't just pick someone off the internet. You wouldn't choose a builder or a dentist that way. Ignore the hype, the scare-mongering and the panic. Use your common sense. Your child may not ever need a tutor. But if he does, let it be a rewarding, mutually fulfilling and memorable relationship. One that shouldn't break the bank or leave scars. You read it here.

Obituaries and How to Avoid Being in Them

Girls' schools, prep schools and even the occasional boys' or co-ed school have been closing at the rate of half-a-dozen annually for several years now. Because recession tends to affect independent schools a couple of years late, we expect such closures to continue. Is there anything parents can do to avoid being caught in a crash?

In troubled times girls' schools are particularly vulnerable. Far more recent – and poorer – foundations, they do not have the resources to spend on flash facilities or to fund everyone's choice of subjects. Many girls' schools have suffered a crisis of confidence over this. In a school with the will to survive, the social and educational benefits of a girls' only sixth form in a school in which you are known should be confidently and unapologetically asserted — by the girls themselves and certainly by the head.

Prep schools face a host of challenges: senior schools looking to the state sector to satisfy the Charity Commission, senior schools transferring to the state sector, grammar schools prevented from expanding, an adverse political climate, reduced funding for diplomatic and military families, improving standards in international schools.

Many independent senior schools have dug themselves a grave with a decade of spiralling fee increases. Even when times are good most parents make considerable sacrifices to pay for their children's education, so recession plus a modest hike in fees can be the last straw.

If the death of a school is sad for us, it can be a disaster for parents. Schools never give much notice of closure – how can they? The moment their state of mind or finance is known, there is a rush for the door. Schools, like marriages, may look harmonious and healthy to the outside world but may harbour all kinds of corrosive and ultimately fatal problems under the smiling surface.

There are nevertheless some runes you can read that may indicate the chances of your chosen school going under. Look out for:

- Falling rolls. For English senior schools, look at the performance table data on our website: you can track how each part of the school has been doing over the last five years. For schools in The Guide, we will note where we are aware of consistently falling numbers. Does the school unaccountably have spaces in every year group, and a willingness to take on difficult cases?

- Poor finances. Schools that are comfortably off generally feel loved and nurtured. A school should look its smartest in September; if no maintenance work or painting has been done over the summer break that could be a warning sign. Look too for copious bursaries and other signs that the school has funds in hand. Likewise, a school unconfident of its future is unlikely to mount appeals for ambitious projects — a new sports hall or music school. Has your school lost the will to live?

- Not sacking troublemakers is a sign, as is cutting corners in the curriculum. Is the head often away drumming up business? Cheap labour: gap-year students can be wonderful, but they are inexperienced and they don't last.

- Loss of self-belief. Many schools have a very particular clientele and image. When a school starts to have doubts, to look a little furtive like someone at a cocktail party who is not sure they want to talk to you, they lose their traditional market and often fail to gain a new one. It takes a strong school to proclaim a steady course.

- In boarding schools, an absence or excess of overseas children. Having no children from overseas at all, particularly in a senior school, can be the sign of a very duff marketing department. More than 20 per cent can make the school an uncomfortable place for the native, unless the school has a segregated facility, as some do.

- A weak head and an unhappy staff increasingly willing to let their feelings show to parents.

The above apply to all varieties of school. Girls' schools are by no means alone in being in an uncomfortable market position. Boarding is in long-term decline, state schools can provide sharp competition, whatever makes a particular school distinctive may no longer appeal to enough parents.

So who is for the long drop? There are no sure-fire ways to see it coming. The battle between schools is fought out over years and fortunes can ebb and flow. A sudden legacy, a new head, selling out to Cognita, a change in fashions or even the relocation of some large employer — all can pull a failing school back into contention. Some independent schools have already joined the state system as academies or free schools and more are applying to do so — an upheaval, yes, but at least the school's still operating. It's not over till the chartered accountant sings.

Is there anything concerned parents can do? If you are really partisan, a talented leader and have a lot of time (and money) on your hands, get involved — school governing bodies can be pretty moribund places, particularly if the bad news has been washing in for a few years. We have seen energetic new brooms make an enormous difference. If you have serious doubts about the stability of your child's school it's as well to prepare an escape route. Check out the alternatives and know who you want to phone should the bad news ever arrive.

UWC ATLANTIC COLLEGE

TRANSFORMATIVE AND CHALLENGING EDUCATION

A UWC Atlantic College education is the beginning of a life-changing journey. Based in a 12th Century castle on the coast of South Wales, United Kingdom, a truly diverse international student body studies for the Atlantic Diploma and learns to respect difference.

The two year course has two parts: the International Baccalaureate academic curriculum, and a parallel co-curricular programme of experiential learning that focuses on global concerns of peace, social justice, physical challenge and a sustainable future.

Through a broad and balanced experience our student demonstrate their commitment to making a positive difference in the world.

Find out more about the opportunities available for 16-19 year olds by visiting

www.atlanticcollege.org

Crammers

A premium option...

Of the 653,000 higher education hopefuls in 2012, 465,000 ended up with places, leaving 188,000 behind. With another bumper crop of applicants this year (2013-2014), that figure could be about to rise, even though there are some 60,000 fewer 18 year olds now compared with four years ago.

Unlike politicians, few students who fail to make the cut first time round will relish the chance to spend more time with their families. Some accept their results, modify their expectations and see what they can get via clearing. Others head back to the classroom for retakes. First port of call for many is their old school. Some, if not exactly overjoyed to see their former pupils hanging around the place like the ghosts of exams past, are happy to let them have another go. Others treat their continued presence as a slight embarrassment. 'I definitely felt they didn't want me around,' says one ex-sixth former, of her mid-league co-ed independent.

So it could be worth thinking twice before you sign up with the dear old alma mater and taking a look, instead, at the many establishments that deal exclusively in the business of grade improvement. They're known familiarly as crammers, more formally as private sixth form or tutorial colleges, and flexibility is their raison d'être.

Some, like Bosworth Independent College, are stand-alone one-offs or part of a small, often family-owned group. Others, like the cosily-named Davies, Laing and Dick, are cogs in a much larger empire. Many incorporate the names of famous centres of learning in their titles though, judging by their actual distance from any spire, dreaming or otherwise, this can on occasion reflect aspirational rather than geographic proximity.

A fair few — but by no means all — are members of CIFE, a loose-knit group founded originally to ensure proper accreditation after the government of the day decided to pull out of the role. (All are now subject to regular inspections.) What they all share is an absence of charitable status (a shock to some parents confronted with the precious gift of VAT on their bill) and large fees, with £16,000 a typical starting point for full-time day pupils. Justification comes in the form of small overall numbers and class sizes, usually capped at eight (sometimes larger for sciences), the quality and experience of the tutors and their sang froid in delivering the goods where – in many cases – more conventional approaches have failed.

What makes the biggest difference, however, is the quality of the tutors. The best won't necessarily have strings of qualifications after their names but will be experienced, dedicated and prepared to put in as much work as it takes to get their students on track.

'When my son fell behind with his assignments, all his homework was supervised,' says one parent, whose son attended a central London college. 'Frankly, it was a relief. Because it's small, you can't get lost and they absolutely know who you are.'

Academic programmes tend to be more about depth than breadth. IBs and the pre-U are a rarity. While there are specialised English language university foundation courses aimed mainly at overseas students, together with specialist entrance exam preparation for medics and others, the world of the tutorial college revolves around A levels.

Despite the abolition of January AS and A2 retakes — from the 2013-2014 academic year, it's summer exams or nothing — colleges are upbeat about the different ways their study packages can be served. Depending on how many grades they need to make up, candidates can either re-do the entire year, opt for a slightly pacier five or six month course starting in January or February or go for broke with an Easter to summer sprint. (CIFE publishes a handy list of FAQs). And, as previously, students can select the units they wish to redo. With careful packing, they can fit in a spot of gap-year gorgeousness, too – though a certain mental toughness is required to follow back-packing adventures with a return to school.

A hard core will spend at least a year there. The super bright can complete A levels (GCSEs too, in many places) in as little as a year, with 18 month and two year courses also on the menu. They can also be good places for those who've had a disastrous first year in the sixth form because, as one website puts it, they're 'immature, distracted, frustrated, heartbroken, or unwell' and want either to start again or switch courses half way through — a breeze following the introduction of a simplified transfer process between exam boards.

There's freedom from much of the enforced esprit de corps that comes with membership of a traditional school community. For the disenchanted, this can come as something of a relief.

But while uniform and pettifogging school rules are out, teaching to the test is quite definitely in. Students can expect frequent meetings with tutors to focus the mind. There's an emphasis on learning skills and revision as you go, with extensive reference to past papers and regular tests — often weekly — to weed out the potential for making silly mistakes. And there's no slacking outside lessons either. One tutorial college expects three to four hours' preparation for every one-to-one hour-long session.

Extracurricular options? While their absence has been a fairly regular gripe (past inspection reports are useful here) things have improved. If a college caters for those young enough (pre-GCSE) to be following the national curriculum, a range of activities must, legally, be provided. Elsewhere, there's considerable variation. As a minimum, many colleges forge links with nearby universities or private fitness centres so students can use their sports and fitness facilities. Others run D of E programmes (Lansdowne College) or organise an annual revue (Ashbourne Independent School).

So which crammer should you choose? Marketed to very different customers, some almost entirely filled with overseas students, others patronised largely by locals, compare and contrast exercises can be tricky.

What you should check:

Expertise in dealing with pupils like to your child.

However impressive the overall A level pass rate, it's essential to ask the college for more detail. A retake student is likely to have very specific needs (a grade or two up in specific modules, an overall climb from a C to an A grade). Be equally specific in your questions. How have similar candidates peformed? What supporting data do they have? Ideally, this should be based on several years' results, especially important as with often small numbers of students in each year group, just one exceptional or disastrous result can significantly skew the percentages.

The minimax effect – the least that can be done for the best results

'We do a lot of number crunching,' says one college. They should be able to advise on the smallest effort required to deliver the best possible grade increase and which units, AS and A2, to focus on.

Who will be teaching me?

Some colleges recruit tutors on a just-in-time basis. 'I was told they didn't know who would be teaching my daughter as they hadn't been recruited yet,' says one mother. Check it out and ensure you meet them first. They may be fine teachers but you need to be confident that the chemistry's there to begin with.

Expertise in dealing with university applications

Some highly competitive courses, such as medicine, expect candidates to be effortless high flyers. Most, including Russell Group, will consider second time round applicants, but it's essential to find out what your chosen university's policy is. Discuss your goals with the college and make sure their advice is based on oodles of past experience.

How they score when it comes to added value

The best colleges are very good indeed, not merely compared with their peers but with UK schools generally. Almost 95 per cent of A level grades from pupils at Cardiff Sixth Form College, for example, were at A*/A (it boasts a substantial overseas contingent). Abbey College, Cambridge and Brampton College Hendon (amongst others) regularly reach 80 per cent grade B and above. However, some are pretty picky when they select candidates. So ask how the different ability ranges perform. Are they all exceptional when they arrive? And how good is the college at helping middling students to punch above their academic weight? Ask for supporting data.

Whether they have a particularly subject specialisation

Some offer a full range of subjects but may lean towards the sciences. Check numbers of candidates sitting each subject so you can get a feel for the balance. Being one of a handful of humanities students in a college of would-be economists could be just your bag, but better to know in advance.

What the opportunities are to socialise

Limited socialising might seem like a good idea to parents of offspring whose year-round partying contributed to their academic downfall. But for the part-time resit student, coming into college for a few hours every week can be a lonely business, so ask how the timetable is organised and whether there are structured opportunities (and space) to meet others.

Whether there's help with the fees

It's expensive. Bear in mind, however, that your money is likely to buy you a substantial amount of tiny group, and often one-to-one, tuition. In addition, many colleges provide help with finances for exceptional candidates who would struggle to meet the fees, so it's always worth asking.

Crammers are not the only route

For those with minimal qualifications but a yearning to go on to higher education, Access courses can bridge the gap. Run by further education colleges round the country, with on-line versions also available (the Distance Learning Centre has a wide range – though attracts mixed reviews) they cover everything from law and politics to sciences and are highly regarded by universities.

One pupil, who missed most of his sixth form studies at his independent day school owing to illness, is now employed by the oil industry in the sort of lucrative post that the pushiest of parents would be hard pressed to sniff at, having completed a science-based Access course followed by a degree at a Russell Group university.

It's no easy option, however. Courses take a minimum of a year to complete and are intended for those aged over 19 who have 'substantial experience of life outside of formal education, gained since completing compulsory schooling,' so it's not an immediate post-school option.

A fair dose of self-motivation is also necessary – something you'll be quizzed about when you apply. You may also be asked to sit ability tests in some areas.

Though you'll have to pay tuition fees (FE colleges in Surrey were quoting upwards of £2,400 to complete a one-year course), help may be available depending on how long you were at school for and what qualifications you have already gained.

The Access to Higher Education website (http://www.accesstohe.ac.uk/) lists numerous Cinderella-style transformations. One full time mother became a midwife; a former waitress is now a criminal barrister. The consensus: if you're determined and focused with plenty of evidence of real life experience gained in the school of hard knocks, Access courses are definitely worth a look.

Oxbridge Admissions

Judge a tree by its fruit, a man by the company he keeps, and a school by the universities it sends its pupils to? Well, you would miss out on the oak, the saint and many wonderful schools for ordinary children, but the level of Oxbridge acceptances is still a pretty good measure of at least some of a school's qualities. You can find full details of each school's Oxbridge successes (and indeed of the other universities that they send pupils to) on our website.

There used to be a joke about Oxbridge entrance. At some colleges, so they said, when you went for interview they'd throw a rugby ball at you. If you caught it, you were in. Until recently, as well as training lawyers, clergymen and educators, the ancient universities were partially run as finishing schools for upper-class young men. This is categorically no longer the case.

Much as the two great universities may huff and puff that they always looked for the best, it has taken a great deal of effort by government to push them into using systems that made this likely. Tests have now, say Oxford, 'been designed to look for aptitude rather than acquired knowledge', and they are moving towards a common and understandable admissions system.

The challenge for independent schools has been to respond to the changed times by equipping their students with such confidence and brilliance that they can triumph over a presumption that they are over-educated and inclined to spend their Oxbridge years partying rather than studying. Many of them have done this very successfully, which is why the percentage of independent school pupils at Oxbridge is still barely below the 50 per cent mark – and indeed why their top pupils (with three A* grades) are more likely than similarly gifted state school pupils to be offered a place.

The challenge for state schools has been to find the time to make their best pupils confident, articulate, sparky, questioning, inventive and learned in the ways of the world while faced with an A level curriculum and marking system that could have been designed to extinguish all these characteristics. A state school that does well in Oxbridge admissions is really something special.

Are these the right universities for you?

For many A Level students, and even more for many parents, Oxbridge is the pinnacle of their academic aspirations, the sine qua non of a university education and a recognised path to fame and fortune. But Oxbridge is certainly not for everyone – even some of the brightest – and it certainly won't guarantee riches, or even a job.

The main criticisms of Oxford and Cambridge are that they are interested in the academic abilities and not in the future greatness of their students, so they draw their entrance criteria narrowly, and that the courses they offer are narrow and (in some subjects) decidedly old-fashioned. Such criticisms might also be cited as virtues — it depends on the individual student.

There are, of course, many reasons to go to Oxbridge, not least of which is the beauty of the architecture, but the primary and central benefit of the education offered here is the tightly focused nature of the teaching. All students are taught by tutorial, either one-to-one or in very small groups. To undergo that intensity of education you need to be thoroughly interested in a specific subject and happy to produce a heavyweight volume of work. Many 18-year-olds are still relatively undecided about their intellectual interests (and ought perhaps to be looking to one of the great US universities) and many too would rather dedicate the period between school and work to a more even-handed balance between study and play (in which case they can join the thousands of like-minded students elsewhere in the Russell group of universities).

No matter how great your passion for a subject, however, there's no point applying to Oxbridge unless you are already extremely well qualified academically. It's not obligatory to have straight A*s at GCSE but, particularly since the ongoing tweaking of the entry requirements, the higher your AS grades the more likely you are to get in – and this will apply in spades if AS exams are abolished. You also have had to have chosen the appropriate A levels — Cambridge in particular is getting very sniffy about some A level subjects.

What you can do to prepare

The best academic schools in the country — the ones that send 10-50 successful candidates to Oxbridge each year — often provide specialist preparation both for the application and for the interview.

'We don't do specific training for Oxbridge entrance,' says Helen Turner, head of sixth form at league-table-topping North London Collegiate School, which sends more than a third of its girls to Oxbridge. 'But what we do offer in year 13 is preparation for a university course in a particular subject, whichever university the girl is applying for. We prepare them to be brilliant at their subject. Everyone, too, has a mock interview with someone from outside the school.'

For those without such well-developed sixth forms, the answer can sometimes lie in the specialist businesses set up to help candidates with everything from the choice of course to interview technique.

'I attended a one-day interview seminar,' says Oxford fresher Jo Campbell, whose Hertfordshire comprehensive provided little in the way of application advice. 'I found it very useful in dealing with the kind of question I was later asked.'

The universities, not surprisingly, are unenthusiastic about these businesses and generally tell parents they are wasting their money. But, while it is, of course, essential to choose a reputable supplier, there seems little doubt that some of these outfits are well staffed with knowledgeable experts who may well further your chances of an Oxbridge place. Look on the web for such as Oxbridge admissions, Oxbridge applications and Oxbridge info.

SENIOR SCHOOLS

Abbey College, London

22 Grosvenor Gardens, London, SW1W 0DH

• Pupils: 130; mixed • Ages: 15–22 • Non-denom • Fees: £17,500–£27,000 pa • Independent

Tel: 020 7824 7300
Email: adminlon@abbeylondon.co.uk
Website: www.abbeylondon.co.uk

Principal: Since September 2013, Rachel Borland, previously principal of Abbey College in Birmingham. She is principal of DLD as well as Abbey College, London, as they increasingly integrate before moving to a single, purpose-built site with student accommodation on Westminster Bridge Road in September 2015. She has previously been principal of an international boarding school in Nigeria, assistant director of studies at the British Council in both Hong Kong and Jordan, and worked at Bath University.

Academic matters: Small classes, capped at 12, but will run courses with upwards of two students. Key subjects are maths, physics, economics, business studies and accounting. Lots of contact time – expect to spend five plus hours in lower sixth and six hours in upper sixth per subject (or eight plus hours per subject if following one year option). Creditable results 2013: 65 per cent A*-B at A level. Strong physics and maths (including further maths), weaker economics, business studies and accounting, which in part reflects language barriers and fewer students rather than innate student ability or problems with teaching. New courses offered include BSc (Hons) in business management awarded by the University of Buckingham (three years), International Foundation Programme (IFP) set at NQF level 3 (one year).

Has a great knack for transforming C grades at AS or A level to A grades via excellent, predominantly traditional teaching and outlook with some modern approaches and styles (ICT, smartboards and learning platform). Interactive studious lessons, students encouraged to question, problem solve and take charge of their own learning – great preparation for university. A reasonable amount of hand-holding and teaching to the test but not for the fainthearted or work-shy – this is intense stuff for those serious about study. Students we spoke to attributed their success to good teaching and always being able to get individual help whenever it's needed; one student added, 'I didn't know what good teaching was until I came here'.

Games, options, the arts: Extra-curricular activities of sister college DLD are available to all Abbey London students. PE lessons for compsulsory school age students are provided in conjunction with DLD. Private music lessons can be arranged. Students are also able to join the local sports centre at a discounted rate. A large number of trips and visits are organised including the Houses of Parliament, London art galleries, Cadbury World and a recent ski trip to Italy.

Background and atmosphere: Established in 1985 as a classic crammer, with students spending a term on retakes in science, by 2000 the college had shifted its focus to cater for overseas and British students requiring two year courses. Now part of the Alpha Plus group, moved from its original base in Notting Hill to the current, leased mansion (part of the Grosvenor estate) in 2005. An immaculate Victorian façade, minutes' walk from the bustle of Victoria Station, hides a thoughtfully transformed interior, complete with fully equipped science labs and specialist teaching rooms. New business centre with state-of-the-art facilities (increasing specialisation in business education).

The crammer element remains, but today accounts for only 10 per cent of all students. Key growth area has been British students underperforming at AS and seeking a fresh start or change in focus. Variety of courses and combinations now offered include: one term retakes; one term AS retake followed by two term A level; five term A level (starting January) and traditional two year courses. Lots of flexibility, prepared to tailor courses to individual.

No on-site catering, but sandwich man visits at lunchtimes and students have own common room.

Pastoral care and discipline: Discipline not an issue: most students come here with one-track minds – success. Pastoral system assists with any issues or anxieties plus usual monitoring and mentoring. Will support and has supported students through tricky times. Lots of help given to those seeking accommodation, be it with a host family or in its own student residence at Urbanest in Hoxton. Plenty of individual support given with university applications including mock interviews with detailed feedback.

Pupils and parents: Wide ethnic mix, increasing numbers of British Asians keen to enter the professions. Traditional recruiting grounds of China and Far East remain fruitful, with sprinkling of white European. Parents tend to be very driven, ambitious and middle class which, for the most part, permeates through to their offspring. Principal or Academic Principal interviews students to ensure college reflects their aspirations rather than simply the wishes of the parents, admitting more than a few micro-manage their children's education.

Entrance: Home candidates, mainly after relative, or complete, failure at AS, often at renowned independent schools. Overseas from a variety of academic backgrounds and stages of education.

Exit: Fifty per cent to business, management and finance and others mainly to engineering. Predominantly Russell Group universities, UCL, City, Sheffield and Nottingham popular destinations. Overseas students focus on ensuring they are accepted at select universities for sought-after courses. One to Cambridge in 2012.

Money matters: Means-tested financial assistance via bursaries taking account of academic potential and need.

Remarks: Does what it says on the tin: few frills or finery. Combination of very good teaching and student endeavour has seen many a sow's ear turned into veritable silk purse; now increasingly a first time choice for the scientific academic. Ideal for the motivated, goal-driven student; ditherers and artful dodgers should look elsewhere.

The Abbey School Reading

Linked school: The Abbey Junior School

Kendrick Road, Reading, RG1 5DZ

• Pupils: 705 girls, all day • Ages: 11–18 • C of E • Fees: £8,790–£13,980 pa • Independent

Tel: 01189 872256
Email: schooloffice@theabbey.co.uk
Website: www.theabbey.co.uk

Headmistress: Since 2002, Mrs Barbara Stanley BA PGCE FRGS. Educated at Glenlola Collegiate School, County Down, university at Belfast and Leicester. Experience as a summer camp counsellor in America led her to take up teaching. Headed Bedford High and Alexandra College, Dublin, before joining The Abbey. Not overbearing or egotistical, quietly businesslike and in control, definitely a thinker and a staunch believer in the benefits of single sex education for girls. Still teaches (geography) when she can and joins field trips. She is married with two daughters and lives in a village just outside Reading. She values the opportunity to serve not only her school but also her local community where she is on the parish council. Keen on hill walking and reading, one of her favourite books is The Poisonwood Bible. She has so far resisted the current vogue to write a 'head's blog', although she did report back during her recent visit to Uganda, 'I'd rather be out seeing things', she says. Parents heartily approve and girls speak in hushed tones of her assemblies – 'she's amazing, really passionate, she never uses notes'.

Retiring in July 2014.

Academic matters: Impressive results at GCSE and A level. In 2013, 52 per cent A* grades and 97 per cent A*-B at GCSE. At A level girls can choose from 26 subjects plus AS critical thinking, the school prides itself on its ability to support unusual combinations. In 2013, 74 per cent were awarded A* or A. The introduction of the IB in 2008 was a brave and forward-looking decision endorsed by a governing body that 'will always choose education over buildings'. Smallish first cohorts means classes of one or two in some subjects; how that's timetabled is one of several Abbey mysteries. First IB results shot the school to the top three UK schools offering this qualification. In 2013 the average score was 39 (average score is 30). All requisite IT, laboratories and specialist teaching equipment present and correct plus innovative 3D teaching in biology. Our guides were very fizzy about the 3D, a lesson in which they used it to study the eye was featured on BBC's Newsround. Curriculum supplemented by trips, visiting speakers, challenging extension work and an excellent library.

Comparisons may be invidious but in this case they're unavoidable. Like non-identical twins, The Abbey and Kendrick Girls' Grammar will always be publically judged in relation to each other and in terms of exam results there's barely a percentage point to choose between them. For many a parent of a bright Berkshire girl finances will decide but while Mrs Stanley is at all times diplomatic she is more than ready to define the value added by an Abbey education. For pupils it's rivalry plain and simple; the best thing to be, we discovered, is the Abbey girl who turned down a place at Kendrick. That's enough of that.

GCSE, IB and A level results were displayed on the 'Abbey in the news' notice board, but no more prominently than cuttings and reports about charity events and gap year projects. While we commend such modesty we managed to discover that 'Abbeydextrous', a team of year 7 girls came fifth in The Times spelling bee national final held at the O2 Arena (the English teacher who took them hasn't stopped smiling since) and sixth formers won the national 2011 European Youth Parliament and Berkshire Young Enterprise. Around 30 with mild SEN receive one-to-one sessions either before school or in lunchtime (no lessons to be missed); small number have EAL support from qualified teacher.

There has been a quiet revolution in the sixth form. While cultural changes such as being allowed to bring coffee into lessons may not seem seismic, loosening the reins to create a pre-university rather than post-GCSE learning experience necessitated 'taking a deep breath'. The difference between school and sixth form is now palpable and girls who would perhaps have left, ready for a change, stay on because the change is here. Itchy feet cured by no uniform, less hierarchical teacher/pupil relations, superlative careers support and magic timetabling to enable endless permutations of A level and IB choices. We chatted to the director of sixth form, a delightful chap who seems to strike just the right balance between informality and high expectations.

Games, options, the arts: The Abbey Edge (can be downloaded from website) is an exhaustive and quite possibly exhausting programme of clubs and activities from Alpha club to jazz dance. It includes an Islamic Union, the chance to learn Mandarin, book groups and news quizzes in the library, drop-in clinics for academic subjects (an excellent alternative to an evening's bad tempered homework trauma), D of E, public speaking, gymnastics, drama, choirs, orchestras, ensembles, cheerleading and golf. Clubs and training take place before and after school and during the lunch hour (and it is just an hour); how on earth girls find time to do all the extra stuff and eat lunch or indeed tea (many are also involved in sports and clubs where they live) is another Abbey mystery. The site is surprisingly uncramped for a town school, loads of green space for full range of running about sports plus excellent indoor swimming pool (early morning swim fit a popular class). Planning application in process for an all-weather sports pitch. Squad training is another pre-school and lunchtime activity with county and national triumphs for teams and individuals. Fixtures are played after school and on Saturdays. Parents are expected to pick up girls who stay on for activities after the buses leave.

Over a third of pupils learn a musical instrument at school and girls make a big noise in both grade examinations and numerous bands, choirs, ensembles and orchestras. There is a major musical production every two years and an annual overseas tour. Drama is very popular and girls we spoke to love the fact that the absence of boys (no shipping in for male roles) means that they get a chance to play all the star parts. There are plenty of opportunities to travel but according to girls, the 'best trip ever', is the annual water sports week in France.

Much is given to Abbey girls and much is expected in return, they are keen fundraisers and the school has developed links with a community and schools in Uganda. Mrs Stanley visited in the summer (reporting back via a blog sent under rather trying circumstances), taking letters from Abbey girls who are now corresponding with their Ugandan counterparts.

Background and atmosphere: It may come as surprise to read that Reading has 'a nice bit', but it does and that's where The Abbey is. It was founded in 1887 as Reading High School, in 1914 it departed from the Church Schools Company and took its present name. The Abbey sits between old and modern houses halfway up a hill that runs between car-dominated Reading town centre and the leafier Victorian villas of the Christchurch Road conservation area. It's far but not too far from the madding crowd and with Reading University close by the general ambience, not to mention public transport links, is pretty appealing. The school is practically next door to both of Reading's massively oversubscribed state anomalies, Kendrick Girls' and Reading Boys' grammars, but while there is some cooperation (careers talks, University presentations) neighbourly relations remain at the polite nod rather than 'come in without knocking' level.

Fairly fragile connection with Jane Austen (school's name taken from a nearby defunct establishment that once educated Miss A for a couple of years) solidified by naming the new arts and humanities block the 'Jane Austen' wing. Old girls apparently horrified when they saw plans to demolish much of the Victorian frontage but less so when the work was completed. The gothic entrance has been retained and old and new blend together pretty well. As with so many schools that have been added to over the years it could be said that the buildings 'lack flow' and some areas are less lovely than others – the sixth form centre looks pretty lived-in and their 'al fresco' dining space is more concrete than courtyard.

Pastoral care and discipline: On every single notice board we saw a simple poster depicting the 'listening tree', a clear diagram that shows girls what to do if they have a problem. Our guides thought that the sixth form 'buddies' are 'really good if you have friend troubles and you can e-mail them if you are shy.' Parents praise pastoral care and girls seemed very clued up on where to go for support, especially the drop-in subject clubs (clinics) held at lunchtime. These were mentioned several times, girls like the fact that there's no stigma attached to them because they offer both extension activities and help with problems. Some parents commented that although happy with the school 'you have to sign up for the Abbey way', implying a certain lack of flexibility, but most we spoke to thought the balance was just about right.

Discipline is maintained via carrots and stickers. Girls aim to 'keep a clean sheet' in their planners (these must be signed by parents), pages clear of marks for crimes against uniform or homework gain house points. This rewards the quietly good, often overlooked by other systems. Stickers featuring the school flower, a magnolia, are awarded for special achievement, these are meant to go in the planner for parents to see but girls often choose to wear them instead. Exceptional effort or achievement (girls and staff) is recognised via a personal card from Mrs Stanley.

Pupils and parents: Hardworking and unsnobby, definitely no princesses here. Many from Reading's business and academic community (university and hospital nearby) and others from Henley, Windsor and Basingstoke. Good transport links: school and public bus network and nearish train station. Believers and unbelievers attracted by the school's Christian values and of course the value added. Former students include Baroness Brigstocke; Elizabeth Taylor (a fine author who really did attend the school, unlike Jane Austen...); Helen Ganley, artist and social reformer and a trio of BBC reporters, Miranda Krestovnikoff, Kate Humble and Sally Taylor.

Entrance: Main entry point is 11 and over half come from The Abbey Junior School. Others from independents (Highfield, Dolphin, Eton End) and local primaries; small intake at 13. Girls sit exams in maths, English and reasoning. Interview with member of staff on their taster day and reference from their current school also taken into account. Sixth form candidates come in for a taster day of lessons in the subjects they want to study at IB or A level. They are expected to gain A*-B in these subjects at GCSE.

Exit: Proper subjects at Russell Group universities. Popular destinations are Bristol, Cardiff, Leeds, Manchester and UCL. Nine or ten a year to Oxbridge. Heavy duty science subjects slightly overshadow humanities choices but English and languages popular.

Money matters: Fees pretty competitive – they have to be. Means-tested bursaries of up to 100 per cent available; academic scholarships (10 per cent) at key entry points. Special awards for music (instrumental tuition paid) and talents in sport, ICT, art and drama.

Remarks: Yes of course they work hard but Abbey girls take things in their stride and manage to do plenty more besides. We sniffed the air and found no trace of the barely suppressed hysteria that can circulate in high-achieving girls' schools (though we suspect legs are paddling furiously below the surface). And the Abbey mysteries? We never did find out how the girls (or their demon timetablers) fit so much into every day. Perhaps it's that 3D science equipment.

Abbots Bromley School for Girls

Linked school: Roch House Preparatory School

High Street, Abbots Bromley, Staffordshire WS15 3BW

• Pupils: 190 girls; 75 boarders, also occasional overnight and flexi-boarders • Ages: 11-18 • Anglican • Fees: Boarding £17,040–£25,725; Day: £4,518–£15,357 pa • Independent

Tel: 01283 840232
Email: enquiries@abbotsbromley.net
Website: www.abbotsbromley.net

Executive head: Since May 2013 Mrs Victoria Musgrave MEd FRSA, following the departure of the previous head and a nasty ISI Inspection report criticising senior management and some of the governors, but praising the pupils and, indeed, the curriculum. The school has been extremely fortunate to obtain the services of the vastly experienced and charismatic Mrs Musgrave, whose cv would fill an entertaining booklet. She is senior professional fellow in educational leadership at Liverpool Hope University, a consultant trainer for the Association of School and College Leaders and visiting lecturer at the universities of East Anglia and Manchester. Over the last 20 years, she has been principal of four state secondary schools in London, Manchester and East Anglia, including Britain's largest state boarding school. In 2006, she gained the title Super Head, resulting in visits to 10 Downing Street. Before being parachuted into Abbots Bromley, she was head of Wymondham High School, Norfolk. While there we wrote of her, 'she is one of the best in the business...they are lucky to have her and should perform increasingly well with her at the helm.' They did, and the Abbots Bromley community will be hoping she has retained her magic. She's also a very experienced teacher, an enthusiastic practitioner of that noble art.

If this sounds too good to be true or like the potted biography of a ruthlessly ambitious bullfrog, think again. Yes, she is impressive and has been very successful in training new heads, improving and developing schools, getting them back on track, boosting morale and self-esteem; no she is not 'pink and fluffy' – anyone who is tired of life should try referring to her as that. She's obviously tough when necessary, is a tireless worker, a straight and practical thinker, confident without pomposity or smugness, and an excellent listener with a good sense of humour. She brushes aside awards like Super Head because she is totally focused on Abbots Bromley and genuinely believes in the school: 'I didn't need to take the job at my age [she has four adult children and three grandchildren] but it's well worth doing. This is a very special school. It just needs a bit more academic rigour and some new appointments.'

She admires the school sufficiently to want to get it back on track. After all, to quote from that critical inspection report, 'Pupils of all ages are highly articulate and confident with good social skills. They show a strong sense of right and wrong and demonstrate excellent behaviour.' So it wasn't all bad, by any means, and Mrs Musgrave is determined to work on that. She's a problem solver and staff, pupils and parents rave about her. She has already addressed the issues raised by the report, which would now read very differently. 'It's amazing what she's done in the short time she's been here,' is the rollicking chorus.

Academic matters: This not a results driven school. It is not obsessed by those ghastly league tables. Abbots Bromley, referred to affectionately as AB, does not subscribe to that immoral and cruel business of kicking out a pupil if her GCSE results suggest that her A level results will damage the school's ranking. When I asked some girls if that happened at AB they looked amazed and replied with tough logic, 'Of course not, you'd be offered more help and guidance.' In the crazy scramble to improve league table ratings we have come across a number of schools who massage pupils' GCSE choices regardless of individual preference. There is plenty of advice and help given at AB but one of the advantages of being a small school – there are about 40 in the sixth form – is that it is possible to tailor girls' needs and aspirations to suit them. The recent inspection noted and applauded that. Instead of shoe-horning pupils into subject blocks, the school, where possible, builds the curriculum around pupils' choices. At best this approach is seen as inspirational and encouraging and not an opportunity for copping out. The words 'good' and 'excellent' are applied more to individuals than to sets of examination results. That said, grade junkies will enjoy a good fix if they look at the range of subject results at GCSE and A level (40 per cent A*/A grades at GCSE in 2013; 63 per cent A*/B grades and 27 per cent A*/A at A level). They are particularly commendable for a school which is non-selective. Girls and teachers seem immensely happy with the opportunities they have to pursue the sciences. In a mixed school they are frequently seen as 'boys' subjects' but here they are pursued enthusiastically. Small classes are greatly appreciated, too. There is a mass of information about subject choices in the excellent booklets that come with the prospectus and results junkies can get a good fix from the results section on the website.

Maths and English are setted for ability but sets are not rigidly static: movement up and down is in response to progress and confidence. Good dyslexia help is available as well as EFL tuition for those 10 per cent who need it. Those we talked to from abroad spoke with genuine fondness of the school, the way in which they had been welcomed and their involvement with dance and other activities. One mother told us of her dyslexic daughter who had struggled agonizingly at her previous school but once at AB had 'taken off. There's such a wonderful mixture of love and expertise at the school. She's blossomed.' Sixth formers help younger girls with maths and other subjects as a genuine extension of that 'family feeling' as well as points towards their Duke of Edinburgh Award.

Games, options, the arts: What makes AB particularly interesting and idiosyncratic is the existence of the Alkins School of Ballet and the Equestrian Centre. These two lungs of the academic body are serious and rigorously pursued, adding depth and variety to a school experience which is genuinely broad and challenging. It's not just a question of donning a frothy skirt and pirouetting around like a fairy looking for a Christmas tree: it is very hard work. Fun for those who like that sort of activity but, be under no illusion, it requires dedication, with a mixture of sensitive response, physical control and courage. Outstanding results for performing arts and dance BTECs. Vocational dance, by audition, involves about eight hours a week; the alternative is dancing for fun, for a sense of release, for 'enrichment'. Both involve commitment, so it's not a case of turning up when you feel like a bit of pas de poisson. Several students have gone on to perform professionally via the Royal Academy of Dance and other prestigious schools. But the excellent director of ballet, a former examiner with the Royal Ballet, and his wife, a former international ballerina, know that the career of a dancer can be cut short and does not last as long as many professions. For that reason they encourage students to do three A levels along with preparing for their BTEC and beyond. 'We want them to have the widest possible choice.' Marvellous equipment – lots of barres and mirrors – but more importantly, fabulous teaching in spacious studios.

The superbly equipped Equestrian Centre is reached via a beautiful tree lined avenue and clearly has everything a budding rider needs to move on to Olympic honours. Indoor, floodlit outdoor, bring your own horse or hire one of the school's – you name it. Girls may learn to ride from six years old and there have been a number of startling successes both at horse shows and with BHS examinations, the top one of which counts for over 100 UCAS points as well as a teaching qualification.

These two activities are more than hobbies: they really do contribute to the well-rounded character of the school. AB is not an academic hot house nor a school for trendy air heads aspiring to have their pictures in Country Life: it is a school which offers education at its broadest and most stimulating. It challenges and nurtures the brain as well as plugging into a lively, creative life of spiritual freedom and energy, artistic expression involving movement in response to music, what the school calls 'enrichment'. The Renaissance was right to combine horsemanship with learning.

Art is exciting and popular with examples of girls' work all over the place, helping to make the passageways of the original 19th century building less formal and intimidating. Plenty of drama, with plays being written and performed by the pupils themselves in house competitions. One wing of the school is dedicated to music, with over 20 individual practice rooms where girls who are now grandmothers practised scales in the morning after cold showers; now there are computers for composing on after warm baths as well as a keyboard studio. Music and singing are very popular, with most girls learning at least one instrument and a much travelled chapel choir – Italy, New York, Paris, San Francisco, Lichfield and – a Cantoria Choir that sings regularly on Radio 4.

Matches against bigger schools, and most are, are played with much zest and skill, with county players in many fields. Another school commented to us, 'Abbots Bromley girls always play with tremendous determination'. 'That's part of the ethos of making the most of our abilities and opportunities,' a pupil told us without a whiff of self-consciousness. Hockey, netball, football, cross country, tennis, swimming, rounders and athletics are all on offer.

Background and atmosphere: The village of Abbots Bromley has a population of fewer than 2000 and has recently been cited in the Sunday Times as an outstandingly good place to live. Most of the pupils and teachers at the eponymous school would agree. There are so many listed buildings in the High Street that the village is preserved at its best: handsome, understated and welcoming. The school itself has two sides: in fanciful terms the mind and the spirit. The academic and intellectual side is what you encounter when you enter from the street and thread your way past the large 1960s building with green copper, hinting at its own age, through narrow alleyways separating the 19th century buildings of the original foundation to the visitors' car park and thence to reception and the head. If you drive towards the equine block, however, you come to the sports fields, the huge Astroturf and the stunning view of Cannock Chase. Here, too, is the grass running track where the school recently had to buy new loudspeakers to make announcements heard above the sound of the girls cheering on their housemates and friends.

The school of SS Mary and Anne is a Woodard Girls' School, one of the oldest girls' public schools in the country. Woodard was unwilling initially to found a girls' school: he couldn't see the point of girls' boarding schools. It is said by some that St Anne's School was founded in 1874 by Provost Lowe, the first Provost of Denstone. Various friends, sensing Woodard's blinkered vision, persuaded him to accept the idea and ultimately he allowed Abbots Bromley into the Woodard Foundation. Six years later, on the other side of the street, St Mary's was founded as a less expensive sister school. The Woodard Schools are religious foundations but Victorian Anglicanism was very class conscious and St Mary's was for the daughters of less wealthy parents. Later ages were more squeamish about such distinctions and in 1921 the two schools on either side of the road became as one. Later they were linked by name as Abbots Bromley School for Girls.

On the St Mary's side of the road there is a splendid injunction to motorists from a bygone age: 'Please do not stand your Motors on This Side of the Road', it reads; on the other side of the entrance is a fiercer notice: 'Private property: no trespassing.' This is the home to the prep school, Roch House, the swimming pool, sports hall and medical centre. The mixture of senior and junior parts of the school contributes to that sense of affectionate unity that pervades the whole place.

The 19th century builders were generous with the size of their windows. Whatever the original motives for such huge windows – wide open at night, no doubt – they contribute much to the rooms, which are airy and spacious. The lovely and inviting library is in the process of being made even more attractive, science labs have been improved, IT is efficient and attractively laid out and the boarding facilities are homely and inviting.

The school chapel is, in keeping with Woodard's principles, the most obvious and memorable building. It has height, majesty and atmosphere and will be even more impressive when the lighting is improved. It is clearly central to the atmosphere of the school and though there is no longer daily chapel for all, one or two girls we spoke to told us in a very natural way that they sometimes went to sit there and think. On Fridays the whole senior school attends Eucharist and 'it's a wonderful place to sing in.' There is an affectionate pride in the chapel and ex-pupils speak most lovingly of it.

Girls we spoke to, and how happy they were to talk, expressed huge happiness and delight in their school. 'If I have children,' said one sparky girl, 'I would definitely send them here.' Others nodded in agreement before she added, 'if I could afford it.'

The sixth form wing, with its delightful common room, cooking areas and comfortable bedsits, offers an induction into university. As part of the practical preparation for leaving home and school, sixth form girls do some cooking and are responsible for their own laundry.

Pastoral care and discipline: The old adage about family warmth and trust in each other is as true and apparent in AB as any school we have visited. It's partly the size. 'I know every girl in the school,' one happy inmate told us. 'That helps a lot.' Girls and staff greet each other with warmth and interest as they move about. We saw some inspirational teaching born of mutual respect and genuine interest. Classes were lively, active and worthwhile, and outside the classroom the willingness of staff to spend time with the girls and listen, advise or help is much appreciated. There are six houses in which there is much scope for interaction across the age range, whether it is in the dining room where houses eat together, playing and watching inter-house sport, performing together in plays and concerts, going on outings and trips. There is a clearly stated anti-bullying policy and girls we spoke to said they felt happy and safe. As far as adults are concerned, girls can turn to their housemistress/master, form tutor, sixth form mentor 'anyone whom they trust.'

Boarding is popular but numerically not as popular as it was, though there are clear signs that interest is burgeoning once more. Younger girls share with three or four others, sixth formers have individual bedsits of a rather higher standard than they are likely to find at university. Girls we spoke to were most enthusiastic about boarding, 'but I can't get my mum to agree,' said one frustrated girl who is stepping up her nights of flexi-boarding. 'Perhaps then she won't notice I'm not at home.' Some parents have moved to be nearer the school. That's always revealing.

Pupils and parents: There is a genuine elegance and style about the girls but they are not remotely pretentious or, to use that word, 'posh'. Those we met were forthcoming without being arrogant and were innately courteous and good fun. Many spoke of the joy of being at AB because 'you don't have to pretend to be anything other than yourself'; they didn't they feel they would be happier at a co-ed school. They love the village and the village seems to love them; dads spoke approvingly of visits, 'do you know of any other school which is bang next door to a jolly good pub?'; mums spoke of the love and support given

by the school and the fact that the girls are happily busy and involved. Those parents who were disenchanted by the previous regime are now coming back on board. The Commemoration Day, when the whole school walks down the centre of the High Street in costume and singing hymns, continues. 'We like the tradition: it's slightly mad but great fun.'

Entrance: Most of the girls at the prep school, Roch House, come on to the senior school for which they are well prepared. Others come from abroad, locally and further afield. Entry is, by and large, non-selective: the school is looking for potential, for girls who will contribute and stretch their potential, for girls who will appreciate the variety of activities on offer. Sixth Form entrants are assessed in English, maths and by interview.

Exit: Some 20 per cent leave after GCSEs. A mix of sixth form destinations from Oxbridge to art school to Royal Ballet. In 2013 leavers went to Oxbridge, Durham, Bristol, Warwick, Leeds, Newcastle, Oxford Brookes, Reading, Exeter, Royal Academy of Dance, Manchester, Nottingham, Cirencester. There is no cloning these girls.

Money matters: The school offers scholarships into year 7, year 9, year 10 and year 12. These may be academic, dance, riding, music, art or sport and children living in the village. Riding and ballet are extras: expect some £800 a term for ballet and stabling around £90 a week. Bursaries may be available. Don't be afraid to ask the bursar.

Remarks: The current head is surely right to see AB as a special school, a school with delightful idiosyncrasies and unique possibilities; a school which really does nurture individuality, offering unrivalled opportunities to pursue dance, the performing arts, music and riding as well as good academic teaching; where girls can choose the subjects which really interest them, uncluttered by social expectations. 2014 is the 140th anniversary of the foundation of the school and the school feels poised to leap into the next decade with 'courage braced and faith rekindled.' There is a new skipper at the helm and a reinvigorated crew. These are exciting times for an exciting school.

Abingdon School

Linked school: Abingdon Preparatory School

Park Road, Abingdon, OX14 1DE

- Pupils: 950 boys, 135 boarders • Ages: 11–18 • C of E
- Fees: Boarding £28,020–£33,540; Day £15,870 pa • Independent

Tel: 01235 849041
Email: admissions@abingdon.org.uk
Website: www.abingdon.org.uk

Head: Since 2010, Miss Felicity Lusk (age: cannot wither her). An organist; director of music in New Zealand schools, moving to Hasmonean High in 1990, rising to deputy head and head of the girls' school. Became head of Oxford High in 1997, where we described her as 'stylish, confident and extremely articulate' – she still is. That colourful and impeccably tailored style (think Mad Men via Buckingham Palace) certainly diverts at least the distaff side of any audience at school functions – much more fun than a sea of suits. Boys predictably noncommittal about what was considered a pretty radical move to appoint a female head. A few mentioned that her assemblies were 'quite short' (we assume this is a positive); one said that she was 'a bit like the Queen', showing her face at most activities but not 'getting really involved' – whether she is expected to dive into a tackle during the rugby or grab a cello during a concert we're not sure.

In her love of music, and her insistence upon the highest possible standards, a perfect match for Abingdon. In her opposition to complacency – 'I constantly want us to evolve and not stand still', as she said of Oxford High – she has found work to do, not without some ruffled feathers and a number of birds migrating permanently. The timetable has been revamped, football introduced and Saturday school abolished (though Saturdays still full of matches and 'other half' activities). At a guess, two-thirds of parents and 100 per cent of boys are delighted.

Her very readable weekly blog at www.abingdon.org.uk/heads_blog, now also featuring terrier, Dudley, wears no makeup: character shines truthfully through. An inspired appointment – we expect this fine and relatively low-profile school to be moved up a gear.

Academic matters: A top rank academic school, but one with a tradition of breadth: in 2013 nearly 63 per cent A*/A at A level (90 A*-B); 83 per cent A*/A at GCSE, slim but comforting tail of lower grades (no properly human community is ever perfect).

Sciences/maths the most popular subjects at A level, with geography (unusually popular and notably successful), history and economics not far behind. For a boys' school, art, drama and languages (Mandarin, Spanish) fare pretty well, as does classics (a department which receives great praise from parents). Latin for first two years, thereafter optional. Classical civilisation popular GCSE choice for those enthusiastic about the history but less so the languages. RS no longer compulsory for GCSE but English literature has been added (used to be considered 'too narrow') – certain amount of reshuffling in these departments may or may not be connected.

Traditional academic focus: an emphasis on the more rigorous IGCSEs, few of the lightweight 'studies' on offer; previous head allergic to 'ologies', but psychology has recently crept in for AS/A level. Some sixth form subjects (eg theatre studies, politics) taught jointly with nearby St Helen's, as is the new general studies course. Practical activities (design & technology, computer programming) relatively underdeveloped as academic subjects – but then 'the other half'.

Setting when CE boys come in at 13 based on exam performance in core subjects, but reassessed at the end of the first year – with maths and MFL reset during year 9 as well. School would say only a small difference in ability and final outcome between upper and lower strata – but these competitive boys perceive it more keenly. Some comment that potential Oxbridge candidates not so subtly identified and polished up quite early on, but one is assured that all is not lost for the late bloomers. General rule is 10 GCSEs taken in year 11, though native speakers of foreign languages may take them earlier.

The quality of teaching and learning by best practice is very much a focus for Miss Lusk, who brings with her a strong culture of peer lesson observation. Boys say that teaching is 'generally good, some inspiring', and that they get on well with their teachers, but they did not seem to be as critical as those in some other schools, given that they are well behaved and work very very hard. Teaching 'well beyond the syllabus, made interesting and relevant'. Room too for the robustly eccentric teacher and here, as elsewhere, those who are not standard issue are usually the most popular.

Classroom learning supplemented by plenty of imaginative day trips, many included in the fees if within UK. Annual classics trip particularly praised – 'way beyond what parents could organise for themselves, well prepared, serious, in the style of the Grand Tour'. Advanced level ancient historians encouraged to write talks about sites and deliver them in situ to the younger boys.

Good learning support – all boys screened, will deal with dyslexia/dyspraxia in children who are fundamentally bright enough to keep up.

The usual methods of regular prep and tests keep boys on their toes and most know how they are faring in relation to others, even if they don't let on at home. Detailed termly reports and regular parents' evenings reveal all. Individual teachers respond quickly to specific enquiries by phone or email.

Games, options, the arts: 'The Other Half', Abingdon's credo for learning beyond the classroom, is an emphatic commitment to breadth in education. Forty pages of stylish brochure lay out the opportunities available and the philosophy behind them. Breadth within breadth: boys cannot do just one sport, or all sport, or indeed all anything, and must 'undertake a period of service-type activity' – classroom assistant in a primary school, charity shop, chatting to grannies among a wide range that is praised by parents for getting the boys really involved.

Sport for all, not just the gifted, though you can just about get away with not taking it seriously after the first few years. The top teams are top notch and the Bs, Cs and Ds are pretty good too. Rugby, hockey and cricket all strong, but come the summer it's the rowers who rule. Oarsmen running the mile down to the beautifully designed wooden boathouse in their pink and white strip pass through one of the more lively residential areas of Abingdon, an educative experience, improving knowledge of the vernacular and self-control. It's all character building and, who knows, may contribute to the Boat Club's string of records and successes at national level (first eight won the Princess Elizabeth cup at Henley for the third year running in 2013). Splendid sports centre with eight lane, 25 metre swimming pool. Four pitches by school, others further away. A good range of other sports, no looking down on those who prefer solo to team play, and Real Tennis (at Radley) a rare delight. Regular foreign tours and training trips for the committed can be effectively compulsory – and often expensive.

Though sport is seriously good, it is by no means everything. Music is fine and widespread, with ring-fenced time to avoid encroachment, lots of bands, orchestras and choirs, with a composer-in-residence too, though it is not much studied as an academic subject. Despite the extended lunch time, parents tell us that it can still be a problem for the sporty and musical all rounder (a type Abingdon favours) to fit everything in. Art and design technology well taught to all up to the age of 14, and those who continue with art achieve strong results at A level.

Drama is enjoyed, not least because of joint productions with St Helen's and St Katharine's, but is not part of the life-blood of the school. The film unit, though, is something extraordinary – a semi-autonomous organisation staffed by professional documentary makers and animators, with industry standard kit. Over 100 adventurous, inspirational and award-winning short films have been created there since its foundation in 2003.

Background and atmosphere: A serene place, even on a gloomy day. Parks and playing fields surround a harmonious assembly of Victorian red bricks. An old foundation (1256), long associated with the Mercers Company. Fine chapel: weekly attendance compulsory, at the inter-denominational end of the Church of England.

Boarding, full and weekly, mostly located in the rather grand houses that form the crescent adjacent to the school. Small dormitories that are remarkably impersonal – each bed with a large, completely unused pin board above it. We have observed this in some other boys' boarding schools – a certain reluctance to provide hostages to fortune or signs of finer feelings perhaps. Well-organised weekend activities for the full-boarders. Food very good – 'great,' said our guides – but everyone seems to rush lunch to get on to whatever else they are doing. The Asian boarding contingent tends to make or order in their own of an evening, local takeaways no doubt grateful for the regular custom.

With a couple of girls' schools nearby, those pupils who want female company do not have to look far; sixth formers have joint lessons, plenty of musical and dramatic co-productions and a shared bus system. Mothers say their sons do better without a lot of girls at the front of the class with their hands up, and generally cluttering up their lives (but then they would, wouldn't they?).

Undramatic uniform of blue blazer, grey trousers and plain blue or white shirt plus any one of at least 30 ties showing allegiance to house, sport or Other Half activity; suits in sixth form. So far, so economic, but watch out if your boy is a team player – anything with the griffin on it hurts. Parent run second-hand uniform shop can really help here.

Pastoral care and discipline: Houses and long, weekly tutorials are the backbone of the system, supplemented by professional counsellor. Pastoral care 'not cuddly, but helpful' – staff are vigilant, and we hear that bullying is stamped on pretty fast; reports too of unusual boys being well supported, the best brought out of them. Not all relish the rough and tumble of the house rooms at lunch time (prefects and CCTV still on the losing side against youthful exuberance), but havens for those who prefer to work quietly. Parents full of praise for lower school (ages 11 and 12); boys are kept at a slight remove from the main school to help them ease into the system.

Good behaviour expected at all times but discipline is kept in perspective, perception amongst boys is that things (especially with regard to hair and uniform) are a little less draconian than of yore. Straightforward sin treated seriously – this is a boarding school in the centre of a town so it needs to be – and it's out for drugs.

Pupils and parents: Most day pupils from within the 20-mile radius of the ('unreasonably' say parents) expensive bus network. Parents usual Oxfordshire mix of academics, medics, IT professionals, many working long hours to afford the fees. About half the school's boarders from overseas – a wide range of countries, and well integrated, those we talked to reported close foreign friends. All in all, they're collected and courteous boys.

Correspondence nearly all electronic and weekly email system works a lot better than letters at the bottom of sports' bags. Active parents' association organises all sorts of social events.

Old boys include MP Francis Maude, actor Tom Hollander, comedian David Mitchell, all five members of Radiohead, and countless others who have proper jobs.

Entrance: A good flow at 11 from surrounding primaries (mostly with the help of the local tutorial network, if only to get used to the exams: seek out a good one via the parents of pupils who made the grade) and preps like Chandlings that teach for the Abingdon School exam. A larger number at 13 from prep schools including Abingdon's own, via a mix of exams.

A dozen or two join at sixth form – Miss Lusk has raised the bar somewhat and it's now generally A grade GCSEs for subjects to be studied at A level. Interview and school recommendation important at all ages.

Exit: Very few leave after GCSE (plenty of warning to parents, if needed). Almost all to university – 15 to Oxbridge 2013, Exeter, Bristol, Manchester, Newcastle, UCL and Southampton also popular. Five to USA/Hong Kong in 2013. A wide range of courses, with engineering and economics prominent; above average numbers choose languages, history and medicine.

Money matters: A range of decorative scholarships, but the money is (as ever these days) in the means-tested bursaries.

Remarks: A premier league boys' school, with a strong commitment to a broad education and academic success. Best suits those robust boys who will knuckle down and do 'a hell of a lot of hard work', but understands that boys need to be amused and not just fed facts.

Acland Burghley School

Linked school: LaSwap Sixth Form Consortium

Burghley Road, London, NW5 1UJ

• Pupils: 790 boys and 465 girls, all day • Ages: 11-19 • Non-denom • State

Tel: 020 7485 8515
Email: genadmin@aclandburghley.camden.sch.uk
Website: www.aclandburghley.camden.sch.uk

Headteacher: Since 2010, Ms Jo Armitage (fifties), previously deputy head of Kidbrooke School in south London. Began her career as an apprentice electrical engineer and then worked on intermediate technology projects in developing countries. A technology teacher, she has worked with the Qualifications and Curriculum Development Agency as well as in two deputy head roles.

Academic matters: A genuinely comprehensive school, with no selection by ability or specialist places. Wide ability range, including more than its fair share of students with statements of special education need. A strong cohort of dedicated teachers. In 2013, 58 per cent of pupils got 5+ A*-C grades at GCSE including English and maths; 21 per cent A*/A grades – achieved through a broad and varied curriculum that focuses hard on the core subjects. Particularly successful Spanish, English, English literature, history and ICT. Offers creative and media diploma. Specialist arts college status is evident in the artwork adorning the walls. Students are now set from year 7 in maths, year 8 in modern languages and other subjects from year 9. They learn French or Spanish, but not both, in years 7-9.

Sociology is one of the most popular and successful A level choices; history, English language, English literature, Spanish, dance, drama, physics and media all strong. A good range of vocational courses, including travel and tourism, art and design and business studies. Part of La Swap sixth form consortium that includes other local schools La Sainte Union, William Ellis and Parliament Hill. In 2013, 49 per cent A*/B grades.

Very good learning support department with effective SEN and EAL teaching and enrichment opportunities for gifted and talented students.

Recent Ofsted report tepid, judging the school as 'requires improvement', citing uneven expectations and lack of clear guidelines in the classroom. General parental feeling is that this is unfair: several wrote to the Camden New Journal to complain that they felt the school is better than when it was judged 'good' by the previous Ofsted. Results over the last couple of years have not matched the high spot of 2011, and some feel that Ofsted went in (during the first week of the autumn term) expecting to find a deterioration in standards.

Games, options, the arts: Staff talk of 'visual literacy as a learning style'. All students are offered instrumental lessons. Excellent drama – offers an A level in performing arts, as well as drama GCSE and A level. Has recently opened a multi-million pound performing arts block including recording studio. Has always had a strong reputation for art, though a parent commented that exam results did not always bear out the excellent work going on in school.

PE is good. No grassy acres, but a large sports hall and a gym – refurbished courtesy of a £1.3 million lottery grant. New multi-purpose all-weather pitch. Students also use Tufnell Park playing fields, the Michael Sobell sports centre and Leaside canoeing centre. Everyone does dance and drama in the first three years. Lots of extracurricular activities, some open to the local community, such as fencing and life drawing.

Background and atmosphere: A very urban school in the side streets of Tufnell Park. 1960s concrete exterior gives on to bright and cheerful classrooms, including a £900,000 learning resource centre stocked with computers, CD-roms and books, staffed from 8am-5.30pm. Two-thirds boys, but makes sure girls not overwhelmed. Girls comment, 'It makes us stick together more. And we have boys as friends, which really surprises girls from single-sex schools.' Older students in particular enjoy the equal relationship they have with teachers – 'There's a feeling of co-operation and mutual respect here,' said a sixth former. 'I expect my views to be valued.' Opened a specialist resource base for autism 2011.

Pastoral care and discipline: Renowned for its peer counselling and anti-bullying service, ABC. Students from year 8 upwards are trained to support others who are having difficulties and to run drama workshops in local primary schools. Students feel this affects the whole atmosphere of the school – 'You get to know so many people you wouldn't usually meet and there's a real sense of community. It makes the school feel safer and more friendly'.

Commended by Ofsted for good behaviour, but inevitably a few students are less interested than others in arriving on time, sitting down and learning. Innovative 'iBehave' approach to behaviour management – students and staff share the responsibility for meeting behaviour expectations. Skilled at supporting students with emotional and behavioural difficulties – learning mentors work with students in the lower years. Focus on these areas has improved behaviour and academic performance at key stage 3.

Pupils and parents: A huge social mix, with plenty of children from the tough local estates and middle class families, who have often chosen it for its friendly co-ed atmosphere over the single sex comprehensives nearby. Around a quarter of students speak English as a second language and 30 per cent are eligible for free school meals – well above the national average. The thriving parents' association runs murder mystery evenings, quiz nights and other social events. Ex-students: Ms Dynamite, Sarah Brown (wife of Gordon Brown), Shazad Latif.

Entrance: Heavily over-subscribed, with a catchment area of three-quarters of a mile. First preference to those with a statement of special educational needs, then siblings, then proximity.

Exit: Up to half leave after GCSEs. About three-quarters of La Swap students to university, including occasional Oxbridge candidates, and some to art college.

Remarks: Creditable exam results from a very mixed intake, remarkable for its art and the egalitarian effects of its anti-bullying and peer mentoring programme. 'It's informal, but with clear boundaries,' said a student. 'The staff are good enough at their jobs to enable them to be friendly.' 'There's a real feeling that if you want to do something, you can,' said another.

ACS Cobham International School

Linked school: ACS Cobham International School (Junior section)

Heywood, Portsmouth Road, Cobham, Surrey KT11 1BL

• Pupils: 760 pupils in senior school, boys and girls; 95 boarders
• Ages: 2-18 • Non-denom • Fees: Day £9,990-£23,150; Boarding £33,460-£40,370 pa • Independent

Tel: 01932 867251
Email: cobhamadmissions@acs-england.co.uk
Website: www.acs-schools.com

Headmaster: Since 2011, Tony Eysele (Natal University BSc; Edgewood College of Education HDE and Heriott-Watt University organisational behaviour degree). Born and educated in South Africa, short stint as a chemist in the oil industry, moved into education to teach sciences. Taught in state schools, then independents – St.Stithians College, Michaelhouse and Herzlia. Head of Helpmekaar College in Johannesburg during its transformation from struggling state school to premier privatised school.

He, his wife and young family moved to Zimbabwe to take on the headship of St. John's College, described by him as 'the Harrow of Harare', to introduce the IB Diploma, making it the second IB school in Africa, while managing precarious relations with the political powers in the country. Concerned for wellbeing of his family, moved to the UK as Foundation director of Lord Wandsworth College, managing the scholarship fund aimed at less privileged students. Wife Cheryl is admissions director at Marymount London; two grown sons, one a teacher, one a professional athlete. Sporty background and reported to be outgoing and likeable.

Aware that his predecessor was a popular head who served for nearly 20 years, and that he has joined a team of experienced divisional principals who have collectively served at Cobham for over half a century. Spent the first year getting to know the lay of the land and building relationships with colleagues and families. Impressed by the very 'hands-on' parent body, who he describes as very open about any concerns they have while at the same time very supportive of the school and staff – says they are the real marketing agents for the school. Has introduced weekly principals' meetings, does regular 'walkabouts' to drop in on classes, meet the pupils.

His goals are to refine and review the co-curricular programme, oversee the building of the new £10.5 million arts centre, which will feature a large state-of-the-art theatre, audit the academic programme with the divisional principals and develop the outdoor education programme. A rather atypical international school head, with unique perspectives on children and education – a most interesting appointment.

Academic matters: American preparatory honours courses (towards American high school diploma), with 14 Advanced Placement courses and the International Baccalaureate (IB diploma) offered in the upper grades, maximum 20 in classes for all grades.

Lower school emphasis on personal progress rather than grades, using carefully designed rubrics assessing progress (that can be readily translated into letter grades for transition to other schools). Very concerned that student gets a truly sound foundation and understands where he has been and where he needs to go, not compete against each other at this age. Strong fundamentals in maths – even those arriving not properly prepared are strengthened by the process (in one example going from 40s to 90s in ERB math scores). Children work well together in teams, share ideas; are mixed well in terms of letting different ones lead, 'even forced into leadership'. Parents report that these are exceptionally empathetic teachers. A certain amount of traditional lecturing in the upper grades, but the school says it encourages and looks for 'proficiency in the Socratic method,' teachers who are excited, engaged in inquiry-based, collaborative teaching and are themselves learners.

The school has always prided itself on frequent professional training in academics and all aspects of dealing with young people. However parents comment that global economic strains have taken their toll on the company that runs the school, and the profit motive has made people cynical. Teachers seem to do the work of two or three and more turnover than in recent years. That means less time for reflection or paying attention to improving systems or working on problems. Yet the students and parents feel that the faculty is the best thing about ACS Cobham, and the faculty seem to feel that way about each other.

Students are placed according to proficiency in maths and languages, mixed but challenged in other classes. Super language choices – courses in nine languages, classes arranged for other languages not offered or in native tongue. Good exam results, especially considering so many EAL students: 2013 IB average point score 33 (out of 45 max).

Special ed assistance is good and getting better – new specially trained teachers in lower and upper grades are particularly good at helping kids deal with learning difficulties and teachers deal with kids' disabilities and different learning styles.

Very strong EAL assistance, both in specific EAL classes and mainstream classroom help. Fifteen per cent of students arrive speaking no English – by ninth and tenth grade may still receive assistance but, by high school, must be proficient to handle the workload.

Games, options, the arts: One of the strongest sports programmes of all the American schools, no doubt because of endless acres of playing fields (and six hole golf course, baseball diamond, tennis courts etc), but especially now because of the 'healthy schools initiative'. Very competent staff run the extensive PE offerings and see to the drop-dead terrific sports centre. Few gyms, clubs, or schools in the world have such state-of-the-art aquatic facilities (computerised touch pads, movable pool bottom, water temp that can change at will depending on activities, UV-based – cleaning all but eliminating heavy, eye-stinging, chlorinated atmosphere), or individual, computer-card operated workout equipment, plus suspended wood floors in the dance studio and gym, in a stunning light-drenched interior that looks like an ocean liner. All hands do sports in middle school, for skill and fun. No wonder the kids have so much energy and look amazingly fit.

By high school, teams are selective (varsity teams compete in ISST competitions around Europe), but so many options (total of about 24 teams in various sports and ages per season) 'Any student in this school who wants to do sports can'. Even by the intensely academic senior year, elective classes are so appealing that most people, including non-athletes, stay in at least one. As everywhere else in the school, teachers come up with an optimum match that fits students' interests while it gives them something they need. Not unexpectedly, excellent facilities and classes for visual and performing arts, community service, like Habitat for Humanity, international academic competitions, clubs, and a million field trips – cultural, historical, or service throughout London and the UK, Europe, Namibia, you name it.

Background and atmosphere: Started in 1972 in attractive 1820s manor house built by Prince Leopold (later King of the Belgians) for his mistress. Finding herself too far from the bright lights of London, she promptly upped sticks and left, but ACS families who move here love it (poor Leopold would have appreciated today's 30 minute train trip to Waterloo). Apart from said love nest and the charming village by the old walled garden, most of the upper school buildings are contemporary, purpose-built and highly functional (of dark brick and rather in the stepped style of 1970s Florida golf condos), a bit dark in the halls, but

the rows of glass in classrooms and dorms help. Additional Early Childhood building housing purpose-built classrooms and office space. Recent state-of-the-art interactive learning centre for classes of all ages, plus new outdoor learning centre to enhance use of woodland environment as a teaching resource.

A closed campus (no one comes or goes along the roads or into the buildings without a pass), which is one of the reasons why appears to be very little concern about things like drugs. In the corridors, students are cheerfully relaxed, sprawled around in the halls with minimal regard for the traffic impediments of long legs and those enormous teenage feet.

It is widely believed that there is no dress code, but in fact there is – enforcement is just a bit listless: the current high school administration reportedly feels that dressing is a form of personal expression (which seems to express itself largely in jeans) and hopes good judgement will be used. Despite the kids being good looking, healthy and relaxed, some parents wish for a less intoxicating mix of hormones and bare midriffs.

Described as a factory by some not used to this particular kind of culture, it is seen as more of a well oiled machine by many on the inside and, although it has its problems, the cogs and wheels usually run pretty well for such a big, complicated place: the grounds and buildings have the liveliness, variety, energy and buzz that are very familiar to students from good, large, urban US high schools.

Pastoral care and discipline: In lower school, family buddies are matched with families of same aged children. Boarders are watched over by a sympathetic team of house-parents, the head of which feels the school nurtures teachers and staff as well as it does students. School rules are clearly stated, with a staged process of discipline depending on severity. Drug offences are dealt with swiftly. A peer group buddy system for students, plus parent, teacher and student training for sensitivity to drugs, sexuality, bullying etc (using self-assessing interactive software, weekly group discussions, speakers) all keep awareness high to catch problems as they arise. School feels it's failed if someone must go; the process even for expulsion is compassionate – concerned with what is best for the child as well as the school.

Lip service is paid to the idea that a culture where you accept responsibility for yourself and others ensures a safe school. However that same assumed self-discipline gives rise to some unease about the busy but largely unmonitored senior room where the oldest students are left to their own devices. Even that wouldn't be a problem, it is felt, if it weren't for a generally lax sense of discipline at the high school level. Most discipline is left up to individual teachers, with a high school head who feels his role is to represent the students' point of view. The fact that the school is 'bursting at the seams' has not improved this situation. It's felt that the lack of discipline has worsened and 'things just fall through the cracks'.

Pupils and parents: Reportedly the student mix is about 46 per cent American (although many say it feels like far fewer Americans these days, making for a more international mix), 11 per cent British, 68 other nationalities. No question the pace and culture of this school is American. When new kids arrive, they adapt easily to the ethos of this caring and open-minded school; accents seem to melt into an American drawl. Students are well-heeled and worldly, and not easily impressed by flashier newcomers who expect to dazzle with riches from afar. Kids alert and amiable with each other, attentive and focused in classes; they love the international diversity, say, 'Someone closed-minded wouldn't like it'.

Lots of high flying expats from the business, finance and sports world; with the odd chauffeur dropping off his young charges (occasionally bodyguards, who then retire to the front gate and unofficially add to the school security jotting down license tags!). Capable, involved parents help throughout the school; enormously successful international parents' committee

A

integrates non-English speaking families, initiating and maintaining contact parent to parent in their own languages – quickly creating a high level of confidence and excellent network of communication. Good parent support seminars, welcoming picnics, transition meetings, and close contact throughout with administration. Families move here because of the attractive town and more space for children, yet easy commuting distance from London. Boarders are often children whose diplomatic or corporate parents don't have appropriate schooling in their current posting, or kids who want to finish here once they've started. There are waiting lists at some of the grades, but admissions tries to accommodate families which can cause the High School to fill to overflowing.

Entrance: Roughly 25 per cent turnover of student body from year to year, but most of it occurs during summer – average stay is three years, due to vagaries of corporate moves. Selective entrance – looking for children 'willing to take on or grow into the challenge, given the space'. School tries very hard to see how they can address any child's needs, whether in achievement, language, or learning difficulties.

Exit: Although college counselling in the past has been very good, of late it's been much spottier, possibly reflecting more staffing problems, with the standard support usually found in such a good American school missing (eg calendar of what to expect through the complex and layered college application, SAT testing process etc).

Nonetheless, students get into a superb range of top universities in the US and the UK (increasingly more in the UK), such as the Ivies, NYU, Georgetown, University of California, Duke, Vanderbilt; and all of the top UK universities, including Oxford, Cambridge, Imperial College, London School of Economics, University College, London etc. Plenty of students have the imagination and adventure to go on to world ranked universities in Japan (University of Tokyo), Europe (eg Stockholm School of Economics) and Canada (Toronto and McGill), to name a few from their impressive list.

Money matters: Financial stability is down to the private corporate ACS owners; no endowment, fees fund the school and include tuition, loan of books, classroom materials, curriculum-related field trips. Quoted boarding fees do not include tuition but do include autumn break holiday trip. Some financial assistance available.

Remarks: A vibrant, buzzy school, the only one of the three ACS schools with boarding students as well as day. 'It's small enough so you know everyone and big enough so you can make new friends.' Most abilities do well here, but those you don't expect to might just thrive. Probably not for the child that gets lost in a crowd, but parents looking for a large, lively, all round and very American school with a great sports programme need look no further.

ACS Egham International School

Linked school: ACS Egham International School (Junior)

Woodlee, London Road, Egham, Surrey TW20 0HS

• Pupils: 190 boys and girls, all day • Ages: 11–19 • Non-denom
• Fees: £6,710–£21,990 pa • Independent

Tel: 01784 430611
Email: eghamadmissions@acs-england.co.uk
Website: www.acs-schools.com

Head of School: Since 2010, Mr Jeremy Lewis BA PGCE. British by birth, raised in Cape Town, degrees from Portsmouth and Nottingham plus a master's in education admin from Bath. Has been in schools from the Isle of Wight to Kuwait, Japan, Hungary and Vietnam. Started as a teacher of humanities, then a progression of senior leadership roles – most recently headmaster of Istanbul International Community School.

Wants to make school a centre of excellence for IB teaching and learning, while broadening and strengthening curriculum. Has extensive IB experience: teaching, coordinating, training; brought the IB to Kuwait in the mid '80s. His Irish wife, Carmel, is a career IB ESL teacher and their two children, both at ACS Egham, are IBPYP and IBMYP products. Believes that more pupils are capable of managing the IB diploma programme than some would say.

His two passions are the idea of developing internationally-minded students and football, both formed during his South African childhood (during apartheid). Sees this as a place where parents, too, are engaged in the children's learning. Held by them as a thoughtful, cheery, reflective and genuine person – a very nice man.

Academic matters: They believe here that every child can succeed, and lots of attention is given to help each student do his/her best. IB programme at all levels – the IB Learner Profile, a guidepost for how learning and behaviour are approached, is everywhere: communicators, thinkers, enquirers, risk-takers, knowledgeable, principled, caring, open-minded, balanced and reflective. Great expectations!

The IB primary years programme inquiry-based, trans-disciplinary approach helps children understand the world they live in, acquire and apply the knowledge. IB middle years programme prepares students for academic rigours of the diploma programme in years 11 and 12, but some say that it is the least understood of the three programmes, and the one that parents question most.

Well-established IB diploma programme with the usual range of courses plus new IB sports, exercise, and health science – introduced thanks to the impressive new sports facility. In 2013 IB results produced an average of 35 points. Most students take the full diploma, although they can opt to take individual certificates without doing the full diploma. IB programmes encourage strong communication skills, teachers give students every opportunity to express themselves and are approachable. One parent said her youngster 'produces impressive PowerPoint presentations and has no fear of speaking in front of a group'. Kids very comfortable with visitors and ready to tell you all about what they are learning or doing, from the youngest pre-schoolers (they're aptly known as 'Scramblers') right up to the second year IB students. A hat design activity going on in an MYP art class was less about millinery fashion and more about design and construction plus fun facts about famous hats in art and history. We learnt a few things we didn't know!

Technology throughout. It's an Apple Mac school and generous provision is rolling out iPad programme in two phases. Class sizes vary significantly across the school and across the subjects. French and Spanish are taught in grades 1-12. The native language enrichment programme gives students the opportunity to maintain their own language. Where viable (minimum of three students of similar ages and levels), mother-tongue languages are supported by additional classes, funded by the school. Eleven currently on offer including most European languages plus Russian, Urdu, Hebrew and Japanese. If fewer than three, the school helps find a tutor with classes paid by parents. EAL programme supports pupils in regular classes with specially trained teachers to help each student acquire basic vocabulary and vocabulary relevant to classroom topics. They make the school fit the child. Limited learning support in the school for mild to moderate needs, but mild special needs support is provided and monitored. Some special needs can be accommodated and each case is assessed by the child study team. If specialists are brought in, parents must assume the costs.

Reports are sent by email, and if any problems, the child study team steps in right away to review all options for help. Each term there are student-led conferences with parents and faculty: the school feels that the student is the main player and should take responsibility for their education. Limited learning support for mild to moderate needs; each case assessed by the child study team and if specialists are brought in, parents assume the costs. ISA (International Schools' Assessment) tests are given to students from ages 8-15, to assess progress and MAP tests (Measures of Academic Progress), a data-led approach originated in the US designed to improving teaching and learning is also used to help students set goals.

The faculty of 85 full-time teachers brings lots of previous international and IB experience. Lewis is pleased that the level of turnover is dropping and teachers are staying longer. In lower school, the quality of the teacher really makes a difference and parents say some teachers are stronger than others. Reports are that overall ACS Egham teachers are much appreciated and well-liked by students and parents are happy.

Games, options, the arts: Healthy mix of sports available: rugby, soccer, basketball, volleyball, cross country, athletics, tennis, golf, softball, baseball, track and field. Impressive new sports facility includes a large climbing wall, a fitness suite, dance studio, two gyms and technology to help students analyse and assess their fitness and technique. The new facilities may see fitness, climbing, dance, pilates and judo introduced. Despite concerns about the smaller size of the school, parents appreciate that chances of making the competitive teams are better. Competition with local international schools and through ISSA meaning some matches in exciting places on the Continent. Lower school offers soccer, gymnastics, tennis and track and field during the school day.

After-school clubs popular for all ages from crafts to model United Nations to sports. Choir has performed at Royal Albert Hall. Artist in residence programme brings in everything from local poets to painters. Annual drama production. Impressive design tech studio – students work with plastics, metal and wood. Parents highlight the rock weekend, a sort of 'battle of the bands' involving everyone.

Mr Lewis' keen to broaden and strengthen students' sense of altruism and responsibilities towards the local and wider community. He is building collaborative partnerships with local schools including two academies. Community service activities include volunteering with Orbis Eye Hospitals travelling with 'flying hospital' to Vietnam and Mongolia, nurturing the school's five-year partnership with a school for street children in Kenya when kids travel out to help in all sorts of ways. Described as 'amazing' by one parent who said, 'this activity created very real connections. Kids want to go back there and become completely engaged. Exposure to other ways of living helped them appreciate their own privilege.'

Background and atmosphere: Located on the fringes of beautiful royal Windsor Great Park, and bordering Victorian icon Royal Holloway College. Campus protected by manned security gates. Illustrious former occupants of the original mansion house include a 19th century Member of Parliament, a WW1 veteran who fought at Gallipoli and his society wife, and wounded WWII heroes who went there for rehabilitation and retraining. Today it is filled with bright and sunny classrooms and offices. Set in manicured gardens, the mansion now shares the grounds with several architecturally-sympathetic modern buildings designed for educational use by ACS.

Much attention in recent years to improving the campus. The buzz is all about the new sports centre, which has state of the art everything PE, with the exception of a pool. General classrooms in the sports centre supplement the school's teaching space to meet the growing enrolment. The lunch room is noisy but teachers supervise and keep under control. Valiant efforts have been made to improve cafeteria service, particularly the flow of traffic; parents say it's probably not adequate yet for the number of pupils at the school. Though the kids grumble in the time-honoured tradition of kids everywhere and describe the canteen as 'boring', once they're actually sitting down to eat 'it's okay'.

The other improvement is the IB diploma centre – exclusively for the eldest students with teaching spaces, offices for both IB coordinator and university counsellors for easy access (plus subtle supervision), lounge with kitchenette with microwave, fridge, etc. for lunch or senior munchies attacks. On the day we visited, PTA was there doing a Macmillan bake sale at school, we loved seeing that they had left a tray of goodies for seniors in the IB centre with 'please help yourself and donate' sign next to a little basket filling up with money. Parents say it's early days but the school is protecting this space for the IB kids and the younger students honour that – 'it's like hallowed ground'.

Plenty of room for everyone to learn and play. Generous art rooms, science labs, early childhood provision is all self-contained and lovely setting for first school experience, beautiful grounds and sports fields. Now that the IB diploma centre is finished, parents would like to see enhancements to science labs, and a 'commons' for middle and younger high schoolers. 'If you ask where the heart of the campus is, there's no obvious answer,' but maybe the new gym will change that.

Two well-stocked libraries and a generous budget of several hundred thousand to meet technology needs. Computers everywhere, high schoolers can bring their own laptops and are given an iPod to use as tools and memory devices. There is 'no uniform, just good judgment'.

Egham is one of four ACS International Schools (three in UK, one new one in Qatar). The schools are governed by a board of independent, non-executive directors (who typically have international and UK experience across a range of areas including education, finance, and law). According to the school's website, the board 'supports the development and the day-to-day operations of the schools'.

Pastoral care and discipline: Despite growth in enrolment, the head strives to maintain a 'small school' feel where teachers and students know each other. Problems are quickly detected and the child study team steps in to review and resolve. The caring atmosphere means that bullying doesn't work here. Parents say, 'there is no anonymity or privacy here so if you are in trouble there's no hiding it.' Health classes, drug and alcohol prevention seminars keep the students informed. Zero tolerance for drugs and drinking – students' unwillingness to disappoint parents largely seems to keeps everyone out of trouble.

Although the school is non-selective, parents say that the culture of the school stresses the importance of hard work and has a way of motivating students. Parents tell of lower school students who want to get on with homework independently and 'without help' from parents. It's not unusual for kids at

IB diploma level to organise themselves into study groups to revise or discuss classwork, but balance is important too and students make room in their lives for pursuing sports, musical interests, etc.

Some parents wonder about the smallish size of the high school and comment that higher numbers of students might mean more resources, more options for musical groups, more scope for sports teams. The all-singing, all-dancing Cobham campus is just down the road and parents sometimes question how much of their fees are subsidising other ACS campuses, including developments in far-off ACS Doha. However, as the school pointed out in response to this comment, Egham has invested a tremendous amount in its own right in recent years. Nevertheless, prevailing view is that Egham's smaller size means that there is a strong sense of community and a family feel.

Pupils and parents: The school attracts 'like-minded' internationally-attuned families who are 'looking for a mind-set, not just a curriculum'. Over 50 nationalities, about 22 per cent US followed by 17 per cent British, nine per cent Dutch, and then the rest of the world. Parents stress there is no predominant nationality or culture and many have chosen Egham for that reason.

The head, also an Egham parent, meets regularly with PTO, does the usual monthly newsletters, and four times each year hosts a forum for parents, taking open questions on any topic – no advance submission required. He's pleased with the strong sense of community at the school – verified through an annual independent parent survey that helps keep him abreast of opinions. 'Welcoming and accepting' are words heard repeatedly about the school community. PTO organises lots of activities to help new parents fit in and a 'family buddy' system gives new arrivals first point of contact in the community and tips like where to get a haircut and buy school supplies. Be sure to ask for a copy of 'Jaguar Tales'.

School bus routes cover areas from Maidenhead and Slough to the north, Weybridge to the east, Frimley and Woking to the south, Wokingham to the west.

Entrance: Non-selective school welcomes students with wide range of abilities. Admission based on previous school records and testing scores, references from previous school, family questionnaires. Academic English required to enter grades 8-12, assessed through a comprehensive English test that can be sent to the current school to administer.

Predominantly expats at the school with about 25 per cent turnover, so there is transiency and hope of a place. Rolling admissions; students admitted year-round. Feeder schools include local area schools but mostly international schools worldwide.

No open days per se, visits by appointment are normally available year round. Parents say that some families are joining ACS without understanding the IB, so ask questions! With the scope and relatively long history of the ACS schools, parents often hear about the school 'on the expat circuit', so that, sustained by ACS International's slick marketing, is what brings parents to the door.

Exit: If children leave before graduation, it is most often due to families being transferred. The school offers the coursework needed to satisfy the requirements for an American high school diploma. University guidance is started in grades 9 and 10, and grades 11 and 12 are given one-to-one advisors to help with the application process. In 2013, students off to universities in the UK, USA, Canada and beyond. Parents are watching to see how a popular teacher recently appointed as college counsellor copes with the dual US-UK university admissions process.

The PSAT is offered to all students in grades 10 and 11. SAT also offered.

Money matters: ACS Egham is privately owned, fee-supported with no endowment. The school relies on income from fees, with surpluses reinvested in the schools to maintain high standards; it is evident that money has been made available to develop the ever-improving facilities and programmes required to serve the growing enrolment. Some parents say the fees are high but that they continue to choose this education because of what it offers. ACS Foundation offers limited needs-based financial aid.

Remarks: The individualised approach to education serves a range of different learning styles and academic abilities. One parent sums it up: 'There are always things you'd like to see done differently at any school, but at ACS Egham my kids are thriving and children are learning, growing and developing. Isn't that what's most important?'

ACS Hillingdon International School

Linked school: ACS Hillingdon International School (Junior)

Hillingdon Court, 108 Vine Lane, Hillingdon, Middlesex UB10 0BE

• Pupils: 580 boys and girls • Ages: 4–18 • Non–denom
• Fees: £9,820-£21,490 pa • Independent

Tel: 01895 259771
Email: hillingdonadmissions@acs–schools.com
Website: www.acs-schools.com

Head of School: Since 2012, Linda LaPine; from the USA; BA (Urban Studies) State University of New York; MPS (master professional studies, special educational needs), Manhattanville College, New York; teaching and principal certification. She was a special needs teacher in New York, also in private practice, before going abroad to International School of Tanganyika, American School in Singapore, Anglo-American in Moscow as deputy head, most recently International School of Panama as director. Now as head of a school that is part of a larger group of four, she devotes most of her time to running Hillingdon, while collaborating with the other ACS heads and board developing programmes and policies for the ACS schools group.

In her words, she came into a good school with no major issues to resolve. After significant developments at ACS Qatar, Egham and Cobham, Hillingdon likely to be the next candidate within the ACS schools group for capital investment, so Ms LaPine is working with colleagues to determine what that might be: strengthening of curriculum, technology, internationalism and/or use of the outdoor environment. 'I am not aspiring for ACS Hillingdon to be a "magnet'school", I just want to provide an overall inclusive educational programme that is a based on a strong school community. Academics are priority, but it's also about the overall family experience, the kids being comfortable and happy, and every child feeling important.' Two daughters attending the school. On contract till 2015.

Academic matters: Take a deep breath before you try to penetrate ACS's patchwork quilt curricula. Start with American-style Pre-K – Grade 5 with international add-ons including some IPC (International Primary Curriculum) units, language and cultural studies to grade 2, then Spanish plus PTSA (Parent Teacher Student Association) -led multicultural weeks (grades 3-5); IB Middle Years Programme with Spanish or French, followed by the last two years of high school with the IB diploma, a fair range of AP courses (11 on offer), ACS-designed high school honours (which is really just 'regular' level, meaning not IB or AP), or a combination thereof. So it combines American school roots with academic programmes, legacies of previous ACS International Schools leadership and drawn from the experiences of the sister campuses – sewn together, with some added layers of internationalism appliquéd on top to embellish the whole work of art. Parents seem happy with what's on offer, and kids are moving forward successfully in their various academic paths.

IB average in 2013 was 34 points, an increase over previous two years, with an 81 per cent pass rate. AP averages was 2.89 points, with 72 per cent earning 3 points or more. There were eight AP Scholars. SAT mean scores were (native English speakers) 517 for writing and 518 for verbal; 580 math; ACT mean was 27.

The early childhood programme is a nice blend of learning-through-play and structure, supplemented by specialist teachers for music, art and PE, and cultural classes. The primary parents are generally happy with the programme, particularly the language and culture classes, and multicultural studies programmes organised by the PTSA. Above all, they like the fact that the primary principal is very much around in the classrooms, engaged with the kids and monitoring progress. One of the few complaints is that some feel that homework is somewhat inconsistent, with more in lower school than middle school. (The school confirms it has a homework policy published in its handbooks).

The high school staff are working with the other two ACS schools to improve counselling on course selection and university and career planning – beginning in 9th grade. Students who are less likely to be successful with the full IB are given some early guidance, leaving it up to the student and family to decide whether to go for full diploma or certificates. About 60 per cent of students go the IB diploma route.

Plenty of up-to-date technology is apparent throughout busy tech labs, with ample use of interactive whiteboards and smart TVs. An Apple school, students from grade 1-12 have iPads issued by the school. The IT team includes three 'integrationists' who help teachers. The IT team is available for students AND even parents who need minor repairs or tech support!

The youngest ones are exposed to languages represented in the school community through the language and cultures programme parents help run. A different language and culture is featured each month, when basic phrases are learned, traditions are explored, food sampled. Spanish taught in grades 3 -5; French offered as alternative option in grades 6- 10.

The NLE (Native Language Enrichment programme – an ACS schools feature) provides mother tongue instruction. With a minimum of three students of similar ages and levels, languages are supported by classes funded by the school (if fewer than three, the school helps find a tutor but classes are paid by parents), scheduled after school for one hour each week. The idea is to maintain reading, writing and oral proficiency; typically on offer are up to 10 languages including Spanish, French, Dutch, German, Arabic and Japanese taught by native speakers. Parents appreciate this but say they'd like to see more, and it can be difficult to enthuse children about taking the mother tongue when their chums are doing 'fun' after-school activities, so they may revert to Saturday schools. At IB level, the provision ramps up as mother tongue language A courses (Japanese, Dutch, currently offered).

Lots of monitoring and MAP (Measures of Academic Progress – a data-led approach originated in the US) tests to track progress. EAL specialists support pupils in regular classes to help each student acquire basic vocabulary and vocabulary relevant to classroom topics. Beginner non-English speakers are accepted up to grade 7; after that some proficiency in English is required. The youngest ones have full-immersion English, with specialists either working alongside the children in the mainstream classroom, or withdrawing them for one-to-one or small group support. For middle and high school, EAL is scheduled during English classes.

Faculty made up of some 17 nationalities, roughly one third each British and US, the remaining from Canada, Australia, New Zealand plus other countries. Average staff age is 40s, and some have been there for quite a long time; average tenure is 7-10 years. The teacher to student ratio is 7.5 to 1. Maximum class size is 20, average 14.

Games, options, the arts: After-school clubs (and some activities offered during lunch) for all ages range from crafts to Model United Nations, Duke of Edinburgh, International Schools Theatre Association, National Honour Society and scouts to sports; there are even middle school magic and Lego robotics clubs. A popular Saturday sports programme for grades K-8 features basketball, tennis, football and baseball. There's been a proposal from the kids for a sleepover in the mansion to see if there's any truth in the rumour that Hillingdon Court is haunted. All suggestions obviously considered!

Quite aside from one parent's comment that sports may not be this school's strong suit, ACS Hillingdon has the highest uptake of the three UK ACS schools: 70 per cent of the students do extracurricular sports. Staff say it's not so much about winning and victory as it is about getting involved, having fun and being well-rounded. But despite all that fun and well-roundedness, the riot of banners and plaques prominently displayed in the gym are testimony to plenty of winning over the years. Recent notable achievements include boys' rugby, basketball and tennis, and girls' basketball and softball. Kids participate in the usual international school sports fixtures, travelling to other countries for tournaments. Sports fields are out in Iver Heath, about a 12-minute bus ride away; an impressive double gymnasium and tennis courts are on-site.

Student art work is exhibited everywhere including revolving exhibitions in the head's office (a proud primary student was in the office taking a photo of this to send to his grandmother), and the centrally-located Bridge Gallery. Most music activities (including lots of music tech and a recording studio) are based in Harmony House; primary music that takes place in the main mansion – in a stunning room with high ceilings, sculpted crown mouldings, cornices, coving and massive windows overlooking the gardens – surely one of the most elegant international primary school music rooms on the planet. Many kids (grades 4-12) take private music lessons during the school day, and various musical ensembles are available for middle and high school students. Hillingdon's Got Talent is hugely popular for the whole school community. In fact, parents described the overall arts programme as 'phenomenal'.

When compared to other local international schools, community service at ACS Hillingdon seems a bit more focused on fundraising for good causes rather than hands-on action. That said, IB students do projects at an orphanage in Bulgaria (running several years now), help in a local nursing home, and also do volunteer activities within the school.

Internationalism is celebrated with lots of support from the PTSA Multicultural Committee and events such as International Spirit Week. Lots of trips locally (starting with a grade 4 camping trip) and abroad as part of the curriculum; middle school trips to Spain or France take place on alternate years linked to the language programmes.

Background and atmosphere: Located in a residential pocket of Hillingdon, a west London suburb on the former estate of Lord Hillingdon, the original Victorian mansion was used during the war as nursing home. Modern buildings added onto the lovingly maintained 19th century house are a bit at odds with the beautiful proportions of the house, but do accommodate the school's many classes and activities.

Entrance through the manned security gates leads to a morning room conservatory, the reception area, a splendid ground floor entry room used for various meetings and events, the admissions office in a beautiful wood-panelled study, and music room and the high school library – several of which overlook the manicured gardens. The aim has been to give the kids access to these beautiful reception rooms, and not to restrict them to the modern parts where most of their classes now take place. The fact that the head's office is not in the auspicious rooms of the original house, but more centrally located at the heart in the school, says something about the school's values.

Lots of nice bright classrooms, generous space for art rooms, numerous science labs, music rooms. Two areas for drama (the auditorium and a smaller mirrored dance or drama rehearsal studio); two libraries, one each for primary and middle/high school, both located in the mansion.

Each section of the school is in a more or less in self-contained area, which parents like. Pre-K and K have their own self-contained pavilion (a calm oasis on the day of our visit) with small library and colourful outdoor play area in a quiet area behind the main house overlooking the gardens. Beyond the gardens are some outdoor sports grounds and tennis courts, and somewhere out there two vegetable gardens tended by students.

Though the school has won awards for its healthy catering, kids say the lunchroom food is 'okay'; but parents love the touch fingerprint payment system as well as the school's flexibility, so kids can buy there or bring their own lunch without the need to handle of money.

Hillingdon is one of four ACS International Schools (three in UK, one new one in Qatar), governed by a board of independent, non-executive directors (who typically have international and UK experience across a range of areas including education, finance, and law). According to the school's website, the board 'supports the development and the day-to-day operations of the schools'. We interpret this to mean that they support the ACS leadership team that meet regularly and consists of the managing director, the heads of finance, marketing, HR, and Ms LaPine and the three other ACS heads.

Pastoral care and discipline: Positive feedback from everyone, including parents, about the strong sense of community. The counsellors are reportedly excellent at helping students integrate into the school and families to cope with the transition to a new country and school, particularly at the primary school level, in addition to supporting the usual issues such as relationships, self-esteem and behaviour. They've also developed with teachers a cyber-safety programme for kids and parents, starting with the youngest children. No mention of serious behaviour issues; good home-school communication; teachers are responsive to emails.

Pupils and parents: About forty nationalities: 34 per cent US, 14 per cent British, and, among many others, a recent increase in families from the Middle East. Parents are made up of a good many corporate expats (particularly finance and pharmaceuticals, many based at Stockley Park), US embassy and other diplomats, and private entrepreneurs, and the international diversity is part of the attraction, according to many parents we spoke to. Some of the British students are repatriating from abroad and prefer to stay in the international school environment with its more relaxed and varied teaching approach. As is true in other London international schools, total turnover is lower than one might expect: about 17 -20 per cent. Families (including staff kids) are staying longer.

A super-active PTSA organises events for parents to socialise and get acclimated with London, and also works with the school to make sure all new families are contacted. Buses are available and covers a wide net: from Maidenhead and High Wycombe to the west, Watford and Amersham to the north, central London to the east, and Heathrow and Windsor to the south. It's a combination of door-to-door or pick up point, and a very good late and late, late bus service is appreciated by families whose children get involved in after-school activities. (Pre K and

K students are not allowed to take the late buses.) Forty per cent of the school's kids are bussed from central London. Parents love the availability of this service, but suggest parents consider realistically the likely travel time.

Entrance: Non-selective; will admit students they feel they can serve and who will benefit from the programme. Admission based on previous school records and testing scores; family statements and references from previous school are preferred, though the admissions director understands that for last-minute summer transfers these are sometimes difficult to obtain. Additional assessment or writing samples may be requested. Academic English required for non-native speakers to enter grades 8-12, assessed through a test that can be sent abroad to the current school to administer. Decisions to admit students (grades 5-12) with diagnosed special educational needs are made in consultation with the specialists. It is sometimes possible – and recommended – that prospective students spend a day in the school.

Exit: Students either leave because of family reposting or graduate from ACS Hillingdon; very few leave to attend local schools. Good college counselling department, helping pupils find the right fit in a more imaginative range of countries than the norm. About 60 per cent of students go to North American universities (eg Boston College, Brigham Young, NYU, Notre Dame, San Diego State, Emory, American in the US, McGill, Uni of British Columbia in Canada); about 40 per cent go to UK (UCL, Royal Holloway, LSE, Warwick, Bath, Lancaster, Edinburgh, Kings); a handful go to countries such as Japan, Australia, Germany, for example Waseda, Keio (Japan), Technical University (Denmark). Most of the UK applicants are IB students, though some AP candidates as well.

Money matters: ACS Hillingdon is privately owned by a for-profit corporation, fee-supported with no endowment. The school relies on income from fees, with surpluses reinvested in the schools to maintain high standards; it is evident that there has been continued investment in the school facilities.

Limited need-based financial aid is available from the ACS Foundation. No big development and advancement programmes; the PTSA does fundraising activities to support school programmes and events.

Remarks: This is a happy, internationally diverse school that is ticking along nicely. A new head with a strong international school pedigree and a special interest in curriculum is bound to bring some changes to the programme once she's had the opportunity to do the prerequisite observation, research and consultation. She'll no doubt want to preserve the positive features of the school. Some holistic soul-searching about this American international educational institution may well lead to interesting developments in the years to come.

Aiglon College

1885 Chesières-Villars, Chesières-Villars, Switzerland

- Pupils: 340 pupils; 305 boarders, 35 day pupils • Ages: 9-18
- Ecumenical • Fees: Prep SFr 30,000-54,000; Senior Sfr 61,000-SFr86,200 • Independent

Tel: +41 24 496 6161
Email: info@aiglon.ch
Website: www.aiglon.ch

Headmaster: Since 2009, Mr Richard McDonald MA (Oxon); obviously a sporty person, strong and wiry, and with his beard could almost be a naval captain. He comes across as a very disciplined man, with a wry smile and twinkle in the eye as soon as you mention his school. Educated at Christ's Hospital and Lincoln College Oxford (studied French and German); taught at Charterhouse; returned to Christ's Hospital to teach modern languages and be a housemaster; became headmaster of Aiglon from 1994 to 2000. Moved on to be director of strategic development at College Beau Soleil in Villars, but returned to Aiglon in July 2009.

After five head teachers in eight years before he rejoined, the leadership of this prestigious mountain school is now in very capable hands. To say that Mr McDonald is passionate about the school and the capabilities of its staff and students would do him a disservice. He literally lives and breathes the school – even eats with the students every mealtime – and has certainly hit the ground running since his return, having obtained IB accreditation almost immediately. He says he is 'vision and inspiration driven, and you can see the results, not only in the move to the IB diploma, but also in his determination for Council of International Schools (CIS) reaccreditation, and the evolving new campus plan which started with the building of the new sports centre.

His staff may see him as overly optimistic but they don't think this is a negative. The students are perhaps still a little wary of him: he has a reputation for being a disciplinarian, not for small things such as a uniform in disarray, but on breaking school rules and therefore trust. He sees a successful student as one who goes on to the best university to which he or she can aspire.

Academic matters: The school follows the British curriculum in years 9 to 11 when all students take GCSEs or IGCSEs depending on their chosen subjects. Students are streamed according to ability in maths, English and languages. The sixth form follows the IB diploma programme. Given the number of different nationalities in the school, around 50, the GCSE results are not bad. In 2013, they achieved 54 per cent A*/A grades. As one would expect, foreign languages are good, but there are notable weaknesses in all three sciences despite excellent facilities.

For a relatively small sixth form, they are able to offer a good range of subjects for the IB diploma – the three sciences, maths, English, humanities, foreign languages (French, German and Spanish, plus Italian, Russian, Portuguese, Arabic, Mandarin and Japanese on a private tuition basis), art, drama, music, plus economics and business. There are also IT and astronomy on offer at IGCSE, with a hope that the latter may become an IB subject in the future. In 2013, the average point score was over 32.

Many students have English as a second language, but thanks to the excellent ESL teaching – a mixture of class and individual support from a team of professionals – this is not seen as a barrier to taking any exams. Around 50 per cent of students go on to US universities, so the school is also an accredited SATs centre, with scores ranging from 1500 to 2150 (out of a possible total of 2400, 800 per exam) for critical reading, maths and writing.

Small classes mean that students get individual attention and can develop at their own pace. Purpose-built classrooms for science, a recently completed modern languages centre in the old post office building, whiteboards and their own computer network system mean students and staff have access to state-of-the-art teaching and learning materials and methods. Students with mild learning difficulties are given extensive support by the learning support department.

Games, options, the arts: A light and airy art studio shows off the talent of many students both in 2D and 3D art. Some students also get the opportunity to display and sell their work in a gallery in Geneva. The music and drama departments allow students to develop other artistic talents. The music department takes over the ground floor of the JCB building, the heart of which is the Oudang room which takes up to 60 musicians. Many students learn an instrument from the traditional orchestral to the bagpipes and many take part in the various college bands, ensembles and choirs. Those less musically talented can get involved with the technical side of the recording or radio studio or the keyboard lab with specialist music computers. The drama department uses the purpose built Exeter Hall and puts on a number of productions annually, including a dance show, and it is also home to the school's Comedy Club. The two departments worked closely together on the last school theatre production Woyzeck, which involved the whole school – students and staff alike.

Stuck on a mountainside, one can forgive the school for not having British style playing fields but they do their best with the limited space available and PE is compulsory for all students. The new sports centre houses a 1,080m multi-purpose sports hall that can be divided into two basketball courts as well as a fitness centre, indoor climbing wall and a cafeteria. The school does well in the SGIS athletics competitions – it must be all that walking up and down a mountainside all day that keeps the students very fit. Football is popular (they do have an Astroturf pitch), as is tennis supported by five courts scattered about the campus, which also double-up as basketball and volleyball courts. Other sports available are swimming, seven-a-side rugby, uni-hockey, golf (the course is just up the road) and of course skiing. Although based in the mountains, the students aren't on skis as much as one would imagine. In winter, students have four hours of skiing a week as part of their PE course, but they are also free to ski on Wednesday and Saturday afternoons. Members of Aiglon's ski race team follow a much more stringent training and competition regime throughout the autumn and winter months and are proud of their successes.

Expeditions or Exes are part of the unique Aiglon experience. Two weekend and one three-day expedition are compulsory for all students each term. In the autumn and summer term these usually involve hiking and camping whilst in winter it's ski-touring. These Exes are deliberately physically (and often mentally) rigorous and challenging but are the one thing that all students seem to remember and talk about with affection. They are however, very strictly monitored and the school has four fully qualified mountain guides on staff. One member of staff remarked that it is these expeditions that forge the special relationships between students and staff and gives them all a great opportunity to get out of school and into the open air to fend for themselves. It is also interesting to note that many of the students go on non-compulsory expeditions at weekends too.

Being a boarding school, there is an extensive options programme (including the very popular astronomy in the Kalouti observatory) which varies depending on the time of year and the specializations and interests of teachers. When asked if they played computer games in the evening, a group of students remarked that with all the other things to do, they didn't have the time or the inclination.

Background and atmosphere: Located in the alpine ski resort of Villars, the school was founded in 1949 by John Corlette, a former teacher at Gordonstoun, and is based on the educational principal of self-reliance developed by Kurt Hahn, Gordonstoun's founder. Originally a boys-only school, it went co-educational in 1968.

Since its founding, the school has grown from a few students and teachers in a single building to an international community of around 350 pupils and 50 different nationalities. In the early years, the school grew by expanding into existing buildings in the village. In the last 20 years, the school has been able to improve the campus with purpose-built junior school premises, the John Corlette teaching building (JCB) and the new Delaware boys' boarding house.

Scattered over the mountainside, some of the buildings have magnificent views of the Alps. There are six boarding houses in the senior school, all single sex, three boys/three girls, with the opposite sex only allowed on the ground floor. One was an old sanitorium, with very 1930s architecture, otherwise think large chalets with lots of wood indoors and out. No British boarding school style dormitories: rooms are usually three or four bedded study rooms, although doubles and singles are more common for the sixth form. Children of different nationalities are encouraged to share a room. Breakfast is still eaten in each house, although there is a cooked breakfast option in the main dining room. Each house has a house captain and inter-house competitions are fiercely fought.

The quality of the food is much improved since it's now outsourced from a proper catering company, with lunch and dinner served in the very chic looking dining room where a lot of the students' art is displayed. There isn't a huge amount of choice, but the food is definitely healthy – salad bar, vegetarian option, invariably pasta and lots of fruit. You'll see fruit bowls scattered around the boarding houses and students are allowed to cook in the house kitchens – home made cakes were seen in all the boarding houses. The students certainly don't starve.

School uniform is informal and practical – white polo neck shirt, cream trousers and when we visited a dark blue sweater with the school emblem – and is compulsory only until the sixth form. (Although it was noted that most of the prefects wore their special scarves or ties and blazers – or perhaps that was just for our benefit.) All the students were well turned out, uniform or not. As well as typical British-style prefects and house captains, there is a head boy and girl, but at Aiglon they are known as Guardians.

Meditations are a distinctive feature of the school – don't think New Age, just a different form of daily assembly. Teaching staff and sometimes guests give a short talk on a specific topic which is preceded and followed by a period of silence. In this day and age, it is unusual for a whole school to come together every morning and the students seem to really appreciate this quiet time of reflection.

Aiglon is also a Round Square school which means they devote a lot of time and effort to participation in community service and work projects at home and overseas. These often humbling experiences give students a strong sense of personal development and responsibility.

Several of the junior school are day pupils, but the girls have a true chalet style boarding house, whilst the boys are in the main chalet. It is a small, nurturing environment, no high pressure, with kids from many countries.

Pastoral care and discipline: Houseparents, personal tutors and most of the staff are on hand to help. The houseparents seem totally devoted to their charges and duties and appear very aware of the difficulties that can arise with different nationalities living close to one another. There is also a well-established PSHE programme in place. Very traditional British boarding school discipline is in place: laps, gating, suspension and even the rare expulsion. Mr McDonald does not hesitate to mete out the appropriate disciplinary action. There is no smoking anywhere on campus, although difficult to enforce over such a widespread area. Wine and beer are allowed for over 17s – a very strict rule given that the legal drinking age for wine and beer is 16 in Switzerland.

There is a zero tolerance of drugs and regular random testing takes place. A strict pocket-money allowance is in place – refreshing to hear, given that most of the students come from very privileged backgrounds. Public displays of affection are discouraged but let's be realistic, this is a co-ed boarding school.

Pupils and parents: Over two-thirds of the students are, not surprisingly, European, with the largest group being British – nearly 14 per cent. The next largest group are Russian (12 per cent) followed by North American (10 per cent) and students from every continent. Around 80 per cent enter with English as their mother tongue or with a high fluency level. A number of more recent pupils are children of alumni. In fact, one student recounted that she and her brother couldn't wait to get to Aiglon, having heard stories about the school from her father and his old school friends. Parents have to have quite a bit of money, whether self-made or inherited, in order to be able to afford the fees, so they form a fairly elite group. However, there are scholarships available for those from more modest backgrounds, including a special scholarship for students from African and Oriental countries.

Entrance: The school has its own series of admission tests, plus an interview with the head, and references from the present school are needed. For admission into the sixth form, satisfactory GCSEs or equivalent are required. Mr McDonald states that Aiglon is a 'de-selective' rather than 'selective' school.

Exit: Hardly any leave after GCSEs. High university fees are not a problem for Aiglon students and around 50 per cent go on to US universities, with the others evenly divided between European and UK universities. You will see a smattering of Ivy League, but also other top schools such as MIT, Stanford, Georgetown, NYU and Tufts in the US, and McGill in Canada. Occasional Oxbridge places – one boy with a Cambridge offer in 2013 went to Harvard instead – along with Durham, Bristol, Manchester, Edinburgh and St Andrews as well as the London University colleges of Imperial, King's, LSE and UCL. Some students stay in Switzerland and go on to the prestigious EPFL (Ecole Polytechnique Fédérale de Lausanne) and hotel schools. One student joined the Moscow State Institute of International Relations in 2013.

Money matters: In addition to fees there are the usual extras, including school uniform and of course ski passes. These do rather add up. Aiglon is a not-for-profit school and gathers funds from full fee-paying students, donations and registered charitable trusts in different countries. The Aiglon College Alumni Eagle Association is also active in raising funds. There is a serious amount of fundraising currently going on to try and bring to life the aspirations of Mr McDonald – a new library and media centre and a performing arts centre are just two of the plans on the drawing-board.

Remarks: Not a school for spoilt brats or prima donnas – the expeditions (Exes) and service projects make sure of that. It prides itself on offering a prestigious education in the broadest definition and, on the whole, it delivers. Highly academic it is not, but the kids do get an all-round education. Students leave here with a strong feeling of self-confidence not arrogance, having been humbled by active service (and not by bullying – something that sets them apart from many of their contemporaries).

Akeley Wood School

Linked school: Akeley Wood Junior School

Akeley Wood, Buckingham, MK18 5AE

- Pupils: 565 pupils, 230 girls/335 boys; all day • Ages: 11–18
- Non-denom • Fees: £12,375; Tutorial Programme £15,675 pa
- Independent

Tel: 01280 814110
Email: enquiries@akeleywoodschool.co.uk
Website: www.akeleywoodschool.co.uk

Headmaster: Since 2005, Dr Jeremy (Jerry) Grundy MA PhD (forties). Educated at Leeds Grammar, then read PPE at St Anne's, Oxford, followed by doctorate at McGill University in Montreal.

He began his teaching career as head of RS and housemaster at St Albans School, before moving to Magdalen College School in Oxford as head of sixth form. He introduced philosophy A level there, a phenomenally successful move. An infectious enthusiast, he is adamant that 'happiness is central to pupils' learning', and that if youngsters 'feel happy and secure in their learning environment', they will realise their potential.

Historically, Akeley Wood had a weak sixth form – only 40 sixth formers prior to Dr Grundy's arrival, but now 129: 'I've always felt that the engine behind a good school should be its sixth form, and that is very much the case here now,' he says. Masses of good PR about the school locally. 'When I arrived I drew up a ten-year development plan, and my view is that the plan will be achieved in half that time.' Recent additions include dedicated sixth form centre, new science labs and classrooms, more interactive whiteboards and full-size Astroturf.

Dr Grundy is hugely proud of the school and what pupils have achieved in recent years. No doubt he has raised standards and, equally important, raised pupils' own aspirations and expectations of what they are capable of. He doesn't teach regular classes but runs the philosophy discussion group, contributes to the sixth form lecture series and frequently pops into classes to observe lessons and contribute to what's going on – 'more on the humanities side,' he says, 'although I have been known to try my hand at scientific experiments!' Also keen to involve himself on the sporting side – he referees school rugby matches and pitches his hand against pupils on the tennis court. Wife, Ginny, teaches art at Akeley Wood and they have two sons who attend the junior school.

Moving on in July 2014 to head Birkenhead School.

Academic matters: Under the aegis of the Chris Woodhead-led Cognita and with the head's leadership, the school is firmly on the up. In 2013, 29 per cent of GCSE results were A*/A, 92 per cent 5+ A*-C including English and maths. Small classes throughout – never more than 20, much smaller in sixth form. A level: 48 per cent A*-B, 15 per cent A*/A, 21 subjects on offer – all the usual, plus business studies, sport studies, psychology, photography, music technology, textiles etc. Setting for maths, science and French. Languages taught are French, German and Spanish. School is one of only 12 in country to be involved in Autology, e-learning system which gives pupils access to more than 200,000 online resources, including textbooks, audio and video.

When we visited it was history week, with a myriad of lessons and activities focusing on the Battle of Trafalgar. A group of year 10s were clearly gripped by an account of Nelson's last moments, while even the canteen staff had been inspired to add ship's biscuits and pease pudding to the lunch menu. We weren't sure how modern-day youngsters would cope with such culinary delights, but school food gets the firm thumbs-up, especially the homemade bread.

IT provision good – two rooms, pupils get 70 minutes a week in Key Stage 3 and many go on to take IT at GCSE and computing at A level. Six science labs and triple and double award science available. Youngsters receive effort and achievement grades every three weeks. New self-assessment system encourages them to look at their own progress and set targets.

Impressive tutorial programme for children with dyslexia, dyspraxia, dyscalculia and those requiring a greater level of support. The classes run parallel to other classes in the year group, catering for a maximum of 10 pupils in each year. System has been widely praised and seems to build youngsters' confidence and self-esteem. One former head boy worked his way from the tutorial programme to win a place at Warwick University to study biological sciences. Some youngsters do study skills instead of talking a second language and can also attend study sessions at lunch-time.

Games, options, the arts: Sport good, with lots of matches against local schools; impressive haul of silverware on display in school cabinet. Main sports for boys are rugby, football, cricket and athletics, while girls enjoy netball, hockey, rounders, athletics and tennis. Equestrian team very successful. Pupils can try other sports at after-school clubs – everything from karate to pilates. Recent sports dome.

Music has grown massively in recent years – around 60 per cent play instruments, very popular at GCSE and A level. School orchestra, wind bands, brass group, choir and rock bands galore. High point of school calendar is Akeley Woodstock, annual rock festival – even the staff band appears on stage, with the head on vocals. Art, textiles and DT all impressive – around eight pupils do art A level each year, large numbers for GCSE. Sixth form has its own artroom while younger pupils get to create their masterpieces in prize-winning art department housed in old stable block. Stunning artwork displayed throughout school.

Drama previously weaker link, but new drama space at Tile House Mansion with flexible lighting equipment, combined with a collaborative approach to the performing arts as a whole (drama, music and dance), has seen new inclusive culture of experimentation.

Young Enterprise and D of E widely taken up, with regular expeditions to the Forest of Dean and Peak District. Annual ski trips and recent visits to Paris and the battlefields of Belgium and northern France. Excellent guidance on universities and careers – the head of the sixth form is the world's living expert on UCAS,' the head boy told us appreciatively.

Background and atmosphere: The school as a whole has seen an enormous £10 million investment from Cognita. Recent IT suites, food technology and art rooms, Astroturf and sports dome – all at the junior school; science lab, IT suite, food tech suite, DT workshop, art room, textiles room, heated sports domes, Astroturfs and new teaching block over the two sites of the senior school. Sixth formers very pleased with their smart new sixth form centre, complete with common room, kitchen and state-of-the-art teaching block, housing 16 classrooms, music performance area and music technology studio.

Main school building is a splendid mock-Tudor hunting lodge set in 22 acres and dating back to 1867. Started out as a traditional boys' boarding school called Hillcrest in 1946 and went co-ed in 1972. Boarding ended in 1980. Expanded in stages. Its junior school and nursery (12 months–11 years) at Wicken Park was acquired in 1988. The 11-13 year olds are at Tile House Mansion and the 13-18s in Akeley Wood.

As we said last time, still a faintly boys' prep school feel to the senior school. Lots of wood panelling, no big assembly area and former billiard room stuffed with electric guitars. Place has slightly cramped feel (while lower school seems huge). Pupils are devoted to the place, though, and say facilities have improved by leaps and bounds since advent of Cognita. 'But I'm really pleased it's still kept its friendly atmosphere,' one pupil told us.

Pastoral care and discipline: School describes itself as 'an unpretentious and civilised environment, where good behaviour, good manners and a smart appearance are paramount'. It prides itself on not being over-regimented or having too many trivial rules and regulations, yet it is crystal-clear in what it expects of pupils. One pupil told us, 'Compared to other schools, Akeley Wood really builds your confidence. It has made me who I am, and leaving it behind will be very sad.' Good PSHCE programme and 'no trouble' with booze or fags. Pro-active drugs awareness talks and strong anti-bullying programme (although pupils say no 'nastiness'). Youngsters well supported by heads of year, tutors, school counsellor and prefects.

Bottle-green/grey uniform up to year 11, own smart jackets/suits for sixth form. Four houses – Hillcrest, Stuart, Pilgrim and Thompson – with house captains, reps from each year and lots of inter-house competitions. House points awarded for academic and sporting achievements as well as effort in the classroom. Head boy and head girl voted into office by staff and pupils. Raft of prefects, with several assigned to help year 7s settle in – although all sixth formers make a point of being friendly and supportive to their more junior counterparts. Some pupils are strikingly modest about their achievements. We were shown round by a boy who had just won a music scholarship to Cambridge and a girl who is a member of Britain's dressage team and an aspiring Olympian. Neither mentioned these triumphs themselves – but their peers spilled the beans! Whole school assembly at beginning and end of term. House and year assemblies every week.

Pupils and parents: Fleet of eight school buses bring pupils in from 25-mile radius – from both rural and urban areas, including Buckingham, Aylesbury, Milton Keynes, Towcester etc. Up to 10 pupils from countries like China, Taiwan and Thailand enter the sixth form each year, living with guardians, staff or local families.

Entrance: Selective. At 11, pupils either move up from junior school (entry is automatic for them, unless head advises otherwise), while others come from range of local primaries and preps. 'We want to ensure that the pupil and the school are a good match, so that we can support and extend them and help them to thrive,' says the deputy head. He adds that low grades aren't necessarily a barrier for pupils entering the school's tutorial programme, but, 'It's vital that they are committed to learning'. All prospective pupils spend assessment day at the senior school. Entry into the sixth form requires minimum of five Cs at GCSE (including Bs in the subjects to be studied at A level).

Exit: Some leave after GCSE for local grammar schools or FE colleges. Virtually all sixth form leavers go to university, choosing vast array of destinations, including Oxbridge, Chelsea College of Art, LSE, University of Maryland (USA), UCL. Recent subjects range from architecture and physics to Assyriology and midwifery.

Money matters: Number of academic, music, art, and sport scholarships available – up to 20 per cent of the fees. Sibling discount across all three Akeley Wood schools.

Remarks: Happy mainstream school that caters for wide range of abilities. Lots of good new-build. Great for boosting pupils' confidence and self-esteem and spotting talents that might have gone undetected elsewhere. Youngsters are happy, engaged and eager to sing the school's praises. As deputy head says, 'It's not the cool thing to be anti-school here.' Akeley Wood is on a roll – and the interesting developments look set to continue.

Albyn School

Linked school: Albyn Lower School

17-23 Queens Road, Aberdeen, AB15 4PB

• Pupils: 400 pupils, 180 boys/220 girls • Ages: 2–18 • Non-denominational • Fees: £6,990–£11,020 pa • Independent

Tel: 01224 322408
Email: admissions@albynschool.co.uk
Website: www.albynschool.co.uk

Head: Since 2008, Dr Ian Long BA AKC PhD FRGS FRSA (fiftyish), who was educated at King's College School, Wimbledon, read geography at King's London and, after a brief spell with Shell (always good to get the outside perspective) worked in a variety of schools – all girls, co-ed, that sort of thing, before becoming head of sixth form at Brentwood, followed by eight years as (academic) deputy head of City of London Freemen's School,

during which time he also did his doctorate (in rural council housing). A lapsed rower and a clever clog who came to a school on the cusp; the previous head had worked miracles, but some were a tad expensive. Has tightened up the finance side. No more babies (staffing ratio hideous) and huge increase in both nursery and chaps throughout the school. 'Always wanted to work abroad' but hadn't quite expected to find Scotland, and possibly Aberdeen in particular, quite so different from his previous experience.

Fair amount of movement in the governing body, new head of the governors 'super chap'. Long runs the school with two deputy heads, one pastoral, and one in charge of timetabling et al. Mrs Karen Thomson is in charge of lower school and the nurseries.

An engaging and entertaining head with a sparkling sense of humour, he is also dead efficient and our request for detailed exam results by subject over the previous three years arrived at our computer before we did. His wife, Gwyneth, was deputy head at Channing School in Highgate, having started her teaching career at St Leonard's School down the coast in Fife as a Latin teacher and assistant housemistress. She teaches classics in the school.

Academic matters: Scottish system: broad range of subjects and results; 53 per cent of Highers grade A in 2013, as were 44 per cent of Advanced Highers; occasional glitches; biology, English, French and maths do well, ditto chemistry and physics. No apparent weaknesses, info systems obviously not yet up and running, but business management and modern studies good. Doing well in the league tables, particularly at Highers (all subjects can be taken at Advanced Higher). German not currently the flavour of the month. Drama with higher level PE now on offer. Spanish (from the upper fifth) and DT are the latest additions to the curriculum. Certain amount of almost individual teaching; the results are impressive (if hardly cost-effective). Strong showing in maths challenge and problem-solving.

Maximum class size 20, with low teens for practical subjects (school says 20, but in practice this is much smaller; most classes are 10/15). Comprehensive computer system, class-taught as well as in suites, laptops abound, pupils can bring in their own. All pupils have their own email and can email homework and queries to staff. European computer driving licence available, keyboarding taught early in the school; some interactive whiteboards.

'Sort of set' maths and English in primary, handwriting important. Jolly Phonics in nursery. All assessed on entry, two learning support teachers cover the whole school, and a pupil's IEP follows throughout their time at school. No problems with dyslexia, dyspraxia and mild Asperger's, and in the past did well for a pupil who was profoundly deaf. No EFL help available as such ('not needed,' says the head), but 'lots of support in the classroom', SEN teacher takes individual groups and double teaches a bit – she is very 'willing' – and was off to help out in a German lesson after we had talked. Scribing, readers and all the rest. No extra charge for SEN help. Digital exams being mooted by SQA, school is investigating voice recognition programmes.

Games, options, the arts: Main games field at Milltimber five miles away – pupils are bused, fabulous athletics track. Now uses Aberdeen's state-of-the-art sports village for a number of sports: athletics, hockey, football, netball. Positive netball and hockey with regional representation and masses of individual sports: national representation in several. With boys now in the senior school, serious thought was given to what sport the boys would play in the senior school: 'Both rugby and football have fervent adherents among parents of the boys, but the latter may be more realistic if we are not to be beaten 80-0 for the next five years. Rowing may be the answer.' And so it is. Boys (only at the moment) are already competing successfully in coxed quads, with footie as a minor – albeit successful – sport. For both boys and girls. Scottish gold medallist coach.

Stunning art department, with a number of pupils going on to higher things in the art world. Very jolly with papier mâché, acrylic and silk screen work. Hot on costume design and much use made of local museums. Always a joy to come here. Strong art and architectural stream. Fantastic music – 'most girls play a musical instrument' – and loads of participation in either choir or instrumental ensembles. New head of music. Good representation in the National Youth Orchestra plus jazz, ceilidh bands. Blues band. Keen drama and dance (Dancercise important). Couldn't do better. Enthusiastic Young Enterprise and highly competitive D of E with oodles of golds. Strong club culture – quizzes, chess, gardening but alas no more Scottish country dancing. Keen on public speaking and debating. Head has encouraged trips: Borneo, Barbados, and cultural tours to Italy. (Some – mainly local – parents, are not entirely convinced of their necessity).

Background and atmosphere: Founded in 1867 by Harriet Warrack, who started teaching girls at home, advertising locally for pupils. Albyn Place (just down the road) became the school's home in 1881, hence the name, and Albyn School for Girls moved to Queen's Road in 1925. The son of one of the gardeners at Duff House, Alexander Mackie was an early moving light, writing books on English (he was a university examiner) and made the school an Aberdeen institution, with emancipated Albyn girls on Aberdeen University student council by 1907. The head was pleased to find his original desk in a passage and it now graces his office (the roll-top concealing all manner of educational detritus).

School based in four attached Victorian merchants' houses, with fantastic ceilings, one well-used library and the predictable garden expansion. Harriet House houses the toddlers, aged 2 to 3 years, while the juniors have a splendid new-build, with classrooms clustered round a splendid hall (with windows on the first floor) giving both extra light and affording entertainment; tiny people were performing a skipping dance during our visit. Lifts in junior school make disabled access almost available everywhere. Kitchen and dining area dramatically revamped, junior school order in advance, seniors pay-as-you-go. Plans afoot for an amalgamated nursery, and a new science block, with better integrated connections between the various houses; the existing school has a strong family feel, but logistically it is a complicated complex of corridors and levels between the houses. Fire doors everywhere. The new-build will be part cantilevered over the existing playground which will have the advantage of deflecting some of the granite city weather. Impressive music department above hall/gym (can accommodate the whole school) in the west end of the school, has undergone a significant makeover. School hopes to increase numbers to 650. Boys started in the junior department in 2005 and have worked their way up.

Pastoral care and discipline: School divided into four quite competitive clans, Douglas, Stuart, Forbes and Gordon, mainly for games. No tutors; pupils can, and do, relate to form teachers and guidance staff when in difficulty. Wickedness equals a yellow card, followed by a red card, usual punishment is an essay. Sense of community – school aims to boost the confidence of the shyest child. Policy of zero tolerance for drink 'n' drugs 'n' rock 'n' roll, so expect to be out for persistent bullying or drugs. Cigarettes and alcohol on school premises = detention followed by exclusion followed by out. 'Bullying is usually changing friendship groups' seems about right, but actual bullying is regarded as a no-no. If there is real cause for concern, then parents are summonsed for a 'discussion'. Queen's Cross church used for Easter and Christmas (Scotland's first gay minister – which upsets some of the parent base).

Pupils and parents: Mixture of professionals – a lot of oil and gas, but farmers and marine engineers in the parent body. The former often have to either move or install their young at short notice. Fair number of first-time buyers; parents can drop off early and pick up late (6.15) for pupils in the lower school but there is an extra charge. International bias, but lots of home-grown ones too; strong middle class ethos with girls neat in check dresses or kilts (any tartan, but proper kilts, not skirts – though we didn't see the full eight yards) compulsory for girls from October to April. Some wear them all year round. Boys are allowed to wear kilts but only a few do, mostly on special occasions.

Entrance: Entry assessment for junior school; however, entry from junior to senior is automatic. Pupils can and do join at any time – throughout the year (assuming space available). Not many come post standard grades.

Exit: Few leave post Highers. Most (98 per cent or so) go to university, often after a gap year. One to Cambridge, a couple to York and the rest to Scottish universities in 2013. Chemical engineering particularly popular and several medics.

Money matters: Incredibly strict scale of rules for payment but (Aberdeen, remember) parents can get a two per cent discount if they pay the whole annual whack within a fortnight of the beginning of the autumn term. Discounts of five per cent for second child from pre-school nursery up, and 50 per cent rebate for third and subsequent children. School 'will do what it can to help parents in difficult times, as long as they are open and talk to us'. Can, and will do, 100 per cent bursary if need be.

Remarks: Now co-ed throughout, this is a school on a roll, small enough for every child to be known as an individual and big enough to offer the best in modern teaching methods.

Aldenham School

Linked school: Aldenham Preparatory School

Elstree, Borehamwood, WD6 3AJ

• Pupils: 560 pupils, 155 boarders • Ages: 11–18 • C of E foundation with ecumenical overtones • Fees: Boarding £18,768–£28,410; Day £13,626–£19,500 pa • Independent

Tel: 01923 858122
Email: admissions@aldenham.com
Website: www.aldenham.com

Headmaster: Since 2006, Mr James Fowler MA PGCE (fifties). Previously deputy head at Highgate, before that head of sixth at Brentwood. He grew up in the area, having attended Merchant Taylors', Northwood, so came with a useful understanding of the neighbourhood and likely clientele. A former choral scholar at New College, Oxford – musicians often make decidedly civilised heads; married with two sons. Impresses immediately in an un-grand way. At ease, clearly highly competent and in tune with his school's very particular and, in this area, rare ethos. Candid and expansive – a solid, astute head to whom you'd have no hesitation in handing your children.

Academic matters: Not for single-minded scholars nor does the head talk about climbing the league tables. When asked whether he is hoping to 'up the academics,' he replies, swiftly, 'If you're asking me whether I want to ensure that all pupils here get the very best out of what we provide, of course I do.' Touché. That said, the academics are good and those who want to get to Oxbridge, and have the brains, will do so. But this is not what Aldenham is about. It takes a broad spread of ability – the fact that most enter at an untestably early age and stay the course more or less ensures that. Later arrivals are refugees from more pressured local schools and come not because of any lack of ability, but because they want school to be about more than that. And it is, here.

Classes are small – we saw, in fact, almost nothing but learning in groups, concentrating faces in friendly fives and sixes. Average class size is 20, down to 11 in the sixth. Setting in maths and science. At GCSE, everyone takes a core of two English, three science, maths, a language, RS, PE and IT, plus options from a predictable list. In 2013, 34 per cent A*/A grades. At A level, a good range of subjects: business and economics popular, as are DT (graphics, resistant materials, textiles), media studies, PE, music, music technology and art. In 2013, 46 per cent A*-B and 24 per cent A*/A grades. Latin survives, as does German – hooray!

Around 12 per cent on the learning support register, the vast majority for mild dyspraxia and dyslexia. Two statemented pupils – mild Asperger's – and provides for them sensitively. Excellent learning support area with several little rooms for one-to-one, much used by the 40-odd overseas pupils who receive EAL help. Praise for provision though head not keen to be known as a school 'for' special needs – which it isn't. More could be done to stretch the most able, as head admits and has plans to do so. Value-added achievement is high and much praise in inspection report for the promotion of independent learning.

Games, options, the arts: The real triumph of Aldenham – the pitches, fields, courts, Astroturf and sports facilities here need to be seen – 110 acres of glorious green belt land stretch away, much of them part of the school's playing areas; the rest gently wooded, cottaged or be-cowed in a way that belies the school's actual position inside the M25. Football is main boys' game in the autumn term, for girls netball and hockey in autumn and spring terms. Spring brings hockey for the boys and summer cricket for boys and rounders for girls. Shooting range, cavernous sports hall plus fitness suite, climbing wall – you name it, they've got it, except, yet, for a pool of their own. Lots of options – athletics, tennis, sailing, fives, judo etc ad exhaustionem. Lots of success too, and tours to lovely places. CCF popular, largely because of the trips it offers.

Excellent art – we loved the ceramic skydivers, the Impressionistic line drawings and witty black 'n' red linocut self portraits which greeted us; DT work similarly ingenious – metal sculpture, pottery, textiles, graphics; very colourful work everywhere. Photography popular, as is working on the production of sumptuous school magazine.

Music thrives and everyone enthuses, especially about 'house music' – clearly an exciting and important annual occasion. Housed in the school's former chapel, cleverly built around so that odd bits of beamed roof or column find themselves in the middle of practice rooms or the recital hall.

Drama housed in theatre designed on a traditional school hall model, ie rectangular, with stage area at one end and stackable raked seating for 130, but allowing for flexible productions and much enjoyed. Refreshing to see a lively list of recent productions with scarcely a musical among them – One Flew Over the Cuckoo's Nest, Speed the Plow, Our Country's Good, Great Expectations, The Taming of the Shrew – along with The Beggar's Opera and, yes, Grease. Someone here cares about real theatre and gets on with it, inspiring others along the way. Good programme of trips and outside speakers. All this activity means that the day school day ends at 5.30pm.

Background and atmosphere: Founded by Richard Platt, a brewer, in 1597. Queen Elizabeth I granted him letters patent to build 'the Free Grammar School and Almshouses' at Aldenham for elementary pupils. The Brewers' Company thereafter had a controlling interest in the school and links remain strong. In the 19th century, the original Tudor building was demolished and replaced by two new schools – one providing an elementary education for the local population, the other a grammar school for fee-paying boarders. What must then have been a remote location and an unpromising one for pupils from all but local farming families is now in prime, protected green belt with the benefit of plenty of well-heeled local villages, prosperous suburbs and satellite towns from which to draw pupils.

The school hit a rocky period a decade or two back, but all areas of the campus have benefited from recent upgrades – new sixth form centre and extension to music school include recreation and study facilities plus classrooms, oak-beamed public foyer and recital room. The green belt location means that the school is in what the head calls 'a leafy bubble' and cannot grow any bigger, and is all the better for that.

Huge range of architectural styles – everything from the attractive Old School building (Victorian gothic with gables, tower, turret and crenellations), beautiful post-WWI library, splendid panelled dining room, depressing mid-20th century municipal style brick and pipework blocks and some sensitive recent building with light, air and heart-gladdening colour, eg languages and media block. Lots of well-kept gardens – each house has one and the head's garden is a gem.

A rather extraordinary chapel – crematorium-like on the outside, started pre-WWII and finished just after – sits over the road that bisects the school. Inside it is vast, white and surprisingly welcoming. School uses it well – eg 'chill-out chapel' – and no-one in the school's mixed population withdraws from services. Stanley Spencer was commissioned to paint altar pieces for the building in the late 1950s but horrified everyone by producing a crucifixion in which he depicted the cross wedged across Cookham High Street 'like a crashed airliner'. The pile of earth in the foreground with the figure of the fainting virgin lying on top was inspired by the pipe-laying operations going on in the High Street. Spencer bemused the boys by telling them, 'I have given the men who are nailing Christ on the cross Brewers' caps, because it is your governors and you who are still nailing Christ to the cross.' The altarpiece was sold to provide much-needed funds in the 1990s and was replaced by a large and striking ironwork cross and dove, which is somewhat less disturbing.

Girls now make up a quarter of the school, aiming for a third. They have their own day and boarding house – last year saw the opening of an additional day one. Lower school children's house, Martineau's, in which years 7 and 8 make a gentle transition from the prep to the senior school, while using all the senior school facilities.

Boarding houses have been recently refurbished and remodelled – no basins in rooms and some lower school rooms for three or four not huge, but good games/common rooms, carpeting throughout, the girls have a terrific kitchen, everyone seems comfortable, the sixth form single rooms are good and a programme of renewal and repainting which is brightening things up. Small school in which everyone knows everyone in a supportive, friendly community.

Pastoral care and discipline: Strong pastoral care – parents comment that their children feel 'looked after and safe'; 'The staff take immense care – there is always someone my son can go to. The fact that all the children have a place in a boarding house, even if they don't board, makes for a really friendly, family atmosphere'. House tutor and/or matron always on duty. 'The staff are wonderfully protective – especially of the girls,' we were told.

Few 'incidents' and school takes a 'sensible' attitude to alcohol, eg a little bar in the new sixth form centre in which they are allowed a couple of beers two nights a week – something they love and wouldn't abuse. Much freedom for boarders to go out at weekends – with permission. Given this freedom, little need to transgress.

Pupils and parents: Day pupils can sign up to one of eight useful coach routes; most come from north, or north of, London, as far away as Hampstead or within walking distance. Most live within 20 miles. Lots of first-time buyers, lots of busy, professional London parents who like the boarding/day flexibility uniquely on offer here. Around 10 per cent Asian, five per cent Afro-Caribbean British, around 25 per cent Jewish, fewer Muslims; about a third of boarders from Germany, then from China, Japan, Hong Kong, Austria and a scattering from elsewhere. School does well to mix everyone up and integrate them.

Parents who send their children here do so for positive reasons and have taken the trouble to find a school which promotes a broad curriculum and a breadth of extracurricular opportunities in a relaxed environment – 'balanced' is the word we heard most often from staff, pupils and parents.

Notable Old Pupils include General Sir Richard Gale, Commander in Chief, British Army of the Rhine, 1952-1956, Jack de Manio, Field Marshal Lord Vincent, Brigadier Michael Taylor, Brigadier Francis Henn, Sir Michael Bett, Sir Denys Roberts, Peter Leaver QC, Dale Winton, Professor Sir Martin Sweeting, Karren Brady, three bishops plus a lot of, mostly legal, worthies.

Entrance: Immense care is taken over this. Head meets all outside applicants – parents and children – a huge job. Forty-five places offered at 11+ for which 130 apply. Those who don't come from the school's on site prep (see review) try from around 15 local preps, eg St Martin's, Edge Grove, Lochinver, Keble etc. A reference from the pupil's present school is sought and all sit school's own tests in English, maths and reasoning. No CE. If interviewees come along after the tests, head sees them 'blind', ie not knowing how they did. At 13+, around 85 apply for the 25-30 places – around five of those offered places likely to be girls. Around 30 -40 in at sixth – many from overseas but must be in tune with what the school is about and achieve at least five C+ at GCSE.

Exit: Around 15 leave after GCSEs – some to schools/colleges nearer home, some to the state sector, a few to employment. Most stay on and leave for a range of universities and courses. The occasional Oxbridge entrant (one in 2013), around half to the newer universities eg Anglia Ruskin to study, eg, business and vocational-based courses, the other half to, eg, Nottingham, Manchester – most, again, to study subjects with a career-orientation rather than an academic basis. A few historians, chemists, archaeologists etc. Some to employment and around 10 per cent to gap years.

Money matters: Good clutch of scholarships and bursaries – academic, musical, arty, technological and sports. Check with school for details.

Remarks: Balance is what you get here – an education and a school life in a balanced and stimulating environment, relaxed, secure and civilised. And in an open and rural-seeming setting that is a barely believable half an hour from London.

Alderley Edge School for Girls

Linked school: Alderley Edge School for Girls Junior School

Wilmslow Road, Alderley Edge, Cheshire SK9 7QE

- Pupils: 550 • Ages: 3-18 • Unified Christian • Fees: £9,834 pa
- Independent

Tel: 01625 583028
Email: admissions@aesg.co.uk
Website: www.aesg.info

Headmistress: Since 2009, Mrs Sue Goff MA (mid-fifties). Passionate, forthright and fast talking, the sort of thoroughly good egg any girls' school would want on their team. Russian and French degree from Durham, where she rowed for the university, PGCE from Oxford, where she rowed for St Hilda's College. Came from deputy headship of Woldingham (RC, boarding), and before that head of languages at Sevenoaks School, to what she describes as 'the ideal school for me, all girls with a church foundation'.

Catholic herself, 'It's hugely important to me – I don't ram it down people's throats, but it's what made me who I am', and talks of developing the good in each girl, thinking of each as 'God's creation'. Parents say, 'She exudes a warmth, yet she's quite a toughie.' Has three grown daughters (and a grand-daughter) and, as part of school's 'joint partnership with home', encourages parents to keep in touch, email and drop in. Tissues on the side in her study bear witness to her listening ear, but she's also not afraid to nudge parents 'with the greatest respect' towards strong parenting themselves. Anti, for example, girls spending hours on Facebook, 'What they do at home does have a knock on effect'. Passionate about enabling each girl to 'go for it; whatever their area of expertise; we're about helping the girls really believe in themselves and aim high, about them becoming confident but not arrogant, not to bring glory to the school but so they get what they themselves deserve'.

Started at the same time as prep head Mr Groves, who she describes as a kindred spirit. Still teaches some French and believes in being 'out there, getting to know the girls – after all, it's all about them'. Plays piano, loves music, opera, ballet and dog, Meggy.

Academic matters: No longer just embracing arms under those who slip through other nets at 11+. In 2013, 90 per cent A*-C at A level; 49 per cent A*/A at GCSE. Cambridge Pre-U can be taken alongside A levels. The ability profile is above average, but recent ISI inspection also described the educational experience here as outstanding and the curriculum as excellent.

Three classes to each year with a maximum promise of 25, and when year 9 classes overfilled they were divided to form additional group. Some sixth form teaching sets are tiny. From year 7, girls conduct self-evaluation and review their own progress. No shortage of computers or study areas, with four ICT suites, a library and designated sixth form computer and study rooms under an apex roof with girders and skylights. Setting for maths from year 7, science from year 9, 'with plenty of chances to change groups if you do well'. Maths clinic every lunchtime, other subjects on various days and girls say, 'The teachers here teach because it's their passion and not just their job'. Pupils are helped with learning difficulties and the head has re-launched gifted and talented scheme.

Games, options, the arts: Three all-weather pitches, two large gyms, a verdant sports field and a modern drama and dance studio with mirrored wall. On sports corridor walls motivational quotes undergird photos of the girls playing sport and a photo-wall of fame celebrates diverse individual successes, some at national level, from horse riding and ice skating to dance, squash and tae kwon do. Teams play in Cheshire leagues with netball particularly strong, regularly reaching NW finals, and a keen football team includes a Manchester City youth player.

Girls say, 'Music here is massive,' with several bands, orchestra and choirs. Keyboard suite, lots of girls take singing lessons. Music exams, success at renowned Alderley Edge Music Festival, celebrated at prizegiving in Manchester's Bridgewater Hall. Art displayed everywhere with particularly exciting 3D models outside main art rooms. The head of art, here nearly 30 years, clearly loves the place, 'and the girls we turn out are so well rounded'. Separate sixth form art room where each girl has own space. Lots of after school clubs, 'best thing about school,' say some girls, trips and exchanges, Comenius European links, D of E, Mock Trial, charity fundraising and links with Kenyan school and women's project.

Background and atmosphere: Founded in 1999 from the merging of Mount Carmel RC convent school on the present site and the Anglican St Hilary's run by the Woodard Corporation from the south end of the village. Now describes itself as an ecumenical unified Christian school with the motto line, 'Aspire not to have more, but to be more'. Prep school on same site and shares some facilities. Compulsory monthly Eucharist is 'boring' in some girls' books, and they're not afraid to say so, but most accept it happily. Four houses named after saints Emilie, Francis, Joan and Hilary, three chaplains, visiting clergy and rallying assemblies; 'We're not turning them all into nuns, but it sets a moral framework and builds positive self-image, esteem and worth,' says head.

Fabulous poster-sized professional photos of the girls at work, rest and play lining every corridor do much the same thing and detract from the uninspiring hotchpotch of red brick buildings once you pass the modern front façade. Girls seem happy and relaxed, corridor manners more hurly burly than stuffy. Breakfast available free from 8am and the dining room is a sociable place where younger girls dine first and staff cluster chatting too. Bread and pastries at break for a nominal charge. Sixth form privileges include not queuing for lunch, 'handy on Friday chip day', a wider range of muffins and buns from their own all day coffee bar and a new 'chill out' common room in which to enjoy them and a natter. An annual highlight for pupils and staff is the house entertainment afternoon, organised by the captains, where everyone performs or contributes backstage.

Pastoral care and discipline: Much emphasis on rewarding good behaviour and effort with certificates, letters home and even chocolate. Merit system includes personal and house points. Referral cards for work related and behavioural lapses – 'We have high expectations and don't stand any nonsense'. Big sister scheme teams sixth formers with year 7s while they settle in. Girls describe friendship and 'knowing everyone' as the best thing about AESG – as one sixth former said, 'We genuinely don't want to leave; this is a school where everybody knows your name'. They're not quickly forgotten, as a leavers' destination board carries large photos of smiling girls (no pouting here) and inspiriting news of where they are now. Parents agree: 'The pastoral care is great – you can ring them at any time'; 'My daughter's extremely happy there – all the girls are so nice'.

Pupils and parents: Overwhelmingly white and middle class, although 20 or so with English as second language. Not all regular church goers, even small minority from other faiths – 'I've not noticed the Christian stuff,' one parent told us. Neat navy uniforms introduced as a new colour when the two schools merged and girls don't seem to push the boundaries – instead they look unspoilt and innocently young, with minimal make up and jewellery. Girls come from as far as central Manchester and Stoke on Trent. Most, however, hail from rural local areas,

so Cheshire set strongly represented, though as one mum put it, 'There are lots of fat cars in the car park, but I'm not the only one who sacrifices to send my daughter here'. Good bus network and near train station; traffic congestion at pick up time.

Entrance: Open to any who are sympathetic to school's ecumenical ethos. By maths, English and verbal reasoning exams, interview and reference, looking for a broad band of ability, girls who'll fit in. Has catch-all reputation of not setting bar over dauntingly high, although head says school regularly turns away girls 'due to their academic profile not being sufficiently high to cope with our academic curriculum'. Entry higher up school includes science and language papers. Half year 7 straight from prep, at home here from the off. Taster day for prospective year 6 girls to really see what it's like.

Exit: Up to 50 per cent leave post GCSE. Most sixth formers straight to university with UCL, Leeds, Nottingham and Aberystwyth all popular. Occasional Oxbridge success. Mix of courses from mechanomics with robotics, pharmacy, history and psychology to childhood studies. The others leave for gap years, which includes a welcome back at school for post A level university applications.

Money matters: Some reduction for siblings. Some automatic academic scholarships, others by application for music, sport and art; a few means-tested bursaries and academic 13+ and sixth form scholarships.

Remarks: Charming girls' school just beyond the very southernmost outstretched fingertip of Manchester's conurbation. A new vigour of academic purpose mingles with the strong Christian ethos that so celebrates and values each girl here, urging her on to be all that she can be.

Alexandra Park School

Bidwell Gardens, London, N11 2AZ

• Pupils: 1,435; 745 boys/ 690 girls; all day • Ages: 11–18 • Non-denom • State

Tel: 020 8826 4880
Email: office@apsch.org.uk
Website: www.apsch.org.uk

Headteacher: Since 2008, Mr Michael McKenzie MSc PGCE (early 40s). Educated at a comprehensive in Birmingham, he read chemistry at Nottingham, then did his teacher training at The Institute of Education. Head of year at William Ellis School in Camden, head of sixth form at La Swap, followed by deputy and associate head at Beal High School in Redbridge. Familiar and comfortable with the school's ethos before he applied, as the founding head had been his teaching mentor. Finds his pupils 'very entertaining, thoroughly enjoyable' and they (and their parents) feel he is a relaxed and positive addition. 'He's always about and knows a lot of the kids by name. He's very on the ball,' said one mother. Married, no children.

Academic matters: Alexandra Park's motto is 'success for all' and the school pulls off the very tricky achievement of being a successful London comprehensive welcoming the full range of abilities and social spectrum. 'Unlike other schools round here, it doesn't pick and choose. It's very inclusive,' says one parent. The intake may be all-encompassing but the academic values remain traditional. 'We don't play any games with the curriculum,' says the head, and the school is notably strong on core subjects. 2013 results at GCSE: 72 per cent got 5+ A*-C

A

including English and maths, with 35 per cent of grades A*/A. Most pupils take 10, including all three sciences. Spanish, French and Mandarin standard languages with Turkish also an exam option for GCSE and A level. Classics also a popular option with more than 120 pupils studying this at GCSE and A level

Has specialist status as a science and maths school and an international school. More than 200 students last year had the opportunity of studying in partner schools in France, Spain, South Africa and China. Mandarin on the curriculum here and is more than token – students can spend time on an immersion course in Beijing, with 30 studying the language pre-GCSE, a dozen or so in the sixth form.

A National Teaching School, indicating the importance the school places on appointing the best practitioners and ensuring they receive the latest training.

Some setting from year 7, depending on the department head – so maths and science are setted, English is not. Arts and media studies – unsurprisingly in this heartland of the media classes – are notably good so, to counterbalance the trend, has opted for a specialism in science and maths, with a dramatic upswing in results. Good vocational curriculum, with BTECs in sport, business, art, salon services and catering, some taught at the College of North East London. 'It means children who might have been less engaged have something positive and interesting to do, and those taking academic exams have the space to focus,' says one parent.

Strong gifted and talented programme (46 pupils with all A/A*s at GCSE in 2013) – pupils take early exams in maths, statistics, astronomy and classics. Also notable SEN support under dynamic head of special needs, with additional support in year 7 for those who've not yet achieved the requisite level in maths and English. Some parents, however, feel the extreme ends attract the bulk of attention: 'I think it would be quite difficult to get support if your kids come in the middle,' said one. 'You have to be very proactive.'

Popular sixth form, now in its seventh year – in 2013, 17 per cent A*/A grades at A level; 32 subjects on offer – strongest include English, French, physics and 'a really happening' history department.

Games, options, the arts: Busy, busy, busy. Specialist music and drama with a media suite and dance on offer. Last year's huge, all-encompassing drama production of The Wiz attracted a cast of 260 kids and staff. Energetic visual arts with A levels in photography, art and product design, plus a creative and media diploma for those wishing to create large-scale projects. Both BTEC and A level music. School choir, with an international schedule. Trips a big feature, with 116 different excursions last year, including a three-week exchange to Beijing, geography in Iceland, French in the south of France, art in Madrid, politics to Washington and design in New York.

Though relatively limited onsite space for sport, games spill over into adjoining Dunsford Park and plenty of variety to suit all tastes. Basketball, football (Newcastle United striker Nile Ranger used to star in the APS team), cricket and netball are main sports, but judo, aerobics, tennis, badminton, wrestling, rugby and golf also part of the offering (aspiring Nick Faldos can daydream their hole-in-ones gazing out from the classroom onto Muswell Hill golf course). Online student newspaper. Eclectic range of after-school clubs includes knitting, astronomy, fashion, pursuit cycling and cheerleading. 'Kids come up with the ideas,' says the head. Good careers advice with visits to universities and higher educational conferences. State-of-the-art sixth form centre, with study centre and purpose-built social space.

Background and atmosphere: Parents lobbied the local authority to create a new school in the area and APS was eventually founded in 1999 on the site of a former FE college. A relatively constricted site, which feels more spacious due to the surrounding greenery of Muswell Hill golf course and Durnsford Park. The original mix of pleasant brick buildings, some from the 1950s, some from the 1980s, have now been joined by a sleek modern extension (winner of a 2006 Civic Trust Award) and the sixth form centre.

Parents unanimous on the remarkably welcoming atmosphere – 'Everyone from the lady on the gate who checks uniform to the school receptionist makes you feel at home'. Even the police officer seeing kids onto after-school buses does it with a smile. Parents also enthuse about the school's multi-culturalism and inclusiveness ('They really try to be for everybody') and genuine concern ('It's far more nurturing than some of the other local comprehensives'). But concern is not cosseting – 'My children came from quite a sheltered primary school, but I feel they've learnt to cope with life here and to cope with London'.

Pastoral care and discipline: Traditional values apply. 'Kids need firm boundaries and it's important for the school to set them,' says the head. 'We expect them to be at school, on time, in uniform, ready to work.' Smart red, grey and black kit is strictly enforced. 'There used to be a gang who wore their uniform in a special way and that's now all ended,' said one parent approvingly. Behaviour in general is good and school hopes to keep it that way by instilling a sense of responsibility. 'We're training pupils to choose to do the right thing.' Misdemeanours promptly and firmly dealt with – 'When my son got into a fight, there was absolutely no messing. They threw the rulebook at him'. Drugs not a notable issue. 'It's bizarre,' says the head, 'at a previous school we had an incident every week. Here perhaps they're more savvy – or more mature.' Weapons, too, conspicuously absent.

Year 7 has its own 'transition manager'. Pupils remain in the same tutor groups for five years with a director of studies for each year. Also supported by learning mentors and counsellors. About 40 pupils with a statement of special needs have mainly cognitive rather than behavioural difficulties and the school copes well with autism, Asperger's and Down's. Communication between parents and schools clearly a strong point – 'All my emails, however trivial, get answered promptly'.

Pupils and parents: Wide social spread, from the comfortable middle-class suburbs near the gates to some of the most deprived kids in the country – 'a high proportion on the cusp of social needs'. Middle classes tend to dominate the PTA, which runs endless jumble sales and bazaars and is strongly involved in the day-to-day running of the school, but the kids themselves mix well. Very supportive parents – 'Parents helped set it up and want to make it work'. The school's popularity has reduced the catchment and the launch of another new school to the east is likely to make the intake more socially homogenous.

Entrance: In 2013, 1450 applications for 216 places. Usual priority to looked-after children, those with statements of special needs and siblings, then distance from the gates, which is now less than a mile. A bulge from adjoining high-achieving primary Rhodes Avenue, as well as from Bounds Green, Our Lady of Muswell, Bowes, Coldfall and Hollickwood.

Majority of existing pupils continue into sixth form. 80 per cent come up from year 11, the rest from other local schools. Open access, provided courses are available and attendance and attitude good enough. External applicants for A levels should have five GCSEs minimum A*-C, with Bs in A level subject choice.

Exit: Some 20 per cent leave after GCSEs. In sixth form majority apply to university; two to Cambridge in 2013, two brothers off to study dance and one girl to RADA; rest to a range from medicine at Southampton to design at Northumbria.

Money matters: Training school and academy trust status bring in extra funding.

Remarks: A notably welcoming place for children (and adults) from a large swathe of the borough. Not an academic pressure cooker but a school with high standards for all.

Alleyn's School

Linked school: Alleyn's Junior School

Townley Road, London, SE22 8SU

- Pupils: 575 boys, 650 girls; all day • Ages: 4–18 • C of E
- Fees: £13,437–£15,867 pa • Independent

Tel: 020 8557 1500
Email: registrar@alleyns.org.uk
Website: www.alleyns.org.uk

Headmaster: Since 2010, Dr Gary Savage MA PhD Cantab (forties). Previously Under-master at Westminster School, joining after 10 years' teaching at Eton, where his roles included head of history, community service coordinator and housemaster of the scholars' house. A historian of 18th century France, has a passion for watching sport (Ipswich Town supporter – he grew up in Suffolk and was state school educated) and for the arts. Has taught himself German, and he and his wife Natalie (a television and film producer) have a pied à terre in Berlin. Would like to encourage in his pupils his own appetite for learning.

'Imaginative...very charming...a good hand on the tiller,' say parents. Certainly a suspicion that he is more elitist in outlook than his predecessors, and parents fear that the school's liberal, creative ethos may be lost. Not so, he insists: 'I want our pupils to do very well in public exams – but emphatically not by turning Alleyn's into a hothouse. I want to expand horizons intellectually and socially without diluting or compromising the Alleyn's ethos. I want to work with not against the grain'.

Academic matters: Used to be the junior partner of the Dulwich triumvirate of schools in academic terms. No longer: the increasing popularity of co-education and a more selective entry has helped its rise up the league tables. 2013 saw 95 per cent A*-B and 72 per cent A*/A grades at A level; 87 per cent A*/A at GCSE. Maths much the most popular A level subject, as one would expect, but otherwise a broad spread of arts and sciences.

The head is 'passionate about non-examined academic enrichment'. He has instituted the Governor's research project prize, which is awarded for a piece of sixth form research – prize-winning subjects have ranged from an anthropological study on ape/human divergence to one on the mating habits of arachnids. He is encouraging a wider range of visiting speakers (the Guide listened to a fascinating talk by a Médecins Sans Frontières nurse; A C Grayling and the Archbishop of Canterbury have been other recent visitors), and has appointed a new KS3 co-ordinator focussing on thinking skills – 'I want to celebrate the life of the mind without compromising our buzz, busyness and happiness'.

Everyone is screened during year 7 to help identify any learning difficulties. At the end of the year, staff get together to decide who is likely to need extra support or an ed psych assessment. Full-time learning support co-ordinator can give individual term-long learning skills courses to those who are struggling. 'They're very quick at picking up when things are not going right,' said a parent. 'We get detailed reports, and I really feel they're on the case.'

Part of the Southwark Schools Learning Partnership, which involves staff and students from 11 state and private schools sharing experiences and working together to improve teaching and learning. Now developing links with the state Sydenham and Forest Hill sixth form.

Games, options, the arts: Has always been viewed as the most liberal and arty of the local independent schools – and, of course, attracts many families from the creative professions. 'Fabulous' theatre (named after a post-war English master who set up the National Youth Theatre) hosts lower, middle and upper school plays as well as many sixth form and visiting productions each year. Full time stage manager and students help with lighting and sound. 'The standard is amazing,' said a parent. 'They've really brought out my son's talents' – though inevitably it can be hard for lesser mortals to get parts in shows. 'But in the sixth form there's much more scope and they can put on their own performances,' said a student.

Large numbers play instruments – flourishing orchestras, choirs and ensembles taking part in master classes and performing at 'astonishingly high standards'. Very impressive art, with many taking it to A level and a very high proportion of A* grades. Not a school that is sniffy about media studies, which has its own well-equipped studio with the latest high-tech editing equipment. Food tech is a GCSE option and there's a popular cookery club.

Enviable sports facilities include new floodlit netball court in the centre of the quad and floodlit Astroturf, alongside sports hall, swimming pool, acres of playing fields. Sport for all but excellence too: whether the 1st XI footballers who recently reached the final of the Independent Schools Football Association cup, the girl who plays hockey for England, the extraordinary water polo teams (boys and girls reached the national finals in every age group and the U14 girls are national champions for the second year running), the fives enthusiasts or the cycling club which meets at the Herne Hill Velodrome. 'There's so much on offer that everyone finds something they want to do,' said a pupil.

Volunteering is important – 'They take it very seriously' – and houses raise funds for their own chosen charities. CCF very popular – opportunities to try gliding, go camping, do adventure training, learn radio communication – as is D of E, with large numbers at all levels. Huge numbers of overseas trips: eg football tour to Germany, geography society expedition to Iceland, religious studies trip to India.

Background and atmosphere: A direct descendent of the foundation Alleyn's College of God's Gift, set up in 1619 by Edward Alleyn, wealthy actor and proprietor of taverns, brothels and bear-baiting pits. Part of the foundation funded Dulwich College; in 1882, the upper and lower schools split, with the lower becoming Alleyn's Boys' School. It became a public school in 1919 and a direct grant grammar school from 1958, until that status was abolished in 1975. At that point it became independent and went co-ed. Other schools within the foundation include JAGS and several state schools.

Pleasant setting in between chic Dulwich village and trendy East Dulwich. Unpretentious red-brick facade of four-storey main building masks the main site, with its landscaped quads and acres of playing fields. A continuous development programme has, most recently, resulted in the dramatic Edward Alleyn building with its state-of-the-art theatre, lecture room, sixth form area and Costa coffee bar. Large sports hall, music school and excellent library.

Parents attracted by its reputation for a liberal, stimulating environment, with its history as a direct grant grammar school and perhaps less pretension than some more traditional public schools – 'We weren't interested in putting our children through a system that gave them an over-inflated view of their position in society,' said one parent. Generous bursaries help the social mix.

Pastoral care and discipline: A very happy place, say parents, with good pastoral care and good communications – 'Any questions get answered immediately'. The head concurs: 'When things go wrong we deal with it carefully, kindly and robustly. We have a strong pastoral setup with many layers, and we all work together to ensure that any children with problems are helped. Everything else is secondary to this.'

Lower school – years 7 and 8 – has its own building, providing a sheltered introduction to the school and, say parents, particularly good individual pastoral care. Year 9 upwards join houses, which give a family feel and opportunities for those who don't make school teams/plays to compete in inter-house events, eg music, drama and sport.

Head reckons only a handful of bullying incidents a year – 'It is a remarkable testament to the ethos of the place' – and parents agree, 'We've never come across any bullying. It probably helps being co-ed, but it is a very well-balanced place'.

Very few exclusions – 'I've had to do a couple of suspensions – for low level disruptions and disengagement – but we can generally get them back on side. Sometimes children give you no room for manoeuvre and you have to say it's not working. But we tackle these things educationally and pastorally from the beginning, and generally the children buy into this'.

Pupils and parents: More bohemian than the other Dulwich independents – 'It's always attracted pupils of journalists, rock stars and theatre people,' commented a parent. The least multi-ethnic of the three schools, probably because high-achieving ethnic minority families tend to go for single-sex education. 'I'd love to see us reflect more broadly the south-east London community,' says the head, 'and I hope that a wider range of families will feel confident applying to us. I don't want us to be a bubble community.' Pupils tend to be 'charming, articulate, incredibly polite,' said a parent. Has produced an unusual number of well-known actors, musicians and writers.

Ex-pupils include actors Jude Law, Nancy Carroll, Jessie Ware, Simon Ward and Julian Glover, director Felix Barrett, musicians Florence Welch, Felix White, Gabriel Prokofiev and Ed Simons, scientists Prof John Isaacs and Prof RV Jones, surgeon Prof Lord Kakkar, editor Kelvin MacKenzie, Air Marshall Sir Christopher Harper and writers CS Forester and VS Pritchett.

Entrance: Main entry at 11, with 125 places and around 500 applicants. Reasoning, English and maths papers. Automatic entry for junior school pupils, but the occasional one who has been struggling may have a probationary year: 'We try very hard to make it work. We will see it through if we possibly can'. Generally a third of year 7 comes from the junior school, a third from local preps and a third from state primaries. 'We like to take as broad a range as possible, but they must be bright enough to flourish, to enjoy the pace and buzz of life here. We're looking for those who will have a fabulous time.' Around 15 places at 13, with science and language exams added in. Interview and school report important. Up to 20 places at 16 (but often fewer) – exams in three prospective A level subjects plus a critical thinking test.

Increasing popularity means that local families can no longer be confident of a place for all their children. Parents who went to Alleyn's themselves sometimes irked to find the academic bar has risen above their reach, with places going to those from all points east, west, south and even north of the river.

Exit: Few leave after GCSE. Nearly all year 13 leavers to university, including Oxbridge and medical schools. Several to art foundation courses, one or two to drama school, a few to American colleges, otherwise mostly to top UK universities to do a huge mix of subjects ranging from natural sciences to social anthropology.

Money matters: Enviably well-endowed with funds from the Dulwich Estate and from the Worshipful Company of Saddlers, which pay for a generous staffing ratio and the ability to carry out a rolling programme of improvements. Some 30 pupils on 100 per cent bursaries and many more on 50 per cent upwards – school fundraising to increase that number. Scholarships (maximum £3000 a year) for music, art and sporting as well as academic excellence.

Remarks: Traditionally a liberal and creative school, beloved of south London media families, which is increasing its academic clout. Parents like the fact the children are 'well-balanced kids with lots to do'. One commented: 'We really feel we landed on our feet – it's a superb school.'

Alton College

Old Odiham Road, Alton, Hampshire GU34 2LX

• Pupils: 2000 • Ages: 16–19 • Non-denom • State

Tel: 01420 592200
Email: enquiries@altoncollege.ac.uk
Website: www.altoncollege.ac.uk

Principal: Since 2004, Ms Jane Machell BA MA PGCE (early fifties). Educated at Wirral Grammar School for Girls and read Spanish and Iberian studies at Southampton University, followed by a master's at Queens University, Canada and a PGCE at the University of Leicester. Joined Queen Mary's College as head of Spanish and rose to head of division via the posts of senior tutor and director of studies. Left to become deputy principal at Brockenhurst College and then joined Alton College as principal. Comes across as a shrewd businesswoman and keen educator in equal measure; keeps her finger on the pulse of college finances as well as a sharp eye on the quality of teaching (has three vice principals to help monitor standards, eg observing lessons). Clearly has an excellent grasp on the education of 16 to 19 year olds.

Has overseen the addition of several new buildings in her time (science, music and the arts) and most recently, the Berkoff performing arts centre. Frustrated by the cancellation of planned government funding for a new engineering building, she got on her bike and launched a fundraising appeal in 2012 to raise £2.4 million in two years.

Academic matters: Offers a very broad range of qualifications to a diverse group of students – anything from Oxbridge to GCSE retakes. The majority of sixth form students study A levels, with fewer following vocational courses. Also educates disabled students from nearby Treloar College.

Excellent range of academic subjects on offer – several young people we met were studying combinations you might expect in any public school sixth form. Achieves pass rates well above the national average. In 2013, 56 per cent A*-B and 80 per cent A*-C grades. Lots of opportunity to mix and match, as also offers A levels in less mainstream subjects such as dance, health and social care, music technology and photography. Some students choose to combine BTEC diplomas with A levels to give their qualifications a more practical slant; others follow the vocational route completely and opt for the extended diploma. BTEC courses include applied science, art and design, business, engineering, graphic design, ICT, performing arts and sport. Those who haven't passed any GCSEs can re-sit them at Alton.

Students say 'sciences are strong' and results back this up; science labs in Beacon Centre are spacious, well equipped and modern. Maths in good health – six maths A levels to choose from. French looks first-rate. Austen building has recording studios for film and media studies, as well as classrooms for English, modern languages and the humanities.

Learning resource centre has well stocked library and lots of individual cubicles for private study – ICT provision excellent: huge, silent room full of screens and students beavering away. Class size averages 19, with a maximum of 26. Statistics backed up by praise from Ofsted, which rated the college outstanding in nearly all areas after two consecutive inspections. Students achieve local and national success – a team won the UK Senior Maths Challenge and law students were finalists in the Bar Mock Trial Competition regional heats.

Outstanding SEN provision, not least for the learning support provided for students at Treloar College (pupils with severe physical disabilities) who study at Alton whilst boarding at Treloar. Dedicated rooms with computers and tables at the right height for students in wheelchairs. Also caters for a wide array of special needs, from dyslexia and dyspraxia to mental health issues and extra help with literacy and numeracy. Has won an Association of Colleges beacon award for its provision for students with special needs – eg creating a sports unit so a disabled student could complete his course by playing boccia in a wheelchair.

Games, options, the arts: Although sport not compulsory, more than 200 students are enrolled on sport related courses and another 200 take part in extracurricular physical activities. One hundred per cent pass rate for the BTEC diploma in sport – 50 per cent with merit and distinction. Large sports hall is located next to playing fields and has a gym with weights and resistance equipment. No swimming pool on campus, but students use Treloar College pool a short distance away. Matches against other Hampshire colleges throughout the year and regularly tops the county schools leagues in rugby, football and mixed hockey. Other teams compete in netball, basketball and badminton in winter, plus cricket and tennis in the summer term. Alternative sports include aerobics, dance, volleyball and women's football.

Michael Gray building houses art and music on three floors; vocational art takes place in two spacious studios on the ground floor, eg fashion design. Top floor is dedicated to A level art, with separate rooms for textiles, painting and drawing. Some very good quality work on display throughout the college and exam results are strong.

Lower floor of Gray Building devoted to music, with individual studios, practice rooms and music technology suites for recording and mixing sound. Music good with all the usual instruments on offer (practice not formally timetabled) – all music and music technology students receive tuition on one instrument free of charge. Visiting peripatetic staff teach nearly 200 students every week, chamber orchestra, jazz band, four choirs (including rock choir) and several instrumental ensembles. Composers' ensemble is on a winning streak – one student won the BBC Proms Young Composers Competition and had her pieces broadcast on Radio 3, while another won the big band section of a jazz competition with her music. College 'jazzers' perform regularly in local festivals and venues, have undertaken a monthly residency in a local pub, performed at the Birmingham ICC and given a short concert tour of France. Two students won places in the National Youth Jazz Collective and others have gone on to study jazz, composition, piano and orchestral instruments at music conservatoires.

Fabulous, modern Berkoff performing arts centre has a professionally equipped theatre, large dance studio with sprung flooring and a busy schedule of performances throughout the year. Stevens Building houses photography studios and darkrooms – one student had her work selected for Royal Photographic Society's International Print Exhibition. Engineering building is distinctly unglamorous by comparison and affectionately referred to as 'the shed'. It nevertheless looked pretty well fitted out to our untrained eye, with lots of practical, blokey activities going on. Sadly, numbers studying engineering stay capped until the new building is built.

Good opportunities for students to flesh out work in the classroom and beef up university CVs – trips to First World War battlefields (English), St Petersburg (art), South Africa (geography), Iceland (chemistry), Berlin (German) and Cuba (photography and biology) organised. Intrepid college students have also got as far as Peru, Tanzania, Bolivia and the Himalayas. Lots of extracurricular opportunities, from Iron Man training in Lanzarote to skiing in Switzerland, chess club, debating society, recreational badminton, grade 5 music theory, first aid and the college magazine.

Background and atmosphere: The first purpose-built sixth form centre in the UK, opened in 1978 with 240 students. It now educates over 2,000 16 to 19 year olds and nearly 900 adults following part-time courses. Over £20 million has been invested in the college since 2002 and new buildings have been added.

Feels more like a university campus than a school. The young people we met value the adult atmosphere and cite mutual respect between staff and students. 'We call our teachers by their first names and we can email them whenever we like,' one told us. Some felt they had outgrown their former schools and said, 'Alton is the right step between school and uni for us'.

University feel continues with college's large refectory serving subsidised meals; also various smaller cafes dotted around where students can buy Fairtrade coffee, sandwiches and snacks. A crèche on site, mostly used by staff but also by a very small number of sixth form students with young children.

Pastoral care and discipline: Big on pastoral care – well organised programme to monitor student progress. Principal recognises that 'myriad things underpin academic successes'. Each pupil has a personal tutor, who reports to a senior tutor, who in turn reports to director of learning. Everyone has weekly personal learning and development lessons in the first year and is issued with an individual learning planner. Pupils touch in and out of lessons via an electronic pass and can monitor their attendance, homework and grades via Moodle (virtual site), which also has plenty of learning and revision resources online; student reps use it to give feedback to staff members. We got the feeling that not much slips through the cracks here.

Gifted and talented programme for around 300 students applying to top universities – focus on interview technique (eg how to cope with being stared down by an Oxbridge don at the far end of a table in very grand rooms) and how best to prepare applications to competitive courses, eg medicine and veterinary studies.

Active student union meets regularly with the principal and organises charity events. Student centre offers counselling and career advice and helps students with higher education choices and contacts for work experience. Few problems with discipline – principal says, 'The vast majority of young people rise to the standards we expect of them'. Quiet garden in memory of former students provides a peaceful space to relax and reflect in.

Pupils and parents: Many pupils arrive from nine partner schools, although a significant number come from other schools in Hampshire, Surrey and West Sussex. Approximately 10 per cent from the private sector, either because they want a more adult atmosphere or a wider choice of subjects (college hosts a special evening for those transferring from independent schools).

Most families live within 20 miles of the college, a few further afield. Ten subsidised bus routes deliver students from destinations such as Basingstoke and Haslemere. Parents choose the college in the hope that it will ease the transition to university, confirmed by feedback from admissions tutors.

Most students are British, although growing number of students from other ethnic backgrounds, one of whom we met (an engaging Russian who spoke excellent English and clearly has a future in politics). Students are mature, focused and fairly laidback; they have clearly made the transition from school to university 'halfway house'. Not perhaps as polished as the independent school product, which isn't necessarily to their disadvantage.

Entrance: Not selective, but anyone missing the applications deadline is very likely to go on the waiting list. Applications invited from November of the previous year to the end of March for entry the following September; everyone is interviewed twice. First interview takes place by the end of April and the second following GCSE results.

College's feeder schools are Amery Hill, Bohunt, Eggar's, Mill Chase, Perins, The Petersfield School, Robert May's, Weydon and St Nicholas' School. Open evenings held in October and March; guidance meetings scheduled in partner schools between November and April. Welcome event for prospective new students happens in July.

Exit: Given the inclusive intake of the college, leavers' choices are broader than most. Has commissioned and produced a highly detailed analysis of its students' destinations, so we can report with complete confidence that 80 per cent of A level pupils, 50 per cent of vocational course students and 98 per cent of art foundation leavers go on to higher education. A very small number (three per cent) chooses further education, eg Sparsholt College or Basingstoke College of Technology, whilst around 13 per cent seek employment.

The most popular university courses are art and design, business, linguistics, biological sciences, law and physical sciences. Top university destinations are the University of the West of England, Bournemouth, Southampton, Brighton, Surrey, Bath, Exeter, Kent and Portsmouth. Seventeen per cent of leavers secure places at Russell Group universities and a few gain places at specialist music conservatoires.

Former pupils include MP Yvette Cooper, actress Catherine McCormack, scientist Jonathan Tucker, musicians Alison Goldfrapp and Gwyneth Herbert, cricketer Chris Wood, comedian Russell Howard and Ben Southall, winner of the Best Job in the World competition.

Money matters: College foundation offers scholarships worth up to £1,000 to those who demonstrate excellence in a particular subject (disciplines have included art, engineering, law, medicine, music and sport). Bursary scheme subsidises the cost of education for families on low incomes and can be used for any purpose, eg paying for the cost of travel to and from college. Award worth £250 is available to students on the one-year art foundation course.

Remarks: Open access sixth form college which offers a broad range of qualifications and provides a bridge between school and higher education to those looking for a bit more freedom to manage their own education. Gets good results and also scoops up those who have fallen by the GCSE wayside. Provides plenty of support, but may not suit someone who needs a hand held at every step.

Altrincham Grammar School for Boys

Marlborough Road, Bowdon, Altrincham Cheshire WA14 2RS

• Pupils: 1,260 boys; all day • Ages: 11–18 • Non-denom • State

Tel: 01619 280858
Email: trichardson@agsb.co.uk
Website: www.agsb.co.uk

Headmaster: Since 2003, Mr T J Gartside MA Edinburgh University (history) (late forties). A calm and understated authority who has led school through £4m of grants and development. Staff like him, boys like him, parents also. Fact is, he's thoroughly likeable; approachable, grounded, without airs, graces or spin; hard to know if he's picked up the character of the school or if it mirrors his, but both are 'good sorts'. Was educated and then taught at Hulme Grammar School for Boys, so this post was a 'coming home' and, with two children still in school locally, he seems settled. 'Where would I find anything better to move on to? And besides, there are always new exciting opportunities and developments, always new challenges', so stagnation is not on the agenda. Quietly ambitious; initial aim was to rival Manchester Grammar School and many would agree the gap has shrunk enough to make deciding between the two at 11 a really tough call, especially for local boys.

Academic matters: Consistently very strong. Last Ofsted peppered with 'excellent' and 'outstanding'. Excellent results in 2013: 79 per cent of A levels A*-B, 53 per cent A*/A; 64 per cent of GCSEs (and most boys take 11) A*/A. All take three sciences, taught in the time most schools give to the GCSE dual science award, many take a language early and boys routinely gain two maths GCSEs as school pilots new syllabus. 'Furthermore,' head says, 'boys tend to rise to where the bar is set,' and while some parents feel 11 subjects is too many, others are grateful subject choices remain wide.

Head delights in really good staff with ability to teach the curriculum with care whilst also enjoying freedom to branch out. Maths and science traditionally strong – science college status, with Olympiad and National Challenge success reflecting this (new £1m physics centre of four labs and a sixth form lecture room). Language college status – French, German, Spanish, Latin, Greek and Chinese in the curriculum, 'and it's not just about the language but the culture too,' say boys. Italian, Arabic and Russian as extras, and a strong community programme of evening classes. Only Greater Manchester school to offer Latin and Greek to A level. Latest addition to the curriculum is food technology, introduced 2011 in a new purpose-built room. Sixth formers praise university application help.

SEN provision responds to needs arising, which are relatively few, mainly dyslexia. Physical access now includes ramps and lifts. Library burbling with activity at lunchtime, no stuffy silence here, instead a happy place and even, on Fridays, live music against the racks of periodicals, quality daily papers, the weekly Spanish El Pais. DVDs to rent, 'and if you take them on Friday you get to keep them for the whole weekend'. 'They're educational,' points out the librarian and, indeed, a few in foreign languages nestle amongst the popular titles.

Games, options, the arts: Sports facilities to die for: The Grammar halls and fitness suite, with views over new floodlit Astroturf, four new tennis courts and 16 acres of fields beyond. Used by the community until 10pm and at weekends, during the day year 11 boys get to lunch behind the plate glass and blue steel. Boys from year 9 up can use the fitness machines and a trainer puts together fitness plans including programmes to support high level sportsmen. Football and rugby enduringly popular, with boys proud to use the Sale Sharks training ground. North of England U13 and U14 champions for tennis. Several England hockey players. Ambitious, 'now we've got the facilities, to become big hitters in the school leagues'. Table tennis also popular – top four nationally in U13s last year.

Parents describe music here as 'excellent' and rejoice, 'It's cool to be musical'. The legendary swing band won the national schools wind band finals and this year the concert band won a gold award in the same competition. Manchester's Hallé Choir recruits here. Private lessons for 12 instruments, strings currently particularly encouraged. No bespoke drama studio, or GCSE, but a recently introduced LAMDA course for sixth formers is proving popular and the acclaimed annual production involves girls from local schools, sometimes in the cast, always in the adoring audience.

Lofty, two storey art room – impressive works bedeck corridor walls. Too many clubs for lunchtime and after school – some take place before the day begins. At lunchtime, a fallow classroom is rare, though the odd quiet space can still be found. By and large, though, this school teems with life with boys engaged over homework, on some of the 433 networked computers (yes, some doing homework) or in a myriad of clubs. Active charity fundraising, community action opportunities. Younger boys marvel as they reel off lists of what they can make in CDT, chess club meets every day and, in a dusty cupboard under the tech block stairs, radio club tunes into global conversations, sticking pins triumphantly in a map of the world.

Background and atmosphere: Celebrated centenary in 2012, with lots of special events. The original redbrick buildings at the heart of school lend a solidly traditional air. The corridors, therefore, are narrow – you take your life in your hands entering the sixth form centre as they pour out for lessons. But if you are not trampled underfoot (and we weren't), they are welcoming. Nowhere seems out of bounds; all ages including staff, mix genially together, and even year 8 guides with a visitor trot happily into the hallowed ground of the sixth form common room. This boasts leather sofas, bistro tables and its own 'servery', where chips and muffins sit unashamed alongside fruit.

Across the corridor, younger boys dine with a smartcard, in no particular order, in the airy Stamford Hall. Packed lunch can be eaten at clubs as well and breakfast is available. Links with nearby St Mary's Church for concerts and services. Academy status since 2011.

Pastoral care and discipline: Parents describe pastoral care as 'really helpful', one new mum praising school for being proactive at keeping in touch when her new starter took time to settle. At the other end, boys who need, for some reason, to apply to UCAS after they've left seem unreservedly welcomed back for help with that. Discipline falls to much respected senior staff, and parents tell us care is taken to fit the punishment to the crime. 'Compared to the girls' head, Mr Gartside doesn't evoke much fear in the students,' say boys, although a Saturday detention isn't relished. 'Boys can make mistakes,' says head. 'The most important thing is that they learn from them' – no histrionics here. Head always in school on Saturdays to support sport and known to be readily available to parents.

Pupils and parents: Unpretentious, middle class. Sixty per cent from up-market Bowdon, Hale and Altrincham, swarming home in green blazers with red trim. Forty per cent from classy Cheshire and the less affluent parts of Trafford borough. A fifth of boys from ethnic minority groups, a third with English as second language, mainly professional families. Ofsted said, 'Diversity is respected and inclusiveness is celebrated by all'; as well as individual faith groups, an inter-faith society called Co-exist. Fair smattering of children of Old Boys.

OBs include local Tory MP Graham Brady, who lent his voice to the refurbishment grant appeal; cricketer Paul Allott and Ian Livingstone, creator of Tomb Raider, Lara Croft and Dungeons and Dragons, Games Workshop and Eidos – new IT suite bears his name after substantial donation.

Entrance: Hugely competitive with four applying for each place. Standards are kept high ('consistent,' says head), using own maths, verbal and non-verbal reasoning multiple-choice papers and a short story, one Saturday in September. Places offered based on bald results, 60 per cent to top local boys, 40 per cent using a wider net. Many are tutored or brought up to scratch in small independent prep schools so playing field isn't level. Head maintains hot-housing won't make the difference (hmm) and counsels against pushing to just pass the threshold and then struggle, and we agree with him there. School does, however, strongly advise familiarity with exam content and format and makes example papers available.

Exit: A couple of handfuls leave and join at sixth form. Ninety per cent from sixth form to higher education to a wide variety of courses. In 2013, 11 to Oxbridge. Vast majority to solid universities – Manchester, Sheffield and Nottingham top the list – to do solid courses: engineering, economics, medicine, maths and computing most popular.

Remarks: Undoubtedly the top boys' state school for miles. Relaxed and happy in its own skin, exudes friendly enthusiasm while producing, after seven happy years, polite, can-do young men. Legions of very satisfied parents – and no wonder.

Altrincham Grammar School for Girls

Cavendish Road, Bowdon, Altrincham Cheshire WA14 2NL

• Pupils: 1,275 girls, all day • Ages: 11–18 • Non-denom • State

Tel: 01619 125912
Email: admin@aggs.trafford.sch.uk
Website: www.aggs.trafford.sch.uk

Executive Headteacher: Since 1999, Dame Dana Ross-Wawrzynski BSc MSc (we settled on fiftyish, as in our last report, so no progress there!), school in Scotland, then Glasgow and Strathclyde Universities – biochemistry and applied microbiology. Taught at Manchester Metropolitan University, All Saints FE College, Central High School for Boys, Loreto School, Manchester, Abraham Moss High School (deputy head), All Hallows, Macclesfield (deputy head).

Hardly lacking in fluency on educational matters, she is a distinguished national leader in education and very successful at raising standards in struggling state schools, as well as supporting maths and language learning in the region – she sees sharing good practice as part of the school's purpose and points out that the benefits accrue in both directions. Consequently a lot of innovative work going on here, in conjunction with Manchester University. Not someone the more timid kind of parent would tackle lightly – 'a very strong character', 'It's made very clear what you will get' – but also said to be approachable and friendly.

As executive head, she relies on her strong management team to handle everyday matters. The headteacher is Mrs Mary Speakman, previously deputy head, at the school since 1991. Although the girls feel they would like to see more of Mrs Ross-Wawrzynski, says a parent, they find her 'great fun' on foreign trips. Husband an architect, twin sons both at Cambridge; enjoys travelling, reading, Radio 4, TV discussion programmes.

Academic matters: A level results consistently very strong – high ranking nationally; 2013 94 per cent A*-B, 73 per cent A*/A. Good numbers for French, Spanish, maths; geography, history, psychology and the sciences popular. Last Ofsted glowed about sixth form: outstanding achievement, teaching and learning.

GCSE very strong across the board and on the up – 85 per cent A*/A. All take nine and follow a programme of enrichment to develop 'all round' skills. Several Good Schools Guide awards for top exam results nationally in various subjects; success in national competitions (science, maths, German).

At key stage 3 all do three sciences, two languages and ICT. Developing personalised and independent learning – gifted and talented identified on entry, but the many opportunities on offer available to all; the Special Schools and Academies Trust is showcasing four of their projects. Average class sizes: main school 25 (up to 29); sixth 11 (up to 19); very good value added key stage 3-4. Plenty of whizzy ICT suites, though not all classrooms have interactive whiteboards (partly as not all the teachers want them, interestingly), but more to come. Has moved to a 10 day timetable.

Most recent Ofsted reckons pupils 'work very hard, concentrate well and behave wonderfully' and praises the high standard of teaching throughout (Dame Ross-Wawrzynski says of her staff, 'They have a passion for their subject, are keen to support all the children and to develop their own practice'), plus teacher-pupil relationships. Many of the girls we met spoke very appreciatively of how generous the teachers are with academic help and university entrance guidance and their excellent exam preparation. Parents say: 'They make the lessons fun and interesting and are very good at focusing the girls and developing their confidence'; 'They work very hard with the less engaged.'

Languages college – very good resources and exam results, work experience in France, Spain and Germany; extracurricular clubs for Russian, Japanese and Chinese plus evening classes in Italian. Science department has national recognition and is working with four schools in Singapore on a sustainability project. A teacher won a national award for innovative development of e-learning, which she very sportingly used on a mega hi tech gizmo for the school. Extra funding from teaching school status benefits students and staff development. A teaching school, so has a leading role in staff training, as well as supporting other schools. Part of Bright Futures Education Trust, a local multi-academy organisation.

Few with learning difficulties/disabilities – mostly mild dyslexia. In class support for statemented disabilities; girls with EAL needs supported by trained sixth form mentors; mild physical disabilities can be accommodated – 'We would take anyone who passed our exams, so long as it was in the best interests of all the girls,' says SENCo.

Games, options, the arts: Standard sports with trendy extras – yoga, trampolining – for years 10-11; national achievements in netball, hockey, badminton, swimming and squash; a football club. Ten music ensembles and a recently acquired upright Schimmel piano (large contribution from the PTA); big concert at the Bridgewater Hall; choir tour to Germany. Plays performed in school hall or drama studio. Dance very popular with two productions each year and girls can undertake the sports and dance leader qualification. Really superlative art, at all ages, in a wide range of media – excellent painting and drawing, fab decorated shoes and bronze jewellery. Food tech, textiles and, unusually for a girls' school, resistant materials.

Astrophysics club for the stellar and zillions more, with sixth former input – they also provide languages support and guidance to younger girls, give taster secondary sessions to year 4 children and help with GCSE maths revision sessions for state school girls. Year 11 and sixth form prefects, a school council,

and girls regularly elected to the UK Youth Parliament. Charity work with Altrincham Boys' Grammar. These girls do it all – glass ceilings look out!

Wide ranging trips abroad (Latin America, Iceland, Russia, Turkey, Cern), exchanges, links with schools in Europe, China, Japan; supports a school in South Africa – has International School award. Biennial careers convention; parents come in to give advice; year 10 careers day and work experience, plus a further week at the end of year 12 (or they can get office experience at school in free periods).

Background and atmosphere: On three sites in the leafy suburb of Bowdon. The main building is 100 years old, with ivy clad walls and an elegant hall. The attractive, compact, main school library has a spiral staircase and black wooden beams – masses of modern teenage fiction and PCs for only half a class, by design, to encourage the others to use books.

A pleasant walk through a park, past all weather pitches and netball courts, takes you to another site, and a third contains the newest development. The sixth have a jazzy orange and maroon common room, their own library and a café. Two gardens and a couple of gazebos, so the girls can eat outside in the summer (their idea).

One girl we met said, 'Stress is a bit of a problem,' because expectations are very high, but others added, 'A teacher will talk to you if she thinks you're putting too much pressure on yourself'; 'The school tells you when you've done well and shouldn't retake all your modules.' They see it as friendly and responsive to their views, obtained via questionnaires, the school council and pupil forums, and have very happy memories of their year 7 'bonding' residential at Boreatton Park. Sixth formers wear smart business clothes, the others dark blue blazers, skirts and jumpers, with white, open neck blouses.

Pastoral care and discipline: Pastoral care a great strength: has a school nurse and a Youth Relate counsellor who visits twice a week, plus a pastoral mentor – 'There's always someone to talk to about your problems'; a sixth form well-being bus comes regularly and a particularly good website area offers confidential help, with a button that alerts the police, who will then contact the school if appropriate – eg in the case of bullying. Praised by a parent for being very thorough and thoughtful in providing for her daughter's particular needs. The lead school in the north west for SEAL (social and emotional education) programme. National Healthy School award; sixth formers mentor the younger girls and in general, 'Girls are keen to help each other'; 'They try to resolve any problems between themselves'. Year 7s settle in quickly – they soon make friends and homework demands are built up gently. An enlightened anti bullying policy – 'Any bullying is investigated immediately; they are very fair'. Very strict on drugs, at school or on trips.

Pupils and parents: Pupils from the local area, from 40-60 feeder schools, all visited in advance by a teacher. About one fifth from a range of minority ethnic groups; very small numbers of EAL; parents mostly 'relatively advantaged' economically.

Good links with parents – information evenings, forums, questionnaires, the comprehensive website with e-bulletins – who are very enthusiastic ('fabulous, a lovely atmosphere', 'You couldn't find a better school'). The girls are focused, thoughtful, happy, confident, articulate and well behaved, appreciative of the way the school is 'always trying to improve itself'. According to the cover supervisor: 'They are very self directed, a pleasure to teach, very respectful and polite'.

Entrance: Takes the top 35 per cent of the ability range, which is wider than most grammar schools. An open day in the summer term for prospective parents to advise on admissions procedure; the waiting list criteria details are available on the website, including the checks made on the residence qualification, so no point renting a second home in the catchment area!

Year 6 tests in September: verbal and non-verbal reasoning and maths; year 7-10: non-verbal reasoning, mathematics, English and a modern foreign language (French, German or Spanish); year 11: maths, written English, written MFL.

Sixth form – four GCSEs at A/A*, including prospective AS subjects, and two Bs, including English. Entry to outside candidates is dependant on being able to offer a timetable in the subjects of their choices. This year 19 external applicants were offered places.

Exit: Year 13: almost all to university, eg Sheffield, Nottingham, Manchester, Leeds, Birmingham and Durham, 19 to Oxbridge, to study a range of subjects – medicine, dentistry, sciences, psychology, modern languages, English and law popular, with a few engineers.

Remarks: Offers excellent academic and extracurricular opportunities, so very good for girls who want to make the most of them. Has been shortlisted for the Times Educational Supplement outstanding secondary school of the year award and attracts many observers – local, national and international. 'The school makes the girls feel they can succeed at any challenges, if they work at them, and can be what they want to be.'

The American School in London

Linked school: The American School in London Lower School

1 Waverley Place, London, NW8 0NP

- Pupils: 1,350 girls and boys • Ages: K to Grade 12 • Non-demon
- Fees: £21,050–£24,550 pa • Independent

Tel: 020 7449 1220
Email: admissions@asl.org
Website: www.asl.org

Head: Since 2007, Coreen R Hester (degrees in English Literature and Education, Stanford University), previously head of Hamlin School in San Francisco. Was ASL's high school principal from 1995-1997, when her children were both pupils there. Early in her career, Mrs Hester taught English at University Liggott in Michigan; she then spent 10 years at the Branson School as teacher, dean, college counsellor, assistant head and interim head of school. Was also previously director of the Western Region Educational Services.

This energetic Californian inherited a well-oiled machine in a newly-renovated campus. She aims to strengthen the already high-qualified teaching staff, is looking at the role of support staff and reviewing the curriculum so that what is taught to five year olds makes sense when they are 15. Highly visible, 'larger than life', with 'lots of presence', she gets lots of praise from parents who describe her as 'so smart and insightful', and couldn't be more approachable. 'She's a great communicator'. 'The impact she has had on the school is huge. She has really upped the game for the teachers. We think the world of her!'

Academic matters: ASL's reputation is tops and an expectation of excellence must be pumped in through the air ducts; parents say that ASL aligns itself with the top US independent and public schools. Classes are no larger than 20 (15 the average in high school) and children are encouraged to take risks and view mistakes as natural learning. To quote a high schooler, 'Being smart is admired here. It's not about showing off, it's about showing what you can do.'

In the lower school the approach is project based, developing attitudes and habits that set up these youngsters for life-long learning. During our stroll through the lower school we saw a full range of teaching contexts – children working one-to-one with teachers and assistants, working in pairs, small groups working collaboratively on projects, whole class groups seated in a big circle on the floor playing a language game, or engaged in teacher-led instruction using an interactive whiteboard. Lower school classes occasionally spend the day at the school's learning centre in Cannon's Park for a day of outdoor and environmental studies.

The middle school programme is designed to develop independence and organisation. While some parents initially worry that middle school begins at grade 5, a tad younger than the norm in many US and international schools, the structure is well designed so that grades 5 and 6 share one floor, and grades 7 and 8 another, facilitating the transition from primary to secondary education. 'Think of it as lower middle and upper middle school', parents say, 'It works.'

High school is preparation for higher education with plenty of options in several subject areas, including over 20 AP subjects, making ASL one of the most prolific AP schools outside the US. In 2013, 234 students sat 673 AP exams in 32 subject areas, 96 per cent scored grade 3 or higher (out of a possible 5). The average SAT I scores are 677 in critical reading, 671 in math and 672 in writing (out of a possible 800 in each). Recent appointment of an all-school curriculum coordinator who is reviewing the entire academic programme from soup to nuts should iron out any kinks has the approval of parents.

Older students say that this is a school where you need to be motivated and work hard. It's more of an unspoken expectation throughout but all confirm there is good support in place and teachers willing to put in the extra hours to help. However, it comes a bit easier if you are pro-active about seeking that help out. One parent says, 'If a child is highly sensitive, it is not always the kindest and gentlest place to be. But if they can access the education, it is a great experience'. All the departments are strong, improvements to language provision previously noted although we have spoken to some dual-language families and kids who say they no longer consider themselves to be truly bilingual having not maintained the other language.

ASL keeps up with US pedagogy, forging strong relations with leading US educationalists, such as Project Zero at Harvard, and not only sends teachers there to learn as part of the school's generous professional development programme but also hosts ASL learning institutes so other educators in the UK and abroad benefit.

Two libraries, very inviting and always busy, parents with volunteering or browsing the shelves themselves. Computer terminals all over and all students have computer classes. Grades 7 and 8 are given laptops which they are expected to master. High school students can bring their own or use those on site.

ASL can handle students with mild learning problems, specialists provide individual support; spaces are limited and there's an additional fee for the programme. One parent we spoke to wanted to dispel the myth that ASL does not deal well with learning problems. Her child's problem, overlooked by previous schools, was diagnosed right away and the SEN team have been 'fabulous'. The English as an Additional Language (EAL) programme helps non-English speakers up to grade 4 come up to speed for better integration in the mainstream. Intermediate and advanced English speakers are integrated up to grade 10. After that, total fluency is required to handle the rigorous academics.

Faculty of 175, average tenure is nine years which is good for international schools. Not only do 75 per cent of the teachers have higher degrees, so do many of the teaching assistants. Despite this longevity of service, a new high school principal, and a new lower school principal and assistant principal joined the staff in 2013. It's early days but parents seem happy with the new arrivals.

Games, options, the arts: Academics are important but so are the arts, sports and other activities, with a growing emphasis on community service. Framed paintings, drawings and photos by former students line the walls, forming part of the school's permanent collection and setting the bar for the arts. Everyone learns an instrument in the band or orchestra and sings in the choir through middle school. These enthusiastic musicians then take up seats in the bands and orchestras at the high school level. Opportunities available to travel in Europe with the choir and orchestras, or with the drama programme. Photo labs and art studios busy throughout the day. The new auditorium looks like a not-so-mini version of the Barbican and it's always in use either for concerts and plays or hosting speakers.

Sports are part of the DNA at ASL but, unlike some stateside schools, sports at ASL complement the academics rather than competing with them. At least 85 per cent of high school students play on at least one school team. There are two gyms, 21 acres of playing fields a tube ride away (students are bussed there though distances means that this is restricted to after-school activities) and a display case filled with trophies leaves no doubt about the school's athletic standing in the international school world.

Special interest clubs too many to mention – all the usual ones and lots of unusual ones, in school and off campus. The PCA funds up to £1,000 for a well-thought-out one-time project put forward by faculty, students or staff. The head also has a fund to support new projects, for example the school's robotics program began this way.

High school students accompanied by faculty members participate in annual spring Alternatives programme choosing between recreational, academic or cultural activities done over four days. Community service with new emphasis on local interaction has 270 kids volunteering in charities and projects based within a few miles radius. They're also building bridges with the nearby comprehensive school thanks to a student-led joint-school Lego robotics club initiative. The kids themselves form lots of service-related clubs that do their own independent fund-raising for good causes they want to support. Students encouraged to assume leadership roles, challenge themselves and take advantage of London. Field trips, not just in London but all over Europe and Africa, organised to broaden perspectives.

Background and atmosphere: Founded in 1951 as an alternative to the British schools for London's burgeoning American diplomatic, military and corporate community, this London city school uses every inch of its space; through innovative planning and fund-raising initiatives they continues to embellish that. Compact brick buildings set on a city block encase the 1,350 student body, which is at capacity. Security fencing surrounds the perimeters and smart security men keep a watchful eye on all comings and goings (no entry without a school pass or photo id). Outdoor spaces adapted to different age groups.

ASL has a strong and active board of trustees in the style of US independent schools. They are active and hard-working and take their role very seriously. The last the big development project added an extra floor, a gym, new labs and a theatre. The lower school has a pod centre for each grade level; classrooms radiate from a central information space housing computers, reading corners and other teaching resources. The middle school students move around between classes more, and the high school is what you would expect: animated kids rushing around halls, definitely happy to be there. Pupil work is everywhere, for example an impressive student-designed notice board about the US elections conveyed both US-essence of the school and the calibre of creativity and critical thinking these kids possess.

Middle and high school classes run for 80 minutes with an hour for lunch. Students bring their lunch or buy it in the cafeteria which is very good, though many in grades 9-12 opt for the off-campus privilege. We hear some grumbles about

pressure on lunch facilities; one parent said she was not particularly happy with the early timing of her lower school daughter's lunch sitting. Lower school students eat a packed lunch (from home or purchased from ASL) in their classroom.

Pastoral care and discipline: It seems that students at ASL work hard and play hard. The kids are motivated to try hard to do their best, to try lots of new activities or get better at the ones they excel at. While allowing for individual initiative and responsibility, the organisation and structure is in place to ensure plenty of support so that no one drifts off course.

Parents report few serious disciplinary problems, saying the school plays it 'close to the vest' and that if there are, they're dealt with quietly and confidentially. School rules not onerous but expectation is that they will be followed and the school will take transgressions seriously. When news circulated about a recent (and rare) cheating incident, the head responded swiftly and firmly. Parents say, however, that teachers and principals are not always consistent doling out the consequences and sanctions which result from misbehaviour.

The school recommends that families abide by US drinking rules – no alcohol for under 21s – which are stricter than those found in Britain, but this is difficult to enforce. If word gets back to the high school dean about a party, he phones the host's parents just to make sure they are aware. At times this makes him more popular with parents than the kids! No dress code, but jeans seem to be the uniform of choice. If you do see the odd shirt and tie, it means a team is off to an away game.

Students arrive at this urban school with different levels of 'street wisdom' and 'stranger danger' awareness. Parents appreciate the way ASL takes pains to speak frankly to parents and kids about the potential problems and equip students with the right skills to protect themselves. A noteworthy issue is that middle schoolers are sometimes targets for muggings in the streets of affluent St John's Wood. Perpetrators are usually other kids looking for the portable technology now standard kit for many students. Nobody ever gets hurt, but it happens a few times a year. Door-to-door bus service available in the morning and after school and also at the end of the after-school programme, covers central, north and west London.

ASL high schoolers do not have an advisory or homeroom teacher, a concern for some parents; instead, a dean of year looks after the year group, working in partnership with principals and subject teachers. In grade 11 deans hand over to the university counsellors, each of whom has a light case load so they can give plenty of attention to each of their charges. Daily bulletins and notices are sent by email to all.

Pupils and parents: The school may be in London but the tone is definitely American – let's call it 'global American'. Eighty per cent of the 1,350 students hold US passports, and half of those are multi-passport holders from dual-national families. There are 50 nationalities in the school and the group of great kids who turned up during break to meet the GSG visitor didn't contain a single American! As a rule, ASL students are bright, curious and confident, and willing to express their views about anything you ask them. But, as one middle school pupil observed, 'international passports do not make a place international, the school is pretty 'American'. The popular award-winning student newspaper The Standard debates this question from time to time. Non-Americans at this school are largely attracted by the academic, social and college counselling preparation for entry into US universities. Lots of 'third culture kids' (professional parents raising children in a country not their own), and ex-pats from the finance world, though the transiency is diminishing as more families stay longer. As one parent said, 'If you are an American coming from another international school, it feels American, but if you are from the suburbs of Chicago or Westchester County, it feels international.

The school has revised its mission statement to incorporate the 'global perspective', and 'bursting the bubble' is one of Hester's goals for the school, which she describes as 'somewhere in the mid-Atlantic'. After 9/11 the school heightened its security and understandably drew inward but now, Hester explains, 'it's time to 'bring ASL into London, and London into ASL' with more intentional planning for programming, including emphasis on community service activities.

There is a perception on the part of some parents that it's economic diversity that is lacking, with concerns that 'too many kids are fretting about the right trainers or Prada handbags, and the presence of a few kids so wealthy that their security guards come to school with them, which is a bit weird.' This is something the school hopes will change through its diversity statement – and a target to grow the financial aid pot to a level equivalent of 8.5 per cent of the tuition income.

It is worth noting that lots of ASL families are there for the second time. Families sometimes choose London as a posting in part because of ASL; it is regarded by many as one of the key attractions of moving here.

Entrance: Admission is based on school records, teacher recommendations and standardised test results (ERB/ SSATs). Turnover is diminishing, with waiting lists at all grades, which means there may not be space for all family members. Unlike other international schools, ASL will only accept applications a year before admission; the first round of offers is made on 1 February. After that, it's rolling admissions.

Huge praise for the school's support for new arrivals – both parents and kids – including seminars, social events and newsletters. 'It's tremendous how much they reach out to pull you in, because they know you are lost.'

Exit: Most students leaving before graduation do so because of family transfers. For those planning to finish the course, university preparation work begins in grade 11 for students and parents. One parent told us that the rumour that everyone has to go to a 'top ten' is untrue. ASL's US Advanced Placements (APs) are welcomed by British universities, and although more ASL students are getting offers from top UK universities, most still opt for the USA. Graduates go on to all the big and little Ivy Leagues, as well as the major state universities in the US (Harvard, Yale, Princeton, Stanford, University of Pennsylvania), the major players in Canada (McGill, Toronto) and British Russell Group unis (Cambridge, Bristol, Queen Mary London). A recent graduate entered University of Virginia as a prestigious Jefferson Scholar with full university funding.

Money matters: Tuition covers textbooks, laboratory fees and all required activities except for the Music Tour for band, orchestra and choir members. There are occasional additional expenses—usually travel—associated with some middle and high school classes. Tuition does not include expenses for trips related to extra-curricular activities such as athletics, Model UN or service learning. Needs-based financial aid is available for tuition and also for school-related trips and activities.

Parents say there is a definite expectation that everyone (including staff) will participate in the school's fund-raising initiatives; this presents a challenging adjustment for some, particularly families who are less familiar with a US independent school tradition. Besides annual funds, there is a major auction every other year ('Think Sotheby's,' one parent says.) Another parent says that the level of importance attributed to the expectation of significant donations is a lingering legacy of previous heads and the days when a family's status at school was, albeit subtly, linked to the size of a financial benefaction, are long gone.

Remarks: In her opening letter to the parents the head spoke about 'striving for the best in American education'. Well, this

school isn't far from that. The resources and facilities are excellent, attitudes are positive and results are good. Bright, curious, motivated kids do well here and those who are in the middle of the road end up surprising their parents.

Ampleforth College

Linked school: St Martin's Ampleforth

Ampleforth, York, YO62 4ER

• Pupils: 585; 495 boarders, girls and boys • Ages: 13–18 • RC (Benedictine), but not all are • Fees: Boarding £30,264; Day £20,133 pa • Independent

Tel: 01439 766000
Email: rf@ampleforth.org.uk
Website: www.college.ampleforth.org.uk

Headmaster: Since 2004, Fr Gabriel Everitt OSB MA DPhil (fifties). Educated at Dundee High School, read history at Edinburgh, then Oxford (first in theology, doctorate in medieval history); ordained Anglican curate, converted 1989, joined Ampleforth community 1990, ordained 1994. Successively head of Christian Theology, housemaster of two houses, third master 2000. A quietly-spoken, thoughtful and candid man, very bright and clear-sighted about how he believes the school should develop. Not a regular fixture on the teaching timetable but makes 'guest appearances' as and when required to do so and observes lessons on a regular basis. Qualified ISI inspector so fully up to speed in driving forward teaching and learning initiatives. Benedictine values fit him as neatly as his habit, which must partly account for the sense of shared purpose within the school.

Retiring in 2014. School is, for the first time, looking outside the monastic community for a new head.

Academic matters: Top of the Catholic league but proud of non-élitist intake – from A stream scholars to IQs around 100, who get extra help with English and maths. Ninety per cent of the slowest workers get three A levels, which bears out the college's mission statement – an extract from the Rule of St Benedict – 'the strong should have something to strive for and the weak nothing to run from'. Determined to stress academic rigour and unashamedly and successfully pushing up A and B grades at A level (2013: 72 per cent A*-B, 43 per cent A*/A), 'though these are not laurels on which we are proposing to rest'; still aiming higher and the value-added score increases all the time, especially at A level. GCSE: 59 per cent A*/A.

They never discard,' says a parent. 'The pupils gain self-respect, the staff have an ability to unlock potential.' Fr Gabriel prudently adds that sometimes pupils cannot or will not cope, 'We try to reach an agreement with parents about them leaving'. Overall aim is for everyone to fulfil, and preferably exceed, their academic ability. The most able are challenged by membership of an unashamedly intellectual discussion club.

Core curriculum plus Christian theology throughout, Latin and Greek too. Half GCSE year takes separate sciences, half (of all abilities) double award. English department now doing IGCSE. Humanities traditionally have more takers and the edge at A level, but maths and science continue to strengthen. English very strong (most get A or B); history and Christian theology regularly successful and enormously popular.

Dyslexics taught 'for the most part' in main stream; additional specialist one-to-one teaching available. EAL provision for pupils whose first language isn't English.

Games, options, the arts: Traditionally powerful games school. Strong first XV, respected throughout the North. Hockey exceptionally strong for boys and girls, netball, lacrosse, athletics (own track), squash, golf (own nine-hole course), fly-fishing, renowned independently-owned beagle pack, shooting (brace of pheasants recently spotted hanging on coathanger outside boarding cubicle). Phenomenal 20 rugby sides – 'We want wide participation in school teams', 10 cricket sides, eight tennis teams, and so on. Sports hall, Astroturf, 25-metre pool. Strong DT and art (centre includes photography and electronics). Very successful voluntary CCF and it has been known for the girls' platoon to teach the boys a tough lesson by winning the CCF challenge. Flourishing D of E.

Music outstanding – Schola Cantorum choir tours regularly, singing in Catholic and Anglican cathedrals, also impressive girls' Schola Puellarum. Talented chamber music group and the biggest school pipe band south of the border, with own Ampleforth kilts. Enthusiastic singing by whole school in the abbey church, though sometimes, by their own admission, 'more Twickenham than heavenly hosts'.

Art is a real strength of the school, hugely impressive work on display – a direct result they say of 'an interaction between inspirational teaching and the environment'. Performing arts theatre (two productions per term) and also smaller studio theatre, popular with pupils, who would like to do even more. Annual pilgrimage for seniors to Lourdes. Own charity, run by students, raised funds to build school in Nepal and to sponsor East European students in school's sixth form. Also several other eye-openingly worthwhile international projects.

A new staff appointment has strengthened careers advice, including preparation for university and after. It's a work in progress but a deliberate and concerted change – 'it's a meritocratic world and our students need to be prepared,' commented Fr Gabriel. Long list of extracurricular activities, including some rarer options such as croquet; also the opportunity to strip down and build a Land Rover. And they usually win the regional school shooting range challenge, 'though not quite sure where that fits with the Benedictine philosophy.' Activities are compulsory between 5-7 pm and though a small number wriggle and squirm, most are happy to take part because apparently 'being busy makes you happy'. This is definitely a busy school – boarding philosophy through and through and even day pupils do everything (except sleep) here.

Background and atmosphere: Founded 1802. Magnificent setting in 3,000 acres of stunning countryside, very calming to the soul with Abbey as its central focus, physically and spiritually. Though fairly remote, 'in fact easy to reach – with some determination – from all parts of the country and world'. Beautiful Victorian Gothic main wing plus Giles Gilbert Scott's huge abbey church and school buildings (1930s), with late 1980s additions. More recent building includes classrooms boarding, houses, theatre, art department and refurbished science and business facility.

Houses vary considerably in character, with deliberate spread of ability – seven for boys and three for girls. Girls originally in sixth form only but co-education now growing throughout school. Charming and articulate boys and girls rub very comfortably alongside each other, the girls raising the bar in a number of areas and the boys raising their game in response. Rolling programme of improvement in boarding houses, 'I have a power shower!' exclaimed one girl proudly. Home from home, clearly, and it matters, especially to the girls. Some girls' houses have nominated 'guardian angels' as peer mentors; varying approach across individual houses, boys tend and befriend as necessary, usually without being asked. A real plus with the boys is that 'this is a place where you don't have to choose between singing in the choir and playing rugby' – it's acceptable, even cool possibly, to do both. Lunch with houseparents each day, central dining room and cafeteria system in use for other meals. Apparently (according to pupils)

'the food is good – for school food', a guarded mix of fierce loyalty and sensitive disclaimer.

School keeps in touch with outside world through excellent lecture programme and far-away projects, eg Chile and E Europe. No exeats except for two in winter term, otherwise half-terms. Handy list of local hotels, restaurants and B&Bs sent to parents in very comprehensive booklet, 'Your Questions Answered'. Not unknown for parents to rent a local cottage during their child's time at Ampleforth. Warmth of hospitality legendary, 'Part of the Rule of St Benedict is to welcome guests as Christ welcomed his'.

Pastoral care and discipline: A key change in recent times is that of the deployment of monastic personnel, there are fewer monks and they no longer perform the role of housemasters. This role has been taken over by families who serve as houseparents – 'very civilising' was the comment. Monks now act as chaplains to the school houses, parents and pupils commend them for being both priests and friends.

Consciences worked on rather than harsh restrictions imposed, all with the aim of turning students into responsible adults. It appears relaxed on the surface; essentially you are 'allowed it until you misuse it'. Fair enough. At the same time, says Fr Gabriel, 'this means clear structure and boundaries; St Benedict was not lax'.

Tough on bullying – those directly implicated and also bystanders – no one ever implicated in bullying can reach the position of monitor at the top of the school, 'a moment of madness can cost you dear.' No uniform as such, but dress code in place.

Pupils and parents: Numbers close to full and consistently so. Pupils from all over the UK and beyond, 30 per cent Yorkshire families, 40 per cent elsewhere UK (often with OA connections), remaining 30 per cent from overseas. Five per cent of overseas pupils are expats, rest mainly European mix of French, German, Swiss, Spanish. The recession has gently pushed up overseas numbers and reduced the number from the rest of the UK. 'We're a long way from London and you have to pass a lot of good schools to get here'. That said, many do, the main attractions being the Catholic Benedictine tradition and – bucking the trend here – full boarding provision, 'the school doesn't empty at weekends'. Scions of top and middle Catholic families (80 per cent); the rest mainly Anglican, but special welcome for orthodox.

There's a sense of comfortable ease between parents and school – 'if you want to be involved and constantly in touch, that's possible, If you want to take a more relaxed approach, then that is fine too'. Former pupils include Rupert Everett, Hugo Young, Lord Tugendhat, Lord Nolan, Sir Anthony Bamford (JCB), Michael Ancram, Sir Anthony Gormley, Lawrence Dallaglio.

Entrance: From a plethora of prep schools, most notably its own – St Martin's Ampleforth. Common entrance (50 per cent), or school test, and interview. Exceptions 'for faith or family', but no one admitted if he or she won't be able to cope with curriculum – even from St Martin's (rare). Sixth form entry: at least five GCSEs at B or above. Non-Catholics expected to take full part in school's religious life.

Exit: Hardly any leave after GCSEs. In 2013, 11 to Oxbridge; Edinburgh and Bristol also popular. Overseas destinations include Stanford University in California, McGill University in Montreal, the University of British Columbia in Vancouver and Trinity College, Dublin.

Money matters: Generous financial help. Academic, music and all-rounder scholarships. Nearly 13 per cent receive means-tested bursary help. In last two years some pupils have attained scholar status after entry.

Remarks: It has been said that people who leave Ampleforth take with them a 'compass for life', a spiritual direction finder, which allows them to hold on to their moral bearings. Three fundamental College aims underpin the thinking and approach here: for parents to call up and say their son/daughter is 'having a whale of a time', to succeed academically and finally, whilst 'not all super pious' – to 'treasure a place in their hearts for the spiritual side of life'. The pupils we met confidently achieved all three.

Parents like and appreciate the 'strong moral feel' of the school 'encompassing faith and learning, as well as 'the welcoming atmosphere'. They describe it as, 'surely one of the most beautiful places to go to school', hoping (and praying) that it can 'live up to the challenge and expectations in coming years', that particular challenge being one of 'raising the bar academically with first rate and inspiring teachers'. School is listening and has taken note.

Anglo European School

Willow Green, Ingatestone, Essex, CM4 0DJ

• Pupils: 1,350 boys and girls • Ages: 11–18 • Non–denom • State

Tel: 01277 354018
Email: enquiries@aesessex.co.uk
Website: www.aesessex.co.uk

Co-headteachers: Since 2005, David Barrs MA BEd Cert Ed NPQH (sixties); educated at London and Bristol Universities and St Paul's College, Cheltenham. Taught in Basildon and Saffron Walden; previously one of the school's joint deputy heads (1994-2005). Interests include the United Nations, cricket, golf and gardening.

Mrs Jill Martin, BA NPQH (fifties); educated at Liverpool University; previously was joint deputy head (with David Barrs) from 1994-2005. Interests include saxophone, piano, reading and gardening.

Apologies for the cliché 'two heads are better than one', but this is clearly the case at Anglo European. The co-heads run the school; they don't 'divide' responsibilities, but are both on hand to take decisions, normally in consultation with the members of the senior leadership who help to ensure things run like clockwork. This leadership model is a legacy of the unexpected death of the previous head; the two deputies, stepped up to take charge, essentially pitching to the governors that they both wanted to share the role. This dream team appears to work beautifully; if one is travelling, decisions aren't delayed, and it leaves both with time to do a little classroom teaching. Parents we spoke to will happily consult either.

The school seems to maintain comfortably high academic standards with a particular international emphasis. Both co-heads have a strong commitment to languages, so we asked what languages both spoke besides English. Interestingly, they both replied, 'none', which is precisely why they are both such strong advocates of the importance of developing linguistic agility in their young charges.

Academic matters: Well-known to many seasoned IB educators as one of the first IB diploma schools (and the first state IB school) in the UK, Anglo European is now celebrating its 40th year. A pace-setter since its inception, it was one of the handful of schools worldwide chosen to pilot the new IBCC (IB Careers Certificate) programme introduced in 2010.

The school's international ethos is evident in significant ways, from the impressive range of languages offered, to internationally-minded teachers, to loads of educational visits and exchanges.

They're introducing the IB Middle Years Programme from year 7, and offer a choice of IB and A levels – or a mix of both. Sets by ability for maths from mid year 7, other subjects from year 8. Competent, knowledgeable counselling to help students sort which programme, or combination thereof, might best suit abilities, university goals, career paths. In 2013, 32 per cent of GCSEs were A*/A and 80 per cent of pupils got 5+ A*-C grades. Average IB point score a very creditable 35; 42 per cent A*-B grades for A level candidates.

One non-negotiable is that all students must continue to study a language all the way through, if not as an IB subject (one additional language is compulsory for the IB diploma), or A level, then as an Asset-examined language (one generally outside the mainstream curriculum). This language emphasis can't be stressed enough. In year 7, students study three languages in addition to English: German, French and Chinese. For year 8, they can continue with German and French, or replace German with Spanish. At the end of year 9, if they are doing well in both their languages, they can begin a third, choosing from Mandarin, Russian, Japanese or Italian. Students who want to take on additional languages, or maintain a mother tongue, may also take lunchtime language lessons (and teachers get lots of praise for their willingness to do this). The parents and students alike talk about this, and truly appreciate the great advantage not only to speak more than one language, but to be spoilt for choice.

The educational exchange visits programme is one of the star aspects of this school. Year 7 students start with a 10 day class visit to a Belgian château with learning activities in France linked to the curriculum. Year 8 students do homestay exchanges with individual host families, whose schools in turn send kids to Anglo European, with students attending classes at the respective schools. The destinations on offer increase as the students move up the school (year 8 to France, year 9 to Spain and Germany, year 10 to Germany, France, Spain, Italy and China), all focused on whatever languages they're learning. Visits aren't mandatory, but very popular. Close to half of the school's 1,350 students participate and return with great stories: clearly a lot of cultural and linguistic learning through this excellent immersion programme.

Citizenship gets a special mention here by all parents we spoke to. Many schools subsume it into the history or PSHE curriculum. At Anglo European it's a 'stand-alone' course encouraging good global as well as local attitudes, all reinforced through the international visits, work placement trips and activities, and the community service programme. One unusual sixth form course is travel and tourism, which is fitting considering the international character of the school.

The choice between A Levels, IB diploma or the new IB Careers Certificate (an interesting blend of academic and vocational courses drawing on IB and A level coursework) or a combination, opens up the most amazing range of possibilities for sixth form, but by no means results in a class system of elites vs non-elites. A level students have the option of taking some IB courses if they wish, for example the Theory of Knowledge course, gaining from the best of both worlds. The sixth formers we met – who represented all three programmes – were confident in the courses they'd chosen, and felt they'd had good advice about the various options.

Classes can have as many as 34 students, but the average is 20. Parents feel the teachers form a strong team, and are themselves international, either nationals of other countries, or repatriating British teachers with international experience. Average age is 40s, and nearly half have been there for over 10 years.

Games, options, the arts: Wide range of extracurricular programmes. Good sports facilities on site – two gyms, a large outdoor field for rugby, cricket, rounders, etc, and a playground for break and other activities. Lots of the usual sports clubs and activities, including trampoline, and some self-defence, but above all Flags, an AE-invented ball game that's a wildly popular break-time tradition. Students say the small swimming pool is 'okay for the younger ones', but serious swimmers prefer to rely on local sports facilities for real work outs. In fact, while one parent said Anglo European would probably not be the best choice for a very sporty student, another mentioned the school's support of a student selected for the England Women's Football (Under 15s) League.

The school has joined an IB scheme allowing 'elite athletes' to do the IB in three rather than the usual two years; other sporting achievements and team victories in rounders, swimming and volleyball are indications of the school's support of sporting excellence. Some 60 students are pursuing the D of E bronze award.

Students say there's lots to do, although sometimes a bit tricky with a long commute for many of them. They also say that many of them are more interested in the community service, citizenship, work placement type opportunities than school-based activities. Drama gets a lot of mentions and seems to involve anyone and everyone (mostly below the sixth form) who is interested in taking part, not just the thespian set that can sometimes dominate in schools. Plenty of musical outlets with bands, orchestras. (One recent graduate has moved on to the Royal College of Music). The Eisteddfod is a popular annual event involving everyone ('Eisteddfod' is a Welsh festival of literature, music and drama) – a sort of school talent show that further extends the school's international ethos – and there is a popular winter arts festival and a Christmas concert as well.

Many of the kids get involved in the World Challenge programme and Model United Nations: the students say that this latter is very much inspired by Mr Barrs' own passion, which must be infectious, judging from the students' enthusiasm for it. He recently arranged for a whole group to go to Geneva to see the UN in action, and this will now become an annual event.

One of the most notable extracurricular features is the school's unique work experience programme. Both parents and students enthuse that this has provided life-changing experiences. The students made a point of commending the school for its continued commitment to this programme, despite recent government budget cuts. There are work placements in both the local voluntary and commercial sectors (restaurants, supermarkets, doctor's offices, banks, a nano-tech lab) and we spoke to students who have worked in New York, Berlin Frankfurt and the South of France. This is a compulsory programme in year 10 and available to any interested student in the sixth form and can be arranged by the school, or by the individual.

Background and atmosphere: Established as a school with an international ethos in 1973 on the site of a former secondary school as part of the local authority's effort to enter into the spirit of Britain's entry into the European Union. At the time Marconi and the Ford Motor Company had operations nearby, employing international and repatriating British families whose children had become fluent in foreign languages, and who were seen as part of the target community for this new school.

In its 40th anniversary year, the buildings look their age – and don't date back to an era renowned for architectural beauty, but rather the typical purpose-built mid-20th century generic state school blue-plan design. They have been well used during these four decades; some of the rooms and public spaces are a bit worse for wear with stained carpets in need of replacement and one or two leaky skylights revealing themselves on the rainy day we visited. But this does not seem to dampen the community's sense of affection for the place, and there is ample evidence of ongoing efforts to expand in response to demand for growth (there are two portakabins), and to modernise, refurbish and redecorate the buildings over the years.

Despite lots of student traffic during break and lunch, the students still seem to try to take care of their space (no excessive litter or books and coats left lying about). The new block under construction that will eventually (by March 2014) replace one of the original buildings is being built with 21st century IT requirements in mind, and will feature the 'COMM' room – a video-conferencing centre where AE kids can link up with other schools worldwide. Sixth form student requests have resulted in wifi provision being installed in their study area. They also have two spaces – one for quiet work and one for 'silent' independent or supervised work.

There are several computer labs around the school, many of which sixth formers can freely access at any time unless they are booked by classes. Younger students use the library. Projectors linked to teacher computers in most all of the classrooms, some interactive smartboards. During our visit we dropped in on year 7s preparing individual computer presentations to introduce themselves at the class assembly. Thanks to the well-liked head of maths, rooms in the maths block are numbered using prime numbers only, and our student guide pointed out a small library collection named after a former maths-loving student, who left his books of maths puzzles and challenges for today's students to borrow. (And they do.)

An outdoor amphitheatre provides a setting for drama or fair weather outdoor classes of all sorts. Throughout the school there are framed plaques and awards going back many years from a variety of organisations (eg World Challenge, International School Award from the British Council, etc), as well as flags representing all the students' nationalities.

Pastoral care and discipline: Despite being a large school, parents we spoke to were happy with the pastoral care and personal attention. They said that despite the occasional fight, bullying, or even the rare instance of drug taking, it is very controlled – 'students regard school generally as a no go area for drugs.' The kids know the boundaries and the school staff seem to know what is going on; they're accessible, communications are said to be very good, the school is quick to respond, every concern is taken seriously, and the follow up is consistent and ongoing.

The kids, too, tell us that their teachers are readily available; emails sent to a teacher at midnight about homework have been known to get a response five minutes later. It seems at least one teacher never sleeps!

Even parents with concerns were very happy with the way the school responded. 'There is a pastoral director for each year group and the kids know they are there for them. Whether it's because of a missing shoe, or the awkward confusion brought on by personal problems, they are like the school's own mums and dads.'The school is really good at fostering independence. 'They embrace it.'

The welcome extended to new students 'was a godsend', one parent told us. For students, especially British kids coming back from abroad, the adjustment is tough but the school makes it much easier. There were plenty of 'Can we help you?'; 'Do you know where you are going?' and 'Are you okay?' comments overheard in the first days of school. The students claim that after a few days, no one can tell the difference between the old and the new students.

The school is rightfully proud of the newly-opened 'sanctuary'. This is a quiet and lovely building set apart from the hustle and bustle of the other buildings for the purpose of contemplation, reflection, discussion and prayer. Funded by parent donations and inspired by the Dag Hammarskjöld meditation room at the UN headquarters in New York, it is a welcome oasis; our Muslim student guide said he'd be returning there in a few hours for his Friday noontime prayer. The school has no religious affiliation, but there is an inclusive attitude that helps foster respect and understanding for all faiths.

Pupils and parents: With around 35 nationalities, this place is truly a little UN community in the heart of Essex, and students come from far and wide to study here. Many people talked about the 'Anglo family' in reference to the kids but also the parent community. The students learn so much about each other, their cultures and beliefs, and parents say they benefit too. One parent remarked that in her daughter's class there are 19 mother tongues spoken. 'We've met families from Brazil, Singapore, Nigeria and France...and when the kids have a birthday party they are quick to remind us about each other's diets, saying one can't eat meat, another must eat Halal, another is vegetarian...'

The great kids we met were adamant that their diversity is accepted, and being different is normal; that's what attracts many of them to the school. There is quite a wide socio-economic range of students from homes as diverse as Essex country mansions and inner-city flats. One parent described it as 'real world'. The head reputedly warns families on the first day that if you don't like allowing sleepovers in various parts of Essex and London, this is probably not the school for you, as the kids do arrange to see each other out of school hours. So many kids use the train to come and go that the school has designated 'train ambassadors' from year 11 and up who supervise their peers, helping to manage the crowd in a special waiting room created for the students within the station, which is a 10-15 minute walk from school through the picturesque village of Ingatestone.

The bus service run by a 'wonderful' private company covers a broad area. Parents say it even ran smoothly during extreme winter weather conditions.

A number commute by train from east London. We met one sixth former who's been travelling up to two hours each way since year 7, and thinks it's definitely worth the commitment. These stories add up to some pretty compelling endorsements. The group of students we met seemed mature beyond their years, yet fun-loving, curious, and proud of their school. There was a genuine sense that these students really appreciate the education they are getting at Anglo European and value what the school and their teachers offer them. Quite refreshing, really.

The parents' association is active; lots of ways for parents to get involved, but no pressure to do so. An alumni association brings former students back for key events, but also for talks on careers, universities, and experiences abroad.

Past students include Douglas McCallum, MD of Ebay, David Abraham – chief exec of Channel 4, professional footballer James Harper, and some actors and musicians of note.

Entrance: Anglo European is an interesting blend of 'local' and 'international' school. As a state-funded comprehensive school (with academy status), they're obliged to enrol local students (feeder schools include Ingatestone and Fryerning Junior School, Margaretting Primary School and Mountnessing Primary School), but there is a priority scheme, with the first three categories being 'children looked after', locals within the three local parishes, and siblings.

Next is the 'international group', and here a point system comes into play with factors such as length of time abroad (and length of time since the overseas experience), ability to communicate in other languages, and extent of the cultural engagement in that context.

There is a very important point that families should know: Anglo European has a 'special dispensation' within the local authority that is highly unusual, possibly unique, within the UK state education system. In order to apply to Anglo European, families need not have proof of local residence. This is a huge bonus as it means that families moving to the UK from abroad seeking an international school can at least apply for places before they arrive.

The admissions secretary, described by parents as 'a gem', patiently explains the process to prospective families who may not be familiar with the system, and she is happy to respond to pleas of help from parents. She herself has lived abroad with her own children, so she is an empathetic ear to have at the end of the phone. Furthermore, with a mobile international

community, and no fees to pay, places become available at very short notice, including mid-year. So, whereas the school is non-selective in terms of academics, it is looking for families who will embrace and support the international outlook.

Exit: Our student guide explains they have regular meetings with UCAS advisors from early in lower sixth to consider university options. There is a Higher Education Superfair with days dedicated to explaining the university admissions process. Students are encouraged to attend local university master classes to get a better understanding of what courses entail.

Enterprise education lessons within the citizenship curriculum provide well-organised learning opportunities working in conjunction with 50 local employers, trainers, and higher education institutions for students from Year 7 upwards.

A good number of AES graduates go abroad to university, thanks in no small part to interest, awareness and richer CVs after so many AES study trips abroad. The university and careers counsellors are well-briefed on both UK and overseas universities. As one sixth former said, her decision to apply to a top Canadian university was based on the counsellor informing her that, with good IB results, she could qualify for a significant scholarship. Alumni are invited back to school events to talk about their experiences, so it seems that, undaunted by foreign languages or new cultural surroundings, these kids are confident to go out into the big wide world for the next stage of their education. The school is developing relationships with universities throughout Europe and beyond as shrewd internationally-minded Anglo European students have worked out that it is now cheaper to study abroad.

Ninety per cent of students go to university, the others go on gap years or take on apprenticeships. Three to Oxbridge in 2013; Edinburgh and Bristol also popular; overseas destinations have included University of California Berkeley, Chinese University of Hong Kong and University of Maastricht.

Those opting to leave Anglo European after GCSEs tend to go to local vocational colleges such as Writtle College for equine and agricultural courses, Colchester Institute, Chelmsford College, South Essex College.

Money matters: There are some low-key fundraising activities organised by the school, the parents' association and the students themselves as part of their philanthropic activities.

The bus service is available at extra cost (paid to bus contractors). The exchange visits incur additional charges, but parents feel they are well worth it, and there is even some means-tested financial support available so that nobody who wants to participate is prevented from doing so on financial grounds.

Remarks: As one parent puts it, you often hear that parents choose a particular school because it fits a certain kind of student. At Anglo-European, there is something for everyone because they really appreciate each student's individuality. When the sixth formers were asked about this, the group endorsed the student who said, 'There is this perception that this school is only good for internationals or linguists, but that couldn't be further from the truth. Everyone benefits here.'

Archbishop Tenison's School

Linked school: North Lambeth Sixth Form Centre

55 Kennington Oval, London, SE11 5SR

• Pupils: 515 boys, all day • Ages: 11–18 • C of E • State

Tel: 020 7735 3771
Email: school@ats.lambeth.sch.uk
Website: www.tenisons.com

Head Mistress: Since 2006, Mrs Elizabeth Sims BEd MA (early fifties), married with two grown-up sons. Previously deputy head at St Saviours and St Olave's. A committed Christian who promotes a caring Christian ethos throughout the school. Her interests include reading and politics.

Academic matters: Generally somewhere between 50-70 per cent get 5+ A*-C grades at GCSE including English and maths. Girls admitted to sixth form, part of the North Lambeth consortium. Cited as an example of good practice in a Lambeth report on raising achievement of Black Caribbean pupils.

Pupils tested on entry to school for cognitive ability and banded into three streams. Class sizes are 29, 22 for those who need most support. Twenty per cent have SEN and either provided with a classroom assistant or LSA in class or withdrawn to a specialist classroom. Those deemed gifted, talented and able (about 25 per cent of each year) learn science as three separate subjects.

Everyone starts GCSE courses in year 9. French is timetabled and Spanish run as a taster course. The extended day gives an extra period of learning for the smartest and plenty are keen to take up to 13 GCSEs – including Latin. Not surprisingly, RS and art are very strong here – the school has specialist arts college status and has a fantastic new sky-lit art studio. Strong links with galleries such as Tate Modern, Dulwich Picture Gallery, Gasworks and the Saatchi Gallery encourage a practical outlook on the art world.

All classrooms have interactive whiteboards and the pupil to computer ratio is about 4:1. Well-equipped DT rooms are popular – great results emerge from them. The library is open and staff available for homework support until 4.30pm. Learning broadened through carefully budgeted school trips.

Games, options, the arts: A game of football starts in the playground as soon as the first two children arrive (about 7.30am). A rooftop fitness suite with sparkling machines is well used and the gym enables on-site PE and basketball practice. Rugby players, athletes and tennis players take the train to the playing fields in Motspur Park, swimming at the Shell Centre pool in Waterloo and the connections with the Oval over the road encourage cricket.

Termly drama productions and music performances; the school choir sings at a number of venues round the borough. Soloists often replace recorded music in the daily assemblies. Individual music lessons are greatly subsidised and bursaries awarded to pupils who gain grade 2 on any instrument. Band and choir practice, guitar ensemble and coursework coaching all take place in after-school clubs.

Public speaking encouraged with in-school debates and practical external successes – a recent presentation of a travel plan to Transport for London and a brief to a parliamentary committee on the needs of street-children in the Democratic Republic of Congo for the charity, War Child; the latter resulted in pupil awards for citizenship from John Moores University and four recommendations being carried out by Lord Alton. Involvement with War Child began during 2005 Make Poverty History campaign and continues with sixth form help on the

development of its website. Locally, an outreach campaign involves pupils with a primary school, special school and a Golden Years group – documented by an impressive student shot and edited DVD.

Background and atmosphere: Founded in 1685 in St Martin-in-the-Fields by the Archbishop of Canterbury, moved to its site opposite The Oval cricket ground in 1929. Boys pour through the gates up to an hour before school and a member of staff checks their appearance – blue blazer for the juniors, black for the seniors. Plain silk ties for prefects and sixth form wear their own smart clothes. No jewellery, trainers nor hats. You can spot the boys with their badged school bags on trains, buses and bikes heading into the Oval – a different coloured crest signifies a different year. This smart uniform and the school's emphasis on polite behaviour have made a real difference to its local reputation.

The boys are respectful and file silently into well-planned assemblies where class members take turns to light the peace candle – this ritual was initiated 'after 9/11 to remind us to be peaceful in all that we say and all that we do'.

Young staff with a low turnover and emphasis on training (inset days and help from the Southwark Diocese Board of Education) ensure a sense of stability; the size of the school (92 intake each year) encourages a family atmosphere, helped by all catering and cleaning staff being on the payroll. The dining room with its healthy food is a gathering point for younger boys – no fizzy drinks, chocolate nor crisps allowed and no vending machines on site.

Pastoral care and discipline: Parents and teachers use homework diaries and one target is set for every subject with three others covering the curriculum, each accompanied by a strategy and a monitoring arrangement. The system is centralised online so that all background information can be pulled up with one click. The school captain, prefects (years 10 and 11), school council (all years) and peer mentoring are all involved in identifying issues such as bullying and theft. A traditional system of detentions, warnings, letters home, form reports and head's reports is used. After this fixed term exclusions, but these rarely result in permanent exclusion.

Pupils and parents: Fifty per cent of boys have English as a second language but very few are not fluent; 25 per cent are Afro-Caribbean, with minority ethnic pupils making up 80 per cent of the entire school, and most are the first in their families to consider higher education. Many parents are looking for a 'mission school' in London, trusting Archbishop Tenison's to continue their children's Christian education while they themselves are doing two or three jobs. Ninety-five per cent attendance at bi-annual academic reviews shows parents are keen to work with the teachers.

Entrance: No catchment area – intake split 70 per cent church attendance, 30 per cent open. Always oversubscribed.

Exit: North Lambeth Sixth Form is a collaboration of three schools in the borough – Archbishop Tenison's, Charles Edward Brooke (girls' specialist media school) and London Nautical (boys' specialist sports school), so the sixth form choices are widened over the three sites. All those who stay on in the sixth form move on to some form of higher education, and most artists gain places at eg Chelsea or Camberwell. In 2013, sixth formers went on to a range of courses including medicine at UCL, engineering at Kingston, theology at Newman College Birmingham and creative arts at Canterbury.

A number of boys from Archbishop Tenison's are awarded bursaries from the Livery Company of the Dyers whilst studying in the sixth form and, over the last three years, a number have been awarded financial assistance from the Livery Company of Chartered Surveyors to help with their university costs.

A

Remarks: A vital school in a deprived area with rising academic results, enterprising teachers and the boys at the centre of everything. The constant celebration of achievement – wall displays, credits, merits, prizes or even just a comment in a homework diary – makes a massive difference to pupils' confidence. The structure of daily worship and parent/carer school communication has proved essential to the growing success of this school.

Ardingly College

Linked school: Ardingly College Prep School

College Road, Ardingly, Haywards Heath, West Sussex, RH17 6SQ

• Pupils: 560 pupils, 325 boys/235 girls, 270 weekly and full boarding • Ages: 13–18 • C of E • Fees: Day £20,925–£22,065 Boarding £27,930–£29,535 pa • Independent

Tel: 01444 893000
Email: registrar@ardingly.com
Website: www.ardingly.com

Headmaster: Since 2007, Mr Peter Green MA PGCE CertRE, a geographer (mid-forties). Began at Strathallan School before moving to Uppingham, where he served first as head of geography and then as boarding housemaster. From 2002, second master of Ampleforth. A rugby-keen Scot, he talks fast, sensibly and a lot, full of good tales and good ideas, anchored by strong faith. Loves his job – always wanted to be a teacher; to be found (by parents, pupils, staff) under the archway at the beginning of every school day. Teenage son at Worth (Worth's head returning the compliment with his daughter at Ardingly) and daughter at Ardingly; married to Brenda, who co-hosts the Thursday prefect dinner.

Strong leadership team with prep and pre-prep heads, lots of new blood recently, but it seems for natural reasons rather than character clashes. Inherited a good financial, environmental and academic foundation for what has been called 'the best kept secret in Sussex'.

Academic matters: Up to six sets in maths and English for Shell (year 9); GCSE subjects include Mandarin, PE and drama plus all the usuals, with over 59 per cent A*/A grades in 2013. Fantastic new language labs on previously ignored floor, subject rooms much more spread out than in the past. Science labs traditional but effective – all manner of ponds and wildlife to use for practicals.

IB offered since 1996, now around 50/50 IB/A level – 36 average point score; 66 per cent A*-B, 41 per cent A*/A at A level, 2013. Students say IB great for those who thrive with exams, new A levels best for those who are crippled by stress and prefer modular work. Parents say school does not pressurise pupils to get highest grades but encourages those who can reach them. Good choice of A level subjects – theatre studies, business studies (popular) along with more traditional options (biology very popular, RS too), languages – French, German, Spanish and Latin. IB big pulling point for Europeans – Germans especially, with exchange rate and government incentives; this will be a safety net for school numbers even in recessionary times. Lots of overlap encouraged between different subjects, combined trips etc. Apparently 'legendary' teachers in English department encouraging creative writing – we imagine Robin Williamsesque invocation of carpe diem?

ICT seen as a tool, big PC suite, ceiling-mounted data projectors, lots of networked computers both in and out of teaching areas – Wifi available in all the boarding houses and the school library. Light, bright and well-catalogued library –

DVDs, books and periodicals; librarian responds with initiative to requests and moans. More staff because of IB, so good pupil:teacher ratio. Long-serving and well-appreciated SENCo who makes sure mild to moderate SEN pupils cope. Success stories include senior dyslexic studying history at Oxford.

Games, options, the arts: Stunning environment in good weather, blustery and gloomy in bad. Pupils really appreciate the surrounding green – from being distracted from personal study by the sight of sheep wandering across a hilltop to being able to go for a run through woods and discover something new. School set in 275 acres, a third of which is let as fields. Newly covered Astroturf pitch used for hockey or tennis (12 courts), plus hard courts, plus use of reservoir for sailing (inter-house competition) and rowing five minutes' walk from main buildings.

More than 80 sports offered during the year, especially successful in cricket, netball, football, girls' hockey, cross-country. Post of director of sports (filled by ex-England rugby cap) seems to be working well – head stirred up tradition by replacing football goals with rugby posts on one pitch... Sports not compulsory but everyone finds something they like (horse-riding is back). Indoor hall and fitness room offering weights as well as state-of-the-art fitness equipment and a personal trainer. Duke of Edinburgh award scheme is popular here, as is CCF – about 25 per cent girls, not just shooting and camping.

Music very strong under charismatic director, voluntary choir of 80-odd invited to sing at St Paul's, St George's Windsor, Chichester, Southwark, Westminster, Paris etc. Peripatetic staff give individual lessons and also perform in the London Philharmonic, The Sixteen and at Glyndebourne. The study of production and recording skills are sourced when needed – but most of pupils' energy is channelled into more traditional forms – string quartets, piano trios, house singing and music competitions.

Drama and art more adventurous; a production per year by each year group and a full school show as well – recently a play that the head of drama had seen win a Fringe First at Edinburgh. Drama team delighted to use projection and non-theatre space to explore pupils' ideas. Art now housed in fantastic purpose-designed conversion – pupils walk through naturally lit and high-ceiling display gallery to get to studios, daily inspiration. Art library, IT suite (with video editing capability), new teacher for animation and video, kiln room, textile room – particularly popular around Leavers' Ball time. Fine art displayed all over campus, art trips to Europe and beyond. DT facilities online in dire need of upgrade.

Background and atmosphere: The jewel in the Woodard crown – 23 independent C of E schools in England and Wales (another 22 state school affiliated), founded in the mid-19th century by Canon Nathaniel Woodard. Moved to this imposing, three storey, H-shaped redbrick building in 1870, high on the Sussex Downs and with marvellous views over the landscape in all directions. Grandly solemn vaulted chapel (stained glass windows in restoration programme) used for weekly Eucharist, whole school and other house assemblies. Not a rich foundation and somewhat shackled by buildings' Grade II listings and doubtful privilege of being in an 'area of outstanding natural beauty'; continuously improving facilities – and ideally keeping more elderly ones like 'a well-scrubbed monastic corridor'. Good management, prudent changes, summer lets, all help to provide major investment (over £11 million in last 10 years) – IB fees paid in euros should help in current financial climate.

Boarding in cluster of three storey houses, moments from main building. All have a house computer (for Skype and Facebook, only allowed at weekends), well-equipped games rooms (Wii for the girls, table footie, snooker, karaoke and X-box for the boys), and kitchens or 'brew rooms'. Girls start off in junior house (all named after old heads) and then in lower sixth are thrown in all together – although they still return to make pancakes for and mentor the girls in their old houses. The boys are in the same houses up until the upper sixth – when both genders mix in one boarding house, Woodard, where the sexes are separated by the Forum (interconnecting doors locked at 10pm), a space with table tennis, table footie, huge plasma (mostly playing music videos unless football, The Apprentice or Skins is on), two brew rooms (where mostly girls make burgers, pancakes, toast, pizza etc) and a bar (open on Saturday night for beer, wine, alcopops and J20s paid for out of house funds).

Boarding facilities best in the refurbed houses, plus the new, co educational, upper sixth, 100-bedroomed (en suite) boarding and day house. More pupils sharing each room (beds, desks, corkboards for posters) in the lower years, age and study load earn you seclusion and a better view – none of the rooms are spacious but all in good condition. Lots of iPod speakers, well-liked matrons, house parents on site to maintain calm.

Lots of tasty and healthy choice in the dining room, monitored by some staff and prefects. Pupils say school is not cliquey (Chinese and Germans groups could form). They seem confident and quick humoured, few exclusive romances – just lots of fun, socialising across years too. Perceived isolation of school is not seen as a negative factor – 'You can get on a train to London and there's so much to do here, you feel exhausted in a good way by the time you get to the weekend'. Very friendly and reasonable both inside and outside school – eg turning up to a parent-hosted party with a crate of Carling under one arm, sleeping bag under the other, cheery cleaning up by all in the morning.

Pastoral care and discipline: Everyone assigned tutor on arrival – pupil's confidante, broker and spokesman and school's link with parents. Can switch if tutor's subject is incongruous with pupil's choices. Thereafter, hierarchy of support/discipline ending at the top. Parents say you'll get an email reply from a teacher within a day and probably a follow up phone call.

Sixth form has dress code, lower forms have uniform – trouser option for girls. iphones not to be used in lessons, laptops only for dyslexics, school email accounts and controls on surfing, some relaxed at the weekend. Head boy and head girl – staff nominate, pupils vote, discussion with housemasters and SMT then head picks – and deputies have weekly meeting with head, prefects' dinner at head's house each Thursday.

Clear drugs and drinking policy – automatic out for class A/B and possible police involvement; second chance over cannabis with testing/counselling/collaboration with parents regimen. Surprising lack of drinking issues for school surrounded by copses/potential shebeens. Flexi-boarding must help, and also responsibility taken early: heads of house in lower sixth, and informal mentoring seems almost instinctive.

Pupils and parents: Forty per cent of pupils live within 50 minutes' drive of the school, 25 per cent come from overseas. IB is prime attraction for Europeans – restricted intake of Germans to 12 per year (but 300 apply). More than 30 other nationalities represented. Parents say great for all-rounders and siblings with different talents.

A broad social spectrum – families are doctors, lawyers, city commuters, diplomats, landed gentry – has entered the Tatler Schools Guide. According to a recent questionnaire, a third attracted by the Woodard ethos; in general families are unpretentious – 'It all feels normal – people might go off on their yachts in the holidays but they won't flaunt it'. Good social network of parents, many used to walk their dogs on grounds after dropping children off – recent dog embargo put paid to that (proliferation of signs to that effect irritates some locals).

Old Ardinians include racing driver Mike Hawthorn, Ian Hislop, composer Stephen Oliver, actors Terry Thomas and Alan Howard

Entrance: Selective via scholarship, CE or other exams depending on point of entry – English, maths, VR tested.

Fifty per cent from the prep, 50 per cent external (St Paul's, Westminster, Westbourne House, Great Walstead, Prebendal, Hurst, state schools). Over-subscribed at present – spaces may appear in current financial climate.

Exit: Some 30 per cent leave after GCSEs, mostly for local sixth form colleges. Rest stay and go on to everything from Oxbridge (three in 2013) to aviation studies at Kingston, University of Southampton, UCL – large proportion to Russell Group or equivalent, some abroad to US, Europe and Canada. Forty per cent take 'constructive' gap year (not much loafing around and working in local pub any more).

Money matters: Academic, music, art, drama, sport and DT awards on offer at 13+ and 16+ various stages – up to 50 per cent tuition remission. Special awards for clergy, Services, Sussex and Old Ardinians' children. Worth scrutinising the literature. Maybe not one to go for if finances are unpredictable – not as strong on tide-you-over bursaries as many.

Remarks: Wide-ranging staff, confident and down-to-earth pupils, beautiful grounds and improving facilities – bit of a mystery as to why more people are not raving about this school, one of Sussex's best-kept secrets.

The Arts Educational School (London)

Cone Ripman House, 14 Bath Road, London W4 1LY

• Pupils: 205, about a third boys, all day • Ages: 11–18 • Non-denom • Fees: £13,350–£14,190 pa • Independent

Tel: 020 8987 6600
Email: pupils@artsed.co.uk
Website: www.artsed.co.uk

Headmaster: Since 2012, Mr Adrian Blake (forties) BEd MAPgDip, formerly the director of teaching and learning at Arts Educational Schools since 2009. Started his career as lecturer in performing arts at NESCOT followed by director of thinking and learning and advanced skills teacher, Greenshaw High School before becoming assistant principal at Lambeth Academy. He is also education consultant for Kestrel Visual Learning and for BEST Education on a range of educational topics.

Mr Blake still works as an actor and dialect coach on acting projects, and is a senior instructor for The British Martial Arts Institute, teaching a range of martial arts disciplines to a wide range of groups. In his spare time he is a keen sports enthusiast and enjoys watching, and even occasionally competing, in team and individual sports.

His aim is 'to ensure that our reputation as a centre of excellence for the arts continues to grow, and that we remain the most academically successful vocational performing arts school in the UK'

Academic matters: 'Arts Educational School is not a stage school. The academic emphasis in the school is equal to the vocational importance and the aim is to produce well-rounded, interesting and interested young people who have the confidence to perform both on stage and in the classroom.' This might come as a surprise to visitors who are surrounded by leotards and leggings, girls' hair scraped into buns, choruses and piano rehearsals booming out of each room. But the complex timetable is firmly balanced and pupils not working on the vocational side are neat in traditional turquoise (known here as 'lagoon') uniforms – which match the classroom doors and look quite demure.

At GCSE, everyone takes biology and chemistry, along with two Englishes, maths – setted from the off – expressive arts, French and three options from a number of blocks – art, dance, drama, geography, history, music and media studies. The most able also do physics. Head of modern langs speaks seven langs himself and would find teachers for any lang a pupil wanted to take. The academic corridors look much as anywhere, and good displays on historical topics make a reassuring change from the glitzy pictures of past productions elsewhere. Around 20 have SEN – mostly dyslexia and, as Mr Price says, 'so many dyslexics can communicate through performing when they cannot on paper'. Wise words. School now runs two parallel courses in the sixth form: a trad A level course along with classes in dance/drama/music or two ASs and two As plus a foundation course in musical theatre, which is now an accredited BTEC. More pupils are choosing to stay on and a number of new students come in at that stage. Ten AS/A level subjects offered – including philosophy, history, photography, maths, history of art and media studies, plus the musical theatre course. Excellent results – 27 per cent A*/A grades in 2013.

Games, options, the arts: On admission in year 7 you choose to major in either dance or drama – but both groups have classes in both subjects. Sport is offered twice a week at the nearby sports centre but, as one parent said, 'The school is so full of energy and they do so much physical activity, neither of our children feel locked in or worried about the lack of outside space' – which is just as well as there isn't any and you'd be wise to go elsewhere if you need to get seriously muddy twice a week. Everyone dances their socks off to take exercise and yoga, 'combat fighting' and dances like hip hop also use up surplus energies. A gym/weights room for the sixth form. Vocational courses include spoken voice, audition technique, text in performance, choreography, expressive arts, dance of all kinds and music. Music is impressive – loads of individual lessons, good resources – now with excellent facilities for music tech and no-one now leaves unable to read music. Everyone has music twice a week. Four choirs, various instrumental groups including a jazz group, and many pupils have private music lessons too. Everyone performs all the time and it is most refreshing to go into a studio and see 13-year-olds, of both sexes, improvising without self-consciousness – no blushful hanging back here.

Three major productions a year – aided by professional wardrobe and set-building staff – and every corridor has racks of costumes just waiting to be donned. Pupils help on the backstage side and learn about the technical aspects of production, as well as film techniques.

Production values are professional and exacting. Unlike at stage schools, however, pupils are not encouraged to have agents and to take off long periods for professional work – school-life and work come first. However, film producers do drop round to choose children for roles – some in major productions, some in ads. The art rooms are a quiet relief and art is a popular GCSE and A level here. Work is varied, colourful and clever. Sixth form now has eight new laptops for photographic work – very popular. Plenty of trips to concerts and galleries.

Background and atmosphere: It's a long, three-storey, plain red brick building, unimpressively occupying about 100 yards of prime Bedford Park along the Bath Road in pricey west London and surrounded by leafy roads housing TV executives in semis which go for £1m++ apiece. Inside it's a different world – once you are past the new turnstile and security system – and security now stops you at each corridor, for which you need an ID card. Plain corridors, plain rehearsal rooms – dozens of them, which all look much the same to visitors, apart from some being black and curtained and others bright and light, but clearly have very different feels to the students, eg 'That's where I do

tap; I couldn't think of acting in there,' etc. A proscenium arch theatre, lots of storage space for costumes and sets, a good-sized, adaptable studio which mimics 'fringe' conditions – everything is geared to preparation for the outside reality.

Students look bright-eyed and busy – you cannot tread water here and drown quickly if you try. Parents rave about 'the positive energy of the place'. Little recreation space – the sixth form has space which acts as a common room but that's it and no outside. Little time for traditional teenage bickering here – 'It's very friendly and you have to work together,' says sage 12-year-old student. A good canteen and good food, though not cheap. Most pupils eat a hot meal at lunchtime – lots of pasta, always a vegetarian option and all prepared on site by unusually friendly staff. Good salad bar. Breakfast daily from 7.45 – a good idea, considering that some pupils commute from as far as Kent or Reading. It's a long day, especially for dance students – 8.30am-5.30pm.

The school shares a building and facilities with the schools of acting and musical theatre. So the foyer and common areas are full of creatively dressed and coiffed students who mingle indistinguishably from the sixth formers. Lots of hugging and kissing and a real sense of cooperation and mutual support. Local area is moneyed and attractive, though we were met by a warning about muggings and the advisability of going around in groups in the evenings. School hires the local fringe theatre, The Tabard, and the excellent Questors Theatre in nearby Ealing for performance space, as well as dance studios at nearby Rambert and other space at Watermans, Brentford. Offers of useful space to the head, please! And a second bathroom for the girls!

Lots of development going on: new studios and classrooms, IT suite, smartboards throughout, ramps and lifts, main theatre completely refurbished (thank you, Andrew Lloyd Webber Foundation), plus a brand new film and TV studio.

Pastoral care and discipline: Ambiance is energetic and purposeful and the emphasis is on self-discipline. Few, having got here, would want to jeopardize their place, and few drop out though some, obviously, realise after a while that the life of a performing pro is not for them. Carefully-structured tutorial system. Students are remarkably focused and learn quickly that success isn't easily won. Drugs, cigarettes and alcohol are seldom a problem at the school because the students are too busy and committed to their chosen courses to have time for such things. Clear policies on all these sins. Pupils appear to love their teachers – 'they aren't "show-bizzy" – they're here to help us with technique'… 'my daughter's science teacher is a hero to her – even though she's not at all into science'… 'the teachers are all so friendly – I mean, not too friendly but just, well, lovely and they are brilliantly supportive'… 'my second daughter isn't into performing but her sister is so happy there, it seemed unfair not to send her too and the academics – more her thing – have been excellent'.

Pupils and parents: From a huge radius round London and very mixed in all ways: the common denominators are talent, a willingness to work, enthusiasm – and parents who can afford the fees. Some sixth formers from far afield are put up in local digs. Very beautiful and talented young people who may have stars in their eyes but definitely feet on the ground. Many parents are in the business and appreciate the school's values – 'the performances are always professional… an excellent training for young aspiring actors and it is most emphatically NOT a Stage School and all that implies,' we were told. 'I wish I'd gone there,' mused one noted actor. Former pupils include Julie Andrews, Sarah Brightman, Darcey Bussell, Martin Clunes, Joan Collins, Leslie Crowther, Janie Dee, Nigel Havers, Cherie Lunghi, Will Young and Glynis Johns and loads and loads of others. Lots of high calibre thesps among current parents – all clearly loving the school.

Entrance: By audition. Pieces prepared for audition depend on which course you are applying for, eg dance solos, drama monologues, sung or instrumental pieces. Then participation in unprepared workshops and classes. Tests in English and maths. Don't come along seeing yourself as the next soap star or Billy Elliot: 'We're looking for team-workers'.

Exit: Some 75 per cent leave post-GCSE to study at institutions that offer the science subjects at A level or to larger, non-fee paying schools.

Majority of sixth form leavers go on to study at drama schools and dance schools in the UK and overseas, including LAMDA, The Central School of Speech and Drama, Bristol Old Vic Theatre School, Mountview Theatre School, Trinity Laban Conservatoire of Music and Dance, London Studios, The Urdang Academy. A few stay on and join the degree courses in the same building. Some to other degree courses at eg Royal Holloway, Birmingham University.

Money matters: No govt or local authority help. The school has a bursary fund to help existing pupils and is currently looking at ways of increasing it. Various charitable trusts might help out an existing pupil in case of collapsed finances but the bottom line is, you'll have to find the fees – which are very reasonable given what is provided.

Remarks: For those who are serious about the work involved in performing arts – with the accent on the work. It's huge fun, but you need energy, commitment and camaraderie. Now with excellent academic teaching too. If you can cut the mustard at audition, you'll have a ball.

Ashbourne Independent School

17 Old Court Place, London, W8 4PL

• Pupils: 225 boys and girls in total (60/40 per cent split) of whom half are in the upper sixth (resits, condensed A levels or special university foundation year), 75 in lower sixth (AS) • Ages: 16–19; plus 25 in the GCSE stream • Fees: £19,800–£21,600 pa • Independent

Tel: 020 7937 3858
Email: admin@ashbournecollege.co.uk
Website: www.ashbournecollege.co.uk

Principal: Since 1981, Michael (Mike) Kirby, BApSc, MSC (sixtyish), who founded the college. Mr Kirby read aerospace engineering in Toronto (he retains a soft Canadian burr) and Birkbeck where he did a Masters in statistics. Very tall, laconic and seemingly inscrutable but a warmth and a smile escape him occasionally and the man is momentarily revealed. After 32 years, unsurprisingly, he and his school mirror each other. Focused, and clear-sighted, he has made a place where little distracts from work but where the work ethic is underpinned by the sense of support felt by the students. His involvement with the students is integral to the day to day running but the touch is light. 'I know a lot of them personally – they can be a bit wide-eyed and innocent but they're just nice kids and they're great fun.' He still teaches maths revision classes – as ever, we applaud – and, unlike many in his position, sees the students very much in their own home context. 'We positively encourage parents to get involved.'

Prominent member of CIFE (the Conference for Independent Further Education) and the British Council Education Counselling Service, he is the owner and proprietor of Ashbourne. This and the length of his tenure make him unique. He is keen that Ashbourne be recognised as a 'bona fide part of the independent school system', hence his resolve not to be the first resort for resit students – though they do come in penny numbers. He launched and continues to steer a pretty effective school.

Academic matters: Most students come for the two-year A level course, although one year and 18 month A level programmes also on offer – these popular with, mostly, overseas students. Separate classes for those AS students who want to improve their grades – a growing trend. However, AS students who significantly 'underperform' – having been warned that they are in danger of doing so – are shown the door. No embarrassment at this – 'We filter,' says Mr Kirby. 'That's how we get the results'. A small middle school offers two year (years 10 and 11) and one year (year 11) GCSE programmes – 25 students at the time of our visit.

At A level, 37 subjects on offer and all taught in small classes – seven is average, 10 is max and even ones and twos for some subjects. Seventy-five per cent of the 2013 cohort's exams achieved A*- B grades, 45 per cent achieving A*-A. Maths much the most popular subject and with the most impressive results – almost all A*-B. Similarly with further maths – 22 takers in 2013. The sciences also taken by many – again with a decent crop of results. Seventeen takers of Eng Lit in 2013, most getting A*-B. We witnessed one Eng Lit class – all girls. Languages holding up well and business here, as everywhere, gaining a more mixed bunch of results. Unsurprisingly, no Latin, no Greek. All language teachers are native speakers. Lunchtime critical theory seminar much-praised and very popular: 'It's way beyond the A level syllabus so you learn about Marx and Freud and feminism and then apply the theories to film and literature. I learned so much from doing it that way,' an A2 student enthused. All lessons are two hours long. Teachers much praised for their enthusiasm and care. Many are long-serving.

Few SEN students with anything other than mild dyslexia/ dycalculia/ADHD and neither building any good for those with mobility difficulties. No SENCO though SEN overseen by affable head of middle school. Mr Kirby says: 'The school is happy to accept those with SEN but makes no special provision beyond arrangements for exams.' A few here have extra exam time, a laptop in exams or a scribe.

Games, options, the arts: Some variance between the college which claims to offer 'a very wide extracurricular programme' and the students, some of whom seem to know little about it – mostly, apparently, the Brits who don't live locally. However, much enthusiasm from those who do partake and especially from those who have gone on overseas subject-related trips with the college. We are told that the college has now appointed an officer who is responsible for student activities and for ensuring that everyone knows about them.

Art is legendary here and the art room – where we were glad to see some mess – was full of concentrating artists and makers of textiles when we visited. Lots of colour and art seemingly derived from diverse influences. College runs a choir but no orchestra/ensembles. Lots of societies – held in lunchtime and after college; good college newspaper written by students. No sport to speak of and some join gyms etc (there's one next door) but, as everyone agreed, it's the price you pay. Very popular Christmas Revue in which virtually all take part – local fringe theatres are hired for these and other performance events.

Background and atmosphere: In two buildings, separated by Ken High Street. 'Old Building' (in Old Court Place) is tucked down a side road – helpfully guarded by two policemen holding rifles (actually outside the Israeli Consulate) – and so discreet, it's very easily missed. Most sixth form classes take place here. 'Young Street Building' in – you couldn't make it up – Young Street opposite houses the middle school and the rest of the sixth form classes including a huge art room – by far the biggest of the school's rooms. Internally, both buildings are pristine – white walls relieved by stylish and undistracting prints and some larger artwork made on site. Plain carpet, bare wood stairs. Sofas only in one common room and the two staffrooms which are as severely workful as the rest of the establishment. There's nowhere to doss, nowhere to hide. You come here, you work. If you want to mess about, you go out. And they do. Ken High Street, the park, cafés and shops – it's all on the doorstep and, if the inside of the school is cramped, up close London is huge, spacious and full of things to do. Students would welcome kitchen space – somewhere to warm up lunch brought from home – daily eating out is expensive – but every inch counts here and the common rooms are small. Lockers only for GCSE, art and photography students.

Can accommodate up to 250 students. Teaching rooms are definitely small. Interactive whiteboards in use everywhere and Mac PCs everywhere too. The 'library' is all Macs and the shelves have text books and uni guides. There is no library. Good music room – again, all tech, as far as we could see though there is, apparently, a piano and a guitar. Good film/media room and photography studio has dark room. At the time of our visit, there were seven students in year 10, 19 students in year 11, 106 students in year 12 and 100 in year 13 – so a decent number of peers from which to find friends and feel a sense of community. A pervasive air of relaxed purposefulness. And a fantastic location.

Pastoral care and discipline: The parents we spoke to paid tribute to the excellence of home-school communications and this is true equally of local or UK-based families and the overseas ones. Few such colleges offer the community feel and nurturing to be found here – strengthened by everyone being on first name terms and easy exchanges of emails between parents and staff. Staff room doors are glazed and usually open – little sense of 'them and us'. Everyone has a personal tutor – the same throughout their time – c20 tutees to a tutor. This is not the place if all you want is processing to achieve results. The staff gain much praise for being on top of their game educationally but also for 'really caring' and being very approachable. Drug use would lead to immediate expulsion but this sanction very rarely used. Probably not your first shot if you've been ejected elsewhere.

Pupils and parents: Students come from both state and independent schools in the UK, as well as from private schools abroad. Around half the students from around 40 different countries – the rest from the UK. Fewer Chinese than hitherto – more now from Vietnam and Malaysia but college recruits from Russia, Botswana, Ukraine and Kazakhstan and elsewhere. All students have to speak good English and must speak English during the school day – even when with compatriots. About 40 per cent of the students have dedicated English-language classes (no extra cost) – up to six per week – however, best not to choose Ashbourne if you need substantial EAL reinforcement. Of the UK students, around third to a half from the state sector. No boarding though college has halls shared with other educational bodies close by and in Hampstead. Some international students' families find their own more local accommodation. Slightly more girls than boys overall and girls vastly outnumber boys in the humanities. Students here don't look like rebels, dropouts or rejects but wholesome and focused – much as at any academic, independent school's sixth form. All relish the social mix and the internationalism. Students on bursaries complement the loaded with no discernible difference. 'It's a bit cliquey,' we were told, 'especially if you're not into smoking and drinking,' but that's what they do at this age – it's part of being a teenager and drugs seem not to feature here, unlike elsewhere. The principal notes that Ashbourne appeals particularly to 'pupils from good local girls' independents who want something different at A level'.

Entrance: January and September intakes makes for flexibility and a great help to those who need time to re-group after, perhaps, mind-numbing GCSE results. Entry via interview – telephone or face-to-face with either principal or director of studies plus a subject-related entrance test. Auditions for drama/music applicants and portfolio for those who wish to pursue fine art – in which the college has a distinguished tradition. Also, most recent school report/grades/predictions and a personal statement. Bs expected for entry to A level courses – though some flexibility. International students must have minimum 5.5 IELTS or equivalent.

Exit: To a diverse list of colleges and university – no processed clones leave here. Oxbridge places and unis abroad not uncommon. Perhaps predictably, London universities, especially University of London colleges, figure prominently, along with eg Manchester University. In the five years prior to our visit, 36 per cent of Ashbourne's students went to Russell group universities. Courses taken mostly point to solid professions and vocations. Many ultimately into law and finance but this is no mere spawning ground for the suited professions. Creatives include artist and photographer Marion Sosa, fashion designer Chau Nguyen, actors Calum Witney and Vicky Pasion, and the writer Dane Weatherman (founder of the literary periodical Black and Blue).

Money matters: Some bursarial help for students of exceptional ability, especially in drama and music, which offer a very few full scholarships.

Remarks: Solid, reliable and effective place to study. Not for socialites, smack-heads or slackers.

Ashford School

Linked school: Ashford Friars Preparatory School

East Hill, Ashford, TN24 8PB

• Pupils: 480 boys and girls; 155 boarders • Ages: 11–18 • Christian but all faiths and none welcome • Fees: Day £14,997; Full boarding £29,997 pa • Independent

Tel: 01233 625171
Email: registrar@ashfordschool.co.uk
Website: www.ashfordschool.co.uk

Headmaster: Since 2005, Mr Michael Buchanan (early fifties) BSc PGCE NPQH. Educated at Downside and King's College London, where he read physics and trained as a teacher. Previously spent 10 years at Highgate School in north London, where he left as principal deputy head. Part of his brief there was to bring in co-education, and he has done a similar job at Ashford with great success. Previously head of sixth form at Royal Grammar School, Guildford. Business-like and charming, he has a passion for physics, sport and choral music – he is a highly experienced, lead ISI inspector. 'very approachable and a good communicator and you know who is in charge', according to one parent. Still teaches and referees sport when he can. Married with two daughters who attended the school; his wife works for a bank in London. He says the whole family felt welcomed from the moment they arrived at Ashford.

He is a 'very good motivator', according to one former pupil, and has introduced the Adventurous Learning programme that is all about taking people – staff and children alike – out of their comfort zone and challenging in all areas, personal as well as academic. It might be trying something new like speaking in front of the whole class and then the whole school.

He 'wants children to develop as self reliant all-rounders who have a sense of responsibility, compassion and teamwork and the resilience to cope with adversity'. He also wants pupils to take responsibility for their own learning and to feel able to make mistakes. Likes every sort of success to be rewarded and feels that learning should be fun. Head and staff lead by example: Mr Buchanan has taken up the euphonium and 40 teachers have taken up other musical instruments to remind themselves what it feels like to be a pupil.

The school has grown by over 150 since he arrived, helped by the massive building boom in Ashford and the fast rail link to St Pancras. He is gradually replacing the ageing school buildings at the same time as driving the rise in academic standards.

Academic matters: Broad intake, results improving year on year. In 2013, 84 per cent A*/B at A level; at GCSE, 74 per cent A*/A. Particularly good results in science and maths. Everyone takes separate sciences from Year 7. All students learn two languages chosen from Spanish, German and French; German most popular. Pupils from abroad also encouraged to take GCSE in their first language eg Chinese or Dutch. Good range of subjects at A level including Chinese, business studies, psychology, textiles, sports studies and drama. In sixth form Russian, German and Spanish offered as a business language (basic language skills, mostly conversation). Very accommodating timetable and school willing to offer a subject to only a handful of students. Digital literacy programme for year 7. A very tech savvy school – radio voting handsets have proved popular and effective – children text answers to the screen anonymously, useful for shy children but also means there is no chance of a snooze at the back of the class as everyone has to participate. Pupils set by ability in core subjects but there is plenty of flexibility and children can be moved up or down mid term if appropriate. No plans to introduce the IB.

Loyal team of teachers who love the challenge and freedom to innovate and are encouraged to use their initiative. Headmaster likes to recruit those with outside experience who can offer something different. Good mix of old hands and NQTs – school runs a leading and innovative graduate teacher training programme. Biology teacher won a UK top teacher award and also organises the school's rock festival, AshBash. A new higher education advisor has recently joined the team to help with UCAS forms and beyond – he was previously a university admissions tutor. The Oxbridge Club provides extra coaching in problem solving and analytical and critical thinking. Lots of language exchanges and trips that help bring learning to life and 'take school work into the real world,' according to one happy father. A level physicists visit CERN.

Some 35 pupils with SEN ranging from organisation skills to severe dyslexia, dyspraxia, dyscalculia and school can support children with physical disabilities, 'The teachers really go the extra mile for a child who struggles – nothing is too much trouble'. No lessons on Saturday mornings but time devoted to sport, rehearsals and activities – day children always happy to come in and it means the boarders are kept busy.

Games, options, the arts: Good sports facilities with two gyms and a floodlit Astroturf as well as a fitness centre and dance suite, indoor swimming pool and all weather basketball court. Cricket played at the local club a few minutes' walk away and a new sports centre opened in 2013 with Sport England specification. Boys' sport now fully developed and there are senior first teams in rugby, hockey and cricket, but fixtures still a bit sparse as other schools are a 'bit slow to twig that Ashford boys are actually rather good at games'. Teams maintained into sixth form and everyone has to take part in a physical activity at least once a week. Yoga and exercise classes popular, especially with the senior girls, along with street and jazz dance and personal survival. Strong house loyalty and everyone expected to take part in house events.

Lots going on in the drama department from house plays and speech and drama recitals, lower school productions and the spectacular whole school summer musical. Active junior drama club as well as technical drama club for those who prefer to keep out of the spotlight. Drama a popular option at GCSE and also offered at A level and school prepares pupils for speech and drama and LAMDA exams. Vibrant music and art departments: head of music is a colourful character who has transformed the musical life of the school; numbers participating have shot up, as has the standard. Tuition on most instruments available from the bassoon to the organ and school has two Steinway pianos as part of the Steinway schools programme. Lots going on: concert band, chamber music groups, string quartet, rock bands, string ensembles, community orchestra. Concerts every three to four weeks. Head wants music to be 'about performance and enjoyment' with plenty of opportunities for showmanship from 'teatime tootles' in the atrium to singing in Westminster Abbey.

Fabulous textiles and 'big and bold' approach to art; several go on to art foundation courses each year. A group of pupils recently designed a stained glass window for a church in the Holy Land and were then invited to install their work in situ. Another group made some wall hangings for the local hospice. 'We do random and different things and let it all come out', says one pupil.

Huge range of clubs and activities, from Lego robotics, to cooking to debating – something for everyone and all have to take part until sixth form. Strong debating team have represented the school at the Oxford and Cambridge Unions' competitions and taken part in the European Youth Parliament at the Foreign Office. Amnesty group won an award for 'Best Fundraising Event in UK Schools' with their 'Dare to be Different Day'. CCF popular and about 12 pupils complete their D of E Gold each year.

Background and atmosphere: Founded in 1898 with the aim that the pupils should play an active role in the life of the town and with an emphasis on 'training and development of character', the school moved to its present site in 1913 and became part of United Learning in 1999 (a group of 31 schools). This brought a welcome injection of cash resulting in new buildings springing up all over the place. Senior school is at the foot of the High Street, approached by a narrow lane and enclosed by high red-brick walls with lawns and greenery stretching down the hill. It's a green oasis in the middle of busy Ashford and quite difficult to find if you don't know where to look. Extensive rugby and cricket pitches are a short walk away. It's an international and friendly community – pupils are expected to engage with school life, and head says he 'does not want passengers on board and expects everyone to take part'. Good food, cafeteria style, lots of choice and healthy salad options. Brightly painted Atrium café a popular meeting place, also open to parents at pick up and drop off time.

Pastoral care and discipline: Strong pastoral care via house system, everyone is allocated a house on arrival as well as a specialist tutor; new joiners in year 7 also have a sixth form mentor. Boarding from year 6 (bussed over to junior school) but very few in this age group. Boarders well supported and cared for; they are also allocated a house and are not allowed back into their boarding houses during the day, which means plenty of interaction with day children. Lots of boarders' activities and birthdays always celebrated. Houses recently refurbished; sixth formers have en suite bathrooms. Six houses, each led by a head of house, a teacher who oversees academic progress and personal development of each child. Children from abroad spend the first weekend of term with a day pupil – helps integration. Close liaison with parents and tutor and regular progress reviews. Lots of leadership opportunities running house events and activities, from community work to the house play.

Pupils and parents: About 70 per cent day children from as far afield as Maidstone, Sittingbourne and Cranbrook (mini bus service). Very few weekly boarders so room for growth here. Families from a broad social spectrum; parents have high expectations and are encouraged to get involved and be part of the community. Twenty per cent foreign nationals, over 24 nationalities and particularly popular with Chinese, Germans, Eastern Europeans and Nigerians – school takes care that no nationality dominates. 'Ashmole is very good at taking kids of any type and getting the best out of them', says a parent, 'and I like the way the school takes trouble to develop the kids' characters as well as the academic side'

Entrance: About 60 per cent come up from the prep school, others from local primaries and prep schools eg Sutton Valence, Dulwich and Spring Grove. Wide ability range – some very bright, others who struggle, but all must have the ability to pass at least six GCSEs. Almost automatic entry from prep school but must be within the academic range. Children joining from other schools sit assessment tests in English, maths, science and non-verbal reasoning and take part in a team building exercise. Preference given to siblings where possible. A further 15 or so join at 13+ via school's own tests. Sixth form entry tested in proposed AS subjects and must have six GCSEs A*-B or equivalent, plus English proficiency test if appropriate. Lots of foreign nationals come for sixth form as well as several each year from local state schools.

Exit: To a huge range of different institutions from Russell Group to modern, including a smattering to Oxbridge over the last few years – broad minded higher education and careers advisor takes huge trouble to guide right student to right course. A few leave at 13+ – no coaching for CE but good relationships with other local schools; handful departs after GCSEs.

Money matters: Academic, music, art, drama and sports scholarships offered – usually 10-30 per cent of day fee. Means-tested bursaries for children of clergy, mostly Anglican but will consider other Christian denominations. Twenty per cent discount for Forces families, discounts for siblings. Church Schools Foundation Assisted Places assessed on a combination of academic ability and financial need, worth up to 85 per cent of fees – offered to those entering in year 7, 9 or sixth form. Short-term emergency bursaries available.

Remarks: A forward-looking school with a strong international contingent which is going from strength to strength, benefitting in part from the huge growth of Ashford town. The school has 'changed beyond belief in the last eight years' and appeals to a wide range of families with its strong pastoral care and adventurous learning programme.

Ashmole Academy

Cecil Road, London, N14 5RJ

• Pupils: 1,465 boys and girls; all day • Ages: 11–18 • Non-denom
• State

Tel: 020 8361 2703
Email: office@ashmoleacademy.org
Website: www.ashmoleacademy.org

Head Teacher: Since 1997, Mr Derrick Brown MA MBA DipEd – degree subjects psychology and business (mid-fifties). Prior to headship at Ashmole, vice principal at Leigh City Technology College in Dartford and then senior deputy at Cranford School – both schools much the size and diversity of Ashmole and in comparable outer London suburbs. Quietly spoken, serious, relaxed and impressively focused on getting things done, he is an outstandingly successful head. Ashmole, as it is now, is substantially his creation, though he pays tribute to the contribution of parents and professionals who have assisted in building both the fabric and ethos of the school. With the site sorted he can now concentrate on the curriculum – 'The beauty now is that we can focus on the rest – music, PE and raising results'. He is supported by a good set of governors who 'want Ashmole to be the first choice over the independents'. Contracted till his retirement, several years away, he has every chance of consolidating Ashmole's reputation as a provider of comprehensive education at its best.

Academic matters: Very strong exchange link with the twinned town of La Raincy, a suburb just outside Paris. Spanish and German are also offered at GCSE and A level, and is becoming more popular. The languages department also offers extracurricular activities in other languages such as Mandarin and Latin

Strong value-added. Entirely non-selective so the results are impressive. Way ahead of the other non-selective schools in the area. Was a specialist science and music school – one of the few schools in the country combining these two specialisms, which says a lot about the ethos. Much is made of the need to teach so that neither sex is disadvantaged and, interestingly, boys here do at least as well as girls – 'It requires a firm, highly structured and disciplined approach with boys but allows girls to show flair and creativity'. Classes are setted in main subjects – 'Mixed ability doesn't work except in certain areas,' says Mr Brown.

2013 GCSEs saw 78 per cent achieving five or more A*-C including English and maths, 40 per cent A*/A grades. A levels: 70 per cent A*-B, 34 per cent A*/A – business studies and French (popular) both 50 per cent A*/A grades, maths 45 per cent and physics 40 per cent. Very strong exchange link with the twinned town of La Raincy, a suburb just outside Paris. Spanish and German are also offered at GCSE and A level, but less popular. No sense here of a science-orientated school ignoring the languages, thank goodness. Science staff come in for special praise from pupils – 'They are so dedicated and help us so much'.

A third of the school has English as an additional language – support in place to make sure they progress, either through extra help or (mostly) in-class intervention. Around a seventh have some kind of SEN – about 1.5 per cent with statements. Learning support are located within their own area providing adequate space that caters for all needs. The weakest 16 per cent drop languages after Year 8, taking BTEC Business instead. These students will have extra support with the basics.

Attractive library but when we visited the stock was woefully thin in many areas and needed major investment. School says it is now fully stocked and regularly used, especially by sixth form.

Games, options, the arts: Wonderfully off for space and facilities: huge floodlit Astroturf court, playing-field, sports hall and separate studio for dance, aerobics and net sports, but no pool. Outstandingly successful in both boys' and girls' football and seems to win almost everything in Barnet championships. Now building its orchestra, with a range of extracurricular clubs and increasing numbers of pupils taking individual music lessons. Music scholarship scheme helps those with talent to develop their skills. Drama popular – big, well-equipped studio – and successful: major musical production each year, standards high and all great fun. Art good and varied – bold colour, lively textiles: we saw some glam evening dresses made by year 10; popular graphics, clay sculpture, fabric painting and photography. Enrichment groups in the sixth offer a choice of cultural, entrepreneurial and environmental activities. School has own radio station. Lots of good before- and after-school clubs and classes.

Background and atmosphere: If you knew Ashmole School in the old days you wouldn't recognise it now. It had survived in pretty dire conditions for years but, on his arrival in 1997, Mr Brown organised the sale of six acres of school land and began a visionary building programme with the proceeds. Design of new buildings the result of collaboration between the school, its very engaged parents and the architect. Re-homing happened in 2004. School, now an academy, buzzes along in smart, functional and not-hideous buildings. New sixth form centre due for completion in 2014. Plenty of outdoor space, sited on rising ground in quiet, residential Southgate – middle class, respectable and easy travel both into and out of London proper.

Proud of itself; everyone works to maintain its shiny smartness. Remarkably free of the litter and chewing gum which seem to breed in comparable schools, it has wide corridors, banks of sensible-sized lockers, spacious classrooms, labs and studios and an air of getting-on-with-the-job. Attractive, functional refectory and sensible menu – much emphasis now on healthy eating and drinking: no fizzy pop. We saw melon being chopped up and bunches of grapes, and wanted to stay and chomp.

The atmosphere is orderly, collaborative, friendly. Classes we peeked into were, for the most part, disciplined and quiet; overall, an atmosphere which encourages work and discourages messing around. Pupils we spoke too expressed a pride in and gratitude to the school we have rarely met elsewhere. 'I want to be a teacher because of this school,' said one.

Pastoral care and discipline: No mobiles allowed except for the sixth form – confiscated if they go off in lessons. Zero tolerance of drugs, weapons and violence – on or off the premises. 'The school is very good about bullying,' we were told by a contented sixth former. Disruptive or abusive pupils are sent to the individual learning room, where they are under supervision, have no contact with their friends and hate it. Two or three days there usually does the trick, but head will exclude for serious offences –– one exclusion in 2012-13 – eg threatening behaviour, theft, fighting and disruptiveness. The result of what reads like a strict disciplinary regime is a school in which pupils feel secure and comfortable and everyone knows the score.

For such a large school, an unusual amount of interaction across the year groups, encouraged by the cultural and charitable activities: pupils feel they have friends in all years. Great faith is expressed in the pastoral care given by the school – certain individual members of staff, eg the school nurse and deputy head, seen as especially approachable and reliable if something needs sorting. General sense of self-discipline and a fostering of civilised behaviour at work here.

Pupils and parents: Vast ethnic mix, as you'd expect, though more Cypriots – Greek and Turkish – than anything else. Main religion is Christianity of all sorts, second is Islam. Mostly working parents so little involvement during the day, but a supportive and hard-working PTA makes big contribution to the school's development and nearly all turn up to parents' evenings. Pupils are cheery, focused, ambitious and involved.

Notable former pupils include Amy Winehouse, former S Club 7 member Rachel Stevens, musician Stephen Sidwell, goalie Mark Bunn, Oscar winning producer Graham King, lead vocalist from The Feeling, Daniel Sells and Channel 5 Tsar Sham Sandhu.

Entrance: Over 1,100 apply for the 232 places – of which siblings will take around 80. You'll get in if you have a sibling there, are a looked-after child or live near enough – otherwise, no chance. Up to 20 music aptitude places; these pupils, along with others who show talent, are placed on the music scholarship programme.

Exit: Around a third leave after GCSEs, mostly for vocational courses elsewhere. Around half of sixth formers to top universities: two to Cambridge and five medics in 2013; others to eg Durham, Warwick, London Universities, Nottingham, Leeds; science, law and humanities are popular too.

Remarks: Slick, sensible and effective. Check out the housing market.

Ashville College

Linked school: Ashville Junior School

Green Lane, Harrogate, HG2 9JP

• Pupils: 510 boys and girls; 105 board (55 sixth form). • Ages: 11–18 • Methodist • Fees: Day £12,090–£12,180; Boarding £21,840–£23,930 pa • Independent

Tel: 01423 566358
Email: ashville@ashville.co.uk
Website: www.ashville.co.uk

Headmaster: Since 2010 Mr Mark Lauder MA (mid forties), educated at Hermitage Academy, Helensburgh, did an MA in English literature and history at the University of Aberdeen, spending his junior honours year at the University of Oregon, Eugene, USA. After graduating he embarked on research at St Edmund Hall, Oxford, where as well as winning a graduate scholarship, he achieved two half blues in rowing. Previously deputy head of Felsted School, Essex, head of history and then housemaster at St Edward's School, Oxford, and before that head of history and master in charge of rowing at Shiplake College, Henley-on-Thames.

Married to peripatetic piano teacher, Caroline, with two sons, both at Ashville College, in junior school. Pupils describe the head as 'having an open door, listening to pupils and making change happen'. Change not so evident to the parents we spoke to – maybe as his approach is 'evolutionary not revolutionary', perhaps early days.

Interests include rowing, rugby, politics and restoring a 17th century Yorkshire parsonage, in between long walks in the Dales and all things Scottish. Believes in whole child development, 'the individual of infinite worth, the social creed of Methodism being the foundation and teacher/pupil relationship the cornerstone'.

Academic matters: Good value-added, especially at GCSE – 47 per cent A/A* in 2013. Science, mathematics, economics and PE all very popular at A level (36 per cent A*/A and 63 per cent A*/B grades overall in 2013). Not a shining star in the league tables, but most pupils exceed predicted potential and very able pupils do particularly well. Good choice of subjects at GCSE and at A level, offering history of art and government and politics.

Average class size 16, maximum 22, dropping to 10, maximum 16, in the sixth form. Years 7-9 follow broad curriculum including at least two modern foreign languages; set for mathematics and languages. For GCSE years, pupils split into ability bands A and B; A are taught Latin and B do extra lessons in English, geography and ICT. Majority take three separate sciences, a few dual award, all at least one modern foreign language.

All year 7 pupils (and year 3 in the junior school) are screened for dyslexia, with further testing and screening as necessary. No pupil has a statement of special educational need, but over 130 pupils receive some additional support for 'mild dyslexic tendencies' – one-on-one support if deemed necessary. Those with dyslexia thrive thanks to the kindly environment and carefully planned programmes of study; indeed in recent years few haven't get the benchmark five A*-Cs at GCSE, and most gain at least a B in English.

Over 60 international students require English as an additional language, mostly taught alongside mainstream English. Target is Cambridge FCE by year 11 and all sixth form sit Cambridge IELTS in year 13.

Games, options, the arts: Facilities – two gyms, 30m swimming pool, fabulous climbing wall, squash courts, fitness room and ample pitches, including a new all weather surface pitch – show importance of sport. Teams and fixtures galore in traditional team sports. All usual suspects on offer plus American influenced disc golf – something for everyone. Director of activities recently appointed to provide even more challenging outdoor opportunities.

Well-resourced and well-used music centre – a third take individual instrumental or singing lessons. An array of choirs and bands, from chamber to soul and jazz to strings. Talented musicians play in the National Children's and National Youth Orchestras, but plenty of playing and performing opportunities for those just starting out too: Verdi Requiem in Leeds Town Hall, Messiah from scratch for charity.

Dedicated art studios and drama facilities always busy. Unusually for a boarding school, a 4pm finish and no Saturday school, but plenty of choice of after-school activities and clubs and supervised prep until 5.30pm. Duke of Edinburgh award scheme available for pupils from year 10. Trip for older students to Malawi ties in with charity fundraising to support the Open Arms Orphanage, which has close links with the school.

Background and atmosphere: Founded in 1877 by the Methodist Church as a senior boys' boarding school, co-ed since 1984. The pleasant, well-maintained site opens up amidst a leafy residential area, with a swathe of pitches and playing fields fringed by the trinity of schools – college, junior and pre-prep – sports centre and boarding houses. Evacuated to Windermere during the war as the premises were requisitioned for the war effort and used by Air Ministry.

Plenty of well-kept facilities – atmospheric Memorial Hall is home to lectures, meetings and some concerts, with larger gatherings filling the school hall. Recent, much-needed, extensive refurbishment programme to most classrooms, with the library now excellent. Investment in ICT infrastructure and hardware and more planned. Co-ed junior and girls' boarding houses recently upgraded. New head of sixth form and changes afoot in academic offering, pupil monitoring and facilities in sixth form centre – so watch this space.

Underpinned by Methodist tradition, a positive, supportive family ethos where pupils feel valued and their voices heard. A genuine sense of community that keeps ex-pupils in contact long after they have left the school gates.

Pastoral care and discipline: Excellent individual pastoral care continues to be a real strength of the school. Head believes in picking up problems quickly to 'fix it small' and then 'partnership between school and parents'. This is recognised by parents, who said that the school 'tried very hard to get it right'.

All year 7 are taken to the Lake District for a bonding weekend early in the autumn term; this receives rave reviews not only from the new pupils but also from sixth formers, who work as liaison prefects and, if assigned to year 7, go too.

School viewed as a day school with boarding – under 20 per cent board, and half of these are sixth form; firmly in the head's sights to improve these statisti85cs. Three senior boarding houses, two boys' and one girls', are comfortably furnished with usual facilities: kitchens, common rooms, games areas and computers.

Approximately one-third of boarders are from South East Asia – this has reduced in recent years. More emphasis on weekly/flexi boarding and more recruitment from the Forces. Girls and boys encouraged to socialise, with trips regularly organised at weekends and half-termly theme evenings. Plenty of activities

on offer after school but all optional. Cultural differences mean not much integration with day pupils after school hours.

Fines if caught smoking, with possibility of exclusion for repeated offences. Drugs: out for supplying or intending to – no issues in recent times.

Pupils and parents: Mainly from local professional and business families, extending from Ripon to north Leeds and surrounding villages. Quite a few first time buyers; Americans from nearby Menwith Hill military base add an interesting dimension. For about 10 per cent of pupils English is not a first language and overall approximately 14 per cent come from a variety of minority ethnic backgrounds, mainly Chinese, Nigerian and European. Thriving Friends of Ashville runs regular, well-supported activities.

Old boys: Ian Dodds (designer of the Moon Buggy), Commander Ian Grieve (head of anti-terrorism Scotland Yard), Jim Carter (Downton Abbey actor), Simon Theakston (director of Theakston's Brewery and chairman of the Yorkshire Agricultural Show) and Peter McCormick (lawyer to the Football Association).

Entrance: For year 7, a day in January with English, mathematics and non-verbal reasoning papers followed by practical activities, plus a report from previous head. Usually a three form entry of 60 pupils, though recent demand has increased this to four forms.

Majority of pupils come from own junior school and nearby preps: Belmont Grosvenor and Brackenfield in Harrogate, Richmond House, Moorlands and Frobelian in Leeds, plus local state primary schools. Six bus routes in operation starting in Leeds, Thorner, Addingham, Ripon and Bramham.

Sixth form entry is via interview and satisfactory reference, minimum five grade Cs with grade Bs in subjects to be studied. Exams, interview and reference are norm for entry at other times.

Exit: Around 25 per cent leave at the end of year 11. About 85 per cent of sixth formers go on to higher education, a couple to Oxbridge, rest to a wide range of Russell Group/redbrick universities.

Money matters: Academic, music, sports, art and drama scholarships are available in the senior school. Scholarships are awarded on entry into year 7, year 10 and sixth form and are reviewed at key stages. Means-tested bursaries of up to 100 per cent of fees are available either in conjunction with scholarships or on a stand-alone basis. Additional discounts are awarded to the children of Methodist ministers and parents in the Forces.

Remarks: A successful all-round day school with a boarding ethos. Plenty of happy pupils in a caring and supportive environment. Academics and teaching being strengthened. Offers a trinity of schools providing seamless transition through each stage of education, obviously popular with many parents and pupils.

Aylesbury Grammar School

Walton Road, Aylesbury, HP21 7RP

• Pupils: 1,290 boys, all day • Ages: 11–18 • Non-denom • State

Tel: 01296 484545
Email: office@ags.bucks.sch.uk
Website: www.ags.bucks.sch.uk

Headmaster: Since 2008, Mr Stephen Lehec BA English and history (Soton), PGCE from St Anne's, Oxford. Previously deputy head since 2006 and before that assistant headteacher at Maidstone Grammar. Married to Penelope, two daughters.

Frank, humorous and energetic, his pride in the school is disarming. He teaches A level and year 7 history, 'dips in and out of' year 7 PHSE and plans to add year 10 economics. 'Teaching commitments keep your feet on the ground – if it's timetabled you have to be there.' Boys were falling over themselves to praise his leadership, marvelling at his ability to know not only their names but also details about their interests. One said, 'He finds time for everybody.' Many had received letters (personal letters, posted to their home address) from him in recognition of their sporting, artistic or other contribution to school life. This is one of Mr Lehec's innovations and recipients from eager year 7s to burly sixth formers think it's 'brilliant'. Other material changes have been the revival of the school magazine and the formation of an alumni association (a very smart move, given the calibre of Old Aylesburians); with academy status granted, plenty more are in the pipeline. He's hot on uniform (ties done up, shirts tucked in), hotter on litter (not a scrap to be seen), hottest on learning.

Gave up playing rugby at a young age (but success of the school 1st XV must be a vicarious thrill), still plays a bit of football, cycles and is getting serious about golf and gardening. He describes himself as a 'voracious' reader of non-fiction and fiction (favourite authors Graham Greene, Iris Murdoch; favourite book The Unbearable Lightness of Being). Admits somewhat ruefully that his wife would say that his main interest outside school 'was school'.

Academic matters: Broad spectrum of GCSE options includes economics, Japanese, Italian, business studies, music, food and nutrition and computing. Curriculum enriched by the benefits of specialisms in science, languages, maths, computing (plus Artsmark, Sportsmark and International Schools awards). In 2013, 65 per cent A*/A grades at GCSE. All take three separate sciences, some GCSEs taken early (languages, citizenship, philosophy of religion) when appropriate. Boys here learn fast and can get through some subject syllabuses in double quick time – for instance all do at least one module of further maths in addition to the GCSE (six students doing one year geology GCSE all got A*). The head says that he is 'looking at the IGCSE syllabuses'.

System of individual target setting has proved very successful; boys set their own academic goals and 'almost always exceed them'. Lessons we observed were lively, challenging and focused: in a year 7 English class boys were eagerly analysing descriptive techniques in Treasure Island; in the well-equipped DT workshop boys were operating lathes and cutting plastics to fashion note holders, assisted by their enthusiastic female teacher. Delicious baking smells drifted from the spotless food technology classrooms – 'The boys have been customising scones,' we were told.

Twenty-five subjects available at A level; 2013 41 per cent A*/A. Sixth formers take general studies or a complementary studies option, GCSE Japanese or Italian, for instance; 'The school likes to challenge us,' observed one.

The school day is made up of five hour-long lessons, a challenge to the doctrine that boys perform best in short sharp bursts. This and smaller teaching groups have had a significant impact on performance in subjects such as English which demand a more discursive approach. Another change made by Mr Lehec was to revitalise the classics department and all boys now follow a 'core classics' course including Latin for the first three years. Boys are frank about the workload, 'There's lots of homework, especially compared to other schools, and everyone wants to do well, get the best grades.' As the head observed, competition thrives in the best possible way.

The SEN team often works with families from the end of year 6 to prepare boys with dyslexia, dyspraxia, Asperger's etc before they start at the school. All are screened for learning difficulties on entry and individual or small group support

provided. Provision is made to accommodate students with visual impairment or physical disabilities. Most able students are catered for with extended special projects, early GCSE entry and Oxbridge tutoring.

Games, options, the arts: Definitely a rugby school (pupils playing at county and national level), but that doesn't stop AGS achieving glory in football (winners and finalists in county cup for several years), tennis (national schools finalists), squash, basketball (their 6'4" coach has taken them to the district and national finals), cricket (tour of South Africa) and national finalists in handball (a new one for us), coached by a former pupil who is on the Olympic team. Fencing, hockey, swimming, table tennis and badminton also thriving. Sports science is offered at GCSE and A level and on-site facilities include a huge multi-purpose sports hall, swimming pool, squash courts (grant from Sport England to refurbish these). Extra pitches just up the road. Two annual skiing trips to North America attract large numbers.

Music, art and drama are all very popular with significant numbers taking these subjects at GCSE and A level; we bearded the head of drama in his studio and he just beamed, 'I've been here 16 years and I love it!' A highlight for one of our guides was when the school put on a cabaret evening at Aylesbury's new Waterside theatre. AGS was the first school to perform there and the evening was a sell-out; musicians and singers performed to a packed house of over 500 and by the end the whole audience was dancing.

This is a school that thrives on all kinds of competition, not just on the sports field. Recent achievements include gold medals in maths, computing and physics Olympiads; Arkwright (engineering) scholarships; Young Enterprise national winners (twice representing UK in Europe) and representation on the England debating team.

Background and atmosphere: Founded in 1598 by Sir Henry Lee, a champion of Elizabeth I. Occupied site in centre of Aylesbury until 1907, now to be found in a residential road somewhere in Aylesbury's one-way system; girls' equivalent, Aylesbury High School, is a near neighbour. The school makes the very best of the buildings it has been given but they're not exactly easy on the eye. Judging by its ubiquity in official photographs, the 'headmaster's lawn', a small square of perfect grass surrounded by lavender hedging, seems to provide the most photogenic view. One of our excellent sixth form guides described the site as 'mix and match' and we defer to him, because he's planning to study architecture.

Inside the older part the parquet floor glows and corridors are half-tiled; classrooms here are straight from central casting with high sash windows and desks facing the front; anyone who has been to school in the last 100 years would feel at home. Newer buildings include fine studio theatre, music practice rooms and recording suite and large multi-use sports hall; other parts are scrupulously clean but with much evidence of careful patching up. Upgrading of science labs under way; next come improvements to the main entrance, a new lecture theatre and IT equipment. Much of the anticipated cost has been raised from parents, alumni and staff – an indication of the school's value to its present and past community. The library is large and bursting with books, the librarian runs reading schemes for years 7 and 8 to 'encourage boys to read books from different genres'. Sixth formers have a common room and snack bar.

House system key to school's character and provides a focus for the boys' keen competitive spirit. Each year the six houses vie for two equally coveted trophies, the Brodie for sporting triumphs, the Watson for cultural and artistic excellence. The competitions for house athletics and the house quiz are held on the same day, thus uniting two cultures and enabling the un-athletic to achieve equal glory. Aylesbury has a co-ed grammar in addition to the boys' and girls' schools, so we asked a group of boys what they thought they gained from single sex education: 'You can be yourself, you don't have to pretend' and 'fewer distractions, more focus and the ability to be more competitive' were the answers. The head endorses this: 'Boys don't have to worry about being cool and aloof; they're not embarrassed to participate in and enjoy singing, music, drama and reading.'

Pastoral care and discipline: The head's aim is for the school to foster an environment of 'well being and mutual respect' – he believes that this is the best medium for successful learning. Emphasis is on 'self discipline' and the positive contribution individuals can make to the community life of the school. Boys feel privileged to come here; expectations are high and behaviour reflects that, but a system of detentions, 'merit holidays' (having to attend school on an inset day) exists for any misdemeanours. According to the head, has been 'the odd exclusion', but no expulsions.

All the pupils we met were courteous and we observed a respectful but relaxed relationship between boys and staff. The whole of the first year is regarded as an 'induction year' and includes a week's residential trip to North Wales. Year 7 boys we spoke to praised the sixth form prefects and the year 8 'buddies' with their silver badges, who are there to help with all the problems and questions they themselves experienced the year before. Pastoral care is spread between tutors, house and year group heads and sixth form prefects are trained in peer mentoring.

Pupils and parents: Active and loyal parents who 'can't do enough'. Boys come from all over, increasing numbers from preps – you'd be crazy not to. Since our last visit when 'no claim' was made to well-known OBs, an archaeological dig has unearthed a rich seam of proud alumni including Stephen Shipperley, co-founder of property website Rightmove; Jake Arnott, author; Tim Besley, member of the Monetary Policy Committee; Shailesh Vara, MP; Peter Rost, MP; Tim Harford, journalist and presenter; Rob Stringer, chairman of Columbia/Epic Label; Ted Cockle, Vice President Island Records UK; Dr Theodore Zeldin CBE, author and historian, and from co-ed days in the 1950s Baroness Billingham and Lynda Bellingham, actress.

Entrance: Via Bucks 11+ test administered by county council. Admission purely on scores, no interview. Boys admitted at 12+, 13+, 14+ via county tests if places available. School interviews and tests for years 10-11. Entry into sixth form requires 362 points from best eight at GCSE and at least B in subjects to be studied.

Exit: Everywhere and for everything. UCAS applications supported by programme of visits and talks from Russell Group representatives and Oxbridge outreach opportunities. In 2013, seven to Oxbridge and seven medics; Nottingham, Loughborough, Warwick, Birmingham, Leeds, Leicester, Oxford Brookes, Bath, Durham and Exeter all popular. Many AGS boys go for engineering, history, business and maths; respectable numbers choose languages, economics, sports and exercise science and biology.

Money matters: Impressive fundraising from grateful alumni, parents and staff enables school to fund buildings and equipment; PTA also funds bursaries for study trips abroad.

Remarks: What kind of boy would fit in here? AGS boys don't have to fit a mould – instead the school seems to bring out the very best in each of its pupils. The many boys we met were spirited, funny, characterful and independent minded; what they shared was pride (not arrogance) in their school and a refreshing enthusiasm to take every opportunity it offers.

Backwell School

Station Road, Backwell, Bristol, BS48 3BX

• Pupils: 1,680 boys and girls • Ages: 11-18 • Non-denom • State

Tel: 01275 463371
Email: mailbox@backwellschool.net
Website: www.backwellschool.net

Headteacher: Mr Julian Baldwin MA PGCE (early fifties), educated at Chichester High School before reading French and Spanish at Queen's College, Oxford. Previously deputy and then acting head during predecessor's illness. Taught for 20 years at Parrs Wood High School, Manchester. Staff view head as 'steadfast, caring and with a sense of humour'. Still teaches and likes to be 'out and about' in the school. Says Backwell is a 'marvellous place in which to work and learn' because of its 'can do' culture. Expects staff to share his commitment to excellence. Since 2011 has been a designated National Leader in Education. Married to Gill, who teaches languages at Backwell; they live in village. Three children – eldest son, Max, graduated from York; Matthew and Kate both went to Backwell themselves and have graduated from Manchester and Sheffield. Head loves sport, literature and cooking.

Academic matters: Over 52 per cent A*-B grades at A level in 2013 and 27 per cent A*/A in 2013, with 22 students gaining at least three A*/A grades; regular Oxbridge places. Boys outshine girls in maths and physics whilst girls perform better overall. In 2013, 63 per cent got five or more A*-C grades at GCSE including English and maths and 34 students got at least eight A*/A. Majority of pupils take 10 subjects, including six options drawn from creative areas, languages and humanities. Nearly half achieve English Baccalaureate annually. Strong in core subjects, especially science and maths, and majority takes at least one modern foreign language to GCSE. A Teaching School with innovative courses for experienced staff as well as new teacher induction and graduate training programmes.

Wider than usual choice at AS and A2. Critical thinking encouraged as an additional AS option in year 13. BTEC in leisure and tourism and creative and media diploma in sixth form, but more demand for academic subjects. In year 7, mixed-ability teaching operates across half the age group with setting in maths from the outset, and in modern languages, science and geography from year 8. Setting by ability increases further up the school. Enrichment programme styled Xtra Bytes runs twilight GCSE lessons in Latin, plus fast-track music. Strong PSHE course with lots of careers guidance. Plenty of computer suites but not OTT, plus Apple Macs for graphic work. Lots of buzz in DT and loads of original designs.

Has a well-earned reputation for special needs including its gifted and talented programme. 'Having the right attitude towards special needs has helped raise expectations of pupils across the ability range,' says head. Puts its money where its mouth is by providing priority accommodation for special needs on ground floor of stunning new building; lift provides wheelchair access to maths classrooms above. We saw one boy with cerebral palsy manoeuvring his wheelchair happily around site (now studying architecture at Cardiff University) and one of 14 pupils diagnosed with Asperger's participating fully in a food science lesson with learning support. Thirty-six children currently with statements, some visually and hearing impaired. All children screened on entry for dyslexia with about 160 currently receiving individualised support. SENCo manages specialist staff including 16 LSAs.

Games, options, the arts: Range of sports (including swimming in years 7 and 8) offered as part of core PE provision, also timetabled in sixth form. Plenty available during extended lunchtime and after school; free late bus for those staying for activities. Pupils use adjacent leisure centre as well as school's sports hall and eight floodlit all-weather tennis courts. No Astroturf but extensive playing fields, which provide room to breathe at lunch-time during drier months. House competitions and some inter-school matches with teams practising and playing after school. Steady flow of representative players at county level. Community sports leadership award is a popular addition for some.

1950s theatre seating 400, and studio theatre for smaller productions in sixth form centre. Outreach work in primaries and participation in local festivals. Full orchestra and range of bands, choirs and ensembles. About 20 per cent of pupils have instrumental lessons and school holds concerts at St George's in Bristol.

Lots of trips within curriculum (art department were at Tate Modern when we visited). Sixth form leavers go on World Challenge expeditions biennially.

Background and atmosphere: Opened in 1954 as a secondary modern; reorganised in 1969 as a comprehensive, with its own sixth form since 1979. In recent years has expanded rapidly and built reputation over a wide area for good discipline and academic success. Carefully concealed but close to village centre. New canopied entrance leads to a modern reception area and spacious foyer, where displays include plenty of art plus evidence of recent school successes. New buildings for special needs and maths (with a multi-coloured roof) and new visual arts studios with vibrant, student-designed art on external cladding. Library is at heart of school life and includes a separate fiction classroom with 7,000 titles, all supervised by a doubly qualified teacher/librarian; equipped with laptops for online quiet study by sixth formers; identikit fingerprint technology used successfully for checking out loans. New-ish sixth form building houses common room, lecture theatre, dance studio and classrooms.

Pastoral care and discipline: Common sense prevails – mobile phones are allowed for emergency use but confiscated if used otherwise during working day. Pastoral system a strength – parents and pupils emphasise how supportive and helpful they find the teachers. One mother described how she received a 'prompt and effective response' when her daughter was subjected to some 'low level irritation' from another year 7 pupil. The large numbers are broken down into manageable units – maintains a separate dining facility for year 7; years 8-11 share two kitchens between their four houses. Sixth formers have their own centre, so GCSE pupils are interviewed regularly by head of house to gauge progress, and sixth formers have lots of support too.

House areas double up as social and teaching space with little evidence of fabric suffering as a consequence. House assemblies in own areas but year assemblies held in theatre. School nurse also monitors attendance and 'uses some discretion' before contacting parents. Nice balance between long-term, experienced staff and younger teachers who move for promotion elsewhere. School council plays part in shaping policies and includes representatives from all age groups, with meetings attended by a governor and clerked by school bursar. Part-time adult mentors help with management of behaviour and learning programmes for relatively small number of disaffected.

Pupils and parents: Predominantly well-behaved, motivated pupils from affluent rural suburbs eight miles south-west of Bristol. Parents expect school to deliver a rounded, orderly, academic education and generally seem pleased with results. Years 7-11 look comfortable and smart in navy sweatshirts over white polo shirts trimmed with house colours. Sixth formers lack 'attitude' and generally wear sensible gear. Presence of a large sixth form helps to 'foster strong work ethic'. 'Some teachers don't believe in homework,' reported younger pupils, but plenty for exam candidates. One girl who was repeatedly 'picked on' at a rival comprehensive said she'd never had a moment's bother here. Active parents' association with fundraising and donations to school's coffers. Former pupils include film director, Kirk Jones, plus loads of media types, academics and sportspeople.

Entrance: LA manages admissions to year 7 – those from catchment area will get a place but heavy demand from elsewhere. Places siblings in same house and takes care to avoid pupils from one feeder school dominating any tutor group. Handles entries into other year groups and sixth form; the latter attracts some from Bristol independent schools.

Exit: Twenty per cent go to FE colleges at 16, much less than from most comprehensives in the LA; a few go directly into employment, but the majority remain in the sixth form. Most year 13 leavers proceed to higher education across a wide range of courses and universities (2013 five to Oxbridge).

Money matters: Converted to academy status in May 2011. Now beginning to use the greater freedoms to the benefit of own students. Parents contribute to school fund to assist with societies and expeditions – financial support available in cases of hardship in accordance with school's comprehensive ethos.

Remarks: Much friendlier than you would expect, given its size. House system ensures pupils in years 7 to 11 have a strong sense of identity. Hugely successful sixth form. Lots of younger, enthusiastic and committed teachers. Positive and reassuring buzz through busy working day confirms how well this place justifies parents' description of it as 'a really good all-round school'.

Badminton School

Linked school: Badminton Junior School

Westbury Road, Westbury-on-Trym, Bristol, BS9 3BA

- Pupils: 435 girls; 180 boarders • Ages: 3–18 • Non-denom
- Fees: Boarding £20,190–£32,070; Day £8,040–£16,920 pa
- Independent

Tel: 01179 055271
Email: admissions@badminton.bristol.sch.uk
Website: www.badminton.bristol.sch.uk

Headmistress: Since September 2012, Mrs Rebecca Tear BSc PGCE (forty). Read chemistry at Exeter University, PGCE at The Institute of Education, London, now completing MA in educational leadership. Taught chemistry at Eggbuckland Community College and St George's Ascot, deputy head at Wycombe Abbey. Wants girls to develop a broad and balanced set of skills and interests. Experience of boarding as pupil, parent and house mistress. Interested in cookery, fitness and music.

Academic matters: Consistently way up in the league tables and so perceived by some as a cherry picking hothouse – vigorously denied by parents, staff and pupils. The intake from the junior school and independent prep schools is broad and inclusive. 'The real value-added strength of the school is that it takes average girls and turns them into high performers,' says a mum with three very different daughters in the school. The bright girls are not made to do more than three A levels and breadth of interest is encouraged – girls do not leave for the holidays groaning under the weight of homework. Younger girls are given a rolling annual introduction to Latin, German, Spanish, Italian, Mandarin, thereby 'cutting the primacy of French'. By the time they are 13 they may choose from three languages.

Subjects are not blocked before the girls have said which ones they wish to do – 'We can't always accommodate all the permutations but we minimise constraints,' says school. Maths and sciences strong. In 2013, 87 per cent A*/A grades at GCSE and 71 per cent at A level. So how are those excellent results achieved? 'I wish I knew,' said an envious head; 'I can't quite work it out myself,' pondered a parent, 'but I think it's because the school is consistent and thorough. As a result there is no great hiatus when it comes to exams.' 'The teachers are enthusiasts,' says a leading academic. 'We enjoy the work,' say the girls, and in the sixth form, 'We're allowed the freedom to work in our own way.' That sense of freedom is central to Badminton – no honours boards, no speech day prize-giving, no trumpeting of individual successes.

Games, options, the arts: 'A few years ago I might have indulged in a mild bleat about the games,' a parent told us, 'but not now.' The facilities are excellent, the girls are healthily competitive in their approach; county and national players. Everyone is encouraged to find a sport they enjoy. Music thrives from its purpose-built headquarters with about 80 per cent learning instruments. Orchestras, ensembles, jazz, choirs, rock groups, quartets. The bright and airy creative arts centre is an exciting place from which are fired inventive and colourful textiles, imaginative jewellery and terrific photography – the overall effect is stunning. Drama too is hugely popular, with up to seven productions a year and opportunities to become involved on and backstage. Lots of trips abroad, some in the company of boys' schools, as well as D of E expeditions.

Background and atmosphere: Founded in 1858, it has always been different. The founder's aim was to give girls as good an education as their brothers. Initially its non-conformist origins and belief in a serious, free-thinking intellectual approach, rather than deportment and sewing, shocked the more staid members of Bristol society. Right from the start it was concerned with the global picture (the first boarder was from the West Indies) and girls were encouraged to think for themselves and not be merely decorous and demure. In 1924 the school moved from Clifton to its current site of 15 acres. Centred around the elegant Northcote Manor with its lovely rose garden and unusual topiary, the campus is full but doesn't feel crowded, thanks to the predominantly light brick and cream paint used for recent additions. Newish 'green' boarding house. Girls are cheerful and friendly (rows of them walking along with linked arms and smiling faces) and the atmosphere is calm and happy.

Pastoral care and discipline: No school chapel but boarders are free to attend church if they wish to. Tutoring is done in year groups. Few rules – the girls seem to be guided by common sense and courtesy with much mutual support. Very, very occasional suspensions. 'A culture of disappointment is what reins in any thoughtlessness,' said the previous head. The sixth form is housed in its own very cleverly designed building: comfortable, homely but not flashy. Sixth formers are trusted and given a lot of freedom. Wearing their own clothes, as opposed to the school uniform, is an outward symbol of this. Head girls are elected by the pupils. 'Discipline really isn't an issue,' we heard over and over again.

Pupils and parents: Pupils still come from all over Europe and the world (20 per cent of boarders). Those from abroad are fully and comfortably integrated and local girls appreciate the opportunity for making international friends. Some mild anxiety expressed about getting the balance right – not too many from the same country – but over 20 countries are involved, so no obvious conveyer belt. Parents come from a cross-section of professions – Bristol is that sort of city – and are happily included in many activities. Famous alumni include Iris Murdoch, Indira Gandhi, Rosamund Pike, Polly Toynbee and Phyllida Law.

Entrance: At all junior levels and then mostly at 11, 13 and 16. Very few from the junior school are denied entry, though they sit the entrance exam at 11 in English, maths and non-verbal reasoning, same as other aspirants. 'They are always prepared to be flexible and genuinely seek bright-eyed all-rounders,' says successful prep school head whose school regularly feeds. Eggheads don't necessarily get in: the school is looking for girls who will fit in and appreciate the idiosyncratic atmosphere and ethos. Entrance examinations in November for 16+ and in January for other age groups.

Exit: All to university and up to 15 per cent each year to Oxbridge; others to eg Warwick, York, Exeter, London universities, Durham, Edinburgh, Oxford Brookes, Architectural Association. Some 25 per cent go on gap years – the experiences gained are reflected in the girls' all-round performances at university, where reports of girls rowing, directing plays, broadcasting and generally getting stuck in. No reports of post A level burn up. Thence mostly into professions. Medicine, science, engineering, finance and law seem to be particularly popular, though, as with everything at Badminton, no pigeon-holing.

Money matters: Means-tested bursaries and the usual range of scholarships (academic, art, music and all-round) on offer at 11+, 13+ and 16+. Foundation awards of up to 100 per cent off fees available for years 6 and 7 (day) and year 9 (boarding).

Remarks: 'Badminton babes', as some boys refer to them with a mixture of awe and admiration, are feisty in argument, independent in mind and spirit, loyal to the ethos of their school, friendly and courteous. Individuality, coupled with common sense, is genuinely celebrated and girls are given freedom and time to develop within a sensitively constructed framework. Don't take too seriously the carpings of envious schools and ill-informed assumptions about Badminton's academic success. Yes, perhaps too many pictures of girls celebrating exam results, but that's only part of the experience. For girls who can handle freedom and match up to high expectations, this school is a beacon.

Balcarras School

East End Road, Charlton Kings, Cheltenham, Gloucestershire, GL53 8QF

• Pupils: 1,345 pupils, 665 boys/680 girls • Ages: 11–18 • Non-denom • State

Tel: 01242 515881
Email: admin@balcarras.gloucs.sch.uk
Website: www.balcarras.gloucs.sch.uk

Headteacher: Since 1996, Mr Chris Healy BA MEd (fifties), educated at Xaverian College, Manchester, before reading history and politics at Nottingham. Returned to Manchester for his PGCE and picked up his MEd from Leicester University whilst teaching in Milton Keynes. Worked his way up through five comprehensives (including deputy headship of Tewkesbury

School and headship of John Masefield, Ledbury) before appointment at Balcarras.

Has raised academic profile here dramatically and is a great supporter of all extracurricular activity. Parents describe him as 'switched on' and attribute much of the school's success to his leadership. 'He knows how to attract the right staff and sorts any problems out quickly,' reported one satisfied parent. An approachable head who knows both pupils and staff well despite the size of the school. A 'head who makes things happen,' say staff, who know he is behind them: last four deputies proceeded to headships. Head regularly undertakes 'pupil pursuits' (shadowing pupils from different houses for a whole day) to gain a pupil's eye view of the school. Keen player in specialist schools' trust and enjoys working with other schools to help raise their standards.

Married to estate agent, Penelope; both their daughters went through Balcarras prior to university. 'Little time for leisure,' he says, but enjoys relaxing at home with his family when he can.

Academic matters: Specialist technology school which outperforms all other Gloucestershire comprehensives, with 88 per cent achieving five A*-C including English and maths at GCSE 2013, 37 per cent A*/A; impressive value-added scores too.

A level results, 68 per cent A*-B, 39 per cent A*/A, place it up with Cheltenham's big name independents and ahead of some of the county's selective schools – quite extraordinary. Over 30 courses through to A2 level in sixth; about 30 take critical thinking. Now offering AQA baccalaureate which involves 100 hours additional input from students. Results are all the more remarkable given that Pates in Cheltenham creams off a proportion of would-be Balcarras high flyers. We met pupils, though, who had turned down the chance to sit for Pates and were glad that they had done so.

Emphasis on lively lessons which hold pupils' interest. Number-crunching deputy has put lots of systems in place to evaluate pupil data and maximise pupil potential. Some parents we spoke to rated maths, business and science departments, whilst others pointed out modern languages and English.

The school's six dedicated ICT suites are well managed and heavily used. DIDA (diploma in digital applications) modular course is taught once or twice a week after school for those who can't be fitted into the timetable. Impressive technology areas underpin school's specialism: usual carousel arrangements to end of year 9, then all pupils pursue at least one technical area to GCSE. We watched an industrious and keen bunch of year 10 pupils in food technology, admired the products of the jewellery option as well as the high standard of woodworking and manufacturing. Some pupils act as mentors in food rooms for weekly visit by different groups from 'feeder' junior schools. We also watched year 8 pupils working in textiles area as part of 'mad hatter's project'.

Modern languages remarkably strong here, with French, Spanish (strong links with Spanish school) and (commendably) Russian holding up well through AS and A2 levels. Eighty per cent choose at least one MFL to GCSE level. Maths strong (60 A level candidates in year 12 and 11 taking further maths); 30 taking physics – all groups taught by qualified specialists.

School benefits from close link with Gloucestershire University education department: six trainees in school at any time. Lots of checks, it seems, on homework and classwork by HODs and senior staff to keep everyone up to the mark.

Well developed individual learning department provides additional help for 10 per cent of pupils who need it. Positive attitude throughout school towards learning support. LSAs assigned to different departments; lots of in-house expertise. Sixteen statemented pupils and several seriously challenged pupils come under the care of this well run department. Sixth formers receive training to help year 7 pupils through paired reading. All pupils are screened for SpLD using NFER and other tests. 'Pupil passports work better than old style IEPs,' says SENCo, who uses them to alert staff to pupils' particular learning needs. Plenty going on to enrich experience for pupils identified as gifted.

Games, options, the arts: Students here revel in the arts: acting, music, art and dance all grab their interest – lots go off to festivals and love getting involved in productions. Highly successful art department – 85 GCSE candidates. We saw exhibition of GCSE examination work which highlighted pupils' range of technical skill and creativity; some of best AS results in country. As many as 40 take art to A2 level with 20+ going on to foundation courses. Four large art studios with plenty of space for different age groups. Some pupils choose to do photography (includes film making and animation) and many work on their art projects during the lunch break or after school.

Purpose built drama studio with separate lighting studio hosts non-stop productions. Second drama studio has been created from former art room. Dance is also popular and takes place in gym or drama studio. Staff say that head is 'terrific supporter of the arts'. 'Fantastic music department,' say parents – eight different ensembles including hugely popular soul band. Two main music classrooms, recording studio and seven practice rooms – terrific buzz amongst musicians when we visited. House music is very popular with input from sixth formers.

Sport is promoted strongly and nearly all younger pupils participate in team games and extracurricular sporting activities. Full size, floodlit Astroturf and good grounds for rugby, cricket, athletics. Boys' and girls' hockey and plenty of tennis/netball courts. So-called 'pavilion' provides a modern space for dance, conferences and presentations. Super sports hall plus fitness suite used by year 10 and above. Pupils rate PE teaching and senior staff will come out to cheer on year 10 rugby players.

Lots of activities at all levels: scores participate in D of E up to gold award; biennial World Challenge expeditions as far afield as Mongolia and Costa Rica. Recent county and area winners in Young Enterprise; sixth formers last year were county winners in ESU Debating Mace, national finalists in Bar Mock Trial at Old Bailey. Annual activities week for years 7-9; camp for year 9 and work experience for year 10 all come at end of summer term.

Background and atmosphere: Positive atmosphere grabs you right away. Despite large numbers, feels like a smaller school. History on this site stretches back to 1958, when the co-ed Charlton Kings County Secondary School moved here. Balcarras was formed in 1986 as a result of a shake-up in the local education system which scrapped single sex schools. Architecturally a product of its era but with lots of modern infilling and a succession of stylish newer blocks to match the earlier ones. The sixth form centre has been extended in response to demand for places; modern languages block and new SEN building.

Lovely playing fields behind and imaginative use of areas between buildings help to give the school a different feel. Whole school has a cared for atmosphere which more than compensates for the utilitarian buildings. We liked the way that the sixth form area interconnects with the main school and the lay-out of the common room where we attended a personal pre-A level assembly given by the head which held students' interest and made good points at a crucial time. Separate computerised study carrels for lower and upper sixth – very impressive and heavily used by students including after school. Well resourced library used by all years, though somewhat small for the number of pupils.

Attractive canteen is popular: lots of healthy eating, good hot meals plus useful 'grab and go' sandwich bars. More pupils cycle to and from school since erection of new cycle sheds and three 'empty car park' days a term when 'even the head cycles to school'.

Pastoral care and discipline: Red hot on attendance – best in county. Strong house system (named after four prominent

Gloucestershire personalities) through main school with seven or eight classes in each year – 'Houses are cornerstone of school's success,' say some. Discipline is based upon committed house staff – for once we saw teaching staff doing lunchtime duties. Senior staff regularly walk the local area to make sure all is well – this goes down well with the community. Commonsense underwrites what goes on – head has to rack his brain to remember last suspension. 'Children don't overstep boundaries,' said one teacher, and we felt staff succeed in creating just the right kind of relationships with pupils, from the youngest to the sixth form.

Pupils and parents: Very mixed lot socially, but switched on to achieving good results whatever their background. Confident, happy pupils who hurry to lessons and work hard when they get there. Sixth formers less interested in Cheltenham's 'spiky' night life than a few years ago, according to head. Sensible, attractive uniform with polo shirts in summer denoting colour of houses in main school and well-interpreted dress code for sixth formers. Those we met were articulate and well-motivated with a confidence based on a 'can do' attitude. Access for disabled – two currently in wheelchairs and one mum spoke of how greatly one boy had benefited from the 'can do' attitude at Balcarras. Sixth formers organise lots of social and fundraising events. Former pupils include modern pentathlete, Jamie Cooke. Really supportive parents who count their blessings

Entrance: Admission criteria have changed to serve immediate catchment area of Charlton Kings. Previously, children living only a mile from the school were losing out to those in villages, now served by Cotswold School or others. 'Seems to be a much fairer arrangement,' says head, but one which inevitably pushes up local house prices. Two Bs and three Cs at GCSE (including English and maths) minimum requirement to enter sixth, which attracts large numbers from local state schools and also from independents.

Exit: Around 80 per cent stay on after GCSE. Ninety per cent to university after A level: five to Oxbridge in 2013; Cardiff popular, also Exeter, UWE, Leeds, Durham, Nottingham, Bath and Gloucester.

Remarks: Here's a school whose success owes much to the head, who moves it onwards and upwards every year. 'Don't ask me to give my son's place up,' joked one father. Great to see a comprehensive raising the bar in a highly competitive local educational market. Must be worth considering a move to Charlton Kings.

Balerno Community High School

5 Bridge Road, Balerno, EH14 7AQ

• Pupils: 800 boys and girls, all day • Ages: 11–18 • Non-denom • State

Tel: 01314 777788
Email: admin@balernochs.edin.sch.uk
Website: www.balernochs.edin.sch.uk

Headteacher: Since 2011, Mr Graeme Sives, whose predecessor, Mr Rory Mackenzie, was in post for 16 years and made a marked impact. His appointment came at a tricky time for Edinburgh senior schools, as cuts meant loss of many senior positions. Mr Sives, a graduate of Dundee with a PGCE from Moray House and an MSC in leadership and management from Glasgow, came to Balerno via Bathgate Academy, where he was a popular head of English and faculty head, and then Linlithgow, where he was

depute for four years. He impresses at first meeting as charismatic and a genuine philanthropist, speaking eloquently of choosing education because he so valued the educational opportunities and inspirations he received himself. Balerno had an excellent reputation but needed to respond to changing circumstances. Some £170,000 down on double-glazing alone, he is determined that 'a good school cannot rest on its laurels'. The school 'is in good nick for a 30 year old' but IT, originally at the forefront of the computer revolution in Edinburgh, is now 'in the dark ages and needs a massive spend which he is seeking to 'manage'. If charm and determination are anything to go by, he will succeed.

Academic matters: An inclusive school with a broad intake. Despite its leafy image, Balerno embraces a socially disparate catchment. Support for learning is run by a team of three specialists plus some really dedicated learning assistants, and Mr Sives is looking to integrate it with the guidance system. There are four guidance depute head teachers, one of whom is in charge of special needs. Scribing, individual sessions and withdrawal from class all available, plus comprehensive tutorial support, use of ICT (laptops available) and extra time in exams. Extra help from dedicated staff for the relatively few non-native English speakers. Six computer suites, used for proper lessons as well as ICT. Teaching is stimulating, if the lesson we took part in is anything to go by. Lots of well-informed S2 students, demonstrating verbal and personal assurance as well as an aptitude for scientific and historical research, acting as well-informed prosecution and defence in a mock trial. Courses on offer to suit all needs – with bags of helpful advice on new Scottish curriculum on the parents' website. SQA results in the top 10 per cent of Scottish state schools so pretty ok for the bright and motivated. ASDAN, vocational courses, business courses etc on offer as well as plenty of homework clubs, exam technique help etc. Mr Sives is developing access to as wide a range of courses as possible to suit all aptitudes and would like to develop this aspect of the already strong links Balerno has with the local community. A huge range of activities includes access to Malleny Gardens (Scottish National Trust) for some work experience.

Games, options, the arts: Despite now being desperate enough for new Astroturf to have raised it in the Scottish parliament, Balerno has an impressive sporting record. Currently, however, outworn facilities on site and sharing Malleny Park with Currie rugby club means that pitches are seldom playable, and hockey and football have suffered as a result. Even so, PE is a strong department and there are althletics, netball and three football teams, all with distinguished records.

Terrific drama – with exam courses at all levels. Lashings of music with instruments of all types resulting in a plethora of groups and choirs – some impressive – plus a trendy and very enterprising pop group doing well-advertised gigs and selling CDs and downloads via the internet. Art rooms were busy with younger pupils in bright yellow aprons, and plenty of artwork around in the curious little outdoor spaces made by the grid-like building structure. Home economics was full of a community group and groups also have access to the Riverside café.

Imaginatively international outlook for a Scottish suburban school, with masses of exchanges including Beijing, Stuttgart, and Budapest, under the Comenius initiative. There is a course in Mandarin as part of the British Council Confucius hub.

There is a huge array of extracurricular stuff from all sorts of sport and the range of outdoor education, Duke of Edinburgh etc you might expect from an independent schools as well as things like debating (at a pretty high level), journalism, Young Enterprise and Stock Market Challenge, trips for most subjects and a fantastic range of productions (West Side Story recently) and concerts. As an 'Eco School level 1' – whatever that may mean – and 'Healthy School level 2', Balerno is not letting the grass grow under its feet.

Won the Lothian finals for Young Enterprise. Work experience for all at S4 and work shadowing in sixth. Parents and school find the positions – a joint effort. Popular clubs post-school, at lunchtime and in the evening: Spanish, web development, electronics and publishing as well as extracurricular dance, snowboarding (Hillend and the real thing), hockey and athletics. Keen charity input.

Background and atmosphere: Has historic antecedents – the charming logbook kept by the principal teacher of St Mungo's Episcopal School in Balerno during the 19th century is a joy: 'Wet and windy all week. One child was blown into the Water of Leith but was fortunately rescued. One child was bit by a dog ... '. The present school was opened on a glorious greenfield site on the banks of the Water of Leith, after several years of 'swithering' in 1983. Somehow in the process the futuristic vision of a community school turned into something resembling a 60s nuclear power station. It's nearly as difficult to get in since the entrance is un-signposted and in an apparently dead-end corner. (The welcome, however, is warm.) Huge long passages, bare concrete staircases with scaffolding poles as banisters and narrow staircases. Much money has disappeared attempting to install ceilings where they were never meant to be and Mr Sives has sensibly given up the attempt and is spending whatever he can get on facilities. The plus factor is a long spacious indoor area which feels like a shopping mall and is wonderful for community events like craft fairs. It also forms a wet weather concourse with access to everything.

The community affiliation provides the school with all sorts of ancillary activities including a serious 20-metre swimming pool as well as some outstanding public areas. Balerno people definitely see it as their school and are proud of its achievements and its role in community education and enterprise.

Pastoral care and discipline: Strong anti-bullying strategies in conjunction with S6. All pupils join one of four houses called after local areas, siblings in same house; heads of houses are in charge of pastoral care and guidance. Tutorial system for all, same tutor throughout the school, good contact for parents on academic matters. Head Start for 'vulnerable' pupils before they begin at Balerno, when the new S1, sixth form and staff spend a week confidence building. S1 pupils also spend a bonding week with their guidance and pastoral staff at one of four residential centres during their first term (Monday – Friday). Regular year group and house assemblies. Head boy and girl play a strong leadership role. School uniform definitely for all, with high standards of presentation demanded.

Pupils and parents: Balerno is right on the edge of the countryside so it attracts every strata of the farming population as well as both comfortably suburban and distinctly urban areas of Edinburgh. About 10 per cent ethnic minorities. Exceptionally well-organised parent council and a PTA raising significant funds.

Entrance: From three dedicated primaries: Dean Park, Ratho and Kirknewton, plus at least 20 others whose pupils request placements. Pupils from outwith the area may have problems with the regular school bus but parents' council helps to provide extra buses.

Exit: A few leave to try their hand in the workplace after S4 (low employment rate), or go on to tertiary education elsewhere. Most stay on for two more years. Seventy per cent or so go on to university; strong links with the local high-tariff universities: Edinburgh, Heriot Watt for science, Aberdeen and Glasgow, plus a tiny trickle to Oxbridge or southern unis.

Remarks: A community school which is learning to use its local roots for the benefit of community and pupils alike.

Balfron High School

Roman Road, Balfron, G63 0PW

• Pupils: 970 boys and girls, all day • Ages: 11–18 • Non-denom • State

Tel: 01360 440469
Email: balfronhs@stirling.gov.uk
Website: www.balfronhigh.org.uk

Head Teacher: Since 2002, Mrs Val Corry BSc (Eng) ARSM PGCE SQH (fifties) who took an unusual course into the heady world of academe. Educated at Morpeth Girls' Grammar School and Imperial College London, where she read metallurgy and engineering, her first job was researcher for British Steel, which she swapped for teacher training at Moray House followed by Grangemouth High and a post partum dabble in ceramics. Then back onto the academic ladder, where she leapfrogged through Linlithgow Academy (she lives in Linlithgow), and Stirling and Wallace High (depute head). She still teaches (physics, PHSE, maths and chemistry); well worn lab coat on the back of her door; 'does people good to see you teach'; and tries to have 'real contact with at least half the school every year' by interviewing pupils individually and in small groups.

Sharp, elegant role model, she has transformed this zinging new school into a 21st century flagship and is totally at ease with the current gov-education-speak (though one or two less savvy locals mutter about 'modern educational mumbo jumbo'...) Oversaw the founding of the Balfron Trust, which was launched in October 2011 – a charitable fund designed to 'enhance the educational, cultural, social and sporting experiences of young people who attend Balfron High School and to promote equality and diversity and to overcome disadvantage consistent with the aims of the school... The School continues to receive sufficient funds for this purpose. However, the funding received is limited and sometimes prevents activities or events that are seen as "extra"; or buying items which enhance experiences.' A bold – if controversial – move which, in these hard times, might well be a wise one.

Academic matters: School has taken to the curriculum for excellence with a vengeance. The three existing houses act as mother-ship for three school-lets (known as schools, following the American model) with a ninth of each year in each school. The form teacher for each year stays with that class throughout their time in school. Class teachers are responsible for the pastoral care of their children and may well teach their form for some seven hours a week, so all pupils know there is someone out there batting for them. Max class size 20 in the first year, in practical subjects and in maths and English in S3, with extra maths and Eng in S3 if needed. Slightly complicated system of mix-and-match with hist and geog (social subjects course) – 'a standard rota used by schools and not complicated', says head; specialist staff from S2. Fiercely academic – 'Not so', says head, 'we do far more here than concentrate on academic subjects' – and high uptake in all advanced higher subjects. Strong science school with marvellous labs (but marvellous everything, see below); biology lab has a greenhouse incorporated into its roof. Labs are an astonishing, carpeted, 90 metres square.

Head thrilled that number of pupils getting five subjects at higher level has grown to nearly 50 per cent over past few years but we have no up-to-date results as school requests its removal from GSG website. Flexible learning not a problem and sixth formers and local adults (evenings) can log on to do distance learning courses; sociology the current flavour of the month. Strong links with Forth Valley College and Skillforce for less academic. Computers abound, three pupils per machine, and emails for all. Whiteboards in every classroom. Problems picked up early, and reported immediately, so that any child finding difficulty should be 'sorted out' quickly – via house meeting, which will include deputy head plus support-for-learning teacher and other appropriate staff, and remedial strategies discussed: professional support, ed psychs pulled in if needed. Qualified head of support for learning plus three others and four assistants in school. This is an inclusive school, capable of dealing with physical disabilities. Terrific library overlooking the atrium, with views out over the games pitches to The Campsies.

Games, options, the arts: School incorporates a fabulous leisure complex with pool, sports hall and weights much used by the local community and open from 7am to 10pm, 365 days a year. (Fantastically fit local community then? – not immediately obvious from mass of adult humanity passing through reception whilst we were waiting!) Excellent swimming (25-metre pool), Astroturf, pitches and athletics track. Masses of games after school, Stirling Council (and the lottery) provide a sports co-ordinator; rugby good – both national and international players in the school, and list of names of all national players of any sport in reception. Art is state of, with every possible medium catered for and finished products creeping onto the walls and a rather chic patio. Computer-linked CDT mass of machines. First year must do home economics, thereafter optional between third and sixth – flash new kitchens with microwaves. Terrific theatre and drama, the theatre available to the community, and masses of music, with local involvement. String, wind and jazz plus Teudan Teth fiddle band, myriad choirs and boy groups plus countless talent shows and clubs at lunch time. Work experience for all at 14. Masses of trips and exchanges, for culture and education (ie skiing is out). Strong links with school in Malawi and a huge amount of exchange – staff as well as pupils. School will underwrite those who can't afford it. Huge amount of charity work and much local involvement, including a guide dog puppy called Faith.

Background and atmosphere: Opened in May 2002 by Helen Liddle, who celebrated the partnership between Stirling Council and Jarvis by sticking the first leaf on the 'school tree of learning', which climbs up the corner of the atrium adjacent to the dining room, where pupils either bring their own or use swipecards (which conceals the free school meals problem – about four per cent). Graduands (to continue the American theme) have their name embossed on a leaving leaf, which is firmly fixed to the 30 foot high tree by the intrepid janitor.

A magnet school. State-of-the-art in every dimension – each subject has a pod of rooms off the main core, terrific views, marvellous outside area (the sun does occasionally shine north of the Highland Line). The school was built under a PFI scheme by Jarvis of Railtrack fame – now bust; catering and maintenance provided by same staff but now employed by SGP and, apparently, 'brilliant'. Magical food with mass of choice. All the rooms are networked for sound (as well as inter/intra netted) and at 10.45am loudspeaker announcements about sin on the school bus, praise for work well done and extra music lessons boom over the speakers. Electronic noticeboard advertising weekend jobs at the local pub. School became a community school proper in 2003 but the old boards still reassuringly in place. School uniform for all: trainers out and shirt and tie back due to pupil demand, atop some of the shortest skirts we have seen this year; smart blue blazers with green trim loaned annually to sixth formers, who must have them cleaned before they are returned.

Pastoral care and discipline: State system of pupil support, good PSHE and anti-bullying strategies in place. 'Balfriending' is a buddy system between first and sixth years which really works. Masses of contact, sixth pick up problems early; incidents are logged, the victim supported and the bully sanctioned –

sanctions range from verbal warnings through 'the imposition of a written exercise' (restorative exercise' = reflections) to temporary or even permanent exclusions and ed psychs etc. Head maintains that most bullying is really just 'a breakdown in relationships'.

Pupils and parents: Huge catchment area: 800 children bused in each day. Good middle class ethos prevails – 'we are a comprehensive school', the head reminds us – combo of real country plus incomers, friendly and welcoming children; few from ethnic minority backgrounds. Enthusiastic parents' council which seems to spend time worrying about 'incidents' behind the (unused) bike shed and why special praise seems to be singled out for athletes. Head stresses that they raise money for the school, help with careers advice and interviews, and work with school to manage road traffic problems.

Entrance: From local primaries, capped at 180, usually 30 or so placing requests.

Exit: Few leave after Standard Grades, around 90 per cent stay for Higher of whom 70 per cent will stay till sixth form. Most to Scottish universities – Ed and Glasgow top of the pops with the odd one or two to St Andrews, and occasional trickle to Oxbridge.

Remarks: Stunning school, happy staff, good work ethos, some of the best views in Scotland. Worth moving to the Trossachs for.

Bancroft's School

Linked school: Bancroft's Preparatory School

611–627 High Road, Woodford Green, IG8 0RF

• Pupils: 855 pupils, 465 boys/395 girls • Ages: 11–18 • C of E, but Jews and Muslims properly provided for; all other faiths welcomed • Fees: £14,130 pa • Independent

Tel: 020 8505 4821
Email: stephanie.wallis@bancrofts.org
Website: www.bancrofts.org

Head: Since January 2008, Mrs Mary Ireland BSc DipEd Member Soc of Biologists, chartered biologist (early fifties). Career began with Proctor and Gamble, but light dawned, she took her teaching qualification and has taught all three sciences and maths in both state and independent schools. Prior to Bancroft's, she was deputy head of Christ's Hospital, before which she had been housemistress at Ardingly and head of science at King's Hall.

Married, with a grown-up musician son, brisk, open, energetic, easy to talk to, attractive Scots intonation. True, professional head, clear about her modernising agenda – lost no time in implementing changes – and as clear about the values upon which Bancroft's was founded and which still inform its ethos. She has clearly been won over by the school and its community, 'The buildings have a wow factor – though I tell parents that they are not what the school is about – but the thing that really appealed to me was the children. They are London children who tell it how it is, multi-racial, striving children who want to do well – they are incredibly competitive. They do everything here that we did at Christ's Hospital, only they cram it into a school day'.

A safe pair of hands – and not hands that mind getting dirty: she cleared up a lunch that slid off a pupil's plate onto the floor when we visited. She is involved, busy and available. Some of her changes not immediately understood by school community, restructuring of the school council and the popular Stars in their Eyes extravaganza being two. Introduction of new Virtual Learning Environment – internet school-home communications system – hit by predictable teething troubles and much groused about, but now a useful asset. She manages to teach some GCSE biology – we applaud. Bancroft's has continued to thrive under her eager eye and hands-on regime.

Academic matters: Notable results across the board (2013 nearly 86 per cent A*/A grades at GCSE) but maths is a star performer by any standards. English more of a spread, despite reports of some brilliantly inspirational teaching. Modern langs getting a boost – all year 7s learn German and Spanish; Russian is an option from year 9; Mandarin recently introduced. Greek and Latin have healthy numbers. Remarkable science results – especially in chemistry. History and geography also impressive. Few takers for art, music and DT – surprising, given the facilities – but a school which takes its academics seriously. No trendy subjects, though drama has seduced its way into the timetable and options list. A particular, enlightened feature is that subjects can be chosen not, as elsewhere, from 'blocks' but from the whole curriculum. If they can manage it at Bancroft's, why not everywhere?

A level results similarly impressive – 89 per cent A*-B, 63 per cent A*/A in 2013. Maths and chemistry popular and successful. Demand for maths and sciences has led to creation of new maths room and science lab. Economics and geography good and, at this level, English also impresses. Greek and Latin survive, though the numbers taking modern langs are, we would suggest, a cause for concern, though may reflect the immense diversity of backgrounds here.

A place where serious learning happens and in which learning is taken seriously. The library, recently revamped with a stylish new mezzanine floor beautifully integrated into the whole, is a proper scholarly resource – not something you see everywhere these days, when for 'library' you can so often read 'IT suite'. Pupils appreciate the library and its staff – 'They are fantastic – they get in anything you need'. Sixth form has a very recent, dedicated library and quiet study area plus university-type lecture theatre – used for societies, debates and visiting speakers. IT everywhere – lots of rooms with new PCs, including a brand new, tiptop language lab, which should give the languages a deserved boost.

Learning support department screens all at 11+ (the prep also screens at 7+). Mrs Ireland appointed the school's first SENCo and has also ensured that all new staff get some training in SpLD. All on the LS register (mostly mild dyslexics) have an IEP and get some kind of individual support – the younger ones come out of different lessons each term and older ones get one-to-one. A TA in class helps those who are happy to be helped in that way. Lower sixth get help to 'develop individual learning skills'. 'They are wonderfully flexible over special needs,' says a parent.

Games, options, the arts: Sports are 'big' and well-resourced. Large playing fields on site plus vast sports hall with 25m pool. Five minutes away is school's own West Grove with pitches, courts, tracks etc. Achievement to match – triumphs in netball, rugby and cricket as well as tours in these and hockey to, eg, New Zealand, Australia South Africa and Sri Lanka. Heart-felt pupil and parental complaints that sport is too elitist – 'if you're not in a squad, they don't give a monkey's' – seen by Mrs Ireland as a priority and B and C teams now being developed, along with soccer. 'We are encouraging more staff to help so we can run more teams. It's something we need to work on.'

CCF is huge, very popular and enthusiastically pursued by those who surprise themselves by how much they get out of it, girls as well as boys – 'It's taught me how to get on with people I'd never mix with normally'; 'It's good that the sixth form help with it – you can have a bit of a laugh with them': not common in what is still, more or less, a London school. Thriving D of E and Sea Scout group with cubs, scouts and explorer sections.

Equally, Mrs Ireland was determined to boost time for arts across the school and has steadily increased provision. Music and drama enthusiastic and popular – annual concert in Drapers' Hall the big annual event, with bands, solo performances and musical mix the main features. Vast range of instruments studied – music maybe more pop and jazz than classical, though we are told around eight classical concerts each year. Drama had a recent fillip with conversion of old gym to good, large new studio and subject now on the curriculum at all levels. Not all musicals here, either – The Caucasian Chalk Circle and Macbeth among recent productions; year 9 and 10 performers taught to fence for their production of The Three Musketeers. Productions at Edinburgh Fringe Festival.

Art, electronics and DT departments produce lively work – we liked the clever clocks, mobiles and the remote control cars and, within the remit of the task, pupils are given their head to be creative with the actual design. Art, exceptionally well-displayed throughout school, originates in one of two brand new studios with kilns and exhibition space – light, spacious and full of quiet artists. Nice ceramics. Art could and should be bigger here – perhaps textiles and photography (on the way), as more than a club?

Tons of trips and tours – though some parental gripes about not enough places on trips for eager applicants. Extracurricular stuff is good, though some cries for more from the inexhaustible.

Background and atmosphere: Founded in 1737 by the Drapers' Company on behalf of Francis Bancroft as a school for poor boys; moved to Woodford from Mile End in 1889 into the present large and imposing red-brick Victorian Gothic revival building – clearly designed to impress, with serious scholarly credentials by architect, Sir Arthur Blomfield, also responsible for Selwyn College, Cambridge, The RCM, much of Charterhouse, The Bank of England, Wellington, Eton Lower Chapel etc etc, as well as an astounding number of parish churches. This is one of his more benign and attractive buildings, with towers, crenellations and oriel windows, a splendid central quad and admirably generous corridors which, though originally intended for 200 boys, still feel spacious for today's quadrupled numbers.

A truly impressive school with twisty, brick staircases and leaded lights which grab eager 10 year olds immediately – 'I chose it because it was like Hogwarts': a unique selling point in Essex, to be sure. Large Great Hall – typical of date and type. Excellent Courtyard Building with colonnaded atrium and sitting area, dining room (all eat together; good food, though popular vegetarian option can run out too fast for true veggie latecomers, we're told), servery and sixth form common room and café: large and well-used. Some typically dismal 1960s add-ons but much better later additions (such as enormous multi-purpose sports hall) and adjoining buildings, eg vast head's house now used for admin and offices too, with head's garden open to everyone for quiet time and 'well-respected'. Very recent physics labs and modern language rooms.

Integral chapel one of the best bits (complete with much-loved chaplain who is 'lovely, a wonderful person for a chat, a laugh and advice – he takes Salsa club'), into which everyone comes once weekly for an ecumenical service. Brass plaques to former heads and a vast stained glass east window set the tone for the services, which are inclusive in all ways, given the mix of pupils. Chapel also used for arts events – words and music etc, a classy extracurricular feature here.

Parental tributes to general efficiency of school and its communications. Sense of order, purposeful activity and common sense all-pervasive.

Pastoral care and discipline: When asked what was good about the school, all the parents and pupils we spoke to – lots – said, as with one voice, 'the pastoral care' – we can't recall such unanimity on any other school feature anywhere. Tributes to the teaching staff, overall friendliness, care and attention given to individuals pour from everyone and are a delight to hear: 'My teacher is amazing – he's given me extra lessons every week. He's ordered in around 30 extra books just to help me. They'll help with anyone – not just the Oxbridge candidates'; 'The teacher gave my daughter as much time as she needed when she was struggling'; 'The staff commitment is excellent; pastoral care couldn't be better'; 'My children love it – they look forward to every day'.

Pupils and parents: From as far away as Potter's Bar, Winchmore Hill and Cheshunt, though most from between 10 and 20 minutes' drive away. Transport from local tube station to encourage pupils to look out of town towards green space for schooling. Vast ethnic and social intake – 'very well-handled by school,' say parents: around 30-35 per cent South Asian, 10-15 per cent Jewish, 40 per cent 'white Essex'. Most parents first-time buyers who 'work very hard to pay fees'.

OB notables include Dennis Quilley, Sir Frederick Warner, Sir Neil McFarlane, Hari Kunzru, Adam Foulds, Yolanda Browne, Andrew Saul, Anita Anand, Lord Pannick QC, Samantha Spiro and Mike Lynch.

Entrance: At 11, 50 come up from the school's own prep. Around 400 apply for 60 additional places. Tests in maths and English plus interviews. In practice around a third of those whose first choice is Bancroft's will get in. Umpteen feeders, though several from St Aubyn's, Loyola and Woodford Green Prep. Around a quarter from state primaries.

Candidates for the sixth form sit the school's own entrance exam in two proposed AS subjects, need six As at GCSE plus the usual references. Around 20 places at this level – very few leave.

Exit: Around 10 per cent leave post GCSE. In 2013, 12 to Oxbridge; Nottingham, Warwick, London, Bristol and Exeter all popular.

Money matters: Fifteen Drapers' scholarships offered annually at 11+ worth a quarter to a half of fees. No means-testing – based solely on performance at entrance exams. Also music scholarships worth half or quarter fees plus free tuition in one instrument. Several Francis Bancroft scholarship awards – means-tested but with a generous financial threshold, worth up to full fees, based on a sliding scale dependent on family income. Bancroft's Foundation set up in 2012 to mark 275th anniversary has already raised significant amounts to increase means tested provision – enough to fund six Foundation scholars.

Remarks: A splendid school, catering for bright children and those who will seize opportunities. Deservedly over-subscribed. Brings glory to Essex well beyond its immediate catchment.

Basil Paterson Tutorial College

Linked school: Basil Paterson Middle School

66 Queen Street, Edinburgh, EH2 4NA

• Pupils: 35 boys and girls. EFL College operates separately on same site. • Ages: 14–19 (but currently some in their 20s) • Non-denom • Fees: On application • Independent

Tel: 01312 253802
Email: info@basilpaterson.co.uk
Website: www.basilpaterson.co.uk

Head: Since 2009, Susan Shaw (40s). EFL qualified and previously director of studies at the Edinburgh School of English. Bubbly and fun, she is obviously enjoying her role as fairy godmother to her students (interestingly, referred to throughout as learners), many of whom may have found school intimidating, chosen the wrong course, suffered absence through illness or been asked by higher authorities to complete their education elsewhere. Shaw aims to bond with learners (tactful at steering), guiding them through both subject and university choices, negotiating UCAS applications, supervising personal statements, helping with clearing (for those who have fallen by the wayside or decided to change unis) and generally looking after their welfare.

Shaw and director of studies, Enrique, select the tutors, some of whom are ful-time.

Academic matters: Edinburgh's oldest and most famous tutorial college, founded in 1929 to offer 'bespoke education for all', comes under the umbrella of the Oxford Intensive School of English (OISE) empire. The answer to many a parent's prayer. Huge number of subjects on offer: Scottish highers, advanced highers and intermediate 2s; plus GCSE and AS/A levels with all three English exam boards. College is an accredited exam centre for SQA, Edexcel, OCR and AQA, plus Cambridge exams on the EFL side.

Edinburgh is rich in tutors, and a team of part-timers cover almost every subject under the sun (psychology currently the poor relation). Maximum class size six, many individual lessons. Flexi-tuition popular, college is open till 6.30 pm, students top up existing grades, study subjects incompatible with the customary five column choices. Most follow the well-worn path to further education. Not an SEN refuge per se, but often the perfect solution for the dyslexic, refusnik (who may well have been bullied), or those previously educated abroad who find a tutorial college more appealing than a conventional sixth form.

Well-equipped (costs extra) lab, art students now opt for trad art colleges. Three hours' tuition per subject for GCSE per week, four or six for Highers/AS levels and Advanced Highers/full A levels. Impressive success rate. Some courses require continuous course work assessment (evaluation and review) and the odd learner may be advised to either change course or level of study. SEN assistance on hand (specialist staff), the SQA now need physical evidence of the need for scribes or extra time, an ed psych report is no longer sufficient. The full-time course includes supervised study as well as a social programme in conjunction with the larger English language wing, not much take up in the latter.

Popular revision sessions during the Easter holidays are regularly oversubscribed.

Middle school for 14-16 year olds opened in August 2012, (GCSE and IGCSEs only) and about to move next door (OISE are big on property and on language schools). The college and middle school share many tutors but are apparently prevented by 'licensing' from sharing accommodation, which would cut down the need for duplicated dedicated classrooms. This is a new one to us.

Background and atmosphere: Two splendid Georgian houses strategically joined together at ground and basement in Edinburgh's posh Queen Street. Some original ceilings still visible, with 12 classrooms of random size, some with spectacular views to the north over the Firth of Forth, state-of-the-art computers (email access for all), student common room and study centre. A dedicated wireless area encourages the use of personal laptops. Place currently needs a spot of TLC round the edges.

College can offer non-local students accommodation through their international EFL host family set-up, not a lot of take-up. Most students are home grown, living with family/ies or in flats in and around Edinburgh.

Queen Street is home to the Edinburgh New Town Cooking School which seemed to us to be a useful add-on, but most prefer the gym at nearby Bannantynes; learners have a key to Queen Street gardens, but use Meadowbank sports centre for circuit training, swimming, tennis and the like.

Pastoral care and discipline: Learners are expected to take a certain amount of responsibility for their studies. Each student and parent/guardian must sign a student support agreement to agree to abide by the school rules. Strong anti-drug bias. Equally hot on time-keeping, regular phone calls both to parents and to students: habitual offenders may be expelled. Homework must be handed in on time, with the threat of remaining on the premises till finished. Regular reports to parents, couple of parents' evenings during the year to 'meet the tutors', compulsory for tutors – on our last visit they were still throwing out the empties – apparently not really a bonding experience for parents.

Pupils and parents: Currently 10 per cent from abroad plus first-time candidates (visa requirements apply for non-Brits); retakes and those hopeful of upping grades. Numbers have a habit of more than doubling during the autumn term as pupils decide to change tack. Most learners fall into the 16-19 age bracket, but the college has students of all ages – up to 70+.

Entrance: Enrolment form must be completed and £300 deposit paid before starting classes. Students are encouraged to meet with the head before starting to discuss subject choices, suitability etc.

Exit: Most to universities across the UK. Past students have gone on to study at (among others) Glasgow, Edinburgh, St Andrews, Aberdeen, Leeds, Newcastle, Strathclyde, Heriot-Watt, University of Manchester, Napier, and Goldsmith's. This year's crop of leavers included a would-be medic to Aberdeen, an ocean scientist to Plymouth, and one to Abertay to study computer gaming (another first for us).

Money matters: Fees are per subject per year and are invoiced termly or by other arrangement.

Remarks: Up and running. An Edinburgh legend still delivering the goods. Numbers usually double between September and December.

Beaconhurst

Linked school: Beaconhurst Junior School

52 Kenilworth Road, Bridge of Allan, Stirling, FK9 4RR

• Pupils: 370 boys and girls; all day • Ages: 11–18 • Fees: £10,626 pa • Independent

Tel: 01786 832146
Email: secretary@beaconhurst.com
Website: www.beaconhurst.com

Headmaster: Since July 2012, Mr John Owen, previously sub-warden (principal deputy head) at Glenalmond College. He is a Fellow of the Royal Society of Chemistry, has been chair of the British Association of International Mountain Leaders for some time, and puts his instructor qualifications in skiing and canoeing to good use.

Academic matters: Small classes, max year group is 30; the 40 currently in transition (P7) are split in two; certain amount of streaming in core subjects. Dedicated tutors from transition, max 14 per group. Italian from junior school (P1) with French and German until S2. Lang labs and 'successful' pupil exchanges. Scottish system: combo Standard, Intermediate II, Higher and Advanced Highers. in 2013, 39 per cent As at Standard, 62 per cent at Intermediate, 13 per cent at Highers and 31 per cent at Advanced Highers. All must do English, maths and courses in IT, core PE, social education, enterprise and young enterprise at S6. Otherwise all the usual suspects, with Spanish club at lunchtime. Product design popular. No classics, strong maths (regulars in Scottish math challenge) and science. Pupils can add to their Higher portfolio or do Advanced Higher in S6. Enthusiastic business admin.

Four computer suites, younger pupils use them too, and whizzo multi-coloured computer in the nursery, where pupils do jolly phonics and only move up to junior school when 'they are good and ready'. Functional looking labs, where, for some reason, offerings from the art dept appear to proliferate (stuck on the door, hanging from the ceiling – apparently they are made in the science labs: a sort of do it yourself atom, 'science department being creative'). Assorted sized, grubby, white lab coats hang from a couple of nearby racks – 'Help yourselves'. Interactive whiteboards abound (we spotted a couple of staff carting two new ones during our interview – 'Cheaper to do it yourself rather than employing a contractor to rig them up') plus data projectors. School heavily into IT and has adopted the virtual learning environment, where pupils can access course work remotely and email both homework and queries to staff.

All pupils assessed for dyslexia and other learning difficulties at J1, though some may have been picked up in nursery. Terrific support for learning, with three support for learning teachers plus a collection of part time qualified (SLAS) assistants throughout (the latter are often older, the qualification takes a year, and they are a 'really valuable support'). Withdrawn, co-teaching – school claims they can 'deal with anything'. Keyboarding skills are mainly enforced in the learning support unit, but touch typing from J1 and 'developed all the way through'. Scribes, readers, extra time in exams, digital exams – you name it: the systems are in place.

Games, options, the arts: Boys' footie team plus hockey teams for both sexes, girls had fun trip to Canada a bit ago. School 'two minutes' walk' from stunning sports complex at Stirling University and makes full use of all facilities – swimming pool, athletics, basketball. Sports students help resident PE staff, regular matches on Sat am. Dedicated sports hall below school dining room with cricket nets shrouding the walls when we visited and available to rent for £150 a pop.

Extensive expressive arts: orchestras, singing for all and really professional drama – compulsory either to perform or to work backstage: brilliant for talent spotting. Choir performs on occasion at Dunblane Cathedral, acclaimed jazz band, some talented young players. Quite small music house away from rest of school for individual lessons. Strong links with Scottish Opera. Charming head of art, who explained she could cover most disciplines – pottery, sculpture, fabric design (but not fabrication), though the offerings on show were a tad mundane: better pieces on the walls around the school.

Geography, theatre et al, trippettes to Glasgow, Edinburgh, wherever. Ski trip to proper abroad, plus visits to Fir Park at Tillicoutry – skiing part of standard grade sport, but not really factored into the Scottish scene: the odd weekend perhaps. High emphasis on (compulsory) outdoor week with real rock climbing, bonding time for prefects at local outdoor pursuits centre; D of E to silver: compulsory. Young Enterprise, work experience. Variety of clubs and splendid charity fundraising with one girl recently arranging a sponsored hair cut (wow!). Hands on charity in India – Beyond Barriers: one year fundraising, next year visiting. No home economics, which seems a missed opportunity.

Background and atmosphere: Number 52 Kenilworth Road boasts a slightly larger site than its neighbours (a random collection of B&Bs and rather grand family homes – the one on offer at £835,000+ went for over a million), but it is incredibly up and downy, with fairly shallow steep steps in all directions.

Windy. For some reason a bus stop-like shelter has been plonked half way up the steps from the science labs to the main campus – 'The weather is awful here,' said our guide, 'and it is really, really useful'.

Assorted collection of fairly pedestrian classroom blocks shoe-horned into what is really quite a small area. Jolly hopscotch and dragons painted on strips of tarmac for youngsters to play on and dedicated nursery area – though no obvious buggies or trikes during our visit (apparently they were garaged). The Cameron Hall is now fully functional and a great asset. The main house (1868 and not that much bigger than its neighbours) which was the original Beacon School for Girls (founded 1919, dreary dame school, had long outlived its usefulness) has been much mauled around (historic Scotland?) and boasts a harum scarum collection of classrooms, store rooms and reception.

A tiny (and admittedly 'much neglected') library boasts computers and a good collection of fiction, but not much for research – we know computers are useful, but paper research is sometimes more rewarding (subject based matter apparently in subject depts). Library open over lunch and post school. Head made much of the (two) comfy sofas, but the sixth formers we met were busy at the table (sums) or the computer, and an outgoing bunch they were too – not often are we asked, 'Where were you at university?'

Beacon School amalgamated with Hurst Grange, a boys' prep in Stirling, to become Beaconhurst in 1976, dropped the boarding and transmogrified into an all day, 3-18 school during the '90s. Chaps, with varying length of hair, and girls neat in (Black) Douglas kilted skirts plus rather expensive looking blazers with bound edges do the school proud. School aiming for eco green flag. Pupil council. No religious bias. Only new dining/sports hall complex wheelchair friendly, but inner driveway makes for a certain amount of accessibility.

Pastoral care and discipline: PSHE throughout, with emphasis on healthy living and 'appropriate progression'. Tutor groups and strong prefect programme interlinked with a four house system – senior pupils take on responsibilities within school and work with younger pupils. Our guide said school was small enough to pick up any possible cliques or bullying.

Pupils and parents: Large number of first time buyers plus amorphous middle class parents. Apart from local small business folk and farmers, some work in oil refinery in Grangemouth which employs a number of non Brits. Fair geographic spread – some bussed in, school mini bus meets train at local station. Congestion problems with collection at tiny car parks – no dedicated visitors' parking!

Entrance: Tinies spend session in nursery and are informally assessed; otherwise two day taster for all – prospective pupil 'buddied' for first day, joining in all lessons, followed by tests in literacy and numeracy and verbal and non-verbal reasoning, with the cognitive ability aspect taken by learning support department. Automatic passage throughout the school thereafter. Some waiting lists.

Exit: Occasional trad family exit to the wider public school system – not many of those; some to Dollar et al for wider choice of Highers (or bigger pond to play in), and one or two leave early for vocational or other reasons, most into some form of further education, with the occasional gap year. Business and sports studies and IT popular, but horses for courses – beauty therapists, civil engineers and medics. Most to Scottish universities.

Money matters: Scholarships available both to those already in school and external candidates. Some form of means-tested bursarial help may be available.

Remarks: Charming little school, grown from a couple of fairly non-performing boarding/day preps to a thriving, fully fledged, grown-up school in the last 24 years. Stunning, little, two class Junior Start, which got a most impressive Care Commission report recently.

Bearsden Academy

Stockiemuir Road, Bearsden, G61 3SF

• Pupils: 1,185 boys and girls (55/45), capped at 210 first-year intake (seven classes of 30); all day • Ages: 11–18 • Non-denom • State

Tel: 01419 552344
Email: office@bearsdenacademy.e-dunbarton.sch.uk
Website: www.bearsdenacademy.e-dunbarton.sch.uk

Headteacher: Since 2008, Mr George F Cooper (forties), who neither wants to talk to us, nor to 'give any more details': he comes from Ayr Academy, where he was depute head and was previously head of English. He was – to quote our informant – 'at Ayr for many many years' and came to Bearsden Academy in the footsteps of the legendary Mike Doig, who turned the school around, following a period of some unsettlement. Cooper faced a serious challenge a few years ago when the school moved to a new site on the perimeter of St Andrews Primary, on the old college site, a term later than planned.

Academic matters: School takes Standard, Intermediate 1, Intermediate 2, Highers and Advanced Highers. (Pupils may also be presented for both Intermediate 2 and 1 instead of the Standard; they have different weighting.) German and French but no Spanish, and three separate sciences; maths and English results 'consistently strong'. Pupils are setted in their second year for English, maths, French and sciences. Not a vast choice of subjects but totally adequate with the non-academic well represented. Most pupils take eight subjects at Standard grade. No details of exam results as 'we do not wish to be featured in your publication'.

Pupils are allocated a guidance teacher during their last year at primary, who acts as tutor throughout their time in secondary. Smashing library which also includes a careers office and much-used sixth form study centre. Six fully-equipped computing/business rooms – the library has a well-equipped computer room – fabulous dedicated space (books being added to all the time). Work ethos is important here, ditto homework, and homework diary must be signed by parent or guardian but pupils can complain 'to their Guidance teacher if they feel that they are unable to cope with homework'.

Support for learning throughout, with learning support staff visiting the linked primary schools to ensure a smooth transition. Four support for learning assistants, who work with children both on an individual basis and in class, scribing if need be; can deal with normal (mild) Asperger's et al, no currently diagnosed ADHD. New-build wheelchair friendly, no (real) problems with profoundly deaf or visually impaired pupils. EAL on hand, over 22 different nationalities in the school, many of whom do not speak English as their first language.

Games, options, the arts: Stunning games hall and, as a community school, this is much used by locals too. Good spread of games pitches; school does remarkably well at rugby, football, with athletics well-represented. Outstanding success in football and basketball. No tennis courts or swimming pool but skiing, snowboarding are popular options, regular trips abroad – the Alps as well as Aviemore. Ex-pupil rower Katherine Grainger won gold at the 2012 Olympics. Superb home economics facility, with pupils learning how to wash and iron, as well as cook and operate electronic sewing machines.

Cultural trips to Paris and Florence and large successful art department, fabric design as well as pure art. Music fantastic, choirs and orchestras of all descriptions, rock band seems to be on the wane. Drama extracurricular but a popular club – pantomime and Shakespeare in alternating years. Long-standing Young Enterprise. Work experience in fourth year, with loads of private placements. Clubs highly popular, and the board game club specialises in esoteric conundrums that make the mind boggle; enthusiastic web club. Massive charity input from seniors in particular, with five-figure sums raised every year. World Challenge Expeditions to Thailand, Mongolia, Tanzania et al.

Background and atmosphere: Now on swish new site. Prefectorial duties include keeping a weather eye on behaviour around school premises. Pupils all neat and tidy in school uniform which is mandatory, with a very strict dress code – no advertising, track suit tops, denim, baseball caps or trainers outwith PE and particularly no football colours or any item of clothing which could potentially cause friction.

Pastoral care and discipline: Exemplary. School has a very positive attitude to bullying – 'Friends against Bullying', senior pupils volunteer to work with the first year group, visit them first thing each day and wear badges indicating that anyone who feels they are being bullied can come to them to discuss the problem. There are also 'supervised' lunch time clubs that youngsters can come to, as well as study-buddies. Chaplaincy team of five – Church of Scotland, Baptist, all take a year each – Church of Rome declines to allow Catholic priests to join this ecumenical team which is a bit odd considering one of the local primary schools (St Andrews) is Catholic and 90 per cent of their pupils come on. Room set aside during Ramadan for prayer.

Strong discipline code, range of punishments, from Behaviour Card which must be signed by all staff, with the ultimate sanction being exclusion. Pupils who persist in being disruptive or who are late are sent to the Behaviour Support Base for the rest of the lesson which they have disrupted and often for the next lesson in that subject; they also have detention at lunch-time. Previous head would exclude but only temporarily; drugs not previously a problem and they were patted on the back by drugs supremo Maxi Richards, who has an input in the senior PSHE programme.

Pupils and parents: Four per cent on free school meals; a good middle class bunch from Milngavie, Bearsden, Canniesburn as well as Drumchapel, north west Glasgow. 'Somewhat' oversubscribed, school has a good reputation and is handy for buses and trains. Priority to siblings, followed by East Dunbartonshire location (distance from front door to front door). Large number of ethnic backgrounds, over 100+ youngsters from non-English speaking families – most Asians and Chinese but Africans, Middle Eastern and east Europeans are well represented. Absolutely no problems with the mix, the school is a 'seriously harmonious group'. Good PTA with parents getting quite deeply involved with the school programme of speakers and interview skills as well as the trad charity role.

Entrance: Automatic from local primaries; then by formula. New arrivals can get immediate entry if space available.

Exit: Only 10 per cent leave post-Standard to do further education elsewhere or go into employment. A few leave post-Highers with university entrance qualifications but most stay for sixth form, notably those going to uni down south. Majority of leavers go to central Scottish universities – no particular bias – industry, dentistry and medicine popular. Regular two or

three to Oxbridge annually. Some to study music, some to art school. Youngsters tend to go straight to uni, but an increasing gap year take up.

Money matters: State, with help on hand to supplement low-income families to go on school trips. Two forms of financial help available to those who stay at school after the age of 16. Footwear and clothing grant for those whose family or guardians qualify as low-income; and the other, the Scottish Executive Education Maintenance Allowance Scheme (EMA), for any pupils living in the area and going to school in East Dunbartonshire.

Remarks: A positive school, firmly setting its sights on the 21st century. Exciting times on newish site; we will watch this space with interest.

Bedales School

Linked school: Dunannie and Dunhurst, Bedales' junior schools

Church Road, Steep, Petersfield, Hampshire, GU32 2DG

• Pupils: 450 pupils: 310 boarders, 140 day. • Ages: 13–18 • Non-denom • Fees: Boarding £31,845; Day £25,035 pa • Independent

Tel: 01730 300100
Email: admissions@bedales.org.uk
Website: www.bedales.org.uk

Headmaster: Since 2001, Mr Keith Budge MA PGCE (fifties). Read English at Oxford. Rugby blue. Previously a housemaster at Marlborough and head of Loretto, 1995-2000. Married with three children. Not your typical head – but then this isn't your typical school, not by a long way. In open-necked shirt, discreetly striped jacket and subtly – though differently – striped trousers and unsubtle candy-striped socks, Mr Budge – Keith to everyone – has slowly, quietly and resolutely established his authority in this school and its diverse, vociferous constituency. He is relaxed, though serious, in conversation. While his commitment to the school and its ethos is measured in expression, it is genuine and profound. Parents criticise him both ways – 'The school isn't achieving academically as it should'; 'Bedales has become more ordinary and interested in academic results at the expense of its traditional ethos'. You pays your money.

Mr Budge treads a narrow – but clear – line between maintaining and improving academics and maintaining and enhancing what Bedales is about. And he is doing it effectively. Witness the appointment of a 'managing head' of Bedales to allow Mr Budge to oversee all three Bedales schools with a view to 'working on the schools' distinctiveness and performance. I am in charge of which staff and students come into the school – ie appointments and admissions. I also come in when disciplinary matters get to a certain point, whether with a student or member of staff – I have crucial oversight of who comes and who goes and I lead on all areas of policy'. Mr Budge is guiding Bedales with the necessary firm grip but light touch.

The 'managing head', since September 2010, is Mr Dominic Oliver, who came from Malvern College, where he was head of English.

Academic matters: Unlike at any other school, students tailor their studies by choosing a combination of GCSEs, the more challenging IGCSEs and the school's unique GCSE alternative, Bedales Assessed Courses (BACs). All three qualifications use the same A*-G grading system. In 2013, 54 per cent of I/GCSE/BAC grades were A*/A.

It gets more unusual as you go further up the school. In Block 3 (year 9) you study a pretty trad curriculum plus one of classical civilisation, German, Latin or Spanish and, crucially 'outdoor work' – one of the unique Bedalian features. From year 10, you take IGCSE courses in English, maths and dual or triple award science; a GCSE in a modern language plus up to two more GCSEs in either history, ICT, music, computing, ancient Greek, Latin or a second modern language. Students also take up to five BACs from a choice of ancient civilisations, art, classical music, dance, design, English literature, geography, outdoor work, philosophy, religion & ethics and theatre.

The approach is cross-curricular and broadening in all respects. 'We had inspirational teachers who were doomed to teach dull and crass curricula,' explains Mr Budge – yes. And parents concur – 'Most teachers are exceptionally dedicated and enthusiastic – they live on site and love engaging with young people'; 'My daughter did the BAC philosophy – she had to produce a massive journal full of her ideas on moral and ethical issues: wonderful'. For those who believe that education should be about education rather than processing and assessment, they can't really send their children anywhere much else. 'And UCAS is hugely supportive,' says Mr Budge. That's all right, then!

A levels persist, though, and nothing too revolutionary makes its way onto the timetable, apart from Pre-U music and an option to complete an assessed piece of independent learning – the extended project. Eng lit, at this and at lower levels, has long and famously been outstanding and the uptake at A level outstrips all else. Art (see below) is also outstanding and popular. Likewise, history attracts the many and with good results. Smaller numbers for languages and the sciences, though those who take maths and drama do well. In 2013, 40 per cent A*/A grades and 62 per cent A*-B.

SENs here mostly consist of mild dyslexia/dyspraxia and affect around 25 per cent. One weekly support lesson – occasionally two – is offered and pupils are not withdrawn from classes. More than that needed and you may want to look elsewhere. Wheelchairs are no problem and school also takes those with hearing/visual impairments and integrates them well. Now has EAL teacher because of increase in overseas students.

'Outdoor work' is key at all levels. Has its own farm – over the five years everyone has a chance to herd sheep, keep bees, learn the skills of fencing, coppicing, gardening, hedging, renovating paths, barns and stone walls, draining and maintaining ponds and all kinds of construction, land management and conservation techniques. We saw home-made coracles, wool being carded and spun, smithing and, unaccountably, a trap that was used in The King and I being lovingly renovated.

Everywhere is green – gardens, orchards and meadows surround and abut the school buildings; we loved the historic timber-frame barns and workshops – turned to all kinds of uses – which one discovers on a ramble around the extensive farm village of the school.

Games, options, the arts: Unlike in other schools, here one cannot detach the outdoor life from the rest. Nonetheless, extensive playing fields and an Astroturf, massive sports hall plus super pool, courts, pitches – everything: sport no longer a bit of a blush and smirk. All have a weekly double PE lesson and all the major sports are offered – even rugby.

Art is uniquely well-resourced and, perhaps, uniquely proficient. Studios and gallery space create a mini art school-within-a-school. The quality of work would do credit to a degree show and we hugely admired the imagination, technical skills, mix of media and the confident handling evident in the work we saw. Life drawing, portraiture, photography, metalwork, pottery, stonework and sculpture, colour and texture experimentation – all impress, along with an informed and liberating grasp of tradition and classical precedents. This is exceptional provision delivered with exceptional dedication and producing exciting results.

Music and drama flourish likewise. Lovely drama studio in adapted workshop, excellent flexible theatre. Productions attract the masses and most enthuse about the last show they were in. They learn production techniques, eg sound and light, too. Music block unappealing on the outside but truly warm and inspirational inside – baby grands everywhere and deep painted walls and dark wood doors. Most learn at least one instrument and lessons are timetabled. Music tech is well-resourced but does not seem here, as in so many other places, to have become what music is all about. Own arts programme coordinator and runs an impressive and inspiring programme of events which brings in top professionals to perform and run workshops – the posters around the place for upcoming and recent events made us feel we were attending a permanent arts festival.

Background and atmosphere: Started by visionary John Haden Badley and his wife in a house called Bedales, near Haywards Heath, in 1893. In 1899 – having begun to admit girls to counteract any undesirable masculine boorishness – they acquired a country estate in Steep and constructed a school – including state-of-the-art electric light – which opened in 1900. Dunhurst – a prep to feed Bedales – was started in 1902 on Montessori principles, and a pre-prep school, Dunannie, was added in the 1950s. No chapel – Badley's approach was strictly non-denominational – hence its attractiveness in its early days to liberals, intellectuals and non-conformists of all descriptions – both British and European. This was contributed to by the coterie of writers, musicians and artists who settled around Steep from the 1920s onwards.

Grew rapidly in the 1960s – the heyday of its a-la-modishness – and became the school of choice for the children of the super-cool. Lawrence Durrell, Simon Raven, Robert Graves, Cecil Day-Lewis, Peggy Guggenheim, Ted Hughes, Edna O'Brien, John Mortimer, Frederick Raphael, Joseph Losey, Peter Hall, Peter Brook, Laurence Olivier, Susan Hampshire, Mick Jagger, Pete Townshend, Sandie Shaw, Trevor Nunn, A.A.Gill, Roger Waters, Twiggy, Hayley Mills and Kirsty MacColl have all been Bedales parents.

Few eyesores – boasts two grade 1 listed Gimson designed arts and crafts buildings (the delicious Lupton Hall, 1911, and the Memorial Library, 1921) and two contemporary, award-winning buildings: the Olivier Theatre (1997) and the Orchard Building (2005). Fabuloso library – would grace an ancient Oxbridge college and makes you want to immerse yourself in the cerebral.

The ethos has survived but there have had to be concessions – has long since taken day pupils, who now make up 30 plus per cent of its population; academic results do count – even committed Bedalians want something on paper – and the informality of its core values have needed strengthening with some more recent rigour. Some worried in Mr Budge's early days that he would dispel the relaxed ethos, but no-one fusses much now. 'Greening Bedales' involves laudable initiatives on many environmental fronts, which other schools would do well to study. Also informs school's policies on trips and exchanges – not just extravagant junkets for the super-spoiled as elsewhere.

Pastoral care and discipline: Unique mixed-age dorms. All in first four years have a lower sixth in the dorm and dorms are for one to five students. Rooms comfortable and friendly – girls' more than boys': 'twas ever thus. '"Boys' flat" (boarding) was designed by a prison architect,' one inmate confided, but it didn't look bad to us and no bars on the windows, for sure. Jolly nice garden, bird tables and bbq. Steephurst, the girls' house, is lovely – the original farmhouse which began the school. Really nice, comfy common rooms – someone here understands about sofas. Bizarre bathrooms in Steephurst – three abutting baths per room: 'You can have a bath with your friends – it gets slightly noisy,' one girl bubbled. 'Pastoral care is really good – they try terribly hard,' a parent said. Good food eaten by everyone together. Upper sixth in own floors in main building – 'Quad' – with kitchens, study rooms (shared with day pupils) and common rooms – inviting and very much a separate world.

Most really love and conform to the 'take responsibility for yourself and get on with it' ethos, though, 'Some people get distracted by all the opportunities and don't work – others don't make enough of the opportunities and doss around,' one wise youngster confided. Very few stay in at weekends and little is laid on – but they have the run of the place and expeditions and outings organised on request. Also 'cosy teas' and 'fireside games'. Own clothes means exactly that – though uniform seems to consist of lots of mini-shorts 'n' tights, track suit bottoms and trainers.

Sanctions for, eg, smoking/drinking/lateness/lying usually means gating. 'It's a brilliant school if you're responsible,' a 14 year old asserted, 'but if you need rules and boundaries, it's not the school for you.' Not many find they can't hack it here. So we were saddened to learn that, in June 2010, the school had dispensed with six of its pupils on account of drug abuse. A spokesman said, 'Six students admitted to drugs offences involving marijuana at the end of last week and all have subsequently left the school as a result.' And again in July 2011, a ghastly end of term fracas resulted in expulsions of three pupils in their mid-teens. Perhaps this is the price to pay for being famously 'liberal', but it seems an awful pity.

Pupils and parents: Money counts now – one of the top 10 most expensive schools in the UK. But Bedales parents understand what the place is about and choose it in preference to the more conventional routes to wisdom and fulfilment, which includes many London families. Pupils are open, friendly and articulate – we met many on our visit and all were thoughtful and eager to explain their school to us. They are genuinely appreciative of what they have and the differences between their school and those their friends elsewhere attend. Very few overseas nationals – perhaps the ethos of no uniform and 'outdoor work' is not what most people abroad associate with a British boarding education! However always a sprinkling of the well-connected, minor royal and generally savvy and liberal from all over the country.

Entrance: Around 55 come up from Bedales' own on-site junior school, Dunhurst; the rest of the 90-strong year group from outside. Many from Windlesham, Highfield, the Thomases, The Dragon, Amesbury, Newton and West Hill Park. Those who want to are pre-assessed 18 months before entry; most thereafter come for a two-day residential in January before entry, plus tests in maths, English and reasoning. Around 75 per cent of these will gain places. As in everything, Bedales is unconventional – 'We back our hunches – we disregard scores when we know someone is right for us'. Many more girls apply for places at sixth form than boys. Assessment via interview – 50 points at GCSE expected (taking A* as 8, A as 7 and so on, based on a nine-subject programme), plus A*/B in A level subjects but, as ever, flexible if they like you.

Exit: Lots of artists to Central St Martin's, Camberwell etc. Rest to every kind of course – many do science, but few linguists – at unis ranging from Edinburgh to Plymouth to Imperial. Six Oxbridge offers in 2013. However recent Old Bedalian mused, 'I wish the school had been more ambitious for me – they didn't push me.' Another regretted that no-one had told her that her choice of A levels would be seen as 'soft' by universities. Mr Budge now setting 'where they go on to' as one of his missions.

Money matters: 13+ scholarships – all means-tested – for outstanding ability in almost anything, plus a separate category for music. At 16, scholarships for academics, art and music and, occasionally, science. Some awards for drama and design at the end of lower sixth.

Remarks: 'If you want an exam factory go somewhere else,' a parent advised. If you want a relaxed, happy and wholesome school with good teaching, real values and a rich outdoor life, look no further. Few Bedalians regret their school days.

Bede's Senior School

Linked school: Bede's Preparatory School

The Dicker, Upper Dicker, Hailsham, East Sussex, BN27 3QH

- Pupils: 800, 450 boys/350 girls; 250 full and 60 weekly boarders
- Ages: 12–19 • Inter-denominational • Fees: Day £19,440; Boarding £27,690–£29,430 pa • Independent

Tel: 01323 843252
Email: admissions@bedes.org
Website: bedes.org

Headmaster: Since 2009, Dr Richard Maloney (late thirties) MA in theology, PhD in educational management. Previously deputy head at Sutton Valence. Married with two young children.

He looks very much younger than his years, an energetic, articulate and a caring man who spent the first couple of terms anything but idle. He is putting his management studies into practice. Says he is 100 per cent committed to the aims of the St Bede's Trust, and the pupil population is inclusive and diverse, even if the door is not as wide open as it once was. He wants to actively address the middle ability range. This will appeal to parents who feel that, while their children were happy, they could achieve more. The head wasted no time in tightening the mesh by appointing a director of academic performance who oversees the setting of motivational targets and monitors pupils' work, with IT systems to track performance.

His aim is 'to maintain the energy, breadth and diversity of the curriculum whilst ensuring students exceed academic potential. I am also ensuring that systems are in place and no child slips through the net.' He feels now is the time to cap the intake. He believes in pupil involvement – during our visit students were involved with the tours and interviews for teaching posts for drama and PE. Can and will jump to action stations to rescue a pupil from elsewhere who needs a new home – and does so with immense humanity, warmth and common sense. Most parents feel this is a good appointment.

Academic matters: Academic deputy head is John Tuson, who has been here since 1993 but took a two-year gap to do voluntary teaching and zoo keeping abroad. He is worthy of mention as the pupils laud him as an excellent and inspirational teacher. Certainly he was enthusiastic as he told us of the work he is now doing under the head and occasionally came up for breath. VA scores revealed that the middle range in years 9 and 10 were below national average and their intention is to double these scores within the next three years. Has put in systems for tracking pupils' performance. New dedicated tutor time to underpin an already strong pastoral system so that staff can keep abreast with individuals' targets. Although this focus is necessary, as some of the middle range of ability were too happy to coast, it would be a shame if Bede's became yet another league table climber, given their remarkable success as a school open to all.

Vast range of subjects on offer at GCSE and A level. GCSEs achieve a spread of results across the grades, as you would expect of a school which proudly takes children of a far wider range of abilities than elsewhere. The number of D grades at GCSE – something less than half the number of As – often reflects the considerable achievement of both pupil and school. A high proportion of Cs. In 2013, 38 per cent A*/A, with particular success in languages, science and art. At A level in 2013, 60 per cent A*-B and 34 per cent A*/A, again with notable success in languages and science. Science department offers nine different courses for GCSE including land and environmental studies – they are perfectly positioned in the heart of East Sussex farmland. A pre-sixth form year is offered for international students to prepare them in English and for the maturity needed at sixth form. Pre-university courses in maths and English for clever clogs but no plans to introduce the IB. Individually tailored learning programmes are central to the success of the school and the flexible curriculum allows for the quirky and boffins to achieve at their own pace.

Well-established special needs dept – this is the school of choice for many children who have SEN: dyslexia, dyspraxia and children on the Asperger's spectrum. Drop-in area where everyone is welcome for help or a chat. As much time spent producing IEPs tailored to pupils who struggle as for the Oxbridge pupil who needs extension work. And they will see an SEN as an opportunity to give support rather than something to shy away from. Most refreshing.

Games, options, the arts: Facilities are nothing short of spectacular. Multi-hall would put most commercial leisure centres in the second league – huge sports hall, squash courts, national size swimming pool. Outside boasts tennis courts, Astroturf, nine rugby and football pitches, netball courts etc. Some serious sport here, especially soccer, where the team recently won the English schools' national trophy from a starting field of 2,400 schools. Also Old Pupils – Clare Wood, Julie Salmon (tennis) Rob Buchanan (rugby), Luke Wells (cricket).

An extraordinary range of choice for their activity programme ranging from the thrilling to the more cerebral, and all pupils are involved four afternoons a week. Elite sportsmen and women have top notch facilities and a tailored curriculum. The Harlequins use their indoor fitness centre for strength and conditioning.

We could be forgiven for running out of superlatives when viewing their art department – they consistently win our top gold award for best school in this category. A real productive buzz in the new studios, awash with outstanding student work. Everything done to the top of the game – ceramics, fine art, photography, graphics, textiles, design technology, sculpting, pottery. Recent new extensions provide a dedicated workplace for each discipline.

Music soon to be housed in a new extension. The musical diary is full of recitals and performances for the choir, jazz band, orchestras at various venues including the village fete, the mansion house etc, so that they share their talents with the community. A healthy mix of choirs, a samba band, rock and traditional bands. Music accessible for all, regardless of ability.

Drama also a vibrant part of each child's life, either as performers, stage crew or audience. Ten or more annual performances to very professional standard with exciting special effects. Department regularly places pupils with RADA, Central School of Speech and Drama, East 15 and the Guildhall.

Background and atmosphere: In the heart of Sussex countryside and continuing to expand by buying more fields from surrounding farms. Has enjoyed healthy growth over the last 10 years and the infrastructure is expanding to accommodate this, the most recent addition being a new dining hall. Presents as a higgledy piggledy mix – the traditional main house extends to elongated, painted beach huts parallel to an impressive new science block with large labs, spreading to new dance and drama studios and finally to fabulous boarding houses. A strong multi-cultural mix with an open and tolerant attitude.

Pastoral care and discipline: Some of the most stylish boarding we know. The entrance is approached via an arched wooden bridge over a pond of carp. This is more like a three star hotel than a boarding house, with the relaxing sound of running water from an indoor feature, an open plan set up with no corridors, no noticeboards, all rooms coming off a large central lobby and upstairs housing flat-lets for the sixth form. Everyone passes matron's room on entry and plenty of smiling personnel around for a chat any time. A hint of the exotic with African lanterns, Tuscan coloured walls, lots of pouffes, all chosen by the pupils on their last African trip (as you do). Two new-ish boarding houses. Each house has three residential staff and one matron.

During the weekend, up to 50 to 75 per cent of full boarders stay, many of these from the international mix of German, Spanish, Russian, Bulgarian and Chinese, particularly in the sixth form. Students are obliged to attend a spiritual meeting of their choice on weekends. Pupils praise the relaxed and caring pastoral staff. Zero tolerance of boys in girls' rooms, although communal living area divides the girls' section from the boys'. Drugs would normally result in an expulsion and they will test if a pupil is suspected of drug abuse.

Pupils and parents: An incredibly large fleet of green minibuses transport pupils across Kent, Surrey and East and West Sussex. Parents come from a range of backgrounds – theatrical, city, farming, popular with families from surrounding countryside. Lunch with a selection of sixth formers provoked a spirited debate about educational liberalism versus traditional education, leaving one in no doubt that this school fosters enquiring minds.

Entrance: Does not describe itself as non-selective: 'Bede's does not top slice but as a mainstream school that offers demanding courses, we are not the right destination for all children... at 13+, pupils must display the potential to pass five or more GCSE examinations at grade C or above and to achieve grade C standard at A Level or its equivalent'.

Admission by interview with the headmaster and reports from previous school. International students have to provide evidence of their English language ability. A large proportion from the prep school; others from schools across London and the south east. At sixth form, students are expected to have a minimum of five Bs at GCSE.

Exit: A handful to Oxbridge (one in 2013); Bournmouth, Exeter, Leeds and Bath most popular universities in 2013; others to eg Edinburgh, Durham, Goldsmith's and University of the Arts. Many leave for careers in media and the arts.

Money matters: Bede's invests in excess of 10 per cent of its annual income in scholarships and means-tested fee remission – academic, art, dance, drama, music and sports scholarships. Prospective students who wish to join outside of the scholarship process are able to apply for means-tested fee remission.

Remarks: The head has a 'can and will do' approach that is infectious and is influencing the SMT to set more aspirational targets for all students, particularly the middle range. A very popular school with huge opportunities for pupils – both the quirky and the conventional. We said, 'Blissfully un-neurotic about where they sit in the league tables', but this is clearly becoming less true.

Bedford Girls' School

Linked school: Bedford Girls' School Junior School

Cardington Road, Bedford, MK42 0BX

• Pupils: 820 girls. All day. • Ages: 11–18 • Fees: £11,445 pa
• Independent

Tel: 01234 361900
Email: admissions@bedfordgirlsschool.co.uk
Website: www.bedfordgirlsschool.co.uk

Headmistress: Since 2010, Miss Jo MacKenzie BSc MSc (late forties), previously deputy head of Ipswich High School GDST. She went to school in Australia (her family emigrated there when she was 5) and studied geography and economics at the University of Western Australia. Says teaching has always been a 'real vocation'. When she returned to the UK she did a PGCE at London University's Institute of Education and, later on, an education masters at Leicester University. Began her teaching career at Bromley High, then progressed to Blackheath High, Alleyn's and Ipswich High.

She was appointed head of Dame Alice Harpur School in Bedford in 2009 and a few months later jumped at the chance to take reins at the newly created Bedford Girls' School – formed when Dame Alice Harpur merged with sister school Bedford High. 'It's a fabulous opportunity to combine the best of both schools and decide everything from scratch,' she says. 'It feels like a new school, but with the history of both. The place has a real heart to it.' Under her leadership, the girls have had a say in everything from the school's new name, uniform and emblem (a stylish, swirly eagle) to the curriculum (including thinking skills and international studies in year 9) and the house system.

Head still teaches geography and in her first year acted as a year 7 form tutor too. 'It keeps you in touch with the girls,' she says. A passionate advocate of girls' schools, she points out that 'girls learn differently to boys and thrive in an all-girls' school. They stay on task, they are encouraged to take risks and they learn about leadership. They don't become anything token.' Head has the chicest office we've seen in a long time – all sleek and modern, with a glass desk and huge vase of white lilies. The vast curved office window looks out over the school entrance, so head doesn't miss a trick. Has long-term partner and lives in house on school site. Parents admire her clear vision for the school and say she's warm, approachable and an impressive role model for pupils. Almost as impressively, she runs marathons (her best time is 3 hours 37 minutes).

Academic matters: In 2013, 38 per cent of A levels were A*/A and 73 per cent A*-B. Around 20 per cent do the IB – average point score 34. Most girls take 11 GCSE subjects – 53 per cent A*/A and nearly 83 per cent A*-B grades in 2013.

Staff are keen that school should offer lively, innovative teaching and we saw some inspiring lessons, including a philosophy class where year 9s stood in a circle to debate their views on the question 'Is it worth risking your own life for someone you don't know?' Sixth-formers like the fact that the school encourages independent learning while giving them a lot of support. 'The basic ethos here is that the school has high expectations, but in a positive way,' one girl said. 'They want us to do well.' Strong links with Bedford School (boys' school down the road and also part of the Harpur Trust), including joint drama, music, debates and CCF.

Year 7s choose two languages from French, German and Spanish, as well as Latin. Maximum class sizes of 24 in years 7 and 8, but this reduces as girls get older. Full-time SEN co-ordinator tests girls regularly – help for dyslexia and dyspraxia available either one-to-one or in small groups.

Games, options, the arts: Keen to make a name for its sporting prowess. Excellent on-site facilities include a floodlit, all-weather pitch, 12 tennis courts, six netball courts, a gym, fitness suite and sports hall. Indoor pool (decked out with jaunty bunting when we visited) and uses pool at former Bedford High site. Main sports are hockey, lacrosse, netball, cross-country, tennis, rounders and athletics, but rowing is growing rapidly in popularity – shares boathouse on the Great Ouse with other Harpur Trust schools. Up to the age of 16 all girls get at least five hours of sport per fortnight and many do loads more – 'We encourage everyone to be active,' the dynamic head of PE told us. Regularly fields four teams per year against other schools and sometimes six.

New music department is now housed in a former architects' practice bought by the school. When we visited, trumpet soloist Alison Balsom had just performed the school's official opening ceremony. Her message to pupils was to persevere, take risks and not give up if they get knockbacks – inspiring advice. Five choirs (four of them open to all), three orchestras, a dance band – something for everyone. Art, textiles and DT very popular – from drawing, painting, printing and sculpture to digital art and installations. Drama is part of the curriculum up until year 9 and can be taken for GCSE, A level and as part of the IB. When we visited GCSEs were about to begin and drama teacher had brought in a good luck cake for her year 11 students.

Own radio studio – year 10 girls broadcast their own 20-minute programmes (music, interviews, debate) every Wednesday morning. Girls encouraged to get involved in Young Enterprise, Model United Nations and D of E. Extended lunch break from 12.35 till 1.45pm so girls can take part in a wide variety of cross-curricular activities. Pupils in year 7 to 9 expected to do two every week, while year 10s and 11 take one. Activities on offer include everything from designing and building a green-powered electric car to knitting, as well as sport, music, languages, culture, book clubs and CCF.

Background and atmosphere: Both merged schools (Bedford High School for Girls and Dame Alice Harpur) founded in 1882, part of the Harpur Trust, a charity benefiting from the legacy of Sir William Harpur, a Bedford merchant who became Lord Mayor of London in 1566, and his wife, Dame Alice. In May every year Bedford Girls' School (owned, managed and supported by the Harpur Trust) celebrates the school's birthday and commemorates Sir William Harpur's generosity. Dame Alice Harpur School moved to present Bedford Girls' School site in 1938 – on the banks of the Great Ouse and a short walk from the town centre. The charity took the decision in 2009 to 'rationalise their provision of education in Bedford to one independent girls' school, one boys' school, one co-educational school and a pre-preparatory school', and so Bedford Girls' School was born.

One parent told us that Dame Alice Harpur (where his daughter was originally) had always been 'very good at making girls feel they can achieve and succeed,' and that the ethos is the same following the merger – 'It has helped my daughter to be organised, confident and happy,' he said. Junior school opened in 2010, senior school in 2011 and whole sixth form in 2012. Has launched house system – very popular with girls, six houses (Austen, Franklin, Parks, Nightingale, Hepburn and Chanel) named after inspirational women. House meetings every two weeks, lots of inter-house competitions and a cup presented at the end of the year.

The girls also helped to come up with the new school's values – which encourage them to be 'bold, imaginative and reflective'. Parents say the merger has been handled well, but admit that integrating two schools 'takes time'. They were rivals in the old days and some girls have stuck with their friendship groups. But new school ran a raft of integration activities in the early days of the merger and they seem to have worked pretty well.

Sixth-formers we talked to showed a fierce loyalty to the new school and said they'd almost forgotten who was where before.

Sixth form girls get an assortment of privileges and responsibilities. They wear smart grey business suits and have their own sixth form garden, plus a café serving coffee, sandwiches and hot food. Open from 8am till 3pm and decked out with metal chairs and a black and white tiled floor, it looks like an upmarket brasserie. Sixth form also gets its own common room – the girls take it in turn to choose the music at break-time (JLS when we visited). Twelve sixth formers voted on to leadership group each year, including head girl, two deputies and house captains. The cohort we met were full of ideas to help incoming sixth formers, including a personal welcome letter, bonding days and a blog. School council consisting of form captains and reps meets once a term. Whole school assemblies held twice a week, as well as year group assemblies too.

Pastoral care and discipline: Five forms per year in years 7 and 8, six from year 9. Each form has a form tutor – girls keep the same form tutor in years 10 and 11 and all the way through the sixth form. Uniform of grey skirt, white blouse, damson jumper and blazer to age of 16, but the head has removed 'petty' rules. Shoes no longer have to be lace-ups, hair doesn't have to be tied back (apart from in science and practical subjects) and pupils are allowed to bring mobile phones into school (junior girls must hand them into their teacher). Behaviour isn't an issue here. Sanctions range from lunchtime detentions through to suspension and expulsion, but the latter haven't been required since the merger. 'The girls aren't goody-goodies, but they want to learn,' says the head. The pupils agree – 'Everyone is quite grown up here,' one told us.

Pupils and parents: Girls come from all over (from as far afield as Luton, Milton Keynes, Northampton, Cambridge, St Neots and St Albans) – by car, train and a network of school buses. Some parents make considerable sacrifices to send their daughters here. 'A few come from fancy backgrounds,' one mother told us, 'but everyone mixes in together.' Communication with parents is good – full report or parents' evening each term, and progress sheets sent home in the October half-term. Parents can ring daughters' heads of year any time – 'It's as little or as much contact as parents would like,' says head. PTA organises a plethora of events, including quizzes, parties and a fundraising ball for 300.

Old girls include the late fashion designer Jean Muir and former world champion badminton player Gail Emms.

Entrance: Not ultra-selective. Main entry points are in year 7, year 9 and sixth form – via interview, assessment and report from previous school. Prospective pupils have informal interview in small groups with the head – 'I'm looking for girls who enjoy learning, girls who have a joie de vivre,' she says – and return a couple of weeks later for exams in English, maths and verbal reasoning. Half of the year 7 intake comes from Bedford Girls' School's own junior school (parents we spoke to were full of praise for the way the transition from the junior to the senior school is handled). The others come from a vast range of state primaries and preps. Ten to 15 new girls join sixth form every year – they need five GCSEs at A*-B (and at least Bs in subjects they want to take for A level or IB).

Exit: Loses a few pupils at 16 – girls who want boarding or subjects not offered by the school. After A level, 95 per cent go to university. One to Cambridge to study law in 2013, and one to Queen's university in Ontario; others to eg Birmingham and UCL. Popular subjects include medicine, biosciences, physics, English and history. Sixth formers told us they felt well supported by their tutors and the careers department in organising work experience, making university choices and the UCAS process.

Money matters: No scholarships (would rather reward excellence via prize-giving at speech day). A number of means-tested bursaries available for academically strong pupils whose parents would otherwise not be able to send them to the school.

Remarks: The merger has got off to an impressive start and the new Bedford Girls' School buzzes with energy, enthusiasm and innovation. A lot of good schools in and around Bedford, but this one looks set to hold its own.

Bedford School

Linked school: Bedford Preparatory School

De Parys Avenue, Bedford, MK40 2TU

• Pupils: 715 boys, 180 full boarders, 75 weekly boarders • Ages: 13–18 • C of E • Fees: Day £16,674 Boarding £27,270–£28,200 pa • Independent

Tel: 01234 362200
Email: admissions@bedfordschool.org.uk
Website: www.bedfordschool.org.uk

Head Master: Since 2008, Mr John Moule MA (late thirties). Young but with a wide range of experience, a head really in tune with his school. Educated at a comprehensive school and sixth form college, he won a history scholarship to Lady Margaret Hall, Oxford, and left with a first. Taught history and politics at Dean Close School, Cheltenham, then moved to Stowe as head of history and later became a housemaster, then senior housemaster. He joined Bedford as Vice Master in January 2006 and, in 2008, when the estimable Dr Evans retired at 60 – earlier than some had expected – was delighted to have his application for the headship accepted. Some parents were slightly wary at first but soon got over it. He has been seen as a definite change for the good, perhaps more approachable than his highly academic predecessor, and all love his informative, monthly newsletter.

Married with three children, two at Dame Alice Harpur and one at Bedford Prep, he is a committed Christian and passionate about the boarding school ethos, which he feels has a positive impact on any school, improves the ability to nurture and provide good pastoral care and enables them to develop 'the whole child'. Mrs Moule 'is thoroughly involved in terms of entertaining and attending school events – we do an awful lot of this!' He felt lucky to have taken over such a good educational establishment where dramatic change was not necessary. He is ambitious for his school, which he feels should be up there with the big names. We agree with him.

Moving on in September 2014 to head Radley College. His successor will be Mr James Hodgson, currently senior deputy head of Magdalen College School. Educated at Wellington College, read classics at Durham; couple of years at Ernst and Young; then PGCE at Cambridge (cricket blue). Six years teaching in Sydney, then joined Tonbridge School as boarding housemaster and director of admissions. Married to Rachel; four children.

Academic matters: Top exam results – 2013 63 per cent A*/A at GCSE; 82 per cent A*-B at A level, with 52 per cent A*/A; IB average point score of 35 (out of a possible 45) – here is a school full of bright boys who work hard under excellent teachers and fulfil their potential. Average class size 19, reducing to groups of eight or nine in the sixth form. Average age of staff 44 and teacher/pupil ratio approximately 1:8. The teachers are focused, enthusiastic and full of praise for the school and their pupils

– no wonder over half have been around over 10 years. Relaxed and friendly relationship between boys and teachers.

Well-structured curriculum. Separate sciences and all boys learn at least two languages (one of which could be Latin) in year 9. For overseas children ESOL takes the place of one of these languages, with about 50 per cent of them taking IGCSE ESL instead of English language/literature. ESOL lessons may be a condition of entry and are billed. Twinning with school in China enables exchanges, joint projects etc.

Sixth form boys opt for either the IB or A levels. Around a quarter to a third takes the IB. This is liable to increase as the school is increasingly popular with European parents, particularly in Germany.

Academic support department helps SEN boys in the way they feel is best for each individual. Two of these boys have offered places at Oxbridge and one boy, who joined in year 10 and was only diagnosed with dyslexia in year 13, obtained straight As at A level. Parents certainly feel that 'they have got it right'. Embryonic plan for a centre of excellence in the pipeline. Would also help G&T children.

Games, options, the arts: Head is passionate about sport and feels every boy should have a chance to be part of a team – 'It is important for everyone to experience training, winning and losing'. Key sports are rugby, cricket, hockey and rowing but lots of others to try, the majority of which enter teams for competitive events. For those who like bangs, an on-site rifle range. International honours in rugby, cricket, hockey, rowing, golf and fencing; have been Daily Mail U15 rugby champions and the East of England U18 hockey champions. Recent cricket tour to St Lucia and to Australia to play rugby. Boat club has history dating back to 1861 and tradition of winning – boys represent Great Britain in junior championships and Old Boys have gone on to row for their universities and their country. This is true of most sports played at Bedford. Even the less athletic boys have fun. The head told us of a boy who just couldn't stop talking about the training and the games he was taking part in – no, he wasn't a high flyer: he was playing for a C team. This is what head feels it is all about. Recent refurbishment and extension of tennis courts and sports pavilion – opened by England Captain and Old Bedfordian, Alastair Cook.

Plenty of individual activities on offer, including swimming (our guide was justifiably proud of the swimming pool), archery, tai kwan do and golf. CCF strong in all three branches, as is the Duke of Edinburgh, these in conjunction with sister school, Bedford Girls', which adds some attraction for the older boys.

Music particularly strong with a state-of-the-art music centre. Several boys read music at university, some Oxbridge choral or organ scholarships, and a horn player got a scholarship to the Royal College of Music. You name the instrument – they can learn it. Lots of choirs, orchestras and bands. Impressive music technology suite, now with facilities including iMac suite and recording studio. Light and airy concert hall. The slightly eccentric, very popular, head of music seems to be able to inspire every boy, no matter how initially reluctant, and they all love it. Parents rave about his ability to open up their children's sensibility and expand them musically. One parent told us that the house singing evening, which the boys take very seriously, is full of extraordinarily good performances and is one of her highlights of the year.

Well-equipped theatre also used by visiting companies. What other school has its own resident astronomer operating from an on-site observatory with a planetarium next door? The resource centres are used by visiting adults as well as lucky Bedford boys. Less displayed art work than at other schools but the facilities are there. Excellent DT labs.

Background and atmosphere: Interesting mix of modern and old, the school's buildings surround the playing fields, giving a green and open feel – country life in the middle of town. An historic school which celebrates its own history but does not hesitate to move into the modern age.

Main school building, gutted by fire in the 1970s – arson, says our guide – was rebuilt to retain its character. The magnificent hall is the focal point, around which classrooms are grouped on four levels. Excellent computer labs, but so far only a few interactive whiteboards. Focus is on teaching, not gimmicks, and, according to parents, it works. Spankingly up-to-date library in its own very modern building – 'It's a great place to work in,' says our guide. Plans to build a new theatre in the old St Luke's Church building and create new science classrooms.

Boarding houses informal and friendly – comfy sofas encourage lolling in front of an enormous television screen. Good sized bedrooms with individual areas for personalisation. Singles for year 13s. Homely atmosphere and caring house parents. 'Our boys are so happy,' said a parent, 'they don't want to come home at weekends.' Few overseas boarders, but no-one complained of cliquiness and parents feel they integrate well.

Whole place has the feel of a country boarding school. In fact, some parents think that better marketing would result in more boarders and that would be a good thing. But that would mean a different development plan: the boarding houses are full.

Innovative and enterprising Bedford School Study Centre. Here, up to 30 international students (boys and girls) spend one to three terms, mostly in intensive EFL, in preparation for entry into a variety of mainstream UK schools. Only two or three a year remain at Bedford, but top guidance and advice is given to all. Full integration at all ages provides an excellent introduction to British schooling.

Pastoral care and discipline: Head is keen on policies – one to cover every contingency. 'They are good for helping to think things through,' he says, 'and for producing a framework for action. I had to expel four boys last term, for drug-related reasons outside school – one learns from these sorts of things.' A parent said, 'They are learning that they have to address the drug problem at a younger age group than usual.'

A good pastoral framework. 'Ninety nine per cent are good at verbalising,' says the sensible and sympathetic, hockey coaching SENCo, who has been at the school for 10 years. Twenty or so boys in each year group who need some sort of help – one-to-one tuition available when necessary, as an extra, of course. 'There's always someone to talk to,' says SENCo, and feels they are quick to diffuse a problem if they spot it brewing. 'These are all very bright children and they often see the answer themselves and say "I should have said or done that" when talking it through with us.' The tutor system also helps. It would seem that they all look out for each other. This was underlined by a parent – 'The bigger boys look after the little ones.' Bullying virtually non-existent.

No student council but senior boys can join committees to discuss academics, sports, arts, innovations and technology. Those wanting to become monitors – and they do, because they can then wear a coloured jumper and brown shoes – have to apply in a written letter.

Pupils and parents: Currently 16 per cent overseas boys, mainly boarders, from 26 different countries including Hong Kong, Germany and Russia. The rest from a spread around Bedford and surrounding counties. Day boys mainly live up to within 40 miles. Ideally suited for boys who are individuals, but extrovert rebels might find it more difficult. Not particularly selective, so all are welcome to try, but those with exceptional learning difficulties unlikely to make the grade – 'They need to be able to cope'.

Long list of notable OBs includes Alec Dankworth, HH Munro (Saki), Harold Abrahams, Paddy Ashdown, John Fowles, Al Murray, Andy Gormasall, Alastair Cook and the reprehensible Lord Haw-Haw.

Entrance: Mainly from the prep at 13 but also from other local schools. Prospective pupils from other preps sit Bedford's scholarship exam and access award assessment papers. Those from state schools are further tested in the key subject areas. Some extra places at 14, then 25 more at 16, which require six passes at GCSE for those going on to do A levels (B grades in the subjects to be studied) or an academic assessment for those following the IB. They rarely turn away day boys – boarding places are at more of a premium.

Exit: Around 10 per cent leave after GCSEs. Thereafter mainly to good universities – UCL, Sheffield, Durham, Imperial, Nottingham, Warwick and Leeds, a handful to Oxbridge; otherwise all over, nearly always in the UK. A broad range of serious subjects.

Money matters: Bursaries and scholarships means-tested beyond 10 per cent. Their own access awards, decided upon following an innovative assessment process that seeks to measure potential to excel – again, means-tested. Head will always talk to parents hit by financial troubles.

Part of the Harpur Trust but financially independent – the Trust now puts its money into other projects around Bedford but continues to govern the school. Has been well run for a long time and is strong enough investment-wise, so no problems envisaged.

Remarks: An oasis in the middle of a busy town, a predominantly day school with a boarding school ethos. An unpretentious school which has everything a boy could need.

Beechen Cliff School

Alexandra Park, Bath, BA2 4RE

- Pupils: 1170, mostly boys but 65 girls in the sixth form. All day
- Ages: 11–18 • Non–denom. Assemblies with Christian theme;
- State

Tel: 01225 480466
Email: headmaster@beechencliff.org.uk
Website: www.beechencliff.org.uk

Headmaster: Since 2005, Mr Andrew Davies, (mid forties), history graduate of University of Sussex. Married to Anne, an assistant head, with two teenage children, one at his school, one at local girls' independent. Career has followed normal trajectory (teaching, head of dept, head of humanities, deputy head) in five local authorities, plus a spell in the commercial sector as principal of Kings International College in Surrey. Has worked in the most and least desirable bits of SW England, so no airs and graces. Direct, engaging and warm, he is passionate about providing his flock with all manner of opportunity to extend and test themselves.

Refreshingly liberated too from some spectres of state education: 'We are not slaves to Ofsted', he says, but with a major success story on his hands, he can afford not to be. Still teaches – he offers GCSE in humanities to year 9 boys in their own time: take-up and results are good. Keen shot, cricketer (coaches both) and general outdoor type who involves himself in school endeavours, such as the Centurion Challenge, 100 mile slog in 48 hours as a Roman foot soldier. Proud of his school, and encourages his pupils to be the same. Well liked and respected by parents, who reckon he's 'good at dragging the goods out of the non-academic' as well as the academic.

Academic matters: Completely non-selective on entry but tends to get more able boys by default. From now on, all year 7s will be assessed with cognitive ability tests on entry to enable better setting than Sats scores provide. Results at GCSE and A level have crept up over last few years and academic aspiration encouraged. In 2013, 73 per cent got at least five grades A*-C at GCSE including maths and English (27 per cent of grades A*/A) with 61 per cent A*-B at A level.

Has specialist technology college status and is a founder member of Bath Educational Trust set up in 2009, a collaboration between Hayesfield School (sister school), Bath University, City of Bath College and global engineering firm Rotork, headquartered in Bath, which aims to 'to provide a better experience for children'. In fact it provides a lot of good practical stuff too, such as far more options post-16, resources and economies of scale in terms of buying power, as well as a smart minibus to shuttle pupils between sites. BET will evaluate its efforts by tracking pupils' early careers until the age of 25.

Thriving and oversubscribed sixth form where IB was offered since 2009 jointly with Hayesfield: those who teach and learn unequivocal in their praise, however suspended for the moment because of modest take-up.

A level choices still extensive at 27 subjects, with the possibility of more at Hayesfield or Bath College. Others can choose Route 2, where they spend a year doing more vocational things at Bath College, along with retakes of English and/or maths GCSE.

Enthusiastic and proactive head of sixth form has gone down well with pupils and their parents. The academically precocious are encouraged to push on and take GCSEs early or AS in year 11; maths and further maths are taught within the same timetable. Most pupils start a second foreign language in year 8 (German, Spanish, Italian) and classics on offer after school. Clearly the message is that pupils will be given extra chances to get ahead, but the onus rests firmly on them. Nonetheless, a few parents worry that a good work ethic is not sufficiently instilled in the boys, and that to be labelled a 'keener' is social death; it is fair to add that the school comes down hard on this. Less able pupils taught in smaller sets and emphasis placed on extracurricular opportunities and successes for those in the bottom set for everything.

Busy SEN department caters for most needs one would expect to find in mainstream, the difference perhaps being that, in tune with the school's general ethos, pupils are expected to take responsibility for their own learning – 'I can't be doing with this excuse culture in education,' states the head. Lessons seem a good blend of purpose and fun, with lots of participation, and hi tech infrastructure to support them. Significant amounts of homework from year 7 compensate for short day – school ends at 3.40pm.

Games, options, the arts: Simply masses on offer, particularly for a state school, due in part to the all-hours culture where so much happens after the school day and at weekends; indeed it is the only comprehensive in Bath to take on the independents at Saturday fixtures. Impressive array of sporting successes in rugby, football, hockey, cricket and shooting borne out by the honours board in the entrance hall, where Amy Williams (GB's only gold medallist in the 2010 winter Olympics) appears, along with fellow Olympian Jason Gardener – and Roger Bannister. Competitive sport taken pretty seriously and winning is encouraged; some parents feel that the school's rugby and cricket coaches select more top players from city clubs than those outside Bath, but the school strenuously asserts that team selection done strictly on merit. Amazing results emanate from barely adequate facilities, though plans advance for a further all-weather pitch. Tennis and athletics in summer. Super sports barn has exterior climbing wall on one end, funded through parental gift aid. Strong links with top notch facilities and expertise at nearby Bath University too. Enough choice for sixth form girls, including rugby, but they say they are not compelled to do anything in the sporting line.

Art and DT have their own well-equipped if dilapidated block – and a committed following producing high quality work. Provision in photography hugely enhanced by the arrival of an industrial printer, bid for by the head of art, who has other grand plans (eg gallery space), if only funds would permit. Music attracts fewer takers, despite avoiding the trap of being a girls' preserve below sixth form, but there's a good range from brass to folk, and they do compete and succeed in the Mid-Somerset Festival, and tour Europe. School recently held its first internal young musician competition. A new music centre is planned – definitely needed. Some plays done in collaboration with the (all female) Royal High; choices like Tartuffe and A Midsummer Night's Dream suggest no lack of ambition. Beechen Cliff also makes its mark locally at Model UN and debating with other schools. Much 'boys' own' stuff goes on in terms of outdoor activities aside from team games: Ten Tors race, Centurion Challenge, D of E and all the opportunities offered at Tir-y-Cwm, the school's cottage in the Brecons, a gem of an asset. All of year 7 go for a weekend's bonding near the start of their first term; thence participation in orienteering, climbing and caving is voluntary. Trips on offer compare well with far better resourced schools, and go beyond the confines of Europe, to Africa for charity work and Canada for ski-ing.

Background and atmosphere: Feels and looks like a boys' grammar, (which of course it was), with a 'perky atmosphere, despite being slightly disgusting,' according to one mother. It became a comprehensive in 1972, after amalgamating with the then boys' secondary modern, and takes its name from the hill on which its 1930s buildings stand. Its future was touch-and-go in 1990, but head and governors mounted a huge campaign ending in the High Court to get it grant maintained status, and keep it open. Beechen remains prominent on the Bath scene in every way, but close up it is very, very tatty: 'We do what we do here despite our buildings, not because of them,' said a sixth former, who went on to wax lyrical about the 'can-do' culture. We agree: one parent left a recent open evening wondering why he had shelled out so much money on independent education for his children, when he could have had so much of it for free at Beechen. Definitely a sense of tradition about the place (boys are addressed as 'gentlemen', 'gents' or 'chaps'), but it's not oppressive: all seem to absorb the values of discipline, courtesy, academic confidence and pride the school promotes, not least in its first ever year book, The Gryphon. Loyalty and considerable affection from its old boys/girls (Old Sulians) and former members of staff come in to teach extra sessions – for love.

The head has beefed up the house system, renaming them after illustrious authors, after whom local roads are also named (this part of Bath is known as poets' corner); introducing a house tie and vertical tutor groups within houses to engender a spot of house loyalty. He's hot on uniform too: boys are picked up on untucked shirts and half-mast ties even outside school, no trainers and wild hair either. Some feel, however, that sixth form girls get away with murder as far as dress is concerned. Food is terrific too: Beechen's award-winning chef has broadened gastronomic horizons no end, producing yummy breakfasts, innovative lunches and buffets for functions from the new facilities he designed and implemented as a result of winning a recent trade competition. Take-up for school meals much higher than average and prices are fair. There's a real effort to source food locally – indeed some of the salad and veg are grown on site by the pupils! Popular snack bar for sixth formers is a tangible sign of the more mature treatment they get. Some parents worry that they are given too much leeway by being allowed offsite in free periods – 'they are still at school after all' – and that staff do not crack the whip sufficiently over punctuality or wasting time in free periods.

Pastoral care and discipline: Undoubted reward culture for all achievement is balanced by traditional sanctions for those who play fast and loose with expected standards, academic or otherwise. Anyone re-interpreting the uniform can expect to receive 250 lines on the vice of scruffiness, slackers get academic detentions on Saturdays. 'Pupils need to see consequences for their actions', as the head says. Parents report good relationships within school and quick response times from staff; the school takes concerns seriously. Sixth formers provide pastoral input to junior boys within tutor groups, in class on occasion and as directors in music and drama. Expectations of them are laid out in the sixth form code they sign before entry. No-one mentioned smoking, drink or drugs – possibly because they are strictly extracurricular?

Pupils and parents: 'Middle class and aspirant, reflecting Bath as a whole', according to the head, who woos newcomers, parents that is, with Pimms and lemonade. Mostly white and very local: the catchment area is strictly drawn. Much emphasis put on the partnership between parents and the school, and it is the sense of shared values rather than class or money, which unites them. The vast majority are totally supportive – 'it really wouldn't suit non-conformists or anyone with authority issues,' said one mother. Strong family connections too. Active PTA runs a gift-aid scheme, whose funds are doled out to successful bidders from amongst the staff or pupils for extras that wealthier schools would take for granted – a climbing wall and better stage lighting, for example. Old Sulians include several sporting greats (see above), as well as Arnold Ridley (Private Godfrey in Dad's Army), Andrew Lincoln (Drop the Dead Donkey, This Life, Love Actually), Curt Smith (Tears for Fears), research scientist, Nobel prize winner and generous benefactor Sir Richard Roberts and the current head of MI6, Sir John Sawers.

Entrance: 162 places on offer at 11, 'without reference to ability or aptitude', to boys living within the Greater Bath Consortium. When it's oversubscribed, precedence is given to normal state sector criteria of boys in care, followed by siblings. Applications taken in October for the following September. Admissions policy below sixth form is rigid – worth scrutinising the local authority website, especially as they prefer applications online. In practice, boys come from nearly 20 different primary schools – and the odd prep. Sixth form entry by interview, but conditional on five GCSE passes, ideally with B or above for subjects chosen for A level.

Exit: Some 50-60 per cent of upper sixth leavers to universities all over the country to pursue a diversity of courses. Exeter most popular recently; also Queen Mary, UCL, Leeds, Edinburgh and UWE. One to Berlin and one to US in 2013. Plaudits from work experience placements indicate that those who start work straight from school are well equipped to do so.

Money matters: Well supported by its parents' fundraising. Less advantaged pupils are able to take part in trips and music lessons by means of a special school fund. Staff keep a sharp eye out for opportunities to bid for or win equipment there is no school budget for; an entrepreneurial culture prevails.

Remarks: A Bath institution and good counterweight to local independents, in that it manages to offer much of what they do – for free, but for boys-only below sixth form. If a fairy godparent were to invest a few million, this would be an outstanding non-selective choice for almost any boy, or sixth form girl.

Belmont House School

Linked school: Belmont House Junior School

Sandringham Avenue, Newton Mearns, Glasgow, G77 5DU

- Pupils: 195: 130 boys/ 65 girls • Ages: 3–18 • Non-denom
- Fees: £4,794–£10,881 pa • Independent

Tel: 01416 392922
Email: admin@belmontschool.co.uk
Website: www.belmontschool.co.uk

Principal: Since 2006, Mr Melvyn D Shanks (forties) BSc DipEd MInstP CPhys SQH, who was educated at The High School of Glasgow, read physics and maths at Glasgow University (a 'lapsed physicist', he still teaches maths 'a little bit') followed by Strathclyde – ridiculously overqualified. Spent five years at his alma mater before coming to Belmont as head of physics in 1990, then deputy head in 1997, and says that, 'The most difficult thing was to move from being in the common room to becoming deputy head'. 'really, really excited', though it was slightly daunting 'becoming CEO'.

Very much on the ball, he has a deprecating sense of humour and showed us round the school with pride. Married, with one son a newly qualified teacher and another in the junior school (who, apart from not giving his father a hug, followed us round with a variety of comments and suggestions). Has appointed a new internal senior vice principal and a vice principal. Keen on staff development and people management, he runs the school with a senior vice principal, the head of junior school, one vice principal and a general manager. No obvious problems in getting staff.

Academic matters: Results have fluctuated but in 2013 pass rate at Highers 83 per cent – 33 per cent of Senior 5 got A grades (better than previous year); Advanced Highers 65 per cent pass rate.

Max class size 20 with core subjects, English and maths in the mid-teens, and most other subjects only nine or ten per class. Setted throughout in English and maths, compulsory to Standard grade along with French (from age 3) and computing. Three sciences, history, geography and modern studies also on offer, plus art and PE (plus German, taught from age 12 but 'not popular'). No classics. Spanish, taught as an exam subject only, pupils can do it post Standard grades, ditto admin and business studies. Eight Standard grades the norm, with Intermediate II an option in many subjects. Most stay on for Advanced Highers and can add the odd free-standing modules in sixth. No particular bias – strong on the science front and on languages.

Whiteboards, digital, overhead projectors – the lot. Keyboarding for all in Transitus. Classroom layout varies according to whim, with juniors either grouped round their teachers or working in standard classrooms. Vast array of cups for academic and personal excellence. Good range of computers, throughout school and not just in suites, two trolleys of laptops motor round classes.

Learning support; all tested on arrival (cognitive ability) – broad intake, and siblings give the school an even broader base. High functioning children with Asperger's, dyslexia, dyspraxia et al are fine, two qualified support for learning staff who follow pupils throughout; either withdrawn from class, or double teaching and strategic advice – free unless ed psych needed. Post-school tutorials in all subjects 'given by all staff, including the principal', from October through May – free. Computers for exams if needed, ditto scribes and readers. Main school (1840 mansion) not that wheelchair friendly (but only six classrooms not accessible). Pupils withdrawn from class, double taught in class if need be and can use the after-school/lunchtime tutorial

system in all subjects if they feel the need. Stunning recent inspection – school could have written it themselves.

Mixed age common room – some of the staff looked as though they were on the wrong side of the desk, but all truly dedicated. 'Granny' was coming in to tell a class of 7 year olds what it was like when she was growing up (we met her – very smart in Burberry she was too).

Games, options, the arts: For a small school they do 'not too badly' at rugby; three girls' netball teams, all play volleyball and basketball. Playing fields some half a mile away – bussed. Keen on tennis and golf, regulars in the British ski championships. Lots of inter-house athletics. Not really a school that does brilliantly in team games against other schools.

Jolly art room, variety of different disciplines, fabric strong and fun fashion on display, kiln, CAD part of the syllabus. Music important – all learn glockenspiel, guitar or drums in six week chunks or they sing. Terrific and popular choir, recently won the Xscape challenge; orchestra (and junior orchestra – based on ability not age) – good charity concert output. Extracurricular drama. D of E well supported. Strong on public speaking and takes part (a little bit) in local competitions, debating club. Oodles of various clubs, Lego popular; eco-monitors.

Background and atmosphere: Founded in the heart of Newton Mearns in 1929, moving to this jolly white stucco building on the Broom estate in 1930. Had magical plans for relocation nearby, turned down on planning, so has now re-grouped, demolished the old wooden hall and acquired a new games hall which is adjacent to the kitchen and doubles for dining (two sittings, takes ten minutes to fold up and stow the tables), junior school pre-orders their lunch for the week and pays with cheque on Mondays, seniors pay as they go. Windows overlook hall on first floor, along with four science labs, plus two IT rooms and a music suite, as well as drama and general purpose classrooms. Splendidly light and airy. Lifts and dead posh loos. Bit of the old rabbit-warren still at the back where juniors are ensconced in highly decorated opening-up classrooms.

Nursery now situated in large modern building in the centre of the campus. On a personal level this editor thinks that the resulting extension has to be the worst of both worlds, with a charming early Victorian villa (gorgeous ceilings, cupola) carbuncalised (as in Prince Charles speak) by a grotesque modern slab of a façade – neither the roof line nor the windows are in any form of harmony with the original: the planners should be shot. After five years of marking time whilst the planners cogitated, the original building had been somewhat neglected. Exterior of original main building now repainted, though some of the floor coverings (1930s lino?) in the classrooms could do with a change. A nice touch: school colours are purple and those chairs that are upholstered around the building are covered in matching purple. After school club for up to Transitus (homework too) 3.20-6 pm, £5 per session. Extensive new outdoor learning space.

Co-ed since 2000 but has always had a policy of having only one school captain as opposed to having head boy and head girl. Good supportive governors.

Pastoral care and discipline: HMI reports, 'The behaviour of children and young people is outstanding.' Not really a naughty school – standard disciplines apply, detentions the favoured punishment. Bullying stamped on, graffiti instantly removed. Buddy system for younger pupils. Pupils have tutors (a promoted position), with each tutor having 20 tutees – possible to change tutors if a personality clash. Strong discipline – children line up in the playground in twos at the end of break: charming. Older pupils open doors and stand aside to let us past. Twice weekly ecumenical assemblies: all faiths represented and holy days celebrated.

Pupils and parents: Good middle-class collection: 10 per cent from the Glasgow Asian population, most of whom have 'strong traditional family businesses'; core of Jewish pupils, smattering of Chinese, broad multi-cultural community. Pupils come from as far away as Ayr, Kilmarnock, East Kilbride, Paisley, as well as nearby Pollockshields, plus one or two from 'north of the river' – buses.

Entrance: 'Low-key informal assessment' for nursery, automatic transfer to junior and senior schools, separate test for children from age 7 upwards based on CAT school reports and interview if necessary. Can join mid term if space available ('We accelerate the entrance process').

Exit: Almost all stay on for either Highers or Advanced Highers. Some (around 10 per cent) may leave post Standard to follow vocational training, others to join the family business. Mostly to Scottish universities – Glasgow popular, Aberdeen, Dundee, Strathclyde, Edinburgh, St Andrews; occasional one or two to Oxbridge but none recently. Tranches of medics, lawyers, vets, accountants, engineers and architects. The odd gap year.

Money matters: Not a rich school, but will do their darndest to hang onto pupils to next public exam if parents who fall on hard times are upfront about it.

Remarks: Super – the perfect local school, works well. Tiny classes, almost a third girls. Dedicated staff. Definitely worth considering.

The Belvedere Academy

17 Belvedere Road, Princes Park, Liverpool, L8 3TF

• Pupils: 725 • Ages: 11–18 • non denom • State

Tel: 01517 271284
Email: info@belvedereacademy.net
Website: www.belvedereacademy.net

Principal: Since 2006 (one year before the school changed from a selective independent GDST school to a state-funded academy), Mr Peter Kennedy BEd Dip Man Ed (fifties), attended Cardinal Allen Grammar School, Liverpool, Christ College Education, and the then Manchester Polytechnic. Head of English and sixth form in a Knowsley comprehensive, deputy head of two other comprehensives in Knowsley, head Ellen Wilkinson High School (mixed) in Manchester, head of Chorlton High School, Manchester. Married, three grown-up children; outside interests include music, sport, travel.

Approachable, affable, humorous; wants to keep the original school's ethos of hard work and high standard of behaviour, attendance and academic results and adapt it to meet the challenges of a mixed ability cohort from all social strata; enjoys seeing the way the girls gain in confidence and blossom in a secure environment with high expectations. Popular with girls ('I love him!'; 'He's cheerful, has authority but isn't intimidating') and parents (including the original ones): 'He's done amazing things...has had a lot of vision'.

Academic matters: Modern foreign languages and science specialisms; lots of tracking and monitoring. Teaching and learning judged outstanding by 2010 Ofsted; teachers seen as friendly, helpful: 'They're amazing – more like friends,' enthused a sixth former. 2013 A levels: over 50 per cent A*-B. Most take four AS subjects plus EPQ; general studies in both years. Wide choice includes business, media, drama and theatre studies, economics, government and politics, classical civilisation, psychology, sociology, music, sport and PE – plans to develop links with FE colleges as less academic girls come through rather than increase the number of vocational subjects and advise them accordingly.

2013 GCSE: 33 per cent A*/A, 85 per cent 5+ A*-C including English and maths. All do at least one MFL, can do three separate sciences, OCR and GCSE IT; also Latin, business studies, performing arts, health and social care, home economics, media studies, PE; bottom band does Study Plus (extra English and maths). No plans to adjust curriculum to improve English Bac league table position – prefers to maximise girls' choice. Study skills and revision sessions offered for one week of the Easter holidays for public exam girls, plus 11 Saturday morning sessions over the year (always full). Mentoring programme for all year 11 students

At KS3 all do French and Spanish and three sciences. Five ability bands from entry on basis of admissions tests (movement allowed) – three high (27/8), one middle (20) and one low (12) which has extra support and a less demanding curriculum, colour coded so not obvious to the younger girls what ability level the colours represent. Setting for maths, English and languages; very good test results, especially maths. Fast track year 9 group starts GCSEs early so could begin AS course in year 11.

Access to network files and lesson materials from home via ICT portal. Top five per cent of gifted and talented identified as well as top ten – extension classes in enrichment time plus in class extension work and supporting of lower ability girls; sixth formers attend Durham University summer school. Massive investment in well-staffed additional support area – has just been awarded advanced inclusion mark. All girls screened for dyslexia in year 7 (and soon in year 12) by in-house specialist; specialist EAL support. Manager feels school could cope with all difficulties.

Games, options, the arts: Has huge modern sports hall plus multi-purpose gym, mini fitness suite; games take place in public park. The usual sports plus tag rugby (specialist coaching), volleyball, basketball, lacrosse, trampolining, dodgeball, aerobics, unihoc, community sports trust leadership award; city success for netball and badminton teams; national gymnastics gold medallist and tai kwondo competitor.

Artsmark Gold: lots of music – ensembles, choir, jazz band, orchestra won a gold medal at the Liverpool Performing Arts Festival; well-equipped music room with space for choir and orchestra rehearsals. Drama studio with flexible seating, annual drama festival – sixth form girls direct younger ones. Spacious dance studio – dance now at KS3, with GCSE to come and eventually A level (performing arts will also become available at A level). Excellent art: mostly painting and drawing with some 3D and print making – current biomedical project has year 12s working with a professional sculptress; art and design plus fine art with art history offered to sixth. Cheerful textiles room – graphic design on the way.

Vast range of activities in lunch hour and enrichment time, at end of lessons three days a week, some organised by sixth – community work, D of E, journalism club (produces school's eletters), comedy (Liverpool being the home city of Alexis Sayle and Julie Walters, after all), bridge, cartoons, debating, chess, conversational Italian, Mandarin, Fair Trade. Annual languages festival including film festival; year 7 and 8 spelling bee; media studies has lively Oscars night; 2011 BBC Schools 'Question Time' national champions. Exciting trips – South Africa, China, World Challenge to Vietnam and Cambodia, Shanghai (to promote Liverpool at World Expo).

Background and atmosphere: Until becoming an academy it was The Belvedere School, a selective GDST independent school. In 2001, a seven year pilot funded by Sir Peter Lampl's Sutton Trust opened up all places on the basis of just merit, with parents paying fees on a sliding scale according to income. Thirty per cent attended for free, it obtained its best ever GCSE results, girls from deprived backgrounds won places at top universities. Still part of the GDST. Numbers have grown steadily from just under 400, with 50-60 in each year group (Mr Kennedy does not want to exceed 850).

Located in the Princes Park area of Liverpool, adjoining a now-regenerated Toxteth, it consists of five linked Victorian (1880) villas plus gardens combined with a new purpose-built extension – the government provided 10 million pounds for capital development whilst co-sponsors, the GDST and HSBC Global Education Trust, each provided half a million. The pleasing décor is predominantly blue (matching the uniform) throughout. A hallway in the original part, with traditional school photos and book cabinets, has stairs lined with framed old war posters leading to the history are. Some very attractive rooms – music, art, the well-furnished and stocked library plus canteen – have large bay windows and original ceiling mouldings and views of the park and gardens. A huge cooking range from the original scullery in a corridor gives its name – the Range – to a meeting place. Outside the canteen is a playground with picnic tables and outside learning space with trees, shrubs and hut, due to be developed into an eco area with a pond. The sixth form have a common room with several royal blue sofas and chairs, plus a private study area. The new part is all very fresh and has modern ICT suites, MFL rooms and science labs.

The girls look very smart in their royal blue blazers and ties with light blue shirt/blouse and navy skirt. They are even required to have navy blue/black school bags and coats, navy blue hijabs and waist belt with purse – gosh, this GSG writer hasn't seen one of those since she was at her own GDST school! Sixth formers wear a black business suit with plain white shirt or blouse. All this, and much, much more, enumerated in the student handbook – this is a school that pays punctilious attention to detail.

The ethos of 'the Belevedere girl' is promoted from the start, by staff and the older girls from the original school; this encapsulates the GDST values of hard work, respect for teachers, leadership qualities and pride in one's school (reminiscent of the American charter schools). Each form has a head and deputy head girl, who hold office for half the year. It is perfectly acceptable to be clever and industrious; the girls don't feel unduly pressured but encouraged to do their best and aim high – 'They want us to do well – if we do our best, they are happy'. They say the school council's suggestions are taken heed of.

Pastoral care and discipline: Very good pastoral care and tight on safeguarding. Bullying not seen as a problem by the girls we met – 'Everyone's friendly – you don't have bullies at Belvedere'; 'The teachers are very aware of social problems'. Sixth formers assigned to KS3 forms, may help individuals with reading; NSPCC training for peer mentors ('buddies'). The girls quickly feel secure and comfortable, according to Mr Kennedy. Thorough behaviour management policy – seems to work, as the girls we saw in classrooms and corridors were all focused and well mannered. All teachers, plus dinner ladies, caretakers, support and office staff, have credit books to reward a range of virtues, leading to certificates, badges, gift/book vouchers, awarded in assemblies; also a traditional prize giving ceremony (but apparently they no longer measure how far skirts are above the knee, as they did in this writer's sixties schooldays).

Pupils and parents: A wide range of social backgrounds; almost one quarter ethnic minority – about half with EAL. From 55-60 primary schools from all over Liverpool, Sefton, Warrington, St Helens and Knowsley plus Hamlet (original Belvedere junior). Web based portal allowing parents to access (some) data on their child.

Notable old girls: Dame Rose Heilbron (judge), Esther McVey (MP), Linda Grant (author), Baroness Morgan of Huyton (has held various public offices). Access to the 50,000 strong network of all GDST old girls.

Entrance: Hugely popular – about 500 applicants for 112 places at year 7 (police needed to control the traffic on test day). All take verbal, non-verbal and numerical reasoning tests; the top ten per cent achievers in the verbal test are accepted for MFL ability promise, the rest are divided into five ability bands (fair banding system) and then reduced by a lottery method. A small number from the old attached prep has an automatic right to a place (until 2015/16); SEN and looked after children criteria also applied.

Sixth form: minimum of five GCSEs at B or above, with at least A/B in prospective A level subjects; takes about 30 external applicants. Plans to build up to 250.

Exit: Roughly ten per cent to FE colleges for vocational courses. Rest depart post A level to a wide range of universities and subjects. Manchester, Leeds and Liverpool popular and three to Oxbridge in 2013.

Remarks: Now 'the school everyone wants their daughter to go to in Liverpool'. An exciting and inspiring enterprise extending the virtues of independent schools to a much greater social range that might be a trailblazer for future struggling ones. Only reservation is that the emphasis on 'the Belvedere girl' could restrict the development of individuality.

Benenden School

Cranbrook Road, Benenden, Cranbrook, Kent, TN17 4AA

• Pupils: 525 girls, all board • Ages: 11-18 • C of E • Fees: £32,400 pa • Independent

Tel: 01580 240592
Email: registry@benenden.kent.sch.uk
Website: www.benenden.kent.sch.uk

Headmistress: Since January 2014, Mrs Samantha Price, previously head of Godolphin School in Salisbury. With a degree from Edinburgh in history of art, she started her career at the Tate before deciding on teaching. Worked at Reading Blue Coat School, King's Canterbury and Hereford Cathedral School before joining Godolphin. She is married to Iori, an army chaplain, and they have two young children. Passionate believer in the ability of an all-girls' school to prepare leavers for life in the modern world and in encouraging a braver, 'risk-taking' culture. 'She who dares, wins!'

Academic matters: Very impressive – pretty much always in the top 50 independent schools nationally and sometimes in the top half of the 50. Small classes, high teacher:pupil ratio of 1:6, a general air of calm and relaxed discipline all contribute. Outstanding Spanish, French and Latin – good to see healthy numbers for Latin and Greek. At A level, good results across the board – of the most popular subjects, biology, chemistry, economics, English, government and politics and history were the stars, with 19 of the 29 mathematicians gaining A*s or As in 2013; 96 per cent A*-B grades overall with 72 per cent A*/A. Some feel the school could offer a greater range of A level options, but the breadth is there if you look for it. Academic enrichment programme – Extend, Excel, Explore – taken by all students on a Friday afternoon.

New £9 million Science Centre opened in 2012, doubling the space available for teaching and practical science. Large uptake in science at A level as a result. Science lecture theatre hosts a wide range of speakers and specialist project labs for Sixth Form and a junior science laboratory suited to teach all three sciences.

School committed to developing modern languages and all girls in years 7-9 – barring real strugglers – take two of French, German, Spanish or Mandarin. Range of minority languages also available. Approach is practical and refreshingly sensible – 'We have loads of trips abroad to bolster the languages'. But also, 'I think children get tremendous confidence from learning how a language is constructed.' D'accord! Eighty per cent A*/A at GCSE in 2013. Good, well-stocked and efficient library. Some feeling among parents of the brightest that academics are celebrated less here than sports and drama, but bright girls we quizzed demurred.

Brightest and those with SEN all supported by study skills department. Extension programme for gifted and talented throughout school. Everyone screened on arrival and individual plans for anyone deemed in need. Thereafter all girls monitored regularly. School acknowledges that dyslexics can be among the brightest pupils, but feels that 'severe' dyslexics will be better helped elsewhere – 'We need to be sure from the beginning that we're teaching in a way that's going to be helpful to them'. Aiming to be wheelchair-friendly throughout, but a large site with ups and downs and isn't there yet – 'We're keen to be aware of what our pupils may find difficult ... We look after our girls in a sensitive, caring way – we can cope with wheelchairs in most areas'. Takes very positive attitude to girls with individual physical difficulties.

Games, options, the arts: Playing fields on the crest of the Kent High Weald spread out gloriously in all directions. Sports hall, fitness suite (open 7.00am-10.00pm and much the most popular facility on site) and 25 metre pool. Everyone plays lacrosse, most play netball and rounders and a choice of 15 or so other sporting activities including ballet, riding, sailing, trampolining and, most recently, rugby. 'Girls love the outward-bound things. Wind-surfing, abseiling – you name it.' Games popular and successful. Lacrosse always top flight and squads regularly in top few nationally. Several county and regional players. Swimming also impressive.

Dance is strong and combines with drama and music to create imaginative and popular events. All given a huge boost with opening of terrific theatre plus dance studio – one of the best school theatres we have seen in terms of space, flexibility, finish and overall specifications. Full time theatre technician – girls learn the range of sound, lighting, stage management. Built on site of old tennis courts and one of a list of major projects that will continue the updating and development programme that is thoroughly and imaginatively under way.

Music wing – music technology is popular now – no-frills and practical, housing teaching and practice rooms. Lively music programme and two-thirds take instrumental/vocal lessons. Special feature is the Hemsted Forest Youth Orchestra, two-thirds of which is Benenden girls, the rest from local preps and seniors – 'Draws talented musicians from the whole area and gives them the chance of playing in an orchestra which is even better than a school orchestra'. Admission 'very much by audition'.

Strong art and design – excellent DT workshops in which 'anything' can be made using 'every possible process' (materials include wood, metal, resin, plastics); computer-controlled gizmos along with traditional techniques – 'We have to hold back visiting fathers,' we were told. Jewellery especially popular. Six art rooms in which we saw good – some outstanding – painting and witty textiles, and particularly liked the sixth form studio with its individual desks and screens for pinning up work in progress – large and successful A level uptake for art and history of art.

Lively cultural programme of events and varied lectures – some compulsory, at which some chafing, and others not, mostly much enjoyed and recalled with appreciation years later, aimed at nurturing more than the narrowly academic. Weekends packed with activities – girls affirm that this has improved beyond recognition in last few years.

Background and atmosphere: In the heart of the Kent countryside, this is real traditional girls' boarding – Benenden Village is a stroll away but offers nothing in the fleshpots line. The site is vast – 240 glorious acres of field and forest overlooking more rolling miles of hills and woodland. The trees alone merit a visit – a fabulous lime tree avenue, broadleafs and a 400-year-old wood are some of the delights of the site. Others include the old walled garden, likely to be reclaimed from the ground staff and restored, and a set of water gardens, recently excavated and restored to form a valuable and beautiful resource for the ecologically-minded. A new eco-classroom has been built, completely sustainable and carbon neutral. The teaching buildings are close and linked at the heart of the site, and boarding houses spread out hither and yon.

No specially distinguished buildings among them, though the main house is a remarkable 1860s re-build of the original Tudor mansion, using brick, fireplaces, panelling etc salvaged from a fire – the overall effect is a kind of Victorian Tudor Gothic. It boasts some reception/meeting rooms and an entrance hall which both impress and gladden the heart with architectural felicities. New science centre contains a junior science laboratory, specialised project laboratories for sixth form project work and 100 seat lecture theatre; also suite of new classrooms for humanities.

Other good things – the wisteriaed 'cloisters', which are a popular meeting place in sunny months, the useful school shop, the large, light dining-room in which food, legendary for the best reasons, is enthusiastically ingested, and the yellow-painted endless corridor, in which excellent – and current – art is displayed. Plus, we are told, school chapel has been refurbished to include a big, new, stained glass window occupying the end wall and specially designed furniture. A beautiful space for small services, recitals or quiet contemplation and prayer. Otherwise most areas are functional in aspect – not a frilly school.

Boarding rooms are good. Still up to seven girls to a dorm in younger years and cramped, but girls assured us they love it. For older girls, single or double rooms – much more spacious and well done, all networked. Good kitchens, games rooms, but plain and sensible – nothing smart or showy.

Pastoral care and discipline: Happy girls – 'It's more like a community than a school,' we were told. 'Your housemaster might be your English teacher – the teachers really care about your pastoral side as well as your academic work.' Most parents concur, though some feel that almost too much latitude is given on occasions – 'They're incredibly indulgent,' felt one. However, 'The house staff are delightful and they are in touch with the real world'; 'My daughter's housemistress knows her so well and is very on the ball' are more common comments. Some feel the divide between the sixth and the rest is too great, but older girls enjoy their privileges and are less inclined to defect to co-ed as a result. Uniform for all, even the sixth, but they're allowed to dress theirs up with scarves etc and, as no-one but each other around to wow, they seem contented.

No serious problems – not one drugs incident for many years. A palpably traditional air about the place, but it isn't fuddy-duddy, and a sensible, balanced approach to life in general prevails. Also a sense of fun – along with the usual school photos, generations have also had fun photos taken, grotesque versions of the real things in which girls dress down, pull faces and adopt extravagant poses. 'Those are the ones my mum frames,' said one, cheerily.

Pupils and parents: All are full boarders, though some go home for weekends; two fixed exeats a term. Flexibility about being taken out at weekends for meals etc. About 20 per cent from abroad, half of whom are expats. Of the other 10 per cent, most are from Hong Kong, with a sprinkling from other Far Eastern countries. Girls attest to a genuine mixing – no segregated groups as elsewhere. This achieved partly via lots of whole year team activities, eg raft building. Solid, traditional clientele – Home Counties and London and from a range of preps – who know what they're paying for and trust their choice. Many daughters of Old Girls; most come here via word-of-mouth recommendation – 'We've not advertised for five years.' Supportive parents who love the place. Grandparents' day and lots of family events, also socials in London and surrounding counties.

Prominent Old Girls include Anne, Princess Royal, Princess Basma of Jordan, Dame Eliza Manningham-Buller, Rachel Weisz, Fiona Shackleton, Liz Forgan, Sue Ryder, Janny Scott.

Entrance: Over-subscribed – lists now closed two or three years ahead. Works closely with prep schools. Pre-tests and interviews at 11 and 13 effectively allow for school to be confident about those likely to make it through entrance exam or CE, those who have a good chance but may need some extra help and those best advised to look elsewhere – school writes along these lines to each individual family. System now pretty streamlined and numbers tend to work out on target. Entry to sixth dependent on exam, interview and current head's report, but few places available as very few leave.

Exit: Hardly any leave after GCSEs. Ten to Oxbridge; Bristol, Edinburgh, London, Exeter, Durham popular for university, some to America. The subjects taken cover the range.

Money matters: Awards of up to 10 per cent of fees in academics, sports, music, art and design, DT and drama available at different stages – 11, 13 and sixth form. Generous means-tested bursaries available, both for those temporarily in need or for longer term support of those otherwise unable to come to the school. Worth exploring. Trust Award bursary programme funding up to 100 per cent of fees for local primary school girls.

Remarks: Everyone's idea of a traditional, upmarket, girls' boarding school, though not remotely hidebound by tradition – cutting-edge and unconventional in multiple ways, in a stunning setting and underpinned with common sense.

Berkhamsted School

Linked school: Berkhamsted Preparatory School

133 High Street, Berkhamsted, Hertfordshire HP4 2DJ

• Pupils: 765: 435 boys/330 girls; 42 full boarders, 25 flexi boarders • Ages: 11–18 • Christian • Fees: Day £15,330–£18,000; Boarding + £6,090–£10,660 pa • Independent

Tel: 01442 358001
Email: admissions@berkhamstedschool.org
Website: www.berkhamstedschool.org

Principal: Since 2008, Mr Mark Steed MA (Cantab) MA (Nottingham – theology) (mid forties). Formerly headmaster at Kelly College, housemaster and head of religious studies at Oundle, before that taught at Radley and The Leys, Cambridge. Three children, one at the school.

He has a no-nonsense approach to change. Improvements, for example to the uniform, computer systems, sixth form block and girls' campus, quickly agreed, all without ruffling feathers unduly. He has his own blog and a determination to overhaul school website and make it much more user- and parent-friendly. 'Amazed by how few schools have a vision' – he

does, though, along with a strong and diverse management team to take it forward. Approachable, energetic and a keen and accomplished sportsman, generally well liked by both pupils and parents.

Academic matters: Adheres to a traditional philosophy of education in seeking to provide opportunities for broad development. The wide choice of subjects at A level – 27 – not to mention the enrichment studies undertaken in year 12, are consistent with this approach. Quantity does not compromise quality, however. In 2013, 53 per cent A*/A grades and nearly 82 per cent A*/B grades at A level. A level art and photography students in the top five nationally for the AQA exam board in recent years. Maths, politics, geography and English are other areas of strength. Care is taken to steer particularly able pupils towards the more academic subjects while others are nudged towards less demanding curricula. The head of sixth form encourages sharp academic focus and pupils to aim high. Staff praised for being readily accessible and other assistance comes in the form of drop-in maths workshops and lectures from leading experts, organised through the local chapter of the Geographical Association, to which the school is host.

While some enter the school lower down having been denied grammar school entry, parents feel that the non-academic would probably not be happy here. Single sex teaching for key stages 3-4 (co-ed in sixth form). As with A levels, results at GCSE have seen improvement over the past few years – around one in three achieve at least 10 A*/A grades; in 2013, 68 per cent A*/A grades overall. Again, good performance in most subjects – modern languages said by school to be on the up with newish head of department. All are required to take GCSE in RS (full course or short course) and many go on to A level. IGCSEs in English, maths, sciences and RS (full course) to ensure they remain challenged, but according to the principal the school is not, and will not become, a 'sweatshop'. The learning support department will conduct assessments if requested and supplementary lessons are organised as necessary. Two ESL teachers.

Games, options, the arts: Receives just recognition for its sporting achievements. It recently won the regional lacrosse championships and former and present pupils regularly represent the country and compete at regional and county level across a range of other sports. Emphasis placed on teaching sport well and ensuring that everyone has fun and is able to benefit. Netball and boys' hockey given new emphasis of late. Rugby, hockey, lacrosse, cricket, football, swimming and tennis compulsory, depending on age and gender. The new sports pavilion has opened up wider possibilities both to pupils and the wider community, including squash, aerobics, yoga, badminton and weight-training.

Over 50 per cent opt to study singing or an instrument of some kind. A talent competition to raise money for charity and Young Musician of the Year are relatively recent additions to the calendar and audiences are overwhelmed by the diversity of talent. The Friends provide Pimms, soft drinks and strawberries for Proms in the Quad, and all leave with fond memories of rousing and moving performances from solo vocalists and musicians – the ever-popular swing songs from the mixed pupil and staff big band ring in their ears. Drama is a popular option at GCSE and beyond and inter-house competitions to encourage all to take to the stage. Some grumbles from parents that staff compete fiercely for pupil time when schedules conflict, but generally a much appreciated aspect of the school – 'My son's speech at our wedding anniversary was faultless. They even found time to teach him public speaking'. May well have honed his dance floor skills too, at the Strictly Come Dancing fundraiser, one of many community events at which the girls and boys come together.

A tour of the school may well take in the historic armoury. CCF is well established and attracts large numbers of recruits

B

each year. The choice between this and D of E is often a hard one, but few can keep up with the demands of both. In addition to special visits, cadets are offered at least one training weekend a month and the D of E expeditions take candidates anywhere from the wet and windswept Lake District to the altogether more clement foothills of the Dolomites. High level of commitment found with a large proportion completing the award.

Background and atmosphere: Christian foundation school which dates from 1541 and amalgamated with the 1888 girls' school in 1997 and the mixed prep the following year. Boys and girls still have their own campuses but some facilities shared. 'Little school feel, big school infrastructure,' says the principal, and indeed a general feeling that all parts of the school come together and meld peaceably with the pretty and historic town.

The Castle Campus, which mostly houses the boys, plus the sixth form, has some slightly scruffy houses and common rooms but these are more than compensated for by the neat grass quad, well-preserved exteriors and assembly rooms, including the grade 1 listed Tutor hall and 19th century Venetian-style chapel. Some modern classrooms and labs and an ultra-swish new dining hall – little wonder parents queue up for those tasty charity breakfasts. Games on the Eton Fives courts provide a popular spectacle and seats under mature trees a traditional girls' meeting place – perhaps not surprisingly, lots of boys milling about nearby.

No-one now suggests the girls, in King's Campus, are hard done by comparatively, enjoying the traditional ('Our art room is more authentic, a Parisian atelier') and the modern – new sports centre and a 500-seat theatre are right on their doorstep, and a more spacious dining hall, chapel and classroom block to the tune of £8 million has now been completed.

Boarding houses are within easy walk of the school and indistinguishable from surrounding privately owned flats. Recently refurbished bedrooms, many en-suite, are comfortable, and tasteful pictures, vases of flowers and modern furnishings give a lovely homely feel to communal areas, with quiet and noisier common rooms to suit your mood.

Smart suit dress code and sanctioning of moderate makeup help prepare sixth form pupils for life after school. Work experience after AS with targeted placements. Good decision making support in the form of advice from teachers, careers fairs and lunches with parents and others to open their eyes to the world of work – in fact introduction to career choices starts much lower down the school, with research, profiling and guidance interviews in years 8, 10 and 11.

Pastoral care and discipline: A community school. Many enter the prep early and stay the course. Up until GCSEs, the separation of boys and girls allows them to be themselves and be less inhibited, while extracurricular activities ensure they are not cut off completely from the other sex. Sixth form very much run along the lines of a college, geared towards preparing pupils for the outside world – many choose the school for all these reasons. A great feeling of pulling together and mutual support pervades throughout. A vertical house system facilitates friendships across and in between year groups – 'This is where we meet to do our prep'; 'We come here to do presentations, sharing our knowledge of specialist subjects'. Spiritual teaching in the chapel, with all faiths welcome.

Pupils wearing smiley badges gather up lost souls and answer questions. On more serious or personal issues, pupils and parents are encouraged to communicate directly with house tutors. Is there bullying? Well, yes, some, but the caring attitude of staff and fellow pupils usually keeps it to a minimum – 'The kids are pretty sensible on the whole'. No real worries about drink or drugs, though recently a discussion forum has been established – 'Schools should provide a moral lead beyond the school boundaries,' says the principal.

Concentration of overseas students in the boarding house doesn't seem to create a divide between them, flexi-boarders and day pupils. Boarders participate in wider weekend school activities and also organise activities and outings tailored to their interests. ESL lessons are offered; visits to London's China Town and markets to buy African foodstuffs reportedly very successful.

Pupils and parents: Generally families live within 40 minutes or so of the school. Small number of MOD and expat families. Number of first time buyers along with the more comfortably affluent. The boarding community largely made up of upper school overseas nationals, mostly from Far East and Africa. Overall mix and town location prevents any feeling that they are living in a rarefied environment. Suits those willing to try everything out and contribute across the board. Pupils friendly, open and fun – 'Well-mannered and a pleasure to have in your house'. The Friends organise regular social events, including coffee mornings. Good chance to meet other parents and put views across to the principal who attends when he can.

Very vibrant OB association with regular sporting fixtures against the school, meetings with fellow professionals, reunion dinners and regular charitable donations to support school activities. Most famous OB Graham Greene, whose father was the school's head. Others include explorer Robin Knox-Johnston, composer Sir Alexander Goehr, Sir Kenneth Cork (former Lord Major of London), Michael Meacher MP, musician Antony Hopkins and actress Emma Fielding.

Entrance: Seventy or so move up from the prep each year. Wide range of feeder schools in Hertfordshire, Buckinghamshire and Bedfordshire, including Abbot's Hill, Beacon School, Gateways, Lockers Park and Maltman's Green School. Home-grown thought to have an advantage but all have to take an entry exam. This comprises verbal reasoning, English and maths testing at 11+ and additional non-verbal reasoning test at 13+. Can enter in years 8 or 10, when testing also takes place. Push to raise the number of girls and even out numbers.

Approximately 40 apply for sixth form from outside. One in two turned away, based largely on GCSE results. Minimum requirement of at least five B and two C grades, which may possibly include a short course (usually RS) with A or B in the four subjects chosen for AS level. A grade required if choices include English literature, maths, modern languages or science. Prospective students meet the head of sixth form and are required to provide a reference from their current school.

Exit: Most go on to higher education, many after a gap year. Seven to Oxbridge in 2013; other popular destinations include Exeter, Birmingham, King's College London, Leicester, Nottingham, Warwick, Bristol and Durham.

Money matters: Fees for extras considered reasonable and fair. Limited number of academic, music, drama, art and sports scholarships available, awarded on merit. Also bursaries in case of need.

Remarks: Combines the best of a single sex and co-ed school. Study with strong spiritual basis and community ethos produces confident all-round achievers.

Beverley Grammar School

Linked school: Beverley Joint Sixth

Queensgate, Beverley, HU17 8NF

• Pupils: 860 boys, all day • Ages: 11–18 • Non–denom • State

Tel: 01482 881531
Email: office@beverleygrammar.co.uk
Website: www.beverleygrammar.co.uk

Headteacher: Since September 2011, Mr Graham Hodson BSc Hons (early fifties). Mathematics degree from Sheffield University and PGCE from Newcastle University. Married with three boys, ages spanning university to pre-school.

Enjoys family time and sporting interests, golf and tennis, a keen walker – in the steps of Wainwright, completed the coast to coast. Teaching career started in the north east before a six year spell in Hong Kong. Returned to Yorkshire in 1995 to work in a further three schools, including Tadcaster Grammar, before joining Beverley Grammar School in 2005 as deputy head in charge of the curriculum.

Is very enthusiastic about the school's recent conversion to an academy and feels that it 'opens up many more opportunities and allows us the freedom to address the financial challenges'. Determined to 'retain the school's open, caring, friendly and successful ethos built upon mutual trust, respect and teamwork'. Parents endorsed this and commented that 'this is what makes the school so special'.

Academic matters: Despite its name, it is non-selective. Rated outstanding in the all recent Ofsted inspections and achieved high performing school award. Specialisms in engineering and cognitive learning.

Joint sixth form with nearby Beverley High School; 20 per cent A*/A and 48 per cent A*/B grades at A level in 2013. Lessons held at both schools so students divide their time between the two. 'I argue that it's a good half-way house between school where they feel comfortable and what it will be like going to university where everything is new,' says head. At boys' grammar classes held throughout the school, sixth form building now used for mathematics – 'Aspirational value of seeing sixth form throughout school,' says head.

Three pathways to GCSE – in addition to statutory core curriculum with additional GCSEs, diploma or vocational courses in conjunction with local colleges. In 2013, 56 per cent got 5+ A*–C with English and maths, 20 per cent of grades A*/A. Success due to excellent differentiated teaching from a committed staff with great pride in the school, options to play to pupil strength and 'can do' philosophy. Differentiated teaching, only setting in maths and modern foreign languages. Learning mentor to keep year 11 on track.

Impressive SEN provision includes two teachers with specialist qualifications in SEN, dyslexia and the autism spectrum and a number of highly trained teaching assistants. Inclusion is promoted, preparing differentiated learning materials and using support within the classroom or alternatively withdrawing individuals or small groups for specialised tuition. The school makes use of volunteers, including parents and others from the local community. Learning support is an option on the sixth form enrichment programme. Access is not easy on the school site, but adaptations have been made to improve this as far as is possible, given the age and layout of the building – lift and stairlifts to access first floor areas. At least one classroom in subject areas has a sound field system.

Games, options, the arts: Strong on sport ('you name it, we do it') – highlights include annual cross-country race. Strong on

music – about 120 have individual music lessons and ensembles galore from orchestras to choirs to rock group. Annual Showcase of talent has replaced the annual drama production, although examination pieces are performed to an invited audience. 'Drama very strong, a real asset to the school,' said one parent. Extracurricular is – well, take your pick: 'If a boy wants a club to be started, we find a member of staff to start it'. On offer all the healthy options, fitness testing and complete range of ball sports. More wacky, the Warhammer Club and BGS Entertainers; just love the no doubt aptly named Rebels' Reading Club.

Background and atmosphere: Founded in 700 AD, England's oldest state secondary school. Cherishes its traditions but prides itself on moving with the times and achieving new goals. Head describes it as 'like moving an ocean liner, constantly making incremental changes, without which it's difficult to maintain momentum'.

On its present site (the outskirts of Beverley) since 1903 and now a mix of the old (a museum of a hall) and the new (the mathematics building, built as the sixth form block). New sports classroom, showers and changing room annex. school library, humanities block and MFL areas all refurbished.

In the main building, look beyond the grubby quarry tiled corridor floor and chewing gum besmirched carpet to the buzz of conversation between lessons, observe the friendly, respectful yet light-hearted exchange between pupil and teacher and note the smile and eye contact from the boy holding the door open – a palpable sense that pupils really enjoy being here.

In response to the sole recommendation in the recent Ofsted, pupils now have greater opportunity to contribute to all aspects of school life through student voice, a democratically elected council made up of representatives from each form. Primary purpose to oversee school and community events but consulted on all school decisions from appointment of staff to school improvements. Valued greatly by the boys we spoke to.

Pastoral care and discipline: A can do philosophy and a 'more carrot, less stick' approach to learning – 'We believe in working hard, but having a lot of fun doing it, so there's a lot of leg pulling goes on in the classrooms. And because we have a relaxed approach to learning, the boys learn because they want to, not because they're being threatened with what will happen if they don't'.

Parents involved at earliest stage over any slips in discipline. School's own social worker may visit child's home to talk over problems. Only one permanent exclusion in three years and exemplary behaviour around school. Creditable reward system of coloured slips/credit cheques which lead to certificates, a monthly cash prize draw and ultimate prizes of badge and special school tie. A mentoring system with a difference to keep learning on track: as well as teachers, mentors can also be volunteers from the community – industrialists, careers advisers, etc – to drum home the value of learning. Head says, 'We use counselling, praise and reward to modify behaviour. We are a happy place where everyone achieves.'

The school's ethos of being friendly, open, caring and successful is underpinned by its SPACE programmes that instil respect, tolerance, empathy and responsibility in the boys and pride in their school. Lunchtime 'pop ins', when careers, health, learning and pastoral staff are on hand, also provide a comfort zone for less confident pupils, together with a strong student support system means little evidence of the macho positioning associated with boys' schools. As one pupil put it, 'The occasional outburst of testosterone is dealt with well here.' No formal links with the girls' high school until joint sixth form – opportunity lost?

Five forms per year group, each representative of one of the five houses. Great effort at entry in year 7 to ensure that forms are as homogeneous as possible. House activity dumbed down due to time constraints, limiting opportunity for vertical integration.

Pupils and parents: Very supportive parents, encouraged to be involved with school from the off (volunteer workforce cleared snow from the school playgrounds). Pupils overwhelmingly from white British backgrounds with few eligible for free school meals or whose first language is not English.

Most pupils enter the school with average levels of attainment, though a number are above average and nearly a quarter have learning difficulties and/or disabilities. Parents of year 7 starters invited to sit with their child for half a day of lessons. One mum, fresh from a science lesson, described school as 'absolutely brilliant. There's such an eagerness and keenness here. It's renewed in my son that excitement for learning'.

Famous past pupils in the twentieth century include Kenneth Annakin, film director, Paul Robinson, England goalkeeper and John Andrew, Anglican clergyman in New York.

Entrance: Deciding factor is distance from the door. Living in catchment area – Beverley and the surrounding villages of Woodmansey, Walkington and Bishop Burton – is pretty much a must, though falling rolls have opened the doors for those living beyond. Heavily oversubscribed and very appealing (from the large number of disappointed parents).

Exit: Nearly 50 per cent left after GCSEs in 2013. Sixth formers to eg Hull, Leeds Met, Leeds, Sheffield, Sheffield Hallam, Bristol, York and Manchester.

Remarks: A heady cocktail – a grown up school that is mature enough to nurture mutual respect, knows its boys, plays to their strengths and delivers, with a dash of good humour thrown in: no wonder boys love it. As one pupil said, 'It's cool to learn.'

Beverley High School

Linked school: Beverley Joint Sixth

Norwood, Beverley, HU17 9EX

• Pupils: 845 girls • Ages: 11–18 • Non-denom; • State

Tel: 01482 881658
Email: admindept@beverleyhigh.net
Website: moodle.beverleyhigh.net

Headteacher: Since 2009, Ms Sharon Japp (early forties), BA in English and sociology from Leeds, MEd and NPQH. Joined school in 1999 as head of English after teaching posts in West Yorkshire schools. Spell as assistant head and then deputy head from 2004. Previous head served for 22 years – governors certainly believe in continuity here.

Neat, pleasant yet guarded, firm but fair, clearly committed to continuing the strong ethos of the school to 'never rest on its laurels'. Has 'been a good new broom' and built a younger management team who are 'as keen as mustard', according to one parent. Respected by pupils and seems by no means to be remote figurehead. Keen for the girls to have every opportunity to play their part in global and environmental issues, from promoting links with overseas schools to supporting the school's gardening club by using produce from their allotment.

Academic matters: Good choice of subject at GCSE, with one MFL and two science standard. Off timetable music, additional MFL and science on offer for those enthusiasts considered capable. Higher and foundation diploma options as well. Subjects are taught in mixed-ability groups, apart from mathematics and languages at key stage 3 and science at key stage 4. In 2013, 76 per cent of pupils got 5+ A*-C grades including English and maths; 31 per cent of grades A*/A. At A level, 54 per cent A*-B and 28 per cent A*/A grades.

Committed teaching staff with an academic tracking and monitoring system that runs like a well-oiled machine. From year 7 to 9, progress leaders track pupil attainment and attitude to learning, using a traffic light system. Managed by an assistant head, a report goes to senior management and strategies are immediately put in place for individual pupils. One parent praised the effectiveness of early intervention for her daughter's mathematics – individual additional twilight sessions for a year transformed her competence and confidence. From year 10, a programme called 'closing the gap' provides significant intervention and support for those who are underperforming.

Pace of work is fast, but hope is to encourage everyone of all abilities. SEN manager uses a team of teaching assistants to give support in the classroom; limited withdrawal, number of pupils with statements in the teens, a provision for visually impaired. Volunteers in years 10-13 give up their free time to help with lunchtime clubs and support in lessons.

Aim is that somewhere around the school, every child's name should be highlighted for some kind of achievement – 'Every girl has a talent and there is a huge expectation and challenge for us all, teacher and pupil alike, to ensure each girl has that opportunity to shine, in whatever domain that might be,' says the head.

Games, options, the arts: Sport very popular – enhanced sports hall shared with community. Good representation at area and county level, particularly in cross-country and athletics. Drama, dance, music and art promoted through the curriculum. One in five have individual music tuition; choirs, orchestras, annual carol service in nearby Minster and summer music concert in St Mary's Church. Currently no joint productions with boys' Grammar School's acclaimed drama department – missed opportunity to strengthen drama? Dance in vogue, with first participation in the national dance/drama Rock Challenge. Inter-house competition mainly through sport and dance.

Technology block and art block provide excellent facilities. Good range and number of clubs meet during the week – rock band to award winning Radiowaves. British Council's international school award – Japanese and Sri Lankan partner schools as well as links with Germany and the Netherlands – and Fairtrade schools award. Highlights of school year include more than 60 trips to places at home and abroad. Fundraising for charities chosen by girls.

Background and atmosphere: Uninspiring frontage onto a main road hiding extensive buildings, grass playing fields and wooded grounds – well maintained with nice touches of hanging baskets and container plants around the buildings. Girls value the buildings and their resources and look after them.

Over 100 years old; the first pupils were mainly boarders in adjacent Norwood House. Much has changed but remains true to its original ideals, reported by the first headmistress Miss Rossiter as: 'The school is designed to supply education of the highest class and to give to girls the educational ideals of the great public schools. Great stress will be laid on the formation of character'.

At the cutting edge of change and adept at adopting the best from new initiatives – became a technology college in the first flush of schools adopting specialist status in technology in 1998. Plenty of computers spread around the buildings, where girls can work unsupervised between lessons; introducing educational use of mobile phones and MP3 players. Holds national healthy school status.

New developments are not a moment too soon. With its small hall, desperately short of large meeting space – in fact the whole school only meets collectively once a year, at the annual carol service in the minster: a real disappointment.

Close links and support from the local authority, particularly with the extended schools team, plus very careful and conservative financial controls, mean that conversion to academy status is not on the agenda at the moment.

A school where teachers give of their best – 'It's all about the children,' says head. 'Teachers are accessible and give an atmosphere of encouragement to the girls,' says one parent, and gave an example of the support her young daughter had been given to take part in a national spelling bee competition – in German. But much is expected of students, too. Classroom noticeboards show details of what pupils need to do to strive always for the next level of attainment – a girl expecting a B grade would never be in any doubt about what was needed to lift herself to an A.

Good staff/pupil relationships result in an atmosphere of maturity and trust. In view of this it is difficult to understand why the uniform skirt length debate, a national phenomenon, was not resolved with pupil cooperation, without the need for parent consultation and public debate. ('Too much emphasis,' said one parent – whose daughters wear the trouser option!) Particularly as fledgling initiative, the student leadership team, covers teaching and learning, communication, links and events – currently comprising one pupil per year group, the team work collaboratively on individual projects, from helping to improve lessons to organising and managing charity events.

Although on campus, sixth form (joint with boys' school, Beverley Grammar) is very much a separate entity. Currently, links with Beverley Grammar below sixth form are almost non-existent – little chance to work collaboratively on projects, enterprises, Duke of Edinburgh etc: more missed opportunities here.

Pastoral care and discipline: The aim is that pupils retain the same form teacher from entry until the end of year 11. Also same progress leader from year 8. Great continuity, but what about personality clashes? 'You try to build a relationship and it provides great life skills,' said one wise pupil. Each form has a captain and deputy, who keep their rôles for a term so that everyone gets a chance at leadership.

Merit system in lower school and good behaviour encouraged in upper school by a points system – students can gain or lose points according to behaviour. Rewards on a sliding scale from a 'wear what you like' day to a trip to a theme park.

Discipline strict but fair and seemingly consistent. Parents are supportive and speak of the good communication they have with teachers – 'We get a mobile phone call if homework is handed in late,' said one. Another talked of her year 7 daughter being mortified by a detention for forgetting to hand in her homework, but agreed with the teacher's stance of 'one rule for all'.

Well-being centre provides a network of support for pupils and their families, incorporating the pastoral team, a nurse, social worker, the SEN manager and the learning mentor.

Pupils and parents: Very supportive local parents encouraged to share school's ambition for their girls. Parents praise communications with the school and feel involved in their daughters' education. Pupils are drawn from local catchment area and take a real pride in their school.

Old girls include Angela Frost CBE, a director at HMRC, a clutch of actresses – Anna Maxwell-Martin and Eleanor Tomlinson – and classical soloist Ildiko Allen. We particularly liked the school noticeboard celebrating latest individual achievements of current and former pupils.

Entrance: Intake of 140 pupils and substantially oversubscribed (nearly double the applications to available places) and draws pupils almost exclusively from catchment area – Beverley and the surrounding villages of Tickton, Walkington and Bishop Burton.

Exit: Around 60 per cent leave after GCSEs. Most of year 13 to university, including one to Oxford in 2013.

Remarks: Never resting on its laurels, a school that is true to itself and its original purpose – to provide excellent education for girls whilst encouraging, supporting and celebrating each individual success. It believes pupil well-being is fundamental to academic success and this, with an atmosphere of high expectation, committed teaching, close pupil monitoring and early intervention, produces creditable results. Strengthening in-school links with the sixth form and more collaboration with partner school Beverley Grammar, below sixth form, would be the icing on the cake.

Birkdale School

Linked school: Birkdale School Preparatory School

Oakholme Road, Sheffield, S10 3DH

• Pupils: 540 in the Senior School; including 50 girls in the sixth form • Ages: 11–18 • Christian, but all faiths welcome
• Fees: £11,163 pa • Independent

Tel: 01142 668409
Email: admissions@birkdaleschool.org.uk
Website: www.birkdaleschool.org.uk

Head Master: Since 2010, Dr Paul Owen, previously academic deputy head at Wellington School in Somerset. Eighteen years' teaching experience, mostly physics but also some IT, chemistry, maths, astronomy and critical thinking. He has considerable pastoral experience (day housemaster) and this, together with his Christian faith, should support continuing commitment to good pastoral care. He lives on site with his wife, Gail, and their three children.

Academic matters: Sciences, maths, English literature and humanities the most popular and successful A levels – 2013 60 per cent A*/A; general studies for all. GCSEs also outstanding – 96 per cent eight or more passes, nearly one third A*. Spanish now on the curriculum and thriving. Greek on offer at lunchtime and can be taken to exam level. Triple award science at GCSE.

Open-door policy in the common room – pupils can approach staff for help at any time. Dyslexia provision costs extra, mild dyslexics only. Huge library, many computer rooms, all linked, with email addresses for all; strong DT presence, subdivided into electronics, graphics and resistant materials. Rather jolly ecology pool and masses of trips for geographers and historians.

Games, options, the arts: Lively school magazine with quizzes as well as the usual sporting achievements. Rugby important here – trips to New Zealand and Fiji. Footie very popular – school has joined the independent schools' competition. Girls do team or individual sport. Thirty metre sports hall and designer gym with weights room. 125 year lease on a sports field some 10 minutes' drive away, complete with £2 million pavilion.

Fabulous art complex, concentrating on perspective when we visited via a rather complicated machine of their own design, 'which never fails'. Truly exciting work – regular As and A* at A level and GCSE, masses of good 3D stuff and the walls of the art department were positively papered in lively pictures: nice 3D guitar and some Modigliani lookalikes. Well-equipped drama studio at Johnson House, with recording capabilities and an impressive wardrobe room. Theatre studies at A level. Much use made of the local countryside with trips to the Peak District, D of E. Whole school supports a school in Nepal, with annual visits both from members and friends of the school.

Background and atmosphere: School founded at the turn of the twentieth century as a boys' private prep school, went up to 16 in 1988, then 18, and added girls in the sixth form in 1996. Moved into current site in 1998 – pleasant bit of Sheffield but hideously complicated campus, embracing Oakholme Road, Ashdell Road, Endcliffe Crescent and Fulwood Road: masses of to-ing and fro-ing between the various Victorian/new-build houses on an incredibly steep site. Good octagonal concert hall; school hall bursting at the seams that doubles as a dining room and badminton court, as well as theatre – extension still planned.

Pupils are encouraged to get involved in a wide variety of lunchtime activities. Separate sixth form block, the Grayson building, which also includes computers. Elegant Johnson House with listed marble fireplaces (£20,000 to replace, said our guide), and RE department on the top floor with a quote from Micah painted on the wall: 'What does the Lord require of you? To act justly and to love mercy and to walk humbly with your God'. Pupils not allowed to go down the main staircase (one-way system). Lockers line the broad passages throughout. As we said before, the atmosphere is lively, scruffy and fun. Steps all over the place – no use for wheelchairs. School uniform throughout – blue, grey and white, with dashing striped ties for the boys.

Pastoral care and discipline: Strong Christian ethos, pastoral care important here. According to the school's policy statement, 'It is the policy of Birkdale School to promote a Christian lifestyle … any illegal use of controlled drugs by either staff or pupils will be treated as serious misconduct' – which is the first time we have seen staff mentioned in such context. Dealing in drugs equals out and no questions. If found using on the premises, the matter is 'taken very seriously' and previous conduct is taken into account. Pupil might be allowed to remain under a strict regime of testing – hasn't happened yet: 'Drugs are contrary to all our teaching'. Smoking on site rare in school, would result in detention, increasing in severity if problem persists. Ditto alcohol. Occasional incidents of bullying are dealt with by (usually) confronting the perpetrator – 'Might suspend', 'Would certainly involve parents'.

Head of year groups plus form tutors for all. Tutors first point of call if a pupil has problems but prefects equally used. Prefects spend a training weekend in the Peak District.

Pupils and parents: Local lads and lasses, many first-time buyers; huge catchment area – parents operate local buses from as far away as Bawtry, Doncaster, the Peak District and North Derbyshire, over a thirty-mile radius. OBs Michael Palin, a couple of judges, a racing driver and an MP or two.

Entrance: Entrance test for all at 11, including those in the prep school, who don't come up 'if it is not the right school for them' – perhaps a handful each year. CE at 13, but tiny intake then. Girls (and boys) join sixth form from many local schools, around 40 each year – five passes at GCSE, with four Bs minimum and at least B in any subject to be studied at A level.

Exit: Excellent careers library and on-line for sixth form. Leeds the most popular university, plus ex-polys, which often offer more esoteric courses: De Montfort, Leeds Metropolitan etc. Four to Oxbridge 2013 – can be more. Business, medicine, engineering, computing and law are popular degree subjects.

Money matters: Not the rich school it appeared to be, having lost assisted places. Certain number of academic scholarships on offer, which can be topped up in case of need. Will carry a pupil to next stage if in real financial need.

Remarks: School has had a meteoric rise from a boys-only prep school to a full blown senior school with girls in the sixth. No current thoughts about girls throughout, though anything is possible. Happily ensconced in Sheffield's education alley – strong and both academically and socially tough.

Birkenhead School

Linked school: Birkenhead Prep School

58 Beresford Road, Oxton, Merseyside, CH43 2JD

• Pupils: 375 boys and girls • Ages: 11–18 • No affiliation but C of E by tradition • Fees: £7,035–£10,320 pa • Independent

Tel: 01516 524014
Email: enquire@birkenheadschool.co.uk
Website: www.birkenheadschool.co.uk

Headmaster: Since 2003, Mr John Clark MA (fifties); read modern languages at Exeter College, Oxford, taught at St Paul's School, head of department at Whitgift, deputy head at Birkenhead 1996. A charming, civilised man; apparent diffidence masks a quiet authority; 'Outstanding,' says a happy parent. He knows exactly what goes on in the school, is respected by pupils for this. A good listener; compares favourably with more pushy and gimmicky heads in his concentration on the proper business of education, his excellent communication skills and readiness to take his position seriously, but not always himself. Not to be detected talking or writing about 'learning platforms'. Loves the 'huge family' of his relatively small school in a realistic, grounded way. Ably backed up by energetic deputy, Mr David Edmunds.

Mr Clark is retiring in July 2014.

Academic matters: Strong pretty well all round, results well ahead of local selective grammars, its main competitors. In 2013 A level: 22 per cent A*/A, 85 per cent A*/B. Majority opt for maths and science (excellent results); largest humanities entries in history, economics and English. GCSE 75 per cent A*/A. Clearly policy of offering (and staffing) wide option range across only three-form entry pays off in terms of small classes and sets, eg language choice from Latin, Greek, French, German, Spanish. Separate sciences for most to GCSE.

Special needs coordinated by staff member, now helped by three part-time learning support teachers. Parents pay for one-to-one tuition. Not much staff turnover – very nice place to teach and live. A general impression of fervent commitment to setting high classroom standards – and indeed to life outside the classroom.

Games, options, the arts: Games record amazing for size of school: cricket and rugby have been strong in the recent past. Most of the usual sports, soccer in sixth form. Senior girls' teams in hockey, netball, lacrosse and rounders. Policy of sport for all, through which individuals find their niche and improve fitness: 'We're not simply interested in natural athletes.' Enormous range of outdoor activities: CCF (all three sections), shared with local RC girls' school; D of E (25 taking gold level); 'biggest scout troop in Birkenhead'. Usual tours and expeditions.

Lively music: choral concerts with Liverpool Sinfonia; much instrumental tuition; chapel choir, claimed unique among day schools in holding weekly evensong during term, involving pupils from age 10 to 18. Active drama.

Background and atmosphere: Founded 1860, became direct grant, then independent in 1976. An unusual campus, hinted at in suburban address. Walking along the four comfortable, tree-lined roads that define the school, you won't guess at the existence of a lively school of 700 lurking behind the screen of large houses and sundry buildings. In fact an agreeable jumble of old and new, including a handsome Victorian chapel and fine cricket field. Years 7 and 8 housed in an elegant mansion, with its own playground and year 8 prefects, helping transition to serious senior school.

At present a handful of girls in the sixth, but they're building up in the prep school and through the school. Co-education originally planned with Birkenhead High School, which has now become an academy, so school is going it alone – to everyone's relief, it seems. Integration of girls has gone smoothly, and should continue; campus is a civilised place, and supervision of all ages discreet but effective. Recent ISI inspection noted 'exemplary' pupils' behaviour.

Liverpool proper may be just across the water, but it feels miles away. The Wirral is a pretty conservative place, and the school is happy with its own traditional elements: little boys wear caps, prefects wear gowns, and the head enters assembly to the head of school's cry of 'School!', whereupon all stand up. Trendy potential parents may not like this.

Recent developments include an extension to sixth form block and improvements to pavilion; a swimming pool is a gleam in the eye. Superb termly newsletter, In Focus, full of pictures, is the brainchild of the head's former PA, who continues to run the school's marketing.

Pastoral care and discipline: Traditional day school system; interlocking staff responsibilities mean it's very hard to fall through the pastoral net – commended in ISI report as outstanding. Report also quotes a boy: 'We don't do bullying here'. One expulsion for drug use in last five years; pupils can be temporarily excluded for rudeness and vandalism – hooray!

Pupils and parents: Pupils mostly from the Wirral and as far as Chester; some walk, some use public transport, many use school bus system shared with Birkenhead High. Pupils seem articulate, confident, happy with work ethos, and yes, a touch conventional. Their alternative sixth form prospectus is worth a read, though hardly very shocking. Parents mostly professional and business, heavily committed to all aspects of school. Flourishing former pupils' society, sharing In Focus with school. Most famous old boy was FE Smith, Lord Birkenhead.

Entrance: Increasingly from own prep – existence of local grammars draws state primary pupils away at 11+. May have been a brief wobble over numbers before the co-education decision, but situation now seems to have steadied, as many parents opt for independent education from the start. Prep pupils not tested at 11+ unless applying for a scholarship – assessed internally, and those not likely to make grade flagged up in good time for parents to find alternative schooling. External candidates tested in English, maths and VR. GCSE hurdle for A levels.

Exit: A few leave at 16+. Vast majority to good universities – most to Russell Group, especially Durham, a handful to Oxbridge each year – to read hard subjects: law, medicine/dentistry, engineering popular.

Money matters: About six academic scholarships a year, a few at sixth form level, some limited-term for music; usually 10 per cent of fees. Birkenhead Foundation Trust bursaries support about eight pupils a year – full remission possible.

Remarks: A confident, humane, non-flashy school in the best grammar school tradition, offering an astonishing array of opportunities for personal development in and out of classroom. Not as driven as some famous ex-grammars in urban areas. It feels nearer Chester than Liverpool, more like Bootham than, say, Bolton. Head's claim of an 'open, happy community' rings true, but parents of young thrusters shouldn't be put off.

Bishop Luffa Church of England School, Chichester

Bishop Luffa Close, Chichester, PO19 3LT

- Pupils: 1430: 680 boys/750 girls • Ages: 11–19 • C of E • State

Tel: 01243 787741
Email: browne@bishopluffa.org.uk
Website: www.bishopluffa.org.uk

Headteacher: Since 2000, Mr Nick Taunt. Read English at Exeter College, Oxford, head of English and the arts at Harwich School, then deputy head of Hedingham School. Married with three children, two of whom went to Bishop Luffa. Eloquent – uses language with lawyer-like precision. 'He's not scary and very calm,' said one pupil. Much approved of by parents – 'he's running a Rolls Royce School on an Austin Maxi budget,' said one in admiration. Most frustrated by lack of time: on a tour of the school, it was like trying to keep up with a sprightly white rabbit in a rather shabby wonderland.

Relishes the power to set the direction for a large school but does not sit in grand isolation: sometimes sits in on lessons and teaches the extended project of the AQA Bacc (which includes critical thinking) in the sixth form. Of his pupils and staff, he says, 'I want each individual to shine' – and this is not limited to the A* sort of shining. His vision for pupils: to develop to be independent, reflective and responsive.

Deeply committed to his school – and education in general – he was appointed National Leader of Education in 2010. Shares expertise and resources with other schools/colleges – 'because we are all responsible for all the young people in the area' – there is a lower exclusion rate in area as a result. Would only leave Bishop Luffa if he felt he had nothing more to contribute: his packed agenda would suggest this is some way off at present.

Academic matters: 'Judgement on grades alone is unhelpful,' says the head. But the grades are excellent for a state comprehensive all the same: in 2013, GCSE: 75 per cent of pupils got 5+ A*-C grades (including English and maths), 38 per cent of grades were A*/A; A level: 65 per cent of grades were A*-B, 37 per cent A*/A. Pupils say there is pressure to do well, but this is from themselves, not the school. 'At the start of the course they do say the grades people got at GCSE last time and you think you'd really like to do that too. I want to get an A to show my parents and teachers that I can do it.' The head says it's important to find the right pressure: these are important times, don't waste them. But it is not an exam factory.

Class sizes 25-30, and remain on the large size in the sixth form. A tribute, then, to the teaching staff that the pupils feel there is so much individual focus on their learning; and that the results are good. 'Inspirational teachers,' say parents. Pupils say teachers are friendly and approachable, and there are only two scary teachers (out of 95). Lessons are lively: there was a buzz of energetic industry, occasionally bordering on boisterous, in classrooms; attentive silence from sixth formers where the teacher was in full flow. The aim is to get pupils to think for themselves: critical thinking starts in year 7 with Edward de Bono thinking hats and is carried through to sixth form with critical thinking in the AQA Bacc. Lateral thinking plays a big part in end of term exploration days: year 7 designed an airline, working in textiles to design a uniform, in food preparation to make light food etc; sixth formers had a 'day of evil', exploring evil as a philosophical concept.

Curriculum not just aimed at those who are academic. Key stage 3 students cycle through all varieties of design & technology: graphics, product design, textiles, resistant materials and food technology. There are two food preparation

B

rooms; in one, purring pupils constructed trifles from their hand drawn designs – some spoon it up on the way home. These rooms are clearly used to the full: cake making even plays a part in further maths, with a chocolate cake holding the current record for tallest further maths cake of the year. At key stage 4, those who want to pursue a different vocational path take day release to Chichester College.

The geography teacher is very popular and successfully converts non-believers – 'my son didn't like geography until he was taught by [the teacher]' – 'he's the reason my son's doing a geography degree.' Budding mathematicians – and those bored by the subject – will be happy with the innovative teaching of mathematics: results are outstanding and there is a high up take of maths in the sixth form.

The learning support department supports not only children with statements, but any pupils with particular needs, including gifted and talented. The four dedicated teachers and nine LSAs provide individual support, group sessions and in-class support.

Librarians work hard to enthuse pupils and staff with e-research and internet safety lessons, as well as an imaginative programme of challenge and award schemes; some way to go yet: just 36 pupils and staff competed in the recent 12/12 Challenge (to read 12 books or write 12 stories). Professional writers present the awards: Andy Briggs and Vanessa Curtis this year.

Games, options, the arts: Two large playing fields, in constant efficient use. MUGA (multi-use games area), climbing wall, and new gym in 2011. 'They really take sports seriously, I thought they wouldn't. It's as good as an independent school,' commented a parent. Year 10 pupils can get a Junior Sports Leader qualification by learning to teach sport to primary school children. Extracurricular activities open to all pupils irrespective of ability: despite high achievement on sports field (pupils compete and win at a national level, and the school has the Silver School Games Kitemark Award for PE) it's an inclusive club at Luffa. Several parents commented with appreciation that their children had been encouraged to participate: 'My son's rubbish at sports, but has become enthusiastic about them, because the sports coach is so encouraging.'

Plenty of non-sporty options: chess club three lunchtimes a week – 'I thought it would be – you know, lame, but it was quite fun,' two film-making clubs, economics society with regular outside speakers, small but lively debating society, and IMPACT- the Christian Union, led by sixth formers, meets weekly to discuss ideas about Christianity and God. Plenty of opportunities for those interested in music: individual tuition, choirs, an orchestra and bands, with concerts and recitals throughout the year.

Keen uptake of Duke of Edinburgh, currently 10 gold, and 20-30 silver and bronze; demand exceeds places. Lots of trips, including French and German exchanges, ski trips, and field trips. Further afield for the sixth formers: Tanzania, Washington and Pompeii.

Arts thrive at Bishop Luffa (it has the Artsmark), and it's not just for those with a natural inclination: drama, for instance, is taught to all pupils across key stage 3 'to nurture confidence and sensitivity.' The new creative arts centre houses music rooms, recording studio, drama and dance studios, and hosts the Bishop Luffa Summer Exhibition: 'Fruition'.

Background and atmosphere: Built in the early 60s with some modern additions since, uninspiring buildings disguise the excellent school within. Cramped conditions – in some corridors you can touch both walls – and it felt a bit dark in places. One parent commented that it is hard to find your way around: year 7s are allowed to be late to class for the first week while they get their bearings. There is a quiet area away from the whirl – 'a good place to go to sort out an argument with friend.' The sixth form area is scuffed and packed; a peaceful interior hub houses a small library with 40 computers (you can bring your laptop and plug it in to the network).

Fun displays of art and textiles: clothes made from anything and everything, a fabric chocolate cake and a pink ring doughnut sitting temptingly at the top of a staircase, while a swan made of white plastic bags flies overhead. As you walk down a corridor a florescent green 3D box appears to float in front of you, the word 'think' written next to it – think outside the box. A grubby green wall looks as though it's waiting for a display: actually it's a wall you can lean on to make shapes – a fidget mechanism for restless adolescents.

Recent work to bring the decoration of classrooms up to scratch – 'a few classrooms are still scruffy,' say the kids. The school is tremendously clean, which is much appreciated by children. Year 7 pupils are particularly impressed by cleanliness after recent exposure to evidently unclean primaries – 'there's no half eaten pizza lying around here.' 'Lit pick' keeps the school tidy – a detention, but also something done during wet break times – 'it's quite fun really'; the head, too, ducks and dives when he spots a piece of litter on the floor.

No religious brainwashing here: the church background shows in the supportive atmosphere. Everyone is important, which is why the two youngest pupils raised the jubilee flag (50 glorious years of Bishop Luffa). The key element is respect, between staff and pupils and in pupil relationships. If you come to Bishop Luffa, you must respect religion, but it's not their brand of Christianity or damnation: the school does have Muslims and Hindus (they can opt out of Communion, but must attend the daily act of worship). However, 'not for you if you are anti-religion,' said one parent thoughtfully.

Food is very healthy; too much so for some: 'it would be nice to have unhealthy stuff sometimes,' said one pupil wistfully; outraged others responded: 'we do have chips on Fridays' – pupils are fiercely loyal to their school. 'The pasta is overcooked,' said a long suffering ex-resident of Italy. But this is lost on most of the kids: Pasta King is so popular it has its own queue. One pupil said, 'sometimes you can be hungry' – apparently what's left by the time the end of the queue is served is not so desirable. Year 7s have their own food queue away from the rough and tumble of the rest. No eating in the wrong place – you get a red slip – but dedicated place for packed lunchers inside, and nice new area outside.

Pupils make their own way to school, on foot, bicycle, or train – 'if I drop him off, it has to be around the corner,' said one parent in lowered voice. Pupils are clearly happy to be there; even if most of them would prefer to be there a bit later in the day. All the pupils we spoke to would like to change the early start time (school day: 8am – 2.30pm). 'It's very hard for teenagers to get up at 6,' said one boy in injured tones.

Pastoral care and discipline: House system provides a sense of belonging and helps children feel secure: support and congratulation at a low key level suitable to the self-conscious age. Pupils assigned to a tutor group in year 7, and stay in the same group until year 13. The day starts with tutorial time and includes a thought for the day. One pupil, who felt his head of house hadn't really appreciated his efforts to change his behaviour, said, 'but I can talk to my tutor. There is always someone to go to.'

Pastoral care is underpinned with imagination: time out of school to visit Dad who works in Gibraltar not seen as a holiday, but essential family time. One parent said, 'They are very sensitive to teenagers. At an options meeting, the talk was not just about options, but also about the fact that kids are growing up and need to have a social life and interests outside school lessons. They really are interested in the whole child.' New year 7s are paired with sixth formers for individual mentoring, and will be greeted by their sixth former outside school on their first morning, so no one goes in alone. One parent commented on her worry when her quiet son started at Bishop Luffa, but how, after a teary first few days, he is flourishing and gaining confidence in its supportive atmosphere. His tutor was in attentive email contact, she added.

Bullying is dealt with quickly, said a parent whose son was a victim, though the head is quick to point out that sometimes it's not so much bullying as thoughtless words. They have a toothpaste assembly to sort this out: it's quick to squeeze out, much harder to put back in again: it's easy to say words...

Disciplinary system: warnings, red slips, then detentions – 'you can get a room 10 for being late' – it's not quite a room 101: no rats or anything scary used to check behaviour at Bishop Luffa. Indeed this school champions a restorative approach to wrongdoing (all staff have been trained), which works well – 'I used to bunk off last year, but I've really tried to turn it around this year.' There are the problems you get with any bunch of teenagers: occasional smoking in the quiet area, the nicking of valuables (one pupil told me your phone or wallet can get nicked during PE if you don't put them in the valuables locker), and some pressure to have the right gear. You can get a red slip for a uniform problem, such as hitching up skirts or under-age make up (light make up allowed from year 11). A Juliano approach to law enforcement – 'some of my friends have just stopped wearing make up,' said one pupil rather wearily. A parent said, 'Not for you if you don't like your child to be pulled up on behaviour – children have to step up and behave.'

Exclusion for swearing at staff, persistent disobedience, smoking or drinking. Drugs at school would result in permanent exclusion – 'because it is important that all the children can feel safe at school.' Eight pupils have been excluded over the last year, with five permanent exclusions in the last 13 years (three of these for drugs).

Pupils and parents: A true comprehensive, it takes all types. Pupils come from the deaneries of Chichester, Arundel and Bognor, and Westbourne. Many middle class, but not exclusively so.

Past pupils include: journalists Jonathan Thompson, Amanda Ursell, Rupert Winfield-Hayes and Charlotte Hawkins (Sky News presenter); theatre director Paul Millar; actors Linus Roach, Rupert Holliday-Evans, Cara Horgan and Nimi March; footballer Joel Ward; investment manager and founder of the Thirty Per Cent Club Helen Morrissey; explorer Catherine Hartley; musicians Jonathan Ansell (of G4) and Zoe Rahman; Rob Shaw, co-founder of Jack Wills Clothing Co; and poet and novelist Sam Meekings.

Entrance: From West Sussex primaries, at 11, 220 places a year, oversubscribed. The vast majority (165) to C of E: prospective parents and offspring need to be regular church goers for two continuous years – 'go from year 3 to be sure of it,' suggested one parent. Thirty places to churches of other denominations, 20 local community places, (no church required) and five special places offered to those in particular emotional need.

Academic sixth form: pupils need to get at least Bs to enter. Around 140 from Bishop Luffa go on to the sixth form, 20 places for outsiders.

Exit: Careers sessions fortnightly from year 7; it's low key and kids can tune it out, say parents, but when you need it, it's there. Around a third leave after GCSEs. Nearly all sixth form leavers to university to university; five to Oxbridge in 2013; some took a gap year; others to London universities, Durham, Bath, Warwick, Bristol, Manchester etc.

Money matters: PFA (Parents and Friends Association) help the less well off pay for school trips.

Remarks: A church school, but not a God club. Principles no one would disagree with: respect for others and helping each person to shine. Excellent results for a state school, but no feeling of being a hot house. Pupils are friendly and polite. Only

downside – the cramped school buildings. One parent said, 'I really feel grateful that my son can go to a school like it. More schools like Luffa are needed! They have a balance between pastoral care and learning, and that is fantastic.'

Bishop Wordsworth's Grammar School

11 The Close, Salisbury, SP1 2ED

• Pupils: 920 boys, all day • Ages: 11–18 • C of E • State

Tel: 01722 333851
Email: admin@bws.wilts.sch.uk
Website: www.bws.wilts.sch.uk

Head Master: Since 2002, Dr Stuart Smallwood BSc PhD PGCE NPQH (early 50s), formerly deputy head. Brought up in Kent and a product of a grammar school like the one he now heads, Dr Smallwood graduated in geology from Leeds and got his doctorate from Cambridge. A brush with the civil service preceded his move into teaching; he has taught in only two schools, though his career follows a conventional path to his current post as head of one of the best state schools in the country. As such, he can press on in pursuit of even greater academic glory without the burden of having to fill fee-paying places; Bishop's offers places only to one in three applicants. 'I only ever wanted to work in this type of school', he told us from his modest, darkly panelled office, where a sheaf of commendations awaited signing on his desk, 'and my aim is to build on this school's particular character and location to create a regional entity'. Somewhat uncompromising in manner, Dr Smallwood is respected by the boys, who describe him variously as 'authoritative', 'dedicated' and 'ambitious for the school'. Married to Charlotte, who teaches English at the girls' equivalent, South Wilts (qv), with a daughter at university and two sons in the school, Dr Smallwood might be found bird-watching, star-gazing or tinkering with his model railway in his spare time; sadly, his failing knees mean no more running

Academic matters: The raison d'être of this top performing school: it's not all that matters here, but nearly. 'Academic excellence for starters,' said the head, when asked about his priorities for the school. Results reflect the high academic bar at entry: in 2013 69 per cent A/A* grades at GCSE, with particular strengths in maths and all three sciences. Oddly, for a specialist language college, language results lag a little behind, despite the requirement to study two languages to the end of year 9, then to take at least one at GCSE. We liked the quadrilingual notices around the school – bon effort! Many GCSE courses start in year 9, and some (maths and statistics often) are taken a year early. At A level, 32 subjects are offered, half of which are taught in collaboration with South Wilts; theatre studies is a new offering. Again, stunning results, with over 44 per cent A*/A and 73 per cent A*/B in 2013. School aims to get 10 per cent to Oxbridge; nine places in 2013. Star subjects at A level are maths, sciences, geography and geology both in take-up and results, again fewer languages including English. Boys talked about the calibre of teaching staff and academic respect, working both ways between them and their teachers: 'They beg you to take their subject for A level,' said one, whilst others praised the amount of support given. 'They fall over themselves to help you,' said another, hot from a one-to-one session on mechanics. We were struck by the keen attention paid to rainfall graphs by a large geography class we dropped in on, but a group of younger boys in a German class were fidgety. One mother reckoned the language teaching is too dry, and inclined to miss the point that language is primarily a means for communication. Some reservations about the science teaching also reached us – a bit old-fashioned and not always right for boys who find it hard.

Standards are kept up by close and supportive relationships between teachers and the boys, and 'by just the right amount of homework, though it might be sacrilege to say it', opined one year 7 lad. The transfer to sixth form is 'an achievement, not a given'; as well as a minimum of six GCSEs at B or above, including Bs for English and maths, there is also a chat with each hopeful about subject choices and possible careers. The head is not above booting boys out if their AS results are not up to snuff but he would do so only if a boy was clearly not suited to post-16 study – 'very rare,' said he – and despite the best efforts of the mentor each boy is assigned. SEN provision caters for the usual range of dyslexia, dyspraxia and Asperger's, and helps boys with difficulties in getting organised, having liaised with feeder primary schools – but it's pretty low profile at this school, we sense.

Games, options, the arts: There is life beyond rugby and cross country, if you look hard, but both these sports are taken with incredible seriousness: 'loyalty verging on the psychopathic and the coach is terrifying', said one mother whose son is proud to play in the 1st XV. The fixture list includes the gamut of schools more closely associated with the game: Sherborne, Bryanston, Millfield, Marlborough, Millfield and other local titans, and top teams get to play at prestigious venues such as Rosslyn Park. Passions run exceedingly high on the touchline, say parents. Cross country also has a massive following and produces successes at county level. All the playing fields are a brisk trot away – the school is truly shoe-horned into a confined space behind the cathedral close – but the boys grumble less about this than they do about the lack of space in the yard to play football at lunchtime. Some parents think the school is 'myopic about other sports' and bemoan the lack of tennis courts, for example, but basketball enjoys a strong following. At least sport-phobes are allowed to hate it in peace and, in sixth form, to spend their Wednesday afternoons in other profitable ways like hospital volunteering; everyone we spoke to confirmed that there will be a group of like-minded boys to hang out with, whether that be geeks, nerds, jocks or eccentrics, which we found reassuring and refreshing. Slackers and rebels won't find too many kindred spirits, however.

Music also very strong at Bishops, as befits a school overlooked by Salisbury Cathedral, the finest, most unified example of early English architecture in the world, with a distinguished choral tradition. Choir sings at school functions in the cathedral and tours regularly, as well as the odd national event like the schools' prom in the Albert Hall, and accompanying the LSO. About 10 per cent learn a musical instrument, taught by a small army of peripatetics. Two orchestras, string groups, wind bands and other ensembles cater for players of all abilities (and possibly none).

Art and drama less important at this somewhat two-dimensional school: many more creative pursuits take place outside the timetable as part of the 40 clubs on offer, and it would not be the right choice for an artistic and delicate flower, reckon parents.

An ambitious range of trips is laid on – as well as destinations one might expect for the linguists, classicists, musicians and (art) historians, rugby teams travel the world. Two ski trips, junior mountain-biking in Croatia or Morocco and a biennial trip to the developing world (Himalayas, Vietnam) add to the offer.

Background and atmosphere: Named after its founder in 1890, who set it up entirely out of his own pocket, and true to its founding principles, the school still delivers an education 'within the context of Christian belief and practice', but this perhaps plays out more in the relationships forged in school than in overt religious observance. It looks and feels like the city grammar school it is proud to be, occupying a very central site accessed through two unmarked entrances. Reception is housed in an ancient coach-house, whose cobbles still deter anyone unwise enough to wear heels. Just as well it's a boys' school, though it was co-ed till 1928. Inside its confines, a remarkable amount of ancient and modern has been crammed, including the chapel, sports hall, a gorgeous new teaching block and – amazingly – some green space. Everyone mentioned the lack of space as the school's only real limitation; we visited on a Wednesday when the place was eerily empty, the boys being occupied on the rugby pitches. But we did spot the lines painted in the yard, presumably to control lunch queues. A discernible air of academic seriousness pervades – 'the boys have to work,' said one mother approvingly – and do substantial amounts at home, particularly in the case of keen sportsmen. Expectations are pitched high – many top universities were represented at a recent careers evening, which included a lecture from a Cambridge admissions tutor. The boys we spoke to unquestionably feel lucky to be there. Parents also appreciate the efforts the school makes to turn them into good citizens, and are generally happy with the quality of reports and parents' evenings. It all feels jolly conventional – and no bad thing, in our view. The boys looked much tidier than many we meet and we did not see any adventurous hair, tattoos or piercings. When asked about drink, drugs and other extracurricular pursuits, one brave soul cited one incidence of drugs he knew about, which he felt had been dealt with the right degree of severity. Not cool in this school, evidently.

Pastoral care and discipline: Boys rate pastoral care highly and reckon there is always someone to talk to when times are hard; heads of lower and middle school came in for particular praise, as did sixth form mentors. The view from parents was mixed: 'I think it's good, but not all of us would agree,' said one. When we brought up the dreaded subject of bullying, the boys looked a bit blank, and confirmed they felt school was 'a safe place to be'. Academic discipline is tight, and a falling off in performance will swiftly be gripped; parents and boys both felt that such rigour would not suit everyone. Commendations for absolute and relative achievement provide a good balance, especially when incentivised with chocolate.

Pupils and parents: Almost exclusively white and middle class, with a tiny proportion of FSM, something the head is not entirely comfortable with and wants to address – as far as this is possible in Salisbury and its prosperous environs. Everyone involved in Bishops appears to share a palpable sense of aspiration, whether in academic, musical or sporting pursuits; 'It suits those who come from families with traditional values,' said a parent. The edgy or unconventional might not feel Bishops was a natural home. Most parents are in professional occupations of some kind

Entrance: Tough, tough, tough. Huge competition for 120 places in year 7 from about 50 local primary schools and some independents. 11+ (school's own test in English, maths and verbal reasoning) is taken with utmost seriousness: 'I've been crammed since I was 4', said one boy with a wink. 'There was no way I wasn't getting in.' The formal process starts in year 5 when the prospectus is sent out to all primary schools within the 'designated area', roughly a five mile radius around the city. Applications are made via Wiltshire council, and the exam is taken in September of year 6. Priority, amongst those who have passed the exam, to looked after children and those on free school meals. School runs coaching sessions as part of its commercial activity (free for those on state benefits), and we imagine that local tutors make a mint. Over 50 arrive at sixth form, with a clutch of good GCSEs at B or (mostly) above

Exit: University applications receive top priority, with the school hosting a university fair attracting all the top names. Also very clued up on summer schools, chances to study abroad and all sorts of ways to enhance applications. One aspiring medic told us his personal statement had gone through 10 drafts before submission. Most jump through the UCAS hoops in their last year, but we were assured that the school continues to support boys who opt to apply post A level. In 2013, nine to Oxbridge and 75 per cent to top universities. Bishops has recently become a SAT centre for entry to American universities; the head has a commendably global outlook. Very few boys thin out after GCSE and those that do are generally seeking more freedom and possibly girls at sixth form college. Distinguished old boys include Ralph Fiennes, Lord MacDonald (ex DPP), Hamish Milne (concert pianist), international rugby players Richard Hill and David Egerton, hockey international John Shaw. William Golding taught at Bishops for 17 years.

Money matters: The school became an academy in 2011, which, after an initial injection of funds, heralds faintly anxious times ahead; its commercial activities include adult non-examined language classes (with a terrific take-up) and lettings such as a non-residential summer school. Interestingly, the boys we spoke to alluded to the careful use of school resources – 'the school does well with what it has', said one. Parents are asked for a termly voluntary contribution to fund extras, gift-aided where possible; 'We're just grateful to escape the burden of school fees!' admitted one.

Remarks: Bishops occupies some interesting territory between the independent and state sectors, and is a member of HMC. As its founder said, 'I should like to found a school which shall be equal to the greatest and best of our public schools' – it seems in many ways he has done exactly that. 'Even if I had had the money for an independent school, I would still have sent my son to Bishops,' said a parent – sums it up, really.

Bishop's Stortford College

Linked school: Bishop's Stortford College Prep School

10 Maze Green Road, Bishop's Stortford, CM23 2PJ

• Pupils: 570 boys and girls; 168 board • Ages: 13–18 • Non-denominational • Fees: Day £16,338–£16,452; Boarding £23,550–£24,714 pa • Independent

Tel: 01279 838575
Email: admissions@bishopsstortfordcollege.org
Website: www.bishops-stortford-college.herts.sch.uk

Headmaster: Since 2011, Mr Jeremy Gladwin BA. Educated at The King's School, Worcester (chorister) and Whitgift School in South Croydon. Graduated from Durham in geography, taught at Shrewsbury School for 15 years, rising to become head of geography and housemaster. Appointed deputy headmaster at the Royal Hospital School in 1999 and headmaster of St Edmund's in 2005. Also an Inspector for both ISI and Ofsted (boarding). Decided to apply for second headship as 'the opportunity to lead Bishop's Stortford College was too good to miss'.

Married with two children and a black labrador. He is a keen walker with a love for the outdoors and ran the Duke of Edinburgh award for many years. Accomplished athlete in his younger days, he particularly enjoys watching rugby and continues to play tennis at club level. Keen interest in all music, especially sacred choral and classical, and is a fine pianist.

Academic matters: Results improving from modest 68 per cent A*/B A level grades a few years ago to 81 per cent in 2013 (54 per cent A*/A) – no mean achievement, considering constitution of cohort remains unchanged. Maths, history, English literature, psychology and physics are most popular subjects, with strongest showing in theatre studies, art, Chinese and economics. At GCSE, a commendable 64 per cent of passes A*/A in 2013, nearly all grades at least C. French for everyone, German for the top three sets; Latin optional, Japanese and Spanish offered in sixth form; GCSE Spanish offered for those with some experience in the language.

Extensive, generously resourced library and good teaching facilities including usual range of ICT. Pioneering use of geographical information system technology and fair few accolades give geography a deserved high profile. School has a new, interactive science centre, designed and developed by the dedicated science department – whizzy, experiential, comprehensible. When we visited, a number of children from local schools were animatedly making the most of this exciting 'must see, must do, do touch' facility.

Pupils have a real appetite for hard work and their efforts are rewarded with merits or, for some, the prestigious '10 club'-tie for A/A*grades at GCSE. Streams and sets for most subjects meet needs of all, including the gifted. Team of two sensitively supports 30 students with mild SEN (charged as an extra), including dyslexia and Asperger's. All international students are offered one or two EAL lessons a week and reach IGCSE level (required for university admission).

Games, options, the arts: Successful sports: unbeaten seasons in rugby and hockey now the norm – then again, they're lucky enough to have England U16 national squad and England senior A team coach (boys' hockey) and legendary rugby coach in their midst. County hockey and district netball and swimming champions – swimming a major sport in fabulous pool; tennis and waterpolo also on offer.

Music strikes a chord, with around 10 per cent of pupils performing to grade 8 or beyond. Good facilities – piano in most boarding houses, recording studio, plenty of airy practice rooms. Twenty concerts a year, including one for pupils, parents and staff, plus a couple of grandioso ventures into the world of opera. Purpose-built theatre seen better days but does the job. Brand-new art centre gives budding Badalocchios room for creativity, composition and exhibition. Trips and tours across the globe including China, Iceland, New Zealand, Africa, St Lucia, Barbados, and a fair few closer to home too. Wide choice of extracurricular activities including D of E, debating (standing-room only for some hot topics) and community work.

Background and atmosphere: Founded in 1868 as a non-conformist boarding school, with aspirations of being 'the Rugby of East Anglia', originally sited on the outskirts of Bishop's Stortford. Despite recent new developments and proximity to town, the 135 acre campus still has a rural feel. Buildings are well maintained with thought given to new additions, though smattering of Portakabins and odd corner seem somewhat incongruous. Boys only (apart from sixth form) until 1995, but opening of new girls' house has seen rise in number of girls to 45 per cent.

Offers termly, weekly or flexible boarding. Full-on Saturday school for all from 8.30am until 3.30pm has its detractors, but most accept it's necessary if children are to make the most of all that's on offer. Food (central dining) improved of late but still odd grumble. Very strong house system – all pupils go into either a day or boarding house, under the care of highly regarded housestaff. 'They're in control and are aware of what goes on and quick, yet discreet, in response,' said one thankful parent. Masses of competitions for everything, from singing through sports to cooking, generate fierce competition and promote house loyalty.

Pupils encouraged to appreciate diversity and to support and applaud each other. Good accommodation, homely rather than hotel, atmospheric and friendly, ensures boarding a bigger hit than ever. Odd parental moan that not all staff are contactable by email, but applause for improved communication with parents.

Regular assemblies, hymns et al, in listed Memorial Chapel; one parent suggested the school should do much more to promote Christianity (school is non-denominational), yet the pupils universally praise the chaplain, citing his thought-provoking assemblies and penchant for 'really smart debates' as a privilege. Excellent careers guidance ensures pupils make appropriate, yet ambitious, choices.

Pastoral care and discipline: Few discipline problems – believes, 'Zero tolerance would result in information embargo; we try where possible to seek to give pupils a chance to get it right'. Admits to odd alcohol issue.

Pupils and parents: Most from within daily travelling distance; boarders mainly from east and SE England but around 10 per cent from Europe and the Far East, 'The blend of nationalities brings a welcome diversity to the college,' says school. A broadening social mix, though not for those seeking county cachet – majority of parents are middle class professionals: doctors, 'something in the City' or lawyers. Parents' association puts on range of activities, many fund-raising, some for fun.

Current pupils have a wonderful skillset: a combination of confidence without arrogance, considered intelligence, an appetite for hard-work and play and a seemingly refreshing openness – truth or bluff, they certainly put us off the scent, for we failed to discover anything untoward lurking in the corridors or under the beds!

Long list of distinguished former pupils includes presenter Andy Peebles, rugby player Ben Clarke, writer Dick Clement and educationalist Professor John Ferguson. The world of espionage features prominently via former heads of MI5, Sir Stephen Lander and Sir Dick White, and Peter Wright, author of Spycatcher.

Entrance: Pupils are selected via interviews, entrance tests and school references; takes a range of abilities, not just academic high-fliers. At 13 majority come from the prep school but takes some 12-15 external entrants annually; small number joins at 14, in time for GCSEs. Some 40+ join in the sixth form – entrance is by interview and written tests; need at least five B grades at GCSE with A*-B in A level subject choices.

Exit: A handful leaves after GCSEs to study A levels elsewhere. All sixth formers head to university, most top choices; four to Oxbridge in 2013 and two to the US.

Money matters: Academic, music, art and sport scholarships offered, plus some assistance for those in financial need. 'A considerable proportion of our income goes on scholarships and bursaries,' says the head. 'If a child is talented but his or her parents can't afford us, we will do what we can to help.' Bursar a happy bunny, following recent benevolent bequests.

Remarks: Had a niche as a strong co-ed independent; now, thanks to a great team, improving results, excellent value-added and quietly determined, friendly pupils, it's nudging comfortably past a number of its competitors. A busy, energetic school, going from strength to strength. Difficult to say who it wouldn't suit; highly satisfied parents tell us school not only finds something each child is good at but does so with aplomb.

The Bishop's Stortford High School

London Road, Bishop's Stortford, CM23 3LU

• Pupils: 1,040 boys aged 11–16, plus large mixed sixth form; all day • Ages: 11–18 • Non-denom, but strong Christian ethos • State

Tel: 01279 868686
Email: office@tbshs.org
Website: www.tbshs.org

Headmaster: Since January 2014 Dale Reeve, previously deputy head of Leventhorpe School, and a maths specialist.

Academic matters: Results showing year-on-year improvement, with GCSE 32 per cent A*/A grades, A level 31 per cent A*/A and 63 per cent A*/B passes in 2013. Business studies and economics strong; two pupils achieved top A level marks in psychology in recent times. Sixth form limited to those with academic bent – anyone seeking sub level 3 should look elsewhere. Usual subjects offered plus film, Latin and critical thinking, with option to study courses such as art textiles through the local consortium. General studies course has attracted speakers including Douglas Hurd, Boris Johnson, Linford Christie and Lord Puttnam.

Class sizes, around 30-32 in the early years, fall to 24-26 for GCSE and 13-19 for A level. Setting by ability begins in year 7 with fast track in maths and French. ICT (received national excellence award) is a fundamental part of the school, and was certainly much in evidence, across all subjects, when we visited. Lots of success in maths, including 10 or so Maths Challenge gold winners annually. See themselves as a research-based school, encouraging pupils to be creative, discuss learning and develop thinking skills. Benefits from having well below average numbers of pupils with SEN (a mere four with statements); those who get through the gates do well here, particularly those with behavioural issues, who profit from the school's order and discipline. Boys feel staff could be less strict and as quick to praise as they are to condemn, but applaud them for their willingness to help solve problems and the time they put into providing activities outside class.

Games, options, the arts: Parents praise the very many extracurricular opportunities offered, everything from regular, and very successful, rugby, football and cricket fixtures (known to field up to 15 teams) through to chess, public speaking, debating, subject-related clubs, D of E and more. Pupils agree, with one perceptive chap saying, 'It's all well and good getting results, but leaving as a rounded person is what really matters, and the extracurricular activities allow for just that'. Music strong – music technology, recording studio and loads of Yamaha keyboards, thanks to school doubling as a Saturday morning venue for budding musicians. Performing opportunities via swing band, choirs, concerts, plays etc plus annual showcase, run by sixth formers, open to all. Head of drama working on an innovative, international project involving seven Dutch schools which will eventually culminate in a joint production. Art success includes work of one pupil selected for display at the RSBA summer exhibition. Number of trips and tours abroad; sixth formers get opportunity to visit far-flung places and take part in social projects via school's Interact club.

Background and atmosphere: School has extensive playing fields and an excellent sports ground (35 acres) some three miles away. Built in the 1950s, utility was clearly the driving force behind the school's functional design. Additional accommodation has been provided in recent years but school bursting at the seams, no more so than in the sixth form centre. We were disappointed to see the friendly caretaker clearing litter from corridors after lunch – shame it was there in the first place; however school is generally well kept; odd area lacks atmosphere and would benefit from displays and a lick of paint, but majority have it just right.

Pastoral care and discipline: High standards of behaviour and dress (blazers de rigueur) are expected from pupils – not a pair of trainers or 'shirt-dress' in sight: bliss! Disciplinary procedures are clearly laid out and a recently established 'sin-bin' – few spend more than a day or so in isolation. Aims to help and support those who find it difficult to conform.

Boys a polite, likable and articulate bunch but not immune from perennial problems of teenage life (self-harm, family problems, bullying etc); younger pupils felt they were left to get on with the transition from primary to senior school and, although work wasn't a big issue, social elements were. School disagrees, saying 'An awful lot goes into this process and this is not a fair reflection'. Wealth of support is on hand via excellent counsellor, structured pastoral set-up and a fantastic community police officer, who, we're told, is simply wonderful with the kids. Boys help themselves too – the active school council addresses key issues of concern; recent successes include the identification, and subsequent elimination, of bullying hotspots around the school; good to see important issues being tackled from the bottom up.

Pupils and parents: Not a comprehensive intake (minuscule percentage qualify for free school meals) – school is in a prosperous part of town, and the parental mix reflects this. Parents a satisfied bunch; as one said, 'If I had to select again, I would still choose to send my boys here'. Many see the school as a cheap alternative to independent education. PTA organises regular events: quiz evenings, race nights, candle-lit suppers etc, and raises impressive amounts of cash. Parents kept informed and involved – imminent move to online reporting set to take parental communication to the next level. Old Boys include Ben Skirving (rugby) and Greg James (Radio1 DJ). The 100 or so girls in the sixth form are a welcome addition, bringing calmness, élan and fresh perspectives.

Entrance: Demand for places far exceeds supply. Has a reputation for suiting the more able, but school insists this is a great school for the academically challenged. Places are awarded firstly on the basis of compelling medical reasons, secondly by sibling link. 10 per cent of places are allocated 'to pupils with a proven aptitude in music or sport', who have to be outstanding in their field. The remaining places are allocated according to where pupils live (the school has a traditional catchment area, defined by postcodes) and primary school attended. Obtain a copy of the latest criteria and study carefully. The co-ed sixth form has 60 places open to pupils who have not attended the lower school – good results, with a minimum grade B in subjects chosen for AS/A2, essential.

Exit: Vast majority of sixth formers to a diverse range of courses at recruiting and selecting universities (roughly a 50/50 split), handful take a gap year, 20 or so to employment. 15 per cent leave at 16, majority to college, to pursue vocational courses. Five to Oxbridge in 2013.

Remarks: With its emphasis on respect, looking smart and working hard, the school's values may appear reminiscent of a 1950s school, but use of technology and up-to-date methodology brings it very much into the 21st century. Suits most, ironically especially the less able or those with difficulties, as they not only benefit from good role models and a house system that allows all to shine, but also the drive to maintain standards means greater help and support for those needing an extra push. Continues to serve locals well.

Blackheath High School GDST

Linked school: Blackheath High School (Junior)

27 Vanbrugh Park, London, SE3 7AG

- Pupils: 290 girls, all day • Ages: 11 –18 • Non–denom
- Fees: £13,410 pa • Independent

Tel: 020 8853 2929
Email: info@bla.gdst.net
Website: www.blackheathhighschool.gdst.net

Headteacher: Since 2000, Mrs Lisa Laws BA PGCE (mid-fifties). Vibrant, dedicated, a head with a mission. Seemingly very relaxed, but determined to make and keep her school at the top, and she is definitely succeeding. She believes in a holistic approach, education of the whole person and the importance of the international dimension in schooling today. In her multi-ethnic, multi-cultural school girls are encouraged to be individuals, to strive for excellence and to look after each other. Parents like the fact that it is not an academic hothouse, yet its results are excellent and right up there alongside all the top South London schools. Mrs Laws is proud that it has been awarded full international school status by the British Council and its partnerships with schools in Europe and the Far East enable exciting and fascinating joint projects. Her vision has brought the school right into the 21st century. It is not a big school but it seems to be able to offer facilities and opportunities way beyond its size. The excellent ISI report bears this out.

Retiring in July 2014.

Academic matters: Small classes, a broad curriculum and an exceptionally wide variety of extracurricular activities enable pupils to get the most out of the excellent teaching available here. Languages and science are strong – our guide is planning to read astrophysics at a top university. She had nothing but praise for her teachers, who she found easy to talk to and dedicated to helping her get the results she wants. Certainly the results, 73 per cent A*-B, 44 per cent A*/A at A level and 93 per cent A*/A at GCSE in 2013, impress. Technology is used to its limits – interactive whiteboards everywhere, computerised laboratories and laptops for every sixth former. Everyone has access to the GDST portal whether working at home or in school.

Confidence-building is deemed important, including risk-taking – outward bound courses start in year 7. European work experience available for all language students. We asked about the IB but they feel they are providing sufficient breadth, and everyone is encouraged to take part in the huge extracurricular programme.

Quick to identify problems, and communication between parents and teachers is good. Children are helped within the system rather than being withdrawn from class although, if needed, additional lessons are available. It is not a school for girls with serious special needs, and anyone applying to join will only be accepted if the school feels that she will be able to cope with the work level.

Games, options, the arts: Own five acre sports field nearby with full size all-weather pitch and lots of tennis courts. Hockey, netball, cross-country – you name it, they can try it. Inter-school matches and competitions here and overseas. Some 95 per cent do the D of E programme, which starts in year 9. Nearly all take the bronze, many the silver and some go on to complete the gold award.

Several different choirs and orchestras, which all are encouraged to join. The year 6 choir has won the Beckenham Festival Award. About 50 per cent learn an instrument; free lessons on an instrument of choice for everyone in year 7. Lots of drama, including backstage and technical, stage and costume design; beautiful purpose-built theatre on site – part of the curriculum from year 7 and available as both GCSE and A level options. Many girls take the LAMDA exams. Inter-house competitions and amazing-looking full school productions. First rate art, ceramics, other 3D work, textiles and photography. Great pictures all over the place and inspired dresses hanging in the senior art room, a relic of a recent fashion show.

Plenty of trips and outings, including recent visits to China, Italy and Spain. The biennial history trip to Russia ensures history remains popular. Our guide was keen to show pictures from a recent art trip to New York. Skiing in Switzerland, singing in Paris, D of E expeditions all over – these girls have opportunities galore.

Background and atmosphere: The first purpose-built GDST school, opened in 1880. Now in larger premises, it maintains the tradition of a thorough academic education for girls for highly competitive fees – a true 21st century version of a Victorian dream. The somewhat plain exterior hides an exciting inside. We followed our guide along corridors in the old and new parts of the building, upstairs to the sixth form's private area and down and around into good sized, airy classrooms, where relaxed, happy-looking girls seemed to be enjoying their lessons and interacting with their teachers, the younger ones all in typical GDST uniform, the sixth form in 'smart enough to wear to the office clothes – no jeans'.

Each corridor is subject grouped. We admired the well-equipped science lab, the biology room with three guinea-pigs, the art rooms, the drama studios, the modern theatre and the huge, fully-equipped sports hall. We saw the brand new cookery room gleaming with stainless steel where sixth formers can learn to cook before going to university, and were amazed by the very grown-up fitness suite. What would the Victorians have thought of the school's digital radio station? We particularly liked the library/resource centre and the language laboratory where a class was working at individual computers electronically linked to their teacher for help and direction. Our guide was very proud of her school.

The students are passionate about green issues and like to keep their teachers on their toes. The school has achieved the healthy schools award and has silver eco-school status. Apparently a winter draught problem, so the sixth form set up a knitting club and knitted excluders for the windows. Their potential is limitless – a sixth former is on the Greenwich Young People's Council and another is a member of the Olympic Legacy Youth Panel.

Pastoral care and discipline: A general culture of support throughout the school amongst teachers and pupils alike and, according to our guide – a bright, confident, lower sixth former – a peer mentoring system that really works. The policy is 'to nurture an enjoyment of learning in an atmosphere of mutual respect and celebration of achievement'. They are sensitive to emotional problems, and the excellent school counsellor supports child and parents alike. A real understanding of each girl is important to them. The house system is successful and the school council gives the girls the opportunity to air their views and feel they really are involved in the running of their school. Stress seems minimal, perhaps due to the fact that they are all encouraged to do yoga or pilates during their lunchtime break. All girls also participate in fortnightly tai chi session.

Pupils and parents: A broad ethnic and social mix with over 25 different languages spoken – 'A real reflection of London's population and a proper preparation for the world they will meet later'. The majority lives locally, Blackheath, Greenwich, Lewisham etc, but others come in from Bexleyheath and Dartford, and the school runs three minibuses, two south of the river to Rotherhithe and to Eltham/Chislehurst, and one north of the river to Canary Wharf and surrounding areas. The common denominator is that all the parents are looking for the best education for their daughters and are willing to make sacrifices to get it. Their involvement and support are manifest. OGs include Mary Quant and Baroness Jay.

Entrance: A lot come up from the junior school. Otherwise predominantly at 11+ and 16+ by interview in the autumn term and examination in January. No sibling policy – every girl is assessed on her own merits. If a space, any child will be welcomed at other times, as long as the school feels that she will be able to cope.

Exit: Between a third and half leave post-GCSE. Range of university courses at mostly good universities eg Oxbridge (one choral scholar in 2013), London, York, Sheffield, Bristol etc.

Money matters: A number of scholarships, for up to 50 per cent of the fees, with an increasing number of bursaries for 50-100 per cent of fees. Always worth enquiring, if your child has a particular talent.

Remarks: 'We are not posh!' they say. Maybe not, but parents are putting the school down as their first choice – girls really want to go here. It is a forward-looking school with traditional values and opportunities for all, providing a well-rounded education thoroughly focused on the future. Here you find the young women of tomorrow being prepared to take their places in an ever changing world. They will be ready.

Blossom House School

8a The Drive, London, SW20 8TG

- Pupils: 179 pupils, 80 boys/ 25 girls in senior school, 16 boys/4 girls in sixth form and 44 boys/10 girls in primary school; all day • Ages: 3-19 • Non-denom • Fees: £26,244–£35,889 pa
- Independent

Tel: 020 8946 7348
Email: admin@blossomhouseschool.co.uk
Website: www.blossomhouseschool.co.uk

Principal: Since its founding in 1983, Mrs Joanna (Joey) Burgess (sixties) DipCST MRCSLT Dip RSA SpLD PGCE. Educated at St Paul's Girls' School and Oldry Fleming School of Speech and Language Therapy. Well known, liked and very much respected locally; married to Paddy, they have four daughters (one teaching at the school) and four grandchildren. Likes to spend her leisure time with her family or playing tennis or golf and socialising. Enchanting, with a wicked sense of humour, the diminutive Mrs B is described by parents as elegant, petite, beautiful and kind, with a steely will. 'Joey doesn't just light up the room – she lights up lives,' said one grateful parent. Another added, 'She runs a great school, is open, approachable and willing to take on suggestions.'

Blossom may be very much Joey's babe, child, teen... but it is clear that everything is child-centred, 'Many are fragile; an unhappy, anxious child is not in a good place when it comes to learning so we have to unpick that'. Pupils are appreciative, saying, 'She speaks clearly, doesn't confuse us and gives really good assemblies.' Her vision, energy, business brain, passion and total commitment steer the ship, but it's no solo voyage – an abundance of willing, first-rate help from the well-oiled engine room. True, we detected a hint that Joey likes control, finds it difficult to let go, 'She isn't perfect, but we wouldn't want her to be – she does what is important, and in her book that includes looking after us too,' say staff. Looking every inch like a lady who lunches, her Friday feasts, laid on for her hardworking team, are legendary, 'We have the most wonderful dos – it is a very sociable school. Joey wouldn't have it any other way – she loves a party'.

Academic matters: Sprinkling of the mature and experienced, but mainly young, energetic, female staff; some come as part of their initial teacher training, then return to hone their skills. Classes are small, typically eight or fewer, with groups of three or four for literacy, numeracy and speech and language therapy. All have an Individual Education Programme (IEP) based on personal learning styles, combined with visual communication aids, such as timetables of the day. Offers a relatively rare, educational-health-emotional package of teaching, speech and language therapy, occupational and physiotherapy, art, music and drama therapy. Structure (which children love), but the aim is to make youngsters adaptable and flexible.

Teaching is multi-sensory, with 'over-teaching', and is linked to an innovative sensory integration programme which helps children regulate and focus: 'It is possibly the most important thing we have introduced'. Every lesson has a learning break, where children head outside for a couple of minutes to exercise and recharge. 'It has made such a difference to their level of concentration'; formats vary according to age but are universally appreciated.

All follow the national curriculum, adapted as necessary. Touch typing from age 7. Pupils grade lesson activities on a scale of 1-3 to indicate the degree of difficulty they experience, giving staff instant feedback and enabling them to adjust their teaching accordingly. Popular projects include 'we are writers', which saw a gamut of poems and prose in print.

Senior pupils make guided exam choices – 'It's a bit like speed dating,' said one enlightened youngster. 'You spend five minutes with staff talking about their subject, then move to the next.' All work towards GCSEs and/or entry level exams, vocational qualifications and practical courses in a range of subjects including art and design, science, maths, English, DT (food or graphic products), media and computer appreciation. Children say they'd like to see GCSE history, German and Polish offered, otherwise diddly-squat on their wish lists. At GCSE, single science and art are among the most successful subjects.

While most achieve many things parents were told (pre-Blossom) they never would, we uncovered the odd parental grumble that older children are not academically stretched. If we are being picky, we suspect some in the senior school might benefit from academic extension and challenge – for example, we saw a maths lesson where teens collectively and impressively identified pentadecagons, icosagons et al, but felt disappointed when they were not then given the opportunity to see basic reflection through to a correct conclusion. However, pushing for academic success has to be balanced against fragile esteems and anxieties – 'What good is a pile of GCSEs if a child is too scared to set foot out of the door?' Indeed.

Games, options, the arts: All youngsters have group music and art lessons – teachers aim to develop creativity, build self-esteem and encourage interaction and communication. Visits to art galleries and plays and sessions in school with artists are popular, but not as frequent as some parents would like. Variety of sports on offer and older pupils are encouraged to work towards Duke of Edinburgh and sports leader awards. Tends to play inter-house sport rather than inter-school, as early outings resulted in crushing defeats and squashed esteems. Not a uniformly popular move. 'My child is sporty and would love the chance to compete against other schools. It's sad, but I guess you have to consider others,' rued one parent.

Background and atmosphere: Situated in a quiet, des-res area, close to Wimbledon Common, started life in the pink house (originally Joey's grandmother's residence), now home to the delightful nursery. Four pupils then have mushroomed 40-fold now, with most located a stone's throw from the original school, in larger, carefully-planned premises. This former care home for the elderly, with good outdoor space, includes age-appropriate play spaces and looks and feels like a small, modern, very well-kept, independent day school (which it is) – 'Joey planned every inch, indoor and out – she knew what was needed: it's fab'. Has all the facilities you could hope for: sports hall, art studios, science lab, well equipped food tech room, music rooms etc.

Pastoral care and discipline: Parents praise the care lavished on their offspring: 'My child loves going to school, the structure, the space, socialising with his friends and the kind teachers'. Many older children arrive feeling angry, let down, stupid and unworthy, so staff unapologetically focus on the individual and work to reduce anxiety and stress. 'We do what is needed – if that is a Theraband on a chair or bluetac to squash, that's fine,' said one therapist, adding, 'Tinies arrive surrounded by chaos and mess. It is our job to untangle. We help them make the links, so they understand their significance to themselves and others.'

All bring own healthy lunches. Eating together, from nursery to 19, is encouraged, with food tasting and exploration very much part of Blossom life. We witnessed the youngest children happily sampling foods of different colours and textures – all the more remarkable when only weeks prior, many had had rigid diets and were reluctant to eat with others. 'It makes family life easier – simple things like trips to the shops, outings, holidays etc are now possible, as well as treats such as trips to restaurants,' say parents.

While children undoubtedly have their moments, we witnessed an abundance of courtesy and encouragement. Being kind to each other is important, as are good behaviour and achievement. Positive steps, however small, are rewarded via a highly-regarded token system. Pupils are controlled but not contained. School rules are simple and clear, 'consequences' rather than punishments for inappropriate behaviour. Three entries in the inappropriate book equals a trip to Joey – 'She doesn't shout, but she does try to help you get it right'. We saw this in action at the start of our visit, when we encountered two male miscreants who moaned animatedly that 'the school was sexist and teachers didn't listen' – yet when we spied them later they were happy, relaxed and smiling. Naturally we tried hard to uncover the alleged sexism, but the best we could muster was a girls' club with no equivalent for the boys.

Pupils and parents: From a wide area of London, Surrey and Kent. Fees reflect the high level of support, but 90 per cent are funded by their local authority. We were particularly impressed by just how articulate some of the older youngsters are, but recognise that talking about and understanding emotions and anxieties are different skill sets.

The active FOBH (Friends of Blossom House) organise an assortment of events including sibling days. School runs numerous parental events including termly curriculum and feedback meetings plus self awareness, and drug awareness sessions: 'It's important we take the blinkers off'. Despite the plethora of events, we received mixed messages from parents – some feel very much part of the school, others less so, possibly because of distance and personal circumstances.

Almost all have nothing but praise for the school. 'We don't just move house, but heaven and earth to be here. We are defensive – we've been through the mill'. Every parent has a story, feels the system is money-orientated, not child-centred – 'Tribunal is expensive, unfair. It is about how good your solicitor is and how many other children the LA have funded ahead of yours. The individual child and their right to an education are missing from that equation'.

Entrance: At 3+ into the nursery; term of their fifth birthday to the junior school; 11+ to the senior school, 16+ to sixth form. Admission at any time, subject to a place, suitability and funding. Progression through the school(s) depends on: progress, what's right for the child and funding. A primary diagnosis of speech, language and communication impairments is required.

Most have additional needs including ASD, dyspraxia, sensory integration difficulties (can cater for the 'fizzy, whizzy' child but not the aggressive or violent), dyslexia (school is CReSTeD registered) and ADHD, occasional selective mute. It is not unusual for youngsters to exhibit a deal of frustration and anxiety as a result of their language disorders, but the school would not suit those whose primary needs are either ASD or behavioural.

Entry is via a detailed three-day assessment followed, for some, by a trial six week period to ensure the child will benefit from a Blossom education. On entry, approximately one third of the nursery children have very limited speech, but thanks to timely, expertly delivered interventions, this reduces significantly as youngsters progress through the school. Quite a few come from mainstream. 'Some cope there initially – they don't look any different to their peers – but as they get older, their difficulties become apparent and frustrations are compounded. It takes a deal of time and devotion for us to get them back on track'.

School says no tablet of stone dictating what child will suit Blossom – it is not only about the profile of the child but also the cohort and group at the time: 'Sometimes we can take children who are a little less able because there may be a peer group who have come through from the nursery with similar needs'.

Exit: Majority stay at 11+, others to specialist schools: More House (Farnham), Moor House (Oxted), The Moat, St Dominic's Godalming, Sibford, St Catherine's. A few to (supported) mainstream state schools: Wimbledon College, Ursuline Convent etc. Recently started 16+ provision – no leavers as yet.

Money matters: More than 90 per cent are LA funded. Hopes to offer some bursaries in the future. Fledgling tribunal fund.

Remarks: Blossom by name, blossom by nature. Regrettably all too many have to tread through manure to get here, but once they do, children flourish and families thrive. 'Without Blossom House I don't think we would have survived as a family – they gave us back our child, our lives'. For the right child with speech, language and communication issues few rosier places to develop, mature and bloom.

Bloxham School

Bloxham, near Banbury, OX15 4PE

- Pupils: 400 girls and boys; 210 boarders • Ages: 11–18 • C of E
- Fees: Day £16,380–£23,205; Boarding £21,270–£29,985 pa
- Independent

Tel: 01295 720222
Email: marketing@bloxhamschool.com
Website: www.bloxhamschool.com

Headmaster: Since September 2013, Mr Paul Sanderson, previously a deputy head and director of curriculum at Gordonstoun. Originally from Northern Ireland, studied at St Andrews University then postgrad qualifications from Oxford and Cambridge. Taught at Lancaster Royal Grammar, Oundle and Carr Hill High before joining Gordonstoun as housemaster. He is married with three children.

Academic matters: Takes children with a broad range of abilities, but brightest and best can, and do, get to top universities (fine to be clever); lets pupils mature and make academic strides without undue pressure. Regular and increasing number of activities for scholars; intensive Oxbridge help on the cards. Striving for academic improvement – A*/B passes at A level nearly 61 per cent in 2013, with 30 per cent A*/A grades; penny numbers taking most subjects but business studies and geography top the popularity polls, with English lit and textiles enjoying particular success. Nearly 32 per cent A/A* at GCSE, 2013. All take IB tech qualification which covers the whole spectrum of ICT skills. Free laptops for all, from 14, with smart internet café on site for fun and games. Attractive, well-resourced library.

CReSTeD DU status, so a great place for bright dyslexics (IQ 120+, maximum 20 in school at any one time), who not only benefit from the direction, ebullience and experience of SENCo but also thrive across the school, thanks to staff awareness, understanding and expertise. Not surprisingly, attracts a number of children with minor needs, and identifies a fair few more (all screened) on entry. That said, only mild needs – Asperger's, ADD, HI, dyspraxia and some medical difficulties – can be met; those with greater needs or requiring regular individual input should look elsewhere; all must be capable of GCSEs and eventual university entrance. Great at motivating those who might otherwise fall by the wayside. As one boy said, 'I've never been a lover of school but found lessons at Bloxham really engaging, especially biology (do ask about the snakes!) and English.'

Games, options, the arts: Wide range of sports on offer: hockey, rugby (regularly fields 11 teams) and netball, through to fives, squash and very serious clay-shooting. Plenty happening on the equine front: a highly-acclaimed polo team, cross-country, showjumping and dressage all feature (no livery on site). Girls and boys participate successfully at national championships in a range of sports on a regular basis and enjoy a couple of overseas tours annually. All play hard, possibly because just as much credibility in turning out for the thirds as firsts. Head praises all great performances but isn't afraid to issue a 'could do better', if needed. Says, 'I challenge a keen sporting pupil not to be fulfilled at Bloxham.' Good facilities: couple of Astros (new one soon to open), modern sports hall (just refurbished), two charming cricket grounds (cricket professional recently appointed). Super indoor swimming-pool, two glass-backed squash courts and climbing wall are much used by pupils and locals. Separate sixth form club-room situated above the cricket pavilion.

The place is singing once again – music facilities and opportunities massively improved and improving; concerts, sung Eucharists, choirs, instrumental lessons and 'Blox-Idol' cater for a range of tastes. Drama is the weak link (handful of plays a year), but with a musical in the offing, this Cinderella subject may soon be given a welcome boost. Purpose-built Raymond Technology Centre offers good facilities; no cooking/home economics yet but it's on the burner; art strong, ceramics exciting, textiles innovative. Young Enterprise, CCF, D of E, successful debating squad, oenology etc – you get the feeling that if something is desired, wherever possible it's either allowed for or will be provided. One parent told us, 'They try to accommodate passions and will flex schooling/times for something really important.'

Background and atmosphere: Founded in 1860 and given to the Woodard Foundation (group of schools originally founded by Canon Woodard to promote muscular Christianity) in 1896. Handsome building of Hornton stone, quarried from below the foundations, with stunning chapel on first floor. The well-maintained school proper is contained in a playing field filled 80-acre campus with a number of outhouses, pitches and buildings, none more than an eight minute amble away. Lower school housed in a magnificent transformation of the former White Lion pub overlooking the main street. Uniform for all, though sixth formers may wear a suit.

A boarding school at heart – day pupils must stay till 6pm but have the option of pursuing activities and heading for home at 9pm. School buses for day-boarders ferry them from convenient pickup points. The week ends on Friday for the lower school, the rest released from 4pm on Saturday. Boarders are 'expected' to be in for the first weekend of term and the first after half term, frequent mass exodus on non-compulsory weekends. Boarding (weekly only) for years 7 and 8 provided in Park Close, a former, rather grand manor house with commanding views and very capable house-parents at the helm. One of the best kitted-out junior boarding houses we've seen – looks and feels like a real family home (which it is). Senior girls' houses smarter than boys', though boys confided they quite like the 'lived in look' – less to worry about. Girls graduate early from dorms to individual study bedrooms while boys more likely to progress to shared studies. Good atmosphere, girls and boys readily mix (intra-house, boy/girl visiting in communal areas only).

Pastoral care and discipline: Many parents choose Bloxham because of its deserved reputation for nurturing and great pastoral care. A caring school with a family feel – children thrive here because, regardless of skills or abilities, they're given confidence and encouraged to have a go. Faith important – emphasis put on living a Christian life in a Christian community, 'actions, rather than possessions'; a goodly showing in RS at GCSE. Lots of systems in place to ensure no-one falls through the net – strong tutorial system via houses, impressive peer listening, chaplain, counsellor etc. Odd grumble by parents about communication with the school but most felt they could readily contact staff, who would swing into action no matter how small the anxiety.

Disciplinary matters usually nipped in the bud; urine testing on demand if drug use suspected, followed by suspension for a week if positive, and random testing thereafter; repeat offences will result in expulsion. Alcohol not a major problem – the villagers complain if they drop litter in the (very pretty) village, and the campus is too busy to find a quiet corner.

First class food, healthy selection, friendly staff and excellent surroundings make dining an enjoyable and sociable occasion; nevertheless staff and pupils vigilant for eating disorders.

Pupils and parents: Most from an hour or so away; lots of first-time buyers. Parents with children in the state sector come because they see it as 'an upmarket alternative', parents from the independent sector because they want a smaller, more local school (as opposed to Stowe, St Edward's, Uppingham etc). Basically north Oxfordshire, farmers, businessmen, Services; eight per cent from abroad – Germans, Russians, Hong Kong Chinese, French, Spanish, plus expats. Produces cheery, confident, polite pupils, interested and interesting.

Entrance: At 11, own test and assessment; CE pass mark 50 per cent; sixth form entrance via interview, report from previous school and GCSE results. Large tranche from state primaries at 11 plus, Carrdus, St John's Priory and The Croft School; at 13 from a wide range including Ashfold School, Beachborough, Bilton Grange, Swanbourne House and Winchester House.

Exit: Small leakage (around 10 per cent) after GCSE. Majority go on to higher education. Great variety – including Russell Group occasional Oxbridge (one in 2013); Birmingham and Southampton popular; range of traditional and exotic courses including PPE, business/marketing, sound production and engineering.

Money matters: Parents in real need still get helped via the dreaded blue form means test. Woodard Foundation can give help in an emergency for children of Old Bloxhamists. Huge collection of scholarships for everything from music, sport (not at 11+), DT, art and academic, for all ages – take as many as you want, at 11+, 13+ and 16+, but will be withdrawn if child doesn't continue to measure up.

Remarks: Being welcomed into Bloxham is akin to being embraced into the heart of the family. As one pupil said, 'You feel like you're wanted; the teachers always seem pleased to see you.' Academically more challenging than before but content, as ever, to take a broad church. What you see is what you get – a cheerful, family school, with Christian values, all mod-cons and the knack of turning out happy and fulfilled youngsters in a quintessentially English setting.

The Blue School

Kennion Road, Wells, BA5 2NR

• Pupils: 1,455 girls and boys; all day • Ages: 11–18 • C of E • State

Tel: 01749 678799
Email: office@blue.somerset.sch.uk
Website: www.theblueschoolwells.co.uk

Head: Since 1999, Mr Steve Jackson (fifties); joined as deputy head in 1989, so has seen it all. Used to teach design technology and PE. Married to a deputy head; three children. Insists on showing new parents and visitors around the school himself. Except us, who were asked not to visit what is already a chronically oversubscribed school. 'A good front man,' said a parent, but 'not engaged in the day-to-day life of the school'. Publicity, website, school profile etc seemingly low on the agenda.

Academic matters: A genuinely comprehensive school. Standards are high at GCSE (67 per cent 5+ A*-C including maths and English in 2013) and consistently good in the core subjects of English, maths and science. Concerns about provision for the less academic at GCSE have been addressed with entry level history and French, and four science pathways to cater for all abilities. Links with Strode College for the more vocationally-minded. At A level (82 per cent A*-C grades in 2013) there is a broad selection of subjects on offer, though – as ever – take-up for modern languages low. Has specialist school status in science and mathematics. Outstanding work in design technology and PE. Much use of ICT within the classroom and brilliant ICT provision throughout. The staff seem genuinely keen to embrace the new technology; they feel ahead of the game due to local company support.

On arrival in year 7, boys and girls are taught together and in mixed ability groups, apart from English and maths where they are setted. At GCSE almost all subjects are setted. Generally little staff movement, and a considerable proportion has been at the school for longer than 10 years, perhaps why one parent said he thought the school was resting on its laurels and that a few teachers were merely going through the motions. A strong belief that if a child is well-motivated then they can do very well here, less so if not. Some think the school should instil a better work ethic early on so children deal better with GCSE pressures.

SEN provision appears to be good, with close liaison between departments and the SENCo and a flexible approach. Pupils struggling with literacy are helped within class or withdrawn for small group work at behest of subject teachers; SENCo runs assessments on request, esp from parents who suspect difficulties. Maths dept more autonomous, with its own specialist TA who sets up in-class/individual/small group sessions according to need. General assessments done in class, which means first week of new academic year can be 'a bit chaotic', until all five sets are sorted out. Bottom sets might number only eight pupils. Pretty well all behavioural issues are catered for, as befits an inclusive school. SENCo says that the school 'does not hunt out children with emotional or behavioural difficulties but tries to support them in their education. However, [parents of] kids on the autistic spectrum hunt us out, even transferring into the area to attend "The Blue".'

Games, options, the arts: Walking into the design technology block feels like entering an art school department – fabulous work and ambitious projects. Regularly wins design awards eg Arkwright Scholarships etc and has established close working links with local businesses for funding and work placements. Bench seating in the historic Palace Fields gardens in Wells was designed by A level pupils at the school. The presence of the sports development centre means that there is a huge choice available in addition to the traditional – including caving and rock climbing actively pursued in nearby Mendips – and the school produces a smattering of county players every year. Music is prominent with orchestra, wind band, jazz band, choir and guitar group – so plenty of opportunity to get involved. Drama a strength with regular productions, and not frightened of tackling ambitious works eg Peer Gynt. Several trips abroad each year, often exotic – witness two World Challenge expeditions, to Africa and the Himalayas, in two years.

Background and atmosphere: Dates back to 1641 when it was established as a charitable foundation via the legacy of local churchman Ezekiel Barkham. The name was adopted over time owing to the blue dyed uniforms provided for the original pupils. A big school plonked in a spacious 33 acres. Slightly elevated position means a fantastic view. Three gyms, a school hall and three dining areas. £2m science block opened by the Princess Royal incorporating six laboratories, prep rooms and a large state-of-the-art ICT facility for use by own students and those from partner primary schools. The 'Blue' theme is carried throughout the décor – blue carpets, chairs, blinds, lino, walls, though 'it all looks a bit tired', said one parent. Work is in hand to make the school more environmentally sustainable, with the lead coming from the unusual 250-person school council, hailed nationally as an example of best practice. Twenty-five council teams raise awareness and funds for what really matters to them, eg Fairtrade, buddying, fitness, cuisine. A great way to demonstrate passion and commitment amongst the young. Dining facilities have won healthy eating awards; in fact 'The Blue' is first school to be awarded FEAST status, by Raymond Blanc no less, which conferred swish catering training facilities for use inside and outside education. Locally-obtained fresh meat and vegetables are used and free chilled water is provided in each of the main buildings. Students also grow some of their own produce.

Pastoral care and discipline: Although a church school, no overt signs of Christianity. An assembly every morning with hymn singing and reading from appropriate texts; however the format is guided by 'worthship' rather than worship. Achievement is valued – every opportunity is taken to publicise (bulletins, posters around the school and regular contributions to local press) and praise. A firm but realistic attitude towards all matters of discipline. Smoking within the building results in a one-day exclusion, as does swearing. The headteacher holds half-termly Saturday morning detentions for students who need redirection.

Pupils and parents: Serves an area of generally advantaged, white, British, English-speaking households; the strong PTA reflects this and raises considerable sums for major purchases, eg a new minibus. Liaison with parents is good, with regular newsletters, meaningful reports and parents' evenings and a recent initiative 'Parent Pay' (how true...) where payment for school meals, trips etc can be made online.

Entrance: Around 250 a year from local primary schools – mainly from within the city of Wells and surrounding villages. Oversubscribed and estate agents don't help this problem. Worth getting a map of the catchment area from the school.

Exit: Over 50 per cent stay on to do A levels at sixth form (though weaker A level candidates encouraged to bail out if AS results disappoint) and, of those, about 80 per cent move on to higher or further education.

Remarks: Solid state option sailing serenely on within a sea of local independents. The emphasis is on motivation and enthusiasm, amply demonstrated by the range of subjects and activities on offer.

Blundell's School

Linked school: Blundell's Preparatory School

Blundell's Road, Tiverton, EX16 4DN

• Pupils: 580: 340 boys/240 girls (360 board/weekly board, rest day) • Ages: 11–18 • C of E • Fees: Day £11,995+; Boarding £16,920–£29,340 pa • Independent

Tel: 01884 252543
Email: registrars@blundells.org
Website: www.blundells.org

Head: Since January 2013, Nicola Huggett MA, previously deputy head at Downe House, and Blundell's School's first female head. Educated at Marlborough College and read PPE at Oxford. Started her career in advertising, moving to teach politics and history at Haileybury, where she was also a houseparent and latterly head of boarding. A keen sportswoman, she has run the London Marathon, played club hockey, captained her college boat club and ridden in international three day events. Married to Spencer, with four children.

Academic matters: Does well, given the broadly comprehensive intake. Top of the tree recently for RS, history and – perhaps surprisingly for rural Devon – languages. 2013 A level: 66 per cent A*-B, 39 per cent A*/A. Spanish and French results superb, science results now among the best in the school. Recently introduced EPQ qualification for the intellectually motivated and curious sixth formers, now very popular. Fifty per cent A*/A at GCSE.

Sixty special needs pupils 'are not overlooked'. 'Some' special provision for dyslexia – one or two sessions a week. Sixty-five per cent of sixth formers have own laptops (50 per cent of pupils in general). School eager to raise intellectual tone, so now more academic societies, a director of studies from Wycombe Abbey, where she was head of history, new honours award system (full colours for service to school, not just for sport), much IT investment. Recently opened academic centre comprising classrooms, IT suites, design and technology and seminar rooms – a £1.5m investment.

Games, options, the arts: Rugby for boys and hockey for girls are the heavyweights. Registrar's wife was an international hockey player and coaches the first team. School says Blundell's has strongest sports teams of any school in Devon – perhaps not too bold a claim as many regional and some national representatives, most recently an England cricketer and a national U15 hockey player, as well as U16 fives champion. All mainstream sports offered, plus strong equestrian team (national champions at the schools' eventing championships at Stonar) and pupils effuse over the delights of kayaking. Fifty acres of playing fields, recent second Astro and all-weather cricket nets, double sports hall, outdoor swimming pool, fitness suite with state of the art equipment.

Harkens to the great outdoors – adventure and leadership programme for pupils in lower years involves eight weekend activities over the year (camp-craft, survival skills, vehicle maintenance, fixing plugs and taps etc), leading toward a three-day expedition in the summer. CCF compulsory for three terms in year 10 (and pupils may carry on to year 13), Ten Tors hike each May a big event and D of E taken seriously, as is Devizes to Westminster kayak challenge.

Particularly strong arts. Very good music department, largely due to long-serving, 'brilliant' director of music and possibly some intake from Exeter Cathedral prep. Choir tours central Europe each year (recently Venice). New building project has doubled the size of the music department and provides an electronic recording studio. An exciting place for drama too – the Ondaatje Theatre (named after OB Christopher, brother of Booker Prize-winning Michael) is a big asset. New, young head of art has introduced a special art status standing for the school's most talented pupils. Drama and art frequently overlap here (the theatre was being used for a solemn session of A level life drawing on the day we visited). Photography also popular. Good workshops (textiles, silver-smithing, cabinet making, engine repairs).

Background and atmosphere: Set in 90 acres, bisected by a busy public road. Dignified collegiate main blocks, cloister and chapel; over the road the newer music block, huge and lovely dining hall, where staff sit among pupils, and the Ondaatje Hall housing theatre, art, photography, pottery. Library refurbished – looks great. Amazing, round Old Boys' pavilion overlooks playing fields – 'The Old Boys paid for it so they could have a perfect view of the rugger'.

Long and illustrious history since being founded in 1604 at the bequest of local clothier Peter Blundell, one of the wealthiest merchants of Elizabethan England. The school's timeline includes 'school used as Fairfax's HQ in siege of Tiverton Castle' (1645), 'maths teaching begins' (1823) and 'schoolrooms heated for first time' (1828). School mentioned in Lorna Doone by (Old Blundellian) R D Blackmore. Moved premises within Tiverton in 1882. Fully co-ed from 1993. Tiverton is 'proud to have it on the doorstep'. Rated as outstanding in each of the six categories in latest Ofsted inspection.

Tawny 'Blundell's tweed' jackets for 13 to 16 year old boys, bright red blazers and navy skirts for the girls; sixth form boys and girls now wear navy blazers. Cars allowed in upper sixth only for going to and from school.

Boarding numbers have doubled in recent times. Seven houses: two girls', three boys', plus School House for 11-13 year olds and – hold on to your seats – a co-ed upper sixth house called Westlake. School House is a sort of middle school within a senior school. Has its own character, own matrons, changing rooms, play areas and structure – own weekend programme (no Saturday school). New, cosy common room, games area, comfortable, redecorated bedrooms (four to six to a room), new computer suite and kitchen.

Girls' houses pleasant, if a little sleepy: single rooms for lower sixth, boys allowed 'just inside the dogrun door' – a quaint reference to past times when Blundell's boys would walk the young hounds for the local hunt. All three boys' boarding houses have been extensively improved over the past three years, with the girls' house due for extensive work in the not too distant future.

Blundell's describes Westlake as a unique pre-university experience, with individual rooms for boys at one end, girls at the other, and both mixing in the central common area. Allows these older students to form new friendships across house divisions and must do wonders for sixth form retention. This arrangement may not suit everyone, but school points out, 'The past seven years have seen significant academic success, and much of this is attributable to the new Westlake project, so it has enhanced the academic focus here'. Separate boys' and girls' common rooms upstairs for slopping around in dressing gowns etc, very important for the girls – 'so we don't have to worry about hair and make up'. Full kitchen, widescreen TVs, no set bedtimes, internet access and basin in each room. Almost everyone boards in sixth form.

Pastoral care and discipline: One or two suspensions for bullying, which shows school is taking it seriously. Drugs not at the top of worry list – not a school where drugs are cool. School says anyone caught with them should expect to be out, but a second chance with regular testing is more likely. No more sixth form bar, but occasional dinner-dance with limited alcohol available. Drunken pupils face temporary exclusion.

Pupils and parents: Wholesome – not much makeup on girls or hair statements on boys. Farming intake has dropped from 20 to two per cent. Parents working in the professions (probably also looking at King's Taunton and Sherborne); increasingly from the West Country (large contingent of boarders from Cornwall, who don't have a lot of choice); many London families relocating to Devon. Some far-flung, including Londoners with local connections. Fair number of Services children. Ten per cent are foreign nationals, from 16 countries, especially Germany – Munich agency sends high-class pupils. Others from Eastern bloc, Japan, Canada. Two full-time EFL teachers – pupils needing extra English get three lessons a week in place of French.

Strongly loyal and supportive Old Boys (school has a busy development office and Old Blundellian Club) include Christopher Ondaatje, Michael Mates MP. Jack Russell (1809-14) of terrier fame – a famous old boy from the 18th century.

Entrance: Official entry points 11, 13 (especially boys) and 16, but other years often possible. CE at 11 and 13 from traditional prep schools (eg Mount House, The Downs, St Peter's and King's Hall) – pass mark 50. Many from Blundell's prep (own 10 acre site on the Blundell's campus; previously known as St Aubyn's, this independent prep was bought by Blundell's, removed and completely rebuilt within it). Good sprinkling from local state schools. Internal and external candidates for sixth form need at least five C grades at GCSE.

Exit: Few leave post-GCSE. Around 90-95 per cent to university – small number to Oxbridge (traditional links through Peter Blundell with Sidney Sussex, Cambridge and Balliol, Oxford), plus Durham, Edinburgh, Bristol, Birmingham, Cardiff, Southampton. Business management, medicine and music are popular career paths, more recently graphic design.

Money matters: Generous number of scholarships – academic, music, art, sport and drama, at different ages. Approximately one-third of entrants hold awards of some sort, up to 50 per cent of basic fees. Foundation awards allow local boys and girls to attend as day pupils. Exquisitely precise fee structure with different prices for boarders, local boarders, weekly boarders, local weekly boarders, flexi-boarders, local flexi-boarders, day pupils and local day pupils (phew!).

Remarks: Distinguished rural school, of ancient lineage, dealing creatively with challenging times.

Bolton School Boys' Division

Linked school: Bolton School Boys' Division Junior School

Chorley New Road, Bolton, BL1 4PA

- Pupils: 925 boys • Ages: 11–18 • Non–denom • Fees: £10,497 pa
- Independent

Tel: 01204 840201
Email: seniorboys@boltonschool.org
Website: www.boltonschool.org/seniorboys

Headmaster: Since September 2008, Mr Philip Britton MBE (fortyish). Unassuming, relaxed and very bright, with a first from Oxford and an MBE for services to physics. Best performance prize from his PGCE at Cambridge, a master's (with distinction) from Leeds in 1998, a secondment to the Institute of Physics advancing the physics curriculum and writing textbooks and, in 2009, an international award for his contribution to physics education. Came here from 17 years at The Grammar School at Leeds where he was head of physics at just 23 and latterly deputy head for five years.

Lives near school with his wife and two sons, both in the infant division, and enjoys the extra-efficient service he receives in local shops from 'his boys' on their Saturday jobs. Loves outdoor pursuits and sailing, 'But first and foremost I like learning and an academic life'. Boys say he's 'young, modern, unorthodox in a good way' and like his GSOH: 'He's funny, self-deprecating and he cracks good jokes in assemblies'.

Academic matters: Results reflect solid education of boys from the top 25 per cent of the ability range. In 2013, 67 per cent A*/A at GCSE and 48 per cent at A level. Long tradition of choosing medicine or engineering so science and maths (the only IGCSE subject, and with setting from year 8) are strong, but humanities and languages also fare well and are popular. Some 20 per cent take two modern foreign language GCSEs, a few take three, helped by native-speaking teaching assistants housed in cottages by the games pitches. Full-time Russian assistant and a biennial trip to Russia. Greek and Latin on the menu with classics sharing sixth form teaching with the Girls' Division.

Six forms of 24 in each year but, by GCSE, average teaching group size is just 17 with a maximum of 15 for A level. By A level most choose heavier subjects – sciences, maths, geography and economics, although some courses are run for tiny numbers. High flyers encouraged to soar with AQA Bacc extended projects, Olympiads and Nuffield scholarships. Head introduced critical thinking at A level, boys also take general studies.

Two libraries, lots of journals, the quality dailies and plenty of computers for working. High-powered staff, lots of PhDs, new ideas and teaching styles from younger teachers. One young pupil told us, 'We've probably got one of the best sets of staff in the country' – certainly boys appreciate teachers' availability and willingness to go the extra mile, and feel that what's expected from them is just that they do their best.

Games, options, the arts: Ten per cent of the timetable is given over to games – 'Boys need to run around and let off steam'. Soccer, rugby and hockey in winter, cricket reigns supreme in summer. Fabulous 25m pool means swimming and water polo are also strong. Two sports halls, one with a climbing wall, a multigym and pitches descending the hill on 'the levels'. 'Our ground staff are brilliant, but we would like an all-weather Astro to practise more to defeat our rivals,' boys say. 'One day,' says head, so it's on the development radar.

Until year 12 every boy spends half a week a year at school's Patterdale Hall on Ullswater. With outdoor challenges and team-building, 'the Patterdale experience' is designed to build character and give lifelong memories. Sixth formers use it for business enterprise training courses. Many other foreign and residential trips including white water kayaking and coast-to-coast cycling.

Music is strong – about half the boys take instrument lessons, annual gala concert at Manchester's Bridgewater Hall. Strong drama too (Sir Ian McKellen was a pupil here) in both a studio and the theatre in the arts centre. Three huge art rooms, one with a kiln, and exciting paintings on display, 'Never a problem finding a cover for the Boltonian magazine'. Special mention for the DT department for building Tenacity of Bolton, a 48 foot sailing ketch just outside the DT department, over 10 years. Over 1,000 boys helped teachers, parents and friends of the school create what's now a mobile outdoor pursuits centre and sailing education resource – 'And MGS (qv) hasn't got one of those,' say boys.

Sixth formers take enrichment classes from car maintenance to finance skills, and all give at least 20 hours to community service, some many more. Heaps of extracurricular clubs and activities – form tutors check that each boy is involved and busy beyond his schoolwork. One parent said, 'Look at the end product: they're so well-rounded – they can talk, they can communicate, they're ready to take their place in the world.'

Background and atmosphere: Imposing, baronial, pink sandstone buildings on 32 acres of well-to-do west Bolton suburb. The Girls' and Boys' Divisions lie either side of a manicured quad with modern arts centre beyond, newly extended junior and new infant Divisions are just down the road, along with a Kidzone building offering care from 7.30am – 6pm and holiday clubs.

Founded in 1516, but re-endowed and rebuilt in 1913 by the community minded, first Viscount Leverhulme. It's spacious and splendid, with magnificent stained glass, sweeping staircases and oak doors and panelling at every turn. It would be easy to slide straight into Oxbridge architecture from here – the buildings themselves seem to imbue boys with an unstuffy self-assurance. Up a little staircase is a rooftop glasshouse, so Hogwartian one might imagine germinating mandrakes. Much teaching is traditional with rows of desks; some labs are refurbished, some not; but the refectory tables and benches certainly feel like a step back in time – although the plentiful grub, prepaid with fees, is bang up-to-healthy-eating date. At the sixth form common room butty bar, Auntie Carol serves bacon sarnies for £1.10 and beans on toast for just 50p, against the telly tuned to a music channel.

Pastoral care and discipline: Discipline is quietly maintained through form tutors and year heads, with a good dose of common sense emphasising owning up, taking consequences and everyone moving on. Few rules, lots of mutual respect, developing 'emotional resilience – stuff happens in life and we want to find the correct place between a traditional stiff upper lip and the arguably modern culture of crying at every opportunity'. Boys encouraged to be 'cheery', as befits leaders of the future. A school nurse available to all in the girls' school building and a school counsellor. Boys feel they have a voice on one of three pupil councils.

Four houses provide a vertical structure for inter-age mentoring. Sons of Old Boys and siblings kept in the same house. Four house days a year with sport, quizzes and board game contests. Fifty-three prizes on speech day, some for community action and outdoor pursuits. Boys stand for teachers and exercise corridor courtesy. Uniform shop on site and open daily.

Pupils and parents: These are good lads, down-to-earth, open and articulate. Half from Bolton, which, head points out, 'is not a northern grit town but middle and upper middle class, a town with considerable affection for the school', and plenty of RP here. Many OBs live in the area and the Old Boltonians' Association is strong. Lots walk to school but nearly half arrive on one of 22 coach routes from North Manchester, Rochdale, Preston, Warrington and rural areas. The wide geographic catchment and one in six boys on bursary assistance give a broad social mix – 15 per cent ethnic minority boys, mainly Asian, reflecting Bolton's make up; some Muslim, some Hindu and a small Jewish presence.

Star in the Old Boys' crown is Sir Ian McKellen CBE, who speaks fondly of the school, but the list includes city bosses, judges, professors and top sportsmen. Sir Harry Kroto FRS won a Nobel prize for chemistry, hence the Kroto Chemistry building at school. Radio presenter Mark Radcliffe, Chess grandmaster (from the age of 19) Nigel Short MBE, Leslie Halliwell, author of Halliwell's Film Guide, Paul Horrocks, editor of The Manchester Evening News, Martin Milner OBE, leader of the Hallé Orchestra, BBC Apprentice finalist Alex Wotherspoon, and Ralf Little who plays Anthony in BBC's The Royle Family to name but a few.

Entrance: Over two applicants per place. NFER VR, NVR and maths tests with school's own creative writing paper in January, interviews and school reports considered, looking for boys who'll get 5s in key stage 2 Sats. A bit of movement at sixth form, entry depends on reasonable GCSEs.

Exit: Nearly all to university, including a few to Oxbridge; medicine and dentistry, engineering, science, maths, humanities and languages all popular. Manchester, Newcastle, Durham, Sheffield, Nottingham, Imperial London and Liverpool particularly favoured.

Money matters: Impressive BSSL, Bolton School Services Ltd, generates revenue for bursary fund from venue hire, catering, the pre-school nursery and by running 12 buses as a coach company. One in six pupils receives bursary assistance, means tested rather than academic scholarship. Financially all four divisions of Bolton School – girls', boys', junior and infants – function as one unit. Lunches included.

Remarks: No-nonsense, solid, traditional grammar school. If you thought, 'They don't make 'em like that any more,' think again and be glad. One mum in a family with three generations of Boltonian men said, 'You can't better this school – it's "belting",' and we are inclined to agree.

Bolton School Girls' Division

Linked school: Hesketh House

Chorley New Road, Bolton, BL1 4PB

• Pupils: 785 girls, all day • Ages: 11–18 • Non-denom
• Fees: £10,497 pa • Independent

Tel: 01204 840201
Email: seniorgirls@boltonschool.org
Website: www.boltonschool.org

Headmistress: Since 2011, Miss Sue Hincks (forties), a graduate of Magdalen College, Oxford, where she achieved a first in modern languages and history. Previously deputy head at The King's School, Worcester. She enjoys choral singing and walking and is a keen theatre-goer.

This is her first all-girls' environment; she says she is thoroughly enjoying working with such intelligent and feisty girls. Feels that Bolton needs to regain its place alongside the single sex heavyweights in Manchester and wants a school

that is very academic but has breadth, and where children leave with fond memories of good times had. Parents tell us she hasn't been afraid to take ownership of the school, and girls sing her praises for attending nearly every school event, including Saturday morning sporting fixtures.

Academic matters: A strongly academic school. In 2013, 70 per cent A*/A at GCSE and nearly 51 per cent at A level. Maths and science particularly strong. DT strong too, with two girls awarded prestigious Arkwright scholarships this year and two full classes running at GCSE.

The sixth form imaginative curriculum enrichment programme aims to broaden and enhance the educational experience and includes sign language, Italian and critical thinking. Alongside the usual, A level options include Greek and theatre studies. Most take four subjects at AS, dropping down to three at A2, although general studies can be taken as an additional A2. Can team up with the Boys' Division to offer subjects where only a few are interested.

Five form entry in year 7 with an average teaching group of 22. This tapers as girls move up the school. Setting in maths from year 7.

Learning support department can't accommodate every SEN as girls must be able to cope with the fast academic pace, but each case is looked at on an individual basis.

Games, options, the arts: Sport is important. Badminton, athletics and dressage all good. School council has been successful in pushing for the introduction of tag rugby and football. Climbing wall and pool shared with Boys' Division, with pool open before school for serious training. Impressive numbers represent town, county and GB in swimming, lacrosse, hockey and cricket.

Drama popular and girls buzzing about frequent productions held in purpose-built theatre.

Music is thriving with over 300 girls learning an instrument. The many bands and orchestras combine pupils from the Boys' and Girls' Divisions, and the jazz band has performed at the Montreux Jazz Festival. Several girls are members of Manchester's Halle Choir.

Background and atmosphere: History dating back to 1913 when the first Viscount Leverhulme endowed two existing schools to form the Bolton School Foundation, with boys and girls sharing a single site. Grand, grade 2 listed, sandstone building which many pupils described as 'just like Hogwarts'. Located a mile away from Bolton centre in 32 acres of greenery. Strong sense of tradition with an organ played in assemblies and prefects in gowns.

A brand new sixth form centre is planned for completion in 2014, which will be shared by both the Boys' and Girls' Divisions, though lessons will still be taught separately. 'The best of both worlds,' states the head. The centre will have Wi-fi access throughout with pupils able to use 'cloud' data storage.

Burgundy uniform liked by girls, but a few parents concerned that the girls looked scruffy. No uniform required in sixth but smart appearance requested. Girls told us that teachers turned a blind eye to the length of skirts and we certainly saw much evidence of this!

Pastoral care and discipline: Peer mentoring by trained members of years 10 and 11 for younger pupils in a specific room on a drop-in basis, with mentors feeding back to staff where necessary. This was much appreciated by pupils we spoke to. Individual circumstances considered when looking at incidents involving drugs and alcohol, but head will expel if needed.

Pupils and parents: Broad socio-economic mix due to the means-tested £2m bursary fund. 'It's no ivory tower,' one parent explained, 'and nor should it be. After all, we want our children prepared for the wider world.' Pupils mainly from Bolton and surrounding areas, many travelling on the bus network shared with Boys' Division. Many pupils from industrious business families, and not unusual for several generations of the same family to come here. One in eight pupils from an Asian background, rising to one in five at sixth form.

Old Girls include Monica Ali, author; Dame Janet Smith, former Lady Justice of Appeal; Baroness Morris of Bolton, Deputy Speaker of the House of Lords; and Anjali Pathak, brand ambassador for Patak's.

Entrance: Around 50 from Hesketh House, Bolton Girls' junior school. Others from local preps and state primaries, often tempted to apply here by the many taster days held for year 5s. Very competitive exam at 11 in maths, English and verbal reasoning, followed by interview.

Exit: Girls go on to study a huge range of subjects at mostly good universities across the UK and abroad – business, law, English, veterinary science, psychology, medicine, dentistry and art foundation courses; a few to Oxbridge.

Money matters: Large bursary fund maintains, as far as possible, the 'principal objectives of the first Lord Leverhulme – that no boy or girl of potential who qualified on academic grounds but whose family were able to offer limited support would be debarred from entry to the school'. School can and will help in unexpected financial crisis. Unusually, no academic, sporting or music scholarships.

Remarks: A traditional, hard-working, down-to-earth school. Less social stratification here than at some of its counterparts in Cheshire – parents commented on how refreshing this was. One mum got quite choked when she said, 'I watched my daughters walk through that arch as little girls and now they're leaving as educated young women, with strong opinions, ready to face a new era.'

Bootham School

Linked school: Bootham Junior School

51 Bootham, York, YO30 7BU

• Pupils: 270 boys, 200 girls; 85 full, 13 weekly and 36 flexi boarders • Ages: 11–18 • Quaker foundation (but other faiths welcome) • Fees: Day £14,595–£15,990; Boarding £16,320–£27,195 pa • Independent

Tel: 01904 623261
Email: admissions@boothamschool.com
Website: www.boothamschool.com

Head: Since 2004, Mr Jonathan Taylor BA (fifties). Read English at Lincoln College, Oxford and has MEd from Sussex. Previously deputy head (eight years) and acting head (for four terms) at Bedales. Not a Quaker but clearly in tune with Friends' ideals; quick-thinking, articulate, unstuffy, approachable and clear-sighted about his vision for Bootham. He describes Bootham as his 'ideal headship' and appears very much at home. His devolved leadership style suits the place – a collaborative and cohesive way of working ('always consider you might be mistaken') encouraging healthy discussion and debate.

Married to Nicola and his interests include the arts, gardening and the outdoor life. Fascinating and engaging in conversation, he displays a real understanding of pedagogy coupled with an endearing ability to put people quickly at ease. He might just be the only member of staff you meet wearing a

necktie, possibly a reassuring touch for new parents, though his brightly coloured striped socks reveal a sense of the maverick within and he is all the more likeable for it.

Academic matters: In recent years school has transformed itself from middle-of-the-road into a Yorkshire leader. Staff aren't exactly sure how this has happened but point to an infectious work ethic ('it's OK to achieve'), backed up by individual attention (Quaker maxim is 'seek that of God in everyone') and powerful sense of community. Academic achievement is 'not the be-all and end-all', say parents, but 'results are good nevertheless'. In 2013, over 45 per cent A*/A at GCSE, 47 per cent A*/A grades and 75 per cent A*-B at A level. Sees itself as a 'premier science school', and results back this up. English and history popular, excellent art and maths. Class sizes throughout emphatically on the small side. Staff aim to fit A and AS combinations round pupils' choices, quite a feat in a smallish school. The approach is 'give them room and they'll deliver', which applies equally to staff and pupils. Staff are an engaged and creative bunch. They have room to breathe here and pupils feel the benefit. 'It's just good practice', says the head modestly.

Specialist science facilities, a music school, art and design studios and an IT centre. Wireless network to help laptop users. Excellent John Bright library much used, recent addition of mezzanine floor adding an attractive additional workspace. Teaching lively and interactive; common claim that pupils take responsibility for their own learning and interrogate their teachers carries more weight here than in many schools – an aspect, perhaps, of the Quaker principle of 'speaking truth to authority' (i.e. don't take it lying down). Has opened its doors by offering masterclasses and summer schools for pupils from other schools, bringing much needed openness across the school community locally and no real surprise that Bootham should drive this. Currently a waiting list for Latin GCSE class for external pupils, all the more impressive as it is run after school.

Wide range of special needs catered for. School goes out of its way to help – ground floor biology lab created to enable pupil with a motor disability to learn alongside her peers.

Games, options, the arts: Wide range of sport on offer. School encourages sport 'as a healthy part of life that hopefully will be continued'. Sport is played by all for enjoyment. Some parents would like a little more rigour in training. 'Testosterone-fuelled heroes don't really fit in here,' said a laid-back senior boy. Tennis and football traditionally popular, swimming (own pool), sports hall with climbing wall, no rugby; teams in all sports accommodate everyone, not just the talented. Despite – or because of – this, plenty of creditable achievement all round; basketball team has been district champion and individual successes include an international fencer, Olympic swimmer, county netball, hockey and cricket squad members and Leeds academy footballers. Playground cricket is the stuff of legend here and a fiercely guarded tradition – one former pupil went on to become a member of the Hong Kong women's cricket team.

Outstanding design work has received national critical acclaim. Vibrant art department, with wonderfully creative pupils' work led by practising and exhibiting artists. Music a major strength. Twenty different ensembles and over 60 per cent learn a musical instrument – mainly for enjoyment but many get to grade 8 and beyond, as well as scholarships to London music colleges. Regular buffet concerts held in main hall. Drama also strong; LAMDA on offer.

Expeditions to exotic places like Bolivia, Peru and Iceland and regular exchanges with France and Germany. School has its own well-used observatory (original William Cooke telescope and lovely polished brass fittings) and boasts oldest natural history society in the country. Hard to be bored here – plenty to do, huge range of extracurricular activities, regular weekend trips and activities for boarders.

A school with a conscience, it's no surprise that Bootham ticks all the boxes as a Fairtrade school. It has the highly-regarded Eco-Schools' Green Flag and can proudly boast that it sends no waste to landfill. BEAST (nickname for Bootham Environment and Sustainability Team) leads the way in reducing the school's carbon footprint, beginning (naturally) in the junior school with mini-BEAST; awarded Eco-Schools Ambassador status in 2013 – one of only 11 schools in the country – for education leadership in eco matters.

Background and atmosphere: Founded in 1823 on liberal, intellectual, tolerant principles. No need to belong to Society of Friends, or even be Christian, but non-credal umbrella, underlined by regular, silent Meetings, does seem to work a kind of magic, and parents willingly buy into it.

Originally for boys only, became co-ed in 1983. Within shouting distance of the Minster and city walls but the only visible part of the school is the fine Georgian terrace and passers-by would be surprised to learn that the site covers nine acres. From the busy main road, look out for the clearly identifiable Bootham blue-green doors, behind which lie a spacious and tranquil campus, with additional buildings gradually edging alongside. The fact that much of the school is hidden from view adds to an air of mystery about the place, yet the irony is that these buildings house some of the most open-minded people you could ever meet. Original buildings are undergoing a cycle of cosmetic updates and more radical facelifts; new arts centre will greatly boost arts provision and free up useful space elsewhere.

This is a largely non-hierarchical place and not rigidly conformist. Relationships between pupils and staff clearly very good – mutual respect is the order of the day. New pupils surprised and impressed by the fact the 'the head will open a door for you'. Parents comment on friendliness of receptionist, catering and ground staff as well as teaching staff. Younger pupils wear a kind of uniform. A dress code for older ones, though it's not immediately obvious, but an impressive alumni list suggests that perhaps it really doesn't matter as clearly clothes do not necessarily maketh the man. Self-run school council is more than a talking shop and can subject authority to awkward questions about how the school is run. 'Not snobby' say parents, who welcome the fact that pupils are 'encouraged to think about wider social concerns and global issues'.

Slight whinge from some pupils about Saturday morning school, but the upside is that the school is in town and so you can make a quick escape to the shops when lessons are over.

Pastoral care and discipline: Given the emphasis on a warm, family-type atmosphere, it would be easy to assume a laid-back, rule-less school short on structure and discipline. Not so. Expected standards of behaviour are clear and 'all the usual systems are in place'. No alcohol allowed on premises, suspicion of drug taking renders a pupil liable to random testing, drug peddling leads to expulsion. The key difference is that pupils here are encouraged to consider the effect of their actions on others and that in itself acts as an effective mechanism for self-control, most of the time. In line with the Quaker ethos, pupils say 'school comes down hard on bullying'.

Good standard of boarding accommodation – possibly better for girls than for boys, but that's not unusual and it bothers the boys less. Flat-sharing for the sixth form (college) girls, which they love and seems sensible in terms of preparation for the future. Good wholesome food, plenty of choice. Day pupils can try boarding in one of many flexible options. Contact with distant homes possible through email and video conferencing.

Pupils and parents: Pupils look like your average floppy-haired teenagers but these are a happy, confident, savvy bunch, probably more comfortable in their own skin than most. A combination of clear yet equitable guidelines and being accepted for what and who you are makes a big difference in these impressionable

years. Prospective parents who found themselves being asked a host of questions by their 'delightfully curious' pupil guides signed up immediately – because 'these were the kind of young people we want our children to be'.

No real parent 'type' – more an attitude. Many children of university teachers and medics, plus a raft of curious first time buyers. Once you've had the conversation and removed any preconceived notions, the Quaker reference point makes lots of sense and clearly appeals. Active parents' association holds regular coffee mornings, walks, lectures and a grandparents' day. Weekly recitals – music, poetry-readings and the like – open to all. Regular Saturday morning gatherings with coffee and croissants at no charge – head and deputy often pop in so can be useful for a catch-up. Some even stay for lunch.

Parents say Bootham is 'addictive' and that 'it gets under your skin'. They appreciate the 'open access to teachers via email, enabling parents to discuss any concerns they may have'. Time and time again it's the 'beyond the academic' bit that parents rave about here. Not that there is any lack of academic rigour, there isn't. It's simply that there is something else, not quite tangible and not appearing in league tables, but you can feel it in your bones.

Day pupils mainly from York and up to 25-mile radius of school. Boarding stands at around 25 per cent, from UK and worldwide, all English-speaking or near-fluent if not. Notable former pupils: include AJP Taylor, Brian Rix, Philip Noel Baker (Nobel prizewinner and Olympic medallist), John Bright (parliamentarian), Stuart Rose (former boss of Marks & Spencer), Silvanus Thompson (physicist), plus 16 more fellows of the Royal Society.

Entrance: A third of the entry at 11 comes from Bootham Junior School, the rest from schools far and wide. Entrants at 11 have an assessment day, at 13 a more traditional exam. For sixth form entry a minimum of seven Cs or six Bs at GCSE required, which must include maths and English. Head interviews all applicants and asks for report from previous school.

Exit: Some 30 per cent leave post-GCSE, mainly to local sixth form college, either for vocational courses or to avoid Saturday school. Many take gap years. Five or six a year to Oxbridge, rest mainly to good universities (Leeds, Sheffield, Newcastle, Warwick) to read 'proper' subjects.

Money matters: Not a rich school: most income generated through fees and fundraising. Some academic scholarships (means-tested), music scholarships (not means-tested) and some special provision for Quaker families.

Remarks: School does well by all and parents say 'differences are celebrated, not shunned or ridiculed'. But don't expect to find a community of meek souls. Far from it. Bootham helps pupils to develop into bright, articulate and considerate individuals. Pupils admit it 'may not suit the highly competitive or the attention-seeker', but having said that, they are quick to add that 'we'd help them to get over themselves...'

Bournemouth School

East Way, Bournemouth, BH8 9PY

- Pupils: 1,060 boys, all day • Ages: 11–18 • Non-denom • State

Tel: 01202 512609
Email: office@bournemouth-school.org
Website: www.bournemouth-school.org

Headmaster: Since 2009, Dr Dorian Lewis (mid forties), previously deputy head at mixed comprehensive, Queen

Elizabeth, Wimborne, notching up experience managing curriculum, doing the National Qualification for Head Teachers. A chemistry graduate from Southampton (did his PhD there too), originating from Wales, taught at Thomas Hardye school in Dorchester until appointed to head of science at Wimborne.

Married with three children in local schools, he relishes his teaching, taking extra chemistry for exam years and thriving on personal contact with staff, pupils and parents. A smiling and reassuringly cuddly demeanour conceals iron determination to get the very best for his boys and a razor sharp awareness of what needs doing. His biggest shock as a new head was the amount of time spent in 'fruitless' meetings, so he immediately set about reorganising the management to produce more 'fruit'.

Feeling the 'good' standards reported in a 2008 inspection left room for improvement, he saw his first year as a 'quiet revolution' – 'Last year a complete development plan for staffing and curriculum, this year the same for buildings'. 'Continuous cohesive management' is his term for galvanising everyone on his 'very talented and capable staff', from the cleaners to the super-efficient business manager, in his own 'velvet revolution'. Indeed, the latest Ofsted report in 2011 judged the school 'outstanding'.

Academic matters: In 2013, 57 per cent A*/As at GCSE, and 67 per cent A*-B, 40 per cent A*/A at A level – only to be expected of such a selective school. Dr Lewis agrees with the inspectors that the teaching, though successful, is pretty traditional – lots of chalk, talk and write; all fine, but needing a little 'oomph', which he is rapidly providing – interactive whiteboards, classroom technology etc – and latest report talks about 'strong collaboration between skilled teachers and enthusiastic boys'. Boys at all levels were clearly engaged with their work and most talked ardently about it.

Classes of 24-31 (24 average) in first three years study the basics plus art, music and technology, with Latin (but no Greek) and French, plus another language chosen from German, Spanish, Italian, and Mandarin Chinese. All take at least 12 GCSEs, with 'fast track' being phased out in favour of the biggest possible bunch of the very best grades ('It's what the unis want').

The 22 plus mainstream subjects on offer at A level include a raft of technologies, government and politics, further maths, psychology and sports science. Results appropriately sound, though was a bit of a glitch in music and, for a specialist language school, the takeup of all but French and Spanish is regrettably low (Dr Lewis has already homed in on this and is 'holding the line' on a compulsory GCSE language for all). Sixth formers can add the Extended Project Qualification (EPQ).

The individual learning needs service is focused mainly on the potential problems of the very bright, coping with a higher than average percentage of Asperger's or similar. Four teaching assistants give in-class and individual support. Lots of personal supervision by designated teacher for children who need 'looking after', and a gifted and talented co-ordinator ensures exceptional students get enough curriculum enrichment and acceleration to keep them on task.

Games, options, the arts: Unashamedly an academic hothouse (some parents would like to see it a bit 'more rounded'), but a vast range of sports, activities and hobbies, all pursued with a determination generated by 1100 plus highly intelligent and competitive boys (and girls in the sixth form). Dr Lewis protests that actually too much rather than too little, but is immensely proud of sporting successes, giving a ball-by-ball account of the final matches of the Glanvill and Aegon team tennis cups (they were runners up in both).

Music is on a grand (and loud) scale, featuring big and concert bands with 50 plus players apiece, lots of brass and much singing. Most years a distinguished performer or two go on to music college. Choirs and singers abound, as to be expected from the school which produced Gareth Malone. The enormous Javanese Gamelan (takes up a whole room), which has highlighted the identity of the music department, is departing for a museum, so perhaps Gareth could come back and identify another area of musical excellence to keep the side up.

Smashing portraiture on show in the music department and a stunning front hall display of one versatile student's work. Art department bristles with artists in residence and has ongoing links with the Bournemouth Arts University College.

Terrific sports centre and all-weather pitches. Football teams in every year group scooped up prizes in local and county competitions, as did the first rugby team. Athletics etc and oodles of cricket. Duke of Edinburgh is pretty new, with Prince Edward visiting to give it a boost. Mammoth CCF with masses of activities for all three services and (another) band with a female bandmaster. Sea Scouts take pride of place in a list of other extracurricular bursting with technological activities (a group built and raced a car) and cultural/arty enterprise (links and visits to Japan/China etc). Loads of chess, films etc etc and a current student won Tesco's junior Masterchef, perhaps spurred on by the shiny cookery kitchens in place for lower school lessons and a pre-uni cooking class.

Background and atmosphere: Born the day Queen Victoria died in 1901, the school moved to its current hallowed portals as WW2 erupted. Only staff and prefects can use the echoing front hall and staircase, where walls groan under notices of awards and achievements. Spectacular for sheer length and solidity and the outsize central clock tower, the buildings are otherwise unremarkable, having been consistently modernised in strict rotation (ie a lab one year means an arts classroom the next), with the result that nothing is really out of date but nothing stands out. Functional new maths block, 'managed in house, which saved thousands', and all mod cons everywhere: wireless computer networks eat money, though don't look spectacular, but all technology is bang up to date. Extensive wooded grounds, including the copse much loved by Gareth Malone, freely available to roam in, since 'Bournemouth boys can be trusted'.

Only the best is good enough here and boys appear to thrive on cut throat competition. Not for the fainthearted, but the feeling is friendly, and boys respond to Dr Lewis's mantra of 'hard work, discipline, smart appearance and respect' by showing real interest – even junior mathematicians seemed enthralled. Most were reasonably tidy, happy to converse and making responsible use of the facilities left open to them at downtimes.

Sixth form (now taking girls) area buzzes with music/TV/conversation/work all going on at once. A helpful sixth form pastoral assistant is on duty at all times to give support on UCAS etc. Masses of older boys at work in the library, with a quiet academic hum and comfortable feel conducive to intellectual conversation or the odd game of chess. It is generously staffed and light and airy, at the top of a newish building with lecture hall and small classrooms, which make it ripe for development into a self-contained sixth form and adult education area.

Sixth formers have freedom to come and go as they please, so their bicycles litter the inner courtyard, chained to any available railings, unlike lower school bikes which are stowed neatly underneath it. Courses such as sociology and drama are taken in the girls' school and the pin-striped sixth form boys socialise freely with their less formally clad female counterparts. Spaces between buildings are nicely got up for sitting in summer and one courtyard has a horticultural feel, though the veg was struggling a bit.

Pastoral care and discipline: A competitive house system complete with tutor groups 'helps you to make friends', as well as providing a forum for informal monitoring of progress and social issues. Uniform is pretty neat, with quite well-cut grey suits (no one looked baggy-kneed) and own choice suits in sixth form, where long hair is a not much used privilege. Prefects on duty in the dining room – Dr Lewis says they virtually run the school.

Discipline, when needed, is firm, based mainly on temporary exclusion, though Dr Lewis has not shrunk from permanent exclusion when absolutely necessary, and the school is successfully draconian about bullying in any form. Parents can get immediate access to the head if he is there (in a curiously unadorned meeting room, since he has opted for a tiny working office). Any whisper of drugs results in parental involvement and appropriate 'severe sanctions'.

Pupils and parents: A broader academic mix than might be expected, especially at sixth form, where entry to courses may be less demanding than some less academic schools. Being Bournemouth, Anglo-Saxons predominate, though an ethnic mix. Flourishing parents' association and a star spangled list of OBs from the '60s comedian Benny Hill to Sir David English of The Daily Mail, Blur guitarist Alex James, educationalist Mike Tomlinson and news reader Mark Austin.

Entrance: No specific catchment, but those outside Bournemouth have to apply via their own LA. Boys admitted by exam process, which starts with an application or 'expression of interest' in September. Testing is year 7 maths, English and verbal reasoning – takes the top 150. Later years admitted by assessment, if a vacancy comes up, but not open to those who failed at 11. Sixth form has extra 50 places and is by GCSE results: six or more A*-B including maths and English.

Exit: Majority to university, including three to Oxbridge in 2013, some to vet/medical schools, general scattering of blue chip and others.

Remarks: Solid as the rock of Gibraltar and nearly as traditional, though Dr Lewis is bringing in some innovative teaching and ideas. His breath of fresh air approach has already transformed the prospectus, made major organisational changes and set some even more ambitious targets. Definitely for the intellectually tough. A school to be reckoned with.

Bournemouth School for Girls

Castle Gate Close, Castle Lane West, Bournemouth, BH8 9UJ

• Pupils: 1,165 girls, all day • Ages: 11–18 • Non-denom • State

Tel: 01202 526289
Email: office@bsg.bournemouth.sch.uk
Website: www.bsg.bournemouth.sch.uk

Headteacher: Since 2004, Mr Alistair Brien (mid-forties), after being deputy head for five years. Educated at The Royal Grammar School, Guildford, read German and history at Exeter before PGCE at Birmingham. Spent his first three years of married life as housemaster of senior girls' boarding house at Keswick School – so clearly dedicated and experienced in shepherding teenage girls – then head of sixth form at the Arnewood School, New Milton. Approachable and easy to talk to rather than authoritarian, his affability covers a meticulous attention to detail and a steely determination for the school to serve his girls well. Parents and girls agree with Ofsted that school is 'led and managed extraordinarily well'. Keen on promoting school ethos and traditional values, with a 'firm but fair' approach to discipline, using carrot (stickers and approbation) rather than stick. Definitely 'prefers seclusion to exclusion' as a sanction, by which he means spending a day under his own supervision.

Regrets that he is now far too busy to continue writing German textbooks. Three children – the two daughters at the school.

Academic matters: An undeniably academic school, basking in recent Ofsted judgement of outstanding in all areas, out to produce scholars and scientists – with considerable success. Awarded specialist status for humanities, more than justified by a comprehensive programme of history (early and modern offered separately at A level), politics, geography, social sciences and psychology, plus religious studies for all at GCSE. Not surprising then that part of the spanking new Spreadbury Building is for social sciences, while RS has had its own building for a long time. More recent designation as a science specialist school attracted funding from the Wolfson Trust for spectacular refurbishment of two chemistry labs, now all singing, dancing and resplendent in saxe blue. One pupil was a national finalist in the young scientist of the year competition. She also pioneered the school's 'big sister' mentoring pairing scheme for pupils – so not just a boffin. Mr Brien agrees with the perception of many parents that the school is 'good' and 'solid' and is working hard to make it 'academically groundbreaking' as well.

All do 11 GCSEs, including triple science and compulsory RS, though outstanding athletes etc are allowed to drop a course to gain training time. Results are spectacular -- 67 per cent per cent A*/A grades at GCSE in 2013, 73 per cent A*/B and 47 A*/A at A level. Exam results, and consequently UCAS points, have improved steadily over the last few years. A small tail of D, E and U grades at A level, accounted for by the open access policy, which allows pupils coming into the sixth form from local schools to pick subjects without having A/B grades at GCSE in them, in the interests of giving maximum opportunity to all.

A levels in theatre studies, economics and business, plus sociology run with boys from Bournemouth School, while PE and minority languages (Spanish and German) are done jointly and girls go to the boys' school for business studies. Mandarin Chinese and Arabic taster courses on offer.

Class sizes average 28 in the first few years, shrinking to around 20 by sixth form. No setting in first three years except for maths. Only around 40 special needs pupils, few of these with learning disabilities, but the school does well by them. The learning centre, with one full-time staff member, currently has a small counselling-style space but is expanding to larger premises. It offers support to any student struggling for personal as well as academic reasons.

Games, options, the arts: Definitely not just an academic sausage machine. Parents report a lively sporting programme with some really competitive teams and something on offer for everyone. Team sports not the centre of life – but then this is a highly academic gifted and talented lead school. Recently introduced football, basketball, rugby and dance proving popular. House system (Mr Brien's initiative) has hotted up sport generally, encouraging friendly competition. A few super-talented pupils notch up national success at sailing, trampolining, dancing and archery. Have been national champions in badminton and also reached national finals in swimming, sports acrobatics and biathlon. PE staff mentor sports stars and are even hoping for a few Olympic competitors. School hosts national netball competitions, though a complete revamp of the gym is on Mr Brien's wish list. Superlative new art studios and pretty solid results at GCSE and A level.

Food technology, textiles and ICT rooms all comprehensively equipped and used by all girls in lower school on a rota basis (another area on the list for re-planning and refurbishment). Music and drama blossoming in the new performing arts centre: 'a cutting edge development'. Regular co-productions with Bournemouth School. Bags of choirs ensembles, orchestras etc. Trips to America, Austria, Belgium etc – link with St Anne's school in Kenya, staff and pupils visit both ways. Debating and public speaking are also very strong with team reaching national finals in the English Speaking Union's contest and the Debating Matters competition, which they claim to be the 'hardest of all'. Impressive list of extracurricular activities includes D of E and belly dancing.

Background and atmosphere: Younger sister of Bournemouth School up the hill and sharing a pleasant green site. Their playing fields meet, sixth form share activities, pupils from both socialise at lunch break and activities like CCF and D of E are offered jointly. Parents think BSG is more pupil-friendly – not just an academic hothouse, gives a more 'rounded education'. Feels like an ambitious school but not a ruthless one. Outward-looking and community-minded, it is co-sponsor with Bournemouth School of new local Church of England academy and recently became part of South West Academic Trust, a group of grammar schools in the south west working with Exeter University.

Distinctly utilitarian sixties architecture has been overtaken by pristine new buildings with good in between spaces which potentially shift the centre of the school away from the unprepossessing front façade – possibly aiming for a new entrance in the foreseeable future. Originally designed to house 700 'young ladies', the current 1100 plus just about fits into the still-evolving complex of new and middle-aged facilities.

Once inside, staff are welcoming, while corridors and classrooms bustle with busy girls. Half of a lovely mural showing the pre-1961 school in central Bournemouth brightens up the reception area wall, with the other half cunningly forming a gallery behind a glass wall. Spacious library is staffed at all times and has a large careers room, also staffed. The new virtual learning environment available via the school's network is the latest addition to technology – state-of-the-art IT is taken for granted here.

Pastoral care and discipline: Pupils and parents endorse the recent Ofsted judgment: 'tremendous clarity of purpose and superb relationships' and 'girls' personal development and wellbeing outstanding'. Sixth formers mentor younger girls and organise the six houses, named after (dead) famous women rôle models. All new year 7 pupils have a 'big sister'.

Pastoral care is delivered in the main by the house system, which has a good reputation for dealing well with problems, including bullying ('mainly the fallout from Facebook'), which is always tackled quickly and generally successfully. Social education in drugs/ internet/ personal relationships etc is provided by heads of houses. Mobile phones turned off in class and confiscated if they ring. Drugs seldom a problem, though Mr Brien would expel anyone selling them. His main weapons, used extensively by staff as well, are listening, talking and discussing. Parents have 'open house' access to head without an appointment every morning from 8-8.15am, otherwise heads of houses are first port of call.

Pupils and parents: Mainly from Bournemouth, but about a third travel from as far as Brockenhurst (east) and Ringwood (north), though Poole (Parkstone Grammar) mops up the western catchment. Parents arrange several bus routes. The canteen opens at 7.45am for parents dropping girls off early, though not after the 3.35pm end of teaching, when the school lets girls stay until 5.30pm. Supportive Parent School Association with lots of social activities raises substantial sums to provide equipment such as the recording studio in the new performing arts centre. Old Girls' Association has just been disbanded as pupils rely on Facebook, Friends Reunited etc. Better known past pupils include Lucy Macgregor (Olympic sailor) and Lisa Dillon (actress).

Entrance: Apply on local authority application form in October. Element of preference for Bournemouth residents though no catchment area – girls can come from anywhere. Around 480 hopefuls sit tests in English, maths and verbal reasoning on a Saturday in September, all vying for 162 year 7 places. Offers sent out in March. Practice papers available to all, and virtually everyone who sits the test will have practised – if you're too lazy to bother, then this isn't the school for you. A few from the independent sector but most come from over 50 state junior schools. Among feeders are Bethany Junior, West Moor's Middle, St Thomas Garnet's Preparatory School and King's Park, Moordown St John's, St Mark's, Queen's Park, the Epiphany and Winton Primaries. Admissions panel takes advice from junior school heads on borderline cases (true for those schools where heads are willing to comment – those opposed to selective schooling can be unwilling to get involved). Forty plus pupils enter at year 12, mainly from local 11-16 schools like Glenmoor and Avonbourne: six A*-C GCSEs the bottom line requirement for entry.

Exit: Fifteen per cent left post GCSE in 2013, but equal number from other schools joined. Vast majority to higher education – Exeter, Bristol, Southampton, Durham popular, six to Oxbridge. A sprinkling directly into employment and an increasing number to gap years. A pretty impressive proportion goes into law, medicine, veterinary and tougher science courses, with a fair share of art, drama etc.

Remarks: A real local grammar with a highly academic but up-to-date curriculum and a surprisingly cosy atmosphere. Certainly not wearing scholastic blinkers.

Box Hill School

Mickleham, Dorking, Surrey, RH5 6EA

- Pupils: 425, including 145 full boarders, 21 weekly boarders
- Ages: 11–19 • Non denom • Fees: Day £15,090; Boarding £22,950–£27,840 pa • Independent

Tel: 01372 373382
Email: enquiries@boxhillschool.org.uk
Website: www.boxhillschool.com

Headmaster: Since 2003, Mr Mark Eagers (fifties) MA PGCE (Cantab) MA (Bath). Educated at King's, Canterbury and Cambridge, where he read history and did his PGCE. Spent 10 years at the United World College in Singapore as head of history – an experience that shaped his thinking and philosophy. Took an MA in education at Bath where he could follow his passion – international education. Previously deputy head at Ardingly. Loves sport, especially cricket; charismatic, energetic and makes things happen. Well liked by pupils and parents and seen as a very good communicator. Married to Jane, who teaches economics and business studies. They have three children, the youngest two at the school.

He has driven through a huge programme of building work and change and has not finished yet. Still some pre-fabs lurking in the grounds – funds being gathered to build new classrooms and a sixth form centre and to rebuild the three day houses (planning permission permitting). A performing arts centre and dedicated sports hall also on his wish list. Quite a traditionalist at heart and a stickler for shirts being tucked in and ties tied, but will listen to what the children are saying. Recently two children asked to study Mandarin, so a teacher was found and they got A and A* at GCSE.

Academic matters: Wide range of abilities – does not pretend to be an academic hothouse but some get extremely good results.

Previously, only offered IB in sixth form, which initially meant a bit of an exodus after GCSEs to pursue A levels elsewhere. Now more staying on for sixth form – lots of presentations and taster days. Average IB points 29 in 2013. Apart from the usual subjects, environmental systems and societies (EVS) proved a popular choice. English, German, Japanese, Russian and Mandarin can all be studied as an A1 language. IB fits well with the Round Square IDEALS of all round education combined with challenges and responsibility, which builds confidence and independence. Now offering a range of A levels again.

At GCSE, 84 per cent got 5+ A*-C with English and maths, 22 per cent of grades A*/A. Science offered as single, dual or triple awards. RS not on the curriculum but is covered in PSHE.

Lots of new dynamic staff, many in their thirties, many attracted by the adventurous activities and expeditions – the headmaster likes to employ teachers with overseas experience. Homework now set via the intranet, so no one can pretend they have not got it. Newly refurbished and well stocked library staffed by a helpful, welcoming librarian and an assistant – a comfortable and popular place to work.

Twenty-five per cent of pupils have some form of SEN, generally mild to moderate dyslexia. Learning support centre has been going for 25 years and everyone has their own IEP tailored to their needs. This usually involves withdrawal from a language lesson for half an hour a week and some in class support – holistic approach: whatever works best.

Games, options, the arts: It is all about building confidence, leadership skills, a sense of responsibility and developing life long interests. The usual team sports on offer – rugby recently introduced. Big focus on individual sports and always on the lookout for hidden talents – will support children's outside interests and give them the chance to excel at anything they are good at, eg European tai kwon do champion, GB show jumper and a 15-year-old skier who won two gold medals. One young jockey was allowed time off from his D of E trip to take part in a race – he won and came back to join the group.

Everyone has to do an activity – anything from the usual sports and drama clubs to fashion, story telling, criminology, the art of pasta making and even circus skills. If someone has an idea, the school will try and accommodate it. Sixth form can't get away with being couch potatoes as have to do an activity for the CAS element of the IB. All years 7, 8 and 9 have to do two weeks of expeditions each year, the cost of which is built into the fees – a great confidence builder and great fun, even for those who were not expecting to enjoy themselves, and very effective for bonding year groups.

The sports hall doubles up as an assembly hall and can accommodate the whole school. Small gym recently refurbished. Small swimming pool used mainly for life saving certificate – any serious swimming done at Dorking Leisure Centre, but school no longer has a swimming team.

Debating a popular option, which, together with the English Speaking Union course, has helped Box Hill pupils do well at the Model United Nations, where the school won a prize for the best delegate in the Human Rights Council. New extension learning club – a voluntary, non-syllabus related session on Saturday mornings to stretch and stimulate children in all subjects.

Music school with a recording studio and mixing deck plus soundproofed practice rooms, all new and shiny and state of the art. For years 7-9 drama, art and music are part of the curriculum. Music timetabled around lessons. Drama offered at IGCSE and theatre studies as part of the IB. LAMDA also popular – several children gain gold each year. Big musical every autumn and an arts festival in March each year – everyone has to be involved in some way.

Dynamic art teaching inspires many to go on to art college – artwork dotted around the school and lining the walls of headmaster's study: a great honour if your picture is displayed in the front hall as the 'image of the week'. Fashion and textiles very impressive and can be studied as an option at GCSE and as part of the visual arts programme for the IB.

Runs three overseas aid projects in Peru, Costa Rica and Africa – aims to send 10 children to each of these projects every year, often proving to be life changing experience. Also involved in other international service projects run by Round Square and organises exchanges with sister schools around the world – some attend the annual Round Square international conference.

Background and atmosphere: Describes itself an 'an independent school in an international network'. Founded as a co-ed school in 1959 by Roy McComish, a master at Gordonstoun. Box Hill is a founder member of Round Square, an international group of schools sharing the philosophy of Dr Kurt Hahn, which puts academic work at the heart of the school but stresses the importance of all round education. He inspired a set of principles (IDEALS – internationalism, democracy, environmental awareness, adventure, leadership and service), all of which call for initiative and responsibility, that is embedded into the Box Hill way of life. Culture of 'have a go', whether academic work, performing on stage, scaling the climbing wall or taking part in expeditions at home or abroad.

Set in 40 acres and centred on a large Gothic Revival Victorian house designed by the architect John Norton, of Tyntesfield fame. Situated in the middle of the attractive village of Mickleham, nestling under the North Downs, not far from the M25, Gatwick and Heathrow and only 40 minutes from central London. Welcoming, large, panelled hall with a fire burning in the grate – still has the feel of an English country house. Good relationships with the village – they share a cricket pitch. Intense programme of refurbishment (new sixth form block under way) but still much to do – contrast of ageing prefabs (due for replacement asap) and state of the art facilities.

House system and small tutor groups mean good interaction and support between the year groups and the school is small enough for everyone to know each other. 'A very nurturing environment and accepting of all comers – very tolerant and inclusive,' says one happy parent.

Promotes the adventurous spirit – when it snowed, some children built an igloo in the garden and were allowed to spend the night in it: can't imagine many schools allowing that. Everything very democratic – sixth form council, student council, boarding council etc. Very active and supportive board of governors.

Weekly boarding very popular – no Saturday school or fixtures, as school feels that weekends are for time to be with the family or relaxation. Plenty of outings and theatre trips etc to keep boarders entertained at weekends. Over 18s allowed to the pub in the village (ID checked by the landlord) and wine is served at the boarders' dinners. Boarders have laptops and wi fi, Skype and Facebook allowed in the evenings. Shared rooms for years 7-11. Sixth form option of single or double rooms – most choose double. All houses gradually being refurbished and rivalry for the tidiest house – but it seems that not everyone has entered the competition! Food greatly improved and now very good with lots of choice – smart new dining hall.

About 45 pupils in the international study centre, mainly in years 8-10 – most stay only for one year until their English is up to speed. The pre-IB course is popular but hard work, as pupils take five IGCSEs plus English in one year. School tries to keep pupils in their correct academic year, but occasionally it is necessary for one or two to take an extra year and sit the IB at 19+. Great efforts are made to integrate pupils with the rest of the school – they live in the same houses and follow the same co-curricular timetable for music, drama, sport etc. Many, but not all, move into the main school at the end of the year.

Pastoral care and discipline: Clear sanctions policy, although some parents feel discipline could be a little stricter, but as one said, 'The children are encouraged to be individuals – and you can't have it both ways'.

Pupils and parents: Deliberate international focus – 25 per cent are foreign nationals; however these are mainly in the 16+ age group; pupils in the lower years mostly from the UK. Students come from 28 countries – quite a few Chinese, lots of Germans, a number of Russians and Ukranians.

Day children come from as far away as Carshalton, Woking, Redhill, Kingston and Horsham – fantastic network of school buses run by a dedicated transport manager which will drop children at their door if possible, a huge bonus for many parents. Aims to produce well-rounded individuals who can contribute to all spheres of life – people who are confident and show leadership and a concern for the welfare of others.

Lots of first time buyers and commuters, some of whom struggle to send children here. Parents can monitor child's progress via Parents in Touch website. Active parents' association which organises fundraising events throughout the year and has recently raised enough money to buy three mini buses. Friday tea with the headmaster once a month – good opportunity to air views and meet other parents. Regular forums for parents to express their opinions, concerns and ideas.

Entrance: Main entry points at 11+, 13+ and 16+ and at any other times if spaces and the subjects fit. Tested at 11+ and 13+ in maths, English, verbal reasoning plus an interview and report from the child's current school.

At 16+ at least five GCSEs at A*-C, with a minimum of Bs in the subjects to be studied at the IB and ideally an A* in maths or a second language for the higher level. Local children come from about 27 different schools, 50:50 state:independent. Those from outside the UK who have not studied IGCSE/GCSE will be required to sit a test in English language, maths and any additional language they wish to study, plus an interview.

Exit: About 50 per cent leave after GCSEs, many to local further education colleges, eg Reigate, Guildford and Colliers at Horsham – sometimes because pupils want to study A levels and vocational courses rather than the IB and sometimes for financial reasons.

Most who leave post IB go on to study a huge range of subjects, from environmental studies at Bangor, international hospitality at Oxford Brooks and archaeology at Durham. Oxbridge does not seem to feature, but a few each go each year to Russell Group universities and a number to art foundation courses. Some international students return to their home countries for prestigious universities in, eg, Paris, Vienna, Munich, Lausanne, USA (political science, psychology, business, law, languages), but many continue their studies in the UK. Universitat Internacional de Catalunya, University of Vienna, University of Westminster and Kent popular in 2013. International relations the most popular course along with Geography.

Money matters: No foundation, so bursaries and money for building works have to come from fees. A development fund being set up to finance the new building projects. Scholarships up to 15 per cent of the fees, considered mainly an honour. Means-tested bursaries available up to 100 per cent of fees. Head keen that everyone should have a chance to come and even persuaded the taxi driver who brought him home from the station to send his child to Box Hill on a very large bursary.

Remarks: You can be what you want to be here and the school will back you to the hilt and give you the confidence to give anything a go. Might not suit someone who does not enjoy the challenges of outdoor activities and expeditions, but even 'pavement pandas' have, much to their surprise, found that spending the night in a cave can be great fun.

Bradfield College

Bradfield, near Reading, Berkshire, RG7 6AU

- Pupils: 485 boys, 280 girls. 680 boarders, 94 day • Ages: 13–18
- C of E • Fees: Boarding £32,190; Day £25,752 pa • Independent

Tel: 01189 644516
Email: admissions@bradfieldcollege.org.uk
Website: www.bradfieldcollege.org.uk

Headmaster: Since 2011, Mr Simon Henderson MA PGCE (an extremely youthful looking late thirties). Educated at Winchester College, followed by Brasenose College, Oxford, where he read history. Teaching career started at Windsor Boys' School, moving to Eton College in 2001, where he was a deputy housemaster and head of history, and on to Sherborne School in 2009 as deputy head (academic). Straight-talking, unpretentious – more technocrat than autocrat, Merkel than Berlusconi, Bill Gates than Donald Trump; stowed his tea mug gripped firmly between his thighs as we conversed. Married to Ali (a civil servant) with four children under the age of 5!

Has introduced the rather fine Bradfield Diploma – a framework for extracurricular activities which aims to make sure Bradfield pupils partake in the lavish range of opportunities on offer. Covers public speaking, leadership, community service, private reading, current affairs, outdoor pursuits, sport, research and a bit of culture. A brilliant way to keep track of pupils' doings – must make writing uni references a breeze. Diploma research topics have included 'Are elite sportsmen born or bred?' and 'Which was worse, Wakefield's initial claims about the MMR vaccine or the media that broadcast them?'

Mr Henderson also ushered in the IB, still in its infancy here, and only pursued by around 10 per cent of sixth formers, though take up is growing. Unlike other schools we know, the IB route here is open to all and the school is keen it not become a ghetto for international pupils or swots.

Academic matters: Where has the old Bradfield gone and what have you done with it? A level results have shot up over the past decade. Sixth form value added scores very good (bearing in mind the school scoops up a nice, fresh sixth form intake including girls arriving from high flying single sex schools). In 2013, 76 per cent A*-B, with 47 per cent A*/A. Head now keen to give a similar boost to GCSEs (51 per cent A*/A grades in 2013). Vast majority of pupils now do three separate sciences at GCSE, with impressive results. Arty GCSEs on offer including dance, textiles and photography (the latter two also available at A level; A level students can also choose film studies or the unfathomable 'science in society'). History, the sciences and maths all achieving well as are modern languages – the latter a bit surprising in this virile school. Newish modern languages block offers French, Spanish, German (quite a few native speakers who come over for the upper sixth year), plus a smattering of Arabic and Mandarin. Latin and Greek both taught. Recent state-of-the-art science centre uses the very latest in sustainable design technology – 13 sophisticated laboratories plus groovy roof garden used for field studies. Around 40 ambitious sixth formers pursue an Extended Project Qualification.

Still, no danger of Bradfield becoming a hothouse, and geeks remain thin on the ground. A few parents feel the school does not always squeeze the best out of its most academic pupils. Has gone a bit Anthony Seldon, with all pupils now taking 'Emotional Literacy and Wellbeing' lessons in years 9, 10 and 11. All take a course in study skills in their first year. The Athena Programme, a lecture-based enrichment programme, broadens sixth form minds. Some 155 pupils receive learning support, most for mild dyslexia. First IB cohort will be examined in summer of 2014.

Games, options, the arts: 'The perfect school for a child who is a jack of all trades, master of none,' one parent told us. The exception to this may be sport, which remains outstanding. Bradfield's football (21 teams!) is the stuff of legend and can be played for two terms, by both boys and girls – some families choose the school for its football alone. Hockey, golf, cricket and even polo also doing very well. Boys won the Micklem Trophy (golf) in 2013, beating Rugby School, Eton and Wellington. The boys' 1st tennis team were runners up in LTA Aegon National Schools' Senior Students Finals 2013. Cricket coaching runs all year via the Julian Wood Academy and several boys play for counties. The 1st XI skipper won man of the series this summer for England U19 and has won a pro contract with Middlesex. Tennis the main sport for girls in the summer and we hear good things about the netball. Lowish numbers of girls means that a talented sportswoman may be playing in three matches a week – good, or not so good, depending on how you look at it. Sports facilities glorious: pristine playing fields, vast sports hall, indoor tennis centre, two floodlit Astros, nine hole golf course, fab indoor pool, dance studio – you get the picture. Masses of minor sports offered including squash, fives, fencing, riding, polo, sailing, shooting, water polo and 'fishing'.

Good to see music riding high. The department is well housed and humming with activity – pupils can practise during activity times and evening prep. Choral music particularly strong and the Chamber Choir travels abroad every year, most recently to Toronto. Instrumental players have taken part in the Music Junction project run by the London Chamber Orchestra aimed at bringing together children from 'diverse backgrounds'. Legendary outdoor jazz evening takes place each June, organised by the energetic head of modern languages – spotlights the jazz band, swing band and individual performances, including by teachers.

Enormous range of art media, taught in a cluster of studios and rooms by a highly enthusiastic and creative team – most practising artists themselves. Pupils here can paint and draw, sew, print, photograph, model, carve and sculpt. No proper theatre, but school productions take place in the Big School or the Studio Theatre. Greek theatre under reconstruction but we look forward to the return of classical productions – in Greek – a tradition that goes back the 19th century. The punishing Interhouse Steeplechase was recently revived, last run in 1948, and in full swing on the day we visited.

Humongous list of co-curricular activities from Shakespeare society to ice skating. The message that overseas trips are less in fashion in these days of austerity chic has not permeated into rural Berkshire so Bradfield sportsmen and women, geographers, musicians, economists ... you name it really... can be found globetrotting. Tennis training? In the Algarve! Film studies? We're off to Hollywood! Even CCF (compulsory in year 10) and D of E teams can be found scaling the rainy heights of Norway and Bavaria.

Background and atmosphere: Bradfield is a village ... and the village is the school. It is cosy – a 18th/19th century hamlet abounding with cute redbrickery, sloping roofs, chapel, leafy lanes and hillside walks. But it is also isolated – no shops, pubs or post office. Founded as a school by the combined local rector and lord of the manor for the education of sons of the clergy in the 1850s. Bit by bit the school took over the village so it includes, in addition to the old school, the old mill which now houses the art department – the stream and mill race still rushing away – and, gloriously, a fabulous arts and crafts manor house with stunning quadrangle and beautiful gardens. The grounds are among the best-kept we know – immaculate; the National Trust would do well to come and learn.

It's a big site stretching across a minor road and, although most teaching happens pretty centrally, fast walking and stout shoes are needed to get from one end to the other. A few privately-owned houses still in the village but most is school-owned and almost 90 per cent of staff live on site. Relatively little turnover in senior staff brings continuity, but also some resistance to change. Average age of staff is 40; 38 teachers have been at the college for more than 10 years.

Relations between pupils are 'mellow', say the kids. None of the pupils we talked to reported bullying. Teachers 'not too pushy' and 'very good at tailoring things to the individual'. Mr Gove would applaud its community-mindedness: Bradfield now sponsors Theale Green, a nearby comprehensive which had been put into special measures by Ofsted. Continues to nurture a 100 year old association with the Bradfield Club – a youth centre in Peckham, London.

Pastoral care and discipline: Vast majority of pupils board ... but you could shoot a cannon through the boarding houses on a Saturday evening without much danger of injury, especially in G House and Stanley House, half of whose inhabitants are day pupils. Still, there are usually over 100 pupils in school on Sundays and the numbers staying in over the weekend climb steadily in the summer term.

All year 9 pupils – boys and girls; boarding and day – start in Faulkner's House, a modern, custom built boarding house with its own dining hall and separate wings for girls and boys. Very popular with the kids, and with most parents who see it as a good transition between prep and senior school and an easy way for 150 new children to get to know each other. A few sceptics less keen and worried about scope for bullying or discipline issues with no older kids there to rule the roost. All agree though that the accommodation is superb, with ensuite bedsits, and usually two or three pupils to a room.

Year 10s move into houses spread far and wide over the wooded site, in which they remain for the next four years – no sixth form house. H House is flavour of the month at the minute (ensuite AND under floor heating!) while D House currently shines at football. Most day pupils stay for supper, prep and socialising, leaving around 9pm – though they are free to leave after lessons at 6pm.

A friendly place. 'We're basically pro-pupil', the head tells us. 'We try to separate the behaviour from the individual and give people a second chance ... but sometimes that needs to be somewhere else.' Doesn't believe in zero tolerance. 'Every case has its own context – there's always a shade of grey'. But no pushovers; five pupils out because of drugs Christmas 2012. Social media sites 'turned off' during lesson times. Alcohol less of a problem here than at some similar schools because most Bradfield pupils go home on Saturday nights instead of into town!

Pupils and parents: Five minutes from junction 12 on the M4 and from Theale railway station; helpful for the chunk of school families that live in London. Also popular with local families and the vast majority of pupils live within an hour and a half of the school. Has not yet been discovered by Chinese and Russians: around 11 per cent of pupils have homes abroad – a mixture of British overseas families and international pupils (from 33 different countries). Boys still far outnumber girls, almost two to one, but the college plans to admit an extra 50 girls from 2015. Top feeders include Cheam, Lambrook, Northcote Lodge, St Andrew's, Broomwood Hall, Thorngrove, Thomas's Clapham, Elstree, Feltonfleet and Eagle House. Former pupils include authors Louis de Bernières and Richard Adams, explorer Benedict Allen, MP Richard Benyon, comedian Tony Hancock (who left school at age 15), actor Claudia Harrison, cricketer and broadcaster Mark Nicholas, Lord David Owen, astronomer Sir Martin Ryle.

Entrance: Tours every Saturday morning – no open days. School says demand for places has 'gone through the roof' in recent years – and our Advice Service can confirm this is so. Now faced with the novel problem of having to select 150 year 9 pupils from an oversubscribed pool. Has resisted raising the CE bar of 55 per cent: 'It would change the inclusive nature of the school – we genuinely believe in things beyond only academic excellence', says the head. Looking for pupils who will take full advantage of opportunities and add 'positive energy', so all candidates are now interviewed. Twice. Children bring a piece of academic work to discuss. No pre-testing, but borderline CE candidates are 'screened' and we have known parents of 12 year olds to be warned in advance that their children are teetering on the borderline. A few children enter year 10 and, unusually, Bradfield admits around 15 pupils into year 11 to do a foundation year before starting A levels or IB.

Some 50-60 new pupils are admitted into the lower sixth. Candidates must be interviewed, submit GCSE predictions (or actual grades) and take a 'General Ability' test in November before year of entry, with possibility for scholarship or award. Places are conditional on attaining a minimum of six B grades, with at least Cs in English and maths.

Exit: Around 15 per cent leave post-GCSE. Then mostly to Russell Group – particularly hot on Bristol and Exeter recently. A couple to Oxbridge, a number to art school, a growing number to universities in the US, Canada or Europe.

Money matters: Not cheap. The prospectus sets the tone when describing 'The Bradfield Experience': 'It's the fun of House Dinners or a netball tour to Barbados; it's the challenge of an expedition to the High Atlas Mountains...' Provides £2m annually in means tested bursaries up to 100 per cent of fees available at 13+ and sixth form. Scholarships awarded for academics, music, art, performing arts (dance and/or drama), sport and all-round ability.

Remarks: An all rounder's paradise.

Bradford Girls' Grammar School

Squire Lane, Bradford, BD9 6RB

• Pupils: 260 • Ages: 11–18 • C of E • State

Tel: 01274 545395
Email: headsec@bggs.com
Website: www.bggs.com

Headmistress: Since Easter 2009, Mrs Kathryn Matthews BSc (mid-forties), educated at Loreto Grammar School in Manchester, then maths and an MA in education at Leeds University. Taught maths at The Oratory, London; deputy head at Gateways School, Leeds. ISI team inspector and governor at Westbourne Prep in Sheffield. Married with three teenage sons. Enjoys theatre, visiting art galleries, reading and rugby union.

Warm and approachable, astute, honest, humorous, in touch with the wider educational world; enjoys teaching maths (does one quarter of a timetable, up to GCSE). Values individual teachers who can enthuse pupils and keen to foster staff talent; wants to maintain the school's high academic standards and enable girls from less privileged backgrounds to succeed. Parents say she deals with problems 'promptly and appropriately' and makes herself available in a flexible way.

Academic matters: Strong on value-added. Consistently good results at A level (78 per cent A*-B, 55 per cent A*/A, 2013) in a surprisingly wide range of subjects for such a relatively small sixth form, with subjects run for just one or two girls; bigger numbers for maths and sciences than arts and languages; excellent art. Class sizes up to 10. Good careers advice and university preparation.

GCSEs also strong (56 per cent A/A*, 2013), especially sciences (all three) and several languages (Greek available); usually

nine taken. Moved to IGCSE maths and science with English under consideration. Business and communication option very popular and successful. Year 10s do a health and safety qualification. All learn Latin in the first three years. Home economics chosen over food technology because of its focus on practical cooking skills and nutrition knowledge. Several awards in national science competitions. Classes average at 18; 23 maximum. Staff described by girls as 'very supportive'; 'They make lessons fun'. Parents say: 'very approachable'; 'They know all the pupils individually.'

Exceptional design and technology department with an inspirational, immensely energetic male head who has procured an impressive amount of industrial equipment for the workshop – Knex, Lego and airfix kits also used, girls make go-karts and pedal cars and enter lots of competitions; also a one-year GCSE engineering option..

Well-led SEN department takes advantage of LA and national resources and liaises well with parents ('They're good at targeting individual needs') and teachers – confident it could handle any kind of difficulty. Dyslexia Action visits half a day a week for assessments and one-to-one/two support (parents pay it directly); also free outside classroom support for dyslexia and EAL – the school is very aware of a growing need to provide the latter.

Large number of computers, but in need of upgrading. Pleasant, well-stocked and used library, with 72 carvings of mice in the Yorkshire Mouseman furniture tradition to spot.

Games, options, the arts: Good facilities include an Astroturf and purpose-built sports hall, but only a half-size swimming pool, with changing-rooms needing refurbishment. Fifteen sports offered – successful in county, regional and national competitions, notably in synchronised swimming (very popular); table tennis teams also strong.

Keen interest in ecology – aiming for Green Flag status. Extensive D of E; debating throughout the school; lots of success in competitions, eg engineering, Young Enterprise, marketing. Sixth formers do community sports leader award, Global Young Leaders, Millennium Volunteers. Wide range of charities. Two – carefully selected – girls visit Auschwitz each year.

High standards in drama, modern dance and art, eg some very elaborate textiles work. About half learn instruments – lots of concerts and clubs (steel pans, jazz, soul). Annual large-scale, themed open day for local primary schools, designed to supplement their curriculum with arts, modern languages and ecology activities, organised by year 10s. Sports and academic trips to Canada, Europe, South Africa, Malawi.

Background and atmosphere: The main, 1930s building is square, with soothing views from corridors of a grassed quadrangle dominated by a huge cherry blossom tree; all the new developments blend sympathetically with the original Pennine sandstone. Seventeen acres of games areas, lawns and gardens. A very attractive, airy conservatory with wicker furniture and large pot plants serves as a waiting area off the entrance hall. The brightly-coloured modern cafeteria offers a wide choice of food catering for all diets. A spacious atrium for the younger girls to relax in with green walls and café furniture and more pot plants. Some recently refurbished classrooms, bright and colourful displays; an orderly, focused atmosphere within. The separate, very attractive, purpose-built Foster Beaver College feels comfortable.

Girls say the school is welcoming and close-knit, not competitive – 'We're encouraged to be independent and set our own goals'; the sixth form is 'like a family'. They are encouraged to take responsibility – elected form prefects, school president with two deputies and sixth form committee, plus school council. A non-selective free school since September 2013.

Pastoral care and discipline: Excellent pastoral care. Small key stage 4 tutor groups. Alert to the usual problems coming from girls putting too much pressure on themselves to succeed, but 'nothing that can't be managed' by working with parents, according to Mrs Matthews. Sensible, enlightened bullying, sanctions and rewards policies.

Pupils and parents: Mixture of middle-class professionals (several doctors) and self-employed plus some working class; ethnically mixed – a large number of Asians, with very supportive parents. Buses from Ilkley, Leeds, Huddersfield, Halifax. Girls are hard-working, articulate, confident, happy, tolerant, enthusiastic – 'mature and intellectually curious', individual and very proud to be at the school, says Mrs Matthews. Bound to become increasingly socially mixed now it is a non-selective free school.

Strong links with parents and old girls, who include Barbara Castle, Rebecca Sarker (TV actress), Jill McGivering (BBC foreign correspondent), Isobel Hilton (journalist) and Pippa Wells (CERN astrophysicist).

Entrance: From preps and state primaries – non-selective from September 2013.

External sixth formers: interview plus five A*-Bs at GCSE, may be separate requirements for specific subjects.

Exit: Just under a half leave at the end of year 11 for local state or independent, co-educational sixth forms, eg Greenhead College. Sixth formers to mostly northern universities – Bradford very popular; several to Bristol and Birmingham. Medical and biomedical subjects lead the list.

Remarks: A very good girls' grammar blending the traditional and modern. It would be enhanced by greater financial resources but gets the really important things right – high standards, very good relationships and a wide range of opportunities. We will watch with interest its transformation into a free school.

Bradford Grammar School

Linked school: Bradford Grammar Junior School (Clock House)

Keighley Road, Bradford, BD9 4JP

• Pupils: 580 boys and 350 girls • Ages: 11-18 • Non-denom
• Fees: £11,490–£11,910 pa • Independent

Tel: 01274 553702
Email: hmsec@bradfordgrammar.com
Website: www.bradfordgrammar.com

Headmaster: Since January 2012, Mr Kevin Riley, previously head of Harrow International, Bangkok.

Academic matters: A powerful, academic school with strong traditions across the curriculum range. Wide range of A levels includes PE, electronics, Latin and theatre studies. Over 49 per cent A*/A grades at A level in 2013 and 62 per cent A*/A at GCSE. School will stand by pupils even if they aren't making the BGS grade. Expectations high, pupils prepared to work hard.

Staff 'amazingly devoted and committed' – and teach sixth formers 'as if they were university students,' said a parent. Low turnover of staff.

Games, options, the arts: Very strong rugby (considerable national success) and netball (in national finals for last three years), cross-country; cricket good too (well, this is Yorkshire, where they take it seriously, like religion), and some outstanding results in tennis, table-tennis and rowing. Keen drama. Music very lively and wide-ranging, both inclusively and at the able top end. Plenty of outdoor opportunities in Lakes and Dales.

Background and atmosphere: School dates back to the 16th century. Formerly a free grammar, became direct grant, then independent. Pleasant, spacious setting on Bradford outskirts, all games on site. Monumental gritstone buildings 'planned with incredible foresight'. Pleasing feel of space to corridors and quads between buildings, all very spick and span. Subjects grouped together in departmental suites. Large modern library and well-equipped IT rooms. Lots of newish buildings including competition-size swimming pool, music school, auditorium, attractive sixth form centre – academic and social hub. Also junior school extension and superb multi-media language centre.

Bradford has changed in recent years, and the school reflects this: Yorkshire chippiness on the way out, replaced by more tolerant, open community. Pupils seem very much at ease with each other and staff, confident and cheerful – though still competitive and fully stretched. Co-education fully established, not a boys' school with girls in it. Head aims to keep the best of the old, and some will find the school quite hierarchical (no bad thing).

Pastoral care and discipline: Lack of self-discipline heavily frowned upon, relatively rare. Theft likely to lead to expulsion. Northern hard-working ethos very much in evidence and plenty of space to let off excess steam. Well-structured, horizontal pastoral care system. Good peer support.

Pupils and parents: Sons and daughters of local professionals and business people; good ethnic mix. Strong parental support – Bradford has always been proud of its grammar school. Large catchment area, efficiently connected by buses and trains, mainly in an arc running NW to SW of city, but also extending into rival Leeds. Old Boys include David Hockney, sympathetic to school, president of recent appeal, Denis Healey, Adrian Moorhouse and Olympic 2012 gold and bronze medal triathletes Alistair and Jonathan Brownlee. Lively Old Bradfordian Association, with more than 5,000 active members.

Entrance: Average school IQ is 120+, so entrance exam pretty selective, but any candidate 'showing sparkle' in any part of exam is interviewed for selection on potential rather than performance. Half of entry (also via exam) comes from junior department (Clock House), which has expanded in recent years and is going strong, tucked away next to main school. Rest of entry mainly from local primaries. Sixth form entrants need 20 GCSE points (A* = 4, C = 1).

Exit: A dozen or so to Oxbridge every year. Nearly all leavers to good universities, majority to read hard/traditional subjects; much medicine and engineering. Popular destinations are Durham, Bristol, Newcastle, Nottingham, Edinburgh, Manchester, Liverpool, Birmingham.

Money matters: Fees kept amazingly low – an unbreakable governors' principle and a tremendous bargain for parents. School doesn't believe in borrowing money for capital projects. Bursaries available from home-grown scheme, funded by Old Bradfordians, Ogden Trust, HSBC, and other corporate benefactors; this enables school to preserve traditional social diversity.

Remarks: First-class, academic and outward-looking grammar school offering high quality, all-round, co-educational education.

Bramdean School

Linked school: Bramdean Preparatory School

Richmond Lodge, Homefield Road, Exeter, Devon, EX1 2QR

• Pupils: 120; ratio of boys to girls 60:40 • Ages: 12–18 • Inter-denom • Fees: £9,720 pa • Independent

Tel: 01392 273387
Email: info@bramdeanschool.co.uk
Website: www.bramdeanschool.co.uk

Heads: Since 1978, Miss Diane Stoneman NAHT (timeless), joined 'some 10 years later' by Mr Tony Connett. Warm-hearted, generous-minded and effortlessly scholarly. To her great regret, she no longer teaches ('swamped by hideous paper work') but in her time has taught virtually every subject. She is also a wonderful artist.

Mr Connett, described variously as a 'maverick' and 'idiosyncratic', is dedicated to the shamelessly old-fashioned virtues of education, daily chapel, good manners and the happiness of the pupils. He is an independently-minded headmaster of a genuinely independent school, prefers common sense and directness to regulations and euphemism. He specialises in a desert-dry drollery designed, perhaps, to deflate the pompous, but no disguising his underlying shrewdness, experience (he had a fascinating life in industry before seeing the light) and his concern for the welfare of the children in his care. The two complement each other and it is typical of their modesty that neither in mentioned on the website or in the prospectus. When asked about that Mr Connett said, 'The school is much more important than its heads.' Actually the two are indistinguishable.

Academic matters: Around 85 per cent of pupils get 5+ GCSE grades at A*-C including English and maths. School website opaque about details, including A level results.

The heads have gathered round them an impressive and enthusiastic staff. The head of physics spoke of his great good fortune in teaching maths and physics A level to small sets – 'They're more like tutorials and if we decide to do a practical as a result of a discussion then we can do it straight away'. All subjects have that intimate feel. The headmaster's love of traditional teaching has not blinded him to modern educational tools. He is no Luddite and the classrooms are impressively equipped with whiteboards and interactive whiteboards plus computers; excellently laid out science laboratories and a large modern home economics suite for teaching cookery and learning about nutrition. All work is closely monitored and recorded in the colourfully helpful prep book with which each pupil is issued. Parents and staff sign and comment.

Games, options, the arts: Subjects are not confined merely to the classroom: as well as reports written on the various expeditions, the termly newsletter has lively articles by subject teachers, designed to link the classroom with the world outside. Challenging expeditions such as the Ten Tors, the Exmoor Challenge and D of E. Staff regularly take 20 or so pupils to the South of France for a PGL activity holiday.

Bright, airy music department complete with electric piano and a suite of Yamaha key boards. Involvement is total and judging by the CD of hauntingly lovely Gregorian chant, the choir is superb. They have broadcast on Sky, CNN and the BBC. Listen out for them.

Delightfully intimate recording studio built (recently) to professional standards with CD and analogue video recording, high band TV cameras and editing facilities. Drama is taught in the lower and senior school and at least one school production each year involving all the pupils. The drama studio has a sprung floor for various types of dance.

Across the road from the school is the games field. In the Lent term football is presided over by Xavier Martin, former coach at the Barcelona FC Football Academy, with striking results; rugby is played in the Michaelmas term and cricket in the summer. Keith Brown, former vice-captain of Middlesex CCC, is overall in charge of games. Girls play cricket, hockey, netball, rounders and athletics. All learn to swim at the nearby university; tennis is also available there.

Background and atmosphere: Founded in 1901, it was bought by Miss Stoneman in 1978, since when much building. All stages of the school – the kindergarten, pre-prep, prep and senior school – are housed in the same area of buildings. The original Regency building, which houses the meeting and greeting rooms as well as the well-resourced libraries, is very handsome. The chapel, designed and built by Mr Connett, is an absolute gem of a building: clear, airy and elegant, with two organs and very fine choir stalls. It is an oasis of tranquillity in a bustling world where the air is loud with the sound of music practice and the shrieks of netball players in the covered sports hall, floodlit for evening activities.

A happy atmosphere pervades the school and the children wear their good manners lightly, greeting openly and courteously. Clearly they are used to talking to adults and the breadth of ages assembled in such a space lends for a genuine family feel. No cafeteria but good home-cooked food and three separate sittings, presided over by teachers and lovely, motherly kitchen staff.

Pastoral care and discipline: The size of the school is a key factor here. Children carry around in their prep books a copy of the all-embracing school rules and expectations and know where they stand. The system of progressing through a series of form heads ensures that staff know their pupils well, 'Can spot unusual patterns of behaviour and lend support and love'. Zero tolerance over drugs and bullying.

Pupils and parents: Parents come from a wide cross-section of society and most live within a radius of 25 miles or so. The end of boarding has inevitably reduced the catchment area, but occasionally people from abroad can be boarded out with designated families.

Entrance: Many come up from the prep. Essentially pupils may enter at any stage: the school is not selective but everyone takes common entrance. For entry into the sixth form, pupils need five GCSEs at A and B grades.

Exit: Numbers leaving post-GCSE vary, but may lose one-third to sixth form colleges. Of those remaining, the majority go on to university, though Miss Stoneham also wishes to encourage training/work opportunities.

Money matters: Fees are very competitive and the heads are justifiably proud of the financial support they offer in a multiplicity of scholarships and bursaries. Don't be afraid to ask.

Remarks: This is an unusual school and will not suit everyone. For some it would be too small; for others its size would attract. Those who talk to staff and pupils may well feel they have stumbled upon an undiscovered jewel, where the aims are high and education lives on. You certainly won't find many other schools like it.

Bredon School

Linked school: Bredon Junior School

Pull Court, Bushley, Tewkesbury, Gloucestershire, GL20 6AH

• Pupils: 230; 20 per cent girls; 60 per cent board • Ages: 4–18; boarding from age 7 • C of E • Fees: Boarding £18,210–£26,460; Day £6,210–£16,875 pa • Independent

Tel: 01684 293156
Email: enquiries@bredonschool.co.uk
Website: www.bredonschool.org

Headmaster: Since September 2013, Mr David Ward MA BEd, previously head of St Felix School in Suffolk. Has also headed Skegness Grammar. A former rugby international, he is a qualified canoeing coach and is interested in sailing, swimming and riding. He is vice chair of governors of St David's College in Llandudno, a school that specialises in dyslexia and dyspraxia using outdoor pursuits.

Academic matters: Maximum 15 to a class but the most we saw was a group of 14. Most classes are much smaller (around seven) and often have a teaching or support assistant alongside. The school's academic results are all to do with value added: while this is emphatically not a special school, a very high proportion of the children here use the learning access centre, and of the 230 pupils, around 90 have diagnosed learning difficulties or statements of special educational need (dyslexia, dyspraxia and communication difficulties are most common). Special educational needs are not regarded as a hindrance – 'Nobody's different, because everybody's different'.

Consequently, children without a learning difficulty are also treated very much as individuals and will, if appropriate, take GCSEs early or pursue particular interests with the support of staff. Lots of kinaesthetic learning resources across the school, with all staff accustomed to dealing with learning difficulties and a dedicated unit of 10 SPLD trained staff working in a purpose built access centre.

In general, children achieve far beyond what they expected – or indeed what was expected of them. All the pupils we spoke to said they were doing things they had thought they couldn't do. In 2013, 61 per cent of GCSE grades were A*-C – mostly down to tiny classes, lots of support, and a carefully tailored programme of subject choices.

As well as the core curriculum of English, maths and sciences, most children take Spanish, art, DT and history or geography. Catering and business studies are also popular. Some will drop a GCSE to use the time in the access centre to improve their learning skills and strategies for other subjects. Others will take entry level qualifications, ASDAN qualifications or foundation level. Individual education plans are built in to lessons with teachers aware of objectives for each pupil.

In the sixth form lots of vocational as well as academic subjects available – level 2 and 3 OCR and BTEC courses in business, sport, agriculture, engineering, ICT and health and social care, as well as A level tuition in most of the usual flavours (English, maths, economics, history, drama, Spanish). The A level range isn't huge, partly because the school is small (20-25 per year in sixth form) and partly because the range of vocational courses is so extensive. Pupils can pick and mix a combination that will work for them.

Strong emphasis on outdoor and practical learning, with all children participating in the school farm – which features a prize-winning bull as well as sheep, poultry, pigs and vegetable growing. All junior students spend time on the farm every week, gaining skills and confidence. Many of the senior pupils take advantage of the farm to study agriculture or horticulture, with the opportunity to take animals to major agricultural shows and help out with the lambing.

The school also now has a 13 acre forest school site and a smaller area of quieter woodland, used in cross-curricular teaching of art, maths, science and English. Parents are sent four sets of grades a year, two with full reports.

Games, options, the arts: Lots of options, with the outdoors at the forefront: mountain biking, rugby, hockey, climbing and swimming. New head intends to expand outdoor education programme. Regular fixtures against other schools. Numbers taking individual instrumental lessons, though not high, are on the rise – currently drums, guitar and woodwind are the most popular. Passionate art staff, an artist in residence, and good art/creative facilities, including sculpting and impressive metalwork shop. Other options after lessons end include needlework, car maintenance, clay pigeon shooting, sugar-craft and lacrosse. Senior students are encouraged to work for awards such as sports leader, basic education leader, British Canoe Union and D of E.

Background and atmosphere: Founded in 1962 by Lt Col Tony Sharp OBE, whose motto, 'The journey is as important as the destination', remains at the heart of the project here. The school is now owned by the Spanish-British education group Colegios Laude.

It is in a rather tucked-away corner of Gloucestershire, in lovely rolling countryside, very calm and peaceful, and built around Pull Court, a rather grand Victorian pile in which many of the children board. The grounds extend to about 80 acres which encompass the farm, forest school, woodland and playing fields etc. Some of the buildings could do with updating; boarding facilities are spacious but a little tired in places; as with many other schools, there is a rolling programme of updating facilities and accommodation. The buildings are full of displays of the children's artwork, and some of the buildings and grounds (notably a new greenhouse, landscaped area and fountain), have been built by the children, who are rightly proud of what they have created. Lots of whole school charity fundraising, walks/runs and swims, sponsorship too of a school in Zimbabwe with practical input from teaching staff.

Pastoral care and discipline: Small tutor groups which meet twice a day. Parents say pastoral care is a great strength of the school – 'They are genuinely bothered – if there is a problem they listen – there is always someone to talk to'. Boarding and academic staff are separate – to give a sense of 'really being at home', and not under the maths teacher's eye when lessons are over. There is a school nurse on site.

Pupils say there is no problem with bullying – anything that arises is dealt with quickly: 'you don't get picked on for being different'. Zero tolerance of drugs and alcohol – not encountered often, but pupils immediately expelled if they cross the line.

Boarding can be full or weekly – about half the pupils board. No Saturday morning school but lots of activities for those who stay including outings, such as paintballing, clay shooting, museum visits, canal boat trips, shopping trips, visits to castles and National Trust sites, Warhammer competitions and so on. There's a new sixth form area, but much of the boarding accommodation, though clean and tidy, is on the basic side.

The food is good: provided by local caterers who are subject to the wrath of the student council if the potatoes aren't up to scratch! Plenty of variety in the menu and a rather stunning view from the lovely light dining room over the surrounding countryside.

Pupils and parents: Some rather quiet pupils, but all speak sincerely about what the school has done for them: 'The tutors help you a lot, they're approachable'. 'They help you so much, you feel confident – you get lots of support.' 'I can keep up now.'

Boarders come from as far afield as Pakistan and Dubai, and from all over the UK. As part of the Colegios Laude group, the school also often has a cohort of Spanish pupils spending a term or two at the school experiencing English culture and learning the language. Day pupils are bused in from all over Gloucestershire and Worcestershire – local families keen on the outdoors, a handful of Services families too. Parents range from celebrities to engineers, professionals and farmers.

Entrance: Via interview and assessment. The school is not a special school and statements of SEN etc are examined carefully. No written tests. Prospective pupils are invited to spend guest days in school and those who might board can stay the night. Open mornings throughout the year. For those with SEN, school will consider both current reports and own assessment to ensure needs can be met by the learning support staff.

Exit: A rising number of pupils (about 70 per cent) stay on for sixth form. Of those, about 80 per cent go to college or university. To a variety of places including Leeds, Manchester, Cardiff, Hartpury College. Range of courses including lots of business, quite a lot of agricultural/environmental, as well as art, criminology, sports management etc. The school seems to produce pupils with an entrepreneurial and creative edge.

Money matters: There are bursaries and scholarships (sporting, arts, academic) available up to 20 per cent, plus 20 per cent discount for second siblings and 40 per cent for third siblings.

Remarks: A small school that rebuilds confidence and transforms prospects for many children with learning difficulties, but also offers unique outdoor learning and practical skills teaching for any child not set on the standard academic course. If your child dreams of farming or sculpture or starting her own business, and wants to spend plenty of time getting muddy in the interim, this could be just the place.

Brentwood School

Linked school: Brentwood Preparatory School

Middleton Hall Lane, Brentwood, CM15 8EE

- Pupils: 1,115 boys and girls, including some 60 boarders
- Ages: 11–18 • C of E • Fees: Boarding £29,385; Day £15,390 pa
- Independent

Tel: 01277 243243
Email: headmaster@brentwood.essex.sch.uk
Website: www.brentwoodschool.co.uk

Headmaster: Since 2004, Mr Ian Davies (fifties), formerly head of St Dunstan's College, south London, and previously head of lower school at Latymer Upper. A graduate of St John's Oxford, theologian, married to a teacher. Likeable, committed, strong on moral values and discipline. An ISI inspector, helps select naval officers for training at Dartmouth for the Admiralty Interview Board and is on the DfE National Advisory Council.

Academic matters: Takes a wider spread of ability than its main competitors – the Chelmsford and Colchester grammar schools – and does pretty well by its pupils across the board. Has been criticised in the past for not stretching the most able but the head points to school surveys showing that the brightest two-thirds get as good or better results as their counterparts at the grammars. 'And the bottom quarter still do well – why would we not want to educate them?' In 2013, 57 per cent of GCSE grades A*/A.

A good spread of A level choices including DT, sport and PE, psychology, theatre studies, ICT; 80 per cent A*-B and 52 per cent A*/A in 2013. Started offering the IB in September 2007. The head introduced it at St Dunstan's and is 'keen on its philosophical underpinning, holistic approach and vision of a "well educated human being",' plus its ability to stretch the most able – average point score of 36 (out of a possible 45) in 2013.

Good learning development department, which includes two full-time SENCos and other trained staff. Pupils are withdrawn for support where necessary and have differentiated tasks in lessons.

The Sir Antony Browne Society (SABS), now open to younger pupils as well as sixth formers, is a forum for the most able pupils to discuss and debate topical issues and is part of a gifted and talented programme which includes other academic clubs and activities.

Games, options, the arts: If you are aiming for the Olympic fencing team (or to play premier division football) this is the school for you. Two fencing coaches are Commonwealth Games silver medallists and several pupils compete at national level. Has won the Public Schools' Fencing Championships for several years. Other pupils represent the country at cricket, sailing, skiing, netball and chess. Large numbers play for the school or their house at the more traditional sports: football, rugby, netball, swimming, cross-country. Acres of playing fields and courts, all-weather floodlit pitch, sports hall with squash courts and excellent swimming pool including learner pool for the pre-prep.

Performing arts block with extensive music teaching, specialist rehearsal and practice rooms and a Sibelius computer suite. One of the largest music departments for a non-specialist school, with large numbers of A grades at GCSE and A level. Some two-thirds of pupils learn at least one instrument; many play in the symphony orchestra, the string orchestra, concert band or Big Band, which has many outside engagements, raising funds for charity. Pupils play in the National Youth Orchestra and National Children's Orchestra. Several choirs and concerts throughout the year.

Plenty of high quality drama, including a production of Les Miserables, praised by John Cameron, orchestrator of the score, as the most exciting he had ever seen. A new 400-seat auditorium houses productions. Art, once in the doldrums, now impressive, as is DT, housed in the Hardy Amies Design Centre with some of his original sketches on the walls.

Huge choice of extracurricular activities, including the largest voluntary CCF corps in the country; popular community service unit. Pupils enthuse about tackling the high ropes course on the CCF summer camp, singing in Siena Cathedral on the music tour to Italy, seeing the Northern Lights during a geography field trip to Iceland, competing in the house pancake race, helping disabled children to learn to ride. Raises some £40,000 a year for charity, mostly via inter-house events organised by pupils.

Background and atmosphere: Founded in 1557 by Sir Anthony Browne, on the site where William Hunter had been burned to death at the age of 19, for refusing to accept the doctrine of transubstantiation of bread and wine into the body and blood of Christ. Browne had sentenced Hunter when a Justice of the Peace for the area, and founded the school as a penance. A school song commemorates the young martyr. In 1622, statutes were drawn up for the school by Browne, John Donne and George Monteigne, Bishop of London, requiring that all boys should be instructed in Virtue, Learning and Manners.

Was a boys' grammar school, principally boarding, for many years. Admitted girls into the sixth form in the mid 1970s and into the main school in 1988. Now has one boys' and one girls' boarding house, for around 70 pupils. Probably uniquely, the boys all get single rooms (varying in size from cubby hole to spacious), while the girls are never more than four to a room. Pupils and parents seem happy with the system of educating boys and girls separately from 11-16, meeting for extracurricular activities.

Seventy-two acre site bordered by woodland, with different departments housed in separate buildings of varying architectural vintage: the Old Big School, which dates back to not long after the school's foundation; the 1867 chapel; the wood-panelled memorial hall with proscenium arch and organ; sixties boarding house; Courage sports centre; red-brick performing arts block. Terraced cottages on the perimeter house up to 50 staff, several of them ANZACs on a three-year stint in the country. A handy journey to school, but with the disadvantage of having one's quiet drink in the garden in full view of any pupils wandering by.

Pastoral care and discipline: Hot on manners and tidiness – 'It's about being clear about expectations. They're expected to be ambassadors for the school inside and out'. Indeed the grounds are pristine and the pupils in general are startlingly well-turned-out, aided by the fact that the Hardy Amies-designed girls' skirt is more or less impossible to roll up at the waist – and very elegant it is too. Hot on pastoral care as well, with senior pupils trained to act as mentors for younger ones and bullying, by all accounts, not a significant problem.

The school is a Christian foundation – 'We take it seriously' – and though other faiths are welcome, everyone must attend chapel once a week.

The boarding houses are run by husband-and-wife teams, who, said the ISI, 'are so committed to the care of the pupils that they have simply extended their own family life to encompass the boarders, providing them with the next best thing to home'. Boarders have access to all the school facilities at weekends, though few formal activities arranged except for Saturday morning matches and some clubs and EFL lessons, and most of the UK boarders go home.

Pupils and parents: Most come from within a 15-mile radius, which includes the idyllically rural and decidedly urban parts of Essex. 'We are very much a local school, and the local community wants us to be part of it.' Boarders include those from further-flung parts of Essex and overseas, from Europe to Hong Kong. The IB is attracting interest from German families in particular.

OBs – who include several teachers at the school – a loyal lot: mailing list of over 7,000. Local ones tend to send their children to the school and many help with careers advice, a mentoring scheme and work experience. The Society of Old Brentwoods runs sports teams, bridge clubs, dinners and outings. Eminent OBs include Sir Robin Day, Douglas Adams, David Irving, Sir Peter Stothard, Griff Rhys-Jones, Noel Edmonds, Jack Straw, Frank Lampard, Jodie Marsh and Sir Hardy Amies.

Entrance: Selective intake at 11, with a small 13+ entry. Around a third comes up from the prep school but must take the same maths, English and verbal reasoning exams as outside applicants. Another third from local state primaries. Applicants who fall down on one of the papers have a supplementary interview to give them a second chance, and those with dyslexia get extra time. Aims to admit those in the top 50 per cent of the ability range. 'We do a good job for high-flyers and for the middle-of-the-road student who might get lost elsewhere.'

Asks for six Bs at GCSE for those who want to move on to the sixth form, 'and nearly everyone gets that. We have a loyal approach to sixth form progression – we will stick with them if they work hard and contribute to the wider life of the school.'

Exit: Thirty or so move on after GCSEs to, eg, sixth form colleges. Nearly all A level leavers to university – eight to Oxbridge in 2013 and five to study medicine; business studies, engineering and economics popular at a range of mostly old-established universities. In 2013, 65 per cent to top 20 universities.

Money matters: Used to be a direct grant school, charging according to income, and offers 10 full-fee bursaries each year as well as up to 25 academic, art, music, sports, drama and boarding scholarships. 'We want a good social mix and are moving towards a means-blind admissions policy. If a child wants to come to Brentwood we want to give them the opportunity.'

Remarks: Extensive grounds and excellent facilities; a handy commute from London. Very strong on all aspects of the extracurricular and provides a well-rounded education for a wide ability range in an ordered environment.

Brighton and Hove High School

Linked school: Brighton and Hove High Junior School

Montpelier Road, Brighton, BN1 3AT

• Pupils: 425 girls, all day • Ages: 11–18 • Non-denom
• Fees: £11,487–£11,550 pa • Independent

Tel: 01273 280280
Email: enquiries@bhhs.gdst.net
Website: www.bhhs.gdst.net

Head: Since September 2012, Jennifer Smith MA, MEd (early 50s), aims to be in post for the long haul after a series of two-to-three year predecessors. An engaging and sensible Glaswegian, she spent the previous 10 years rising to deputy head at Wilson's, a state funded selective all boys school in Sutton. She still commutes south from there, her husband goes north to his headship in London and their daughter is at Sutton High (one of the 28 other members of the Girls' Day School Trust). It was the vision of Helen Fraser, the CEO of the GDST, and the way she engages with political debate in a non-stuffy way, that really attracted Ms Smith to her first headship. 'It's about building resilience in girls' learning and confidence, while also very important to give value for money. My main aim is for each girl to know that we care for her and about her progress.'

Earlier challenges include five years as a head of English at an all boys grammar, in her late 20s (and the first years of GCSEs) and a vital role in the turnaround of the ranking of Wilson's results. She uses her daily train journey to Brighton to blog for the school website – part of the 'technical explosion' she spearheaded in her first year, with a new online portal and online reporting. She doesn't teach the timetable at present, but does cover lessons, watches teaching and does duty in the canteen, using that time to hear suggestions from the students – and act on them eg new transparency in the behaviour system and a consistent 'tariff of discipline'.

Academic matters: Academic results excellent with 79 per cent A*-B grades at A level, 47 per cent A*/A, and 60 per cent A*/A grades at GCSE in 2013; dedicated staff passionate about their subjects. Bright, stimulating, independently minded, confident girls – a description approved by parents, staff and the local general public. Pupils are very conscientious and pile the pressure on themselves, but are encouraged to progress as individuals. Parents wonder at the results without overt peer rivalry – they feel it is extremely supportive, all of BHHS want everyone to succeed.

Touchscreens or interactive whiteboards in practically every classroom, enable and encourage pupils to share centre stage with teachers. Pupils say the use of these and the online portal with past papers and learning tools really simplify catching up on classes and revision. Assessments for dyslexia and dyscalculia provided by the school and support for moderate cases via newly appointed full-time SENCo (who also teaches chemistry). Online reporting should now ensure that a diagnosis of dyslexia is attached to pupils through all subjects, in the past communication about the need for extra support has broken down.

Science is very popular, young and dynamic rather than geeky – the worktops in the revamped labs wouldn't look out of place in a kitchen showroom in Hove. Each sixth former has her own tray of instruments and test-tubes, encouraging responsibility and continuity. Latin is taught all the way through, first French then a choice of German or Spanish, while maths and English are also strong with great use of external resources, whether it is a Cipher Challenge, guest author or theatre visit. The combined alumni of the GDST help to encourage aspirational and concrete links with world outside lessons, the pupils are busy and keen on learning, aware that their choice of single-sex education may already have given them a leg up.

Careers programme impressive with close links with the local careers service and employers, and free psychometric testing in year 11 and the school organises work experience at the end of that year too. There are enterprise activities in all years, the Temple Project Qualification (the school's version of an Extended Project Qualification) and an intensive programme of visiting speakers, all of which apparently makes writing your personal statement for university application easy, although it may take you until then to realise that all these experiences are rounding out your character…

Sixth form has the biggest space in the whole school – although the numbers are small at present. This means very focused teaching and a real family atmosphere for those that stay, with plenty of experience coaching and mentoring the younger girls. Traditionally over 50 per cent leave, many to the range of great (free) FE choices around Brighton where there are more A Level choices on offer externally eg media studies and vocational ones. Many BHHS girls have been there since the age of 3 or 4 so are keen to spread their social wings and learn with boys, although some regret leaving when their A level results are not so impressive as those who remain. Ex-students, with their male friends, can pop (and sign) in to visit the sixth form centre from the nearest FE college, BHASVIC.

Games, options, the arts: Great modern sports hall with disabled access and the normal rainbow of court lines, layered nets and trampolines, also two outdoor netball courts and Astroturf at the junior school. Netball and athletics are the most successful teams, but the track record is spread like the matches between independent and state sectors opponents. Sport is good but it wouldn't be the reason to come to this school. The pleasant walk to the courts in St Ann's Well Garden is enjoyed by tennis players, girls are minibussed to Roedean to swim, and the fitness studio is hugely popular – especially with the sixth form. However, the dance studio next to it appeals across all years, with one mirrored and one glass wall and all dancers with their eyes on the highlight of the year, a performance in a central Brighton venue. Drama also well taught in dedicated studio with professional lights and mixing desk, doubles as make up and dressing room in the whole school productions.

Art department is beloved and productive – a microcosm of the ideal atmosphere of the school where teachers listen to individuals and then encourage each one to stretch themselves beyond their own expectations. 'It doesn't feel like a lesson, the teachers let you decide.' Officially it occupies two floors in a separate building with a darkroom and a Mac for photography (at A level) but the students' work is placed all over the school, is changed regularly and entices visitors to follow it to the source. Design technology also impressive with great use of acrylics and projects that range from concept to marketing. Likewise, home economics' projects are all encompassing eg tasty biscuits in enticing packaging and a level 2 food hygiene award – very useful for a summer job in a café.

The music house is next in line for a revamp, at present a rabbit warren of slightly shabby rooms – good for splitting up and doing individual work but not very inspiring for those not already passionate musicians. However, full range of peripatetics, three choirs, two orchestras and a jazz band – as well as a biennial school musical – so the proof is in the packed performances, not the woodchip. Also hosts Springboard, the Brighton and Hove Performing Arts festival.

Background and atmosphere: The original building (the Temple) became part of the GDST schools in 1880 – still central to the site, with pillars said to represent inverted cannons. Cluster of contemporary extensions spread out from this, wonderful height and light in the science block, other subjects spread between new and old buildings. Year 9 have a separate block near the netball courts and then the sixth form centre and canteen are over a (narrow) public road from the main house – Brighton's youth mayor is in the sixth form at present, so she aims to present a case for a pelican crossing, typical example of a BHHS girl's can-do attitude. Main hall, used for two assemblies each week and performances, has retractable seating – when we visited, a vicar had just given a thoughtful address; apparently she has to be good since there are a fair few sceptics in the student body. The canteen is a smaller area, children eat in sittings with a good choice of hot and cold and a snack bar where crisps and sandwiches can be bought with fingerprint activated pocket money. Staff eat in the sixth form centre canteen.

Main library is peaceful, with high ceilings – the sixth form can work there or in their own centre, computer access to the online portal as well as shelves of books. The sixth form are allowed phones but the younger ones are not allowed to use theirs during the day – it is a busy site, so there wouldn't be much chance in the five minutes when the girls flood the corridors and stairs between lessons, racing back to the basement locker room to get more books or their sports kit. Uniform for the younger years, with small earrings and no bracelets – the sixth form can wear what they like.

A strong ethos of charitable giving with a 'Guild' collection every Wednesday, where pennies are collected by reps in each form room. This all adds up and is given to two chosen charities per year. The charities are pitched by the girls at an assembly, so almost always have a personal motivation behind them, and the students use all their initiative to raise funds through other events eg a fashion show.

School council is also influential, with suggestions and complaints fed up through reps in each form. The same system operates in the GDST as a whole, so a case for change in BHHS would be pitched by a student rep to the Trust governors.

Pastoral care and discipline: Strong pastoral support system with form teachers and sixth form tutors and year heads – set up for easy communication and accessibility. A mentoring service for younger girls – BLOBs – is an old acronym for Best Listeners of Brighton Schools. This really works, and is made easy by the amount of inter-year, inter-house contact through drama, sport competitions and end-of-year entertainment. Imaginative PSHE – we have encountered this in other Trust schools: the special events and whole days given over to topical issues all help to raise awareness and assist pupils with self-expression on current affairs.

School nurse on site, at the heart of the school near the basement locker room – parents and girls really value that common sense support; it eliminates the drama from long-term health conditions. Families really appreciate the frequent personal letters home from the head celebrating individual achievements. At the other end of the spectrum, some parents talk of bullying not dealt with swiftly enough in the past, however, the new head appears to be a fresh broom.

Students see themselves as a recognisable type, 'a BHHS girl through and through' – plenty of room for spirited girls but everyone is aware of the opportunities that the school gives them, so they are ambitious, organised and self-motivated. The head girl team is an example of the way cooperation and communication is fostered within the school – and links to organisations outside it.

Pupils and parents: Probably 70 per cent from Hove with the rest from Brighton, Pulborough, Eastbourne, Worthing, etc. Buses from Patcham, Worthing and Lewes. A real social and ethnic mix – artists, creative industries, investment bankers, local vicar, teachers – and, due to competitive fees, a good economic mix. Busy parents, both normally working to afford the fees, or taking some help from grandparents.

OGs Karen Pickering MBE, Olympic swimming gold medallist, Claire Hicks MBE, director of Impact Foundation, businesswoman Heidi Cooper, Beth Cordingley from The Bill, several recent University Challenge competitors.

Entrance: From a wide range of local maintained and independent schools and also the junior school. A recent 23 per cent rise in the intake at year 7 is hoped to swell the sixth form numbers. GDST entrance assessment for the main school – selective, but not super selective. At junior level a range of tests – see children at play and interview them. Entry at sixth form requires five GCSEs at C grade or above, with A or B in subjects to be taken at A level; girls come from The Towers, Warden Park, Shoreham College.

Exit: Some 50 per cent leave post-GCSE for the FE college next door, BHASVIC – the very wide of subjects and boys in the classes are enticing. Another 10 per cent to other FE opportunities – often it is a financial decision for the families. University destinations included one Oxbridge in 2013, plus eg Durham, East Anglia, Sussex, Canterbury Christchurch, to study a wide range of courses from law to fashion journalism to physics.

Money matters: Means-tested bursaries at year 7 normally awarded in rank order of performance in the entrance exam (50-100 per cent of fees); academic and music scholarships (10 per cent of fees) also available. More bursaries at year 12 and also another eight scholarships (10 to 30 per cent discount).

Remarks: Parents say it produces empowered, confident, clever girls – but not cocky ones – 'education rather than status'. Has suffered in the past through comparison to its noisy neighbour, Brighton College, both by staff and onlookers – now hopefully in an era where it is certain of its own value and ethos, with individual encouragement producing fantastic results and grounded girls.

Brighton College

Linked school: Handcross Park School

Eastern Rd, Brighton, BN2 0AL

• Pupils: 975 boys and girls, 100 in lower school, 325 boarding and 650 day • Ages: 11–18 • C of E • Fees: Day £14,130– £20,400; Boarding £27,390– £35,880 pa • Independent

Tel: 01273 704200
Email: registrar@brightoncollege.net
Website: www.brightoncollege.net

Head Master: Since 2006, Mr Richard Cairns MA (mid forties). Left Oxford with a first in history; his path to Brighton led him

through a law firm in Australia, a Palestinian refugee camp, Stewart's Melville in Edinburgh, The Oratory in Reading and the deputy headship of Magdalen College School, Oxford. The list of achievements/accolades in his tenure is staggering – it includes the opening of Brighton College Abu Dhabi; a rise from 147th to 16th in the UK academic rankings; a doubling in boarding numbers; a trebling in applications; a huge new building programme; the acquisition of Roedean Junior School and Handcross Park Prep School; an ISI inspection report with outstanding in every category; The Sunday Times Independent School of the Year.

Keen not to take the credit for this all by himself but has built a teaching and management structure that ensures that ideas and initiatives can be sparked and grown – whether inside or outside the student body. That type of attitude is magnetic – for pupils, parents and staff. He sees himself and the college as a mix of tradition and modern – that was the design brief for the decorating team that were part of the recent revamp but it goes much deeper than the furnishings. 'I want every pupil to be who they want to be – as I say to them in assembly [pupils agree he does, and they remember it ...] "If I try to be him, who will be me?".'

Plenty of other schools trying to tempt him away – the governors recently agreed to a 10 week international trip, he says 'to give me thinking time for the next seven years'. It was a global reconnaissance mission visiting universities in the US and Canada as well as potential twin schools in Finland, Sweden, Singapore, Ontario and Hungary. Such symbiotic connections are characteristic of this head – and they appear to stem from a dedication to improving education wherever he can use his influence or initiative. He kicked off his tenure with compulsory Mandarin lessons – but in doing so also connected with Kingsford, an East London school that was doing the same. Out of this link grew the London Academy of Excellence (LAE) in Stratford, East London, the first new sixth form free school academy in the country, helping kids from disadvantaged backgrounds to get into university by making sure they pass the right A levels – with a powerful independent school sponsoring one of each of the major subjects eg Brighton College sponsors economics, Eton does English, Highgate does maths etc.

Has high expectations for his pupils, wanting them to be excited in the classroom for the 200 days a year that they come to 'this place of learning' and is keen for them to leave to begin careers rather than just enter a profession (no matter how elevated). He teaches history to all of the fourth form – meeting every child, marking their work. They report creative punishments from him for inattention eg writing a whole story about a turtle, or a poem about the girl the note was being passed to. Less formally, he has breakfast with the prefects and invites sixth formers to dinner. The pupils love getting to know the head in this way (one of seven children, he certainly knows how to cope with a large dinner table) and relevant issues, ranging from divorce to cricket, often emerge casually. Refreshingly and realistically, he's not shy of stating financial figures to his pupils either – from how much the new boarding developments cost to how much he would need to be sponsored to run the Big Balls relay for charity.

Academic matters: Shining results, and they keep getting better: In 2013, 96 per cent A*/A at GCSE, 96 per cent A*-B and 74 per cent A*/A at A level; this is up with the best in London too – years of consistent improvement in results (and counting). One of top value-added schools. Twenty-six subjects offered at A level. A 60/40 split arts/science at A level; biology, chemistry, economics and maths are particularly popular (the latter taken by about two-thirds of the pupils). About a quarter do four A levels all the way through. Advice given to A level students is integral to their choices: a year group assembly on careers and outside speakers (John Major, Boris Johnson, Viv Richards, David Dimbleby, David Starkey, Jeremy Paxman, Michael Gove, Matt Prior ...) visit in a Wednesday afternoon slot. Each department runs both a course-specific and a general Oxbridge activity, which obviously pays off, with a record number of pupils heading up to Oxford or Cambridge.

Staff are sparky and motivated – attracted by the charms of 'London by the sea' and being part of a school that's going up and up. An appraisal system is at the heart of the classroom: the kids fill in an online questionnaire on each teacher which gets fed back to the head of department who in turn gives a summary to the director of studies. So sub-standard teaching should not slip under the radar and many teachers turn down career progressing jobs elsewhere to remain. Quirky and effective teaching is respected by the pupils – whether it is their Mandarin teacher throat singing on You Tube, or a video of a worked through past paper available for maths A level revision. The Story of Our Land course combines history, geography, philosophy and religion for the third form – when talking about an invasion force coming over the cliff, study the geography of that cliff, or debate the merits of the Muslim or Christian standpoint while looking at the Crusades. This is in line with Michael Gove's draft national curriculum – and has surprising parallels with a Steiner main lesson.

Languages are popular, not just through the Mandarin innovation – compulsory in the pre-prep since 2007 and now a GCSE option (all A* grades so far), with graduate students from Chinese universities to assist – but also Latin, French, Spanish, Russian, Italian, German and Greek. The burgeoning Mandarin option is now confirmed as a USP, with the school being awarded Confucius Institute status by the Chinese Government as a centre of excellence for the teaching of the language – the first such honour for a UK school. The school-wide recommendation of only nine academic GCSEs (with at least one other being artistic or creative) encourages a good balance between academic and extracurricular – as does lesson time between 8.30am and 4pm being sacrosanct, enabling an extra five hours a week for music, sport or dance.

All new pupils attend a literacy class and the dyslexia centre is nationally famous, specifically helping around five per cent of pupils. English is taught within the centre (instead of a second modern language) for years 7-11 in small groups, individual help available in sixth form. Taking complete control of English makes a huge difference, removing embarrassment and stress. School actively seeks out and welcomes the bright child with dyslexia, dyspraxia or dyscalculia. Entry based on recent education plan report, CE assessment morning (observed in groups) and interviews by head and excellent head of centre. Approximately 50 taught in centre, also supports the prep school students. Group work means that children become fantastically supportive of one another, concentration on remediation with younger ones and study skills with older. Time to finish tasks is not an issue – a good end product motivates students.

The bright library has a mezzanine level and is used to provide quiet working space for the sixth form frees. The dedicated sixth form centre also has computers but is generally more social. There's a comprehensive intranet with update alerts sent by email and text. Saturday morning revision classes on offer in the holidays, mostly to boost confidence before exams. Class sizes average 18 up to GCSE; after GCSE, the average is eight.

Games, options, the arts: Year groups of 150 mean that someone will always be into the same thing as your child. Everyone has to do dance, PE and drama. House drama, house song and up to 15 different productions a year (including visiting companies, A level and GCSE performances and Commedia dell'Arte). Dance boasts 100 per cent A at A level and A/A* at GCSE in a state-of-the-art performing arts studio (outside classes offered to the community). Six-strong faculty teaches over 72 dance classes a week. Examinations taken in ballet, modern, tap and jazz, and the school boasts boys' street dance, modern and tap

groups from junior to senior level. The Montague studio is two minutes' walk away.

The music school (scheduled to open in September 2014) can only improve an impressively productive performing arts department. Half the pupils have one individual music lesson per week from more than 40 visiting music teachers and 22 music groups rehearse weekly: choirs, orchestra, rock groups, concert band and various chamber groups, with participation in the National Chamber Music Competition as well as tours to Prague and Moscow. Ex-parents miss going to the performances.

Two hugely popular and innovative sixth form house competitions stem from the entrepreneurship programme and Strictly Come Dancing. The former gets academics and creatives developing a business plan together, each team competing to win £3,000 to commercialise their idea – previous winners have been a parking app and a device to stop babies knocking hot tea over. Strictly ensures boys are valued for more than just sport – the biggest applause in Monday morning assemblies is drawn by the most unconventional achievements.

Purpose-built spaces for art, photography and DT mean all is in place for the making of beautiful art and design – there are still some lessons when the pupils get to watch a video for low maintenance inspiration, but the proof of the art is hanging on walls around the campus.

Sport is enormously important here, all pupils taking part in games twice a week – rounders, netball, tennis, cricket, swimming and rugby possible on campus, otherwise it's a minibus to the college's Jubilee Ground, with six rugby pitches or two cricket grounds, further floodlit netball courts, a pavilion and three hockey Astroturfs nearby. Withdean's athletics stadium also hosts fixtures; each weekend sees some 300-400 children involved in competitive matches. National trophies in rugby (1st XV unbeaten in Sussex since 2007) and netball (Sussex champions and national finalists), and leads the county in athletics. Cricket for both sexes is a great strength – three former pupils play in the current England women's team.

Community service is a vital part of school life: every week, pupils visit elderly people and help disabled children, or teach pensioners how to use a computer; Make a Difference Day (MADD) sees every single member of the college out serving in the community in more than 100 different activities, from cleaning beaches and clearing scrub to sorting clothes for charity. Throughout the year the school raises money for local charities (including Whitehawk Inn, Rockinghorse, Chestnut Tree House) and those further afield (Romania, Kenya, Sri Lanka, India).

Background and atmosphere: Compact campus in Kemp Town, just four blocks from the sea front. Imposing buildings purpose-built in 1840s by Gilbert Scott (designer of St Pancras Station and the Albert Memorial). The school has spent £35 million in the past five years on an award-winning School of Design and Technology and new teaching block for English, new language suites, two new boarding houses, two new sports pavilions and an award winning Smith Café, where boarders can meet in the evening, health centre and staff common room, and a new boarding house. The most popular part of this are the places where the boys and girls get to hang out casually together instead of signing in and out of each other's boarding houses.

Sited to the east of the landmark pier and pavilion, the school succeeds in being fashionable, practical and innovative – the lack of Saturday morning school means that everyone can have a full weekend and the chance to be part of the town instead of just being educated within it. This could put some parents off, since Brighton and Hove, like many seaside cities, has its fair share of addicts, drunks and loons. However, we've heard no reports of pupils happening on any of these and most sensible local parents realise that their children are going to come to Brighton at the weekend anyway, and it is far better that they feel comfortable in their favourite cafés, bars and shops rather than loitering round Churchill Square ... Officially, there is a square patch of Kemp Town streets where pupils can stroll for 20 minutes of an afternoon, in a group, as long as they sign out. However some definitely sneak a walk to the beach – they feel it's their right considering the prospectus proudly features pupils enjoying this out of bounds place.

The children are thoughtful and articulate – we visited on the day of Thatcher's funeral and got into a discussion with a group of 13 year olds about whether people would dislike her so much if she had been a man who had implemented the same policies. The head picks an individual each Monday to share a random act of kindness in assembly – this type of awareness is at root of the school's ethos which goes a fair way to balancing the social mix here. As in all schools, cliques could be described if you were looking for them but the most popular are not necessarily the richest or prettiest; difference is respected and often admired. The pupils are aware that they are privileged. The sixth form wear smart business-like clothes with some restrictions that are flouted when girls fancy tottering on high heels. They can drive themselves into school but must use street parking – high council parking charges are unpopular, with parents driving to attend chapel as well.

The whole school benefits from a good sense of the outside world, whether it is through exchanges with schools in Russia, Africa, America and Australia, the perspective offered by pupils from an inner-city school or the opportunity to twist their tongues round a year's worth of Mandarin Chinese. A link with Kingsford Community School in Newham, East London, began with the heads' discovery that they shared a desire to make Mandarin mandatory, and has grown into an HSBC sponsorship of three Newham pupils' education in Brighton for a year. Sixth formers buddy up with pupils at the London Academy of Excellence and share study tips via Facebook (boarders allowed 10 minute slots) and email.

The chapel, just big enough for the whole school, is used three or four times a week for secular and multi-faith assemblies as well as Christian ones. Tradition still holds firm here (the oldest public school in Sussex) with the heads of school taking it in turns to sit alone in a pew, yet the chaplain is entertaining and eccentric – a new hymnal was an opportunity to get houses to each prepare a song and belt it out in competition.

Pastoral care and discipline: As the head comments, this is 'a town school that is part of the real world, not apart from it'. At the beginning of every term he reiterates the ground rules on theft, bullying and beyond: expulsion and no second chances is the line on drugs and the security at the school gates is tight, yet cheery.

Weekly boarding is extremely popular because there is no Saturday school – full-time boarders can avoid the school curfew if they stay with local families at the weekend who take responsibility. Pupils can return from home by 9.30 on a Sunday night or on a Monday morning – there are buses to outlying towns. A report is emailed home every three weeks and there are parent meetings – although some parents report not much time for parent feedback. Those needing the most help definitely get it – those who are motivated enough to dance between options will attract it too.

The head of the lower school and the headmaster meet every single registered pupil in their own school before they enter Brighton College. This reduces the fear about attending a new school and gives the pastoral staff a heads-up on what house and friendship group might suit a newbie. The little ones arrive three days before the rest of school and go on a treasure hunt to help them get their bearings. The transition to the upper school is another focus point for the empathetic head of lower school – moving from being one of 40 to one of 150 under the shared care of tutors and houseparents.

One lower school house and 13 others when the post common entrance cohort enter, 325 boarding and 650 day – about 70 children in each so a good chance to develop cross year

relationships. All of the youngest year in each senior school house share a tutor – as pupils grow they are matched with another for GCSEs and then A levels. Majority of housemasters and housemistresses are married and parents report incredible empathy for the fallout from tricky family and financial situations. Pupils learn how to iron a shirt, sew on a button and hold their own at a dinner party through house activities – really useful preparation for university admission and beyond.

Any bullying is dealt with speedily and with emotional intelligence – no homophobia or racism, some teasing but real respect for individuality. Two options at meals and dishes containing wheat are labelled, the school is nut free. Food is also available in the Smith Café and Café de Paris below the dance studio – and the houses all have kitchens for an emergency stack of toast for a starving teenage boy.

Pupils and parents: A great social mix from the children of butchers to highbrow TV presenters, successful entrepreneurs and a smattering of Conservative MPs; 33 per cent boarding, most weekly, but seven per cent overseas (five per cent Asian). Less than one per cent black pupils (reflects demographic of Brighton). Lower school just under 50 per cent from Brighton state schools, also many from London schools that stop at 11. Head ensures that useful parent contacts are wound into life of school in way that benefits both– from Leon providing soup recipes for sidelines at matches to a stylist helping with a fashion show. No Saturday school (weekly boarders can leave Friday 4pm, return Monday am) is popular with parents. School buses from towns ranging from Crowborough to Eastbourne with express services for weekly boarders Friday evening and Monday morning from Tunbridge Wells and Chichester. Pupils are cheerful, enthusiastic, friendly and polite and have an easy, relaxed relationship with teachers – at the top end of the school they feel part of a wider community, again, good preparation for life outside.

Entrance: Placed first nationally in league tables amongst co-educational schools, inclusive not exclusive. CE pass mark still 55 per cent – whether from coming from prep school or externally; will rise to 60 per cent in 2015 with a minimum of 55 per cent in English and maths.

Emotional intelligence used in assessment of intake for Brighton College Prep so a maximum of five out of 60 each year do not go through to the college – they must be the bright side of average or they will not be happy here – and those who disrupt the learning of others won't fit in either.

Around 30 pupils come all the way through from the pre-prep, a further 15 or so from the prep, 40 from the lower school (these don't take CE). Seventy more from 54 other preps including St Christopher's, Hove and Handcross (now run by Brighton College).

Dynamic head of lower school has worked hard to build brilliant enrichment days for Gifted and Talented at local primaries – practical lessons in science labs, language work and unique experience of a senior school. All of this very attractive alternative to Brighton state school ballots.

Around 70 new pupils at sixth form (B+ grades at GCSE are essential), mostly from Burgess Hill, Brighton and Hove High School, Eastbourne, Hurst and Lancing.

Exit: A handful after GCSEs to local sixth form colleges, almost always for financial reasons. One hundred per cent of A level leavers to university. Around 16 per year to Oxbridge (record breaking 23 in 2013); others to eg Bristol, Manchester, London unis, Bath and Edinburgh. Famous Old Brightonians, including Peter Mayle (writer), Lord Alexander of Weedon (lawyer and banker), Lord Skidelsky (historian and politician), Laurie Penny (writer), David Nash (sculptor), Matt Prior and Holly Colvin (cricketers), Sir John Chilcot (chairman of the Iraq Inquiry), Sir Michael Hordern (actor) and Jonathan Palmer (racing driver), testify to range of successful careers which may ensue.

Money matters: At a recent open morning, parents were wondering about what extras Brighton College might offer to justify its fees being higher than rival local schools' despite its limited campus space – half an hour later they were totally sold, having been treated to a Commedia dell'Arte take on the drama, a taste of Strictly Come Dancing by sixth formers and the heads of schools speaking about the high quality lessons. Many parents struggle to pay the fees but bursaries and up to 20 academic awards (5-50 per cent off basic fees), five music scholarships (up to 30 per cent off), art, drama, dance, sport and all-rounder awards (up to 25 per cent off) and a DT scholarship (up to 15 per cent off) are available at 13+.

Registration fee of £110, then hefty deposits for accepting an offered place from £1,750 (day) to £13,750 (overseas boarders). Only refundable if pupils don't pass the entrance exam. Deposits retained to cover extras charged in arrears, balance refunded on exit from the school. Extras include £270 per term per musical instrument, £260-£1,125 per term for the use of the dyslexia support centre, £1,325 per term for English as an additional language.

Remarks: Happy, broad-minded town school for children and families who are keen on learning – producing fantastic results and sparkling individual success stories. Pupils are encouraged to achieve as much as they can, so you'd never be bored, but you could end up with too much on. Bold ideas fostered in student, staff and parent body, all the while anchoring the opportunities enabled by the fees in real world experience. Detractors of the school (often parents of ex-pupils at the prep or pre-prep) see it as too results focused, with some families turning to outside tutoring to enable their children to get into the College. CE pass mark will be raised to 60 per cent in 2015, fuel for the fire of those who judge the school to be top-slicing to climb the results ladder, explained transparently by the school as a tool to manage the high volume of applications.

Bristol Grammar School

Linked school: BGS Infants and Juniors

University Road, Bristol, BS8 1SR

• Pupils: 940 boys and girls, all day • Ages: 11–18 • Non–denom
• Fees: £12,840 pa • Independent

Tel: 01179 736006
Email: recruitment@bgs.bristol.sch.uk
Website: www.bristolgrammarschool.co.uk

Headmaster: Since 2008, Mr Roderick MacKinnon BSc PGCE (early fifties). Educated at Aylesbury Grammar School before reading engineering at Leicester. From university followed father into army – commissioned into Royal Artillery and promoted to Captain. Returned to Leicester for PGCE, then to teach science at The Minster School, Southwell. Head of physics at Tiffin Girls', then deputy head at Colchester Royal Grammar School for four years before promotion to headship of Bexley Grammar School, where he remained for 13 successful years.

Somewhat reserved initially but is actually warm and personable with an infectious passion to educate. Believes that 'a rising tide carries all boats' and that school's role is to enable effective learning. No children from former marriage but 'wonderful father figure' around school, say colleagues. Parents say that he is 'prominent' and 'a breath of fresh air'. Listens to parents' and pupils' views and 'will go out of his way to give individual pupils a few words of praise when they do well,' said one admiring mother. Realistic about pressure as a head – limits himself to teaching learning skills and is out of

school as little as possible. Hit headlines when he took IGCSE into Bexley GS – adding to debate over standards at key stage 4. Needed little persuasion to move to BGS, where he has more academic freedom to up the tempo. A lover of history, country walks and classical music.

Academic matters: In 2013 48 per cent A*/A grades (77 per cent in A*-B range) at A level – commendable, given the large numbers involved. At GCSE, 74 per cent of entries at A*/A. Parents choose BGS because it is 'serious about standards,' said one father. Head has moved candidates into IGCSE: first came maths, then English, history and sciences – means to stretch students better, though head insists that school is 'not an academic hothouse'. Aims at quality rather than quantity in terms of entries and doesn't express groups. EPQ in the sixth form.

Parental opinions on teaching standards vary: general satisfaction and one parent described her daughter's teachers as 'inspirational'; criticism, though, of weaknesses amongst some of the 'old guard'. We sat in on an A level English lesson in which inspired teaching steered the discussion to undergraduate standard.

Full curriculum in years 7 and 8 includes Latin for all; Greek, German and Russian appear as options in year 9; 26 subjects currently studied in sixth form to A2 level. Successful DT department now extended to food and textiles; super work in product and graphic design witnessed by impressive displays. Pupils set own (mainly high) targets for themselves in this and other subjects. Year/subject bases fringe open areas; junior school pupils share same site at present – not ideal, we thought, though little ones seemed unfazed and get to use a range of senior school facilities. Expect homework from the outset here – properly monitored and marked; builds up to three subjects per night plus GCSE coursework by year 10. Internal exams for years 7-10 in summer term used for assessment purposes.

Selective nature of school does not preclude some SpLD needs – SENCo to co-ordinate support for SpLD mainly in junior years. Honours programme main stimulus for 100+ gifted and talented pupils, but general diet is rich and varied.

Games, options, the arts: Excellent sports facilities include Failand complex (a 20 minute minibus ride away): two floodlit Astroturfs, a vast expanse of pitches, low ropes (assault) course in woods plus wow factor, £2m sports pavilion which outdoes any other Bristol school and accommodates up to 350 players, with super changing and recreational facilities. Large-scale participation on Saturdays in inter-school competitions as well as on weekly games day. Heavily used modern facility on site includes super glass-back squash courts, a dauntingly vast climbing wall (professional outside staff lead this activity) and full size sports hall. Graveney (an old boy) Room is the dance studio, also used for judo and other activities. Cricket pros come in for net practice, fitness suite heavily used by older students and effective use made of salle for fencing (school has specialised in this sport for many years). We watched mixed junior PE class – lots of fun with young, energetic staff. PE now an option at A level and GCSE. Outstanding girl athlete has reached international level, current independent schools' judo champion, national fencers and plenty of representative team players in variety of sports.

Large numbers doing art so quirky new base on Elton Road bursts at seams – high quality work on display here and around school but no separate gallery as yet. Head of art (previously at Dulwich College) places emphasis on 'giving pupils their creative voice'; lots of print-making and timely expansion of digital art.

Next door we found a vibrant music department (apart from 'vanishing violinists') with all you would expect from a large school: main orchestra with lots of offshoots in terms of ensembles, jazz band, woodwind, brass groups etc. Twenty main concerts/competitions during the year. 'My daughter has taken up the sax and loves it,' glowed one mother. In addition to individual lessons, pupils in years 7-9 have two class-based music lessons per week; option choices for GCSE (much use made of Sibelius software and Macs for composition at this level) and beyond. School rents one of Bristol's premier venues (St George's) for annual concert, where works like Schubert's Unfinished get the full BGS treatment.

Drama is high profile with approximately 10 students a year taking A level – Mackay Theatre (opened by no less a person than Sam Wanamaker) provides professional-standard studio space with enough fold-away seating for most productions plus pro-standard sound and lighting; house plays each year and full scale musical biennially. HoD also manages 'stage crew', which takes all-comers to work behind the scenes. Major sixth form drama at end of winter term (recently Michael Frayn's Noises Off was very successful) and lively outside pantomime in summer term performed by years 7-9 in amphitheatre. Fringe Society performs at Edinburgh Festival. Head keen to put new performing arts centre at top of his wish list. Dance and DT (food and textiles) now exam options (although academic choices predominate).

D of E and Ten Tors get loyal following. Leadership a big thing here with co-ordinated visits and leadership diploma in the offing; recent expeditions include Peru, the Arctic and Morocco: sparked great interest in supporting education for girls there (over £20K raised in four years to build girls' hostel). Activities programme one afternoon per week in years 7-11; lunchtime and after-school clubs include mentoring, debating, textiles, chess and a whole lot more.

Background and atmosphere: School founded in 1532 by the Thorne brothers – Bristol merchants made good. School motto: 'ex spinis uvas' ('from thorns to grapes') makes a play on their name. Other benefactors (some of whom are linked to Bristol's slavery-based prosperity) have been downgraded – witness re-naming of newly opened Thorne entrance after effective lobbying by school council (meets six times a year and exerts a real influence) against school's now blackballed choice of Tyndall.

Shoe-horned into site it has occupied since mid-nineteenth century. Disparate collection of buildings covers whole gamut of architectural styles (trademark Pennant stone with Bath stone edges much in evidence); unexpectedly peaceful despite central Bristol location. Modernised science wing, new classrooms for art and music and upgrading of music practice rooms are all recent developments. Impressive (now double-ended) glass entrance doors lead into central Victorian building, with stairs sweeping up to what must be one of the grandest school halls ('Great Hall') and greatest settings for school dinners in the land.

Full school assembly a weekly tour de force: former headmasters stare down from gilded frames on panelled walls, whilst current one speaks from rostrum flanked by senior staff and pupils. Unexpectedly intimate style in assemblies given grand setting – a real sense of a family gathering, we felt. School (all wear daffodils) goes en masse annually to cathedral for Charter Day service and singing of school song in Latin. Successful allocation of outdoor spaces for different age groups – includes one sitting out area with skylights over DT department below: a most successfully designed area opened in 1994. Ownership of six adjacent Victorian villas in Elton Road provides a variety of characterful outposts for modern languages, music and art. Lots of long service medals amongst staff – more than most day schools.

School is ICT savvy: plasma screens keep everyone up to date with events and diary; 11 suites of PCs dotted around site and smartboards are used to good effect – we watched enthusiastic year 9 Russian class learning vocabulary with a difference via one: Russian word lists constantly changing on the screen prompted enthusiastic pupil participation. Four laboratories per subject in science – all high spec. School library is best we've

seen in south west – open until 6.00pm, it clocks nearly 500 pupils a day through its turnstile; hub of BGS literary activity. Recent outside speakers have included Michelle Paver, Jeremy Strong, Michael Wood, Frances Kay, Michael Morpurgo and Sir Ranulph Fiennes.

Well turned out collectively – 'Individualism shines through ideas,' says head, who praises pupils' world awareness and consideration. Pupils 'love their house fleeces enough to go to the local shops in them,' said one teacher. Lunch now served in the Great Hall; choice/standard seemed fine; breakfast club operates daily for pupils and parents before school; pupils generally use topped up smartcards to pay for meals. Great careers suite; world of work day in year 9 and user-friendly approach to resources backed by full-time head of careers to guide and encourage: 'Follow your passion,' she urges sixth formers.

Pastoral care and discipline: Boys still outnumber girls but the latter thrive here too, from what we observed. 'Phlegmatic boys helped my daughter cope better with stresses of exams,' explained one mother, who thought single sex would not have been helpful. Kind introduction to senior school life provided in induction programme – head of year 7 visits every feeder school; pupils have taster day in summer term prior to entry.

Parents get email contact with all staff – works well, say parents. Pupils placed in one of six colour houses (named after their heads) which operate form-wise for years 9-11. Well established peer mentoring system which is effective and has reduced teasing. Staff use restorative justice to good effect and school is short on petty rules. Pupils are happy and girls especially 'make friends quickly,' said year 7 mothers. Overlap between heads of houses (still all male, we noticed) and year heads works to pupils' advantage with lots of co-ordination over pastoral concerns and academic needs. 'Misconception is that BGS is too big, but family atmosphere of the house system addresses that,' we were told. No overall house championship.

Sixth form has own centre which successfully combines a social area (café open until 2.00pm daily) with facilities for private study; 30 tutorial groups of 10-12 students; experienced head of careers on hand to guide as necessary. BGS prides itself on its small-scale approach through its house system within context of a big school, and parents like way any problem is sorted out quickly.

Pupils and parents: Broad profile in terms of ethnicity, majority from professional background including high number of academics. Parents' evenings 'reflect how teachers really know pupils', and lots of social events throughout year. Strong alumni association and former pupils include Lord Franks, Nobel laureate Sir John Pople and Rabinder Singh QC.

Entrance: Applications accepted at any stage for entry to all years except 11 and 13. January entrance examination principally for main entry (132 pupils) at 11+. Half annual entry comes from BGS Juniors and remaining 60 or so places from up to 30 primary schools across city and beyond. Combination of multiple choice verbal and non-verbal reasoning tests plus papers in English. Acceptance on basis of performance on tests, interview with staff to discuss interests and school work, confidential report and predicted grades. Some candidates called for interview with head to assess for Scholars' Programme. Interview evening for sixth form applicants according to proposed A level choices – offers conditional on GCSE results.

Exit: Around 10 per cent leave post GCSE (eg for state alternatives or financial reasons). Sixth formers to a wide range of universities including 13 to Oxbridge in 2013.

Money matters: Not a hugely wealthy school, but has come through the post-assisted places era well and is able to give bursaries and scholarships to 10 per cent of pupils. Scholarships, usually worth 10 per cent of fees, for year 7 entry – 13 on academic merit, one for sport and one for creative and performing arts – and year 9 – four on academic merit, one for sport and one for creative and performing arts.

Remarks: Proximity to university creates a useful sense of 'an educational continuum', commented some parents. A school where care is 'profound rather than superficial' – something we picked up from all those we consulted and where 'it's cool to be bright'.

BRIT School for Performing Arts and Technology

60 The Crescent, Croydon, CR0 2HN

• Pupils: 950, all day • Ages: 14–19 • Non-denom • State

Tel: 020 8665 5242
Email: admin@brit.croydon.sch.uk
Website: www.brit.croydon.sch.uk

Principal: Since June 2012, Mr Stuart Worden, BA, MA, GTP. Forties. Previously school's director of theatre, though involvement stretches back, one way or another, almost to its foundation in 1991. Before that, was all over the place (literally, not metaphorically – he's highly organised) as, like so many of school's staff, has combined education, education, education with production, production, production. Though past isn't yet mythologised, may yet happen, given that when whistles through key moments of his career, 'the years change each time,' says affable minder.

First act of our (possibly world exclusive) version opens in Chichester, where, the 'first and only' theatrical type in his family (brother, also in education, got there by more conventional means), he was taken on regular trips to the theatre – 'virtually at the end of my road' by 'lovely' mother. Was hooked, particularly by the language, leading to writing/producer roles with everyone from the National Theatre to the Royal Exchange Manchester, Playwrights' Co-operative and Working Title Films.

Teaching cropped up early on, too, with FE/HE posts on the film writing MA course at Sheffield University in 1990 as well as a spell as drama teacher at Lansdowne College in Kensington, reprised during two years at the Chichester College of Technology in 1991-1993.

May not look like conventional head (he's creative industries smart, down to intelligent glasses) but is meticulous when it comes to rock solid efficiency of school administration. His ethos is creativity within a framework, from the details (photographic ID for visitors, lessons that run to time or he'll want to know why) to the big things – buildings, new and refurbished, that are no architectural folly but really work.

Wants students to leave not just with creative potential on the way to being realised but equipped with hard-headed entrepreneurial nous to back it up (there's praise in literature for a student's massive on-line following).

His long term involvement in community arts – helped create Steam Industry, a theatre for all initiative – has also led to blossoming of school's outreach programme which is increasingly varied and demanding, though also, he stresses, 'purposeful and long term.' Virtuous circle, too, as those seeking to make career in the area can opt for community arts practice BTEC qualification – developed by school and so far unique in the UK.

Pupils work with hospice patients, asylum seekers and rape victims and also act as talented big brothers and sisters to pupils in new, much-needed primary that Mr Worden helped get off the ground – projects naturally including a home grown musical. BRIT Kids, for local children 8-15, includes community classes and free performances at local Ashcroft Theatre, themed day for tinies, too.

He attracts huge praise from staff. 'He's professional, a good leader, very polite, expects high standards and is very positive,' thought one, speaking for everyone else.

Pupils, too, like his friendly, hands-on approach. 'When I needed help with recording for radio, he was like, "give me a minute and I'll do it",' said one. As a result, takes a while for everyone to work out who he is, particularly those whose previous experiences with authority figures were of a bruising nature. 'He doesn't give out a principal vibe,' says year 11 pupil who had only recently clocked who he was.

Older pupils, though, had no problems with identification. 'Love the way he comes round, sits with us and chats,' said sixth former. 'Not like any principal I've met,' reckoned another. 'He makes an effort to talk.'

Perk of job is 'daily' feedback about pupil success (during GSG visit, it was smash hit involvement in London Fashion Week). As to qualities required by prospective student, he's 'not sure' where talent features in the equation or passion, either, come to that. Instead, stresses importance of being 'nice and kind. Creativity and the arts need you to be open and then you should be willing to share your skill with others. I think that's a special quality.'

Is regularly asked whether school might extend to cover wider age range or sprout satellite versions in the regions. Likely to remain a one-off, he thinks, an 'extraordinary' place that does far more than equip pupils for careers. 'Parallel with that is the sense that the school goes to so many people and uses the arts to enrich their lives.'

Academic matters: Wouldn't be hard to see school as a giant performing arts centre with added classrooms. Not that 'straight' academic teachers would thank you for the description, or principal, come to that. ('Not a Fame Academy' a recurring leitmotif in literature).

Staff are either traditional types who 'come here because they think it's the right school to teach at and want to be part of what we're doing here' or creative industry professionals who want to teach 'in a place that specialises in what I'm skilled at,' thought principal. No passengers: choreographers, film makers, playwrights, composers all welcomed but need to commit to training: on the job GTP programme is particularly popular.

Academic staples are bunched together, with sociology, humanities, science and musical theatre in East Wing (actually the main building of Old Grammar school – pay attention at the back). While inevitable focus on performance can make it seem as if you're never more than two minutes from a rehearsal, rooms are well-soundproofed to avoid stardust leakage into classes.

Staff work hard to harness pupils' energy, GCSE groups enjoying animated discussions on causes of youth crime in lively sociology lessons, maths teacher moving us along from fidgety class, distracted by visitor. 'This is a creative enterprise,' says young, happy-looking teacher.

Once here, it's a hard place to leave. Teachers, like pupils, praised 'inspirational' atmosphere – latest arrivals include new head of costumes, fresh from Eastenders – and warmth that 'sucks you in'. Though no coloured hair (something of a pupil speciality, though 'they get over it after the first year'), they span the gamut from blouse and skirt to finest beard, bomber jacket 'n' red trainers combo.

Star quality tends to reside in BTEC results. Full-on approach makes results extra impressive. In years 10 and 11, pupils take BTEC level 2 diplomas (counting as four GCSEs) as well as following well-equipped and solidly taught GCSE classes in core subjects – some streamed, if ability range demands it, subjects broadly EBacc-themed.

Given intake at year 10 – nerve-wracking standing start for any teacher – results are spectacularly good when it comes to performance-related topics such as dance and drama, and pretty respectable in the must-do areas, too. At GCSE (or equivalent) remarks lifted numbers gaining five A*- C grades including English and maths to just north of 70 per cent up after slight dip in 2012, maths back to 74 per cent at grades A*-C though still lagging behind Eng lang and lit, both up in the mid 80 per cents.

Inevitably, still greater pressure for sixth form, with BTEC diploma (choice of broadcast and digital communication, community arts practice, dance, interactive media, music, musical theatre, technical theatre, theatre and visual arts and design) the starting point with rich rewards – over 90 per cent gained at least one distinction in 2013 compared with just under 70 per cent in 2012 for all.

Everyone also takes additional AS or A level(s) (15 subject choice) or additional BTEC qualification. Results largely respectable here, too, A*-B once again closing in on 50 per cent as they did in 2011 (slight dip in 2012), a few pupils coming slightly adrift in English Literature (most popular subject) and maths.

Welcome flexibility allows teachers to devote whole days to some post-16 BTEC modules. 'Means you really get to learn,' thought one, approvingly. Course options can lead to slight difficulties: not everyone, for example, is drawn to the sewing that's currently a must-do part of the visual arts and design and technical theatre arts courses – though discussions are currently under way on possibility of evolving a stitching-light option.

For those needing extra help – there's screening for all during May induction day – terrific SEN is a huge strength, generously accommodated, areas including cosy, cushioned area and Smartboard-equipped classroom – 'keeps sense of routine' – where struggling pupils (SpLD biggest need, also some ASD and ADHD) get parallel lessons at slower speed, multisensory approaches added 'until it works'. Most staff 'very supportive and recognise that approach builds self-esteem'. Doubters (and there are a small number) are won over by success stories, including pupil who went from U to A* in English GCSE.

Whatever the choice, it's a full-on commitment, eminently do-able for the already organised, efficiency step-change required for those who aren't, and a tough old regime for all which can come as shock to anyone expecting straight drudge for drama swap.

'Same as any old school but one where there's less time for academic subjects,' thought slightly jaded year 11 boy. Even with sensible timetable structuring separating academic and performing arts days, extra workload means 'you need to push yourself and get ready to learn.'

Games, options, the arts: Stuffed with opportunities for performance and just about everything that goes with it, arts naturally the main drain on space, from eight music rooms, all sound-proofed (plus innumerable additional rooms for individual lessons – drums, vocal, keyboard, bass all popular) to two theatres – one, Obi (as in benefactor Sir Maurice Oberstein rather than Kenobi) complete with two storey barn doors to make scenery shifts from adjoining scenic workshop easy peasy.

Textiles/costume design space in main building a pleasure to experience, too, recently remade with retractable door splitting teaching space, allowing GCSE students to spark off older pupils.

Hands-on stuff rules, however. Literally so in case of portable appliance test, pupils shinning impressively up ladders to check the lights. 'Need to understand what's dangerous,' said teacher (and a useful all-purpose teenage rule, too).

With students billed by specialism, (dancer x and musician y) in school literature and so much going on, can sometimes be hard to know where lessons end and the extracurricular begins. Even college awards nights become performances, most recent complete with Great Gatsby staging and X Factor style audience votes (which would brighten up more conventional speech days elsewhere no end).

Driving everything is all-round enthusiasm, fuelled by wide range of sixth form specialisms and staff contacts – brilliant, of course – with some interactive media students, for example, getting chance to work with Aardman studios.

Sixth former taking BTEC in technical theatre had had a ball working on Tim Burton-inspired costumes for 'Hamlyn', put on in local theatre and one of 40 productions through the year ranging from Artaud and Brook to Brecht, Caryl Churchill and much in the way of full-blown Shakespeare, many others with words and scores written by the staff and/or pupils.

Traditional educational add ons far from absent, however. Duke of Edinburgh runs conventional course (though Jack Petchey awards – imaginatively awarded for academic rather than community service excellence in years 10 and 11 – do not). Sport isn't neglected either. School has own Olympian to its name, and while council has hung on to school's (small) sports field, necessitating relocation of sports day (and other fixtures) to nearby Norwood Lakes, the keen have school gym – somewhat battered but serviceable – for basketball (popular girls' team, which meets on Mondays, 'vicious', thought year 13 boys, admiringly).

Background and atmosphere: Patriotic acronym is down to British Record Industry Trust – great and good still feature on governors' list – and whose funding and influence led to school's foundation in 1991 (after Mrs Thatcher, fearing creation of home for resting thesps, had been won round – or so the legend goes).

They're hugely proud of what they've created, says principal, and with good reason. Despite growth of vocational training colleges covering the 14-19 age range, school remains a one-off, the only free (prospectus uses capitals to emphasis) performing arts and technology school in the country, state funded but outside LA control.

Set within easy walk from Selhurst Station – not likely to become new Hoxton any time soon – school, though not an obvious looker from the outside, is full of thought, care and taste when it comes to the interiors. Inevitable tired corners mainly in vintage old school building (site originally housed Selhurst Grammar), one of three of varying styles and vintage. Newest, light and bright, is very plush indeed though smart rooms and corridors largely rule throughout the site, with plenty of tarting up (paint 'n' porthole doors even in otherwise non-refurbished areas, for example).

Feel is urban grit, rather than Surrey Downs (even feels like a long way to leafy South Croydon) with undeniable pressure on space. No pupil common rooms, for example (one year 11 girl had asked teacher to keep an eye on possessions during the day – gladly done, too) – immaculate carpeting in many corridors provides comfortable sitting space for the needy (speckly stone finish remains in original school building) with one student sitting by banked lockers busily sorting out vast pile of music.

Little in the way of school jargon, bar slightly confusing names. (Blue Block, though lovely, isn't blue). Main (and alias-free) building, built new for school's opening, has been substantially refreshed. Features include internal windows opening out on to corridors (principal's office too, at his request, providing a window on to the world), walls liberally decorated with high quality art (everything from Aboriginal-motifs to Banksy lookalike and delicate Japanese figures disporting themselves against parchment backdrop).

Academic year, too, is unusual with five eight-week terms, interspersed with fortnight breaks. Officially 'best supports delivery of the curriculum and ensures students return refreshed', though according to one teacher, production demands mean 'you'll often find students coming in over the holidays'.

With the exception of occasional overt whackiness – bins spray painted in wild array of colours following theatre teacher's guerrilla decoration initiative over the summer holidays – what dominates is sense of all-through professionalism.

And while absence of uniform, bells (and whistles, at least off stage) may not tend towards the norm, expectations certainly do, with teachers unlikely to indulge in too much time-drift as 'students will tell you when break is,' reckoned one.

Pastoral care and discipline: It's a busy old day, lights up 7am, not dimmed until 12 hours later. Though 'no-one will be here all that time,' says principal, some will operate in unconventional hours – drama and dance students, for example, warming up in the early hours before auditions or classes, studios booked up way in advance so pupils can edit their films.

Outstanding attendance, particularly at sixth form level, testament to commitment but also in stark contrast, in some cases, to pupils' unhappy educational experiences elsewhere. Several talked about feeling 'like outsiders' in other schools. Here, blend of rigour and tolerance seems to suit everyone. 'I felt I'd found people like me,' reckoned one sixth former.

'We think it's a good place to be looked after,' says principal, who is particularly proud of large scale speed meet and greet induction where grizzled year 11 veterans help newly arrived year 10s to settle in.

Body image can (predictably) be an issue, countered by strong message highlighting the glory of the individual, school stressing its more unconventional successes such as Adele to ensure that identikit size nothings aren't touted as the only aspiration worth pursuing.

On-site counsellors, presence discreetly advertised to students via form tutors, provide additional back up, while healthy eating (just about the only niggle otherwise superlative inspection report could find) is now a major school focus, with year 10 science pupils reporting on savoury snack fat content to year 13 dancers, canteen staff challenging pupils 'in a friendly way' if appear to be opting for unhealthy/minimalistic lunch (those on free school meals compelled to have healthy meal, though 'it's not about being a dictator but guiding and supporting,' thought staff member).

Staff enforce gentle discipline – students in library, verging on slight chattiness in quiet zone, were instantly quelled by (silent) entrance of smiley but no-nonsense librarians. Creativity within a framework something of a necessity, especially with school jam-packed, recent BTEC additions adding another 200 to sixth form so 'as much as can take without bursting,' says school.

May be a timetable but there's 'no "you will do this number of hours" – it's their school,' says principal. Adds up to atmosphere that engenders sense of independence combined with professionalism – a lesson for the future, as with sixth form pupils given permission to leave lesson to conduct library research, but with return time and teacher expectations clearly outlined.

Pupil voice is heard loud and clear, too, in everything from 'almost daily' cake sales to fundraise for forthcoming productions to active student council which recently voted to ban environment-unfriendly disposable cups at lunchtime, 'commit to bringing in refillable bottles'. No wonder giant painted portrait of the blessed Jamie on wall of bigger canteen dispenses saint-like smile like a South American folk hero by way of inspiration.

Pupils and parents: Education should be accomplished without removing innocence along the way, thinks principal. 'Friends assume it's going to be like Fame, but it's really down to earth,' felt sixth former, though performers in particular exhibit healthy dose of chutzpah and aren't backwards in coming forwards, adding in a couple of pirouettes and a solo on the way in – we enjoyed early morning dancing huddles outside dancing

(professional-looking gurning, too, in one case) – and tales of close harmony rivalry in the canteen.

Though unified by drive – 'at an ordinary school she'd be the leader of the pack, here, she's in a class with 30 of them,' reckoned mother of aspiring dancer – school community otherwise diverse. Families range from chimney sweeps to the loaded, many drawn from immediate area, which is 'socially complicated,' says principal, characterised by side-by-side pockets of affluence and deprivation – eligibility for free school meals is above the national average, and school also runs 'BRIT loves Selhurst' campaign, offering free tickets to locals.

Entrance: Not for everyone. One talented singer-songwriter had opted instead for Guildford ACM. 'They advertise it as once you go there, 75 per cent of your future career is done, but I know it's hard work.'

Some find the place for themselves – press coverage is pretty much non-stop. One girl, now in sixth form, paid first visit to keep friend company and ended up the one with the place.

A minority very local (15 per cent from Croydon), though vast majority (75 per cent) from South London, remaining 10 per cent, selected on raw talent, not postcode, can come from anywhere in UK. (School stresses desire to avoid impossibly long journeys, somewhat spoiling effect with X-Factor winner Leona Lewis, quoted as describing two-hour round trip as 'so worth it').

Oversubscribed all the way through, less so for those entering in year 10, massively for sixth form. For 14 year olds seeking place in year 10, process less daunting, though useful to muster clear ideas on what pupils would gain from coming here.

Technical courses based on portfolios followed by workshops the norm. Inevitably stressful for would-be performers. 'She got recalled, she cried, she stuffed up in her first audition and thought "that's it" – but got in,' said parent who felt school wasn't looking for fully formed talent (there are rumours of already successful child stars being turned away) but 'something in kids that they can bring out – they don't necessarily want someone who's completely polished and finished and looking for it as a way into the next big thing,' A fair comment, thought school. 'It's about unlocking potential rather than a finished product.'

Exit: In a handful of cases, some year 11 pupils may not make the sixth form, most after discovering that love for performing arts has worn off. 'Might get to age 16 and think, I don't want to be a dancer – I want to do something else with my life,' says principal. 'They might just change and that's a good thing.'

At least 90 per cent, sometimes more, do carry on into sixth form, and almost everyone, even those who leave post-16, go on to further and higher education elsewhere – most recent extreme example swapping bright lights for animal husbandry.

Principal stresses proof that employability issues amongst the young can be triumphantly overcome. According to school survey, 70 per cent of past pupils end up working in creative industries. A few are household names but this is definitely not yardstick of measurement. All, says principal firmly, are superstars even if not household names because 'are the best box office manager or record label executive.'

School's well-designed vocational courses, with an eye and a half on the future, help speed the process along. Community-related courses, for example, lead to a virtuous circle, helping local bodies and in the process raising future trained community facilitators – a growing area for well-regarded HE courses such as Central School's applied theatre and education BA degree. Others end up at RADA, Central School of Speech and Drama, Rose Bruford, Drama Centre, East 15, Bristol Old Vic and LAMDA, or head off to university – Kent, Manchester and UEA amongst them.

Once through, you'll find their words, music, performance, directorial and backstage talents just about everywhere you look, from fashion shows to musicals, national theatre to community arts, in the UK and internationally.

Remarks: Vocational dazzler with some academic bright lights as well. An educational showstopper, and one you definitely won't want to walk out of half way through, which tempers sprinklings of stardust with lashings of nuts and bolts reality checks. That's what they say. We secretly think it's like collecting every school's coolest kids and putting them in one place. If we could set this review to music, we probably would.

Brockwood Park School

Brockwood Park, Bramdean, Hampshire, SO24 0LQ

• Pupils: 75, all boarders • Ages: 14 –19 • Non denom, enquiry about all aspects of life encouraged. • Fees: £18,860 pa
• Independent

Tel: 01962 771744
Email: enquiry@brockwood.org.uk
Website: www.brockwood.org.uk

Co-principals: Since 2006, Mr Adrian Sydenham and since September 2013, Dr Gopal Krishnamurthy. Mr Sydenham has taught psychology at Brockwood for over 10 years and holds master's degrees in modern languages, environmental planning and international criminal justice.

Dr Gopal has spent most of his life, since the age of 4, as a student and teacher at Krishnamurti's schools in India, the UK and the USA. He was a student, mature student and staff member at Brockwood and teaches physics and maths as well as being co-principal. He has a PhD in education, MAs in education and philosophy and a BA in physics.

Why two principals? 'We'd like to avoid the notion of the heroic head.' They both, in common with all residential staff, are committed to the teachings of Jiddu Krishnamurti, inspirational writer and speaker on philosophical and spiritual subjects.

Academic matters: Exams 'are not our main thrust', says school, with understatement, 'but are seen in perspective alongside things like yoga, working in the garden, and care of rooms' (all compulsory). No GCSEs. The school uses Cambridge International Exams for A levels, OCR, Edexcel and AQA and mixed results are achieved – in 2013, 18 per cent A*/A and 45 per cent A*/B grades (hard to draw out any trends from such a tiny number of students). Some retakes taken at local sixth form college and many pupils will be returning to their home countries for higher education, so British exams not the be all and end all but do need to be recognised in Europe.

No fixed academic timetables into which pupils must slot – each programme is created afresh for each child with plenty of scope to concentrate on a single passion. An 18-year-old musician we met had secured two free days a week to spend on intensive piano work. Another had dropped all academic subjects to study only art, yoga and pottery. Others were focused on more traditional subjects.

No pressure; no punishments if homework is not done; lots of one-on-one teaching. SEN support offered on individual basis – one weekly session is partially covered by the fees, further help is charged for. ESL for overseas students who need it. Computers discouraged but permitted. 'K Class' compulsory once a week to study Krishnamurti, held in soothing white carpeted room with scatter cushions. Lots of sitting on floors here. 'Inquiry time', when the whole school gets together to discuss a theme – eg why are we vegetarians?; why do we value silence? – a core part of education.

Staff comprise renaissance men and women, most teaching two or three subjects at any given time. So some teaching inspired, while some a bit patchy, 'and teachers can suddenly head off on sabbatical or stop offering a subject,' said a parent. Non-residential specialist teachers are brought in to fill gaps.

Games, options, the arts: Health and fitness, yes – games, no. Some sort of exercise is scheduled twice a week (gym with fitness equipment). Not keen on competition, no prizes. Has been known to play football against another school, but never in anger. Music inspiring and given space to flourish, with two concerts a year and a variety of instrumental lessons offered. 'It's not about excelling,' a teacher told us. 'It's about a feeling of enjoyment.' Five pianos, a drum kit and a recording studio on hand – pupils can record their own albums. Art barn, designed by Keith Critchlow in the arts and crafts Cottage style, is the fine art centre. Dance, drama, photography, pottery – all the arts – thriving.

Background and atmosphere: Founded by Krishnamurti in 1969 with a gift of £40,000. This was meant to be his retirement fund – instead he bought Brockwood Park and 40 acres of inspiring, serene grounds within South Downs National Park. Still has the same gentle feel he would have liked, with the main building housing admin, classrooms and girls' dorms. Beautiful octagonal assembly hall used for silent meditation before breakfast, whole school meetings (twice a week) and concerts. A huge rambling and impressive library with interesting selection of books, eg on alternative medicine. Boys' rooms, 'the Cloisters', surrounding small pond – exceptionally nice, like a boutique hotel (though boys speak of noise reverberating through the thin partition walls and single glazing). Seven new and beautiful interconnected boarding pavilions now provide extra accommodation.

Originally set up to be international, fully boarding (no day pupils, and pupils may stay over half terms) and small, and has remained so to this day, 'But we could get a bit larger,' says school. Has softened its early ascetic, socialistic ethos, when staff were discouraged from having children of their own, yet remains curiously spartan – no TV, 'except news and football' on one aged set 'that receives three channels'! No cleaning or kitchen staff – all members of the community, including teachers, do their own laundry and help clean/clear tables/wash up meals.

Kitchen fully vegetarian and mainly organic. Smaller 'eco-kitchen' available to the students. Garden and greenhouses lovingly tended by all, produces everything from pumpkins to sweetcorn – all eaten at the school. Seeds are gathered for the following year. Twenty chickens provide eggs. Care for the environment a priority and recycling given its own room. Roughly 10 'mature students' (early 20s) an important cog in the Brockwood wheel – they do the cooking and some other work within the community in exchange for room, board and the opportunity to study and bask in Brockwoodian tranquility.

Pastoral care and discipline: No school rules – instead pupils and parents sign an 'open letter', a group of agreements including meat-free diet, attending morning meeting, staying in rooms after 10pm and no smoking, alcohol or drugs. No automatic punishments for anything – everything open for discussion. 'Fear is a destructive force in education. Take away fear and authority and pupils can be creative, willing to try things. It's important to discover what they love to do,' says Bill. Relationships, getting along in a community, solving problems are key. Drinking a big no-no, whatever a pupil's age: this may be the first school we have visited where drinking and smoking are highly uncool. All that said, does have to expel the odd pupil, for the usual reasons, and can be tension between providing structure for younger pupils and freedom for the 18 and 19 year olds.

Some 30 members of staff, plus the mature students, live on the campus and students work and live alongside them, the school's greatest strength – or a weakness, depending on how you look at it. Telephone numbers of school's 'independent listener' and Childline prominently displayed around the school.

Pupils and parents: International – 15 out of 75 from the UK, none local. Others Spanish, French, German, Dutch, Danish, and then from literally everywhere. Everyone looks quite normal – not much inclined to purple hair or facial piercings – and impressively verbal, eloquent and softly spoken. Most pupils come from families with an interest in Krishnamurti. Others find it on the web (key words vegetarian, holistic or alternative). Some parents consider Brockwood Park alongside other alternative schools, eg Bedales, Frensham Heights, St Christopher's, the Steiners (especially Michael Hall), Summerhill (A S Neill got some of his educational ideas from Krishnamurti). A few come from Inwoods, the 'small school' within Brockwood Park grounds educating 30 children age 4-11 (started as a school for staff children). Estimates that around 1400 men and women have now been educated at Brockwood Park and keen to involve them more in the school through workshops, fundraising etc.

Entrance: Same process for prospective pupils and for staff – a trial week followed by a meeting of the school community to share impressions of the visitor. Up to a third of applicants are turned away. Maturity is the essential qualification according to the pupils – 'We won't take someone who ruins the community'. Despite unorthodox ethos, most definitely not a magnet for alienated teenagers. 'We're low profile, and don't want to be a sink school for problem kids.'

Exit: Students leave equipped for life, though not necessarily for higher education in the UK. However most students will go to university, either straight away or eventually – frequently overseas, especially the USA.

Money matters: Fees kept low. All residential staff are paid the same (frugal) salary so are, in effect, subsidising the running of the school. One third of pupils receive some level of bursary.

Remarks: Uplifting and unique school with the modest aim of completely transforming consciousness and creating a new human being. 'The bar is set high,' said one member of staff. 'Feels a bit like an academic retreat,' said a student trying to sum up the school's ethos. Or a kibbutz. The sort of school that changes lives. Intellectual curiosity will flourish here – but exam results may be elusive.

Bromley High School (GDST)

Linked school: Bromley High School (GDST) Junior Dept

Blackbrook Lane, Bickley, Bromley, Kent, BR1 2TW

• Pupils: 600 girls in senior school • Ages: 4-18 • Christian, non-denom • Fees: £14,022 pa • Independent

Tel: 020 8781 7000
Email: admissions@bro.gdst.net
Website: www.bromleyhigh.gdst.net

Head: Since 2010, Mrs Louise Simpson (early forties) BSc, PGCE, married with one daughter, educated in Wales and Ireland. She has had an exciting career in teaching at Ratcliffe College and Gresham's, then as head of biology at King's Rochester and deputy head at Brighton College. Having worked with Richard Cairns and Anthony Seldon, she has brought some dynamic education management skills to Bromley and has worked hard to make the school more welcoming. She has established a new community service programme to help the school integrate with the local community.

Off in July 2014 to head St Paul's School, Sao Paulo, Brazil.

Academic matters: Academic results consistently high – 74 per cent A*/A at GCSE 2013; 84 per cent A*-B at A level, with 53 per cent A*/A. Science and modern foreign languages remain particularly strong and a number of girls go on to study these at top universities. Modern foreign languages department has links with France, Germany and Spain and arranges much better than average exchanges, visits and work experience placements. Recently awarded the British Council's full International School Award. All subject areas have dedicated heads of department who ensure high standards and excellent results. Parents say the teaching is solid and fairly traditional, maths teaching is especially impressive and a top subject choice in the sixth form; school adds that staff changes have led to more diverse teaching styles.

The head and her senior management team work extremely hard to make sure that the curriculum is really flexible, so girls can have as much choice possible in all the age groups and fit in extra GCSE subjects if they want. Smart modern classrooms and sparkling labs inspire the girls to work hard and care for their environment. All pupils have a personal tutor who tracks their progress and sets targets with them for their academic and personal development on a regular basis. Well-stocked library looking out onto woodland provides an inspiring place to work before and after school.

Two part-time SENCos provide additional support on a one-to-one basis for pupils with specific learning differences and run study skills programmes for all pupils. EAL is available as required.

Games, options, the arts: Great opportunities for the sportswoman here – acres of space, athletics track, three hockey pitches, including an Astroturf which can be hired by local clubs. Pupils frequently win awards at national, county and borough level across athletics, gymnastics, hockey and netball, tennis and swimming; cricket enjoying great success. Ms Simpson was once a national level rower herself. A number of specialist coaches are employed to enhance sporting opportunities via school clubs. Indoor swimming pool and gym which is made available to staff and families out of school hours. Duke of Edinburgh scheme rapidly expanding (over 100 pupils involved), annual World Challenge expeditions, and international cultural exchanges to Asia and China for sixth formers.

Performing arts and dance studios recently updated to create an incredibly clever and versatile performance space. Offers dance GCSE. Regular in-house drama and music festivals and pupils achieve distinctions in LAMDA and ABRSM exams, including musical theatre. Music department to be enjoyed, producing a lovely range of concerts; everyone is encouraged to learn an instrument or join a choir. International tours for the various choirs and orchestras and a yearly middle school music tour to Paris. Art work is of a very high standard, some talented GCSE students do really well, textiles and photography recently introduced as A level choices for budding artists.

Background and atmosphere: Originally founded in 1883. In 1982 moved to its present 25 acre site, complete with woodland and a lake. Cool, calm atmosphere pervades the corridors, which are lined with noticeboards announcing forthcoming events and successes. One area is dedicated to the school's history and a gallery of portraits.

General impression is of a busy and active school. School tells us the uniform is 'not dreary and maroon any more – we have a smart new grey blazer and maroon/grey check pleated skirt for the seniors and a pretty maroon/grey check tunic for the juniors – the girls and parents love this new uniform'.

Recent £1m refurbishments include sixth form common room, dining room and swimming facilities.

Pastoral care and discipline: All pupils have a personal tutor whom parents can contact at any time to discuss pastoral or academic matters. Democratic elections run for the selection of a head girl, two deputies and senior prefects. Sixth form girls can train as peer counsellors and access to a professional counsellor on a drop in basis or by appointment. Older girls are encouraged to mentor younger pupils and gain work and life experience by helping in the junior school. Updated home-school communications.

Pupils and parents: Predominantly local families, however some travel from all over Kent and south London. Parents mainly hard-working types from the professional classes, small social and ethnic mix. Dedicated parents organise the active PTA, running fund-raising events and the school bookshop. Parents' forum discusses school issues and aims foster good working relationship between staff and parents.

Old girls include Margaret Hodge, Susanna White, Prof Joan Walsh; Richmal Compton was once a member of the teaching staff.

Entrance: 11+ competitive entrance exams involving creative writing, non-verbal and verbal reasoning, an interview and reference from junior school. Sixth form entrance requirement is a minimum of six GCSEs A*-B grade.

Exit: Some 30 per cent leave at 16+ to attend co-ed sixth forms or local grammars. Most sixth formers go on to higher education, mainly good universities; one to Oxbridge in 2013; others to a range to study eg medicine, maths, music, art, ancient history and architecture.

Money matters: Everyone sitting the 11+ entrance exam is automatically entered for academic scholarships – music and sports scholarships also available in year 7, for year 9 entry and year 12. Sixth form scholarships for art, music, sport and academics. Means-tested bursaries, Founders awards, are available up to 100 per cent of fees.

Remarks: A selective school, offering a wonderful range of opportunities to widen horizons and develop new interests. Suits academically able girls with lots of drive.

Bromsgrove School

Linked school: Bromsgrove Preparatory School

Worcester Road, Bromsgrove, B61 7DU

- Pupils: 910, 535 boys/375 girls, 365 full boarders; 45 weekly boarders • Ages: 13–18 • Middle of the road Anglican • Fees: Day £14,175; Boarding £19,775–£29,985 pa • Independent

Tel: 01527 579679
Email: admissions@bromsgrove-school.co.uk
Website: www.bromsgrove-school.co.uk

Headmaster: Since 2004, Mr Chris Edwards MA (late forties). Educated at Merchant Taylors' School and Merton College, Oxford (first class honours in English). Married to Karen, no children. Formerly head of English at St Paul's School in Sao Paulo, Brazil, then deputy head and acting head of Stowe. Intelligent, straight talking and charismatic without being smug. An exceptional head and deeply committed to the school – 'It's a joy to be here,' he told us.

He has increased pupil numbers by 300 – 'I've promised the governors I'm going to stop now.' Sees Bromsgrove as a place to add value across the board, not just in academe or sports.

Growth in the school has enabled a huge building programme – 18 new science labs, a glorious sports hall, beautiful boarding houses. Bromsgrove International College in Thailand was opened in 2005.

Parents describe head as visionary, hugely talented and endlessly energetic, as well as funny and kind, while staff say he is very supportive. A great lover of music, literature and travel and, our spies tell us, a gifted pianist.

Off in July 2014 to head the United World College of South East Asia.

Academic matters: Small classes, outstanding teachers and high expectations produce some very impressive results. Prides itself on value added – not least because it competes for pupils with the King Edward VI foundation schools in Birmingham. Not highly selective on intake but makes a very good showing at GCSE – 56 per cent A* and A grades in 2013.

Facilities for all subjects are very good, in many subjects outstanding. An impressive library, careers and IT complex with lots of well-lit desks and plenty of natural light and space. Range of modern foreign languages available, including Italian and Russian. Latin and classics on offer. All pupils take IGCSEs in English, maths and sciences. Most take 11 subjects at GCSE.

Of the 900+ pupils, over 400 are in the sixth form. Offers both A levels and the IB. A level results are excellent across the board with 89 per cent A*-B grades and 61 per cent A*/A in 2013, and particularly strong results in economics, maths, languages, design and PE. A wide range of subjects available, including politics, drama and design technology. The IB is a recent introduction (the first cohort completed it in 2011) and the head and staff are passionate about it. At present about 20 per cent of the sixth form take the IB. Initial results were somewhat disappointing, but the second batch and third averaged 35 points, with a half of candidates achieving a bilingual diploma in 2013. Whether parents will catch the enthusiasm of the staff remains to be seen.

While not by any means a hothouse, pupils need to be up to the mark and ready to push themselves to make the most of what it offers. Possibly not a school for the very timid, children battling with dyslexia or those with other less 'mainstream' learning profiles.

Games, options, the arts: Outstanding standard and range of sports. For a start it has fantastic facilities – 25m swimming pool, two Astroturfs, dance studios, gym, new sports arena and lots of playing fields, netball and tennis courts. It also has excellent coaching – recent coaches have included Paul Mullan, the England under-18 rugby coach, and James Fair, the international hockey player. Three Bromsgrovians in current England rugby squad. Cricket has had its share of caps; also a large number of students who play representative sport in hockey (Bromsgrovians represented Great Britain and Germany at the 2012 Olympics), netball, swimming, fencing and show jumping. Plays to win. That said, you don't have to be a sporting demigod to represent the school – A to D teams for most sports and development squads, so enthusiasm and application all it takes to get stuck in.

A wide range of activities on offer from jewellery making to RADA classes, film club and debating. The CCF is strong – a proud history of achievement in the Services (five VCs are commemorated in the school chapel). D of E Award is very popular and other forms of community service are strongly encouraged.

Unique Saturday morning programme – optional for most pupils (compulsory for staff). Offers a vast array of intellectual, cultural and physical activities, from Oxbridge extension lessons to ethics, first aid and table tennis. According to pupils, 'Everyone comes in,' and staff reckon take up of even fairly esoteric activities is very high.

After some time in the shadows, music is now coming on in leaps and bounds – more than 30 a year now take it at GCSE. Lots of opportunities to play in orchestras, informal concerts, chamber and chapel choirs, pop, and jazz ensemble etc. The school choir has recently performed in St Paul's Cathedral and St John the Divine in New York. A new music block is next in the head's sights.

Gorgeous DT/art block with excellent woodwork and metalwork facilities, beautiful light studios. Great textile work and paintings on display.

Background and atmosphere: Founded as a charity school in the 15th century, re-founded in the reign of Edward VI and substantially reinvigorated in the 17th century (some lovely original buildings still extant). The 100-acre campus is situated in the centre of Bromsgrove but has no feel of a town centre school – very spacious, landscaped and looked after with great care. Despite the enormous building activity (including the rebuild of the off-campus sixth form boarding house) and the very significant increase in pupil numbers in recent years, does not feel overcrowded. The house system seems to prevent pupils from feeling swamped.

The school tradition is middle-of-the-road Anglican – twice weekly chapel is compulsory but with the emphasis on ethos not denomination. All faiths and none are welcomed.

Very happy buzz, well ordered, with polite and focused pupils. Puts great emphasis on pupils being themselves and not trying to fit into a particular Bromsgrove 'shape'. Whether the passion is for sport, aviation, engineering or music, pupils are encouraged to be their best and given the resources they need to try out their ideas. 'We do what we think is right for the pupils regardless,' say staff.

No bells between lessons and although the atmosphere is relaxed, uniforms and bedrooms have to be kept neat and tidy – spot checks carried out. Staff wear gowns to chapel and detentions are held in a panelled 17th century hall, where wrongdoers have to explain themselves to staff in front of the head boy and girl, so in some respects quite a traditional feel. Day and boarding pupils pretty equally split – good balance between the two. Day pupils participate enthusiastically in weekend activities.

Pastoral care and discipline: All pupils are divided into houses – houseparents and their tutor teams (roughly one tutor to 10 pupils) provide daily input, support and oversight. 'We can tell from the way they walk in whether they're looking forward to the day or not,' say staff. Houses are furnished and designed with great attention to detail, have a home from home feel and very good boarding facilities.

School has team of trained student listeners and pupil-led anti bullying policy. Pupils say bullying not an issue, all staff are approachable and that any issue would be 'picked up straight away'. Parents praise the school for its 'positive input and affirmation of the children', excellent communications and ethos. 'It's about creativity, not ego,' one told us. 'The school delivers good citizens. No one gets pushed into a mould.'

No second chances for pupils who break the rules on sex or drugs – very few do. 'We have an ethos of responsibility and good behaviour,' say staff. 'The pupils are very good at self policing.'

Pupils and parents: Pupils are a delight – happy, enthusiastic, unpretentious and genuinely keen to take on responsibilities and contribute to the school and the wider community. Optional Saturday classes are full, huge enthusiasm for the vast array of extracurricular activities. A large local catchment from Worcestershire, Shropshire, Warwickshire and Birmingham, and boarders from all over – Italy, Germany, Russia and China. Most UK parents are professionals, middle class and Midlands-based. A significant number of Forces families. Staff say parents

are very collaborative and supportive. Not many landed gentry – and this is not a school where a title would cut much ice.

Entrance: For the senior school entry is via the school's own test or CE. The largest cohort come from Bromsgrove's own large prep (700 strong), whose pupils are assessed informally and most of whom progress to the senior school. Others come from local schools. Entry to the sixth form is massively oversubscribed – GCSEs at B or above essential.

Exit: Few leave after GCSEs. Virtually all sixth formers to university, with three-quarters gaining places at top universities – Durham, UCL and Exeter particularly popular in 2013.

Money matters: Scholarships, though available, are nominal and carry kudos, not cash. However bursaries, strictly means-tested and worth up to 100 per cent of fees, are available to the right candidates. Serious about enabling access for those who would benefit from what it has to offer.

Remarks: A remarkably impressive and exciting school, driven with imagination and dynamism by an exceptional head. Produces engaged, friendly, unstuffy and highly successful pupils who thrive within an excellent academic and pastoral environment, with national standard sports. 'We are free to do what we think best because we're under the radar,' says the school. We don't think they will stay under the radar for long.

Bruton School for Girls

Linked school: Sunny Hill Preparatory School

Sunny Hill, Bruton, Somerset, BA10 0NT

• Pupils: 250; 80 boarders • Ages: Girls 2–18; day places for boys 2–7 • Non-denom with Christian ethos • Fees: Day £4,875–£13,620; Boarding £16,065–£22,890 pa • Independent

Tel: 01749 814400
Email: admissions@brutonschool.co.uk
Website: www.brutonschool.co.uk

Headmistress: Since September 2012, Mrs Nicola Botterill BSc MA NPQH (mid forties). Degree in geography from Middlesex Polytechnic, master's in geography in education, Fellow of the Royal Geographical Society and RSA. Taught at Wallington Grammar School for Girls, Ashcroft High School (head of geography), head of geography and house, director of marketing and studies, then second deputy head at Putney High School, deputy head at St Mary's Calne.

Has always had an interest in ICT and the use of technology in the classroom, outdoor education and value of fieldwork. Avid traveller, lecture, theatre and cinema-goer, with interests in archaeology, geology, arts and crafts, photography, art galleries, DIY and gardening.

Plans to 'bring in the outside world', develop sixth form and nursery, provide day girls with dedicated spaces to study and beds in the boarding houses. 'Global awareness is essential for the girls in this fast-changing world and technological understanding is key for future success. I believe in the importance of critical and creative thinking.'

Academic matters: Has continued to achieve best public examination results in Somerset even in post assisted places era. In 2013, 37 per cent A*/A at A level; courses run subject to demand. Sensible balance struck between new and traditional subjects – eg classics plus French, German and Spanish all available, as well as psychology, drama and theatre studies.

Recent dip in sixth form entry, but numbers creeping up. Maths and sciences particularly strong but good results across board testify to positive work ethic.

We were struck by the variety of schemes, awards and initiatives: not many small schools have three language assistants or a postgraduate researcher in the science department. Top results reached by international pupils in unglamorous but vital IELTS exams. In 2013 57 per cent A*/A grades at GCSE- strength in core subjects. Average class 15 girls in years 7-9; 13 in years 10-11 and eight in the sixth, though many groups smaller (eg three girls taking A2 economics). Modern languages popular – visits start with 40 year 8 girls spending a week boarding at Maison Claire Fontaine in Burgundy; GCSE Spanish students visit Seville, plus individual exchanges in France, Spain and Germany. Taster sessions in Mandarin.

Three-quarters of staff female with 15 teachers on staff over 10 years. Girls rate help given with university applications and careers, with OGs involved in talks and local firms such as Westland giving 'real' experience to sixth form physicists. Home bred courses for gifted and talented. Top award for year 10 student in recent national mathematics contest. Our teachers 'go extra mile,' say senior girls.

New SENCo from state sector: support to wider range of girls, especially in spelling and number work, follows them seamlessly from prep to senior school. Improved sense of inclusivity means school 'would consider' mild Asperger's, says SENCo, but site unsuitable for visually or physically challenged.

Games, options, the arts: Parents like 'the broader perspective' offered. Strong PE and games with plenty of fixtures at all ability levels. We watched as year 7 ergo rowers practised in fitness suite, aiming at repeat gold medal performance in national indoor championships. Lots of staff coaching teams after school. High quality floodlit Astroturf and tennis courts; dance studio and large gym provide for most sporting needs. Outside grass area reserved mainly for athletics in summer. Hilly surroundings make for a testing cross-country course. Tag rugby now proving very popular thanks to expert staff coach. County players in netball, hockey, tennis, pole vault and cross-country. Fifty girls took part in last ski trip to French Alps. Recent hockey tour to Singapore and Malaysia scored a hit.

No shortage of choice when it comes to activities: self-defence, beauty therapy and the much vaunted Leith's cookery course, to name but a few. Public speaking includes even international pupils: English Speaking Board advanced certificate and LAMDA awards.

Music school, built 30 years ago, has proved more than 'fit for purpose': large rehearsal space for choir and/or orchestra plus effective soundproofing between practice rooms. Fourteen peripatetics – instrumental and singing. Healthy sized choir (which we saw practising after school) is one of 17 music groups that meet weekly, plus frequent tours to Europe and around southwest cathedrals. Year 10 student recently had rôle in fully staged Pergolesi opera, La Serva Padrona. Year 11 girl danced lead in English Youth Ballet performance at Yeovil's Octagon Theatre. Successful art department in airy studios – visual evidence of homegrown talent around school, but no gallery, alas! Annual arts week includes book character day and poetry slam competitions. The Gleam (echo of Tennyson and also school song), school's lively magazine, largely product of girls' input (hooray!).

Lots of year 10 girls go for D of E bronze award and some tackle silver and gold in sixth form. Keen group of riders uses local stables but no on-site equestrian facility yet; now hosts hunter trials; good results obtained in: inter-school show jumping including success at national level and one girl selected to represent GB at three-day event in Ireland.

Background and atmosphere: Founded in 1900 by Henry Hobhouse and William Knight, head of Sexey's School in Bruton.

Sunny Hill might not always live up to its name weatherwise but a warm enough atmosphere. Enjoys great location on edge of small town. Incoherent collection of buildings but it doesn't seem to matter. Science block works well within and new studio theatre even looks good from outside too. Mellow 'old house' building lends an almost collegiate feel from main road. Much is being done to improve look of the place including landscaping an amphitheatre in the heart of school. Carpeted corridors help soften noise; chairs in assembly hall suggest surplus stock from an Indian restaurant but serve a purpose. Small-scale rather than grandiose with refreshing lack of pretension.

Regular assemblies, links with local church, annual Cranmer awards, Christian union and confirmation suggest healthy spiritual ethos for those who seek it, but otherwise not overtly religious. Long days with many present after lessons for activities but no Saturday lessons. Lots of Saturday sport and varied programme for boarders (many of whom choose to stay back).

Pastoral care and discipline: Well ordered school with staff quick to troubleshoot if necessary. Parents' view is that 'school is very strict in policies' but only needs to weigh in very occasionally. Seniors good rôle models for juniors: organise impressive range of competitive, social and fundraising events. Triumvirate of senior girls (who run 'open door' policy and a peer mentoring scheme) seen as a stepping stone for juniors and help to nip potential problems in the bud. We liked the first term tutorial setup for year 7 when they are 'babied a bit' by senior staff. Everyone seems happy with food arrangements – attractive dining area, sensible range of healthy options.

Deputy head oversees boarding and pastoral arrangements. Realistic attitude to boys, who can visit 'on ground floor only' of senior boarding house. Mumsy housemistresses with assistants to mop fevered brows where necessary. Separate house tutor groups for years 7-9, 10 and 11, then sixth form. Girls divided into 'halls' for competitions. International girls scoop double bedrooms on grounds of accumulated clobber.

Pupils and parents: 'Girls come out confident and speaking up for themselves,' said one ex-parent. We met a group of unusually articulate year 10 girls who were all positive, whilst their seniors were well informed, poised and able to 'think on their feet'. Commendable initiative shown by ex-Cheltenham Ladies' teacher in charge of eight girls who spent summer in Tanzania building houses for Habitat for Humanity charity and more recently, a summer trip for sixth form girls to India to work in an orphanage (funds were raised partly through quiz nights in local pubs). Girls come up with some original ideas for raising money for other charities (eg Children in Need and Goodwill Villages in India) and eco projects – Bruton has been awarded the Eco Schools' Green Flag twice for environmental initiatives in school. Overseas pupils requiring EFL teaching capped at 10 per cent.

Old Girls include Ethel Knight (UK's first female vet) and Clarissa Farr (current head of St Paul's Girls in London).

Entrance: Own entrance papers in verbal and non-verbal reasoning for 11+ and 13+ entry (about 10 girls enter year 9). Minimum of five Bs at GCSE to get into sixth. Over 90 per cent transfer from prep to senior school at 11+. Growing entry at 13+ welcomed by head. Tradition of some entrants from state primaries. Overseas applicants tested in English and in subjects they want to study in the sixth form.

Exit: Fewer tempted away at 16+ as tales of regret filter back. Sixth form leavers to eg biology at Bath, journalism at Cardiff, fashion PR at London College of Fashion.

Money matters: Fee levels what you'd expect without too many extras. Discounts for siblings and Services. Keen to fund more bursaries.

Remarks: Success without frills – not trying to prove anything and more inclusive than one might expect, given its academic reputation. Has everything you'd look for and more besides. 'Good value for money,' report satisfied parents.

Bryanston School

Bryanston, Blandford Forum, DT11 0PX

- Pupils: 675, 385 boys/ 290 girls, 585 full boarders • Ages: 13–18
- C of E • Fees: Boarding £32,214; Day £26,415 pa • Independent

Tel: 01258 452411
Email: admissions@bryanston.co.uk
Website: www.bryanston.co.uk

Head: Since 2005, Ms Sarah Thomas (early fifties). A GDST girl hailing from Birkenhead and proud of it, Ms Thomas read Lit Hum (classics – the proper kind with Greek) at Oxford, before becoming an articled clerk to a notary public. Both her parents taught, but their entreaties not to follow in their footsteps clearly fell on deaf ears, for she left the law to do her PGCE at King's College London, before longish stints at Sevenoaks and Uppingham. All that formative experience of co-ed boarding has equipped her admirably for Bryanston. 'A female head is just a part of who we are, and the best part of my job is recruiting outstanding staff', she says. We found her a (charming) force to be reckoned with, whom we can imagine causing stuffier members of HMC to choke on their sherry. 'Splendid', say parents, '100 per cent approachable, with fine powers of judgment'. Ms Thomas makes a point of keeping her hand in at the chalk-face – everybody has to do Latin in the first year, and a fair few take it on to GCSE; a brainy minority do Greek as well.

Ms Thomas' husband teaches at nearby Hanford and writes children's books and plays; they have two daughters at university. In her precious time off? 'reading – for its peaceful aspects and the opportunity to lose myself in other worlds', she says, plus walking her dog and cooking.

Academic matters: Not desperately selective, with an expectation of 50 per cent for each subject at CE – but what marks this school out is the way academic life is structured. The timetable contains assignment periods for each subject alongside lessons, where prep, further study or one-to-one sessions with the subject teacher take place – the latter ominously named 'correction periods'. In the first three years, assignment periods are supervised by the subject teacher, providing access and extra help outside lessons. Academic progress is tracked more tightly here than in any school this editor had seen: weekly assessments are provided by each subject teacher and entered on the e-chart, the online mark-sheet to which parents also have access. All assignments (prep) are set to be handed in a week later, so being organised and learning to manage a workload is a skill learnt early. 'The tutorial system ensures success,' says the school: each student is allocated a tutor for the duration of his/her time at the school – so far, so conventional – but these individuals do so very much more than that somewhat over-used term suggests. 'We tutors deal with the academic, spiritual, moral and act as a kind of PA', said one. Parents greatly value this and tutors' accessibility both to students and parents. SEN provision supports what goes on in class: each department appoints a staff member to liaise with learning support. One-to-one tuition is available; all help offered is discreet and without stigma. School claims to 'deliver for every child we admit.'

So does it pay off? At GCSE in 2013, 57 per cent A*/A grades, which puts school on a par with local independents such as the Sherborne schools, where entry requirements are higher. 'My daughter got results beyond our wildest dreams', raved one mother, who also reckoned that Bryanston had been perfect for all three of her children, with differing abilities and interests. Visual arts of all kind very popular and successful, as is Latin and Greek; results suggest as much enthusiasm as aptitude for Latin, but it is heart-warming to see such a resurgence in classical languages. School keeps a Greek theatre tucked away in its extensive grounds, and the JACT summer school in Greek – of formidable repute – for all-comers is held here. At A level, 81 per cent graded A*/B and 54 per cent A*/A in 2013, but value-added shows up strongly against comparable schools. Business studies and English are the most popular choices, sciences hot on their heels, followed by art and design in its various forms. History and geography have a moderate following; modern languages surprisingly little, along with music and drama. First IB results in 2014.

Games, options, the arts: The scope is amazing – clearly something for the most idle couch potato. All the sports and facilities one would expect in a school of this type feature (rugby, hockey, netball, cricket, tennis, rowing) and both hockey and lacrosse are on offer in consecutive terms. Luscious grounds stretch down to the river Stour, where rowing of increasing seriousness takes place out of a beautiful new boathouse designed by an OB and keen oarsman (sadly we weren't shown this). New arrivals learn navigation skills and how to survive a night in the open – useful for those times when they get lost in the grounds. A carousel of adventurous options takes place in the second year, comprising (amongst other things) falconry, canoeing and rock-climbing. Riding might seem quite mundane; we were bemused not even to be shown the stabling, indoor and all-weather schools, or cross-country course on our visit. Keen riders can bring their own steeds. Sailing in the school's own fleet of Lasers in Poole harbour. School is notable local and national player in a variety of sports. OBs include Phil de Glanville.

The art at Bryanston hits you between the eyes as you walk in. Enormous canvasses adorn the long walls of each of the central corridors in the main building: the scope of the department and amount of available hanging space, plus the skills and dedication of teachers and students, mean the most ambitious projects can be executed. The art department is divided into 2D and 3D; both aspects enjoy a passionate following and are fabulously resourced. Best work of both past and present pupils has twice been showcased in Cork St (no less). School's reputation for a creative curriculum is well deserved, and fulfils the aspiration for 'the joy of the abundant life' which an early headmaster articulated.

Music and drama (both excellent and ambitious in scope) tend to be avidly pursued for the love of them, rather than chasing yet another GCSE. The 600 seat Coade Hall measures up as well as any school theatre facility, indeed visiting theatre companies stage performances here. Usual musicals (Cabaret, Guys and Dolls in recent years) sometimes include a showing for prep schools – canny marketing! Annual play for each year group (eg The Crucible, Pride and Prejudice in a specially adapted version). Much student-led drama, and our guides enthused about house drama, where even the most reluctant performers tread the boards. Music is top notch, and will be further enhanced when its new facility opens in 2014. The 300 seat concert hall, and stage large enough to accommodate a symphony orchestra, umpteen practice rooms, recital rooms, recording studios and enough sound-proofing to keep the rock bands away from the string quartets will probably rival anything in SW England. Let's hope they are generous with it. Again, any musical whim can probably be accommodated – if not here, then where? Over a fifth of students sing in a group or choir: we heard the first rehearsal of one of mixed age and mixed ability during the lunch hour, and tuneful and enthusiastic it was too. Musicians perform all over the place, including London and abroad – the dance band to Paris, the chamber choir and orchestra to Florence. All students have to learn a musical instrument in the first year, which may be where the enthusiasm and lung capacity to play the bagpipes starts – there is even a pipe band. 'What the musicians did in the hols' was an interesting little aside in the school's extensive literature; one boy's attendance at a course at Berklee College in Boston helped him gain a place on its coveted degree programme.

Extracurricular activities are taken seriously here in pursuit of the abundant life – there is everything from Accessorise (jewellery) to yoga, and a choice of four out of more than 100 is compulsory in the first two years.

Background and atmosphere: Exceedingly long drive through woods leads eventually to a baby château perched on a rise overlooking the river Stour. Modelled on Menars in the Loire valley by Norman Shaw, the house had to be sold to meet the death duties of Viscount Portman after the family had lived there for just 30 years. In 1928 a young Australian school master bought it and founded the school on traditional and modern principles – et nova et vetera, as the motto says. Going co-ed in the early 70s was well ahead of the trend, and Bryanston has kept its reputation for blazing a trail – 'Just don't call us progressive,' said the head, with a visible shudder.

Acres (400) of grounds and beautiful bold modern additions surround the house, which aside from the diggers and heavy plant constructing the new music school, make a harmonious whole. Inside, two long parquet-floored corridors dotted with sofas in the main house give the continuing impression of being fortunate residents of a mansion, though everyone looks more purposeful. Even the staff and visitors' loos were contained in a spacious cloakroom with leather armchairs in which to retreat from the fray... Teaching spaces are high spec, particularly the science labs, with their wet and dry areas in the newish Sanger building, named after a double laureate biochemist and OB.

Three boarding houses are contained within the main building, the rest scattered over the grounds immediately around the main building. Accommodation is comfortable rather than de luxe. Everybody eats centrally in the delightfully refurbished dining hall, and the food is all it's cracked up to be: we sampled the excellent salad bar but the hot choices and puddings all smelt and looked scrummy too. Rather cool café in lieu of tuck shop sells smoothies, cookies, pizza and other appealing fare; houses also have kitchens for making snacks and drinks. When we asked about the long walk into Blandford, students looked slightly blank – why would they need to do that when everything is at school?

Pastoral care and discipline: Exceptionally good care is taken of all students. Newbies meet their tutors on arrival at school, and the team formed between him/her and the housemaster or mistress (known as a hsm, to rhyme with bosom) is a tight one. It seems as though it would be hard for any unhappiness or falling off in performance or morale to go unnoticed. Each house has a distinct character and students are placed in them according to a process 'akin to Hogwarts' sorting hat', according to the head. Boys spend a year in one of two junior houses; girls go straight into the house in which they will spend their whole time at the school.

We liked the understated but definite sense of a spiritual life at Bryanston, led by the chaplain. As well as the church in the grounds, there is a dear little chapel in the vaults of the main house which acts as a calm retreat from the hurly burly of life going on outside its open doors. One parent told us her son had 'quietly gone off and got himself confirmed', slightly to her surprise (but pleasure).

The persistent reputation for unchecked behaviour and general licence, drugs in particular, has been slow to die, but one parent briskly dismissed it as 'quite unmerited'. According to the school and the parents we spoke to, any involvement would result in immediate expulsion – and the kids know it. A civilised and age-appropriate view is taken of alcohol for sixth formers 'carefully monitored under adult supervision,' says school. Any misdemeanours are 'harshly dealt with,' a mother confirmed. The school rules and regs fit on one side of paper and are unequivocal and up to date, eg 'Computers/I-pods/MP3s must not be used to watch films, play games, listen to music in lessons, prep and after lights out'. For a school with a dress code rather than uniform below sixth form, we found the students tidier than at many other schools: the drill is a coloured polo shirt with a sweater with black or navy trousers or skirts; more leeway for sixth form.

Pupils and parents: When asked if she could sum up a Bryanston pupil, the head said no she couldn't, though one hallmark would be 'someone comfortable in their own skin', who would enjoy being a part of things. We were actually allowed to meet very few, just the head boy and girl who showed us around, who were of course charming and very much on-message. As for the parents, quite a range professionally from doctors to financiers to creative types, but they struck us as exceptionally thoughtful about their children's education. The geographical spread, in common with many schools, has contracted so that Bryanston is really a south west school, though with a significant minority coming from London and the south east, and a handful from the furthest reaches of the UK. A few from overseas.

Notable OBs include Lucian Freud, all the Conran boys, Mark Elder, John Eliot Gardiner (who sent his daughter too), Ben Fogle and Emilia Fox.

Entrance: There are130 places at 13+ via CE (50 per cent expected in all papers) or by Bryanston's own papers from an amazing number of prep schools. Close links forged with preps and prospective parents; instead of open days with a cast of thousands, the school arranges group visits for 12 or so families, as well as individual visits. Registered pupils are also invited to various events in the two years before they arrive. Between 25-30 new students arrive at sixth form for which 50 points at GCSE are required, after a day of tests (maths, English and abilities) and interviews at the school. Existing pupils also have to meet the points requirement, waived only in very exceptional cases.

Exit: Around 10 per cent leave after GCSEs. Nearly half of upper sixth leavers apply to university once they have their results. The head of sixth form is all for this, and has tweaked the school's UCAS process to accommodate it. University strategy starts with tutors early in lower sixth and the vast majority of students do go on, whenever they apply. 'Less formal relationships between staff and students mean they are confident enough to bounce up to them and ask for what they need,' he says of the application process. About half take gap years.

Degree courses, interestingly, tend to be conventional choices (business in various forms, history and English – but classics too – hurrah!) in conventional places: Bristol, Leeds, Oxford Brookes and UWE. A sprinkling of medics, linguist and politicians too, plus around 10 per cent to art foundation courses. In 2013, two Oxbridge offers, four medics and two vets.

A few gripes about careers and higher education guidance at AS level from parents; whilst they like the rather unpressured approach to UCAS, they feel alternatives should be more clearly spelt out. Newish head of sixth form appointment is grounds for optimism, however.

Money matters: Fees in line with comparable schools but some items appear on the bill as extras, unusually, such as stationery, art and DT materials. Scholarships across a range of disciplines including DT and ICT to a maximum of 25 per cent of fees. Bursaries on application.

Remarks: Stunning school with unrivalled facilities and a great deal of latitude and encouragement for students to explore any aspect of academic, sporting and artistic life which takes their fancy. Too much too young? Possibly. A great deal more traditional than its reputation would suggest, but myths can take a long time to break down. We could not find any detractors, try as we might!

Brymore School

Cannington, Bridgwater, TA5 2NB

- Pupils: 140, 115 boarders, all boys • Ages: 13–17 • Inter-denom
- Fees: Boarding £8,790 pa Day-free • State

Tel: 01278 652369
Email: office@brymore.somerset.sch.uk
Website: www.brymoreschool.co.uk

Head: Since 2011, Mr Mark Thomas, previously acting head. Mr Thomas was confirmed as head after holding the reins after a turbulent period which saw the suspension and then departure of his predecessor.

Academic matters: Brymore's three Rs are 'resilience, responsibility and resourcefulness'. Doesn't mean that traditional three Rs are neglected – quite the opposite. We spoke to parents of able boys who have not suffered academically by moving to Brymore: 'He studies better because of the practical work,' commented one happy dad. Slower learners do particularly well here. 2013 saw 88 per cent achieving 5+ A*-C grades (27 per cent including maths and English).

Lower ability boys 'clamour for extra help,' say staff: many boys see Brymore as a 'second chance'. Engineering, agricultural and horticultural subjects occupy one-third of timetable and lead to an NVQ qualification alongside GCSEs. We were mesmerised watching self-confident year 10 boys pouring molten metal into moulds and then knocking out their castings – awesome! Drawing office and computer lab (mainly for CAD work) enhance DT facilities. Year 12 students opt for either a BTEC first award in an agricultural subject or level two NVQ in engineering. Art, dual science and geography sit alongside core GCSE subjects. RE and PE provide half a GCSE each. No MFL after year 9.

Outstanding special needs provision lies at heart of school's recent academic improvement. 'Financial support needs to be maintained,' pleads SENCo. Staff are given specific guidance by SENCo for each of the lower ability groups (where staff: pupil ratio is 1:7). Fast-track phonic revision for these boys in year 9 using a multi-sensory approach. SENCo always on look-out for suitable non-fiction to interest boys. Dedicated specialist staff (three f/t and five p/t teaching assistants – each of whom specialises in a subject area – plus three LSAs to 'plug the gaps'). 'It's all about relationships at Brymore,' explains the exuberant SENCo, who has to take on some entrants with reading ages as low as 7 on entry. SEN expertise ranges from SpLD to ADHD and Asperger's. About 30 boys are on SEN register plus loads more with difficulties of various kinds.

Learning support in every prep session and reading offered before school and at lunch-times. Learning mentor helps to 'retrack' individuals and also works with small groups. Staff encouraged to use target-setting and self-assessment. Boys are generally 'up for it,' says SENCo, who promotes literacy as 'relevant to life'. 'Message gradually sinks in,' she says with a smile.

Six-day timetable of 54 lessons: each of 35 minutes; doubles and triples for practical subjects. No options beyond year 9, so parents must be sure that what is on offer is going to suit. School puts maximum 24 boys in top (B) set of each year, 20 in middle (R) and 16 in lower (Y) one. An 'average ability' boy leaves with five or six GCSEs and an NVQ qualification. Post-16 provision poised for possible expansion.

Games, options, the arts: Sport is important at Brymore with emphasis (in keeping with school's ethos) upon team rather than individual effort. Most boys play rugby ('We give Millfield B teams a good run for their money,' says head and fixture list looks impressive). Hockey attracts about 20 boys, and cross-country is particularly strong with boys doing school's three-and-a-half mile ('Chads') course at least once a week. Failure to do this or missing fitness sessions results in team deselection. Super athletics: Brymore has been Somerset champions for 19 consecutive years and dominates under-17 age group. Hefty representation at county level; hammer, pole-vaulting, cross-country, road running and walking make nationals – two boys currently representing England. Multi-purpose hall used for volleyball, table tennis etc. Enthusiastic golf, fishing and mountain biking. Caving and karate current favourites.

One mum runs chess activity; staff take boys deer and badger watching on nearby Quantocks; also popular for hill walking and D of E (bronze and silver) expeditions. Annual ski trip still draws great support. Young farmers' club. Business incentive scheme linked with Barnardo's offers year 12 chance to gain experience whilst raising money for charity. Little music or drama outside the curriculum, though some boys have peripatetic drum or guitar lessons.

Background and atmosphere: The Brymore School of Rural Technology was established in 1952 for sons of Somerset farmers on an impressive 60-acre site on the edge of Cannington, between the Quantocks and Bristol Channel. A half-mile tree lined drive affords first sight of extensive farm buildings and impressive new accommodation. Head has been given mandate to 'change the culture but retain the ethos'. Two newish (50-place) boarding houses and recent refurbishment of existing Dickensian provision in main house. Mini dormitories for four boys apiece plus common rooms and staff quarters. Should sell boarding concept more easily to nervous parents.

Main building the 17th century mansion originally owned by a notorious Civil War figure, John Pym, Oliver Cromwell's right hand man. The original stable yard complete with clock tower has been converted to sizeable metal and wood workshops, plus two blacksmiths' forges and foundry to industrial standard. No wonder the ghost of John Pym still roams this part of the school (sound of restless horse hooves on cobbles at night)! Motto: 'diligentia et labore'. Together with a spur motif it forms school crest, visible on blazers (worn for formal occasions and for assembly every morning).

Boys bid for plots to grow vegetables in impeccably-kept one-acre walled garden dating from 1753. Pupils are responsible for upkeep of entire estate: tree-pruning, grass-cutting, weeding, planting flower beds all lead to an NVQ. A self-financing farm is at the heart of this unique set-up – lambing a flock of 50 ewes, rearing free-range chickens, beef cattle and pigs ('more of which should end up on boys' plates,' complained one mum) and milking cows at 6am on a crisp winter morning are essential parts of the learning. 'Backing a tractor through a gateway and getting 10 out of 10 in a spelling test are of equal value here.' Prince Charles visited in school's golden jubilee year – no doubt a 'home from home' for HRH.

Pastoral care and discipline: No written rules. Staff talk 'with' rather than 'at' boys; no raised voices when we visited. Loads of patience which boys appreciate. Common sense and co-operation paramount – we watched a new boy being offered spontaneous, genuine help in a DT lesson from an older hand. Great! Teenage boys without that sullen, 'back off' expression and no backchat. Lots of friendly conversations overheard in and out of classrooms. Yes, really! Sloppiness not appreciated here – especially by boys appointed (after interview) as heads of department on the farm. 'Boys thrive on the level of responsibility they're offered at Brymore – you don't get it elsewhere,' emphasised one father.

Tidy appearance underpinned by common-sense dress code – once assembly is over boys don black sweatshirt or working rig. Hooray! Inter-denominational; assemblies usually include a hymn, but we watched a clever video presentation by head on the power of advertising which got boys laughing first thing. Older staff than in most schools, but younger blood may fill current vacancies. In addition to kindly matrons (who provide 24 hour health cover) boys have access to two counsellors who visit regularly. Tasty grub and plenty of it, with only one caveat mentioned above. Two deputies and head all residential. Some teachers described as 'quirky' by parents; boys rate them highly. Staff give loads of time outside the classroom.

Pupils and parents: Head takes boys who haven't thrived in mainstream. Not everyone a wurzel – some from London; one or two overseas and around 50 per cent from Somerset. We met boys from the Isle of Rhum and Northumberland, which suggests that 'word has got around'. Mixed bunch socially but mostly boys used to 'doing what they're told'. Head marched 12 of them down to barber's at beginning of term – 'Uniform includes head and feet as far as I'm concerned,' he asserts. Assembly has retro look – shirts tucked in and ties properly knotted. Boys learn independence – 'After a few weeks at Brymore my son told me to stop fussing over him at home,' said one mum, whose enthusiasm for the school has resulted in friends sending their sons to Brymore too. 'If your son is a day boy, you have to be prepared to pick him up at odd times,' said another mum, whose sons like to stay late for activities.

School takes exhibition trailer to county shows but mostly admits through word of mouth. Boys here don't have to be farmers in the making, but a love of the open air and practical work are essential. What kept impressing us was the level of concentration and co-operation on practical tasks around the whole school. Former pupil teaches blacksmithing: great role model for boys who can see how the practical Brymore education can be basis for a successful business in later life.

Other OBs include MEP Neil Parish, Mark Irish – England U21 rugby player, Julian Anderson – world windsurfing champion.

Entrance: Approximately 60 boys admitted at 13 plus the odd one at any stage: when we visited, two boys had joined year 10 after spring half-term. Day boys (head now refers to them as 'out boarders') will need to board when on farm duties. All boys quizzed on their 'suitability for boarding' – the school's only selection criterion. Current one year post-GCSE course open to applicants from outside. All must accept six day week.

Exit: Over 70 per cent to further education colleges such as Lackham, Sparsholt, Kingston Manward, Duchy College, Cornwall or closer to home – Canninton College and Bridgwater. 'Brymore boys often get fast tracked at college,' said one farmer dad. Some boys progress to degree level. Some into apprenticeships, others to work-based learning or employment. Many former students now run their own businesses.

Money matters: Boarding fees being increased slightly (quantum improvement in boarding facilities seen as justification for this). Some pupils obtain educational grants from home LAs.

Remarks: Deserves wider recognition and should be heavily oversubscribed. A unique boarding school with a sense of purpose and a special atmosphere. By no means a boot camp

– boys treated with respect. When pupils leave, staff 'see no resemblance to the boy they were sent'. Look no further if your son isn't afraid to get stuck in and is currently feeling swamped by worksheets and undervalued in a 'rubbish' school.

Almighty fracas in September 2010 resulted in change at the top – though character of previous head widely appreciated in the school community and unbesmirched. Perhaps some understandable tension between what Brymore offers and the 'pupil protection at all costs' policy of the local authority? The governors have invested much trust in Mr Thomas and it is to be hoped that he delivers.

Burford School

Cheltenham Road, Burford, OX18 4PL

- Pupils: 1,180 boys and girls (85 board, the rest day) • Ages: 11–18
- Inter-denom • Fees: Boarding £9,000–£9,600 pa; Tuition free
- State

Tel: 01993 823303
Email: head.4040@burford.oxon.sch.uk
Website: www.burford.oxon.sch.uk

Headteacher: Since 2008, Mrs Kathy Haig BA MEd (forties). Educated at Burford School (her family lived at nearby Shipton-under-Wychwood), followed by Leeds University, where she studied food science and nutrition. Taught at schools in Hull, Keighley and Preston before moving to Ellesmere Port Catholic High School in Cheshire. Spent 12 years there, rising to become deputy head. 'I consider myself fortunate that very early on in my career I realised I wanted to teach,' she says. Still teaches GCSE health and social care to years 10 and 11 (four periods a week) – 'I like teaching,' she says. 'It's what a school is about.' Chatty, full of ideas and keen to stress the pride pupils take in their school. Married to management consultant and has two children, one of whom is a pupil at Burford.

Academic matters: Rural comprehensive with rare boarding element (one of only 30 or so state boarding schools in the UK). Offers wide range of subjects to wide ability intake. Setted on ability for maths, science and languages. Overall GCSE grades well above national average – 64 per cent got five plus A*-C grades including English and maths, 25 per cent A*/A grades, in 2013. At A level, 53 per cent A*-B grades and 23 per cent A*/A. Total of 23 subjects on offer at A level, including business studies, economics, PE and sports, psychology. Most youngsters take at least nine GCSEs. Homework plays integral part, with parents asked to sign children's student record books once a week up to GCSE.

Learning support unit, housed in own block, was judged outstanding in recent Ofsted report. Deals with wide range of special needs (dyslexia, dyspraxia, Asperger's, year 7s who arrive with lower than average reading ages) and helps pupils achieve.

Was a specialist science and technology college – good for cash. All year 7s do French, with German and Spanish on offer from year 8. Group of 11 to 14 year olds recently linked up with Oxford University students to learn Latin. Two computer suites and all do ICT. They're also ahead of the game when it comes to cookery lessons – teach food technology. One vocational course – applied business studies – for year 12s (business and communication studies, word processing etc). Average class sizes around 25 up to GCSE, 15 in sixth form.

Games, options, the arts: Lots of wonderful green space and very committed sports staff. All pupils get one PE lesson and one games lesson a week – hockey, football, rugby, netball, tennis, athletics, keep fit and dance. Gym in main school, separate sports hall (only building large enough to house the whole school), rugby and hockey pitches, tennis and netball courts etc. Loads of matches with local state and independent schools.

Light, airy art block with different areas for art, design and technology, textiles. Stunning work on show in foyer, from wall-mounted magazine racks to stylish jewellery and ceramics. One pupil even made a ferret house! Drama is popular. Around 20 took part in national Shakespeare Schools' Festival, performing a 21st century version of The Taming of the Shrew. Around 25 per cent of pupils learn a musical instrument – everything from classical to jazz and rock. New drama studio and learning centre.

Impressive library, with more than 23,500 resources and own website. Pupils encouraged to read for pleasure as well as work, with authors Jacqueline Wilson, Anthony Horowitz and Charlie Higson getting the thumbs-up. Book of the week on display at front desk. After-school homework club held in library three times a week.

Voluntary extracurricular clubs held every lunchtime – most keen to participate. 'We do everything from sailing and skiing to dance and computer clubs,' says head. Good takeup for D of E – around 75 year 9s doing bronze award. Lots of year 12s do Young Enterprise and year 10 engineering pupils regularly involved in Formula Schools, where they get the chance to design, build and race model cars at Silverstone. Many trips to foreign climes – rightfully proud of its 14-year tie with a school in Uganda, the longest-running reciprocal exchange link with a school in Eastern Africa.

Background and atmosphere: Founded by charter in 1571 and still celebrates Charter Day in November every year. Has been on present 36-acre site (also owns 40 acres of farmland) since 1949, when Burford Grammar School was enlarged to form Oxfordshire's first comprehensive school. Maintains many old grammar school traditions, including house system, prefects and uniform for all but sixth form. Head girl and boy voted for by staff and sixth formers. Main school situated on the busy A40 on edge of beautiful Cotswold town of Burford (just over an hour from London on a good traffic day). Original building has been vastly added to and site is a maze of interconnecting buildings, although a chirpy year 8 assured us, 'You soon get the hang of it'.

Around 80 boarders live in Lenthall House, a listed building in the town itself. Behind the honeystone walls, it's a bit of a Tardis, with modern facilities and warm, cosy rooms. Boarders come from all over – from Oxfordshire to Hong Kong. Boarding places highly sought after. 'I could fill the boarding house three times over,' admits head. 'It's a safe environment and a kind of halfway house between school and university.' Weekly and full boarding available.

All pupils (and staff) belong to one of four houses named after school founders – Falkland, Heylin, Warwick and Wysdom. Fiercely competitive, with contests ranging from creative writing and fashion to Monopoly and ultimate frisbee. House points given for homework, effort, presentation etc. Pupils attend assembly twice a week. School council with two representatives from each form. Sixth form housed in their own block, with common room and study area. Pupils reckon food is 'very nice', with daily choice of hot meals, pasta, salad, sandwiches and vegetarian options. Cashless system, where they use swipe card to pay for school dinners.

Excellent induction programme for new pupils. Year 13s get special training to act as peer mentors to year 7s. Teaching assistants on hand to guide the youngest to classes in early weeks. Year 7s also get a three-day residential trip to the Isle of Wight during their first week as part of their settling-in process. Year groups divided into eight forms, each with own tutor.

Smart uniform (black blazer with school crest, black trousers/skirts, house tie and white shirt) for younger years. No uniform for sixth form – but expected to dress 'appropriately', ie no flip flops, T-shirts with offensive logos, ripped trousers etc.

Pastoral care and discipline: Well-defined rules set out in excellent student record book – smart navy hardback given to each pupil at start of each year. Contains everything from equipment needed for school, spelling lists and tips on how to present classwork to home-school partnership agreement and what to do if the school bus is late. School's central tenet is that 'everyone will act with care and consideration to others at all times', and it seems to work. Head runs a tight, stable ship, with pupils comfortable and secure within a firm list of dos and don'ts – dos include using 'polite and courteous language', while don'ts include not distracting others. 'It's not an overly strict school, though,' a sixth former told us. 'We get treated like grown ups.' Those wanting to talk about problems can go to their tutor, head of year or any other member of staff – plus school counsellor who's on site three days a week. Firm policies on drugs, drink and smoking and school anti-bullying policy crystal-clear.

Pupils and parents: Wide variety of backgrounds, from quite posh to disadvantaged. Buses (some local authority, others organised by parents) bring children in from 10-mile radius, including Lyneham, Kingham, Carterton and Witney. Pupils very polite – they open doors for visitors and behave well; 'This is a school where staff can teach,' says head. 'It's not about crowd control.'

Old pupils include Gilbert Jessop (cricketer), Simon West (film director) and Alice Freeman (rower).

Entrance: Over-subscribed, but children living in catchment area and attending one of Burford's nine partner primary schools virtually guaranteed a place. Around 35 per cent come from outside catchment area, though, with priority given to those with siblings already at the school. Head says it's always worth prospective parents talking to her and explaining why they want their children to come. Number of year 7 places has been upped from 200 to 210. Some new pupils also join higher up the school, particularly in sixth form.

Exit: Around 50 per cent leave after GCSEs, for local FE colleges, apprenticeships or to join family businesses. About 60 per cent of sixth form go to university – to read everything from astrophysics to naval architecture (one to Oxford in 2013).

Remarks: A happy comprehensive school that offers a good, all-round education and some boarding places too. Pupils are keen to do well, know what is expected of them and rise to the challenge admirably.

Burgess Hill School for Girls

Linked school: Burgess Hill School for Girls Junior School

Keymer Road, Burgess Hill, RH15 0EG

- Pupils: 340 girls, 55 boarders • Ages: 11–18 • Non-denom
- Fees: Boarding £25,500–£25,950; Day £14,250–£14,700 pa
- Independent

Tel: 01444 241050
Email: registrar@burgesshill-school.com
Website: www.burgesshill-school.com

Headmistress: Since 2006, Mrs Ann Aughwane (late fifties), graduated from Loughborough, joint honours maths and education, previously deputy head of the school and prior to this head of mathematics at Guildford High. Interrupted her career to be a maths research associate at Edinburgh University.

An affable, generous-hearted, 'mother hen' character, always ready with a hidden stash of luxury biscuits and chocolates and thus a magnet for a tête-à-tête with the girls, who describe her as very supportive and approachable. Understandably proud of the school and its reputation for excellent teaching and results, and works to improve any aspect that may need some TLC – which includes the pupils. 'We passionately believe that the girls will thrive in our care, and even those who come to us lacking in confidence will emerge victorious'. At odds with the hot-house image that sticks to the school like glue – 'Academic rigour, while very important, must also be matched with getting the best out of every girl, whatever their aspirations, be it lawyer or a sailing instructor in Australia. Entry to our school is not judged on whether they're clever enough but whether the school can meet their needs'.

The day we arrived was an assembly on 'celebration' with a lot of clapping. The school is selective but not overly so, and she has the motto 'Open every door, as you don't know where it may lead, surprise yourself and try things new'. An article for Sussex Life on her work/life balance has proved difficult, as some of her 'work' includes going to musical concerts, art galleries and trips abroad to support the girls while they build extensions to a maternity unit for their Kabbubu village charity. Tough – but someone has to do it.

Enjoys theatre, walking and 'craft things' – whilst she makes no claims to being an artist, can talk art, music and sport. Surgeon son, lawyer daughter and husband 'learning to retire'. Retiring herself in July 2014.

Academic matters: Very strong and consistent year on year, gaining excellent results and a reputation as one of the best schools in Sussex. Has become more selective over recent years while not altering entrance criteria at all. If you're wired for work, then this school would be a great fit. GCSE 71 per cent A*/A in 2013; A level 81 per cent A*-B, with 42 A*/A in 2013. Girls strongly encouraged to take two facilitating subjects (ie subjects that bear weight with Oxbridge and Russell Group) – almost one third of all entries in science and mathematics. History and psychology also popular.

Recently piloted at AS level the extended project qualification (EPQ), which involves an independent research project and provides a useful bridge between school and university level work. The GCSE version of this provides pupils with an enrichment activity and 'allows some pupils to fly,' says academic head. They also do an Olympic games cross-curricular course to develop cooperative and management skills. The head of chemistry comes from an engineering consultancy background and now thinks 'teaching is the best job in the world'; this sentiment is echoed by many of the staff.

Aims to cater for special needs within the classroom, only occasionally withdrawing a pupil for special help – believes differentiation means no child slips through the net. Both parents and children have mixed views on this – some experiences do not tally with the school's. The parental chatter is that trying to deal with specialised needs in class does not give sufficient help, and the less academically ambitious can slip under radar. The head cites value-added data to show approach works well, and clearly some students with special needs have thrived. Many parents wax lyrical about the support for able pupils.

Games, options, the arts: No rolling acres but the site has more than adequate facilities considering its proximity to the town; both quality and quantity much improved since our previous visit. It now has five tennis/netball courts, athletics field, Astro and refurbished sports hall. The Triangle leisure centre, with swimming, squash, badminton and more Astro facilities, is close by. The A teams are competitive and do well on the local circuit and nationally. Some parents remark that if you're not in the A team, 'you don't get a look in', but the fixture list seems reasonably extensive and inclusive. A dedicated 'sport for all' coordinator focused on helping individuals find their niche rather than just concentrating on teams – tag rugby, football, basketball and Zumba introduced as options (although little in the way of dance); rowing, sailing and golf available nearby. Girls doing gold Duke of Edinburgh expeditions are overseen by the head of the junior school, who is training to be a mountain leader.

Fresh, wood-clad art block, with light and spacious studios displaying exciting and thoughtful compositions – good to see an increasing interest in the creative subjects by the Asian students. Offers textiles and resistant materials; staff discuss their subject with animation; plenty of local involvement with the local festivals. Several take art A level, with excellent results – some go on to St Martin's, Falmouth or Brighton. Royal Academy outreach life drawing programme; annual life drawing day; work displayed on the Saatchi schools' website.

Spectacular drama productions in different genres, some involving boys from Haywards Heath sixth form college; many girls help backstage. Recent productions include Cabaret and We Will Rock You, so 'slightly out of my comfort zone – but that can only be a good thing,' says head of music. Workshops, public speaking classes, visiting professionals give Shakespeare workshops. Lovely sounds coming from the music block, which now houses the new music technology suite. An array of choirs and ensembles performs a range from Brahms to Lady Gaga.

Girls rate the quality of careers advice very highly. Nothing low key: unique careers-focused business trip to Hong Kong. Speakers include ex-apprentice finalists, business leaders and management professionals; annual networking dinner where girls can practise formal business interaction with various professionals.

Background and atmosphere: Founded in 1906 as a co-educational day school by a group of parents, the PNEU (Parents' National Education Union). It became a girls' school in the 1920s, grew steadily and moved to present site in 1930. Now an independent trust. Located some 20 minutes from Gatwick, walking distance from town and 10 minutes from Brighton.

An eclectic and attractive mix of buildings, of varying red brick and turn of the century architecture, many recent wood-clad additions, a central glass atrium linking different departments, new science and sixth form blocks and, most recently, Wolfson language suite. The 14 acre site still retains pockets of gardens, attractive quads and a sense of well-manicured elegance. The staffroom is reminiscent of a five star hotel, with many matching sofas and plush carpets – you expect uniformed maids and waiters to be on tea service rather than the staff rushing through with piles of books. All this filters through to the girls, giving a productive and civilised atmosphere.

Modern, spacious and well-equipped sixth form centre with common rooms, kitchen, IT suite and study rooms. 'The new recruits and boarders fit right in like a glove,' says a parent. The school council suggested room for improvement with the food, which has been sorted: new head chef, great choice – we had a particularly scrummy lunch.

Pastoral care and discipline: Says it has never had any issues with drugs or alcohol – just a couple of incidents of girls smoking. Any bullying 'is dealt with sensitively,' say parents. It's cool to work here, so boffins readily accepted. Some talk of too much academic pressure; others thrive on it. Generally unreserved support for the way staff handle any misdemeanours, but the girls evidently respond to and facilitate a fair and civilised code of conduct.

The two boarding houses, Silverdale and Avondale, are period residences on the outskirts of the site. Some 54 boarders, the majority Asian, some Spanish, some Kenyan and a couple of English; the head would like to expand the range of nationalities. No full boarding below year 7, although girls can take advantage of the flexi boarding provision from the age of 9. The common rooms, with Nintendo and Wii, kitchen, pool tables, piano and IT rooms are large and pleasant; a pagoda and gardens surround the boarding houses.

Summer barbeques in the gardens go down well. The boarders may walk into the town, and have exeats with the day girls, although the Asian girls tend to stay self-contained and spend much of their weekend working. They were not forthcoming when asked about any weekend jaunts, though they do take part in plays and productions specially for boarders. They receive some extra language support if necessary.

Pupils and parents: Pupils are a welcoming, friendly, confident, smart and well-rounded bunch, ready to debate and up-beat about their experiences of school. The fees are relatively moderate, so parents are a mix of shop owners, teachers, pilots, media professionals, GPs and consultants. Girls are mainly local and from as far south as Worthing, as far west as Horsham, Crawley and surrounds. Eighty per cent of boarders are Chinese.

Some notable old girls include Haydn Gwynne (actress), Holly Willoughby, Caroline Atkins (cricketer) and Dr Francesca Happe (world authority on autism).

Entrance: Selective but not overly so – average ability upwards. Automatic entry from junior school as long as head feels they can cope with the work. Entry by examination, interview and references. Head looking for capable and productive girls but says, 'We have our fair share of characters'. Exams in maths, English and verbal reasoning; informal interview.

Exit: Nobody is evicted for poor GCSE results, but may be some tactful interventions if school feels someone would not cope. Some 60-70 per cent stay for the sixth form, with some moving to co-ed schools and others joining from state schools and abroad (the last capped at a third). Latest leavers to Royal Northern Music College, RADA and Central St Martin's as well as eg maths at Bristol, international relations at Leeds and management at LSE.

Money matters: A generous number of means-tested bursaries. Academic and music scholarships are open to girls entering years 7, 9 and 12, mostly for between 10-25 per cent of the day fees. Art, drama and sports scholarships for entrants to year 9 and sixth form. Girls can accumulate awards but these cannot exceed 50 per cent of the full day fees.

Remarks: A very good and civilised school that is consistent in its delivery of excellent results across the board. Successful in producing confident and resourceful girls who are ready for challenges and willing to give back to the community.

Bury Grammar School Girls

Linked schools: Bury Grammar School Boys; Bury Grammar Junior School (Girls)

Bridge Road, Bury, BL9 0HH

• Pupils: 470 girls; all day • Ages: 11–18 • non-denom
• Fees: £9,333 pa • Independent

Tel: 01617 972808
Email: info@bgsg.bury.sch.uk
Website: www.bgsg.bury.sch.uk

Headmistress: Since 2003, Mrs Roberta (Bobby) Georghiou BA Med (fifties). English graduate from Manchester University.

First headship. Previously deputy head of Westholme School, Blackburn and before that, head of English at Bolton School for Girls. Two grown-up daughters, one of whom went to BGSG. Is also an ISI inspector and on the GSA council.

Mrs Georghiou has overseen substantial improvements during her tenure, with an impressive new arts centre close to completion and plans in motion for a sixth form centre. The development of the arts centre was precipitated by the enforced demolition of a crumbling section of the school. She admits it was daunting at first but a bleak moment when weighing up the figures was quelled by an intrepid sixth former who offered to sky dive to raise funds. She raised a staggering £10,000 and inspired an impressive variety of other fundraising events. An emphasis on charity work is a feature of the school and, as the head told us: 'It's a school tradition to rise to challenges. The swimming pool was built with funds raised during the Great Depression.'

Head regarded with much affection and respect by pupils and staff alike. Smiley girls jostled to open doors for us as we walked around the school. Head has an easy manner but one suspects there is a lot of paddling beneath the surface; one parent described her as a 'pocket rocket'.

Academic matters: This is a hard working school with high value-added scores. In 2013, 45 per cent A*/A grades and 77 per cent A*/B at A level, and 72 per cent A*/A at GCSE. No IB; maths IGCSE available for some. Wide range of options available at A level – 28 subjects on offer with some less mainstream subjects jointly taught with Bury Grammar School for Boys. Class sizes are small and extra support is available in lunchtime clubs or one-to-one sessions. 'The school quickly identifies and addresses areas of weakness', according to one parent. The results are strong, especially in maths and science. Psychology, taught by the SENCo, is also successful and popular. Only a handful of mild SENs, no statements and no one requiring extra time despite the thorough support available. Head says school 'doesn't discriminate'.

Although languages are strong at GCSE, only a handful take them at A level, despite smartly refurbished language suites and pictorial evidence of lots of trips and exchanges. Surprisingly few pursue art or music to A level, but perhaps this will change with opening of the new arts centre and improvement of facilities.

ICT suites, and technology in general, has been overhauled. Interactive white boards are everywhere and fully used – even by teachers of a certain age. Apparently some viewed them with reluctance until, as one pupil said, 'they realised what they can do and now they are all really enthusiastic.'

The environment is disciplined but the classes are relaxed and buzzy, with lively discussion encouraged. We witnessed a debate about the Second World War in a history class – much laughter despite differences of opinion. Humour is important in the teaching and some of the staff could give alumna Victoria Wood a run for her money. Parents told us that good relations between staff and pupils get the best out of even the most timid girls.

Ample individual support is given to sixth formers when choosing courses and working through the UCAS process. 'They really care where you go', one pupil said. Old girls come back to do interview practice – a great idea.

Games, options, the arts: Facilities include five new netball courts, on-site games fields and a shared swimming pool at the boys' school. Teams compete locally and across Manchester. Less sporty girls are encouraged to participate and for the younger years, squads are enhanced by clubs. Occasional taster sessions for less mainstream options, including fencing and martial arts.

A variety of music groups, with some of the choirs and orchestras run jointly with the boys' school. The standard is high but there are opportunities for the less gifted to join in. One parent said, 'My daughter's life now revolves around her music but it was the school that recognised and brought out her talent.' Every year the two schools stage an ambitious musical production – 'spectacular', according to a parent.

Impressive choice of lunchtime activities from D of E to street dancing, Lego robotics and knitting. CCF, long established at the boys' school, has recently been extended to the girls and is increasingly popular. One pupil assured us that 'you actually cope better with your workload when you're busy'.

Lots of opportunities for foreign travel, with language exchanges, skiing and music trips, all organised well in advance (payments broken down to make them as accessible as possible).

Background and atmosphere: Independent but with a traditional grammar school feel, rooted in the local community with a strong sense of the pragmatic Lancashire character. Parents say school is friendly, welcoming and 'truly genuine'. School was founded in 1884 and amalgamated with the boys' school in 1906. Boys moved to a separate site across the road in 1965. Strong links are maintained, with some combined teaching in the sixth form and a variety of shared activities. The two schools also share kitchens and both dining rooms are in the boys' building. The girls' prep and mixed infants are on the same site and although separate there is plenty of contact with the younger children.

School doesn't have a grand entrance and the maze-like feel of the buildings, which have been developed and added to over its century of existence, was amplified when we visited by building work. Leading off the beautiful old hall – 'the school's soul,' according to the head – with war memorials and portraits rooting it in its history, the new arts centre certainly looks to the future. Airy, bright and sharply modern, it offers much-needed accommodation to the art and textiles department and will bring the library into the heart of the school. New sixth form centre for boys and girls will include classrooms and common rooms.

Public spirit is a fundamental here. Every form gets a charity to support and members are encouraged to work as a team to raise funds. Environmental concerns are taken ultra-seriously, with as much as possible recycled. Salad boxes are salvaged from the kitchens by the school's eco club and given to the gardening club to use as seed trays. Lights are turned off. The healthy eating tuck shop thrives, although someone stuck up 'RIP' when the vending machines were taken away. Not that the school needs a vending machine – they have cake sales galore.

Pastoral care and discipline: The school is proud of its pastoral systems and the general view from parents and pupils is that they are right to be so. Queen bees don't thrive here, whether they are held in check or just don't come. A parent who moved her daughter, previously bullied at another school, told us she was grateful for the subtlety and extent of support given and impressed at how quickly she settled and gained confidence. When we visited it was notable how at ease the girls were with each other. Lots of teamwork, clear codes of conduct and a small environment where all are known as individuals. Unacceptable behaviour is swiftly dealt with and a parent described the school as a 'tight ship where expectations are clear'.

School council is proactive and the girls definitely have a voice and ability to bring change. The school uniform has been redesigned with the girls opting to change their distinctive pale blue jumper for a more ordinary navy version, lighter blazer and 'more flattering' skirt.

Pupils and parents: Predominately local but girls do travel in from as far afield as Rochdale and Prestwich. Backgrounds are broad and culturally diverse but this is not a glossy school and the fees represent significant outlay for most families. Parents are very involved with an active and thriving PTA.

Entrance: At 11, exam papers in maths, English with essay and verbal reasoning plus reference from previous school and an interview – all granted equal importance. Head told us that, 'some of our highest flyers at GCSE were unremarkable in the exam but demonstrated their potential in the more relaxed interview'.

Exit: Some 40 per cent move on after GCSEs. Sixth formers don't head very far to university – Lancaster the most popular in 2013, followed by Edinburgh, Keele and Leeds. Head of sixth form believes this is gradually changing and more are looking to study further afield. Medicine and science are particularly popular, plus degrees targeting professions.

Money matters: Means-tested bursaries available; they operate on a sliding scale and are strictly monitored, always with home visits. Awards are based on a combination of strong academic performance in the entrance exam and financial need.

Remarks: A happy school that really cares. The nurturing family atmosphere gets results and produces girls who are both mature and confident. Down-to-earth, academic girls will do well here.

Caistor Grammar School

Church Street, Caistor, LN7 6QJ

• Pupils: 655, 305 boys/350 girls; all day • Ages: 11–18 • Non-denom • State

Tel: 01472 851250
Email: admin@caistorgrammar.com
Website: www.cgsonline.org.uk

Headteacher: Since 1996, Mr Roger Hale MA PGCE FRSA (early 50s). Attended Huddersfield New College, Trinity College, Cambridge, London Institute of Education (MA in education management). Taught history at Haberdashers' Aske's School, Elstree; head of history at Queen Elizabeth's Boys' School, Barnet; head of sixth form at Tewkesbury School, Gloucester; deputy headmaster Caistor Grammar School (has just clocked up 20 years at the school). Ex-Ofsted inspector; sits on various local and national committees including the Association of School and College Leaders, the Education Funding Agency, Grammar School Heads' Association.

Very energetic, talks at a rate (we were scribbling furiously to keep up with him), friendly, humorous, tremendously enthusiastic about the school and not at all pompous (target of wet sponges for YE fundraiser; came as Napoleon on fancy dress day; has a pleasantly cluttered, small study with chintzy curtains and lots of old whole school photos; accompanied year 7s and 8s on a very muddy bushcraft weekend). He knows all the pupils (writes a comment on all their assessments and reports), by whom he is liked and respected, and is a lover of tradition who is not pining for a new build, because he values the contact with the school's past, and the existing buildings 'help keep our feet on the ground'. Wants pupils to be 'well taught in a way that makes them love learning', to do 'qualifications that matter and prepare them for the next stage in their education' and to develop as individuals. A hands on, highly visible head – loves teaching (takes a year 10 group for history) and stands in the yard in morning and afternoon breaks. Married with a son and daughter; enjoys walking and gardening.

Academic matters: In 2013, 80 per cent A*/B and 48 per cent A*/A at A level. Options include classical civilisation, sport and PE, government and politics, RE (philosophy and ethics). Sciences, maths, Eng lit and history particularly popular and strong; DT and MFL good too, but small numbers, as with art, music, RS, PE and ICT (no performing arts/theatre studies); good uptake of class civ. Strong GCSE across the board – 59 per cent A*/A in 2013; 10/11 taken: must do a language, three sciences, RE; German, history and statistics the most popular options.

Outstanding for teaching and learning in latest Ofsted, which is far from common. According to Mr Hale, staff 'have a passion for helping pupils to do the best they can', endorsed by pupils we met – they are 'outstanding', 'fabulous' (sixth former), 'They have their own personality', the history teachers are 'really brilliant' and make lessons very exciting. Two termly assessments for effort and achievement and the longest comments we have ever seen on yearly reports; parents are given lots of data so they can see how their child is doing in relation to the year and their own prior achievement. Girls do surpass boys in their results but not all the time and not by much, and boys here exceed boys nationally.

SENco qualified to test for dyslexia (provides free individual support with spelling) – can accommodate anyone who passes entrance test, will deal with them on an individual basis, but nature of school site (lots of steps, some narrow corridors) would make it very hard for someone with a permanent physical disability. Doesn't screen all children for dyslexia but scrutinises test results in year 7 to identify any significant discrepancies and contacts all parents re any special needs at entry; in class support possible but kept minimal to suit children's feelings about it; G and T programme.

Games, options, the arts: Specialist sports college since 2004 and hub school for regional schools' sports partnership, lead school in Lincs for national school games initiative; awarded Sportsmark seven times. Medium size sports hall, modern fitness suite, two extra indoor spaces for PE; two netball courts (year 9 girls county champs); extensive playing fields (two plus floodlit Astro) with pavilion half a mile away.

Plenty of timetabled sport for all: usual sports – lots of fixtures – plus orienteering, archery, martial arts, water sports; individual achievements at county, regional and national levels, eg swimming, riding, sailing; close links with local sports clubs and other organisations. Outdoor pursuits residentials, abundant trips – skiing, netball tour to Barbados, football to Holland, Germany for World Cup, sixth form to Senegal and China.

All key stage 4s do level 1 sports leadership award in lessons; various other leadership awards; year 12 students have hosted and led county conferences for secondary children. Astonishingly, four students chosen to carry 2012 Olympics torch (one donated hers to the school) and ex-head boy was one of the seven younger generation athletes who lit the cauldron in the opening ceremony (surely a record for any school). A girl's design for the Paralympic mascot one of 12 national winners.

Much improved music accommodation, including fully sound-proofed drum practice room; music taught throughout key stage 3, exams at GCSE and A level if wanted. Orchestra, choir, several instrumental ensembles; timetable suspended for day of annual house music competition. Sixth formers do Trinity/Guildhall performing arts awards.

Although no theatre nor drama/dance studio, school play and house drama competition are high profile – most recent production, Les Miserables (performed in town hall) much acclaimed. Possibility of doing dance GCSE at another local school. Good results for GCSE art but low numbers at A level. Modern food tech room – cookery club, lessons for sixth formers, entries in Future Chef comp.

Lots of encouragement to get involved in the wealth of extracurricular activities – 'The teachers are very good at pinpointing your special talent and encouraging you to develop it'. Busy D of E; excellent school newspaper, with lively and entertaining articles and colour photos and illustrations – won Best Newspaper in the prestigious national Shine competition, with praise for the 'sensitive handling of the death of a teacher'; sports newsletter; masses of clubs, eg eco, Amnesty International, chess, pottery, Czech for beginners, global student forum, public speaking, Young Enterprise. Extensive range of trips – outdoor pursuits, London, Ukraine, Iceland; France, Germany and China exchanges; link with schools in Senegal and Morocco.

Many house activities run by students and leadership opportunities in performing arts, literacy, languages, maths. Awards evening is a wonderful celebration of the great range of achievements in and out of school – the ones you would expect plus solo gliding, volunteering at the Olympics, being the Young Mayor of North Lincs, working with young disabled athletes, even a trophy for moral courage.

Very good careers programme from year 7 – year 8s have a Real (jobs) Game day; all do work experience in year 10 and year 12s encouraged to find placements too; all year 11s interviewed by head about future plans. Annual events to develop employability skills – enterprise days, sixth form challenge of industry conference, newspaper days, plus visiting speakers. Year 13s praised help with university applications and interviews.

Background and atmosphere: Founded 1630 by Frances Rawlinson, Rector of South Kelsey. In 2000 became a foundation school, then converter academy 2010. String of outstanding Ofsteds (grade 1s for everything in the last one) – the only school in Lincs to have been included in Ofsted's Hall of Fame on four occasions; 2002 became a beacon school (for academic excellence), twice received a School Achievement award. As a high performing specialist school became humanities college as well from 2008; gifted and talented lead school. Much bemedalled – Charter mark status twice; investor in people six times; healthy schools and international school awards.

Situated close to centre of Caistor, a small market town. Trad red brick buildings a mix of 17th century and 1930s, '80s and '90s styles. Some of the labs are limitingly small – about to start work on a new building with better science facilities. Reasonable ICT resources; very new food tech room. On two sides of a close around the attractive, ancient parish church, which gives rather a homely feeling (despite the view of the burial ground). Original ironstone hall with oak panelling and ceiling dating from 1631 in daily use – an impressive environment for detentions. Smallish library with pedestrian decor has lots of engaging fiction but narrow range of magazines and newspapers. Some drab corridors, enlivened by many attractive photos of pupils' activities and art.

Modest sixth form centre in Casterby House, once a large private residence – we thought some of the common rooms looking the worse for wear could do with a makeover, but were assured by Mr Hale that the students 'like them the way they are'. More dull décor in the cafeteria but good choice of food made on site from local ingredients (much more important in the scheme of things) and a highly regarded catering manager – students enthused about the Xmas dinners (upmarket veggie dish too). Small garden with very attractive paving to commemorate an assistant head and lab technician.

Ethos of 'strive' and 'excel', in the words of one of the younger pupils, with 'a great sense of fun' (parent); friendly, supportive, harmonious community with friendships across years, small enough for everyone to be known and treated as as an individual – witness a handful of year 12s re taking their AS year to improve their grades; 'There's a huge ethos of respect, for teachers and each others, that permeates throughout' (parent); big focus on leadership from an early age, with opportunities to develop confidence in public speaking. Even has a very engaging school cat. Christian flavour – annual one day seminar for year 12s to engage with ethical and political issues. Active, highly regarded school and sixth form councils; views of parents, staff and pupils canvassed via regular questionnaires.

Three houses – lots of competitions, often organised by sixth formers, including a pancake race. Uniform is black, grey and white – girls can wear 'formal black trousers' instead of a skirt; sixth wear office-type clothes. We were charmed by the sartorial diversity displayed, including a three piece suit with fobwatch and bow tie; winkle picker shoes and a stylish red and black floral number – evidence that individuality can be expressed.

Pastoral care and discipline: Usual structure of form tutors led by heads of different parts of school. Rules emphasise reason and consideration for others. Not heavy on sanctions – extra work, 'the occasional detention', but 'takes an extremely hard line' on drugs; 'When problems arise we try to involve parents at an early stage'. Head sets great store by smartness – untucked shirts now a thing of the past, thanks to the head of the pastoral system, who has also tightened up on classroom behaviour – 'zero tolerance policy,' says Mr Hale approvingly. Pupils say (reassuringly): 'You know where you are'; 'The head's more likely to have a talk with you than punish you'; 'People behave well from respect rather than harsh rules' (sixth former).

Counselling service plus drop in health clinic. Sixth form prefects and volunteers act as student counsellors, attached to lower forms – younger pupils trust and have a high regard for them. Very little bullying as open site, staff much present and Mr Hale 'gets involved if there's any bullying'; any such issues are dealt with in an understanding way; 'There's always a teacher you like you can talk to'; code of cyber conduct being written by school council. Good induction for year 7s includes sleepover in gym (good for bonding with classmates and teachers) – new children settle easily, even if coming alone from their primary school. Rewards for good behaviour and work – £10 gift vouchers for winners of many merits.

Pupils and parents: Mostly white British, reflecting local population; over half from catchment area. LA school buses for years 7-11 (sixth have to pay a contribution), plus parent-organised transport for some out of catchment areas (can cost over £1000 a year). Active Friends' Association – parents involved in activities and fundraising; the ones we spoke to very happy with the teachers, friendly atmosphere, well-organised parents' evenings and regular communications ('Parents feel valued and are seen as partners in their children's education'). Very thoughtful, articulate, appreciative and polite pupils.

Most notable Old Girl is Dawn French, 'But I'm sure there'll be many more quite soon,' says Mr Hale.

Entrance: Organises own admissions procedure (close to that of other local grammar schools) – two VR tests taken in September (results available before deadline for LA preference form); takes top 25 per cent of ability range. Year group of around 94 – over-subscribed. Need to live within 6.5 miles of Caistor on or before September 1 of year of application – goes by highest score, then highest score for out of catchment area candidates.

Years 8 and 9: similar VR tests; year 10: VR test plus maths and English papers. Sixth: minimum five A*-B at GCSE, at least B for would be AS subjects plus C in English and maths – about 15 join from outside.

Exit: Some 15-20 per cent leave post year 11 for nearby sixth form/FE/agricultural colleges to do vocational/performing arts courses not on offer at Caistor or to join family businesses.

Almost all year 13s progress to often very good universities; 2013 two to Oxbridge; others to eg Newcastle, Sheffield, Durham, Nottingham, King's College London, Edinburgh, Exeter, Leeds, Warwick, York, as well as less high-powered ones, to do a tremendous breadth of courses – sciences/medicine, history, social sciences, law popular. Others to the Forces or jobs with training.

Remarks: A very strong contender if you are after sound academic values and achievement, with firm discipline allied to encouragement of talent and individuality, plus a good dollop of heart.

Cambridge International School

Cherry Hinton Hall, Cherry Hinton Road, Cambridge, CB1 8DW

• Pupils: 250 • Ages: 3-16 • Fees: £9,900–£11,760 pa
• Independent

Tel: 01223 416938
Email: admissions@abelards.com
Website: www.cambridgeinternationalschool.co.uk

Principal: Since 2006, Harriet Sturdy, PhD, educated at Perse Girls, read history at Durham before heading to Glasgow (PhD), Department of Child and Adolescent Psychology. Forty-something, hands-on, friendly, knows all the students by name and their backgrounds, what classes they are taking, why they are there. She splits her time between the two campuses. Trim and energetic, full of blue-sky thinking about future developments while at the same focusing on minutia of day-to-day logistics, stepping in to cover classes, signing the kids up for a new activity or competition, personally delivering new computer hardware. Married with one son and one daughter. 'There are plenty of traditional teachers and schools in Cambridge. I want to create a school where teachers are able to take risks and are given freedom to be bold and try new things. You can't make a difference if you don't.'

Academic matters: CIS follows the International Primary Curriculum (IPC) in the infant and junior departments. The IPC is cross-curricular and topic-based in its approach, drawing on the national curriculum for maths and English, but using resources from Australia and New Zealand for reading. Secondary department follows national curriculum leading to a mixture of IGCSEs and GCSEs in years 10 and 11.

Despite its small size, CIS offers 22 GCSE and IGCSE options and tries to be as flexible as possible with the timetabling. Some take the IGCSE exams, particularly in languages, before year 11. In 2013, 45 per cent A*/A and 75 per cent A*-B grades. Interestingly, maths results tend to be stronger than languages. Classes are small, maximum of 15 in the infant department, 16 for juniors and secondary though some IGCSE option classes are smaller. Parents appreciate the inclusive nature of the school and the fact that each pupil, regardless of personality or learning style, is respected and treated with importance. Comments convey the same theme, 'individual attention to the needs of all', 'tailored to each child', 'children can learn at their own pace', and 'my child is challenged because she works at her own level'.

Much attention given to language learning. Spanish and French are offered (in addition to ESOL) from junior school. Mandarin introduced in infants and gradually spreading with some juniors and seniors taking as well. Big emphasis on mother tongue instruction, a large display boasting all the languages spoken and taught greets you at the entrance to the junior school. This presents some timetabling challenges but parents say the school works hard to resolve these. At certain times the junior school resembles the Tower of Babel, with every nook and cranny occupied by small groups of children learning a different language. One British parent, delighted that her child is studying three languages, noted that at CIS children seem to have a better facility to learn other languages because they are surrounded by students who speak up to three or four. On offer are Mandarin, Dutch, Swedish, Norwegian, Danish, French, German, Spanish, Greek, and Italian. Basically, it's 'language on demand' with the Cambridge academic community providing the requisite teachers. Pupils enter and win national language competitions. Unusually for an international school, CIS students also excel at Latin. Perhaps not surprising given its proximity to the University of Cambridge, the school has won several Latin competitions including the Cambridge Classical Association Latin Reading Competition.

The school can support students with mild learning needs because of the small class sizes and individualised approach, and there are two support teachers in place. CIS also has the advantage of its nearby sister school, Holme Court Cambridge, for those students with more significant special needs. Parents of SEN students speak highly of the attention given to their children.

Staff are international too: just over half are British (most with experience abroad), the rest from all over including USA, Canada, South Africa. Average age low 30s. All seem genuinely happy to be working in this unique school in a city internationally renowned for scholarship and academic excellence. Teachers are encouraged to take initiative, to think 'outside the box' in order to respond to student interests and to make good use of experiential learning opportunities. Parents say staff 'keep an eye on each child, they pay attention and are quick to help'.

Games, options, the arts: Cherry Hinton (infant and junior school) is bursting with displays of children's art, including large sculptures and mobiles created collaboratively by class groups. At The Temple (senior school campus) there is a little building with newly converted loft dedicated to art. Drama is also on offer for all, with annual productions. Primary children study recorder and ukulele, individual music lessons are available and there are orchestras on both sites.

CIS is proud of its 'Forest School' programme based on the Scandinavian model of using the natural environment to develop personal skills. In the wooded grounds pupils explore flora and fauna in their natural settings and outdoor activities teach problem solving and collaborative lessons. Infant classrooms open directly onto this green teaching space.

Parents and children are happy with the range of clubs on offer. At the junior school Lego is popular; netball and debating get a special mention at the secondary. Others include cooking, musical activities, maths and science clubs. Sports are recreational and competitive, no 'fair weather' athletes here, the stalwart cross-country runners are out rain or shine, pounding through the grounds and fields of the surrounding area. Other sports include hockey, tennis, basketball, football, table tennis. The school participates in the Cambridge School Sports Partnership and pupils relished the irony of their international school team winning the junior cricket competition.

A business enterprise activity in the secondary is giving students hands-on practical experience in starting their own companies, organising shareholders and investors, negotiating with local business professionals and arranging events to boost their income such as catering, car boot sales and punting trips on the Cam. D of E awards scheme in place. The school has a long-standing commitment to the Kasiisi Porridge Project to provide daily meals to children at a school in Uganda and the student council also organises activities to raise funds for local charities.

Plenty of field trips – London museums, Stratford-upon-Avon – plus residentials for the secondary pupils. Students practice journalism in School Report, first writing, then reporting the news which is filmed in the local BBC Cambridge studios. Code Club is a run by a network of volunteers who go into schools to teach children computer programming. Considering the school's proximity to the epicentre of Britain's IT industry, this gives students exposure to cutting-edge thinking.

Both campuses offer hot lunches or children may bring their own. At Cherry Hinton Hall the hot lunches are brought in and served, whereas at the senior school they are prepared on site. CIS offers a breakfast club at no cost, plus after school homework supervision or clubs that are handy for working parents.

Background and atmosphere: Dr Harriet Sturdy is a second-generation educator, inspired by her parents, the 'Brangelina' of their day, who opened their own school in Cambridge when they found that their nine multi-ethnic, adopted children were not always received by the local schools with open arms: Sancton Wood School became their 13th child. Sturdy became involved when she returned to Cambridge after completing post-doctoral work in Glasgow, to sort out family and school affairs following the early deaths of her parents. (Sturdy's father was a Cambridge academic who in his free time helped his wife with the business side of the school.) She branched out to start a nursery school when her first child was born and then opened a special needs school, Holme Court, with her brother, Daniel. Taking the family concept of 'inclusion' to the next stage, she and Daniel opened Cambridge International School in 2006. Daniel has moved away but returns regularly to support the strategic thinking and business affairs of the school. Very much still a family enterprise, Sturdy's son and daughter went to the school and her husband teaches Latin and Spanish. Besides Daniel, three of her 12 siblings work there as teachers, administrators or support staff.

As a proprietor Sturdy is free to make plans which seem to come to fruition when the time is right; developments occur when the family feel that the 'finance' and 'idea' stars align. In its short history, CIS has grown onto two campuses about 15 minutes apart. The infant and junior departments are at Cherry Hinton Hall, a former council owned early Victorian house built in the Tudor style set in a lovely parkland. Besides classrooms of all shapes and modest sizes, it has a small library with a rather limited collection. In the extensive grounds there are play areas, games fields and an allotment.

The senior school is at The Temple campus in Abington, also set within lovely secluded grounds featuring all-weather sports pitches and a sensory garden. The attractive large pink house, relatively modern despite its more traditional style, contains classrooms, ICT lab, science lab, a small careers and university counselling hub and the study room. There are smaller buildings in the grounds for art, recently extended into the loft space, and science. Growth in numbers has meant that the library was sacrificed in order to create more classroom space, so the books are now housed in the study room which is available to pupils during free periods. A marquee (legacy of the previous occupants who ran the place as a wedding venue) extending from the main house into the garden serves as an interesting venue for meals and assemblies, though this will be replaced by permanent buildings in due course. PCs and laptops throughout the secondary campus plus a well-equipped computer suite. Newly acquired Apple Macs installed in media lab where pupils engage in filmmaking.

Pastoral care and discipline: The school has a strong sense of community and an authentic family atmosphere, no doubt because it is a family-run school. New pupils soon settle and become part of the group. Pupil prefects and houses contribute to the sense of team spirit. Older pupils struggling with school or personal issues can see the counsellor who knows them all and/or make use of a newly-created space for some quiet down time. No major discipline issues reported.

Pupils and parents: There are 40 nationalities in this small community representing a wide range of socio-economic backgrounds. Just under half are British, the rest are from expat families working at the university, medical research, NATO, and firms in Cambridge's 'Silicon Fen'. Children live in Cambridge or villages within a 30 mile radius, taking advantage of the bus and inter-campus shuttle services. Owing to the small numbers, this service is not yet as convenient as parents might wish, but new routes have been added. Pupils look happy and comfortable in their uniforms and are confident speaking to visitors.

Parents seen as partners and encouraged to share their expertise in any way possible, talking to classes or at assemblies about national or religious celebrations, countries of origin or cultural matters. 'It's always easy to see evidence of learning at the school', say parents, 'and yet it is not rigid'. No board of governors but the Cambridge International Parents Association (CIPA) provides an informal means of communicating suggestions and concerns to the owners. Everyone gives high marks for communication and accessibility, to Dr Sturdy in particular.

Some local families, including Brits who join CIS by default when unable to get places at their preferred state schools, opt to stay because they find the experience so positive and the international character of the school a real bonus. They enjoy welcoming and getting to know families from other parts of the world. The school occasionally has pupils from abroad who live with families in the school in a homestay arrangement, those who do this seeing it as another learning benefit for all concerned.

The school has nearly grown to capacity and there are no immediate plans for significant increase in numbers. The plan is to preserve the family feeling by having single form entry in primary, two form in secondary. The school has applied for ISI membership to broaden the CIS network of professional and pupil opportunities.

Entrance: Broadly non-selective though older pupils need to be able to cope with IGCSE. Report and reference from previous school if applicable. It's a simple process, something appreciated by a parent who commented, 'I could not conceive of making my child sit through a two-hour grilling and exam to get in to school'. The school is young and still growing but once it reaches capacity a more formalised admissions process will likely follow. Waiting lists for some year groups although the school will do what it can to accommodate newly-arrived families. The parent community helps newcomers adapt to the school and to the Cambridge area, sensitive to the challenges of adjusting to a new country. Teachers and classes send pre-arrival emails to welcome new children coming from abroad.

Exit: Although the school does not have a sixth form, they provide a careers and counselling programme and advise pupils about their next move. Pupils who leave are generally relocating abroad or moving on to local schools, although one parent who enrolled here because her preferred Cambridge school was oversubscribed says that now she would never dream of moving her daughter until she finishes. After IGCSEs pupils go on to study for A levels or IB at local state or independent schools or occasionally to FE programmes.

Money matters: CIS is a young school without legacies or endowments but will consider making financial aid available to families needing support. If a pupil and CIS are a match, the head is reluctant to allow financial challenges to stand in the way. One parent said, '(the system) appears to be pretty informal, but the impression is that if someone is struggling to meet the fees, the school wants to help.'

Remarks: This is a young, 'quirky in a good way', school that is clearly providing a solid education to a niche community in Cambridge. For parents keen on exposing their offspring to a more international perspective, this school provides a fabulous opportunity to meet and learn with children from different countries.

The Camden School for Girls

Sandall Road, London, NW5 2DB

• Pupils: 970; all day • Ages: 11–19 • Non-denom • State

Tel: 020 7485 3414
Email: csg@camdengirls.camden.sch.uk
Website: www.camdengirls.camden.sch.uk

Headteacher: Since 2010, Elizabeth Kitcatt BA MA (Institute of Education). Ms Kitcatt has been at the school for 15 years, joining from Parliament Hill School, where she was head of English. At Camden, under the previous regime, as well as teaching English, she was deputy head, responsible for 'teachers' professional development' and 'school improvement planning'. Looks a bit like Delia Smith and has the same reassuring, measured presence. Clearly strong on detail, but generally considered rather more cautious and less charismatic than her predecessor. 'She's a bit bland,' said one long-term parent. 'She's quite a lot stricter, but otherwise seems to have made little impact.' Determined to maintain the school's high standards and inclusive approach. Enjoys singing in her spare time.

Academic matters: Camden is one of the country's most successful comprehensives. In 2007, Ofsted rated it 'outstanding' in every respect (except attendance) and commented that 'it rightly deserves the outstanding reputation it has among parents and in the community'. In 2013, 80 per cent of GCSEs were graded A*-C, including English and maths. But the sixth form is the jewel in the crown and A level results are stellar, with 76 per cent A*-B and 45 per cent A*/A grades. 'Top class curriculum,' says Ofsted, and that includes a hard-going compulsory core at GCSE of English, maths, science, philosophy and theology, physical education, French or Spanish and PSHE. Mixed-ability classes of about 28 pre-GCSE, 20 in the sixth form, and work carefully monitored with individual targets set at the beginning of each year. Homework, too, taken seriously, with detentions for slackers.

The sixth form decidedly less mixed-ability than the lower school, as only those who make the grades make the transfer. The curriculum here is traditional and academic with classical civilisation, history of art, ancient Greek, economics and philosophy supplementing the mainstream subjects. ('Softer' options such as media studies and DT are only taught to AS Level). Extended Project Qualification (EPQ) also popular. Intellectual stretching taken even further for Oxbridge aspirants with after-school 'masterclasses' covering everything from the Economic Downturn to The Wasteland. Much inspired instruction, particularly in the sixth form. 'It's like an old-fashioned grammar school,' says one parent. 'The teaching is really rigorous.' Lower down, there are those who struggle with more challenging pupils. ('Some teachers just can't control the class,' said one year 9 parent. 'There are subjects where my daughter has completely given up.') Though sciences are well taught with strong results, this is a noticeably arty school – possibly not the ideal place if medicine is your ultimate goal (only one trainee medic in 2011). Special needs well catered for, with sensitive individual support in class or by withdrawal in small groups. After-school homework club for dyslexia and spelling. Middle-class parents, too, tend to pick up the slack when students flag.

Games, options, the arts: 'Art and music are fantastic here,' said one mother with two daughters, one artistic, the other musical. Most parents (many in the media) agree. The school has specialist music status with dedicated music places at both 11 and 16, and this pool of talent forms the core of two orchestras (including a 70-piece symphony orchestra), various chamber music ensembles, three choirs, a wind band, a jazz group, a jazz choir and a recorder group. Both music and music technology offered at A Level. Energetic and dedicated head of music. Art, too, is incredibly strong ('Art is really big in this school,' said one student fan) with powerful work on display throughout the halls and a glorious traditional art studio (formerly the gym), with a suitably bohemian skylight, as well as a pottery studio. Textiles equally vibrant. Art is the fourth most popular A Level choice (after English, maths and history) with a good number of A*s. The keen also use the EPQ to extend their range (a short film made by a student was recently shown on the South Bank) and about 20 per cent of leavers go on to art-related degrees. Drama too – with the already professional among the sixth form – is strong, with an annual Broadway show and sixth-formers mounting their own production. (Stage management is offered as an enrichment activity and last year one pupil left to take up a recording contract.)

Sport, on the other hand, is probably not the school's forte. An on-site gym, outdoor netball court and attractive dance studio are supplemented by excellent facilities at Cantelowes Park, a few feet from the gates, but play-up, play-up and play the game is not really the ethos here. Plenty of clubs from art, technology and modern languages to specialist make-up and knitting, and sixth formers devote Wednesday afternoons to 'enrichment studies', ranging from creative writing to personal finance and tag rugby. All the more traditional ornaments, too, including a sixth-form newspaper and a debating society. Though there's plenty going on, you do have to be self-motivated to make the most of it. 'My son was supposed to do football as an enrichment activity,' said one mother, 'but no one monitors it. He just has Wednesday afternoons off.' School trips (Austrian tour for musicians, ski trip) and work experience abroad organised annually.

Background and atmosphere: Camden, founded in 1871 by Frances Mary Buss, is an iconic school in the history of education. Buss – and her limerickly-linked counterpart, Dorothea Beale, who founded Cheltenham Ladies' College – were responsible for establishing three of the great landmarks in women's education. Buss founded North London Collegiate in 1850, and then, specifically for girls of more modest means, Camden, which opened in 1879 and until 1920 (when it established its own sixth form) regularly sent scholarship girls on to North London for sixth form. The school went comprehensive in 1977.

Relatively restricted site with a motley collection of buildings, from the high-ceilinged, large-windowed Victorian through 60s concrete to red-brick modern. Good facilities with new science labs, a well-stocked library, modern computer rooms and classrooms and a building finished in 2004, which houses design technology, English and music. Socially, the atmosphere is relaxed but purposeful. 'I was at quite a strict girls independent school before I came to Camden in year 10,' said one sixth former, 'and I much prefer it here. You're treated like an adult.' Good food – pasta and garlic bread, curry – at reasonable cost.

Pastoral care and discipline: Deliberately few rules, but Ms Kitcatt is generally noted for having tightened up on the detail, clamping down on latecomers and absentees. 'Camden Compass' spells out the behaviour code, but generally a strong sense of trust and girls are 'let out into the unknown' from year 9. That doesn't mean, however, their activities remain unobserved. 'The one time my daughter was absent without leave, you knew immediately,' said one parent. 'They really have the girls sussed,' said another, with a daughter who'd encountered considerable difficulties. 'I really feel they listened to my worries.'

Highly praised induction programme eases new pupils into the sixth from, where the approach is definitely 'young adult',

with signing in rather than register and no requirement to be on site during study periods. 'We see it as transition between school sixth form and college,' says the head. Loose-rein it may be, but a strong team of tutors oversee 18 students each and offer advice on everything from study skills to gap years. Elected prefects organise the leavers' ball and help out younger girls. Parents in general think the outcome is all that could be desired. 'It's a terrific environment and produces really feisty girls, who are encouraged to think for themselves and question.'

Pupils and parents: 'Camden girls have a sense of their place within the world that is immediately recognisable,' says one former head girl, and who could dispute her standpoint? 'Girls are confident beyond belief,' said one parent with a more ambivalent view. Camden is a cool school, an obvious haven for the daughters of the north London, left-leaning media classes. Current and former parents include the sculpture Antony Gormley, Random House chief Gail Rebuck, and Tate Modern director Sir Nicholas Serota, and old girls in the same style number Sarah Brown (wife of Gordon), Professor of Networking Julia Hobsbawm and actress Emma Thompson. The mainstream here is street-smart and sociable and frequently blessed by names like Hermione, Indiana and Genevieve. But while all participate in the uniform non-uniform of skinny jeans and stylish footwear, this is not a socially homogeneous institution. The school serves a catchment where the proportion of those eligible for free school meals is well above average, and it educates a plentiful sprinkling of refugees and asylum seekers, from Kosovo to Kurdistan. 'It's multi-dimensional and multi-ethnic,' said one mother. 'It's an urban experience, but excellent.' In the sixth form, there's a significant influx from the independent sector.

Entrance: At 11 – unless you have an SEN statement, are in local authority care, have a sibling still at the school or are a talented musician – you will have to live no further away than 0.982miles of the school entrance 'in a straight line as the crow flies'. Even then you'll have to sit a 'banding' test (40 minutes of verbal and non-verbal reasoning) to ensure all classes are of mixed ability. Once the four bands are established, 28 places are offered in each band according to the general criteria. Camden is definitely one of those London schools which people move house for (and sometimes only pretend to move house – a naughtiness the school clamps down on firmly). If that's your plan, living within a few feet of the gates is your only sensible course of action. At 11, there are eight music places awarded independently of all other criteria. Music candidates take a multiple-choice aptitude test to whittle down the numbers, then the top 60 are invited back for a five-minute audition. In the sixth form, Camden goes co-ed, admitting a further 150-170 new pupils (from about 1000 applicants), no more than half of whom can be boys. Once again siblings are given precedence (but only if the sibling is still at the school on the date the applicant starts). Other places are dependent on distance from the gates, academic references and GCSE grades, predicted and actual (documentary proof required for all three). Grade Bs essential in at least five subjects, including maths and English language. At this point, a further 15 music places on offer to those who play 'an orchestral instrument to a high standard.'

Exit: Quite a number leave at 16, either because they don't make the grade or because they prefer a sixth-form college, apprenticeship or employment. Vast majority of leavers at 18 to further or higher education, including several to Oxbridge and occasional one to Harvard. Art foundation and music schools also very popular.

Money matters: Camden is a voluntary aided school and, as such, has to contribute 10 per cent to its buildings costs. Parents give generously and there is an annual fund-raising appeal, with monthly donations from £10. Plenty of further fund-raising activities, too, where celebrity watching is the order of the day.

Remarks: One of London's best and coolest schools. Suits the self-motivated, self-assured, creative individualist, particularly those who might find the atmosphere elsewhere pettifogging and unimaginative.

Canbury School

Kingston Hill, Kingston Upon Thames, KT2 7LN

- Pupils: 57, 47 boys/10 girls. • Ages: 11–16 • Non-denom
- Fees: £14,355 pa • Independent

Tel: 020 8549 8622
Email: head@canburyschool.co.uk
Website: www.canburyschool.co.uk

Head Master: Since 2002, Mr Robin Metters BEd (late fifties). Teaching career spans 30 years. He was principal of Woodside Park International School in North London for 16 years before taking over at Canbury. Married with two grown-up children, enjoys sports, particularly sailing and golf. Time permitting, he is keen to join in sporting activities with pupils and is an enthusiastic spectator at all school events.

Academic matters: Small, inclusive school catering for children who would not necessarily thrive in large comprehensives. Good range of subjects on offer; the majority of pupils take around nine GCSEs. Considering it is non-selective, results are impressive, especially for maths and English. Options at 14+ now wider with additional GCSEs subjects. In 2013, 14 per cent of pupils got 5+ A*-C grades including maths and English; 11 per cent of grades were A*/A. Small class sizes enable teachers to provide that ever important individual attention, – staff pupil is ratio 1:7. Sensible amount of homework with clear guidelines for each year and an optional homework club.

A number of children with SEN, mostly dyspraxia, dyslexia and mild Asperger's/ASD. One-to-one support with specialist teachers in-house to ensure individual needs are meet. Local speech therapists and occupational therapist work with the school as required. English as a foreign language tuition is also provided on a one-to-one basis or small group, depending on the needs of pupils.

Games, options, the arts: Excellent range of sporting activities for a smaller establishment, so something to suit everyone's tastes. Takes advantage of the numerous local sporting facilities in Richmond Park, Kingston and on the Thames for sailing, canoeing and rowing. Cross-country running is a major sport in which pupils compete successfully and everybody gets the opportunity to learn to swim.

Visual arts are strength – colourful expressive art displays and many different media are used; parents say three-dimensional design, ceramics and collage are particularly popular. Class music is taught for the first three years and some children have individual instrumental tuition and enjoy performing in informal concerts. Drama taught mainly through small group work with an emphasis on developing communication skills and building confidence. Younger pupils tend to be the actors, with older ones taking on technical roles and directing the productions.

A variety of clubs run at lunchtimes and after school, table tennis, karate and arts being popular. Good variety of excursions and field trips arranged each term for all to help pupils develop new interests – prides itself on taking the children out and about.

Background and atmosphere: Founded in 1982 by John Wyatt, accommodated in a large Edwardian house on Kingston Hill. Whilst the site is compact, it has the advantage of backing onto Richmond Park, where many of their sporting activities take place. Recent renovations include a new science lab changing facilities and complete redecoration, the IT suite and art room recently made over too. Fully accessible – able to consider applications from children with physical disabilities. An educational charity administered by a board of governors whose aim is create a genuine community where individuals can be happy and motivated to achieve their maximum potential. Despite pupils being hard at work, calm and less formal atmosphere in comparison with many other schools.

Pastoral care and discipline: Pastoral care is high on the agenda to ensure well-being and self-esteem. Caring – everyone treated as an individual and taught to feel good about themselves and their abilities. Form tutors are always available to deal with any day-to-day problems, home work diaries are used to convey messages between home and school. Two members of staff are trained counsellors and pupils have a school council. Clear set of school rules are presented in a booklet, The Canbury Code.

Pupils and parents: Mostly professional parents from all walks of life and a range of backgrounds, both international and UK based. Families tend to be fairly local from a five mile radius from Richmond to Weybridge, handful come from central London. A school council is run by staff and parents to raise funds for the chosen charity of the year.

Entrance: At 11+ pupils spend an assessment morning at the school. Places are offered following a meeting with the headmaster and satisfactory reports from previous schools.

Exit: At 16+ most choose to go to further education colleges, Epsom, Esher and Guildford. A few opt for sixth forms at local schools, eg Coombe Girls'.

Money matters: Both current and prospective pupils can apply for means-tested bursaries.

Remarks: A good choice for children who require a sympathetic approach to their education. Definitely fills a gap in the education market, comment parents. A positive and warm atmosphere, where everyone is made to feel welcome.

Canford School

Canford Magna, Wimborne, Doset, BH21 3AD

- Pupils: 380 boys, 250 girls (250 boys board, 130 day boys; 175 girls board, 75 day girls) • Ages: 13–18 • C of E • Fees: Boarding £29,640; Day £23,166 pa • Independent

Tel: 01202 847207
Email: admissions@canford.com
Website: www.canford.com

Headmaster: Since September 2013 Mr Ben Vessey BA MA MBA (forties), previously senior deputy head at Christ's Hospital. Four years in the City as an oil and gas broker before moving into education. He was head of history at first Dauntsey's and then Millfield before joining Christ's Hospital. He is married to Harriet; they have three young sons. A passionate sportsman, particularly keen on rugby; has coached at various levels. Also musical and has performed in a couple of large choral pieces in recent years.

Academic matters: Do not be fooled by the relaxed and informal atmosphere that pervades, even when A levels and GCSEs loom – some cracking good teaching is going on and the staff we met were fizzy, fun and focused. What's more, pupils seemed to acknowledge and value that, frequently volunteering respect and affection for their teachers – even when out of earshot. The excellent relations between staff and pupils which really do seem to exist at Canford are founded on trust and willingness, as much in the classroom as outside of it. Indeed these divisions are frequently invisible: whether it's the school lobster sloughing his shell, wounded seahorses finding solace with the biology faculty, brown trout being launched into the river, setting out for Lyonesse in search of Thomas Hardy and Tennyson, down to St Ives for painting and artists, much of what is taught and disseminated involves wholeness. This is not gimmicky stuff: it's education in the round, education for life.

Statistically-minded league table bibbers ought to be impressed by the results published in the prospectus pack and on the internet: they make good reading. GCSE and A level results are right up with co-education schools with more illustrious names – 2013 88 per cent A*-B at A level, 68 per cent A*/A; 75 per cent A*/A at GCSE. Considering the breadth of intake, that speaks volumes.

New boys and girls try every subject available in a kind of academic circus including Connections, a non-examined course in every year group involving PSE, citizenship and general knowledge. Everyone takes a language at GCSE – very, very few people drop below a B. The system precludes cutting out subjects too early and gives a far more realistic foundation from which to choose A levels. Breadth, breadth, breadth.

Facilities are good: glorious library, innovative new IT room, lively DT space (more girls than boys taking A level this year – so one in the eye for critics who say that co-education polarises subject choices), good science laboratories (55 per cent in the lower sixth doing sciences – 'The quality of teaching for the sciences is one of the best-kept secrets in Dorset,' says a delighted parent). Languages are 'fun' and imaginatively taught but numerically not as popular; music and art results excellent (the latter taught by the man who runs the first XV).

All this is supported, encouraged, broadened by visiting authors and scientists, poets and politicians: fresh air from without as well as expeditions and trips abroad, trips to the theatre and other places of interest – no boundaries.

Good provision for those with learning difficulties. Learning skills can replace a GCSE and help with dyslexia is in-house and available on a one-to-one basis.

Games, options, the arts: Notable successes on the games field at every level. Rugby, hockey and cricket for boys; hockey and netball for girls are the main team games, though a sizeable number of boys and girls take to the river and propel themselves backwards as fast as they can. Some recent successes at Henley and more local regattas, and a magnificent feat on the part of a boy who recently sculled over the Channel only 10 minutes outside the world record. A Royal/real tennis court (not many of those around), a delightful golf course as well as numerous Astroturf pitches and a huge sports hall with room for indoor cricket nets, indoor hockey, weight-lifting, dance practice rooms – everything. Newish indoor swimming pool.

The CCF is popular but not compulsory, with an exciting assault course and the opportunity for challenging expeditions; alternatively, younger pupils take part in conservation project work, while the majority of sixth formers are involved in a local partnership project such as working with disabled young people or helping teach science and languages in local primary schools.

The Canford Northam project is a more ambitious community project with an inner-city youth club in Southampton – always the outside world beckons. Nowhere is this more obvious than with the Canford Partnership which, founded with money raised from the sale of the Assyrian bas-relief, annually sends parties of young Canfordians to orphanages in India, Argentina and Tanzania. Pupils raise money over the year and then visit with practicalities and spirit, helping to build tangibly and, as importantly, build bridges of understanding and friendship. Staff and pupils are 'humbled by the experience' and feel they have a 'clearer and wider window on the world'. Again, this is not a gimmick, rather a life-enhancing experience.

Music is terrific and has been for some time. Concerts for all and by many abound; a great number play instruments and are encouraged to perform at any standard. Drama – in the hugely attractive Layard theatre, built specifically for teaching purposes but home to travelling thespians and countless home grown productions – is lively, innovative and popular. 'Anyone can get involved, from actors to lighting and sound boffins', and they do. Art flourishes in a minimalist building designed by a previous art master, offering a wide range of media from oil paintings and ceramics to glass work and objects from abandoned cars. Creativity, the courage to experiment and challenge boundaries, individuality and skilled draughtsmanship are all in evidence. The building is open at weekends.

Background and atmosphere: Dull would he (or she) be who failed to respond to the beauties of Canford and its landscaped grounds. Here, where a building of some sort has stood since the Domesday book, is a monument to the ambitions of the Guest family of GKN fame and Sir Charles Barry, architect of the Houses of Parliament inter alia. The Norman origins remain in the evocative John of Gaunt's kitchen, no longer used for the purpose, and the delicious church in the grounds, too small to take the whole school but used for smaller gatherings. The main building is 19th century at its most baronial. Eating is enjoyed within a magnificent Great Hall where in 1888 Edward, Prince of Wales, danced after a ritual slaughter of birds at a shooting party. Nowadays cafeteria meals offer a wider choice of good food with breakfasts allegedly 'amazing'. Founded in 1923, great names from the past are given to key buildings but sit lightly on the superb modern buildings dotted around 250 acres complete with wonderful arboretum, a constant source of delight and research. That, and the river with its suspension bridge and mill pond offer a whiff of Eden – as well as teaching aids. The beautiful surroundings play an integral part in this purposeful paradise and it's all only two hours by train from London. A newish teaching block includes eight classrooms for economics, business studies, classics and chemistry, ICT suite and two laboratories for physics and chemistry.

The three day houses are mixed and a day pupil told us that they feel integrated, though many go home at 6pm. The most interesting accommodation is within the main buildings – School House, for instance, has a State bedroom, wonderful old rooms and a maze of corridors. More recent house accommodation is well designed, with good chilling out areas and kitchens, computer rooms and study bedrooms for older pupils. Girls have bright and airy accommodation comprising single and double bedrooms with wash-basins, sewing machines and areas for socialising with the boys. A recent group of inspectors described the accommodation as 'outstanding', not a word that is selected lightly from their bland vocabulary.

Prefects are chosen less for their role as bloods, more for their ability to identify minorities and to care. All this supports the feeling that the aim of the school is to promote well-rounded citizens rather than slaves to league tables. The head of school is chosen after a series of interviews and prefects act as conduits between staff and pupils – no swaggering. Pleasant tuck shop known as 'the grubber', much to the delight of the press when the Assyrian bas relief was recognised as genuine, complete with holes from darts. Excellent health centre makes up for not having house matrons living in, and an impressive sixth form centre.

The overall feeling we got was of space and friendliness, with pupils ready to talk and laugh, all very happy. Special mention for the sixth former whom we discovered lolling on a sofa reading Dante on his ipod – at least that's what he claimed.

Pastoral care and discipline: The matter of child protection once more drew that rare word 'outstanding' from the inspectors, something which did not surprise our guides – 'There are so many people you can talk to if you're worried or unhappy'. Each house has a married houseparent, three tutors (one resident in each boarding house) and a matron. Bullying is very rare, though, not unusually, can be some jostling to establish pecking order among the first year. The point is, no one need feel isolated. An official counsellor and a listening service for those who feel some objectivity is required. Sixth formers choose their own tutors – not necessarily from a subject teacher – and meet regularly.

Zero tolerance policy on drugs (though our guides couldn't remember the last incident); illegal drinking, though dealt with firmly, is more of a challenge. Smoking, it is said, is no longer a problem. Senior pupils may, with permission, visit the fleshpots of Wimborne for dinner on Saturdays and are required to show restaurant receipts. Reins are lightly held but never dropped.

Pupils and parents: Not an international school nor, surprisingly, a national school. The school is 'content to remain below the radar' and pleased that the majority come from less than two hours away – 'It makes it easier to get to know the parents if they are regular visitors'. A smattering come from London and six per cent of boarders come from the Channel Isles. Some foreign nationals – a few from the far east, from Africa and Europe – but by no means the shopping trolley loads imported by some schools. Day pupils can come and go by bus, and for them occasional overnight accommodation may be offered; senior pupils may use their own cars. The school does not empty at weekends – indeed for 10 weekends of the year pupils are required to stay at school; otherwise arrangements for home leave are sensitively handled. The majority of parents come from local professions with a high preponderance of medics. Those to whom we spoke appreciated the contact they have with the school.

Entrance: Pre-assessment in year 7 leads to the offer of a conditional place. Fifty-five per cent at CE is the benchmark, though the school will exercise its discretion in favour of potential flagged up by prep school heads. Relations with prep schools are good and this year's batch of scholars came from 20 different schools – over 40 on their books. About 30 join annually post-GCSE.

Exit: Ninety-six per cent gained places at university 2013, with 89 per cent to Russell Group and 1994 institutions. Bright pupils are encouraged to set their sights at Oxbridge – 'It's a healthy challenge' – and 15 got places in 2013.

This is a school which is not overly fussed about league tables, so isn't in the business of weeding out pupils who may bring them down a little – providing they are really striving for their potential. Occasionally the school will suggest some would 'do better in a different environment', but that's usually enough to do the trick. Traditionally strong on engineering and medicine, but an increasingly wide variety of subjects are read at over 30 different universities.

Money matters: A range of scholarships is available at 13+ and into the sixth form.

Remarks: This is a very special school. Superb facilities in an almost matchlessly lovely environment; first-rate teaching with pupils who really do seem to find joy through achievement. A school of opportunities with windows open to the world outside. Unpretentious and sensitive, at ease with itself but without a trace of smugness. A school which can hold its own with the most popular in the country but one which has, perhaps, benefited from not being fashionable. The question is, for how long will that bonus remain with them?

Canon Slade CofE School

Bradshaw Brow, Bolton, BL2 3BP

• Pupils: 1,680 • Ages: 11–18 • C of E • State

Tel: 01204 333343
Email: contact@canon-slade.bolton.sch.uk
Website: www.canon-slade.bolton.sch.uk

Head: Since 2006, Canon P Williamson BSc MSc PGCE CPhys MInstP (late forties). Taught physics. Was assistant head here from 1994, moving to headship of Holy Trinity Senior School, Halifax in January 1998, returning as head in 2006. Describes himself as a practising Christian and parents say, 'He brings a real Christian influence'. Pupils remark that he always attends drama performances, 'He's so encouraging; he treats us like adults; he doesn't shout at you but tries to work with you'. That he loves the job is evident – 'To be the head of Canon Slade is the best job in the world; I'm here until I retire, I love the place'.

Academic matters: Intake from the whole ability range yet results consistently well above average – 83 per cent got at least five A*-C including English and maths at GCSE, 32 per cent A/A* grades, 2013. At A level, 58 per cent A*-B.

Performing arts particularly strong, reflecting specialist college status; top school nationally for the AVCE vocational performing arts for boys and pupils regularly hit the top five per cent of results nationally at all levels in drama and dance, as well as in modern languages. ICT results were notably disappointing in comparison, but school says they are greatly improving thanks to new head of department, new computer suites and plenty more computers around the school for use in private study. Ambitious gifted and talented programme. Target setting through all years – 'You've got to be prepared to work hard here,' say pupils, 'but they don't leave anyone behind; everyone's encouraged to do their best'. Pupils praise teaching staff, who're 'always on hand at lunch time and after school to give extra help and run extra revision classes before public exams'.

Annual 'walking on water' competition, with physics department giving teams £50 from gifted and talented budget to design and make shoes that'll race across the surface of the swimming pool. History trips to European battlefields and language exchanges with France, Germany and Spain as well as with twin schools in Germany, Spain and Japan. Latin available at both GCSE and A level, even for just one student – 'We'd be loath to give it up,' says head who, along with senior staff, dons his gown every morning for assemblies.

Games, options, the arts: Specialist college status for performing arts with extensive opportunities. Drama and dance studios with full length mirrored walls, new state-of-the-art sound recording studio with full time technician and school hall with traditional stage for renowned high standard productions. Over 20 per cent of pupils play an instrument and contribute to more than a dozen varied ensembles and Young Musician of the Year competition as part of school arts festival. 'We're sympathetic to those offered contracts with theatre companies or orchestras,' says head, 'as long as their academic life doesn't suffer.' Extensive art rooms are ripe with fruit of pupils' labours – 'You have to knuckle down in here,' they say, 'and we've got our own kiln'. Range of design and tech rooms full of beavering students and from the food tech room a view of the out-of-bounds pond that's protected habitat for an endangered gold-crested newt population.

PE offered at GCSE and A level – 'We've got fantastic sports facilities and loads of opportunities,' say pupils. New changing rooms and a state-of-the art health suite, together with two new classrooms. Half yearly sports assembly for handing out colours – some blazers groan with these. Bright, clean refurbished 17m indoor swimming pool also used by staff three times a week. Pool, floodlit Astroturf, gym and studios all used by local community. Footballer pupils enjoy workshops with Bolton Wanderers FC. National level cross-country success due in part to school's 57 acres which include 'agony hill'; national schools' finals hosted here. Several national athletes including two on Olympic cycling talent programme, a modern pentathlete and a water polo player; senior girls national biathlon champions.

Dozens of extracurricular clubs, 'The car park in early evening is full of parents collecting children from after school drama, music, sport and other clubs,' says head. Pupils also busy with D of E, Young Enterprise, community service and substantial charity fundraising. Lots of awards including Artsmark Gold, Sportsmark, Investors in People, Leading Edge Status, Excellence in Mentoring among others.

Background and atmosphere: Founded in 1855 by Canon James Slade for 'classical and moral instruction in conformity with the principles of the Church of England'. A lifesize oil still oversees the hall and the annual Founder's Day service commemorating his death is much loved by all. A girls' school opened in 1879 and the two joined in 1902. The current buildings grew up decade by decade from the 1950s as a direct grant grammar school and then a C of E voluntary aided comprehensive, with selective entry ending in 1978. Modern, airy chapel. School says significant redecoration and refurbishment – including 'state-of-the-art changing rooms' and 'new, very smart lockers' – has improved the 'grotty bits' the pupils used to complain about. Pupils are proud of their good reputation in the wider community.

Pastoral care and discipline: Distinctive Christian ethos. Full-time chaplain and team described as being 'at the heart of this community of 2,000, which is his congregation'. Each day a different form group has communion service in the side chapel and all have daily Christian assembly, form prayers or service in main chapel. School motto, Ora et Labora, the imperative forms of the Latin literally translated as 'You must pray and you must work', sets the ethos. 'It's no mistake that the prayer comes before the work,' declares the head, and pupils say, 'Oh, yes, most people are real Christians here but the Christian stuff isn't pressurised'. Ofsted said, 'Pupils' spiritual, moral and cultural development is excellent.' Pupils describe the school as caring with very little bullying. 'We have a low threshold of tolerance for poor behaviour,' says head. 'If we deal with low-level problems like undone top buttons, the rest takes care of itself. We don't tolerate a child being cheeky to a teacher, and if they were to swear at a teacher they'd be excluded.' Detentions and contacting parents are first steps, followed by isolation in school and eventually exclusion. Pupils say, 'Isolation doesn't teach anything – it just causes aggravation,' but parents like the firm hand, saying, 'The children have a healthy respect for the discipline system and the teachers.'

Sixth formers describe their common room as relaxed and friendly. Newish sixth form directorate has given students much greater say on dress codes, management, activities etc via 'student voice' of sixth form council and prefects. Numerous societies and action teams set up.

All carry ID badges which double as pre-paid cashless catering cards for breakfast, break and lunch, which pupils describe as 'very healthy – whoever heard of a tuck shop that only sells fruit?' before admitting they can buy fair-trade chocolate as well. Long outdoor queues for the canteen mean that some flout rules by eating packed lunches in playground to delight of scavenging seagulls who rake through the litter – latterly greatly reduced by sixth form eco action group working with school council.

First four years wear green blazers, year 11 graduates to black sweatshirts as transition to smart casual, 'but no denim', of sixth form. New intake, 270 in 10 forms, has outdoor pursuits bonding, lower sixth an induction day of Pennine pursuits.

Pupils and parents: Pupils come from far and wide from seven LAs – Bolton, Manchester, Salford, Bury, Blackburn with Darwen, and as far afield as Lancashire and Yorkshire. Over 1,000 travel on fleets of public and school buses and public trains, some 700 under their own or parental steam. The low percentage of ethnic minorities does not reflect the catchment areas but may, head admits, 'reflect the church-going population. Our pupils have a head start because most of them come from stable homes where their parents want them to do well'. Lower than average percentage eligible for free school meals.

Entrance: Not for those ambivalent about the Christian faith. Children from committed Christian families with a lengthy proven track record of regular church attendance stand the best chance of bagging one of the heavily over-subscribed places. Points given for church attendance as verified by an ordained minister and places offered to the 270 applicants with highest scores through LA co-ordinated system which matches offers with children's given choices. Entrance to sixth form is based on GCSE performance and not on faith criteria. Over 50 per cent of pupils stay on to sixth form taking 90 per cent of places. The rest are also oversubscribed and attract a broader ethnic mix as other faith groups are drawn to overall ethos of school.

Exit: Some 60 per cent leave after GCSEs. Ninety per cent of year 13 to university, three-quarters offered first choice, respectable number to Russell Group, one or two to Oxbridge, with good success for medicine.

Remarks: Fantastic opportunities for performing arts and deserved success from hard work across the board in a caring and unstuffy but distinctly Christian atmosphere.

The Cardinal Vaughan Memorial RC School

89 Addison Road, London, W14 8BZ

• Pupils: 920 boys, plus 130 girls in sixth form; all day • Ages: 11–18 • RC • State

Tel: 020 7603 8478
Email: mail@cvms.co.uk
Website: www.cvms.co.uk

Headmaster: Since 2011, Mr Paul Stubbings, previously deputy head, appointed after a row over admissions criteria between the school governors and the Westminster diocese – the diocese objected to the parental involvement criteria as discriminatory against poorer parents – which resulted in a purging of the governing body, injunctions and a stalemate resolved by a governors' U turn and Mr Stubbings' appointment (very popular with parents).

Academic matters: Consistently impressive results and school makes no bones about aiming for academic excellence in its comprehensive intake. School has specialist status in mathematics and IT and computing is BIG here – though some would like to see computer science on the curriculum in addition to IT. A level results 87 per cent A*-B grades in 2013. Range of subjects offered not immense but includes economics, music tech, philosophy and sociology. It has to be said that the 'newer' subjects do not attract vast numbers. School also offers applied A level in business – Bs for most. Most popular – and successful – A level subjects are maths and Eng lit – both astonishingly good. GCSEs – again not a huge range of options – French and Spanish now the only modern langs though Latin thrives and Greek is up-and-coming. Most popular subjects are engineering – a double qualification – French and ICT. Everyone takes RS. in 2013, 63 per cent A*/A grades overall – and remember this is a comprehensive school.

This degree of success is not achieved by having independent school sized classes. In the lower school class sizes are 28-30 though music, DT, art and IT groups have 20 pupils. At KS4, class sizes vary but core subjects are taught in groups of 25-30. Most sixth form classes are under 20. Girls and boys seem to achieve similarly though there are some mutterings about AS candidates being 'encouraged' to drop subjects rather than continuing to A2 if it is felt they are unlikely to do well. Accolades abound – the Vaughan is in the top 20 of just about every league table – often near the top. It is regularly named 'top Catholic comp in the country' by those who have such plaudits to give away. Parents and pupils, for the most part, add to the encomia. No-one could eulogise the school's shiny new facilities – apart from all the IT stuff – or accommodation. The level of achievement here is down to the quality of the teaching and the staff and pupils' pride in the place. We heard of 'lovely teachers', the good monitoring of progress and much high praise, especially, of the music dept. Bright pupils speak warmly of their 'inspiring' teachers – 'they are amazing – best in the business' – and they mean it.

All applicants are tested – to ensure that school takes across the ability range and to better enable banding once they arrive. School takes 'more than our fair share of statemented children' and it is a beacon of hope for those parents of children with significant difficulties, seeming, as it does, to offer real education in a compassionate community. Majority with SEN, though, are mild dyslexics and dyspraxics. Who goes where is decided, of course, by the LA but school is concerned about the sheer additional physical space taken by extra LSAs who accompany some of the children with more severe SEN. And this is understandable. Many rooms are small and rather poky and corridors are not spacious. Busy SENCo and others give in-class support but parents give mixed reports. One parent felt that her dyspraxic son's problems were picked up very late and that the support he was subsequently offered was barely adequate. Similar reports from others. School, however, tells us that such comments are 'vastly outweighed by parents delighted with our SEN arrangements'. School unashamed of its high octane essence. 'Here we have traditional, hothouse academic teaching. It can be a bit of a shock for those who come in from outside.' G and T pupils offered Greek – where else in the state system is this a growth area?

Games, options, the arts: Very little space on school premises. This is hardly uncommon in London, but it cannot help the potential for the school's sporting excellence to parallel its academic prowess that, for the most part, games depend on a coach trip 30 minutes away to Twickenham – a major part of any school day, however inspiring the location when they get there. Games, nonetheless, played with immense energy and enthusiasm and, especially on the rugby pitch, are done well. Cross-country also popular and successful – especially for the girls; rock climbing and indoor rowing equally so – four rowers offered schols to train for 2012. Football and basketball also played with vigour and rigour. Complaints of too little sport in the recent past now being remedied.

Over 30 per cent of pupils receive individual music tuition and music is a glory of the school – now enhanced by superb new space and facilities on the top floor – big rehearsal/recital rooms, lots of practice rooms and music tech facilities which must induce composing even in the tone deaf. All under a busy and smiley head of dept. Lots of ensembles include the popular Big Band. Schola Cantorum – the celebrated choir – tours and gives concerts all over the place. In London, this includes Westminster Cathedral, Westminster Abbey, St John's Smith Square, The Royal Opera House – they recently provided the boys in Turandot – The Barbican and the Queen Elizabeth Hall. Outside the UK, this includes Italy – all the grandest places in Rome – plus Spain, Greece, Holland, Germany, the USA and France. In 2007, they sang High Mass at Notre Dame. The Schola now has its own Songschool – just like in a regular cathedral choir school – in which the choir rehearses – a real boon. Drama, never a strength here and not an academic subject is, however, enthusiastically pursued and results in popular productions of, mostly, musicals. School's original main building began life as a theatre and we wondered why so little use is made of it in this way – the stage and gallery are intact, if a little dog-eared. Good art – we liked what we saw of the ceramics, sculpture, mobiles, printing et al – lively creative stuff – and equally good DT – wood, metal and plastic work. Lots of imaginative and rewarding extra-curricular trips and visits – especially for the musicians – parents glow.

Background and atmosphere: The Vaughan is located in posh Holland Park – wide, quiet streets lined by well-appointed Victorian villas and mansion blocks. Shepherd's Bush, on the other side of the monster roundabout round the corner, is a world away, whereas Kensington High Street – about 15 minutes walk the other way – seems a natural neighbour. Founded in 1914, the school is a memorial to the third Archbishop of Westminster, Herbert, Cardinal Vaughan. It began life as an independent school with 29 pupils but became a grammar school in 1944 and a comprehensive in 1977. Girls were first admitted to the sixth form in 1980 and their presence – 'an adornment to the school', according to previous head – is established. No chance of going co-ed throughout – simply no room. The original building – Addison Hall – was a musical theatre, but its exterior – possibly what attracted its purchasers – is more reminiscent of a Rinascimento palazzo in pink stone. It now boasts an entrance with highly-wrought grillwork in which the school's motto, Amare et Servire, and crest are displayed. 'The Old Building' as it is known, houses years 11-13. The 'New Building' was built in the 1960s and much added to since then. It has an attractive exterior with a pretty little garden and an impressive reception area which abuts the main hall – full of pupils on supervised private study when we visited – no 'free' periods here. DT and IT are housed in the Pellegrini Building, named after a former head. Some roomy places inside but the overall impression is of a rather cramped school with little space – especially outside – and many rather bleak areas. Most rooms have air-conditioning but we almost passed out in the heat of some of them. Few rooms or corridors have displays or much colour and the ambiance is not so much monastic as a little neglected.

Situated in these leafy, pricey avenues, you'd expect an upmarket local school population. But it isn't so. School takes from all over and the only common denominator is a commitment to the Roman Catholic faith. Previous head was wearily, but pugnaciously, defensive of the charge of being socially or academically elitist. He wrote, 'people ask why our pupils' performance goes so far beyond national averages. After all, our top results at A level and at GCSE, over the last five years, have improved six times more than national results. Is it because, as some would like to believe, we "cherry pick" pupils from privileged backgrounds? I don't think so. More than 18 per cent – almost a fifth – of those boys who achieved such staggering results at GCSE last year were on free school meals. The national average of pupils on free school meals is 14 per cent. So much for the slander that the Vaughan is socially selective.' Maybe the slander persists because the staff wear academic gowns – must be anathema to Dave Spart, head of St Jargon's, and those who pump out new brainless 'initiatives' every morning.

The life of the school is imbued with its Roman Catholic inspiration. Everywhere are photographs of pontiffs, cathedrals and the school's own choir singing in various glorious cathedrals. Year groups go on retreats at Tyburn Convent and at Farm Street and the school day and week are punctuated by regular Mass, confession, Benedictus, angelus and so on – all lessons begin and end with the Sign of the Cross and some teachers have prayers in each of their lessons – to a degree rare even in RC schools. But there is also a spirit of enquiry. Vaughan pupils address seriously 'the Dawkins Delusion', 'the problem of Free Will' and 'the Just War theory'. Philosophy pupils attend Heythrop College for talks on philosophy of religion, epistemology and ethics and theology pupils explore the history of Israel. The ethos is embraced and warmly defended by pupils when appropriate. They are aware of the privilege of being here and of the secular – and other – pressures that might have it otherwise. While most parents express great satisfaction with the school in general, we heard a few murmurs from those who are less than ecstatic. 'It's fine as long as all goes well'... 'they're not brilliant at dealing with problems'... 'they're not great at getting back to you' – (school says, 'we pride ourselves on excellent communications with parents and prompt responses to their queries') – and 'it's best for the really bright'. School warmly disputes this too. And most are truly grateful for what they receive.

Pastoral care and discipline: Discipline is tight but, by now, so well-established that it works and few transgress. Sixth formers have more latitude though their common-room is open only at breaktimes. Occasional bullying is 'firmly and speedily dealt with'. Zero tolerance of drink or drugs is seldom tested. The occasional idiot caught smoking in the streets – sixth form pupils are allowed out of school in breaks – is punished. We saw lots of Vaughan pupils out and about and they definitely do not frighten the horses. 'Old-fashioned good manners' expected and, in general, displayed. The atmosphere is orderly and we saw only quiet classes. Catholic ethos underpins everything and is palpable. Sex ed taught 'by the RS dept for the moral side and the science dept for the biological details'. Four houses – Campion, Fisher, Mayne and More. Real sense of camaraderie between pupils.

Pupils and parents: Pupils come from a wide area covering most of London, some from as far away as Hertfordshire and Surrey. Around half are from ethnic minority groups. Some 30 per cent speak English as an additional language. Here the offspring of a few of well-heeled 'old' RC families from Kensington learn alongside those of their Filipino, Portuguese or Spanish live-in domestic staff and the children of Irish immigrants from Wembley, in a context hard to find elsewhere. Parents very appreciative of parents' evenings when teachers come to find them rather than the usual ghastly queuing for a two minute slot with a glazed-eyed teacher. Notable former pupils include actors Richard Greene – Robin Hood in earlier days – and Roger Delgado, footballers Bernard Joy of Arsenal and Fulham and the last amateur to represent the England national football team, Paul Parker and Eddie Newton, novelist Helen Oyeyemi and comedian Dominic Holland. Also WWII flying aces Donald Garland VC and Paddy Finucane DSO and recent Olympic rowing gold medallists Martin Pross and Gary Herbert. Many seem, however, to have worthy careers in the City.

Entrance: Pupils come from over 50 schools. Around 725 apply for the 120 places at 11+. At sixth form, around four apply for every

place. Most of the sixth form entrants will be girls – lots from Sacred Heart – and the entrance requirements at that stage are academic, rather than devotional – As and Bs in the subjects they will study in the sixth. School has long been (in)famous for the rigour of its admissions' criteria and stories abound of devoted little church-goers being rejected on account of imperfect catechism or knowledge of parables. 'Nonsense!' bellows school. Early baptism, weekly attendance at mass, Holy Communion – all are taken for granted in applicants; no mention now of the 'family involvement' that was so contentious. Applicants split into three ability bands, 12 music places.

Exit: A regular mighty handful to Oxbridge, all doing solid subjects at real colleges. Most of the rest to heavyweight universities to do heavyweight subjects – law at King's, maths at Imperial etc and a sensible fistful to eg sports psychology at Bournemouth. A notable number to architecture and engineering. Some 20 per cent leave after GCSEs – most to join other schools, a few to employment, another few to other RC colleges.

Money matters: Voluntary aided. School asks for a voluntary contribution of £300 pa for the Governors' Fund and the vast majority stumps up – some more, some less but no-one comes after you if you don't. A few instrumental bursaries for sixth form entrants who must have reached at least grade 6 on an orchestral instrument.

Remarks: A unique opportunity, not to be missed if you can meet the requirements and stay the course. The kind of school parents everywhere cry out for and few, very few, ever find.

Caterham School

Linked school: Caterham Preparatory School

Harestone Valley Road, Caterham, CR3 6YA

• Pupils: 880 (475 boys and 405 girls), of whom 165 board • Ages: 11-18 • United Reformed Church; open to all • Fees: Day £14,991– £15,690; Boarding £27,771– £29,277 pa • Independent

Tel: 01883 343028
Email: admissions@caterhamschool.co.uk
Website: www.caterhamschool.co.uk

Headmaster: Since 2007, Mr Julian Thomas, BSc MBA FRSA (early forties). Graduated in computer science from King's College, London. Subsequently took PGCE at Queen's College, Cambridge, and MBA in educational leadership at University of Hull. Spent five years in the City with Lloyds Bank and BP but moved into teaching after 'an epiphany' at Liverpool Street station in the mid 1990s – 'I realised there was more to life than what I was doing; I wanted to make a difference'.

Before taking over at Caterham, he worked in several independent schools, including Portsmouth Grammar, where he was director of studies, and Hampton (boys' school), where he was second master. Delighted to be head of Caterham – 'I walk around the school and think, wow, what a wonderful place!' Full of enthusiasm for his task; aims to make Caterham the best it can be – 'The goalpost has moved. A few years ago we wanted to become the best co-ed boarding school in the south-east; now we are aiming to be one of the finest co-ed schools in the UK'.

He not only is young but also looks it – parents love to tell how they thought he was a sixth former when they first saw him, though such stories are probably embroidered for dramatic effect. Think fresh and enthusiastic – Tony Blair when he was popular. 'Highly capable and caring,' says ISI. Parents feel he played himself into his headship very well, took things

C

gently, not changing things for the sake of it, but has put his own stamp on the place. Collegiate approach to management and has a top-notch senior management team. Pupils like him (he squeezes in some teaching when he can, drops into classes all the time) and he's generally seen as a good ambassador for the school.

Married with two children, both pupils at the prep school next door. In his spare time 'gets a buzz from endurance activities', walking, trekking in Nepal and the like, loves sport and is qualified to coach rugby, cricket, hockey and netball. Has also written six maths textbooks.

Academic matters: Now among the UK's top independent schools, out-performing many of its more famous rivals, yet strangely still just under the radar. At GCSE in 2013, 78 per cent A*/A. At A level, one of the top 70 independent schools in the country – 88 per cent A*-B and 63 per cent A*/A.

Maths and science are stand out subjects here (triple science the norm). The biology and physics departments have received a several GSG awards for A level results over the past few years. French, German, Spanish, Latin and Greek offered to GCSE and A level. ICT taught both as a discrete subject and across the curriculum, with 620 computers for pupil use throughout the school day, all networked and with email and internet access.

However, Mr Thomas is quick to stress that academic success must not be the pupils' only achievement – school's watchwords are 'An education for life'. Parents agree that the school gets the best out of all the children – not just the super-academic. Also on the curriculum are study skills such as speed-reading, research techniques, typing, all designed to give students the edge out in the real world. The first independent school to be awarded Thinking School status by Dr Edward de Bono – too detailed to explain here, but it involves planning thinking processes using coloured hats. Children we met understood it perfectly; school offers courses to enlighten confused parents. No plans to introduce IB, but IGCSE offered in English, maths, sciences.

First class teaching team works hard to engender a passion for learning. Parents describe it as dynamic, dedicated and (again) youthful. Lessons are enjoyable and lively, not all chalk and talk. Great head of science, wearing a bright pink overall when we saw him, and pupil guides proudly announced he had new labs designed to his specification. Lots of on-going staff training and opportunities mean turnover is low. Class sizes in first three years average 20-24, dropping to 15-20 for GCSE teaching and usually eight to 12 for sixth form. All the facilities, resources, bells and whistles you would expect for the money. Oozes prestige.

Not huge call for SEN provision (a handful) but around 90 pupils have learning difficulties and disabilities. A TA for the visually impaired and some one-to-one teaching. A dyslexia specialist is available. Inclusive system of study buddies sees older students passing on their experience to the younger years – anything from straightforward subject help to other issues like time-management. Eighty or so pupils receive EAL support.

Games, options, the arts: All strong, in keeping with school's aims to develop all-rounders. Sparkling achievements on the sports field are just as impressive as the academic results. Priority sports are rugby, hockey, cricket, lacrosse and netball, with many teams winning regional awards, but lots of others on offer, from athletics to tae kwon do. Sport is taken seriously but not just for the elite – everyone encouraged to have a go.

Drama has a fairly high profile and is improving. Impressive performance space but no dedicated studio. Music next on Mr Thomas's list for development. Up to 30 per cent of pupils currently learn a musical instrument (exams can be taken) and plenty of opportunities to perform. But although lots get involved in high standard school and house productions and concerts, only handfuls take music and drama at GCSE and A

level. Better take-up of art and design, with pottery, textiles and photography offered.

Both D of E and the CCF are thriving – pupils regularly win armed forces scholarships. All told, around 35 clubs and societies, from chess to debating, kit car challenge popular. 'Put us up against any school and we'd win for sheer range of activities on offer,' challenges Mr Thomas.

Background and atmosphere: Situated in 80 acres of leafy loveliness in a wooded valley of the North Downs, south of London, just inside the M25. Approach is via a quiet residential road of substantial houses. Main school building is an attractive, Victorian, red brick building looking out onto its own impressive playing fields, hills beyond. Inside a preponderance of tiling and brick – looks nicer than that might sound. Modern science block and sixth from centre.

Boarding facilities recently upgraded. Years 7-9 in good sized, six-bedroomed rooms, thinning out as they rise through the ranks to qualify for single, ensuite accommodation by upper sixth. Ofsted pronounced the boarding offering as 'outstanding' – in fact some university halls may be a come-down. Homely atmosphere – lots of staff live in and build up good relationships with their charges. Growing requirement for flexi-boarding acknowledged and accommodated wherever possible. Boarders do really well here where their life is fun, but well-structured. Prep every night under controlled conditions and then checked – boarders get great results. Staff delighted as TVs and computer games gather dust – too much else on offer: loads of sport and special events.

All the pupils smartly turned out, business suits for sixth formers. A happy, vibrant place, where students are enjoying, rather than enduring, their days. Nice easy atmosphere – always visitors around, parents welcome, teachers used to having their classroom doors opened mid-lesson.

Pastoral care and discipline: Standards of behaviour are high ('exemplary,' says ISI) and pastoral care is top-notch, based on the principle of mutual respect. Any problems dealt with quick time and head says he would never punish a significant misdemeanour without getting to the root cause – a holistic approach. Mr Thomas says he's conscious that young people get a maelstrom of mixed messages in today's media and can get caught up in a 'cool to be cruel' culture. He sees his school as the counter-balance to that – 'I want to show the pupils that kindness and courtesy matter'. Staff set the tone, aiming to turn out 'nice people that parents and school can be proud of'. Need we add zero-tolerance of bullying, drugs and drink – all non-starters? Minor demeanours dealt with by way of warnings and gating – practical things like litter duty, rising to detention. Suspension and expulsion obviously the end game – but both are rare events. Pupils generally have good relationships with teachers and other staff. School linked to URC, but it's a light touch, no Christian exertion, all welcome.

Pupils and parents: Parents are really supportive of this place – it's not unusual for 500 spectators to support Saturday fixtures. Largely a local school – 70 per cent travel less than five miles to school – but other day pupils from up to 30 miles away (plenty of school buses and good transport links with mainline station just a 15 minute walk). Boarders from 25 different countries, including UK, but significant numbers from East Asia and Eastern European countries.

Parents from a wide mix of professions and businesses. Successful and productive parents' association has a good time raising significant sums for the school. Old Cats (boys so far, as school only fully co-ed since 1995) include Geraint Jones (organist, conductor); Angus Deayton (television presenter); Sir Alan Moncrieff (first Nuffield professor of child health); Sir Arthur James (Court of Appeal) and recently cricketers Ali Brown, David Sales and James Benning. Old Cats a big feature

– turn up at all the events, plays, fixtures, magazine launches, giving the current pupils a real sense of their school's history and traditions.

Entrance: Academically selective, mainly at 11, 13 and 16. Own exam used (English, maths and verbal and numerical reasoning) plus interview and report from current school (Common Entrance for setting at age 13). For sixth form entry, six GCSEs at grade A (grade B for existing pupils moving up).

No special skills or religious requirements; school has URC affiliation but pupils of many faiths within it. Thirty per cent of intake from state schools (plus 10 per cent to sixth form).

School's main feeder is Caterham Preparatory School, which provides around 40 pupils in year 7. Others are The Hawthorns, Hazelwood, Oakhyrst Grange, St Mary's C of E Junior School, Sevenoaks Preparatory School, New Beacon School and Copthorne School.

Exit: Around 10 per cent leave after GCSE, generally because eg drama or art specialists, or for financial reasons. All sixth form leavers to university, 10 per cent to Oxbridge, most of rest to other top tier destinations eg Bristol, Southampton, Exeter, Warwick, York etc.

Money matters: About a third of pupils receive either scholarships or bursaries. Scholarships and exhibitions awarded at 11 and 13 (academic, art, music, sports and all-rounder). At 16 academic, art, music, sport, science and drama are available. Most represent 25 per cent of fees with academic scholarships of up to 50 per cent. Boarding/international scholarships are also available. All 11+ and 13+ day pupil candidates are automatically considered for academic scholarships, but specific application forms are required for other scholarships. The number offered varies each year, but essentially funds are available equivalent to 10 school places.

School also has a bursaries scheme for children of United Reformed Church clergy, for families in the Forces or those on a low income. There is a new, fully funded sixth form bursary named in honour of slavery abolitionist William Wilberforce, who was a friend of the school's founder and a subscriber to the school, giving Caterham 10 guineas a year.

Remarks: A classic independent school – great results, large, leafy grounds, good facilities, strict discipline, polite, charming and well-informed pupils. You can see what you are paying for here. It's on the up and pulling ahead of the pack now.

Central Newcastle High School

Linked school: Central Newcastle High School Junior Dept

Eskdale Terrace, Newcastle upon Tyne, NE2 4DS

• Pupils: 600 girls, all day • Ages: 11–18 • Non-denom
• Fees: £6,918–£11,178 pa • Independent

Tel: 01912 811768
Email: cnhs@cnh.gdst.net
Website: www.newcastlehigh.gdst.net

Headmistress: Since 2006, Mrs Hilary French MA Oxon MEd PGCE NPQH (fifties). A historian. Four years as deputy head at Teesside Prep and HS, followed by five years as head. Married to Durham University lecturer with one daughter. Welcoming and approachable, she is determined to shrug off any hint of the 'little bit aloof, closed door' image she feared the school had gained. Has adopted more open approach, welcomes closer links with parents. 'I think people thought we closed the doors and got on with it – don't question us. We are very different now.' Masterminded a £5m plus revamp which also physically opened up the school, particularly the entrance. Knows every girl by name and aims to produce confident girls able to achieve their potential. On the board of Centre for Evaluation and Monitoring, which 'helps me keep a finger on the pulse of education'; current president of the Girls' Schools Association.

Appreciates that the girls may well have a 'portfolio' career, but believes that a good, sound education built on moral values, respect, courtesy and hard work will stand them in good stead. Attitude is to build self-confidence, celebrate successes and the rest will follow. Loves the buzz of coming to school and meeting the girls and working with them and their parents. Girls and parents like her. 'She is very warm and approachable and that now sets the tone for the school,' says a parent.

Will become head of Newcastle High School for Girls when it opens in 2014, a merger with Newcastle upon Tyne Church High School.

Academic matters: Works within the A level system but has an extended enrichment programme which includes the AQA Baccalaureate. Reviews curriculum every year to meet needs of new intake.

Four class intake and all the way through from year 7, roughly 20-25 per class, 25 maximum. Smaller groups for sets and options. Setted in January year 7 for maths and year 8 in English, speedy set for languages, who then take the relevant GCSE early. Beyond that no further streaming. 'We are already selective so they start out at a certain level and we don't want to move them around too much. We don't want any of the "not in the top set" attitude that can make you feel a failure.'

SENCo, whose knowledge is 'encyclopaedic', carries out individual assessments and girls with learning difficulties are supported. Formal extra support comes at extra cost, less formal support not charged for.

Huge variety of subjects on offer at A level; the best girls' school in the area for GCSE/A levels. In 2013, 73 per cent A*/A grades at GCSE. Philosophy for all. Strong classics; outstanding results in the sciences, which explains why many go off to be doctors and vets – more than half take three separate sciences at GCSE. Good library, computers all over. Exchanges to France, Germany and Spain and languages equally strong; digital language lab in a separate building. New library, art school, ICT resource centre, sixth form common room, English school (strong success in debating) and an additional state-of-the-art science lab. sixth form work area; 85 per cent A*-B, over 60 per cent A*/A at A level, 2013.

Improvements to outside grounds have improved the girls' leisure facilities. 'We are not a hothouse that crams girls – you can see that by walking around. We give them 100 per cent commitment, build their confidence. Success comes from that. We are an academic school, but you can almost take the academic side for granted. It is the rest that makes the school. We want the girls to be part of something that is exciting, vibrant and lively,' says head. Parents agree, 'The school provides a good, rounded education.' Students appreciate their opportunities and the help they get, 'The teachers are fantastic – you feel like you want to go round and thank them one by one'.

Happy with single sex success, 'Egos are fragile and the girls need the space to have a go, make mistakes without living up to any stereotypes. When they go on to university they are streets ahead of their co-educational sisters in confidence and ability to tackle the outside world, not timid, shy girls'.

Games, options, the arts: Very strong in sport; ethos of everyone gets a turn, but success on a national stage is celebrated – examples include hockey and netball tour in South Africa; national representation in netball, cross country, biathlon, swimming, squash.

Dance now offered throughout the school including at A level; newish dance studio. Recent development linked the music school to the super sports hall and created new drama studio. 'Music is stunning,' says the head. Subject has own building with keyboards, a fine wigwam-shaped recital hall and recording studios. Drama includes regular full school productions played at city centre professional theatre. Dazzling arts curriculum: ceramics, jewellery making, photography, fine art etc and a lot of fabric work. Girls run their own fashion shows.

D of E very popular, one of the largest participating schools in the area; navy and army CCF with field days and camps. World Challenge trips to Tanzania, Chile and India; sports tours to New Zealand and Australia; ski trips to Europe and the US.

Background and atmosphere: Founded in 1895 and set in a selection of new-builds and converted Victorian villas. Big investment in opening up the school has paid dividends, now less stuffy. 'I think environment is important because you spend a lot of time here and it needs to be fresh, tidy and modern.' Away from main building, a former synagogue with fabulous stained window gives stunning light for art department – filled with art and models. Close to metro station/main roads for ease of access. Stage used to take up half the hall and has been removed to allow a whole school assemblies, also a multi-use space to include dining at lunchtime. Recent ISI Inspection report littered with 'excellent' and 'outstanding'.

Merging with Newcastle upon Tyne Church High School in September 2014 to form Newcastle High School for Girls – a flagship school for the Girls' Day School Trust.

Pastoral care and discipline: Excellent PSHE with full new programme; year heads in charge of pastoral care and monitoring progress, keeping an eye on individual ups and downs and safeguarding the 'quality of life', plus form teacher/tutor, plus qualified counsellor. Anti-bullying policy – but it 'isn't a problem', as girls have respect drummed into them from the off. Merits and demerits promote the good and punish the bad. Girls educated about the risk of drugs.

Pupils and parents: Solid middle class intake from throughout region as far as Alnwick, Co Durham; loads of professionals and very wealthy parents, but no snobbery in the playground. Rich mixture of regional accents and healthy mix of different cultures. Working hard to engage parents more – 'You want to be invited in to see what your daughters are doing at times when you can get there' (head). Using pastoral system to underpin better communication – heads of year and form teachers take the lead. Email is a favoured communication tool for 'hard-pressed, working parents'.

Transition from junior to secondary is sensitively handled with little ones offered an 'experience day' and then 'big sister' sixth formers help them settle in. 'They very soon blossom from the opportunities that they get and are soon coming in via the metro like all the others' – head. We picked up that it isn't so quite so easy to settle in if you are joining the school from a different junior school and not from CNHS's own. School says in response that it 'organises several induction days and team building exercises to make sure that the girls new to CNHS get to know all the other girls and settle in quickly.'

Articulate and friendly girls. School uniform, flat-soled shoes, all very smart. Sixth form in their own clothes, though some students would like uniform there too. 'I would prefer to be in uniform; I think it's nice when everyone looks the same,' a sixth former told us – interesting.

Entrance: Natural progression from own junior school and competition for other places is fierce. Entrance exam and interview to get in at year 7. If 10 leave post-GCSE, then 10 more come in.

Exit: Under 10 per cent leave post GCSE. After A level, five to Oxbridge in 2013; also York, Birmingham, Edinburgh, Nottingham and Leeds. Medicine a popular career choice, plus other sciences, regular stream to art colleges.

Money matters: GDST funds bursaries (all means-tested annually).

Remarks: Having lost the 'aloof' accusation that apparently affected the school, pretty much doing everything right. Produces confident, bright and articulate girls without the 'like' and 'whatever' attitude of others of their age-group. Marvellous.

Centre Academy

92 St John's Hill, London, SW11 1SH

- Pupils: 50 boys and girls; all day • Ages: 8–19 • Non-denom
- Fees: £24,000–£38,000 pa • Independent

Tel: 020 7738 2344
Email: info@centreacademy.net
Website: www.centreacademy.net

Principal of the Centre Academy Schools: Since 2007, Dr Duncan Rollo BA MA PHD (sixties), born in Scotland, raised in the USA. A professor of English in the States, he returned to the UK some 21 years ago. Awarded postdoctoral fellowship LSE; has penned numerous articles on various aspects of education and written three books on effective communication.

Popular with parents, personable and empathic with a can-do approach that, say parents, has made a real difference. Knowledgeable and charming, an expert on SEN matters, he is also refreshingly honest – if mistakes are made or something needs improving he takes it on board.

Head teacher: Since 2011, Mrs Vikki Langford BA MA, highly experienced in SEN and holds a variety of qualifications, including graduate certificates in dyslexia and Asperger's Syndrome. Particularly interested in the use of language within the world of autism.

Academic matters: Small classes averaging five or six pupils enable group work as well as individual teaching. Every effort is made to adapt the curriculum to the needs of the individual with timetables monitored daily by tutors. Broadly follows the national curriculum to year 9 (age 13), thereafter GCSE, USA high school diploma or vocational courses – whatever suits; the continuously assessed American system works particularly well.

A well-regarded work experience programme runs with additional guidance provided by Connexions, and university applications are wholly successful. Own in-house language and occupational therapists and all staff attend regular specialist training sessions. Pupils are confident about their learning – in recent years almost all have achieved A-C in GCSE English. The quality of teaching is on the up – that's not just our observation: a recent Ofsted inspection highlighted some outstanding elements.

Games, options, the arts: Annual trips to adventure camps, places of interest and, for older students, overseas. No on-site sports facilities, so pupils make full use of the local sports centre and nearby playing fields. Drama important, not just for fun but for supporting language and communication skills too, with the neighbouring church hall providing much-needed space for the expressive arts. Art studio is a hive of activity – traditional drawing, painting and sculpture offered alongside weaving and embroidery; plenty of opportunities to develop fine motor skills and concentration. Regular clubs include arts, sports and community service offerings.

Background and atmosphere: Founded in 1974 and housed in an attractive Edwardian, but small, building with limited outdoor space close to a busy road. A well-equipped ICT room, small science lab, art room and a new library are evidence of a continuing programme to improve facilities. Welcome plans are afoot to replace part of the property with theatre facilities and a gym. Had some bumpy times, probably not helped by the size of the building and its location, but the arrival of Dr Rollo and more recently Mrs Langford have calmed the waters. An active school council is helping to revitalise the community spirit and a smart new uniform promotes pride and identity.

Recently opened a new school, Centre Academy East Anglia, near Bury St Edmunds. Similar ethos and programmes, but also has a boarding facility for 8-16 year olds.

Pastoral care and discipline: At the heart of the pastoral care system is a preventative approach to everyday problems – everyone has a mentor whom they meet with three times a day. Many of the pupils have not fared well in other schools and so clearly appreciate the friendly staff; one boy confided, 'This is the first school where I have felt confident enough to ask the staff questions without fear of getting into trouble'.

Life skills are an integral part of the curriculum, with pupils encouraged to use their initiative and get involved, hence the recently-opened pupil-run tuckshop for break times. A highly experienced counsellor runs an impressive support team. Home-school links considered essential; masses of help given with organisational skills, and homework can be completed at school during the daily prep period.

Pupils and parents: Complete mix from all over London and home counties, but with an international flavour – mostly British with a few from USA, Europe and the Middle East. Around 70 per cent are funded by LAs.

Entrance: Admission from 9+ years, then as places become available; caters for a range of needs including milder autistic spectrum disorders, dyslexia/ADD/dyspraxia and complex processing difficulties. Eccentricities can be managed but not aggressive or violent behaviour. We've heard mutterings from a few parents that the school isn't always receptive when making initial contact and can be 'funny' about sending out information. We raised this with Dr Rollo, who promised to investigate – his concern clearly about the distressed parent who is seeking a school like this, rather than any over-riding marketing concerns. He did note that the prospectus is not sent to parents until he has had a brief phone chat to ascertain the appropriateness of the school for the child. Officially, first step is to have a conversation with Dr Rollo to check the school is what you are looking for. If all agree it may be suitable, the next stage is to send in the relevant documentation, eg medical and psychological reports. The family will then meet with Dr Rollo, and the child will be invited to spend two or three assessment days. Assessment is two-way, to see how the child copes and to ensure the school will be able to meet particular needs. If the trial period does not work out, Dr Rollo will try to assist with finding an alternative placement for the child.

Exit: A few return to mainstream schooling before the end of Key Stage 3. Eighteen plus mostly to university, odd one to FE college; UK universities have been happy to accept the four-year USA high school diploma as an equivalent to GCSE and A level.

Remarks: Special strength is its wholly individual approach and dedication to preparing pupils for their future and beyond. A unique school that recognises one size definitely does not fit all.

Channing School

Linked school: Channing Junior School

Highgate, London, N6 5HF

• Pupils: 415 girls, all day • Ages: 11–18 • Non-denom (Unitarian)
• Fees: £15,255 pa • Independent

Tel: 020 8340 2328
Email: admissions@channing.co.uk
Website: www.channing.co.uk

Headmistress: Since 2005, Mrs Barbara Elliott MA PGCE (early fifties) a Cambridge linguist. Taught previously at St Albans Girls, St Columba's College (boys), East Barnet comprehensive, Aberdeen College of Commerce and Haberdashers' Girls – an impressively varied career. She is relaxed, engaging, sophisticated, capable, retaining a faint Lancastrian directness in her voice; the proud mother of four sons and someone who clearly relishes the charge of so many 'lovely' girls. Has a very level-headed view of her school – 'It's an intellectual place but we're not ferociously competitive. Everyone can try everything – they're not stopped from doing things just because they're not good at them'. 'Mrs Elliott is wonderful' is pupil and parental consensus.

Academic matters: Trad academic curriculum – everyone takes two Englishes, maths, science and a lang at GCSE; popular options are art, business and communications, geography, history and Spanish. Exceptional results in English lang and additional science; 85 per cent A*/A grades overall in 2013. Teaching reckoned excellent across the curriculum and nice small classes.

Again, no surprises at A level – 20 options, economics well-established and exceptionally successful; the teachers are examiners and 'they know how to deliver'; 96 per cent A*-B, 74 per cent A*/A in 2013. Apparently, the first girls' school to offer an AS in financial studies. Other popular subjects are English and maths, but no slouches among the disciplines. German, Latin and Greek survive, art flourishes and science numbers are highly respectable – clearly no fitting a mould here.

Staff very much given their head to choose the syllabuses they feel best suit their pupils – IGCSEs now taken in English, sciences and languages – and encouraged to pursue their own continuing education, always a good idea. ICT embraced enthusiastically with suites of Apple Macs and girls produce 'unbelievably sophisticated presentations and assemblies'.

No-one with a statement but around 22 girls with an IEP, all supported by additional learning co-ordinator. Most have mild dyslexia or processing difficulties. Everyone screened on entry but 'our classes are so small the staff pick up quickly on any problems'. No withdrawals and girls 'access guidance and support' in lunchtimes and breaks. Wheelchairs would be difficult here as main school building is on five floors with narrow stairways and no lift. Apparently no-one hitherto with an ASD – 'So far they haven't applied'.

Games, options, the arts: Most done on site – PE mostly in the main school hall, has courts and pitches, though the girls also walk to Parliament Hill and Stanhope fields for broader pastures. No cavernous sports hall yet – major building project in progress to provide a new sports hall, music school and performing arts theatre – but good multi-gym and, all in all, no deprivation of facilities.

Lovely relaxed art studios at the top of the building with unique views right across London. Textiles, computer graphics, dark room, printing, drawing and painting – all with a rare freedom and sense of exploration. We saw no prescribed, formulaic work here – much inventive and witty. We liked, especially, the sculptures made out of white straws – a brilliant skeletal snake and a very scary skull. Music reportedly exceptional; lots learn individual instruments and are genuinely enthusiastic – sixth formed their own a capella choir recently, just for fun. 'They have wonderful instrumental teachers,' enthuse parents. 'They fasten onto what an individual child could be good at and nurture it.' Drama a major school preoccupation – good, lively productions with mass involvement, also studied eagerly up to GCSE and A levels.

The Highgate location is a dream for luring in visiting speakers – in the week we visited had played host to Carol Ann Duffy and Kazuo Ishiguro. Diane (Kindertransport) Samuels was writer-in-residence at time of our visit and school now appoints its own 'poet laureate' – not, we understand, rewarded with the traditional butt of sack but £200 to spend at High Tea of Highgate: sounds good. Clubs galore, very much following the current enthusiasms of girls or staff. 'It's whatever we've got and,' says head, 'whatever you want. If there's an appetite for something we're very happy to run it.' Sixth form girls would like more opportunities, they told us – once-weekly enrichment classes enliven their studies but, seemingly, they have immense appetites for new things and could take more. Duke of Edinburgh Award pursued with as much gusto as everything else – 14 (out of 38) year 13 girls taking the gold award when we visited. Lots of charity activities which combine do-gooding with fun. 'The school really promotes initiative,' girls told us.

Background and atmosphere: Occupies a considerable frontage along Highgate Hill, yards down from the shops and easy-peasy if you live anywhere in this chic and desirable London village. In 2010, it celebrated its 125th anniversary and has a fascinating history. Founded in 1885 by a Unitarian minister and two of his congregation – daughters of a banker and Egyptologist – for the education of the daughters of Unitarian ministers, it remains the only Unitarian school in the country. Unitarianism, which originated in Hungary, fosters liberalism, religious tolerance and democracy and its tenets still inform the school's atmosphere today, though Unitarians themselves are thin on the ground. The present head of RE is a female Unitarian minister. 'If I come up against a sticky problem, I will sometimes look at what the Unitarians said,' says Mrs Elliott. The school was named after an American – William Ellery Channing – who, Mrs Elliott informed us, 'has a lot of useful things to say about education and women's rights, and the school always listens to extracts from his lectures on our Founder's Day in early July'.

The main building itself is attractive internally, though a rabbit warren away from the few spacious rooms – you go up and down narrow staircases and through little corridors that must take some time to learn. Plenty of remnants of the gentlemen's houses the school buildings once were – good marble fireplaces, elegantly paned windows and cornicing here and there – but it feels cosy and homely and lively displays of girls' art everywhere which warm the heart as one scurries along.

Library is housed in a good, light room overlooking the high street – modern furniture, airy and well-stocked. We loved the ceramic models of shops on the High Street behind the librarian's desk. Three other buildings on site house the main hall, classrooms, the sixth form centre with kitchen and separate canteen – we have never seen so many coffee mugs anywhere – IT suite, gym/theatre and sports facilities.

Reasonable amount of outside space given village location, and a rather tragic small garden with a greenhouse and chicken run. But we did visit in late November – 'If you come in the summer it's amazing,' girls assured us. And Mrs Elliott confirms that the organic garden and chickens have fed the real appetite the girls have to become 'greener'.

Pastoral care and discipline: House system recently reintroduced here as elsewhere – always a giggle for this ancient writer, who recalls the abandonment of such things in the '60s when they were seen as reactionary and divisive. 'We love it!' bubble the girls. 'You meet so many girls in other years and it's such a good way to get everyone more friendly' – competitiveness here is clearly less than ruthless. Palpably friendly relations between staff and girls and a relaxed and collaborative feel pervades lessons. Girls evidently glad to be here and seldom rock the boat. 'My daughter had a problem,' a mother told us, 'and the school was magnificent. I cannot speak too highly of how they dealt with it.'

Pupils and parents: Mostly local but they come from all over north and central London as well as Herts and Middlesex. Predominantly white middle class, but a good sprinkling of everyone else too and everyone melts and blends happily together.

Old girls include Baroness Cox, Peggy Vance, Tanya Moseivitch, Harriet Sergeant, Eileen Hulse and Princess Sarvath of Jordan.

Entrance: In addition to the 20-odd who come up from the junior school, takes 60 external candidates at 11+; around 350 apply via the North London Consortium of Schools' entrance exams. About 120 places offered. Joiners from all the local preps and primaries – from around 100 schools. Head or member of senior team meets all prospective parents. At 16+, minimum of six Bs needed including A*/A in A level subjects. Well worth trying for a sixth form place here and many do. Occasional places occur and school keeps a list of hopefuls whom they contact and assess as appropriate.

Exit: A few leave each year for co-ed schools or sixth form colleges (and some scoot back pretty quick.) Thereafter, to serious courses in good places – 2013 five to Oxbridge; Bristol, Leeds, Nottingham and Edinburgh also popular. Several economists, English also popular, but otherwise they cover the range.

Money matters: Academic and music scholarships up to 10 per cent of tuition. Bursaries up to 100 per cent of fees – means-tested.

Remarks: 'Never forget,' reads the text over the sixth form centre, 'life is expecting much of you and me.' Thus said Miss Matilda Sharpe, one of the founding sisters. Its gentle exhortation characterises this school in which all is relished, much achieved and nothing forced. A parent told us, 'They get their Oxbridge places but in a different way.' Hard to imagine a better start for an outgoing, lively-minded girl.

The Charter School

Red Post Hill, London, SE24 9JH

- Pupils: 1100, 610 boys, 525 girls • Ages: 11–18 • non-denom
- State

Tel: 020 7346 6600
Email: info@charter.southwark.sch.uk
Website: www.charter.southwark.sch.uk

Head Teacher: Since September 2013 Mr Christian Hicks.

Academic matters: In 2013, 72 per per cent of pupils got 5+ A*-C grades at GCSE, which is excellent given the range of children, with 30 per cent of grades A*/A. Focus on learning and achievement at all levels – many children have feelings of minimal self-worth, though the most able pupils do as well at GCSE as in many selective schools. It's not enough to be a good teacher here – you must have an amazing range of skills to motivate children. Many of the staff are outstanding and choose to be here despite more lucrative offers elsewhere – job satisfaction must be very high. Most are in their 20s and 30s (the older ones are those in management positions), some have only ever worked at The Charter School, others have come from a variety of establishments including business and industry. The Charter School has been declared outstanding twice in a row by Ofsted.

Class size is around 25 at KS3, drops to 22 at KS4 and, in the sixth form, ranges from six to 20+. Everyone is setted from year 7 in English, maths, science and MFL. Bespoke streaming in years 10 and 11. Subject study always has a practical aspect: in English, when looking at poetry from different cultures, you might kick off with a two-minute interview of your neighbour to find out where they come from – with the reassuring discovery that very few children or members of staff, whether black or white, have a parent of wholly English descent.

School zones dedicated to different subjects, eg humanities, citizenship, science, maths, communications. Latin available and Mandarin offered to around 180 pupils in KS3, now extended to KS4. Citizenship classes strong. At A level in 2013, 60 per cent A*-B grades. School now offers the Extended Project Qualification with 67 per cent of projects graded A*-B in its first year.

Practical links with local businesses encourage realistic choices after school. The school has won every business and enterprise competition that it has entered in the past two years – flyers for The Charter's own Dragon's Den were pasted everywhere when we visited. Strong business links with King's College Hosptial, PwC, SJ Berwin and IPC Media being key partners. Mentor scheme for students from year 10 upwards, with over 100 business mentors offering support. Science is very strong with excellent results in triple and single science subjects.

Experiencing teaching from the other side of the desk through peer-to-peer mentoring is very popular here. Pupils see the effort that goes into preparing and evaluating a lesson and the value of clear target-setting – encourages empathy and concentration. This takes place in English, business, maths, science, languages and art. Language Leaders in year 7 teach French and Spanish to local primary school pupils, and Sports Leaders in all year groups help out at a range of primary schools.

Parents of children with SEN see the school as a place where their kids will be supported whatever their needs – the school has full wheelchair access. The Charter takes about five per year group though successful SENDIST appeals may push this number up. There is nonetheless, great tolerance among the pupils of their peers' complex needs – if it is explained to them that a boy might cry out without warning, they just take it in their stride. The library is light and well-equipped with different areas for KS3, KS4 and sixth form – SEN students and their LSAs can also work in this space. There are lots of books on CD and tape and listening posts with beanbags (memorably, an ADHD student became so relaxed listening to a story that he curled up on one and nearly fell asleep).

Games, options, the arts: Sports facilities have been transformed from the worst to among the best across Southwark state schools; school leases neighbouring playing fields and new changing rooms. Football very strong (links with Millwall, Fulham and others) and rugby and cricket getting stronger – beating Dulwich College being the goal (a tall order, given the regular practice on gleaming pitches that the private school provides). Strong links with Dulwich Cricket Club – the school's first team were Southwark Champions in 2012 and i2013. Top class coaches run after-school clubs in eg table tennis, basketball and triathlon boxing, tennis and girls rugby. Well-connected parents provide opportunities such as swimming club at JAGS. This has resulted in students representing their country in table tennis, swimming and cycling. D of E offered from year 10.

When we visited, the GCSE art show was being hung in the entrance atrium, and all manner of people – from facilities manager (painting a stand) to the head (had his eye on a new painting for his office) – were involved. A fashion show was planned on a catwalk around the paintings to showcase the textiles. Impressive progression of work and peer-to-peer mentoring in art classes. Music department has plenty of keyboards and hundreds of children have private lessons; percussion is particularly popular. Year 7 children can win scholarships to pay for individual music lessons, and Southwark Youth Orchestra is in residency. Whole school (including staff) takes part in a yearly production (most recently Romeo and Juliet). Hall, a smaller, dedicated theatre and drama studio used for productions.

Background and atmosphere: One hundred metre drive (no smoking on this either) off Red Post Hill up to security gates of school (everyone has a swipe card for ID which also enables them to pay for or get free school meals) which is shared with JAGS's sports ground. A school has been on this site (right by North Dulwich train station) for years but, after being closed due to poor behaviour in two previous incarnations, this one came about in 2000 after an 18-month campaign by local parents. They wanted a local community school that would give an education to rival independent neighbours James Allen's Girls' School (JAGS), Dulwich College and Alleyn's.

The building has been revamped (rather than rebuilt), meaning that the hot pink walls of the entrance cohabit with the impressive dedicated reception area. The canteen has been refurbished and is bright and airy. Pupils pay for meals using the latest payment-recognition technology. The courtyard has also been revamped. Classrooms are light and clean, the corridor floors have been re-linoed in bright colours and very little graffiti to be seen, but still some points which suggest the school was designed more as a middle-class planner's fantasy rather than thorough detailed analysis of its pupils' needs. The site is compact (the playing fields were sold off in the 1980s, so now girls from JAGS play lacrosse just over the fence…) but the available space is being re-assigned with input from the school council, including the installation of an outdoor gym.

Involvement of the pupils in the running of the school is obviously vital to its atmosphere: this ranges from children conducting interviews with prospective teachers, through their re-design of the school uniform and building use to their evident ease of communication with the current teaching body. It's a south London hub school for student leadership, with year councils and a vigorous and positive school council – no political apathy here; everyone votes. It's also a hip place for teachers to work, so a lot of young staff who have their own social life (based around Dulwich Village and East Dulwich). You hardly hear a member of staff shouting – you have to like children to work here and if you don't, you won't last long.

A transparent-walled cyber café is shared by sixth formers and staff and is in use at all times of the day. The main dining room seats 180 and the queues and sittings are self-organised. Twenty-five per cent eat packed lunches outside in the adjacent courtyard under the 1970s mosaic or in the main assembly hall, which has specially-designed tables for the purpose. Each year has a 20 minute assembly weekly and a key stage one twice a term – no full school gathering.

This school aims (according to Ofsted and locals, successfully) to create a haven of peace/calm/civilisation for children whose journey home may often involve interactions with those from less disciplined schools and those who may have been excluded. For some children there are few rolemodels for manners or educative application in their home environment.

Pastoral care and discipline: Complex behaviour management system with non-teaching behaviour officers as well as an inclusion manager who helps pupils reassess their attitudes to learning and behaviour. Three learning mentors are linked closely to the behaviour manager and two separate pupils' support units for KS3 and 4. Children are given three warnings in class before being sent out – at this point both teacher and pupil have to go through a process of restorative conferencing. The hierarchy of discipline goes through year leaders to directors of learning (one each for KS3, 4 and sixth form) and the head only deals with exclusions. Basically, pupils can't just be thrown out from this school if their attitude does not fit the ideal work ethic; skilled tactics must be employed instead – they are, and they are working. In-house counselling service available to deal with less noisy problems.

Hoodies and caps are banned, taking away a layer of anonymity and disguise from teenagers. One stud per ear, no mobiles or mp3s and all staff addressed as Sir or Miss. Inflexible line on drugs, violence and smoking: after being caught smoking, a pupil must report to a meeting room on entry and exit to the school, and if they continue after that they will be excluded. Staff barred from smoking on site too. School police officer shared with Alleyn's and JAGS (every Southwark secondary school – state or independent – has one assigned) present for part of every school day. Multi-agency contact (with YoT, CAMHS, social services etc), an educational welfare officer and preventive activities like circle time and an anti-bullying project.

Pupils and parents: 70 per cent from Dulwich Village and East Dulwich (privileged) and the rest from the neighbouring estates; 50 per cent white with majority of the non-white Afro-Caribbean or African – few Asians. With a near 50 percent gender split, boys and girls happily mix and share successes and feel very prepared for adult life when they leave. Complete range of ability in the children, over three per cent with statements. Participation in the Black Pupils' Achievement Programme brought up the question of how to groom people to stand for election to the board of governors – the confidence issue is not just restricted to pupils

Entrance: Biggest group from Dulwich Hamlet Junior School (The Charter takes more of their year 6 – about 75 – than any other school), and four other main primaries. Totally oversubscribed (1200 applications for 180 places) with the head's secretary very experienced in dealing tactfully with desperately keen parents. Transition methods are held up as a model example locally.

Exit: Virtually all stay on for sixth form or go to Southwark College for more vocational options or a change of environment. Sixth form has reached full home-grown capacity and everyone who applied for university got a place (98 per cent to their first choice). Many to Russell Group as well as Royal Academy of Music, Royal Veterinary College and medical schools. Two to Oxbridge in 2013.

Remarks: One ex-head who went on to advise the government, another head-hunted for a fresh city academy, a local MP who is now shadow minister for the Olympics and London, a BBC documentary about discipline in the classroom – this school is held up as an example in many worlds. It is a truly comprehensive school and parents praise the commitment of teachers to getting the best out of individual brains. The pupils look you in the eye, are sparky, involved and really grow during their time here. A small number enter with some pretty big problems, but when they leave they are all good citizens.

Charterhouse

Godalming, Surrey, GU7 2DX

- Pupils: 665 boys; 135 girls in sixth form. All board except 31 day boarders and 29 day pupils in the new Sixth Form House
- Ages: 13–18 • C of E • Fees: Day £23,865 pa; Boarding £32,925 pa
- Independent

Tel: 01483 291501
Email: admissions@charterhouse.org.uk
Website: www.charterhouse.org.uk

Head Master: Since January 2014, Mr Richard Pleming, previously head of Wrekin College. in Shropshire. A Cambridge scholar, he has taught at English at Eton, St Paul's Boys and St Edward's Oxford. He is married to Rachel Crowther, a doctor and novelist, and they have five children.

Academic matters: Brainier and brainier – 2013 saw 78 per cent of (I)GCSE grades A*/A (42 per cent A*). Has bravely embraced IGCSEs – thought by many educationalists to be superior to GCSEs – in English, all sciences, maths and history. Maths, history and economics vie for most popular choice among A level students, followed by all three sciences and English. The school's dissatisfaction with A levels (not rigorous enough, inconsistent marking, not convinced by the AS/A2) has caused it to look about for alternatives. Now many departments teach the Cambridge Pre-U and all public exams are taken terminally, freeing up the summer term of the lower sixth for teaching, and the IB offers an alternative for those wanting a broader course of study. Amalgamated results are available on the school website but it will not give us separate grades for the three alternatives.

Frank about being academic first and foremost. Two hours' prep per evening in the first years and builds from there. We are told that the average class size in the lower school is 16.61 (not to be confused with 16.60 or 16.62), though they can go as high as 24. Sixth form more intimate. Fifty-two teachers have been at the school over 10 years – amazing what subsidised housing will do for staff retention – but lots of important recent appointments.

Around 60 pupils have mild SEN; one pupil statemented. An English teacher is in charge of SEN – mainly mild dyslexia, which head notes is common among the scholars. So SEN not a bar to achievement here, but certainly not a school one would seek out for a child with learning difficulties.

Games, options, the arts: A football school – Charterhouse, recent winner of the ISFA Boodles Cup, is credited with inventing the art of dribbling, which emerged because boys were confined to playing their ball game within the cloisters. 'It's such a relief not to have rugby-worship ruining everyone's life,' said a mother with a second son elsewhere. For a traditional school, enlightened when it comes to games choices. 'Yearlings' must trudge through the major sports but even they take part in a minor sport each term. From then on choice is paramount – 'I gave up hockey in my second year,' our guide told us – unless you are required to play for a school team. Variety of sports on offer really is unbeatable and includes riding, rackets, rowing and even a little rugby for sixth formers (one school rugby team). Plenty of inter-house activity and A-F school teams means that not only the superstars get to take part. Girls' main sports are hockey, lacrosse and netball. Sports hall that was state of the art when built over a decade ago now looks – well, state of the art.

Eager to celebrate culture as much as sport; you can now win house colours for art, music, drama and every Under School pupil must attend three cultural events per term. Head of music has raised the standard of choral music enormously and is well liked. One of the few public schools that can cope with a genuinely talented musician but, if your child wins a music scholarship, be aware that the time commitment will be immense – for some 'unmanageable'. Everyone happy with the art department at the moment, though pupils described it as free and innovative while management stressed its focus on good old drawing and painting. The director of art has won the BP Portrait Award. Photography also very good. Ben Travers theatre no longer as impressive as it once was, now that so many schools have built similar versions, but still an asset. Much competition each year to be chosen as part of the school's delegation to the Model United Nations in the Hague. D of E and CCF, of course. The Royal Marines Section has won the prestigious (and very tough) Pringle Trophy three times; the RAF Section has camped in the US and South Africa.

Background and atmosphere: Founded, together with an almshouse, in 1611 by wealthy businessman Thomas Sutton on site of an ancient Carthusian monastery, hence Carthusians. Moved to the current site atop a hill just outside Godalming in 1872. Public schools are always torn between the competing necessities of saving money (this is a school) and appearing elegant (this is a lifestyle) but Charterhouse manages to exude good taste at almost every turn, barring the odd plastic chair. Gothic spires, turrets and mellow stonework; cricket pitches flat as a mirror. Girls admitted into sixth form since 1971, as was the vogue, but one of the few such schools not to then extend co-education down to age 13 (and emphatically will not be doing so).

Loaded with historical touches, eg cloisters built as memorial to former pupils who died in the Boer War, main school chapel built in 1920s to commemorate 700 Carthusians who died in the Great War. We note, however, that the Charterhouse Museum no longer features on the school tour – most of the treasures from antiquity that it housed were sold to fund the rebuilding of the (beautiful) library. Hoping to create an endowment to ensure school can not only prosper but also admit able pupils of modest means including 25 'public benefit boys'. Also considering slight increase in the number of sixth form girls.

Pastoral care and discipline: List of school rules informs us that a 'sack attack' and 'debagging' are both unacceptable. Rules regarding prep: 'Should a beak not arrive at a hash you should remain and work quietly for the remainder of the hash. At the next strike of the school clock, it is the duty of the member of the division highest in alphabetical order to inform both the beak in the nearest hashroom and the headmaster's secretary of the beak's absence.' Quite. School also publishes exceptionally clear statement of principles and practice that lays out every detail about how the school works in less than three pages (much less entertaining to read). Twelve houses including new-ish sixth form house, Fletcherites. Saunderites, Verites, Gownboys and Girdlestoneites are in the heart of things in the original school buildings. The New Houses, a collection of modernistic multi-storey '70s blunders, have stoically weathered the decades – and have been rewarded by coming back into style, or nearly. Boys fiercely loyal to their houses and all think theirs best. Girls do prep and socialise in their ('boys') house (one upper sixth girl is currently head of her house) but leave around 10pm to go home to their boarding accommodation. Upper sixth girls all board in Chetwynd: extremely nice; all individual bedrooms. Lower sixth girls in one of four homely houses – rotate each term. Boys not allowed anywhere near.

Girls wear attractive black skirt suits and the occasional black trouser suit. Many come from all-girls' schools and appreciate being able to start fresh with other girls, rather than entering a co-ed school where girls have already forged friendships. Also like the more university-style existence here. And the boys. Presence of girls helps to tone down teenage boys' tendency to macho excess and dilutes bullying. Pupils may go into Godalming – not London or Guildford – two afternoons a week. 'Pub leave' only for over-18s with permission; school has own sixth form bar open to over-18s from Christmas onward. Lots of social events, bands playing, wince society etc. Can be a robust environment, and school is strict if perhaps unimaginative on bullying. Comes down hard on vice, especially drinking. If a boy is suspended for bad behaviour, it is treated as a final warning – 'I never suspend twice'. Recent appeal by family of expelled boy upheld school's decision. Pupils are tested if a suspicion of drugs. If drugs found in system the pupil may be expelled. If the pupil is suspended, he or she will have to submit to random testing for the rest of their time at school and will be expelled if a second test is positive. Currently around a dozen 'second chance' boys (drugs or alcohol). The handful of day boarders must stay at school each night until at least 9pm (can be much later). Parents warn that the 24/7 demands of the school make it virtually impossible to be a day pupil unless you live less than a mile away. Boarders may pop home most Saturday nights but must be in on Sunday if needed.

Pupils and parents: Girls here do not HAVE to be attractive, confident and from a well-heeled family – but it certainly helps. Ditto for boys, though they are more of a mixed bunch. We watched boys earnestly trudge round the school clutching ring binders – something that would have been considered impossibly uncool a decade ago. Little in the way of trendy hair, no piercings etc. Mostly from south London, Surrey, Sussex and Hampshire; 20-30 from ex-pat families, 10 per cent foreigners in the under school with more joining in the sixth form. Long and distinguished list of Old Boys: Joseph Addison, John Wesley, William Thackeray, Ralph Vaughan Williams, Robert Baden Powell, Robert Graves, Jonathan and David Dimbleby, Rachel Portman, who was the first female composer to win an Academy Award (for the 1996 film Emma) and had a premiere of her work at the BBC Proms. And who could forget Peter Gabriel and the rest of the lads in '70s art-rock band Genesis?

Entrance: Around 125 chaps enter year 9 – most take CE or scholarship exams, but school has own test for boys coming from an alternative universe (state schools or abroad). Register at least three years before entry. Guaranteed places offered two-and-a-half years before entry based on satisfactory report from prep school (conditional on 60 per cent CE pass). Parents then asked to fork out deposit. In November of year before entry, parents pay a second deposit and commit themselves to Charterhouse as their first choice school. Around 15 boys (mainly from abroad) and 50 girls enter at sixth form, most with a tidy stack of mainly A* and A GCSEs. Much oversubscribed for girls' places. Some prospective parents of girls put off by school's coolness of manner – 'You get the distinct impression when you apply for a girls' sixth form place that they are doing you a favour rather than vice versa'. Selective examination and interview for sixth form places conducted in the November of the year prior to admission.

Exit: Almost all stay on for sixth form – one boy a year might be asked to leave at the end of his first year if attainment and effort are not up to scratch, two or three ditto after GCSE mocks, after much consultation with parents.

Almost all to higher education: 20 Oxbridge, many to top universities, eg Leeds, Bristol, Newcastle, Durham, UCL, Exeter, Manchester, Nottingham, Edinburgh, to take great range of courses – engineering, maths and science very popular, followed by social sciences and humanities, then business management, modern langs, law and arts. US universities increasingly popular – Yale, Harvard and University of Pennsylvania amongst 2013 destinations.

Money matters: Fees (slightly) lower than Eton – so no joke. Intelligently aware of the danger that public schools could eventually price themselves out of the market. Hopes that fundraising may provide a future source of support for the school so that fee increases can be kept under control. Scholarship exams sensibly late in the year (May). Ten Foundation scholarships worth 10 per cent of the fees, plus five exhibitions worth five per cent. Probably the only school in England to offer a closed award available only to – wait for it – sons of lawyers. Peter Attenborough awards for all-rounders, plus music, art and sports scholarships also available. At sixth form, several academic awards, plus music (generally, and also particularly for organ) and art. School offers bursary programme for bright but genuinely needy boys 'in keeping with the intentions of the founder Thomas Sutton'.

Remarks: Traditional public school with all the trimmings. A class act from top to bottom. 'An academic school,' said a boy, 'that would be wasted on someone who was merely academic'.

Charters School

Charters Road, Sunningdale, Berkshire, SL5 9QY

• Pupils: 1700 boys and girls • Ages: 11–18 • Non denom • State

Tel: 01344 624826
Email: charters@chartersschool.org.uk
Website: www.chartersschool.org.uk

Co-Headteachers: Since 2009, Mr Martyn Parker and Mr Richard Pilgrim (fifties). Appointed as deputy heads at Charters in 2000, they worked together so well that when the previous head, Dame Marcia Twelftree, retired, they decided to apply for the headship as a team. The result is a highly successful partnership, liked and respected by pupils and parents alike, who describe them as 'involved, approachable, very supportive'.

Richard Pilgrim, who also teaches physics here, has been at Charters 29 years and proudly declares, 'I can honestly say the school has never been as good as it is now.' Married with three teenage children, likes reading and the outdoors and describes himself as 'a lapsed French horn player'. ('He's very talented!' puts in his colleague.) Martyn Parker is married with two grown-up children, and worked briefly in local government before coming into teaching 29 years ago. An English teacher, who also still teaches here, he signed up for a science GCSE last year 'because I realised how much I don't know' and taught himself. ('He got an A!' adds Pilgrim.) A very well-matched couple, who even finish each other's sentences.

Academic matters: Extremely good, and getting better all the time. GCSE and A Level results consistently put them in the top 20 per cent of state schools nationally, and that includes the grammars. In 2013, 54 per cent of A level grades were A*/B and nine per cent A*; 82 per cent of pupils got 5+ A*/C grades at GCSE including English and maths. All the more creditable, given the non-selective intake: children with a reading age of 6 rub shoulders with potential Oxbridge candidates, but, say heads, 'it's really important for us that we cater for all abilities; the school is comprehensive and will remain so.' Curriculum is therefore very broad. Traditional GCSEs and A Levels still very popular, but are offered alongside BTECs and NVQs, with the less academic KS4 pupils able to study off-site subjects such as motor vehicle technology and construction. French and Spanish are both taught to years 7-9, and we liked the way that all signage in the school was trilingual. Latin offered to G&T students. Facilities in all teaching spaces are up to date, with both Macs

and PCs available for students to use. Really excellent library and sixth form study area, accessible to students from 8am to 6pm, and guarded by the thoroughly lovely Miss MacDonnell, who, our guides assured us, was the reason that 'it's always this quiet.' Everyone we spoke to lauded the staff as enthusiastic and knowledgeable, with one boy falling over himself to give praise: 'The teachers here are really up for giving everyone and everything a go.' He went on to describe how one of the English teachers, who happened to be a law graduate, was teaching him and his friend GCSE law as an extracurricular, simply because they'd asked if they could do it. Parents confirmed that 'studious children are accepted and congratulated by other children.' A sixth former commented, 'The school doesn't put you in a bubble; they emphasise independent learning here.'

Games, options, the arts: Charters became a Sports College in 2002 as part of the specialist schools programme, which entitled it to receive extra funding for sports-specific teaching and facilities, provided this was used to drive the whole school forward. The Coalition axed the programme in 2010, but sport remains central to Charters' success and their facilities are excellent: seven tennis courts, full-sized hockey pitch, two Astroturf pitches, and two sports halls including basketball court and weight-training facilities. Every year group has 10 hours of sport per fortnight, and out of 70+ extracurricular activities offered each week, 40+ are sports and dance related. As well as the more traditional football, netball, etc, sports such as golf, trampolining and skiing are all available to do off-site. Although the school scores some impressive successes on track and field, much of what's on offer is intended to be fun rather than competitive, so that all pupils are catered for. It clearly works. As one satisfied parent observed, 'My daughter loves the sports. She's never home from school!' Both heads very positive about the value of sport to education as a whole, adding 'We don't have an obesity problem here!' And we could see, as we walked about, that they really didn't.

Annual drama productions in purpose-built drama studio are popular, and music is strong too, with choirs, orchestras and a broad range of instrumental lessons. Extremely varied programme of trips, both day and residential: the school jointly owns Tirabad Outdoor Educational Centre in rural Wales, and sends parties there throughout the school year. All the pupils waxed lyrical about the good times they'd had at Tirabad, with several calling it the best thing they'd done at Charters. Other destinations have included Spain, the USA, Sri Lanka, Beijing, Rome and Paris. Strong D of E programme, and lots of clubs – science, creative writing, debating, chess, etc.

Background and atmosphere: Established in 1958 as a secondary modern with 400 children, Charters became comprehensive in the 1960s to cope with increased demand and remains committed to comprehensive ideals. Became an academy in 2012, say heads, 'because of the benefits of self-determination. We're less subject to the whims of education.' Since its beginning, the school has occupied the same site in an affluent, leafy suburb of Ascot. The uniform is sensible and unfussy, the modern(ish) buildings clean and businesslike, and there are a number of very pleasant green spaces in which pupils can sit and chat. Highly regarded by locals throughout its history, the school exudes purpose, cordiality and calm. All the students we spoke to said that they'd made plenty of friends here and that it was a very welcoming place. 'The people are open and friendly here'; 'The teachers help you get to know people'; 'My son has had a good time at Charters'; 'My children love all their teachers and find them very approachable,' were typical comments.

Pastoral care and discipline: Outstanding on many levels. The Maine Centre offers on-site support for any child with medical, social, bereavement or emotional issues and is fully staffed throughout the school week. Any pupil can drop in there with or without an appointment; students praised it as 'fantastic'. The school has also been a centre for physically handicapped pupils since 1981, and is fully equipped with ramps, lifts, etc. It works closely with a nearby autistic school, and provision for its high number of statemented children is excellent. Horizontal tutoring system, with tutors remaining with their charges from year 7 through to year 11 wherever possible. School has been nationally recognised for the leadership opportunities it provides for its students. Incidents of bullying are 'quite rare', according to the pupils, who also said that such occurrences were dealt with 'very well, very quickly and with an iron fist'. 'I've never, ever felt unsafe at this school,' added a year 9 girl. Year 11 prefects are all encouraged to take pastoral responsibility and, say parents, develop into mature and thoughtful young adults. A concern about discipline in their child's tutor group was raised in one quarter, but this appears to be exceptional: sixth formers we spoke to emphatically denied that there had ever been such issues during their time at the school and seemed genuinely shocked to hear otherwise.

Pupils and parents: Very much a product of the locality, with about 87 per cent of students from white British families, but high employment in the area has meant that families from all ethnic backgrounds are moving here in increasing numbers. Very broad social diversity, with deprived Bracknell pupils being bussed in alongside those from advantaged Ascot. Very strong parent support for the school.

Entrance: With 500 applicants for 240 places, the school is heavily over-subscribed. As an academy, Charters is now its own admissions authority, but it buys in admissions admin procedure from local authority and the usual criteria apply: statemented children, proximity, siblings, etc. See the school's website for details.

Exit: After year 11, about 25 per cent to local colleges or to employment. The rest continue into the Charters sixth form, where 90-95 per cent go on to a wide range of universities, including Russell Group ones. A small number of Oxbridge successes each year – seven in 2013..

Money matters: State-funded academy, with a budget of £8.5m. Government bursaries available to disadvantaged post-16 students who would otherwise be unable to continue their education.

Remarks: An admirable and humane school, with some of the sparkiest, brightest, most articulate and most delightful students it's been our pleasure to meet. Successfully holds its own against its glossy independent neighbours, and is preferred to same by many parents. If we hadn't lived in Crystal Palace, we would have sent our own children here.

Cheadle Hulme School

Linked school: Cheadle Hulme School Junior School

Claremont Road, Cheadle Hulme, Cheshire, SK8 6EF

• Pupils: 1,110 boys and girls; all day • Ages: 11–18 • Non-denom
• Fees: £10,344 pa • Independent

Tel: 01614 883330
Email: Registrar@chschool.co.uk
Website: www.cheadlehulmeschool.co.uk

Head: Since 2010, Ms Lucy Pearson BA (early forties). Educated at Keble College, Oxford, where she read English literature and

language, followed by an Open University teaching degree. Previously deputy head at Wellington College in Berkshire. She opened the bowling for the England women's cricket team from 1996 to 2005, consistently a lead wicket-taking fast bowler and player of the year in 2000 and 2003. Not surprisingly, she still coaches cricket at Cheadle Hulme.

Charismatic and dynamic, a huge champion of co-education – 'There are so many lessons to learn for boys and girls being educated together,' she says. 'Many children just don't fit the mould in single sex schools. Our function isn't to prepare just one type of child. There is a robustness about co-education. It teaches children about human interaction.' Clearly very ambitious for the school, she says that it has 'the potential to be outstanding at everything. We can be more forward thinking, more modern, more exciting'.

A father told us that 'she's really energised the place,' and pupils reckon she is 'friendly and chatty' and 'fun, but not a pushover'. One boy remarked: 'She's at everything, even Saturday sporting fixtures. I was on a battlefields trip in France and she even turned up there.'

A former member of the National Youth Choir, she loves reading and walking her dog, Frankie.

Academic matters: Continues to have good exam results – 60 per cent A*/A grades at GCSE in 2013 and 44 per cent at A level (79 per cent A*/B). However, although exam results are ultimately the paymaster, the head says that 'there must be fun in education. Hard work must be balanced with support'. Pupils appreciate the wide range of teaching styles the school employs and comment that teachers are very approachable. All subject areas hold weekly clinics – pupils can drop in if they need assistance and regular revision classes are held for those taking exams.

Regular effort grades have been introduced to ensure no child slips through the net. All pupils in the upper sixth take extension classes to gain depth in subjects unrelated to their A level work. IGCSEs and Extended Project Qualification (EPQ) available in some subjects and the Pre-U offered in philosophy, business studies and economics.

The school has seen a rise in popularity recently and prep schools are reporting more pupils turning down places at other prestigious independents to take up places here. As a result, an extra form introduced to cope with increased demand. Although head denies any desire to keep climbing the league tables or for the school to become more selective (it currently has a broader intake than some of its competitors), does seem to be a move to broaden and enrich academic opportunities available to pupils.

Full time head of learning support can cope with mild to moderate SEN, as long as pupils can cope with the curriculum. Pupils assessed on an individual basis.

Games, options, the arts: Drama is very popular and has its own studios. Many performances take place in the atmospheric, but slightly cramped, Holden Hall. Music is outstanding, with many orchestras, choirs, a cappella group, concert band, ensembles, samba and rock bands, to name but a few.

Successful sporting teams, but still plenty of opportunity to get involved if you don't make the teams. Many pupils represent their sport at club, county and country levels.

Vast array of extracurricular activities on offer, including school's own radio station, film club, table tennis and a charities committee.

Background and atmosphere: Established in 1855 as a co-educational school for 'orphans and necessitous children of warehouse men and clerks'. Expansive, leafy grounds have a collegiate feel. Pupils look very at home but seem purposefully busy. The main stately Victorian building sits comfortably next to their modern counterparts with their spacious, airy classrooms. Year 7 has own block to ease the transition from little to big school. Sixth formers have their own common rooms and butty bar, but the few we spoke to grumbled that their facilities could do with a revamp. Smart bottle green and black uniform, changing to navy blue in the sixth form.

Food gets a big thumbs-up. Plenty of good quality options to choose from in the canteen (which boasts stained glass windows and high tech finger print recognition system). 'Grab and go' lunch bags available for pupils too busy to queue.

Pastoral care and discipline: Parents can't praise the pastoral system highly enough. One mother, whose son found adjusting to senior school life very difficult, said that staff were fantastic, often taking the time to ring her in the evening.

Sixth formers act as peer mentors to new year 7s, to help them settle and give them someone to talk to. 'It was brilliant,' one boy told us. 'I could ask him lots of questions that I felt silly asking a teacher.'

Pupils and parents: Mainly from south Manchester, Cheshire and Derbyshire. Parents are mostly professional and from a cross section of backgrounds. Now starting to pick up more Asian families, who have in the past tended to choose the Manchester independents. Extensive bus routes, plus a pick up and drop off service from the local station.

Notable former pupils include MEP Chris Davies, BBC political editor Nick Robinson, political correspondent Lucy Ward, BBC broadcaster Katie Derham, political correspondent Stephen Day, soprano Susan Bullock, Labour peer Lord Dubs and actor Daniel Rigby.

Entrance: Competitive entrance exam at 11 in English, maths and verbal reasoning, followed by separate interviews with pupils and parents.

Exit: Three to Oxbridge in 2013; others to eg Durham, Sheffield, Nottingham, Leeds, Newcastle and UCL.

Money matters: Substantial bursary fund makes a Cheadle Hulme education a reality for many families. No academic scholarships, but sports and music scholarships offered for year 7 entry, plus music scholarship also offered for sixth form.

Remarks: A vibrant, action-packed school that is rapidly increasing in popularity. Pupils are bright, well supported and gently cared for to achieve their best.

Chelmsford County High School for Girls

Broomfield Road, Chelmsford, CM1 1RW

• Pupils: 895 girls; all day • Ages: 11–18 • Non–denom • State

Tel: 01245 352592
Email: office@cchs.essex.sch.uk
Website: www.cchs.co.uk

Headteacher: Since 2007, Mrs Nicole Chapman. Born in Burgundy, France, but says she feels 'like a local girl', having relocated to Essex soon after gaining her licence ès lettres (BA honours equivalent) in English with Spanish and French at university in Tours. She has a son and two step-children and joined CCHS after six years as head of a girls' grammar school in Gravesend, Kent – 'They're slightly less super-selective there,' she says – and before that a mixture of challenging and high-achieving grant-maintained and foundation schools.

Perspicacious and single-minded, she is certainly a safe pair of hands for Chelmsford's stellar girls' grammar and is revered for her tough stance on standards ('Girls here are delightful, but they will take advantage if you let them'), inspiring them to greatness ('Being the leaders of tomorrow is something of a mantra here') and her tireless scouring of the state's coffers to make sure that her super-bright girls have access to the best possible facilities and resources ('They deserve them,' she says, simply). Some new pupils – and their parents – admit to being slightly startled by Mrs Chapman's determined approach, but she has impressed with her willingness to re-visit the issue of uniform just a few years after the introduction of an unpopular design and her efforts on the funding front are much appreciated.

Academic matters: A real star of the league tables, twinkling brightly among the UK's top 10 state – and outshining all but the most hefty-fee-ed of the public – schools, one of just a rarefied handful of secondaries in the country to have triple specialist status – modern languages, technology and music. Academic achievement is famously sky high, with eleven A*s at GCSE common and regular achievers of four As at A level. in 2013, 53 per cent A*/A at A level and nearly 86 per cent A*/A at GCSE.

No wonder then that parents, from the London boroughs to the coast, get themselves in a twist when it comes to priming their daughters for Essex's notorious 11+ entrance exam, leading to a frenzy of tutoring that, for some academically-promising girls – or those with clued-up parents – can begin as early as year 4. Rumours of occasional drop-outs, but the vast majority of girls are genuinely of the intellectually-gifted variety and relish the challenge. 'There are girls here who have been coached through the exam and then struggle, but we do our best for them,' says the head. 'It's sad because it does dent their confidence.'

Unsurprisingly, given its specialist status, sciences and languages are particularly strong, and this despite the decidedly outmoded facilities – 'a triumph of good teaching and bright pupils over an increasingly unsuitable complex,' says the head, who is working hard to rectify the situation with a new £2.5m modern foreign languages block and a plan to add more labs.

Girls cite the single-sex environment as a factor in their willingness to throw themselves into the more traditionally male technological pursuits, without fear of opprobrium. All learn French, German and Latin, and a growing trend towards internationalism at the school saw the introduction in 2009 of the IB, including ab initio courses in Italian, Russian, Spanish and Mandarin, to which AS students are also welcome. 'IB as a package is ideal for bright, hard-working girls who want to stand out from the crowd,' says the head. She is at pains to point out, though, that she has no intention of going over to the IB completely – specialism at A level suits many at CCHS, particularly those who have a clear idea of a future career in a narrow field. That said, the head is anticipating a settling in period as the IB becomes established. 'Understandably, parents here can be slightly reluctant about change and we'll need to convince them'. Average point score of 37, out of a possible 45.

Games, options, the arts: Despite the academically-biased two-week timetable, which means that the necessary enrichment subjects can be confined to one hour-long lesson a fortnight, less bookish pursuits are also encouraged at CCHS. Every half-term a cross-curricular enrichment day sees all students off timetable working on an extended project or activity, often off site. PE is compulsory all the way to the top and years 7-11s have two one-hour lessons a week. At least one sporty club every lunchtime and every day after school including gymnastics, fencing and trampolining, alongside team games. Tennis, netball, hockey and athletics are particular strengths – collects trophies from national and district competitions.

About a fifth of the school learns a musical instrument – the orchestras and choirs are of a frighteningly high standard. Art is also pursued with enthusiasm and amazing talent. The list of lunchtime and after-school clubs reads like a novel – every department makes a contribution. French film club, football, netball, musical theatre, hockey, cross-country, netball, junior choir, history society and debating are just a fraction. Also student-led professional societies for future doctors, lawyers and the like are evident. Lunchtime is an hour so plenty of time for a 30-40 minute activity and then food, though girls often combine to save time.

Chinese has been introduced as an after-school club – plans to shoehorn it into the curriculum: link to China through the British Council immersion initiative, and as Essex is twinned with the Jiangsu province, partner school in Nanjing. Unusually for a girls' school has CCF – shared with the boys at King Edward VI Grammar School down the road. Long and commendable tradition of community service, with almost all sixth formers involved and girls forming strong bonds with local special schools and retirement homes, often giving up their free time to continue beyond the prescribed sessions.

Background and atmosphere: A traditional red-brick Edwardian grammar school on one of the main roads into the county town of Essex, will bring back memories for any grammar school girl of the last century. Opened in 1906, it has remained largely unchanged since, save for some tacked-on additions and the impressive music centre, complete with a recording studio, which, as the head says, 'shows up the rest of the school'. New languages centre has freed up space at the rear for an extension to the science block and a new sports hall, which is severely lacking. The swimming pool was recently refurbished; all-weather hockey pitch and playing fields. The performing arts block is a real asset with a large drama space, and sixth formers have their own house for relaxation and study. A café has recently been set up to encourage girls to eat food cooked on-site rather than frequenting the local takeaways.

Pastoral care and discipline: In a close-knit community of fewer than 900 girls, discipline is hardly an issue. Stress, however, is – pastoral care evident across the board. Parents thrilled by their daughter's 11+ success are often reluctant to airlift her out of such a rarefied social milieu in favour of the local state secondary, so Mrs Chapman focuses her efforts on helping flounderers to rise to the intellectual challenge of CCHS through close monitoring, confidence-building and occasionally making adjustments to individual curricula, lightening the GCSE burden. A specialist mentor spends lunchtimes supporting girls who are not performing as expected, because, says the head, 'We have to make sure that the girls enjoy being here and do well. They need to keep up with the pace and cope with being among very bright girls, so we often have to work hard to build self-esteem – there is a self-fulfilling prophecy about the bottom end of grammar schools'. Despite parental grumbles about teachers who warn that a B is nowhere near good enough, Mrs Chapman asserts that the pressure often comes from the girls themselves – those who also have friends outside of school are better at keeping perspective.

When we visited, 44 students were noted on the special and additional needs register – the vast majority with identified medical or pastoral needs. The register is reviewed termly with student progress managers – staff are made aware of changes and additions and encouraged to report worries about any students not mentioned.

As might be expected, ordered atmosphere – students take responsibility for their property and their actions, work confidently and are extremely self-motivated. Behaviour policy sent to all students on entry and parents asked to sign an agreement outlining the expectations that the school, the parents and the student all have of each other. A logbook is used to record homework and as a regular channel of communication between form tutor and parents, who monitor progress and commitments and comment as necessary. A

mature staff with an average age of nearly 45 is on hand to address concerns. Canteen lunches are promoted, as much for the social opportunity as the nutritional value.

Pupils and parents: Hard working and very able girls from supportive homes travel up to three hours a day to CCHS – no specific catchment area here. Consequently the ethnic mix does not reflect that of the immediate locality and almost a tenth of students have English as an additional language.

Entrance: Applications are on the up but, despite rumours in the press, the extra numbers are coming principally from the state sector, which pleases Mrs Chapman – 'We don't want to give the impression that we are a free alternative to independent education – grammar schools exist to provide an education for the very brightest, whatever their background'. Girls have come from more than 200 feeder schools over the past three years, and although a few years ago almost half were from preps, that proportion is now down to about a quarter.

Admission no longer by the Essex 11+ exam but instead by tests 'designed to measure comprehension, vocabulary, verbal reasoning, non-verbal reasoning and numerical reasoning skills', prepared by Durham University's Centre for Evaluation and Monitoring, and intended to be tutor-proof (no practice papers available). Tests still held in September (initial results in October). Places are offered by the local authority on national offer day in March to the 120 girls who have performed best in the selection tests and not been offered a place at a higher preference. A waiting list stays open until the end of the autumn term. Occasional vacancies further up the school are filled by inviting all girls on the waiting list to sit a test.

Vacancies in the sixth form – often created by girls being tempted away by the mixed sixth form at the local boys' grammar – are readily filled and a further 30 places are made available, bringing the sixth form year group totals to around 150.

Exit: Only a smattering opt out of higher education while more than 85 per cent win places at their first choice of university. In 2013, 14 to Oxbridge and nine medics; King's College London, Cambridge, Birmingham and UEA most popular destinations.

Old girls worthy of particular note include the United Nations' first woman Under-Secretary General Dame Margaret Anstee, Dragons' Den dragon Rachel Elnaugh, sculptor Catharni Stern and BBC correspondent Emma-Jane Kirby.

Remarks: An intellectually stimulating environment that gives a flying start to the brightest of girls.

Cheltenham College

Linked school: Cheltenham College Preparatory School

Bath Road, Cheltenham, GL53 7LD

• Pupils: 640: 390 boys/250 girls; full boarding: 450, flexi boarding: 65, day: 125 • Ages: 13–18 • C of E • Fees: Boarding £31,851–£32,751; Day £23,868–£24,768 pa • Independent

Tel: 01242 265600
Email: registrar@cheltenhamcollege.org
Website: www.cheltenhamcollege.org

Headmaster: Since 2010, Dr Alex Peterken BA MA DEd (thirties). Three children, one a chorister at Salisbury Cathedral School, two at Cheltenham College Junior School; he enjoys choral singing (bass) and walking in the Cotswolds. Dr Peterken was educated at The Prebendal School, Chichester where he was head boy and head chorister, thence to Eton College as a Music

Exhibitioner. BA in theology from Durham, MA in educational management from London and a doctorate in education from Surrey. After 11 years at Charterhouse where he was head of higher education and careers and latterly housemaster of Saunderites, he joined the College in 2008 as deputy head and still teaches in the religious studies department.

Referred to admiringly as 'the man with the plan,' he fearlessly embarked on a programme of significant changes when he took up the headship, building for the future on the school's traditional strengths. Has he succeeded? 'It's the same but better,' we were told over and over again, so that's a yes. Genial, very youthful (one of the youngest HMC heads) and delightfully unstuffy, he teaches half a term of RS to all the first years and sits in on lessons, 'not at the back; I sit next to the pupils and ask questions.' Pupils can visit Dr Peterken, without an appointment, before chapel each morning; he wants to know what's going on, what's exercising his charges. While there may not be queues at his door at 8 in the morning, all the pupils we spoke to said that they 'felt listened to'.

Academic matters: In 2013 57 per cent A*/A at GCSE. IGCSEs are offered in maths, English literature and science and were recently introduced for history and geography. Maths, English, DT, music, history and science results are particularly impressive. 2013 A levels 47 per cent A*/A grades. Dr Peterken has no time for the excuse 'you can't do all things well', and while there are no plans to become more selective or chase league table rankings, there is a strong drive to enrich the academic opportunities for all students via a broader approach to the curriculum and programmes that enable pupils to learn more effectively.

Lessons are 35 minutes long and the new two-week timetable is, apparently, much less confusing than its eight-day predecessor. We saw thoughtful group work (boys and girls at separate tables) in Latin and a biology class where all but one were learning to love leaf mould and get to know its inhabitants. Our visit was early in the term and the biology teacher was still enraptured with her versatile refurbished labs.

The sixth form has received considerable attention with the introduction of an independent learning project for the lower sixth designed to extend and deepen subject knowledge (offered in addition to the EPQ). The College is also the first UK independent school to run an innovative accredited leadership and life skills course in the sixth form based on Sean Covey's book 'The 7 Habits of Highly Effective Teenagers'. Pupils can choose from 24 A level subjects including textiles, theatre studies, history of art and Latin and Greek. Critical thinking can be taken as an AS.

One of the assurances Dr Peterken and his team gives is that no pupil is allowed to 'slip under the radar'; academic problems are tackled promptly via an 'academic support plan' drawn up with the pupil, parents, housemaster, tutor and subject teachers. The head is also very keen for pupils to learn from each other: disorganised pupils are assigned a buddy to help them on the path to order; older and wiser pupils give talks along the lines of 'Things we wished we'd known ...'

EAL pupils attend an induction programme prior to the start of the academic year and are supported by two EAL specialists. Learning Support Department caters not only for those with mild dyslexia, dyspraxia, ADHD etc but also ensures the gifted and talented are suitably challenged. The role of this department extends to the whole school, overseeing initiatives to develop the learning potential of all pupils.

Main school library has just been completely revamped, its wonderful tiers of gothic windows pour light onto new shelves and lounging readers. Banished with the old furniture is conversation; a kind of un-modernisation which, according to our guides, has been welcomed by all. Even more enticing than golden silence are the iPads mounted on black metal plinths that pupils can use to search the library catalogue which does not, we are told, extend to Angry Birds.

Games, options, the arts: Dr Edward Wilson the Antarctic explorer was educated here and no fewer than three intrepid members of staff (one of whom is director of activities) have climbed Everest – surely some kind of a record. While the hills and fields of Gloucestershire offer little to challenge explorers or mountaineers, pretty much everything else is available to fortunate Cheltonians. The first ever inter-school rugby match was played on the school's splendid pitch in 1844, overlooked no doubt by the confection of a pavilion that resembles a miniature Brunel railway station. In the summer this perfect pitch, which won the College's groundsman Groundsman of the Year award, plays host to the venerable Cheltenham cricket festival.

County and national triumphs in rugby, hockey, cricket, tennis, rowing and polo; coaching for all abilities is now 'much more professional' and even third and fourth team matches are keenly contested and enthusiastically supported. Rackets (a forerunner of squash) is one of the more arcane sports on offer and the College has won the national championships three times and is consistently in the top four. Golf, swimming, water polo, dance and fitness are part of the exhaustive (and exhausting) sports programme as is yoga, a surprising hit with the boys; apparently it is very effective for rugby injuries.

CCF, Young Enterprise and D of E are all enthusiastically tackled, the latter being offered in its less common cycling, horseback and ski-touring options in addition to the usual walking challenge. Service activities take place every Wednesday and volunteers give their time locally at schools and residential homes. Longstanding links with Kenya see College pupils working on projects there, often carrying this on into gap years.

Art, music and modern language teaching takes place in the rather grand neo-classical surroundings of Thirlestaine House, a former gentleman's residence. Its original features – huge mirrors, chandeliers, ornate cornices and radiator covers – have survived generations of school children (just) and create a suitably bohemian home for the creative chaos of art and pottery studios. The long gallery is venue for exhibitions, lectures and public events. Two students have recently gained places at RADA for costume design and backstage training courtesy of the outstanding DT department while another gained a place for acting.

Forty per cent of pupils learn a musical instrument and while this is a lower uptake than comparable schools the figure is increasing. Chapel and chamber choirs plus orchestras, bands and ensembles must keep that 40 per cent pretty busy. One of the listed buildings nearing completion is the theatre that will reopen as an up-to-the-minute performing arts centre complete with dance studio, green room and, less predictably, a plaster frieze of the Parthenon uncovered during refurbishment. School and house plays and reviews are hugely popular, everyone is encouraged to get involved either performing or backstage.

The College also plays its part in Cheltenham's cultural life, participating in the annual festival fest. The combined choirs of the College and Dean Close opened a recent music festival. Harmony with nearby Dean Close and the Ladies' College is described as 'cooperative' with pragmatic sharing of visiting speakers, careers events and collaboration between international students' societies. Pupils are more forthright, acknowledging and enjoying the rivalry.

Background and atmosphere: Beautiful mellow Victorian gothic buildings along Cheltenham's busy Bath Road undergoing final stages of major re-vamp – grade 1 listed status an expensive headache but good news for Gloucestershire's stone masons and other master craftsmen. It's easy to see why visiting Americans (NATO base nearby) get a touch of the vapours, it's every inch the English public school. Public areas certainly getting the five star treatment though classrooms remain workaday and well used (all have requisite IT and smart boards). Stonework not the only area revamped: Dr Peterken has installed a duo of deputies, one pastoral, one academic, a director of learning, a new head of sixth form and 30 new members of teaching staff. Numbers, like results, are rising and a modest increase in places (about 40) is planned, as is another girls' boarding house. Students and parents tell us that much has changed for the better, not change's sake. Singled out for mention were improved home school communication and relations between teachers and pupils. Interestingly, members of staff said that they thought this had always been one of the strengths of the College but our sixth form guides were very certain that things were different and teachers were 'much more involved and friendly'. The staff we met lived up to their billing and were indeed friendly, funny, charmingly young fogeyish in a few cases, and clearly enjoying both the teaching and strong sense of community at the College.

Pastoral care and discipline: Pupils start each day in the glorious chapel, no doubt energised for study by the famously enthusiastic hymn singing. This is such a feature of College life that a recent group of upper sixth leavers asked if they could record themselves in the chapel singing favourite hymns as a parting memento. The house system is everything here, for boarders and day pupils alike; each is a community within a community and fiercely competitive. Every house has its own character and distinguishing traditions such as prefect blazers and boaters (worn with pride apparently). Houses are in residential roads just outside the campus perimeter – separating 'home' and school is considered very important: the head encourages pupils to adopt a professional attitude to school, 'it's a place of work', whereas houses are a home from home, informal and a place for relaxation. Parents are encouraged to join in with weekend or social events and are pretty much in agreement with Ofsted's conclusion that boarding provision at the college is 'outstanding.'

Housemasters/mistresses first in line for problems whether academic or social and liaise very closely with teaching staff to ensure 'joined up' care. Older pupils train for peer mentoring responsibilities and can often pick up on wobbles before they become serious. Mobile phones (aka 'the biggest headache') only allowed in houses and, along with laptops, must be handed in before bed. If a housemaster overhears parents being berated or harangued – not uncommon in a school population that is totally teenage – he will challenge (hooray!). The writing of proper thank you letters (to former prep schools, weekend hosts and the like) is another courtesy expected of pupils. In addition to a matron each house has a resident tutor who hosts academic 'clinics' outside school hours. Christowe, one of the original Victorian boys' boarding houses, has been beautifully decorated by the current housemaster and his wife (an interior designer) and there's not a whiff of the institutional in the first floor family rooms. As with all of the boys' houses, 60 or so boys live here, sharing for the younger and single rooms for sixth formers. The common room and library are full of house memorabilia (house names a constant in the College); fascinating archive photos and a mini museum all foster a sense of continuity and house identity. Wonderful cushions decorated with the piratical house insignia of skull and crossbones were a gift from a parent. Clubby red-painted snooker and games room much admired. Ashmead, one of the girls' houses, was built round a garden quad with secure key pad entry system, lovely light bedrooms and civilised socialising areas. Boys are allowed to visit for film evenings and the like – apparently rom-coms are rather favoured, a guilty pleasure that cannot be indulged in their own houses. The housemistress heads off cliques by splitting up prep school groups and changing room-mates each year. All residents meet twice a day – a practical system that also enables staff to observe shifting dynamics. House staff and prefects alert to meal skipping and similar warning signs when 'faddy could

tip into eating disorder.' While most pupils come from similar backgrounds staff are alert to potentially insensitive displays of conspicuous consumerism – affording one the unexpected chance to ask a parent to 'take back the mink'.

Some pupils disgruntled about recent tightening up on trips into Cheltenham town centre – now only Sundays unless there's a legitimate need. Head has responded to parents' view that since the school offers so many activities, 'hanging around in town' need not be a supplementary option. Bath Road still in bounds for banks, supermarkets and cafés, not that the last should be necessary – food is plentiful with lots of choice: salad bar, curries, carvery and good puds served in the former chapel and 'legendary' bacon rolls and snacks dispensed by the very friendly ladies in the tuck shop. This is a town school and necessarily takes firm line on drugs, drink and similar misdemeanours. Sixth form privileges are realistic – at 17 pupils can go out for a meal at an 'approved' restaurant; at 18 they may visit a similarly endorsed pub. The sixth form social room in the main school has a café/bar; 'we have to prepare them for life beyond school', one housemaster told us.

Pupils and parents: Good mix of first time buyers, second generation Cheltonians, Forces and international. Around 18 per cent from outside UK – 30 countries represented. Not snobby or excessively label conscious. Many boarders are from local area or within a few hours of Cheltenham. Children don't have to grow up too fast here; they're down-to-earth, polite and confident without being arrogant. 'It's not a London school', one parent said approvingly. Uniform of navy and cerise plus usual complexity of ties generally adhered to, all pupils wear own choice of pastel shirts; boys' individuality expressed mainly via hair.

OCs include Rageh Omar, journalist; Tim Bevan, film producer; General Sir Michael Rose; Nigel and Jack Davenport, actors; James Whitaker, royal correspondent; James Stout, world rackets champion; Sir Alan Haselhurst MP, deputy speaker of House of Commons, The Right Hon Lord Anthony Colwyn CB and the Norfolk Coroner, William Morris. Several events marked the centenary of Dr Edward Wilson who died with Scott in the Antarctic in 1912.

Entrance: Increasingly competitive. Most via common entrance, 40 per cent from own junior school, others from plethora of localish preps including Beaudesert Park, Abberley Hall, Pinewood, St Hugh's, Hatherop Castle, The Dragon, Bilton Grange, Moor Park and St John's on the Hill. Entrants from state schools take exam (papers in English, maths and, where appropriate, French); sixth form candidates require at least five B grades at GCSE and must sit papers in subjects to be studied.

Exit: Around 20 per cent leave after GCSEs. Most sixth formers to higher education. Handful to Oxbridge (three in 2013), most to Russell Group universities with Manchester, Cardiff and Bristol current favourites; others to eg Oxford Brookes, UCL, Edinburgh and Royal Holloway. Most popular subject choices: biological sciences, economics and management, history, engineering.

Money matters: Scholarships (usually 30 per cent) and exhibitions (between 10 and 20 per cent) offered at 13+ and 16+ in academic, art, DT, drama (13+ only) music and sport. All-round award may be made at College's discretion. Additional means-tested bursaries also available.

Remarks: Radical modernisation does not always fit easily with old traditions, whether architecturally or educationally, but as the scaffolding comes down and the builders' vans leave, one feels that Cheltenham College is emerging refreshed and ready for a new era. This school is a happy, spirited community inspiring real affection and loyalty in its members.

The Cheltenham Ladies' College

Bayshill Road, Cheltenham, GL50 3EP

• Pupils: 850; 640 board, 210 day • Ages: 11–18 • Christian but welcomes and respects all faiths • Fees: Day £20,442–£23,247; Boarding £30,450–£34,302 pa • Independent

Tel: 01242 520691
Email: enquiries@cheltladiescollege.org
Website: www.cheltladiescollege.org

Principal: Since 2011, Eve Jardine-Young MA (thirties). Educated in Malawi, won a sixth form scholarship to the school she now leads, a place she credits with, 'changing her life profoundly.' After graduating in engineering from Cambridge she worked for Ove Arup (structural engineers) before moving into teaching. Taught economics at Radley, moved to Epsom College where she was housemistress and head of sixth form, thence to Blundell's as director of studies. Married, her husband also works in education. Hobbies include reading, music (she is, apparently, rather a good pianist), gardening and a talkative cockatoo.

Her appointment surprised some, but the CLC Council has a record of selecting left field candidates although they've only had to choose 11 since the school was founded in 1853. Ms Jardine-Young described the protracted recruitment process as: 'Extraordinary, the Council are very involved and take their responsibility extremely seriously.' Ms Jardine-Young lives up to her name and looks scarcely old enough for such a heavy mantle (or such big shoes, albeit worn with the previous owner's blessing). When asked if she felt the weight of history on her shoulders she said she saw her responsibility as, 'stewardship, not of buildings but of tradition and future potential.'

So far Ms Jardine-Young has wisely kept her head down, watching and learning the ropes of the mighty ship CLC and we don't expect her to turn up in the press any time soon banging the drum for girls' schools. Her experience in both single sex and co-ed establishments keeps her diplomatic on this subject, 'at their best, both systems work very well'. The words most often used by parents and girls to describe the new principal are 'friendly,' 'approachable' and 'sincere' and indeed she is; talkative she may be but she is not a loose cannon so we wondered why a marketing person sat in on our interview. Apparently it was for 'training purposes.'

Ms Jardine-Young is her own woman and, in the best possible way, has not yet developed a headish persona. She isn't fixed, she likes exploring ideas and thinking aloud, but don't be fooled, she brings a formidable intellect to her alma mater. Nostalgic talk of a Proustian flashback courtesy of the smell of varnish is followed by discussion of the school's institutional 'meta language'...'while we rightly praise girls who achieve, do we give enough thought to what it means to be a winner? Do we articulate other values frequently enough?' She brims with excitement and vigour and her commitment to and passion for the school shine through. She says she has plans. We can't wait.

Academic matters: League tables may come and go but CLC's academic record remains mighty. In 2013, 88 per cent A*/A, with 64 per cent A* at GCSE. At A level an impressive 71 per cent of passes were at A* or A, 90 per cent A*-B. Sciences, maths, economics, history and English by far the most favoured subjects but there are plenty of options and small numbers take Japanese, physical education, theatre studies, classical Greek and history of art. It's early days but so far the IB results are extremely strong: points average of 38 in 2013; over 40 per cent of entrants gained 40+ points (out of 45). School crowned top IB girls' boarding provider in 2012. Recent golds in chemistry

and biology olympiads and finalists in the national maths team challenge. It must be said that, as in similar schools, pupils from the Far East raise the bar considerably in subjects such as maths and music. We have also heard from several sources that for some a popular summer holiday activity is subject extension classes in Hong Kong. The principal says, 'We're not producing clones, the model of exam grades at any cost leads to mental brittleness.' Try telling that to the tiger mothers.

The year 7 music lesson we observed was pretty serious, girls working at a high level, keen to answer questions, otherwise quiet and diligent. IB French – a debate on the uses of philosophy – was a bit livelier. The science labs looked like those in a university, girls in white coats utterly engrossed in their experiments. Parents tell us that while the prevailing mood is indeed serious there are 'inspirational' teachers and the girls enjoy their lessons. Average class size is 16 (seven in the sixth form), progress is monitored closely and girls move up or down through sets as necessary. The brightest may take one or two subjects early but most do ten or so GCSEs at the normal time and in their stride. Parents impressed by proactive way in which teachers identify any problems and put solutions (extra lessons etc) in place swiftly. Pupils must learn to manage their time from day one – not only do they have to get to and from house to school promptly but they also have free periods for music lessons/practice and homework.

Small numbers with EAL or SpLD, mainly dyslexia. Specialist support for girls who need help with study skills, literacy and mathematics, but clearly CLC is not the place for those with significant problems and the school is frank about this. Most areas of school fully accessible by wheelchair but distance of houses precludes all but a day pupil in these circumstances.

Games, options, the arts: Full programme of music and drama – size of school means there are opportunities for all who wish to perform; impressive results in LAMDA and music exams. Up to 50 music scholars (abandon hope if you're not grade 8 or diploma at 11) must delight the ears at concerts and lunchtime recitals. College's jewel in the crown is the new arts centre, the Parabola (it's in Parabola Road). Just across from main school, it has a 300-seat theatre, dance rehearsal rooms and small gallery primarily for school use but also hosts public shows and exhibitions. It's carving out a niche as a venue for new writing and experimental theatre, the type of thing that attracts a bijou audience, in Cheltenham at least. The town's many festivals also provide plenty of opportunities for cultural enrichment.

Impressive plate glass and metal arts building, school often has artists and writers in residence too, most but not all, women. Super textiles dept (school produced designers Katharine Hamnett and Amanda Wakeley) sadly Marie Celesteish with only three or so girls taking it beyond GCSE. Cornucopia of extra-curricular options as one would expect but school is explicit in warning girls that academics must come first. Strong tradition of charitable doings: prefects nominate three UK and three international causes to fundraise for each year. Pupils also volunteer to work at St Hilda's East, the charity established in 1889 by the 'Guild' (alumni association, now 10,000 strong) in London's East End. 'What,' we asked naively, 'is Hilda patron saint of?' Answer came there none but a few red faces and a Google later we discovered that she is saint in charge of learning. Old girls who work at City law firms also do pro bono work for the charity. We doubt Miss Beale would recognise today's East Enders but the area served by the charity is still very deprived and there remains much for the Cheltenham Ladies to do. Closer to home there is a well established community links programme and girls from year 11 upwards are to be found all over the locality helping out at homeless shelters, animal sanctuaries, primary schools and retirement homes.

Sports acreage and facilities (partly open to public) are pretty good and about to get even better when the sports hall extension is completed. This will enable sports such as hockey, tennis

C

and lacrosse to be played all year round. Notable individual achievements in athletics, tennis, skiing, riding; team sport triumphs more frequently at county level although recently CLC has got through to national finals in hockey, tennis and dry slope skiing. Most agree that sport not in premier league with few opportunities for the C,D,E team players to turn out (given size of school there must be a fair number of these). Some physical activity compulsory all the way through with Zumba and Pilates for the less sporty from year 5, but the sixth formers we saw were hardly rushing to the gymnasium. Wii Fit in houses may be more popular. On the other hand we hear of considerable efforts made to find something for the keen but not so able to participate in. The school is most successful at national level in equestrian sports, with a girl in the GB under 16 team and talented riders competing for India and Australia. Not sure the school can take direct credit for this. Gloucestershire with its links to the European riding scene may have been a deciding factor. There's no stabling at the school but girls may keep their mounts 20 minutes away in Leckhampton. Polo is played at Birdlip.

Background and atmosphere: Miss Dorothea Beale led the school (including a nursery and a teacher training college) from 1858. She was a suffragette who pioneered women's education at a time when biology had to be code-named 'human geography' to stop irate fathers taking their girls home because to learn about such things would make them unmarriageable. Not content with revolutionising women's school education, the astonishing Miss Beale also founded St Hilda's College, Oxford. What would she make of today's Cheltenham Ladies as they sweep all before them, outperforming most boys and becoming leaders in their chosen careers? Ms Jardine-Young says that the College has become, 'more open, less introspective,' since she was a pupil there. Her aim is to take that forward and enable girls to 'become more adventurous learners, prepared to succeed but resilient enough to cope with failure.'

The main entrance to the College is on one of Cheltenham's wide boulevards. If it weren't for girls in PE kit massing on the steps it could be mistaken for a corporate HQ and, with 800+ pupils and over 600 employees, in one sense that's what it is. Behind lies a glorious quad, three parts Victorian Gothic creeper-clad grandeur, one part grim 1970s concrete modernism. Miss Beale wanted her girls to learn in surroundings as beautiful as those boys had been favoured with for hundreds of years. The original fabric of the College with its wonderful chequer board marble corridor, grand library, mullion windows and arts and crafts frescoes was thus as much a political statement as a seat of learning. The teaching rooms we saw were in the main functional and surprisingly anonymous. You couldn't tell you were at such a legendary school unless you happened to be daydreaming and looked out of the window (and we're sure that never happens).

On the day of our visit there had been something of a non-story in the national press about 'draconian guidelines' issued to ensure that 'mufti' (or home clothes) were sufficiently modest. School rather twitchy about this and we never did get the chance to ask girls what their opinion was. Parents say they resented the tone of the letter rather than its content (some outraged by both). Many admitted that they were pleased to deflect responsibility for discouraging tiny shorts etc onto school. Uniform is pretty dreary though - the most enthusiasm we could elicit from parents was that 'it does the job.' The good people of Cheltenham may have nicknamed the girls 'greenflies' but something a little less evolved, 'algae', perhaps, would more precisely describe the shade of the green skirts and jumpers. Sixth formers may wear navy pin-stripe trousers although to this reviewer the effect of these with regulation shirt and jumper is a curious half-bank worker, half-schoolgirl centaur. But away with such frivolous concerns, we feel the disapproving shade of Miss Beale urging us to look at the bigger picture. She's right, of course.

Pastoral care and discipline: This is a big school and the house system works well by breaking it down into manageable units - roughly 60 girls per house. Whole school meets every day in the Princess Hall for prayers, notices etc. Houses, most substantial and Victorian, but pleasingly not too unsympathetically subdivided, are scattered in nearby leafy residential roads and strings of Ladies' College girls walking to and fro are one of Cheltenham's perennial sights (hence, perhaps, worries about unsuitable attire on mufti days). Some houses are quite a hike away, conveniently making sensible footwear a must. Fair bit of road crossing necessary and this concerns new parents as girls travel in unaccompanied groups. Girls eat all meals in their house, a buffet lunch is available in the main school for those taking exams or with commitments that use up travelling time. Each house has its own chefs but meals are planned centrally - economies of scale no doubt, also cuts down on lunch envy - girls get to choose favourite menus. Eating environment and food seemed pleasant enough in the houses we visited. Significant boarding refurbishment project planned and to enable this a new junior boarding house has been acquired into which each house will 'decant' in turn.

Younger girls' dorms spacious and very jolly with home duvets, under-bed storage and lots of photos and personalisation. At the foot of every bed was a brightly coloured tuck box. Single rooms for older girls are small but characterful, many with inspiring views. A place in one of the old-fashioned 'cubs,' dorms where beds have a curtain around them, highly coveted. Parents full of praise for pastoral care whether for boarders or day girls - house mistresses in particular singled out for responding to e-mail/telephone calls by return. Incidents - friendship issues or bullying - nipped in bud equally promptly we hear. Girls bring their own laptops but internet use is heavily monitored. Boarders may use social networking sites from year 3 up out of school hours. The sixth form house we visited was originally the indefatigable Miss Beale's teacher training college. With its elegant library (plus wireless of course), it is intended to be a 'halfway house to university.' Girls may come and go with more freedom but the academic tutors and house mistresses liaise to minimise girls pushing themselves too hard and staff on each floor listen out for late night working.

Pupils and parents: So sorry to undermine a popular cliché but we encountered no braying Henriettas or snooty aristos, just normal girls - friendly, unaffected and full of fun. Our year 9 lunch companions were sweetly excited about how much they 'loved going to Waitrose' (store has wisely established itself as the nearest supermarket) and triumphant that they had persuaded the local ice cream van to call at their house. Some observe (as did we) that nationalities tend to stick together both in and out of lessons - inevitable perhaps - and a look at the results lists in the excellent school magazine tells its own, by now familiar, story of the formidable Chinese work ethic.

Whispers on the GSG grapevine that the school is not quite as fashionable with metropolitan parents as once it was but London is still the home city of boarding majority. In the main, parents are the usual spectrum of by no means rich professionals who choose the College because of the opportunities it offers their bright daughters. Several mentioned that they valued the school's relative conservatism and high expectations in a world of declining standards. All said that the pace is fast; too fast for a few.

Entrance: Entrance exam at 11+ (English, maths, VR). 'Please don't coach,' the school begs parents. 'We can spot the child who has been coached.' We imagine most parents have their hands over their ears and are singing loudly. At 13+ exams in maths, English, science, VR and French (if previously studied). For entry to the sixth form girls must sit exams in the subjects they wish to study.

So what exactly, we quizzed the head of admissions, does CLC look for? All girls take the same exam, thus candidates from outside the UK must have a very high standard of English. Every admission is considered on an individual basis; a girl's extracurricular interests are an important factor. The message from parents is, if you think it will suit your daughter, have a go. One told us, 'my daughter wasn't top in her prep school but she got a place and is loving it.' CLC wants girls who 'accept that they are joining a community.' Families are strongly encouraged to visit several times so that they know 'what they are getting.' Indeed families are under nearly as much scrutiny as girls themselves. Great importance is attached to what the school calls, 'generosity of spirit' – interpret that as you wish. Roughly 25 per cent from outside the UK (ex-pats as well as foreign nationals), many from the Far East, and the IB programme attracts strong candidates from Europe and South Africa. The 200 day girls keep school's Gloucestershire roots strong.

Exit: A few leave post-GCSE but most stay on and benefit hugely from the higher education and careers advice provided by the school's Professional Guidance Centre. Support includes subject mentors to aid with further reading and personal statements, interview training and the opportunity to talk with Guild members about university and career choices.

In 2013, 71 gained places at Oxbridge, rest to Russell group or abroad (US Ivy League increasingly popular choice). Careers of old girls give a flavour of what Cheltenham ladies do next: heaps of lawyers, MPs, medics and scientists. They include Nicola Horlick (financier), Cheryl Gillan (Conservative MP, Secretary of State for Wales), Rachel Lomax (first woman Deputy Governor of the Bank of England), Dame Mary Archer (scientist), Lisa Jardine (historian) and Rosie Boycott (journalist).

Money matters: Plenty of 'merit based awards' and scholarships for eg academics, art, sport and music. 'Limited amount' of funding for means-tested bursaries and some help for families of current pupils in financial difficulties. Bursaries intended to widen access to College are 'carefully awarded' to girls who would benefit from a College education. Principal very keen to extend opportunities in this area.

Remarks: A top flight school with strong traditional values and a clear sense of purpose. For the bright and energetic all rounder this school offers an exceptional education that is both broad and deep, with endless opportunities for fun and enrichment along the way.

The Cherwell School

Marston Ferry Road, Oxford, OX2 7EE

• Pupils: 1815 boys and girls, all day • Ages: 11–18 • Non-denom • State

Tel: 01865 558719
Email: head@cherwell.oxon.sch.uk
Website: www.cherwell.oxon.sch.uk

Head: Since 2010, Mr Paul James MA (Cantab) NPQH (late 30s). Appointed first as deputy then acting head at early departure of the previous incumbent. Previous experience includes deputy head at RGS High Wycombe and head of middle school/assistant head at Magdalen College School, Oxford. Read natural sciences at Cambridge and is a keen triathlon competitor, medal winner at European Age-Group championships. Married with two primary-aged children. Chairs the Oxford University Department of Education internship team, which broadens the school's links with the academic life of the city.

Fresh and energetic in manner, he has won back the parents' confidence, 'brought a rigour to things that the school needed'. Current parents feel he makes himself visible at parents' evenings and proud that he answers all their emails. He heads a staff of nearly 120, mentors some year 11s and appears in the classroom when needed – he recently described the responsibilities of a head's position to develop some year 9 students' understanding of People in Power; even willing to declare his salary, when asked. He expands warmly on his vision for the school as one that leads by example in the local community. Useful experience in a variety of settings, grammar, independent and maintained schools, has enabled him to lift The Cherwell to a position where it holds its own with many local independent schools.

Academic matters: Cherwell has maintained its place as one of the best state secondary schools in the county, oversubscribed and building on its impressive sixth form reputation. It offers a breadth of subjects at GCSE, both academic and practical, from dance to product design. The science specialist status, attracts large numbers who pursue physics and further maths in sixth form. History and English are popular and all take citizenship at GCSE. German or Spanish and French are supplemented by trips abroad. Maths is set in year 7, but other subjects are mixed ability. In 2013, 71 per cent 5+ A*-C grades, including English and maths. Post-GCSE there is an extremely wide selection of A level and vocational courses, including health and social care, science in society and BTECs in sports and engineering. A*-B pass rate has risen over last few years from just under 50 per cent to 61 per cent in 2013. As the head says, 'You can't come here and be bored'.

Nearly 75 per cent of students go on to sixth form, the other places being eagerly taken up by locals from nearby maintained and independent schools. Strong results and Oxbridge places as well as interesting subject range attract fierce competition for places.

Very inclusive school: dynamic learning support department manages fluctuating numbers on SEN register, can be as many as 300. Two resource bases run within the school: hearing impairment and communication and interaction, which are filled from county-wide referrals, with over 20 specialist teachers and clinicians. Hearing-impaired students attend mainstream classes, some in sound-proofed classrooms, with additional support, such as laptops, to access curriculum. Resource bases integrate children into mainstream where possible so the students are 'very used to children dropping in and out of their classes'. In addition, The Base provides specialist support for students with behavioural difficulties and 'fragile' students at specific times, although not on a permanent basis. Vulnerable students have access to behaviour management professionals and counselling, as well as a range of activities and courses. Bases are valued by all, which 'enhances the inclusive nature of the school'. Empathy and support for peers are qualities specified in The Cherwell Code, displayed round the school. Students with identified needs are visited at primary schools and benefit from a programme of transition into the secondary site, above and beyond the taster day for prospective year 7s. Word on the street, however, is critical of the level of dyslexia support within the school. The 23 per cent of accelerated learners have access to their own gifted and talented officer.

Games, options, the arts: The school spreads over two sites, each with access to games fields, netball and basketball areas and tennis courts, as well as three gyms between them. In addition, the local Ferry sports centre and rugby club are a stone's throw away, resulting in strong rugby teams for both men and women, football and indoor racquet sports. Under 15s are national basketball champions. Parent grumbles that the school has a 'chip on shoulderish' attitude to cricket, given that there are so many pitches and teams to play with locally. Wheels are the thing here, however. The school boasts first place in the 'cycling to school' league with an advisor on hand to new entrants to advise on bike routes. The lively Cycle Club enjoys links with national cycle associations, and offers bike polo, grasstrack and BMX training, as well as bike maintenance courses open to the whole school. Not surprising to find a professional skateboarder among the alumnae. Sadly, with a pool next door, the school has not the funds to offer swimming lessons, which is a shortcoming in a city sited on a river.

Art, music and drama are taken by all year 7s, and offered as choices at GCSE and beyond. Extra-curricular music is popular, with a choice of gospel choir, chamber choir and a guys-only barbershop for singers, several bands and a full orchestra which performs impressively in local churches. One year 12 boy recently conducted the orchestra in his own trumpet arrangement. Scratched corridors are livened up with exciting art work (a tea-bag evening gown greets you in reception) and artwork spreads out over the ground, literally, with a pavement drawing project. The younger years take advantage of Oxford's rich museum, gallery and library treasures, while older years also visit London exhibitions as part of the GCSE or BTEC courses. The 'Chicken Project' combines business studies with a charity fund-raising venture bringing agriculture to a South African village; proceeds go towards education. This was also embraced by the science department, which hosted a cross-curriculum research study into chickens' colour preferences. After-school clubs are popular, to inspire the students in anything from rowing to chess (old boy is an International Chess Master!).

Background and atmosphere: Outshone by the architectural beauty of nearby independents, this is a diamond in the rough school. An organic collection of modern buildings, some dating from 1963, when the school was founded, make up the North Side (key stages 4 and 5) while a more homogeneous building for the younger years sits across a busy road, connected by a frescoed tunnel. Wide fields and the meadows of Marston surround the students and direct access to a long bicycle boulevard protects them from the traffic. Once you have located the main entrance in the smart sixth form block, the welcome is warm and genuine. What started out in the 60s as a small secondary modern is now an academy and a leader in Oxfordshire partnerships drive, with an active programme to share expertise with local secondary schools and raise standards in primary ones.

Pastoral care and discipline: Discipline, in particular absenteeism, has seen the greatest change under the current head. There is now a clear rewards policy familiar to all students, which has been effective in reducing exclusions and keeping standards of behaviour high. All the students I met seemed motivated by the Amazon vouchers they earn for success, academic and non-academic; and happily none seemed to have had experience at the other end of the scale: solely problems with equipment and lateness. Parents of students joining at sixth form reported a 'sink or swim' culture, which teaches students to 'run their life a bit'. Those that can, do well; those that can't are now monitored closely by a full-time inclusion and attendance officer. Recent change to written reports system means they are sent home rather than entrusted to the students. Each year group has both a teaching and non-teaching head, for day-to-day worries, as well as a mentor system using teachers and people from local community; the head see individual cases, himself. Bilingual buddies are assigned to new starters from overseas who have language support needs, and peer monitoring is also used. As one parent said, 'It is very good if your children are keen and get on with it; if you are easily distracted, you're distracted'.

Pupils and parents: Around the school, you hear the healthy hum of discussion, as students move between the sites and nearby Summertown shops, where the older ones hang out at lunch. Others use the popular canteen or take advantage of the multi-gym. Students span a wide range of social, academic and socio-economic backgrounds, with above average numbers of English as second language speakers. Catchment families range from university members, medics and white-collar professionals to Oxford's more vulnerable families; but all benefit from the active parents' groups raising money both for school building projects and charity. The United Nations feel is reinforced by the lack of uniform. There is a three Bs rule for girls (decent covering of body parts beginning with B) and a 'no low slung pants' rule for boys, but otherwise anything goes. The by-product of this informality, according to the head, is a strengthening of staff/student relations. Interchanges I overheard were spirited and challenging but this side of respectful. Famous alumnae include Rachel Seiffert (writer); Tom Poster (winner of BBC Young Keyboard Musician of the Year) and Yasmin le Bon (model).

Entrance: Oversubscribed from a dozen or so local primaries within Oxfordshire LA, except for the two resource bases which take students with statements and by referral. Sixth form causes a stir in the local community by attracting students from excellent independent schools, persuaded by wider range of options, perhaps funkier than they have been used to as well as greater independence. One parent remarked, 'They get more of a taste here for what is to come at university'.

Exit: Nearly 80 per cent go on to A level, either at The Cherwell or at local FE college. Some 95 per cent of sixth form leavers go to university; rising numbers each year to Oxbridge (14 in 2013). Dazzling range of subjects taken at university, reflecting vibrant mix of sixth form, but science subjects are popular, as well as history and maths. Three to medical school in 2013. Careers counselling starts early and guidance to popular vocational courses; a few go directly to employment.

Money matters: Head welcomes the recent academy status as 'protection from the difficult financial climate'. Large sums raised by PTA, when needed, including helping to fund a library in SE Asia by taking advantage of school's links with the Bodleian

Remarks: The Cherwell fulfils its slogan, 'A Centre for Opportunity'. The vision and commitment of the new head has made it a contender in the competition for Oxford's brightest children. It offers an exciting range of subjects and activities geared to the real world; a lively melting pot of students who span the social spectrum and staff who know how to get the most out of this diversity. The result is articulate and worldly leavers, many of whom achieve good results. Those who can't ignore disruption do less well.

Chew Valley School

Chew Lane, Chew Magna, Bristol, BS40 8QB

- Pupils: 645 girls; 550 boys, all day • Ages: 11–18 • Non-denom
- State

Tel: 01275 332272
Email: enquiries@chewvalleyschool.co.uk
Website: www.chewvalleyschool.co.uk

Head: Since 2003 Mr Mark Mallett LLB MA PGCE (fifties). Son of a Methodist minister and educated in both independent (Kingswood, Bath) and state sectors, (Reading School and Maltby Grammar), he read law rather reluctantly at UCL, before having a

Damascus moment, as he put it, whilst visiting a friend teaching English in Algeria. Back to the London Institute for his PGCE and MA before wanderlust took him to Borneo for VSO. Since then, his belief in comprehensive education has shaped a career in two of the best in the west, Backwell and Chew Valley, as well as a foray to the north, QEH Hexham.

Bearded and charming, Mr Mallett believes a liberal education should be an entitlement for all, and expresses his concern about 'the narrowing of education, albeit in a laudable attempt to drive up standards'. Resisting the lure of academy status, Mr Mallett gained foundation status for his school in 2010, working with the LA 'from a position of equality, rather than subordination', as he expressed it.

He retains a passion for English, which those he teaches say is infectious, and which can be seen all over the school, with apposite notices on pertinent doors: 'If music be the food of love, play on' to the music dept., 'Exit, pursued by a bear' to the playground. 'Fabulous teacher', we kept hearing. Keen musician, sings weekly at City of Bristol Choir and enjoys opera and theatre. Married to Deborah, a former language teacher now training to be a Methodist minister, with 2 grown children, a daughter at Oxford (choral scholar) and a son in his gap year.

Parents and pupils give him a universal thumbs-up, as do Ofsted, who graded the school outstanding in all but 4 out of 31 measures in 2011. 'I'm still walking on air' says Mr Mallett, whilst paying generous tribute to his staff.

Academic matters: Success across the board, particularly impressive for a non-selective school. Everyone does either French or Spanish in year 7, star performers are identified, fast-tracked and encouraged to take up German in year 8. Maths setted from the start, science in broad ability bands, everything else mixed ability groups. GCSE results have risen steadily over the past few years – in 2013, 64 per cent got five plus A*-C including English and maths, 22 per cent A*/A grades. The study camp, run in the Easter holidays, must help. Not flattered by government value added measures due to the trad profile of the exams taken here.

A level results are very good too, with 55 per cent A*-B grades, 27 per cent A*/A in 2013. Strongest subjects seem to be maths (including further maths) and sciences, sociology, psychology and drama. Twenty-nine subjects offered at A level. Academics are taken seriously here: Oxbridge hopefuls are assigned external mentors from amongst the governors or local businesses; the AQA baccalaureate (A levels, AS critical thinking and EPQ) is offered and pupils present their EPQ submissions at a special evening. But the school does not want 'Oxbridge to be the achievement we shout loudest about': it's as much about making sure that the more vocationally bound get the courses they want too. Around 25 per cent of the GCSE cohort take an applied route. The G&T register records prowess in all sorts of areas, not just brain-power.

Parents largely content with academic offering, though one mentioned frustration with just five minutes laid on with each subject teacher per year, and felt that there could be more precision for individuals, eg 'What does my child have to do to get an A*, rather than an A?'. SEN provision universally praised: totally free of stigma, and housed in a series of rooms which act as a safe haven for those who find the hurly-burly and unstructured nature of break-times difficult, or for those who want a quiet place to knock off coursework. (The library isn't always as quiet as pupils would like, they told us). School has 12 per cent recorded as SEN; out of 100 or so, 18 have statements. Some vexation that disruptive kids without statements cannot be given the help/means/resources to bring about better classroom behaviour – a common complaint in tightly-resourced state schools.

We found lessons lively and engaging, particularly a Spanish one, where pupils were building complex sentences with towers of books. A sixth form PHSE class engaged pupils in a discussion of student finances. Marked work was displayed on the walls, showing off both pupils' and teachers' expertise.

Games, options, the arts: Stacks on offer, appreciated by everyone. Chew Valley's rural location and 30 acre site mean masses of pitches, tennis courts, an Astro and gardens. All usual sports feature, plus girls' rugby and sailing on nearby Chew Valley Lake. Pupils enjoy busy fixture list with local schools plus links with community clubs and Bath University for facilities (eg 50m pool) and specialist sports teaching. Team performance is impressive, yet still some parents grumble that the 'sports just don't compare with independent schools'. Extracurricular outdoors-y stuff also offered by committed staff, such as Ten Tors and D of E. Gym and sports centre on site shared with general public, which reduces cost. Certainly enough sport beyond traditional games to keep everyone happy, including a committed and successful cheer-leading group – we could hardly squeeze into the PE office for pompoms.

School has had performing arts status since 2003, and is strong across the board. As well as terrific debating, public speaking and plays (As You Like It, Guys and Dolls, Ubu Roi suggest there's something for everyone), music is described as 'amazing' by one mum (around a quarter of pupils take extra music lessons and achieve grade 8 in some cases).Ensembles range from orchestra, flute group, to brass, folk and all the way to rock band; singers can choose from several choirs and less formal set-ups. Dance dept (which caters for boys too) puts on own festival which attracts the twinkle-toed from primaries, secondaries and even universities on occasion. Regular prizes from annual Mid-Somerset Festival.

Visual arts appear as rather a poor relation to its all-singing-all-dancing siblings. Both art and DT facilities looked well-loved and used, and school has in the past curated the LA's schools' art exhibition, yet all that unadorned breeze block inside the school was crying out for some vibrant canvasses. More on show please!

No poverty of ambitions in terms of expeditions, however: Chew Valley pupils have recently been to India, to Lesotho and to Honduras, where two new bird species were identified.

Background and atmosphere: Looks like the 50 year old secondary modern it once was, with a clutch of undistinguished low level buildings – with the exception of the stunning new sixth form block overlooking the lake. Chew Valley has enjoyed a well-deserved reputation for excellence for many years and now has a building to reflect it, with teaching space, seminar rooms and a café, where students were hard at work when we visited. School is fortunate to have so much green space, enough to grow veg and to keep chickens, who reside at Cluckingham Palace.

It all feels buzzy and purposeful, in fact we were practically trampled by chattering kids en route to various destinations – no flattening themselves against the wall as the head sweeps by. This lack of undue deference meant lively and stimulating conversation with pupils who identified clearly what they love about the school (range of stuff on offer, encouragement to start clubs or activities, great relationships with staff, school grounds and their use as outdoor classrooms), and what's on their wish-list (proper performance space which does not double as dining hall, better stocked library). Lunchtimes are very busy with clubs and the Learning to Lead programme – a very upswept version of a school council, with over 100 pupils 'working in teams with real power and responsibility'. The wind turbine in the grounds which supplies some of the school's power, the healthy meals in the canteen and the residents of Cluck House are evidence of their work. So significant has this been that team members have been to two national conferences to talk about how it's done. Parents like it – as long as there are enough willing volunteers to run all these teams. Charities extremely well supported through various team-based initiatives also.

Bad behaviour is dealt with by the behaviour support teacher: 'We will not have our lessons disrupted,' states the school. Time after time we were told about the family atmosphere and the tremendous loyalty ex-pupils feel; parents value the fact that the school provides the climate and opportunity to try things out: 'My child has found a real delight in drama which has had a knock-on effect in English,' said one mother, 'they really do blossom in all sorts of ways'.

Uniform is practical, cheap and standards are enforced. Sixth formers wear whatever they like.

Pastoral care and discipline: Generally judged to be exceptional, and not just by Ofsted. School has had designated home/school liaison officer for the last 10 years, who dragged herself in from her sickbed to talk to us, and who acts as a point of contact for parents; matters raised are then referred on to the right person – medical, academic or pastoral. This highly rated lady can also refer troubled pupils to external sources of support, as well as advising parents in crisis. Some services eg counselling are brought into school because of its rural location and provided from Lake View, an unobtrusive building in the school grounds designated for small group teaching.

Parents and pupils appreciate clarity on the perennial irritants of fags and booze, and the more insidious matter of drugs; school says none of it presents a great problem, but won't stop short of exclusions – fixed term or permanent – for those who transgress.

No-one mentioned bullying, but all parents we talked to praised the speed and quality of the school's response to any issues they raised. The prevailing climate seems to be one of praise, far and above blame.

Pupils and parents: Predominantly local – school serves the 120 square miles of the Chew Valley and is a key feature of the community. Wide-ish economic mix of families of modest means – 'There's rural poverty even in Chew Valley,' says the head – all the way to Bristol professionals who choose to live south of the city, and who may well do so on account of the school. A few refugees from south Bristol schools, most of which are 'well rough'. One young man told us he had gone off the idea of his local school when someone threw a chair out of the window during a lesson the day he visited. Not exactly ethnically diverse – this was about the only note of criticism Ofsted could muster.

We found everyone we met bright, articulate and positive. Parents actively encouraged to be part of school life – there's an enthusiastic School Society which raises funds and puts on events – but some felt that even greater use could be made of parental expertise in applying for grants etc. All report good communication, and appear genuinely committed to and grateful for the education Chew Valley lays on. Former pupils include John Garden (keyboards in The Scissor Sisters); recording flautist Nicola Woodward and professional percussionist Justin Woodward.

Entrance: At year 7, 196 places and demand outstrips supply. Majority of intake will live within 'school's area of prime responsibility', but some places will go to out of area applicants. Check LA (Bath and NE Somerset) criteria with care. School sits (awkwardly) on the borders of two other LAs, South Bristol and North Somerset. At sixth form, a minimum of five GCSE grades A*-C to include English and maths is required.

Exit: Four to Oxbridge in 2013, 22 students to Russell Group, Durham Sheffield and Birmingham popular.

Some fall-out post GCSE to employment or to sixth form colleges. By that stage the urban temptations of Bristol (St Brendan's, City of Bristol) or even Norton Radstock college exert a pull – and they put on huge range of courses. Of those who stay on, a handful start work, another handful take gap years and the majority go to the university of their first choice, covering a great range: four Oxbridge 2013, others to eg Durham, Sheffield and Birmingham. UCAS preparation is thorough. Degree choices are many and various – from accounting to tourism, via Chinese studies and a notable attraction to earth sciences.

Remarks: A model of comprehensive education, this school truly serves all the interested parties in its community. 'A private school without fees', 'If I had my time again, I would definitely choose Chew Valley' say parents. About as good as it gets – worth moving for.

Chigwell School

Linked school: Chigwell Junior School

High Road, Chigwell, Essex, IG7 6QF

• Pupils: 420 pupils; 27 full boarders in the sixth form • Ages: 13–18 • C of E but welcomes all • Fees: Day £10,785–£14,985; Boarding £24,675 pa • Independent

Tel: 020 8501 5700
Email: hm@chigwell-school.org
Website: www.chigwell-school.org

Headmaster: Since 2007, Mr Michael Punt MA MSc PGCE (forties), a physicist who lives on site with his wife Gill and their three sons, one of whom attends the school. His calm and positive influence is palpable throughout the school, although he modestly describes his many successful initiatives as 'just tinkering'. Parents know better, saying he's 'approachable, liked and respected'. One even tells the tale of a parent who was torn between three schools for her child but plumped for Chigwell on the basis of meeting Mr Punt.

Academic matters: Excellent results – 2013 75 per cent A*/A at GCSE; 75 per cent A*-B and 47 per cent A*/A at A level. ISI inspectors praised 'pupils' positive and conscientious attitude to learning and their excellent relationship with the teachers'. Experienced, dedicated staff and a free choice of options outside of the core subjects are major factors, says the head, who is keen to offer a wide range at A level, including those required for a broad choice of university courses, to pique the interest of his academically inquisitive students. History and geography are the long-established favourites here and good results can be credited to an experienced department, says the head. Economics, maths and sciences are also strong at A level but drama and DT are on the rise too, enforcing Chigwell's reputation as a place for the all-rounder.

Maths IGCSE is taken – pupils are setted 'loosely' in year 7 in preparation. Three-quarters take separate sciences at GCSE – sets for these start in year 9. New heads of languages and English recently appointed to boost takeup and results, which have lagged behind the other subjects in the past. English is set in year 10 and languages are now more popular choices for GCSE and A level, thanks to the early introduction of Spanish and German in the junior school.

One of Mr Punt's most successful recent innovations has been the change of lesson length from 35 to 50 minutes, which has increased teaching time for sixth formers and given teachers the scope to introduce more pupil-centred activities.

Dedicated SENCo – junior school pupils screened on entry, further testing in the senior school. Learning support used mostly in the junior school. High ability students developed beyond the classroom with extension activities.

Games, options, the arts: Parents are pleased with the balance of academic work and life experiences – 'Valuable pursuits such as art, drama, music and sport enhance the atmosphere of positive competition,' says one.

Seventy-five acres of playing fields surround this small school but indoor facilities are relatively modest in comparison to many of its peers – unfancy sports centre and small outdoor swimming pool. Hockey strong for both boys and girls, set to build with recent Astro. Competes well on the football pitch and numbers several county players in netball and cricket – own all-weather nets. PE pursuits are rotated half-termly, eg basketball and badminton. Golf is played at the nearby club and sixth formers can visit the local gym or use the on site fitness equipment.

The drama centre is an eye-catching red-brick building with impressively professional facilities – foyer big enough for pre-theatre drinks receptions; rehearsal and teaching rooms, 200 moveable seats; two productions a year and sixth form play. A dozen students each year take drama A level with great success. Music very inclusive – every other pupil learns an instrument, annual Prom concert open to all, house music competition, Young Musician of the Year event, performances by many ensembles.

Huge choice of extracurricular activities, from D of E and scouts to art exhibitions and the inspiring and thought-provoking talks run as part of the Williams Project, named after philosopher and Chigwell alumnus, Bernard Williams.

Background and atmosphere: Set on the approach road to the historic high street, founded in 1629 by the Reverend Samuel Harsnett, the local vicar, who became Archbishop of York and Chancellor of Cambridge University. Today the original red-brick schoolhouse forms the centrepiece to this pretty village of neat buildings, punctuated by gardens and quads planted with blooms and trees. The surrounding playing fields stretch as far as Epping Forest and give a rural aspect to the school and some lovely views from the windows of the attractive, low-rise teaching blocks. None of the facilities are more than an easy and pleasant stroll apart. The music block is positioned centrally, so the odd note and phrase float across the greenery, and the drama centre is a well-designed modern addition. When we visited, the new dining hall, sixth form coffee shop and kitchens were under construction and the pupils were excited to be taking their meals in the Harry Potteresque main hall. The new food facilities were later declared open by Michel Roux. Plans for a sixth form study centre.

The 1920s chapel was built in tribute to fallen alumni and is a mainstay of life here. Twice weekly services embrace all the beliefs represented at this multicultural school and speech day includes a passage from each of the six major world faiths – integral respect and sense of community. 'This is a happy school,' says the head – does seem to be a sense of harmony at work. No need for intrusive bells to mark the change of lessons – pupils make their way around the school in an ordered fashion and newbies of any age wear a plain tie so they can be spotted and helped when in need, in typical caring Chigwellian fashion.

Has own nomenclature for year groups, from removes (year 9), through lower fifth, upper fifth and lower sixth to middle sixth (year 13). Intranet – Chigwell's Gateway – heavily relied on for submission of homework and essential admin such as notices and timetables. An electronic noticeboard system is also well used – life seems to flow in a stress-free fashion.

Pastoral care and discipline: 'Excellent' from ISI for pastoral care – easy to see why. A strong four-house system, and staff who 'really know their pupils', according to the head, mean students are comfortable in the knowledge that they are being 'looked out for'. Promotes a society in which everyone takes responsibility for each other and the wider environment.

Sixth form students from abroad valued for the insights they provide into other cultures and ways of life. Mostly from Central and Eastern Europe and China, encouraged to give talks on the issues affecting their homelands, the only ones to board in four homely houses on-site – their constant presence gives

the school a lived-in feel. Boarders are also attached to a day house and take a full part in activities there.

Food is said to be plentiful and good, with healthy options and popular themed days – children spoke enthusiastically of tasting lobster on seafood day, and sausages were dished up all round to celebrate St George's Day. The uniform is smart and sober – kilts or plain trousers with a navy blazer, though the sixth formers wear office attire.

Pupils and parents: This leafy, middle-class suburb is spoilt for choice education-wise, with several good fee-paying schools on the doorstep and some of the best grammars in the country a short hop on the train away. Even Old Chigwellians admit to investigating the competition before signing up their offspring, but one was pleased to note, 'The school has retained one of its key attributes – to ensure that pupils attain their potential'. Equally, though, appeals to first-time buyers, notably British Asian families who are attracted by the excellence in maths and sciences, and those who see Chigwell's strength in 'creating confident, well-rounded people'. Although this is undoubtedly an affluent area, and children are drawn mainly from a four or five-mile radius, the head is aware that families often make sacrifices to send them.

Slightly more boys than girls in the seniors, but as the juniors are now 50-50, set to change in the future. The pupils we met fell over themselves with helpfulness and had a relaxed, confident air. Parents have many opportunities to speak informally with staff about their children's progress and well-being at breakfast get-togethers and afternoon teas, and the Friends of Chigwell put on a programme of social events.

School minibus service runs from Theydon Bois and Epping, bringing pupils to school in the mornings – hopes to expand routes in the future.

The list of distinguished alumni includes William Penn, Sir Arthur Grimble, Austin Bradford Hill, Edward Vulliamy and Sir Bernard Williams. Sir Alan Sugar lives virtually next door and his grandsons are pupils here, as were their fathers.

Entrance: Most come across from the junior department; very few vacancies at 13. At 16 no advertised places – those moving up to the sixth form are expected to have achieved at least Bs or above in six GCSE subjects and A/A* in their A level choices.

Exit: 'Students here have high aspirations,' says the head. Very few post-16 leavers. In 2013, six to Oxbridge, four overseas; rest to a range from Leeds to Bath to King's College London.

Money matters: Academic scholarships available at 11 and 13 years; scholarships for art, drama and music offered at 16. Means-tested bursaries available.

Remarks: A relaxed and happy school with a real family feel; a very civilised place nurturing confident, caring all-rounders.

Christ College, Brecon

Brecon, Powys, LD3 8AF

• Pupils: 210 boys, 150 girls. 230 boarders; 130 day pupils • Ages: 11–18 • Christian • Fees: Boarding £18,270– £24,510; Day £13,275– £15,870 pa • Independent

Tel: 01874 615440
Email: enquiries@christcollegebrecon.com
Website: www.christcollegebrecon.com

Head: Since 2007, Mrs Emma Taylor MA (early forties). Educated at St Antony's Leweston and Canford. Exhibitioner at New

College Oxford (PPE). Previously philosophy, religious studies and economics teacher Stowe; housemistress Canford; deputy head Dean Close. Seriously bright, wears it lightly but it shows in both what she writes and in what you see going on here, for this, you will find, is a school with a curving bow wave. Unstuffy, capable, effective. Shrewd in her strategic vision: understands her market and dreams not of bigger but better. Has already topped the school up and lifted exam results. Does not shy away from decisions which, in a school which venerates tradition, can elicit dismay – an example: school colours are no longer the exclusive reward for good sports but are now conferred – following a painstaking justification process – on high achievers in anything.

A terrifically good sport in her own right, an indefatigable supporter of absolutely everything that goes on: 'She's everywhere!' Widely liked and admired. Has fostered links with the local community. Likes to know what parents think and, as one avowedly difficult mother told us, usually responds to an email within the hour. Her husband is a modern linguist, currently a house husband. Two daughters, one at the school.

Academic matters: For reasons of geography and demographics CCB – as they call it – is very much its own place. Small schools are normally for children who aren't terribly good at school, need to 'develop at their own pace'. If that's what you're after, don't shortlist this one. Intake is unusually comprehensive, always will be, and the sixth form is annually boosted by switchers from other schools, state and independent, and overseas students – the lack of a good local sixth form college is a great help here. The top end is seriously bright – handful to Oxbridge annually – with those not so bright not so very far behind. Results, hitherto thoroughly respectable, are on the up, seriously good by any standards. An eye-blinkingly good crop of A* grades at A level (15 per cent in 2013, with 44 per cent A*/A; 54 per cent A*/A at GCSE) and just a tiny number of failures: Mrs Taylor has managed to lure some really good teachers here.

Small class sizes, even for an independent school – in the sixth form some are minuscule, possibly a little too much so. Meticulous monitoring. Academic pressure is insistent, but 'the teachers aren't on your case the whole time'. A 'per ardua ad astra' culture pervades all areas of life here and, in the classroom, they seem to be getting it about right – cheerfully perspiring students are the ones who work best; parents are more than happy with the bottom line.

Subjects studied all untrendily academic, plus Cymraeg. For any school this is a good range, with no concessions to soft options. Can be the usual small-school timetabling snags, though. Exceedingly strong maths, good science, superb art and photography – no weak areas. Modern languages in stormingly good shape under the influence of marvellous head of department. Classrooms are bright and, given the school's income stream, commendably well equipped. The new science block is a class act as is their new Centre for the Creative Arts (opened in September 2013) – simply stunning.

SENs mild to moderate mostly – you must be able to work independently; anything more severe only if allied with high intelligence. One SEN teacher, a full-time, unusually well qualified member of staff whom the mother of a dyslexic boy instructed us in a manner not to be contravened to praise to the skies. Her classroom is not a self-pity inducing ICU – more a pit stop. Highly flexible, she can see any student as and when for as long as necessary – a reminder that remedial intervention is more about the interaction of two people than the administration of clinical nostrums. Sixth formers, particularly, like to use her for study skills support. And what about this – no extra charge for her services.

Games, options, the arts: To wake up and gaze at the new day here is to lift your eyes unto the hills (it's probably raining again), for, verily, they are all around. If that makes you quail,

go some place else – fresh air is what these boys and girls gulp much of. And here we come to another peculiar quality of the school: where anything to be done it's all hands to the pump, your school needs you – it's a small school thing. Opportunities are more plentiful, necessity for involvement more urgent, which could be a recipe for desperate, heroic failure if results didn't prove otherwise. As the boys and girls like to say here, they punch above their weight, an assertion borne out by a rugby victory just before our visit over a school three times its size. The heritage sport is rugby, unsurprise unsurprise, and it's well coached. 'There are three of us who've played to a fairly decent level,' explained a former Ireland international. For those who do not get off on rough-housing it in mud opportunities as diverse as fencing and riding. 'Whatever you're good at they really get behind you,' said one boy.

Rugby remains pre-eminent, but only just – other sports are coming up fast. Are girls playing a demure second fiddle? No way – their achievements actually place them at a higher level than the boys. Hockey and netball are outstanding, and it doesn't stop there – students are to be found doing all sorts at county and international level. You've got to be impressed, you really have.

No school for a laidback child – masses on offer outside the classroom and plenty of expectation to do it. A school this size is especially sensitive to the enthusiasms of its teachers, so kayaking is strong, as is mountain biking. As are all manner of outdoor pursuits activities, and D of E. With its army links – Brecon is HQ of the army in Wales and some parents are based at, er-hem, Hereford – the CCF is taken massively seriously.

On the culture front, music is top-notch, with eight choirs (eight, for heaven's sake), and the singing in chapel has to be heard to be believed. Lots of ensembles, Thursday lunchtime concerts, links with Welsh National Opera and Brecon Cathedral, plus a fiercely contested inter-house competition in which all take part (a competitive element to most things here). Drama is well done. Art is incredibly strong, photography a glory. Best of all, boys and girls get to do all sorts of things they normally wouldn't – your country needs you, you see. Look, there's the captain of the XV in a surplice.

Any school community stands in danger of being inward looking. They counteract that by inviting the local community to use the school's facilities (charity commissioners well pleased), cultural exchanges with China and Japan and school trips to all corners in the holidays.

Background and atmosphere: Founded in 1541 by Henry VIII on the site of the sacked and wracked Black Friars' church, victim of the Dissolution. The choir of the original chapel survives – well, some of it: it's been Gilbert Scott-ed – and the splendid refectory. Students are touchingly proud of this ancientness, as of the crowned 'h' tag, which is the school's logo, and of the fact that the chapel where they meet every morning has been worshipped in continuously since around 1250. The ancient buildings are architecturally charming, the rest of the campus unremarkable but easy enough on the eye. The 19th century big school is now the library. The new science block, with its dry-stone outer wall, is undeniably handsome. A campus feel. It's not at all a swanky place – the Welsh don't do grandeur; its appeal is its human scale. And its ravishing setting, of course, bang in the middle of the attractive market town of Brecon, washed on its eastern fringe by the excitable river Usk.

Recently awarded the best possible inspection grades in all three areas examined by Estyn, the office of Her Majesty's chief inspector of education and training in Wales.

Pastoral care and discipline: Boarding remains strong, always will – Forces families particularly want it and numbers are trend-buckingly high. It accounts for the social tenor of the school. Boarding done badly is the stuff of fag-roasts; done well it is what you see here: warm relationships between pupils of all ages and between pupils and staff. It's a marvellous sense of community, it really is – even inscrutable strangers like this Guide are enfolded from the word go. Add to that a strong responsibility felt by older pupils to give something back, testament to a regime of vigilant, humane supervision.

The school's small size is just one factor, and it enables a brand new year 7 away from home for the first time to feel comfy at once. They have their own house, the year 7s and 8s, a jolly, caring place run by husband and wife houseparents, with occasional reinforcement by specially assigned senior boys and girls, for whom it is a proud duty. Everyone here is known by everybody else. One parent lauded the inability of her spotlight-averse son to elude attention. Parents and pupils alike agree that pastoral care really is very good. A most touching and illustrative emblem of social health here is the custom of pupils leading most morning chapel services, where they often share highly sensitive personal experiences – you wouldn't do that if you didn't feel you were among friends. Accommodation is adequate and up to date, with room sharing up to the end of year 11, and single study bedrooms for almost all thereafter. Food meets general approval.

This is the sort of school which embraces differentness only so long as it's allied to a strong dynamic. Rebels, hangers back and bunkers off do not find a social niche – discipline is observable and bought into. They're a bit square, that's one way of looking at it. Or are they? One parent with current experience of a big, smart school, reflecting on this, was inclined to wish for more dabblers in radicalism, more what you might call racy sophistication and worldly wiseness. Then she reflected on the grottiness of teen nihilism and all the perils inherent – and came down firmly in favour of Christ College. What best equips your child for the world as it is? That is the question. Well, these boys and girls are far too busy and sunny-minded for substance abuse for sure. Damn it, the highest estimate of cigarette smoking we could elicit from the pupils was two per cent. Heavy-handed discipline is rendered unnecessary by a strong, consensual sense of purpose. Buck that, though, and you're out.

Pupils and parents: Most from within 50 miles, from primaries and preps in Wales, the English marches and further east. Parents are businesspeople, professionals, farmers and army officers. Some expats. Around 17 per cent of pupils actively recruited from abroad, especially Japan, China, Hong Kong and other Asian and European countries. A steady annual inflow of sixth formers from Germany – they come for a term, that's what they intend, then stay on for the year, even two years. Also a little contingent of Nepalis, sons and daughters of Gurkhas.

So it's a pretty good multicultural mix, but how English, how Welsh? A strong Welsh flavour, as you might expect – some pupils come from Welsh-speaking homes and a lilt in the voices of many of the teachers. Also a significant English presence. The head, English as can be, puts it this way: she wants everyone to be imbued with 'a sense of place, a sense of history', while a Welsh parent pronounced the school 'sufficiently Welsh'. In truth, they all rub along perfectly happily – simply not an issue. All nationalities well integrated – we were impressed by the number of Chinese boys, customarily prone to solitariness, who play rugby. And, gosh, they do all love to get together to sing those Welsh hymns.

Former pupils include Tori James, polar explorer and adventurer; Peter Watkins, film director; Simon Hughes, Lib Dem; and Jonathan Smith, playwright and author of The Learning Game – a book you should read.

Entrance: Three entry major points: around 30 arrive at year 7, 20 at year 9 and 30 at year 12. At years 7 and 9 an entry exam: English, maths and an IQ test. At year 12 you need six GCSEs at C minimum. Taster days in addition to open days, overnight if you wish. Greater pressure for places now than has been – a

broad church, for sure, ability wise, but no pushover. Parents say the school is very good at assigning boys and girls to the right house.

Exit: More or less all to university. Two to Oxbridge in 2013; others to study eg civil engineering at Surrey, zoology at Bristol, technical theatre at the Guildhall and sports science at Anglia Ruskin.

Money matters: Scholarships and bursaries for the able and deserving needy. The full fee is astonishingly good value, a tribute to astute management – around 25 per cent less than flagship competitors and, what's more, no inescapable extras. This does emphatically not make it a poor relation.

Remarks: A damn fine little school with a well-satisfied core constituency, by which it is well known. Lacks cachet? If that's what gives bang to your buck, you'll look elsewhere. If it's first-class boarding you're after, you ought to have at least one small school on your shortlist and this is an excellent candidate, reached by roads more rapid than you'd think, through ravishing countryside. Here's a school which inspires affection and admiration in both equal measure and in spades.

Christ's Hospital

Horsham, West Sussex, RH13 0YP

• Pupils: 870: 815 boarders • Ages: 11–18 • C of E • Fees: £0–£28,200; Day £14,610–£18,300 pa • Independent

Tel: 01403 211293
Email: enquiries@christs-hospital.org.uk
Website: www.christs-hospital.org.uk

Head Master: Since 2007, Mr John Franklin BA Dip teaching MEd admin (mid-fifties), came from nine years of headship at Ardingly. Born in Australia and quietly-spoken yet firm, his experience is spread across both hemispheres – six years as a deputy at St Peter's Adelaide, the oldest school in mainland Australia, prior to that an English teacher and acting housemaster at Marlborough for three years. Kim, his wife, teaches English part-time and he tutors a wide range of pupils full-time. He mixes with the pupils by walking the school and sports pitches (with or without his dalmatian and golden retriever) and by maintaining an active presence in dining hall each lunchtime.

Lots of fresh blood in his senior management team: a new bursar, a couple of new deputies, a new chair of the school body – a chance for governance structures to be brought into the 21st century? After 450+ years, CH finally has its own governing body, legally separating the school from the foundation. Behind the scenes, the head is integrating his five-year development plan with the foundation organisation and also planning on increasing the number of teaching staff. On the pupils – 'To say emotional baggage holds some pupils back explains the problem but does not excuse it. Every child must be happy, achieve their academic potential and have a rounded education'.

'I am a great improver': he's implementing much of what proved so successful at Ardingly – a more organised and supportive tutorial system; he's already tightened up discipline. Made major changes to the governance and organisation in 2011 and there is now active recruitment of some fee-paying pupils, both day and boarding plus small numbers of overseas pupils brought in to broaden horizons and add greater diversity to the pupil mix.

The school is being marketed during his headship (a first), resulting in increased numbers of worthy applicants, more donations and more teaching staff aware of what CH is up to.

Academic matters: Junior class sizes up to 25, down to 20 in core subjects at GCSE and fewer in option groups, 10 or 11 for A level or IB. GCSE subjects chosen at end of year 8 – must choose history, geography or theology & philosophy and French, German or Spanish. A level pupils study four subjects at AS and three to A2 (some do four or five A2s). The IB Diploma arrived 2011 – uptake strong and growing. In 2013, 71 per cent A*/A grades at GCSE, 37 per cent at A level; IB average 35 points.

Weekly chapel and tutorial periods; upper sixth get weekly lectures on topics ranging from Picasso's Guernica to David Scott's experience as an astronaut. A voluntary programme of optional academic activities including, eg, politics, debating, critical thinking and architectural appreciation. The whole campus including all pupil rooms can access the Wi-fi network; all encouraged to use own laptops/tablets for work and play, provides machines for those in need.

The campus is arranged by subject blocks, all with high ceilings and plenty of space and equipment, including science and language labs. The ugly sister is the IT department – the 15 classrooms above it are soon to be replaced with a new classroom block and resource centre. A small SEN unit with two SENCos; plans to expand this with a part-time assistant.

One main library, with a 16th century painting (cut to size in the move from Newgate a century ago; unfortunately the signature was a casualty of this trim) and a mezzanine level with extra computers. Art and humanities have their own specialised libraries which are open for evening work, as are all academic departments, providing support.

Games, options, the arts: Huge choice of extracurricular activities. The pupils have to decide what they can fit in, with more personalisation as they move up the school, a preparation for university life. The main sports are hockey, netball, football, rugby, cricket and tennis – the sports centre is dual use with the public, 25m pool, double-sized sports hall, six squash courts, spin bikes, split-level fitness suite, vending machines and a café. A scout hut, CCF and D of E on offer too.

A 500-seat theatre, modelled on Shakespeare's Globe, with padded red benches instead of the standing yard. Used by travelling drama companies as well as the school (contemporary dance as well as curriculum-relevant plays). Music has a respected and talented director who's very good at encouraging even the coolest Grecians to sing their hearts out in chapel. Learning is certainly not all grade-focused – four organs, we saw a couple of harps, 140-strong chapel choir, orchestra, jazz ensembles and marching band that performs at the Lord Mayor's Show (and plays everyone into lunch daily).

Energetic art department, successful and focused on working on pupils' own ideas, which produces an enormous range of work. Three floors of bright and naturally-lit space, an artist in residence, art historian, three full-time staff, print-making, kilns, a sewing room (which is so popular it may expand and textiles re-enter the curriculum), a computer suite (although the primary source of each project is drawing, digital images are always involved) and a library full of glossy books – all open from 7.15am to 10.00pm. Art has always been good here but department now co-operates much more freely with others – joint trips with philosophy, business studies, DT to New York, Rome etc. DT department occupies almost as large a space and is just as well equipped with a laser cutter, a graphics area etc.

Background and atmosphere: Moved to the current 1,200 acre campus in 1902, into a building designed by Sir Aston Webb (who also did the façade of Buckingham Palace and King's College, Cambridge) to house 1,000 pupils and Ingress Bell. Fascinating school history – a museum on site dedicated to

it, under-visited at present but rumours that this will change. Since most of the main buildings were constructed over a century ago, an ongoing conservation programme.

The covered cloisters that enclose the quad are studded with commemorative marble plaques alternating with padded felt noticeboards detailing sports teams. The chapel and dining hall face each other across the quad. Lunch served in two sittings, food is good, choice of hot and cold, apparently a chef's theatre to show off the back kitchen skills – £8 million update of the facilities in progress.

The uniform has hardly changed since Edward VI founded the school in 1552 in Newgate – the britches are a bit less itchy, senior girls can wear tights – yet pride in the mustard coloured socks and figure-disguising Tudor coats is obvious – current pupils reckon that 95 per cent of them would vote to keep it. A bit more individuality in hairstyles and jewellery, and after lessons are over you can change into contemporary clothes.

CH runs in three-week blocks before a leave weekend – some children don't want to or can't go home; they can stay in or get matched with a friend and spend the weekend with their family – 'There's no one way to be a CH pupil'. This diversity is the school's strength – whatever obstacles or advantages your home life might present, everyone is equal as soon as they tie on the bands of their uniform. The new 'deps' (deputy Grecians, lower sixth) probably find the acclimatisation most difficult. Pupils learn within the first year to live with a huge range of personalities, which stands them in good stead in later life. Well-adjusted, confident and accepting children.

Pastoral care and discipline: Chapel services are important – not least because it is a space big enough for up to 840 pupils to gather on Tuesdays and Sundays. The school was founded partly in response to a sermon preached by the Bishop of London – and sermons are still powerful today; even if every pupil is not touched, they definitely pay attention. Lots of children here whose parents or carers are ill or struggling, so faith can be a real touchstone.

Eighteen boarding houses – 16 single sex ones along The Avenue and then two co-ed built in 2000. Each is looked after by a married couple (practically all of the 90 staff live on site), often with their own families, so that every child gets a taste of parental and sibling relationships that may well be lacking in their own home. A recent revamp has left these boarding facilities sparkling – no junior shares a room with more than three others, big common rooms with ping-pong and snooker, bright kitchens, a phone room (for the first two years everyone hands in their mobile at night). Every new arrival gets a nursemaid in the year above, and this relationship produces a family tree stretching across year groups.

The two Senior Grecian houses (the nomenclature comes from the sixth form historically having to study classics) would be the envy of any university student. Often more space than the children might have to themselves at home – big windows, a sink in each (senior's) room, double-height communal spaces, bowls of fruit, kitchens shared between eight, a BBQ on the deck, a little library area with a piano and students' art displayed. A third of the Grecians might be in long-term (more than a year) relationships with each other – no peer pressure to do this. The proximity of co-ed living space means that sex could be problem, but the co-ed nature of the full school normalises boy/girl relationships.

Minor misdemeanours mean getting up for 7.15am and a dress parade. Mini-detentions on Sunday am, the big one is on Saturday night, and a card system which restricts free time by having to sign in – for smoking, bullying, drinking alcohol. Apparently the new senior management team is particularly strict on smoking and 'night walking' (previously popular with the boys). 'Swearing at the staff is unacceptable' (suspension) and continued difficulties will result in a behaviour contract between the pupil, parents and school – a line drawn in the sand. Drugs

– class A or supplying – mean immediate expulsion with the involvement of the police; for cannabis there will be one chance, after which the ongoing drug testing policy is implemented. Family circumstances are always taken into account – parents really appreciate consistent and accessible staff.

Pupils and parents: The pupils know they're lucky to be here – for everyone who gets in, four or five are turned away. Accepts pupils from all over the UK, in reality about 30 per cent from London, 30 per cent from Sussex, 30 per cent SW and home counties, rest from Scotland, Wales, north of England (most from further afield enter at sixth form, but only if they have some extended family in the SE). Historical links with Richmond, Newbury, Reading and Twickenham – the towns on the route of John and Francis West (17th-century scriveners) to Christ's Hospital. A small but growing number of pupils now come from Europe or the Far East.

Only 42 per cent of pupils have both parents resident at home and lots of aspiring middle class and freelancers. Some of these would appreciate more potential for communication with each other outside school. Parents, even those of children who have left, will spread the word via posters and leaflets in doctors' surgeries etc.

Pupils are drawn from all walks of life and the majority enjoy some form of means-tested bursary. Less than 10 per cent of the pupils pay the full fees (their parents want their child to come to a school that's a good social mix and reflective of society); everyone else pays a fraction according to their means. If CH does its job, then former pupils will be ineligible to send their children to their alma mater, unless they pay the full fees.

Famous Old Blues (the dead ones have boarding houses named after them) include Coleridge, Middleton, Peele, Barnes Wallis, the cricketer John Snow, comedians Mark Thomas and Holly Walsh, the academic Alan Ryan, the conductor Sir Colin Davis and the MP Martin Linton.

Entrance: Most at 11+, 25-30 at 13+ and 45-50 after GCSE. No feeder schools, but a very good relationship with south of England primaries and preps. Introduction days for schools are held twice a year so that the staff can imagine what type of child will thrive at CH and so talk to interested parents in their areas. The initial application form elicits lots of information about family circumstances and finances – from the previous school, the local church, social services; the staff in the admissions office are at the end of the phone to answer questions and baffled or swamped parents really value this.

The child also completes a form and comes to the school for a residential initial assessment – with a maximum of 249 other hopefuls. They stay in one of the boarding houses and spend two days experiencing chapel, English, maths, verbal and non-verbal reasoning, an interview, sports and a chance to demonstrate special skills such as music or art. Mild dyslexia and dyspraxia accepted but competition is fierce – only one in five applicants gets a place. The foundation advises on the best method of entry: presentation (by individual governors or corporate bodies, RAF, Guy's Hospital, the Church), special categories (specific areas of residence, parental occupation) or competition (most pupils). No preferential entrance requirements for siblings.

Exit: Some 10-15 per cent leave after GCSE for vocational courses; over 90 per cent of sixth formers to university – the Upper Grecian houses are a real stepping-stone to life there. In 2013, 11 to Oxbridge; York, Manchester, Leeds and KCL popular; medicine, archaeology, sport, classics, law, music, maths degrees. Artists seem to take it in turns to go in posses to Wimbledon, London College of Fashion, Central St Martin's.

Money matters: Currently 13 per cent pay nothing and 30 per cent pay between 11 per cent and 25 per cent of full fees. Parental contributions are assessed on the total family income of the home in which the child resides, interest and dividend payments plus a percentage of any financial and other assets above £25,000. Most DSS benefits are included but not housing benefit, disability allowance and carer's allowance. Reviewed each year, discounts for siblings within school. Tudor-style uniform is free. Extras include £20 pocket money per term, music contributions (means-tested again), a dictionary and a Bible. CH has a big endowment but, like every other school, lives beyond its means. Curriculum-based trips are partially funded by the foundation, means testing applies. Old Blues provide travel grants for gap years etc.

Remarks: In the words of the head, 'This is the most noble school in the country' – it is the only independent school that escapes the state school prejudice when attracting principled teachers. The Old Blues are incredibly loyal and you can see why – with 75 per cent of them in the top quartile of income in their later life, CH turns many lives around in an unpretentious and joyful manner; admirable work.

Churcher's College

Linked school: Churcher's College Junior School

Ramshill, Petersfield, Hampshire, GU31 4AS

• Pupils: 1060; 45/55 girls boys • Ages: 4–18 • Non-denominational Christian ethos • Fees: £8,400–£12,375 pa
• Independent

Tel: 01730 263033
Email: enquiries@churcherscollege.com
Website: www.churcherscollege.com

Head: Since 2004, Mr Simon Williams BSc (biology, Durham) PGCE Cambridge, MA education management (forties). Previously deputy head of Warwick School, he started his career teaching biology and rugby at King's College School, Wimbledon, where he was also assistant housemaster, followed by a stint as head of science at Newcastle-under-Lyme School. Married to Alison, an accountant, who is a strong supporter of all the school events; they have two sons in the senior school and a daughter who attends the nearby junior school.

Full of energy, he remains very much a hands-on head – once a week he fulfils the role of a classroom assistant at the junior school, teaches PHSE to year 7, getting to know everybody in the new intake, and general studies to older pupils. He has an eclectic range of interests in the arts, carpentry and, of course, sport, having been a keen rugby player and worked as an outdoor pursuits instructor. At weekends he can be found refereeing school matches or simply spectating and cheering on various sporting events.

Academic matters: Academic results produced 45 per cent A*/A at A level, 75 per cent A*- B, in 2013. At GCSE, 65 per cent A*/A. Traditional school offering lots of added value; equal importance is given to each area of the curriculum and pupils appear to be flourishing. Everybody's progress is regularly monitored; from year 8 pupils move into ability-related sets for some subjects. Maths teaching is notably good and pupils say it's a subject they really enjoy – quite a rare comment from schoolchildren. Young mathematicians have great successes in both local and national competitions and Olympiads, and the most able can take GCSE and AS early. Pupils study separate sciences; four new science labs, bringing the total to 12. All study at least one modern language with good grades being achieved in Spanish, French and German.

Sixth formers have a good selection of choices at A level, along with general studies and life skills programme. Students benefit from classes in cookery, first aid, self defence and the ever important personal finance, the aim being the young people will go on to university well-equipped for coping with life as well as their studies.

Humanities have an admirable reputation amongst pupils, offering some interesting and unusual trips to enhance educational experiences, bringing events and prose to reality. Up-to-date technology throughout the school includes a digital photography studio; pupils can access school computers system from home, so no excuses for not doing your homework.

SEN: Small department run by two members of staff both with specialist qualifications, work with colleagues to assist them in differentiating lessons to meet pupil needs. One-to-one literacy support and study skills available, also hearing loop. All year 7s are taught study skills and touch typing classes are on offer.

Games, options, the arts: Boys' two main winter sports are rugby and hockey with cricket in the summer; girls' main sports are netball and hockey and in the summer it's rounders. That said, oodles of other minor sports and options – anything from tennis or golf to horse riding. Over 20 acres of playing fields; on-site facilities include Astroturf and indoor swimming pool. Certainly an outdoorsy school – superb range of expeditions and sports tours: younger pupils start with camping trips in the UK, moving on to mountaineering in Montenegro or possibly trekking and canoeing in South America. Large numbers of pupils take advantage of the D of E scheme, CCF and World and First Challenges; younger pupils can join the school's own outdoor activities club, OSCA.

Orchestras and ensembles galore run for all abilities of young musicians; jazz and blues bands, string quartets and various choirs have an impressive local reputation and tour both here and abroad. Lots of class music lessons; the music centre is visited by over 20 music teachers each week offering tuition on more or less any instrument from the harp to the piccolo. Big open-air summer concert is of a very high standard and a popular annual event.

Upbeat drama department encourages students to write, acting and direct their own plays, junior and senior drama club members can get involved with everything to do with a production. Cooperation between artists, musicians and theatrical types makes for a great combination of set designs, costumes and acoustics, leading to very professional performances. Good number take a range of LAMDA examinations. Nice light art studios, fine arts and design and technology look stimulating, the next artist in residence is a sculptor. Huge design and technology studios, large enough to accommodate students wanting to build their own racing cars and bikes. Extensive selection of clubs and societies both at lunchtimes and after school.

Background and atmosphere: Founded in 1722 by Richard Churcher for Hampshire boys, so they could be educated and apprenticed to masters of ships sailing for the East Indies. Continues its tradition of rowing, sailing and things military – every year they send a team on the Ten Tors expeditions to Dartmoor, a test of endurance, navigation and survival skills. Naval heroes' names are all given to school houses.

During most of the 20th century was the local grammar, until the local authority withdrew support and it became an independent fee paying school. Pioneers of co-educational establishment – the first girls arrived in the sixth form in 1980 and they became fully coed in 1988. Comfortable atmosphere boosting the can-do attitude – pupils definitely understand meaning of 'nothing ventured, nothing gained'. Staff, parents and pupils contribute to some lovely, colourful garden areas including a butterfly garden, which go towards promoting positive feelings to work and play. Sixth form centre with its own pool room, conservatory and garden to relax in. No uniform, but expected to dress appropriately, smart jacket and trousers/skirt or suits.

Pastoral care and discipline: Pupils are split between five houses. House captains and sixth formers act as peer mentors to younger members of their house. Form tutors are always available to pupils and their parents for day-to-day matters. Pastoral care system is eager to develop each young person's sense of responsibility for themselves and others. The buoyant extracurricular programme sees sixth formers getting involved with and encouraging younger children to try out new things and develop many different skills. The school's aim is always to work in partnership with parents and develop good relationships between staff, parents and pupils. PHSE programs are regularly reviewed and staff say they find student feedback invaluable. Confidential email helpline for students who want to contact pastoral staff.

Pupils and parents: Mostly local and fairly well-heeled; pupils come from an approximate 25 mile radius around Petersfield; lots of pickup points for the school coaches around Surrey and West Sussex. Parents have the opportunity to become deeply involved in school activities; they can train as volunteers to help with countless outdoor pursuits events and Duke of Edinburgh – a committed and enthusiastic bunch. Fortuitously, lots of arty types as well, who help out with theatre productions, costume making and concerts, even joining in as instrumentalists. Very definitely a family based and community school. Buckets of highly successful fundraising for charitable projects all over the world. Green Day helps staff and parents promote awareness amongst pupils of wider international and environmental issues. Old Churcherians society produces quarterly news magazine. Good few actors, journalists, England rugby union players and businesspeople, eg Tiny Rowland, are amongst the alumni.

Entrance: Main entry to the senior 11+ and 16+, a few places available at 13+. At 11+ and 13+ entrance exam in maths, English and verbal reasoning, followed by an interview with the headmaster and references from current school. At 16+: interview, reference and candidates' GCSE results.

Exit: At 16+ around 20 per cent move to state sixth form colleges. At 18+ all to university or art college – Exeter, Loughborough, Reading and UWE all popular; one or two to Oxbridge and several medics most years.

Money matters: Scholarships are awarded on the basis of performance in the entrance exam, usually between 10 and 25 per cent of the fees. Music scholarships and a number of music exhibitions to cover instrumental tuition fees. Sixth form scholarships for academic excellence and exhibitions for excellence outside the classroom. Bursaries of up to 100 per cent are means tested and reviewed every one or two years to ensure they are awarded to those most in need of financial assistance.

Remarks: Very successful all-rounder school which understands how to balance its curriculum to bring out the best in all its pupils, be it physical, musical, artistic, dramatic or academic. Exceptional value for money, for an action packed service.

Churston Ferrers Grammar School

Greenway Road, Churston Ferrers, Devon, TQ5 0LN

• Pupils: 900 boys and girls; all day • Ages: 11–18 • Non-denom • State

Tel: 01803 842289
Email: secretary@churston.torbay.sch.uk
Website: www.churstongrammar.com

Headteacher: Since 2007, Mr Robert Owers BA PGCE CFES NPQH (forties), educated at Gaynes School, Upminster, before reading history at Warwick. Taught at two large co-ed comprehensive schools in Essex before promotion to deputy headship at top performing Chelmsford County High School for Girls. Limits his teaching here to general studies and 'learning to learn'; appointment raising school's academic profile in Torbay area. Parents feel that he is making positive changes to make pupils more independent in their learning. 'Approachable and relaxed style,' commented one mother. Lives locally with wife, Justine (who teaches drama part-time at CFGS), and their two children. Strong background in sport: represented his university and Essex schoolboys at football; plays cricket locally. Able, energetic and communicative head who is intent on moving this school into the top five per cent of co-ed grammars.

Academic matters: In 2013, 38 per cent A*/A and 73 per cent A*-B at A level, with honours fairly evenly spread between departments rather than relying on a few 'big guns'. Sixty per cent A*/A at GCSE. Good value-added education – pupils leave with better results than parents often anticipate. Head is keen to provide 'more than the exam treadmill', but knows that good grades matter.

Obtained foundation and specialist humanities status. We were particularly impressed by the geography department – video conferencing with an adopted school in Peru was not something we had expected, nor partnership over climate change with schools in Spain, Finland and Estonia involving foreign visits and hosting a final conference at Churston. MFL department also makes good use of this facility as well as own computer lab.

D & T includes food technology to GCSE and textiles (annual 'catwalk' fashion show has become a popular event). 'My daughter has really been encouraged in her art from year 7 upwards,' said one mother. Usual carousel arrangement for practical subjects in years 7 and 8; product design a popular A level subject.

Recent gold medallist in British Biology Olympiad and top student in the country for chemistry. Similar successes in national maths contests too. Academic needs of every pupil are taken seriously and include re-jigging the timetable if necessary: 'They really care and do what's best for the individual,' commented a parent. Twenty-three subjects on offer at A level, including good numbers in psychology, sociology and business studies. Six computer suites and plenty of smartboards, but not overburdened with ICT.

Learning support is taken seriously: two pupils are currently statemented, with access to a designated LSA according to need, and a number receive individual or small group help for SpLD outside the main timetable. Initial screening occurs when literacy issues are raised by the English department, but further diagnostic tests are paid for out of learning support funds, using an outside agency.

Games, options, the arts: Sport is a big deal – good facilities and some successful teams. Top sporting strength is basketball, winning two national championships, thanks to two England coaches on its staff. Football, netball, hockey and athletics also produce county and some national players. Enterprising individuals achieve sporting success outside school – recently in national tae kwon do, octopush (underwater hockey) in Portugal and south coast coastal rowing.

High quality productions are always a sell-out. Eye-catching artwork; dedicated computer suite in artroom. Recent year 11 involvement in community art project with primary school pupils at nearby Greenway House culminated in impressive exhibition. 'Music is improving,' say parents: orchestra and choir perform at festivals as well as in-house concerts; wide range of lunch-time and after school musical activities.

Sixth formers encouraged in public speaking. Serious about environmental issues and has a thriving Force for Change movement. Dedicated Combined Cadet Force for year 9 upwards, managed by armed forces sergeant. Organised trips through CCF – BTEC award in public service part of scheme; D of E (to gold standard) and Ten Tors (35 and 45 mile teams) only available through CCF. Other recent school visits include exchanges with French and German schools, a dozen sixth formers going to Russia, rugby tour of South Africa and expedition to Kenya.

Background and atmosphere: New learning resources centre (named The Cube) catches the eye before one steps into the attractive, modern entrance foyer. Very relaxed atmosphere is immediately obvious – a non-invasive 'beep' indicates each lesson change and pupils move more calmly than in most schools. Set on the edge of a picture postcard Devonshire village, the only co-ed grammar for the Torbay area. Surrounding tranquillity interspersed with idyllic Railway Children style steam train running alongside school – originally a popular mode of transport to it and still used by some.

Extensively developed since opening in 1957 – lots of new classrooms (including modern languages suite), well-equipped science labs, plus sports hall with fitness suite, drama studio and assembly hall. Sixth formers have own study and social area (extended by them during a recent summer holiday) – new centre opened very recently. Pleasant café ('the Greenhouse') for civilised sandwich eaters and the like which also serves up pasta in a variety of forms. Smallish outdoor heated pool and lovely playing fields plus hard courts for netball and tennis. No Astroturf as yet.

Strong links with Lucre in Peru – Fair Trade calendar with proceeds going to the Peruvian primary schools that produced the art work; active in local community and lots of national charity giving: Childline (from sale of blue ribbons during national anti-bullying week); Leonard Cheshire Foundation, shoe boxes for Children in Need and others. Commitment to sustainability includes termly newsletter going digital and six recycling zones around school. Latest Ofsted outstanding for all 36 categories.

Pastoral care and discipline: Ask parents why they choose Churston and they'll reply 'pastoral care', which they rate as 'much better than at neighbouring grammars or comprehensives'. Five groups of 26 pupils placed in houses at beginning of year 7. Experienced pastoral team provides guidance and support; year 11 prefects trained in listening and restorative justice. Problems are 'dealt with promptly and effectively'. Active school parliament. Smoking and drugs policies adhered to, with some good educational input too in these areas. Minor bullying problems resolved by bringing together those involved. Parents, teachers and staff alike view atmosphere as 'friendly but purposeful' and relationships as 'easygoing and relaxed'.

Pupils and parents: Modern grammar school pupils – no longer in blazers. White shirt, tie and school crested sweatshirts for years

7 to 11 (flexible dress code in sixth form). Size means everyone gets to know each other – 'very friendly,' say pupils. Twenty-five feeder primaries including Brixham, Dartmouth and Paignton. Year 5 primary pupils are introduced via a one day induction and in-coming year 7 have an induction week at the end of year 6. Parents can e-mail school; termly reports and well organised parents' evenings. Parents say that the school 'knows its pupils and encourages them to excel without undue pressure'.

Entrance: Foundation status allows school to set part of tests itself. Around 250 first choice applicants for 130 places in year 7. Apply through LA, with supplementary application form direct to school. English, maths and verbal reasoning tests; those only passing two of the three will be ranked in a border-zone that takes account of additional academic information from the primary school. Between 30 and 35 students from Brixham and Dartmouth Community Colleges join sixth form (six B grades at GCSE the minimum requirement) annually.

Exit: Few leave after GCSEs. Two to Oxford in 2013; Plymouth most popular uni, followed by Southampton, Bournmouth, UWE, Cardiff and Keele.

Money matters: Online 'parentpay' system means trips and activities can be paid for with credit and debit cards from home.

Remarks: Caring and close-knit – feels more like a rural comprehensive than a grammar but delivers the goods academically. Strong pastoral system, increasingly effective teaching. A lovely example of 11-18 co-education working well.

Cirencester Deer Park School

Stroud Road, Cirencester, GL7 1XB

• Pupils: 1,005, boys and girls, all day • Ages: 11–16 • Non-denom • State

Tel: 01285 653447
Email: enquiries@deerparkschool.net
Website: www.deerparkschool.net

Head: Since 2003, Ms Chiquita Henson. Read English at Sheffield, PGCE at Bristol. Has taught at Deer Park since 1989 and was deputy head from 1994. Friendly, open and very professional, she was described by a pupil as 'not scary but she gets respect'. Just managing the school's awards and status changes must be a full-time job, but she teaches the occasional lesson and goes on a weekly 'learning walk' where, unannounced, she observes teaching and learning in a particular year group and 'feeds back to staff'. Beyond school she is involved in consultancy, initial teacher training and is trustee of a local educational charity. When asked what makes a good teacher she opts for 'vocation and inspiration, people who give their knowledge but also a little bit of themselves'. Seems to give Deer Park considerably more than a little of herself – parents praise the school's strong leadership team, though a few felt that the head was sometimes 'not so visible'. Free time is for family, catching up with reading and travel.

Academic matters: The head describes the school's successful application for academy status as a 'challenging journey', motivated by a vision that went 'beyond money'. She states that 'greater autonomy will ensure the school maintains its broad curriculum and personalised learning (highly valued by parents and Ofsted)'. At a time when less fortunate schools are having to narrow their focus, academy status allows Deer Park to keep as many qualification options open as necessary.

Results are strong – 2013 GCSE 65 per cent five plus A*-C including English and maths, with 29 per cent A*/A grades. Students for whom this route is not suitable may opt for BTEC First Certificate (continuous assessment, equivalent to two GCSEs) in practical subjects such as applied science, art and design, sport, performing arts and business. Other vocational subjects such as hair and beauty, motor vehicles and childcare are currently offered as part of the 14-19 curriculum. Whatever their qualifications are called, when they leave at 16, the school's aim is that pupils will have become 'independent learners and creative thinkers'.

Five lessons of 60 minutes per day are arranged into a two-week timetable. Occasional 'standstill days' when year groups go off timetable and focus on one topic such as slavery – organisations who work in the field run creative activities and the children work collaboratively. The aim is to encourage the pupils to see how different subjects link together and to 'build learning power'.

Lunches are staggered to give lower years plenty of outside time and avoid competing football matches. Pupils are setted by ability in year 7 for maths and for languages and science in year 8, but this is flexible. Year 11 pupils are given targeted revision lessons according to predicted grades. About 20 per cent choose to do triple science, with the rest following the dual award or BTEC route. Modern languages on offer are French, German and Spanish.

Big focus on applied and independent learning: we saw a drama lesson where pupils were being gently prompted to evaluate and improve their own performance. In a science lesson pupils were using computers for research, learning about reliable sources – 'We're taught that books are often the most reliable,' said our guide. Pupil teacher relations are respectful and relaxed, and in classes we observed pupils were not distracted from their work by visitors. Two parents' evenings a year, one with the child's tutor, the other with subject teachers; a few grumble that it's not always possible to meet all teachers at the latter, but agree that staff respond very promptly to emails or phone calls.

Parents very positive about the way in which the school organises personalised learning. Individual targets are agreed, these are monitored and if a pupil falls below, help is arranged straight away to get them back on track; the most able children are also stretched and given extension tasks – no coasting allowed. Others appreciate the way that 'resources are shared equally' – in other words, every child gets attention, not just those at the extremes.

Learning support team base is next door to the artrooms. They work with 13 statemented pupils, another 140 or so are on school action programmes. Provision in place for those with visual or hearing impairment or mobility problems. Highly regarded and successful LIFT (Learning in the Fast Track) scheme is an intensive programme that uses synthetic phonics to improve literacy skills of children who join with low reading ages.

Games, options, the arts: Lots of the above via timetabled lessons, lunchtime and after school clubs. Choir, orchestra, jazz and steel bands perform locally and abroad. All encouraged to take up an instrument (though our fine year 10 guides had managed to resist). Rehearsals were under way for a summer concert and our visit was accompanied by some very tuneful musicianship. Major whole school production every two years, auditions for the next, The Wiz, advertised on electronic notice-boards.

Wide programme of inter-school sports fixtures with success at town and county level. Year 11 students can become games captains and take a course to develop leadership skills that they put into practice running clubs and teams. Our year 10 guide seemed to do every sport on offer and had enjoyed umpiring cricket matches at nearby primary schools. Huge sports hall supplements outdoor space. Colours for sports displayed in trophy cabinet.

Resistant materials GCSE class was boys only (apparently two girls taking it in the year above) and girls outnumbering boys in graphics, but lower down the school all get a chance to try out art, DT, food technology, textiles etc. All must take one creative subject at GCSE – the parent of one boy who would not 'naturally have chosen anything arty' is now very enthusiastic about GCSE catering. Students' photographs, paintings and ceramics displayed everywhere, with no danger of being overshadowed by sixth form talents.

Background and atmosphere: Take a deep breath (the information on the school's website is pretty thorough), and click the link to 'history'. This school is a fascinating palimpsest of every change of government and educational dogma since the 1960s. The head has been here long enough to greet direct grant schools coming back in the 21st century as academies – granted academy status in 2011. Also displayed on the website and in the reception area are more badges than on Baden-Powell's sleeve – logos for local, national and international initiatives (no wonder graphic design is such a popular GCSE option). Became a technology college in the early 1990s – a smart move resulting in generous provision of PCs in dedicated 'faculty' IT suites, supplemented by iMacs for music technology. Has also been awarded Schools of Creativity status and a Sportsmark. So, does all this result in an identity crisis? The head is pragmatic, 'Specialisms enable the school to develop a curriculum that is as broad as possible, going beyond core subjects'.

In place of a motto has a rather gnomic phrase beneath its name: 'More than a visible curriculum'. It may not be catchy, but the key words here are 'more than' – the head is determined to grasp every opportunity that's going to broaden and widen the educational experience of local children. Not culturally diverse – the head feels that the award of International School is particularly important: trips abroad are made available to pupils who wouldn't normally get such opportunities.

Mainly 60s buildings with later more or less appealing additions, surrounded by trees and an enviable acreage of playing fields, tennis and netball courts, plus an Astroturf pitch that keeps games going all winter. It's a shame that on the day we visited the path to reception was decorated with discarded wrappers – the school does everything it can with plenty of bins and litter patrols, but on this occasion the packaging seemed to be winning. Head observes wryly that the children are passionate about global environmental issues, but dolphins and rainforests are clearly more engaging than boring old tidiness closer to home. Multi-purpose main hall serves as theatre, venue for whole school assemblies, dining room and occasional gym. Newer Atrium is a light modern space used for exhibitions and socialising at break. Kiosk selling sandwiches, drinks etc probably source of litter – nowhere else to run to at lunchtime (unless you want to visit the Royal Agricultural College over the road).

Current uniform is smart navy blue polo shirts with school badge and black trousers or skirts, but revamp in the pipeline. Pupils will be involved in the process and head plans a fashion show to launch the new look. Parents we spoke to not convinced that this will put an end to girls customising skirts à la mode when 'girls from all the other schools do it too'.

All classrooms display yellow posters with the school's 'golden rules' about behaviour and attitude in lessons; also prominent in teaching rooms and on the website are the 'four Rs': resilience, resourcefulness, reflectivity and reciprocity. The head says that these 'form the core aims of teaching and learning'. They're fine words, and we think we know what she means.

Pastoral care and discipline: Strong belief in 'harnessing the student voice' – collaboration with pupils has resulted in refurbishment of lavatories and even the move of a whole department. Students felt that the languages faculty was a little isolated, so it was relocated closer to the centre of the school;

the result was an increased take up of modern languages. No rules as such – instead the whole school has put together 10 'standards', which are regularly reviewed. Transgression results in traditional sanctions, ie detentions for late homework or low-level disruption. Where possible fixed term exclusions (they send the wrong message) are replaced by an 'alternative to exclusion'. Has an inclusion centre for children who need to be out of lessons or for hospital educated children and others who require a gradual supported entry into mainstream lessons.

Discipline doesn't seem to be a major problem – although on our visit we saw a couple of disgruntled pupils standing outside classroom doors, the prevailing atmosphere was studious calm. Our guide said that although this is a large school, she had felt 'recognised as an individual' from day one. Another pupil said that when she came to Deer Park she didn't think she was good at anything, but with the help of her teachers she has discovered that she is.

Pupils and parents: Mixed, as one might expect. Plenty of middle class parents with 'high expectations', who chose Deer Park because it is truly comprehensive (nearby Stroud and Cheltenham operate grammar school system). One such said that the choice of Deer Park over a grammar for her children had 'never felt like a compromise'. Pupils also drawn from less privileged pockets of Cirencester and beyond, but below national average for free school meals. Slight fall in roll (demographics the culprit here) means parents can apply from out of catchment and pupils travel in from as far as Painswick, Stroud and Cricklade – school and public bus services deliver.

Former pupils include Olympic rower Peter Reed and Joe Harris, 18, youngest elected councillor in the country.

Entrance: Approx 33 primaries feed CDPS, but some of the smaller village schools will only be sending one or two per year. Our guides said that most joined the school knowing at least a few other pupils – plenty of partnership work with local primaries promotes smooth transition.

Exit: Nearly all stay in education; many move to next door Cirencester College and some to school sixth forms in Stroud or Cheltenham.

Remarks: Education reforms come and go, and Ms Henson and her team have played a long and successful game on behalf of the children of Cirencester to ensure that their school remains at the forefront of comprehensive excellence. Academy status brings new challenges, but Ms Henson is determined to keep the broadest possible curriculum. Resilience is one of the school's 'four Rs' – Deer Park works hard in order that pupils leave prepared to tackle whatever the future may hold with optimism and confidence. Apply now, before the birthrate rises.

City and Islington College

283–309 Goswell Road, London, EC1V 7LA

• Pupils: 1,350 students, roughly 60 per cent girls, 40 per cent boys • Ages: 16–19 • Non-denom • State

Tel: 020 7700 9333
Email: courseinfo@candi.ac.uk
Website: www.candi.ac.uk

Director: Since 1999, Ms Keren Abse (fifties). Has a BA in English, an MA in history and a PGCE in English, all from the University of Sussex. Taught at Reynolds High School in Ealing and Quintin Kynaston School in Westminster before joining what was then

Islington Sixth Form Centre in 1984, as English teacher and then deputy director. Praised by Ofsted for 'exemplary' leadership.

Academic matters: An inner London sixth form college, nicknamed Candi, that takes in a very mixed student body, often with modest GCSE grades, and sends most of them to university. 'The staffing makes our institute special. We have high expectations of the staff and they are very enthusiastic.'

English has extensive enrichment activities such as theatre trips and creative writing workshops. Science, with a heavy emphasis on practical work, is growing in popularity year by year, in contrast to national trends. Offers Italian, German, Spanish and French – an unusual breadth of languages for the state sector – taught in state-of-the-art language labs. It will never be amongst the top league table performers but adds huge academic value – 2013 73 per cent A*-C grades, just under 50 per cent A*-B. Most popular subjects tend to be English, psychology, sociology and media studies. A parent commented approvingly that the college was willing to run advanced extension English classes for just two students. The A level choice is huge: 37 subjects ranging from electronics to Turkish. Has offered the IB since September 2010.

Nearly all the teaching is mixed ability, though weaker science and maths groups that can have extra sessions. Gifted and talented students are identified and encouraged to take part in a range of extension activities. A few students, mainly from linked Islington schools, retake GCSEs – many have arrived from abroad fairly recently, most stay on to take A levels.

Links with several universities. Queen Mary, for example, runs a mock interview programme, Sussex organises a media residential school and City contributes to the law support group. Has a 'partnership for excellence' with University College, London, committing both to work closely together. Staff have developed strong links and students have lectures and masterclasses in subjects ranging from electrical engineering to geography, plus UCL library cards; weekly 'medics link' programme of lectures and meetings; UCL students run an astronomy club. 'One of our key strengths is the effort we put into encouraging students to apply for higher education. Many come from families with no culture of going to university. UCL doesn't drop grades for us, but increased numbers of our students are applying there.'

Around 10 per cent of students speak English as an additional language – many are refugees – and get excellent support: some who arrived in their teens with little or no English gain top A level grades. One student who had come from the Congo three years before got a place at Oxford to study maths. Drop-in academic writing facility open all week for advice.

Games, options, the arts: Sport is not high on the agenda here, though a five-a-side football/basketball pitch round the back. But a varied enrichment programme on Wednesday afternoons, which includes a range of scientific and political speakers, student magazine, robot club and street dance. Art students visit Rome, politics students go to Brussels, plus many local outings to theatres, ballets and galleries – 'We put a lot of effort into enrichment, as many of our students would never visit the theatre or ballet otherwise'.

Spacious, top floor art, photography and design studios, with lavish facilities and plenty of imaginative 3D, textile and artwork on display. Dance, music, drama and theatre studies plus performance studies all A level options. Own well-equipped performing arts centre, with two studios that open into a theatre space – whole college musical each year. Students have also worked with companies ranging from the Welsh National Opera to Rambert Dance Company and Comédie Française.

Background and atmosphere: The sixth form college is part of City and Islington College, which also includes the centres for business, arts and technology; lifelong learning; health, social and child care and applied sciences. The other four centres, on sites around Islington, concentrate on vocational courses for adults as well as teenagers.

Moved in 2003, from two Victorian buildings close to Holloway Road to a £9.2m landmark building somewhat akin to a cruise liner moored alongside Goswell Road near the Angel. The Kalwall finish appears white, translucent and calming during the day and glows at night – abundant glass, giving views across the City from the sixth floor.

'If you wonder what's happened to all the money spent on education over the past few years – well, it all seems to be here,' commented a parent. All rooms are linked to the internet, all classrooms have projectors linked to computer, video player and whiteboard. It is accessible throughout for people with disabilities and has a good range of specialist equipment.

Pastoral care and discipline: A sixth-form college, with an atmosphere to match and lighter touch than most schools. 'You need to be self-motivated,' said a parent, 'because they won't stand over you.' However particularly praised for its academic support, with students' progress carefully monitored and regular reports to parents. The discipline is strict, with no quarter for bad behaviour, but very strong pastoral care from tutors and student counselling and advice service. Highly rated for its equal opportunities and support for disabled students.

Pupils and parents: From over 100 schools right across London, particularly Islington, Hackney, Haringey and Tower Hamlets, with a huge cultural and ethnic mix. Around three-quarters of students are from ethnic minority backgrounds ranging from Bangladeshi to Turkish.

Entrance: Acts as the sixth form for six Islington secondary schools that do not have their own. These students get first priority, providing they apply by the end of the spring term and gain the requisite GCSE grades. All courses require at least five grade Cs – applications usually close early in February. Applicants must include a reference from their school and attend a course guidance interview. Final enrolments take place once students have received their GCSE results, in the date order in which they applied.

Exit: Around 80 per cent generally go on to higher education, including several to Oxbridge – four in 2013, and seven to UCL. In total, 45 to Russell Group universities to study courses ranging from medicine, law and philosophy to astrophysics. The others go on to a range of jobs, some applying to university later on as mature students. Many students stay at home while studying for financial or cultural reasons – the most popular universities are London ones, including Westminster, Middlesex and City. Sussex is the highest ranking outside the capital. Business and related studies top the list of degree subjects, followed closely by English and media studies. Art foundation courses are also popular.

Remarks: A beacon in an area with historically poor educational achievement. Its student body mirrors its inner-city location and many arrive with lower than average GCSE results. But excellent teaching, wonderful premises and strong support mean that most leave for university with creditable A levels (or, in future, IB results) under their belt.

City of London Freemen's School

Linked school: City of London Freemen's Junior School

Ashtead Park, Ashtead, Surrey, KT21 1ET

- Pupils: 880 pupils, 50 boarders • Ages: 7–18 • Inter-denom
- Fees: Boarding £24,192; Day £11,250–£15,066 pa • Independent

Tel: 01372 277933
Email: admissions@clfs.surrey.sch.uk
Website: www.clfs.surrey.sch.uk

Headmaster: Since September 2007, Mr Philip MacDonald MA. An Oxford classicist (in his fifties) with a long career in education: experience in single sex and co-ed schools, day and boarding. Married with four teenage children, all pupils at CLFS. His previous post was nine years as head of Mount St Mary's College, Derbyshire. In his palatial office, he exudes self confidence and experience. He is 'very interested in the idea of educating the whole person' and explains this as 'including sport, drama, debating, music, providing wider opportunities for children to find fulfilment and thus happiness'. Parents find him 'quite aloof and reserved', feel they don't know him, one saying, 'I wouldn't know him if I passed him in the street'.

Academic matters: Very good results year on year at both GCSE and A level – 2013 79 per cent A*/A at the former, with 56 per cent A*/A, for the latter. Not a pressured academic hothouse. Parents are universally complimentary about the teaching, singling out physics, English, politics and business studies – 'Teachers fabulous, with lots of them there a long time'; 'Teaching is excellent and without high pressure'. Superb teaching facilities housed in the Haywood Centre (named after the previous, long serving and very popular head). This hub of the senior school is an airy and attractive, well-equipped block of classrooms, IT and multimedia rooms plus a large library open until 6pm for individual study.

Not a first choice school for a pupil with significant SEN, and ask lots of questions for a child with mild SEN just to make sure the school can help. SEN support is limited – head tells us very few pupils with statements. He would ask parents to consider whether this is the right academic environment for their child – he feels it 'may not be suitable for pupils with formal SEN statements'. A parent of a mildly dyslexic pupil reinforces this view saying, 'There is little specialist help, but teachers are kind and supportive and do the necessary such as extra time in exams; maybe it wouldn't be suitable for a child who is quite dyslexic.' A head of learning support provides help within the curriculum for mild needs, such as a slow reader, and support classes are available for children who are struggling in English. A parent of a pupil accessing this help praised it saying, 'The kids call it the remedial class, but they have a very positive attitude towards it.' Mr MacDonald tells us they have had hearing impaired children and wheelchair users and says the issue is, 'Can we enable a youngster with special needs to access the curriculum?'

Games, options, the arts: The stunning facilities are not aged and beautiful but very much contribute to an environment which cannot fail to impress a pupil (or perhaps even more their parents). Sports facilities are outstanding and would compete easily with the best of the public school fraternity. Glorious and extensive grass pitches, huge Astro pitch for tennis, football and hockey, a vast sports hall, an enviable 25 metre indoor swimming pool, two squash courts and a multi-activity room for table tennis and aerobics. Sport is well and truly part of life here – parents report a 'massively active programme but it's not forced' and sport is 'made fun not a chore'. Very much a 'come and try' atmosphere, rather than a 'team place or else'

school. For the seriously sporty, A and B teams are fielded in the more popular sports. Most fixtures are scheduled on Saturday mornings and squad members are required to attend.

Drama occupies as central a position as sport, both within the curriculum and in extracurricular clubs. A hugely enthusiastic head of drama (who maintains a dedicated drama website for the school), plus more terrific facilities including a professionally equipped theatre, mean plenty of productions. Good GCSE and A level results and some impressive acting alumni. Music is encouraged, with plenty of choirs, ensembles and an orchestra putting on about 30 performances and concerts. Musical theatre productions performed to sell-out audiences in a nearby 800-seater public venue are described as 'great' and 'the highlight of the musical year'. Students' artwork of a high standard is displayed around the school and the art and design technology facilities, like all of the facilities, really are top class.

A huge range of lunchtime and after-school clubs cater for all tastes and interests. Senior pupils run some and can even start them on their own initiative. Trips out of school include an annual whole school visit to the City of London to celebrate the school's close ties with the City, plus many regular field trips both locally, within the UK and abroad – the list of destinations is long.

Background and atmosphere: Founded to educate orphaned children of the Freemen of the City of London, owned by the Corporation of London. Support staff are employed by the City of London and governors are largely from the Court of Common Council (ie City officialdom). The Corporation provides financial support for capital projects, which helps to keep fees to a minimum. HR, planning and management all operated by the City, which leaves the head and school free to run and manage the education – 'a burden lifted!' says Mr MacDonald, who describes the Corporation as 'forward looking with a long term view, also traditional and a little bureaucratic'. 'A little bureaucratic' may be something of an understatement – all our interaction with the school was slow and slightly difficult. The admin side worked like an old fashioned office, hierarchical and by the book – one gets the impression the whole school probably works like that, as everyone ultimately refers to a more senior authority.

Ashtead Park's 57 acres are owned by the City of London Corporation and the grounds are subject to open spaces regulations. Expansive, formal and well kept, with zebra crossings and double yellow lines, the City of London coat of arms on railings and bins really do make it feel like a London park. The feel is of a campus with pupils moving between various buildings. Parents particularly appreciate the 'beautiful setting' and 'great atmosphere to work in'. The 'mansion house', in grand country house style, houses music practice rooms and the dining room (rather small and old fashioned) plus reception rooms, offices and girls' boarding. The girls' accommodation in the main house is by no means trendy and high tech – in fact, quite the opposite: rather old fashioned and fusty. Boys' boarding house is a rather uninspiring building due to be completely renewed.

Boarding is part of the school's statute and must be provided. (To this day a small number of 'foundationer' places – they have their fees, be it boarding or day, met in full.) However, boarding is not like at other boarding schools – it is used almost exclusively by pupils from abroad (vast majority of boarders are sixth form entrants). The boy boarders are from Hong Kong and Russia, apart from seven English pupils. All the girl boarders are from Hong Kong or the Far East. The girls' housemistress said she had to make them 'stop working sometimes and go out for a walk' – they are under immense personal and family pressure to succeed. With their very strong work ethic and extremely high standards, the boarders are often culturally different from the local day students.

All pupils and staff are in one of the three houses – good opportunities for positive relationships between age groups.

Each house holds a weekly assembly and accumulates merits through music, sporting and other achievements and good work to win the annual house competition. The sixth form has its own centre and is run 'almost like a separate school'.

Pastoral care and discipline: Parents are positive, describing pastoral care as 'excellent' and 'second to none'. Pupils have a daily tutor group and parents are encouraged to get in touch if they have any issues – they feel 'It's made clear who is responsible' and they 'always have somewhere to go – staff have an open door policy'. The spirit of the school is respectful and listening and pupils are encouraged to be kind and helpful. Parents and staff describe it as 'a family school with lots of siblings across it', the environment is 'caring and very friendly', ' Boys and girls mix well' and 'They grow up to be rounded on gender issues'. Pupils report that 'staff treat them with respect', which sets a good example and gives them self confidence. Senior pupils mentor juniors and volunteer as class prefects and to run extracurricular clubs.

Discipline is laid down in clear policy and stuck to firmly; bullying is not tolerated. Incoming pupils sometimes find the regime initially rigorous as they learn the rules, but it is seen as fair. Parents say 'no bolt out of the blue – problems are flagged up early' and it's the 'right balance'.

Pupils and parents: Pupils neither scruffy nor especially tidy – just nicely ordinary. Despite our request to be shown round by a pupil, we were, unlike at most schools, put firmly in the hands of the marketing manager. Both boys and girls we met en passant were communicative and pleasant when asked questions. Pupils predominantly from surrounding Surrey towns of Ashtead, Epsom, Banstead, Leatherhead, Esher and Cobham, but some travel down from south-west London and even a couple from north London. School transport from most of these local areas plus a shuttle bus to Ashtead Station help parents avoid the school run.

Families from a wide range of backgrounds – plenty with both parents working. Parents say this 'adds to the rounded normal feel of the school'. Many find the variety comfortable, with lots of ordinary families. Definitely not posh, does not even try to compete with its neighbour Epsom College. Some parents we spoke to were positively anti 'the four wheel drives and mothers dressed for tennis one upmanship' of some other local schools. 'Everyone is friendly', parents can get involved if they want and regular parent and family socials.

Entrance: Entry to the junior school via entrance exam, school report and interview. Sixty places at year 3, increasing to 80 at year 7. Majority enter the senior school directly from junior school with no entry tests. Parents love the fact their children can go straight through from the junior school and see this as a major advantage, to dispense with 11+ and CE worries. A further 25-30 are added from local preps including Downsend, Danes Hill, Cranmore and Lanesborough. Entry is competitive with screening tests at 11 and 12 confirmed by entrance exam or common entrance at 13. Head is pleased to add a little variety from other schools to 'leaven the mix'. Sixth form entry on predicted GCSE grades, school report and interview – about 20 join, including overseas boarders.

Exit: About 10 per cent leave after GCSE to taste life in a sixth form college or another school. Those who stay expect to go to university and do, mostly to Russell Group; some 10 per cent to Oxbridge, other current favourites Bristol and Birmingham.

Money matters: Generally perceived by parents to be excellent value for money and cheaper than other comparable schools in the area. Academic and music awards at 11, 13 and sixth form available to current pupils and incomers. Means-tested bursary awards, sponsored by the City Livery Companies and often tied to certain professions. A very small number of children of Freemen who have lost one 'family breadwinner' parent attend completely free as Foundationers.

Remarks: A good, solid school, not quirky or elitist, in fact quite the opposite. It does what it says on the tin: genuinely providing pupils with wide opportunities and an all-round education including consistently good academic results, without a hothouse atmosphere.

City of London School

Queen Victoria Street, London, EC4V 3AL

- Pupils: 950 boys; all day • Ages: 10-18 • Non-affiliated
- Fees: £13,803 pa • Independent

Tel: 020 7489 0291
Email: admissions@clsb.org.uk
Website: www.clsb.org.uk

Headmaster: From April 2014, will be Sarah Fletcher, previously head of Kingston Grammar School. An Oxford historian, she has also been deputy head at Rugby and taught at Wycombe Abbey, St George's Montreux, Habs Girls' in Elstree and Lawrence Sheriff Grammar in Rugby – an admirably varied career with child protection, housemistressing and Pre-U experience along the way. We described her at Kingston as 'softly spoken, sparkly, diplomatic and clever.' She has two grown up sons.

Academic matters: An academic school of high expectations rather than high pressure. 'You work as hard as you need to work,' said a sixth former. 'You know who is good at what – and you accept that.' 'They welcome your strengths, whatever they are,' said a parent. Talented linguists can take French or Latin GCSE in year 10, whilst also studying Russian or Greek. Musicians, too, can take their subject a year early and some boys do additional maths alongside maths GCSE. In 2013, over 90 per cent of I/GCSEs were A* or A; at A level, 37 per cent A*, and over 73 per cent A*/A.

'Most departments have at least one amazing teacher,' said a sixth former. A good mix of long-serving and newer staff. Strong emphasis on science in the sixth form – several boys coming in from linked state schools with science scholarships; history also extremely popular, with numbers taking it to A level second only to maths.

Excellent support for those with mild dyslexia/dyspraxia – 'It needs to be mild or they wouldn't cope' – with 100 or so boys receiving extra help in small groups. 'It's wonderful and very low key,' said a parent. The building is accessible for wheelchairs, but so far only boys with a broken leg have made use of this.

Games, options, the arts: In Tardis-like fashion, the compact-looking school building encompasses a sports hall, gym and swimming pool as well as squash courts and fencing salle. Seventeen acres of playing fields a half-hour coach ride away and a couple of concrete playgrounds on site. 'When I looked out before school this morning there were four cricket matches, a football game and some basketball going on,' said a sixth former.

Teams have reached London cup finals at cricket, football and water polo, and the school fields teams in 12 competitive sports, including golf and sailing – 'Sailing suits our boys because you need a mixture of intellectual and physical aggression and you don't have to train too hard'. Pupils have represented their country in fencing and table-tennis in recent years, with recent successes in football and athletics. School's sporting profile increasing, with more teams in the lower years playing matches against feeder prep schools.

But it is fair to say that the average City boy is not a fanatical sportsman. He is likely to be equally interested in debating, singing in the choir, playing Warhammer. 'We push debating and public speaking because it makes the boys more thoughtful and considered. It counters any yob culture.' Zillions of clubs before, during and after school: Model UN (with annual conference); railway society (with its own model railway room); Jewish society (generally involving food); Square Mile club (with eminent speakers such as Jeremy Paxman, John Bercow and Nick Robinson) et al. 'I'm very keen on being an outlooking school. The boys will have to make their way in a global setting.'

Pupils in year 9 get to know their city well on eight visits to, eg, the Museum of Surgery and the Globe. Over 140 other school trips ranging from a Chinese exchange to geography field trips to India, Iceland and Cuba. European work experience in year 12. Extremely popular CCF, with hundreds of pupils learning to fly, going camping at home and abroad, skiing, canoeing, driving powerboats – 'It was one of the best things I've done at school,' said an ex-pupil. Community service is an alternative and charity fundraising is high profile – over £58,000 raised for READ International.

The school theatre was revamped and drama is strong, with frequent theatre visits and many productions in conjunction with City of London Girls' School. Joint orchestras and choirs, too, bolstered by the choristers who join at the age of 10. The music is 'fantastic', said a parent, and a sixth former agreed, 'If you're good you become sucked into the music department and your life revolves around it'. Two terms' free instrumental tuition for everyone in the younger classes.

Background and atmosphere: Has its origins in a 1442 bequest of land to support the education of poor men's sons. This endowment became so valuable by 1834 that it enabled the Corporation of London to found City of London School in Milk Street, near Cheapside. Unusually for the time, it was a day school that did not discriminate against non-Anglicans and offered a practical and progressive education which included science and English (as opposed to classical) literature. It moved to Blackfriars in 1879 and to its present red-brick purpose-built facilities in 1986.

Wonderful site with many balconies and windows looking out across the Thames to Tate Modern, adjacent to the (alas, no longer) Wobbly Bridge, with St Paul's right behind. Very urban, very buzzy. Keen on outreach – staff seconded to help East London state schools with maths, sports, drama etc. Boys not cosseted, expected to be independent, used to getting about London on their own from the age of 10 upwards. A teacher recounts approvingly how she overheard a group of 11 year olds, who had finished exams early, organising their own trip to a pizza restaurant across the river to celebrate. 'The boys are immensely proud of being part of the City of London,' said a parent.

Some boys who joined at 13 found it took time to integrate; they also mention an atmosphere far less pressured than their prep schools, with time to coast for a while.

Pastoral care and discipline: Strong anti-bullying culture. Pupils report some scapegoating in the younger classes, but no physical abuse, 'And people soon grow out of it'. 'They work very hard to deal with it,' said a parent. 'It's a very welcoming place. There's space for all sorts of diversity – black and white, rich and poor.' By general consent a complete lack of racial tension. Clear expectations, rules strictly enforced. 'It's relaxed but firm,' said a pupil.

Pupils and parents: Extremely cosmopolitan. Few local families so nearly all travel in by tube, train or bus, from all points but particularly north and west. The huge catchment area and generous bursaries encourage a rich ethnic and social mix

emanating from St Albans to Mile End. 'It makes teaching RE very interesting. In a class of 20 there will be a hundred different opinions, and they educate one another about their own religions.' OBs include Daniel Radcliffe, Peter Ware Higgs, Julian Barnes, Lord Levine, Kingsley Amis and Herbert Asquith.

Entrance: Takes around 40 boys at 10, some of these Temple Church or Chapel Royal choristers on scholarships. The main intake – about 60 boys – is at 11. Around 60 per cent of these come from state primaries. Another 45 come in at 13, almost entirely from prep schools. Now examines and offers places to 13+ candidates in year 6, so no chance of a retake for those who don't make an 11+ place.

Around 15-20 join the sixth form, often with science scholarships, and mostly from state schools, including linked schools Stepney Green and St Thomas the Apostle.

Exit: Around 12-15 leave after GCSEs, almost invariably for state sixth forms. Nearly always gets 20+ Oxbridge places (19 in 2013), with the vast majority of the rest going to Russell Group universities (88 per cent in 2013), many to read science or engineering.

Money matters: A good place to try for a scholarship or bursary – total of 106 full fee, means-tested bursaries throughout the school, plus 30 academic, sports and music scholarships a year.

Remarks: Very urban, very happening, very cosmopolitan school that achieves high standards without undue pressure and produces independent, outward-looking boys. 'We're happy as Larry,' said a father. 'We'd recommend it to anyone.'

City of London School for Girls

Linked school: City of London School for Girls (Prep School)

St Giles' Terrace, London, EC2Y 8BB

- Pupils: 700 girls; all day • Ages: 7–18 • Non–denom
- Fees: £13,866 pa • Independent

Tel: 020 7847 5500
Email: admissions@clsg.org.uk
Website: www.clsg.org.uk

Headmistress: Since 2007, Miss Diana Vernon BA PGCE (forties), who comes from a headship in the rolling green acres of Woldingham School in Surrey, and was previously a housemistress and biology/business studies teacher at Downe House. However, the City is familiar territory, as she once worked nearby in PR and she comes across as very much a PR professional: smart, dynamic, ambitious, keen to extol the merits of her school. 'She's fantastic...really wonderful...down-to-earth,' say parents. 'She's made huge efforts to get to know all the girls and they really like her.' Girls concur, 'Even in the first week she knew people's names. She's something very good that's happened to our school.'

An excellent manager – 'I really feel she takes things on board and will follow them up,' said a parent. She has instigated popular breakfast meetings for parents from different year groups – 'Because the girls all make their own way here, you don't see parents much. It's useful to put faces to names and I want them to feel that they can come in and see us when they need to. And it helps them to know what's going on here. We haven't been singing loudly enough about what we do'.

Although she has taught entirely in independent, selective, girls-only schools, mostly country boarding schools, she was inspired to become a teacher whilst a governor of a south London comprehensive. She feels that City's location is one of its great advantages – 'right in the heart of a vibrant, cosmopolitan city. You can visit the Tate Modern during an art class and it's very easy to attract interesting speakers'.

Off in April 2014 to head the Methodist Ladies' College in Melbourne.

Academic matters: Up there with the top selective schools – 81 per cent A*/A grades at A level in 2013, with maths, history and English the most popular subjects. Praised for imaginative teaching methods. Everyone does two modern languages from year 7, choosing between French, Spanish, German and Mandarin, and studies at least one to GCSE. Some take Spanish a year early – most get A*s – then start the AS course. In 2013, 96 per cent A*/A grades at GCSE and nearly 78 per cent A*. Top set mathematicians do additional maths alongside GCSE maths, and everyone studies three single sciences. Teaches thinking skills to year 10 and 11 pupils, who can take the AS exam alongside GCSEs: 'It's good for university assessment tests and interviews and I like to give them the opportunity to be stretched'.

Part of the East London Schools' Consortium, exchanging good practice with other girls' independent and state schools, and hosting the Urban Scholars Intervention Programme Saturday school – some 60 gifted and talented state school girls from surrounding boroughs follow a varied programme encouraging them raise their aspirations and attainments.

Games, options, the arts: Music particularly vibrant, with numerous orchestras, ensembles, groups and choirs, many run jointly with City Boys. 'It's very inclusive,' said a parent. 'Anyone can go along to the orchestra and they all get a good experience of performing.' Most peripatetic teachers come from the nearby Guildhall School of Music. High quality art and DT – the innovative coffee tables in the reception hall were designed and built by a student. Often produces Arkwright engineering scholars. Plenty of drama – 'lively and good,' said a parent – again, often in conjunction with the boys' school.

'It's not the place for someone who wants to chase a ball around playing fields,' said a pupil, 'but they do pack things in.' It particularly suits those who shine in the compact arenas of swimming pool, netball court and gym, with successful swimming, fencing, gymnastics and netball teams. Diving, canoeing, climbing, running and water polo are other sporting options, alongside cricket, hockey and football on the new five-a-side Astroturf pitch. City girls always make up a large proportion of the City of London team for the London Youth Games and pupils have represented England at karate and fencing.

Makes good use of its central London location, with numerous outings to museums, art galleries, concerts and theatres, as well as strong connections with City banks and businesses. Sixth formers set up and run lunch-time clubs ranging from Asian society to cheerleading, with plenty to choose from. Residential trip destinations range from Bideford to Beijing.

Background and atmosphere: Founded in 1894 with a bequest from coal merchant William Ward as a school for girls that 'would correspond, as near as may be, to the City of London School …. making all proper allowance for the difference of the sexes'. It moved to its purpose-built, five-storey, Barbican home in 1969. Uncompromisingly urban, surrounded by multi-tiered flats and office blocks, it shoe-horns in everything from a food technology room to a multi-gym and sixth form centre with pool table, beanbags and computer suite, looking out over a khaki-coloured lake. Corridors are lined with noticeboards crammed with information.

Buzzy, busy atmosphere. Girls are encouraged to be independent; nearly everyone arrives by public transport. 'Our girls are pretty savvy. We give them support and advice on dealing with potential problems and they're streetwise in the nicest possible way.' Plenty of emphasis on ambition and women

in leadership, with City mentors, visits to City institutions and talks by scientists and journalists, bankers and army officers.

Joint activities with City Boys include concerts and plays, lectures, careers conventions and mock Oxbridge interviews, plus social events organised by parents for the junior classes – 'By year 9 they prefer to organise their own social life'.

Pastoral care and discipline: No easy ride academically – but the pressure to succeed comes from students as much as staff. 'There's a focus on academic success,' said a pupil, 'but everyone wants to do well. And staff are aware of other things going on in your life apart from work, so you feel supported.'

Four houses give a strong sense of identity and belonging, as well as opportunities to get involved in drama and sports competitions. Strong pastoral support – 'They do look out for them,' said a parent. Parents can even log on to keep tabs on what their daughter ate for lunch and what she has to do for homework.

Pupils and parents: Girls travel from Chelmsford and Croydon, Bromley and Buckinghamshire, though the majority are the children of 'North London intellectuals and City bankers,' said a parent. A fair social and ethnic mix – 'It's a melting pot of girls,' says the head. 'They learn to respect each other and value other people's opinions.' Girls tend to be independent, opinionated and ambitious, inspired by the location of their school.

Entrance: Part of the North London Consortium, which sets joint maths and English exams each January. Applicants to City also sit GETINTU – a computer-based cognitive test – in November. From some 500 applicants, 280 are interviewed, to choose an intake of around 70, who join the 20 or so coming up from the prep school. Has now abolished its year 10 intake in favour of four, rather than three, year 7 classes. A few girls join the sixth form.

Exit: A fair outward trickle after GCSEs, mostly to co-ed state or private sixth forms. All sixth form leavers go on to university, art or music school – 20 or so to Oxbridge; Bristol, KCL, UCL, Durham and Edinburgh popular; history, politics, philosophy and languages amongst the most common degree subjects.

Money matters: Scholarships and bursaries help support 23 per cent of pupils. Academic, drama, art and music scholarships, generally worth £1,500 a year, available at 11 and 16, plus means-tested bursaries – 'We have a strong means-tested programme, so we have the flexibility to give bursaries to those who need it'.

Remarks: Vibrant, ambitious, high-achieving school in the centre of London, producing confident and articulate girls.

Clayesmore School

Linked school: Clayesmore Preparatory School

Iwerne Minster, Blandford Forum, Dorset, DT11 8LL

- Pupils: 260 boys (140 boarders), 165 girls (110 boarders)
- Ages: 13–18 • C of E • Fees: Boarding £30,837 Day £22,560 pa
- Independent

Tel: 01747 812122
Email: mmccafferty@clayesmore.com
Website: www.clayesmore.com

Headmaster: Since 2000, Mr Martin Cooke BEd (Hons) FCollP (mid-fifties). A St Paul's chorister before boarding at Monkton Combe from where he went to Bishop Otter College, Chichester as an organ scholar and graduated with a Sussex degree in music and education. Began career at Bembridge School, Isle of Wight where he was director of music for fifteen years, ten of them as deputy head. 'A great leader of people,' confided a teacher. 'Has put Clayesmore on the map,' commented one father. 'Instills a sense of goodness,' added the mother of a boarder. Had a huge input at the prep for six years prior to landing senior school job. We have rarely met a head who is more hands on. Works closely with lovely wife, Eleanor. Both their children (Adam and Anna) went through school successfully. Describes his hobbies as music in general, playing the organ and information technology: he is an Apple aficionado and seldom far away from his iPod, iPhone or iPad. A human dynamo with an endearing touch of eccentricity, he reckons that running a music department was excellent training for headship. Enjoys playing for whole school services and will let rip on chapel organ when he feels so inclined. Has certainly lifted school out of its nineties doldrums and stamped his personality on it. His ambitious 2020 vision to provide more state of the art facilities seems achievable in light of school's recent track record.

Academic matters: 'Not in business of boosting league table positions,' says head though both GCSE and A level results exceed admission level expectations. In 2013, 49 per cent A*/B grades at A level and 27 per cent A*/A; 28 per cent A*/A at GCSE. Year groups of around 100, six sets in core subjects. Interesting variation in English (not met elsewhere) where both top GCSE sets in English are co-ed but lower sets are single sex: 'works really well,' we were told by HOD. Pupils setted in French, science and maths (some entered for IGCSE). Spinney Centre has classrooms for geography, history, business studies and careers, all bristling with the latest computer technology. Welcome flexibility in A level choices and new subjects being added (psychology the newest arrival). Gracious library is well stocked and boarders can study there until 9pm. Adjacent ICT room gleams with Apple hardware in constant use. Launch of VLE facility will give every pupil own screen on school network. DT facilities are good (large workshop with CAD-CAM router and separate graphics studio). Various examples of recent projects on display including a 'storage tyre on wheels' design used in pre-prep. DT students get to try their hand in real world outside (eg with local craftsman David Bowerman). We saw (and smelled) yummy nosh being prepared in food science area: pupils working towards BTEC award. HOD runs valued activity (usually as part of CCF programme) for autistic pupils from nearby Forum School. Good take up for languages (French, Spanish and German all available to A level) and Latin also on menu. Language teaching facilities include a digital lab; foreign visits and exchanges are well established. Geographers go to Iceland for fieldwork, scientists have been to CERN, Geneva.

New business centre replicates a trading environment and gives a further boost to success of business studies and economics. BTEC qualifications in ICT, hospitality, sport plus travel and tourism keep less academic on board for sixth. Small classes and switched-on teaching account for upward drift. Sixth form essay society and evening lectures broaden horizons; careers teaching includes HE visits and will shortly move resource base to new business centre.

By no means a specialist SpLD school but provides outstanding learning support for children with slight to moderate learning difficulties: 14 staff (all fully qualified), superb learning support centre (LSC) atop Jubilee Building which includes a lecture hall and IT hub as well as individual teaching rooms. School proud of getting dyslexics into top universities: 'my son has flown since joining Clayesmore and has overcome his dyslexia,' chirped a very satisfied mother. Mrs Anne Cowley has recently been appointed Head of LSC for both prep and senior. All children are assessed, by an educational psychologist if needed. About 35 per cent of pupils have some form of support, and a 'tiny number' have serious needs. 'Children don't have to have a label,' said

SENCo. Progressively more group lessons which are a fraction of cost for 1:1 help. Pupils generally come out of language classes, extra sessions can be timetabled if necessary, everything and anything to help. Good communication between LSC staff and subject teachers: 'have moved to software that supports every teacher in every classroom.' Support for most able too though labels such as 'gifted and talented' are seen as divisive. CReSTeD specialist unit category: listing essential for Forces children, who will be deprived of 'unlimited help indefinitely' otherwise. Strong EAL too, with up to six hours a week, either individual or in pairs. Extra charge for both based on level of need. Academic staff hold frequent meetings to assess pupils' performance and communicate any steps taken quickly to parents.

Games, options, the arts: All pupils do sport three times a week and have access to great facilities. Year 9 pupils are expected to try out in major sports. As pupils move up through school there is greater flexibility: non team players generally find their niche by year 11. Impressive fixture lists with some notable successes against bigger schools. A sprinkling of county players, some individuals reaching national levels eg in athletics, and cross-country plus nationally successful orienteering team. Locals share impressive leisure complex: indoor pool, gym, squash courts and modern fitness suite. Sixth formers get free membership for out-of-school sessions. Open swimming in evenings is popular. A few élite swimmers train daily from silly o'clock. Floodlit Astroturf for hockey, tennis and netball. Expeditions on Dartmoor and more ambitiously to Everest base camp, Borneo and Malawi. Regular sports tours abroad (one in pipeline to India). CCF facility includes a rifle range, army and RAF sections for pupils in years 10, 11 and sixth form. Many opt for D of E: high medal haul including golds. Sailing at Ringwood and horse-riding also part of sports programme.

Exciting music happens in purpose-built department run by committed director, assistant and 14 peripatetics. Pupils have scored 100 per cent success in music exams up to diploma level over last 15 years (including 24 at grade 8 in last three years). Concert band has raised staggering £50K for charity over last six years. Regular music tours with singers and instrumentalists: choir has sung at St Mark's, Venice. Next stop for musicians: Helsinki and Tallinn. School welcomes visiting artists: latterly David Owen Norris. Sophisticated electronic keyboards and recording studio useful for A level music technology. Regular representation in national youth choirs and orchestras. Composition master class in Salisbury, loads of internal concerts, ensembles for strings and woodwind, brass group, flute choir. Recent performances have included Marriage of Figaro and Dido and Aeneas.

Four staff currently involved in teaching drama including dynamic HOD whose youthful appearance belies his age. A level theatre studies and three major school productions a year part of varied and inventive menu. Many pupils get involved on technical side; costumes department particularly professional and is overseen by ex-Star Wars wardrobe mistress. Auditioning for Hairspray when we visited and puppets hanging up in green room were for enacting Russian folk tales – quite a skill manipulating puppets. Dance based in social centre and drumming in band room nearby. Masses of tripettes: Bristol, the Old Vic, London. 'reading plays' give access to more pupils: can perform in costume with script in hand. Mystery plays at Christmas.

Outstanding art department focuses on championing individuality and creative thinking. Separate village location in former primary school increases the counter-cultural feel: pottery, painting and drawing and sculpture all have discrete spaces. Lively HOD and a real sense of bustle and fun. Sixth formers have a dedicated work space. Latest addition is iMac suite for digital art. We liked the displays of art around the school and admired some senior students' work. End of year exhibition gains universal plaudits. Regular trips to galleries in London and Paris.

Keen Greenpower group of pupils won prize for best engineered vehicle at Goodwood meet for electric cars. Recyclers aplenty: eco committee run by geography department.

Huge range of extra activities four afternoons a week and all staff expected to run at least one. Pupils can do anything from fencing and yoga to textiles and pottery.

Background and atmosphere: Vaguely reminiscent of his gothic revivalist Natural History Museum, the main house (completed in 1878) was designed by Alfred Waterhouse and built for 2nd Baron Wolverton as his country seat. Founded in 1896 by Alexander Devine, school moved to 'Clayesmore's promised land' in 1933 after earlier incarnations in Middlesex, Berkshire and Hampshire. Set in idyllic 62 acre site of well-maintained grounds including a lake (complete with kingfishers and swans) in rural Dorset north of Blandford Forum in the lee of ancient Hambledon Hill.

Overriding impression is of a self-contained and happy extended family. Prep children and seniors (often elder siblings) co-exist happily cheek-by-jowl in these beautiful surroundings. Recent additions include Jubilee Building (nine science labs, ICT and learning support) and the even newer Spinney Centre. We were surprised at the lack of a zebra crossing (not for lack of trying on school's part) to get across busy A350 to reach picture postcard village of Iwerne (pronounced Euan) Minster where Devine house (for boys) and the quirky art department can be found. Pleasantly airy dining-hall serves wholesome nosh with copious salad and vegetarian options Good cross-cultural influences include a celebration meal for Chinese New Year. Lovely chapel not quite large enough for increased size of school: one house drops out weekly for Friday service, trad Sunday morning service for boarders. 'School is radically different from five years ago,' claimed deputy head (formerly head of English at Cheltenham Ladies') who pointed to a 'growth mindset' amongst staff. Huge techno buzz: staff ICT training and frequent 'blue-sky thinking'.

Pastoral care and discipline: Head reputedly keeps a tight lid on discipline supported by his deputies and pastoral staff. Rare suspensions for more serious behaviour problems but general ethos one of carrot rather than stick. Tutors (sixth formers choose their own) meet pupils weekly. Christian tradition important (school has Anglican chaplain) but not overbearing.

No dip in boarding (60 per cent of pupils) over last eight years. Experienced set of married houseparents lend distinctive flavour to each of the boarding houses (three boys' and two girls') – all on site except for Devine in former village rectory (where sixth form head of house had cooked a roast lunch for 32 boys the Sunday prior to our visit). Five boys live in a separate house nearby known as 'number four' under the supervision of an adjacent tutor. All round boarding facilities for boys and girls warrant inspectors' recent praise. No separate day houses: works well in school which is majority boarding. Medical centre provides 24 hour cover with permanent nursing staff.

Variety of boarding spaces – most year 9 rooms are five or six bedders, older ones get threes and fours and sixth form either share study bedrooms or get their own. The Capital is sixth form social area with a café (open from 10.30am for paninis, milk shakes etc) down in the London underground-themed basement of main house. 'Watching TV after games a favourite form of relaxation,' sixth formers told us. No alcohol served during week though prefects are granted pub leave on Friday nights. Social centre cum tuck shop for years 9-11 is next to music school and opens up after prep; stages open mic nights etc. Great efforts made to have fun weekends for boarders, including discos, talent contests and popular sixth form parties – houses take turns to organise. Saturday shopping trips organised to gentrified Blandford or Shaftesbury. Southampton shopping mall is most popular destination (for staff too). Duty staff organise Sunday excursions after chapel to local places of interest such as Bath.

Pupils and parents: Has become a serious contender on local circuit: we met pupils who had preferred Clayesmore's more intimate atmosphere to impressive facilities elsewhere. Good mix socially: unpretentious lot with some brainboxes but mainly honest citizens who work hard and tend to outperform expectations. A recent sixth former gained selection for Global Young Leaders Conference in Washington as well as a place at Oxford. School minibus service covers all points of the compass within a 25 mile radius with some parents ferrying to and from pick-up points from further afield. Can sometimes stay over if late night activities, weekly boarding OK (casual boarding if space available, charges apply). Senior pupils can bring their own cars. About five per cent are London refugees, a good sprinkling of ex-pat children (Forces, diplomatic etc) plus a small number of foreign students – eg Russia and Germany. No great green wellie influence. Staff-parent meetings timed to coincide with start of two-night exeats. Friends of Clayesmore raise funds for all manner of projects and needs. Clayesmore Society promotes 'The Clayesmore Season' a year round extravaganza of wider social and cultural activity for family and friends. Electronic reports and newsletters keep parents well informed. Interesting list of former pupils includes former Beatles manager, Brian Epstein; Stephen Joseph (pioneer of theatre in the round); TV artist, Tony Hart; Queen's orthopaedic surgeon, Sir Rodney Sweetnam.

Entrance: 'Ring Margaret', (head's words) to arrange initial visit (you'll be assured of a tour with pupils and a chat with head). Common entrance at 13+ (places not conditional once offered) for those from prep schools, interview with the head. Flexibility over admissions: school likes to take whole range of academic ability. Sibling friendly: 'if Frank can come so can Phyllis,' we were told. 'Willing all-rounders' and 'kind and thoughtful people' are particularly welcome. Just under half come from own prep with rest from 20 or so local (and some not so local) prep schools: Forres Sandle Manor, Hordle Walhampton, Highfield, Durlston Court, Port Regis, Dumpton, Sherborne Prep and Castle Court figure large plus a few from maintained schools. Rash of academic, music and art scholarships, several species of all-rounder awards made each year. Sixth form entrants (from a variety of state and independent schools) need five A/C passes at GCSE.

Exit: Some leave after GCSEs for state alternatives. Sixth form leavers head mainly to higher education: a surprisingly steady trickle to Oxbridge, more to Russell Group and then a host of other university destinations. From previous year's list we picked out Arabic and Middle Eastern studies at Exeter and motor sport technology at Oxford Brookes as indicative of the wide range of choices. Some Forces, some vocational courses. School turns out vets, medics plus strong art, drama and music stream.

Money matters: Not bargain basement but oodles of scholarships to compensate and help shallower pockets – sixth form up to eight, with a minimum of four reserved for those not presently in the school, others for local candidates (means tested), plus internal, and music (string players preferred). Scholarships, exhibitions and bursarial help for academics, music and art for entry into senior school at 13 (continuity awards operate from 11 to A level via the prep school) and more means tested awards. Closed bursaries for serving members of the Forces.

Remarks: Likely to impress from the moment the prospectus (like no other) drops through the letterbox. Lives up to its new marketing image surprisingly well and possibly exceeds it in human terms. Head has made all the difference. Probably what a boarding school should be: not oversize, caring, happy and successful across all ability levels. Ten out of ten for effort.

Clifton College

Linked school: Clifton College Preparatory School (The Pre) + Butcombe Pre-Prep

32 College Road, Clifton, Bristol, BS8 3JH

- Pupils: 715 pupils, 445 boys/270 girls; 340 boarders • Ages: 13–18
- C of E but pupils from many faith backgrounds • Fees: Boarding £28,200–£32,985; Day £21,525–£22,725 pa • Independent

Tel: 01173 157000
Email: admissions@clifton-college.avon.sch.uk
Website: www.cliftoncollegeuk.com

Head Master: Since 2005, Mr Mark Moore MA (late forties). Educated at Wolverhampton Grammar School and Downing College, Cambridge, where he read English, captained the university Eton Fives team and was world champion. A wonderful all-round games player who converses intelligently and interestingly about sport – 'He really understands games players,' said a hero-worshipping hockey player – but absolutely not a hearty. In fact he's a mighty talker on a range of subjects and is refreshingly iconoclastic about a number of educational issues, including league tables and some individual A levels. Teaches A level English – 'I love it'. One bright boy described him as a 'brilliant' teacher.

Engaging, witty, a strong advocate of co-education (girls have broken the breathless hush of the Close for 25 years and he has taught at Marlborough), he is committed to a 'broad church' in terms of entry into the school. Passionate about Clifton and its traditions, though with a clear eye to 21st century needs: he has a shrewd eye on the global scene – 'We have boys and girls from over 20 countries' – and is keen to inculcate an understanding between different faiths and nationalities. 'He may appear a little aloof,' said one senior boy, 'but he doesn't miss much.' He listens to pupils' initiatives and they feel encouraged. Above all he expresses a real affection for, and interest in, the pupils and a sympathetic understanding of rogues. Has instituted a school council. He and his wife, Jo, a fabulous cook with a wicked sense of humour, entertain a lot: staff, praepostors' (prefects), pupils of all ages, prep school heads and visiting lecturers.

Amidst all this they have four children, two boys and two girls, all within the various stages of the school. After Marlborough he had seven years at Eton followed by 11 years at Radley, where he was head of English. This is his first headship, though he's no greenhorn in terms of schoolmastering and has worked under some illustrious heads.

Academic matters: Good teaching (and preparation at prep schools) has resulted in good value-added at GCSE. A broad range of subjects with non-examined courses designed to feed the all-round pupil and a balance of art and sciences, the latter mostly taken separately. A thoughtfully flexible timetable allows for great diversity of subject choice. In 2013, 68 per cent A*/A grades.

A levels offer a broad spectrum of subjects from psychology to Chinese and from ancient Greek to sport and physical education – in total 31 subjects. No sense of narrowing down to A levels and breadth is encouraged – most choose four, some more. In 2013, 19 per cent A*/A and 75 per cent A*-B grades. Bright pupils are served well and less bright pupils are encouraged to reach their potential and made to feel good by doing so. As one grateful mum said, 'Pupils are never discouraged from pursuing a subject because they might not do very well and so lower the school's position in the league tables. Help and advice is given, but it's individual rather than political.' 'The school offers exemplary help and advice with university entrance,'

said a senior university don who is also a parent, 'and the co-curriculum stands them in very good stead when it comes to balancing the different aspects of university life.'

For dyslexics and others with learning difficulties, excellent one-to-one teaching where the emphasis is on support and building self-esteem. Evidence of the success of this programme lies in boys and girls who have had learning support and then won Oxbridge places.

Games, options, the arts: Beyond the classroom it offers an extraordinary range of activities with amazing facilities. In the pursuit of manly chivalry, it was one of the first schools in the country to make sport compulsory; now the damsels have joined in for different reasons – such a range on offer that 'everyone can find something they are good at,' said a satisfied parent. Rackets, fives, squash and tennis courts abound. A sports hall with indoor cricket nets, an indoor swimming pool, a huge gymnasium bursting with instruments of torture and one of the most beautiful cricket grounds in England. There, year after year, WG Grace piled on the runs, and in the summer of 1899 schoolboy prodigy Arthur Collins made the highest individual score in the history of the game: 628 not out. The crowded score book is on view in the prep. In the winter term, rugby is played, including the oldest rugby fixture between schools in England, Clifton v Marlborough, the Governor's Cup, first competed for in 1864.

That's just on the Clifton side of the river. Cross over by the thrilling suspension bridge – even Cliftonians don't swim across – and you come to Beggar Bush (safely referred to as BB). There, under the expert eye of the head groundsman, an old Cliftonian, stretch acres of playing fields with new international-standard Astroturf hockey pitches, a covered pitch allowing year-round tennis and netball, 24 tennis courts, a Real Tennis court, a new fitness centre with pavilion for entertaining, all open to the public at set times. When we visited, huge earth-moving machines like prehistoric monsters were filling in dips and valleys with building rubble for, inter alia, a full-sized all-weather rugby pitch. Girls' and boys' hockey thrives and produces its generous crop of internationals and county players who regularly go on tours as far away as South Africa and Australia. Rowing on the Avon, and further afield in Plymouth adventurous mariners can experience The Moosk, a 55ft gaff-rigged yawl built in 1906 and fully restored.

So much for burning up physical energy. What of the creative juices? Music and drama thrive. The new Joseph Cooper Music School is proving a huge success. The building is stuffed with pianos and practice rooms as well as modern technology in the shape of synthesisers and computerised composition suites, plus recording studio. Choirs, ensembles, orchestras, bands abound and perform regularly; the chapel choir sings nationally and internationally.

Named after old Cliftonian Sir Michael, the Redgrave Theatre, a surprisingly spacious building which offers little hint of its opportunities from the road, hosts over 40 productions a year including visits from travelling thespians. Pupils are in the National Youth Orchestra and the National Youth Theatre. The house drama week, a festival of pupil-produced plays, is hugely popular with everyone, including parents, and offers opportunities for anyone keen to participate. Musical productions eg Les Misérables. A room in one of the houses has been converted into a ballet and dance studio where even the 1st XV have practised for a musical! Art and ceramics are stunning (look at the prep school art to see the talent being fed through).

The Close, with its statue of Earl Haig and striking war memorial to those killed in the Boer War, to say nothing of the haunting arch commemorating the dead of the two world wars, is constant reminders of Clifton's connection with the Forces. The CCF is large and girls participate as enthusiastically as boys. D of E is very popular – own property in Wales as base for orienteering and walking weekends. Mountaineers cling on to rock and heather all over the world. Everyone is involved in some sort of community service. Overseas expeditions have included Arctic Circle, Borneo and Ecuador.

Background and atmosphere: The Victorian buildings, conveying as they do the impression that Clifton College has been around for much longer than its foundation in 1862, are very handsome – especially where the stone has been cleaned and the brick repointed. The jewel in the crown is the Percival Library, modelled on Duke Humfrey's mediaeval library in the Bodleian. It has been tactfully refurbished, combining traditional scholarship with information crunching: elegant bookcases in the body of the building; functional banks of computers in the foyer. Evidence of further improvement is everywhere: a scrappy old dump has become a new all-weather play area, tatty old tennis courts have been made playable. The science school has been totally refurbished, offering the latest new facilities.

After its foundation and the early building, set about building or buying houses – thus Houses are houses, for the most part. Recent improvement has resulted in bright and airy rooms equipped with modern accessories – running water and power points, for instance – plus comfortable lolling space with plenty of sofas and armchairs. 'Home from home,' said one happy girl. Day pupils have their own houses and enjoy all the amenities of boarders, minus the bed and breakfast, with facilities for sleeping over if parents are out gallivanting. The head has introduced matrons for each day house, which has not only improved the medical backup but also added further depth to the counselling and befriending in houses. New houses for the girls reflect the increase in numbers. Traffic (if that's the right word) between houses for boys and girls is civilised and, of necessity, restricted. CCTV cameras are thicker than on the M1 but that, we were assured, is to catch or deter Burglar Bill.

Overall a bustling, friendly atmosphere and pupils smile and greet. We heard of a boy currently at a big, powerful London school itching to join Clifton at sixth form – 'The kids are so normal there'. Big School is a big dining room but with small tables and attractively presented food – consumption does not disappoint. A newly created café in the chapel crypt complements the school shop, called, inevitably, Grubber.

Pastoral care and discipline: A town school, unless you're at BB. Not far from the leafy suburbs and impressive houses, Bristol offers its attractions and its temptations. The newly appointed Marshal, a man who used to work in counter-espionage, is responsible for overall discipline, rule keeping and self-restraint. Eighteen year olds are allowed to visit certain pubs with strict provisos – 'They guard that privilege jealously'. Staff say that, by and large, the pupils are pretty sensible about visiting pubs and clubs. One pupil we asked shrugged his shoulders with a grin – no animosity there. Sanctions are in place, so is trust.

The chapel is a monument to 'muscular Christianity', complete with stained glass window depicting a cricket match, the game of life. A popular and charismatic figure, the chaplain ensures that the chapel remains a focus of spirituality and a forum for discussion and discovery, eg when we attended a service, a group of boys were talking about the many facets of love – they were sensitive and unflinching in their treatment of the topic.

An effective tutoring system based on the houses – pupils spoke with appreciation of the friendly atmosphere and good relations they enjoy with the staff. Above all they appreciate the way they are allowed to develop as individuals. Interestingly, pupils spoke warmly of the support team: the porter, the ground staff and the secretarial branch.

Pupils and parents: Parents, mostly professional, come from a cross-section of society working in media, law, engineering, academia, and lots from the Forces. Day pupils are on the increase. Boarders make the most of the flexi, weekly and full boarding options and the proximity of Bristol Airport has brought cohorts of Europeans from further afield. The strong, historical Jewish connection brings pupils from Lithuania and neighbouring countries, even from Siberia – a cosmopolitan school and celebrating it.

Famous old boys include three Nobel Prize winners, seven winners of the VC, two Field Marshals and scores of gentler participants including LP Hartley, Sir David Willcocks, Trevor Howard, Simon Russell Beale, John Cleese, John Madden and Richard Foster – the list is impressive.

Entrance: Seventy per cent enter from the prep school – communication between the schools is effective so the entrance exam is for setting purposes. Common entrance is pitched at 50 per cent and potential. Own exams for pupils applying from the state system or abroad. Few leave after GCSE and the sixth form is massively oversubscribed.

Exit: Some 10 per cent leave after GCSEs. Despite lowly entrance requirements, most sixth formers go on to first choice universities over a wide geographical area: 12 Oxbridge in 2013; 80 per cent to top universities.

Money matters: Scholarships, awards and bursaries are awarded for the usual things, and discounts available for children of Forces and the clergy.

Remarks: In many ways Clifton can be summed up by its excellent magazine, one of the few which can be read with interest even by strangers, containing a scholarly interest in the past and a celebration of the present. With such a variety of good schools in the area, it has got to work hard to justify its expense and its less tangible position in the market. For many it's the dinner party school, watched closely and much discussed. Inevitably gossip throws out unattractive stories hinting at a certain arrogance, even a degree of philistinism – extraordinary when you see the standard of art, music and drama. After a brief period dedicated to climbing the league tables, has returned to teaching for potential.

These are exciting times for Clifton. It is not yet riding the crest of the wave but a huge wave is building up. There could be some good surfing.

Clifton Hall School

Linked school: Clifton Hall Junior School

Clifton Road, Newbridge, Edinburgh, EH28 8LQ

- Pupils: 340 boys and girls, all day • Ages: 11–18 • Non-denom
- Fees: £10,125 pa • Independent

Tel: 01313 331359
Email: headmaster@cliftonhall.org.uk
Website: www.cliftonhall.org.uk

Headmaster: Since 2005 Mr Rod Grant BA PGDPSE (early forties). Came from Hutcheson's where he was principal teacher of English, responsible for literacy. His original brief at Clifton Hall stretched through primary to S1. School had already started an all through policy, but had anticipated adding pupils year on year. At our last visit he promised, he would stay until 2015 at least: but with a 'youngster' in the school, this timeline doesn't look too likely – NB: George Watsons, Robert Gordons and Heriots are due to lose their heads this year, and feelers have been out, Grant admitted to being a tad 'unsettled' but has no thoughts of leaving, nor of expanding beyond 400. During our discussion it was difficult to keep his eyes straying from assorted young playing random hockey in the walled garden outside his office window.

From Prestwick in Ayrshire (where he has a second career as a 'property developer' – he lets out his flats there), educated at Merchiston, read English at Edinburgh, but abandoned this to join his brother in a wine bar venture. Returning to academia, he completed his degree at the Open University (having, in the interim, been housemaster at Drumley House School – deceased – in Ayrshire; his blog is highly entertaining), doing his PGCE at Paisley and cutting his teeth at a state primary in nearby Broxburn.

Less than three months into his headship, Grant was faced with a fire sale when approached by the governors of the tiny failing St Serf's school (94 pupils aged 5-18, lousy prep inspectors' report, mediocre senior report) suggesting a merger – and, after much gubernatorial activity, the schools amalgamated in September 2008. Huge amounts of dosh were spent converting previous dorms into classrooms – for 20 – but they look a bit squashed with 16 or 17, installing fire doors and the like, and awaiting an invasion. Which hasn't stopped. The school roll has increased by 184 per cent, 'the highest', Grant said proudly, 'in Scotland'. Double wowser. Pupil pin map shows a huge spread, from Galashiels in the borders to Falkirk, East Lothian and north of the Forth, numbers from Edinburgh. School picked up 19 from the demise of St Margaret's; buses from there, buses all over.

Certain amount of new build, some good, some bad, and some just plain ugly. Most resemble farm buildings, but then we are in (very basic) farming country. Mega £4m+ scheme in pipeline to cover the games pitches to the right of the drive with a combo 400 seater theatre, full basketball pitch and collection of classrooms. This editor suggested sinking the basketball pitch and the theatre (neither need daylight) and revamping the workshop and classrooms. The games pitch, charming club house and happy young playing hockey enhance the drive to the castle; though the less said about the monstrous carbuncle of a theatre workshop in the north west corner the better. Does what it says on the tin – but more suited to a building site than in plain view of the [Grimms] fairy tale 1857 Bryce Castle. Cladding is easy on the eye.

Rumours rife about the £1.7 million the merger realised – Grant is not so upfront, 'We spent what we got'. New kitchen adjacent to games hall, which doubles as dining room. Very fancy pants sports pavilion, all singing and dancing – the games facilities are let occasionally.

Popular weekly coffee mornings for parents, good catch up time, and a boon for the lonely or just plain concerned. Grant's common sense view on bullying – and now cyber bullying since our last visit – and some of the wilder health and safety regulations ought to be circulated round the head's grape vine. His wife, Helen, teaches in the junior school; they live on site.

Academic matters: Grant doesn't do league tables: nor do we: biased and adjusted, the biggest scam on earth. Nor does he do bells. Same form taker throughout for all in senior school. Set for maths from S2 (stops the boredom factor), otherwise parallel classes, no streaming. We found a brace of S4 classes studying John Steinbeck's Of Mice and Men. Simultaneously. Good pupil interaction, inspired relaxed teachers. Proper French, German and Spanish from P5 (aged 10). All the usual suspects plus admin, geology, philosophy and media studies in S5 and S6. Free choice for highers et al, Eng and maths essential, otherwise list preferred subjects in choice order. Grant promises to run a course if only one taker. Two computer suites (one Apple, one PC) used by all for timetabled lessons as well as IT – networked, intranetted, wireless. Labs designed by science staff, complete with prep room and adjacent scientific classroom. School follows Scottish system. No problem with absorbing the new national qualifications

Two dedicated SENCos: one in junior and t'other in senior school, plus an assistant. Pupils either withdrawn from class individually, in groups or offered dual teaching. Can cope with minor physical handicap – senior classrooms are upstairs – and Asperger's (mild).

Games, options, the arts: Team games on every available speck of green greeted our arrival. Cunning junior rugby/football goal makes Heath Robinson look like Einstein. But what fun.

Enthusiastic music; two were studying advanced higher music in the former chapel during our visit, whilst a hotch potch of students were writing, directing, producing a piece on Marilyn Monroe. We suggested blow heaters. Peripatetic staff. Exciting art – intricate dress design. Strong focus on preparing the young for the real world; and pushing creativity, practical nuts and bolts as well as the academic. Eco committee – school recently gained Green Flag status. Charity involvement via houses – children choose their own projects. Pupil council, with reps from every class and Eco council, with reps who suss out what the school can do to improve the environment. At our last visit we were sceptical about proposed outdoor classroom under pupil construction (in Scotland?). But they did it, with a combo of straw bales on larch and lime rendered (pupils wore rubber gloves). Wow.

Gym (with bars and benches) doubles as dining room, three sittings, takes two and a half hours (external caterer). Charming swimming pool, timetabled lessons for all (local primaries use it, scuba club one night a week and disabled group at weekends). Parents were watching a group of 5/6 year olds' swimming lesson during our visit. Senior school a bit dodgy on team games, though lots of clubs (judo, ballet, fencing, swimming) – no tennis courts seen. Sports facilities can be hired out by locals. Nine hole par three golf course on horizon but no all-weather pitch as yet.

Background and atmosphere: Clifton Hall is a magical Bryce house, complete with impressive oil paintings and the odd bit of antique furniture, in 54 acres of child-inspiring grounds off the Newbridge roundabout – the junction of A8, M8 and M9. A boon for parents to the west of Edinburgh, who can either take advantage of the school buses, which leave Bathgate, Livingstone, Newington and the West End of Edinburgh daily at 8am (departs at 5pm each evening) or drop off their poppets on the way to work, school open 8am to 6pm. The lodge at the entrance, previously let for not much more than a peppercorn, is now a humming café (post nat 5s only) generating £1000 plus a term.

Happy young sunning themselves outside when we visited, unaware that Euphame Macalzean, heiress of Clifton Hall, burnt alive in 1691 for witchcraft, has regularly been seen visiting her old nurse near the lodge.

Founded as a boarding boys (only) prep school in 1930, school became a limited company in 1964, thence weekly boarding, thence day, followed by girls, pre-prep and nursery. Clifton Hall had already started taking senior pupils before the amalgamation with St Serfs; ideally placed, it has all the vibes of a grand public/prep schools, games pitches, busy swimming pool on site, surrounded by (climbable) trees, contained, secure and with none of the health and safety issue of boarders.

First thing you see, even before you enter the school proper, is a show case of last year's trophies: an Olympic torch, carried by one of their youngsters and nestling cosily beside a Scotland under 16s rugby cap, and a fiddle score. The hall (good Victorian panelling) is decorated in French; and while the somewhat hotch potch configuration of class rooms is in good heart, we noticed the parquet flooring in the music room, labelled Library, former chapel (and quite obviously originally a billiard room) was ready for a spot of TLC.

Senior, junior and nursery all have their own dedicated playspace, the head can watch from his study – has been known to invite concerned parents to watch their darlings at play. Weekly menus handed out to all, so parents don't cook the 'same for their tea'. Lots of parent participation.

Previously painted in rather jolly primary colours, particularly in the basement, school has opted for uniform blue, and, despite our previous comments, the whole place looks bandbox fresh. The gorgeous doo'cot was about to have serious input from Historic Scotland. It didn't.

Pastoral care and discipline: Head has common sense attitude. Small enough school to care – tinies walk down school paths hand in hand. Matron sign still visible on first floor door. Children devised own set of Golden Rules (representatives from each class on pupil council) – each pupil must have both a request and a thank you.

Pupils and parents: Huge catchment area. Eighty-five per cent plus first-time buyers, ditto two working parents. A complete mix. The occasional parent follows the trad route, prep at 8 and senior school at 13, but most stay the course. FPs (aka CHOPS) include Rory Bremner, Jim Clark and Jamie Bruce Jones of Caledonia Play, designer of the splendid wooden castle in the nursery garden.

Entrance: Mainly through the (non-selective entry) nursery – a proper nursery school (member of the Edinburgh City Partnership Scheme) with many of the children wearing uniform, and junior school. Otherwise first come, first served, assessment to pick up glitches. Overbooked for nursery and first few years of primary. Space sometimes available in the senior school. Will accept pupils at any time; gentle school, a number from maintained sector who have been bullied (cyber bullying the new head on the block: trollig). Grant reckons to have a good 'conversion' rate of potential parents, emailing them within three days of interest being shown, and keen on first names. Regular parents' evenings. Two/three per cent ethnic mix.

Exit: Most to some form of higher education; most stay in Scotland. Aberdeen, Heriot Watt, St Andrews, Edinburgh, Glasgow, Robert Gordons, Oxford. The odd gapper.

Money matters: Fees include almost all extras; trust fund on hand to pick up financial hiccups 'for a year or two' – 'safety net' rather than 'safety blanket'.

Remarks: Wowser. 'School is going places and it is growing,' was what we said last time. Governors very bullish, and so they should be. Head has maintained and increased momentum: the school roll is now a whopping 332, nearly half junior and half senior plus nursery.

Clifton High School

Linked school: Clifton High Early Years and Junior School

College Road, Clifton, Bristol, BS8 3JD

• Pupils: 250 boys and girls, 10 boarders; • Ages: 11 –18; • Non-denom, Christian ethos • Fees: £8,730–£12,435 pa • Independent

Tel: 01179 730201
Email: admissions@cliftonhigh.bristol.sch.uk
Website: www.cliftonhigh.bristol.sch.uk

Head of School: Since 2008, Dr Alison Neill (early fifties), a former research scientist with long service at Clifton High – started as a biology teacher and worked her way up via head of sixth form to head of school. Parents describe her as fair, kind and taking a personal interest in the children, 'And amazingly elegant at the same time,' said one. Works with her executive team, Mr Tony Richards, head of early years and junior school, and Mr Guy Cowper, the director of operations in charge of business matters.

Long years at the school haven't made Dr Neill narrow-minded: some radical rethinking has gone on since she took on the headship, from the move to co-education at all ages to the links between different parts of the school. Even the head's office was not sacred: down came the curtains to let the light in – possibly a symbolic gesture as much as an interior design choice. The head says the decision to admit boys to the secondary school was triggered at least in part by her disappointment at having to send her own son elsewhere at 11, but that personal feeling was backed up with intensive research into current educational thinking and visits to other schools practising different models of co-education.

Academic matters: Not an academic pressure cooker, but results are good for the intake – in 2013, 52 per cent A*/A at GCSE, and 40 per cent A*/A at A level – and small classes mean plenty of support is available. A few bright stars in each year, but staff stress they are even prouder of those who struggle to achieve hard-won Cs and Ds at A level and go on to higher things. GCSE and A level options are as flexible as possible, with no option block system.

Parents talk about a 'sense of fun' underlying the serious academic work, which could be seen on our visit with a year 8 class firing rubber bands at a ball during a physics lesson in a practical demonstration of forces.

Boys and girls are taught separately in years 7-9 in the core subjects of English, maths, biology, chemistry, physics and ICT, and in modern languages in year 7. Pupils are organised into mixed gender groups for all other subjects and all other years – the diamond edge model. Parents and teachers seem happy with the system so far – seen as a good compromise for parents wanting the best of both single-sex and co-ed education.

Languages a strong point – carousel system for trying out French, German, Spanish in years 7 and 8. Wide range of overseas trips, full-time native speaker assistants for each language. Latin is strong and popular (helped by an innovative head of department); Greek is no longer officially on the menu, but may be offered on demand if a group within a year is desperately keen. Classical civilisation an option at A level. Science provision is good – large numbers taking biology A level, possibly helped by a popular and young head of biology, but takeup of other sciences also increasing. Business studies, psychology and IT available if enough interest.

The special needs coordinator makes sure that everyone is screened periodically so dyslexia and other issues can be picked up at any stage, and individual or small group help offered, but school does turn away some needing more support than it can cope with. Physical disabilities adjusted for as far as possible, but the age and layout of buildings make accessibility an issue.

Games, options, the arts: Drama is popular and inclusive – regular productions for all school levels are 'very creative'. Option of extra speech and drama lessons during school hours (leading to external exams) for the keen and many take drama at A level. Lively musical scene, with most instruments offered and several chamber groups, plus school choir and orchestra.

New multi-user games area for eg hockey, netball, basketball, tennis and five-a-side football. Gym and swimming pool on the main site, but playing fields off-site on a large development shared with the university at Coombe Dingle, with good modern and spacious facilities including indoor sports courts and more outdoor tennis courts. The full-size swimming pool is a perk not available to most of the other independents in central Bristol.

Increasing numbers of boys mean that the school can now field full rugby or cricket teams for inter-school sports, and it has arrangements with sports clubs sharing the Coombe Dingle pitches to augment the options available. Tennis players have the example of old girl, Jo Durie, to look up to. Head of school games (boys) making his mark throughout the school and head for girls also recently reappointed.

Historically stronger on food and textiles than the more masculine variants of design technology, but that is changing. The lower years curriculum for textiles has been rejigged for gender neutrality with the advent of boys – less fashion, more kites and other items – and some new options have been introduced, such as graphic design and music technology.

Background and atmosphere: Boys now 40 per cent of total in every year group and well represented in all areas of school life. Teaching staff still female-dominated (roughly two-to-one ratio), but more men being recruited, eg heads of boys' sport, food technology, history and government and politics, plus of year 9. Pupil numbers now steady or rising after earlier dive. Teachers and parents rave about the school's warmth and friendliness, partly due to its size but also deeply rooted in its attitudes and culture.

Has expanded from its original cluster of impressive nineteenth century houses, with various less attractive twentieth century additions around a central lawn. Cramped in parts, but the use of space is efficient, and the heart of Clifton location helps keep the image upmarket. Classrooms and corridors look a little shabby in places, but all the equipment you would expect, from interactive whiteboards to computerised language labs, and it is clean and well-lit. Seven recent IT suites plus Apple Mac musical technology suite and performing arts centre, including cinema.

Everyone from junior and senior schools (staff included, though on separate tables) has lunch in the cheerful hubbub of main school canteen – a good choice of hot and cold meals, plus salad bar (more limited choice for the little ones). Also a cafe opening on to a courtyard for breaktime and after-school snacks. Sixth formers have own eyrie in the main building: study and common rooms with Wifi (all issued with laptops) and a more grown up feel.

Pastoral care and discipline: Pupils generally agree that staff are approachable and relations friendly, and parents full of praise for the firm but caring attitude of the staff – 'No one gets lost in the crowd,' said one. Pupils encouraged to talk to any member of staff they choose about a problem – they don't have to stick to their own tutor if they find another teacher more sympathetic. The school nurse (shared with the lower school) has a suite of rooms and is there for anyone who feels unwell or needs a chat.

Sixth formers assigned as peer mentors for years 6 to 8, seen as the peak danger years for bullying. Bullying is taken 'very seriously' – school uses strategies to build resilience, and tries to work through issues openly with dialogue.

Discipline system of merits and demerits in place, most often used for handing in work late or not at all – three demerits lead to a detention – but apparently most staff rarely use them.

Boarding has shrunk from whole-school to now only being offered in the sixth form, with a handful of boarders living with local families rather than on-site, but school says it is keen to promote the boarding option (new boarding coordinator recently appointed).

Pupils and parents: Family backgrounds are varied, but on the whole not as wealthy as those driving past the school to Clifton College up the road, or as high-pressured as the ones at some of the single-sex Bristol girls' schools. Lots of sibling groups and some second or even third generation pupils. A large proportion of the staff send or have sent their own children to the school, including the head, which can be seen as a vote of confidence. The big shift to co-ed doesn't seem to have fazed the parents – only one apparently upped and left in protest – and most are supportive of the thinking behind the diamond model.

Old Girls include Jo Durie, Sarah Keays, Mary Renault, Stephanie Cole, Elizabeth Filkin and Bernice McCabe (current head of North London Collegiate).

Entrance: Intake is from a wide range of local primaries throughout the junior years and at 11, with some movement from other Bristol and regional independents. Boys joining the upper school under the new system include some first-timers, but also some sixth formers who spent their primary years at CHS. Entry for outside pupils at 11 via tests in NVR, maths and English, plus a chat with the head – informal for most, more formal for scholarship or bursary applicants.

Progression from the junior school is automatic, with only those hoping for scholarships taking the entrance tests. Potential scholars are identified from entrance examination and interview by the head. Any juniors seen as unlikely to make the grade are given plenty of warning, usually at least a year or so before they would need to make a move. Sixth form applicants taken on the basis of GCSE results or predictions, previous school reports and interview; some may be asked to sit in-house tests in relevant subjects.

Exit: Most stay on after GCSE, though a few have always opted to leave for co-ed sixth forms – too early to see the effect of the arrival of sixth form boys – or to take up subjects not offered. Nearly all to some form of higher education at the whole range of universities and art colleges.

Money matters: Not a rich school, but enough in the pot to help 30 or so pupils a year, with support ranging from token academic scholarships to full assisted places or bursaries for three or four. Fees are in line with the other Bristol day schools.

Remarks: Bouncing back from a rocky patch, with a dynamic head, closer integration with the early years and junior school and boys throughout the senior school and sixth form. Still not an obvious choice for seriously sporty boys, although this is changing, but sporty girls have plenty of scope here, and the relaxed, friendly atmosphere and small class sizes have plenty to offer for more academic or arty types of both sexes. 'There's a very calm and grown up feeling,' said one girl.

Cobham Hall

Cobham, Gravesend, Kent, DA12 3BL

• Pupils: 160 girls; 90 full time and 3 weekly boarders • Ages: 11–18 • Multi-faith • Fees: Boarding £22,800–£28,750; Day £15,090–£19,100 pa • Independent

Tel: 01474 823371
Email: enquiries@cobhamhall.com
Website: www.cobhamhall.com

Headmaster: Since 2008, Mr Paul Mitchell BSc in maths and PGCE from University of Newcastle (early fifties). Previously deputy head at St Mary's School, Cambridge, and before that taught at Royal High Bath, Godolphin in Salisbury, Radley College and in the state sector.

Early on, a keen interest in sport a factor in his career choice, granting him the flexibility to keep at the top of his field as an international pentathlete – he represented Britain for 10 years. Now often to be found out of hours at the stables with his two horses, but brought his enthusiasm for sport to the school. Not someone to put too much emphasis on this or that standard, far more on the individual and how each can find their niche and come to life at the school. Keeps tabs on them all. He speaks with disarming candour and while evidently fiercely loyal to the school and conscious of economic realities, you feel his genuine openness and his appreciation of openness in others. 'I'd approach him about anything, but he'd probably know and have done something about it already,' we were told. Unmarried.

Academic matters: IB introduced in 2009, in keeping with the traditional internationalism and Round Square ethos of the school. (A Levels phased out at the same time and are now no longer offered.) Since then, sixth form intake has increased slightly, suggesting that both IB and the one-year pre-IB course may be a draw for overseas parents. UK parents also prize the broad, values-based education that the IB promotes, but so far Cobham's average IB points score has been under-whelming: 29 in 2013, which wouldn't get you a place at Russell Group universities. At GCSE, 50 per cent A*/A grades in 2013. However, parents don't seem overly concerned and are quick to mention cases of teachers generating interest and unexpectedly good results in particular subjects. The school's mantra and Round Square motto is 'There's more in you than you think', and with small class sizes (12-15 in the lower school, middle 10-12 and a small sixth form) enabling a high degree of individual attention, parents are confident that staff bring out the best in them, in and outside the classroom. Students were warm in their praise of staff: 'They care about us so much.' 'They're really encouraging and they go out of their way to help you.' 'My grades have got much better since I came here,' were typical comments. Over half awarded a bi-lingual diploma.

The Susan Hampshire Centre (student support department) caters for pupils requiring learning support. Predominantly, pupils using the centre have dyslexic/dyspraxic tendencies or Irlen Syndrome (a condition which affects the way the brain processes visual information). For each, an IEP drawn up covering literacy, maths and study skills, according to their needs. Two specialist EFL teachers.

Games, options, the arts: Head says that the school was somewhat at the 'egg and spoon race' stage a few years back, but this is changing. The girls enjoy their sport and relish a more competitive approach and the greater focus on field and track. Notable recent successes in the biathlon, high jump and 1500m. Some new specialist sports coaches; enthusiasts enabled to go to county netball and local hockey club training. Rounders also popular, and if that doesn't tickle their fancy, always badminton, dance, zumba, aerobics and swimming.

Just under half the pupils study a musical instrument or sing and have the opportunity to join instrumental groups and one of four choirs. Regular lunchtime concerts and a major performance each term in the fabulous Gilt Hall. Drama is evidently innovative and fun – inter-house drama and music festivals every other year in which all have to participate. Being an extra during the filming of Wild Child at the school must also have been a real thrill for some.

Good sporting and other facilities include an indoor heated pool, indoor and outdoor tennis courts, dance studio and fitness suite. Bikes encourage the girls to be more active. Well-equipped theatre and, judging by the art and sculptures on display, artistic talents well catered for. Programme of lunchtime and after-school clubs and, at the weekend, film, culture and shopping trips keep boarders occupied.

In truth, none of these activities nor the D of E is out of the ordinary. What excites most is the school's membership of the Round Square and the opportunities for adventure that it creates. It's obviously a subject of much discussion and anticipation amongst the girls, who come up with varied fundraising ideas – fashion shows, bake sales and sponsored cycle rides – to enable them to travel to and support community projects in far-flung places. School exchanges and international conferences also a regular feature. Parents love all this character-building and eye-opening stuff plus the sense of security which comes with the school's 40 year Round Square association and vast international network.

Background and atmosphere: Cobham Hall is only a short distance from Ebbsfleet International railway station (London, St Pancras 17 minutes) and major motorway links, but passing through the gates is like entering a time warp away from the noise and bustle of modern life. A Grade II listed Elizabethan building comes into view, all more modern classrooms and boarding houses discreetly tucked away out of sight so as not to detract from the 150 acres of beautiful parkland. The buildings are made accessible for various events during the year and, in the spring, the grounds are open to the public, who can gaze in awe at the carpet of flowers. Inside, many rooms are beautifully preserved with the help of English Heritage, and scattered about with wonderful nonchalance are portraits of past owners, framed historical documents, and even a horse-drawn carriage resting idly at the end of the Independent Learning centre.

Since its establishment in 1962, has had internationalism at its core, and cultural integration and enrichment are still very much a part of life here. On Friday nights pupils tell stories from around the world, and assemblies feature explanations of different religious beliefs and traditions. Nonetheless, as one pupil put it, it does feel a bit of a 'bubble community', a small world of its own. No bad thing, say parents of, in particular, younger pupils, as it allows, indeed encourages, them to develop a strong values-base on which to build their future lives.

Pupils are proud of the community and individuals' achievements and, through the various student committees and leadership structures, play an ongoing and important role in promoting them. If they didn't like the head – and most do – arguably they would have themselves to blame: after all, they interviewed him before he got the job.

Pastoral care and discipline: 'We're a close community. We all know each other and everyone has the freedom to be who they want to be.' Quiet, outgoing, musical, academic, sporty, the school accommodates all, bar perhaps those who want to break away and form their own group. It has a gentle and friendly atmosphere with real thought and care taken to ensure that, whatever your background, you settle in well. In this nurturing atmosphere even the shyest gain confidence.

Sixth form boarders live in dedicated houses, with cooking and other facilities to reflect their greater independence. Younger full-time and flexi-boarders have bedrooms in the main school building which are comfy and spacious. Little touches like putting a teddy in a flexi-boarder's bed, the big sister system to look after newcomers and peer mentoring are examples of how the girls look out and care for each other. Day pupils are encouraged to try out boarding as part of the induction and get five free nights per term – part, perhaps, of the school's current strategy to tip the balance more in favour of boarding. This, and the fact that many day pupils stay late, means no great day/boarder divide. Some parents comment that it would be good if boarders were invited out more regularly but, with 80 per cent or so staying in at the weekends, it is rare for anyone to be at a loose end.

Discipline is 'tough but fair'. Incidents of a serious nature are rare, as is bullying, problems mostly limited to minor fall-outs, perceived as inevitable amongst teenage girls. Where parents have had concerns of this nature or in relation to academics, they find staff accessible and responsive.

Pupils and parents: 'Outside, they think we're all posh but we're not,' says one girl. This is backed up by a parent's observation: 'There's anything from old bangers to Rollses coming up the drive each morning'. A 50/50 mix of international and UK boarders. Living in a small community while acquiring a good level of English is clearly a strong draw amongst the 32 nationalities represented.

Parents say pupils are polite and chat quite happily with them in a relaxed and mature way. They are supportive of each other in work and play and tend to just get on with whatever they are tasked to do. In the all-girl environment, parents celebrate that little pressure to grow up too fast. Sixth formers wear suits; few uniform infringements lower down school.

The Unicorn (parents) Association is very active and welcoming – 'You almost have to beat them off'. Regular teas before exeat weekends, coffee mornings, school events, art exhibitions, salsa and jazz evenings provide ample opportunities to meet other parents. The wide catchment area can otherwise make this and sharing transport difficult.

Former pupils include BBC newsreader/journalist Mishal Husain, Alex Crawford, foreign correspondent/journalist, and Kate French, who represented Britain in the 2012 Olympics pentathlon.

Entrance: At 11+ and 13+ applicants sit maths and English assessments, provide a report of recommendation from their current school, attend an interview and take part in group activities. Those wishing to enter the sixth form (both internal and external applicants) sit the IB entrance examination. A further 15 or so girls every year come from various countries for a term or two specifically to improve their English.

Exit: Approx 45 per cent move on after GCSEs, mostly to larger mixed schools or sixth form colleges. The introduction of the IB has had little impact on sixth form numbers. Of those staying on until 18, a small minority take a gap year. Most pursue further studies in their countries of origin or in the UK at a variety of universities and colleges from Nottingham Trent to Queen Mary.

Money matters: Discounts are available for daughters/ granddaughters of old girls (Elders). Reductions for those staying on in the sixth form and discounts for Forces families, diplomats and families working for UK charitable trusts overseas. Bursaries and scholarships available. Fees for extras are considered reasonable and no extra charge for day pupils on boarder taster weeks or for breakfast and supper when they are involved in clubs.

Remarks: A friendly and caring environment with strong international links and the premise that everyone achieves, given belief and support.

Cokethorpe School

Linked school: Cokethorpe Junior School

Witney, Oxfordshire, OX29 7PU

• Pupils: 660 boys and girls; all day. • Ages: 4–18 • Joint C of E and RC foundation • Fees: £15,975 pa • Independent

Tel: 01993 703921
Email: admissions@cokethorpe.org
Website: www.cokethorpe.org.uk

Headmaster: Since 2002, Mr Damian Ettinger BA MA PGCE (forties). Educated St Joseph's College (Beulah Hill), Universities of Manchester and Surrey (theology and philosophy). Previously head of theology and housemaster at Downside and before that at Prior Park College, Bath. Teaches theology up to GCSE and philosophy in the sixth form. Voluble and delightfully opinionated, his passion for Cokethorpe and all it can do for its pupils is undimmed since our last visit. We searched high and low for evidence of squashed laurels in Mr Ettinger's wood-clad study but found none.

We cannot recall touring a school and hearing the head's name mentioned so frequently: 'They were Mr Ettinger's idea – some people didn't get them at first but now everyone loves them,' (of the delightful metal animal and bird sculptures that pop up on lawns, walls and roofs) or, of the excellent termly newsletter, The Ocellus, 'Mr Ettinger set that up'. The Trafalgar-inspired fourth plinth in the courtyard? You guessed it – Mr Ettinger and his ideas again. It is this vision and energy that have driven the renaissance of Cokethorpe, making it now a first choice school for many. He is pretty frank about the changes he made when appointed, 'Learning support was dictating the culture of the school'; LS now at roughly 10 per cent and, as a result, 'is much more effective'. He wants Cokethorpe pupils 'to exhibit the old-fashioned virtues of kindness and decency' and challenge the current trend of laddishness in both boys and girls. Big on manners, he restored proper plates, cutlery and glasses to the dining hall against advice and, guess what, the sky didn't fall in.

Among the buzzier bees in Mr Ettinger's bonnet is the question of 'why kids lose enthusiasm for science' – one way of tackling this at Cokethorpe is links with nearby Rutherford labs so that teachers can go and play with the latest equipment and bring their renewed enthusiasm back to pupils. His pipedream is an 'interdisciplinary science park approach to teaching'; also on his wish list are a new theatre, music school and dedicated examination hall.

Mr Ettinger is something of a jazz buff and reviews for Jazz Journal. When asked what he would do if he were not headmaster, he claims he would like to run a garage (he owns three classic cars and has recently done a welding course), but we think something of the architect manqué is there too. He's big on 'sightlines', and the extensive (and expensive) building programme has been managed with real vision – new and old flow together in productive harmony. He pays tribute to his second in command and the 'hands on' governors and is grateful not to be 'shackled by internal politics'.

Mr Ettinger, who describes himself as a 'Roman Catholic of the English variety', is married with five children (ages 23 to 9), his wife teaches IT at a nearby FE college – 'The fact that she isn't involved in the day-to-day running of the school allows me to go home and be a typical family man'. When asked what car he would be he points to a model on his desk – 'That one, a brown Ford Cortina Mk 3'.

Academic matters: Solid results – in 2013, 27 per cent A*/A and 63 per cent A*/B grades at A level; nearly 38 per cent A*/A at GCSE. The long-term concerted effort to instil academic rigour is clearly paying dividends, but the head is by no means complacent, claiming that although he doesn't want to depart entirely from Cokethorpe's valued reputation as an inclusive, family school, there's room for 'nudging' things up.

School is changing to IGCSEs for most subjects, but IB has been considered and rejected. Instead, Mr Ettinger's sights are on widening what is currently a trickle into a regular stream of pupils heading for Oxbridge and leading American universities. Most popular A level subject choices are currently the Oxbridge-unfriendly PE, business studies and psychology, but geography, maths and science not far behind. Relatively small numbers taking languages and English.

One of the first schools to introduce Cambridge pre-U for history (with excellent results) and same for other subjects (English, modern languages, economics and philosophy) arriving shortly. Impressive general studies programme of visiting lecturers and other extension activities for sixth form, including English literature recitals where staff hold forth on matters of literary interest.

Lessons we observed were, on the whole, pacy and inclusive – small classes (average 14, max 20) should mean nowhere to hide, but perhaps muttering at the back will always be with us. Work we saw was very helpfully marked with positive comments and constructive criticism.

About 10 per cent, mainly pupils with dyslexia or dyspraxia, receive specialist individual support (up to three hours per fortnight) and liaison between teaching staff and the LS department ensures pupils' needs are met in lessons.

Games, options, the arts: Cokethorpe is indeed fortunate in its spacious grounds, and maximum use is made of these for all sports that require acreage – rugby, football, hockey, cricket and even golf. Strong inter-house competition in addition to matches with other schools means that all get a chance to participate at some level. County champions in rugby and hockey, and county and national representatives in athletics, cricket, tennis, netball and cross-country. Particularly strong record of national successes in clay pigeon shooting and kayaking. Climbing wall but no swimming pool – 'Everybody thinks it should be on my wish list but it isn't,' declares the head, so wet stuff takes place at Brize Norton. Standard issue large echoing sports hall with gallery gym – our guides described this (and practically everything else Cokethorpean) as 'amazing', but we thought the gym rather macho. It is, they conceded 'mainly for the rugby players', but girls' only sessions too. An hour at the end of each day and extended Friday lunchtimes are for over 50 'AOB' activities such as salsa dancing, bird-watching – surely pretty rewarding, given the sylvan setting – poker, touch-typing and archery.

DT and art benefit from spacious well-appointed workshops – some great examples of student work on display including beautifully turned and decorated paddles. Art, photography and textiles are offered at GCSE and A level. Music for all and to a very high standard – we liked the way it is unavoidable even for those who do not play or sing: pupils give lunchtime music recitals, madrigals on May Day, a singing category for all in the inter-house competition, and the choir sings grace from the gallery to dining pupils below every Wednesday. An award-winning school jazz band and termly gig nights are a very popular platform for the less classically minded. Drama offered both as part of the curriculum (theatre studies) and as an AOB option; two main school productions a year including a summer Shakespeare and plenty of house plays keep Cokethorpe's thespians busy.

Days are long – buses leave at 5pm for what can be an hour's journey home – and an enormous amount going on. Add to this field trips, workshops, charity fundraising, competitions, homework, weekend matches and Saturday morning performing arts academy – it's no wonder parents tell us some pupils can fall behind.

Background and atmosphere: Founded in 1957 with 14 pupils, the school occupies a Queen Anne mansion surrounded by 150 acres of serene, manicured parkland complete with ha-ha and ancient trees – recently reduced by 10, thanks to a tornado that ripped through (fortunately on a bank holiday). The Vanbrugh-style mansion, where the first Viscount Harcourt entertained literary fellows Swift, Dryden and Pope, is now home to admin, head's study and the junior department. Entrance hall and public areas uncluttered and notably free of pupils' artistic endeavours (an absence more than made up for in rest of school), all the better to appreciate the original Georgian lines perhaps.

Behind the mansion in its cobbled mews is, wonder of wonders, The Grove, a Costa Coffee outlet serving free drinks and snacks (fruit, biscuits etc) to sixth formers. This venue also used as 'philosophy café' hosting talks and seminars. Our guides were immaculate in the sixth form 'business dress'; what manner of business some of the other Costa denizens aspired to we can only speculate, but the head prefers a degree of individuality to abandoning the dress code altogether. Teaching and learning for the seniors is in new-build academic departments arranged round a quad, a fab library and luxurious sixth form centre – lots of glass and metal successfully merging modern with the mellow Cotswold stone.

Another architectural triumph is the double-height dining hall – the head fought planning, not to mention health and safety, to get the huge baronial fireplace installed; it must be quite a sight at Christmas. We stood in the gallery and looked down on refectory tables and benches beautifully designed in plain solid wood and thought of all the cabbagey subterranean school watering holes we have had the misfortune to visit. In fact the food does also appear to be 'amazing'. Lucky, lucky Cokethorpe.

Smart pin-striped trousers and skirts, navy jumpers with gold trim – it's a challenge for the determined fashionista to tweak a uniform like this but, bless 'em, they do. Perhaps, like a wise parent, the school picks its battles, and rather than being too stuffy about minor infringements, sets its sights on encouraging the major virtues such as tolerance and respect for others. Interestingly, the head might prefer pupils to channel their rebel spirits into 'underground magazines and the like'; he expressed a nostalgic regret for the absence of such.

Pastoral care and discipline: Cokethorpe is a joint Roman Catholic and Church of England foundation and pastoral care has long been seen as a strength of the school; pupils to whom we spoke endorse this – 'It's a real community – everyone knows everyone else and looks out for each other'. Rules and useful information including school policies on bullying helpfully set out in the pocket-sized Blue Book issued to all pupils. Head keen to maintain family feel and will 'bend a little' to accommodate siblings of varied abilities. Having pupils aged 4 to 18 on the same site certainly seems to foster an atmosphere of mutual support and it's hard to imagine any child passing through anonymously.

Pupils and parents: Subsidised buses pick up 70 per cent of pupils from 22 routes encompassing Swindon, Oxford, Brize Norton and Didcot. School population not ethnically diverse – reflects local demographic (any episode of Midsomer Murders will give you the idea) and parents are the usual mix of professionals and first time buyers. Pupils seem to be a sparky bunch.

Entrance: Increasingly popular, not just because independent co-ed options in Oxfordshire are pretty limited – roughly two candidates for every place. Senior school (age 11): interview, tests and observed activities. Candidates for 13+ offered provisional place on basis of pre-test, conditional on satisfactory performance in CE. Sixth form requires A* to C in maths, English and science plus 'good' grades in subjects to be studied at A level.

Main feeders are local state primaries and independents such as The Manor, Chandlings, St Hugh's, The Dragon, New College School, Abingdon Prep. Cokethorpe has an 'association' with nearby Westfield House Nursery School, from where a number of children enter the reception class every year.

Exit: A fifth leave post GCSE. At 18, to a wide range eg nursing at Oxford Brookes, economics at Manchester, history at Exeter and sports coaching at Canterbury.

Money matters: Lots of means-tested scholarships/bursaries of all kinds – academic, art, music, sports, drama, classics, modern langs and all-rounder. Minor schols for two years from 11. All gauged on exam performance and interview with head.

Remarks: Cokethorpe is an interesting study in just how long the tail of a school's former reputation can be. Even now, 12 years from Mr Ettinger's year zero, one still occasionally hears it referred to as a 'soft option' (but this is Oxfordshire, where 'soft' is a relative concept). Prep school heads know different and the days of, 'Never mind – there's always Cokethorpe,' are long gone. This is a thriving, energetic school; several parents mentioned they liked it because it is a less stuffy, more grounded place to learn than some of the competition. As a relative newcomer, Cokethorpe has been able to cherry-pick some of the more appealing traditions of older establishments and make them its own, forging ahead with all the positive benefits of modern co-education in a classical English setting.

Colchester County High School for Girls

Norman Way, Colchester, CO3 3US

• Pupils: 550 girls, all day • Ages: 11–18 • Non-denom • State

Tel: 01206 576973
Email: office@colchestergirls.essex.sch.uk
Website: www.cchsg.com

Headteacher: Since 2010, Mrs Gillian Marshall, previously deputy head at the mixed comprehensive Notley High School, Braintree. Has also had extensive experience in selective schools.

Academic matters: The buzzy, bright girls here have fought their way through the rigorous consortium of selective schools in Essex 11+ exam, the cream of the crop. French and German are begun in year 7, Latin kicks in in year 9 and Spanish is an option from year 10. Pupils must take at least one of French or German to GCSE, and may keep on with any of the other languages too. Sciences are taught separately from year 8 and are popular A level options – reflecting CCHS's status as a specialist college for both science and languages.

Taking 11 GCSEs is the norm – 82 per cent A*/A, 2013. A level results are impressive across the board – 88 per cent A*-B, 63 per cent A*/A; 90 per cent of those taking it regularly achieve an A in maths. Everyone studies critical thinking, and takes the AS exam during years 10-11. Such stellar achievement in all areas can cause anxieties, but bringing perspective is something the school does well, according to parents.

Only 20 girls are on the school's SEN register and a variety of needs are represented. An assistant headteacher takes on the additional role of SENCo and support is generally offered on an individual basis – no in-class assistance as the school does not have teaching assistants. However staff themselves are constantly updated on individual students' needs, and the school works closely with students, parents, the student advisor and external agencies, if need be.

A recent Ofsted report was largely flawless – with a barb about a requirement for more publicity about charity work, smacking of desperation to find a hole to pick. Nevertheless it ruffled the feathers of the school, which retorted, 'Initiatives here are for educational purposes, not to tick a box'.

Games, options, the arts: Numerous musical groups, ensembles and choirs, many instigated by the girls themselves. Drama also strong – when we visited an external drama coach was taking a class in the hall for a lively session. The lack of facilities does not hamper the girls' sporting performance – they like to win on the hockey pitch, netball court and athletics track. While the élite are picked and trained in squads, those with more enthusiasm than talent have many active clubs to choose from, including dance and fencing. Most clubs take place at lunchtimes due to travelling home arrangements – huge range, from the academic and the vocational to the fun, some run by senior pupils; staff are generous with their time and encouragement. D of E is thriving.

Background and atmosphere: Founded at the turn of the century but relocated to its current site, a campus setting on a quiet road a mile from the centre of Colchester, in 1957. A collection of rather characterless buildings typical of that era,

which have to be made the best of. The main teaching block is chilly in winter and boiling in the summer, despite an attempt to insulate the vast windows. The superb new m-School encompasses the 'music, mathematics and mind' departments. The 'mind' is the critical thinking department, which has a showcase high-tech i-lab where students scrawl their thoughts on the wall and then recall them at a later date for further study. The music department has two large teaching rooms, a recording studio and a computer suite fitted out with Apple Macs, keyboards and composition technology. Maths has – well, what do mathematicians need, anyway?

Sixth formers have their own common room and private study area. Gym is pleasant and high-ceilinged. Playing fields on-site, though rather bleak. Picnic benches are arranged on the scant greenery in between blocks for girls to gather on at breaks.

The girls rave about the food – a one-man band buys fresh every day and even tries out recipes suggested by the girls. A bright dining space serves hot and cold food, paid for in the old-fashioned way, and girls who have lunchtime clubs can request cold food to be speedily collected and eaten wherever is most convenient.

This is an ordered environment, but without the stuffiness that extremely academic schools sometimes find it hard to avoid. Cloakrooms are reassuringly untidy, although each year group has PE bags in a specific colour and lockers for books.

Pastoral care and discipline: With so much talent in a relatively small space, CCHS could be something of a pressure cooker environment; however, the strategy is to use PE and PSHE lessons to teach coping skills, approaches to revision and even breathing exercises at crucial times.

The girls themselves say they feel well supported by the staff, who are generally long-serving and move up through the years with their charges as far as the sixth form. Girls appear to get along happily together. Self-discipline is exemplary – the system of detentions is rarely called into play.

Pupils and parents: Girls here come from around 65 different primary schools across central and north Essex and south Suffolk and from varying backgrounds. A handful have English as a second language, although their fluency has enabled them to get through the entrance exam. Statemented pupils tend to have hearing or sight impairments.

Keeping in touch with parents is not easy, given the geography, but there's a monthly eNewsletter; parents are largely supportive of school events, also raising money for badly needed new buildings.

Old girls include gardener and writer Beth Chatto, Olympic gold medal winning sailor Saskia Clark and MP Stella Creasy.

Entrance: One of the top-performing schools in the UK, it's no surprise that places are highly sought-after, though seemingly less of a scrum than at the grammars closer to the capital. Entrance is granted to those 112 girls who choose the school and perform the best in the notorious consortium of selective schools in Essex 11+ exam, one half verbal reasoning, the other maths and English in equal part.

The minimum entry requirement is four As and two Bs for all the students coming into the sixth form, including English language and mathematics and grade A/A* in the subjects to be taken at A level; many travel from far and wide, some lodging in Colchester for convenience.

Exit: Around 40 per cent leave post-GCSEs. Only one or two choose not to go on to university – 10 to Oxbridge in 2013; York, UAE, UCL, Sheffield and Bath popular. Law, medicine and academia established career paths.

Remarks: A relaxed and purposeful academic school, where self-motivated high-achievers are gently steered towards success.

Colchester Royal Grammar School

Lexden Road, Colchester, CO3 3ND

- Pupils: 850 boys and girls (girls in sixth form only), all day, apart from 30 sixth form boarders (boys only) • Ages: 11–18
- Christian • Fees: Boarding £10,200; (day free) • State

Tel: 01206 509100
Email: info@crgs.co.uk
Website: www.crgs.co.uk

Headmaster: Since 2000, Mr Ken Jenkinson (fiftyish). Educated at Danum Grammar School, Doncaster. BA in French and German from University of Leeds and MA in French from University of Sheffield. Started his teaching career in a Doncaster comprehensive, then moved on to Blundell's, where he was head of modern languages. Five years as deputy head at Colchester Royal Grammar before becoming head. Enjoys sport (football, rugby and cricket), travel and spending time with his family. Authoritative but pleasant and friendly manner with pupils. Married to Jackie, a librarian currently working as a school secretary. Two daughters.

Academic matters: Extremely high academic standards. No setting in years 7 or 8, French and maths setted from year 9 – 'But this is only a question of pace,' says the head. 'Set 4 pupils will still be expected to achieve A* at GCSE.' French and Latin in year 7, choice of German or Greek in year 8. One of the very few state schools to offer Greek to A level – for a state school, an above average number go on to study classics at university. Fantastic results at GCSE and A level – in 2013, 84 per cent A*/A grades at GCSE and 75 per cent at A level.

Occasional SEN pupil with physical disabilities or Asperger's; any EAL pupil will have had a high enough standard of English to pass the selection tests.

Games, options, the arts: Cricket and rugby particularly strong. Regular fixtures against state and independent schools. Netball, and now rugby, as well as racket sports and fencing for the sixth form girls. Many other sports available as extracurricular activities including athletics, sailing and weight-training. Also plenty of non-sporting activities. Great music department with loads of opportunities for any pupil with any musical ambitions.

Background and atmosphere: Directly descended from a Colchester town school that existed in 1206 and was granted royal charters by Henry VIII in 1539 and Elizabeth I in 1584. Set in an affluent residential area of Colchester, the main buildings date back to the late 19th century. Latest additions, which include new blocks for history, classics and art and renovated music and drama facilities, fit well with the attractive old school buildings. The new George Young Building serves as a concert hall, performance studio and lecture theatre. Lovely, well-tended gardens of a standard unusual in a state school, featuring quiet and private sitting areas for pupils. Extensive playing fields five minutes' walk from the main school and a heated outdoor swimming pool. Two boarding houses with a mixture of single and double bedrooms; family-style facilities, five resident staff members for the 30 boarders. The uniform includes a vivid purple blazer not very popular with the boys (school begs to differ); no uniform for sixth formers but smart dress required.

Pastoral care and discipline: Generally very high standard of conduct and not many discipline problems. Punishments include loss of privileges and lunchtime and after school detentions. Few expulsions in the head's time at the school. Zero tolerance of drugs – possession leads to expulsion.

Pupils and parents: Years 7-11 mainly from Colchester and surrounding area, but pupils travel up to an hour each way each day, sixth formers from further afield. The boarding house caters mainly for those who would have too far to travel to school each day and pupils from abroad; very popular in Hong Kong – a member of staff visits the country each year to interview potential sixth formers. Very active parents' association raising funds for the school.

Old Boys include Telegraph columnist Giles Smith, economics commentator Tim Congdon, costume designer and double Oscar winner Jim Acheson, founder of Freeserve, John Pluthero and former BBC education correspondent Mike Baker.

Entrance: Highly competitive 11+ exam – 50 per cent verbal reasoning, 25 per cent English and 25 per cent maths. 'Places will be awarded in rank order to the top 96 boys in the order of merit who have named Colchester Royal Grammar School as a preference.' The exam is set by the consortium of selective schools in Essex, which has 12 members, and is held in November at the school. Candidates do not have to live in Essex. Four places available for entry to the school in year 9, but the competition is stiff – report, plus tests in maths, English, science and a modern language.

Minimum of four A and two B grade GCSEs for entry into sixth form for internal and external candidates. The 80 or so external entrants (half of them girls) also require a school report and must satisfy the school's academic requirements. Candidates for sixth form boarding places must meet the academic requirements first. Overseas boarders must be British or EU passport holders.

Exit: Hardly any leave post-GCSEs. Sixth formers virtually all to university; 30+ to Oxbridge most years – 20 to Cambridge alone in 2013, and another 20 to medical school.

Remarks: One of the country's top selective boys' state schools, rivals many independents. Any academically able and hard-working boy (and sixth form girl) should thrive here.

Colfe's School

Linked school: Colfe's Preparatory School + Pre prep and Nursery

Horn Park Lane, Lee, London, SE12 8AW

- Pupils: 460 boys and girls • Ages: 11–18 • C of E • Fees: £14,184 pa • Independent

Tel: 020 8852 2283
Email: head@colfes.com
Website: www.colfes.com

Head: Since 2005, Richard Russell (fifties), previously deputy warden of Forest School. Educated in Ireland and went on to read classics at Cambridge. He started his career as a Latin teacher; teaching initially attracted him as it would allow him to pursue his interest in archaeology and attend digs during the long summer holidays. Knows everybody and what they're up to, teaches Latin to year 7. He spent 15 years at Sevenoaks coordinating the IB programme; however, he has never thought it particularly suitable for Colfe's and is a great fan of A levels. A professional and pleasant person, say parents, easy to get on with and ambitious for his pupils. He lives in Blackheath with his wife, who works in the City. Nowadays holiday times see them heading for their house Sicily, where they make their own olive oil.

Academic matters: Exam results heading upwards every year – 54 per cent A*/A at GCSE in 2013, with particularly strong showing in maths and science, and 37 per cent A*/A at A level. Maths, English and the sciences are popular closely followed by economics and history. Most take nine or 10 GCSEs including a language, choice of German, French, Spanish or Latin. Whole school aim is to make classes active and stimulating; everything is in place for high flyers who might be heading for Oxbridge but also for those who might need to go more gently. Setting for maths, sciences and languages. History and maths departments are particularly strong performers; provision for accelerated learning groups for additional maths qualifications. Sixth formers can take Extended Project Qualification. Students with mild specific learning difficulties are supported by specialist staff. The library is a well-used resource, full-time librarian who also doubles up as head of careers, open until 6pm, during Easter holidays and to students on study leave. Outstanding advice and guidance on selecting courses and universities. The school recently ran a conference to introduce the option of going to university in the Netherlands. Most science labs recently refurbished.

Games, options, the arts: Arts and sports are strong all round, structured to suit all tastes and talents. 'Sport for all' policy means there is something for everyone, be it dance or being a member of one of the successful rugby teams. On-site facilities including a gym and 25m swimming pool, which hosts swimming galas, kayaking, water polo and lifesaving courses for year 10s. Additional large playing fields are a few minutes away by minibus on the Sidcup Road. Former Surrey and Kent opening batsman coaches cricket, and athletes often selected to represent Greenwich in the London School Championships. CCF with its unique Army Air Corps unit popular as is D of E, with many progressing to Gold award.

Large art department includes printmaking equipment, a kiln for ceramics and a dark room. Parents comment on the energetic drama department; pupils encouraged to write and produce their own plays. LAMDA classes, stage management and technical theatre skills all on offer; impressive variety and number of productions. Up-to-date music rooms and individual soundproof practice studios; swing bands, orchestras, and choirs galore. Huge range of clubs and societies to join: particularly popular are maths, chess and debating along with many inter-house competitions, quizzes, drama, sports and concerts. Regular outings, theatre visits and trips abroad; sixth formers visit the Gambia annually to help build and maintain a school. Good participation in the arts, but relatively small numbers go on to take these subjects at A level, drama and media studies taking the lead over art, design and music.

Background and atmosphere: Founded in 1652, to educate 'the poor boys of Blackheath' by the Rev Abraham Colfe of Lewisham. Later the school was left in the trust of the Leatherseller's Company, whose livery members make a majority up today's governing body. The school was evacuated to Tunbridge Wells during the war and then to Somerset, finally returning to London in the early 70s as a state boys' grammar for a few years before opting to go independent as opposed to becoming a comprehensive. The school became fully co-ed in 1999.

Corridors adorned with pupils' work and achievements; atmosphere is positive and busy with smartly dressed, friendly pupils and helpful staff. Bleak, utilitarian brick buildings softened by shrubs and trees. New sixth form centre is next on the buildings expansion agenda, as accommodation is currently quite tight.

Pastoral care and discipline: Pastoral care continues to be excellent and very much part of the school's ethos. Well-established house system; everyone attends regular house tutor meetings; years 8-11 are in vertical age groups, sixth formers and year 7s in separate groups. There are lots of opportunities for leadership and mentoring within the house system to help pupils develop maturity, gain confidence and a range of life skills. Frequent house activities and competitions ensure everybody is involved in the school community. School nurse and independent counsellor. Parents say home school links are encouraged and the head of pastoral care is always available to speak with them. One commented that pastoral staff have done well in creating a supportive and caring atmosphere. Pupils seem thoughtful and considerate to others, older pupils particularly good at mentoring younger ones.

Pupils and parents: Mainly professional types from Blackheath, Lewisham, Lee and more recently other areas accessible via train links. Head is keen to recruit from as varied a pool as possible, so a lot of effort is made to encourage children from state primaries as well as independents to apply. Big old boys' and girls' society runs a number of activities and fundraising events. Everyone is invited to the annual service in memory of the founder Rev Colfe. A good all-rounder school producing an interesting range of pupils going into many different careers. Interesting alumni list reflects the school's diverse range: Brian Fahey, composer, John Hayes, energy minister, Peter Howitt, actor, Kenneth Grayson, first professor of theology at Bristol University, to name but a few; alumni include actors, novelists, musicians, politicians, scientists and sportspeople.

Entrance: 11+ interview, reference from current school and exams in maths and English. Sixth formers are offered places on the basis of an interview, reference and predicted GCSE grades.

Exit: Small number leaves at 16+ for sixth form colleges. At 18+ pupils move to many different universities with around 50 per cent to Russell Group and several to Oxbridge, music schools and RADA.

Money matters: At 11+ and 16+ scholarships, means-tested awards and bursaries are available for drama, art, sports, music and academics. Around 20 to 30 per cent of pupils receive some form of fee subsidy.

Remarks: Pleasant, relaxed atmosphere. Provides a high standard of education without being overly competitive. Its focus on individual successes and promoting a balanced approach to life and learning is not to be underestimated in today's hectic world

Collingham Independent GCSE and Sixth Form College

23 Collingham Gardens, London, SW5 0HL

• Pupils: 220 in total: 30 in GCSE department, 190 over two years in senior department; roughly 50/50 boys and girls • Ages: 14-20 • Fees: £17,100–£18,225 pa • Independent

Tel: 020 7244 7414
Email: london@collingham.co.uk
Website: www.collingham.co.uk

Principal: Since 2012, Dr Sally Powell BA MA PGCE (early forties), a London and Oxford English specialist, lively, welcoming, delightful. Has notched up a not inconsiderable 10 years here (in fact many staff are of long standing and committed to the place).

Mr James Allder BA, a geographer (fortyish), is deputy principal and director of studies; an enthusiastic skier and snowboarder. Mr Paul Bilic MA, a linguist, oversees the GCSE department in Queen's Gate.

Academic matters: You go to Collingham for two things – the academics and the sense of being independent while, in reality, being nurtured and carefully monitored. The place, though, stands or falls on its teaching – 'We integrate modern methods with traditional teaching – the emphasis is always on the teaching; the rest is back-up.' So don't come here if you want wall-to-wall technology – not that it isn't where it's needed: interactive whiteboards in, eg, geography rooms and students port their laptops hither and yon. Facilities for both digital and trad photography indicate an imaginative approach and a small IT room right at the top of the school for the actual teaching of it. Twenty-nine GCSE subjects and an extraordinary 36 A level subjects offered. Generally around 30 per cent A*/A grades at A level; some 40 per cent get 5+ A*-C grades at GCSE.

All A level subjects taught in designated subject rooms, which are functional, not over-crowded with displays or other distractions and well-maintained. At GCSE, the average class size is five and never more than nine; at A level much the same, though, depending on what subjects you choose, you can be taught one-to-one – great for the students, and the teachers like it, too, of course. GCSE students usually in college 9.15am-6.00pm; AS students get 20 hours of teaching weekly, A level students get 18. 'GCSEs are brilliantly taught,' one recent alumnus told us. 'I was rescued.' A few more popular classes – no room is huge – are rather cramped, but no-one minds much.

Learning support tutor sees those with SEN difficulties (charged extra) and subject teachers also do one-to-one as needed. Probably not for those with more than mild dyslexia or similar. Up to eight hours' weekly EAL support.

Games, options, the arts: Art produces an impressive range of work in many media, given the fact that only one small studio, with intense and dedicated ('fantastic' and 'amazing,' students told us) practising artist, whose domain it is. 'I'm interested in teaching them to be artists – to express themselves in art,' he imparted, and students love it here. Corridors and stairwell round about display varied work in many disciplines – we liked especially the horse mobile made from cleverly coloured twisted paper. Twelve GCSE and 20 A level art students at the time of our visit – testament to the small is beautiful as successful ethos.

No sport, apart from student-organised football in the park one evening a week and some take themselves to a local gym. Clubs run if someone wants to run one, so debates happen one year and not the next. Drama is enthusiastic and curricular – classes take place in the Study Room, a small studio theatre is borrowed for exams and exam prep. Theatre studies trips to London shows. Citizenship course involves a good range of mind-broadening trips. Skiing and walking trips plus an annual concert. But you won't come here if the extracurricular life is what feeds your roots – this is a plus for most here: 'There's nothing to distract you from work'.

Background and atmosphere: Modest and understated six-storey house in Collingham Gardens – an equidistant five minutes' walk from Gloucester Road and Earl's Court tube stations in an unshowy bit of west Kensington; has been a school of a sort for much of its 130 years, having previously accommodated Gibbs' Prep School until the mid-1970s. So it is quite remarkable that the building retains many attractive features and is maintained in such a way as to preserve that sense of its being a house, not an institution – friezes, cornices, attractive mirrors and chandeliers about the place and a minimum of ghastly fluorescent tubes, sludge-coloured paintwork and other municipally-inspired excrescences. In the black and white tiled hallway are little tables with students playing chess – no, they weren't put there to impress us: it is student-inspired and a student-pursued activity. The splendid first floor drawing room – now the Study Room – is library/exam/private study area, where, when not in use for exams, students go between taught periods to do homework etc. The individual subject rooms have small specialised book collections.

No outside space to speak of – a small patio at the back – but students are encouraged to use Kensington Gardens or Holland Park in the summer, not more than 15 minutes' walk away. Earl's Court is not devoid of bars and cafes and students know where they are. Tiny cafeteria in the basement, rather like the art room, produces range and quality of food in inverse proportion to its size: aroma of frying mushrooms nearly did for us – until we opened the door to the chemistry lab further down the basement corridor (very labby labs here).

The GCSE building in Queen's Gate Place – all white Regency elegance – accommodates most of the needs of the smallish contingent of students at this level. Supervision and monitoring very important here for students as young as these; the school secretary has an important pastoral role – this is a significant commitment to the other site and its, on occasions, perhaps more vulnerable denizens. Several full-time academic staff – the place succeeds largely on account of the inevitably close and trusting staff:pupil relationship which develops: 'We combine a homely, personal feeling with cutting edge teaching'. Interestingly, the families of the two founders still own the College – this contrasts, perhaps significantly in terms of ethos, with the much larger concerns which own most other tutorial colleges in central London.

Most students live locally, though some from further off stay with family – 'We love grandmothers'; a few overseas students board with host families. 'If we get it right, we can restore the spark they may have lost at their big schools' – many come having failed to thrive at their public schools, through sickness, bullying, perhaps some gentle eccentricity or simply just not being happy. 'Some who may have loved prep school boarding can just outgrow it...We hope to be a village school in the middle of Kensington.' It doesn't feel quite like that – too much general sophistication in the air – but in terms of the smallness and closeness of the community, it is spot on. Seen by many as providing a dry run for university without the sense of being cast adrift that some experience there.

Pastoral care and discipline: Punctuality is important – you are signed in for each class, not at the start of the day, and parents are called within 15 minutes in the case of no-shows. But you don't need to come in early if you don't have a class – think what that means to a 16 year old! A few smoking Collinghamers lurk on the pavement and College is pragmatic – 'We don't allow it on site and we don't like it, but we'd rather they do it where we can see them. Everywhere they are, we are'. Clear sanctions for those who don't work and occasional expulsions if they just won't. Not an option for druggies or bullies from elsewhere, 'We're too small to be a second chance saloon'. But, 'We are very happy to take anyone who's been ill or in a muddle, sensitive souls who need individual attention, perhaps if they've had an eating disorder – we will look after them'. Expulsion for drinking or drugging or bullying here virtually unheard of.

Parents have open access to their child's tutor – easy communication. 'They rescued my son,' one mother told us. 'I can't speak highly enough of their care.' 'The teachers are incredibly friendly,' an A level student told us. 'I was welcomed with open arms.'

Pupils and parents: You have to be able to raise the cash – and some pull out all the stops to do so – but it's cheaper than boarding. So everyone from global bankers to school secretaries, and the students mix, seemingly seamlessly. No scope for ostracising oddballs here – everyone accepts and is accepting. Considerable range of ability too. Very few join from the state sector. Roughly 60:40 boy:girl split. Notable leavers include Minnie Driver and, more, recently Georgia May Jagger.

Entrance: Interviews, references from current/previous school and, if necessary, an exam – 'They've got to want to work with us'. Can take people at any time, so great for relocaters and those who've just gotta get out – flexible.

Exit: Practically all to university. In 2013, two to Oxbridge; others to London, Leeds, Newcastle and Bristol.

Money matters: Given the small classes and the individual care and attention, it's not as much as you might think. But one-to-one is charged extra by the hour, exams and materials for practical subjects likewise extra, so do check what you sign up for. Some bursaries in case of need.

Remarks: 'I am so happy here,' one bright A level spark told us. 'I'm with a lot of clever people; we're brilliantly taught. Everyone is perfectly normal – they just didn't like the regimentation of school life.' A fabulous opportunity to regroup and get on track if things have gone awry – and a good place for friendships too. Some come back years after to see staff. A gem.

Coloma Convent Girls' School

Upper Shirley Road, Croydon, CR9 5AS

- Pupils: 1080 • Ages: 11–18 • RC • State

Tel: 020 8654 6228
Email: webadmin@coloma.croydon.sch.uk
Website: www.coloma.croydon.sch.uk

Headteacher: Since September 1995 Maureen Martin (fifties), BA economics and history, then additional RE and education management qualifications. Whilst on foreign postings with her family had a varied teaching career in international schools, including deputy headships at Alice Smith International School, Kuala Lumpur and El Collegio Britannico, Mexico. Grew up locally and attended Coloma as a child.

Bounding with energy and ideas, deeply committed to educating all young people to the highest possible level, equally committed to ensuring the staff access additional qualifications and attend continuous training programmes. Much-admired by the local and school community, she will make time for you, but she can be hard to catch as she is so very busy. Alongside all her sterling work at Coloma, she is executive principal at The Quest Academy – Coloma Trust, a non-denominational, co-ed secondary school in Croydon. She has also been involved in transforming the lives and education of primary school pupils by taking their school out of special measures.

Academic matters: In 2013, nearly 95 per cent of pupils got 5+ A*-C grades at GCSE including English and maths; at A level, 34 per cent A*/A grades and 68 per cent A*/B – constantly in the top 30 comprehensive schools; specialist status for music and science. Every pupil is tracked and monitored throughout their school career to ensure that they are taught and learn properly and achieve their potential. Subject teaching across the curriculum is considered to be very strong; where weaknesses are identified they are dealt with swiftly.

Years 7 to 9 are mixed ability, with setting from year 8 for maths and sciences. Staff continually research and develop ways to assist pupils' learning and much time is given to researching

work-related courses and activities. Head of economics has recently introduced the personal finance GCSE to ensure the girls understand how to manage money as well as the consequences of redundancy, unemployment and recessions. Language choices are French, German, Spanish, Latin club and Italian in sixth form; annual European trips and home-stays are arranged. Further developments include establishing a modern foreign languages network so good practice can be shared. Dual award or three separate sciences as well as food and nutrition can be studied in well-resourced labs.

Full-time learning support coordinator oversees additional support in maths, English and study skills, including organisational and life skills. Specialist staff visit the school to provide one-to-one tuition as required. Reading ages of new entrants are assessed as part of tracking and monitoring scheme for each individual pupil. Those identified as struggling to make progress, regardless of ability, are offered support.

Inclusive sixth form centre aims to suit many, offering 28 A level choices, IB diploma and Cambridge Pre-Us; development plans include introducing some further BTEC/diploma courses. Sixth formers gain experiences and skills from an extensive range of extracurricular and enrichment opportunities on-site and in partnership with other schools. Well-established tradition of public speaking, debating, musicianship and business enterprise; the girls scoop countless prizes at competitions and national events.

Whole school benefits from a managed learning environment – web tools are used to enrich learning, access homework and help home-school communications. Good mixture of male and female staff, a number of whom have dual roles, scholarly and generous types who are willing to share their skills and talents throughout the school.

Games, options, the arts: Exceptional and active music department: about 400 pupils learn an instrument; two orchestras, several choirs, including gospel choirs, and large instrumental ensembles. Regular winners of awards at the National Festival of Music; around half the pupils belong to one of the choirs, which tour and perform all over the world. As a specialist music college the school has developed additional recording, composing, and performance facilities and provides courses in music technology and performing arts. Over 40 musical and dramatic events are organised every year in-house, at the Fairfield Halls and beyond. Recent performing arts centre means whole school play reinstated, aiming to include all ages and talents, staff welcome too.

Range of sporting options; standards are high, netball, lacrosse and tennis admired and a number of girls go on to play for local and national teams. Indoor and outdoor facilities for all weathers, football and cricket clubs increasingly popular, 3G floodlit pitch. Dancers were recently invited to perform at Sadler's Wells. Duke of Edinburgh Award scheme runs and CCF is available as a joint venture with neighbouring Royal Russell School. Year 9s go on very popular annual trip to a trust house in Austria, where pupils can ski and spend time in an Austrian school.

Background and atmosphere: Founded in West Croydon in 1869 by a Belgian order, the Congregation of the Daughters of Mary and Joseph, led by Reverend Canon Van Crombrugghe. Opened with three nuns and one pupil; after a couple of years they moved to a larger house. 1965 saw the move to the present large, leafy site on the edge of Shirley Hills, and in 1978 the convent became an RC comprehensive. Ever developing and striving for excellence by keeping in step with modern educational demands, has high performing specialist status and had science specialism. A bright, clean, hard-working environment, highly structured but also welcoming and inclusive.

Celebrated its 140th birthday with a huge party in the Royal Festival Hall, music specially composed by Howard Goodall. The celebrations were widely attended by members of the convent, school, friends and old girls, who are also active in helping to fundraise for school enterprises. As a Roman Catholic foundation, has special ethos: 'Every member of the school community is motivated to see that they can make a positive difference through love, commitment and service. Prayer, respect for one another, integrity, kindness and compassion are greatly valued'.

Pastoral care and discipline: Some girls feel the school rules are a bit strict, but most parents and pupils feel pastoral care is thoughtfully planned and helps to ensure everyone feels equally valued. Home-school contact is thought to be very good, with most documentation provided in 'read friendly' format. Full-time pastoral manager supports staff, ensuring the daily well-being, behaviour and progress of each pupil. Hand-picked counsellors visit the school and referrals can be made to other agencies. The PSHE programme is boosted by outside organisations and special issue days. Girls learn to be considerate, reflect on others' feelings and the possible consequences of thoughtless actions. Staff and pupils join disabled children on the annual Easter pilgrimage to Lourdes

Pupils and parents: No particular catchment area or feeder primary schools. Girls come from all over south London, Kent and Surrey. Hard-working, motivated and committed Catholic families who wish to support their daughter's education, along with all the charitable projects Coloma is involved in. Champions of fundraising, staff, pupils and parents organise a magnificent number of events for school buildings, equipment and numerous charitable projects. Events manager assists the charity committee coordinating events from concerts, fetes, readathons and quizzes to the annual rag week, which alone can raise as much as £28,000. Helps to fund a school in Uganda, in addition to supporting other charities at home and abroad. Pupils very pro-active in creating new ideas and opportunities to fundraise – Christmas fête has included an ice rink. Unsurprisingly, many ex-pupils choose to work in education, social and caring professions.

Entrance: At 11+ non-selective; statemented and looked-after children and then a points system to assess practising Catholic credentials. Entry into the sixth form includes students of other denominations and faiths who are in sympathy with the ethos of school

Exit: Around 30 per cent leave post-GCSE for local colleges or co-ed schools. About 85 per cent of sixth formers to university: one to Oxbridge in 2013, others to eg Leeds, Sussex, Loughborough, King's College London and Bournemouth.

Money matters: Parents encouraged to donate monthly via school's 'Pass the Baton' scheme, and most do.

Remarks: Truly remarkable school for its vision, academic achievements, charitable activities and contribution to society. Considering it operates on a budget less than 40 per cent of an independent school, must also be commended for economic genius. Produces well-rounded, articulate and innovative young women.

Colyton Grammar School

Whitwell Lane, Colyton, Devon, EX24 6HN

• Pupils: 825 pupils, 460 boys/ 365 girls • Ages: 11–18 • Non-denom • State

Tel: 01297 552327
Email: admin@colytongrammar.devon.sch.uk
Website: www.colytongrammar.devon.sch.uk

Head Teacher: Since 2008, Mr Paul Evans BEd MEd FColl T (early fifties) who served 11 years as deputy head at Colyton, after which he viewed the applicants for headship and decided he had better apply unless he wanted years of work to go down the drain. Clearly the governors and local authority agreed with him! Born in Plymouth, he did a biology degree at Exeter and PGCE at St Mark and St John before teaching in Newbury and Reading where he became head of department, then of science and eventually of Faculty at Theale Green school in Reading. He saw Colyton as something of a homecoming but originally intended to stay only for about five years. His first day put paid to that idea because just walking down the corridor, everybody smiled at him.

He and his wife, an assistant head in a local school, live nearby and he loves walking and is a keen photographer. A tall welcoming man with a quiet sense of humour under his unassuming exterior, he is obviously liked by his pupils who refer to him, respectfully, like a friend. Immensely proud as he is of the school's outstanding academic record, he insists that it is the breadth of education that really counts, believing that pupils gain as much from experience of masses of school activities and from working on their own research topic for the extended paper for the AQA English Baccalaureate as from getting the four (usually) excellent A levels which will qualify them for uni. He modestly attributes the school's success to a series of sensible decisions taken at the appropriate time

Academic matters: Unusual, even revolutionary, in that pupils do two years at key stage 3 and two at GCSE, which leaves them with three for A level. Most do four plus general studies, with an impressive 64 per cent of all entries getting A/A* in 2013 and nearly 90 per cent A*/B. Despite the accelerated curriculum, GCSE results are also outstanding – 83 per cent A*/A grades in 2013. Results are spectacular considering that, though selective, this is not one of the super selective warhorses. Everyone takes GCSE maths, English lang and lit, three separate sciences, French and RS, plus at least three others.

A level is enriched by the Baccalaureate, which means that pupils also do a personal research paper, critical thinking AS level and programme of community service and awareness, which is integral to their studies. While, as a qualification, this does not increase their chances of a good university place, it gives them a head start in writing their UCAS applications and makes them independent learners – and they seem to enjoy it.

German offered as a second lang, though not a big takeup, and Spanish only as a non exam activity together with Japanese and Latin (though some do take them to GCSE). DT, product design (fantastic DT facilities, though the school doesn't reckon it's one of its strongest subjects), sport, psychology, drama and business studies available, but no economics or engineering, though enterprising pupils have been known to teach themselves subjects such as scientific engineering, with successful results.

Everything is superbly equipped. A rolling modernisation programme has kept everything pretty well up to date, with oodles of computers for class use and in study areas (including some smashing Macs in the music department courtesy of performing arts) and a further IT infrastructure on the way. New labs, music, technology have been added to the site and recently a food technology lab, plus major refurbishment of other technical facilities. Friendly library with librarian or helpful parents on hand and a really efficient lending system, which nonetheless considers books being read more important than books being back on shelves. Cosy corner has subject based academic journals for specialist to browse – and they use it.

Minimal SEN needs, though school accepts and provides for pupils with specific needs, profoundly deaf being a case in point.

Games, options, the arts: Definitely a school for the all rounder. Huge value attached to extracurricular, which none the less happens mainly in the long lunch hour, because of the scattered catchment (travel difficulties) with only sport, some music and film club regularly after school. Lots of good sports facilities, tennis, hockey, netball and other all weather surfaces all fully occupied at our visit time, and a state-of-the-art sports hall shared with the community who have access during the school day as well as evenings etc. Beautiful sprung floored studio, impressive main hall with everything from cricket nets to TV playback for analysis of performance (PA again), all maintained and cared for by pupils and community users alike. Masses of success in all sports: teams and individuals have an impressive record in East Devon, in netball, tennis, athletics, rugby, badminton, football (girls and boys) and cricket, and also feature regularly at national level in tennis, netball, rugby sevens etc. Lots of outdoor stuff, with a regular crop of D of E golds, as well as Ten Tors. Colyton pupils have starred in every thing from British maths and science Olympiads and poetry competitions to cycle building and mock trial teams, in all of which the school's entries have hit the jackpot.

Music pretty strong and much loved by pupils with three or four big choirs, orchestra and smaller groups set up as interests change. Fantastic new music block equipped with all singing and dancing Mac computers for composing and music quizzes and well as a recording studio, lashings of instruments including smashing new Yamaha Grand pianos provided by the Parents' Association. Lots of adventurous choral stuff on a grand scale with composers Alexander Lestrange and Will Todds conducting own works as well as major trad items like Messiah and Mozart. Though there is a very big take up of instrumental teaching and GCSE music, not many take A level, presumably because of the pressure to do career subjects rather than for lack of enthusiasm. Drama is in the old school hall, now equipped with proper, raked seating, and there are annual productions, recently featuring Shakespeare musicals based on Winter's Tale, Comedy of Errors (taking advantage of some conveniently gifted twins), as well as more serious productions. Modern, airy and impressive art department filled to the brim with work in all media: fascinating pottery sculpture outside the door, some very accomplished painting and portraiture and recently the school has been 'excited and privileged' to have its own sheep and lamb, in the style of German architect Friedensreich Hundertwasser, included in the multi-coloured flock 'grazing ' outside Exeter cathedral.

There's not much you can't do at Colyton because anyone with an interest can set up a group, so astronomy, Christian Union, Carnegie (book reviews) etc vie with the usual suspects: Young Enterprise, chess, dance et al, not to forget the extremely enterprising Green Society, which was one of the first tranche of green flags winners and keeps it end up by organising house energy saving contests and building a bug hotel called the Crawl Inn in the field behind the school. Trips abound, music and art doing alternate UK and foreign visits, while a recent initiative is inspecting English vineyard ecology with a view to doing the same in France and Germany under Exeter University's 'Life in the Vines' scheme. The expected range of foreign exchanges. history/geog fieldwork, ski trips and theatre visits.

Background and atmosphere: From the outside, unremarkable, except for the difficulty of actually finding it, hidden as it is among fields and woods along extremely narrow lanes, the school is a pleasant collection of low pink brick buildings. The pretty front façade and cloistered original buildings date from the thirties when the school moved from Colyton town, where it had originally occupied the church porch. It was started in 1546 by the 'feoffees' of Colyton for the benefit of boys of the town, when Henry VIII allowed them to keep the land he had seized from them on condition it was used for the benefit of all.

Once inside the main school, rooms are roomy though low (seagulls tap dance on the flat roofs), and different sections of the school are separated by grassy areas edged with flowers though which one eventually reaches the main campus. This is extremely attractive and beautifully planted with lavender, roses and shrubs in raised beds with outdoor seating areas for the canteen, called 'Take That!' The huge Cotrill hall, originally a barn, on one edge, provides an assembly space, big enough for the whole school, which meets thrice weekly as well as a concert and exam hall. The long-term pipe dream is to replace this with a really practical performance space. Whole school assemblies typify the family feel of the school. Pupils have a sense of being grounded in the community, emphasised by the war memorial, which they honour annually, and by the presence of local people and parents in the sports hall and libraries, as well as by the close knit house system and schemes for prefects mentoring younger pupils.

Plenty of new buildings with spanking new labs (the very latest for food technology) technical department and language labs, all situated, like the two sixth form houses, in domestic looking buildings surrounded by gardens, which enhance the villagy feel of Colyton. It also feels very calm despite the masses of activity in all areas.

The sixth form common rooms, though jam-packed at break times, were buzzing gently, not noisy, and the only litter evident in the entire visit was a postage stamp size scrap of paper under a table crowded with chatting youngsters. From one of the English rooms in the upper sixth house (year 12 and 13 are together, while year 11 has its own transitional house), there is a glimpse of the sea over the hill, as well as swathes of maize, pasture, trees and hedges.

Pastoral care and discipline: Pastoral care is extensive and provided by the school houses: Ash, Beech, Cedar and Oak. In lower school each of the four forms in each year constitutes a house tutor group, though from GCSE onward the form ceases to be a teaching unit. In the three 'sixth form years' the groups are mixed for pastoral supervision, though house loyalties and responsibilities remain. A school counsellor to provides help and supports and trains sixth formers to mentor the rest. Pupils and parents say (and the inspection report endorses) that the atmosphere of trust in the school is such that any problems between pupils are quickly shared with staff, so the bullying policy and code of sanctions are rarely needed. No culture of 'don't tell on your mates' means that bullying hardly happens and any 'name calling or that sort of thing' is dealt with at once. Sanctions are mainly detention with the ultimate for serious crime being 'head's detention' on a Saturday with the threat of exclusion to enforce it. Lots of time spent training new pupils to respect the facilities evidently works very well. Minimum supervision 'because it's not needed in IT rooms, break times' etc. Pupils teachers, ground and canteen staff all seem to function like one big, and happy, family.

Pupils and parents: Pupils come from all over East Devon as far as Exeter one way and Bridport and Chard the other. No school transport but a combination of public and private transport provides a pretty comprehensive network. Pitifully minimal free buses only to those further than three miles for whom it is the nearest school. Very British on the whole though a few enthusiastic families have moved into the area, one even from China! Uniform, strictly adhered to for years 7-10, is black trousers/skirts, white shirt, school blazer and tie. Years 11-13 have choice of black, navy (or dark grey trousers for boys) and jackets, cardigans with blue and white striped shirts worn with quite informal interpretation of the rules in the handbook – head is allowing a fitted shirt for girls to be worn outside skirts! Canteen is open for breakfast but not after school and pupils can stay till 5 or for matches or the occasional after-school activity, but most rely on the post-school buses. Dividing the school day into only four periods timetabled over a two weeks means that less time wasted, so more than an hour is free for lunchtime extracurricular and tutor time. Small body of supportive parents (with its own excellent website) does masses of fundraising (£40,000 for new pianos) and a range of services in library etc. Parents commend the school's initiative and openness and think that, if choice is limited by the school's size, it's more than made up for by flexibility and support. Singularly few carps and those mainly about food, uniform and contacting teachers. There is a simple but evidently effective school home agreement, an annual full report and a termly summary of achievement and commitment grades.

Entrance: At 11: not limited to a catchment area but strictly by exam in order of merit for those who qualify by passing the NFER verbal reasoning plus NFER maths and/or school's own English paper. Oversubscribed by about 3-1 and about half who qualify get in. Apply initially via Local Authority but parents also have to apply direct to Colyton for the familiarisation/ practice test day. Head advises that it's useful to do a few trial tests to see how they work but insists coaching doesn't help. Admission to sixth form is post GCSE (with equivalent of eight C grade including maths, Eng and two sciences) to year 11, which means that hopefuls would have to extend education by a year.

Exit: A few, or none, drift off after year 11 to sixth form college, where they have to repeat a year. Impressive tranche to Oxbridge – 14 in 2013 – and top universities (Durham and Warwick popular in 2013), with bags of lawyers, doctors (14 in 2013), vets along with the odd theologian, neuroscientist or astrophysicist, plus a few to art or music.

Money matters: Lots of extras, trips etc and no support for transport.

Remarks: A gem of a school! Truly academic because pupils are interested, happy because everyone trusts each other, unpressurised because of excellent organisation and fun because it combines pleasant surrounding with adventurous activities. Lucky East Devon!

Comberton Village College

West Street, Comberton, Cambridge, CB23 7DU

• Pupils: 1445 boys and girls • Ages: 11–18 • Non-denom • State

Tel: 01223 262503
Email: thecollege@comberton.cambs.sch.uk
Website: www.combertonvc.org

Executive Head: Since 2001, Mr Stephen Munday CBE MA PGCE (late forties). Read economics at Cambridge. Previously director of sixth form and deputy head County High Saffron Walden. Still somewhat young-looking and refreshingly unaffected – reference to the recent outstanding Ofsted provokes a boyish glow. Well liked by all, his tendency to deliver morning assemblies with a fair amount of movement is affectionately

referred to as 'the Munday dance'. Attends all those conferences that successful heads seem to frequent and has worked for the DfE on several projects. However, he still maintains a strong interest in economics and tutors sixth formers who pursue an economics research project as part of their pre-U or Extended Project Qualification – his spacious, egalitarian office is home to a rather menacing portrait of hero Keynes, a gift from a past pupil. Received an honorary doctorate from Anglia Ruskin University in 2009 and a CBE in 2013, both for Services to Education. Married with three children and a regular church-goer. Enjoys playing sport, mainly golf these days, and supports Everton 'even though they don't often win'.

Academic matters: Mantra of achievement backed with an array of targeted interventions – 'They do jump in if kids are underachieving'. Cracking GCSE results for a comprehensive: 42 per cent A*/A and 80 per cent five plus A*-C with English and maths in 2013; first lot of sixth formers achieved 21 per cent A*/A and 54 per cent A*/B grades. Pupils value contributions from their peers and lessons are predominantly interactive – teacher-led questioning and comments from the floor the norm.

Impressive commitment to languages, with Spanish taken by all and productive links with schools around the globe. Top sets have to take a second language but, according to a mole, this can be 'a bit of a disincentive' if interests lie elsewhere. Gifted and talented are stretched with extension work plus after-school options – AS economics, history and critical thinking as well as an additional maths qualification. Hard workers who aren't necessarily academic can follow vocational pathways.

Self-contained suite of rooms, within the main body of the school, is home to the calm, well-resourced SEN department – a welcoming refuge for those with educational or emotional needs. Intelligent, flexible approach with pupils attending mainstream lessons as much as possible – 'Our philosophy is neutral', and they really do 'look at what's best for the individual'. Extensive list of supportive strategies range from in-class teaching assistants to music or Lego therapy.

Up to 12 pupils with Asperger's syndrome, not necessarily from within catchment, are based in two diminutive mobiles with cheery pots of flowers softening the entrance. Work here is centred on the development of social skills while as many lessons as possible are taken in the mainstream. Good understanding that little things can upset and staff readily adapt to remove potential barriers – 'We might need to find a room where there isn't a sciency smell'.

Games, options, the arts: 'Sport is the best,' enthused our tour guides. Not overly competitive according to parents, but varying degrees of sportiness are well served. All the usuals plus PE and dance at GCSE and/or BTEC – an individual timetable can be seriously weighted in the direction of sport. Inclusive and popular approach for the older ones. Choices include off-site golf, skiing or rowing and 'leadership' – pupils take part in sport or dance and deliver sessions to children in feeder primaries. Good facilities: several large gyms (with one for trampolines), Astro, outdoor swimming pool and dance studio where a hip hop dancer recently ran two classes – 'so much fun'. Sporting pictures done by pupils add a touch of colour to the corridors. Sports clubs are 'never cancelled because of a lack of numbers. There's usually a waiting list so we have to get our names down quickly'.

Music is enjoyed – 'We can relax but still get the work done'. Gospel, blues and reggae feature and end of term concerts, in the new performance hall decked with tiered seats, showcase musicians who're 'worth a watch'. If BTEC and GCSE art are taken in tandem, timetables can be heavily biased for the arty – 'Our son is thrilled by the quantity and quality of it all'. Pleasing to see GCSE after school for those who can't fit it in on their main timetable.

Voluntary activities and clubs run from 3-4pm every day with 75 per cent attending something sporty. Mandarin and Latin plus D of E, which goes from strength to strength – by the time they leave around half will have taken bronze, and if any pupils have started gold, the enthusiastic teacher in charge has made arrangements for completion at Comberton.

Background and atmosphere: Founded in the 1960s as a village college, it's continuously grown to meet the needs of several hugely popular rural villages close to Cambridge. Became an academy, and opened a sixth form, in 2011; now part of the Comberton Academy Trust, which also includes the new Cambourne Village College – many of the Comberton staff work across both schools, and Comberton executive principal has the same role at Cambourne. Neighbouring Melbourn Village College has also joined the Trust. The wider community is a gentle presence and is seen using sporting facilities or visiting a branch of the local building society based in the reception area. Functional, unassuming buildings are in good repair, and amazingly we didn't spot a gob of gum anywhere – 'We just don't,' according to a pupil. Fresh, well-ordered feel to the place.

Excellent induction programme makes sure that 'new children aren't totally at sea' whilst the team of year 10 and 11 mentors and system of keeping the same form tutor all the way up reinforce a perception 'that there's always someone there for you'. Pupils encouraged to be independent and responsible – all have opportunities to succeed, and when they do ample recognition. Has yet to develop the distinctive character which prompts leavers to say more than, 'We'll miss our friends,' but this should come now that the new sixth form for 350 students (major £7 million state-of-the-art building) has bedded down.

Healthy eating promoted – 'We only get chips one day a week' – but parents say there's a lack of choice for the end of the queue and 40 minutes isn't long enough for a lunch break. Given the numbers involved and diminutive serving stations, they have a point. Head won't make major changes but has instigated ways to use time efficiently, eg cashless payment with debit cards which are topped up away from the dining area, quality vending machines and additional outlets serving hot soup and baked potatoes.

Pastoral care and discipline: 'We don't feel intimidated here' – a big school which manages to make pupils feel at ease. No herding in the corridors and staff a visible presence during break and lunch time. Each year group tends to congregate in their own designated, clearly delineated outside area where large sweeping canopies give shelter from the elements. Pupils have a say via the school council and they've promoted recycling – no litter anywhere – and helped devise a school uniform which solves the problem of dangling shirts and low slung ties: neat, pale grey polo shirts and sweatshirts with yellow trim and school logo top black trousers, but – a shame – year 11s are allowed black sweatshirts – a popular but depressingly sombre ensemble.

Children are actively involved in drafting behaviour policies and the sorting of issues tends to be pupil-led. Parameters are clear and detentions known as MODs or SODs, an interesting acronym for 'serious offence detention', deal with most transgressions. Permanent exclusions, usually relating to illegal substances, very rare. Parents fully back the non-negotiable policy of zero tolerance.

Pupils and parents: Confident, cheerful children who know the value of education. Predominantly middle class with relatively few from ethnic minorities. Parents move to the area because of the school and pay a premium to be in catchment – stories of sealed bids or camping in rented accommodation until a property comes on the market aren't unusual.

Entrance: Admission criteria in order of importance: resident in catchment, sibling, from a feeder primary. Popularity of the school and new builds in catchment have made entrance a potential nightmare. Lots of appeals and on the odd occasion busing of Comberton children to a different secondary. New comprehensive in Cambourne should help solve the problem.

Exit: Vast majority (75 per cent) to one of the sixth form colleges in Cambridge, but own new sixth form now open and has proved popular from the outset. Of the first lot of sixth form leavers, a strong minority to Russell Group universities.

Remarks: The popularity of this well-organised comprehensive is justified. High standards and enthusiastic staff. A sixth form gives the finishing touch.

Concord College

Acton Burnell Hall, Shrewsbury, SY5 7PF

- Pupils: 225 boys, 250 girls; 415 board • Ages: 13–18 • Inter-denom • Fees: £30,300 pa • Independent

Tel: 01694 731631
Email: admissions@concordcollege.org.uk
Website: www.concordcollegeuk.com

Principal: Since 2005, Mr Neil Hawkins MA (forties). An experienced schoolmaster, whose former jobs include head of history at Sevenoaks, where he also coached cricket. Immediately prior to Concord he was director of studies at The Leys School, Cambridge. A graduate of the university there, he read history and, even more importantly, 'saw this lovely lady during the first lecture I attended and invited her back to my rooms for tea afterwards'. The lovely lady, Vanessa, now Mrs Hawkins, keeps an eye on the girls' welfare and teaches geography. Students we spoke to described her in the same words as her husband had used.

Engaging, warm and welcoming, with a bubbling sense of humour and an air of inner calm, Mr Hawkins clearly delights in being at Concord – 'As a historian, it is wonderful. Look out there. Over to the right the castle and to the left the Parliamentary barn'. As principal, he talks with infectious enthusiasm about the students, the staff and the whole setup, cheerfully and convincingly dealing with common misconceptions of the college.

'He really cares about us,' said a student. 'He knows our names, comes into lunch every day and asks us how we're getting on and he listens to our answers. That is why so many student-led initiatives are implemented.' 'He certainly has his finger on the pulse,' said one parent. The right man for the job, and during his reign the college has gone from strength to strength.

Academic matters: The very smart coffee table prospectus – brochure might be a better word – has eye-watering pictures of the beauty of the setting, the excellent facilities and, prominently, masses of statistics. So, too, does the website, so rather than make this entry read like a company report, we highlight unique features. The impressive statistics are freely available elsewhere.

To an extent the school owes its continuing success to statistics. It is, after all, an international school. Parents and children living abroad and searching for the 'best schools' are bound to look closely at league tables and take note. Older, more distinguished, schools may rely on their historical reputation and the perceived social advantages that go with them, but affluent parents from abroad – and 85 per cent of the students are from overseas – are pragmatic in their approach and will go for what appears in those ghastly league tables. Above all, they want to see results, and where better than in those league tables? Concord, not surprisingly, trumpet theirs. In terms of results they are hugely successful, regularly up in the top five of co-educational schools, out-punching many public schools in Shropshire and beyond. 'But,' says the principal, 'I always tell prospective parents and pupils we're not a crammer. We offer so much more.'

And here's the interesting thing about Concord's success compared with so many traditional schools jostling for position in the market place. It uses its results (78 per cent A*/A grades at A level in 2013, and 75 per cent A*/A at GCSE) as an initial attraction and then displays its full range of wares; many other schools display their wares first and then speak quietly, sometimes rather defensively, about their results. Both approaches can stimulate doubts. Visitors to Concord may have them allayed.

In the sixth form students choose to study either three or four subjects to A level plus one or two subjects to AS level. Unsurprisingly, maths and sciences are the most popular subjects, but the principal has been keen to broaden the academic scope to include European languages, history and geography. He cites two Oxford PPE students and a Cambridge historian in recent years, along with other Oxbridge successes. Clearly such possibilities exist, though the humanities at A level are unlikely outstrip maths and the sciences.

The junior school has expanded to over 150 pupils, including a number of local day pupils, some of them from nearby prep schools. The parent of a local girl, who had turned down the offer of a scholarship from a nearby public school, told us that her daughter was ecstatically happy and had grown immeasurably in confidence. 'The best thing we ever did was to send our daughter to Concord, the first school she has ever attended where she has been really happy.' One prep school head we spoke to was full of the praise for Concord's 'delightful' pupils and the amazing facilities.

Initially they follow a broadly balanced curriculum in the lead up to GCSE, which starts in earnest in their second year. Core subjects are mathematics, English and the three sciences. They can then choose from a further range of subjects including English literature, history, geography, economics, Spanish, French, German, Latin, art, photography and music to study to GCSE.

We had a fascinating series of tours into specific areas of the school, all conducted by different groups of students from the junior to those in their last years. So we were able to talk in depth with some 16 students. They were uniformly open and fresh in their enthusiasm for talking about their school and clearly immensely happy. Not the faintest whiff of arrogance, cynicism or world weariness. Impossible to winkle out a serious complaint and no, the principal had not bribed them. What emerged, with a strength which might surprise some, is that it is 'cool to be clever and to work hard'. Nothing conceited about this, no smugness about recognising they had academic talents, no hint of intellectual superciliousness. They just seemed to delight in their talents and the opportunities to exercise them.

Just as well – academic study is unashamedly and vigorously promoted as the most important aspect of the college. Every Saturday morning students in year 10 and above sit internal tests to give them as much preparation as possible for the public examinations. Some may gasp in horror, muttering 'crammer, crammer', but it does not seem to the students to be force-feeding. One very impressive girl told us it was just to ensure they were 'conceptually sound' – a memorable phrase. This was the same girl, incidentally, who told us, ' I chose to come to Concord because my school in Singapore was too relentlessly academic.' We asked about the pressure to perform well in these and the public exams. 'The pressure does not come so much from the teachers', we were told. 'We are disappointed with ourselves if we do badly.' So is it self-imposed pressure? The boy we asked just chuckled – it was obviously a silly question.

It is sometimes suggested, and some league tables seem to confirm it, that confronted with bright, dedicated girls, boys tend to shrug their shoulders and switch off. Not so here, it would seem. The boys we met and witnessed were perfectly happy to admit how keen they were to do well. It is interesting to note that in 2011 the boys out-performed the girls at GCSE, and did the same at A level in 2010.

Games, options, the arts: One of the frequently repeated criticisms that circulate in Shropshire and beyond is that Concord has impressive facilities for sport but no-one uses them. The few football teams perform reasonably well in local leagues; rugby is on the decline. Sport is offered as a recreation, not a religion. That's not to say no interest. One boy told us that when a football match is on the television in the senior school commonroom (the West End), a visitor might think that Concord was a girls' school – not a boy to be seen (all watching the game). Squash and basketball flourish – we were shown the results of a three-figure thrashing the latter team dished out to a famous local public school; archery, badminton, tennis, athletics, water-polo, fencing, riding, climbing and mountain biking are on offer, with some county players. A huge and impressive sports hall, but really enthusiastic games players should look elsewhere. Lower sixth form students must now attend some physical fitness sessions – mens sana in corpore sano is not completely ignored.

Over the years the school has spread out to include some or much of the village of Acton Burnell, and there in the attractive village is one of the jewels in the Concord crown: the art building. This has no architectural merit at all beyond being functional – the jewels are kept inside, where we saw some inspirational work completed and in progress. Evidence of much imaginative and creative work in textiles, ceramics, photography, painting and graphics. Art is increasingly popular, partly because, 'It uses another part of your brain and needs a different sort of concentration', partly because an increasing number of students want to go on to study architecture and, every bit as popular a reason, because it is fun.

Wonderful, wonderful music school, with as good a concert hall as any we have seen. Now well over 100 students take music lessons and more than 60 sing in the choir. A student recently won the Shropshire Concerto competition and for the last two years over 200 students have been involved in charitable fundraising concerts. We were lucky enough to attend an evening concert, which was memorable not just for the high standard of the singing and playing (by all ages), but also for the obvious enjoyment shared by participants and audience alike. A short and entertaining play followed, written and produced by a student. We've seen slicker productions, but it was performed with huge intelligence and zest.

The philosophy club is hugely popular, as are Scrabble, bridge, international societies, charity club, Outreach (voluntary work) and the choir. One Eastern European boy told us, 'In my country, if something is voluntary we run out of the door and into the street. Here I am interested and I go, perhaps because it is voluntary.'

Background and atmosphere: As the principal observed, he has a beautiful view from the window of his study in the handsome eighteenth century building at the heart of the school campus. It is also of historical significance, since the thirteenth century ruined barn housed what is often referred to as the first meeting of a parliament where the Commons was seriously represented, summoned by Edward I. It gave the principal the opportunity to write that the Princess Royal in 2010 may have been the first member of the royal family to visit since 1283. T S Eliot would have delighted in the Elizabethan tomb in the parish church erected, to Sir Richard Lee, an ancestor of Robert E Lee – here, the intersection of the timeless moment.

The main house, which appears magically out of nowhere as you approach through the lanes of very rural Shropshire, was built in 1814 by a prominent Catholic family who, during the Napoleonic war, gave sanctuary to the Benedictine monks who later went on to found Ampleforth, Downside and Stoneyhurst.

Do the students know about all this history ? Well, clearly they know some. Telling us about the excitement and beauty of the fireworks display on the recent 5th November, one of them pointed to the ruined walls of the Parliament Barn and said, 'We succeeded this year.' Others volunteered how much they liked the beauty of the surroundings and the elegance of the main building – 'It does make a difference'.

Over the years, a village of new buildings has grown up around the campus, nearly all of them in keeping with their surroundings. The overall effect is aesthetically pleasing, blending in with the glorious wooded hills that back on to the house – no battle here between beauty and utility. The new, bright, fascinatingly-designed library is a necessary enlargement to the wonderful early nineteenth century Gothic chapel which used to house the books, but now offers comfortable chairs and computers in its new role as a commonroom. In a room off the chapel (firmly locked) we were told there was a ghost – that is unconfirmed

The school was founded in Sussex in 1949. Nearly 25 years later it moved to its present site and four years later the college accepted girls for the first time. In 1983 it became a charitable trust with a board of trustees, and in order to attract the most able students a substantial scholarship programme was introduced. So nothing hasty about the way in which the school has evolved – no shoring up, no swift changes of direction, just steady building, in every sense.

It is an obviously happy school. Staff and students greet one with a smile of welcome and reveal themselves as friendly, easy conversationalists. Like puppies, if the analogy may be excused, they seem to know no fear but greet with an open freshness, expecting the same in return. This is clearly the result of mutual respect and affection between students and staff, where an impressive mixture of long-serving teachers and young risers. Students obviously cherish the strong sense of community. They had touching stories to tell about the warmth of the welcome they experienced on arrival for the first time – 'I was very anxious as the taxi drew up, but everyone was so kind when I went inside the building that after ten minutes I suddenly remembered my parents were still in the car'. Another younger girl felt that their shared learning of English drew together students from varied backgrounds and languages.

They showed mutual physical respect – no jostling and shoving, no groups of no-good boyos huddling in the corner planning their next escapade, no boisterous calls, but plenty of vivacity and liveliness, natural courtesy without enforced restriction, boys and girls walking freely together.

Pastoral care and discipline: The high profile staff involvement is benign rather than military, with a lack of silly idiosyncratic school rules. None of the 20 or so students we asked could come up with any obvious bone of contention. They feel they are listened to and, in return, accept what has been arrived at, often through mutual consent. Trust is at the heart of it all. Smoking and drinking can lead to rustication and eventually expulsion; involvement with drugs leads to instant dismissal.

The 17 boarding houses, some in the village just beyond the school gates, are comfortable and well laid out; the houseparents are warmly appreciated. The superbly roomy and comfortable commonroom, the West End, is a popular rendezvous, encouraging school rather than cliquey house friendships and contributing to the sense of community. The food is astonishingly good and in generous proportions and variety – we know of no other school where the dining room is thickly carpeted.

A unique feature of the school is that overseas pupils can – and up to 250 do – stay on during part of the Christmas and all of the Easter holidays, as well as half term holidays, at no extra expense.

Pupils and parents: Past pupils remain deeply loyal to their school and frequently send their children to follow in their footsteps. Asians predominate, but a strong African contingent and a burgeoning number from Eastern Europe – in fact about 40 nationalities. A number of local day pupils from a variety of backgrounds has further increased the diversity.

Entrance: Day and boarding applications welcome for year 9, year 10 or year 12. The school is unashamedly selective, especially for year 12 candidates.

Exit: An impressive array of top universities. Twelve to Oxbridge in 2013, with economics, law, maths and medicine all popular subjects; others to eg Durham, Warwick, King's London, UCL and Imperial.

Money matters: The school is generous, though not profligate, with scholarships. Details on the website.

Remarks: Those who prefer the chapel and team games approach of the traditional public school won't wish to consider Concord, as in many ways it is the antithesis. Students who seek an excellent academic grounding particularly, but not quite exclusively, in the sciences might be attracted. Those who see the future as global rather than merely western should be interested: international friendships are there for the making. A school where intellect and academia are celebrated, but not at the expense of personal happiness. It really is more than an exam factory – it could be the start of a great adventure.

The Coopers' Company and Coborn School

St Mary's Lane, Upminster, Essex, RM14 3HS

• Pupils: 1384 boys and girls, all day • Ages: 11–18 • Christian • State

Tel: 01708 250500
Email: info@cooperscoborn.org.uk
Website: www.cooperscoborn.org.uk

Head: Since May 2013, Dr David Parry, formerly deputy head, who took over when previous head David Mansfield moved to lead Dulwich College Beijing. Was deputy of the school since 2005 including a stint as acting headteacher. Dr Parry was involved in setting up the school's link with Canterbury Christ Church University and also works with the University of London as a visiting research associate.

Academic matters: You 'can expect to do well', said Ofsted in its most recent response to pupils, and so they do. Learning takes place in a culture of success led by passionate and well-qualified teachers (ratio is 17 to 1), who clearly benefit from the school's third and most recently awarded specialist status, as a teacher training school (the other two are sport and humanities). School has therefore consistently achieved near top GCSE results nationally and the proportion of pupils achieving the highest grades is significantly above the national average – 85 per cent of candidates gained five or more A*-C passes including English and maths in 2013, and 37 per cent of grades were A*/A. They are especially strong in English lang, English lit, mathematics and art and design, but pupils do exceptionally well in RS, DT, textiles technology and music, with generally 100 per cent pass rates.

At sixth form pupils are offered a wide curriculum of traditional subjects but are also introduced to new courses – media studies, psychology and politics. Popular choices are the sciences, esp biology, business studies, history, maths and psychology. In 2013, 60 per cent A*-B and nearly 32 per cent A*/A grades.

Curriculum options are as standard for most schools that follow the national curriculum with years 7 and 8 studying all 10 subjects but a second MFL introduced in year 8. Work on careers is introduced for year 9s. At GCSE pupils study mainly full course GCSEs but the school also allows them to choose one or two short GCSE courses. Popular choices are history, German, geography and sport/PE but fair numbers also choose Spanish and French.

Pupils are setted only for maths, at the end of year 7. From year 7 to sixth form, homework is considered an essential part of shaping pupils' academic experience, particularly in relation to independent learning and thinking skills. School says 'regular homework would be equivalent to an extra year of education with consequent benefits', so expects parents to support their children's completion of homework and to sign their homework diaries. Parents are informed of what is expected at the beginning of each school year.

Despite high results and a NACE award for its gifted and talented programme, the school is working on improving grades. Reason for this is that teacher assessment at KS3 shows that most pupils start well (all achieve the nationally expected levels 5 and 6 in English, maths and science, with a fair number achieving level 7 and even 8 in mathematics, which is outstanding) and Ofsted notes that even better progress at key stages 3 and 4 is possible. Having recognised this the school introduced TRIPS – a Tracking, Reporting, Intervention and Planning System to monitor progress and 'early indications' of change look successful. Parents receive regular TRIPS reports (at least every half term) showing an academic target grade, pupils' present attainment grade and an effort grade, enabling all three parties to monitor progress and make any necessary interventions to keep grades on track. Underachieving pupils receive support from either the SEN department, LSAs or learning mentors. Just six per cent currently receive some type of extra support and less than one per cent of these have been statemented.

Games, options, the arts: Games and PSHE remain compulsory throughout the school years, even at sixth form. PE is outstanding with pupils winning many national competitions: 'There have been many times when we were behind and looked unlikely to win, but we won', observed former head, capturing pupils' exceptional achievement, resilience and aptitude for sport and learning in general.

Pupils enjoy a rich curriculum ranging from circuit gym training to trampolining, cricket and netball to indoor rowing. Coopers Cats has received natural recognition as an outstanding star programme for athletes, so lots of opportunity to be stretched. Sports and athletics have been so successful at the school that several teams often represent the school at national and international events and pupils took part in the opening ceremony for the 2012 Olympics.

Well-equipped art studios, arranged as individual cubicles where pupils have their own designated area in which to work. Its 'open house' policy approach encourages independent work, along with the clearly outstanding levels of work on display, creates a wonderful 'art school' atmosphere. Pupils consistently have work displayed in exhibitions around the country.

Music and drama are also both strong here. Drama recently was among the top 10 per cent for value-added scores in schools across the country. Pupils take part in several national ensembles and theatrical events. Connection to the Worshipful Company of Coopers means there are various concerts and events throughout the year. Around 250 pupils have instrumental lessons in school and at least another 50 have lessons outside school. Standard is high, up to grade 8, and students with exceptional achievement attend the Guildhall and Trinity Saturday College.

Huge range of extracurricular choice. Pupils are expected to get involved in music, drama and sport as well as the academic curriculum since school feels this has a great impact on the sense of culture and engagement. 'There is something for everyone,' said a year 11 pupil. Before and after and school lunch time clubs cover almost every conceivable area, from chess to fishing (under music alone there are 28 weekly activities including four wind bands, two orchestras, four jazz bands, a swing and brass band, five choirs and numerous rock bands). Several clubs have been instigated and are run by pupils.

Overseas trips are important. Language trips (year 8) and exchange trips (year 10) support Spanish, German and French but there are many others eg a rugby trip to New Zealand and a tennis trip to Florida, plus other trips to explore interesting places such as Namibia and Botswana. Year 12 and 13 pupils visited Madagascar to build a secondary school block. The school is developing links with China. Pupils praised the language exchange programme: 'They match you really well so you have lots in common and are able to make real friends, which is a good motivation for wanting to actually have a conversation'.

Background and atmosphere: A rich history dating to 1536 when it was first established as a free school for boys. Its name came in 1552 when the Coopers' Company was asked to take over the running of the school. It was then located in Stepney, Tower Hamlets. In 1891, it joined foundations with the Coborn school for boys and girls and remained at sites at Mile End and Bow until the school moved to Upminster in 1971.

At its present location, situated a good distance from the main road amid 25 acres of greenery, and home to a pond visited by ducks and geese, the school very much resembles an independent school. However, because 'the school's been here since 1971 ... it needs improvement,' and modernisation and development have seen new buildings regularly erected since the 80s, the latest being a sixth form block. Other smaller but notable modern developments include a solar panel roof, i-desks (computers that pop up out of the desk) and a laser cutter, with which pupils confessed: 'we have gone to town'. The outcome of their efforts is the various metal placards signposting the DT, textile technology and design and art departments. 'The best way to protect the future is to design it,' says the laser-cut sign on the front of the main DT building, as if to help create an atmosphere of vitality and aspiration for future success.

Pastoral care and discipline: Organised by heads of year. Years 7-11 form tutors are responsible for about 30 pupils, who remain in the same form group throughout the five years. Sixth form tutors look after about 20 students each. School tries to create a good mix with external entrants to the sixth form easily assimilated. Two forms allocated to each of three houses, a system which helps create vertical links as well as the horizontal year groupings. The school also selects school captains from year 12 pupils, who must apply for the position. These are prestigious positions and the selection process includes interviews by the head. The one boy and one girl selected hold office throughout their final year. Whole school council plays a key role in the decision-making processes – including the appointment of senior staff. Pupils are given a sense of importance and are consulted on important developments, 'because it won't work if the students don't like it'.

Peer to peer mentoring, and around 150 sixth formers work with younger pupils. Very high expectations of conduct. Parents and students report an effective response to the few incidents of bullying and racism; they are dealt with quickly by form tutors and heads of years. The school's approach to remedying problems is to get those concerned to accept responsibility and consequences for their actions. Bad behaviour is just simply 'uncool'. Instead pupils exhibit very positive attitudes to learning and life. 'We do try to look after each other, standards are high, it's tough love and there is a genuine sense of commitment.'

Pupils and parents: Mainly white middle class and clearly aspirational. A 'Christian school with an eclectic mix from all recognised world religions'. Pupils seem proud of their school and very contented. In a day when many young people seem to take what they have for granted, it was refreshing to meet a group of pupils who seemed extremely appreciative. They clearly thrive on their many opportunities for responsibility – 'you have these free periods and you soon learn that you need to work independently, so you use it to complete essays and extra research'.

Everyone is welcoming – greeting visitors with smiles and hellos, saying thank you, holding doors open and even singing to themselves as they pass by. Many parents are supportive of the school and help out at school events. Active PTA of about 30 members, very good for a secondary state school. They arrange various fund-raising events including a monthly sale of supermarket vouchers to parents and staff which enables school to raise over £10,000 per year to buy eg a minibus.

Entrance: Unusually large number of feeder schools (around 100 from the boroughs of Havering, Brentwood, Billericay, Basildon, Tower Hamlets, Newham, Barking & Dagenham, Redbridge and Thurrock) due to the school's historic links to East London and wish to preserve the principles of the Coopers' Company and Coborn Educational Foundation.

No doubt this helps intensify competition for places – over 800 applications for just 180 places and a fair number go to appeal. Priority to looked after children and then aptitude for sport. After this it's children connected to a Christian denomination or affiliated to one of the other three recognised main world faiths. Then siblings at the school, children with exceptional needs that the school is best placed to meet, those living locally and then those outside the borough.

Most stay on to the sixth form after GCSE. Around 50 places for students from outside but again, massively popular with over 300 applications. Applicants need at least eight A*-C grades to be considered for a place, to be sympathetic to the school's Christian character and be willing to uphold its 'Love as Brethren' ethos by giving time to serve the school. Oversubscription criteria prioritise looked after children, highest predicted grades and then availability in specific sets.

Exit: One-fifth leave after GCSE. Around three-quarters of sixth formers to university (nine Oxbridge offers in 2013). School provides a range of opportunities to prepare for post-school eg science pupils attend conferences, workshops, competitions and special events at Nottingham and Cambridge. Many go on to study pure science subjects and vocational courses such as medicine, veterinary science and dentistry. Other popular subjects include psychology, economics, architecture, art history, journalism, politics and theatre design.

Money matters: The school allocates £10k to assist pupils that need help and also provides music and sports grants of up to £500.

Remarks: An impressive and dynamic school that prepares pupils for success. Dazzling reputation in the local community and the word on the street blames it for increased house prices in the Upminster area. World class in true sense of the word.

Copthall School

Pursley Road, London, NW7 2EP

- Pupils: 1,160 girls, all day • Ages: 11–18 • Non–denom • State

Tel: 020 8959 1937
Email: enquiries@copthall.barnet.sch.uk
Website: www.copthallschool.org.uk

Head: Since 2005, Ms Jane Beaumont, BA (Oxford) PGCE (London University's Institute of Education). Started her career at Copthall as an NQT in the early 1990s and has not strayed very far since. Although she came into education 'late', she was assistant head/director of sixth form at Acland Burghley school for 10 years and deputy head at both The Compton and Fortismere schools. 'I live locally and that's very important. I know and understand the local community.' Her husband is head of a Redbridge comprehensive school.

Down to earth, forthright and likeable. Her abiding passion for the job, even in her eighth year, is evident in the way she enthusiastically bounces through our meeting (metaphorically speaking), and is on top of all the facts, figures, statistics, Ofsted reports etc. However, it's not just about making the grade for this head – she also takes a genuine interest in the wellbeing of her girls. 'Around a lot', is what one of the parents told us. Another says she marvels at her dedication, 'she's always the last one to leave and will wait at the bus stop until every one of her students is safely on the bus.' One pupil told us, 'When she asks you how you are, you know it's because she really cares and it's not just meaningless words.

The product of a single parent family who went to 'tough schools', but got herself to Oxford University, Ms Beaumont says the experience 'has informed my career and made me passionate about the power of education to improve lives.' She is a firm believer in a strong educational background for a broad spectrum of pupils; 'I love the fact that Copthall is a genuine comprehensive school with children from all backgrounds and abilities. I find it amazing how ambitious most of them are in their learning, and we are here to get them to realise this ambition.'

Academic matters: In the top 20 per cent of schools nationally for student progress recently. All the more admirable when one takes into account that there are 60 different spoken languages at home and 22 per cent of students on free school meals (compared to 16 per cent nationally). Good solid results – 2013: 58 per cent of pupils got 5+ A*-C at GCSE including English and maths (where value-added is very good), 32 per cent A*/A grades. Organises some learning by ability rather than age.

A good range of traditional and non-traditional options, including food tech, ICT, childcare, and a City and Guilds level 2 diploma in beauty therapy (equivalent of five GCSE grades A*-C). Wide range of A levels with maths, biology and chemistry all popular (as elsewhere, few opt for physics); 32 per cent A*-B grades in 2013, 15 per cent A*/A. Psychology and sociology also get large numbers of takers. Non-traditional female subjects like sciences and technology are stronger than in many 'mixed' environments. This is something the head is very proud of – 'the fact that there is such a good up take across the range of sciences, arts, humanities and technical subjects, allows us to have an unusually wide range of subjects offered at A level for a sixth form or our size.' Has leading practitioners for history, dance and business education.

Copthall has specialist business and enterprise college status and this is embedded across the curriculum: 'Our mission is that our students will leave Copthall prepared for the constantly changing world of work.' Plenty of opportunities to develop business acumen. These may include raising money for a World Challenge expedition (this year Malaysia), baking and selling biscuits or creating a new children's card game called 'Shuffles', enabling team members to develop production, finance and marketing skills amongst others. PHSE includes modules in personal finance.

The school is 'committed to educational opportunity and inclusion.' It needs to be – approx 32 per cent of students are on the SEN register. The SEN co-ordinator also liaises with outside agencies. One parent said, 'They're really on top of this. My daughter is dyslexic and she is offered a lot of support including extra reading classes and a scribe for exams.' Reading is a priority here. The school analyse who is and isn't taking books out of the library. Actively encourage parents to read with their children, especially in families where English isn't the first language. Everyone is tested in year 7 – those in need get extra help in class or in small groups. Five teaching assistants manage year 7 and 8 pupils with complex needs who require full-time support. Learning co-ordinators keep an eye on pupils' progression and those who are struggling with work and behaviour may embark on an intensive programme in the inclusion centre, which puts most back on track. The school has converted many parts of the building to make them wheelchair accessible. Two stair lifts and two wheelchair lifts have been installed and a number of classrooms contain height adjustable furniture.

As with many large comprehensive schools, a healthy amount of self motivation is required to succeed. One parent expressed concern about her daughter's education at the school: 'I do worry that pupils at the lower end of the spectrum could slip through the net.' However, she continues, 'in many cases the school's GCSE results don't reflect the hard work the teachers put in.'

Games, options, the arts: Plenty to do. A wide range of practical subjects on offer including art, DT and performing arts, with small classes for practical subjects. Good facilities and well-equipped DT and art rooms. Astounding pieces of art work on display in the art room, although some pieces which deserved to be mounted on feature walls were slightly hidden from view. (One student in particular could've given Dali a run for his money).

Strong on dance and drama. Great success in ballet and selected students have taken part in a programme with the English National Ballet (Impressive wall displays of student performances). Drama very popular too with lots of performance opportunities in school and regular trips to theatre companies including the Old Vic, Sadler's Wells and Regents Park Open Air Theatre. The school runs a summer school for selected year 6 transfer pupils every year. The theme, purpose and pupils differ each summer depending on need, for example literacy and numeracy etc. Active and diverse music department with extracurricular groups that include rock band, guitar club, a 'glee' choir and a year 11 a capella group.

Big on sports – perhaps inspired by the well known stadium down the road. GCSE PE is an option and as well as the traditional competitive sports, pupils are offered trampolining, zumba, yoga, rowing, basketball and the option of cheerleading for the Saracens Rugby team,that now uses Copthall Stadium for its games. Own sports hall, netball courts and hockey pitches, with Copthall swimming pool and Power League Football Centre down the road. Links with local sports clubs are used to offer a wider sporting curriculum. Inter-form and inter-school matches, lunch-time clubs, and keen sportswomen join Barnet sports clubs. Athlete and commonwealth medal winner Nadia Williams is an alumnus.

Background and atmosphere: Named for Copt Hall, the local 17th century manor house, opened as a grammar school in 1936 and merged with Woodcroft School in 1971. It became a girls' comprehensive in 1973 and operated as a single school on two separate sites, until extensive rebuilding enabled its amalgamation on one site in 1996.

Copthall is situated on the corner of two roads. Page Street is a leafy, pretty road with posh secluded houses and the promise of great things. Indeed the facade of the school from this perspective is of an imposing brown brick building with a large feature window which sits in a decent forecourt. Turn the corner into Pursley Road and the picture changes. This is a very busy, nondescript road, redeemed slightly by the vast playing fields opposite the school. In the morning, one is faced with a sea of green, as the Copthall girls descend from the bus and make their way into the main entrance.

Enter the building from this side and you could be forgiven for thinking you had entered an NHS hospital. The reception area is large and airy, but sterile and very blue, with a large semicircular reception desk, where we almost expected to pick up our prescriptions. Above the waiting chairs, there is a large television screen with informative bulletins for students and a particular emphasis on healthy eating.

This school is a bit of a hotchpotch of the old and new, and we weren't really sure where one part began and one ended. The original part of the building is fairly dark with narrow corridors and high windows. There was a distinct lack of charm or character in this part of the building, which could partly be rectified by adding some personal touches – more student displays on the wall, a good injection of colour etc. Enter the school hall for a trip down memory lane. It probably hasn't changed since the 50s, which is intentional, the head assures us. This does lend a certain nostalgic charm to it and clearly word has spread as it has become a popular filming venue, which can add Call the Midwife to its recent list of credits.

On the positive side, a cash injection has allowed for some very nice elements. A pretty secluded courtyard where sixth formers can study or have some quiet time, a fully equipped beauty salon for those taking the beauty course as an option, a superb, fully mirrored dance studio with a sprung floor, a large, well stocked library and a decent sized (purple) business suite.

Students also took the initiative to design the façade of a new building a couple of years ago. They decided on a 'green vine' motif and had the brainwave of turning each leaf into a national flag using different shades of green – representing the various nationalities in the school. The effect is a beautiful variegated pattern.

Plans are underway for the Copthall School expansion programme (12 new classrooms planned for 2014), and the school is due to expand by one form of entry from September 2014. One parent expressed concern about this expansion and told us: 'I understand the necessity for creating more school places, but I'm worried how the school will cope with getting even bigger, and how it will impact on the individual.' Indeed it is hard to imagine how another structure could be cramped into this one site – the only plus side being that they may have to finally remove the demountables in the school's forecourt, which have well passed their sell-by date.

Pastoral care and discipline: Discipline a high priority especially with regards to uniform. One parent said, 'Have you met the head? Even I feel like straightening my skirt when she passes by.' Clearly Ms Beaumont has little time for nonconformists – the school prospectus says it all; 'students will be asked to remove nail varnish at a cost of 20p....if students opt to have piercings (eg nose studs), this must be done at the beginning of the summer holiday, so they can heal and be removed for the start of school in September.' The result is a well turned out bunch of girls in a smart, dark green tartan uniform (a far cry from this editor's Copthall schoolgirl days). Any desire to out-individualise each other is done beyond the school gates.

Mostly nice, well-behaved girls (a couple of the classes we passed sounded a few decibels louder than possibly acceptable). Permanent exclusion rate is very low, averaging one a year. In most cases it is students who didn't start at the school in year 7. Strict on attendance and punctuality. The education welfare team works closely with the school to highlight the importance of this. An attendance of no less than 95 per cent a year is expected as is a prompt 8.35am start. Early school finish at 2.55pm (Gove would choke), but only a 35 min lunch break: 'We have a staggered lunch break to cater for four sittings so that students get a freshly cooked meal.'

Much has also been done to combat bullying, which in a school of 1,200 girls is almost a sad inevitability. Student services situated in the heart of the school is open to any vulnerable student throughout the school day. Peer mediation, buddying and anti-bullying council also help to protect more vulnerable pupils. Learning co-ordinators, many of whom are non-teaching heads of year, are employed specifically for the pastoral needs of students.' One parent said, 'I had a child who was bullied when she first started the school, but it was dealt with promptly and sensitively and there are no issues any more.'

What the school lacks aesthetically, it certainly makes up for in its infrastructure. 'Inclusion' is a word used by many of the parents we spoke to. There is an admirable amount of information for parents including informative weekly newsletters and three reports a year. One parent told us, 'we don't lack for information here.' A conscious effort has been taken to include parents from multi-cultural backgrounds who may find integrating a challenge. Ms Beaumont instigated a group last year for 30 parents which ran for 12 weeks and was completely funded by the school. As a result of its success, the plan is to make it an annual event.

Various incentives for students to perform are given throughout the year. The pièce de résistance is a Celebration Evening held at the end of the school year to recognise exceptional achievements in different subjects. One parent said, 'This is something my daughter really aspires to achieve and it motivates her.' Encouragement is extremely important, the head believes, 'if you get the pastoral stuff right, everything else will fall into place.'

Pupils and parents: A great ethnic and social mix with lots of middle class girls and those from tough estates – 'we don't have large numbers from any particular ethnic minority or social class, which gives us a nice breadth of views.' Parents mostly very supportive; very active PTA and parent governors – strong sense of parental inclusion. One parent told us, 'My daughter had the option of going to a selective school, but when we weighed it up we felt that Copthall provided everything she needed, academically and socially.'

Entrance: Heavily oversubscribed school – approx 496 applications for 180 girls in each group. (This will change from Sept '14 when the school expands). Organised by the LA, with looked-after girls and those with particular medical or social needs first on the list, followed by siblings or those with a brother at their partner school Christ's College. Remaining places are offered on a geographical basis – generally less than a mile and a half away. Some 30 to 40 join the sixth form from outside.

Exit: Around 40 per cent of the year leaves after GCSEs, mostly for local colleges, many to follow vocational courses. Over 80 per cent of sixth formers to university (most of the rest to FE colleges), generally one a year to Oxbridge. Others to study eg medicine at Manchester, history at Warwick and aerospace systems engineering at Coventry. Good work experience and careers advice.

Money matters: Barnet is officially viewed as leafy suburbia and thus not in need of urgent government cash for, eg, replacing portable classrooms. Stable staff, but turnover not helped by the fact that they can get inner-London weighting just a few miles south. Supportive parents help with raising cash.

Remarks: Good, solid, highly inclusive local school with a strong sense of community. Plenty of scope for developing a

bent for science, languages or making a million at business, while picking up performing arts or food technology skills along the way. We hope its expansion in 2014 will not dilute its ethos.

Cotham School

Cotham Lawn Road, Cotham, Bristol, BS6 6DT

• Pupils: 1280; mixed • Ages: 11–18 • non–denom • State

Tel: 01179 198000
Email: info@cotham.bristol.sch.uk
Website: www.cotham.bristol.sch.uk

Head: Since 2005, Dr Malcolm Willis (fifties). First degree from University of Wales, and doctorate in education from the University of the West of England. He held a previous headship in Swansea. Ambitious and businesslike, but approachable, say parents.

Academic matters: Results are good for the broadly average ability intake: 2013 63 per cent five plus GCSEs including English and maths at A*-C, 28 per cent A*/A grades; at A level, 65 per cent A*-B and 34 per cent A*/A grades.

The sixth form – North Bristol Post 16 Centre – has been a joint operation with nearby Redland Green School since the latter opened in 2007. Sixth form options cover the full academic range, apart from classics. Music, dance, drama and performing arts are popular, but biggest subjects are maths and English.

Most classes are mixed ability up to GCSE, but maths is setted from part-way through year 7, and pull-out groups for those needing more support in core subjects. About a third of year 11 take separate science GCSEs rather than core science, and a handful of BTEC courses are offered in business, sports, art and ICT.

Half assigned to do French and the other half German from year 7, and the majority continue to GCSE; Spanish is the optional second language. Latin not offered in the main timetable, but twilight classes are available for those who are interested.

Enrichment schemes for the brightest ones include participation in local and national maths challenges, where Cotham holds its own against many of the local independent schools. Maths was an official specialism, along with ICT.

A specialist, nine-person inclusion/SEN team with its own suite of rooms looks after the 150 or so pupils with special needs, most of them minor.

Games, options, the arts: Dance is the big thing here – specialist school for the performing arts, with a particular strength in dance, so everyone dances for at least the first couple of years. Lots of performances, some to a very high standard, and a fair number take it as far as GCSE or further. Drama in and out of school hours is popular and inclusive.

Music also good – not many schools can boast a complete gamelan orchestra set-up, on top of the more conventional facilities. About 10 per cent of students take private music lessons at school, and practice rooms are available for use at lunchtimes.

Not the sportiest of schools, but plenty going on for the keen. The gym is large and modern; space for outdoor games on site is limited, and more of it was eaten up in the recent redevelopment, but everyone gets a chance at team sports at shared sports fields a coach ride away. The school's performance in less mainstream sports – badminton, basketball, athletics – is respectable, and occasional successes in rugby and netball.

Outdoor pursuits are a strength, despite the inner-city location. Good take up of the Duke of Edinburgh award and a high standard achieved. Also a good track record in the Ten Tors challenge.

Background and atmosphere: Started as Cotham Grammar School in the 1930s but was on a downward slide in reputation and results even before it turned comprehensive in 2001. Under the current head, Ofsted ratings have moved up from satisfactory to good to outstanding, and the school's reputation has soared, making it one of the most oversubscribed in the city. Converted to academy status in 2011, despite some parental opposition.

Shifts in admissions policies and catchment areas have changed the school's character over the years, and the glut of independent schools within a mile or two means some of the brighter potential recruits are skimmed off before entry. The improving reputation may be changing that, although two former independent schools turned academies are also attracting students from the core catchment area. Responding to demand by adding an extra year 7 class every year from 2011, so school will eventually expand to around 1600.

A massive rebuilding and refurbishment programme just squeaked in before the Building Schools for the Future initiative was abolished, so well-designed new buildings with modern labs and art rooms, and the original 1930s building (housing mainly maths and languages) is looking refreshed and more user-friendly. Next on the wish-list is a larger capacity hall, as the one in the main building cannot hold the whole school. Flexible performance spaces get plenty of use for school shows as well as by community groups. The library is large, well-stocked and well-used.

Cotham's half of the shared sixth form is based in a Victorian house along the road from the main school, although A level teaching is scattered over the whole site, and for some classes involves a 15-minute walk to Redland Green. The timetable allows for a steady stream of teenagers walking back and forth between the two at break times.

The site is a bit cramped for the expanding school population, but well-planned, with covered outdoor areas for eating and conversation, as well as areas of grass and tarmac. School food – all 'fairly traded' – is 'pretty good', but the dining room is tiny for the pupil numbers, so many bring packed lunches. No one is allowed off site at lunch time until the sixth form.

Pastoral care and discipline: A big school – and getting bigger – so a few parents mutter about children getting lost in the crowd, and what they can get up to unsupervised in hidden corners of the site at break times. The head is seen as aiming for a tough but fair stance on discipline and generally as succeeding, with a robust bullying policy and low tolerance for disruption. Uniform – logo sweatshirts and black skirts or trousers – can come across as a bit scruffy.

Form tutors are the first stop for pastoral issues, but a school counsellor to help with problems arising at home as well as in school, and anyone can use weekly drop-in sessions with the counsellor, nurse or outside agencies specialising in drugs, alcohol and sexual health.

Does its best to make transition from primary school easy and has close contacts with feeder schools. Most year 7s will already have spent time at Cotham getting involved in dance programmes while still at primary school, and they get a 'bonding' outdoor activity trip early in the year.

Pupils and parents: As wide a range as you would expect from a school with a catchment stretching down to edgy inner-city areas on one side and over to the arty Georgian terraces of Clifton on the other. Students speak 27 different languages – a broad ethnic mix. Lots of academic, medical and media parents (the school is close to the University of Bristol, the Bristol Royal Infirmary and the BBC). Some parents say the Clifton kids tend to stick in one group, the Somali kids in another and so on, but others report more mixing as time goes on.

Entrance: No changes planned under academy status: non-selective intake, applications through the local authority, and priority depends mainly on distance from the school, with a mapped area of first responsibility.

Exit: Around a third to Russell Group universities, including a few to Oxbridge and a few medics.

Remarks: A thriving comprehensive with an arty urban atmosphere, dealing well with local and national challenges, but the pace of the last few years' improvements could be hard to maintain, even with the academy status.

Craigholme School for Girls

Linked school: Craigholme Junior School

72 St Andrews Drive, Pollokshields, Glasgow, G41 4HS

• Pupils: 410 girls, all day • Ages: 3–18 • Non-denom
• Fees: £4,485–£10,407 pa • Independent

Tel: 01414 270375
Email: admissions@craigholme.co.uk
Website: www.craigholme.co.uk

Principal: Since 2004, Mrs Gillian C K Stobo MSc BSc (mid fifties). Moved from High School of Glasgow, where she was educated herself. Glasgow through and through, she read chemistry at Glasgow University and did her Dip Ed at Jordanhill. After 'a bit of teaching', followed by about 10 years raising a family, she joined the High School as part-time chemistry teacher in 1993, progressing to head of chemistry, then assistant rector, but still finding time to complete her MSc thesis on learning support for able pupils. Now working on her doctorate – quite a role model.

Severely smartly suited, her impressiveness is lightened by her warmth and genuine passion for girls' education. She runs the school with the senior management team of junior and nursery heads plus the business manager, seeing the school as a 3-18 unit, friendly, purposeful, with success rooted in 'knowing what girls need and providing it right through from the nursery'. Well versed in 'education-speak', she focuses on 'the real and different needs of girls' widely varied modes of learning', concerned for the 'mismatch between technology in school and how the young actually use it'.

Backed by 'a strong board', she has moved the school forward, managing the inspirational £2m sports development in Pollok Park (home of the Burrell collection) and hopes that, if it becomes a training venue for the 2014 Commonwealth Games, it will put Craigholme even more firmly on the map.

Academic matters: Still a determinedly academic and very Scottish school using Scottish Standard Grade, Intermediate 1 and 2 (subject heads taking decisions on which best prepares for Highers), Highers and Advanced Highers. Despite small numbers will put on Advanced Highers for individuals, though contact time may be reduced and pupils use Heriot Watt's internet-based Scholar for support.

Impressive results (2013: pass rate 100 per cent for Standard Grades, 93 per cent for Highers; 27 per cent of S6 girls got A passes in three Advanced Highers) and small classes (12-16). French at four for all, with German from S2 and Spanish from S1, though classics have gone the way of all flesh. Specialist science and art using senior facilities for J7. Strong emphasis on science, taken as three separate subjects all through, perhaps at the expense of history etc, which is studied in rotation in S1 and 2. Chemistry offers an S6 forensic chemistry module, human biology at Higher and Advanced Higher is 'particularly well suited to pupils interested in the biomedical sciences and professions allied to medicine'. Physics runs a supporting engineering club.

Smashing light-filled study library with permanent staff to hand, tucked attractively under the eaves with every conceivable study aid. It goes without saying that computers and high tech equipment, interactive whiteboards et al support every aspect of teaching, as well as a discrete computing course. Classrooms well planned into subject specific areas and light, pastel painted and modern, for all their pretty moulded ceilings, elegant Edwardian windows and tasteful white blinds.

Dyslexia screening with trained help and ed psych support. Sizeable Asian intake seldom in need of help with English. Pupils are given individual or in-class help as appropriate and the school 'prefers looking for pupil's alternative strengths to flagging weakness'.

Games, options, the arts: Teams, choirs, orchestras, clubs in all disciplines travel to every corner of the globe. A choral trip to China, Florida (choir won at a Disney festival), Vietnam with geography, not to mention regular Paris, Aberfeldy, Lake District, London and more local trips for both the usual round of D of E etc and curriculum enhancement. Strong music department has forged links with China, Argentina, Africa and Australia, hosting visits when no trips happening.

Both the school, and indeed sport for women, have become higher profile in the surrounding area with the appointment of a school-based community sports coach, with Craigholme spear-heading holiday sport camps, sport for Asian women and training for the 2014 Commonwealth Games. Hockey, tennis and athletics have dominated with bags of success, and recently new facilities have allowed pupil initiative to pilot other areas such as netball.

Drama including Shakespeare much in evidence in both junior and senior school, thanks to the Mitchell Theatre's festival. Home ec has smashing new facilities which have tempted year 6 back to do a cake-icing module – supposedly great training in manual dexterity: for dentists!

Background and atmosphere: Three affluent Victorian residences have been cunningly joined by purpose-built stone and glass halls to form a nearly harmonious whole. Large reception rooms and linking social spaces, including a multipurpose assembly hall, amongst airy classrooms and useful gathering points. The three houses are linked by the Dungeon, a subterranean passage, rightly named, despite cream paint and gaudy lockers. This provides wet weather access to all the buildings, gives a café, common room and acres of cloakrooms, cheerfully crowded with girls in unusually tidy scarlet blazers and Craigholme tartan kilts. Plans afoot, but currently on hold, 'because of the recession', to make the redundant gym hall into a canteen and provide much-needed play space and an extra classroom, which would create a real asset from a depressing though valuable area. Recent social space, The Hub, for older girls to have lunch and socialise in.

Girls like the food. Up to S4 cafe attendance is compulsory, though packed lunches are allowed. Sixth formers more forthcoming than younger girls and clearly enjoy their roof top common room. Unanimously enthusiastic about the school, they insist that being all-girls is no curtailment to social life in a city environment. Seeming very much at home, they take responsibility for granted – not really surprising since some had been at Craigholme for 14/15 years. Almost every inch of wall space crammed with evidence of activity, with a strong sense of the relevance of education to the local and wider community, and vice versa – news reporting a recurrent theme with the seniors; BBC Newsday contribution echoed in the J7's complete newspaper, a cross-curricular medium for some really exciting learning.

Pastoral care and discipline: Houses – Scottish castles – run vertically from start of junior school and evidently evoke competitive identity, though form teachers are first point of contact for parents. Bullying prevented by careful placing and management of vulnerable pupils rather than by sanction. Teachers' care for and knowledge of individual pupils and their needs is evident. A minimum of major problems thanks to monitoring, small tutorials and good PSE.

Pupils and parents: Largely affluent middle-class catchment spread over south side of Glasgow, with three school buses and a good train service bringing girls from as far as Cumbernauld to Ayrshire, including some areas north of the Clyde. Number of first-time buyers and ethnic minorities. School open from 8.30am to 6pm. Supportive parents raise funds for the Foundation and give their time and expertise to extend the pupils' life skills.

Amongst past pupils are scientist Rosalynne Watt (won the Siemens prize at Cambridge while doing PhD and the Institute of Physics Young Researcher in Combustion runner-up), paediatric emergency physician Joanne Stirling, artist Sally Carlaw, crime novelist Louise Hughes, ex-editor Scottish Field, Claire Grant and TV journalists, Victoria Lee and Carla Romana.

Entrance: Assessment for all, even the nursery. Main entry points J1, J7/6 and S1, though a few join S5/6. Despite the exam, will take girls 'who have abilities in other areas'. Sample papers not available, as 'potential rather than achievement' is the key. Numbers steady during recession, though the entry pattern has changed, with parents nervous of committing from the start of J1.

Exit: Few fall out along the way – the majority of girls from juniors form a core of about half of S1. Top universities Glasgow, Strathclyde, Nottingham, Edinburgh to study eg dentistry, mechanical engineering, architecture, business; also some to eg Michigan State University, Laine Theatre Arts School and American Academy of Dramatic Arts.

Money matters: Not a rich school but will support parents in financial crisis. Approachable attitude encourages early consultation about potential problems. All assistance is means-tested rigorously (including capital/investment income). Bursaries mainly for S1 entrants and those whose circumstances change

Remarks: Still a nice school with nice girls in a nice part of Glasgow. Impressive staff and up-to-date, open-to-change teaching and leadership.

Cranbrook School

Waterloo Road, Cranbrook, Kent, TN17 3JD

• Pupils: 440 boys, 315 girls; 250 board • Ages: 13–18 • Non-denom • Fees: Boarding £10,986–£13,179 pa; Day free • State

Tel: 01580 711800
Email: registrar@cranbrook.kent.sch.uk
Website: www.cranbrookschool.co.uk

Head Teacher: Since September 2012 Mr John Weeds, formerly principal of Reading School. A Cambridge classics graduate, he has taught at both state and independent schools.

Academic matters: High quality intake and good value added, but a spread of lower grades too. In 2013, 59 per cent A*/A grades at GCSE and 49 per cent at A level. A wide (but notably academic) range of A levels include Latin and music technology. Computer studies and psychology available to AS level. Students can also take vocational A levels through link with Angley School up the road.

Has been a specialist science school for a number of years – popular, separate sciences for all at GCSE, and good labs. Results good but not spectacular. Increasing uptake of all three sciences at A level, with chemistry being particularly popular with the girls. A community science and astronomy society uses the school's new observatory, which is equipped with several telescopes. Also a specialist language school – French, Latin and Spanish on offer; only 20 per cent take a language A level: better than average but room for improvement. Does notably well in French. Overseas students including Chinese given the opportunity to take GCSE and A level in their native language, but any teaching is done outside the curriculum. Strong humanities: history particularly so at all levels, plus politics and geography. Setting for maths and French – some children can take these GCSEs early. Large, well-equipped kitchens for pupils to learn food technology. Lower sixth are all required either to take a critical thinking AS level or do an extended project, which encourages independent learning.

One part-time SEN teacher and a part-time assistant – will accept those with academic or physical special needs so long as they would 'benefit from a grammar school education', ie generally mild dyslexia. Irregular sessions mainly to give pupils strategies for coping. They do have one statemented child and another joining, but remarkably few pupils overall are recorded as having any level of SEN.

Games, options, the arts: Philosophy of sport for all, and they do it well. Lots of opportunities for everyone, compulsory games once a week plus various sports clubs. All the usual sports – several teams and matches. First XV rugby team very successful. Recent rugby and hockey tours to New Zealand and Fiji. Outdoor heated swimming pool, squash courts, Astroturf for hockey and tennis, plus sports hall with dance studio, climbing wall and multi-gym.

Active music department with a director of music and 16 peripatetic music teachers. About 180 children learn an instrument. Orchestra, big band, two choirs as well as various chamber music ensembles and rock bands. The performing arts centre has music teaching/practice rooms, a chamber music room, music library, recording studio, concert rooms and drama studio. The Queens Hall is the home of the drama department and is a fully-equipped and recently refurbished theatre, largely run by the pupils but also used by outside touring companies. Annual house play festival as well as junior, senior and whole school productions.

Lots of extracurricular activities, sixth form lectures and visits, plus a number join Young Enterprise Scheme, setting up and running their own business. Students in the lower school are expected to take part in two extracurricular activities, whilst sixth formers are encouraged but not compelled to get involved. Active CCF, both an army and RAF section, with an annual camp, regular field days and adventurous training camp. All required to do two weeks' work experience after GCSEs.

Background and atmosphere: Founded in 1518 by John Blubery; in 1574 Queen Elizabeth I granted the school its Royal Charter, still displayed in the library, and the school began its life as the 'Free Grammar school of Queen Elizabeth in Cranbrook'. Centred on School House, a fine Georgian mansion, 70 acres of buildings, gardens and playing fields close to the centre of Cranbrook. Co-ed since 1972.

Went through a period of complacency and was seen to be resting on its laurels, but things seem to have tightened up recently and pupils' academic progress now monitored more closely, although one parent said that it still needs a bit more 'oomph'. Particularly suits proactive self-starters who do not need to be spoon-fed – if children want to do something, they need to make it happen. Struggling children are spotted early and high achievers well managed. Sixth formers given lots of responsibility – running clubs, committees, technical support in computer rooms, specialist help with lighting in the Queen's Hall etc. Good food – very pleased that they have recently managed to recruit the chef from Benenden School down the road.

Pupils seem have a lot of fun here and a thriving social life. Lots of opportunities for foreign adventures – link with a community in Tanzania, every other year a group of pupils go out to work alongside local people, places much sought after and pupils have to earn money to pay their way: lots of money-making projects set up in the local area in run up to the trip. The Tanzanian teachers are then invited to come to Cranbrook to work alongside class teachers. Exchange partnership with a school in Kerala, South India, plus trips to battlefield sites, Paris, Vienna and many more. British Council's International School Award for bringing the wider world into the classroom through a range of international projects.

Pastoral care and discipline: Strong house system for day pupils and boarders. On arrival, each child is allocated a tutor who will monitor academic and activities programme as well as social progress and work closely with the head of house. Effective mentoring system in place; some senior pupils opt to become 'listeners' and are trained by the school; a local counsellor to hear and help those with personal difficulties. Although non-denominational, close links with the parish church – the vicar of Cranbrook is an ex-officio governor of the school (religious education studies continue into the sixth form). Bright, airy, well-decorated houses for boarders, some in small dormitories but most in study bedrooms. Activities are laid on for them at the weekends and many go out to stay with day children.

Pupils and parents: Parents tend to be middle class professionals – some London commuters, some local. Generally interested in their children's education and hugely supportive of the school. Strong links with parents – frequent parents' evenings and assessment reports sent home regularly. Parents encouraged to contact the tutor whenever the need arises. Very few families on benefits and very few super-rich either.

Confident, natural children without arrogance, well-spoken, chatty and polite. They are expected to get on with it – those who are highly motivated and well-organised get the most out of their time here: independence is strongly encouraged.

Boarders tend to be either those just outside the catchment area who cannot get a day place plus a number from London; about a third of boarders from overseas – anyone with a British passport or right to residency can get a free education, includes Hong Kong Chinese, Nigerians and anyone from the EU. EAL tuition is offered free of charge to anyone who needs it.

Old Boys include: astronaut Dr Piers Sellers, Harry Hill, Tim Smit of Eden Project fame, Sir Charles Wheeler and sports commentators Peter West, Brian Moore and Barry Davies.

Entrance: Competitive entrance at 13+ (unusual for a state school). Objective NFER test (verbal and non-verbal reasoning) plus school's own papers in maths and English. Set against top 25 per cent of national ability range. Always over-subscribed, but even more so in the current economic climate. Very rare for places to become available in years 10 and 11.

May be some extra places available for sixth form entry but no guarantee of this, especially for boarding. Minimum requirement of seven Bs (but in reality pupils are likely to achieve far higher grades than this), plus a letter from the student's current head and a meeting in the spring term before GCSEs. Anyone who does not achieve seven Bs at GCSE is asked to leave.

Day pupils must live within 8.5km radius from the school on normal roads – ie no cutting through forests in 4x4s, as has been tried in the past – and houses reputedly cost £20,000 more within the catchment area. This policy is very strictly adhered to – if a child has already joined the school and the governors discover a fraudulent or deliberately misleading application, the child may be asked to leave. Transfer between boarding and day and vice-versa depends on places and the 8.5km catchment area still applies. Slightly different admissions procedure for boarding places and often marginally less competition, but the pass mark remains the same.

Owing to the 13+ start many children have been to private prep schools – lots from Dulwich Prep, Cranbrook. About 30 per cent from Angley School in Cranbrook – these will have come from local state primaries and spent two years in the fast track at Angley before taking the entrance exam at 13+. Angley understandably does not want to lose their brightest and best at this stage and does not prepare them for the exam – parents tend to get outside coaching. Contrary to popular belief, not a quota system from Angley – first past the post wherever the child comes from.

Exit: Virtually none leave post-GCSE. Some 95 per cent of sixth formers to university – 10 to Oxbridge in 2013; lots of help with personal statements and interview practice etc.

Remarks: Feels like a public school – indeed many local parents choose it over public schools even if they can afford fees. Does not have the hothousey atmosphere of the other grammars in the area and pupils appear relaxed and even laidback, but must be lots of paddling under the water to get the results they achieve.

Cranleigh School

Linked school: Cranleigh Preparatory School

Horseshoe Lane, Cranleigh, Surrey, GU6 8QQ

- Pupils: 400 boys, 220 girls; about 70 per cent board • Ages: 13–18 • C of E • Fees: Boarding £31,830; Day £25,950 pa
- Independent

Tel: 01483 273666
Email: enquiry@cranleigh.org
Website: www.cranleigh.org

Headmaster: Since 1997, Mr Guy de W Waller, MA MSc PGCE FRSA (fifties), educated at Hurstpierpoint, read chemistry at Worcester College and educational psychology at Wolfson College. Cricket and hockey blue. Former headmaster of Lord Wandsworth College. Obvious enthusiasm, energy and self-confidence. Clearly doesn't feel he has to impress anybody – PR machine definitely switched off the day we looked round; also a tendency to be rather glib and flippant (he doesn't have much time for this guide!). Describes himself as a 'frustrated housemaster – definitely not a career headmaster'. Feels that co-ed schools 'reflect the world we live in'. Has no doubts that school is doing it right – right balance of boys and girls, right approach to education. Describes the school fondly as 'this crazy place with heart'. Still teaches chemistry and philosophy – believes being in the classroom 'focuses you'. Likes to be kept informed and involved with pupils and says, 'The key is to have a good team in place'.

Cuts something of a controversial figure amongst parents – variously described as 'charming, dynamic, running a tight ship' as well as 'distant, arrogant, autocratic, doesn't listen to parents', and all range of comments in between. Has in the past been criticised for rather resting on his laurels, but the last year alone has seen the opening of a huge new academic centre for science, modern languages and maths; the opening of a four-storey art and design building; the addition of a (fourth) all-weather sports pitch and a complete refurbishment/extension of the cricket pavilion. For others, he can do no wrong.

Retiring in July 2014. His successor will be Mr Martin Reader, currently head of Wellington School in Somerset. He has an English degree and MPhil from Oxford, where he was a keen rugby player, and was deputy head of Reigate Grammar before moving to Wellington. He is married to Amanda.

Academic matters: Although academia is not wholly what Cranleigh is about, results have improved greatly of late, not least because of the introduction of girls throughout the school. At GCSE 2013, 62 per cent A/A* grades. At A/AS level, individual strengths vary from year to year, but drama, economics, English, history, languages, maths and the sciences usually up there with good grades. At A level in 2013, 81 per cent A*-B, 54 A*/A. Head says that pupils 'don't have to be superstars,' but one parent commented that the academic side is definitely hotting up and 'B and C students may struggle'. A SENCo screens all entrants, support offered for those who need it – one-to-one sessions which cost extra.

Games, options, the arts: 'Sport is a very important part of just about every Cranleighan's life,' says head. The sheer range of sports available is staggering – really something for everyone. Facilities extremely impressive – 100 of the 200 acres of the school land given over to playing fields – and include the Trevor Abbott sports centre, four all-weather pitches, one of which converts to 12 tennis courts in summer, to add to the other 12 courts (all packed with Wimbledon wannabees when we visited), indoor and outdoor swimming pools, cricket and rugby pitches stretching as far as the eye can see, championship standard squash courts, six Eton fives courts, nine hole golf course, stables with own horses (pupils can bring their own horse(s) if desired), and so on. Key sports include rugby, cricket, hockey, lacrosse, netball, tennis and athletics. Football nowhere near the same emphasis as rugby – might put off a soccer-mad boy. Opportunities for all levels of talent – parents with non-sporty but enthusiastic children say that they really enjoy what they do. But certainly don't bother applying if your child absolutely loathes sport.

Art generally praised, but one informed parental critic 'wasn't that impressed'. Drama particularly strong with fantastic theatre facilities (very professional tiered auditorium) and a new technical studio, and lots of chances to perform throughout the year in a variety of different shows. Musically, opportunities vast, with choirs, orchestras, individual instrument tuition, concerts throughout the year. Interestingly, though, music not hugely popular at either GCSE or A level.

Head does not feel the description 'after-school activities' is apt for Cranleigh: 'It's not an expression that fits with our ethos as here, after-school activities equal going to sleep – you have to be careful not to say "going to bed" in a co-ed school'. Quite! However, call it what you will, other than sport, the options are wide-ranging and children have lots of opportunities to fill their day – 'Too many,' says head.

Background and atmosphere: Founded in 1865 for farmers' sons, going through something of a renaissance and currently wildly fashionable – 'The school has become very popular since Guy Waller became head,' was how one prospective parent put it. Another described how it was her daughter's 'dream come true' to get in. Set in stunning grounds, it certainly fulfils every expectation of an English boarding school. Beautiful, impressive façade – breathtaking architecture which continues inside to the chapel, library, quad.

Six houses: four boys', two girls'. Boarding houses seem well designed – the newer ones obviously more swish with bright and airy feel; dorms (generally sleep four) for younger pupils (individual rooms for older ones) on the whole seem like the typical teenage bedroom – posters on wall, clothes strewn everywhere, but a homely atmosphere. Dining hall atmospheric, pupils help themselves from a choice of food – 'Rather like motorway services,' says head.

Boarding actively encouraged – majority do board, not out of necessity but desire to engage in all the school has to offer. If you are looking for a school where the kids are home at 4.00pm lounging around and chatting to parents, forget it – this is not the school for you. Absolutely key at Cranleigh are the sporting/extracurricular opportunities and a long school day – whether boarding or not. A parent of a day pupil commented, 'She loves the social whirl and doesn't want to come straight home.'

Pupils encouraged to eat, sleep and breathe Cranleigh and are busy from dawn till dusk – school day is from 7.30am until potentially 9.00pm at night. 'If they really want to go home after that, they can,' says head. Everyone expected to participate in the school fully and the head very pro boarding and quite disparaging of what he calls 'five day' schools.

Everyone has Saturday school virtually every Saturday, and over a third of boarders stay at the weekend – although one boarding pupil said, 'We all go home at the weekend,' so it depends what a particular peer group does. A number of parents we talked to felt should be more weekend exeats. 'My children aren't usually home till 6.30pm on a Saturday, which makes going away for the weekend or seeing friends very difficult,' said one parent of day pupils. Boarders need to be back by 7.00pm on a Sunday, so an even shorter weekend for them.

Pastoral care and discipline: Christian values underpin school society. Huge crackdown in recent years on sloppy discipline – drugs definitely not tolerated in any way; two boys expelled recently for possession, although 'those expulsions surprised nobody,' says a not particularly shocked parent. Personal possession of alcohol and smoking also big no-nos leading to a variety of sanctions, including gating and detentions. Persistent offenders suspended. Sex education, not surprisingly, quite high up the agenda here and romantic attachments between pupils definitely discouraged. 'Inappropriate' sexual behaviour leads to suspension or expulsion.

Head says whole feel of school is 'more like a university' and that pupils will need self-reliance. Pupils' daily pastoral care managed within each of the six houses and weekly meeting between head and tutors allows specific problems to be discussed. Bullying tackled via the tutorial/house system where pupils can talk in confidence. Individual housemasters and housemistresses have their own views on mobile phones, going out etc – it's the luck of the draw ('Nonsense!' says the head. 'The only variation is whether the house actually collects phones overnight/during prep').

Surprisingly, considering tough line on transgression, school not a pageant of well-turned-out pupils – lots of customised uniform in evidence and funky hairstyles. Sixth formers wear suits – but for some the word 'suit' is ambiguous, and Mr Waller is trying to tidy them up. All this trendy dishevelment and urban cool seem a bit incongruous in such glorious surroundings.

Pupils and parents: Interestingly, for a predominantly boarding school, parents tend to be from quite a small, local radius (certainly no more than 30 miles the norm) – and it's not unusual for parents to actually live in Cranleigh. Parents are 'a mix of backgrounds,' says head – although as the school is hardly cheap, presumably most are well-heeled (though Mr Waller keen to stress that a significant number have bursarial assistance). One parent said that school is 'like a movie set – full of beautiful people,' and certainly pupils are particularly cool souls who come across as mature, self-possessed individuals.

Entrance: Entrance list opens in May, two and a half years before September entry. Candidates and parents interviewed for interests/values/aspirations – conditional offers based on these and prep school reports, pending CE results. Very oversubscribed so can afford to be choosy about who gets in.

Head looking for pupils who 'enjoy being at school and have the capability to be interested in a wide range of things'.

For entrance to the sixth form (about 15-20 come in at this stage) the expectation is to have gained six points at GCSE, with two points for an A* or A grade and one for a B grade. Also at least a C grade at GCSE for maths and English language. Candidates will also be interviewed and reports sought from previous head.

Exit: Up to 20 per cent leave post GCSEs, for 'places offering more diverse AS/A2 courses than us', but the vast majority stay and go on to a wide range of universities. Five to Oxbridge in 2013 (three to study law); Bath, Bristol, Nottingham, Exeter, Loughborough and Oxford Brookes all popular.

Money matters: Fees by no means cheap, but most parents seem to feel that 'you get what you pay for' with the huge amount on offer. Scholarships available – academic, music, art and the Eric Abbott for candidates of 'strong academic ability and at least one other area of excellence', eg sport/drama etc – up to a maximum of 10 per cent of fees for the top awards. Other than that you'll need to remortgage.

Remarks: Hugely popular school with lots on offer, strong academia and mega street cred. Ideal for the sporty, energetic, sociable and independent child.

Croydon High School

Linked school: Croydon High Junior School

Old Farleigh Road, South Croydon, CR2 8YB

- Pupils: 375 girls, all day • Ages: 11–18 • Non–denom
- Fees: £13,899 pa • Independent

Tel: 020 8260 7500
Email: admissions@cry.gdst.net
Website: www.croydonhigh.gdst

Head: Since May 2010, Mrs Deborah Leonard MEd, BEd (forties). Deputy head of Nottingham GHS, arrived towards the end of the academic year as acting head for the following year after only brief tenure of predecessor. Previously deputy head of Thetford Grammar and head of PE and school development at King Edward's Birmingham. Her master's is in management and learning and she is passionate about girls' education. A very keen sportswoman, she has been a national league hockey coach and plays golf. She grew up in the Lake District and enjoys climbing and walking.

Academic matters: GCSE results excellent – 67 per cent A/A* grades, the rest mostly Bs. Good all-round education with a strong performance from the science, maths, English and modern foreign languages depts. French, German, Spanish and Latin offered; talented linguists can take up to three options at GCSE, putting linguists on a par with the scientists. Newly-decorated, bright, clean science and language labs, with recently updated resources. Parents report very solid teaching in maths; quite a few go on to take maths and further maths at A level. A tracking and monitoring system recently introduced to help move towards more individualised learning, the aim being to ensure everyone meets their potential. Year 9 girls encouraged to try out subjects and choose a balanced mixture of GCSEs before making A level choices – always guided towards their strengths.

Subject choices at A level now expanded; in 2013, 55 per cent A*/A and 83 per cent A*/B grades. Sixth formers link with Whitgift and benefit from a good range of sporting, artistic and

C

practical enrichment activities. Accessible careers centre which maintains links with outside agencies; girls also encouraged to get involved in voluntary work, help run school clubs and undertake some supervisory roles with younger children.

ICT centre and library stay open until 5 pm, library is run by a much-appreciated and knowledgeable librarian, who facilitates book groups and a number of other literary related activities. Pupils volunteer to assist in the library, designing information posters and leaflets. Girls say library comfortable to work in, with desks overlooking attractive grounds, a popular place to be – good stock of books, audios, periodicals and DVDs.

A few wobbles recently on the staff front but we hope now settled down. Reasonable mix of long-serving and new, younger staff. Part-time SENCo organises some additional support provision which includes screening and study skills for all age groups.

Games, options, the arts: Something for everyone – energetic sporting calendar: hockey, netball, tennis, cross-country, rounders and gymnastics. School has won the netball national finals 14 times in the last three decades and is successful in many other national events. Large sports centre, which doubles as a private club, houses gym, sports hall, dance studios and pool, where the highly successful swimming teams train. Recreational sports include badminton, self-defence, table tennis, aerobics and salsa. D of E award scheme thrives, also regular field trips as well as adventure holidays, music tours and skiing. Year 7 go to an activity centre in Devon for a week of outdoor activities.

Traditionally strong music, say parents – instrumental tuition available on most instruments including tuba and harpsichord. Wonderful choirs, orchestras and bands in-house and Fairfield Hall concerts are always a sell out, musicians are involved at local and national levels. Own annual chamber music composition competition judged by an external adjudicator. Music and drama departments work together to produce spectacular musicals each year. Surprisingly few choose to take music GCSE or A level, a shame for such an innovative group of musicians. Art teachers continue the open-door policy so pupils can use facilities – which include pottery studio and dark room – outside timetable classes.

Girls also get out and about and take part in national and local competitions; enthusiastic debating groups and year 7 made it into the finals of a recent national spelling bee.

Background and atmosphere: Founded in 1874, the school moved in 1966 to its present purpose-built site, which accommodates the junior and senior schools. The buildings, which are rather utilitarian from the outside, provide excellent well-proportioned rooms. Spacious landscaped grounds supply superb sporting and recreational space for both juniors and seniors. A few well-loved school pets enjoy the grounds too. Comfortable atmosphere pervades, possibly influenced by the many links encouraged between older and younger girls. All appears to be quiet and purposeful.

Pastoral care and discipline: School code of conduct is included in pupils' yearly planners; school rules are mostly common sense or based on health and safety requirements. Sixth formers train as peer listeners to befriend younger pupils. No outside counsellor, however referrals can be made through the school nurse. All girls are encouraged to look out for each other and respect each other as individuals. Teachers are available to pupils on a drop-in basis first thing in the morning..

Pupils and parents: From around 70 feeder independent and state primaries. Catchment area stretches from south London to rural Surrey, although the majority lives within a five-mile radius of the school. Pupils come from a range of backgrounds, mostly professional; proportionate racial mix with around a dozen different nationalities attending. Link with Shenzhen in China, so a small number of Chinese students are able to live locally to attend the sixth form. PTA runs fundraising events and sixth form fashion show often raises around £4000 for charity.

Alumnae: Jacqueline du Pré, Helen Chadwick, Elizabeth Laird, Jean Ure, Jane Warr, Marilyn Cutts, Rabbi Helen Freeman etc etc.

Entrance: At 11+ annual entrance test in November and informal interview with the head or deputy. All those offered places attend a special induction day during the summer term before entry. At 16+, interview, report from the previous school and seven GCSEs, B grade for subjects to be studied at A level, A grade for mathematics, chemistry, physics and modern languages.

Exit: Around 30 per cent leave at 16+, mostly for co-ed schools or state sixth form centres and colleges. Great majority to university, a handful a year to Oxbridge (four in 2013); Nottingham, Durham and Manchester popular, otherwise anywhere from London to Edinburgh. Combined degrees becoming particularly popular, eg engineering or law with a modern language.

Money matters: Standard GDST scholarships and bursaries are available. Music, art, drama and sports scholarships for year 7 entrants. Jacqueline du Pré music scholarship and sixth form scholarships.

Remarks: Consistently good results across the board. Pupils appear highly-motivated and accomplished, but maybe too rigorous a place for a more sensitive soul.

Culford School

Linked school: Culford Preparatory School and Pre-Prep

Culford, Bury St Edmunds, Suffolk, IP28 6TX

• Pupils: 670 girls and boys; 200 board in senior school • Ages: 13–18 • Methodist foundation • Fees: Day £16,995; Boarding £25,500–£27,255 pa • Independent

Tel: 01284 385308
Email: admissions@culford.co.uk
Website: www.culford.co.uk

Headmaster: Since 2004, Mr Julian Johnson-Munday (late forties). Educated at Norwich School and Leicester University, where he read English. Previously housemaster at Cranleigh and deputy head of Mill Hill (during his tenure he studied for an MBA at Durham). Unpompous, affable manner but makes no bones about the clear direction of the school and the setting of targets for staff and pupils. Is intent on raising the school's profile and has overseen a busy programme of building. Seeks to maintain and support the school's boarding provision (currently over 50 per cent) and is not enamoured with flexi boarding options, as he believes they could compromise a vital spark of the school. His wife, Jo, is the school's marketing and foundation director and they have one son.

Academic matters: Strong performance at GCSE (41 per cent A*/A grades in 2013) and A level (24 per cent A*/A, 54 per cent A*/B) – impressive considering school is not ultra-selective. Head remains calm about occasional downward 'blips' in results, saying with disarming frankness that 'year groups do vary in ability'. Average class size is 17 (seven in sixth form) with setting in the core subjects of mathematics, English, sciences and languages. All pupils study at least one modern language (French, German and Spanish on offer) with Latin available as a GCSE option too. In mathematics, high ability pupils take IGCSE in year 10 (all gain A*/A) and additional maths in year 11. Science is very strong and has superb facilities; roughly half do separate sciences at GCSE. Learning support has its own department and is well resourced.

Pupil support across the curriculum is arranged either on a withdrawal basis or outside the timetabled day. A popular programme of seminars and tutorials with high level speakers for the gifted and talented and potential Oxbridge punters.

The school day includes eight periods (four on Saturday), plus after school activities. Day pupils don't leave until 5.30pm.

Games, options, the arts: Outstanding sports provision includes a 25 metre indoor pool, floodlit Astroturf, games pitches galore, fitness suite and squash courts. The indoor tennis school attracts students from all over with its elite training programme run by professional coaches. Similar regimes are now available for rugby, hockey and swimming. Many pupils train for and take part in athletics events at county and national level and the whole school does two 80 minute periods of sport each week.

New theatre and dance studio are well used, with two major productions each year (some taken to the Edinburgh fringe) and plenty of choirs, orchestras and ensembles. Large numbers take instrumental or singing lessons and a pupil recently won a choral scholarship to St John's College, Oxford. Art and design are strong subjects in the school with good results at GCSE and A level. Plans are afoot to improve the present facilities.

Background and atmosphere: Sublime setting in 480 acres of landscaped parkland, complete with Grade I listed bridge and gardens designed by Humphrey Repton. The main building, originally owned variously by the Cadogan and Cornwallis families, is 18th century. The school moved to its present site in 1935 and has maintained the original fabric to a high standard and made full use of its assets. Lord Cadogan's morning room is the head's study – complete with distracting vistas of the park. The grand visitors' lavatory installed for a visit by Edward VII is still in situ, together with a photograph of the royal visitor. In the grounds, a series of newer and, for the most part, well designed buildings house classrooms, science laboratories, sports and boarding facilities. High standards of maintenance throughout are helped by generous bequests from old pupils – a notable feature.

Unhurried, almost relaxed air about the school. Excellent staff/ pupil relationships, plenty of banter, easy but respectful. Headmaster greets pupils by name. Girls' uniform, featuring an ankle length pleated skirt, could be a turn-off for some, though we were told by pupils that it is 'comfortable and cool in summer'. Parents describe the school as a 'hidden gem.'

Pastoral care and discipline: One of the school's great strengths, and the one most frequently mentioned by parents, is the care of pupils. Tutors and house staff deal with everyday matters but the headmaster keeps himself very well informed and can be the key figure at a moment of crisis. 'My son was confused about his future,' one father told us. 'The headmaster took him out for a walk with the dog and that seemed to sort everything out.' Emphasis is on consideration for others – kindness and politeness towards staff as well as to other pupils, and few discipline problems.

Pupils and parents: Majority of pupils are drawn from professional and business families from within a radius of 50 miles. They include a fair sprinkling looking for a different pace from that offered by some of the other local schools. About 20 per cent of boarders are Forces children and just over 10 per cent from overseas, including a cohort of 10 from Germany, who attend for a year. Families are tremendously loyal and many pupils are the children of Old Culfordians.

Entrance: At 13, admission is by examination, school report and interview. Around three-quarters join year 9 straight from Culford Prep, with the remainder coming from local state and prep schools. The school report and interview are as important as the exam result – the head knows what he is looking for. Sixth form entrants need seven good GCSEs, with at least Bs in the subjects to be studied at A level.

Exit: Almost all go on to university, with good numbers to Russell Group institutions, and Oxbridge increasingly on the radar (one entrant in 2013).

Money matters: A complex web of scholarships and exhibitions available at main entry points (normally worth between 10 and 20 per cent of the fees). Academic, music, art and sports awards are on offer, together with bursaries for the financially hard-pressed. Reductions for Forces children and siblings. Overseas pupils charged at a slightly higher rate.

Remarks: A thriving, happy school with excellent foundations and confident leadership. It deserves to be better known than it is.

Dame Alice Owen's School

Dugdale Hill Lane, Potters Bar, Hetfordshire, EN6 2DU

• Pupils: 1,450 boys and girls • Ages: 11–18 • Non-denom • State

Tel: 01707 643441
Email: admin@damealiceowens.herts.sch.uk
Website: www.damealiceowens.herts.sch.uk

Headteacher: Since 2005, Dr Alan Davison (fifties). Read theology at Durham and gained his master's and doctorate in education leadership at Leicester University. Started his teaching career in Brent, became head of Notley High School in Braintree and then of Mill Hill County High School in Barnet. Spent two years working for London Challenge, developing the leadership strategy across the capital's schools. Always planned to return to headship though and was delighted to be appointed as head at Dame Alice Owen's. 'I am a firm believer in system leadership,' he says, 'but I very much missed the day-to-day work in schools.'

A vastly experienced head, he sees academic excellence as the key to his school's success. Rather than making sweeping changes at Dame Alice Owen's, he was clear from the outset that continuity was a real strength of the school and set out 'to build on the excellent work of my predecessors over the last 400 years.' Staff and parents reckon he's done just that. 'He's a head who gets things done,' a father told us. On the morning of our visit the school was full of year 6 visitors and their parents. The head whizzed around like a whirlwind, answering questions about everything from the length of lessons (an hour) to the number of applicants per place (more than six for each one). Places are so sought after that the first thing he says to new pupils every September is 'well done. You made it.'

School never advertises or parades its achievements. It doesn't have to. As head says, 'We are happy with what we are doing and people hear about us by word of mouth.' Asked the secret of the school's success he told us: 'It's about hard work, enjoyment and achievement. We expect all the students to do well. Everything is possible – that's the way we approach it.'

Focused and energetic, he cycles to school every morning ('it's only four miles,' he says) and stops year 7s in their tracks when he abseils down a zip wire during their three-day PGL trip every September. He still teaches three periods a week (mainly maths, DT and IT) and reckons it's key to staying in touch with what's going on in teaching and learning. 'Heads can become very remote,' he says. 'It's lovely to get back in the classroom.' His wife is a professor at UCL and they have four grown up children, one of whom is a maths teacher. Outside school he enjoys the theatre, skiing and football. Originally from Whitley Bay, he's a keen Newcastle United fan.

Academic matters: Dame Alice Owen's has high expectations of its pupils – and they rise to the challenge. Almost 40 per cent of youngsters are selected by academic ability or musical talent and results and facilities are more than a match for local independent schools. In 2013 more than 64 per cent A*/A grades at A level, and more than 88 per cent A*/B grades. Eight-three students achieved straight A*/As, while 18 got three or more A*s. Wide range of academic A levels, with maths the most popular, followed by chemistry. Some students choose to do the EPQ too.

At GCSE more than 65 per cent A*/A grades in 2013. School specialises in science, music and languages and pupils either take triple science or core and additional science. All take a language from year 7, then add a second in year 8. Most do two languages at GCSE. French, German and Spanish on offer and for keen linguists Italian, Mandarin, Japanese, Russian and Latin can be arranged too. Regular trips abroad, including staying with host families in year 9 and study trips in year 12.

Parents say their children are encouraged academically and given lots of homework, though there's plenty of help and support in place. Most recent Ofsted report commented that staff were 'willing to go that extra mile' and it seemed that way to us. Sixth formers, for instance, were full of praise for the support they get with UCAS forms. Each student is assigned a UCAS tutor and they meet at least once a week to discuss university applications. Philosophy teacher is pioneer of revision methods and several pupils said they'd been encouraged to learn what worked for them individually – everything from mind maps to spiral learning. Very few behaviour issues, say the teachers. 'The children are very motivated and focused,' said one. 'You can really teach your subject here. You don't have to dwell on managing behaviour.'

Maximum class sizes in years 7 to 11 are 32, with seven or eight groups per year. In years 7 and 8, mainly mixed ability, apart from maths. From year 9 English and languages are set. In the sixth form, class sizes range between 12 and 20. Approximately 100 pupils on the SEN register – learning support team works alongside them in lessons. Sixth formers encouraged to offer additional support once a week too.

Games, options, the arts: A very sporty school, with a huge expanse of games pitches, large sports hall and floodlit Astroturf. Boys play football (the year 9 team won the national final a few years back), rugby, hockey, cricket, athletics, gym, badminton and basketball while girls do football, netball, hockey, badminton, athletics, tennis, rounders and cricket. School produces lots of talented cross-country runners – perhaps not surprising with 35 acres of grounds to run around in. County and national representatives in many sports.

Superlative music. The school marked its 400th anniversary in 2013 by hosting a sell-out concert at the Royal Albert Hall. There was also a service of thanksgiving at St Paul's Cathedral – 'the whole school got the train and we walked from Moorgate to St Paul's,' said a sixth form girl. 'I don't think I'll ever forget it.' Approximately 400 pupils learn an instrument and there's all manner of orchestras and groups to join, from flute ensembles and chamber choirs to jazz quartets and soul bands. School boasts a host of grade 8 musicians and several play in the National Youth Orchestra.

Art is popular, with about 80 pupils a year taking it at GCSE, 25 at AS and 15 at A2. Four large studios filled with easels, tables and work filling every inch of the walls. Regular drama productions, including lower school play for years 7 to 9 and upper school production for years 10 to 13, all performed in fabulous Edward Guinness Hall. Plenty of other extra-curricular activities to choose from – 147 at the last count, so something for everyone, including D of E and World Challenge. In 2012 a dynamic group of budding engineers designed, constructed

and raced their own miniature Formula One car and went on to win the national F1 in Schools competition. They topped that by becoming runners up in the world finals in Abu Dhabi. Lots of photographs of their triumphs on display.

Background and atmosphere: School was founded in 1613 by Dame Alice Owen. Born Alice Wilkes, she narrowly missed being struck by a wayward arrow when she was young and vowed that as soon as she was rich enough she would do something for posterity as a mark of gratitude. Fifty years on and thrice widowed, she used her wealth to establish a school for 30 boy scholars from Islington. She entrusted its running to the Worshipful Company of Brewers, which for the last four centuries has supported and encouraged the school.

A girls' school was added in 1886 and in the late sixties, a search was made for a new location. The school moved to its present site on the edge of Potters Bar in 1973. To this day Dame Alice Owen's takes immense pride in its history. All year 7s receive a crown (now a £5 commemorative coin) at a ceremony at the Brewers Hall in the City of London. Older pupils receive annual 'beer money' till they leave (£1 for year 8s, rising to £6 for year 13s). Dame Alice originally instructed the governors to visit the school annually to inspect the pupils' progress and this still forms part of the annual open day and prize giving. In the early days the scholars collected flowers to make buttonholes; today pupils in years 7 to 11 wear white carnations while sixth formers sport red carnations.

School is modern and purpose-built, surrounded by woods, fields and a lake. Lots of new buildings in recent years, including the concert hall, maths, art and DT centre and cricket pavilion. When we visited new science building well underway. Atmosphere everywhere is purposeful, busy and friendly. Effective school council (which has its own Twitter account) has achieved a myriad of changes, from more water fountains to a café where older pupils can buy sandwiches and paninis (a sort of mini Subway). Food gets the thumbs-up – hot food, vegetarian options, salad bar, jacket potatoes, sandwiches and chips served once a week. Pupils pay via fingerprint scanners and can sit where they like in a large, airy dining room which boasts a life size model of Dame Alice Owen (sculpted by Sir George Frampton, best known for his statue of Peter Pan in Kensington Gardens) in one corner.

Pastoral care and discipline: Pupils say they feel at ease and able to be themselves. They see their form tutors for 20 minutes every morning, with sessions ranging from checking homework diaries to discussing risk-taking, the use of the internet and bullying ('not a massive issue here.') Tutors hold regular progress reviews with their tutees. Reports sent home twice a year plus parents' consultation evening once a year. If pupils have done particularly well at something a 'well done' postcard is sent home.

Fairly nondescript black and grey uniform though girls get to wear jaunty red jumpers. School rules stipulate 'no jewellery, piercings or ornamentation of any kind' and we didn't spot any. Sixth formers, clad in smart office wear, are enthusiastic about their outfits. 'The novelty of wearing a suit hasn't worn off yet,' grinned a year 12 boy in a stylish floral tie.

School gives sixth formers a greater degree of independence, with five study periods a week for year 12s and ten for year 13s. 'We're encouraged not to waste them,' said a sixth form boy. 'Actually, it's nice to be in an environment where people work hard. There is a real work ethos here.' Sixth formers have their own sixth form centre, with common room, kitchen and SALC (student access learning centre). Head boy, head girl and four deputies meet the head every week and there's a raft of school and form prefects.

Pupils and parents: Pupils travel from far and wide – not just from Potters Bar but also from Enfield, Barnet, Hatfield, South Mimms and Islington. The youngsters we met seemed industrious, grounded and as keen as mustard. One boy told us: 'When you look forward to coming to school you know it's good.' Another remarked: 'It's a very positive atmosphere. The teachers are very enthusiastic about their subjects they are teaching and you can't help but fit into that pattern. Everyone works hard and feels very proud to be here.' Lots of distinguished former pupils, including Gary Kemp (and three other members of Spandau Ballet), Madness guitarist Chris Foreman, Sir Alan Parker, Dame Beryl Grey and Joss Ackland. A framed letter from Gary Kemp on the wall in reception declares he's 'proud to be an Old Owenian.' Spandau Ballet gave their first performance in the school hall and a commemorative plaque is planned.

Parents are an eclectic mix – media types and factory workers to company directors and teachers. They are hugely supportive (hosting fundraising events, quiz nights and a summer ball) and all keen on the idea of an academic, non-exclusive school.

Entrance: Unusual admission rules. School is semi-selective and vastly oversubscribed – around 1,300 children compete for 200 places each year. Special needs and looked after children take priority, then 22 who live closest to the school and siblings of pupils already at Dame Alice Owen's. Ten places for musical aptitude, 65 awarded on academic ability (tests in English, maths and verbal reasoning), 20 places for children living in or attending school in Islington, then staff children and other children nearest to the school. Children taking the entrance exam and music tests must live in one of the school's designated local priority areas.

Around 500 compete for around 30 additional places in the sixth form. Applicants come from local state and independent schools and need in the region of six A*s at GCSE. Slightly more girls than boys in sixth form.

Exit: Around five per cent leave after GCSEs. After A levels virtually all to higher education. Eighty per cent to Russell Group universities and 27 to Oxbridge in 2013. Lots to UCL, Imperial, Bristol and Durham. All manner of subjects – from medicine and engineering (43 per cent go on to study science) to economics and politics. 'Our students are eclectic in their interests,' says the head.

Money matters: Funded by government as an academy but also gets money from the Dame Alice Owen Foundation (The Worshipful Company of Brewers is the trustee), fundraising events and donations.

Remarks: 'Positive, energetic and progressive' – that's how one of the teachers summed up Dame Alice Owen's and we agree. This is a gem of a school, where teachers can teach, pupils work hard and parental support really makes a difference.

Dame Allan's Senior Schools

Linked school: Dame Allan's Junior School and Nursery Linked school: Dame Allan's Girls' School

Fowberry Crescent, Fenham, Newcastle upon Tyne, NE4 9YJ

• Pupils: 665; 400 boys/265 girls • Ages: 11–18 • Christian foundation • Fees: £10,782 pa • Independent

Tel: 01912 750608
Email: enquiries@dameallans.co.uk
Website: www.dameallans.co.uk

Principal: Since 2004, Dr John Hind (early fifties), PGCE MA (history) from Downing College, Cambridge, MEd (Newcastle), PhD (history) Durham. Previously deputy head of Kingston Grammar and before that at Durham and Exeter. Approachable,

speaks enthusiastically of 'our family of schools' and believes in instilling a 'can do' mindset rather than creating an academic hothouse. Approaches each pupil with 'Let's work together and see where we can get to'. Parents commented that 'he runs a tight ship' and whilst 'a little distant', both parents and pupils have 'warmed to him over time'.

Has made considered, evolutionary changes to remove segregation between the boys' and girls' schools, while retaining their separate identities – most recent, a management restructure to shed traditional boy/girl school delineation. Now has two vice-principals, Alan Hopper for academic and Janet Middlebrook for pastoral, with teams from both schools reporting to them.

Married to Ginny, a dentist, with a family of two daughters. Outside school, a keen campanologist and member of the conseil d'administration of the Relais de la Mémoire, an international organisation founded to keep alive WWII memories in order to promote reconciliation and understanding in Europe and beyond.

Academic matters: Pupils split into single sex schools from age 11 to 16 (co-ed for most extracurricular activities other than sport) before returning to co-ed sixth form, though all are housed in the same buildings. Benefit of single sex teaching adapted to the recognised differences in learning styles of boys and girls, though teachers shared across schools (adaptability tested on recruitment). Subjects are zoned in different parts of the building so integration is inevitable and allowed.

Good subject choice at GCSE with dual award or single sciences, dance and drama; nine subjects as standard. In 2013, girls 62 per cent and boys 50 per cent A*/A grades at GCSE. At A level, choice of 30 subject with enrichment programme, including TEFL and sign language courses. In 2013, combined sixth formers got 46 per cent A*/A grades. Personal tutors for sixth form; younger pupils spoke of 'approachable teachers who run out-of-class surgeries and help with time management problems'. Individual learning needs and abilities are identified; reporting system of attainment and effort valued by parents, though some felt could be more 'push and stretch' for the most academically able.

Learning support mainly takes places out of lessons, ideally outside normal curriculum. Currently a charge is levied.

IT is good and investment in infrastructure currently being considered – to BYOD or not to BYOD (bring your own device). Pupils from year 10 told us they found single-sex teaching 'took off pressure in the classroom', but 'plenty of opportunity to get to know each other before sixth form through joint activities, like educational visits and Duke of Edinburgh'.

Games, options, the arts: A wealth of opportunities abound. Excels in music with diversity from chamber choir to ceilidh band and just about everything in between. Pupils perform with National Youth Choir and achieve success in national competitions.

Dance is 'right here, right now', as demonstrated in aptly named annual show and impressive, purpose-built dance studio. Not only success for pupils as Youth Dance England finalists, but takeup even extends to the first XV, as part of their training programme. Lots of performance opportunities, from informal lunchtime recitals and studio performances to major school productions; from pupils performing at the Edinburgh Fringe to the choir members singing with the Bach Choir at Newcastle University.

Sport is valued as much for its inclusivity (everyone gets chance to represent school) as its excellence. For half a century boys have represented their county at rugby, but recent success in squash (girls' success in National Schools competition), swimming (girls recent National Schools champions) and cross-country (representing Northumberland in English Schools competition). Range of sports on offer is dazzling, with weightlifting, archery, tennis, running, taekwondo and netball having all produced internationals. Sport transports away from muddy fields of Tyneside to tours in, for example, South Africa and Italy (rugby), Barbados (cricket), Canada (hockey and netball).

Outdoor and leadership education feature strongly, providing increasing challenge for younger pupils and leadership roles as they move up the school. Duke of Edinburgh silver and gold are available from year 10 upwards.

Real adventure is further offered by World Challenge participation – has seen pupils go to Uganda, Kenya, Bolivia, Mongolia, China and the Indian Himalayas. Exchanges flourish to France, Germany etc and in Relais de la Mémoire – joint initiative with French, German and Polish schools to nurture continued learning about and respect for victims of war and holocaust.

Lots of lunchtime and after school activities including the more unusual – clog dancing, eco panel, electronics and fencing. Challenge and success in business-related competition – recent finalists in Bank of England's Target 2.0 and winner of RES Young Economist of the Year. Parents speak of 'individualised opportunities' for each of their children, resulting in 'confident and capable' young adults.

Background and atmosphere: Founded in 1705; girls' school believed to be one of the oldest independent girls' schools in the country. Founded by Dame Eleanor Allan, daughter of a city goldsmith and widow of a wealthy tobacco merchant, to provide a 'proper' education for 40 poor boys and 20 poor girls. Keeps that ethic but has shaken off the pre-1980s segregation of girls at one side, boys at the other.

Current buildings date from mid 1930s, cushioned on all sides by surburban housing and fronted by a green playing field, a snug oasis amidst the mid-war semis. An airy, modern entrance leads to functional ground floor corridors, made interesting by the display areas on the walls. Well resourced and accommodated art, dance, music and sport; library refurbished in recent years to include areas for careers clinics, science and sixth form study. Good sixth form common room and study accommodation, separate enough for independence – with well-placed sixth form staff teaching and office space to allow discreet observation. Lower down school space is at a premium and one girl told us, 'The dream would be a common room for each year'.

Strong sense of community and family – pupils at ease in a friendly atmosphere. Cherishes church links – historically the cathedral school, and retains links with St Nicholas' Cathedral and Church of SS James and Basil. Places community, charity/fundraising work on a par with academic and sporting achievement.

Separate houses in boys' and girls' schools, though move afoot to 'pair' houses in each school – currently used almost exclusively for sporting competition. Dr Hind feels both schools 'still need a separate identity'.

Pastoral care and discipline: Form teachers/tutors perform pastoral role in both schools. Trained counsellor to listen to any particular problems, with confidential referrals from school nurse. An effective pupil counselling system called Link, where sixth formers provide a listening ear and guiding hand. Flexible merit system keeps pupils on course. Typically a demerit is a warning sign, two prompts letter home and three invokes detention. Pupils report zero-tolerance of bullying and drugs.

Parents and pupils find any problems dealt with promptly, fairly and effectively. An inclusive school that doesn't give up easily on pupils with behavioural problems.

Pupils and parents: Wide social mix – 'money matters' to many parents working hard to afford fees. Catchment is Newcastle and hinterland (Tyne Valley, coast, Durham area, plus wider north east). Pupils mainly from Dame Allan's Junior School (good transition programme for year 6), state primary and middle schools, Newcastle Preparatory School and Choristers

Durham. Most have English as first language, though several speak another language at home.

Old boys/girls include Sir David Lumsden, Ian La Frenais, Elizabeth Fallaize (pro-vice-chancellor of Oxford University) and more recently Ellie Crissell (TV presenter and journalist).

Entrance: Entry is at 11 to senior schools by January assessment in English, maths and verbal reasoning, followed by an interview. Sixth form entry conditional on GCSE results and at least a A, for external candidates, to study a subject at AS level.

Exit: Some 80 per cent stay on for co-ed sixth form. Nearly all go on to university – two to Oxford in 2013; rest to mostly northern unis eg Newcastle, Leeds, Edinburgh, Durham, Manchester, York.

Money matters: Scholarships of up to 50 per cent of fees awarded on entrance examination results. Participating school in Ogden Trust science scholarship scheme. Music scholarships also available. Means-tested bursaries awarded up to 100 per cent of fees if needed. Though not a rich school, eight per cent of pupils currently receive bursaries.

Remarks: A diamond in shape and in character, pupils encouraged to and do take full advantage of many opportunities to learn, travel and develop. No flashy jewels here, pleasant but functional buildings nestled amongst residential housing. Stiff local competition, particularly for girls – Dame Allan's tries harder. Community and family values ingrained and the individual pupils nurtured.

Dane Court Grammar School

Broadstairs Road, Broadstairs, Kent, CT10 2RT

- Pupils: 1,200 boys and girls, all day • Ages: 11–18 • Non-denom
- State

Tel: 01843 864941
Email: admin@danecourt.kent.sch.uk
Website: www.danecourt.kent.sch.uk

Head of School: Since 2012, Miss Maureen Wolloshin (late forties). Joined from the independent Ipswich High School for Girls, where she was deputy head. Before that she was lead advanced skills teacher at Langley Park and Crown Woods schools in south London.

Grew up in Leeds with an ambition to be a baroque chamber musician. Studied at Leeds College of Music and Trinity College of Music in London, then became a professional oboist, playing for the English National Opera North. But a stint playing six nights and two matinees per week in My Fair Lady sounded the death knell for a career in music, and she became an education co-ordinator and music therapist at the Maudsley and Bethlem psychiatric hospital, before moving into teaching.

She now plays the ukulele, and downtime finds her enjoying the rich folk music scene in the pubs of Broadstairs. Home is a one mile cycle ride from school, where she has fulfilled a dream to live with a view over the sea.

Parenting two daughters, now grown up, taught her that 'firm kindness is better than firm discipline' she says. It also gave her 'common sense and perspective'. Perhaps this is best demonstrated by her refusal to sweat the small stuff. She takes a relaxed approach to minor uniform infringements, and isn't worried if students are logging onto Facebook on their own devices during breaks. 'They have to go through the school account, and I have never had fewer problems with cyber bullying than here because it is monitored,' she says.

Wolloshin is responsible for day-to-day running of the school, while Mr Paul Luxmoore oversees this school and King Ethelbert as Executive Headteacher. The Dane Court and King Ethelbert Trust sponsors Cliftonville Primary and Ellington and Hereson schools.

Academic matters: The school converted entirely to the IB in September 2012, 'because A levels have proved not fit for purpose, and students with an IB are more likely to gain a place at the best universities', Wolloshin says. Students can choose between the more academically focused diploma or the careers certificate, which is a vocational version and offers courses such as applied business, sports science, and health and social care, alongside the core subjects.

It's an intense programme but Wolloshin says: 'Busier students get better grades. They will only have two to three free study periods per week, but once they get into the rhythm of working at that pace they really enjoy it.'

Not all parents are happy about this change. One comments: 'It feels as though the sixth form has suddenly gone comprehensive, offering vocational courses as well and I feel our children are ill prepared for the IB through our style of education which is not European style. They have been narrowing their studies and heading towards specialisation since year 9.'

English, science and maths departments are strong, and sixth formers rate the history and politics departments. Parents say languages are an area of concern, and Wolloshin agrees, calling that a 'fledgling' department. A newly appointed languages head and staff are charged with turning the department around. French, German, Spanish, Italian and Japanese are on offer.

The school is an academy and a designated teaching school, and Wolloshin maintains that its teaching standards are extremely high. 'I've always thought that in any school there will be one-third of staff who need intervention. Here there are just a couple who let the side down and need support', she says. There's strict internal scrutiny on the quality of teaching, with staff involved in peer observation and improving lesson standards.

Results 'reflect the community' Wolloshin says. She points out that in the Thanet area, there are around 40 more grammar places than children reaching the required standard each year. 'You would expect to see 100 per cent A* to C at GCSE in a grammar, but that is almost impossible to achieve in our community,' she says. 'The current year 11 didn't all pass the Kent test. This year will be the first time that every pupil in year 7 passed the test.'

Given that context, the school delivers well – 2013 results show 94 per cent of pupils achieving 5+ A* to Cs at GCSE (including English and maths), with 42 per cent of GCSEs at A* or A. Sixth formers take their studies seriously – 'You're expected to work hard here', they say – and a couple make it to Oxbridge each year. In 2013, 27 per cent of A levels were graded A*/A, with 51 per cent at A* to B. Those taking the IB achieved average points score of 34.

Games, options, the arts: Arts are a real strength, reflecting a community where many musicians and artists make their home. There is exceptional art on display, and photographs outside the theatre show professionally costumed and staged productions of Grease, Annie, and Midsummer Night's dream.

Broadstairs has a big reputation for folk music, hosting an annual festival and performances in its pubs every night. There are a lot of musicians among the parent body which in turn encourages the children – lessons on a wide range of instruments are provided, and as we pass the peripatetic music rooms Wolloshin points out, 'The equipment is well respected, the doors aren't locked'.

Overseas tours include a 10 day trip to teach in Namibia for the sixth form, a pastoral trip to Bonn for year 8s, skiing, and departmental trips to Valencia, Iceland, Ypres, Paris, and New York.

Sporting teams do the school proud – both girls' and boys' football teams regularly reach the Kent Cup final. Girls came ninth in the country at the National Rugby finals at Twickenham, and the school table tennis team are national champions. Those who aren't selected to play for the school have an opportunity to compete in house sporting events. Those who aren't enticed by team games can take part in extracurricular sports such as rowing, rock climbing, orienteering and mountain biking.

Parental reports on sports provision are all good, and one mother of two pupils comments: 'The sports department is outstanding; it has been really good both for my child who isn't good at sport and the one who excels at it, they've both been encouraged and it has built their confidence.'

Background and atmosphere: One of the lucky few to see renovation under the Building Schools for the Future programme, before it was scrapped by the coalition. A £20 million rebuild and refurbishment completed in 2011 has created a spacious and natural light-filled campus, which appears at once industrious and serene. It's the kind of building you walk into as a parent and immediately cross your fingers and hope everything else is right.

The aim of the programme was to create inspirational buildings to make pupils feel valued and worthwhile – and in this case it works. Walking into the central atrium, it looks more like the offices of a prosperous technology company, and it's not hard to see how this motivates children more than the grimly oppressive Victorian architecture of many schools.

At break time we saw students milling around the big central space are queuing at the coffee bar, sitting in comfortable chairs chatting in groups, looking over their notes prior to exams. There's no regimentation, and they look more like university students. 'They are being informally supervised,' says Wolloshin, 'the senior staff offices overlook this area'.

There are six open plazas, each hosting a house base. Each plaza or hub is also a curriculum area base, and has labs or classrooms leading off from a large central study space. The plazas are open at break for their house to eat lunch in, play games, or do homework.

The sixth form has a distinct area in each house plaza and in the central atrium, but there's been a deliberate decision to integrate them more with the rest of the school. 'We wanted to move away from having a sixth form common room, away from that clique, now they help with supervision across the school,' says Wolloshin. 'Everyone mingles more now,' agree the students.

One plaza houses a computer room with 80 machines which is open at lunchtime, before and after school for homework or general use.

Pastoral care and discipline: There's no uniform for the sixth form – jeans and shorts are in evidence. Younger pupils are in uniform, but with the hitched up skirts, shirts hanging out, and make-up which drives some heads to apoplexy. Wolloshin refuses to worry about it. 'I try to avoid using uniform as discipline. I'd rather have untidy students who have a good relationship with their teachers. Otherwise it leaves all interaction being about uniform. Our students are not always the neatest, but they're happier for it,' she says.

It's evident that pupils are relaxed around her, there's no shrinking away as she walks down the corridor. She dishes out praise as we walk around the school, and her soft Leeds accent make her interactions sound motherly. 'That's brilliant, you clever girl', Wolloshin tells one pupil carrying an impressive cake she has just produced.

Recently established house system is used to entrench a sense of community, and the first thing pupils see as they walk through the front doors is a screen displaying live house point totals. A house cup and book tokens are awarded to top performers.

Students who cross the line are dealt with by a restorative justice system. 'It's not a punitive approach, we urge people to do the right thing', says Wolloshin. 'We talk to them, and we listen to them'. Lots of the students have had training in peer mentoring and they will meet with the pupil concerned, he or she will also hear from other children what their actions felt like to them. 'We avoid people being told off in public', says Wolloshin. One student who has transferred to the sixth form from another school finds the atmosphere very different. 'Everyone here is a lot nicer, and there's a lot more respect,' she says.

Pastoral care is delivered through a mentoring system that is popular with both students and parents. 'I really like mentoring, it allows us to have time with our form tutor and if you have a problem you can go to them about it,' says one girl. A parent with two children at the school concurs. 'The pastoral care is excellent, they are supported really well,' she says. Another parent wishes more detail was conveyed home, saying: 'I don't feel we get enough information. There were plans for a computer system, where parents would be able to see for example if their child had been late for a lesson, or got a house point, which looked like it was going to be good but it never got off the ground.' School says this system will be introduced in September. But one mother has found staff 'very accommodating' when she has needed to discuss anything, saying: 'It's a real advantage that you can ring up and a teacher will call you back or see you to sort out any problems.'

Pupils and parents: 'The worst thing we have to deal with among pupils is complacency. There's a lack of self-belief that comes from living in this area, a lack of experience of being stretched and challenged', says Wolloshin. The deprivation in the area and scarcity of jobs – 3,500 applied for 180 jobs at Primark – means that students see no future for themselves, and 'we have to do a lot of work on confidence building,' she says. These social problems are compounded by London boroughs buying up cheap housing in the area in which to place their overflow social housing tenants, and clusters of Eastern European immigrants settling in the area 'which causes huge tensions and a lot of resentment. We have to do a lot of work with students on equality and understanding', she says.

Wolloshin describes the parent body as mixed, with some finding themselves in challenging circumstances, but says the vast majority are supportive. In surveys, 98 per cent of parents said it is a good school and they are happy with the education their child is getting. A parent we spoke to commented: 'I work in a junior school and I always recommend it to parents there'. Pupils agree that it's a pleasant environment. 'It's a nice community, everyone is happy and friendly,' says one.

Entrance: There are two grammars in Thanet – this is considered the better one and is oversubscribed. 'There are 70 appeals to hear this year,' Wolloshin says. Students come from more than 30 feeder primaries.

School is currently over planned admission numbers in every year group, so joining mid-way depends on a place coming up. Pupils can join in the sixth form, and need six Bs and two Cs at GCSE to do the IB Diploma, and three Bs and two Cs to do the IB Careers Certificate.

Exit: Around 40 per cent leave after GCSEs. Usually 80-90 per cent of sixth form students go on to university, but Wolloshin says numbers are dropping since the increase in fees. Four are going to Oxbridge this year, as well as some to Russell Group universities, and others to Canterbury which enables them to live at home. 'There's a lot of support to help them make university choices,' says a parent.

Remarks: This would be a great fit for the child who doesn't respond well to authoritarian, old school regimes. Everything about the school, from the building to the head's attitude, speaks of treating the pupils respectfully, on the assumption that they will behave maturely.

Children are not publicly bawled out for misdemeanours, instead they talk through their actions with their peers. Expensive equipment isn't locked away – why should it be, there's no assumption that the kids will damage it. And the physical space looks more like a university, which in turn creates the expectation that this is a place for serious learning.

Dauntsey's School

West Lavington, Devizes, Wiltshire, SN10 4HE

- Pupils: 790 boys and girls; 40 per cent board • Ages: 11–18
- Inter-denom • Fees: Boarding £27,585–£31,260; Day £16,365 pa
- Independent

Tel: 01380 814500
Email: info@dauntseys.org
Website: www.dauntseys.org

Head Master: Since September 2012, Mr Mark Lascelles (mid forties), previously lower master, and temporary acting head of King's School Canterbury – something of a rough ride. He was educated at Shrewsbury School and Durham, where he read geography and was keen and proficient in cricket and football to county level and beyond. Now he only plays social cricket, – frustrating, as he is very competitive. Back at Shrewsbury for a further 17 years, he became a housemaster and coached many of the Shrewsbury teams before joining King's School in 2009. He is married to Amber, a teacher and graduate of Durham, who was a national level canoeist. They have three young daughters.

Mr Lascelles is stunned by 'the quality of pupils' at Dauntsey's, not just their academic level but their genuine niceness and the energy injected by having an intake at 11: something he had 'missed out on before'. He sees Dauntsey's as a collegiate school, for families who understand about good education, and are not blinded by fashionable pretension.

So far both the curriculum and the classrooms are quite traditional (he promised not to make changes during his first year), but the stunningly high level of pupil satisfaction registered in the recent ISI inspection bears witness to the excellence of the teaching. Parents like him and say he is accessible, listens and takes a personal interest in all pupils, meeting the school bus every morning and being a friendly presence at most activities. He had a hard act to follow and is very different to his predecessor, 'but has finally mastered the art of feeding biscuits to paddling canoeists as they pass in the Devizes to Westminster race!' Out of school he enjoys travel, skiing, reading and theatre – and is rapidly developing a taste for musicals, which is just as well as Dauntsey's is about to put on Sondheim's Into the Woods followed by Mamma Mia.

Academic matters: Over the last few years Dauntsey's has come up quite a few pegs in the academic stakes and has a pretty impressive record for a 'not overly selective' school – though of course success breeds demand which ups the ante. In 2013, 50 per cent A*/A grades at A level and 76 per cent at GCSE – mostly IGCSEs which, pupils say, 'prepare better for A level'. Big Cheeses of the school world locally should look to their laurels or Dauntsey's might pip them at the post. Curriculum includes a four language carousel of French, German, Latin, and Spanish for the first year from which two or three languages may be chosen. Other languages – Mandarin, Russian, Japanese, Greek, Arabic etc – are done in extracurricular time. Native speakers are encouraged to take exams in their own languages.

Three science IGCEs for two-thirds of the year group; the rest do dual award science (three sciences taken as two GCSEs). Spanking new science labs full of GCSE groups practising practicals. A spectacular full size skeleton monoplane hangs in the hallway and the charming courtyard with super bosky pond has raised beds crammed with Japanese anemones.

No limits on choices at A Level. DT (resistant materials), in a whizzy new class room, with new courses in psychology, history of art and English language starting. Outstanding in maths and further maths and more than sound across a very wide board including theatre studies, music technology and class civ as well as the mainstream stuff.

Class size around 16 in GCSE years. Busy SEN department with three full-time staff, providing help, within the timetable but at extra cost. Mainly helps mild dyslexia and offers a safety net for the organisationally challenged but, 'If pupils pass the entrance exam,' says the head, 'it is rare for us to say we can't cope with their special needs'. Impressively wheelchair friendly (even disabled wet-room showers!) for a school with no current need for it. Thirty or so need and get EFL tuition, which is thrown in as part of the special enhanced international fees. Efficient IT taken for granted, having virtually reached IT saturation point, though pupils are pretty impressed that free standing printers at convenient points access and print from their personal files activated by thumbprint. Pupils register by thumbprint too for afternoon school, but house staff like to lay eyes on everyone in the morning.

Games, options, the arts: Sport is definitely big and timetabled three times a week. Boys' and girls' hockey, rugby and cricket doing pretty well at county and regional level. Football played in senior years, tennis, for all, and netball, for girls, all tackled competitively. A smart-looking rugby pavilion graces the grassy expanse in front of the main school and new sports pavilion is planned, which is nice for the girls.

Girls regularly send a hockey team to South Africa to match the triennial rugby tour of the Australia, and there is no shortage of opportunity. The recently acquired Mercers' field has extensive pitches, 'levelled by computer,' pupils say. Archery happens there but was elusive on our visit, though we spotted the coach's van. A huge range of 'strenuous pursuits' available in the 'long break'.

Situation alone gives Dauntsey's a whiff of bracing contact with the great outdoors, focused, during our visit, by the whole school cross county race. The delightful lower school guides, when asked what happened to non-sporty people, didn't think there were any. Some parents feel that the less talented enthusiasts need more chances to play in teams, even against each other. Masses of expeditions like the Brecons Challenge and a long distance canoe race from Devizes to Westminster. Moonrakers, a third year programme, offers all sorts of outdoor adventure challenges (at no extra cost), and the more ambitious Dauntsey's Mountaineering and Expedition Society travels to the orphanage they have adopted in Romania or visits their contacts in Bhutan. Lots do D of E though they skip Silver because of exam pressure.

Solid rather than spectacular facilities – indoor swimming pool, two handsome Astros, sports hall, athletics track a hike away – a source of grumbles for a few, macho fitness area with scary weights and levers currently getting a facelift and a bit more space. Too unusual to omit is the sailing club. No Optimists or Fireflies on a pond for Dauntsey's, which has bought a 100 year old Tall Ship, the Jolie Brise. Pupils competed in the Fastnet in 2013 (she actually won the first in 1925); they also cruise more lazily off the Isle of Wight. Everyone gets a go in mixed teams of eight and parents are envious.

What the music department lacks in size it makes up in enthusiasm – multitudinous groups of every genre happily play away, certainly more than 20 groups timetabled – choirs, orchestras bands. It needs a bit more space. A good take up of instrumental tuition on every instrument ever invented makes for plentiful concerts with some mature and accomplished performance. Practice sessions timetabled for junior boarders.

There is serious drama – King Lear is probably as serious as it gets – when enthusiastic performers can be weaned away from everyone's first love, the many enormous school musicals and 'extraordinary performances' which sometimes even make it to London theatres. Smashing A level results in theatre studies. The multi-function 'memorial' school hall has really good lighting and equipment thanks links with the West End. Plans are a foot to refurbish it with better seating (sinking into the floor) though it would be a pity to end such bizarre juxtapositions as the stately school altar, sanctuary and organ at one end and a stunning full size white puppet cow at the other. Annabel's, the well-equipped drama studio, has everything needed to launch careers via the Edinburgh fringe and such venues. Good and popular dance studios too – it's in the curriculum – with a few boys taking part.

Across the playing field, the chimneyed art block has a deceptively arts and crafts look but is full of all the relevant IT and pottery things. It's about to get an upgrade to make more space and dark room for photography planned for A level. Head of art keen on observational drawing. Bags of school trips – modern languages to Spain and France, geography to Iceland, RS to India, Adventurers to Bhutan, skiing in Italy

There's not much you can't do at Dauntsey's, which is probably just as well for 300 or so boarders marooned in a leafy backwater.

Background and atmosphere: Founded in West Lavington in 1542 on the deathbed largesse of William Dauntsey, master of the Worshipful Company of Mercers, the school opened in 1895. Mercers' Company still provides six governors, occasional generous financial help and annual knees-up for its associated schools which include an unlikely spread from St Paul's Schools in London – both boys' and girls' versions – to Peter Symonds College (state sixth form in Winchester), two new academies and The Royal Ballet School.

The advantage to being almost at the back of beyond is that Dauntsey's has plenty of room to spread itself – a seven hole golf course at the Manor House (co-ed boarding for juniors) who undoubtedly get the prettiest building. Some choose to ramble home through a lovely mile of so of woodland path, from which their Victorian mock Tudor mansion welcomes them at 4.30pm into a spacious galleried hall with inviting sofas round blazing fire in winter, to take tea and delicious looking scones and cake. It's a spick and span version of Hogwarts, with its long oak tables and panelled common rooms smelling of furniture polish rather than 60 small boys and girls. Dormitories are functional but spacious with lovely views, weekends full of well planned, child friendly activity, mostly on the spot.

Lawns and trees enhance the setting of the handsome main school building, and the recently redesigned reception area is reminiscent of a five star hotel with its glass topped tables, comfortable furniture and well lit pictures changed regularly by the art department – and it is nice to see the artist's names. Other facilities are more functional, but very well maintained. Perhaps a bit countrified for some hardened Londoners – until 1930 the school was known as Dauntsey's Agricultural School.

Dauntsey's has mushroomed, to the extent that buildings jostle haphazardly with an increasing number of lawned and planted milling-about spaces between buildings, so the brightly coloured maps at every corner are necessity not decoration. A young pupil claimed to have taken only a week to find his way about. What impresses is that it has absolutely every facility a school should have but nothing extravagant. Boarding houses (single sex), both old and new are exceptionally spacious, some with en-suite facilities and all have kitchens, workspace and proper recreation area. A sixth former described it as 'certainly better than adequate but not quite luxury'. Day houses get

D

everything the boarders have except the bedrooms and the juniors have their own similar on-site day centre.

The most spectacular feature is a superb bright and airy new library –which must say something about academic priorities. Some exposed desks/computers down the centre of the building may not be everyone's cup of tea (where do they hide the sweet packet?) but more sheltered study space is available upstairs plus round tables and comfy chairs for a good read. Fooling around can be done in the cyber café or in the tuckshop. Lessons finish at 4pm and it is technically possible for day pupils to creep off then, but most stay on for prep or take part in clubs or sports until the mass bus exodus at 5.30pm. Boarders have two hours of prep in the evenings, one just before and one after supper.

Uniform is as expensive but not more than most. Girls have a rather limp blue check skirt with blue blouse and pullover. Boys in blue shirt and grey-blue jacket. No uniform in sixth form but smart-ish dress required (suits or chinos, tie and jacket for boys and at least a nod towards formality for girls) – quite widely interpreted. The reversible black and white rugby shirts are just being phased out for smart though less popular mainly white ones which wash better but get smelly very quickly. The busy school shop has an endless supply to lend to those who forget games things. The San is modern and inviting with quiet places to sit and suffer and comfortable looking bedrooms. Pupils definitely value the care given there, including counselling.

Pastoral care and discipline: Much less privilege orientated than many schools, so apart from the 17 Club, which is the hub of sixth form social life, and biscuits at morning break, sixth form and prefects live and work alongside the upper school and take a full part in house life. Relationships between year groups are definitely flexible. Responsibilities taken seriously by prefects and captains of houses, who are selected by head and staff. Drugs get immediate expulsion and pupils know it. Apart from that, 'rules are', pupils say, 'a matter of common sense', though a new rule book is issued each year. The comments they made on 'how far into the opposite sex house' they are allowed showed they had a pretty shrewd idea of what is and is not acceptable. They also emphasised the trust between pupils and staff.

The pastoral system functions through the houses, in which the house staff and at least four assistants act as tutors to about 60 pupils. Parents say problems are handled successfully and with great sensitivity.

Pupils and parents: Not toffs on the whole, more local families, farmers and small businesses, with quite a number from state primaries or first time buyers. Lots of professional families with two parents working to earn the fees. International intake widening from Hong Kong and Russia to a wide spread of countries: Europe and beyond. Fifteen bus routes from Salisbury (south), Swindon (north), west to Frome and east to Hungerford and Andover, which puts them into competition with a number of good grammar schools as well as some top independents. Being just over an hour from London, Bristol and Southampton makes boarding pretty accessible from UK or abroad. Breakfast provided for all-comers in the pleasant dining hall. Boarders have to be there by 8.15. Buffet service with spectacular and popular 'live cook' every day and all meals in on the fees though not compulsory – a few chose to use the house kitchens though the dining room was full, although it staggers sittings.

Entrance: At 11+, from state schools and a few preps, entry is by Dauntsey's own exam (maths, English, VR and optional music auditions). Selective in that they accept about the same standard of candidates as Salisbury Grammar, according to the head. At 13+ they take mainly boarders from prep school and some from abroad via 13+ CE or scholarship exams, with very few day places at this stage, adding an extra two forms. Feeders include Chafyn Grove, St Francis (Pewsey) and St Margaret's (Calne), All Hallows and Thorngrove plus many local state primaries. Everyone sitting an exam at 11+ is automatically considered for a scholarship and around 15 pupils out of 80 admitted get some sort of award.

Some 50 pupils join the school for sixth form, around a third from abroad – a minimum of three A and three B grades at GCSE is required from UK pupils, plus interview.

Exit: A trickle – up to 15 – leave after GCSEs mainly for local sixth from colleges. Good proportion to solid science, medicine, languages etc courses at uni and a respectable number to Oxbridge (six in 2013).

Money matters: Much more aware than many schools that parents' resources are not infinite. The vibe from parents is that day fees here particularly good value for money. A few nice touches: music lessons cost the full whack for first instrument but less for second and subsequent ones; a 10 per cent reduction for siblings who are boarding at the same time (a very sibling-friendly school). Mercers' connection is a help when it comes to funding building projects but not a bottomless pit.

Remarks: It's in there competing with the heavies but still unpretentious, with feet firmly on the ground. Parents value its special atmosphere, rooted in being reasonably non-selective, both academically and socially. Steadily improving results and facilities are putting Dauntsey's among the front-runners in the area. Its friendliness, breezy campus and outdoorsy image belie a focused academic purpose, which encompasses arts and sciences, though it doesn't inhibit the pupils from having a pretty good time. Dauntsey's is fab.

Dean Close School

Linked school: Dean Close Preparatory School

Shelburne Road, Cheltenham, GL51 6HE

• Pupils: 480 pupils, 250 boys/230 girls; 290 board • Ages: 13–18 • C of E (Anglican Foundation) although all denominations welcome • Fees: Day £21,645; Boarding £23,580–£30,960 pa • Independent

Tel: 01242 258044
Email: registrar@deanclose.org.uk
Website: www.deanclose.org.uk

Headmaster: Since 2008, Mr Jonathan Lancashire (late forties). Read maths at Cambridge, taught maths at Radley, then qualified as a chartered accountant. After a spell as bursar at Rishworth School he moved to Dean Close in 2000. Dean Close is most fortunate to have a head with experience in matters educational and fiscal; as several people remarked to us, he is, indeed, the 'right man for the times'. His wife is head of history and politics at Cheltenham Ladies' and they have two children at university.

Mr Lancashire is urbane but approachable; a sharp dresser, he says he is a country boy and pig farmer manqué but, if he is, we're talking Lord Emsworth, not Neil Carter. He still teaches four maths lessons a week and plans, with some trepidation, to branch out into lower school physics. 'It's good for the pupils to see that the head will have a go,' he says. He enjoys sailing and climbing and, because modern life 'leaves spiritual things neglected', is undertaking a pilgrimage to Santiago de Compostela in small sections. Dean Close sixth form participants (boys and girls) in a recent Tough Guy challenge – a nine mile run and grueling assault course – were very surprised to find they were competing against their headmaster. Having previously been a spectator, he decided that he would rather take part than watch, even if it meant floundering in the mud being out-performed by his pupils. He believes that 'an important part of being a head is a willingness to be the fall guy', but qualifies this with 'occasionally'. Parents impressed by his 'quiet authority' and what seems like an uncanny ability to be everywhere. 'He turns up to every event,' they say. 'He's always there.'

Academic matters: Solid results for all at GCSE and A level and though year groups vary, the trend is upwards. The head says that the school looks for 'attitude as well as aptitude', a statement that demonstrates his confidence in the school's proven ability to develop and boost its pupils.

Twenty-two GCSE subjects offered, with most taking 10 or 11, smallish numbers for classics, Latin and Greek. 2013 GCSE/IGCSE: 60 per cent A or A*. Physics and music very strong at A/A* level. Separate sciences and maths results consistently very strong with cohort taking AO maths too. English, maths, separate sciences, history and DT IGCSE on offer. At A level, 72 per cent A*-B, 43 per cent A*/A. Once again the mathematicians are light years ahead with A*As – whatever it is they put in the water in the maths department should be bottled.

Classes are small, between 15 and 20 (12 in the sixth form) and teachers, according to one parent 'work with each child's individual abilities', and, according to another, 'achieve miracles'. Mild SEN (dyslexia, dyspraxia) catered for and EAL is taught in individual lessons or groups.

The head is proud of the extension programme for sixth formers designed to help them develop critical thinking skills, engage with different ideas and 'confront non-standard stuff'. A critical essay competition open to the whole school is judged by an external adjudicator and keenly contested.

Games, options, the arts: Hockey is the game here for boys and girls, with seemingly every team vanquishing all comers, including the likes of Millfield, to become county champions and national finalists. One of our guides was a rugby fanatic but realistic about his school's performance against the big names: 'We're probably not near the top'. Emphasis is on everyone getting a game – at least three and up to five teams for every year group. A pool, gym, rifle range, dance studio and climbing wall and, in addition to acres of playing fields, a large covered pitch so the younger children can play outside whatever the weather.

Equestrian sport is an increasingly popular option – this being Gloucestershire, a handy polo club in nearby Birdlip where riders can learn this sport from scratch. Teams take part in schools show jumping, cross-country, eventing and dressage competitions, with individuals competing at national and international level in all disciplines. No stabling, though, so you'll have to leave the pony at home.

Music here was described by one parent as 'second to none' – all are encouraged to take up an instrument or sing. Practice sessions are not timetabled but schedules are agreed with music tutors, which apparently results in more productive practice. The music school houses teaching and practice rooms and the Prince Michael Hall, used for concerts and public speaking. Hosts of chamber ensembles, rock bands, choirs and orchestras and musicians perform locally and nationally. Regular tours have taken them to Paris, Venice and New York. A strong tradition of Oxbridge organ and choral awards; the boy choristers from Tewkesbury Abbey's Schola Cantorum (stars of many a CD) are educated here. In residence is the new head of strings, the celebrated Carducci Quartet.

Art, too, has its own purpose built 'school' and exhibition space. Results at GCSE and A level are strong, a good proportion go on to continue their artistic education in some of the country's most acclaimed art colleges, including Central St Martin's, Chelsea, Camberwell and The Slade, and further afield such as the Charles Cecil Studios in Florence. Sixth form artists have allocated spaces where they can leave out works in

progress. The art school's BonBernard Gallery is used to display both pupils' and professionals' work.

In addition to a studio theatre and a large amphitheatre in the grounds, fortunate thespians can also tread the boards of the Bacon Theatre, a 550 seat venue that wouldn't look out of place in small town. Named after former headmaster, Christopher Bacon, it hosts at least eight school plays a year, a major musical such as Les Misérables or Guys and Dolls every two years, as well as numerous professional productions; lecturing luminaries including Judi Dench, Samuel West and Peter Hall. In addition to GCSE and A level theatre studies, pupils are prepared for the RADA and LAMDA examinations up to diploma level. The school theatre company, Close Up Theatre, has performed sell-out plays at the Edinburgh Fringe for several years.

Add to the above a huge choice of clubs and societies, CCF training, D of E and a community action programme where pupils work on projects locally and abroad (building a school in Uganda) – it's no wonder boarding (or 'day' boarding, two nights a week) is so popular with local pupils: they don't want to miss out.

Background and atmosphere: One parent described the atmosphere at Dean Close as 'relaxed yet achieving' and that just about sums it up, rather more succinctly in fact than the colour printing fest of promotional literature – considerably more quality photography, paper and gloss than other schools we've visited and needing its own Dean Close carrier bag. School mags, The Decanian and Young Decanian, are similarly shiny and flawless and perhaps just a little corporate. The school is more humane and down to earth than its brochures let on; the pupils we met were charming and grounded – one said that the best thing about school life was being part of a 'community of individuals'.

Occupying 50 green acres just beyond the centre of Cheltenham, it could be quite a daunting place but somehow keeps the protective ethos of a small school on its big site. The main school is a familiar mix of Victorian and later additions – although it is by no means short of the latest smartboards and ICT equipment, we were delighted to see a well-stocked library like an upturned boat and a wonderful high ceilinged history classroom with piles of books, walls covered in posters and a makeshift display of shells (exploding variety) and a tin helmet. And was that chalk dust floating in the shaft of sunlight coming from the tall windows? Probably not. The head has plans for a major redevelopment in the heart of the school, 'a radical approach to teaching space' (plus a new swimming pool) – we hope the history classroom's days aren't numbered.

The dining hall serves hearty home-cooked food with plenty of choice, pupils and staff eat at refectory tables with a fine view of the grounds. Boys and girls we spoke to were generally positive about the meals – several said they thought the food had improved while they had been there. Boarders can supplement with toast, hot chocolate and other snacks they prepare in the kitchenettes.

Pastoral care and discipline: The principles of Christianity form the moral heart of the school and for some this is a deciding factor, but 'no pressure' to get involved beyond cultural Christianity. One parent, not a churchgoer, was positively evangelical about what he identified as the 'spirit and energy' of the school. Our guide, who was very involved in this aspect of school life, said, 'It's not uncool to be a Christian here.' A whole school evensong in the chapel every Friday and voluntary communion and Bible studies plus a pupil-run Christian Union. The popular female chaplain organises various programmes to develop pupils' spiritual awareness.

No significant behaviour problems – main challenge, according to the head, is day pupils, who very occasionally get into trouble 'off-site' at Cheltenham's seedy dives. (Are there any?) Testing for any suspected of substance abuse; immediate dismissal for dealing. School takes a 'cultural approach' to bullying and staff vigilant for anything, even if it's just chit-chat, that may make a child feel isolated. Head very hot on challenging what he feels is a contemporary fashion for sexist put-downs. Prefects trained to look out for anyone feeling wobbly. Parents we spoke to describe pastoral care as 'fantastic', 'The staff genuinely care about the children'. A few grumbles from parents of day pupils, who wanted more opportunities to discuss their child's progress than the termly meetings with staff, but all agreed teachers were approachable and quick to respond to queries.

The girls' boarding house we visited was light and modern with glass brick floors in the corridors. Rooms were reassuringly untidy (inspections on Sundays), customised with posters, photos and plenty of home from home clutter. 'Keep calm and carry on' seems to be the motto de choix on many walls. Sixth formers have single rooms with linked ensuites and plenty of Cath Kidston bunting. Fourth form prep is done in separate study areas and monitored by sixth formers. Downstairs are squashy sofas with bright red cushions, board games, puzzles, a Wii, DVDs and music. Saturday night is film night. Boys' boarding similar standard but less bunting, and sofas evidenced rougher treatment.

Pupils and parents: A good number of boarding parents are first-time buyers – the lack of old boy snobbery is a big draw. Significant numbers of Forces and diplomatic families are delighted to find a school where all their children can be educated together. School keen to stress its 'local' character, but even pupils whose parents live within bus distance elect to board when they get older (both our guides fell into this category). Mix of established families and London defectors has energised population in recent years. Roughly 15 per cent from overseas but no dominant nationality.

Famous Old Decanians include Tom Johnson and Pete Brown, rugby players; Hugh Quarshie, actor; George Adamson, author of Born Free; Francis Bacon, artist; Lord Bernard Ribeiro, former president of Royal College of Surgeons.

Entrance: 'Quite accessible,' according to the head, but two applications for every place; he adds that one of the qualities Dean Close looks for is curiosity, children who will 'have a go' and embrace every opportunity the school offers. Pupils enter at 13 from the school's own prep and after common entrance from others such as Pinewood, Beaudesert Park, Hatherop Castle, Prior Park, St John's-on-the-Hill. Sixth form entrants are accepted on the basis of three subject-based papers with VR or EAL.

Exit: Majority to Russell Group, handful every year to Oxbridge (five in 2013), plus a few to art college and drama school. Popular subjects: engineering, accounting and finance (no surprise there, given calibre of mathematicians) and geography; favoured institutions currently Bristol, Bath, Oxford Brookes and Exeter.

Money matters: Described by more than one parent as 'value for money'. Scholarships and exhibitions for 13+ and 16+ entry awarded for excellence in academics, music, sport, art, drama, DT, plus a few for 'all rounders'. Small number of 100 per cent bursaries for those who 'could benefit from a Dean Close education'.

Remarks: Dean Close is a warm and welcoming school, aspirational without being snobby and secure in its strong moral and social values. As one of our guides said, 'You don't have to be a type to fit in here – you just have to be keen to give everything a try.'

Devonport High School for Boys

Paradise Road, Stoke, Plymouth, PL1 5QP

• Pupils: 1,150 boys • Ages: 11–18 • Non-denom • State

Tel: 01752 208787
Email: headteacher@dhsb.org
Website: www.dhsb.org

Headmaster: Since 2008, Mr Kieran Earley BA MA NPQH (late thirties) educated at John of Gaunt School, Trowbridge, before reading English and drama at Bangor and PGCE at Bath. Has studied part-time for multi-disciplinary MA and further educational qualifications. Family roots lie in the Navy and in Plymouth – had to pay back Navy university scholarship when he decided that his future lay in the classroom rather than at sea. Began teaching English and drama at Bishop Heber High School, Cheshire, then took a year out to run Sound and Fury – Shakespeare and music educational workshops; next came a year at King's College, Madrid, then three appointments in Cheshire over eight years, culminating in assistant headship back at Bishop Heber. Deputy head at Torpoint Community College for just two years prior to current appointment.

Ideas man with vision; pupils and parents welcome his energy and involvement. 'Has settled in very well,' they say. Compared first year at DHSB to 'drinking from a firehose' but seems to be surviving. Boys 'like him' and add that he is 'out and about', talking to them and to staff. Married to maths teacher, Alex, with three sons currently at their village primary school in Cornwall. Looks young for a head: he's on a mission to see DHSB achieve 'outstanding' levels in all areas. Aside from time with the family, he enjoys playing football and cricket for local teams.

Academic matters: Consistently good results at GCSE (2013, 51 per cent A*/A) and A level (63 per cent A*-B). Head is raising the academic bar and appointed deputy from Torquay Boys' Grammar to help achieve this. After a massive brainstorming exercise involving staff, parents, governors and pupils, head has condensed key stage 3 curriculum to years 7 and 8. This exercise has involved a lot of cross-curricular dialogue and some radical thinking. Setting from year 9 where Latin (compulsory still in years 7 and 8) becomes part of a mini option scheme. Mandarin introduced from year 8. Curriculum shake-up at junior end allows more time for boys to get into their key stage 4 workload (all boys study 10 subjects to GCSE plus RE and PE). Astronomy now a GCSE option.

Parents say that maths and science teachers are good at getting pupils to 'think out of the box'. Boys generally take four or five AS subjects in year 12 and three or four A levels in year 13. Head has plumped for AQA baccalaureate to extend sixth form curriculum – projects in the pilot group included producing and performing in a Pinter play and sustainable building. As a G and T opportunity, offers level 2/3 diploma courses and Young Apprenticeship schemes in engineering and art (granted school specialist engineering status and judged as high performing at it).

Obtained a second – languages – specialism in view of its European studies centre in France and its new engineering-based relationships in Germany and other countries. Numbers opting for languages in sixth is on the increase and all take at least one MFL to GCSE. Hooray! Lots of languages initiatives with 50 boys participating in an on-site Chinese enrichment day and some boys selected for Euroscola day at European parliament in Strasbourg.

Third specialism granted in field of applied learning: this is developing a more independent and innovative learning community and giving boys the opportunity to develop workplace skills in proper industrial contexts.

Sixth formers can study alongside girls at other schools in the consortium, which also includes Notre Dame, St Boniface and Eggbuckland. Teachers' rôle increasingly that of facilitator: we watched sixth form English class directed into research and composition using individual laptops. Psychology growing in popularity; science and maths seen as strengths alongside engineering. New virtual learning platform (FROG) allows pupils to access work from home and includes a facility for uploading work and having it marked electronically.

Boys are screened for SpLD and SENCo operates from a cottage on site which also provides a useful sanctuary for any needing it. School ('lynchpin of the citywide campus,' says head) provides lead for gifted and talented programmes in science, maths and engineering across the city.

Games, options, the arts: Strong sports tradition – enviable record at county, regional and national levels. Consistent local success in a dozen sports. Nearby civic pool is used for swimming. Hockey off campus for 50 boys involved – Astroturf is high on head's wish list. Cross-country and orienteering take place either on Dartmoor or at picturesque Mount Edgcumbe Country Park.

Lots of engineering activities – eg a team of year 8 boys recently won best use of electronics award in a national competition for remote controlled 4x4 vehicles in schools. Art, taught in refurbished studios, popular at GCSE and A level and also operates as a club activity. Music is based in a separate house on site which includes a classroom, recording studio and individual practice rooms. After school activities include school orchestra, swing band, choir and rock club – recent production was Joseph and the Amazing Technicolour Dreamcoat. Drama gaining popularity: good numbers taking GCSE and A level courses and making advantage of splendid new theatre with pull-out seating for 300. Separate ATC building on school grounds with participation from both within and outside DHSB.

Wide range of before and after school clubs from robotics to rock climbing; involvement in Plymouth youth parliament and local success in ESU competition. D of E and both 35 and 45 mile teams for Ten Tors (on doorstep) perennial favourites. SW regional champions in Schools Challenge. Up to 400 (including year 7) benefit annually from school's own French centre at Uzel in Brittany where, for under £250 for five days, pupils get to practise French and participate in orienteering, canoeing and riding. Other recent trips abroad include art to Paris, skiing on Jungfrau and classicists visiting Rome and the Bay of Naples. Sino-DHSB co-operation includes a link with Xiuzhou Modern Experimental School.

Background and atmosphere: Founded in 1896 by first headteacher, Alonzo Rider, to give educational opportunity to able boys from less well off backgrounds. Aims reflected in school motto: 'prorsum semper honeste' ('forward always with integrity'). New mantra is 'helping families raise their sons', as school adjusts to 21st century changes in technology and the learning environment. Moved to its present site in 1945 to occupy a huge Grade 2* listed building which had formerly served as a prison during the Napoleonic wars and as a hospital during WWII.

Some of the interior remains rather barrack-like and battered, but recent additions and improvements include the new Edgcumbe theatre, library and sixth form centre plus an attractive refectory. Sports hall and fitness suite are heavily used; five engineering workshops – all boys take at least one D&T subject. New food technology base currently under construction. ICT used throughout school (universal access to digital teaching resources) with departmental laptops and four IT suites. Extensive playing fields for a city centre school provide some room to breathe; tight packed buildings, however, mean boys can move relatively quickly between lessons.

Pastoral care and discipline: Strong pastoral care team includes heads of year; six houses, into which boys are placed on entry, with one form per house. Separate head of sixth form. Purposeful atmosphere and a real effort by staff to sort out any problems quickly – 'Come down heavily on wrong-doers,' say parents. One mother praised way that school had helped her son overcome insensitivity from his peers. Still a bit scruffy at the edges, but boys gain confidence as they progress.

Devonport Voice is the school's initiative for incorporating pupil opinion and is gaining momentum with its vision of 'words into actions'. Head recognises achievement in fortnightly full school assembly: recently noted successes range from six D of E gold awards and grade 8 piano to a national indoor rowing champion and year 7 boys raising over £1K for Lepra charity.

Pupils and parents: New initiative has been to appoint a parent support adviser – a welcome move, given the very mixed social catchment including Chinese and other ethnic groups. Supportive parents with an active PTFA – initiatives include fundraising discos and a link with a local charity shop to recycle school uniforms, to help reduce excessive growth spurt costs. Pupils travel from within 750 square-mile catchment area. Parents from the three Plymouth grammars have organised contracts with local bus company for eight double-deckers to bring children from the city's neighbouring districts. Boys from 160 feeder primary schools desperately want to come here and often pressurise their less committed parents. Takes up to 12 per cent of Plymouth's boys.

Old Boys include Sir Austin Pearce, chairman of British Aerospace, a smattering of admirals, professors, current Bishop of Truro and Anne Widdecombe's dad.

Entrance: Written English paper (comprehension and composition), two multiple choice papers on maths and verbal reasoning. PTFA organises a 'mock paper' at £30 a shot – real thing is held on two successive Saturdays. Oversubscribed: candidates selected on basis of their score, which is standardised. Transfer into all other years (except 11 and 13) is possible, dependent upon availability of a place and satisfaction of entry criteria.

Exit: Almost all stay on post GCSE. Majority to university – in 2013, 11 to Oxbridge, seven medics and two vets. South West universities popular – Exeter, Plymouth, Bristol, UWE, Bath. Generous sponsorship from Engineers' Employers' Federation and BAE Systems results in large number heading into engineering and science courses.

Remarks: Moving from the traditional into a more modern concept of selective education. Good local reputation for turning out worthy citizens.

Devonport High School for Girls

Lyndhurst Road, Peverell, Plymouth, PL2 3DL

• Pupils: 805 girls • Ages: 11–18 • Non-denom • State

Tel: 01752 705024
Email: dhsg@devonportgirls.plymouth.sch.uk
Website: www.devonportgirls.plymouth.sch.uk

Head Teacher: Since March 2009, Mrs Anita Hemsi BSc MA (Ed) PGCE NPQH, previously acting head.

Academic matters: High standards – 99 per cent got 5+ A*-C GCSE grades including English and maths in 2013. Choice of 20 A level subjects, further options including politics, psychology, sports studies and media studies – part of a consortium, the

Link Partnership, which allows more timetable flexibility. English, the sciences and maths are particularly popular A level choices and students often sit additional Institute of Biology British Olympiad exam. French, Italian, Latin, Spanish and German available at GCSE and A level and new language block supports this. Budding engineers invented collapsible mobile platform to lift equipment on and off ships, which has been adopted by the Royal Navy. Weaker achievers or students with SEN receive ample support.

Games, options, the arts: Thriving basketball squad. Dance taught in main school hall. Sporting stars have made national squads in hockey, netball, basketball, swimming and athletics, and improved sporting facilities are likely to further boost success. Music is a strength, with more than a third of girls playing an instrument and achieving grade 7 or 8 by year 10. Flourishing orchestra and choir perform a carol concert in the city church each year. Drama group teams up with St Boniface College for Boys and Devonport High School for Boys for annual production. Active Christian Union. Duke of Edinburgh available elsewhere through local YWCA; windsurfing and sailing offered through school.

Background and atmosphere: Founded in 1911, moved to its present purpose-built site in 1937. The redbrick building is off a busy road opposite parkland. No great views and access by car is somewhat puzzling. Originally built for three forms of entry but since expanded to four – still waiting to dispose of 10 temporary classrooms. Low turnover of staff – teachers almost seem relieved to be here, 'Pupils listen and like to learn'. Sixth form has own centre with kitchen and study. Every girl has access to internet and own email.

Pastoral care and discipline: Good level of care and support; discipline is a 'quiet word in their ear'. School nurse and youth counsellor from Youth Enquiry Service run weekly drop-in sessions. School council instead of prefect system – each form elects a member. Girls have been sent home for minor incidents but no exclusions in previous head's 15 year history; letter sent home to parents if caught smoking. Sixth formers expected to dress as if at work; body-piercing items must stay home. Everyone in school is 'expected' to contribute to school's chosen annual charity. Good attendance record and extremely positive attitudes.

Pupils and parents: Attracts girls from some 50 feeder schools in Plymouth, west Devon and south-east Cornwall. Many professional parents from doctors and nurses to lawyers and scientists.

Entrance: Plymouth exam: multiple choice and written English. Pupils admitted in the order of their exam score until the maximum intake of 120 is reached. Sixth form entry is open on interview to students who have achieved at least five GCSEs at grades A*-C, with B grades in subjects (or equivalent) they wish to pursue at A level – 46 average point score.

Exit: Some 85 to 90 per cent migrate into sixth form, others move away or choose vocational courses. A few go into modern apprenticeships. Most continue to further education, although gap years popular. About four Oxbridge candidates annually. Cardiff, Exeter, Bristol, Southampton and London universities are favourites.

Remarks: Currently preferred choice for parents wanting single-sex selective education for girls. Students seem well prepared not just for academic success but also for life after school.

DLD College

100 Marylebone Lane, London, W1U 2QB

- Pupils: 340 boys and girls • Ages: 14–21 • Non-denom
- Fees: £17,500 pa • Independent

Tel: 020 7935 8411
Email: dld@dld.org
Website: www.dldcollege.co.uk

Principal: Since September 2013, Rachel Borland, previously principal of Abbey College in Birmingham. She is principal of both DLD and Abbey College in London, as they increasingly integrate before moving to a single, purpose-built site with student accommodation on Westminster Bridge Road in September 2015. She has previously been principal of an international boarding school in Nigeria, assistant director of studies at the British Council in both Hong Kong and Jordan, and worked at Bath University.

Academic matters: A small minority of pupils are there to do one-year GCSE courses, the rest one- or two-year A level courses. College offers a GCSE programme geared for SEN students, also retake courses of varying length, up to one year. Maximum class size 10. Commendable results from a mixed ability intake. Most GCSE students take seven subjects, from a limited list that includes the basics plus French, religious studies, art, graphics and drama. Russian, Chinese, Spanish, Italian and German are available via individual tuition. In 2013, 72 per cent of grades A*-C.

A level students get a choice of 35 subjects, including music technology, photography, film and media studies, sociology, psychology and languages, in more or less any combination. Art, economics, religious studies and philosophy are consistently popular, alongside English and maths; 52 per cent A*-B grades in 2013.

Some students are disaffected when they arrive – 'But it is unusual for them to be anti-education after a few weeks. It's important to fit the right course to the right student. Because of the small class sizes they get lots of individual feedback and huge amounts of encouragement, and most start making progress very quickly'.

The college can cope with a wide range of special needs, generally picking up several previously undiagnosed cases each year. Most students need group support with study and essay writing skills; individual help is also available at extra cost. 'Our SEN students get more or less the same level of results as the others – due to getting the subjects right and plenty of support. Apart from English for academic purposes, students can also have individual sessions with our SENCo.' Accredited by CReSTeD, whose most recent report speaks of it as a unique school.

No quarter is given academically – 'We will not accept scrappy work. We believe in raising standards and in helping students believe they can move up to the next level'. Many staff are from Oxbridge and some come from non-teaching backgrounds – the theatre, the City, the BBC. 'They work unbelievably hard,' said an insider. 'They put in a lot of effort for the students.' The most recent ISI report reports that students like being at the college and are very happy with the personal support that they receive.

Games, options, the arts: A surprisingly arty college – A level art and photography are two of the most popular and successful subjects and several students are refugees from high-powered academic institutions where the creative side is less valued.

The main aim of most students is to pass their exams – extracurricular activities are not high on the agenda, except for those in plays and sports teams. A level students, in particular, often work long days. However, all GCSE students play curricular sport at local centres on Friday afternoons, including football, basketball, tennis, netball, dance, rock-climbing and aerobics – sports clubs and matches after school. The DLD youth theatre puts on two performances a year; the house band – organised by the drummer of Van der Graaf Generator, who is also the music technology teacher – plays well-attended gigs; film, Duke of Edinburgh Award, EPQ, debating and art clubs.

Background and atmosphere: Now one of 17 schools owned by the Alpha Plus Group, founded in 1931 to provide tutoring for Oxbridge and Colonial Service entrance exams. After World War II it began to specialise in A and O level teaching. In 2004 it moved from Notting Hill to light, airy, refurbished premises in Marylebone, with an 80-seater theatre, recording studio, three art studios, science labs and photography studio.

Informal atmosphere, closer to a college than a school, with staff and students on a first name basis. 'They're unfussy about clothes and about students in clinches on the stairs,' said an insider. 'But academically they're pretty tough. Students don't get away with things.'

Pastoral care and discipline: Strong pastoral system. 'Many students have had a shifting lifestyle and it's a real haven for them,' said an insider. 'There is a lot of respect because students know we care about them.' A register is taken in every lesson and parents are texted or emailed. Each student has a weekly meeting with their personal tutor to talk about progress and future plans; five directors of studies working closely with the personal tutors. Tough sanctions for misusing drink and drugs – those under suspicion are sent for drugs tests, to general parental approval. 'There are a few troubled and troublesome students,' said a parent, 'but most buckle down eventually.'

'Occasionally there are students we don't manage to turn round. Then we'll often suggest to parents a gap year in the middle of the sixth form, preferably working in Waitrose. It concentrates their minds on the consequences of failing to work and the difference in maturity when they come back is often amazing.'

Sanctions include supervised study; also a system of verbal and written warnings based on employment law. Bullying is taken very seriously – 'They don't care about superficial things,' said an insider, 'but on work, drink, drugs and bullying they clamp down very quickly'.

Pupils and parents: Most students have come from private schools. Some have had enough of boarding; some have been ill; some have found their previous school too rigid or too stressful. Others come from peripatetic diplomatic families. Some lack confidence and need to learn good working habits. Most thrive in the informal but structured atmosphere.

Entrance: Those going into the sixth form need a minimum of five grade Cs at GCSE; if they haven't passed maths or English they will need to retake these. Everyone is interviewed and previous schools are asked for references. The college will not consider students who have been disruptive elsewhere.

Exit: A few GCSE students move on elsewhere – perhaps to state sixth form colleges – but most go through to the sixth form. Those aiming at Oxbridge are given an intensive course including lectures, seminars, mock interviews and individual tuition – one to Cambridge in 2013; one to Queen's Belfast and one to uni of British Columbia; others to LSE, UCL, King's College. Extra help also for potential vets, doctors and dentists, via a bespoke medical programme. Wide range of degree courses, with business, management and finance being the most popular, also art foundation, mechanical engineering, sports and exercise science.

Money matters: Several scholarships available, worth 10-100 per cent of fees, plus bursaries.

Remarks: Good at stimulating the very bright as well as re-motivating the disaffected. Informal atmosphere with strong staff/student relationships underly a structured regime where everyone is kept up to scratch.

Dollar Academy

Linked school: Dollar Academy Prep and Junior School

Dollar, Clackmannanshire, FK14 7DU

• Pupils: 1227 pupils, of whom 70 board • Ages: 11–18 • non-denom • Fees: Boarding £20,637 – £24,669; Day £7,974–£10,665 pa • Independent

Tel: 01259 742511
Email: rector@dollaracademy.org.uk
Website: www.dollaracademy.org

Rector: Since September 2010, Mr David Knapman BA (maths) MPhil (forties), previously deputy head of Hampton School in London, where he still has a foot on the property ladder. At Hampton he established a non-nonsense reputation but was also notable for his work with charities and the local community. Educated at Morrisons, 'doon the road', followed by Sheffield and Exeter. Married to Brigitte with two sons (younger one in the school). His mother lives in Dunblane and 'is my fiercest critic; she keeps her ear to the ground'. Plays tennis regularly and enjoys 'playing the piano badly'. Wife also a teacher, came from a country background and is 'pleased to be in Scotland', they like walking the hills and are planning to tackle Ben Lomond this summer (Munro bashing very popular around here).

They live in a stunning Georgian street which houses a collection of school buildings – much in demand by film crews no doubt – we yomped to the burn to see Mylne Bridge (built and named for the local minister and first rector, who opened the school in 1818, to give him a short cut to the kirk) and were told that if it 'weren't for that pine tree, we could see Castle Campbell' (we googled it – it is pretty impressive).

Has a dry sense of humour: when asked how his son felt about moving to Scotland he explained that the bribe of a new puppy had been more than sufficient, though he is coy about the exact species (we suspect a spot of Mr Heinz 57). Hugely enthusiastic and 'very popular – going down well' and 'doing just fine,' say our spies. Sits in on classes, walks round every day and never misses a match, concert or play. Boarding numbers going up and examination results at a record high last year.

He was mentored by Dr Ken Greig, rector of Hutchesons Grammar in Glasgow (we hadn't realised that heads had mentors too) who seems to have grown a beard in solidarity. Certain number of staff changes; new assistant rector, 12 new staff, including Rob Moffat to coach PE (previously coach to the Edinburgh rugby squad, he was dismissed in 2011 'as the team failed to progress up the league table' – doubt if Dollar is quite in that league, but rugby here has a long tradition – three former pupils currently members of the Scotland squad), a mixture of young and old teachers, housing not cheap in the Dollar area but it is the perfect place for families.

Academic matters: Strong academic tradition, particularly science with a compressed science option on offer for 14-16 year olds and large numbers for medical school; English and mod langs good too, German and French more popular than Spanish; Latin, Greek and classical studies (heroes for zeros) all on offer and four dedicated classics teachers. All three langs from junior school plus some Japanese, Russian, Italian, philosophy, car mechanics and other jolly options. Broad streaming for English (with EFL if needed), tight setting for maths and mixed ability in most subjects, plus. Large business department offering economics, business management, finance and accountancy.

Rector and/or senior staff have a 20 minute meeting with every pupil (and their parents, who usually keep stumm during the interview) to discuss their personal subject choice. Pupils choose the subjects they want to study and classes are worked round them, rather than the trad system of block choice. There is a distinct emphasis on the academic rather than the vocational.

School follows a mixed bag of courses: standard grades (about to become national 4 and 5) intermediate I and II; highers, advanced highers and the Scottish baccalaureate – which doesn't seem to have many followers outside Dollar.

Classes of 6-24. Efficient support for learning in place; one-to-one, small groups and support learning in class all on offer. Variety of reading methods on offer, but jolly or unjolly come to that – phonics in the main. School has a positive approach to those with ADHD: pupils can drop into the dyslexia centre at any time. Serious homework, carefully spelt out in a smart little green book full of info for parents which interestingly persists in referring to the school as the Academy. 'Whatever else, we expect that all pupils in the Academy should have enough work to occupy their evenings and any child who indicates otherwise misunderstands.' Not quite all singing and dancing new computer system (school report says 'could do better'), touch-typing for all, strong on techy subjects – most to advanced higher level.

Games, options, the arts: No sport is compulsory. That said, boasts a first XV rugby team unbeaten for the first seven years of this century. Regular tours to Europe and further afield: Canada, Japan, Italy et al. Shooting 'phenomenal'; always a strong showing at Bisley. Hockey hot stuff. Numerous individual county reps in major and minor sports – golf, skiing and badminton, as well as more esoteric activities such as shotput, curling, table tennis, equestrian vaulting (gymnastics on horseback) and triathlon (NB Clackmannanshire ain't that big). Mass of games fields, 63 acres of school grounds, much used hall and swimming pool. Amazing circular Maguire Building – sports, arts, drama – million pound bequest from FP Brian Maguire; formidable school art on display and used for external exhibitions too – even the Scottish Examinations Authority asked for a painting for their new premises. Second bequest from the Price family resulted in a new 5.3 metre inflatable for the navy section. All weather surface was opened by Linda Clement, Scottish Ladies' hockey captain. Presumably by bullying off.

Strong volunteer CCF – good following, not just because of the trips to Canada. Three pipe bands, who all sport the Campbell tartan; the B band was third in the national CCF championships this year. Two orchestras, jazz bands, oodles of choirs; the annual Christmas concert in the Usher Hall was a sell-out with almost 2,000 in the auditorium. Drama timetabled with masses of productions – the rector believes that 'pupils gain confidence through performance'; lots of smaller concerts – 'six performers, 30 in the audience'; that sort of thing. Hot on debating, all sorts of trophies as well as representation in the winning Scotland team at the 2012 world champs in South Africa – a tour de force. Ballroom dancing on Fridays; participants learn Latin American and rock 'n' roll, Japanese dancing the latest wheeze but no medals for this nor for Scottish country dancing. Prize winners sport their bronze, silver, gold or Scottish Awards proudly on their blazers thereafter.

Munro bashing, D of E, exchange and trips, work experience at home and abroad, go-kart racing at Knockhill, skiing, motor mechanics, surfing, falconry. Clubs for everything, usually post school, late buses nightly. Fabric technology timetabled. Over 70 options in total; terrific facilities; powerful charities committee (15 mile sponsored walk raised over £50,000, staff, parents and doggies all included). Cooking for sixth formers and boarders.

Background and atmosphere: Captain John McNabb, a former herd boy who rose to become a ship's captain and, latterly, a ship husband – literally looking after ships in port – died in 1802, leaving half his fortune, £55,000, to found a school to educate children of 'the parish wheir I was born'. Rumours abound whether the monies came from slavery or piracy but they were certainly augmented by bribes from ship owners eager to be first past the post. After much shilly shallying, the Rev Andrew Mylne, a trustee, commissioned Playfair to build a 'hospital' which finally opened in 1818. The first co-ed in Scotland. McNabb's corpse was rediscovered in the 1930s and proudly brought back to Scotland, and cremated. Gruesome or what. His ashes are entombed in the wall above the main Bronze Doors; this has to be the only school in the land where pupils pass under the founder every day. By 1830, the grounds at Dollar had become an Oeconomical and Botanical garden, boasting some of the rarest trees in the country – certainly the most northerly tulip tree, as well as a Corsican pine, and specimen sequoias. Pupils originally had their own plot of garden, though we are not sure whether this was for ornamental purposes or whether they were expected to augment the school kitchen. The interior of Playfair's original building was gutted by fire in 1961, which allowed a certain amount of internal rearrangement. Zinging concert hall (the Gibson Building), improved science block. Current wish-list includes a new technology, engineering science and earth science building – to be built out of 'funds'. The grounds are open to the public daily. And the library is no longer lollipop pink.

Formerly a direct grant school, Dollar became independent in 1974 – a day school, with an international boarding element. Easily accessible from most of Scotland and just a short hop from the Forth Road Bridge and Edinburgh Airport. The boarding houses are small, no more than 40 in each; all three have had recent million pound facelifts, stunning. Wet weather a feature of the place and masses of matches are rained (or snowed) off, (school says very rarely due to new all-weather Astroturf courts and pitches). NB The school uniform includes beanies (first time ever for us on a clothes' list) and macs with fleecy linings. Rector says he doesn't mind what they wear on their heads, as long as they are warm.

Pastoral care and discipline: Automatic out for drugs. Lousy work equals detentions post school or early morning – dead unpopular with parents, plus out if 'The pupil is not deriving benefit from being at the school or indicates by his/her conduct that he/she does not accept the rules of the Academy.' Pupils not particularly streetwise – 'Pupils have a reasonable amount of self-knowledge but on the whole they are not young people obsessively interested in the major interests of the day; it is no bad thing for them to remain children for a little longer'. Victorian values, with clear rules; many of the petty restrictions have been done away with, and the kilt may be worn by chaps at almost any time, though most prefer to be 'breeched', except for dances or reels.

Pupils and parents: The vast majority comes from within a 30 mile radius – impressive number of buses, plus Forces children and a contingent from the Scottish diaspora worldwide. Dollar itself has the reputation of having the highest percentage of graduates of any town in the country. School has a long tradition of looking after the children of tea-planters, missionaries and engineers – still. Perhaps a tad parochial and 'mercifully' free of Sloanes. Exceptionally strong and active FP network, including Sir Frank Swettenham, the first Governor of Malaysia, Sir James Dewar, the inventor of the vacuum flask, and the sculptor, George Paulin. The governing body is mostly FPs, which ensures that the place has freedom to develop but an awareness of its history shapes the thinking – no bad thing.

Entrance: Usually at 11 or 12, by examination, which is quite selective. Generally over-subscribed for entry at fifth and sixth forms; each case individually considered; good GCSE or Standard grades required plus good refs and an ability to put something into the school. No open days as such – parents and prospective pupils are welcome to visit at any point of the year, which gives the opportunity to see the school in action.

Exit: A handful to Oxbridge each year. Otherwise most students head for the Scottish universities: Edinburgh, St Andrews, Glasgow, Aberdeen, with under a quarter going south or abroad. Low gap year take up: either a reflection of the recession or the 'get on with it' mentality. The chairman of governors and his wife have set up a trust with more than £1 million to encourage the youngsters to take up challenges involving travel. If that doesn't persuade entrepreneurs overseas.

Money matters: Collection of means tested-academic bursaries at 11 and 12, plus ESU, Forces and boarding bursaries (usually means-tested, with tuition not covered). Fees very reasonable; governors tough on non-payers.

Remarks: Very sound – this large, solid, co-ed school provides education in the best Scottish 'get on with it' tradition, facing the 21st century with the expectations and values of an earlier age, mercifully free of most of the excesses of the 60s. 'Robust teaching and meritocracy' are important here. Up there with the best of the merchant schools, though possibly 'not quite so trendy'.

Douglas Academy

Craigton Road, Milngavie, G62 7HL

• Pupils: 985 boys and girls • Ages: 11–18 • Non-denom • State

Tel: 01419 552365
Email: office@douglas.e-dunbarton.sch.uk
Website: www.douglas.e-dunbarton.sch.uk

Headteacher: Since September 2008, Mr Seamus Black MA (fifties), educated at St Xavier School, Coatbridge (a local-ish lad then), read Italian and French at Glasgow University and came to the old Douglas Academy for a year – 'to get to know the traditions', having been previously deputy head of Shawlands Academy. He still teaches when he can and is often 'out and about' – a wandering head, he keeps a beady eye and is incredibly proud both of the new school and of the 'high quality' of his staff and 'pupil attainments'. Keen on parent involvement, he runs the school with a management team of seven, including the head of music. He also talks incredibly quickly and is very on the ball. Married, his family lives in Dunbarton.

Academic matters: A strong school – results consistently high and the HMI report is peppered with 'very good's. Three sciences on offer, many take two, pupils do well in science and maths challenges. French and Italian, Spanish option at sixth form, plus Mandarin. Fair amount of autonomy in employing staff, 'But if there are teachers free within the authority, then we have to take them' (an iniquitous system that caused much grief to England – high time it was abandoned here too); otherwise school advertises and can make its own appointments.

Regular success across the board at Standard Grades, music specialists take both Standard and Higher music without fuss and, 'effortless'. Specialists take 'specially tailored courses', but see below. Most pupils get a 'variety pack' of eight subjects at Standard Grade, including core subjects; most stay on for Highers and Intermediate courses, and a 'goodly proportion'

stay for Advanced Higher – school responds to 'the needs of the pupil': a certain amount of mix and match with Intermediate grades. Asterisked (ie outstanding) performance noted in history, modern languages, art and English.

Staff visit local primaries and meet new pupils the term before they hit big school. Children are setted for maths in October of their first term, and for some other subjects in their second year. Classrooms equipped with IT, interactive white boards and learning wall, as you might expect with a top notch new build: teachers happy and au fait with the most modern of facilities and the results speak for themselves.

Extensive support for learning, with a strong team which offers both guidance and support in class, offering help for the brightest as well as for those with learning difficulties, and with an acknowledged expertise in Asperger's.

Games, options, the arts: Does well at rugby, hockey and athletics – 'strong competitive edge'. Not for layabouts – a doing school. State of the art, all-weather rugby, football and hockey pitches, huge games hall plus two gyms, fitness suite, much used by the community, who also do evening and keep-fit classes here. Tennis, cross country course. Mass of charity involvement (beat the High School of Glasgow) and national award winners.

Became a centre of excellence for music in 1979 and boasts a first orchestra of 'almost professional standard', plus an outstanding chamber orchestra, senior wind band and second orchestra – very full (60+), which often has first year pupils playing, as well as non-music specialists. Chamber choir, junior choir, senior choir, who swept the board at the most recent Glasgow Music Festival, with the former beating the adult section to boot. On a par with St Mary's Music School in Edinburgh. Music lessons carry a nominal charge for non-music specialists, and local concerts are always a sell-out, particularly the annual Christmas concert at St Paul's in Milngavie. Almost equal numbers of boy and girl choristers: serious senior choir, the junior one is merely 'good' but, by any other school's standards, it would be outstanding. Most of the music staff have top jobs in Scotland's orchestras and choirs. Adjectives tend to fail when dealing with centres of excellence, but take it as read that any superlative would be inadequate.

Pupils follow the normal curriculum, but 20 per cent of their time is spent on music. Music specialists come from all over Scotland, Ullapool to Newton Stewart, and their chosen instrument can be in any discipline from fiddle to piano. No quotas for entry, around about eight or 10 annually, currently 49 dedicated music scholars, places free and open to all (help given with transport), with pupils from further away boarding at Dalrymple House (about 75 per cent), opposite the Botanic Gardens in Glasgow's west end (they share with pupils from the centre of excellence for dance at nearby Knightswood). Two homework tutors.

Background and atmosphere: Superlative new build in old school grounds with magical views of the Campsies to the north. Transition was more or less 'seamless'. School dress equals blazer (S6 pupils), white shirt/blouse, school ties, trousers or skirts and no trainers – 'Parents and pupils have high expectations'.

Pastoral care and discipline: Team of ministers from local churches involved with school. 'Drugs not an issue' and good (state) guidance system in place ('highly effective'), plus link tutors who have informal relationships with the pupils, offering both emotional and social support. Clearly defined rules about bullying and loads of staff backup – 'good extended team'.

Pupils and parents: No 'significant number' from ethnic minorities and no problems with religious festivals – 'praying (as in five times a day) never an issue'. Parents 'feel welcome', and good fundraising and pastoral parents' association in place.

Entrance: Four associated primary schools, one of which is tiny and rural. Pupils from (the Catholic) St Joseph's may come here, and almost all do, or they may prefer to be bused the 30 minutes or so there and back to the local secondary Catholic school in Kirkintilloch. Excellent child-orientated joining handbook.

Exit: Most Scottish universities.

Remarks: Stunning state school for musicians, which moved to a split, new, fantastic, state of the art campus in 2009 – worth moving house for if you are not in the catchment area, even if you aren't a musician. Exam results impressive and getting even more so. Outstanding recent HMI report. Strength through knowledge, the school motto, very much a byword.

Dover College

Linked school: Dover College Infants and Juniors

Effingham Crescent, Dover, CT17 9RH

- Pupils: 125 boys/100 girls; 105 boarders, 7 weekly boarders
- Ages: 11–18 • Broadly Christian but all faiths welcome
- Fees: Day £6,495–£13,755; Boarding £15,450–£27,150 pa
- Independent

Tel: 01304 205969
Email: admin@dovercollege.org.uk
Website: www.dovercollege.org.uk

Headmaster: Since 2011, Mr Gerry Holden MA PGCE, previously headmaster of Rendcomb College. Educated at St Augustine's High School, Edinburgh and St Andrew's University, where he read medieval and modern history, followed by PGCE at Oxford. Started teaching at Wolverhampton Grammar School for Boys, then became head of history at Forest School. Ran the history department at Millfield, and then appointed as deputy head at Frensham Heights. ISI inspector and edits a publication about sharing excellent teaching practice. Married to Liese, whose photographs are displayed around the school; they have a grown up son.

An experienced headmaster who knows where he wants to take the school. 'He has masses of new ideas and there is always lots going on', says one sixth former. 'He has made such a difference to the school and has so many aims and objectives – he really wants to school to succeed,' says another. Very engaging and charming, he has a comfortable and easy relationship with parents, pupils and staff. A flamboyant character with a penchant for brightly coloured socks and handkerchiefs and a flowing red St Andrew's gown. 'Perfect for the school', a happy parent told us. Good on the marketing side and is 'very good at promoting the school and has a wonderful way with the kids' – certainly the numbers have increased since his arrival. Believes in developing skills beyond the academic, especially confidence and resilience. 'Because confidence matters' has become the motto of the school and he firmly believes that 'with confidence the world opens up to all sorts of possibilities'.

Keen to give everyone a chance at leadership. He is 'a fan of people trying things out and into giving pupils responsibility,' one pupil told us. Has tightened up discipline and 'made everything fairer', which has, interestingly, met with general approval from the children. The phasing out of Saturday morning lessons, leaving the day free for matches and activities, seems to have been greeted with universal approval. A keen sportsman, he coaches the 3rd XI football team and acts as referee at some fixtures.

Academic matters: A broad ability range – 50 per cent A*/B grades at A level and 91 per cent of pupils got 5+ A*/C including

English and maths at GCSE in 2013. Sciences taught separately for the dual award. Good range of subjects offered in sixth form. The introduction of BTECs in sport and PE, travel and tourism and health and social care has meant that more are staying on for sixth form. Apart from the usual subjects, GCSEs offered in health and social care, PE and business studies.

About 12 per cent need some sort of SEN – lots of help available, from help with study skills to more intensive one to one help. A very dedicated team of teachers who 'go the extra mile' for the children and focus on individual learning styles. 'I could not believe how much trouble the teachers took with my son,' says one mother. Small classes – 12 to 14 for GCSE and sometimes only six for A level.

Has welcomed international students since 1957 and the International Study Centre opened in 2001 – total immersion in English plus lessons with peer group in maths, ICT, DT and sport. Depending on the level of English, pupils prepared for Cambridge Preliminary English Test (PET), IGCSE or IELTS. All international pupils are integrated into the main school. Some start in International Study Centre and move over when ready. Others join the main school on arrival. About 50 pupils need some sort of EAL support.

Games, options, the arts: The usual sports – football, hockey, netball etc. Cross country popular and successful (Dover College hosts a big inter-school event each year). Aerobics, basketball, sailing with Dover Sailing Club, swimming at a local pool. Everyone given a chance to shine and 'teachers are always trying out new people for sports and giving people a chance to showcase their talents'. Sport compulsory up to sixth form and most carry on after that. Most girls continue with sport but fitness classes, dance and yoga also popular. Not a school with acres of rolling fields but has its own pitches as well as an AstroTurf, sports hall, dance and fitness suites and a basketball court. 'Some of the sports facilities could do with a bit of a makeover,' say some parents. Link with Canterbury Christ Church University's sports department ensures a steady supply of recently qualified sports teachers who 'refresh the department and bring new ideas'.

Lots of music, including chamber orchestra and ensembles. Members of the local community often play in the orchestra and the choir sometimes sings evensong in Canterbury Cathedral. Tallis Music School has been relocated and refurbished and now provides soundproof pods, a recital room and teaching rooms.

Strong arts. Textiles, art and photography offered at A level. Particularly good photography – annual photographic competition also open to parents and fabulous photos displayed around the school.

Huge range of activities – from belly dancing and debating to madrigals and horseriding. Leadership activities, including D of E Award (up to eight gold awards a year) and Young Enterprise, all designed to build self-confidence. Strong emphasis on community and charity work. Senior pupils can get involved in the Ukraine project. A group raises money for the charity and then spends two weeks in the Ukraine refurbishing an old people's home, running a sports camp for disadvantaged children and chopping logs for the elderly. One parent describes it as 'a life changing experience for my son, who realised for the first time what true hardship is'.

Background and atmosphere: Founded in 1871 by a group of local businessmen who wanted Dover to have its own public school. Housed in the grounds of the 12th century Benedictine St Martin's Priory, an oasis of green in the middle of Dover with wonderful views of Dover Castle and nestling behind the famous white cliffs. Went co-ed in 1974 (one of the first boys' schools to do so) and now almost 50:50. Although much of the original priory was destroyed by Henry VIII, there is still a feeling of history. This is despite the hotchpotch of buildings added over the years, from late Victorian houses to the uninspiring

D

modern. The school has the only Norman refectory in Britain – still used for its original purpose and doubles as a concert hall and theatre too.

Dover College is a small local school with an international dimension and a strong sense of community 'where everyone knows everyone'. We heard comments like 'it's not overly posh but perfect for where it is' and 'it's a local school with a kind and caring environment which understands the kids' needs and gets the best out of each pupil'.

Christian foundation. Chapel is physically and spiritually at the heart of the college but all faiths and none are made to feel welcome. Three services a week, including Friday afternoon chapel.

Pastoral care and discipline: 'Because confidence matters' is the motto of the school and huge emphasis is placed on personal development and building pupils' confidence. 'I am confident that the school has the control of my children's wellbeing and promotes good social skills and ethics,' a parent told us. 'I am very proud when people comment on how well mannered my children are'. Well developed tutorial system and house staff and prefects have finely tuned antennae for drugs and alcohol. Head likes to bring together the students and the non-teaching staff. For example, the kitchen chef is also linesman for the 1st XI football team, a minibus driver is the referee and the estates manager runs D of E.

Years 7 and 8 are housed separately in the priory which ensures a gentle introduction to the senior school. All houses mix day and boarding so everyone gets to know everyone. 'It's nice to mix with different years because then you get to make more friends', a pupil told us, although another said 'some nationalities still stick together and keep themselves to themselves'. There is 'major house loyalty' and lots of inter-house events – music, sport, drama and the keenly fought house conker competition. All boarders have supper together at the weekends. Entertainment, theatre and shopping trips organised although many are happy 'just chilling with their friends' and catching up with schoolwork.

Pupils and parents: Day children tend to be fairly local and many are ferried to school via a network of minibuses. About 30 per cent from abroad (30 nationalities), 10 per cent service families (including a number of Nepalese families who serve locally with the Gurkhas). About 10 per cent of local children choose to board 'because it's fun'.

Huge range of abilities – some children very bright whilst others struggle to get five good GCSEs. 'A lot of the kids are not that academic but the school brings out the best in them', says a parent. The emphasis on building confidence produces comfortable well-adjusted children who are happy to strike up a conversation with anyone, but without a hint of arrogance. Life is full on here and as one pupil said, 'sometimes we are just too busy as every teacher wants you to do their thing'. Even so, they seem to love every minute of it.

Prefects given lots of responsibility and say that 'it is important to act as role models to the rest of the school'. They apply in writing and are then interviewed by a panel chaired by the head. Lower sixth enrichment week takes the pupils well out of their comfort zone and often a few previously hidden talents come to the fore. Pupils have to stage a senior management meeting, role play a crisis, take part in an Apprentice style marketing project and film a debate – all in one day. Parents like to feel involved. One mother told us that her children 'are treated in a caring and understanding way and I can talk to the teachers whenever I want'. Head has worked hard to develop lines of communication with parents and sees the relationship as a partnership overseeing the children's education. Parents kept up to date with events via parent portal and social media sites.

No typical Old Dovorian, although many are entrepreneurs who have made their own way in the world. They tend to keep in touch. Former pupils include composer Dai Fujikura, Sir Frederick Ashton, X Factor supremo Simon Cowell, film producer Guy East and various ambassadors and military figures.

Entrance: Almost non-selective. School has its own 11+ test in November before entry for setting purposes only and head likes to interview everyone. Will take children who might fail elsewhere and give them the confidence to succeed. Only turns children away if they won't be able to cope. Most join at 11+ from the junior school and local primaries. A few come in at 13+ from prep schools like Northbourne Park, Spring Grove and Wellesley House. About 25 students join the sixth form – mainly from abroad. Pupils can join at any time if there are spaces, except into year 11.

Exit: About 25 per cent leave after GCSEs, mostly to the state system. Sixth formers head to a range of universities. Not many to Russell Group but a wide variety of courses – recent choices include sports and exercise science at Canterbury Christ Church, pharmacology at Bristol, hospitality and tourism at Surrey, civil engineering at Nottingham, equine studies at Sparsholt, computer games technology at Portsmouth. Lots of help with UCAS – careers adviser knows pupils well and 'keeps expectations realistic'. Not many take a gap year.

Money matters: Range of awards offered, including 11+ scholarships in English and maths, 13+ scholarship awarded on strength of CE and 16+ scholarship on strength of GCSEs. Academic, art, music, sport and all rounder scholarships on offer. About a third of local pupils on some sort of scholarship or bursary. Not a rich school and bursaries come from fee income but school does what it can for those who encounter unexpected financial difficulties whilst at the school.

Remarks: Not hugely academic and nor does it pretend to be, but this is a happy, relaxed place where the building of self confidence underpins everything the school does. It's high praise indeed when a sixth form pupil says, 'I have been very happy here and can't fault it'.

d'Overbroeck's College

Linked school: Leckford Place

The Swan Building, 111 Banbury Road, Oxford

- Pupils: Sixth form – 260 boys and girls (boarding and day); Leckford Place (11-16) – 160 boys and girls (day only); One year GCSE programme at International Study Centre – 40 boys and girls • Ages: 11-19 • Non-denom • Fees: Sixth form – £19,785 (day) to £30,030 (boarding); Years 7 to 11 Leckford Place – £13,710 (day only). • Independent

Tel: 01865 310000
Email: mail@doverbroecks.com
Website: www.doverbroecks.com

Principal: Since 1996, Mr Sami Cohen BSC (fifties). Educated in Baghdad, then moved to London at the age of 17 to do his A levels. Read chemistry and French at Leeds University – the course was created for him and sparked a lifelong passion for 'breadth' in education. Followed in the footsteps of his mother and aunt, who were both teachers, and began his own teaching career at d'Overbroeck's in 1979 – two years after sixth form was founded. Moved to Paris in 1992 before being invited to return to d'Overbroeck's as principal four years later.

Charismatic, focused and approachable, he is particularly proud of opening the college's 11-16 arm in 2005, transforming d'Overbroeck's from a sixth form college into an all-through 11-19 school. 'We are able to offer each age group an environment that suits that particular age group,' he explains. 'We are open to a reasonably wide range of abilities and we value people with interests and enthusiasms. We want everyone to have a well-rounded, lively education, to be able to laugh a lot, to make great friendships and to feel that they have personally grown, developed and flourished.'

A keen linguist (he speaks French, Italian and Arabic), he no longer has time to teach these days – 'which saddens me.' Knows all the students well and is a familiar presence around the college's two sites, constantly stopping to chat. Pupils address teachers by their first names at d'Overbroeck's so he is 'Sami' to all. 'I'm totally immersed in the life of this place,' he says. 'There's a lot more I feel I can contribute.' Wife Emily is an EFL specialist and they have three daughters. The elder two both attended d'Overbroeck's and are now students at Oxford and UCL while the youngest is a pupil at the Dragon.

Academic matters: Academic results continue to go from strength to strength. In 2013 58 per cent of A levels were A*/A, with well over a third of students achieving A*/As in three or more subjects.

Sixth form offers 35 subjects at A level (all the usual, plus others like film studies, history of art, philosophy, sociology, photography and communication and culture). Unlike some schools (and thanks to nifty timetabling) students can choose virtually any mix of A levels. 'The key to students' success is getting the subjects right,' says the principal, who encourages students to choose the subjects they'll enjoy and do well at. 'There is no subject combination that we rule out,' says the academic head of sixth form. Alongside their A levels some sixth formers take the AQA Baccalaureate, which comprises an extended project, AS critical thinking and enrichment programme. Lower sixth students must get a minimum of CCCD grades at AS level to continue into the upper sixth – college reckons that if youngsters don't achieve this they're unlikely to cope with the rigours of A2. Good support for the tiny handful who don't manage this hurdle though and in some cases students retake the year.

Principal says the college appoints teachers 'who know their subjects inside out', are enthusiastic and care deeply about teaching. Lessons are informal, engaging and interactive, with teachers constantly checking that everyone has 'got it' before moving on. The students we met were unanimous in singing their teachers' praises. 'You won't find better teaching anywhere,' one girl told us appreciatively. 'I switched to economics quite late and my teacher stayed behind for an hour every week to help me catch up, from the day I started till the week my AS exams began. I've never found teachers who care this much.' Another said: 'The teachers want the best for you and it makes you want the best for yourself.'

GCSE results are good too. Fifty-three per cent A*/A grades in 2013, with maths, biology, chemistry, physics and drama particularly notable. Most pupils take ten GCSEs, including three separate sciences and at least one language. French, Spanish, Latin and classical civilisation on offer but school can organise German, Japanese, Mandarin and Russian if required (the benefits of having the dreaming spires of Oxford close by).

Academic ethos is the same in both sections of the college. 'We are an academic school,' Mark Olejnik, the genial head of Leckford Place (the lower school), told us, 'but we want children to enjoy their learning. Happiness is the very essence of what we do here.' Learning support offered for mild dyslexia and dyspraxia at no additional charge. Sixth form teachers have been known to spot issues that have been missed by previous schools and target appropriate help for students. Class sizes are small – no more than 15 up to GCSE and an average of seven at A level. There's an emphasis on discussion and confidence building throughout, with pupils encouraged to offer their views.

Games, options, the arts: School has worked hard to offer a broad range of sports and activities. Sport isn't compulsory for sixth formers but students are expected to do at least one extracurricular activity in the lower sixth – everything from hockey, rugby and netball to film club, yoga and first aid available, plus Young Enterprise and D of E. Lower sixth students also have compulsory enrichment programme – variety of outside speakers, from university professors and admissions tutors to writers, scientists and entrepreneurs.

d'Overbroeck's doesn't have its own playing fields but makes the most of the extensive facilities across Oxford. This seems to work well, with students being ferried by minibus to Oxford Brookes (which has an Astroturf, fully equipped sports hall, fitness gym, squash, badminton and basketball courts, climbing wall and more) and other sites. Similar approach to sport at Leckford Place. Year 7 and 8 pupils get three hours of games a week while those in years 9, 10 and 11 have two hours and 20 minutes of timetabled sport.

Drama is a delight, with younger pupils teaming up with sixth formers to stage major productions like Les Misérables and Peter Pan. At Leckford Place pupils have a double lesson of art and a double lesson of music each week. When we visited a group of year 8s were studying 'impossible architecture,' designing fantastical creations that would give our most eminent architects a run for their money. Many go on to study art in the sixth form and one parent told us: 'I am an artist myself and can say that my daughter has been brilliantly taught.' Eighty students take individual music lessons – all levels (beginners to grade 8) and everything from the violin to electric guitar. Recitals by pupils are often held at the Jacqueline du Pré auditorium at St Hilda's College, as well as regular concerts for students of all ages in the hall at Leckford Place. Music and music tech are popular at A level too.

Debating and public speaking are hugely popular. A team of year 9 pupils recently reached the national final of the Youth Speaks public speaking event. 'Opportunities are thrust on you here,' one of the team told us. 'It really makes you want to participate.' Loads of school trips, including recent summer expeditions to Namibia, Iceland and China for year 10 to 13 youngsters, annual ski trip and visits to theatre productions in London and Stratford-upon-Avon and the Rutherford Appleton Laboratory, one of the UK's national scientific research centres.

Background and atmosphere: d'Overbroeck's is 'a mushroom-shaped school' – the place gets bigger as it progresses up the age range. It started out as a sixth form college, founded in 1977 by French and Spanish teacher Malcolm van Biervliet, who was head of languages till he retired in 2007. Invited to speak about the college's ethos he said: '...friendship is a cornerstone in the d'Overbroeck's structure, contributing to the happiness of staff and students alike, and thus making the process of teaching and learning a more enjoyable and symbiotic experience.' Staff and students agree that his vision still holds true today.

Sixth form is housed in two large Victorian villas in leafy north Oxford, complete with stained glass windows, tessellated floors, classrooms, library, student common room, admin offices and a large garden at the back. Students doing science A levels walk up to Ewert Place in Summertown while the performing arts department is based round the corner in Leckford Place. Lessons are 65 minutes long and sixth formers get 15 minutes in between to get to their next class.

There's a real buzz everywhere you turn – lots of lively chatter, teachers and pupils on first name terms and an informal and energetic atmosphere throughout. No dining room but local caterer sets up shop in common room to sell sandwiches, paninis and drinks at lunchtime. Lots of students stroll up to M&S or Taylors in Summertown to buy lunch – they're spoiled for choice. 'This is a relatively informal environment,' says the principal. 'We don't stand on ceremony but there are clear boundaries and we have high expectations of the students.' Youngsters heartily approve. 'It's not stuffy here at all,' a girl told us. '

D

Most lower sixth boarders live in one of two co-ed boarding houses close by (20 places at 106 Banbury Road and 18 places at Hayfield). Double rooms with en-suite bathrooms at 106, singles with shared bathrooms at Hayfield. Girls and boys live in separate 'zones,' but meet up in communal areas for meals and socialising. Houseparents cook supper, lend a friendly ear to boarders, oversee the 7 to 9pm study periods and make sure everyone is in by the 10.30pm curfew (11.30pm on Fridays and Saturdays). Upper sixth boarders live with host families, all carefully vetted and regularly inspected. There's also a privately run girls' boarding house – Benson's.

d'Overbroeck's opened its lower school in 2005, snapping up a Victorian building in nearby Leckford Place previously occupied by Phil and Jim's, a local state primary. A ten-minute walk from the sixth form, the site is compact but makes the most of every inch of space. The lower school now boasts an ingeniously designed main building, with a galleried library resembling the upper deck of a ship, light and airy classrooms and a social area with a vivid pink wall, café tables and glossy blue lockers. The original school hall next door is used for lunch (wholesome meals dished up by nearby St Hugh's College), assemblies and theatrical productions. Leckford Place numbers are now approaching 160 (maximum would be 175), with two forms in years 7 and 8 and three from year 9.

No uniform for sixth form but year 7 to 11 pupils wear smart navy polo shirt or jumper with college logo. 'Apart from that they can wear their own clothes,' says the lower school head. 'As long as they are reasonable. No purple hair, hoodies, hats or nose piercings.' He admits that being called by his first name took a bit of getting used to though principal and students reckon it enables everyone to be themselves.

Pastoral care and discipline: Pastoral care is widely praised. Sixth form students are assigned their own director of studies (universally known as a DOS) – usually one of their subject teachers. Youngsters talk to them about academic and pastoral matters, with academic progress, attendance, punctuality, work rate and general wellbeing closely monitored. 'I see my DOS everyday,' one boy told us. Parents get a progress report by email every six weeks. Pupils can also talk to a trained college counsellor if they prefer and many turn to the college's dynamic young social organiser – a huge asset to the college who organises everything from film nights to barbecues. 'We are strict about the things that we need to be strict on,' says the principal, and students and parents concur with his words.

Firm rules on alcohol, drugs and smoking. No drugs tolerated – offenders asked to leave immediately. Students say bullying 'just doesn't happen here' and that unlike many other schools 'there is no sense of being considered cool or not cool.' 'Everyone is included,' a sixth former told us. 'It's a really friendly place.'

Sixth formers say that d'Overbroeck's has got its priorities right and appreciate the fact that it doesn't impose pointless rules and regulations. 'If you want a school that makes you go to chapel and has an army of prefects this probably isn't the right school for you,' one boy remarked. The college is firm about pupils being prompt for lessons and handing work in one time. Students who are ten minutes late aren't allowed into the class at all and an email is immediately sent to their parents. The only gripe we heard from sixth formers was the lack of lockers – a perennial whinge.

Form tutors are the first port of call at the lower school, with tutor groups meeting everyday and staff holding meeting every week to discuss pastoral issues. Head of Leckford Place stands at the school gate every morning to greet pupils – 'even in the pouring rain,' said one girl. 'It makes you feel really welcome.' Younger pupils we spoke to praised everything about the school, from the small class sizes, 'fair' rules and chocolate cake ('it's not overcooked') to being able to email teachers for help and getting answers back in double-quick time. 'You rarely have anyone in a bad mood here,' said another pupil. 'And I'm not just saying that.' Leckford Place has its own car-themed house system – Cooper, Morris and Austin – but unlike more traditional establishments these focus on environmental matters and fundraising for charity as well as competitions and sport.

Pupils and parents: Pupils are an eclectic mix of high achievers and grafters. Year 7 pupils generally arrive from local primary schools while year 9 entrants tend to come from Oxford preps like Christ Church, the Dragon and New College. No boarding at 11-16 – most live in Oxford and surrounding villages but some travel from as far afield as Wantage, Faringdon, Swindon and even Warwick. More boys than girls in lower school but a few more girls than boys in the sixth form. Post-16, equal numbers of day pupils and boarders. UK students come from a vast range of schools (both state and independent) while international students fly in from more than 30 different countries, including Italy, Spain, Russia and China. A handful of very clever Thai government scholars every year too.

College makes a big effort to keep parents 'in the loop.' Parents we spoke to appreciated its 'modern, unstuffy approach,' 'family atmosphere' and 'emphasis on the important things.' 'My son never enjoyed school until he came to d'Overbroeck's,' one mother told us. 'But he has thrived and been happy here right from the start. He'll be very sad to leave.'

Entrance: College is selective but principal emphasises that pupils have 'a reasonably wide range of abilities.' Alongside the academic requirements staff are looking for students 'who will enjoy the environment and make the most of it.'

Main entry points are year 7, year 9 and sixth form. At 11 and 13 applicants take internal assessment tests in English, maths and non-verbal reasoning, plus a short interview and reference from current school. 'We are looking for potentiality,' says the head of Leckford Place.

At 16 prospective students have an informal interview (they can also sit in on a few lessons if they wish) and need eight A*-C grades at GCSE, including maths and English. College also stipulates that pupils need at least a B in subjects being taken at A level while those doing maths need at least an A at GCSE (further maths needs an A*). International students sit written English language test (and maths test, where appropriate) and their level of English must be strong enough for the courses they want to do.

Exit: At 16, two-thirds of Leckford Place pupils move to the sixth form (a few head to local state schools like Cherwell and Cheney and in recent years three girls have moved to Magdalen College School's co-ed sixth form). At 18 virtually all go to university – UCL, LSE, Bristol, Leeds and Manchester currently the most popular destinations. Ten per cent to Oxbridge most years.

Money matters: A range of academic, art and performing arts scholarships for pupils entering years 7 and 9 (up to 20 per cent of tuition fees). Academic, art, performing arts and environmental scholarships available at sixth form level (up to 50 per cent of fees).

Remarks: d'Overbroeck's has made its mark in Oxford as an exciting and forward-thinking place to be. Along with top-notch teaching and rigorous academic standards the sixth form helps students to achieve impressive results and make lifelong friends along the way – the ideal stepping stone between school and university. For younger pupils Leckford Place is fast making a name for itself as a lively, happy environment that fizzes with energy and ideas.

Downe House School

Cold Ash, Thatcham, Berkshire, RG18 9JJ

- Pupils: 575 girls; 565 boarders • Ages: 11–18 • C of E
- Fees: Boarding £31,830; Day £23,040 pa • Independent

Tel: 01635 200286
Email: correspondence@downehouse.net
Website: www.downehouse.net

Headmistress: Since 1997, Mrs Emma McKendrick BA PGCE FRSA (late forties). Educated at Bedford High and at the universities of Liverpool and Birmingham (German and Dutch). Previously at The Royal School, Bath, where she had been i/c careers, sixth form, a house and deputy head before becoming head in 1994. Remarkably young when appointed to her first headship – that this was so is to the credit of the school's governors. She is soft-spoken, stylish, somehow very grown up, calm and relaxed. Her office and the room in which she receives visitors is a joy – windows on three sides so she can 'see everything', bright, light and tasteful. Parents – who tend to be deeply passionate about the school and many of whom are Old Girls – sigh with pleasure: 'She is excellent, on top of everything'; 'She is miraculous – I can say nothing against her. She is so professional, warm, and has a sense of humour. One cannot but be in awe of her, but you love her too'.

Academic matters: Has opted for Pre-U in preference to A levels in all but a few arts subjects. The reasons are admirable – more teaching time with no AS exams getting in the way and the capacity to focus on real teaching and learning. 'It really has made a difference to my upper sixth,' says the head. 'They are forced to be more independent. They are far better served by the Pre-U in terms of coping with what they will get at university.'

In 2013, 75 per cent A*-B grades and 62 per cent A*/A at A level, and 82 per cent A*-B equivalent (grades D1 – M2) at Pre-U. Maths very popular, with biology and English close behind. Good numbers for Latin and the odd taker for Greek. Politics, photography and economics offered along with history of art, plus all the trad subjects. Wide range of languages including support for home ones. Eighty-six per cent A*/A at GCSE. Blissfully small classes – school teacher:pupil ratio is an enviable 1:5.4: this is nurturing indeed.

Most teachers highly praised, many seen as 'inspiring'. Learning skills support given to those with mild dys-strata plus those who need extra help with organising themselves or time management. Also stretching help for the most able. Hopeless site for anyone in a wheelchair – the buildings are too scattered and the site is too up and down for this to be possible. EAL support given where needed – 35 in receipt of individual help when we visited.

Games, options, the arts: That the extracurricular life of the school is run from its own sizeable woodland cabin in the heart of the site with designated staff tells you everything. Every kind of opportunity is offered here – from trips to The Royal Opera House to playing lacrosse for Berkshire, to preparing soup for hungry people in South Africa from sackfuls of bones fresh from a slaughterhouse. Lots of visits from outside speakers, who clearly inspire and motivate. Much lively and imaginative charitable activity – often with the boys from Radley. Excellent drama – again, often with Radley – generously supported by Old Girl, Geraldine James, who opened the performing arts centre and has been known to take aspiring actresses under her wing. Two recent successful auditions for the National Youth Theatre. Successful and popular debating.

Sports are many and varied and include, for older girls, Pilates, fencing and golf. Several girls are England lacrosse players – lax taken more seriously here than other sports. Internal competition between houses seemingly counting more than fixtures against other schools. Art is lively, though housed in the least attractive building on site – great range of activities: we loved the individuality of work in textiles, ceramics and woodwork, along with truly impressive painting. Ballet, modern dance, tap and hip hop on offer and around half the girls take speech and drama. Practically all of them learn at least one instrument. 'They all do so much extra,' a parent told us, half-admiring, half-concerned. 'They do whack on the pressure – the girls themselves, that is.'

Houses clearly of immense importance here – friendly but significant rivalry in all areas of school life. Lots of trips at home and abroad – all with sound educational or charitable purposes. Most exciting, memorable and generally aaaahed over is the term spent in every girl's second year at the school's own converted farm in the heart of Perigord. Those who join the school in year 9 seem to spend the next five years biting their lip at having missed an unforgettable experience. A seasoned sixth former told us – as if it were obvious – 'Oh, we never stop talking about it.' It's about French and French life, cuisine, charity work, community and living ensemble.

Background and atmosphere: Founded in 1907 by Olive Willis, its first headmistress, as an all-girls' boarding school. Its first home was Down House in the village of Downe, Kent – formerly the home of Charles Darwin. The school outgrew the house so Miss Willis bought The Cloisters in Berkshire – its present home – on a high ridge which provides occasional views over distant downs. The Cloisters – still at the heart of the school – comes as a surprise. Built by Maclaren Ross for an order of Spanish nuns, who named it The School of Silence, it has an arched walkway linking most of the classrooms which – with its white walls, arches and terracotta pantiles – is incongruously Moorish in the heart of Berkshire.

However, the school has grown many newer buildings – boarding houses, specialist blocks etc – around the main building and the site is now extensive – many buildings nestling amongst trees, woody areas and neatly planted beds. All maintained by 'little green men' who hover around the site on electric car-lets. No architectural gems here – nor any monsters – though a few blocks lack charm. The whole has a sense of modest purposefulness – described by one mother as 'almost spiritual'.

All but a handful of local day girls are full boarders. Lessons until 12pm on Saturdays are followed by sports, so everyone signs up to the full boarding life. Saturday evenings are spent in rehearsal, at concerts, trips to theatres, cinemas etc. Sundays include trips, D of E activities and chillin'. The uniform is standard school green skirt, shirt and jumper, though the sixth form still cling to their floor length black skirts – 'They wear them so they can keep their pyjamas on underneath,' one mum told us.

Pastoral care and discipline: 'Completely faultless,' a mother said of the pastoral care. 'The house staff are very responsive and email you back at once.' 'When people complain, things do get done,' another vouchsafed. 'We've been bowled over by the pastoral care,' said yet another. 'The attention to detail is extraordinary – almost obsessive. Nothing is too much trouble.' One boarding school veteran told us that the boarding staff were much the best she'd ever come across. The boarding houses themselves are much loved. We relished the dressing up boxes in the junior houses.

First year girls are in one of two houses, one onsite and the other in the village, though this may change with developments afoot – the village house would be mourned by many. New individual personalised tutor system for years 7 and 8. Second to 5th years are in mixed age houses – dorms are mostly

D

spacious; singles and doubles for the older girls are homely and attractive. Everywhere is properly carpeted and curtained. Fresh flowers abound – no sense here that 'nice' areas are just for show – this is home and it feels like it. All houses either wireless or with network points.

Sixth form houses are exceptionally well designed and furnished. Pigeon holes for girls' post and newspapers; sofas, careers areas, meeting rooms, kitchens. Girls can be independent here, if they wish – no wonder so few leave after GCSEs. All have a personal safe in their rooms. Further extension to and enhancement of the boarding facilities planned.

The loveliest school dining room we have seen in over 100 schools – proper tablecloths on round tables seating six to encourage time over meals. Food – 'We make all our own bread and sausages and buy in the absolute minimum' – which occasions rhapsodies in the girls.

Some sense that the sixth form centre separates older from younger girls and work still to be done on integrating those who arrive after the first year, but this is tricky in girls' schools everywhere. Very few discipline problems – smoking sighed over as 'an occasional safe rebellion which one wishes they wouldn't do', and illicit drinking looked upon as a threat to a girl's personal safety – 'You need to be safe, to look after yourself and to preserve your dignity,' the head reminds them. No drugs incidents within memory and the very rare girl who 'cannot stop being unkind has to go'.

Pupils and parents: Girls from all over the UK and beyond; increasing numbers of daughters of alumnae. Seven per cent from overseas – mostly from the Far East but also the US, Nigeria, Kazakhstan. Parents solid middle class, usually with boarding backgrounds.

Exceptionally impressive list of notable alumnae includes: chemist and educator, Rosemary Murray, Geraldine James, Clare Balding, Mary Midgley, Elizabeth Bowen, Priscilla Napier, Anne Ridler, Audrey Richards, Sophie Conran, Lulu Guinness, Fru Hazlitt, wildly different comics Miranda Hart and Laura Solon, Hannah Wright – pioneering barrister, Jenifer Hart – pioneering civil servant and Oxford don and Aileen Fox – pioneering archaeologist. Oh – and Kate Middleton. A rare degree of loyalty amongst alumnae – few schools excite more affection, it seems, and many keep in touch. Mrs McKendrick fosters this in imaginative ways, enlisting Old Girls to support newbies in their professions, eg an established barrister mentoring a recent alumna in her pupillage. A considerable attraction to potential parents.

Entrance: Lists close at 110 applicants and head interviews all those over four days, during which all are tested in maths, English and reasoning. They also participate in drama and sports activities et al to see whether they're happy and likely to fit in with boarding life. Eighty then invited to sit CE for the 60 available places. At 13, around 65 are assessed similarly for the 35-odd places. Girls from 180+ preps/primaries have joined Downe in recent years – from all over the UK.

At 16, it depends on how many are leaving but usually around 8-10 places for the 'huge' number who apply. Applicants sit the school's own papers and the strongest are then interviewed, the best offered conditional places. Seven I/GCSEs at B or above expected including A*/As in sixth form subject choices.

Exit: Most to top universities, eg Bristol, London, Warwick, Exeter, Leeds, Edinburgh, with around 10 per cent to Oxbridge. Some to universities in the US. Popular subjects include science/medicine, psychology, history of art, MFL, economics, politics, RS, business related degrees plus music and creative arts.

Money matters: Scholarships for sports, arts and academics more of an honour than a significant contribution to fees.

Bursaries up to 100 per cent of fees plus additional help available for the right applicant.

Remarks: Archetypal traditional girls' full boarding school turning out delightful, principled, courteous and able girls who go on to make a significant contribution to the world. As one parent said, 'We couldn't be more thrilled.'

Downside School

Stratton-on-the-Fosse, Bath, BA3 4RJ

- Pupils: 355 pupils; 280 full and 7 weekly boarders • Ages: 11–18
- RC and Christian • Fees: Boarding £22,539–£28,374; Day £14,154–£15,747 pa • Independent

Tel: 01761 235103
Email: registrar@downside.co.uk
Website: www.downside.co.uk

Head: Since 2003, Dom Leo Maidlow Davies MA BD STL (mid-fifties), a Benedictine monk who has been at Downside man and boy, departing only to read archaeology and anthropology at Cambridge in the '70s, and theology at London and Rome in the '80s. Since then, he has taught classics as a novice master, been a housemaster and still teaches RS to the sixth form. His steepled fingers, intense spirituality and learned air thinly veil a delightful sense of humour and turn of phrase: Downside is undoubtedly a Catholic school 'but I don't need a beauty parade to see just how Catholic pupils are'. Working out of a charmingly messy book-lined study overlooking the quad, he appears to enjoy the right degree of respect and warmth with his flock. His faith is at the centre of everything he does: 'The glorification of God is important and this school does not tuck a little bit of religion away on the side', yet he is much in tune with the transient preoccupations of the young and addresses them with apparent sensitivity. Commercial necessities and front of house are well handled by his management team, an effective foil to this most cerebral of men, yet some parents feel that he should exhibit more honest-to-goodness leadership, particularly in dealing with less than effective teaching.

Retiring in April 2014. His successor will be the school's first lay head, Dr James Whitehead, currently second master at Worth. Educated at Stonyhurst College and Oxford University, he worked at Downside from 2004-2007 as head of English and director of studies (his Catholic credentials are exemplary, says the school). He has also taught at Radley. He is a fellow of the royal Society of Arts, and passionately interested in literature and sport. He is married to Nicola, and they have two daughters.

Academic matters: Beefed up in recent years, especially at at A level, with 74 per cent A*-B and 48 A*/A in 2013; creditable GCSEs, too, at 59 per cent A/A* some of which is attributable to the previous determined director of studies, who insisted on a 50 per cent average at common entrance (since 2006). A new director of studies now in place 'to give us a further shake-up', and 'has introduced a new system of ambitious target-setting' The Year 7 pre-assessments mean that CE is no longer the usual benchmark for admissions; also new entrance assessments for year 10 and year 12.

Value-added particularly strong here. Subjects offered at GCSE and A level are 'properly academic and recognised by leading universities'; this causes some pupils wanting more choice and/or creativity to bail out for sixth form. Most take 11 GCSEs, including at least one modern language; RS compulsory for all but the most alienated foreigner. Some parents critical of academic snobbery, eg a society for Oxbridge pupils (only).

School says, 'There are a range of academic societies for all pupils and each faculty coordinates its own Gifted programme.'

A tutor is assigned to each pupil – they're around the houses during prep to offer sticks/carrots as appropriate. Grades every half term mean progress can be closely tracked and problems dealt with; lots of additional support sessions on offer. Academic societies in every year group exist to 'ignite an appetite for higher achievement' (a very Benedictine aspiration) and essay prizes for all subjects and year groups. Refurbished library is enough to provoke intellectual endeavour in anyone. Wifi operational but some parents worry that ICT is an add-on, insufficiently integrated into lessons. 'They're asleep on IT,' said one dissatisfied dad. School says 'We have a new ICT manager who is working hard to change systems and upgrade protocols'. Brand new iMac suite – not before time: pupils reckon that 'humanities far outstrip sciences'. School points to 'significant improvement in GCSE science results in 2013'.

Claims 'long experience of supporting pupils with mild special needs, especially dyslexia and dyspraxia', though points out that pupils must be able to cope with a mainstream academic curriculum, albeit with one-to-one support where needed. Dedicated unit which also caters for moderate learning difficulties and some behavioural issues. Its low profile assures discretion to its users. Follows Cambridge ESL course and all EAL pupils – even those only here for a year – leave with an English qualification.

Games, options, the arts: 500 verdant acres mean pitches almost as far as the eye can see, plus tennis/netball courts, a running track and new Astro. As well as traditional rugby, hockey, football, cricket, tennis for the boys and hockey, netball, tennis and rounders for the girls, more exotic activities are on offer. Sailing now takes place at least one afternoon a week, with the school having dinghies at nearby Shearwater. Super sports hall and beautifully refurbished swimming pool accommodate those less keen on the great outdoors. Philosophy tends to be team participation for all, rather than winning at all costs, (though 1st XV 'repeatedly victorious' at the time of writing), and there's an upscale fixtures list. Some parents feel that the approach and organisation could be considerably sharpened up. Top players can join local clubs and county/regional squads. Thriving CCF, compulsory for part year 9; D of E and Ten Tors popular too, but Downside maintains a proud and distinguished military tradition.

Pupils' art adorns the walls of the main building's wide corridors, with their quaintly wonky parquet floors; art block totally refurbished. Innovative work in all media and remarkable photography, some of which appears in the school's own publications, oeuvres of extraordinary glossiness – and paucity of content, but school says 'we have the annual Raven magazine which records all events/ sports/ house reports etc from the whole year.'

Drama very strong and they're fortunate to have a theatre seating 600, with a stage built wide enough to perform Gilbert and Sullivan, in the days when it was fashionable. Plays put on for all age groups and in each house once a year, and everyone gets involved, on or off the stage. Fantastic music and art provision mean enough competent players, singers and set designers to ensure productions are almost always pupil-led.

Music outstanding – and so it should be, with the prospect of singing mass every Sunday in the sublime setting of the abbey church. The Schola Cantorum performs major choral works throughout the year and has several CDs under its belt. No less than four chamber choirs of only 16 voices each (boys, girls, mixed, junior) invite only the especially talented to audition. Players shine too, either in the orchestra, chamber groups or the pipe band. Organists lucky enough to have two quality instruments to play on site. More contemporary fare trumpeted at the battle of the bands and charity showcase, shared with nearby Writhlington School, but considerable feeling that modern and/or alternative music (eg folk) should get more airtime than it does. Oddly enough, music tech pretty good after recent investment and pupils now encouraged to create own rock bands with Saturday concerts organised every term.

Background and atmosphere: Rearing up from the surrounding countryside, the abbey is visible for miles around and dominates the sleepy, slightly run-down village of Stratton-on-the-Fosse. The present, somewhat austere, buildings date mostly from 1814, when it had become safe for Catholics once more to provide education in England, but the school is over 400 years old. The spiritual life of the monastic community permeates the very fabric of the school; this veteran of many schools had never experienced anything quite like its atmosphere. As the head remarked, 'It would be hard to leave Downside without a sense of what a spiritual life was'. The monks are vital to the life of the school; some teach and their presence in the chaplaincy is particularly valued, but their role is one of influence rather than power. Some 80 per cent of the pupils are Catholic; those that aren't are asked to 'recognise the distinctively Catholic nature', but a few feel somewhat sidelined, including parents, who chose the school for its pastoral care and spiritual grounding, yet resent the distinction being drawn. Nonetheless, these aspects do not disappoint, and the way in which the school lays down the foundations of faith – whatever the pupils then go on to make of it – is widely praised; 'an anchor for life', as one father put it.

Atmosphere and setting remain distinctly traditional, helped by wonderfully anachronistic uniform which includes, at various stages, black jackets and pinstripes for the boys, and for the girls classic mid-length kilts and red or black jumpers as well as grey jackets (even in sixth form, astonishingly); girls' uniform designed by a committee of mothers. Sports kit cooler, if lurid. Magnificent though slightly gloomy refectory, serving unspectacular food when we visited (school assures us 'a new catering manager has seen food improve significantly both in standard, quality and quantity with varied and delicious menu'); some complain there isn't always enough of it for hungry boys at supper time, but the theatre café opens in the evenings, filling any gaps, and there are kitchens in all the boarding houses. Gripes about food or any other matter raised at school council. Strong house allegiance to all of the houses for boarders and day pupils; no longer a separate house for 11 year olds – boys now join Powell, girls Isabella House, with their own separate areas. In common with most boys' schools, no change at sixth form.

The girls' arrival in 2005 has breathed new life into the place, 'the making of it', according to one mother of three sons, though a few dissent! 'We are no longer preparing boys and girls for different roles,' says the head, then adds 'but our primary purpose is not to produce chaps who will be useful to the economy'. Oh dear, not too many sons and daughters of Old Gregorians in the pipeline then...'We are a popular choice with Old Gregorians,' says school. However, a palpable family feeling about the place. Parents also like the notion of service the school promotes. It does all feel rather insular though, and remote from modern life. Certainly wouldn't suit more urban types, which is perhaps why some parents choose it! inter-house socials and some with outside schools, but some parents feel strongly that a small school so rurally located definitely needs more. Downside has determinedly kept its ethos as a full boarding school, with 85 per cent boarders and a full weekend activity programme. Some day pupils elect to spend much of the weekend at school; when we visited, everyone was preparing for a Roman banquet on the Saturday night – no stuffed dormice, we hope.

Pastoral care and discipline: Excellent pastoral care and tolerance for the individual produces happy kids, some of whom have found Downside a refuge after the rough and tumble of other schools: 'My daughter is respected for who she is and her confidence restored', said one relieved mother who moved her from the local state offering. Each pupil has a tutor to oversee academic matters but they liaise closely with house staff, so that the overview is seamless. Policies strive for consistency; there is a dedicated head of pastoral care. Problems of smoking and drinking are 'manageable' – the school aims to educate the pupils though the pitfalls. Parents are kept informed of all but the most minor misdemeanours and sanctions tend towards privations at weekends, such as detention, gating or the wearing of uniform. Pupils report some inconsistencies in the awarding of punishments, but they agreed that owning up was likely to be in their best interests, both in this world and the next. No reports of inappropriate relations with the opposite sex; perhaps all that moral guidance pays off.

Achievements of all kinds are celebrated at house or school level; certificates in 'seemly Latin' are handed out at headmaster's assembly six times a year, along with sporting colours and caps. He marks lesser successes with a hand-written postcard, a nice touch.

Downside, in common with other reputable institutions, has weathered storms of historic abuse cases in recent years, but the ISI report of 2012 found safeguarding 'excellent'.

Pupils and parents: Lots of different backgrounds and educational experiences united by 'common values and aspirations to a spiritual life' – plus Catholicism in majority of cases. Strong family ties. A certain amount of Catholic snobbery but not so much social – this is not a flashy school. Most enjoy a good and mutually supportive relationship with the school, though some report that 'feedback is not always welcomed, let alone acted upon'. The pupils struck us as articulate, thoughtful, focused (though not alarmingly so) yet somewhat unworldly, seemingly immune from the teenage temptations of sex, drugs and rock 'n' roll. (Perhaps not in the holidays.) Mostly local families, but increasing numbers from London, fleeing the intense competition for places at decent schools, or metropolitan distractions. A sprinkling of foreigners, 10 per cent or so.

Entrance: Entry below sixth form has had a shake-up. Entry is now only into years 7 or 8 (curiously year 6 too in the past), via the Downside Assessment Test, a computerised aptitude test with no possible preparation, with assessments in maths, English and general reasoning, plus interview and reports from the previous school. Nonetheless, all pupils still sit common entrance or common scholarship in year 8 – results determine sets in the senior school. Conditional places sometimes offered to less confident performers, who then have to 'pass the CE exam threshold', currently set at 50 per cent across all subjects. Normal whirligig of open/taster/induction days. Sixth form entry depends on interview, previous school's reports and references and tests in subjects intended for A level. B grades at GCSE, but As for sciences, are required to pursue any subject to A level.

Exit: A little fall-out after GCSE, mostly pupils seeking a wider or more vocational choice at A level. Later, almost all to higher education – wide range of universities: two Oxbridge offers in 2013 (one to read theology at St Benet's Hall, following a long line of OBs); others to eg Bristol, Cardiff, Manchester, UCL, Warwick, York, The Wharton Business School USA. Approx a third take gap years and apply post A level, something the school encourages – we hope it offers the same degree of support over UCAS forms as it does to those still present. Director of studies intends to track leavers' destinations more closely in future – more information would be useful.

Money matters: Fees in line with, if not cheaper than, comparable schools. A 'substantial number' of scholarships and exhibitions available, the size and distribution of which

are at the head's discretion. Usual offer of music, sport and all-rounder, plus choral awards of anything up to 50 per cent of fees. Discounts of up to 15 per cent for scions of Old Gregorians and 10 per cent for siblings, also means-tested bursaries.

Remarks: A culture of aspiration, whether spiritual or academic, pervades this rather rarefied school. Sheltered by the abbey and guided by its faith, pupils are cocooned from less welcome bits of modern life and allowed to concentrate on acquiring a thorough intellectual and spiritual toolkit, and to grow up in their own time, with idiosyncrasies intact. Very special, and not for everyone we suspect, but a great choice for practising Catholics and those seeking strong spiritual direction in a school.

Dr Challoner's Grammar School

Chesham Road, Amersham, Buckinghamshire, HP6 5HA

• Pupils: 1,310 boys; all day • Ages: 11–18 • Non-denom • State

Tel: 01494 787500
Email: admin@challoners.com
Website: www.challoners.com

Headmaster: Since 2001, Dr Mark Fenton MA MSc PGCE PhD. Now in his mid forties, became head in his early thirties and remains an ebullient and boyish figure, with a nice sense of irony, passionate about his school and about delivering an education that isn't all about exam statistics (one of the few heads we've met who genuinely doesn't have the figures at his finger tips). Educated at Brentwood School, Essex, followed by Peterhouse, Cambridge, where he read history, graduating with a first. PGCE at the Institute of Education, then squeezed in his PhD (on how parents choose schools) while already working. Started out at Chelmsford, at a mixed comprehensive, then taught history and politics at King Edward V1 Grammar School for six years, rising to assistant head. Then deputy head, Sir Joseph Williamson's Mathematical School, a grammar school in Rochester, before proceeding to Dr Challoner's as one of the country's youngest heads.

Feels the school he took over was not only run down but a bit insular and old-fashioned. He has spruced it up physically, socially and academically, transforming its traditionally élitist (some would have said arrogant) approach to one where 'intelligent awareness' is the norm. 'Now it's a softer place,' he says. Wants the education he provides to be 'broad-ranging and rounded', to teach about perseverance, responsibility and risk – 'I want boys to be able to reflect on what they've done; I want them to understand collaboration.'

Parents feel he has come tightly to grips with the organisation; most find him very approachable – 'When it snowed and half the boys couldn't get in, he just said, "Right, let's go out and have a snowball fight," and the teachers all joined him.' Continues to teach (citizenship to year 8, politics A level) and, according to one father, knows 'endless boys' by name. Recently appointed a national leader of education by the National College for School Leadership, one of about 100 heads in the country.

Academic matters: Now Buckinghamshire's top-performing grammar and consistently in the top 20 nationwide, though not a school where undue pressure seems the norm. Breadth considered a desirable commodity – Dr Fenton believes that the more pupils learn the better they become at learning. Most take 11 GCSEs, with a compulsory language and humanity plus four options. Two-thirds take four A levels – 'research shows that if you take four subjects you do better in all four'. 2013 70 per cent of grades at GCSE A*/A; 84 per cent A*-B and nearly 60 per cent A*/A at A level.

Specialist status in science – 'The science teaching is incredibly strong,' said one parent – and carts away loads of awards from the Royal Society of Chemistry. Second specialism in languages. 'We asked: where is there most scope for improvement? Boys and languages can be a bit of an uphill struggle; we wanted to put it front and centre in an innovative way.' As well as French, Spanish and German, Mandarin and Russian now offered as sixth form options and language teaching approached in a creative fashion using music to help aid speech rhythms, plus cultural enrichment days and work experience exchanges abroad.

The head is an enthusiast for more adventurous teaching and learning methods all round – 'The point is for them to work things out and then explain how they've done it'. Staff are trained to understand boys' strengths as learners and boys do specialised induction days in years 7, 10 and 12 devoted to reflection on learning. Teaching (and indeed everything else) praised as excellent in recent Ofsted inspection (though one parent felt the school was still stronger on the science side than on the arts). Twenty-five A level options. Standard classes of 30 in the early years, 20-30 at GCSE, 15-20 higher up. All teachers are involved in SEN and, if necessary, an individual education plan will be drawn up, with some individual tuition where required.

Games, options, the arts: Sport played at top competitive level – 'We knew the school was academically strong,' said one parent, 'but our son wouldn't have survived if it hadn't had good sport as well and he absolutely loves it'. Headmaster very keen on cricket, which is reflectively buoyant. Regular sports tours abroad – football to Holland, cricket to the Caribbean. Very successful soccer team, hockey up and coming. National finals of the under 19s squash; national junior cross-country champions. Annual activity week lets boys try out the more unusual sports, like climbing and golf. Sport for all with house competitions and lunchtime clubs; facilities include two sports halls, a floodlit all-weather pitch, a fine cricket square and pavilion.

Music also hugely strong with a good boys' choir, professional standard jazz band and swing band operated jointly with the matching girls' grammar school down the road. Lots of other co-ed activities, including lively drama – annual drama, musical and senior play. Debating enthusiastic and strong. Wide range of stimulating education visits (geographers to Iceland, historians to Washington DC). Six houses with plenty of inter-house competition in sports, music and science.

Background and atmosphere: Founded 1624 under the will of Dr Robert Chaloner (sic), former rector of Amersham and Canon of Windsor. Moved to present site in 1905, when it became co-ed. Due to expanding numbers, girls got their own premises in 1962. The boys' school is still focused round the 1905 core but has expanded higgledy-piggledy, with a motley mix of buildings from creaky '50s to state of the art 21st century. Not the most coherent or beautiful site, but well equipped with the requisite facilities to house and stretch its 1300 or so bright and well behaved young men. New sixth form centre and library.

'Excellence with integrity' is the school's motto – it prides itself on the responsibility it gives to pupils. 'This school respects students, gives them responsibility and trusts them,' said one. Very active student council – 'It teaches negotiation and leadership,' says the head. 'We regularly consult students and student groups undertake research, then present their findings to the senior leadership team. It work across the ages and helps them understand both research and presentation.'

Sixth formers given considerable degree of freedom – attendance compulsory till lunch, then free to go if no lessons. Large number of boys given official responsibility in the sixth form, with 60-80 elected prefects, head boys, house captains etc. Boys supervise lunch with walkie-talkies and mentor new boys. Healthy hot lunch for younger pupils, sixth formers have their own café with slightly less PC snacks or leave the premises to make their own eating decisions. Blazer and standard tie pre-GCSE, own suit and tie of authority thereafter.

Pastoral care and discipline: In general, a sensible, well behaved lot ('I'm sure there must be drugs, but I've never seen any evidence of them,' says one long-term mother). School confronts traditional problem areas head on. 'We bring in search dogs unannounced and have a drugs counsellor,' says the head. 'Since we introduced this policy five years ago, we've not had a single drugs related incident.' One or two challenging students and usual tiresome teenage misconduct, treated firmly but with understanding. 'One boy couldn't fit a pornographic film on his memory stick so he tried to upload it onto the school computer,' says the head wryly. 'He got a one-day exclusion. I don't mind the odd misdemeanour but I get fed up when they can't learn from their mistakes.' Pupils themselves have drawn up the bullying charter, displayed in every classroom. Student development team and support staff with a counselling qualification.

Pupils and parents: Solid middle-class parents from the surrounding solid middle-class landscape. Ethnic minorities (about 15 per cent) and free school meals very much less in evidence than elsewhere; nonetheless parents and pupils range from the very poor to the significantly well off. Coaches deliver boys from more remote spots but the school also nicely near the tube.

Entrance: All applicants take the Buckinghamshire Test (the best score of two tests in verbal reasoning) and anyone who gets 121 (with 141 the top mark) is entitled to a grammar school place. Technically, this means the top 34 per cent will be eligible, though occasionally successful candidates will fall below the benchmark, including some boys who qualify through the appeals process. Catchment area is defined by the council. Ever-more-heavily oversubscribed, it used to take boys from more than seven miles away, now rarely more than six miles – don't even think of applying if you live out of county. Twenty places for external applicants at A level – candidates must have 386 points from their best eight GSCEs, plus at least a grade C in English and maths. Some subjects have additional specifications.

Exit: Very few leave post-GCSEs. 'When we offered our sons the choice of any independent school they wanted, day or boarding, they all decided they'd prefer to stay at Challoner's,' says one mother.

Around 10 per cent to Oxbridge; Southampton and Exeter very popular, then Birmingham, Nottingham, Bristol, LSE, Leeds. One or two venture abroad. Strong in maths (several recent years have seen as many as eight or nine students go on to Oxbridge to read it), science and engineering (22 on assorted engineering courses), but all academic areas well represented.

Money matters: Strong PTA fundraising, but parental financial support is optional rather than press-ganged.

Remarks: An outstanding boys' grammar school, particularly strong in science, which produces well-qualified, level-headed, responsible adults, able to fit in anywhere. A friendly, purposeful, down-to-earth place, where boys enjoy a good social life with their peers and the neighbouring girls' grammar school.

Dr Challoner's High School

Cokes Lane, Little Chalfont, Buckignhamshire, HP7 9QB

- Pupils: 1,075 girls, all day • Ages: 11–18 • Non-denom • State

Tel: 01494 763296
Email: office@challonershigh.com
Website: www.challonershigh.com

Head: Since 2011, Mr Ian Cooksey MA (Oxon) MA (Lond) FRGS (late thirties). Educated at Queen Mary's Grammar School in Walsall and Magdalen College Oxford, where he read biological sciences. Has spent his career in the state sector, first at stellar grammar Tiffin School, Kingston upon Thames, where he rose from biology teacher to assistant head. Moved as vice principal to Tomlinscote School, Frimley, before being charged with taking King's International School, Camberley, out of special measures, which he successfully achieved. Came full circle back to a state grammar when he joined DCHS as head, the fourth in an eight-year period.

Married with two small children, Mr Cooksey says there was 'lots to retain and preserve' when he joined the school, with his first task being to move the school from a good to outstanding Ofsted rating. Keen to drag DCHS into the future with pioneering technological advancements across all subjects (year 7s now issued with laptops) and to further improve independent learning skills amongst the girls. He is strongly against 'spoon feeding pupils through the curriculum' and keeps his hand in with two periods a week in the classroom with sixth formers.

Proudly describes the girls as 'brilliant ambassadors' for the school and as such has decided to take a back seat at open evenings for prospective parents and let the pupils do the talking. Parents – some of whom have seen a few captains of this large and well established ship – wait with bated breath to see what this keen mountaineer (he is currently climbing all of Scotland's Munros) will bring to the school now he has his feet well and truly under the table.

Academic matters: DCHS regularly hovers around the top of regional and national state school league tables. Five classes of 30 in each year group, with setting from year 9 in maths. Strong results at GSCE (79 per cent A*/A in 2013) and A level (59 per cent A*/A and 86 per cent A*-B in 2013) with unanimous agreement amongst parents and girls that maths is the greatest academic strength of the school. The number of year 12s choosing to take further maths as a 'twilight course' in their free periods is testament to this, with girls describing their maths teachers as 'inspirational' and 'unbelievably thorough'.

Languages also 'fantastic' according to pupils, with French and either German or Spanish from year 7 and Latin from year 8; in year 9 girls choose two of the three they have studied so far, with many taking two languages at GCSE. Mandarin on offer from year 12.

Good breadth of subjects available at both GSCE and A level, with strong take-up of biology, chemistry and maths at A level partly due, according to head, to 'external factors' driving girls to make themselves more employable but also to his 'amazing team of teachers' some of whom have been with the school over 30 years. Religious studies currently most popular subject at GSCE, again due to 'outstanding' teaching staff, and other humanities are taught with 'integrity and enthusiasm', according to parents. Fairly large take-up of English literature at A level, although there are a few grumbles from parents about 'patchy' teaching in this core subject.

Games, options, the arts: PE mandatory from years 7-11, with all the usual suspects (netball, hockey, athletics and gymnastics) taught to a high standard by enthusiastic staff. Sport popular both on and off curriculum, with a sports leadership programme in place for years 12 and 13 and a junior athlete education programme for those competing at county, national or international level. DCHS successfully competes at a high level across the board, including more marginal activities like fencing, basketball and rowing in its armoury. Cricket, football and rugby also on offer for the brave at heart and girls' achievements outside school are also commended. Majority of sports clubs are free, with just a handful (such as rowing, fencing) charged as an extra.

Huge range of artsy extracurricular activities on offer (again, mostly free) with an impressive array of ensembles for all levels from the music department, including a swing band which tours with the boys' school biennially. Budding performers are spoilt for choice, with constant opportunities to sing, dance and act on offer, the highlight being the annual joint musical production with the boys' school, hosted by each on alternate years. There are also opportunities from year 10 for girls who wish to learn technical sound, lighting and set building. Excellent arts and technology faculty, with quality work festooning the immediately surrounding area, although it's a pity this doesn't make its way further into the school.

Complementary studies in Italian and Russian on offer for sixth formers, with Russian and Mandarin also available to years 8 to 13, with one of the Russian groups working towards a GCSE. There's also D of E and fiercely contested debating, with regular trips to the Oxford Union and external lecturers from the worlds of business and government visit the Economics Society. In short, something for everyone, although parents occasionally comment that they would like girls to be pushed to do more.

Unbelievably long list of school trips for all year groups, from curriculum based and language exchanges to a PGL for year 7, a Raleigh trip to Tanzania for year 12 (with girls expected to raise funds to travel and work for charity) and a biennial history trip to Russia for year 13.

Background and atmosphere: Founded in 1624 by Dr Robert Chaloner (sic), becoming co-ed in 1906. Girls hived off to Little Chalfont in 1962 (the boys' school, Dr Challoner's Grammar School, is a few miles away in Amersham). Tucked away amongst prime South Bucks real estate, DCHS is a blot on the greenbelt comprising a mix of 1960s buildings with more modern extensions added in the 90s. Plus points are an outdoor amphitheatre, used for summer term performances, and an impressive number of multi-purpose spaces including a large, modern sports hall; assembly hall; gymnasium and sound-proofed drama studio, all excellent for the school's large and active performing arts community.

Subject to restricted state budgets, the fabric of DCHS lacks many of the gleaming facilities one might expect in a leading school, but has a dilapidated charm all the same. In the words of one parent: 'it's truly a state school, but it all somehow works.' No vast games fields or state of the art pool but the girls achieve highly in sports – ironically, particularly swimming – nonetheless. The library and sixth form common room would benefit from major facelifts and pupils lovingly describe the school as 'cramped' (and the loos as 'dreadful!') but the head says there are plans afoot to address this in the mid-term with the addition of a new sixth form centre (donations to the £3-4 million fund needed gratefully received).

Despite ferocious competition for places, parents of more junior pupils report a surprisingly relaxed and happy vibe rather than a hothouse feel, although the consensus is that quiet souls might struggle initially due to the school's sheer size and pace. Parents of younger girls generally agree that the 'whole child is nurtured'. Pressure ramps up from year 10, though, when girls are expected to sing for their supper and deliver nothing less than A grades; not a school where 'just doing your best' is good

D

enough, with those in years 12 and 13 expected to put in up to five extra hours a week of independent study per subject on top of an already heavy homework load.

Pupils say they are given 'a lot of freedom' and there is a feeling of trust and ownership around the school, with girls given free rein of the buildings – including the computer labs – at break times. New TV screens, displaying 'digital posters' and other information for pupils are scattered through the corridors (a pupil-led innovation). In the words of one girl, 'every voice is heard here'. Collegiate relationships between staff and pupils are notable by initiatives such as 'sine nomine', a society which enables the girls to perform good deeds anonymously, such as cleaning the school bus or decorating the staff room at Christmas.

Pastoral care and discipline: Incidents of poor behaviour are, in the words of the head, 'very rare'. No permanent exclusions in living memory and only a couple of temporary exclusions more recently – for smoking, which has a zero tolerance policy. More emphasis, therefore, is placed on pastoral care which is described by parents as 'very good'. Friendship issues (that's bullying in girl-talk) are kept in check with befriending schemes between year groups and a 'big sister, little sister' initiative, with older girls able to mentor junior sports squads or tutor younger ones if they are struggling academically.

Girls have the same academic tutor for their whole tenure at the school, and for greater personal problems they can make a confidential appointment with the school counsellor. Popular termly discos with the boys' school enable them to let their hair down in a safe environment.

Hugely successful house system encourages mixing and co-operation between year groups. A head girl 'team' is elected each year, with one head girl and nine deputies, each looking after a specific aspect of the school ranging from innovation and student voice to press and PR. Very professional glossy school magazine put together by pupils, showcases girls' talent in writing features, poetry and short stories as well as photography and artwork.

Word has it that teacher/parent communication has 'greatly improved', with parents now able to email individual teachers via the school office. Parents receive a weekly newsletter, including a check-list of information that should have been passed on by pupils. Girls receive the weekly Hedwig Post by email to keep them abreast of what's afoot around the school.

Pupils and parents: The intellectual standard is the common denominator here, with entry dependent on success at 11 plus, now administered by a conglomeration of the county's grammar schools following collective achievement of academy status. Despite the affluent surroundings (around 20-25 per cent join annually from prep schools), the school is both socially and ethnically diverse, albeit with a very small number eligible for free school meals. Excellent bus service (around £10 a week if school is not your closest) from surrounding areas morning and afternoon, but parents need to be on hand to collect after later activities.

Middle class parents like the fact that the school makes their children more aware of different social situations. Those of pupils entering the sixth form from the independent sector say the diversity was an 'eye opener' for their girls, but largely take this as a positive step towards life after school.

Entrance: Selective. Catchment changes on an almost annual basis, dependent on number of applications and how many make it through the 11 plus. Lots of finger-crossing (not to mention ferocious tutoring for years in advance) by hopeful year 6 parents for those 150 coveted places. Entry requirements mean that unlike most state schools, girls may join in ones or twos from their junior schools, forcing them to integrate and make new friends quickly. Even the largest feeders only send between 10 and 15. Watch this space for changes in selection procedure now DCHS has achieved academy status and no longer has to kowtow to the local authority. Currently preference given to siblings and, for the first time in 2013, also to those qualifying for free school meals.

Around 30 additional places open up in year 12, attracting girls to apply direct from other grammars, independents and the brightest from the community schools (comps in old money). This is oversubscribed and girls are selected on GCSE results (minimum of two As and four Bs required, with As or Bs in chosen A level subjects). New sixth formers receive a baptism of fire into this independent learning environment and are expected to hit the ground running, which can be a shock for some, especially those from cosseted independent schools. Top grades are expected from the get-go and pressure is intense at this stage

Exit: Ninety-five per cent on to higher education. A large proportion (around 70 per cent) to Russell Group universities; seven this year to Oxbridge. Nottingham. Bristol, Birmingham, Leeds, UCL, UEA and Sheffield all currently popular.

Money matters: State maintained. Parents invited to make a voluntary contribution of £365 per year to the Challoner's Girls' Foundation to enable the school to fund a variety of initiatives such as pupil laptops. Very active parents' association helps out with regular fundraisers.

Remarks: Full of bright-eyed go-getters who give their private school peers a real run for their parents' money. The Challoner's brand continues to live up to expectations for parents lucky enough to have both 11 plus results and the moveable feast that is the catchment in their favour, although those who have been pushed through the 11 plus may face a tough challenge.

Drayton Manor High School

Drayton Bridge Road, London, W7 1EU

- Pupils: 1590; mixed • Ages: 11-19 • non-denom • State

Tel: 020 8357 1900
Email: adminoffice@draytonmanorhighschool.co.uk
Website: www.draytonmanorhighschool.co.uk

Head: Since 1994, Sir Pritpal Singh BSc MA FRSA, educated at Highgate School and London University, where he read chemistry (mid-fifties). Previously deputy head at Cranford Community School, prior to which he was head of chemistry, head of science and head of year in various other comprehensive schools, mainly in London. His own schooling (DMHS has academic links with Highgate) and, perhaps, his current school's early history as a grammar, underlie his approach, and grammar school virtues seem subtly to strengthen this non-selective comprehensive. Premier league football clubs could learn from Sir Pritpal's career. Put a good man in a moderately-achieving school and let him get on with it for long enough to find a vision, amass the means and expertise to realise it and then build on it. The high-flying Drayton Manor High of today is the result and Sir Pritpal – along with numerous other honours and awards – was knighted for services to education. Supported by many long-serving staff, notably the senior deputy head – here since 1983 – he is relaxed, candid, softly-spoken, smiley, winning in manner, and, though wholly on top of 'initiatives' and the latest government plans, is refreshingly free of edu-speak.

His tenure has not been without controversy. In 2008, he went head to head with Ealing Council over admissions. Accused of trying to select middle class children, the school was vindicated and the result is an admissions policy which allows children to come to Drayton Manor if it is the nearest school to their home. See below for explanation of what seems obvious. In 2011, the school was granted academy status. The attempt to seek parental opinion was only a partial success – very few replies. 'I like to think it was that they trusted us,' remarks Sir Pritpal, somewhat beadily and probably correctly. Those parents who do involve themselves are appreciative – 'he runs a tight ship... his staff are happy and, mostly, they stay... he is always there at parents' evenings and events ...'.This last is significant as some 'superheads' more or less disappear from the day-to-day life of their schools. Staff likewise pay tribute – 'he has added to the culture of the place and made it what it is today; it was hard work, especially on standards and behaviour. He took us back to the fundamentals and it has worked'. Drayton Manor struggled for decades but now, under professional management and sound educational principles, it is giving the local independents real competition.

Academic matters: Now outperforms other Ealing state schools and some of the local independents at A level – this reflecting, but only to some extent, the academic bar to A level courses. Thirty A level subjects on offer plus extensive Wednesday afternoon enrichment programme which includes EPQ and citizenship courses worth half an A2.

Latin survives at GCSE with excellent results, though struggles at A level; German also battles on; best language results in French at GCSE and A level. Separate sciences at GCSE with exemplary results – much parental praise for staff, also in history and English. Starry A level results in government and politics, history, English, media and further maths. Overall, results impress – 65 per cent A*-B grades, with 35 per cent A*/A, in 2013. A few non-A level sixth form courses available for those who don't make the grade at GCSE – site and facilities don't allow for more. At GCSE 2013 67 per cent of pupils got five plus A*-C including English and maths, with 27 per cent of grades A*/A.

Setting in maths from year 7, in science and languages later on. Enlightened approach re setting – 'We don't have an ideology – we look each year at what will work best' – and parents praise the flexibility of pupils moving up and down as appropriate. Library not huge for the size of school – good stock of popular fiction plus smallish, though interesting, stock of subject books. Parents say, 'I've got a lot of time for all the teachers – they require grammar school standards: our children have achieved even more highly than we had hoped, due to them'; '˜They like lively discussion to promote learning.'

Twenty-one per cent have some type of SEN – 22 per cent in years 7-11: support is rigorous, systematic and professional under head of inclusion. Good links with primaries, baseline assessment on arrival, SENCo involvement with subject and class teachers and constant target setting and monitoring make for unusual progress. Thirty-four statemented children, 290 on school action or school action plus; eight with an ASD, 157 with MLD or SLD and 61 with behavioural or social difficulties. EAL support offered on a withdrawal or in-class basis, mentoring, masterclasses, tracking. Inclusion centre takes children on a last warning and is staffed by 'our best teachers', who offer individualised teaching to 'develop positive behaviour for learning' – a narrow curriculum, taught in small groups in 'a nurturing environment'. Those identified as gifted and talented are monitored by the intervention department, who check they are sufficiently stretched and challenged.

Games, options, the arts: Great range of sports, much success. Sporting ambition fostered in teams and individuals. Lots of showings in the higher levels of Middlesex tournaments and beyond – boys' 1st XI won the Middlesex Cup; both girls' and boys' football teams reached English School national finals last year. Netball and dance also outstanding. Onsite provision of numerous hard courts and field supplemented by nearby pitches – the best for a state school in Ealing, we are told. New all-weather surface in the offing. Lively drama, culminating in the key stage 3 expressive arts festival (art, music and drama) every summer including the inter-house drama festival, the Shakespeare Schools festival and the school production attended by many of the feeder primaries as part of the transition programme. A good idea. Art is produced by an enthusiastic minority but we were not wowed by what we saw; most work, however, to be done on music where the talent has yet to be harnessed and developed. 'We're determined for it to be of the highest standard – we are working very hard behind the scenes,' says the head, acknowledging the problem. However, a flautist is part of the National Youth Orchestra and has performed nationwide. Food tech, DT and textiles all with specialist provision. New arts building – the Sir Montague Sharpe Building – about to open (January 2014). Lots of trips and visits – we are particularly pleased to see London theatres featuring prominently. Also, impressive range of speakers from the Big Outside.

Background and atmosphere: Began life as a grammar in 1930 and has the solid, handsome building you'd expect, though now supplemented by later blocks of varying quality around the central piazza – tastefully developed in recent years during multi-million developments, including large scale refurbishments to buildings and sports facilities and new science labs. Outstanding is the Frances Moore Building named after much-loved deputy head. Impressively broad corridors. Venerable trees, well-tended shrubbery beds and a few hanging baskets greet the visitor and the reception area is more friendly smiles than forbidding security measures. Pupils are well-turned out, the place is in good nick and we saw little litter. Classroom after classroom was engaged in orderly and seemingly quiet, collaborative work. Few eye-catching displays – though some good, blow-ups of current pupils are an attractive feature – little to distract and a purposeful, no frills approach pervades the school. Lots of IT; trad school hall used for productions and gatherings. Good new-ish dining hall with new caterers and excellent and popular food – a particularly wide choice and reasonably priced – though we wondered about 'chocolate peanut butter cheesecake......! All foods prepared on-site using fresh ingredients – healthy options predominate. Sixth form have a common room for each year – spacious, well-used and appreciated. Pupils have a cleaning rota! Some sense that house system is underused and that pupils have little idea what those outside their immediate circle do. The head sees the truth in this and says, 'we're on to it.'

Pastoral care and discipline: 'We've had one smoking incident on site in the last 10 years,' says the head. One of two permanent exclusions or 'managed moves' annually for persistent disruptive behaviour. Very rare drugs incidents – 'they know that if they do that they jeopardise their own future'. Good structured pastoral care system, mentoring, buddying, quick pick-up on problems. We heard no reports of bullying not jumped on and dealt with. 'Care, courtesy, consideration and integrity come before anything else,' says the head. Staff call each other 'sir' and 'miss' as they pass in the corridors. Parents praise the inclusive atmosphere – 'everyone is included in awards, not just the high achievers but those who've made progress. The ethos encourages aspiration'. Also appreciation of the disciplined approach – 'they are hot on punctuality and attendance' – and the efficient staff-home communication. Uniform and sixth form dress code seemingly adhered to – though they don't look like automata either. Much in place to guide towards post-school life though some students felt it needed to start earlier and be more pro-active. Again, Sir Pritpal, wonderfully undefensive in the face of criticism, sees this as something he is happy to address – new careers coordinator now appointed.

Pupils and parents: From a very narrow chunk of Ealing these days as the school's popularity and reputation have grown. With a catchment area that takes in everything from the neat Edwardian terraces opposite, the detached grandeur of the Victorian houses a few hundred yards to the east and the council estates of west Ealing and Hanwell, the mix could not be richer. A vast range of backgrounds – 57 different home languages spoken and 34 per cent have English as second language. Lots of after-school classes, notably in ESOL and English, offered to parents alongside other support classes. Pervasive culture of aspiration melds and blends and whatever background you came with, you leave with a sense of your own potential. Notable former pupils include Lord Justice Sir Michael Fox, Martin Rowlands, artist/producer Steve McQueen, Jay Kay, Rick Wakeman and 'if I hadn't been a footballer I'd have been a virgin', Peter Crouch.

Entrance: Vastly over-subscribed. Lots of siblings. Usual local authority criteria apply but the court case won in 2008 means that children will gain a place at Drayton Manor if it is the nearest school to their home. In practice this means that if you live a mile from the school but it remains the nearest school to home, then you will have priority over children who live half a mile away but have other schools from which they can choose. Some 50 per cent come from five local primaries – Drayton Green, Hathaway, Hobbayne, Montpelier and North Ealing. Odd disparity in local population and in other local schools means that all years have more boys than girls. Entry to the sixth form depends on five good GCSEs including English and maths as well as other stipulated grades depending on your choice of A level – most subjects requiring Bs at GCSE. These requirements apply to existing students and to applicants from outside.

Exit: Around a third leave after GCSEs – to employment or vocational courses elsewhere. Virtually all sixth form leavers to university – six to Oxbridge in 2013; several vets, medics, dentists and pharmacists; quite a few engineers; Brunel, Queen Mary's, Westminster and Sussex popular.

Money matters: An annual £10 contribution is asked for.

Remarks: Get clear about the admissions policy and move house. This is about as good as it gets.

Driffield School and Sixth Form

Manorfield Road, Driffield, YO25 5HR

• Pupils: 1,790 boys and girls • Ages: 11–18 • Non-denom • State

Tel: 01377 253631
Email: office@driffield.e-riding.sch.uk
Website: www.driffieldschool.net

Head Teacher: Since September 2012, Mr Simon Jones, who was acting headteacher during his predecessor's secondment to the National College for School Leadership. He joined the school as deputy head in 2005 and is married with four children.

Academic matters: Headline 5+ A*-C GCSE grades including English and maths at disappointing 57 per cent in 2013, due largely to stubbornly low English language results – school assures us it is on the case, with whizzy new head of department driving improvements. A level 40 per cent A*-B grades. Every single child is tracked in every subject all the time. Teachers log progress of pupils every four weeks on an electronic registration system. Computer flags up any student who fails to make hoped-for progress and hapless pupil is brought up to speed in

whatever way the school decrees, be it extra homework or late study. Child is attached to a mentor – a teacher designated to get them instantly back on track. Parents love it, school loves it, even students accept it's for their greater good – apparently. And it's not all bad news for pupils – the mentor can negotiate deadline extensions etc for a student genuinely snowed under.

SEN dept, now called Student Services (ie inclusive), can cope with (almost) any learning difficulty from moderate to severe – the entire dys-strata, ADHD, plus severely (rather than profoundly) deaf (the school operates a sound field system). Some 200 children on the register with IEPs for all including 49 with statements. One-to-one, one-to-two, small groups, anything from one hour to three hours a week, alpha smart (computers) – in and out of school, and all networked. Eighteen teaching assistants, all highly trained; most remedial help is provided in class, but occasional one-to-one, max one and a half hours a week, but 'can buy in more'. Very accommodating – 'Can adapt to different needs'; special co-ordinator for their able, gifted and talented programme too.

Games, options, the arts: International recognition for performing arts. Winners many times of international Rock Challenge competition for dance, drama and music. Strong on sport, particularly cricket, rugby, hockey. Thriving Duke of Edinburgh scheme. Range of activities outside lessons excellent. Extracurricular activities given priority because of rural catchment area where, for many children, school is core element of their social life.

Background and atmosphere: A whopper of a school, among the biggest in the country, set in a vast 40-acre site and with most of the students' home villages in the Yorkshire Wolds. Feels less like a school, more like a campus, not least in sixth form which boasts own internet café. School only 50 years old but has just spent millions on new design and technology, specialist performing arts and ICT blocks, with imminent building of new sports hall and swimming pool.

Biggest asset? Its own residential studies centre in the North York Moors National Park for everything from geography field trips to intensive study seminars. Pupils encouraged to use school with its 600 plus internet-linked computers out of hours. Doors open at 7am and library is open until at least 7pm, sometimes later. Children can go home for a meal, then catch special late bus back to school for more study or activities before school bus takes them home again.

Pastoral care and discipline: Potential for feeling swamped enormous as intake mostly from small rural primaries. Problems prevented by putting students into six houses and having registration forms comprising six students from each year group. New pupils instantly taken under wing of older ones – one of many ways school encourages responsibility. Sixteen-year-old student governor says views of pupils are taken seriously: 'They really listen to us'.

Discipline tight – school prides itself on standing no nonsense. Will not tolerate pupils disturbing lessons and disrupting education of the majority.

Pupils and parents: Parents from wide range of backgrounds, but many have caught school's ambitious bug and work hard to support it. Pupils' progress reports to parents three times a year and full report annually. Newsletters to parents via email so no chance to 'lose' that letter about extra homework. Parents' briefing evenings about, for instance, study leave.

Entrance: Seriously over-full and only takes pupils from 130 square mile catchment area.

Exit: Most stay on to sixth form and then to universities including Oxbridge.

Remarks: A beacon state school combining innovation and risk-taking to fire up the ambitions of a whole community. Recently designated a specialist maths and computing school.

Dulwich College

Linked schools: DUCKS (Dulwich College Kindergarten and Infants School); Dulwich College: The Junior School

Dulwich Common, London, SE21 7LD

• Pupils: 1,295 boys. 105 full time boarders; 25 weekly • Ages: 11–18 • C of E • Fees: Day £16,455; Boarding £32,208–£34,188 pa • Independent

Tel: 020 8693 3601
Email: info@dulwich.org.uk
Website: www.dulwich.org.uk

Master: Since 2009, Dr Joseph Spence BA PhD (fiftyish), previously headmaster of Oakham. Was Master in College at Eton from 1992-2002, so had charge of the scholars, one of the top academic jobs in independent education. A history and politics graduate, he is disconcertingly multi-talented: he writes and directs plays, has written several books on Anglo-Irish history and culture, and plays sport 'quite well'. A personable, enthusiastic and charming man, he is married to a lawyer, with two sons and daughter. 'Great news for the college,' say parents.

His predecessor spent much time and energy on developing Dulwich College franchises overseas; he is clear that 'my job is here. I value our commitment to the Dulwich College schools abroad, for they are impressive and can enhance our reputation, and I want to develop real educational links with them, but my focus is SE21'. He is keen for the three foundation schools (the others being JAGS and Alleyn's) to work more closely together and has formed closer links with JAGS.

Of the boys-only environment, he says: 'It's only when you leave the co-education setting that you realise how much social engineering you have had to do to avoid gender stereotypes. Here, you don't have the issue of having to persuade boys to be in the orchestra, the choir, the play.'

He is 'determined to harness the history of this place. I want to give everyone a sense of pride in where they find themselves and an understanding of the status of our extraordinary College. I want to make it as good as it's ever been by the 400th anniversary in 2019'.

Academic matters: Dr Spence feels that Dulwich has been punching slightly below its weight academically. 'I don't want us to be a pale imitation of St Paul's or Westminster. We take the top 15 per cent of boys – in terms of academic ability, they take the top five per cent – but you can do as well here as if you were in the top five per cent. I am committed to the cause of learning beyond the classroom (and away from the test), but we must never lose sight of the academic basis of our work.'

The academic basis isn't bad – 83 per cent A*/A grades at GCSE in 2013, with sciences and languages still looking particularly strong and English, previously thought to be a weaker link, having delivered 82 per cent A*/A. Maths is the most popular A level, sciences and economics close behind, undoubtedly influenced by the scientifically-minded boarders from China and Eastern Europe. Over 90 per cent per cent A*-B at A level in 2013, 66 per cent A*/A across a remarkably wide range of challenging subjects.

Screening for dyslexia in years 7 and 9, with some boys referred for an ed psych assessment. Learning support dept helps those diagnosed with a learning difficulty, who may use a laptop at school and in exams.

Dr Spence's first job was to look at the 13-16 curriculum and iron out any kinks in the system, eg over-rigid setting which resulted in an aptitude for science being a pre-requisite for the fast-track French course. No plans to introduce the IB but has set up the Dulwich Diploma, which is similar in its outlook: four A levels, an extended essay and a real commitment to service, plus attending the master's series of five lectures a year. 'I will write to every admissions tutor about the Dulwich Diploma to make sure they know what we are doing.'

Games, options, the arts: 'Extraordinary work going on beyond the curriculum.' Sport has always been a big deal here and the greater academic emphasis won't change this. Seventy acres of playing fields include two full size all-weather pitches and an athletics track plus numerous courts and pitches, a swimming pool and a vast sports hall. Rugby is a major sport – 40 teams play regular matches – and has spawned quite a few international players; boys also compete at football, hockey, cricket, badminton, golf et al. They fence, they row (boathouse on the Thames at Putney), they play water polo. Most recently an evident encouragement of another sport at which Britain has begun to excel: cycling – plans for the College to support the redevelopment of the Herne Hill Velodrome. As in most large and sporty schools, boys need major talent to make the top teams.

Edward Alleyn theatre hosts numerous performances by all age groups, including one big upper school production each year in conjunction with JAGS, and inter-house drama competitions. Theatre studies an A level option; though not drama GCSE. All art staff are practising artists. Plenty of artistic options from ceramics to animation. Music also strong with lots of orchestras, bands, ensembles and choirs – including the college chapel choir – playing and singing in regular concerts, in such as St John's, Smith Square and the Queen Elizabeth Hall.

All year 7s visit the school field centre in the Brecon Beacons for hiking, rock-climbing, canoeing etc. D of E, scouts and CCF popular; huge variety of clubs and societies. Lots of language exchanges, sports, music and drama tours, field trips, trekking, sailing and skiing expeditions.

Background and atmosphere: Founded in 1619 by the wealthy, flamboyant actor and businessman, Edward Alleyn. He set up the foundation, Alleyn's College of God's Gift, and endowed it with the ancient manor of Dulwich, including considerable land. Part of the foundation funded the education of 12 poor scholars by resident Fellows. Its successor charity, the Dulwich Estate, owns what land remains and distributes its surplus income to the schools within the foundation, which include Dulwich College, JAGS, Alleyn's and several state schools.

The college moved to its present site in the mid 19th century; the main buildings are grand, confident Victorian redbrick, embellished with stucco worthies in cream niches. They include such treasures as the panelled great hall, the masters' library and the Wodehouse library (PG is an Old Alleynian), with archives including 'the largest and most important collection of material on the professional theatre and dramatic performance in the age of Shakespeare to be found anywhere'. Ernest Shackleton is another OA, and the James Caird – the terrifyingly small boat in which he sailed the stormy southern ocean from Elephant Island to South Georgia – is berthed in the North Cloisters.

New landmark building, the Laboratory, under construction – will house 21 new science labs, IT suites and junior school wing plus 240 seat auditorium. Designed by Grimshaw architects of Eden Project and Cutty Sark fame.

Not a school you could walk past without noticing. The manicured pitches surrounding the (mostly) gracious buildings give the impression of a country public school or traditional university campus. But the boys – 30 per cent of whom receive some sort of help with fees – cheeringly reflect their multi-ethnic south London environs.

It is part of the Southwark Schools Learning Partnership, which includes five state and three independent schools working together on a huge range of projects. Also sponsors the new Isle of Sheppey Academy – a mutual learning relationship which is likely to include the College helping with aspects such as modern languages and Oxbridge preparation whilst learning from the Academy about innovative teaching methods.

A multi-national arm franchises three schools in China and one in Korea, and an events and enterprise element runs the school bus network and rents out the college facilities for, eg, wedding receptions. This helps to bring in funds for improving facilities and increasing bursaries, and should provide opportunities for international exchanges.

Pastoral care and discipline: Boarders in a small minority here – 130 out of around 1,300, mostly sixth formers and many from the Far East. They inhabit swish boarding houses – sixth formers have their own rooms with en suite bathrooms – and can take advantage of all London has to offer at weekends. Dr Spence has plans to develop boarding further, increasing weekly boarding and integrating boarders better with the day boys. 'We have the feel and the facilities of a boarding school, and we need to make more use of them. I'd like to widen our appeal beyond the Far East and Europe.' Houseparents work hard to create a home-like atmosphere. All the boys are members of day houses, which provide opportunities for making friends and mixing with boys in other year groups, to say nothing of competing against one's peers at anything from sport to chess to debating and recitation.

'They're pretty good at motivating boys who don't want to work,' said a parent. Those found with drugs are out, say college rules, but not heavy-handed on this. Will give a second chance to boys excluded from elsewhere who are keen to join in the wide range of activities. It is perhaps inevitable that with such a large college we will hear concerns about certain aspects of pastoral care. However, we believe that the master and his heads of school are unflinching in their determination to avoid complacency in an area of school life which has been commented upon favourably in successive ISI reports.

Pupils and parents: Mostly local, though many take the buses run in conjunction with three other local schools – providing excellent opportunities for socialising, say boys. Good ethnic and social mix, including, of course, the international boarders, though it is fair to say that the core clientele is the solidly middle-class families of the Dulwich/Blackheath/Greenwich/Clapham surrounds. This is a very large school and particularly suits confident boys who don't need encouragement to take advantage of all the off-piste opportunities.

OAs include PG Wodehouse, Sir Ernest Shackleton, Raymond Chandler, Lord George of St Tudy, Bob Monkhouse, Lionel Barber, CS Forester, Karol Sikora, Graham Swift and Michael Ondaatje. The school has produced more than its fair share of international sportsmen, including England Test cricketer Trevor Bailey and the England and British Lions rugby player, Nick Easter.

Entrance: Takes 70 boys into year 7, plus around 60 coming up from the junior school. All applicants take maths, English and verbal and non-verbal reasoning tests; junior school boys must pass the tests but are not competing for places with outsiders. Another 60 join year 9, again after English, maths and reasoning tests. Those trying for an academic scholarship must also take French, science, history and geography papers. Up to 40 places, mostly boarding, for outsiders joining the sixth form. These largely go to international students, many from Hong Kong, assessed by entrance exams. UK candidates – like boys already

in the college middle school – must get A*/A GCSE grades in their four A level subjects and at least two more grades B or above, including maths and English.

Exit: A few – virtually none in 2013 – likely to trip over the sixth form entrance requirements and leave after GCSEs. Nearly all sixth form leavers to university, including 18 to Oxbridge in 2013; London University colleges, Bristol, Durham, Newcastle, Nottingham, Manchester and Warwick popular; one or two to American and Hong Kong universities. Medicine, economics and engineering particularly common degrees.

Money matters: Academic scholarships of between 10 per cent and a third of fees available to boys joining in year 7 and year 9. Music scholarships, of up to a third of fees plus free tuition on two instruments, also available at year 7 and year 9. Art scholarships of up to 10 per cent of fees and sports scholarships of up to a third available at year 9 and year 12. Means-tested bursaries also available, all but a handful from year 7 and above; about a third of boys have some sort of help with fees.

The 1940s-60s was the era of the Dulwich Experiment, when the school offered free places, funded by the local authority, to boys who could pass the entrance exam. 'I've met hundreds of 60 to 80 year olds who benefited from those and wax lyrical about the school and what they got from it,' says Dr Spence. 'We need a new Dulwich Experiment, with a move towards needs-blind admissions.'

Remarks: Huge operation that manages to encompass sixth-month-old babies and 18-year-old school leavers, to say nothing of franchises in the Far East. Exudes a traditional public school ambience of stalwart Victoriana amidst enviable manicured acres, but houses a cheerfully diverse mixture of south London and international boys. The Master is intent on upping the academic ante whilst encouraging the vast range of activities outside the classroom, and drawing on the sense of history that enriches the Dulwich College experience.

Dunraven School

94–98 Leigham Court Road, London, SW16 2QB

• Pupils: 1300 day boys/girls–50/50 (plus 56 in new linked primary) • Ages: 11–18 • Non-denom • State

Tel: 020 8696 5600
Email: info@dunraven.org.uk
Website: www.dunraven.org.uk

Principal: Since September 2003, David Boyle (forties), BA NPQH FRSA. Married with a young daughter. A north Londoner by birth, 10 years at Dunraven have made him a thoroughly naturalised Streatham man, and proud of the success he's done so much to create. 'My main interest is work,' he explains (although he concedes a liking for literature and cinema) 'and after work, my family.' Under his energetic leadership, the school has achieved creditable results, and acquired a bewildering array of designations: High Performing Status, Beacon Status, Advanced Healthy School Status, Investors In People status – and on it goes. Along the way, it's become the most popular school in Lambeth with seven applicants for every place. Parents describe him as an excellent manager and highly effective communicator. The secret of his success? 'I love what I do,' he shrugs. 'And I like working with people who enjoy what they do.'

Academic matters: Dunraven recently celebrated yet another set of 'best yet' results at key stages 3, 4 and 5 – testament, says head, to the commitment of 'a fantastically creative and hardworking staff team.' GCSE results are significantly above both local and national averages, with 77 per cent of students achieving 5+ A*-C including English and maths, and the sixth form was rated 'outstanding' by Ofsted. In 2013, 82 per cent of A level grades were A*-C and 27 per cent A*/A. Expectations are high. 'We start from the premise that the children will do well, and might do even better than we think.' Younger pupils are kept aware of how well the older ones are doing, and the benchmark is set higher each year. 'We're aiming for "astounding",' says head, with a modest smile.

The curriculum in key stages 3 and 4 is broad and balanced, thanks to what's called the Dunraven Baccalaureate: English, maths, science, humanities, languages, and all the arts, because 'the kind of learning opportunity you get through the arts is invaluable.' Other subjects are also offered, notably DT, ICT and PE/dance. Visiting teacher from Westminster comes in every week to teach Latin, which is proving a popular option at GCSE and A Level, but we thought the language provision could have been broader. French and Spanish are offered, with the G&T students given the chance to do both; but there used to be Mandarin. The impressive sixth form (230 students), housed in its own new purpose-built centre, is the most successful in Lambeth, and offers a wide range of academic and vocational courses – A Levels, BTECs, GCE applied and the AQA baccalaureate. All Dunraven year 11s can apply to study there and most do, but places are sought after and are not guaranteed. Strong enrichment programme of activities, both on and off site, includes theatre and opera visits, excursions, exchanges, competitions, and residential trips abroad.

SEN provision is excellent and enlightened. The school has its own on-site speech therapist, whom we came across energetically pummelling a child with cystic fibrosis ('Just clearing his lungs!'), and parents were full of praise for the SENCo, who was described as 'fantastic', 'works like a Trojan', 'highly empathetic'. 'We felt that our child was properly supported throughout her time here,' was a typical remark.

There were parental murmurs about their child being unable to study all his/her preferred subjects at GCSE due to timetabling issues (a problem not unique to Dunraven), but the majority of feedback was overwhelmingly positive. 'My child left with a love of all his subjects, based on great teaching,' was one comment. 'There is rigour in all that Dunraven does,' was another, and everyone we spoke to praised the 'constantly rising level of academic achievement.' The children agree: 'The teachers are good and you learn stuff,' said a cheerful Y7 boy, who'd been temporarily sent out for being cheeky. 'You make friends, you learn, every class is suited to you,' added a strikingly poised Y10 girl.

Games, options, the arts: You can do almost any sports here: in addition to football, rugby, cricket and basketball, there are opportunities for badminton, fencing, swimming, diving the martial arts, boxercise, trampolining and ice-skating (using facilities at Crystal Palace). Engagement with games remains good throughout KS4. Drama, dance, art and photography are all popular, and the Soul Choir enlivens many a local church concert. Music is also strong, and the excellent Play It Live initiative, part-funded by the local authority, enables the children to work regularly with professional musicians.

Background and atmosphere: The school is approaching its 100th anniversary, and now has an attached primary school – the first reception children started in 2013 and will move into their permanent £5 million home in September 2014. Originally founded with a bequest from the Earl of Dunraven, it expanded onto its present site in 1950, moved into the Philippa Fawcett College in the 1970s, became grant-maintained in 1993 ('A very important decision for the school'), and gained academy status in 2011. £20 million mixture of rebuild and refurb (under the last government's Building Schools for the Future initiative) now complete, including new sixth form centre. Some very inventive touches, including the use of recycled shipping containers for new buildings, which look incredibly smart and cost half of what was originally planned.

Smart blue and grey uniforms, own clothes for sixth form (with a requirement to be 'respectable'). Students work purposefully, and – during our visit, at least – an air of orderly quiet prevails. The pupils we met were polite and helpful. Even the malefactors hanging around outside the classroom who'd refused to go in, for reasons they were unable to articulate, knew what was expected of them. After chatting to us about how much they liked their school really – 'It's fun here...there are nice trips... a good after-school club, something to do every day' – they filed in equally to begin geography.

Pastoral care and discipline: Considering the size and diversity of this school community, we were impressed at how calm and purposeful the students were. The emphasis everywhere is on courtesy and consideration, and the pupils confirm this: 'The people are nice. The teachers are good and you learn stuff.' Parents praise the staff as 'incredibly supportive', and any bullying is dealt with swiftly and effectively with 'restorative justice' sessions and behaviour contracts. Very low turnover of staff tells its own successful story.

Pupils and parents: An inclusive, socially and ethnically mixed intake that reflects the diversity of the area.

Entrance: Entrance tests put children into one of five ability bands; the school, which is heavily over-subscribed, then takes 20 per cent from each band, allocating places in line with its (non-academically selective) admissions policy.

However, in response to local demand, Dunraven is also developing a two form entry primary phase, to be housed in the newly refurbished Mount Nod Road site. The first reception children came through the doors in September 2013, and will have an automatic right of entry to Dunraven Senior when they reach year 7. It's well worth living on a building site for. From his temporary office in what was the janitor's bedroom, the head positively radiates excitement: 'This provision will eliminate the trauma of secondary transfer. Everyone will benefit. We'll be able to offer expertise and opportunities to enrich the primary experience, and their different pedagogical approach will increasingly influence us.' Heady times indeed.

Exit: At 16, the majority (65 per cent) progress to Dunraven sixth form; a few move to local sixth form colleges, training etc. At 18, nearly leavers go on to university, with an increasing number of top university successes every year, including Oxbridge (two deferred places in 2013), Imperial, Bristol sussex and Queen Mary. The rest take a gap year, or have a lead into work of some kind. Head says, 'The aim is to get to the end of Y13 with a choice.'

Money matters: EFA-funded academy since August 2011, and in receipt of many grants and awards in recognition of its academic success and work for the community.

Remarks: A dynamic, exciting, successful school community. Proof that you can have a comprehensive school that works for everybody.

Durham High School for Girls

Linked school: Durham High School For Girls Junior School

Farewell Hall, South Road, Durham, DH1 3TB

• Pupils: 335 girls, all day • Ages: 11–18 • C of E, accepts all faiths and none • Fees: £6,780–£10,725 pa • Independent

---

Tel: 01913 843226
Email: headmistress@dhsfg.org.uk
Website: www.dhsfg.org.uk

Headmistress: Since September 2012, Mrs Lynne Renwick BEd (early 50s). Returning to her roots, born in Durham, read history and education and spent a short period working for the National Trust. Moved between independent and state sectors; Tadcaster Grammar; Walton High School for Girls in West Midlands; head of history at GSA British girls' school in Peru; spent time in Japan as part of a British delegation of educators. Head of humanities at Dixon's City Technology College in Bradford, assistant head at All Saints School in York, principal of Our Lady's Abingdon, Oxfordshire. ISI inspector, member of the professional development committee of GSA, former governor of Cranford House School, Oxfordshire.

Says that she 'loved teaching in all girl schools and knew she wanted to be head of one'. Believes that Durham High girls are 'comfortable in their own skins and moulded in a positive way'; they find being in an all girl environment 'just so easy'. Keeps in touch by lunching with groups of girls twice a week.

Married to a freelance illustrator working in advertising and design; no children, but five nieces ranging from teens to twenties. Very interested in conservation of old houses and architecture, loves ice skating – for the past five years has been on the ice between 6.30 and 8.00am every Saturday morning, mastering dancing and keeping fit. Also enjoys reading, hill walking, travelling and interior design.

Academic matters: Consistently the highest performing school in the county and came out particularly well in the English Bacc league table. A levels: 39 per cent A*/A; usual subjects plus psychology, sociology, Latin, Greek, classical civilisation, sport, theatre studies, art and design – a notable range for such a small sixth form. Impressively, almost half do maths and sciences, EPQ taken – no slacking from these girls.

2013 GCSE: 77 per cent A/A*, with particularly good sciences, fine art, textiles, history, Greek, Latin and music. French, German, Latin and newly introduced Spanish at key stage 3. Does well in maths, business and Latin and Greek speaking competitions. Astronomy offered extra sessional for high flyers. Very good ICT provision, with area for enrichment and extension activities on school website. Max class sizes: 24 (key stage 3), 20 (key stage 4), 14 (sixth form), but can be a lot smaller. Girls spoke appreciatively of teachers' personal approach and the amount of individual attention they get.

Parents speak highly of teachers who 'build relationships with each child individually and get to know what makes them tick'.

Well-resourced library; reading groups for each year; organised annual event of Big Book Bash for year 7s with 10 local schools. Supervised homework club available until 5.30pm. Qualified SENCo can test for dyslexia, works closely with staff, advises on individual needs and liaises with outside agencies. Gives individual support outside the classroom at a cost to parents. Says school could cope with any special needs apart from severe behavioural difficulties and that these girls do very well (endorsed by latest inspection report). EAL specialist support offered at a cost.

Games, options, the arts: The usual range plus cricket, rowing, golf, karate, skiing, rock climbing, basketball, sports coaching awards – encouraging participation as PE compulsory. Sports tours – next destination Sri Lanka. Regional and national success with some individual national high flyers (gymnastics, tumbling, fencing and netball); 1970s sports hall, netball courts and playing field on site – others hired off site.

Durham High's alive with the sound of music. Over 50 per cent of girls take instrumental and singing lessons. Lots of music exams, no competitions or festivals though performance opportunities abound; choirs, orchestra, ensembles, lunchtime concerts, and of course, cathedral connections. Well resourced music technology room – music GCSE popular. Big productions tend to be musicals, but straight plays too, plenty going on in all parts of the school – drama studio fully utilised. The seniors' play is performed at the Gala Theatre in Durham – the school's drama studio stage is, cleverly, the same size, to facilitate the transfer. A year 9 panto toured 25 primary schools; dance performances, too.

Very good art – students' work has been shortlisted for the Royal Academy online exhibition for A level candidates; also textiles, graphics, pottery, photography club. No food tech, though, which girls would like, but after-chool cookery club and survival lessons for sixth form. Largest D of E centre in County Durham for the Gold Award, community service, big Amnesty International group, eco activities, school council re-launch. Sixth form enrichment programme covers IT, philosophy, politics, debating, Young Enterprise. Buddying of younger girls by older ones, who help with academic work (eg basic maths and reading), produce their plays and lead their activities (all good personal statement stuff). Healthy competition through house activities, drama, singing and sports; also used for charitable fundraising.

High quality careers and post-school preparation though focused on university. Task-based enterprise day for years 7 and 8 involves teamwork and workplace scenarios; participates in Durham's future business magnate programme in year 8; Young Enterprise and work experience in year 12.

Background and atmosphere: Opened 1884 in the centre of the city as a C of E school. Moved to leafy outskirts down the road from university science suite in 1964 – all purpose built. Additions since then – sixth form and art accommodation, science labs, ICT and library building, sports hall and attractive two storey brick buildings, one housing a performing arts studio, music room and classrooms and another the junior school – ring the single storey originals. Lengthy flight of gentle steps leads down to the understated entrance providing a disappointing vista of flat roofs – dispelled once inside by wide corridors, bright and airy classrooms, a veritable Tardis.

A compact site, yet sufficient hard play areas, playing field and well wooded grounds; swimming pool, all weather pitch and fitness suite all accessed off-site. Nursery and junior girls situated near to the seniors, contributing to the secure, friendly, family feeling. Two ICT suites, a greenhouse for the biology lab, large, well-resourced library (every year has a reading group), pleasant quiet room with modern stained glass windows. Roomy sixth form common room, kitchen (university survival cooking classes on offer) and study areas on edge of campus in building shared with art and design facilities.

The sixth form wear dark suits – the rest sport dark green jumpers and blazers, choice of yellow and green tartan kilt or skirt. Wide choice of healthy food in dining room used by all from 3 up. Lunch arrangements and uniform only negative comments from the girls we spoke to – was ever thus.

All girls means just that here, from nursery to sixth form. Social and debating events with local co-ed schools, Oxbridge preparation with co-ed Durham School on offer.

Christian values lie at the heart of the school, embedded in daily school life with regular religious assemblies, a school chaplain, annual whole school communion, baptism and confirmation preparation and Christian Union.

Great continuity and commitment post school days; ex-pupil teachers, governors and parents. Parents an daughters agree that 'there is a feeling of belonging, a mindset to want to do well and a shared set of values amongst the pupils.'

Pastoral care and discipline: Last inspection praised excellent pastoral provision. Childrens' mental health high on teachers' agenda. Without exception, girls spoke of support and encouragement from teachers; being known well; talents spotted; confidence built. Supplemented by trained counsellor plus school chaplain.

Common to girls' schools, we were assured that bullying and discipline is not a problem. 'Our values spread amongst everyone,' said one, accompanied by nodding heads in unison. They are confident that teachers would sort it if anything did occur – 'there is always someone to go to if you are upset'. PHSE advocates being a 'telling school' and anti-bullying; respect shown by staff integral; parents value the updates on contemporary national issues. Head says, 'proposed changes in behaviour policies shared with the girls as part of review process'.

Well thought out transition for year 7s – a welcome ceilidh and preparatory outreach work with feeder schools in science and Latin plus a joint drama production. Buddying system with year 8s, several joint activities through year to cement relationships. Sixth formers act as 'big sisters' to younger ones. Sixth form piloting mixed tutor groups of years 12 and 13 with positive response

Pupils and parents: Pupils from a wide range of backgrounds from Durham and a broad area around the city, from state and independent schools; some EAL. Extensive bus service – to be widened further. Very satisfied, actively supportive parents who are regularly consulted by the school and kept up to date with weekly news bulletins; information booklets and website – in head's marketing radar. Thoughtful, mature, articulate girls. Notable old girls: Wendy Craig (actress). Joanna Burton (opera singer), Wendy Gibson (TV presenter).

Entrance: 11 and 13+: exams in English and maths, interview and school report; takes above average ability. Sixth: five A*-Bs at GCSE including English and maths, with at least B in prospective A level subjects (A grade for some), school report and interview; about 10 join.

Exit: Up to 40 per cent leave after GCSE for other sixth forms, mainly local high performing state schools. Almost without exception sixth form leavers to university; one or two to Oxbridge, Northumbria University popular, as are Durham, Leeds, Edinburgh and Newcastle. One thespian to the States to study musical theatre.

Money matters: Scholarships/exhibitions at 11, 12-14 and 16+: academic, sports, music, performing arts; 10 per cent clerical fee remission, a scholarship for daughters of practising Christians of any denomination based on RS test. Means-tested bursaries up to 50 per cent of fees to girls in about the top half of the ability range – gives over 10 per cent of senior school fee income to these. Sixth form: scholarships worth 100 per cent of fees for very able girls whose parents could not otherwise afford the fees; Ogden Trust scholarship (100 per cent of fees); academic scholarships up to 50 per cent on the basis of exams in two chosen subjects; music scholarships and exhibitions; drama, performing arts, art and sports scholarships; clerical bursaries.

Remarks: High performing (academic, theatrical and musical) single sex school. The only all girls' day school in Durham and looking to an increasingly wide catchment. Bedrock of Christian values where every girl matters and talents are discovered and nurtured in a close knit community.

Durham School

Linked school: Bow Durham School

Quarry Heads Lane, Durham, DH1 4SZ

• Pupils: 635 girls and boys • Ages: 11-18 • Church of England but all faiths welcomed • Fees: Day £12,360-£15,450; Boarding £17,685-£23,790 pa • Independent

Tel: 01913 864783
Email: enquiries@durhamschool.co.uk
Website: www.durhamschool.co.uk

Headmaster: Since 2009, Mr Martin George BA MBA (mid forties), educated at Durham School and Manchester University (politics and modern history), then 10 years in the army, 10 years at Newcastle under Lyme School (director of studies), 2004 King's School, Tynemouth (deputy head, i/c pastoral care). Relaxed, humorous, genial, energetic – clearly a good sport, as he let pupils throw wet sponges and buckets of water at him while in the stocks for charity. Popular with parents, who see him as a moderniser who values the school's traditions (but we don't know if he is encouraging the head boy to exercise his right to grow a beard and keep a goat on Masters' Green) and very approachable – 'His door's always open'; 'A good listener and very willing to help'; 'He's passionate about the school – he's proud of all the children; they're part of his extended family'; sends handwritten notes to congratulate pupils on special achievements. Teaches a year 9 history group and A level politics; wants school to produce happy, confident and successful – in a wide sense – pupils. Involved with CCF and running club – seriously fit, he raised an impressive sum for Help for Heroes by doing the Hadrian's Wall Run (83 miles); also enjoys cycling, gardening, music, travel. Wife works in learning support department; two children at Durham School.

Academic matters: A level nearly 29 per cent A*/A, nearly 53 per cent A*-B in 2013, probably why Mr George wants to develop academic aspects of the sixth form ('more rigour', a study centre, supervised study time, more intellectual societies). Choices include economics, politics, psychology, philosophy and ethics, classical civilisation, PE, theatre and business studies, but no EPQ (under consideration) or AQA Bac. Very good support with university applications.

GCSE results nearly 38 per cent A*/A (down on 2012 figures of 44 per cent). Separate sciences, Latin, classical civilisation, drama, music, PE, DT and graphic products; most do at least one MFL (French, German, Spanish) and all do short course RE. German or Spanish added to French in year 9 (can also do Latin); language awareness days, with themed meals. Most recent inspection praised pupil-staff relationships, teaching and use of monitoring, but commented on some marking inconsistency, which school is addressing (though we did see some exercise books that were closely corrected but lacking in encouraging comments). Classrooms tend to be traditional, with just one computer plus projector (only a few interactive whiteboards), some darkish, but also some new ones and some modern ICT facilities.

Strong learning support department – well qualified, flexible, sensitive; can cope with most needs apart from severe behavioural problems; the spread out nature of the campus could be a problem for anyone with major physical disabilities. Screens all new entrants for dyslexia and ESL, if from overseas (extra charge for ESL – full time specialist – and learning support sessions); trains other staff. Thorough going gifted and talented policy – systematic identification and monitoring, early maths GCSE, fourth A level and extra, challenging activities.

Games, options, the arts: Astroturf, swimming pool, sports hall, playing fields, very good rowing facilities and access to top flight coaching; individuals and teams successful at regional, county and national levels. One of the oldest rowing clubs in the country (dates from 1847) – the whole 1970 crew represented GB and has current international stars. Water polo taking off in a big way, ski team reached finals of English Schools' Championships, a GB fencer; also cross country, golf, squash, boxing, rifle shooting, wind surfing, climbing (games compulsory in sixth). Girls have more chance of being in teams through being in a minority.

Very accomplished choral singing – TV appearances, radio broadcasts, including Radio 4's Sunday Worship (we heard this and thought it excellent), and a number of CDs; orchestras, jazz band, rock group; concerts at The Sage, Gateshead and Durham Cathedral plus foreign tours. High level art and drama – Shakespeare and big musicals, modern studio theatre.

Wide choice of activities – cake decorating, fashion design, jewellery, model and soft toy making, dance, electronics, D of E, CCF (all three sections); for the more cerebral: Italian, current events, poetry; participates in BBC School Report (writing news bulletins and reports) and the lively and entertaining school newspaper, The Durham Eye, printed in house, has reached the finals of a national schools media competition. Careers education now expanding.

Lots of fundraising for charity and foreign trips – staff and pupils seem to have bags of energy and enterprise; World Challenge to Mongolia, Africa, India, Latin America, Borneo, rugby tour to Australia, girls' netball tour to Gibraltar, rowing camps in Belgium and Norway, winter walking in Scotland, ski trip to France – phew, we need to have a lie down at the thought of all that activity!

Background and atmosphere: One of oldest schools in the country – goes back to Cardinal Langley's re-founding of Durham Cathedral in 1414; at the end of the last century became more or less independent of the dean and chapter. Originally situated on Palace Green, next to the cathedral; moved to present site on other side of River Wear, 1844, only five minutes' walk from city centre. Has the feel of a traditional rural boarding school, with lovely views of sports fields and gardens containing many mature trees, although the majority of the pupils don't board (day ends at 6 pm); several mellow sandstone buildings either side of lawns leading to the hill that ascends to the chapel. The 98 steps all commemorate old boys who died in the two world wars; on Remembrance Day the whole school lines the stairs at twilight, holding candles, while a wreath is laid on the memorial plaque, which must be very moving. Stunning view of viaduct, cathedral and school from the top. 1926 traditional chapel with pews etched with the names of all leavers. Further up is the Astroturf and beyond, up again, are rugby pitches, so you need to be pretty fit just to get to them.

Girls introduced into the sixth form 1985, became fully co educational 1998. Five vertical, single sex houses: three boys', two girls', three for just day pupils, three with boarders; full, weekly and part time possible – full starts year 9. Each house, located along a street outside the main campus, has studies (shared or single), common rooms, kitchen and leisure facilities, recently upgraded; strong sense of community, house captains and monitors (prefects). Boarding provision graded good in inspection – relaxed atmosphere, flexible eating arrangements on Sundays, plenty of activities. Good range of food (we can recommend the home-made veg soup), but boarders we met wanted a more substantial meal later in the evening, after their sports training.

Chapel plays a central role – four assemblies a week; also services and concerts in Durham Cathedral. Various school councils – the junior council wrote an unofficial guide to the school. Parents say it's fine to be successful, academically or otherwise, and like the competitive element provided by the house system – 'They all get very involved'; 'The school finds where the individual can develop and works with it'.

Pastoral care and discipline: Pastoral care centred on form tutor and house staff, plus chaplain – rated outstanding by inspection, which glowed about relationships in general and moral and social development. Bullying not seen as a problem – pupils we met felt should it occur, it would be dealt with quickly and effectively (school would exclude if necessary), anti cyber bullying policy devised by staff and pupils. Senior prefects and school and house monitors support younger pupils – 'It's a very caring environment: the house system works very well'. Monitors (prefects) now selected through written application and interview. New children have an acquaintance day in the summer term before entry, an induction day just before term starts and a 'buddy' in their house when they arrive. Prep school pupils will also have used the senior school facilities regularly and visited for a day in year 5.

Pupils and parents: At 11, about half from prep school, most of rest from state primaries; at 13 and 16 from a range of state and independent schools. Many of day and weekly boarding pupils from within or close to Durham, others from as far as Sunderland, Newcastle or Darlington. A range of ethnic and financial backgrounds but mostly professional or self employed. Several of boarders from overseas (including Forces children) – most from Hong Kong, mainland China and Germany.

Plenty of contact with generally satisfied parents – monthly e-letter, website, academic diaries, meetings, a parents' forum. Forthcoming, well mannered, confident pupils – the phrase 'nice middle class kids' springs to mind.

Entrance: At 11+: short tests in English, maths and VR; 13+: all have to take tests in English and maths plus short interview. Above average ability but a wide range. Sixth form entrants need five GCSEs at B or above with a minimum C in maths and English.

If overseas applicants can't sit the entrance exam, they can get in with a school reference, but need a good level of English – for sixth need level 5 IELTS. Some stay in sixth for three years – special programme for first year. Has top rated tier 4 Boarding Sponsors' licence.

Exit: A small number leave at the end of year 11 for vocational courses or jobs and a few at the end of year 12, after some more maturing. A wide range of subjects (including drama and music) and universities, with a good proportion to top ones (one to Oxford in 2013, to study fine art); Newcastle, Northumbria, Durham, Bristol, York, Teeside and York St John popular. Civil and chemical engineering popular choices as well as art and psychology.

Money matters: 11+: academic and music exhibitions, drama and sport scholarships. 13+: academic and music exhibitions and scholarships; drama, sport, art and DT scholarships, plus internal academic scholarships. 16+: the above plus organ scholarship; external Burkitt scholarships and exhibitions, awarded on basis of papers in two chosen subjects with general paper and interview(s), and internal scholarship for a non-scholar with outstanding GCSE results.

Sibling, Forces and clergy discounts. About 150 pupils have means tested assistance and 105 non-means-tested admissions scholarships.

Remarks: Fees are relatively high, but parents we spoke to felt the school was worth it, in particular because of the extracurricular and pastoral virtues. Work to do on the academic front, but produces well rounded, decent young people, who have opportunities to develop a wide range of talents to a high level in a supportive, peaceful and very attractive environment.

Dwight School London (Upper School)

Linked school: Dwight School London, Lower School and Kindergarten

6 Friern Barnet Lane, London, N11 3LX

• Pupils: 210 boys and girls • Ages: 11–16 senior; 16–19 IB Diploma Centre • Non–denom • Fees: £15,420–£17,925 pa • Independent

Tel: 020 8920 0600
Email: admissions@dwightlondon.org
Website: www.dwightlondon.org

Head of School: Since 2005, Mr David Rose (fifties) CertEd BA MAEd LPSH. Married with two grown-up daughters. Softly spoken, clean shaven, well dressed, relaxed, very approachable and much travelled. The majority of his teaching experience has been overseas, including headships in Cyprus, Germany and Houston. Extremely enthusiastic about the school, which he took over as, apparently, the fourth head in four years. He's brought much-needed stability that has led to the strengthening of the three IB programmes, and improvement to school discipline. He's overseen renovation of some of the school buildings and facilities and the introduction of a new special educational needs partner school, and has put Dwight on London's international school map. He really enjoys working in the 2 to 18 through-school situation.

Academic matters: Runs the IB programme at all levels – in 2013, average point score 32 (out of possible 45). Average class size in upper school not normally more than 15. Although they would rather a child moved up through the school, they will prepare children for common entrance etc if required. Years 7-11 follow the MYP. Years 12 and 13 follow the IB programme according to ability, some pupils opting to follow individual courses which produce certificates (acceptable for university entrance) rather than following the full diploma programme.

Languages are well catered for – French is introduced in the nursery section, Spanish in year 7 and Italian is an option at diploma stage. Computers all over the place. Interactive whiteboards in every classroom with linked Macs. Wireless technology enabling laptop use anywhere. No RE, though they say this is covered in global studies and most religious festivals are celebrated, which was evident in photos round the school. Homework regarded as important and students are expected to fill in their diaries and keep to deadlines; can be done in school out of hours.

Computer database covers every pupil, profiling, recording progress, enabling and tracking accurate parental contact. Parents also receive a chatty newsletter from the head at the end of each week, not only containing news but also updates on extracurricular activities available both to their children and themselves. Excellent website.

Most learning difficulties, or learning differences, as they prefer to call them, catered for; good specialist teachers. Would accept a statemented child but not one with disruptive behavioural difficulties. The QUEST Programme aims to 'teach children with different learning styles to function successfully and independently in an academically challenging mainstream setting'. Sessions are mainly one-to-one but some class based time if relevant. Holmewood House is the new partner school that is able to admit students with more complex learning issues.

English as an additional language (EAL) regarded as essential for children with two non-English speaking parents – two to five lessons a week, one to one or in a small group depending on needs. Native language sessions also provided; special teacher brought in if necessary – Greek, Japanese etc. Would be reluctant to take a non-English speaker after year 8. Language Heritage Day once a year when everyone speaks their own language. Not only over 35 different nationalities represented by the pupils but also 15 amongst the full-time teachers.

QUEST and intensive EAL run as separate programmes with costs ranging from £870 to £2,995 per term depending on extent of need.

Games, options, the arts: Games obligatory once a week per year group – sports field five minutes away by minibus and has use of Trent Park sports hall. Tournaments not only with local schools and nationally but also overseas – recently cricket in Barbados and football and netball in Antigua. Lots of clubs from chess to martial arts – kendo very popular at the moment – to cater for compulsory activity sessions. Emphasis put on 'healthy exercise' – shirkers beware!

Good music – about 25 per cent learn an individual instrument, orchestra, chamber group and lots of different bands. Very excited about setting up a link with the Barnet Symphony Orchestra; loads of different instruments in the music room, classical and modern – no excuses not to try. Several soundproofed rooms for individual tuition.

Lots of outings to concerts, theatres and galleries as well as trips home and abroad. The Model United Nations Conference of course features, and an annual exchange with the Dwight School in New York, but perhaps the most exciting thing the older children have done is help build a village in Cambodia: not only did they organise events to raise funds but some of them also went out to lend a hand.

Background and atmosphere: School originally founded in 1972 by Dr Stephen Spahn, director of the Dwight School in New York, and Sir Maurice Bowra, Warden of Wadham College, Oxford. Is now fully owned by the Spahn family. Dwight London, which followed the establishment of Dwight New York, is part of a group that now has campuses in Vancouver Island, Seoul, Beijing, with Shanghai on the horizon. Dwight students are eligible to participate in Dwight Global Leaders, a summer gathering of high school students from all over who come together to develop leadership skills and learn about social entrepreneurship.

Dwight London is on four sites in two locations. The upper school (nearest tube Arnos Grove) consists of Dwight and Jubilee Hall, both of which are purpose-built. Dwight was, once upon a time, Friern Barnet Grammar School, and a few traces of this still remain in scruffy corners and inter-connecting classrooms. Five minutes' walk away, Jubilee Hall is a bright, modern building originally created solely as the IB centre, but recent modifications now enable both buildings to be run in sync. Classes are timetabled to minimise movement between the sites, which has improved the general timekeeping and removed excuses for tardiness. All children below year 10 are escorted between sites. Good playground outside Dwight and lovely common room for the diploma students in Jubilee Hall.

Apart from the laboratories and studios, all classrooms non-specific and spacious. When we were there, the library was being used for an English class discussion concerning the amount of television watched – soaps, of course, but not too much, as far as we could gather. Other pupils working quietly at computers in a different area only looked slightly distracted. Enthusiastic teachers and pupils wherever we went, all happy to explain what they were doing. Although a lot of the classrooms seem to be at sub pavement level, no lack of light.

The dining area has been completely modernised since our last visit – now with a coffee shop style cash cafeteria. Food all brought from the kitchens in the lower school 10 minutes' drive away. A huge plasma screen on one wall broadcasts the news or other teacher-selected items. Year 10 upwards are allowed to make use of the local cafés if they prefer to, with parental permission, of course.

Fantastic art studio overseen by a huge golden eye. All sorts of different creations, paintings, sculptures, models – lots of inspiration from an enthusiastic teacher. Both disciplines of sight and sound expanded in a galleried computer studio overlooking art and music rooms, where Macs are used for creating music, animation and design.

The whole school seems to buzz with exciting projects – children in the physics lab enjoying experimenting; lovely creations in the DT studio, including great clocks made by the younger students; a drama studio in a dark and mysterious room entirely surrounded by black curtains: 'Double, double, toil and trouble'.

Pastoral care and discipline: Strict conduct code – IB philosophy of intercultural awareness and respect for the individual thoroughly in place. Very few rules otherwise needed. Mobile phones allowed (upper school only) but have to be left in the school office. A system in place should problems occur and a counsellor who is apparently popular and fully occupied. Communication links between teacher and parent encouraged and always available.

As each new entrant is individually assessed, transition is normally easy. A child will be placed in the class relevant to stage of learning, even if this occasionally means (temporarily) out of year (for example when arriving from a different hemisphere country). With such a mixture of nationalities and backgrounds and the ethos of respect for all, settling in is not usually a problem.

Pupils and parents: About two-thirds local north London and just beyond. The rest expats working in industry, embassies or high commissions and the occasional university lecturer. No-one normally more than 30 minutes away. School bus service provided at extra cost. Most families have an international background, usually one English-speaking parent. Nationalities include Japanese, American, Chinese, Australian, Swedish, Indian and Greek. Parental involvement encouraged, whatever their experience and talents can provide. Large range of presentation and social events arranged each year.

Entrance: Mainly in September but can also join at other times of the year if required. Interview and report from previous school only real requisites. Many come up from the lower school but others from other local schools or overseas.

Exit: Mainly to university, a lot London based but some overseas – occasional one to Oxbridge, others to, eg, Edinburgh, Manchester, the University of British Columbia, Exeter, Queen Mary and University College London.

A careers guidance service – all take the Morrisby test. The link with The Dwight School is extremely useful for those wishing to attend American universities – the head also has an extensive knowledge of US schools. Business and languages are probably the most popular subjects, but science is also an option and they are beginning to make greater in-roads into the arts.

Money matters: A variety of scholarships for talented students: academic, music, sports and citizenship. Bursaries for needy students, £500 to £1000 a term, but they will keep a child at 100 per cent if a crisis arises. At the moment two boys from West Ham football academy on sports scholarships and at least one talented musician – flexibility seems to be the name of the game; finances ultimately dependent on the owners' wishes.

Remarks: Ambition to be the number one international school in London. Good management structure and an enthusiastic team of teachers operating the IB programme with imagination and zest. Students enthusiastic, controlled and happy.

Eastbourne College

Old Wish Road, Eastbourne, BN21 4JY

- Pupils: 360 boys/270 girls; 310 full boarders • Ages: 13–18 • C of E • Fees: Day £19,750–£19,830; Boarding £29,760–£30,090 pa • Independent

Tel: 01323 452323
Email: admissions@eastbourne-college.co.uk
Website: www.eastbourne-college.co.uk

Head: Since 2005, Mr Simon Davies (mid-forties). Previously vice master at Bedford school, prior to which he was head of biology and senior housemaster at Abingdon School. Married with children; wife runs a literary charity, is involved with school publications, and hosts dinner parties for new staff. Two of their three children attend the school. Mr Davies is affable, approachable, intelligent, warm, unpretentious, you get the feeling you can trust him (even though he was previously a derivatives broker in the city, 'but not something he ever intended making his career'). Described by some as an inspirational biology teacher.

He enthuses about what education should and should not be. It emphatically should not be about league tables and measurement. It should be about 'how well a child does in relation to his or her ability and aiding them make their choices'. He asserts that his school is 'selective but not highly selective' and the school measures success more in value-added terms than in absolutes. He has hundreds of conversations with pupils, parents, staff to ensure this message is communicated and he listens to what others have to say. He likes the school to be relaxed, never casual and always purposeful. He makes a point of getting to know the pupils and parents and can very impressively recount details of pupils past and present.

He quotes de Bono – 'there's no point being brilliant if you're brilliant at the wrong thing' – and believes too many schools proclaim their brilliance at just the wrong thing. 'We are not the Chelsea Flower Show', but more in tune with Capability Brown, ie not an exhibition of bloom on show for a short burst but developing saplings that will continue to grow and fruit for years to come.

Academic matters: A wide sweep of subjects at GCSE (can take French, German, Portuguese, Spanish, Latin and Greek). This freedom of choice is evident through the curriculum, eg a pupil can study many creative subjects such as architecture, textiles, music tech and not be bogged down with subjects that he/she is not interested in. A real strength of the school is the value-added – from the academically gifted to those for whom academic success is tough: time and again pupils entering with Bs and Cs emerge with As. In 2013, 61 per cent of grades were A*/A.

School aims to include all SEN pupils where possible but specific provision for mild dyslexia, G&T and TEFL. One full-time and one busy part-time teacher. All children are screened on entry. Individual SEN lessons are charged for.

No separate cost for the G&T provision, however, which is department specific, eg BioSoc for biology; DT entered a RIBA parliamentary design competition (finalists). A G&T coordinator monitors the challenge to these pupils and each department has its own one. Since the introduction of A* for A level a '100 per cent club' for the élite achievers. Academic whole school societies for G&T, eg Hayman society, the New Academy and Casson society etc (details on website).

Not a huge breadth of A level subjects – no psychology, sociology, politics. May consider politics if they found the right candidate, but few requests from parents or pupils for 'pop' subjects such as psychology. So a traditional curriculum is what traditional parents want? 'Not so,' say a few parents, more on offer at A level would be interesting, eg Italian was taught inspirationally to GCSE but the plug was pulled for A level, much to the disappointment of some fired-up pupils. IB programme not on the horizon here. In 2013, 50 per cent A*/A grades.

School feels they are ahead of the game in the way they use and integrate ICT through the curriculum. Reports are produced online every three weeks, showing pupils' grades for effort and achievement. Science block is new, sporting 12 laboratories and some of the most spacious we've seen – results accordingly exceptional.

Worth a mention is the level and scope of the DT work. Housed in a large new block, staff have commercial and industrial backgrounds. Has won GSG DT and textiles award – after a trip around the many rooms, it is easy to see why. Many pupils leave to study project design, textile engineering, architecture etc. School works closely with renowned local architects, professional designers, who offer constructive criticism. Excellent architectural models on display, pupils designing a local House of Parliament when we visited, soon to be followed with a design for Westminster to be displayed on site. Fantastic range of high tech equipment that industry would die for, 50 per cent takeup for GCSE. At present building cars with sustainable themes, green power, and a lot of awards for resistant materials use, graphics etc.

Games, options, the arts: Strong at the top level, plenty achieve national status and some international and offer excellent competition on the local circuit. Two good recent appointments. A level 5 rugby coach and a head of netball raising standards. Fives, shooting, swimming, recent addition of fencing, golf are taken up by more senior pupils if team sports are not for them. Most are engaged on a daily basis and the school fields many teams for some fixtures; some consternation that the less conscientious and the D of E team can slip detection and be seen munching pizzas in town! 'There's a certain glamour for the first XV and those that excel in sport but 'if the child doesn't jump at the school, then the school doesn't jump at the child'. The manicured rugby pitch dominates the front of the school but the main sports fields are a five minute drive away.

Some interesting art work on display. Graphics not offered. Plenty of drama productions and musical events, bands, choirs, rock and swing bands, soirees in the houses etc but again it would be prudent to enquire what is done for the pupil who is reluctant to raise his head above the parapet. Plenty is open to the community, clubs, societies etc, eg silver surfers' club whereby the pupils act as agents to help ageing locals with ICT skills. CCF and D of E flourishing. Fertile links with local sports clubs so that facilities are shared, and they host regional prep school rugby and hockey tournaments – good outreach for prospective pupils and talent.

Background and atmosphere: The seventh Duke of Devonshire founded the school in 1867. The current Duke is President of the Eastbourne College Council along with other influential Eastbourne residents. The school is not socially exclusive but rooted in the Meads community. Main school is an imposing red-brick building, amid an aesthetically pleasing mix of others, old and sympathetically new and ensconced in the heart of Eastbourne. No ivory tower feel, though it is fronted by a large pitch and bordered by five-storey Victorian houses and retirement homes. There is constant traffic of hearty pupils hotfooting around the perimeter hurrying to lessons. It is close to the railway and next to Devonshire Park, home to the pre-Wimbledon Men's and Ladies' Tennis tournament. Themed dinner parties for the sixth form, catered for by the college. The standard of food is very good, excellent range of choices, although pupils impressed with lunch but were critical of teas. Plenty of inter-house competitions, concerts, soirees etc.

Pastoral care and discipline: Very, very strong indeed, very nurturing, excellent loops of communication with pupils, parents and staff, definitely the throbbing pulse of the school, and possibly why it is so successful at reaching all abilities. Head of boarding came from Sevenoaks and thus brings plenty of experience. He believes the boarding works so well because they focus on 'character and relationships which are fundamental to the way the school is run'. Parents and pupils concur that pastoral philosophy is backed with action and not self-promotion. Good system of buddies and sages for the new boarders. The school is run as a full boarding school, 50/50 full boarders to day boarders. No weekly boarding. Now more flexibility for day pupils: minibuses leave at 6pm and 8pm so pupils can choose when to go home each day and 'organise their work, co-curricular activities and family life most effectively for them and their families'. School revolves around the house: all pupils are registered in the common room of their house, assemblies, announcements are all made in house. The boarding houses are all spacious, light; all have good facilities with their own garden. They each have a tuck shop run on a profit basis; one house bought two goats for an Indian community. Junior boarders share three to five to a room, reducing up to the sixth form, where they have large single rooms. House parents or matrons are the first port of call for any confidences.

A generally wholesome and happy bunch, they give the thumbs up to the quality of boarding staff and to the blend of home and school it achieves. 'Good manners go with the turf and discipline has been tightened up,' says one parent. 'One strike and out' policy for drugs brought into the school and socialising between sexes is kept strictly to the common room (perhaps more vigilant these days since the embarrassing incident reminiscent of Notes on a Scandal captured on a pupil's mobile phone!). It was testament to the head that the incident was dealt with deftly and didn't become a major media event. The head remarks here that this happened a few years ago and is not representative of life at Eastbourne.

Pupils and parents: Varied social mix. On one side you have the Sussex Downs and the rolling Sussex countryside. It attracts families wanting a boarding-style education. The international contingent makes up only eight per cent of the school – Chinese, Nigerians, Germans. These students integrate properly and don't stay in packs. Flourishing parents' and friends' society that organizes social functions.

Entrance: Overseas pupils are accepted provided their level of English is proficient. Candidates for year 9 entry sit CE or the college's own entrance exams or scholarship papers. The hurdle for sixth form is B grades or better at GCSE. About 30 pupils enter for sixth form from surrounding state or private schools.

Exit: Mr Davies talks candidly – clearly his less academic pupils aren't also-rans to be sold down the river and replaced by clever-clogs from other schools at sixth form. Very small number leave post GCSE (10 per cent or so). At 18, mainly to a mix of redbrick, Russell group and vocational colleges; three to Oxbridge in 2013. About a third take a gap year; Durham, Edinburgh, Exeter Leeds and Newcastle popular over the last few years. Rather a high proportion of girls leave to study public relations, business, media related studies, leisure management.

Money matters: The school is full although could accept a few more at a push. Scholarships available for most subject areas and a foundation director oversees the fundraising and bursary fund. He is aiming to build a pot by contributions from parents and staff to allow financial help to the struggling. The headmaster introduced the idea of all staff contributing the price of a pint per week to the fund. This equates to approx £250 a week and thus £15,000 a year. This philanthropic pint fund consequently translates to a) a full bursary for a fortunate and worthy pupil and b) a thirsty staffroom! The fees remain highly competitive by comparison to other full boarding schools. Music scholars receive free tuition, international students pay EAL fees as a lump sum arrangement diminishing year by year.

Remarks: Good for all abilities and school is snug in its own skin. More about developing integrity in the pupil than about clawing its way up the league table, but equally relishes seeing top notch scores from those capable of such.

Edgbaston High School for Girls

Linked school: Edgbaston High School for Girls Preparatory Dept

Westbourne Road, Edgbaston, Birmingham, B15 3TS

• Pupils: 480 girls; all day • Ages: 11–18 • Christian ethos and respect for all traditions • Fees: £10,704 pa • Independent

Tel: 01214 545831
Email: admissions@edgbastonhigh.co.uk
Website: www.edgbastonhigh.co.uk

Head Mistress: Since 2006, Dr Ruth Weeks BSc PhD (mid-fifties). Formerly head of Redland High in Bristol, a city with possibly an even more ferociously competitive educational environment than Brum, and which has clearly schooled her in what needs to be done to up the admiration factor for this arguably under-appreciated school. Not a PR hot-airhead by any stretch, but has a good story to tell – she's improved communications admirably, started an excellent weekly e-newsletter, and holds informal coffee mornings where parents can drop in and sound off. A wholly unterrifying sort of head, nothing of the dragon about her at all. Easy, charming, sincere, principled and, phew, bright. She's a chemist and finds time to teach years 7 and 13. A Brummie by birth and breeding, she has come home. Married, two daughters.

Academic matters: Everyone knows that it's the King Eds that do best, so does that make Edgbaston a plucky but undeniable second best? A good many unsentimental parents clearly think so and migrate at 11+ if their child can get in. They nevertheless leave behind lots of good brains and, increasingly, best brains, because this school does things the way more and more parents loyally like. Raw scores demonstrate good teaching all round. Superb value-added scores more than merely attest to this. In 2013 70 per cent A*/A at GCSE, 69 per cent A*-B at A level, with 44 per cent A*/A. Real breadth here, with girls going on to do the whole range of subjects at university from medicine to fashion. Science and maths are strong, art simply stunning. They still do Latin and Greek, resist silly subjects but listen to their girls, so soon home economics and perhaps digital photography will add to the (excellently taught) PE and psychology. IT excellent and everywhere. Mild SENs only.

Games, options, the arts: Passionate about enrichment – who's not? – but a lot goes on here outside the classroom. They're a sporty lot and, though a city centre school, the four-acre site enables them to play a good range of games including football. Sparkling new pool, sports hall, all-weather pitch. Dance and drama are strong in their seriously fabulous new performing arts centre. Masses of lunchtime clubs. Music is pervasive and everybody studies it all the way through.

Background and atmosphere: Non-denominational but with Quaker and Unitarian roots and a Cadbury connection, where elements of no-nonsense nonconformity linger. Utterly unpretentious. Friday assemblies are spent silently listening to music. Strong emphasis on charitable work. School population almost matches the city's racial mix and the girls we spoke to were totally colour-blind. Single sex education has always been very much a Birmingham thing, a good thing for those whose culture and religion require it. The school is unable to lay on halal lunches but provides a salad alternative. Assemblies offer up praise to God, but no specific God – each to their own. In this affectionate environment it works.

Comely 60s buildings erected when the school moved from the city centre, with a charming recreation of the old reception room inside and some very fine portraits of former heads. The prep school is separate, integral and shares the same ethos. This is the cleanest, shiniest, un-school-smellingest school you'll ever see – it really is remarkable. Splendidly resourced classrooms, very civilised meeting areas. The setting in this leafy suburb, bang next door to the Botanical Gardens and among university buildings, is highly agreeable.

With an investment of £3.5 million, the school has significantly improving facilities with a new extension which includes a new state-of-the-art sixth form centre, library, classrooms and a fitness suite.

Pastoral care and discipline: Pastoral care here is a major strength. In addition to tutorial support, senior girls mentor younger ones. Girls praise teachers for the individual attention they give. It's an un-cliquey place, they assert – impossible, you would have thought, in a girls' school, but the influx of new girls at 11+ brings about a healthy remix. This really is a notably inclusive, supportive environment and, of course, small size is a factor. The girls wholeheartedly buy into the ethos.

Pupils and parents: Pupils come from all over Birmingham and an outer ring which takes in Redditch, Kidderminister, Tamworth and Stourbridge, so some long journeys here – that tells you something. Increasingly popular with university lecturers. Thriving parents' association, Edgbaston High School Parents' Association (EHSPA), who organise everything from second-hand uniform sales to social jollies.

Current high achievers include Molly Dineen, filmmaker; Lydia Hislop, racing correspondent for The Times; Professor Sally Davies, director of research and development at the Department of Health; Robyn Jones, Credit Suisse Outstanding Woman in Business; Philippa Lett, top model; and Kate Williams, author and TV historian. Quite a spread.

Entrance: Starts at two and a half. Entrance tests at 11 and other years when places are available. Entry to sixth form non-automatic, but departures hardly ever happen. This is a selective school, it's no pushover and it's nudging its bar upwards.

Exit: Around a third leave after GCSEs. Seven to Oxbridge in 2013; others to eg Durham, Nottingham, LSE, Leeds and Birmingham to study eg Russian, medicine, law, graphic design and biomedical science.

Money matters: Not a rich foundation, but very keen to reach out and help where it can. Bursaries available – ask about them – and some scholarships. Fees more or less on a par with rivals.

Remarks: Anything but a sink-or-swim sort of place – lots of rigour as well as kindness. An easy school to be very fond of, waking up at last to the need to proclaim the good news about itself, a matter of urgency as straitened times return.

The Edinburgh Academy

Linked school: The Edinburgh Academy Junior School

---

42 Henderson Row, Edinburgh, EH3 5BL

- Pupils: 1025, 705 boys, 320 girls • Ages: 2–18 • Non-denom
- Fees: Senior £9,765–£12,126; Junior £7,182–£8,871 pa
- Independent

Tel: 01315 564603
Email: admissions@edinburghacademy.org.uk
Website: www.edinburghacademy.org.uk

Rector: Since 2008, Mr Marco Longmore BA, Edinburgh historian (early forties). Previously senior deputy head of Alleyn's School (qv) prior to which he taught history and modern studies at George Heriot's School, and then moved to George Watson's College as head of history and modern studies.

Elegant, relaxed and exuding confidence, Mr Longmore reports a 'management restructuring' with two 'senior deputes' to cover senior (senior depute rector) and junior school (headteacher) and further depute rectors in both. The senior school is re-divided into 'transition' (11/13), middle years (14/16) and sixth form (17/18). New heads of these areas, plus assistants, manage academic and personal supervision, 'supporting families and allowing information giving and gathering'. This provides a 'sense of progression' and more effective 'delivery of the school's as well as the parents' expectations'. The word in Edinburgh indicates that this may be a necessary move.

An enthusiastic sportsman with a keen interest in theatre and public debates, Mr Longmore believes so strongly in the values of the 'co-curriculum' (stressing the 'co-' rather than 'extra-' curriculum) that he has started a rector's book of outstanding achievement so he can personally acknowledge this. He and his wife, Karen, have two children, both in the school.

Academic matters: Hybrid public exam structure with GCSEs for all across the board, followed by either Higher or AS and then A levels (A2); children showing an interest in a Scottish university are encouraged to take Higher English. Those with a target of A levels and/or university in England might go for the AS route, depending on the subject.

Overall, results pretty strong, English, maths and mod langs particularly, and most subjects good at A level with new A* above the national average. In 2013, 92 per cent A*-C, 19 per cent A* at GCSE and 92 per cent A*-C, 46 per cent A*/A at A level. Science department invigorated by new science building and numbers going on to science-based subjects at university high. Business and finance courses also growing in popularity as new head of dept hits his stride and now popular at university. History and modern studies hit a wobble last year, but school reports dynamic new head of dept already having a strong impact.

Sport and PE are popular and getting good results. Latin and music have small uptake but terrific results and school keen to keep such subjects in exam years to retain breadth. French, German and Spanish all doing well in big department and Chinese Mandarin introduced on a trial basis. Good range of subjects at Higher, though some parents find it frustrating that specialist subjects not available (such as Russian, law or psychology). Depute rector says that no-one has expressed an interest in these subjects for some years but, as with Chinese Mandarin, school will consider introducing those where there is sufficient interest.

Staffing levels good. New appointments made and turnover has been steady with lots of internal and external appointees. Some changes made as a result of recruitment from another Edinburgh Independent school (St Margaret's) that closed. Feedback from parents very positive: the academy was very dynamic and supportive in assisting, and built a special one-off curriculum for S4 group.

Expect a broad academic range of pupils. Junior years largely mixed ability with the exception of maths and English. Further up the school, teaching groups defined largely by blocking scheme, though set by ability where possible. Maximum class size is 24 in younger years though generally lower. Support for learning department is strong and growing. Support spread between extraction and collaborative teaching in classes and pupils with learning difficulties are treated positively. Results commendable given the mixed intake, 'but,' says the rector 'remember that a C or D grade may represent a great triumph for an individual and the others things they achieve in sport or music, for example, are also hugely important'. The top end of the exam list will indicate the school's expectations of academic children. The tradition of 'dux', the brightest boy or girl in the school (Magnus Magnusson was dux in his day), is extended to include wider group of high achievers, the Dux Club.

Games, options, the arts: The school tradition for providing a mini squad for the Scottish rugby side continues and this year is no exception, with usual rash of caps, would-be caps and waiters in the wings. Merchiston and The Academy celebrated the 150th anniversary of their annual match – the longest-running fixture in world rugby – with a slap-up dinner at Murrayfield, which raised £34K for Hearts and Balls (sic) which fund-raises for rugby injuries. (Merchiston won – but only just!). Two years ago, the Academy won the Brewin Dolphin National Schools U18 Cup.

Main games field beside the junior school with its fantastic (community) sports hall shared with lucky local residents. No pool (Mr Longmore says the wish list is still under debate) but specialist weights and gym and two new all-weather hockey pitches. Girls now have their own competitive teams in sports such as hockey, netball and athletics. Emphasis is on mixed sex sport for the girls, though the boys retain their, admittedly distinguished, team identity.

Outstanding art department with notable achievements in every discipline, brilliant ceramics; life class in the evenings a popular option. Dashing but philosophical young head of art said that this year's theme is Substance and Appearance. The department, complete with tools, books and other comforts, occupies a central space. Music outstanding, all-singing and dancing. Superlatives from our informants reach awesome proportions. Lucky singers and orchestra just back from a tour of Sorrento. Any pupil learning an instrument can play in concerts 'even if it is only three notes and child has been learning the trombone for three weeks'. Concerts outstandingly professional (the odd radio concert). The senior school chamber choir won the Songs of Praise school choir competition in 2011 – the first Scottish school to do so.

Drama immensely enhanced by the sympathetic conversion of the lovely old physics building to a state-of-the-art performing arts centre, the Magnusson Centre for Performing Arts (£2.5m): theatre and dance studio with girls' and boys' showers and changing for every imaginable activity below. Inside is breathtaking, though original features have not been vandalised: outside some additional curious tiled 'ears' provide ventilation for the new activities.

CCF hugely popular (everyone has to join, including the girls) – great flurry of battledress and airforce blue evident on Remembrance Day; piping particularly strong, with successes in both quartet and trios. Keen D of E; lots of hobbies – jewellery-making the most recent, attracting boys as well as girls – and good charity input – the charity committee does a massive amount of fund-raising (£16.5k for four local and national charities) and even the last rector was known to take part in a charity sleep-out. Well, Mr Longmore?

Background and atmosphere: Lord Cockburn and Sir Walter Scott founded school in 1824 amongst others. Built in traditional Edinburgh-inspired sandstone (Greek mode), the Greek motto on the main portico reads, 'Education is the mother of both wisdom and virtue'. Buildings in main school a mixed bunch, some obviously designer-inspired additions, including a fabulous oval assembly hall, plus a mass of add-ons as well as classrooms and impressive new labs around huge bleak tarmac courtyards, although new seating and planting across the school helps to soften the traditional yards. Pleasant gardens surround the administrative areas. Stunning music department. Look for generous Edinburghoisie-sponsored libraries etc; successful FPs remember their font of learning with pride. Boarding houses, now sold, have made a good nest-egg for further developments (still to be prioritised). Planning permission currently being sought for refurbishment of existing sport pavilions and a new pavilion, plus new reception area for visitors and admissions in senior school. School owns a field centre in Angus.

Boys wear bright blue blazers; girls, when visible, look neat in a tailored version. All-through co-ed at the academy is cold news now. Girls now 29 per cent in both senior and junior, and 50 per cent in nursery; entry applications indicate an increase but it still looks and feel like a boys' school. Feedback from parents indicates that this is changing, however.

School sold five (disused and needing money spent on them) tennis courts several years ago (little boxes built on them) which caused press comment, and built the James Clerk Maxwell science building, which is now fully functioning. Outstanding interior with exciting scientific photographs forming whole walls, tiptop labs, colour-coded to match the textbook coding of red for chemistry, blue for physics and green (of course!) for biology, which also boasts nature garden complete with pond and a magically beautiful fishtank embedded in the entrance hall wall.

£2 million upgrade of nursery school, also housing juniors up to second year, recently completed. 'very well received,' says rector. Numbers of pupils at the junior school had fallen and girls have taken up the slack. The new-build also houses after-school care for juniors available up to 6pm. In 2012, a £1.5 million project for new classrooms in the Junior School commenced.

Pastoral care and discipline: Pupils divided into four 'divisions' (houses), pastoral care via depute rector (pastoral and personnel), heads of year plus form takers (class teachers); good PSHE. Head ephor (prefect) is a key link with rector and school. School 'not complacent that drugs are confined to an area south of Princes Street', or 'stop at the railings – incidents do occur'. No automatic exclusion unless dealing is involved. 'If at all possible we give the pupils a second chance'; parents are involved. 'Pupil may forfeit the right to remain in the school (for a varying length of time).' City temptations are close. One or two teeny reports of bullying still around, but really just aggravated teasing and no more than any nit-picker might expect.

Pupils and parents: All sorts, with a large traditional intake of the Edinbourgeoisie. Small tranche from abroad, mainly Europe. Rector and head of junior school keen on playing down traditional middle-class image of the school – hence extended and very popular nursery hours and 8.00am breakfast for seniors. On the whole, pupils are pleasantly self-confident and polite – occasional uncouth youth but not more than teenage adolescence. Robert Louis Stevenson and Archbishop Tait of Canterbury are FPs, as are partners in many of Edinburgh's institutions today. As girls still outnumbered by boys parents may be a little hesitant to send the less confident.

Entrance: Traditionally patronised by the great and the good of Edinburgh (the Edinbourgeoisie) and does well by them, plus an increasing number of first-time independent school buyers (around 40 per cent). Entry handbook makes ages and stages for entry very clear, despite the contortions of language and ingenuity required to make the Scottish and English education systems fit into a coherent whole. Girls' advent has, as expected, increased the application rate (for both sexes we understand) but not changed the system.

Exit: 'Around 90 per cent' to various universities, roughly 60 per cent to Scottish, the rest elsewhere, with fewer recently taking a gap year first. Steady trickle (three in 2012) to Oxbridge – as ever, sciences and engineering feature strongly, with creative and social subjects on the increase. Art something of a speciality. Enlightened careers department (rector again: 'very very good'). Quantities of embryo lawyers, doctors and merchant bankers, plus, it has to be said, a plethora of pupils going off to university to read engineering, physics, technology, English, modern languages, sports studies, history, international relations. 'What they do thereafter may be different – but they are not cloned down the three routes which you mention. Some into the professions, but progressively more into art, drama, interior design and administration.' School can manage SATS (for American universities). Unconditional offers from Scottish universities based on Scottish Highers taken in (lower) sixth year do not always make for academic concentration in seventh (upper sixth) year.

Money matters: Good crop of scholarships for musicians and academics plus means-tested bursaries; school may support pupils in financial difficulties in a number of ways depending on the circumstance, until the next practical exit point. 'No endowments per se – majority of scholarships and other bursaries come out of fee income.' Familial discounts for third child (and more). The Edinburgh Academy Foundation's primary goal for next year is to support the annual giving programme. Bursaries are means tested up to 100 per cent fees in line with OSCR expectation.

Remarks: Now the dust of the transition to co-educational has settled, the Academy emerges as a popular school with huge potential and rapidly improving facilities. Girls are now 29 per cent of both junior and senior – not perhaps for the shrinking violet, but well worth watching.

Edinburgh Steiner School

Linked school: Edinburgh Steiner School – Lower School

60 Spylaw Road, Edinburgh, EH10 5BR

- Pupils: 250 boys and girls • Ages: 3–18 • Non–denom
- Fees: £7,860 pa • Independent

Tel: 01313 373410
Email: admissions@edinburghsteinerschool.org.uk
Website: www.edinburghsteinerschool.org.uk

Chair of the College of Teachers: No head as such – role of chair is rotated: current chair, Philip Shinton, has been in position for a year. Major educational decisions are taken by the college of teachers and executed by the school's management team in conjunction with teachers. The bursar, board of trustees and college of teachers are responsible for finance, admin and building development. Forget trad hierarchy – teachers in the Steiner Waldorf world 'share responsibility and authority for the daily running of the school and the educational programme'.

Academic matters: Pupils start each day with a 'wake-up call': rhythmic time/or morning verse followed by the main lesson, a two-hour slot when 'topic blocks' are covered in four-week chunks: astronomy, philosophy, history of architecture, whatever. These are not necessarily exam fodder, but the Open College Network (OCN) recommended that the 'narrative's' main lesson be 'accepted without amendment and accredited' – OCN levels 1 and 2 are equivalent to A or B/C at GCSE.

New classroom, learning support base and library. School says, 'Pupils are encouraged to read widely and to make full use of the extensive range of academic resources available to them in the libraries, galleries and museums of this wonderful city'. 'Pupils make a day book for each subject': the one we saw was beautifully illustrated and the pupil concerned could hardly fail to understand angles after many diagrams and pages of colouring.

Spanking new computer room, though computers still thinner on the ground here than in many schools; most classrooms equipped with computer-generated projectors (they 'ripped out the whiteboards,' we were told) and computers not encouraged (nor telly) till age 14, either at home or at school. Computer lessons include deconstructing and reconstructing old PCs as well as designing websites (school one impressive).

As in Europe, formal education starts at 6, with pupils reading first from what they themselves have written (having been 'familiarised' with the letters), and learning both French and German. (Those who join the school later may have to take extra lessons, and pay extra to catch up.) Five-week trips to proper French and German Steiner schools – funded by pupils themselves via jumble sales/pizza cook-ins and the like. No 'real' homework until aged 9.

Classes of about 20, brighter pupils can leapfrog, and vice versa; EAL for older foreign nationals (charged), the younger ones pick it up as they go along. 'Huge learning support' – regular testing for all for dyslexia et al in lower school and again on entry to senior school at 14, some pupils with statement of needs. School follows a multi-sensory approach with the emphasis on co-ordination and 'curative' specialists. Qualified staff in both lower and upper school, plus one 'floater'. General dyslexic (dyspraxic etc) help is covered within the fee structure, but if parents request extra, it costs. School has reputation for a caring environment.

Offers GCSEs, Standard grades, Intermediate I and II, Higher, Advanced Higher and AS levels. The normal two-year GCSE syllabus is studied over one year, with maths, English, German and French GCSE taken aged 16, followed by humanities, the sciences and art at 17, and either Highers or AS levels at 18. Though no academic selection, results are good in general, some seriously good. Strong German and French. In 2013, 90 per cent overall pass rate for Highers and Advance Highers, and 100 per cent for Intermediate courses (classes 10 and 11).

Lots of practical science with hands-on lessons taught in rather antiquated labs – everything taught 'experientially and children learn by doing'. 'By teaching science, art and religion in this integrated way, we hope to implant in our young people a holistic view of life, so that they may regard the world with understanding and serve it with respect.' Loads of exchanges globally with other Rudolf Steiner schools.

Steiner teachers are trained in-house – this is one of four training centres. Prospective disciples come from all walks of life: some are former pupils, some former parents and some come from trad teaching backgrounds (sometimes they stay with Steiner and sometimes go back to mainstream). The part-time course is spread over three years and includes an introduction to Rudolf Steiner and anthroposophy, the esoteric science, Goethean science and artistic practice (and this is in the first year), plus Parsifal: Biographical Questions with Reference to the Grail Legend, eurythmy, creative speech, painting drawing etc. During the second and third year all must do teaching practice.

Games, options, the arts: Small basketball court, cricket and hockey; seven-a-side rugby at Meggetland 'dead popular'.

Timetabled PE and gym, acrobatics a recent addition – pupils wear Steiner tee shirts and track suit bottoms. Hall used for gym, theatre etc. Options and the arts integrated into syllabus – art exam results consistently very good. Fabric design, weaving, knitting from age 6. Music and drama ditto and inclusive. Cooking lessons for all, baking in kindergarten during our visit.

Background and atmosphere: Three trad Edinburgh Victorian villas, in a residential area, set betwixt George Watson's extensive campus and various parts of Napier University. Various modern additions, exciting Swiss chalet for tinies. Mother and toddler group. Parking 'borrowed' from a church opposite, though masses of parking meters on road outside. Three acres of tidily shoe-horned campus, children playing anywhere and everywhere, neatly segregated by age. Proper pupil gardens. Every bit of space is used, some tatty areas, nothing precious – the whole place smacks of a lack of funds, though the paths are better maintained than previously. (School protests, as 'work is ongoing to renovate classrooms'.) Pupils' work on display adds interest to otherwise lacklustre classrooms, with a huge and amazing felt hanging in the main reception area. Christian school, everyone enjoyed a Michaelmas feast the week before our visit, other faiths' holy days celebrated.

Steiner schools do not follow the (now largely historical) orthodox attitude to education, but treat each child as a blank canvas to be filled with interlinking academic, artistic and practical information, delivered in such a way as to incite curiosity, encourage creativity and an awareness of others. Has long been regarded as a 'school offering alternative education to somewhat scruffy children in hippy clothes, who took no exams and pretty well ran riot'. However, since the Scottish government introduced their much vaunted curriculum for excellence, has become an educational flagship, albeit an holistic one. To quote The Scotsman: 'All schools strive for innovation but one that does more than strive is Edinburgh's Rudolf Steiner. It lives and breathes innovation'. The educational philosophy that Rudolf Steiner put into practice in 1919 for the children of the employees of the Waldorf-Astoria cigarette factory has finally come home to roost.

School lunches, 90 per cent organic (following the principles of Steiner's bio-dynamic organic movement), locally sourced, menus provided and prepared daily by older pupils. Lunch price quite reasonable; the seniors, with a nod towards encouraging enterprise, make a modest profit on the lunches, which they use to pay for their end of term trip.

Holds an open day one Friday each month and visitors (usually prospective parents) are welcome and allowed into classrooms while lessons are in progress.

Pastoral care and discipline: Small school, variety pack: some pupils come up via kindergarten, others join for logistic or other reasons further up the school. Staff are caring bunch. One child asked to leave in 'living memory'; otherwise does its best to bring out the best in each and every one, 'instilling life-long learning'. We were surprised to see one pupil eating a banana in class.

Pupils and parents: In addition to Steiner aficionados, parents are a disparate collection of mainly middle class enthusiasts who are fed up with, or whose children do not get along with, other local schools. Plus some 'out-boarders', pupils from further afield, who stay with local families, plus some exchange students from Rudolf Steiner schools elsewhere, as well as those from non-Steiner schools.

This is a hands-on school and parents are expected to contribute during the term, as well as 'helping with redecorating etc' during the work week at the end of the summer term. Relaxed dress code – no uniform; a (very) general policy states that pupils should be clean and tidy – no logos, football strips, ripped jeans, hair colour or excessive jewellery; fairly impressive standard of makeup on some of the older girls; no hajibs (by choice). Pupils are comfortable in the company of visitors, happy to chat and share their work, interests and aspirations – no obvious teenage angst or reticence here – and quite honest about how they were bullied at their last school.

Entrance: Suck it and see: visit school, take child to interview, with a second and longer visit if need be. Pupils come throughout the year, at any time, either through kindergarten or, often, age 12, when they have either discovered problems with their current school or need to have their self-confidence boosted.

Exit: Ninety-five per cent of pupils leaving at the upper end of the school go on to some sort of further or higher education: a wide range of academic and vocational courses, from marine science at the University of the Highlands and Islands to the British Racing School in Newmarket, mathematics at St Andrews, drama at Stevenson College, law at Aberdeen University or English at Napier University. Oxbridge 'not out of the frame', but doesn't figure recently. Gap years popular, furthering the Steiner philosophy wherein journeying is an important part of life.

Money matters: £20,000 available for those in financial need. Steiner aficionados are currently working with the Scottish Government and Edinburgh LA to secure state funding for these schools.

Remarks: Founded 70 years ago, the Edinburgh Rudolf Steiner offers cradle-to-grave, still slightly alternative education, with some brilliant teaching and perfect for the child who finds the trad schooling system difficult.

Egerton–Rothesay School

Durrants Lane, Berkhamsted, Hertfordshire, HP4 3UJ

- Pupils: 100 boys/40 girls • Ages: 50 aged 6–11; 180 aged 11–16 • Christian; all faiths admitted • Fees: £14,028–£19,971 pa
- Independent

Tel: 01442 865275
Email: admin.dl@eger-roth.co.uk
Website: www.eger-roth.co.uk

Headteacher: Since September 2013, Mr Colin Parker BSc DipEd PGCE (fifties). Studied at Oxford and Exeter Universities; was a senior officer in the Cunard Line and taught maths and computing at Bishop Fox's School in Taunton before joining Egerton-Rothesay in 2003. He has been head of maths and business studies, head of house and head of upper senior school here. Interested in broadcast media – he was a freelance sports journalist for the BBC in the 80s – and supports Watford FC. Married to Chisa, a translator; they have one daughter.

Academic matters: Has a speech and language centre (Rainbow Centre) in a modern, purpose-built block – well provided for in terms of staff and equipment, for children from years 1-5. High staff:pupil ratio and children are kept busy with every opportunity for learning. They follow the national curriculum but extra time is given to their language and communication. They then join what remains of the original prep school (Springboard) for years 4-6.

Springboard feels like a very small prep school with slightly old fashioned facilities and teaching methods but, here again, very high staff:pupil ratio means that everyone performs to their best. Children banded according to the amount of support they need, so some will have lessons in very small groups with several learning support assistants, while others may manage in classes of about 10 or 12. Those having extra support – almost all – come out of lessons for weekly individual support sessions, though plenty have more, including speech therapy, occupational therapy, as well as seeing the educational psychologist, who is in school several days a week.

The senior school has specialist subject teachers and an impressive range of subjects and choices. All take maths, English and science to GCSE (if necessary at entry level). In 2013, 48 per cent of overall grades were A*-C. We witnessed a geography class with only two GCSE students, so students not limited by numbers opting for a subject. Modern languages a strength, with work on the walls of a good level and pupils mentioning excellent teaching. The specialist art and technology rooms are slightly cramped, but the work comes out plentifully. Drama and PE clearly very popular – over half the children choose these subjects for GCSE. Almost all take ICT to either GCSE or the ICT short course. Several children use laptops and all are encouraged to learn to touch type.

Sixth form now up and running – plans for an interesting and varied curriculum with preparation for life after school.

Games, options, the arts: School clubs take place on Friday afternoons (too many children take the school bus to be able to have after-school clubs other than homework club, available every evening). The range of these creative learning activities is enormous and unusual – from clay pigeon shooting to puppetry, snowboarding to golf. Each term pupils sign up for the club they want to join – these are across the age groups, encouraging mixing between the years, mentoring and tolerance. These larger groups allow for sharing of ideas not only in the school council but also when creating plays, magazines, plus for sports teams.

Compulsory PE all the way through, but not necessarily competitive nor a team sport – sport is fairly limited (by the children's abilities rather than the space or will of the school). Matches with other schools and huge excitement if they ever win, but mostly great pleasure just to be out there representing the school. About a third learn a musical instrument – flute, guitar and, more unusually, percussion and jazz keyboard.

Background and atmosphere: Two private prep schools based in the centre of Berkhamsted Village were amalgamated to create Egerton Rothesay. The current site was bought in 1988 and now the entire school is based on a spacious piece of land just outside the village. The original 1988 buildings are showing their age and some of the learning support teaching and the educational psychologist are based in Portakabins. However two purpose-built, attractive, new buildings funded by the sale of one of the old school buildings from the centre of town – gym/dance hall, teaching and tutor rooms for the older children and the purpose built, cheerful, one storey Rainbow Centre for children with language and communication needs. The classrooms are mostly small since few in a class, with much individual or small group learning. Still owned privately and clearly not wealthy – one has the feeling that money is being spent on teachers and individual support rather than facilities.

Pastoral care and discipline: Pastoral care is hugely important in a school with so many special needs and contributed to by a relational youth worker who acts as a listening ear and independent adult, as well as a chaplain. The children say no bullying and they feel safe. Small classes with little room for ill discipline – children who are grateful to be here and respectful as a result.

Pupils and parents: Virtually all have additional support needs – currently 57 out of 177 have a statement and all have access to specialist provision that takes place within school hours. Large team of specialist support teachers including five speech and language therapists and an occupational therapist, as well as an educational psychologist based at the school, though other specialist teachers come in to teach individual lessons on a peripatetic basis. Parents speak of the huge relief they felt when they found a school where their child could feel normal rather than anxious. Children who were too scared to go to school being gradually resettled into the classroom. Parents, on the whole, are simply grateful to have their children happy and flourishing and take pride in the achievements and progress made at school, spoke of the gentle manner with which their children are treated. Catchment radius of 25 miles – many take the school buses.

Entrance: A school for the dyslexic, the dyspraxic, those with dyscalculia, mild or moderate learning difficulties, ADD and Asperger's plus communication needs, but not moderate ADHD or EBD. Reasonable wheelchair access – can deal with mild physical disabilities. Entrance considered on a case by case basis – the headteacher looks at paperwork on the child and writes a profile, the parents visit the school and meet with the headteacher, the pupil visits the school over a few days, and only then is a decision made on whether the school can provide the right support for that child and a place offered.

Exit: Pupils leave with a good range of GCSEs and the large majority have gone on to take A levels at sixth form colleges or other schools, with a small number to work or vocational courses. Some now staying on for new sixth form.

Remarks: Feels lively and active yet caring and safe, providing an education tailored to each child's needs and abilities. It aims to provide additional support to children who would not succeed in mainstream schools and to increase their confidence, allowing them to push their boundaries and leave with qualifications to enable them to flourish outside this accepting and unassuming school.

The Ellen Wilkinson School for Girls

Queen's Drive, London, W3 0HW

• Pupils: 1,450 girls; all day • Ages: 11–18 • Non-denom • State

Tel: 020 8752 1525
Email: office@ellenwilkinson.ealing.sch.uk
Website: www.ellenwilkinson.ealing.sch.uk

Acting head: Since September 2013, Ms Rachel Kruger.

Academic matters: In 2013, 65 per cent of students got 5+ A*-C grades at GCSE including English and maths (25 per cent of exams with A* and A grades). English, sciences, languages (including Arabic and Latin) all strong. A specialist maths and science college – a healthy proportion take maths, biology and chemistry A level (increasing numbers opting for physics with plenty of A grades). Arabic, further maths, psychology and philosophy are recent additions to the A level choices. In 2013, 49 per cent A*-B grades at A level. Several vocational options at level 2 and 3, including business studies, travel & tourism, health and social care and ICT. Runs maths and science taster sessions and masterclasses for feeder primary schools, with excited pupils trying out practical experiments in real science labs.

Some 50 per cent of students speak English as a second language – EAL support is excellent. 'Most speak English enough to be understood. The difficulties arise with subtleties of language – maths terminology, for example.' So both English and EAL lessons focus on the specifics of language, and learning foreign languages can help with sentence structure. Drama is particular helpful for some girls who get little conversation practice outside school because their close female relatives do not speak English. Good SEN support, in and out of the classroom. Extracurricular gifted and talented enrichment activities. Scores very well on value-added basis, and is probably the best-performing Ealing school that does not select on academic or religious grounds.

Games, options, the arts: PE facilities have been transformed by new sports and performing arts building. Plenty of outdoor space, with grass and all-weather hockey pitches and netball/tennis courts. Sport is popular and high on the agenda – 'Because we're an all-girls school it's cool to be sporty'. Successful basketball and netball teams, lots of clubs, eg dance, trampoline, badminton, ultimate frisbee, inter-form matches. 'We do competition here. We celebrate people taking part but we reward winners too. Students need to be resilient.'

Art studios ablaze with papier mâché, silk screen printing, life model drawings. The (smallish) canteen is decorated with exotic designs created during the year 7 arts and crafts day. Everyone does drama in years 7 and 8 and a fair number carry on to GCSE and A level. Plenty of performance opportunities: Christmas musical extravaganza, school musicals, year 12 pantomime, orchestra, rock band and choirs.

Gardening is a popular club – paths are lined with daffodils and crocuses, flowers bloom in brightly painted pots, herb gardens and vegetable gardens. Other clubs include Amnesty, debating, chess, film. Students go on geography field trips, D of E, language exchanges; they take part in mock bar trials, science, technology and maths challenges, debating competitions, classes with visiting artists, musicians and actors.

Background and atmosphere: Named for Mancunian Ellen Wilkinson, who was a Labour MP during the '20s, '30s and '40s, one of the leaders of the Jarrow March in 1936, and became the first female Minister for Education in 1945. The school sits amidst comfortable, leafy, mock-Tudor suburbia, though few pupils live in the immediate vicinity. Brick buildings, mostly one or two storeys high, flanked by grass and flower beds planted by the gardening club, with a tube line running behind a high wall round the edge of the playing fields. New sixth form centre and study rooms, library and resource area.

The only all-girls state school in Ealing. 'This makes them unselfconscious: they're happy to sit and make daisy chains in the summer, they're keen on science and sport, they're very appreciative of each other. They don't grow up quite so quickly.'

Pastoral care and discipline: Well-ordered. Girls are put in one of four divisions – similar to houses – and stay in these throughout their time at the school. 'It's like having a smaller school within a bigger school, with a family feel.' For some girls from difficult backgrounds, school is the most stable aspect of their lives, and discipline is based round 'catching them being good'. Learners of the Month are celebrated, awards for perseverance and commitment. Most are well-behaved girls, who give the school a good name. A member of the audience during a recent class trip to the National Theatre wrote to the school to praise the exemplary behaviour of its students.

Pupils and parents: Great ethnic mix, with around 20 per cent white, 20 per cent black, 20 per cent Asian and 20 per cent Arabic. The rest come from a variety of backgrounds, eg Polish, Chinese. Most of the well-heeled residents in the immediate vicinity patronise independent schools, though some Japanese girls from the local enclave join the sixth form. So the catchment area tends to spread along the local tube lines and bus routes.

Entrance: Increasingly oversubscribed, with over 600 applicants for 216 places. Priority to siblings, looked-after children and those with specific medical or social needs. Then 10 per cent from linked Ealing primary schools. Other Ealing primaries get next preference, with the remaining places filled by those living nearest. In practice, this probably means less than two miles away.

About 40 girls from other schools join the sixth form each year, with a baseline of 5+ A*-C GCSE grades for A level courses, including Bs in their A level subjects. Those who don't make the grade can take level 2 courses..

Exit: The 30 per cent or so who leave after GCSEs tend to go to mixed sixth forms or colleges, or follow vocational courses elsewhere. A few high-fliers are lured by scholarships to local independent schools.

Sixth form leavers mostly go on to university, with a trickle to Oxbridge, but some potential students find it socially alien and the majority stays in London. Imperial is particularly popular. Also SOAS, Kings, Queen Mary and Royal Holloway, London; Liverpool, Brunel, Leeds, Lancaster, Sussex and Anglia Ruskin. Biomedical sciences, business and law figure highly, with English close behind.

Remarks: An increasingly successful and popular school. Huge social and ethnic mix, egalitarian traditions. Stable staff, nice girls, few discipline problems. For many pupils it is a haven and a springboard to academic success.

Elmhurst School for Dance

249 Bristol Road, Edgbaston, B5 7UH

• Pupils: 110 girls, 80 boys; majority boards • Ages: 11–19 • Non-denom • Fees: Boarding £23,091–£24,894; Day £18,015–£18,672 pa • Independent

Tel: 01214 726655
Email: enquiries@elmhurstdance.co.uk
Website: www.elmhurstdance.co.uk

Principal: Since September 2010, Ms Jessica Ward BA dance theatre, post-graduate diploma in dance performance, QTS, NPQH (early thirties). She started dancing at the age of two and continued to study ballet and other dance throughout her school years. Degree from the Laban Centre (now Trinity Laban); joined the resident company, Transitions, where she taught as well as performed, and gained her post-grad diploma. Set up dance department at Islington Green School (whilst also head of year) – dance now a high-profile GCSE and BTEC subject in the school, which has a 40-strong boys' dance company. Then worked for EdisonLearning (sic), an educational services provider, as part of its senior management team, at Turin Grove secondary school in Enfield. Described by Ofsted as a 'highly effective leader'. Has also run workshops for trainee head teachers and created programmes for Teachers TV. Phew – all this by her early thirties.

Keen for Elmhurst students to leave with high academic achievements as well as outstanding dance skills, and comments: 'I look forward to strengthening our relationship with Birmingham Royal Ballet even further, to place Elmhurst firmly as a centre of dance excellence in Birmingham, the UK and beyond'.

Academic matters: First and foremost a ballet school but academic studies do still matter. Regularly found midway down the schools' top 500 league table, also winner of three Good Schools Guide awards (for dance and performing arts, inevitably). But still reasonable results for a school with no

academic selection and a timetable spotlighting vocational training. In 2013, 67 per cent got 5+ A*-C grades including English and maths at GCSE; 28 per cent A*/A grades at A level. Usual curriculum subjects as you'd expect, but with science only as a double award and French the only language choice. As principal explained, 'French is the language of the school – it's the language of ballet.' Most students take six core GCSEs, another two from a list of options plus RE short course. English taught as additional language to lots of overseas students. Some learning support for mild to moderate dyslexics.

Subject choices at A level very restricted due to nature of three-year sixth form, which is heavily vocational. All graduate with qualified dance teacher status (the national diploma in professional dance is degree level), plus A levels in, say, art, music, French, English literature or GCSE office skills. No science. Previous principal insisted the curriculum is 'broad and balanced'. As the prospectus points out, 'In the event of a career cut short by injury or a change of aspiration, they (non-vocational qualifications) constitute a reliable insurance policy'. Lots of non-ballet careers followed by former pupils would seem to support this.

State-of-the-art ICT room, also interactive whiteboards in bright airy classrooms, well-stocked library as well as plenty of books in departments and boarding houses. Class size 30 max, with English and maths streaming in GCSE years. Six-day week starts at 8.20am, finishing at 8pm after prep – five meal or snack breaks during that time.

Games, options, the arts: Exclusively classical ballet since move to Birmingham – tap, contemporary and jazz only taught as appendages to ballet rather than disciplines in their own right. Superb dance studios with slightly sprung floors rarely out of use. Surrounded by both external and internal windows so young dancers can get used to being on show. World-class dance teachers under the artistic directorship of Desmond Kelly OBE. Each class has own piano accompanist. Closely associated with Birmingham Royal Ballet and students perform with the company on a regular basis: 'It's the kind of experience dance students would normally only be able to dream about'. BRB director David Bintley CBE also school's artistic advisor.

Fabulous 250-seat theatre at hub of school which is hired out for summer school/conferences. Great evidence of artistic ability on show, with students' own work adorning the walls. Sports necessarily limited. No team sports like rugby or hockey but students put through Sthenos body conditioning (exercise) programme and allowed to use neighbouring school's swimming pool. Can also kick a football around school grounds. Music, not surprisingly, extremely popular – around 200 individual music lessons (both instrumental and vocal) a week as well as class music for all for the first three years, then music as GCSE, AS or A2 option.

Background and atmosphere: Relocated to Edgbaston area of Birmingham in summer 2004 from its former home in Camberley, Surrey, the culmination of five years' planning and building. 'We believe it's the first purpose-built ballet school in Europe for this age range,' says school. Originally set up in 1922 by Helen Mortimer as the Mortimer School of Dancing, re-named Elmhurst Ballet School in 1947. Uncertain future in Surrey forced total rethink – its now purpose-built, edge-of-city campus is the glorious result and 2005 winner of Birmingham Civic Society's new building prize. Vocational (dance) faculty built up from scratch. Move had total support of parents, pupils and governors. Two other bits of Camberley relocated – an old painting of the former Elmhurst and a bronze Girl with Otter standing outside a boarding block. Designed so dance studios and classrooms form ring around theatre, while medical centre and boarding houses do same around small outdoor amphitheatre.

Two nurses, two medical care assistants and two physiotherapists on the payroll, so help always on hand.

E

Treatment room always busy as the least twinge is quickly repaired. Never a dull day on site. Constantly buzzing with visitors (Friends of Elmhurst were sitting in on dance classes the day of our visit and you could hardly move without bumping into a governor or two) but students plough on regardless. The overall impression was of complete contentment – the smiles never stopped coming.

Even though the aroma emanating from the school bistro smelt like school dinners, the food looked very different. Choices ranged from salads to curries to jacket potatoes and pupils sat at tables with plates piled high. 'We have our own catering team so we have total control over diet and nutrition,' says the school. 'We take eating disorders very seriously and our menus are regularly reviewed by a leading dietician.'

Each boarding house has live-in houseparent and resident tutor who are responsible for daily health and welfare issues. The students have a comfortable common room, kitchen and communal areas within each house. Year 7 and 8 boys live next to the medical centre, year 9, 10 and 11 boys next door and year 7,8 and 9 girls in the adjacent house, all sharing double rooms, while year 11 students have spacious single study bedrooms with en-suite shower-rooms. An off-campus house five bus stops away for the first year sixth formers (with resident members of staff). Students in 6:2 and 6:3 live in rented flats and houses: 'It gives them the independence they need at that age'.

Pastoral care and discipline: Pastoral care primarily the responsibility of tutors and house-parents, also taken on by everyone – older pupils help and support younger ones. Bullying quickly stamped on through mediation rather than sanctions, both sides (including parents) brought together to sort it out. Would have zero tolerance of drugs if they became an issue, but school stresses, 'There are no drugs'. In such event, the course pursued would be 'negotiated withdrawal'. Discipline generally not an issue either – the discipline students show in the dance studios spills over into their daily lives. (Certainly true, if the state of classrooms and study bedrooms is anything to go by.) Head of pastoral care told us, 'The difference is that all our students want to be here. They know how lucky they are to have a place here and they're happy.'

Pupils and parents: Numbers up significantly since move to Midlands, especially among the boys – put down to the Billy Elliot effect. Both boys and girls are bright, cheerful and totally focused – 'They have an emotional maturity you don't normally find in youngsters of that age'. Come from far and wide – 13 nationalities represented. Full range of backgrounds dictated by sliding scale of fees support – 'The children blend together seamlessly because they have one thing in common – the concern with excellence'.

OBs and OGs (known as Old Elms) include actresses Helen Baxendale, Hayley Mills, Juliet Mills, Jenny Agutter and Joanna David, singer Sarah Brightman and ballet dancers Dame Merle Park, Diana Fox and Isobel McMeekan.

Entrance: By audition only. No formal academic test. Selection made on 'perceived potential' and 'commitment' rather than technical brilliance – 'That can be taught, but this isn't a place for recreational dancers'. Auditions held between October and March (fee non-refundable). At least 12 applications for each place, so youngsters really need to be something special. Big sixth form intake to replace those weeded out.

Exit: Around 20 per cent lost before sixth form to dance careers or other vocational schools more suited to them. Regular assessments throughout school career will have identified weaker members, who will be directed elsewhere. Ruthless, maybe, but school explains, 'We're all about producing classical ballet dancers. It's a very demanding art form and there's no point in giving youngsters false hope'. Of those who stay the course, most each year secure contracts with international ballet companies before leaving and 95 per cent are in professional employment within six months of leaving.

Money matters: One of eight specialist schools that get government support through music and dance-aided places scheme. Receives funding for 102 aided places across lower school, and sixth formers helped through national dance and drama awards. Means-tested support given to most gifted and eligible 11 year olds, with funding continuing until end of year 11 if youngsters get through artistic appraisal in year 9. When visited, had 145 students on state scholarships. Fees not extortionate compared with similar specialist schools. Few extras include text books, exam and audition costs, and any medical expenses not covered by compulsory medical insurance.

Remarks: A very special place for very special students. It was easy to forget at times that Elmhurst was, in fact, a school, as pupils looked happier than they had any right to be! Certainly not a school that would suit all, though, but then that's the whole idea. Only the best need apply – it's as simple as that.

Eltham College

Linked school: Eltham College Junior School

Grove Park Road, Mottingham, London, SE9 4QF

• Pupils: 575 boys plus 60 girls in the sixth form; all day • Ages: 11–18 • Christian Free Church • Fees: £14,046 pa • Independent

Tel: 020 8857 1455
Email: mail@eltham-college.org.uk
Website: www.eltham-college.org.uk

Headmaster: Since 2000, Mr Paul Henderson BA FRSA (mid fifties). Educated at the Leys School, Cambridge, Nottingham University and postgraduate certificate in education at Cambridge. Captained first X1 cricket at school, at university and played in first XV rugby too. Taught at Norwich School for 15 years, where he was director of studies, head of classics and, for a brief while, acting deputy head; then second master at St Albans for six years before taking over headship of Eltham College. Keen sportsman and loves singing.

Says that perhaps the most important things that he does are 'employing staff and getting children through the door'. Teaches everyone in year 7, so that he can get to know them. Comfortable with what is being done at the school and feels that it is an exciting place to be. Believes now 'a good balance of stable staff and young newcomers'.

Feels strongly that the school has an important role to play in the community and has built up good relationships with local state schools. Introduced a community scholarship, targeting over 20 primary schools that are within a mile and a half's radius. Extremely excited about the links they are forming with schools in China and elsewhere. Parents find him approachable and like the general open door policy of the school. Married with two grown-up children.

Retiring in July 2014. His successor will be Guy Sanderson, currently deputy head of Reigate Grammar. Read PPE and modern history at Oxford, began his career in the City, then trained as a teacher at St Paul's Boys' School. Has also taught at Whitgift and City of London schools. A keen open water swimmer, skier, and church elder in Sussex. Married to Laura, a headhunter; they have three children.

Academic matters: As results show (2013 A level: 73 per cent A*/A and 91 per cent A*-B), a highly academic school where pupils are stretched to the limits of their abilities. Yet, parents tell us, this academia is nurtured into them and they are taught to be well-organised and to want to succeed. The teaching is, on the whole, parents say, 90 per cent excellent – teachers are always prepared to give extra help and support if a pupil asks for it. Teacher/pupil relationships appear relaxed and respectful.

Broad curriculum and the school works hard to identify the particular strength(s) of each child and build on them. Languages very strong, many taking two or three at GCSE level. French and Mandarin compulsory in year 7, German in year 8 and Spanish can be taken up in year 9. Latin also compulsory in years 7 and 8 and all do short course in GCSE RS. The three sciences studied separately unless circumstances exceptional. 'Science is fun,' we were told by a boy. 'All theory is backed up by experiments.' Maths and science are taken as IGCSEs. Three streams in each subject, according to parents – 'top, middle and could-be-better': no-one here is 'bad' at anything. 2013 GCSEs: 73 per cent A*/As.

Full-time learning support teacher. All new pupils screened on entry for possible difficulties and, if anything arises, parents immediately involved and a programme devised. Support and encouragement is part of the school ethos and, according to parents, communication is easy and as frequent as necessary. When we asked about G and T, we were told that really every child in the school is gifted or talented and that, because of the huge range of activities in the school, everyone should be properly stretched. Also that teaching is always done to the top level, on the assumption that all are perfectly able – we're not sure that parents of middle-of-the-road, less motivated boys agree or are happy with this.

Games, options, the arts: Sport is considered an essential part of school life and everyone is encouraged to participate. With 60 acres of playing fields and an all singing, all dancing sports centre, something for everyone. In the sixth form it could be just table tennis, but before that rugby, hockey and cricket are tops and played competitively at all levels internally, against other schools and nationally. Also regular overseas tours. Plenty of other options as well; the girls have a couple of strong netball teams; foil and épée fencers recently qualified for the British Championships and even a golf team. Swimming also popular. Duke of Edinburgh Award scheme followed to gold level, though parents said the expedition costs seemed rather high. The less sporty can still find their niches and are encouraged to excel in their individual talents.

Plenty for budding thespians. Drama is on the curriculum for all in years 7-9 and can be taken at GCSE and A levels. Productions range from Shakespeare to blockbuster musicals, so something for everyone and a great theatre in which to perform. Pupils thrilled with the experience of taking shows to the Edinburgh Festival.

Music very impressive. Chances for everyone to join in – the head thinks it is good for teamwork. Lots of choirs, orchestras and jazz bands. About 65 per cent learn an instrument. A parent said she makes a point of going to every musical occasion and is in total awe of their capabilities. Apparently choral singing an exceptional strength, several pupils are members of local and national youth choirs. The trebles have international engagements and performed with Sir Simon Rattle and the Berlin Philharmonic, also at the BBC Proms. On the last night of the Proms, music and picnicking in the grounds – a popular end of year event.

Great art on display in the main entrance hall and elsewhere – lots of talent here. On average a dozen take art A level, all getting A*, A or B, mostly As. Sculpture displayed outside along route to junior school. The Gerald Moore Gallery for modern and contemporary art is a new centre for learning used by the school and wider community through exhibitions and an outreach programme.

A multitude of trips or, as they call them, journeys every year: art galleries and museums at home and abroad, adventure courses for younger pupils and advanced D of E, languages in their countries of origin, geography, biology, history, theatre, music – any excuse for adventure. This school really does believe in breadth, encouraging research and getting out and about and exploring the world. Some of the sixth form even went cycling in China and younger pupils are scheduled to take part in exchanges with schools in Beijing. Parents praised this cultural aspect and are exceptionally happy with the organisation of language exchanges.

Background and atmosphere: Originally started as a small boarding school for the sons of missionaries – still a strong Christian foundation, with the importance of caring for the community and travelling far and wide part of its ethos. Since moving, in 1912, to this elegant 18th century mansion surrounded by green fields, it has grown in size, stopped taking boarders, introduced girls into the sixth form and become thoroughly part of the 21st century, opening up great opportunities for today's youth. Yet its aims are still very much the same: to produce polite, caring, focused young people ready to go out into the world knowing what they want and where they are going.

Buildings very much the usual mixture of old and new. The central hall and the chapel, where pupils attend a service every morning, could not be more traditional, but the surrounding classrooms and buildings are bright, up to date and contain every modern technological element. Good resource centre for languages, excellent science labs, computers everywhere. Several exciting projects, particularly perhaps the 'green car challenge', voluntary at any age, where, every other year, students design and build an electric car to run at Goodwood. Wow!

Hard-working atmosphere prevails. Reasonably turned out, well-mannered pupils smiled at us wherever we went and looked thoroughly involved in their lessons, whether mechanical or creative. Excellent library, the use of which is built into the curriculum, with quiet areas for study and where prep can be done before going home. A green oasis in the middle of busy, bustling SE London that still has a bit of a boarding school feel about it. A warm welcome greets anyone walking across the threshold, and the enormous statues in the central courtyard, representing power and speed (they came from the old Tricity Building in the Aldwych and were donated by, amongst others, old boy Dr Gerald Moore), illustrate the sense of purpose that exists equally amongst pupils and staff.

Pastoral care and discipline: Comprehensive anti-bullying policy and zero drug tolerance. Parents sign contract outlining, amongst other things, acceptable behaviour in school. Fairly strict, disciplined environment. Tutors expected to know everything about the children in their care. Pastoral team meets weekly to discuss potential or ongoing problems. Popular school nurse always available for chat. Head of girls for those in sixth form. Communication lines between school and parents excellent, problems answered promptly. House system also enables peer mentoring.

Pupils and parents: Solid SE London, mainly from within five-mile radius. Good social mix with a wide range of backgrounds, all keen to ensure good education for their children. Lots of working mums – pupils can be dropped off at 8.00am if necessary. Several school buses ferrying backwards and forwards. Lots of social occasions for parents to meet and mingle.

Ex-pupils include early sons of missionaries, Eric Liddell, Olympic runner, after whom the sports hall is named, and Mervyn Peake, author of fantastic Gormenghast trilogy. More recently, Major Phil Packer, military hero, and Jim Knight, ex-minister of state for schools.

E

Entrance: Seventy-five places at 11+, of which about 50 per cent come from the junior school, the rest from about 60 local primary and private schools. Occasional spaces at 13+. Girls included in 16+ entry which increases the sixth form by about a third. School insists no specific quota. Head interviews all candidates, looking for those that 'want to have a go'. Says 'sponges' would not do well here – pupils need to have drive and really want to do well. Regards interview as most important part of entry process.

Exit: Pretty well all to top universities. Nottingham, Bristol, Warwick, Durham, Exeter and Oxford most popular over last few years.

Money matters: Up to 20 academic scholarships available at 11+ and 15 more at sixth form level for art and drama. Also several for music and sports. Bursaries available for the needy. Apparently fundraising in last few years has been very effective, so the money is there – five to six per cent currently benefiting from bursaries. The school would like this to continue and grow.

Remarks: An academic arena for those who know what they want and are willing to give anything a go. For children with enquiring minds, adventures to be had, the world to understand, chances to learn, to give to others and to grow. Those who are kind, considerate and passionate about something will flourish here, but the insecure, and those who need more than a gentle nudge, may not get as much out of it. Fantastic opportunities here for grabbing; boys and girls emerge with a well-rounded, worldly education, ready to take whatever chances life may give them.

Emanuel School

Battersea Rise, London, SW11 1HS

• Pupils: 445 boys/320 girls, all day • Ages: 10–18 • Christian Foundation • Fees: £15,735 pa • Independent

Tel: 020 8870 4171
Email: enquiries@emanuel.org.uk
Website: www.emanuel.org.uk

Headmaster: Since 2004, Mr Mark Hanley-Browne MA (late forties). Educated St George's College, Weybridge, BA in natural sciences at Oxford then PGCE at Cambridge. Previously, taught at Sevenoaks for five years, assistant master at Charterhouse for nine years and deputy head (pastoral) at Highgate for seven years. Enthusiastic and ambitious, has led the school forward and academically upward, making some 'dramatic changes' along the way. Particularly proud of three new computer suites named after old boy, Sir Tim Berners-Lee, creator of the World Wide Web.

Is 100 per cent pro the A level system and has no intention of introducing the IB. 'Specialising at 17/18 is the right timing, four subjects is enough. After all, they will have to specialise even more at university. And we do quite a lot of the extras the IB offers, more self-motivated research and involvement in charities and community support.' Believes that all children should be doers and really want to participate; 'the child who is quite good at everything but not excellent at something' would not really fit. All prospective pupils interviewed which he believes is the most important part of the entry procedure; woe betide anyone lacking a focal interest, no matter how bright he/she may be. Parental views seem to vary. Some say he is 'a bit aloof', others say 'affable', 'approachable' and 'often seen about the place'. Married to Rachael, who works for an American business school. They live locally.

Academic matters: Seems to be steadily pulling its socks back up again. In 2013, 51 per cent A*/A grades at GCSE and 39 per cent at A level, with 71 per cent A*/B. Head 'not in the least interested in league tables' and has withdrawn from them. He feels that he is giving his pupils a far broader, all-round education than exam results alone can possibly show.

Parents certainly happy with the experience their children are getting, 'The teaching quality is good', and the staff 'dedicated and supportive', particularly the heads of year, although they also spoke about some finding it difficult to keep control over classes. The head says, 'Getting good staff has been my top priority.' Pupils feel that, on the whole, teachers are 'brilliant and inspiring' and several new ones in the last few years who are 'great'. The majority of children in the first year (6) come from local primary schools and parents feel are probably disadvantaged where maths and French are concerned, but they seem to catch up quickly enough.

Certainly the facilities are all here – science, language and design technology labs plus computer rooms all spankingly up to date. We saw children working with wood and metal, experimenting with science, heads down solving mathematical problems; they all looked happy, positive and intent, with relaxed looking teachers keeping them absorbed. Classrooms are well equipped with the latest technological aids.

An active, imaginative learning support department has its own room with computers and other important aids, alongside a team of specialists who also have their own area of teaching, so are also fully involved in school life. Open door policy when possible but chaplain always around to act as counsellor as well. Pupils are assessed and continuously monitored with constant parental consultation. As far as practical, tries to keep one-to-one sessions out of lesson time – head doesn't really like children being withdrawn from classes. Also runs a homework club after school for those who need help. Between 12 and 15 per cent have mild learning difficulties.

Games, options, the arts: Fantastic sport, music, art and drama – this is where the school really wins hands down. Rugby, netball, rowing and cricket their major sports – the teams compete at all levels both at home and abroad with many successes.

On-site games fields, access via a private gate to the facilities on Wandsworth Common plus 14 further acres of sports ground at Blagdons, near Raynes Park; own fantastic sports hall which includes a climbing wall, exercise rooms, ergometers, as well as a PE classroom; large swimming pool which pupils say is 'great', but changing facilities 'pretty scruffy' – we believe this is one of the head's next update plans. Huge boathouse at Barnes housing 45 boats – no wonder so many Emanuel pupils win sporting awards at all levels, from local to international, and some girls and boys even go on to represent the country in their chosen field. All do pretty well in (what they deem) minor sports as well – athletics, swimming, fives, rounders, dance and tennis.

Music and drama very strong. Several orchestras, bands and choirs – something for everyone. Pupils we talked to particularly keen on number and variety of bands. Children sing in the National Youth Choir and play in the National Youth Orchestra. Plenty of chances to learn individual instruments – we were told 250 music lessons given weekly. Concerts and recitations regular events, have even put on Bach's St John's Passion.

Very excited, when we were there, about current production of Oliver! – plenty of parts for everyone. Pupils said drama department 'very brave', presumably for putting on ambitious productions – certainly they have the facilities. We would probably say that to put on Tom Stoppard's Arcadia was pretty brave, but they did, and it was a great success. Another of the head's projects was to widen the theatre – new theatre opened in May 2013.

Art studios amazing – recent project on 'passions and obsessions' produced fascinating results. Enthusiastic teacher with equally eager pupils. Head is a great art fan and views the school as a showcase – certainly everywhere we went pictures hung on walls, and apparently lots more also stacked in storage rooms: some really wild and wonderful. Says he commissions pictures from students every year. Lots of trips, home and abroad, to expand their horizons – singing in Venice a recent highlight.

Background and atmosphere: Originally richly endowed by the Dacre legacy in 1594, there's a courtyard in the middle of the main building dedicated to three Queen Elizabeths. The first on the throne at their foundation; the second who planted the central tree, Queen Elizabeth, later the Queen Mother, in 1951; the third, her daughter who made a royal visit in 1994. Surrounded by glass, this is typical of the traditional/modern mix in this school. Old buildings house modern facilities and new buildings grow up out of old ground. The library, which could be said to be the hub of the school, is a good illustration. With silent areas behind glass and a circular staircase leading up to an archive room full of school history, it is a great place for pupils to gather for meetings, research or quiet study. A good learning resource centre. Librarian relaxed and welcoming, pupils often stay to do homework there; which would explain why one parent said her daughter never seems to bring much home. Its renovation one of the head's decided successes.

Main building originally a Crimean war orphanage, taken over by Emanuel in 1883. Although, internally, it has been through many changes, the chapel, on the first floor, remains and assemblies held there daily. This is still a Christian school bearing Christian values and commitment to the community outside as well as within. Pupils are polite, open and, according to those we talked to, have good relationships with their teachers. Also spoke positively about their headmaster. Year 9s talked about team building, peer mentoring and the way older years interact well with the younger ones. School council seems to help this, as does the house system. They say school seems to recognize what each child is good at, really promote it and thus create confidence. Out of the mouths of babes. Must be good. Whole place feels happy, friendly and welcoming. Parents say school good at making sure course work is done on time otherwise 'big trouble'.

Split of school day seems to work well with two classes before a short break, then two more before half an hour's assembly and two more before lunch at 1.15. Excellent food, say pupils, good choice, but queuing system not good if you are late. Lovely to have tables outside in summer. Sixth form thrilled with their new common room and café (only open at certain times and not for lunch), very grown-up. Whole sixth form area with all its own facilities is brill. Parents say very friendly and lots of activities and involvement for them as well.

Pastoral care and discipline: Tutor system combined with house system and easy access to head of year ensures that any problems that arise should be spotted and dealt with quickly. We asked pupils where they would go if they needed to talk to someone sympathetic and they agreed that it would probably be the head of year first and then the chaplain. Chaplain also has sixth form team to help him when necessary. Christian ethos is important and responsibility for others would seem to be endemic. Big emphasis on being part of community and charitability. Natural interaction and mutual respect between teachers, pupils and year groups does appear to be working.

All pupils carry conduct cards recording homework timetables, commendations and misconduct records – five commendations and you get a chocolate, but get a misconduct signature and you have to start again. Beware of getting five misconduct records, Saturday morning detention looms.

Separate, comprehensive policies on bullying addressed to parents, teachers and pupils. This is something almost bound to occur, in some form or other, in a school full of alpha boys and girls. The majority of parents we talked to were not worried

and felt that school handled problems well. However, some think there should be zero tolerance and, at the moment, don't feel this is happening. Most praise the pastoral care whole heartedly but a few doubts remain over the handling of difficult or sensitive cases.

Pupils and parents: Mainly local, 85 per cent from within three mile radius. Typical south London mix. Many working to make sure their children get a good education.

Ex-pupils include Michael Aspel, Andi Peters, Michel Roux, Issey Cannon (recent member of under 21 England women's cricket team) and Peter Hain.

Entrance: Competitive at 10+, 11+, 13+ and 16+. Must get 55 per cent in entrance test and show special aptitude somewhere. Good command of English, both written and spoken, essential. Priority for siblings as long as performance report from previous school OK. Popularity has surged, recently 500 applicants for 85 places at 11+ and 700 overall. Interview mandatory. Must have special interest but need not be academic. They are looking beyond pure academia.

Exit: Around 20 per cent move on after GCSEs, if they didn't make the grade or would rather go elsewhere, but most stay for A levels. One or two a year to Oxbridge (two in 2013), majority to Russell Group and other good universities – Exeter, Leeds, Manchester, Newcastle and Bristol most popular recent choices.

Money matters: Lots of bursaries, not only academic but also music, sport, art and drama. Varying degrees of financial support. Strong bursary fund, constantly growing aiming for self-perpetuation. Big fund-raising drive with ex-parents. Governor of the school, James Wates, created special fund; six children benefit from his bursaries at the moment.

Remarks: An amazing campus to find in an urban area close to Clapham Junction. For parents who can scrape the fees together, in a borough sadly lacking in good secondary schools, it is ideal. For sporty, arty, musical children, the opportunities to expand their talents and their horizons are all here.

Epsom College

College Road, Epsom, Surrey, KT17 4JQ

• Pupils: 465 boys and 235 girls with 240 weekly/full boarding boys and 135 weekly/full boarding girls. • Ages: 13–18 • C of E
• Fees: Day £21,255; Boarding £28,383–£31,098 pa • Independent

Tel: 01372 821234
Email: admissions@epsomcollege.org.uk
Website: www.epsomcollege.org.uk

Headmaster: Since September 2012, Mr Jay Piggot, BA MA PGCE. Early fifties. Previously headmaster at alma mater Campbell College, Belfast between 2006 and 2012, and, before that, put in 17 years at Eton (clearly a hard place to leave) starting as assistant master in 1989 and becoming house master 10 years later.

Not bad going given that it was only his second teaching job: his first, immediately after completing his MA in English Renaissance literature at Liverpool, was at Millfield, where he taught A level/Oxbridge English.

Career success undoubtedly assisted by personality and appearance – quietly dashing, though doesn't overdo the leading man business. Gimlet vision, too – noticed and swiftly dealt with errant piece of rubbish – a very small plastic wrapper, only one in otherwise immaculate grounds.

Lordy, lordy, what a popular man he is. Pupils – 'a joy,' he says – say he makes an effort to know names, comes to matches and makes with the social chit chat. Biggest vote winner, however, are the birthday cards – otherwise sophisticated international pupil clearly thrilled with his, particularly handwritten signature – cynic had checked authenticity with damp finger just to be sure. Parents also like what they see. Innovations all welcomed. 'very proactive behind the scenes and has pushed through some sensible changes,' says one. Definitely a step up from predecessor. 'School ran well but didn't have the personality.'

College was already known to him before the headhunters came a-callling, and found vision, ethos and commitment very much to his taste. Younger son, a keen golfer, moved with him (older brother is going great guns at Eton).

'Would love' to teach again and might when has got through current to-do list, which is lengthy. Getting shorter by the minute, though. 'Some heads would take a while to work out what they were going to do,' says teacher. 'He's made lots of changes already.' Popular changes include axing of seasonal timetables, originally to make most of winter light, but cause of mega all-round confusion to all.

New for 2013 was high profile reintroduction of matrons into the houses, an Eton-inspired development that's brought a caring, maternal touch (thus far, all women) to details such as tracking down missing shirts and sewing as well as control of rowdy element.

Of even greater significance has been academic shakeup, still on-going, starting with observation of every member of staff since he arrived, followed with ISI-style feedback. 'A privilege,' he says. (We're sure they feel the same). Many stay for years. No wonder, with perks headed (for many, though not all) by housing either on-site or within a few minutes' walk. 'My wife told me we're not going to move,' said one. Given Epsom property prices, you can't blame her.

In addition to the introduction of heads of year, designed to add missing link identified in recent inspection, he's also not going to stand in path of old-timers who could be moving on to greater things elsewhere, while rejigging weak spots including A level languages and biology and GCSE English literature. Dynamic incomers, including former Uppingham head of modern foreign languages – similar developments in science – are being brought in together with fledgling new generation of bright young things adding oomph to lessons (occasional dullness one of few inferred criticisms in last inspection report).

Still more shaking up to come, however, essential given school's previous sleepiness and 'red-hot' competition – Wellington, Cranleigh and Charterhouse as well as St John's Leatherhead and Reed's School.

Bumping up interior life of school is part of the process, with Eton's dawn to dusk (and beyond) intellect-boosting programme the inspiration for mind-expanding programme – expect more pupil-organised drama, musical and debating activities (medical, history and politics societies are already on the go) sparking impassioned discussions that ramp up the intellectual temperature from tepid to mercury-busting.

Mark of success? Would like popularity of places to increase to the point where competition for boarding places as strong as for day hopefuls.

Academic matters: One of formerly mid-ranking schools to have substantially upped game in recent years. Fun lessons got pupils on the go, literally so, with movement minus the music, A level students standing up for miracles (theology) and marginal cost (economics) – everything, in fact, but their rights.

Parents, while agreeing with head that some teachers are 'past their best', think generally offset by vast majority who are 'engaging, personable and, most importantly, able to motivate. They appear to love their subjects and to enjoy teaching and the company of the children – none of these are a given in my experience.' Megawatt enthusiasm often a game-changer,

especially at sixth form level. Sciences score particularly high conversion rates. 'Was my dream to be a translator – now it's chemistry,' said pupil.

Ability to devote time to all (an impressive 55 hours contact time a week) means that 'there are no lost causes,' says head. Plentiful tracking and feedback means pupils know where they are and how they can improve, feedback seamlessly integrated in lessons. 'We put down our comments when we've had a test and it gives teachers a good idea of where we are,' said sixth former.

Though class sizes aren't teeny tiny – average 20 for GCSE (maximum 23) and between 10 and 12 at A level (15 max), with pupil to full time teacher ratio of 8.4, school is consistently good when it comes to added value, setting in maths, banding in languages and sciences (where small group of less able students might do GCSE dual sciences rather than IGCSE triple). No-one takes 'silly' numbers of GCSEs, says senior teacher – aim is to ensure good grades in manageable quantities. Currently, results generally very good given relatively mixed intake, with around 70 per cent A*/A grades at GCSE; 79 per cent of A level entries graded A*/B and nearly 56 per cent A*/A in 2013.

Good, largely traditional subject range, almost ology-free – 'nothing against psychology but it just isn't us,' says teacher – though language options now include GCSE Mandarin, originally for overseas students but now open to all.

Hugely dynamic head of DT is also bumping up recruitment, particularly amongst girls, by ensuring that environment, full of technological marvels – though it's pupils' superb mortice and tenon joints and chamfering skills that help pull in the A* grades – is also tidy ('was grubby and fragmented') with plenty of wood-turning (apparently the secret of cross-gender appeal).

Big feature is Extended Project Qualification (EPQ), a mini-dissertation that, at best, combines originality and staying power (recent topics include carcinogens in food and madness in Henry Vlll's court – separately). Worth the effort. One pupil, down an A level grade and out of university course, called department head and used hers to talk her way back in again.

No doubt that attracts the very able – one pupil, exile from leading girls' school, delighted to be somewhere that praised good work rather than training spotlight on pupils only when failed to deliver top grades – though one parent queried its suitability for the truly brilliant. 'Might be a bit too comfortable,' she thought. 'It's a broad church and some kids are too bright [and] shouldn't be there.'

Extra scaffolding where needed, with clinics all the way through the school in all key subjects and teachers not just present (many live in) but in many cases 'always available.' That said, school isn't geared up to cope with anyone with more than mild learning difficulties. Of the 100 or so pupils with SEN, none is currently statemented, SpLD the overwhelmingly dominant need, though have coped with (mild) ADHD as well.

Plenty of emails home and 'progress reports every three weeks,' ensure that everyone knows what's going on, while lengthy school day (finishing 6.00pm) incorporates sufficient free periods for the organised to sock it to the homework.

And though definitely not a hothouse, with initially gentle place startling to alumni of non-stop pushy preps, school gets praise for stress-appropriate levels of pushing tailored to each child. 'They know which way to push,' says mum of recent leaver. 'The teacher told my child that she "might get an A in biology GCSE, but I don't think so".' Nettled, daughter was spurred on to do just that.

Games, options, the arts: Sport success plentiful – boys' and girls' rugby sevens regular regional winners, lots of post-school success, too (five OBs play for Harlequins), ditto hockey (mixed seniors won Surrey U18 competition), as do minors with 2012 Captain of Golf driving his way to Stanford Golf Scholarship (first European for over 10 years, says school) and shooting.

Facilities generous – including swimming pool – and, in case of one of two sports halls, close to giant-size (even better when new sports pavilion up and running), two cracking sports halls, one giant sized, six squash courts, a swimming pool and a fencing salle, No partridge in pear tree (but would undoubtedly be doing a few press ups if there were).

Outside, timetable pushes variety – first years will have both outdoor and inside sports in an afternoon and, further up the school, non-standard sports can be done off site – riding, for example, and, until school got its own, wall-climbing.

Range ensures that 'you're not penalised if you're not sporty,' thinks a mother, with matches, for all. 'Sport is very important, whether you're A team or D/E/F team material,' agrees another parent.

Sports captains, rated by the rank and file – 'positions are well earned,' thought one – have a real say in team structure. 'You can discuss team composition with the coach and that's good,' thought pupils.

Termly activity sheet encourages pupils to experiences shock of the new. One boy, initially dreading jive dance, discovered instead that was 'that sort of person' – and loved it.

Plenty head for D of E, room for all (can add more staff if demand is high). CCF feather in school cap – one of oldest and biggest in country, teeming with facilities, (we liked esteem-heavy 'confidence' rather than assault course). Wears success lightly – numerous impressive sports cups casually behind bars with the guns).

Arts also attacked with relish. Music felt to be 'on the ascendant,' thought teacher, with lots of instrumental lessons – drums, singing, electric guitar and piano the biggest sellers, some reaching diploma level; challenging, performance opportunities ranging from low stress impromptu recitals to high quality productions including The Cunning Little Vixen and excellent chapel choir, masses lining up to audition – a macho-free area, reckoned year 4 and 5 pupils. Those not making the grade can 'let voices develop' in non-selective Glee Club instead.

Visual arts, recently upgraded, feature confident, instantly recognisable year 9 pictures of Kew Gardens – one of many trips. Everybody gets out a lot, DT excursions to real factories (Brompton bikes to Henry vacuum cleaners) so popular that school staff sign their Sundays away, too, school chef enjoying outing to Cadbury's as much as pupils.

Background and atmosphere: Altogether a civilised place to be, starting with laid-back parking regime, permitted along one side of the one way road that winds round the lush green campus (new upper sixth drivers are vetted by the head), imposing chapel at its heart.

Though patron is HM the Queen, not a high-society institution. Started life as the Royal Medical Benevolent College, a charitable Good Thing, helping the relics of deceased impoverished medics.

Strongly Victorian in spirit and execution – most buildings completed between 1850s and 1920s. School wasn't welcomed by all, overt charitable status 'distasteful' to recipients, reckoned contemporary letter to Lancet.

Took boys for the first 120 years or so (sisters presumably expected to marry their way to economic success); girls added 1996 largely as emergency recession-busting tactic (local area had suffered heavily and pupil numbers had plummeted).

Now, of course, school wouldn't be without them and they're on almost equal terms in the sixth form (77 to 92), though minority partners in other years. Desired ratio is 60:40 is, thinks head, about right, ensuring girls have the same options as boys, particularly when it comes to games. 'All get the chance to contribute,' he adds, firmly. No complaints from girls themselves, or parents, so seems to be working.

Though it's all 19th and early 20th century authenticity from the front with 'real wow factor,' thought parent, sold on first visit, tasteful modern extensions stretch back a considerable distance to the rear (current bursar, a woman, was a former architect and it shows).

Behind public face is 'pupil world', the second sweep of buildings where most of the teaching takes place. Modern additions – humanities building particularly palatable – don't jar (though some areas, like maths and theology blocks could be nicer, and almost certainly will be when funds permit).

Boarding houses, dotted round the site, vary, some already done up to the nines – matching up to head's aspirations to equal best in Britain – to others channelling best of 1950s (slightly yellowing paintwork, campsite-style loos, basins and shower) though even here, being overtaking by creeping snazzy-ness (decking and glass) that will dominate when facelift is complete.

When it comes to décor, different departments exhibit endearing idiosyncrasies – from pot plants in chemistry lab (and sign announcing 'nudisme interdite au delà de cette limite') to blue-painted English rooms (also notable for friendly clutter of framed posters and attractive display boards already filling up nicely in second week of term) while modern languages is all-purple (even down to lampshades). Black wall in one of physics labs, however, is for sensitive experiments and 'not because we're pandering to goths,' explains larger than life department head.

Technology warmly embraced with wi-fi throughout (and 'extreme' internet safety settings triggered by word 'Middlesex') and the Hub, new high tech room where lessons can be recorded for posterity.

Tradition equally enjoyed but not pointlessly so – most of original medical artefacts and stuffed animals that once dominated science rooms have gone. 'Antiques dealer took the rest,' says teacher, cheerfully.

Pastoral care and discipline: Seniors a strong force (and will be even more so once head succeeds in replacing current sixth form block with something altogether spiffier). Take turns to lead assemblies that are so far removed from commonplace fare that we had to double check that searingly articulate reflections on 9/11 were being delivered by sixth form girls. It appears effortless. No wonder – it's been in rehearsals since June, points out the friendly chaplain.

Older pupils keen to stress that 'hierarchical system associated with traditional English boarding school, pitting year group against year group' is 'a terrible idea' and will pitch in to take sides if older boys show signs of picking on younger ones. 'It's part of our role and it works.'

Little in the way of serious misbehaviour, however, with just two pupils 'withdrawn by parents' (expulsion by face-saving euphemism) in senior teacher's 15 years. Drugs tissues in both cases, though it's very rarely the end, behind the scenes second chances often possible. Day to day, class silliness and late homework the main issues, reckoned pupils, with escalating sanctions – lines, notification of tutors, warnings, departmental then school detentions – rattled off by all.

Lots of rewards, too – from pizza or chocolate for work-related merits and distinctions to privileges of seniority – sixth form day girls cited joy of leaving sports kit on shelves in study rooms instead of trekking, when younger, to go to separate storage area.

Sensible trouble-preventing measures include half-termly dorm swaps and plenty of weekend activities for full boarders, from trips to Thorpe Park to house evenings and bowling. ' Never lonely because lots going on,' said sixth former.

And though house system (separate for day and boarding pupils) engenders ferocious sense of competition (choir contest in particular), it isn't carried over into lessons, 'which stops it becoming tribal,' reckoned parent.

Buddy system helps combat homesickness (most reckoned that worst was over within first week), one house even creating own surrogate family, one year group per generation and organising popular old fashioned sports day as an ice-breaker. Here, too, matrons, add much appreciated extra tea and sympathy layer (housemistresses – always academic staff – can 'sometimes be more of figure of authority,' thought sixth formers.')

Pupils and parents: Predominantly local intake with vast majority of pupils including 95 per cent of UK boarders, living within 10 to 15 miles. School keen to expand the range but, meantimes, results in happy fusion of streetwise Londoner with leafy Surrey-ite, reckoned teacher – cool without the ennui.

Masses of staff have own children here (has peaked at 40 or so). One parent we spoke to who'd opted for local alternative thought numbers were excessive – though appeared to be a lone voice.

Working mums – far more these days – were something of a feature to the point where socialising tends to feature nights out to ensure 'you don't feel out of the loop,' thought career-driven mother.

Cosmopolitan feel added by international component (largeish at 15 per cent) drawn from Hong Kong, Malaysia, Russia and Korea, though many more from western Europe. For the 10 per cent who are non-native English speakers there is a structured EAL programme in place, but they're fully integrated into the curriculum says the school, 'right from day one'.

Malaysian numbers unlikely to be affected by opening of sister school in Kuala Lumpur in September 2014 – first foray into pastures new, as 'there will always be pupils who want a UK education,' reckons school.

Entrance: School is after all-rounders with several strings to their bow and 'fair share of the bright pupils'.

Once a second choice regular, increasingly a bill-topper, recruiting from over 40 preps and state schools, likely to increase as it extends reach beyond its traditional feeders (Danes Hill and Downsend, Shrewsbury House, Aberdour and Feltonfleet feature prominently though no official feeders). Full-on charm offensive attracting south west London schools.

Main intake (around 130 candidates) in year 9, with January pre-test in year 6 (VR – scores of around 118-120 the norm – NVR, English and numerical skill plus interview), same again (minus NVR) for non-prep candidates in January of year 8. Lots of scholarships on offer, over 230 currently, 43 (sport, art, drama, music and all-rounder) at 13+, value between £500 and £1500 pa.

Boys' day slots normally full by the end of year 6, boarding fills up last, best hope for last-minute applicants though gap closing. Once 'day pupils were brighter and more studious' than boarding pupils, thought one insider. No longer the case.

If no joy at 13+, small number of places at 14+ (three to five only, English, maths and NVR tests). Second biggest influx is post GCSE with 45 to 50 joining the sixth form, following VR, NVR and numerical skills tests plus interview. Push to up state school numbers (currently around 20 per cent of the total) as a way of 'supplementing the ratios'. Some haggling after AS results with handful of pupils whose D and E grades give cause for concern. Repeating year not an option, dropping a subject can be the solution.

Exit: No shortage of ambition, most achieving first choice unis, with six to Oxbridge in 2013 (though 'should be more,' reckons head); Bristol, Nottingham, Leeds and Exeter also popular. Economics and finance followed by business, geography and sociology popular though, despite high quality art as A level option – and photography just added – it's currently not being pursued as a degree option.

Money matters: Annual bursary spend close to £750,000 on up to 100 per cent of fees. Possible additional financial support for families with medical connections through the Royal Medical Foundation, based at the school, though since 2000 a separate legal entity.

Remarks: Mark of success, reckons head, will be when boarding – effectively last chance to buy before London – matches pressure on day places. With demographics and parent power going his way, could be done. 'A brilliant school for my son,' said

parent. Another commented that school had got everything there was to get out of her son. 'You really can't ask much more than that'.

Ermysted's Grammar School

Gargrave Road, Skipton, BD23 1PL

• Pupils: 810 boys • Ages: 11–18 • State

Tel: 01756 792186
Email: admin@ermysteds.n-yorks.sch.uk
Website: www.ermysteds.n-yorks.sch.uk

Head Teacher: Since 2008, Mr Graham Hamilton BA PGCE (early fifties), educated at Netherhall Comprehensive in Cumbria, Ripon and York St John University (English and geography). Taught in state schools in the Lake District for 18 years, attaining senior management level, then the latter at a far more challenging comprehensive in Bradford, which 'turned me into a better manager and leader', followed by deputy headship here for three years. Introduced the school council and is keen to incorporate its suggestions; wants to turn out 'well rounded, active citizens and autonomous learners with a lifetime's love of learning' and to raise the boys' aspirations, eg boost their confidence at Oxbridge interviews.

A hands-on head, highly regarded and well liked by parents ('very can-do – sees opportunities rather than obstacles and will go out of his way to be helpful') – supervises an IT room during the lunch break and covers lessons, firm but not a shouter, described by boys as 'a personal head; he's always around the school – he knows everyone's names, takes an interest in everyone's work and appreciates our achievements'. Good sense of humour, interested in honest self-evaluation, independent minded (won't make modern languages compulsory for the sake of enhancing their English Bac league table position at the expense of classical languages and civilisation), thoughtful and unassuming, inspires confidence that he will do his best for the school in the face of worrying funding cuts – he feels very responsible for protecting its 500 years of tradition.

Enjoys walking, reading, theatre and cooking – has introduced food tech at KS3 because he wants to ensure boys have 'survival skills' and can cope when away from home. Wife, Mary, works for a charity, two teenage daughters, one at Oxford University, the other at Skipton Girls' High School.

Academic matters: A level: high achievers – 2013: 72 per cent A*-B with 46 per cent A*/A; most do four along with general studies; AQA Bac (very good EPQ results); last Ofsted rated teaching outstanding. Non standard subjects: Latin, classical civilisation, economics (the room presided over by three plaster gnomes sitting on the window sill – the Gnomes of Zurich?), psychology, critical thinking. Also government and politics, drama and theatre studies, PE and French, open to the Girls' High; will run subjects for just one or two students. Strong maths, chemistry, biology, economics, English language and literature, German, history. The very bright have been taking first year Open University courses as well (YASS modules) through science specialism funding – alas, no longer available. Average class size: 18-20. A parent we spoke to felt some of the teaching could be 'more dynamic and contemporary', but others were very happy – this is an area the school is keen to improve on.

Deputy head/head of sixth on top of his game: writes brilliant guides – comprehensive and entertaining, to boot – on success at sixth form, choosing universities, writing personal statements and Oxbridge interviews; the latter consists of detailed accounts of past boys' experiences, plus feedback letters about unsuccessful applicants from admissions tutors, and kept me absorbed on my train journey home from Skipton to Sheffield – and very nearly to Doncaster! All students have a mock interview with a professional. Success at national competitions, eg science Olympiads, Maths Team Challenge, Great Shakespeare Debate.

GCSE also strong – 2013: 61 per cent A*-A; sciences (all do three separate ones – became science specialist college 2009), PE and RS stand out. Sets can be up to 32 but bottom ones 10-12. High KS3 performance; can take GCSE in astronomy. Lots of science enrichment: links with Leeds University, Salters' Festival, summer camps. Very good value added stats. Plenty of IT – choice of exams – but no wireless networking yet; trialling use of netbooks in English department. Two modern language teachers considered the best in the county by the LA advisor, French and German nationals as assistants.

Focused, well behaved boys in the library and any classes we observed. The ones we spoke to appreciative of teachers: 'Even the busiest teachers can always find time for us', 'They can't do enough for you', 'They tailor the teaching to the individual, not the whole class', 'In the sixth form they let you learn in your own way...they are almost like your friends'.

SENCo able to cover a wide range of special needs but no specialist support available, unless a boy is statemented – differentiation within classroom strategy. Whole school approach to dyslexia – teachers use dyslexia friendly techniques with everyone; will test if requested, but also piloting initial screening of all year 12s with in house test. English department runs extra sessions of literacy support at KS3.

Games, options, the arts: 1992 sports hall with cricket nets and climbing wall plus mini fitness suite, but limited land, so uses town leisure centre to supplement playing fields and for swimming. New pavilion with sixth form common room in prospect. The usual sports plus cross country (very strong at county level and current national fell running champs), climbing, orienteering, basketball, badminton, golf, archery. Traditionally a rugger school, though less emphasis on it now; very keen on cricket, played in all weathers (county level success); became Yorkshire hockey champion without its being a school sport – just went in for the competition and won it; sports leader and rugby refereeing qualifications; can do community action instead of games.

Large, well resourced music room; 'brilliant' big band, managed by 'unbelievably dedicated' teacher – European tour; rock groups, barber shop, plus the usual. Music and drama done with girls from the High (as well as year 10 German exchange) – often musicals, also Shakespeare Schools Festival; several study drama, music and music technology at university and drama schools.

Though art and design exam results are undistinguished, the art we saw was very accomplished and interesting, suggesting the boys are given plenty of freedom to be original; a large, light art room, with a number of connected small rooms used for displays. Modern technology building – manufacturing, resistant materials, electronics, graphics, and now food tech in a new room. Lively school magazine with long, humorous articles.

Work experience in France and Germany, trips to Peru, Iceland and plenty of opportunities for the sixth to boost their personal statements with community work, mentoring junior pupils, helping with sports day at a primary, charity fundraising, teaching at their partner school in Sri Lanka (also cricket and dance tour there), World Challenge.

Background and atmosphere: Preserves a sense of its past as well as being as up to date as funds permit. Voluntary aided – founded 1492 (or possibly 1468) by Pater Toller, Dean of Craven, moved 1875 to present site. 1910 sandstone extension with old wrought iron railings; school bell from original school on display; old boardroom with wooden bookcases housing antiquarian books and portraits of old headmasters. More recent additions all designed sympathetically by the same architect, creating a harmonious effect.

Modern CDT facilities, science labs and classrooms and multi purpose new refectory with extra-large interactive whiteboard displaying 24 hour news. Good choice of food (healthy school status) which sixth can use as a common room in the afternoons – staff on hand to serve coffee and yummy looking flapjacks. Multi-purpose hall for assemblies and drama performances inter alia, plus small organ; well resourced library with rather fetching maroon and orange decor and separate sixth form learning resource area; amazingly clean and tidy loos (which we don't usually get shown with such pride!). Only has one covered play area. Most classrooms are large and light.

Informal motto is 'aiming for excellence', and 'It's OK to work hard – the school runs on the work ethic,' a boy told us. The normal amount of pressure to achieve you would expect in a grammar school, but a spirit of 'friendly competition' and 'You set your own targets'. Not solely focused on academic success and a feeling that 'you are free to be who you are', 'It's a personal school', 'Everyone dumps their bag anywhere and feels it's safe', 'There's a strong community sense'. Keen to get feedback, from boys (on teaching and learning, PSHCE, bullying) and parents before changes are introduced. Sixth formers can go into town at lunchtime and study at home if they have a free half day.

Pastoral care and discipline: 'The boys' welfare is central,' said a parent. Clear explanation of behaviour expectations and sanctions in boys' planners. Good anti-bullying policy – bullying not seen as an issue by the boys we met: 'It's never mean or malicious', 'The school is very good at managing it – they crack down on it'. Twelve year 10s trained to support lower school boys. Teachers seen as very approachable: 'Your form teacher is always there if you've got a problem', 'There's always someone you can talk to'.

Pupils and parents: Boys come from Skipton and a wide area beyond, from over 50 primary schools. Mostly middle and working class with a small proportion of ethnic minority. The boys we met were delightful – very thoughtful, sensible and unassuming, ranging from sensitive, reformed man (the head boy elect) to a school team member Dr Arnold would have approved of. Active PTA. Maths and science events for parents plus access to evening GCSE astronomy class. Old Boys include Iain Macleod (politician) and Simon Beaufoy (scriptwriter of The Full Monty).

Entrance: 11+: VR and non VR tests; takes well above average ability, but quite a broad range for a grammar, extending to the top 30 per cent; much private tutoring by parents. Over subscribed – uses siblings rule, distance from school; can try exam again for years 8-10 if spaces.

Sixth: up to 15 per cent (20-22) from other secondaries. Need six A*-Cs at GCSE, with B in would be A level subjects (A for maths), but flexible; also interview with head of sixth and tour of school plus meetings with other teachers (all part of selection process) – hugely oversubscribed.

Exit: The great majority stay on for the sixth – about 10 per cent leave after GCSE for, eg, apprenticeships, employment, RAF or FE colleges, to do vocational courses or different A levels.

Nearly all sixth formers to university; seven to Oxbridge in 2013, other popular destinations Durham, Sheffield, Lancaster, Exeter, Bath, Birmingham and Newcastle.

Remarks: Skipton can be described as a sleepy market town, but this school produces very able boys capable of getting to the top, who may need a bit of pushing to do so. It is getting a great deal right in a wide sense, if the boys we met are typical.

Eton College

Eton, Windsor, SL4 6DW

- Pupils: 1,300 boys (all boarding) • Ages: 13–18 • C of E
- Fees: £33,270 pa • Independent

Tel: 01753 671249
Email: admissions@etoncollege.org.uk
Website: www.etoncollege.com

Head Master: Since 2002, Mr Anthony (Tony) Little MA PGCE (late fifties). Educated at Eton, read English at Corpus Christi, Cambridge (where he was a choral exhibitioner), and did his PGCE at Homerton. An ultra-experienced head – after teaching English at Tonbridge and Brentwood, he was head of Chigwell for seven years and then head at Oakham for six. Warm, approachable and down-to-earth, he has proved to be an excellent and innovative head man (as pupils call Eton heads). He reckons Eton boys are 'the kind of people who roll up their sleeves and get things done' – and he's exactly that type himself. Boys can turn up to see him without an appointment between 8 and 8.30am any weekday morning, and despite his hectic schedule he manages to teach philosophy and ethics to the lower sixth. 'It's therapy for me,' he claims. Also makes a point of meeting every upper sixth (B block) boy for a one-to-one chat in the summer term they leave. It takes 12 days, and, as he says, 'I get a snapshot of a generation'. Enjoys his job hugely – 'There are days you could do without, but on the whole it's good fun'. When it comes to his own future he has 'no long-term plan', but jokes that 'at some point I will fall off my perch'.

Takes particular pride in Eton's focus on pedagogy and the 'outward-facing' way it has widened access to boys from all backgrounds. 'We do not want to be a finishing school for the titled and rich,' he declares. He started a partnership between Eton and six local state schools, and from September 2013 will oversee a new initiative enabling up to three boys from disadvantaged Liverpool backgrounds to spend two years at Eton. School is one of eight independent schools involved in the launch of the London Academy of Excellence in Newham, the first sixth form college to be built under Michael Gove's free schools programme. Wife Jenny is very involved in school activities and they have a grown-up daughter who works in advertising. Hobbies include music, theatre and, in his words, 'Norfolk'.

Academic matters: First class all round. Tutor for admissions told us that it's seen as 'cool' to be academically successful at Eton – but they're not giving out latest results. Majority of boys take A levels, but Pre-U offered in a growing number of subjects too. Maths is most popular subject at A level, followed by history, RS, physics and economics. School doesn't have plans to offer IB – 'The advantage of the IB is breadth,' a master told us, 'but we feel that the boys get that breadth anyway through the options on offer.' As well as their main subjects, sixth formers choose two additional options – a wealth of choice, from philosophy to Portuguese.

At GCSE, most boys take 11 subjects, including at least two of the three sciences. IGSCEs taken in sciences, languages, maths, history, music and DT. Fabulous languages department – nine languages taught, including Arabic, Japanese, Mandarin and Russian (department will soon move to new £20 million quadrangle, complete with 22 classrooms, two language labs and a library). Younger boys in classes of 20 to 22 (setted from ability from their first year and up to 14 sets per year group), with smaller class sizes as they get older. Total of 35 lessons (called schools at Eton) a week, but most boys have some free periods. Pupils have internal school exams in Michaelmas and summer terms. Youngest boys get an hour of prep a night, and two to two and a half hours as they progress up the school.

Full-time teaching staff numbers 150 – a good mix of old and new, and more women teachers than before. School is keen to encourage boys to be independent learners and boys get sessions on time management, study skills and exam technique. Rather than instructing pupils, 'You must do it like this,' school asks boys, 'How do you think we could do this better?' All pupils have a tutor and they meet once a week in small groups (maximum of six) at their tutor's house. Same tutor for first three years, then boys choose their own sixth form tutor.

Has invested heavily in SEN support – an educational psychologist spent a year setting up and coordinating the SEN unit and training staff. Around 50 to 60 boys receive regular learning support for mild to moderate dyslexia, dyspraxia, dysgraphia – either one-to-one or in small groups. All boys assessed during their first term and any whose results give cause for concern get extra help.

School reports are meticulous. All subject masters write reports for every boy they teach. These are sent to tutors, who add their own reports, then to housemasters and finally to parents. 'You get a pretty good idea of how your child is doing,' says one appreciative mother.

Games, options, the arts: Excellent – every extracurricular activity on offer, including cookery lessons from top chef (and provost's wife) Caroline Waldegrave. 'The opportunities are phenomenal,' a father told us wistfully. 'I only wish I'd gone there.' Sport remains superb, with facilities (and results) second to none. Boys must commit to a main sport every term – football or rugby in Michaelmas term, hockey, rowing or the Field Game in the Lent term and athletics, cricket, rowing or tennis in the summer. A raft of minor sports on offer – from Eton's own Wall Game to beagling. Unlike some schools, head encourages boys to continue with sports through exam terms.

Dazzling art department (the Drawing Schools), with marvellous open aspect over playing fields – one of the best we've seen. Remarkable and challenging work, beautifully executed and displayed. When we visited, eight boys were off to do art foundation courses after A levels. Paintings by the likes of Anthony Frost and Patrick Heron hanging on walls, collection of ceramics donated by an old boy, art library, CAD suite, two 3D printers – the place definitely has the wow factor. Music is brilliant too. Department attracts the brightest and best in the country via its music scholarships. Around 1,300 instrumental lessons a week and regular and very polished concerts held in concert hall.

Not surprisingly, with starry alumnae like Hugh Laurie, Damian Lewis, Dominic West, Eddie Redmayne and Tom Hiddleston, takes drama very seriously indeed. The drama department has its own full-time designer, carpenter and manager, plus a part-time wardrobe mistress, and puts on a plethora of school and house plays, some led by teachers, some by boys. When we visited, eclectic forthcoming productions ranged from Cyrano de Bergerac to Flames over New Jersey, a play co-written by a pupil and member of staff.

Huge number of outings, visits and field trips, and good provision for pupils post exams. CCF very popular – army is the biggest single employer of Old Etonians (including Prince Harry, of course). Vast number of clubs and societies, with top-notch speakers, often launched and run by the boys themselves. 'We give boys confidence in themselves,' says one beak. 'We treat them as adults and they get a lot of responsibility quite young.' Recent activities range from a charity cycle ride to raise money in memory of Horatio Chapple, the Eton pupil who died in tragic circumstances in Norway, to a spectacular fashion show (attended by Dame Vivienne Westwood, no less) staged by a boy with ambitions to be a fashion designer. 'I would have worn one of his ballgowns,' an impressed mother told us.

Background and atmosphere: Founded in 1440 by Henry VI (sister college of King's College, Cambridge, which was founded a year later). Seventy King's Scholars still live in the original buildings (most elegant dining hall and ancient classroom with original benches and graffiti). Buildings of mellow old red brick, medieval courtyards, grounds running down to the Thames, boys in tailcoats and white bow ties hurrying to lessons – the whole place looks like a film set. Magnificent chapel built by Henry VI and a second chapel for Lower Boys. Has appointed an imam and RC chaplain, Jewish and Hindu tutors on the staff too.

Twenty-five boarding houses, including College (for King's Scholars). Single study bedsits for all from day one. Huge variety of rooms and décor. The rooms we saw were pretty salubrious – one housemaster we met drew the line at 'floor-drobes'. Sanctions imposed for messy rooms range from laundry duty to black-bagging, where boys' possessions get stuffed in a bin bag and the culprit must pay a fine to get them back. All rooms networked and school endeavours to teach boys about responsible computer use. Boarding houses scattered either side of the High Street and beyond. Houses are known by the names of the housemasters in charge. They are in post for 13 years, so the names of the houses change with them.

Boys wear tailcoats and stiff collars – apart from office bearers, who wear proper wing collars and white ties. Brilliant for posture, as boys stuff pockets in their tailcoats with essential school kit, pulling even the most round-shouldered teenagers straight. School uniform not as expensive as you might think – good second-hand trade, both boy-inspired and via the school tailors in the High Street. Fancy waistcoats worn by the school prefects, or to give them their proper title, the Eton Society ('Pop'). Pupils don't wear tails across the bridge to Windsor any longer – much informal changing and half-changing (putting on a jacket rather than tails) after lessons. Teaching staff mostly live within 600 yards of the school, which creates a 'good sense of community'.

Lively atmosphere. Every day is structured and active, with boys and beaks constantly on the go. Beaks wear gowns for their three-line whip coffee break – Chambers – when one beak will attract the attention of another by tugging at his gown. Has its own traditional (and ever-evolving) school language: terms are 'halves', weekly tutor sessions are 'private business' and boys who aren't King's Scholars are Oppidans – luckily, a helpful glossary on the school website to explain all. Excellent school mags (The Chronicle, The Junior Chronicle) which are sold on high days and holidays for commission. All boys now have mobile phones and discount-available laptops.

Pastoral care and discipline: Still the traditional school it always was, but broad-minded, outward-looking and liberal in principle. Boys who get into trouble are given lots of support. Clear policies on drugs, alcohol and cigarettes. Any boy caught using, selling or possessing drugs 'will go,' says head firmly. But if a suspicion that a pupil may be dabbling with drugs and is prepared to talk about it, school takes 'a different route' – parents are informed and both they and the boy are asked to sign a contract, offered counselling and subjected to lectures and random drugs testing. Alcohol less of a problem now ('tiny numbers,' says school) but smoking is still there – though less than in co-ed schools, according to head. For first offences, smokers pay fines to cancer charity and will 'go on the bill' – Eton-speak for when a boy misbehaves and is sent to the headmaster or lower master. Boys have limited (but increasing with age) rights to go into Windsor and further afield – but only with their parents' permission.

In the boarding houses dames keep a weather eye on the boys, stay in contact with parents and run domestic matters. 'They are the co-runners of the houses,' a housemaster told us. 'They're not emergency first aid SWAT teams.' Older pupils volunteer to mentor new boys and answer questions like how to cope with the volume of work or what to do on Sunday mornings. House common rooms equipped with table football, pool table and TV. Lots of inter-house competitions. Half the houses offer in-house catering while boys in the others eat breakfast, lunch and supper in a large central dining hall. Lunch is a formal, if speedy, affair, with grace said at the start and finish. 'The houses are like little schools within a house,' a father told us. 'Everyone says their own house is the best.'

Pupils and parents: 'There isn't a typical Etonian,' the tutor for admissions told us. 'It's a very big school but it isn't one homogenous block. It's a school that is vastly more socially and culturally diverse than it's ever been.' He reckons that the boys who thrive are those who are 'curious, prepared to try out new things, have a love of learning and a deep-seated desire to get on'. Around 20 boys a year from state schools and 12 per cent from overseas – Hong Kong, China, Russia, Germany, France, Italy, Nigeria and the US.

The boys we met were a sparky bunch who cited the sports facilities and the friendly atmosphere as the best things about the place. Boys say they aren't bothered by being at a single-sex school – girls from St Mary's Ascot, Wycombe Abbey and St George's Ascot team up for some drama productions and, as one chirpy pupil told us, 'We can meet girls in the holidays'. Asked whether you have to be a boffin, gifted sportsman or one of the lads to get the most out of the school, Eton insists not. 'A boy who wouldn't say boo to a goose when he arrived got really involved in theatre lighting and sound while he was here,' a master said. 'By the time he got to 17 he was so respected that he was cheered admiringly every time his name came up at the end of performances.' A mother said that even though boys need to be 'self-starters and able to keep up with the work', the school suits different types – super-bright, sporty, quirky, you name it – and boys don't have to be utterly brilliant. 'My three sons are all quite different,' she told us. 'But they have all been very happy there and done well.' Another parent described it as 'an extraordinary school, with amazing opportunities', though, given its size, 'perhaps not the place for wilting violets'.

The fourth of June (aka school speech day) is as buzzy as ever, but the mass of royal watchers have gone. A huge mix of families – 'We have boys whose families live in castles and boys whose families live on inner-city estates,' says head. Lots of first-time buyers, along with sons of Old Etonians.

Notable Old Boys listed on school website – illustrious roll includes Hubert Parry, David Cameron and 18 previous prime ministers, loads of politicians (Eton provost William Waldegrave, Nicholas Soames, Douglas Hurd, Boris Johnson), Captain Oates, the poets Gray and Shelley, Princes William and Harry, a clutch of journalists (Charles Moore, Nicholas Coleridge, Craig Brown), plus chef Hugh Fearnley-Whittingstall, rower Matthew Pinsent, counter-tenor Michael Chance and Edward Gardner, musical director of the English National Opera.

Entrance: Around 1,000 candidates for 250 places – from more than 100 different schools. Entry procedure appears to be working well (the traditional 'put his name down at birth' regime was abolished in 2001) and the parents we spoke to expressed firm approval of its thoroughness. The head man once took the exam himself – 'I did pass, but did rather better in the oral part,' he told us last time round. Pupils must be bright enough to cope with the academic demands of the school, but Eton is also looking for boys with spark, flair and potential who will thrive in a boarding environment.

All prospective applicants assessed in year 6 – ultra-detailed assessment includes verbal reasoning, numeracy, perceptual potential, interview and school report. Five-strong committee spends two days assessing the candidates, and out of 1,000 boys assessed at the age of 11,250 will be offered places (conditional on passing CE or, for boys at state schools, Eton's own exam in year 8). Another 80 are placed on the waiting list. School recognises that by assessing in year 6, system may penalise late developers, so stays in touch with school heads and gets feedback on near-miss candidates. Successful candidates visit four boarding houses and list their choices – 80 per cent get one of their top two preferences.

Scholarships are a central part of the school – around 20 per cent of boys receive some form of financial support. Scholarship boys include 14 King's Scholars (decided on academic merit alone), plus New Foundation scholars (boys joining Eton from state schools) and many more.

To progress into the sixth form boys need a minimum of six A grades at GCSE, although in reality this is easily exceeded by all of them. Twelve sixth form scholarships offered a year – only for boys from state sector or independent schools lacking sixth form provision.

Exit: Loses one or two after GCSE – mainly those who opt for co-ed or day schools. At 18, virtually all progress to higher education. PPE, PPS, philosophy and theology the most popular subjects, followed by history/history of art, science and engineering. Between 65 and 100 a year to Oxbridge, others to Russell Group and increasing numbers to American universities, the majority Ivy League.

Money matters: Pots of money and assets. Stunning setting means school has a popular sideline from films (The Madness of King George etc). Can afford to (and does) have everything of the best. Pays its staff very well indeed. Aim is that finances shouldn't be an obstacle to any boy who is offered a scholarship and a large number of bursaries for parents who can't afford the fees or have fallen on hard times. Regular subsidised summer schools – rowing a popular option for prep school wannabes.

Masses of public activity – the rowing lake at Dorney is used nationally for training international rowers (and for the London 2012 Olympic rowing and kayak events), and the athletics hall and swimming pools (indoor and outdoor) are much in demand by locals out of term time. Currently on a mission to raise £50 million to fund further bursaries – has raised more than half so far.

Remarks: Still the number one boys' public school. With teaching and facilities that are second to none, Eton produces bright, purposeful, articulate young men with a sense of ambition and self-worth. School is far more forward-thinking and outward-looking than many realise and really does encourage boys to make the most of the dazzling array of opportunities on offer.

Exeter School

Linked school: Exeter Junior School

Victoria Park Road, Exeter, EX2 4NS

- Pupils: 710 pupils, 430 boys and 280 girls; all day • Ages: 11–18
- C of E • Fees: £9,795–£10,857 pa • Independent

Tel: 01392 273679
Email: admissions@exeterschool.org.uk
Website: www.exeterschool.org.uk

Headmaster: Since 2003, Mr Bob Griffin MA (fifties). Educated at Wallington High School for Boys, then Christ Church, Oxford, where gained first in modern languages (French and Spanish). Taught at Markham College in Lima before becoming head of modern languages at Haileybury. Came to Exeter from RGS Guildford, where he was second master for five years.

Pupils like him, staff respect him and parents rate him. 'One of the school's real strengths,' we were told by one mother. Another said he 'combines warmth with gravitas' and 'empathises with wider parental concerns'. Still teaches a little and often covers for staff absences. Solid, no-nonsense kind of skipper who keeps his ship on an even keel. Cares deeply about his school and doesn't look ready to move elsewhere. Takes time to get to know everyone and 'just joins in'. Head's wife works at nearby university. Daughter moving into tertiary education from Exeter School, while son is in sixth form. Popular with pupils we met, who described him as 'fair' and 'not beyond a practical joke or two'. Enjoys all things Hispanic, walking on Dartmoor and choral singing. Believes in steady development of facilities rather than headline grabbing expansion. Proud of pupils' achievements and of how school has raised its game.

Academic matters: Top notch results are 'just a part of what the school does well,' say parents. In 2013, 56 per cent A*/A at A level and 80 per cent (a new record) at GCSE.

Not a hothouse, but slackers will be pulled up sharply. Regular reporting to parents (includes early warning on promotions and demotions) is a cornerstone of the school. More of an old grammar school work ethic, which most parents relate to easily. Larger top sets (up to 24) in languages and maths allow the less able to get more individual attention in lower sets (10 to 14). Inequalities of choice in modern languages now resolved by a carousel of two terms each in French, German and Spanish in years 7 and 8. Broad choice of options at GCSE, plus RE for all. Twenty-five subjects on offer at A level. Maths and science lead school's results tables but performance is impressive across the board.

Laboratories (all 12 of them) date back to 60s but have been upgraded in terms of kit. Classrooms we saw were all equipped with interactive boards and digital projectors. Staff appointments from state and independent sectors are handled with considerable care, so mix of youth versus experience is about right.

Experienced learning support co-ordinator provides help where needed; staff and parents now realise that special needs cross the whole ability spectrum. Dyscalculia is handled within maths department. 'Pupils are delightful,' says special educational needs coordinator, 'and average ones leave with a cracking set of results.' Strategy sheets for pupils receiving support are updated twice termly and are available through school intranet to all staff. Recent needs addressed include a registered blind pupil, hearing impaired, cystic fibrosis and mild autism.

Amazing programme of enrichment activities – mock trial on day we visited – centred around Crossing club for seniors (includes Oxbridge entrance preparation) and Catalyst club for middle school.

Games, options, the arts: Busy is an understatement here, with large numbers of pupils and staff occupied after school and at weekends. All main games are played well, teams at all levels and pupils reach county, regional and occasional national representation. Older pupils branch out into wider range of sports. Strong PE staff (five full-time in senior school), some extra performance coaches where required and loads of support from rest of staff. Large and modern sports hall with well-equipped fitness area upstairs, dance studio, squash courts and a climbing wall. Kayaking hugely successful. Other leisure activities include croquet and ultimate frisbee.

Extensive sports fields with Astroturf and a variety of hard surfaces for tennis and netball. Outdoor heated swimming pool in centre of school. Some parental concern that a successful sporting year group could be hard to 'break into' if children joined it later. Sports tours overseas are well subscribed. Annual Ten Tors challenge is taken very seriously (more candidates than places available ensures competitive edge) and involves teaching and ancillary staff as well as parents (former Rifles Lieutenant Colonel leads the school's campaign) over a number of weekends.

Music particularly strong – nearly half the pupils play an instrument. Choirs, jazz bands, orchestras provide glittering programme of concerts throughout the year. One parent said her children had found the approach to music 'too serious', whilst another said that hers had 'flown musically' since joining. Choral society pulls in staff, parents past and present and pupils for high profile performances in Exeter Cathedral. Other concerts are charity fundraisers. Some reach top grade/diploma level and regular participants in national choirs or orchestras. Outreach work at local state primary school involving input from sixth form musicians. We witnessed a lunch -time rehearsal for the junior orchestra – 'work in progress,' we concluded, but range of levels and instruments showed strength in depth.

Good art studios (doors open from 8am to 6pm), with plenty of talent in evidence. Potential quickly harnessed by experienced staff and displays in exhibition gallery bear witness to this. Drama has been headed by a couple who arrived from Paris over 20 years ago – inventive, diverse and of a high standard. Wide range of productions for seniors (most recently Pirates of Penzance) and juniors, with performances in main hall. More intimate pieces in drama studio, which has raked seating.

Strong CCF contingent attracts about two-thirds of pupils, though some opt for D of E or community service. Visits and trips abound. Recent ones include year 9 battlefields visit to France and Belgium which involved over 100 pupils, annual art visit to St Ives, geographers in Alps spending a day on the Argentière glacier, joint classics and geography visit to Bay of Naples (taking in Solfatara volcano and Pompeii).

Background and atmosphere: Founded in 1633, originally for sons of freemen of Exeter. Collegiate feel attributable to famous Victorian architect William Butterfield (who also designed Keble College, Oxford). Links to city's St John's Hospital account for presence of one of three surviving Blue Boy statues over doorway of Exonian Centre (houses archives and provides meeting space for governors' meetings etc). Twenty-five acre site is only a mile from city centre and provides views to open countryside and Haldon Hills beyond. Recent fill-ins and additions have been skilfully matched with original brickwork. Central tower (in brick not ivory) houses office accommodation and staff rooms and is especially well integrated. Major £1m+ building programme has produced new sixth form centre, rebuilt music school, new art studio and free-weights gym in sports hall.

Post-war school became boys' direct grant reverting to independent status in 70s. Girls appeared at sixth form level in 1980; fully co-ed since 1997. Present ratio in favour of boys looks set to stay, given proximity of two well-established girls' schools. Girls we spoke to thought co-ed worked well and was 'a better preparation for later life.'

No hint of toffishness, though range of extracurricular activities is more akin to an expensive boarding school. Pupils at all levels look smart; some flamboyance evident amongst sixth form boys in particular. Generally busy but occasionally relaxed sixth formers can choose how to use their free time. Many go to the well-equipped and refurbished library, while others choose to work in the sixth form centre study room and/or hang out in the comfy seating in the large common room next door (breaktime bacon butties a particular favourite). More than adequate school lunches served to majority of pupils (only 20 per cent opt for packed lunches) in multi-purpose hall.

Pastoral care and discipline: Senior staff visible around site outside lesson times. Sixth formers allowed off-site at lunchtimes, but most don't have time. Mainly self-managing discipline, given school's positive approach, but potential troublemakers risk being weeded out at end of year 11. School marshal, alias CCF instructor, pops up unexpectedly and helps to ensure order. Well established house system monitors

progress and well-being. First line of contact for parents through heads of house now made much accessible through email. Parents praise this system and say that 'a response is always forthcoming quickly and any query investigated'.

Combination of a weekly assembly in the main hall (PowerPoint presentation with a moral twist followed by extensive laudations for conquering sports teams when we visited) for the whole school. Smaller chapel and other gatherings for houses are well established. Sixth form has own programme, with outside speakers plus lots of HE and careers input.

Pupils and parents: Predominantly from professional families. Bright and 'expected to deliver' academically. Popular as a 'family choice' for sons and daughters. New year 7s all go on early residential weekend to an outdoor education centre at Dartmeet. Senior pupils (many have come right through from the junior school) provide leadership in hands-on rather than authoritarian way. Sixth formers we encountered were refreshingly articulate and enthusiastic. Extensive playing fields good for letting off steam. Mobile phones (which are allowed if used sensibly outside lessons) were hardly in evidence. A few pupils cycle to school.

Former pupils include Olympic yachtsmen Stevie Morrison and Ben Rhodes, former MP David Bellotti and actor Matthew Goode. Other alumni range from explorers, businessmen and military to media people. ESPA parents' support group) is very active, with social events and fundraising through year.

Entrance: School report and January examination (no longer required for most junior school pupils). School considers potential as well as achievement. Entry from prep schools and others at 13+. Sixth formers selected by GCSE results (minimum of six grade Bs at GCSE), school reference and interviews. Catchment area spread far and wide and includes over 60 feeder schools, but mainly within a 20 mile radius.

Exit: Around 20 per cent leave after GCSEs. Two to Oxbridge and seven medics in 2013; rest to a range of destinations and courses.

Money matters: 'Honest to goodness value for money', with flat fee from 11-18. 'Typically, both parents work and grandparents may chip in,' we were told. Range of awards at 11, 13 and 16. Governors' means-tested bursaries help parents unable to afford full fees. Special awards from local benefactors and Ogden award for one sixth form entrant. Improvements and developments made through good housekeeping rather than borrowing.

Remarks: Unpretentiously successful. Offers a stimulating learning environment with every opportunity for boys and girls to play and work hard.

Fairley House School

30 Causton Street, London, SW1P 4AU

• Pupils: 180 boys/girls; the number of girls/boys does vary quite a bit on a month by month basis; all day • Ages: 5–14 • Inter-denom • Fees: £28,500 pa• Independent

Tel: 020 7976 5456
Email: office@fairleyhouse.org.uk
Website: www.fairleyhouse.org.uk

Headmaster: Since September 2013, Mr Michael Taylor BA PGCE FRGS.

Previous principal, Jackie Murray, is now school's principal educational psychologist.

Academic matters: Regularly inspected and accredited by CReSTeD, the register for specialist schools with provision for dyslexia and SpLDs. Pupils are split into a junior department – five to nine years – and a senior department – 10 to 14 years, class size usually 8-12 pupils. The main emphasis being on numeracy and literacy, everyone is put into a small group to match their ability and skills for maths and English and rejoins their class for other subjects. Children are taught to understand their own learning styles and shown strategies to overcome barriers to learning to achieve their targets. The aim is to return children to mainstream schools as soon as they are able, which has great success in doing. Test results such as Sats are very respectable, especially from children who can have quite pronounced difficulties.

Every child has an IEP which is regularly reviewed by the trans-disciplinary team to monitor progress and ensure that individual needs are being catered for. Mornings start with exercises; depending on the individual, this could be physical, orthoptic or attention focused. All the classrooms, including the science lab, are buzzing with activities, visual reminders and clues, anything that is memorable: models made by the children, word banks for a current history topic or colour coded parts of speech. Every teacher has specialist qualifications which ensure that all classes are fully accessible and multisensory. 'Having teachers who are nice to you and understand has changed my life,' said a 10-year-old. The learning support is an integral part of the whole school approach to teaching. The transdisciplinary approach is used across the curriculum, helpfully allowing therapy delivery to be linked to specific subjects and development. Homework is colour-coded to help with the organisation, and deadlines must be met to prepare the children for returning to mainstream school. Help and advice is on hand for those who get stuck.

Depending on the individual needs of the pupil, speech therapy and occupational therapy are incorporated into classroom learning, art, drama and sports. Younger children will be making 'ch' out of chocolate buttons whilst older ones are baking round pies to help understand and remember the mathematical sign pi. Children are taught to touch-type once they have achieved a reading age of approximately eight years. In-house speech and occupational therapists run their own sensory integration programmes and motor coordination classes. The therapy staff organising the motor coordination classes have been specially trained in America and continue to attend training in the USA to keep up to date.

Games, Options, the Arts: Wonderfully imaginative art displays line the corridors and even the ceilings are decorated in many areas of the building. Pupils make their own ceramic tiles depicting various scenes from history and also design and execute murals. The most recent addition is the newly-built art studio and kiln room. The children enjoy a great variety of artistic activities including textiles, fashion, design and technology, sewing and puppet-making.

A range of sports – all the traditional ones, alongside canoeing, fencing and yoga. Although doesn't have its own playing fields, they make good use of local facilities at Battersea Park and the Queen Mother sports centre. Music and drama are taught as separate subjects and integrated into other curriculum areas to help children develop good communication skills. Everyone is encouraged to learn a musical instrument and the school runs its own acting awards and music medals scheme. Parents pack into the termly dramatic and musical productions.

Extra-curricular activities include museum and theatre trips along with a wide choice of lunchtime and after-school clubs. Club options change regularly depending on the clientele and demand.

Background and atmosphere: Founded in 1975 by a speech therapist, Daphne Hamilton Fairley, as a charitable trust in memory of her oncologist husband, killed by an IRA bomb.

The upper school site, originally a church, has been cleverly converted into a four-storey building. The junior school pupils are housed in a Victorian infants' school in the shadows of Lambeth Palace, backing on to Archbishop's Park, complete with sports facilities and an adventure playground for the children's use. Both buildings are well decorated, with a lot of space dedicated to the children's achievements, visual timetables and fantastic works of art. The atmosphere is purposeful, peaceful and well organised, encouraging pupils to be themselves. Lots of smiling and cheerful faces – nobody should feel the odd one out here.

Pastoral Care and Discipline: Structured mentoring system involving 18 members of staff to whom children can refer themselves. Aim is to work in a strong partnership with parents to help ensure things do not go wrong for pupils due to simple misunderstandings. Seems to be working, as parents feel pastoral care has improved over the last few years.

Pupils and parents: From all over London, and a few from the edges of the home counties. Everybody and anybody affected by neuro-diversity. By all accounts, lots of very supportive and enthusiastic parents who are keen to get involved with school activities. Most recently the parent group has fundraised to update and restock the school library. Weekly newsletters, back-up information on the website and parents can use a communication book or e-mail teachers. Comprehensive, well-designed website, but not 'read friendly' as yet.

Entrance: Children are invited to spend two days here, where they will have a transdisciplinary all-round assessment to ensure that the school will be able to meet their needs. After the assessment, parents are provided with reports from an educational psychologist, speech therapist and occupational therapist and then invited for a conference to discuss how the school can help and support their child. Assessments cost £250-£850. In the event of the school not being able to offer a place they will suggest other options to parents.

Most pupils have a diagnosis of specific learning differences, usually dyslexia and/or dyspraxia and the related conditions ADD, ADHD and Asperger's. Also able to accommodate some pupils who have non-conventional learning styles and find mainstream schools inaccessible.

Exit: The average stay for pupils at Fairley House is approximately two/three years. Some return to junior schools, eg Newton Prep, Eaton Square, The Hall, Northcote Lodge; older day pupils to Portland Place, Davies Laing and Dick, Royal Russell, Thames Christian College. Boarding choices include St Christopher's, Millfield, Sibford, St Bede's, Bloxham and Bedales. A few return abroad when their families move back.

Money matters: A few bursaries are available for trainee teachers. As yet, unable to offer bursaries to pupils, but will assist parents with tribunals and the statementing procedure. Approximately 26 per cent of pupils have a statement of special educational needs and are funded by their local authorities.

Remarks: Certainly good value for money, but the fees are terrifying and beyond the reach of many without local authority funding. A remarkable school for its holistic, multi-sensory and transdisciplinary approach. A beacon for children with learning and processing differences and parents who have been tearing their hair out trying to cope in other situations.

Farmor's School

The Park, Fairford, Gloucestershire, GL7 4JQ

• Pupils: 1,200 boys and girls, all day • Ages: 11-18 • State

Tel: 01285 712302
Email: dtaylor@farmors.gloucs.sch.uk
Website: www.farmors.gloucs.sch.uk

Headteacher: Since September, 2013 Matthew Evans, previously deputy head of the Henry Box School in Witney. Has won a national teaching award for achievements in enterprise education; his first leadership post was coordinating a school's business and enterprise specialism.

Academic matters: A comprehensive school taking the full ability range and achieving very good results: 85 per cent get five or more GCSEs at A*-C (69 per cent including maths and English). At A level over 80 per cent A*-C, with over 10 per cent A*. Sciences very strong throughout, as are languages (French and Spanish plus Latin at GCSE). Art and design students do extremely well at A level, as do English, business, sociology and media studies. A great strength is range of subjects – 24 at A level plus a handful of vocational subjects, including engineering. Specialist teachers for every subject.

Lots of enrichment activities at all stages outside the standard curriculum. Well-organised library with full time staff, plenty of PCs – 350 networked throughout the school; pupils can access their own work and also have protected internet access for appropriate study. Dedicated spaces for sixth formers to study and or socialise.

Good support for those needing additional help, especially with literacy – mostly delivered in class, but on a withdrawal basis if need be. Classes are not small – 25 to 30 is not unusual in the lower years, but smaller for GCSE years (around 20) and sixth form groups. Good careers advice – the school has Investor in Careers status, with a week in year 12 dedicated to post-18 options.

Games, options, the arts: Good sports facilities – though no swimming and no all-weather surfaces – but rugby, football, hockey, netball, basketball, tennis, cricket and athletics, with many representatives in county teams and regular wins in district and county sports. Plenty of space to run about in. The local on-site sports centre is shared by the school and local community.

Wealth of foreign trips, mostly sports and language related – including destinations such as Ecuador, Paris, Berlin, Iceland and Russia as well as World Challenge trips to Bolivia and the Galapagos Islands – organised by enthused staff and, says the head, very well supported by parents. A great drama studio with plenty of lighting and sound equipment – a proper green room etc. Performing arts GCSE growing in popularity, a recording room and practice rooms for musicians – in fact quite a buzzing music block; about 150 take individual music lessons and plenty of opportunities to join in choirs and orchestras. Regular concerts and dramatic productions. Young Enterprise and D of E are also popular

Background and atmosphere: Founded in 1738 with money left by Elizabeth Farmor and Mary Barker to educate 50 boys in Fairford – a picturesque Cotswoldy town in a predominantly rural area. Girls were admitted in 1815, became fully co-educational in 1922. Originally in the centre of town, in a building now the community centre, but in 1961 it moved to its present site in 18 acres of parkland a short walk away, becoming an 11-18 comprehensive in 1966 and an academy in 2011. The 1960s buildings are showing their age rather – not least because 1200 pupils are now being accommodated in a building originally designed for 400. The head says keeping it all in order is 'a constant battle', but some very good new buildings too. An impressive business teaching facility and very good, new science labs.

All parts of the school are well ordered – no tatty displays – though possibly more could be done to show off some of the excellent art and textiles work (which has netted amazing A level results but is not prominent round the school). Staff say, 'We can do challenging work with the pupils because the standards of behaviour are so high and pupils want to learn and do well.' Pupils say the teachers are 'fantastically supportive' and that even in this sizeable school, 'you're never anonymous'. Lots of emphasis – from staff, pupils, parents and head – on the quality of relationships all round.

Pastoral care and discipline: Clear rules, well known and observed. Head says most pastoral issues arise from families under pressure rather than disobedience or disruption in the classroom. Tutor groups of about 30. The atmosphere is unflustered and orderly. Lots of links with external agencies where needed, school counsellors available, peer counselling and buddy reading schemes to promote good relationships and support between pupils at different stages. Drugs/ alcohol etc 'less of an issue than ever' – school takes 'a very strong line' if any misuse is discovered.

Pupils and parents: Intake from Fairford, surrounding villages and as far away as Swindon. A wide social mix, from those who are struggling to the comfortable county set. Parents are very supportive, with an active and positive PTA. They praise the school's good and frequent communication, say staff are very responsive to individual pupil's needs and that pupils, though well supported, are expected to 'get on with it' – high expectations in a friendly environment. Pupils are polite, motivated, personable, fairly well turned out and very pleased to be at Farmor's. They speak with great enthusiasm about the approachability and commitment of the staff, and their willingness to offer support and help.

Entrance: Has doubled in size over the last 10 years and now 'as big as we can get' – impressive, considering that the local demographic dip would have predicted a fall rather than a rise in school numbers. A fairly large catchment – some children travel in from the Wiltshire borders. Truly comprehensive – 'no selection of any description' – though all come with their Sats scores and are put in sets for maths, science and languages (not for English).

Five A*-Cs at GCSE needed for sixth form, with Bs preferred for A level choices, although some leeway allowed. About half the sixth form (which numbers 150 per year) come from other local schools (mostly those that don't offer sixth form provision).

Exit: Around 50-60 per cent stay on for sixth form, with most others going on to vocational courses, some to sixth form college in Cirencester. Most A level students continue their studies at university, although that profile is changing in the current climate to include apprenticeships and management training. Over 35 per cent go to Russell Group universities with business, sciences and art very popular subjects. Favourite destinations include Cardiff, Nottingham, Bristol, Exeter, Swansea and Manchester. A few to Oxbridge.

Remarks: A comprehensive school in the best sense: opportunity and encouragement for every child at the right level and a genuine partnership between pupils, parents and staff.

Felsted School

Linked school: Felsted Preparatory School

Felsted, Great Dunmow, Essex, CM6 3LL

• Pupils: 300 boys/235 girls; boarding contemporary (3 nights) – 215; weekly (5 nights) – 120; full (7 nights) – 115 • Ages: 13-18
• C of E • Fees: Boarding £24,825–£28,185; Day £20,383 pa
• Independent

Tel: 01371 822605
Email: ado@felsted.org
Website: www.felsted.org

Headmaster: Since 2008, Dr Michael Walker MA PhD PGCE (early fifties) previously head of King Edward's in Chelmsford, where he spent 18 years, rapidly rising up the ranks. Before that head of history at Gresham's School. Sought-after to share his expertise at regional and national level. Despite having massively impressive credentials, he places great value on tapping into others' ideas and experiencing for himself all aspects of the school. Pupils and members of the newly formed parents' forum cite numerous examples of proposals implemented. He's made a point of staying overnight at each house in turn, has risen to the challenge of singing and dancing on stage – 'I was utterly petrified' – and will compete cross-country against a sixth former to raise money for charity. All combines to make a strong leader who has injected new thinking and set out a clear path while reportedly remaining approachable, open, kind and low-key.

Academic matters: Not overly selective, but each year a solid cohort achieves top grades across the board in both A levels and GCSEs. In 2013, 48 per cent A*/A grades at GCSE; 60 per cent A*-B, 25 per cent A*/A at A level. Known for its success in psychology, but pupils do well in other subjects – Latin and modern languages, history, maths, science and art, to name but a few. More generally it has the reputation of bringing out the best in all. IB now taking off amongst quite conservative local families – currently about a third of the sixth form opts for it: 33 average point score.

Parents recoil at the thought of its becoming an academic hothouse and support increased focus on individual educational plans, with the aim of ensuring maximum academic success – but not at the expense of other activities. Recent increase in number of classroom assistants to support the process. SEN pupils, of whom about 45, often take one fewer GCSE, to allow time for more personalised support. EAL teachers also on hand.

Streaming in the lower years and class sizes are kept small – between 15-20 up to GCSE – and often considerably smaller in the sixth form. Staff development encouraged. Recently staff and pupils were asked to suggest what constituted a good or outstanding lesson and the findings have been discussed openly with all – can but add to the pressure to deliver.

Games, options, the arts: Traditionally sporty. It has produced some outstanding cricketers and Olympic athletes. Games fields and facilities stretch as far as the eye can see. Currently has a tennis player in the top 10 nationally. Hockey, cricket, rugby and netball all strong with regular success at regional and national championships. If you don't make the teams, no shame with lots else on offer to keep you fit and occupied. Emphasis very much on participation, be it in sports, regular music events featuring individual talent, the many choirs and orchestras (30 per cent are involved in music of some kind), drama or in the wealth of extracurricular options which make for very full days and busy weekends. Not perhaps for the retiring, ill-organised or easily-wearied type. Huge take up of D of E – at the last count

no fewer than 26 gold awards in the upper sixth – and 220 enrolled in CCF.

Very much accords with the head's ambition of becoming a Round Square school promoting IDEALS – internationalism, democracy, care for the environment, adventurous pursuits, leadership and service. In addition to much-appreciated local community activities and links to disadvantaged communities in East London where pupils have been busy promoting cheerleading, the school is reinforcing developing world links. Students queue up for opportunities to break the 'Felsted bubble'. They include visits to the partner school in Ethiopia and jumping aboard a former pupil's Magic Bus which supports children in the slums of Mumbai.

Background and atmosphere: Traditional, yet progressive, it feeds off its history but is not hidebound by it. Founded in 1564 by Richard, Lord Riche, Lord Chancellor of England, the school's original Guild Hall is still in use with other, later, attractive Grade I and II listed buildings scattered throughout the village, interspersed with well-tended lawns and sports fields and cut through by the quiet Dunmow to Braintree road. Most recent additions include the music school and the sixth form centre – a great space to access the net and meet informally or at regular social events where the odd glass of wine is permitted. Overall impression of being a happy, happening place with parents content to be swept along for the ride.

Pastoral care and discipline: Recent tightening up on uniform and behaviour welcomed by parents and local businesses alike. Swift and decisive action when bullying and other misdemeanours uncovered, although, in truth, such incidents are relatively rare. Good relations between parents, pupils and staff enhanced by the introduction of clearer reporting systems and a new atmosphere of openness and purpose. Standardising flexi-boarding arrangements has overcome some earlier problems concerning integration of full and part-time boarders and there are robust measures in place to help new and international students settle in. Although many local boarders disappear at the weekends, the stayers-in are rarely short of invitations to stay with local families, outings or on-site activities to fill their time.

Two day and eight boarding houses, four for boys and four for girls. Separate upper sixth form boarding houses. Year 9 board in pleasant shared accommodation – all other years have single rooms though some choice of double rooms if pupils prefer it. Homely common room areas and studies.

Pupils and parents: We hear that Essex is proud of producing self-starting, entrepreneurial and independent spirits. Parents value the fact that 'they're not sausage making' and champion these qualities at the school. Pupils range from the highly-driven and academically-orientated to the more fun-loving and easy-going, but all pretty down to earth. Characteristics of the typical Felstedian recently assessed, based on feedback from various parties, include being ambitious, motivated, accepting challenge and being self-aware.

Long list of notable OFs includes English test cricketer John Stephenson and General Sir Richard Dannatt, until recently Chief of the General Staff. Huge diversity of talent is reflected in the senior positions and success OFs have achieved in science and medicine, the military, politics and public service, academia, business, sports and the media.

While most live within a couple of hours of the school, it is increasingly attracting London-based families. Taking advantage of its proximity to Stansted Airport, international students make up some 20 per cent of pupils – getting towards the high end amongst schools in this guide. Lots of Germans do IB and a similar number of students from China, Hong Kong and all round the world.

Entrance: Many come up from the prep. Other popular feeder schools are Holmwood House, Heathmount, Orwell Park and Edge Grove. Those taking CE are required to obtain 50 per cent in each paper. Others take a verbal reasoning test, interview and submit a confidential report from their current school. They may take tests in maths, French and English for setting purposes. The same is true at 14+ entry. At 16+ there is a similar entry procedure and pupils are required to obtain six GCSEs at grade B or better including B grades in the subjects being pursued. Pupils who do not have English as their first language will be assessed by the head of EAL.

Exit: Around 90 per cent stay on to the sixth form. After A level most to good universities such as Exeter, Durham, Nottingham, Newcastle, Birmingham, King's London, and a sprinkling to Oxbridge (one in 2013). Business-related subjects, medicine, humanities and the sciences popular.

Money matters: Academic, music, sport, art, design and technology or drama and all-rounder scholarships offering up to 20 per cent or £1,000 off the fees are available at 13+ and 16+. There are some assisted places up to 100 per cent on a means-tested basis.

Remarks: Real sense of excitement as head avidly goes about canvassing views and implementing change to fulfil his vision of making Felsted 'a leading independent boarding and day school, regionally, nationally and internationally'. Well on his way, from what we hear, with parents welcoming a renewed focus on academic performance but not at the expense of individualism and quirkiness. All agree – it's one to watch.

Fernhill School

Fernbrae Avenue, Rutherglen, Glasgow, G73 4SG

• Pupils: 160 girls • Ages: 3–18 • RC (but all faiths welcome)
• Fees: £8,976–£9,300 pa • Independent

Tel: 01416 342674
Email: info@fernhillschool.co.uk
Website: www.fernhillschool.co.uk

Head Teacher: Since October 2012, Mrs Theresa Hayburn, previously depute head of St Andrew's and St Bride's High School in East Kilbride. Has 20 years' teaching experience, including over 10 years working with Scottish Qualifications Authority as marker, setter, moderator and external assessor, and also as an associate assessor with Education Scotland, taking part in school inspections.

Academic matters: 'Does very, very well', firmly rooted in the Scottish exam system, doing S grade, Highers and, increasingly, Advanced Higher; though some subjects (English, mod langs and Latin) use Intermediate 2 instead of S grade. This is an academic school, which offers a full curriculum, results are pretty impressive – very good pass rate at all levels (Highers 84 per cent in 2013, Standard, Intermediate 2 and Advanced Highers all 90+). 'A wonderful spirit of team work' pervades and pupils 'work well together'. Teachers can give real personal attention to pupils of all abilities. Five Highers the norm, with no formal examinations in drama or home economics, but music now up to Ad Higher.

Huge investment in IT over the past five years, keyboarding for all, flat screens, local area network, and 40 stand-alone machines. Computing is offered as an exam subject up to Ad Higher level. Staff all dual qualified and can book computer suites for lessons. Two interactive whiteboards to date and around the place.

Humanities well taught and good SEN provision. Pupil support taken very seriously and – from evidence of results gained from a mixed ability intake – very effective.

Games, options, the arts: Amazing range of sports on offer – rugby for primaries of both sexes, plus all the usual girl-affiliated activities: netball, volleyball, hockey; house matches as well as inter-schools friendlies. Size means team sport tends to be participative as well as competitive; for primary athletics had a clean sweep at the South Lanarkshire track events. Parents are enthusiastically involved in annual sports days, keen swimming at a local swimming pool nearby (absolutely stunning after another refurbishment) and successful cross-country team. Saturday sports for teams. 'Staff are brilliant at encouraging star quality athletes,' though high fliers tend to go to local clubs for high-level training etc.

Some clubs post-school and a wide variety during lunch. Chess popular, debating important, poetry a recent successful addition. Masses of woodwind and violins, the occasional trumpeter and pianist and, at last, an orchestra, formed just as Mrs Sexton arrived and going from strength to strength. Lots of group playing and house competitions – music is fun here. Regular trips to the Royal Concert Hall in Glasgow and last year a choir trip to Paris. No drama – as yet: 'Basically this is an academic school'. Airy all-purpose art department including fabric and fashion design, 'band-box smart into the bargain'; pupils design the fabric and follow all the way through to the finished item – impressive.

Background and atmosphere: Perched beside a golf course close to the Cathkin Braes, the central Victorian family home, overlooking the city of Glasgow, nestles in nine 'nook and cranny' acres. Private and very secure with locked gates. It was founded in 1972 as a primary school and pushed the leaving age up – demand and supply. Classrooms added when necessary, though the main quad is splendidly uniform. Two more recent teaching blocks are smart and practical, while the collection of cabins and smaller classrooms was brightened with boxes and baskets of flowers on a summer visit.

Runs on Catholic ethos – pupils deliciously polite, tons of praise for all and oodles of cups awards and prizes for a various activities. Immaculate – strap shoes, caps for boys and round felt hats for girls, even with their summer dresses and long white socks. Strong links formed between senior girls and primary pupils, with buddies at break time. Packed lunches, hot lunches Wed/Thurs, most pupils eat lunch in the hall but senior girls have a bit more privacy in their own common room.

Pastoral care and discipline: Founded on respect for other people and 'treat them properly' ethos reinforced by anti-bullying assemblies and workshops in first and second year secondary. Of course girls sometimes fall out, but no real bullying. Strong PSE and MRE (social and religious education in old speak) programmes, four houses and tutor system in place. Drugs, smoking and alcohol awareness days. Drugs simply don't happen – a very particular ethos and catchment which means that on the whole children stay children and enjoy their childhood.

Own chaplain and strong links with the local community. All practising RC pupils are prepared for the sacraments of first communion and confirmation within the school. Primary school staff are all practising Catholics, but not essential for teachers in the senior school; non-Catholics may be excused services. Welcomes all: Hindu, Muslim etc – no religious or sectarian bigotry. The Asian pupils celebrate their feast days and the school acknowledges other faiths with understanding and respect.

Pupils and parents: From all over – some travel quite a long distance: North Lanarkshire, Ayrshire, buses. An oasis of middle-class respectability. Can leave pupils from 8.30 am, which is handy for commuting parents, but no after-school care (the buses again).

Entrance: Entrance assessment and interview for all pupils – looking above all for potential.

Exit: Some leave directly after Highers in S5. Gap years for some post-Higher; 95 per cent go on to university, usually in Scotland. More now staying on for S6 and Advanced Highers. Selection of degree courses including law, medicine, dentistry, plus some traditional academics and business – impressive for a small school.

Money matters: Financial assistance is available and always means tested. Chair and deputy chair of the board of governors review bursary provision.

Remarks: Still a school serving a very specific Catholic heartland population, but will accept pupils of all faiths – looking for girls only (senior school) and strong moral values. Ideal, of course, for a wide range of children needing small, loving and caring environment with the benefit of a strong religious backbone, but this is an academic and adventurous school with 'some pretty lively pupils and a fantastically committed staff'. Difficult to find – one of Glasgow's well-kept secrets.

Fettes College

Linked school: Fettes College Preparatory School

Carrington Road, Edinburgh, EH4 1QX

- Pupils: 285 boys, 270 girls; 410 board, rest day • Ages: 13–18 • Non-denom • Fees: Day £22,170; Boarding £29,160 pa
- Independent

Tel: 01313 116744
Email: admissions@fettes.com
Website: www.fettes.com

Headmaster: Since 1998, Mr Michael C B Spens MA (sixty), educated at Marlborough and Selwyn College Cambridge, where he read natural sciences. Came to Fettes after five years as head of Caldicott, having previously spent 20 years at Radley where he was housemaster and taught geology, after a short spell in business. The transition between junior and senior schools is always an interesting one but Mr Spens has weathered his double change with charm and élan – one might say nonchalance, but that would be harsh, and misleading; quarter is not easily found here: there is a tightly-wound spring beneath the cultivated appearance of charm and relaxation. Expect zero tolerance on the drugs front, 'The students don't want it around', and the Fettesian druggy alcy image no longer makes headlines in the Scottish press. Fettes is challenging all-comers as Scotland's school of choice, surprisingly, even on the day front, 'And we're more expensive than the others,' says the head – but then we are talking Edinburgh (think mink and nae knickers). Married to Debbie, they have three children (one at Fettes, one on a gap year and one at university) and a much-loved labrador ('Kiwi, because she's all black'). Charismatic, vibrant, fun. Fettes and Mr Spens are zinging. Currently forefront of the campaign to keep Scottish independent schools' charitable status and all over the Sunday papers.

Academic matters: Almost all heads of departments have changed during the past few years – 'new young staff', 'very good', 'strong', 'Edinburgh is a strong draw'; and, having played the Scottish versus the English system along with all the other big players, added the IB in 2006. Pupils can choose whether they want to specialise, therefore do A levels (2013: 80 per cent A*-B, 51 per cent A*/A), or take the broader IB syllabus: excellent results – average score over 36, 25 per cent scored over 40 points. At GCSE, 69 per cent A*/A grades.

Three sciences on offer throughout, plus trad French, German and Spanish, as well as Mandarin (available for beginners as well as for native speakers). No particular bias – physics, chemistry, history and geography outstanding at GCSE level, maths and English almost equally strong; results in all disciplines equally impressive at A level. Art results outstanding throughout the school. Tranche of outstanding French GCSEs taken early. Strong tradition of classics; government and politics and history of art available at A level. Broad range of subjects, but not the biggest take up at A level in langs, classics or further maths.

Foreign pupils with minimal English are no longer accepted willy-nilly, unless they happen to be particularly bright or have siblings in the school. EFL is on hand, but pupils who don't have 'a pretty good working knowledge of English' are encouraged to do an English lang course before they arrive (Edinburgh School of English is popular).

Good staff:pupil ratio. 'Computers zooming ahead' – wireless networked throughout, with all senior school students having their own laptop.

Games, options, the arts: Wide range of opportunity for games. 'Rugby is strong, though no longer a religion' (73 blues to date). Needle matches with Glenalmond and Merchiston on the rugby field and Strathallan in hockey. Lacrosse impressive, girls play hockey and netball as well; sixth form not forced to play team games at all – 20+ other sports including swimming and aerobics also available. Big sports centre and swimming pool providing a wide range of other sports, old pool now an exam hall/ceilidh and disco area.

Music 'a huge strength' with loads of bands, orchestras, three choirs and a string quartet etc etc, two popular concerts in spring and autumn plus carol service all in aid of charity. Keen drama with imaginative productions, pupils often perform at the Edinburgh Festival (and win awards). Frankenstein the most recent production with over 100 pupils involved. New art centre in pipeline (still) and 'very inspirational head of art' (another one, if you follow) recently appointed. Pipe band popular. CCF, community service, D of E etc. Masses of trips, everywhere, for everything.

Background and atmosphere: William Fettes (later Sir William), the son of an Edinburgh grocer, made his fortune during the Napoleonic Wars when 'he became Scotland's leading contractor for provisions for the army'; his only son died in 1815, and William in 1836. Whilst he had originally intended to found a hospital, he later 'decided to create a school for orphans and the needy'; and – after prudent investment – the trustees decided that with £166,000 in the kitty, there were enough funds to acquire land, and both build and endow a school: Fettes opened in 1870 with 200 boys.

Vast Grimms' fairy-tale of a building, turreted and with acres of wood panelling and shiny black floors (are they granite or stone flag underneath the tarry surface?) purpose-built in 1870 by Bryce. Part of the main building still has the original steam-driven heating which starts up twice a day with alarming groans and wheezes – ripe for the engineering museum methinks.

Various Victorian edifices scattered about the school's wonderful 90 acre grounds plonk in the middle of Edinburgh. 'School uses Edinburgh much more now,' says the head. Spectacular development after school sold 'redundant' acres to build Fettes Village, a collection of neat little boxes which splits the games field and provided the cash for much-needed expansion. The collection of new and converted buildings that house the new prep department are much bigger than they look from the outside, an example of space well used, and about to be extended. New posho boarding house – Craigleith, dead modern – to accommodate the expanded sixth form which is due to increase by 25 per cent. The sixth form centre houses 125 upper sixth pupils in two identical wings (surely this should be 126 or 124?) each with their own individual room and provides a transition between the disciplines of school and uni with pupils being able to cook their own meals if they want to.

The school has gradually metamorphosed from famous trad boys' school to genuinely co-ed. The flavour has changed from home-grown Scots to more exotic (school says ' 75 per cent UK, 15 per cent British ex-pats, 10 per cent foreign nationals with over 40 countries represented in this').

Pastoral care and discipline: Despite colourful stories in the Edinburgh press in past years – drugs, booze, etc, grossly overstated, says the head – there is a clear framework of discipline that is well understood by all. This is a school with a zero tolerance policy on drugs. Edinburgh is the drugs capital of the north and running a school in the middle of it is no joke. Under-age drinking is an acknowledged problem. Three tier system on the discipline side: housemaster/deputy head/head = rustication/formal warning and suspension or expulsion. Ditto smoking. Very clear house-visiting rules – no overt demonstrations of affection; bonking equals out. And yes, they do lose the occasional pupil for all these misdemeanours, ditto bullying. Strong anti-bullying ethos. Prefects very responsible – imaginative anti-bullying code involves culprits writing down what they must or must not do and signing it. Expulsion is always an option.

Pupils and parents: School topped up with many non-Brits in the bad old days, now the mix is veering more towards the British norm but still collections of exotic foreigners – Russians, Chinese, Japanese, Americans, Ukrainians, but fewer Bulgarians than previously. Increasing numbers of locals and Scots from all over. 'Pupils from 40 different countries, East European connection sadly dropping off.' Very strong old Fettesian stream, plus loads of first-time buyers, intellectuals etc etc. Good vibrant mix. Old Fettesians include John de Chastelaine, Ian McLeod, James Bond, Tilda Swinton, Lord Woolf and Tony Blair – remembered fondly for 'his acting ability'!

Entrance: CE or school's own exam for those not coming from UK preps. Approx 40 students a year join the sixth form after GCSE elsewhere, currently much sought after as pupils pile in from other, mainly Scottish, schools.

Exit: Hardly any leave post GCSE. Most to university – 2013 popular destinations include Bristol, Glasgow, Edinburgh, Leeds, Oxford and St Andrews to study eg engineering, English, maths or law.

Money matters: Well-endowed with scholarships including academic, music, sports, all-rounder, piping, art, up to 10 per cent of fees. Also means-tested bursaries: 'The level of these awards depend upon parents' financial means and can cover up to the full value of the fees'.

Special (Todd) bursaries for Old Fettesians, 12.5 per cent discount for Forces (not so many of these around). However risks being stripped of charitable status by the Scottish Charity Regulator if it does not make fees more affordable for lower income families.

Remarks: Undoubtedly the strongest school in Edinburgh – possibly riding too high? To quote one governor, 'It is better to have a challenge, otherwise we become complacent'. Head adds, 'No danger of becoming complacent; the most dangerous thing in a school is to stand still.' Exciting cosmopolitan mix in an exciting city.

Fine Arts College Hampstead

England's Lane, London, NW3 4YD

- Pupils: 140 boys and girls • Ages: 14–19 • Non-denom
- Fees: GCSE £17,685; A level £17,625 pa • Independent

Tel: 020 7586 0312
Email: mail@hampsteadfinearts.com
Website: www.hampsteadfinearts.com

Joint principals: Nicholas Cochrane and Candida Cave (50s). Both studied at the Ruskin School of Drawing and Fine Art, Oxford. Cochrane then went on to work for the Old Masters Department at Christies. The pair started teaching at a tutorial college and found 'we were quite good at inspiring people'. The decision to set up a college of their own was something that just 'came about', but clearly had a market, and has grown steadily ever since. Nicholas Cochrane teaches fine art, while continuing to exhibit with The Royal Society of Portrait Painters. (In 1999 he won the Prince of Wales's Award for Portrait Drawing.) Candida Cave, too, remains a practising painter and playwright, while teaching art history. Parents and pupils are great fans of their warm and relaxed approach. 'Candida Cave is what all parents dream of in a teacher, but think they'll never meet,' said one. 'She's imaginative and nurturing, but not a push over. My daughter just fell in love with her.'

Academic matters: A very broad, almost exclusively, arts-based curriculum (no science in the sixth form, though a few mathematicians). The visual arts remain, as one might expect, exceptionally popular. Photography is the number one subject choice (80 students this year) but also large numbers for fine art and art history, English literature, textiles, graphic design, film studies and media studies. The fine arts approach provides a strong traditional grounding (from classical busts and life models), which leaves many students with strong enough technical skills to bypass foundation courses. (The college also runs a two-term post a level portfolio course, to ensure preparation for art degrees and art college is tip-top). An extensive curriculum (29 subjects in all) of liberal arts, social sciences, modern languages (French, Spanish and Italian), and classical studies (Latin, Greek, ancient history and classical civilisation), can be taken in virtually any combination. Strong results overall (36 per cent A*/A and 69 per cent A*/B in 2013), with English and fine art particularly stellar. Exceptionally high 'valued added' between GCSE and A Level (fourth highest in the country) produced by caring teaching in small groups (classes never exceed nine).

'My daughter had failed spectacularly at two fee-paying schools,' says one appreciative mother of a daughter now at a Russell Group university. 'She thought she was a dunce until they took her under their wing. They produced an incredible turn around and she went from Cs to As.' Since 1994, the college has also offered GCSE, with two year groups of about 20 in all. 'We find there's a real need in year 10,' says Candida Cave, 'particularly when schools start saying, you should drop this or that.' GCSE subjects include biology and some physics but probably not the place for nascent medics. In 2013, 48 per cent A*/A grades. Staff long-serving and enthusiastic (including three ex-students and Candida Cave's daughter), with a fair proportion who also have alternative lives as professional artists, film makers, etc. Teaching style relaxed but enthusiastic; student style, co-operative competition. 'It's very much teaching in discussion, they want to impress each other in a nice way,' says Candida Cave. Good information given to parents and pupils about progress, with fortnightly reports and two parents' evenings. Rated outstanding by Ofsted in latest report.

Games, options, the arts: Plenty of opportunity to display talent, with an annual art exhibition, music and drama recital, and short films shown at the local Everyman Cinema. (One girl was recently runner-up for the Young Film Critic Award at Bafta). Loads of outside speakers and cultural outings, with annual study trips to Florence, Paris and Venice. Not at all a hierarchical place, and students organise their own entertainment – 'a certain number tend to take the lead each year' – including charitable fund-raising (for Breast Cancer awareness, the Red Cross, a local hospice) and other social events. Certainly not the ideal environment for the sporty (and few here care) but GCSE students have fencing lessons plus PE at a local sports centre and the College's long-standing football team plays against other sixth-form colleges. Popular table tennis, too, on site.

Background and atmosphere: Started in 1978 in the YMCA in Tottenham Court Road, teaching art and art history. 'We started because there wasn't anyone else specialising in the arts,' says Candida Cave. Moved to Belsize Park in 1982, and then, in 2002, added a converted Victorian dairy, which now forms the hub of the school, providing rambling lateral space around a cobbled courtyard. A good mix of classrooms (some more spacious than others) and excellent studio space, for art, drama, photography (with its own darkroom for traditional-style printing) and media studies. The atmosphere is intentionally informal and teachers are called by their first names. 'The college was very much founded as a bridge between school and university. Many students come here because they're looking for something more flexible.' Students congregate in the common room, where free coffee is on offer, but no food supplied on site. Some bring sandwiches, the majority visit the multitude of local eateries. Dress code vaguely artistic and bohemian (the odd fur gilet and extreme make up, the majority in UGGs and tracksuits), but kept well within limits. 'If it offends, we tell them to dress properly. It's just common sense.'

Pastoral care and discipline: 'What we liked about the college,' said one parent, 'is the industrious informality. They take the job seriously, but don't wear it too formally.' Pupils' work and well-being is immaculately monitored. Everyone has a personal tutor, whom they see for an hour and a half each week. The tutor goes through reports, helps with essay-writing and advises on university applications. All GCSE pupils sign in at 9 and again at 1.30. If pupils are not in class an email is sent to parents within half an hour. 'Pupils turn up because they want to,' said one parent. 'But, equally, they know that if they can't be bothered to turn up, the attitude will be, don't bother to come back.' Most have no problems with this. 'I've never been to a school before where all the other pupils want to learn,' said one boy. Students sign a contract of behaviour, so know exactly what is expected, and misbehaviour, social or academic, is followed by an oral warning, a written warning, and then a parental meeting. 'We've not excluded someone for eight to nine years, and not even suspended anyone for a long time,' says Candida Cave. 'We're run here on mutual respect and they do seem to rise to that.' Most see the college as a place where they can be confident concerns will be dealt with quickly and in confidence. Definitely a haven for those for whom more boisterous or insensitive environments have just not worked. 'The college made my daughter believe in herself. I feel I owe them,' said one parent.

Pupils and parents: A mix of mostly local professional/artistic families, who tend to be profoundly relieved that their children have found such a civilised and creative niche. Some of those who come to do GCSEs have previously been educated abroad. Others have had enough of boarding school, or failed to fit into more conventional schools. Alumni include Orlando Bloom and Helena Bonham-Carter.

Entrance: All applicants are interviewed with their parents and the college makes offers based on two criteria: candidates 'really want to be here' and 'they intend to go on to higher education'. Minimum five GCSEs with C or above, but this liberal benchmark is generally well exceeded, not a few arriving garlanded with a multitude of A*s. Most from local independents and leading boarding schools, a few from the state sector and schools further afield.

Exit: A generous sprinkling into every permutation of arts and media – from film studies and fine art to fashion retailing and creative writing – but also to marine biology and international relations. One to Oxford in 2013 to study English; Leeds and Birmingham popular destinations.

Money matters: One scholarship of 100 per cent (based on academic merit, a statement of why they deserve a scholarship, and an interview). Two of 25 per cent may be given for outstanding exam performance at GCSE ('We wanted to show we appreciated their intelligence.') A limited number of bursaries awarded to students who have previously been educated in the state system who would not otherwise be able to afford private education.

Remarks: A low-key, calm and friendly place, with strong teaching and results, particularly in the arts. Ideal for the 'arty, urban misfit' who has wilted in a more conventional environment.

Forest School

Linked school: Forest Preparatory School

College Place, London, E17 3PY

• Pupils: 750 • Ages: 11–18 • Anglican Foundation • Fees: Prep £10,200–£11,829; Senior £15,081 pa • Independent

---

Tel: 020 8520 1744
Email: info@forest.org.uk
Website: www.forest.org.uk

Warden: Since 2009, Mrs Sarah Kerr-Dineen MA. Read English at Cambridge followed by postgraduate study at Oxford and NPQH. Taught at Open University, Kelly College, Oxford High School (where she was an acting subject head) and St Edward's Oxford (where she was housemistress and responsible for the pastoral care of 80 girls, then director of studies). Senior leadership team of about eight. Sees herself as 'a teacher, not a CEO', and despite the school's size, treats her job as if she was 'running a small school and knowing every pupil', believing that the 'way to keep a school from becoming impersonal is to keep units of care small'. Nevertheless, as warden she is strategic in approach to building this 'happy school': you 'set a vision but then look at how to express that at every stage – there's no point saying you have a vision to be one thing and then not doing anything to live up to it'. She still teaches, including all the year 7s, has pupils to lunch weekly and the youngest pupils are invited to come to the house where 'they learn to appreciate the significance of the school's history.' Parents say, 'It's a very well run school' and describe its leadership as 'first rate'.

Academic matters: 'Both of my daughters are scholars,' said one very pleased parent. Single-sex teaching in this co-educational environment 'creates a study environment that boys and girls feel comfortable with and which enables them to achieve their best', says school. Teachers are committed, about a third of them have been here more than 10 years and all of them are specialists in their subjects; also large number part time eg music, drama and dance specialists. Most pupils are of above average ability. They do well across the board, notably in English, history, geography, maths and the sciences. From year 8, some setting occurs for maths, English, MFLs and science. There is a free choice from French, German and Spanish. Latin is taught to all pupils during the first two years, then it becomes a GCSE option along with ancient Greek.

In 2013, 50 per cent A*/As at GCSE, and 71 per cent at A level. Extended projects, which allow GCSE and A level students to flex their academic muscles beyond the norm, are popular. With topics and titles such as 'A legal definition of torture' and 'Love and the Adversary' (a treatise on the representation of Satan in English literature), pupils demonstrate their capacity for critical thought.

Courses in both the boys' and girls' schools run broadly in line with the national curriculum. This leads some parents to make the same complaint heard of state schools, that lessons can have 'too much focus on teaching for success in the sometimes dull GCSE syllabus rather than to wider lateral thought ... but I think this is what happens everywhere'. Hence, by and large, parents also prize the school for its 'good academic expectations but not [being] too pushy'. As one parent echoed, 'I don't consider that [my daughters] are always adequately stretched, but the humanities and arts subjects appear to be particularly well taught', adding that they had turned down places at more academic schools in favour of Forest's 'more balanced experience'. '

The number of academic challenges, competitions, tournaments and Olympiads these pupils enter is dizzying: maths challenges, chemistry masterminds, physics olympiads, and even the informatics olympiad – where pupils have competed in Thailand against the best young computer scientists in the world.

Trips to eg the Battlefields, Munich (history), Devon (geography), China, Russia, Japan oand the USA.

Majority of pupils stay on at sixth form where courses include classical civilisation, government and politics (with visits to key places in London, Washington DC and New York, and supported by guest speakers such as Iain Duncan Smith, John Bercow, George Galloway and Nigel Farage), philosophy (a popular university choice) and economics. The A level economics department has links with the City of London, the Economics Association and Institute of Economic Affairs.

Extra support for those who need it; school publishes an excellent guide to independent study to help struggling pupils find their own answers or at the very least to formulate thoughtful and clear questions before asking for help.

Games, options, the arts: You will find them all here: aerobics, basketball, cricket, even fencing. Extensive playing fields, netball and tennis courts, various pitches, a sports centre housing two heated swimming pools, cricket nets and a fitness suite. At sixth form, PE covers sports psychology, history and exercise physiology. Pupils can try out other sports eg karate, cross-country and golf during activities afternoons and house matches. Several record achievements gained at county, regional and national level in netball, rounders, hockey, tennis, badminton and athletics.

A large (one of the largest in London) and busy music department with over 700 instrumental and vocal lessons a week. Every pupil has the opportunity to try out an instrument free of charge and pupils are encouraged to take the lead in musical activities, often leading to specialisms. With seven orchestras, 10 bands, 14 choirs and more than 40 specialist teachers, numerous opportunities to perform. School is extensively equipped with practice, recital and technology rooms. On the day of our visit one of the bands was preparing for a lunch time concert in the chapel, the norm at this school that presents more than 80 concerts and other performances a year both in and out of the school. Tours take place in the UK, Spain, Italy, Netherlands and France and the school regularly sends pupils to major conservatoires. Regular choral and organ scholarships to Oxford and Cambridge.

Drama and art also taken seriously. The purpose-built Deaton Theatre seats 350 and has state-of-the-art lighting and sound equipment. Pupils act in large-scale productions and learn design or technical skills. As part of the house drama competition, they can select, cast and direct their own productions. A long tradition of excellence in drama with present and past pupils making successful careers in this area (the West End show Stomp was founded by former pupils) and pupils have been involved in many well known television and theatre productions, including East Enders and The Bleak Old Shop of Stuff for the BBC, and a West End production of Oliver! Art and design studios are well-resourced and pupils allowed to develop their passion outside classroom learning hours.

Co-curricular opportunities in sport, music, drama, dance and visual arts. CCF linked to the Royal Green Jackets offers field days, annual camps and weekly training. The Duke of Edinburgh Award is popular. Other opportunities include student-led societies, video production, languages, musical theatre, and journalism. Pupils also take part in raising money for charity, in public speaking competitions, and community work such as visiting the elderly and riding for the disabled.

Background and atmosphere: Old and new exist side by side here. It is close to the bustling City of London and yet surrounded by the quietness of ancient forest. The St John the Baptist chapel, where pupils regularly congregate for services and other events, is at the heart of the school and reminiscent of a history that goes back to 1834 when it began with just 22 pupils. Although Anglican in tradition, the outlook is ecumenical to cater to the broad range of backgrounds, faiths and cultures. Pupils enjoy this and say 'It is good to have the school come together and talk about different faiths.' Alongside the old, are new buildings like the Sylvestrian Leisure Centre, built with the aid of a 'buy a brick' fund-raiser organised by the parents' association, used by the public at weekends and was a quiet camp for Team GB during the 2012 London Olympics, and the Martin Centre for Innovation, with digital teaching and learning facilities for the whole school.

Pastoral care and discipline: Form and house groups, headed by a housemistress or master, provide a sense of belonging and stability. Because classes are small, community atmosphere is strong; 'pupils are well known individually by the staff,' say parents. Pastoral care gives each child 'the support they need to progress socially, morally and academically'. Housemasters and mistresses stay with a child through his or her time at the school and are there to advise on any aspect of school life. This continues at sixth form. Pupils are allocated a tutor who oversees academic progress, helps with university applications, and advises on careers.

There is heavy emphasis on the code of conduct in the school prospectus: 'all observed behaviour, which indicates a lack of mutual regard, will be fully investigated', 'the school stands firmly against any form of verbal or physical bullying or any behaviour which is intended to cause distress to pupils', and the 'Warden may require the permanent exclusion of a pupil if, in her opinion, it is in the interest of the pupil of the school community'. Approach is good lines of communication. 'Children are encouraged to talk and are listened to' and to report incidents of bullying to an appropriate person, says school. 'Where bullying is detected, we acknowledge our responsibility to support both the bully and the victim'.

Parents say, 'Bullying – the school deals with this very well'. Others say 'We hear mixed things about how long it takes the school to home in and deal with these issues; but no direct experience'. Most say their children learn 'in a secure, supportive and encouraging environment'. 'The children know they are lucky but they don't see themselves as special', warden says. 'If children are not happy they won't learn, get that right and the grades will come.'

The best thing about being at the school, said a pupil, is the 'diversity, I like the mix, staff are kind, they encourage you to do the best you can do.'

Pupils and parents: A diverse ethnic mix. They come from the surrounding east and north London and Essex areas. Most are the children of professional parents and no-one speaks English as a second language. Past pupils include actor Ian Beale and cricketer Nasser Hussain.

Entrance: Most from the prep move to the senior school at 11, joined by a large number from other state and private schools (English and maths tests). Variable numbers admitted at 13+ depending on spaces.

Exit: Nearly all to university, including six to Oxbridge in 2013.

Money matters: Bursaries and scholarships – academic and music awards at 11+, academic, music and sports at 13, academic, art, music, drama and sports at 16.

Remarks: A happy school with committed staff, and pupils who clearly display a strong sense of independence and enjoyment of school life. While remaining true to its traditional roots, this is a forward-thinking school, humane and open-minded, with both feet on the ground. Its clear grasp of the rich inter-relationship between the curricular, the co-curricular and the pastoral ensures children do well.

Fortismere School

Linked school: Blanche Nevile School

South Wing, Tetherdown, London, N10 1NE

• Pupils: 1,700 boys and girls; all day • Ages: 11–19 • Non denom
• State

Tel: 020 8365 4400
Email: office@fortismere.org.uk
Website: www.fortismere.haringey.sch.uk

Headteacher: Since 2010, Mrs Helen Anthony BA MA PGCE (forties), previously head since 2006 of Central Technology College in Gloucestershire. Studied English at Liverpool and Keele, PGCE at King's College London. Had a number of teaching and leadership roles in London and Gloucestershire before joining Central Technology College, which was then one of the roughest boys' schools in the country. She brought it back from the brink of closure and transformed its rating to 'good' (Ofsted talked of a 'remarkable journey').

She has imported to very middle class Fortismere some of the tactics that had wrought improvements in her previous setting, such as a hard line on punctuality, attendance and litter. She clearly has a steely determination and is evidently not a head to be trifled with, though on our tour a pupil did not hesitate to buttonhole her to check she had signed a form for him. 'very hard working and ambitious,' say parents. Mother of two daughters.

Academic matters: A large proportion of bright, motivated pupils and also a greater than average number of pupils with SEN, with a relatively small mid range. In 2013, 39 per cent A*/A grades at A level, with 71 per cent A*/B. Similarly strong at GCSE: 50 per cent A*/A grades, and 81 per cent of pupils got 5+ A*-C grades, including English and maths.

The previous head had introduced setting for every subject from year 7; this has been loosened, but school still sets early for maths and science, whilst English is taught in mixed ability classes. 'I trust my faculty heads on that, but they must show that it works.' Relatively low class size of 24.

Everyone learns French or Spanish in year 7 and promising linguists are offered Mandarin or German in year 8. They are encouraged to take two languages to GCSE; around 80 per cent of pupils take at least one. The top 60 per cent are encouraged to take triple science GCSE.

Teaching standards mostly very high with the odd exception, say parents. 'They expect of lot of the students – I think they push them very hard. They encourage and extend them, particularly with the personal projects in the sixth form.'

Reporting system to parents 'has improved. They tell you what your child's target is, what level they're performing at now and whether that's okay. I've mostly found teachers very responsive when I've emailed them.'

The sixth form admissions criteria are 'closer to a grammar school', with at least five B grades at GCSE required for A level, and As for certain subjects eg maths. The small number of vocational options, with five C grades at GCSE as a boundary, include music technology, ICT, business, media and sports science. School also teaches classical heritage and global perspectives Pre-U courses.

Maths a very popular A level, alongside history (teaching dubbed 'exceptional' by parents) and English. Respectable numbers pursuing biology and chemistry, and – as one might expect in this liberal, intellectual area – philosophy, psychology, government and politics and sociology, though linguists disappointingly few.

'Amazing' preparation for Oxford, said a parent. 'It was all very low key, but there are several young Oxbridge graduates teaching at the school, and they ran workshops, put on seminars, did mock interviews, and put pupils in touch with other students who'd been through the process recently. It was all there, but it was up to the kids to push themselves that much further.'

With its large, segmented site and high pupil numbers, possibly not the most suitable school for children with learning difficulties, but many choose it nonetheless, 'and we do a very good job with them'. Those with statements – and there are a relatively large proportion of these, mostly with autistic spectrum and behavioural issues – have their own teaching assistant. However, 'we try to keep away from TAs velcroed to children', and they are included in class work as far as possible, with small group sessions to help them develop independent learning skills. Linc team helps those experiencing learning difficulties – temporary or permanent. The secondary department of the Blanche Nevile School for deaf and hearing-impaired children occupies an impressive building on the site. Some of its pupils join in the main school activities.

Games, options, the arts: Fabulous new music block, with recording studios, composing and practice rooms, plus multi-use performance spaces, mirrors the importance of the subject here (though few take it to A level). Symphony orchestra, big band and several choirs; community choirs and orchestras include parents as well as children; hosts Saturday music school. 'We play a key role in the local community.' Head doesn't envisage the abolition of music aptitude places having any effect on the quality of music-making in the school. 'We have always had a lot of hugely musical students – it comes with the parent body.'

Impressive displays of art and fabulous photography coursework around the school on our visit, plus bright papier mâché aliens and rats created by younger year groups. Photography a popular A level and one can see why. Drama also 'massive'. 'We're a very artsy school. It's our natural default setting.' 'Fantastic' production of Little Shop of Horrors included the actual plant from the West End show; sixth formers regularly take productions to the Edinburgh fringe, and help with GCSE drama performances.

Sports stars used to hone their talents largely outside school, but sport has been bolstered by increased amounts of time in the upper years plus the introduction of Colleges, or houses, which run weekly inter-college competitions and encourage non A team players to get involved. However, parents report that it is possible for the less athletically inclined to avoid breaking into a sweat, and it is fair to say that reports of sports team triumphs do not feature largely in school newsletters. Sports hall, tennis/netball/basketball courts, acres of playing fields and 'very popular' table tennis tables. The head would dearly like the renovation of the 'stagnant' disused swimming pool to be her legacy, but financial constraints seem likely to stymie this ambition.

Another innovation is whole school enrichment sessions every other Wednesday afternoon, with a choice of 87 activities from yoga to cooking to science. All the staff, including admin staff, are encouraged to join in. An assistant head who was a dancer in a previous life runs a tap dancing club; the head runs a Born to Teach? training course for year 12, which includes planning and teaching lessons in primary, secondary and special schools.

Large range of trips includes 'brilliant and very well organised' week in Beijing for Mandarin speakers, exchange visits to France, Spain, Germany, Senegal and India ('though you do have to queue up at 7am with your cheque to get a place on the popular ones,' commented a parent), D of E, outdoor pursuits in the Brecon Beacons, ski trips, field trips and cultural visits. A steady stream of authors, scientists, politicians etc comes to give talks; librarian organises team of pupils to shadow Carnegie medal deliberations, reading and reviewing shortlisted books; teams enter debating competitions.

Background and atmosphere: Large site amidst leafy Muswell Hill Edwardiana has been the setting for a series of schools of all sorts, including private, state grammar and comprehensive. Fortismere was formed in 1983 by the amalgamation of Creighton and Alexandra Park Schools (another Alexandra Park School has since opened nearby). Site includes a hotch-potch of buildings from its various incarnations. North and South Wings linked by a quarter-mile pathway round the playing fields that can resemble a storm in the North Sea in inclement weather. Accommodation beginning to show its age, but bright and cheerful. Head has encouraged a multitude of notice boards – with college news, photos of trips, information on clubs.

Very much a community comprehensive with a relaxed atmosphere (subject to 'behaviour for learning' sanctions), and pupils strolling around in jeans and tee shirts. 'Proudly non-uniform', though with a veto on revealing too much skin or underwear. 'It's part of the ethos for children to be able to express themselves,' said a parent.

Pastoral care and discipline: Good transition system, with year 6s spending three days at the school in the summer term getting to know the site and teachers. Has recently introduced vertical tutor system, with 18 pupils of different ages from the same college in each group replacing old form tutor system. All staff – including admin staff – are tutors, 'which enables us to have small groups, and also increases student respect for non-teaching staff'. Mixed reviews from parents and pupils, some enthusiastic whilst others feel that the system needs time to bed in and become a tradition, and that they would prefer to spend the time with their peers.

Student leadership team, which includes head boy and girl and their deputies, has a meeting with the head each Monday. 'It has already had a real impact. They really challenge us about why we do things, and it makes me think about structures.'

Head's introduction of zero tolerance for lateness and absenteeism has shocked some families and delighted others,

with one parent terming it 'draconian.' 'The behaviour here was good, but I thought it could be better,' says the head. 'If you are disrupting the learning of others, that is not negotiable. Parents complain, but when I tell them their child is stopping other people learning, they find that hard to justify.' She refuses permission for holidays in term time: 'We get a lot of poorly relatives in far flung places towards the end of the Christmas and summer terms.' In response to pupils' requests for carrots as well as sticks, Vivo system gives house points for helpfulness, participation, tidiness etc and is widely reported in the newsletters.

Pupils mostly very happy and have good relationships with staff, but some parents feel that the pastoral system is variable. Some teachers 'do resolve your issues,' said a parent, citing the 'novel and interesting solutions' to stress suggested by her daughter's college head. However, 'I had a very unsympathetic reaction from the school to a family death. I found their policies very inflexible.' 'They didn't seem to be sensitive to the needs of my younger daughter,' said another parent, whose children had joined from a different education system. 'I really didn't feel she got the support she needed, and I felt that no-one had an overview of the situation. I also had no response to a very carefully worded email about a pastoral issue that had upset her.'

Permanent exclusions rare, and usually for persistent defiance or repeated breaking of behaviour policies. Will swap recalcitrant pupils with other local schools. 'We're good at managed moves – they can be very effective.' Will also use outside providers such as local boxing and football academies for those who clearly need a different approach. 'We prefer to try something different before moving to permanent exclusion.' A parent commented: 'There are some wild and woolly kids, but they don't tend to disrupt classes.'

Pupils and parents: Largely affluent, liberal, middle class families – artists and musicians, writer and actors – plus quite a few looked-after children. 'It is a very political school. I have to remember that parents don't just read the Guardian – quite likely they write for it too,' says the head. These are mostly cool kids, relaxed and confident, proud to be at Haringey's most popular comprehensive. 'My daughters' friends are lovely,' said a parent. 'They meet up to study and all help each other.' Ex-pupils include soul singer Michael Kiwanuka.

Entrance: Takes 243 pupils into year 7. Those with an SEN statement naming the school – and there are many of these – will automatically get a place. Then priority to children in care, those with particular medical, social or emotional needs, and siblings, with the remainder by distance, usually less than half a mile.

Takes 110 or so outside students into the sixth form, from state and independent schools. Requires 5+ A*-C GCSEs for vocational A levels and 5+ A*-Bs for academic A levels, with higher grades for certain subjects eg maths, from internal and external students. Those who don't get at least three D grades at AS are liable to be directed elsewhere.

Exit: Small numbers move on after GCSEs, generally for more vocational courses elsewhere. Nearly all sixth form leavers to university: Sussex, Leeds, Manchester and Bristol the flavour of the moment; 10 to Oxbridge in 2013 and six medics. English, philosophy, psychology, maths, law, geography all popular.

Money matters: Very active parents' association, the FSA, which underwrote the refurbishment of the sixth form centre.

Remarks: A popular and high-achieving comprehensive that successfully includes those with difficulties as well as extending the most able. Head's vision is for it to have 'an active mind, a finger on the pulse and a big heart.'

Framlingham College

Linked school: Brandeston Hall Preparatory School

College Road, Framlingham, Woodbridge, Suffolk, IP13 9EY

• Pupils: 245 boys, 175 girls; 240 boarders, 175 day pupils • Ages: 13-18 • C of E-inter-denom • Fees: Boarding £27,029; Day £17,373 pa • Independent

Tel: 01728 723789
Email: admissions@framcollege.co.uk
Website: www.framcollege.co.uk

Headmaster: Since 2009, Mr Paul Taylor BA. Read history and politics at Exeter University. Formerly lower master (deputy head) at King's School, Canterbury, and before that director of sport at Tonbridge School. Very friendly, charming without overdoing it and a good listener. Aims to 'produce a decent, rounded human being who looks you in the eye' and believes the school's good performance should be better known outside East Anglia. Wife, Amanda, is secretary of the Framlingham Society and they have four children – two at university and two at Framlingham.

Academic matters: Performs well at both GCSE and A level, though not highly selective – strong commitment to pupils of varying ability. In 2013, 62 per cent of A levels were A*-B and 36 per cent A*/A. At GCSE, 46 per cent A*/A grades.

SEN provision well established. Emphasis on supporting the pupils' needs – a register (updated termly) is kept to inform staff across the curriculum of any difficulties. Timetabled access to small group and individual tuition avoids pupil withdrawal from mainstream classes. All pupils must be capable of following the academic programmes at GCSE and A level. Provision for ESL also excellent – separate classes as well as individual tuition. Facilities well thought out, well designed and un-flashy. Exceptional library and design and technology building. Classes kept small, average size 12.

Games, options, the arts: Excellent provision for all sports. Artificial surfaces, new indoor pool and fitness centre (well used, especially by girls) – hosts many tournaments. Sport is important – all pupils take part competitively, whatever their level of ability. Music and drama popular too. Brand new theatre/performance studio and many pupils take drama options at GCSE and A level. Well attended regular public performances – pupils recently took The Importance of Being Earnest to the Edinburgh Fringe. Concerts held in local churches – Framlingham and Orford, as well as Ely Cathedral. Big takeup for D of E, with numbers reaching gold awards. Curriculum also supported by extraordinary plethora of clubs and activities.

Background and atmosphere: Founded in 1864 in memory of Prince Albert, Queen Victoria's husband (his statue takes pride of place at the front of the school). Imposing Victorian main building in stunning setting, perched on a hillside with a gorgeous view across the valley to 12th century Framlingham Castle. A variety of buildings added over time, none of them particularly distinguished, but well planned to make good use of beautiful and extensive grounds. Stupendous view of the castle from many perspectives (head has bagged dress circle view from his first floor study).

A tone of respectful informality throughout. Pupils well-mannered and noticeably calm, even at lesson changes and in the dining hall at lunchtime. Boarding houses well planned and comfortable enough, though girls' quarters, unsurprisingly perhaps, are more home-like and with better decoration. Pupils come and go with their own swipe card; most go home at weekends, unless from abroad.

Pastoral care and discipline: Policy of incorporating day pupils into boarding houses is now well established and a great success. Many pupils do 'occasional' boarding. A parent told us: 'I can email the housemaster directly if my daughter wants to board at short notice – on the same day on occasion.' Anti-bullying posters dotted around school and any incidents picked up on quickly. 'The housemaster got to the bottom of the matter on the same day,' said one parent, 'and the boys are still together in the same house.'

Keeping sixth formers in the house system creates opportunities for leadership. As a relief from house responsibilities, sixth formers have their own common room and social areas – plans afoot to create a technologically sophisticated sixth form centre. The school's 150th anniversary in 2014 is a launch pad for this and other initiatives. The head rightly lauds excellent pastoral track record but emphasises that 'the family is more important. Schools can over-claim for themselves'.

Pupils and parents: Pupils are mainly drawn from middle class East Anglian families. In some cases, several generations have attended the school. A strong body from abroad, notably Germany and the Far East. Head sees the school as poised to appeal as much to the Oundle and Uppingham market as to its Norfolk and Suffolk constituency. Excellent reputation locally and no problems recruiting.

Entrance: At 13, pupils from Brandeston Hall, Framlingham's linked preparatory, accepted 'on the nod' – assuming they can cope with the academic rigour of the college. CE and interview for everyone else, though tests in core subjects (English, maths and non-verbal reasoning) can be arranged for pupils from schools that don't do CE. The interview is key and head also takes prospective pupils' school reports seriously.

Significant numbers enter after GCSE, with places offered conditionally on the basis of an interview, school report and a minimum achievement of seven A*-C passes at GCSE/IGCSE or equivalent. Overseas candidates also sit tests in English and maths.

Exit: Almost all go to university, with traditional universities well represented. Head is aware of need to identify and support Oxbridge potential early – one off there to study medicine in 2013. The place of careers advice is stressed – he believes it should be seen as separate from the university application process. Parents rely on the school as an expert resource.

Money matters: A range of scholarships awarded for outstanding academic, musical, artistic and sporting excellence at 13+ and 16+. Further means-tested bursarial help is available as needed. Reductions for siblings and Forces families.

Remarks: A well run, unstressful school, with happy pupils and high levels of achievement in all areas.

Francis Holland School, Regent's Park

Clarence Gate, Ivor Place, London, NW1 6XR

- Pupils: 450 girls, all day • Ages: 11–18 • C of E • Fees: £15,810 pa
- Independent

Tel: 020 7723 0176
Email: admin@fhs-nw1.org.uk
Website: www.fhs-nw1.org.uk

Headmistress: Since 2004, Mrs Vivienne Durham MA (fifties). Prior to her arrival at Francis Holland, much-loved deputy head at South Hampstead High and had taught at Guildford High and Haberdashers' Girls, where she headed the English department. Deservedly one of the most popular heads in the business, loquacious, enthusiastic, fervent in her belief in 'education' rather than in specifically 'girls' education', highly articulate and jolly good fun. She is a people person writ large, but also a clever strategist and manager of resources. You want to give her your daughters and we spoke to no-one who regretted having done so. 'Mrs Durham is very caring, very switched-on and really nice to deal with,' vouchsafed one grateful mother, who spoke for many. The staff clearly love her too and the girls plainly see her as a role model. We could quote much of what she says but will settle for: 'I've never seen an online facility which could replace a good human being in the classroom'. She is infuriatingly svelte and chic and married to the former head of University College School.

Academic matters: Small classes – especially at A level – are an almost USP here. No class is bigger than 25 and, in the sixth, 14 max – many are far smaller. For a relatively small sixth form offers a creditable range of subjects including economics, history of art and psychology. Most popular subjects tend to be art, biology, English, history and maths; the best results in RS, politics, geography, history of art and art. Economics less strong. Theatre studies offered at A level though not at GCSE. Outstanding results in many subjects – 57 per cent A*/A in 2013. Extended project (worth half an A level) can be taken in addition to A levels and challenges the most able.

GCSEs and, increasingly, IGCSEs (81 per cent A*/A) also include a good number of options – most popular are history, art and geography. Wisely, allows girls to take either three separate sciences or double science – we approve.

SEN support is generally by withdrawal or out-of-lesson individual support. Most of those who receive help are mildly dyslexic/dyspraxic but additional support also for those perceived as G and T. Three-strong 'learning enhancement' team. 'We give girls extra support the entire time – it's simply part of what we offer,' says head, and parents concur, 'The girls can refer themselves for support and there's excellent liaison between the subject staff and the team'.

But the academic input here is far more than just good teaching. Weekly lectures by outside speakers open to all from year 9 up. Lots of trips hither and yon and good use made of privileged location and the proximity of the odd museum, House of Parliament, Bank of England or three.

Games, options, the arts: Minutes from Regent's Park, where most sports take place. Onsite is a tiny Astro playground – good for netball shooting practice but no more – but a good sized gym, fitness suite and, surprisingly, basement swimming pool, opened 1996, somewhat improbably, by Old Girl Joan Collins – swimming one of the more competitive sports. Sport compulsory for all, but lots of choice by the time you're in the sixth and Zumba is a recent, popular addition – along with yoga and the use of the fitness suite.

Art is exceptional here – lots of it lines the corridors and we felt inclined to snaffle some of the best pieces to hang at home: really attractive, skilful, imaginative work. Top floor now houses the two studios, plus kiln, dark room, and printing press; views over the grey slate, Georgian rooftops and grey, steel satellite dishes must inspire artistic freedom, as it clearly burns bright.

Music also housed up here, though you'd not imagine the few small rooms result in the level of skill and performance managed by the girls here. Seventy per cent learn at least one instrument. Orchestras, choirs – large and chamber – and other ensembles thrive and surprise. Annual concert with the boys of Harrow School is a highlight. Music and drama combine to produce major annual show, plus drama competition – these draw in most, one way or another, though more drama – especially in the upper years – would be appreciated by many. Young Enterprise and Duke of Edinburgh Award scheme both thrive, along with more than 70 clubs and activities.

Background and atmosphere: Founded by Canon Francis Holland in 1878 at the instigation of his wife, Mary Sibylla, an interesting woman, mother of six, who pushed for the education of 'girls from the middle and upper classes' and later converted to Roman Catholicism. The second school with Canon Holland's name was founded shortly after just off Sloane Square; the two schools still occupy their original sites and are run by the same foundation. Sibylla's letters were published by her children and make for touching reading.

Minutes from Baker Street and Regent's Park, the main building is a classic 1900s redbrick school – smallish classrooms, corridors, lots of floors and a wonderful hexagonal hall with three galleries and lots of polished wood. But the Tardis cliché really applies here. From the unassuming outside, you can't imagine how the school could accommodate more than a few dozen girls, but inside it goes on and on and has some surprisingly spacious areas. The library is also a decent size and has acquired a new area for computers in addition to the trad bookshelves and table space. Sofas and armchairs – we approve of that too. The stock is good, but some updating might inspire more to use books along with Google.

The hall – used for all major events – is not an ideal performance space but has extendable staging and clearly works. The acquisition of the adjacent Gloucester Arms pub and its consequent reopening in 2008 as the Gloucester Wing has been a major advance – Mrs Durham is on the lookout for a further property to enable further expansion, not in numbers but in facilities. Now possesses two good art studios, seminar rooms and a splendid, well-used lecture theatre. The old saloon bar is a useful space for drama work, charity activities and talks. School is an admirable mix of traditional and up to the minute – computer system renewed in 2011 and everyone now wired in and up, as you'd expect.

Right at the top is the sixth form area and it's super – lots of space, though it can get crowded at breaks – with a roof top garden, a workroom, silent study area and commonroom with cooking area, sofas and lockers. Staff allowed in to pop marked work etc into sensible pigeon holes. School is accessible – lift enables wheelchair-users to get almost everywhere, though some corridors and steps make odd corners impossible.

The food is 'the best in London' – certainly the salads were lusciously inviting, as were the plates of fruit – pomegranates, passion fruit and melon slices: drool! Kitchen staff clearly popular with sixth formers – 'They are so kind – they bring us up hot chocolate and muffins,' we were told, and that really is kind, as four flights of stairs are involved.

Pastoral care and discipline: Universal praise for the pastoral care – 'The school could not be more supportive'; 'The staff are incredibly sensitive and caring. They are firm when it's needed, but you are always supported,' parents told us again and again. 'The staff are inspiring – they are more than just academic: they look after the whole child,' is another theme'. Heads of year have overall responsibility and a counsellor visits weekly. Home and social difficulties – as anywhere – but few discipline problems; Mrs Durham the ultimate arbiter.

Backup for practical as well as emotional needs: 'The UCAS support here is amazingly impressive,' an Oxbridge hopeful told us. 'The school has been so on top of everything – you get at least three teachers helping, loads of sessions; our head of sixth is amazing and she makes us feel completely secure in how we approach our applications.'

'I want them to be confident and self-possessed but not trumpet about it,' asserts the head. 'We are absolutely about nurture. We are kind and academic. Kind is central.'

Pupils and parents: Interesting mix. Professional families from all over – hence the higher than usual incidence of relocating ins and outs that results in places appearing at odd stages: academics, medics, thesps and financiers, as you'd expect. The very rich – 'There are a few "princesses" in the sixth form,' muttered one or two parents – along with those who struggle to find the fees.

Notable Old Girls include Theresa Villiers, Joan and Jackie Collins, Tamara and Petra Ecclestone, Emilia Fox and Holly Branson.

Entrance: From over 170 preps and primaries. Majority from Pembridge House, Bute House, Sarum Hall, St Mary's, Hampstead, St Christopher's, Hampstead, St Christina's. Applications via the North London Consortium – exams in English and maths plus interviews. Oversubscribed of course, but as for many parents whose daughters also apply to the other powerhouses in the area the school, for all its virtues, is not always the first choice, a good chance of a place at 11+ if your daughter is able and would fit in. Location in central London means that relocating families come and go more than elsewhere and places often occur in other years – it is always worth a call.

At 16+ very few are taken – Mrs Durham has a sizeable sixth form and is not straining nerves to cram in more. Perhaps two to three places awarded to, perhaps, 20-30 applicants. A/Bs needed at GCSE.

Exit: Around 10 leave after GCSE and head for mixed sixth forms, notably Highgate – some come back. Mrs Durham is not the head to throw you out if you have problems or your GCSEs disappoint – 'We take them in at 11: we'll stick with them till 18'; also several families whose daughters have found refuge here from unhappiness elsewhere.

No identikit FH leaver – 2013 fledglings went everywhere including American universities, Bristol, Durham, Edinburgh, Leeds, LSE, UCL, as well as Oxford and Cambridge.

Money matters: A few bursaries and scholarships and worth enquiring, but, like most girls' day schools, not munificently endowed.

Remarks: Your clever daughter will be well taught and will do as well here as anywhere. Your shy and gentle soul will be loved and encouraged. Definitely no hothouse but a school that warms and nurtures. A gem in the heart of the metropolis.

Francis Holland School, Sloane Square

Linked school: Francis Holland Junior School, Sloane Square

39 Graham Terrace, London, SW1W 8JF

- Pupils: 315 girls, all day • Ages: 11-18 • C of E • Fees: £16,125 pa
- Independent

Tel: 020 7730 2971
Email: registrar@fhs-sw1.org.uk
Website: www.fhs-sw1.org.uk

Headmistress: Since September 2012, Mrs Lucy Elphinstone BA PGCE FRSA (fifties). Educated at Barnstaple Grammar School, Devon, and Newnham College, Cambridge (English). Started teaching after other careers – publishing, bookselling, counselling, hospitality, ghost-writing, property development (partner in building firm with husband). Wide teaching and leadership experience – from 3 to 18 years. Started educational career in Scotland – head of a Montessori pre-school, head of English and director of studies in two prep schools, director of drama at Fettes College, head of English at King's College, Taunton, head of sixth form and senior leader at Downe House. Four adult children. Keen on skiing, tennis, riding, singing, piano, theatre, reading, painting.

Her vision is 'to prepare young women for the challenges of the workplace in the coming decade by creating an environment which develops skills and character, not just academic ability'. Aims to develop girls' 'flexibility, initiative, creativity, enterprise, resilience, optimism and grit' by introducing more opportunities for service, fundraising, leadership, teamwork, invention, sport, learning about business, intellectual challenge (via Extended Project Qualification), studying with boys, debating and public speaking.

Academic matters: In 2013, 70 per cent A*/A grades at GCSE and 48 per cent at A level. Traditional teaching approach 'not for the unmotivated'. Many teachers on staff over 10 years but not fossilised – plenty of young too. Sympathetic to mild special educational needs but no specialist provision, although links with the Kensington dyslexia centre – 'We couldn't take anyone who was academically challenged'. Staff track individual pupils where help may be needed and parents are kept informed.

Won't be drawn on singling out any particularly strong subjects – 'It's a small school and therefore dependent on the girls in each year' – but looking at the last three years together, it's clear that French, Spanish and German are all strong and popular, English and maths are popular; five or so a year take sciences to A level. Latin and Greek offered to A level, with students keen to read classics at university. Will facilitate exams in languages for those who speak them (a number have, eg, Russian and Spanish as their mother tongue) but doesn't offer it as part of the timetable. Small class sizes – typical sixth form class is six to eight; further down school 15 the norm.

Games, options, the arts: Passionately committed ballet teacher who has been there forever; Princess Margaret competition held internally each year; lots of links with the Royal Ballet School. Music and drama also strong – regular concerts in St John's, Smith Square and choir trips to, eg, Prague and Venice. Strong emphasis on community work – girls recently raised over £10,000 auctioning, among other things, a Tracy Emin mug, to fund schools in Malawi and India. Closer to home they work with the elderly in a charitable settlement in Battersea.

The Duke of Westminster unveiled Carmel Hall, the school's new performing arts centre, formerly home to The Grosvenor

Club, a working men's club. It provides top notch music and drama facilities (including 10 music practice rooms) plus a stunning double-height performance space – a really major boost for the school.

Sport – netball, rounders, hockey, athletics – takes place mainly in Battersea Park (home of the annual sports day), but has the luxury of one netball court on site that doubles up as a playground for the junior school, also a well-equipped gym. Inter-house competitions in both sport and music.

Lovely, bright, airy library where the younger girls can be found curled up on beanbags reading. Lots of help and encouragement with career choices – old girls come back to talk about their work and no hesitation in taking advantage of the range of expertise among parents. London walks; theatre trips; visits to galleries as well as a well-patronised D of E, bronze or silver level.

Background and atmosphere: Impressively spacious, light-filled school on residential road behind Sloane Square. Wide staircases where considerate girls walk sensibly. An intimate school with lots of space. Relaxed and comfortable sixth form common rooms with the obligatory magazine pictures plastered over the walls. Bright, functional and well-equipped classrooms. Netball court in the centre of the school separates senior from junior school. Late 20th century blends well with – recently decorated – 1881 portion (including recently extended school hall with stained-glass windows). Affiliation with St Mary's Church; no special emphasis on religion.

Pastoral care and discipline: 'Excellent,' enthuses the recent ISI report, commenting on the 'pupils' attitudes to learning' and the 'relationships with one another and with their teachers'. Effective systems managed by the deputy head and form tutors ensure that 'nobody escapes attention'. School would not shirk from suspending, but only in extremis, 'for, say, vandalism or deliberately lying or cheating – not that there have been any cases of these'. For lesser offences, detentions (married with a rewards system). Not a huge number in detention each week – 'a sign that they work'. Clear and defined boundaries minimise any escalation of problems. Girls stand up when a teacher enters the room.

Clear communication channels for parents; open-door sessions timetabled twice a week for those who want them.

Pupils and parents: Confident, articulate, self-aware girls who sparkle and appear to have fun while getting their work done. Daughters of doctors, captains of industry and TV presenters, as well as Russian magnates and Saudi royalty. Pretty uniform – (some very small) grey skirts with blue and white check blouse. King's Road-style own clothes for sixth formers.

Old Girls include Vanessa Mae, Jemima Khan, Rose Tremain, Jane Fearnley-Whittingstall and Anya Reiss, who won the Evening Standard Most Promising Playwright, the youngest playwright to have a play performed at the Royal Court.

Entrance: 'We are not the most selective school in London,' though more people chasing fewer places each year (currently eight applicants for each place not taken by the 50 per cent coming from the junior school). Many sisters but no sibling preference. Part of the North London Consortium Group One. Written exam in English and maths at 11, plus interview and attendance at two lessons for assessment. Places do occasionally arise further up the school, especially in years 8 and 9 when the odd girl might choose to go off to boarding school.

The brightest from the junior school tend to choose to go to the more pressured competition, but this is not universal.

Exit: Around 10 per cent leave post-GCSE. Almost all to university – a few to Oxbridge; also American universities. Some choose the London College of Fashion or the Royal Ballet School.

Emphasis on matching the pupil to the right course with a wide range of destinations. Courses from law, medicine and maths, marketing and advertising to journalism, psychology and history of art.

Money matters: Three bursaries up to full fees at 11+, 14+ and sixth form. Academic and music scholarships also available and help for clergy daughters. Drama and art scholarships available for sixth form.

Remarks: A traditional school that is relaxed in its approach, but not at the expense of academic excellence. No longer the option 'for your less bright daughter', but brings out the best in girls who might flounder in a larger, less personal, establishment. If your daughter is fiercely competitive, then probably not the school for you – here standards are encouraged to come from within.

Frensham Heights

Linked school: Frensham Heights Junior School

Rowledge, Farnham, Surrey, GU10 4EA

- Pupils: 370 pupils in senior school, 90 Boarders • Ages: 11–18
- Non-denom • Fees: Boarding £22,620–£26,340; Day £16,125–£17,790 pa • Independent

Tel: 01252 792561
Email: admissions@frensham-heights.org.uk
Website: www.frensham-heights.org.uk

Headmaster: Since 2004, Mr Andrew Fisher BA MA (forties), educated at Geelong Grammar in Australia (where his father was headmaster) followed by the University of New South Wales (history and Eng literature) and a master's in education management at Sheffield. Came from Wrekin College in Shropshire, where he rose through the ranks to become deputy head. Married to Catherine, with two young children who are not in the school – 'As the son of a head, grandson of a head and nephew of a head, I realise that they must have a bit of a life outside school'. Teaches 14 year olds, loves teaching. 'Children only get one chance', 'School should be the best experience they ever have', 'Students should get the chance to make mistakes'.

Appointed a deputy head academic whose job it is to 'ensure that all pupils fulfil their potential – not with the eye to any league table but to them not wasting their own time, other pupils' time or their parents' money'. 'Several got quite a bump when head kept his word by not allowing them up into the next year as they had not worked hard enough. It has had a remarkably salutary effect.' Personable and fun; pupils say, 'He's OK,' (highest form of praise), 'You can hear him whistling in the morning' – but not apparently later in the day. Probably a people person rather than a builder.

Academic matters: In 2013, 70 per cent A*/A and 42 per cent A*/A grades at A level – science and maths strong. Most take at least two, some take three, a few only take one. Vast range of different and busy A levels, eg photography, which can also be taken as an extracurricular subject at GCSE.

Drama, dance, music, art, 3D design, DT and sport options at GCSE. In 2013, 42 per cent A*/A grades overall. Setting in maths and science but not other subjects to avoid labelling perennial slow-streamers. 100+ pupils receive support for mild specific learning difficulties and virtually all get extra tuition. Parents interested in personal development, not league tables. No classics nor RE after age 14 (pupils thought they might like it). Some good, unconventional teaching, using drama etc to get the message across. Average class size 17.

Lower school classrooms are dotted along the ground floor of the converted and much-expanded stables, IT in the hayloft (powerpoint presentations the norm), ditto (but not the same hayloft) busy multi-media library, well-used with audiobooks, videos and appealing paperbacks, and classical music buzzing gently in the background. Ceramics everywhere. Library is open till 6.30pm – points for laptops; teaching sessions on how to run a library and use a catalogue, along with quizzes and games for 13+, make this one of the more imaginative libraries we have visited.

Games, options, the arts: Head keen on sport – his employment of the ex-director of performance at Southampton football club revolutionised the fortunes of the school football teams. Sport is improving enormously – 'both in the quality of the schools against whom they play (for instance boys' matches v Eton, Winchester and Charterhouse) and in the results they are achieving – several sides are unbeaten'. Games compulsory twice a week, whole class play the same games up to sixth form, when they can choose. All the usual games, but probably not the place to send a prep school rugby champion (no rugby) – boys play soccer, hockey and cricket, girls hockey, netball and rounders, plus minority sports, led by tennis, basketball etc. One or two already involved in colt county cricket, new all-weather nets, Astroturf. Sport's profile seems to be achanging – apparently the original cricket ground was laid down by the Charringtons in 1900 so that Daddy could play and Mummy could entertain the Prince of Wales.

The most terrifying high frame ('It looks even higher from the top,' said Andrew) which combines every conceivable Superman movement plus some that even stuntmen would be amazed at. Woods filled with serious and popular climbing frames: Jacob's Ladder impressive. School was the first to be licensed as a centre for outdoor education, and 'The ropes course is partly about personal challenge, but it is actually far more about respecting and supporting others, and taking responsibility for one's own actions, which is why it is a timetabled lesson'. Forges strong staff/pupil links and is much used in summer by business workshops. Forget convention: this is the most imaginative playground we have ever seen – traditional gym looks Neanderthal by comparison.

Certain amount of D of E, but not the religion you find in many schools. Expeditions important, huge range – staff 'give up weeks of holiday time to take pupils to the Red Sea and the Sahara'. Trekking, camping, mountain climbing, survival skills, first aid. Lots of weekend trips away for boarders which day pupils can join – most sound rather scary.

Intimidatingly good performing arts; the building itself has won oodles of awards, with several pupils in current TV programmes and films. Award-winning dance in stunning dance studio: shiny black floor, wall of mirrors and no shoes allowed. New, rebuilt, slightly surprising music centre (fires are in fashion at Frensham: this time it was a squirrel which apparently ate the wires – horrifying photographs of the detritus left by the blaze) has a glass roof in the main auditorium, which means that it is almost useless sound-wise when it rains and like an oven when the sun shines. Fortunately the house itself boasts a glorious ballroom which can be co-opted for concerts.

Music strong, with loads of opportunities to play and sing, including an annual concert tour abroad. Twenty-two peripatetic music staff, some of them international performers, two orchestras, three choirs, string quartets, masses of concerts and a soirée in June – for some reason they also teach the bagpipes. More ceramics dotted all round the place, with children's art on every wall, everywhere – the main hall, the passages. 'We like having our work on show – it is very encouraging,' said our 11-year-old guide. Not quite big enough art department (extension probably on next wish-list), but some

superb results – glorious pupil-designed panther in foyer of the performing arts centre.

Background and atmosphere: Founded in 1925, a school ahead of its time: co-ed, capable of taking children virtually from cradle to university, with no uniforms, bullying, competition, housepoints nor prizegivings. Creative learning and thinking important, plus the arts – think Bloomsbury in the country. Teachers and students all on first-name basis. Vague dress-code – 'We do insist on more formal dress when the occasion demands' – but no overt fashion dictates.

Magnificent Edwardian pile, built by a brewery magnate, set in beautiful 100+ acre grounds with stupendous views – over 50 miles on a clear day; Frensham Ponds just over the hill. Massive outside use of performing arts centre, which was set ablaze by an electrician's halogen light just days before it was due to open. Fair amount of new build and lots of titivating eg newish sixth form centre. Also new drama and photography studios and extension to music school to include new recital room/recording studio.

No chapel or assembly, but morning (sic) talks on Monday afternoons, varying from the 'enlightened to the mundane'. No Saturday school, day pupils may leave at 4.10pm on weekdays; behaves much more like a day school than boarding school except in the sixth form; probably not ideal for full boarding lower down. Boys' houses across the road, girls live in the main building in recently renovated rooms.

Pastoral care and discipline: Very nurturing pupil/teacher relationships with teachers widely available out of school hours – 'If you get a bad mark, it's easy to discuss it with your teacher,' said a pupil. Mentors counsel younger students – 'nice and easy to talk to'.

Strict about getting prep in – discipline is taken seriously. No smoking; bar twice a week, school gets cross if drink overdone. Drugs the same perennial problem – though head will always give everyone a second chance, even to taking on pupils dismissed by other schools, but immediate expulsion if caught indulging on school premises. Pupils with a drug history coming from other schools must agree to a contract, and will be subject to regular – periodic – drugs testing; one out last year.

Pupils and parents: Pupils come from state and independent schools in Surrey, East Hampshire, West Sussex and the A3/M3 corridor into south west London. About seven per cent expat and no more than 10 per cent from overseas. Unusual international dimension, echoing the founders' international conscience, with the head keen on bringing overseas children into a 'parochial part of Surrey'. Large numbers of those whom we met lived 'within two minutes' of the school, and neighbouring villages are rapidly becoming school annexes.

Lord Moser is an Old Boy (he came as a refugee from Nazi Germany). Many from the arts, publishing, film, entertainment, design etc. Also academics, professionals and IT people. Annual parent-teachers' meeting, which doesn't seem quite enough, plus parents' committee 'which meets each term to discuss matters of common interest'. (Fly on the wall stuff that.)

Entrance: Mainly at 3+, 11+, 13+ or 16+. Assessment, interview and school report at age 10 (or below). Entrance exam required for the older children. Considerably 'oversubscribed for our January entrance exam. There will therefore be those who are not offered places. But, and it is a big but, the selection will never be just about academics – the reason why we have our own entrance exam, the reason why we offer all pupils the chance to show us skills/interests they have, irrespective of whether these skills are of themselves scholarship standard'. Success in sixth form entrance exam, and subsequent offer of a place, subject to obtaining six Cs or better at GCSE; A or occasionally B required in subjects to be studied at A Level.

Hates to turn anyone away – 'The worst thing you can say to anyone is: you failed. So we encourage families to disclose all problems before getting as far as the entrance process'. Some children come here from schools where they were not happy.

Exit: Around 55 per cent leave after GCSEs. One to Oxbridge in 2013; others to eg Bath, Durham, Imperial, Birmingham, Lancaster, Plymouth, Queen's Belfast, Central St Martin's, St George's Medical School, Trinity Conservatoire.

Money matters: Scholarships have, for many years, been restricted to £750 (£450 exhibitions). Means-tested bursaries available for those whose parents would not otherwise be able to afford a Frensham Heights education. Enterprise Company that helps the school to make a bob or two letting out facilities like the outdoor education centre to visiting schools. Also does a brisk trade in weddings, and competitive music festival and summer schools contribute to funds.

Remarks: Schools with a liberal outlook are thin on the ground so, if this alternative education appeals to you, then Frensham, with its emphasis on freedom and friendliness, is worth considering – particularly for the transfer of an unhappy child or those who do not fit neatly into the traditional system.

Frewen College

Rye Road, Northiam, Rye, East Sussex, TN13 6NL

• Pupils: 105 boys and girls; 36 boarders • Ages: 7–17 • Non-denom • Fees: Day £14,070–£22,410; Boarding £21,699–£31,110 pa • Independent

Tel: 01797 252494
Email: office@frewencollege.co.uk
Website: www.frewencollege.co.uk

Principal: Sine 2006, Mrs Linda Smith BA PGCE PGCert Asperger's syndrome (sixtyish). Has held a number of senior management posts in both the maintained and independent sectors. She sees her value to the school in growth in numbers of children boarding, technological improvements and the development of creative arts in the curriculum. Her main focus for the future is on developing its role as a centre of excellence, to share good practice and provide training, and to improve the facilities. In this she is supported by an experienced and very committed business manager and bursar, Jeremy Field, who has set in motion ambitious plans for continued development of the facilities. Also supported by a deputy who has been here for 30 years and a senior master who has been here for 27. Not that no new teachers – drama, maths – but a core of very settled and experienced ones.

Academic matters: Specialises in supporting dyslexics and dyspraxics with the associated speech and language difficulties such children can have, as well as a number of children with Asperger's syndrome. The majority have statements with a range of needs, though mostly they have severe literacy needs. Comorbidity, numeracy difficulties, poor memory and slow processing also all common. Children almost inevitably arrive at the school with poor self-esteem and a lack of confidence that it works unceasingly to improve. They do not take those whose primary problem is ADHD or MLD, nor those with profound speech and language problems. The nature of the building and its unalterability (planning regs) do not allow for wheelchair users to come as boarders.

The separate junior school for years 3-6, in a house opposite the main one, is spacious and incorporates classrooms and a small hall. The 12 junior children, in two classes, were calmly eating in the main school with all their teachers when we visited – giving the impression of a large family lunchtime.

At year 7 most move into the main site, though a few each year have so successfully caught up they are able to rejoin mainstream education elsewhere, some passing entrance exams to local independent schools.

In the main school, small class sizes (around six to eight – often with two adults) persist and all the classes we visited were relaxed, with everyone seemingly absorbed and involved. Parents feel that it is the small class size that makes the school excellent for their children – allowing teachers to work with them individually. New science labs are about to be built, though already a fully-fitted laboratory for combined science. Touch-typing, predictive text and voice-recognition technologies have all been introduced (Dragon Naturally Speaking and Write On Line used). The importance of ICT is apparent, with every pupil achieving a distinction in the latest set of coursework-based OCR level 2 ICT qualification (equivalent to a GCSE A*).

Most students take five or more GCSEs – in latest exams, 45 per cent of grades were A*-C. Classes include daily whole-school literacy sessions, with all staff and pupils involved in intensive sessions in very small groups.

Almost all the teachers and teaching assistants have SEN qualifications – very important to the head, who regularly gives training herself to other schools. Specialist therapists as well – for occupational, sensory integration and Johansen auditory therapies – and two child psychotherapists. Speech and language therapy is of growing importance. Having so much support organised within school – including the counsellor, whom children can choose to refer themselves to – led one parent to say that she was finally allowed to be just a mother to her child, rather than the organiser of all their therapies.

Two IT rooms and a therapy room for small groups or one-to-one, which is used for 'time out' space, especially for Asperger's children, for whom class activities can be stressful. Speech and language therapy room and one for occupational therapy. Therapy is included in the school fees, either as specified in the statement or from the pupil's individual education plan, prepared by the school in collaboration with the pupils and their parents.

The separate rooms for occupational and other therapies supplement the underlying ethos that skills are integrated into all areas of school life. An individual pupil's targets may be to 'make eye contact' or 'develop turn taking or sharing'; the primary goal for each child is to act in a socially acceptable way or learn to make themselves presentable, plus prepare for life outside school. One parent said that her child's goals were integrated into all their subjects, lessons and life at school, and it was this integration that allowed for progress. This vision for the pupils' future lives is evident also in the way careers lessons are taught in years 10 and 11, the fact that work experience is so important and the care taken in finding schools, colleges or training after GCSEs.

Games, options, the arts: Large, but not heated, outdoor pool used for kayak practice in winter and swimming in summer in the exquisite gardens at the back of the house; no sports hall, though good use is made of a local community sports hall. Facilities include a cricket field, football and rugby pitches, tennis/basketball/netball courts, an all-weather, floodlit, five-a-side football and hockey pitch, orienteering and cross-country trails; the fitness suite is being moved to a nearer and updated building. The 60 acres are the setting for a 17 school cross-country championship, as well as being used by the local primary school on a regular basis. The outdoor education department is greatly supported by antipodean students who come on their gap year and stay at the school, raising the sporting possibilities. GCSE in PE and Duke of Edinburgh Award scheme are both popular.

The most popular option subject is art – hardly surprising, given the enthusiasm and professionalism of the art teacher (a former senior lecturer from Camberwell College of Art) amongst the art staff. Excellent results in art GCSE, with some pupils going on to art colleges.

Half the children learn musical instruments, music GCSE encouraged – six pupils currently studying it. The music teacher was so proud of the school that when we visited, we were told that the school should be in the 'best schools guide, not just the good schools guide'. Individual music playing is also popular – on any musical instrument the child wishes, including jazz keyboard, singing, sax. Some bands, but not enough children for an orchestra. Drums are taught by a teacher who is an ex-pupil. One parent said that her child had been given a music scholarship so she could continue to have music lessons they could not afford – not because she was the best player, but because it was so good for her confidence.

Home economics/cookery/food and nutrition are taught to all pupils up to year 9, since it is seen as a life skill, though some six are currently going on to take GCSE. Recognises the importance of independence and self-sufficiency – boarders are expected to join in making Sunday lunch each weekend.

Background and atmosphere: The main house, formerly called Brickwall, is quite stunning – and a bursar's nightmare. The 1617 black and white Jacobean façade, original leaded lights 'n' all, fronts some quite splendid plasterwork ceilings; 17th century, painted, oriental, leather wall-coverings; concealed staircases, with who knows what behind, plus a ghost called Martha – the poor darling ran out with her nightie on fire and expired on the onion patch c1752 (bursar assures us fire precautions have been improved). The house came with numerous family portraits, other paintings, furniture and artefacts, the curatorship of which is an abiding feature of the school's management.

Fierce English Heritage regulations constrain what can/must be done to alter or preserve. This is especially true in the chess garden, where the topiary is a glorious Sissinghurst/Knole-style garden with a knock-out mix of beautifully planted borders and formal yeweries – maintained by gardener with RHS silver gilt medals and supported by a small team of gardeners, including another ex-pupil. Converted stables house a number of departments, and the 'temporary' classrooms are gradually being replaced and altered. The main change will include a proper hall for assemblies and plays (especially with the new drama teacher).

Far from any towns and not easy to get to, the advantage being a mood of calm and spaciousness and lack of tension. In order to stay near, the head and the deputy live in the village, though pupils come from much further afield. This feels like a public school, with its historical and eccentric building. Boarding has just been upgraded hugely with the alteration of a house for the girl boarders – fresh, spacious and homely – with a view from the sitting room over more luscious gardens and woods. The boys are still up winding stairs and back corridors in the main building, but their rooms are bright and cosy, with several extra rooms for hanging out – games, books, music, kitchen space to make snacks in, as well as a large television.

Displays around the school are not only of academic and art work – much emphasis is placed on the importance of team playing, supporting each other. A poster by a pupil states that 'Frewen is good for friends, teachers, food, sport and happiness' – a clear indication of priorities. Has named the four school houses after dyslexics the children will know and associate with – Jamie Oliver, Steven Redgrave, Richard Branson, Nigel Kennedy.

A real asset is the catering department – it provides a really good range of healthy food, adapting to the 15 different special diets and requirements of the pupils, eg home-made biscuits are left on separate plates – nut-free, gluten-free, dairy-free: each child gets a biscuit, just a different one according to their individual requirements. Recognises the importance of teaching good eating habits and keeping children healthy, and works hard to ensure that children make appropriate choices – something that is made easier where the pupils are boarders and food management and consistency can be maintained.

Pastoral care and discipline: 'Makes an effort to understand the child,' according to one parent, with an established pastoral system but, clearly, 'Anyone can talk to anyone if they want to'. Deputy head deals with most behavioural problems – few problems severe enough to reach the head. One parent said that since joining Frewen, she no longer had to speak to teachers about her child's concerns, since 'children have a good relationship with their teachers and can speak to them directly'. Another child said, 'Teachers are strict but always clear and fair'. No evidence at all of vandalism or litter when we visited. A sense of a whole-school approach here to general welfare: 'Everyone understands the difficulties,' said a teacher – pupils work with maintenance and kitchen staff on work experience, terrific for self-esteem. The three ex-pupils who are employed by the school are certainly good as role models.

Pupils and parents: About half from neighbouring East Sussex and Kent, most of the rest from other local authorities, helped to school by a minibus that collects from Waterloo for boarding. Growing number of pupils from abroad, whose parents are grateful to find a special needs school where their children can board – from Hong Kong, France, Singapore; also a contingent from the Forces.

Boy to girl ratio is 68:32, a matter of particular interest to the bursar, who is not convinced more dyslexic boys than girls, just less diagnosis of dyslexia amongst girls – working towards 50:50 mix of boys and girls. Parents mixed in all ways, largely realistic about their children's aspirations, and school works hard to foster links. 'The first time she has real friends,' was a comment from one parent about her child being at ease in her peer group.

Entrance: Initial meeting with parents to find out the needs of their child, then the child comes to visit. All therapist and medical reports are collected in and pored over by the school admissions team – including the SENCo and boarding staff – to evaluate and see if they can match the child to the class in terms of needs and peer group. Two or three evaluation days by child in school – the head says that classes are too small and intimate for this entrance procedure to be done any less meticulously. Children taken from 7 years old, with boarding possible according to the child's maturity and readiness for it.

Exit: Most to some sort of further education – usually a practical, vocational or art course at a local college. Some straight into work. Given the educational difficulties of some of these young people, an encouraging record: for at least the last six years, all have gone on to further education, job training or employment, and many regularly come back to visit.

Money matters: No scholarships (though music lessons supported if needed), but means-tested bursaries may be made available in cases of need. Bursaries for Forces families. Around 70 per cent per cent are pupils with statements, paid for by local authorities; rest are Forces, from abroad or privately funded.

Remarks: A country house with extensive grounds makes it feel more like a holiday home than a school. An ideal setting for the confident, dedicated and enthusiastic staff to gently encourage the best in every child and a safe place to board. Consistently outstanding Ofsted and good CReSTed and LA inspections. If the school feels you're 'a Frewen child' and takes you, they'll give you of their best.

Friends' School

Linked school: Friends' Junior School

Mount Pleasant Road, Saffron Walden, Essex, CB11 3EB

- Pupils: 230 boys and girls; 40 full boarders, 15 weekly boarders
- Ages: 11–18 • Quaker • Fees: Day £15,720–£15,915; Boarding £19,845–£25,770 pa • Independent

Tel: 01799 525351
Email: admin@friends.org.uk
Website: www.friends.org.uk

Head: Since September 2013, Anna Chaudhri MA Cantab, PGCE, early fifties, who took over from Mr Graham Wigley, head since 2006. Scholar of Robinson College, Cambridge, she attained BA 1st Class Oriental Tripos and an MA. Research Fellow of Clare Hall, Cambridge, specialising in Caucasian literature, before taking her PGCE. Began her teaching career as a German teacher and examiner for Cambridge Arts and Sciences, then taught German at St Paul's Girls' School, before moving to Chelmsford County High School for eight years as head of German and careers. Deputy head at Friends' School from 2009 before being appointed head. Her husband is emeritus reader in physics, Cambridge University, and they enjoy music, walking and travel.

She is a published author of several research articles on Ossetic literature and editor of two books on related subjects.

Says that Friends' strength lies in its size – 'in a setting where many schools are tending to expand, form consortia and provision at sixth form is often in large colleges, offering a multitude of courses but to very large classes, Friends' is a small but strong community, where all efforts are directed towards getting the best out of each pupil'. She is described by parents as 'fair, calm and very approachable' and is known – and celebrated – for her high expectations of the children in terms of behaviour and learning. 'She also has a freshness, which is unexpected,' says one parent. 'She says things like, "we'll just have to think flexibly about this one, but I'm sure it's possible".'

Academic matters: 'We offer a standard range of academic subjects, which allow successful progression to higher education and employment,' says head. 'Our education is, however, inclusive and supportive so that our pupils leave us as well-rounded young adults, with a good moral compass, ready to contribute to society.' For a school whose policy is to select as wide a range of pupils as will fit into its relatively small yearly cohort and will benefit from its curriculum, Friends' does extraordinarily well. There is a rejection of the tyranny of league tables and no policy of withdrawing borderline candidates in order to improve statistics. Small classes – two form teachers per form, and the intake of 30 in year 7 is divided into three forms of 10; three sets in maths and science by year 9. Value-added is above average (more than a whole grade across the board for many students) and maintained year on year, though the numbers achieving five or more GCSE A*-C grades including English and maths necessarily fluctuates from 70 to 90 per cent depending on who's in the year group (76 per cent in 2013). There's a free choice of GCSE subjects and no Ebacc obligation – 'our pupils are individuals and we want them to achieve the best they can without shoe-horning them,' explains head. Cosy sixth form (most tutor groups only six) attracts those who can't face 'factory farm' sixth form colleges nearby. Groups vary in size for A levels (sometimes as few as six, though 18 in the biology class when we visited) and several new subjects recently added, though the weightier subjects such as further maths and science remain as popular as art and photography. In 2013, 48 per cent A*-B and 25 per cent A*/A grades.

Member of the National Association for Gifted Children – caters for the more able as well as special needs. Three specialists in a separate study centre with six assistants for class-based work. Dyslexics predominate but mild Asperger's, impaired hearing and occasionally a statemented pupil can be accommodated. School bumph suggests now a cap on the number with needs in each year group and head won't admit anyone she feels the school can't support well. Established ESOL department.

Games, options, the arts: Friends' regularly slays the local giants on the sports field. Cricket, rugby, hockey, trampolining... 'There's a real percentage opportunity,' says head. 'In a small school with a lot going on, children get more of a chance to try everything.' At least half of pupils represent their school at some sport or other. Sports hall with sparklingly refurbished swimming pool in which each year group has a term of lessons. Two or three gappies help out. Spacious campus has acres of playing fields, hard tennis courts and a 25-metre swimming pool. D of Eers travel further afield.

Music is taught at least once a week all through the school and is a popular choice at GCSE and A level. Around 70 per cent learn an instrument but practice sessions aren't timetabled. The many instrumentalists make use of a large rehearsal space and there's a concert every term involving a rotation of the school orchestra, choirs and ensembles. Annual house music competition is a lively affair by all accounts.

Drama studio was full of seniors rehearsing Daisy Pulls It Off with gusto when we visited, on stage as well as behind the scenes. Annual plays for years 3 and 4, 5 and 6 too and the keenest thesps join drama club.

Workmanlike art studios with some impressive pieces – notably a display of teachers' faces interpreted bravely by their students; a couple every year get into art college. Artist in residence. DT room has a laser cutter as well as the usual CAD/CAM equipment.

Extracurricular programme has been re-energised of late and was praised by recent ISI inspectors for its breadth – from fashion and textiles club to industry days. A recent bank holiday weekend prompted a boarders' trip to Paris. Clubs and activities go on at lunchtimes and after school and there are residential trips and more elaborate journeys – geographers to Iceland, for example. 'They get to do lots of things that we did as children and still fit in the academic work,' says a parent, gleefully citing Easter bonnets, maypole dancing, yoga days, forest school and a long list of trips.

Background and atmosphere: One of only seven Quaker schools in the country. Founded in 1702, this well-travelled school began life attached to a workhouse in Clerkenwell. Lifted off to Croydon and, when typhoid threatened, settled on the present site donated by two Friends. Wide barren drive curves up to an imposing Victorian edifice supplemented by several additions of various vintages. Last summer, paths around the campus were upgraded and grass tennis courts nurtured. Land on the school's perimeter was recently sold off for housing development but this hardly impinges on the school's feeling of space, with open areas right in the middle and dotted with picnic benches. Proceeds from the land sale contributed to the new junior and early years building. Sixth formers congregate in a civilized double height space and appreciate the annual Ikea budget – helps build a sense of shared responsibility.

Generally, the atmosphere of an unpretentious grammar combined with a small county school with tight community ties. With its well-worn, old-fashioned feel, a place where individuality is cherished, catered for and celebrated. 'My child said joining Friends' felt like "getting into a warm bath" after his previous, enormous rather impersonal school,' says a parent. Certainly an impressive modern application of the traditional Quaker values, which are kept alive on a daily basis. Year 7s visit Bourneville, where they learn more about the Quakers (as

F

well as visiting Cadbury World). Parents admit to being slightly irked by the modesty of the place – 'they don't like to trumpet their successes as is not Quakerly, but I guess that the product is more important than the PR,' says one.

The Quaker commitment to 'stewardship' is also driving a refurbishment of the tattier parts of the school's buildings. Now the paths have been spruced up and hedges lowered to create a more open and spacious feel outdoors, there are plans to tackle the heating system and windows and to increase the school's use of renewable energies and its general sustainability. There's also a move towards new technology – the ICT room is a veritable orchard of Apples and a new VLE is up and running.

Pastoral care and discipline: 'Quakers have been educating the individual since 1702 – it's only now that everyone else is catching up!' points out head. Indeed this is where the Quaker ethos comes up trumps. Pupils truly feel that their school values them and they in turn value it, and each other. Certainly the fact that the emotional and personal well-being of the children is paramount is palpable. Support and encouragement abounds. There's also a welcome sense of stillness in an increasingly frenetic world – school meetings and assemblies begin with a moment of quiet reflection (which the head admits she misses at out-of-school engagements) and it's easy to see why this is a school that suits school-phobics or those bullied elsewhere. A mentoring scheme for year 11s – who select a teacher who'll be there for them if things get a bit much – is a safety net much appreciated by some in particular. No uniform for sixth form nor, in line with Quaker principles, any prefects – a quartet of senior scholars represent their peers.

Just three houses – Merell, Tuke, Lister – but lots of competitions and an easy way for all ages to mix. 'Year 7s can talk to year 11s here,' confirmed our guide.

Relatively short day with a 4pm finish, after an 8.30am start. Lunch is a choice of the hot meal of the day, pasta or sandwiches, and at break-time pupils pay for their own sausages rolls and paninis.

Truly flexible boarding with full boarders catered for as well as those who pitch up for the odd night, and around 60 pupils taking up the option.

Banned substances aren't 'condoned'. Where illegal drugs are concerned, cases are considered individually, but expulsion or suspension plus future random testing are likely outcomes.

Pupils and parents: 'I am not a Quaker but I love the idea of Silent Assembly and the emphasis on looking for the good/God in everyone, which runs counter to some of 21st century popular culture,' says a parent. Indeed Friends' pupils are candidly chatty youngsters who do recognise strengths in themselves (and others) and don't see areas of difficulty as weakness. Only a sprinkle of teachers and pupils from a Quaker background, though the governing body is still essentially Quaker. Day pupils come from a 30 mile radius – Cambridge is 20 minutes away – and boarders from London and the Eastern counties. Parents mainly professional and entrepreneurial. Some nine per cent are international students from around the globe – Asia, US, Eastern and Western Europe (a 35 year tie with German schools) – and are fully integrated into the English boarding school way of life. Location is a plus – 80 minutes from Heathrow, 30 from Stansted – along with the attention to pastoral care and no Saturday school, so plenty of trips out at the weekends.

Old scholars include BBC Blue Planet producer Martha Holmes, rock star Tom Robinson, Lord Newton of Braintree, educator extraordinaire Naomi Sargant and quite a few of the Rowntree clan. Alumni organisation now numbers more than 3,000 and they're kept in touch with a termly newsletter and invitations to school events.

Entrance: Thirty come in at Year 7 (60 per cent from Friends' Junior, the rest from Dame Bs, Howe Green House, Heath Mount, St John's, St Faith's et al, as well as local village primaries), swelled by another 10 in year 9 (from St Faith's, St John's and overseas). Entry is by interview and – not desperately difficult – assessment (evidence of intellectual potential to achieve C or above at GCSE). A third of pupils stay on to A level and any new sixth formers are generally from overseas.

Exit: Post-16 exodus to sixth form colleges beginning to slow as A level curriculum broadens. About a quarter tend to take a gap year or go straight into employment, and the rest make it to their chosen universities, including Russell Group and art schools.

Money matters: Nobody who could benefit from a Friends' education should be discouraged from applying on the grounds of finance, says head. Fifteen per cent of pupils receive means-tested bursarie, and scholarships are dished out to those arriving in years 7 and 9 for academic excellence, art, drama, music and sport. Sixth form scholarships are at head's discretion (maximum £2000) for those who contribute substantially to school life. Quaker bursaries for Quaker families.

Remarks: Calm, caring place for individuals who benefit from bespoke push, stretch and support.

Gateways School

Linked school: Gateways Preparatory School

Leeds Road, Harewood, Leeds, LS17 9LE

- Pupils: 200 girls • Ages: 11–18 • Non-denom • Fees: £11,385 pa
- Independent

Tel: 01132 886345
Email: gateways@gatewayschool.co.uk
Website: www.gatewayschool.co.uk

Headmistress: Since September 2012, Dr Tracey Johnson BSc PhD PGCE (early forties). Born in Ontario, Canada, educated at Glenlola Collegiate School; University of St Andrews (science), Cheltenham & Gloucester College of Higher Education. Physics teacher and housemistress at Cheltenham College, deputy head at Lord Wandsworth College. Married with two young sons. Enjoys skiing, cycling, running, reading.

Academic matters: In the top five per cent nationally for value added. Creditable A level results – 2013, 28 per cent A/A*, 67 per cent A*-B, physics very strong. Small groups, even just one or two girls; usual staples plus a wide range of options for such a small sixth. AQA Bacc, Extended Project Qualification, Greek, critical thinking and citizenship AS for the very bright. Girls praise teachers as 'like friends', helpful and stimulating; lessons involve lots of discussion, independent thought and learning, with students giving powerpoint presentations on smartboards. They like the small classes and the absence of boys – 'We're more focused'; 'We don't have to worry about getting things wrong in class'; 'What you look like isn't so important' – and appreciate the help with university admission: mock interviews with an academic from Leeds University or a businessman from London, followed by feedback with a score.

2013 GCSE 42 per cent A/A*; IGCSE maths; all do a foreign language, humanity and creative arts subjects; ICT, RS and IGCSE (double award) science started in the summer term of year 9. All take three modern foreign languages in year 7, then two or three in years 8/9; Latin for all in years 7-9, when they also do some 'stepping up days' involving mixed age group work. Classes average 16 – we saw very focused pupils. Very good facilities across the board.

Exceptionally thorough gifted and talented provision across the school, including maths and music master classes, creative arts workshops, after school Mandarin classes, thinking skills, Greek and Latin GCSE, early entry public exams, national competitions.

Learning support received high praise in the latest inspection report: the qualified co-ordinator meets regularly with heads of departments, children are supported in class or outside in individual or small group sessions. Can cope with autism, dyslexia, dyspraxia, physical impairments – will take statemented children if their needs can be met.

Games, options, the arts: The usual sports – particularly strong netball (recent Barbados tour) – and lots of extras, such as climbing, orienteering, football, trampolining, tag rugby, with very successful gymnastics to international level; sports leader award popular. Modern sports hall with fitness suite; no swimming pool but outings to, eg, a driving range, golf course, following girls' suggestions.

The music centre is a converted house from the Harewood Estate, well equipped with keyboards and computers; new suite complete with recording studio. Plenty of performances, at school and in the community; a singing master class. Very attractive hexagonal theatre with versatile seating and a small drama studio in the main building – ambitious plays produced, such as The House of Bernarda Alba; A level play outings to London, Stratford and northern theatres; LAMDA very popular. High level ballet achievements, with visiting companies doing dance performances and workshops. Good art; all key stage 3 pupils do food technology and textiles, including how to use a machine.

Impressive sums are raised from ambitious charity projects, such as a fashion show and 200 mile cycle ride, organised by the girls, for the Leeds homeless, Russian orphans, African school children, Amnesty International. Sixth formers do local volunteering (all), help with clubs throughout the school, run the school council and develop cooking skills in readiness for university. Participation in lots of competitions, school, house and external, with outstanding success in regional business enterprise competitions; also hosts breakfast business networking conferences. Duke of Edinburgh popular; the whole school writes, illustrates, designs and publishes their own book; a parent and daughter book club. Green flag/Eco schools award renewed twice – some school food is grown in their own kitchen garden. Lots of trips abroad, plus outward bound residentials for years 7-9; Cambodia expedition; recent International School award.

Background and atmosphere: Situated in the village of Harewood, between Leeds and Harrogate. Began as a small prep in Leeds in the early 1940s, moved to its current site 1947, started secondary level 1960s. The eighteenth century main building was originally a private home belonging to the Harewood estate – much wooden panelling and banisters; elegant, well decorated classrooms looking out onto hills; the particularly attractive library has pine shelving, comfortable chairs for reading and a large study space above with a sloping pine roof; also some darkish, rabbit warreny corridors and a large, cheerful, year 11 common room on the top floor. The sixth have their own cosy relaxation and study area in the cellars – two rooms with beanbags, more pine and a small kitchen, as well as another pleasant study room; all have their own desks and access to two computer suites (study areas recently revamped). The new, low buildings are very harmonious, the courtyard at the back having a farmyard feel (complete with pungent smells from a nearby farm – but not every day, we were assured by Mrs Wilkinson).

The uniform is cherry red blazers with red and black check skirts. The sixth wear a tailored suit with knee length skirt/trousers and are allowed jewellery, nail varnish and loose hair. Prefects (not staff) wear academic gowns in assembly, which they see as 'quite cool, like Harry Potter'. Girls view the school as happy, secure, friendly and welcoming to newcomers. The learning co-ordinator described them as very tolerant of anyone with special needs: 'They see the person, are very supportive, protective and generous'. Has introduced a pre-A level foundation course for international day pupils. The sixth formers value the school's intimate character, which affords them so many opportunities to undertake responsibilities and develop their talents.

Pastoral care and discipline: Pastoral care a very strong feature, based considerably on the amount of individual attention girls receive and how well their teachers know them. Parents feel any problems are handled quickly and effectively; a trained, experienced teacher acts as a confidential listener for girls with emotional problems; all year 7s have two mentors – a year 9 and a sixth former. 'There is always someone to talk to if you have a problem,' we were told by a girl.

Pupils and parents: A range of cultural backgrounds; parents are predominantly managerial/professional. Pupils mainly from Leeds and environs, covering a wide geographical area: Harrogate, Wetherby, Otley, Ilkley, Boston Spa. Good links with parents – ready access to head and staff, regular newsletters, a termly magazine, The Gate Way. Girls are open, enthusiastic and articulate. Henrietta Hill (human rights lawyer) is an old girl.

Entrance: Year 7: tests in maths, English and (on line) non-verbal reasoning, and an interview – only for external candidates; takes girls of average and above average ability.

Sixth: need six GCSEs at A*-C with at least a B in subjects to be taken at AS level. Small numbers, but on the up, and leavers often return.

Exit: A third to a half leave post GCSE for maintained schools and colleges. A broad range of universities and subjects, several to Russell Group – Nottingham, Exeter, Northumbria and York popular; subjects range from medical sciences to physics to languages.

Money matters: Scholarships up to 30 per cent of fees – academic, music, drama, sports; an exhibition scholarship for all round contribution to school life and high academic standards plus in extracurricular areas; a foundation scholarship for able girls living close to the school; more than one scholarship can be won. Also means-tested bursaries.

Sixth – academic scholarships up to 20 per cent of fees based on total GCSE points score; exhibition scholarships up to 20 per cent for high GCSE achievement plus all rounder ability and contributing to a number of areas of school life.

Remarks: A high achieving, close knit school in a very pleasant, secure environment, with a strong awareness of the wider world and offering a wide range of extracurricular opportunities.

Gems Bolitho School

Linked school: GEMS Bolitho Junior School

Polwithen Road, Penzance, TR18 4JR

- Pupils: 98 boys 77 girls • Ages: 4-18 • C of E • Fees: Day £11,100-£14,760; Boarding £18,300-£28,000 pa • Independent

Tel: 01736 363271
Email: enquiries@bolithoschool.co.uk
Website: www.bolithoschool.co.uk

Headmaster: Since September 2013, Mr Gordon McGinn Cert Ed (60),who previously taught maths at Kings College School

Wimbledon for 34 years, whilst also coaching hockey, cricket and golf. His partner is an artist and he has two grown up children.

Academic matters: Global outlook created by a former inspirational head, who introduced a bi-lingual stream in French for years 4 to 8 in 1997 and the IB in 2000, long before many other schools. Four French staff deliver history, geography and ICT en français, and the timetable is tweaked to build in eight intensive language lessons. Parents choose this option for their offspring, who then take GCSE French one to two years early. Beguiling lessons – we could have stayed all day. Everyone else follows the usual curriculum, leading to IB only in the sixth form – does not offer A levels.

Anyone from abroad coming in with poor English can take up the offer of the intensive English section, where they are with their peers for English, maths and sciences but sometimes taken out of other lessons to be taught separately by EFL specialists, to bring them up to speed.

Pupils typically do 10 GCSEs out of 21 subjects (including four languages) offered – psychology, Chinese and PE theory are added to the usual selection: not bad for such small school, where a typical class maxes out at 15 or so. Results sometimes sparkle, but vary tremendously from year to year: five plus A*-C percentages including English and maths (81 per cent in 2013, with 25 per cent of grades A*/A) depend on cohort and on year groups of only 40 or so. Has been county science champions, despite ancient facilities.

IB average point score generally under 30 – don't forget, though, that this is a completely non-selective school, with a high proportion of SEN children, around 25 per cent, so great added value. Staff think that the IB myth – that it's only for the super-brainy/industrious – needs breaking down: 'It's an all-ability course,' they assert; small classes and high levels of learning support get even the least promising candidates through its rigours.

Strong SEN provision with a dedicated SENCo and teaching space – they do their best by pupils, some one-to-one lessons. Some difficulties can be tested for in-house and extra time in exams requested as necessary. Most cases are mild. The other end of the scale is accommodated too: one exceptional linguist has Arabic lessons from a peripatetic.

IT skills seem good – it's a core GCSE subject, integrated throughout the curriculum and delivered from laptops which travel round the school on trolleys, as well as from two IT suites.

Games, options, the arts: Performing arts traditionally strong, especially musical theatre, where funky choices such as School of Rock are popular with everyone. Straight drama given a shot in the arm by including it as a GCSE. Good take up for music too, with just under half the pupils taking instrumental or singing lessons, nine ensembles, several musical events in and out of school and six county players, one of whom also plays in the National Children's Orchestra. Music in particular is seen as an entrée to Penzance life and as a way dispelling any sense of town and gown.

Sporting options are a mix of the trad and the not so trad – capitalises on its coastal setting to offer sailing, surfing and windsurfing alongside rugby, hockey, football and netball. Parents reckon the school 'does extraordinarily well for its size' – the first school ever to win the ISA netball and rugby 7s tournament in the same year (distinct echoes of David and Goliath). Close links with local Pirates (of course) rugby club. Swimming, which has produced county standard swimmers, at local leisure pool (and sports hall) next door – on good enough terms with them to host an invitation gala there. However the pupils complain that the pitches slope and not enough facilities or people to make viable teams.

Nonetheless enough to tempt those whose sporting bent take them in other directions, such as riding, running, badminton,

tennis, table tennis and indoor rowing – for any future gig-racers perhaps, as it's Cornwall. Enthusiastic outdoor pursuits teacher recruits for Ten Tors and D of E bronze and silver (gold to follow), and charming whole school effort on sponsored coast to coast walk, in which everyone – tinies, grannies, staff, dogs – takes part. 'Does wonders for morale.'

Background and atmosphere: Housed since 1918 in the beautiful, granite, former Bolitho home in a leafy Penzance road where the camelias and magnolias were in full blast when we visited – this setting surely captivates. But oh, what shabbiness awaits behind the façade! A miserable collection of additions, Portakabins and sheds (one such add on laughably called the West Wing) are mercifully hidden from view behind the house. Badly needs some investment in infrastructure, especially science labs – new nursery building and impressive sixth form centre have been prioritised; new prep building.

Has endured turbulent times since its founding as a C of E High School for Girls in 1889 by the Woodard Corporation. It became St Clare's in 1928 and was snatched from the jaws of closure in 1995 by parents, who made it charitable and co-ed and re-launched it as the Bolitho School. Bad and unprofitable times befell it again recently, which led, after a period of damaging uncertainty, to its purchase by GEMS in 2010. What rather commendably persists, though, is a stubborn sense of 'business as usual' and family atmosphere: one parent reported that children had no idea their school's future was so dodgy.

Despite its size, truly a Penzance fixture, which has made great strides recently in integrating itself into civic life, taking part in Mazey Day, the culmination of the west Cornwall midsummer festival, and other local events. As the second largest private employer in the town after Tesco, some disquiet when closure loomed.

Its size does mean that everyone knows everyone within school, and the fact that all eat in the same modest dining room reinforces that. We took a very good view of the boarding staff, who clearly know their charges well as individuals, so are able to give just the right degree of latitude. Accommodation is homely, if not smart, for all below sixth form, where boys and girls are housed on separate floors of the main house. Each boarder has his/her own room and use of a kitchen where they cater for themselves at weekends, plus communal space to hang out. It's all wireless, so conducive to study too. Houseparents are at pains to treat sixth formers as the young adults they soon will be.

Pastoral care and discipline: New pupils are randomly allocated into one of three houses with fine Cornish lighthouse names, though without a physical base; all members of staff are attached to a house. Discipline is not a huge issue, apparently, so carrots predominate over sticks. Credits are given for good work or trying hard; these are converted into house points, which are handed out for all manner of good things, along with commendations and certificates. Misdemeanours reduce house points, but the slate is wiped clean of these every term, whilst credits accumulate all year. Smoking, alcohol, sex, drugs and the fleshpots of Penzance hardly mentioned, so not too much of a problem then, we guess. Some parents report an anti-boy bias: the girls can do no wrong and 'When we do get told off, we just cry!' said one little miss (school feels this overstates the case).

Pupils and parents: The catchment in Penzance is inevitably three-quarters fish, so pupils come from near and far, bused in from neighbouring communities in south west Cornwall. A handful of foreigners, mostly from Asia, but a trickle from Germany too, where they like the English IB; a recent inspection commented favourably on wide cultural diversity within the student body. Has relied on its reputation locally to fill its places, but that may change with possibly more ambitious marketing from GEMS.

The pupils we met were unpretentious, tolerant, articulate and not especially sophisticated, their parents a mix of the well and not-so-well off. All were very positive about and loyal to their school, despite recent ructions and and changes of head. However, A levels and 'more pupils' came up over and over again on their wish list. Most notable OG is Rosamunde Pilcher, whose novel Coming Home depicts life at the school between the wars.

Entrance: Completely non-selective and 'entry is possible into any year group at any stage,' says the school, sounding slightly desperate. That said, usual entry points are years 7, 9 and 12, although it operates as a primary (reception to year 5), middle (year 6-8), senior (year 9-11) and sixth form. Pupils appear to blend, fit in and find friends easily wherever they come from. Transition between stages is automatic. Admission is by application form and look-see.

Exit: Eighty plus per cent leave after GCSEs, as only IB offered at sixth form – many to local(ish) behemoth Truro College, which provides 60 AS/A2 subjects in any combination and thousands of mates to do them with. The more vocationally minded might choose Penwith College with its wide range of alternatives to A levels or IB.

Of year 13 leavers, 75 per cent or so get to the universities of their first choice – and what a diverse range they are, from a number to Oxbridge; Durham, Manchester, Navy College, to universities in the USA, Germany, Paris, Hong Kong and Switzerland. Not many take gap years.

Money matters: Fees reasonable for what the school offers, but a costly education for a comparatively isolated and economically deprived part of the country, especially with the excellent and free Truro College 30 miles down the road at sixth form. Fees on a graduated scale, depending on age. Scholarships offered for academic, sporting, musical or artistic excellence – and a £500 incentive for any parent recruiting a new pupil to the school.

Remarks: Doughty little school with an international outlook and feel, as befits a setting so near Lands' End, but which has been through some rough waters recently – and not for the first time. Definitely needs a strong hand on the helm to plot a firm course for its future identity and stick to it, for at the moment it feels apologetic and not quite sure which star to steer by.

George Abbot School

Woodruff Avenue, Guildford, GU1 1XX

• Pupils: 1,960 boys and girls • Ages: 11–19 • Non-denom • State

Tel: 01483 888000
Email: office@georgeabbot.surrey.sch.uk
Website: www.georgeabbot.surrey.sch.uk

Executive Headteacher: Mr Daniel C Moloney BEd MA FRSA (fifties), head since 1999, is now executive head of George Abbot and nearby Kings College school. Married with two children. Very experienced head – was top man at Feltham Community College before the headship at George Abbot. He is full on, not pretentious nor posh but enthusiastic and proud of his school. In his businesslike office, the school's coat of arms (Latin motto) and a painting of Archbishop George Abbot juxtaposed between an array of students' spectacular artwork and photography, encapsulate the school and the man as the best of both tradition and modernity. Parents recognise his impact on the school, reporting he is 'very dynamic and controls the school well', and, 'He has business management drive – the school has developed hugely in his time'. Parents and children respect

his 'personal presence and confidence'. He is all praise for his 'fantastic management team' and feels 'a school this size would take a long time to change'.

Head of School since 2012, Mrs D Cooper.

Academic matters: A strong academic performer in the state sector. Ability setting starts at 11 and is used increasingly in core subjects. The academic focus of the school, reported by parents, pupils and staff alike, encourages hard work and good practice – work must be handed in on time and no lessons missed, tardiness is quickly followed up with a 'pink slip' requiring an explanation from the pupil, a second will trigger a letter home. Pupils feel 'They keep an eye on you'. Progress monitoring is strictly applied with pupils and parents involved in review and target-setting. Action is taken to bring on pupils who are not performing well, everyone matters equally.

Plenty of options – 33 GCSE subjects and 34 at A level. In 2013, 85 per cent of pupils got 5+ A*-C grades at GCSE including English and maths; 29 per cent of grades A*/A. Not surprisingly, a huge variety of art and design subjects and photography (very popular at both GCSE and A level), but English, maths and science by far the most popular. Good to see that science and maths are booming. At A level, 32 per cent A*/A grades and 58 per cent A*-B in 2013. NVQ options in the sixth form for less academically able.

Head says, 'SEN children have the highest value-added of any group in the school,' and credits this to a 'dedicated team, including the director of SEN and a SENCo who came from a specialist school'. Reading, spelling and learning styles are tested on arrival. About 10 per cent of pupils receive help. Withdrawal support in small groups, provision including 'units of sound' programme for dyslexic students and a strong centre for up to 15 visually impaired students. Gifted and talented pupils are catered for with specific summer schools and an 'extensive enrichment programme' overseen by two specialist staff. The 78 children with EAL requirements have provision in liaison with the local authority.

Games, options, the arts: Arts of all sorts are top notch. Fantastic displays of mature work abound and pupils, not just the artists, really enjoy these surroundings. Past pupils who progress to art foundation courses are all too aware of the advantages GA provided and put their success down to 'plenty of funding, plenty of space and good teaching'. Music also very popular – 'Playing an instrument is a very Guildford thing,' a performing arts teacher told us. More than 200 pupils learn an instrument up to grade 8 and perform in school and outside, everything from chamber music to Guilfest (Guildford's answer to Glastonbury).

Sport is the only area of repeated disappointment for parents, though the school says, 'A recent independent parent questionnaire indicated a fairly high level of satisfaction with the sport in the school'. Facilities look good, plenty of fields, a huge indoor sports hall (doubles up as the Surrey County Cricket Centre, a result of partnership with Surrey County Cricket Club), a brand new Astroturf pitch, plus smaller halls and a fully-equipped gym. Turns out teams for football, rugby, netball, cricket and athletics, pupils display colours on their lapels and honours ties won for sports. Yet many parents feel sport is lacking: 'There's not enough time in the national curriculum'; 'Lack of sport is just part of the state system'. Sports are seen as mainly an after-school activity relying on pupils' own commitment.

An enormous list of lunchtime and after-school activities covers curriculum subject catch-ups plus extra arts and sports, some run by sixth formers earning a sports leadership award. These are all optional and pupils can get away with doing none. One parent suggested, 'It might be better if they were encouraged to do more.'

Background and atmosphere: Buildings are institutional blocks but well-maintained and equipped, positively dripping with gleaming new Apple Macs and the like. The huge size of the school is managed by splitting it effectively into four sections – year 7, years 8 and 9, years 10 and 11 and the sixth form. Each has its own dedicated building and each year group has its own playground. The year 7s are particularly cosseted: with their form rooms in a dedicated building, they have their own loos and garden as well as playground and eat lunch separately from the rest.

Sixth form is housed in a new building, shared with performing arts. Relationships between teachers and students are more adult at this stage, but it still feels like school and some move to colleges for 'more independence'. Leavers 'graduate' at a student-organised ceremony at Holy Trinity Church and 'G Live', celebrating A levels plus community work, D of E and other awards.

Atmosphere is calm, controlled and ordered. Pupils are expected to work hard and parents are expected to support the ethos. Head's view is, 'If you don't like or value uniforms, discipline and manners, then don't come here'. The spirit is can-do and friendly, with very little negativity. Pupils and teachers respect each other and 'understand that people are good at different things'. It's egalitarian, provided pupils work hard and to the best of their abilities: 'They are all concerned with how well they are doing and they don't stress the teachers by messing about'.

Our guides on the day frequently mentioned making appointments to see tutors or advisors and booking work sessions in libraries or on computer stations. The whole place is buzzing with a managed, grown-up way of working – pupils need to operate within the systems and take responsibility.

It's not particularly parent-friendly, but parents put that down to the size and increased pupil independence at secondary school. Some parents criticise lack of ready access to teachers – just one day a year when you get a 5-10 minute slot with each one, otherwise the form tutor is the single point of reference. The school, however, says that parents are advised that they can contact the school and make an appointment at any time throughout the year to meet with a member of teaching staff – 'There is also a clinic held on the first Monday of each month, where parents can attend without an appointment to meet with a member of the senior leadership team'.

Pastoral care and discipline: Parents say GA doesn't seem to suffer from discipline problems, 'They deal with the one or two difficult children and don't seem to have the critical mass that makes classes uncontrolled'. Pupils have the same year head through years 8/9, then 10/11, ensuring they know each other well. Clear, confidential processes to deal with bullying; no-one we spoke to had had any experience of bullying, though they felt it would be dealt with very quickly. A resident youth worker is available 'to talk to you about anything – home, school, whatever'. One parent, describing how his child had been suspended for involvement with drugs, told us, 'The head was very supportive and helpful through this traumatic time. The school process kicked in, involving counselling for parent and child.'

Pupils and parents: Located in a middle class area of a largely middle class town. Families here reflect that – the vast majority is motivated and aspirational. The head regards his competition as the independent sector and parents feel they are very similar to families at local independent schools. Even pupils see themselves as more 'like independents' and 'definitely the best state school around'. Sixth formers describe themselves as 'all quite intellectual', 'motivated and hardworking, few slackers or chavs', 'Pupils all rub along and respect each other'. The head says that '50 per cent of the local secondary heads' children are pupils at GA'.

Entrance: As an academy, the school is its own admission authority. However, it works closely with the local authority to administer applications. Like all Guildford schools, it is heavily oversubscribed, over 800 applicants for 300 places. In practice about 50 per cent of places are taken by siblings, statemented and looked after children, who all automatically get in. Mr Moloney says, 'If you live in the immediate area you're likely to get in,' and he optimistically tells parents wherever they live that if they feel GA is the school for them, then apply. Main feeders Boxgrove, Bushy Hill, Burpham and Holy Trinity are all linked through community events and the local extended school confederation.

Selective sixth form entry, stated requirements five A-C GCSE minimum but, in practice, much more – five A*s plus other subject specific requirements depending on A level choices. Some 25/30 join sixth form from outside – popular with private school pupils (looking for a piece of real life before university?), but it operates very much as a school rather than a sixth form or FE college.

Exit: Less than one third leave at 16 – mostly for local FE or sixth form colleges, some to work. After sixth form, vast majority to university, huge range of courses and locations including many top universities.

Money matters: Attracts funding as a successful school and applies for whatever is available, running on a budget of over £10 million. Outstanding fundraising by PTA, eg towards new buildings and the Astroturf pitch. International links mean many opportunities for trips abroad which parents pay for, though funds to ensure no-one is excluded.

Remarks: Large, successful comprehensive academy in affluent area providing a modern, ICT-led curriculum which works for all sorts – the bright and less so. Particularly suitable for arty, media interested children and those who sit comfortably with the school procedures and systems. Very real option for the sixth form for cash-strapped parents of private school children.

George Heriot's School

Linked school: George Heriot's Junior School

Lauriston Place, Edinburgh, EH3 9EQ

- Pupils: 1,565 boys and girls, plus 30 in nursery • Ages: 11–18
- Non-denom • Fees: £6,867–£10,299 pa • Independent

Tel: 01312 297263
Email: admissions@george-heriots.com
Website: www.george-heriots.com

Headmaster: Since January 2014, Gareth Doodes (thirties), previously head of Milton Abbey School. Read history and was a choral scholar at St Andrews, PGCE at Cambridge. Has also worked at Taunton School and Oakham. An accomplished musician, he is married to Jess, and they have a young son.

Academic matters: Not easy to extract detailed examination results (by subject by grade) – so keep asking. Solid results at all levels. Advanced Highers 45 per cent A and 94 per cent A-C 2013. Maximum class size 26, 'but usually much fewer'. Classes streamed early, setted for maths at nine; also for English from 11. Steeped in 'Euro-awareness', a sort of Euro-starter course at eight, with either French, German or Spanish at 10. A second language can be taken at 13. Strong sciences across the board but actually no particular bias. Eight Standard Grades the norm; Latin available to Standard and classical civilisation to Higher level is surprisingly popular.

Finely-tuned support for learning but limited in the amount of help they can give – will not take children with a formal statement of needs except in 'exceptional circumstances', but

G

any child with a suspected problem is seen by the support for learning department, which then swings into action. Both withdrawn and team teaching on hand, either individual or in small groups. School will bear the cost of extra lessons and may, in certain circumstances, cover the cost of an outside educational psychologist – they have their own, who is free. Can cope with ADD/ADHD up to a certain degree, Ritalin is not an issue – 'We would consult with parents to see how their children might be best served'. EFL lessons are charged for. Computers all over the shop, loads of new suites.

Games, options, the arts: This is a games school. Outstanding rugby and cricket and girls' hockey very powerful; games played at Goldenacre, along with all the other Edinburgh schools mafia; FPs use the pitches too. Pupils bused across Edinburgh, cross-country running and rowing are favourite alternative sports – the school has a boathouse on the canal. Badminton and extracurricular football are all in the frame, plus fencing and very good swimming – a small training pool on the (very cramped) site, but basically they use the baths at Warrender.

Drama now timetabled and taken at both Standard and Higher levels. New head of music recently appointed, which has done wonders for this department – choirs as well as a variety of chamber and other orchestras. Art streaking ahead, and photography on offer, but not to exam level. Sixth year does voluntary service, working in the nursery, helping with lower primary pupils and outside placements, eg the outpatients at the Astley Ainslie.

Background and atmosphere: George Heriot, jeweller to King James the VI (and I), who had started business life in a booth by St Giles, left the princely sum of £23,625 'for the building of a hospital' (ie a charity school) on a 'site at the foot of Gray's Close', for boys whose fathers had died. Fabulous ogee curved-roofed towers, the place was first inhabited by Cromwell in 1650 and, whilst principally designed by William Wallace, the magical inner-city school can boast of almost every important 17th century Scottish architect – finishing with the court favourite, Robert Mylne. Claims to be the longest-inhabited school in Scotland. Magnificent Pugin chapel revamped by James Gillespie Graham in 1837; pupils still sit on backless benches. A rather snazzy library in the lower half of a hall has been disastrously (school rejects this epithet – not surprisingly) split in two to provide a concert hall above. While all schools are perennially short on space, this is the most blatant piece of architectural sacrilege we have ever come across.

Founders day celebrated with 'buskins' (garlands) round the founder's statue on June Day. The foundation was feudal superior of great tracts of Edinburgh, and has close links with Donaldson's hospital for the deaf (the school's after-school club is held there daily). The hospital became a school in 1886, changed its name and the 180 foundationers were joined by paying pupils, but the 180 registration marks are still visible in the quadrangle. Boarding was phased out in 1902 and girls admitted in 1979; became fully independent in 1985. FPs are known as Herioters.

Fantastic views of Edinburgh Castle but the site is cramped; hence has recently purchased a site from the Edinburgh College of Art and planning permission has been granted for a new sports centre. A new sixth year common room and café – plans for the site include expansion of the music facilities. Uniform for all, different ties for prefects and sixth. Trips all over the shop in every discipline.

Pastoral care and discipline: Code of conduct equals school's rules, which parents and pupils have to sign, based on 'personal safety, safety for others and respect for others, property and the environment'. Ladder of sanctions. Good PSHE team who are proactive in reducing tension, both sides must face up to an issue. Persistent misbehaviour and not responding =

out; detentions and discussions with parents more normal. Occasional suspensions, no real problems with drugs, alcohol and cigarettes. Concern if school work suffers, no random drugs tests. Church of Scotland chaplain; school uses Grey Friars Kirk (of Bobby fame) for services.

Pupils and parents: Sturdy middle class lot, Edinburgh-average ethic. Thriving parents' association.

Entrance: Tests (English, maths, VRQ) at primary and senior level, including from own junior school; predicted grades for pupils joining post-Standard Grades.

Exit: Regularly four or five to Oxbridge (six in 2013) – runs induction weekends down to Oxbridge along with St Mary's Music School to familiarise pupils with the collegiate system, otherwise mostly to Scottish universities. Some leave after Standard Grades, either to employment or further education elsewhere.

Money matters: Felt the loss of assisted places keenly but is pretty well back up to speed. Foundation still provides 100 per cent bursary for 'children of primary or secondary school age, who are resident in Edinburgh or the Lothians, whose father has died and whose mother might not otherwise afford the cost of private education'. Raft of other bursaries and scholarships, will keep children in place during financial crisis – but rather depends on child for how long.

Remarks: Thunderingly good inner-city school in a spectacular position, doing what it does do well.

George Watson's College

Linked school: George Watson's College Junior School

67-71 Colinton Road, Edinburgh, EH10 5EG

• Pupils: 2,323 (boy:girl ratio 53:47) • Ages: 12–18 • Non-denom
• Fees: £6,825–£10,074 pa • Independent

Tel: 01314 466000
Email: admissions@gwc.org.uk
Website: www.gwc.org.uk

Principal: Since 2001, Mr Gareth Edwards MA (late fifties). Educated at Tudor Grange Grammar, Solihull, and read classics at Exeter, Oxford. Taught at King Edward VIth Edgbaston, before becoming head of department at Bolton Boys, and vice principal of Newcastle-under-Lyme School. His Scottish experience started as head of Morrison's Academy in Crieff. Though instinctively charming and open, he is reluctant to talk about himself, being utterly opposed to 'the cult of the headteacher.' As he says: 'In a school this size one person can give a steer, but it is the strength of the team that matters.'

Retiring in July 2014. His successor will be Mr Melvyn Roffe BA FRSA (mid forties), currently head of Wymondham College, and before that head of Old Swinford Hospital. Read English at York, studied education at Durham. Married with a son and daughter.

Academic matters: Academically, a highly successful school and also groundbreaking in that it offers from the IB, as well as Scottish Highers and Advanced Highers (SQA), with the odd A level (music and art) thrown in). The only Scottish School offering this particular combination. At S3/4 Watson's is still offering Intermediate II, having rejected the new 'Curriculum For Excellence's National Level structure on the basis that it does not give a sufficiently strong foundation for further study, sacrificing depth to breadth.

G

Head points out that Watson's curriculum for S1 and 2 is certainly broad and gives access to further study in two languages and three sciences. French, German or Spanish or Chinese from S1, plus Latin for all in S2. Sciences are studied in rotation with chemistry and technology in S1 and biology and physics in S2. As well as the usual suspects, economics, business studies, religion and philosophy, health and food tech, plus PE and games, are all fitted in by means of a cunning seven-day cycle – forget the day of the week just remember today's number! Setting in maths and English for S1 and languages from S2 but otherwise largish classes of 25, with 20 for practical subjects. All pupils study maths, English and a language as exam courses, with a wide choice for the further eight they can take.

The IB students have to commit from the beginning of S5, as it is a two-year course – six subjects, three at each of two levels roughly equivalent to Higher and Advanced Higher, plus a big theory of knowledge course with an extended essay and time allocated to creative things and service. Mr Edwards says it attracts the polymaths, and not necessarily all the brightest. Of 15 IB candidates in 2013, eight achieved 36 points or more (out of 45). At Advanced Highers, 55 per cent A grades, at Highers, 52 per cent As. Pupils certainly feel they do well and offers were pouring in from up-market universities at the time of our visit. Our two prospective medic guides were waiting anxiously as medic offers usually come in last.

Strong maths department with masses of Higher and Advanced Higher takers. Max class size 25 but 20 (as ever) for practical subjects. Fantastic technology centre devoted almost entirely to electronics. Phalanx of up-to-date labs for all three sciences (taken seriously to the extent that there is only straight biology, no human or social options). Provision of every sort of educational IT goes without saying. Trad langs: French, German, Spanish and Italian, plus huge Mandarin following, Russian if required (but no automatic 'catering' for ethnic langs). Lashings of exchanges and native speaking assistants. Help available ESOL for non-native English speakers.

George Watson's has been instrumental in the development of SEN in Scotland and retains its excellent reputation. It is 'not selective' by ethos (head likes the nickname Morningside Comprehensive) and prides itself on identifying potential problems (has its own educational psychologist). Drop-in centre caters for the brightest as well as those who need oodles of help, or just a short sharp explanation with some bothersome subject. Heads of special needs in both junior and senior schools, plus assistants in class (usually in junior school) and either one-to-one or group sessions. No charge. One of a few schools to teach study skills throughout the school; literacy skills on offer when needed. Sixth formers with good Higher passes help out and also scribe. Help too, from scores of parent volunteers who – amongst other activities – record text onto tapes.

Careers advice starts from 15 upwards, beginning with the usual Morrisby testing used by independent schools (pupils thought it was quite helpful) to help make informed choices when deciding on five or six subjects from the choice of 26. Extension modules and additional subjects available for the last year. Classics and classical civilisation, media studies a sixth form option. Frequent professional development training for all staff throughout the school.

Games, options, the arts: Rightly famed as a rugby school, this is an ambitiously sporting place. The pool (complete with redundant but historic chimney) and one sports hall have recently reopened after a lengthy renewal programme and there are copious further facilities. Watson's runs the Galleon sports club, open to other organisations as well as the school and local community, complete with dining and accoutrements at the Myreside pavilion as well as every kind of sporting venue. A plethora of sports clubs of just about everything you could think up, for both primary and secondary, with list of successes at all levels for the standard school sports, football, hockey etc and a swathe of other activities.

Rowing, for instance, achieved European medal status. The Galleon offers extensive and exciting holiday clubs and activities, supplementing all year round and after-school care.

Both senior and junior World Pipe and Drum Champions recently with pipe teams touring Japan. Unrivalled choice from about 80 clubs and societies: 20 sports clubs, four orchestras, three bands, musical ensembles and several choirs, plus organised games, strong drama and no lack of engineering etc, with teams building and racing their own Formula cars. Something for absolutely everyone. Impressive and extensive art department. School trips abound at home and abroad. Popular third year 12 day project which, our guides said, had been a seminal experience and terrific bonding with contemporaries. This backpacking marathon, which tests staff and parents as well as pupils, is currently celebrating 50 years of expeditions by attempting to bag all 283 Scottish Munros – only 24 left to go at time of writing.

Background and atmosphere: George Watson, merchant and financier, left a legacy of 12 grand in 1723 to provide 'post-primary boarding education' to the 'children and grandchildren of decayed Merchants of Edinburgh and of the Ministers of the Old Church thereof,' with a preference for those with the surname Davidson or Watson. School opened in 1741, operating under the aegis of the Merchant Company until the mid 1980s, having moved to current site in 1932 (after a period in the wilderness) and amalgamating with George Watson's Ladies College in 1974.

A splendid and impressive façade, so extensive that the Pentagon or Hermitage spring to mind, charmingly softened by trees and sweeping lawns/games fields. H-shaped listed building, unashamedly institutional with acres of shiny floors, wide corridors and polished oak. The enormous school hall forms the link between the long two-storied runs of classrooms etc at front and back. Breaktime confronts visitors with battalions of teenagers, all remarkably welcoming and relaxed. The easy rapport between staff and pupils is noticeable, despite the impossibility of knowing everyone with such large numbers.

Vast 50-acre campus includes variety of pitches, plus art, junior and nursery schools in a somewhat random selection of architecture. Huge dining hall operates a swipe card system for pupils from P4 up. Parents can top these up on-line via their credit cards; school provides packed lunches or hot/cold menu which is published on their website, though only for pupils and parents. Like Watson's itself, the website is of such a scale that it isn't always easy to find what you want.

Pastoral care and discipline: Oddly, pastoral care does not feature at all on the school website, nor can one find the policy statements that most schools put out. What is there and is evidently effective and respected is a seven-point school charter devised by pupils.

The ethos of respect for others means, in practice, our guides explained, that fighting is not tolerated and seldom happens, ditto bullying. A tried and tested system manages this huge school, with two year heads per year group following pupils all the way through the school. First year pupils keep the same form teacher for two years; the next three years follow suit and pupils then choose their tutor.

Sixth formers are actively involved throughout the school. Strong anti-bullying policy, parents immediately informed and consulted if child is involved, and are apparently impressed by the help given in difficult situations. Detentions plentiful, but expulsion rare. Regular training for specialist guidance staff who help with listening and advising.

Pupils and parents: Popular (in the trad sense of the word) Edinbourgeoisie, wannabes and incomers taking for granted that it is Edinburgh's top school. Pupils certainly appear motivated and purposeful. Very much a local school, though some travel quite a distance – buses from East, Mid and

West Lothian. Boarding now defunct. Strong PA with bags of fundraising functions etc.

Former pupils include Sir David Steel (The Right Hon Lord Steel of Aikwood), Sir Malcolm Rifkind, Sir Chris Hoy, former Scottish rugby internationals Gavin and Scott Hastings, broadcasters Sheena McDonald and Martha Kearney and eco-sculptress Angela Palmer. Older generations may be more impressed by Sir Basil Spence, Rebecca West, Martin Bell and Sir Eric Anderson, previously provost of Eton.

Entrance: Majority come from junior school. Assessment before entry at all levels; where places are in short supply, academic achievement and presence of siblings already in school both count. Entry at 12 and upwards is by selection where vacancies arise, taking maths, English and verbal reasoning papers along with interview. Waiting lists at some stages. Fresh blood post Standard grades (more come than leave). The introduction of the IB means there are a few more places available for S5 as these courses are not quite full.

Exit: Around 90 per cent plus stay on after Highers for further studies. 90 per cent plus go on to higher education. No details were made available about individual leaver destinations but 80 per cent go to Scottish universities and a regular five per cent to Oxbridge.

Money matters: George Watson's Family Foundation: primarily for 10/11 year olds, though awards available in junior school and current pupils 'may apply for short-term help at any stage.' Means-tested. Will keep a pupil to the next public exam in extenuating circs, plus extra help for those with a 'recognised learning disability.' A range of up to 11 academic and two music scholarships each year: 25 per cent. Sports bursaries, Enablement Fund and the school is part of the Ogden Trust Science Scholarship Scheme. Numerous short-term or long-term bursaries for those in need; with assistance for more than 120 pupils. In 1997 the school's own foundation was established to further the original Watson credo and has recently funded the new music school extension, the GWC Centre for Sport and a lift for disabled students. Fees can be paid monthly by direct debit.

Remarks: Something of a Leviathan and definitely all things to all pupils and parents, with a distinguished and deserved reputation. Communication with parents and pupils said to be effective and every pupil treated as an individual. Big is beautiful in that very few schools can offer quite such a diversity of experience and opportunity in and out of the classroom. Size has also meant that it is groundbreaking in educational areas such as SEN and the IB.

Giggleswick School

Linked school: Giggleswick Junior School

Giggleswick, Settle, BD24 0DE

- Pupils: 225 boys/160 girls, 220 boarding • Ages: 11–18 • C of E
- Fees: Boarding £18,615–£28,650; Day £15,930–£19,620 pa
- Independent

Tel: 01729 893000
Email: enquiries@giggleswick.org.uk
Website: www.giggleswick.org.uk

Headmaster: Since 2001, Mr Geoffrey Boult BA. Read geography at Durham University. Previously a housemaster at St Edward's, Oxford and head of geography at Cranleigh School. Married to Katie, four daughters, one current and three former

Giggleswickians. Refreshed after a three-month sabbatical has taken on the mantle of Chair of HMC North East. A friendly, good-humoured, youthful figure, well-liked and respected by pupils, accessible and conspicuous on the school campus. Has developed a love of life in the north; appreciates the straightforwardness of northerners, well represented on the parent body. A committed Christian and keen sportsman, once a county hockey player, now enjoys coaching games and indulging his passion for golf. Has improved academic results through emphasis on individual target setting and lowering entry to age 11, blends academic performance with the breadth of opportunities that Giggleswick offers. Feels that if he has 'achieved anything it has been to give the school confidence'.

Moving on in July 2014. His successor will be Mark Turnbull MA, currently deputy head of Eastbourne College. Studied geography at Liverpool University and did an MA in London; taught geography at Sevenoaks, where he was also head of department, housemaster and head of boarding. An active hockey, cricket and rugby coach, he has led charity and international projects, and is married with three children.

Academic matters: In 2013, 42 per cent A*/A grades at GCSE and 28 per cent at A level (56 per cent A*/B). Improved academic standards 'spectacular with the same intake,' enthuses the head, due to personalised learning, with setting in French, maths, science and humanities, focused learning support and 'aspire' programme for gifted and talented. Combined with individual monthly assessment of effort and attainment measured against targets, with tutor sessions to motivate further improvement. All available on-line to pupil and parents, together with full reports three times a year. Success breeds success and has allowed the school to turn down the odd pupil.

Broad curriculum with separate sciences and a taste of three modern foreign languages and Latin in year 7, reducing to two language subjects by year 9. Choice of 19 GCSE subjects – usually nine or 10 taken. Committed staff, a blend of age and experience who 'provide inspiration to the pupils and are very positive and caring'. 'A pretty impressive bunch' a general view from parents, articulated by one. Small class sizes, less than 20, and significantly smaller groups, down to four pupils, study a selection of the 22 A level courses offered. Sixth form enrichment through the Extended Project Qualification plus Open University YASS modules – offered alongside A levels for those who require stretch and challenge. Most interests and abilities catered for though those wanting to pursue purely vocational courses are directed elsewhere at 16. No massaging of results here – if you study for a subject you sit the exam. 'Failure not necessarily a bad thing,' says the head. 'Sometimes it can provide a much needed wake-up call.'

Special educational needs support tailored to individual need and provided through support in the classroom on the whole. Full time special educational needs co-ordinator and successful buddy system where older children with experience of a learning difficulty mentor younger ones. EFL provided (two to four lessons a week), one to one, in study periods, but anyone arriving from abroad must have a basic level of English.

Lots of computers, including some in each boarding house; every pupil has email and a computer link in their study bedroom.

Games, options, the arts: Rugby, cricket, cross country and hockey loom large in the (very full) fixture list. International coaching over the past few years has led to such success that the school has had to drop traditional fixtures in search of more competition. With impressive investment in indoor and outdoor sports facilities almost any and every sporting interest is covered. Seven hard and three grass courts, together with the opportunity to train in Portugal, ensure continued popularity of tennis.

Keen drama started by Russell Harty – several OGs and some pupils active in the profession, but luvvies and their tantrums not tolerated. The Richard Whiteley Theatre, named after the late TV presenter, who was an old boy and governor, provides a suitable and flexible venue for such recent diverse productions as We Will Rock You and Alice in Wonderland.

Art and design taken seriously – a real strength with good facilities across the disciplines, resident artist changing annually, impressively ambitious design work allowing some pupils to skip university foundation courses.

A third of pupils learn an instrument (some play professionally), heavenly chapel choir and lots of bands regularly tour home and abroad. Plenty of opportunity to perform in front of a home crowd with a programme including recitals, concerts and annual Rock Concert, not to mention the fiercely contested 'themed' inter-house Singing and Speaking competition.

Highly productive CCF unit, compulsory in year 10, and those that carry on can gain Silver and Gold Duke of Edinburgh Awards and earn an additional four A/A* GCSEs through the CVQO Public Services BTEC scheme, in addition to military qualifications. Making the most of its glorious Dales location, outdoor pursuits activities abound; conservation projects and all the usual opportunities too.

Background and atmosphere: Set in the western margins of the magnificent Yorkshire dales beneath an imposing limestone escarpment, 60 minutes' drive north of Manchester and Leeds (so the brochure says!). Founded in 1512, moved to present site in 1869. Attractive buildings overlook Giggleswick village beneath the fabulously restored chapel, complete with landmark copper dome, a fitting reward for the walk up the steep hill.

Immaculate and comfortably sized school campus (big enough to be roomy, small enough to retain a real sense of community) with a calming oasis of lawn in its midst. Happy, relaxed but purposeful atmosphere, knots of pupils engaged in conversation amongst themselves or with staff. Polite and smiling welcome from everyone; a real sense of community.

Promotes a real 'can do' philosophy, encouragement and support for pupils to have a go at anything and everything. Evening prep, activities, clubs, house events, rehearsals and sports practices mean its a 12 hour school day, with little respite on Saturdays. All the pupils we spoke to seemed to thrive on it, though Sunday evening chapel was popular for the lie in it provided! Not surprisingly, day pupils opt to use their bed in their boarding house on occasions – for a fee.

Recent sympathetic development has included the Richard Whitely theatre, sports halls, all weather pitch, upgrade to classroom facilities and at the heart of the school, the wonderful Sharpe library, where there's always a buzz of activity. IT suite and internet café are popular venues for nightly prep.

All meals eaten in the modern dining hall (cafeteria system, separate sittings, lots of choice and pupil endorsement that the food is good). Boarders can supplement with toast, hot drinks and other snacks they prepare in the house kitchenettes (girls' facilities more extensive than boys' – surprise, surprise!).

Sixth form centre with bar on the edge of the main campus– current cohort trying to find ways to make it more 'happening'. Alcohol allowed at weekends but consumption strictly monitored.

Pastoral care and discipline: Parents see pastoral care supported by medical centre, school doctor and chaplain as a major strength. They describe pastoral care as 'fantastic', 'the staff are dedicated and genuinely care about the children'. Correspondingly, there are no significant pupil behaviour problems, though lack of accessibility to temptation in this rural location may help. Chapel is an integral and important part of the school but faith more important than denomination and appreciated by a number of parents who believe 'it adds a special personal spiritual experience'.

Thorough drugs checks (this is no-nonsense Yorkshire) – sniffer dogs brought in termly; compulsory drugs testing used on known and suspected offenders and anyone dealing faces immediate expulsion. Smokers required to attend cessation clinics.

More traffic from boys to girls' houses, visits welcomed but permission must be sought to move away from public areas. Behaviour between sexes 'should not cause embarrassment to anyone'. Staff vigilant for anorexia and similar – system in place to check on pupils suspected of skipping meals, including height/weight monitoring and meal attendance cards.

School engenders a non-bullying culture and staff vigilant for anything that may make a child feel isolated. Sixth formers charged to look out for anyone feeling wobbly. House masters maintain good communication links with parents.

Seven houses – four boys', two girls', one junior (years 7 and 8 together with junior school boarders). Different character to each of the boys' houses (not surprising with 500 years of history), not so for the girls. All pupils allocated a bed, room mates usually a mix of day and boarding. Small dorms for years 7 and 8, study bedrooms for years 9 and up, shared until year 11 (boys) or sixth form (girls). Senior house staff tutor years 7-10, with pupils choosing their tutors from year 11. Exeats – four a term.

The boarding houses we visited were comfortably furnished and in good order though the boys' evidenced more wear and tear. Rooms were reassuringly 'lived in', personalised with posters, photos, soft toys and general clutter. 'Keep calm and carry on' seems to be the universal mantra. Sixth formers play an important role in the smooth running of the house and are rewarded with single rooms. Year 9 prep is done in separate study areas and monitored by sixth formers. Common rooms, displaying fine examples of residents' art, are filled with squashy sofas, board games, puzzles, a Wii, DVDs and music. Strict rules on TV watersheds but Saturday night is film night.

Pupils and parents: Some 55 per cent fully board, the rest are local children from a large catchment area; school transport system. Numbers stable though reduction in boarding. Recession has seen families release property equity by moving to the area – children remain as day pupils; parent commutes to work. Healthy 60:40 ratio boys to girls. School fully co-ed since 1983. Seventeen per cent overseas, 16 per cent expats and Forces – popular with all these. Parents in business and the professions. OGs: James Agate, Richard Whiteley, William Gaunt, Sarah Fox. OG society well established on the internet.

Entrance: Not a great problem – at age 11 Giggleswick entrance exam, at age 13 normally CE together with interview and previous school's report. Entrance into sixth form is by a minimum of five GCSEs at grade B; around 35 new sixth form entrants per year. Giggleswick Junior School, the main feeder for Giggleswick at age 11, is situated on the campus.

Exit: Around 20 per cent leave after GCSEs. Sixth formers to a range of mostly northern universities; three to art foundation courses and one to music college in 2013, plus three to universities abroad.

Money matters: Scholarships and exhibitions for academic, all round achievement, sport and music are awarded at 11+, 13+ and sixth form, with art at 13+ and sixth form and sixth form only design, drama. There are 15-20 awards annually, ranging in value from 10-50 per cent of fees a year, the majority for 20-25 per cent. Means-tested bursaries can increase fee reduction to 75 per cent for scholars who could not otherwise take up an offered place. School has benefitted from large gifts from OG Norman Sharpe and more recently Graham Watson (late governor).

G

Remarks: An 'all round' education with support and encouragement across a spectrum of academic and extracurricular activity, for any willing to take on the challenge. It is a warm and welcoming school with no sign of snobbishness (as you would expect in Yorkshire); secure in its strong moral foundations. As one of our guides said, 'you just have to be prepared to give everything a try, and if you fall out of line there's always someone to help pick you up.'

The Glasgow Academy

Linked school: The Glasgow Academy Dairsie

Colebrooke Street, Glasgow, G12 8HE

- Pupils: 295 boys, 265 girls • Ages: 11–18 • Non-denom
- Fees: £9,930–£10,770 pa • Independent

Tel: 01413 425494
Email: exrel@tga.org.uk
Website: www.theglasgowacademy.org.uk

Rector: Since 2005, Mr Peter Brodie MA (Oxon), PGCE (fifties). Educated at Abingdon, with a master's in English from St John's, Oxford, followed by a PGCE at Oxford and a (later) master's in education management (part-time) at Canterbury Christ Church University College. 'A good intellectual training exercise,' he told us. He came from King's Canterbury. 'Let's not talk about me, let's talk about the school. I haven't changed.' But boy, the school has 'improved and moved forward.' An inspired appointment, he runs the school with a senior management team (OK, yawn, yawn) but Brodie spreads his net wide. The new deputy rector comes from Buenos Aires and the next is coming from Oakham, neither of which is next door.

Efficient chain of command, with a can do, will do approach. 'Peter comes up with ideas, and leaves us to get on with it,' say staff. Mass of new staff, but one or two older ones still in situ so 'good mix in staff room.' Encourages staff to do further training. Our chauffeur to the Milngavie site was doing a school-sponsored master's in education.

He is also dead efficient. As we said last time, he is the only head who, when faced with a barrage of questions to which he did not instantly know the answer, left detailed info for us to collect with the rest of the bumf from his office. This time he pre-empted us, and we left with a couple of trees' worth of facts and spread sheets, including all the exam data and a jolly CD plus an earlier GSG print out neatly annotated in green biro. Chalk is in the blood – his father was a headmaster and his mother taught PE.

Bubbly, enthusiastic and fun. Keen on teaching with the 'wow' factor and passionate about 'encouraging children to make the most of the opportunities school can provide.' Brodie believes strongly that 'a culture of high expectations combined with good pastoral care helps children grow in confidence and achievement.' Quite. Sees every pupil each year with 'three bits of work, selected by themselves,' and whilst he finds himself bamboozled by the computer programmes with which he is presented by S1 and S2, he adores the mini-films they make. But then, in a previous life, he was the arts festival manager, and produced numerous plays.

Still potty about postcards, the rector had 2,000-odd printed from the best artwork on his arrival. Several reprints later, he delights in sending pupils cards to congratulate them on any success – a good bit of art, an interesting essay, debating victories (national champs for last two years), sporting achievements, you name it. He has done much to reinforce the house system, appointing oodles of new members of staff, plus eight new heads of houses ('stunning appointments,' he told us).

Academic matters: School follows Scottish system. Computer suites all over and hot on programming. School is wireless and pupils can email queries and prep to staff. Science labs and lots of add-ons (next step is creation of a dedicated science block with an egg-shaped auditorium, which will hold an entire year or house, and loads of glass-fronted labs and chill out areas). Expansion of numbers (50 more on the books for next year) ditto classrooms means average of 17 in senior school (S1 – S3) with fewer for practical subjects. Minimum class size – one. Roughly 14 pupils per class post standard grade, nine in S6. Sciences, computing studies, and geography strong at standard grade, huge numbers doing biology and maths (intermediate 1 and 2) as well as Highers and Advanced Highers. Maths set in P7/S1. English and humanities impressive, with a gratifying take-up in French. Spanish on offer, but not much take up to date. A number of French/Spanish come for a two-year stint (parents on secondment to Iberdrola, down the road). Native speakers (any language) encouraged to take Highers in their mother tongue. Both candidates got As in Latin Higher last year; no takers for Greek. Product design on offer, with variable uptake. In 2013 60 per cent A*/A at GCSE. Highers: 79 per cent A*-B with 54 per cent A*/A.

Links with both Glasgow and Strathclyde Universities – Italian at the former and lab work at both. A vast and complex sixth form guide details both academic and ancillary courses available. Rector keen to 'raise the academic bar.'

Childcare qualification for sixth formers, who can take the early education and childcare SQA intermediate 2, which includes the REHIS certificate in food hygiene (essential qualification for work in restaurants or commercial kitchens). Trenchant mentoring involving sixth formers, who also help out with the tinies. Home economics popular at sixth form level – part of the life skills course.

Good SEN pickup. Psychological and spatial memory and reasoning for all from P1, and other year groups assessed on a rolling basis. Remedial help on hand, laptops in evidence and extra help in exams. No problems with children with ADHD. Support for learning much in evidence – learning support based in purpose-designed refurbished accommodation, with trained support staff in both senior and prep. Support is mainly lesson-based with teaching assistants, though child will be withdrawn either for one-to-one or small groups if necessary. Drop-in clinics manned by different people each day. No shame in popping in for a quick explanation. Good buddy system, with senior pupils helping out where necessary (slightly more girl mentors as far as the three Rs are concerned). Good dissemination of information. All staff aware of individual teaching strategies for those on the help register. No extra charge for remedial lessons. No problems for the visually challenged – extra large print.

Games, options, the arts: School mag lists a myriad of sporting successes. Sixteen sports, 18 internationalists, Olympian reps, that sort of thing. Individual sports too – badminton, rowing (pairs champions) and 30 ergs. Rugby school (more than 100 former pupils have won Scotland caps). Four playing field areas with Astroturf, floodlights, some hundreds of metres apart from each other at Anniesland (the home of many Glasgow independent schools' playing fields). Plus an all-weather pitch in the middle of the campus. Recently acquired extra ground from Jordanhill – bought a bit and share a bit. Hockey, cricket, footie, athletics, as well as tennis. Games are important here – zillions of inter-house competitions as well as inter-school matches. Rugby and hockey tour to Belfast in 2013.

Masses of inter-house activities at lunchtime – 'a hundred ways to win points for your house.' Outstanding pipeband, with lots of exposure – duty band at Murrayfield for a Scotland vs England match, Kelvinhall etc. CCF non-compulsory but still popular. D of E – trillions of golds. Trips almost everywhere, in every dimension (art as well as skiing). New dedicated expedition leader organises outdoor activities, weekend expos: rock climbing on the Costa Blanca, mountaineering in the windy north of Scotland (scary photograph in mag). Language trips all over. The rector feels a real need to get the Glasgow young out of their cosy environment and see the big bad world outside.

Music is strong, with choirs for all, orchestra, string, wind band and various ensemble. Concerts back on form and dynamic head of music is spearheading musical resurgence. More than 500 individual music lessons a week, from harp to clarsach. Twenty-three visiting music staff. Recorder for all aged eight and nine, plus keyboard at 10 and 11 (plus drums, guitar and base guitar). Unusually, school prefers the Scottish music exam syllabi. Over eighty musicians to New York recently. Planned music tour to the Netherlands in 2013.

Drama timetabled for past three years. Two sets currently for standard grade and a popular crash Higher and Advanced Higher (pleasing results). Fiddler on the Roof and Hot Mikado the most recent productions, with West Side Story in the wings.

Spectacular art and stunning artroom at the top of Colebrooke Terrace. Pottery, fabric and every conceivable discipline. Strong follow-through to art schools all over. Some of the most imaginative school art we have seen – walls lined with this year's art and not just a conglomerate of previous years' goodies. Again, unusually, school prefers the English exam system for art. Huge number of girls doing design technology, though this may have something to do with the dishy member of staff in charge (still)!

Background and atmosphere: School founded as a limited company in 1845 (the oldest fully independent school in Scotland). Re-constituted as a memorial to the 327 staff and pupils killed in the First World War. Merged with Westbourne School for Girls in 1991. Based on the banks of the River Kelvin. The Glasgow underground system is but 100 yards away, and the western end of the M8 a busy quarter of a mile distant. The handsome Glasgow sandstone main building is surrounded by music, humanities and science blocks, with random play areas scattered about. The two-storey computer linked library (The Well) is hub of the school. Pupils study here during their free periods, and can ask for any book or any DVD to be ordered.

The school is extending its campus into Colebrooke Street, where 'SciTech', a £10 million science centre (due to open in 2015) is being constructed. To the north, the £6 million prep school curves round the banks of the River Kelvin. It has awesome classrooms and canvas-covered roof top (theatrical/social) space and stunning chrome-studded glass walls over the precipitous drop.

Fifty-minute lunch break is filled with inter-house and club activities and only S6 pupils permitted to leave school grounds. Good assembly (Cargill Hall) and dining hall complex, with vending machines (carefully controlled) and good buffet catering. Pupils have eating cards so parents can check up exactly what their little darlings have been eating. All pupils wear uniform – the senior girls natty in kilts incorporating the Westbourne colours. Five Higher successes entitle pupils to decorate their blazers with a blue ribbon (quite a lot around). Sixth form have a duplex chill-out area on two floors in the old 'writing room.' Serious debating at the Gavel Club. Terrific booklet of information for parents includes info on how to pack/carry your back pack (no more than 15 per cent of your bodyweight), an incredibly detailed clothes list and a code of conduct at sports fixtures for pupils, parents and staff.

Pastoral care and discipline: Pupils are allocated one of four houses, through which much of the extra-curricular activity is channelled. Each house has a male and female head, plus PSE and anti-bullying procedure in place. Popular house points system, including debating and music. All pupils advised on Facebook strategy – rector concerned that online grooming is a real threat. Strong chain of command – heads of year and tutors for all (who stay with the pupil throughout their time at school.

Each tutor has 11 or 12 tutees whom they see for 'at least' 10 minutes every morning. Good pastoral structure in place and it works. The occasional theft – 'Yes, we're into sin,' said the rector, but no recent problems. Suggestion box – mainly used by first two years of senior school, and dealt with by the deputy rector. Positive behaviour committee. School council. School into Fairtrade and very eco-aware. Sixth form gets wide range of lectures from a variety of speakers, including forensic scientists, MSPs, reps from Department for International Development, uni professors and fire brigade. God equals total exposure from a raft of faiths – pupils actively encouraged to contribute to themes for the week. RE is not an exam subject. Hot on charity fund raising. Links with school in New Delhi.

Pupils and parents: The usual Glasgow mafia. Excellent links with the west and M8 conurbations. Good PTA, basically sound middle class. Loads of former pupils' children, plus first time buyers. Buses from further afield. Old pupils include Sir Angus Grossart, Niall Ferguson, Sir Jeremy Isaacs, Lord Vallance, Sir James Barrie, Donald Dewar, Sir John Cargill Flashman creator George MacDonald Fraser and singer Darius Campbell.

Entrance: Largely automatic from junior schools – school's own test. Some incomers at sixth form level. They need grade 1 at standard level for courses to be studied at Higher level, plus interview with rector or his deputy and department heads. Newbies can arrive at any time assuming space available. Occasional waiting lists.

Exit: Trickle post Higher, ie at S5, otherwise most stay till S6, either for advanced highers or adding to their existing portfolio. Ninety-four per cent plus to universities, fewer to south. Oodles of medics. Five or six regularly to Oxbridge (three in 2013). Law popular, ditto business and engineering.

Money matters: The school has worked hard to get comprehensive bursary scheme in place – the hope is that 'financial need should never prevent anyone.' Emergency fund may be available to help with trips. Will certainly keep pupils to next available exam stage.

Remarks: A good solid school, with an exciting and dynamic head moving seamlessly through the 21st century. Should not be overlooked under any circumstances.

Glenalmond College

Glenalmond, Perth, PH1 3RY

- Pupils: 230 boys, 165 girls, of whom 85 per cent board
- Ages: 12–18 • Ecumenical within an Episcopalian foundation
- Fees: Boarding £21,960–£29,295; Day £14,970–£19,965 pa
- Independent

Tel: 01738 842000
Email: registrar@glenalmondcollege.co.uk
Website: www.glenalmondcollege.co.uk

Warden: Since 2003, Mr Gordon Woods MA (Oxon) PGCE (fifties), educated at Durham, head boy. Previously housemaster, head of geography and second master at Shrewsbury, he is still a geographer at heart and was horrified by the GSG access map (this editor's youngest having nicked her Tomtom and we do like belt and braces). A keen stroke (with the winning Oxford lightweight crew in 1976 and 1977), he has taken up golf (nine hole course in house) and mellowed into Perthshire in true Glenalmond tradition. His wife, Emma, directs her energies into producing the ultimate OG cookbook, with more than a

G

little help from the current crop. Two children, a doctor son and a daughter with a peach of a job in London. Warden Gordon has 'absolutely no thoughts of retirement'.

As a human geographer, Woods is 'passionate about geography and the part that the subject can play in the way the other half lives. You must always look outwards'. No longer teaches but has a girl tutor group. Breakfast with new pupils still on the agenda plus lunches with the lower sixth. Charming and articulate, he is pleased with the school roll: 395-396 next week, with the imminent arrival of yet another refugee (this time from south of the border) but often, recently, from schools rather closer to home. Believes 'Glenalmond needs to be outward-looking and not just outward bound, to retain a strong sense of its own past but to be modern in its approach to pupils and parents.' 'Seeing boys and girls through the teenage years has to be a three way partnership – pupils, parents and the school'. Five years ago the wish list included a medical and well being centre, another girls' house, better sports facilities and a revamped theatre. New vertical girls' house in the offing, with 20/25 extra rooms to be added to Cairnies, currently home to 15 year olds (but see below). 'The last four or five years have been spent planning, and we have just (August 2013) appointed a new director of development'. And about time too, though you need both dosh and confidence to move on.

We were pleased to meet a younger breed of staff and housemasters including the dishy new housemaster at Skrine's, the odd wrinkly of course, but beards/designer stubble and blazers prevail. Wowser.

Academic matters: Follows the English system. Only. An astonishing 24 subjects on offer at A level, including ancient history (two candidates last year), D&T (12) and PE (three). No current Greek scholars; but three Latin-ists, one Russian and one Dutch. Couple of musicians, one of whom scored D, and, as ever, one taking music technology (one – 'one of the relatively few schools to offer this as an examined subject'). Seven presentations in French. Pleasing number of candidates in the usual suspects – maths, English, history, and geography the strongest both in candidates and success, though the odd D creeps in. Economics popular, government and politics available. Science strong – science and maths block is awkwardly placed on the slope to the north of the main complex and connected at various levels, the traditional build-it-by-numbers confection we see so often, with tubular rails and bog standard three-level classrooms. Some excellent science results, but school still leans towards the arts; religious studies A-level equals philosophy and ethics. D&T rather the poor relation. Suspect the syllabus may be in a state of change – it can't make sense to present so few candidates in so many subjects in not a very large school, which is what we said last time too.

Setting in the third year – core subjects still set individually, four sets. Loads of class related trips. Recent timetable revision resulted in longer lessons and a fortnightly rotation.

New heads of art, chemistry, English, lang, maths, geography, biology, history of art and learning support; collection of buzzy young staff around, though still one or two who reckon that teaching at Glenalmond is 'a way of life'. Contractually, staff must live on site (now allowed to live off site for three years before retiring), which makes it more difficult to get part-timers.

Two computer suites tick the boxes; internet access in houses (nannynet, intranet, wireless), 10-fold increase in broadband speed. Fibre optics, JANET, two networks throughout school, apple and PCs, computers in classrooms. Laptops all over the place. Software used to detect fraud with pupils downloading coursework from elsewhere (does it work, we wonder?).

All screened on entry. Dyslexia support represented at meetings of heads of departments. Certified ed psych's report needed for extra time in exams; SENCo and three fully trained dyslexia staff, plus classroom assistant – 'strategies for life as well as time management'; can deal with most of the dys-strata

– 'loads of one-to-one lessons', dedicated learning support room. Prep club more or less acts as a drop-in centre for instant help, from prefects as well as contactable tutors ('we can knock on most doors at any time' said one sixth former.)

Originally dubbed the scholars club, exclusively for scholars and exhibitioners, the William Bright Society (WBS) runs both a lecture series (open to all including parents) and a thinking series – variety of erudite texts: this year by Hobbes, Locke, JJ Rousseau, Paine, Declaration of Independence etc: read, digest, discuss. WBS now attracts a wider base, with nominees from form takers/housemasters (this editor was flattered to be asked but wasn't quite sure she was up for 'induction and pseudoscience'). Additional programmes include long term academic planning, Oxbridge prep, and research programmes with local unis.

Most of the male chauvinists are now a thing of the past – 'Hope so,' said Woods, (who prides himself on being 'somewhat understated').

Games, options, the arts: Half term letter summer 2012 announced that because of 'ealth and safety considerations, needle rugby matches with Strath and the like were to be abandoned (well, school had lost comprehensively that year 79-0 to Strath, 52-7 to Loretto, and 67-0 to George Watsons). Certain amount of grief amongst the rugger bugger fathers: relief for mothers. We understood, from a prep source, that the aforementioned schools had been known to 'educate' hefty chaps from the southern hemisphere during the rugby months in the northern hemisphere and vice versa; and that the Strath team weighed more than the Scottish one. Watch this space.

Boys' hockey coming up fast, girls' hockey and lacrosse strong, ditto tennis and netball. Sports are a key part of life here and daily participation is compulsory (the constitutionally disinclined can get by with a spot of umpiring), regular interruption by vile weather. Rich in all-weather, spectacularly floodlit pitches. School majors in outdoor pursuits activities and uses its site to good advantage – all sorts of activities: conservation projects, Munro Club, full-bore shooting as well as clays, indoor and outdoor. 22 range, Scottish Islands Peaks Race, skiing with regular trips to freezing Glenshee (a number of past and current members of Scottish ski teams – own artificial ski slope was 'ealth and safety-ed), curling a not too surprising newcomer, own nine hole golf course at Cairnies (golf scholarship), sailing. Several gold D of E assessors on staff – hugely popular option, with trips to Norway and the more rugged parts of the USA. Fishing (on the River Almond).

Terrific CCF (Coll has strong army links) – fifth form CCF (both sexes) now an option but compulsory in fourth form, regular camps throughout term popular ('important to be serious about it,' said our 15 year old guide; 'looks good on your CV, and helps with your DofE'). Oy? We think skool should be fun. Strong emphasis on leadership training: more cadets for officer training from Glenalmond than any other school in Scotland. Granny bashing, or community service for non militant sixths. Mass of add-ons: chainsaw course, first aid at work; food hygiene course (essential if you want to work in food industry in the hols). Masses of charitable fundraising: 100 mile sponsored walks. That sort of thing.

Head praised new head of art, who has two splendid pics of his own on the wall. Ok, early in the year, but we were less than convinced by either the layout of the department, nor the pupil work. Some ceramics to die for. Computer links with the outside world. Lifeclass.

Imaginative drama with musicals top of the pops. Recent refurbishment and remodelling of the theatre. Costa coffee shop in theatre foyer (and jolly good it was too).

Strong music assisted by new chapel organ: we just missed choir practice. Resident vicar looks strangely '70s and could do with a haircut. Two pipe bands, which hotshot on the charity front: played at Lords for England/Australia International.

Background and atmosphere: Known to the pupils as Coll. Founded in 1847 by Prime Minister Gladstone, Scotland's oldest, most elegant school. Spectacular self-contained quad with cloisters, centred on the chapel (with its surprising spiral staircase) set in immaculate 300 acre estate surrounded by some of the smartest grouse shooting in Scotland. Several modern additions stuck round the back, including Basil Spence music block, science and maths block. Gorgeous library (chapel of learning, 'natch), well stocked (real old collection as well as lots of modern stuff) inviting armchairs; media area downstairs. Jemma Pearson bronze of Gladstone unveiled summer 2010.

The mixed sixth form common room was crowded, noisy and relaxed. This proper boys' boarding school took girls at sixth form in 1990 (last ditch saloon) went 'all the way' in 1995; admissions now running 50/50. Currently five boys' boarding houses and three for girls (45 per cent girls).

New boys' boarding house – Skrines (old one has been converted into learning support centre) one of the smartest houses we have seen in a long time – 'the largest single investment in the school's history' – providing bedroom and communal accommodation that the school claims is 'comparable with the best in Britain' (which has to be QE). Decent-sized single rooms and huge four bedrooms for the youngest with good wide corridors – still blighted by the site of the garage. According to the bursar at the time, housemasters wanted garages close to the house: sure, but housemaster's wives would prefer a view from the kitchen.

Architect obviously took his eye off the ball – the showers – nasty plastic sort of triangular things – are rapidly showing signs of wear (well, boys will swing from the shower rails). Ditto the silly islands in the Brew rooms – most now gone. The lighting in the Brew rooms is sensor controlled, which makes television viewing and film nights a health and safety hazard. (Ladders required to baffle the sensors – geddit? Ladder climbing not allowed.) Warden sez 'this is not a health and safety hazard' and that the architect also designed the accommodation at Stirling University – 'nuff said.

Fifth form girls (ie GCSE year) move to a previous boys' house, Cairnies (now upgraded), quite distant from the main campus, adjacent to the golf course – same architect. The aforementioned showers, whilst in better heart, are too small for girls to wash their hair in (think about it) they much prefer to use the old fashioned (which school thought had been abandoned) five bath, power shower room in the basement instead.

The double bedrooms are smaller than cabins in steerage on a not very good shipping line – not enough space for a rabbit to work, far less girls studying for their GCSEs, though, in mitigation, it has one of the best common rooms we have seen. We await developments with interest. This had to be the worst million pounds spent anywhere. Warden maintained 'this is an unreasonable remark, as the overwhelming reaction from girls and their parents to the accommodation in Cairnies' (no bedrooms on the ground floor, bars on ground floor windows, deserted at night! Scary stuff) 'has been wholly positive.' Not from my contacts it ain't, and if it is so powerfully appreciated, why are there plans to turn it vertical?

Boys and girls mix socially during the day and after prep in school, but not in each others' houses, although moves are afoot for each house to have a co-ed common room for limited access. Sixth form bar on Saturdays; Scotland is unique in that sixth formers are allowed access to booze plus grub under 'well monitored circumstances'.

Glenalmond is remote – (Warden sez 'only an hour from the centre of Edinburgh: this ex-racing driver-trained ed has never done it in that time) and rather set apart from the world – you can't just wander round at will. Shopping bus to Perth twice a week, in house tuck shops, with variable hours. Fixed exeats on either side of half term – 'Parents have free and welcome access to their children at any time and can take them out on Saturdays and Sundays (after chapel)'.

Informative school prospectus (an earlier prospectus could have been a VisitScotland guide to Perthshire, not at all the sort of thing to impress grannies, who might well end up footing the bill); jolly handy supplement goes into enormous detail. Weekends said to be more organised. Boy and girl joint heads of college, which scares the pants off OGs.

Magical dining room with good buffet hot/cold – we had a delightful chicken tikka. Interestingly, there is a hospital-type antiseptic hand wipe machine at the exit to the dining room; most used it, but shouldn't it have been at the entrance? Apparently there are 'also three at the entrance to the dining hall'; we must have missed them.

We toured Goodacre's. Pupils graduate from individual tables in prep room – overseen by prefect – to desks in their dorms, and one lucky fourth form dorm had four beds, two showers, two basins and a loo – how's that for ensuite? At age 14? Pupils can use the clothes washing machines when matron doesn't need them (sock bags). Good games/telly room, book case in corner bung full of books, DVDs, games. Housemaster previously in the real world with Price Waterhouse, has written the seminal IB text book on business and economics, professional tutor with the uni of Buckingham, laments the little uptake he has from pupils who want to study economics and business studies. This is a waste of opportunity and yet school/GSG web site indicates that many current students are indeed going down that line.

Pastoral care and discipline: Previous high jinks some time ago have resulted in a massively impressive, tightly worded code of behaviour which covers everything from cycling without a helmet to public displays of affection between pupils, as well as extensive drugs etc document – 'Smoking is a major social gateway to the smoking of illegal drugs. The College may regard persistent tobacco smoking as a reason for asking parents and pupils to agree to future drug testing'. These documents are unique in our experience and we are slightly concerned that sometimes alleged offences may be judged in black and white – the HMI boarding report was rather fazed by it too. Warden thinks school is 'pretty clean at the moment' though he did touch wood as he said it. Pupils and parents 'receive a copy of the Code of Behaviour Expectations, Encouragement and Sanctions'. We didn't.

Basically: random drugs testing on suspicion, out if positive; smoking equals house gating, Warden's gating and letters home, followed by suspension. Smoking in a building equals suspension even for the first time. Drinking to excess in permitted zones equals Warden's gating, followed by bans and possible suspension, no spirits allowed in the (local) recognized pubs and watering holes. No bringing alcohol back to school under any circumstances. Local keepers still complain about empties and other detritus on the neighbouring grouse moor. (We like a tad of spirit!)

No reported bullying – head of boarding both neutral and approachable. Anorexia said to be less of a problem – couple of girls under watchful eye, but nothing serious. Jury still out on how to deal with cyber bullying (trolling).

Pupils and parents: Scotland's school for toffs – 'Jolly nice parents' says the warden. Traditionally, Scottish upper middle and middle class, army, Highland families. About 20 per cent locals and 21 per cent foreigners from all over, plus seven per cent expats. All real foreigners must have guardians, via parents or contacts, or school will fix 'em up with guardianship agencies 'with whom we have worked successfully in the past'. EAL in place. Number of first time buyers, though trad parents are coming back in handfuls. Girls float daily in tweed jackets and black skirts, and long tartan kiltettes for best; chaps have moved from grey shirts to white, and look at tad like refugees from the local state school with their often outgrown grey bags and blazers. Tweed coats for sixth form only. Full kilt with short tweed jacket for best. Second hand shop.

This is seven day a week boarding; the 50 day boys and girls stay to 6pm most nights and 9pm on Wednesdays, Saturday morning school with match play if required in the afternoons; odd bed available – up to 15 a term at 20 quid a night. More ecumenical than an Episcopalian foundation might imply – 20 per cent Catholic, who are prepared for confirmation, plus Church of Scotland.

FPs (known as OGs) a generous bunch, include Sandy Gall, Robbie Coltrane, Miles Kington, Allan Massie, David Sole and Andrew MacDonald (Train Spotting fame), Adair Turner (former chairman of FSA), Charlie (Lord) Falconer, erstwhile flatmate of Tony Blair – who was at arch-rival school, Fettes.

Entrance: Own entrance exam at 12, most at 13+ via CE, oodles from Belhaven, Ardvreck, Craigclowan, St Mary's Melrose, Malsis and Aysgarth, with a clutch from Cargilfield, Mowden etc, as well as state primaries or overseas. Entrance not a difficult hurdle at the moment ('academic threshold 50 per cent'). Department heads visit primaries/preps and do 'fun experiments' pour encourager.

Sixth form intake need six passes at national five or GCSE or entrance test and previous school's recommendation; a number from Germany.

Exit: Hardly any leave post GCSEs. Three to Oxbridge last year, most of the sixth formers whom we met were determinedly heading Oxbridge-wards. Majority to university or some form of higher education – Glasgow, Edinburgh, Exeter and Newcastle popular, ditto Forces. School has been assiduous in filling in our bits and bobs on line, a great help, and unusual.

Money matters: Discounts for siblings of 25 per cent, a whopping 50 per cent for fourth child, 10 per cent for children whose parents are in the Forces and Fil Cler bursaries for offspring of the clergy. Otherwise myriads of bursaries, means tested, from five to 100 per cent. Music (including piping), art, sport, plus all round scholarships. Latest wheeze is for individuals to sponsor deserving but needy pupils by direct giving (anonymously).

Remarks: This editor christened Glenalmond 'the Eton of the North' in our first edition: serious glitch caused downturn in numbers, girls were introduced and Glenalmond started regaining momentum: however during our last visit we were concerned that the warden had fallen into some dreadful Perthshire lethargy; he seemed to have gone off the boil. But lo, there has been a transformation. Back and bubbly, Woods is positively on a roll. Ditto numbers. Girls more confident (complete with rash of pearl ear-rings and sophisticated make-up) and altogether more girl-like – rather than honorary boys as previously. School says: 'In last HMI inspection, 2009, we were rated as excellent for improvements in performance', well it would, wouldn't it? We wonder why it took the warden 10 years to turn Glenalmond back into the sort of place non-first time buyers are prepared to boast about.

Godalming College

Tuesley Lane, Godalming, Surrey, GU7 1RS

• Pupils: 1,700 • Ages: 16–18+ • State

Tel: 01483 423526
Email: college@godalming.ac.uk
Website: www.godalming.ac.uk

The Principal: Mr David Adelman BA (fifties). Educated at Hampton Boys (then a grammar school) and Trinity College, Cambridge. An historian by training, he's the son of another, Paul Adelman, whose well-regarded works include a history of the Labour party. You can pick up his own slim volume, Signs of the Times, on Amazon. Previously deputy principal at Esher College for five years and before that at Haywards Heath College for 14, starting as a history teacher and rising first to director of curriculum.

Somehow finds time to teach history of art (every senior manager is also a subject tutor). Parents, who don't tend to see much of him ('like other heads – you meet them once when you're being shown round, get on with them so well you feel you could invite them to tea, then you don't see them again until speech day') but praise his professionalism when they do. 'Comes across very well,' says one. Students, privy to far more of his informal side, have a slightly different take. 'You listen to him in assemblies and think, come on David, that's not the real you,' says one. 'Goofy' was another (affectionate) description.

Has been pivotal in setting up a group to represent sixth form college interests in the face of increasing funding uncertainty, but he's a private person who doesn't care to share personal details with GSG (biographical information was unearthed after extensive research conducted with, we hope, appropriate historical rigour) and declines to be interviewed. A shame as he's clearly an engaging personality and a highly effective leader, too.

Academic matters: Students flock here from state and private schools for the teaching quality and results. Open access means just that. Five GCSE C grades theoretically opens the door to the 40 A level subjects on offer (including BTEC equivalents), though Bs and above are required for maths and sciences and 'the better the grades, the easier the transition,' says college.

Half way house courses such as AS Use of Mathematics offer a way in to an otherwise out of reach subject, while access courses for anyone not achieving entry grades first time round provide second chance GCSE essentials including English, maths and science, together with BTEC starter courses. Add one year express language courses and a good range of not-to-be-sniffed-at BTEC National Diplomas – lots of distinctions and merits, new subjects regularly added to the roster, most recently hospitality and entertainment – and there really is something for just about everybody.

Results very good, given such a wide range of courses and aspirations; in 2013, 34 per cent A*/A grades at A level and 73 per cent distinction or merit BTEC Nationals. Most take four AS and three A levels, some more, with a compulsory second year add-on, most themed to your main subjects and ranging from EPQ (extended essay) to hip-sounding rock school award.

Compared with the general run of schools, the humanities are notably popular. English literature heads the pack, followed by history (more girls than boys opt for 16th century, vice versa for modern variant; relative size and excitement of modern ordnance plus the Philippa Gregory factor could be at work). Sciences a little below average in popularity but still strong, with a budding biologist one of four British Olympiad winners, and physics, though boy-dominated ('they often see the maths so easily,' says tutor) inspiring a few girls to enrol on engineering courses afterwards.

Good languages, French most popular. Enticements include a week's work experience abroad, though German students have yet to bite. 'I offer every year but…' says slightly doleful tutor. Good spread of the more modish subjects (world development, media and film studies courses) – one classroom converts into bijou cinema for home-grown film screenings.

Overall, though, the arts have it, performing or static, from textiles (a largely though not exclusively female enclave) to dance, art, drama, and theatre studies, all exuding top grades (in some cases, nothing but). 'Imagine being able to dance for A level. It's amazing!' enthuses parent. Quality is taken as read – one art student is a BP portrait award entrant – and jaw-dropping displays of talent abound, off the walls when it comes to dance and drama; on them elsewhere. Inspirational tutors who talk to each other as well as the students (blindingly obvious, you'd think, but very definitely doesn't happen everywhere) and are universally praised for going beyond the call of duty.

Unsurprisingly, special educational needs – all sorts – are enthusiastically welcomed as are physical disabilities and far more than lip service is paid, with specialist support for everything from Asperger's to ADHD and cerebral palsy. Lots of lifts, while one learning support room is deep in heart of English block (a big 'welcome' sign drives the message home). Independent learning centre (aka library, but with reams of added features) houses drop in centre catering for anyone requiring a bit of tlc. Add some in class and individual support together with smallish teaching groups (average of 15 to one, though there's considerable subject variation) and the bottom line is that the lost are unlikely to stray too far without being brought back into the fold.

Games, options, the arts: 'If all you're doing is thinking about exams, you're not going to get an all-round education,' says principal. Timetabled enrichment activities and a choice of 20 or so extracurricular activities from Amnesty International to zumba. D of E notably popular. Sport lives up to the colossal gorgeousness of facilities (sports hall is the size of a small school all on its own) with strong swimming, football and rugby squads and national championship-winning netball team.

Arts won't disappoint either. Two theatres in frequent use by dance and drama companies, noted for high octane, large scale productions, often involving local school and community groups. There's a host of talented musicians, too.

Background and atmosphere: Twelve acre campus that's truly handsome and everything the most demanding parent could ask for. Large but easy to navigate. The main building, all recessed lights and colourful but restrained carpets set against pristine white, is a delight to walk through. Just about every subject is now housed in luxury.

'Big but tight knit,' says the principal. Not for anyone who wants the 'more custodial setting,' as he puts it, of a smaller scale school environment. Much talk of recreating yourself, resulting in enjoyable stylistic differences between the philosophy set (highly articulate, sitting cross-legged, guru-like, on their desks during open day) and the buzzy drama and music crowd (big on hand gestures and hair flickage).

'It's a place of serious study. One student turned up late for lessons just to be noticeable. In her old school, everybody would giggle. Here, everybody rolls their eyes. They're not impressed,' says parent.

Pastoral care and discipline: Personal tutors, the first port of call for help, are seen weekly and are expected to know their charges well. Supplemented with regular one-to-one sessions with subject specialists. Relationships generally are excellent.

There's a clear three strikes and you're out policy, though few go off the rails and exclusions are rare. 'You are expected to mature and we will be on your case if it doesn't happen,' says the principal. 'When my child was falling behind I got a pretty swift email saying she needed to hand in her work,' says a parent. 'The problem was dealt very quickly once I was made aware of it.'

Pupils and parents: Intake reflects the affluent, middle class demographics of the area. Old Boys and Girls are an extrovert bunch, including comedians Ben Elton (who opened the new performing arts centre) and Rufus Hound, together with actresses, Drop the Dead Donkey's Ingrid Lacey among them. Current generation of funny, articulate pupils seem to be carrying on the tradition, though attempts to shock by the small group on Godalming Station, identifiable by orange 'can I help you?' badges from open day, noisily speculating on the quality of mathematicians' love lives (limited, they felt) left surrounding bourgeoisie anything but épaté.

Entrance: Guaranteed places for linked Waverley federation schools Broadwater, Glebelands, Gosden House, Rodborough and Woolmer Hill, no matter when they apply. For others, used to be a first come, first served scrum until admissions policy was changed, making prospects of a place nearly as good for those attending Bohunt School, Fullbrook School, Midhurst Rother College and Weydon School, as long as they submit applications towards the end of the September preceding year of entry.

For all other applicants, distance from college is the deciding factor, though things aren't as gloomy as they might sound. 'In the past, though not this year, we have been oversubscribed,' says principal. Students can come from as far away as Clapham.

Exit: Around a third of A level students to UK's top universities, while some 80 per cent go on to higher education in some way, shape or form. Some subjects excel: 60 per cent of chemistry students, for example, make it to Russell Group universities, Oxbridge or the Royal Veterinary College.

Vocational courses feed through nicely as well, on the whole, though universities, blowing hot and cold, don't help – two were havering over whether to continue accepting diploma in childcare and education as an entry qualification after experiencing a high drop out rates amongst students recruited elsewhere. College was limbering up to make forceful case against. 'We'd argue that our higher levels of pastoral care make it very unlikely,' says tutor.

Remarks: Modern surroundings, excellent results, committed tutors and enthusiastic, ebullient students. One student was worried about going on to university not through fears about demanding course but because 'it might not live up to the standards here.'

The Godolphin and Latymer School

Iffley Road, London, W6 0PG

• Pupils: 750 girls; all day • Ages: 11–18 • Non-denom
• Fees: £17,280 pa • Independent

Tel: 020 8741 1936
Email: registrar@godolphinandlatymer.com
Website: www.godolphinandlatymer.com

Head Mistress: Since 2009, Mrs Ruth Mercer BA (late forties), read history at London University and is passionate about the subject – 'One of the reasons I chose to teach', she says, 'is so that I could continue to learn history'. Previously head of Northwood College, where, after a bumpy beginning, she was a considerable success. She grew up in Preston – her northern accent is just discernible after years of teaching in independent London girls' day schools – head of history and politics and Notting Hill and Ealing for 12 years, deputy head here at Godolphin from 1998 until 2002 and thence to Northwood College which she ran for seven years.

Married to the deputy head of Greenford High Comprehensive in Ealing; they have two teenage children, both at single sex schools. 'I practise what I preach,' she says. Wholeheartedly committed to single sex education: 'We fail both boys and girls if we educate them together because we can't meet their very different needs,' she says. Succeeds the highly respected Margaret Rudland after 23 years, but since Mrs Mercer was her deputy until 2002, staff here knew what they were getting and, as one said, 'We were thrilled with her appointment – she is so hands on'.

Thoughtful, honest (prefers careful accuracy to hard sell) and tactful, Mrs Mercer is serious but clearly enjoys humour and is not afraid to join in and make a fool of herself, whether it be in the chorus of Mamma Mia directed by the girls or in a fitness contest, organised by the students, clad in blue wig and hood. Teaches history to year 7 – 'I need to know what the girls are like as learners as well as individuals'. This is a head who rolls up her sleeves and gets on with it at the coal face. During her first two terms she shadowed several classes, sitting with the girls, doing all the set tasks – 'quite a challenge when you are in a GCSE chemistry lesson and you haven't done chemistry for aeons'. It was an invaluable exercise, one of the results of which was the appointment of a thinking and learning coordinator (a refreshing departure from the usual 'teaching and learning'). She identified that teaching here needs to move away from the didactic – 'predictable hoop-jumping isn't training them for the real world'.

Popular with the girls, who appreciate her warmth and friendliness. None of the parents we spoke to had much, or indeed any, contact with her. They don't seem concerned. As one parent put it, 'She may tweak a few things but she isn't going to screw it up'.

Academic matters: Examination results are impressive – 77 per cent of A level results at A*/A in 2013 and those doing the IB achieved well too – average point score of 40 out of a possible 45. English literature, history, maths and biology particularly popular, with chemistry and history of art close behind. A level choices include philosophy, government and politics, music technology, Russian, classical civilisation.

IB take-up varies but Mrs Mercer is a great fan because it makes girls think ('exam technique has dumbed down A levels') and is right up the street of your typical self-reliant and busy Dolphin (that's what girls here are known as – past and present). All A level students can now do an extended project so they can be as stretched (nearly) as much as the IB candidates. In 2013, 92 per cent of GCSE grades were A or A*.

Over 50 per cent of staff have been here for over 10 years, 25 per cent of staff are men (not bad for a girls' school). Some parents comment on how results driven the school is – As are expected the whole time and 77 per cent is a poor mark. One mentioned her horror when parents were told in the November of their daughter's first year – two months in – whether their daughter was meeting her expected targets.

Positive noises from the girls. Teachers are supportive and always available to help, they say. No tutor system, however, and, as one parent pointed out, there is no one person who knows your child really well academically and has done all the way through so you can have a productive discussion with them about, say, their choice of A levels.

Full-time individual learning needs coordinator (Mrs Mercer doesn't like using the pejorative sounding 'special needs'). Needs mainly on the mild to moderate dys-strata and organisational skills, though have had statemented children in the past. Each case will be judged individually but girls here need to be able to stand the pace. 'All our girls are Gifted and Talented,' says head and the aim is to constantly stretch and stimulate them with the quality of the lessons. No extra charge for extra help.

Games, options, the arts: If your daughter is passionate about sport but gawky on the pitch probably not the school for her. Although the teams – hockey and netball in particular – are strong, if your daughter isn't picked she is likely to get sidelined – a common complaint among parents. Astroturf (floodlit) hockey pitch, courts for netball and tennis – all on site and girls here are competitive and keen. Involvement rapidly declines for the not so sporty and as they move further up the school – one girl told us there is very little sport beyond year 10. Fencing, yoga and pilates as well as rowing (they share a boat house with Kings, Wimbledon). Not much swimming though they do have use of Latymer's pool.

Drama and music are a different story – very inclusive, ambitious and hugely popular. Girls take responsibility for a number of shows throughout the year – producing, directing and acting in them. Splendid new facilities housed in the Bishop Centre (nothing ecclesiastical meant by the nomenclature – it is in fact named after Dame Joyce Bishop, headmistress until 1963, but building is made up of St John's Church together with the vicarage, which school acquired in 2008). Concerts and theatrical performances take place here with state-of-the-art lighting and seating facilities (though one parent controversially complained that the acoustics were terrible and you couldn't see a thing – 'that's now been fixed,' school assures us). The Rudland Music School is connected to the Bishop Centre by a bright glass corridor. First class facilities for music playing and music making – you can burn discs in high tech studios, store your instrument in a discreet but secure locker and practise in comfortable soundproofed music rooms. A joint orchestra with Latymer Upper School as well as various choirs, ensembles and bands including a jazz band. 'You can get involved even if you have no musical talent whatsoever,' said one pupil, approvingly.

Art is strong. One girl commented that it was best thing about the school. Pottery a little disappointing. They still have a kiln but no longer have any wheels.

Huge range and number of trips – domestic and global – whether it be classics trips to the British Museum, Bath or Athens, skiing in the US or trekking in the Sinai desert. Swimming is not the only contact girls have with Latymer Upper. They go on French and German exchanges together and sixth formers do joint work experience in Versailles and Berlin.

Impressive amount of work in local community, especially with the elderly. One old Dolphin fondly remembers that her first experience of the indignities of old age was while she was at school here helping old ladies onto the loo. A 'social services' team led by about seven girls in the sixth form coordinates whole school charitable efforts – every week they choose a different charity. They raise money by any means possible – cake sales or charging fellow pupils to watch all the staff perform Mamma Mia during lunch break.

Background and atmosphere: Built as a boarding school for boys in 1861, became an independent day school for girls in 1905 and evolved, through different state-aided statuses, before turning independent again in 1977 rather than becoming a comprehensive school or being closed down altogether. Situated at the end of Iffley Road in W6, it's encased by hectic Hammersmith on one side and leafy Brackenbury on the other. There is a definite churchy feel to the architecture.

What was formerly St John's Church is now the Bishop Centre. The original buildings are yellow brick Victorian, with some distinctly church-like windows and a formal panelled assembly hall. Recent yellow-brick additions blend in fairly harmoniously and have provided science labs and art studios, a pottery room, computer studies rooms and language labs. 'I like the way different buildings have different feels,' said a pupil. The ecology garden is used in biology lessons, there's a quad with pond (plus dolphin statue) and a courtyard where girls can eat lunch in warm weather. The spacious top floor sixth form centre resembles an airport lounge with roof terrace and tuck shop. 'We feel privileged to come up our own staircase to our own room,' said a sixth former.

Although almost every girl we spoke to said they loved the friendly and supportive atmosphere, a number of parents complained of an 'us and them' attitude from the senior staff – 'they prefer to support the teachers rather than sympathise with the concerns of parents,' said one. That said, it is universally acknowledged that school responds swiftly when something can be done.

This is a close knit community where there is mutual trust between staff and pupils. Girls here are real joiner-inners – for many of them the school day runs from 7 in the morning until 8 at night. They are given a lot of responsibility and there is healthy contact between younger and older girls. One parent described the atmosphere as buzzing. We would have to agree.

Pastoral care and discipline: Head says behaviour is good, and better than when she was here as deputy seven years ago. No instances of drugs found in school: if they were, each case would be dealt with individually, but likely to result in expulsion. Regular surveys about bullying – school council (chaired by head girl – with one member of staff – the rest are girls) produced its own anti-bullying strategy, recently revised to incorporate facebook cyber-style bullying.

Sixth form can go out to Hammersmith at lunchtime – a privilege that can be withdrawn for bad behaviour.

Mutterings among parents about poor communication – 'it's hard to get hold of teachers' – and one said that her daughter's form-mistress hardly knew her: 'They only have 10 minutes with the girls in the morning'. A parent of a younger girl said she was still working with the reputation of the school as being a good one rather than what she has experienced – 'I wish I knew what she was doing in the day,' she said.

Pupils and parents: Parents are professional – city types and lawyers, a few in media and publishing. Ambitious with high expectations. Not as much diversity as there used to be in the days of Assisted Places, though school tries hard with a bursary fund to maintain some socio-economic spread. Lots of Gucci and Fendi handbags at the school gates as well as the odd chauffeur dropping off a daughter of a Russian magnate. Quite a high number of children from the States and France who live in SWs 1 and 3. A few from Ealing, Kew and Richmond and a small number from north London, otherwise it's largely local.

Girls are feisty, confident, independent and grounded. Not afraid to stand up for what they believe in and their teachers let them – its part of the mutual respect that is so valued here. It's cool to be clever and to be responsible. Timid girls tend to blossom, and enjoy – as one parent put it – the slightly Victorian approach to structure and boundaries. Not many of the hair flickers in Starbucks in Hammersmith will be from Godolphin, and one old Dolphin – also a current parent – pointed out that it's fine for girls here to have chunky thighs and to use the wrong hand cream. Old Dolphins include Nigella Lawson, Davina McCall, actresses Kate Beckinsale, Jemima Rooper and Samantha Bond, writer Sarah Dunant, Professor Dame Susan Greenfield, architect Julia Barfield and singer Sophie Ellis-Bextor.

Entrance: Competitive – about 500 each year apply for a 110 places. About a quarter from state primaries, large number from central London preps – Pembridge Hall, Bute House, Thomas's – over 100 schools. Member of group 2 of the North London Consortium of girls's schools that set common maths and English exams. All girls are interviewed twice. 'We place a lot of emphasis on school report and interview,' says head. 'We are trying to get at potential, do they have the ability and willingness to think for themselves – are they teachable?' adding how depressing it is when they ask what they do in their free time and are told that most of it is taken up with tutoring. A pretty high standard of raw ability is required if they are to keep up with the fast pace of lessons. Siblings will be turned away if not they're not up to it.

Exit: A small number – about 10 per cent – will leave after GCSE to go to eg Westminster, or boarding schools – Marlborough, Wycombe Abbey, Cheltenham Ladies, ('but we bring in at least that number,' says head).

After A level or the IB almost all go on to the most selective Russell Group Universities; five to Oxbridge in 2013, three to McGill University in Canada, one to Trinity College Dublin; others to Dubham, Bristol, Exeter, SOAS etc.

Money matters: A development director raises funds, particularly for bursaries. School will make every effort to ensure that no-one has to leave because their family has fallen on hard times. One or more music scholarships at 11 and music and art scholarships in the sixth form.

Remarks: A stimulating school that does its job well. Produces independent, confident (rather than arrogant) girls that are looked after but appear to be looking after themselves. An excellent choice for your busy daughter who loves to join in.

Godolphin, Salisbury

Linked school: Godolphin Preparatory School

Milford Hill, Salisbury, SP1 2RA

• Pupils: 345 girls; 60 full boarders, 65 weekly boarders • Ages: 11–18 • Christian foundation • Fees: Boarding £25,290–£27,024; Day £18,528 pa • Independent

Tel: 01722 430511
Email: admissions@godolphin.wilts.sch.uk
Website: www.godolphin.org

Headmistress: Since January 2014, Mrs Emma Hattersley, previously deputy head pastoral at Sherborne Girls. She studied music at Durham University and trained as an opera singer at the Royal Academy of Music. Has also been housemistress at Canford School. She is married with three children.

Academic matters: Standards are high and parents comment on academic 'atmosphere of purpose' and 'motivated girls who want to succeed.' One parent added, 'punches well above its weight for a local school', and observed that results are especially good given that the school doesn't set the bar too high on entry.

Very good A level (64 per cent A*/A grades in 2013) and GCSE results (75 per cent A*/A) helped by small class sizes; no option blocks at GCSE allows flexible subject choices. Fifth year girls take six IGCSE core subjects in English, maths, a modern language (French, German or Spanish) and science, adding three further subjects for a total of nine. Options include Latin, drama, music, RS (popular), food technology, design technology and art, and recent additions geology, statistics and computing. The most able take three separate sciences plus full complement of extras to gain 10 GCSEs.

New 'reBEL' programme offers third years the chance to try out new subjects eg politics and develop independent learning, critical thinking and entrepreneurship skills.

Taster A level sessions are on offer in the fifth year and girls feel they get good advice when choosing; option groups of complementary subjects are created around each year's choices. Some changes allowed if girls don't get it right first time. Sixth formers full of praise for their teachers' willingness to go the extra mile on their own time. 'We're really going to miss them when we leave.' Most subjects are strong; excellent results in sciences, with a good crop of A* and A grades in arts subjects also. Girls say the only fly in the ointment is that formal tuition in ICT peters out early; school says ICT tuition is 'top of the agenda'.

Scholars' programme helps broaden learning, and individual progress reviewed annually by the head; scholars (and other pupils if interested) meet on Friday afternoons for talks, eg corporate Britain, the mathematics of poetry, the science of diamonds and UK prehistory. 'The thing I really love about this school is that it's cool to be clever,' enthused one. Up to 15 per cent of girls have educational psychology reports; extra maths and English for anyone falling behind.

Games, options, the arts: Lacrosse is top of the sporting agenda, with hockey, netball, swimming, tennis, cross-country, athletics and riding also on the 'official' list. School claims that sport here can be enjoyed for 'fun, fitness and by fanatics'; one parent commented that there was 'too much emphasis on winning in first year', while another said her daughter's 'confidence in sport had gone up stratospherically', so clearly balances out. Lots of optional sports clubs, from fencing and volley ball to zumba; small fitness suite occupies adjacent room to fabulous 25-metre swimming pool. First lacrosse team won U19 National Schools Lacrosse Championships two years running.

Music excellent, with over half of girls taking instrumental and singing lessons – all the usual instruments on offer and many learn more than one. Lessons rotate through the timetable for years 1 to 4, and are scheduled outside academic lessons for years 5 and above. Around 80 take music exams each year and the majority passes with merit or distinction. We did feel slightly sorry for sensitive musicians playing in Rose Villa in winter (most music taught here); feels a bit damp and Dickensian and soundproofing between rooms isn't great – head says a planned fundraising campaign will set aside capital to refurbish the building. Modern, circular Blackledge Theatre makes up for these shortcomings with a wonderful central performance space, ringed by music rooms with good acoustics. Used for concerts, drama productions, debates and talks by visiting speakers. There is a school orchestra, concert and jazz bands, plus a good range of instrumental ensembles including string, wind and brass trios, quartets and consorts. Vocal ensemble reached the finals of BBC Songs of Praise School Choir of the Year competition; has also won Barnardo's Choir of the Year and performed in the Royal Albert Hall.

Fantastic art block lures the arty, academic girl who might otherwise have gone for Salisbury's grammar school. Two spacious studios for drawing/painting, with separate rooms dedicated to textiles, ceramics, photography and 3D; another smaller room full of iMacs for graphic design. Working artists regularly visit and set projects for GCSE students; hugely enthusiastic art teacher (would happily have talked for hours) described field trips and artwork in detail. Art on display is outstanding; fabulous paintings all over the place (one girl had even managed to sell her work in a local gallery) and excellent A level displays.

Plenty of other opportunities outside the classroom for girls to add to their CV: CCF and D of E programmes run by willing volunteers and local defence firm Qinetiq partners an engineering scheme (girls worked on designing video equipment to record weapon drops). Debates take place with boys from Bishop Wordsworth Grammar School. Over 60 clubs at lunch time and after school include the usual and unusual, eg bell-ringing, sugar-craft, Japanese and Mandarin.

New Women in Business programme invites upper school girls to put together a business project and bid for £10,000 start up capital donated by local investor.

Background and atmosphere: Founded in 1726 from a bequest made by Elizabeth Godolphin, school opened its doors 100 years later with the admission of eight 'orphan gentlewomen' into its first home, the private residence of the headmistress; moved to its present 16-acre site on Milford Hill in 1891, 10 minutes away from the cathedral close and city centre. The original building is now the main school hall, with newer buildings squeezed on to almost every available square foot of those 16 acres; traditional grass playing fields are at the heart of the campus. Somehow, school's hilltop setting prevents it from feeling cramped and overlooked. Buildings have been placed sympathetically and there is even room for a car park (manic when there is an event involving the whole school).

Most visitors blink twice when first confronted with an army of girls going to and fro in their royal blue 'pinnies' (worn over full school uniform) but girls seem genuinely to love them and regularly vote to keep them. We suspect this reflects the 'incredibly middle class, sensible families' which gravitate towards this school, but really no bad thing as everyone looks uniformly neat and tidy. Girls don't hesitate to express themselves through their hairdos (locals recognise 'Godolphin girl hair' at 50 paces).

Boarding recently restructured to include years 5 and 6 in the prep school, and boarders now join a house according to age: junior (9-13), senior (13-16) and sixth form (16-18). Boarding houses being completely refurbished and still a work in progress; study bedrooms are comfortably spacious with plenty of storage and common areas. Shared dining hall adjoins junior and senior houses; sixth form house has its own kitchen. Sixth form centre provides areas for study, leisure and careers advice plus Costa Coffee café. Drive to attract more boarders is paying off; numbers are on the up (welcomed by girls and parents alike as both would like more integration) but as a result flexi-boarding is becoming more difficult. 'You have to board more than three nights to get your own bed.'

A dizzying programme of extracurricular activities, known as Godolphin Plus, is run by academic staff seven days a week; some activities compulsory for those staying in and for everyone up until 5pm, whilst others are optional. Activities vary according to age, eg cooking and mug decorating for younger girls, with quiz nights and poetry evenings for older ones. We confess to wondering how staff keeps energy levels up, but looks like enormous fun! House parents supervise boarders' extra activities and keep a beady eye on prep. Friendly, informal rivalry encouraged between the houses, with 'bake-offs', sports matches and performing arts competitions taking place throughout the year.

Pastoral care and discipline: Parents full of praise for 'excellent' pastoral care provided by school. 'Girls talk to their tutors rather than bringing problems home,' said one parent. 'Matrons are lovely', said another. Teaching staff say they are always on the lookout for anyone looking a bit miserable. By the same token, the school is prepared to take action if a member of staff is not cutting the mustard and therefore pre-empt unhappiness. Mutual trust between girls and staff ensures that the privilege of walking into town (allowed in groups from year 3) is rarely abused; nor are there any problems with smoking, drugs or alcohol. 'There simply isn't the culture here.' Contact with boys is encouraged; socials arranged with Winchester College and Bishop Wordsworth boys' schools from third year up (closely chaperoned). Sixth formers allowed a glass of wine or champagne (tightly controlled chit system operates) at their parties and can entertain male visitors in the boarding house until 10pm. Parents say that the school 'listens to its pupils'. Above all, a very friendly place; 'sitting in the car park, one sees girls walking along, skipping along, all smiles and cuddles – it's a very happy school.'

Pupils and parents: Until recently, mostly local families but this looks set to change with the rise in boarding numbers. As international students are capped at 17 per cent, school will probably continue to attract the daughters of middle class professional parents, eg doctors, lawyers and business people. 'No toffs here', chirped one parent, backed up by another who opined that 'this isn't a school for the upwardly mobile.' Doubtless true, but the large vehicles in the car park and 'designer mufti' on weekends might still make it a bit tough for those scraping together every penny for fees to feel completely comfortable here. Sixth formers are relaxed, articulate and self-confident, clearly allowed to grow up to be themselves; at the same time, younger girls don't leave childhood behind too soon. Old Girls include Jilly Cooper, Minette Walters, Dorothy

Sayers (three boarding houses renamed after these writers), together with Deborah Mearden, Amanda Brookfield, Lousie Beale, Charlotte Longfield and Katie Knapman.

Entrance: At 11+, 12+, 13+ and sixth form. Registered pupils invited for a preview day and night in the autumn term, before taking entrance exams in the spring term. Girls come from school's own prep, plus other local prep schools such as Leaden Hall, Salisbury Cathedral School, Farleigh, Chafyn Grove, Princes Mead, Stroud, Twyford, St Swithun's Junior School, Forres Sandle Manor, Finton House, St Thomas's Prep and Cheam.

Exit: Around 30 per cent leaves after GCSE, to local state schools and sixth form colleges. Most sixth formers go on to higher education; a good handful chooses art foundation courses. Russell Group universities loom large in the list of leavers' destinations, five to Oxbridge in 2013; others to eg Bath, Bristol, Leeds, Manchester, Exeter, Warwick, Oxford Brookes. Courses range from archaeology to criminology, philosophy, theology, maths and medicine; a few opt to study music at a conservatoire or follow a vocational course, eg occupational therapy. Around a quarter takes a gap year.

Money matters: Scholarships at 11+, 12+, and 13+ for outstanding merit or promise in academic work, music, sport or art (13+ only). Awards are worth 25 per cent of boarding or day fees. In sixth form, scholarships awarded for all of the above plus drama. Additional bursaries may be awarded to scholars in case of financial hardship. Six Foundation Bursaries (worth 70 per cent) are offered to orphans in need of financial support, when one parent has died or whose parents are separated or divorced. An Old Godolphin Association Bursary (25 per cent) is occasionally available to the daughter or granddaughter of a former pupil at the school. Entrance bursaries are available to all eligible candidates (including at 14+) in order of registration.

Remarks: A wonderfully nurturing school which gets very good results and provides a kind and supportive boarding experience. Girls who might feel overwhelmed in an academic hothouse are just as likely to flourish here as the confident, independent types who don't mind the heat. Scholars' programme has introduced a slightly more competitive edge, but most unlikely to become a pressure cooker or lose its warm and caring ethos; should keep going from strength to strength.

Gordon's School

West End, Woking, GU24 9PT

• Pupils: 740 pupils, 380 boys, 360 girls; 125 full and 70 weekly boarders • Ages: 11–18 • Inter-denom • Fees: Boarding £14,607; Day £6,483 pa • State

Tel: 01276 858084
Email: registrar@gordons.surrey.sch.uk
Website: www.gordons.surrey.sch.uk

Head Teacher: Since September 2010, Mr Andrew Moss BA MEd NPQH (forties). Started teaching in 1992 and has worked in a variety of boarding and day schools, including most recently a headship in a Cognita independent school. Before that he was a deputy head in Hampshire, and deputy, director of studies and housemaster at Wymondham College (also a state boarding school). 'He's a breath of fresh air,' said one in the know, 'bringing the school forward, without losing the best parts.'

He's less of a father figure than his predecessor, who transformed Gordon's from plodding to premier league, but is equally enthusiastic about this rather unusual school. 'I'm in the best of both worlds,' he says. 'We have the sort of heritage and behaviour you'll typically see in an independent, but with more grounded, authentic people around, people from all walks of life.'

Every parent we spoke to described him as 'professional', then variously as 'dynamic', 'pleasant' and 'ambitious', although some admitted they did not know him very well yet. 'He speaks well at meetings, seems a good manager and has a very business-like manner,' said one, 'but he hasn't put himself out to get to know people'. Yet all agree he has a good handle on the school and is well-respected by pupils, from whom he'll take no nonsense. 'If he told my children to jump, they would simply ask "How high sir",' said one. Interviewed by pupils in the school magazine, they said of him; 'His signature stern, tough chapel talks have become synonymous with his presence itself'.

He's undoubtedly got strong ideas, but does use staff and parents as a sounding board and talks about 'empowering people' and 'decentralisation'. 'You can't build capacity all by yourself,' he says. 'You need good people to get involved and play a role in ideas and delivery'. Wasted no time in making his presence felt – investing in several projects including building new and revamping existing facilities, improving reporting systems and assessment methods and sorting out better communications with parents.

Keeps a finger on the pulse by taking PSHE lessons on economics and finance once a week. Has two children of his own (both at the school) and is a keen skier in his spare time.

Academic matters: Among the very best state offerings in the country, with an academically rigorous curriculum. It is an all-ability school, for which pupils are not selected via entrance exams, yet its results are top notch. In 2013 85 per cent of pupils achieved five or more GCSE A*- C grades, including English and maths, with 42 per cent A*/A grades. At A level in 2013 27 per cent A*/A grades.

Its secret? Head puts it down to school's balance of traditional and modern methods – everything from reading out loud and spelling tests, through to use of peer assessment and mini whiteboards. Parents like its size (small), the emphasis on setting (rather than mixed-ability teaching) and its boarding school ethos.

Although two-thirds of its pupils live at home, the school is structured as a boarding school, with these 'day boarders' (as they are known) organised the same way as the wholly residential boarders in an extended school day. So everyone is in a house, with house parents, and following the same programme, including supervised homework, until 7.30pm.

Everyone is set for English, maths and science (out of four) and also for languages in years 7 and 8 – a language is compulsory at GCSE; either German, French or Spanish. Class sizes average 22, maximum 30 with a ratio 12:1 pupils to teaching staff. Lowish requirements for additional support, some seven per cent have one to one EAL help and four per cent have statements of special educational need, led by full time SENCo and delivered in small groups and individually. 'Although it's a regimented place, the school does adapt well to individuals', said one mother. 'They are very good at saying, this person has issues, let's sort him out – and I've seen some children really blossom here'.

They plough through the work, books filled at a pace and there are plenty of practice papers and timed tests to make sure everyone is well prepared for GCSE. 'The new linear exams will suit us,' says AM. 'In fact we will gain as our work ethic is all about keeping it together to the end'. School has never been keen on the 're-takes' culture which fuelled much of the GCSE discontent.

Parents praise a strong and disciplined teaching team with high expectations that pupils will be self-disciplined to work hard and be courteous at all times. Good systems in place ensure that nobody slips through the net. 'Monitoring is really good', said one parent. 'If someone isn't working at the expected level they will be pulled into a clinic to get them up to scratch'. One of AM's tasks has been to improve the process still further, with more informative, more frequent reporting, particularly for key stage 4/5. On top of an effort grade, pupils now receive target and working grades and every half term they receive significant feedback on what they need to do next. Lessons are fairly formal, there's an atmosphere of calm, but pupils are fully involved. Word on the street is that supply teachers find covering lessons at Gordon's a pleasure – they do not get ripped to shreds as in some state schools.

Homework is 'reasonable' – homework diaries are an important part of keeping on top of everything, really well used, signed every week by parents and school. 'They have to have it with them at all times and it's great for day to day communications, gets them organised and responsible,' said a parent. 'It's almost like the children are on report at all times,' said another. 'But it's for good comments too – they can get a stamp (like a gold star) and sometimes we'll get a note from a head of department or a house master if they've done something wonderful'. Evidently the regime can be stressful for some; 'My son cried for half an hour when he lost his homework once,' one mother said.

Around 180 at sixth form take 'facilitating' A levels (serious subjects that will win students places at Russell Group and other leading universities). No vocational qualifications on offer. 'We retain those for whom the sixth form is suitable,' says AM. Parents like it that sixth formers are not allowed off-site during teaching hours, so are more likely to work during their free periods – school calls them 'study periods, there are no frees'.

Ofsted rate school as 'outstanding'; its glowing report is littered with superlatives like 'exceptional' and 'beyond excellent'.

Games, options, the arts: It's all going on, both during the school day and as extracurricular options. After what would be the end of the school day at most state schools, the extended day here begins with 'period 6' – anything from sport to cooking, calligraphy to mountain biking or ultimate Frisbee. It's compulsory, and costs some £6400 a year, although if pupils have a bona fide after hours activity not available at the school there will be a dispensation.

Masses of sport on offer, with good facilities on site – more than 40 acres of playing fields, and all the usual football, rugby and hockey pitches, to the less usual (for a state school) shooting range, Astroturf and indoor heated swimming pool. Gordon's teams are happy to take on the toughest opponents and often play independent schools. Next on AM's wish list is a new sports hall – you don't doubt he will get one. 'Sport is a great release for everyone here' said one mother. 'There's so much for them to do so that it's not all about pure academia. It's more of a lifestyle, there's a total mix of ages on the parade square after school and always someone around to kick a ball with'. 'I love that my son's outside instead of on his X box,' said another. 'The amount of physical activity is great.'

There's a huge emphasis on D of E, with some 90 pupils achieving awards every year and lots of it at the much tougher gold end of things. 'Bronze is one thing, but getting stuck into a trip to Borneo is quite different form working in a charity shop for an hour a week,' said AM. 'It's quite striking how many golds we get, in fact we have organised 40 overseas trips in the past 10 years'. And all three forces are represented in Gordon's combined cadet force – quite a feat to manage a naval unit in land-locked Surrey.

Great tradition of hard-fought inter-house competition gets everyone involved, regardless of ability; not just in sport but also in art, music and drama, with specialist facilities for all – an outdoor theatre is the latest addition. There are two annual art exhibitions and two full scale productions every year. Music

very big, as well as an orchestra, choir and concert band, there's a pipe and drum band which, together with marching practice, is a major focus of the school.

Background and atmosphere: Ceremony and discipline is in the DNA of Gordon's, which was founded in 1885, at the behest of Queen Victoria, as a national memorial to General Gordon who was killed at Khartoum. The reigning monarch has been the school's patron ever since.

Every pupil learns to march and takes part in every one of the eight parades and chapel services held each year, accompanied by the previously mentioned pipes and drums marching band. There is marching practice every Friday, and once a year pupils go to London and literally stop the traffic when they march down Whitehall to the Cenotaph, ending up at the bronze statue of General Gordon on the Embankment. Although right up the street of the keen musicians in the band, it can be rather a chore for the others. 'I wouldn't say the marching is universally popular, but they get used to it – it's just what they do, everybody does it, it's part of Gordon's,' said a parent. 'And in fact after they have left school I think that trip along Whitehall will be a really special memory for them.'

Day to day things are rather less regimented, but all very orderly – AM likes to describe the atmosphere as 'purposeful calm'. The school is built around a large quadrangle, quite bare and military in feel, with the odd bench here and there, where the students hang out during break and lunch if they are not in their houses. Alongside the original Victorian buildings are some less pretty 1960s additions, and (much better) 21st century facilities, including the new music and drama centre, science block and sixth form centre. Classrooms are large, light and spacious, in both the older and newer buildings, and well resourced. Stunning chapel, built in 1894, which houses numerous school treasures, including a book which lists the names of all the Gordon's boys killed in the two world wars. Pupils are never for a moment in any doubt about their school's heritage.

There are five day houses and four residential houses – all well used by both day and full boarders, who mix well. Boys and girls are allowed freely in each other's houses, but no boy is allowed upstairs in the girls' boarding houses and vice versa. Boys' houses with pool and table tennis tables, girls centred more around comfy sofas and bean bags. Full boarding houses include common rooms, study areas and dormitories with study/bed units – all homely and understandably more relaxed and not as tidy and regimented as other parts of the school. Ofsted's inspection of boarding facilities pronounced them 'outstanding' in every respect. One boarder said that he doesn't 'go home' in the holidays, saying that he and his parents considered the school to be his main home.

Pastoral care and discipline: A very disciplined place; 'Without good order there can be no learning in the classroom,' says school. Generally not much allowance for anyone stepping out of line, but for those obedient souls happy to stay within the set boundaries there are plenty of rewards and responsibilities on offer. Pupils quickly pick up on what's expected of them at Gordon's – they get it and are generally hardworking and appreciative of what's on offer. 'It's brilliant fun' and 'not one horrible teacher', our tour guides told us. They don't even seem to mind their 'boarders' duties' – vacuuming and emptying the bins.

School terribly keen on simple good manners, insists that pupils are courteous and considerate of others. Similarly picky about uniform. If a girl's skirt is deemed too short (and we didn't see any) she will be given a week's grace to get a new one. Everyone attends the chapel twice a week. Very close companionship among pupils who say they trust each other. New peer mentoring system working well. Need we mention zero tolerance of bullying, alcohol, drugs and associated misdemeanours? Strong culture of 'telling' to house parents and tutors is encouraged from the off. One longstanding parent convinced it's the combined support from house parents, tutors and teachers that underpins the academic success here.

Pupils and parents: Although it's a state school, most parents have money, certainly parents of boarders who have to cover the boarding fees. Parents of day boarders must be able to afford the £6000+ day boarding fees and will be in a certain socio-economic demographic to live in the catchment; of necessity they must live practically next door and some will move house to get this education for their children. 'We may have spent time and effort moving so close, but we saved on tutoring for entrance to a selective school and are continuing to save a fortune in comparison to the level of fees we'd pay for an independent school now,' said one. Aside from these locals, parents are a huge mix of professional, diplomatic and Forces. Weekly boarders typically live within an hour's drive, full boarders come from all over the UK, with about 10 per cent from overseas.

Pupils seem friendly, happy and very proud of their school; all regular young people, not quiet and cowed by the rules and regulations, but confident and ambitious types who seem to thrive in the order of everything.

Parent/school communications have improved – still a way to go, but would have been more of a criticism a few years ago. Text messaging system, emails, more frequent newsletters and bulletins are all AM innovations and remodelling of website is next on his 'to do' list.

Entrance: Tough. There are typically 400 applications for the 100 year 7 places on offer and around half of these are generally swallowed up by siblings. Non-selective, so no entrance exams. Around a third of places go to full or weekly residential boarders, prioritised by 'need to board'. This usually means children from Forces families from the UK and overseas – the school foresees increasing numbers of such children following recent changes to legislation.

For admission as a 'day boarder' think purely of location. Catchment varies but typically you'll need to live no further than 600m from the school. Mother of a baby was enquiring when we visited and local estate agents are well used to dealing with desperate parents who've left it rather later, but want to move next door. A small number of places allocated each year to children with statements of special educational needs.

Some additional places are available for the sixth form, where the entry requirement for both existing and new pupils is five GCSEs A*-C (including English and maths) with Bs for subjects to be taken at A level.

Exit: Most stay for the sixth form, then on to university; one to Oxbridge in 2013. A few head off at 16 for more vocational courses at nearby Brooklands College.

Money matters: The education is free, but parents pay for the boarding, and even parents of day pupils (called 'day boarders') must pay for the compulsory post 3.30pm element of the day, house system, Saturday school, lunches and teas. Some bursaries available.

Remarks: A very different state offering – more like a private school without the price tag and elitism. Committed to traditional values, high standards, good discipline – doesn't share its 'semper fidelis' motto with the US marine corps for nothing. Those happy with the 'heads down and work' ethos are rewarded with an all-round top notch education, pastoral care par excellence and enviable opportunities for sport. Suits focused, self-directed types, rather than a rebel who would be exhausted by the discipline. It's a school for achievers – a child with no oomph or aspirations would be lost among these go-getters.

Gordonstoun School

Linked school: Aberlour House the Junior School at Gordonstoun

Elgin, Moray, IV30 5RF

- Pupils: 425 boarders, 65 day; boys and girls • Ages: 13–18
- Inter-denom • Fees: Day £12,420–£24,651; Boarding £20,199–£33,285 pa • Independent

Tel: 01343 837837
Email: admissions@gordonstoun.org.uk
Website: www.gordonstoun.org.uk

Principal: Since 2011, Mr Simon Reid BA (English) (50), a South African who read English at the University of Witwatersrand. Came to Britain in 1985 because he, 'wanted to teach English literature in the country where it was written'. Comes from Worksop College where he was deputy head, having started his UK teaching career at Brentwood School, thence Stowe, and Christ's Hospital (housemaster for six years). His wife, Michele, is French, the family bi-lingual. Two young, one at uni and t'other in sixth form at Gordonstoun.

Enthusiastic about the Round Square ethos, Reid upbraided us when we spouted our usual mantra: please could we have results by subject by number of pupils by results… with a sharp, 'for some pupils a B or a C in any subject is a triumph in itself.' We know, we know academia is not what Gordonstoun is about, but we like to trace trends. By the time they leave, 'Gordonstoun pupils should know about service, face up to challenge, be capable of leading, globally aware, resilient not arrogant', which is fine and dandy as far as it goes. Focus is useful. Perhaps it should be adopted as the sixth Gordonstoun commandment? We reiterate our editor's brief, why should anyone send a child to any school when they have no idea about the academic strengths and weaknesses of the place.

Academic matters: 'Students are here for the whole broad experience'; 'The balance is important'. Huge range of ability from children, from those 'at the lower end of the academic scale', to all A* candidates. Gordonstoun boasts a pass rate A-E (99 per cent last year since you ask: most schools only mention A-C). 'A level results recorded the highest number of A*/A passes and saw 95 per cent of students gain entry to the university of their choice,' in 2011. 'School getting more academic,' says the head.' We requested detailed exam results, by subject by grade as we always do: 'We do not publish our exam result on an annual basis but a copy of the average over the last three years is attached. What is worth noticing this year is that the highest number of students achieving above their predictions, whether that is at A* level or below. This is far more important than detailed examination results and highlights the distinctiveness of our broad curriculum and ethos'. Native speakers can do A levels in their own langs. Classes setted for maths and English from 13. Networked computers throughout, wireless connection in all boarding houses. Bespoke international citizenship course new kid on the block, Reid takes it at top end: not PSHE or RS but 'examining real problems against a global background'. Good remedial support – all pupils screened on arrival. Will scribe for exams. EAL available at all levels.

Games, options, the arts: Community service is important at Gordonstoun. All do service training aged 16 and choose which discipline to follow: the fire brigade (the most popular), mountain rescue, coastguards, canoe life guards, ski patrol, first aid, technical, marine training and rescue, conservation, pool life guards. Number of exchanges with other Round Square schools – Canada, Germany, Australia. Local projects and joint international expeditions to India, Sinai, Thailand,

Kenya, Honduras to work on conservation/ecological schemes. The latter are expensive – students are encouraged to fund raise to meet own costs. Outdoor pursuits expeditions, sleeping in snow holes, add a whole new dimension.

School has its own 80 foot sail-training yacht, Ocean Spirit of Moray, timetabled sailing weeks (when the weather can be 'pretty wild', according to the skippers, ditto the crew). Tall ships' race a regular feature; school has a new 28 foot training cutter and a rash of new lasers (which could make for interesting sailing).

Mainstream games on course but long distances to other schools for matches cause problems. Reid says 'school plays locals and rugby league'. New sports hall opened in March 2013 by Olympians Heather Stanning and Zara Tindall. Those over 16 can be in charge of swimming pool and do life guard training. Outstanding Ogston theatre, new extension, performing arts studio with sprung dance floor. Newest drama studios look stunning. We were shown the previous green room, now a storage area of monumental proportions, in detail; how anyone finds anything in the place goodness only knows. Par hazard, our guide was the daughter of a long time friend; our other guide was a most charming clever-clogs about to hit global mathematical hotspots (from Norfolk, full blown scholarship). A level pupils lead dance workshops in local primaries. Each year group has 'headmaster's reels' of a Saturday, with a caller. Head not yet been known to wear the kilt.

Trips all over – Europe, Australasia, points west. Magnificent art, lots of disciplines, graphic design impressive. Particularly strong DT with pupils learning not only to make lights but also cost them effectively.

Background and atmosphere: Founded in 1934 by the German educationalist, Kurt Hahn, Jewish refugee, founder of Salem School in Baden-Württemberg and believer in educating and developing all aspects of children, not just the academic. Grounds and setting lovely – half a mile from the Moray Firth with cliffs and beaches nearby, and not as cold as one might think (Gulf Stream). Gordonstoun House is a former residence of Gordon-Cumming of card-cheating fame. Beautiful circular stable block (hence Round Square) houses the library and boys' house. Cunning music rooms round exotic chapel (shaped like an open book – magnificent, but repairs to the pews are sadly botched).

Head is masterminding a £10.5 million (apparently no problem getting dosh) 'refurbishment' of the Round Square boarding house and making the old building above accessible to all 'by creating a curriculum centre for international and spiritual citizenship'. We are not actually quite sure what this means – sounds a tad like new-labour-speak, and to think it was not that long ago we found a couple happily bonking in one of the alcoves (which was, perhaps, in view of many many previous incidents – more in keeping with the spirit of the place).

Certain amount of re-jigging houses; girls' houses bung full, but some boys' houses (sixth form particularly) could be busier. The lease on Duffus House at the entrance to the school will be given up within the next five years. Houses spread all over, some quite a hike from the main school (you would never guess they were originally army huts). Minimal exeats – distances are huge, but pupils often do not want to go home, regular socials (by block on Saturdays), films and formal dinners. This is a school that has to make its own entertainment. Prospectus lists nearby hotels, B&Bs (with prices) and ways of getting to school (a good four hours from Edinburgh but less than that flying from London). Non-stop social life which swings right through the holidays – caveat for Southerners.

NB planes from nearby Lossiemouth (currently under reprieve) 'the largest and busiest fast-jet base in The Royal Air Force'. Low flying planes screech overhead about every three minutes (strangely, and this editor has visited Gordonstoun five or six times, this is not a memory we have of previous visits).

The young say you get used to them after a while. Reid says: 'This is not accurate. They are not allowed to fly directly over the school and only take off over the nearby runway two or three times a day unless they are on a major exercise'. Okay, but they seemed to be only hundreds of feet above the games field nearest to the swimming pool every couple of minutes.

Pastoral care and discipline: Occasional problems with drugs smoking and alcohol (not to mention the P word) – 'not totally whiter than white'. No automatic expulsions; pupils get alcohol or smoking points, and head negotiates with the parents. 'Not accurate, head manages according to Gordonstoun code of conduct', according to Reid. 'The Code of Conduct is not on our website but is posted to every parent before their child joins the school and is re-sent if there are any changes', in other words, the goal posts have changed. Drugs: straight to the head, usually straight out. Will take pupils who have had to leave other schools: contract in place. Head tough on perpetual offenders, particularly bullies – 'Children have eventually had to leave the school as a result', said the previous head. Commendably clear rules. Girls and boys can visit each others' houses but only allowed in the opposite sex's 'mixed common room'. (sounds a blast) and nowhere else. Each pupil has an academic tutor, boarders have houseparents and assistant houseparents in every house. Shopping bus to Elgin on Friday, but only the upper sixth can visit on Saturdays and can 'have meals out in the evening'. Head removed our previous comment that Elgin can be pretty rough and has had a serious, and we mean serious drug problem in the not too recent past. God worshipped in a Christian fashion, more than lip-service to other faiths. Local minister can prepare for confirmation. (Principal would prefer we changed this to 'prepares for confirmation'.)

Pupils and parents: A third English, a third Scottish and a third from the rest of the world – wide diversity of students, some deeply rich, some less so, with the less so benefiting from serious scholarships. Numbers of first time buyers. Parents dropping off their young have been known to stay, 'for a few days'. FPs include royals; William Boyd; Eddie Shah; the composer of 'The Flower of Scotland' – Roy Williamson; Martin Shea; Alan Shiach; Lara Croft; Sophie Morgan, who commentated for Channel 4 for the Paralympics; 2012 Olympian gold medal winner, rower Heather Stanning. Numbers currently (Reid changed this to 'marginally') down, particularly boarding boys and day pupils.

Entrance: Pupils come up through the junior school, Aberlour (usually automatically, at 11), Ardvreck, Cargilfield, Belhaven (under the new management) and prep schools south of the border. Assessment for those joining at year 10 (about 10 each year) and influx to sixth form. Pupils are assessed both academically and for personality. Odd places sometimes available for pupils, 'at any level of the school for short periods – although not normally less than one term'. Keen to keep up its intake from outside Scotland – may pay travel/hotel bills for prospective parents. Gordonstoun challenge – usually in June – invites UK prep schools to send teams of four or five, all expenses paid for a three day jamboree at Gordonstoun. The idea, of course, being that the little darlings will be so impressed, that whatever school they had previously considered will be cast aside. (NB in previous times Gordonstoun gave scholarships to all prep heads' children regardless).

Exit: 'Non-stimulated young' and even some less academic young have been known to leave Gordonstoun at sixth form level to study A levels elsewhere, either at other schools or crammers. Around 15 per cent don't aim for university but for family business (fair number of local farmers – as opposed to landowners), vocational training, though not, we think, the Forces. Otherwise to universities all over: Newcastle, Leeds, Bristol and Edinburgh eternally popular, occasional Oxbridge entrants.

Money matters: Set fee; parents can 'opt above', and some do, 'notably so'. Scholarships and bursaries awarded after means-testing. Hardship fund. Success of flourishing international summer school helps with dosh. Fundraising doesn't seem that difficult. Stunning new bursaries for children of fisherfolk. Second hand clothes shop. Picked up the tab when Aberlour House was closed in 2004 (it was losing money); the buildings were sold and funds realised more or less paid for the stunning new build, Aberlour, in the grounds.

Remarks: Children and parents appear happy. Fashionable, co-ed outward-boundish boarding school with vast range of pupil backgrounds, not overtly academic, though current head vows it is getting more so. Recent HMI/Care Commission (Feb 2011) inspection awarded 'excellent' for two out of the five categories and 'very good' in the remaining three. Increasingly popular, Aberlour prep school in the grounds has been an enormous addition. Budget airline flights to nearest airports popular with southern-based families as well as those further afield. Regular direct links from Inverness to Amsterdam: Aberdeen to Frankfurt, and thence to points global. It is still a long drive from Edinburgh and Glasgow.

The Grammar School at Leeds

Alwoodley Gates, Harrogate Road, Leeds, LS17 8GS

• Pupils: 1,200 boys and 1,100 girls • Ages: 3–18 • Non denominational • Fees: £8,001–£11,691 pa • Independent

Tel: 01132 291552
Email: admissions@gsal.org.uk
Website: www.gsal.org.uk

Principal and Chief Executive: Since 2010, Mr Michael Gibbons. In his fifties, he has been head of Queen Elizabeth Grammar School, Wakefield. He read history and completed a PGCE at Kings College London.

Academic matters: Academically selective and well up in league tables – 86 per cent A*-B grades at A level in 2013 and 70 per cent A*/A at GCSE. Generally a longer male than female tail but very good showing in value-added terms. Good girls' entry in science and maths at A level and GCSE; size enables school to lay on many language options (German, French, Latin, Greek, Spanish). A choice of almost 30 A level subjects. Most pupils relish the academic challenge and appreciate support of well-qualified and dedicated staff (teacher:pupil ratio across whole school is 1:10). A real sense of intellectual purpose about the place. Up-to-date library and IT facilities support teaching. All pupils screened for dyslexia on entry; some help given thereafter. Many new teachers appointed in recent years, committed to coeducational school.

Games, options, the arts: Boys had strong reputation in traditional team games (frequent representation at county level and beyond in rugby, and, this being Yorkshire, the 1st XI tend to moonlight in the tough world of league cricket). Football now an official game, taking advantage of both social trends and vast playing fields on new site. Girls' standards have risen (equal users of two huge Astroturf pitches), reached national finals in U14 and U18 netball. Lacrosse taster, mixed hockey, football too, and plenty of other sports, including strong cross-country. Visits to outdoor centre in splendidly wild upper Teesdale centre part of everyone's curriculum. Voluntary CCF, scouts and D of E also on offer.

Girls' school had outstanding art tradition, which continues; boys no sluggards either. Strong food technology department – boys much in evidence in cookery club. Exceptional music: classical, folk, jazz, and 60 per cent learn an instrument. Lively magazine – ambitious and satirical writing, plenty of humour. Good drama, no more need for one school to 'lend' pupils to the other for productions. Very good debating (national successes).

Background and atmosphere: Girls' school (LGHS) founded in 1876 by Yorkshire Ladies Council for Education, while the boys' (LGS) was founded in 1552 when Sir William Sheafield left £14.13s.4d. to found a school 'for all such young scholars, youthes and children as shall come to be taught, instructed and informed'. New premises were found in 1624, and in 1857 increasing numbers prompted a further move to a site a mile from the city centre, with confidently gothic ecclesiastical buildings – now part of Leeds University – designed by EM Barry, brother of the then headmaster and member of the famous architectural family. In 1997 lack of space and pressure of curriculum brought the governors' courageous decision to build a completely new school, under Dr Bailey's predecessor, on the north edge of Leeds.

Result is a very handsome set of buildings, 'a blend of function and quality', designed by an architect who did imaginative work at the previous LGS site, incorporating (according to one senior pupil) 'the longest school corridor in Europe'. Vital historical bits from the old buildings are incorporated – few if any major schools start with an advantage like this (visitors are wafted by lift from reception to the elegant administrative area and invited to admire the campanile, piazza and porte-cochère). Though purpose-building didn't come cheap, fee increases over the last four years have been 'comfortably below sector average'.

Recent building in preparation for merger includes new science, maths and music provision, departmental suites, a dining hall and a sixth form common room; a second sports hall and extension to theatre are planned. Each year group has its own common room and now more intimate sheltered areas for association – something probably more appreciated by girls, who miss the cosier atmosphere of the old LGHS, which gave rise to a strong sense of community. Most (younger) boys have simpler needs, connected with space to kick a football around.

Impression is that all pupils are determined to make the new school work and, in fact, don't always recognise problems that may exercise staff and parents. A buzz of confidence in the air as pupils move about the generous and well-lit circulation space; parents comment on the civilised consideration pupils show for each other. Strong house system throws girls and boys of different ages together for communal activities – not only sports competitions but also maths, masterchef and music.

Girls and boys aged 11 to 16 are taught separately (the so-called 'diamond' system), but pastoral and social activities are in a mixed environment. Sixth form is completely coeducational.

Pastoral care and discipline: Both schools had excellent systems and much thought went into new structures, firmly established from day one, and more generously staffed than formerly. Head keen to point out that a big school doesn't mean big units, just a lot more small ones; heads and deputies of each year located in offices next to their groups, to keep a benign eye on things.

Pupils and parents: From Leeds and a wide arc to the north, well served by public and school-run bus routes. Significant proportion from ethnic minorities, notably Asian, and a strong traditional Jewish element, all reflecting area's cultural diversity. Doesn't serve only the wealthy – bursary fund on its way to second million. Parents generally supportive, many typically outspoken Yorkshire. Former pupils include Dame Pauline Neville Jones, journalist Jill Parkin, comedian Barry Cryer, poet and playwright Tony Harrison, singer Robin Blaze, Gerald Kaufman MP, Ricky Wilson of the Kaiser Chiefs, and golfer Colin Montgomerie (who has given a sports-weighted bursary).

Entrance: Mostly from own junior school (tinies still in Rose Court on original LGHS site, 7-11 located with senior school) and local primaries, some from independent preps. Selection by usual in-house exam, interview and report. Some places available at 16+, heavily over-subscribed since merger; minimum five grade Bs at GCSE demanded including, where appropriate, subjects applicant wants to study in sixth form.

Exit: Nearly all (predictably) to higher education in well-established universities: 17 to Oxbridge in 2013. Very few leave after GCSE. Gap years popular.

Money matters: A number of means tested bursaries available at age 11, a few at 16; a few academic/music scholarships 'for exceptional potential'.

Remarks: Created in 2008 as merger of two excellent single-sex schools, Leeds Grammar and Leeds Girls' High. Despite careful four-year preparation there were bound to be differences of approach in first year (more among staff and parents than pupils?) to be reconciled. Girls and boys react differently to discipline and surroundings; one parent of girls found rules 'boy-centred', another's daughter welcomed the wide extra-curricular range. But a fresh identity undoubtedly being forged with both constituencies being taken seriously and suspicions of a male takeover diminishing; much responsibility here on the senior management team and breaking down a 1,500+ school into manageable and pupil-friendly units (see above). All in all, a remarkable school, drawing fully on excellence of both former parts. For many families, it makes sense to have children educated in the same place.

The Grange School

Linked school: The Grange Junior School

Bradburns Lane, Hartford, Cheshire, CW8 3AU

- Pupils: 630 boys, 520 girls, all day; • Ages: 11–18 • Christian
- Fees: £7,515–£10,050 pa • Independent

Tel: 01606 77447
Email: office@grange.org.uk
Website: www.grange.org.uk

Headmaster: Since 2005, Mr Christopher Jeffery (early fifties), BA. Read history at York. Previously deputy head at The Perse School, Cambridge. His wife is a nurse. Three children, all educated at The Grange. Very involved in the local church, plays the piano and guitar and composes music in his spare time. Fast talking and energetic. Passionate about the school and what it offers. 'Wild horses wouldn't drag me away,' he says. 'This place fits me like a glove.' Prides himself on remembering everyone's name, something commented on by both pupils and parents. 'He's so supportive and approachable,' one mother told us. 'He doesn't distance himself.'

Academic matters: Very good results. At GCSE 89 per cent A*/A in 2013. At A level in 2013 86 per cent of papers were graded A*-B; 63 per cent A*/A, placing the school as one of Cheshire's top academic performers. The head puts this down partly to real academic choices. The school doesn't turn its nose up at offering subjects such as graphic design and IT at A level. 'We need to prepare children for where the world is going,' he says. Logic lessons from year 7.

Many pupils we spoke to said the homework load was very heavy and that homework timetables often weren't followed.

However, some parents reckoned this prepared their children for the real world. The school denies any hothousing.

All sixth formers participate in an enrichment programme one afternoon every week, designed to broaden and balance the academic experience. Options include cookery, photography, community work, RocketBall and bridge. Extra support is available for pupils applying to Oxbridge or to universities abroad, and special workshops for those wishing to study medicine and engineering. There's a gap year co-ordinator and a small bursary fund for youngsters embarking on purposeful projects that make a difference to others during their gaps years. 'Service is extremely important,' says the head. 'Pupils are privileged to be here, but with that comes responsibility.'

SEN assistance is provided by a full time SENCo, as long as pupils can access the curriculum with no in-class support. All year 7s and sixth formers are screened for SEN.

Games, options, the arts: Amazing £3.6m purpose built theatre, of which children are rightly proud, used all year round for drama and stages yearly productions. House drama and art competitions.

Full range of sports, with pupils playing for country in polo, baseball, football and rowing.

Music department brimming with life and has received much investment. Housed in its own block with specialist classrooms, music technology suite and peripatetic teaching rooms. Orchestras, choirs, ensembles and lunchtime concerts give pupils plenty of opportunity to perform. House system mingles age groups for drama, music and sport. New sports hall under construction.

Background and atmosphere: Senior school was founded in 1978 due to prep school parental demand. Previous heads have concentrated on exam results but Mr Jeffery says that 'now we're firmly established we can offer more and move in different directions.' School has planning permission for further building, including a new sixth form centre, due to be completed in June 2014. Some complain that the canteen is too small. Pupils say there's 'not enough choice' and the need to pay cash causes long queues.

Pastoral care and discipline: Parents and pupils praise pastoral support offered by staff. 'All the teachers are so helpful and friendly,' one boy told us. 'But if you go off track they'll push you back on.' One mother we spoke to had a child with a long-term illness and lauded the support she received. Peer support in designated room by ChildLine trained prefects.

Pupils felt that bullying was rare but when it happened was handled well. 'Of course bullying happens,' says head, 'but we deal with it swiftly and undramatically.' He added that 'eccentrics tend to fit in well here – there's a place for everybody.'

Smart grey and green uniform, although many of the girls we spoke to bemoaned the flesh coloured tights.

Pupils and parents: Pupils come from a 25 mile radius in mid-Cheshire and as a result are mostly white, middle class and wealthy. The school offers an extraordinary number of foreign trips and although the head points out that some families are 'making sacrifices to find the fees,' pupils we spoke to didn't feel that funding these trips was an issue. The school has found it difficult to persuade families living nearer to Manchester to consider sending children here instead of travelling into the city. They are trying to tackle this with more advertising and have seen a 20 per cent increase in external applicants for year 7.

Parents are very involved in school life – raising funds, helping with sport and providing work experience. A parents' Christian group prays regularly for the school.

Entrance: Four-form entry, with 65 per cent coming from the school's own junior department. The rest come from local state primaries and other independent preps. Entrance exam consists of computerised papers in maths, vocabulary, critical thinking and reasoning and written papers in English and verbal reasoning. This is followed by a personal questionnaire.

Exit: Almost all to university, some after a gap year. Lots to Leeds, Birmingham, Edinburgh and Nottingham in 2013. Five to Oxbridge. A few to universities abroad.

Money matters: Fees are in line with other north west independent schools, but beware, exam fees aren't included. Very small bursary fund, plus a limited amount set aside for academic scholars. Music scholarships available in year 7.

Remarks: Although often overlooked, The Grange is really starting to make its mark. An excellent, friendly school, providing a sterling education. A must to consider if you are looking for a co-ed in mid-Cheshire or south of Manchester.

Graveney School

Welham Road, London, SW17 9BU

• Pupils: 1,955 boys and girls • Ages: 11–18 • Non-denom • State

Tel: 020 8682 7000
Email: info@graveney.wandsworth.sch.uk
Website: www.graveney.org

Principal: Since 1989, Mr Graham Stapleton MA (early sixties). Read history at Cambridge and started teaching at the school 40 years ago when it was Battersea Grammar School. Married with two grown-up children, his hobbies include reading (20th century American novels) and listening to jazz. He has the air of a history professor about him. No immediate plans to retire as he wants to stay and oversee setting up of new Tooting Primary School. 'Fantastic and inspiring', declares one parent. 'He really cares about each and every student'.

Academic matters: School is regarded as one of the top 200 state schools in the country. In 2013, 63 per cent A*/B grades at A level, with 36 per cent A*/A. Thirty-five subjects available at A level – English literature the most popular and film studies recently added to the list. In 2013, 75 per cent of pupils obtained five or more A*-C grades including maths and English at GCSE, with 45 per cent A*/A grades. Focus is on the academic subjects. Some 85 per cent of students take triple sciences. RE is a compulsory GCSE. All students study a foreign language – French, Spanish or German (with Latin and Mandarin available as twilight subjects – before or after school).

Students need to achieve five A*-Cs (including maths and English) to stay on into the sixth form. If they don't get these grades they have to leave (on average 20 per cent don't stay on). Those with poor AS level results are advised to find alternative courses.

Pupils are divided into ability bands as soon as they enter the school in year 7. They are banded largely by English scores and then set for maths from year 8 onwards. Extension programme for those nominated by teachers (includes PE, music and art as well as English, maths and science). Some concern from potential parents about what school is like for those who don't get into the top band (extension group), but anecdotes from current parents say that the next band (upper) is also very high achieving. 'Whichever band your child is in, the teachers will push them to achieve their best', says one mother. 'They seem to have a knack of finding out what motivates your child and then

encouraging them'. There is movement between the bands so no need to panic if your child is not in the extension group. However some parents complain about the high number of students in the extension classes – up to 33 in some cases.

High number of students with special needs (55 with statements) – 'because we have such a good reputation', explains the principal. SENCo and various learning mentors look after these students.

Games, options, the arts: Everyone is encouraged to take part in team sport and play for their form or house. Sports include rugby, football, volleyball, netball, cricket, tennis, athletics and basketball. One parent complained that there is only one timetabled session of games per week but principal stresses that all students are encouraged to take part in one extracurricular sports club after school. Even PE classes are streamed, so students get chance to play with others of similar ability.

School puts a special emphasis on music. All children eligible for free school meals get free music tuition. Around 350 learn an instrument at school (taught by peripatetic teaching staff) and more learn outside school. Each year around five students are members of the London Schools Symphony Orchestra and some students go on study music at university or music college. School orchestra has 40 students, and choir has 70. All encouraged to take part in a musical event or production. When we visited, rehearsals were in full swing for annual sixth form production – Annie Get your Gun (with 200 students taking part).

Background and atmosphere: School became an academy in 2011. It is spread out over two campuses so despite its size (around 2,000 students) it doesn't feel overcrowded. Formerly a teacher training college, the original Georgian building (now rather scruffy) houses the art department. Other buildings have been added on over the years. School was due for refurbishment before government budget cuts so now looks rather tired.

When we visited at break time, students were orderly and well behaved. Pupils all stood up when principal entered class – emphasis on good old-fashioned manners. No lockers, so pupils have to carry everything round with them, complained one parent.

School meals fantastic – delicious food and good selection, though some grumbles about the lengths of the queues. Lavatories rather ghastly, and few and far between. Some are shared by both sexes (one side boys and one side girls) which many parents find unsuitable, particularly for adolescents (although principal says the unisex toilets are popular with students).

Pastoral care and discipline: Teachers really do seem to care about each and every student. When we visited we came across the head of art berating an A level student for not completing his coursework. Afterwards she confided, 'he'll get an A* but he needs to understand that he has to put in the work.' This attention to detail is followed through at all levels. We also met a year 11 student being mentored by the principal to ensure that he gains the all-important five A*-C grades at GCSE. 'Are you making sure your homework is handed in on time?' he enquired. 'Mostly', mumbled the student.

Pastoral care is very good and students with difficulties are mentored by students higher up the school who have been through the same experiences.

Pupils and parents: Parents include middle class arty types and a good cross-section of the local community. Pupils in the extension group (those selected by ability) travel from further afield whereas others live locally and walk to school. Pupils are proud to belong to the school. 'Now I'm at Graveney I believe I can do anything', a year 9 student told us proudly.

Entrance: For year 7 entry all applicants take the Wandsworth year 6 test. This selects top 25 per cent (63 pupils out of 2,000 who sit the exam), and then 75 per cent selected on proximity to school. Sibling policy now applies to all pupils, including ability places (although it does not guarantee a place in the extension group: pupils still have to take the test to see which class they go into).

Most students stay on for sixth form but there are an extra 150 open places (for which school receives 1,000 applications). Many students join sixth form from the private sector, especially from single-sex schools. 'I think they want a more culturally diverse environment', says the head, 'and of course at that age they want to meet the opposite sex'.

Exit: Some 10 per cent leave after GCSEs, perhaps because they haven't achieved the crucial 5+ A*-C grades. Around 30 per cent to Russell Group universities (including 11 to Oxbridge in 2013). Remaining 70 per cent to variety of other universities and music, art and drama colleges.

Remarks: Pupils who manage to get in are assured of a top class education in a socially mixed environment. Local parents often turn down places at schools like Alleyn's and Dulwich if their children manage to get places here.

Greenhead College

Greenhead Road, Huddersfield, HD1 4ES

• Pupils: 2,200 boys and girls • Ages: 16–19 • Non–denom • State

Tel: 01484 422032
Email: college@greenhead.ac.uk
Website: www.greenhead.ac.uk

Principal: Since September 2013, Mr Anton McGrath BA PGCE Cert SPLD, previously vice principal since 2008. Educated at Bury Grammar School and read geography and German at Aberystwyth; has worked entirely in sixth form sector. He has a son and a daughter.

Academic matters: College is one of three in Kirklees: each specialises in a different sphere. Hence Greenhead offers science, health and social care and business studies at applied level, as well as A and AS levels in law, government and politics, maths ad infinitum, humanities, sciences, psychology, philosophy and sociology. French, German, Spanish and Italian on offer, but no classics or esoteric languages – yet. Sciences particularly popular, with over 800 entrants for both biology and chemistry in 2013, and over 1000 for maths (the latter particularly successful too, with 24 per cent A* and 57 per cent A*/A grades). Overall, 41 per cent of grades A*/A in 2013 and 67 per cent A*/B.

Good takeup for OCR (RSA) qualifications. Average class size below 20 for A levels and 21 at AS. Most students opt for four AS and three or more As. College will also 'investigate the possibility' of grafting on extra subjects if 'sufficient demand' and space. A level general studies for 'almost all'. Also offers extended project and critical thinking to give further evidence of academic excellence for demanding universities. Head employs staff who are 'experts in their field', and it shows.

No real break between some lessons – the distances can be quite far – but no bell and a business-like but sensibly relaxed atmosphere prevails. Students have ample room to study and socialise – the library is peaceful and well banked with computers; they can chat and study in the reading room and use a main hall area as a common room.

Seems to have twin pillars of success. Firstly, the open door policy, where students always have access to staff and rarely find a staffroom door closed to them. Friendly staff cluster in subject rooms during their free time and any pupil can walk in and ask for help: 'These are young adults – we don't shut ourselves away in adult rooms and leave them in the corridor'. Secondly, the college's own value-added system developed by Kevin Conway and now built upon and widely followed. It picks up students who are falling behind or deserve particular praise very early and, most particularly and without rancour, helps bring teachers who are performing below par up to scratch.

They take students with mobility, visual and other difficulties and provide good support for learning – this is, after all, state-funded. Prospective students are advised to contact the college's learning support coordinator for advice prior to admission, so any specialist support or facilities can be put in place (strives to meet all reasonable requests).

Games, options, the arts: Recent fitness room, all-weather sports field and changing room block. No large sports hall of their own but has use of one. Major playing fields are five minutes' walk across the park. Strongest football side in the county, cups all over the place, squash, netball, rugby (both codes), basketball good (boys and girls), hockey – popular; spectacular success in tennis. Olympic skier Fiona Hughes is a former student.

Enormous art rooms in £2 million building, shared with law and business – walls drip with creative work. Music is very strong with the orchestra, plus jazz, string quartets and choir the subject of much pride. Helped by impressive music department with full recording gear and Apple Macs. Vibrant drama, often with play rehearsals at 7.30am as well as pm and at weekends.

Serious enrichment programme. College has 130 teachers and all offer an enrichment subject from a bewildering choice, from creative writing and first aid to power yoga, critical thinking, swing music, poetry, boxercise, archaeology, Scrabble, climbing, golf, skiing, Freudian psychology, D of E – in fact if a teacher can teach it, you can do it – plus hints on how to handle Oxbridge. Every student must attend one course, but if you don't fancy any of them, then start your own. Excellent work placement programme – 588 placements last year, home and abroad. Happy to bring in experts to college if the right placement doesn't present itself – 380 on work-based projects.

Background and atmosphere: A very busy college; tight on space, which makes lesson changeover a little bit London Underground, but the students love it and enjoy being right in the centre of Huddersfield, close to train and bus stations and shops. A former girls' school, it has grown physically and in reputation. A 10-year plan embraces further new facilities – including the new maths and science building, opened by HRH Duke of Kent. Thanks to five lifts, most areas are now fully accessible. Student union, self-elected prefects.

Pastoral care and discipline: Pastoral system is another secret of success. Twenty-two staff have tutor duties and plenty of time is set aside for students to take up tutor guidance. PSHE for all. College will exclude for violent or abusive behaviour, smoking 'not tolerated'. Students with problems can make an appointment to see a counsellor, and they do. No racial tension. Students report that the college is not cliquey – no sense of all the sports 'jocks' sticking together, for example. Regular 'whole block' assemblies – unusual in most sixth form colleges.

Pupils and parents: Lots of middle class, but a good cross-section and a better than usual success rate in turning round fortunes of youngsters who did not fare especially well at GCSE. Strong work ethos. Huge catchment area, about two-thirds of the students come from partner schools. Students enjoy not calling the staff 'Sir' or 'Mr' and like coming to college. One told us, 'My friends at other colleges don't want to go but I want to come, otherwise I would miss out.' Their only gripe is a lack of space.

G

Entrance: Regularly 40 per cent oversubscribed, so apply well before mid-February of the year you want to go to. Fed by 12 local partner schools in the same catchment area and around 55 other schools nearby on a placement basis. Places allocated on the basis of interview, plus results of mock GCSEs and school reports. Six per cent from the independent sector. Open days for year 11 students and their families.

Exit: Aspirations are high here. Over 90 per cent go directly to higher education, including 34 to Oxbridge in 2013 and over a third to Russell Group unis; very strong medical bias – at one point the college was responsible for one per cent of the new medical intake in the country. Five per cent take a gap year (and then go presumably to higher education) and rest to work. Musicians may choose the Northern College of Music or the Conservatoire but, equally, may decide to go to university first and then study music full time.

Money matters: Some students are entitled to an allowance (student bursary fund) to enable them to access sixth form education.

Remarks: Up there with the very best state and independents. Superb student/staff relationships foster an excellent, enjoyable learning environment. Turns out successful students again and again, whatever qualifications they first arrive with.

Gresham's

Linked school: Gresham's Prep School

Cromer Road, Holt, NR25 6EA

- Pupils: 490 boys and girls 290 full boarders • Ages: 13–18
- C of E • Fees: Boarding £29,250; Day £22,425 pa • Independent

Tel: 01263 714500
Email: registrar@greshams.com
Website: www.greshams.com

Acting headmaster: Nigel Flowers, deputy headmaster, is overseeing the school after the abrupt departure in December 2013 of previous head Philip John.

Mr John, who had been headmaster at the school since 2008, issued a statement in November 2013 to say he was leaving early 'for personal reasons and to spend more time with my family'. He also said he had 'some immediate health issues that need attention', and that he was 'very proud' of the achievements since he came to the school.

Nigel Flowers has been at the school for 22 years and is a former pupil. The school is in the process of appointing a successor to Mr John, who will probably start in September 2014. The new head will need to be an experienced fan of the IB system, and probably have a cosmopolitan outlook, since the school's decision to cease offering A levels from September 2015 is likely to increase its popularity amongst sixth formers from overseas.

Academic matters: Setting in various subjects and on the whole small classes where children 'don't get lost in a crowd'. Parents speak of a generally unpressured approach where pupils are allowed to go at their own pace – 'The focused kid who wants to learn is thrust forward'. Ten to eleven GCSEs for the majority; in 2013, 91 per cent of pupils got 5+ A*-C grades including English and maths, with 50 per cent of grades A*/A. Strong performances in maths (which offers fast tracking) and English literature.

For the sixth, at present A levels or the IB, however, from September 2015 will only offer the IB. Good results in most areas – 51 per cent A*/A grades at A level; IB: average point score

of 35 (max is 45). Relatively low interest in languages – however, compulsory for all as part of IB. Standard facilities spacious and perfectly okay.

Good noises re learning support, given instead of language lessons (three languages compulsory until year 10 – some in the centre do one, two or none). Parents feel the school doesn't want to advertise just how good they are – that's our impression too. Cap on numbers imposed by the number who can be accommodated in the cosy unit. Sympathetic, well qualified staff (two full time, four part time, plus one who delivers ESL) provide a 'sounding board for all sorts of needs' – dyslexia, dyscalculia, dyspraxia, mild Asperger's and ADD. 'It's a pyramid – there's a big drop in numbers after years 9 and 11 and pupils only need an occasional visit once they are in the sixth.' Strong links with the junior school, screening for new entrants, IEPs for each child, offer of scribes, readers and voice activated computers. Charges according to the number of sessions in the unit with a cap of £500 at term. Also applies to ESL.

Games, options, the arts: Outdoorsy lot who appreciate the inclusive ethos and huge number of teams. Hockey (girls and boys) and cricket particularly strong – rugby still to find consistent form. Ample number of pitches and tennis courts, well used Astroturfs and swimming pool, four refurbished squash courts and a rifle range (justifiably trumpets awards gained by members of the rifle club and the achievements of two pupils who, between them, have been British Junior Ladies champion four years running). Weights room, gym and rowing machines for extra exercise and sailing for those who feel the call of the water.

Flourishing D of E with healthy number of gold and silver awards. Other options include BASC course (British Association for shooting and conversation) and the CCF. Drama is big here – 'Outstanding – it blows me away,' gushed a parent. The Auden theatre (the real thing with dressing rooms, professional lighting and sound systems) hosts a tremendous variety of performances given by touring companies – well attended by locals and free to pupils. Also a venue for numerous school productions – we enjoyed an impressive offering produced and played with great brio. Music also valued. Wide choice of instrumental tuition (approx 40 per cent have lessons) plus various orchestral, band and choral activities. Rather crusty music facilities upgraded in time for the 2013 Britten centenary.

Grown-up art block with decent studio space. Oil paints from the start and life drawing on a regular basis. Large canvases all over the place – strong, confidently realised representational images. Some 3D work and a new kiln recently installed. Regular artists in residence and exhibitions in the foyer – all very positive.

Background and atmosphere: Although founded in 1555 as a free grammar school, it wasn't until the 1890s that it became something more. Somewhat random development of the 170 acre site (including 90 acres of woodland) makes for a fair amount of walking – all but the upper sixth have to use a bridge which straddles a road into town. Structures vary from listed to unattractive. Solid Edwardian classroom blocks, a sizeable chapel and The Big School, a rather fine hall with polished wood floors, rub shoulders with the thoroughly modern Auden theatre and now listed 'temporary', '20s, thatched huts (scruff shacks). Everywhere spotlessly clean. Comfortable atmosphere. Friendly, relaxed relationships between pupils and staff despite some predictably unpopular tightening up (sixth have to wear suits and girls are meant to tie their hair back – one or two still manage the tousled look).

Inter-house competition important but doesn't hinder cheerful social interaction (most have known each other since they were tinies in the junior school) – sixth whizz off to congregate at the BOP (bar on premises) with the rest flocking to Dave's Diner for a burger and fizzy drink. All allowed into Holt three times a week – charmingly sedate country town.

Boarding houses on a rolling revamp programme – some more homely and cared for than others. Full and weekly boarding with over 40 per cent day pupils – working hard to promote full boarding and parents say weekend activities have improved. Some houses can empty if nothing going on, so worth checking which have a higher proportion of full boarders.

Day and boarding pupils are integrated with the former having a base and or bed in boarders' rooms – flexi boarding isn't encouraged ('We're not a baby sitting service,' according to the head) but when activities are full on, pupils can stay the night. Large dining hall where pupils eat at house tables – staff have a table of their own. Adequate buffet fare with vegetarian option – for hungry moments packets of squadgy white bread can be toasted and buttered in the house kitchens.

Pastoral care and discipline: A small school where everyone knows everyone. Positive interaction between year groups and approachable staff (tutors, house parents, school counsellor and multi denominational school chaplain) – parents say issues are dealt with promptly. Some pupils find going from junior to senior a big leap, but others relish greater independence and a chance to take responsibility for what they do – new bods are 'buddied'. Polite (lovely to find door holding is de rigueur), biddable lot. Sixth formers have sessions on stress; a clear anti-bullying policy. Zero tolerance re illegal drugs. Pretty tough on boozers (although over 18s are allowed to visit The Feathers with permission) and pupils found in their company can expect to be punished. Same applies to smoking.

Pupils and parents: Fresh faced, friendly girls and boys – their 'confidence comfortably worn': more upturned collar and bleached rugby shirt than Vivienne Westwood. Most come from East Anglia, Lincolnshire etc – getting that all important driving licence makes getting home for the odd night or two a breeze. Twenty per cent foreign nationals in the sixth (strong German contingent). In the main parents involved in farming, law, accountancy etc.

Old Boys include Sir Stephen Spender, W H Auden, Benjamin Britten, Ben Nicholson, Sir Christopher Cockerell (inventor of the hovercraft), James Dyson, Lord Reith, Prof Alan Hodgkin and Stephen Frears.

Entrance: Fifty per cent CE plus interview. Keen on siblings but only if 'up to standard'. Eighty per cent come in from own prep school (parents wonder if its popularity means that cherry picking will make the school more 'academic'). Rest from local preps or maintained sector.

For the sixth form six GCSE A*-C with B grades in subjects to be taken in the sixth. IELTS minimum score of six, or equivalent level of ability.

Exit: Around 30 per cent leave after GCSEs. Trickle to Oxbridge (five in 2013), otherwise all over the place with heavyweights well represented – Newcastle, Imperial, Warwick, Bristol, Edinburgh, York, Oxford Brookes and Loughborough most popular. One to Bocconi University, Italy, in 2013.

Money matters: Worshipful Company of Fishmongers, with whom has close links, gives generous scholarships – recent launch of Gresham's Foundation will help fund new builds and bursaries. Twelve academic awards (up to 100 per cent 'upon demonstration of financial need'), in addition to art, drama, music, sports and all rounder. Sixth form scholarships (academic, art, music etc) for those who've done fantastically well at GCSE and haven't already received an award. Annual award of £1,500 for maths genius and £750 for pupils who 'undertake voluntary work through Student Partnership Worldwide'. For pupils whose parents have fallen on hard times does its best to help them through until next public exam.

Remarks: Has been known as an unsophisticated public school where parents have valued a broad education without an over pressured, hot house atmosphere. Introduction of the IB is making its mark – should broaden outlooks – we say the school's attractiveness to a wider, out of county audience. An interesting time ahead.

The Grey Coat Hospital

Greycoat Place, London, SW1P 2DY

- Pupils: 1,010 girls, 40 boys in the sixth form • Ages: 11–18
- C of E • State

Tel: 020 7969 1998
Email: info@gch.org.uk
Website: www.gch.org.uk

Headteacher: Since 2011, Ms Siân Maddrell (forties) BA, previously first vice principal of Pimlico Academy. Read French at Durham followed by PGCE at Oxford; started her teaching career at Grey Coat, eventually becoming head of modern languages and one of the first advanced skills teachers in the country. Moved on to Elliott School, then became assistant headteacher at Acland Burghley before joining Pimlico. Enjoys sports, reading, going to the theatre, travelling and spending time with her family – she has two young sons.

Academic matters: Twice rated 'outstanding' by Ofsted. Excellent exam results in 2013 with benchmark 85 per cent of students achieving 5+ A*-C grades at GCSE including maths and English; 43 per cent A*/A grades. At A level, 62 per cent A*-B grades and 28 per cent A*/A. GCSE and A level results are impressive for a comprehensive intake – very few failures in any subject. Specialist language college and training school. Vibrant and well thought of school, strong teaching staff who are open to new ideas and methodology. 'An enthusiastic and committed bunch,' claim parents. Evening Standard Award for academic excellence is proudly displayed in the head's office. Particularly dynamic languages department offering a good range of choices; girls do particularly well in French. Pupils selected for their aptitude for languages can study three languages by year 8, one of which is Mandarin. European and Asian exchange programmes are run with other schools along with 'culture of the month'. The school also works with local primaries who teach foreign languages. Pupils are encouraged to do well with incentives such as 'mathematician of the month' and debates are welcomed. Single and dual award sciences on offer; girls now benefit from lovely new modern science labs at St Michael's, the upper school site.

Excellent ICT facilities integrated across all curriculum areas. The sixth form open evening is run as a road show, attracting prospective pupils from all over London from both the state and independent sectors. A small number of boys join at sixth form. 'We come for the friendly atmosphere and better facilities,' say boys. Active careers department with business mentors and careers road shows. Head has arranged a link with Westminster School so pupils can study subjects, such as Latin A level, not available at Grey Coat. A head of special needs, a number of learning support assistants and a programme for gifted pupils.

Games, options, the arts: Sportsmark – amazingly successful sports, considering the limited facilities, run by a dedicated head of sports. They make the best of the small on-site space; pupils use the outdoor facilities at Battersea Park and local pool. Recently national champions of cricket, they have produced national football and cricket players. Hoards of trophies for almost everything. Year 9 have the option of doing junior or community sports leader qualifications or a BTEC in sixth form. Strong music and drama, four large choirs that have performed at the Albert Hall, wind band and strings group. Instrumental tuition is subsidised by the school's Foundation. Theatre studies A level and drama GCSE are becoming very popular, several plays are produced annually. Successful competitors in the Mock Magistrates and Bar competitions. Huge list of lunchtime and after-school clubs to choose from, D of E awards and community service programmes also run. New arts building houses facilities for drama, music, art.

Background and atmosphere: Founded by concerned parishioners to reduce crime and get urchins off the streets in the days when the parish of Westminster was considered a den of iniquity. In 1701 the governors purchased an old workhouse to set up a school to provide education, board and lodgings and care (hence hospital in the name) for 40 boys and 40 girls. Benefactors' portraits still hang in the Great Hall. There was a murder in 1773 and a rebellion against the dreadful conditions in the school in 1801. In 1874 The Grey Coat Hospital became a day school for girls led for some years by one of the great pioneers of education, Elsie Day. The lower school continues today on the same site, St Andrew's. An additional site, St Michael's, houses the upper school. Both premises have gyms and libraries. The school is increasing resources and facilities for sixth form students.

Pastoral care and discipline: Girls are expected to be responsible for themselves and considerate to others. Good community feel with plenty of opportunities for spiritual and moral development. Long tradition of caring and solid Christian values; other faiths are also welcome. Older girls have the opportunity to take on serious responsibilities and serve the school. 'Everyone gets a chance to be involved here and staff are approachable,' say pupils. Sensible set of school rules aimed at producing conscientious young people. Many past pupils return for the annual school celebration service in Westminster Abbey. Strict uniform code.

Pupils and parents: Big inner-city mix, few locals, pupils come from all over as catchment is anyone living in the dioceses of London and Southwark. Popular choice for the children of education professionals. Streetwise, polite and (mostly) sensible, hard-working girls, plus a handful of boys in sixth form.

Entrance: At 11+, 15 selective places by exam for girls showing an aptitude for languages, then standard LA criteria – 25 per cent band 1, 50 per cent band 2, 25 per cent band 3 with priority given to practising C of E families and siblings.

Exit: At 16+ one-third leaves to follow vocational courses or A levels elsewhere, mostly because the school does not offer the A level courses they want; a few to work. At 18+ most to university, a third to Russell Group – London, Durham, Bristol; three or four to Oxbridge.

Money matters: The Parents' Guild raises money for the school and charity, keeping up the long tradition of serving the community. Parents are asked to contribute a small amount of money on a monthly or annual basis.

Remarks: Ever popular, the pioneering spirit lives on, as does the tradition of care. Regularly on Ofsted annual list of 'outstanding providers' of education and care.

The Gryphon School

Bristol Road, Sherborne, Dorset, DT9 4EQ

• Pupils: 1,645 boys and girls • Ages: 11–18 • Church of England • State

Tel: 01935 813122
Email: office@gryphon.dorset.sch.uk
Website: www.gryphon.dorset.sch.uk

Headteacher: Since 2007, Steve Hillier MA PGCE (late forties). Educated in Wiltshire and read geography at Cambridge before embarking on a teaching career in various community schools up and down the land. Of his appointment to the Gryphon, his first headship, he says, 'All the moons aligned: it was a community school with a sixth form in the west country'. Under his rule, the school has gone from strength to strength (and graded 'outstanding' by Ofsted), providing a valuable counterweight to the considerable avoirdupois of the local independents (Sherborne School, Sherborne School for Girls, Leweston). 'The only difference between us and them is class size', he states, bravely, though no-one could deny the amount of cross-fertilisation between all the Sherborne schools. Mr Hillier also does all manner of worthy things with North Dorset Schools and Somerset Academies in terms of leadership and funding expertise; the Gryphon became an academy in 2012 'to enable us to keep doing what we are doing now', as he put it.

Parents rate him for the job he does though they do not feel that they could get to know him easily – heads of year have far more of a bearing on school life – but they appreciate his presence at most school functions. 'He's everywhere and nowhere at the same time – quite scary, really,' opined one sixth former. We found him expansive and relaxed on his home ground, and justifiably proud of what goes on there. Mr Hillier is married with three sporty children, two at neighbouring Gillingham and one at university; he and his family enjoy active holidays walking and exploring sites 'where history meets geography', and he is a sometime Bath Rugby season ticket holder.

Academic matters: Commendable results by any standards and particularly for a non-selective school. Vibrant, ambitious sixth form with significant influx from other schools has offered vocational options alongside A levels such as, for the last two years, Level 3 BTEC courses, where two-thirds were graded Distinction Plus in 2013. At A level, a sharp increase in the grades awarded in 2013 (34 per cent A*/A and 62 per cent A*/B) means Gryphon students going on to Oxford (head not unhappy about the fact that the Gryphon sends more to Oxbridge than Sherborne and Sherborne Girls combined), several other Russell Group universities and to read competitive and rigorous subjects such as medicine and dentistry. At GCSE, results were spectacular in 2011, with languages ancient and modern (Latin is taught by a visiting member of staff from Sherborne School) and music very strong. A dip in 2012 was rebalanced by the best ever results in 2013, with 31 per cent A*/A grades, against a backdrop of falling results nationally. Good showing in vocational choices too, with almost everyone passing almost all BTECs and diplomas taken, and 100 per cent pass rate in ASDAN's Certificate of Personal Effectiveness. Academic commitment is expected from the off; some parents feel that too much homework is given in year 7.

Pupils speak very highly of their teachers: 'approachable, passionate about their subject, willing to give up their time'. Maths, economics and art were singled out for particular praise – we were less sure about the guillotine in one history class room. Library and computer provision modern and well-resourced, some excitement about the imminent trial of iPads as a portable learning resource reinforces the importance the school places on e-learning.

The proportion of students with SEN is higher than average; we suspect because of the school's excellent provision, which includes a 35-strong SEN team all of whom have their own particular expertise, plus a dedicated space 'the blue room' where the troubled and overwhelmed can withdraw when it all gets a bit much. Here, sessions on self-esteem and anger management are run alongside more conventional catch-up sessions in literacy and numeracy. All new arrivals are screened on entry and school maintains close links with local services such as CAMHS; efforts are made to intervene early and to investigate causes behind disruptive behaviour, rather than merely dealing with it.

Games, options, the arts: The breadth and enthusiasm for sport and the arts make The Gryphon an all-encompassing school and the recipient of the Artsmark gold award. Its site on the edge of Sherborne means ample space for pitches, courts, Astroturf and a leisure centre with fitness suite and sports hall (which could do with updating, say parents), also available to the community at certain times. An outdoor pool has been filled in, but swimmers use the indoor facilities of the two independents in the town. Usual offering of rugby, hockey and netball (where some teams are coached by local club coaches) branches out into golf, basketball, karate, shooting and solo star-dance up to national standard. School also has a show-jumping team in this horsey part of the world, though set up and run by parents. Participation rates are high – two hours PE per week are timetabled up to year 11 with options changing every six weeks, 'and there's a team for everyone', according to our small guide, a keen netball player. At the weekly enrichment afternoon for sixth form, sport is the most popular choice at whatever level; members of staff and some sixth formers took part in a 10K Christmas Pudding run for charity. School an undoubted presence in the local sporting scene – 'nakedly competitive,' said one sixth former, grimly – which takes on all comers with relish, particularly the local independents, and with considerable success. The Sports Award evening is a highlight in the school calendar.

Music a real strength here too, in this most musical of towns; school benefits from close relationships with the abbey and the other Sherborne schools, all of whom contribute to the Sherborne Symphonia, a joint orchestra, and lots of other collaborations. Success on the national stage too, with high rankings in the BBC Songs of Praise Choir of the Year and students gaining places in the National Youth Choir and Orchestra. But the school celebrates its own music too, with two full concerts, a carol service in the abbey and a European music tour every year, for both singers and players, and numerous opportunities inside and outside its gates.

Drama and film-making also prominent: musical theatre the runaway favourite with recent productions of Les Misérables, Oliver! and West Side Story, but more adventurously, a version of Dr Faustus updated to 80s London and a feature film of Far from the Madding Crowd in recent years.

Art and design of similarly high standard; some stunning furniture made by recent A level students would grace any avant-garde shop window. 'We're not spoon-fed – we're encouraged to develop our own ideas', said one A level artist. Younger ones work with textiles, food and resistant materials in rotation; school boasts a professional catering kitchen alongside its art and design studios. Photography also popular, and much work is exhibited locally.

Background and atmosphere: Founded in 1992 out of an amalgam of local schools, the Gryphon's undistinguished buildings were purpose built for 800 or so, and now house double that number. (The gripe we heard from everyone was lack of space: considerable congestion in corridors at peak

times and no room for lockers). Planning is under way for a new teaching block, however. Outdoor sitting space with nice wooden tables and benches a precious overflow, but surely bleak in midwinter.

Even though it is but 20 years old, the school feels agreeably traditional in terms of its expectations, aspirations and values, reflected in its naming after an ancient and noble mythical beast, denoting intelligence and strength. The gryphon appears on the uniform navy blue sweatshirt and all published material – strong branding indeed. School rightly makes the most of its position as Sherborne's secondary school by holding prize-givings and carol services in the abbey.

Relationships between students and staff, which are collaborative and supportive without crossing the boundary into familiarity, are universally praised: 'I want this to be an island of civility, not a shouty school,' states the head. Even the newest/youngest/shyest students feel as though they are recognised as individuals. School appears to cater for all comers: 'I've got one very bright one, one really naughty and one not very bright and it's suited them all,' said one frank mother.

Parents report mostly good communication from teachers via email (it could be sharpened up when a child is absent, for example), but that parents' evenings are a scrum. A local church which has outgrown its premises meets every Sunday in the conference room, and one of its clergy has been appointed chaplain three days a week, but the school does not feel overtly Christian. That said, we did not spot much religious or ethnic diversity, but significantly a few years ago one student felt moved to start a campaign called 'I am Me', celebrating difference and amounting to a powerful statement against bullying – an initiative which gained her a national award.

Pastoral care and discipline: Exceptional. School has UN 'Rights Respecting School' status and expectations of behaviour are laid down with positive reinforcement under the guidelines which grace every classroom – 'catch them being good' is a policy statement, and the prevailing culture is one of reward and recognition. 'Teachers are good at making us feel our age and giving us the right amount of responsibility, but they don't nag', said one older boy. Everyone we talked to commented on the close eye the school keeps on healthy relationships between students, and a sixth former remarked on the sense of community between the staff. Sanctions, which are not applied in haste, take the form of detentions of increasing length and seriousness.

Pupils and parents: Mostly white and relatively to very prosperous – school has a lower than average percentage of free school meals – and with a genuine commitment to education and a sense that they are fortunate indeed to be at The Gryphon. Masses bussed in from anything up to 20 miles away; 'I was determined to go to The Gryphon, even though we live out of catchment,' said one new girl. Several teachers from local independent schools send their children; yet more blurring of the lines between the Sherborne schools. The students we met were jolly, chatty yet thoughtful – and pleased with their lot.

Past students of note from this young school include two actors (Sam Dorsey and Ben Hardy), one rising star in film production and another at Bath Rugby.

Entrance: Officially 240 places for year 7, which are almost always oversubscribed by 30 or so – no wonder the place is such a squash. Most come from nine partner primary schools but a quarter of the intake from outside the (largely rural) catchment area; this is a highly regarded school locally. Though transition arrangements appear to be good once the kids arrive at school, at least one parent felt more effort could be made to reach children coming from outlying schools.

At sixth form, nearly 40 per cent arrive from local state and independent schools; entry requirements are five GCSEs at grade C or above to include maths and English, preceded by an interview in the spring. A level choices in maths, the sciences and languages require a B at GCSE. Some 95 per cent of sixth form students stay on to complete year 13. 'They're knocking at the door to get in at sixth form', remarked one mother.

Exit: A few leave after GCSE to pursue less academic courses at Yeovil College. Practically every sixth former accepted to university of first choice; UCAS guidance gets top marks from students; a few take gap years.

Remarks: Super much sought-after school at the very centre of its community taking on the Sherborne independents. Truly a model of comprehensive education at its best – a place for all comers, which children and parents set their heart on, so it bulges at the seams.

Guildford High School

Linked school: Guildford High School Junior School

London Road, Guildford, GU1 1SJ

• Pupils: 635 girls • Ages: 11–18 • Christian • Fees: £14,250 pa
• Independent

Tel: 01483 543853
Email: Guildford-Admissions@guildfordhigh.co.uk
Website: www.guildfordhigh.surrey.sch.uk

Headmistress: Since 2002, Mrs Fiona Boulton BSc PGCE NPQH MA. Previously deputy headmistress and, before GHS, teacher and housemistress at Stowe and Marlborough. Mother of three school-age children, Mrs Boulton is very keen on work/life balance and carefully keeps her own work and home lives separate. However, she obviously thrives on spinning many plates at once, finds the challenges 'enormous fun' and describes the vibe in the staff room as of 'friendship and mutual support'. She has picked her staff to work together and expects the same commitment and plate-spinning knack from them too. Over the 10 years she has been at the helm she has 'aimed to make GHS outstanding in every area with no weak links', seeing this as the best way to compete with the wealth of other local girls' schools. She hates the suggestion that GHS might be considered an academic hothouse and is certain that is not the experience of any of her pupils, citing the sheer range of activities on offer here. Girls are very fond of her, whilst also being 'slightly scared'; she can silence the full school hall by just walking in. Parents value her honesty about the pressures to expect for their daughters in each year.

Academic matters: Academically outstanding: results-focused culture plus a strong and empowering sense of expectation in the girls leads to top performance at GCSE and A level, permanently in the upper echelons of national league tables. In 2013, 93 per cent of GCSE grades A*/A and 88 per cent of A levels. Predicted grades are tracked throughout senior school and show an average increase of 1 to 1 grades.

Mrs Boulton describes her pupils as 'some exceptional girls, but the vast majority are bright and enjoying life', and puts their success down to 'fabulous staff, supportive parents and it's cool to be clever'. Younger pupils echo her describing 'great teachers, you can ask them anything, nothing is seen as stupid to ask', whilst sixth formers tell us 'teachers will spend as long as you need to explain anything', describing one-to-one sessions fathoming some tricky maths or English dilemma. The girls are taught how to learn, think and debate rather than what to learn.

At 11 girls choose two of French, Spanish or German; all girls have three years of Latin and separate sciences are studied throughout school. Additionally philosophy, Mandarin, touch-typing, Adobe photo-shop and current affairs are covered on a rotational basis throughout the first three years. Innovative information booklets give a complete insight for parents and pupils as to expectations and curriculum in each school year, including guidelines for parents on how to help at home; these booklets are typical of the professionalism and clarity of everything at GHS. Parents describe the culture as 'driven' and ' focused'; they feel it's taken for granted that girls will cope academically.

The first three years involve less homework (Mrs B recommends using a timer) and more fun trips out; the pace steps up at the start of GCSE courses in year 10. Girls need to be motivated and organised to take it all in their stride; one parent felt 'you could sink quite quickly', although there are few casualties. No homework is given over the holidays allowing a complete break mentally to 'create balance and perspective'; parents, pupils and staff really appreciate this.

A tiny number of girls have SEN, but the pace here suits only the most able and provision for SEN is simply to ensure 'staff take into account specific learning needs'. The few for whom English is an additional language are sufficiently fluent not to require additional support.

Sixth form is a breed apart: girls say they feel different, are treated differently and have a different experience – all important to keep the interest levels up for pupils who may have been at GHS for 10 years already. The sixth formers have their own house, with teaching rooms, a quiet study room and a large, funkily furnished common room complete with kitchen for lunch or snack-making. Really buzzing with clever, confident, animated young women concerned with everything from the latest heels to the meaning of life.

Games, options, the arts: Sport is a significant part of school life; although it doesn't capture all the girls, there is genuinely something for everyone. Main sports are lacrosse and netball, though many more are timetabled – swimming, gymnastics, athletics, rounders, football, badminton, yoga, dance. Standards are incredibly high in the top school teams (county or national) and girls who are not at these hugely committed levels may lose interest in the main sports by the time they are 15 or so. Mrs Boulton tells us 'we create lots of opportunities for sport' and there is an enormous array of unusual fitness options, Taekwondo, fencing, indoor climbing and, the latest addition, Zumba. Indoor rowing was started a couple years ago, became very popular and in true GHS fashion they won two golds and a silver at the National Indoor Rowing Championships. About 100 metres up the road and overlooking Stoke Park is the newish sports centre. Home to a fab pool with electronic touch timing, it also houses an sports hall (within indoor netball court, so no freezing evening training sessions), a fitness centre for the 16+, and a large social area for comfortable match teas, meetings and sixth form parties with the boys from the Royal Grammar School (half a mile away).

Music is another big part of school life with hundreds of individual lessons taught weekly by specialist teachers. There are plenty of opportunities for performance with the many choirs, ensembles, bands and orchestras, including some at very high standards. A joint choir and orchestra with RGS boys toured Italy in 2012, performing in Verona and Venice.

Opportunities for drama include the annual panto written and directed by lower sixth and performed by year 7. Girls from year 10 up may audition for the two main productions a year (one with the RGS boys), whilst years 8 and 9 take part in a Shakespeare Festival – each form puts on a play with girls directing and acting, eight plays in all over two hectic days.

Parents marvel at the commitment required of their daughters to take part in so many activities, at such high standards, 'some girls do everything – but it's difficult'.

Extracurriculars are covered by an enormous array of clubs. On the first Friday of each term girls sign up for clubs and groups in music, sports, creative arts, science, cooking, language, maths, cartoon, reading, board games, textiles; just about everything is covered and girls can do something extra every day.

Background and atmosphere: GHS is the jewel in the crown of United Learning, which owns 11 independent schools and sponsors 17 academies in the maintained sector. The school is run by Mrs Boulton and her team rather than centrally, but with the advantages of a wide group of other United Learning heads, teachers and managers to consult over best practice, as well as a central budget to draw from for major projects.

The school is located where Guildford town centre meets leafy Victorian suburbia. Buildings are a mix of old and new, though all very well maintained. There's always something being added or improved: the sports centre a few years ago, then an attractive large house next door was purchased and converted to provide sixth form teaching rooms as well as some welcome garden space, and the latest, just going to planning, will be a music block.

Hugely positive attitude to school and academic work throughout the place. Pupils value their abilities and want to make the most of themselves; their mission is to work hard and get good results. Respect for each other is evident in the way girls interact and the general lack of nastiness. Parents describe GHS as 'an exciting and buzzy place to be' and say 'if you have an ability the school will find it', and everyone celebrates all success without resentment. No-one treats others differently if they're in lower sets, but make no mistake, this place is not for the faint-hearted, over sensitive or needy; it would not be comfortable to just scrape in and bump along the bottom. Pupils need to be robust to make the most of everything on offer.

Pastoral care and discipline: Girls' first port of call for help and advice is their form tutor, followed by their head of year and the deputy head. However, pastoral care is seen as the shared responsibility of all staff and girls know they can talk to any of them. Importantly, there are clear procedures for communication amongst staff including regular updates, pupils' records and a 'TLC list' in the staff room for any special situations. Mrs Boulton is particularly proud of the individual care, especially in unusual and tragic circumstances.

The atmosphere amongst the girls themselves is genuinely supportive and respectful. Parents say there's little of the nasty bitching often associated with all girls' schools. Inevitably there is a bit, but the school deals with any quickly and works hard to prevent it. Occasional fall-outs amongst these strident and feisty individuals, but no out-and-out bullying.

School rules, listed on the website, are pretty sparse; maybe these pupils are just too busy to be rebellious. Very few detentions seem to be given; when we visited our young hosts hadn't heard of any girl getting a detention and were quite shocked at the thought of it.

Drugs, drinking, legal highs – Mrs Boulton tells us there have been no issues during her time here, though she recognises that as a day school she is not involved with the girls' weekend activities. She explains girls are taught 'decision making, how to extract yourself from difficult situations and how to act' so they may look after themselves.

Seventy per cent of the girls arrive by public transport, mostly train, which parents find 'fantastic and convenient' even for later leaving times with after-school activities. A 'buddy system' links new girls with existing pupils who travel from the same home rail station; the buddy accompanies their charge to the school door for as long as is required until they are confident.

Pupils and parents: Families from a wide catchment both geographically and socially, though the majority are solid middle class with both parents working; not flashy, more grounded with plenty of common sense and less touchy-feely than some of the other Surrey girls' options – not many with ponies! Parents are very on-board with the work hard, play hard ethos to achieve top results.

There is no specific type of girl for GHS, says Mrs Boulton, 'there's an eclectic mix of personalities'; the emphasis is on respecting each other's differences, 'it's OK to be yourself'. She feels any type can find a niche here whether sporty, musical, an all-rounder or a quiet bookish girl. The parents we spoke to had a variety of daughters and concurred they all fit in; the rider was they needed to be focused, motivated and pretty robust. When we looked around the girls were a confident, ebullient lot, comfortable in their own skins and with the business of learning; not show-offish but definitely proud of their school and achievements.

Little or no evidence of customising uniform or wearing make-up or nail varnish. Girls all neat and tidy in their practical, rather than lovely, uniforms. Sixth formers in own clothes but still workaday and no eye-boggling fashions.

Notable old girls a surprisingly arty lot – portrait artist Jane Allison, playwrights Ella Hicks and Lucy Prebble, actress Celia Imrie and TV presenter Louise Roe.

Entrance: GHS describe itself as 'an all-through school with natural progression junior to senior', thus girls from the junior school take around 40 per cent of senior school places at 11. For the others, entrance assessment is over one full day early in the Lent term comprising an exam based on the national curriculum, one hour of English, creative writing plus comprehension, and one hour of maths, from addition and multiplication through to problem-solving. Candidates are interviewed by the headmistress or other senior teacher. No trick questions; Mrs Boulton describes it as 'a friendly chat about yourself'. The process is very transparent with the aim of creating a level playing field for entrants of all backgrounds, looking for individual's skills not previous teaching standards. About three applicants for each of the 60 available places, and competition is tough as the school's reputation puts off unlikely candidates. Big range of feeders, with almost a quarter of girls entering from the state sector. Independents include Rowan, Hoe Bridge, St Ives and Halstead; state juniors include Cleves, St Paul's, South Farnham, Pyrford, Horsell, Holy Trinity and Bushy Hill.

In the lower sixth there's a maximum of 10 places available. Girls sit three one hour papers from a choice of subjects plus a general paper and an interview. Entrants are expected to have at least eight good GCSEs with A*/A in their chosen A level subjects.

Exit: High aspirations plus lots of school support – including a dedicated higher education advisor – means girls generally get what and where they want. Each year around 20 per cent go to Oxbridge; equally popular is Durham, followed by a long and varied list of good UK universities. Most popular courses are medicine and languages of all sorts, but there's an enormous range including chemical engineering, psychology, art, politics and veterinary medicine.

Money matters: Scholarships worth up to a third of fees. Assisted places available at 11+, bursaries for daughters of the clergy and for any sixth formers, all assessed on financial need. Small sibling discounts of five and 10 per cent.

Academic scholarships equally available to incomers and existing pupils; all sit the 11+ or 16+ entrance exams if they wish to apply. So although girls may move from junior to senior and into sixth form without taking any exams, if they wish to have a go at scholarship they do need to sit the entrance exams alongside the external candidates. In reality only the few truly shining stars do so.

Music scholarships similarly available to internal and external candidates. Girls at 11+ must be at least grade 4 on an orchestral instrument and on piano and at 16+ grade 8 on two instruments or one plus singing at chamber choir standard. Lots of clear and encouraging information available, but only worth it with a real musical talent and dedication.

Remarks: Outstanding at every turn, providing a superb education, not just fantastic exam results but a whole positive and enquiring approach to life, the universe and everything. Girls need to be very bright and hard working to make the most of the opportunities. In return the school will uncover all talents, make the most of every iota and send girls off with confidence and a fistful of accomplishments

Gumley House RC Convent School, FCJ

St John's Road, Isleworth, Middlesex, TW7 6XF

• Pupils: 1,180 girls; all day • Ages: 11–18 • RC • State

Tel: 020 8568 8692
Email: general@gumley.hounslow.sch.uk
Website: www.gumley.hounslow.sch.uk

Headteacher: Since 2012 Mrs Ewa Kolczymska, previously deputy head.

Academic matters: For a non-selective state school, very good results. Compares extremely favourably with local and national averages. Comes top in local league tables. In 2013, 34 per cent A*/A grades at GCSE and 58 per cent A*-B at A level. On vexed subject of AS levels, head feels weaker pupils benefit from leaving school with some qualification but regrets loss of free study periods, 'so essential for independent learning'. Designated as a high performing specialist school and has a languages specialism.

Very committed to special needs provision. Two fully qualified teachers and 14 learning support assistants. SENs catered for include physical difficulties, learning difficulties, ASD, dyslexia, Down's Syndrome. To make sure that they miss nobody, policy is to screen for literacy at the start of year 7 and organise support as appropriate, eg literacy tuition, in-class support, reading clubs or monitoring, as appropriate. Preferred method of support is in the classroom – where possible tries to avoid withdrawing girls from subject lessons. Classroom support now widely accepted by staff and students alike. No stigma associated, in fact the girls often ask for it. Wheelchair access throughout the school seen as part of ethos – 'We encourage concern for the disabled, the marginalised and the needy'. Sixth formers involved in helping younger pupils.

Games, options, the arts: Netball, hockey and athletics very strong – regularly wins all local tournaments. Eight tennis courts, a new all-weather surface hockey/football pitch set in spacious 10 acres. New dance and fitness studio (very popular), new drama studio. Thriving orchestra and plethora of private instrument lessons on offer.

Background and atmosphere: Founded in 1841 as a school and convent by the Faithful Companions of Jesus. The Queen Anne house surrounded by lovely grounds creates a peaceful oasis in west London. Strong support from parents, 'We couldn't run it without them'. Superbly equipped library in former chapel (just

the place for inspired contemplation), sensational octagonal assembly hall for whole school events. Despite rigorous religious requirements at entry level, the atmosphere is cheerful and tolerant with no hint of religious oppression.

Pastoral care and discipline: Prides itself on discipline. Truancy very rare. Emphasis on strong school/home links. Distinctive uniform worn with pride. Strong emphasis on religious, spiritual and moral formation of pupils. Very supportive staff.

Pupils and parents: The catchment area covers a wide area of west London from Southall to Twickenham so a broad mix of intake. Most parents make a voluntary contribution to the school's development fund each month.

Entrance: Non-selective academically at age 11. However (and here's the rub), girls and their parents must be practising Roman Catholics (written proof required from parish priest), and that means attending Mass every Sunday. Other entrance criterion is distance from school. Heavily oversubscribed; head has no plans for further expansion – 'We'd rather like to keep our grounds as they are'.

Exit: Quite a few to Russell Group universities, to do subjects including mechanical engineering, Japanese, law, English, history, biological sciences and maths.

Money matters: Voluntary aided so run by head and board of governors. Funded through the local council but parents' contributions (voluntary) keep it running as a Catholic school, provide extra facilities and offset maintenance costs.

Remarks: For a budding Mr Bennet who is also a fully paid-up member of the Catholic Church, now would be a good time to visit an estate agent in Isleworth. An excellent school in lovely surroundings, which will give all your daughters a good education – well worth a visit.

Haberdashers' Aske's Boys' School

Linked schools: The Haberdashers' Aske's Boys' Preparatory School & Pre-Preparatory School

Butterfly Lane, Elstree, WD6 3AF

• Pupils: 1,200 boys; all day • Ages: 11–18 • C of E • Fees: £15,867 pa
• Independent

Tel: 020 8266 1700
Email: office@habsboys.org.uk
Website: www.habsboys.org.uk

Headmaster: Since 2002, Peter Hamilton, MA (fifties). Educated at King Edward VI Grammar School, Southampton and Christ Church College, Oxford, where he read modern languages (French and German). Taught at Radley before becoming housemaster and head of languages at Westminster. Then to King Edward VI Southampton, as head. Still teaches regularly: 'You need to keep your hand in' – a philosophy he clearly applies to learning as well, as he spent a recent sabbatical in Morocco studying Arabic: 'It's a fascinating language'. When not expanding his linguistic range, he likes riding and hill walking, windsurfing and fast motorbikes – 'I have a death wish,' he jokes (confirmed, perhaps, by his support of Southampton FC). Like his pupils, business-like, energetic and intelligent. Feels his contribution has been to 'reinvigorate' an already high-octane offering (a viewpoint clearly shared by the Independent

School Inspectors, who recently found the school provided 'an outstanding educational experience'). Two daughters, one with his French wife, Sylvie, an osteopath.

Academic matters: This is a top-of-the-league-table school and no one has ever been heard to voice the opinion: 'Exams aren't the most important thing'. Exam success is a priority – to the school, pupils and parents (who occasionally sneak off and get their children to sit extra exams elsewhere). 'Grades matter,' says the head, 'because they let parents know that most doors will be open to their sons.' And certainly few that aren't flung wide on the basis of these consistently high results – in 2013, 79 per cent of A levels A*/A. GCSEs are seen merely as 'a hurdle to get over' (boys soar over the bar, with more than 94 per cent of GCSEs A*/A in 2013). Quality not quantity, however, is the head's guiding principle – exam numbers are kept to a manageable nine or ten at GCSE, three at A2. ('Unless you're taking further maths, they discourage you from doing four,' said one sixth former.)

The head is also a traditionalist as far as the curriculum is concerned, undistracted by the IB, the Pre-U or the EPQ: 'We don't muck around. A levels serve boys very well'. That said, he feels the A* has not really solved concerns about 'stretch and challenge', an issue addressed at Habs by teachers taking pupils well beyond the specifications – 'We really ramp it up at A level'. Both pupils and parents are appreciative of the effort – 'Nearly every teacher is a good teacher,' said one recently departed student. 'Some are truly exceptional and inspiring. You hardly ever see a bad teacher.' Parents agree: 'My two sons have had consistently good teaching,' said one.

Though maths and economics are by far the most popular A-level choices, sciences and arts are equally strong. A language carousel is offered in year 7, with four taster tongues (Latin, German, Spanish and French). Italian and Russian are added for GCSE. Some subjects set on ability from year 9 – a good thing, say parents: 'There are boys here who are just light years ahead'. At A level, something of a cultural divide, with the sciences dominated by Asian pupils. Year 7 can be tricky for those not already in training for the school's intensive regime and those from homework-free primary schools can sometimes feel daunted. They soon learn, however, to take it in their stride.

Games, options, the arts: Whatever boys do here they do well – as a strong an emphasis on the extra-curricular as the academic – 'It's a work-hard, play-hard place,' said one parent. Sport is played energetically and competitively – excels at cricket and waterpolo (national champions). As well as the usual team effort (a rugby and hockey school), individualists can enjoy athletics, orienteering, badminton, shooting and golf.

Two-thirds play a musical instrument – music and drama have always been taken seriously, with a demanding choice of work (think Brecht, Arthur Miller and Shakespeare, rather than High School Musical) and a high calibre of performance. Excellent facilities include one of the country's few operational fly towers and a well-used drama studio. (The school has a notable history of creative talent – recent alumnae include Matt Lucas, Sacha Baron Cohen, David Baddiel and Booker nominee, A D Miller.) Some adventurous art work, too, with a series of individually painted cow sculptures dotted round the site.

Characteristically, the more intellectually demanding pastimes also attract a high turn out, so plenty of chess champions and debating-cup winners. 'Our boys can talk for England,' says the head. Wide range of activities, mostly at lunchtimes, with a fair number of brain-stretchers, including crosswords and Scrabble. Community service is given a strong emphasis – 'We try to make them realise that being gifted brings the responsibility to put something back into society,' says the head.

Background and atmosphere: Opened in 1690, endowed by wealthy merchant haberdasher, Robert Aske, for the benefit of less fortunate members of his profession. Founded in Hoxton, it moved to Hampstead in the early 20th century and then, in 1961, to its current spacious 100-acre site in the grounds of Aldenham House in Hertfordshire. The attractive 17th-century red brick mansion, once the residence of banker and influential botanist Vicary Gibbs, remains the core of the school. As well as the undoubted delights of its rolling rural expanses (the house and grounds served as the backdrop for '60s television series, The Avengers), notably well-equipped, with a medley of well-planned and well-laid out buildings – 'The facilities are superb,' said one parent. The library is perhaps one of the most attractive features – spacious, bright and busy, with enthusiastic and knowledgeable staff.

One of the school's advantages (and sometimes disadvantages) is its secluded location, giving the feel of a country boarding school (or 'outer space,' as one pupil put it tartly). With the exception of a few sixth-former drivers, most boys arrive in the morning and stay firmly put until they are ferried home by parents or coaches at 4 or 5pm. The house system is strong here, particularly in the lower school, where boys are taught by house, and remains a focus of exertion throughout. (This is a competitive school, particularly early on, when who beat whom at what is a regular conversational gambit.)

'Diversity' is a word the school could have invented. The entire spectrum of belief is celebrated weekly with 12 individual assemblies covering everything from Hindu, Buddhist and Jain, to Jewish, C of E and secular. Most are led by the boys themselves and all pupils, whatever their persuasion, are welcome to attend whichever they choose. Most try out at least one alternative to their own faith (bagels seem to be a big selling point in attracting custom for Jewish assembly). 'The school is very good on multi-cultural,' says one parent, 'with strong friendships across all the ethnic and religious groups.' Extensive network of prefects in the sixth form, elected by the boys. Food generally considered 'very good', with a new 'grab-and-go' area and sixth formers able to stock up in their own commonroom.

Pastoral care and discipline: These are bright, well-behaved, motivated boys – disciplinary issues are seldom a concern. A ferocious work ethic is necessary to survive happily at this school and the push from parents, particularly of the Tiger variety, tends to be as strong as that from teachers – 'We don't have arguments about homework here,' says the head. Parents agree: 'Boys work very, very hard'. Discipline is firm, however, with detention for minor misdemeanours (like forgetting your swimming costume), and prep not done to a satisfactory standard. 'Boys like to have boundaries,' say the head. 'I see myself as a benign despot.' Problems regularly seen elsewhere are not really part of the culture – 'People make mistakes, of course, but we rarely see anything malicious'. London's usual temptations tend to remain safely outside the gates – 'If they're brought in, there's zero tolerance. The boys know what's expected'.

Pupils and parents: Primarily the affluent and aspiring professional classes, reflective of the north London/ Hertfordshire borders in which the school sits. (An extensive network of coaches imports boys from St John's Wood to Luton, Harpenden to Ruislip.) The school has traditionally had a significant Jewish core, who still represent about 30 per cent. This has more recently been overtaken by Asian families, who now make up about 30/40 per cent of the intake. Whatever their ethnic origins, these are families where the mantra 'education, education, education' is not simply spin. 'They know education is important to the future of their children and are full square behind them,' says the head. Some feel this can lead to a view that the only set to be in is the top set. Boys don't generally wilt under the pressure and come out positive and polite, self-assured without being self regarding. The list of illustrious old boys is long and includes Simon Schama, Sir Nicholas Serota, Sir Martin Sorrell, Damon Hill and Brian Sewell.

Entrance: The main intake is at 11, when the school sets its own exams in English, maths and reasoning. About 600 apply for 100 places (in addition to those coming up from the prep school); 300 recalled for interview, which takes place in groups and individually. 'We don't mind crooked profiles,' says the head. 'If someone is outstanding at maths, we can cope with the fact that they're less good at English.' That said, a school where a high percentage of successful candidates will already be at, or near, the top of their class. At 13 plus, 70-80 apply for 20 further places, with exams in English, maths, science, French, humanities and an optional Latin paper. At 16 maybe a handful of places to cover gaps left by leavers – entry by interview, a general essay and – for those wishing to study maths – a maths paper; minimum of 6 As or above required at GCSE.

Exit: Many to top universities Durham, Edinburgh, UCL, Imperial, Bristol, Bath and Birmingham. An impressive 46 to Oxbridge in 2013. Large numbers into the professions – medics, law, vets and dentists. 'Parents want practical careers for their boys,' said one father.

Money matters: Fees not outrageous by any means, but money tends to be dealt with penny by penny and extras are added regularly to the bill. Some 200 boys are on scholarships of between 10-30 per cent of fees. Bursary help also available, ranging from 5 to 100 per cent.

Remarks: A school which prides itself on identifying talent and building on it. Not the place for free spirits or those who want to muck around, but an outstanding offering for the bright-eyed and directed.

Haberdashers' Aske's Hatcham College

Pepys Road, London, SE14 5SF

• Pupils: 1,030 boys and girls • Ages: 3–18 • Non–denom • State

Tel: 020 7652 9500
Email: reception@hahc.org.uk
Website: www.haaf.org.uk

Principal: Mr Declan Jones LLB PGCE NPQH of the all-through 3-18 academy. Has had 14 years of senior leadership experience and is an executive member of the Haberdashers' Aske's Federation 'Three Schools One Vision' leadership team. Has extensive experience in developing initiatives to deliver school improvement and a special brief for assessment and ICT across the Aske's Federation. Lots of contact with pupils and parents and is the visible face of the College's leadership team. Teaching and learning of the highest quality are his priorities. He is married with two young daughters, both in secondary school.

Since 2011, Chief Executive of Haberdashers' Federation is Adrian Percival. Takes up the reins from Dr Liz Sidwell CBE, who has been appointed as schools commissioner for England. Started his teaching career in physics in Staffordshire in 1987, progressing to become headteacher of an 11-18 comprehensive school in Oxford in 1999. Subsequently moved into a national role in school improvement delivering government education policy from 2005 until this appointment in 2011. Now oversees this considerable empire, aided by a heavyweight senior management team. Each school and site has its own principal and senior leadership team. His portfolio includes strategy, finance and monitoring standards and leadership on consultancy.

Academic matters: Entrance selection criteria assure a spread of ability and, given that, the results are good. Boys and girls taught separately until the sixth form – little to choose between the sexes' achievement at GCSE level. Neither the usual differences in subject choices, which is refreshing. In 2013, 71 per cent achieved five or more GCSE grades A*-C including English and maths, with 22 per cent A*/A. Good range of mainstream subjects including Mandarin. A selection of students does a foundation course in Latin in year 9 – an option thereafter.

At A level, 52 per cent A*/B and 26 per cent A*/A grades in 2013 – popular subjects include psychology, English literature, maths, history. Music technology facilities are excitingly better than any we have seen elsewhere – studios for making videos and music production alongside the solid, traditional stuff. Had specialism too in ICT. A whole technology building has ample facilities: 'You can always get access to a computer,' said a techie sixth former. Innovative idea is to take PCs apart and rebuild – to see how they are made: brave! One class was the most over-heated classroom we have ever been suffocated in.

DT good – intoxicating scent of wood surrounded us as we enjoyed the collaboratively workful atmosphere in the workshop. Food technology resources also good – pastry-making classes we observed were noisy but focused. Art is lively – we admired pâpier maché animal heads and solid painting techniques in two good-sized studios.

Around one in seven pupils on the SEN register, about half supported in class and around a quarter has additional support with specialist teachers or learning mentors. About 25 pupils with statements for a range of physical or other needs, including ASD, in which the school has a minor specialism; they are supported by the inclusion team, which works alongside the SEN staff. SENs taken and dealt with seriously. Three new lifts to assist wheelchair users. Gifted and talented team supports the very able.

Games, options, the arts: Five minibus minutes away are its 14 acres of playing fields: two rugby pitches, two football pitches, seven tennis courts and a sports hall – a rare asset for an inner city school of any denomination, comparing well with facilities offered by many fee-paying schools. Range of outdoor games includes rugby, rounders, softball, hockey, cricket and football – equally popular with both sexes. Indoor activities on offer include volleyball, badminton, sports hall athletics, weight training, basketball and trampolining. Huge multi-purpose sports hall plus gym with all the machines you'd expect. Results are impressive, especially in rugby, athletics and cross-country.

Arts and crafts, including textiles, lively and intelligently taught with good results. Good black and white portraiture, lino cuts, paper lampshades and other imaginative work. Music is strong and has had much investment. Suite with practice rooms, though no designated recital/performance space, but school uses neighbouring church for performances. However musical life zings – 40 plus public musical events annually, 400 pupils sing in choirs, chamber groups (including two string quartets and a piano trio), orchestras and ensembles, along with bands of all descriptions. Composer in residence. Eleven pupils are members of the London Schools' Symphony Orchestra, more than 60 attend special Saturday classes at the colleges. All students are given the opportunity to receive free instrumental tuition, on condition they attend one of the choirs or ensembles.

Drama is taught throughout – very popular at GCSE and A level. A purpose built studio has been completed and plans for an exciting outdoor performance space under way. Junior drama festival every year plus several drama productions in the upper school, some of which are performed in local theatre venues. Recent productions include Coram Boy, The Turn of the

Screw, A Christmas Carol and Dracula. Added bonus of being able to loan costumes from the National Theatre costume store, which is just up the road.

Background and atmosphere: Complicated. One of the Haberdashers' 'family' of 10 schools, fee-paying and state, plus one grammar in Shropshire, now federated with an academy. The governing body is made up of committed, knowledgeable and serious educationalists, with a determination – hence the acquisition of Malory, reputedly 'the worst school in the country', and its transformation into Knights Academy, plus in 2009, Monson (which had notice to improve from Ofsted in 2008) – to grow and develop more schools on the successful model that is Hatcham. Became an academy on the understanding that federation with Knights, six miles away, was agreed – the impact on the area is substantial and promises most interestingly.

Hatcham itself is divided between three sites – Jerningham Road, which houses the lower school, in a huge Victorian redbrick edifice, typical of its time; Pepys Road – 15 minutes' walk up Telegraph Hill to a similar building, only in quieter, leafier surroundings, where the older pupils are (and the site for a new free school), and the primary, at the Mornington Road site whilst its Hunsdon Road site is rebuilt. All buildings have the air of the great old-fashioned grammars they once were – honours boards in the great hall etc – but innovation thrives – swipe card system in the canteen. The sites are linked by a constant minibus shuttle, though older pupils can walk. The streets are lined by solid and attractive Victorian houses, the area looks affluent and well-established – but an alarming incidence of muggings, around one a week on pupils, mostly for their mobiles, we were told.

All sites are well-kept and every opportunity to cultivate and maintain a little garden area for sitting outside or small class lesson has been seized. However outside space actually on-site is very limited. Good lecture theatre a real boon and well-used. Classrooms are, in general, not silent, but the buzz is collaborative and amiable. Work gets done here and in relaxed and co-operative style. Rated outstanding by Ofsted in latest report.

Pastoral care and discipline: A house system here – and it plays a rôle in every aspect of college life. Pupils like it and feel a real sense of belonging. Strong PSHCE establishes ethos and works preventatively. Anti-bullying website, mentoring by senior pupils, peer counselling and mentoring. Small tutor groups and individual transgressors dealt with individually – no inflexible policy. No exclusions for drugs in two years prior to our visit, no random testing – seemingly no need. Staff/pupil relations respectful and appreciative.

Food in canteen eaten by most looked excellent – stuffed peppers, hot puddings, salads, sandwiches – and dead cheap too.

Pupils and parents: Pretty reflective of this cosmopolitan and socially mixed area – 60 per cent of pupils are white, around 25 per cent black; a high proportion are Turkish, Chinese or Yoruba speakers; total of 36 first languages spoken at home by pupils. It all seems to make a relaxed and homogenous whole. Parents wildly supportive.

Famous former pupils include Lord Soper, artist Rowland Hilder, dambuster Sir Barnes Wallace, actor Rafe Spall, newsreader Fiona Bruce, footballer Shaun Wright Phillips, fashion designer Georgina Knight and numerous other sportsmen and women.

Entrance: For a place in year 7 has to be named on the local authority common application form plus completion of an additional information form for the College, which is a 3-18 academy, so children in year 6 of the primary phase have automatic entry into the senior phase.

All applicants take a non-verbal reasoning test and the score achieved places them into one of nine ability bands. No point in coaching for the non-verbal reasoning test as it takes children from all abilities.

Exit: Around 40 per cent move on after GCSEs. Four to Oxbridge in 2013; rest of sixth form leavers to a wide range from Bristol and Manchester to Coventry, Kent and Greenwich.

Remarks: The most over-subscribed non-selective state school in Great Britain.

Haberdashers' Aske's School for Girls

Linked school: Haberdashers' Aske's School for Girls, Junior School

Aldenham Road, Elstree, Hetfordshire, WD6 3BT

- Pupils: 890 girls, all day • Ages: 11–18 • Inter–denom
- Fees: £11,484–£13,554 pa • Independent

Tel: 020 8266 2300
Email: admissions@habsgirls.org.uk
Website: www.habsgirls.org.uk

Headmistress: Since September 2011, Ms Biddie (Bridget) O'Connor MA (fifties). Educated at St Helena School, Chesterfield, read classics at St Hugh's College, Oxford, followed by PGCE at Sidney Sussex, Cambridge. Taught classics at Francis Holland, head of it at Old Palace School, Croydon. Moved to Haberdashers' Aske's School for Girls as head of classics and sixth form, then deputy head. Headship at Loughborough High School for nine years before being welcomed back. Married with one grown-up daughter. Enjoys reading, cooking, creative arts, walking and her home in France. Says she is 'looking forward to continuing the excellent reputation Haberdashers already has for excellence, not only in academic work but also for developing the whole person.'

Academic matters: Results are consistently stunning and place the school firmly in the top tranche of every league table – 2013 97 per cent A*-B at A level with 81 A*/A. Popular subjects are history, maths, biology, Eng lit, chemistry – with results to relocate for, especially in the first two. GCSE: 94 per cent A*/A (has girls getting into the top few nationally).

No surprises in the curriculum, though relatively few of those who take a language in the sixth form continue after AS level. Languages well-supported and resourced and girls who meet lang teachers in the corridors are expected to address them in the appropriate demotic. IT also well-resourced. Few take art A level, which must be disappointing, given the quality of what is produced here and the top results for those who do. Sizeable contingent, however, take technology and get top results – justifiably from what we admired in the workshop.

Everyone assessed on entry – mostly mild dyslexia. Later the occasional girl with organisational or processing problems is identified and given support by individual learning department. Screening in years 7 and 9, and an annual week of subtle observation in all year groups to pick up on any other problems. SENs not big time here: one-to-one support given and all those with an identified need have an agreed individual learning plan to help them and their teachers address that need – reviewed regularly.

Games, options, the arts: The school is alive with the sound of music – 90 per cent learn at least one instrument and grade 8 is nothing unusual here. The symphony orchestra – 50 strong – is made up of mostly grade 8 students; music tours abroad and occasional musical productions with the boys next door, such as a joint concerts. Bands of all kinds – plenty for those who are not at grade 8 but just love doing it – and top-notch facilities, including for music tech. Superb recital room, though we wondered at the choice of black and white tiles – the only unharmonious aspect.

Music and art share a block with an excellent atrium used for displays – we saw some terrific sculptures and models, evidence of an uninhibited freedom of imagination and a thrilling creativity. No textiles, but pottery, and it was good to see that actual drawing is alive and well here – all the basic skills in good heart and joyous to find that girls attend life classes just for the love of it. Superb DT, taken to A level by academic girls who produce knock-out designs and have fun doing it.

Drama very strong – the middle school play the week before our visit had a huge cast; something found for all who wanted to be involved and the pictures suggested an exuberant performance, costumed with flair and ingenuity. Productions large and small, conventional and alternative, dot the calendar.

Vast sports hall (though no dance studio). Lots of outside space. New pool and fitness suite a great asset. Lots of sporting prowess – teams excel in gymnastics and synchronised swimming and individuals at badminton, lacrosse and athletics. Lacrosse is main winter sport, with netball and swimming; summer is tennis, athletics and plenty of opportunities in everything from football (popular), cricket and dance. Popular D of E. Trips everywhere and of all kinds. Opportunities galore and parents like the way, 'You can dip in and out of things just to give them a try'. Delicious things like The Thinker society.

Background and atmosphere: Take your satnav. Probably easy to locate when you know how, the two Habs' schools occupy a vast site moments from the M1, but down a country road where you'd least expect to find them. It's a bit like an industrial park when you arrive – security barrier, car park etc – with the splendour of the main Victorian building that is now the boys' school's admin hub to your left, and the heart sinks gently at the sight of the girls' school's main building – a featureless, rectangular block on which the only decoration is a plaster shield with the motto 'serve and obey'. Inside, however, it is light, spacious and comfortable, and one wonders why an architect who could get so much right made so little effort to produce something with a more inviting exterior.

In 1689 Robert Aske (Master of the Worshipful Company of Haberdashers) left £20,000 to found a school and almshouses in East London. After several moves and expansions, the girls' school moved here from west London in the early '70s, following the boys, who had taken over Lord Aldenham's estate, big house and all, a few years previously, so excellent hall into which whole school can fit. Good sixth form provision, though the girls feel their – vast-seeming to us – commonroom is too small. It has its own canteen – a boon in a day school. The privilege of this amount of space – 55 acres – for London-based children is unique, as is the happy co-existence of two single sex schools, which combine when appropriate and provide, for many, the best of both worlds. Parents like the fact that the sexes can meet in such a civilised way – and they do, at lunchtimes, at the gates – and join up for shows etc, but live and learn separately.

The atmosphere is cheerful, collaborative and civilised, with a genuine relish for what can be done here. We have yet to see more smartly turned-out staff, which somehow adds to the sense of politeness and self-respect that permeates the place.

New building development plan will include a new dining room and substantial changes to the catering arrangements.

Pastoral care and discipline: Parents are happy – one with children at both schools felt, 'The girls have more freedom, the boys are more regimented. The teachers are very approachable and put themselves out to deal with an individual's problems'. Girls agree and, for the most part, staff and girls relate easily – though high standards of behaviour are insisted on and some may chafe a bit. We witnessed one girl being met with a very stony-faced mistress at the staffroom door when she asked for a teacher, calling her 'Miss' rather than 'Mrs'. Clear policies on narcotics and bullying. Zero tolerance for drugs in theory – head has not had to put it into practice. Bullying 'is not acceptable full stop,' says head. 'If the parents or the girl tells us, we will do something very fast.' Little evidence of any such problems here and girls look happy. One told us approvingly of the lack of petty rules in the school. As one parent said, 'The school allows you to be what you are.'

Pupils and parents: Maze of coach routes brings everyone from everywhere – around 100 pick-up points from St John's Wood to Winchmore Hill to Welwyn, Harpenden, Watford and Ruislip. Result is a highly diverse ethnic, social and cultural mix which, head says, 'We really value'. Weekly split assemblies – Christian, Jewish, Hindu/Jain/Sikh, Muslim and humanist – and, wonderfully, you can choose which you want to go to on any given Thursday. Girls quizzed about friendships between people from different cultures look bemused. Said a parent: 'What really sells Habs' is the girls – confident but not cocky, willing to give anything a go and masses of positive energy.' Old Girls include BBC's Charlotte Green, Vanessa Feltz and shoe designer LK Bennet.

Entrance: Fifty come up from junior school, the rest from local preps and state juniors. A four or five form entry annually – around 450 apply for about 115 places. Exams in English, maths and VR – those who perform best invited to interview. A few admitted at sixth form level if they've got what it takes.

Exit: Under 10 per cent leave after GCSEs. Most popular universities are Oxbridge (22 places in 2013), Bristol, Nottingham and London Universities. Fifteen medics in 2013; geography, history and law next most popular subjects.

Money matters: Means-tested financial assistance (average is £6,000+) annually, including free places. Also academic scholarships for up to half fees, including music awards. No discounts for siblings.

Remarks: This is what girls' education in the modern world, at its best, is all about.

Haberdashers' Monmouth School For Girls

Linked school: Inglefield House

Hereford Road, Monmouth, NP25 5XT

- Pupils: 315 girls; 110 board (full and weekly), the rest day • Ages: 11-18 • Christian foundation, non-denom • Fees: Day £9,660-£12,870; Boarding £18,171-£26,460 pa • Independent

Tel: 01600 711100
Email: admissions@hmsg.co.uk
Website: www.habs-monmouth.org

Headmistress: Since 2008, Mrs Helen Davy (fifties), was head of Cobham Hall, where laid foundations for move to IB. Read modern history at Oxford, followed by postgraduate study at

King's College, London. Then worked as a radiographer at the Royal Free Hospital for four years before beginning teaching. Has taught history, history of art and politics at Roedean and The Towers Convent School. Before Cobham she was head of the faculty of cultural studies and acting senior mistress at Roedean. During a career break she ran a small fine wine business and still retains an interest. A warm and enthusiastic person who seems to be very much in touch with the outside world. Married, no children; her husband, a biodiversity enthusiast, now retired.

Off in April 2014 to head Havergal College in Toronto, a leading Canadian girls' school. Her successor will be Mrs Caroline Pascoe, currently head of Truro High School for Girls. She has a microbiology degree from Bristol University, was a member of the GB rowing squad at the 1992 Barcelona Olympics and an officer in the RAF Volunteer Reserve. She has worked in the Himalayas and still leads high-altitude trekking expeditions. She is married with a son.

Academic matters: Examination results excellent at both GCSE and A levels, sustained over the last five years. Nearly 76 per cent A*/A grades at GCSE in 2013; nearly 53 per cent at A level. Art, modern languages, maths and sciences popular choices. At sixth form offers over 30 options in conjunction with Monmouth School – co-ordinated timetable and many shared classes. Sensible use made of new technology to support traditional teaching. Learning support available on an individual/shared basis from suitably qualified staff. Study skills taught to equip students for independent learning throughout the school.

Games, options, the arts: Keen on a rounded education and has nurtured a diverse extracurricular programme. Drama and dance popular, with first-rate facilities also used by the local community. Wide range of sporting options includes lacrosse, hockey, rounders, rowing, swimming and tennis; several PE staff are international players. Well-equipped sports hall, pool with magnificent views, floodlit all-weather pitch and well kept playing fields encourage girls to become involved with sport – we watched some of the younger girls respond with St Trinian's-like enthusiasm during a sports lesson. Girls represent Wales in various sports on a regular basis.

Duke of Edinburgh Award popular as well as local community service. Fundraising has enabled the school to undertake projects in Africa to help local schools improve their facilities. Girls join the CCF at Monmouth School. Strong art department evidenced by work shown throughout the school – on entering one of the art rooms we were confronted by the surreal image of a host of small ceramic Adams and Eves. Annual interhouse Eisteddfod embraces a wide range of skills and activities. Music flourishes – 50 per cent take lessons on an instrument or voice, choirs and orchestras give girls a chance to shine, some current pupils in the Welsh National Youth Opera.

Background and atmosphere: School founded in 1892 to complement Monmouth School, whose foundation dates from 1614. It was funded by the original bequest of local man, William Jones, a member of the Haberdashers' Company who made his fortune in Russia. The livery company is responsible for the school and provides financial support. The original late Victorian buildings are set on a hill overlooking the market town of Monmouth. Over the last 10 years facilities have been improved with sympathetic modern additions, including a glassed atrium linking some of the buildings together.

Flexi-boarding available. Younger girls board in the main school in three or four bedded rooms. Older ones are based in a purpose-built boarding house with sixth formers having study bedrooms. New sixth form house with 45 en-suite study bedrooms. Accommodation is spacious and bright and includes plenty of space for both study and relaxation.

Well-developed programme of after-school and weekend activities. Food is good and served in a comfortable dining room. Uniform for all pupils – badges on jackets worn with pride. Good mix of female and male staff. The girls sometimes gently tease the latter – of course.

Pastoral care and discipline: The aim is to make it a happy place. Pastoral support available from a number of sources: effective peer monitoring of younger pupils by trained sixth formers; heads of year or house; form tutors and school chaplain. Bullying is rare – the girls have good and supportive relationships between themselves. Reserves the right to search for drugs, but this has never been a problem.

Pupils and parents: Wide range of parents including first time buyers of independent education. Catchment area is south-west England and south-east Wales. Becoming more popular with overseas parents; fewer pupils from Monmouth itself than in the past. Former pupils include Lisa Rogers, Sandra Huggett and Jackie Ballard MP.

Entrance: A third from their own prep school, Inglefield House, a third from other preps and a third from state schools. Entry at 11 by entrance exam, an interview and school reports. At 13 by common entrance or own exam. Sixth form entrants must have five GCSE passes at grade B or above and be interviewed.

Exit: Around 20 per cent leave after GCSEs. Sixth formers to a wide range of destinations including Oxbridge (three in 2013), Yale, Bath, Bristol, Durham, Guildhall School of Music and Drama, London, Edinburgh and Hong Kong.

Money matters: Has replaced about a third of the government assisted places scheme and offers a number of scholarships. Fifteen per cent of pupils receive some help with fees. While day fees are now in line with similar schools, boarding fees are very competitive.

Remarks: Friendly school that produces feisty young women.

Haileybury

Hertford, Hertfordshire, SG13 7NU

- Pupils: 765 (435 boys, 330 girls); 475 boarders • Ages: 11–18
- Christian foundation • Fees: Boarding £18,516–£29,190; Day £14,568–£21,924 pa • Independent

Tel: 01992 706353
Email: registrar@haileybury.com
Website: www.haileybury.com

Master: Since 2009, Joe Davies MA (Cantab) PGCE (fifties). Educated at Christ College, Brecon, then St John's College, Cambridge, where he read history. After graduating, he worked in the City for a year but 'hated every second,' so returned to Cardiff (where his father was an academic) to do a PGCE. 'I'd wanted to be a teacher from the age of 14, but thought it was too drippy to go straight back to school.' Teaching clearly in the blood, since two brothers and three of his four grown children are also in the profession.

Taught at Tonbridge, where he became a housemaster, then deputy head of St John's School, Leatherhead, before taking on his first headship at Sutton Valence. Stills teaches history to the higher level IB. He feels his achievement at Haileybury has been to increase the emphasis on academic performance, while placing ever more significance on the extra-curricular. Sets a good example. A keen cyclist and marathon runner (who has recently completed the Venice marathon with his wife and two of his children), he also enjoys cryptic crosswords and reading history.

Academic matters: A famous name in public school education, Haileybury has in recent years become equally well known for its enthusiastic participation in the IB. 'We began in 1998 because it promised a broader curriculum and a boost to boarding, but we're now totally idealist,' says the head. Today about 110 sixth formers follow the diploma programme, with about 40 arriving each year specifically to do so. A levels, however, are still very much on offer and the school does very well in both sets of exams, with 37 points a fairly standard average in the IB, and very pleasing results at A Level (54 per cent A*/A in 2013). Biology chemistry and history notably strong. Though not the easiest things to run a school with a dual set of qualifications, this is managed by highly-qualified staff (including a hefty sprinkling of doctorates), who generally teach across both systems. The ISI commended the 'often outstanding' teaching.

Lower down, IGCSEs in just about everything, with 59 per cent obtaining A*/A in 2013. Here, all do a compulsory core of maths, English language, science and RS ('because of its philosophical and ethical bent'). Languages include Italian, French, Spanish, Latin and Classical Greek, with German also taught to the 15 or 20 native speakers taking the IB. Pupils are set in maths and languages from year 7, science and English from year 9. Reasonable numbers who require some type of learning support (typically 50-80), with two teachers to address their needs, one a specialist in language, the other in maths. A small number, too, have extra help with English as a second language. Overall high aspirations, with sane expectations. 'They work hard, but it's very unpressured,' said a parent. 'They expect you to try your very, very best.' Relationships with staff particularly good, both in and outside of the classroom.

Games, options, the arts: Co-curricular activities are very much part of Haileybury's raison d'etre and the school has an outstanding reputation for both sport and choral music. Sport compulsory for all throughout, with games afternoons twice a week and matches on Saturday. Plenty of teams too, often from A-D, so everyone gets a chance to show their mettle. Those who aren't fans of the playing field can do 'something less taxing,' with options including aerobics, badminton, trampolining, rowing, rackets, golf and sailing (which currently boasts one girl who sails for Great Britain). Though boys triumph in hockey and football (where the school play in the Boodles Cup) and girls in tennis and lacrosse (competing at county and national level), rugby and cricket remain the 'communal sports.' 'Boys' rugby is the main thing,' said a girl, and the whole school turns out to cheer on rugby matches played on the front field. Facilities can only be described as superb, with a bright, modern pool, two Astroturf pitches and a professionally operated tennis club in the grounds. The rackets court is also considered one of the finest in the world and plays host to the world rackets championship.

The school has a 30-year tradition of exceptional choral singing and won the BBC Songs of Praise School Choir of the Year in 2005 (it has reached the semi-final twice since then too). 'One of the things I enjoy most about the school,' said one parent, 'is the Christmas concert. It's just magnificent.' Chamber choir of about 30 ('very intense,' said one member) plus larger chapel choir of about 90. Wide range of other musical opportunities, from jazz bands to concerts and musical theatre. Twenty peripatetic music staff. 'You potentially can do any instrument,' said a teacher. 'We currently have pupils studying the steelpans, jazz piano and the organ.' The stand-alone music building, which already enjoys a charming beamed concert hall, is undergoing a £1m refurbishment.

Art taught in its own large, light, purpose-built building, which not only caters for those doing GCSE or A Level, but for leisure enthusiasts, seven days a week and in the evenings. Offers 2D and 3D, print, ceramics, photography and textiles,

with exams tailored to individual interests. Dance lessons on offer for about 100 keen participants in jazz, ballet, street and tap, plus an annual dance show. 'Fantastic drama,' said a pupil, listing an energetic range from house drama to full-school musicals, which take place in the well-equipped studio theatre.

An abundance of trips. Sport (South Africa) and music (Slovenia, Prague and Venice), plus charity and subject specific (Uganda, Tanzania, Vietnam, and Sinai), as well as more modest outings to battlefields and cultural events.

Wednesday afternoons are devoted to community service, D of E and CCF for years 9 to 11, broadening out in the sixth form to take in activities like photography and web design. One extended weekend each term devoted exclusively to D of E and CCF (which flourish in equal numbers). Plenty of societies and lectures. Model United Nations particularly popular and the school recently played host to a world conference with 800 delegates. The head, who feels strongly that co-curricular activities build up life skills, has devised a specific year 9 programme which includes such fundamentals as Outward Bound skills and life saving.

Certainly you wouldn't enjoy the school if you weren't happy with a busy life. 'Everyone encourages everyone else and invites them to get involved. It's very full on,' said one pupil. 'You do have to learn to plan your time to fit in all your commitments, but you go to bed feeling fulfilled.'

Background and atmosphere: The school was designed in 1806 for the East India Company by William Wilkins (also responsible for the National Gallery and Downing College, Cambridge) as a training college for civil servants bound for India. In 1862, after the closure of the college, it was taken over by Haileybury, to be transformed into a public school for families in the professions and services, amalgamating, in 1942, with the Imperial Service College. The first girls were admitted in 1973. Today the school continues to occupy an impressive 550 acres of rural Hertfordshire, complete with magnificent neo-classical university-like buildings constructed round a traditional quadrangle. Later additions are sympathetic and well designed, with most subjects benefiting from purpose-built space. Beautiful, well-stocked and well-used library. 'If they don't have a book, they will get it for you.'

The school remains a Christian foundation with an Anglican chaplain who officiates in a domed chapel of cathedral-like proportions. Though Haileybury is ethnically and religiously diverse (with a fair number of Muslims, Jews and Hindus) everyone must attend services four or five times a week. 'It's here they learn the values that hold the school together,' says the head.

Charity work is taken seriously and the Haileybury Youth Trust, first set up in the East End in 1890 by Old Boy Clement Attlee, has been working with impoverished Ugandans since 2006. It has been commended by the UN as a model of a small-scale charity, patenting a brick now used for buildings schools, kitchens and water towers.

Two further Haileybury branches now operate in Kazakhstan, the first British public schools to be opened in Central Asia. These help underwrite bursaries for UK-based students.

Pastoral care and discipline: The school essentially operates as two schools, a more-or-less self-contained lower school, running as a day prep from 11 to 13; and an upper school, from 13 to 18, which is very much a boarding school, with a full day of lessons and sport on Saturday.

From year 9, about 70 per cent of pupils board, with a sizeable chunk of weekly boarders who leave late on Saturday and return on Sunday evening (except for five or six weekends annually, when all remain). Boarding ethos even for day pupils, who stay till 6.30pm and have their own beds at school. Seven boys' houses, five girls'. Four recently built, with light, bright rooms, the rest older but updated. All sit amongst pleasant greenery and house 55 boarders, overseen by a housemaster or mistress, plus a resident tutor. In the early years, eight to 10 pupils share a large, subdivided space; from year 11, single or shared rooms.

Girls do their own laundry, boys have theirs done for them. 'They think girls prefer that arrangement,' justified one pupil. Active inter-house social life and plenty of weekend activities for full-time boarders, with Saturday film nights and Sunday trips. Plus 'a lot of people have flats in London' or visit local pupils (with beneficent parents). Parents ('my son's housemaster is just wonderful – warm, jolly, intelligent, everything you could hope for in a male role model') and pupils ('my housemistress is the most reasonable woman') praise the boarding care.

Not a grand school in atmosphere. 'It's cosy and terribly, terribly happy,' says one parent. 'You could not think of a better place to have your teenager running around.' Food comes highly commended. 'It's one of the things people rave about,' said a sixth former. Three compulsory meals a day (plus an optional snack on games days), but with plenty of choice. The new Costa Coffee, a latter-day tuck shop, is 'the' place to congregate. Manners are formal (new pupils jump to attention, teachers are addressed as Sir) but not stiff. All pupils wear uniform, tartan skirts and blazers in the junior school, plain navy suits in the sixth form.

Discipline runs the usual gamut from detention to permanent exclusion. Drugs dealt with firmly. First offenders are suspended for a week, and regularly drugs tested thereafter, second-time offenders are expelled – though the head 'can't remember excluding someone.' Strong prefect system, with 30 to 40 college prefects given additional responsibilities and privileges (more flexibility in uniform, better rooms, pub visits).

Pupils and parents: Largely from the surrounding counties – Hertfordshire, Essex, Buckinghamshire, Cambridgeshire. In general parents are 'City folk, business people, successful professionals' and as most live reasonably nearby, more involved than usual at boarding schools. Large numbers from Europe for the sixth form, particularly Germans and Italians; a trickle from Haileybury's sister schools in Kazakhstan. Pupils are happy, confident, friendly and balanced.

Entrance: Fifty in year 7, a further 60 in year 9. Unusually, also a healthy intake (10 to 20) in year 10. Typically 50 new pupils enter the sixth form, including about 40 from overseas. At this juncture the school is heavily over-subscribed, with about three applicants for every place. Entrance tests at all levels in maths, English, verbal and non-verbal reasoning. Year 9 entry pre-tested by negotiation with the prep school 12 or 24 months in advance and CE used for setting. 'We are looking for somebody who wants to do their best, is B+ to A* academically and will throw themselves into the co-curricular,' says the head. Wide range of feeders includes Heath Mount, Edge Grove, Lochinver House and Keble.

Exit: About 10 to 20 leave after GCSEs, often for local day schools. Post A Levels and IB, it's mainly to Russell Group universities (most popular choices include UCL, Durham, Nottingham, Leeds, Bristol and King's College London), and increasingly, to Europe and the US. About 12 each year to Oxbridge (split evenly between A Level and the IB). Good range of specialist advisers, for Oxbridge, medical school and North American universities. Three or four to art college.

Money matters: Music, sport, art, and all-rounder scholarships of up to 30 per cent of fees, plus a range of (generous) means-tested bursaries.

Remarks: A dynamic and energetic school, with a long established, successful IB diploma programme. Haileybury actually achieves what many boast about, a well-rounded education. Great fun for those who want to be involved in everything it has to offer.

Hall School Wimbledon, Senior School

Linked school: Hall School Wimbledon, Junior School

17 The Downs, London, SW20 8HF

• Pupils: 250 boys and girls • Ages: 11–16 years • Non-denom
• Fees: £13,224 pa • Independent

Tel: 020 8879 9200
Email: enquiries@hsw.co.uk
Website: www.hsw.co.uk

Headmaster: Since 1990, Mr Timothy J Hobbs MA (fifties), educated at Eastbourne College and St Andrews, where he read medieval and modern history. Abandoned accountancy training in favour of a teaching post at Hill House International Junior School, which he left six years later, encouraged by parents, to set up his own school – the original Hall School Wimbledon Junior School. (In 1999 his brother Jonathan joined as principal of the junior school.)

Unmarried – except to the school, which TJH (as he likes to be known) hates us saying, but no better way to describe his passion and dedication to the place. An avuncular figure with quite old-fashioned (in the nicest possible way) sensibilities. He's a stickler for good manners, a strong advocate of books over computers and likes the children to be outdoors in the fresh air as often as possible. Alongside such Blyton-esque objectives, he espouses a rigorous and thorough approach to teaching, tested weekly in his personally devised homework system.

Works tirelessly at the sharp end and consequently gets to know every child very well. Does some teaching but, more pertinently, personally leads the many school expeditions – basically count him out for the summer term: he's 'on tour'. Traditionally has baked every pupil a cake for their birthday – 'a great way to focus on that child for half an hour and think about their needs in the coming year,' he says. But less keen on thinking about their parents – he's not interested really: he's all about the children. 'I've never met him,' said one mother who has been at the school a couple of years. 'He's very nice,' thought another, rather vaguely. 'But you'll never see him glad-handing at the gates.' TJH happily defends his position, 'I can't know and run the school properly if I'm seeing parents all the time: I have some excellent staff who do that. I am keen that parents speak to the right person to deal with their questions/ concerns. If that person is me, then I will meet with them.'

Opinionated on occasion, one gets the impression that it is his way or the highway – you either buy into his ethos of the school or go elsewhere. Admits he dislikes detail and dealing with the minutiae of running a school – 'He does tend to wander off,' agrees the school secretary – but he's absolutely your man for some blue-sky thinking, pushing the envelope, outside the box type of approach. Cutting something of a maverick figure, he and his school have a local reputation as being quirky; although actually he and the whole setup is much more traditional than reputation would have it. Outside school, he is interested in culture, particularly art, which he collects and hangs at the school.

Academic matters: For a largely non-selective, mixed-ability school, does extremely well. The ethos is that learning should be a pleasure, not a chore, and that exams are not the be all and end all – as the prospectus says, 'Thought is the most important activity taking place at our school'. So no teaching to the test, other than, obviously, complying with the requirements of the GCSE and common entrance syllabuses. A nod to the 'spirit and content' of the national curriculum, all combined in school's own Work Programmes.

Pre-GCSE the core curriculum includes English, maths, French, German, science, history, geography, religious studies (including a chunk of philosophy), art, DT, music and drama. At GCSE the timetable will be written around that year's cohort. No ICT GCSE (see below) or PSHE, which is covered 'more naturally' during conversations on school trips, lunchtime and as part of the RS syllabus.

Children are encouraged to believe that all subjects are equal – poetry as valuable as science – with no more praise given to a mathematician than to a pianist than to an athlete. 'It sounds ridiculously clichéd, but we do faithfully honour the individual,' says TJH. Forget the league tables and think about the value-added. 'Some of our children will leave with a full set of A*s, while for others a collection of B and C grades will be a personal triumph and just as worthy of celebration.'

IGCSE is preferred in science – largely because they are, in school's view, 'more child-friendly – we are an international school after all'. Certainly the language used is simpler, making them more boy-friendly perhaps. 2013 27 per cent A*/A overall at GCSE.

Homework is relevant, contained and limited to 45 minutes a night, all designed to reinforce what has been taught in the classroom. It's a system of the school's own devising called Flints. Based on a 'little and often' philosophy, the pupils get bite-sized exercises in four or five different subjects every night and are then tested at school on Friday morning in what is called 'a Flint Wall'. Some parental feeling that CE children pushed a little harder than the rest – which would be unsurprising. Hard to over-emphasise the importance of Flints, which are an enormous part of the school – 'My child is quite obsessed with them,' says one mother. Certainly parents can see exactly what is going on (particularly valued by those overseas). 'It gives trust and comfort that their children are being prepared at the highest level,' says TJH.

One area where children may not be so highly skilled is in ICT – TJH is not a fan but, bowing to the modern world, such technology is tolerated and available, with laptops permitted where it helps a dyslexic child. School dropped the ICT GCSE because it felt the syllabus did not deliver and was genuinely not useful. Computers available in classrooms, two dedicated ICT suites. TJH prefers that children are trained to use books as a resource. But it is worth noting that the Flint system is a highly sophisticated computer-based one, so although anti-ICT for its own sake, the school isn't exactly advocating chalk and slate – it's more of a philosophical position. DT is also not strong – really only facilities for woodwork and the subject falls off the curriculum after year 8.

The school says it has average numbers of special needs children for a private school. Lots of dyslexia, so surprising to hear from one parent that her child's dyslexia was neither picked up nor sympathetically handled – don't assume school has it covered. TJH says, 'HSW is diligent about not labelling children, hence possible explanation for this comment. Every child is assessed annually.' SENCo (praised by a parent) who tries to meet most needs within the classroom – inclusivity is everything here. Nearby Kingston upon Thames and New Malden have large Korean and Japanese communities and a third Hobbs brother has links in the Far East – reflected in school numbers. Predominantly female staff with several long-standing members steeped in Hobbsism.

System of deputies and senior tutors aims to devolve power down from the head. For the future, a sixth form is on the cards – parents would welcome it and school is similarly keen to get stuck into A levels, but space limitations make it no-go at the moment.

Games, options, the arts: Lazybones and other such slackers need not apply. Get your children used to the great outdoors – they will be thoroughly aired here with lots of sport and all sorts of clubs. Every day begins with a wakeup call of 30 minutes' circuit training from 8.30am and loads of sport is timetabled throughout the week – some each day, bad weather rarely stops play. Rugby, hockey and netball feature large – no swimming facilities, though, and no playing fields on site, but extensive playing fields and sports facilities nearby. More chances for girls to play in the teams as fewer of them in the school. Fantastic place for netball – borough champion, long established tour to New Zealand extremely popular. Boys' rugby tour to NZ recently added. TJH admits to feeling 'rather galled that Epsom, Cranleigh and Millfield get credit for having international players who are actually former HSW pupils who got their first touch of a ball with us'. The Levels, new play/ sports facility at the junior school, used for PE programme and training ground for strong climbing tradition – lower circuit level provides two parallel obstacle courses and upper climbing level includes a traversing wall.

Drama in its many different forms runs through the timetable for all years. Every child has a role to play in his or her year group's annual performances and learns that production, lighting, costume and makeup are just as important as starring roles and comic cameos. Also dance laid on for girls. Well equipped music studios and peripatetic teachers offer vocal, guitar, piano, woodwind, percussion, music theory and music technology lessons, plus an orchestra, choir and various ensembles. A long day school day helps the children fit it all in.

Hard to overstate the importance of field trips at this school – usually in the summer term and always led by TJH. They are educational – picking up on the history and geography of whatever location, eg Northern France and D-Day landings – but also provide an opportunity to talk through PSHE-type issues, undertake physical challenges and bond as a group.

Background and atmosphere: All very civilised. Original Victorian building has nice features including a 'country house-style' library filled with giant bean bags, although as one parent pointed out, the bean bags are more in evidence than the books. And no librarian – all a bit strange for a school that claims to value books so much. Not a glamorous place, and some of the newer parts (from 1980s and '90s) are a bit dismal (the school tells us that they have been recently redecorated), although all floors are carpeted and windows curtained to minimise nasty ambient noises. Walls are decorated with original artwork, including TJH's own collection. Not much of the children's work around the place – although we did visit early in a new term. Classrooms are of different sizes, but space is well used and no feeling of crush and cramp. Unusually for a secondary school, years 7, 8 and 9 stay put and the teachers come to them; from year 10 the more traditional set up of children moving around.

The place is boy-heavy – school says 60/40, but perception is more 70/30 as you walk around; it varies throughout the school, some years more boy-dominated than others. Although school says it desires equal numbers and a new campaign recently launched to increase numbers of girls to 50:50 by 2020, lots of very good girls' schools in the area make for strong competition. TJH says he is very mindful – and keen to change the fact – that some girls might not come to the school because of male feel to the environment. But no nasty role-modelling – children will see TJH gardening, cleaning and even hanging curtains.

An active place – outward bound-style uniforms say it all. Nice to see children (admittedly year 7s) actually playing at break time rather than skulking around trying to looking cool. Balls allowed – or rather encouraged – and we can't believe this place would have any truck with conker-bans and the like. 'They really celebrate childhood here,' says a parent. 'When it snows they are told to get sledging.' Similarly, where many schools would have a ban on running, here running outside is good.

Forty-five minute break mid-morning and a similarly decent break in the afternoon – on both occasions your child will be encouraged to get fresh air. Freshly cooked food for lunch. As well as a birthday cake large enough to share with their class and take a piece home, every child is given a Christmas present by TJH – 'They are simple acts of kindness to show each child that they matter to us'.

TJH conscious that some wariness exists over family owned schools and is keen to stress that the place is not a 'Tim Hobbs' production – 'There's a proper structure here, with Jonathan (TJH's brother and head of junior school) and I each supported by a very able deputy and a system of senior tutors'. We feel it would be some deputy that made much headway against a Hobbs brother – though TJH disagrees!

Pastoral care and discipline: TJH extremely strict on all interaction at the school, proud of the fact it is 'a very safe place', and of course its small size makes it reasonably easy to monitor. 'I've found that the school watches the children very closely, particularly as they get older,' said one mother. Few rules, mainly commonsense. The fact that TJH displays his own art collection around the place speaks volumes – obviously no vandalism. 'We spend a lot of money on making the school nice and comfortable; they wouldn't write on their parents' walls and we don't expect it here either,' he says.

Little call for punishments as children quickly understand what's expected of them – 'We try not to create pointless barriers and rules'. But action will be taken if necessary – a child was expelled a few years ago for bullying, which the school 'loathes' and is the ultimate no-no here, widely defined to include even ignoring somebody: this place is very inclusive. Parents all mentioned how their children grew in confidence at the school. If somebody does do wrong, staff are 'shocked and upset' rather than angry. No detentions – school would not want to send a message that break-time activities were not important and could be dispensed with at will. Ever evolving, at one stage considered providing make up lessons for the girls – in reality, probably no better way to put girls off the whole idea!

Pupils and parents: Sixty per cent from the rather prosperous local area – which is roughly mid-way between Raynes Park and rather grander Wimbledon. Others from Kingston, New Malden, Dulwich and Clapham, with a couple from Kensington, Knightsbridge, Barnes and the like, so a fairly up-market clientele, including the odd famous name. Children of all shapes, sizes, nationalities and abilities – parents similarly mixed bunch. No PTA or sports days (by design) so not the easiest place to get to know other parents, particular if you haven't been at the junior school – though the school doesn't accept this comment.

Entrance: By assessment at 11+ – applicants spend a day at the school: interview with deputy, English and maths assessment and they take part in drama, music and games activities. 'We're watching for behaviour too – it's quite an elaborate process,' says TJH. Prides itself on seeing the good in all. Consequently this can involve two or three meetings with parents – all handled by long-serving deputy. 'While there is no such thing as a HSW child, we are looking for a good match.' Regular 11+ open mornings (four Tuesdays each term).

Exit: About 10 per cent fall out at 13 after the common entrance group leave. Pupils go all over the place – locally to King's Wimbledon, Lady Eleanor Holles and Westminster, alongside further afield Winchester, Cranleigh and Millfield and St John's Leatherhead. All out at 16, eg to Epsom College, but not to one particular school/sixth form.

Remarks: A happy school, brave enough to take on children that other London schools might well turn down. Children who are a bit eccentric will be comfortable and accepted here. A humane place that concentrates on all-round development (not just academia – so not for league table obsessed parents) and turns out confident, personable, polite and physically fit teenagers.

Halliford School

Russell Road, Shepperton, Middlesex, TW17 9HX

- Pupils: 425 boys, with girls in sixth form; all day • Ages: 11–18
- Non-denom • Fees: £12,450 pa • Independent

Tel: 01932 223593
Email: registrar@halliford.net
Website: www.hallifordschool.co.uk

Headmaster: Since 2002, Mr Philip Cottam MA (fifties), previously a senior master at Stowe, housemaster at Sedbergh and an officer in the army. A historian (still teaches). Two grown-up children from his first marriage and an adult stepson from his remarriage. A most excellent mixture of the military and the human – 'Knows his mind – no dithering'. Energetic and enthusiastic, 'old-fashioned in such matters as punctuality and hair style', but 'someone you can drop in on impromptu'; 'charismatic, knowledgeable, fair'. Bookshelves full of military history, photographs of skiing and avalanches on the walls, theatre and concerts his recreations.

Knows all his pupils by name, passionately interested in their doings and welfare and expects all his teachers to be the same. In the last 10 years this attitude has permeated the school and become the source of its principal virtues.

Focuses on development planning, recruiting (pupils and staff), marketing, academic life and pastoral care. His deputy, Richard Talbot, covers day-to-day operations, organisation and discipline. Retiring in July 2014.

Academic matters: Not the local academic top stream, but very much a place where an academic boy, suited to a smaller broader school, can flourish. 'My son was allowed to be smart, punctual and bright, and was not teased much.' Entry requirements having been pushed up a few years ago, exam results have now reached very respectable levels: 34 per cent A*/A at GCSE in 2013; 15 per cent A*/A at A level and 46 per cent A*/B.

Value added looks good, too. 'There was one boy who did not quite pass our entry exam, but I gave him a place as he was a brother and there was also something about him. I warned the parents there was a distinct possibility that he might not do very well at GCSE (I still have the letter I wrote). He achieved nine A*/A grades at GCSE. It was all about confidence and late development.'

All take Latin in the early years, and all are expected to emerge from GCSE with a pass in a modern foreign language. A good range of subjects at A level, with less of an emphasis on the sciences than is usual in a boys' school.

Generally focused on bringing out the best in each child, with a great deal of personal attention when they falter in their progress. Immediate, easy and deep support for everyone with specialist support being extended with an appointment of a full time special needs teacher. Online assessment on arrival to confirm, diagnose and update. Plans organised for those who need it: for most this means making staff aware, for those who really need it specific support from the new specialist teacher. We spoke to one parent who was fizzing with pleasure at having her dyslexic boy looking forward to a maths exam.

Games, options, the arts: Every boy leaves here as an initiate of the national male religion of sport, and many with an eye on the priesthood. Rugby and rowing have the largest temples, but a wide range of minor gods, all well provided for. Sport binds this community together and gives the boys confidence and comradeship. Much excellence, but it is participation that counts, and parents report that even those with no noticeable sporting talent or bent join in, enjoy the experience and feel comfortable.

Sixth form girls get to enjoy the sporting atmosphere, but not, unfortunately, to participate in much of the competition.

Drama way out of the ordinary. Excellently resourced, with a fine small theatre. Highly regarded by the boys (several of the sporting champions are keen participants), wide enjoyment of participation, a strong tradition of technical theatre, easy integration with academic subjects on, eg, Shakespeare, superb exam results and many going on to take theatre-related subjects at university level.

Music and art both very strong and engagingly taught. Several parents commented on the strength of support for their son's musical talents and the school's willingness to allow practice to infringe on lesson time. Expanded facilities in a pleasingly designed new building (still a building site when we visited). By no means all boys' schools have this dual enjoyment of sport and the arts – it has always appeared to us to be a great strength in readying boys for the world. Lots of other extracurricular activities, with a strong emphasis on human engagement.

Background and atmosphere: A Georgian house, looking across a busy road to the Thames, surrounded by classrooms and other school buildings in a pleasing and coherent style. Lots of sports fields behind, much used.

'A happy, disciplined family'; a very pleasing collection of young men, relaxed, easy to be around, but clearly accustomed to hard work; 'Individuality respected, not ground down'. Everybody, particularly staff, expected to look out for others and to deal with, or find someone to deal with, problems when they find them. 'Will give a boy a chance to turn around and will bring the shy out of themselves.' A number of parents told us that their son's confidence had been really boosted after just a few months at the school – 'He was encouraged to give his all, given responsibility'. Not, in practice, a perfect system – 'It happens with some teachers, not others; sometimes you have to chase', but the impetus from the centre makes sure that it happens in the end. The school is probably around its maximum size if this approach, reliant on human interactions rather than numbers and systems, is to work – but it is excellent while it does.

Those girls who arrive for sixth form seem happy and successful: well worth a look if you think your daughter might enjoy the company of a very civilised and respectful gathering of boys.

Staff enthusiastic, 'happy to join in with pupils' activities, really know the boys well'; 'approachable and not at all stuffy, and really seem to get the balance right so that things are not regimented, more relaxed but respectful'. Good communications with parents; yearly questionnaire gets a good response. Staff eat (the passable) lunch with pupils.

Pastoral care and discipline: All wound up in the general structure of support and expectations, with excellent results. 'Bullying quickly dealt with.'

Pupils and parents: Parents largely local, hard-working. Pupils bright-eyed, engaging, unstressed, but get the work done. 'Confident, but not cocky. Self-assured, but not in a mean way,' said a parent, and that's the way they appeared to us too. Girls very much at home. Not a place that would suit someone who does not want to join in or who loves mucking around.

Entrance: Has upped pass mark to 50 per cent, with a noticeable effect on results, but will still take brothers who miss the grade if the school thinks they have a reasonable chance of keeping up with the pace. Cares more for the interview than the marks alone. Half come in from state primary schools: some practice in verbal and non-verbal reasoning recommended.

Exit: Quite a flow after GCSE to local colleges for more vocational provision, the odd one to more selective schools'

sixth forms, but those (75 per cent or so) who stay on almost all go to university, with a notable interest in drama, media studies, engineering and sciences. A few to grand universities, a few to sports scholarships in the United States.

Money matters: Sensible fees, plus some scholarships and bursaries.

Remarks: A sporting, harmonious school, comfortable in its role as part of the local Championship, doing very well for the boys (and sixth form girls) that it suits.

Hamilton College

Linked school: Hamilton College Junior School

Bothwell Road, Hamilton, ML3 0AY

• Pupils: 400 boys and girls • Ages: 12–18 • Christian (multi-denom) • Fees: £8,823 pa • Independent

Tel: 01698 282700
Email: principal@hamiltoncollege.co.uk
Website: www.hamiltoncollege.co.uk

Principal: Since 2008, Miss Margaret Clarke BSc MA education SQH, (fifties), formerly vice principal at Hamilton. Before that she was depute head teacher at Harris Academy, then director of ICT and head of post-primary education for learning and teaching, Scotland. She was not around at our visit, but her staff speak of her enthusiastically as a friendly person whose priority is dealing with pupils and parents. She sees the school as 'a learning community where the values of respect for others, tolerance and integrity are encouraged within a caring Christian ethos'.

Academic matters: The school 'has high academic expectations' and, using the Scottish exam system, offers Standard grades or Intermediate II at S4 (most pupils do eight subjects plus Intermediate 1 RMPS), generally five Highers at S5 and a combination of Highers and Advanced Highers at S6. French, from J5, German and Latin, from SI, on offer. All three sciences taught from S1.

Results are solid at S grade and Int II with high spots in history and chemistry. RMPS for all at Int I has an excellent pass rate. Most take English and maths Higher and the school 'usually manages to meet subject requests at Higher and Ad H'. Some non-core subjects such as business management, PE, technical studies etc on offer. School says take up of Ad Highers is growing. Classes fairly small; year groups of 70ish split into four and setted for maths, English, French etc. Loads of competitive triumphs too: with impressive victories in maths challenge and the Gilbert Murray Classical Essay competition amongst others.

Learning support team with qualified helpers gives both in-class and separate help to dyslexics etc, the team working closely with teaching and pupil support (guidance) staff and with parents. Staff relate personally to small groups so 'no one should slip through the net'. Lots of internet help with 'Moodle', an online course management service via the school website.

Games, options, the arts: Impressive record of art school entry (lots to Glasgow) and some distinguished past pupils. Walls zing with really exciting work, often killing two birds with one stone by using a theme from literature or even chemistry. The art room has a fantastic outlook and is jam-packed full of pupils' sculptures, photography etc. The slightly self-effacing modesty of the art teacher does not conceal the fact some outstanding work happens under his skilful care.

Music up to Ad Higher with a good wide range of instrumental teaching and bags of opportunities to perform in orchestras, choirs, groups, musicals and foreign trips. Choirs and orchestra tour the Black Forest with a mixed programme, as well as concerts and drama in school in local churches etc. Drama especially active with entries to Glasgow Shakespeare festival (Hamlet). No exam courses, but Victoria College, London Certificate of Speech and Drama.

Football (girls and boys, but not together), rugby, hockey (girls just had their first trip ever – to Ireland), netball etc – with lots of after school practices and matches. Bullish athletics with juniors winning locally and a Scottish national long jumper, ditto swimming. Scarcely surprising with a really good indoor pool and games hall and two gyms to practise in. School teams are battling in national competitions but lots of opportunities for tip top players in local clubs, as well as some inspiring input via the school: playing with Glasgow Warriors, inviting Hamilton Academical player to visit etc etc.

Most extracurricular clubs, sport and some orchestras after school for juniors and seniors. The extracurricular booklet, complete with timetable to be downloaded from the extremely efficient website, includes 40 plus activities like chess (hosted regional championship), book club, stocks and shares group, Young Enterprise (for older pupils) and entrepreneurs (for younger ones), ski club (trip to Austria), press review and Scripture Union...

Loads of curriculum based visits locally and abroad – Auschwitz recently via Holocaust Memorial Trust. D of E started recently, with lots of bronze and silver hopefuls looking to gold soon and a fair share of outdoor activities/trips. Debating and public speaking just getting going again.

Background and atmosphere: Probably the starkest school building in the Scottish independent sector – a pale blue shoebox with bright red signage rising oddly behind some spectacular ornate railings (a relic of the former Hamilton Palace) but with stunning views and masses of space overlooking Hamilton Park race course. The pitches are actually in the middle of the track, reached by a tunnel. In spite of its appearance the school, a Christian foundation, originally one of a group of three started in the Manchester area, was jolly lucky to get a redundant '60s teacher training college complete with terrific (then – and still pretty good now) games facilities, lovely indoor pool, stunning hall and purpose-built large light classrooms. The central assembly hall holds the entire school and its banks of 'in the round' eating and magnificent pyramidal wooden roof make it a really good auditorium space, well equipped and much used by the school and external lets.

Inside is purposeful with busy pupils. The central space and upper floors belong to the seniors, with the juniors and nursery on the ground floor of each 'wing', separated from the central space by the hall on one side. On the other is a spacious courtyard with an ecological greenhouse made from recycled plastic bottles and lots of garden equipment – takes ecology seriously. It also prides itself on its health promotion and has a gold award from Lanarkshire. The library and dining area run along the back of the building next to the racecourse, both huge with masses of glass. The rather bare dining room is 'heaving at lunch times' and the library is open to students at intervals and after school, as well as in constant use by classes during the day after school. A spectacular glass box, perched on a vast expanse of flat roof, is the staffroom, which must reach equatorial temperatures when the sun shines – but fortunately this is Scotland!

The junior school and nursery, however, are crammed with colour and activity, using every spare inch of wall and floor space. The senior school, with its wide corridors and huge entrance hall, complete with LCD display showing lunch menus ('which

pass the Gold HPS standard with ease') and other bits of vital school info, is well maintained, despite a few dark stair corners. It all feels a bit institutional and functional, but clearly does function very well as an institution. The overtly Christian ethos encourages lots of charity fundraising and a very impressive 'Transform' project with a school in Burkina Faso, involving annual visits by groups of sixth formers and reciprocal trips for teachers. Part of this initiative, providing internet facilities for the school, has was featured on BBC World News.

Pupils wear burgundy blazers, with blue braiding for prefects and pale blue shirts, black trousers for boys and Lindsay tartan for girls. Ties for all – striped for boys and plain for girls – plus tracksuits and cagoules in house colours for games: quite a pricey item and uniform policy is strict.

School day is from 9am to 3.15pm (juniors), 3.45pm (seniors) with buses leaving at 3.55pm but 'wraparound care ' in the nursery starts at 8am and ends at 6pm at an extra charge. Aftercare for juniors till 6pm.

Pastoral care and discipline: House system delivers most of the pastoral care, plus each child is allocated an individual guidance teacher. Inspectors recently commended this. Form teachers also help. The prefect team are appointed and have to apply and be interviewed. Head prefects 'do a lot', including representing the school at outside functions. Staff think discipline is good and few sanctions are needed – 'Bunking off school just does not happen'. Smoking – couldn't remember catching anyone in school, but zero tolerance, and if pupils are seen smoking outside school or in town, parents are contacted. Drugs 'not a problem', but would result in permanent exclusion. Stringent mobile phone policy, available, like most other Hamilton info, on the website, says phones will be confiscated for the day – 'We're just trying to get them to use them sensibly'. Bullying not a big problem, 'But, as everywhere, it happens,' so a raft of measures – sanctions (see policy on website), counselling, life skills programme, meetings with parents.

Pupils and parents: Huge catchment area taking in most of the south side of Glasgow and Lanarkshire, with extensive bus routes to Lanark, Biggar Kilsyth, Cumbernauld and East Kilbride. Intake multi-ethnic. Friends of Hamilton College, a very go-ahead body, fundraises for school equipment and does charity stuff too. It has recently donated a (second hand) cardiovascular fitness suite (huge) much used by pupils, staff and parents.

Lots of famous arty former pupils including Katie Leung (acted Cho Chang in Harry Potter); Lorna Ritchie, set and costume designer (worked for Jonathan Miller); and Blair Thompson, Scottish artist and winner of numerous awards (in The Herald's top 20 Scottish artists) – all of whom started their careers in Hamilton's art room.

Entrance: Mainly to nursery, J1 and S1 but will accept at any stage. Entry assessments for all.

Exit: Most juniors move up, a few drop out after Standard grade (S4) and again after Highers (S5), though the past few years have seen more staying on to S6. The majority to university, mainly Scottish, though the very occasional to Oxbridge or other English ones. Some to further ed and apprenticeships or work in family businesses.

Money matters: Not a rich school but well managed. Bursary scheme up to 100 per cent strictly means-tested and awarded by committee of governors etc. Will try to help a family in sudden financial trouble. Discounts of 10 per cent for second, 20 per cent for third and 40 per cent for fourth child and 25 per cent+ sibling discount for 'full time Christian workers'.

Remarks: Not to be ignored! A good solid school, perhaps a little old fashioned but now at the leading edge in Scotland for its use of ICT in learning teaching and admin'. Sound, good value for money, and certainly worth a look if you live in the area or in oversubscribed East Renfrewshire. 'Exceptionally positive' recent inspection. It may not be beautiful, but it is certainly useful and might even be exciting.

Hampstead School

Westbere Road, London, NW2 3RT

• Pupils: 1,300 boys and girls • Ages: 11–19 • Non-denom • State

Tel: 020 7794 8133
Email: enquiries@hampsteadschool.org.uk
Website: www.hampsteadschool.org.uk

Headteacher: Since 2006, Mr Jacques Szemalikowski MA BSc PGCE NPQH CPhys MinstP (early fifties). Positively explodes with energy, a dynamo. Five minutes in his company and you are left exhausted. With four young children of his own, this guy is driven. He is here to make a difference, and in his seven year tenure as headmaster of Hampstead School, he has.

A graduate in astrophysics, and a teacher for 25 years before his first headship at The Warwick School, Redhill, Mr Szemalikowski is somewhat old school in his principles and discipline. A misbehaving student can find themselves holed away for the day in the exclusion zone, 'our naughty step' – a small building situated at the back of the playing fields. He makes no apologies for his rigorous approach to education, both for his students and staff members alike. His mantra is 'Every child can achieve, every child will achieve, whatever it takes' – and he does what he can to ensure this is not just hot air. He organises trips to Oxford so that his students can be aspirational: 'I want them to know this can be for them too. I want them to be the movers and shakers of the modern world.'

His staff are not allowed to rest on their laurels either. He doesn't do 'good' – he wants outstanding from his staff and they are expected to attend weekly regular after-school workshops, which have been running for the last four years, in order to achieve this (the latest Ofsted report commented that there 'wasn't yet enough outstanding teaching.') A recent high turnover of staff, he says, was testimony to their 'tremendous training' which secured them promotional posts in other schools. Like him, don't like him, 'I'm not here to be popular, I'm here to get the job done.'

Hit the headlines recently for reporting the student author of a blog critical of the school to the police and to the universities where he hoped to study.

Academic matters: 2013 saw 63 per cent of pupils achieve 5+ A*-C grades at GCSE including English and maths. No mean feat when you consider that nearly half the pupils are bi-lingual (63 different nationalities), five per cent are statemented and nearly 40 per cent are on free school meals.

Equally impressive are the 2013 A level results, with 73 per cent A*-C grades, 43 per cent A*/B and 18 per cent A*/A. In the top 20 UK state schools for continuing into science A levels after GCSE. Big emphasis on science, and there is the option of triple rather than double science for students who attain at least a level 6 at the end of key stage 3. Maths, too, is strong and the school is very involved in maths challenges with students achieving above national average numbers of gold, silver and bronze certificates. The school also offers free Saturday school maths masterclasses for gifted mathematicians from years 5 and 6 of local primary schools.

English and media are popular subjects, and students also have the option of learning Arabic and Italian (as well as French and Spanish). Bi-lingual homework support is offered. Pupils have six BTECs to choose from including catering and hospitality, and a wide variety of A Levels including three new ones in philosophy, creative writing and culture and communication. No subject is offered at GCSE level which can't be carried through to A Level. 'We don't stream, we set, so there is movement', the head points out. Maths, English and science setted from year 7. Every faculty in the school has a remunerated teacher responsible for gifted and talented children. There is a clear focus on standards and students are tracked from the moment they arrive. They have individual charts and are monitored six times a year. As soon as a student starts to slip, staff want to know why. An appreciative parent commented that the school is 'quick to congratulate children if they've done well – very good at praising.' Strong curriculum support and SEN help, notably those who arrive with little English, and catch up is rapid: 'assessors couldn't tell the difference between SEN students and non-SEN students', we were told.

Archaic-looking but well-equipped classrooms, most notably the music department, where a large cash injection has meant up-to-date technology. Through their status as a technology college they have been able to implement a £0.5 million upgrade to the library, creating an independent learning centre combining traditional library resources with new technologies. (That said, the library is actually quite scant on books itself). Masses of extracurricular activity perhaps also reflects the academic ethos of the school: the school's debating society has had spectacular success in Model United Nations – with ongoing victories both as a delegation and individuals. Involved in Jack Petchey Speak out Challenge and has a Youth Parliament.

Games, options, the arts: Fizzes with activity – plenty to do. Music is popular and heavy investment in this department has meant that each of the school's 1,300 students is offered the opportunity to learn a musical instrument. Pupils can choose to join a wide variety of musical activities, including senior or junior orchestra, guitar orchestra, jazz band, junior choir and many more.

Enthusiastic drama – great onsite replica fringe theatre, partnerships with the Hampstead Theatre Club, Royal Court and Tricycle all help to inspire; a few students had extras parts in the Dustin Hoffman movie Quartet.

Strong sport, particularly football, basketball and table tennis. The football team won the Bliss Inner London Cup in 2012, becoming the first Camden school to win the trophy; the girls' basketball team won the Under 15 Championships in 2013. A team of students and staff also recently completed the 56-mile London to Brighton bike ride. Limited playing fields, but somewhat redeemed by its other on site facilities including a basketball/netball court, a dance studio, a fitness suite, a multi-use Astroturf and an on-site pool (that could do with some love).

The plethora of extracurricular activities includes gardening (they have an allotment which grows produce for the catering department), poetry, rugby, dance and aikido clubs, plus several music ensembles. For the more dedicated student, those who lack quiet space at home and those who need extra help, there are after-school homework sessions.

Background and atmosphere: Hampstead Schmampstead – this school is no more in Hampstead than Arsenal (FC) is in Arsenal! Situated in between colourful but definitely not posh Cricklewood, Kilburn and semi-posh West Hampstead, you can see the flag before you see the school. Red and emblazoned with the school logo, the flag waves proudly high above this impressive large red-brick building. The main building, formerly the old Haberdashers' Boys' school, was built in 1908 and indeed on first appearance promises great things.

One is immediately struck by the amount of banners displayed on the building's facade: 'Best ever GCSE results', 'read more, earn more, learn more', 'Leaders of tomorrow' and so on. Mr Szemalikowski, who has been on three trips to the USA (Chicago, Boston and DC), says it's very much an American thing to do: 'It reinforces key aspirations at all times.' Tear your eyes away, walk up the ramped approach, through a plate glass entrance into a fairly modern foyer and see more slogans – this time on a wall-mounted flat screen TV, and from the wisdom of Galileo: 'Measure what is measurable,' the theme of the week.

Mosey on through the foyer to a vast concrete, central open air atrium faced by a modern teaching block and broken only by a dark and reedy pond – 'there are fish in there.' Mr Szemalikowski smiles brightly on our tour. The school was due for a substantial rebuild in 2011, but sadly the national school redevelopment scheme was axed by the coalition government. Refurbishment started and ended on new loos – £125,000 spent on giving them a spruce up as 'the test of any state school is its loos', says the head. (Although why the staff room is right next to them – the mind boggles).

A well-equipped ICT and catering block (with industrial spec kitchens) looks in stark contrast to the rest of the school. Good sixth form centre with huge common room overlooking the central atrium. Lucky sixth formers can feast their eyes on yet more banners – this time displayed on the walls around the central atrium – (did we mention Big Brother?) Wheelchair access throughout – the school is completely DDA compliant. There is a disability resource which can cater for up to seven students with complex needs. These students are fully integrated into mainstream lessons.

This is a big, sprawling campus, and easy to lose your bearings, especially for new pupils coming from little primaries. Lest you forget where you are, fear not, everything is logoed – from school water bottles to the dustbins, another of the head's ideas of constant reinforcement of group identity. Pupils are a mixed and diverse bunch, but all seem to share a common loyalty towards the school and enjoy being there. One 13-year-old pupil told us: 'I love the responsibility they give us. I was on a panel to help elect the last deputy head of the school.' Badges are awarded to students who meet standards and display good behaviour – bronze through to platinum. Get platinum, you can have lunch with the head! Students' pride in their school is evident in the total lack of graffiti, vandalism and litter.

Commendable efforts to involve the outside world and lots of whole school charity work. An appreciation of the diversity of the school is prevalent – Black History Month, Gay/Transgender Month, a recent trip to Auschwitz, to name but a few. The school culture involves loads of celebration and reward of achievement and improvement.

Pastoral care and discipline: If punctuality and attendance ain't your bag, this ain't your school. Mr Szemalikowski and the entire senior management team are at the gates to greet pupils from 8.40am, after which sluggards have to report individually. (Early risers' club offered from 7.30am onwards for an extra cost of 50p). Attendance has improved dramatically since Mr Szemalikowski came on board. He is completely intolerant of any absence during term time (other than illness) and allows pupils two days a year for religious holidays. 'Every day counts', is another of the school's slogans.

Head reintroduced uniform to the school, and according to an ex-student, it has made a huge change – 'now everyone is on a level playing field.' Different ties denote whether or not a student has been trained in peer mentoring, and any student feeling vulnerable can approach those who have. Automatic exclusion for fighting, drugs, alcohol or carrying a weapon (as was recently the case with a student found to be carrying a knife). The head walks around daily to keep in touch, and lo and behold, if a student is wandering aimlessly in the grounds, they are stopped and questioned – and only when Mr Szemalikowski is entirely satisfied with their response are they sent on their way. Good level of security – brings to bear the stark reality that you are in an inner-city school.

However, despite Mr Szemalikowski's robust attitude to discipline, one parent says, 'it doesn't go far enough'. She feels that students are given too many chances, although she does acknowledge that the exclusion zone is a good deterrent – 'my daughter was in there once, and has said she won't be going there again.' (It is a small outhouse building, which can hold up to six students at any one time, with no contact with their peers for the whole day). Classes seemed to be well behaved for the most part – with the exception of the odd class joker – and a good level of concentration in what they were doing. PE, however, was on the very raucous side.

Non-teaching heads of year are another of Mr Szemalikowski's brainchilds. The idea is that the heads of year are there solely for the pupils' welfare needs and not to be distracted with marking homework. It works brilliantly, one parent enthused. 'It means that if I have any concerns about my child I know I can contact the head of year, and they are always available to speak to, no matter what time of day.' Year common rooms are 'exclusive to Hampstead School' – the idea being that year groups can eat together at lunchtimes and the heads of year have their offices in there and are always available at lunchtime too.

Buddying, mentoring and restorative justice schemes all bolster pupils' sense of security, and bullying is rigorously kept in check. 'The House', situated a stone's throw from the Exclusion Zone, is a cuboid block on the perimeter where you go if you are troubled – or troubling – and is well staffed with welfare workers, counsellors and other supportive types.

Recent school awards include: UNICEF Rights Respecting School (Level 1) Award; Pupils' and Parents' Achievement for All Quality Mark (first school to achieve this and now a national roll-out school).

Pupils and parents: From moneyed West Hampstead, to recent refugees in temporary housing, the demographic is diverse – all the more admirable when one considers how far the school has come. One pupil told us, 'I love the fact that one of my best friends is black, the other wears a hijab'. A real feature of the school, we were told, is that no ethnic groups predominate. Nineteen per cent is white British – the largest group.

Former pupils include Sadie Frost, Rachel Yankey, Julia Drown MP, Alec Bogdanovic, Jake Lensen, Tobias Hill, Zadie Smith.

Entrance: From up to 71 primary schools (no named feeders; totally non-selective), and covering three boroughs – Camden, Brent and Barnet (admissions, managed by Camden) – the school is now oversubscribed in every year. One parent, a born and bred Cricklewood local, remarked how the school used to have a 'terrible reputation', and no right-thinking parent, given the choice, would have sent their kids there – but she said, 'that's changed since Mr Szemalikowski came on board'. Oversubscribed sixth form both from internal and external candidates. Twenty year 12 places are available to external applicants that meet the entry requirements – which vary according to the level of course they want to pursue.

Exit: About 70 per cent stay for the sixth form, the remainder go to other colleges and sixth forms. Some 70 per cent of sixth formers move on to an impressive range of higher education – from chemistry at King's College, law at Bristol and maths at Leeds to a paid apprenticeship in aerospace engineering with Air Bus, at University of Surrey (which was big news because the student beat a large number of applicants for the prestigious placement). One former student has become an international DJ and producer as a result of studying A level music at the school.

Remarks: The head's energy and vision has already worked wonders on this school. A melting pot of culture and diversity, and a whole host of activities to keep even the most ardent child interested. However, this school ain't for the faint hearted – large and imposing, and big on discipline and punctuality. In need of a massive cosmetic make-over (Mr Gove!)

Hampton Court House (Senior School)

Linked school: Hampton Court House (Junior School)

Hampton Court Road, East Molesey, Surrey, KT8 9BS

• Pupils: 190 boys and girls • Ages: 13-16 • Strictly non-denominational • Fees: £14,361–£15,591 pa • Independent

Tel: 020 8614 0857
Email: admissions@hchnet.co.uk
Website: www.hamptoncourthouse.co.uk

Head: Since 2011, Guy Holloway MA, heads the senior school. He studied at King's College School, Wimbledon, before reading English at Peterhouse, Cambridge. He is a passionate educationalist, fascinated by how children learn and the vastly different approaches to education across the world. For several years he was a volunteer with Save the Children UK, working with disadvantaged children aged 6 to 12. He spent many years in Paris, first at the international PR firm, Burson-Marsteller, and then at the Ecole Active Bilingue, where he was head of English in the section Britannique, teaching A level and preparing his first students for Oxbridge, whilst simultaneously creating chaos in the section Française, teaching his beloved classe de seconde. He was part of the 1993 founding team which opened the Harrodian School, where he was director of studies. He runs a weekly seminar – a comprehensive history of music course for all children in years 1 to 8 – and teaches GCSE psychology. His interests include piano, record collecting (vinyl LPs of 1950s and 1960s), concert-going, foreign travel, languages, mathematics (statistics), chess, film directing, and theatre (has directed over 30 plays).

Founder, proprietor and head of junior school is Lady Eliana Houstoun-Boswall ISIT (Paris) ('mid-sixties,' she says, though she looks more fabulous at that age than anyone who runs a school has a right to). Educated at the Lycée Français, New York (clearly a formative experience – good and bad – and one she vividly describes), then Georgetown University, Washington DC. Thence to a postgrad course at L'École d'Interprètes, Paris. A linguist herself, she has a precision and elegance of diction one seldom hears. In addition, her convictions and educational principles – wildly idealistic though some may think them – are articulated with an intensity that is hard to resist. They are expressed with characteristic fervour on the school's website – pour yourself a glass of something expensive and settle down for a treat.

Eliana (as everyone calls her), has two children of her own, both involved in the school – her daughter teaches English to the tots and her son is finance director and chairman. She co-founded and ran The Harrodian School (qv) – achievement enough, you might think: starting schools was never a push-over. Having gone into property with her husband and made a bit of a pile, after the divorce she bought Hampton Court House – an extraordinary estate with a fascinating history (see below) and took three years and more than £1m to bring it up to the standard required for educating the young. One cannot but admire the courage, drive and vision which did this solo. However, some parental feeling that a board of governors/trustees might lend a guiding hand, to the benefit of the school community in general.

Academic matters: Languages, the arts, civilised values and culture reign here. DT is now much better resourced than hitherto, but if you are a parent for whom computer expertise and a solid career in the City are the ultimate goals, via a rowing blue and an MBA, this is probably not your school. If you want your child to be a linguist, to study academic subjects with values attached, to learn about art, music and to develop individual interests in a liberal, relaxed atmosphere, you'll probably love it. And that is what you will get if your offspring is bright, motivated and responsive to opportunities. At GCSE, an admirable range of options for so small a cohort includes five languages – old and new – and business studies. We watched an attentive and large class of year 11, seemingly all girls, doing psychology.

However, results thus far are highly variable. In 2013, only 32 per cent of GCSE grades were A*/A. This can be accounted for, in part, by the number of children with mild dyslexia supported by the school. It is also explicable to some extent by the emphasis on arts – drama especially – and the expenditure of some pupils' effort and time in these rather than academic areas. Also, the emphasis is on self-motivation, if you don't want to work no-one exerts much pressure – and this may also be true of some pupils' families. In addition, a lot of coming and going – both staff and pupils have had an unusually high turnover, though we are assured that more staff are now here to stay. Additionally, the school has, until now, positively encouraged – well, at least, enabled – its brightest and best to leave at CE, so it is hardly surprising that the results – even given the heady atmosphere – do not impress.

Things will change, as Eliana wants 'more discipline and rigour' and acknowledges work to be done. She accepts, reluctantly, the need to become more 'establishment – while keeping the ethos of happiness', and clearly the intellectual and cultural values will not be sacrificed to a galumph up league tables – and grace à Dieu for that. But Latin and Greek and the languages, art, music – all acknowledged to be superb – flourish here, and year sizes are so small that virtually individual timetables can be made for those who need them – for now. IT now well-provided for with a designated room full of Macs with big screens. Teachers – many from abroad – provide intellectual clout, though some parents feel that, while they may be clever and knowledgeable, some are not 'teachers', either by qualification or by inclination.

School very accepting and inclusive of SENs. SEN department consists of a SENCo who comes in three days and as needed plus two others, one trained and the other very experienced. They work in small groups or one-to-one, as best suits the child. Nineteen per cent of pupils on SEN register – mostly mild to moderate dyslexia but school will support ADHD and dyspraxia. Ofsted praised good use of IEPs. Invitingly crowded and well-stocked, smallish library with views over the park, but so cold that the teacher giving an individual lesson in there did so in coat and scarf.

Games, options, the arts: Arts are strong, strong, strong and part of the feel of the place. Art seen as anything but a discrete subject – rather very much part of the philosophy that underpins the educational approach. Delicious things like the band kit set up in the old ice house in the garden, music everywhere – around half the pupils take individual classes and everyone throws themselves into drama and art. Music department comprises professional, practising performers – an impressive list – and children here are clearly exposed to the best. Several of the ones we spoke to had performing ambitions and clearly no shyness about such things prevails here. This confidence also evident in the manner of the children as they move around the school and address each other and the staff.

Sports rather more haphazard – coaches and courses seemingly come and go, but a considerable range of games and challenges are undertaken, from kayaking on the Thames – what an asset a river is! – to fencing, fitness and a newly launched D of E initiative. Some older pupils with especial gifts teach the younger ones – guitar and dance were mentioned. Chess is a big thing here – a specialist teacher on the staff.

Background and atmosphere: Built in 1757 by the gloriously named George Montague Dunk, second Earl of Halifax, the house is stunning. Its entrance hall – as pictured on the prospectus – has to be seen, columns, gallery, ceiling fireplace 'n' all. To say nothing of the view over Bushy Park, the proximity to Hampton Court itself and the fabulous neighbouring houses on the little lane one drives down to reach the gate. The lake, grotto and ice house in the garden were added in 1771 and, when his lordship died, the house was left to his mistress, Mrs Donaldson, and, on her death, to their daughter. Nice work if you can get it. The house then passed through a succession of tenants and, in 1871, was sold to Marmaduke Blake Sampson, City correspondent of The Times and Argentine consul in London. He built the picture gallery, later a ballroom and subsequently concert room. Then a further century of lettings and sales – among them to the tea-planting Twinings – until, in the 1980s, it became a Save the Children home for refugee Vietnamese boat children. You couldn't make it up.

Eliana bought it in 1998. The school began in 2001 as a pre-prep and prep but, as the first pupils got to leaving age, it seemed natural to continue into the complex realms of senior education. Sixth form planned for 2015.

'Satisfactory' was the term favoured by Ofsted in its inspection report of early 2010, in relation to almost every aspect of the provision, also recording 'inconsistency' in the teaching styles and approach. Hence the arrival in 2009 of Mr Tristram Jones-Parry as 'advisor', charged with upping the academics, improving 'systems' and generally beefing up all-round discipline.

Children of all ages mix and mingle – lots of hugging in break time, which we liked. No uniform, though 'you have to look presentable' – and they do: rather more here than in many uniformed schools where the rules are stretched to the scruffy limits. The teachers too – some in suits, others very casual, but no-one pushing at the boundaries. Happy parents love the 'warmth and liberality of the ethos – it's just what we wanted. Not perfect but so much better than a hothouse'. Mixed parental reports on school admin and general efficiency – but we had a sense of this, as other areas, being tightened up.

Pastoral care and discipline: Discipline is expected to come from within rather than be imposed. School's philosophy is a belief that all – pupils and staff – should be treated equally and with respect. Politeness and good manners are insisted upon and bullying, we are told, is not countenanced, though some parental feeling that, on occasions when it occurs, the bully is accorded rather more TLC than the bullee. School aghast at this allegation, but reports of bullying not adequately dealt with reached us more than once. On the other hand, we learned of other such incidents which were swiftly and sensitively sorted.

'It's a wonderful place for children thought elsewhere to be unteachable,' we were told and, assuredly, children who need space and air can breathe here and find that perhaps they do want to learn after all. But some don't last here either and the school's open door policy occasions, perhaps, a less stable – though very accepting – community than has been good for it. Staff a mix of the 'very laid back and the over severe,' parents told us. 'Some are wonderful with the children and really make the relaxed, first-name thing work. Others can't hack it and leave. I've heard teachers swearing at children loads of times.' We witnessed a cheerful confrontation between a teacher and a genial but recalcitrant fifth former on our visit – amicable and polite, but clearly a conflict between equals rather than one in which authority was firmly exercised. Children with a more mature understanding of personal relationships will think they've come to heaven.

Pupils and parents: Popular with French families for obvious reasons, though some grouse that the French is not truly bi-lingual which, with the breadth and transience of the school population it could hardly be by senior stage. Pupils from a 30 mile radius – school bus collects and deposits. Attracts the unconventional, the liberal, the arty. Lively Friends of HCH have outings, balls and shopping events to support both school and a Sri Lankan orphanage. Annual Blood Lust Ball occasions a wide range of parental reactions.

Entrance: Via interview with candidate and parents, plus maths and English tests. Eliana and Mr Holloway must be satisfied that the pupil and family are in sympathy with the school's ethos and approach. From Cameron House, Hill House, Wetherby and local juniors.

Exit: As diverse as you could imagine. Leavers to Kingston Grammar, UCS, Hockerill Anglo-European, The Brit School, Hampton, DLD, Bryanston, Halliford, Westminster, Hurtwood House, Latymer Upper, Richmond or Esher Colleges, Wellington, Eton, City of London. Some few unaccounted for.

Money matters: Up to three scholarships – academic, music, arts – annually, worth 10 per cent of fees max – all 11+ candidates automatically entered.

Remarks: Ideal place to grow and learn for those who will thrive on the relaxed and civilised values of the place. Hitherto seen as a refuge for those who couldn't get on elsewhere – sometimes the obstructive or wayward – but this is likely to change now, though the head will continue to take on those with something to offer that may not be conventionally academic. And so he should.

Hampton School

Linked school: Denmead School

Hanworth Road, Hampton, Middlesex, TW12 3HD

• Pupils: 1,200 boys; all day • Ages: 11–18 • Inter-denom
• Fees: £15,990 pa • Independent

Tel: 020 8979 5526
Email: admissions@hamptonschool.org.uk
Website: www.hamptonschool.org.uk

Headmaster: Since September 2013, Mr Kevin Knibbs MA (forties), previously principal deputy head. Read history at Oxford and won two football blues; was head of lower school and senior master at Bolton School Boys' Division before joining Hampton in 2007. Has helped the Hampton U15 football team to national success and keenly promotes rugby at the school, including the building of the new all-weather pitch and strengthened links with the London Wasps.

Academic matters: A consistently tip top performer locally with already good results moving onwards and upwards. At GCSE, number of A*/A grades has been rising markedly – 90 per cent in 2013 – putting the school amongst the top independent schools in the country. At A level in 2013, 94 per cent A*/Bs and 74 per cent A*/As keeps the school in the top 25 – without anyone being asked to leave after GCSE (and very few choose to), so no large intake of high-flyers into the sixth form. The in house Hampton Extended Project Qualification now forms an important part of the broad sixth form enrichment programme. Although the school is no slouch on the Oxbridge front, with 31 places last year, many parents see the absence of a hothouse atmosphere as a strength (and one of the reasons why they choose the school). Wide range of subjects on offer with plenty of take-up in languages and science subjects.

H

IGCSE science and maths are taught – no coursework and more testing. Some boys take one or two GCSEs early. Setting is organised to ensure that no boy is in the bottom set for all subjects – 'No Hamptonian should, nor does, see himself as a bottom set boy,' explains Mr Knibbs. Year 7 boys choose between French, German and Spanish. Latin is compulsory until year 8. The launch of Mandarin is a proven success.

Average class size on entry is 23/24, though the size of teaching groups is often much less, with nine or fewer for German GCSE not uncommon. Sixth form sets are in single figures to low teens. A modern extension houses English, technology and art, and the myriad of machinery and art equipment gives the impression of being very well used, as are the various IT suites. All boys can now access their computer-based work files from home. A state-of-the-art teaching block, the Atrium, houses 11 fully-equipped classrooms and an additional biology lab. All classrooms have Apple TVs and digital projectors and most staff and many pupils have iPads.

The library is welcoming, open even in the holidays, and extremely well-stocked. Careers advice has a high priority and is impressive (although one parent bemoaned lack of advice for A level choices) with efforts being made to think more globally. Plenty of females on the staff. Average age of staff 37 and they are top drawer – plenty of Oxbridge graduates and PhDs. Several old boys also to be found in the staff room. Turnover never out of single figures.

Special needs are catered for free of charge through a head of learning support, but the school is cagey about how many boys or how much work this entails – delve deep if you want to send an SEN boy here. Provision for children with English as an additional language is negligible.

Games, options, the arts: Sport is very strong: 16 current boys have won international honours for England or GB at nine different sports. All the necessary facilities are on site, apart from the new boathouse shared with neighbouring girls' school, Lady Eleanor Holles (LEH), a mile or so away. Each boy chooses the sport he wants to play – a key success factor, according to the school: 'The boys taking part are there because they want to be and there are none who don't, which makes for higher quality sessions'. All sports spawn international players.

The ideal school for a budding Beckham: unlike most private schools, football is a major sport here with the U15 and first XI winning the Independent Schools Football Association Cup in 2012, the third time for the first XI. Have also twice won the inaugural ISFA Fair Play trophy in recognition of on field conduct and respect for officials. Rugby has taken off in similar leagues recently with the first XV having won the Esher President's Cup and the inaugural U18 Topflight International Schools' Shield, and the first XI having been named Rugby World Team of the Month. New all-weather pitch is apparently a 'unique facility' as accredited for football and rugby. Rowing is big, big news – one of the leading UK schools (check the provenance of the Oxbridge Blues next Boat Race day). Notably strong in cricket, the first XI winning the 50/40 league for several consecutive years. But not all brawn and no brain – chess thriving: up to four teams playing matches each week.

Music takes many forms and can be at a very high level. Has recently had its first BBC Young Musician of the Year finalist, now at the Royal College of Music on a full scholarship, and three organ scholars in residence at Oxbridge, as well as several choral scholars. Plenty of light-hearted groups and joint performances with LEH each term too. Drama productions sometimes shared with the girls but often all-male affairs. The recent 450 Hall (it actually seats 400 – built to celebrate the school's 450th anniversary) was designed as a centre of excellence for the performing arts and is an exceptional facility both for the school and for use by the outside community.

The list of co-curricular activities is so long that you wonder how they can all be fitted in, especially since most boys, reliant on the school coach service, go home promptly at 4pm. The answer is the extended lunch hour – where plentiful and reportedly high quality food is served over a long enough period to fit around all the clubs. In addition to all the extracurricular activities, a very popular lunchtime programme of eminent speakers – politicians, businesspeople, academics, media figures and famous old boys: Dr David Starkey is on the list of speakers as well as Jeremy Paxman, Zac Goldsmith, Iain Duncan-Smith and John le Carré, and don't forget Tara Palmer-Tomkinson. The boys who are busy at their sports clubs don't know what they're missing!

Similarly, so many trips and activities in the holidays you wonder if the boys ever see their families. Beware – all these jolly jaunts are not included in the fees. For those desirous of helping their fellow man plenty of opportunities for helping in the local community, as well as links with African communities in Uganda and Malawi. Jointly with LEH won first place in the Barnardo's People Recognition awards for their Saturday activity club for children with disabilities – all the result of a huge commitment from the staff to the wider curriculum.

Background and atmosphere: In the heart of suburbia surrounded by houses and other schools. Parents can breathe a small sigh of relief – girls may be nearby but not a shop or pub in sight. Superbly spacious grounds; buildings not an architectural gem though well-maintained and constantly being updated. Loads of outdoor space – quads, gardens and playing fields which many boarding schools would envy. Interiors are light and airy and remarkably tidy – even the corridor outside the rowing ergo rooms presents kitbags in a long, neatish row. The sixth formers are proud of their common room with its own café selling vital sustenance at break time and a flatscreen TV tuned to Sky Sports.

Claims to be the first school in the country to go 'climate neutral' through off-setting emissions caused by its daily running. Climate Care, the link company, offsets through projects including renewable energy and energy efficiency schemes in Southern Africa and India and forest restoration in Uganda. Has its own bore-hole for irrigation of its playing fields, solar panels and a wind turbine. Continues to raise pupils' awareness of climate issues – the boys conduct regular audits of the school's energy consumption.

Formerly a state grammar school (went independent in 1975); about 50 per cent of the pupils come from state primary schools, and is fully committed to a large 13+ entry from prep schools. Many of the parents were not independently educated and definitely not a school for Hooray Henrys, although within school the boys look the part in blazers and ties (even in the sixth form). However, the minute they leave the school gates the shirts become magically untucked and the ties unknotted – these guys know the meaning of 'grunge'. A marriage here of public school ethos and London lads.

Proximity to Lady Eleanor Holles is supposed to provide 'the best of both worlds' – single sex teaching means that monosyllabic 14 year olds are not intimidated by garrulous girls, but, 'The boys certainly know what girls are,' says the head. The two schools have audited their joint activities with a view to expansion. Hampton has also established sixth form management courses with Surbiton High.

Pastoral care and discipline: New boys at 11 are given as much help as possible to settle in with their peers – an overnight team-building exercise is very popular, with boys returning 'raring to go'. Similar jaunt for 13+ entrants. Mentors from the upper school are allocated to newcomers. New boys are closely monitored and any who are found to be struggling with work or organisation given special support and help with study skills. Counselling is readily available; a parent whose son had an extended illness felt that staff went the extra mile to ensure an efficient return to school – 'He was even met at the door by the head of year'.

Assemblies celebrate a range of achievements – concentration on success is more important than telling the boys what they have done wrong and exceptional work is presented to the head. Stringent illegal substance policy – expulsion is a serious threat.

Pupils and parents: No obvious Hampton boy but, if you want your son to be kept busy, here is an environment to suit all sorts. 'Like most things in life, it's what you put in that counts,' says one parent, 'and most people in the Hampton community both give and consequently receive a lot – it might not be the right school for a boy if he's not the type to roll up his sleeves and join in.' Delightfully suburban – no smart cars, champers and party frocks here on prize-giving day but a nice mix of keen mums and dads from a wide range of backgrounds. All faiths represented and celebrated, according to the head. Huge west London and Surrey catchment area bolstered by the extensive school coach network shared with LEH. Socially, neither the boys (nor LEH girls!) complain about bussing, but parents take note – it's not cheap, and be prepared to spend hours in the car at weekends to pick up and deliver from far flung friends' houses. Once a Hampton boy, always a Hampton boy – contacts with ex-Hamptonians are strong.

Entrance: Two thirds come at 11 (mostly from state primaries) and one third at 13, from more than 200 schools. (Denmead School is part of the same foundation but is no more 'tied' than any other.) Majority of 13+ candidates are pre-selected at 11, then need 65 per cent at common entrance. Four applicants for every place at both 11+ and 13+ entry.

Advance place exam available for 10 year olds to avoid the scramble at 11, but boys who don't make it early are encouraged to re-sit with no prejudice. Both the 11+ and 13+ pre-tests consist of three papers: maths, words and reasoning, English response and composition. Locally, the tests are perceived as demanding – according to the school, 'The entrance exam is designed to identify innate ability rather than to test what has been taught or coached'. The local private tutors, who make a tidy sum coaching for this and other school exams, would no doubt disagree. Acceptance is based on school's own exam, interview and school report combined with an age allowance. What is clear: it is not enough just to be academic – the school also assesses 'a pupil's likely positive contribution through good behaviour to the aims, ethos and co-curricular life of the school'.

Acceptance at sixth form is based on at least six GCSEs at A or A*, interview, school report, personal statement and written assessment.

Exit: Tiny numbers leave after GCSEs. Almost all sixth formers to top universities or medical schools. In 2013, 31 to Oxbridge, though not all the brightest choose to apply – school is relaxed about this. Bath, Bristol, Nottingham, Durham and Exeter all particularly popular; increasing numbers to US, often on academic or sporting scholarships; also Dublin, Belfast, Sydney, RADA and Central St Martin's.

Money matters: Academic, all-rounder, art, music and choral scholarships. Means-tested bursaries.

Remarks: A super outward-looking school keen to preserve its strengths (not about to go co-ed), but ready to embrace change if it will further educational achievement. Ideal for high calibre all rounders, but don't think of sending toffs, tremblies or tearaways.

Harris Academy

Perth Road, Dundee, DD2 1NL

- Pupils: 1110 boys and girls, all day • Ages: 11–18 • Non-denom
- State

Tel: 01382 435700
Email: harris@dundeecity.gov.uk
Website: harrisacademy.ea.dundeecity.sch.uk

Headteacher: Since 1997, Mr James Thewliss BSc PGCE (fifties) who was educated at Broadhurst High in Motherwell, read geography at Glasgow University and did his PGCE at Hamilton College. Previously depute head at Dalziel High in Motherwell and before that depute head at Wallace High. Very experienced, a chap who knows the area, married, with two children, both now up and flying. Charming, articulate and fun, 'Love this job – I cannot believe how lucky I am to have it. Everyone thinks I am nuts'. It's not so easy to get good staff, fairly high turnover.

Academic matters: Well above average: no particular bias, but with around 50 per cent of all pupils leaving after Standard grades (most go to Dundee College) it is a little difficult to give an accurate picture. Smashing results for those who do stay on to sixth form – way above national average (though with 38 per cent with three Highers – or better – it's not that hard a target to beat). Masses of computers etc, all heavily used, with waiting systems in place if need be. Impressive library with yet more machines, class teaching on computers as well as IT. Pupils do keyboarding and basic ICT skills and use the skills in presentations: power point, sound, film-making, animated flow charts. Max class size (legal limit) 33, but down to 20 for practical subjects.

First couple of years all study English, maths, science, history, geography, modern studies, home economics (magic), technology (great) plus one modern language: French, German or Spanish. Latin on hand, but no Greek. Streaming after first year when a fast track for English, maths and modern languages comes into force. Teaching disciplines are a combination of individual, small group, whole class teaching and discussion. Strong learning support.

School attracts a number of ethnic minorities whose parents are billeted to the local university, hospital or area, 14 currently in the school. Russian, Bengali, Urdu and Cantonese the most frequently spoken at home – native speakers can take these at standard grade. EAL is taught by the special educational needs team, and the HMI thought they were a bit stretched. Pupil support staff co-teach where necessary in class, but 'Such support may result in a revised elaborated or alternative curriculum and include individual or small group tuition'. Supported study includes homework clubs, and a teacher is available early on Tuesday mornings or Thursday evenings to help pupils with problems. Good encouragement, too, for the more gifted. Terrific use of external facilities. HMI also a bit dissy about homework – the amount, the marking et al, but that was some time ago, and the results of the recommendations are not yet available. The HMI other comment which concerns us is that brighter pupils 'do not appear to be sufficiently stretched'.

Eight Standard grades for all as far as possible. Languages, humanities and modern studies above average and good showing in the Scottish and UK Maths Challenges; ditto the Dundee Enterprising Maths competition. Inspiring programme of lectures from outside speakers. Serious advice for all pupils on which road to take. Good choice post Standard with the option of intermediates 1 and 2 as well as Highers and Advanced Highers in a raft of subjects, plus tourism and hospitality at standard grades. Regular assessments and good parental feedback.

H

School is an important cog in the education of children in the autistic spectrum and takes 10 pupils (never fewer) by request and allocation from the west of Dundee and the city itself (Morgan Academy takes those who live East of Dundee). These pupils are scattered across the age range, and school only accepts the next pupil when space becomes available. 'Lovely laddies' (mainly boys, but that's the nature of autism) all have individual educational programmes which are regularly monitored and amended. Some are totally supported individually and educated in the base (only one currently); others attend mainstream lessons but may be entirely supported in class, or allowed to attend certain classes for a short period – eg physics: in mainstream for six weeks, and then back to the unit. Most take Standard grade maths and all have speech and oral communication. School OK for physical handicaps – 'Only one lift, but there are ways of moving round the school'. The base is popular with 'normal kids' who choose to join those in the autistic spectrum at lunchtime – a reverse integration. Many of these pupils will go on to Elmwood College in Fife, where the school has close links.

Games, options, the arts: Games fields half a mile away, gyms on site plus swimming pool. Large sports complex off-site. PE timetabled and impressive lineup of games (extra-curricular) including the very popular rugby, hockey, football for boys and girls, athletics, basketball (enthusiastic coach) water polo etc.

Art, as you might imagine, deeply computer-linked: ceramics, painting, ICT, no CAD as such but the facility to use computer based design. Computer suite in art room, home economics, metalwork area, all computer based and hands on. Mass of instrumentalists, music strong and popular with ceilidhs and rock concerts (including FPs) – huge charitable input, 'everything and anything'. Choirs, bands, orchestras. Popular theatre club, though not available as an exam subject, despite pupils' requests. Outstanding debating, thrashing all comers; vibrant YE and truly popular D of E, with a whacking list of gold, silver and bronze successes. Not the longest list of clubs we have ever seen, but thoroughly active, mass of trips abroad: humanities with proper exchanges popular.

Background and atmosphere: Founded in 1885 and 'the oldest public school in Dundee', moved to the handsome granite building in 1931, school then added on a hotchpotch of flat-roofed excrescences in the '60s. Thirties classrooms elegant and airy, with corridors wide enough for children and their bags to pass; '60s nasties – apart from the inevitable flat roof drip – boast beastly narrow passages, scarred by teenage bookbags. Stunning views to the south, with really quite a lot of playground. Tiny dining hall in basement, next to library, students wait their turn in a surprisingly orderly queue at the 'red line'. Work experience at 14; some – less academic – pupils can study vocational subjects; access courses in communication and maths or apprentice-shops locally.

Complete rebuild planned by council. School decanted to a temporary home at the former Rockwell Academy site in Lawton Road in 2013 – for three years if all goes to plan.

Free school meals (but the cafeteria is cashless). Help with school uniform (school provides the basics ex-stock) and trips. Grants available. If pupils stay for fifth year the odds are they will stay on to sixth: five Highers the norm.

Pastoral care and discipline: Sixth formers buddy first formers – 'very protective and good anti-bullying strategy'. Strong PSE reinforced by RME. Pupils are divided into four houses, and the pupil support strategy is handled by house representatives, each house having two guidance and two support-for-learning teachers. Terrific inter-house competition, both in the academic and the sporting field, with marks being allocated for each and house championship fiercely fought over.

Defined sanction system: if pupils disobey one of five clearly defined rules, then they 'may be excluded for up to three days' for continuous disobedience, and head will meet with the parents. He 'is not prepared for disruptive children or anti-social behaviour' to permeate the school and would much rather produce 'decent sensible sensitive citizens' who are a lot 'more use than an anti-social chemist'. To this end (and this is a first for us) he has installed a splendid reward system (Pavlov eat your heart out). Each pupil (who has the school code drilled into them during their first week, 'so they can't say they don't know what is expected of them') is given a personal plan which must be stamped at the end of each lesson. Pupils earning 250 marks are awarded a certificate, can skip an afternoon's school and see a film of their choice – and get a Mars bar. 500 stamps qualify for a silver certificate and a free ticket for Megabowl; gold equals a trip to Alton Towers, with a certain amount of parent input, and platinum a three day trip to London. Platinum winners have to have their cards stamped after almost every lesson to qualify – head just loves these trips. Links with top year of feeder primaries – guidance staff and teacher visit regularly (HMI reckoned the school 'could try harder') and first year pupils all decamp with their teachers to Falkland Youth Centre for bonding and team-building stuff.

Pupils and parents: A mixed bunch, some here briefly, charming and well-mannered. Good parental support and school booklet encourages this. Farmers, business people, as well as the university and hospitals. FPs include Donald Findlay QC, Bruce Milan, James Crabb (accordion player), the footballer Christian Daily and the much beloved George Galloway – who does not even receive a mention in the FP online site under 'government'. (Should we have checked 'media/television personalities'?)

Entrance: Always full. Pupils come from five main feeders with a couple of dozen placement requests annually. Certain amount of logistical movement. Standard rules about addresses and siblings.

Exit: Either post Standard grade, or (usually) post sixth form. Some 70 odd per cent to universities, mostly to Scotland but the occasional trickle to Oxbridge. Inspired careers advice.

Remarks: Inspirational. An outstanding head – pity he can't inspire the building with as much enthusiasm as the children.

The Harrodian School

Linked schools: Harrodian Preparatory and Pre-preparatory schools

Lonsdale Road, London, SW13 9QN

- Pupils: 435 boys and girls • Ages: 13–18 • non-denom
- Fees: £16,305–£18,750 pa • Independent

Tel: 020 8748 6117
Email: admin@harrodian.com
Website: www.harrodian.com

Headmaster: Since 1999, Mr James Hooke BSc Hons PGCE (early fifties – yet could still be mistaken for a sixth former here, only smarter and slightly more conventional). Educated up the road at Hampton, read geography at Leeds and then straight to the City as a banker. Soon became bored and took off to Latin America, where he taught at St John's School in Buenos Aires. Impressed the former head, when he arrived here in 1995, with his knowledge of languages and very soon became deputy head. His youthful appearance belies a steady, practical and considered approach. He loves the job and is totally committed to the pioneering ethos that is being achieved here. His daughter and son are both at the senior school. One parent commented that he seems to float around the place – no one is very sure what he is doing to steer the ship. His subtle touch seems to be effective, though – as soon as the slightest problem is brought to him, it's swiftly and decisively resolved.

Academic matters: High standards without undue pressure is the consistent message. 'Children can learn at their own pace and grow in confidence,' was the observation of more than one parent. Streaming in English, maths and languages. As it becomes more academically selective at every entrance point, and the image that this is a school for the clotted cream of society starts to fade, the results continue to make dramatic improvements. Seventy-three per cent A*-B at A level (40 per cent A*/A) in 2013 and 54 per cent A*/A at GCSE – impressive stuff.

Those with SEN, so long as they have mild to moderate needs, are well looked after. A team of ten support staff run by the experienced and highly praised SENCo work closely with mainstream staff. Pupils are taken out of sport or Latin to the appealing suite of rooms tucked away at the top of the main building for mostly one-to-one attention. No formal programme for the gifted and talented – this is not pegged onto learning support. 'We don't like the implications of branding a child as gifted and talented – it sends the wrong message to others.'

Maverick and colourful members of staff from all walks of life who, unsurprisingly, thrive in such a civilised environment. Muttering among some parents about the high turnover of antipodeans, but Mr Hooke is keen to point out the cultural diversity and energy young Australians bring. Average age of staff is young – 35 to 40 – and 20 have been there for more than 10 years.

The curriculum is mainstream with a heavy emphasis on modern languages – key to a civilised life; how refreshing. All learn French to a more or less bilingual level, taught wholly by native speakers. They can also do Italian, Spanish and German; Japanese, Chinese etc are available by arrangement. Latin and religious studies survive – can offer Greek for those who want to do it. Media and business studies are popular. Graphic design recently introduced as an A level option.

ICT is well provided for – gleaming Apple Macs in three spacious rooms dedicated to ICT as well as in various key rooms around the school. Everyone has a lesson a week and are encouraged to use it in other academic areas. Interactive whiteboards making slow progress – some but not many. We speculated that the founder's penchant for York stone took precedence but were told firmly that his resistance to state-of-the-art teaching technology is based on educational principles – children get enough screens at it is; he wants to avoid any interference in the teacher/pupil oral interaction.

Overall good, and promising to become better and better – 'Academic bar is being raised each year,' says head.

Games, options, the arts: One pupil remarked that she contemplated going to boarding school but realised she didn't need to – she could go to the Harrodian. The sense of space (25 acres of pitches, courts, play areas and gardens) and the emphasis on getting plenty of exercise and fresh air (they carry on even in torrential rain) are central to the Harrodian experience. Winning isn't, however: lots of fixtures in traditional sports, as you would expect, but competition isn't the main focus – 'It would be wrong to thump a team 12-0,' says head, and one parent remarked that sports day was a bit of a joke: plenty of races but no one with really any idea of what's going on. 'It's more about happy kids enjoying themselves.' Mr Hooke is keen to counter that while they have an inclusive approach – A, B, C and D teams – the A team is competitive. Plus a highly-qualified team of sports coaches, high tech equipment that can record a match so you can replay it MOTD style to comment on technique, as well as the best sports equipment.

Building work is soon to commence on a swanky sports hall which will provide a gym as well as fencing salle and dance studios. In true Harrodian style it's not just the conventional that is on offer either – a smattering of glamorous options, eg a racing ski team will compete in France and attend a three day training camp; golf is being developed at Dukes Meadows; yoga, karate and self-defence as well as boxercise and volleyball. Small but heated outdoor pool in attractive colonnaded courtyard – only open April to October.

Lots of dynamic and bubbly music – from opera (The Magic Flute recently performed by the prep school) and musicals to the hugely popular Battle of the Bands judged by a celeb from the music industry. Bands allowed to record CDs on site and make their own photographed cover. Intimate recital/theatre studio with fixed raked seating and individual practice rooms housed in the music school, which bursts with activity of all kinds – three senior choirs, orchestra and smaller groups. A less-than-confident guitarist may be called upon to accompany a singer in assembly – while excellence is recognised and valued, it's not over-lauded.

Drama is dynamic and innovative. Pupils here are confident about getting up on stage and often take the initiative themselves to write and perform, eg comedy sketches. One boy in the prep school took a few terms out to perform in the film of Peter Pan. Artistic endeavour is encouraged, opportunities valued. Art happens in three different rooms around the site – all equally pleasantly cluttered; 20 per cent take art at GCSE, impressive photography and graphics studio – we saw haunting models of WW1 soldiers recreating the carnage of the trenches. Very little cookery, textiles club popular with girls in the prep school but not much evidence of it in the senior school. DT markedly absent – surprising in such a creative school.

Background and atmosphere: As eccentric as you would expect. In a previous incarnation it was the country club for Harrods employees. Sir Alford and Lady Houstoun-Boswall – a couple with a vision – bought it in 1993 (pipping The Lycée and St Paul's Boys' at the post), he the eighth baronet, she an American multi-lingual teacher, headmistress and restorer of historical buildings (see Hampton Court House), and proceeded to create a dream – a co-ed school run according to civilised values in a civilised environment to produce relaxed, happy children. The original intention was to create a prep school but two-way expansion occurred and now it runs from four to 18. Strong sense of family ownership and involvement – Sir Alford's sister, Mrs Moore, lives in a flat in the school and has a pastoral role, he has an office and comes into the school most days and his elderly mother can be spotted eating lunch in the dining room with the children.

The dream appears to have been realised – this is one of the least institutional schools we have visited: no sign of industrial carpets and concrete here. York stone courtyards embellished tastefully with inessential but elegant and stylish jeux d'esprit – little fountains and stone vases, olive trees, loggias and parterres. Spacious reception areas with sweeping staircases, three piece suites nestled on landings and in comfortable corners. No signs, no bells, no uniform, and no common rooms for staff or pupils ('reduces the chance of any whispering behind doors,' says head). Real three course lunches eaten on tablecloths in a dining room that could seamlessly become a ballroom. A coffee shop, complete with open fire, latte and floor to ceiling plush curtains (no crisps, no coke). And yes, the children are relaxed and are happy and seem surprisingly unspoilt by the privileges they enjoy here. We heard tales of some children returning, having left, and others ecstatic when they didn't get into another school.

Pastoral care and discipline: We were fully prepared to witness a level of chaos – not a bit of it. One parent described the discipline here as 'contained liberalism but certainly not lax'. Boundaries are clearly defined and pupils respect that, while enjoying an unusually equal and positive relationship with staff. If you miss homework you will be given a detention; these can take place on a Saturday morning (when no school) but the number of detainees is small – a reflection, we were told, of how well the system works. Zero tolerance on drugs – 'I have expelled children for drugs and wouldn't hesitate to do so again,' says head. Pupils have a mature self-regulating approach but it's not the place for someone who persists in pushing the boundaries – 'They wouldn't fit in,' says head.

Pupils and parents: Increasingly trendy media and fashion types from central London, with a fair helping of celebrities, but the core group of middle class professionals from affluent Barnes are still here too. A few first time buyers who are coming to grips with what is meant by a Russell Group university. Plenty of money, though – not many families here are scraping to find the fees and this is reflected in the lavish activities and trips that your child will want to attend. Children less bothered than their parents by this – thank goodness – and are confident, relaxed but polite, and relishing the space and the stimulation of the place.

Entrance: Huge waiting lists for the pre-prep – 'It's getting to the stage that you may wish to plan your caesarean at the beginning of the month,' we were told, with only a slight hint of irony. Non-selective. Strong sibling policy. Competitive at 8+ and 11+ and for occasionals. 11+ applications from a huge range – local state primaries as well as local preps; 'Girls' schools are less sniffy now,' head said. Becoming increasingly competitive – 250 applicants for 20 places. Two-thirds of candidates are interviewed, in some cases on the strength of an excellent school report notwithstanding a poor exam result. Despite evident delight at the quality and calibre of applicants in recent years, head keen to preserve the ethos of not creaming and cramming.

Takes a few more at CE. Entry to the sixth requires six or more Bs with As in the subjects chosen for A level. Standards less stringent for internal applicants.

Exit: A decreasing few at CE to trad boarding schools (Eton, Harrow, Charterhouse, Marlborough, Wellington etc) and the odd one or two to single sex London day schools (St Paul's Girls', King's College School etc). Will lose a few in the sixth form to, eg, tutorial colleges and boarding. Most leave for good universities, including a few to Oxbridge (none in 2013), after A levels to read a well-balanced mix of arts and sciences, creative and practical courses.

Money matters: Fees pretty average for location and what's on offer, but very little help available to pay them – limited bursaries (the funds are kept for a crisis) and no entrance scholarships. Academic awards are offered at 13+ and 16+.

Remarks: The secret of this unique place is undoubtedly out, as the gap continues to narrow between its local reputation – a country club for kids – and the experience of those on the inside – it's possible to achieve high standards without being tense and worried about doing it. The challenge will be how the school manages to maintain that ethos, as competition to experience such a delightful way to learn and grow becomes ever more fierce.

Harrogate Ladies' College

Linked school: HLC Highfield Prep School

Clarence Drive, Harrogate, HG1 2QG

- Pupils: 345 girls (155 full boarders) • Ages: 10–18 • Anglican
- Fees: Boarding £24,360–£30,845; Day £14,370 pa • Independent

Tel: 01423 504543
Email: enquire@hlc.org.uk
Website: www.hlc.org.uk

Principal: Since 2013, Mrs Sylvia Brett BA MA (forties). Read theology at Durham, followed by masters in philosophy and religion. Taught RS and was sixth form housemistress at Royal Masonic School, then became lay chaplain and head of RS at Caldicott Boys Preparatory School. Head of lower school, RS teacher and year 7 housemistress at Downe House before being appointed as sole deputy at Roedean.

Married to Justin, a classics teacher, and has one daughter. Her interests include music (singing and piano), art, swimming, family and friends.

Academic matters: Good and improving – regularly registers individual subject results in top five per cent nationally. In 2013, 46 per cent A*/A grades at A level and 74 per cent A*/B at GCSE. Strength is with mathematics and sciences (especially physics), a particular bias in the sixth form, but modern languages are fine – normally only the odd D at GCSE, otherwise all A*-C. Only a handful (three or four per language) opt for modern languages at A level but achieve good results. Over the past four years, 32 per cent of girls have pursued a business-related degree course. Launched 2010 in purpose built business suite, the Business School has increased business-related subjects to include accounting, business studies, economics and psychology. Wider purpose to promote enterprise and entrepreneurship throughout the school.

Teaching is generally very good – friendly good-humoured staff and girls feel both known and supported. As one parent said, 'My daughter has loved every minute – the environment, the work ethic and the dedication of the teachers.' Practical subjects good too – impressive art throughout the school and girls using a wide range of complex design and technology equipment, with an after-school group delighting in dismembering an old moped for spare parts for their go-kart. Well-equipped food technology room used up to GCSE – A2 available if demand. Enrichment programme for first year GCSE and sixth form to widen horizons in preparation for higher education. Plenty of IT facilities and ICT available as GCSE. Class size maximum 20, average 12. Reports always discussed with head or tutor prior to being sent home. Displays everywhere – a striking balance of pupil work and thought-provoking material, alongside posters from house captains rallying the troops.

Overseas students encouraged to sit exams in their native language, additional English language tuition available (and certainly encouraged) at no extra charge. EAL students used to sit IELTS rather than GCSE English, but pilot study of integration with mainstream English classes in years 10 and 11 has proved highly successful and will be the way forward. Some SEN, usually mild to moderate dyslexia, catered for out of the classroom on an individual basis by specialist teachers.

Games, options, the arts: Sport, the life-blood of the school, is keenly pursued by all. Lacrosse ('lackie') is king – current holders of northern schools' lacrosse title with good representation at county and regional level. Tennis – under 13s Yorkshire schools' champions. Good, much-used, sports facilities include plenty of tennis and badminton courts, multi-gym, 25-metre pool and an enormous indoor general-purpose sports hall which doubles up as a venue for social events, speech day etc.

An extensive extra-curricular menu embraces golf, sailing and ski trips as well as keen D of E and masses of charity and community work. Interesting business breakfast club and model United Nations. Burgeoning participation and success in Leeds Young Enterprise. Also boasts a flourishing ham radio station (call sign GX0HCA) – historic triumph was a hook-up with the Mir space station and the International space station.

Dedicated music house accommodates ensembles galore, from samba to string. Music is a real strength and majority of girls learn an instrument or two. Choir ran away with prizes at the Harrogate Festival, features on BBC Radio, at cathedral services across the land and on tours, Eastern Europe being a favoured destination. AS and A level theatre studies on offer, with plays and productions acted out in the suitably-equipped drama studio. Curriculum supported by regular trips to concerts, theatre and cinema. Many girls take LAMDA lessons (honours and distinctions the norm). Careers education taken seriously – two weeks' work experience for all followed by presentation and lunch.

Background and atmosphere: School founded in 1893 on a nearby site and is one of the Allied Schools. Within walking distance of the busy town centre, in the heart of Harrogate's leafy prime real estate, originally part of the Duchy of Lancaster. The pleasant Victorian mock-Tudor buildings with sympathetic additions blend gently with the locality. C of E (own chapel, resounding hymns et al) in small doses for all without exception. Brand new assembly hall will be officially opened in 2013 to mark school's 120 year anniversary. Separate sixth form centre in main school complete with common-rooms, study centre, kitchens, AV room etc with use of business school café. Unique sixth form studies valued by girls as their space and used for personal study until 9.00 pm each evening. Food is now provided by external catering company, which has seen a marked improvement in the choice and quality of meals available; recently refurbished dining room. Staff and girls dine together in main dining room, self-service with occasional formal dining.

School council meets regularly, though girls would like it to be less of a talking shop and to exert more power. A new uniform (predominantly navy) has been introduced throughout the school whilst keeping the traditional green cloak. Dress code for sixth form – business wear, recently more rigorously enforced.

Pastoral care and discipline: Manners strictly monitored. Occasional links with other schools, but not into creating artificial exposure to boys. Drugs and similar problems uncommon and treated with firmness – head retains discretion, expulsions rare. Health centre, specialist counsellor, tutors and staff all on hand to help if things go wrong.

Four well-presented boarding houses each have generously-sized attractive study bedrooms, a common-room centred on the TV, kitchen and games room. Up to four share a room in lower school, but most sixth formers have their own room with internet access for all in studies and bedrooms. Friendly comfortable feel, not snobbish or overtly feminine, girls mix well with the sense of a supportive sisterhood. Girls are encouraged to mix across the ages with a buddy system operating for new pupils. Flexi and weekly boarding as well as day and full boarding, weekends brimming with trips and activities.

Upper sixth housed in Tower – a half way house between school and university where pupils prepare and eat breakfast and a couple of evening meals in house and have greater freedom than lower down the school (team building exercises at start of upper sixth aid the bonding process). At 16+ girls are allowed out one night a week.

Pupils and parents: Mostly from Harrogate and the environs. Number of boarders from overseas, especially high number in the sixth form, though work in progress to widen intake and balance ratio. Hong Kong, USA, China, Thailand, Spain, Brunei, Germany, France and Baltic Republic currently being marketed. All faiths and none in the school. Parents predominantly from the usual professions, many Harrogate notables, also self-employed and some farming families, popular with the Forces. Turns out informed, assured, polite and articulate girls, cooperative rather than competitive. Strong OG network, including Anne McIntosh MP, Jenny Savill (author), Juliet Bremner, Claire King, Henrietta Butler and most recently Laura Winwood, former president of the Oxford Union. Working hard to encourage more recent leavers to stay in touch.

Entrance: Own entrance test (maths, English, verbal reasoning) taken on assessment day, together with reports from previous school. Main entry points are 11, 13 and 16 but school flexible. Highfield Prep is the linked feeder school. Minimum five GCSEs at grade C or above required for entry to sixth form, international pupils tested in English and appropriate subjects.

Open days: taster day in October, sixth form open day November, boarding taster in January, general open day in June.

Exit: Historically large numbers at 16 leave for local state or independents (29 per cent in 2013) and influx of international pupils, many Chinese. Recent culture shift – majority of day pupils staying and wider range of international boarders. To a widespread selection of universities, including London unis, Exeter and Bath, though northern locations, eg Durham, Edinburgh and Manchester, feature strongly. Occasional Oxbridge candidates.

Money matters: Academic scholarships of up to 25 per cent of fees. Regular Forces scholarships of up to 15 per cent. Music (in form of lessons) and honorary scholarships in art, sport, drama and all-rounder also awarded. Bursaries up to 100 per cent at governors' discretion.

Remarks: An 'in-town' girls boarding/day school that shouts 'girl-centred' education, is proud of it and walks the talk. A new whole school approach aims to provide a 'traditionally modern' experience for its pupils. A convincing start to re-balancing the school, with sixth form retention and diversifying overseas pupils. A tide of change and one to keep on the radar.

Harrow School

5 High Street, Harrow on the Hill, HA1 3HP

• Pupils: 820 boys (all board) • Ages: 13–18 • C of E (but 'significant' number of RCs) • Fees: £33,285 pa • Independent

Tel: 020 8872 8007
Email: admissions@harrowschool.org.uk
Website: www.harrowschool.org.uk

Head Master: Since 2011, Mr Jim Hawkins MA (forties). Educated at King Edward VI Camp Hill School for Boys in Birmingham and read maths at Brasenose College, Oxford (he was a year above David Cameron and knew the PM slightly). Did PGCE at Oxford before first teaching job at Radley – perfect combination of teaching maths and coaching rugby and rowing. Head of maths at Forest School in Walthamstow, then deputy head at Chigwell School. Prior to Harrow he was head of Norwich School for nine years – 'a fantastic school in a beautiful city.' Norwich went co-ed during during his headship but there are 'no plans' whatsoever to follow suit at Harrow. 'We are very happy as we are,' he says firmly.

Proud of the fact that Harrow enables boys to enjoy being boys. With a plethora of activities from dawn till dusk he reckons the school suits 'the kind of boy who wants to take the opportunities we offer and throw himself into things.' He says education at Harrow goes 'way beyond the exam syllabus' and that there's 'no better place for the really bright boy with a strong attitude towards life and learning, the sort of boy who is going to contribute and soak everything up.' School sends loads of boys to Oxbridge but head is equally proud of those who 'work jolly hard to get their As and Bs. They are some of our great successes.' When we asked who the school wouldn't suit he was unequivocal. 'It wouldn't suit someone who wanted a sixth form college sort of experience. Harrow is a highly organised, very busy school and it's very clear what the demands are.'

Dynamic, focused and urbane, with dashing good looks. Still keeps his hand in at the chalkface by teaching 'a bit of maths' to the youngest boys at the start of the academic year. 'It's really nice to have 40 minutes when you are focusing on something entirely educational,' he says. 'The key thing as a head is to find ways of interacting with the boys. Without that you lose touch with reality.' He makes a point with having lunch with boys and in the 'beaks' dining room' when he can. Very sporty – he rowed for Oxford's lightweight crew and was captain of Brasenose rowing. Ran the 10-mile Long Ducker, school's annual charity race from Hyde Park to Harrow, in 90 minutes, though laughingly admits that the director of studies did a faster time.

Loves his job, although he admits 'the highs are very high and the lows are quite challenging.' Says there are three main educational areas he wants to develop. First is the 'super curriculum' to encourage academic scholarship above and beyond the timetabled curriculum, research, independent thinking and university-style learning. Second is to look at preparing boys even better for university – he's already appointed a five-strong universities team with specific knowledge of Oxbridge, medicine and the US universities – and third is to concentrate on 'leadership and service.' School is already very active in local community (links with primary schools, tea parties for elderly, projects with Mothers Against Gangs charity etc) but head would like to do more. 'We want the boys to understand that leadership and service go hand in hand,' he says.

Wife Zoe is an artist and they have a young daughter. They live right in the heart of the school (along with their newly acquired cocker spaniel puppy) and regularly invite boys for breakfast – 'bacon butties and croissants.' Enjoys music, sport, reading and the theatre.

Academic matters: Teachers, parents and the boys themselves describe Harrow as an 'academic' school and results are impressive. Harrow's results don't appear in league tables – head says he's fed up with the 'one-dimensional snapshot' they deliver. At A level in 2013, 74 per cent A*/A grades and 89 per cent A*/A at GCSE. IGCSEs taken in English, French, German, Spanish history, maths, and biology, with chemistry and physics about to follow suit. Twenty-seven subjects on offer at A level – all the usual, plus business studies, government and politics, history of art, music technology, photography and theatre studies. Maths the most popular subject at A level, with two-thirds taking it. Half the boys do four subjects at A level rather than the usual three (one boy recently did nine). Sixth form electives are new innovation for lower sixth pupils – a chance for boys to experience university-style teaching in specialist areas. Cerebral subjects on offer include aspects of medicine, ancient philosophy, super physics, great economic thinkers and aesthetics (jointly taught by head and head of art).

Dazzling array of languages on offer – French, German, Spanish, Italian, Russian, Turkish, Polish, Japanese and Mandarin. All three sciences are compulsory at GCSE. School has its own observatory with three telescopes and astronomy offered as a GCSE. At GCSE classes range between 14 and 20 pupils while at A level they are between 10 and 12. School caters for mild dyspraxia and dyslexia. One-to-one help given off-timetable, with cost varying from nothing at all to £30 per hour depending on the level of support required. Dedicated band of teachers (or 'beaks' as they are known at Harrow) includes many writers of scholarly books. Women make up 15 per cent of staff.

Games, options, the arts: There's no doubt about it, Harrow is a very sporty school, with hordes of teams regularly trouncing their opponents. Sport played five afternoons a week, 32 sports on offer and director of sport encourages even the less enthusiastic to 'have a go' at something. Main sports are rugby, soccer, cricket and Harrow football. The latter is played with a pork-pie shaped ball which absorbs the wet and can be propelled by any part of the body. Even though it's played in the depths of winter and is a very muddy affair the boys love it and only wish more schools played it (Harrow is the only one). When we visited pupils were counting the days till their Harrow football match against an OH team. Last year lots of their fathers had played and there was even one grandfather in the side – 'but we were very careful with him.'

Vast expanse of playing fields, sports centre with indoor climbing wall, weights room, 25m pool and sports hall, courts for tennis, rackets and squash, nine-hole golf course and Olympic-sized running track. School boasts national champions in rackets, fencing, fives and judo, two boys playing rugby for England and number of cricketers playing at national and county level. The mother of a gifted sportsman was full of admiration for the way the school nurtured her son's sporting talent whilst keeping him focused on his academic studies and helping him achieve stellar grades. 'The school sees each boy as an individual and were very supportive and flexible,' she told us.

Head of music admits that when he arrived eight years ago there was a perception among rival directors of music that Harrow was 'an old-fashioned school where little value was placed on music and the arts.' To his delight he found the reverse was true and there's a 'wealth of musical talent.' Half the boys learn musical instruments and 50 per cent of these achieve grade 8 or better by the time they leave. Practice sessions timetabled for younger boys. Loads of orchestras, choirs and strong tradition of singing (see below). More than 100 concerts a year, with recent performances at the Royal Albert Hall and Royal Festival Hall. Steady stream of boys to top universities and conservatoires to read music too.

Excellent Ryan Theatre seats 400 and is used for school and professional productions but annual Shakespeare productions take place in the beautiful arts and crafts Speech Room. A huge, wood-panelled half-moon, it boasts authentic Globe-style staging and seats the entire school. Wonderful art and, befittingly for a school where photography pioneer William Fox Talbot was a pupil, photography. There's no lounging around with nothing to do at weekends either – scores of extra curricular activities to choose from, everything from the Alexander Society for boys interested in military history to the Turf Club for horse racing fans.

Background and atmosphere: Harrow is one of only three all-boys, full-boarding schools left in the UK (along with Eton and Radley). Boys have been educated here since the 13th century but the school was founded in 1572 under a royal charter granted to local farmer John Lyon by Elizabeth I (Lyon's, the newest boarding house, is named after him). The aim was for the school to provide free education for 30 local scholars, a number later increased to 40 by the governors. School sits in picturesque Harrow on the Hill, surrounded by 400 acres and with panoramic views across London – of it, yet remote from it, as we said last time. On a clear day you can see Canary Wharf from the head's study and it's just 25 minutes by tube to Green Park. Visitors to the undulating school site take note – flat shoes are a must.

School is steeped in tradition and history. The 17th century Old Schools contain the beautiful Fourth Form room, with names carved into every inch of panelling, from Byron to Robert Peel. It's also where Professor Flitwick's charm classes were shot in the first Harry Potter film (lots of tourists gazing admiringly when we visited). The stunning Vaughan Library, designed by architect Gilbert Scott (he also created London's St Pancras Station) has chess sets on tables and stays open late during exam periods. War Memorial Building commemorates the 633 OHs who died in the First World War. You can't help but be profoundly moved by the Alex Fitch Room, an Elizabethan wood panelled room with stained glass windows and a Cromwellian table, given by a grieving mother in honour of her 19-year-old son after he died in the First World War. She asked that it should be used for the purpose of boys meeting their mothers and that a light should always be left on over her son's portrait. Plaques and memorials commemorating quirky events are everywhere. Charles I rested here while preparing to surrender and little inclines have memorable names like Obadiah Slope, wittily named after Trollope's unctuous Barchester Towers character.

Harrow Songs are legendary. No Harrovian, either past or present, fails to mention the strength of feeling they engender and the lump in the throat they provoke. Songs have been an important part of the school since 1864, when the head of music wrote the first song, and they are considered to be 'a unifying force.' In November each year the whole school assembles in Speech Room in honour of its most famous alumni, Sir Winston Churchill, for the Churchill Songs. Like rival Eton, school has its own jargon. 'Skew' is a punishment, 'tosh' is a shower, 'tolley up' is permission to work late and so on.

Pastoral care and discipline: Pastoral care is meticulous, with highly structured system of resident housemasters, assistant housemasters and matrons. Harrow's 12 houses are integral to the school and boys are fiercely loyal to their own house. Some houses are regarded as stricter than others and parents we spoke to said it's important 'to pick and choose carefully.' One of the houses – West Acre – is the subject of an ITN documentary series, following the life of the school for a whole year. Housemasters in post for 12 years and as well as doing most of the admissions assessments each gives their house its character and reputation. They also work round the clock – 'at the beginning of every term I say to my wife "see you at the end of term,"' one housemaster told us with a grin.

We visited two very different houses – Druries, which dates back to the 1790s and is a maze of charming nooks and crannies, and the ultra-modern Lyon's, or the Holiday Inn, as a few wags have nicknamed it. 'It's the best piece of real estate around here,' joked one boy, hugely appreciative of its light, airy, five-star rooms. 'There's room for us to move around and not cause too much havoc.' Each house has common rooms, games rooms (kitted out with plasma TV, pool and table tennis tables), garden and 'yarder,' an area where boys can run off steam and kick a ball about. Two boys sharing is the norm in the first year but by year 11 (or even earlier) they get their own room, complete with desk, shelving, computer and, occasionally, en-suite shower. All pupils' names etched on wooden house boards, with head of house's name picked out in gold. Boys can make toast and heat up soup in their houses – 'and the more ambitious make Pot Noodles,' said one boy. We trust he was joking. Meals are eaten centrally and food gets a firm thumbs-up – from us too, if the lunch we had with sixth formers was anything to go by. Boys are allowed to go out for a meal with their parents on Sundays but there's no weekly or flexi-boarding. Two weekend exeats in the autumn and spring terms and one in the summer.

Harrow takes a pragmatic approach to technology and social media but the boys are so busy there isn't much time to sit around and play computer games. Pupils understand that bullying is 'completely unacceptable' and head says that it has plummeted, 'not down to zero, but pretty close.' School does a bullying survey every winter and housemasters, year group tutors, matrons, two school chaplains, health education tutors and school psychologist pick up on most things. Discipline is clear and firm but the place feels pretty relaxed, with boys knowing exactly where they stand. 'You are given freedom but if you abuse the freedom you would be punished,' one boy told us. Zero tolerance on drugs and use or supply in term-time or holidays means expulsion. Anyone found with spirits suspended and warned while smoking is handled through 'escalating sequence of sanctions imposed by housemasters.'

Smart uniform of dark blue jackets (bluers), grey flannels (greyers), white shirts and ties, plus, of course, Harrow's infamous boaters. Boys wear them or carry them and either love them or loathe them. They're allowed to write their names and draw pictures on the inner rim and spray them with varnish to protect them. Members of Philathletic Club (school's top sportsmen) get to wear bow ties. Sunday wear is black tailcoat and the whole kit and caboodle.

Pupils and parents: Pupils come from all over and school is proud of its 'broad and varied intake.' We said last time that it's the sort of place where a Yorkshire farmer's son will be sharing a room with the offspring of a City banker – and it still holds true. Between 10 and 15 per cent are progeny of OHs, while 20 per cent are from overseas (some ex-pat, others from vast range of countries – 40 at last count). Twenty-five with EAL requirements. Most boys are C of E but there's a 'significant' RC community. Small numbers of all other main faiths or none.

The boys we met were engaging, appreciative of the fine education they get and very proud of their school. 'It doesn't give you a sense of entitlement, just a great responsibility to give something back,' one boy told us, while a sixth former who'd joined from a state school at 16 said that he'd been 'pushed and challenged' and that there was 'a lot more opportunity for debate' than at his previous school.

Parents reckon the school suits all-rounders who work hard and like sport. 'It's very disciplined and the boys are busy all the time so they have to be organised,' one mother said. 'There isn't any time to get up to any mischief and the boys are really tired by the end of term. There's a real camaraderie about the place and the boys make life-long friends. I can't fault it.' Another reckoned that even though it's 'strict,' any boy would thrive at Harrow, as long as they can cope with being in a large school where they won't necessarily be 'king pin.'

Long and distinguished list of former pupils – seven former prime ministers (including Sir Robert Peel, Lord Palmerston, Stanley Baldwin and Sir Winston Churchill), 19th century philanthropist Lord Shaftesbury ('a towering figure – we refer to him a lot,' says the head), Jawaharlal Nehru, King Hussein of Jordon, Lord Cardigan (who led the Charge of the Light Brigade), General Sir Peter de la Billière, plus countless other men of military renown (20 holders of the Victoria Cross and one George Cross holder). The arts and sciences are equally well represented, with a dazzling list of luminaries including Lord Byron, Richard Brinsley Sheridan, Anthony Trollope, Terence Rattigan, John Galsworthy, Cecil Beaton, Edward and William Fox, Richard Curtis, Benedict Cumberbatch and James Blunt, plus Crispin Odey (one of the UK's most successful hedge fund managers), Julian Metcalfe (founder of Pret à Manger), cricketer Nick Compton and Tim Bentinck (better known as David Archer).

Entrance: Very competitive. Around 600 apply for the 160 places on offer at 13. Prospective pupils are assessed at the start of year 7, through tests, interviews and school reference. Offers are made – subject to CE or scholarship exams 18 months later. Sixty per cent expected at CE. 'Some weight' given to sons of OHs and boys' siblings – 'but brothers don't automatically get in,' said a parent. Boys arrive from more than 100 regular feeder schools. All-boys' boarding preps like Caldicott and Cothill top the pack but others from a myriad of co-ed and day schools.

Total of 24 new pupils a year into the 340-strong sixth form. Candidates need at least seven or eight A*/A at GCSE but many will have straight A*s. Candidates write a CV, plus letter to the head explaining why they want to come to Harrow, and take tests in their proposed A level subjects. The best attend a day of interviews and assessments.

Exit: Ninety-nine per cent to university – 24 to Oxbridge in 2012 and most of the rest to Russell Group. Increasing number opting for Ivy League universities in the US and other top international institutions.

Money matters: School has given franchises to Harrow Beijing, Harrow Bangkok and Harrow Hong Kong, with a fourth likely to follow in the next few years. These are all successful enterprises carefully monitored by Harrow and also fund generous bursary schemes at home.

Wide range of scholarships and bursaries at 13 or 16. School offers means-tested bursaries of up to 100 per cent of fees to pupils who win a scholarship of any sort. Up to 30 scholarships a year for academic excellence, music, art or talent in a particular area (normally worth five per cent of fees). There are also Peter Beckwith scholarships for gifted and talented boys whose parents can't afford to send them to Harrow. Two awarded each year to boys aged between 10 and 13 – these can cover fees at a private school from the age of 11 and Harrow fees from 13.

Remarks: Parents looking for a top notch, blue chip, full boarding, all boys' school will be hard-pressed to beat Harrow. This is a school on top of its game.

Haydon School

Wiltshire Lane, Eastcote, Pinner, Middlesex, HA5 2LX

- Pupils: 2,030 boys and girls; all day • Ages: 11–18 • Non-denom
- State

Tel: 020 8429 0005
Email: info@haydonschool.org.uk
Website: www.haydonschool.com

Headteacher: Since 2006, Robert Jones (mid forties). Read economics at LSE and taught in Hong Kong for four years before returning to the UK. Moved to Haydon in 1999 and quickly moved up the ranks to become assistant head, then head. Married to drama teacher. Two sons – one in his 20s, who has just finished at university, while the other is seven. Originally from Manchester, he's a huge Man United fan and looks rather like an ex-professional footballer himself. Still plays football and coaches Ascot United under 7s (his son plays for the team) and keeps fit by running a number of half marathons each year.

Academic matters: Specialist language and applied learning college. Seventy-one per cent of students achieved at least five A*-C grades including maths and English at GCSE in 2013 (31 per cent A*/A grades). Language provision is excellent, with students starting off with French and Italian or Spanish and German. Options for taking on further languages (such as Mandarin and Latin) higher up the school. 'Around 100 opted for Mandarin this year,' says the head proudly. Forty per cent take two foreign languages at GCSE.

More than 30 GCSE or BTEC options. 'We want to offer as broad a curriculum as possible,' explains the head. Applied learning specialism allows the school to offer a wide array of courses, from Greek to construction. 'There is a broad range of subjects offered,' one parent told us.

All KS3 teaching (apart from maths and technology) is in mixed ability groups. 'We believe this gives all of our students the best possible chance of achieving their best,' explains the head. Parents like the fact that class sizes are around 25 but some would prefer more streaming though. 'At present in year 7 there is streaming just for maths,' says one parent. 'I would like to see this extended to other key subjects such as English and science as is practice in other local schools'.

At A level 58 per cent A*/B (27 per cent A*/A) in 2013. Again, a wide choice of subjects available. Parents praise the quality of teaching and particularly the revision lessons offered around exam time. Students need six GCSEs at A*-C (including maths and English) to study four A levels. Those who do not have a minimum of a C in English or maths are able to retake these and can study three A levels.

Twenty-two statemented students. One SENCo and a team of learning support assistants support these pupils. Also a special centre where students can be taught in small groups. When we visited we met a group of students learning to express their emotions through the making of Star Wars masks.

Games, options, the arts: School has scored successes in a host of sports – at both local and county level. Particular strengths are rugby, rounders and indoor athletics and there is even an ultimate frisbee team in the sixth form. New sports hall opening in September 2014.

Haydon has benefited from new facilities in recent years, including £5 million art and design building and £2 million music and performing arts centre (three music rooms, drama studio and music mixing room. plus one-to-one teaching rooms). School has two orchestras, jazz band, samba band and wide variety of other music groups. Four big concerts a year as well as annual musical or play.

Thriving art department achieves excellent exam results. Students can study art, textiles and photography at A level. Lots of school trips too – to France, Germany, Italy, Peru and Swaziland.

Background and atmosphere: School is situated on the edge of the Northwood Hills in Pinner, with spacious playing fields. Rather nondescript 1950s buildings – originally two grammar schools that merged in 1977. Haydon became an academy in 2011. Lots of building work going on when we visited.

Food in the sixth form cafe is so good that the staff choose to eat there. Food in the canteen for the rest of the school has less favourable reports but new caterers were about to be appointed when we visited so this will hopefully improve. Some of the toilets need a little TLC but these are in the process of being refurbished. 'The boys' changing rooms are a real state,' one student told us, but we weren't shown these on our tour. We were very taken with the pool table and primary colours in the rather groovy sixth form common room though.

Pastoral care and discipline: A new positive reward system has recently been introduced. 'The reward system is a great motivator,' one parent told us. "My child strives to get good news notes, commendations and other rewards.' Meanwhile a year 8 student said: 'I really look forward to the awards assembly. It's a way of showing how hard we are working.' One of the top awards means pupils get a special lunch with the head (mums sadly aren't eligible to compete for this award).

Students excluded for threatening behaviour or repeated disruption in lessons (four permanent exclusions last year). Parents are happy with school's approach to behaviour. 'I have always found that a high level of discipline is maintained from the minute the children arrive at the school,' said one. When we visited, students seemed well behaved and friendly.

Pupils and parents: 'Haydon has a really good reputation round here,' a student told us, 'and all my friends at other schools wish they were here.' The school offers both pupils and parents a chance to voice their opinions – parent voice group meets four times per year.

Entrance: Most students live locally (within a mile or so to the school). Admissions criteria are: children in public care, then siblings, then children living nearest to the school, then employees' children. An additional 60 students join in the sixth form.

Exit: A quarter of pupils leave after GCSEs – for college, other schools, apprenticeships or employment. Around three-quarters of sixth formers to university, and about a third of these to Russell Group universities, including one or two a year to Oxbridge.

Remarks: A friendly comprehensive that really does cater for all, with strong vocational courses as well as the more traditional A levels – all taught to a high standard. 'I would have no hesitation recommending Haydon,' said one parent. 'I feel my children are lucky to attend the school.'

H

Headington School

Linked school: Headington Preparatory School

Headington Road, Oxford, OX3 7TD

- Pupils: 805 girls; day, weekly and full boarders • Ages: 11–18
- C of E • Fees: Day £14,352–£15,801; Boarding £24,252–£30,591 pa
- Independent

Tel: 01865 759113
Email: admissions@headington.org
Website: www.headington.org

Head: Since 2011, Mrs Caroline Jordan, previously head of St George's Ascot. She was educated at St Helen's and St Katharine's, read geology at Oxford and did a PGCE in science at Manchester University. Was head of sixth form and deputy senior housemistress at Wycombe Abbey before joining St George's. Married to Richard; one teenage son.

Academic matters: Parents say happily that they can take a back seat and rely on the school to keep the girls on track – 'It's fair to say that my daughter is of average ability and the school has pushed, focused and nurtured her to get top grade GCSEs'; 'They get good results without serious pressure'. In 2013, 78 per cent A*/A grades at GCSE. Sixty-four per cent A*/A grades at A level in 2013, with a very good take-up for biology, maths and chemistry – 'I'm a chemist, so I know it's important'. Geography is another popular subject. The 2013 IB cohort achieved an average score of 38.

The school is 'not aggressively selective' and can accommodate those with mild dyslexia and dyspraxia. It has on occasion welcomed pupils with sight or hearing problems and one with cerebral palsy. Extra help is usually included in the fees, unless it is 'very specialist and very frequent', in which case it costs £30 an hour. Foreign students can get help with cultural English from the EAL department. Everyone is given achievement and effort grades six times a year and decides in consultation with their teachers what to aim for in the next half term – 'In the younger years we are much more interested in the grades for effort'.

Games, options, the arts: Rowing is 'sensational,' said a parent – 'the total sporting strength of the school. They all row at national level.' The newly-opened floodlit Astroturf pitch (six years in the planning) has revolutionised ball sports, which have been known to take second place to rowing. Enthusiastic teams compete at netball, hockey, rounders, fencing, cross-country etc and seven are county champions. Sports hall, fitness suite, swimming pool and assault course in the woods that fringe the site.

Light, airy, galleried art and design building with a dark room, kiln and history of art room. Plenty of impressive artwork on display including ceramics, photographs and textiles. A good take-up for art and history of art at AS and A level, and several students each year go on to art foundation courses.

The impressive Headington Theatre is used by outside companies as well as school thespians, with concerts, dance displays, musicals and plays alternating with school fashion shows, comedies and lectures. School drama is 'excellent', say parents, often in conjunction with the boys of Magdalen College School. Music school boasts state-of-the-art equipment including electronics studio and recording studios, airy teaching rooms for individuals, ensembles and full classes, and performance spaces both indoors and out.

The house system encourages everyone to take part in inter-house sport, music and drama competitions. 'It's one of the best things about the school,' said a pupil. 'You get to know people from all the different years and it's all organised by the students.' Pupils agree that the emphasis on so many different activities makes Headington special – 'You join because you've heard the music or the drama's good, then you find that so many other things are too'.

Background and atmosphere: Founded in 1915 by a group of evangelical Christians to provide 'a sound education for girls to fit them for the demands and opportunities likely to arise after the war'. It occupied various large houses in Headington before moving to its present site, the main school built in neo-Georgian style in 1930 amidst 26 acres of grounds, including four boarding houses. It is still run by a Christian foundation and boarders attend Sunday church services run by a lay chaplain – 'But it is very open – a service may be on a theme such as thinking about others and all the girls are happy to attend'.

Around a third of the school boards, half of the boarders from abroad. Full, weekly and flexi-boarding with different age groups in different houses. The younger girls, some from the prep school, share bright, cheerful dormitories with posters and teddies abounding. Nationalities are mixed and girls move room each term to prevent cliques forming – 'They can ask to share with particular friends but don't always get it'. Older girls get twin or single rooms and increasing freedom, with permission to go out for a meal or off to the pub. Instead of gap year students, now employ graduate assistants in the boarding houses, mostly en route to PGCE courses. Plenty of activities to keep homesickness at bay – from table tennis tournaments to chocolate fondue evenings and London theatre visits. Some older girls who live nearby choose to board for the last year or two to prepare for going off to university.

'My daughters have both been incredibly happy there,' said a parent. 'I haven't got a bad word to say about it,' said another. 'We get on really well with most of the staff,' say sixth formers. 'They look for good things in everyone.'

Pastoral care and discipline: Drugs, alcohol and smoking all banned on school premises; the head feels that alcohol is the greatest threat to teenagers generally. Strong pastoral support system includes mentoring by part-time staff, who see those in need of extra care once a week for perhaps six weeks at a time – 'It can make a real difference to have that injection of extra attention and it seems to get them sorted fairly quickly'. Anyone can book an appointment with the school counsellor – 'She's really great,' say students.

The school keeps in close touch with parents – 'A student is a jig-saw puzzle – different people see different parts – and we may ask how things are going at home if she doesn't seem to be performing as we would have expected. And sometimes parents need reassurance, especially if she is their eldest child'. One parent praised the school's reaction to a family crisis: 'They were excellent, very calm and supportive, and arranged for her to board for a week until things blew over'. Another, whose daughter was off sick for some time, commented, 'They were amazing and very understanding when she came back.'

Plenty of effort is put into encouraging foreign students and other boarders to integrate with day girls, with everyone joining in international evenings and events such as the rock challenge dance competition – 'We find out what the shy girls are interested in. The Brunei girls, for example, performed their national dance'.

Pupils and parents: From some 30 countries, including Brunei, Hong Kong, Italy, Russia and Australia. Day girls come from a 30 mile radius, with quite a few weekly boarders from London catching a coach which drops them right outside. A mixture of different backgrounds including wealthy country people, professional parents and academics. 'They're a nice bunch of normal girls,' said a parent. OGs include Baroness Young, Julia Somerville, Lady Longford, Christina Onassis and Emma Watson.

Entrance: Ninety-six pupils join the school at 11, of whom about 40 have come up from the junior school. Another 15 or 20 come in at 13. These have all sat common entrance. About half the new entrants at 11 are from state primaries – some 58 different feeder schools. Not ferociously selective – about two applicants for every place. Sixth form applicants sit exams in their chosen A level subjects and are expected to get at least six A*/B grades at GCSE. Overseas applicants all sit exams, including an EFL paper if English is not their first language. Twenty girls from Hong Kong join the sixth form, chosen by the head from a field of 100 – 'They integrate much better now we interview them all personally'.

Exit: Most GCSE students go through to the sixth form. Around 10-15 move on to co-ed sixth forms or sixth form colleges. All sixth form leavers to university, about 10 per cent a year to Oxbridge (eight in 2013), with a good proportion going for science/medical degrees, and a few to art foundation courses.

Money matters: Academic, art, drama and sports scholarships all worth £300 a year; music scholarships for tuition on one instrument and a Loft Simson music scholarship for tuition on two instruments for an exceptional candidate.

Means tested bursaries of up to 100 per cent of fees are available to applicants for entry at 11, 13 or 16, and Forces/C of E clergy bursaries also available.

Remarks: A happy school that manages to turn out girls with admirable exam results without undue pressure and with rich extra-curricular experiences along the way. 'The staff make sure that life's not all about work,' say students happily. 'You leave school with so much more.'

Heathfield School

London Road, Ascot, SL5 8BQ

- Pupils: 200 girls; all full boarders • Ages: 11–18 • C of E
- Fees: £30,348–£31,041 pa • Independent

Tel: 01344 898343
Email: registrar@heathfieldschool.net
Website: www.heathfieldschool.net

Headmistress: Since 2009, Mrs Jo Heywood BSc PGCE (early forties); a chemist. Began her teaching career in a large

comprehensive in Surrey, thence to St Mary's, Ascot – a shuttlecock's flight away. She stayed there for eight happy years as teacher of chemistry and head of house. Concerned that she should not become 'complacent', she moved down the road to Heathfield in 2005 to become deputy head (pastoral). When her predecessor, the late Mrs McSwiggan, became ill, Mrs Heywood became acting head and, after Mrs McSwiggan's death, the decision of the school's governors to appoint her to the headship was a popular one with, it seems, the entire school community. 'She's so Heathfield,' one girl enthused – 'she understands the homeliness and the traditions.'

And it is not hard to see why they wanted her. She is the fourth head in ten years and is in it for the long run. She 'knew everyone' and was ideally placed to bring ambitious aspirations in terms of academic attainment, stability and personal commitment to a school she already loved. She provided, however, more than much-needed continuity. She is a warm, commonsensical head with youthful enthusiasm, generosity of spirit and a firm belief in what Heathfield is all about, which are just what's needed here. 'She's lovely,' said a parent. And she has taste – her refurbished room is peachy and beautiful: hits exactly the right note. Heathfield survived the previous difficult decade in remarkably good shape. A good long spell of steady renewal and growth is already proving successful in restoring this unique school back to full health and stability.

Academic matters: Warm, friendly and positive atmosphere, striving for every girl to be the best she can be. Small class sizes enable girls to thrive. Offers a wide range of subjects at GCSE, including accounting, further mathematics, classical civilisation and Latin. Mathematics popular and successful. Creative talent is encouraged with art and design, textiles, photography. Single sciences, geography, religious studies, art and design and drama stand out; also strong English and mathematics. In 2013, 42 per cent A*/A grades at GCSE and 44 per cent A*/A at A level.

Games, options, the arts: Everything done with energy, enthusiasm and friendly collaboration. Core sports are netball, lacrosse, tennis and athletics but loads else on offer, in particular the school's equestrian strength. 'We punch above our weight,' says Mrs Heywood – 'around 15-20 now play polo, we have some fantastic show jumpers and around 15 per cent now ride.' Team successes in several sports and notable individual stars include an international skier, national skating and lacrosse players. 'We will always help if they need to go away to play their sport,' says the head, as if it were quite the most normal thing in the world.

Many school trips and tours to exotic places. The inviting cookery room encourages girls to roll up their sleeves. Everyone learns cookery in the first three years, no-one does in years 10 and 11 (except for leisure) but very popular Leith's course available in the sixth. The cookery room is also used imaginatively – we observed a biology class learning about micro-organisms in food. Yum!

The school's theatre (opened by Mother Winsome, late of St Mary's Wantage and diplomatically named St Mary's) seats 300 and includes drama room, music rooms (including music technology) and attractive conference room. Drama is adventurous and strong, considering the small forces available. Theatre balcony cleverly overlooks sports field – rather like the grandstand at Lord's. Textiles and photography are exceptional and art in general is varied, imaginative and surely outstanding, again, for so small a school. Masses to do at weekends, though, according to parents, 'this is when good friendships become great'.

Background and atmosphere: Founded in 1899 by Eleanor Beatrice Wyatt, who began by starting small schools for girls in London but, on deciding that out of London would provide a healthier environment, acquired this 18th century house, built in the style of a restrained Italian villa for the Paravacini family. Off the main road out of Ascot – very discreet sign: you need to know.

The white-painted, modest exterior belies the pleasures of the interior – most notably the splendid drawing room now given over to the lower sixth as its privileged common-room. Elsewhere, the interior of the main house provides unremarkable but pleasant accommodation with some distinctive attributes – the classrooms are huge for these small numbers and most now boast areas with comfortable chairs and sofas as well as the usual desks and tables. The common-rooms are exceptionally well-appointed – every year has one – though girls would always like more, of course. The upper sixth kitchen looks more like a real family kitchen than any school kitchen we can remember.

Beautiful and rather special chapel of which the girls are clearly proud and in which they spend ten minutes each morning. Dining room now less formal – no more top table, thank goodness. Food definitely good. The grounds are charming – lots of huge trees and plenty of space everywhere. Virginia creeper and other sensitive planting around its buildings old and new (newer ones are low and attractive) make these real gardens. In a unique and privileged location just outside Ascot (which has a station), six miles from Windsor and Eton (Windsor bus stops at school gate), 20 minutes from Heathrow, 30 minutes from London, this school has a relaxed and country house feel and everything is on an inviting human scale.

Merged with St Mary's Wantage in 2005. Lots gained in terms of dosh from sale of Wantage plus a few migrants and some excellent staff. Mrs Heywood always keen to invite St Mary's Old Girls, in the hope they may come to feel at home in their land of adoption.

Heathfield now the only small boarding school for girls in the UK. Rightly proud of this unique status and all that it offers to the right family. Numbers are on the rise – though not too much. Boarding is good – everyone who wants to has a single room from year 10 upwards and dorms for those below. In the year 10, you get a trial week in the upper sixth bungalow – such fun and sense of independence engendered by this canny move that very few leave after GCSEs: they can't wait to experience the freedom and fun the top year enjoys. They are allowed to cook their own meals and do their own washing – quelle joie!

Pastoral care and discipline: A successful four-house system – Austen, de Valois, Seacole, Somerville – felt by girls to have improved inter-year relationships in general. All but the upper sixth wear uniform – trad navy with blue tie; upper sixth wear their own clothes. Quaint system of 'bows and bearings' – badges for conduct and manners, kindness, deportment etc – apparently much prized: girls wear these and other honours in long chains down the front of their jerseys. Very few disciplinary concerns. Focus always on the individual. 'The school could not have been more helpful when my daughter joined at an odd time,' a parent told us. 'Instead of disciplining people,' said a sixth former, 'Mrs Heywood tries to help them.' 'The head of boarding has been here for ever,' said another. 'She knows every trick in the book. She can read your mind.'

Excellent pastoral support within the full boarding system but no rigidity – 'If the dog or the horse has died, we're not so Dickensian that we won't let them out for pastoral reasons'. Girls enthuse – 'Our house mothers are so lovely!' Friendships lauded – 'We all get on – you have to in such a small community'; 'It's so nice knowing everyone'; 'You can't afford to be cliquey here'. 'The teachers are on the side of the girls and get the best out of them.' Proper support for boarding families includes transport help and luggage storage.

Pupils and parents: Lots of daughters, nieces and granddaughters of Old Girls. But newcomers too – all drawn by the palpable sense of tradition and, now, a sense of a school firmly in the 21st century – in many ways – while weird, anachronistic things like writing real letters still encouraged. Not falling into elephant traps into which so many others have been lured – 'We've been through a bit of a time and we could fill the school with overseas pupils, but we're not going down that road,' says wise Mrs Heywood. Fifty per cent from London, 20 per cent from Home Counties, 15 per cent from overseas – everywhere: no dominant nationality. Up-market clientèle – this school has lost none of its cachet, though parents claim, 'It's not for snobby show-offs – the girls are lovely and natural: they have no "London edge".' Lots of social stuff with Eton, Wellington, Radley and Harrow.

Entrance: Around two applicants for each of the 18 places at age 11. The usual academic tests but much emphasis put on the head's report from current school. Strong intake at 13. At 16, around 10 or so join to replace those who have left.

Exit: Around four per cent left after GCSEs in 2013. A lively list of sixth form destinations and courses includes economics and accounting at Edinburgh, architecture at King's College, philosophy at Loughborough, maths at City, law at Universidad CEU San Pablo, Madrid, drama at RADA and history at Trinity College Dublin. Definitely no stereotypes here.

Money matters: A few bursaries available to means-tested applicants; the Old Girls' Association also offers financial assistance to deserving cases. Academic scholarships awarded, though these dish out prestige rather than dosh.

Remarks: Unique now in offering traditional, full boarding for lucky girls in a close, happy, small community with all mod cons and opportunities. Sensible, sound and super.

Heathside School (Weybridge)

Brooklands Lane, Weybridge, Surrey, KT13 8UZ

• Pupils: 1,280 girls and boys • Ages: 11–18 • Non-denom – but affiliated to the diocese of Guildford • State

Tel: 01932 846162
Email: sburoni@heathside.surrey.sch.uk
Website: www.heathside.surrey.sch.uk

Principal: Since 2009, Mrs Anne Cullum BA in English, PGCE NPQH (forties). Previously in Shropshire and Staffordshire and moved to Surrey in 2001. Head of sixth form at George Abbot, Guildford, before joining Heathside as vice principal. At the school for a year before taking over as acting principal, encouraged to apply for headship proper and won the job ahead of external candidates. She's no nonsense, working hard to move the school forward, strategic, but recognises and is respectful of the school's history. While the previous longstanding head was a tough act to follow, Ms Cullum rattles through a long list of initiatives and projects, which reflects some feeling that school had rested on its laurels for a while. She stresses the work on curriculum changes and that the school is now a real mover and groover within the county. Sits on several education and policy committees and councils. Consensus among parents is that she is doing a grand job and is good for the school. 'She's a fantastic head,' said one mother.

Of course in a place of this size many parents who have not had personal dealings with her and have only heard her speak in public, where she does not shine – she's better one-to-one. School expresses surprise at this and says she loves doing assemblies etc. 'She's not a huge personality,' says one mother. But another reported that her son and his friends described her as 'a legend' after spending time with her on a school ski-trip. Parents also appreciate little things she has done, like improving home/school communications and tightening up on uniform standards. Married and has two teenage children, not at Heathside – 'They would never want to be at the school where I worked,' she says, laughing. Outside of school she spends time with her children and enjoys reading and sports, particularly skiing and aerobics.

Academic matters: Gets very good academic results which put it up with top-performing comprehensives nationally. From a non-selective intake, over 82 per cent of pupils gained five or more A*- C passes including maths and English in 2013, 36 per cent at A* and A. At A level, 64 per cent of the grades were A*-B and 32 per cent A*/A.

Heathside is a technology and modern languages college, so that pupils now buck the trend and all take Spanish, French or German at GCSE. Three language assistants, all native speakers. Huge emphasis on English and maths, which are seen as absolutely core – some subjects are more equal than others. Anyone who joins sixth form without maths or English GCSE will have to add it to their timetable – 'They do it until they pass it' is school's attitude. Good takeup of solid traditional subjects like history, geography and single sciences. 'We encourage them to choose subjects that have credibility,' says Ms Cullum. Lots of specialist teachers, even in physics where a national shortage. Parents feel very confident that Heathside will deliver for their children.

School received 'outstanding' grading in latest Ofsted inspection for both the main school and the sixth form. Head has revised the curriculum radically and first fruits of this appear in a subsequent Ofsted inspection of English which found the school's achievement here to be outstanding in every respect, with standards well above average. Similar drive now being applied to monitoring and improvements in other subject areas. 'I am always asking "how good is the learning?" and I want to look at any weaker subjects and develop them so that every area is outstanding,' said Ms Cullum. Staff are skilled up, valued and consulted, and generally only leave to take up promotion or if moving aboard. Parents pleased that teaching is consistently good, homework always marked, and describe staff as 'enthusiastic' and 'great'.

Some complain about the number of GCSEs – as many as 12 – school insists on: a GCSE in technology is compulsory (either graphics, textiles, resistant materials, electronics or food technology) and very time-consuming. Students are grouped with others of broadly similar ability and setted for maths. Reorganised and re-setted in year 9 in readiness for GCSEs. Critical thinking from year 10 for accelerated groups. 'It seems to be streamed for everything,' says one parent. 'Great if your child is clever, but I do worry that the less bright ones will find themselves in a class with the disruptive pupils.' Average state school class size of 31 maximum, dropping to 26 by key stage 4.

Sixth form is up against strong local competition, but has a reputation for high-quality teaching – most stay on and do well. Great takeup of science at A level, politics, only English lit, no English language, critical thinking to AS. Pupils in search of vocational courses head next door to Brooklands College – the sixth form offers 'academic' A levels only. Dedicated sixth form block, newer than the main building, ground floor shared with main school but, as you go upstairs to sixth form proper, you are greeted by leavers' desirable destinations posted up on the walls to inspire others.

EFL provision as needed (not much – it's hardly multi-cultural) and a special needs facility on site within the learning resource centre, though most support is classroom-based. School says it teaches all its students in a 'multi-sensory way, responding to specific learning difficulties by offering different learning styles'. The SEN area supports students further by offering clinics to sort out subject-based learning needs. No specific testing on entry. Teaching assistants and higher level teaching assistants help in classrooms, with over 30 pupils receiving one-to-one assistance. Can cater for most needs, including visual and hearing impairment – some classrooms equipped with induction loops. Access for the physically disabled, including a shower and treatment room, dedicated loos and lift, ramps everywhere – aiming to make whole school accessible.

Games, options, the arts: All valued and well executed. Sport and music strong and locally renowned. Very sporty place, success in rugby has come out of nowhere – year 11 boys have won rugby scholarships to Rugby and Millfield, one plays for Harlequins. Runners up in U15 boys' national squash competition. Plenty of football and cricket. Netball is main sport for the girls. Lots of other activities on offer – from athletics to volleyball – though one moan that, despite the long list of offerings, effort is concentrated on rugby players.

Drama department beefed up by addition of a second specialist teacher. Music very good – hundreds of students get involved, everything from individual lessons to school orchestras and choirs, productions and after-school clubs. Duke of Edinburgh very strong and completion rate good. Fantastic trips, sports tours in Europe, footballers to David Beckham Academy, Gifted and talented regularly off to special events. Always loads going on and students encouraged to give it all a go – 'The opportunities here are second to none,' said one parent. Everyone does some community work, eg in a retirement home, other school, or hospice.

Mrs Cullum says, hand on heart, Heathside has the best links with industry and business she's ever known – certainly the effort is huge here: for example Glaxo Smith Kline helps with science and BP sends over 30 staff for a work experience day, conducting mock interviews with students, mentoring and giving help with CVs etc. Lots of (Ofsted highly praised) governors drawn from local businesses. Geographically fortunate, also has links with local businesses like Mercedes, Honda, McLaren.

Background and atmosphere: A happy school where staff are committed and students generally enthusiastic. Despite large numbers not a scary place for a tiny year 7 – friendly and caring, though over-crowded: most of the buildings date from 1966, when the school was built for just 500 students (students are rather buffeted along the corridors). It's a bit grotty in places, but not much that some plaster and paint couldn't fix and not because nobody cares – rather it's a classic case of a school being under-funded and/or prioritising elsewhere. A £6.5 million building programme is scheduled for completion in 2016 when school returns to eight forms of entry; science labs and PE changing rooms already upgraded.

School tries to cope with high numbers by a system of dual break times and having just a short lunch break ('Helps keep order,' agrees one mother) and some teaching is done in the hall. 'It's not the best environment,' says another. Ms Cullum not delighted with our previous description of 'scruffy and unkempt' – 'We spend a lot of time trying to improve what we have got and I'd like that taken out,' she says. But it is a factor that parents might note, though evidently, given the high standards in other areas, not a deal-breaker for those clamouring to get in. 'You overlook the shabbiness of the buildings when you see the children's happy faces,' said one mother.

The school's situation is better, down a quiet lane, opposite a cemetery and playing fields, surrounded by trees. No access down the lane for drivers at school start and finish times – parents are asked to drop at the top. Fifteen minutes from station, lots walk – the lane is awash with a sea of students in their cobalt blue blazers at the start and finish of the day.

A good feeling of community around the place – echoes of a primary school atmosphere where key staff know the students and really engage with them. 'The children must believe they can do what they want to do,' says Ms Cullum. 'We tell them they can achieve whatever they want.'

Pastoral care and discipline: All good and recently revised. Dedicated, non-teaching student support staff on hand for administration in this area, eg contact with parents, monitoring attendance and dealing with emotional issues. Parents happy that school is responsive and proactive about any issues raised.

As everywhere, a few difficult pupils, but not huge numbers and the school has a reputation for trying hard with them. It's strict but fair and sanctions are explicit. Full time exclusions have halved in the last couple of years – it's taken seriously. For example, students in isolation were previously based in a room on a main corridor, attracting too much of a buzz – they've now been moved right out of the way and have no chance to revel in their notoriety. The school's code of conduct, 'Give respect/gain respect', is well known to all. The 10-strong senior leadership team is seen around the place, not remote.

Generally pupils' behaviour and attitude to learning are good – it's OK, even cool, to be clever here. School repays that with ethos of 'listening to the student voice'. Head girl and boy, prefects and house system all recently introduced. Successful mentoring programme. Pupils fairly smart – no uniform in sixth form.

Pupils and parents: Middle class, reflecting local area. Lots could afford to send their children privately but choose Heathside instead – whole families go through. Equal numbers of boys and girls – a friendly bunch, motivated to achieve. Engagement from parents is good, for example 60 plus to a recent presentation on introduction of house system and in recent parent/governor elections six applicants for one vacancy. The five unelected candidates all went on to ask how they could help the school in other ways, prompting Mrs Cullum to think about developing an area where parents can offer support somewhere between governors and Friends of Heathside, the PTA. Parents raise a huge amount of money for the school, at the same time PTA offers an enjoyable social aspect with usual mix of quiz nights, parties, murder mystery events and so on. Recently their funds paid for refurbishment of reception and new projectors in classrooms – necessary as fewer than half have interactive white boards.

Entrance: A real scrum to get in here from Weybridge, Walton and Hersham area. Parents prepared to go down the private route will try their luck here before shelling out fees. Average of 700 plus applications for 210 places. At 11+ students join from up to 20 primaries, but predominantly from Ashley C of E (Aided), Cleves School, St James C of E. Strong links with its primary feeders – employs staff to go into them on a weekly basis. Otherwise usual sibling and distance criteria in operation. Reduced from eight to seven form entry in an effort to sort out overcrowding; numbers going back up in 2016, as the current primary school bulge reaches it. Currently selects one tenth of intake on basis of aptitude in music, sport and science and technology (known as 'challenges').

To join the sixth form, students need five A* to C GCSEs, including at least a B in subjects for A level – recently some 25 external applications.

Exit: Up to half leave after GCSEs. Sixth form leavers to a range of universities. In 2013 two to Oxbridge, ten per cent to Durham and others to Nottingham, Southampton, Leeds, Birmingham, Manchester, Bristol, Loughborough and more.

Remarks: A happy school with high standards. Unpretentious, offering its students a good all-round experience. Winning combination of committed staff and eager students – state education as it should be.

The Henrietta Barnett School

Central Square, London, NW11 7BN

• Pupils: 690 girls; all day • Ages: 11–18 • Non-denom • State

Tel: 020 8458 8999
Email: admissions@hbschool.org.uk
Website: www.hbschool.org.uk

Acting headteacher: Mandy Watts is holding the fort following the departure of Oliver Blond to head Roedean. The new head, Mrs Del Cooke BSc MBA NPQH (early fifties), will take over in September 2014. She is currently head of Sir William Perkins School in Surrey. Maths graduate with MBA in educational management, her broad experience covers the comprehensive system, sixth form college, adult education and boarding at Cranleigh, where she was head of maths, housemistress and finally deputy head. Interested in music, she plays a number of instruments, including self-taught bassoon. Married with three sons.

Academic matters: Consistently top or very near the top of the A level league tables, Henrietta Barnett seems to achieve that position without any of the obvious pressure found elsewhere. 'It's very uncompetitive,' said one parent. 'It's much more about collaboration and co-operation.' In 2013, 95 per cent A and A* at GCSE, 77 per cent A*/A and 95 per cent A*-B at A level. Dedicated band of long-serving teachers teach clever and motivated girls. Most do nine or 10 GCSEs, four or five AS, three or four A2s. Results strong across all subjects. A good range of languages. French and German for all in year 7, Latin for all in years 8 and 9. Plus ancient Greek and the recently added Spanish. The school has updated the curriculum in a number of other ways, bringing in drama in the early years and enrichment courses at A level. The bias at A level is currently towards maths and the sciences, though French and English have a healthy representation. The school wants to improve the balance. Goodly amount of homework – 'But they're not driven hard. It's the engagement with other people that makes them think. They should be excited in the classroom.' Three form entry. Class size 24-31 in early years – with no setting except in maths – falling to 10-13 in the sixth form.

Games, options, the arts: Possibly not the most sporty school and certainly somewhat handicapped by its restricted grounds. However, 2011 saw the opening of a large multi-purpose Astroturf court in the newly landscaped grounds for netball, hockey, football and volleyball to be played on site. Four tennis courts, two polished but petite gyms, a new fitness suite with a range of exercise equipment and a variety of pitches available on the nearby Hampstead Heath extension. Two double periods of games a week, with a wide variety of exercise alternatives, including golf, swimming, rock climbing, orienteering, fencing, box exercise, yoga, Pilates and dance.

Has music college status (with English as a subsidiary). 'This is a very clear area of excellence and part of the majority of children's experience, which goes beyond subject teaching.' Very active music department. Specialist music house for peripatetic lessons, with its own music library. Eleven or 12 music groups meet each week, with teachers and pupils playing together. Music status brought new performance space, a music technology suite, a band room and a rehearsal space for rock music.

Previous head, with his wide experience of the independent sector, made a determined effort to broaden the extracurricular offering, with more drama, inter-school debating with local independent schools – 'The girls can be a bit shy and it helps to build up their confidence' – plus an artist-in-residence working on site all year. 'You need to work at building up confidence, self-esteem and achievement beyond the academic. They will all leave with good qualifications but we have to teach them how to make a success out of life.'

School trips, through each subject department, take every year group out once a year. French and German exchanges. Lots of day trips. Founder's week, held in the summer, provides an entire week of outings. Own field study centre in Dorset, which every pupil visits for one week during their early years at the school.

Background and atmosphere: Founded in 1911 by formidable social reformer Dame Henrietta Barnett, who wished to establish a school to educate bright girls regardless of their means. Housed in architecturally stunning Grade II* listed buildings by Sir Edwin Lutyens, the school sits, like a minor stately home, in a calm and soothing sea of green. The floors are polished parquet, the windows as high flying as the pupils, and the overall effect is of light and airy rooms straight out of an Angela Brazil novel. Nonetheless, parts of the building are fairly down at heel – the result of a long shared ownership with the local adult education institute. The school is gradually reclaiming the territory and buffing it up. 'The building is beautiful and the girls are very proud of it but it's not entirely fit for modern purpose.' A £7.5m government grant paid for the complete refurbishment of the science wing, and a music and drama school and art and DT centre opened in 2011. The school is now even more desirable.

Pastoral care and discipline: 'They're very well behaved and always do their best. Discipline is hardly needed here.' Polite and friendly girls are treated as adults from the word go, rules are explained and pupils tend to live up to the high expectations. Elected student council – which helps choose the head. Tutors in sixth form for groups of 10, seen individually to ensure problems, both academic and pastoral, are dealt with promptly. Junior and senior school have their own assembly halls for non-denominational assemblies, plus twice termly whole school assemblies.

Pupils and parents: Girls bright, curious, well-supported and very keen to learn. When the school was founded the intake was largely local but, since the arrival of league tables, the catchment has broadened considerably (now a parent-run bus service to cater for those who can't easily get here by the restricted public transport). Wide ethnic mix – about a fifth Indian and a fifth white, the rest from serendipitous backgrounds. Well below average number on free school meals. Girls work unusually well together. 'There really are no cliques here,' said one parent with a daughter in the sixth form, but after-school social life is not necessarily as vibrant as elsewhere.

Entrance: One of the most competitive entrance tests in the country with 1000+ girls applying for 93 places. NB Register by late July; tests in September. Two papers: verbal and numerical reasoning, and English and maths extension questions (this second paper is only marked for the top 500 performers in the reasoning test). 'It's fairly straightforward, but we do try to challenge the most able'. Pupils come from 50-60 primaries. A further 40-45 places (with approximately 100 applicants) in the sixth form with six A grade GCSEs minimum requirement plus As in intended A level subjects. Girls coming up through the school must also meet this requirement.

Exit: Around 10 per cent leave after GCSE to go on to larger (co-ed or independent) sixth forms. Eighteen to Oxbridge in 2013. Lots of medics, dentists and biomedical scientists. Specialist UCAS adviser helps girls through their university applications and helps raise expectations of what can be achieved – 'We want to keep the blinkers off'.

Money matters: A grant of £7.5m has provided a music and drama school, an art and design & technology school and

refurbishment of the science block. Recent refurbishment of maths, English and history departments has been completed as well as newly landscaped grounds and multi-purpose games area. An active PTA and a parental support scheme to which many parents regularly donate.

Remarks: One of the top academic state schools in the country, providing a gentle, inspiring education in a wonderful setting for very clever girls.

Hereford Cathedral School

Linked school: Hereford Cathedral Junior School

Old Deanery, The Cathedral Close, Hereford, HR1 2NG

- Pupils: 505 boys and girls; • Ages: 11–18; • Christian Foundation;
- Fees: £12,270 pa; • Independent

Tel: 01432 363522
Email: admissions@herefordcs.com
Website: www.herefordcs.com

Headmaster: Since 2005, Mr Paul Smith BSc. Originally a zoologist (undergraduate at Manchester, postgraduate at KCL), his first teaching post was at Rugby, followed by stints at King Edward's School Birmingham and as head of science at Haileybury, then second master and acting head at Portsmouth Grammar School. A softly spoken, friendly, but determined character. Married with two daughters.

Works hard at getting to know every child and speaks of teaching as a 'humbling experience'. Insists on the importance of staff respecting pupils and not becoming 'myopic' about children who don't fit a particular mould. Emphatic about the importance of strengthening relationships through extracurricular activities. Pupils say he is 'nice, funny, witty and approachable'. Staff say he is 'calm and considered – you can ask him anything'.

Very keen that the school should be 'all round' – not, for example a music academy or languages specialist. Looking to broaden the horizons of the school and has introduced a small number of international homestay boarding students in the sixth Form

Academic matters: Strong academically, with 51 per cent A*/A and 76 per cent A*-B at A level in 2013 and 60 per cent A*/A at GCSE. At A level, English, modern languages, history, art, music and RS all do very well. Good results in sciences too – no really weak areas. Nice range of A levels – the usual suspects plus Latin, history of art, philosophy and ethics.

As well as receiving half termly grade reports for effort and achievement, with target grades included from year 10, pupils have to fill in a self assessment form every term that is completed alongside their reports – something parents value highly. Staff say this is not a crammer and that the range of abilities is reasonably wide. Nonetheless expectations are high.

All students take maths (top sets take two AS modules in year 11), two English, and short course RS as compulsory GCSEs. Some 60 per cent take triple award science and the remainder dual award. The vast majority take French or Spanish, although a handful use the curriculum time for learning support. An additional three subjects are chosen from a range of options, GCSE Japanese is offered as an extracurricular addition, and the school is about to introduce Mandarin.

Interactive white boards in most classrooms, school email used to set and receive work – although traditional means are also used, and there is good access to PCs within school for those who wish to use them, including a dedicated area in the sixth form centre. A well-stocked library with its own small IT suite and a galleried, silent study area. Welcoming and evidently well used, also the venue for the school's book clubs, debating club and film club.

Learning support is well organised with all children MIDYIS tested on entry and supported as necessary, either within class or small group withdrawal. A sense of 'open door' for any wanting assistance. Pupils say they can go into the learning support unit for 'anything and everything'. A handful of International students in the sixth form, all of whom are tested on entry, have EAL timetabled into their week.

Games, options, the arts: Art, music and design are simply outstanding here. The A level results (100 per cent A*/A grades in art in 2013) speak for themselves, and the quality of work on display is excellent, varied and innovative. Complemented by a small but very well-resourced history of art department. Beautiful, naturally lit studio for the use of sixth formers and large light rooms for the lower years. Textile work is also beautiful.

At the other end of the design spectrum, the DT workshops (for both resistant materials and electronics) are well kitted out. Some interesting project work, and DT seems to have been fairly successfully sold to the girls, who make up around 25 per cent of the GCSE cohort.

Music is a central part of school life. The school remains the choristers' school for the cathedral but aside from that there are masses of choirs, chamber ensembles, jazz bands and piano trios as well as a music technology club. About half of all pupils take instrumental lessons, and the school is a choral power to be reckoned with. The senior girls' choir (Cantabile) was the winner of the senior children's choir section of the Llangollen International Musical Eisteddfod in 2012.

Sporting success is seen as important but participation is also perceived as a means of increasing pupils' confidence and strengthening relationships. Successful teams fielded in rugby (two Welsh U18 players in recent years, cricket (a number of county players – the girls' cricket team have played at Lords several times in the last few years reaching the finals of Lady Taverners indoor cricket competition), hockey (boys and girls – county and regional players), netball, rounders (two England players) and tennis. Football has also now been introduced for boys and rowing is popular too. Large and well-equipped sports hall. Fencing and swimming also available as options. Spacious, well-maintained sports fields are a 15 minute walk from the cathedral green (slight moan from pupils who have to walk there and back); netball courts are close, though not actually on site.

Unusually, CCF is compulsory in year 10, and many stay with it into the sixth form. It runs a huge range of courses including leadership, sailing, gliding and diving. There is a regimental dinner, summer camps, annual field days. The school also runs an annual trek for year 12 students to the Annapurna range in Nepal where it supports a local school. D of E also well supported.

Extracurricular clubs in just about everything – including mycology, Japanese, New Testament Greek and (reassuringly) board games. Definitely a school where all interests are catered for.

Background and atmosphere: Herefordshire is a deeply rural county, and Hereford itself has something of the quiet county town about it. It is impossible not to feel slightly removed from the cut and thrust of the 21st century here. The school, originally for choristers of the 12th century, is set around the stunning cathedral green, and the splendours of the cathedral lend a special flavour to the place. That connection (the chaplain is a minor canon of the cathedral, as well as teaching full time) gives the school an implicitly Christian flavour and pupils clearly appreciate the depth and beauty of the place.

Quite traditional in feel. Monitors (prefects) wear gowns to chapel, as do academic staff. Services are held four times a week in the nave, and much of the musical and artistic excellence of the school seems to feed off the cathedral tradition of creative and artistic expression. Good spaces between the buildings, which are a combination of listed glories and more modern blocks (such as the sports and dining halls). But for all the leafy tranquility, the school is a very busy place, with lots to do, lots going on, and great enthusiasm from top to bottom about the possibilities 'out there'. One of very few schools whose pupils can claim to have founded a charity with a national ambit (The Little Princess Trust). And there is another under construction. Pupils evidently feel that not only do they have a responsibility to do the right thing, but also that they have the capacity to make a difference.

A very pervasive family atmosphere – the school runs from 3-18, so lots of siblings, many parents are Old Herefordians, and many staff educate their children here, so the community is remarkably tight.

Pastoral care and discipline: Pastoral care is evidently a very integrated part of school life – four school houses, each with eight tutors, so tutor groups are small. Academic staff are positively encouraged to run extracurricular activities and to strengthen relationships and pastoral links through them. Parents are encouraged to email academic and house staff with any queries, and say that any concerns are dealt with 'instantly', and 'children are kept too busy to have time for cyber bullying'.

Pupils say there is no problem with reporting bullying and getting it sorted out if it arises, but that it is rare. They also say that the school system of detentions is applied consistently, but that need of it is infrequent. Staff say they have very little to deal with on the disciplinary front.

Pupils and parents: Pupils are an absolute delight – very supportive of one another, articulate and appreciative. Comfortable in their own skin, but not full of themselves. Extremely positive about the school and proud of their achievements, but no trace of entitlement or arrogance – if they are a little on the quiet side one gets the impression that this is a result of not having to shout in order to be heard. Parents are a combination of local farmers, businesspeople and professionals. Many attended the school themselves. Busy, supportive PTA. Parents say, 'All children have something special – and here the teachers help them find it', 'The school builds self confidence' and 'identifies needs quickly', both academically and pastorally.

Entrance: Selective, but with Herefordshire school numbers in a demographic dip, cannot afford to be hugely so. Most of the junior school pupils end up here, and unless there is a particular cause for uncertainty, are offered a place without taking the entrance tests. All external candidates at 11 examined in English, maths and VR. There is also an interview for every candidate. Successful candidates at 11 can defer their place to 13+ if happy in a prep school elsewhere, and there is also a separate entry procedure at 13 (not CE). For the sixth form at least six Bs at GCSE and at least Cs in English and Maths GCSE are required plus references, interviews etc.

Exit: The majority stay past GCSE and into the sixth form though a few go to the local, and very well thought of, sixth form college. Four to Oxbridge in 2013 (from an upper sixth of around 65) plus lots to Russell Group – especially Bristol, Cardiff, Leeds, KCL. A good mix of subjects – including dentistry, physics, veterinary science, law, history, business and economics. A number too taking fine art and music. Not many into electronics or ICT.

H

Money matters: Academic scholarships worth 15 per cent of fees available at 11+, 13+ and 16+. Other scholarships worth 10 per cent of fees for music, sports and all rounders (also for art at 13+). A number of bursary awards and some Ogden Trust bursaries for science students joining the sixth form. Previously a direct grant school and actively fundraising to broaden access.

Remarks: Justifiably growing more self-assured, a school with a great deal to offer and an ethos of careful, thoughtful, nurture. Much to impress, with truly outstanding arts and music, a wide curriculum, a great sense of community service and genuine commitment to developing courage, confidence and a sense of adventure in even the quietest child.

Hermitage Academy

Cardross Road, Colgrain, Helensburgh, G84 7LA

• Pupils: 1,400 bpys and girls • Ages: 12–18 • Non-denom • State

Tel: 01436 672145
Email: enquiries@hermitageacademy.argyll-bute.sch.uk
Website: www.hermitageacademy.argyll-bute.sch.uk

Head: Since 2007, Mr Geoff T Urie (forties), who was educated at Paisley Grammar and read geography at Glasgow University. He first came to the school as depute head before spending a couple of years at Ardrossan Academy – 'I had to come back to move to the new campus'. He runs this conglomerate with a depute and staff of over 100: no apparent difficulty with getting new teachers. He is proud and welcoming and was pleased to spend some time with this editor, who dropped in out of the blue.

Academic matters: Scottish system. All do Standard grade English and maths (for which they are setted) plus personal and social development, PE and RE. Three sciences throughout. Courses on offer vary between foundation, general and credit levels – huge choice from graphic communication, hairdressing, home economics, motor vehicle engineering (City and Guilds), woodworking, as well as uniformed and emergency services (popular), terrific fashion and textile, design, health and food, plus product design, baby sitting and accounting, and all the usual subjects. Maximum class size 30, but in reality much lower – with half below 20. French, German and Spanish offered to exam level, Spanish and Italian lunch time clubs as well. Exam results show a pleasing number getting good grades.

IT everywhere, whiteboards and overhead projectors. Student planner and fairly strict homework expectations, can email queries to staff, much use is made of GLOW and HABIT revision programmes. Help on hand for weaker students – two dedicated teacher plus the support team (this is an inclusive school, with some pupils getting a mega amount of help) led by 'a DHT pupils' support and 11 principal teachers, as well as 10 principal teachers of guidance and a principal teacher of support for learning'. Learning support either short sharp bursts out of class ('the kick-up' room), or assistance during lesson time. IEPs where necessary and good links with Get It Right For Every Child, the local partnership agency which oversees what happens next.

Games, options, the arts: Splendid sports hall with electronic scoring, two proper gyms with ropes and strong gymnastic following; terrific dance studio, weights room – 'busy all the time'. No pool (uses local one, but currently under refurbishment), two football pitches plus Astroturf, tennis courts. A couple of football players spent some time training with AC Milan – which has to be a senior mega moment. Sports activities are, in the main, extra-curricular – massive amount

nonetheless (funded through the Active Schools programme), with senior pupils helping official coaches and enthusiastic (and successful) involvement in football, swimming, athletics and golf. Three Peaks race, Young Enterprise (rather jolly tartan recently accepted and registered with the Scottish Tartan Authority, scarf currently on sale, but watch this space). Activity days and rash of clubs.

Big school, big bands: symphony, wind, brass, swing with samba on the cards. Choirs, and hefty trad Scottish in/output with fiddlers, Gaelic choir and pipe band. The best fabric ever, ditto fashion design. Drama – latest offering Casualty Jane. Amazing record of charitable activity. Has strong links with Comenius and different European schools – Germany, the Czech Republic, with loads of trips in every discipline.

Background and atmosphere: Drop dead gorgeous modern building in stark black and white opened a few years ago – built to hold 1,700 and not currently full. Overlooks the Clyde – all singing and dancing. Long wide passages, two huge spaces (architects of new school builds always seemed to economise here) with a splendid ground floor dining hall: holds 1,000 and, when we visited just as lunch was finishing, it was quiet, orderly and remarkably tidy – the cleaners had perhaps one small waste paper basket full of detritus; stage at one end with ancillary green rooms and storage, professional lighting and rather posh red plush curtains. Pupils operate a swipe card system which disguises any free school meal stigma. Glorious assembly hall above (seats 1,300, sound-proofed and used for exams as well), stunning views with amazing decorative mega pipes at roof level – probably nothing more mundane than the central heating system but it looks 22nd century stuff.

Terrific library with cunning circular window roof lights (head always coming in and turning lights off in the interests of economy, forgetting that those furthest from the windows are then studying in the dark). Library pupil-led – everything state of the art, can't fault it. Vast car parking area, see-through bike sheds hold 80 bikes (but you can't smoke behind them). Head had rather hoped that the local fuzz would turn up to 'keep an eye' at admission time, and is not quite sure whether he is pleased or disappointed that they refused: not enough naughtiness apparently. Traditionalists are happy that the old HS (Hermitage School) shield has made the transition, as has the wheel of the Lucy Ashton, which for so many years greeted pupils at the previous academy.

Pastoral care and discipline: Managed by group of depute head teacher and heads of every year, plus dedicated guidance teachers. Strong PSE; pro-active anti-bullying strategy in place with all newbies being given an anti-bullying card, 'It's OK to talk'. Sixth year pupils active in Friends Against Bullying – their photographs are displayed on notice boards, and oodles of anti-bullying programmes in place. The odd exclusion. School uniform for all – prefects wear red ties.

Pupils and parents: Everything from farmers to local business folk, to Forces personnel based at nearby Faslane – inclusive in every possible way. Strong parent-teacher body.

Entrance: Some placement requests, otherwise school has 10 linked primaries from as far as Arrochar, Cardross and Kilgreggan; also has 'close links' with Parklands School in Helensburgh, which is Catholic – pupils might well be expected to attend an RC secondary RC, but 'find it more convenient' to come here. Operates a 'hooked on Hermitage' programme – masses of to-ing and fro-ing by learning support and subject teachers; all P6/7 pupils spend two days at Hermitage in June to meet their guidance teacher and S6 buddy, plus two pupil/parent evenings throughout the year. Serious input into changeover – works well.

Exit: Impressive careers advice which extends beyond a pupil's time at school. Currently some 170 pupils in sixth year – about 85/90 per cent stay on after Standard grades, of whom a further 90 per cent stay on thereafter. Latest statistics show that some 60 per cent either went into further or higher education.

Money matters: Funding available for essential (or non essential, come to that) trips for those who couldn't otherwise afford it.

Remarks: Impressive new build, inclusive school – appears to work exceeding well.

The Hertfordshire & Essex High School and Science College

Warwick Road, Bishop's Stortford, CM23 5NJ

- Pupils: 1,075, mostly girls; boys in the sixth form • Ages: 11–18
- Non-denom • State

Tel: 01279 654127
Email: admin@hertsandessex.herts.sch.uk
Website: www.hertsandessex.herts.sch.uk

Headteacher: Since 2009, Mrs Cathy Tooze, previously head of Hadleigh High School in Suffolk. Positive and authoritative, her manner is relaxed, though you feel she can be firm when the situation demands. Her husband works in telecoms and they have two teenage sons and a young daughter, which helps her to see things 'from the parental perspective,' she says. She spends her leisure time with the family, who particularly enjoy watersports and skiing holidays together.

Academic matters: A very successful school, a particular feat given the fact that it is totally non-selective. Eleven GCSEs the norm and 81 per cent 5+ A*-C, including English and maths in 2013. 'Quality rather than quantity,' says the head, who puts the exceptional grades down to 'exceptional standards of teaching and learning' and the very positive work ethic. But, she adds, 'This is a caring school, not an exam factory.'

The traditional curriculum certainly works well for the students, many of whom are of an academic bent, but modern aspects too and new technology is embraced where appropriate. Teaching is very hands-on. Pupils are set targets with progress tracked three times a year and each has a mentor to get them back on course if they should stray. 'This is how we notch up the outcomes,' reveals the head. 'We can raise expectations just that little bit higher every time.'

Generously staffed, and good admin support allows teachers to spend more time in the classroom and less on pen-pushing. All teach their degree subject, which, the head says, means they are focused, committed and keen to broaden the students' experiences through a huge variety of trips and extra-curricular activities. As a science specialist college, it's maybe no surprise that science success is high – many take triple science, which stands them in good stead for A levels. Languages are growing in popularity. French is setted from year 7 and compulsory until year 9, and Mandarin has recently been introduced. Working closely with the local Polish community to enrich the curriculum further. Media studies and sociology are attracting students' attention and, for many, the technologies are a good contrast to the more academic classes. Top sets can number as many as 28, but the lower classes are often much smaller.

Very wide choice of subjects at A level, particularly as part of the local consortium, which pools its resources to host minority interest subjects. In 2013, 80 per cent A*-B grades. Herts & Essex offers dance, further maths and German. Although

undoubtedly a timetabling nightmare, this scheme allows for great breadth. Psychology is another popular A level option. Sixth formers have a half-day of enrichment on Wednesday, which includes D of E, pilates, extra languages and sport, and also listen to struggling readers in year 7.

Assesses the needs of all students on entry and monitors their progress closely throughout their time. A whole school approach to learning support – able, gifted and talented students are identified, in addition to those who will benefit from individual learning plans, plus differentiated learning materials to provide educational challenge for all students. Where a student has a particular need (for example, a visual impairment) learning materials are adapted and staff training put in place, so that all teachers are fully aware of the adaptations they can make to their planning and preparation to ensure access to the curriculum. Four teaching assistants timetabled to offer both in-class support and some small group literacy sessions. Ground floor access is good throughout the site. Where some of the school buildings are inaccessible to wheelchairs above ground level, rooming considerations are taken into account when timetabling.

Games, options, the arts: Sporting facilities are good and the students take full advantage of them. Netball is a strength – girls recently represented the east of England, coming third in the under-16 national championships. Tag rugby, pilates, yoga and judo are popular and indoor rowing is an unusual forte. Sixth formers continue with their interest in sport and the boys compete well on the football and rugby fields. Hard courts for tennis, netball and basketball, four rounders pitches plus a football pitch onsite, as well as a 25m indoor pool and dance studio. Has its own large playing fields with hockey pitches and a grass running track five minutes' walk away.

Art taken seriously – makes use of the Rhodes Centre in the town for exhibitions, raising the school's local profile. Work displayed in public places throughout the school too. Large numbers attend art clubs and workshops. Good use made of proximity to London and Cambridge, with their wealth of art galleries – visits by students independently, or with their families, also encouraged. Students are inspired to produce work that is original, personal and skilful; A level options in art, art and design and fine art printmaking.

A separate music school across the road is a hive of activity. One of four local schools to give entry to eight pupils who show exceptional musical aptitude at age 11 – 'It's about an innate aptitude for music, not experience,' says the head. Plenty of other students with musical ability entering through usual channels, though – 10 per cent learn an instrument. The head describes the concerts as 'breathtaking'; several choirs, an orchestra (the only one in a state school in the town) and ensembles for regular playing practice.

An International school – a genuine focus on global citizenship. Close links with a school in Uganda – teacher exchanges and an annual trip for year 13s. New similar arrangement with a school in India, thanks to student fund-raising. Leadership partnership status, which involves staff, students and the community in sharing good practice. Benefits include staff mentoring, coaching programmes and many student leadership opportunities.

Background and atmosphere: Dating back to 1909, the original buildings, in a leafy residential road just a mile or so from the town centre, have the feel of a grammar, though in fact The Bishop's Stortford Secondary School for Girls was opened to prepare girls for a career in teaching for a fee of £3 a term. In 1944 fees were waived and the school was granted self-governing status by King George V, who presented a portrait of himself that hangs in the impressively panelled school hall to this day. New teaching blocks have been added in the intervening years and a house over the road was acquired to make a very suitable music school.

Sixth form study rooms, English classrooms and an exhibition space added recently, but no more expansion on this site, as planning permission is being sought for brand new buildings, in conjunction with the boys' Bishop's Stortford High School, on green belt land in the town. Local residents unkeen. With a burgeoning local population, a need for a new location, points out the head, and the planned huge swimming pool and eight-court sports hall will also be available for community use. The intention is for the girls' and boys' schools to remain discrete entities in separate buildings, and although a whisper of sixth forms being merged, this is yet to be decided. But crossovers and joint provision to the benefit of all concerned, says the head.

Pupils are often canvassed on their opinions – recently asked if they wanted to change their distinctive uniform of brown kilt and beige jumper: the response was a big 'no', although the hemline was raised slightly. Sixth formers are expected to turn up in suitable business dress.

Pastoral care and discipline: Pupils known individually and closely mentored. Leadership is strong, with a head boy and girl as well as a swathe of prefects and a school council. Sixth formers are trained as peer mentors who support pupils lower down the school by acting as 'buddies'. A form per year for each of the five houses – a tradition – with competitions in sport and music, but no need for rewards for good behaviour, says the head – 'It's just expected'. She reports no real discipline problems, although an immediate one-day exclusion rule for use of bad language. A recent annual pupil survey showed they felt safe and were confident any bullying would be properly dealt with.

Pupils and parents: Parents realise that their children are spoilt for choice in Bishop's Stortford, with several very good state secondaries right on their doorstep. Herts and Essex is often picked ahead of the local fee-paying institutions, with the traditional approach to education and the largely single-sex environment a vote-winner. 'Students here want to learn,' says the head, and girls and sixth form boys strike one immediately as being focused and sensible, with a very savvy attitude to their studying and related future prospects. Very supportive friends' association, a pro-active governing body and a parental forum, which has real input into changes of direction and provides feedback. Parents are kept in touch with newsletters four times a term, and any requests to see the head are usually granted the next day.

Entrance: Except for musical and sporting stars, non-selective – regularly three times as many applicants as year 7 places. Medical and social grounds for entry are prioritised, then looked-after children, then siblings. Ten per cent of places are reserved for students with an aptitude for music and sport and their development is monitored throughout their school career.

Not many pupils leave, so very few spots open up in other year groups. New sixth formers occasionally bring a younger sibling with them. Any gaps that do materialise are filled from the 'continuing interest' list, in accordance with the admissions arrangements, with those with siblings already in the school jumping to the top.

Sixth form entry is by four pathways, depending on the number and quality of GCSEs amassed. Pathway one requires seven As or A*s for those who are on course for an Oxbridge or Russell Group exit. These usually number about 50 students, who sit five ASs and are mentored for the top universities. Pathway two is for the 60 students who have Bs and above – they have the choice of most of the A level subjects on offer. Pathway three, where Herts & Essex's own students are prioritised above external applicants, requires Cs and above at GCSE – they're offered about a dozen, less academic A level options, including health and social care, applied science and sociology. Pathway four is the diploma course, offered at local consortium schools. 'It's about setting children up to be successful,' says the head.

Applications from boys for year 12 are on the up, but the head is keen to cap the number admitted at a third of the sixth form population. The offer of philosophy and ethics, Latin, media studies and film studies combined and the science specialism draws them in, and many transfer from the local Anglo-European school, which only offers IB.

Exit: Roughly a third leave after GCSE. 'There's always a number of students for whom we don't have a provision at sixth form, but there are great courses elsewhere that suit better,' says the head. 'The focus is on getting to the university of choice and that isn't going to be accessible to everybody.' Straight A* students at GCSE are expected to go all the way to the top universities and all-round skills prepare some for Oxbridge entry – a handful every year (four in 2013), more than other schools in the town. Twenty per cent or so to Russell Group. Durham, Bristol and the US are favoured choices.

Remarks: A positive learning environment for hard-working girls and sixth form of both sexes, striking a balance between traditional values and a modern approach to individual attainment.

High School of Dundee

Linked school: High School of Dundee Junior School

Euclid Crescent, Dundee, DD1 1HU

- Pupils: 340 boys/335 girls • Ages: 11–18 • Non-denom
- Fees: Juniors £7,515–£8,775; Seniors £10,665 pa • Independent

Tel: 01382 202921
Email: admissions@highschoolofdundee.org.uk
Website: www.highschoolofdundee.org.uk

Rector: Since 2008, Dr John Halliday (early fifties) previously head of Albyn School (qv). Educated Abingdon School, followed by BA in Germany, linguistics at Exeter and PhD at Cambridge on German and Austrian satire in WW1. Married with three children, two now at university and one at school in Edinburgh, he misses the buzz of teaching but compensates in other ways. In a large school this takes positive effort – interviewing achievers in any field, helping with sport, playing in the orchestra (as an accomplished viola player) and attending all school occasions. After a baptism of fire at Rannoch, (now defunct) which he, none the less, remembers as 'inspirational', he initiated coeducation at Albyn School in Aberdeen with a resulting huge increase in numbers. Easy on the eye and quietly confident about his role in Dundee, despite plunging in with an almost completely new senior team (he had a hand in the appointments) and facing a triple anniversary for the school. 'Like Dundee,' he says, 'the school is modest about its achievements, which are considerable.'

The same is true of Dr Halliday. His first task has been to build a strong close management team, which includes his much valued bursar, and to improve internal communications through more regular meetings. Keen to develop an 'integrated curriculum' making the 'co-curriculum' more co-ordinated and giving a range of opportunities to take account of multiple types of intelligence, and to build teamwork, leadership and self reliance. 'Not just ticking boxes but trying to systemise' it all, while maintaining Dundee's high academic tradition. This should improve prospects, especially for middle ability students. A new performing arts centre is a high priority for him and space is available, though plans not yet formulated.

Academic matters: A Scottish school through and through, with high expectations, using Standard Grades and Intermediate 1 and 11 followed by Highers and Advanced Highers. A solid range of subjects with French from year P6. Results pretty good generally, and spectacular in modern languages, chemistry, history. Most teaching in mixed form groups but English, maths and languages are set. English department was delighted to have two finalists in the Pushkin Prize for short stories. The take-up in French, Spanish and German has improved and is outstanding in history, which, understandably, gets its fair whack of the S1/2 curriculum, not being reduced to a share of rota system as in many schools. English and maths Highers taken by the most with good grades. Not much take up for Latin and minimal for Greek (on offer, plus Russian in S6) but a good range of marginal subjects – sociology, technical studies, PE, managing environmental resources etc – together with some academic toughies – philosophy, economics – and respectable numbers taking all sorts of maths specialisms: stats, mechanics etc. Class sizes from three or four to mid-20s. Masses of techno equipment – PCs, internet link via Abertay University etc and trolleyed laptops for class use in the junior school. S6 can do enhancement courses at Dundee University.

Learning skills centre with three dedicated staff provides support and specialist teaching in junior and senior schools for 'mild to moderate specific learning difficulties' (dyspraxia, dyslexia, ADHD, mild Asperger's). Early intervention encouraged. Support also for the super bright. Few need ESOL which tends to be given in class at primary and rarely needed at secondary. Much-used library, with areas for different ages and activities and full time librarians on hand who also arrange multifarious library talks and activities.

Very good exam results in 2013: 58 per cent of Highers and 59 per cent of Advanced Highers grade A.

Games, options, the arts: Pupils mostly bused to games in the multi-million Mayfield sports centre, though swimming is in the Dundee University pool. Strong rugby, girls' hockey, netball and athletics, tennis, cricket etc etc. D of E has really flourished with 16 achieving gold. CCF, a pipe band – with girls as well as boys – riding and skiing teams (the latter swept the board at recent schools championships) are the tip of an iceberg of physical activities from line skating to golf.

Art department, chilly with a garret view of intriguing Dundee roof-scape, serves curriculum and co-curriculum using, for instance, the skill of the textile classes to teach the scarf making club, while the jewellery class – with boys as well as girls – gets help from the enthusiastic chemistry department in decorative fusing of metals. Music very strong with concerts in the town and a musical production biennially – Dido and Aeneas as a bit of a contrast to Tin Pan Alley! Numerous orchestras, groups and choirs.

Drama strong with productions at all levels. Art, music and drama all available as exam subjects up to Advanced Higher with some very good results, so we wait with baited breath for what they can do if the new creative arts centre materialises. Formidable debating in true Scottish school tradition helped by the fact that the debating coach also manages the Scottish schools debating team.

Background and atmosphere: This is school in the grand tradition of Scottish education, founded in 1239, making it over 770, and eventually receiving its charter from Queen Victoria in 1859. Princess Anne followed her great grandmother's example by visiting to mark the double celebrations 175 years on. The High School is a City 'treasure' and has a governing body drawn partly from the City's great and good, the 'Guildry' and 'Nine Trades', partly elected from among parents, past pupils etc and some co-opted for their skills.

The neo-classic, portico-ed façade, beloved of Scottish school architects (a little grubby) sports the celebratory banners designed by a sixth year pupil. Completely surrounded by some of Dundee's better buildings (including the newly opened McManus Gallery much used by the art department) it faces a huge half-moon of tarmac, elegantly railed, and fiercely patrolled by janitors to provide a safe recreation area during school-time but open to parents, who would have no hope of parking in Dundee at the end of the school day.

The impressive Doric front is flanked on one side by the 1880s Margaret Harris Building, once the girls' school, which now houses the juniors, and the on the other the (ex) Trinity Church, which provides a hall (not big enough for the whole school), the ground floor library and attic drama space.

Departments are cunningly grouped in a collection of buildings, some quite grand, gradually accumulated along Bell Street and curiously interspersed with courtyards, one of which sports tall, thin climbing wall. Roomy and light teaching rooms, plenty of space, though not much greenery. Pupils mill about, open, friendly, and happy to talk about their work. Some corners/staircases a bit dark and 'schooly' but most bright and clean, though neither corridors nor pupils are unnaturally tidy! Boys wear navy blue, while girls wear 'softer' grey blazers with a grey Dundee High tartan skirt. The tartan looks best as pinnies for the tinies. Blazers up to £90 in larger sizes, but a parents' thrift shop.

School recently acquired former post office building in Dundee's city centre, just yards from the campus, and plans to transform it into cutting-edge performing and visual arts centre housing music, drama, art and design departments.

Pastoral care and discipline: Four vertical houses, with continuity from juniors to seniors, run by guidance staff, have two forms each in each year group, the guidance teacher being the first point of contact for pupils and parents. Despite freedom to go into town at lunch breaks, the rector reports far more phone calls from citizens complimenting the helpfulness of pupils than complaints. No spectacular problems but guidelines are clear – suspension for first offence for smoking and the like, while a pupil with drugs can expect to be expelled.

Pupils and parents: Some 50 per cent from Dundee, 50 per cent from Fife, Angus and Perthshire, up as far as Forfar and Blairgowrie etc, with five different bus routes. A mix of farmers, professionals and people working for universities and hospitals. Pupils can bring own cars but not drive others. Former pupils include William Wallace, AL Kennedy. Lord Cullen and Lord Ross, and more recently Andy Nichol, Mark Beaumont, Frank Hadden and KT Tunstall. BBC's Andrew Marr had a short spell in the juniors.

Entrance: By assessment at all stages, with two-thirds coming into seniors from juniors. Demand and waiting list not much hit by recession, though bursary applications are up.

Exit: Few leave post S4 and S5. Almost all to university, generally Scottish with a smattering of Oxbridge and other English ones.

Money matters: The very first school inspected and passed by OSCR (Scottish charity regulator), the school gives about £700,000 in bursaries every year (approximately 13/14 per cent of its annual turnover). Bursaries, all means-tested, are normally awarded to form 1 but applications from current parents in financial trouble will be considered. Stringent means-testing for all. Number of independent trusts which also give financial support to individuals in the school. No specialist scholarships for academic, art, music sport etc.

Remarks: Still a warhorse of a school, doing an impressive job for Dundee and its surroundings. The fine tradition of Scottish education is alive, well and living (independently and at a price) in Dundee. New developments eagerly awaited.

The High School of Glasgow

Linked school: High School of Glasgow Junior School

---

637 Crow Road, Glasgow, G13 1PL

- Pupils: 685 boys and girls, all day • Ages: 10–18 • Non-denom
- Fees: £9,228–£10,605 pa; • Independent

Tel: 01419 549628
Email: rector@hsog.co.uk
Website: www.glasgowhigh.com

Rector: Since 2004, Mr Colin D R Mair MA Cert Ed (fifties), who was previously depute rector here. A classicist, educated at Kelvinside Academy, St Andrews, Glasgow and Cert Ed at Jordanhill, thence to The High School in 1976. He became depute rector in 1996, having previously been head of classics and housemaster. Charming, affable and well-versed in the ways of the school, he reluctantly relinquished his teaching role when he became rector but 'would be keen to cover whenever the chance arises'. 'Nice idea,' he says, 'couple of classes when I can.' He would also be keen 'to help out on either the cricket ground or rugby pitch' and hoped that being rector wouldn't 'make him too remote' from the school itself' (not a chance, says this editor, who has met him on earlier visits to the school). He now finds himself on the touchline each Saturday, where pupils and parents alike 'get his views (on everything) instead of rugby'. Far from complacent, the school continues to outperform expectations. Mr Mair is seriously strong and sits on SLS, and represents SCIS and SLS on the UCAS standing group (which is enuff initials for anyone).

Academic matters: A thunderingly good school on all fronts. Eight Standard grades now the norm for all, though these are interspersed with Intermediate II: English, maths, the sciences particularly strong, though perhaps chemistry hasn't been returning quite so many As as, say, physics or human biology – but a thumpingly good department nonetheless. Strong and successful following in French, German, Spanish and Latin. Pleasing lack of 'studies', drama called drama (up to advanced higher) and not theatre studies, ditto classics (which of course may not be the same thing as classical civilisation) with varying numbers doing modern studies, business management, information systems and economics with equally varying results. Good to see fashion and textiles to advanced level, though tiny trickle, as with home economics, but tranches doing art and design with pleasing number of A grades. Occasional glitch but nothing to worry about. Geography and history notably high on the wow factor but impressive results in all disciplines, and not apparently too many problems with silk purses and sows' ears. In 2013 just over a third of Standard Grade pupils gained eight or more grade 1 or A passes. Eighty-four per cent of pupils gained five or more Higher passes (38 per cent grade A) and at Advanced Higher 80 per cent A/B (60 per cent A).

Streamed in maths throughout and English from S2, then banded for langs, bright pupils extended, five maths sets, Latin for all first two years, French and German throughout, Spanish offered at third year and as a crash course in the sixth year. Business management popular. Serious and successful representations as ever in last year's Olympiads and 58 awards in the intermediate maths challenge, including 17 gold, and 38 with 15 gold in the junior challenge. Fewer girls than boys doing Higher physics, though still a few. Stunning new lab conversion (all those flat roofs – though everything has to be well checked as school built – not on green field – but close to previous coal workings) with old labs amalgamated to provide both working and practical areas, Greenhouse re-attached to new biology lab on second floor; school offers human biology as well as the 'normal' option, and pupils can take this as a crash subject in their final year at school – useful for those entering the medical profession (Glasgow University is popular for medics). Dedicated sixth form labs where pupils can leave their experiments up and running (under supervision if required). Approx 30 per cent follow science-related courses. One of the best sixth form handbooks we have come across, complete with university entrance requirements and advice – other schools would do well to copy. Huge variety of subjects and options – sewing for all – fluffy toys and embroidered lined denim bags in the lunch hour. Max class size 26, with 20 for practical subjects.

Excellent and organised learning support throughout, with masses of liaison from junior school, and good follow-on in all disciplines. Head of learning support is also SQA special arrangements co-ordinator (extra time in exams et al), with mass of experience, she comes from the state sector, plus part-time colleague, double teaching, some drop in help, scribing, good record of tracking children with problems and following up. Dyslexic pupils from junior school teamed up with senior pupils for the first two years, to encourage and help them with any organisational difficulties and with homework etc. Impressive library, computers everywhere; dedicated for the fifth and sixth form only, during their study time, but all pupils can and do use them during their lunch break.

Games, options, the arts: School surrounded by 23 acres of games fields and car parks; masses of district, county, country players (Olympic representation) and tranches of representatives in almost every discipline. Regular rugby/hockey trips to Canada. Huge range of activities, including sailing, skiing (trips to the States popular) as well as D of E. Cultural trip to China in 2009 and visit to Cuba in 2010. Visits to elderly and strong links with local group of autistic children. Lots of charity projects, often house-based. Masses of popular clubs, lunchtime and post school. Our lunchtime trip round the school found a host of impromptu debaters, charity organisers and proper choir practices.

Impressive debating skills – silver mementos of previous glory all over the shop: The Observer Mace, the Cambridge Union, the Oxford Union and ESU. Regular finalists including ESU finalists last year. D of E enthusiasts and much encouragement.

Massive and exciting drama and music, trips all over the place. The former in super new purpose-built studio – always interesting to have the theatre on the first floor (drama very much a whole school thing, with the home economics dept doing costume and the art dept the scenery). Full-time teacher of drama. Mass of sponsoring – the Fraser of Allander lecture room, Wolfson Foundation in Science and such-like. Regular spectacular productions. 'really exciting music department', which has won chamber music awards in recent years. Smart new music practice rooms with mirrored walls. Choirs and orchestras abound, trips abroad, travelling for competitions and the like. Fauré Requiem in Paisley Abbey and orchestral/choral concerts in Glasgow University Chapel highly acclaimed. Lord (Norman) Macfarlane, who is deeply involved both with the school (at both levels) and with the Kelvingrove Art Gallery re-incarnation has involved each with the other, and High School pupils regularly took part in lunch time performances at Kelvingrove during 2009, when the organ was being re-furbished. Sparky art department with a gallery, but not much take up at higher levels – work is a serious matter in the west. Rector challenges this, saying 'an encouraging take up at Higher levels with pupils regularly going on to art colleges'. 'Art on the up'. Study skills for all plus time management, politics and interview skills in sixth form.

Background and atmosphere: Founded as The Choir School of Glasgow Cathedral in 1124, gained grammar school status during the 15th century and became a high school in 1834. Despite its high academic standing, school was closed by

Glasgow Corporation in 1976. An appeal launched by the High School Former Pupils' Club funded the new purpose-built senior school on the sports ground at Anniesland Cross, already owned by the FPs, and the new school opened the day after the old school closed – a triumph. The High School merged with the former PNEU dame school, Drewsteignton, in Bearsden, three miles away, now the junior school. New history, The Town School, by Brian Lockhart, just published, is detailed in the extreme, but even he did not appreciate that the original Drewsteignton (which formed the basis of The Junior Dept of The High School of Glasgow) was not originally a girls' boarding school (it was underwritten by this GSG writer's grandfather, so she has inside knowledge) but as a day school, with originally four pupils (my mother was one) and there were so little funds available, that pupils were taught to read and write on trays filled with sand!

The flat-roofed building at Anniesland has expanded considerably; with new additions sprouting all over the place (usually on the roof), though fortunately without any obvious loss of playing fields. Square split level assembly hall, artificial floodlit pitch, new stand complex which incorporates an impressive and well-used club house plus school dining room ('with caterer from heaven'). Sixth form area houses coffee shop and loud music as well as dedicated computers and work areas. School uniform for all, with girls in tartan skirts. The old house system remains, with each house having its own particular area in the school.

Pastoral care and discipline: Highly defined house system with colours but not names carrying on from junior school, siblings follow siblings into the same house. PSHE largely house-based with house staff playing a major role in extra-curricular and social activities. Transitus (11/12 year olds) pupils are lovingly tended with lots of back-up from junior school, particularly with learning support.

The Rector has enormous parental support and says that he 'is not complacent, but no problems'; no recent drugs cases, though a couple have been asked to leave in the past for going OTT, but certainly would expel if drugs were brought into the school. 'Staff beady eyed'. Suspensions for 'major offences'. Otherwise punishments range through sanctions, lunchtime detentions, clearing up litter (black bags) to school detention after school on Fridays.

Excellent blue booklet on promoting positive relationships – good PSE step guide, practised from the junior school. Jazzy new format school mag.

Pupils and parents: Ambitious, strong work ethos, almost half come from the affluent Bearsden/Milngavie complex and the remainder from different parts of Glasgow and outlying towns and villages, plus Helensburgh. Good trains from Coatbridge drop pupils at Anniesland. Bus system, some pupils from Ayrshire, the Trossachs (aka the edges of Argyll). Popular amongst the middle classes. Pupils can and do drive to school, large pupil car park. The geographic jump from the centre of Glasgow to the West End has changed the bias of the school, which now has fewer Asian and Jewish pupils (no synagogue in the West End), though a significant number from the South Side. Still large element of first time buyers plus one or two recently arrived Europeans. Previous pupils include Bonar Law, Sir John Moore of Corunna, Campbell Bannerman, Lord Macfarlane of Bearsden, Sir Teddy Taylor, Lady Cosgrove and Lesley Riddoch.

Entrance: At 10 and 11. Automatic from junior school (qv), otherwise three times oversubscribed – 50-60 applicants for approximately 32 places at Transitus and 30-40 for first year. 'Healthy uptake'. Odd vacancies in most years, own entrance exam, small number after Standard Grades, 'not many, really'. Fifth year candidates should have grade 1 passes in virtually all

their Standard grade exams, or As at GCSE if they have come from England. Sixth year entrance based on exam results and school reports.

Exit: Virtually all to degree courses all over, with a fairly high (90) percentage to Scottish universities, a regular few to Oxbridge (5 per cent in 2013) and about 15 per cent going elsewhere. About 10 taking a gap year this year (out of 94), but numbers rising. Work experience popular and all sixth year encouraged to undertake community service. No particular bias in career – medics, engineers, accountants, IT course, lawyers, possibly less enthusiasm for the humanities.

Money matters: School sympathetic to genuine problems, no academic scholarships but 50-60 bursaries awarded on a financial need basis (and Rector is pleased when he can help pupils of a suitably high calibre in financial need). On-going bursary fund.

Remarks: School on a roll, going from strength to strength. A remarkable success story – and, as we said before, a high school truly worthy of its name.

Highgate School

Linked school: Highgate Junior School and Pre-Prep

North Road, London, N6 4AY

- Pupils: 1075 girls and boys • Ages: 11–18 • C of E • Fees: £17,475 pa • Independent

Tel: 020 8347 3564
Email: admissions@highgateschool.org.uk
Website: www.highgateschool.org.uk

Head Master: Since 2006, Mr Adam Pettitt MA (late forties). Oxford modern and medieval linguist. Taught French and German at Eton, Oundle and Abingdon and was second master at Norwich School. Has French wife and school-age children and is quite the most interesting, eloquent and thought-provoking head this veteran GSG reviewer has met in many a long school visit. Propelled by a sharply focused and incisively articulated moral and educational philosophy, Mr Pettitt is spare, brilliant and energetic. He must be an exacting – though supportive – man to work for. His pupils can only benefit from his firm commitment to outreach to schools and to those without their advantages, to placing an understanding of language at the heart of modern languages and to educational values rather than exams and results. The results will follow where this approach leads. Parents are unstinting in their praise. The most inspiring head we've met in years.

Academic matters: Mr Pettitt has a refreshing disrespect for the bodies deserving of it: 'You choose the exam board on the basis that it will have the least distorting effect on the way you want to teach' – bingo! In 2013, 86 per cent A*/A at GCSE and 46 per cent A*/A at A level. IGCSEs now in English x 2, sciences, langs and history and many subjects now opt for the Pre-U as an alternative to A levels. This can only enhance the nature and quality of learning. English and langs the first to head this way. Mr Pettitt the 'de facto head of MFL' at the time of our visit so langs getting the oxygen they needed and number of takers is sure to rise. Mandarin now through to sixth form. Maths much the most popular A level and, with further maths, has impressive results. Also strong are English, art, Latin, all sciences and RS. Tiny numbers take theatre studies, Greek, classics, music – school does not offer music tech nor other popular 'modern' subjects eg textiles, psychology and lose a few post-GCSE on that account. Number of subject options (24) felt by some to be a little limited, given the size of the sixth form and some sixth would like more drama and art. However, good innovations include the 'knowledge curriculum' and 'critical method' courses. Lively, student-led conferences. Mr Pettitt takes all criticism on the chin and, given that after his seven years in post (at the time of our visit) over 70 per cent of the staff are his appointees, this – as everything else – is fast developing.

Head's inclusive approach is just that: 'The quality of the way you learn is critical and every child's experience is equally important... Every day is important – I am most interested in the way each one of us teaches and learns...' IBAC – Independence through Buzz, Aspiration and Collaboration the new acronym around the place. So this is not the school that was, nor the one people think they know. The fabric – see below – is radically changing and the character equally so. This encapsulated in the sane and sensitively individualised approach to SEN. The Victorian main building is not good for those with mobility problems though school says 'we will try to make it work by moving our routines and schedules as far as we can.' Director of learning support covers all three schools and is a renowned expert in autism. The support for all conditions and syndromes as they emerge is individual, tailored, supportive and 'concerned with management rather than labelling.' The very few with EAL needs are usually the very bright.

Games, options, the arts: Blessed with playing fields and space beyond the dreams of other London schools. If the educational philosophy and general zip in the place doesn't inspire you, the sporting facilities will. Girls' sport, some feel – school disputes – still catching up with boys'; football and netball still pre-eminent but plenty more on offer and played hard. Sports hall, pool, weights, Astroturfs, squash courts – it's all here. No country school could offer more.

Interior activities also privileged and currently being transformed by an enormous rolling building project that will add considerably to teaching space but also, it is hoped, to an eventual sixth form and arts campus. Drama and music thrive – many productions, concerts of all kinds and tours – art a little undemonstrative at the time of our visit but some lively colourful work around. Mills Centre provides studio and gallery space. Cultural life better displayed in the admirable school publications – professional-looking periodicals on history, politics, science, theatre and thought written and produced by pupils. Terrific range of clubs (they include 'vinyl and philosophy,' beekeeping, LBGT soc and feminist society), trips, exchanges and tours – extra-curricular is praised by many but not fully taken advantage of by all. 'I used to feel that some pupils' cultural references were limited to Arsenal: great though that club is, I want them to see and know so much more,' comments Mr Pettitt, happy to stress to parents that while these opportunities are on offer it is up to them to take them up!

Lots of charitable and outreach activities for both staff and pupils – several staff now working at local state schools as part of community partnership work. This very much part of the Pettitt ethos – outreach is not a box ticking necessity here but an essential part of what it is to grow into a valuing and valuable person.

Background and atmosphere: A school with an up and down history. Founded as the Free Grammar School of Sir Roger Cholmeley, Knight at Highgate, in 1565 – former pupils still known as Old Cholmeleians. Became Highgate School in the late 19th century – and no longer free. The chapel, undergoing terrific refurb at time of our visit, 'complete brick by brick restoration, new roof, stained glass windows repaired and cleaned, apse painting restored etc; lighting and heating to render God's work less chilly and gloomy,' in Mr Pettitt's inimitable phrases – and main buildings are 19th century. Some impressive bits – old gothic central hall with Norman arches, leaded lights, wrought iron balcony and cantilevered ceiling and splendid new Sir Martin Gilbert library in old assembly hall. A real library which, unlike so many schools' learning resource centres, actually has books in it, alongside all its rows of PCs, and an atmosphere to encourage concentration and study.

By the 1960s, the school buildings (some considerably less felicitous), including boarding houses, were spread over the heart of Highgate Village – the premier north London suburb whose denizens refer to it as 'the village' and who are, understandably, rather smug about living there. Charter Building (2012) adds new subject rooms in a five-storey glass cube. All very high tech – interactive whiteboards and PCs everywhere. The whole site is now a mix of the new, light, glass-bound, airy and stylish, and the old, rather shabby, small passages and dark areas along which school operates a clever one-way system – but all likely to look a great deal smarter and more coherent in the next few years. Much tramping up and down the hill between the main buildings and the Mills Centre, playing fields etc and each day sees orderly crocodiles with professional chaperones trailing along.

School suffered during the 70s and 80s and took time to recover its reputation. Girls joined the sixth form in 2004 and year 7 in 2006, and the whole school is now fully co-educational and fully rehabilitated. A Christian foundation and an inclusive one, with multi-faith assemblies and speakers from different religions on a weekly basis. House system – 12 houses – but no fanatical exclusive loyalty to these, rather a friendly rivalry in competitions etc and designed to encourage the mixing of year groups. 'It's a family school,' a parent told us. 'Not everyone is terrifically academic, though they really make the scholars work. They are very encouraging to everyone.'

Pastoral care and discipline: We saw only absorbed and concentrating classes with lively teaching. Discipline, as pupils gratefully pointed out, is not dependent on the whims of individual staff but 'whole school,' ie you know what is coming to you at every level should you transgress. Very little transgressing these days and we have seldom seen so few uniform infringements – everyone is smart.

Small classes 'very well-monitored,' say parents. 'It's extremely well-run,' we were told. 'We are kept fully informed and have lots of email contact with staff,' another told us. 'The teaching staff are so enthusiastic and they really care about my children,' another enthused. Occasional loutishness clearly frowned on by majority of pupils who are a civilised lot. 'We have sent all our children there – they're so different academically and in their characters – but all have been happy.'

Pupils and parents: From a wide area of north and more central London, though most live near, if not within walking distance. 'Not ruthlessly elitist,' as one parent put it but lots of city lawyers, accountants etc with clear idea of what they want from the school. Pupils friendly, happy and articulate. Most seem proud to be at the school and keen not to jeopardise their futures. Notable OCs include Rt Hons Charles Clarke and Anthony Crosland, Michael Mansfield QC, Johnny Borrell of Razorlight, Ringo Starr's son Zak Starkey of Oasis and The Who, Orlando Weeks of The Maccabees and DJ Yoda, Phil Tufnell, Sir Clive Sinclair, Alex Comfort, Nigel Williams, Sir John Tavener, Barry Norman, Gerard Manley Hopkins and Sir John Betjeman. Doubtless, Old Girl Cholmeleians shortly to make their marks.

Entrance: Wildly oversubscribed at every stage – on a scale we see most commonly with the grammars. Six hundred apply at 11+ for the 70 places available when the junior school pupils have been accommodated. At 13+, 180 compete for 25-30 places. At 16+, 120 for 30. At 11, around 60 per cent from state primaries and 40 per cent – mainly girls – from local preps. At 13+ mostly boys entering from the obvious preps – Arnold House, Devonshire House, The Hall, Keble etc.

Exit: Around a dozen, mostly boys, leave post GCSE to, mostly, Camden School for Girls, which has boys in the sixth. Around 90 per cent gain places at their first choice university – mostly Russell Group, Bristol and Birmingham being the most favoured; some now head to top US universities. Good numbers to Oxbridge each year. Economics, English and languages are popular subject choices.

Money matters: Scholarships – music and academic – at all usual entry points and now purely honorary. 'Much kudos, but not just to the particularly brainy but to those who exemplify scholarship (persistence, creativity, setting own agenda, leading learning in the classroom, originality),' stresses head. Bursaries up to the value of ten 100 per cent fees available each year and most go to those who get all or most of that amount. School makes extensive efforts via primary school visits etc to reach those who need to know.

Remarks: A new school in all but site and name – co-ed, modern, delivering a first rate education to the lively minds and limbs lucky enough to get in.

Hills Road Sixth Form College

Hills Road, Cambridge, CB2 8PE

• Pupils: 2,000 girls and boys • Ages: 16–19 • Non-denom • State

Tel: 01223 247251
Email: cwalker@hillsroad.ac.uk
Website: www.hillsroad.ac.uk

Principal: Since 2008, Mrs Linda Sinclair BA (early fifties). Languages and linguistics at Essex, followed by three years in banking. Retrained as a teacher with most of her career at Hills Road, teaching economics and business studies. Became deputy principal in 2003. Definitely not a big 'I am'. Instead a democratic, likable manager – someone who's able to field questions with a beguiling smile and placatory answer. Some new initiatives – nothing radical – coupled with a resolve to maintain high standards and keep this huge, fluid place running like clockwork. She says, 'The college caters for ambitious students,' and her intention is to ensure they're 'provided with the right tools for the next stage'. She keeps in touch with students by regularly visiting lessons, organising discussions with groups of students and attending extra-curricular events. She also does a small amount of teaching.

Academic matters: Nothing but praise for this side of college life – whatever they tell you, Hills Road is chosen first and foremost for its academic credentials. High expectations all round – a remark that 'A C grade really isn't good enough' sums up the thinly-disguised view of many. Bright, focused, super-keen young adults who relish a challenge. 'Firm but fair', well qualified staff. Lunch time surgeries in all subjects for extra help. Top notch facilities in every department plus trillions of computers. All in all, perfect ingredients for impressive results – 51 per cent A*/A, 80 per cent A*/B in 2013. Outstanding status awarded by Ofsted and regularly tops the league tables as the highest achieving sixth form college for points per examination entry.

Over 40 A level subjects on offer. Every student takes at least four AS subjects in their first year – seems to be very little give here. History is popular, but the crowd pullers are biology, chemistry and maths (which gets praise from everyone – 'They're always finding new material and addressing individual needs', 'There's always someone there waiting to offer help' and 'If I went into teaching I'd like to be like Mr X'). In their second year many still take four subjects.

Alongside core subjects, first year students start the Extended Project Qualification, which is completed in the autumn term of the second year. This is an opportunity for students to develop and realise an advanced level project entirely of their own devising.

At some stage during their time at Hills Road about a quarter of the students will seek help from the excellent study skills centre, which deals with everything from time management, handwriting and essay-writing skills to ESL, dyslexia and Asperger's syndrome. It also provides assistive technology, in-class support and timetabled sessions.

Games, options, the arts: Year 12 students must attend at least one enrichment session once a week – something for everyone and real appreciation for the level of choice. For the physically active, 30 different options – all the usuals plus the possibility, if enough interest, of rustling up provision for something new. Regular representation in national teams and a couple of Olympians (hockey and triathlon) and Paralympian (Goalball). Sizable cricket hall bedecked with droopy nets, five professional indoor tennis courts, sports hall, squash court, fitness suite bulging with muscles and, just a hop away, 10 acres of sports fields and a brand new pavilion. Alternatively drama (it flourishes in the small but perfectly formed Robinson Theatre funded by a millionaire old boy), music (range of ensembles and good facilities) or art, which regularly hosts an artist in residence.

Huge number of student-led clubs and societies, some funded by the student council – we fancied ultimate frisbee or global citizenship. Young Enterprise and community service going strong. D of E as well but, as students have until they are 26 to complete all the elements, it isn't clear how many actually go on and get gold.

Work placements in Germany for linguists coupled with worldwide visits and exchanges, including links with partner school in Mthatha, explain recent International Schools award, which acknowledges the effectiveness and diversity of links.

Background and atmosphere: One glance at the sophisticated, no expense spared prospectus and the message comes over loud and clear – this is 'niversity': nine-tenths university or, as one mum put it, 'university with someone still doing the washing'. These are students – the central area is the quad and the place to meet is the buzzy student café, which could sit quite happily in a shopping mall. Continual coming and going of the multitudes – students love the freedom of only having to be on site for timetabled lessons – makes a sense of cohesion or belonging difficult to achieve. Students say the first two weeks can be daunting, but guidance from day one ensures almost all come to flourish in this heady mix of independent learners. Many find it's the first time they can get something from 'school', whilst others have found friendship with like-minded souls – spods, boffs and swots don't have to keep their heads below the parapet: they can fly.

'We're not interested in the past – only the students' future,' said a big honcho, so we'll do the history bit. College started life in 1903 as a selective grammar – nearby Perse complained to the government and tried to get it closed down. Relaunched in 1974 as a co-ed college for 600 sixth formers. Subsequent ballooning to 2,000 now makes the place a giant, bright pond – the original buildings have been neatly linked to tasteful, well designed modern blocks. The main student social areas, The Hub and The Link (both recently refurbished), are now wifi enabled cyber cafés with modern décor, leather sofas and student artwork.

De luxe pluses are contacts with the university and a stream of celebrated speakers – Stephen Hawking, John Major, Lord Dearing, Zandra Rhodes, Sir Martin Rees, the Astronomer Royal, and Tony Juniper.

Pastoral care and discipline: So much is 'up to the student' and, although they 'won't let you drown', students have to take responsibility for their learning and post A level plans. Self-discipline is a prerequisite; subtle reinforcement comes from the super-efficient pastoral system based on daily email contact and 16 specialist tutors, who have offices in the student guidance centre. 'Luck of the draw which tutor you get' – the best are 'fantastically helpful' or 'always there for you while you cry'. No hope of swaps if things aren't quite so positive – one or two seem to 'only think about academic individuality' – but, as one pragmatist said, 'You only have to see them once a week, so you sit there and put up with it'.

Adult behaviour is expected and most meet expectations – strict rules re attendance for lessons and meeting of deadlines are made clear from the start and regular 'goofers' (non attenders, to you and me) who don't change their ways are 'helped to find alternative routes'. Concerns can be voiced through the student council, who've been consulted on most college rules – two members are on the board of governors. 'As there's not much missing', focus is on fund-raising for charity and social functions – freshers' disco and two annual balls are highlights of the year.

Pupils and parents: Mature, generally biddable bunch, who have academic aspirations. Some commute a considerable distance – buses stop outside and it's a 10 minute walk to the train station. Cyclists living over three miles away can apply for a termly £30 incentive to be green.

Some 85 per cent of students from maintained sector in and around Cambridge. The rest lured (finance and freedom oft quoted reasons) from independents (especially the Perses, Leys and Kings Ely). Parents (they're likely to sniff at Classic FM and laud Radios 3 and 4) are involved, committed and tremendously ambitious for their offspring. Former students include prominent government officials, Anil Gupta (director of the TV programme, Goodness Gracious Me) and Tom Heap (journalist and BBC presenter).

Entrance: Becoming increasingly selective – B or better in subjects or related subjects for proposed A levels ('better' is more realistic, given level of over subscription and academic credentials of most). Priority for those from the Cambridge 14-19 partnership area. Feeder schools are contacted to gauge applicant's suitability. Reference also required, with predicted grades, behaviour, level of commitment and ability to make the most of opportunities being key. Guidance (non-selective) interviews for all qualified in-area candidates (parents are included and are under no illusions as to how hard students will have to work) – a phenomenal feat, given the numbers. However not all entrants from outside the area (most come from within a 30 mile radius of the college) are interviewed.

Exit: Effective programme for budding medics, vets and dentists, plus full-time careers advisor and several tutors with relevant expertise. Almost all to degree courses at a wide spread of institutions – Leeds seems to be the new Nottingham. Good numbers to Oxbridge (lots make post-results applications) – admission tutors come in to talk to students. College will help with gap year arrangements and about a third take up the option. Small proportion don't last at Hills Road, but retention rates are well above sixth form college norms.

Money matters: The college has 'outstanding' financial status and has also been very successful in recent years in bidding for a number of QIA grants to support innovative projects and share good practice.

Remarks: Powerful, top of the range sixth form college. An exciting place, especially for bright, questioning go-getters who are ready for some independence. Not quite as fizzy for the faint-hearted or less than determined.

Hockerill Anglo-European College

Dunmow Road, Bishop's Stortford, Essex, CM23 5HX

- Pupils: 850; 310 board • Ages: 11-19 • Non-denom
- Fees: Boarding £10,629–£14,379; Day £0–£5,661 pa • State

Tel: 01279 658451
Email: admin@hockerill.herts.sch.uk
Website: www.hockerill.herts.sch.uk

Principal: Since September 2013, Mr Richard Markham, previously director of studies at Marlborough College. An Oxford historian and former international hockey player, he spent most of his career at Marlborough, where he led the introduction of the IB and taught history and history of art. He was also a deputy housemaster and master in charge of hockey.

Married with two children. He is also a former international hockey player who represented Wales. Continues to play hockey and enjoys cycling and golf.

Academic matters: One of the most successful comprehensives in the country. In 2013, 57 per cent A*/A grades at GCSE and 94 per cent of pupils got 5+ A*-C grades including maths and English.

A school of two halves – the sixth form is significantly different in composition to the GCSE years. Post-16 pupils who can't manage the high academic bar (minimum three As and three Bs in the subjects they wish to study) or prefer the narrower range of A level go elsewhere. That leaves about 50 per cent of those who come in at 11, topped up with a significant intake of local and international high fliers. Pupils at this stage select Hockerill because of its outstanding offering in the IB (it is the top IB state school in the country – an average point score of 34.6 in 2013 and 10 per cent obtained 40 plus points, excellent by any standards) and these are the type of pupils looking for a broad ranging and demanding education. Those who choose this route seem to love the stretch and demands it requires. 'IB rocks,' said one.

Hockerill is certainly not an easy ride at any stage and you would only be interested in the school if you had both a very positive attitude to hard work and to the study of modern languages. 'We are an academic school in an increasingly competitive world. We tell year 7 if you don't want to work hard and study hard, this is not the place for you,' says the head. Two languages are compulsory from the off, as is Saturday morning school – this is a boarding school after all – and there's prep a plenty (two hours a night by year 10). The Hockerill pupil profile is of the high-octane variety – 'A typical student here will take GCSE languages early and triple science, but will still manage to play college rugby, involve themselves in Big Band and do CCF,' says the head. 'They will be fully involved and totally knackered.'

Seven languages on offer – including Japanese and Mandarin – and 'immersion' plays a big part in the school's approach with subjects other than languages taught in a second tongue. In year 7, music is taught in French; in year 8, geography and history. Top linguists also undertake a three-week exchange in which they live with a local family and go to a local school. 'My daughter has now done two exchanges, one to Japan, which was fantastic,' said one parent. By year 8 almost all are fluent and early GCSE language grades in year 10 are all As and A*s.

The school follows the IB middle years programme, which means all pupils continue with a language, arts, and technology. In year 10, all undertake a personal project, demonstrating their ability to carry out independent research, and this project – on anything from cookery, to fashion, video, film – is used as part of their application for the sixth form. This, however, is not just a school for the academically outstanding. 'My children are of completely different abilities,' said one mother, with two at the school. 'My son is a bright boy, but not academic. Originally, we thought there was no way can he could cope with the language requirements. But it is a small school and really nurturing and he has been put in a small class with those of lower ability. Sixth formers come in and help out and all the teachers understand his difficulties.'

Games, options, the arts: The IB attitude demands you get involved and pupils here take that diktat seriously – over 70 clubs (including fencing, ballroom dancing, public speaking and a knitting group). Saturday school adds a bit of timetable leeway, but the mood is involvement and a significant number of pupils choose some after-lesson activity every day. 'In year 7, they are encouraged to do at least two activities,' said one mother of two. 'My children tried fencing, basketball and cross-country amongst others and enjoyed them all.' Sport keenly played – against both state and private schools – and school teams hit well above their weight. 'We do much better at games than our size would indicate,' said one sixth former proudly. 'Our rugby team is as successful as schools with 10 times the number to pick from.' Boarding pupils particularly praise staff support. 'Teachers will come out and coach even at 9 or 10 at night.' Music well supported with a musical technology department and a multitude of concerts. International trips are a fundamental part of the school's philosophy and, as well as language exchanges, there are regular journeys to India and Rwanda. The global theme underlies everything and popular in-school pastimes include Amnesty International and mock United Nations.

Background and atmosphere: Compact and leafy site close to Bishop's Stortford town centre with an attractive mix of Arts and Crafts, '30s and contemporary buildings, including a new boarding house. Boarding schools are a relatively rarity in the state system, but this is very much first and foremost a boarding school, with two large senior boarding houses pre-GCSE and another for those entering the sixth form. (Teachers have flats within the boarding houses.) The school's calendar is similar to a conventional independent boarding school, with longer holidays to allow boarders to return home for two weeks at October half term, three weeks at Christmas and nine weeks in the summer. Pupils make good use of the extra time – 'It allowed me to go to China,' said one. Boarding houses are bright and well maintained and all pupils have a study bedroom, sharing till year 12, then winning their own private space in their final year. Classrooms are quiet, teachers politely addressed. Very strong community feel, with everyone getting involved. 'Not just a place to be – a place where you grow up,' said one remarkably mature young man. Strong sense of mutual respect between teachers and pupils: 'Teachers give a lot. We want the knowledge and the teachers help us to learn'.

Pastoral care and discipline: Orderly and calm, neat and self-disciplined, a school with a traditional approach. Pupils wear uniform throughout (blue in the lower school, black and white in the sixth form), and wear it conventionally ('I said to one boy, you'll get a haircut in half term,' says the head – and you know the boy will). Teachers expect to be called Sir or Mam. Even in the boarding house neatness is the rule and regular room inspections ensure that pupils keep their belongings far more tidily than at home. No one seems to have a problem with this – 'We have very traditional expectations,' says the head. Few serious disciplinary matters. The head has seen no permanent exclusions and only one two-day fixed term exclusion. 'Parents feel the school is responsive to any concerns – 'You always have one or two issues,' said one, 'but whenever we've gone to them about anything, it's been sorted out efficiently.'

Pupils and parents: This is primarily a white and middle-class school, though by no means all English. 'There are a lot of international parents,' said one international parent. 'It's not just the boarders – you hear so many different accents even amongst the day pupils.' Those eligible to apply include anyone holding a UK or European passport. Forty per cent come from overseas, with significant numbers from China and Hong Kong as well as from mainland Europe. Pupils are poised, articulate, mature and confident and very proud of the community they live in. Parents are grateful – 'We felt like we'd won the lottery when our daughter got in,' said one.

Entrance: Seven hundred apply for 120 places in year 7, 200 for 130 places in year 12. Hertfordshire residents are allowed four choices at year 7, and you can use two of these to apply for both a day and a boarding place. Those looking to board are interviewed – away from their parents – to assess how well they would adapt to life away from home. Places are allocated on the basis of siblings, future boarding need and distance. More applicants for day places than boarding, but either way a considerable queue – 'Pupils at fee-paying boarding schools wait until a place becomes available and then jump,' says the head.

Exit: Around 40 per cent leave post GCSE. Some prefer A levels, some no longer want Saturday morning school. Post IB, very high level to Russell Group and other top universities. A few looking to North America as well as to leading European universities. The school has recently appointed a student counsellor to help pupils apply for universities overseas and a marketing company to scour international universities for details of all courses taught in English. 'We need to encourage our students to look beyond the UK boundaries,' says the head.

Money matters: Much cheaper than a conventional independent boarding school, with boarding fees stretching from just over £10,500 to just over £14,000. Also offers a 'day boarding' option, at about £5,500, which means pupils can be dropped at school at 7.15am and picked up post-prep at 9pm, undoubtedly an asset for those living at a distance or working long hours.

Remarks: An exciting well-run school, with a orderly atmosphere, that demands a lot from its pupils not only in the classroom but outside it – and generally gets it.

Holland Park School

Airlie Gardens, Campden Hill Road, London, W8 7AF

• Pupils: 1,330 boys and girls • Ages: 11–18 • Non-denom • State

Tel: 020 7908 1000
Email: info@hollandparkschool.co.uk
Website: www.hollandparkschool.co.uk

Head: Since 2001, Mr Colin Hall BA PGCE (early fifties). What he inherited was a disenchanted fiefdom, with low attendance, low academic performance and more than its fair share of inner-city problems. 'Standards are not high enough,' lectured Ofsted crisply, and 'behaviour is unruly'. Since his arrival, Mr

Hall, an energetic terrier of a man, has worked 14-hour days and six-day weeks to transform the school into one of Britain's 'most improved'. The 2011 Ofsted described Hall's leadership as 'inspirational', and few would disagree.

Mr Hall attended Durham Wearside Grammar School, read history at Sheffield, followed by a PGCE at Cambridge. Started out as a history teacher, before transferring to English at Thurston Community School (now College) in Suffolk, then at Harrogate High School in North Yorkshire. Rose rapidly through the management ranks, firstly as director of sixth form at King Edward VI Morpeth, in Northumberland, then deputy head at Cheney School in Oxford. First headship was Longford Community School in Feltham, Hounslow, a tough inner-city school, where he quickly drove up GCSE results from 16 per cent A*-C to 40 per cent before being headhunted for Holland Park. The school he joined was on the verge of special measures and it soon became apparent that Mr Hall and existing staff were not on the same wavelength. 'My job involved assisting people's passage to places where they might flourish,' is his velvet-glove description of those 'ugly' times. His own views are clear and consistent – 'Adults run the school. That's what makes it a safe and agreeable place to be'. Describes his job as an obsession: 'I'm not good at the work-life balance. This is a passion, the best thing I could have ever done with my life'.

Academic matters: In 2013 87 per cent of pupils got 5+ A*-C at GCSE including English and maths and 38 per cent of GCSE grades were A*/A. Has a banded intake, with four bands selected on the basis of verbal and non-verbal reasoning before entry. All are then re-assessed in the middle of their first term and setted for each subject. It's clearly a method that works, but some students find it creates a 'them-and-us' mentality. The quality of the teaching is strong and the dedication of staff unquestioned. 'I'm looking for robust teachers, open minded, passionate about what they do, with an energy beyond their subject,' says Mr Hall. 'If children love a subject, it's because of the person who's teaching it.'

Pupils have nothing but praise for the staff. 'The teachers are really, really dedicated,' said one sixth former. 'They'll stay in school till 8 or 9. Even on their birthday. They never take a day off.' Teacher development is very much part of the programme. Younger staff observe their more experienced colleagues and can take specialist courses on the weekend for aspiring leaders. 'Once you've found them you want to hook them,' says Mr Hall. Preparation and monitoring are meticulous. Classrooms are laid out in advance of lessons. 'It's about rigour and order' – and that applies to students, who all have chic student planners for parents to sign weekly.

The school has a humanities specialism and English is its lead subject. The approach to the curriculum is relentlessly innovative. Latin is on offer for GCSE and A level. Dance, music and drama taught as separate subjects in years 7 and 8. Modern languages are French and Spanish ('We tried Italian and German, but they didn't root'). GCSE is a three-year programme, in which most students will already have acquired their 5+ A*-C grades by year 10 ('They can see the end point more quickly'), leaving year 11 to focus on a wider diversity of choice including early A level study.

Sixth form is now, as always, primarily academic, with some very small classes ('It's like a free private school,' said one pupil). Results are on the up, with 70 per cent A*/B, 38 per cent A*/A in 2013. English and maths most popular A levels.

Parents cannot praise SEN highly enough. Some 220 pupils on the register of emotional and learning needs, overseen by the SENCo and 15 teaching assistants in specialist accommodation.

Games, options, the arts: Hall wants Holland Park to be a 'life-transforming institution' and has worked as vigorously to develop the extra-curricular as the academic. Art rooms are large, light and lively. Highly praised director of dance, collaborates with several dance companies including English National Ballet. Poet Simon Armitage is a friend of the school, as is the writer Alan Bennett (one of its houses is named after him). Music, with new teachers and increased funding, is an ever more popular choice at GCSE and pupils have performed at the Royal Albert Hall.

Sports facilities in the new school (opened in November 2012) are exceptional, including a 25m competition swimming pool and extensive specialist multi-surface outdoor spaces. Sport is important (and recognised by a Sportsmark award). 'Sport can build up or destroy confidence,' says the head, who recruited a new leader from the independent sector to up the ante in rugby and introduced rowing at Barn Elms rowing club. The cricket team has played at Lords and Ampleforth.

Amongst the wide range of clubs available, sports fans can do football, rugby, cricket, judo, baseball, gym and swimming. An annual garden party celebrates outstanding sportsmanship. School trips, too, are seen as a foundation pillar of the education and are underwritten by a £1m trust, enabling for example every child in year 7 to visit Stratford (for Romeo and Juliet and dinner in a restaurant), year 8 to Rome, GCSE historians to Berlin and Auschwitz, A level geographers to Iceland and Sicily. 'The trust enables us to benefit the children of families who don't have those kind of resources.'

Background and atmosphere: The original school building was designed by the architect of the Royal Festival Hall, Sir Leslie Martin, and built at the then astonishing cost of £1m, it opened in 1958 as one of London's first purpose-built comprehensives. The school, set in eight leafy acres of London's most costly square footage, has always been controversial and Kensington locals weren't entirely happy with its arrival. Naturalist Peter Scott (who claimed the children would frighten away nightingales), John Betjeman (who worried about the trees), and the High Commissioner of South Africa (who feared for his garden parties at nearby 'High-end') were only a few of those who inundated The Kensington Post with their concerns. At the time, the feeling was that the school would 'reduce Campden Hill to Earl's Court'. Early fears, however, were soon confounded. The school quickly attracted high-profile, left-leaning pioneers convinced that state education was the answer for a more egalitarian age.

Celebrated former peer and socialist minister Tony Benn transferred his two oldest sons from Westminster and Charles Jenkins, son of Labour cabinet minister Roy, joined the sixth form from Winchester. Hardly surprising, then, it was soon dubbed 'The Eton of comprehensives'. In the '60s and '70s, became increasingly progressive and undoubtedly cool (Anjelica Huston was a pupil, as were the children of the Marquess of Queensbury), but the '80s and '90s were not so kind, and cool turned to chaos.

Today, its pristine, £80m, light-filled classrooms are once more an oasis of well-ordered calm. The corridors are polished, the reception ornamented with fresh-cut flowers and the pupils themselves, in smart grey suits, would do credit to any independent school brochure. 'The environment,' says Mr Hall, 'is part of an attitude, a landscape for learning. It transmits that we care about young people and, as a result, students want to work hard and feel they belong.' Certainly students are proud of their school – 'It's a shining hall of hope,' said one; 'a fantastic place to be,' commented another. The brand new building, opened in November 2012, has added outside space, a 25m competition pool, dance studios, state-of-the-art music studios, bespoke furniture and a more compact and SEN friendly interior. An architectural gem, designed by Aedas in stone, glass, copper and bronze. 'It's a wonderful privilege to open a brand new building and launch it for children,' says the head.

Pastoral care and discipline: Where once mayhem, now tranquillity, and pupils higher up the school notice it most. 'When I came here it was completely chaotic – now it's an incredible school,' said one year 12 boy. 'There is a very special thing about the school, an openness and willingness,' says the head. 'Pupils behave with good grace and enthusiasm.' They definitely feel comfortable here. 'It's very close knit, like a family. It looks after the kids and cares about how you are,' says one. The head aims to create a safe and secular, humanist community and instil a sense of spirituality – 'We live in such a ready culture – we don't want to replicate what happens out of school'. Pupils meet weekly in their house (Anderson, Baker, Bennett, Chappell or Seeley) for assembly, and listen to choral music and poetry – 'Not because its of use in exams, but because it takes them beyond their everyday passions'.

Praise is very much part of the mix and an annual awards dinner, Perfect Tense, recognises outstanding achievements, attitude and contributions during the year. Award winners' portraits ornament the corridor walls. Vertical tutor groups exist for a better understanding across the years ('and less bullying,' said one pupil). Behaviour is good – 'Students are friendly and welcoming and express pride in their school' (Ofsted 2011).

Pupils and parents: From a vast range of ethnic backgrounds (90 languages spoken). Fifty per cent speak English as a second language, about 10 per cent are refugees, mainly from Somalia and Eastern Europe. Around 50 per cent are actually English by origin and language but, as was the original intention, investment bankers ('We felt the head was a great leader, a visionary person. We took a gamble, but we're delighted with it') and intellectuals (Will Self) are once more happy with their local state provision.

Entrance: One thousand apply for 240 places. Banding tests held in November/December. The school operates a sibling policy, then distance from the gates. Makes every attempt to ensure parents understand that if you live more than a mile away, your chances of entry are slim. (Last year 60 appeals produced only one extra place.) There are 24 Art Aptitude places each year; applicants sit an aptitude test and are subject to different entry criteria.

All sixth form applicants, internal and external, are interviewed by an assistant head, who leads the sixth form. Places offered on the basis of a school report and predicted grades. A*/As required at GCSE in the subjects the student wants to study at A level: 'It's not absolutely rigid – some students are bored at GCSE'. Year 11 students the school wants to retain are wooed with 'an extra bit of love and a series of suppers'.

Exit: A large number leave post-GCSE – 75 per cent in 2013 – for sixth form/FE colleges with different curricular offerings or work-based training. Whilst the school is totally comprehensive, the sixth form is 'an unashamedly elite institution' demanding A*/A GCSE grades. Lots of sixth form leavers to London universities eg Imperial College, King's College, Queen Mary and UCL. Others to Oxbridge (three in 2013), Nottingham, York, Warwick, Edinburgh, Manchester and more. All have one-to-one guidance on university choice and a programme of visits, with time and effort put into personal statements and developing 'cultural capital'.

Money matters: Now, as always, Kensington and Chelsea's flagship comprehensive, very well funded by the borough.

Remarks: A school which has gone rapidly from 'could try much harder' to 'outstanding' (Ofsted 2011), under a dynamic and inspiring head. Now, once more, a model cosmopolitan, inner-city comprehensive. Suits those, according to one student, who are 'hard-working and opinionated, who strive to do their best. It's not for someone with a blasé attitude'.

The Holy Cross School

25 Sandal Road, New Malden, Surrey, KT3 5AR

• Pupils: 940 day girls • Ages: 11–18 • RC • State

Tel: 020 8395 4225
Email: hxs@holycross.kingston.sch.uk
Website: www.holycross.kingston.sch.uk

Headteacher: Since 2001, Mr Tom Gibson MEd NPQH BSc DipEd,(forties). Educated Wimbledon College, read physical education and sports science at Loughborough University. Previously taught at St Joseph's, Beulah Hill, Glyn ADT and St Gregory's, Kenton. Married to a fellow teacher, four children. Well-experienced in different areas of education, a pleasant, unassuming gentleman who has brightened all horizons.

Academic matters: A mostly long-serving, committed staff of all age groups delivers an 'innovative curriculum' and the 'quality of teaching and learning is outstanding' (Ofsted). Class sizes are around 30. A level results improving (76 per cent A*-C in 2013; 18 per cent A*/A) and with a high level of value-added. GCSE results consistently over 75 per cent 5+ A*-C including English and maths (79 per cent in 2013). Awarded Specialist Science College status in 2003, which enabled the school to develop its provision in science, maths and ICT. Independent working habits are encouraged. A £5.4 million building project has provided excellent facilities for drama, music, science and IT. Sports hall and dance studio opened in 2007. The sixth form is in partnership with a local boys' school, enabling them to offer a wider choice of subjects – much appreciated by pupils and parents. SEN and EFL are catered for by specialist teachers throughout the school.

Games, options, the arts: Two garret-style studios provide an inspiring setting for art and DT. A hard-working music teacher is making new waves with the orchestra in a state-of-the-art music suite, and individual instrumental tuition on most instruments can be arranged. The school trains year 10 as Wimbledon ball girls. Creative drama department in purpose-built drama facilities is growing – many do GCSE. Duke of Edinburgh Award Scheme along with an extensive selection of after-school clubs, including astronomy and young engineers.

Foreign language exchanges to France and Spain plus opportunities such as working in orphanage in Thailand, trips to Lourdes, skiing, year 7 camping trip and a music tour to Europe.

Background and atmosphere: The Sisters of the Holy Cross founded the school in 1931. It became grant maintained in 1993 and in 1999 became a voluntary aided school within the diocese of Southwark. The original buildings have been much added to and updated. Caring and moral values help deliver a smooth, organised atmosphere. Whilst Roman Catholicism predominates, all other faiths are welcomed. Pupils are encouraged to be involved in the community through voluntary work.

Pastoral care and discipline: Sensible school rules – girls are expected to be mature and aware of others' needs; all have form tutors. Strict uniform code – girls ticked off if not properly dressed. Sixth form pupils expected to be self-disciplined and present themselves well.

Pupils and parents: Good ethnic mix; 90 per cent are Catholics. 'We are from all walks of life here, professionals to refugees; most are somewhere in the middle.' The common interest is a well-balanced and Christian education. Serious PFA.

H

Entrance: Pupils come from a wide catchment area. First preference to practising Catholics. 148 places available in year 7.

Exit: Currently 80 per cent of students return into the federated sixth form, with 15 per cent moving to local colleges and a small number to the world of work.

Remarks: With a young and dedicated head, a school for parents to watch develop. October 2007 Ofsted stated that Holy Cross 'is an outstanding school. Christian values and concern for others are at the heart of its work.'

Howard of Effingham School

Lower Road, Effingham, Leatherhead, Surrey, KT24 5JR

• Pupils: 1,580 boys and girls; all day • Ages: 11–18 • Non-denom
• State

Tel: 01372 453694
Email: Howard@thehoward.org
Website: www.thehoward.org

Head of School: Since 1999, Rhona Barnfield, MA BSc (late fifties). She is the executive head both here and at Thomas Knyvett College in Ashford, which is run, like Howard of Effingham, by The Howard Partnership, a not for profit, two-school (so far) federation.

Mrs Barnfield's title matches her appearance – top to toe executive with confident voice, hairdo, little black dress and red jacket, topped with pearls and matching brooch. Gravitas a-plenty.

Rare amongst heads, she appears to have no existence outside her current corporate role (or not one easily accessed via normal sources). Enquiries elicited the barest of bald facts – that she chairs assorted education-related committees in Surrey (and is a whizz on budgets), is an experienced schools inspector and lives in nearby Tadworth. As to interests, family or even previous career, the rest is silence (she doesn't do interviews).

A fab front-woman at public-facing events, she has become 'more of a figurehead,' thinks one mother. Day to day management is the remit of Mrs Helen Pennington, BSc, NPQH.

Mrs Pennington, the former deputy head, has been the head of school since September 2012. A jolly-looking, hands-on presence, with the air of giving you her fullest attention while struggling not to think about all the other things she should be doing, Mrs Pennington heads up the six-strong senior team. Though a long-serving teacher with more than a decade's experience at the school, year-long absence in 2009 to 2010 on secondment to Ofsted, followed by troubleshooting support at assorted struggling schools means she's not as well-known as she will undoubtedly become. Those in the know give her the thumbs up with 'nice' the starting position on the ratings scale.

Academic matters: Long-held reputation for excellence. 'The school got its first Oxbridge success when I was here,' says one parent, and manages consistently good results against stiffish local competition. School intake, with a largish contingent from motivated and relatively affluent families must help (though as lower results from similar schools in other equally well-to-do areas demonstrate only too well, certainly no sinecure).

School isn't about to let the demographics take the strain, and takes considerable pains to choose high quality staff who are passionate advocates for their subjects – and the school. Teaching the sixth form is seen as a particular perk. 'We fight to do it,' says one member of staff, while pupils are full of praise. 'They're fantastic' says one. 'They went to top universities. They

don't just choose anyone.' Staff are young, too. 'I struggled to see who were the sixth form and who were the teachers,' says a disconcerted though admiring mother.

If educating younger children is felt to be slightly less fun, there's no sign of it, bar the occasional pupil blogger's comment (one is particularly scathing about foreign languages to-the-test GCSE teaching – though this is more a comment on current exam system than the school's interpretation of it). Plenty of lively lessons (an hour's session is standard here), including rousing chorus of 'Je me lève, je me lève, je me lève, lève, lève,' to the tune of William Tell Overture. 'We do as much practical work as possible,' says Mrs Pennington, as corroborative chemical odour drifts from science lab. 'Our aim is to make sure that the pupils go home more tired than the teachers.'

All that energy translates into healthy numbers of GCSEs as the goal for most and results that are frequently good and often exceptional. In 2013, 83 per cent of year 11 pupils passed five or more GCSEs at A*-C including English and maths. Plenty on offer for the very academic (Latin from year 9) and the more practical-minded, with catering studies GCSE, for example, pulling in around as many as French.

Good range of vocational qualifications (children's care to vehicle maintenance) also offered either by the school or at local college as GCSE alternatives/additions (lots of BTECs, with plenty of mixing and matching).

With its gifted and talented designation, you'd expect school to be good at helping the high flyers, as indeed it is. Nit-pickers might question how the less able are faring. With early setting (for maths and languages in year 7 first term and humanities, English and science added in year 8) the aim is for each to receive according to need. While number crunching puts school fourth in the county for across the board progress (and comfortably amongst Surrey's premier league state schools for GCSE and A level results), government data shows that only a third of low attainers are making 'expected progress in maths' at key stage 4 (compared with 82 per cent of middle and 95 per cent of middle and high performers).

There's some weeding out post-16, though most make it through to sixth form, which sees between 20 to 30 joining from other schools. More than 59 per cent of A level grades were A*/B and more than 31 per cent A*/A in 2013. Plenty of flexibility, with BTECs in science and business studies (amongst others) providing an alternative to those drawn to the subject but not necessarily suited to A level course.

School listens and will add new subjects if demand and resources are there. Dance has been introduced, while geology, a recent newcomer only rarely on offer in state sector, is attracting small but highly motivated numbers. Once discovered, it captivates, with almost half current batch of students planning to continue after school. Given joys of 'going down mines, yomping around in Land Rovers and finding your own ammonite,' says jolly teacher, who can blame them?

Parents testify to thoroughness of approach. School may be big, but there's no hiding place if work is slipping – with a plethora of remedial help to put things right. 'One parent told us: Though it's a busy school, it's extremely well managed. There's constant feedback. When my daughter was doing her GCSEs, her mocks didn't go brilliantly. Straight away, pupils get a mentor, someone checking and they do revision classes.' It's less the three Rs than two Ts – tracking and target setting, with pupils knowing exactly where they stand and what they should be capable of.

However, computer doesn't always say 'no' if pupils are desperate to take subjects (particularly at A level) which results to date suggest will be a stretch, though proof of commitment to the extra work required will be sought.

Same rigour applies to learning or additional needs (around five per cent are statemented or supported with school action plus; two per cent have a different first language). Inclusion department (three rooms with range of resources) provides support in and out of lessons. There's also a supervised lunchtime homework club and small, sensitive touches including a sign outside the learning resources centre offering (subtly worded) selection of coloured overlays for those with dyslexia.

Games, options, the arts: Two hours a week devoted to sport. Facilities include a giant sports hall which, though locked and empty on the morning of our visit, hosts many and varied activities. Year 7s offered gym, dance, netball, athletics, and tennis in lesson time and a decent range of clubs (and plenty of others, like Glee, chess and art, that cultivate mind over muscle). Rugby is currently the school's biggest bragging point, with year 7s becoming 2012 national schools champions, beating Castleford High School at Wembley.

Sports teachers, as young and energetic a bunch as you could wish for (distinctly twitchy if they haven't exercised at least one set of muscles within last 30 seconds) confirm the growing popularity of PE as a GCSE and A level option, and are (unusually) prepared to travel to assess pupils whose talents (in riding, skiing and swimming) lie outside standard range. D of E also on offer.

It's not just the brightest and best who dominate matches, though parental rider is that keenness isn't always felt to be enough – sheer numbers (and concentration of activity during lunch break) make dogged determination to get noticed an essential. Additional weekend activities (such as Sunday netball) help to 'balance things out.'

No such issues with drama – slick productions (one for key stage 3 pupils, one whole school) have the adjectives flying like bouquets. Subject is also increasingly popular as a sixth form option (boys as well as girls), with two recently making Oxbridge on the strength of it.

Richness of offerings inside art and DT departments reflect willingness to invest in pupil creativity. 'How can you stifle it?' asked Mrs. Pennington, pointing to large clock (A level DT project) that could have hung with pride at Waterloo Station. Equally impressive art, including Chagall-inspired paintings and delightful Chinese scrolls, by pupils in years 10 and 7 respectively, reinforces the point – as does high percentage of art A level students who go on to foundation courses. Creative impulses even extend to sewing machines featuring bios of leading designers as inspiration, with one GCSE textiles masterpiece – a gorgeous, Union Jack-emblazoned horse blanket – unmissable clue to one pupil's out of school interests.

Sixth formers are speedily drawn into range of CV-friendly activities. They include working with year 7 and 8 pupils and getting involved in busy student committee which runs everything from Christmas ball to sale of Valentine's Day carnations.

Background and atmosphere: Green-looking at the front (lots of grass and a playing field) but an abundance of tarmac round the back and a bleak-looking netball court, though there's some carbon offset with a fair few mature trees dotted around. School owns adjacent playing fields and even manages to house a complete (though separately run) nursery school in its grounds.

Inside, with the possible exception of its smart sixth form block, not a place you'd pick on appearances alone. Paint choices don't always help though old girls at open day thought the décor had improved since 1980s, when purple doors were the norm.)

But though school might wear every one of its 70 years rather less well than the average pensioner, results and esprit de corps are proof positive that outer appearances are no guide to inner beauty, with strenuous efforts made to overcome physical limitations.

Nautical references are everywhere (school is named after Second Lord Howard of Effingham, commander of the fleet that defeated the Spanish Armada in 1588). There's an end of year Ship's Log and year groups divided into Arks and Royals. Aptness of imagery extends to organisational efficiency that keeps everything ship-shape and Bristol fashion, ensuring that potentially unwieldy numbers are tightly organised: with the exception with (very minimal) giggling, large (ish) classes were well behaved and corridors devoid of stragglers and lost souls. Those out of class on official business must carry teacher-issued authorisation.

Sense of order pervades waffle-free school literature (sensible 'behaviour for learning' rules include beginning and end of lesson uniform checks and need to stand behind chair until invited to sit down by teacher). Notices firmly (but nicely) reinforce the rules. 'Tie knots should be level with top button, not tummy button', urges one.

Pastoral care and discipline: Highly rated by parents. 'My child had the same form tutor from year 7 right up to her GCSEs, and she was wonderful,' says one parent. Year 7s are eased in very gently, with support from trained-up year 9 mentors, one teacher per subject, their own area at break time and earlier lunchtime to give them a few minutes' head start on the mêlée.

Not bullying free, though the advent of the new head may, it's hoped, result in more successful approach to the inevitable girls' friendship issues that cause the majority of problems. Robust school structure means there are 'lots of different channels you can go down,' say parents. 'The first point of call would be the form teacher, then you've got head of year, head of subject, deputy head and then the head.'

Pupils, too, praised staff accessibility – felt to be good throughout the school and exceptional in the sixth form. 'You can go to anyone,' says one. 'They're very sympathetic.' Flexible, too.

Parents says it's a kindly place, with plenty of rewards for effort (there are twice termly doughnut mornings for year 8 stars, for example), but the school is 'no pushover.' 'If there's a piece of GCSE coursework that hasn't been handed in, you know about it,' says one parent. Similarly, privileges higher up the school are substantial but must be earned. Sixth formers start by having to be in at the same time as younger pupils, though later on, after demonstration of requisite commitment, they may enjoy a lie-in if they don't have early lessons.

Sixth formers, who wear own clothes, can melt away into own common-room for R and R, bizarrely furnished with railway platform style slatted metal benches on one side, soft seating on the other. At the other end of the age range, plenty of thought goes into ensuring that younger pupils have gradual exposure to shock and awe of older bods. They eat in junior canteen (lots of nice-looking food though five a day message may not be getting much of a look in: single bowl of fruit fights losing battle with table groaning with trays of desirable-looking cakes).

Outside, field provides handy overspill for older pupils, weather permitting. When it doesn't, overcrowding is ever-present hazard, though with lots of other space open for business, including some covered areas and quiet courtyard area with staff providing informal supervision outside, and well-used learning resource centre and cyber café inside, there's usually somewhere else to go.

As to the future, school's acquisition of academy status in 2011 was followed days later by plot of land opposite going up for sale. This prompted speculation (according to local paper snitch) about whether or not head planned full-scale move and rebuild, followed by demolition of current site. Despite a few mutterings about corporate aspirations gone mad, parents would be thrilled.

Pupils and parents: Sea of white faces for guided tour. Proportion from local independents rose substantially during last recession and well-spoken, committed parents abound. Pupils are a well-behaved bunch who reflect general propriety of the area (move into Horsley and you'll be given a list of potential babysitters in your welcome pack – it's that sort of place). Friendly, with parents and pupils praising sense of community and ease with which new friendships are made. 'My daughter had been at an all-girls school which was very small, so at first it was a bit of a shock to the system but she's really glad she went there now,' one parent told us.

No wonder prospective mothers are keen. 'I've got two – this is the arty one and this is the sporting one,' says one at sixth form open evening, thrusting sons forward at deputy head in the manner of a determined saleswoman.

Entrance: Predictably over-subscribed. Eight catchment areas give a clue as to the complexities of 240-place year 7 entry.

Admissions officer is a 'guru,' says the school and probably needs to be (knowledge may be passed down the generations with runes and a silver chalice). Basically, anyone living in Horsley (East and West) is in, ditto Howard-facing Fetcham inhabitants (others are more likely to slot into Leatherhead secondaries). Those with siblings at the school can do a certain amount of queue jumping (though there's a move to restrict priority status to those living within catchment area). Combination of proximity and attendance at feeder primaries (Oakfield, Eastwick, St Lawrence, The Raleigh, The Dawnay and The Royal Kent) is the next best bet.

For sixth form, net is cast a bit wider. School welcomes applicants from a range of private and state schools – and gets them. While Bs and Cs will get pupils in, they might struggle to meet the demands of most academic courses. School, however, spends considerable time juggling ability, projected results and aspirations and ensuring that suggested course fits the bill.

Exit: Some leave at 16, many for vocational courses at Guildford College or Nescot College in Epsom, others for Godalming College. Of the 183 in each sixth form year, well over 95 per cent stay in education, with around eight each year making Oxbridge. Assortment of subjects and destinations, including handful each year doing medicine or veterinary science. New BTECs may, it's felt, open up new, more hands-on courses ('not to be sniffed at – the Russell Group isn't everything,' was the message).

Remarks: Quality education from a serious-minded and effective school. Bright, motivated pupils in particular will blossom, with minute attention to detail ensuring that, for an educational oil tanker, it does well not just with high seas but Bs and As, too.

Howell's School, Llandaff, GDST

Linked school: Howell's School Junior School, Llandaff

Cardiff Road, Llandaff, Cardiff, CF5 2YD

- Pupils: 770 (all girls to year 11); co-ed in the sixth form; all day • Ages: 11-18 • Non-denom • Fees: £6,976–£11,913 pa
- Independent

Tel: 029 2056 2019
Email: admissions@how.gdst.net
Website: www.howells-cardiff.gdst.net

Principal: Since March 2007, Mrs Sally Davis BSc PGCE (late forties). Educated at Bassaleg Comprehensive School, Newport and Bedford College, University of London, where she studied geology. Taught at a number of inner London comprehensives before joining Howell's as deputy head in 1992. Bubbly personality who consults with her management team but appreciates the buck stops with her. Married to a teacher and has two children.

Academic matters: Results remain strong – 85 per cent A*/Bs at A level, with 58 per cent A*/A in 2013 and 72 per cent A*/A (at GCSE. Science is very popular. The range of subjects available has expanded in recent years. The average class size is 18-20, with many smaller groups. Staff a mix of young and older teachers. We sat in on a practice for a debating competition and it was clear that pupils are encouraged to ask questions.

A clearly defined SEN policy, and Dyslexia Action Cymru has an on-site satellite on the campus. Parents are expected to pay for any SEN referrals. The needs of moderate dyslexic/dyspraxia pupils can be met. Also procedures in place to identify gifted and talented pupils and ensure they are academically stretched.

Games, options, the arts: Examples of pupils' art are shown all round the school. Drama is popular and we sat in on a very lively improvisation session. Over half the school play an instrument, many at county or national level. Concert hall and practice rooms are well used by the many choirs, orchestras and groups. An annual Eisteddfod is held which encompasses a wide variety of activities designed to give as many pupils as possible a chance to take part. The spirit and history of Wales is alive here and well supported by both parents and staff.

Sport taken seriously. Apart from lacrosse, hockey, netball, tennis, athletics and swimming, rugby has been introduced for the sixth form boys. Fencing, badminton, cross-country running and dry skiing among other sports available.

After school activities are well supported and range from ballet to Mandarin. Duke of Edinburgh award a firm favourite. Award-winning careers advice programme with a dedicated careers coordinator supported by outside speakers and the GDST Minerva network, which offers a supportive scheme for sixth formers including on-line information and practical training courses.

Background and atmosphere: Merchant Thomas Howell on his death in 1537 left a large sum to the Drapers' Company for the benefit of orphans. Howells, founded in 1860, benefited from this legacy. Joined the Girls' Day School Trust in 1980. A short distance from the centre of Cardiff off a busy road, the campus is more extensive than first appears. The main buildings have a Hogwarts look about them with a Grand Hall complete with fresco, turrets and impressive staircases. Improvements and extensions have been added over the years as required. Younger pupils wear simple but smart uniform. Sixth form have no uniform but a dress code. Good food with plenty of choice. Multi-cultural entry with over 30 different languages spoken. Communication with both pupils and parents is given a high priority – examples of this include a revision guide for parents, regular newsletters, messages sent by Schoolcomms and handbook for new pupils. A buzzing feel to the school – pupils seem keen to learn and enjoy what is on offer. The sixth form college is based in two Victorian houses, over the road from the main campus. Sixth formers are treated more like university students and have space both to study and chill out.

Pastoral care and discipline: It is made clear to pupils that the school expects them to take responsibility for themselves and to respect others. Strong anti-bullying policy is part of a proactive pastoral system. Drugs, alcohol and smoking not an issue but will be dealt with severity if found.

Pupils and parents: Catchment area from Cardiff to Newport, Bridgend and the Valleys, with buses provided. Wide range of backgrounds, which makes the school socially inclusive. Many first time buyers of independent education. Notable former pupils include Baroness McFarlane of Llandaff, Professor Rosalie David, Emily Barr, Jane Crowley QC, Lucy Cohen, Linda Mitchell, Jemma Griffiths the singer, known as JEM, Charlotte Church and Hannah Mills, who won a silver medal for sailing in the 2012 Olympics.

Entrance: Entrance test for year 7 in maths and English. The principal then interviews all candidates being considered for a place. Entrants to the sixth form are expected to have a minimum of six grade C GCSEs and above, including grade B or above in their chosen A level subjects, and are also interviewed

Exit: A few leave after GCSE. Majority go onto a wide range of universities – Bristol, Exeter, Swansea, Cardiff, London and Durham being popular choices. In most years several to Oxbridge (three in 2013). Medicine, dentistry, veterinary sciences, law and engineering are among the more popular degree subjects (12 got places to do medicine in 2013).

Money matters: The GDST Minerva Trust and the Thomas Howell Trust support means-tested bursaries. Currently about 20 per cent of the senior school receive them (some are 100 per cent). Also a small number of scholarships.

Remarks: A school that nurtures the pursuit of learning and the arts while celebrating Welsh culture.

Huish Episcopi Academy

Wincanton Road, Langport, Somerset, TA10 9SS

• Pupils: 625 boys, 615 girls • Ages: 11–18 • Non-denom • State

Tel: 01458 250501
Email: office@huishepiscopi.somerset.sch.uk
Website: www.huishepiscopi.net

Principal: Since 2013, Andrew Davis BSc PGCPSE NPQH (forties). His degree is in applied science and he is particularly interested in astrophysics, climatology and sedimentology. Was principal of Dawlish Community College for seven years (school became one of the highest performing schools in Devon during his tenure). Previous posts as deputy principal at Exmouth Community College, one of England's largest schools, assistant principal at Plymouth High School for Girls and head of science at Holyrood School in Somerset.

Main interests are in developing teaching and learning and curriculum design to raise standards of achievement and ensure that schools 'are designed around the students as an individual rather than the student fitting the system.' Married to a teacher and has three children. His outside interests are family, cycling and reading.

Academic matters: Clearly benefiting from its new academy status, with its new sixth form the icing on the cake. Operates two distinct bands in years 7 to 11. Two top ability groups identified within each band for English and a number of other subjects. 'Tight' setting in maths and science. Impressive approach to foreign languages, with lots of effort made to broaden horizons. Global Gazette magazine is published annually and highlights new initiatives like Mandarin classes. Most pupils try a second language from year 8 and continue with one or two languages from year 9. Some take Latin as an extra.

Three vocational BTEC National Diploma courses available. Sixth form students are encouraged to take up the Extended Project Qualification. GCSE results have improved consistently; in 2013 60 per cent achieved five or more at grades A*-C including English and maths. Mathematics results were the highest for years, with 77 per cent achieving A*-C. A level results in 2013 saw 45 per cent A*/B grades and 19 per cent A*/As. Good results also at key stage 3 and school is in top 25 per cent nationally in value added tables. Lessons we saw in years 8 (German) and 11 (history) certainly held pupils' interest and used lively resources to full effect. Parents say teachers 'work incredibly hard' and

pupils latch on to those who show 'passion for their subject.' Much effort has been put into training and recruiting staff to teach to A2 level. Head of sixth form came from similar role in Bristol and has made huge impact. We saw an AS English language class that involved students in careful analysis of material and perceptive discussion with their lively teacher.

Timetable works on basis of a 50-lesson fortnight with maths, English and science getting seven, six and five lessons respectively at key stage 3. Strong emphasis on ICT – laptops on trolleys available on demand and new sixth form IT hub bristles with iMacs. Science is well funded and generous laboratory provision allows pupils 10 lessons of science per fortnight at key stage 4. Strongest candidates take triple science. Around 20 per cent A* at GCSE in chemistry, with maths almost as good. Study centre is a continuing multi-media success and at the heart of the school's learning. Pupils actively involved in book selection, reading for pleasure lesson in years 7 to 9 and a scheme for accelerated reading. Recent Readathon raised £1,500 for Roald Dahl Foundation (£300 given back in form of new books for library).

At GCSE, along with compulsory subjects, pupils choose four from 16 optional subjects. Class sizes vary according to subject and ability. Large labs accommodate up to 32 pupils in top sets, allowing lower ability groups of 16 to 19. Less flexibility in other core subjects. Links with Yeovil College enable some pupils at key stage 4 to follow vocational courses such as engineering and animal care. PSHE course where topics include dealing with stress and depression.

All year 7 children are screened for specific learning disabilities on entry. Close liaison provides plenty of information beforehand from feeder primary schools. Special educational needs co-ordinator works with whole staff to support pupils within normal timetable. Eighteen learning support assistants work alongside mainstream teachers (some work in specific subject areas). Special needs include Down's syndrome and cerebral palsy. Pupils with Asperger's syndrome get help with socialisation and use of free time in school.

Games, options, the arts: Longstanding reputation as a sporting school, especially in boys' football, rugby, girls' hockey and cross-country. Huge numbers involved on extra-curricular basis. Pupils achieve individual representation at area level and school has produced national champions in athletics and high national placings in cross-country. Participation stretches to biathlon and inter-school swimming. Young leaders award for years 8 and 9 gets pupils to direct younger ones in sports activities. PE/sports studies is a popular GCSE/ BTEC option. School shares its purpose-built leisure centre with locals (a real bonus for this rural community). It includes fitness centre, dance studio and superb squash courts. There are also floodlit multi-use outside courts, a heated 25-metre open air pool, extensive playing fields, plus full size all-weather pitch for hockey or football. Sixth formers get free use (even out of school hours) of the leisure facilities (now managed by school).

Music has come on leaps and bounds in recent years – choirs, jazz band, orchestra and lots of instrumental tuition. New drama studio with raked seating – recent productions include I Hate Shakespeare and Moulin Rouge. Lower school hall doubles up as a drama studio for younger pupils.

Artwork is well displayed throughout school (fashion a particular interest). Innovative and enthusiastic department succeeds in getting students into specialist art and design courses. Wide range of extra-curricular clubs and activities (some payable), including badminton, parcours and Taiko drumming. Loads going on at lunchtimes and after school. Busy schedule of fieldwork and trips overseas – recent expeditions include AS art, history and French students to Paris and year 10 to 13 linguists to Brussels (funded partly by the EU) to attend a session of the European Parliament.

Background and atmosphere: School motto is 'Conemur' – Let us strive – which head feels is as appropriate now as ever. Was in first group of 30 'high performing' schools to be offered academy status. This has resulted in extra funding and coincided nicely with the addition of a sixth form. 'Independent school education without the fees,' suggested one member of staff. Single-storey red-brick front to school dates from 1939, with seven subsequent additions behind. Eye-catching sixth form wing ('illuminated walkway looks particularly impressive from the main railway line at night,' said students) has transformed look and feel of the school since we last visited. East wing contains art suite, photographic studio and media hub. Conference suite provides flexibility for talks or use as a teaching area. Still feels like a small school from the front entrance, but on entering the sixth form there is a definite 21st century ambience. Twenty-one new classrooms and three new science labs have been added recently. For many years was a 'lovely secondary modern,' able to go comprehensive slowly and steadily. Certainly not nine-day wonder, it has built up a reputation locally as a school which 'gets the best out of children.' 'You very rarely hear shouting,' said one teacher whose experience elsewhere had obviously been very different.

Smooth transition arrangements for children moving up from primary schools – a concert by primary schools was in rehearsal on the day we visited. School opens up inside like a Tardis, but the original appeal of the place hasn't been lost. Main assembly hall (which doubles up as a canteen for years 9-11) has been refurbished but can only accommodate one year group at a time. Corridors are congested during lesson changeovers given recent increases in numbers but hour-long lessons limit pupil traffic and enhance work ethos.

Pastoral care and discipline: School believes in dealing with any issues quickly and emphasising positive behaviour. 'It's about removing barriers to learning and supporting pupils in their achievement,' explains assistant principal. Golden rules are set out for all. School council is active and helps allocate rewards. Year 7 head oversees transition from primaries and visits all feeder schools. One mother of a shy daughter praised the way 'staff even visited our home during the holiday before she joined to reassure her.' Ten tutor groups for about 260 year 7 entrants. Year 10 and 11 pupils act as form friends to years 7 and 8. Prefects are chosen from years 10 and 11 (sixth formers play no formal disciplinary function in the secondary school). Tutors follow pupils from year 7 to 11. No house system but inter-form events by year group range from year 7 benchball to whole school cross-country. Recovery room operated for any pupils withdrawn from lessons. Attendance is carefully monitored and there is a close watch on cyberbullying. Mobile phones aren't allowed for secondary pupils – 'but we don't go looking for them,' say staff. School has taken over former parish rooms to provide a discrete student guidance and learning centre (caters for up to 40 pupils) – under dynamic staff leadership and tackles head-on the educational, emotional and social needs of the disaffected few. Additional support for all pupils includes health clinic run by NHS nurse, careers adviser, part-time counsellor and family support worker.

Pupils and parents: A genuinely friendly place. Secondary pupils and sixth formers come from a 200 square mile catchment area. Increasingly oversubscribed. Copes well with all types. Local professionals don't need to fork out on costly alternatives,' one mother told us while another said: 'We moved here from London having been tipped off about the school.' Sixth formers have worked hard to create a good social and student life. We were told that some who started at colleges soon had second thoughts and came running back to join the new sixth form. From 60 in its first year, more than 100 entrants a year now and look set to rise. Parental views are sought and involvement is maintained through regular newsletters. Turnout at parents' evenings is usually about 90 per cent. No formal parents' association but lots of support for events throughout year. Huish-i is being developed as a virtual learning environment and forum for communication with parents.

Standard school uniform, including a blazer. Most girls opt for trousers in the winter. Generally well presented, with some scruffiness at the edges. Sixth formers we saw were dressed sensibly and not on a fashion parade. School day finishes at 3.20pm, with armada of coaches to ferry pupils home. Pupils' contributions valued at all levels. 'Lead learners' are identified and 'learning without limits' programme has set up links with Sekondi-Takoradi School in Ghana. One year 8 boy is currently leading a successful Amnesty group, while others run an environmental action team. Prize-winning school garden, healthy eating programme and lots of eco initiatives. Chair of school council is member of UK youth parliament. Democratic to a T elections held under single transferable vote system. Pupils are even involved in interviewing new staff.

Interesting array of former pupils include fashion designer Alice Temperley and Bob the Builder creator Sarah Ball.

Entrance: Parents move to be within the catchment area (includes about 30 villages across mid-Somerset). Twenty per cent of pupils come from outside the catchment area – by straight line distance from the school.

Exit: Sixth form opened in 2010 so there's no set pattern yet. But so far some 50 per cent of pupils progress into sixth form and then to university. After just three years of operating, students have gone to both Oxford and Cambridge, with other destinations including Exeter, Bristol, Falmouth and Bath. The other 50 per cent leave for colleges, apprenticeships or employment.

Remarks: This trail blazing 11-18 academy in rural Somerset just goes on improving. The new sixth form is the icing on the cake.

Hurst Lodge School

Linked school: Hurst Lodge Junior School

Bagshot Road, Ascot, SL5 9JU

- Pupils: 135 girls, 50 boys (aged 3-18); 23 boarding (weekly and flexi), 160 day • Ages: 3-18 • Non-denom • Fees: Senior Day £13,740 pa; Boarding £22,290 • Independent

Tel: 01344 622154
Email: admissions@hurstlodgesch.co.uk
Website: www.hurstlodge.co.uk

Principal: Since 2013, Miss Victoria (Vicky) Smit BSc (forties). Had an earlier stint as head between 1998 and 2011. But, concerned about the propriety of being both co-owner and head (her brother, Sir Tim Smit, started the Eden Project and the school belonged to their mother), she appointed another head in her place for a brief period. It didn't work and Miss Smit is once again head.

This former Hurst Lodge girl, who 'has been 23 years in the place,' bounced into our meeting in rather fetching wellies, waterproof trousers and trackie top. She had been helping out at Hurst Lodge's Forest School and was clutching a wet teddy – which she handed to her assistant with the comment that 'he needs to have his bum dried.'

Previously worked with the army and a team of agricultural management consultants but helped her mother move the school in 1999 and never left. A Forest School leader (younger Hurst Lodge pupils learn how to take risks in the real world), she has undertaken 'multi-discipline training' (which sounds a bit like being qualified in common sense). A joy – rather like the best possible Girl Guide, favourite aunt or big sister. She bubbled with enthusiasm, giggled and waxed lyrical and we positively skipped round the school, hopping up the odd staircase to avoid being mown down by busy children. (Our notes actually say: 'bubbly, bouncy, loving').

Academic matters: Not a Russell Group route. School is non-selective and mixed ability. One third are on the SEN register – the majority are on the dys-spectrum: dyslexia, dyspraxia, dyscalculia, plus Asperger's, high functioning autism, ADD, ADHD, epilepsy, diabetes. Mild Tourette's, but no pupil who 'would disrupt the balance of the class' is accepted. All children with SEN are assessed prior to entry. Taster for all, sometimes two or three tasters (and usually after the third, the answer is no). Two SENCos, eight staff with 'SEN commitment,' tiny caring classes (10 the norm for GCSE, max 18).

Children are withdrawn for support from mainstream classes – between one and five lessons per week (charged as extra, same as individual music lessons). Some statemented children have learning support assistants in class and a number of students attend sessions with the speech therapist. Timetables are adaptable, nothing is written in stone. Gifted children either work with the class above or attend special extension classes. EFL support on tap. The odd GCSE module taken early. Parents and guardians invited along to relevant assessment meetings with ed psychs and SENs, co-training sessions and open discussion with and by all concerned with any particular pupil's problems. Regular reports home and school hopes that parents will be upfront about concerns and vice versa. School both small enough to care and big enough to pull punches.

Academic change is in the air and new enhanced sixth form programme comes on stream in September 2014. This will have 'a slightly different focus' and include business studies, English, history of art, Spanish, French, environmental studies, art, textiles, photography, drama, and music. One hundred per cent success rate at A level, with 70 per cent As; Eng lit, science, maths, psychology, PE and fine art. At GCSE a full range of subjects on offer, with excellent results. Double science, triple science, interactive white boards, computers, everything you might expect from a mainstream school.

Difficult to quantify results from such a tiny cohort. Some subjects offered as IGCSE or BTEC, which school says gears 'subject delivery to individual need.' Given the mixed ability intake and the large numbers with real problems, these results are phenomenal. For most, each exam passed, at whatever level, is the result of a massive joint pupil/parent/teacher input and a huge boost to self esteem and morale.

Students take an average of 11 GCSEs each, 'as in 10.5 GCSEs each, of which seven are academic and three and a half arty.' Wide range of traditional academic subjects alongside more vocational stuff – dance and performing arts. BTEC in childcare, in-house nursery and placements available (next step perhaps to follow Norland into self-defence?)

Pupils say that teachers go out of their way to explain things and really take time. 'We get lots of attention; our teachers are amazing,' we were told. School practises a total immersion approach – if, for instance, the history project is the Tudors, then it is Tudor in the artroom, Tudor exploration in geography, Shakespeare, Marlowe and probably lampreys for all at lunch time.

The most recent ISI inspection found the school to be 'excellent.' So did we, and we loved the idea that the principal would happily cancel all lessons to have a gigantic snowball fight. Or get the entire school to make kites and fly them one windy day, while the music department blasted 'Let's go fly a kite' on mega-megaphones.

Games, options, the arts: Terrific. Halfway to a stage school, with all students studying performing art (including ballet and modern tap) until the age of 14 – boys too. Hair workshop (dancers' buns – natch) and make-up lessons. Some pupils combine school with performing in the West End, while others take part for the hell of it. Two amazing (odd floor surface – slightly bungey) dance studios which link up to provide the most impressive performance space. Huge LAMDA take-up. Large numbers go on to further dance, ballet, modern, tap and jazz, ditto drama. Southern circuit national drama heats held here. Principal is the Independent Schools' Association National Arts Co-ordinator and in charge of national drama, art and essay competitions. Eighty per cent of pupils learn a musical instrument and most take voice lessons. Recording studio onsite.

Mind-blowing creative arts, undoubtedly amongst the best fabric/art portfolios we have seen in any school. Outstanding. We were seriously impressed by a quilted memory box with fabric detail of professional standard. Artwork round the school wasn't that bad either and sewing machines and cookers vied for space in the art/craft room. Life class, computer aided art, photoshop. Practical cookery lessons preferred to the more theoretical food tech – optional at 15 and compulsory for sixth formers. Ceramics, sculpture and animation (there's also a wowser YouTube video on line of Buff Orpington eggs hatching as part of school's eco project).

International sportsmen/women (and an Olympian or two) are allowed two weeks off for competitions during the year. Swimming important – school has open air 25m pool, surrounded by child inspired gardens. Lifesaving, tennis, footie with the local village club on Saturday, riding Tuesdays, polo Thursdays, netball, hockey, rounders, karate and athletics, judo.

Pupils grow veggies in a polytunnel, and a nearby pen is full of weird and wonderful ducks and chooks (their eggs currently off the agenda until six weeks after worming). This is a hands-on smallholding and we were constantly interrupted during our tour by little people asking 'if they could help feed the hens.' The head replied: 'tomorrow we have to put cream on them. Do you think you could hold them?' Bees – and school makes own honey. For many pupils, this hands-on approach to life beyond the classroom or their (sub)urban roots is their first taste of how the other half lives.

Learning for life classes important throughout, but particularly at the top end where pupils are prepared for the world outside. Strong links with the Eden Project started by Tim Smit, and work experience there, as well as on the school's own smallholding. This is sustainability education at its best.

Pupils are taught interview techniques (and what to wear), public speaking, sex education, first aid, flower arranging (well, you never know), deportment, proper etiquette, how to lay a table, which glasses to use for what wine and how to reply to formal invitations (might be quite clever to offer a level 2 food hygiene certificate so the little darlings could get proper paid holiday jobs). Staff brainstormed to come up with a list of skills that proved most useful in later life and this programme is the result.

Mega collection of after-school clubs. School estimates that only about 20 per cent of pupils go straight home after school – all the others (usually fortified with a cake and drink from the canteen) stay to do extra activities. Dance of all descriptions, ballet, tap, jazz, modern. Pupils can take a GCSE after hours, if they can't fit it into their time table, plus all the usual sport, arts and crafts, gardening, electronics, public speaking, and polo. Staff stay on too; mathematical challenge popular plus knitting, touch typing...

Background and atmosphere: Founded as a dance school in London in 1942 by Doris Stainer, a formidable woman with a cane. The school has grown and moved several times since then – to its current 22-acre site on the outskirts of Ascot in 1997.

Main school building is nostalgically Victorian with extensive add-ons, including kindergarten, classrooms and studio block. The tiny chapel – now used for choir practice – has rather fun stained glass and a very low door to ensure that one slightly bolshy incumbent actually made obeisance to the altar.

Children deeply involved in the food they eat and catering staff happily join them at mealtimes to discuss future menus and their respective nutritive values. This is an all-embracing outlook on education, celebrating every achievement and keen to boost self confidence. Supervised homework, limited access to the internet and constant advice regarding social media and cyber-bullying.

Flexi, or weekly boarding. Three/four to a room (the most recent conversion still smelled of paint during our visit, having been subdivided the previous week) and a third boy joined the other couple of boarders three weeks into term. Pupils can start at any time assuming there's space available and with the taster caveat previously mentioned. We much enjoyed a short chat with the (married) housemistress who tries to make life as homelike as possible, organising trips to the cinema, board games, bread making, barbies and 'going off-site.' In-house wickedness equals discussion, followed by 'house chores.' Buddy system of the same age for new boarders. Girls have a splendid dolls' house, and Wendy house and boys their own common room. Waiting list for boarders at some ages.

The recent addition of boys is gradually having an effect. It started when one boy – a sibling – was taken on to help a family in need and snowballed from there. A third of pupils are boys, most of whom, to be honest, are in the junior school But as the school has only advertised its co-ed credentials since 2010, numbers should grow from here on. Three boy boarders as we write. School ain't for all boys though. Unsurprisingly, it's the fathers who have the biggest problem with hearing their sons may be dancing (optional for boys as they may choose an alternative such as sport or technical lighting), but could suit some gentler souls who might flounder in a large, male-dominated environment.

Pastoral care and discipline: Ofsted found pastoral care to be 'exceptional.' Not many rules – they are summed up as 'accept everyone.' Pupils have a good relationship with staff – friendly but respectful. One of the worst sanctions is apparently that head is 'disappointed.' Polite pupils stand up when teachers and visitors enter a room.

Small boarding house upstairs in school proper, max 38. Students can board from the age of 9. Weekly or flexi boarding too and odd night for £55. Small size means the students have friends of all ages and it's run like a large family, with students and staff sitting down to breakfast and supper together. Ofsted reckoned the boarding provision to be 'outstanding.'

Non-denom, 'global mix'; Church for Christmas, synagogues visited, comparative religion taught (though veggie not kosher). Proper wrap-around care, from brekky at 7.45am to supper at 5.45pm. Assembly for all on Tuesdays, plus the odd parent. Neat tartan pinafores and tweed hacking jackets for all.

Pupils and parents: Locals from a 30-mile radius. Boarders from Birmingham, Cornwall, plus a fair sprinkling from overseas, Korea, Japan, Africa. Working parents appreciate the good before and after-school care provided. Boon for all: 'There's so much laid on here that I don't need to run myself ragged taking them to activities outside,' one told us. 'They can even have some tea here and then do their homework. It's a real help.' Number of first time buyers, plus old girls' children. Notable old girls include Duchess of York, actresses Juliet Stevenson and Claudie Blakley and TV presenter Emma Forbes.

Entrance: Non-selective, but 'pupils need to fit in to the class without altering its dynamic significantly,' says principal. Twelve-year-old would-be pupils spend a day here, with papers in English, maths and reasoning – more of a placement test than entrance exam. At all other times, they spend a taster day (or two or three: ditto those with SEN hiccups) at the school, during which they will be assessed 'to ensure that they can access the school's curriculum.' Special needs children are assessed by the learning support team who need a copy of their last ed psych report/statement. No place offered if the school reckons they can't offer the right kind of support.

New pupils welcome at any time throughout the year assuming there's space available (often from the state sector in the run-up to Christmas or in instances where eight/nine-year-olds are overwhelmed by transition to independent preps).

Exit: Chaps sometimes leave at 11 for trad preps, including Woodcote House, Hall Grove and Papplewick. Over half of girls leave after GCSEs, many for art college or performing arts courses, leaving a tiny sixth form. In 2013, three on gap years, one back to Japan and others to places like Cardiff, Regent's University London, London Contemporary School of Dance and Central Saint Martins.

Money matters: Academic, dance, drama, music and art scholarships on offer. Be warned that there are extras to pay – LAMDA exams, special needs support, after-school care etc. Discounts for siblings and Forces families. 'Lost a few' in the recent recession, but numbers are stable, with rather more refugees from the state system.

Remarks: It is not often that this long-time Good Schools Guide editor comes out of a school with a happy buzz that lasted all the way back to London, and even now, when faced with the computer, still feels that all can be right with the world. A happy mainstream school that's not afraid of a special need or two. And it doesn't have to be anything major – also good for helping pupils who just need a little bit extra individual attention to help them succeed, whatever their talents. Unusually strong performing arts programme. No amazing sparkly facilities, just spoonfuls of common sense and human kindness.

Hurstpierpoint College

Linked school: Hurstpierpoint College Preparatory School

College Lane, Hurstpierpoint, BN6 9JS

• Pupils: 400 boys/330 girls, 100 weekly boarders, 285 flexi boarders • Ages: 13–18 • C of E • Fees: Boarding: £24,030–£30,240 Day £20,325 pa • Independent

Tel: 01273 833636
Email: registrar@hppc.co.uk
Website: www.hppc.co.uk

Headmaster: Since 2005, Mr Tim Manly BA MSc (mid-forties). Educated at St Edward's Oxford followed by Oriel College, Oxford where he read classics. He had always wanted to go into the teaching profession and after six years as a headhunter in the City and an MSc in industrial relations from the LSE, he went to Cambridge to do his PGCE at the age of 30. Says it was the best decision he every made and has never looked back. Spent six years at Sevenoaks, where he became head of classics and housemaster, before moving to Oakham as deputy head. Married to Henny; they have four children in the school.

He arrived when Hurst was treading water and has taken it from strength to strength and increased the numbers from 630 to 1,030 (for all three schools). He has raised the intellectual atmosphere, but 'feels that academic achievement is not an end in itself but a key to future success – life is about personal bests and engaging with opportunities'. Manners, civility and courtesy are his personal crusades, and pupils are strongly encouraged to write thank you letters and reply to invitations. He is a man of extraordinary energy who does not believe in down time, apart from the odd brief escape to his cottage in Wales. Feels there is no room for complacency as things can slip very quickly. The staff room has been revitalised, and about 70 per cent of teaching staff have joined since he took over. One pupil said, 'The headmaster makes people want to do well for him'. His door is always open and he knows children and parents by name.

Academic matters: In 2013, nearly 40 per cent A*/A at A level, 65 per cent A*/A at GCSE. Strong sciences and maths at A level. Pupils can do A level in their native language eg Dutch and Polish. IB offered since September 2011 – first exams in 2013 when students' average point score was 36.6. The school offers the A1 language paper in German. The head would like to see the IB embedded as a viable alternative to A levels and would like about 40 to choose IB each year whilst 100 do A levels. About 30 per cent of A level students take the Extended Project Qualification. Need to get an A or A* in GCSE in subjects to be studied at A Level or IB.

Challenge grades are particularly popular with parents. Based on IQ tests, an ambitious but, with hard work, achievable grade is set at the beginning of each academic year. Children are assessed through challenge grade reviews every three to four weeks and these, accompanied by teacher comments and a graph to plot progress, are emailed directly to parents. 'Problems are picked up as soon as they arise and there are no nasty surprises,' says one happy parent. Children meet their tutors each week to discuss academic progress. There is a strong work ethic throughout the school; children are set extra work during the holidays and half term and are encouraged to take initiative and responsibility in all aspects of their lives.

Good SEN department with three full-time and four part-time teachers – about 15 per cent of pupils need some support, mainly for mild dyslexia and dyspraxia; this is charged for.

Foreign nationals who want to join the sixth form are screened for English before arrival. EAL compulsory for anyone who needs it and is included in full boarding fee for international students. Although there is a well-stocked library, the use of text books is diminishing in favour of electronic media; increasingly, work is done on subsidised iPads, and the academic block bristles with Apple Macs. Plenty of careers guidance – sixth formers are given interview skills coaching and help with writing cvs. Parents and pupils can attend presentations on UCAS and there are gap year fairs and seminars. All are encouraged to take part in Young Enterprise initiative where pupils have the opportunity to create and run their own business – they were the local prize winners for best company in 2011 and 2012. OJ Club of former pupils very supportive of the careers programme and many come back to make careers presentations and offer executive shadowing schemes.

Games, options, the arts: Games are compulsory in the first year but after that, those who hate team sports can do something else eg outdoor pursuits or health-related fitness programme monitored by the school. Lots of enthusiastic teachers mean that most people find something they enjoy – biking, surfing, kayaking, sailing etc. Everyone has to do at least three exercise sessions a week, reducing to two in the sixth form, and most girls keep going with sport. Minor sports include fencing golf, shooting, triathlon, power-walking and riding – Hurst sponsors the annual schools' competition at Hickstead. House and inter-school competitions in the major sports and many minor sports eg water polo and cross-country running. 'Everyone has a chance to play in a team if they want to – the school will put together a team and find a fixture.' Everyone encouraged to have a go and 'you don't have to be good but just have fun' – it

is hoped pupils will find a sport they want to continue after they leave. Lots of sport played at county level and occasionally pupils are selected to represent their country.

Vibrant music department with orchestra, jazz band and wind band as well as various ensembles and quartets; some 140 in the choir and about half learn a musical instrument. Class music compulsory in Shell (year 9) and the whole school is involved in some way in the annual house music competition.

Huge range of activities from car racing to rock climbing and all Remove (year 10) do silver Duke of Edinburgh award through the CCF. The school has set up a farming project in conjunction with Plumpton College with pigs (one of the pigs is used for the Boar's Head Feast), chickens, fruit trees and a conservation group where children can learn countryside skills like hedge-laying. The aim is that they discover what they enjoy and develop life-long hobbies and interests.

Art room open to all – not just those studying for public exams. Photography, textiles, ceramics, sculpture graphics as well as drawing and painting. Drama is offered at GCSE and A level as well as an extra-curricular activity. There is a Shakespeare play each year and a musical most years as well as lots of small productions in the drama studio – often student directed. There is a playwright in residence with weekly workshops for those who want to write for theatre.

Dance compulsory for Shell (Year 9) and is also offered at GCSE and A level. Increasingly popular with boys and girls – contemporary dance, breakdancing, hip hop, street dance all offered. Trips all over the world – community expedition to Malawi, cultural exchange to China, plus subject trips to eg Italy, Barcelona, Iceland.

Background and atmosphere: Founded in Shoreham in 1849 by the educational pioneer Nathaniel Woodard. It moved to its present purpose-built site in 1853 and the chapel was finished in 1865 – a beacon of Victorian muscular Christianity. Set in 140 acres, with views to the South Downs and surrounded by playing fields. From a distance it could be mistaken for a monastic community, but this first impression belies a vibrant and forward-looking school. Constant updating and refurbishment – science and DT blocks refurbished, and new academic quad, second Astroturf completed in 2011 and new digital library underway

The mantra 'achieving your personal best' permeates all aspects of school life, not just academic but also participation in sport and clubs, activities and social relationships. When the school was founded in the 19th century, 'ancient' ceremonies were introduced to give it a feeling of tradition and history. There are banner ceremonies and on Ascension Day, everyone climbs the nearby Wolstonbury Hill for a special service, and the headmaster distributes 'Lowe's Dole', money left by the first headmaster for the choir. The Boar's Head procession and Feast at the end of the Michaelmas term, when a boar's head is carried through the cloisters accompanied by the choir singing a 16th century hymn, is one of the highlights of the school year.

Pastoral care and discipline: About 55 per cent board to some degree – mostly flexi, often three nights a week, but 100 weekly boarders. Full boarding not offered until sixth form and tends to be for foreign nationals. There are 10 houses up to lower sixth divided into day and flexi-boarding – with a strong system of pastoral care and communal responsibility and a tradition of inter-house competition. There is a robust anti-bullying policy, a representative from each year group in each house sits on the school council, and house guardians are chosen for their approachability to discuss any social issues within the house. The lower sixth act as prefects, mentor the younger children, are responsible for the day-to-day running of the houses and supervise prep and lights out. Sniffer dogs and random drugs testing from time to time – all sounds a bit alarming but Hurst does not have a drugs problem.

Upper sixth has its own house, St John's, which is set apart from the main school buildings and is more like a hall of residence where everyone has their own study bedroom. Co-ed, with girls and boys in separate wings, which are alarmed at night. Students have their own common-room, kitchen, computer room and laundry room. They run their own lives, but are not cut off from the rest of the school, and organise school functions and charity events; all the sixth form have to do some form of community service.

Hurst is a Christian school and the chaplain plays a major part in school life, but Christianity is not imposed on anyone. Pupils encouraged to recognise spiritual dimension and to develop a strong moral compass and sense of duty. Compulsory Friday evening chapel marks the end of the school week. No Saturday school, just sport, activities and play rehearsals.

Pupils and parents: Around 95 per cent live within about 45-50 minute drive. Head wants to keep the school local with an international dimension. Tweeded landed gentry, city commuters, medics and local farmers and businessmen. Good network of school minibuses run morning and evening from as far away as Hove, Copthorne, Lewes, Seaford, Forest Row and Horsham. 'very parent friendly, and school bends over backwards to make life easy for parents,' says one working mother – the weekly and flexi-boarding option and no Saturday school particularly popular. Parents particularly praise the very good communication via emails and newsletters and the regular parent-teacher meetings Active parents' association runs social events – coffee mornings, barbecues, inter-house quizzes and the Christmas fair.

Famous former pupils include Admiral Sir Michael Boyce, chief of the defence staff in the Gulf War, various MPs and ambassadors, former general secretary of the National Association of Head Teachers, Sir David Hart, actor Michael York and film director Ronald Neame.

Entrance: Not hugely selective, with 55 per cent pass rate at common entrance. Keeping a fairly broad church becomes increasingly difficult as the waiting list grows. School's own exams in English, science and maths for those coming from schools which do not prepare for CE. Doesn't cull after GCSEs. Many come up from Hurst's own prep school; others come from local prep schools, eg Windlesham House, Great Ballard, Dorset House, Great Walstead, Pennthorpe, St Aubyns, Westbourne House and Handcross Park. Some from local primaries and a few from London day schools. Some 40-50 join in sixth form. Need an A* or A in subjects to be studied plus a minimum of a C in maths and English or the equivalent in home country. Occasionally spaces in year 10 at start of GCSE course – entry by school's own tests. Almost at capacity, with waiting lists in some years – does not want to get much bigger as will grow out of the chapel – already building a gallery.

Exit: About 20 per cent leave after GCSEs, often to go to sixth form colleges – do not lose any to competitor schools. Send to a wide range of universities (most to Russell Group and 1994 Group), including several to Oxbridge each year (five in 2013). Others to a good range of universities to do eg medicine and veterinary science, others to more creative courses eg theatre studies at Leeds, creative writing at Royal Holloway and music production at Leeds College of Music. About half take a gap year.

Money matters: Means-tested bursaries, sibling discounts and special bursaries to help children of former pupils. Range of awards at 13+ and for the sixth form – academic, art, sport, drama and IT worth up to £1,600 per term can be topped up by means-tested bursaries. Also means-tested bursaries to take a child to the next stage if parents experience financial hardship.

Remarks: A school which is going from strength to strength under the strong leadership of its dynamic headmaster. It is now the first choice for many parents who would traditionally have sent their children further afield. We tried hard to elicit negatives from parents, but everyone was universal in their praise. Fantastic value added, where each child is tracked and challenged to reach their full potential in all areas of their lives, and where they are encouraged to push themselves beyond their comfort zone.

Hurtwood House School

Holmbury St Mary, Dorking, RH5 6NU

• Pupils: 325 girls and boys. Mainly boarders • Ages: 15–18 • Non-denom • Fees: £24,501–£36,750 pa • Independent

Tel: 01483 279000
Email: info@hurtwood.net
Website: www.hurtwoodhouse.com

Joint Headmasters: Mr Richard Jackson MA (late sixties). Began working in marketing, then became a prep school master before founding Hurtwood in 1970 in a National Trust rented house with 17 pupils and a dream. He wanted to recreate what he views as the idyllic prep school atmosphere of security and discovery for A level students. He feels that at 16 it is time for a change and seeks to bridge the gap between school and university. His drive, enthusiasm and inspiration have got the school to where it is today and he admits he will never totally relinquish his day-to-day involvement in its organisation, not, that is, 'until I am taken out in a box'. His wife, Linda, is school bursar and currently responsible for catering and domestic arrangements.

Cosmo Jackson BEd (fortyish), his son, came straight from Bristol University to work for his father. No attempt at any other career for him – he knew exactly what he wanted to do and his enthusiasm and flair are equal to it. It is difficult to discover the division of labour – both talk about their school projects and achievements with excitement and well-deserved pride. Perhaps Cosmo says 'my' a bit more often – he is probably more involved with the day-to-day administration – but they still seem to be a team and it is very much a family concern. His wife, Tina, teaches history and assists with careers. They have two children, currently at local prep schools. Will one of them want to carry on the family tradition? That is a question yet to be answered.

Academic matters: Excellent results all round – small classes and top level teaching have proved a recipe for success. In 2013, 67 per cent A*/A grades and 89 per cent A*/B. Interestingly art, maths and psychology were top performers in the A* stakes.

Large range of available subjects that can be combined any way desired – for instance biology and chemistry could go with theatre and music, if that is where a student's talents lie. Theatre and media studies are the most popular, with maths, business studies, art and English literature coming close behind. Good languages and sciences as well.

Although the general appearance would seem rather liberal, the structure is certainly not. All students are graded weekly and their progress carefully monitored by tutors and teachers, a system designed to keep everyone on their toes. Parents appear to really like this – they can review their child's performance at any stage and know he/she is not lagging behind.

No specific special needs help, but a co-ordinator for dyslexia, and extra lessons can be provided where necessary. Extra ESOL lessons available, plus a one year foundation course with GCSE options for overseas pupils needing a more intensive introduction to English, and an introductory summer course for foreign students.

To encourage breadth of experience, each student has to spend specific times each week on subjects in which they are not taking exams, a programme imaginatively called 'Enigma'. This is compulsory and they are not allowed to miss sessions. The Enigma range is enormous – life skills, fitness, media, arts: a student's creativity is challenged and channelled.

Games, options, the arts: Games are an option, not compulsory, but a variety of sports/activities is available every afternoon and they do manage to produce enough teams to play external matches and go on overseas tours. Playing fields and all-weather courts. Termly outdoor pursuits expeditions.

Perhaps the greatest strengths of this school are its media and theatrical facilities, which are to die for – a theatre with a revolving stage, roll up seating, totally professional lighting and sound equipment; as Richard Jackson says, 'Could be the Donmar'. These students learn all aspects of film making, theatrical productions, music and dance – someone really keen could do up to 12 hours' dance, on top of his/her academic studies. Performing, shooting, recording, cutting, mixing – studios for everything, and they do the lot with spectacular results, often up to professional standards. A utopia for creative minds – no wonder they have such high pass rates in theatre studies, media studies and music technology.

Great art, textiles, design – modern and traditional: here are some talented students being well taught. In 2013, 50 took art A level and 30 got A*s. Look at their website and you will understand why.

Background and atmosphere: As you drive along narrow leafy Surrey roads, following outward bound style directions, finally turning into a drive marked inconspicuously Hurtwood House, you begin to slightly wonder whether you have made a mistake and this is someone's private residence – it does not feel like a school. Cars parked outside the house and a fleet of buses, presumably fresh from ferrying students from their not-too-distant boarding houses to the place where they will spend the rest of their day – no-one is allowed back to their house during school hours – but absolutely no institutional feel and no sense of nearby easily reachable towns with irresistible attractions beckoning vulnerable teenagers. No transport – this school is a big protected place (from the parents' point of view) where you can learn and be yourself (from the students').

The main house, a huge country mansion perched high in the Surrey hills with fantastic views across to the south coast, has an old fashioned feel about it. Walk in and ahead you'll see an elegant staircase leading to students' comfortable informal accommodation – at least two to each bedroom; turn left and you'll be let in through a secure plate glass screen into the central hall. At the far end, leather sofas and a gigantic television set, perfect for showing examples of school productions etc.

The classrooms, laboratories and studios are all very cleverly built into the grounds, below the eye-line, some underground. A feeling of wonder grabs as you walk round the performing arts complex and meet students animatedly editing film, mixing sound, working creatively in a set-up bound to enthuse 17 and 18 year olds – their idea of heaven. Walk into the classrooms, all at ground level, and you find small informal groups with their teachers, some interactive whiteboards (only where they will be used properly), some pupils using laptops – technology is there, where it is needed, and bang up to date.

At break time students sit casually on steps and walls chatting – no uniform, most of them in jeans but looking tidy. All students join at the same time so no one is coming into an alien environment – they make friends quickly. As a stepping stone between school and university this seems a good place to be.

Pastoral care and discipline: Housemasters, in-house tutors, personal tutors – students have plenty of people to talk to and are being constantly monitored. The atmosphere is grown-up and informal – staff are called by their first names. No prefects which, the Jacksons say, together with the fact that all the students are new at the same time, eliminates serious bullying. Zero tolerance of and random testing for drugs. Three things that are totally unacceptable, says Richard Jackson: bullying, drugs and stealing.

No organised activities at weekends – theoretically they can all go home, but often drama rehearsals for the next production, so the houses are never totally empty. Permission always needed for exits. Staff purport to know where anyone is at any time.

Pupils and parents: Young people who have got fed up with school, want a change, are artistic with ambitions in the world of television, cinema and theatre, whose parents can afford to send them here, a lot boarding for the first time. Twenty-five per cent from a broad overseas spread – currently about 25 different nationalities.

Entrance: Non-selective. 'We interview each candidate,' say the headmasters. 'They must want to come to the school.' No-one expelled or suspended.

Exit: Some to drama school or art college, others to trad universities, Leeds, Bournemouth, Sussex, for instance, to read media related subjects, or UCL, Manchester, Imperial etc for economics, languages and the occasional biochemistry or engineering degree. Sixty per cent to Russell Group; a few to Oxbridge.

Money matters: Fees pretty high, but what else would you expect with all these facilities? Worth checking on available scholarships, some for performing arts and some for maths/science. A possible scheme in the air, with support from parents, to include less privileged children.

Remarks: Clearly this is for the seriously creative student, though it also caters for the seriously academic – over 150 students studying maths or further maths. But the creative part seems to dominate and some might find it all too much. For those looking for change, needing smaller classes and lots of nurturing or wanting somewhere to expand their creativity, it could be just the right place. A different and exciting environment, somewhere that develops confidence and encourages disciplined methods of learning – young people discover that hard work creates happiness and fulfilment. A place where 'students can make things happen and school can make things happen for them'.

Hutchesons' Grammar School

Linked school: Hutchesons' Grammar Primary School

21 Beaton Road, Glasgow, G41 4NW

- Pupils: 1,000 boys and girls • Ages: 11–18 • Non–denom
- Fees: £8,234–£10,230 pa • Independent

Tel: 01414 232933
Email: admissions@hutchesons.org
Website: www.hutchesons.org

Rector: Since 2005, Dr Ken Greig MA (Oxon) PhD (fifties), a geologist by inclination and (maths) teacher by trade. Educated at George Heriots in Edinburgh, (Dux), a first at Oxford plus a PhD in practical geology and a stint with BP as an exploration geologist. Previously head of Pangbourne (and part of HMI team). Married with one child still in the school and a daughter reading history at Cambridge, he and his wife are settled in south Lanarkshire (which must be a bit of a daily trek).

'Our Dr Greig is absolutely super – everything we wanted, and good looking and charming into the bargain'. (He is all of that – and now sports the fashionable shorty beard: three up from designer stubble we understand.) Greig has proved a breath of fresh air for Hutchies, which was a riven community; he has achieved what many believed impossible, the school is visibly cohesive, with departments co-operating and a 'much better atmosphere in the common-room'. Time spent 'binding the community together', improving the ethos to make the school more at ease with itself is never wasted'. Coffee in the common-room on Fridays is a popular sounding ground and not just for mixing up departments: 'there's just the danger that the separate departments will become isolated because of the size of the school and the geography of the building', but also for thrashing out future plans: the new drama building – three stunning rehearsal rooms – is a triumph of co-operation.

Rector (and senior colleagues) sit in on lessons (though no longer one a day); with a follow up lesson for both teachers and pupils: 'a way of getting to know them all as people'. Quite a number of staff changes recently, but fewer than one might expect: reasons for digging in may be that staff 'are happy to stay where they are' and feel 'lucky to be in this school' (and so they might, for not only do all staff get opportunities to go on courses, at home and abroad, they are also offered aromatherapy and massages – we suspect for free, but it wasn't mentioned). No matter, the rector has seen them all in action (each ad is oversubscribed with applications), and apologised for the delay in getting copy back to me 'because I have been interviewing' so all this might change. New senior depute (from Abingdon) and a head of classics (from Bradfield).

Greig runs the senior school with a senior depute rector plus four deputes, one of whom is known as director of curriculum (overseeing academic and ancillary activities including the arts) and one 'director of ethos'. Christine Haughney, previously head of Calderwood Lodge in Newlands, a former Hutchie parent, heads the primary at Kingarth Street.

When pressed, the rector admitted to 'not resting on his laurels' (the new drama studio had yet to be formally opened) and though flat roofing (as in building on) is not currently on the agenda, his next ambition is to reclad the existing buildings – an interesting mixture of 60s at its worst and some rather imaginative brick work.' A piper (in trews rather than the kilt) and a golfer, Greig would rather be known for his geological yomps than his prowess at either of the former: 'rusty', 'don't practise enough'.

Academic matters: Formidable results; strings of As in highers with pupils regularly getting six or more in S5 (ie fifth year) – 65 per cent A grades in 2013 – and many staying on to top up with extra Highers, Advanced Highers or A levels in sixth year, despite the fact that they will already have university entrance qualifications in the bag. A 'mixed economy'; heads of departments choose whether A level or Scottish syllabus and teach accordingly – in all cases two years' study is truncated into one. A level maths, history and economics (government and political studies) outstanding – scads of A grades at Higher with almost a third of year group notching up five or more A grades. Thirty-one got six Highers at grade A, eight all at Band 1 in 2013, a feat achieved by only 33 pupils nationally. 'This could only be achieved by high quality teaching and commitment,' says the school. 'With the forthcoming SQA changes the Hutchie culture of consistent hard work and genuine understanding will be more vital than ever.

Special interest courses in sixth year – Italian, Portuguese and survival cookery (plus own cook book).Results per pupil make other schools quake with envy and broad enough pupil

base to offer a moving feast of ancillary subjects. Classical Greek comes and goes, head of classics may just make Greek a serious Higher contender. Vast classics department – Latin compulsory till third year. This is senior stuff. School is open early and late, staff will hold individual drop-in sessions if needed. Biology no longer top of the pops (pupils do human biology too) – maths, English and chemistry head of the pack; pupils encouraged to take as wide a spread as possible – and they do. Only French, German and Spanish on the language front. Native speakers can take Highers in their own tongue. Language labs, satellite TV.

Double-decker library at the forefront of technology uses finger print recognition and is stacked with as many DVDs (Shakespeare on film) as books, and computers everywhere intranetted and internetted. No EFL, 'they've got to have good English to access the syllabus' and no setting for first year – 'Got to find their feet first, this is a big step' – though set for everything thereafter. All pupils screened at 11 and any problems with reading and writing picked up by SENCo, who will 'work within the context of the class', no withdrawn lessons, but fierce academia means that those whose dyslexia holds them back academically may be either screened out or given the tools to succeed – Hutcheson's primary department particularly hot on this. Class sizes of 20/25 at bottom end of the senior school, reducing in number as specialist subjects kick in.

Games, options, the arts: Sports stadium opened a few years ago on old playing fields at secondary school which now incorporates impressive Astroturf hockey pitch and international training standard Tartan athletics track. Astroturf hockey pitches at Clydesdale ground adjacent to the school, plus international standard cricket ground. Pupils are bussed to Auldhouse for rugby. No swimming pool on site (problems with old coal minings underneath); huge sports hall with fitness centre and gym (certain amount of public access required – as ever – by over vigilant planning Hitlers, but school has succeeded in restricting this to evenings only). All the usual games – rugby almost a religion, county and country representatives abound. Hockey (couple of staff in the UK Olympic squad) etc, plus rowing (Rector was a rower, but 'not enough hours in the day') and '25 sporting options'. Curling growing in popularity – Olympic win did wonders for the sport. Trophies in every discipline.

Good and busy drama – consistent finalists in the Scottish drama and music festivals. Three big productions each year. Expect even more emphasis on drama when new building gets into its stride – all three classrooms were in use during our visit including five senior students watching a somewhat raunchy version of As You Like It upstairs.

Terrific music, school does A level music, deeply unhappy – as are the majority of music departments in Scotland – about the Standard and Higher music syllabus ('Scottish music exams not that hot'); several orchestras, pipe band, jazz. No CCF; granny bashing and masses of charity work popular; recent links with local state schools – the Mark Scott Leadership for Life Award was set up 'after the tragic sectarian murder of Mark Scott' in 1995, school works in partnership with the RC Holyrood school (NB Glasgow can be as sectarian as Northern Ireland in places).

Art fantastic, with kiln, fabric design plus home economics – though no huge number doing the latter. Raft of other options: pupils can do advanced driving (fairly strict rules in place about driving other pupils), archaeology, first aid, Italian and Portuguese. Lots of trips abroad and pupil exchanges. D of E et al. Photo montage on website of trips to Paris, Italy, Switzerland, Australia and Spain – mostly subject based, sports tours, but just the occasional jolly.

Background and atmosphere: Both Hutcheson's Hospital and School were founded in Ingram Street in 1641 by the brothers Thomas and George Hutcheson (the latter was Glasgow's first banker). In 1841 the school moved to the 'quietness of the situation, good air, roomy and open site' of Crown Street in Glasgow's Gorbals, before moving to leafy Pollokshields in 1960, five minutes from the M8 and a doddle from either side of the river. Good local buses, ditto train service. Amalgamated with the girls' school in 1976 (the primary then moved into the girls' school at Kingarth Street, but see below) and went independent in 1985; the board of governors is full of the great and the good of Glasgow: the Merchants House, Hutchesons' Hospital, the Trades House plus the Church of Scotland Presbytery, some ex-officio, some co-opted, 'who have got their act together' – could one say at last? Ex-officio boards can be very elephant in the room-ish.

Large, wide open corridors, huge blocks of classrooms. Super chunks of new-build on what is basically a sixties flat roof horror; masses of photographs, good pupil-inspired art. Subjects are grouped either horizontally or vertically, superb – if dated in places – facilities. New labs. Dining area extended, still pretty busy at all times.

Hutchies acquired the adjacent United Reformed church at the turn of the century. Active during our last visit, the dwindling congregation has now joined up with the church down the road, and the school has full use of this brilliantly converted space, complete with internal stained glass window, red Glasgow sandstone walls (one of them new) and comfy red purple and grey chairs (originally for the congregation). The church hall has transformed into an auditorium with collapsible seating – school not sure now how they ever managed without it – which is home to weekly sixth year lectures, Talking Points, held on Friday mornings and ranging from Mindpower: Fact, Fiction and Fakery via The Genetics of Engineering to Eating Disorders. The series is open to all by ticket – mega wows. This is architecture at its best, creating an entire music centre with practice rooms in the crypt and all manner of exciting performance space, plus a computing centre – for computing lessons rather than for use as an alternative teaching area: 36 networked computers. Would that all schools could be so imaginative. It is also a popular fund-raiser, let out for weddings, bar mitzvahs, conferences.

Weekly assemblies are divided by year group – the rector delivers four assemblies a week, two to each group. Individual year groups hold separate assemblies on alternate days elsewhere. 'The trouble with such a large school,' said Greig, is 'there is nowhere large enough to take the whole school at the same time.' School operates on swipe cards – the original cashless economy: pupils top up their cards and use them to buy lunch (very good, lots of veggies and salads), breakfast or whatever. Pioneered no fizzy drinks from vending machines. School uniform in regulation black and white – no obvious anomalies that we saw.

Pastoral care and discipline: Divided into four fairly loose houses for games, competitions and the like. Seniors 'buddy' littles when they join senior school. Strong emphasis on PSE, with fatigues or detention in place for minor wickedness, though individual teachers may set their own punishments – the ultimate deterrent is expulsion. Tutors for all over a two-year period. Rector admits to 'a bit of bullying', but strictures in place to combat it, and his own children, who moved here from the south of England, 'found it a friendly place'. Miscreants' parents 'would be invited to withdraw their children'. NB Hutchie pupils are expected to maintain the same high standard of discipline when they are beyond school premises. Not overtly Protestant, the pupils have many gods.

Pupils and parents: A mixed bag – 'social, ethnic and economic A-Z'. Cosmopolitan collection of parents, about a third bus their children daily – over 20 miles – from Paisley, Renfrewshire, Lanarkshire, north of the river, Ayr and Falkirk, courtesy of good road links and school bus service. Occasional 'real' foreigner. Long tradition of having a significant number of Jews – separate assemblies on Thursdays; perhaps 10 per cent from Asian backgrounds. Muslims may go to the mosque at lunch time

on Friday, have separate lessons for gym and no problem with scarves (though girls eschew dancing). Recent assembly had a Muslim, a Jew and a Protestant all discussing charitable giving.

Number of FPs' children. FPs include John Brown of the shipyard, plus John Buchan, Russell Hillhouse, Carol Smillie, Ross Harper, James Maxton, Richard Emanuel, Lord McColl, Ken Bruce, Lord Irvine, Olivia Giles, RD Laing, Lord Adair.

Entrance: Either from local prep or (usually) state primary, the odd refugee from other independents. One hundred a year more or less automatic up from the primary school, plus 100 extra (all pupils then get mixed up), otherwise by written test. Admission for all usually in August but, if space available, can join at any term.

Exit: Ninety-five+ per cent to universities: Five to Oxbridge in 2013 – an impressive list of firsts (and double firsts) from all graduates. No real enthusiasm for gap, education is a serious business in Scotland – particularly as many parents, often first time buyers find the current economic climate difficult. Most to Scottish universities, but 50 per cent fewer applicants this year to unis south of the border – the tuition fees you understand. A couple to LSE and UCL in 2013.

Money matters: Currently discounts for siblings, around 40 full-fee bursaries and some prizes for sixth formers. More funds being actively sought. All bursaries are means tested. But 'there should be no bar to a really able pupil profiting from a Hutchies education' – full bursaries are not unusual. Certain amount of concern recently when Hutchies failed the OSCr test, but this is now a thing of the past. We were amazed that Hutchies failed the charity trap, we are not talking about some overblown dame school, but one of Scotland's leading academic ones: what planet are the charity boys on? It took an inordinate amount of time to unscramble. For info: Hutchie's income was over 14 million quid last year AND you only get a four per cent discount if you pay five years in advance (with a five per cent per annum projected increase built in). Remember that founder George H was a banker.

Remarks: Awesome. Fiercely academic but pupils achieve their impressive grades from a fairly unselective background. Traditional teaching with enormous breadth, at its very best and using the most up to date tools available. As a previous rector said, 'It's cool to succeed here' – no change in that. Thomas and George would be proud.

Hymers College

Linked school: Hymers College Junior School

Hymers Avenue, Hull, HU3 1LW

- Pupils: 385 boys, 375 girls • Ages: 11–18 • Non-denom
- Fees: £9,621 pa • Independent

Tel: 01482 343555
Email: enquiries@hymers.org
Website: www.hymerscollege.co.uk

Headmaster: Since 2006, Mr David Elstone (early fifties). Read history and geography at University College, Cardiff and has taught at a variety of independent schools (including six years as depute rector at Hutchesons' Grammar School in Glasgow).

Unceremonious and determined, with a good sense of humour and plenty of drive. He was described by one parent as 'immensely caring'. Has brought in 'massive changes' and as one parent told us, he has 'kept the high standards but relaxed the whole school down'. Passionate about education and helping young people to become better learners.

Passion extends to Bristol City football club. A former cricket and hockey master, he maintains his interest in cricket and is a member of the MCC. Married with two sons.

Academic matters: Academically selective on intake, 'though not as selective as most grammar schools'. Standards and expectations are high and exam results very commendable. Little, if anything, to match it locally.

In 2013, 45 per cent A*/A grades at A level and 71 per cent at GCSE. Broad curriculum includes Latin. Streaming in maths only until year 10. French, German and Spanish on offer, though linguists in the school would appreciate even more choice. Traditional offering at A level including general studies and the EPQ. At GCSE pupils take a minimum of eight subjects, though more on offer if desired (and able).

The four Rs of educationalist Guy Claxton's Learning Power are fundamental to learning here – resourcefulness, resilience, reflectiveness and reciprocity. The head told us: 'We needed to be more flexible in our teaching methods and personalise the learning experience for our pupils. Teaching has changed dramatically in school. We offer a traditional curriculum but it's not what is taught but how it is taught. We need to help to make our pupils' learning secure'. There has been investment in modern technology, a multi-media language laboratory, whiteboards and iPads for teachers.

Fewer than 40 pupils in school have SEN or a disability. Year 7 pupils are given a screening test in year 7 and individual learning difficulties identified through teacher observation too. Personal learning plans are drawn up via one-to-one work, where pupils are assessed, in agreement with parents. A specialist programme of physical exercises for children needing further learning support has 'had a profound impact in the classroom', says the head. A member of the junior school staff has been trained to deliver the programme.

Programme of careers advice starts in year 7, building up year on year to work experience and careers convention in year 11. Year 12 students use Centigrade programme and there is interview training and a series of sixth form lectures given by experts from a variety of professions, business and industry.

Games, options, the arts: Where talent is recognised (whether in sport, music or the arts) pupils are given support and encouragement but are expected to demonstrate commitment and be prepared to put in extra time and effort after school and on Saturdays. Opting out isn't an option. Games compulsory – rugby and cricket for boys, hockey (notably successful) and netball for girls, tennis (very successful) and athletics for both. Pupils well represented in national competitions.

Successful and nationally recognised music department, with representation in the National Youth Choir. Nearly 40 per cent of pupils take voice and instrument tuition. Free instrument loan for an indeterminate period. One of the highest number of pupils in the country taking ABRSM exams. Lots of performances by choirs, ensembles and orchestras – in-house and at venues like Beverley Minster. Drama is thriving – subject is included in year 7 and 8 curriculum and offered at GCSE and at AS level. Recent productions in 200-seater Judi Dench Theatre include The Magic Flute and Dracula and involved music, art, design, business and electronics departments.

Debating and Young Enterprise very active. D of E scheme regularly attracts over 100 pupils a year. Army Cadet Force (voluntary and after-school) popular with 30 or so members. Sporting and music tours on offer but with a maximum cost to pupils of £1,000 – a nod to the economic downturn.

Background and atmosphere: Opened in 1893 as a school for boys. School's founder, the Reverend John Hymers, a Cambridge fellow and Rector of Brandesburton, left money in his will for a school to be built 'for the training of intelligence in whatever social rank of life it may be found among the vast and varied population of the town and port of Hull'. The school has remained true to founder's intent, with below average fees and over 120 pupils receiving financial assistance through means tested bursaries funded by own endowments and The Ogden Trust.

Pleasing approach to the main entrance, which overlooks well-maintained playing fields, all-weather pitches and even a lake for keen ornithologists. Belies first impressions: when stepping inside you are immediately confronted with a view of the traditional assembly hall, lined with doors of carved wooden lockers ajar and adorned with sports bags, spilling items of PE kit, books and papers. It does get better, particularly in the new facilities.

Careful financial management (and some generous benefactors) has enabled extensive recent investment in new theatre, sports hall, sixth form centre, junior school and swimming pool. Attractive and sympathetic to the original buildings, though perhaps at the cost of refurbishing the older ones. Plans afoot to build a new music facility and learning resource centre.

The school manages to attain high levels of academe whilst pupils remain relaxed and happy, seemingly not under pressure. Parents allude to the changes under the current head (comments like 'it's not such an intense school') and praise the dedication of staff and their excellent relationship with the pupils. School's ability to identify talent and encourage pupils to shine, praised by parents, as well as the differentiated teaching. 'All are catered for', said a mother with three very different daughters at the school.

School has cultivated links with the local community. Lots of outreach programmes for pupils while the head sits on a number of local trusts and the court of Hull University. Has helped to raise perception of Hymers in the city.

Pastoral care and discipline: Pastoral care is a real strength of the school. It expects high standards and pupils don't disappoint. All fairly relaxed for much of the time. Parents speak of 'mutual respect and trust between pupils and teachers' and feel well informed. They told us that staff are accessible and problems are dealt with effectively. Pupils are well looked after and look after each other. Buddy system very effective – mentor training for year 12 on active listening and giving advice. Mixed tutor groups in sixth form promote collaboration and cohesion.

Bullying taken seriously – not just for victim but also to change behaviour of bully. School counsellor on hand. Pupils can expect to be expelled for serious misdemeanours, such as bringing drugs into school, but no expulsions for 10 years.

School consistently has equal numbers of boys and girls – in dining room we observed lots of mixed groups across the age range in conversation. According to our sixth form guide there's 'plenty of girl power' here.

Pupils and parents: Large catchment area – Hull, East Yorkshire, North Lincs, buses in all directions. Reflects the lack of ethnic diversity in the area. Wider social spread than most independents, due mainly to generous bursaries and lower than average fees. Many parents are first-time buyers, ranging from professionals (preponderance of medics and educators) to owners of local takeaways.

Pupils are open, bright, positive and enthusiastic. They value the academic support they receive and close friendships they make.

Entrance: For entry at 11+ pupils sit competitive exams in maths, English and verbal and non-verbal reasoning, plus interview. Four-form entry, 108 places in all (about 30 for external pupils, remainder transferring from own junior school). For sixth form, five GCSEs at grade B or above required. About 12 or so enter at 16, replacing the similar number of leavers.

Exit: Between 80 and 90 per cent stay post-GCSE. A good handful to Oxbridge each year; the rest, head to a gamut of English universities, with northern Russell Group strong favourites. Half study science and mathematics related degrees. Medicine and healthcare sought after too, with an equally consistent show of economics, business and social studies.

Money matters: About 15 fee remission places per year – all means-tested bursaries, some full fees.

Remarks: Hymers is an unpretentious place. School has maintained high academic standing yet managed to relax intensity in recent years, though high expectations remain for commitment and ambition. Pupils are confident, well prepared and proud of and valued for their successes across any number of disciplines.

Ibstock Place School

Linked school: Ibstock Place School, Prep and Kindergarten

Clarence Lane, London, SW15 5PY

• Pupils: 935 (530 boys, 405 girls); all day • Ages: 11–18 • Inter-denom • Fees: £13,200–£17,025 pa • Independent

Tel: 020 8876 9991
Email: registrar@ibstockplaceschool.co.uk
Website: www.ibstockplaceschool.co.uk

Headmistress: Since 2000, Mrs Anna Sylvester-Johnson BA PGCE – known to all as 'Mrs SJ' (late fifties). Previously head of The Arts Educational School in Turnham Green, prior to which she taught at The Lycée and before that she was head of English at The Green School for Girls in Isleworth. An interesting and eclectic mix. Chic, svelte and very much in control, she is a mix of smiley and steely. That she has made the school the success it is today is beyond doubt. The splendid new-build that has transformed the school and the elegance and taste with which no visitor could fail to be impressed will be a lasting monument to her drive and commitment.

Academic matters: IGCSEs in all core subjects now. A distinctive feature – and one of which we approve – is the insistence that all take two languages at IGCSE. German, Spanish, Mandarin, Italian, Latin and Greek – on offer, which we applaud. French popular and the most successful and the vast majority take this plus Spanish. Eng lit results outstanding, as are the results for those who take individual sciences, though dual award candidates' results weaker and parents report problems in the science dept which, school tells us, are now resolved. Geog and hist are popular options with most results A*-B. Overall, 74 per cent of I/GCSEs A*/A grades in 2013 but some surprising disparities in results.

Ibstock's sixth form is a relatively late bird and is still spreading its wings. It began in 2006 and its size now reflects its growing reputation and success. Philosophy, psychology and economics offered alongside the more trad subjects at A level – biology, English, psychology and maths being the most popular. All sixth formers now take the Extended Project Qualification. In 2013, 48 per cent A*/A grades and 80 per cent A*/B. Small sixth form means, mostly, small classes – a definite plus.

Parents praise school's flexibility in moving pupils between sets when appropriate. No specific learning support unit but school supports mild dyslexics, dyspraxics and Asperger's children. Learning support – at an extra charge – given to 69 pupils at time of our visit. This school is assuredly not a haven for those who would struggle elsewhere and anyone who

applies with this is mind 'is under an illusion from the distant past when the school was hippy-dippy!' One-to-one EAL support given to a few. The site overall would be tricky for a wheelchair user but the corridors – especially in 'new school' – are wide and easily navigable.

Games, options, the arts: 'We believe in competition – children are inherently competitive,' says Mrs S-J and plenty of opportunity to compete – in sports, debates, drama, you name it – in and out of school. Good cross-curricular initiatives, much public speaking and sensible trips to worthwhile places. Usual range of sports supplemented by good range of extracurricular opportunities. Notable individual successes in many competitions and sports – representatives in several national squads. Music, art and drama all thrive – 'the teachers put a lot of time into the arts side,' parents told us – and a warm sense of encouragement to try things out – witness the lively art and DT we enjoyed.

Background and atmosphere: In a nook on the edge of Richmond Park, between plush Sheen and the louring Roehampton modernist blocks of the late 1950s, sits the quite lovely Ibstock Place House, built in 1913 by Frank Chesterton (cousin of the more famous GK) and which was the home of the Duchess of Sutherland until 1920, during which time she was Mistress of the Robes to Queen Mary. She indulged her considerable taste in decorating the house, however. Between 1925-45 it was owned by the Paget family who brought in many mod cons eg a telephone system and a swimming pool. After three years of being requisitioned by the Ministry of Supply for scientists engaged in top secret work in radar development, the house was, in 1945, bought by the Froebel Educational Institute as accommodation for its 'demonstration school' – to practise the principles of the pioneering educationalist, Friedrich Froebel, whose fearsome bust still supervises the school gardens.

Rapid growth led to the building of the kindergarten and prep school buildings and various other add-ons until the quite magnificent extension to the main building – 'new school' – in 2011. The main building gave the new one something to live up to. Generously proportioned, elegantly decorated, now embellished with grand mirrors, large vases of opulent flowers, rugs, sofas and general country house elegance – all this must exert a civilising influence on young minds and spirits. New school – housing classrooms, labs and staff workrooms – is similarly appointed – ceramic tiled, spacious, with civilised loos and ample locker room, energy-saving lights etc – it is well-thought-out, tasteful and inviting. A sense of pride pervades the place and well it might.

Good, two-floor library with up-to-date stock, big chairs and a view of the school's 'woods'. Woods, orchard, 'bike city', two all-weather surface pitches and little garden make up main site's 10 acres of attractive outside space. 'Over the road' reached by a clever bridge is school's sports hall, drama studio, art room and two large pitches. Not the easiest school to get to – school runs pro bono minibuses for senior school pupils from Barnes Common station in the morning and after school from 4.00-6.00pm. Several public buses stop on Roehampton Lane, a short walk through the university campus. The popularity of 'bike city' is testament to the number of senior school pupils who cycle to school. Otherwise, you'll need a school run partner or three.

Pastoral care and discipline: Universal praise for the pastoral care and parents largely reported 'very happy children'. House system is key to the school and all appreciate the vertical groups in houses which make for a family feel. No drink incidents in anyone's memory, likewise few other discipline problems and bullying 'instantly dealt with – our investigations are always very thorough'. Some parental grumbles about high staff turnover – to the seeming mystification of Mrs S-J and definitely not seen as a current problem. Immensely sensible 'no bag' policy. You take your bag to your locker, take out what you need and can't go back for the next two hours. Result – no-one bashes you with a rucksack in a corridor, no heaps of bags at entrances and everyone has to think ahead. Hooray! Very attractive and sensible uniform worn, by most, with style and decorum.

Pupils and parents: The vast majority from the Putney, Roehampton, Richmond, Sheen areas. However, school contained children from over 250 junior schools when we visited, the most coming from Sheen Mount, East Sheen Primary, The Roche and Putney Park – after the school's own prep, that is. Active PTA and parents praise home-school communication. Parents a mix of professional, artistic, City and everything else. Notable former pupils include Emily Blunt, Nigella Lawson, Frieda and Nicholas Hughes and, head girl in the then top year, at the age of 13, Iris Murdoch.

Entrance: Register asap. Everyone interviewed for 11+ and all sit papers in English, maths and reasoning. Hugely oversubscribed. Some 500 children try for 90 places at 11+. At 13+, a few places for which there are 40+ candidates. At 16+, around 30 apply for around 10 places. A minimum of 57 GCSE points required plus As in A level subjects.

Exit: Bristol, Exeter, Nottingham, Leeds, Sussex and London unis particularly popular, with a good scattering elsewhere, from classics at Exeter and sport and recreation management at Edinburgh to yacht and powerboat design at Southampton Solent. Generally several to art foundation courses. Four to Oxbridge in 2013.

Money matters: Some academic, art, drama, dance, music and sports scholarships at 11 and more at 16 – value between 5-50 per cent of fees. Bursaries means-tested here as everywhere.

Remarks: Attractive school offering something rare – an all-through coeducational education in an inner London suburb. Improving academics. Turns out thoroughly nice young people.

Ilford County High School

Fremantle Road, Ilford, Essex, IG6 2JB

• Pupils: 955 boys, all day • Ages: 11-18 • Non-denom • State

Tel: 020 8551 6496
Email: enquiries@ichs.org.uk
Website: www.ichs.org.uk

Headteacher: Since 2010, Mr Michael Capon (fifties) BSc, BEd, MA Ed (Mgmt) NPQH. As well as management, head studied mathematics, geography and computer education. He started teaching in Cambridgeshire. After this his career spaned head of subject at a girls' grammar in Kent, head of mathematics faculty at a comprehensive on the Isle of Wight where he joined the leadership team as director of studies and, finally, a 16-year-spell at St Martin's School in Brentwood, Essex, as deputy headteacher responsible for the curriculum, the sixth form and finally for quality assurance. During this period he was also an associate consultant on sixth form issues with the local authority in Essex.

So this is Mr Capon's first headship and first single sex boys' school. He is a deep thinker, driven by something more profound than the desire for good exam results. In fact he spent the first year in this post thinking and observing. Mostly his thoughts were about how '[grammar] schools like this work and how you can make them better', making use of his more 'comprehensive philosophy and experience'. 'No doubt it is a good school, gets good results', but, he said, it is 'interesting to see how grammar schools make valued added progress, and not to pre-judge'.

He is troubled by what he terms as 'a misguided view' that the purpose of schooling is to get good exam results. Like many heads of other grammar schools he is concerned about the intake; that the cohort should not be overly made up of pupils who get a place just because they have been tutored to pass the entry test, but because they have natural ability and would benefit from the grammar school experience. He is concerned with identifying and producing young men who are able to demonstrate skills and attributes, 'like responsibility, resilience, ability to think outside the box, to question ... and ... to tackle new information and knowledge they have never met before'. Such young people may end up with a grade A* or a grade C but 'they can't half think'. Given such a choice, 'Which would a university be more likely to give the place to?' head asks suggestively. 'GB plc needs innovative thinkers. You can be the best scientist in the world but if you don't have a creative idea you're not going to get anything new, all you are going to do is regurgitate previous knowledge.'

Evidently, the time he took to sit and think about such issues paid off as the school registered a value added indicator of 1037 in 2011, a year after he joined. According to the value-added measure ALPS, the school is ranked in the five per cent of top schools for A levels. All this despite national funding cuts shortly after his arrival that meant reducing the senior leadership team from eight to five. The average age of teachers across the school is 48 with at least 30 who have been working at the school for 10 years or more.

Academic matters: Head has made it his business to remind these boys that the five A* to C benchmark is a myth if they think 'that's all I need' because it 'doesn't open any doors at all'. The context here is five A* to A grades, 'as that's what the Russell Group universities are now able to cite as an entry requirement. It depends on what your aspirations are, the head says, but in this environment, 'for these boys, it's five A* to A' at least'.

So the boys excel right across subjects at GCSE (61 per cent A*/A grades in 2013), with strongest results shown in the sciences, mathematics and the humanities subjects. Pupils said all boys here enjoy maths. Their enjoyment is reflected in grades: over 95 per cent A* or A at GCSE. Many of them, 80 at present, study maths and further maths A level. English lang may not look as strong with A* to A results almost halved at 49 per cent, but the fact that most other results were awarded Bs and just 13 a C gives a fuller picture of boys doing commendably well. The picture is similar for English lit. Still, all three science subjects feature equally strongly in results. These very able pupils also take part in maths olympiads and competitions in chemistry and physics.

The humanities are supported by field trips and other visits. French is offered as a first language in year 7 and from year 8 pupils study either German or Spanish as well. Languages are compulsory at the school in key stage 4, and about 11 choose to study two choices to GCSE. few continue to A level, but we did meet one student who took on the task. He said, 'It is good to study a language at A level. It's a challenge.' There is lots of support for learning with European trips and work experience opportunities. The school is developing partnerships with schools and colleges in Germany, Spain, Switzerland and Denmark.

At A level popular subjects are biology, chemistry, economics, mathematics and physics; other subjects on offer include computer science, English, geography, history, government and politics, and psychology. Most stick to academic rather than creative subjects. In 2013, 83 per cent A*/B and 54 per cent A*A grades. Subject-based reviews help to monitor each subject and data tracking to monitor pupil progress helps spot and tackle underperformance, not that there is much of that here, according to parents. The school was rated Outstanding by Ofsted at the last full inspection. Maximum class sizes, at 30 (and 22 in the sixth form), are at the upper end. Teacher-pupil ratio is about 1:17. The school caters for some 560 pupils with EAL requirements 'with in-class targeted intervention and in group support'. There are about 32 pupils across the school that receive SEN support from learning assistants. So, there are challenges, some of which you would not find at other schools with comparable grades.

This school has received many acknowledgments of its achievements and several awards, including Leading Edge School. Highest Performing Grammar School in Mathematics. The school achieved International School status from the British Council in six months. The school has historic links with Southern Africa so is 'seeking to see if there is any residue [connections from past links] there', and it is actively seeking to develop links with India and China to explore alternative learning styles.

Recently, the head has been asking questions like, 'If we started with a blank sheet on what makes a good student, what would it include?' 'How can we produce students who think outside of the box?' and 'Why should a university choose one student over another?' As a result the school introducing inquiry-based learning into year 7 in to help develop pupils' aptitude for critical thinking, leadership and responsibility. The plans have gone down well with parents and governors, except for one complaint: 'My child is in year 9, isn't he going to be disadvantaged?' The head's response is, 'that is a difficulty with change'.

Games, options, the arts: Sporting trophies for cricket and swimming, and a Sportsman of the Year award, all point to an environment where sport is taken seriously and given plenty of room for expression. Pupils enjoy taking part in swimming galas and pointed out to us the 'basketball court where we play football'. They explained, 'There is space for both but the football is the most popular though cricket is what we are best at, we tend to do well at cricket.' At the entrance to the sports hall is a notice board invitation to follow the PE department on Twitter to keep up with fixtures, lessons, inter-house competitions and results. There is plenty to report on, given the substantial provision in all the major sports and activities (from ultimate frisbie to indoor rowing and rugby). On-site facilities include an artificial cricket strip, two football pitches and a 400m running track. The sports hall itself houses a heated swimming pool. There are also four badminton courts, a full size basketball court, with two small courts and provision for volleyball, five-a-side football, and tennis. Upstairs there is a fitness/weights room, an aerobics area, a viewing gallery and a 'theory room for people taking GCSE or A level'.

The head describes the curriculum as 'very academic', saying, 'We have not gone down the road of media and other modern subjects but we do support art, music and languages. They are harder to maintain financially, but to have a school like this not having subjects like these in some form is unthinkable.' Drama is compulsory for year 7s as part of the English curriculum, and they all take part in an annual production, but after that it disappears from the curriculum.

Those students who do choose art produce rich, bold and inspiring work, much of it on display in corridors throughout the school. It includes drawings, paintings, photography and sculpting. Curriculum is enriched by visits to national museums and art galleries.

Provision for music is as rich as sport, though it is not so popular as an option. Around 62 pupils have timetabled music lessons and some exceptional talent can be found here. Some lessons take place at the Redbridge Music School and specialist music teachers visit to teach. Pupils have plenty of opportunity to develop their gifts on piano, violin, cello, double bass, saxophone, drum, voice and more through orchestra, jazz ensemble, choirs and various bands. There are concerts and performances in London and abroad. Few pupils take art or music A level.

Extracurricular provision across the school is rich, with clubs, groups and ensembles covering every interest. There are debating societies, rugby, sailing and indoor rowing clubs and for those wishing to stick to the academic, clubs to deepen awareness of astronomy, philosophy or physics.

Background and atmosphere: The school was founded in 1901 as Park High Grade School. It was a boys' and girls' school back then and located in Balfour Road. The boys' school split in 1929 and moved to its present location in Freemantle Road in 1935. This is a built-up residential area but the school has a secluded feel. The building is traditional, with beautiful oak stairwells, large wooden boards with lists of past notables – headteachers, year captains and the like – and display cabinets. The cabinets line either side as you enter the reception area and show off a big collection of plaques and trophies a reminder of the sort of school this is. They include awards for the Bank of England and Times Interest Rate Challenge, an Acknowledgement of Educational Excellence in Academic A Levels from Edexcel, an award from Help the Aged for helping to unite generations, and, most impressive of all, an award for best A level results achieved by boys taking critical thinking at an English grammar school, from the Good Schools Guide.

The school layout resembles two adjacent squares, with two stories of classrooms organised around these in circular fashion. This makes it very easy for new pupils to learn their way round as where you start is usually where you will finish. Near the front is 'the hall where assemblies happen – we have them in the afternoon,' a pupil explains, 'and variety nights where students and teachers perform'.

The atmosphere is bustling and lively, especially in the music department where boys frequently practice and experiment. A new learning resource centre and library was opened by the author Chris Ryan and has remained true to the celebration of literature with regular live and video conference talks by visiting authors. Other talks also take place there, including, for example, one for students interested in medicine, organised by York University. The school is planning further expansion, including an enlarged sixth form, which will increase funding. Building work will provide more independent study space for the sixth form.

Pastoral care and discipline: Parents comment on being drawn to the school by its 'ethos of competitiveness and success... it nurtures the boys and prepares them for the future'. Sometimes it is just the small things, like planners 'to ensure their homework is completed on time and all timescales are met' and the even distribution of that homework across the week. A parent said this allows his son time to complete and hand in work. This helps because 'He has music and drama lessons outside school in the evening and on weekends, which he enjoys. He also does sports two days a week.'

Noticeboards for each house, year and department keep pupils updated... 'notices on helping out, tours, linguist of the month...' Department specific news is also tweeted and there is a Facebook page for prefects.

Pastoral care arrangements at the school have moved from a horizontal year-based one to a vertical house system. There is a head of house and a team of five form tutors who work with and support pupils as they progress through the school. Form tutors are generally responsible for pupil welfare and progress. The new system provides greater opportunity for the boys to develop stronger skills in leadership, mentorship and responsibility, plus opportunities to develop relationships across year groups, right to sixth form. Pupils report that keenly-contested form sports competitions have been replaced by equally high-spirited house competitions.

Year 7s receive peer mentoring from older pupils in year 9, 10 and sixth form. 'They're a bit of a role model for the younger kids, someone to look up to...' and 'if you have any problems settling in you [can] go to see them.' For one pupil, who joined at sixth form, this was 'one of the things I liked when I came, people always willing to help'. He told us that bullying, or rather the lack of it, was another nice surprise for him, as at his previous school 'fights were a common occurrence. It was a radical change for me; since I've been here I haven't seen one'. 'The school has a strict anti-bullying policy,' said another sixth form pupil who has been at the school since year 7. 'I haven't really come across many cases of bullying in the school. I think most boys are fairly clued up that it's wrong.'

It is this reputation for strict discipline that was given by several parents as one of the school's strong points. They said, 'the boys are well behaved', the school has 'a good approach to bullying' and 'I do not hear of any violent incidences at the school.' Evidently there is the occasional event, but 'in that one experience the head of house got in touch quickly to explain the situation; it was quickly settled. Thankfully my son has not had any further incidents and we hope it remains that way.'

Pupils and parents: Overall, pupils come across as happy and well-adjusted. They come from a wide mix of ethnic backgrounds, and from the borough of Redbridge and surrounding areas like Waltham Forest, Newham, Barking and Dagenham. They range from bubbly, stumbling and oblivious year 7s making their way between lessons, to the year 11s who showed us around and were articulate, mature and friendly. One told us about the cooking lessons the school organises for sixth formers to help them prepare for university. He said: 'I think I am fairly confident for a boy of my age.' He then added, with honesty, 'I can't fault it and I have achieved as good a grade as I can. I didn't motivate myself as well as I could have before but now I've put my foot down.'

The majority of parents believe their children are being well taught and that all round provision at the school is good, although one mentioned that it would be nice to see pupils involved in more volunteer work and fundraising and more 'events such as leadership conferences, etc' to stimulate boys' minds. There is an enormous sense of relief at having got a place at the school, which is unsurprising given that it is the only boys' grammar in the borough. One parent said that the school 'has lived up to our expectations'. They appreciate the 'emphasis on all-round development and not just academics'.

There is a parents association that helps to raise money for resources at the school but, like many high schools, it dreams of getting more involved. 'The general trend here is that parents do not get involved,' said an active parent, 'they are of the feeling that once their child is in the school that is all they need to do. The school is not greatly funded and some parental support could help pay for things that are needed. It's not only about the fundraising but the community spirit, which I am afraid is very lacking.' Head understands that 'parents have busy lives' but says 'in some cases parents don't get involved enough, we still have parents you never see other than at parents' evening'.

Mr Capon is more anxious about boys whose parents 'have unrealistic aspirations for them'. His main message to parents is that it is about the education, not just the grades, 'about the breadth of roundness'. It is not just pupils that need to learn to think outside of the box, parents do too. 'If a boy's real interest and passion is for humanities and not science, fine, as that it is where they will get real satisfaction and achievement.' He tries to instil into both parents and pupils that, 'If you want to do engineering at university you can't just concentrate on maths and physics, your GCSE profile needs to be high quality across all 10 subjects, you can't afford to have A*, A*, A*, ..., A, C. It is the quickest route to an admissions tutor's waste paper basket.' Most parents get this and some have little sympathy for those that do not. One said, 'there are always a few parents who do not take this on board, despite the school's best efforts, and end up disappointed when their sons fail to get into their chosen university.'

Notable former pupils include Raymond Baxter, TV personality (Tomorrow's World), Sir Trevor Brooking, footballer, and David Miller, Deputy Chief Inspector of Air Accidents.

Entrance: A selective school, though head does not think it is as selective as many of the other grammar schools in Essex. Nevertheless, more than 850 boys in the borough of Redbridge and nearby compete for the 120 places available each year by sitting the 11+ examination. The test is administered by the London Borough of Redbridge. School manages its own admission to the sixth form, with places offered dependent on predicted GCSE grades.

Exit: Almost all (some 85 per cent) stay on to sixth form. Leavers go on to study subjects such economics, architecture, dentistry, medicine, law, physics and engineering. Majority choose to study in London at eg King's College and UCL. Six to Oxbridge in 2013.

Remarks: A school that delivers a high standard of education and produces young men who seem well prepared for the wider world. Somehow seems to be a victim of its own success, constantly having to grapple with the challenge of how to progress and maintain its impressive record and position among high performing secondary schools. However, this situation is tempered by a very likeable head who constantly manages to find better ways to articulate what the future of good education should look like.

Immanuel College

Linked school: Immanuel College Preparatory School

Elstree Road, Bushey Heath, Bushey, Hertfordshire, WD23 4EB

• Pupils: 520 boys and girls • Ages: 11–18 • Jewish • Fees: £13,866 pa • Independent

Tel: 020 8950 0604
Email: admissions@immanuel.herts.sch.uk
Website: www.immanuelcollege.co.uk

Head Master: Since April 2012, Mr Charles Dormer MA (mid-forties), previously head of the King's School, Grantham. Born in New York into a third generation Jewish-American family, and initially educated there and in Florida, he has dual American and British citizenship. He studied English at Magdalen College, Cambridge and has taught in independent schools and selective state schools for 24 years.

Academic matters: The focus of the school is the provision of a nurturing education centred on a core of Jewish studies. Very small classes (18 pre-GCSE, as little as three or four at A level) mean all pupils are well known. 'The small classes meant my daughter reached the top end of her ability,' said one mother. Though selective at 11, the academic range is reasonably broad, albeit skewed to the more able. In 2013, 55 per cent A*/A grades at GCSE and 65 per cent A*/A at A level. Probably works best academically for the child who needs close care and attention, rather than the one who needs academic extension. 'I had two children in the school,' said one parent. 'My daughter got a very, very good set of GCSEs; the school really added something she would not have got elsewhere. My son is very able and I'm not sure it stretched him.' Some concerns, too, about curriculum monitoring at A level. Considering the Pre-U and 'revisiting' a discussion on the IB – 'Though we don't really feel it suits our learning profile. It's not good for those whose maths is wobbly'.

Boys and girls are taught separately years 7-9 – 'Girls need a respite from male competitiveness and being scrutinised,' says the school. Independent learning project in year 8 to develop research and study skills. Years 10 and 11 now setted and co-ed. IGCSE in maths, history, music and science. Top set takes triple science IGCSE.

Jewish studies a fundamental part of the curriculum. Modern Hebrew taught in years 7, 8 and 9 and students have the option to study biblical Hebrew as well as textual Jewish learning. Three religious study options for sixth formers: A level RE with Judaism and ethics; preparation for Jewish life and an intensive textual course (some pupils go on to study at yeshiva and seminary). Secular A level options include sociology, theatre studies, PE, maths and psychology.

Lively, relaxed engaged teaching and excellent teacher-pupil relationships. Once appointed, teachers (half of whom are not Jewish) tend to stay. 'There are some very, very good teachers,' said one parent. Good and caring special needs provision (with two teaching assistants) for both physical and learning difficulties. Despite the upstairs-downstairs site, a specially adapted lift makes all things possible. Outstanding specialised support and individual learning plans.

Games, options, the arts: Art particularly vibrant, with good numbers going on to places at leading art schools and art rooms packed in lunch hours with pupils polishing their portfolios. Music part of the core curriculum but only a handful take it at GCSE. Potential young talent fired up with an American band and subsidised music lessons. Three concerts a year, two drama productions.

Not a school where parents prioritise sport and high-level competition certainly not part of the creed. School, however, wants pupils to reach a decent level in all their hobbies 'to improve their quality of recreation'. The sport on offer has improved in recent years with a keen young staff who arrange some 250 fixtures. Football played with enthusiasm and success, good showing in basketball. Boys offered football, basketball, tennis, athletics, cricket, badminton and trampolining, girls football, netball, rounders, tennis and dance (very strong). Adequate rather than inspiring facilities: prettily-positioned running track, well-used tennis courts.

A strong and enthusiastic following for debating. Teachers contractually bound to help out with the extra-curricular and school trips definitely a strength. The whole of year 9 to Israel, the entire year 12 to Poland. 'The four-week trip to Israel is a real bonding experience. It creates friendships for life,' says one parent.

Background and atmosphere: Founded in 1991 by the then Chief Rabbi, Immanuel Jacobovits, who wanted to establish a religious school to rival some of north London's most famous academic names. The core of the building is a magnificent turreted Victorian pile (formerly a convent school) described by Pevsner as sitting atop its 11 acres of Hertfordshire green belt like a 'Harrogate Hotel'. The original high-ceilinged rooms with their elaborate plasterwork are still in use for art classes and classrooms. Plenty of later additions. This, however, is not some pristine show home, rather a comfortably shambolic family house.

Unlike some of its Orthodox state school competitors, it has a more modern approach to the faith – 'We study contemporary literature and a range of religions'. Not as academically competitive as the private schools it was set up to rival, it provides a more intimate and nurturing atmosphere. No bar and bat mitzvah programme at the moment, but under consideration. Programme of social action in Jewish and wider community a high priority. but the list of charities funded seems long and all-encompassing. Friendly and encouraging community in a protected and protective environment. 'Because of the size, it has a real family feel,' said one parent. School aims to turn out 'young people who are kind and confident, know themselves and help others. They understand where they are going, have a loyalty to being Jewish and a relationship with their faith that is going to continue'. Food is kosher, healthy, appetising. Staff share pupils' dining room, which offers a calm and orderly place for all to sit, eat and enjoy civilised conversation.

Pastoral care and discipline: Pastoral care very fine tuned. Head of year plus four tutors in year 7, designated pastoral leaders in years 8 and 9. Deputy heads constantly available to pupils and parents (as, indeed, is the head). Prefects are self-selected – those who are keen to take on responsibility apply for the post and are interviewed. Once appointed, they play a large part in the life of the school, helping younger pupils to read Hebrew, organising social events and charity fairs. Prayer is a fundamental part of the ethos – years 7-11 have compulsory prayers every morning before class. For sixth formers, prayer is primarily voluntary, though compulsory before the major festivals.

Not a school where discipline is a significant issue. Certainly no serious concerns about drugs: 'We have a programme of education – we'd be mad not to – but it's a day school and it's common sense for pupils not to put themselves in a position of vulnerability'. Some after-school detention but it's not prominent – 'Teachers are very good at classroom management'. Inconsiderate car parking by sixth formers tends to irritate the locals.

Pupils and parents: Applicants must be Chalachic Jews, as defined by the Chief Rabbi's office, but after that the school takes in the full spectrum, from the seriously observant to those who don't attend synagogue but have an attachment to the Jewish way of life. Particularly popular with Sephardic Jews. Pupils tend to be articulate and creative – 'They're nice, decent kids, not too cool or street smart,' said one observer; parents affluent professionals from a broad sweep of north London and Hertfordshire. Coaches bring them in from near (Bushey and Pinner) and far (Hampstead Garden Suburb, St John's Wood.) Coaches at 4.15 and 5.45pm – pupil groupings at school often divide into coach-journey buddies.

Entrance: Selective entry but not overly so. School aims to take those 'who can pass GCSE at grade C or above. We're looking for someone eager to learn, excited by being on the planet. We want someone curious, rather than just academic'. Small intake into the sixth form.

Exit: Good preparation for universities – series of seminars after AS, plus tailored individual advice. On our visit a sixth former was searching through university courses with the deputy head and being warned about how courses might suddenly disappear – 'No stone is left unturned. We find courses that suit pupils' strengths'. Also prepares students for any additional tests required for degrees such as medicine or law. In 2013, two to Oxbridge. Birmingham, Nottingham and Leeds popular destinations too. Many do their gap year in Israel.

Money matters: Not a rich or well-endowed school. Some symbolic scholarships, but most extra money used to help those who have hit rocky times. Entrance exhibitions in art and music of up to £2000 a year. Some scholarships of up to half the fees.

Remarks: Produces confident and well-qualified young people with a deep understanding of their faith.

SENIOR SCHOOLS

Impington Village College

New Road, Impington, Cambridge, CB24 9LX

• Pupils: 1140 in years 7–11, 305 pupils in the sixth form • Ages: 11–19 • Non-denom • State

Tel: 01223 200400
Email: office@impington.cambs.sch.uk
Website: www.impington.cambs.sch.uk

Principal: Since 2007, Mr Robert Campbell BA PGCE MPhil (mid forties). Married with three school age children (two at the College themselves). This English graduate, who has quickly climbed the educational ladder and already has a previous headship under his belt, is seriously conscientious and totally wedded to the job. Pro-active, direct and thoughtful, he's a great believer in inclusivity and is good at promoting IVC (Impington Village College). Acronym speak occasionally pops up, but as his vocation is to be active within the school, he doesn't sit on committees or live behind a desk – currently teaching GCSE English. Interests include fiction, history and music – he plays the guitar and clarinet. Also an international orienteer who has represented England and hopes to do so again. On top of all of this he often runs to school from Cambridge Station. As someone who has 'endeavoured to be everywhere for everybody', he must be, as one parent commented, 'Superman'. We rather agree.

Academic matters: A school with a split personality. Pre-sixth a happy, sound community comp where the ordered teaching environment lauds the bright and gives sensitive help to the less able. Comments from parents that some have learned to be middle of the roaders are countered by the head. He assures us this is a thing of the past now, two tutors per form – the learning tutor and assistant learning tutor stay with their charges all the way through – making under-achievement less likely.

At GCSE, a solid performance given the mixed intake – 71 per cent with five or more A*-Cs including English and maths in 2013, with 27 per cent A*/A grades. Students start key stage 4 in year 9. Applied learning schemes for those in this year and above. Courses in catering, construction, life skills, hair and beauty – a salon on site. Has specialist language status – it provides a French teacher for local primaries and has a clutch of European teachers on the staff. All in year 7 learn French and Spanish. Option of Spanish and Japanese at GCSE and Russian in the sixth. Greek, Italian, Latin and Chinese also on offer and some fast tracking for super linguists. At the other end of the scale, the sensible alternative of an international award, which increases awareness of other cultures.

Now to the extraordinary sixth form, where 75 per cent take the IB – introduced in 1991 – with most of the rest taking A levels in the arts. A bona fide international college with a well regarded head and students from 33 nations – 'The way international students raise expectations and level of competition is an eye opener for the home cohort,' commented one parent. In 2013, the average IB point score was 32, and 68 per cent of A level grades were A*/C.

'Hugely inclusive' place – a quarter have special needs. The spacious, purpose-built Pavilion provides a perfect base for SEN and treatment centre for those with physical difficulties. Where appropriate, designated lessons and/or in-class support. In addition, boasts an IDEAL unit which provides 25 places for young adults with moderate to severe learning needs, including those with Down's syndrome. Some of the 25 are from out of catchment – the rest LA referral. All join mainstream pastoral activities and, where appropriate, mainstream lessons. We were impressed with the positive interaction between some of the IB students and members of the unit.

Games, options, the arts: Verdict from the punters is that 'sport is brilliant', and appreciation for staff who not only put in extra time but are also scrupulously fair when selecting teams is unanimous. Has a Sportsmark award – a fine choice of team and individual games at all levels. Pupils are encouraged to try everything and boys genuinely enjoy dance lessons in the sprung floor studio – an enthusiastic ex-pupil has returned to teach in the school which inspired him to dance. Games not compulsory in the sixth – enthusiasm for team sports found lower down the school seems to fizzle out.

Performing arts are particularly strong – a composer, fine artist and professional dancer have been in residence in recent years. Impressive drama: excellent and often challenging performances – not many places where you'd find a production of Antigone by Sophocles put on by year 11 GCSE students playing to a full house. Workshops run by external talent, ballet classes before school and a post 16 School of Performance.

Introduction of two-weekly timetable has given more time for extracurricular activities. Lots of clubs including an active Amnesty International group. D of E is very popular (several gold awards each year) with the IB requirement of 150 hours of community service readily accommodated. Many trips overseas and international exchanges – a year 11 student recently gained a scholarship to spend five months in Japan.

Background and atmosphere: On the outskirts of Cambridge, founded in 1939 under a scheme (devised by Cambridgeshire's education secretary Henry Morris) where rural England was to be provided with educational and social centres serving all ages – continues to offer adult education and maintains a sports centre open 364 days a year from 6am to 10pm. Walter Gropius, of Bauhaus fame, designed the main building which, although jaded on the outside, still makes an interesting architectural statement, particularly in the curved wing where the head has his office. Large entrance hall serves as the 'prom', where younger children congregate and happily chatter. Newer buildings radiate across the ample site.

Good facilities including indoor pool, impressive sports centre with first-rate gym and sauna, library with a sound proofed sixth form area, a history department set around clusters of computers and an editing suite with top notch equipment. Children are well behaved and appear pleasantly relaxed in this straightforward, well-tended environment. Jolly touches give a lift to otherwise bland spaces – cronky metallic structures donated by a local sculptor and bright graphic images in the year 7 eating area. Improved, healthier food and cheery canteen. A shame children have to buy water and relatively little space for eating at tables – but giant leap into the 21st century with 'vericool' (note the creepy name): a finger print recognition system which has effectively cut queues at tills and signing in points. Orwell and 1984 come to mind, but pupils, predictably, think it's 'cool'.

Sixth, who don't wear a uniform, have their own building with a buzzy, welcoming common room. New mezzanine floor hasn't done much to alleviate crowding and the head hopes for a new centre to accommodate ever increasing numbers. Community spirit is strong and charitable events abound – a project to raise money for children in Ghana has already given some the opportunity to go to school. Students have also been to Bangalore to help the street children.

Pastoral care and discipline: Caring, friendly atmosphere predominates – true to its egalitarian principles, no prefects: very Impington. All have access to a male or female counsellor – a great help with stress and all sorts of problems. Bullying isn't swept under the carpet but dealt with straight away – as one pupil commented, 'This is a big school and we are children'.

Students and a teacher recently refined the behaviour policy and volunteers are involved with a mentoring scheme. Highly rated community support officer, employed by the school, is based in the college – 'He's an excellent rôle model, onto mischief in and out of school, and works with the child, their family and the college, and every school should have one,' enthused the head. 'Absolutely brilliant,' commented one mum.

Pupils really feel they have a voice. Large, unelected and active student council, co-ordinated by a member of staff, is open to all. Head believes in being firm but fair and developing pupils' sense of responsibility towards the college. Very rare permanent exclusions. All cases are looked at individually and support is given to students and families, but the policy re banned substances is clear.

Pupils and parents: Parents of 11-16 year olds range from Cambridge academics to the seriously underprivileged. In the sixth form, pupils come from all over: some are local, others from a range of countries – mostly in the EU. International students and those from outside Cambridgeshire are housed (carefully) with local host families. Sixth formers we met (of several nationalities) were delightfully open, mature and self motivated – 'The work is extremely challenging and we have to work hard, but the atmosphere in this school is so good that I really regret having holidays. It is just a wonderful school'. Praise indeed from someone who's come from abroad.

Entrance: At 11 from local primaries in catchment. Over-subscribed but appeals often succeed, boosting class sizes above the target level of 28 (20 in the sixth).

Majority of new sixth formers either international or from local schools. Four distinct courses in the sixth. For the selective IB, pupils need to be well motivated and have an average B grade profile at GCSE; according to a sixth former, 'if students don't work that's their problem – they'll sink'. For A levels – mostly arts based – normally five Cs or better. For the School of Performance, which provides a vocational training for those planning a career in dance, theatre or music, academic qualifications aren't an issue, but students are informally auditioned and are likely to take one or two A/AS levels. Special post-16 one-to-one course for those with severe learning difficulties.

Exit: At 16 around 70 per cent move on to local sixth form colleges (Hills Road, Long Road etc) for wider range of A levels and vocational qualifications. International sixth formers to a wide range of mostly European universities; local students to eg Cambridge Regional College, University of East Anglia, dance and drama schools.

Money matters: No fees unless non EU families relocate to the area. Entitlement to free education – or assistance – is determined by the visa status of parents.

Remarks: An exciting, forward-looking place which has much to offer all sorts. Energetic head looks set to make pre-sixth equal to the sixth form, where the international cohort makes IVC exceptional within the state system.

International School of Aberdeen

Linked school: International School of Aberdeen, Preschool and Elementary

Pitfodels House, North Deeside Road, Pitfodels, Cults AB15 9PN

- Pupils: Upper school (grade 6 to grade 12) – 120 boys/140 girls
- Ages: 11–18 • Fees: £17,875–£20,020 + £2100 capital fee pa
- Independent

Tel: 01224 730300
Email: admin@isa.aberdeen.sch.uk
Website: www.isa.aberdeen.sch.uk

Director: Since 2002, Dr Daniel Hovde PhD (fifties) who came to the granite city from the jungles of Sumatra where he was head of an International Services contract school, contracted to Chevron. Before that he taught in the Canadian Academy in Japan, which was founded as a missionary school in 1913 and was home to some 35 different nationalities. Married to Karol, a counsellor with the school (they adopted their daughter in China whilst in the far east), educated in Seattle, studying history, social studies and (majoring in) education from Washington State University, followed by a master's in education and a doctorate in educational leadership – 'It seemed to take forever'. He taught in between his lengthy education and was pleased to come to Aberdeen, as it was 'the right size and make-up for himself and his wife and good for the daughter' – they could 'all work in the same place'. Delightful, outgoing and friendly, he runs the school with a pair of principals and positively bounced this editor round the school (as he had the previous one). No change here, except he has added two more bows to his string: he is now an avid Munro bagger, and force majeure, an architect manqué. The new build is spectacular, with not a little input from the head, who, when we asked him about summer holidays, said they weren't – and we went round the building, 23 days into term, when the website with maps and all hadn't been changed.

Academic matters: School nominally follows the IB, but they also cover High School Diplomas. Most pupils do the IB diploma and average 33 points (33 in 2013). Pupils get Advanced credit for having taken the IB, but it is by no means suitable or even needed by all. Some Standard grades taken 'for curiosity benchmark'. Fair mish-mash. Massive amount of to-ing and fro-ing; over 35 nationalities are represented in the student population, 32 different languages spoken, most pupils come for two or three years, some only for one, and 'odd one beyond five'. Pupils go on the roll of honour (spelled, of course, 'honor') society if they have done well in the realms of academe, leadership and service. All very American and fairly in your face, with a strong emphasis on service.

School is divided into three distinct parts: elementary – pre-school to grade 5 (ie 10 year olds), middle school (grades 6-8) and high school (grades 9-12). Each department has its own distinct area in the school, with tinies having a splendid enclosed play area on squidgy tarmac.

60 per cent of all staff are British 'local' hire, with husbands in oil, or 'just living here', and 40 per cent have a mixture of backgrounds, from English-speaking countries in the main, though native speakers employed for Spanish and French (the two languages offered for IB) plus Dutch mother tongue (think Shell). School appears to run as a commune with no heads of departments, plus two counsellors. Whilst senior pupils seek advice from staff, younger pupils are ambivalent about whether they go to a teacher or an older pupil ('natural helpers') for

assistance. EAL where necessary – three dedicated teachers. Roughly 30 pupils in each year group, 13/20 per class. Choices accelerated, and learning support available – two dedicated members of staff. School is brutally honest – if pupils need more than 20 per cent support per week, then they will have to go elsewhere, ie local mainstream.

Games, options, the arts: Stunning sports wing housing a double gymnasium, huge games hall, fitness centre, multi-purpose spaces, 25 metre six lane swimming pool, much used by locals – as are the gym/games facilities, fitness suite and multi-gym. Terrific outdoor sports area: two all-weather basketball courts (teams play internationally), tennis courts, facilities for football and golf (which they also play internationally and in the Scottish League) plus volley ball. Teams visit London, Stavanger, Spain and Portugal as well as running their own internal league. Cabinets of shining silver in previous school not yet up, but dedicated space available in canteen/rec area.

Terrific music space, with recording studios et al. No orchestras but number of instruments taught, ditto choirs – pupils make music outside school. Rather clever computer programme which goes red when you hit the wrong note – deeply popular. Serious theatre which replicates the one they lost – magical acoustics – plus black room, an infinite space used for theatre or odd parents' meetings; history of lavish drama. Impressive art all over and whizzo new artrooms with outside area for really mucky stuff; external kiln. This is all things for all people – quadruple wows all round.

High charity presence: sleepovers for the homeless, shoe-box appeal and the eight year olds visit local 'rest' homes and read and perform to them. American boy scouts, cub scouts, girl guides and Brownies, but no D of E.

Background and atmosphere: School founded in 1972 by Mr McCormick and bought by the oil companies in 1980. The latter own the buildings and oversaw the negotiations with Aberdeen town council, who had to approve each and every bit of the new build, but the oil consortium underwrote the school (and undertake all the improvements – wish lists et al), leasing the buildings to the school for a peppercorn. The school is run by a charitable trust, with the members of the board being appointed in proportion to the number of employees' children in the school at one particular moment. A local solicitor sees fair play. School owns 16 acres of land, with nine acres of games fields off site.

The (unsigned) reception area is through the much revamped late Victorian (1881) Pitfodels House, which boasts double glazed curved windows (a first for this editor, who is quite into houses) and beautifully replicated mouldings (wood) leading to the street (see below). Two wings on either side of the library, one for the games area and one for the classroom block. Very light and airy, with hidden lights wherever from south facing windows – in the roof, on the staircases – which seem to float with exciting banisters; 40 huge magically filled classrooms – the junior ones interlinked so that classes can combine if need be; wide passages with a mass of gossip areas, comfy seats – gosh!. Pupil pics abound, so not that soulless. The landscaped gardens contain a mass of car park area and sport a splendid if somewhat surprising three storey granite tower, thought to date from the mid 17th century.

New build is based on a village street, with the library as the hub – a glorious double decker library with a random collection of computers – plus, of course, dedicated computer rooms elsewhere. The canteen, at the end of the street boasts both bog standard school seating and high level tables and chairs, plus cafeteria style seating. Pupils revel in the ability to be both grown up and silly at the same time. The new chef has turned school catering around – now making a healthy profit. Children have an account but can buy outwith. (NB Peanut butter not allowed – epi-pens and de-fib machines on hand.) At the end of the street an eight metre climbing wall and, when the cafeteria peripherals are pushed to one side (all the side boards are on wheels), school has a huge entertainment space for exhibitions and the like – cunning.

Pupil lockers (high enough off the ground for them to put bags under) line their respective teaching areas and are still decorated in rather uninspired wrapping paper on their birthdays. Lots of happy birthday singing at lunch. Much talk of how super Scotland is, and a certain amount of Celtic indulgence. Trips all over the shop.

Pastoral care and discipline: Head anxious to dispel the myth of spoilt little rich boys; keen PSE and strong RME. Guidance by clans or houses. Staff are trained in different cultures and dealing with people in a different fashion (how things are done at home) – 'Kids are kids'; 'Knock on wood – no overt bullying, but quite a lot of teasing'. No bullying because of habits, more 'teasing because of personality traits' (his words not ours). Drug presentation evenings, and head has – 'Oh yeah, on occasion' – disciplined and suspended (never expelled) miscreants for a day or two: details of all suspendable offences in handbooks, complete with list of drug test cut-off levels. Head keen on independent study and motivation, and no gum may be chewed in class.

Pupils and parents: No school uniform, but of course everyone conforms – we were, though, slightly surprised to see a seven (?) year old in mini skirt with high heels and sparkly tights.

Most students arrive via school bus. Good parent contact with weekly newsletters. Recent influx of locals, who pay a lesser fee. With the new build, which is a couple of miles closer to the centre of Aberdeen, school is actively canvassing for more locals.

Entrance: Whenever. Slightly undersubscribed, could hold 600.

Exit: Universities in America and Britain the most popular, with a few heading to study in the Netherlands and Canada too. Others to Imperial, St Andrews, Aberdeen, Glasgow, Robert Gordon', Hull York Medical School and West Scotland in 2013.

Money matters: Fees paid by oil companies, otherwise one or two non-oil American expats, bursaries and financial aid available so that school more reflects the cost of a 'normal' British school. IB academic scholarships available for final two years.

Remarks: We previously said, 'Smashing school – an eye-opener,' but never expected that our next visit would indeed be the result of smashing the school. It had, in 2006, been ten days into building their new gym, which would have released their old gym to become a theatre, when Aberdeen County Council announced the route of the new ring road – straight through the old school. But now? We are (un)reliably informed that the new build (which is fantastic) cost £51 million – and it looks it! Wow! Wow! Wow!

Totally logical, of course, to follow an international programme but, with such an influx of non-native teachers, it might be possible for a family to be billeted in Scotland for a year or so and experience no native culture at all. Thank you for sharing.

International School of London

Linked school: International School of London – Junior

139 Gunnersbury Avenue, London, W3 8LG

- Pupils: 365 boys and girls • Ages: 3–18 • Non-denom
- Fees: £19,750–£22,500 pa • Independent

Tel: 020 8992 5823
Email: mail@ISLLondon.org
Website: www.ISLLondon.org

Head of School: Since 2009, Mr Huw Davies, Oxford University MA (PPE) PGCE. Has long experience at ISL: previously deputy head, IB diploma coordinator, higher education advisor, history and Theory of Knowledge teacher. Generous with his extensive IB knowledge and experience, is an IB consultant to prospective IB schools and often on authorising teams for IB schools worldwide. A man of few words, he comes across as an archetypal British ex-history master, yet he clearly has a foot firmly in the international education world. Parents did not have a lot to say about Mr Davies; he is possibly more engaged in the behind the scenes day-to-day school management and the big-picture strategic jobs (school refurbishments, increased capacity for growing demand, mother tongue programme etc); delegating more of the 'front of house' interactions to his teachers and principals.

Academic matters: The school offers the IBPYP, IBMYP, IBDP continuum. Some high school students opt out of the full diploma, earning instead an ISL high school diploma. There's a good selection of IB courses, with more online through Pamoja Education.

Primary students have specialist teachers for music and PE; art is taught by class teachers. From middle school, specialists teach art, drama, music and PE (through Grade 10). Strong level of support in primary classes with plenty of assistants for classes that can number up to 20.

The major draw for every single family we spoke to is the 'terrific' mother tongue programme. It may cost extra depending on numbers, but mother tongue classes are offered primary through to high school with about 16 IB languages leading to the added advantage of a bilingual IB diploma. If a new child's language is not on the list, they will try to find a teacher. EAL support is also strong.

Some primary parents prefer the slight 'delay' in reading for younger children when compared to the local English schools. For families coming from countries where formal schooling begins at age 6 or 7, ISL's gentle introductory literacy approach at age 5 is more comfortable. However, others comment that while they're very happy at ISL, the range of English fluency may have an effect on the academic pace and rigour compared with other independent schools.

Laptops are lent to students and kept at school, so away from school students access their work online. Interactive whiteboards or smart tvs in many classrooms. We noticed there weren't as many students 'connected to devices' as is seen in other London international schools – for better or worse.

Engaged and cheerful children everywhere we went. A parade of primary students with yummy sandwiches headed to the dining hall, leaving behind open exercise books in their classroom, with individually written recipes for 'my favourite healthy sandwich' (part of their health living unit using hands-on IBPYP approach); youngest children eating and chatting while teaching assistants circulated attentively; middle school students debating the value of democracy and advantage of a student council that can organise fun activities in preparation for an upcoming assembly; CDT students sawing away at wood; art students busily tidying up their room to head to the assembly...everyone looked settled and at ease. Great esprit de corps apparent from fact that the entire secondary participate in assemblies.

IB results steadily rising in recent years; average point score in 2013 was 33; just under half earned bilingual diplomas, far above the international average.

Parents generally happy with communication with the school. There's good overall consultation. Some say response to emails are occasionally inconsistent: while issues raised in an emails seem to be addressed by staff, parents aren't always kept informed of the follow up. The parent of a younger child was surprised when parents were not invited to accompany children to see the classrooms on orientation day. Parents new to the IB curricula sometimes may struggle if they don't attend the parent education events provided by the school.

With families coming from so many different national education systems, everyone has his own idea about the 'right way' to do things. Managing these expectations and helping children adapt is part of the ISL challenge, and for the most part, parents report they do a great job.

Approximately 90 teachers, average age is early 40s, with several part-time language teachers. About 15 have been there for over 10 years.

Games, options, the arts: There's a mix of after-school clubs, though some primary parents would like there to be more, and juggling after-school pick up can be tricky if a younger sibling has nothing to do. Usual international school sports such as volleyball, football, basketball and tennis, and triathlon offered too, with international tournaments. Primary PE and sports take place on site in the hall, small playground, or neighbouring park. Secondary kids go to a nearby sports centres or the park. Weekly swimming for all up to grade 10 at Brentford Leisure Centre. One parent suggests ISL may not suit the 'uber-athlete'; 'it's fun and competitive to a point, but for serious athletes, families join local sports clubs.'

Private instrumental lessons schedule during the school day, with ensembles practising after school. ISL takes advantage of London as a vast field trip opportunity; early in the year there's a week when nearly everyone from grade 4 vacates the school for three to five day trips. Some incorporate team-building to integrate newcomers; in the middle years they're language-related (Beijing just added). Only the youngest and the IB students (except those on a biology trip) stay behind. Primary parents tell us that the idea of sending their 9 year olds off on a residential trip 'takes some getting used to'.

Many community service opportunities on offer by school, and students also organise their own. One returned to her native India to volunteer in a school for the summer. ISL has work experience programme for all grade 9 students; the school helps organise, or parents and students find their own placement. Though they're a bit young to work, it can inspire their thinking about what IB courses they may select. For one student it also led to summer job opportunities and a gap year project after graduation.

Background and atmosphere: A secondary school founded in north London in 1972, ISL was one of the first authorised IB diploma schools in the country. The school merged in the late 80s with the International Community College, a primary school founded by the Marakem family, becoming a full 4-18 school and moving into a former Catholic school on the North Circular Road in west London. The school is still owned by the Makarems, who recently opened schools in Qatar and in Surrey (buying Shell's former Dutch school). The group is managed by Amin Makarem, the founder's son, who oversees the leadership team of the three schools. Parents say the ISL's quite independent of the other two; not much inter-school activity at student level apart from some sports competition between the Woking and Surrey, but we hear more collaboration is planned.

446   SENIOR SCHOOLS

The building would not win any architectural prizes, but it is undergoing a major refurbishment to modernise and make more it attractive. The primary is located in an annex rented from the next-door church; the school reports that it has no plans to relinquish this space even when the refurbishment is completed. ISL is a rabbit warren of hallways and stairwells with every nook and cranny utilised – the staff room, practically in the rafters, is a hive of energetic teachers planning and conversing in umpteen languages – a very positive vibe.

The school definitely needs sprucing up; it's not easy to see any rationale to the arrangements of secondary school classrooms or corridors and public spaces. Possibly due to building works under way, the school can feel cramped and disorganised. The head and school leadership team are considering how to reconfigure the classroom arrangements once the refurbishment is complete.

The primary lunch room is uninspiring, and the play area out front is basically a hard surface to run around and play a few ball games on, though as a result of the construction, the kids are going to the park more, which is a lovely treat and very handy. The school is protected by secure gates.

There's a two-level art room and a photo lab, a great CDT classroom, functional science labs of a certain age, a useful multi-purpose hall, a library (which will be relocated after the refurb) and lots of multi-use classrooms of various sizes. Middle and high school students share classrooms and primary share some of the language and specialist classrooms; primary parents reassure us that it's a happy family atmosphere, and of course the teachers are always supervising youngsters as they move through the building.

But the likelihood is that if a family visits ISL for the first time after seeing other international schools in the area, the facilities and environment may not quite measure up. One parent said that when they first drove up to the school, 'we could have cried', but having got past that, it was their first choice school, and they are very happy there. Despite the tight spaces, the students are friendly, polite and seem to move through the building in a pretty organised fashion, and it bodes well for world peace if kids of 50+ nationalities can get along so well in these relatively cramped quarters. The strong message coming from parents is 'don't be put off by first impressions'.

The school is aware of its limitations, hence the renovation programme. They are also always on the lookout for suitable additional space, and if the appropriate solution were found, they might relocate the IBDP to its own centre. Families considering ISL may bear this in mind, and that other schools in urban London face similar challenges when planning ahead.

Grades 11 and 12 may leave campus for lunch, early years eat in their classrooms, and everyone in between eats in the dining canteen. Parents we spoke to say their children prefer to take lunch from home over the optional lunch programme booked termly. Door-to-door bus service is available; with growing London traffic problems, they strongly recommend that families choose from neighbourhoods like Kew, Chiswick or Ealing.

Pastoral care and discipline: The strong sense of community provides a solid foundation for the behaviour and discipline in the school, which is of course guided by the IB Learner Profiles. The school handbook directs parents to home room tutors for everyday matters, or the divisional principals, with more serious or school-wide concerns then directed to the head. Some less IT-savvy parents seem to be having some teething problems with a new online communications system. But their main concern is the welfare of their children, and as one happy parent said, 'at ISL children are treated like royals.' No big discipline worries came to our attention.

Pupils and parents: Possibly the most international school in the city if not the country; ISL's students come from 55 countries – the largest single group representing only 13

per cent. It creates fertile conditions for developing open-mindedness and international understanding for students, as well as parents and faculty. With many dual-national families, some kids hold as many as three or four passports. Parents love this environment where 'if you speak several languages, you're not unusual'.

Parents are also drawn to ISL by its smaller size and the friendly and approachable staff, who they credit with helping children settle in so easily and comfortably, knowing 'how to manage the adjustment for children coming from very different school systems'. Teachers are approachable and deal with new children individually (and also help parents with tips to manage the family transitions). At ISL, this is more than marketing hype.

We hear that families interact socially outside of school; ISL parents believe that having their children learn to understand peers from all backgrounds is a huge advantage. Parents of older students report that their children meet at weekends, and most are happy for them use public transport to arrange this; week nights are spent at home with their noses in the books.

Very active PTA; many families regard the school as the heart of the community. They plan outings and orientation activities for new parents. Parents arriving mid-year are welcomed with newcomer's events and even English language lessons. One parent told us of a group of families who regularly take weekend trips around the UK. (Another said she sometimes feels there are more activities for parents than for the kids.) PTA got praise from everyone we spoke to.

Most are expats on temporary assignment in the UK, many based at the nearby Brentford business park or growing hub of international companies in Hammersmith, or one of the many embassies. A number live within easy distance of the school, which makes managing the social life a bit easier, and parents know one advantage of living away from the centre of London is that their money goes further – bigger houses, bigger gardens.

Entrance: Rolling admissions allows students to apply from all over the world, all year round, although there are waiting lists for some year groups. Apply before Easter to improve chances. Admission is determined by previous records, a teacher reference, student and family questionnaires. Interviews are always welcomed (required for IBDP). No testing (English language is assessed after admission); students with special educational need to provide diagnostic assessments used to determine whether the school can properly serve the student. Non-English speakers with good academic reports are admitted up to Grade 10. During interviews there's a lot of discussion about the mother tongue programme and the possible fees for this service.

Although the school does not comment on a sibling policy, parents say they make an effort to ensure all children in a family get a place. Admissions director gets high marks for his thoroughness, efficiency, responsiveness and care, and he can tell you about every student in the school. Though on first impression he may appear somewhat diffident, with his many years' experience working with ISL families, 'he knows his onions'.

Exit: About 70 per cent of graduates go to UK universities, although more now applying to American universities. Some return to their home countries and ISL has a long history of helping students find the right fit in a wide range of countries – an important consideration for families. Even students who earn the ISL High School diploma gain entry into UK universities. Very occasionally, a student may leave ISL to pursue A levels. The largest numbers of graduates have gone to Edinburgh, Oxford, Warwick, UCL, King's, Imperial, St George's Medical School and Queen Mary; overseas destinations include Tokyo Science University, Kyoto University, Keio McGill, Technical University of Budapest, University of Chicago, University of Texas, Bocconi

Milan, and Ecole Superieure du Commerce. An impressive list, but parents are advised to ask the school specifically about the more recent successes.

Money matters: No scholarships as such as most pupils have corporate support, but school will keep a child in extreme circumstances if a family financial problem arises.

Remarks: A school with a solid academic track record that has clearly won over the hearts and minds of its many international families. Many organisations, not to mention a few world leaders, could learn a lot about fostering global understanding from this school.

Ipswich High School

Linked school: Ipswich High Junior School

Woolverstone, Ipswich, IP9 1AZ

• Pupils: 430 girls • Ages: 11–18 • Non-denom • Fees: £11,574–£11,736 pa • Independent

Tel: 01473 780201
Email: reception@ihs.gdst.net
Website: www.ipswichhighschool.co.uk

Head: Since September 2013, Ms Oona Carlin, previously deputy head (academic) at Putney High, and before that head of chemistry at the Royal Masonic School. She studied chemistry at Imperial College, and has taught at a range of schools, including two years at the English School in Bogota, Colombia. Once a county level hockey player, she still plays regularly, and recently captained Windsor Ladies.

Academic matters: Continues to maintain its position as top academic school in the county – and value added is well above average. In 2013, 62 per cent A/A* at GCSE. Combined science at GCSE plus the popular, recently introduced sports science. Good selection of mainly academic subjects at A level – 41 per cent A*/A in 2013.

Keen learners and high expectations – parents are impressed that best practice starts from day one. Generally traditional, not unduly pressured approach. Problems are spotted quickly and plenty of support, especially in maths, where groups are small. In the sixth form help is there if needed, but 'We're encouraged to be responsible. It's good preparation for uni'.

SEN provision isn't a feature but 'children with learning impairments aren't disbarred – they need to show potential or be of above average intelligence'. A specialist comes several times a week to provide support in English and develop study skills, whilst maths support is given at lunchtime by a member of the maths department.

Games, options, the arts: Plays hockey, netball, tennis and rounders, with county champions at several levels. Fine facilities including a top notch sports hall and swimming pool which is open to the public out of school hours. Lunchtime clubs for all year groups, whether in the main teams or not. Fencing on offer and extracurricular provision in sailing and riding growing – has its own equestrian team.

Over one third of the school have singing or instrumental tuition and annual concerts at Snape Maltings are 'fantastic'. Drama is strong and popular – a generous theatre. Parents enthuse over recent appointments and innovative approaches which have 'pushed standards to the highest levels'. Self-contained, spacious art department with a dedicated sixth form area. Students can take A level critical and contextual studies or squeeze in an additional GCSE. Predominantly two dimensional work that's expressive and well informed.

Range of extracurricular activities mainly at lunchtime. Gold D of E has a good take-up. Food studies welcomed back onto the curriculum with purpose-built cookery rooms – taught to years 7 and 8 as part of their core curriculum and available as an extra lunch time or after-school club for all other year groups, and the sixth form as part of their co-curricular enrichment programme. Interesting development and one we will follow with interest to see if it is emulated elsewhere.

Background and atmosphere: Founded in 1878, this GDST flag flier 'nurtures alpha females in a lovely way'. A fair ethos where manners and respect foster good relations between staff and pupils – a civilised and harmonious place. The idyllic out-of-town site, home to the school since 1992, provides something of an oasis away from the pressures of everyday life. Girls genuinely appreciate their surroundings and, despite those cutting easterlies, relish the freedom to roam over most of the 80 acres of parkland, with its grazing sheep and slopes on the edge of the Orwell. All the buildings, including the central hub, a Grade 1, pedimented, be-urned Georgian pile, are well loved, and not a spot of litter to be seen. The same is true of the sixth form area at the top of the main house where students have their own work-station and laptop. They also have a comfortable common room with pool table and bistro kitchen kitted out with café style furniture, dishwasher, fridge and microwave – all very grown-up. Sixth formers also have a minibus service at lunchtime, three times a week, to go into the county town, Ipswich.

Lunch in the old orangery is a chatty affair, food is plentiful and healthy. Sixth use a separate dining area which overlooks the grounds and River Orwell beyond, but each half term are invited to a meal in the smaller of the two libraries and are introduced to guests who share knowledge of the world of work. 'We're encouraged to meet new people and speak confidently,' said student. No uniform for the sixth – cerise and grey for those lower down, with compulsory (very popular) smart grey blazer for years 7-11.

Pastoral care and discipline: No houses – inter-form competition instead and a tutorial system which is at the heart of effective pastoral care. Mentoring for year 7s, who are befriended by a senior girl, plus societies and clubs where a healthy mix of year groups. Girls know who to seek out if the need arises whilst 'shrewd teachers see beyond the veneer'. Unobtrusive discipline with few serious problems. Theoretical zero tolerance of illegal substances has yet to be tested.

New initiatives are run past the girls and the head listens to their thoughts and ideas. Eco issues, driven by the pupils and a deputy, are high on the agenda – a 'blitz week' with the school monitoring its energy use and making an effort to keep consumption to a minimum alerted all and brought amazingly positive results. An organic vegetable plot, tended by the girls, is being developed and it's planned to provide cut flowers and produce for the canteen.

Pupils and parents: Mostly local girls from a wide catchment with 60+ pick-up points for coaches – the journey, lengthy for some, is seen as part of the school's social life. Families very mixed – strong professional contingent and quite a few in farming. Charmingly unaffected girls.

Entrance: At 11. Majority from the junior department. Another 35 or so from state or independent juniors. Entrance tests in English, maths and verbal reasoning – plus school report.

For the sixth – five GCSEs with B or above for AS subjects, except for maths where the requirement is A/A*.

Exit: Around 50 per cent leave after year 11, some of the brainiest to the free alternative over the county divide. Post A level a few to Oxbridge (four to Cambridge in 2013), with most of the rest to heavyweights – healthy spread of courses. No starry OGs (though one leaver off to RADA in 2013 so watch this space...) but a significant proportion are highly successful in a range of professions.

Money matters: As one of the 24 schools of the Girls' Day School Trust, the fees represent excellent value. At 11 and 16 a few scholarships awarded on merit. Academic, art, music, drama and sports scholarships at 11 and 16 for up to a quarter of the fees. Means-tested bursaries, awarded on need and academic merit, up to full fees. Short term assistance available if needed.

Remarks: Definitely not a girly place but echoes of an august girls' boarding school, especially in its setting. Highly desirable for the down to earth academic.

Ipswich School

Linked school: Ipswich Preparatory School

Henley Road, Ipswich, IP1 3SG

• Pupils: 740; 470 boys, 270 girls; includes 36 boarders • Ages: 11–18 • C of E • Fees: Boarding £18,759–£23,289; Day £11,478–£12,582 pa • Independent

Tel: 01473 408300
Email: registrar@ipswich.suffolk.sch.uk
Website: www.ipswich.suffolk.sch.uk

Headmaster: Since September 2010, Mr Nicholas Weaver BA (late thirties). Read engineering at Jesus College, Cambridge. Previously deputy head (academic) at Portsmouth Grammar, and before that taught physics at the Leys School, Cambridge, the Royal Grammar School, Guildford, and Radley College. Tall, elegant, with an approachable, unruffled manner. He is keen to develop what he calls the 'growth mind-set' – a strategy for developing the potential of all pupils, with a particular eye on those identified as academically able. The Academic Excellence Programme is designed for this 'elite' group, although open to all comers. Changes to senior management structure have resulted in a more streamlined, collegiate approach; all posts are now advertised externally. He is married and has three children, all at Ipswich Prep.

Academic matters: Pupils are encouraged, even pushed, to work hard. Whilst not an academic forcing house, there is no place for coasting. The brightest of the bright will be fast tracked – lessons before school for some and there is a programme of enrichment, including lectures and seminars, geared specifically at these pupils – 'We are hoping the head doesn't over-do all the elitism and Oxbridge stuff,' commented a parent. Homework is now called PSC, which stands for Preparation, Stretch and Consolidation – 'No one remembers,' said several. Though selective, the school has quite a wide ability range, but despite the head saying, 'we recognise the hard-won B grade', there are not many of these in evidence. In 2013, nearly 69 per cent A*/A grades at GCSE. Spectacular results in Russian, with over 50 per cent awarded an A* (out of a cohort of 42); illustrates perfectly that inspirational teaching is what it is all about. The head has made clear his priority to raise all teaching in the school to this exceptional standard. A level results equally stunning, with nearly 51 per cent A*/A grades. School expects pupils to have the solid achievement of an A grade at GCSE for subjects studied at A level, and the sixth form is no place for

slacking, with compulsory enrichment programme alongside ASs. No demand here for IB, as curriculum seems to be diverse enough.

All year 7 entrants are tested for SEN, but as this is a selective school, the needs identified will often be to do with organisation, mild dyslexia, or for ESL, for which support is offered outside the timetabled day. Head has introduced drop in clinics at lunchtime so any pupil can seek help informally.

Games, options, the arts: A recent shift in emphasis in referring to the 'co-curricular' rather than the 'extra-curricular', with a designated assistant head in overall charge (formerly head of sixth form). First division player in all the team sports – frequently area and national finalists, most recently in hockey. Sport is for all, and the school often fields teams from A – D. Other sports on offer, and played highly competitively, include karate, sailing and equestrianism. Also entered a winning pair in the national finals of Eton Fives. School recently bought nearby sports centre, complete with sports hall, fitness gym and floodlit Astroturf hockey pitch.

Music is taken seriously, with a third of pupils taking individual instrumental lessons and a variety of orchestras, choirs and ensemble groups which perform throughout the year. The Chapel Choir, besides a regular slot singing Evensong at St Paul's Cathedral, tours both at home and abroad. The Annual Ipswich School Festival of Music brings internationally-renowned musicians to perform at the school in master-classes and workshops. Drama GCSE is also offered also as an enrichment sixth form option (no theatre studies A level) and several productions are staged throughout the year. The sixth form recently performed Seussical-the-Musical, based on the works of Dr Seuss. Thursday afternoon activities include CCF and Duke of Edinburgh plus a long list of clubs and societies including photography, journalism and robotics. If the club isn't already there, it can be started.

Background and atmosphere: The school has occupied its present site since 1852, but it has a medieval foundation (Cardinal Wolsey is an illustrious Old Boy) and the school's history is well-recorded and treasured. In addition to the original, rather gloomy Victorian structure there are some fine and functional 20th century buildings which adjoin each other by a series of passages, steps and covered ways. Later additions include the sports facilities and sixth form building, which overlook the playing fields – a focus for relaxation as well as sport. There is a school chapel and a library of exceptional quality and design with windows by John Piper depicting the seasons. The boarding house is a short walk away, occupying its own grounds in a suburban road. Everything is well cared for and maintained. Odd fusty corners in the older part of the school offset by displays of pupils' work, posters and subject information. Pupils by and large polite rather than courtly but clearly intent on their pursuits. Straight-forward uniform policy, with sixth formers allowed the latitude of wearing their own clothes. Conformity seems natural here though 'slight oddballs have been successfully integrated'; especially if they are clever.

Pastoral care and discipline: Usual house and year group tutorial system with a separate identity for years 7 and 8, each form keeping the same tutor. The school chaplain, a full-time member of the teaching staff plays a key part in the pastoral set up. The matron has her room strategically placed near the hard play area, a reassuring presence at break and lunchtimes. There is a strong expectation that pupils are well organised and can cope with the pressure, though all know where to turn if in difficulties. Despite the city location, little flouting of rules, and a system of merits and detentions seems to keep the odd backslider on track. Occasional serious offenders dealt with firmly.

Pupils and parents: Mix of farming, professional and business families from the rural reaches of East Anglia together with those from Ipswich itself or other towns, mostly in Essex. Quite a lot of parents are London commuters. Extensive network of bus routes bring many pupils to school, and of the 40 or so boarders over half come from overseas, mostly Europe and the Far East. Boys continue to outnumber girls by about 2:1 in years 7 to 11; the influx of girls to the sixth form – often from the nearby GDST school – gives a better balance, though girls remain in a minority. Pupils appear to be well able to cope with the rigours of the school; perhaps not ideal for those lacking in confidence or who thrive on pushing the boundaries.

In addition to Cardinal Wolsey, notable Old Boys include the author and illustrator Edward Ardizzone, physicist Sir Charles Frank and the writer Rider Haggard (King Solomon's Mines).

Entrance: The majority join at 11 (year 7) with many coming up from the prep. All take the same entrance exam (results are used to organise setting in year 7). A report from the pupil's present school and a chat with the head are also required. At 13 (year 9), another 30 or so are also admitted via common entrance or school's own exam. Pupils do need to have above average ability to pass and to flourish. Entry to the sixth form requires six GCSEs with at least Bs, preferably As in chosen A level subjects.

Exit: Majority leave for university with a leaning towards the Russell Group, particularly Leeds, Birmingham, London and Warwick. Several to Oxbridge and the head is keen to push up numbers.

Money matters: Queen's (academic) Scholarships equivalent to 50 per cent offered at 11 and 13, based on pupil's performance in the entrance examination plus interview. Means-tested bursaries can cover the full fees if necessary. Scholarships are also available in music, art and sport at 11 and an all-rounder at 13. A full range are offered at sixth form, together with a number of means-tested bursaries.

Remarks: A well run, urban school, with many opportunities for bright, motivated pupils to excel.

Italia Conti Academy of Theatre Arts

23 Goswell Road, London, EC1M 7AJ

• Pupils: 20 boys and 80 girls; all day • Ages: 11–16 • Inter-denominational • Fees: £12,975–£15,990 pa • Independent

Tel: 020 7608 0047
Email: admin@italiaconti.co.uk
Website: www.italia-conti.com

Head: Since 1975, Mr Clifford Vote. Educated at universities of New South Wales and London (economics, psychology and education). Previously taught in secondary schools in Australia. Affable Aussie with a more or less lifelong dedication to the school. Regular team member for Independent Schools Inspectorate and board member of the Council for Dance, Education and Training.

Academic matters: Theatre schools are not judged primarily by their academic results, but the school performs creditably; more than 17 per cent A*/A grades at GCSE in 2013. Learning and behaviour, said the ISI, are 'overwhelmingly good or very good'. The school recognises that for its pupils the vocational parts of the day are the most important. 'They get academia more or less by default without realising. The fact that most of them get through eight GCSEs at an average of grade B is a huge achievement.'

Everyone takes English language and literature, maths, single science, drama, dance, history, French and art GCSE courses. Those 'who demonstrate a profound incompetence in a subject' may be allowed to drop it, and several from each class give up French, a few history or art. Maths is strong, science greatly improved, French rather weaker. 'Modern foreign languages depend on cumulative learning: because they spend so much time on vocational subjects, our children are more inclined to flit from topic to topic.'

Most teaching is mixed ability, though maths is mostly taught in ability groups from year 8 upwards. 'Mixed ability in small classes harnesses the ability of children to learn from each other as well as from the teacher, which is a huge advantage for children who have problems with didactic forms of teaching.'

The academic entrance test is largely diagnostic: 'They cover the curriculum in half the time available to normal schools, so they must be reasonably bright'. They must also be willing to learn: 'In our small mixed ability classes a few children who weren't interested would have an appalling effect. They're training for a career that will offer them an extraordinary range of experiences: they don't have the right to circumvent their academic obligations.'

Limited SEN support, so can take few dyslexic children. 'We just don't have the space to accommodate more staff. And there is a huge amount of help available elsewhere; I would advise parents to spend their money on that rather than our fees.'

Games, options, the arts: Art is very successful, especially in view of its cramped space. The ISI praised its 'creativity, vitality and sense of industry', and nearly everyone who takes the GCSE gets a good grade. No sport – performance is the raison d'être here, and half of each school day is spent dancing, singing and acting. While some classes, clad in traditional blue school uniform, get down to maths coursework or studying the Second World War, others in leotards are rehearsing for a modern dance exam or putting together a performance. The skills, teamwork and dedication are outstanding. No theatre on site – in July the whole school decamps to Wimbledon for a week to mount 'a humdinger of a production' of variety performances, demonstrating a phenomenal range of musical theatre skills.

All the pupils are represented by the Italia Conti agency and are not permitted to attend auditions except through it. But although many of the pupils have appeared in Harry Potter films and the like, outside professional work is not a major part of the school experience – 'Whilst you're out working you can't be in class learning technique, and those who are out too much won't be up to the standard of training we offer at 16 plus'.

Background and atmosphere: If you climb the steps of an office block opposite the Barbican to find dance students practising moves in the reception hall, you are probably at Italia Conti. This is the oldest theatre arts training school in Britain, founded in 1911. It grew out of the first production of the children's play, Where the Rainbow Ends. Italia Conti, an established actress with a reputation for working with young people, was asked to take over their training. The play was a triumph, and the school was born in basement studios in Great Portland Street. Now it shares nine floors of an ex-office block in the City, traffic roaring by outside, with over-16s doing full-time performing arts courses. Classrooms are cheek-by-jowl with practice studios; students training at the barre have views over the City skyline.

Pastoral care and discipline: Self-discipline and team-work are an integral part of performing arts training, and the pupils are in the main so delighted to be at the school that discipline and relationship problems are few. Many of the vocational classes are mixed in age groups, with older pupils acting as mentors and rôle models. A full-time matron deals with medical and emotional upsets. 'They learn to live the lifestyle of a performer, which is partly about having the skills but also about being able to cope with success and rejection.'

Pupils and parents: About half the pupils have already attended the associate weekend schools in places like Chislehurst, Guildford, Wokingham and Tunbridge Wells, so a strong southern home counties contingent. Pupils are confident and friendly – 'Socially, they are amazing. I expect them to be able to get their own way nicely. If people want to be with you, there are few obstacles to a successful career'. Ex-pupils include (amongst many) Noel Coward, Gertrude Lawrence, Patsy Kensit, Tracey Ullman and Leslie Phillips. More recent graduates include Danny Bayne, Newton Faulkner, Claire Goose and Kelly Brooke.

Entrance: The 12 associate schools act as feeder prep schools, though pupils audition successfully from a wide range of backgrounds. Around 12 or 13 pupils come into year 7, with more joining over the next few years, to a maximum of 20 in a class – 'very few live within five miles, so it tends to take persistence for them to persuade their parents that they're old enough to make the journey'. The academic test is largely diagnostic; students also prepare a song, two speeches and up to three types of dance – 'We're looking for exceptional ability in one and trainability in all three'. All those who are considered right for the school are offered a place – 'We try hard to select children who will thrive. The school would be purgatory for children without the physical abilities'.

Exit: A few transfer to state or independent sixth forms to do A levels, but the vast majority move on to the one or three-year intensive performing arts courses in the same building run by the Italia Conti Academy of Theatre Arts. One of these, the three year performing arts course, produces 'audition ready' graduates with a degree equivalent national diploma in professional musical theatre from Trinity College, London. Government dance and drama award scholarships are available for this course.

Money matters: A number of full and part scholarships for children from the associate schools. No open scholarship auditions. Some charities help to fund places.

Remarks: Children with a talent and passion for performance will thrive here. 'It's a wonderful place to grow up,' says the head. 'There's so much to see and do and so many talented people to emulate.'

James Allen's Girls' School (JAGS)

Linked school: James Allen's Preparatory School (JAPS)

East Dulwich Grove, London, SE22 8TE

• Pupils: 785 girls (senior school); (1,080 ages 4–18); all day • Ages: 11–18 • C of E Foundation but all are welcome • Fees: £14,700 pa • Independent

Tel: 020 8693 1181
Email: henrietta.kiezun@jags.org.uk
Website: www.jags.org.uk

Headmistress: Since 1994, Mrs Marion Gibbs BA MLitt FRSA CBE (fifties). Read classics at Bristol, where she also did her PGCE

and part-time research. Was an HMI and has also inspected for Ofsted and the ISI; has been awarded a CBE for services to education, especially partnership work with state schools. She has taught in state and private schools including Burgess Hill and Haberdashers' Aske's School for Girls. A passionate classicist, she has been an examiner and written books on the subject, and teaches citizenship, Greek, Latin, Greek mythology and classical civilisation to different age groups – 'How can you manage your school if you don't know all your pupils and where they are coming from?'

A highly efficient operator, particularly good one-to-one. 'She's dynamic, she's sensible, she knows what she wants and achieves it,' say parents. 'If there's a problem, she's on the phone, you're straight in there, and it's dealt with very quickly.' Girls say: 'She's a brilliant head. She knows everyone's name and what you're doing. She's in tune with the students – we are her focus.'

Academic matters: Teaches Pre-U English literature – 'It allows the girls to read more widely and really develop their critical skills' – and some subjects, eg English and maths, have moved to IGCSE for a better course; otherwise the school is still committed to A levels and GCSE – JAGS girls like to choose their own subject combinations so the IB is not for them. A very strong showing, with 85 per cent A*/A, 98 per cent A*/B at A level in 2013, and 94 per cent A*/A at GCSE. A wide range of languages offered to GCSE and A level, including Italian, Russian, Spanish, German and Japanese, with a good take-up at A level. Maths, biology and chemistry are other popular A level subjects, alongside English and history. 'Our daughter has learned to work hard without pressure from us,' said a parent. 'She's had some fantastic, enthusiastic teachers who have really inspired her.'

A few girls have mild dyslexia/dyspraxia and the school has also accommodated children with sight/hearing problems. It does not provide one-to-one help, except for those with a statement of education need, but the SENCo liaises with staff and parents to ensure that girls are coping within normal classes, are provided with, eg, laptops where necessary and get extra time in exams if they are entitled to it.

Part of the Southwark Schools Learning Partnership, which includes five state and three independent schools working together on a huge range of projects. 'A real partnership is organic. It develops out of shared interests. We all have something to learn from one another. If we're having a theatre company or a speaker in, or a training session, we'll invite other schools over, or we may go to them.'

Games, options, the arts: Several pupils said they had chosen the school for its music – indeed, a huge variety of orchestras, choirs, ensembles and groups to choose from, playing in over 30 concerts each year. 'There's something for everyone, whatever you play,' said a pupil. Ralph Vaughan Williams and then Gustav Holst were the school's first two music teachers. Planning permission has been granted for a community music centre (active fund-raising in progress), to be open to the community after school and at weekends as well as for school use during the day. Art also very strong, including fabric and textiles, with six art rooms and several students most years going on to art foundation courses. 'The art department really pushes you,' said a pupil. 'You learn such a lot.' Drama is 'exceptional,' said a parent, including joint productions with Dulwich College and trips to perform at the Edinburgh Festival.

A very sporty school – plays an extensive and generally successful programme of inter-school matches, with house competitions giving the less physically-talented a chance to shine. One pupil commented, 'You have to be really good to play for the school.' PE GCSE and A level options. Facilities include a sports hall with squash courts, multi-gym and new state-of-the-art 3D climbing wall, a dance studio – 'We do everything, from flamenco to Bollywood to street dance' – and an elegant swimming pool with a large spectator area, plus extensive playing fields, artificial turf and courts. A wide range of sporting opportunities in the upper school, including ice skating and dry slope ski-ing.

Background and atmosphere: Part of a foundation established by talented Elizabethan actor, Edward Alleyn, which includes Dulwich College and Alleyn's School. The school was founded in 1741 by James Allen, a Master of Dulwich College, as a free reading school for local poor children. He died five years later, leaving a bequest to secure his school's future. It has been girls only since 1845 and moved to its present site in 1886.

Much development since, culminating (so far) in rather swish dining room and Deep End café in what used to be the swimming pool. Grammar-schoolish dark wood stairways and window frames in the older parts contrast with light and airy glass, white paint and pale wood in the newer areas. Fabulous library, dance and drama studios, 200 seat theatre, labs and DT rooms, walls lined with notice boards crammed with photos, lists, cuttings and posters.

But best of all are the 22 acre grounds, where girls are free to wander at will during break times, which, alongside sports pitches and courts, include botanical gardens (originally planted over 100 years ago by pioneer ecologist and head of science Dr Lilian Clarke), engagingly shaggy woodland and wetland areas, and even a tree-lined country walk. Also a bridge over the railway line which runs through the grounds, with views down the line to North Dulwich station. The school has its own environmental manager who runs a biology club, welcomes children from nearby state primary and special schools for nature trails and pond-dipping and spreads the ecological word to other schools in the area.

The head is keen for the girls to share their privileges with the wider community – 'You need to get in the habit of giving something back. We're training them to roll up their sleeves and do something'. So, as well as sharing their sports and other facilities with other schools and local people, girls are encouraged to visit the nearby Cheshire Home, work with Romanian children with special needs, help with the Saturday literacy scheme for local children and join Kids Company children in their art activities.

Pastoral care and discipline: Unashamedly old-fashioned over behaviour: no bad language, no graffiti, no chewing gum. Best suited to girls with no great inclination to rock the boat. Has excluded permanently for bringing drugs to school and temporarily for physical violence and being caught smoking more than once. 'If there's any chance of pupils misbehaving outside school, they'll be down like a ton of bricks,' commented a parent. However, the head says that sanctions are rare, 'We're tough, but we don't have a lot of discipline issues'.

A many-tiered pastoral system which includes form tutors, heads of year and the two school nurses, who are also trained counsellors. Girls say they like having a range of people they can go to for help but report most people rub along well together. However, some felt that occasionally, stressed students are not noticed and that the pastoral net does have the odd hole. The school says it has worked very hard to improve pastoral care over the last few years and keeps a look out for stress and anorexia, 'But they do mostly enjoy their food. When we banned sweets and cakes from the tuck shop, they came up with charity cake sales'.

In the main school girls are usually allocated forms according to their houses, with staff and students getting together in fund-raising events such as sponsored space hopper race, teacher karaoke, film-and-cake club. Sixth formers have vertical tutor groups, including year 12s and year 13s, so the younger girls can learn from the older ones' experiences of going through the UCAS process.

Pupils and parents: Diverse ethnically and socially, with plenty of girls on bursaries and some 50 home languages. Girls are bright, buzzy, focused. 'They come out very confident, streetwise kids,' said a parent. 'They're used to standing up for themselves and arguing their point.' They travel in from a wide area by train or bus, mostly from south of the river but increasing numbers from the north (12 minutes by train from London Bridge). OGs include Anita Brookner, Lisa St Aubin de Terain, Dharshini David and Sally Hawkins.

Entrance: Hot competition. Everyone is interviewed in the autumn term; maths, English and verbal reasoning exams in the spring term. Around a third comes up from the junior school, and some 40 per cent of new entrants are from state primaries. Sixth form entry for outsiders depends on entrance exam, GCSE results, school reference and interview. Generally 10 or so join at this stage.

Exit: Around 10 per cent a year leave after GCSEs, mostly for co-ed sixth forms. A level leavers virtually all go to university: usually 20+ to Oxbridge, a few to art college, the rest largely to top universities to study anything from drama to dentistry.

Money matters: The last part of James Allen's bequest was used to establish a Scholars' Fund to replace the abolished government assisted places in 1997. Eighteen James Allen's Bursary places, which can pay for up to full fees plus help with uniform, lunches and school trips, awarded each year. School also gets an annual grant from the Dulwich Estate, which pays for more scholarships and bursaries. More than a third of pupils are on some sort of financial assistance. Up to 20 scholarships at 11+, including music, art and sports awards. Major scholarships of £1000 pa and minor scholarships of £500 pa can be means tested up to full fees. A few 16+ scholarships of £1000 awarded on the basis of GCSE results.

Remarks: High-achieving school at work and play, with a strong social conscience. Suits bright, well-ordered girls who are keen to get involved. 'You feel really proud that your daughter's at JAGS,' said a parent. 'You know she's set up for life.'

James Gillespie's High School

Lauderdale Street, Edinburgh, EH9 1DD

• Pupils: 595 boys, 540 girls • Ages: 11–18 • Non-denom • State

Tel: 01314 471900
Email: admin@jamesgillespies.edin.sch.uk
Website: www.jghs.edin.sch.uk

Headteacher: Since January 2012, Mr Donald J Macdonald BSc MBASQH Dip Ed (fifties), previously head of Liberton High (school's exceptional progress under his watch resulted in an invitation to 10 Downing Street). Has taught science at a range of Scottish schools including Knox Academy and Portobello High. Married, with two daughters; lists golf, fishing and Scottish malt whisky amongst his many interests.

Academic matters: Class size 30 (20/25 for practical subjects), setted early for maths in the September of their first year, second year setted for English. Three separate sciences for all from the third year onwards. No classics, but French, German, Spanish and Urdu, a growing number also learn Gaelic (a feeder school where pupils do all subjects in Gaelic). All languages are taught up to Higher level. School does mix of Nationals, Highers, Advanced Highers and A levels for physics, art (in order to form a portfolio), Urdu and geography – an interesting diversification for a state school. Excellent support for learning, dyslexia, dyspraxia, and help with exams, both withdrawn from class and team teaching in class. ADHD is OK – 'Most reasonably well-behaved'. 250 of the pupils come from 40 different countries – 'the most diverse population in Scotland': EFL available (free) for all who need it. CDT is 50/50 craft and design and all computer-based – 350 computers in the school. Recent BECTA award for best website.

Games, options, the arts: PE and swimming off site; Meadowbank stadium used for PE and extensive after-school activities. Football, rugby, hockey pitches about 1.5 miles away at Kirkbrae – pupils are bussed. Games are basically extracurricular, girls' football and netball are popular. Short lunchbreak, 45 mins, so few lunch clubs – pupils mainly go to the local cafés and carry-outs. Massive music uptake, with carol service normally held in the Usher Hall, over 500 regularly on the stage. Senior orchestra, junior orchestra, lessons free. DT, libraries and PE area. Strong, spectacular art, photography, impressive fabric design. Huge dance area, media popular with lights and editing studios, three drama studios. Wizard home economics department – better than most homes we know. Trips all over the place, in many disciplines – skiing, Paris for art, historians to the trenches, geographers to do glacial research in the French Alps.

Background and atmosphere: Founded in 1803 as a result of a legacy from James Gillespie, 'a wealthy Edinburgh manufacturer of snuff and tobacco', who was born in Roslin. Started with 65 students and one master and led a peripatetic existence. At one point the prep school for the Merchant Company's secondary schools. By 1908 had a roll of over a thousand, including girls, and offered secondary education under the aegis of the Edinburgh school board, moving to Bruntsfield House, just off The Meadows, in 1966 and going fully co-ed in 1978. The earliest building on this site dates from 1300, and the current building, Bruntsfield House, was built in 1605, with later additions and improvements. Sir George Warrender, whose family was to be awarded the title Bruntsfield, bought the house from the original owners and was intrigued to find that if you hung a sheet from every window you could access from the inside, still sheetless windows outside. A secret room was discovered, with blood-stained floor, ashes in the grate and a skeleton under the wainscot. The Green Lady haunts the top storeys to this day.

The head has a grand office in the main building, with a spectacular ceiling and an impressive fireplace, almost exactly replicated by the music room not quite next door. Now surrounded by predominantly 60s-type classroom blocks, relieved by swards of green and mature trees with a singular clock in the middle of the campus which, despite thousands spent on renovation, will never work properly as the hands were found to be too long. It remains as a memorial to the follies of the architects of the day, though interestingly, nothing but praise for the design. The campus is hidden amongst decent Victorian tenements – more grass and trees than you would expect. Woefully short of space – a certain frisson when the local electricity board sold an adjoining substation without first offering it to the school, which desperately needs room to expand. Rebuilding of new school has now started; senior pupils take classes in the nearby Darroch centre in Gillespie Street for the duration.

Pastoral care and discipline: Follows the state guidelines – good PSHE, good anti-bullying strategy in place: 'We get the youngsters to talk it through … We bring them together and get the bully to accept their behaviour is wrong'. 'No current problems' with cigarettes, alcohol or drugs, but will exclude on either a temporary or permanent basis if necessary. Last head only ever made two drugs-related temporary exclusions, but it would be permanent if any hint of dealing. Also out permanently for a violent attack, though temporary exclusion for 'physical violence'. Homework books which must be signed by parent or guardian. No uniform, which is going slightly against the current Edinburgh trend – 'If it ain't broke, don't fix it'.

Pupils and parents: Free intake, so diverse: 47 languages spoken. Large number of professional families (Marchmont is a popular area for the university) plus 'a significant group of working class, with relatively poor backgrounds'. Huge ethnic mix, with some girls wearing the chador – they may well do PE and swim wearing full leggings and long-sleeved T-shirts (though parents can ask to withdraw their daughters from these lessons, few do). Lifts being installed next year for wheelchair-bound pupil, minor physical handicaps OK. Strong parent/teacher involvement.

Entrance: First year capped at 200; catchment area recently re-drawn but some places still available by request – very popular, with pupils from as far away as Penicuik and Musselburgh. Obliged to take children on a first come first served basis, waiting lists. Certain number of pupils who have obtained university entrance elsewhere in the independent sector join in sixth form for Higher Still (and a better chance at Oxbridge).

Exit: Number leave after Standard Grades, either to further education or work; good proportion to universities, mainly Scots, studying medicine, science, art college, followed by social subject and music in that order. Annual trickle to Oxbridge.

Remarks: Can't fault it.

JFS

The Mall, Kenton, Harrow, Middlesex, HA3 9TE

• Pupils: 2,060 boys and girls • Ages: 11–18 • Jewish • State

Tel: 020 8206 3100
Email: admin@jfs.brent.sch.uk
Website: www.jfs.brent.sch.uk

Headteacher: Since January 2008, Mr Jonathan Miller BSc MA NPQH (late forties). Educated at Carmel College and Imperial College London, he has been at JFS for many years. A former head of chemistry and head of science, he was responsible for planning the school's timetable and IT strategy when it relocated to Kenton, also deputy head. Articulate and highly respected, considered even handed, even tempered and level headed, well able to preserve the happy balance which exists between pupils of a wide range of religious observance within the school.

Academic matters: A very large comprehensive that compares favourably with many grammar schools in terms of results. In 2013 52 per cent of A level grades A*/A, while 81 per cent of students gained 5+ A*-C grades including English and maths at GCSE, and more than 47 per cent of grades were A*/A. School graded 'outstanding' by Ofsted in latest report in every one of the 39 judgements made.

New pupils are admitted into 10 accelerated or mixed ability tutor groups and all subjects are set by ability in year 8. Both upper and lower ends are given unusually strong support. The gifted and talented have accelerated classes from year 7, while the large special needs department – with over 80 statemented children – has its own suite, six special needs teachers and six permanent teaching assistants. Those struggling at the bottom of the middle band are perhaps the least well served. French for all in year 7, Spanish for all from year 8. IT bang up to the minute, with interactive whiteboards in every classroom. Science, too, unusually well equipped with 15 laboratories.

First-rate, highly sought after, academic sixth form with around 550 pupils, housed in its own discrete space (though with some lessons taught in the main school). Large expansion of the curriculum at this point, with applied art (including photography and graphics), economics, business studies, psychology, sociology, childhood studies, theatre studies, media studies, politics and critical thinking added to the GCSE basics. Masterclasses, too, for the 25 or so Oxbridge candidates, including some pupils from neighbouring boroughs.

A core of long-serving staff provides some outstanding teaching in all subjects. 'A child who wants to work could not receive a better education anywhere in the country,' said one mother, whose son recently left for a top-flight university. Teaching is carefully monitored, with videoing of lessons – prides itself on its continuing professional development and places the training of teachers from a number of teacher training institutions high on its agenda: about a third of its trainees stay on as teachers, so few problems with recruitment.

Games, options, the arts: Outstanding range of facilities, which include 14 acres of playing fields, two sports halls, a dance studio and a multi-gym for students and staff. Games lessons focus on athletics, ball games, gymnastics and dance.

Strong music department – all students take music in years 7, 8 and 9 and about 15 per cent also take instrumental lessons with visiting staff. Ten practice rooms, keyboard laboratory, recording studio, two specialist classrooms, plus music masterclasses. Large auditorium which seats 900, plus a concert hall for 450. Amphitheatre for outdoor concerts and performances. Five interconnecting art rooms, plus a sculpture terrace. Media studio with professional standard film and television equipment and an editing suite. Well-equipped library.

Annual reading festival and poetry competition. Excellent range of school trips, including Poland (for sixth form Holocaust studies), Israel (year 9 residential scheme), Prague, Strasbourg, Flanders and Paris. Duke of Edinburgh, Young Enterprise. Kosher kitchen with a healthy and balanced diet – no other food can be brought into school.

Background and atmosphere: The largest Jewish comprehensive in Europe, has a particularly distinguished history and tradition. Founded originally in the East End in 1732, it had, by the 19th century, become the largest school in the world, with 4000 students, mainly poor Jewish immigrants. Bombed in WW2, it was re-built in Camden Town in 1958, but by the time it transferred to Kenton in 2002 the accommodation had, in the words of its previous head, become a 'cesspit'. Perhaps previous head Dame Ruth Robins's most significant achievement was guiding the complex negotiations which secured the large and leafy site in north-west London and overseeing the design and building of the new school, with its light, modern buildings, wide curved corridors and state-of-the-art technology. Has a strong family feel – often parents, grandparents and even great-grandparents are former pupils – with an outstanding sense of continuity, community, warmth and commitment. The social side of school life is particularly prized by parents and most students enjoy coming to school and make life-long friends.

Pastoral care and discipline: Blue and white uniform, which meets the demands of the most Orthodox – so girls in skirts with arms covered, respectful necklines and 'no ironmongery', boys with heads covered with skull caps (albeit some only when they see the head approaching).

In such a large school, the organisation of the pastoral side is of vital significance. On entry, the intake of 300 is subdivided into 10 groups of 30. Each student joins a tutor group and is assigned a tutor – who stays with them throughout – a year manager and director of studies, so three adults looking after

every child. Also buddy and peer-mentoring systems. The ethos is strict, determined but kind – discipline is certainly not a major issue, with quiet and orderly classrooms. Famous detention room – Room 17 – for any persistent offenders and a designated behaviour team to deal with transgressors. 'One or two per cent take up all the time, but I don't know of a single child we haven't turned around,' said the previous head.

Outlook and practice is Orthodox and one of the key aims is to further Jewish values. Very strong Jewish studies programme – 'outstanding,' says Ofsted – and all take GCSE in religious studies. Modern Hebrew and Israel studies are included as part of the Hebrew education programme. Accelerated GCSE in modern Hebrew. Daily services, led by students. Wonderful light, purpose-built synagogue with delicate stained glass windows, where volunteers teach additional Jewish education to the most Orthodox.

Pupils and parents: A very broad spectrum of religious belief, from 'those considering rabbinical studies to those who've never seen a candle lit on Friday night'. Nonetheless, you would probably not feel comfortable here if you didn't want your child to be involved with the Jewish experience. Indeed, for some non-practising parents, it offers a religious opportunity they feel they can't provide at home. 'We're not observant,' said one mother, 'and one of the nicest things about the school was that it enabled my son to have a bar mitzvah.'

Entrance: Some 700 applicants for 300 places. In 2009, following a much-publicised court case, the applications process altered and it was forced to abandon the principle of giving priority to those children who are Jewish according to the religious principles stated by the Chief Rabbi. Instead, in common with other Jewish schools, it now gives priority to those who meet a test of religious practice. Parents for year 7 places have to provide a certificate to testify to synagogue attendance, evidence of a formal Jewish education and/or of family activity in the Jewish community. Places awarded on a points system, which also applies to siblings and external applicants for the sixth form. Those applying for admissions should study the criteria carefully.

Exit: Around 10 per cent leave after GCSEs. Of those who stay on for sixth form, a sizeable majority go to Russell Group universities. Eight to Oxbridge in 2013.

Remarks: An outstandingly well-run comprehensive, with a warm and well-ordered atmosphere, in bright and spacious modern buildings. Ideal for those looking for a strong education within a secure environment and Jewish cultural tradition.

The John Lyon School

Middle Road, Harrow, HA2 0HN

- Pupils: 580 boys, all day • Ages: 11–18 • Non-denominational foundation, welcoming pupils of all religions • Fees: £15,540 pa • Independent

Tel: 020 8872 8400
Email: enquiries@johnlyon.org
Website: www.johnlyon.org

Head: Since 2009, Miss Katherine Haynes BA MEd NPQH, a mathematician (fortyish). Miss Haynes was the first woman to be appointed head of an HMC, boys only, school – a notable milestone. Previously head of maths at Warwick School (qv), prior to which she held the same post at Edgbaston High (qv). This is a look-you-straight-in-the-eye-plus-firm-handshake head, one whose palpable intensity of purpose masks, you feel, warmth and a sense of fun. She is articulate, forthright, focused. 'What a school provides needs to match its location... I want teaching that is dynamic and energetic, that enables boys to learn in the way that is best for them.' She is realistic about the physical limits of the school site – 'It's a question of going with what we can do rather than "what if?"' Perhaps less visible about the school than her popular and relaxed predecessor, Miss Haynes initiated a crackdown on 'standards' and discipline from day one – clearly a bit of a bombshell for some but appreciated by most. All recognize that 'she is keen to do good things with the school'... 'she is going to up its game' ... 'she's obviously keen to do her best'. Whatever uncertainty and scepticism might have rippled through the school on her appointment, it sure as anything isn't there now and parents, staff and boys look puzzled at the idea that a woman in the job is unusual. She has taken on an interesting school at an interesting time – boys' only day schools are thin on the ground these days. In her hands, John Lyon is a school of which north west London is going to sit up and take notice.

Academic matters: Mainstream trad curriculum. Maths much the most popular A level subject with majority getting A*/As. Chemistry, history, religious studies and economics also with good uptake and results mostly in the A/B band. Biology more of an A-C spread. Few modern linguists – nothing unusual there in a boys' school – though Spanish now an ab initio option with French which may strengthen both. School also offers psychology, drama and music tech at this level. In 2013, 95 per cent A*-C at A level, nearly half A*/A. At GCSE, likewise, no curricular quirks. In 2013, 61 per cent of subjects taken gained A*/A. Maths IGCSE taken and results are impressive – all but nine of the 93-strong cohort achieved A*-B. All three sciences also very strong with over 90 per cent A*/A. The Englishes now IGCSE and get mostly A*/B. Latin & Roman Civilisation taken by year 10 pupils with strong results. German now, sadly, dead. No obvious weak areas. Able to take advantage of big brother school up the hill, ie Harrow, for individual language specialisms among other perks. IT hitherto seen as integral to learning in general and not as 'a subject' but this is changing – all take it in the first two years – no shortage of computers about the place – and an A level in the subject is 'probably on its way'. No DT though – simply not possible given the constraints of the site and, seemingly, no pupil or parental pressure to bring it into what otherwise might be seen as a natural home.

Learning support dept works in classroom and via withdrawal. Around 60 on the register at the time of our visit. Mainly assists dyslexics and dyspraxics – of a mild to moderate kind – and has boys on the ASD spectrum too. Site is a bit up and down but most is accessible and wheelchairs are 'not impossible'. We grilled many parents and boys and no subject is seen as weak – most staff, in fact, praised for the support they give. Library full of PCs and much fiction. Somewhat eclectic stock otherwise and what appeared to us an unusual cataloguing system.

Games, options, the arts: Drama clearly lively and popular – possibly not unrelated to the fact that girls from several chic local schools eg St Helen's, Northwood College and North London Collegiate compete at auditions to play opposite the boys in big, well-appointed, productions. We witnessed some younger boys improvising with none of the coyness and self-consciousness common elsewhere at this age group. Provision is good – two studios and the big hall, though no performing arts centre here – no space. Parents enthuse about productions. Music also exceptional despite unglamorous accommodation – school musters all manner of ensembles and boys play a great range of instruments. Good to see, alongside the bands and R and B, a motet choir and string ensembles. Music tech growing. 'The standard of music and drama is amazing,' a parent told

us, 'the last concert was so moving I came out in tears.' Art in a series of studios and some good displays of pupil work here and there in otherwise rather uninspiring corridors. Good to see art done by staff on display – and not just by art staff. Sports hall – though not of the cavernous size found elsewhere – and provision otherwise is good – impressive fitness centre, excellent pool, playing fields up and down the hill and much borrowing of Harrow's fields and pitches also enhances opportunities. Cricket an exceptional strength. Lots of popular expeditions – sporting, educational and charitable – classroom building in Uganda, India and Vietnam occasioned particularly zesty response – along with mountaineering in the Alps.

Background and atmosphere: It's tucked into a winding road on the Harrow hill, still reminiscent of the quiet leafy village this must have been. Harrow School dominates the hill and its fields and structures abut John Lyon's, but this is a happy brotherly co-existence, and the cadet school benefits in many ways from the senior. School sits on the edge of two conservation areas which concentrates creative thinking as far as development is concerned. The main school building is Victorian gothic. One small new-build – under the 'estate strategy' – enabled it to change its designation from housing economics and dining to become a new sixth form centre which opened in September 2012. It includes a dedicated sixth form work space with state of the art IT facilities, as well as a space for relaxation. Pretty arts and crafts villa now the admin hub. Most corridors, painted white under fluorescent lighting and with municipal carpet, are pretty stark. Good-sized school hall, with picture windows and views on two sides. The site is not spacious and few buildings delight the eye but it doesn't feel crowded – partly because of the surrounding pitches and fields. Limited space means that the population has to stay at more or less its present size – the relative smallness of the school seen by all as a great attraction. Parents are united – 'everyone knows everyone – they all mix, older and younger, especially on the school bus and all are very accepting of each other'... 'sport and drama means they make good friends across the age groups'... 'because it's small they get a lot of individual attention and that develops and strengthens their confidence'. Three-quarters eat school food which, reportedly, 'could be better' and assuredly needs a more comfortable home. Atmosphere is healthily but not aggressively male – good number of women teachers probably helps. Parents pay tribute – 'the school is very good at bringing on their confidence'... 'it's academic but not pushy'... 'it's an academic school but people aren't separated into geeks and jocks'.. 'not cliquey...everyone is treated equally'... 'good at parent-teacher contact'. 'My son is very happy there.'

Pastoral care and discipline: All lessons start and end with boys standing for the teacher – we approve. Year 13 boys are peer mentors for the younger boys – trained and monitored by professional school counsellor. Clear disciplinary structure – detentions and brief suspensions sort most problems and these are mostly related to late work or behaviour. Two exclusions since Miss Haynes's advent – both for unacceptable behaviour. Drugs/smoking/drink infringements seemingly unknown. Bullying managed by prevention so very little goes on. Self-discipline is the ethos and it seems to work. Pupils clearly proud to be here.

Pupils and parents: Huge ethnic and social mix reflecting the local area. Thirty-odd home languages. Around two-thirds a mix of Asians – mostly Indian. All seemingly mix and co-exist with the school needing to do very little to help it along. An overall ethos of work and collaboration does all that's needed. Most live within two miles of the school but they do come from further afield eg Ealing, Hounslow, Watford and Bucks. Five bus routes. Noted Old Boys include actors Julian Rhind-Tutt and Timothy West, writers Geoff Atkinson and Liam Halligan.

Entrance: Main feeders at 11+ are Alpha Prep, Reddiford; at 13+ St Martin's, St John's, Quinton Hall, Clifton Lodge. At 11, c60 places and c40 at 13. Heavily over-subscribed at both levels. Selection via exam – an online test and an essay at 11. Then an interview with some mental maths. At 13, exams in maths, English and science plus optional papers in eg history, geog or RE. Plus interview. At 16 there are additional places and well worth applying. A grades needed in A level subjects and a decent spread of good grades overall.

Exit: A range of subjects and universities – economics, IT, business, engineering, biomedical sciences and dentistry loom large. Mostly to Russell group or plate glass – several to London colleges, one or two to Oxbridge. Lots, seemingly, reapply post A level results – better matching their results to their choice of course, perhaps, and school offers good support.

Money matters: Good number of bursaries – all means-tested. Scholarships worth up to £2,000 remission of the tuition fees in academics, sports, art & design, music, drama and all-rounder. If you have a gifted son and no money you could get a fabulous deal here.

Remarks: Solid, sound and sensible. Deserves to be far better known.

Jordanhill School

Linked school: Jordanhill School Primary

45 Chamberlain Road, Jordanhill, Glasgow, G13 1SP

- Pupils: 590 boys and girls, all day; • Ages: 11–18; • Non-denom;
- State

Tel: 01415 762500
Email: info@jordanhill.glasgow.sch.uk
Website: www.jordanhill.glasgow.sch.uk

Rector: Since 1997, Dr Paul Thomson BSc PhD Dip Ed (fifties), educated at Dollar Academy, thence to Glasgow uni for a combined honours in maths and physics plus (later) a PhD, having done his Dip Ed at Jordanhill, once next door, but now consigned to the John Anderson campus. Thomson's meteoric career path found him appointed as one of the youngest heads in Scotland, that apart, he has a fearsome intellect and spouted facts and figures faster than most heads we have met, adding all the while 'that it is available on the web page', and a member of the Board and Advisory Council of the SQA. Keen to 'improve the educational environment', he has masterminded a mega building programme since our last visit extending the refectory, constructing an all weather pitch (much in use during our rather damp visit) and building (and we suspect doing more than a little designing) a stunning new classroom block – the South building (replacing what was once a gloomy collection of classrooms). He has also transformed the hall – but see below. Unlike many heads, Thomson regards these developments as 'a pupil necessity and therefore worth spending time and thought on', rather than as an end in itself to glorify Jordanhill and his own cleverness in getting the funding.

Jordanhill is the only direct grant-aided non-special school in Scotland, and runs its own budget, as does each department. A block grant comes from the Scottish Government Education Department to whom the school is answerable. Thomson regards himself quite rightly as a CEO, working 'with the staff' and running the place with a budget of £5,200 per child per annum (used to be more, but what with recent cuts...). He obviously misses teaching; his entire demeanour changed during our tour round the school: whenever we found a child to be talked to – about anything – gone was the efficient question-answering model and in its place appeared an interested smiley friend. (He also does all the 'early' UCAS references.) But youngsters apart, we suspect he does not tolerate fools with ease (he thinks he has 'mellowed a little' recently). He also picks up emotional flack, and, after our whistle-stop tour of the new developments we coffee-ed in the staff room (young, vibrant, get the picture?) where a teacher related how much help he had been given when he had 'found it all too much': still at the school, he now has a gentler job.

Academic matters: The school is inclusive: the most successful state school (albeit grant-aided) in Scotland. Four classes of 25 (rather than the trad legal limit of 33) with practical classes of 15 (max 20). Some setting in maths and French. French from primary, Spanish on offer from age 14 to Advanced Higher level. Langs taught via a star system, when the whole class fills the chart they get French breakfast (croissants perhaps?).

School has offered Scottish Bacc since 2009/10 for science and languages, as well as Advanced Highers. In S5 80 per cent of pupils passed three or more Highers in 2013 while 48 per cent passed five Highers. More than 50 per cent passed one or more Advanced Highers.

Arrangements on hand for non native-speakers to have help with extra English (ESOL) and take exams in their native langs, through Shawlands Academy, the Punjabi and Urdu centres etc. Gaidhlig and Gaelic are both listed, though not taught at Jordanhill; pupils studying Cantonese, Greek, Italian, Latin, Mandarin, Russian or Urdu may well be able to include them in their bacc programme. Special needs well catered for – 'If they can cope then we will take them, unless their needs are such that the school cannot accommodate them'; some pupils have records of needs. SEN students have open access to networks; three dedicated staff work across primary and secondary schools, plus five pupil support assistants, scribing where necessary. Paired reading with sixth formers wherever; support sessions during lunch, after school, in the evening, this is tailored formally structured study support. Standard testing for all aged eight – 13: English, maths, spelling, VR; anomalies picked up early and ed psychs called in if necessary.

Public exam results across the board streaks ahead of other Scottish (and Glasgow) schools in particular, and an astonishing 84 per cent of pupils stay on for second year sixth. Masses of external activity, much to-ing and fro-ing with local unis and colleges: higher psychology in partnership with Anniesland College, in the evenings. School is well used. Regular successes in quizzes and competitions both nationally and abroad.

Overhead projectors; white boards as standard, school both hard wired and wireless: computers (400+ of them) in every discipline, in the art rooms, wherever. Trolleys of notebooks motor round classrooms. Rector adds 'School has ICT mark and previously won ICT leadership reward'.

Homework clubs and some homework online. Ditto supported study. Several groups of pupils doing research projects have direct links with staff. Power point demos by all, from P7; P6 and rest of junior school observe before a general discussion on the quality of the presentation with either the rector or other members of staff. (Rector's face lit up like a beacon when he described this). Debating and public speaking timetabled for 11-13 year olds. Loads of interaction. Evening support classes for exam years, labs are open at lunchtime and post-school. Good modern library, more computers and even more in the careers department. Lifts and ramps all over the shop.

Games, options, the arts: Impressive number of playing fields, or use of them. Certain amount of mixing and matching amongst the Anniesland educational fraternity, with Jordanhill having bought the Laurel Park (which closed before amalgamating with Kelvinside) hall (two gyms and a sports hall), whilst Glasgow

Academy owns the Laurel Park games pitch. With me so far? School owns one rugby pitch, uses one from the uni, and has a couple of footie pitches on a 75 year lease from Strathclyde uni. Not bad for a non-independent school on an inner city site. The impressive all-weather pitch is home to the Hillhead Hockey Club, who train and play here.

Fantastic games and oodles of caps – capped pupils wear green ties; colours gold collars, half colours gold stripe etc, and can be awarded for team, individual, musical success or any international representation. Pupils also wear date badges and can end up looking a little like a Christmas Tree. Trad games: rugby, hockey, football, cross-country running and athletics.

Stunning north-facing art department in the South building, certain amount of art on display, magical fabrics, fabric jewellery new kid on the block. Kiln and new silk screen machine in place. Sculpture and good CDT.

Drama strong, top two years do a show for the whole school, and drama timetabled P6 – S2. Current cuts mean part-time drama coach only, higher drama link up with Knightswood Secondary. Inspiring music, with specialist staff from P6 up. 'The best music department in the country,' says the rector. 300 plus pupils play an instrument, 26 different ensembles, serious orchestras. All swinging, and particularly keen on composing. Concerts popular with parents. Outstanding music results. Pupils won a prize with their first film.

Clubs for everything, chess particularly popular. Hot on debating, and citizenship. Home economics a serious contender, more post-Standard grades, when students also study international cuisine (head's face lit up again). 'Healthy take-up, both home economics rooms refurbished'. Deep envy from this editor.

Ambitious outdoor education programme with pupils spending afternoons or weeks away depending on year group; costs, but funds available for those who otherwise couldn't afford to go (less than two per cent free school meals in the senior school as opposed to almost 30 per cent for the rest of Glasgow). Senior pupils have a bi-annual trip to the developing world, part project part tourism. World Challenge. Oodles of trips abroad: Euroscola at the European Parliament in Strasbourg, Paris, Spain, Denmark and points west. Massive charity involvement – both fund-raising and community work in the locality. Jolly school mag written by pupils, staff and FPs, clearly laid out with brilliant editing, comes out twice a year, easy to read, with none of the trendy under shadowing that doting grannies find so irritating (not to mention GSG editors).

Background and atmosphere: Founded in 1920 as a demo school for Jordanhill College of Education became direct grant in 1987, having narrowly escaped closure in 1969. Handsome classical grade B listed building. Rector has stunning panelled offices (think Eltham Palace); huge classrooms with high ceilings and wide pupil-proof corridors have had a makeover (well, most of it has). The hall has been brilliantly elongated – parquet flooring matches, the wall bars have gone, lighting in place and sloping floored chairs (if you follow) being installed during our visit. Blackout blinds. Acid etched glass panelled doors to die for, actually, most of school has natty oak doors to die for (though not yet the cupboards). Fantastic development of the somewhat miserable building previously owned by Strathclyde uni, bought by Jordanhill and transformed into one of the most exciting class/art/spaces we have seen. This bright 15 room classroom block, with north facing art room and huge atrium on the ground floor, has been neatly dovetailed in. We were confidently told the atrium had a popular foodie kiosk in the corner; with our luck, it was unmanned during our visit. Much used as a drop-out zone; each pupil has a lockable locker and there are cunning (quite light) moveable circular seats. Good informal performing space; the balcony above overlooks. The next development was a £150,000 revamp of the adjacent

science building with support from the Wolfson Foundation (£40,000).

School surrounded by (some) games pitches. The high fence which divided the school from the college is now a thing of the past, as, indeed is Jordanhill College. Now amalgamated with Strathclyde uni, it moved (lock, stock and barrel) in 2012 to the John Anderson Campus under the westering of Glasgow Cathedral. Following demolition of the random collection of 'temporary' classrooms, the magnificent David Stow building is now exposed to the west in all its glory. The planning process for future developments is under way: flats are mooted for the main build, but school uses the imposing and important Francis Tombs Hall within for high days and holidays which may throw a spanner in the works. And of course the games pitch is inalienably zoned educational. The total potential development land would appear to be 16.6 hectares (out of 21) at 16 houses per hectare, and the ongoing discussion is as much tree and flora protection as infrastructure. There is talk of the games pitches being administered by The Charitable Trust of Jordanhill school. Chicken and egg: school may have to grow to accommodate new potential pupils.

Strong links with local Jordanhill parish church. Strong links too with Glasgow state schools – joint improvement meetings for staff and pupils, whilst the latter have a joint pre-vocational programme, plus Your Turn project involving pupils across the city. Pupils from other schools can come to Jordanhill to pick up the odd Higher or Advanced Higher not catered for in their own schools.

Pupils are neat in brown uniforms, but decorated as above. Tinies wear charming green pinnies. Efficient and fairly unforgiving uniform guidelines in the prospectus supplement. Headscarves not a problem. Sixth year have a dedicated study room. JOSS operates an after-school club for tinies in the nearby church hall.

Pastoral care and discipline: Four houses – the heads of houses are guidance staff with combined office and interview rooms. Pupils meet with their tutors for 10 minutes each day; the latter are responsible for PSE. School policy is to clamp down hard on any form of bullying. Neither the rector nor his predecessor have permanently excluded; a clearly defined code of sanctions, including letters home, litter duty (brill) and detention. Regular links between sixth form and littles – combined reading and the BFG club. Minister from Jordanhill parish church takes assemblies, but this is an ecumenical school, with all religions' festivals observed – rector is keener that pupils learn 'to conduct themselves properly in church' and understand other faiths (by, eg, visiting local synagogues, mosques and temples) rather than pay lip service to any particular religion.

Pupils and parents: Serves a predominantly owner-occupier area – professionals, who form an enthusiastic parent-teacher association, with parent volunteers in primary department and loads of fund-raising. Nine per cent ethnic minorities. Cashless buffet (looked good); young may not buy food for others. Only pupils above S3 allowed off campus for lunch. Fairly sensible set of rules: and equally clear list of sanctions, most requiring parental signature.

Entrance: Traditionally, 33 pupils are added to those who come up from primary, thus four classes of roughly 25. Inclusive, by address, over-subscribed, waiting lists. Siblings get priority. Some places may become available in odd years, ditto (never advertised) available post Standard grades. First come, first served, as long as you meet the entrance criteria and, in the case of advanced Highers (or SBacc) if the subjects you want to take are already full, then you must try elsewhere.

Exit: Some 75 per cent to university. Trickle to Oxbridge (one in 2013), a few to universities down south (two in 2013) – Imperial for engineering, Liverpool, Manchester, the odd musician to the Royal Academy of Music, and tranches to art school, with or without a foundation course. But most stay in the west of Scotland. Dentistry, medicine and veterinary school all popular.

Remarks: Outstanding, with an inspirational, slightly left of centre rector (though mebbe – perish the thought, he might have mellowed just a tad). Better resourced than many schools in the independent sector – and it's free. A beacon – Glasgow independent sector eat your heart out: Jordanhill should be compulsory viewing for the lot of you.

The Judd School

Brook Street, Tonbridge, TN9 2PN

• Pupils: 1,030 boys • Ages: 11–18 • non denom • State

Tel: 01732 770880
Email: enquiries@judd.kent.sch.uk
Website: www.judd.kent.sch.uk

Headmaster: Since 2004, Mr Robert Masters BSc maths first class from Reading University and PGCE in maths with games from Bristol. Previously taught at two boys' grammars in Gravesend and Torquay (where he was deputy head). Mid-forties, looks as if he could still keep up on the hockey pitch but prefers cryptic crosswords and jogging these days. Parents can find him somewhat aloof and, while some speak of the encouragement he's given their bright lad, others wonder if he would know them. We suspect he keeps closer tabs than he lets on – he smirks as he points to the glass bookcase in which he can observe unnoticed their comings and goings. He is praised for attracting substantial resources and has robustly and controversially protected the school's lack of catchment area. His personal commitment to his ideals is also apparent. 'Our pupils should leave able and willing to change the world with intelligence, good morals and ethics.' Married with three children.

Academic matters: With a high entry standard at 11+, excellent GCSE results (76 per cent A*/A in 2013) and at least 15-20 Oxbridge offers the norm, there's no doubt that this is the domain of the fiercely able. 'It does them no favours to tutor them to death to get in. Once there they'll struggle,' say parents, with peer pressure and the workload pretty relentless (snow closures no respite). Nothing most boys can't cope with and they generally thrive on the challenge. It's a place where you're expected to take the initiative and focus on the job at hand and, though closely monitored in the early years – teachers are praised for gaining a good understanding of individuals' strengths and weaknesses – later on some might be allowed to slip behind. Parents of the more applied enthuse about the support received from the high calibre and dedicated staff. Pupils too. 'I only half mentioned I was interested in a book and the teacher had ordered it for the library.' Its specialist status in science, maths, music and English also helps make it an exciting place with doors opened to local primaries and others.

Success is celebrated but the benchmark set high. The talented are singled out through a one to watch section in the school magazine and those attaining the top GCSE results receive a letter welcoming them to the sixth form. Says one parent, 'By any external measure, on academics and in other fields, pupils outperform, but some fail to get a sense of just how good they are and lack confidence'.

Unlike other local grammars, has stuck with a fairly traditional curriculum. German is obligatory in year 8, other standard language offerings being French and Latin. Says the head, 'We want to make sure that everything we do, we do well'. There's streaming in maths and some get the GCSE out of the way early, freeing up additional time to pursue wider interests, which all are expected to maintain. Alongside GCSEs all study a non-examined subject – forensic science and philosophy being just two of the subjects on offer. In the sixth form four or five AS, and three to five A levels is the norm with 67 per cent achieving A*/A and 91 per cent A*-B in 2013. At the end of year 11 the school loses one or two wanting to do IB, but the head has no plans to introduce it, championing A levels as an opportunity to specialise and considering the A* grade challenge enough. Lots of free study periods and self-discipline required in the upper sixth, which is well ingrained in most by then. Some parents wish for a little more hand-holding as university options are considered.

Individual and group support is available to those not up to scratch in English at lunchtime and in other subjects too, for example through mentoring. The school is increasingly experienced in SEN and integrates dyslexic, other mild SENs and the exceptionally gifted and talented within the classroom. It also caters well for those with physical disabilities.

Games, options, the arts: Most boys love their sport and there's no excuse in the younger years, when the school fields several teams in each sport and anyone turning up is guaranteed a game. Later it can prove difficult to carry on and, in some parents' views, pupils are given insufficient encouragement. Lots of rivalry with county grammars and independent schools, it holds its own in rugby, cricket and positively excels in athletics, cross-country and rugby sevens – it's one of the top state schools in the country. Pupils also receive national recognition in other sports – rowing, sailing, swimming (though the school's pool is said to resemble a biology lab and has long been out of use), table tennis, judo and taekwondo being but some examples. At lunchtime any thought that shirts can be kept tucked in and uniform neat are dispelled, as you witness hordes of boys kicking around a football or doggedly defending a basketball net.

Music is another area of real strength. 'I think my son's sometimes overwhelmed by the opportunities to get involved and perform and I have been simply spellbound by the standard of the choirs and orchestras.' The school gives about 30 concerts each year with pupils also involved behind the scenes, using the technology lab in the well-equipped music block. Individual lessons are scheduled to ensure pupils rarely miss the same lesson twice. Drama is less prominent and not offered at A level, although sixth formers do stage productions regularly, doubtless made easier by the influx of girls to take on female parts. Annually more than 100 pupils pursue D of E bronze award with 20 or so going on to attain gold. Many also distinguish themselves in the CCF while others partake in the school's well-developed outreach programme in maths, science, music and sports.

Background and atmosphere: The school retains strong links with the Worshipful Company of Skinners, which established the school in 1888 to provide an affordable alternative to Tonbridge School. It moved to its current site in 1896 and is ten minutes walk or so from the railway station, on the southern outskirts of the town, near other schools and colleges with its sports fields bordered by housing estates. It's a hotchpotch of buildings, dating from the late 1800s and 1920s, and interspersed with recent additions, with a somewhat scruffy, collegiate feel, not without charm. The Atwell building, housing geography and maths, was completed in 2009 and, together with the modern music block, sports hall and all-weather pitch, compensates for the irritation of long lunch queues due to the lack of hall large enough to accommodate whole school events. Planned improvements in number of science labs, with old ones being refurbished. Moving around, there's a fairly relaxed feel, with boys huddled in groups and bags strewn about.

Pastoral care and discipline: Early on boys are left in no doubt that they are expected to work hard. If you don't do well enough, you take the test again and work handed in late lands you a detention. Most soon get used to it and toe the line.

Socially early days can also be a little tough as boys settle in with their peers from a wide range of schools. The mixing up of classes after a year is also sometimes a challenge for the shy, but different tutors are allocated to look after pupils as they progress through the school and parents find them and other staff responsive to concerns raised.

Minor infringements on uniform and the like tend to be played down, the embarrassment factor of clearing lunchtime tables often being all that's required by way of punishment. Parents are expected, and generally do, take the lead on issues such as drink, smoking or drugs and, on the rare occasion they feature, parents say they are dealt with swiftly and conclusively.

Girls are jokingly said to be a civilising influence in the sixth form and are briefed on what to expect in a predominantly male environment. They seem to hold their own and soon integrate, judging by the smiles and buzz of purposeful activity in the sixth form common room. Prefects and heads of houses are appointed and older pupils act as mentors to the younger years, some wearing 'listener' badges or manning a room where pupils can go during lunch to play board games or to discuss problems. The house system is also designed to promote cross-year contact and a sense of community.

Pupils and parents: Parents tend to aspire high for their offspring and to be active supporters of their efforts, in whatever field. Pupils are keenly aware of the academic credentials that accrue when they get into the school, but this rarely spills over into arrogance. Most are open, friendly, direct, supportive of each other and keen to engage, the reticent or disorganised generally being those who make less of their time there.

The parents' association is active and organises regular events including coffee mornings, a popular football fiesta in the summer term and well-attended bi-annual ball.

OJs include Terence Lewin, Former Chief of Defence Staff and Admiral of the Fleet, rugby player Martin Purdy, Cecil Frank Powell, Nobel Prize winner for physics and Humphrey Burton, head of music at the BBC.

Entrance: Parents are advised to put it as their first choice and competition for the 125 places in year 7 is very stiff. There are usually in excess of 500 applications. In recent years, around 80 applicants have got full marks in the 11+. Preference is given to those in local authority care and then high-scoring applicants; distance is only invoked as a tie-breaker, outraging some schools and parents in the county (though on average only 15 students join from out of county each year).

About 50 external candidates come in at sixth form; many are girls from local grammars, with a requirement of four GCSEs at A grade or above. In practice, two-thirds of entrants have got five A*s or above. Again, places are much sought after and may become more so as nearby schools switch to the IB.

Exit: Rare that a pupil does not go to university either directly or after a gap year. Approximately 45 apply to Oxbridge each year of which, in 2013, an awe-inspiring 20 received offers (and achieved them).

Money matters: Many parents and former pupils contribute readily and generously to the Development Fund, contributing half of the £2.4m cost of the Atwell Building. There is a quiet presumption of affluence which at times results in grumbles over fund-raising requests, and the cost of trips: 'Could they not ski in Europe?' There is a Hardship Fund but pride deters some from making requests.

Remarks: Offers an exceptionally good education for the unashamedly bright and motivated. The opportunities to shine are there for those who want to take them but no mollycoddling for those who don't. Says one sixth form prefect with a brother at a nearby independent school, 'My parents still can't quite believe they've got all this for free'.

Kelly College

Linked school: Kelly College Preparatory School

Parkwood Road, Tavistock, Devon, PL19 0HZ

• Pupils: 350: 200 boys, 150 girls; 50–50 day/boarding • Ages: 11–18 • Anglican foundation but all faiths and denominations welcome • Fees: Boarding £22,650–£26,985; Day £12,150–£15,450 pa • Independent

---

Tel: 01822 813100
Email: admissions@kellycollege.com
Website: www.kellycollege.com

Headmaster and principal of the Kelly College Foundation: Since 2008, Dr Graham Hawley BSc, PhD, PGCE (early forties). Educated at Mill Hill School, followed by Durham and Exeter. Not a pin-stripe suited, hands on lapels, sound bite delivering headmaster of the bullfrog sort – a modest and gently amusing conversationalist who listens sensitively ('He really understands us,' said one of the girls) and has sane and realistic ideas about Kelly College and its constituents. After a spell at Ardingly as housemaster, he moved on to Warwick School as deputy head – a job 'I was surprised to be offered'.

He was even more surprised to be offered the job at Kelly, but 'if there is an opportunity....' Was attracted to the school for its most obvious qualities: its size, the location with its natural beauty and the opportunities it gives the young for enjoying childhood. 'For the most part the young here are gloriously unsophisticated.' Those initial attractions are what continue to sustain him.

'Before I discovered plankton' is an unusual paragraph opener from the headmaster of an independent school. Dr Hawley's first class hons in natural sciences and his doctorate have taken him to solitary places: the west coast of Scotland, Devon, Cornwall, India, Bangladesh and Sumatra. Do not think Gussie Fink-Nottle – think someone who is highly intelligent and articulate, with a close eye for detail and the willing ability to notice and pay attention to everyone. Everyone we spoke to, from ground staff and cooks (those vital people) to pupils, staff and parents, spoke of the head's interest in and concern for individuals – 'He stands outside every morning and greets us by name'. Married to Rachel; they have two delightful children who attend the school.

Moving on in July 2014 to head Loretto School in Edinburgh.

Academic matters: If you are interested in those ghastly league tables you may be disappointed. 'Education is not about league tables' – a point of view expressed by an increasing number of heads who no longer enter their schools. Kelly is one of those. In 2013, over 63 per cent A*/B and 32 per cent A*/A grades at A Level, with nearly 39 per cent A*/A grades at GCSE. This is not a selective school when it comes to academics – 'We will ensure that pupils do as well as they can, but we are not an exam factory,' says the head.

Class sizes are small – sometimes very small at A level – and without exception pupils we spoke to were full of praise for the extra help offered by their teachers when necessary. A good range of solid academic subjects on offer, with excellent language and IT areas. Parents spoke of the expert and sensitive advice they had had from staff when trying to help their children choose the most suitable subjects for them. Still a school of thought that says, 'Better to go further afield if you want a real academic education,' but that lobby is 'less vociferous these days,' a very satisfied parent told us. Parents and pupils speak very highly of the help given to those with special needs.

Games, options, the arts: For those in the know, has an awesome reputation for sport – particularly swimming. The list of champions and Olympians is impressive – endless county and national champions and five 2012 Paralympic medal winning swimmers. But it does not feel a hearty place: it is old fashioned enough to insist on old-style school blazers with ribbons and badges festooned all over athletic gods and goddesses, but musicians, artists, thespians and prefects can be equally decorated – the school is just good at celebrating and acknowledging. The groundsmen look after the pitches marvellously, but we felt it was significant, or at any rate interesting, that all these successes came without a sports hall. Stories were told of opposing teams begging to be allowed to leave the Astroturf over the road and play inside, only to be told, 'We don't let the weather interfere'.

On the other hand, a splendid and most interestingly designed performing arts centre with superb facilities for music, drama and debate – to say nothing of interval entertainment. Close by is the art building with evidence of creative painting and pottery. Outdoor activities are legion. We were left gasping in admiration at the number of boys and girls who had completed the 125 mile canoe marathon from Devizes to Westminster; completed the Ten Tors race; trained as divers, rifle shots and mountaineers. So much to do and so much enthusiastic willingness to have a go. Many pupils achieve qualifications in the Duke of Edinburgh awards and participate in the CCF (all three contingents).

Background and atmosphere: Very close to the attractive town of Tavistock, with its historical connections with the Duke of Bedford, who donated the land, founded in 1877 by an Admiral Kelly. Sculptured into the side of the hill overlooking Dartmoor, the main building is a wonderful example of what Victorians felt a public school should look like. The result is long corridors with Gothic archways, stone floors, wide staircases, mullioned windows: all very Hogwarty but generously softened with skilfully chosen colours, pictures, honours and, when we visited, wonderful heraldic banners as part of that year's theme, created by the younger children with enthusiastic support and encouragement from the seniors – a tribute to the universal friendliness pervading throughout. That really is one of the impressive aspects of the school, which must account for such keen willingness in so many activities. Handsome library presided over by enthusiastic librarian; slightly forbidding but impressive chapel, used four times a week. Boarders spoke enthusiastically of the sixth form centre and the activities arranged at weekends. Flexi boarding is very flexi.

Attractive new buildings higher up the hill behind the Victoriana, one of them the delightful Conway House where the 11 and 12 year old boys and girls live in comfortable harmony before joining the senior houses. 'It's a good way of settling in,' one of them told us, 'and the staff are very friendly.' As for the co-ed question, has been doing this for nearly 40 years and it all feels very relaxed and natural.

Pastoral care and discipline: Lunch in the dining room (excellent Yorkshire pud) was a good insight into the relationships between staff and pupils – clearly mutual respect and genuine affection, with enough of both to allow friendly banter on occasions. The pupils themselves were forthcoming, friendly and honest in their conversation with us. While accepting that bullying was always a possibility, they felt that the tutorial system in place was a good safety net and protection – always someone to talk to; ISI categorised the standard of pastoral care as excellent in 2012. Pretty sensible school rules based on common sense – 'We don't have much trouble,' said one senior member of staff.

Pupils and parents: Parents come from a broad spectrum of professions and choose it for a variety of reasons. One said to us, 'Kelly is famous for its swimming. My son can swim but hates it. But he gets stuck into lots of other things and that's the point. I take the view that excellence breeds excellence. It's good to have it around.' The pupils we met and observed were open, friendly and trusting and we noticed how much interaction existed between the different age groups. It really did feel like a family – even the bunch of genial rogues we spoke to were very friendly, funny and loyal.

Entrance: About 50 per cent of entries into the first form come from Kelly Prep, just down the road. Academically the emphasis is on literacy and numeracy, with as much attention paid to potential as to knowledge. Entrance at sixth form is based on GCSE results (or equivalent) – normally about 20 new sixth formers joining each year. The important thing is to be alert, bright-eyed and willing to be taught. That applies as much to rugby players as potential Nobel Prize winners.

Exit: About two-thirds go on to the sixth form. Nearly all of these to university with a trickle to Oxbridge. Popular universities include London, Bristol, Bath, Southampton, Manchester.

Money matters: Scholarships and bursaries are available. Naval and Forces families may receive 10 per cent discount – don't be afraid to ask.

Remarks: A delightful, small and happy school which offers wonderful opportunities to anyone who is prepared to get stuck in, where effort is rewarded and friendships flourish, unhampered by bogus sophistication and false glitter.

Kelvinside Academy

Linked school: Kelvinside Academy Junior School

---

33 Kirklee Road, Glasgow, G12 0SW

• Pupils: 360 pupils (205 boys/155 girls) • Ages: 3–18 • Interdenom • Fees: £10,230–£10,830 pa • Independent

---

Tel: 01413 573376
Email: registrar@kelvinsideacademy.org.uk
Website: www.kelvinsideacademy.org.uk

Rector: Since January 2012, Mr Robert Karling BA, MBA (distinction in education management), SQA (accelerated route) (fifties). Comes from King Edward VII and Queen Mary School in Lytham, where he had been principal since 2003: the school had been involved in a particularly vicious amalgamation (including a bleach-chucking incident), which must have been unsettling for all. Previously depute rector of Morisons. He read history at Edinburgh University and both he and his wife, Julia, who teaches art, are thrilled to be in Glasgow; they have two boys at Nottingham university. His valediction from KEVII & QM spoke of his 'qualities of leadership, decency, clear convictions, restraint and selflessness'. Karling, with a gentle sense of humour and clear aims, says how pleased he is in a school where he can 'know all the pupils', and how touched he was by 'the great warmth of the staff'; he found the young to be 'delightful, modest, impressive young men and women'. He teaches history, helps on the games field, is involved in the school play and edits the school mag; aims to re-vamp school values ('modernise and expand') and has put a 42 point development plan to school governors, and staff, who seem unfazed.

We asked, as usual for 'results by subject, by numbers of takers, by results and by grade for the past – preferably three years, but last year would be good'. Karling replied with the following: 'Thank you very much for visiting Kelvinside Academy and for sending us your draft. We are delighted that you are impressed and you have said many very good things about us. On reflection, however, we do not wish to be included in the Good Schools Guide. While the factual accuracies are correctable (they weren't), I don't think the wording in a number of places is right and there are a number of statements which are not relevant. I think it is better to decline inclusion in the Guide politely and wish you continued success in the future.' (Well at least it is in plain English – as is their masterful website.)

Karling's comments echo – almost word for word, the dissing of the Guide and Kelvinside's inclusion by the previous head but one, John Broadfoot, who was rector for almost a million years – well not quite, but just a tad out of the 21st century perhaps? Whilst 'the two sausage machines' referred to by the rector, even in the current dismal economic climate, continue to attract pupils by the score, it would appear that the marketing of Kelvinside may possibly have lost its way.

Academic matters: Follows the Scottish system, with national 4s and fives; 'happy with it and working our way through'; 'not much point in making a fuss', writing some of the papers (national 4s only). No intention of following the IB route. Pass rate (A-C) for pupils sitting five Highers was 97 per cent, with 50 per cent of results at A grade. Pass rate (A-C) at Advanced Higher was 85 per cent, with more than a third of results at A grade.

Max class size 20, four parallel classes, upper school setted for English, maths and modern languages: French from age five, German and Spanish from transitus (ie: P7). No classics. Native speakers can take exams (highers etc) in their own lang, school will pull in tutors, though those needing EFL must get help outwith school. Business/enterprise, business management popular with 12/13 year olds who follow through with some spectacular success with Young Enterprise: best wheeze was Kelvinside teddy bears.

Head is rejigging the IT infrastructure, moving to on-line marking and getting rid of paper. NB grannies who v often pay bills like prospectuses and tend not to be too good on line. New head of digital learning, school moving to wireless, with net books and tablets surrounded by a virtual learning environment in both junior and upper school. Super computer complex which includes a multimedia lab 'that anyone can use' FRONTER; and a small lab for the website, with conference and digital enhancing facilities. Personalised learning for all.

New head of learning support too, every child assessed on entry, glitches firmly knocked on the head: one to one sessions, if necessary, otherwise small groups, from juniors up; trained teachers in each faculty. Free. Drop-in sessions, parents can drop in too, drop-ins for homework. School will 'bend over backwards' to help individual pupils'. Phoenix Club, 'enrichment activities' – for those who prefer non-sweaty stuff; plays, ballet, opera and film, discussion. Stretching the mind. Good work-shadowing arrangements for 14/15 year olds.

Pupils from the state Cleveden Academy a bare half mile away join the odd science and English lesson, use games fields at Balgray: works to both schools' advantage.

Games, options, the arts: Small school, so everyone who wants to, gets a chance to shine. Loads of music – masses of tinies carrying instruments bigger than themselves were struggling off to junior orchestra when we visited, a lovely sight. 'Huge numbers, string, wind, full and junior orchestra, jazz group, one or two (four to be exact) pipers; Sibelius in music tech dept. Award winning string orchestra, good showing in Glasgow Music Festival. Expressive arts important: drama timetabled and impressive in the Gilchrist Hall. Thoroughly Modern Millie, Jekyll and Hyde (for which 80 young auditioned). Heaps of extras. Liberal studies include a wide range of classes – philosophy et al. Psychology, cooking long since abandoned (shame about the latter). Photography plus all the usual suspects in the art dept. Fabric, fashion, textiles. Life drawing in the Botanic Gardens (could be chilly). CAD.

Balgray playing fields, less than a mile away, opposite the boating pond: Rugby and cricket powerful, girls play hockey. PE is mixed and can be taken by staff of either sex' ('no issues'). Rowing (pace Katherine Grainger) has tremendous support, academicals in the Glasgow Schools boat, and currently doing heads of the river (Clyde). Two serious gyms, fitness suite. Cleveden Academy use games pitch, which now has a posh Miller Drummond pavilion: about to celebrate its first fundraising breakfast as we write. School expects happy fundraising from enthusiastic parents – and gets it.

Trips all over, both for sport and fun; rugby tour to Paris, Holland for hockey. CCF compulsory for all for one year, thereafter voluntary, all three services. Popular shooting range in the attic, and country reps. Skiing both at home and abroad, country reps again. DofE and camping at Rannoch costed into fees, dedicated specialist out-door member of staff.

Background and atmosphere: Kelvinside Academy started life in 1879 in the elegant Grade A building by James Sellars, now much expanded, but still with wide passages, high ceilings, ornate assembly halls. The school was re-named, The Kelvinside Academy War Memorial Trust, after the Great War; and war memorials for FPs who died in both wars line the main school stairs. Glasgow was awash with the building of splendid temples to learning during the 1870s/80s; many have dropped by the wayside, some have changed hands, but Kelvinside remains a beacon to an earlier age. Numbers have increased; school, co-ed since 1998, includes junior and nursery, the latter based in a couple of posh Kelvinside villas across the road. Plans on the cards to transform these into a sixth form house; move nursery across to main building and roof over part of the frankly disorganised area at the back of the school proper to form a social area.

Parents can drop off early/ collect late (late waiting till 6pm), brekky from 8am. Rather a fine double-decker library. Stunning new Gilchrist Theatre opened in Kennedy Mall (Nigel Kennedy was major donor). Outside caterer, pupils have to opt in, meal times staggered (halal not a problem); sandwiches eaten in the Mall, kiosk with salads, rolls, fruit on sale.

Proper charity work undertaken by school which raises funds for conventional charities but also help out at the pointy end with the Glasgow soup kitchen (hands on: most indigents aged between 30-60; often ex-cons, drug addicts, with health problems). This is community out-reach at its best: one staff for every two pupils. Juniors clear up the river Kelvin (Friends of the River Kelvin) and spend time gardening for the elderly.

Pastoral care and discipline: House system strong, house tutors remain with their charges throughout pupils' time in school. PSE important. Regular assemblies, often taken by prefects; year group assemblies, school ecumenical, but Carol service, Easter celebrated, as well as Remembrance day, Jewish, Muslim high days and holidays acknowledged. 'A certain amount of smoking' – 'We flush the smokers out'. Karling expelled three boys for dealing on site in his second term. Counselling on hand but miscreants are probably out anyway. Will take pupils thrown out from other schools, who must agree not to take drugs during their time at Kelvinside. Rector 'doesn't believe in random testing or contracts'; always tells parents. Cheating, stealing 'can lead to suspension; bullying can lead to good-bye'. School boasts 'a strong partnership with parents'. Robust bullying policy overhauled: cyber bullying a 'real worry'; that, and grooming. Holiday club to help with baby sitting problems.

K

Pupils and parents: Middle class, professional, a significant number of first-time buyers, lots of travelling. From Gairlochead, the Trossachs, to Dunlop in Ayrshire. Bus from Newton Mearns/ Southside (Clyde tunnel useful). Selection of ethnic minorities, but then Glasgow is a city of growth. Parental poll: most seem pleased with current incumbent, but 'after John Broadfoot was here for so long', and then to have two changes in less than in four terms'. Unusual to find fence-sitters in the education world. Particularly in Glasgow.

Good fundraisers, from posh balls to burgers on the games pitch. 'very welcoming' said Karling. Second-hand shop run by parents. And one of the best websites we have come across, not a fancy pants word amongst them. The joy.

Pupils can drive themselves to work with permission, usual caveats about pupil only and no friends. FPs include Sir Tom Risk, erstwhile governor of The Bank of Scotland, Sir Hugh Frazer of the eponymous department store, Lord Rodger, high court judge, the (increasingly thinning) spike-haired violinist Nigel Kennedy and rugby player Ritchie Grey (not to mention Harry Rottenburg) and gold Olympian rower, Katherine Grainger (though she didn't take up rowing until she hit Edinburgh uni).

Entrance: Through the nursery, or wherever; traditionally at 5, 11, 12 or sixth form level. Not academically selective – by interview and assessment, previous school report, five standard plus at A for subjects to be taken at higher level.

Exit: Over 80 per cent to universities – usually Scotland; Edinburgh, Glasgow, Aberdeen, Dundee, St Andrews, Strathclyde and Heriot Watt popular in 2013. Lots of medics, engineers, lawyers, but also softer subjects, child-nursing, and event management as well as marine sciences and pharmacy. Not a lot of gappers.

Money matters: Usual discounts for siblings, collection of bursaries and more wished for. Bursaries, many of whom go to pupils from Glasgow's east end, are rigorously means tested, private detectives, wardens, the lot. Rotten Foundation (as in Harry Rottenburg, 1875, who invented – amongst other things – the original starting block, first used in the 1948 Olympics) unfailingly generous. Scholarships = hefty book tokens not cash.

Will help 'wherever possible' if financial difficulties occur; 'not a problem', 80 per cent pay by direct debit, and discount if parents pay up front for the year.

Remarks: Strong traditional school, takes tinies through to upper sixth, seamless, co-ed, back under firm hand after a little wander in the wilderness (rate my teachers tells all). School became co-ed 1998 (the last of the Glasgow schools to combine), when Laurel/Park amalgamated with Kelvinside (which was grant-aided until 1985). Numbers (as fairly prevalent in independent sector at this moment) a tad down. Smaller gentler school, 'not the sausage machine of the ones on either side'.

Kent College

Linked school: Kent College Preparatory School, Pembury

Old Church Road, Pembury, Tunbridge Wells, Kent, TN2 4AX

- Pupils: 450 girls (including 75 full boarders and 10 flexi boarders) • Ages: 11–18 • Methodist but other faiths welcome
- Fees: Seniors: Day £17,322; Boarding £27,924 pa • Independent

Tel: 01892 822006
Email: admissions@kentcollege.kent.sch.uk
Website: www.kent-college.co.uk

Headmistress: Since 2008, Mrs Sally-Anne Huang MA, MSc, PGCE (late thirties). Educated at Bolton School for Girls and Lady Margaret Hall, Oxford, where she read classics and English, then PGCE at King's College, London. Married to Alexis, a management consultant whom she met at Oxford, two young sons. Spent six years at Sevenoaks School, where she taught English and classics and was latterly a housemistress. Moved to Roedean as sixth form housemistress, then senior housemistress and spent four years as deputy head before moving to Kent College. Has raised the academic standards and increased numbers and would like to raise standards still further, but is determined to keep a wide ability range. Has a very good relationship with the girls and operates a genuine open door policy so girls feel comfortable to go and see her at any time.

Academic matters: Apart from the usual subjects, film studies, product design (textiles), food technology, drama and theatre studies, psychology and PE are offered at A level. In 2013, 68 per cent A*/B grades and 36 per cent A*/A grades. GCSEs 49 per cent A*/A grades. Option to take all three sciences separately or as a dual award. Inspirational textiles teacher has taken the subject to new heights. Science is strong and a pupil recently won bronze in the International Chemistry Olympiad.

RE taught to all up to the sixth form and all younger girls take food technology. Healthy eating is covered in PSHE. The careers department is proactive and helpful and sixth form attend a higher education preparation programme with weekly sessions on interview technique, gap year planning, money management etc. Due to the recent increase in pupil numbers, several new teachers have joined, so a healthy mix of new younger teachers and others who have been in the school for many years. Plenty of male teachers – two are housemasters. Good support for minor learning difficulties and good communication between learning support and mainstream teachers.

Games, options, the arts: All the usual sports – girls have competed at national level at swimming, hockey and gymnastics and are U13 south east area cross-country champions. A gymnastics academy is also open to outsiders on Saturdays. Outdoor activities seen as important and the school has appointed a head of outdoor education who oversees the Duke of Edinburgh programme and various adventure trips at home and abroad. A 'confidence course' has been built in the grounds which includes a scramble net, a 12 ft wall and a 30 ft abseil tree – school officers in sixth form have a team-building weekend using the course. Sixth formers are required to take part in sport for one double period a week but this could be trampolining, aerobics, aquarobics, Salsa or more mainstream team sports. Everyone encouraged to get involved.

Lots of clubs before and after school and at lunchtime, from tae kwon-do to public speaking lessons and clay pigeon shooting, and girls are encouraged to initiate activities and start clubs, eg a street dance club and gospel choir. Astonishing that they can fit so much into a day. They are even good at bee keeping – the school's honey was commended at the National Honey Show.

Top two years have enrichment programme where they work in a small team on a project of their choice to gain a Record of Achievement by the Open College of the North West. This could be producing the school magazine or a cooking course leading to Leith's certificate in food and wine, an extended essay or community service. Young Enterprise scheme where they can run their own business for six months, working in mixed groups with other local schools. Charity Committee organises fund-raising events. Plenty of opportunities to hone public speaking skills and look at the bigger picture in World AIMS (Action in Methodist Schools) Weekend, where such issues as the arms trade, climate change and development are debated, and at the Global Students Forum and model United Nations events in Tunbridge Wells and Bath. Women in Leadership conferences are held annually with outside inspirational speakers; girls also debate subjects such as 'Are women taking over the world?' – lots of thought-provoking and challenging stuff. Dan Snow, John Sergeant and Sandi Toksvig were recent visitors. Drama impressive with whole school productions in the purpose-built Judi Dench theatre – 'The school has very high expectations of the girls and they always seem to step up to the plate'. Their highly acclaimed opera, Carmen, was their most ambitious production to date. Music on the up with a modern music centre and Apple Mac computer suite where girls can compose. LAMDA and English Speaking Board exams and every girl will speak in at least one assembly a year.

In 2012 they celebrated school's 125th anniversary with a weekend film festival, Victorian day and grand summer ball. Lavish art and library centre with large open plan library, art studios, kiln room and exhibition space on the horizon.

Background and atmosphere: Founded in 1886 in Folkestone and moved to its present site in Pembury, just outside Tunbridge Wells, during World War II. Managed by the Methodist Independent Education Trust's board – but with a very light touch. Also has its own governing body, half of whom are members of the Methodist Church or members of a Christian church. Methodists state that their schools aim to be 'caring, family communities committed to the development and full potential of each individual, having regard for their personal attributes as well as their academic aspirations'. Kent College certainly does this and caring for the individual is central to the ethos of the school – each girl's well-being is paramount.

Modern and well-designed boarding houses and classrooms cluster around the original baronial style Victorian house and everywhere has a light and airy feel. Huge amount of refurbishment and number of building projects with new science labs and IT suites completed, plus expansion of sixth form centre. £4 million art and library centre, including café, studios and exhibition space, opened in 2013.

Pastoral care and discipline: The school has a warm and welcoming atmosphere and girls are happy and relaxed while leading incredibly busy lives. A strong Christian ethos is a subtle part of the routine – girls are expected to take part in assemblies but the celebration of other religious festivals is an integral part of school life. A spirit of tolerance and respect is part of the ethos. Relaxed and comfortable girl/staff relationships. The tutor system ensures any problems are picked up early – mentors are allocated to girls who struggle; also a school counsellor. Girls are supportive of each other across the year groups and the house system means that different year groups pull together in sporting competitions and charity work. Day girls are allowed in the social areas of boarding houses and encouraged to try flexi-boarding, and older girls help supervise younger ones at bed time. New girls are integrated quickly and attend an induction programme which includes an overnight camp in the school's orchard. Discos, socials and joint productions with local boys' schools are popular.

Pupils and parents: The school seems to breed great enthusiasm and loyalty. Twenty per cent of boarders from overseas, eg Nigeria, China, Russia, Thailand and mainland Europe, but nationalities carefully balanced and trouble taken to prevent cliques forming. About 25 children need extra help with English. Around 20 per cent of boarders from Forces families. School sees itself as a small global community. No typical Kent College girl, but they do have a great zest for life and want to try everything, are extraordinarily confident with a 'can do' attitude and are encouraged to surpass their expectations and believe that they can be anything they want to be – yet no hint of arrogance. They come from as far as Bromley and Tenterden – good network of school buses. Wide variety of parents from all walks of life – great tolerance of difference – but mostly from business and professional families. Famous old girls include the Countess of Wessex and Sarah Sands, editor of the London Evening Standard. Good links with parents, who feel involved at every step. Active parents' association who organise social events throughout the year – a ball, coffee mornings, new parents' social evenings and a pamper evening. Also a thriving old girls' association and active Friends of Kent College Association, which includes ex staff, parents and governors.

Entrance: Not overly competitive – broad intake and can cope with a wide range of abilities as lots of individualised care. Most enter at 11+ and attend the entrance day in the November before entry, when they are interviewed and sit the school's own exams in English, maths and verbal reasoning. The school also requires a letter from the girl's current head. Entry at 12+ and 13+ with exams in the January before, when they are also tested in science and French. A taster day and overnight stay are strongly encouraged. Those who come up from the prep school also have to take the test. Sixth form entrants need six GCSEs at C or above and A*, A or B grades in the subjects they wish to study at A level. Children come from a wide range of local prep schools and primaries including Holmewood House, Rose Hill, Sevenoaks and St Michael's, Otford.

Exit: Up to 20 per cent leave after GCSEs, usually for the co-eds, eg Sevenoaks or boys' grammars. Sometimes girls come back and have been known to repeat the lower sixth year rather than stay somewhere else. Most go on to some form of higher education to a huge range of destinations, from pharmacology at Edinburgh, chemical engineering at Cambridge, land management at Royal Agricultural College, Cirencester, retail marketing at Loughborough, Spanish at Oxford, criminology at Cardiff. Lots of help with UCAS forms and personal statements and Oxbridge preparation lessons including interview practice with a local boys' school.

Money matters: Academic, music, drama, art and sport scholarships offered at up to ten per cent of fees. Means-tested bursaries also available.

Remarks: Has improved hugely over past few years – numbers up, recent glowing report from the Independent Schools Inspectorate. Girls leave with great self-confidence and strong sense of purpose.

Keswick School

Vicarage Hill, Keswick, CA12 5QB

- Pupils: 1,075; 545 boys, 530 girls; all day except 45 boarders
- Ages: 11–18 • Non-denom • Fees: Boarding £8,685 pa; Tuition free • State

Tel: 01768 772605
Email: admin@keswick.cumbria.sch.uk
Website: www.keswick.cumbria.sch.uk

Headmaster: Since September 2012, Mr Simon Jackson MA (Oxon) MEd FRSA, late thirties, previously deputy head, only the eighth Head in the last 115 years. Educated at the Royal Latin Grammar School in Buckingham and St Catherine's College, Oxford, where he studied biological sciences. Did his PGCE at Wolfson College, Oxford and MEd at University of Gloucestershire. Married with a young family, he is youthful, well-respected, hugely bright and enthusiastic; 'we plough our own furrow here'; he clearly enjoys the freedoms brought from academy status and doubtless wouldn't have it any other way. A scientist and outdoorsy type, he commands respect from all and sundry and you can see why – he has a real presence about the place and wraps enormous charm and an intelligent approach to education around it.

Academic matters: Results at GCSE and A level remarkable across the board in view of non-selective comprehensive entry. At GCSE 73 per cent of pupils got 5+ A*-C grades including English and maths in 2013; 31 per cent A*/A grades; English, maths and science do especially well. Unusually, separate sciences taught by specialists to almost all pupils – school has been awarded science specialist status and was rated outstanding in every respect in a science survey inspection in 2012. Setting in most subjects from year 8, working towards 10 GCSEs as the expected norm. French or German taught in year 7, two languages (or more) for most after that. In 2013, 37 per cent A*/A grades at A level, 82 per cent A* to C; new buildings opening 2014 will allow an increase in the range of A levels on offer. Leadership and volunteering opportunities are encouraged and welcomed to add breadth. A useful Parents' Guide to Home Learning (aka homework) is on the website. Some provision in small department for SEN – other local schools specialise more in this area.

Teaching styles lean towards the traditional. Staff are an interesting bunch; 'inspiring people create aspiration,' says the head; an unusually high number have had previous professional lives (a doctor, a lawyer, an engineer and a journalist to name but a few) and came to teaching via a road to Damascus moment. Most stay forever – and not just for the stunning view from the staffroom window. Parents and pupils appreciate staff commitment and teaching quality; school has leading edge status and is a hub for teacher training, attracting interest (and admiration) from far and wide.

Games, options, the arts: Regular successes in sport at county level; all the usual sports on offer, played at a seriously competitive level; 'See you later Sir, we're off to win,' say girls to the head as they set off for a hockey match. Sports fields overlook Derwentwater; large sports hall on site and lots of tennis/netball courts. No swimming pool; the outdoor pool was closed a long time ago due to health and safety legislation, but open water swimming in the lake is surprisingly popular, and for those unafraid of heights, the school even has its own dry ski slope. Professional coaching via links with local sports clubs has enabled talented pupils to excel even further, with former pupils (male and female) now competing successfully at national level.

Music thrives – much instrumental and singing tuition, very successful choir and orchestra and various other ensembles. School is about to purchase a baby grand piano for the main entrance for passing pupils to enjoy during break. The jazz band is heading for commercial success; you can even hire them for your wedding.

Drama is very strong and is about to become even stronger with the provision of new facilities in 2014. School works closely with the Theatre by the Lake and a week-long 'iPerform festival' is a whole school treat each July.

The John Muir award for conservation is undertaken by everyone; beyond that the surrounding mountains and lakes create a whole realm of opportunities to get seriously wet and/ or muddy with canoeing, raft-building, orienteering, sailing, rock-climbing, fell-running, horse-riding, mountain biking and skiing all on offer.

Interestingly, many of the extracurricular clubs and activities are organised and run by the pupils themselves – they can suggest it, manage it and become the budget holder for it should they so wish. One boy is already proving himself to be commercially astute, making money from an app business he runs alongside the computer programming club and his school work. There are clubs a-plenty; having the Lakes on your doorstep brings so many challenges and opportunities, far too many to list. The theatre group and astronomy club allow you to experience a world far beyond the Lakes, as do numerous overseas trips and an annual German exchange.

Background and atmosphere: As old as Cambridge University, though considerably less well known to all but the locally wise, this school has evolved through the centuries to become one of the top comprehensives in the country. Now, as an academy, it is essentially independent in all but name (and tuition fees); the views alone from this place are worth more than any pupil premium. Originally founded mid 14th century by a local vicar, the boarders still attend the church where it all began. Re-founded in 1898 by Victorian pioneer Cecil Grant, who surprised everyone by creating a coeducational school and also opening a sister school in Harpenden. The Queen has visited three times to date; this is a place that attracts much admiration from interested academics and inspectors alike, and is running out of shelf and wall space for the number of cups and national awards it has won over the years.

On the present site since 1996 on the outskirts of town, it is a mix of buildings, old and new, with more planned and approved for the near future – so the builders are a regular feature here. This is an ambitious place; it has so much, yet wants more, please sir, as soon as funds allow. More boarding provision would be welcomed by both the school and those on the waiting list for places: they could easily triple the size of the boarding house and then fill it overnight.

Despite the size and space needed to accommodate the 1,120 pupils, the teaching site is compact, the music house and sports fields are just a short walk away. Plenty of IT provision; pupils scan in for registration and use of biometrics allows school to be a cash free zone, with lunch and any equipment extras payable directly with parents able to top up from home. Classrooms are attractive and well-resourced and mostly more attractive in than out; the weather can be bleak here and external decor can and does take a hammering. Impressive art and design on display in circulation areas.

The school motto – 'Levavi Oculus – I Lift My Eyes Up' – is taken very literally in your first year here. Part of the induction for the year 7 intake is to climb Skiddaw, which at 932 metres above sea level and the fourth highest mountain the England, is no mean feat. Surely after that nothing at school will ever feel daunting again, but that's the point, school is proud and defiant in its claim that the pupils here 'are not risk-averse'.

Plenty of civic pride about, big on community spirit and strong sense of identity. Locals benefit from a shared use of (some of) the facilities and this, alongside neighbours in close proximity, keeps the school ever mindful of its public image locally, which is no bad thing.

Pastoral care and discipline: School majors in its 'sense of community' mantra. Lots of talk of 'partnership'; high expectations are made clear from the outset and pupils play ball. It's a large school yet manages a small school feel – you are known here. School claims pupils are self-disciplined but, realistically, they are teenagers and there is a real sense that someone is always watching. Clearly lots of fun to be had outdoors, but they mean business inside the classroom and pupils get the message early on. Mobile phones are not allowed, unusual but sensible – that said, nobody checks, the need to do so hasn't arisen, yet.

The pastoral system is straightforward, clear, and appears to work. Even though the boarders are a small percentage of the whole, it adds a sense of all-round care and helps to shape the ethos; Ofsted recently rated boarding school outcomes and boarding provision as outstanding. Boys and girls occupy separate floors in a shared boarding house; rooms are two, three or four bed and equipped with all the basics, there is a shared common room for younger pupils and a separate one for sixth form. Plenty for boarders to do; there is evening prep with tutors in school followed by a raft of optional activities, trips to the cinema and theatre and organised outings every weekend. Originally intended to accommodate children from remote settlements and the Forces, the boarding list is now made up of UK and EU passport holders from all over the world.

Distinctive and traditional green and maroon uniform for all, including sixth form. Smart crested blazer worn proudly by younger pupils, a few shirts hanging out further up the school but most look smart.

No room for complaints about the food; school boasts the national catering manager of the year and lays claim to the best puddings in the country. They also cater for local primaries as well as running four food outlets on site ('it's a bit like M&S,' says one boy).

Pupils and parents: A whole fleet of school buses, plus excellent local transport (Keswick is a good transport hub and therefore more accessible than you might have thought), helps to attract pupils from a very wide area. This brings an unusually broad social intake from right across the Lake District and out to the industrial belt of west Cumbria and beyond. Although most travel by bus, some parents are prepared to drive many miles a day to get here. 'We had a school just down the road', says one parent, 'but our daughter visited here as a Brownie, remembered it well and knew instantly it was the place for her...and no regrets, it's well worth the drive'.

Pupils are a busy and breezy bunch – focused academically yet still finding the energy to go above and beyond. A recent seven minute long lipdub video speaks volumes – they know how to have fun but they know what they are doing and do it well. They might be surrounded by sheep, but no sheep-like behaviour here – there is a big world out there and they aim to play their part in it and make the most of it.

Old Keswickians act as mentors to older pupils, providing advice on university and career pathways and bringing a welcome voice of experience to teenage ambitions and aspirations.

Entrance: No entry tests, though asks for recent report from current school, for information but not selection. Preference given to siblings, prospective boarders. Out of catchment applicants considered on strict basis of distance from school. Many of the feeder primaries are remote village settings and the school works hard on induction days to make new pupils feel welcome – especially important if you are the only one from your school. Further intake into sixth form, minimum requirement of five A*-C grades, including English and maths, with entry requirement of B grades in maths and sciences.

Exit: About 15 per cent leave after GCSE and a further 10-15 after year 12. Ninety per cent of year 13 leavers go on to university, including a handful each year to Oxbridge, and 10 per cent of leavers go on to study at university abroad.

Money matters: Interestingly, and unusually, scholarships available in biology, geography, music and drama, so do ask.

Remarks: It's an ambitious place – you can take the academics as read, but the adventurous, creative and often entrepreneurial spirit is what gives it the edge. Think of it as Richard Branson meets Bear Grylls with Stephen Hawking thrown in for good luck, and you are some way to finding the heart of the place. And of course, that goes for the female equivalent of those guys too – there's no shortage of female high-flyers, from the girls' rugby team yet to concede a point to a UK champion downhill skier and mountain biker – plenty of impressive girls feature here.

Kilgraston School

Linked school: Kilgraston Preparatory School

Bridge Of Earn, Perthshire, PH2 9BQ

• Pupils: 320 girls (including 125 full boarders). • Ages: 2–18 • RC, but plenty of non-Catholic pupils (including Muslims) • Fees: Day £14,925; Boarding £25,455 pa • Independent

Tel: 01738 812257
Email: headoffice@kilgraston.com
Website: www.kilgraston.com

Principal: Since September 2012, Mr Frank Thomson (mid-forties), previously deputy head of Mount St Mary's College in Derbyshire. Educated at Ampleforth, has two Cambridge masters degrees (in philosophy and land economy, and the economics and politics of development). Worked in accountancy before taking up teaching; has spent two decades working in Catholic schools around the UK.

Academic matters: No longer so sleepy – academic record on the up, which has helped the school roll grow by 50 per cent in the past five years: now full, with boarding oversubscribed.

Runs primarily on the Scottish system, with standard grades followed by highers and advanced highers in sixth form. One hundred per cent A/B grades achieved in highers in 2013 and 87 per cent A/B grades in advanced highers. Certain number of fast track standard grades in French and English. Science on the up with new head of physics, new science block; old labs being converted into a sixth form centre (funds in place). Efficient remedial unit (CReSTeD WS); specialist teachers for dyslexia and dyspraxia – one-to-one teaching and EFL on offer. Lang labs popular. Many exchanges, French, German and Spanish (both pupils and staff), via Sacred Heart network.

Games, options, the arts: Impressive 25m swimming pool complex, sports hall (fitness suite and climbing wall) faced in sandstone, with niches echoing those in the stable building (well converted into prep school with attached nursery) – historic Scotland at its best. Wide choice of sports. Eight floodlit tennis courts, international-sized, all-weather, floodlit hockey pitch. The only school in Scotland with equestrian facilities on campus – 60m x 40m floodlit manege and livery. Coaching by Olympians and internationalists.

Strong drama, and inspired art – 'going from strength to strength'; the art department overlooks the Rotunda and boasts an enormous computer-linked loom. Exciting ceramics, regular master classes. D of E, debating, leadership courses. Music centre in the attics, with keyboards and 14 individual sound-proofed study rooms; guitars and stringed instruments everywhere (and hanging from the walls); sound recording studio. Writers' group. Cooking and brilliant needlework – the girls make their own ball gowns for the annual ball with Merchiston. Dedicated director of weekend and outdoor activities encourages all sorts of co-curricular options such as whitewater rafting, canoeing, sailing.

Background and atmosphere: Founded in 1920 – one of 200 networked schools and colleges of the Society of the Sacred Heart. Moved to the handsome red Adamesque sandstone house in 1930, set in 54 acres of parkland (though to be brutally honest it does look a bit like a grand pony club camp when you go down the drive); masses of extensions including spectacular Barat wing, light and airy with huge wide passages. New science centre opened in 2013. Previous head removed many of the statues of saints from the Central Hall, feeling this would be an excellent place 'to show off some of our superb artwork'. Indeed pupils' work does look smashing, but school looks a bit bleak (we liked the saints – they filled the gaps better).

Bedsits from third year, tinies' dorms divided into individual cabins. Some serious investment in the dorm areas; moderated WiFi access and single rooms with washing facilities for girls from age 12.

School stops at 4.10pm on Fridays for day and weekly boarders, but masses of alternative activities for those who stay. Computers, games hall/courts, art, music and sewing rooms open throughout the weekend. God important here – most attend assembly and mass on Sundays, Feast days still special.

Pastoral care and discipline: Sacred Heart ethos prevails – staff enormously caring, 'will go the extra mile'. Pastoral conferences every week, independent counsellor on tap, bullying handled by BFG (Big Friendly Group). Disciplinary committee, gatings, suspensions, fatigues round school for smoking. Drinkers are suspended and a not-so-recent problem was 'nipped in the bud'. Will test areas, not girls, if drugs suspected – the girls here are not the dozy lot they used to be. Charming little handbook for new pupils full of helpful advice. Girls not as street wise as they think they are – tendency to cover woolly pulleys with badges. In sixth form.

Pupils and parents: Trad boarders from all over Scotland and beyond (London and overseas). Day children from Fife, Dundee and Perthshire, Stirling. Buses. Numbers of first time buyers: 'useful little school, just south of Perth...'

Entrance: Not that difficult, although boarding places currently at a premium. Scholarship exams in February. Junior school entrants also do CE. Otherwise 11+ from primary schools and 12+ from prep schools. Pupils can come whenever, half term if space available. Sixth form entry – 'good Standard grades/GCSEs to follow A level course': pupils from overseas or local state schools and are steered to 'appropriate' levels of study.

Exit: A few leave after Standards/GCSEs. Nearly 90 per cent of girls to university. In 2013 nearly two-thirds to Russell Group universities. Edinburgh, Glasgow, UCL, Durham and Warwick popular, plus St Andrews, Aberdeen and Dundee. Three per cent to Oxbridge and some to study abroad. Quite keen on gapping.

Money matters: OK financially – the nuns left rich pickings – as evidenced in the current capital investment programme (swimming pool, new theatre, bistro-style dining room, international-sized all-weather hockey pitch etc).

Up to 10 academic, art and music scholarships. Also riding, tennis and sporting scholarships. Almost one-third receive assistance of some sort. School is 'good at finding Trust funding' for those who have fallen on hard times. Livery £50/£30 winter/summer if used by school, otherwise £85 per week (which is cheap) plus all the other accoutrements – shoeing, vetting, worming, special feedstuff.

Remarks: The only all-girls' boarding school left in Scotland, popular. Small, gentle, not overtly Catholic, splendid facilities. Popular prep; we previously said 'Scots parents see it as a viable alternative to St Leonards', the latter is no longer in the frame having gone co-ed, huge numbers of day pupils at both.

King Alfred School

Linked school: King Alfred Lower School

Manor Wood, 149 North End Road, London, NW11 7HY

- Pupils: 615, all day, 50:50 boys:girls • Ages: 4–18 • Non-denom
- Fees: £12,624–£15,219 pa • Independent

Tel: 020 8457 5200
Email: admissions@kingalfred.org.uk
Website: www.kingalfred.org.uk

Head: Since 2003, Mrs Dawn Moore (mid-forties) BSc MA (London) PGCE. Grew up in Nuneaton (daughter of a teacher), where she attended Higham Lane School, before proceeding to UCL to study genetics. PGCE at the Institute of Education, MA in education management at Kings College, London. Started at King Alfred as a science teacher in 1986, recognising at once that this was somewhere she felt at home: 'On my first visit, pupils came up to me and said, "Hello. Who are you? Can we help?" They weren't afraid to talk to adults. It was so different from my teaching practice'. After having her two daughters (now in the senior school), she took a couple of years off. Returned as a part-time science teacher, then deputy head – 'There was no favouritism. I had to apply for every job'.

A warm, unpretentious enthusiast, completely committed to the school's ethos, 'Dawn' operates an open-door policy and knows most children, from the tinies to the sixth form, by name. Parents see her as an intelligent, anchoring presence: 'Dawn is wise and good at putting your mind at ease,' said one. 'The head is lovely,' said another. A trained and practising schools inspector, in her limited spare time she loves reading and cooking.

Academic matters: A school where exams are famously not the priority. Pupils sit no formal exams until year 10, although each subject has its own testing process to ensure students are ready for GCSEs. That said, prides itself on being able to teach to the highest standards – 'If a child can get four or five As, we'll get them there,' says the head. Pleasing results at GCSE (most pupils take nine), with 51 per cent A*/A grades in 2013; equally solid at A level, with 41 per cent A*/As. Exams may not be the focus, but 'personalised learning' definitely is, and parents feel happy that every child is treated as an individual. 'We have no idea who the clever children are,' said one. 'All are special – they're not compared to one another.'

Not a vast range of subject choice at GCSE (only curriculum languages French and Spanish); good variety at A level, with 24 options, and every attempt is made to accommodate any combination. The classroom approach, as with the whole-school approach, is relaxed – 'Teachers are not that strict,' said one senior school pupil. 'It can sometimes take quite a long time for lessons to begin, but you're still motivated to work.' Homework

K

and marking, however, can be a bit too relaxed for some – 'The school believes that children should be children,' said one mother. 'I like the fact that it doesn't force them to do two hours a night, but sometimes I think they could push a little more.'

Sixth form particularly strong in the expressive arts (photography amongst the best in the country) and arts subjects (English, history); scientists generally find themselves in a minority. A few vocational options post GCSE (business studies and music technology) – 'Some children are not ready to leave school at 16,' says the head.

Additional support is available for students with mild specific learning difficulties – individually, in groups or in class. Students are monitored throughout their time at the school. Teachers build up a picture of pupils' learning profiles and identify those who might require specific intervention.

Games, options, the arts: Known for its creativity and the strength of its visual arts teaching; all lower school classrooms have ovens for baking; own forge. Thriving drama, with theatre, 'black box' studio and masterclasses often given by parents who are themselves leading lights in the profession. Music, too, is popular, with orchestras, band and ensembles of all kinds. Two well-stocked libraries, one for seniors, one for juniors.

Sport played enthusiastically, but 'go, fight, win' is not what this school is about. 'We don't have a first 11 in each year – often we just have a mixed-ability team,' says the head. The spirit, however, is strong, and an eager crowd turns out to support the home team. As well as the usual ball sports, sails three (school-built) boats on Welsh Harp. Games aside, for a London school an outdoorsy place. The large central playing field is at the heart of the campus and even on the rainiest day is filled with fresh air enthusiasts. Considerable emphasis on self-sufficiency. Den building very much part of the experience and whole-year camping trips take place from year 4.

Extracurricular, too, is core. In the senior school, years 7-11 required to make their choice from a wide range of activities, from pottery to golf; sixth form options include screen-writing for films, emotional intelligence and Mandarin. Strong commitment to volunteering throughout, with pupils helping out at the local special school and raising significant sums for international causes (including building a school after the tsunami in Sri Lanka). Good careers advice (which kicks off in year 7) helps with GCSE and A level options and UCAS applications pre- and post-A level. As one might expect, green is high on the agenda – one of the first schools to introduce solar panels and recycling bins. Delicious, exclusively healthy lunch with plenty of fresh salads, yoghurt and water.

Background and atmosphere: Founded by parents in Hampstead in 1898, original aim was to provide an education based on what was best for the child and encourage learning for its own sake. Part of the progressive movement, sees its kindred schools as Bedales in Hampshire and St Christopher in Letchworth. Moved to its current site, a leafy patch of north London opposite Golders Hill Park, in 1921, and has recently expanded, with a school building for the infants across the road from the main site at Ivy Wood, once the home of Anna Pavlova. Attractive, if compact, grounds, with a mixture of periods and styles (new fitness studio, music and drama block, lovely arts and crafts dining hall) grouped around a central village-like common. Star attractions include a wooded amphitheatre, an arbour (Squirrel Hall), formed from the sheltering branches of two ancient chestnuts, and a diminutive farm, complete with chickens, ducks and bees.

The original ethos – liberal, progressive, egalitarian, child-centred – remains core to the school's values today. Parents and pupils agree that the needs of each child are foremost – 'They try to act very holistically. They look at the individual and find out what makes them shine'. In many respects, too, operates as a large extended family, without the rigid age divide found elsewhere. 'It's a really friendly school,' said one year 9. 'Older

kids look out for younger ones and you'll see sixth formers play with year 7s'. 'Most children seem to enjoy their time here' – 'They skip into school every day,' said one long-time parent. 'Even after the holidays, they can't wait to get back.'

New Fives Court lower school building opened in 2011 – includes auditorium, cutting-edge art technology room with kiln and multi-purpose room for food science, rural studies and general science. ICT suite, learning support area and lower school library upstairs.

Pastoral care and discipline: Has always believed in minimal rules and flat hierarchy. Teachers are called by their first name, pupils are expected to be self disciplined, co-operative and self-motivated. Head sees the mutual respect between teachers and pupils as one of the key strengths of the school, 'We trust them to be sensible'. The expectation, too, is that wrongdoing is likely to be an accident – 'We enable children to learn from their mistakes. There are no quick sanctions. It has to be worked through. Equally there are few re-offenders'. Those who cross the line between liberty and licence – 'being irresponsible in the science labs' or 'putting others in danger' – are given a 'blue form' and sent to the head. Children can be devastated – 'I've seen 16-year-old boys cry,' said a member of staff. Offences too serious to talk through – inappropriate behaviour towards their peers, bullying – can result in suspension. Expulsion for drugs on the premises, but head can't remember the last incident and the school has a 'huge' drugs education programme. 'The kids are pretty mature about sex and drugs,' said one parent. No uniform or dress code, but pupils tend not to push the boundaries, preferring standard-issue jeans and jumpers.

Four counsellors – 'We know what's out there and make it our business to be pro-active'. Help too from other pupils – peer mentoring, school 'Cits', pupils' council. The end result is a happy bunch of kids. 'I've seen other parents go through miserable teens,' said one mother with two teenage children at the school. 'King Alfred teaches them a lot of confidence.' Non-denominational – pupils of every faith and none.

Pupils and parents: An arts and media favourite, parents often choose it for its informality and creativity. 'They come from both ends of the spectrum,' says Dawn Moore. 'There are those who are so liberal they think we're conservative and those who are conservative with a small "c".' Popular, too, with former pupils. New converts are often those who disliked their own, more traditional, schooldays: 'I'd have killed to go to a school like this,' said one. 'They make it such fun.' Pupils, mainly from the wealthier suburbs of north London (Hampstead, Golders Green, Highgate, Muswell Hill), are confident and articulate and expect to be given equal weight as adults. Quite a large international contingent – Americans, South Africans, Israelis, Swedish, Germans, Spanish, Italians.

Entrance: For entry at 4, names down at birth, then first come first served (100-200 apply for 40 places): 'We go down the list'. New entrants come for a half-day assessment, are interviewed by the head of the lower school and observed by teachers – 'We soon pick up on how they function'. Seventy or so apply for a handful of places at 11 – 'A lot of thought goes into the mix of classes'. Not highly selective at A level – four GCSEs minimum for those already in the school, five for 12 or so newcomers, with A*-B in chosen subjects. All candidates, however, interviewed to ensure they'll fit into the school culture.

Exit: One or two leave in year 6, a third or so post-GCSE – 'Some children have been here since they were 4 and it's quite a long time to spend at one school,' says the head. About 90 per cent to further education, a good chunk (8-12 each year) to art foundation, then to the full spectrum of universities. One to Oxford in 2013 (human sciences), others to eg Birmingham, Bristol, Manchester, Sussex, York and Warwick.

Money matters: Though not particularly well endowed, attempts to keep fees as stable as possible while keeping facilities up to date. No scholarships, a small number (about four) of means-tested bursaries in year 7 and sixth form.

Remarks: A kind, liberal, creative school that suits the self-starter, the sophisticated and the artistic (pupils and parents). Will get the best out of most children, but possibly not ideal for those who require competition in the classroom or on the games field. Good, too, for the square peg and those who might find a more traditional environment oppressive. Not a school for parents obsessed with league-table position or those looking for children who jump to attention when an adult enters the room.

King Edward VI Five Ways School

Scotland Lane, Bartley Green, Birmingham, B32 4BT

• Pupils: 1,180 girls and boys, all day • Ages: 11–18 • non-denominational–broadly Christian • State

Tel: 01214 753535
Email: office@kefw.org
Website: www.kefw.org

Head: Since September 2012, Mrs Yvonne Wilkinson BA PGCE NPQH (late forties), previously head of Gateways School in Leeds. Geography degree from Northumbria University; taught at a variety of schools including the Algarve International School; was first ever female deputy and acting head at King Edward VI Five Ways before joining Holy Trinity School Worcester as head. Husband Robin is a national award-winning canal narrow boat designer, boat builder and engineer; two children. We described her in her previous post as 'dynamic, very capable and self-assured'.

Academic matters: Very good indeed. In 2013, 50 per cent A*/A grades at A level and 81 per cent A*/B. No weaknesses but particularly strong in English and economics. All usual subjects on offer plus sixth form additions of psychology, philosophy, government and politics, classical civilisation and media studies. Pupils take three single sciences. All study two languages from French, Latin, German and Spanish from year 7. All now begin GCSE (or IGCSE) in year 9 and take some AS in Y11, all take GCSE RE or citizenship in year 11. All sixth formers take AS/A2 or IB, together with A2 general studies and critical thinking. IB introduced (alongside A level) in September 2011.

Classes average 25 in the main school, reducing to 20 at A level. Extra help on hand in most subjects. Maths workshops/clinics held four days a week, not just for standard help but for fun and to develop skills too. Only a handful are identified as having special needs, two with statements. Support given as needed.

Games, options, the arts: Good sports facilities including sports hall, sports pavilion (doubles as additional lunch area), immaculate, county standard cricket pitch and own pool (recently refurbished to include sound and light system for aquarobics). A brand new, large, state-of-the-art fitness suite. Climbing very popular – superb indoor climbing wall built when one in locality closed. All usual sports. All belong to a house; range of competitions held weekly – lots of sports, spelling bees, Call my Bluff etc. Art shows recent signs of improvement (including a new conservatory studio). New high spec drama studio, dance studio and music technology room. Food tech offered to younger years. DT ordinary, nothing

spectacular. About a tenth learn an instrument in school, with a handful playing to grade 8 standard. Good drama – seven productions a year.

Lots of trips to everywhere, for everything, emphasises 'Five Ways, five continents' – growing number of international links in Africa, India, China, New Zealand and Chicago. Plenty of extra-curricular on offer including D of E, chess, and debating – something for everyone, whatever their level of talent or expertise.

Background and atmosphere: An aided, co-educational selective school, one of the seven King Edward Foundation schools (all bursarial work carried out jointly), founded in 1883. Funded by the state with additional help and funding from the Foundation. Moved from Five Ways to current 30-acre site on the southwest tip of the city in 1958. Formerly a grant maintained school, became co-ed in 1998. Has been designated a high performing specialist school, also specialises in science and humanities. School is a centre for The Royal Geographical Society and the Ordnance Survey. Became a 'converter academy' in 2011.

Immediate area deprived but bordering open countryside – views of the reservoir and fields mingle with small terraces and high-rise. School steadily being smartened, still has feel of a 1950s grammar (the odd scuffed edge) but more building, renovation and development in the pipeline. Super, well-kept grounds (full-time groundsmen work particularly hard). Pupils enjoy being at the school, say a good atmosphere and it's possible to have fun with their teachers.

Pastoral care and discipline: Firm discipline – anti-social behaviour not tolerated. Pupils say they get lots of support but also do a lot off their own backs. Designated counsellor but they are encouraged to talk to whoever they feel comfortable with. Peer tutoring being introduced. Assembly hall complete with fabulous church organ can, and does, accommodate the whole school, all seated since the opening of a 200 seat balcony. Three whole school assemblies a week including a traditional Christian assembly complete with hymn (nice touch).

Pupils and parents: Pupils travel from all over Birmingham with some 40 per cent from outside, primarily Worcestershire and the Black Country. Expected social and ethnic mix – super origin chart on display shows many pupils' families originally from Ireland and India, handful from Africa, smattering from America and the Caribbean. Getting smarter (will push as far as they dare) but frequent uniform purges keep most looking reasonable ('We will smarten them up,' insists the school). Active Five Ways Old Edwardians Association. Notable OEs include: Kate Ashfield (actress), Ben McCarthy and Ben Wright (BBC journalists), David Cannadine (historian), Michael Checkland (Director General of the BBC) and Tom Butler (Bishop of Southwark).

Entrance: Competitive – 1,800 pupils vie for 150 places at 11. Pupils accepted by strict rank order of scores, no interviews, no concessions for siblings or proximity to school, though parents do appeal. No fixing to get 50 per cent girls (more boys than girls apply, school roughly 40 per cent girls, thanks to popularity of girls in sixth form). All applicants need to complete a grammar schools of King Edward VI application form and the LA preference form supplied by their resident LA. Each of the King Edward VI schools counts as a separate choice. Occasional places at other times.

Approximately 70 places per year for sixth form. Applicants tend to have straight A*/As; some will have missed the boat first time around but worked extremely hard to earn a coveted place. Head enthused by additions, says they tend to be hard working and diligent, give a bit of a kick to some pupils who may have rested on their laurels.

Exit: Majority leave at 18 – around 95 per cent to traditional universities, rest take a gap year. Seven to Oxbridge in 2013.

Remarks: A top-flight, state, co-ed grammar school that competes well, but not quite on an even footing, with independent rivals. Very much about the education, not the school, a bargain for the middle classes, gives wings to the able but less well off.

King Edward VI Grammar School, Chelmsford

Broomfield Road, Chelmsford, CM1 3SX

• Pupils: 870: 805 boys, 65 girls in the sixth form. All day • Ages: 11–18 • Non-denominational • State

Tel: 01245 353510
Email: office@kegs.org.uk
Website: www.kegs.org.uk

Headteacher: Since 2008, Mr Tom Sherrington BSc MSc NPQH (forties). Previously head of secondary section at the British International School, Jakarta (a high performing school, we're told). Also deputy headteacher at Alexandra Park School, Haringey, and assistant headteacher at Holland Park School, Kensington. His interests include writing and performing music, playing guitar and piano.

Academic matters: In terms of academic achievement one of the top 10 state grammars. In 2013, 84 per cent A*/A grades at GCSE and 55 per cent at A level (not including general studies, which is taken as a compulsory subject). Outstanding commitment from staff who, according to a parent, 'go a thousand miles beyond the call of duty and don't just stick to the curriculum. They give a proper education'. 'Teaching isn't obsessively focused towards exams,' and a love of learning is engendered right from the word go. Younger boys enjoy 'creative lesson plans' (Blackadder used to illustrate a point and volcanoes made from bicarb of soda) whilst older pupils, according to a sixth former, are 'challenged and taken to another level'.

Extensive use of computers in all subject areas, each of which has its own website with lesson resumés and question sheets – big boon for team players who miss a lesson. Awards for those who tot up the most effort marks. 'The school values you if you try your best. We had a letter from the maths department praising our son for the work and effort he'd put in this year,' said a mum. Some feeling that the odd coaster slips through the net, but head is adamant: 'Every child gets the provision they need – we try to find out what's causing a block'.

Very few have special educational needs but a SENCo for one-to-one assistance and ILPs – visual impairment, dyslexia, dyspraxia and Asperger's syndrome are accommodated. Understanding, inclusive approach – 'circle of friends' sometimes recruited to look out for particular individuals.

Games, options, the arts: Not known as a particularly sporty place, but rugby's faring well and full range of fixtures in all major sports. Sixth get the chance to play squash or swim at the local sports centre. Multigym, for all comers, recently opened after representations from the unteamy, who wanted somewhere to let off steam.

Welcoming art department – veritable Aladdin's cave crammed with lively work, especially by the younger ones. New music block – parents are impressed with the standard of concerts and way their children enjoy this side of school life. D of E, CCF, trips and good selection of clubs enrich beyond the curriculum. Best for those who live nearby – a long journey home can thwart involvement.

Background and atmosphere: Founded in 1551, nearly 350 years before it settled on the present site close to the town centre. Last 100 years have seen numbers increase eight-fold and buildings, permanent and 'temporary', added behind the original low-key red-brick frontage. Absolutely no frills, though. Library housed in the school's first hall – beanbags for the younger ones and friendly librarian who, according to a pupil, 'has an encyclopedic knowledge of every book'. The Darwin Centre – sixth form centre – is a three storey state-of-the-art building containing a spacious study area, high-tech careers library, classroom and spectacular sixth form social area on the top floor. The project was funded by a legion of extremely generous donors and is the largest and most rapidly off-the-drawing-board-onto-the-foundations building project of any state school in the country.

Strong sense of community where the acquisition and sharing of knowledge exude from every pore. Contented, well-behaved kids are absorbed in the learning process. Typical boyish inattention to sartorial matters (although a recent uniform drive has smartened them up significantly) but no deviation from the standard white shirts and black blazers – customised with a bright red stripe round collar and reveals. Plain blazers for boys and girls in the sixth with a free choice of shirt colours.

Big drive to improve school lunch has seen fizzy drinks banished and an emphasis on locally sourced meat and veg. Accessible web site gives menus for the term and clear indication of the odd dish that hasn't been prepared in house.

Pastoral care and discipline: Full-time counsellor on hand if help is needed. General perception that boys are nurtured – 'Any difficulties are identified early on and strategies are given to help,' said a parent. Transition to the school can be difficult, but parents find staff approachable and understanding. Slightest sniff of bullying is instantly investigated – support from staff mentors, who are available at any time. Active school council encourages a high level of civilized co-existence and lack of confrontation – 'My son's hair was slightly off the wall after the summer holidays. I was impressed with the way they managed to agree on a compromise,' commented a parent. But no exception to clear rules regarding banned substances – Mr Sherrington is determined 'to preserve social order within the school'.

Pupils and parents: Pupils from as far afield as some London boroughs. Diverse parent body – range of occupations and backgrounds. Old Boys include Lord Fowler, Simon Heffer, Grayson Perry.

Entrance: Hugely competitive. In recent years, over 800 of the brightest examined for the 112 places. Parents say at least a couple of years of coaching are a must. Wide catchment area with over 60 feeder schools – prep and primary.

Almost all on to the sixth. Minimum four As, four Bs – plenty of warning that this is non-negotiable.

Exit: Virtually all to university – on average 16 per cent to Oxbridge, and UCL also popular. Lots of medics. Spread of locations and courses – the traditionally demanding dominate.

Remarks: Inspired approach towards teaching. Staff are passionate about their subjects and students thrive in an atmosphere where it's cool to study.

King Edward VI High School for Girls

Edgbaston Park Road, Birmingham, B15 2UB

- Pupils: 565 girls; all day • Ages: 11–18 • Non-denom
- Fees: £10,935 pa • Independent

Tel: 01214 721834
Email: ct@kehs.co.uk
Website: www.kehs.org.uk

Principal: Since 2013 Mrs Ann Clark. Educated at Bradford Girls' Grammar School and Girton College, Cambridge, where she achieved an entrance scholarship to read modern languages. Has more than 25 years' experience in secondary and university education and was previously deputy headteacher of Heanor Gate Science College in Derbyshire.

'KEHS has an outstanding tradition of excellence,' she says, 'both academically and in the rich extra-curricular life of the school. I want the girls who come here to aim high, work hard to achieve their potential and seize all of the opportunities that are presented to them.'

Married, with two children.

Academic matters: Outstanding academically for decades, one of the country's top academic schools (placed at the pinnacle of league tables. Sixty-two per cent A*/A grades at A level in 2013). Superb, innovative, vibrant, creative teaching and an ethos of hard work. Biology, chemistry, maths and English are currently the most popular subjects – Latin not far behind. RS well liked, 'We get to debate politics and religion – it's really very exciting'. Practical and problem-solving activities aplenty including 'paper clip physics' and participation in the education engineering scheme. Good Schools Guide award for the best independent girls' school for A level business and economics, and also for classics, proudly on display. Many staff of long standing – excellent, lovers of teaching, passionate about their subjects, want girls to delight in the joys of learning, not be suffocated by the confines of exams and assessments. Lots of individual attention – help is available from all and any staff at all times.

Wide academic syllabus. Maximum class size 26. Over 60 per cent of pupils take A level sciences (and must follow a non-A level English course); one third takes arts (and must follow a non-A level maths course) and one third mixed. General studies taken as fifth A level – and girls get mostly As in this too. Russian, Italian, German and Spanish on offer. Classics department flourishing and innovative. School moved to IGCSE maths – 'Much more fun and challenging,' we're told. In 2013, 88 per cent of GCSE grades were A*/A.

Nine science labs, two computer rooms – equipment recently upgraded, super library (with high numbers of girls opting to study in school during exam period). Classrooms double as subject rooms, with old-fashioned desks in some, but filled with pupils' work on display – we particularly liked the facial symmetry and golden ratio in maths. Some classes taken with King Edward's School (qv). 'Outsiders sometimes think teaching here must be a soft option,' commented one member of staff, 'because all the girls are bright, but the fact is that a little doesn't go a long way – they lap it up and want more.' Girls are adept arguers and class discussion and debate are encouraged from the earliest forms.

Games, options, the arts: One of the few schools where enrichment is genuinely as important as the academic. Plenty of trips, masses of fund-raising and community service, including Bolivia as part of World Challenge. Swimming outstanding,

formidable hockey teams. Netball, tennis, athletics, fencing, basketball; good, strong dance group; aerobics popular. Girls picked for county squads in several sports, 'They get madly keen'. Good facilities: sports hall, Astroturf, squash court, fitness centre, pool. No sports day, GCSE PE on girls' wish list. 1983 Centenary art and design block filled with textiles plus traditional painting and superb ceramics (we liked the busts produced for A level). Girls combine A level art with science and arts subjects.

Music and drama now greatly enhanced by the opening of The Ruddock Performing Arts Centre, shared, as with much else on this site, with the boys of King Edward's School next door. Impressive auditorium, good-sized and well-equipped drama studio, dance studio, good foyer space and attractive glass frontage. Many concerts, plays and dance productions – most shared with the boys from over the drive; school symphony orchestra outstanding but lots of performance opportunities for all levels. Drama/theatre studies shared – popular, challenging and deservedly famous under 'very professional ... inspirational' (according to latest Ofsted) and extraordinary teacher, due – to much wailing and weeping – to retire in 2014. Productions big and small to top standards. Music also outstanding – combined again. Fabulous video technology room with TV cameras, full editing suite, mixing etc. Younger pupils do compulsory creative living, a carousel of ceramics, still photography, electronics, food. Older students are encouraged to do non-exam courses such as sports leadership, video or food technology. Careers advice and work experience all on offer (records kept of university interview experiences and past UCAS personal statements to help current applicants). Stacks of extra-curricular: debating, creative writing, living history and film-making a mere flavour.

Background and atmosphere: Part of the King Edward Foundation group of schools (all bursarial work carried out jointly), founded in 1883 and followed King Edward's School to present site in 1940. Shares same architect – campus is a pleasing blend of red brick plus usual later additions; feeling of space and calm inside. Direct grant school until 1976. Girls wear uniform until sixth form, when free rein is given to fashion. Perhaps the happiest and most cohesive staff we've come across – that they are valued (collegiate approach, equal professionals doing different jobs) and encouraged to pursue their interests, not tied down with policies, paperwork and the latest government initiatives, must surely be significant. Part of graduate teacher scheme: 'This is a good place to learn to teach,' says head.

Pastoral care and discipline: Liberal outlook – girls of all ages trusted and encouraged to take and share responsibility. Staff hold a short weekly meeting to discuss concerns, but have 'been very lucky'. Girls follow a pastoral care and personal decision-making programme and can discuss problems with any member of staff. No prefect system, no head girl, no houses (many girls say they would like houses, especially for sports competitions). No school drugs offence policy – 'Any cases would be dealt with on an individual basis'. No exclusions or 'asked to leave' during current head's tenure. Recognises they also have to help high fliers deal with failure. Staff send girls cards wishing them luck in their exams – a nice touch. Good parental contact. In principle, parents can contact senior staff, head or her deputy 'certainly within the hour', if it is clearly an urgent matter (other schools please note).

Pupils and parents: Seriously bright children of professional families, middle to lower middle class. Not the tidiest bunch we've seen, not particularly girlie girls; they are confident, savvy, happy to get stuck in and share responsibility. They take learning seriously (absolutely fine to be clever), live life to the full but enjoy it and have fun along the way. Shares transport system with boys at King Edward's; girls come from as far away

K

as Lichfield, Bromsgrove, Wolverhampton, Solihull. 'Not a school in this league for miles and precious few anywhere,' say parents. Approximately 35 per cent ethnic minorities, as you might expect – no problems here. Ecumenical outlook. Active school council – black jumpers and recycling among recent initiatives. Established OG society; currently working to draw more Old Girls into today's school community.

Entrance: School's own very selective test 'designed to test the children, not their teachers' (nice one). School spends two weeks searching the completed tests 'for potential, not raw marks'. About half come from state primaries. Tough entry post-GCSE (and girls are 'warmly welcomed' at this stage) – school's own exam in relevant subjects, plus interview and previous school's report. By their statutes girls have to be resident in the area of the West Midlands with their parent(s).

Exit: Very few after GCSE (having the boys next door removes the urge to fly off to a co-ed), and does not throw girls out for doing badly at GCSE but stands by its commitment to them. Five to Oxbridge in 2013 and the rest to the top range of universities – Birmingham, Manchester, Exeter, Bristol, Leeds, Sheffield etc, almost always to their first choice. After university to the professions, arts, media, industry, business; school records 'noticeably more and more high achievers – no glass ceiling'.

Money matters: Assisted places have been replaced by an 'equivalent governors' means-related' scheme – up to 14 places a year. Academic scholarships up to the value of two full-fees at 11 (not more than 50 per cent per pupil).

Remarks: One of the country's top academic girls' city day schools, turning out a long line of academic high-flyers, and an example to the grammar school tradition of how this can be combined with breadth, civilisation and fun. Only for the seriously able and talented.

King Edward VI School (Southampton)

Linked school: Stroud, the King Edward VI Preparatory School

Wilton Road, Southampton, SO15 5UQ

• Pupils: 585 boys, 390 girls; all day • Ages: 11–18 • Non-denom, with C of E ancestry • Fees: £13,095 pa • Independent

Tel: 023 8070 4561
Email: registrar@kes.hants.sch.uk
Website: www.kes.hants.sch.uk

Head: Since 2002, Mr Julian Thould MA – Pembroke College, Oxford (mid fifties). Surprisingly, for this overtly scientific school, his subject is history with a passion for medieval castles, evidenced by some detailed scale models in his office, including an intricate one in chocolate, that he was judging for a year 7 competition. Worked in industry before a teaching career in some top schools, Westminster, Cranleigh and King's Worcester, until appointed to his first headship at King Edward VI. Impressively well organised but definitely approachable, he believes children do best when they are happily occupied. Hence the exciting co-curricular programme, which not only attracts some to the school but also encourages enthusiasm, enjoyment and ambition that spills over into academic work.

Parents say he runs a tight ship and nothing is too much trouble. During his 10-year tenure he has had the whole of the inside of the school refurbished. Everything gleams, from the highly polished blue lino in the wide corridors to the cream

paint, which looks universally new. Prolonged search could only find some chipped paint in the music department (all those bulky instrument cases!) and shabby props in drama. The governors have bought much-needed space in form of the Wellington sports grounds on the edge of the city. Also new is a residential outdoor centre on Dartmoor, used as much for reading and study groups as for adventure activities. PHSE has been another priority, plus more facilities both for pupils needing extra support and for the unusually gifted, with a fully-qualified team of special needs teachers and a care team of three nurses, counsellor and chaplain.

As a dedicated educator and a parent himself, with one child still in school, and three at uni – medicine, history and earth science – he feels himself identifying with parents' concerns and in touch with their children. Even his personal interests veer towards the educative. As a Francophile, his enthusiasm takes the form of accompanying the summer trip to Normandy. Though he cites keeping fit by cycling and walking as his personal interests, books and reading are central, exemplified by his insistence that all pupils share this and spend an hour's reading time each week in the library – appreciated by most students, though one 'real reader' said it was infuriating since whatever he really wanted to read was always at home.

Over the past 10 years the school has grown, with just under 40 per cent girls – there are some whizzy girls-only schools in the area. The head is especially keen on the extensive projects in science, reading, languages etc which staff and pupils run with local state primaries. It encourages links, and there are good bursaries for the less privileged. He still has plenty of plans up his sleeve: upgrading of art department, theatre and music rooms is planned in the immediate future.

Academic matters: 'All our pupils are bright enough to do three sciences and a language,' says the head, and certainly exam results speak for themselves. The swathes of A* s at GCSE are in maths and the sciences (66 per cent A*/A grades overall in 2013), with maths also multi-starred at A level but there is a fair sprinkling at all levels in every subject in the wide and demanding curriculum (88 per cent A*/B grades and nearly 69 per cent A*/A in 2013). In the lower school everyone has a go at two mod langs and Latin and carries on with one modern plus at least one other (either modern, Latin or Greek) until the end of third year. At GCSE everyone takes RS early (a bit reluctantly at present though with tip top results – this is due for a change). All do three sciences and a language with the option of three further subjects, adding up together with maths and English subjects to a total of 10.

There are routes to either three or four A Levels in sixth form with everyone doing 'foundation studies' as well. Pupils can do subjects not taken at GCSE, except of course in maths, science and languages where knowledge is cumulative. Despite the excellence of the arts and humanities, most choose maths and science. In one group of 10 pupils all but one claimed maths a favourite subject and, incidentally, RS as the least. 'You can get maths done and either you understand it or you don't.' Work ethic is strong with pupils saying 'it's great if you do well but no one is afraid to ask if they're struggling with something'. Possibly science and maths are so popular because there are so many medical/scientific families, and it's what the school is known for. But the head says, 'Look at the results. There's a better success ratio!'

Sixth formers clearly have high expectations and are appreciative of the support the school gives them. The classes we saw had a quiet buzz of interested discussion and pupils talked about their work with serious enthusiasm.

Games, options, the arts: Art is exciting with masses of multi-media, sculpture, abstract, photography flourishing and due to expand with the advent of a new head of art with an impressive photographic career. Some really good art going on; also some frustration within the department that comparatively few take it beyond GCSE.

Music certainly lively and enthusiastic. A very impressive a capella choir organised by the sixth formers was rehearsing during our visit as well as the strings boning up on Prokofiev for an orchestral concert. Lots of pop and light music as well, and students doing music technology on equipment resembling aircraft consoles. A few get to National Youth Orchestra standard and there are lots of tours, concerts, festival triumphs, high-powered workshops and masterclasses etc. Drama also popular with several performances annually, musical and other. Some are in the lofty great hall with its airy but formal atmosphere and acres of honours boards and some, such as a recent History Boys, in an intimate theatre in the round, professionally lit and equipped and due for expansion soon.

The importance of sport is emphasised by the school being fronted by sports fields, both grassy and green Astro-turfed. The cavernous sports hall is flanked by a new dance studio much used by the girls, though even the boys do a dance module in the third year. Some of the girls' games, compulsory for all, are really fun and a chance to unwind from a tough curriculum, but for many it's serious business. Fantastic record in netball (girls), hockey (both girls and boys) and cricket at county and regional level. Rugby is less strong, 'but a keen coach'. Masses of individuals achieve in fencing, sailing, rowing, swimming etc and there's strong support for athletes of all varieties. Double Olympic sailing gold medallist Iain Percy was here, also Keith Wiseman (past chairman of the Football Association), John and Simon Francis (county cricketers), Dudley Kemp (England rugby cap and past president of the RFU) and Rob Moore (hockey Olympian). Parents like the Saturday fixtures – they keep 'em out of town.

Fifty-plus clubs, many as intellectual as the most academic parent might hope, but some with a distinctive King Edward's twist to them: the Byron Society, the German Magazine Club, the Scamp Club (concerned it seems with codes and code-breaking). The Green Team is busy planting veg and its work has now been crowned by the award of a Green Eco Flag. The recent appointment of an assistant head of co-curricular to coordinate it all demonstrates both how important this aspect is to the school and how incredibly well organised – essential if pupils are to fit it all in.

Real training for social awareness too, with masses raised for charities by the 'charity commission' – £25,000 plus per annum in a huge variety of enjoyable ways – and pupils enjoy the contact they have through educational programmes with local primary schools: 'It's a real pleasure to be able to help someone with reading or science'. Lots of D of E – gold awards – and a plethora of trips enthusiastically promoted by staff. 'Good staff – good at their job, ' a parent commented.

Background and atmosphere: A historic foundation funded by William Capon for the poor scholars of Southampton, under royal charter from the boy king, it opened a year after his death in 1554. The present buildings date from its return from evacuation in Poole during WW2. From the outside it still looks like a post-war grammar school, despite acres of grass and smart blue railings all round – a recent really efficient security and check-in system is in place. Inside, it feels distinctly sophisticated and academic, with the acres of polished lino and slightly institutional coat of arms set into the front hall floor. Everything is geared to a comfortable, work-friendly environment. The atmosphere in the attractive sixth form centre, with its elegant metal arches, break-time snack bar and constantly manned careers offices, positively invites hard work. 'You can get more done here in an hour than in a whole evening at home,' an upper sixth boy commented.

Lots of recent refurbishment in the science zone part funded by the Abraham Trust. No shortage of money, so a new all singing and dancing technology centre and of course appropriate IT everywhere – iPads just coming in for the art department.

Recently acquired the Stroud School in Romsey, one of its main feeders, now known as Stroud, the King Edward VI Preparatory School.

Pastoral care and discipline: Terrific rapport between pupils and staff, especially amongst sixth formers. Prefects, known as Prepositors, and heads of houses patently feel part of the team running the school, and the head boy talks as eloquently as the head in the video clips on the website. Collaboration is key, with school council having a say in major decisions and undertaking research into pupils' needs. They take credit for the streamlined but inviting dining arrangements. Good healthy fare with svelte sixth formers tucking into old-fashioned nursery puddings – too busily occupied to put on weight! Rules on uniform etc are strictly observed, keeping the confrontation points at a superficial level. It must work since they look pretty smart, including the non-uniformed, 'dress for work' sixth form. Pastoral care run through tutor groups drawn from one or two years depending on age and stage. PHSE stresses intelligent responsibility. Lots of drugs education. Head more concerned about 'legal highs' – alcohol etc – and pupils' awareness of what they are doing to themselves. Sanctions range from detention for minor infringements of rules to expulsion, short suspension and investigation, testing for drugs. All staff get pretty extensive pastoral training and meeting times to coordinate concerns. The school assumes an intelligent attitude from pupils, and all rules and policies are clearly laid out with relevant explanation in the student diaries.

Pupils and parents: It's efficient and serves the large proportion of local medical and academic families, with very small ethnic minority proportion. The huge catchment area is right up to Andover and Winchester to the north and edging Portsmouth and Bournemouth east and west. Seventeen bus routes, all energy-savingly full, with major routes doing a second evening run for after-school activities. Locals, including the head, use bikes. Lots of community-minded parents run a PTA (the KESSoc) with second hand shop, social stuff etc. Most can't find anything but good to say of it.

Recent old Old Edwardians range from Hugh Whitemore (playwright and dramatist) and Michel Vickers (pop group Manfred Mann) to Michael Langrish (Bishop of Exeter), Ian Bruce (president of the RNIB) and Sir Edward Abraham FRS (Oxford academic – ground-breaking work on penicillin and synthetic antibiotics). Also His Honour Judge David McCarraher, Sir Michael Bichard and Her Majesty's Ambassador Richard Kinchen MVO.

Entrance: Known to be hard enough to put off unrealistic would-bes but still about two try for every place. Exams in maths, English and reasoning plus interview and report from previous school. Half from state primaries, and around 25 local independents. Sixth form entry asks for six GCSEs at grade B including English and maths but possibly getting a bit more competitive after a bumper crop of super bright applicants. Pupils from the newly acquired Stroud prep school compete on equal terms with the other entrants – no special preference.

Exit: About 70 per cent go through to sixth form. Almost all to Russell Group universities – the cream. Around 10 per cent to Oxbridge.

Money matters: Bursaries, means-tested, 100 per cent remission for the most deserving. Scholarships, academic (up to 10 per cent) and creative arts (up to five per cent) of the fee. Entry at 11, 13 and sixth form. A tight budgeting school with a policy of never borrowing to build. Always has enough cash in hand to cope with any eventuality

Remarks: At first sight a juggernaut of a school, but definitely more upmarket than its grammar schoolish image. Everything done thoroughly and well, as its confident, lively and hard-working pupils attest. Certainly worth the commute from Andover!

King Edward VI School (Stratford-upon-Avon)

Church Street, Stratford-upon-Avon, CV37 6HB

• Pupils: 630 pupils (boys aged 11–18 and girls aged 16–18) • Ages: 11–18 • State

Tel: 01789 293351
Email: office@kes.net
Website: www.kes.net

Headmaster: Since 2010, Mr Bennet Carr BA FRGS (forties). Undergraduate studies in geography at Queen Mary's College, London, then PGCE at Institute of Education, followed by The Bishop's Stortford High School (head of geography and sixth form, assistant head). Influential deputy headmaster of St Olave's Grammar School, London (Sunday Times State School of the Year 2009) for eight years.

Enjoys the independence that has come with academy status and likes being at a small school where he can get to know pupils and be 'at every production, every concert and every match.' Fanatical about small details making a big difference (shirts tucked in, skirting boards retouched every Friday evening). Parents say he has hugely improved communication. Married with two daughters.

Academic matters: GCSE and A level results are very strong. In 2013 80 per cent of GCSEs were A/A*. At A level, 50 per cent A*/A and nearly 82 per cent A*/B. English and French Departments have chosen to follow the Pre-U rather than A Levels, as they believe it better suits the needs of their students (no immediate plans to extend this to other subjects). A growing range of A levels – the 'usual suspects' plus PE and Greek. Psychology added to the A level offering from 2013, and uptake has been enthusiastic.

KS4 is spread over three years. This allows additional classroom time for curriculum enrichment and, alongside slightly extended lesson times of 45 minutes, gives more time for teachers to extend and enrich learning in the increased time available. All boys take English, English language, maths, triple award science, a language (French, German, Spanish or Latin) and RS as compulsory GCSEs, with three options (which include Greek and ancient history). Two DT options at GCSE (electronics and resistant materials).

At A level, as with many boys' grammar schools, sciences, maths and further maths are popular. Economics, geography and history also well represented. A good few take German and one or two take French and Spanish. Regular reports and half-termly grades, together with target challenge grades, including marks for punctuality, attitude in class, homework etc. As a state school, classes are not 'independent sized' – 28 in years 7 and 8. From year 9, when options are chosen, numbers tend to drop to around 20. At A level, groups are much smaller and the head says: 'I will run an A level course for one student if it's the right subject for them.' Students say expectations are high and teachers are 'always there' if they need help.

Brightly lit and well-stocked library (temporarily housed). Very good ICT facilities and Moodle for homework/research etc. SEN provision not huge but the school does have boys with mild dyslexia, dyspraxia, and Asperger's. Students performing below their personal challenge grades are supported in a variety of ways, including mentoring by senior staff and older students. SEN students are identified, monitored and supported and SENCo works with the school nurse, parents and outside agencies as appropriate.

Games, options, the arts: Sport is important – and well supported. Rugby is still strong and the new director of sport is a former professional player. Rowing, fencing, cricket, athletics and hockey are also offered to a high level. A fantastic sports hall (also used for assemblies, concerts, school productions etc), with a proper fencing piste. Very large and lovely playing fields a mile up the road to which the boys walk. Although the school is naturally keen to excel, all are encouraged to join in. Boys can choose whether to be in 'participation' or 'performance' groups. A-D squads in rugby, so room for more than just the successful handful. Rugby and cricket tours, both in the UK and overseas.

As you'd expect, drama features strongly. There is a lovely drama studio and lots of productions within the school, using, among other venues, the Guild Hall where Shakespeare himself would first have seen and participated in stage plays. Very strong link with the RSC and the school is able to access its expertise, costumes, and even its stage on occasion. As well as the 'usual' drama activities, the school has also run Edward's Boys for the last 10 years (a company exclusively producing 'boys' plays' from the early modern period – the only one in the world to do so). Run by the deputy head (pastoral), it has a growing reputation. In a one-off break from their boys' plays repertoire, they performed Henry V at the RSC Swan in 2013. Not many schools can pull off a trick like that.

Lots of music. Previous head's policy of offering a free term of instrumental tuition to every year 7 boy has been maintained as 'sheer genius' by current head, because of the enthusiasm and talent it unleashes. School runs more than 20 choirs, orchestras and chamber ensembles and offers lessons in all mainstream orchestral instruments. About a quarter of the boys take music GCSE, a handful at A level, and in 2012 two went on to study music as undergraduates.

Some lovely art work, and a good, well-lit studio, though facilities are not outstanding. Separate, small building for A level students, where each has his own space to spread out. Some impressive A level work on display. Not a huge subject for the school (about 20 per cent do it at GCSE). Much of the design enthusiasm seems to be channelled into DT, offered in resistant materials and electronics, where the boys get very thoroughly stuck in. Around 40 per cent take DT at GCSE, and there are large, well-equipped, buzzing workshops.

D of E is popular. Most boys take bronze and many go on to higher awards. Lots of other clubs, including debating, bellringing, astronomy and Greek.

Background and atmosphere: Known (inevitably) as 'Shakespeare's School,' this is a place where the history is not so much sensed as inhabited. Classes are still taught in the half-timbered 'big school' where Shakespeare himself would have studied – a fabulous room with an extraordinary beamed and cantilevered ceiling and ancient desks pitted with centuries worth of schoolboy initials, all still in situ. This sits directly over the Guildhall, where Shakespeare's father presided as the high bailiff (mayor) of the town. Until very recently this was used as the school library but is now being renovated for less intensive uses, such as small concerts and drama productions. Just next door is a gorgeous chapel with 15th century wall paintings, where weekly assemblies are held.

New reception area has made the entrance to the school much more welcoming for parents and visitors. Boys are expected to form part of the welcome team. Beyond the Tudor glories, much of the school consists of fairly unremarkable 20th century blocks, but these are well maintained (the head won't tolerate anything less) and serve their functions well. New sixth form space with its own café, which bucks the generally utilitarian trend. Labs are modern and properly kitted out. Halls, studios and ICT suites are impressive.

Sitting in the heart of Stratford, just a couple of minutes walk from the RSC and the river, the school is very much in the heart of the town and significant effort has been made recently to increase positive contact between the students and the local community. As well as involvement with the RSC there is an expectation of service to the town, through the talking newspaper, local hospice and a school for children with special needs. The students know that their conduct and appearance will be noted for good or ill, and seem very keen to make a positive impression.

The head lives within the school campus and says he rarely leaves the gates between Sunday night and Friday so there is a sense of constant input. The general atmosphere is one of students who are proud of their surroundings – thoughtful, engaged, purposeful and confident (but far from cocky).

Pastoral care and discipline: Pastoral care is at the heart of the school. Second deputy head focuses exclusively on pastoral issues and there is also a school counsellor who visits weekly. Careful induction of the year 7 boys with a buddy system and from year 8 vertical tutor groups are operated within four houses, enabling support and good relationships between different year groups. Pupils mentor one another and raft of 20 elected prefects and five senior prefects must explain at interview why they think they are fit for the job of head boy.

Students say there is 'practically no bullying' and that they would intervene immediately if they saw anything going on. 'The most important things we're learning are to work as a group and be part of a wider community,' we were told. No significant issues with alcohol, drugs or smoking.

Tight control of uniform (the headmaster is regularly spotted at bus stops checking that the boys' top buttons are done up), and boys stand when visitors enter a room. That said, the atmosphere is friendly. Boys say staff are very helpful and always available if they need support. Parents told us that the boys' happiness comes first and that the head makes it his business to 'be everywhere' and ensure that everyone feels valued.

Pupils and parents: With a catchment area that takes in Coventry, Solihull and part of Banbury, as well as some fairly leafy Cotswold villages, there is a wide mix of background and outlook. Some farmers' sons, many from professional and academic families. The boys are courteous, confident, thoughtful and articulate. Currently four per cent EAL pupils. Parents are engaged and astute, very supportive of the school and heavily involved in fundraising for sports, performing arts, and school facilities. They clearly feel confident that their sons' potential is being nurtured and prized here. Old boys (apart from Shakespeare) include Reginald 'rex' Warneford VC, poet Richard Spender, actor Tim Pigott-Smith, musician Neil Codling (Suede) and the biblical scholar Arthur Peake.

Entrance: Year 7 entrance tests are administered by the local authority (for this and the other four Warwickshire grammars). Distance from home/siblings not taken into account. Currently about three applicants per place, although this has been rising. Girls admitted to the sixth form from September 2013 (up to 25 out of an intake of 100), with around three applicants per place. For sixth form, at least eight strong GCSEs required (4A, 2B, 2C) with As expected in their chosen AS subjects.

Exit: A few leave post-GCSE (10 per cent in 2013). Most stay on to take three or four A levels (some take five). After A levels boys leave to do everything from classics at Oxford to apprenticeships at Jaguar Land Rover. A strong selection of universities, including four to Oxbridge in 2013, lots to Russell Group to study a wide (science heavy) variety of subjects. Recent choices have included medicine, veterinary medicine, maritime science, aerospace engineering and zoology, as well as history, economics, law and international relations.

Money matters: Three voluntary groups run by parents raise substantial amounts (used to assist boys who may not, for example, be able to afford sports tours or the right kit for D of E). The students say there is no sense that you can't ask for help, 'even if its just a day trip that costs £30,' and that they all fund raise together to reduce the costs of major trips and exercises.

Voluntary contribution to school fund of £365 (a pound a day) per family each year – used to subsidise extra-curricular life. Plentiful leaving scholarships awarded to A level stars (these contribute to their first university term). Additional leaving scholarships available for specific subjects, such as veterinary science and medicine, plus numerous other awards.

Remarks: A flourishing school that is developing an impressive offering under imaginative leadership and achieving results that will turn many independent schools green with envy. A brilliant place for bright boys to flourish, with great emphasis placed on provision for all – from sporty to geeky. Ensuring the boys' happiness is regarded as an essential precursor to academic accomplishment.

King Edward's School (Bath)

Linked school: King Edward's Junior School + Pre-prep and Nursery (Bath)

North Road, Bath, BA2 6HU

• Pupils: 675; 245 girls, 430 boys, all day • Ages: 11–18 • Non-denom • Fees: £11,955–£12,150 pa • Independent

Tel: 01225 464313
Email: headmaster@kesbath.com
Website: www.kesbath.com

Headmaster: Since 2008, Mr Martin Boden MA (late thirties). Educated at Bolton School (where he was asked back to teach after his PGCE) and Jesus College, Cambridge, where he read French and German. Spells at Cheadle Hulme School and Bradford Grammar as head of modern languages preceded his arrival at King Edward's as director of studies, whence he was appointed head, after a turbulent period with three heads in six years – a boy wonder. Married to head of geography, Jane, with an infant son.

Proud of grammar school career and academically very ambitious for his school. It shows: as director of studies he redesigned the school day to lengthen lessons to 60 minutes, necessitating a move to a two week timetable to 'underline philosophical aim of depth in education'. Something's clearly working – KES is up there in the top 100 independents. Anxious to dispel local reputation as hothouse, however, by taking every opportunity to flag up everything else the school does: he claims its stunning results are attributable to 'the quality of the teaching', not merely the innate ability or industry of its students.

Although relentlessly on-message when we visited, we did uncover a keen footballer – 'Though I have learnt to love rugby since coming to Bath' – and the drummer in the staff band. Parents reckon he is straightforward (what you see is what you get) and professional and respect him, not least for his intellect and ability to think strategically – though some feel he has yet to perfect the art of delegation.

Academic matters: Strong across the board. In 2013, 80 per cent of GCSE grades and 63 per cent of A level grades A*/A. Prominent

Oxbridge entrants boards (eight or so per year) draw the eye on the way in, setting the tone and expectations. 'The school takes great pleasure in its rude academic health,' states the head, who also claims intake is not off-puttingly selective. That myth will take some dispelling locally, where it still prevails. Nonetheless, pupils are not pushed into taking absurd numbers of public exams: the norm is nine or 10 GCSEs, four subjects at AS, dropping to three at A2 in most cases. A small group of enthusiastic year 9 classicists is now able to pursue Greek as well. IGCSE for several subjects including maths and separate sciences. A level options have been enlivened by trendier non-trad additions like photography, but intellectual rigour is applied and delivered here too.

SEN provision has been massively developed since we last reported – the head says, 'It has been embraced by pupils, parents and staff'. Learning support now has its own department, one of whose staff has close links with the junior school. 100 per cent screening for year 7 has just come in. Individual support lessons in school time as a chargeable extra (after assessment), but the head concedes that the school would find it hard to accommodate severe cases of dyslexia, dyspraxia or dyscalculia.

Games, options, the arts: Sport is king here and woven into the fabric of the school. Keenly competitive rugby, hockey, football and netball: fearsome local reputation extends to cricket, tennis and athletics in summer. Much participation at county level, some at national, and individual quirks accommodated, such as pole-vaulting and the Devizes to Westminster canoe race. Indoor sports complex, Astroturf and an athletics track on site, grass pitches a mile away at Bathampton. No swimming pool, but close enough to the university's superior set-up. Head conscious of managing the tension between winning at all costs v sport for all. Sixth form options include walking the inhabitants of the local dogs' home, as part of community service.

Drama an increasing strength: one recent Old Edwardian, Tom Payne, has become a star of stage and screen, and at least one production has been to the Fringe. Music facilities small, uninviting but high tech. Staff mad keen, though, and try their best to enthuse: recent appearances of the highly selective chamber choir, 16 in number, and the non-auditioned one have been very well received and instrumental groups gain plaudits at the Mid Somerset Festival. Notable individual successes too (eg National Children's/Youth Orchestra, fast track GCSE group getting all A/A*), yet music still seems to have an undeserved image problem for non-participants.

Visual arts emanate from a well-used department with an enthusiastic following and a fantastic annual exhibition. Graphic design and photography well catered for with their own designated space, and DT has its own bang-up-to-date CAD/CAM workshop. Loads of trips every year, mostly Europe but recently Kenya as part of Global Schools Partnership, and Antigua for the cricketers. Very active CCF, Duke of Edinburgh awards and Ten Tors Challenge teams, plus an annual activities week, remove pupils regularly from the confines of Bath. Charitable initiatives undertaken with typical seriousness of purpose.

Background and atmosphere: Ancient grammar school founded in 16th century but wears its history lightly, if at all, having abandoned its historical but unsuitable buildings right in the city in the 1960s in favour of the southern slopes. Buildings scattered over a steepish site: largely functional but not beautiful, exceptions being Nethersole House, a Georgian mansion housing the parts the head's visitors will see first, plus history, politics and classics, and B block, a sensational high tech teaching space. Some parts could do with smartening up, such as the dining hall and locker spaces – cheerless in winter, we suspect; short on common-room space below sixth form. Food gets thumbs up, though – all done in-house with plenty of hot and cold choices. Impression is busy busy busy, but not frenetic. Lessons have a real buzz: no-one's snoozing at the back. Actually they wouldn't be allowed to – academic commitment and performance are what count here, though, as the head is so keen to point out, that's not all that counts.

The shortish day – lessons end at 4.00pm and even the keenest are shooed out of the library by 5.30 – means most clubs – over 60, from the cerebral Aeolian (the hot air club?) to the practical Young Life Savers – are fitted into lunchtimes. Take-up is reasonable and pupils say everything they want, but some parents worry that that 'there is too much time to hang about and obsess'. Earlier reputation for being two dimensional (ie kids who weren't bright and/or sporty didn't count) gradually fading, though some pupils reckon this is not a school for nonentities, passengers or those without particular skills or gifts. It is certainly cool to be clever here, and an air of academic seriousness is quite discernible. The head conceded, when pressed, that children who don't throw themselves into their work and at least some of what is on offer at KES might not thrive.

Personal independence and eco-conscience encouraged too: large numbers of pupils make their way to school by bus, train (school runs a shuttle service from the station), bike and on foot; space for sixth formers to park. Lively social scene after hours with other Bath schools, but partying which invades the groves of academe, literally or otherwise, strongly discouraged.

Pastoral care and discipline: Strenuous attempts to rid itself of persistent reputation for being tough seem to have met with some success – current pupils and parents praise support given to them, particularly when the going gets rough, academically or otherwise. Pastoral deputy head and p/t chaplain from the Bath Abbey on board. We witnessed one teacher truly going the extra mile with an evident straggler in her lunch break; apparently discussions about pupil welfare predominate over crosswords and gossip in the staff room too. Inordinate trouble taken not only by tutors but also by subject teachers over personal statements. Academic expectations are high, but pupils are helped, not bullied, into meeting them by effective tutors, who enjoy just the right kind of rapport with their charges.

Senior management occasionally exercised over pupil behaviour in town on Saturday nights and not afraid to expel those who supply drugs. Sixth formers are expected to be rôle models and mentors to the lower school: in lower sixth they can try out the rôle of deputy prefect for three weeks before standing for election. Forty per cent of upper sixth then become prefects, with 10 or so senior prefects, from whom a head girl and boy are appointed.

Pupils and parents: Wide social and economic cross-section coming from a 25 mile radius, with a refreshing lack of snobbery for an independent school. Pupils are articulate, open and direct but without brashness, and they are proud of their school. The head likes to remind them that having all those opportunities does not make them better people. Parents are academically ambitious for their children ('But not at the expense of all the extras,' he says) and support the school in all it does, including active fund-raising for extras; interestingly, one said it was hard to 'give the school money', so determined is it to be financially independent. Amazingly few gripes of any description. Most famous Old Edwardian is comedian Bill Bailey. Older notables have reached prominence in industry, academia, finance and the military.

Entrance: At 11, 90-or-so places up for grabs by passing an entrance exam in maths, English and verbal reasoning. Fifty per cent of the intake comes from its own junior school, tucked away at the top corner of the site, nearly all the rest from a range of local-ish primaries.

Some 25-30 places offered at sixth form, conditional on good GCSE passes (A/A* desirable for A level subjects), interview and references from previous school. Sixth form entry tends to attract more girls, who even up the numbers and give the sixth form a genuinely co-ed feel.

Exit: Vast majority to university of first choice with few gap years, including five to Oxbridge in 2013. Exeter, Durham, Cambridge, Leeds and UCL most popular, followed by Oxford, LSE, Imperial, Edinburgh, Manchester, Sheffield and Southampton. Wide diversity of degree courses but medicine and geography particularly strong. Sports and art-related degree choices also feature. A sixth left after GCSE in 2013.

Money matters: Widely acknowledged by parents to be a 'complete bargain', for the calibre of teachers and range of opportunities it provides. Approximately 15 per cent of pupils receive means-tested bursaries, total fees in exceptional cases. Bursary forms routinely given to prospective parents; the head very keen to encourage able but impoverished candidates to apply.

Remarks: Bath's most academic co-ed school, where bright, confident, motivated achievers will thrive on the constant intellectual stimulus it provides in and out of the classroom. Totally unpretentious in site and clientele, with the feel of a grammar school, but edgy – for Bath. Specialises in producing independent thinkers.

King Edward's School, Birmingham

K

Edgbaston Park Road, Birmingham, B15 2UA

- Pupils: 830 boys; all day • Ages: 11–18 • C of E/multi–faith
- Fees: £11,250 pa • Independent

Tel: 01214 721672
Email: admissions@kes.org.uk
Website: www.kes.org.uk

Chief Master: Since 2006, Mr John Claughton (pronounced Clawton) MA (mid-fifties). A proud Old Boy of King Edward's, he spent 17 years as a master at Eton – 'I could have been a lifer' – and a short spell as head of Solihull School before his dream role came up, 'the stars aligned' and he found himself in charge of the cherished school halls of his youth. Married with three sons (two of whom have been at King Edward's), he went to Oxford (a double first in classics, with two publications under his belt) and played county cricket for Warwickshire.

Claughton's enthusiasm for King Edward's (KES) is tangible. As we sit in his wood-panelled office, he jumps up frequently, rarely finishes a sentence, but eagerly holds forth on his ambitions for the school and his firm belief that 'it should be a place for bright kids, not rich kids'. By his own admission, he often cocks up on speech day 'so the parents know I'm human'. According to parents, he 'runs a tight ship' and 'does not suffer fools gladly'. His door is always open – we were kept waiting for half an hour as our meeting was bumped to accommodate a parent who had dropped by with concerns about his son. Quite right too. As one parent attests, 'He is the most passionate and accessible school head I have ever come across in my time as a parent. He has always replied to an email that I have sent, no matter how big or small the query or what time of the day or week.'

Academic matters: In September 2010, the IB replaced A levels and in the second year of results, pupils averaged 37 points, with a good median score across all subjects at both Higher and Standard Level. Only Standard Level maths dipped below the 5 point grade. Five pupils at KES achieved the maximum score of 45 points, achieved by just 111 students out of 127,000 who took the IB worldwide in 2013.

Switching to IB was a risky move for the school and it's still early days to gauge the long-term impact on admission numbers. Judging by the social media debate, some parents clearly have hesitations about the switch from A levels, but Claughton is unswerving in his defence of the IB: 'It offers a breadth of knowledge and intellectual challenge for students,' he insists – and he's certainly endorsed by such impressive early rounds of results, even though the switchover has clearly been a stressful period for staff.

In 2013, 89 per cent of GCSE grades were A*A (68 per cent A*) – a record result. Academic achievement is a clear priority. That said, an emphasis on fun and practical learning is still in evidence – Maths Olympiads, robotics competitions and field trips aplenty (including recent visits to Pompeii and Guyana and rugby tours to Malaysia and China).

Games, options, the arts: Drama is legendary, with the senior annual productions – often hard-hitting musicals with casts of thousands – being the must-see event of the year. Much of the performing arts outside lessons is joint with the girls' school (King Edward V1 High School for Girls), so there is a large pool of both student and staff talent to draw on, but even so, it knocks spots off anywhere else in the region and possibly nationally. There are lots of other productions through the year too, so masses of boys and girls get involved. 'Of course, we audition, so not everyone can tread the boards,' says the director of drama, who works across both schools, 'but if they are really keen, we find them plenty to do backstage'. The end result is that far more boys go off into theatre-related courses than you might expect in such a conventionally academic school.

There is music everywhere. From the swing bands to the choral society to the symphony orchestra ('up to National Youth Orchestra standards,' says one parent), boys are surrounded by opportunities to hear or participate in high quality music. The only down side of all the fabulous music and drama is that boys report going to university can be a bit of a let down. 'Not as good as school,' is a comment often heard from Old Boys who have taken the dedication and talent as the norm throughout their KES days.

The unswerving professionalism of the whole thing is enhanced by the new Ruddock Performing Arts Centre, which is shared with the girls' school. Named after its benefactor (old boy, successful financier and chairman of the Victoria and Albert Museum, Sir Paul Ruddock), it includes a stunning concert hall – 'acoustics are as good as Birmingham's Symphony Hall,' says the justifiably proud head of music – a drama studio kitted out with the latest technology, and a dance studio with views over the university botanical gardens and girls' playing fields, saying loud and clear, 'We take the arts seriously'.

Main school sports are rugby, hockey, cricket and athletics, but there are more than 20 sports to choose from in total, including water polo, where the school enjoys national success. Thanks to the glorious 50 acre site, the school has six rugby pitches, five cricket pitches, an outdoor athletics track and a new £2m hockey Astro pitch. The elite squads are national standard and the school is in the middle of a massive spend on facilities (construction of an indoor sports centre is the next big-spend project in the pipeline). 'I think the sports department felt a bit miffed when the drama and music had so much lavished on them', said one parent.

The list of extracurricular activities is long and deliciously idiosyncratic. There is a Living History Society (again gaining from being joint with the girls' school) that is the only historical re-enactment school group in the country. They hold their public gripped at many a historic building event. Then there is a Graphic Universe Society, Agora, the joint philosophical society, the Parliamentary Society and so it goes on, all led by wildly enthusiastic members of staff and senior boys.

Background and atmosphere: Founded in 1552 by King Edward VI, and now the flagship of the King Edward Foundation group of nine Birmingham schools, including King Edward VI Camp Hill, an excellent grammar and the school's main academic local rival. The school moved to a famous Charles Barry building in 1836, but this was demolished and the school has occupied its current 50 acre site since 1936. It sits next door to the King Edward VI High School for Girls, sharing some facilities as well as a healthy social life (while waiting in reception, we watched a procession of nervous boys drop Valentines cards in a special box, to be collected later by one of the girls).

The original red-brick buildings – interiors slightly scruffy with chipped paintwork and scuffed floors ('our corridors have got the shiniest floors of any school I know,' says Claughton) – sit at the heart of a growing network of shiny new-builds, including the £5m modern languages centre. Honours boards align the walls, there's constant activity in the corridors and a feeling of fun and friendship prevails. Formalities are conspicuous by their absence and on our tour, a caretaker tidied a patch of lawn, ready for the scattering of a local benefactor's ashes: 'Miss Davis – she went to the girls school but believed in what we are doing here in terms of assisted places – and so left us £2 million', explains the chief master. He has driven an outstandingly successful fundraising programme, raising £15 million in the last six years, an incredible feat for a day school during a recession.

Pastoral care and discipline: In their first few weeks, new boys – or 'Shells' – receive lessons covering areas such as bullying, safety on the journey to school, how to manage homework and even how to find their way around school. Ongoing PSE programme covers sex and drugs education. John Claughton believes drugs are less of a problem than 10 years ago and stress is now a more worrying factor affecting boys. Some of the teachers are trained in counselling and the school has an Open Door Youth Counsellor who comes to school once a week. Parents describe the pastoral care as 'exemplary' and 'outstanding'. Head of pastoral care, Mr Howard, is singled out by one parent for 'his dedication and commitment to make KES a happy and healthy environment'.

Pupils and parents: Many of the boys are from Birmingham and surrounding areas but some come from as far as Walsall and Derby. Some 60 per cent of boys are from ethnic minorities. No boaters or wing collars here – so not for parents (or pupils) who enjoy a bit of pomp and formality. The boys we saw hurtling through the corridors were a bit scruffy, and there was plenty of noise but the enthusiasm and ambition was infectious.

Parents' comments are resoundingly positive, although some respondents to a recent school-commissioned survey flagged the need for 'more frequent and informative feedback on their son's progress'.

But when it comes to the bigger picture, parents seem reassured. As one mother of a current year 10 boy comments, 'As a parent, you are made to feel that your son counts and is important – not just another number, lost in a large school.'

Old Boys include two Nobel prize winners, the painter Edward Burne-Jones, politicians Enoch Powell and David Willetts and writers from JRR Tolkien to Lee Child and Jonathan Coe (who both recently spoke at the school).

Entrance: Highly competitive – 700 candidates for 125 places at 11+. Entrance tests in English, maths, verbal reasoning. Five or so places available at 13+, and another six to 10 places for sixth form entry, dependent on interviews, GCSE predictions and headteacher's report. Academic and music scholarships available (50 per cent funded) as well as means-tested assisted places – now 35 a year. About 30 per cent of pupils are given financial support through these schemes and 10 per cent have free places.

Despite healthy competition from other Foundation schools in the area, demand is high and parents warn about the tough entrance exam. 'I don't think it would suit a boy whose academic ability is below the range – possibly getting to the school by cramming and coaching,' comments one parent of a son on an assisted place.

'KES is excellent if your child is clever and hard-working but not so if they start to struggle to keep up', says another parent, 'it can be a bit sink or swim'.

Exit: Twenty-one Oxbridge places in 2013, including seven to study medicine there (and eight elsewhere). Other universities include nearby Birmingham (a two minute stroll across the road), Exeter, Nottingham, Durham, Leeds, Cardiff and Imperial. A pretty broad split between sciences and humanities. A few parents voiced concerns about how well the IB would serve their children when applying for UK universities where A levels are still the norm, but so far, such concerns are clearly unnecessary.

Money matters: The school is admirably committed to continuing to increase the number of assisted places available. More than half of latest applicants applied for one. The King Edward Foundation chips in £1.2m towards these and successful fundraising has contributed another £5m+.

Remarks: The exuberance and drive of the place hit you the moment you walk in the door. What it lacks in shine and ceremony is more than made up for in energy and ambition. Switching over entirely to IB with no transition period was a bold move, but so far, the signs are good. No hushed corridors or austere masters here. It's less about the polish and more about the passion. Diverse, caring and fun but underpinned by an intellectual rigour and clear pursuit of excellence.

King's Bruton

Linked school: Hazlegrove School

Plox, Bruton, Somerset, BA10 0ED

- Pupils: 220 boys, 95 girls; 225 board, 95 day • Ages: 13–18 • Christian • Fees: Boarding £27,948; Day £20,004 pa
- Independent

Tel: 01749 814200
Email: office@kingsbruton.com
Website: www.kingsbruton.com

Headmaster: Since 2009, Mr Ian Wilmshurst MA PGCE (mid-forties). Educated at The Edinburgh Academy, where he was head boy, then Pembroke, Cambridge, where he read geography. Started career at Highgate as geography master, house tutor and games coach, then back over the border to Merchiston, where he was a housemaster for five years, as well as teaching geography and coaching 1st XV rugby, before promotion to deputy headship at The Royal Hospital School in Suffolk. Wants to breathe more commercial realism into a school which has perhaps sometimes suffered the financial consequences of misplaced priorities. Married to Helen, who helps with the marketing, is a tutor and runs the equestrian activity. Their two daughters are at Hazlegrove.

Head's strong sense of justice has already rattled a few cages, but most parents are behind his disciplinary stand and feel that he 'will raise profile of the school'. Wants to improve academic standards (which head doesn't?) whilst keeping the school's traditional warmth. He sets all King's pupils the three challenges of 'do your best academically, make the most of your talents and look after each other.'

'Not afraid to change things,' reported pupils (who 'really respect him') whilst parents thought he would 'pull up on any sloppiness.' Claims not to be ambitious personally. Parents say that 'he is a very nice man' and 'much more personable than first impressions might suggest.' Enjoys hill walking, the odd round of golf and time out with his young family.

Academic matters: Consistent if not superlative – school admits a wide spectrum of ability. Thirty-five per cent A*/A grades at GCSE in 2013 and 42 per cent A*/A at A Level. IGCSE is offered to all pupils in maths and to most able as separate sciences; two out of three languages on offer can be chosen in year 10 – teachers choose courses to play to pupils' strengths with brightest sitting 10 subjects. May not match high flyers in Bath or Bristol but delivers more than King's parents often expect.

Head of teaching and learning – a new post created to focus on stretching the more able and to improve independent learning. Pupils are fast tracked (eg scholars in Latin, which is still offered within timetable for year 9 and at A level but is taught as an activity at GCSE) where appropriate, flexible timetabling to meet individual needs and expanding provision for gifted and talented. Thirteen AS pupils currently involved in Extended Project Qualification; some introduced to this and to philosophy in year 9.

Huge range of subjects (17 or 18) in year 9; small class sizes a great plus point; setting in core subjects. ICT is not taught as a separate subject; lots of computers and smartboards but some subjects have been ICT shy, it seems; good use is made of intranet in some GCSE (eg sports studies) and A level (eg geography) work. Surprising location of food technology (very popular with boys – 10 pupils currently taking AS) in science building rather than with DT. School benefits from involvement in Mid-Somerset consortium to bring new blood into teaching from other backgrounds – two trainee teachers currently on this GTP programme.

Valued learning support department (it has a long tradition here) with its inviting base conveniently located alongside the library. Head of learning support is keen that pupils receiving help are 'not seen as different'. She helps organise the annual ISC conference on SEN and is very experienced at managing provision: 20 to 25 per cent of pupils currently receive some measure of support. All entrants are screened for reading comprehension, spelling and processing speed. Numeracy is covered from within maths department and two teachers are employed to work with EAL pupils (currently over 20 of 80+ overseas pupils receive support with English). Insists that Bruton's learning support is not about 'old ladies in cupboards' but aims to enable pupils to 'make the most of their talents'.

School also offers level 3 BTEC certificate, broadly equivalent to one AS level. Says that 'for students who find the A level examinations challenging, BTEC provides the alternative to enable them to achieve bite-size tasks which will lead to larger assignments/assessments.' BTECs available in health and social care, hospitality and sport.

Games, options, the arts: Sport (compulsory three times a week including Saturday) counts for a lot – 10 per cent of pupils have performed at representative level. Tennis players reached girls' and mixed finals nationally; other recent national finalists include biathlon and gymnastics plus top equestrian events. Sports teachers are ex-internationals, including professional hockey coach; loads of teams in major sports; increasingly attracting girl athletes; universal participation in some events (eg annual cross-country). Opportunity to shine in a team at King's as opposed to being one out of 200 overlooked players elsewhere. Large sports hall with gallery and fitness suite; two squash courts, fives court, acres of playing fields and Astroturf.

Swimming at nearby Sexey's or Hazlegrove. Range of sporting activities (from archery to trampolining) offered throughout the week.

Strong art department (14 currently in A2 group) with good studio spaces (including photographic studio) for exciting range of work and new school and community gallery, thanks partly to success of recent art auction. Sixth form curriculum includes life drawing and history of art also on offer. Music (includes music technology to A2 level) is very popular; about 150 pupils currently play an instrument and opportunities to perform include big band, chapel choir, string orchestra and military band (which recently took part in Lord Mayor's Show in London). Big band goes down a storm at annual black tie dinner dance, 'Swing into Spring', for parents and friends. Battle of the bands and open mic evenings for the extrovert. We listened to lovely chamber choir, which presents range of modern and traditional music with high level of competence; also barbershop and close harmony groups, all under director of choral studies. Lots of concerts each term. Drama offered to A level with productions put on by pupils at all levels in impressive Fitzjames Theatre.

CCF very well established: gliding, sailing and camps all feature regularly, with some opting for D of E programme instead. Varied and extensive activities programme covers everything from girls' cricket or rugby to Arabic and Scottish reels. Recent visits include year 9 to the World War One battlefields, language students in Barcelona, lower sixth to Paris, biologists at Nettlecombe Court near Exmoor and historians experiencing Nuremberg and Leipzig.

Pupils raise money for charity and annual sponsored endurance challenge in Morocco (organised by the chaplain) funds gap year students (to the tune of £1k+ each last year) who go out to Salem in India to work at a Christian orphanage. School's rural location makes work experience difficult to organise and all but a few miss out; successful careers convention for year 12 involves former pupils in giving advice and information. Strong local links exist mainly through weekly community service, which involves 65 pupils working with groups ranging from primary pupils to senior citizens. Innovative international committee organises events such as European Languages Day and Chinese New Year.

Background and atmosphere: Mellow yellow stone wonder located at centre of this unusually scholastic country town, in shadow of landmark Dovecote. Founded in 1519 during reign of Henry VIII, shut its doors after only 20 years and was then re-opened in 1550 under Edward VI – difficult for pupils here not to have a sense of history. Straddles busy road to Castle Cary – no zebra crossing yet to make crossing it safer – and sits conveniently alongside main railway line to south west. Has added buildings (eg impressive Hobhouse science centre and 'badly needed' reception area) without destroying the harmony of older ones. Old House (complete with turret added by a former housemaster) is oldest part of school whilst smallest boarding house of seven is Arion – a girls' house. Neighbouring parish church doubles as school chapel twice a week; assemblies are held in beamed Memorial Hall: recently refurbished, thanks to +£90K raised within King's community in memory of Ben Ross (see below). Adjacent John Davie room (used for small functions, concerts and meetings) could be next on the list. Purpose-built, inviting music 'hub' provides for individual and group lessons.

IT is wireless networked throughout school; separate computer rooms available for classes or study periods. School intranet includes useful lesson notes and reviews for pupils. Excellent, active library works closely with English department (eg accelerated reader scheme) to get even the most reluctant reader involved and lots of literary happenings (eg on national poetry day, world book day etc). All boarding houses bar one have been upgraded or refurbished and last one is on track for summer 2014.

Dynamic and popular chaplain (doubles as a rugby coach) insists he's not tried 'to do anything clever' but has upped the Christian vibes here with 'TGI' – a weekly get together – plus drop-ins at lunch-time. Nothing forced – which goes down well with the neutral majority. Definitely a major element in building a positive ethos at King's (chaplaincy programme described as 'vigorous and popular' by inspectors). Since 2010 there have been many staff changes and in September 2013 25 members of staff were under the age of 30.

Large, airy dining area provides wide range of menus and since January 2013 a new range of hot salads are now available. Pupils can cook up own food in houses after prep and are provided with basic rations.

Pastoral care and discipline: 'Family atmosphere' is what attracts parents and pupils – 'friendly children and good mixing between year groups' praised by one father. 'Fantastic pastoral care', said one mum, whose son is now in fourth year of boarding. Some pupils trained to act as mediators where cases of harassment arise. Well established PSHE programme includes sessions on stress management to help pupils cope with exam pressures. Medical centre provides for day pupils and boarders; free physio sessions on offer for all those sports injuries and visiting counsellor to provide additional support.

Smoking less of a problem these days (we didn't have time to check behind the bushes) but rigorous sanctions for those discovered. Sixth form club serves alcohol on Wednesday, Friday and Saturday evenings for an hour or so; junior common-room a great success: we were told that 'friends just click with each other here'. Head 'takes all circumstances into account' before applying sanctions in areas such as drugs or illicit sex. 'Outstanding' latest Ofsted report for level of care, praise for boarders' activities and leisure resources, safety, achievement and enjoyment of school.

Pupils and parents: All-round traditional education sought by King's parents is steadily moving towards a more focused academic one. Sophisticated incomers appreciate it as much as locals, who prefer its 'slight scruffiness' to more lah-di-dah alternatives. Pupils appear confident and purposeful – apparently they get ('unfairly,' they say) occasional anti-toff flak at inter-school events (eg annual Bruton's Got Talent). Boarders are in vast majority and though girls are well established here (first admitted in 1969) they remain outnumbered by boys two to one. Internet savvy parents can enjoy seeing sports and other activities on school's 'gallery' (thanks to input from a local parent employed to provide all the visual media) even if they can't attend functions in person; regular newsletters and 'plus one card' sent to parents via house staff whenever an achievement has been recognised.

Long list of worthies going back to Hugh Sexey – auditor to Queen Bess and James I and founder of still extant Sexey's Hospital in Bruton. Lots of military top brass (including more recently Air Chief Marshal Sir Peter Squire) plus less worthy William Dampier – a 17th century explorer and buccaneer – and author of Lorna Doone, RD Blackmore. Also The Sunday Telegraph's Mandrake, comedian Marcus Brigstocke and Sergeant Ben Ross – killed by a suicide bomber in Helmand, Afghanistan, who became the first Brutonian to be killed in action since the Korean War.

Entrance: About half of Hazlegrove's leavers move to King's. Remainder from Chafyn Grove, Perrot Hill, All Hallows, Port Regis and a host of others. Wide ability range as parents tend to choose King's for its own sake rather than its league table position.

Exit: Some 80 per cent go on to sixth form. Nearly everyone to higher education – half to Russell Group universities, one to Oxbridge in 2013 and remainder to every which course anywhere.

Money matters: Twenty per cent discount for Forces families. Fewer scholarships (still available for academic, sixth form and music) than previously but increased number of means-tested bursaries. Year 9 rugby scholarship programme launched recently.

Remarks: 'Fairly useful,' said one dad clearly not given to hyperbole, whilst another parent stressed how King's 'does very well at catering for a wide range of ability'. Parents like the family feel of King's – its safe setting and sense of traditional values make it a popular choice. Moving forwards in curriculum terms but should guard against losing its warmth in a drive to be more ambitious.

King's College (Taunton)

Linked school: King's Hall School

South Road, Taunton, Somerset, TA1 3LA

• Pupils: 165 girls, 265 boys; 100 girls board; 175 boys board – the rest day • Ages: 13–18 • C of E • Fees: Boarding £28,440; Day £19,140 pa • Independent

Tel: 01823 328204
Email: admissions@kings-taunton.co.uk
Website: www.kings-taunton.co.uk

Headmaster: Since 2007, Mr Richard Biggs (mid forties). Much admired at his previous school, Lancing, where he was deputy head and, for a time, acting head. Prior to that he was director of studies .and a house tutor at Magdalen College School, Oxford. Degrees from the Universities of Cape Town (BA in physics) and Oxford (MA in maths and philosophy), where he was a Rhodes Scholar. Very bright, but not intimidatingly so; he has a wonderful sense of humour and has made a tremendous impact on the school. 'Inspirational and on the ball,' says one delighted parent; ' He's brilliant,' says a pupil. 'He knows everyone's names and leads from the middle.' An interesting concept, but as we toured around, it became clear what was meant. He pops up everywhere: joining campers over night and staying, watching on the touchline, attending plays and concerts, teaching top maths sets and generally wandering about, observing and encouraging. Prep school heads and teaching staff at the college, alike, talk of his energy and interest in what they are doing.

Shrewd, open to ideas and clear about implementing the best, he has a refreshing vision for the school and is on the way to implementing it. He is ably supported by his charming wife, Sarah, and their two young children, who attend King's Hall.

Academic matters: 'There are far too many exams and too much attention paid to league tables,' says the headmaster. 'I'm less interested in the grades than the process of learning away from exams. I want teachers to be passionate about their subjects.' A new third form curriculum has been devised to make it stimulating and not merely early steps towards GCSEs. The head of English tutors the young scholars, inspiring and challenging; prep is not sacrosanct and can be used for rehearsals and discussion groups: pupils are encouraged to plan and use their time effectively. The dismissal of league tables is not a defensive game founded on sour grapes: separate sciences for most at GCSE and value added is very impressive, a clear sign of good teaching and hard work. In 2013, 56 per cent A*/A grades at GCSE and 39 per cent at A level. The school enjoys strong links with Exeter University and beyond, performing well academically, but not for the sake of league tables.

Games, options, the arts: Flourishing. Games are taken seriously ('But there's no embarrassment if you're not all that good – you can always find something you can do'). Has won National Schools Sevens (rugby) twice, designated a centre of excellence by the English Cricket board (the legendary Dennis Breakwell still reigns supreme), successes at fencing, cross-country, netball, hockey. Outstanding newish swimming pool.

Senior School Choir of the Year in a BBC Songs of Praise; wonderful jazz CD with other musical delights sent out to prospective parents. Newish art building, a clever adaptation of an old house, with stunning work being produced under inspirational head of art and artists in residence. Newish theatre and drama studio. Absolutely amazing DT. Superb building for it – and how well it is used: cars stripped down and repaired, inventions mushrooming, skilfully drawn up plans converted with real craftsmanship. No wonder they have won the Good Schools Guide Award for design and technology four times.

Has just opened a Leith's accredited cookery school.

Background and atmosphere: Founded in 1880 to mark the 1,000th anniversary of the death of King Alfred – pleasing ecclesiastical Gothic complete with obligatory tower. A hundred acres of good playing fields and, by and large, interesting new buildings. A member of the Woodard Corporation – regular services in the large, plain but impressive chapel with its popular chaplain. Services are varied, with scope for open discussion as well as more formal worship. Very fine Gothic dining hall and the Woodard room is an excellent facility for concerts, functions and conferences – when we were there, it was bursting with a very lively careers seminar. Thanks to the generosity of an OB, funding has been made available for a brand new, IT-rich modern library. Popular sixth form centre with attractive alpine-looking bar. The overall feeling of the school is warmly friendly and it was not unusual to see pupils of different ages chatting away convivially – that is, when they were not tearing about.

Pastoral care and discipline: Seven houses, two recently built, mixed day and boarders. Day pupils are welcome to stay over night, by prior arrangement, and we were told of several instances of that which resulted in permanent boarding. Boarding is very popular: weekend activities are arranged by houses and boarders are expected to be in residence for most weekends. Those we spoke to were delighted to be so. 'Weekends are the best time of the week,' said a young boarder, and then grinned sheepishly. This is a school which takes boarding seriously and where the boarders are absolutely not day pupils who live too far away to go home. As far as discipline is concerned, common sense and courtesy really do seem to prevail, though the authorities are not stupid!

Pupils and parents: This is not an overwhelmingly grand school: more aspiration than pretension, reflected in the clientele. A number come from the Forces, others are from business, farming etc. Ten per cent come from abroad. The parents' association is active – indeed one of the things we noticed when talking to parents was their loyalty. OBs include Geoffrey Rippon, cricketer Roger Twose, rugby internationals Tom Voyce and Matthew Robinson, historian John Keegan, singer and broadcaster Alexandra Edenborough and children's broadcaster Dominic Wood.

Entrance: Via common entrance or VRQ at 13. Fifty per cent or so come from King's Hall, the excellent partner prep school just out in the country; the rest from a wide geographical area: Exeter and Salisbury Cathedral schools, Jersey, Port Regis and around. A number enter at sixth form.

Exit: Most to university – science, engineering and medical degrees all popular. 2013 destinations included Oxford (law), LSE (actuarial science) and Southampton (aeronautics and astronautics).

Money matters: Academic and sports awards of a third fees at 13. Several music scholarships, plus art, drama, DT awards. At sixth form: sports, music and academic scholarships held in November each year. Special scholarships for those from state schools.

Remarks: A sound, well-balanced school, sailing exciting waters with a very able skipper at the helm.

King's College School (Wimbledon)

Linked school: King's College Junior School (Wimbledon)

Southside, London, SW19 4TT

• Pupils: 840 pupils (including 75 girls in the sixth form); all day • Ages: 13–18 • Anglican foundation with own chaplain • Fees: £18,900 pa • Independent

Tel: 020 8255 5300
Email: admissions@kcs.org.uk
Website: www.kcs.org.uk

Head Master: Since 2008, Mr Andrew Halls MA (early fifties), previously head of Magdalen College School, Oxford, prior to which he was deputy at Trinity in Croydon and head of English at Bristol Grammar School. An impeccable trajectory. All preceded by a Cambridge double first in English, which is always encouraging. When you meet him you can see how well it fits him. Spare and fine-featured, quietly-spoken, assiduous and gently donnish without any of the waspishness that can accompany the brilliance – he is 'the compleat headmaster'. He is driven by the soundest of educational values. Hence his preparedness to modernise and innovate, even if the owners of tender toes squeal a bit, and hence his willingness to fight on behalf of pupils if he thinks any injustice has been done to them in public exams – as happened with an IB subject in 2011. A man of high principle and warm enthusiasms – especially for the partnership programmes undertaken by his school, real partnerships with local, national and international communities. You sense that the initiatives all schools need to take to maintain their charitable status are undertaken here from genuine conviction and principle, not just expediency.

Married to a fellow teacher, Mr Halls has two daughters. He is deeply proud of the school he inherited and to which he is devoted, and he pays tribute especially to his 'generous' staff and the generosity of spirit he finds in the school as a whole. He was a precociously young head when appointed to his first headship, to which he brought energy, vision and courage. Now, he is a wise and experienced leader – one who, seemingly, leads discreetly rather than with PR as his priority. The only parental criticism we heard of him was that they didn't know him or see him much. But one suspects he is discreetly everywhere. No questioning his quiet, dedicated authority and the clear assuredness of his vision. An exemplary head.

Academic matters: King's – or KCS as it is as often known – used to offer only the International Baccalaureate, but reintroduced A levels in September 2013, citing the A* grade as a way of recognising exceptional performance. Mr Halls takes a balanced view and, though convinced of the IB's worth and breadth, is no blinkered zealot. Consistently excellent IB results. In 2013, the co-ed sixth form pupils averaged 40 points out of 45, and nearly 86 per cent of higher level grades were 6 or 7.

League tables of results can be read any number of ways, but at least two – the Daily Telegraph and the Times – when gauging success in A level, IB and pre-U results all together placed King's as the fourth highest ranking sixth form in the UK in 2013. The IB has been seen as a great draw for those who enter at 16 but as a mixed blessing by others. One long-serving parent – who was full of praise for the school – said, 'I sent my boys there despite the IB rather than because of it,' and another told us, 'We think it's fantastic and most can manage it, but it isn't for everyone'. However if you take it on, you can be assured that you will be taught it here as well as it can be taught, it will flex to support your weaker areas and challenge your strengths as they should be challenged. 'The IB is so much work – I don't dare tell my friends at my old school – but I do even more extra-curricular stuff because we are all so busy all the time. I didn't know I could do so much,' enthused one girl.

At GCSE – most now take IGCSEs – 96 per cent of grades were A*/A in 2013 and 75 per cent of boys got 10 or more A*/A grades. A number take many more, often adding a new language in year 11 – Russian or Italian. Most also take additional maths GCSE – in 2013, 91 per cent of takers gained the top grade. No weak areas. Maths pretty amazing – A* for 143 of the 161 candidates. Penny numbers of B grades in most subjects and virtually no Cs in anything. At all levels, the range of options is impressive. At IGCSE, pupils have choice of six mainstream languages; individuals also catered for – around 80 have English as an EAL. We enjoyed the notices on language room doors – eg 'Chiudere la porta!' Parents and pupils full of praise – 'The teaching is fantastic and the classes are very small... My sons have an excellent bantering, relationship with their teachers – it gets even better as they go up the school'. Excellent academic library with displays changed weekly plus private study reading room.

Around 10 per cent have some kind of SEN, though none with statements – mild dyslexics/dyspraxics by no means in the majority in this cohort: motor skills difficulties, emotional and communication problems and the more severe dyses all taken on and supported individually in class or via withdrawal, as needed.

Games, options, the arts: Powerful and impressive on all fronts and the advent of sixth form girls has given them an extra edge. A bit of a sporting breeding ground – in team and individual achievement they figure prominently in many activities, most notably perhaps in tennis, rowing, rugby, athletics and football. New sports pavilion; on-site sports hall, pool, courts (recently refurbished) and pitches – and additional 'fantastic' facilities in West Barnes Lane. Opportunities for travel include D of E, endless sports camps, languages trips and exchanges, history, geography and classics visits – nothing obviously OTT and unnecessarily spoiling for the over-privileged. Excellent list of outside speakers/visitors brings the great outside and its challenges into school, eg Prof Sir Lawrence Freedman (think war studies and the Chilcot Commission), Mike Atherton, Simon Russell Beale, Carol Ann Duffy and Andrew (Churchill) Roberts all popping in.

Music, art and drama really exceptional. We found the art unusually expressive and free – especially rare in what is predominantly a boys' school – and felt quite exhilarated by the wit and life in what we saw in many media. We quite liked the fact that it was a bit messy too. Drama is legendary – the school takes shows to Edinburgh and sells out. Beautifully staged shows in the main theatre and little ones in the drama studio. Music likewise – housed, as so often, in less than shiny accommodation, but producing outstanding performances and performers in many genres. Chamber orchestra tour to Spain, concerts in St John's Smith Square and St James Piccadilly, The Cadogan Hall and St Paul's Cathedral. Debating and many other activities offer far more than your average teenager could do in twice the number of school years he has.

Much made of the school's partnerships with local state primaries and seniors. Sixth formers teach Latin at one and football at another; lively participation in the 'aspirations' programme, designed to help less privileged children raise their sights.

Background and atmosphere: Founded in 1829 as a junior branch of King's College, London – hence various ties still extant, eg the shared school and College colours. The move to Wimbledon was made to accommodate more boys – just over 200 – and 1911 saw the school being granted its independence. Junior school opened in 1912 and, since then, the school has grown and flourished abundantly. Its history – we visited in its anniversary year – is proudly, though not in-yer-facedly, celebrated in displays around the school, and most interesting it is too. Controversially, the sixth form has admitted girls since 2010 – not controversially inside the school (it seems an unqualified good thing) but clearly, the hard-working local and less local girls' schools are less than thrilled. The boys are converts, 'We were very excited at the idea of the girls coming – it was a bit awkward at first but everyone has come together now'.

The school faces a quiet corner of Wimbledon Common; the main building is solid, Victorian red brick. We often describe a school's setting as 'leafy' – this is about as leafy as a top London senior school can get. Its neighbours are the imposing detached houses of the very prosperous and the more modest 18th century terraces and pub which still evoke a villagey feel. Behind the main building, the extent of the school surprises. Many later buildings – mostly functional rather than architecturally glorious, but the site overall is a pleasure to encounter. Vast, classic Great Hall with organ, WWII commemorative tablet, Gothic window and splendid beamed ceiling – all as Hogwarts as you could wish. One-storey wooden music practice block – 'It arrived on a lorry and they just planted it there – quite surprising!' Most subjects in their own blocks or corridors. Good displays in most areas – we liked the maxims, eg 'Forgetfulness is the parent of poverty', which stimulate thinking, though we were told that some displays hang about rather too long. Wind turbine and solar panels contribute some power. Courtyards, much attractive brick paving, sculpture – notably that which marks the school's adoption of the IB with all its internationalism (Japanese stone lantern, African stone and wood pieces, Chinese lions etc) – and clever and well-tended planting make for a relaxed and pleasant place.

First stage of a major development and refurbishment programme has just been completed with the renovation of the Great Hall entrance. Further plans include a new classroom block, new music school and additional sporting provision.

Pastoral care and discipline: House system valued and relished by most. Also tutor groups, in which a pupil remains for his entire school life. System makes for a sense of security and consistency and ensures that you are known – valuable when it comes to UCAS forms. Parents praise the supportive atmosphere – 'It's been very good for my boys, who are all very different,' we were told. Although, 'The success of the system depends entirely on the tutor – we've been very lucky, but it's not been so for everyone'. Some parents of boys who enter at 13 feel more could have been done to integrate their sons and help them make friends, but this has now been addressed by the appointment of a 'brilliant' head of middle school – a long-serving head of house, who has 'transformed' their integration. Much parental praise for general school organisation, home-school communications and school's skill in picking up problems - 'They're usually onto it before you are,' we were told. 'If you get there early – at 7.00am – the car park is full of staff cars – they put in a huge amount of extra effort.'

K

School officers chosen via application, election and interview – the positions are coveted and hugely prized. Counselling service and chaplain to pick up birds with broken wings, but it seldom gets that far. Separate faith assemblies once a week. Smart plain suits and shirts for the sixth allow for some individual expression and no-one looks like a clone. Vast sixth form common-room with TV, all-day coffee bar and a range of seating from the upright, austere I'm-here-to-work kind to the flop-on-a-sofa-just-leave-me-for-a-bit kind. Large dining room serves wide choice highly appetising food which almost all eat – staff and pupils ensemble.

The girls we spoke to were incredibly happy and none seemed to regret their move. 'We're much more modern – we feel more grown-up here,' was the consensus – but then of course, they didn't stay at their previous schools to experience the sixth form there, did they? They positively relish the house system – 'It was a joke in my old school' – and are wowed by the 'team spirit'. Perhaps a lesson for the girls' schools here – many of which cling to the idea that houses and team spirit are somehow olde worlde and passé (as indeed, they once were).

Pupils and parents: A real mix – as you'd expect: academic and professional parents alongside first generation immigrants with bright offspring on bursaries. Common denominator is brains and enthusiasm and they come from a very wide area. Good range of bus services means you don't have to grind through the traffic. Impressively eclectic list of former pupils (OKs) includes Sabine Baring-Gould (wrote Onward Christian Soldiers), Dante Gabriel Rossetti, philologists Sweet and Skeat, Robert Graves, composer Robin Holloway, traitor William Joyce, the Beeb's Alvar Liddell, Roy Plomley and Mark Urban, actor Ben Barnes, musician Marcus Mumford and no fewer than five VCs.

Entrance: Most boys – around 90 – come up from the junior school. Everyone else needs to be registered by the end of September in year 6, and then sits a pre-test the following January. They come from everywhere – 300-odd lads take this for 60-odd eventual places. Pre-test in maths, English and reasoning. Around 150 of the best performers are interviewed. Interviews are a) general and English-related and b) science and maths focused. Around 100 are then offered places conditional on CE results or King's own scholarship exam.

At 16+ they admit girls – 'very, very clever girls,' an admiring mother of boys told us – from a range of girls' schools, though predominantly Putney and Wimbledon HSs, usually attracted by the IB, or from Godolphin and Latymer, which does the IB but for a far smaller cohort. All 16+ applicants take tests in English, maths and a general paper and then have four interviews. The vast majority taken at this stage are girls, reflecting the greater number of applicants as well as their performance in the assessments. Roughly four applicants per place.

Exit: A few leave post-GCSE, often in pursuit of A levels (likely to become even fewer in future). The rest stay on and leave for the top universities – 50 to Oxbridge in 2013, the rest to London University colleges or heavyweight provincials, eg Durham and Bristol, to do traditional subjects. Increasing numbers heading across the pond – eight to the USA and Canada in 2013.

Money matters: Good range of scholarships and bursaries considering that, unlike the ancient foundations not so far away, this is not an endowed school. Increasingly, here as elsewhere, money being diverted into means-tested bursaries to attract the bright but broke. Well worth enquiring – up to 100 per cent fee remission possible in certain cases.

Remarks: It makes every kind of sense to get in early – the competition for places at 13+ being so tight. By any standards a top school offering an exceptional education under a notable head.

King's Ely Senior

Linked school: King's Ely Junior

Barton Road, Ely, Cambridgeshire, CB7 4DB

• Pupils: 445 boys and girls, including 135 boarders • Ages: 13–18
• C of E • Fees: Day £18,009; Boarding £26,070 pa • Independent

Tel: 01353 660700
Email: enquiries@kingsely.org
Website: www.kingsely.org

Head: Since September 2013, Mr Alex McGrath BA PGCE. Educated at The Manchester Grammar School and Durham University, where he read history. Despite a vocational pull to teaching, he began his working life as a police officer before taking up a temporary post at St Bees School, Cumbria. Keen interest in writing, fly fishing, Russian history, rugby union, marathon running, drama and fine art. Married to an artist; they have three children. Tall, smart, unapologetic about his own 'free' education at one of the UK's premier schools (MGS was a direct grant school at the time), it's evident he wants youngsters to feel similarly passionate about their learning and wealth of opportunities. Keen they receive a real education not a spoon-fed, tick-box, experience.

Arrived at King's Ely following a shortish and somewhat difficult tenure at Leighton Park, first as head before being replaced by a colleague – we suspect wrong place, wrong time with some difficulties and issues outside of his control, rather than anything untoward, and are pleased to see him taking the helm once more. Prior to that he was deputy head at Trent College. At Leighton Park he was described as 'polite and thoughtful, measured and reserved'. Parents of miscreants were impressed with his 'firm but fair and thoughtful handling of their off-spring'. We liked him – said he was 'refreshingly honest and not into educational claptrap or spin' – and have high hopes that he will become a leading light at King's Ely.

Academic matters: Though increasingly selective at 11 and 13, the bar is not quite so high as for certain of the Cambridge schools close by. Considering the reasonably wide ability range, the school is achieving very respectable and frequently glowing results. Pupils are setted for most of the core subjects; close attention is paid to individual progress, and though not an overly pushy school, 'drifting along with little effort will be spotted', a mother remarked. Twenty-four subjects offered at GCSE (54 per cent A*/A in 2013) including single sciences, Latin and geographie (geography in French). Religious and moral philosophy is compulsory. Thirty-one subjects offered at A level with business studies, mathematics and psychology all popular, and 34 per cent A*/A grades overall in 2013. Those with specific educational needs, such as dyslexia, are well accommodated. There is individual support available, together with a drop-in clinic, and a close eye is kept on subjects chosen at GCSE, with a flexible approach to certain subject choices allowed.

King's Ely International prepares pupils with sufficiently good English to be able to enter UK independent schools, including this one. The classrooms and boarding accommodation are separate, but the head is encouraging greater fraternisation with the main school: 'It can only benefit all pupils'.

Games, options, the arts: A strength of the school is what happens outside the mainstream academic timetable. Tremendous range of opportunities, from rowing at 6:30am to singing in cathedral services. Music predominates, with more than 50 per cent learning an instrument, and ensembles, choirs and orchestras galore. The girls' cathedral choir recruits from the senior school, for which there is a 33 per cent reduction in the fees, with bursaries available if needed, as the girls all board. This is the first scheme of its kind in England. It will be interesting to see if the idea is taken up by other co-educational schools connected with cathedrals. The choir sings regular cathedral services, as well as touring and performing elsewhere. The musical training given to these girls will prepare them for advanced study and choral scholarships at university.

Sport remains central and important, though perhaps 'not the be all and end all as at some schools,' said a parent. Besides regular hockey, rugby and so forth, there is an emphasis on the more recondite sports, especially rowing, which is taken very seriously. The school has its own boathouse, pupils keen enough to be up with the lark and even some Olympic potential.

The Ely Scheme (Outdoor Pursuits Programme) runs compulsorily in year 9, optional from year 10, and many continue. Teaches self-reliance, responsibility and leadership skills. The teaching facilities for art and design are impressive – as is the teaching. Eye-catching displays of recent work are quite outstanding and several pupils, thus encouraged, go on to study at prestige institutions, notably in fashion and design.

Background and atmosphere: Occupies a sublime position adjacent to the cathedral, partly within the close itself, but largely in a sprawl of buildings (some medieval, others purpose-built) nearby. Glimpses of the cathedral, the Ship of the Fens, tantalise from many windows, notably from the head's office, in the Old Palace; hard for conversation to compete with the romanesque masterpiece behind. The cathedral's presence is both seen and felt, but the school also has a close relationship with the town through a variety of initiatives with other schools and local organisations. Frequent road-crossing is managed by pupils safely and with aplomb – it is just part of school life. Other buildings include The Monks' Barn, which houses the dining room (think National Trust restaurant – food, if anything, even better) jolly atmosphere, staff eating with pupils. The library has been re-ordered, also within the ancient fabric, but retains a monastic feel. Boarding houses are clean and comfortable, rather than deluxe. Girl choristers have their own boarding house, complete with grand piano in the common room. The Old Palace (former residence of the Bishops of Ely) is now a sixth form centre, with boarding space for 26 girls.

Pupils and parents feel they are listened to, and heard. The school council, a forum to discuss new ideas, is taken notice of by the powers-that-be.

Pastoral care and discipline: The Christian foundation of the school has a strong influence on the community. Rules are few, though strictly enforced particularly for those boarding, but there is an atmosphere of trust. The head is very aware of the pressures on pupils and feels 'peer perception' can be 'the hardest nut to crack'. Emphasis on enjoyment as well as achieving.

Pupils and parents: Largely professional, business and farming families, drawn from surrounding Eastern counties; Kings Lynn and Cambridge both send cohorts (quick, easy train services). School believes 'it is in no-one's interest for pupils to travel more than half an hour each way'. Overseas contingent (about 12 per cent) including those in the King's International Study Centre. Past pupils include Alan Yentob, the tenor James Bowman and Olympian Goldie Sayers.

Entrance: Own exam at 11 (to prep school) and at 13+, through a common entrance style exam (or common entrance itself). About 75 per cent come up from the King's prep and the remainder from a mixture of local-ish schools, Barnardiston, South Lee and the Cambridge prep schools. Numbers well up and competition for places is increasing. Entry for the sixth form – minimum of six grade A*-C passes at GCSE with at least Bs in chosen A level subjects.

Exit: Clutches leave after GCSE – often to Hills Road in Cambridge or other sixth form colleges. Post A level, the majority leave for Russell Group universities (business studies and management are very popular), with a significant number going to colleges of art and design, such as St Martin's in London. Gap years on the increase.

Money matters: Variety of scholarships awarded at 11 and 13+. Choral scholarships of 33 per cent of fees for ex-boy choristers who remain in the school choir and senior girl choristers. Other reductions for clergy and Forces families and top-up bursaries for those in financial need.

Remarks: The school has an atmosphere of purposeful learning, and provides plenty of opportunities for all types to shine. A strong, happy school where the Christian ethos is taken seriously.

King's Rochester

Linked school: King's Preparatory, Pre-Preparatory and Nursery School

Satis House, Boley Hill, Rochester, Kent, ME1 1TE

• Pupils: 300 girls and boys; mostly day; 10 per cent board • Ages: 13–18 • C of E • Fees: Boarding £27,000; Day £8,835–£16,635 pa • Independent

Tel: 01634 888590
Email: admissions@kings-rochester.co.uk
Website: www.kings-rochester.co.uk

Principal of King's Rochester and head of the senior school: Since September 2012, Mr Jeremy Walker MA, previously head of sixth form and senior manager at Berkhamsted School in Hertfordshire. Educated at Sherborne School and read theology at Oxford. First teaching post at Bishop Stopford School in Northants, then a housemaster, head of religious studies and head of theory of knowledge at Ardingly College, West Sussex – like King's, Woodard schools.

He is married to Harriet and they have two young children children, who have joined King's prep and pre-prep. He is keen on running and golf; also loves music, art and drama. 'Thanks to my children, I like to think I am quite good at Mario Kart on the Wii.'

Academic matters: Good academic results in general, particularly value-added. In an area known for the quantity and quality of its grammar schools, does remarkably well by its academically broad mix of pupils. Unique feature is German – taught to everyone from reception upwards and taken at GCSE at 13 and at A level, by those who choose to, at 16. Other languages include French, Russian, Latin and classical Greek. These are well supported by lots of trips and exchanges, including the D of E gold award. Results correspondingly impressive. 2013 GCSEs: 43 per cent A*/A. Refreshing to see no mandatory three sciences here, though one is compulsory and many take more. IGCSE sciences, maths, music and German – seen as a return to the rigour lost in the persistent dilution of the current curriculum. Everyone takes RS. The Diploma in Digital Applications at GCSE level in preference to standard ICT courses, as it allows pupils to develop projects actually using their IT skills – eg designing websites etc

At A level, 24 subjects including geology, Latin, classical Greek, economics and PE. In 2013, nearly 90 per cent A*/C and about a third A*/A. English, maths, economics, biology, chemistry, geography, DT and RS the most popular, with a spread of results. General studies for all. Small classes at this level and a collegiate feel mean that most pupils perform beyond expectation.

Team of qualified educational support teachers supports the pupils who have some kind of special educational need – mostly mild dyslexia, though school happily accommodates and makes provision for those with educational needs and physical disabilities where possible. Good sprinkling of gifted and talented too. An attitude of inclusiveness, can-do and helpfulness – pupils are assisted in class, through withdrawals and with IEPs.

Games, options, the arts: Main sports are rugby, hockey, netball, rowing, cross-country, fencing, swimming (in school's super pool) badminton and cricket. Netball shines in the honours lists and individuals achieve highly in rugby, otherwise a mix of results, but all played with huge enthusiasm on the school's beautiful, centrally sited pitches. Skiing is excellent – two nationally placed teams; shooting also on offer, with D of E and CCF. School has own sports centre five minutes from main site and principal recently introduced raft of sports scholarships.

Music is exceptional – this is a cathedral school and the chapel is the Rochester Cathedral, which dominates the site. Every morning begins there and glorious music is a given for the lucky congregants. Lots of ensembles, concerts and musical occasions of all kinds. Art is good and DT inspired – both achieve highly, though a smaller range of applied arts available here than elsewhere, perhaps. Performing arts very strong – lots of high quality productions despite lack of actual designated studio/theatre. Loads of clubs – around five choices each evening.

Background and atmosphere: Remarkable, and something of a surprise even to Kent locals who never penetrate the venerable and picture-book centre of Rochester. King's is the second oldest school in the country, founded in 604. It is at the heart of ancient Rochester; the cathedral and the castle all part of the mix of buildings – Norman, Tudor, Georgian, Victorian, 20th century and very recent indeed – which make up the school and its environs. Sixth formers housed in The College, a 17th century gem/Victorian gents' club – panelled and painted rooms, beautifully furnished, immaculately kept and self-policed, an education in civilised behaviour in itself. Pop into the cathedral while you visit and find the mural painted in honour of the school's 1,400th birthday – see if you can spot previous head peeping out of a window.

Round about is the less glamorous, also less recognised Medway region, which includes both deprived and highly privileged areas – this breadth and diversity appropriately reflected in the school community. Venerable buildings, now equipped and furnished to highest level, and several new ones which set standards for elsewhere. One of the most recent is the conference centre 2006 – elegant, with a super-dooper IT spec and imaginative decorative features, providing a versatile space for gatherings big, small, formal or relaxed. Purpose-built pre-prep 2000 is a model of what a pre-prep should be. New girls' boarding house (see below) similarly classy.

The whole place is beautifully maintained. It looked its best on the day we visited – all gorgeous colourful borders against old brick walls on a sunny July day – but it's immaculately kept and standards of appearance – for flower-beds and pupils alike – are high. Standards high altogether – behaviour, manners, respect, courtesy, consideration, order are the core values inculcated. A feeling of space, at odds with the reality in some respects, and no-one looks crowded here. Pupils value the school's history and tradition as well as its determination to make the 21st century

facilities second to none. 'The atmosphere's really friendly,' said one sixth former. 'You couldn't get better.'

Pastoral care and discipline: Unashamed Christian ethos and equally unashamed valuing of and respect for the faiths of others. Everyone takes RS to GCSE, but it is taught from an ecumenical point of view and Buddhists, atheists and everyone contribute to chapel services and the spiritual life of the school. Each day begins in the cathedral, where the service is 'always challenging and provocative, as it's crucial to understand religion and its impact on society'. Three chaplains available and the prospectus says, 'The pastoral, sympathetic care of each child is the responsibility of every member of the school staff'. House system and everyone has a house tutor who monitors all aspects of tutees' life.

Boarding is small but offers as much as many full boarding schools, along with a close family feel. The boarding houses – central on the site and surrounded by gardens and nice touches like a barbecue and picnic tables – are exceptionally well-furnished – all carpets and fresh paint, and the rooms, especially the new ones, are large, have four data points each and excellent en suite bathrooms. Nicer than average common-rooms with vast plasma TVs, games etc. PC suite. We met several happy boarders. Half remain in school at weekends and exeats are allowed every weekend. Lots of activities and trips. Good food all freshly prepared and a very varied menu. We were especially impressed with the boarders' supper menu – not just soup and a roll, as so often elsewhere, but the works in three courses and very munchable.

Discipline is tight but the manner is relaxed, and pupils and parents pay tribute to a rare degree of tolerance and community spirit in which oddballs flourish alongside the sports captains and Oxbridge hopefuls. A parent volunteered, 'I like the healthy eccentricity which is also one of the most important aspects of any education.'

Pupils and parents: From up to 30 miles away and increasingly from the smarter Kent towns, eg Tonbridge and Sevenoaks. Also from the less manicured Chatham and Maidstone and towards east London. Everyone from old Kent families with centuries-old school connections to first-time buyers of private schooling, often second generation immigrant families who value the all-round start in life the school offers. Boys no longer outnumber girls in most years and a better balance is being achieved. Parents deeply involved and organise events with passion and fervour. Pupils a mix of the very bright for whom public school was always the only option to numbers of 11plus near-misses whose families scrape up the necessary and, seemingly, never look back.

School publishes Eminent Roffensians – a fascinating social history – said ORs are a stirling mix of the military, the divine, the artistic, the athletic and the bizarre. Among them are Richard Dadd, artist and parricide, composer Percy Whitlock, actor David King, Rt Hon John Selwyn Gummer MP and his brother, Peter, now Lord Chadlington, and lots of brigadiers.

Entrance: Via interview and test, though school sees itself as broad ability academically. Many come from the prep school on site but increasing numbers join at 11 from feeder schools. We met happy 18-year-olds who'd been there since they were four – the sense of cohesiveness derived from a shared childhood was palpable. Intake at all ages, although mostly at 11 and 13, though no rigid pass mark at CE. Some arrive for the sixth form – often refugees from the grammars. School takes great care to look at the individual child and his/her circumstances and every candidate is seen by one of the school heads.

Exit: Virtually all to university to study the full range of academic and vocational subjects. A handful to Oxbridge most years; rest to a range of Russell group and other universities.

Money matters: Good range of valuable scholarships – up to 30 per cent minimum remission, means-tested up to 75 per cent, for King's Scholars. New sports scholarships and all-rounder award aimed at good academic performers with extra strengths in art, drama, sport or music. Also means-tested awards and awards specifically for those from the state sector. Scholarships for specific aptitudes, eg music and organ playing. Remission also for clergy, Forces families and siblings.

Remarks: Rigour and compassion blend in a classy school which, were it in Wiltshire or Berkshire, would be turning them away in coachloads. This is a gem of a school.

The King's School (Chester)

Linked school: King's Junior School (Chester)

Wrexham Road, Chester, CH4 7QL

• Pupils: 980 girls and boys • Ages: 7–18 • C of E, cathedral foundation • Fees: Juniors £8,814; Seniors £11,499 pa
• Independent

Tel: 01244 689500
Email: admissions@kingschester.co.uk
Website: www.kingschester.co.uk

Headmaster: Since 2007, Mr Chris Ramsey MA (late forties). Previously head of King's College, Taunton, deputy head at Cranleigh, head of languages at Wellington College. Educated Brighton College and Corpus Christi, Cambridge. Quick thinking, fast talking, intensely communicative in person and via his weekly blog. Rocked the boat initially with his energetic challenge to the status quo, but all seems plain sailing now. Not expecting further squalls from big changes to curriculum in 2011, 'we've been two and a half years planning for them and by and large the whole community's on side'. Three children in school from the juniors to the sixth form. He's 'thought provoking, very interesting, a very good teacher,' pupils say 'and he's at every performance, engaged with everything'. Pastoral and academic deputies also very much involved in senior team leadership of this big school.

Academic matters: Extremely ambitious, no complacency here with big changes to stay ahead of the game. Strong at GCSE with 73 per cent A*/A. Since 2011, IGCSEs in languages, sciences, maths and music. Pupils also sit just nine instead of ten subjects, from a choice of 21, 'aiming for quality not quantity', with a stronger 'enrichment programme' from Mandarin or astronomy to community service. In sixth form no more distracting January resits (just the summer) and a big emphasis on LVI extended projects. The whole school has moved to a two week, five daily period timetable. A levels in 2013 achieved 89 per cent A*/B grades, 64 per cent A*/A.

Pupils are quick to give 'fulfilling my potential' as a top reason for coming here and praise the teachers for being 'interested in what benefits us as a person across the board, especially the heads of department; being passionate about their subject is instilled in the life of King's'. Teachers must expect head to pop in to lessons, 'to take an interest, be visible, be encouraging', in a spirit of respectful, constructive criticism. Aside from traditional academic prowess, provision for music, art, DT, ICT etc is temptingly good including a state-of-the-art 3D photocopier for realising CAD (computer aided designs). Yearly Arkwright scholars reflecting splendid DT; plenty of prizes in other national Olympiad challenges.

The bright modern library, open from 8-5.30, attracts 800 visits a day to its 16,000 resources, which include 85 journal subscriptions. During our visit in exam season there's a convivial but studious burble of joint revising here, and in fact elsewhere, too, in corridors and round the entrance foyer art exhibition. Plenty of computers everywhere, whiteboards and netbooks in some classes.

Games, options, the arts: 'What I love about King's, a senior pupil told us, 'is the plethora of opportunities here'. He's directing his own production of Waiting for Godot in the new theatre, using two weeks of the summer holidays to rehearse his cast. Will this be his extended project? 'Well it could be, but I also want to look into whether Dostoevsky deserves his reputation as a dark author; personally I don't think he does so I want to argue his case'. Yes, he hopes to read English at Oxford but, outwardly at least, he's modestly not expecting an offer. The whole school is buzzing about the new (2011) Vanbrugh Theatre which has 250 foldaway raked seats, 200 seats in the stalls and a gallery, plus, up a spiral staircase, thespian dressing rooms complete with light-flanked mirrors.

Every weekend some 140 pupils make the most of the boathouse and coaching on the Dee, continuing a 134 year old rowing tradition. King's grows a steady supply of national rowers, most recently Tom James, 2008 Olympic medallist and Olivia Whitlam, world U23 champion 2007 and 2008 Olympic finalist, and makes its mark at the National Schools' Regatta. Fiercely competitive in all sport from excellent facilities, 'the only thing missing is lacrosse' say pupils. Acres of pitches, courts, floodlit Astro and tradition of inter-house sport so all can take part. The 18m pool is the only facility seniors seem luke-warm about, 'it's a bit jaded, only big enough for the juniors really'.

Fabulous music school boasts bright recital hall with floor to ceiling apex windows, recording studio, classroom full of computers and six individual practice rooms. About half take individual instrument lessons in school and pupils enthuse 'if there's an instrument you want to play they'll find a teacher for it'. Twenty-five orchestras, ensembles and choirs, including Schola Cantorum, which leads services in the Cathedral. The music head, described as 'fantastic' by parents, has direct phone and email on school website. CCF here was 150 years old in 2010 and there's a minority but well-worn path into the armed forces from King's. Over 120 other activities from D of E (80 per cent take bronze, about half silver), Model United Nations, charities, and clubs from Scrabble to meteorology.

Background and atmosphere: Founded by King Henry VIII in 1541, the school left its city centre cathedral site in 1960, and in 2011 celebrated 50 years on the Wrexham Road site just inside the city's by-pass. Today school rents 32 verdant acres from the Duke of Westminster. A generous school flag flies from the copper-capped tower, fluttering over rangey modern buildings in spic and span grounds. Beyond the secure reception area that's open all year the atmosphere is purposeful and businesslike, and the classrooms spacious. The dining room and one or two corridors form bottlenecks at busy times but polite pupils naturally wait their turn, holding doors open for adults. And despite the throng of life and busy corridors, in the middle of it all a happy duck and drake rear their annual brood in one of two attractive quads.

Pastoral care and discipline: Pupils describe this as 'a very friendly school' and parents praise the effort made to help children settle in here at all levels. Prefect and sixth form mentoring and form tutors form backbone of pastoral care. Last ISC inspection mentions 'the excellent relationships between pupils and staff...engendering an atmosphere of trust and security'. Emphasis on integrity and honesty so, for example, under 13s who give false dates of birth to start a Facebook page are asked by school 'what does that say about you as a human being and is that the sort of human being you want to be?

K

Their Facebook pages usually disappear after that'. Regarding network communication generally, head urges pupils to 'be kind, be kind, be kind'. Strong cathedral links endure, although the feel is of a Christian school with a small c. One of two weekly assemblies includes a two minute 'Quite Interesting' public speaking slot for pupils to share their interests, 'to develop a zest for learning'.

Achievement is recognised in many areas, 'not just for the goal scorers and A*s'. Choosing not to fulfil responsibilities, such as not storing bags correctly, brings the consequence of sanctions such as detentions, simple as that, but discipline doesn't seem to need to be heavy handed; it's a pretty civilised community. A full time nursing sister and assistant staff the sick bay.

Pupils and parents: Proportion of girls has grown to 35 per cent (40 in the 2011 11+ intake) since their arrival in 2003 and the school now feels properly co-ed with girls of all sorts, not just robust pioneers. Despite school becoming more image-conscious under Mr Ramsey, pupils remain disarmingly normal and charming, a very nice bunch. Head describes intake as 'very varied, we don't just have one type of boy or one type of girl' and says 'we don't have many girlfriend and boyfriend issues, the atmosphere is just cordial and friendly'.

Largely middle class and white, professional or farming backgrounds. From Chester and Cheshire, the Wirral and North Wales, in their distinctive navy, green and white striped blazers and ties. Sixth formers move on to crested navy blazers with ties denoting activities and status and senior prefects get to wear academic gowns for special occasions. Conveniently for parents there's a uniform shop on site. Less convenient they tell us (to a man) is the car park jam up at collection time; 'there are 1,000 pupils here, we try to keep it moving but it's a big school and parents just need to accept they have to be patient,' is head's response. Many use fleets of buses, some shared with Queen's. The glossy Herald news and annual King's Eye celebrate the many varied happenings here.

Entrance: From the juniors by continual internal assessment. From elsewhere by 11plus exam in January, with English, maths, verbal and non-verbal reasoning and an interview. Selecting from the top 25 per cent and looking for the brightest 100 regardless of gender. Sixth form requires A* or A in intended subjects and seven GCSE Bs or above. Assessments for the junior school at 7+.

Exit: The opening line on school website states, 'From your child's first day at The King's School at seven years of age, we are preparing them for graduation and beyond'. University is unapologetically assumed from the off and school prides itself that over half go on to a university from The Times Top 30 list. Annual handful to Oxbridge, four offers in 2013 and 11 to medicine and dentistry. Sixth form support for course and university choice very strong, with all UCAS applications submitted by end of October.

Notable old boys include TV's Martin Lewis, Ronald Pickup (actor), Nickolas Grace (actor), Sir John Vanbrugh (architect), Steve Leonard (TV vet), Freddie Owen (cricketer) and Admiral Sir Peter Dennis who, after leaving in 1730, reportedly invented mayonnaise, and eight Olympians – four in 2012 including gold medal rower Tom James MBE.

Money matters: About 80 senior pupils receive some kind of means-tested bursary; 10 have free places, with plans to increase bursary provision to help more pupils over next decade, returning somewhat towards school's founding principles of helping 'poor, friendless boys'. King's Scholarships awarded during first three years; others in sixth form. Lunches compulsory adding £660 a year.

Remarks: Purposeful, confident co-ed school with top-notch facilities and acres of space, producing uber-capable young adults who're nevertheless, friendly and unassuming.

Kings' School (Winchester)

Romsey Road, Winchester, SO22 5PN

• Pupils: 1,650 boys and girls, roughly 50:50. Boarding (boys only): 18 • Ages: 11–16 • Fees: £9,501 pa • State

Tel: 01962 861161
Email: kings.school@kings-winchester.hants.sch.uk
Website: www.kings-winchester.hants.sch.uk

Headteacher: Since 2013, Matthew Leeming. Educated at Westminster School and St John's College, Durham. Taught geography at schools in Liverpool, Lincolnshire and Peterborough before moving to Hampshire. Spent six years as deputy headteacher at Brookfield Community School, then appointed headteacher of Crofton School in Stubbington. Married, with two children.

Academic matters: Impressive results considering not an academically selected hothouse. In 2013, 83 per cent of pupils got 5+ A*-C at GCSE including maths and English and 39 per cent of grades were A*/A. Lessons bridge the academic with the practical; German, Italian and Latin all options, as are health and social care and photography. Good preparation for the outside world. Purposeful atmosphere.

Games, options, the arts: Excellent facilities for every sort of activity. Thanks to careful budgeting and a well-conceived application to the National Lottery, a fully flood-lit Astroturf pitch and large multi-surface flood-lit playing area with six tennis courts and space for basketball and netball. Recent large sports centre which links the new swimming pool and sports hall; beautiful cricket pitches.

Recently took over the management of the nearby Tower Arts Centre, a very attractive Victorian water tower, considerably refurbished with a new stage, up-to-date lighting and sound system, a printing press and art studios. We saw some extraordinarily beautiful creations in the art department, where pictures were being assembled for GCSE; impressive work in the excellently equipped science and technology department and a thoughtfully designed business centre for sustainable businesses – companies set up and run by the pupils with help and interaction from business partners. Everywhere you look the work of pupils is celebrated and held up for inspiration and admiration.

Background and atmosphere: An amalgamation of two under-performing single sex schools, linked into one 25 years ago, in a leafy and spacious area of suburban Winchester with views over the downs. The older parts – the original girls' school – have long, narrow corridors, once dark and forbidding, now enlivened and enlightened with pictures, posters, photographs, many reproduced and blown up to giant size, thanks to the school's printing press, one of its sustainable enterprises; also more modern buildings with wider corridors.

Pastoral care and discipline: 'About 97 per cent of the pupils want to be taught,' said one teacher. It shows, but without any dampening of youthful noise and energy. Moving about the school, the decibel count is healthy; once lessons begin it is appropriate.

A designated school for pupils with physical disabilities – to stand in the middle of the school when pupils are moving to

K

different classrooms between lessons is to witness very movingly how well this aspect of Kings' concern works: compassion and understanding are manifest in this intelligently run school.

Pupils and parents: Lots of grateful local families and mostly happy pupils – one 11 year old boy gasped out, 'I just love this school!' Another older boy announced he was 'pleased to be leaving,' but added with a grin, 'It's been quite good, though' – high praise from an adolescent. Pupils greet and smile and in conversation reveal themselves articulate and relaxed – it was difficult on occasions to remember we were talking to 16 year olds and not sixth formers. On the whole town and gown work well together – one local described the school to us as a 'lovely lot'.

Entrance: The prospectus gives information about entry, administered by the Hampshire County Council, so no control over who comes to them. Parents express preferences – consistently the most over-subscribed school in the area – but the council ultimately assigns pupils to one of the three secondary schools in the area. Thanks to shifts in local demographics, parents may now apply from outside the official catchment area. Always appeals and waiting lists. Children or families who have a serious medical, physical or psychological condition receive preferential treatment for admission. A boarding house for around 30 pupils, some of whom come from abroad.

Exit: Some 95 per cent go on to Peter Symonds Sixth Form College, a few to other sixth form colleges and the remainder to vocational courses. Interestingly, some stay on in the boarding house because they like it so much.

Remarks: By any standards an outstanding school – if all state schools were as good as this, the HMC would be a much slimmer body.

The King's School (Worcester)

Linked schools: King's Hawford School; King's St Alban's School

5 College Green, Worcester, WR1 2LL

- Pupils: 930; 505 boys 420 girls • Ages: 11–18 • C of E
- Fees: £11,682 pa • Independent

Tel: 01905 721700
Email: info@ksw.org.uk
Website: www.ksw.org.uk

Headmaster: Since 1998, Mr Timothy H Keyes MA (fiftyish). Educated at Christ's Hospital, read classics at Wadham College, Oxford, then PGCE at Exeter. First headship. Came from Royal Grammar School, Guildford, where he was second master, having previously held classical teaching posts at the Perse, Whitgift and Tiffin. A committed and active Christian. Says, 'I think that's important because the school is run on Christian principles.' But keen to stress all faiths 'welcomed and valued'. Sings with Worcester Festival Choral Society, also a keen campanologist. Sits on the board of UCAS so able to give solid advice on higher education. Outgoing, friendly and infectiously enthusiastic – he's a man on a mission. Knows all pupils by name and what's going on. 'I'm interested in every one of them,' he says. 'I hope they know that.' The friendly face of authority, but not a soft touch. Wife Mary Anne teaches maths and science to juniors (King's St Alban's) and takes Christian Union club. Two sons – both in higher education. Lurcher, Tess, rounds off family unit.

Retiring in July 2014. His successor will be Matthew Armstrong MA PGCE, currently an assistant head of Charterhouse. He studied modern and medieval languages at Oxford, and renaissance studies and English literature at Birkbeck College, London. He has previously taught at Winchester College and been a business analyst for McKinsey & Co. He is married to Kate, and loves running, skiing, mountaineering and chess.

Academic matters: Selective though flexible intake with generous approach to lower entry exam marks if child excels in other areas. Much emphasis placed on 'unlocking potential' and pupils 'doing the best they possibly can'. Class size maximum 24 with setting introduced pre-GCSE in maths and English. May be more setting in future but not much, as head believes it can be 'demoralising'. At GCSE 70 per cent of papers graded A*/A in 2013; 83 per cent A*-B grade at A level (54 per cent A*/A). Maths and sciences (separately or as dual award) consistently good at both GCSE and A levels. Modern languages, English, art and music similarly impressive. Interesting observation by head. 'GCSEs and A levels are very important but their shelf life is very short,' he says, their main use being to secure university places. 'It's our responsibility to produce people who can work in teams, manage themselves, take responsibility, who can lead and who are well-balanced.'

Options include drama, music, and theatre studies. Now offers A level politics and AS level critical thinking. Classrooms bright, freshly painted and well organised with mixture of eyes-front and huddle teaching according to year group. Changeover from boarding to day school freed up loads more rooms, giving lessons new lease of life and increasing year (but not class) sizes. Science labs in typical 1960s block but labs themselves have all been recently re-fitted with great effect. Recent award-winning £2m library – central to academic life and fully integrated with a very active careers department – it is well-stocked and e-friendly putting bytes on more equal footing with books. Elsewhere computers much in evidence. Dedicated IT rooms as well as classroom provision. Recent new art school, DT department and lecture theatre. Specialist help for mild learning difficulties only.

Games, options, the arts: Awarded Sportsmark Gold in new millennium. Sport an important part of school life – 'but not an obsession', says head – with fine facilities like sports hall, fitness suite and 25-metre pool, also used by outside bodies. Games played once a week (twice in the earlier years). Very competitive and successful – in particular the girls' rowing eights (recent national champions); new boathouse just completed and new sports and performing arts centre (the SPACE) will open in September 2014; an impressive rugby XV and sevens, strong cricket, hockey and netball. One recent leaver plays rugby for England and one won an Olympic gold and silver in rowing. Dance a popular activity among both boys and girls.

Outstanding art – and lots of it. Might have been the unsung hero a few years ago but deservedly celebrated from the rooftops now. In recent GCSE exams, 17 students from King's have been among the best in the country. Art school in separate building secreted behind red brick wall but visitors discover a paint-splattered Aladdin's cave inside. Extremely high-quality work. Work shown off well in dining hall, around school and in specially designed and lit gallery.

Much music, as you might expect at a choir school. Eighteen boy choristers boost ranks of cathedral choir (until voices break so most come from junior school). Over 100 musicians, three school orchestras (two pupils recently in National Youth Orchestra), two school choirs, a wind band and brass group. Two school organs for pupils' use. Oxbridge organ and choral scholarships not unheard of. Flourishing drama department. Newish 310-seater theatre in frequent use for plays, concerts and big screen presentations. A full-time theatre manager adds an extra dimension to the activity.

Plenty of opportunities for travel, home and abroad. King's accepted onto EU-funded Comenius Scheme, which involves joint projects with schools in France and Germany. School's own outdoor pursuits centre in the Black Mountains hugely popular; art and language students, historians and geographers also venture far and wide. National finalists in Young Enterprise Scheme and awarded the UK's first 'Centre of Excellence' in 2011. Very involved in local community (sixth formers help young readers at local primaries and host events for the elderly and for a local special school) and further afield (young Nepalese student sponsored through university). Extra-curricular can mean anything from chess club to climbing the Himalayas. Innovative relationship with a local comprehensive based on shared extra-curricular activity and common ethos. The school day might not be long (8.30am to 3.50pm) but it's certainly packed. School remains busy until 5.30pm each day.

Background and atmosphere: Superb green setting under the watchful gaze of Worcester Cathedral, founded in 1541 by Henry VIII after the suppression of the priory. Described by the head as 'an oasis of calm' at heart of busy modern city. Head sees this location as of great benefit to pupils, enabling them to build relationships with leading city institutions and businesses. Oldest part is 14th century former monks' refectory now serving as vast and imposing assembly hall. Despite school's great age, no school motto (dismissed as fatuous by head). Closest it comes to one is Greek inscription (translated for us by classicist) on heavy oak assembly table: 'I learn what may be taught; I seek what may be found, and I pray for what heaven may grant.' (Well, that just about covers all eventualities.)

Despite hundreds of years of history and tradition, it feels refreshingly unpretentious. School completely co-ed since 1998. From early age, pupils encouraged to look beyond school gates, to try new things and help those less fortunate. Keen communicators internally and externally. Slightly stodgy but worthy annual school mag The Vigornian, supplemented by a twice yearly 'K' Magazine, and more upbeat weekly bulletin newsletter via email. King's underpinned by two junior schools – one right next door (King's St Alban's) shares senior school facilities; the other (King's Hawford) lies to north of city in country setting. Have own individual heads but Mr Keyes is supreme head.

Pastoral care and discipline: Pastoral care still run, unusually but very successfully, along boarding school lines, based on old house system. Newcomers at 11 put into forms of 20-22 for first two years to make friendships and settling in easier. For remaining five years pupils assigned to one of eight houses (around 80 per house, 16/18 in each year group) with six tutors per house responsible for pastoral issues (staff paid extra to take on this role). Sixth formers act as mentors for younger pupils. Active school council and pupils also have voice through elected monitors and sitting on food and uniform committees. Imaginative team-building events early in the year for new pupils. Pretty hot on rules – suspension for smoking and drinking (even in Worcester city centre). Drugs more complicated: automatic expulsion for dealing, final warning for using. 'We are very tough when we have to be,' admits head. Best summed up as firm yet fair. Parents always contacted and consulted, particularly in rare cases of bullying. Daily matters of appearance, behaviour, punctuality and so on dealt with through system of coloured papers issued by staff which collectively give overview of pupils' activities.

Pupils and parents: A fairly mixed bag. Reputation for old money but far more professionals and new money these days plus a number of strugglers. Many give generously towards bursaries for current pupils and are supported by a professional and effective Foundation Office which coordinates alumni activity. Large numbers of former pupils return each year to share expertise and the benefit of experience, some as part of Barnabas Group (leaders in their fields who address full school assemblies). Annual fête or charity walk regularly raises tens of thousands. Parents prepared to travel some distance too since King's went day (Stratford, Birmingham and Evesham, to name but a few), with school coaches from Evesham and Malvern and a morning shuttle mini-bus from the north of the city junior school, King's Hawford. Many pupils use the train or local public bus services.

Pupils smart, interested but above all confident – from the youngest up. Well-mannered, not afraid to speak up, enthusiastic. 'We are not seen as having a mould,' says head. 'We turn out interestingly different characters. The example set by sixth formers to younger pupils is superb.' OVs (Old Vigornians – they take their title from the Roman name for Worcester) include TV presenter Chris Tarrant and comedian Rik Mayall.

Entrance: Entry exam at 11+, with papers in maths, English and verbal reasoning (qualifying for those coming up from the two junior schools, competitive for external candidates). Between 130 and 140 new places at 11. Own entry exam at 13+ – vacancies vary in number each year but usually between five and ten places. School looking for 40-50 per cent minimum pass but considers all-round performance and potential. About 25 places fall free each year in sixth form – at least five Bs and two Cs needed at GCSE. Entry to junior schools also selective. Chorister voice trials held throughout the year. A good voice is not enough in itself to win school place.

Exit: At least 95 per cent to higher education with a few heading for Oxford and Cambridge (six in 2013). Medical studies perennially popular, as are languages, art, drama and mechanical engineering. Few losses post-GCSEs. No weeding-out policy to improve overall A level results.

Money matters: Good crop of academic and music scholarships (worth up to a third tuition fees) up for grabs in the junior schools and at 11, 13 and 16. Boy choristers awarded 50 per cent scholarships by cathedral to cover their time in the choir. Head says, 'the school will do its very best to make sure no chorister has to leave after that scholarship ends.' Growing number of bursaries available, with assitance of up to 100 per cent of fees. Big appeal under way to make more funds available (growing at 15 per cent per year), recently boosted by single gift of £1 million. Small discount for third and fourth siblings.

Remarks: Big enough to offer much, small enough to keep it personal. Individual choice and achievement count for a lot here, with boys and girls given the right mix of guidance and freedom to discover their own strengths. A real feeling of relaxed respect among students and staff with co-operation seen as the key to reaching goals. 'It's quite simply a lovely school,' says one parent. Very well thought of locally (even by those who haven't got children here) and much sought after. Book early.

The King's School Canterbury

25 The Precincts, Canterbury, CT1 2ES

- Pupils: 821; 453 boys, 368 girls (626 board, 195 day). • Ages: 13-18 • C of E • Fees: Day £24,270; Boarding £32,235 pa
- Independent

Tel: 01227 595579
Email: admissions@kings-school.co.uk
Website: www.kings-school.co.uk

Headmaster: Since 2011, Mr Peter Roberts MA PGCE (early fifties), previously head of Bradfield College for eight years. He was educated at Tiffin Boys and read history at Merton College, Oxford where he got a first, followed by a PGCE at London Institute of Education. Started teaching career at Winchester as head of history, then also as master in college. Always immaculately dressed – 'sometimes a 'vision in tweed and sometimes besuited'. He is super brainy and regarded as 'quirky and eccentric but with a good sense of humour and perfect for the job – we would not want anyone who was run of the mill' says a happy parent. A thoughtful academic 'who works unbelievably hard and is always out and about with his dog.' He attends every play, recital and concert and even attends the matrons' meeting; describing his job as 'vastly enjoyable.' Teaches the Shells (year 9), 'when he can'. Says he was struck by everyone's enthusiasm about the school when he first arrived and 'listened to the constituent parts'; he has now set out his vision for the future and what he considers to be the 'essence' of King's. Major projects include the acquisition of the Malthouse which will be converted into a performing and visual arts centre, and a Victorian primary school which will house the new science centre.

The headmaster describes the ethos of the school as 'interactive osmosis' 'it is the richness, the diversity and range of our lives here that makes it distinct and special.' He feels the school 'gives a strong sense of belonging, a realisation that King's helped to make them (the pupils) what they are' and 'this creates the wish to give something back in return' and sees the atmosphere of the school as 'like a massive confidence-building machine'. Expects very high standards from the children at every level and has tightened up on discipline, manners and presentation. Each week the Roberts invite 15 different pupils, one from each house, to lunch in their private dining room. Much expected too from staff and light being shed on the few pockets of less than good teaching.

Married to Marie, an elegant and accomplished Frenchwoman who was head of department at two large state schools and, in addition to teaching French and German, is also a harpist. They have three daughters. Enjoys spending time in France where he sails, practises calligraphy and paints watercolours

Academic matters: The pursuit of academic excellence is at the heart of everything the school does but co-curricular activities given equal weight and pupils have a 'rich' day. The brightest take some GCSEs early, allowing a head start on AS subjects; the less academic may drop a subject at GCSE. Pupils encouraged to take a creative subject like art, drama IT or music alongside academic subjects. In 2013, 86 per cent A*/B at A level with 15 pupils getting 3+A*. Over 90 per cent A*/B at GCSE (IGCSEs for most subjects). Strong across the board and languages particularly good – mainly taught by native speakers and housed in the Old Palace. Sciences popular – female head of science and five out of the seven physics teachers are women. Most subject combinations can be accommodated even if some have to be taught outside the timetable. School always looking at ways to stretch the most able and curriculum constantly adapted. Currently 27 subjects to choose from at A level (including geology) and advanced extension awards in most. Astronomy offered as a GCSE along with Italian, Russian and Mandarin GCSE ab initio in sixth form. Strong work ethic and 'Children do not seem to realise how much they cram into the day, it is just normal for them,' says one mother.

Pupils encouraged to think about their broader academic profile and alongside AS levels there are enrichment subjects such as critical thinking; perspectives on aesthetics; globalisation and science and the extended project. Careers advice starts in the first year on a drop-in basis and fifth form have timetabled careers periods to help with A level choices and beyond.

Stunning William Butterfield designed library (1848) is centre of academic life with a hushed and studious atmosphere and combining the best of the old and new with 30,000 books and a range of periodicals and European newspapers as well as DVDs and online reference sources. It is a great source of pride and always staffed and open every day until 10pm and at weekends. Somerset Maugham and Sir Hugh Walpole both left their personal libraries to King's.

About six per cent need extra help, mainly for mild dyslexia, and any pupil can ask for help with study skills. Probably would not suit anyone with bigger difficulties and some parental concerns that children do not get as much support as they need. EAL for a handful of pupils but all must be fluent on arrival. No plans to introduce the IB.

Games, options, the arts: Acres of playing fields about 15 minutes' walk away as well as a modern sports centre incorporating pool, indoor courts, climbing wall, café and gym – more akin to the smartest private leisure centre than the school sports department. Huge choice of sports – girls' hockey thriving with 15 girls in the English hockey training system. Cricket and rugby going from strength to strength and several boys have been selected to play for Kent U18s; school has also produced several international fencers. Rowing on the up for boys and girls after a period in the doldrums and old boy Tom Ransley won bronze at London 2012. Sports coaches include England cricketer Mark Ealham and Olympic hockey player Jennifer Wilson. Not everyone represents the school in matches but still play sport for 'fitness, health and fun' and most people find something they enjoy. Everyone is expected to get involved and participation is everything – 'you don't have to be brilliant but just give it a go and have fun.' Sporting trips all over the world – rugby in Argentina, cricket in Grenada and netball in South Africa.

Long tradition of excellent drama and music and anyone involved is definitely awarded 'cool status.' Fab new music school – over half the pupils learn at least one instrument. Symphony orchestra plus numerous bands and ensembles, the pupil run jazz club is particularly popular. Plenty of choral groups, from the Crypt Choir which tours annually, most recently to China, to the choral society which is open to anyone who enjoys singing including parents and staff. 'Wherever you go around the school there is always music coming from somewhere'. Masses of drama both on and off the curriculum – house plays, GCSE and A level productions, drama competitions, fashion shows, full school plays – 'Wherever there is a quiet corner, you will find a rehearsal going on,' as well as regular theatre trips to London. Busy art department housed in twelfth-century priory has a different artist in residence each year. New photographic studio and pottery centre opened by old boy Edmund de Waal.

Huge range of activities continues into sixth form – anything from academic societies with visiting speakers to mountain biking, cryptic crosswords, debating and the Model United Nations. CCF once again a popular option. Community work and volunteering are central to school life and are often part of Duke of Edinburgh Award and include teaching science in local primary schools, riding for the disabled and help with swimming for disabled children.

The famous King's week at the end of the summer term is the highlight of the year for pupils and parents alike and is a festival of music, drama and dance with events being staged in all corners of the school every day for a week – parents and friends come bearing picnics and it is a major social event culminating in Commem Day and the leavers' ball. 'The quality and variety are phenomenal' and there is everything from Shakespeare, classical concerts and jazz as well as a lighter touch provided by the house harmonies. Those not involved do not feel excluded and have as much fun as those taking part.

Background and atmosphere: Set in the shadow of Canterbury Cathedral and part of a world Heritage Site, this has to be one of the most inspiring settings for a school. Founded in 597 when St Augustine arrived in Canterbury and then re-founded as The King's School during the reign of Henry VIII after the dissolution of the monasteries – not many schools can produce a list of headmasters going back to 1259. Beautiful ancient buildings and cloisters and immaculate gardens with the busy city life going on just beyond the gates. Pupils enjoy the contrast and the fact that the city with its shops and cafes is on the doorstep and say, 'it makes us feel part of the real world'. The headmaster says the combination of the cathedral and a vibrant student city 'grounds the children in a wider reality'. The school sponsors the Folkestone Academy and lends its facilities to the wider community.

Took girls into sixth form in 1970s and went fully co-ed in 1990. Six boys' and five girls' boarding houses plus three day houses and a smaller sixth form girls' house in a variety of architectural styles from the thirteenth century Meister Omers to 21st century Grange. Half the houses clustered round the cathedral and the other half across the road on the St Augustine site where they have their own dining hall. Pupils equally happy to be in houses in either location, most popular houses booked up years in advance. A close knit community, 'it's got everything, the spiritual dimension from the cathedral and a sense of beauty and history'. Former pupil Michael Morpurgo said, 'King's is like a university designed for younger people.'

Pastoral care and discipline: Smart uniform worn throughout the school, pinstripes, wing collars and a jacket – and a brooch for the girls. All look very professional and businesslike; monitors wear purple gowns and are, unsurprisingly, known as 'Purples'. Astonishingly busy day, one of the first lessons the children learn is how to plan their time, but there is still room for lots of fun. Strict rules and punishments regarding drugs, alcohol and parties and children know where they stand. Strong Christian tradition and moral values. The main school services held in the Cathedral but different religious and cultural backgrounds recognised and valued.

'Children have a healthy respect for each other and are generally self-regulating regarding bullying and other misdemeanours' and honesty and integrity are highly valued. Pastoral care comes in for particular praise from the Independent Inspectors. Big effort to address everyone's happiness with several staff/pupil committees to ensure all have their say. Boarding houses friendly and welcoming with areas where pupils can make their own snacks and relax. Small dormitories for younger children and individual study bedrooms for sixth form. Large and popular social centre open to the whole school during the day and to sixth formers in the evening. Food consistently praised by all. Three flexible exeats per term means there is always plenty going on at weekends. Sixth form given more freedom and are allowed to book supper leave in Canterbury.

Regular communication with parents especially through housemasters and house mistresses. Good interaction between year groups facilitated by mixed age tutor groups and mentoring from older pupils. New 'Shells' have a top year mentor. Day children and boarders mix well and 'you can't tell the difference' according to one pupil.

Pupils and parents: A good mix socially and culturally with a wide catchment area – popular with locals, London and county sets and Foreign Office families and increasing numbers from abroad. About 12 per cent foreign nationals. Doesn't really produce a type but pupils are articulate, well rounded and very supportive of each other, appearing genuinely to celebrate each other's achievements. 'The finished product is amazing' according to one mother, 'the boys and girls are charming, personable, not shy or arrogant and have a great sense of fun but are still ambitious'.

The recently formed King's Society, a cultural, social and educational society for parents and friends now comprises over 300 families. Members organise lectures, music recitals, tours of the Cathedral with the Dean and social events. Old boys and girls include potter and writer Edmund de Waal, astronaut Michael Foale, Patrick Leigh-Fermor, Christopher Marlowe and William Somerset Maugham, supermodel Jacquetta Wheeler, Olympic silver medallist and world champion rower Frances Houghton and Anthony Worrall-Thompson.

Entrance: At 13+ by common entrance. School's own exam and an interview for those who have not been prepared for CE. Occasionally spaces in year 10. About a third come from Junior King's but they still have to take the same exams as everyone else. Rest from a range of Kent and Sussex prep schools and London days schools. Pass mark has recently been raised to 60 per cent but school likes to keep families together and takes an enlightened view if someone is borderline. It is also possible for pupils to take an entrance exam to Junior King's at 11+ which would guarantee entry to the senior school – they would still have to take CE for setting purposes. About 30 join in the sixth form with entrance by competitive exam and interview in Nov before entry with minimum of 7 Bs or equivalent at GCSE. Seven Bs required to move into sixth form and 3 Cs at AS required to stay for A levels.

Exit: About ten a year leave after GCSEs usually to local schools or London day schools. Most sixth formers depart to top universities -15 per cent to Oxbridge with most of the rest going to Bristol, Edinburgh, Durham, Exeter, Leeds, Newcastle, Manchester and Nottingham and an increasing number to the American universities and Trinity College Dublin. Languages, sciences and economics/business management most popular degree subjects recently. Between 10 and 15 to medical school each year.

Money matters: Up to 20 King's Scholarships and exhibitions as well as music and sports and art scholarships, all with a rigorous selection process and worth up to 10 per cent of fees. Three or four sixth form scholarships awarded for outstanding performance in the sixth form entrance exam. Greater emphasis on bursaries – the King's foundation has been set up to fund both scholarships and bursaries and allocated over £1 million a year. Parents means tested annually and can receive up to 100 per cent of full boarding fee.

Remarks: Thriving academic school with highly motivated pupils – 'The children never stop – I do not know how they fit everything into their day and still have time for a busy social life,' says one parent. Not a heavily religious school but the Benedictine tradition of care for body, mind and spirit is very much in evidence.

K

The King's School in Macclesfield

Linked school: The King's School in Macclesfield Infant and Junior Division

---

Cumberland Street, Macclesfield, SK10 1DA

- Pupils: 715; 315 girls, 400 boys; all day • Ages: 11–18 • C of E
- Fees: Infants £7,740; Junior £8,520; Senior £10,770 pa
- Independent

Tel: 01625 260000
Email: admissions@kingsmac.co.uk
Website: www.kingsmac.co.uk

Headmaster: Since 2011, Dr Simon Hyde MA DPhil (late 40s). Born in Macclesfield and an Old Boy, degree in modern history at Oxford, doctorate there and at the University of Bonn plus a bit of teaching, history master at Loughborough Grammar for three years, swift ascent to senior teacher and head of humanities at Oakham, deputy head at Haberdashers' Aske's Boys, Herts, for seven years, where he was responsible for school development and strategic planning.

Approachable, balanced, financially shrewd, good sense of humour, ambitious in a realistic way for the school, appreciative of staff. High approval rating from all the parents we spoke to, who praised his communication skills – 'a breath of fresh air', 'very impressive and dedicated', 'terrific...not a strutter...makes the parents chuckle in the first five minutes'. Has seized the opportunity to make a number of new senior appointments (enjoys full backing of governors) – young energetic types: previous deputy head (who, sadly, died in Dr Hyde's first year) replaced by two, one for academics, the other i/c development – 'to take a long view'; overall director of sport; head of IT (much to do here). In his first year taught a year 10 history and lower sixth politics group to establish his teaching credentials to staff and pupils – clearly loves teaching.

Very keen for school to be centred in the local community – working with council to support its regeneration plans, encourages sixth form outreach work with feeder primaries and community use of facilities. Wants to acquire funds to invest in infrastructure improvements (new Astro and sports centre, better IT) and extend bursaries, and to raise academic expectations (without losing any of the fantastic extra-curricular opportunities) – pleased by stronger than ever 2012 results, in a more stringent year for marking. Would like the pupils to 'look smart and have fun'.

Not married. Judges national and international debating competitions (ran the regional ESU Mace and judges at world schools comps). Interested in German culture and likes reading historical and detective fiction (the classy Swedish kind, Henning Mankell's Wallender series, so definitely on the side of the angels).

Academic matters: Diamond structure – co-ed infant and junior school, single sex years 7-11, co-ed sixth. Very consistent at A level – 2012: 76 per cent A*-B, 42 per cent A/A*. Wide range of academic subjects (no IB nor vocational options) including economics, business studies, government and politics, geology, psychology, philosophy, sport and PE, computing as well as IT, Latin and classical civilisation (small but steady numbers). History and psychology very popular, then biology, economics, maths, chemistry; no drama, but can do theatre studies in year 13 extended studies programme, which allows a fifth AS in, eg, critical thinking, or LAMDA, public speaking, Japanese, sports leadership qual; all complete ECDL then too. Max class size 15, but year 13 sets can be as small as 5. Much proficient use of electronic whiteboards throughout, but we enjoyed the English language class demonstrating that low tech skilful questioning can also engage students successfully.

GCSE very consistent too – 2013: 98 per cent gained 5 A*-Cs including English and maths, 30 per cent A*/A; all do at least nine, with a modern lang (Spanish most popular); can do separate sciences; options include drama, religion and philosophy (excellent results); all work on ECDL. Gender divide closing here (but not at A level).

Very broad curriculum in year 7; 17 subjects, including three modern langs (French, German, Spanish – several native speakers on staff), choose two in year 8, two or three in year 9; setting in maths from year 7; max class size 25; children encouraged to go beyond homework. Separate sciences in year 9 and have to choose two from art, music, technology and drama. Praise for teachers from a disconcertingly poised and articulate, very new year 7 boy – 'They're fun and good at what they do'; 'They're firm but help you understand,' added a voice from year 9; 'You're encouraged to learn independently, not just rely on the teacher,' from a year 13. According to parents, the teachers know their pupils well as individuals, expect them to work hard, do the best they can, but recognise not all will excel. Various kinds of commendations for especially good work or effort – certificates, letters and postcards to parents, assembly presentations. Several computer suites, huge language lab in girls' division with masses of PCs.

All departments impressively active outside the classroom – workshops, trips, lecture visits, science shows, exchanges; success in a wide range of external competitions; psychology department has 'adopted' a female Bonobo at Twycross Zoo. Lively English – strong creative writing, eg slam poetry workshop, literature quizzes, play trips, videoed performances of book reviews for World Book Day by year 7-9 classes, participation in BBC News School Report Day; trip to BBC at Salford for boys to work with film making equipment.

Scholars have extensive enrichment programme – eg extra modern language in year 9 or Latin; some activities run by sixth formers, who create and deliver workshops at feeder junior schools; residentials on very stimulating topics going well beyond the curriculum for years 8-11.

SENCo confident school can accommodate mild versions of dys-strata, Asperger's, ADD/ADHD, visual and hearing impaired plus physical disability (but boys would find the last more problematic, owing to the geography of their part of the site). She is a qualified dyslexia and literacy specialist, with two p/t dyslexia specialists and TAs for class support, in and outside class. Fifteen pounds an hour for individual dyslexia session (pairs possible); all departments have a member of staff who links with learning support department. All year 7s and later entries screened for dyslexia. Well resourced generally – school, 'happy to provide what's needed'. Homework club at lunchtime provides refuge for less secure pupils.

Games, options, the arts: Very strong sports – 25 acres of playing fields (main ones for matches, Derby Fields, one mile away); Astros with floodlighting; four new netball courts for girls; boys' and girls' divisions have large gyms but no modern sportshall (yet). Wide range – the usuals plus golf, sailing, orienteering, fencing, skiing: caters for the keen and those who just want enjoyment. Very successful rugby (boys and girls), hockey, trampolining, netball and cheerleading: witness a cabinet crammed with elaborate, glittering red, blue and silver trophies (no English modesty here) – a shelf literally collapsed beneath their weight; riding, swimming (despite having to use the town's leisure centre). A 2012 women's Team GB gymnast, two girl British biathle champions; several pupils represent their county or region. Girls' sports facilities recently upgraded, boys' getting same treatment – will include county-size Astro, half-size Astro, cricket nets and four tennis courts.

Music huge and very impressive – full and string orchestras, various bands, including jazz – Big Band highly regarded

K

locally; various choirs; lots of concerts at school and in the community; participation in youth orchestras (Halle,Wigan jazz, Stockport symphony, guitar ensemble). Some in Cheshire and national youth choir; recent tour to Budapest. Wide range of music including film, blues and barbershop.

Unusually ambitious plays produced – Cyrano de Bergerac, Candide, The Rivals, Arturo Ui (a girl took lead role, another plays in first cricket team); biannual musical; art department creates excellent sets and props. Whole school productions plus separate boys' and girls' ones; years 8-10 panto.

Tremendous multi media art (we saw more 3D than 2), displayed throughout the school – we were struck by some interesting glass work (own kiln, gets remnants from local window company), very realistic cakes made of coloured felt on a stand and expressive year 8 ceramic masks. A level students have produced video and sound installation exam pieces. Annual residential in North Wales; twelve students selected for Cheshire GCSE gifted and talented residential. Busy DT – talks, trips, competitions, eg Lego League.

Heaps of (mixed) societies and activities – D of E, sixth form community action, sound technology, arts and philosophy soc, European youth parliament, Amnesty International, debating, fair trade, Arabic. Vigorous financial arm – Young Enterprise, investors club – 30 teams across the three divisions competed in student challenge, sixth form economics department honoured by Bank of England for ten years' outstanding contribution to their National Target 2.0 competition. Sixth form council; charities and social committee raises thousands of pounds; sixth formers help run clubs for younger pupils in senior and junior schools. Good careers programme – work experience week for all in year 10, more possible in sixth form, one full-time careers officer.

Fab trips – Cerne, skiing in Colorado (pricy), chateau study week in Normandy for sixth form linguists (tasty), also (mixed) chateau trip at end of year 7 (memorable); year 13s can do work experience in France with a company, returning just before their oral exam. Rugby tour to Canada, hockey to South Africa, history trip to China, diving in Egypt, World Challenge to India. Very testing outdoor activities trips – coasteering (involves jumping off cliffs into the sea – must be heart stopping for parents), canoeing, surfing; mixed ages for these leading to friendships across years. The pupils we met all very appreciative of this wealth of opportunities – the only downside was finding enough time to fit in all they wanted to do.

Background and atmosphere: Founded by Sir John Percyvale, Lord Mayor of London, in 1502, as a grammar school. Moved to present site in 1854; in 1946 became independent fee paying school. Girls were introduced into the sixth form in 1986 and in 1992 new girls' and (by now) co-ed junior divisions established in refurbished ex-Macclesfield High School in Fence Avenue, about a mile away, followed by infant department in 2007. Lovely views of the Peak District (but some drab corridors in the girls' section). C of E with ecumenical ethos.

The boys' and sixth form campus is very large, mostly pleasant redbrick or sandstone and harmonious modern additions around a central green fringed with trees. A bridge over a street leads to recent £2.5 million sixth form block and practice pitches. Colourful, attractively cluttered Alan Cooper library with masses of magazines and DVDs as well as books, wooden beamed sixth form study area on upper floor, honours board for First World War war dead on wall, with an OB's medals beneath it. Separate junior library with lots of fiction. 'The school will get you any magazines, newspapers and books you need,' according to a sixth former. Sixth have common room, study area and cafe in own centre.

Separate girls' division (370 girls, three forms of 25 per year) and boys' (500 boys, four forms of 25) reduces gender stereotyping re subject choices – several boys choose art and girls maths and science at A level – and allows flexibility of teaching approaches; year 11 house captains and prefects allow more and earlier opportunities to develop leadership skills, eg mentoring younger pupils, supplemented by plenty of co ed activities and trips.

Academics well balanced by the extra-curricular – head of boys' division observed that the introduction of music at start and end of assemblies encouraged respect for more than just sporting prowess: all achievements celebrated. School council meets every three weeks, issues frequent questionnaires to canvass views, proposals heeded. Parents and pupils feel it has a friendly atmosphere. Food praised for quality and choice (smart cards used); sixth allowed into town in lunch hour.

Dr Hyde should be happy, as almost all the pupils do look very smart – indeed we wondered whether one very elegantly turned out sixth former in suit with waistcoat was a member of staff (but were relieved to see at least one boy with a tie veering towards half mast).

Pastoral care and discipline: Thoughtful transition – year 6 taster day (our year 11 tour guides still remembered their fish, chips and chocolate cake lunch); year 7s said older pupils very helpful if you get lost; bonding form residential trip early in first term. Sixth formers train as peer supporters for years 7-9. We were assured bullying not a problem – the school would stop it immediately: 'It's something King's wouldn't tolerate because it just shouldn't happen'. Mixed age activities encourage general friendliness and there's 'always a teacher you can talk to about problems', as well as the nurse or heads of year. Sixth in tutor groups of 12; induction morning and welcome evening organised by year 13s for new year 12s.

Pupils and parents: Extensive catchment area, about 20 mile radius – lots of bus routes, 10 minute walk from train station to both sites. From own junior school, prep schools and a wide range of state primaries; three quarters white British. Lively, confident, happy and energetic pupils. According to head of girls' division, 'Quirkiness and slight eccentricities are liked', girls of different types 'rub along well' – but they need to want to learn, to be happy.

From various backgrounds (majority professional, some farming families and a sizeable minority of blue-collar workers) – 'very rounded parents,' one told me; AstraZeneca based locally, also commuter belt for airline companies at Manchester Airport. Praise for speed of response to queries – 'totally fabulous lady in the office, who will put you in touch with everyone you need to communicate with'; 'Teachers get back to you soon if you phone'; email alerts, regular letters with email addresses of people to contact.

Entrance: Exam mid January – English, maths and VR for years 7-8; plus science and languages for year 9; the last minus VR for year 10 plus interview with child and parents. Belongs to Greater Manchester Consortium of schools, so follows its timetable for year 7 applicants (check deadline dates on website). Roughly 10 -15 per cent entry to sixth from outside – need at least four As and two Bs at GCSE, plus interview (parents as well) and reference from current school.

Exit: Less than 10 per cent leave post GCSE – mainly to take vocational courses at FE colleges; girls may want a more relaxed, less structured atmosphere.

After A level students depart to a wide range of universities – Liverpool, Leeds, Manchester, Newcastle, Nottingham, Durham, Birmingham popular; three Oxbridge 2013 (current hopefuls praised help with preparation). Largest numbers for business/ economics/accounting; then biology, followed by geography, psychology, law, engineering; two scholarships (UCLA and Imperial) in 2013.

Money matters: Means tested bursaries – strong performance in entrance exam needed; scholarships for outstanding performance – worth £1200 pa; two music scholarships awarded at time of entrance exam worth £600 pa towards cost of musical tuition – need at least grade 3. Quincentenary bursaries for new sixth formers. Sibling discount.

Remarks: Interesting marriage of traditional values – suggested by cabinets of silver cups, old whole school photos and honours boards in reception – with progressive educational approaches. Dedicated, astute head augurs well.

Kingston Grammar School

London Road, Kingston Upon Thames, KT2 6PY

• Pupils: 825 (455 boys/370 girls) • Ages: 11–18 • Non-denom
• Fees: £16,020 pa • Independent

Tel: 020 8546 5875
Email: registrar@kgs.org.uk
Website: www.kgs.org.uk

Head: Since September 2009, Mrs Sarah Fletcher MA PGCE, an Oxford historian (late forties) and, according to parents, a breath of fresh air. She came from a deputy headship at Rugby where she had been for 12 years. Previously taught at Wycombe Abbey, St George's Montreux, Habs Girls' in Elstree and Lawrence Sheriff Grammar in Rugby – an admirably varied career with child protection, housemistressing and Pre-U experience along the way.

Mrs Fletcher is pretty, softly spoken, sparkly, diplomatic and clever – one of the new breed of heads we are meeting more frequently, now that governors have learned that women can do the job superbly without being remote administrators and while being warm, human and effective. A 'can do' head, she has plans to 'green' the school, ie to landscape and plant it so as to soften its somewhat austere aspect – we approve. She's also smartened up the pupils. Parents say, 'She is wonderful. She has lots of new ideas and is only holding back so as not to overwhelm people. She's good at consulting – she really wants our views.' And pupils agree – 'Her door is always open. She wants us to come in'. Under Mrs Fletcher, the school is opening up in all ways – 'I believe in creativity, independent learning, helping people to think for themselves and stretch themselves. I want opportunities for everyone'. An inspired and confident head for an inspiring and confident school.

Moving on in April 2014 to become the first female head of City of London Boys.

Academic matters: Now does IGCSEs in maths, English, sciences and languages. No Pre-U yet, though under consideration as an alternative to A levels. Maths is popular at both levels and results are outstanding – pupils praise the brilliant teaching, and even those who say they aren't mathematical find it hard to resist. Eng lit, physics, biology and history also star. Smaller take-up in langs despite good teaching. Department currently musters 14 languages. Greek taught in collaboration with Tiffin Boys. In 2013, 63 per cent A*/A grades and 87 per cent A*/B at A level across the subjects; 77 per cent A*/A grades at GCSE. No great surprises in the curriculum, though sports studies and theatre studies offered at A level. A few pupils yearn for cookery. IT seen as a tool, not an end in itself – all sixth formers take the European Computer Driving Licence.

Learning support department helps those on the dys strata, mostly mild, a few moderate. Learner profile compiled for all children seen by ed psych or specialist teacher – school a great believer in constant monitoring and tracking to ensure progress. Site pretty accessible and school will put itself out to support mobility if needed. Lots of laptop users and open to those with aural/visual impairment – 'so long as they can cope with the site'.

Impressively stocked library, actually called 'the library', not 'the resources centre'. And books actually used – most reassuring. Pupils praise their teachers and librarian unreservedly – 'They will always run extension classes if you ask'; 'They'll order anything in for us'. Parents praise the academic ethos – 'It's not pushy, but they do get the results'; 'They really encourage them to think for themselves'; 'They're quick to pick up on people's talents and nurture them – even talents the children didn't know they had'.

Games, options, the arts: In an area full of good schools – and some of them are free – this is what gives Kingston the edge and makes it the first choice even for those whose children are super-bright and might well gain a place at a local grammar. The extracurricular opportunities here are seemingly limitless or, at any rate, fill a 40 page booklet. Half a dozen activities pre-school, a dozen or more in the lunch break and a further dozen after school make for a busy, busy life. Pupils we spoke to said they stay after school every day – though this, of course, not true of everyone. Loads of trips (local, national and international), an excellent programme of outside speakers and an expanding sports programme ('One of our newish teachers, an ex-army officer, thinks anything is possible') which includes girls' football, now countering erstwhile grumbles of sport being only for the best. Netball no longer a poor relation but zooming. Boathouse on the Thames provides rowing option – 'It's huge!' we were told. CCF very popular with the first year's cohort, tails off thereafter, though masses of opportunities for RAF flying, summer camps (very popular) and some get scholarships to Sandhurst at the end. The Cage – two onsite courts with soft surfaces – due for upgrade, but most sport takes place on the Fairfield – a field behind the main site – or off-site at Ditton Fields, a bus ride away. New stress on community service to people, locally and beyond, less fortunate than themselves. Older pupils admit, 'It's a bit of an eye-opener' for those who had, hitherto, looked inwards rather than outwards.

Music acknowledged to be outstanding. Music tech new and burgeoning – already growing out of space – but trad music also supported, though small academic uptake. 'We want music that will appeal to everyone but which has a high class end.' Drama, well-housed in excellent, flexible and well-equipped performing arts centre, produces classy shows, including annual Shakespeare festival and real plays – good to see something other than High School Musical and Grease for once. House drama, Ad Lib and annual dance fest much enthused over, even by boys.

Art and DT are exceptional – masses of workshop/studio space and we drooled over brilliantly conceived and executed mini-dresses made from eg sweet papers or exquisitely embroidered canvas. Professional quality furniture made by GCSE class, perspex clocks and clever ceramics make you want to get your hands gummy. Previously blank walls now acting as showcases for pupil work – a welcome and humanising change. The list of national awards, prizes and achievements across the extracurricular spectrum fills several pages.

Background and atmosphere: In the midst of Kingston's tarmac tangle, it's fine if you know your way but, if you don't, leave an hour or so to locate it and then park – no parking on site and even the staff have an efficient system of sharing lifts and spaces. The school itself looks like a real old-fashioned grammar on the outside – solid, brick-built and purposeful – though, once you get inside, the modernisation and bright, light spaces change one's initial impression. The trad grammar style persists in the school hall from your parents' childhood, with honours boards, memorial tablets to those who fell in the two wars and faint echoes of 'Praise my soul the King of heaven' lurking in the curtains. Space is certainly not lavish here, though the school is less cramped than some of its central London peers.

Pupils wear white shirts and black or grey uniforms – they look sensible and tidy. 'They have really cracked down on very short skirts – they want everyone to look smart. It's made a huge difference,' we were told by one rather elegant sixth former. About half the school eat school lunches, acknowledged to be much improved and gaining support – it looked good to us, and lots of choice. The place feels relaxed and welcoming. Pupils like the house system, which enables friendships between the years – 'We feel far more like a real community now'. Good café for sixth form – into which staff also pop ('It's OK – they don't come in in large numbers') – with TV, stereo system, drinks and snacks. Good home/school IT links – email used all the time now, we were told. The most appallingly ear-lacerating school bell we have ever heard.

Pastoral care and discipline: Good system of heads of year and form tutors – 'They get to know you really well' – but discipline scarcely an issue here – 'They're really hot on bullying'; 'They've always got time to talk to you if you've got something you need to sort out'. Misconduct marks, summons to head of year, rare Saturday detentions generally all that's needed. No smoking, drink or drugs problems that anyone can recall. 'The pastoral care is extremely good,' a parent told us. 'They're quick to pick up problems and keep parents in touch. It's in the culture of the place.'

Pupils and parents: From only around a three mile radius, so they probably know how to navigate Kingston's surreal road system. From over 150 primaries – some 65 per cent from state schools.

Notable former pupils include Edward Gibbon (The Roman Empire one), Michael Frayn, Jonathan Kenworthy, James Cracknell, Neil Fox, Andy Sturgeon (imaginatively roped in to help with the reshaping of the school's landscape) and 2012 Olympic gold medal rower Sophie Hosking.

Entrance: The main entry points are 11+ and 16+ with some spaces available for 13+ entry. An option to sit a 10+ deferred entry examination in year 5 to secure a place in year 7. More or less equal number of boys and girls arrived at through merit, not engineering. Interview seen as important, 'We are not academically exclusive in our selection – we look for potential'. School works closely with the feeder schools – especially at 13+ so as to not to encourage unrealistic applications – 'We don't believe in disappointing people'.

Exit: They spread over the country. In 2013 destinations included Nottingham, Bristol, Newcastle, Birmingham, Exeter, Manchester, Durham, Warwick, Bath, Imperial, King's and Leeds – and a few to art school. Annual sprinkling to Oxbridge – 13 in 2013. Biggest range of courses you could imagine.

Money matters: Scholarships worth 10 or 20 per cent of fees available at all entry points and awarded on results of tests. Bursaries worth up to 100 per cent of fees also at all entry points and means-tested. Worth a serious look if you are local, clever and strapped.

Remarks: Great school, great future.

Kingswood School

Linked school: Kingswood Prep School

Lansdown Road, Bath, BA1 5RG

- Pupils: 715 boys and girls; 535 day, 180 boarding • Ages: 11–18
- Methodist • Fees: Day £12,759; Boarding £23,958–£27,498 pa
- Independent

Tel: 01225 734200
Email: admissions@kingswood.bath.sch.uk
Website: www.kingswood.bath.sch.uk

Headmaster: Since 2008, Mr Simon Morris MA (Cantab) modern and medieval languages, especially German (late forties). Educated at Ipswich School, then a spell in the City after Cambridge – 'But in my heart of hearts, I always knew I'd be a teacher'. Despite exclusively independent school career, has taken pains to cut the mustard by doing his PGCE and NPQH, the latter quite unusual amongst independent school heads. Previously deputy at St John's, Leatherhead, via housemaster and head of modern languages at The Leys and head of German at Warwick School.

First ever non-Methodist head of this Methodist school – openly C of E but embraces Wesleyan philosophy of service. Might seem unassuming but isn't: passionate about instilling high but attainable standards in every individual – in everything they do. Married to Caroline, who teaches modern languages in the school and has lots of state school experience. Three children, all pupils here. Supported by triumvirate of deputies, all good foils to the others. Takes junior PHSE programmes as a chance to stay in touch/get to know the newly arrived. Visible, approachable, welcome and frequent spectator; keen cricketer. Appears to have 'gone down brilliantly' with parents and sixth form, in particular. Firm of handshake and of purpose, a round peg in a round hole.

Academic matters: Strong performance across the board. In 2013, 55 per cent A/A* at GCSE and 50 per cent A*/A grades at A level. Vies for second place in Bath league tables with Prior Park (Kingswood edged ahead last year), behind local academic hothouse, King Edward's. Must do really well on value-added, then, for a school which claims not to be 'narrowly selective'. Masses of choice, with 23 subjects to choose from at GCSE and 26 at A level. Languages lag behind in terms of take-up, despite German being compulsory alongside French in year 7. Two languages too much pressure, some parents think.

Main teaching block (The Ferens) utilitarian and colour coded inside according to subject. OK labs and lots of IT throughout. Unlovely but much loved sixth form block (The Dixon) houses some teaching, the HE and careers department, studies and chill-out space, including a kitchen. Magnificent Gothic splendour of a library enough to make anyone work; sixth form has Perspex platform of privilege at far end. Cosy seminar room at entrance.

Not a huge number of diagnosed SENs but one-to-one help on offer (paid as extra) for those who need it. Head keen to take 'any child who can access the Kingswood curriculum', including those with dyslexia and on the autistic spectrum. Inclusive, non-stigmatised provision. Head's personal experience informs his attitude.

Games, options, the arts: Plenty of pitches/courts/Astroturf, flattened out on three levels of alarmingly sloping grounds, imaginatively named lower, middle and upper, the latter a short minibus ride up the hill. Usual rugby/hockey/tennis terms for boys, hockey/netball/tennis for girls, but tempting options too for the less sportingly inclined, eg the slow running club(!). Not queuing up to show us the swimming pool.

Strong links with Team Bath at the University – makes good use of its facilities and expertise. Sport taken seriously but no discernible 'jock' culture – in fact current captain of rugby also a musician of note. New pavilion on the Upper, which also hosts Bath Rugby Club in this rugby-obsessed city. A 2012 swimmer's timetable has been pared down to fit training in; a promising young golfer is also in the slips.

The arts generally acknowledged as outstanding and have their own awards ceremony. Charming arts and crafts style studio produces works of exhibition standard in all media; a local gallery has chosen more Kingswood work than from any other Bath school. Sixth formers and staff wear enviable monogrammed smocks.

Music school a super light space boasting a top-notch recording studio and an 'inspirational' head of music who embraces everything from Bach to the Beatles, and whose students recently recorded for Children in Need at Abbey Road. Something for all performers of all styles and standards. Drama right up there too, with proper theatre as well as a studio. Productions for all ages, which neighbouring schools attend, plus a massively popular comedy club for (brave) aspiring stand-ups. Shows are collaborative, with pupils involved with writing, producing, publicising as well as performing. Theatre also twice a venue for BBC Question Time.

Background and atmosphere: The only school founded by John Wesley (who believed that education should engage the heart as well as the head) and first ever Methodist one, spawning over 700 across the world since. Moved from Bristol in the early 1850s because of unreliable water supplies and has occupied an imposing pile of purpose-built Victorian Gothic on steep northern slopes above Bath ('Satan's throne', according to Wesley) ever since, almost opposite the Royal High School. Other buildings of varying degrees of age and beauty are dotted around its 140 acres of manicured grounds, including the chapel, too small these days to house the whole school, which gathers for religious and secular assemblies in the theatre. Not at all horribly worthy, as its history might indicate.

Has managed to hang on to the feel of a co-ed boarding school with day pupils. A long day for everyone (5.30pm finish after activities or, rarely, prep) and mixed day/boarding houses from year 9 right up to upper sixth. No Saturday school but good activity programme for boarders, plus usual sporting fixtures on Sat pms. Littlies spend their first two years in Westwood, a gentler introduction to the big school. Boy and girl boarders occupy separate floors of immaculate dormitories for six to eight, out of bounds to day pupils, who share the slightly dark living space downstairs. Room sizes go down while mess goes up in the six single sex senior houses, where the feel is cosier and autonomous. Space for occasional over-nighters.

A spirit of service (to the school/local/global communities) expounded by the head and lived out in the school, eg by close involvement of sixth form with junior pupils, lots of unglamorous charitable stuff in Bath as well as abroad, eg bricklaying in Malawi – Uruguay at planning stage. Green credentials measure up too: holder of Eco-Schools Green Flag, fluttering proudly from flag pole; in-house (and excellent) catering sources as much food as possible locally or from Fair Trade; sustainable development committee currently looking at ground source heating, reducing food waste and an improved travel plan. Head talks convincingly of 'our responsibilities to the planet'. Right mix of respect and banter between pupils and staff, and pupils at the top and bottom of the school – 'They really look after each other,' said one mother, echoing several others. Central dining in splendid Gothic setting helps all 600 pupils get to know each other.

Sees itself as an innovator amongst Bath schools, eg Model UN, and quite keen to show them how it's done. International flavour: pupils come from 15 countries, but an eye is kept to see that no one nationality dominates and all get an essentially British boarding experience. Pupils love it – 'I've got friends all over the world,' declared a sixth former, with an eye to his gap year.

Pastoral care and discipline: 'Outstanding,' according to parents; 'They're just so nice to each other – and that goes for kids and staff,' said one, whose son fled bullying at another school (it gets zero tolerance here). Touchy-feely stuff not at the expense of academic rigour or general endeavour, however: expectations are laid down early and slacking discouraged. A clear system of sanctions looks good on paper, but we didn't find anyone who would admit to being on the receiving end of it. Emphasis definitely on support and redirection, rather than on chastisement, and all felt help for any problem was very much on hand.

Pupils and parents: Moderately to exceedingly affluent but not especially posh. Wide range of professions amongst parent body, offspring of (more successful) actors, musicians and sportsmen/women amongst pupils. 'Incredibly supportive – and reasonably demanding,' says the head. Pupils are engaging and confident without arrogance, and startlingly uncritical of their school. Most come from north side of Bath – crossing the city at peak-time is hideous and plenty of provision south of the river.

Entrance: Fifty per cent from own prep school, some from other prep schools mostly north of Bath, good few from local (excellent) primary school, St Stephen's, where they have strong links and collaboration. Maths, English and non-verbal reasoning tested at 11+ to try to ensure fairness; coaching not expected and discouraged. Head sees all entrance papers.

Exit: Virtually all go through to sixth form. Most to university (86 per cent in 2013). Handful to Oxbridge and to art and music colleges, others to diverse degree choices all over Britain.

Money matters: Good value for what's on offer: third cheapest in Bath with lots of extras thrown in. Some parents resent those long holidays, which can be a problem for those working so hard to fund it all. Academic and special talent scholarships offered at years 7, 9 and lower sixth. Head keen to increase bursary provision throughout.

Remarks: Super school which has finally gained its place in the competitive galaxy of Bath secondaries. Setting and atmosphere suggest privilege without pretension; particularly good for budding performing or visual artists who require results too. Takes the best of Methodist philanthropy and adapts it for a secular multi-cultural world. Truly global in feel and outlook for an English school.

Knowl Hill School

School Lane, Pirbright, Woking, Surrey, GU24 0JN

- Pupils: 65; 20 girls and 45 boys; all day • Ages: 7–16
- Predominantly Christian • Fees: £15,789 pa + therapy
- Independent

Tel: 01483 797032
Email: info@knowlhill.org.uk
Website: www.knowlhill.org.uk

Principal: Since 2005, James Dow Grant MA Ed (sixties). Began his career in direct grant grammar schools, before moving to specialist schools in 1978 to work with children affected by specific learning difficulties. Spent four years as deputy head at Knowl Hill, then took over the headship from Angela Bareford, who cofounded the school in 1984 after being unable to find a suitable school for her own dyslexic son. Head is passionate about up-to-date academic research into specific learning difficulties and has a particular interest in specialist software. Parents say he has bags of experience and empathises well with the pupils and the difficulties they may have experienced.

Academic matters: All pupils follow the national curriculum, modified in some cases, and are divided into year group classes of around eight. In addition, each child has individual tuition for their specific area of difficulty as required. Pupils are equipped with laptops, taught to touch type and have personalised coloured graphic timetables. SENCo oversees IEPs, which are regularly monitored and shared with parents.

Full range of subjects studied, alongside a particularly strong ICT and art department. Good mixture of male and female teachers – most have mainstream and specialist qualifications and have developed a diverse multisensory and flexible range of teaching strategies. A holistic approach to each child is seen as paramount to ensure they reach their true potential; this also helps to eliminate any self-esteem problems.

Huge range of specialist software includes programmes to help with boosting short-term memory, poor auditory skills, sequencing and number operations. Everyone up to year 8 follows a SPLAT (specific learning and therapy) course that targets their needs and may involve speech and language and occupational therapy. Therapists also work alongside teachers in some lessons to ensure that every child is accessing the curriculum. Foreign languages are usually an area of difficulty for most of the pupils, so they aren't compulsory but can be organised on an individual basis.

Some pupils are reintegrated back into the mainstream system. Pupils who stay on work towards a range of national qualifications to GCSE. Those who aren't able to cope with GCSEs can take foundation entry level examinations and ASDAN qualifications. Some older students also attend vocational link courses at local further education colleges.

Games, options, the arts: On site facilities are limited but a games field and tennis courts opposite the school enable pupils to take part in a full range of sports. Swimming lessons are held at a nearby sports centre. All pupils take part in weekly drama lessons. These incorporate guidance and life skills training to help students develop greater awareness of day-to-day problems and strategies to cope with them. Pupils put on their own performances and are encouraged to write their own plays and sketches. A music therapist runs a listening programme to help youngsters develop the auditory skills needed to listen effectively and communicate well. Class music has been through a bit of a lull, but this is about to be rectified. Language therapist and teachers run social skills and communication groups – keen pupils can take the English Speaking Board exams.

The art and design department is the jewel in the crown. Pupils can choose from a range of courses, including woodwork, textiles, pottery, digital or analogue photography. The department's success is highlighted by pupils taking AS and A level art and design subjects early and an impressive number go on to study arts courses at a higher level. Lunchtime clubs on offer, as well as a daily homework club at the end of the school day. Educational trips are part of the curriculum – they are designed to help pupils build independence and social skills. There are also optional trips to Outward Bound centres and abroad.

Background and atmosphere: Set on the edge of the peaceful village of Pirbright, the school site is thoughtfully designed and compact. The original building, an attractive redbrick Victorian schoolhouse, has been extended, with a two-storey art and performance block added in 2003. Outdoor areas include the playground (which doubles as a sports area), an adventure playground with climbing equipment and a picnic area for summer lunches. Staff and pupils are approachable, friendly and caring.

Pastoral care and discipline: Head ensures that staff are well trained in all aspects of pastoral care and fully aware of the psychological impact a specific learning difficulty can have. Social and emotional development is on an equal footing with academic attainments. The school also promotes strong links within the community, parents and other schools (independent and state). An independent counsellor visits the school every week to work with the children in a safe and confidential environment. The counsellor is available to both pupils and parents on an appointment or drop-in basis.

Pupils have their own school council which meets regularly to discuss day-to-day issues and a head boy and a head girl are elected every year.

Pupils and parents: Children come from a range of backgrounds and nationalities. Fairly large catchment area includes Surrey, Hampshire, Berkshire as well as the outskirts of London. Many share lifts to and from school and Brookwood station is a few minutes' drive from the school.

Entrance: All applicants have specific learning difficulties, dyslexia and the overlapping conditions. From 7+, prospective parents and children are invited to visit the school and must provide relevant medical and psychological reports outlining the child's specific areas of difficulty. The school also has close links with local authorities and will accept suitably statemented children.

Exit: At 16+, the majority go on to further education colleges, with arts, ICT, construction, mechanics and horticulture among the most popular course choices. A few students move to a school sixth form to study A levels or BTECs.

Money matters: Several means tested bursaries of up to 50 per cent of the fees. Around 70 per cent are statemented and funded by their local authority.

Remarks: A caring specialist school that aims to produce responsible and capable young adults who know where they're going. The success of the school empowers pupils to be able to make choices about their own futures.

Knox Academy

Pencaitland Road, Haddington, East Lothian, EH41 4DT

- Pupils: 390 boys, 425 girls, all day • Ages: 11–18 • Non-denom
- State

Tel: 01620 823387
Email: knoxacademy@knox.elcschool.org.uk
Website: www.ka-net.org.uk

Head Teacher: Since 2012, Mrs Sarah Ingham BD PGCE, (forties, but looks like thirties). Joined Knox Academy in 2001, previously deputy head. Educated at Bolton School Girls Division and St Andrews (BD), Herriot-Watt (PGCE), Glasgow Caledonian (post-grad counselling and supervision diploma) and Edinburgh (post-grad educational leadership and management certificate – the headship qualification). Cor. She taught religious and moral education at Kirkcudbright Academy and Currie Community High School, where her husband Charles still works. A star –

K

bubbly and fun, with splendid auburn locks and trendy eBay shoes. 'I love it, the best job in the world,' she says of her role. She took this editor with enormous pride to see her pièce de résistance, Tots and Teens, a proper nursery where embryo nursery nurses – not to mention a whole raft of other teenagers – help to look after local youngsters (from three up: nappies not a problem) for £1 per session. Mothers meet in the food court for coffee at collection time – a boon for stay at home mums.

A great believer in giving service back to the community, the head runs the school with a £3 million budget. A new housing estate is in the offing at Leatham Mains, so pupils are capped at 800. New build is at the planning stage, five new classrooms to be added to this already expanded school (need a compass to negotiate). Can choose own staff – 'interview, choose and watch them teach: no good spending half a million on someone who can't perform.' Oodles applied for a PE post last year, 15 or 16 for geography, but not always that big a choice. The 'good young female physics teacher' is a real bonus. This is devolved management at its best.

Academic matters: Keen on curriculum for excellence, the school is inclusive. Thirty pupils per class, 20 for practical stuff, and streaming in maths. (Busy maths club, popular with high flyers). Does well – strategies in place throughout.

S3 pupils have the choice of including literacy, numeracy or The Prince's Trust (which covers both, but includes life skills, independence and team work) as part of their personal curriculum at national 4 level. Massive choice at S4, including practical woodworking and hospitality (practical cookery). Oddly enough, not a lot of take up in computer games design. Otherwise, expect the usual subjects, with alternatives of enterprise and employability, personal development and volunteering – to be chosen with advice from tutor. Refreshing to find a school where academic attainment is not the be all and end all. That said, the school punches well above its weight both in national and East Lothian exam results. Spectacularly.

Three dedicated guidance staff, plus two learning support; help in class if needed. Pupils with mild(ish) SEN are catered for. SEN and guidance staff work together and share a bright passage of individual rooms; pupils with special needs 'do not necessarily attend all classes,' special computers with huge type available for the visually challenged and laptops to help the dyslexic. Mixture of 'learnings' on hand, with support either on an individual basis or in class. Youth worker provides pupils support to deal with 'any difficulties' and 'help and support transition into the real world'. Inclusion and integration is the name of the game. Deaf, registered blind (striped pillars) and wheelchair friendly.

No particular bias academically. French and Latin only (the very occasional trip to Rome) in the language department, occasional odd lang clubs – depends on staff interest. English and maths essential for all at all grades. School has been working towards the new curriculum for five or six years and – unlike smaller establishments – embraces national 4 and 5 with enthusiasm.

Impressive list of Highers, including administration, business management, music and religious, moral and philosophical studies. Also available at Advanced Higher level, along with a host of other options. This is a school that caters well for the academic and the ordinary mortal. Pupils list five out of 23 subjects offered in order of preference, with a couple of reserves: a timetabling nightmare, but how sensible. Optional Easter holiday revision weeks at all levels.

Raft of computers – 40 in the computer department, a further 60 in the business education department, more in the jolly library, which has rather noisy air conditioning and also houses the careers department, plus a couple of laptop trolleys. The careers officer comes once a week and pupils can either just pop in or make an appointment for one-to-one consultation.

Games, options, the arts: PE timetabled and on offer to higher level – huge following. Games fields onsite, all the usual suspects – rugby popular, volleyball, basketball, hockey, netball, girls' and boys' footie teams and golf (one chap currently on the East Lothian fast track and more than 100 volunteered to pick rubbish at the 2013 Open at Muirfield this year). Badminton courts, climbing wall, fives court. School currently swims in the local Aubigny centre and does remarkably well in competitions – good support from the East Lothian sports development officers. Physical activities coordinator based in the school manages the huge (and we mean huge) outdoor education department. Outstanding athletes on the sports leadership skills work programme get time off to train.

Sixth formers have a team building weekend early in the year, and pupils not on exam leave have an activities week: from extreme sports to visits to Paris, the Alps, Italy and London, day trips to Edinburgh, the Dynamic Earth, spooky Mary King's Close or the Science Museum in Glasgow. Italy, Prague, Amsterdam on the cards, with seniors heading to New York in a couple of years and 30 off to China for a month. Home-based options include hospitality and fishing; digital films have rather fallen by the wayside. Myriads of trips abroad; Young Explorers' Trust et al, D of E and sixth year do an hour's community service each week.

Superb music in the old building. Musicians give two concerts annually, oodles of orchestras, choirs, and bands. Popular pipe band. Drama, panto at Christmas and well used dance studio. Stunning art department – good selection of paintings in view. Magical and inspirational fabric and hatting department, plus ceramics and all the rest. Home economics equally buzzing – the smell of newly baked bread was mouthwatering. School seriously into Europe – representatives went to the first Youth Eco-Parliament in Berlin. The Alice Burnett twinning scholarship is popular and school encourages languages via a language week (the whole school goes French, Italian or Latin for the week). Good links with France, Italy, Finland, Sweden and now Rwanda. School recently gained its second British Council International School Award, the first Scottish school so to do.

Citizenship course is 'part and parcel of the curriculum.' School council has a training day for all, with proper speakers and a grown up agenda. All do work experience at S4 (the school has a core list of placements if pupils can't find their own). Pupils have to write letters of application and go through the whole gamut – excellent practice (though Knox will step in if all else fails – and will even supply steel-capped boots, if that is what it needs). No charge, unlike some schools south of the border.

A few years back, the school won the BBC Schools' Question Time and pupils were involved in producing a televised programme. Good YE extends as far as 13-year-olds, who have moved on from decorating flowerpots to board games. Always tried out on the head first. Profits go to charity – school is keen on 'the big traditional charities' like UNICEF and locally they support the sick kids' hospital.

Background and atmosphere: The most recent in a line of education establishments in Haddington, dating back to 1379. The previous school, dedicated to John Knox at the end of the 19th century, still boasts a statue of him in the grounds and has been converted into sheltered housing for the elderly, some of whom may have come here in their youth. School moved to its present site in the 1930s – loads of additions since. The assembly hall, bigger before the recent additions, is currently 'ealth and safety-ed' at 500.

Blue new-build looks spectacular (cleverly organised so that the gym and sports hall will be available to locals), with access to the dining hall. Food here is good – healthy eating a priority (eat your heart out, Jamie Oliver), though to be honest, the cooked menu was a little drear; salad bar and sandwiches. Regular exposure to different cultures. Thai food for all, Dim Sum for a day.

Dress code for all – white shirts, school ties and black trousers or skirts, black jeans now an acceptable alternative. School blazers mandatory for S5 and S6, gold braiding for prefects.

Pastoral care and discipline: Twelve minutes each morning for all with their tutor, short messages and encouragement. Head is keen on mantra of wisdom, engagement, respect. Tutors emphasise responsibility and attainment – pupils should try to 'punch above their weight.' Strong on service, volunteering. Equally strong on discipline, with letters home to parents and detention the ultimate deterrent.

Pupil points system where pupils can gain or lose points and receive certificates once a certain level has been reached. Proactive anti-bullying strategy – zero tolerance. Zero tolerance too on the drugs front (not so sleepy Haddington has a fairly hefty problem). Sixth formers do a buddying routine with first year pupils, and keep a watchful eye for the dreaded b...y word.

Pupils and parents: Eclectic, though predominantly white middle class, like its catchment. A mixture of East Lothian farmers (usually well founded), the butcher, the baker, the candlestick maker, plus a home grown cache of third generation unemployed and a recent influx of Eastern European refugees. Certain number of recent refugees from the independent sector.

School conceals a 'long demographic' – real deprivation in some areas (school has funds to assist with emergency clothing, allowing those who absolutely can't afford it to join in activities week, with help from John Watson's Trust). Surprising nine per cent on free dinners. Around 80 to 90 in S5 and S6 qualify for the weekly £30 EMRA payment (means tested and quite complicated).

Supportive parent-school partnership and KASG (Knox Academy Support Group), an excellent and effective fundraising initiative. Parents' evening once a year for each year group.

Entrance: Automatic from King's Meadow Primary, St Mary's Roman Catholic Primary in Haddington, ditto Yester Primary in Gifford. The rest by placement requests (a lot of those).

Youngsters come for a couple of taster days the term before they are due to start. Head wishes there was some way of keeping cusp birthday children in primary for another year to help them develop with their peers.

Exit: Good follow through to S5, with much higher proportion staying on to S6 and university entrance (most choose Scotland). The odd gapper and the occasional Oxbridge candidate.

Of those who leave at 16, some go on to FE elsewhere, others into industry. According to Skills Scotland, East Lothian has the highest proportion of school leavers going directly into employment. School website advertises apprenticeships with hints on application processes (would suit a winter leaver).

Remarks: Excellent. No adverse comments from any of our contacts. So go for it, but make sure you are in the catchment area first, and watch it, the catchment area shrinketh.

La Sainte Union Catholic Secondary School

Linked school: LaSwap Sixth Form Consortium

Highgate Road, London, NW5 1RP

• Pupils: 1,200 girls, all day • Ages: 11–18 • RC • State

Tel: 020 7428 4600
Email: general@lsu.camden.sch.uk
Website: www.lasainteunion.org.uk

Headteacher: Since 2008, Mrs Maureen Williams (forties). Educated at a convent school in Hampshire, read English and medieval literature at Exeter University before taking her PGCE at Digby Stuart College, Roehampton. Taught English at St Joseph's College, Croydon and La Retraite Roman Catholic Girls' School in Lambeth, before taking over from long-serving head Sister Teresa and becoming the school's first lay principal, charged with a mission to gently modernise while maintaining the traditions of La Sainte Union. A calm and competent presence, no doubt the school's illustrious tradition remains in safe hands. Married to a senior probation officer, she enjoys running, walking and good food in her spare time.

Academic matters: One of Camden's top-performing schools. In 2013, 77 per cent of pupils achieved 5+ A*-C grades at GCSE including English and maths, with 34 per cent A*/A grades – a significant achievement for a school with no academic selection, and not reached by any fudging of the exam system. Pupils here take a demanding curriculum, with nine and half subjects kept going until GCSE, including a compulsory modern language, ICT and RE. Has specialist status in science and maths and 25 girls a year take all three sciences. Everyone, however, benefits from the science enrichment programme with a multitude of speakers from UCL and Imperial College (both of which offer work placements). 'Many of the girls come from backgrounds where there is limited experience of higher education,' says the head. 'The programme raises their aspirations.' Science results have improved significantly, though A level physicists are still a relative rarity. Setting in maths from year 7, broad banding in science, English and languages (French and Spanish) from year 8. The gifted and talented are led along at a brisk pace, taking some subjects early and adding to the basic diet with astronomy, geography, Italian and statistics. 'The school has some really clever girls,' said one mother, 'and they really nurture them.'

All abilities and interests, however, are well catered for, with young apprenticeships and diplomas increasingly popular. 'Not everyone has to be brilliant, but everyone has to achieve what they can,' commented a parent. 'They say, this is your goal, go for it – but not everyone's goal is the same.' About 70 per cent proceed to the sixth form, which forms part of the popular local consortium of four comprehensives, La Swap. A commendable 47 per cent A*/B grades at A level in 2013, though results post-16 are not quite as starry as at GCSE. 'We could raise the entry requirements,' says the head, 'and attract a higher ability cohort, but we know we can achieve these results without doing so.' Some 20 pupils have statements of special needs, including one with Down's; has wheelchair access by means of lifts. 'They try to help everyone,' commented one parent.

Games, options, the arts: Music is a particular strength ('Super,' says Ofsted) and is based here for the entire consortium sixth form. The standard of singing is unusually high with a 'talented' voice coach in residence. Whole school enthusiasm manifested in a 130-strong gospel choir (a Tour Choice, which performed recently in Barcelona Cathedral), a year 11 jazz band and a strong chamber choir. About a third of pupils take individual instrumental or voice tuition.

Definitely not a 9am-4pm place – 50 clubs operating, before, during and after lessons, everything from rowing and trampolining to keep fit and cookery. For hard-pressed working parents, the homework club, with supervised study before and after school, is a real boon – as it often is for girls. Thriving art department. The spacious walled grounds include a decent range of pitches, made full use of for two hours' compulsory weekly sports, including rounders, netball, athletics, basketball, trampolining, football and aerobics. 'There's no sitting on the side here,' says the head.

Background and atmosphere: One of a number of schools founded by the Sisters of La Sainte Union de Sacre Coeur, a teaching order founded in the early 19th century. The Camden school has now been in the borough for the past 150 years. Housed in a gracious Victorian building (with later additions), maintains the stately and soothing presence of the former convent boarding school it once was. The classrooms in the main block are light and high-ceilinged, the floors polished to a mirror sheen, the gardens to the rear are elegantly laid out with a small orchard and an ample stock of summer roses (sensibly, girls are required to keep to the path and admire from a distance).

Though now very much a modern comprehensive, with a broad intake of practising Catholics from across the capital, still has the purposeful air of calm you might expect from its history. The last teaching sister departed in 2010, but the tradition of the founding order and those of the Catholic faith are well maintained. 'We see our mission as promoting the values of the gospel and spirituality, preparing children for a life centred on Christ, celebrating the sacrament and providing links with other parishes and the international LSU community,' says the head. Has its own pretty chapel and pupils attend mass once weekly on a rota. Founder's Day is marked with mass – and ice cream.

Pupils wear the distinctive uniform of tartan kilts and white stockings with pride – and recently voted to retain this particular tradition. Strong sense of community, both local and international, including its sister school in Tanzania. Vocal school council (with elections for president and vice president) has its say on bullying and school food as well as uniform.

Pastoral care and discipline: Despite its affluent north London location on the lower slopes of Highgate, intake is anything but indulged – 65 per cent of pupils from low income families, 10 per cent on free school meals. The student population reflects the Catholic population of London – a third speak English as an additional language; a sizeable percentage are first and second generation immigrants from Nigeria, Ghana, the Congo, Poland, South America and southern Europe. Parents are active in their own churches and in the school. 'There is a real sense of community,' said one. No linked parish but many families attend nearby St Joseph's, Highgate and St Dominic's in Kentish Town.

Pupils and parents: 'This is an inner-city comp,' insists the head, though anyone dropping in from outside might be excused for thinking the term doesn't match the orderly space within. Behaviour is generally exemplary but, for those who stray, bad marks and detentions, as well as fixed-term exclusions. Girls with difficulties are certainly not left to fend for themselves. 'Some girls are from families with real problems and they would rather be at school on weekends and holidays than at home,' says one mother. 'This is a safe place to be.' Offers both parental support and additional help with behaviour management and conflict resolution. Teaches about the temptations of drugs and alcohol but drugs are not a significant issue, at least on

site. Problems mainly concern friendship disputes that change social boundaries. Good induction day in year 7 brings pupils from disparate locations and homes together. 'My daughter has really blossomed here,' says one happy parent.

Entrance: 180 girls admitted to the heavily oversubscribed year 7, mainly from Catholic primary schools. No selection on ability but must be practising Catholics baptised in the first year, then able to demonstrate regular church attendance for at least three years. Pupils arrive from seven boroughs – from Walthamstow to Barnet – as distance is measured by public transport rather than metres from the gates. Eighteen places offered on musical aptitude, with an objective test and a small audition. Entry to La Swap sixth form requires a minimum two Bs and three Cs for A level. All girls who enter between 11-16 base themselves at the school for the sixth form.

Exit: About a fifth to Russell Group universities, with UCL a favourite option. Popular subjects include English, history, business studies and art foundation. Medics get specialist coaching for BMAT tests. One or two to Oxbridge each year, including medicine.

Money matters: Despite the fact that two-thirds of parents here are on a joint family income of £30,000 or less, most manage the £100 a year voluntary contribution. 'Parents are very generous' and very active, constantly raising funds with second-hand uniform sales etc. 'This is not a rich school,' said one, 'but the school and parents make every effort to give the girls the opportunities that others might take as a given.'

Remarks: A calm and orderly universe, demanding (and getting) high standards of achievement from girls who might not always be expected to reach this high.

The Lady Eleanor Holles School

Linked school: The Lady Eleanor Holles School, Junior Department

Hanworth Road, Hampton, TW12 3HF

• Pupils: 880 girls; all day (690 in the senior department; 190 in the junior department) • Ages: 7-18 • C of E • Fees: £13,050–£16,200 pa • Independent

Tel: 020 8979 1601
Email: office@lehs.org.uk
Website: www.lehs.org.uk

Headmistress: Since 2004, Mrs Gillian Low MA Oxon PGCE Cantab (mid fifties). An alumna of North London Collegiate School, she read English at Somerville, then dipped her toes into corporate management before wisely turning to teaching. She began with EFL in Italy – well, you would, wouldn't you? She came to Lady Eleanor Holles following six-year tenure as head of Francis Holland, Clarence Gate, prior to which she had been deputy at Godolphin and Latymer. An impressive and tailor-made run-up for her current role. Mrs Low is an ISI team inspector, has been a governor of three schools and is a past president of the GSA. She has two daughters and a son, all in their twenties. She has now seen an entire cohort of girls through the senior school and, in 2011, presided over the 300th anniversary of the school's foundation. She is definitely the head you want to have charge of your daughter. Sensible, of sound and confident judgement, easy to talk to and plainly a real human being. With the aid of a 'rigorous and passionate' staff, she runs an outstanding school with the commitment and professionalism it requires. Seen by parents as 'a great promoter of the school' and as 'leading from the front,' she inherited a special place and, when the time comes, will leave it stronger and brighter. A top head.

Retiring in July 2014.

Academic matters: Few do education better and it's done via thrilling, not drilling. Outstanding results by any standards – ranked 9th in the Financial Times A level table in 2012 and seldom slips much below that. Committed to A levels rather than the IB or Pre-U, the school ups its academic offering at the top end via the AQA Bacc and the Extended Project Qualification, plus an enrichment programme. Maths the most popular A level. Relatively few take modern languages despite exemplary results – German flourishes here as nowhere else we know. Good range of new sixth form subjects – eg classical civilization, psychology and economics (in which virtually all get A*/A). 2013 saw 83 per cent of subjects taken gaining A*-B. GCSEs similarly outstanding – 95 per cent A*/A with less than one per cent below a B grade. Grown-up attitude to all subject areas exemplified by the regular Focus newsletters published by the school – excellence aimed for across the board. A culture of enquiry and exploration fostered throughout.

Few with more than mild learning difficulties here, though SEN support is embedded and SENCo is abetted by a specialist who's in school four days a week. One-to-one when needed and lots of support. Seriously good school to consider if you have mobility problems or are wheelchair-bound – flattish site, lifts and wide corridors, plus can-do approach.

Games, options, the arts: Legendary for sports and the facilities here are second to none for a girls' day school. Some parents choose the school on the strength of the sports – academics, what's that? Lacrosse the main winter game and played to win – which they do. We heard about the first lax team's match against the first rugby team from Hampton – sounds a hoot. Rowing also a speciality – a welcome rarity in a girls' school. Sports tours – to Barbados and America in summer 2012. We visited at a time when the arts were surviving in annexes and temporary accommodation, pending the unveiling of a splendid new performing arts building with theatre and purpose-built or cleverly converted space for art, drama and music opened in 2013. This will mean the rehoming of sixth form commonrooms and other amenities and will involve a considerable – though highly desirable – upgrading all round. Drama here is seen as 'brilliant' even with the current facilities, music is exceptional – The Holles Singers were BBC Youth Choir of the Year in 2010. We enjoyed the art we saw – particularly the ceramics – although we felt that far more of it could be displayed around the school. Also lively textiles, but only to GCSE. The extra-curricular life of the school is exceptional – especially so for a day school. Parents enthuse – 'there are so many opportunities – a huge amount going on all the time'.

Background and atmosphere: The school was established in 1711 under the will of Lady Eleanor Holles, daughter of John Holles, 2nd Earl of Clare. This makes it one of the oldest girls' schools in the country. It began life in the Cripplegate Ward of the City of London, then moved to other premises in the City till 1878, thence to Mare Street in Hackney (that building now houses the London College of Fashion). The current school, purpose-built and designed in the shape of an E, opened in 1937. Such a long history is scarcely uncommon in many of our great public schools but rare in girls' schools. A palpable pride underpins the place – made more palpable by the great 300th anniversary celebrations of late 2011. The staffroom has seen many distinguished names. They include Pauline Cox, former head of Tiffin Girls', Margaret Hustler, former head of Harrogate Ladies' College, Cynthia Hall, current head of Wycombe Abbey, and Frances King, current head of Roedean, who all taught here.

Very long, horizontal, featureless and functional, the two-storey main building doesn't delight the eye but then again, it doesn't offend it either. Inside, the corridors are wide, the rooms are light and everywhere is well-kept. The place is somewhat hospital-like with its lengthy corridors and polished wood floors. The pupils insist though that 'the thing that brings it alive is the girls' – which is fair enough. Excellent sixth form centre features small teaching rooms – ideal for a history seminar or session on poetic form. The sixth form library somehow exemplifies the whole. It's light, overlooks the pitches, is exceptionally well-stocked and has neat tables for study and rows of PCs. But while the stark white walls (one, admittedly, temporary at the time of our visit) allow for no distraction, it's pretty Spartan and cries out for more display. Big main library, again well-stocked, especially with classic and modern fiction.

Focused and purposeful atmosphere. Girls are well-turned out in grey uniforms and the sixth formers look fresh and neat in casual dress. A sense of order pervades throughout, including the monitoring and assessment of pupils' progress. Parents praise the ethos of the place. 'it's cool to be clever and cool to be good at sport,' said one, while others told us: 'it's a real all-round school. You've got to be bright to get in. They don't mince their words and you've got to keep up. They expect a lot from the girls from an early stage – they have to take responsibility for themselves. If you don't turn up for a practice, you don't stay on the team'. Strong links with Hampton School – the boys' school just across the playing fields. They share a boathouse, coach service and drama. Girls take a typically pragmatic attitude – 'it's very helpful in debating – it makes a huge difference having to do it in front of boys as well,' they said.

Pastoral care and discipline: House system was introduced in 2008 and is going great guns. 'I was surprised,' says head, 'by how quickly it got into the routine of the school. It expands the range of extra-curricular activities and the opportunities for leadership and taking responsibility'. The girls themselves enjoy getting to know older and younger pupils and the houses make for greater cohesion and community. This is continued through outreach work and the increasing involvement of alumnae. Much praise for the pastoral care system – a clear structure and everyone knows who to go to. All heads of year have their own offices. Good system of buddying, and a feeling that no transgressors would get away with it for long. No noteworthy sins of the drink/drugs/fags kind and minor bullying problems are dealt with swiftly. A culture of openness means that it's all right to tell someone if you're not happy. Academic monitoring also praised. 'They've always recognised that my daughter has potential – the teachers are patient, encouraging and they've helped her to reach the point of realising just how well she can do,' one parent told us. Everyone likes the food – a huge range of options.

Pupils and parents: From a wide area – Acton to Woking, and all points in between. Families are mostly professional and clever and increasingly ethnically diverse. Lots of parents have boys at Hampton – a good mix. The common denominator is a valuing of what this school offers.

Entrance: Around a third come up from junior department, the rest from schools like Newland House, Twickenham Prep, The Study, Bute House, Holy Cross Prep, Kew College. Girls come from as many as 40 different schools, including a wide range of primary schools. Four to five applicants for each place. Tests in maths, English, non-verbal reasoning and a general paper. School also sets its own exams for sixth form applicants. No GCSE hurdle here. 'We trust our judgment,' says staff, who look at exams, interviews and reports from current schools. Grateful parents of girls who came through 11+ selection are impressed by the process. 'It was by far the most individual interview system,' one told us. 'It was slick and in 20 minutes they seemed to have learned everything about her'.

Exit: Relatively narrow range of universities, perhaps resulting from word of mouth and established traditions. Over recent years, on average, 80 per cent to Russell Group universities. Destinations include Oxbridge (14 in 2013), Durham, Bristol and London. A couple to Trinity College Dublin and the USA. No limits to what they study – good courses in everything. Notable old girls include Lynn Barber, Charlotte Attenborough, Carola Hicks, Annie Nightingale, Saskia Reeves, Jay Hunt and Gail (University Challenge) Trimble.

Money matters: Drive underway to increase the number and value of bursaries. Means-tested and reviewed annually. Academic scholarships worth up to 10 per cent of fees at 11+ and sixth form level. Arts scholarships up to 10 per cent, plus free instrumental tuition.

Remarks: 'It's been just what we hoped for,' one mother told us, while an imminent leaver sighed happily, 'I've enjoyed every day'.

Lady Lumley's School

Swainsea Lane, Pickering, YO18 8NG

• Pupils: 1,005 boys and girls • Ages: 11–19 • Non-denom • State

Tel: 01751 472846
Email: admin@ladylumleys.net
Website: www.ladylumleys.n-yorks.sch.uk

Headteacher: Since 2007, Mr Richard Bramley. Former deputy head at Chelmsford County High School and recently advisory teacher in Islington, North London. Wife also teaches. Daughter and son in sixth forms in Chelmsford. Loves the school and enjoys every minute of his headship. Believes that everyone in the school community can be inspired with a love of learning and, by being so, maximise his or her life chances. Pupils say, 'He's lovely!'

Academic matters: Sound GCSE and A level performances; 75 per cent A*-C grades at GCSE in 2013 and 43 per cent of A level grades A*/B. No prima donna departments here – school claims its strength is quality of teaching across the whole curriculum, especially at Key Stage 4, and Ofsted largely backs that up. Strongest performances consistently in the basics – English, maths and science. Able linguists given the option of taking GCSE French a year early, with German to follow in year two. Early results impressive.

Also does well by less academic pupils – 15 and 16 year olds can take a double GCSE in engineering, studying partly off-site with engineering firms. Others opt for GCSE health and social care, drawing on links with GPs and hospitals – would-be paramedics, chiropodists etc please note. Vocational path can continue into sixth form with packages including modern apprenticeships. Students encouraged to pick and mix, customising education to boost chances of achieving career goals. Strong, award-winning careers education and guidance, and work experience programmes.

Games, options, the arts: A specialist sports college with extensive sports facilities in a glorious rural setting. New fitness suite and floodlit all-weather pitch used by pupils and local sports clubs with benefits to both. Sports hall, gym, good athletics facilities, all helping to encourage all-round sporting achievements. Drama taught in every year group and those with a musical interest can join the orchestras and choirs. All the usual extra-curricular clubs and societies too, but pupils have to risk indigestion to join. One downside of a sprawling catchment area is that buses whisk pupils away at the final bell – makes for busy lunchtimes, with sports practices, science clubs, revision workshops and even dreaded detentions all competing with the sarnies.

Background and atmosphere: Set on the edge of the market town of Pickering, a mix of every architectural style over five decades. Built in the fifties, the older buildings are offset by a newish £1m+ administration block, sixth form and community learning centre, with a conference centre for use by school and community. Besides, who couldn't live with a bit of dodgy 50s architecture, when the view is of sweeping school grounds framed by countryside, with even the puff of an old steam railway in the distance? Good disabled access, including lifts.

Biggest surprise? Classroom doors are left open during lessons and all you can hear in the corridors is the teacher's voice. Cloakrooms have been replaced with lockers with a key for pupils, which have been very successful. Even the morning rush into school is orderly. No school-run congestion because of the buses and an uncanny absence of the teenage sillies.

Pastoral care and discipline: A no-nonsense school which sets high standards and expects pupils to meet them. 'It irons out problems before they escalate,' said one parent, which seems, to use a third metaphor, to hit the nail on the head. Unacceptable behaviour is dealt with quickly and efficiently. Students are given 'cool off' time, which can include that most excruciating of all punishments – writing a letter of apology.

School policy to keep children busy, in and out of lessons, and 'treat them like human beings', giving them the courtesy of decent catering, clean toilets and graffiti-free walls. Strong on caring and community, and rolls up its sleeves to practise what it preaches. School still collects food to make into harvest festival parcels and gets pupils to deliver them to nominated neighbours over many miles – one of a dying breed, we suspect.

Pastoral care boosted considerably by Lady Lumley's Education Foundation, named after its founder, an Elizabethan landowner. Her bequests to the school mean that it can still spend upwards of £20,000 a year on pupil support, from subsidising trips to encouraging pupils' projects. A very nice carrot indeed.

Pupils and parents: A true comprehensive, drawing from an area of affluent professionals and farming communities – lots of the Range Rover set, but also its fair share of children from disadvantaged homes. Good rapport with parents, who receive a report in every term of every year. Pupils' progress tightly monitored with regular tutorials – no hiding place here. Parents talk of a happy school and are pleased with children's achievements.

Entrance: Living in the catchment area is the only way to be sure of a place. A whopping 22 per cent of pupils come from further afield after winning appeals, but if your heart's set on Lady Lumley's, you might have to move house to get in – people do.

Exit: Almost 60 per cent of pupils stay on into the sixth form, expected to increase as vocational courses expand. Around 85 per cent of sixth formers go to university. One to Cambridge in 2012.

Remarks: A solid school which feels part of the community it serves. Recent letter from newly qualified graduate thanks school for giving out-of-class tuition to him and others who needed that extra push: 'It has made all the difference to my future. You made me feel I was somebody and I could achieve my goals,' he writes. Says it all.

Lady Margaret School

Parson's Green, London, SW6 4UN

• Pupils: 725 girls; all day • Ages: 11–18 • C of E • State

Tel: 020 7736 7138
Email: admin@ladymargaret.lbhf.sch.uk
Website: www.ladymargaret.lbhf.sch.uk

Headteacher: Since 2006, Mrs Sally Whyte BA French and Russian, PGCE NPQH. Formerly deputy head at Dr Challoner's High School in Buckinghamshire and assistant principal at Exmouth Community College in Devon. A charming, cheery lady who undoubtedly has the school firmly under control and clear plans for the future – Ofsted praised the 'exceptional capacity of the recently formed senior leadership team'. 'This is a lovely school to be head of,' she says.

Academic matters: Traditional, rigorous teaching produces invariably good results (English was rated outstanding by a recent Ofsted subject inspection) – 'We're now fully staffed with excellent teachers'. Everyone – except the few girls with statements of special educational needs – takes a foreign language to GCSE and RE is also compulsory. In 2013, 91 per cent of girls got 5+ A*-C grades including maths and English; 48 per cent of grades were A*/A. English literature, history, mathematics, biology, chemistry are the most popular A level subjects. Art and design subjects also have a very strong showing. The sixth form is expanding with a new state-of-the-art building which has allowed the introduction of new subjects at A level, including economics, psychology and music technology. In 2013, 41 per cent A*/A grades and 71 per cent A*/B grades at A level.

Missed an 'outstanding' rating in the latest Ofsted inspection because of variable progress between subjects and year groups – the most and least able have tended to make the best progress. The head, however, is beefing up the systematic monitoring of each girl's academic progress so no-one should be overlooked in future. 'They add tremendous value in a lot of cases,' said a parent, 'as long as the girl is not resistant to having value added.'

The girls with SEN – mainly dyslexia – are well looked after, with excellent targeted support. Very few with behavioural difficulties – they would be likely to struggle in the traditional, closely-regulated environment. 'Parents tend to realise that if their daughter's not going to be able to cope here, it's not right for her to come.'

Games, options, the arts: Art and textile design are popular and successful A level subjects, with a high proportion of A grades, and quite a few pupils go on to art college. Plenty of impressive art on display. Music 'permeates the whole of the school', and large numbers learn instruments. Plenty of ensembles and choirs – a musical production such as Annie or Oliver! every other year. Inter-house music, debating and drama competitions. But performance space is limited – no drama studio or theatre and no drama GCSE or A level.

Not ideal for the sports-mad child – facilities on-site are limited to some tennis/netball courts and a gym (yoga, basketball and dance amongst activities on offer), though older girls use the local sports facilities. Netball, rounders and football matches – 'We play and achieve well'. Amazingly, 15 girls took GCSE PE in 2012 and four took it at A level.

Background and atmosphere: Has its origins in Whitelands College School, founded in 1842. In 1917, when Whitelands was threatened with closure, the Second Mistress, Miss Enid Moberly Bell, and other school staff 'rescued' a large number of pupils, who joined the new Lady Margaret School, named after Lady Margaret Beaufort, mother of Henry VII, founder of St John's and Christ's Colleges, Cambridge.

The school is in three listed Georgian houses facing leafy Parsons Green, with a gym, hall, impressive technology block, classrooms and landscaped garden beyond. A £6 million programme to expand school to accommodate four-form entry now underway and will include new classrooms, larger dining facilities, improved accessibility etc.

Very strong sense of community, happy atmosphere, tightly regulated; parents comment that it has the feel of an old-fashioned girls' grammar school.

Pastoral care and discipline: A traditional school with a strong Christian ethos and pastoral imperative that includes taking on girls with health and social problems. A parent commented, 'They have an impressive record of nurturing.' Strict about uniform, homework and manners, and everyone takes part in collective worship in the mornings, 'Though the Muslim and Jewish girls I know feel extremely valued,' said a parent. A very few short term exclusions, virtually none permanent. 'The vast majority come here wanting to work, get exam results and have fun.' The PHSE programme covers careers, study skills, citizenship, sex, drugs, alcohol etc.

Pupils and parents: The intake reflects the surroundings of this very leafy part of south west London. The revised entrance system has changed the make-up of the school. 'But there's still a critical mass of well-supported, compliant girls,' said a parent. Incredibly committed parent body, plenty of whom could have afforded to go private. Some impressive fund-raising goes on – the latest summer fair day raised some £20,000. Pupils strongly supportive of each other, confident, lively. OGs: Janet Street Porter, Jill Saward, rape law reform campaigner.

Entrance: Sixty-seven places (called foundation places) are reserved for girls who have been to a C of E church on a regular basis. The other 53 are open places. The main criterion is walking distance to the school. Everyone takes a maths and English banding test and is placed in band 1 (top 25 per cent), band 2 (middle 50 per cent) or band 3 (lowest 25 per cent), with places allocated in those proportions. A few places go to those with an SEN statement and looked after children. Very oversubscribed – over 500 applicants each year for the 90 places. NB You must complete and return both the local authority common application form and the school additional information form.

Those hoping to go through to the sixth form must have at least six A*-C grades at GCSE, including B grades in the chosen A level subjects; mathematics, languages and sciences need A grades. An increasing number of girls join the sixth form from other schools.

Exit: A few don't make the grade to go through to the sixth form and some go off for a wider range of courses – 'We offer quality but not quantity'. Nearly all sixth form leavers go on to university, over 40 per cent to the élite establishments over the past five years (fourth comprehensive in the country on this basis), including five to ten a year to Oxbridge.

Remarks: Small, traditional, friendly church school with high standards and family atmosphere in a quiet green setting. The social mix is changing but, in this part of London, it will always attract a high proportion of bright, hard-working girls, and the head is not letting the school rest on its laurels.

Lancaster Girls' Grammar School

Regent Street, Lancaster, LA1 1SF

• Pupils: 925 girls; all day • Ages: 11–18 • Non-denom • State

Tel: 01524 581661
Email: lggs@lggs.lancs.sch.uk
Website: www.lggs.org.uk

Headteacher: Since September 2007, Mrs Jackie Cahalin BA (forties), a historian, three previous years as deputy head at LGGS, only the ninth head in the school's 100+ year history. A friendly, calm yet authoritative presence, she clearly enjoys the company of the girls, and this appears to be reciprocated.

Academic matters: Very sound – one of the top 20 schools nationally, aspirations to be in the top 10. Tremendous results at GCSE (75 per cent A*/A grades in 2013). A levels very impressive too (75 per cent A*/B grades and 47 per cent A*/A grades in 2013). Strong languages (French, German, Spanish), has language college status and more recently international school status awarded by the British Council. Latin before school – 'dawn Latin' – is over-subscribed.

Large numbers of girls opt for sciences in the sixth form, skill and interest level being strengthened by studying three separate sciences at GCSE. Maths is the most popular A level subject. Marked technology emphasis (specialist status); sponsorship and collaborative projects including Arkwright scholarships; enviable technology and IT teaching provision. High computer count, interactive whiteboards everywhere ('Lots more than the boys' school,' say the girls). Able staff (about one third men), age profile creeping upwards – they don't want to leave, and you can see why.

Games, options, the arts: By their own admission, not the best sporting facilities, essentially due to lack of space. Sports fields five to 10 minutes away from school. Astroturf pitch and new fitness suite and dance studio. Dance flourishing, with many clubs run by the girls themselves and after-school GCSE dance classes. Sport is important and keenly played, especially hockey and running (representative successes). Much variety beyond these, including rugby, fencing and swimming. Old-fashioned gym brought up to date by the addition of an immensely popular Wii fit screen. Music strong and multi-form, house music competitions one of the girls' favourite annual events. Joint ventures in music with boys' school; also drama and public speaking. Largest centre in the area for D of E. Strong international links include a link school in India and World Challenge to Madagascar. Plenty of European overseas trips and exchanges and representation at science fairs in South East Asia.

Background and atmosphere: Founded 100 years ago on central site, with more modern additions and surrounded by private houses. Very limited parking and limited outdoor space for play or socialising. However, site restrictions have brought about some inspired and resourceful use of space, as buildings are updated and transformed according to the changing needs of the school. Newer additions include impressive technology, cooking and IT areas, and a brand new sixth form centre with large study area.

Girls appear very academically focused – they have earned their place here and tell us they are 'eager to learn and like the fact that they don't have to wait for others to catch up'. Busy girls, hardly a moment when they are not occupied, thriving on the many challenges and opportunities. Hint of academic snobbery from a few – a little dismissive of 'less academic' subjects at A level; however 'You can be yourself here,' they say, and appear happy in that. The head concurs – 'Girls are braver in lessons in an all girls' school and it's OK to do your homework and to take on leadership roles.' Girls genuinely feel they have a voice on the school council and have been actively involved in uniform updates. Has a healthy eating award and food is 'pretty good', with plenty of choice for all. Was grant maintained, now has academy status, which allows a degree of control over its destiny, including (vitally) academic selection.

Pastoral care and discipline: Usual form tutor system, backed up by heads of key stages, works well. Relaxed but far from lax – great emphasis on trust, self-discipline and good old-fashioned standards of behaviour; make-up, nail varnish, piercings and hair colour all forbidden – the girls know and, for the most part, respect code.

Pupils and parents: Straightforward girls who are proud to be here and keen to get on and to do their bit for society. They want to do well and make their mark on the world, and it's not hard to believe that they will. Wide range of parental backgrounds, not surprising in middle-sized county town. Parents rightly assume high academic standards but also value the 'what else?' factor – year 7 parent says her daughter settled easily and well, despite friends going elsewhere, thanks to good pastoral care on transition from primary school. Another parent, with three daughters through the school, places huge value on the 'real-life perspective' of the place provided by numerous opportunities to interact with students both from the local boys' school and overseas, via inter-cultural exchanges.

Entrance: Four-form entry and heavily oversubscribed at 11+. Admission is 'according to ability and aptitude' – tests in maths, English and VR. Entrance exam in September and results come fairly speedily to aid the admin selection process. First chance goes to inhabitants of Lancaster and District (map available from school), then residual places to families living outside these. If at first you don't succeed, try again later – up to one third of post-GCSE year group has entered from other schools, with only a minimum qualification of five or more GCSEs at B and above; this is a huge attraction – draws from local maintained schools and the independent sector.

Exit: Very few leave after GCSE, but up to 100 join the sixth form. Almost all go on to higher education – seven students to Oxbridge and 10 to medical school in 2013.

Remarks: Awarded 'outstanding' in four consecutive inspection reports, a confident, sought-after and successful state grammar school. A place where, despite (because of?) the smallish county town background, girls are encouraged to look outwards as well as inwards, resulting in refreshingly open-minded, ambitious and worldly-wise young women.

Lancaster Royal Grammar School

East Road, Lancaster, LA1 3EF

• Pupils: 1,050 boys (including 50 full boarders and 115 weekly boarders) • Ages: 11–18 • Christian foundation • Fees: Boarding £9,000– £9,900 pa; Day-free • State

Tel: 01524 580600
Email: sknight@lrgs.org.uk
Website: www.lrgs.org.uk

Headmaster: Since September 2012, Dr Christopher Pyle MA (Cantab) PhD (Cantab) NPQH (forty), previously a deputy head of the Perse School, Cambridge, and before that their head of geography. Very much a Cambridge man: did his geography degree and PhD there. Particularly interested in glaciers, hydrology and climate change. Briefly a manager at Anglian Water before taking up teaching. Married to Sally, a maths teacher, with three young sons.

A keen runner, he has also completed the Devizes to Westminster canoe race for charity, and is a fan of the Lakeland fells. He has been churchwarden and PCC member of a large Anglican church.

Academic matters: Superb tradition – regularly near top of table for state grammars, strong value-added results. Aiming high taken for granted, as is the graft to support it. In 2013, nearly 50 per cent of A level grades A*/A; nearly 63 per cent of GCSE grades A*/A. Very much the traditional grammar school ethos, challenging boys to 'fulfil their potential in a competitive environment'. Narrow ability range, so no setting (except maths and French) up to GCSE; class size averages 28. Maths outstanding, stronger classics than in most independents. All do technology up to GCSE – school has technology, languages, mathematics and computing specialisms. Sciences taught separately up to GCSE and all three are popular sixth form options. Most pupils do four A levels, a third manage five, general studies taken as read, literally, as it's not taught, but the school teaches an enriching life course, developed internally but partly lifted from the IB, which can include anything from leadership to conversational Italian to the lyrics of Bob Dylan. Special needs (eg dyslexia, Asperger's) looked after in-house. The especially gifted are stretched by further enhancement schemes and wide-ranging extra-curricular provision.

Games, options, the arts: Team games rather than individual sports dominate here. Strong rugby and cricket, taken seriously – they beat most independents. Frequent tours – Hong Kong, Australia, Japan, Barbados and sometimes High Wycombe. An impressive list of other sports, plenty of outdoor pursuits in nearby Lake District and rowing on the Lune leading to some successful pairs at Henley. Much encouragement to join in – couch potatoes don't seem to figure. Music popular, regular drama productions (often with sister school in Lancaster). Very good art and design results.

Background and atmosphere: An ancient foundation, in existence by 1235 and endowed in 1472. Took the decision to become an academy in 2011, to provide greater autonomy. Queen Victoria donated £100, hence its 'Royal' tag – and the school still receives the same amount (sadly not index-linked) annually from the Duchy. Buildings gather around a crossroads on hilly East Road, 'possibly the most academic crossroads in the northern hemisphere' – PE to biology means crossing two roads but doesn't worry the boys and 20mph speed limits are enforced. Mixture of Victorian houses and purpose-built blocks, leading to impressive newer additions (science and business/design centres, new boarding houses). Parking is tricky but most walk or use public transport.

Though it in most ways resembles its independent competitors, it differs in that not much money to do the things that the private sector usually takes for granted. It doesn't matter, of course, since the school concentrates on the important transaction of the classroom, but it does mean the place can look a touch untidy at the edges. Real sense of history and tradition about the place: 'Juniors love wearing blazer and tie,' says Mr Jarman. Boys scuttle purposefully between classrooms that range from slightly tired-looking to smartly refurbished. Older parents will be reminded of the grammar school of their youth – 'no-nonsense, no-frills,' says one successful and grateful old boy. An ambitious and exciting 50-year master plan is attracting support from old boys – a real drive here that leaves you in no doubt that it will happen.

Boarding gives the school an edge and identity and attractive new facilities have understandably brought a resurgence of interest. Younger boys have a splendid boarding house with views to die for and a back garden of immaculate cricket pitches. Dorms are cheery, comfortable and well-furnished, with sitting rooms and homely kitchens for tea and toast after school. Seniors are housed in a very attractive and well-designed conference centre-style building adjoining a Victorian villa, with comfortable ensuite single studies alongside relaxed sitting rooms and a modern kitchen, allowing the boys both privacy and companionship as and when required.

Pastoral care and discipline: Boys respond to the no-nonsense direct approach of staff in a school that thoroughly understands them. The school looks to recruit 'schoolmasters' (of either sex) rather than 'teachers'. Heard the saying, 'They don't make them like that any more'? Well, they do here, apparently. Thorough care systems for both boarding and day work well – pastoral staff heavily committed to pupils' welfare and relations between boys and teachers admired by parents and inspectors. High personal standards expected. Not much evidence of real wickedness; school suspends for possession and would expel for dealing – and the boys know it.

Pupils and parents: Lancaster is a city with a small town feel – boys come from every walk of life and are a very genuine mix. Still 'the school on the hill' to some, yet no wish for this to become a middle class enclave – rather it is open to any boy, from any street, who can cope with living and working alongside a future Oxbridge don. Local day boys given preference; about 40 places go to those further afield. Boarders come from all over but must be a UK subject or have an EU passport and a UK guardian. Boys and parents very proud of school and its regional standing. One parent – 'No child of mine would ever go to a boarding school' – absolutely delighted to see her son thriving both academically and relishing life as a boarder also. Parents are easily persuaded to contribute regularly to the development programme – not a burden, given free day education and bargain boarding fees. Old boys include Prof T Hugh Pennington, microbiologist; Kevin Roberts, CEO Worldwide Saatchi and Saatchi; Jason Queally, Olympic cycling champion; Brigadier Alex Birtwistle, foot and mouth star; Tom Sutcliffe, journalist and Sir Richard Owen (dinosaur man).

Entrance: By oversubscribed competitive exam at 11 (English/maths/reasoning). Three strands of entry: local day, regional day, boarding. Boarders considered separately but all 'must be of an aptitude and ability suited to an academic curriculum'. All leave at 16 and then reapply for sixth form places: 'Tell us why we should give you a place here' – great practice for university UCAS or even the real world. Regularly increasing intake at 16 and growing interest from independents for sixth form places – grab a boarding place whilst you still can.

Exit: A few leave after GCSE; vast majority to good universities, mainly in the Midlands and North, eg Durham, Edinburgh, Manchester, St Andrew's, Warwick and York, though some dipping a toe into southern universities such as Imperial. In 2013, 16 to Oxbridge.

Remarks: Buoyant, selective grammar school with big reputation in the region; chiefly a day school but also offers excellent boarding provision. Has managed to retain marked degree of independence within maintained system, offering a curriculum above and beyond the norm, including classics – 'If we don't offer it, which state school will?' says the school. A wide range of extra-curricular activities which, according to a parent, 'suit a boy's needs extremely well'. Unashamedly academic but takes all-round education seriously and delivers.

Lancing College

Linked school: Lancing College Preparatory School

Lancing, West Sussex, BN15 0RW

- Pupils: 545 (345 boys, 200 girls); 325 boarders • Ages: 13–18
- C of E • Fees: Day £21,780; Boarding £31,020 pa • Independent

Tel: 01273 452213
Email: admissions@lancing.org.uk
Website: www.lancingcollege.co.uk

Headmaster: Since 2006, Mr Jonathan Gillespie, read languages at Cambridge, taught languages at Highgate school; head of modern languages, then housemaster at Fettes College. Feels experience as head of department and housemaster means he knows what he is managing from bottom up, which is helpful. Married to Caroline, former civil servant, now part-time website administrator and full-time mother and taxi driver to their two sons. Parents say they seem to attend everything ('exhausting to think about,' said one parent feelingly), and that he is a strong presence.

Relishes being head of an independent school – means he can make the right decisions for his pupils. Says Lancing is about helping pupils become who they want to be.

Moving on in September 2014 to head St Albans School.

Academic matters: Very good, consistent performance at GCSE and A level: 54 per cent A*/A grades at GCSE in 2013; at A level, 53 per cent A*/A grades, 78 per cent A*/B: great results from a virtually mixed ability school. Not top grades at all costs: pupils are set a target appropriate to them, and there is celebration if the target is met; whether that target be a C or A*. 'Not an exam factory, so doesn't attract those sort of parents,' says the head, and one parent commented that they opted for Lancing over a more academically pressurising competitor. Tremendous value added at Lancing – pupils achieve exam grades they wouldn't have dreamed of.

Core subjects are always streamed, others usually so (where numbers allow). Class sizes around 18 in years 9-11, down to a maximum of 15 in the sixth form. Maths is outstanding, popular with pupils and excellent results – a triple maths A level student enthused about the teaching, and useful weekly drop in sessions. Pupils give good reports of history too. Super science labs, remodelled in last few years, although science results not outstanding. Great well-stocked library with mezzanine level of computers. There are plenty of languages on offer: French, German, Spanish, Italian, Greek, Latin – pupils start with two languages in year 9, and must continue with one until GCSE. German and Chinese strong. A jolly year 9 German class showed off their iPads (now standard issue), which come into their own when teaching languages: teachers can set oral homework, and iPads will correct pronunciation; no more lost homework since pupils are emailed assignments.

Two reports during each term with grades for each subject, and a full written report at the end of term. Early remedial action if someone is falling behind – 'no one falls through the net'. An extremely busy learning support coordinator supports around 80 pupils with mild to moderate learning difficulties (mostly mild dyslexia), of whom 35 require continuous one-to-one support (at extra cost); full-time learning support teacher just joined. Not much in-class support.

Games, options, the arts: School week covers six days, so four afternoon sessions for options – pupils here like to keep very busy. One afternoon a week students choose between CCF or community service. Drama is popular, even with non-actors – some of the academic hard core work backstage for light relief.

Theatre seats 180, retractable seating means it's possible to play in the round, and make an orchestra pit in part of the old swimming pool on which the theatre was built. Drama GCSE, but not enough takers for A level. About 15 productions a year – modern punk Romeo and Juliet about to get under way. Also an open air theatre.

Plenty of games sessions (down to twice a week for sixth formers), with lots of choice – focus on football, hockey, netball, cricket and tennis, but lots of other options, even for the not keen – 'I get by on yoga,' said one. One boy said he came to Lancing because it's a football school – other public schools generally favour rugby. Extensive playing fields, tennis courts, Astroturf pitch and swimming pool. Plans for a super new sports centre – planning permission granted, and fundraising making good progress. And for those who love animals, farm is a sports/activities option – a sport hater/animal lover could exist blissfully at Lancing. The farm has really developed in the last couple of years, and includes rare pigs, alpacas, lamas, lots of cuddly smalls and sheep – kids can get permission to stay out late and help with lambing. Meat from the farm has started feeding the school this year, and they are experimenting with a market garden with the aim of supplying veg too.

The music department is housed in standard 60s fare, but is staffed by teachers full of love for their subject and incredibly enthusiastic about sharing that love with pupils. Their scruffy studies overflow with sheet music; one, curiously, with a child's road layout mat on the floor and a dog in the corner – who's apparently won over many recruits to music. 'They are mad,' said one pupil kindly, 'but we have a great time.' Plenty of practice rooms, which only get too busy at Associated Board exam times. Drum kit handy for those who want to pop in for a jam. Glorious choir (lovely CD – Surrexit), and numerous orchestras and bands. Lunchtime concerts most weeks, and a big concert every half term. Many continue to patronise the music block even if they don't take the subject, and around 300 learn instruments. 'It's all about joy in music making,' said one teacher – there is certainly much delight taken in music here. One parent, who encouraged her reluctant son to join the choir, says he enjoys it more than he ever (as a teenager) would admit – 'It's a very special thing to be part of.'

Art is a strong area: housed in a contemporary purpose-built centre, full of light, with eager students keen to show off their amazing work: everything from oils to an installation of hanging clingfilm, called 'Urban' – clay room and kiln, printing, etching, photography and fine art – 'Waterfront was our first topic this term, so we went to Venice' – where else? Older pupils have their own areas, so don't have to clear up paintings under way – the spacious rooms feel full of many little studios. Weekly drop-in art sessions for those who have never lifted a brush, or keen artists who just haven't got enough time to follow an art course. Art at every turn throughout the school – one house has turned the curve at the bottom of a stairwell into Venice.

Great DT centre, with examples of GCSE and A level work which wouldn't look out of place in a designer furniture store, along with a few quirky ideas – for dog owners who feel all that bend and throw is just a bit too energetic, how about an automatic dog ball launcher? Again, those who don't continue with this option can nevertheless return to pursue DT as a hobby.

Background and atmosphere: Grand old buildings of Sussex flint, dating from 1848, with elegant quads and huge chapel standing on the hill overlooking the rolling Downs. In this beautiful setting, it feels distinctly public school, but it's not as cut glass as all that. Clearly impresses parents – 'They're experiencing things to do with heritage and a sense of history which seep into their experience and become something they value.'

A Woodard school, it has a strong Christian tradition, still very much in evidence. No skipping weekly chapel here, for conscientious objectors or other faiths – 'It might not be something they carry on with later in life, but at least they have been exposed to it – like maths,' said a teacher. Although a Christian school, they are not out to convert you – pupils of all faiths or no faith are welcome here. It's more about the values of Christianity, and in particular caring for each other. The service is a wonderful thing to experience – inside, the chapel is glorious and the voices of the choir soar – only St Paul's cathedral has a higher ceiling. High church with plenty of bells and smells and the accompanying pageantry – it must seem like a foreign land to some, and service delivery was on the dry side. Pupils seem to attend quite happily though, girls wrapped in 19th century style cloaks of house colours; boys just cold. Over half troop up for communion or a blessing. Pupils assure me that a fair number attend voluntary chapel – held in the crypt daily before breakfast. One parent said she felt doing the communal thing is very important – apparently leavers miss most their time in chapel.

About two-thirds of pupils at Lancing are boarders, and the head is clearly a strong advocate of boarding; certainly boarders seem very happy and enjoy having a wealth of activity available on their doorsteps. Modern, comfortable accommodation, although you won't find the gold taps one parent was hoping for. Years 9 and 10, two to four in a room, from year 11, single study bedrooms. Shared rooms are filled to capacity with beds and desks, but the pupils don't object to cosy conditions: one sixth former told me how much she missed sharing a room with friends – 'I've been with them since I was 13 – they are like my sisters.' Day pupils can board for a night free if they are at school after 9 pm on school business, such as play rehearsals, which pleases parents.

Friends can visit house communal areas – although pupils often go and chat out on the quads after dinner. Houses have common rooms (with Sky +), squashy sofas and views over rolling countryside, and kitchens with daily deliveries of bread, spreads, and fruit for any time consumption. Each house has an IT room, and wifi throughout; one house has a sweet shop open in the evenings. Sixth formers have their own common room and kitchen – 'It's the best thing about the house.' School cafe opens at break, in the afternoons and evening.

There is a rather splendid dining hall – could almost be a back-up chapel should something happen to the other one, with long wooden tables and oddly discordant plastic chairs. Wide range of food available, nice, but not remarkable on the day of our visit – one pupil said it 'goes up and down a bit.' Sixth formers can skip breakfast in the dining hall and cook their own.

The sixth form is not for those who want to scruff around in jeans and tee shirts for a couple of years – smart business wear is expected here, with more responsibility as prefects or house captains, and more independence, in organising time in and out of school: year 11 and sixth formers can go into Brighton, and they're considering allowing the sixth up to London. In common with the rest of the school, some fabulous trips on offer: the travel section of the school magazine resembles a highly desirable travel brochure.

Pastoral care and discipline: Parents say it is 'like being part of a community with a strong family atmosphere.' Well-defined house system with a network of people taking care of pupils. As well as housemasters/mistresses (the first point of call for parents), there is a matron on hand, year 10 'uncles' and 'aunts' for new year 9s, and the peer support system provided by sixth formers. If all this fails, 'there is always a teacher you get on with particularly well'. Pupils admit to feeling a bit homesick for a few weeks, but say it quickly wears off. At break time, kids troop back to their house common room for squash and biscuits: some kids pop in and straight out again, others sit and chat to matron and other house staff. It is a moment away from

work – like having a break with your mum. Matron – 'We are their family here.'

Parents feel discipline is 'not in your face'. Seems to work, but quite gently done. Approach 'firm but fair'. One mum says the balance must be right, because the kids are so relaxed about going to school. Bullying, drug and alcohol abuse not generally a problem, but will be dealt with severely. The one pupil who could recall an episode of bullying was clearly startled by how strictly it had been dealt with.

Communication is good where a parent has a concern – email or telephone contact will lead to a rapid and thorough response. Parents say school is very welcoming and encourages parents to feel involved. There is some small tension between the parent who felt that parents of day pupils require more communication (than those of boarders), and the head's feeling that 'occasionally helicopter parents need to be told to buzz off in the interests of their child.' This does feel like a school where parents should be prepared to step back a bit, and let their child take responsibility for themselves.

Pupils and parents: Fits oddballs – we met some pupils who were strongly individual but seemed very happy at Lancing. 'Not for the inert,' said one teacher, 'nor for one-dimensional academic types,' said another. Pupils from Lancing Prep and other prep schools in the area. Parents generally middle class professionals, city types, and around 20 per cent from overseas.

School runs its own buses, routes to suit need from the surrounding area, and shuttle between Lancing College and the prep.

Former pupils include playwrites Sir David Hare, Christopher Hampton and Giles Cooper, lyricist Sir Tim Rice, novelists Tom Sharpe and Evelyn Waugh, Shakespeare scholar and writer John Dover Wilson, singer Sir Peter Pears, Archbishop Trevor Huddleston, TV presenter Jamie Theakston, Sir Christopher Meyer, Charles Anson, Dr Rana Mitter, Sir Roy Calne, Stephen Green (Baron Green of Hurstpierpoint) and Alex Horne.

Entrance: Gently selective – mid 50 per cent pass rate at CE, with separate assessment for those from the state sector. For the sixth form, need good GCSEs and school reference, interviews and tests.

Some 20-30 places for girls at sixth form, 10 for boys.

Exit: Around 20 per cent leave after GCSEs. After A levels a few to Oxbridge, lots to London, many to Russell group, others all over. Increasing interest in universities in the US.

Money matters: At 13, academic, music, art, drama, sports and all-rounder scholarships, up to half of fees, which can be augmented depending on family circumstances. Sixth form awards – academic, music and art, up to a third of fees.

Remarks: A friendly and beautiful place to grow up in. Pupils are happy, and unselfconsciously themselves. This is a place where individuals will flourish, and there is evidently great care and attention to ensure this is so. Not for those who like to take things easy – a culture of keeping busy.

Langley Grammar School

Reddington Drive, Langley, Slough, Berkshire, SL3 7QS

- Pupils: 1040; girls and boys • Ages: 11–18 • Non-denom • State

Tel: 01753 598300
Email: school@lgs.slough.sch.uk
Website: www.lgs.slough.sch.uk

Headteacher: Since January 2010, Mr John Constable BSc (forties), was deputy head of Wycombe High School and before that posts at Sir William Borlase (Marlow), Watford and Aylesbury Grammars. If his CV seems to show a trend, then no surprise to learn that he is a 'classical grammar school boy', the product of a town grammar in Suffolk (but no, he isn't related). Not quite a seamless move from learning to teaching – he took his degree in engineering science and management at Durham and worked for Unilever for a couple of years before evolving into that highly prized creature, a physics teacher. Acknowledging polarised opinions on the subject of grammar schools, he believes that, when it works, the model, certainly as represented by Langley, still has the potential to transform lives. Married with two young children, he sails, is a qualified dinghy instructor and cub scout leader, enjoying the chance the latter gives him to work with younger children. Other interests are hill walking and photography. 'It's hugely important to do other things,' he says.

This is his first headship, at a school where there are 10 applications for every place and which was declared 'outstanding' by Ofsted; so, where does he intend to go from here? '"Outstanding" doesn't mean perfect,' he says – scope to 'review the curriculum' and boost students' independence. So far, so virtual; if he has more specific plans (beyond building works) he's not letting on. Immensely likeable, quietly charming, he is also understandably guarded – these are early days and one feels that he is keeping his powder dry.

Academic matters: Among the top state grammars in the country and highly valued locally, a school where expectations are high. A specialist maths and computing school. Over 60 per cent A*/A grades at GCSE in 2013 and 74 per cent A*/B grades at A level. Such results are particularly admirable given that, on entry to the school, 40 per cent of students have a first language other than English. Booster classes in English, particularly essay writing skills, and by the end of key stage 3 the majority of pupils exceed expectations. The library plays a key role in this – its indefatigable staff organise all kinds of initiatives to get everyone reading widely; its SOAR (switch off and read) Fridays for years 7-9 are a great idea: all electronic distractions are disabled and 10,000 books regain their rightful place as the library's main attraction.

Very strong in all academic areas and formidable in maths. An 'expectation' that the majority will take three separate sciences at GCSE and most do so, along with choices from the wide range of arts, technologies and languages (French or German). No Latin or Greek here, but classical civilisation is an option for GCSE and plans to offer it at AS level. Psychology, sociology, philosophy and ethics and law all offered at AS and A level. Head is considering IGCSEs but 'has yet to be convinced'.

Classes are broadly similar in size to those in other grammars – 30 at key stage 3, mid 20s for GCSE subjects – but the prevailing air of studious quiet is enough to indicate that at Langley this is not a barrier to learning. As the head comments, 'Part of that is us, part of that is because the majority of our students come to us well-motivated and with a respect for learning.' On our visit the view in every classroom was of heads bowed or hands up – 'You've got to like your book work,' commented one of our guides. Small number on SEN register, mainly for dyslexia or other SPLD, and students' individual needs catered for by SENCo, a gifted and talented coordinator and school counsellor.

Games, options, the arts: Music and drama facilities are spacious – the main sports hall can accommodate the whole school – and professional looking; foundation status means it can make its own choices about how to spend money and, notwithstanding the science and maths bent here, sport and the arts are impressively resourced. One of our guides said of the sports facilities, 'It's only when you go to away matches that you realise how lucky you are.' Whole school drama productions, house and school concerts are a key part of school life; instrumentalists are served by the borough's peripatetic music teachers and a recent push to encourage take-up of brass instruments has apparently been successful. Not surprisingly, chess is particularly strong, as the silverware in the trophy cabinet in reception goes to show, but Langley is equally successful in the less cerebral sports. 'This is not a rugby school or a hockey school' – the aim being to offer the widest possible range to appeal to the maximum number of students. Two hours of timetabled sport a week is augmented by plenty of lunchtime and after-school activities and matches; the girls' basketball team has been county champion for two years in a row. Sixth formers can also earn money working in the huge sports centre – facilities are open to the local community out of school hours.

Background and atmosphere: Sitting comfortably among quiet residential roads, the grounds and immediate vicinity are immaculate – not a crisp packet or drinks can anywhere to be seen. Presents a smart, purposeful face to the world both outside and in. This isn't an ancient foundation – built in 1956, the style is post-war municipal Brutalist, softened with age and summer bedding. Inside, the original core buildings are beautifully maintained with gleaming linoleum and polished wood. Fortunate to be surrounded by plenty of green space and playable surfaces are extended by a floodlit all-weather pitch.

A 'redundant' strip at the edge of the site was sold for housing in order to finance a significant building programme. Classrooms have the requisite whiteboards, computers etc, and even in the older parts everything is scrupulously clean and well maintained. In the corridors, subject notice boards are up-to-date and colourful, but pupils' work is not prominently displayed in public areas. A much-needed refurbishment and extension of the dining room was under way when we visited – the student council was involved at all stages of its design ('including the colour scheme,' remarked the head) and attended all presentations. This cashless café style area, with small tables and squashy sofas, will provide a continuous service, including breakfast, with the emphasis on healthy eating. Sixth formers can eat in the common-room or outside at picnic tables. The food is, apparently, much, much better than it used to be.

Slough's education system is rather mix and match – of the 12 secondary schools in the borough, four are grammars. According to Mr Constable, 'interesting philosophical differences regarding selection, but heads are working together very effectively' to raise standards for all. Not much in the way of philosophical difference if you talk to parents or locals though: residents are fiercely proud of these schools and the opportunities they offer young people. Even parents we spoke to whose offspring did not get into Langley are refreshingly unchippy. Local primaries don't teach to the 11 plus, but Langley is involved in a great deal of outreach work with younger children, especially in the area of IT, to share the school's equipment and expertise. It also actively supports three non-selective schools, with senior staff involved in training NQTs and peer mentoring schemes, and contributes to another partnership (readers are being spared an alphabet soup of acronyms here) aimed at raising achievement in a group of local schools.

One is struck by how calm everything is. Bells have been abolished and pupils walk quickly to their next lesson chatting quietly in groups – no crowd control needed here. Green blazers with the school insignia for boys, green jumpers for girls, traditional enamel badges for positions of responsibility worn proudly. Sixth form uniform smart variations on a theme of monochrome.

Yes, this is a focused and academic school, but it is not inward looking – it has been awarded International School status for its 'outstanding development of the international dimension in the curriculum' and sixth formers in particular are very enthusiastic in their fund-raising for charitable causes abroad.

Pastoral care and discipline: The head describes his school as a 'good mix' and the student population as 'harmonious', and pupils we spoke to confirm this. Understandably, the ethos of the institution is broadly secular – no religious clubs but plenty of discussion supported by an assembly programme of visiting speakers. The response to bullying is 'prompt and effective' action by tutors and heads of year. In addition, a peer mentoring scheme for which pupils are trained and a website that allows students to report incidents or request support anonymously. Staff are energetic and experienced, just the right combination of new ideas and old wisdom, and pupils receive a high level of pastoral support, particularly in the first couple of years when boys and girls arrive from unusually diverse geographical (the school has no catchment area) and cultural backgrounds. Our year 13 guides had fond and grateful memories of the buddy system which pairs small groups of new pupils with a sixth form mentor.

A 'fairly traditional house system' (head) with lively inter-house sporting fixtures and music competitions with external judges. No school bus – public transport network here pretty good – but a car share scheme operates too. School day ends at 3.15pm and a full extra-curricular programme of sport and other activities takes place after this and in lunch hours. Some funding is available to support the purchase of uniform or pay for trips in cases of hardship.

'Code of conduct' and the 'usual range of sanctions' for those who break it. Major transgressions are rare – a commendable zero racist incidents, for example. The head believes in tackling any potential problems head-on and claims that he and his senior staff spend as much time as necessary face to face or on the phone to parents.

Pupils and parents: Pupils enter from a wide geographical area and over 80 primary schools. About 40 per cent come from Slough borough but, because the school is close to the boundaries of other authorities, 'out of borough' entrants can also live relatively nearby. Two-thirds of the intake from what are officially described as 'minority ethnic groups', just over half coming from Asian/British-Indian backgrounds. Pupils are charming, polite and very proud of their school.

Entrance: Verbal and non-verbal reasoning papers taken in November. Slough is not a selective authority, so parents must opt in for their children to take the test set by a consortium of Langley and two other grammars. Places are allocated according to rank order of performance, thereafter distance from school is only possible advantage. Coaching? 'Of course there is,' says the head. Roughly 20 sixth form places for external candidates – admission on the basis of GCSE performance and specific grades stipulated for A level subjects chosen.

Exit: Mainly Russell Group universities, King's College London and Imperial particularly favoured. Overwhelmingly science, medicine, engineering and computing, but some choose other traditional academic subjects such as history or English – nothing remotely fluffy. Not as many as one might expect applying to Oxbridge – the head believes work to be done here. Gap years are not the norm and the school continues to provide support for pupils after they leave, especially those who delay university entrance.

Remarks: Huge local pride in Langley and the other Slough grammar schools – it seems that the noblest ideals of the old fashioned grammar survive here untarnished. Perhaps because of its location, relatively untroubled by sharp-elbowed incomers looking for a private education on the state. Hard working, serious minded school – indeed one feels that pupils sometimes might need to be encouraged to look up from their books and spend a few minutes day dreaming. Langley is at the heart of its community, providing invaluable opportunities and changing lives – as a charming sixth former remarked, 'If you're willing to give everything a go, it's all there for you and the teachers help you to achieve'.

Langley Park School for Boys

South Eden Park Road, Beckenham, BR3 3BP

• Pupils: 1,690 (boys 11–18 and girls 16–18) • Ages: 11–18 • Non-denom • State

Tel: 020 8639 4700
Email: office@lpbs.org.uk
Website: www.lpbs.org.uk

Headteacher: Since 2013, Steve Parsons MA. Previously worked as senior leader in various London schools and most recently spent seven years as deputy principal at Dunraven School in Streatham.

Academic matters: Intake is non-selective. Boys join in mixed ability tutor groups, then 'tightly setted' for subjects – seven entry forms divided into 10 ability-based learning groups. Head very enthusiastic about this, and the school's results explain why: English language GCSE is consistently in the top five per cent nationally and success in maths and science is impressive. Specialist status in maths and computing, with links to other schools to offer master classes. School re-introduced engineering at GCSE and A level five years ago, and now has its first Oxbridge success with the subject. Also won the Spirit of the Event Team Award in the Shell Ecotec Challenge (designing a fuel efficient car) three years running. In 2013, 83 per cent of pupils got 5+ A*-C grades at GCSE including English and maths, 31 per cent of grades A*/A. At A level, nearly 65 per cent A*/B and 28 per cent A*/A grades.

Head actively recruits teachers from the top universities, training them at Langley. The result is a good mix of experienced longer-serving staff and dynamic newcomers. Students rave about them: 'The teachers are really helpful', 'They always help you out if you ask them', 'Languages here are fun, really in-depth', 'Science lessons are great', 'The staff are fantastic – I've never met one I didn't like' are just a few of the comments we received. Culture of going the extra mile, combined with imagination and innovation: Bobby George, the darts champion, was booked to give a masterclass in mental maths. Thriving co-ed sixth form, which girls leave the independent sector to join.

Excellent SEN provision, with statemented pupils completely integrated into school life. Gifted and talented programme for more able pupils, whose results compare favourably with those from grammar school. 'All three of our sons have blossomed here,' said one parent. 'We couldn't be happier.' 'My daughter loves it,' added the mother of a sixth former. 'She's so much more confident now.'

Games, options, the arts: 'We're the only state school who's played Eton at Fives!' enthused head, adding, 'We got slaughtered.' Notwithstanding, sport here is very strong, rugby and hockey particularly so – a boy described the recent rugby tour of South Africa as 'unbelievable – I'd recommend it to everyone'. Links with professional sportsmen keep the profile high; gold Sports and Artsmarks. Art is truly amazing – OB Henry Mee's mural is still there from 1973, and has been joined since by hundreds of remarkable and thought-provoking artworks, all by students and all proudly on display. Drama and music both flourish, with regular productions, choral tours and concerts – Catfish Blue, the school's jazz group, did well at the National Festival of Music for Youth and went on to play the Royal Albert Hall in the Schools' Prom. 'The performing arts are huge drivers of motivation and confidence,' head believes. All boys learn to ride a horse at the end of year 9. Lots of trips abroad and dozens of refreshingly different extra-curricular opportunities, including comedy club and fly-fishing.

Background and atmosphere: Previously the Beckenham and Penge County Grammar, became comprehensive in 1976 and moved out of Penge. At beginning of 2012 moved to new £38.5 million building just east of previous site; new sports facilities opening in early 2013. Co-ed sixth form since 2001 started with seven girls, now has 181, and has, head says, 'Transformed the feel of the school, hugely benefiting both our learning and our extra-curricular' – adding, endearingly, 'Girls are brave, you see'. Staff/pupil relationships extremely good and head really does know every child in the school by name. Uniform is smart and smartly worn, formal dress for sixth formers.

Pastoral care and discipline: Described by one student as 'excellent', and parents endorse this. 'The head doesn't just sit in his office – he's out there setting the tone,' said one father, and everyone we spoke to praised the staff and the example they give. Students are expected to be courteous, cooperative and sensible. Sixth formers given responsibilities such as library and lunchtime duty and helping younger pupils settle in.

Pupils and parents: Drawn from the immediate locality, mostly Beckenham and West Wickham. 'A nice area – we are privileged,' admits head. Majority of parents are aspirational, expecting their children to work hard and do well. Students likeable and down to earth. One turned down a place at a local independent school, because 'Langley was friendlier'.

Entrance: School is massively over-subscribed at 11 – only siblings and those living less than 1.07 of a mile away can hope to get in. Predictably, local house prices reflect this. Priority also given to children in care.

Exit: Around 75 per cent of boys stay on at 16. At 18, most go on to university and usually get their first choice. Between two and four Oxbridge successes most years.

Remarks: A wonderful success story of a school. Comprehensive education at its very best.

Langley Park School for Girls

Hawksbrook Lane, Beckenham, Kent, BR3 3BE

- Pupils: 1650 pupils; Girls only in years 7–11; co-ed in sixth form
- Ages: 11–18 • Non-denom • State

Tel: 020 8663 4199
Email: info@lpgs.bromley.sch.uk
Website: www.lpgs.bromley.sch.uk

Headteacher: Since 2011, Dr Anne Hudson, MA BA PGCE PhD, fifties. Though local – lives in nearby Beckenham with husband Stuart, a retired teacher (no children) hence appeal of current job – this is her first professional move into suburbia. Was previously head of Central Foundation Girls' School in Tower Hamlets, her fifth inner-city comprehensive, the other four co-ed and all universally on the up with one – Dunraven School in Lambeth, where she was deputy head – teetering on cusp of outstanding inspection score.

Precise (always a pleasure to encounter 'syllabi' in briefing notes), energetic – a keen cyclist who misses 'therapeutic' 24-mile round trip commute to last school – and articulate (diction so crisp you could serve it with dips at a cocktail party), she's notable for a jaw-dropping back story that's more Cry the Beloved Country than Être et Avoir.

Raised in Southern Africa, put aside early dreams of being a teacher when was sent to boarding school in 1970s segregated Zimbabwe – 'if we went to town, my best friend and I weren't allowed to sit at the same table' – and was confounded by 'boring history lessons' about Tudor and Stuart goings-on in distant England while civil war, raging on doorstep, was completely ignored. After dropping out of English and French degree at University of Cape Town, signed up for 'voluntary work' with Namibian resistance until deported to UK by South African-controlled government. You hope for tales of derring-do with bandolier over shoulder and grenade clenched between teeth but 'not heroic,' she insists, as 'they deported lots of bishops, too.'

While working at Namibians' London HQ by day, took BA in economics by night followed by an MA in history and, teaching aspirations rekindled, a PGCE at Institute of Education (and has since been awarded a PhD in education by Leeds University). Started career as history teacher in Enfield with 'rusty' French on the side, criss-crossing London's eastern reaches to take up ever more senior posts. Spent seven years as assistant head at Deptford Green School in Lewisham, famed for transformation from near write-off to teacher's pet under headship of establishment darling Sir Keith Ajegbo, who also nudged Dr Hudson into studying for a doctorate ('an accident' she says, modestly) after she had accumulated a thesis's worth of raw data on whether citizenship can be a whole-school specialism. (Apparently it can.)

Teaches some PSHE and GCSE history lessons and is a highly visible and hands on presence – 'my sister saw her clearing rubbish round the garden,' says awed year 7 girl. Parents, who don't know her that well, equally don't see this as a problem – gives out direct email address and is a reliable presence at school events- 'walks round saying "hello" at parents' evening,' says year 7 mother.

Desire for headship born not so much from personal ambition as clear-sighted grasp of its benefits – 'I could see that having power in the school could help you shape things.' Style is going down a storm with the pupils, who without exception cite reinstatement of own clothes day, banned for five years after bullying incident, as biggest achievement to date (Dr Hudson, you'd imagine, would hope for a legacy with a little more gravitas). Many (unprompted) praised her cheerful, high-

L

profile presence round school. 'I've spoken to Dr Hudson at least three times,' marvels year 11 girl. 'I didn't talk to the old head once.' 'She's far more relaxed,' confirms a parent.

Academic matters: The reason parents send their daughters here. 'It was the academic side that appealed,' says one, who moved house specifically to secure a place. Plenty to shout about, too, with GCSE A*-C pass rate including English and maths 83 per cent in 2013 (head's publically declared goal is five good GCSE passes for all by 2020), and 40 per cent A*/A grades – particularly high percentages in single subject sciences and fast track languages, both reserved for most able.

Good news continues in sixth form. While new vocational courses are being added to roster that currently includes business, travel, health and social care with aim of broadening appeal (almost the only 'could do better' in otherwise glowing inspection report) the emphasis, says head emphatically, is unapologetically skewed 'towards the more able students'. Results – 48 per cent A*/B and 23 per cent A*/A grades in 2013 – prove the point.

Success doesn't, however, come at expense of the 200 or so pupils with special needs, many speech and language related (about 20 have statements). Good-sized and centre stage learning support unit, home to two key workers under direction of deputy head with SEN background, is widely appreciated as a whole school safety valve offering help for anyone under pressure.

Add enthusiastic teachers, including one working her socks off to spark discussion on ethics of designer babies amongst slightly somnolent GCSE biology class, and the technology head extolling the wonders of the computer programmed laser saw that cuts anything (Goldfinger would be envious, though less fussed by its ability to add detailed floral motifs) and it sounds like roses all the way.

Well, up to a point, Lord Copper. There's the odd wilting bloom. Success in some small but perfectly formed subjects (GCSE music, growing fast, consistently secures 100 per cent Bs or higher) is balanced by occasional whole-subject wobble (applied science a case in point). And despite GCSE success in languages, one of school specialisms – others are technology and sport – numbers die away post 16, with totals for German, French and Spanish scarcely into double figures (reflection, sadly, of national malaise). It's not for want of trying, what with Mandarin and Latin both available as popular lunchtime and after-school clubs, and the 150 EAL students, many bilingual, able to take community languages as additional GCSE. Currently, advanced linguists who take French GCSE early follow a slightly waffly culture-related programme with some cake-making but little academic bite in year 11. Head's plan to move them on to AS level work may help though, judging by less than encouraging results in other schools, it may not...

Then there's the little matter of boys' school next door which clocks near identical GCSE results to its neighbour – 'girls should do at least six per cent better,' says Dr Hudson – and is also seen as the place to go for sixth form sciences. Resulting mini brain drain especially in chemistry and physics is cause for concern but could soon be reversed with appointment of whizzy new head of science who comes with tried and tested Pied Piper-like A level recruitment skills. Shouldn't be rocket science – sixth formers who ignore hype and stay on for science are glad they did. 'Class sizes are very big in the boys' school – I knew the school and the teachers and the course seems to suit me,' says one.

Head wants everyone (including staff) to up game, crunching primary school data so hard you can almost hear it squeak in effort to identify budding talent from arrival in year 7 and laying down the law with clear minimum academic goals for pupils (with hope, of course, that these will be routinely exceeded). 'Boys are often deluded about their own potential, whereas girls tend to underestimate themselves,' says head,

crisply. If she has her way, however, certainly won't be the case for much longer.

Games, options, the arts: Sport highly rated. 'Amazing,' says one pupil. Lots to do and places to do it in, large if slightly sombre sports hall and gym inside; five tennis courts and an all-weather pitch in addition to five acres of green space outside. Old Girls include Ellen Gandy, 2012 Olympic 100m butterfly finalist, and with current pupils making literal waves in diving and even water polo, and figuratively in squash, could be first of many.

Favours the competitive (lots of wins for netball and hockey squads in local championships) so 'you need to push yourself,' says parent. Theoretically, however, something for everyone and if the timetabled sport doesn't do it for you there's probably a club that will, from yoga to fencing. 'They really shine. You name it and they'll have it,' says pupil.

Robust though sport is, tends to be swamped by performing arts which have pirouetted across website and ousted match results from shared on-line notice board, replacing them with close-ups of recent and seemingly non-stop round of acclaimed productions. Frequent high-quality, whole-school collaborations between dance, drama and music include large cast versions of Annie and Alice in Wonderland, which have gone down a storm, while with around 300 students learning instruments, there's a decent range of ensembles, too, including 50-strong jazz orchestra which recently toured China.

Mini Brit academy feel never stronger than with dance: tap and street offered, but classical ballet a particular strength, masterminded (and frequently choreographed) by three dance teachers whose remit covers everything from hit versions of Twilight and Beauty and the Beast to GCSE, A level and, coming soon, BTEC courses complete with glamorous overseas revision courses, all apparently done without drawing breath. Indeed, a new dance studio was recently opened by Deborah Bull of King's College London. Motto, unsurprisingly, is 'anyone can dance' though, as sixth form boys as yet unconvinced, male performers are currently imported from next door.

In addition to 'look at me' events, lots of looking after others, with pupils from year 9 onwards lending a hand at local primaries while year 12s, who have Wednesday afternoons free thanks to miracle of timetable coordination, can opt to fill them with voluntary work, often as part of thriving D of E programme, open to all though you'll only get the go ahead if you're doing 'what your predicted grades say you should be,' says one. You can't keep staff away either: science teacher – a 'bundle of energy,' says head – awarded MBE for educational work in community.

Background and atmosphere: In its 90-year history (last 50 on current leafy site), school has had several Time Lord-like incarnations, beginning as a county girls' school, becoming a grammar in 1945, a comprehensive in the 1970s and achieving the full collector's set with academy status in 2011. Connections with the past haven't been sloughed off, however, with original society for Old Girls (known as Adremians) still going strong. There's also traditional, ultra-smart uniform much cooed over by outsiders, less so by current parents faced with dry-clean-only blue piped blazer and hard-to-press pleated tartan skirt. 'I get granny to iron it,' confesses one.

School design, mid-20th century standard issue, features main two-storey main building with separate blocks for drama/sport, science (11 perfectly decent labs), sixth form and technology (newest and nicest of the lot with six well-equipped workshops), together roughly framing three sides of large and picnic table studded if slightly bleak courtyard (the main R&R outside area until student council secured leave to use 'head's own garden', a green and pleasant space round the corner). Effect is pleasant and unintimidating. New girls get maps and are quickly at home – in some schools you feel satellite tracking and emergency rations wouldn't come amiss.

Everyone now very nice about multi-million pound newly rebuilt boys' school (similar name, no relation – though in dim and distant past may once have shared sixth form – something there's no desire to repeat). Wasn't always thus. Dr Hudson's predecessor fought plans all the way to Supreme Court and won what turned out to be pyrrhic victory as second application was nodded through shortly afterwards. Bridges now mended, cordial relationships re-established and girls offered use of new facilities, notably the hear-every-bat-squeak acoustically advanced auditorium – 'when boys aren't using it,' says head, without apparent irony. Big brother (though a benevolent one) rules.

Make do and mend philosophy only goes so far, however. Head has planning permission for new music block, and an additional floor on top of sixth form building (including café and social facilities) has just opened.

Surprisingly little sense of over-crowding, and there's even a whole school assembly once a term or thereabouts – though 'if it were all boys, there would be accidents,' says head. (One pupil confessed to eating outside 'even when it's raining' just to get away from it all). Children seem to move in mysterious ways (possibly by converting themselves to compressed data format at busy times, more likely by learning to keep elbows in when using corridors). It's particularly noticeable at break, when what should be a scrum for the food and drink somehow isn't.

Mood is welcoming, helped by delightful, off-beat art displays (ceramic artichokes on sticks, anyone?) partial door 'n' floor refurbishment (light wood/portholes combo gives vaguely Nordic/nautical feel depending on preference), and homely areas including large, book-lined library, well used in and out of school hours, which hosts termly themed parties complete with cakes to keep reading top of mind when 'other things step in,' says librarian, diplomatically.

Pastoral care and discipline: Four houses; Lambda (yellow), Kappa (blue), Sigma (red), and Gamma (green) – fortunately no Brave New World Epsilon – as much an admin tool as a motivational one, used for imposing a little organisational clarity on eight form entry – it's two forms to a house (block booking, no arguments) and little sense of feverish competition 'except on sports day,' say girls.

Friendship issues inevitably the biggest problem cited by parents, especially lower down the school. 'They look so grown up,' says worried mother who mentions daughter's need to apply defensive makeup following pressure to fit in.

If there is a problem, overwhelming pupil consensus is that there's always somebody to talk to – 'even the canteen people are friendly,' says one – and staff are often very popular, with tears on departure, though 'a few scare me, and I'm the parent,' says one mother.

Relationships improve the further up the school you go. 'Students do have problems with teachers – no school's perfect but mostly they're great and there if you want them,' adds another. Discipline, though firm, is considered: if there's out of character bad behaviour, staff will 'try to find out where you're coming from first,' says year 11 pupil, with exclusion very much a last resort and help provided, wherever possible, in situ.

Officially, form tutors are first point of contact, often staying with same group for several years. Parents praise ease of communication – teachers are listed in pupil planners and there are individual email addresses for all, up to and including head. 'If you expect other members of staff to give out their contact details you should be willing to do the same thing,' she says.

Highly effective school council, a model of its kind, 'lets teachers know what students are thinking, rather than what they assume they are,' says pupil, and gets things done – broken soap dispenser that had languished for weeks in one of toilets was 'fixed within days' after complaints. It's helped by involvement of sympathetic teacher who 'is on our side but is honest and will say if we're asking for outrageous things.' Youngest girls have as much of a voice as senior pupils and an

equal chance of being chosen from full meeting to present ideas to head. 'You even hear what sixth form are doing,' says one.

Pupils and parents: Tight catchment area means many new pupils arrive with others they know. While behaviour is 'fairly standard for teenagers these days; you stop for 10 minutes to let them cross and nobody says thank you,' harrumphs slightly gloomy local, her experience seems exception rather than rule: on morning of visit no sign of anything other than almost universal good manners – lots of hands raised in salute to waiting cars as girls (boys, too – a symphony in blue and burgundy respectively) arrived in their hundreds.

In school, too, doors are routinely held open and there's general sense of courtesy towards others (helped, quite possibly, by numbers of teachers in corridors – though a benevolent rather than sentry-like presence).

Parents are necessarily local, many the hard-working exemplars praised by politicians of every hue. As a fair percentage commute to jobs in London, don't necessarily see much of each other, although with quite a few events (first class fireworks display, for example) 'opportunities to socialise are there if you want them,' says one.

Entrance: Large school, tiny catchment area (has shrunk to under a mile before now though normally hovers just over). Means that despite size of intake (240 places in year 7) it's routinely oversubscribed and there's always a waiting list.

Pupils come from nine or so local primaries (Oak Lodge, Marian Vian, Highfield Junior, Pickhurst, Unicorn, Balgowan, Clare House, Hawes Down and St Marys Catholic Primary) though feeders in name only as attendance is no guarantee of place and distance (barring standard priority given to looked after children) is king.

Estate agents testify to school's popularity. Parents vote with their square feet. 'We specifically moved to get a place,' says one (though other more dubious practices aren't unknown either).

Three-quarters stay into sixth form, again oversubscribed (minimum of 10 places available to external candidates, usually more in practice) and, like majority of local schools, co-educational, though boys so thin on the ground (around 20 a year) that spotting them not unlike real life version of 'Where's Wally?'

A level places dependent on securing minimum of seven GCSE passes (about 50 turned away at application stage) with minimum B grades in four including chosen AS/A level subjects, A*/As preferred for toughies like chemistry and teacher recommendations for languages. Anyone opting for performing arts will also need to pass audition.

Exit: A third or so who leave post-GCSE stay close, some moving to boys' school next door (with a few, who don't care for the size, moving back) while a very few opt for selective grammars like St Olave's and Newstead Wood or independent schools like Trinity School in neighbouring Croydon. A few head off to larger colleges to study work-related courses, though head keen to slow exodus of less academic – should have 'right to continue here even if not high flyers,' she feels.

No compromises when it comes to onwards academic journey. Almost all make it into higher education, nearly all first or second choice universities with Bristol, Leeds, Warwick, Southampton 'all popular,' says head of sixth form, and the most able encouraged to try for Oxbridge – normally a couple of places each year and the same again for medicine. Law, business and administration, biological sciences and creative arts and design (including music and drama) head the list of subject choices, with maths and English not far behind and a light dusting of languages and engineering.

Brand new Careers Academy 'will provide specific advice and guidance backed up with seminars, careers days, contact with employers and practice at interviews and skills'. School

L

'has been commended for its outstanding preparation of UCAS applications.'

Remarks: Short on square feet but, remarkably, feels as if has enough breathing space for everyone, helped by honest, intelligent leadership, enthusiastic staff and pupils who seem happy to be here and for the most part do well – a real breath of fresh air.

Lansdowne College

40-44 Bark Place, London, W2 4AT

• Pupils: 250 • Ages: 14-19 • Fees: Range from £3,360 a year per GCSE for up to 4 GCSEs, to £18,520 for a 3 subject, 1 year A level course • Independent

Tel: 020 7616 4400
Email: education@lansdownecollege.com
Website: www.lansdownecollege.com

Principal: Since 2010, Mr John Southworth BSc MSc Eng. Not the usual background for a head: he spent 20 years in the army before joining the Perse School to teach engineering-based DT. After various promotions over 10 years there he ended up as director of co-curriculum. His wife still teaches at the Perse; they have four teenage sons.

Not a schmoozy head: 'We do what it says on the tin,' he says of the college's offerings. 'I try my best to provide what parents are paying for.' Parents comment that his army background shows through in his bluff manner: 'He's very much his own person. He said exactly what he thought, and it turned out to be right.'

Gives the impression of being a tough manager. 'He must have an eye for recruiting good staff,' said a parent, 'and I get the impression they all toe the line.'

Academic matters: There is a small GCSE cohort of some 40 pupils, but this is essentially a sixth form college offering one and two year A level courses plus short retake courses. With the demise of January retakes, it now offers February to June courses. 'They can come to us in September to sort out UCAS, then go off for a gap few months before getting down to work. We hope they'll come back with renewed vigour.'

Colleges like this stand or fall by the value they add, and Lansdowne claims an average one to two grade increase at A level on its short courses. 'We're expert at getting people with Cs up to A/Bs. And at getting Cs for people who were predicted to fail.' Classes are tiny: six is average, with one or two not unusual, especially for more esoteric subjects such as Russian, Japanese or geology. In 2013, 25 per cent A*/A grades at A level. Around half of these results were from retake students and half from those who did their entire A level course here. Maths is the most popular subject, with large cohorts also for biology, chemistry, English, psychology and economics. Courses range from accounting to graphics to philosophy.

The college starts in year 10, teaching core GCSE subjects plus a carousel of options, but the GCSE course runs over one year and most join in year 11.

Passing exams is the raison d'être here – students are 'very focused on achieving examination success', said Ofsted, mentioning 'interesting and challenging lessons' – and tutors make sure the foundations are in place. 'They went back to basics, and kept repeating them, but they did make her enjoy her subject again,' said a parent. Teaching focuses on exam technique. 'Because time is so short, we have to concentrate on ensuring they know how to get the best results – to understand

what examiners want,' says the principal. 'They have to know how to tick the boxes.' Students have weekly exam practices in the hall where they will sit the real thing. 'If they do it once a week they don't panic when the time comes.' GCSE and lower sixth students have at least three hours a week of supervised study periods. No exam study leave or June half term: 'We run our own revision programme. We teach right up to the last exam in the last subject.'

Abilities range from those who have failed first time round to those who need top results for competitive courses. 'But in a small class this range doesn't matter. Stronger students tend to pull up the weaker ones. If you put all the C grade students together they tend to stay at that grade. However, if we find we have a particularly weak group we may add on extra lessons.'

The college rarely accepts students with statements – 'we don't have the facilities or staff' – but has improving learning support, with a third of students on the register. 'We've just bought 25 new laptops for those who need them.'

Very flexible timetabling – organised by the principal – means the college can offer any combination of its 47 A level and 27 GCSE subjects. It also enables sports stars or those with medical problems to fit in lessons round other commitments. 'Every single timetable is written for an individual. And they are organised for the convenience of the students, not the teachers.'

Many of the teachers have higher degrees. 'This sector attracts highly qualified staff, because every class is an exam class.' Ofsted rated the college outstanding, commenting on the 'very wide and flexible range of courses' and the teachers' 'excellent knowledge of their subjects'.

Runs a medics' programme for those aiming at medicine, dentistry, pharmacy or veterinary degrees, and Easter revision courses, with plenty of individual careers advice and help with UCAS applications.

Games, options, the arts: Plenty of creativity going on, with GCSE drama students rehearsing their devised piece during our visit, photography and artwork adorning the corridor walls, a bright north-facing art studio, graphics room and 'fantastic' photography department with its own dark room.

GCSE students have one PE lesson a week, the football team plays in a league, and there are ad hoc rugby and netball teams. There's an annual ski trip, a chance to do the Duke of Edinburgh Award, and a post-exam activities week that includes paintballing and a trip to Thorpe Park, 'to say thanks for working so hard'. In the autumn term, GCSE and AS students spend Friday afternoons visiting museums, galleries and other London sites or listening to outside speakers. They go ice skating, bowling and to the cinema together. There's a Christmas party and a summer ball, organised by the student council. However, it is fair to say that these students' main focus is on their studies, and no-one joins the college for its extracurricular offerings. As a parent said, 'You're not going to go there for the night life.'

Background and atmosphere: In a quiet back street between Notting Hill and Queensway, the sixties building could be an anonymous block of flats. Inside is a maze of classrooms, science and language labs, art and photography rooms. Noticeably, whilst there is a study centre with plenty of computers, magazines, reference material and past exam papers, there is no library. It is bright, but one parent commented, 'You have to fight the look. There's not a frill to be had.'

Originally a primary school and community centre for the neighbouring synagogue, it became a college in the late '70s. Once individually owned, it is now part of Astrum Education, which also includes Duff Miller and Chelsea Independent Colleges, and is owned by private equity firm Sovereign Capital. Happily, the firm is prepared to invest in the infrastructure, and building work to create more classroom space and freshen up the fabric is planned for the short summer break. No common room but students socialise in the canteen and on the small outdoor patio area.

Pastoral care and discipline: Relaxed atmosphere – 'having no uniform breaks down a lot of barriers' – but a stringent approach to punctuality and attendance, with a register taken at the beginning of each lesson. The college has a full time attendance officer who will phone or text any missing student, then their parents. Each student has a personal tutor who keeps an eye on their well-being and progression. 'Because our groups are so small we can keep tabs on things and deal with any problems quickly.'

The college will expel for smoking drugs repeatedly. 'If they're caught once they're suspended; if they're caught again they're expelled. I can't pretend it doesn't happen – we are in central London. It's the worst day of my life, but I do have that ultimate sanction, and there's no shying away from it.'

Pupils and parents: A mix of backgrounds, including around 13 per cent international students from countries ranging from Kazakhstan to Libya, a percentage liable to increase over the next few years. Some pupils come from state schools in year 11 for intensive small-group GCSE tuition, others are recent arrivals in London. Some have been ill or been asked to leave their previous school. Most join the sixth form to improve on previous grades.

Entrance: All applicants are given a tour and interviewed by the principal or vice principal. 'We ask about their background and how we can help them.' The college is not selective, but will look at previous exam results.

'It was the tutors who convinced us when we looked round,' said a parent. 'They told us it would be hard work for our daughter, and could be lonely, but they thought they could get her through. And they did.'

Exit: Of the GCSE students, around 50-60 per cent stay on for A levels. A level students nearly all to university: occasional one or two to Oxbridge; around half to top universities ranging from Durham to Sussex to SOAS.

Money matters: Several means-tested bursaries and academic scholarships up to 40 per cent of fees awarded each year, the latter via the autumn scholarship exam.

Remarks: Extremely good at its job, which is concentrated and detailed preparation for passing exams. Few frills or frivolities. 'It's a sleeves rolled up place,' said a satisfied parent.

LaSwap Sixth Form Consortium

Linked schools: Parliament Hill School; Acland Burghley Schoo; William Ellis School; La Sainte Union Catholic Secondary School

William Ellis School, Highgate Road, London

• Pupils: 1300 • Ages: 16–19 • Non-denom • State

Tel: 020 7692 4157
Email: laswap@williamellis.camden.sch.uk
Website: www.laswap.camden.sch.uk

Joint Head Teachers: La Swap is a sixth-form consortium composed of four neighbouring comprehensives – Parliament Hill, La Sainte Union, Acland Burghley and William Ellis, and the heads of the four schools (Ms Susan Higgins of Parliament Hill, Ms Maureen Williams of La Sainte Union, Ms Jo Armitage of Acland Burghley and Mr Sam White of William Ellis) share the headship. They meet monthly to plan a strategic overview.

Academic matters: These four comprehensives, geographically within a few hundred yards of each other, created an amalgamated sixth form to provide the widest possible subject variety and range of qualifications. Lucky sixth formers here can study a remarkable 39 A levels, as well as BTECs, NVQs, a certificate in childcare and GCSEs (for those who need further preparation before going on to A levels). About 80 per cent of students follow a purely academic course, the rest sit vocational exams, but those who want to can mix and match. In 2013, 18 per cent A*/A grades and 46 per cent A*/B grades at A level. The consortium's strengths lie in vocational subjects, the visual arts (with consistently outstanding results) and arts subjects, like RE, media studies and English. Still possibly not the ideal location for scientists.

Teaching (with over 300 teachers) is enthusiastic, knowledgeable and well prepared. 'We've generally found the teaching to be very good,' said one parent, 'though, as always, you'll get the odd dud.' Some criticism for not always taking into account the wide range of ability in this relatively unselective sixth form, but not all would agree – 'In my classes, some people have 10 A*s and others mainly Cs, but I haven't found that a problem,' said one boy. All students are allocated a base school but most study on a number of sites. Some subjects are taught on all the sites, the more rarefied – philosophy, textiles and dance, for example – on only one.

Each pupil is given target grades on entry based on GCSE results and is carefully tracked thereafter, with good exam preparation and help with study skills, as well as twice yearly reports. 'The communication with home is excellent,' says one parent. 'If my son has done something well they email me. Equally, if he's not doing his homework, they'll let me know.' The academic side is clearly complex, but well organised. 'I wanted to change one of my subjects early on,' said a pupil. 'I went to see the head of year and it was sorted by the end of lunch hour.'

Games, options, the arts: The extra-curricular here is a significant part of what La Swap has to offer, being as varied and extensive as the academic range. The generous enrichment programme – which largely takes place on Wednesday and Thursday afternoons – provides 35 options, from ballet and debating to theatrical make-up, D-jaying and maths master classes. Off-site sports include sailing and climbing. The programme is not compulsory, but everyone is encouraged to have a go, regardless of previous knowledge or expertise.

Background and atmosphere: The four schools (La Sainte Union, an all-girls' Catholic school, William Ellis, an all-boys' former grammar school, Acland Burghley, a co-ed comprehensive, and Parliament Hill, an all-girls' comprehensive) decided to unite their sixth form offering 25 years ago. Each school retains its distinctive ethos and pupils generally enjoy the change of pace. 'I really like the different atmosphere in each school,' said one. All four schools retain the pupils they take in at 11 and each has its own director of sixth form and heads of year.

One great plus of the model is the half-way house it offers between school and sixth-form college. 'My daughter originally wanted to leave and go to college,' said one mother, 'but once she'd started at La Swap, she found the teachers treated her with more respect and she was given much more responsibility for her assignments.' The advantage for students who opt for continuity is that they remain in familiar surroundings while meeting new people and conquering new horizons. 'In the earlier years, my daughter's friends were all local,' said one parent. 'In the sixth form, she suddenly had a whole new set of friends from all over London.' New students, however, don't feel excluded – 'I felt everybody was in the same position as I

L

was,' said one. 'People had friends from their original school, but they didn't know anyone from the other schools.'

La Swap is careful about taking both existing students and recent arrivals to a more independent level of study, with a well-planned induction programme, including a thorough briefing on the outline of each course and relevant dates and department procedures. Students like the friendly, laid-back but organised approach and strong sense of community.

Pastoral care and discipline: All students register at their base school, where they take most of their lessons. Here they have a head of year and a tutor who monitors their work and well-being, with regular interviews to discuss problems and set appropriate targets. Also a confidential professional counselling service and regular PSHE, with outside speakers, group work and discussions.

Pupils and parents: Students, from a huge range of ethnic and social backgrounds, apply from a vast swathe of north London. Despite the consortium's leafy surroundings on the eastern edge of Hampstead Heath, all four schools are inner-city comprehensives with a socio-economic intake reflective of the term. Generally, pupils are confident and mature and get on well.

Entrance: LaSwap has about 1,300 places on offer. Eight hundred of these generally go to existing students; a further 300, however, are available for students from schools outside the consortium. The entrance procedure is intricate and careful attention must be paid to every step and date. First step is to register interest online by the end of the autumn term. Then, armed with a ticket and a parent, prospective candidates attend the open evening in January. Applications must be submitted by post or by hand in early February – those who miss the deadline are immediately put on the waiting list. All applicants who meet the deadline are offered an interview at the school in February or March to discuss subject choice and given conditional offers based on GCSE grades. Those with offers must attend the one-day induction course held before the start of the summer holidays, when summer assignments are set. Post GCSE results, further interviews and places are confirmed.

Exit: About 400 students go on to 60 universities to study 50 different subjects, from medicine and accountancy to drama and international relations. About 20 per cent to Russell Group universities. A large contingent to leading art colleges, mostly to the University of the Arts, London (Central St Martin's, Chelsea, Camberwell and London College of Fashion etc). A handful to Oxbridge – four in 2013.

Remarks: A good compromise between school and a sixth form college, with an extraordinary range of subjects on offer. Tends to suit the motivated and the self starter, but not ideal for those who will be distracted by studying on a number of sites or who require the disciplined parameters of a school sixth form to function at their peak.

Lathallan Senior School

Linked school: Lathallan School

Brotherton Castle, Johnshaven, Angus, DD10 0HN

- Pupils: 190 boys and girls (120 in seniors and 70 in juniors).
- Ages: 13–18 • Non-denominational • Fees: Day £16,329; Boarding £22,386 pa • Independent

Tel: 01561 362220
Email: admissions@lathallan.org.uk
Website: www.lathallan.org.uk

Headmaster: Since 2009, Mr Richard Toley BA MPhil PGCE (forties), who joined Lathallan in 2006 as director of co-curriculum from the nearby High School of Dundee. Educated at The Merchant Taylors School in Liverpool, followed by St David's Lampeter (where he met his wife). MPhil at St Andrews – down the road – and PGCE at Strathclyde. He and his wife live on site, with their two small young. Catapulted into the headship, (he had an 18 month apprenticeship, but didn't know what was in store for him) he is comfortably confident in his role. (We just popped in for a quick check on our way down from Aberdeen, so he couldn't have mugged up facts or figures. As if). School moved from being 'just' a prep school with a hugely popular and often over-subscribed nursery in 2006, to building up a senior base year by year. On one of our visits we were shown exciting plans for a huge new build, but caution overcame enthusiasm and the governors reined back, revamping under-used dorms in the attics, reconfiguring some of the girls' dorms and converting the freed-up first floor dorm space into spectacular classrooms (some with basins still evident and some with basins nattily concealed in cupboards. Still there in 2012). An historian, charming and relaxed, Toley teaches classics (as in classical studies) and history 12 periods a week in the senior school. Resplendent in green socks, we talk in his office/drawing room filled (so it appeared) with dragons – the current passion is warhammer – and a familiar (slightly battered) Boule cabinet. Impressive collection of uber-powerful governors plus parent-governors, 'tremendous backing'. Toley coaches rugby and cricket.

Mr Toley runs the school with Duncan Lyall, head of senior school and James Ferrier, head of junior school (qv). Duncan Lyall, BSc, PGCE, (forties), an Edinburgh lad, read mechanical engineering and teaches maths. Married, with a young son, he came to Lathallan from Peebles High School, having previously taught in both the borders and Aberdeen.

Academic matters: Scottish curriculum: 17+ subject options at all levels. Recent results encouraging, good scattering of As across the board in both higher and advanced higher. Mixture of highers, and intermediate 2, plus standard grades, the latter disappear next year to be replaced by national 4s and 5s. Toley quite relaxed about this change, 'we will work our way through'. Mandarin – whenever. French, Spanish (native speakers), not a lot of take up in the former – though two outstanding results in higher and advanced higher, with a couple doing Spanish at standard grade. Latin from aged 11 (classical studies at higher and advanced higher), crash course in Italian – offered at higher level, but no take-up – plus the usual suspects: maths, English, three sciences, history, geography (pleasing and popular), business and classical studies, art, PE and drama, and managing environmental resources (MER). Results are penny numbers, occasional glitch, but these are early days, and the school is non-selective. Civilianship the latest addition – ie how to open doors, ladies first, that sort of thing; school is talking to exam boards as to how they could make this an examinable subject. Think finishing schools, think nanny, think how clever.

L

All assessed for dyslexia et al on arrival at senior school, juniors are checked 'carefully' and if obvious, they get a 'proper test'. Two dedicated learning support staff, one to one, clusters, or co-teaching. Costs the same as a piano lesson. Back-up for the bored and the brightest. Class sizes around 13 (maximum class size 16), pupils streamed for maths and English which are taught in refurbished classrooms in the castle, interactive whiteboards all over. IT impressive – Dell computers all over the shop with Apple Macs in senior school. Science is in a hotchpotch of temporary buildings beside the nursery complex: the staff whom we met are young, enthusiastic and fun. Loads of new staff, 26 permanent staff on the books and six part-timers. Specialist staff for junior school. No apparent problem in attracting staff, though cheaper for them to live further south – the Aberdeen catchment area is pricey.

Games, options, the arts: Music everywhere – bagpipe boxes all over the porch and hall when we visited, both girls and boys in pipe bands much in demand for charities and have entertained Princess Anne of late, played in the Angus show, the Glamis gathering, Hollyrood parliament etc. Pipes and Drums played at the battlefields in Belgium and compete in the Royal Pipe Band Competitions. Scottish country dancing no longer has parental input; marvellous photographs in the porch of a junior Scottish country dancing lesson – note the kilt loops and the ecstasy on the faces of the young. Strong drama: new head of music previously with Aberdeen Youth Theatre, no orchestra per se (yet) but wind and ceilidh bands.

Toley has introduced a new formal schoolwide traditional PE programme, which, 'through age-appropriate indoor exercises aims to improve co-ordination and mental agility both in and outside the academic classroom' (sounds a tad Steiner-ish).

Thrashing all comers in under 16 rugby 7s, new games pavilion under construction (board member head of SRU); 7s rugby team off to Dubai later this year, but 'mainly it is regional' with all points south of Gordonstoun. All seven plus year olds play sport daily, tennis courts double up for netball (Astroturf), ten acres of playing field overlooking the North Sea and own beach (bracing), plus refurbished gym. Lots of jolly rugby trips and girls' netball tours. Sea at the bottom of the garden, but no sea sports – too rough.

Head of outdoor education is Monro-potty, 'probably climbed them all three times' says Toley. D of E timetabled. First two years of senior school spend six days in the mountains, mountain rescue, navigation (shades of roundsquare). Skiing, both at home and abroad.

Background and atmosphere: Founded in the imposing Victorian Brotherton Castle in the early 1930s. Originally a traditional boys' boarding prep school, set in 62 acres of woodland and catering, in the main, for 'the folk over the hill'; now a thriving nursery through to advanced highers co-ed school offering full time, weekly or flexi-boarding. Bruce houselets guard the corners of the long abandoned formal garden which makes a splendid play area. Influx of foreign boarders since full boarding re-opened: 30 boarders housed in separate wings of the castle (previous staff quarters), co-ed boarding tidily arranged, mainly oily children, from Thailand, China, Spain, Nigeria, Russia. Scottish Guardian Overseas Association oversees them (and individual guardians have to pick up the flack if their charges are sent 'home', ie gated). Some locals, bed and breakfasting available. Regular exchange programmes with 'smallish' schools in Canada, Switzerland and Australia, the latter were enjoying their six weeks in Angus during our visit. More than 25 clubs, 'we rotate them' says Toley.

Library and resource centre in main building with classrooms and nursery in bright converted stable block with massive additions. Some lessons in temporary classrooms. Masses of eco-input. Newly refurbished common-room for senior school pupils. School uniform provided in house, with rather jolly fleecy waterproof jackets which staff wear too. Staff all have to take the minibus test.

Pastoral care and discipline: School small enough for every child to be known (cherished is a word that comes to mind if it didn't sound so soppy), strong anti-bullying policy. Occasional gatings for wickedness, no child yet asked to leave. Civilianship a popular subject. School is 'bespoke, focused'.

Pupils and parents: Increasing number of first time buyers, FPs, very supportive, strong parental input, parents will drive many miles out of their way to drop off their tinies in the nursery. Return buses for older children from Stonehaven, the Edzells and Aberdeen with coaches from Brechin and Montrose. Aberdeen business community plus local farmers, commuters, usually from within one and a half hour radius (which takes you to Dundee). Rob Wainwright an old boy, ditto Ian Lang (Lord Lang of Monkton). Niche school: perfect for the occasional non-performing refugees from bigger trad schools: Fettes, Merchiston, Robert Gordons. Children thrive in the smaller environment. 'We care'. (Those parents to whom we spoke fell into the latter category. Their relief was palpable.)

Entrance: At any time to any year group if places available, many come via the prep. Otherwise form 5 (P7: 11, 12 year olds). Taster day. Informal tests in English, maths and verbal reasoning, but not a selective school. Numbers up from prep school, 10/12 a year. Currently full first three years of senior school (and nursery and pre-junior school ie ages 5 and 6).

Exit: Tiny trickle leave for trad independents age 13, otherwise the odd re-location. Sixth formers head in the main to the Scottish unis: St Andrews, Edinburgh, Aberdeen, Heriot Watt, Stirling and Glasgow.

Money matters: Money matters 'under control', up to 100 per cent bursaries (and extra help if necessary). Second-hand clothes shop. Will keep child if parents fall on hard times with the usual caveat of being up front about the problem.

Remarks: This is the tail that wagged the dog. We have visited Lathallan over the past 20 odd years: six headmasters. This was a school which had – quite frankly – been toiling. Sometimes it had a nursery which took babes from two months, sometimes from three years. In any case it was a boys' boarding prep school with an increasingly dismal roll call (even after they took girls and day pupils) and a glorious view. Two, or was it three? heads ago, the brave decision (we thought nuts) was made to expand, on a year by year basis, to become a fully fledged school, with highers and advanced highers and all. We were wrong. Very wrong (and we won't rehearse further the various decisions down the line). Remarkable success story.

The Latymer School

Haselbury Road, London, N9 9TN

• Pupils: 1370, equal balance of boys and girls; all day • Ages: 11–18 • Non-denom • State

Tel: 020 8807 4037
Email: office@latymer.co.uk
Website: www.latymer.co.uk

Headteacher: Since 2005, Mr Mark E Garbett (late fifties) MA (Cambridge) MEd NPQH. Plenty of experience in academically strong schools, including a previous headship at Stretford Grammar School, Manchester; five years at Skegness Grammar

School and Royal Belfast Academical Institution; and a spell as head of maths at Framlingham College. All helps, though Latymer 'is much more selective, you're teaching very bright young people all day, every day, you've got to stretch them, you've got to be on top of your game to generate that respect that you know what you're talking about'. Head supported by three deputies and 82 full-time staff, all with degrees in their specialist subjects (pupil teacher ratio is 17:1). A down-to-earth maths teacher who likes high standards, Mr Garbett 'still teaches two classes each year' and, in his fourth decade in education, loves the fact that 'I still get new questions' from students. He likes teaching and likes children, 'really important because just occasionally a parent comes across a teacher in a school and has this idea that that teacher doesn't like children. We can't have that here'. This helps with selecting new teachers: 'If I ask a teacher in an interview, "Do you teach chemistry or children?", I am really interested in their answer.' Since he has recruited around 60 per cent of the current staff since joining the school, child-friendliness level is evidently high. Head describes his position at Latymer as 'the best job in education – who would want to be secretary of state?' He finds the many opportunities to meet parents – at welcome evenings, parents' evenings, concerts, sports sidelines, one-to-ones – 'enjoyable, except for the time when I was foolish enough to volunteer to sit on a bucking bronco at an International Food Festival'. He fell off. Has two daughters, plays the piano, sails and runs.

Academic matters: Good GCSE results making it the top performing school in Enfield borough and within the top six per cent in London. Very good A* to A results in maths (98 per cent in 2013); English lang and English lit (72 and 57 per cent respectively); and the three sciences (biology, 87 per cent; chemistry, 83 per cent; and physics, 88 per cent). Pupils must choose a MFL from French, German (both very popular), Russian or Latin (not so popular) plus a humanity subject or religious education. ICT is not taught as a separate subject but incorporated across the whole curriculum.

Years ago a decision was made to reduce the number of GCSEs to nine to ease the stress on pupils and so that 'school life can be enjoyed for itself'. The recent introduction of triple GCSE science increases the number to 10 but head still thinks it important that academic success is not at the expense of 'a life outside school'.

At sixth form the school offers 'nothing apart from an unashamedly academic programme', so no vocational subjects here. The majority stay on at sixth form but another 50 join from other schools, so exam rates at 88 per cent A* to B grades is commendable. Having a larger than normal sixth form means the school 'can teach a big range of subjects, which smaller sixth forms struggle to offer'.

Parents agree that the school is 'very good academically' and it certainly makes plenty of effort to reward academic achievement across all years. Year 13s are awarded in specialist subjects too, such as mechanics, statistics and government and politics. Pupils who do not gain a subject prize have the opportunity to be awarded either a Latymer Lodge or school prize for gaining a high aggregate at A level. There are also open awards for special achievements in spoken English, creative work, instrumental performance, music composition and fieldwork. Prizes are awarded for service to the school in music, debating and service to the community, thus plenty of motivation to strive and to win here. 'They will take your child through the process and your child will pass the exams,' one parent stated confidently. Another said, 'I believe that both my children have been encouraged and guided to fulfil their academic potential. Classroom teaching is supported with a range of visits and activities to inspire as well as stretch.'

Where pupils have a special learning need, they will find help through one of the two SEN teachers: one helps to 'identify those pupils whose needs require support in the learning process', and the other 'helps support children with particular gifts or talents'. Around 350 pupils have EAL requirements and of the 29 pupils identified as having a special educational need just three have a statement; the remainder have support such as 'school action' or 'school action plus'.

Games, options, the arts: More than 17 different sporting activities offered (from athletics and badminton to volleyball and ultimate Frisbee). Notable achievements include winners of Enfield Schools Hockey Champions and Enfield Football Cup, alongside a number of other firsts, seconds and thirds in regional finals for netball, tennis and cricket. In year 10, when pupils have the opportunity to specialise, and at sixth form, they can also take squash, golf, swimming, orienteering and dry-slope skiing in addition to the normal range of sports on offer. The school encourages active lifestyles and rewards pupils' enthusiasm for sport with a number of awards that recognise outstanding achievement both in and outside of school. These include hockey, football (for girls, not boys), netball, cross-country, rounders, tennis and cricket. All pupils have the opportunity to spend a week at Ysgol Latymer (the school's outdoor sports centre located in Snowdonia National Park in Wales) for activities such as hill walking, orienteering, climbing, abseiling and canoeing.

Latymer once had an art specialism and so the subject has a strong presence outside the department, with work on display around the school and cross-curricular contributing (for example, year 9s painted the background scenery for senior drama productions of My Fair Lady and Hairspray). Experts visit to do talks and run special workshops in oil painting and sculpture, and the department runs visits to the London Institute, Tate Modern and Tate Britain as well as to Barcelona and Paris. As a result examiners have commented on the good grasp pupils have of contemporary artists.

Drama is supported by trips out and really plays out hugely in the big theatre productions that take place at the school each year: a main school production in November, a junior production in July, and the house drama competition every other year. The language and drama curriculums are supported by school journeys and exchanges through links with Russia, France and Germany; there have also been exchange visits with the Mwambisi school in Tanzania; geography is supported by trips to a range of destinations including Iceland, classicists to Italy, artists to New York, skiers to the French Alps, canoeists to the Ardeche, music to Austria, Belgium, Germany, the Czech Republic and other places in Europe; sports to Holland and Italy. There have been other trips to Nepal and India and Malawi, and every other year there is a sports trip to Barbados.

In music, 'considerable opportunities exist, both in the curriculum and in extra-curricular activities'. Many activities – piano, violin, clarinet, recorder, horn and voice – played to a 'very high quality, culminating in the almost professional standards of some of the most able pupils'. A quarter of the pupils learn a musical instrument at standards ranging from beginners to beyond grade 8. As pupils advance through key stage 3 they focus on 'practical music-making wherever possible' covering projects on classical, jazz, pop and world music, with regular assessment every half term. There are five orchestras ranged from grade 3 to post grade 8, a concert band and several choirs. They perform at school concerts and many are invited elsewhere, such as the National Festival for Music.

Latymerians enjoy a rich range of extra-curricular activities that shape life at the school; parents value its contribution to their personal and social development. House theatre and music productions; over 60 different clubs and teams run before, during and after school, and at weekends. Clubs cover art, gardening, chess and more. There is a Young Enterprise group, an economics society, a Christian union and clubs whose sole purpose is to raise funds for less fortunate children in developing nations while pupils learn more about their lives.

We are told that the school's Amnesty International group is 'the largest and most active school group in the country'. The LAFTA (Latymer Awards in Film, Television and Advertising) is a fun and creative play on the Oscar-style awards ceremony.

Background and atmosphere: Tradition creates the atmosphere at Latymer. It was established in nearby Church Street in 1624 at the direction of Edward Latymer, a City merchant, who bequeathed certain property to trustees on condition that they were to cloth and educate 'eight poore boies of Edmonton'. His, and the 'generosity of the many others since', are remembered each year on the school's Foundation Day. Pupils are proud of this tradition and seem enthusiastic about the events that keep it alive. The school's motto – Qui Patitur Vincit (Who Endures Wins) – aptly sums up the spirit of the school, and is the title of the annual talk to the school (head's given it seven times so far and says it's a 'feat to bring a new twist to it'). The school moved to its present location in 1910.

On the day of our visit it seemed very quiet, apart from the hum and beat of instrumental practice (including drums) in the music department and a flurry of students preparing for the school's major production in the Seward Theatre downstairs. Built on three acres of land and flanked by 12 acres of playing fields, which separate the school from the main A10 road, it looks deceptively small from the front. There are a number of outbuildings around the main one, added at various times over the school's life and capturing its spirit of progress: the great hall (1928), which seats over 1000; the gymnasia and technical labs (1966); a performing arts centre (2000) and a sports/dining hall complex (2006). In 2010 the high-tech multi-purpose Seward Theatre (performance space, auditorium, media studio, art gallery and drama theatre) was opened. The school also has a number of rooms dedicated to specialist teaching, for example, a suite of 12 science laboratories, six fully equipped technology rooms, and specialist ICT rooms with wireless networks, an intranet and access to remote access learning. There is a large library, with separate learning resource and careers centres. Sixth formers have a large common-room and quiet study area.

The school's traditional atmosphere is maintained by the old students' association (there is an old boys' football club and old students' badminton club). Ex-students are very much involved school life, participating in school events, contributing to lessons, presenting school awards and setting up special funds. There is a rich sense of celebration of the past: each year a whole school assembly is organised for the 'grand Act of Remembrance' in honour of Latymerians who died in the two world wars. They sing the national anthem, read from the Bible, listen to a talk about war life and have a 'blessing suited to a multi-faith audience' pronounced by a local reverend. There is a book listing war casualties in the library, which pupils proudly pointed out.

Pastoral care and discipline: The 180 pupils in each year are organised into six form groups, and each form group belongs to one of the six house groups. They remain in these groups throughout their school lives, meeting daily for registration and form periods, including, in the lower years, PSHE lessons delivered by the form tutor. Each year group also has a head of learning (first point of contact for parents concerned about progress) who, along with the deputy head of learning, also acts as mentor.

Pupils also have 'a wealth of information on the intranet to help them achieve a healthy balance,' said a parent.

House culture is strong. Each has a senior pupil to lead, democratically elected. Activities are organised by senior pupils and used to inject a sense of comradeship and teamwork across all year groups, and to make new year 7s feel fully inducted into life at Latymer. They do this via sports tournaments and various competitions such as cake-making, drama and music. 'Equally importantly', houses also 'operate non-competitively'

to organise community service activities and to help raise funds for charity (one house group raised over £80 in 20 minutes for Water Aid by taping water bottles to themselves). Together, this creates 'a strong sense of coherence and team working' among pupils at the school.

Pupils are expected to abide by the school rules and the home school agreement they signed with their parents on joining the school, but the school views 'self discipline resulting from wanting to learn' as a more important deterrent for poor behaviour. Although behavourial problems are rare and 'dealt with swiftly by the head of learning or form tutor', one parent did say she thinks the pastoral care side of things 'is not as strong as the focus is on the academic side'. However, other parents say pastoral care is excellent: 'Not only do my daughters experience excellent teaching, they also benefit from being at a school with a firm commitment to pastoral care. They feel safe, secure, confident and happy. While the academic side is challenging, it is not to the exclusion of everything else.' Another said she has 'always felt comfortable emailing teachers direct if I have a concern or question'.

Pupils and parents: Anyone and everyone who is 'very clever', though the school wisely lists acceptable postcodes in its admission criteria. This includes half from Enfield, then from a wide surrounding area which takes in Hackney, Islington, Tottenham and Essex. Old boys include footballer Johnny Haynes and Strictly Come Dancing host Bruce Forsyth.

Entrance: Only those 'deemed capable of achieving higher grades of GCSE are considered' at this highly oversubscribed, selective school. Selection is by the NVR test as well as literacy and numeracy. A parent said 'it used to be harder to get into' but 1700 typically apply for the 186 places, so many are still disappointed. Priority is given to looked-after children and those who live in designated postcodes areas in the boroughs of Hackney, Waltham Forest, Haringey and Enfield. Offers also made to around 20 students who show 'exceptional musical talent and achievement' akin to Grade 5.

At sixth form, 95 per cent stay on. An additional 50 places are allocated to pupils from other schools bringing the size of the sixth form to 234. Sixth form is also oversubscribed with around 440 applications for these 50 places. Places are offered to students who achieve at least six GCSE grade As, including the subjects they wish to study at AS level; they must also pass the Latymer test and live in one of the designated postcode areas.

Exit: Around 95 per cent go on to university or other forms of higher education in music and art. The school does not 'push Oxford or Cambridge though plenty apply, and plenty get offers' (34 in 2013). Others go on to study mathematics, the sciences, medicine, law, economics and the humanities at UCL, Imperial College, King's and other major universities. Very few – one or two – leave to go straight into employment.

Money matters: The Latymer Foundation offers some financial assistance to pupils experiencing hardship.

Remarks: A peek back in time shows that some well-known former pupils like Baroness Claire Tyler (chief executive of Relate), footballer Johnny Haynes and Sir Bruce Forsyth CBE all did well here. Pupils clearly still do. This is a zealously traditional school with a highly likeable yet firm-handed head and pupils who show a healthy balance between hard work and play. There is some effort to keep with the times but the head's view is that 'If it ain't broke don't fix it'. Ofsted has a similar attitude and in its last report described the school as outstanding.

Latymer Upper School

Linked school: Latymer Prep School

237 King Street, London, W6 9LR

• Pupils: 1,175 boys and girls (49 per cent girls); All day • Ages: 11-18 • Non-denom • Fees: £16,485 pa • Independent

Tel: 0845 638 5800
Email: registrar@latymer-upper.org
Website: www.latymer-upper.org

Head: Since September 2012, Mr David Goodhew – read classics at Oxford and previously deputy head of Durham School. He inherits a school in good heart and a considerable investment of trust that he will maintain its new-found spirit.

Academic matters: Results have steadily improved, though Latymer has yet to achieve as highly as its intensely selective intake would lead you to expect. A levels in 2013 saw 88 per cent A*/B grades and two-thirds A*/A grades. GCSEs were 94 per cent A*/As.

New curriculum rolled out in 2010 looks both worthily innovative and imaginative, now though some chafe at the lengthy double lessons – now 90 minutes long: 'It's fine if it's your favourite subject, but if it isn't...'. Designed to improve educational value in general with, it is hoped, knock-ons for results which, while good, remain a notch short of stunning. A few parents of the brightest feel that Hawking Minor is less than stretched, but this may change now. Most teachers highly praised and much admired. Sixth form teaching seen as especially good – along with excellent careers and university advice: 'My son's tutor made all the difference'.

Parents enthuse about the learning support department, which is 'excellent and run by two most wonderful women'. 'My son can go before school, during lunch break or after school,' one told us, gratefully. 'We don't pay for this extra help,' another acknowledged. 'And my daughter can take her homework or anything else she needs help with.' School reckons on around 10 per cent needing some kind of support, mostly dyses, a few ASDs; will lay on help in year 7 for temporary EAL if needed.

Games, options, the arts: Sport is notable and famed throughout the western (London) world! On-site provision is limited, though sports hall, fitness suites, pool and two tarmac courts find nesting room here. Main school games take place 15 minutes away in Wood Lane and the lack of on-site facilities offers no impediment to the school's legendary prowess. Rowing and football are particular strengths, but all pursued with vigour and success.

Four good-sized studios pump out impressively free and imaginative art across the media, and similar creativity informs the lively work done in DT – very professional jewellery made in silver smithing club; two lasers, a furnace and a brazing hearth – even an anvil – enable skill and experimentation of a high order. 'We prepare them for a future in architecture, product design or engineering,' we were told. But also, 'It can be a fantastic release to heat something to 1000° and beat the hell out of it.' Quite! All take DT, art, music and drama to end of year 9 and then, somehow, choose. Music is powerful, with any number of bands and ensembles large and small in wildly various musical modes – from Latin to chamber choirs and a full orchestra. Outstanding standard over all. Likewise drama – taken seriously and executed professionally.

Lunch hours are packed with activities and all pupils – especially the first three years – encouraged to take on as much as possible. Quite astonishing range of extra-curriculars on offer – we counted nearly 100. Good range of outside speakers.

Everyone drools over the trips – 'Amazing – far better than at my last school,' enthused a recent arrival. 'I've been everywhere – fantastic trips to South Africa, Egypt, Argentina.'

Background and atmosphere: You could miss it, crouching unobtrusively behind a low, gothic arched wall on the south side of the rather dingy King Street between Chiswick and Hammersmith. It occupies a rectangular plot between King Street and the roaring A4 into London (you don't notice the roar, we are told, after a month or two) under which runs a cunning subway, through which the children troop to the prep school, the sports hall, pool and, rather surprisingly if you're not quite sure where you are, the River Thames. The Latymer boat house nestles underneath (opposite the St Paul's Boys' one) and the school is a rowing powerhouse. The main building dates from 1890 (hence the red-brick gothic); smart newer buildings abut it now and the old tarmac car park has recently been reborn as an attractive 'piazza', popular for chillin'. Other onsite outside space is minimal but no-one is given much time to miss it.

The school began in 1624 and boasts a tablet commemorating its founder – Edward Latymer (a wealthy puritan, who pledged funds on his death-bed to educate and feed 'eight poore boies') – set into the outer wall, in piam memoriam etc. Old style main hall, complete with honours boards, WWI and II memorial tablets (always heartbreaking), stained glass and large portraits of former heads. Brown glazed tiles very much set the tone in the main building – smooth wood and big windows more the mood in the good new buildings. Performing arts centre, connected to older arts building by two glazed bridges, has enhanced provision in all subjects, especially music. Good-size, flexibilissimo studio theatre. Block with ground floor library (exemplary – has the feel of a top quality municipal resource but is exceptionally well-stocked and, when we visited, was stuffed with silently working pupils, who genuinely did not look as if they'd been bribed) and three floors of science, plus small lecture theatre. A pint pot here now accommodates a quarts-worth of space – cleverly done.

The site has been softened in recent years by planting with a design sense lacking hitherto. Spacious sixth form common-room reminiscent of an airport lounge with TV, sofas and vending machines. Sixth form also have a rather swish café bar – open to others too, but it oozes cool that would be wasted on the young. Dining hall serves excellent food, though lunch time is a crush. Organising 1100+ pupils in this limited space inevitably results in log jams and queuing at all changeover times, but it's pretty good-humoured and everyone shrugs.

Pastoral care and discipline: Considerably improved under previous head – but then it needed to. Parents applaud, 'My son keeps being late and they make him stay in – which I approve of'. Veteran parents who have witnessed the last years' changes concur, 'The discipline is stricter now, which is right because things quickly get out of hand'. Some older pupils chafe under what they see as a harsh régime – 'If I didn't have to come to early registration, I could have an extra half an hour in bed, which would be of real educational value,' one cherubic sixth former vouchsafed, earnestly. 'They're very anal about stuff like that,' a friend chimed in – while parents rejoice behind the cornflake boxes. School discipline is pragmatic and effective – 'Drink, smoking, drugs and bullying? We have them all, and anyone who says they don't is lying through their teeth'. Has expelled and will expel pupils if drugs are brought into the school, and the good of the school as a whole will always prevail. Likewise with bullying – 'We have an open culture here. The bully thrives on silence and fear. If a child is feeling belittled or upset, there is always an avenue he can go down,' and it's not just words – pupils say it really is like that now. Much praised system of older pupils mentoring the younger ones. The sixth formers sense a real change when they reach this elevated state – 'The staff really make an effort to get to know you and work with you... I've had endless individual help'. Boys and girls now wholly integrated and it feels like a proper co-ed – 'You don't ever feel the boys have been there longer,' a sixth form girl affirmed.

Pupils and parents: West London and fringes – most from within 30 minutes' travel, though a recent influx from the Kensington end of things. It has few competitors, being the only co-ed with an academic reputation for miles around. The school of choice, therefore, for the educated middle classes, from fat cats to media types on short contracts. At 11, around half come from state primaries – providing local tutors with most of their annual income. Parents praise much-improved school-home communication, 'They always get back to me quickly'.

Entrance: Most of the school's own on-site prep come up. Around 50 per cent from local primaries. Some 800 candidates for the 130 places at 11+ – boys slightly outnumber girls. Usual English, maths, reasoning and interview. At 13+, around 45 sit for the seven places on offer. At 16+, around 185 candidates for about 50 places. School requires minimum four GCSEs at A including the subjects to be taken in the sixth.

Exit: Everyone pays tribute to the careers and uni advice. Oxbridge, Manchester and London are top choices. Thirty to Oxbridge in 2013 and increasing number to US or other top international unis. A few annually to art, music or drama schools, otherwise medics, economists, engineers and linguists. Several actors among its famous alumni – Hugh Grant, Alan Rickman, Christopher Guard, Imogen Poots, Mel Smith, Gus Prew; also heavyweight musos Walter Legge and Raphael Wallfisch, plus Pete Townshend's dad, who was expelled; a few notable sportsmen plus politicos Kulveer Ranger, Keith Vaz, George Walden, the Beeb's Joshua Rozenberg and local MP Andrew Slaughter. Also Heston Blumenthal, Dr Hilary Jones and Lily Cole. Appealing mix on Old Boys' nights, no?

Money matters: Getting increasingly generous. Around 70 pupils on 100 per cent bursaries and more planned.

Remarks: Summed up by a year 13 girl – from the first cohort of girls to go all through, 'It's a really academic school, but not just academic – it's a real all-round school. I've loved it. I've had a ball.'

Lavant House

Linked school: Junior Lavant House

West Lavant, Chichester, PO18 9AB

• Pupils: 95 girls; 20 boarders • Ages: 11–18 • C of E • Fees: Day £13,680; Boarding £21,528 pa • Independent

Tel: 01243 527211
Email: office@lavanthouse.org.uk
Website: www.lavanthouse.org.uk

Headmistress: Since 2013, Mrs Caroline Horton BSc MEd NPQH. Previously deputy head at Parkstone Grammar in Poole, Dorset. Educated at Leeds Girls' High School and King's College, London and began her teaching career at Queen Anne's School, Caversham. Taught at The Maynard School for ten years before becoming head of maths at St Margaret's School, then assistant head at Torquay Girls' Grammar School.

Married to Mark, with three sons.

Academic matters: Small and traditional school with a broad range of abilities. Head says that more academic mentoring as well as pushing each girl's grade boundaries is achieving academic success. However this school is about much more than the sum of its results. Because of its small numbers it can accommodate individual needs and thus the value-added is high. When working on their GCSE options the girls are required to rank their subjects on a scale of one to 10 and a flexible timetable is constructed to include their choices. This flexibility extends to A level, eg classes of just one for Spanish and economics. Science rated as very good by the pupils and staffed by enthusiastic teachers. Because of the small numbers in the labs (now being updated), 'a high proportion of time can be spent on experiments and a lot of practical work; the pupils really engage and get involved'. Art and media popular and results good. French is taught from year 1, Latin from year 7 and Spanish from year 9. All staff have SEN awareness training and are kept up to speed with any emerging problems, which are 'nipped in the bud,' we're told. New learning centre for G and T as well as mostly dyslexic pupils – specialist SEN teacher and TEFL teaching for foreign students (but very few international students). In 2013, 36 per cent A*/A grades at GCSE and 22 per cent at A level.

Games, options, the arts: Facilities are good for a small school – an outdoor pool, three netball courts (soon to be resurfaced), a good old fashioned gymnasium plus hockey pitches. Main sport is netball – they do well on the local circuit and 50 girls are taken each week to the West Sussex netball club to train. Separate stables on the periphery of the school – many girls own horses and love to ride at weekends. Active Duke of Edinburgh Award scheme, with the school being perfectly placed for such ventures amongst the Downs.

Music is crucial for the head as she develops more ensembles, string groups, orchestra, a harpist, an emerging flute group – bearing in mind the size of the school, this is some achievement. Art is a big strength – pupils' work adorns every available nook and cranny and is housed in a long light studio with some exciting textiles on display. Offers the unendorsed GCSE course that includes digital photography, printing, some sculpting. Fine art and textiles; new food tech facility. They make good use of the neighbouring Pallant House gallery for visits and workshops and are introducing an integrated arts evening in the summer term – a production of varying scenes performed around the lovely grounds, particularly the orchard, to include the music, art and drama department. Many girls take GCSE drama – not many performances, however, as teacher feels drama should be more about process than performance. Abundant trips to, eg, nearby Goodwood House, Fishbourne and Bignor Roman villas, Chichester Theatre, plus trips to Auschwitz, Flanders battlefields. Year 9 spends a week off timetable exploring the tunnels, cellars, roof spaces and ice house of Lavant House and plenty of camp outs at school.

Background and atmosphere: A former large country house – Dora Green founded the school in 1952 originally for her own children, one of whom is still on the board of governors. The main building is a mix of flint and 18th century red brick, with spacious rooms and well-tended grounds. Additions of studios, a cottage, the Scott Building, named after the last headmistress, and multi-purpose large hall merge well with surroundings. The school is approached on a long path surrounded and cushioned by the Sussex Downs and fields of horses and stables. A long terrace to the rear provides a safe and pleasant place for afternoon teas and evening barbeques. Teachers love teaching here, and why wouldn't you? The deputy head was internally appointed six years ago and has been at the school since 1980.

Some 20 boarders housed in the eaves of the main house; rooms are cosy, fastidiously tidy, with some unattractive wall colours, although apparently chosen by the girls themselves. Flexi-boarding is very popular – plenty of beds to cope. Accommodation ranges from single rooms to dormitories of seven for those that like company. Four sixth form boarders who have their own small cottage in the grounds – individual rooms with a small sitting room and kitchen. Plenty of activities and outings for the boarders; the head of boarding is also, very usefully, PE trained and thus sets up stool ball, swimming, croquet, rounders etc. A safe path that the girls can ride their bikes down to West Wittering beach – the stuff childhood memories are made of. Food is good with a daily large salad bar, vegetarian and dish of the day. Warm family feel throughout the school.

This is an established school, grounded in Christian values – a traditional grace said before lunch. To some this may be non-PC, but the head is unapologetic, 'as this is what our school represents'.

Pastoral care and discipline: Head of pastoral care is also the head of art and says the care is about constant communication with the nurse, counsellor, matron, staff and parents – 'The most important thing is that the staff are approachable, so that any girl can talk through a problem'. Discipline is not a problem – 'No teacher needs to raise their voice here: a raised eyebrow is enough,' said one parent.

Pupils and parents: A broad social mix described by one as 'ranging from the country wellies to the Gucci brigade'. One parent chose the school after bumping into a group in the Chichester Theatre car park – 'The school minibus arrived, the girls disembarked and we found ourselves walking into the theatre with them. We noticed how well they conducted themselves and how very appropriately dressed they were, not very made-up but an assured and classy set of girls – an encounter of more value than all the marketing'. Another parent chose the school because of the amount of back-up literature and details of events etc sent to them after their visit, keeping them totally in the loop: 'They were too attentive to be resisted'. The girls mix well and feel they are very supported and not inhibited from being themselves – 'It's cool to be clever or not,' say some girls. Day girls come from a radius of 20 miles, boarders further afield, some Forces children and small handful of overseas boarders, mainly from France and Spain, and at present two Chinese pupils.

Entrance: Pupils can and do join at various stages, mainly 11 and 13. Formal assessments in maths, English, NVR (11+) and science (13+). Entry to the sixth form is dependent on GCSE results (the fact that the school does not stipulate specifics here indicates flexibility).

Exit: More (some 80 per cent) now stay on to the sixth form and then to diverse destinations: e.g. Edinburgh, Sussex and Plymouth in 2013. Links with an Australian independent girls' school, Abbotsleigh – exchanges after sixth form (the girls' rooms overlook Sydney Harbour).

Money matters: Music and academic scholarships offered at 11 and 13. One fully funded place for year 10 and year 11 based on academic merit and parents' financial situation.

Remarks: Small size of this school its huge strength – very flexible in accommodating individual pupils' needs. It can cope with the academically able, although that is not its raison d'être. You can rely on good manners, integrity and the well roundedness of these girls.

Leighton Park School

Shinfield Road, Reading, RG2 7EE

- Pupils: 490 (320 boys and 170 girls); 135 board • Ages: 11–18
- Quaker (all faiths welcomed) • Fees: Boarding £24,072–£29,730; Day £15,759–£19,089 pa • Independent

Tel: 01189 879600
Email: admissions@leightonpark.com
Website: www.leightonpark.com

Head: Since 2013, Mr Nigel Williams. Nigel has worked at the school for 18 years, in a variety of roles, most recently as deputy head. School says he is committed to the Quaker testimonies of peace, integrity, equality and simplicity.

Academic matters: Solid, not stunning, results but school takes a broad range, stands by its charges, lets them pursue passions and has been known to make silk purses from the proverbial. In 2013, 65 per cent A*/B grades at A level with an average point score of 32 in the increasingly popular International Baccalaureate. At GCSE, 36 per cent A*/A grades. Almost half A level students take maths – a strength of the school – and about a third physics or chemistry. Extensive labs a hive of animated activity when we visited – frequencies and vibrations in physics, reaction times in chemistry, buzzing and busy. Excellent art and design, English lit good. Modern languages flagged by parents as a 'could do better' with few if any boys taking at A level. First name terms (used throughout) can make it hard for staff to establish themselves but most do so with great aplomb. A few staff moved on, some for promotion, some retired, others by mutual agreement; new blood well-received. Smallish classes, good facilities, multi-media languages centre, well-appointed maths building, great workshop space for DT. Religious studies (called 'beliefs and values') includes philosophy of Quakerism. Reading important, jolly library with squishy bean-bags and themed, artful displays prepared by a librarian passionate about inspiring others to read. School regularly hosts visiting authors, and even produces and prints its own books and anthologies.

Intellectual rather than academic in approach: pupils are encouraged to question, think, experiment and to challenge ideas. 'We do more than just learn, we consider implications,' said one girl; another added, 'Leighton Park lets you be an individual, even giving you metaphorical rope to almost hang yourself with, then steps in at the critical moment, if you haven't saved yourself.' In line with the Quaker ethos, head is keen to create a professional learning community and subscribes to the view that 'teachers should be guides on the side not sages on the stage'. Had a major push on improving accountability and upping expectations. Monitoring, recording, reporting and targets emphasised with 'portfolio of progress' to highlight the good and the gaps. No intention of ceding to sausage machine, 'We expect pupils to question and to challenge, but they have to take ever-greater responsibility for their learning too.' Some parents concerned cerebral push might spoil the nature of LP, others guardedly approve, 'If it focuses staff and students without strait-jacketing, allows them to continue to explore their learning and doesn't pressure the way some other local schools do, it will be fine.' Procedural tightening addresses odd moan about communication. 'In some ways the lack of hover encapsulates the beauty of LP but in others it doesn't cut mustard – there have been lots of last minute assessments and squeezing things in, so better planning is welcome'; another added, 'It wasn't helpful to hear your child had gone from A to D at the end of an academic of year'. Precisely.

Approximately 20 per cent have mild to moderate needs (mainly on the dys-strata but ADHD, Aspergers, VI, HI okay). Super Individual Learning Centre (ILC), with its refreshingly generous rooming and good, nurturing team of experienced staff, operates an open door policy, with students dipping in as required. 'Support isn't a life sentence, we don't tattoo it on their forehead,' says learned SENCo. Not the place for complex needs, no classroom support, no TAs and usually max withdrawal of one lesson per week. Pupils expected to work hard to develop skills and coping strategies. Hottest ticket in town is the frequently gate-crashed ILC party. Parents of new pupils report fantastically speedy, school-wide help, understanding and support. 'My child is bright but has organisational and processing problems. Unlike his previous school, they were on to his difficulties immediately, working on strategies, putting systems in place and keeping me informed.'

Games, options, the arts: 'It's so much fun here' say youngsters; prospectus is crammed with exciting accounts of extra-curriculer options – D of E, art club, debating, Amnesty International, textiles, Young Enterprise, house competitions a mere flavour. If what you fancy isn't on offer (how can that be?) then pupils are encouraged to start a club. Odd parental moan that some advertised activities don't always run – some organised by pupils who later bail out, others lack a critical mass to make them happen. Art good and innovative; we loved the statue in the quad, the painstaking work of a GCSE student. Glowing reports of magnificent music and compelling dramatic productions with orchestras, ensembles, choirs and performance opportunities aplenty. Impressive list of county sportsmen, sports and fixtures galore. Floodlit Astroturf and super games pitches but gym aged and sports hall on wish list. Super 25 metre indoor pool. Trips and tours to everywhere for everything – possibly jars with school's Save the Planet group (inspired by 'ecologist in residence')? Sixth Special on Friday afternoons welcomes a range of dynamic speakers and much debate.

Background and atmosphere: Founded as a public school in 1890 to educate scholars for Oxbridge, nicknamed 'the Quaker Eton' at the time, it still has style but in a modern, forward-thinking kind of way. The 'old school' is a fine Georgian building with a gracious reception area; outside, a small lawn and ha-ha date from its origins. Sixty acres of parkland – a welcome oasis of greenery; calm and (mainly) elegant buildings provide a welcome change from Reading's maze of tarmac, cheek by jowl with the University of Reading, close to M4 corridor and Heathrow. Grounds much used, most recently for an enchanting Gruffalo trail, engineered and designed by LP pupils to enthral children from local primaries. Wonderful calm atmosphere, Quaker ethos permeates pupils' psyche – look for good in others, pupils (and active PTA) raise loads of money for charity, second chances common.

No Saturday lessons – so lots of weekly boarders, (flexi on request) – plenty for weekenders to do. Day pupils often stay for supper and prep. Operates on boarding school lines; fierce house loyalty with sports, music and competitions galore. Generous, well-kept, homely accommodation, one junior house (years 7 and 8), and four co-ed senior houses – all with kitchenettes, games rooms etc. 'There's an ease and maturity of friendship between the sexes which stems from the co-educational houses,' says head. There was certainly a great buzz and friendly, welcoming atmosphere when we visited, day students seamlessly integrating with boarders and much mixing across ages. Sixth form centre – The Caradon Centre – has areas for IT, careers, study and relaxation as well as kitchen and meeting rooms plus own garden. Wonderfully civilised, trendy Oakview dining facility offers great range of tasty, wholesome, healthy meals and treats.

Pastoral care and discipline: Universal acclaim for excellent pastoral care, each child assigned a tutor who oversees their well-being and progress. Mutual respect of pupils and staff is palpable but that doesn't mean kids get an easy ride. Tougher stance than many schools on transgressions, drugs, alcohol etc. 'The difference is, those who err are disciplined but once they have served time for the crime, they are allowed to move on'. 'My son had a couple of run-ins but still made it to prefect, I think other schools would have marked his card.' Low incidence of bullying, most disputes self-resolve. 'My daughter has a huge group of friends and a great social life, kids care about each other.' Good careers advice; sixth form staff praised, 'They continued to help my son even after he left.' Staff encourage pupils to think about and question their choices, 'Even if you are a dead cert for Oxbridge they won't push you into it, they want what's best for you, not what looks good for school.' Parents say, 'All schools have bumps along the way but staff at LP are always ready to listen, to be open-minded with the interests of the child paramount.' Recently smartened uniform policy a hit with us – navy for younger years, business suits from Y9 up.

Pupils and parents: Smart, friendly and quickly at ease in our company, pupils were happy to share their views on the school, warts and all. 'More history, chocolate and sports,' were frequent requests from forthright, younger boys; 'less sport,' said a lone female voice, happy to go against the grain. Older girls, setting up a lunchtime food stall, fund-raising for good causes, gave an eloquent account of their work and aims. Lots of schools talk about individuals but there's no stamp or typical LP child – lots of quirky kids, plenty of off-piste discussion but no truck with showy, ostentatious behaviour. Element of compromise means those who need continual, clear boundaries would struggle. 'Expect periodic engagement in brutally frank discussions; some youngsters can be outspoken, challenging ideas and conventional thinking', say parents. Won't always pick the best pupils to do something – give chances. All major faiths represented, five per cent Quaker. Large number of feeder preps and primaries mainly from Berkshire, Oxfordshire, Hampshire and Bucks. Twenty per cent overseas from 24 countries, including USA, China, Australia, Europe. Parents from a range of professions, lawyers, business, IT and university professionals plus media types. Old Leightonians: Sir David Lean, Sir Richard Rodney Bennett, Jim Broadbent, Laura Marling, Eliza Bennett, Michael Foot, Lord Caradon, Lord Frederick Seebohm and a fair clutch of MPs plus Rowntrees, Cadburys, Clarks, Reckitts, Morlands and Frys.

Entrance: January entrance tests for years 7-10 (alternative dates if needed) in maths, English, non-verbal reasoning. Pupils chosen on previous report, interview and reference from current head. At sixth form about 35 enter from outside with at least six A*-Cs and A*-B grades in chosen subjects (A/A* for maths).

Exit: Most to university, Imperial, Kings, Exeter and Warwick the most popular. About 20 per cent take a gap year. Four to Oxbridge in 2013 and some to specialist colleges eg RADA, conservatoires etc. A few leave at 16 for sixth form colleges.

Money matters: Several major and minor awards for art, music, drama and sport. Means-tested bursaries. Friends' schools' bursaries available to those with Quaker parents. David Lean Foundation awards one annual scholarship for 100 per cent of day fees, for academic excellence.

Remarks: Stuck unapologetically to revered, old-fashioned values of encouraging independence of thought, creative thinking, collective spirit, spine and responsibility. 'Their voices are heard, they learn to cope with life but in a comfortable environment where they can make mistakes. It's this distinctive preparation for real life that makes LP different.' Parents talk of

L

the leap of faith: 'It doesn't suit everyone; it bucks the pressure-cooker trend, evident in so many schools in this area, yet they still get the result'. 'My son wasn't a conventional learner and struggled at GCSE yet staff were patient and in the end he soared, achieving top grades. I am not sure he would have done so elsewhere'. Ideal for the confident, considered, articulate intellectual with a mature outlook, but equally those who've had a knock, find their feet and are encouraged to fly.

Lenzie Academy

Myrtle Avenue, Kirkintilloch, Lenzie, East Dunbartonshire, G66 4HR

- Pupils: 1,240 boys and girls (50/50 split); all day • Ages: 11–18
- Non-denom • State

Tel: 01419 552379
Email: office@lenzieacademy.e-dunbarton.sch.uk
Website: www.lenzieacademy.e-dunbarton.sch.uk

Head Teacher: Since 2011, Mr Brian Paterson BA PGCE (late forties), previously head of Abronhill High. Educated at Paisley Uni, his PGCE was in modern studies and economics at Jordanhill. He taught in Glasgow and Lanarkshire before doing eight years as principal teacher, firstly at Harris Academy, Dundee and then at Boclair Academy, East Dunbartonshire, where he also spent seven years as depute head teacher. He has been a marker and setter for SQA, an educational consultant for the BBC and a writer of educational materials.

From a Glasgow background where pupils left school at 16 and university was not an option, he is grateful to the teachers who encouraged him and wants to gives something back, feeling it is his civic duty. Not attracted to a more lucrative career though he once 'wobbled for ten minutes'! Life is now pretty full on at school – recently included being the murder victim in an ASDAN project – so down time is spent mainly as a taxi-driver for his children, one still in primary and one in sixth form, both in East Renfrewshire plus a daughter at Strathclyde. He likes to play football twice weekly in the staff seven-a-side club but getting away for some hillwalking at weekends is a bit of a pipe dream. Having run an academic school at Abronhill he sees himself as having taken on the challenge of making a school with a pretty distinguished record into something of real excellence. His go-ahead SMT of six deputes are unlikely to allow many bottoms to get stuck on laurels. Very clear on priorities, he will not waste energy on problems that are likely to resolve themselves or are not resolvable.

The immediate plan is a £650,000 facelift – a complete paint job (not before time); school is also being comprehensively re-roofed and getting new doors for all entrances and the tired looking football/ hockey pitch outside the school is getting a new all-weather surface. He is strengthening the house system, giving pupils more responsibilities and making things more competitive in the academic sense not just in sport. Tracking and monitoring are being sharpened up so he can quickly spot weak areas or potential failings. Longer term he wants to build up drama and has his eye on how to make more studio space, if funds permit. Grass will certainly have no chance under his purposeful feet!

Academic matters: Classes currently at 30, with eight forms per year group (capped at 240). Uses the Scottish SQA system – in 2013 S grade and H grade results kept school in top 10 per cent of schools in Scotland. Advanced Higher results impressive too, with significant increase in performance. Impressive range of subjects on offer, even in comparison with the best of the independent sector. Most teaching areas a bit trad to look at

but some top notch equipment everywhere. Nice to see as many boys as girls in Higher design and engineering, however battered the benches. They clearly know their own minds.

Plenty of pupils do three sciences at S grade, while the bulk do two and no one is allowed to get away without one. All do one modern foreign lang to S4, currently French or German, with Spanish just starting up, though no Latin, Italian or eg Mandarin, even in clubs. The advantage of size is that there are over 30 subjects on offer for S5/6 many of them at four different levels: Advanced Higher, Higher, Intermediate I and II. This range is further increased by distance learning, so there isn't much limit to what you can do, especially as flexibility includes letting pupils take subjects at other local schools if the timetable won't fit. Plugged into Strathclyde and Heriot Watt's SCHOLAR learning programmes and into the local consortium.

A magnet school – pupils from other (state) schools come to Lenzie to study Highers and Advanced Highers not available in their own. Stunning computer studies results at all levels and the school has a record of jolly good results over a number of years in maths, all three sciences, art and design and health and food technology. Interactive whiteboards much used. Results, already pretty spot on, have generally improved in response to tighter monitoring and academic mentoring programmes.

SEN well staffed – monitoring is good and still improving. A supportive culture in school includes a scribes' and readers' club. Provisions vary from year to year as children with severe difficulties, either physical or intellectual, attract appropriate help. This is a totally inclusive school by ethos.

Over 100 pupils do not have English as their first language (speaking 31 different languages) and extra help and EAL are available. Homework club at lunch time and super supported study scheme post school – 200 pupils regularly stay on – when pupils can access the ICT suites.

Games, options, the arts: Apart from a huge – though not as huge as originally planned – games hall built in 2001 and two pitches on site (currently getting the new Astroturf), provision looks a bit limited but the school uses local club pitches five minutes away to impressive effect and offers all the usual sports, with some enthusiastic players including a national athletics champion. Lots of way out stuff too: outdoor education, a successful sailing club and even collie racing!

Art department is very go ahead with 2 Higher photography course, portraiture with a real artist, Andrew Ratcliffe, and masses of work going on with colour. Vibrant displays in the art rooms and some smashing mosaic murals all over the school to brighten it up. Vocational courses in tourism, textiles, hospitality and so on, there's even one in cake decoration; all put on as serious opportunities in Scotland's current economic climate.

Music is big too with plenty of classical and quite a few groups on the performance side and academic on offer up to Advanced Higher. No pipe band but plenty of electronics just coming in despite the expense! Huge production every year with Guys and Dolls the most recent.

Background and atmosphere: Unremarkable 1960s buildings, now looking distinctly retro, date from when the school moved to a roomier site from a square set, stone building in Lenzie, which is now the primary school. Pleasant brick court in one wing with a sadly rundown garden (but grass won't grow there we were assured!); inside corridors are wide and classrooms really light and spacious. The other wing has such narrow passages that that a one-way system is essential but it's brightened by the work and info put up by various academic departments. Lenzie hasn't had the benefit of the funds lavished on its snazzy neighbours in Bearsden and Kirkintilloch but there's lots of ground around the school for development and already an inviting patio for sitting out, when the Scottish weather allows!

Nice smart new dining hall with gallery for social use and carrels for study, plus every possible device to make it a multifunctional centre. No pre- or post-school cafeteria, though the area is open to early comers from 8.15 and school is open til 6 or so when community use starts.

Main hall is desparately dingy but brightened up on our visit by a comprehensive 'Hopes for the Future' inter-disciplinary learning display from an S2 project. Terrific programme of renovation is on-going but the formerly plentiful 'glory holes' have been eradicated and there are endless lockers everywhere. One room is now being transformed into a dance studio/fitness suite.

Pastoral care and discipline: Guidance is done in forms and a teacher stays with the class as it goes up the school. The six deputes are year heads and meet with the guidance teacher once a month to discuss every member of each class thoroughly. Not much need to use the bullying code but it's there and the occasional fight calls for extreme sanctions – mainly expulsion for a day or so. Behaviour guidelines classify bad behaviour in three levels; the third gets a 'demerit' reported to parents and if Mr Paterson gets his way this will also go into competitive house records.

Mr Paterson is tightening up uniform and there's a smart new (remarkably inexpensive) navy blazer with green braid and new school badge (the old one was all wrong and blazers were baggy). We saw a few coloured hairdos and nose rings and some very short skirts. Everyone seems to wear just about anything for games.

Pupils and parents: The pupils we met were polite and quiet and staff friendly and concerned. There are pupil councils for each year group consisting of two pupils from each class and this is being co-ordinated with house councils which will help socialising to be through all age groups.

Quite a large proportion come from ethnic minorities, since local universities attract staff from abroad. Majority of parents from the locality and 'leafy Lenzie' is fairly upmarket. Parents are supportive and run a Friends of Lenzie Academy (FOLA 125) which does a great job raising funds for the school. The Parent Council is supportive of the school's activities and developments.

Entrance: Entry is capped at 240, of which usually 130 or so are locals. Some apply from outside the area which now includes part of a huge newly built estate, most of which is outside the actual catchment area but so close that those applying are likely to get priority.

Exit: Most pupils stay on until S6, with a few leaving at the end of S4 and S5. About 75 per cent to HE/FE, mostly Scottish unis with three or four to Oxbridge each year and the rest normally to training or work. Statistics show a few 'lost', ie no work or training, but these are usually 'gap year students.

Remarks: A whacking great school with a dynamic head and tremendous possibilities, already doing a grand job for 'leafy Lenzie'.

Leventhorpe School

Cambridge Road, Sawbridgeworth, CM21 9BY

- Pupils: 1,190 boys and girls; all day • Ages: 11–19 • Non-denom
- State

Tel: 01279 836633
Email: education@leventhorpe.net
Website: www.leventhorpe.net

L

Headteacher: Since 2008, Mr Jonathan Locke (forties), degree in maths from the University of Wales and PGCE from Cambridge. A keen rugby player forced to retire through injury, he now spends his free time running and cycling but also enjoys relaxing trips to France with his language teacher wife Celine and their two young children. A natural communicator, he believes that 'Whenever you make a decision it's impossible to see it from every perspective – someone's opinion always hits you from left field, so that's why it's important to speak to as many people as possible to make sure all opinions are taken into account'. To that end he's 'freely available and very approachable to parents and children,' says one parent, and hosts a listening lunch every month to sound out the staff on new developments, gripes and suggestions. Another parent comments, 'He holds discipline and achievement high on his agenda but encourages all aspects of a young person's development.' His positive approach to education is certainly infectious, and his efforts to ease the curriculum into a more pupil-centric way of thinking have been very well received.

Academic matters: Sats results determine setting for new year 7s in some subjects, and these are checked up on throughout years 7-11 – 'It's fluid,' says head. Year 9 is an 'enrichment year' with pupils offered a broad choice of subjects: additional literature in English, experiments in sciences plus a vocational option, PE theory, philosophy, sociology – refined when the time comes for GCSE option decisions. A very wide selection of subject options at GCSE – some clever timetabling software ensures that 95 per cent are able to study their chosen combination.

Enthusiasm high and reflected in results – in 2013, 73 per cent got 5+ A* to Cs including English and maths at GCSE, with 25 per cent A*/A grades; at A level, 54 per cent A*/B and 24 per cent A*/A grades. Open University modules can be studied alongside A levels and this – and the fact that the place is buried in computers – typifies the ethos of independent learning. In fact it provides one of the largest school OU cohorts in the country. 'Our aim here is to encourage pupils to take ownership of their education and to develop a sense of responsibility that will transfer to further and higher education and into the workplace,' says the head.

Games, options, the arts: A new, state-of-the-art leisure centre boasting a vast sports hall, dance studio, fitness suite, flood-lit Astroturf, classrooms etc is extremely well used. Leventhorpe does well on the sports field and makes the most of close ties with the local cricket and rugby clubs.

Music facilities are 'reasonable,' says the head rather generously, but even so music is thriving: 300 students have lessons, a school orchestra and a choir that goes on tour every few years – the staff choir shows the way. Musical aptitude places are available to a handful of year 7s from out of the area, and free lessons encourage them to develop their talent. A few go on to music college each year.

The art rooms are hives of colourful activity and the annual fashion show gives young designers the chance to strut the catwalk in their own creations. The expanded sixth form provides a pool of leaders for activities: they have revived the student council themselves and take it very seriously, recently having the casting vote on the restructuring of the school day.

Background and atmosphere: A collection of rather plain 1960s buildings – has the advantage, though, of being nearly all single-storey with wide sunlit corridors and classrooms off. This makes for an easily navigable, light and airy school with few bottlenecks and plenty of space for displays. Being set back from the main road just on the edge of this small town and backing onto playing fields and farmland, it has a tranquil, rural aspect.

Well-resourced by state standards – impressive ICT suite with pop-up monitors and a face-recognition registration system in the sixth form block, for instance. Food technology is an increasingly popular option since the completion of new kitchens. New learning resource centre under construction.

Although this is a sizeable secondary and pupils come from a scattering of villages on both sides of the Herts-Essex border, it has a small-town community spirit. Pupils seem proud of their school and coming here is generally a given – 'Why go anywhere else?' asked one pupil in bafflement. Uniform is fairly traditional – blazers and white shirts with a kilt for girls and plain trousers for boys, sixth formers smart in business wear with suits for both and ties for the guys. The overriding impression is one of purposeful industry – and smiling faces all round.

Pastoral care and discipline: House system is all-pervading and trumpeted through distinctive ties for boys, the house name embroidered on girls' shirts and coloured blazer badges. Pastoral care is funnelled through the tutor and head of house, and sixth form mentors look out for year 7-11s. As well as inter-house competitions, achievement in the classroom is rewarded with points for the house and the totals are eyed with enthusiasm. Celebration of success is key – the Headteacher's Commendations are listed every fortnight in the school newsletter and achievements of both pupils and staff are highlighted. 'It's through rewards that behaviour can be modified, not through sanctions,' says the head, but is quick to point out that the school has very few problems with discipline and pupils on the whole are purposeful and law-abiding.

Except in the case of major misdemeanours, exclusion is eschewed in favour of 'inclusion' – a day spent working under adult supervision in isolation on school premises: 'A day at home can be seen as a reward,' says Mr Locke. Minor transgressions are dealt with by tutors. Although mobile phones may be brought to school, using one in lesson time leads to confiscation and a call to a parent to collect the offending item from Mr Locke himself. Bullying is dealt with effectively – the heads of school run a listening panel of senior prefects and trained student counsellors to support any pupil who feels they might be affected. No exclusions this year and the Thursday after-school detention session is the only one – generally fewer than a dozen children in it.

Pupils and parents: Since the arrival of Mr Locke, parents have appreciated being kept in the loop with increased school-home communication and a constant dialogue. Pupils are dispatched with PDAs to canvas opinions at parents' evenings. Feedback informs school policy: 'If a parent posts a message via the school website saying that they think standards of appearance are going downhill, we post a teacher on the gate to check uniform the following Monday morning'. Parents generally appreciative – an interactive revision night, when parents and pupils were instructed by three key subject teachers on revision techniques and useful websites, was singled out for praise.

Entrance: Children from eight feeder primary schools in Sawbridgeworth and the surrounding villages – usually a place for every child in the catchment who wants one. In response to local demand the school has recently increased the number of places it offers each year to 180. Eighteen places for children with musical aptitude from outside the catchment, who sit a standardised test in common with other good state schools in the local area, and are then encouraged and often financially supported in their musical endeavours.

Scraps over good sixth form students with sixth forms in Bishop's Stortford and Harlow: two Bs and three Cs, including at least a C in maths and English at GCSE, to get in.

Exit: About 70 per cent to own sixth form, which has ballooned of late from 200 to 320, due, says the head, to 'good marketing and fantastic results.' Some 85 per cent to university, including two to Oxbridge in 2013; several to medicine, dentistry and law. 'They don't just want students with a string of A*s,' points out the head. 'It's their ability to conduct themselves and communicate, and that's what our curriculum develops for everyone.' A strong link with the head's alma mater, Cambridge, with good preparation and support for those anticipated to make the cut.

Remarks: A very businesslike establishment with a forward-thinking head who seems likely to take it to greater heights. An innate sense of community – pupils take pride in themselves and their school.

Leweston School

Linked school: Leweston Prep and Pre-Prep School

Sherborne, Dorset, DT9 6EN

• Pupils: 235 girls; 110 boarders (full and weekly) plus up to 20 flexi • Ages: 11-18; plus co-ed prep on site for ages 2-11 (girls may board from year 3) • RC–but the majority are other denominations • Fees: Boarding £22,350–£27,360; Day £16,560–£17,265 pa • Independent

Tel: 01963 211010
Email: admissions@leweston.dorset.sch.uk
Website: www.leweston.co.uk

Headmaster: Since 2006, Mr Adrian Aylward MA (Oxon) MBA PGCE (mid fifties), educated at Worth School and Oxford, with a PGCE from Kings College London. A meteoric rise in corporate finance led to his appointment as CEO at the tender age of 29 – 'Maybe I did it well because I never did it seriously', he admitted – but it is clear that he does take headmastering rather seriously, and indeed does it rather well. 'The decision to teach was the first one I ever consciously took, rather than being carried along by events', he says. A PGCE in his early thirties preceded a teaching career entirely in Catholic schools, with the exception of his NQT year at the Royal Grammar School, Guildford: this is a man for whom faith is a central part of his life. Some parents reckon he is a little removed from the day to day running of the school (though he swears he knows every girl in it) and recognise the strong team that backs him up, but all enjoy his intellect and eccentricity. (We love the Latin tags on the school literature.) Very sharp, very frank and very funny (gales of unseemly laughter emanated from his beautiful art deco study when we were talking to him) and clad in a racy and un-headmasterly red sweater, Mr Aylward seems well-placed to carry on turning over stubborn perceptions of Leweston as second best to Sherborne Girls: 'We're very different schools', he avers 'and we are now seen as a genuine alternative and ready to take them on in terms of boarding and academics'. Married to Caroline, he has one daughter at Bristol, one at Leweston and a son at Downside.

Academic matters: Very much on the up. Results in recent years show a steady rise, with an especially successful spike in 2011. In 2013 72 per cent A*/B grades at A level and 52 per cent A*/A. Pre-U is offered alongside A levels in music, history, English and history of art, and results are sound, with very few girls getting below a C or equivalent. Twenty-three subjects on offer at A level, with compulsory courses in various things which round out the syllabus, including the global perspectives part of the Pre-U and the extended project. School justifiably proud of the fact that 90 per cent of applications to medical school have met with success in the past five years. At GCSE, 69 per cent A*/A grades in 2013. Ten subjects out of 20 on offer is the norm; a language and RS are compulsory. Some subjects can be taken early. The fact that the timetable can be tweaked to accommodate any combination of subjects is a huge plus – and very much to the director of studies' credit. Value-added scores are particularly high for Leweston, placing it in the top five per cent of schools nationally at GCSE and top 10 per cent at A level. Greater numbers being interviewed for Oxbridge and recent success in the British Maths Olympiad all add to the sense of a school whose academic star is in the ascendancy. Parents enthuse about maths, English, Spanish, geography and music in particular.

SEN provision deals with mild end of normal issues, including ADD and ADHD, but can accommodate moderate learning difficulties. All girls tested for SEN on entry and school has CReSTeD status. The gifted-and-talented are not neglected either. EAL also catered for; in fact huge enthusiasm voiced for the school by overseas girls.

Games, options, the arts: Conventional offering of hockey, netball and tennis enlivened by squash and badminton courts and, recently, by the transformation of the gloriously sited outdoor swimming pool into a year-round facility by the construction of a perspex roof with retractable side panels. Over 40 green acres go some way to explaining the school's success in track and field events, particularly cross country and, interestingly, football. Three sportswomen of international standing in 2013 indicate a school which punches above its weight. Horse-minded boarders can have their mounts at livery: riding lessons can be arranged in either of the two arenas at the school, and teams take on other schools at dressage, show-jumping and eventing. Some kind of sport is compulsory for everyone, including sixth form – all activities are registered. Quite apart from the benefits of exercise (to work off the excellent food), compulsory sport, 'gives girls the opportunity to try out different things, and instils a sense of commitment', says the head. All levels of D of E also available.

Music is a key part of school life and the lure of nearby Sherborne, with the abbey (home to the carol service) and its joint Schools Sinfonia Orchestra is enough to make any school raise its game. Three recent top performers achieved diploma-level music. A variety of ensembles provide somewhere for any aspiring or shy musician to play or sing, and the joint forces of music and drama come together to produce a musical, most recently 'Sweet Charity'; also collaborations with Sherborne School, plus other male bastions requiring girls. Good showing in Dorset and beyond, notably at the Mid Somerset Festival in Bath for music, drama and recitation. Art and design strong too; we particularly liked the textiles, whose remarkable creations would (and do) grace any catwalk. In fact there is an increasingly well-trodden path to colleges of fashion from Leweston. Many sixth formers take up the option of Leith's basic certificate in food and wine with gusto – a professional qualification and simply essential for those stints as a chalet girl in one's gap year – while all girls have to do survival nutrition and cookery.

Background and atmosphere: Founded originally in Sherborne in 1891 by the fearsomely named Religious of Christian Instruction (a group of nuns hailing from Ghent), the school moved to its current home three miles away in the Palladian manor of Leweston in 1948, which was purchased from the Rose family (of lime juice fame). A palpable sense of Catholicism still prevails, but not the nasty exclusive you-can't-take-communion-here kind; we felt that girls of any faith, and possibly none, would be welcomed. No nuns these days, but the chapel is central to school life, and the tiny exquisite 17th century Trinity chapel in the grounds hosts smaller weekday masses.

Pleasing mansion of golden ham stone sits at the end of a long drive through the park, somewhat marred by later necessary additions, some of which (eg classrooms round the back) are barely fit for purpose, say parents. They are also well aware that the facilities, 'don't compare with Sherborne Girls', although a welcome new sixth form den with a café and wi-fi has just been opened. Somehow though the relative modesty and make-do-and-mend feel rubs off on the girls, who are appreciative, charming, bright and definitely going places. 'I chose it for my daughter because of the kind of girl who goes there', said one mother, herself an Old Antonian, as former pupils are called. A very accepting culture was also widely praised – of girls from abroad, and of personal quirks, for example – making it a place where girls can truly be themselves, whether that means not growing up too fast, or fleeing bullying at other schools. 'I am thrilled that my daughter has been able to do loads of sport, which she loves, instead of being made to stick just to academics and music, which she's good at', said one happy mother, 'and she's been able to stay younger for longer'.

The social pressures of being right in Sherborne with 600 boys are of course less marked at Leweston, but some parents feel that more use should be made of opportunities for joint productions and sports training, and voiced faint irritation at the fact that there is a 10 per cent sibling discount between Sherborne and Sherborne Girls – but not with Leweston. The head, however, says firmly that his school is back in the game, with joint trips to Cordoba and New York, as well as musical, dramatic and social endeavours.

Pastoral care and discipline: Discipline was not mentioned – these girls seem a biddable flock – but pastoral care gets a big thumbs-up. High staff:pupil ratio at 1:7 means no-one feels out of her depth without a life-belt. Boarding has had a shot in the arm and numbers are rising, now standing at about 50 per cent. 'There was some lack of clarity about it', said the head, 'but putting all the junior boarders in one house has improved matters.' School could still do with more local boarders – there needs to be a critical mass', according to one mother, who also remarked that her daughter did not enjoy staying in at weekends – weekly boarding is an undoubted trend. Interestingly, Leweston was one of only 10 schools recently chosen to trial the new BSA Boarding Skills Award, a kind of D of E of boarding (but without the yomping): 'to be used as a currency for employability alongside academic results', according to those who devised it. (Everyone passed.)

Pupils and parents: The majority, nearly 80 per cent, British; a sizeable minority of girls from SE Asia and a good mix of Europeans make for a reasonably cosmopolitan feel to the place. Most UK residents are very local; one mother said she felt at a disadvantage coming from Hampshire, as it was hard to get to events during the week. A sprinkling from London, 2 hours away by train. All we met seemed down-to-earth and unpretentious, with realistic expectations of school and life generally.

Entrance: At 11, 13 or into sixth form, but at other points by arrangement. School sets own entrance tests at 11 (academic, numerical and perceptual reasoning), relies on Common Entrance at 13 and on six 'good GSCE passes' at sixth form. Everyone has an interview with the head. Scholarships in art/DT, drama, music and sport offered along with academic ones.

L

Exit: A few pull stumps after GCSE, possibly in search of boys. Those who stay are glad they did; in fact we were told of one girl who tried a neighbouring school but headed hot-foot back to Leweston after a couple of weeks. University choices span the length and breadth of the land, with a variety of degree courses, from English and history of art to maths and medicine. Spanish most popular as language degree course. Eminent old girls include Kristin Scott-Thomas, Erin Pizzey and Serena de la Hay (whose Wicker Man can be seen from the M5).

Money matters: Cheaper than many competitors by over £1000 per term for boarding in some cases. Scholarships to the value of 10-30 per cent, 50 per cent for three scholars of exceptional ability across all disciplines at 11+.

Remarks: Gaudere and bene facere, rejoice and do well, so says the school motto: Leweston girls certainly do both. Hidden gem in a sleepy hollow, definitely meriting a look from those seeking to escape the glitzy rat-race that some girls-only education has become.

The Leys School

Linked school: St Faith's

Trumpington Road, Cambridge, CB2 7AD

• Pupils: 560; 335 boys, 225 girls (370 boarders, 190 day) • Ages: 11-18, plus associated prep St Faith's 4-13 • Methodist/inter-denom • Fees: Boarding £20,235-£27,780; Day £13,185-£18,480 pa • Independent

Tel: 01223 508904
Email: admissions@theleys.net
Website: www.theleys.net

Headmaster: Since January 2014, Mr Martin Priestley, previously head of Warminster School. Studied PPE at Oxford; interests include singing, writing and playing squash.

Academic matters: Traditionally middling but in recent years results have been shooting up. In 2013, 69 per cent A/A* at GCSE – vast majority take separate sciences, physical ed (pupils see it as a big plus that it can be taken regardless of other options) and religious studies (compulsory) taken in year 10. At A level, 43 per cent A*/A in 2013 – strong results from maths, physics, geography and history. Sets for maths, languages and sciences. Parents appreciate the breadth of talents and ages in the staff room and agree that teachers are very 'clued up'.

Indeed a much sharper focus on the academic in recent years, most notably 'learning beyond the curriculum' through a greater use of extension work, often making the most of the talents of Cambridge University postgraduate students who inspire the most able Leysians. Pupils are encouraged to take personal responsibility for their learning – only one hour a night designated prep time, for example, but an expectation that free time will be managed effectively to get it done. 'It's a balance between ensuring good exam results and developing the skills for future learning and responsibility.'

School doesn't flaunt its SEN credentials (dedicated department with three staff, one full-time) but garden variety learning difficulties well supported. A realistic view taken on entry as to 'which children will prosper here and which will not.'

Games, options, the arts: It would be an understatement to say that games are important here. Some real high-flyers – currently numbering national rugby and hockey players (girls and boys),

plus a champion equestrian team and keen rowers. School participates in the Cambridge University leagues for some sports and gifted athletes are assured of top level competition. Swimming and rowing are strong. Top-notch facilities are an attraction – first-class sports hall (shared with local sports clubs), floodlit Astroturf hockey pitch (converts into 12 tennis courts in the summer), recently extended fitness suite, newish pavilion, boatyard on the Cam. Sport sessions three afternoons a week and after school too for the enthusiastic; however, a more flexible approach now being taken to talents, with those whose are not most in evidence on the field of play being allowed to spend a portion of games time in the music practice room, drama studio, art room or wherever their star shines brightest. Many other activities too – 'our son is taking cookery very seriously,' said one proud parent.

The bright Rugg Centre is the hub of all things artistic – studios, DT, photography and ceramics. Art goes from strength to strength – two finalists in as many years in the Daily Telegraph/Saatchi Gallery art competition and some stunning exhibitions in Cambridge. Serious musicians are now being attracted – many joining from the Cambridge college schools with a strong musical tradition – and there's a large and high quality orchestra, string and wind groups, choir and even a parents' singing group. Distinctions aplenty in LAMDA exams and regular school plays and performances. Heaps of school trips, including scientists to Canada, geographers to Iceland, classicists to Pompeii and Naples, linguists to France, Spain Germany... Also many visitors in, notably authors to inspire the literature group to get reading.

Background and atmosphere: Opened in central Cambridge in 1875 with 16 Methodist boys. Red-brick Gothic buildings, modern additions, sporting facilities and a dotty miniature railway (with several halts) ring central playing fields. £9.5m Great Hall recently completed – science and performing arts centre comprising assembly hall, theatre, drama and dance studios, science labs, art exhibition space and a café – its architecture bridges the gap between old and new buildings either side. With additional games fields nearby the school has an ample 50 acres.

Went co-ed in 1994 and maintains a roughly 60:40 boy:girl split. The majority of pupils are boarders – girls in a modern block with balconies (for sunbathing) and potted plants. Home boarders, 13 and up, have all the advantages of boarding but with breakfast and sleep at home – the best of both worlds according to many pupils and their parents – and travel outside of the infamous Cambridge rush hour (it's longer than an hour). Day pupils are off home by 4.30pm but many stay till 6pm.

A robust community of a small school. Approachable house staff (some with babes and buggies) add to the family feel and students are trusted to go off into the city centre from an early age – repaid by invariably returning when stipulated. Bikes are welcomed (this is Cambridge after all) and some houses have communal bikes to borrow. Sixth formers pop in and out of the city as they please and have their own club at school, open for an hour or so every evening after 9pm and serving beer and wine (with a strict limit).

Girls' uniform, pre-sixth, recalls the school's wartime evacuation to Pitlochry – Mackenzie tartan kilts – but there's no rigid dress code for either gender in the sixth form and the school tracksuit (attractive dark and light blue) seems most favoured attire.

Pastoral care and discipline: Parents and pupils are impressed by the pastoral care – the key to its success is the system of one-to-one timetabled tutorials with informal top-ups whenever needed. Housemasters and prefects unearth any problems before they have a chance to take root. Parents report that they often see teachers in general discussion with pupils. Chaplain is popular and much in evidence – parents as well as pupils appreciate his support. Christian ethos is strong and chapel two or three times a week in various permutations of pupil groups (day pupils less keen on the occasional Sunday attendance).

Training for prefects focuses on 'developing antennae for any difficulties' and is all about student welfare. 'There's a real consensus here about what matters in education. If we can get the pastoral care right, then all else will fall into place.'

Discipline is seen more as an opportunity to guide than to punish. No problems with substance abuse for quite a while. Pragmatic approach to bullies but most misdemeanours seen as issues for pastoral care.

Pupils and parents: Mostly UK residents – just 12 per cent from foreign shores, mainly in sixth, though good ESL on offer – and the vast majority live within an easy two-hour commute of Cambridge. 'No PR disasters' in recent memory and boarding is now more popular than ever among UK students – any day boy or girl who leaves before the sixth (local state super-sixths are the alternative) is usually swiftly replaced by a boarder.

Parents are 'not exclusively green wellies,' – in fact a good mix of local academics, scientists, medics and many escapees from the capital. Good effort on the part of the school to draw in the parents – parent rep per house and a PTA that is extremely active for a boarding school.

Their children are in the main self-assured and overwhelmingly relaxed and comfortable in their skins. The Leys is appreciated locally as the 'rounded' option (speaks volumes about the perception of the alternatives) and certainly burgeoning personalities are given free rein – the school is small enough to cater to the individual and does it well. There's no 'Leysian type,' says head. Old boys include Martin Bell, Sir Alastair Burnet, Richard Heffer, mathematician Sir Andrew Wiles, J G Ballard.

Entrance: At 11 and 13. Half the intake crosses the road from St Faiths (same foundation), and the rest is made up of arrivals from preps such as Cambridge's King's and St John's, as well as Dame J Bradbury, Orwell Park, Barnardiston Hall, Aldwickbury and a steady recent trickle from Heath Mount. Own entrance exam in English, maths, verbal and non-verbal reasoning and a report from the previous school at 11+ and 13+, but no interviews apart from for scholarship candidates. Personal qualities are rated as highly as academic attainment and many considerations. Entry for the sixth is usually a bare minimum of five Bs at GCSE, but most external applicants are armed with a mix of A*, A and Bs. Around 80 per cent of sixth form boards.

Exit: Most day pupils and a few home boarders switch to excellent, local sixth form colleges at the end of the fifth (any boomerangers are graciously re-accommodated, usually with a day place). Majority of sixth formers head to university, with a fair number taking gap years. Russell Group most popular of course, especially Edinburgh, Leeds, Nottingham, London.

Money matters: Scholarships slashed to five per cent of fees and only for two or three great brains at 11, with talents in music, drama, sport, DT and all-round considered at 13 and sixth form entry. Fee concessions for those who need them and special bursaries available for Forces families, Old Leysians and Methodists. Each year a bursary is made to one Methodist boarder from the City of London through a link with the Wesley's Chapel community.

Remarks: Comfortable school where young people are given the support and space to stretch out and grow into their personalities.

Lincoln Minster School

Linked school: St Mary's Preparatory School

The Prior Building, Upper Lindum Street, Lincoln, LN2 5RW

• Pupils: Senior school: 230 boys/250 girls (including 85 boarders). • Ages: 11–18 • inter-denominational • Fees: Day £11,997; Boarding £20,664–£23,982 pa • Independent

Tel: 01522 551300
Email: enquiries.lincoln@church-schools.com
Website: www.lincolnminsterschool.co.uk

Principal: Since 1999, Mr Clive Rickart BA PGCE, previously head of the prep school from 1996, when the United Church Schools Trust merged the Cathedral School for Boys, St Joseph's School for Girls and Stonefield House School. Prior to this was boarding housemaster at Stamford School and head of Oswestry Junior School. Much to be proud of here. 'A modern take on traditional values' is how he describes it and there is plenty of evidence of both. His grown-up children are former pupils and you can tell that he loves this place. Warm, welcoming and unassuming, yet with a sharpness of vision that has brought real growth and development during his tenure. Much praise from parents for his 'commitment and sincerity and the principle of considering what is best for the children that guides his every move'.

Academic matters: Large, spacious, airy classrooms and eight impressive labs in the new build, some with far-reaching views across the Trent plain. All very well-equipped with state-of-the-art IT equipment creating an environment that's clearly serious about teaching and learning. There is a real pride about the place with plenty of quality work on display and a general sense of order and rigour all wrapped up with warmth and bonhomie. Wide corridors with carpets and plenty of natural light create an almost corporate feel – more business-like and less school-like than the norm. Parents recognise the importance of the huge value added by this mixed ability school – seems it is down to strong pupil/teacher relationships and lots of individual support and attention as and when required. In 2013, 48 per cent A*/A grades at GCSE and 49 per cent A*/B and 24 per cent A*/A grades at A level. The three sciences are taught in rotation at key stage 3, then separately and fully beyond that, leading to plenty of As and A*s in triple sciences.

French and Spanish taught, other languages occasionally on demand as extra-curricular options. Basic range of subjects on offer at GCSE with most studying 8 or 10 subjects. Wider range of subjects at AS and A2, all the usual trad subjects plus a few less common ones such as graphics, psychology, sociology and travel and tourism.

Average class size 17, max 24. Pupils say teachers have 'an infectious passion for their subject'; typical is the Earl Grey Society – other teas (and biscuits) are available – an extracurricular activity run by the English dept offering university seminar-type sessions to discuss a shared love of literature and broaden both reading and horizons. There is a clear work ethic; teachers look busy and focused, as do pupils, but no sense of hothousing. A chilled out common room for sixth form sits alongside a silent study area, with a teacher on duty and plenty of uni prospectuses and careers advice around to guide and inspire.

Easy access to the local university brings additional academic range and scope; use of their library for sixth form extended projects, master classes and an introduction to engineering are all there to be experienced and enjoyed. Mild and moderate learning difficulties catered for; around 80 identified as SEN, a handful have statements, rest mainly dyslexia, dyspraxia, occasionally ASD. No extra charge for specialist support.

Games, options, the arts: Music plays a very large part in the school's curriculum with its close relationship to the cathedral – they say you don't have to be musical to come here but it 'still touches you'. The director of music's role is (uniquely) divided between the cathedral and school, which provides 40 choristers (20 boys and 20 girls), so standards are incredibly high, with a number of orchestras, bands and groups making for a busy concert programme and occasional radio and TV appearances. Cathedral choristers enjoy a busy life and can be day or boarding; choral scholarships available, normally 50 per cent off full fees (boarding and tuition). Choir rehearsals take place on four weekday mornings and weekends are carefully balanced with 'a busy one followed by a lighter one' to allow for a life outside school. Chamber choir performed on Howard Goodall's chart-topping album Inspired in 2013.

GCSE express music course for year 9 pupils allows them to complete the full course two years early. Cookery is an adventurous experience here: teacher is ex-military so only for the brave. Butcher a chicken? 'Why not? After all, it's cheaper than buying chicken portions so great prep for uni,' say grinning pupils. Wealth of extracurricular choices in addition to the music options; all the usual plus rarer alternatives such as rowing and remote-control car club. 'Flamboyant' head of art so plenty of wow factor in that department, stunning work on display. Drama is thriving and all year groups are encouraged to take part; it's 'taken seriously here,' say staff and taught to A level.

Sports field is a short walk away in Lincoln's conservation area and the newish sports hall and new Astroturf have fuelled the school's already high standard of team and individual performance. Rugby and hockey are king, but football, netball, basketball and tennis also popular. 2013 saw plenty of success in rugby 7s as county plate winners in three age groups and county champions in U15 girls' cricket. Also has riding teams who compete regularly at events across the country and just to prove this really isn't an unsophisticated backwater at all – polo now on offer and growing in popularity, with parents too, who particularly enjoy the après polo activities. Sailing offered as an extracurricular activity; a high level of involvement in the Duke of Edinburgh Award Scheme and a very full outdoor and adventurous programme; Young Enterprise regional finalists.

Small-ish city but school has big ideas and knows that there is a big world out there so no sense of isolation. Rugby tours to Italy, geography trips to Iceland and Switzerland, annual ski trips and more besides extend opportunities to explore and learn about the world beyond – but these are grounded young people, fundraising to cover their own costs is not unusual here and is to be admired. Project India is a venture close to their hearts, working to provide essential aid in Southern India. Sixth formers visit for up to three weeks at a time to create buildings for the deaf, community cafes, clearing land for fruit farms and teaching English, with the occasional cricket match thrown in just for fun.

Background and atmosphere: Formed in 1996 through a merger of the Cathedral School for Boys, St Joseph's School for Girls and Stonefield House School. In 2011 St Mary's Preparatory School merged to form the new preparatory school. As part of United Learning (formerly UCST), it now houses 800 pupils across three sites with 76 boarders housed on 11-18 site. Bucking the trend with boarding on the increase, a few Forces children remain; boarders are a 50/50 home-grown and overseas mix; full, weekly or flexi boarding all available. Boarders live in a period house in the historic quarter; unsurprisingly a number are choristers, though not all. Plenty of investment in boarding, it's holding its own in a dwindling local market and recent investment is paying off as boarding houses are revamped and refurbed on a rolling programme; big expenditure on girls' boarding in 2010, more in 2013. Serious funding in this area indicates a real commitment to boarding into the future. Weekends

for boarders involve cinema, theatre, ten-pin bowling trips, barbecues on sunny evenings and the annual summer camp is a real highlight; midweek there are plenty of opportunities to join a smorgasbord of school activities, go swimming, learn karate or join the Guides or Scouts.

Christian-based but attracts all faiths and none. Religious services (including communion) held at the Minster, but not an issue, nobody pulls out. Five school houses, named after cathedral cities, attract fierce loyalty and healthy competition between pupils of all ages. A mix of building styles and eras, some rented from the Dean and Chapter; hugely attractive and spacious new buildings sit cheek by jowl with the old; a converted Victorian school building is wonderful for drama with its bell tower, leaded windows and brick arches and sits alongside a stunning contemporary £10million music school, recital hall and sports hall. It is hard to tell which are school buildings and which are not: they all seem to intermingle across this concentrated historic quarter of the city, which includes the Minster and, interestingly, a school-owned pub. The profits from the pub provide useful additional funds for scholarships; anxious parents need not worry, it's not a place for pupils but thirsty locals can enjoy a drink here, safe in the knowledge that they are supporting a good cause.

Unsurprisingly in this somewhat ancient and crowded setting, car parking is extremely limited. Apart from special occasions and evening events, when the playground can be used, it's street parking for all. Sixth-formers bemoan the lack of parking (and the army of zealous local traffic wardens), wise parents manage it by avoiding the journey altogether and sensibly taking advantage of the school transport: 12 buses carry pupils in from all directions, as far afield as Nottingham.

Pupils (unprompted) tell us that 'the food here is very good' – huge spacious dining room, part of which becomes a café at breaktime, all very civilised. Themed lunches are popular, especially Italian day.

Pastoral care and discipline: Good manners are important, as is respect, 'bullying, incorrect uniform and chewing gum are big no-nos,' say pupils. All seems quite low key but take it as read that anything more serious than that is prohibited and brings severe reprimand. Tutors are always on hand to help pupils and answer parents' concerns. A pupil mentoring system works well and means that prefects, too, are approachable, even by the younger members of the school.

'Business wear' is the order of the day for sixth form and they are an unusually smart lot. Below sixth form it's a uniform with an attractive and distinctive striped blazer (a view not necessarily shared by pupils) for both boys and girls. Good to see so many sixth formers in school during our summer term visit – it's unusual during what is normally regarded as a term of study leave by most schools. It's a healthy sign when pupils are offered taught revision classes and extra individual tuition right through and up to exams, and wisely they grab it with both hands – they simply want to be here.

Pupils and parents: Large number of first time buyers with a mix of professionals and business people – farmers, hospital and university staff, Siemens employees – most working locally, plus a fair-sized commuter set heading to London and other cities beyond the county borders.

Parents tell us that they like the fact that this is a 'through school' ie 3-18, and are also fans of the school's commitment to 'old-fashioned principles of respect, discipline, manners, consideration of others and kindness – right from the earliest stages'. Parentmail system keeps them up-to-date with info and news.

Thoroughly charming yet sensibly grounded pupils, hardworking and ambitious, unafraid to look you in the eye and chat easily. Notable former pupils include: Jack Harvey (motor racing), Lizzie Simmonds (Olympic swimmer), Alice Ross (pastry chef at Michel Roux's le Gavroche), Sophie Allport (renowned ceramic designer and business woman), John Scarborough (Education Officer, Cameron Mackintosh).

Entrance: The majority of pupils come from the Minster's own prep school; other popular sources include St Hugh's Prep, Woodhall Spa and Highfield's Prep, Newark, plus a myriad of other prep and junior schools. External applicants attend a personal assessment day in January, the intention being to indicate and understand the breadth of ability or potential, although entrance is not based purely on ability.

Exit: Eighty per cent go through to sixth form. A wide variety of university destinations in 2013. Award-winning virtual careers library, which can be accessed from computers outside the school, is a tremendous resource for leavers.

Money matters: Well endowed under the auspices of United Learning. Scholarships for academic, art, music and sport. Means-tested United Learning assisted places.

Remarks: Forget preconceptions of Lincolnshire being a flat and remote county: you can commute to London from here without too much difficulty, indeed many do; and the school occupies a magnificent setting high on a hill overlooking the rooftops of the historic quarter of the city with views of the Minster from (almost) every window. A happy and successful product of a four-way merger, no doubt tricky at the time but thriving now that the dust has well and truly settled and the place ticks like a well-oiled machine.

Lomond School

Linked school: Lomond School Junior Department

10 Stafford Street, Helensburgh, G84 9JX

• Pupils: 290 boys and girls (65 boarders) • Ages: 3–18 • Non-denom • Fees: Day £9,240–£10,080; Boarding £22,020 pa • Independent

Tel: 01436 672476
Email: admin@lomondschool.com
Website: www.lomondschool.com

Headmaster: Since August 2009, Mr Simon Mills BA (fortyish), formerly senior deputy head at The Portsmouth Grammar School, where he greatly enjoyed working with Forces families and developing a high value co-educational school. Cambridge geography graduate, worked with BP Oil. Boarding housemaster at Stamford School (also head of department) and Blundell's School. Grew up in St Andrews and educated in Perthshire. Married to Ruth, a primary teacher, three children, all at Lomond School.

A great believer in developing young people to their fullest potential and a strong supporter of the extra-curricular life of the school. Passions include skiing, windsurfing, sailing, golf and all things outdoor. Academic extension, strong pastoral care, pupil leadership and developing a wide co-curricular programme are of greatest importance to him.

Moving on in July 2014 to head Robert Gordon's College.

Academic matters: Setted in English, French and maths at the age of 12, French taught from five, German from 11. Huge range of subjects on offer, including such esoteric ones as graphic communication, modern studies and business management, as well as French, German and Spanish. Three sciences. Latin GCSE taught by video conference link and distance learning. School

takes Intermediate 2, National 5, Higher and Advanced Higher. In 2013, 45 per cent A grades in Advanced Highers and 46 per cent A grades in Highers.

Maximum class size 20. Sixth form were working supervised (which is unheard of at that age) in the library when we visited. Homework very important – children keep a diary and expect to do at least two and a half hours each night in their Standard Grade year. Has strong links with private schools in China, Germany and US. Computers everywhere, networked, and all have access to the internet; keyboarding skills for all, electronic interactive whiteboard presentations for all by all. Tutors for all. Good learning support (and provision for those with dyslexia, ADD or ADHD). English as a Second Language on hand.

Games, options, the arts: Huge playing field just along the (tree-lined) road. Full-sized floodlit Astroturf hockey pitch. Rugby and hockey the two main winter games, with tennis, cricket and athletics in the summer and oodles of add-ons. Swimming in the local pool, option of squash, riding and badminton. Inter-house matches popular. Mass of lunch time clubs, D of E popular and, of course, sailing, The Scottish Islands Peaks Race, Lomond Challenge (a beastly tough triathlon) – not a school for sissies. New games hall, adjacent to the Astroturf, includes badminton courts, climbing wall, dance studio, fitness suite and indoor cricket lanes. Further development to include another smaller Astroturf.

Traditional Scottish music important – clarsach players, fiddlers, pipers and singers are in regular demand. Strong music, based in the old stables – one wall entirely covered with guitars, not just for decoration, judging by the enthusiasm the guitar teacher generated. Recording facilities in place. Big bands and chamber orchestras, over 20 instruments on curriculum with some 150 individual lessons. Sparkling art department, with old school desks press-ganged into use. Huge variety of disciplines – photography with spit-new kit, magical screen printing, jewellery making, as well as the more prosaic (which it wasn't) sculpture, painting and etching. Tremendous enthusiasm here – enchanting flower costume, complete with design, basque and wings, made for last summer's play, on show. Strong drama.

Background and atmosphere: Based on the northern edge of the posh, sleepy, seaside town of Helensburgh, originally housed in a series of Victorian villas. Present school is an amalgam of Larchfield, founded in 1845, and the girls' school, St Bride's, founded in 1895. The schools combined in 1977; later a stunning re-build. The resulting school is a curious combination of old and new, with three floors replacing the original two and subject rooms being grouped in series. Most impressive – massive amount of glass, super new dining hall, good gym and terrific entrance hall with glorious views out over the Clyde. Burnbrae now the most modern boarding house in Scotland – boys and girls share the same building but are separated by a state-of-the-art security system using biometric readers. All pupils wear uniform (kilts for females) – neat and tidy with ties and a thoroughly purposeful air.

Pastoral care and discipline: Strong anti-bullying procedure in place – the 'no blame' circle appears to be the most effective. Confidential suggestion boxes all over the school are really part of the anti-bullying programme. Good PSD programme. CCTV cameras throughout. Children not 'given a lot of rope', eg any substance abuse leads to suspension, 'pending a discussion of their school future'. Dealing equals straight out. Smoking is apparently 'not happening just now', but smoking in uniform is 'not on'.

Pupils and parents: An upmarket lot – solid middle class, from the surrounding area (they organise the buses), some from as far away as Glasgow. Number of Forces families (Faslane naval base next door) and some from further 'round the bay' send their children here (the local state school thought to be too state). A few mainland Chinese usually come for most of their secondary schooling, plus connection with Germany, whence the occasional pupil comes for a year or a term – not much take-up of Scots going to Germany in exchange.

Bonar Law was educated at Larchfield, as well as John Logie Baird – his school report, displayed in the dining room, apart from showing that he was 14th out of 14 in maths, expresses the hope that he will eventually 'go on and do something with his life'!

Entrance: Either up via nursery or from local state primaries.

Exit: Usual dribble away after Standard Grades and could fill up the resulting places several times over, trickle leaves after Highers; some, eg those going south to university, tend to stay and do their Advanced Highers. Most will end up at university – 2013 destinations included Glasgow, Strathclyde, Highlands & Islands, Paisley, Glasgow Caledonia, Edinburgh, Dundee, Heriot Watt and Aberdeen. Usually two or three to Oxbridge. Many take gap years, particularly the Chinese option, where girls and boys have their fares paid, receive two-thirds the normal salary and teach in China for a year, complete with lessons in Chinese.

Money matters: Not a rich school. Will support pupils in financial difficulties; an increasing number of means-tested bursaries (up to 100 per cent) available at the age of 10 and 11 and post-Standard Grades.

Remarks: A jolly, busy school, perfect for those who want to keep their children at home without the hassle of going daily to Glasgow.

L

The London Oratory School

Linked school: The London Oratory School Junior House

Seagrave Road, London, SW6 1RX

• Pupils: 1,380; all boys except for 50 girls in the sixth form; all day • Ages: 7–18 • RC • State

Tel: 020 7385 0102
Email: registrar@los.ac
Website: www.london-oratory.org

Headmaster: Since 2007, Mr David McFadden BSc MA (fiftyish), a round peg in a circular hole. An Old Boy, began his career here, thence to Australia, where he spent 20 years teaching and, ultimately, headmastering. His previous two schools were Aquinas College and the Christian Brothers' College in Fremantle.

Mr McFadden retains an Aussie twang with a characteristic Aussie candour and relaxed confidence which we found engaging and reassuring. He has a clear sense of his school and what he wants to do there and, while paying tribute to his long-serving and much-admired predecessor, made pretty radical – and generally approved of – changes in his first, fast-moving year. It was not a honeymoon. He has been extraordinarily busy, engaged, among much else, in a huge consultation process to find out what the school community sees as priorities for change. This led to an impressive and far-reaching strategic plan – a massive agenda of 'things to do'.

Boys, parents and staff enthuse: 'He's very involved'; 'He's exceptional ... dynamic ... very approachable'; 'He seems to know what you're thinking ... and (most importantly) the lunches are heaps better'. We can't think of many heads we know who better fit their posts and we look forward to a further flourishing of this unique institution.

Academic matters: Selective only on the grounds of Roman Catholic practice – the level of academic achievement is usually remarkable. Parents and boys attribute the results to good teaching, high expectations and the discipline which, though too strict for some, clearly pays dividends. Teaching is assuredly excellent in general, though with some serious failings here and there. Excellent showing in new English Baccalaureate, as already long established that all pupils take mathematics, English, three separate sciences and MFL for GCSE and a very significant proportion study history and/or geography. Languages do exceptionally well here – refreshing in a boys' school; especially heartening to see German thrive. A level results in 2013, 65 per cent A*-B and 42 per cent A*/A grades.

Parents and pupils pay tribute to the 'challenging' curriculum, which makes a virtue of teaching beyond the syllabus, and to the efforts of the staff, who see strugglers individually and dollop out support and encouragement. The less academically able are offered a sixth form course in advanced business – a hybrid of two A levels and an AS, leading to qualifications in business and computing, a practical alternative to a sixth form college course for those who can't bear to leave. Classes felt by some to be too big, especially at sixth form level. However overall standards are high, high, high, to the extent that, in the recent Sutton Trust report, it was ranked top amongst all non-selective state schools, second amongst all selective state schools and 30th amongst all schools, including the independent schools.

SENs catered for – attracts standard numbers of the usual spread of needs: a few with Asperger's but no other ASDs at time of our visit. In-class help along with withdrawal where appropriate. Wheelchair-friendly and SENs seen, in general, as just part of life.

Games, options, the arts: Outdoor space is in short supply and boys are bused to Barn Elms – a round trip of not much less than an hour. Rugby is big here, with six teams in the first form alone and more than 20 in total – becoming more available to all. Mr McFadden speaks of 'heart and hand' – seeing the development and nourishment of all parts of a pupil as central to his education. Rugby played mostly against the independents and at weekends, so a big commitment for the privileged few. Weights, water polo, rowing and basketball are other main activities at present; also a good, well-used, on-site, 17m pool. World Challenge, a popular activity since 2002, has more participants than any other school in the country – state and independent – and sends boys on exciting, self-financed trips of a lifetime. Also popular is D of E. CCF perhaps the biggest in any state school, both army and RAF – tours, camps and expeditions of all kinds. Lots of sixth involved in community work – helping at local schools and care homes, at soup kitchen on Saturdays, at the offices of a local charity etc.

Music is very big, fuelled by those who come up from the Junior House, all of whom have exceptional aptitude. Some 600+ pupils learn at least one instrument. Bands, choirs and orchestras thrive and are well-housed in the arts centre. The Schola is a choir of professional standard and considerable significance in the world of RC – and secular – music: three visits to Rome in as many months, including representing the Vatican in Al Gore's LiveEarth initiative. They record for films and TV and are regarded with deserved respect. They were one of the main choirs at the mass for the beatification of Cardinal Newman on the Papal visit to Britain.

School's on-site arts centre is an impressive asset and includes stunning 300-seat galleried theatre in which full scale shows are mounted – Pirates of Penzance in production when we visited. Good display spaces – a stimulating photo show by member of staff was good to see, along with a vast Paolozzi

Brutalist sculpture. Pupils go on to study art/art history or architecture at prestigious institutions. But art/ceramics/DT etc not much in evidence – more of their efforts around the school would help the ambience and encourage les autres. No photography or textiles on offer, though both are available in extra-curricular clubs.

Lots of overseas trips in the holidays – foreign exchanges, cultural and historical visits. Rugby tours to far flung places and singers and instrumental players performing far and wide.

Background and atmosphere: Founded by the Oratorian Fathers, 145 years old. It moved to its present site and buildings – in the lee of Chelsea FC's massive stadium – in the 1970s and has worn surprisingly well. Some rooms and corridors, notably in the sixth form areas, are dilapidated but, in general, the place was imaginatively designed and feels looked after. We liked the brick courtyard with its lead flashing. Newish block provides English department classrooms, learning support rooms and a function room to aid parental involvement. Has the look of a less than well resourced independent school, but the faces of the boys and staff belie that – an air of engagement and pride, a sense of collaborative energy and achievement which transcend the physical shortcomings and lack of space in some areas.

Some clearly unsatisfactory aspects – lunch (now good and with vegetables, though no sandwich option) is eaten in house rooms, which are also used for teaching after the metal grilles are rolled down and the servery disappears. Some year groups have no social space to speak of and are cramped and crowded. The large sixth form common room doubles as a fencing salle. Much of the school has a rather austere feel, which you couldn't describe as 'monastic' and, therefore, perhaps, good for the soul. We felt it to be bleak when we visited but, since then, the paintbrushes have been out and more displays put up, which must lift the spirits. Recent extension to and major refurbishment of main teaching block.

The chapel, opened in 1992 by Basil Hume and dedicated to St Philip Neri and St Edward the Confessor, is simple in design and has a warm and gentle feel. Major ceremonies held in the famous, huge, Italianate Oratory Church in South Kensington. The Catholic ethos underlies all aspects of the school but not obtrusively or obsessively – it is simply a given and central also to Mr McFadden's plans to develop the community involvement of the school. Long-standing commitment to local primary schools and charities – such as SURF and the SVP soup kitchen – with sixth formers carrying out voluntary work and the music department involved in outreach programmes..

Pastoral care and discipline: Discipline is acknowledged to be tight – rules are strict and enforced strictly. Any mobile phones spotted on the premises will be confiscated and have to be collected by parents. Eight boys were expelled or left in Mr McFadden's first year after two cannabis smoking incidents. 'You need a clear-cut policy, but you have to have a listening ear and heart.' The approach is 'compassionate', but zero tolerance for physical violence – automatic suspension for anyone who tries to sort a problem by 'raising a hand against someone else'. House system encourages friendships between the year groups and boys in the sixth can mentor those younger who need support over a subject or a problem. Parents warmly praise the staff for their pastoral care, especially the deputy heads – of whom one has been in the school for 20+ years since the start of her career and the other who is a past pupil of the school. Head keen to grow the 'heart and hand' of each boy – to integrate his learning into what his life is about, both individually and in terms of his service to the community.

Pupils and parents: From a vast geographical area, most London boroughs, inner and outer – some leave home at 7.00am to come here. Over 50 languages spoken at home; serious Roman Catholicism the only – but unifying – common denominator.

Parents are warming to head's drive to involve them in all ways – social, educational and practical. Parents' groups for sports, music and food and more to follow. Reports are now termly and home-school contact far more a normal thing, though some complaints persist of parents not being kept in touch. Children appreciate the knock-ons of greater parental involvement and find it supportive and helpful. The boys themselves are relaxed, friendly, ambitious and hard-working. Classes are head down and concentrating. We heard no raised voices, saw few inattentive faces. Pupils have a sense of pride in themselves and in the school which one would wish to see replicated everywhere. The only boy who wouldn't like it there, we were told, was someone who didn't want to involve himself.

Sixth form girls are no mere modern import designed to boost results. They date back to a link with a girls' school in the 19th century and were incorporated into the sixth in the 1950s after a merger. Their numbers are small but, says head, 'They add so much to the school'. It was good to see girls and boys out and about in the lunch hour clearly in relaxed friendship and at ease – no cattle market or points system here. Notable former pupils include Simon Callow and Haley Atwell. Oh – and David McFadden.

Entrance: Simpler than hitherto, but heart-sinking for anyone other than an assiduously practising Roman Catholic family with lots of community involvement. In fact, don't bother to apply unless you are a pillar of your local church and known to your priest, who will have to vouch for your bona fides – both pupil's and family's. Admission process involves completing the school's Religious Inquiry Form and a local authority Common Application Form. Eight hundred plus apply for the 160 places. Junior House boys transfer automatically and parents praise the seamless transition. Sixth form also over-subscribed. Forty places for girls attract 200 applicants and, again, the RC credentials are what counts, plus 'expected performance at GCSE and suitability for an A level course which will be sought from each pupil's current school'. Likely applicants are invited to a 'course suitability meeting'. Girls join from Sacred Heart – virtually the whole year applies – Gumley, the Ursuline Convent and a few from Lady Margaret's.

At time of writing the school has been instructed by the Schools Adjudicator to change its 'unfair' and complicated admissions policy which rewards far-sighted parents who have performed long-term service to their local Catholic church.

Exit: Most stay on after GCSE; almost 400 in sixth form. Regularly wins Oxbridge places covering the range of disciplines (six in 2013). Otherwise to good universities everywhere to read everything. Refreshingly few silly subjects pursued – these pupils have been properly taught and sensibly advised.

Remarks: Much that is excellent, but also much potential for building this school – in bricks and mortar terms as well as educationally and spiritually. Destined for stardom.

Longridge Towers School

Berwick-upon-Tweed, Northumberland, TD15 2XQ

• Pupils: 170 (50/50 boys and girls) • Ages: 11-18 • Non-denominational • Fees: Day £7,476–£11,682; Boarding £22,554–£23,799 pa • Independent

Tel: 01289 307584
Email: pupilsadmissions@lts.org.uk
Website: www.lts.org.uk

Headmaster: Since 2009, Mr Tim Manning BA, mid fifties, a Londoner who chose to study maths at Bangor and liked it so much that he did a PGCE in order to stay on for an extra year and 'found when I got up in front of a class I just loved it'. Then King Williams College on the Isle of Man was looking for a rugby playing maths teacher. He joined Longridge as head of maths in 1993, became deputy head in 1995 and was appointed head in 2009 on the sudden departure of his predecessor. A keen rugby player (played for his uni and looks the part) and golfer, he has encouraged excellent sport with remarkable success. Justifiably, he is bursting with pride at the highly complimentary Independent Schools Inspectorate report issued in 2011, which praised academic achievement and the activities programme, commenting on his outstanding leadership and the provision for personal development. He firmly attributes success to his strong management and pastoral care teams but has clearly worked wonders himself in a fairly short time. Living within walking distance on what was once the Longridge estate, both his children went right through the school from early years to university.

Academic matters: All through school from 3-18, with French started at seven and German at 11. Spanish, Italian and Latin as extra-curricular but can be taken at GCSE, as can Chinese. Wide range of GCSE subjects with flexible timetabling based on the needs of each particular year group so that 95 per cent get to take what they want. English, Eng lit and maths for all plus six other options (can include three – or two – separate sciences or science and additional science.) Usual subjects plus ICT, CDT (done in a well-equipped but basic hut in the grounds), sports studies, drama and music. Consistently sound record of 'passes' with a good sprinkling of A and A* in biology, maths and a few in Eng lit and elsewhere. Almost everyone takes drama and IT, both with solid results and no significant weaknesses, though art a bit up and down. In 2013, 74 per cent of pupils got 5+ A*-C grades including English and maths; 21 per cent of grades were A*/A.

At A level, 49 per cent A*/B grades and 26 per cent A*/A in 2013. Choice includes the usual subjects plus economics with business studies, sports science and further maths; general studies AS for all now replaced by critical thinking after rather iffy results; while psychology can be taken at AS over 2 years. Dusting of A*/As across most subjects and a consistently solid 'pass' rate but also quite a smattering of C/D. Inevitably small groups – will put on a mainstream subject for one pupil in sixth form. Anyone with 5+ Cs can take A/AS though B preferred in subject concerned.

SEN support offered mostly by individual withdrawal with personal education plans used to keep teachers aware of needs. English help for pupils from China etc and efforts to provide extra stimulus for the very bright.

Juniors start from early years foundation stage (tiny classes of 5 to ten only) on Oxford Reading Tree, supplemented by lots of Jolly Phonics and Ginn letters and sounds.

Classrooms pretty modern with a few interactive whiteboards and computer projectors, lots of IT including laptop trolleys for use in amazingly antiquated though very adequately equipped labs. The smartest lab is in the junior school building for 7-11s. Called Stobo after a benefactor, the junior school is still clean and new looking with state of art (though cheerfully decorated) classrooms, cloakrooms and hall etc. Early years to junior 3 have humbler but thoroughly refurbished quarters absolutely brimming with colour, imaginative stimulus material and even recorded birdsong. A pleasant fenced outdoor area for tinies and some smashing all weather play equipment, in enthusiastic use.

Games, options, the arts: Sport flourishes with highly successful seven-a-side rugby reaching finals in county tournaments – they struggle to produce a top-level full team from a small co-ed school but are outstanding in sevens. Recent leaver runs at Scottish, English and Great Britain under 20 championship level, soccer just starting, lots of hockey for girls with several county players, a school champion skier and masses of opportunity for basketball, volleyball, badminton, cricket, tennis, curling (Scottish school finalists) etc. Spacious sports hall (takes a marquee inside for prize days and dances,) defunct swimming pool left by previous convent school so minibuses take them to Eyemouth pool but grounds lend themselves to hosting local cross country etc. Pipedream of a new Astroturf hockey pitch is still pretty distant.

Lots of choir, orchestra, jazz groups etc with star pupil in Northern Youth Orchestra but little take up of academic music beyond GCSE. Informal lunchtime concerts much enjoyed by all. Special centre for peripatetic music in a pretty Gothic house in the grounds which the previous head rejected as a home. Drama in the round in strange theatre converted from former convent chapel, with jazzy lighting, provided by the enterprising parents' 'school development association'. Recent production is Billy Liar. Art seems a bit marginalised in a building seven minutes walk from main school but is looking to a new art teacher to hot it up next year. Head's ambition is to reincorporate this in a new sciences and practical subjects building. The school is now full and seemingly growing, so he hopes to revamp abandoned plans for new labs into a more inclusive facility.

Boundless activities! Almost all day pupils including juniors stay till 4.40 for an hour of activity which can include supervised study, tutorials, extra coursework or teaching. Falconry is clearly the latest craze – the juniors couldn't stop talking about it – but also the tip of an impressive iceberg: archery, athletics, lacrosse and other sports, debating, wildlife gardening (with a good muddy pond), Yoga, a new Radio Longridge, Science and Engineering clubs, cheerleading, war games and lashings of other things. Head comments that having rearranged activity times, to suit staff and pupils better and the staff can do what they really like. Bags of trips: German exchange, sport to Canada, South Africa, Iceland etc. Charitable links with Borneo and others. D of E for seniors and Adventure Service challenge for juniors.

Background and atmosphere: The extraordinary Victorian Tudor extravaganza built of sandstone ashlar in 1880s for Sir Hubert Jerningham, a liberal MP, on the estate inherited by his wife Annie Liddell was designed to impress (it does!) by the Buckleys who redid Arundel Castle. It features battlemented stone chimneys, magnificent great hall, now for concerts, with hammer-beams sporting snarling monsters with grotesquely bared teeth, an imperial staircase and an elaborate portico added to shelter the Prince of Wales' carriage (though history is silent over whether he actually arrived to use it) all making Longridge the grandest house in the area. Set in 80 acres of parkland, it became a hotel, then in 1949 an Ursuline Convent school. In 1983 it was re-structured as the co-educational Longridge Towers School. In a fantastic rural setting with imaginative use of the castellated grand areas, the school also has the problem of making stone staircases, high ceilings and a warren corridors work for 21st century education. The original library had a

L

cunning makeover with a gallery providing working space and banishing the previous nightmare scenario of children on ladders to glass (non-safety) fronted bookcases. There's lots of help on hand and an ambitious programmes of visiting authors etc. 'Service wings' house boarders, dining rooms and kitchens – some tasty dishes (pupils actually like it on the whole) made on site with a few home-grown veg. Boarding on two floors (girls above, boys below) has spacious mostly two-bedded rooms, some with en suite showers. Their height makes them a little stark though inmates are allowed locked doors and a free-ish hand with posters and personal paraphernalia. Pleasant and well-planned recreation room, with spotless kitchenette and generous supplies of luscious fruit. All obviously well used and well cared for but lots of echoey passages and stairwells, improved by pupil art work (not always the right way up though it's hard to tell!) Most noticeably some stunning Aboriginal hangings done for a drama liven one of the central stairways. Everything clean and mainly litter free, well used and not unnaturally tidy.

Pastoral care and discipline: Independent Schools Inspectorate really praised pastoral care. Qualified nurse in boarding and system of tutors and year heads (form teachers for juniors) and three school houses which run vertically through juniors to senior school. Pupils respect and value system and genuine interest of staff, so problems are picked up quickly and children tend to monitor and report issues like bullying before they become serious. New junior school council is prized by pupils. Plentiful contact between all ages with seniors helping with reading and games. Unusually friendships across year groups are not uncommon, especially valuable in such a small and variable boarding situation. Strong sense of community enhanced by boarding and also by the school's involvement with its neighbourhood. Activities provided supplement rather than compete with local amenities such as junior golf. Pupils are ready to take responsibility as elected prefects etc within and without school. One sixth former even combines his school duties with being chief coastguard for Lindisfarne.

Pupils and parents: Masses of bus routes bring pupils coming from a scattered area which includes not only Berwick on Tweed, the surrounding boarder country in both England and Scotland but also the Holy Island (Lindisfarne) population, whose children need to board on days when the tide cuts off their journey too or from school. Hence boarding has a special wing for them where siblings can be together and the provision has a more temporary feel than the full termly boarding, though they share its amenities and supervision. So boarding at Longridge is more 'flexi' than most and the population fluctuates. Boarding seems to be on the increase with about 32 current maximum and applications going up. A few boarders from abroad, mainly China, otherwise a largely British intake.

Uniform is in a state of flux though everyone looks quite smart. New blue blazers, white shirts, grey trousers and knee-length straight skirts with prominent kick pleats in blue, white and grey tartan look neat and innocuous, while tinies wear blue and white cotton summer dresses.

Parents run a dynamic programme of events and raise significant amounts for equipment etc. Governors take an active interest in the school and the local worthies, whose families give the names to houses etc, support it with visits and interest.

Entrance: By assessment at all levels but school will take anyone capable of benefiting from what's on offer. Since Longridge pupils come from Scotland and England with different systems involving changes of school at 7, 11, 12, 14 and even different age cut off points, September for England but February for Scotland, need careful induction and class sizes are unpredictable. Just starting a class for three year olds in response to local demand.

Exit: Some leave from juniors at either 11 and 12 (English and Scottish systems!) mainly to to independent, Ampleforth, Merchiston Castle etc, though not usually to local state schools. There is more than at trickle after GCSE to local and Newcastle sixth forms and a few to independent boarding. Those who stay to upper sixth go mostly to uni, a few to blue chip and a surprising quota of sports degrees. Some to academic courses too.

Money matters: Not a rich school but awards available for academic (up to 50 per cent), sporting (up to 10 per cent) or musical (free tuition) excellence are offered to those qualifying by exam, achieving county sports honours or by audition. Pupils from Holy Island are sponsored by the local authority, which would otherwise be unable to provide adequate hostel accommodation.

Remarks: Small, with all the advantages of good supervision, care, close-knit community and friendliness a small school can give. Copes very well with the disadvantages of scale, so pupils do not lose out on activities, subjects etc. Berwick-upon-Tweed is jolly lucky to have this alternative at hand!

Lord Wandsworth College

Long Sutton, Hook, Hampshire, RG29 1TB

• Pupils: 535; 345 boys/190 girls; 95 full boarders, 95 weekly boarders, 100 flexi boarders • Ages: 11–18 • Non-denom
• Fees: Day £18,930–£19,920; Boarding £25,350–£28,140 pa; Flexi boarding (3 nights) £20,670–£22,668 pa • Independent

Tel: 01256 862201
Email: admissions@lordwandsworth.org
Website: www.lordwandsworth.org

Headmaster: Since 2010, Mr Fergus Livingstone (mid forties). Brought up in Oxford (schooled at St Edward's), came to English by playing Mark Antony in Julius Caesar, and still switched on by drama. Read English at Cambridge, straight into teaching at his old school, then at Eton for 10 years, head of English and housemaster at St Paul's School in São Paulo, head of English at Bishop's Stortford College at a time when that school was rising from obscurity, deputy head of Rossall from 2005 when that school was rescued from imminent extinction. Has, in other words, been well trained under some fine headmasters.

Commands great affection from parents. Always there on the touchline or at plays, always listening, always interested, always knows your name. A sure touch in dealing with bullies and supporting the parents of the victims and the perpetrators (not that this is a frequent happening). A good communicator, say parents: 'you never feel left in the dark'. His idea of discipline is a firm hand on the shoulder rather than a bludgeon – though pupils clearly feel the hand to be a steely one. Enthusiastic, an academic underneath. Paxmanesque.

A builder, with plans for the school both in education (notably reflective about character development) and architecturally. Has been improving things generally, say parents. A rugby and hockey nut, and a sportsman generally. Married to Gudrun, an Icelandic opera singer. Three children.

Academic matters: A good, broad, mid-range school, and a good place to be a bright kid – they are well rewarded for working hard, half a dozen Oxbridge candidates each year. 'He is being well stretched, and has taken to classics to our great surprise', a parent told us. Lots of setting – from the start, five sets for maths – but not a pressurised place: 'he's pushed enough, but not too much'. Plenty of homework, but can be done before you go home. 'Do the basics beautifully' is the mantra that Fergus Livingstone learned from Stephen Winkley, his headmaster at Rossall, and has put into fine effect here.

Forty-seven per cent A*/A at GCSE in 2013. About half take all three sciences – twice the proportion of boys than girls, which shows up at A level too, sadly, especially in physics. Sixty-five per cent A*/B at A level in 2013, and 35 per cent A*/A; art, geography, English and languages relatively popular, compared to similar schools, with business studies, economics and psychology on the rise.

Chirpy, well thought out, involving teaching much appreciated by pupils. Parents say teachers are engaging and effective, know their pupils well – 'staff put so much into the school'. All live on site, several miles from the nearest village (though there is a pub just outside the gates), so quite a community.

Very keen on the AQA extended project: feel that it develops breadth and intellect, can be dropped if it proves all too much, plays to LWC pupils' strengths, and shows them up beautifully at Oxbridge.

Screening for learning difficulties in the first and third years, and in the lower sixth. Dyslexia the commonest, followed by information processing problems. All teachers briefed on the particular needs of each child, and generally this works well.

Games, options, the arts: Takes sport seriously and keenly. One parent we talked to remembered, and who would not, their son's yomp in the Welsh mountains in filthy weather. Nonetheless, you won't be sidelined if sport is not your thing. Not large enough to be sure of beating all-comers, and is just as interested in the C team as the A. Rugby (but no football), cricket (a close relationship with the MCC, tour to Sri Lanka, and match teas to sigh for on glorious summer evenings). Determined that girls' sport should be great too – hockey coach in the GB Olympic team. Netball and, in the summer, rounders and cricket (hurrah!)

Minor sports include swimming (25m pool and you can do scuba training here), squash, badminton, tennis, horse riding. Will support pupils whose performance takes them out to county competitions and above – swimmer, fencer and showjumper included currently.

A strong push underway to improve and extend all arts provision. 'Focus on the co-curriculum' is another Winkley motto and the headmaster clearly intends to add substantially to the quality and quantity of an already decent provision.

Art itself is already a most inspiring department, popular and with excellent exam results (almost all A* or A), aiming to help pupils explore their talent rather than corral them into standard styles. Pupils participate in teaching – discussing how to approach new topic areas. Short on computing support, more said to be on the way. Art and sport a common mix of enthusiasms.

Drama clearly much enjoyed, the centre of school life for some pupils and an enjoyable part of it for most. An ambitious list of productions – Ayckbourn, Pinter, Shakespeare. English teachers involved in drama activities – encourage scriptwriting. Lots of have-a-go. Few take A level though (none in 2012), the result of a staff hiatus of a few years ago, but good cohorts now coming through (14 in the current fifth form). A new dance studio being used to effect, boys being drawn in by house dance competitions etc.

Music provided in fine quantity and improving quality: two thirds of juniors take lessons in school, half that number in the senior school, but not notably important to the life of the school.

Strong CCF, linked to RAF Odiham with aerial results. D of E – an accredited awarding centre so not reliant on external assessors. Expeditions to all corners of the country.

Computer programming just getting going. DT keen and reasonably well provided for. No science club. As our school reports often said, 'could do better', but in LWC's case there are improvements afoot.

Pupils encouraged to do a lot – and 'those who do, do better academically too' say parents. Pupils set frequent 'challenges': anything from cooking to Karate – to broaden their experience. 'There do not appear to be waiting lists – they seem to get into an activity as soon as they want to'.

Background and atmosphere: Created in 1912 under the will of Sydney James Stern, Lord Wandsworth. Twelve hundred acres of Hampshire chalk down were bought as a refuge for agricultural orphans, the occupations provided drifting gradually away from manual to academic toil, taking fee-paying pupils soon after the last world war. Well spread out in these rather bare uplands, looking much like a 20th century Hampshire village, never inspiring in its architecture but not offensive either. Main campus pleasingly higgledy-piggledy. Glorious feeling of surrounding space, though children not allowed unsupervised access to the wilder bits, or the working farm.

The care of orphans remains central to the school's identity and ethos, though with the current dearth of gruesome agricultural accidents the school no longer asks for a farming background. Foundationers, as they are known, make up 10 per cent of the school population, are heavily supported financially (about eight per cent of fee income is used, with the full support of those paying, for this purpose), and fit seamlessly into this unpretentious school. As long as Foundation candidates are up to the school's entrance standards they are chosen on the basis of need, not performance: the objective is to do well by the children, not flatter the school's exam and sporting performance with imported superstars.

Parents speak of an immensely friendly school, the head of personal growth and character. And, with the inevitable exception of the boys' changing rooms, it smells good too. 'The school understands parents, opens its arms to them, says "how can we help – how can you help". Lots of parental involvement with the school as a result. 'I am as much a part of LWC as my son is'.

School runs from 8.15 in the morning to 4.15 in the afternoon, but it rarely works out that way. What with activities (so many, so well run, so enthusiastically enjoyed), and friendships, and homework, and boarders to set the pace, parents report days that run till 8 or even 9.30pm – and then there's the flexi-boarding: occasional nights at any time and at short notice, but if you contract for three nights a week you get 'your own bed' (we think this means a dedicated bed, rather than not having to sleep top to tail) and competitive rates.

Boarding in comfortable houses: nice study/recreation areas (mostly), restrained decoration, comfortable dormitories with engaging personalities – but too many blank pinboards and animal-free beds. No nasties, a certain amount of mess and tubs of Promax and Diet Fuel for the sports-mad boys. Mixed-sex house (but separate dormitories) for the first two years, separate houses thereafter.

Weekends properly provided for, with trips and films. The film 300 is a favourite with the boys: 'an inspiring story about duty and loyalty, courage and honour' or, according to A O Scott's review, 'about as violent as Apocalypto and twice as stupid'.

Pastoral care and discipline: Head set out to help children mix – senior pupils lead junior activities, for instance. Has worked, we are told: parents and pupils say there are no cliques and schoolfriends span academic, sporty, arty, their own houses and others, as well as across years. 'Everyone just gets on with each other'. Parents speak of the real attachment between house parents and their charges and praise tutors too. Staff also involved and helpful – pupils and parents email them at all times of day and evening and get quick answers. Staff know immediately (systems, not memory) who else is involved with each child, and so can pass on news, views and worries quickly.

Not a school where sin flourishes in any obvious way – pupils are trusted, and act accordingly. Not a boozy school – the boys asked that the 1st XV tour to South Africa was dry, as they didn't want to get dehydrated! Smoking is not tolerated. A pupil who persisted would be asked to leave.

House life is important. 'Once pupils touch base there they are left to their own devices', parents say. Form strong friendships. Girl/boy relationships respectful and civilised. They don't tend to couple up. Sex is forbidden.

Very occasional soft drug issues have been dealt with sensibly. Food raved about by pupils, but by no means gourmet.

Pupils and parents: Parents mainly middle class, many new to independent education. 'I chose LWC because I work hard and could not fit in with the state school day, but I had not realised what I was getting. My son comes home from school asking "can I do this can I do that?" There is so much more going on that it seems to generate another culture'.

Pupils are 'well rounded, decent people who understand themselves and have a social conscience'. Confident. Not dreamers. Grounded. 'Well balanced, confident, level-headed, quite polite'; 'comfortable in their own skins', 'ready for life', 'can manage their day, talk to people', 'have a broader toolkit than just the academic' say parents. The ones who showed us round were a real pleasure to be with. Lots of hearty folk, but you don't need to be robust to flourish: we heard several parental stories of shy kids, or loners even, the ones who 'always end up at the bottom of the rugby scrum', who have been picked up by the school, set challenges, helped to make friends and generally brought out of themselves.

Old Sternians, as they are known, include Jonny Wilkinson (as you will not fail to notice if you tour the school).

Entrance: From Amesbury, Eagle House, Yateley Manor and a wide range of prep and state primary schools. Bus services from as far as Winchester, Bagshot, Churt, Crookham, Hindhead, North Waltham and Yateley.

Likes all rounders. Entrance exams 'not horrific, but neither are they a doddle' say parents. In the centre of the local independent school academic scale, taking children who are average and above. If you are coming from a state school, use a tutor to familiarise your child with the style of the exam questions.

Exit: No hoofing out at 16 unless you do so badly at GCSE that A levels are not a realistic option, but nonetheless about a third leave then, mostly for one or other of the excellent local state (and hence free) sixth form colleges. Barring accidents, all who remain here for the sixth form go on to university – 2013 destinations included Imperial, Edinburgh, Liverpool, Bristol, King's, Newcastle. Two to Oxbridge in 2013 (innovative and effective support from the school). One fifth take a gap year.

Money matters: Ten per cent of pupils supported by The Foundation. Means-tested awards restricted to British children who have lost the support of one or both parents through death, divorce or separation, and whose surviving parent (if there is one) has not formed a new relationship. The order of priority is: 'children who have an identifiable boarding need, the need for pastoral care and support, the need for stability and security in a structured environment, the candidate's home and family situation, the ability to cope academically, integrate socially and contribute to the college community, the family's financial circumstances'.

Remarks: Long known to us, never before thought worth a place in the Guide, Lord Wandsworth was an Ugly Duckling whose spring has arrived in the shape of a fine headmaster. Well on the way to Swan-dom.

Lord Williams's School

Oxford Road, Thame, OX9 2AQ

• Pupils: 2,150 boys and girls; all day • Ages: 11–18 • Non-denom • State

Tel: 01844 210510
Email: office.4580@lordwilliams.oxon.sch.uk
Website: www.lordwilliams.oxon.sch.uk

Headteacher: Since 2005, Mr David Wybron MA (fifties). Previously, deputy of lower school, then deputy head overall before becoming acting head. He joined in 1991 as head of humanities and still teaches a history GCSE class. Read history at Swansea University and taught in Cambridgeshire and Great Missenden, Bucks before arriving in Thame. He exudes a serious-minded confidence and dependability that comes from long experience as a head. Married to a secondary school head of department with a son at LSE and a daughter training with a London law firm. He is rightly proud of his school's good reputation and has ambitions to continue at the current high standards, whether in winning university places or fitting a 16 year old for a good apprenticeship. 'I'm pleased the school is judged to be outstanding, the next challenge is to keep it there'.

Academic matters: More than 55 per cent got 5+ A*-C GCSE grades including maths and English in 2013, and above average results generally. Additional science, art and design, English and history are popular choices at GCSE; French, German and Spanish languages as well as a range of tech options from electronics to food – we found a disembowelled car engine in one of the work rooms. A levels are a major success, with nearly 42 per cent A*/B grades in 2013. Wide range of subjects at all levels, taking advantage of the partnership programmes with other schools to offer anything from academic subjects, strong in sciences and maths, to practical alternatives dance, sport/PE and health and social care. Class sizes don't exceed 30. If there was a weakness, one mum felt, it was that a child would achieve what they expected, but not more.

Seventy per cent of students go on to sixth form (boasts biggest sixth form in Oxon) joined by students from other local schools including Bucks grammar schools, who are attracted by the size, range of courses and good reputation. There were reservations by one parent about the intake at sixth form. 'Some kids didn't really want to be there... and were a bit of a distraction.' However, head felt it was evidence of a supportive and inclusive school – 'we don't make children move if they are not getting A/B grades.'

Teaching staff turn over at a healthy rate, but are organised and professional, according to one parent, and 'make you feel proud of the teaching profession'. Energetic both in and out of school day, some taking adventurous trips abroad or answering emails in the evening and at weekends. Parents felt they showed a refreshing and realistic attitude about the qualifications needed for life rather than for the top university places. 'It's easy when you throw money at it or have a swanky headmistress, but here they are working with budgets that are incredibly challenging'. Slight regret that this meant library wasn't open every day after school.

Comprehensive in the best sense. There is a hefty learning support department, with 400+ on SEN register and over 30 specialist teaching assistants. The ambition is to encourage students to independent working both academic and social, so teaching assistants are rotated throughout the school week. The reputation for learning support is widespread, with families known to have moved to the area to make the most of the specialist provision. The department can be accessed voluntarily by students wishing to catch up with classwork. In addition, there is a resource base for ASD, separate admission requirements, with visiting clinicians. Integration into mainstream classes is tailored to the individual, but students we met were very comfortable with inclusion, to the extent of barely noticing it.

Games, options, the arts: Sports specialism status remains, although now not of any financial advantage – one parent remarked, 'sports college doesn't appear to be that organised' – more to highlight the healthy mind, healthy body ethos. Acres of green and pleasant fields, supplemented by three new Astroturf pitches, athletics track and rugby pitch make up the site; students also pop into Thame Leisure Centre next door in their lunch hour and for year 7 swimming lessons. More unusual options include handball and girls' football. Head delighted that it is the only state school to play an annual cricket match with the MCC. Old boys lists a number of professional footballers and rugby players among them.

Dance and drama is also popular, and has picked up Artsmark awards. There's a snappy new performance studio for concerts and plays and a versatile exhibition area for art installations. Our guides were enthusiastic about their clubs and surgeries in the lunch hour, even 'catch-up' clubs as well as debating and gymnastics. Musicians take individual instrument lessons on a rotation scheme, but numbers who take up an instrument are not great. There is an annual 'singer of the year' competition for the lower years and musical ensembles for the older students. The Duke of Edinburgh would be tickled pink to hear how many Tamensians attend his award courses (about 200) and the head rolls up his sleeves to muck in on the residential weekends: 'You've got to be different things at different times'.

The exciting World Challenge displays the school's breadth of vision, offering the chance for the older students to experience a cultural trip overseas, including India, Africa and the Far East, to the envy of the parents. One week at the end of the school year is Ace week, given over to extra-curricular activities, which may be anything from car maintenance to camping and water sports.

Background and atmosphere: One glaring inconvenience: the school occupies two sites, a couple of miles apart. The older site on Oxford Road is for key stage 4 and sixth form and the newer site at the other end of the charming market town for key stage 3. Commuting is done by staff, not students, and timetabled, although one parent griped that the split site caused a few delays in classes. Head's vision for the school is to bring it all into one camp, after some horse-trading with the local authority.

Wandering through the leafy grounds of the upper site, you wouldn't guess you were in such a large school. The stately old schoolhouse with sunken lawn, now the sixth form centre, is surrounded by low-level newer buildings in a variety of styles, like a university campus. The school was established in 1559 by Lord Williams of Thame with connections to New College Oxford. Portraits of the venerable old headmasters still peer out from the walls of the old building, and antique scholars boards add a sense of heritage. The history is kept alive by the famously active alumnae, The Old Tamensians, who meet regularly at the annual founder's weekend, 'more like in independent schools,' says the head. I saw present-day students, visibly engaged in their work and pastimes, intent on study but with a healthy hum of discussion; all but sixth form tidily presented in their popular maroon polo shirts and hoodies.

Pastoral care and discipline: Head projects confidence about dealing with bullying and problem behaviours, 'I don't duck things', and happy that he has a strong team for pastoral issues, including support officers and home/school link workers. One parent commented the system of reporting was superior to other schools, another that there was a 'high level of responsiveness' that had been missing at her child's previous grammar school. As well as face-to-face parents' evenings, tutors keep in touch by email, and one parent was chuffed to have received a post card for her child's outstanding work. Head was savvy about new technology, defining it as a new challenge to schools: 'There is always a surprise; this job is never boring'. Students were familiar with straightforward points system for rewards and discipline. Good behaviour is rewarded by watching a film or a paintballing jolly. Poor behaviour, after a series of warnings and detention, could incur a short period of 'solitary', but as my student guides said, 'if you do it once, you don't want to do it again'. Parents agreed that the process worked and kept the school's standards high. Transition into the school at year 7 is managed by taster days for all; extra visits for SEN children, and a week-long summer school of fun activities to taste it and see.

Pupils and parents: Varied social backgrounds: some academic, some rural and some from more deprived areas, but real sense that it reflects the local community. Statistically, lower than average numbers on free school meals and ethnic minority students but higher numbers of SEN, due to the Resource Base. At the time of my visit, and rather surprisingly, there were no children requiring EAL support. One of the first schools to recognise 'young carers' and set up support system for them. Students are agreeably confident, articulate and appeared attentive and focused in the lessons, 'always so courteous and pleasant,' said a parent. They are proud of the links with a twin school in The Gambia, which involves cross-curricula expeditions and cultural visits. New parents are encouraged to join the Lord Williams's Association, and get to know one another and the head at the meetings. Old students include Restoration dramatist, Etherege; a clutch of poets and composer, Howard Goodall.

Entrance: Oversubscribed from local primaries within Thame and Chinnor; also takes Buckinghamshire applicants from over the county border. The Resource Base is filled by students with statements and by referral. Separate sixth form entrants take a range of routes, some from independent schools.

Exit: Up to 70 per cent go on to sixth form. Others follow courses at FE college or start apprenticeships. Most leavers at sixth form go to university, with half a dozen a year taking up Oxbridge places. One parent was delighted at the broad-minded attitude of the senior staff to university destinations: 'If you don't get in (to Russell Group university) it's not the end of the world'. Careers counselling starts in year 10 and students are encouraged to make an appointment at any time after that, if needed.

Money matters: Converted to academy in September 2012, which head hopes will go some way to protecting the cuts in funding all secondary schools face. Lord Williams's Association (parent-led) helps with fund-raising and the students themselves raved about class competitions to collect for the Gambia school.

Remarks: 'Lord Bill's' is a modern comprehensive with traditional roots. An experienced and egalitarian head runs a tight ship over two sites, maintaining steady standards whilst keeping an eye out for trouble. The school is 'a broad church' – academic success, alongside a healthy mix of sports and arts, as well as insightful pastoral support. Said a parent, 'A caring, community school that turns out decent people'. Quite definitely a competitor to the independents and grammar schools over the tracks.

Loreto Grammar School

Dunham Road, Altrincham, Cheshire, WA14 4AH

• Pupils: 1050 girls • Ages: 11–18 • Catholic • State

Tel: 01619 283703
Email: admissions@loretogrammar.co.uk
Website: www.loretogrammar.co.uk

Head Teacher: Since 2006, Mrs Jane Beever MA PGCE NPQH (early forties), first lay head. Educated at a Catholic grammar in Liverpool, read French and Italian at Liverpool and Leeds universities; previously deputy head at Loreto. Head is also a national leader in education.

Easy to talk to and approachable (weekly drop in time for parents), humorous and realistic. Girls value her knowing them all by name and the interest she takes in them at chance meetings. Believes in providing a structured environment with clear rules but is very mindful of individuals – 'We are a very human establishment'. Enjoys walking – 'but my outside interests are mainly Loreto, in England and abroad!'

Academic matters: Specialisms in science and maths. Glowing Ofsted re curriculum, achievements, teaching and learning, sixth form and relationships – girls develop an affection for their teachers; a number we met expressed appreciation of their teachers' friendliness, helpfulness, generosity with their time and skill ('amazing teaching').

In 2013, nearly 72 per cent A*/B grades and nearly 42 per cent A*/A at A level; especially strong chemistry, Eng lit, art and design, geography, government and politics, Latin. Offers 30 subjects (will run them for just one to three students) including ologies, economics, Latin, sports science, textiles and resistant materials (but not food tech, which some girls would like). All do a general RE course with broad-ranging outside speakers, eg Loreto Sisters working with trafficked women (led to girls' active involvement in a local campaign) and street children in India.

Continually improving, high GCSE achievement – in 2013 61 per cent A*/A grades; outstanding RS and expressive arts, very good separate sciences (increasing uptake), English, Latin, geography, music, art, food tech, textiles. All do RS and a modern foreign language (Spanish and German too).

Successful in the usual national academic comps, plus engineering, Mandarin Chinese speaking, Model United Nations and film script writing, at regional or national level.

Five forms of 30 at key stage 3 (setting in maths, science and mod langs from year 8), reduced to six forms of around 25 at key stage 4; sets of 12-20 for A level. Well-endowed with modern ICT and science facilities and a developed VLE (eg revision chat rooms). Very focused on constant improvement – uses independent advisors and involves girls.

Well-qualified, sensitive and innovative SENCo – would try to accommodate all needs, including physical disabilities (a blind student did very well), but mostly focused on dyslexia (no extra costs).

Games, options, the arts: Limited space on site for sports and PE – just trad gym plus school hall and a few all-weather courts; sports grounds with Astroturf close and uses nearby leisure centre eg for swimming. Not that this holds the girls back – success at regional to national levels in standard sports plus several individuals at national level in eg gymnastics, karate and boxing, with a world champion kickboxer to boot.

Impressive music – high level choral singing (Canatamus group regularly in TV recordings), major annual concert at Manchester's Bridgewater Hall. Large drama studio with upper level and much stunningly good art – check out the gallery on the school's website and prepare to be bowled over; a well-established, full-time artist in residence. We were particularly taken with the sparky school magazine, Loreto Life – more impressive creative pieces than we often see and plenty of humour.

Wide-ranging choices in the additional life skills courses – at key stage 4 including self defence, voluntary work via the St Vincent de Paul Society, teaching science or helping with enrichment groups in primary schools, web design; for sixth formers EPQ, general studies, AS science and society or critical thinking, career-linked programmes such as Medlink and vet Medlink, Headstart courses in STEM subjects.

Various clubs and competitions and substantial sums raised for charities, notably their sister school in Kolkata, India, where sixth formers visit bi-annually; exchanges to Spain, Italy, France and Germany; two enterprising Chinese girls present their own regular local radio show. Leadership encouraged at all ages; the school council, says head, 'has teeth – and they show it!'.

Background and atmosphere: Under the trusteeship of the Sisters of Loreto, the school's origins derive from foundress Mary Ward, a splendid sounding 16th/17th century Yorkshire nun who pioneered early experiments in the Christian education of girls, convinced they should have the same opportunities as boys, since women 'could do great things if men would stop making them believe they could do nothing'! She set very high standards of teaching in her schools and her ideas were developed by two remarkably enlightened and innovative 19th century sisters.

Began as a small private school in the YWCA quarters in Altrincham, 1909, with four nuns as teachers; 1946 registered as an independent grammar school for girls. In 1972 the prep and grammar schools became separate; 1997 awarded grant maintained status, then became a voluntary aided school in the Trafford LA, 1999. Specialist maths and science college 2005; now an academy (girls consulted too).

Its fundamental values of truth, justice, freedom, sincerity, joy, excellence and internationality derive from Mary Ward's vision of a life of service – 'No half measures – no half women' – and are physically visible around school, as well as in the strong sense of a supportive community based on mutual respect, plus the national and international extent of its concerns – all take part in a weekly current events quiz and it belongs to a network of over 120 Loreto schools in different countries (has an international school award). Seeks to turn out 'women of courage who are alive to the needs of humanity and committed to making a better world' and, according to a parent, 'instils confidence in all the girls'. Their Catholic faith is central – daily worship in the form of class, year and whole school assemblies, services and masses, plus retreats.

The architecture is a blend of traditional and modern – the quirky 90 year old part is the original convent, with pleasant red brick façade, much wood within, a central 'Crush Hall', where the student services desk is sited, and very special chapel decorated in white, blue and yellow, graced by stained glass windows above half height alabaster arches, a floor-to-ceiling modern tapestry and very comfortable chairs (no austerity here) – clearly a much cherished space. Some classrooms lack space and the narrow corridors can get congested, but the girls we saw in transit behaved very sensibly.

The most recent building, containing refurbished science labs and ICT suites, is only some 10 years old, with a new third storey. The sixth have an attractive, fresh common-room and the library has also been upgraded – lots of fiction and other well-used-looking books; a small 'chill out zone' furnished with bean bags and comfy chairs; access to PCs and laptops – very focused girls at work.

The uniform consists of dark blue skirts with cream blouse/shirt, tie and very, um, striking blazers with navy blue, gold, white and maroon stripes: a full classroom made this editor

L

think of a convocation of outsize maroon wasps. Girls say they make them look like deckchairs, but we were assured, 'You get used to them,' and one admitted she had become fond of hers. Business wear for the sixth. Drop-off time parking to be avoided, as a few schools bunched along the road.

Pastoral care and discipline: High praise for pastoral care in inspection reports and from parents we spoke to – the usual structures plus a lay chaplain and access to an external counsellor. Year 12s mentor year 7s, who also have a year 8 'buddy' when they start. Taster visits and a 'marvellous' open day for year 6s, plus transition programme for post-18 planning.

Focus more on relationships than rules – girls treated as individuals; exclusion very much a last resort. Discipline not 'a major problem', according to head and deputy head – 'It's very rare for a girl to kick against the traces'; 'friendly but firm – they have a healthy respect for the staff' (parent). Various rewards, eg celebration lunches ('We see good food as very important' – head), Fantastic Fridays (weekly meeting with head for academic achievers), Bright Stars (recognition for the less outstanding but steadily virtuous girls who might otherwise go unnoticed).

Pupils and parents: Four or five main Catholic feeder primaries, plus 30-40 smaller ones – Altrincham, Manchester, Stockport, Warrington and beyond. A broad range of socio-economic and ethnic backgrounds but majority from high social class areas; almost all baptised Catholics with a few of other faiths – has had a Muslim head girl. Happy, secure, polite, considerate, supportive, serious-minded girls.

Parents in general very pleased – 'Can't fault it', 'absolutely delighted' (mother of four) – and Mumsnet concurs, though one had wanted more detailed support with medical school application. Plenty of contact, eg newsletters, e access to girls' progress, open weekly Mass, invitations to science activities, and their views sought regularly.

Entrance: Governing body controls decisions re admissions, Trafford LA co-ordinates. Takes top 40 per cent of ability range. Very over-subscribed – main requirement is to be a baptised Catholic child; also uses baptised other faith, placing in exams and distance from school.

Year 7: closed NFER tests in VR and English plus closed school tests in creative writing and maths (no practice papers available).

Sixth form: just dealt with by school, not LA; 15 places for external students, who 'will be expected to support the ethos and values of the school' – need at least six GCSEs A*-B including English and maths; above criteria for over-subscription.

Exit: Some girls leave after GCSEs (a quarter in 2013). Has a partnership with Loreto College in Manchester, so girls can do a subject there and the rest in school. Almost all to university for a broad range of subjects – English, history and business common. Around two-thirds to Russell Group – Sheffield, Newcastle and Manchester popular, seven to Oxbridge in 2013.

Remarks: Exceptionally high standards reached in all endeavours, in an orderly, nurturing atmosphere that does not exclude humour and originality. Kindness rather than competition prevails, with a deep awareness of the spiritual dimension.

Loretto School

Linked school: Loretto Junior School aka The Nippers

1-7 Linkfield Road, Musselburgh, EH21 7RE

• Pupils: 430 boys and girls, takes boarders • Ages: 12-18 • Non-denom • Fees: Boarding £18,690-£28,590; Day £14,040-£19,440 pa • Independent

Tel: 01316 534455
Email: admissions@loretto.com
Website: www.loretto.com

Acting head: Since April 2013, Elaine Logan MA PGCE (fifties), state educated, started her teaching career in the state sector, followed by English and drama at Dollar Academy. Moved to Loretto in 2001, becoming housemistress of Holm House (and gathering a host of 'Compliance, Inspection and Child Protection' qualifications on the way) before becoming assistant vicegerent in 2012. Married with three children, two of them at Loretto, she lives with her (now retired) husband a couple of miles from school. She took over after the surprise resignation of Peter Hogan, five days before the start of the 2013 summer term. The IT savvy former head did much to kick Loretto into the 21st century and we are delighted that this process is continuing, though not necessarily with the same emphasis. Acting head is pushing a virtual learning environment – all pupils from form two upwards have access to lesson plans (the new approach went live in September 2013). 'The staff have embraced it tremendously,' she says.

The only female HMC representative in Scotland, she is much enjoying her unique tenure ('but I often used to dep for Peter, so it's not all foreign'); keen on 'reflective practice' – which sounds a tad Steiner. She still has tutees (no gender bias), teaches all first year in senior school, form two drama, and A level theatre studies. Unashamedly 'child centred', she 'likes children' and is charming and chatty.

From September 2014 new head will be Dr Graham Hawley, currently head of Kelly College, Tavistock.

Academic matters: Monthly tutorial assessments are, 'minuted and followed through', with pupils and parents but see above and watch this space. School follows the English system – GCSEs for all, plus AS and A2s. Best exam results ever in 2013-23 per cent A* grades at GCSE and 16 per cent A* grades at A level. No (current) thoughts of moving to the IB, but goodness knows what is going to happen in the world of academe over the next few years. Classics back on stream but not – currently – offered at A level. Goodly selection of top end passes; maths, physics strong as ever, but Eng lit and art in the ribbons; v strong German (native speakers perhaps?). Music a tad sad exam-wise in the last few years, and not many sporting heroes... (as in PE successes as opposed to on the pitch).

Traditionally strong on science and engineering, humanities, government and politics (number in both cabinets recently); business studies creeping up the ladder, plus economics, French and Spanish. Boy/girl ratio pretty even across the field, Russian and Mandarin available at all levels, native speakers encouraged to sit for qualifications in their own langs, tutors can be pulled on if necessary. Three sciences standard at GCSE, though one can be dropped for art.

Setting in English, maths and languages, most subjects from third form. School recently became an Associate school of the Royal Society, which sounds pretty grand but only lasts two years. Apparently girls no longer set the academic bar, 'it depends on the year group'. The staff we met were all bright, bubbly and enthusiastic. ESL (extra cost) and learning support available throughout. Drop in centres, 'staff very helpful' said head boy.

L

Special societies for clever clogs. Smartboards in classrooms and networked computers everywhere, including study-bedrooms. Eighty pupils each year in sixth form. Impressive visiting lecturer programme, usually one per week, members of upper sixth regularly give lectures too; interview practice for all.

Games, options, the arts: Singing as ever good and keen: the whole school sings in the war memorial chapel choir and performs at the Schools Proms at the Royal Albert Hall. Music improving in leaps and bounds, with orchestra and jazz band, most of the second form (ie 12 year olds) study one or more instruments. The pipe band performed with Sir Paul McCartney in Liverpool last year. Wow! The first all-Steinway independent school in Europe – Steinways throughout campus (other schools please note). Drama on the up – theatre studies taken at all exam levels (sprinkling of As at A), school is a registered LAMDA centre. Art scholars do life classes, screen printing and textiles. Campus and online Loretto radio station as well as all singing and dancing recording studio.

PE is an examinable subject, strong sport – girls' athletics and lacrosse do well; the appointment of a head of girls' games has given it a real impetus. Impressive string of wins on the rugby pitch over the last few years has put 1st XV firmly back in the top league. Fine all-weather court, new Olympic blue Astroturf at Pinkie (pretty garish), and acres of playing fields. Canoeing in the Musselburgh lagoons, but not a lot of use made of the sea itself (enthusiasts sail in North Berwick).

The golf academy is flourishing, currently number one in Europe (school has a long tradition of senior golfing FPs), and golf is professionally coached throughout the school, with all pupils using top class practice facilities on campus, including a nine-hole Huxley all-weather putting green. Rounds are played at the local Craigielaw, and Archerfield down the firth. Rash of success over the years, older pupils' lessons re-jigged to accommodate coaching; three golf scholarships to leading American universities to date; wins in many county championships. Summer residential golf camps are run to encourage new golfers to apply (ie as pupils at the school). Variety of trips and exchanges, for pupils, and for staff.

Background and atmosphere: Founded in 1827 in the 'honest toun' (which is why Pinkie House had the first electronic gates in Scotland), and bought by Hely Hutchison Almond in 1862 (a distinguished scholar of unconventional convictions – Scotland's answer to Dr Arnold). Loretto went fully co-ed in 1995. The traditional East Lothian ochre-coloured buildings straddle the A1; on occasion, the tunnel below is used for sailing boats…don't ask, it needs to be flooded first. Slightly disjointed campus with various outbuildings, including The Nippers and a wodge of playing fields north of the river Esk. Rolling plan of refurbishing houses and a certain amount of tinkering location-wise. School house has become the day centre. Pinkie House, with its important painted ceiling in the gallery under the roof, has a particularly gruesome extension and is home to some of the sixth form boys who have obviously driven out the ghost of the first Lady Seaton, Green Jean, wife of Alexander, who jumped from the gallery (there is a most unflattering portrait of her on the main staircase). The gallery itself, dissed by Historic Scotland as a dorm (too much sweating) is now a function room (roof repaired, 45K worth of fire alarms and sprinklers, bank of loos), licensed for 120, temporary kitchen available – that sort of thing. Lesser rooms converted into rather grand exam centre and extra lecture rooms.

Linkfield, previously a pupil led bar (ah, those were the days), now houses the CCF and outdoor centre etc. CCF for all, navy and army only. Current prospectus (not enuff words, too many pics for grandparents – who like more words if they are to pay the bill, and many do) about to be replaced by zinging new edition with proper words and descriptions. If one is brutally honest, whilst the CD and memory stick are super, in the real world of

marketing grandparents/parents, particularly first time buyers, like to leave the prospectus lying around – it sure beats ducks on the wall! Very jolly map at back is spoiled by beastly black arrows to Pinkie House and Junior School and there is, as yet, no mention of the new Eleanora Almond girls house – arranged by apartments – which was due to open on the High Street the day after our visit (it had been ready for months, but the Care Commission had been a little tardy in inspections). Holm House (with lift for disabled access) and Balcarres, for girls, are adjacent to the (small) sports centre, junior girls' house and girls' sixth form house. Study bedrooms in sixth form house. Senior common rooms for sixth form with a certain amount of male access; barbecues are popular at the girls' houses and attended by all. Girls' boarding bung full, certain availability for chaps (but not dead empty you understand). The Yard (under staff supervision) is the new social centre for sixth form weekend shenanigans.

Kilts on Sundays – some remnants of the traditional uniform remain. Red jackets the norm for all, with navy collars distinguishing sixth form: 'just get it sewn on, no need for new blazer'. Still no ties for daily dress. An absolute ban on any form of platform heels – no more 'tottering on the asphalt'. Second hand shop.

'The CRC (communication and resource centre) now houses a modern sixth form centre – designated areas for independent academic study, university admissions, individual tutoring and socializing'. Quite. This was formerly a disaster area with unusable polychrome covered computers on the first floor, it's now a jolly library with all sorts of nooks and crannies in the midst of the main school campus, useful when time is too short to get back to study bedrooms, and a good resource centre. Must have had more money thrown at it than you would believe, and finally, it works! 'The aim is to create an ambience more like a university's and provide good opportunities to develop leadership skills'. Yah

Full boarding, weekly boarding, flexi-boarding plus day pupils, the latter particularly well integrated. Buses from all over: East Lothian, central Edinburgh, the Borders and more in the pipeline. School operates a six morning, three afternoon schedule; day pupils can and do go home during the week at 4.30pm if they have no further activities (otherwise it is 6.30/8.30pm).

Sixth form boarders can get permission to go into Edinburgh on any night of the week 'providing that their work is in order'. They can go to a film, the theatre, concerts (rock or otherwise), and the upper sixth can go racing in Musselburgh, all of ten yards from main school entrance. The young told this editor that they take taxis home after partying in Edinburgh and charge it to their parents' bill, this has been kyboshed by the head and buses are gaining in popularity. Younger boarders take the school bus of a weekend to Kinaird Park, which houses a collection of utterly desirable shops – a great improvement on Musselburgh. This is a chilly corner of East Lothian and the east wind whistling across the racecourse from the North Sea is an almost permanent feature (head is not so sure, and boasts of the Musselburgh micro-climate).

Pastoral care and discipline: Zero tolerance for drugs no longer the norm – pupils are not automatically out for being caught actively using any drug; though they are for dealing. 'Each case treated on its merits'. No random testing unless pupil has been suspended and is back on probation. The GSG wonder about 'legal spikes'. School is tough on persistent bullying ('We spend hours on it – please don't use the word "tough" '), cyber bullying the next kid on the block. Recognised ladder for punishments, no longer entirely in the houseparents' domain: breathalyser, gatings, rustications and out for alcohol; gatings and letters home for smoking. NB pupils can be expelled both for their own misdemeanours or if their parents have 'treated the school or members of its staff unreasonably.'

Pupils and parents: Usual Scottish collection. Not a lot of foreigners; representatives from 21 countries currently (penny numbers); large number of OLs' sons, daughters and grandchildren, some of whom join for the sixth form only. Numbers of first time buyers, particularly amongst the day crew, who see Musselburgh as a viable alternative to going all the way into town. Not really a Sloane/Charlotte Ranger school. OLs include a gang of MPs, Lord Lamont, Lord (Hector) Laing, Andrew Marr and Alastair Darling.

Entrance: Own entrance exam or CE from Scottish and northern prep schools; 20 per cent of pupils come up from The Nippers en masse. Special exam and interview for those from the state sector or from overseas. Around 50 per cent now day, outstanding 20 per cent increase in boarders during the last few years, with more boys coming in sixth. Six GCSEs at C and above for entry into sixth form, with As in subjects to be taken at A level. Scholarships and bursaries are available.

Exit: Ninety-seven per cent or so to tertiary education, with a sporadic Oxbridge trickle.

Money matters: Scholarships for academics, musicians, drama, art, sport, golf, plus scholarships for those from the state sector and for those coming up from The Nippers etc etc. Bursaries rigorously means tested (private detectives, that sort of thing) but the fiercely academic Almond Scholarship, worth 100 per cent plus is income blind. Sixth form scholarships and bursaries awarded to those 'who have deserved well of Loretto'.

Remarks: Famous Scottish co-ed public school that has embraced day pupils to combine the best of both worlds: trad boarding with robust day option. Small enough to gentle those in need of nurturing and big enough to compete with the rest of the Scottish pack. And with an almost unbeaten XV...

Loughborough Grammar School

Linked schools: Loughborough High School; Fairfield Preparatory School

Burton Walks, Loughborough, LE11 2DU

- Pupils: 1010 boys; 60 boarders, 950 day. • Ages: 10–18
- Christian–non denominational • Fees: Day £10,725; Boarding £23,115 pa • Independent

Tel: 01509 233233
Email: registrar@lesgrammar.org
Website: www.lesgrammar.org

Headmaster: Since 1998, Mr Paul Fisher MA (mid-fifties). Came via Prior Park College in Bath and Marlborough College before becoming headmaster of Mount St Mary's College and thence to Loughborough. Married to Helen, who teaches Spanish and French in the school, with two boys. Read classics at Christ Church, Oxford, where he won a cricket blue, played for the university second XV and ended up as president of Vincent's, the élite sporting club of the university. Later he played cricket for Middlesex and Worcestershire. Has run the London and Paris marathons.

A naturally modest man – we had to prise his sporting triumphs out of him – he is not a red-faced hearty nor the lapel-tugging, bullfrog sort of headmaster who booms out educational edicts from Olympus. The word 'fun' appears more often than 'leagues' in his vocabulary. Thoughtful and quietly spoken, his main concern seemed to be how, with so many boys in the school and such a compact day, he can get to know them

better. He lunches with them as often as time allows, seeking 'ground level information' and 'taking the temperature of the day'; he teaches RE to year 10 pupils, 'Islam and philosophical things, such as free will', and 'wanders around a lot,' as one boy put it. 'An excellent listener,' one parent told us; 'surprisingly accessible,' said another.

The day we visited, the A level candidates were attending their last day of lessons before retreating for study leave. An ideal opportunity, one would have thought, for hearing the truth about the headmaster and the school. Without a flicker of hesitation, all the boys we approached spoke glowingly of the whole set up, including the headmaster. 'Lightness of touch', 'good sense of humour,' 'is interested in us' were the sort of comments which cropped up over and over again. Judging by the easy banter that staff and head were indulging in over the very good lunch we had in the boys' refectory, relations with staff are good, too. It certainly feels a very happy school.

Academic matters: As with much we encountered at Loughborough, the academic programme is carefully thought out. For the first three years the emphasis seems to be on learning for pleasure – or the pleasure of learning. Breadth rather than an exclusive drive towards good grades is the aim; a genuine wish to stimulate a sense of enquiry and wonder as well as accumulating knowledge. Clubs and societies outside the classroom seek to support that – see the list of clubs and activities below. 'We aim to eliminate any barriers surrounding the classroom,' one member of staff told us. All boys take nine GCSEs in addition to a further programme of religion and philosophy, PHSE and outside activities. Some Latin and less Greek is taken at GCSE and Latin is on offer at A level.

The excellent website and prospectus give generous information about the academic side of the school. Those who thrive on statistics can positively gorge themselves, revelling in small percentage differences between the popularity of subjects from year to year and the percentage of A and B grades. They will see that, in general, the sciences, maths, politics and economics seem the most popular, but they will also note that 28 A level subjects are on offer and they do not include raffia dolly making or flower arranging. Breadth of choice is encouraged and where difficulties arise matching a pupil's choice of subjects, the school will seek to accommodate. For those who still insist on reading league tables, Loughborough scores well. In 2013, more than 59 per cent A*/A grades at GCSE and more than 51 per cent at A level. Facilities in support of their enlightened approach are excellent, with a delightful and much-used library – not quite as big as it looks in the pictures – a superb language laboratory and a state-of-the-art new science complex; new maths building under construction.

Games, options, the arts: Plenty of sport and healthily enjoyed, 'though you don't have to be good at sports to make friends,' a youngish boy told us. Rugby probably the most popular game but has also had some notable successes at football, both locally and at international level, cricket, cross-country, basketball and tennis. In addition to pitches close to the school buildings, about 40 acres of specially-levelled games pitches, a cross-country course and a grass athletics track near Quorn, about four miles away. Pupils are driven there and back. The scene from the superb pavilion is most impressive.

Extra-curricular activities include a thriving CCF section, the popular D of E award scheme, debating, chess and bridge, the last three obviously helping to break down any barriers that might surround the classroom. Bridge, in particular, popular and successful, with players moving on to national and international honours. We were assured 300 chess players – amongst other things, a thinking school.

An excellent drama studio, of which the school is justifiably proud, leads on to 'stunning productions' in conjunction with the girls' High School. The new music school, run by a wildly enthusiastic head of music, has seen more and more people learn instruments (year 6 pupils all do). Singing is increasingly popular and the choirs and orchestras go out and about nationwide and overseas.

Background and atmosphere: Founded in 1495, moved up to its present site in 1850 and now part of Loughborough Endowed Schools, sharing the delightfully spacious and leafy campus with Loughborough High School for girls and Fairfield School, the co-educational prep. Though independent of each other, the three schools share the same governing body and a number of facilities.

For those parents who cannot decide between co-ed or single sex Loughborough could be the answer. The main quad with its Tennysonian Tower and cherry trees is a delightful fusion of old and new buildings blending in sensitively across the centuries. In fact, the whole campus feels more like a university, an impression confirmed by the school's approach to the pupils, who are treated as burgeoning adults. Sixth formers, currently having their designated centre upgraded, may have lunch in the school refectory or in town and the house system is designed to be 'healthily competitive and fun' (that word again).

Boys come from a wide variety of ethnic backgrounds, but diversity seems genuinely celebrated and seen as an opportunity to enlarge mutual understanding. Boys look you in the eyes and smile. They seem very much at ease with each other and the staff – that includes non-teaching staff as well. The departure of the head groundsman after nearly 40 years of loyal service was marked by a ceremony at the top of the tower while below the entire school gathered to cheer him – a real community.

Pastoral care and discipline: 'I think the best thing about this school is that they trust you,' a leaver told us. Another said, 'I'll be a bit sad to leave but I'm ready now. I think they've prepared me well.' He then added wryly, 'Well, I hope they have.' Small tutor groups, not selected on purely academic grounds, help form friendships and understanding not only between pupils but also with staff who seem, in general, much appreciated – 'They always seem to have time to help, even the weird ones'. A good anti-bullying policy in place, but all the boys we spoke to said that it really wasn't an issue and that they felt supported and understood. One or two offered the theory that going home in the evenings helped diffuse any tensions. All sixth form boys are made prefects, giving them a sense of responsibility and belonging; senior prefects are elected by the boys concerned – a system which seems to work well and is another example of the important part trust plays in the running of the school.

Two separate boarding houses run by housemasters with their own families, both in the heart of the school. School House, for senior pupils, has room for over 30, of whom about 65 per cent are from at least five different countries. The rest tend to be Forces children. Housed in a delightfully quirky mid-19th century listed building, it was the headmaster's house, as witness the mosaic floor in the hallway and the welcoming Latin message over what was originally the front door – ask the housemaster to translate, if you can't: he is primed. No longer a green baize door – he and his wife (a teacher) live cheek by jowl with their extended family. The boys' accommodation is approached via an amusing rabbit warren of stairs and passageways and comprises shared bedsits before seniors gravitate to rooms of their own. Pleasant recreational facilities as well as kitchen and laundry. A resident house tutor. The genuine family feel is further enhanced by the cleaning ladies, some of whom see their posts as hereditary, obviously care about the boys and know them well – another example of that community feeling.

Denton House for juniors (10-13 years) takes up to 18 boarders and is decorated cheerfully and imaginatively in a building which was once a private house and still retains that feeling. In addition to full boarding, flexi and weekly boarding are welcomed when space is available. Lots of weekend activities on offer. Occasionally boys choose to do a stint of boarding in order to help them feel even more at home in the school. Pupils from abroad receive support and encouragement from the housemaster's wife, a trained EAL teacher. Cautious noises about increasing the amount of boarding and both buildings are in line for refurbishment.

Pupils and parents: Not a school for toffs; one which absorbs about 25 per cent of boys from ethnic minority backgrounds and a wide cross-section of parents. The ones we spoke to felt involved and part of the community. Buses come in daily from a radius of about 20 miles as well as the local area. Boys return home at 4pm unless they are staying on for extra-mural activities. Approx 35 boys from Hong Kong and mainland China as well as other parts of the world. An impressive variety of famous old boys testifies to the feeling that Loughborough does not do pigeon-holing.

Entrance: By own examination at 10,11 and 13 or CE at 13. Selective, more on the grounds of suitability than academic ability. It does not set out to be a specialist school for learning difficulties but all boys are screened for dyslexia on entry and help is available from learning support. About 50 per cent of pupils come from Fairfield, Loughborough's prep school, and the rest from primaries and other preps. Caters for pupils who transfer at age 10 by having a year 6 class which is integrated into the senior school to prepare them socially and academically for continuing into year 7.

Sixth form entry is based on GCSE results. Conditional offers made after interview with the headmaster, report from present school and predicted GCSE grades. Overseas pupils are required to sit examinations in those subjects they wish to study at A level.

Exit: About 10-15 per cent leave after GCSE, usually in pursuit of courses not available at Loughborough. Virtually all sixth formers go on to university: 10 to Oxbridge and 14 to London unis in 2012; Durham, Exeter, Birmingham, Bath and Newcastle also popular. No outstanding subjects, but a greater proportion reading for science-based degrees than the humanities.

Money matters: A number of scholarships at different levels are available – don't be afraid to ask. A 25 per cent boarding fee remission for Forces children.

Remarks: A civilised school at ease with itself but constantly looking to improve. Ask to see a copy of the regular newsletter from governors to parents and guardians, a document which aims to keep the whole community aware of the thinking behind decisions and aspirations – not many schools do that. A happy school where boys are encouraged to pursue worthwhile individual goals, while having fun. Highly regarded locally and by connoisseurs further afield. A special community preparing boys sensitively and intelligently for university and beyond.

L

Loughborough High School

Linked schools: Loughborough Grammar School; Fairfield Preparatory School

Burton Walks, Loughborough, LE11 2DU

- Pupils: 600 girls; all day • Ages: 11–18 • Non–denom
- Fees: £10,191 pa • Independent

Tel: 01509 212348
Email: admin@leshigh.org
Website: www.leshigh.org

Headmistress: Since 2011, Mrs Gwen Byrom BSc MA PGCE (early forties). Lots of varied experiences and qualifications gathered during her ascent to the headship of Loughborough High. She read biochemistry at Manchester University, followed by a master's degree with the Open University. Later she added psychology to the quiver of subjects she is qualified to teach. Has taught in a grammar school in Kent, then head of junior science at Solihull followed in fairly quick succession by Bedstone College, Roedean and, most recently, Cheltenham Ladies' College as vice-principal (pastoral). If you trawl the internet, you will find very complimentary words from some ex pupils about Mrs Byrom. She says that Loughborough High is the best place she has ever taught at with the best staff she has ever worked with. 'This is the place for me. This is what I've been dreaming of.'

Teaches philosophy to year 7 to get a feel for the girls as they come into the school. 'I love the interaction and I want them to have the confidence to express doubts about what I say and to argue with me, me the head. We discuss a wide range of issues and I think that helps them to know me better. It certainly helps me get a feel for the pulse of the school. I hope these lessons are perceived as enrichment. They certainly are for me.'

Girls we spoke to said how approachable she is, what a good listener. One group described her as 'mumsie', a term which clearly surprised, if not baffled her. We've heard headteachers called worse things. Keen on single sex education, which is just as well all things considered. As a scientist she is aware that girls in single sex schools are more likely to pursue the sciences than in a mixed school where sciences are perceived by boys as their prerogative. Overall she seems to have gone down well with parents, who speak appreciatively of her thoughtful, gentle approach. Some query whether she is fierce enough, whether she is as determined about league tables as she 'should be'. Others say 'she is a motivator, not a battle-axe, and there are more important things than league tables.' There's a compromise lurking there.

When we asked about plans for the future she became tremendously excited about iPads for everyone. Faced with an ageing Luddite who shamelessly prefers books, she visibly turned up the heat arguing with something that WB Yeats might have called 'passionate intensity.' It was a magnificent and sincere performance. As one worldly father said, 'Oh, she's got bottle'.

Married to a physics teacher who is on her staff. Four children.

Academic matters: Loughborough High doesn't feel like an academic oven nor an intellectual boiler: it does feel like a skilfully used slow cooker where the right temperature serves to permeate the ingredients with interesting tastes and infusions. GCSE and A level results are clearly published for interested parties to see and analyse and in today's climate, where schools are increasingly run as businesses and driven by targets, it is right that staff and pupils should celebrate good results (77 per cent A*/A grades at GCSE and 63 per cent A*/A at A level

in 2013, in case you are interested). But that sort of success doesn't seem to be what this school is really about; that's not what seems to unite teachers and pupils in mutual respect, interest and concern. There's plenty of talk in schools about 'happy family atmosphere.' Loughborough High certainly has bags of that, but what is more interesting is the palpable feeling that genuinely shared academic interests and concerns hint at another level of happiness and satisfaction. Neither seems at the expense of the other. That's what comes over as the heart of the school. And that doesn't happen by chance. It involves hard work and attention to detail; it requires genuine love of learning and enquiry from teachers and pupils alike.

Potential parents can look at the website and see the results, the choices available and the variety of opportunities beyond the classroom, but that's not what impressed us most. We witnessed a fabulous teacher who described herself as being 'as nutty as a fruitcake' enthuse and encourage a group of sixth formers who were trying to decide what topics they wished to work on for their EPQ during the summer holidays. Music Therapy, The French Revolution and Literature, a fiendishly difficult sounding science investigation: 27 girls were volunteering to pursue their chosen topic over the summer holidays. They were liaising with teachers to act as personal tutors over the holidays. The decibel count was high and happy. These were not necessarily what Australians call Pointy Heads: they were girls of spirit and zest, girls who might, as one teacher put it, jump in puddles.

We heard girls talking about the wonderful help given in choosing universities and the right course; we heard teachers saying what fun it was to teach such lively and interested girls, 'though they can drive you mad'; we heard girls talking about the extra help teachers were prepared to give. 'Everyone realizes how lucky we are to have so much support,' said a girl. It was a feeling echoed over and over again. In the splendid library we met a girl reading Plato's Symposium for pleasure and keen to discuss it and another bursting to talk about Churchill and the Gold Standard; we saw some thrillingly exciting textile work, inspired by a teacher who would have been totally camouflaged in a herbaceous border. And to extend that theme, the breadth and number of GCSE subjects on offer – 23 in all – ranging across a very wide spectrum suggests the thoughtful planning of a skilful plants person who wants people to wander and pick whatever delights.

There was the faintest whiff of cordite and revolution amongst those artists who wanted to do more art and design but felt they were being prevented by the preponderance of maths and science. To give a shake of the statistical pepper pot, it is interesting to see that in the last three years GCSE art textiles had 46 candidates; A level textiles in the last three years had five. We heard a whisper that something might be done about that. One final glance at those stats – they can be mesmerizing – is that in the last three years 89 candidates have sat biology, 95 chemistry and 13 physics. But enough. There's more to Loughborough High than digits.

As might be expected, the facilities are excellent; the teaching superb.

Games, options, the arts: The recently refurbished Astroturf, a huge area, is shared with the boys – though not simultaneously. Hockey, netball, cross country, tennis, athletics, rounders, soccer and cricket. Plenty of county players and more, though the delightful girls who showed us round said that they found the games too serious and just wanted to take exercise. So they went to the gym. No shame in that. Music is phenomenal. Housed in a superb modern building it isn't, actually, but it feels as if it is, the centre of the whole Loughborough complex. Inside there is a wonderful sense of activity and involvement orchestrated by the seemingly tireless music teachers. 'Music is what makes my daughter so happy at Loughborough,' a father told us. 'None of our family is musical but my daughter has taken to singing and loves it. It's been the making of her.' In fact there are 15 choirs, including a senior choir of 120. Overall it is a thrilling place. Other extracurricular activities include the Duke of Edinburgh Award, in which over 70 girls are involved; debating, chess, bridge – the latter particularly popular. The girls we spoke to were thrilled that they are now allowed to join the CCF section. It is a sombre thought that one of the first women officers to be killed in Iraq was a former pupil.

Background and atmosphere: Founded in 1850 and one of the oldest girls' grammar schools in the country, it is now part of the Loughborough schools empire that includes the boys' grammar and Fairfield Prep, run by a central governing body. But, important this and fiercely protected, each of the three schools on the very handsome campus is autonomous. Boys and girls do some lessons together – politics and psychology, for instance – and they share the music school, but overall they have separate identities with their own teaching blocks and accommodation. For those parents who cannot decide between single sex and coeducation this might seem the perfect arrangement. As for the atmosphere, it is purposeful and friendly. Girls seem very much at home in the sensitively run set up and 'we are given the opportunities to air our views.' There is a wonderful variety of meals in the excellent dining room with cheerful, friendly kitchen staff contributing to the overall sense of well-being.

Pastoral care and discipline: Over and over again we heard comments about how friendly and helpful the staff are; how they are helpful not only with academic matters but with social and personal confusions. 'There's always someone to turn to,' seemed a subliminal refrain. There are anti-bullying guidelines in place but girls looked astonished at any suggestion they might need invoking. There is a genuinely warm and mutually shared feeling of interest and respect between staff and pupils.

Pupils and parents: Pupils come in from a 40 mile radius covering Leicestershire, Derbyshire and Nottinghamshire, and we have heard stories of families moving to be nearer the school. Parents we spoke to felt involved, consulted and considered. 'You can be sure of straight and honest feedback from staff at parents' evenings,' one father told us, 'none of that politically correct foggy stuff. What's more, the teachers really know the girls.' That certainly sounds refreshing.

Entrance: About 40 per cent of entries come from Fairfield, the Loughborough prep, the rest from local state and private junior schools. Intakes for year 7 are assessed in English, maths and verbal reasoning; the next three years the same plus a foreign language paper. Entry into the sixth form is via GCSEs, reports and interviews. Typically A or A* grades are required for those subjects to be taken at A level plus at least five B grades which must include maths, English and science. No wonder they get good A level results.

Exit: Up to 18 per cent leave after GCSEs for a variety of reasons: boarding, sixth form college or a subject which is not on offer at Loughborough. Girls told us that very few left because they were fed up. Three to Oxbridge in 2013, 11 to study medicine and lots to Russell Group universities. Much success with university places in a variety of subjects: sciences are popular, plus philosophy, politics, modern languages, classics, music and architecture.

Money matters: There are a number of scholarships and bursaries available. Don't be afraid to ask.

Remarks: The best of both worlds with superb, inspirational teaching and alert, interested girls. Not a hot house dedicated to clawing up league tables, expelling anyone who doesn't contribute to that, but rather a genuinely academic school where learning is prized and pursued with a measure of joy and satisfaction. A very happy school. A very good school.

LVS Ascot (Licensed Victuallers' School)

Linked school: LVS Ascot (The Licensed Victuallers' Junior School)

London Road, Ascot, SL5 8DR

- Pupils: 470 boys and 260 girls • Ages: 11–18 • C of E • Fees: Day £14,475–£16,005; Boarding £25,830 pa • Independent

Tel: 01344 882770
Email: registrar@lvs.ascot.sch.uk
Website: www.lvs.ascot.sch.uk

Headmistress: Since 2010, Christine Cunniffe, MMus BA and almost completed MBA (forties). Three children, all at the school (husband does the 'mummy bit' at parent evenings). Personable, open, quietly assured and one of what seems like growing number (or should that be band?) of musicians to forsake lieder for leadership. Other careers have beckoned. After university, had close brush with the law (professionally speaking, that is) securing postgraduate traineeship with Slough-based legal practice only to succumb to alternative role as pianist to fashionistas and London high society (think white baby grands and late nights in plush hotels). Four years in, realised that though 'loved life, not what I wanted to do when I was getting older'. Putting aside renewed yearnings for law when husband-to-be pointed out years of study ahead, she tried her hand at teaching and loved it from the off, going straight in as head of music, first at a Stevenage school, then St. Bernard's, a selective co-ed grammar school in Slough. Joined LVS Ascot as ambitious director of music in 2003 (school, which had no choir when she arrived, was performing Vivaldi's Gloria at Eton College Chapel just two terms later).

Overcame crisis of confidence in first year as head when numbers dipped (they're now on the rise again), confessing all in school magazine – unusual if not unprecedented openness for a head – which, she feels, sends useful message to pupils. 'You have self-doubt. I thought, the children are going to face problems in life, so why pretend it doesn't happen?'

Is considered by parents to be doing a good job though some would like a greater presence and more speechifying at major school events. 'She needs to be seen and heard a bit more...you've got to be the front runner, Urain Bolt-ish and get up there if you're a head with over 1,000 pupils and fee-paying parents,' says one. Pretty visible during the school day though, the more so as job comes with house in grounds (she also has west London bolthole for change of scene). 'I'm not one of those people who hides behind a closed door; there's no point.' Doesn't teach but asks boarders to choose lessons for her to observe every week, and on day of visit was in gym encouraging sixth formers flagging half way through 56-mile sponsored row for charity. 'I said, "I'll be your Mrs Motivator".'

All parents have her email address, a useful barometer as 'they'll only bring something to me directly if they are really upset,' and doesn't shy away from taking criticism on the chin. 'I don't want people to tell me what they think I want to hear but to be honest.' Pleased, she insists, to get lots of 'forthright' comments when recently invited parent group in for dinner and presentation on proposed introduction of heads of year to help raise academic bar through better tracking and target setting.

Own experiences make her sympathetic to late developers. 'I experienced problems at about 13 and it's made me passionate about not giving up on a child until we have exhausted all areas,' though firm when line has to be drawn – handful of children have been asked to leave during headship. 'The boundaries are like an elastic band – you have to know when it's going to break.'

Like Mary Poppins, will go when mission is accomplished. 'I'm a realist. If, after five years, I think my job's done, I'm not going to stay around.' Not necessarily to another headship, either. 'I might just become a lawyer after all,' she says.

Academic matters: Though tolerant, school isn't the place for skivers. 'The school's a hard runner... and they want the exams. Non-selective doesn't mean an easy ride,' says a parent.

Exam results compare well with local competition – GCSEs in 2013 a creditable 32 per cent at A*/A, good in anyone's money for non-selective school, let alone one so large. Ten the norm though whittled down to nine for some students with learning difficulties who fill the time with extra English and maths support. Choice of around 20 subjects, nothing showy (there's no Latin or classics, for example). English, maths, French or Spanish and science/environmental science all compulsory with options including German, humanities, all the sciences, media/business studies, art and PE.

Sixth form options broad and getting broader, with law and psychology recently added to the roster of around 30 courses. Students will need GCSE B grades or better in chosen subjects though vocational courses such as ICT and sport also available for those of a more practical mindset. Mixed ability intake makes the 55 per cent of A levels graded A*/B in 2013 even more of an achievement.

Head on mission to ensure that ability is unearthed and nurtured earlier through advanced data crunching and addition of heads of year to management team. 'We haven't even scratched the surface with gifted and talented children,' she says (something also picked up in recent inspection). School's strength thus far has centred on bringing low achievers up to snuff (several heart-warming stories of pupils helped up the academic ladder to top exam grades) and parents like the approach, big on encouragement, small on class sizes – average teacher to pupil ratio of one to 12– and low on hothouse forcing (definitely not the school's style).

Games, options, the arts: School's philosophy is that there's something for everyone and brave attempts are made (with help of extensive range of activities, all bar four included in the fees) to keep participation rates high all the way through the school. A dip in current year 10 and 11 girls' teams reflects lack of numbers rather than interest.

Approach, strong on inclusion and optimism – sports honours board runs to 2023 – is recognised by award of Sportsmark Gold and helped by cracking facilities including two games halls, larger with climbing wall and cricket nets, smaller with cushioned floor for happier landings in judo and high impact sports. Enticing heated pool is well used, offering all-ability training at 6.30 am three times a week, while thumping pop music from upstairs broadcasts presence of well-equipped fitness suite, predictably popular with older boys. Has recently set up elite golf academy for sixth formers which combines coaching at a nearby club with a BTEC in sports science.

With recent wins in judo, swimming and rugby, achievement counts but so does nurturing, for B as much as A teams so not seen as also rans. Felt by some parents to handicap the single-minded. 'Everyone gets a game which is to be encouraged but [can be] a drawback if you really want to excel at one sport,' says one.

Head would like greater take up of outdoor activities and has appointed ex-marine who 'doesn't sleep and likes to live in tents,' to make it so. With shortly to be re-jigged timetable incorporating two additional sessions a week for all (year

9 upwards can do as part of D of E, open to as many as are interested) expect substantial increase in fresh air intake.

Vibrant artistic life is similarly wide ranging (though indoor-based) with ringing endorsement from award of Artsmark Gold to prove it and enthusiastic support from (literally) all-singing, all-dancing staff who aren't averse to taking to the boards as hoofers in zingy, highly regarded productions like Hairspray and Bugsy Malone. (By all accounts do a mean version of 'Teacher, leave them kids alone' too).

With five choirs, numerous ensembles including rock school, and around a third of pupils learning instruments, some to diploma standard, performance is shifting from niche activity to sizeable minority occupation. Possible that numerous pianos lurking in school nooks and crannies (some boarding houses have several) are conveying subliminal positive message; whizzy music tech studio probably better recruitment ad. Admittedly, boys in years 10 and 11 remain somewhat shy and retiring – 'Music's not a cool thing to do,' says pupil – but some at least are drawn in again at sixth form (though the need to pep up UCAS forms with wholesome balance of activities is, they confess, also a factor).

Background and atmosphere: Site was formerly home to Heatherdown, an ultra-traditional prep school for chaps and David Cameron's pre-Eton alma mater with own miniature steam railway. It was demolished in 1982 after Licensed Trade Charity (LTC) which runs school, founded 200 years ago to support drinks trade employees, made such an advantageous sale of previous premises in Slough to well-known supermarket chain that could fund construction of what prospectus claims is the 'most modern boarding school in the UK'.

It comes complete with LVS branded drainpipes and school houses named, delightfully, after major drinks brands, leading to such pleasing sentences as 'this year saw the introduction of many new staff and students to Guinness,' in school magazine.

And yes, lovers of mellow brickwork may need to recalibrate their aesthetic sensibilities when it comes to the exterior (think sheltered housing designer meets Etch a Sketch addict – prospectus sensibly avoids any full-on shots of the facade). However, it's well worth the effort as school lacks neither charm nor character and is stuffed with quirky touches from the formal (two back-to-back reception desks, one glitzy for corporate visitors to charity HQ, the other, smart but workmanlike, for school traffic) to the relaxed (skeleton of dolphin in science lab, Garfield soft toy clasped lovingly between jaws). There's tradition, too – the 25 acres of grounds with rustic bridge spanning small but perfectly formed lake prove the point – but exists primarily to serve a purpose (lesson bell all but abolished after it broke five years ago, ending mid-sentence rush for the door and making teachers so happy that was never re-introduced).

Thoughtful layout now approaching 30th birthday may no longer be at cutting edge of school design but fundamentals still apply, noticeably the way space-intensive subjects like performing arts get the room they need in central location rather than being consigned to outer reaches of site, while related subjects are housed together making navigation a breeze – at least if you're a pupil. 'It's the adults who struggle,' says passing teacher.

It's all well cared for, too – maths display board with cracked plastic cover is rare exception ('Children pick at it without realising they're doing it,' explains staff member) and nicely spruced up where required. Two out of the four boarding houses are now plushness personified – others should follow within the year – with full-size beds and colour-matched walls, carpets and curtains chosen by pupils. Palettes err towards predictable blues in boys' boarding house though biggest difference is in communal areas where girls arrange smart leather sofas close together to maximise eye contact and conviviality, boys in contrast opting for side by side seating for maximum cheering-on potential during pool matches.

Add lively art room with wall-to-wall high quality work (intriguing bronze-effect sculpture floats above plinth), busy, popular DT department with more saws than you could shake a freshly trimmed stick at and fabulous learning resource centre; light, airy and staffed by team of affable universal aunt and uncle types who always have a giant jigsaw on the go and live for research – 'You need a bit up here and to love finding things out,' says one – and easy to see why purpose-built practicality gets parental thumbs up. 'Some private schools try to make the best of the [space] they happen to have such as a former chambermaid's room being used as a biology class room, [whereas] LVS have great class rooms built to deliver good lessons,' says a father. Boarding house staff, particularly those with experience of compromise Victorian conversions, are similarly enthusiastic. 'A breeze to run,' comments one.

Pastoral care and discipline: Highly regarded focus of pastoral care is the tutor group system with same teacher responsible for child's well-being throughout school career. Works well given high percentage of old-timers (figuratively speaking) on staff – 40 out of 340 have been there over 10 years – and is liked by parents and pupils. 'They have a vested interest in you as a person, you're more than just a pupil,' says 17-year old.

In contrast, tribal Yin to sensitive tutor group Yang is a house system that's far more than convenient administrative format. Pitting combined boarders – normally three houses strong (four including juniors) against three teams of day pupils, it's a focal point of school life, with fiercely contested matches generating 'as much rivalry amongst the [teachers] as pupils,' says member of staff.

Not as daunting as it sounds, however, given universal insistence that loyalties do not cross into lessons nor escalate beyond friendly rivalry ('It's just banter,' confirms sixth former). Day pupils can also cross to other side by signing up for occasional one-off boarding sessions and there's added flexibility with extended day, including meal and the run of learning resource centre, popular with working parents.

For boarders, it's all about fine-tuning to achieve delicate balance between homely family feel (thoughtful inclusion of year 8 boarders with juniors for extra cosseting) and early detection of transgressions. Morning lethargy beyond normal teen parameters can signal OTT late night laptop/mobile use (enormous phone bills arriving at parental home the other telltale sign). Controlled independence, such as giving year 11s separate kitchen and TV 'so they don't have to watch the same thing as year 8s,' explains teacher, is carefully cultivated.

Keeping idle hands (and brains) busy is the priority. 'We don't want boarders sitting around, twiddling their thumbs,' says pastoral head. Especially true of weekends when minibuses, booked by the hour, swap returning sports teams for boarders off on assorted excursions (shopping, films and bowling all popular) with departures and arrivals as precisely coordinated as flight control at Heathrow.

Pupils and parents: A nice, un-showy and straightforward bunch, pupils are thoughtful rather than introspective, articulate but not glib, and fond of school (in touch with emotions, too – one burley and soon to be ex-sixth former has admitted to welling up when contemplating imminent departure). Start of term, says one, 'feels like you're going home rather than just going back.' There's affectionate tolerance for teachers who, they say with preternatural (but approving) gravitas, 'want to have fun but in a sensible way'.

As in other schools, pupils on show to visitors usually the top dogs. Here, cheeringly, they may only recently have had greatness thrust on them and reformed Horrid Henries stand as much chance as card-carrying Perfect Peters of getting their day in the sun. 'Prefects aren't just the "right" people,' explains one of the current glorious band of brothers (and sisters).

Families cover socially and economically broad spectrum from royalty to socially deprived (borne out by range of parental cars at drop off – five and six figure off-roaders rubbing fenders with elderly mid-range saloons). Mix of working parents/career mothers, but either way are generally friendly and polite; won't hesitate to come forward if there's a problem, though occasional hothouse impulses 'are squashed quite quickly by the school,' says approving mother.

Entrance: At 11+ majority from school's own junior department with assorted state and private schools supplying the rest. Also small but significant international component, with 30 overseas students from as far afield as China, Russia and Korea and 40 or so from ex-pat families, many in Forces.

Families are attracted by all-through co-education, cracking facilities, local reputation and complete absence of entrance exams unless you're after a scholarship, academic worth a not-to-be-sniffed-at 50 per cent off fees; music, art, drama and sport a slightly less headline-grabbing £1,000 a year, in which case standard hurdles apply.

Once settled, pupils tend to stick around. '..We were never going to take the boys out unless we needed to,' says mother. Locals form large proportion of the clientele and, while job mobility means some degree of coming and going each year, there's not as much as you might suppose. Around 50 per cent of pupils stay on into sixth form ('places will only be offered where deemed appropriate by the head of sixth form, director of studies and head,' says admissions policy) with incomers, including first time boarders from local day schools, plugging the gaps. 'In my [elder] son's year, I'd say that 80 per cent went... all the way through,' says parent.

Catchment area extends 15-20 mile radius or so to Reading in west and Maidenhead up north, compass points ably covered by seven school bus routes (some over-subscribed, so worth checking). Head is on a mission to spread the word elsewhere so expect increasing numbers of refuseniks from super-selective London fringes, deepest Berks and Bucks.

Exit: As you'd expect given breadth of intake, pupils take corresponding range of university courses from the solidly academic – medicine, law, economics – to the more vocational, including photography and journalism. Many secure first rank uni places including one or two to Oxbridge some years. Cardiff, Oxford Brookes, Bournemouth, Southampton and Warwick most popular in 2013. Old boys and girls end up as community stalwarts, many as successful entrepreneurs or 'something in the City'. Few facts and figures to back this up though with-it marketing manager is making good the omission with 'where are they now?' campaign.

Money matters: Ten per cent discount for siblings (but only third onwards and then only while all three attend school), 15 per cent off for MOD employees, including five per cent early payment discount and a 20 per cent reduction for anyone who has worked in the licensed drinks trade for five years or more.

School tries to keep budgeting simple with many senior school clubs and activities included in the fees – rowing, riding, sailing and ballet plus individual instrumental lessons and one-to-one language or learning support are the main extras. Means headline fees are just that, with minimum of extras buried in the frequently expensive small print.

Remarks: All-comers welcomed in this well-equipped, friendly and unpretentious school that combines non-traditional exterior with timeless values and makes non-selectivity the starting point for success rather than a justification for its absence.

Lycee Français Charles de Gaulle

Linked schools: Lycee Français Charles de Gaulle (British Section); Ecole de South Kensington (Primary School of the Lycée Français); Ecole Marie d'Orliac; Ecole de Wix; Ecole André Malraux

35 Cromwell Road, London, SW7 2DG

• Pupils: 3,900 (including primary and nursery school); all day (but see below) • Ages: 3-18 • No religious affiliation
• Fees: £5,898–£10,791 pa • Independent

Tel: 020 7584 6322
Email: inscription@lyceefrancais.org.uk
Website: www.lyceefrancais.org.uk

Proviseur: Since 2012, Mr Olivier Rauch. Degrees in history and geography from University of Lyon as well as Agregation (French civil servant educational leadership qualification). Previously head of lycée in Rabat and a lycée in Toulouse (which included a preparatory programme for the prestigious Grandes Ecoles). Started career as a history and geography teacher. Married, with three grown up children who live abroad.

Urbane and distinguished, he is confident in his preparation, knowledge and previous experience of running large French lycées, yet a touch of humility makes for easy conversation. He's also head of the three satellite primary feeder schools.

One of his major concerns is the launch of a new school in Wembley. He and his leadership team are working on the bigger problem of how to redistribute London's French school-age children into satellite French schools, and how to use the space this would free up at Charles de Gaulle – more student lounges, common areas and specialist classrooms. However he knows families worry how the inevitable change in location for some might affect them.

Another goal is to assess the anomalies between the French baccalaureate and A levels that seem to impede his leavers' entry into some British university courses (medicine for example). And if that weren't enough, he's also planning the school's centenary in 2015.

Parents comment that discipline has improved since head's arrival – he thinks this may be a result of his close communication with students via the student council.

Academic matters: Lycée Charles de Gaulle is the premier French school in Britain and one of the largest in the world. The raison d'être is to provide French education leading to the French baccalaureate, regarded by many as one of the most robust school-leaving qualifications there is. With many dual national French-English families enrolled, the Lycée also offers GCSE and A levels.

The French model has the following divisions: maternelle (reception and year 1), primaire (years 2-6), college (years 7-10) and lycée (years 11-13). In primaire and college, the school offers the French curriculum in French. From the final year of college (year 10) students either move over to the British section to do GCSEs and IGCSEs followed by A level or continue through to the French baccalaureate. Parent perspectives on the Lycée vary significantly depending on their own cultural expectations of what constitutes a school education, but most parents seem to feel that overall the kids are well taught, learning lots, enjoying the challenge and loving the school's international community.

Primary class teachers do everything (including art and PE), specialists support IT and music. The quality of the art is down to the creativity of the teacher but we've heard of some great stuff with cross-curricular projects and older classes partnering with younger ones. Parents say there's 'frequent assessment and evaluation' so a struggling child is quickly identified. A

primary parent with British school experience describes the French system as 'less flexible, but of high standard.' Class sizes are about 28, with an assistant in each class. Classroom arrangements are fairly traditional, with desks in rows, though we saw some more varied arrangements.

College is another story. Some students entering college come from schools where the entire enrolment is less than the year group they are joining. Students move around for different lessons in what one parent described as an 'anonymous teacher environment.' Students have advisers whom they see for maybe 30 minutes per week and there's no expectation of pastoral care on the adviser's part. They monitor pupils' progress through frequent assessment and parents are kept informed. The problem is that it's public knowledge, so if you are bottom of the heap everyone knows, which can take its toll on the self-esteem of less confident pre-adolescents. The survivors – and there are plenty who thrive on the mounting pressure – develop strong independent skills and learn to manage their time and work successfully, which is one of the attributes French parents expect to see.

The French curriculum is followed in the French section for the oldest students (confusingly called the 'lycée'). In year 12 there are three French baccalaureate pathways: economics and social science, literature and science, where the subjects studied vary as does the number of hours devoted to each. The word is that there is pressure from both school and parents to go down the prestigious science route. Because so many students are fluent in English, many do a GSCE in English within the French bacc stream.

The international version of the French baccalaureate (which follows the French bacc curriculum but has more courses in English and leads to the same official French bacc exams) has recently been introduced, so it's too soon to evaluate. (Not to be confused with the IB Diploma). Students join this programme in year 10; transfer from this programme into the British section is only available in year 12 and depends on availability of space. No 'bacc-light' – this programme reputedly demands an even heavier time commitment than the regular bacc.

The British section offers the GCSE/A level pathway. Students must be fluent enough in English to manage. Discipline is also an issue– nobody with a rap sheet gets in. Occasionally this route is apparently recommended for students who may not succeed with the French bacc.

Year 10 pupils do a wide range of about 10 courses, including French of course, but also a third language (pupils are spoilt for choice – Italian, Spanish, German, Arabic, Russian, Greek and Latin on offer). French IGCSE exams are compulsory, which pleases parents, though there seem to be some questions about timing with kids sitting exams too early.

In year 11 students generally drop one or two subjects as they get into their AS level and A level subjects. Parents rave about the maths, chemistry and physics, but suggest that those interested in the arts tend to look elsewhere (French education is not noted for intellectual autonomy or commitment to creativity, which are fairly fundamental for art). French and PE are compulsory until year 13; from 2015, A level French will be taken in year 13.

Deciding which route to choose – French bacc or British A levels – can be daunting. Those opting for the British tend to be dual nationals, non-French who joined the Lycée because their kids were in a French system and Anglophile French families setting down permanent roots in the UK.

The appeal of the French bacc is its strong global reputation, with its slavish commitment to developing intellectual rigour. But it's hard work, rigid, requires lots of memorisation and absorbing of new information. 'The French system crams knowledge into your brain – and we know the brain is a muscle that can be stretched,' says one French parent.

But some French students aiming for a UK university question the need to do the full-blown bacc when they can focus on more specialised A levels. Plus it's no secret that class sizes in the British section are smaller (about 12 compared to 28 to 30 for the French section) and the teaching style is more conducive to project work, class discussions and debates.

The French bacc classes, 'no wishy-washy child-centred approach,' are more traditional, 'cruelly elite' in a 'sink or swim' learning environment. 'Teachers instruct with minimal empathy. You listen and absorb the learning, which can be a challenge for students with strong personalities inclined to engage in debate and, God forbid, challenge the teacher.' Then there is the matter of 'loyalty to French heritage.' If they move to the British section some families lament the move away from the French educational tradition, even though it may be the right decision educationally. British section kids have more time for extra-curricular activities. Places in the British section are competitive; with the Lycée full to capacity, expansion of this programme seems unlikely. But more French students are considering the advantages of the A level university pathway, so there are more applicants than spaces.

Ongoing discussion amongst parents about A level results. The small size of the A level cohort means there are limited courses offered and timetabling clashes can prevent kids from taking the courses they want, leading some frustrated families to change schools after GCSEs. It has also been suggested that some French parents whose children are in the British section have a hard time overcoming the 'pedagogical cultural divide' between the French and British systems; they simply don't understand the flexibility that British teachers have in delivering the curriculum.

The governance and management structure of the Lycée is naturally focused on the French curriculum. For a British deputy head, finding a way to sit within that institutional culture is undoubtedly a challenge. Although the policy of rotating the head makes sense for Lycées worldwide, it probably has an impact on attention to GCSEs, A levels etc in the British section. Each new head has to get up to speed with the whole (and for them, anomalous) British programme, along with all the other challenges of running such a large institution. It's a steep learning curve for even a top educationalist.

French bacc results are excellent, above the French national average. For each of the three streams the overall 2013 pass rate was 99 per cent and 92 distinctions out of 235 candidates.

A levels are by comparison less impressive with 57 per cent A*/A grades. French A level results could be more impressive, given the context, although the school points out that students only have three hours a week for French and take the exam a year earlier than other schools. GCSE results show 69 per cent A*/A grades in 2013 (no I/GCSE French results for 2013 because none taken). Parents think this differential in results between the French bacc and A level has been taken on board by the head.

Although French nationality, language and heritage is the common denominator here, some kids are not completely fluent in French. It's full immersion, so if a child isn't capable of fully functioning in French by the age of five, parents say they'll struggle when reading and writing begins. Others move their children out as they get older because parents lack sufficient French language to fully support them – unless they have a French-speaking nanny at home to sustain the French speaking day and supervise homework. English as a second language is taught from primary, with some setting for levels in consideration of the native speakers. In college, students are streamed for English. Other languages are available but no mother tongue instruction other than French and English.

For students with special needs, the educational psychologist and speech and language adviser recommends what sort of specialist might help manage the student's learning (dyslexia is not uncommon) but the school itself does not provide much support in-house. School has disabled access in all but one building but the logistics of the daily timetables and student movements mean that students with mobility challenges would struggle here.

Many teachers (average age early forties) are civil servants, with professionalism and benefits for which French teachers are renowned. Forty-five per cent have been at the Lycée for more than 10 years.

Games, options, the arts: On Wednesdays, primary classes end early but extra activities like cooking, crafts, IT, sports and games are offered. Human Rights Club, Justice in the Heart and House of Students are student-led activities the British and French section students do together, but French section students have less time to devote to these.

Curriculum-related residential trips abroad include India, Berlin (history), Paris (Comédie Française), Greece (classics), Venice (Italian), New York (art), Moscow (Russian). Compulsory work experience programmes in years 10 or 11 are organised by parents.

A few hundred students do sports, many on Saturdays at the sports facility in Raynes Park, competing against London schools and schools abroad. There's a school sports day but parents warn: 'Don't expect to get a ribbon unless you place first, second, or third...' Music is popular, with ensembles, orchestra or choir to choose from.

Background and atmosphere: School was founded to serve London's French population, but also to further France's 'mission civilisatrice' – making French culture and education available to the Brits. During the Second World War it became the home of the Free French and the head sits in the office once occupied by General de Gaulle, so the school's name has meaning. British section was created 60 years ago to offer the French programme in English, but the differences in the French bacc and A levels meant that a marriage was not practical, so the British section sits within the organisation as a 'stand alone'. Over the years the Lycée has spread and now occupies a city block across from the Natural History Museum. If approaching the area during pick-up you'll think you've alighted at the wrong end of the Eurostar.

Part of the AEFE (Agency for Teaching of French Education Abroad), the Lycée is one of more than 100 overseas schools directed by the Ministry of Education and is governed by a committee including the French ambassador and other diplomats. Heads are rotated, with posts lasting up to five years. British section is managed by Kelvin Zane, dapper ex-deputy-head of a London comprehensive, whose fluid command of French has enabled him to adapt to this large French organisation. His UK experience is invaluable when it comes to matters such as child protection and Ofsted.

Facilities have been renovated to absorb increasing student numbers – a combination of inter-connected newbuild and Victoriana and using lots of cheerful colours. Buildings open out at the back to play area shared by all ages. Parents say 'it looks confusing, but the kids figure it out in a day or two.' Primary is in a building shared by upper classes on the top floor. There's a large hall for dramatic and musical performances, music and art rooms; PE is outside in the central yard, at local sports facilities or own grounds in Raynes Park. The yard has large canopies with seating areas to provide all-weather cover; no indoor play area.

A large library mushrooms over several floors, separated into college and lycée sections. Classrooms have desks in traditional rows. Computers in the libraries, study rooms and computer lab, but not much evidence of technology inside the classrooms.

Lunch is served in a bright, clean cafeteria. Youngest have their own lunchroom; lunch is compulsory unless there are extraordinary dietary needs. Varied three course menu looks just short of Cordon Bleu by usual school standards. Considering that the chef turns out more than 2,500 meals a day, the food looked and smelled very appealing; fish always on offer for those with Kosher or Halal preferences.

School also boasts an impressive medical centre, staffed with sympathetic nurses and a full-time doctor. Parents are happy with home-school communication, and it's easy to have a quick chat with the primary teacher at dismissal. The formal communication cycle is 'front loaded' with year-group parent events at the beginning of the year; after that it's up to parents to seek out the teachers – but they'll be in touch if there's a problem.

Pastoral care and discipline: With such an enormous student body, parents' reports are mixed. Some parents insist the kids 'don't get lost, are well looked after,' while others say that once in college students are 'a number and their teachers hardly know them.' For students joining college, the school tries to put them in classes with three designated friends to ease the 'culture shock' of coping with the sheer scale of the Lycée. This is less a concern for rising Lycée primary students already familiar with the environment.

Playground attendants are a prominent 'French' feature – supervisors keeping an eye on everyone. College students may leave campus provided they have parents' permission (most don't); in the top years most go out for lunch. A nifty school diary is issued to track home-school communication; the back cover has every student's photo, identification and timetable so anyone trying to slip out can be identified and sent back to class.

The children are cheerful and polite; primary teachers remind them about the importance of greeting people respectfully. No lockers – backpacks are stored here and there. No reports of any significant behaviour issues; everyone knows what is expected. If students fall short, they may be given more homework or required to attend school on Saturday. School psychologist offers counselling for students. Secondary school year group leaders have offices in their own sections of the school, with a secretary to manage the 300 or so kids in each level.

Parents warn that drop off and pick up can be stressful. By staggering start and finish times the school manages the flow of traffic pretty well under the circumstances. But parents need to be prepared for the possibly overwhelming feeling of chaos and confusion at the start.

Pupils and parents: The French connection is the common denominator. Predominantly French nationals with at least one French parent, also a significant number (about 20 per cent) dual nationals (British/French); small proportion British. Other nationalities include Canadian, American, Italian, Spanish, Lebanese, Moroccan and Russian. Many parents are in London on short-term assignments – diplomatic, financial services, media, industry. The generously subsidised fees (not available in the British section) widen the socio-economic net, attracting families who may not normally aspire to private education. Parents prefer this more realistic reflection of society to the rarefied atmosphere of economic privilege that they associate with many London independent schools.

Students come from all over – some with long commutes on public transport but they feel it's worth it. In some cases the main wage-earner commutes to France or travels internationally but the family has chosen to stay in London in order to keep the kids at the Lycée.

The APL (parents' association) organises after-school activities, raises funds, supports the athletics programme and serves as a sounding board for issues of community interest. Some non-French speakers say it's difficult to become involved. Eclectic list of 'vieux garcon et filles' includes Jacqueline Bisset, Natasha Richardson, Gyles Brandreth, Lady Olga Maitland, Roland Joffé.

Entrance: Registration process begins around April of the entry year, with decisions sent in early May. Highly over-subscribed,

entry is described as 'a nightmare, haphazard and chaotic.' Families normally apply to other schools as well; some start off elsewhere to await an offer. There's a priority list of criteria: children of French diplomats, siblings (in primary only), children from another official French school (locally or abroad), including students following the CNED (the French distance learning programme), then any miscellany of Francophones fortunate to get in.

Siblings trump everything else in primary so families bank on getting one tiny first foot in the door, knowing the others are pretty much a shoe-in. One French national tells us she put her children on the waiting list from the earliest time allowed. Her eldest was unsuccessful but a few days after the term began the younger one was offered a place, posing a dilemma for managing two-school runs simultaneously. When she explained this to the school, they somehow magicked up a space for the second child.

Best tip for locals is to transfer from one of the official AEFE Ecole Homologuée nursery schools such as Ecole le Hérisson, L'Ecole des Petits (Fulham) or La Petite Ecole. Feeders for primaire entry include the annexe schools – Wix (Clapham), South Kensington, Ealing and Fulham. Year 7 feeders include Ecole Jacques Prévert, L'Ecole Bilingue, L'Ecole des Petits and L'Ecole de Battersea. For year 10 (British section) and year 11 (French section) it's the new Bilingual College in Kentish Town (CFBL). Beware though – not all schools with emphasis on French language are official AEFE schools, so check the Lycée's website if you're banking on this as your golden ticket. Families do move on so vacancies arise mid-year, but school always refers to the waiting list. According to one successful mother, 'this is the only hope for a local family wanting their child to go to the Lycée' and requires strategic planning of Napoleonic proportions.

No admissions testing and once a child is in, parents have no worries about future entrance exams such as 11+ or CE.

Exit: The Lycée prides itself on its careers department, with advisers specialising in UK, US and French universities. Careers counselling begins in year 11; a major careers forum involves experts and university reps from three continents. Some parents feel more coordination is required to rationalise the Lycée exams and Oxbridge and Russell Group entrance criteria and more focus needed on writing UCAS personal statements.

Roughly one quarter go to French universities, with 10 per cent of bacc graduates gaining entry into the Grandes Ecoles. British destinations include Oxbridge, Bath, Imperial, UCL and other London universities, Warwick, Durham, Edinburgh. US universities include McGill, Georgetown, Columbia. Some to other countries and a few do gap years.

Money matters: A 50 per cent AEFE subsidy (except for those in the British section) makes for bargain tuition by London standards. Some welfare grants, bursaries – and APL has been known to rally when a family falls on hard times.

Remarks: This is a huge institution yet parents say children are happy, well taught and love the cultural diversity. The waiting lists are testimony to the school's overall success. With the French and Francophile population growing daily, it seems that the entente cordiale is alive and well in this petit coin of London.

Magdalen College School

Linked school: Magdalen College School Junior School

___

Cowley Place, Oxford, OX4 1DZ

___

• Pupils: 670 boys; all day; 80 girls in the sixth form • Ages: 11–18
• C of E • Fees: £14,096–£14,628 pa • Independent

___

Tel: 01865 242191
Email: registrar@mcsoxford.org
Website: www.mcsoxford.org

___

Master: Since 2008, Dr Tim Hands BA AKC (theological diploma) DPhil (fifties), current chair of HMC and previously head of Portsmouth Grammar, where he carried through many ambitious and imaginative ideas. A state school pupil turned down by Cambridge ('I was told by the careers adviser at my grammar school that I wouldn't get to university at all'), he read English at King's College, London, then went on to St Catherine's, Oxford, followed by Oriel, where he ended up as a lecturer. He became housemaster at King's Canterbury, then second master at Whitgift School. He comes from a long line of teachers, including both parents and an ancestor who was schoolmaster on HMS Victory. Likes sport and music – was co-leader of the London Schools Symphony Orchestra and conductor of the Oxford University chamber choir, Schola Cantorum. The author of several books about Victorian literature and teaches English A level.

'He's very approachable. Pupils and staff all like him,' said a parent. Another commented, 'He comes across as very human and down to earth, not at all in an ivory tower. It must be very hard to be a head in Oxford where lots of your parents are masters of colleges and they all have very high expectations.' Married to Jane, a solicitor; two sons.

Academic matters: 'This is a school full of A*s,' says the head, and its results are undoubtedly up there in the firmament – 74 per cent A*s and 95 per cent A*/As at GCSE, and over 91 per cent A*/A grades at A level in 2013. This can, commented a parent, make a child feel that getting an A is an abject failure. However, another recounted how kind and helpful the school had been when her son achieved (relatively) duff GCSE results – 'They were very positive and he felt they were on his side'.

A strongly traditional school in many ways. It was founded as 'a school of the university and within the university' and is focused accordingly. Everyone does three sciences (though one parent commented that 'actually my son would have preferred to have been able to do another humanity instead') and classics is a given – 'They take it for granted as a way of training the mind'. A narrow range of subjects – philosophy, politics, further maths and now economics are the extra A-level options.

However, says the head, 'our curriculum is on the other hand quite liberal.' One afternoon a week in the lower sixth is spent on Waynflete studies (the school was founded by William of Waynflete), which involves a series of talks by experts in their fields on anything from world economics to swine flu. Pupils then choose their research topic (generally, but not always, closely linked to their likely university subject) and are taught initially by lectures and seminars at school, then in individual or paired tutorials by university academics.

By common consent very high teaching standards – 'My son finds virtually all the teaching exciting and the staff are very interesting and helpful'; 'You have a real sense that they are on the boys' side. My son says, "The masters are really cool – you feel that they love their subjects."' Hard work is expected – 'It's not for the academically idle' – and certainly the previous head hauled the school up through the league tables. 'Lots of the boys have sisters at Oxford High, and their parents felt that

they should be achieving the same high grades,' said a parent. Most parents agree that their children are not hot-housed – 'They don't feel that their noses are to the grindstone' – but they are expected to buckle down and work long hours at home. However, the mother of a talented sportsman was impressed by how flexible the school was prepared to be over his training schedule – 'There was a good symbiotic relationship, and he didn't let them down'.

Games, options, the arts: Compact site, which includes a sports hall with a multi-gym and floodlit tennis courts. The 13 acre School Field is just over the Cherwell – rowers can launch straight from the school – and it also has access to a range of college and university sports grounds, hockey pitches, athletics tracks and swimming pool. Support for sports is excellent, with a number of high flying sports professionals on the staff, eg Philip DeFreitas (England) for cricket; Grant Seely (England Sevens, Northampton Saints) for rugby; Todd Williams (Australia) and Andy Watts (England A and Reading) for hockey; and Sadie Lapper (England) for netball. The main team sports are rugby, hockey and cricket. Sixth form girls play hockey, netball and tennis – with sailing, rowing and badminton also popular. Pupils have competed in national teams at hockey, shooting, rowing and sailing, and many school teams are county champions. The school has exceptional successes at sailing – in 2013 they won the National and International Schools' Team Racing Championships, RYA National Youth Team Racing Championships and National School Sailing Association's single-handed team racing championships.

The junior school recruits the 16 Magdalen College choristers and music is an integral part of life in the senior school too. Singing is particularly strong, as one would expect, with several choral societies and choirs. Choristers sing from the top of Magdalen Tower on May Day morning, Madrigals Society sings from punts on the river, the Oxford Sixth choir sings in a variety of venues in Oxford. Also orchestras, bands and ensembles. 'The standards are fantastic. A lot of pupils are incredibly talented,' said a parent.

Drama scholarships have been introduced in 2013, but drama is not a GCSE or A-level option (yet) – 'We don't have the facilities. But we will have'. The school hall doubles as a chapel and theatre, with an altar and stained glass windows at one end and a stage at the other. Has a collaborative project with Oxford Playhouse, now in its third year. Performs large-scale musicals – including Sondheim's Sweeney Todd and the world premiere of a sung Lord of the Flies – as well as works by playwrights as diverse as Pinter and Shakespeare, but the head has greater plans. 'By 2016, the quartercentenary of Shakespeare's death, we want to have established ourselves as a performing centre for early modern drama – Shakespeare and his contemporaries,' he says. 'We have already put on a fantastic performance of As You Like It on the School Field, and we are planning a new modern theatre'.

An annual Arts Festival has been running since 2009. Last year speakers included Baroness Sue Campbell and Rupert Everett, as well as children's author Julia Golding. There are also concerts, lectures, theatre, tours, films, workshops and an art show – 'We want to liberate all the creative forces around us'.

Background and atmosphere: Founded in 1480 by William Waynflete to educate choristers and prepare other boys for Magdalen College. Former masters include Cardinal Wolsey, former pupils St Thomas More and William Tyndale. It moved in 1890 from its original location in Magdalen College to its present site just the other side of the bridge, opposite St Hilda's. Buildings of a variety of pedigrees, from the School House, built in 1893 and now housing the junior school, to the 2008 New Building, which includes the swish canteen (serving rather tasty lunches), up to date ICT centre and fabulous top floor art and design rooms with views to die for. Like other former direct grant schools, it has the feeling of a city grammar rather than

M

a public school, with a relaxed approach to uniform and heaps of schoolbags in random corners – 'We're a little Byzantium, situated where east meets west, where Cowley meets Oxford, very multi-faceted and multi-ethnic'. An overtly Christian school, with non-denominational services in chapel every morning. Pupils can opt out, but very few do. 'I like going to chapel,' said a sixth former. 'The whole school gets together, and people enjoy singing.' Pupils are relaxed and friendly – 'They don't have that public school arrogance,' said a parent. 'A typical Magdalen pupil is high achieving but modest.' 'Most pupils can find a niche here,' said another. 'There's such a mix: bookish, geeky ones, sporty extroverts – they're not clones. It's fine to be eccentric.'

Pastoral care and discipline: Pastoral care is 'a speciality,' says Tim Hands. 'It is the part of the school of which we are most proud, and I sense it has been fantastic for a long time. We have a light touch – we're disciplined and liberal simultaneously. Lessons can go from quite chatty to silent concentration when necessary.' The pastoral system is based round the six houses, which are organised by home location and compete at sports, singing, debating etc for the house cup. Expulsion (rare) for theft, systematic anti-social behaviour or involvement with drugs. A parent commented: 'When we've raised any issues they've been prompt and sympathetic. They're worldly-wise about what teenagers get up to.' 'They run a tight ship,' said another, 'but pupils do need boundaries.'

Pupils and parents: Mostly academic and professional families, including some who are scarily high-powered on the academic front and quite a few who struggle to afford the fees. 'You're not up against much "big money",' said a parent. Many Oxford pupils, but private buses serve far-flung areas such as Abingdon, Wantage and Banbury. OBs include (amongst many) Ivor Novello, Sam Mendes, Misha Glenny and Ben Goldacre.

Entrance: At seven by maths and English papers plus observation lessons in small groups. At eight and nine by tests in English, maths and verbal reasoning and an interview. At 11 by maths, English and verbal reasoning tests and an interview. At 13 by common entrance for prep school boys, after pre-test in year 6. By school exam for state school and other secondary school boys at 13 – maths, English, verbal reasoning and French. For the sixth form, by verbal reasoning test and interviews. Pupils are expected to get A* GCSE grades in their chosen A-level subjects; incomers – mostly girls – generally have at least six A* grades.

Exit: A few leave after GCSEs, mostly for local state sixth forms. Record Oxbridge figures in 2013, with more than a third (47) of A-level leavers to Oxford and Cambridge (preparation apparently 'super-delux'); the rest nearly all to other top universities, including Bristol, Durham, Imperial, Warwick, KCL, Nottingham, Leeds, UCL, Newcastle, Birmingham, Exeter, Edinburgh, Manchester, St Andrews, Bath and LSE, and further afield to Valencia and Boston. Sciences probably more popular than humanities, anything from aeronautical engineering to cognitive neuroscience.

Money matters: Scholarships and exhibitions for academic and extra-curricular excellence – modest amounts, but can be topped up by means-tested bursaries. Choristers get a 66 per cent fee remission. Will generally try to help families who fall on hard times.

Remarks: Up there with the top of the academic high-fliers. Uses its Oxford connections – intellectual, sporting and creative – to the best advantage, creating a niche where sports stars and geeky bookworms are equally at home. 'I feel the school is in safe hands,' said a parent. 'It's a very impressive place.'

Malvern College

Linked school: The Downs Malvern

College Road, Malvern, Worcestershire, WR14 3DF

• Pupils: 670 pupils (300 girls/370 boys); 80 per cent full boarding and 20 per cent day pupils • Ages: 13–18; prep 7–13 and pre-prep 3–7 • C of E but ecumenical • Fees: Day £21,264–£21,927; Boarding £33,081–£34,239 pa • Independent

Tel: 01684 581500
Email: enquiries@malcol.org
Website: www.malverncollege.org.uk

Headmaster: Since 2008, Mr Antony Clark MA HDE (fifties), previously head of Gresham's School for six years – 'When I hit 50 I thought it was time to move on or stay for ever'. Educated in South Africa and at Downing College, Cambridge, where he read history and narrowly missed a cricket blue, he was head of two demanding multi-racial schools in South Africa before he took over Gresham's. Friendly, open, intelligent and modest ('My predecessor did much of the strategic planning from which we are now benefiting'), he has brought 'stability and leadership' to a school which had been through choppy waters and was relieved to have him at the helm. 'We know where we're going now,' says one member of staff; 'Just what we needed,' says a grateful parent. 'What we like about him,' said a sixth form girl, 'is that he has instituted more rewards for success. It isn't just sporting activities which are acknowledged now – he notices a lot, and it feels good.'

His wife, Brigitte, has built up the family law section at the law faculty at the University of East Anglia and teaches there three days a week. 'Pretty good for a recycled South African,' says the head, adding with a twinkle, 'I'm very proud of her'. A good rôle model for the girls, she is much more than a mere consort adept at pouring tea and making small talk – boys and girls who know her enjoy her company. The Clarks share the view that education should include 'fun and laughter' as well as appreciating the capacity of the individual within a group. 'Malvern has suffered from over-governance,' says one local prep school head; 'But not any more,' says another. He is not a grey anorak sort of head and examples of his integrity are widely admired.

Academic matters: The second school in the country to adopt the IB and runs it alongside A levels – 50 per cent study each. Statistically minded parents reading through the welcome pack (prospectus and DVD) will love all the facts and figures. Up front about its academic results and deserves to be: the good results are right across the board: English and maths, business studies and languages all do well, as do the sciences – separate and dual. Little Latin at A level; Greek at A level and IB. Recent introduction of a three year build up to IB and A levels, largely aimed at bringing non-native speakers up to scratch to prepare them for the English system – lays firm foundations for the subjects taken at the highest level. In 2013, 37 per cent of A level grades were A*/A while the average IB score was 36.5 points.

Very good facilities – orchards of Apple Macs stretch over the campus and obvious efforts to fully incorporate the use of computers in a creative and positive way, encouraging intellectual curiosity rather than relying on them to give quick answers. This is evident, for instance, in the art school and very impressive library, as well as the whiteboards and reactive whiteboards in all the classrooms. As befits a school which pioneered the Nuffield Science course, good laboratories (a Nobel prize for chemistry was won by an old boy early in the last century). The teaching areas are bright and purposeful and

M

the teaching 'lively and encouraging,' says one satisfied dad. 'Pretty good,' agreed an A level student, who probably meant much the same. As far as learning difficulties are concerned, one pupil we spoke to was full of praise for the help he had received with his dyslexia. The overall impression we received was that help with more serious difficulties was less apparent, though bags of sensitive advice and support.

We detected that running the IB as well as traditional A levels was not all plain sailing – not difficult to identify a touch of tribal rivalry between the two camps: pupils we met indulged in healthy discussion/arguments over the comparative merits of each. One argument says that the IB stultifies extra-curricular activities and produces breadth at the expense of depth; the other side appreciates the breadth of IB and that their last term ends at half term. Everyone commented on the nigh impossibility of playing for a senior cricket team while working for the IB. Perhaps most important is the thoughtful and expert guidance from heads of department, housemasters and teachers in general, acknowledged by pupils and parents alike. Only one pupil commented wistfully, 'I wish we were all in the same boat together,' and added, 'for social reasons.' One interested observer with a professional interest in Malvern spoke of 'boringly studious Europeans dampening the atmosphere'. In reply, the school talks of celebrating its global links and actively seeks to promote understanding of the world beyond, not merely through the IB community service.

In an attempt at tackling what the headmaster refers to as 'the boredom many bright pupils feel', he has appointed a school-friendly academic development co-ordinator with special responsibility for challenging and extending the more able pupils. The aim is to identify particularly gifted and talented pupils and encourage a lively sense of intellectual curiosity. Numerically Malvern is top-heavy with a large sixth form and the wish is to inculcate a 'mini university feel' – in the academic sense, of course. A burgeoning partnership with Hereford Academy, including an annual scholarship into the sixth form.

Games, options, the arts: In the history of Malvern, the decision to play rugby in the winter term and football in the spring – implying, as it does, a greater importance attached to rugby – is comparatively recent. That has not yet proved an unqualified success, though younger teams are performing excellently. The partnership with Worcester Warriors offers pathways or development to those who show particular sporting talent. Has opened a large sports complex complete with indoor cricket school used by Worcester CCC, which contains a double sports hall, 25m swimming pool, climbing wall, squash courts, fitness suite and shooting range. The two rackets courts have been recently refurbished and now offer tournament quality standards for play. Wonderful cricket pro strives to maintain Malvern's reputation as a cricket school. Already an abundance of sporting and outdoor opportunities, and in the midst of the hockey and lacrosse a very successful girls' football team.

Much opportunity for music making – the music school is housed in a wonderful Victorian monastery with the cells providing atmospheric practice rooms approached via an impressive staircase. Lots of concerts – orchestral and smaller groups as well as choral. Close by, a handsome church now serves as a concert hall as well as a venue for lectures and meetings; the crypt has recently been converted into a hugely appreciated sixth form chilling out centre with an attractive bar, supervised by staff.

The art school is pretty dreary from outside but inside positively fizzes with creativity and energy under its dynamic director. Genuinely exciting examples of work, all over the campus and constantly rotated, are testament to the high standards achieved and a feature of the school. Fine art most popular, though the variety of media pursued is wonderful. The DT building, linked to the art school with an amazing bright, glassy staircase with bags of display areas, is heart-lifting. Functional and inspirational building within which cars are constructed and developed and budding designers are encouraged to stretch the boundaries of possibilities. Both buildings are open at the weekends and used. One boy told us, 'I virtually live here.' Popular at GCSE.

Strong CCF and D of E with plenty of opportunities for adventure, not least at the school's cottage in the Brecon Beacons, which everyone attends during their time at the school. Much community service.

Background and atmosphere: Founded in 1865, quickly expanded – now 11 houses scattered around the 200 or so acres, terraced out of the Malvern Hills. Justifiably famous for its setting, it is not just a country school, as it is so often labelled. True, the town of Malvern doesn't give the impression of bright lights and the lure of sin, but the school does not feel out in the sticks. No whiff of fertilizer drifting over when the wind is in the wrong direction; no distant sound of cattle winding slowly o'er the lea – in fact, the approach past handsome Victorian villas feels a little cramped, as you thread through the parked cars. Once through the tower of the main entrance, however, the scene below is breathtaking and there it does feel like a country school. So although it isn't a city school, by any means, it does benefit from the proximity of the town and can play both cards. Pupils appreciate the town's change of atmosphere and one girl told us how excited she was to be sitting in a café with her boyfriend when Simon Callow walked in. (The town's theatre, only yards from the school, stages a wide range of productions before going on to London and is much appreciated by staff and pupils.)

Has been fully coeducational for 20 years and feels happy with it. Pupils still eat in houses – a recent move to go for central feeding was met with fierce and triumphant resistance. The advantages of this – especially with a good catering company in overall charge, so none of the old business of starting the month with caviar and ending with baked beans and last week's bread – include the homely feel of guzzling with chums, the opportunity for house parents to observe behaviour and feel the atmosphere, and for girls to be girls/boys to be boys. Socialising areas downstairs for boys and girls, otherwise it's strolling in the grounds or tea in the town. 'The staff treat us with great maturity and sense,' said an apparently serious pupil. We were lucky enough to have lunch twice and to appreciate not only the very good food but also the excellent company of the pupils, clearly used to talking to alleged adults.

Two new boarding houses have been most sensitively built with 21st century pupils in mind within a 19th century ambience to accommodate growing numbers. Younger pupils sleep in small dorms with separate studies before graduating to bed sitters. Day pupils are attached to boarding houses and flexi-boarding is available when room.

Science school currently being built – official opening in 2015, to coincide with the school's 150th anniversary.

Pastoral care and discipline: As with so many boarding schools, revolves around its house system. Parents we spoke to were almost unanimous in praising the quality of the house parents. A few little gripes, as expected, but an overall appreciation. Each house has a resident house tutor and house assistant; one of the spin offs of house feeding is that members of staff lunch in different houses on different days of the week, which means they get to know a wide circle of pupils outside the classroom and vice versa.

Junior pupils are assigned a tutor up to GCSE; thereafter they may choose their tutor – and not necessarily one who teaches their subject. The attitude to bullying is clearly laid out, as is the complaints procedure. The safeguarding officer regularly visits the houses, is known to all and freely available for consultation and support. Pupils who wish to become involved with peer mentoring and how to listen. A good safety net is in place and no one need ever feel isolated – time after time we heard that from pupils.

The policy on drugs is clearly displayed and well known to pupils. Personal sympathy and offers of help will be shown and counselling offered, but basically, if you're dealing or caught in possession, you can expect to be expelled. Testing is an option if reasonable suspicions are aroused. Drinking is dealt with on a graded system from sin bin to red card; smoking is also dealt with on a graded scale leading to rustication. Above all common sense and the law of the land are the guidelines.

Pupils and parents: A good cross section of parents, mostly from the professional classes. Forty per cent of pupils come from abroad and from 27 countries – lots from Europe and an increasing proportion from Africa; an annual clutch comes every year from Germany, mostly for two years (now a German Old Malvernian on the Council). The international feel lies easily – pupils talked openly about the pleasures of getting to know children from far flung corners of the world. A smiling and greeting school, from the excellent porter to the pupils who showed thoughtful courtesy when directing us.

Entrance: Initial dealings are with the legendary registrar. Once registered, entrance is via CE (50 per cent pass), scholarship or, in the case of children from state schools, a paper set by Malvern in English, maths and science. Thirty per cent from The Downs Malvern, the school's associated and updated prep school, the rest from some 25 other prep schools. About 50 to 70 sixth formers join every year either via entrance papers in the subjects they wish to read at A level or IB or the scholarship.

Exit: Nearly all go on to sixth form. Almost all sixth-form leavers to university (about 20 per cent after a gap year), including around 10 per cent to Oxbridge (five to Oxford in 2013), around half to Russell Group universities and a strong minority overseas (the majority to the US) eg Yale, Stanford, Princeton, Cornell, Brown, Johns Hopkins, Berkeley and Columbia in the US and McGill in Canada. Economics/business and humanities/social sciences most popular.

Money matters: Scholarships are available for a wide variety of talents at 13 years old. Bursarial help is available after means testing – don't be afraid to ask.

Remarks: Has shown a degree of flair and imagination, reaching high standards without ever reaching the peaks – perhaps it has been slightly off the boil over the last few years. The prospectus speaks of entering 'an exciting phase of development' – certainly the current mood is buoyant. It needs to be, with so much financial investment, in these tricky times. Recent interest has grown dramatically. Perhaps, as someone has suggested, 'The giant is awakening' – watch for Brobdingnags in Worcestershire.

Malvern St James Girls' School

Linked school: Malvern St James Girls' School Preparatory Department

15 Avenue Road, Great Malvern, WR14 3BA

- Pupils: 430 girls (including 215 boarders) • Ages: 4–18 • C of E
- Fees: Day £8,310–£16,425; Boarding £16,005–£31,005 pa
- Independent

Tel: 01684 584624
Email: admissions@malvernstjames.co.uk
Website: www.malvernstjames.co.uk

Headmistress: Since 2010, Mrs Patricia Woodhouse BMus. After studying music at London University, started professional life as a freelance musician, composing, singing and conducting, before moving via a brief period in the City to the world of education. Has been involved in 'all sorts' of schools over the past 20 years. Director of music at Wimbledon High School, sixth form housemistress at Queenswood, deputy headmistress at St Mary's Wantage and formerly headmistress at Abbots Bromley School for Girls. A governor of Bloxham School, and an ISI Inspector. Very enthusiastic, passionate about the school and the girls: 'The school serves the girls, not the other way around', 'we're equipping them for life after university', and loving being where she is: 'I've found my school – I'm so lucky'.

Academic matters: Good results both at GCSE and A level. At A level in 2013, 85 per cent A*-B and 67 per cent A*-A. At GCSE, 60 per cent A*-A. Most girls take 10 or 11 GCSEs. Many sixth formers also take SATs for the US universities. An increasing use of IGCSEs to stretch the girls and increase flexibility. The head is 'not tempted' by the IB but promotes the school's education enrichment programme, running alongside the A level curriculum, which has been designed to give the girls the opportunities, especially in terms of creative thinking and learning resilience, to glean many benefits traditionally seen as an 'IB preserve'. The school also offers critical thinking for years 10 to 13.

Lovely facilities – an excellent purpose-built science block, beautiful and spacious art block, good drama studio and plenty of computers for girls to use in class and for prep. Virtual learning environment allows submission of work online to teachers. Small class sizes – never more than 18. Well organised and supported prep time at the end of each school day.

Teaching is highly responsive to the needs of individual girls – the school has an excellent reputation locally for untangling able girls whose dyslexia/dyspraxia has been a stumbling block to them elsewhere, and learning support is woven into the school structure. 'We welcome the full spectrum of learning profiles.' One-to-one support is available for dyslexia, dyspraxia and EAL at extra cost.

A good choice of modern foreign languages at GCSE and A level, and a modern language at GCSE is 'as close to compulsory as it can be'. French, Spanish, German, Chinese, Russian and Latin taught. A well-stocked and well-set-out library with specific areas set aside for sixth formers. Academic reports are termly, with progress checks every half term.

Games, options, the arts: Fantastic sports facilities – newish and splendid sports hall – and plenty of opportunities to make use of them. Where girls show exceptional promise and talent in sports (currently national representatives in lacrosse and golf) their curriculum commitments will be adjusted to allow them to flourish on the sports field. Growing an equestrian team who make use of the facilities at Hartpury Equine College. Many outdoor pursuits also supported – not least by virtue of being at the foot of the Malvern Hills. Lots of girls involved in Duke of Edinburgh too.

There are plenty of opportunities to get involved with music groups or to take individual lessons. Very good drama facilities, and for those interested in life a step beyond there are debating societies, involvement in model UN, volunteering opportunities at local schools, fund-raising for local charities and so on.

The lovely artwork on display around the school deserves a mention, and the textiles department produces some breathtaking pieces. Girls who want a go at pottery, painting, stitching or drawing will have a ball here.

Background and atmosphere: The school is well situated in the centre of Malvern, directly opposite the train station, in the building which was once the Imperial Hotel. The surroundings are lovely, with the hills stretching up behind the town, and the buildings feature lots of high ceilings, generous rooms and well-lit spaces. Younger girls seen skipping about chatting and hopping, older girls seem calm and happy. 'We'd notice someone walking round with her head down (or her nose up) straight away.'

The atmosphere is calm and relaxed but with an underlying energy and a sense of fingers on the pulse. Small enough at 420 for the headmistress to know every girl by name. The school has a full-time chaplain and there is a sense of respect for and interest in a diverse collection of girls from varied backgrounds. A mixture of UK and overseas students, although the head has now capped the number of international students. Pupils come from the very local to the far-flung – Thailand, Brunei, Russia and Nigeria amongst others.

Day girls are well integrated into the boarding school feel – with each day girl assigned to a boarding house and many using flexi-boarding either regularly or occasionally. There is no Saturday school but plenty to keep girls busy at the weekends. Boarding is done by age group with a prep house, two houses for years 9-11 and two sixth form houses. Boarding houses are well set up and comfortable, with plenty of space and privacy for older girls, and nice common-rooms.

Food is good – recently brought back in house to improve standards and, according to our sources, successfully so. There are always Halal and vegetarian options available and the staff eat with the girls.

A strong commitment to sharing facilities with the local community. The school is well liked by the locals, who say the pupils are polite and never give any trouble. Few rules, relatively late curfews by comparison with other local boarding schools – the girls are given a lot of responsibility, self-discipline is encouraged and the girls respond positively. A family atmosphere – 'the school is all about good relationships'.

Pastoral care and discipline: Pastoral care permeates the structure of the school, with school staff and older pupils committed to maintaining the highest standards. Prefects are trained as 'sixth form listeners' by Childline and know exactly what to do and when to pass concerns on to staff. Prefects are elected by a combination of sixth form and staff votes. Zero tolerance of drugs – but head has 'never had to deal' with drugs at the school. Sixth formers are encouraged to attend and host dinner parties with members of other nearby schools. Alcohol consumption is restricted to two glasses of wine on such occasions, but not allowed on school premises otherwise, though 18 years olds are allowed to go to local pubs.

Prefects, head and parents all say that bullying 'does not happen'. Girls are allocated to small tutor groups of about 12 and each form also has a prefect. The head says, 'There is nowhere to hide', and the combination of house staff, peer support, small classes and an open door policy 'from the head down' mean the girls always have someone to talk to. 'We train the girls to manage themselves and the girls are comfortable being themselves.'

Girls of all ages mix well and the head makes time to have teas and dinners with small groups of them so that she can get to know them better.

Pupils and parents: Pupils and parents come from all over the place. Day girls live up to an hour away (minibuses from very nearby and also from Hereford and Ross-on-Wye). Some boarders are local too; about a quarter of pupils are from overseas. The girls we met were cheerful, polite, welcoming and thoroughly enjoy being at the school. Parents say, 'It's lovely, friendly and happy – and every teacher is up to speed'.

Clara Furse, the first woman chief executive of the London Stock Exchange, the late HRH Princess Alice, Duchess of Gloucester and the childcare expert Penelope Leach are former pupils of St James's School, while Malvern Girls' alumnae include the writer Aminatta Forna. More recent former pupils include BBC correspondent Hannah Hennessy, journalist Elizabeth Day, surgeon Abbie Franklin and city high flyers Helen Freer and Elizabeth Sharpe.

Entrance: Prospective pupils are interviewed by the head – via Skype if need be – and all face formal assessment tests. Formal interviews and often quite a long 'courtship' including taster days etc. Prep department provides a growing number into year 7, with others coming from local primaries and prep schools (boarding and day) like Hatherop Castle, The Elms, Abberley Hall, Godstowe and The Croft. At 11, girls sit cognitive ability and comprehension tests, while others do common entrance at 13. Main entry points are years 7, 9 and sixth form. Girls looking to enter sixth form must take a written paper in one of the subjects they wish to study at A level and a general essay paper. All international students must take an EAL test. Not highly selective, but girls 'must be intellectually curious, with a good IQ' and 'able to benefit from what we offer'.

Exit: Most stay on after GCSEs. Virtually all sixth form leavers to university. A handful to Oxbridge (four in 2013), and a good number to Russell Group destinations. Places at Imperial College, UCL, Durham, SOAS, Edinburgh, St Andrews, Warwick etc. A variety of courses incorporating everything from veterinary science to film production, but with a strong representation in sciences, engineering, economics, business and politics.

Money matters: The school offers a number of academic, music, sport, art and drama scholarships, which are worth between 10 and 20 per cent of fees. Bursaries are also available and may be combined with scholarships. The maximum bursary/scholarship combination available is 40 per cent of fees.

Remarks: A school that is different, 'not tethered to league tables', with a lovely relaxed atmosphere, yielding impressive results in the classroom and on the sports field. Happy, confident girls and staff.

M

The Manchester Grammar School

Linked school: The Manchester Grammar School Junior School

Old Hall Lane, Manchester, M13 0XT

• Pupils: 1,280 boys; all day • Ages: 7–18 • C of E links, but basically non-denom • Fees: £11,055 pa • Independent

Tel: 01612 247201
Email: general@mgs.org
Website: www.mgs.org

High Master: Since September 2013, Dr Martin Boulton, previously under master (deputy head) of Westminster School. He studied at Manchester Grammar in the sixth form, then spent time working in the mining industry in South Africa, before studying mining engineering at Nottingham University. He gained at PGCE at Manchester University and taught physics at Sherborne School before joining Westminster in 2001. His interests include mountaineering and gliding, and he is passionate about school sport.

Academic matters: Commonly regarded as the outstanding boys' school in the region. Very starry A level results – 93 per cent A*-B in 2013, with many brilliant individual performances – and a particularly wide choice of languages, including Italian, Spanish and Russian (some parents would like Chinese too); electronics growing. Maths and sciences the biggest hitters, with biology more popular than physics (perhaps in preparation for careers in medicine), then history, languages and English, followed by economics, geography and politics. Psychology and theatre studies only available in the IB programme (began 2008). Strong results here with an average of 41 in 2013, even a boy who obtained full marks, a spectacular achievement – in top 10 of UK IB schools; a wide choice of options and due to run in conjunction with Manchester High School for Girls.

IGCSEs in most subjects, to offer extra challenge, and possibility of taking Extended Project Qualification in year 11 (usually a sixth form exam). All do a foreign language, even Mandarin Chinese; curriculum extras include philosophy and critical thinking. Again, large numbers of superb results – 85 per cent A/A* for the last six years, with 90 per cent in 2013. Homework expectations are from up to six hours a week in year 7 to 16 hours a week for the lower sixth. Classes of 20-26 till the sixth form, where sets are considerably smaller. Much success in all kinds of national and international competitions, from chemistry to classics to code breaking.

These are boys who are eager to learn, and teachers of distinction who write on and have a passion for their subjects – understandably, they find it a hard school to leave. Our sixth form tour guides spoke eloquently about the 'vibrant learning environment' and the knowledge, enthusiasm and expertise of the staff, who 'like us to learn the subject, not just pass the exam' and are happy to take their pupils extensively beyond the syllabus. Correspondingly, boys are expected to show independence by, eg, going further than what has been covered in the lesson in their homework. Parents appreciate the 'good mix of different types of teacher'.

Well regarded by the LA for the support given to boys with learning difficulties. SENCo confident they can accommodate a full range of special needs; withdrawal for, eg, dyslexia support, individual or small group, with no extra charge, but boys who need laptops expected to provide their own.

Games, options, the arts: Various pitches and courts, a huge sports hall, gym, two multi gyms and swimming pool. The gifted and ambitious thrive – 'Second to none,' said a happy parent – through top level coaching, leading to major match success in a great array of sports up to international level; exceptional water polo – has had five boys in the GB under 16 team – plus an under 19 world duathlon champion. Boys who just enjoy sport offered a diverse set of options – golf and softball as well as martial arts and sports leadership awards.

Excellent music – own organ and two grand pianos; larger music school planned for 2015. Has links with the Halle Orchestra, whose Children's Choir rehearses here; a biennial concert at St John's Smith Square, London. Winners of national competitions and Oxbridge organ scholarships; singing tours. Mainly classical with some jazz.

Recent, very well-equipped drama centre with theatre and two studios. Year 7s and 8s compete in 20 minute Shakespeare productions and perform in local primary schools; older boys have put on A Funny Thing Happened on the Way to the Forum, Tartuffe in French and Oedipus (in translation). Collaboration in drama and music with Manchester High and Withington Girls' Schools.

Outstanding art in a variety of media displayed around the school, in a small, central gallery, on an outer window sill of the three storey Parker Art Hall – models of Wallace and various owls – and, unusually, on the refectory walls. However, only a small number take art at A level. We were deeply impressed by the sophisticated and witty writing in the hefty school magazine, Ulula – 168 pages, no less – and fabulous photography. The New Mancunian newspaper has won several national awards.

One hundred and thirty clubs and activities, with much input by the boys, include the existentialist forum, robot and film-making. Talks from very elevated visitors – politicians, professors and presenters, often Old Mancunians. Energetic fund-raising for charity, eg the 100 mile dash for Pakistan involving the whole community that raised £30,000; a marathon boy swimmer raised £37,000. Supports two colleges in Uganda and maintains a long-standing tradition of local community service – large numbers do outreach work in state schools. The sixth form has an extensive enrichment programme – practical options such as cooking on a student budget (how to make real soup) alongside nourishment for the mind, such as preparation for an alphabet soup of university admissions tests (HAT, LNAT, ELAT). Lots of far-flung trips and treks – Iceland, China, Peru, Africa – as well as weekend treks closer to home, plus camps and activities weeks at the school's three residential sites.

Background and atmosphere: Outstanding last two ISI inspections. Founded 1515 by Hugh Oldham, Bishop of Exeter, who also contributed handsomely to the establishment of Corpus Christi College, Oxford, to 'educate able boys regardless of their parents' means'. Moved from the city centre in 1930 to its present site, in a largely residential area of Manchester. Became a direct grant grammar school 1944, reverted to independent status in 1976 – the first in the country to react with a bursary appeal when the assisted places scheme ended in the late 1990s and the only one of five independent schools to pass every section of the Charity Commission's public benefit test unequivocally. Delivers free talks to schools and groups in the community.

Entry is past playing fields and through a tripartite arch beneath a clock tower cupola. Impressive reception area with wooden panelling, portraits of past High Masters, a marble bust and leather sofas. Built around a quad, to help early pupils from deprived backgrounds feel more comfortable at Oxbridge interviews, with an internal cloister. Trad Memorial Hall with organ and dark panelling. Well-resourced Paton Library plus separate Alan Garner Library (he maintains links with the school) for the younger boys with masses of fiction; own bookshop, too. Some drab corridors, however, and the sixth form facilities could be more lavish. Stands in 26 acres with an area full of wildlife used for teaching (the Rectory Woodland) containing a diverse population of birds including great spotted woodpeckers, rose-ringed parakeets and an owl. School

M

motto is: Dare to be wise – many owls of various shapes, sizes and materials to be found throughout. Religious assemblies for different faiths open to all.

Strong focus on academic achievement but parents say, 'It offers so many different opportunities, there's a niche for everybody,' and boys we met were confident bullying not a problem – 'Most people know where the line is'. However, we have heard reports of boys perceived as in some way odd being teased in an unpleasant way, and of disturbingly laddish behaviour witnessed outside school – some parents believe standards have slipped from past heights. Those who thrive need to be resilient, self-motivated and well organised.

Uniform is blue blazer, grey trousers and blue or white shirt; sixth form wear suits with free choice of shirt colour. Food 'very varied and good,' we were told, and efficiently organised dining hall; lunch in a bag available for busy boys. Butty Bar with snack food for sixth, open from 7.30am.

Pastoral care and discipline: Focus more on rewards – eg commendations sent home, boy-friendly prizes, the 'wise old owl' badge for marked improvement, general 'good egg' awards – than sanctions, eg litter collection and detentions. Reasonable alcohol and drugs policy – automatic permanent exclusion for supplying or trading, but more flexible for using; might employ random drug testing.

Boys assured us if they had a difficulty they would see their form tutor, head of year or another teacher they trusted. Staff seen as friendly and supportive in the main – 'They want you to do your best but they aren't breathing down your neck'. A large number of sixth form boys mentor younger ones and assist lower and junior school form tutors – most become prefects – and all new pupils are matched with a 'friend' who lives near them and can accompany them on their school journey for their first few days.

Thoughtful transition arrangements for year 7s and a very helpful guide for lower school parents; two full time (and one part time) nurses – the lead nurse is also a trained counsellor. Praise from parents for the help given to a number of boys with 'difficult problems – they did their best for them and brought out the best in them'; however a question mark was also raised in our mind about how flexible the school would be on occasion and how effectively it communicates boys' special needs to all their teachers.

Pupils and parents: Mainly business and professional backgrounds but very mixed socially, thanks to the bursary scheme, and ethnically. Most from Manchester and the surrounding area, also from far afield – Preston, Sheffield, Buxton, Stoke on Trent (school shuttle bus service from the railway station plus Cheadle and Altrincham). Confident, articulate boys who enjoy their rich school life. No embarrassment about being academic here and plenty of scope for wit, fun and quirkiness. Parents consulted via forums; plenty of contact through emails, newsletters, weekly bulletin on the website.

Famed for producing a great range of very clever and individual high flyers. Old Mancunians include: writers Thomas de Quincey, Robert Bolt, Alan Garner; Nobel Prize for Chemistry winner JC Polyani; pianist John Ogden; National Theatre Director Nicholas Hytner; actors Ben Kingsley, Robert Powell; broadcasters Michael Wood, Martin Sixsmith; cricketer Mike Atherton; several prominent figures in academia, medicine, business and finance.

Entrance: Automatic entry for junior school boys. Much thought has gone into the assessment process, designed to identify the genuinely very able, as opposed to the highly tutored, and to be fair to state school boys. Admissions days for external year 7 applicants, who come in groups of 12, are held from late September to early January, during which they take part in various engaging activities including learning new topics, with tests on them, and group work. Also tests in January in English and maths, including verbal and non-verbal reasoning, plus extended writing (past papers with answers and advice on how to use them as preparation available on the website). Previous school reports considered too; will do Skype interviews for boys living abroad. Results at the start of March. Usually takes half from prep and half from state schools.

Sixth form: average of A in GCSEs/IGCSEs plus A/A* in A level subjects; external candidates also do written tests in would be A level subjects (free past papers provided), plus interview(s) and reference from current school – plans to introduce year 7 type assessment days here too. Takes 12-25 – a lot of flexibility: 'We would never turn away a good boy'.

Exit: Around six per cent leave after year 11 to do vocational courses at sixth form/FE colleges or because they fail to meet the very stringent sixth form entry requirements (but school says some flexibility here for hard workers).

Large numbers to Oxbridge (20-30 a year) but boys now opting for Ivy League and Russell Group universities as well – one of the top boys' schools for entry to the élite UK universities (very successful for medicine). A wide range of academic subjects studied.

Money matters: Discount for siblings and reduction if whole year's fees paid in advance. Bursary fund of close to £20 million supports over 220 families – has one of largest schemes in the country and has just launched a new appeal aiming for £10 million by 2015; additional hardship fund for trips and emergency fees support.

Ogden Trust and HSBC scholarships for state school applicants to sixth form, which can be combined with a school means-tested bursary up to full fees.

Remarks: One of the leading boys' schools in the country. Offers huge extracurricular opportunities and an academic education going far beyond the constraints of the national curriculum and exam syllabuses, together with the pleasure and stimulation to be had from learning with, and from, equally gifted and motivated students. In the words of a sixth former, 'There's a tingle here – everyone has an idea on their mind.'

Manchester High School for Girls

Linked school: Manchester High School for Girls Preparatory Department

Grangethorpe Road, Manchester, M14 6HS

- Pupils: 680 girls; all day • Ages: 11–18 • Non-denom
- Fees: £10,287 pa • Independent

Tel: 01612 240447
Email: administration@mhsg.manchester.sch.uk
Website: www.manchesterhigh.co.uk

Headmistress: Since January 2009, Mrs Claire Hewitt BSc (late forties). Educated at Wakefield Girls' High School, chemistry degree plus PGCE from Sheffield University. Taught at Harrogate Ladies' College, Fulneck School, Sheffield High becoming deputy head and, in 2005, head of King Edward VI Grammar, Louth. Trim and very crisply turned out, but the air in the head's study has significantly softened. 'We love her so much, she's really friendly,' girls enthuse. Teaches chemistry to all year 7s and passionately committed to single sex education, 'I know where girls do better', but glad the High Master of neighbouring Manchester Grammar concurs that collaboration's a great thing. Enthusiastic about Man High's curriculum 'meeting the needs of young women entering the 21st century global workplace' but 'all the time maintaining positivity, having fun'. Proud therefore her staff can also let their hair down, for example in a recent Strictly-style 'dance with your teachers' charity talent show. Popular for having brought back jumpers after she saw girls shivering in just blouses and blazers – 'she listens,' girls say; 'a quick win,' she demurs. Married to an MGS old boy, no children but a doting auntie, she's a keen cyclist who loves music.

Academic matters: Outstanding results keep school high in league tables with 94 per cent of A levels scoring A*/B in 2013 and 68 per cent A*/As. At GCSE, 87 per cent A*s and As and at both levels lower grade tails are negligible. Awarded International Baccalaureate IB World School Status in 2010, the average point score was 38 in 2013 and school has been 'working hard to communicate with universities'. Broad choices with Latin and PE to A level. Twenty per cent take Latin GCSE, 10 per cent dance and all take GCSE short course RE. Four form groups each year of some 28 girls, with smaller teaching groups. Great facilities – plenty of ICT provision, two state-of-the-art language labs, and stunning sports complex. Sparkling modern science labs, just two remain what the girls call 'retro'. Chemistry strong and popular here and a couple of years ago a Man High girl was crowned world no 1 female chemistry student in the International Chemistry Olympiad, going on to study natural sciences at Cambridge. The chem labs have arguably the best views of the neighbouring park through huge windows. Textiles and art overspill meanwhile dwell in two prefab huts. One parent described the DT here as 'girlie', but school points out that for each of the past five years one student's gone on to study engineering. Girls very proud of their libraries, one studiously silent, the other a burble of information gathering and team work. Well-used subject clinics with girls praising teachers for giving up their time. Some 23 girls receive extra help from a variety of sources including a designated learning support coordinator and heads of year. The especially gifted and talented are well supported; for example one outstanding mathematician's ability warranted one-to-one maths lessons from an early age; she eventually represented the UK in the International Maths Olympiad. 'You've got to be willing to work hard here' and 'we do put pressure on ourselves,' pupils say; 'but girls here are ambitious for their futures and definitely career orientated'.

Games, options, the arts: State-of-the-art sports complex with climbing wall and five star viewing gallery. Bright air-conditioned multi-use dance studio, extensive fitness suite for older girls and staff and top-notch 25m indoor pool. U14 national champions at water polo with six regional and three England squad players; perhaps it's practising with the very successful Manchester Grammar teams? Strong hockey and tennis and a GB runner too. Junior sports awards for community service. Super music house with 13 practice rooms and three class rooms. Over 400 girls take instrument lessons including a clutch of harpists. Comenius choir exchange with Sweden and Austria in 2011. Drama studio has floor to ceiling views of gardens and black-out drapes. Main hall fits all seniors on stacking tiered chairs that can roll back for exam season. School is own D of E awarding authority; large numbers of awards at all levels. Model United Nations, Mock Trial, Young Enterprise, strong community links and a student run paper, 'Onward'. Many joint activities with Manchester Grammar boys higher up school; drama, music, debating and other societies, reciprocal rose delivery on Valentine's day and Man High's sports day held on MGS grounds.

Background and atmosphere: From burgeoning jasmine in immaculate flower beds (in summer at least) to elegant lily

arrangements in reception this school is fragrant with the sweet smell of success. The latest ISI inspection speaks of all here 'sharing in a vision of excellence in everything they do'. Girls in a painting class or eating lunch on the benches amongst floribundant rose bowers are becoming accustomed to a very civilised lifestyle. The classrooms are spick and span and even the extensive locker areas neat and tidy. Respectful girls in cream and black open doors and stand for the head and there's no corridor chaos here. The only bottleneck is the lunch queue; lunches compulsory for years 7 and 8 but after that the arrangements are laid back with pay-as-you-go needing £2 or £3 a day or the option to bring your own. The modern architecture (school was rebuilt after extensive WW2 bomb damage) and bright airy accommodation enjoy verdant views of manicured lawns, pretty gardens and an internal quad with a clipped box parterre. The leafy backdrop of Platt Fields Park makes it almost impossible to imagine that Manchester city centre lies just beyond Rusholme's vibrant curry mile. Lots of brothers go to nearby MGS and buses serve both schools, as well as arch rivals Withington Girls. Unashamedly ambitious and without doubt fulfilling its 1874 founding objective 'to provide for Manchester's daughters what has been provided without stint for Manchester's sons'. The termly glossy High Flyer magazine celebrates individual and collective achievements.

Pastoral care and discipline: Peer and staff hierarchy for pastoral care. Head describes school's size as just right, 'any bigger and you lose sight of individuals, any smaller and you compromise on opportunities.' School nurse in four-bed sick bay opposite head's study is often first port of call for worries or problems. Late homework slips, detentions for chewing gum but generally they're an amenable bunch. One parent praised school for working hard with her 'wayward adolescent daughter'. Girls feel they have a voice through school council and because the new head stops to talk to them in the corridors. Caretakers live on site and school is approached down its own cul-de-sac drive with car park barriers and security doors with cctv. No barbed wire visible but it feels very secure. Staff enjoy being looked after by staffroom staff, brownies and a fruit bowl, plus their own work and resource room with computers. Frequent sightings of orderly strings of prep girls in yellow gingham add an aaah factor.

Pupils and parents: Hugely culturally diverse, 20 per cent Muslim, strong Jewish contingent with a third experiencing one of 40 other languages in their home lives. Assemblies also include Christian, Sikh, Hindu, humanist and secular options. From all over Greater Manchester and beyond, mostly from professional families with both girls and staff mentioning the huge proportion of doctors' children here. Much celebration and role modelling of old girls' achievements and careers, with a strong network for contacting those who might be helpful. Significant can-do message constantly re-inforced.

Old girls include, famously, Cristabel, Sylvia and Adela Pankhurst; assorted businesswomen such as Clara Freeman OBE, Marks and Spencer's first female executive director; Merlyn Lowther, the Bank of England's first female chief cashier, whose signature was on every bank note; leading lawyers such as Ann Alexander, who acted for the families in the Shipman case; Judy Finnigan, of Richard and Judy fame, Lucy Higginson, editor of Horse and Hound magazine, Labour MP Louise Ellman and GB fencing star Megan Lomas. Plenty of less daunting rôle models too in entrance foyer hall of fame, where distinctly non-celeb girls doing great things for charity are also featured.

Entrance: Academic selection of clever and very clever girls at 11 initially by exams; maths, essay, comprehension, verbal and non-verbal reasoning. Then interview when girls are asked to bring something of interest to talk about, and primary school

M

report. Whittling down three applicants per place, about half from state primaries. Promotional DVD professionally designed.

Exit: Impressive and solid leavers' destination lists mostly to first choice of university eg Leeds, Liverpool, Birmingham, Edinburgh and King's College London. A regular handful to Oxbridge (six in 2013). Pupils praise careers service which is integrated into life from year 8, includes aptitude testing and careful individual support for subject choices and future plans; certainly the careers room always seems to be active.

Money matters: Ten per cent, about 12 girls a year, receive some bursary or scholarship help; many very quietly although some speak positively and publicly of their assistance as part of the new £2 million Pankhurst Bursary Appeal. Twenty per cent discount for third child in school.

Remarks: Beautiful setting for unashamedly ambitious education, high expectations and positive mental attitude; in school's words, 'shaping the next generation of remarkable women'. Girls here expect strong careers but there has been a mellowing and this generation's route to the top seems more likely to come from intelligent hard work than from sharp elbows.

Mander Portman Woodward (MPW)

90-92 Queen's Gate, London, SW7 5AB

• Pupils: 480 boys and girls • Ages: 14-19 • Non-denom
• Fees: £19,656-£23,973 pa • Independent

Tel: 020 7835 1355
Email: london@mpw.co.uk
Website: www.mpw.co.uk

Principal: Since 2010, Steven Boyes BA, MSc, PGCE (mid-forties). First became principal in 1997 and now back at the helm after four years, during which he has worked on a number of development projects for the MPW Group. Read geography and English at Lancaster University before going on to do a master's degree in management sciences. He has subsequently published articles on aspects of physical geography and is a textbook reviewer for two publishers. He was a senior A level examiner for over a decade and is a serving inspector for the Independent Schools Inspectorate. Was appointed chairman of the Council of Independent Further Education (CIFE) in 2010. Married to a lawyer, Melanie, with two children. A former county level squash player, he still plays a variety of racket sports and golf. Other hobbies include collecting crime novels and political biographies and crosswords.

Academic matters: You can take or retake GCSEs and A levels here, in one or two years or even a over a term. You can also come in for after-school private tuition, for a week's revision course at Easter or for extra Oxbridge preparation. Never more than eight in a class and those retaking in a year are taught in a different group from those in the second year of a course. Will run courses for single students but with half the normal teaching hours – 'If you're being taught one-to-one you whizz through the syllabus'. Many GCSE students are studying A levels at the same time; 34 per cent A*/A GCSE grades in 2013.

A staggering range of 43 subjects in any combination at A level – from ceramics to geology to statistics. The 'reassuringly expensive' fees fund a high enough ratio of staff to students to provide a genuinely personalised curriculum, with staff willing to set extra practice work when necessary or go over tricky subjects with individuals after lessons. 'And because the classes are so small, they can stop and explain anything you don't understand,' said a student. In 2013, 71 per cent A*/B grades and 35 per cent A*/A.

The latest ISI report commented on an over-reliance on worksheets and model answers at the expense of independent learning, though most classes we saw involved staff and student discussion. 'I felt the comment was a bit unfair,' says the principal. 'If you are providing someone with a one year A level, you have to do it in ways reminiscent of the old crammers. But pedagogy needs to be increasingly diverse. I was amazed when I arrived by the quality of the teaching staff here.' MPW stands or falls by its exam results and university places and a high proportion of staff are also public examiners – 'This can be a double-edged sword: great expertise but sometimes too great a focus on exams'.

Students get plenty of timed tests and exam practice. Parents are kept up to date with twice-termly reports and can also log in to see test results, what homework has been set and whether or not it has been done – 'particularly useful for those who are overseas'. They are also encouraged to pick up the phone to personal tutors whenever they have a query. 'They put themselves out to be helpful,' said a parent.

Helping students get into Oxbridge was MPW's original raison d'être, and it has added medical, veterinary, dental and law school applications to its expertise. Indeed, it publishes books on these and several other related subjects. It provides interview practice, seminars and specialist preparation for university entrance tests, plus detailed guidance on completing UCAS forms. 'The director of studies was very helpful over my son's personal statement,' said a parent. 'I didn't get involved at all, which was such a relief.'

Historically, SEN help was not high on the agenda. But the principal has appointed a head of academic support – 'I didn't want to ghettoise particular learning difficulties' – who is a qualified educational psychologist. Staff are being trained to use academic support plans and set appropriate targets for students, such as always writing down verbal instructions – 'We're not an SEN school but I think everyone is getting something out of having a SENCo. It is a growing area of need'.

Games, options, the arts: Offers fine art, ceramics, photography, textiles and graphics, separately or combined into a single A or AS. Art and ceramics studios, two darkrooms and a well-equipped history of art library. Organises two exhibitions each year, with work by ex-students at art college or university on display alongside pieces by current students and staff, and helps those aiming at art college to put a portfolio together. Art historians visit Florence or Paris as well as local galleries.

A donation from a grateful ex-student now at Cambridge has re-equipped the theatre studies studio, used for extra-curricular activities such as yoga as well as examination practicals. The Winter Ball is becoming an institution.

Sport is not a major part of college life, particularly in the sixth form, where it is voluntary – GCSE students have one compulsory and one voluntary session a week. However free membership to the nearby gym is extremely popular and there are enthusiastic football and rugby teams. Netball is, by popular request, another option.

Background and atmosphere: Founded in 1973 by three eponymous Cambridge graduates to offer small group A level retake and Oxbridge entrance tuition. Now greatly expanded, with sister colleges in Birmingham and Cambridge, it occupies three listed stucco buildings in smart South Kensington, where enviably large sums have evidently been invested in facilities and decoration.

Buzzy but relaxed atmosphere, with staff and students on first name terms, no dress restrictions and a lack of petty rules

– 'You're not going to be told to do your tie up or tuck your shirt in here'. Some students find it hard to make friends, since communal activities and space are limited and fellow-students may be there for only a short period of time. 'But everyone's very friendly,' said a parent, 'and my son really likes all his teachers – they treat him like an adult.'

Pastoral care and discipline: 'I feel they're actually concerned about you,' said a student, 'which I never felt at my last school.' Personal tutors, who have a light teaching load, are responsible for students' work and welfare – 'Too often schools divide up the pastoral and the academic. Our tutors are a one-stop shop for parents – the buck stops with them'. Parents are full of praise – 'They are very open to any kind of discussion. And unlike his previous school, we get lots of communication'.

Despite the relaxed atmosphere, strict about turning up on time and getting work done. Registers are taken at the beginning of each lesson and the registrar is liable to phone absconders' parents, even if it is 3am where they are. 'It is very difficult not to work here. We are a very disciplined place. We give masses of homework and you get a lot of feedback. The students always say that MPW stands for "makes people work".'

Will expel for 'any involvement with drugs on or off the premises', violent behaviour or even persistent smoking in the vicinity (fair to say that groups of illicit cigarette smokers were conspicuous by their absence). 'If you're clear about boundaries most will push it as far as the limit, then stop. Parents never say we didn't warn them.'

Pupils and parents: Virtually all from independent schools. GCSE students tend to be recent arrivals from abroad – 'Lots of foreign students come in by chauffeur,' commented a parent – or those who have had differences of opinion with their previous school. A level students may have outgrown boarding school, lost confidence in their previous school or had medical problems. An increasing number transfer into the upper sixth after disappointing AS results elsewhere. Plenty of diplomatic and business families.

Entrance: By interview. Will never take anyone who has been expelled for drug-taking, but will consider perpetrators of long-term low-level misdemeanours or one-off mistakes. GCSE applicants take English and maths tests: those applying to join year 11 may be advised to go into year 10 to build up their skills or English fluency. A level applicants generally need at least six grade Cs at GCSE, with Bs in their A level choices, but can retake English or maths if necessary alongside AS levels. Those whose English is not fluent can study EFL alongside other subjects until they catch up.

Exit: Some 90 per cent of GCSE students go on to the sixth form. Around five per cent a year to Oxbridge and up to 10 per cent to medical/dentistry/veterinary schools – 'As a non-selective school we do very well across all subjects. We have good connections with medical and dental schools, and they know we know what we are talking about when we recommend a student'. Around half to Russell Group universities.

Money matters: Scholarships and bursaries of up to 100 per cent at all levels by competitive exam.

Remarks: Relaxed, collegiate atmosphere combined with a strict attitude to attendance and work. Small classes, great flexibility, plenty of communication with parents and a strong emphasis on what it takes to pass exams and get into university.

Manor House School

Linked school: Manor House School Junior Department

Manor House Lane, Little Bookham, Surrey, KT23 4EN

- Pupils: 160; all day • Ages: 11–16 • Christian non-denom
- Fees: £14,310 pa • Independent

Tel: 01372 458538
Email: admin@manorhouseschool.org
Website: www.manorhouseschool.org

Headmistress: Since 2008, Miss Zara Axton BSc PGCE (forties). A varied teaching background – starting with maths in a Catholic comprehensive and progressing through to four years at Kent College as pastoral deputy and head of sixth form.

She tells us she has an open door to parents, is informal and likes to meet people 'by being around'. She describes her input so far as having 'slightly rebalanced towards the academic, reviewed processes and sharpened up', whilst also maintaining the nurturing and fun ethos. We found her very comfortable when she talked about her thoughts on the school – she is proud of the girls' only status of Manor House and 'would worry about girls' self confidence in an environment dominated by boys'. However, she was decidedly not relaxed nor keen to talk about herself. Her 'more reserved approach' (than the previous head) has meant that she cuts something of a controversial figure among parents. Some we spoke to have yet to warm to her or were reserved about her – largely because they all felt that they did not know her and that she has yet to make her personal presence felt. On the other hand, one parent told us, 'I like her and she had brought in good ideas and changes. Anyone new will upset a few people, often the vocal ones'. 'I really like her,' said another. 'I find her approachable and my daughters go in for a chat with her.' All parents we spoke to felt she was generally running the school well.

Academic matters: The range of abilities is genuinely broad, from high flyers who want to work without pressure to those who struggle with academia. GCSE results are excellent from such a spectrum, pitching the school well against the local competition – 52 per cent A*/A grades in 2013. Most popular GCSE subjects are art, Spanish, French and geography, less so the sciences. High flyers in English can take GCSE a year early. Nice to see plenty of vocational options at GCSE – food and nutrition, child development, art, music, PE and drama.

The head feels all abilities are catered for 'because we teach in small groups and have stable staff who know the girls well'. About 27 per cent of the senior school teachers have been there more than 10 years – a few taught current pupils' mothers and clearly have great affection for both the school and the pupils. Some staff movement with the arrival of Miss Axton – commonplace as all new heads make their mark; also as the school only has pupils to 16, young ambitious teachers would have to move on if they want to teach A level. Class sizes average 20 – parents all agree good academic results are gained by small classes and the small scale of the school, telling us, 'The girls are a bit spoon-fed,' but the work ethic is positive and 'being clever is OK, not geeky'.

The full-time head of learning support provides help to girls throughout the school (junior and senior), individually or in small groups. No SEN assessment on entry but about 10 per cent are referred by their teachers for additional help; anything more than a couple of sessions are charged extra. Girls have a positive view of the help they are given at all levels.

Games, options, the arts: Sports are a big part of life here – all the usuals and matches most afternoons for A through to

M

D teams whenever possible, so most gain match experience, much appreciated by parents and girls. Games teaching widely praised, 'The PE staff work incredibly hard'. Some girls very involved and with excellent results. On-site outdoor facilities (including pool) and sports hall good; changing rooms for each year dotted around school, but no showers, which can be a problem for the older girls.

Music, art and drama all enjoyed as part of the fun, have-a-go ethos. Busy, inspirational art room buzzing with girls and their pretty and impressive artworks. Drama is praised by parents as very strong with a 'wonderful teaching team' – girls of all ages take part in productions both on stage and backstage. Newish director of music is 'young and full of enthusiasm'. Individual music lessons taught by a variety of peripatetic teachers, standards range from beginner to grade 5, the majority at grade 2 or 3, with plenty of opportunities for performance in school.

Background and atmosphere: Housed in a classically beautiful Queen Anne house set in formal gardens and parkland, tucked away in a surprisingly quiet and leafy Surrey lane close to the busy A3 and M25. The house can be hired as a wedding venue via a completely separate events company. The lovely gardens, sweeping lawns, as well as the 'safe feeling' location, are much appreciated by parents and many of the girls. Inside, the house feels as much like a rather grand home as a school, with a central staircase leading up to classrooms on the upper floors. Behind the main house are a number of newer blocks housing the art room, school hall (doubling as a theatre and gym) and classrooms for the oldest girls and, separately, the nursery and preparatory sections. Unusually, a well-equipped home economics department – girls are taught nutrition and diet as well as child development and textiles, and good old fashioned sewing.

Truly a through 2-16 years school – little, if any, separation between early years, juniors and seniors: it is one community, a major 'USP' the school uses to differentiate itself from the competition. Although the juniors and seniors do have some separate playing areas, they are involved in each other's school lives on a daily basis, with most of the senior girls having a role – prep and subject prefects, house and sports captains – with responsibilities across the whole school. They are greeted with excitement, hugs and kisses by the juniors, who love the seniors to bits. Miss Axton describes it as 'a small, friendly, nurturing school where everyone is known'. Parents generally like the small size, especially at the younger end, feeling, 'It's a good choice for a quiet child,' but sometimes find that 'in such a small environment one girl can upset the applecart'. Delightful website (in fact one of the best school websites we have seen) with loads of pictures of happy smiling girls, gives a real flavour of the place.

Pastoral care and discipline: 'To love is to live' is the school motto and generally fits well – girls all know each other and are friendly across age groups. The girls we met on our visit were charming, polite and confident without a hint of precociousness. Huge praise from every parent we spoke to for the pastoral care – 'second to none'. Parents describe the caring environment as 'cosseted' and 'like being wrapped in cotton-wool', acknowledging that a few find it too much so in their latter years – although Miss Axton says, 'No parent or girl has ever raised this with me'.

A counsellor visits for one day each week, providing confidential advice and support for both girls and staff. Issues of potential teen angst – alcohol, drugs, eating disorders, cyber-bullying, self esteem – are covered in class. The head reports very few problems, explaining they work 'with clear policies and consistent boundaries' and discuss bad behaviour and its effect. Parents tell us, 'Girls who have been particularly unpleasant are taken for a chat'; Miss Axton says, 'I can assure you these are not cosy chats! I do, however, give them the right of reply and the opportunity to put the situation right.'

Pupils and parents: Parents choose it to avoid the academic pressure and competition of the 'Surrey schools mafia' – they are a varied and non-judgmental lot who mix comfortably. They feel Manor House suits 'girly girls', 'quiet girls' and families who are 'not too pushy'. Plenty with family ties, mothers who are old girls, as well as lots of sisters. Girls look fresh faced and tidy, with swinging pony-tails and sensible skirt lengths. Not for the wild child, the rebel or rule breaker: she would stick out like a sore thumb.

Pupils come from around a 10 mile radius from Epsom to Guildford, school minibuses pick up in the morning. No home bound school transport is laid on, but a minibus runs to Effingham Station before and after school.

Entrance: Most girls move seamlessly through from the junior to senior school here; the largest external intake is at 11, with pupils coming from a scattering of local state and independent schools. An entry testing day is held in January prior to entry in September – verbal reasoning, English and maths and an informal interview with Miss Axton. She also chats to parents; she's looking for girls 'who want to be here' and the school accepts a wide range of abilities, from the very academic to those whose interests are in other areas of school life.

Exit: All girls leave after GCSE, mostly to study for A levels. Leavers' destinations in 2013 included Claremont Fan Court School, Esher College, George Abbot, Godalming College, Hartpury College, Howard of Effingham, Hurtwood House, Prior's Field, Reed's, St John's and Tormead. A few head in different directions such as child care, hairdressing or the arts. A few jump ship at age 13 – particularly girls who have been at Manor House all through nursery and juniors.

Money matters: A few scholarships of limited value at 11, including one for the top state school joiner. Annual means-tested bursaries are available, in line with the school's charitable status, for new and existing pupils, theoretically covering up to 100 per cent of fees, though the head is keen to manage expectations. Applications for bursaries need to be made by February for the following September and involve a home visit as well as consideration of the pupil's contribution to school life.

Remarks: A charming, small, friendly school, ideal for girls who need a caring environment to reach their full potential, be they very academic or otherwise. Wholesome unpretentious girls mix with other 'nice' girls (no fears they would lead each other astray). Pupils work hard, play hard and form friendships for life – a school, which though fully embracing the new, harks back to a wonderful bygone era. Think Enid Blyton's Malory Towers (without the boarding) – in the nicest possible way (think, but do not say: the head takes huge exception to the comparison).

M

Mark College

Blackford Road, Mark, Highbridge, Somerset, TA9 4NP

- Pupils: 69 boys, 6 girls; • Ages: 10–19; • Non-denom;
- Fees: £19,488–£48,783 pa; • Independent

Tel: 01278 641632
Email: markcollege@priorygroup.com
Website: www.priorygroup.com/markcollege

Principal: Since September 2010, Michelle Whitham Jones, BSc PGCE MEd NPQH. Married with an adult son. Has taught children, for over 15 years, from ages 2-19, in both mainstream comprehensive and SEN – SBED, PMLD, SLD, MLD, ASD, specialising in physical disability and language disorder.

Academic matters: Takes boys and girls of 'average and above average ability' with specific learning difficulties associated with dyslexia and language disorder. CreSTeD 'specialist provision' status and chosen by DfE as a beacon school for dyslexics. Some real experts amongst staff with all the right training and experience; school geared up for students getting information from sources other than books. On site speech and language therapist, occupational therapist and art therapist. Students follow national curriculum with core subjects including English, maths and ICT. Assessed at beginning of year 10 to determine level of help required (eg reader and/or scribe) in public examinations. In most cases students choose three more subjects from DT, food tech, PE, geography, history, drama and art.

ICT support makes sense for dyslexics with voice activated software (highlight a word and you hear it) to help get good ideas down on paper. Academic input 'second to none', according to one father who fought an expensive two year battle with his LA to get his son funded. Students say teachers, 'try different ways' to explain things and recognise their difficulties in reading, self-organisation etc. Meets challenge more often than you'd expect to get students GCSE grade C in English (most enter school with reading age of 7) and pupils attain well above national average in maths and humanities; most come out with pleasing results overall. Sixth form offers seven A levels on site, plus a full range of subjects which can be chosen from Strode College, with full support given for pupils' dyslexic needs through Mark College.

Good ICT suite, pupils may use own laptops in classrooms. Boarders can use their own laptops in boarding house internet lounge.

Games, options, the arts: Wednesday fixtures either with local comprehensives or schools on Independent Schools' Association circuit. Students see themselves as sporty (school has won Sportsmark award with distinction). Good-sized sports hall on main site with much used multi-gym; games pitches visible on other side of main road, plus a new addition of nine hole golf. Pupils compete nationally in cross country and some county representation in athletics, rugby (sevens particularly strong) and cricket. Twenty per cent of pupils learn a musical instrument: piano or keyboard, electric guitar or drums, but no choir or orchestra. Cosy library and television room is used by students during breaks.

Art department has expanded into purpose built cabin; much artwork on display (including in principal's study). Drama recently relocated into own studio with outdoor stage. DT is housed in own building allowing for spacious workshops and teaching space. Teaching kitchen opened in 2012. Laboratories and classrooms aren't large but work well here – we were impressed by the quality of lessons seen and especially by positive vibes between staff and pupils. Parents say plenty of sport and practical activities like car club are just right.

Background and atmosphere: Founder, Steve Chinn, taught dyslexics in USA before opening Mark College as a leap of faith in 1986. School has grown like Topsy but remains unpretentious and relatively small scale. Recent acquisition by Priory Group to become their flagship dyslexic school is allowing school to 'upgrade and expand'. Administrative offices, staff room plus some teaching and boarding facilities centred in listed, red-bricked Mark House. Cluster of converted buildings all close by on peaceful 24-acre site lined by splendid trees and backing onto farmland. Easy access to junction 22 on nearby M5 enables frequent visits (now in MPVs more than in minibuses) to coast and nearby towns for shopping at weekends etc. Dining hall accommodates whole school and is used for assemblies. Pupils say food OK – best at weekends when numbers are smaller.

Pastoral care and discipline: Mainly long-serving, experienced staff, with some young care staff and teachers. Parents comment on 'good pastoral support'. We saw boarding arrangements with privacy for older boys and girls plus common rooms with recreational and some self-catering facilities. Small dorms in Mark House for younger pupils help them to get to know one another. Head of care lives on site; married house managers with dogs etc make for a homely atmosphere. Most year 11 students become prefects with extra privileges in return for duties; withdrawal of extra tuck or early bedtimes used as sanctions but heavy discipline uncommon.

Pupils and parents: Unpolished but engaging boys and girls who get along well with each other; school raises self-esteem and it shows. Complete social mix here; many have chequered earlier school history; a few from overseas. Lessons designed to cope with short attention spans: ADD 'goes with the territory', according to principal; she won't accept emotionally disturbed pupils or severe Asperger's. A few day pupils stay for prep before going home and can arrange to sleep over.

Entrance: Parents send educational psychologist's report and statement is present before initial visit is arranged. Prospective pupils carry out a trial at school for informal assessment. Normally one class entry (maximum eight pupils) in years 7 and 8, with two classes or more in years 9-11, but this varies – when we visited over one third of boys were in year 10. Some each year from specialist dyslexic schools, eg Appleford in Wiltshire and Belgrave in Bristol.

Exit: Most stay on or go to schools on CreSTeD register that offer continued support, though some leave already able to cope with mainstream 16+ education.

Money matters: About 40 per cent of pupils receive post-tribunal LA funding; remainder fee-paying, but many parents can't afford full five years. We hope that fees will be maintained at their current 'reasonable' levels and feel that current principal really wants this – time will tell.

Remarks: Now with girls. Focused and specialist teaching; size and setting allow a committed and interestingly diverse staff to, 'achieve what they set out to do'. Lucky ones who get here (after what has often been an impossible situation in mainstream education) often 'enjoy school for the first time'.

M

Marlborough College

Marlborough, Wiltshire, SN8 1PA

- Pupils: 920 boys and girls; 900 full boarders and 20 day pupils
- Ages: 13–18 • C of E • Fees: Boarding £32,280; Day £27,420 pa
- Independent

Tel: 01672 892300
Email: admissions@marlboroughcollege.org
Website: www.marlboroughcollege.org

Master: Since 2012, Mr Jonathan Leigh. Educated as a chorister at St George's, Windsor before moving on to Eton College and then Corpus Christi College, Cambridge, where he was a choral exhibitioner and read history.

Previously head of Ridley College in Canada and before that head of Blundell's School (where he introduced full co-education, promoted flexible boarding and brought a local prep school on to the campus) and second master of Cranleigh School. Married to Emma, also a Cambridge history graduate.

Academic matters: Now offering A levels, the IB and the Pre-U – something for everyone. That is really the keynote here in general – a wealth of opportunities of all kinds. In 2013, 58 per cent A*/A grades at A level and Pre-U; at GCSE, 79 per cent A*/A grades. Options include astronomy – school has the Blackett Observatory which houses the best telescope in any UK school and everyone gets a chance to use it in year 9. Outreach also brings in users from local primaries and preps and various other groups – a real gift. 24 A level options include four mainstream languages, business, classical civilisation, DT and (very popular) politics. Surprisingly few – compared to elsewhere – for music tech. Massive numbers for English lit, biology, history and maths.

Excellent innovation is 'Form'. Children in the first year – 'Shell' – follow a course which integrates English, history and RE, all taught by one teacher. Sounds like real education – is anyone in government listening? The IB – 'We won the Common Room over' – now getting under way, with an average of 35 points in 2012. The Master was keen because of its international perspective, because it 'offers a safety route in case A levels get further devalued', because of its 'philosophical attraction' and the 'remarkable intellectual challenge' it offers the Common Room. Good new staff intake – many from the top London day schools. Exceptionally high teacher:pupil ratio. Excellent library – a delight for the mind and eye.

Around one in nine pupils have some kind of learning support – three full-time SEN staff see them either one-to-one, in-class or withdrawn; some is free, some charged for, eg lots of individual support. Very extensive site but can and will accommodate wheelchairs – ramps and general access recently upgraded.

Games, options, the arts: Terrific games – aided by good staff (including former captain of Leicestershire cricket, an Olympic gold medallist) and fabulous facilities which include a swimming pool, 25 metres long, with an adjustable floor – either sloping or deep for diving: everyone we spoke to told us about this. Individual and team successes in, particularly, fives, lacrosse, rugby, netball, hockey and football. Has produced 38 rugby internationals and four England captains. Football coached by pros from Swindon FC, lacrosse by former England international. Lots more including shooting, polo and everything else you can think of.

DT excellent – we saw wonderfully creative artefacts derived from field trips, eg litter bins, benches and butterfly feeders. Casting in all kinds of materials here. Thirty per cent of DT A level candidates are girls. Art everywhere – art school a big, bright, airy place full of eager beavering. Art a serious matter here – great tradition of history of art (see Old Marlburians below): seen as culturally and intellectually central to the ethos. Film editing suite, photography, varied and imaginative ceramics.

Superb music under outstanding, internationally renowned head of department, with wonderful facilities. Everyone involved in some kind of music and around half learn one or more instruments: 'They've encouraged my wholly unmusical boys to play instruments – inspirational teaching'. Concerts in and out of college, and a good range of music here: not just guitars and drums but the real thing – along with guitars and drums. Recent concert of opera scenes impressive. Drama – lots of quality performance space – also outstanding: recent productions from a York Mystery play to The Seagull and A Winter's Tale.

Moving towards a surer sense of its place in the outside world. One knock-on will be a greater emphasis on socially responsible trips – 'rather than super-charged tourism', a loss for some but addressing the gripes from some parents who feel that the very expensive trips the school has offered are, of necessity, exclusive. Plenty to do at weekends – though some feel could be more for the less academic and non-sporty. Loads of trips and tours – art to NY, geography to Tenerife, Russian scholars to St Petersburg, netball to Barbados and 'wilderness trip' to S Africa. Oh to be a child again!

Background and atmosphere: Founded in 1843 for the sons of the clergy for the south of England. Imposing red-brick quadrangle, with elegant Queen Anne building at the head of the court, contrasting with Memorial Hall built after World War I, and archaeologically important earthwork known as The Mound in the middle of it all. Mix of interesting buildings from all eras since includes vast and glorious chapel in late Victorian Gothic – perhaps the most impressive we know; pupils clearly proud of it. Also the War Memorial Assembly Hall – 'the best piece of American campus architecture this side of the Atlantic' – with a stunning theatre rather like the Harrow 'Speecher'. Extraordinary features here and there, eg a real Egyptian mummy, found by some pupils in a store cupboard, now glass-cased in the foyer of the languages and classics department. Grounds and gardens are beautiful and include the Master's garden with a quite wonderful vast beech tree, under which we saw a glorious pool of mauve crocuses.

Has its own argot – the year groups, for instance, are: Shell = year 9, followed by Remove, then Hundreds, then, prosaically, sixth form. Wide range of views from parents: 'In some ways it's very progressive,' we were told. 'In others it's incredibly dyed-in-the-wool and needs to move into the 21st century.' Most agree that the end result is a well-mannered, sensible young adult.

New-ish head of upper school upping the notion of service in the school's extra-curricular activities – going some way, perhaps, to meet the complaints of some parents who feel the school is too inward-looking and insufficiently socially responsible. Witness latest new-build, which has solar panels and a ground source heat pump – 'This is the way society ought to be moving'. School has opened a branch in Malaysia – not a franchise but a real partner, and much exchanging is intended. Also a new international study centre.

Pastoral care and discipline: Fifteen houses – six for boys, five for girls and four mixed (though the sexes are segregated on different floors, wings etc). This is, in all ways, a full boarding school, though a very few local day pupils also attend. No plans – or pressure – to offer weekly/flexi boarding. Provision varies – pupils move rooms each term with no choice of room-mates, but a feeling that this works well and prevents exclusiveness. Good kitchens ('brew areas') and lots of excellent single rooms for the older pupils. Some houses have decision-making, democratic 'year group councils'. Good common-rooms – TVs, sofas, PCs, and everywhere is intra netted. 'Outhouses', ie those houses which are more than five minutes away, have their own dining rooms, where breakfasts and dinners are taken. Lunches and all meals for everyone else in vast dining room – 'Can feed 1500 in one and a half hours'. Food good. Excellent on-site medical team – surgery held daily. Good support for travel arrangements at start and end of terms.

All parents we spoke to emphasised the importance of getting into the 'right' house. In other words, visit, ask questions, be sure it feels right. Girls' boarding – for which we have previously reported that you needed to be 'robust' – now seemingly 'fantastic': we heard only ecstatic reports. Not so, in all cases, boys' boarding. Much of it also 'fantastic' and house staff reported 'lovely', though too many reports of the housemaster being 'so lovely but not strong enough' kind. Also reports of bullying not properly dealt with, far too much cavalier nicking of other people's possessions and a careless attitude among staff over such things in some houses. We even heard reports of 'initiation rites' still current in one or two houses – not quite the roasting over an open fire, but still not acceptable. (College assures us that these matters are being dealt with.) Some parental feeling that the dame system for younger boys could be more caring. In other houses, not enough care taken to ensure boys get to bed early enough. New Proctor has a responsibility for fair discipline across the whole college community.

Plans to up the number of girls, but not by much: 'It wouldn't work – the girls would steam-roller the boys'. True, the girls who come in for the sixth do balance the numbers and seriously impress. They generally go into a mixed house 'so as not to disrupt friendship groups' – for example on an upper floor over the junior boys. Lots of rules in school almanac – dress code largely adhered to, but rules on mobiles only in houses in the evening clearly now 'relaxed'. Ongoing boyfriend/girlfriend relationships manifest in the way some pairs had their arms around each other – very sweet, we thought, and nice that they don't feel it has to be hidden. Out for dealing drugs, a one-chance testing policy otherwise. 'We make plentiful use of breathalysers and we've a drive on smoking at the moment – there's too much of it.' Only good reports of sixth form boarding, but clearly work still to do lower down.

Pupils and parents: All the girls we saw had uniformly long hair and were very pretty. A generally relaxed feel, though a certain prevailing sense that you still need to be 'tough' if you're a boy and young. Families largely traditional boarding types, though much new money and some few from overseas. Notable OMs include William Morris, Anthony Blunt, John Betjeman, Nicholas Goodison, Wilfrid Hyde White, James Robertson Justice, Lord Hunt (of Everest fame) Francis Chichester, Peter Medawar, Louis MacNeice, Siegfried Sassoon, James Mason, Bruce Chatwin and Frank Gardner. Along with synods of bishops and masses of generals, brigadiers etc. Oh, and Sam Cam and Kate Middleton were here too.

Entrance: Visit any time after birth. Three years prior to entry go to an Open Day, visit houses, chat to housemasters/mistresses; then come back in the September two years before entry to see more houses and have more chat; then apply by November 5 in year 7, at which point the College will write to your child's prep for an assessment, which will count for 50 per cent of the total one. Individual arrangements are made for overseas pupils or those at primaries, but all candidates are assessed at the College. Ten per cent of assessment via the 'Durham test': an ingenious online reasoning/number skills exercise – 'very expensive' and very subtle, 'much more accurate than CE'. It even takes into account dyslexia and dyspraxia. Remaining 40 per cent from interviews. Official CE pass is 60 per cent, but this is flexible – 'We don't want to be an academic hothouse'.

Don't hear that too often. Around half the applicants get places. For sixth form entry, a minimum of six GCSEs at B, including English and maths.

Pupils from everywhere, but many from Cheam, The Dragon, Farleigh, Highfield, Port Regis and Windlesham.

Exit: Not all parents impressed with careers and university guidance – 'We had to do it all on our own,' we heard. However careers now being given a shake-up by being moved to the centre of the college. Around three-quarters take gap years. Manchester, Bristol and Leeds the most popular destinations for several years now; much the most popular courses are in history, art history, modern languages. Annually between 15-20 to Oxbridge (16 in 2013). Very few to the London colleges and no sign yet of an exodus across the pond as elsewhere.

Money matters: Lots of awards at 13 and 16; unusually generous provision for a) Forces children, b) clergy children. Worth getting ordained for, but also worth getting the booklet – far too much up for grabs to describe here.

Remarks: The quintessential English boarding school, now moving towards a more international, more modern future.

The Mary Erskine School

Linked schools: ESMS (Erskine Stewart's Melville School); Stewart's Melville College

Ravelston, Edinburgh, EH4 3NT

• Pupils: 750 girls (almost all day) • Ages: 11–18. (Separate entry for junior school) • Non-denom • Fees: Day £9,726; Boarding £19,023–£19,512 pa • Independent

Tel: 01313 475700
Email: admissions@esmgc.com
Website: www.esms.edin.sch.uk

Principal: Since 2000, Mr David Gray BA PGCE (fifties), who was educated at Fettes, read English at Bristol, where he did his PGCE. Taught English in a Bristol comprehensive, before moving to a language school in Greece, then taught English and modern Greek at Dulwich College and was head of English at Leeds Grammar, before heading Pocklington School in East Yorkshire, for eight years. Since the Stewart's Melville vast conglomerate forms the largest independent school in Europe, it is not surprising he feels he is in a position here 'to give something back to Scotland, having been away for almost a quarter of a century'. Brought up in Inverness, he is proud of his Scottish roots and sees himself and Stewart's Melville/ Mary Erskine as at the 'most exciting cutting edge of Scottish education', and stresses that he's the first overall principal who is actually Scottish. Mr Gray spends part of the week in each school. We visited him at his base in Mary Erskine, where he was busily involved in compiling a history of the school for his teaching contact with the girls.

Very much a hands-on head, the principal reckons to keep sane (and fit) by swimming and jogging at 7am each morning, and is a familiar sight as he cycles between the two campuses. He also 'works the room' quite beautifully – 'We all think we know him well and that he knows our children almost as well as we do,' said one father (a gift no doubt inherited from his politician father?). Keen on promoting self-confidence in his pupils, he sees himself as an 'educator' and is teaching English and coaching cricket at Stewart's Melville. After eight years he feels pleased that the school has 'become a gentler place' and that the 'children are wedded to our ethos of reasonable,

M

sensible behaviour'. No need for draconian action on the discipline side recently – when silliness occurs, 'the student body can be very conservative on behaviour,' while parents 'don't want to be ashamed of the school'.

Mr Gray runs the twin senior schools with two deputy heads and the head of the co-ed junior school, Bryan Lewis, who is also vice principal. Mrs Linda Moule took over as deputy head of The Mary Erskine School in August 2009; she was previously vice principal of New Hall School, Chelmsford. Mr Neal Clark, depute head of Stewart's Melville for the last ten years, describes himself as a 'grammar school boy, in tune with Scottish social culture'. All school facilities have been upgraded in the last ten years, 'so future plans are for maintenance rather than development'.

Academic matters: The principal and three heads have agonised together over the pros and cons of single-sex v co-ed. All four speak with the same passion – and often the same phrasing – of their 'best of both worlds' system. Boys and girls educated together at junior school, separately from age 12-17 – gains for girls (being able to get on with learning) and boys (feeling free to talk about poetry etc); then the social etc gains of co-education for the sixth year and all activities. 'Not a highly selective school' – however described by an educationalist as a 'grade one academic machine'. Classes of up to 25 (20 for practical classes) setted, with groups subdivided to extend the most able.

School has embraced the new Advanced Higher in depth – greater analysis, independent study, projects and dissertation. Mr Clark – though pleased that this year's SMC sixth year averaged two AH passes – would like three to be the norm. Recent results show a pleasing number of As and Bs across the board in both schools, with some outstanding successes in history, sciences and maths. Advanced Higher results in 2013: 43 per cent A. Higher results also impressive (84 per cent A-B; 63 per cent A in 2013), particularly at MES 'on the languages front' and for SMC in history and geography. French, German, Spanish and Latin on offer to Advanced Higher Grade.

Since 2002, Standard Grades phased out (except drama) in favour of Intermediate 2 (which is based on the same assessment pattern as Highers). Results pretty impressive here too.

Very good links (still) with the Merchant Company, which provides masses of business breakfasts and connections with professional firms around Edinburgh. Single IT network across all three schools with 'massive schools' intranet', interactive whiteboards galore and close on 1000 computers. Biology department links with the horticultural department of the world famous Edinburgh Botanic Gardens. Impressive careers structure across both schools and excellent library facilities. Pupils can sign in for private study.

Schools combine for sixth form, most extras and pastoral structure. In the interests of integration, sixth formers have to take academic courses from both schools – a feat resulting in limitless (almost) variety of course permutations, miraculous timetabling and quite a few bus journeys. Outstanding back up for those with learning difficulties – school has its own educational psychologist; 'some on Ritalin'; 'will never abandon anyone'.

Games, options, the arts: Big is beautiful, providing a list of over 75 different clubs for all, from goldsmithing to Greek, costume design to curling and cross country, lunchtime and post school – popular. Major sports have separate clubs for ages/stages and 27 rugby teams. Good at football too. Girls prefer hockey and basketball, still better at shooting than boys, and both sexes join the voluntary CCF (trillions of girls, over 400 members in all). A second super new floodlit Astroturf at MES, 'so everyone gets a chance'; dramatic wavy roofed swimming pool (at Stewart's Melville) with co-ed sixth form slump-out room adjacent, new gym (at MES), cricket pavilion (MES again). FPs and current pupils share sporting facilities at MES; extra games pitches at Inverleith.

Needle matches in almost all disciplines, with FPs representing both county and country across the board.

Incredibly strong drama – regular performances at the Edinburgh Festival and throughout the year at the Playhouse etc. Masses of every sort of orchestra. New £2.5m performing arts centre's opening splash was Snowman composer, Howard Blake, and Scottish Chamber Orchestra. Centre took 12 years in the planning – seats 800 with a 'retractable' stage and dividing walls, replacing the old assembly hall, which was huge and impressive, and jolly nice in its way. Pupils can learn to fly and ski (Hillend and the real thing: the Alps, Canada). Brilliant debating team – regularly the Scottish Debating Champions and European Youth Parliament finalists; SMC has represented Great Britain abroad all over the shop. Good home economics. Art spectacular – dramatic artroom atop MES (with adjoining pottery and greenhouse).

Background and atmosphere: Stewart's Melville campus is based round the magnificent David Rhind-designed Daniel Stewart's Hospital, which opened in 1885 and merged with Melville College in 1972. Fairy-tale Victorian Gothic with a cluster of necessary modern additions, surrounded by ever-decreasing games pitches and car parks. The old chapel is now a library, complete with organ and stained-glass windows. Stewart's Melville is also home to the senior department of the junior school – see separate entry.

Mary Erskine was founded in 1694, as the Merchant Maiden Hospital, moved to Ravelston in 1966, changing its name to The Mary Erskine School, and amalgamated with the boys' school in 1978 (girls wear charming Mary Erskine tartan kilts). MES clusters in decidedly 1960s architecture – with now quite a lot of more modern extensions, round the pretty but sadly overwhelmed Ravelston House (1791): swimming pool, tennis courts, games pitches, Astroturfs etc, the last much used by FPs. The nursery department and the youngest classes of the junior school are also based here – see separate entry.

Smart dining room complex serves all juniors and 80 per cent of seniors opt in. Sixth form coffee bars with stunning overview of school and pitches.

Two boarding houses, Dean Park House and Erskine House, furnished like large (and very well-equipped) family houses and based on the edge of the Stewart's Melville campus. Tremendous family feel – boarders are encouraged to invite friends home, caring house parents, only 56 boarding places.

Regular buses from East and West Lothian and Fife service both schools, which operate as one, under the auspices of Erskine Stewart's Melville Governing Council. Each school, though, is fiercely proud of its individual heritage.

Pastoral care and discipline: Both schools have a tutorial system for the first year, followed by house system in upper schools. Houses are common to both schools and house competitions have mixed sex teams. Good links with parents. Brief is that 'all children have a right to be happy here'. Code of conduct established by consulting pupils so 'they know exactly where they stand'. Excellent anti-bullying policy: wary pastoral staff and peer-support group 'with professional training' stop 'children slipping through the net'. Sophisticated PSE programme right up the school, including study skills. Buddy system for those coming up from junior schools.

Automatic expulsion – 'zero-tolerance' – for those bringing in illicit substances – 'Those on the periphery of the same incident will not necessarily be excluded, but can come back in as long as they agree to random testing'. Smoking 'unacceptable and pupils suspended'. Alcohol 'not an issue in school'.

Pupils and parents: Edinburgh hotch-potch of New Town and suburbs, with many first-time buyers and lots up from England. Siblings and FPs' children. Taking over a third of Edinburgh's independent secondary pupils, it's less élitist and perhaps less dusty than some city schools. Children living far out can spend the night when doing evening activities. Parent-teacher group ('the red socks brigade') slightly better organised into a Friends of the School group – fundraising, ceilidhs, 'good cash cow'.

Entrance: At 11,12, 13 or sixth form – otherwise 'by default'. Automatic from junior school. Entrance assessments held in January but can be arranged at any time. Waiting lists for some stages but just go on trying. Entrance to upper school is by interview, plus school report plus GCSEs/Standard grades (five credit passes for S5 entry.) Numbers up overall.

Exit: Minimal leakage pre Highers; most sixth year (96 per cent) go on to university (gap years growing in popularity, especially for girls), most opt for Scottish universities but a few Oxbridge (2 in 2012), London, Bristol etc. SATS (for American colleges) not a problem. Art college, music/drama are popular alternatives.

Money matters: Scholarships/bursaries available, some linked to the Merchant Company, others sibling directed. 'No child will be left wanting in a (financial) crisis.'

Remarks: A glance at the school mags, Merchant Maiden and The Collegian, sums it up: bags of boys' poetry, multiple hockey, rugby and cricket teams, Oxbridge places, fabulous art, photos and writing, plus fascinating glimpses from boys and girls reporting on the same activities with subtly different views.

An outstanding school: happy pupils, happy staff – focused on self-development with impressive results.

Marymount International School

George Road, Kingston upon Thames, KT2 7PE

- Pupils: 260 girls; day and boarding - Ages: 11–18 - RC (but all faiths welcome) - Fees: Tuition: £17,520–£20,020; Boarding supplement £12,290–£13,720 pa - Independent

Tel: 020 8949 0571
Email: admissions@marymountlondon.com
Website: www.marymountlondon.com

Headmistress: Since 2010, Sarah Gallagher MA (mid-forties). Educated at a convent school, she studied for her degrees at University College Galway. Previous teaching and leadership posts at boarding and day schools including Queensgate, Lord Wandsworth College, most recently St Leonards-Mayfield School, taught in Rome. Dips in to teach Latin at Marymount from time to time.

Attractive, stylish and poised, she is articulate and empathetic in her interactions with others, strategic in her approach. The girls say she is 'busy and important' but also approachable. 'Ms Gallagher is so intelligent that you just think to yourself you could not possibly have a conversation with her, but when you do she is lovely.' Can picture this head on Mastermind or in the finals of a schools' edition of 'Strictly'. Husband also a teacher, two daughters at university. 'I want to build on the strength already here, a tremendous appreciation for learning and its significance in the school and its application outside school. The girls are learning for life; building character and community is integral to this. It's an exciting place to work, parents and students are committed, the philosophy of the IB and RHSM and Marymount London are all compatible.'

Academic matters: Marymount is a Catholic secondary girls school offering the IB Middle Years (MYP) and IB to an international community. The first (1979) girls' school in the UK to take up the IB in Britain, Marymount's grade 6-10 curriculum

is built on solid institutional foundations. In 2013 pupils scored an average of 34.71, with more than 20 per cent earning 40+ points. Last year one candidate achieved a perfect score (45), a result attained by fewer than 0.2% of students worldwide and several other Marymount girls have achieved similar in previous years.

No resting on laurels, they've been reviewing the MYP to align it with IGCSE content, ensuring all topics are covered in the IBMYP context by end of grade 9. Gallagher wants parents to be assured of MYP rigour, the priority is to be learning-driven, not taught to the test. Range of IB subjects and results is excellent. Lots of sciences, 'and we do lots of field trips', say the girls. The school is offering a relatively new IB course, environmental systems and societies, which satisfies either the IB science or IB humanities requirement. 'My sister likes geography and science so it's perfect for her.' Marymount's MYP covers the broad spectrum of disciplines, with the interesting addition of philosophy to introduce the girls to, 'the language of philosophy', before they embark on theory of knowledge at diploma level. As would be expected, religious education is also a key part of the programme.

School prides itself on the wide range of languages offered. Extra mother tongue support in German and French in grades 6-8 dependent on enrolment. Parents warn that languages are sometimes subject to demand and in a small school it's not always possible to satisfy all requests for second language. It seems that there are mixed messages here and prospective parents are advised to discuss this at the early stages to clarify. The school does its best to support girls in working out alternative options – as one pupil explained, 'a friend who speaks Thai is taking IB Thai mother tongue; she's self-taught with the help of a tutor'.

The school is wireless throughout; iPads now in grades 6-9 and will move up the grades as pupils progress; girls were excited to show off the first new Mac TVs, there are more to come. The library has undergone a complete refurbishment – it has 9,000 volumes and membership of London Library enhances the collection.

Classes never more than 16 and many, particularly at diploma level, only four to six, fewer still for languages. Some classrooms are designed with small seminar-style groups in mind.

The teaching faculty is an international bunch, average age forties. Pupil-teacher ratio is six to one and staff seem to know most of the girls, affirming parent comments about supportive and nurturing environment with a caring individualised approach. Low turnover and enough long-termers to provide a cohesive core. Plenty of support staff and school nurse on site.

Mild/moderate learning difficulties and other issues managed collaboratively by the learning resource coordinator, teachers, parents and students themselves. Lots of individualised support throughout the school and the girls themselves were quick to talk about peer tutoring offered during free periods or after school.

The enrichment programme for able students has about 40 on the register. These students are invited to apply to programmes sponsored by Ivy Leagues (Stanford, Yale, Princeton, Johns Hopkins) and top tier UK universities. Additional provision includes extra-curricular activities as well as resources which are made available to students for independent study and wider reading.

Games, options, the arts: Mix of competitive and non-competitive sporting activities available for all grades on and off site. If the school does not offer a particular sport they will help connect with local teams. Marymount is part of the International School Sports Association and they have produced an impressive record of results in soccer, badminton and tennis at championship tournaments hosted by member schools in different parts of Europe. One pupil training with the Chelsea ladies' development squad and several play with the Richmond Volleyball Club. When girls were asked why they

M

chose Marymount, one replied that she came for the sport and when you hear that one of their football trainers is with Chelsea, no prizes for guessing which team Marymount girls support.

Musicians have plenty of opportunities to play in ensembles and chamber groups. About 20 per cent take private instrumental or singing lessons; school boasts a 100 per cent pass rate in grade exams. Entry to the choir is by audition and choristers participate in school concerts and annual tours to European cities, performing in major churches and cathedrals. Teachers encourage girls to perform in local festivals and competitions.

Drama is inclusive and the entire community builds up to a major production each year; in true girls' school tradition male roles are played by the girls. Keen thespians can participate in ISTA (International School Theatre Association) festivals and when we visited girls were buzzing about their weekend ISTA trip to Stratford upon Avon. LAMDA examinations offered. Visual arts seem focused on painting and photography –the girls tell us that the art teacher is an inspiring photographer. Framed art by generations of pupils displayed throughout the school.

Consensus is that the most fun of all is the 'international day', when everyone shares their culture and cuisine.'The Japanese do the best, and the [boarding] girls are already planning even though it's still months away'! Zumbathon – a fundraising activity involving the whole community beeping and bopping, swinging and swaying to music, was also highly popular and yielded no casualties.

As a Catholic IB school, community service involves everyone at Marymount. Middle school do environmental projects that include cleaning along the bank of the Thames. Older girls volunteer in local activities including soup kitchens and schools and further afield join other RHSM students in projects working with children in places such as Zambia. All students take part the spiritual life of the school and attend an annual retreat. Girls of all faiths come to Marymount and this provides opportunities for students to learn about other beliefs and traditions; care is taken to ensure that everyone feels comfortable at Mass and prayer. We visited on a Hindu feast day and the girls said they had started the day with a Hindu prayer; Muslim girls wear their headscarves with confidence.

Background and atmosphere: Established in Kingston in 1955 by ten nuns from the Religious of the Sacred Heart of Mary (RSHM), sent by the Eastern American Province. Mid-19th century French founder of RSHM aspired to provide charity for all classes through schools, homes and orphanages that worked interactively across socio-economic barriers. Schools opened in France, Ireland, Portugal, England, the US and later Latin America and the rest of the world. The first sisters who came to Kingston started a 'year abroad' programme for US university women, then a school offering the US secondary school curriculum. Early seventies saw the arrival of Sister Anne Marie Hill, a determined Irish mover-and-shaker, well known in international education circles and now executive director of the network of schools. She introduced the IB making the school more relevant to its growing international student body and reflecting RSHM's original ethos. During the noughties Marymount had a series of heads as RSHM grappled with transition to lay leadership and during that time the board of governors was created.

In Ms Gallagher the sisters seem to have found the ideal head who brings continuity at the top, leading the school from strength to strength thanks to the partnership forged with the RSHM sisters and the board she describes as 'independent and experienced'. Enrolments are at an all-time high and it's all-systems-go for development plans aimed at enhancing programmes and facilities. School works closely with the other Marymount partners under Sister Anne Marie's guidance,

meeting every 6-8 weeks to discuss areas such as strategic planning and communication. Increasingly involvement with the international network of RMSH schools – 19 worldwide – is now bringing more opportunities to the pupils.

The school is based in an affluent part of Surrey occupying a large Edwardian house plus various more recent additions connected by walkways. Elegant grounds with lawns, manicured flowerbeds and sculpted hedges. 'The teddy bear topiary sold me', says one dad, 'How can you not love a school that has teddy bear topiary?' (We presume he had already consulted the GSG about minor details such as teaching and pastoral care.) Main house with original wood panelling and stained glass, is head office and reception. Oldest boarders have the spacious shared bedrooms above and the remaining nuns living in a wing just off their hall. Sisters no longer teach but are very much part of the fabric of the school, occasionally eating or sharing cocoa and study evenings with the girls. The nuns are loved by the girls and parents appreciate their presence.

Modern blocks house multi-purpose classrooms, the library and university and careers counselling rooms. Another block has the gym (floor replaced recently), music rooms and auditorium for assemblies, all-school Mass, drama. Yet another has more dorms, cafeteria (food is 'so-so', particularly at weekends), classrooms, infirmary, student lounges. A new quasi-Scandinavian wooden structure houses more small tutorial rooms just right for the many language classes and designed with IB language examination conditions in mind. Most of the buildings surround the garden and have big windows that bring the outdoors in and give a refreshing sense of space and light.

Boarding rooms and facilities are clean and pretty tidy. Boarding areas are kept locked during the school day unless a girl has a reason to be back in her room. The school's proximity to Heathrow is an attraction for boarding parents, the girls say that the school's proximity to London is the attraction for them! Small school chapel is used by boarders and local community alike and plans to re-develop and open the ceiling to the rafters and heavens above are underway.

Pastoral care and discipline: Spiritual values underpin the ethos of Marymount, rooted in the mission of the RSHM, 'that all may have life'. These values are made explicit on the website, even the most casual browser will see them on every page, running alongside photos. School welcomes girls from all faiths but we think it might not be a comfortable environment for the girl who has none.

Plenty of support available at the school: academic, social, emotional and personal; more expertise called upon if necessary. The headmistress is well briefed and aware of anyone who may be feeling overwhelmed, unhappy, unsettled. Girls say she shows genuine interest.

Parents Association hosts a welcome back family barbecue during the first weekend of the school year when boarding parents are there dropping off daughters so they are able to meet day families. One parent said the school went out of its way, allowing their daughter to board temporarily so she could start at the beginning of the year, before the family transfer to London took place. Another described how the teachers made an effort to encourage her daughter to join the orchestra for a big performance, even though her late arrival meant she had missed several rehearsals.

Clear procedures allow boarders off-campus freedoms to visit friends and family while ensuring their safety. One guardian who has long looked after boarders during half-term breaks told us that some older girls feel the school is too strict. She helps them, and their far-off parents who hear the grumbles, appreciate that the school is being understandably cautious and not at all unreasonable. Worth mentioning here that the school also takes weekly boarders from local (ie London) families and it is sometimes possible to arrange short-term boarding for day girls whose parents travel. Two exclusions in the last three years of boarders who, after several warnings, broke the rules about leaving campus.

Pupils and parents: Marymount girls are internationally diverse, cheerful, articulate, academically motivated, quietly confident and as a bunch, quite enchanting. More aspirational then ambitious, they love their school and really enjoy having peers from all over the world. They look out for each other, especially new ones, and although one day girl says she wishes there were more ways to get closer to the boarders, everyone, including day parents, feels that the day girls and boarders are pretty integrated.

The girls are reflective about the realities of being in a single-sex environment. They feel they are able to focus more on learning, but they would like to find a 'partner' boys' school and the student council have made some moves in this direction. Trouble is that 'all the boys' (schools) seem to be taken', but they have not given up. Gallagher is a big advocate of the girls' school advantage, having also worked in mixed schools. 'When adolescent girls become interested in boys, it can be frustrating to see how much they measure themselves against the approval of the boys in the group. Without that distraction they can develop as intellectually rigorous learners, they are their own people.'

The families that choose the school value the ethos of school, its Catholicism and internationalism, but are equally attracted to the IB. There are 40 nationalities in the school, British representing just over half. Other significant groups are German, Spanish, Japanese, Chinese, US, Australian, Korean and Italian. The numbers within these groups are balanced very carefully to facilitate integration. The school bus service extends into London to Sloane Square and more routes are under consideration.

Parents association organises events including outings for parents which are appreciated by newly-arrived expats.

Entrance: Local families are urged to attend one of the open days. Inbound expats on 'look-see' trips to London may book appointments. Girls' admissions based on availability and a review of school reports and teacher references. The headmistress interviews all girls prior to offering a place. English language fluency is required with exceptions made for younger students for whom English is a second language. Most classes have waiting lists so best to apply a year in advance though there is some turnover so you could be lucky.

Local feeder schools include Holy Cross, The Study, Fulham Prep, St. Agatha's, The Grove, The Old Vicarage, The German School (Deutsche Schule London), Putney Park, Garden House, Unicorn School, Cameron House, Ursuline School. Day girls come from most SW London postcodes including Richmond, Wimbledon, Putney, Chelsea, South Kensington.

Exit: Small number leave to do A levels elsewhere. Most head to university and the chart we saw on the college counsellor's wall listing every 12th grader's destinations confirms that they are applying to many countries. Counsellor stays in close contact with parents, especially boarder parents, about each girl's plan and the process they must follow depending on the country of their destination. PSAT and SATs also offered.

In 2013 two to Oxford, with the rest going to Bristol, Durham, Cardiff, Exeter, Nottingham, UCL, Warwick, York, Royal Veterinary College, Royal Holloway, Central St Martin's London, Manchester, Surrey as well as universities in Ireland, Japan, Hong Kong, Switzerland and the US.

Money matters: School has no endowment so financial stability is maintained by tuition and fundraising initiatives. 'Being an international school and in the current economic climate, we need to be sure we are guarded and forward looking – we can't

rest on our laurels.' The PA also fundraise for activities that support the school and pupils.

Scholarships (academic, art, music, drama, sport, community service) for grade 6 and 8 students. Some offered for grades 10, 11 and 12. Some financial aid available for means-tested students. About 20 per cent of the pupils benefit from this.

Remarks: Successfully serves a niche market of internationally-minded families seeking a girls' school with a Catholic ethos. In the words of one parent, 'We've been over-the-top-happy. The school provides excellent support and people from all over the world fit in and are welcome there.'

The Maynard School

Linked school: The Maynard Junior School

Denmark Road, Exeter, EX1 1SJ

- Pupils: 365 girls, all day • Ages: 11–18 • Non-denom
- Fees: £11,268 pa • Independent

Tel: 01392 273417
Email: admissions@maynard.co.uk
Website: www.maynard.co.uk

Headmistress: Since 2009, Ms Bee Hughes, after seven years as deputy head of Hitchin Girls' School and a wide-ranging career including fifteen years in Hong Kong at Island School and West Island School (where she captained and coached national hockey team). Strong academic background: has an MBA and was heavily involved with University of Cambridge initial teacher training programme. Teaches in senior school, and philosophy in the extended studies programme in the sixth form.

Academic matters: Consistently excellent results: In 2013 85 per cent of papers were awarded A*-B at A level (60 per cent A*/A). At GCSE 72 per cent A*/A. No Sats. No early entries – 'Girls should enjoy GCSEs,' says head. Outstanding maths department (two-thirds take it beyond GCSE). Further maths plus good number continue subject at university. Sciences strong too – modern labs and dedicated staff. We watched a year 10 biology group conducting chromatography experiments to test for food additives. Outstanding English department also bags top grades. Twenty-three subjects taken to A2 level, plus AQA Baccalaureate – lots of small sets. Food science (super refurbished facility) and textiles have regular takers but DT as a separate subject disappeared some years ago – accommodation apparently unsuitable; a pity, we thought.

Commitment to learning support has helped make school more inclusive. SENCo (an OG) fell into post by default but has made it her own. Only one girl statemented (with hearing impairment) but 35 girls currently have 'profiles'. Full assessment for SpLD and look-out for difficulties in maths. Free learning support generally offered when first required. ESL teaching as required. School counsellor comes in to see girls on regular basis. Head believes shape of day is important – three hour-long lessons in morning, long lunch break for activities, then assembly and two further lessons. We liked the idea of lower 3 (year 6) girls having lessons in senior school prior to transfer at 11+. Parents confirm younger Maynardians 'aren't overburdened with homework'; head has wanted girls to get as much as possible done in lessons. Fair enough – especially given distances many of them travel daily.

M

Games, options, the arts: Art and music housed in separate building, provides creative hub at centre of school. Separate sixth form art studio allows girls to spread work out as they like. Dark rooms for girls specialising in photography (not a separate A level, however). Two other spacious art studios for younger girls, plenty of strong and imaginative work on display. Music strong at all levels, 'charismatic teaching,' say parents. Some win music scholarships to specialist colleges and universities. Three orchestras, three choirs, plus a chamber orchestra and choir, jazz and wind bands, then various ensembles. Summer and autumn concerts and lots of less formal recitals. Six practice rooms and pianos everywhere.

Mostly in-house drama productions (handy little drama studio tacked behind main hall where major productions take place). Drama studied for GCSE and A level. LAMDA exams; girls participate in Exeter Competitive Festival each spring. When we visited girls were recovering from four successive nights of Sweeney Todd production. Girls and parents excited about recent appointment in drama: professional actor who has appeared regularly on TV and on stage. Sounds promising.

Surprisingly sporty for an academic school. Three on-site netball and tennis courts. Super-sized sports hall and magnificently refurbished gym, where we watched 30 or so sixth formers going through kick boxing paces led by a Rambo-like male instructor. Phew. Other activities include fencing, golf and aerobics. Girls walk to external swimming pool but are bused to nearby university Astroturf for hockey. National reputation for netball and basketball.

Overseas visits have included Russia, Iceland and, more recently, Borneo. Annual ski trip to Austria (travel by coach to save parents money and use British instructors who 'understand what is required'). World Challenge – 20 girls spent a month in Ladakh in summer hols. Work experience abroad is popular and gap years taken in far-flung places. Young Enterprise well established and Maynardians participate in European Youth Parliament each year as well as public speaking competitions. Ten Tors and D of E hugely popular. Loads of voluntary and charity effort, especially in sixth (eg Singing for the Brain – Alzheimer's charity; helping at hospices or schools for deaf or partially sighted). Popular weekly ESP (extended studies) programme for sixth form provides a wide choice from animation or ethics to self defence and sign language. Girls see it as a welcome change from formal studies. Sixth formers claim they 'can concentrate better in all girls' school' and that they 'motivate one another'.

Background and atmosphere: Founded in 1658 so school celebrated 350th anniversary in 2008. Moved in 1882 to its present 'island' site close to main competitors and a stone's throw from city centre. Former incarnations included boarding and direct grant status. Blue Boy statue commemorates historic link with St John's Hospital Trust, which still provides money for bursaries. Non-denominational and proud of it. 'Might seem a bit chaotic sometimes, but girls have a whale of a time and produce wonderful results,' declared one parent. Assemblies (sixth formers attend and take one assembly a week) generally have a Christian theme, though we watched year 9 girls performing classical Greek Lysistrata (somewhat censored). Lovely piece about women's power over men, though a shame one of the Greek 'women' dropped her 'baby' on stage – laughter all round. Girls and staff clearly on side with performers.

Attractive mosaic floor tiles create a sense of continuity with past generations. Honours boards around newly-refurbished main hall also echo past glories. Some fine new buildings – Pring, Ryan and classroom block, the Murdin Link – infill every available space; garden of reflection (created in memory of a girl killed in a train crash) and rose garden provide welcome intrusions of nature into an otherwise congested site.

Not overrun by computers, though good IT facilities in main and Pring buildings as well as in attractive sixth form centre and a new IT suite in the Link building. Laptops available for girls where needed. Recent building provides five extra classrooms and includes a lift for disabled access. State-of-art learning areas with 'nice clean lines'. Girls love reading and well stocked libraries are popular. Celebrating world book day with a competition – turn your classroom door into a book jacket, a novel idea, we thought. Low staff turn-over (many have 20 plus years' service). About a third male – 'I appoint whoever is best,' says head. 'The Maynard is a teaching paradise,' said one new arrival. 'It's bliss to teach in a place where pupils are enthusiastic,' commented another. Parents talk up school's friendly staff and atmosphere and confidence it inspires.

Pastoral care and discipline: Girls encouraged to behave responsibly. Rare misdemeanours dealt with sensitively by staff. Zero tolerance of bullying. Persistent bullies will be suspended, counselling provided. Smoking not tolerated ('by girls,' we were told) on or near site, let alone worse substances. Tutorial system overseen by heads of year responsible for academic progress and general welfare, girls see tutors twice daily. Carefully structured and monitored PSHE programme in all years. Plenty of careers teaching and hand holding through UCAS minefield. Two weeks' work experience for all girls at end of year 11. Innovative careers fair held in October – 'Jobs for the Girls' for girls across the city. One head girl and three or four deputies elected by peers and staff attend annual GSA leadership conference. Year 11 girls and below held to high standards of appearance, though uniform is practical rather than fussy – no tie, blouse designed to wear over kilt.

Year 10 girls trained to act as one-to-one peer supporters for year 7. School council run by head girl team comprises two reps from each form. Recent victories include return to 'proper' cutlery in dining-hall and better provision for storing kit on site. Small dining hall provides good choices including daily vegetarian and salad options – 'Girls love the meals,' said one mum. Some bring sandwiches – especially if they're busy at lunch-time. Sixth formers can make own snacks or go into city centre (few do). Lunch-time clubs run by sixth formers for younger pupils (see entry in Junior section). 'Sixth form atmosphere more like university,' say girls, who clearly enjoy comparative freedom and being taught by staff they know well. Parents praise way staff motivate their daughters and 'give extraordinary amounts of time'. Girls are 'encouraged to do lots of things and are recognised for their achievements'.

Pupils and parents: A really mixed bunch. One third from city, remainder from as much as 50 miles away: Plymouth, also Taunton, Barnstaple, South Hams and Lyme Regis. Parents operate successful bus schemes to serve main Exeter independents.

Most parents are professionals, business people and university types. Very few overseas. Lack of pretentiousness. We liked fact that girls give feedback to head when prospective staff are interviewed. Parents help with careers advice etc and say, 'There is never a feeling of not being wanted'. Parents' association does plenty of fund-raising and socialising. Old girls include Professor Dame Margaret Turner-Warwick – first woman president of British Medical Council; Claire Morall, author, short-listed for Man Booker Prize 2003; Diana Brightmore-Armour, MD Lloyds TSB corporate banking division.

Entrance: Admission from seven to 15 is by entrance assessment and interview. Selection not just on academic results: girl with artistic potential was offered a place on basis of her portfolio though she had some weaknesses. 'Now her schoolwork has improved too,' said head. GCSE grades and interview for sixth form. Seamless entry from junior school with no further qualifying hurdles to clear between lower 3 (junior) and upper 3 year 7 (senior). Feeder schools include local state primaries plus Exeter Cathedral Prep, St Peter's, Lympstone and The New

School, Exminster. Head likes school being used by outside groups (eg sports clubs, Stagecoach and local churches) at weekends.

Exit: Virtually all sixth form proceed to higher education. Some leave after year 11 (for financial or other reasons) and are replaced by new arrivals. High proportion to Russell Group universities, three to Oxbridge in 2013.

Money matters: Governor assisted bursaries pay up to 45 per cent of fees for those in need. Two scholarships and two exhibitions awarded annually for music for years 7, 8 or 9. Sixth form scholarships are available for academic, music, sport and art. Sibling discounts offered. Governors deal sympathetically with extreme hardship. Sourcing trust funds has been very successful to support students. No major endowments.

Remarks: Leaves you with a good feeling. Academically successful but not at expense of friendly atmosphere. 'We chose the school because we liked the finished article,' said one mother. Girls have loads of support from one another as well as staff. Girls are 'kindly and thoughtful'. Parents seem relaxed and trust school to do a good job.

Mayville High School

Linked school: Mayville High School Junior Department

35–37 St Simon's Road, Southsea, PO5 2PE

• Pupils: 490; 240 boys, 250 girls; all day • Ages: nursery 2 years 9 months–4; pre-prep 4–7; junior school 7–11; senior school 11–16 • C of E • Fees: Senior £8,760–£8,835 pa • Independent

Tel: 023 9273 4847
Email: enquiries@mayvillehighschool.net
Website: www.mayvillehighschool.com

Headteacher: Since 2013, Linda Owens BEd (sixties). Was headteacher at Mayville from 1994 to 2008, during which time she oversaw the move from girls-only to 'co-education with a difference' – boys and girls taught in separate parallel classes. Firmly believes that unless children are happy, relaxed and have self-respect, they put up barriers to learning – so she considers a positive environment for pupils as the key to success.

She has given up skiing in France and looking after her grandson to return to Mayville for one academic year to ensure the school and its procedures are in the highest order, ready for the appointment of a new head in September 2014.

Academic matters: Boys and girls are taught separately for main subjects and the school's two-form entry means there's a boys' class and girls' class in each year group. Wide ability range, with mild to moderate dyslexia a speciality – the school has four highly trained dyslexia teachers. Lots of bright sparks too, but many who have wilted in more bracing environments respond well to the nurturing of a small friendly school. Mayville allows children to prove they are good at things. Not too much testing and no KS2 Sats as some children have fled here from all that.

Classes small – maximum of 24 in senior school, with some groups in single figures. History, geography, plus some drama, dance and music in mixed groups, but core of English, maths and sciences separate – 'because boys and girls learn differently'. Very keen on individual learning styles and giving homework differentiated for varying abilities. School achieves sound results for able children and has an impressive success rate in subjects taken by all – maths and Eng language and literature. Good mathematicians do statistics as well, with

considerable success. Nearly half do three separate sciences, the remainder doing dual award. Low-ish take up of languages (some dyslexic pupils drop French at KS3) but French and Spanish offered. Technology popular and well-equipped and plenty of IT and interactive whiteboards etc. Choices for GCSE tailored to fit needs of each group. In 2012, nearly 32 per cent A*/A grades at GCSE.

SEN is exceptional: well staffed and impressively organised. Provision made for the gifted and talented. Sensibly, Mayville only undertakes what it can do well, so very severely educationally challenged are not accepted.

Parents report that children's achievement and confidence improves – 'beyond our wildest dreams,' one told us. Highly qualified teachers do all the right polysyllabic things – multi-sensory, kinaesthetic etc, but above all they make the children feel they are achieving. A further six teaching assistants give classroom support. One parent commented of his son: 'He thought he was an idiot, but now he's ready to take on the world.' The combination of small classes, one-to-one teaching, kind, helpful teachers, setting and achieving their own targets and more time in school (a longer day with shorter breaks and more learning time) seems to work wonders for both the strugglers and the bright sparks.

Games, options, the arts: Sport four times a week, lots of fixtures with other schools, masses of enthusiastic teams. Only one netball court on site (used by one year group after another in staggered break times) but a massive playing field eight minutes away by minibus. Mayville is also a major user of the local authority sports centre just behind the school, so facilities are surprisingly plentiful.

Drama and performance skills something of a speciality. Dance for all, including specialist lifting classes which get the boys on board. All pupils can take part in anything, with everyone fully engaged and 'needed as part of the team.' Music block looks tiny but was purpose built and has whole class space and three practice rooms. It was locked on the day we visited 'because it wasn't the music teachers' day' and is crammed into what looks like a garage space, but there is now an orchestra (masses of flutes but a bit short on strings), choirs, jazz group and rock bands. All juniors are given experience of recorder, a brass instrument and violin and many of them go on to take up instruments. Biggish list of after-school clubs – St John's Ambulance, sport, digital photography etc are all well attended – plus supervised homework. Open from 8am till 6pm, 50 weeks a year, with holiday clubs for Mayville pupils only.

Background and atmosphere: Almost 500 pupils from three to 16 are crammed into five town houses and a bungalow, but even so, the place doesn't seem squashed. All four to 11-year-olds are now in purpose-built classrooms. Airy all-purpose hall, largish classrooms, new library, design technology area and SEN centre.

The rest of the accommodation is well used – even a bit battered in places – but neither parents nor pupils mind. Parents know they get excellent value and children respond to kindness and good teaching by trusting the staff and each other. The school has been in this collection of seaside villas, two streets from the sea, since before 1900. Has been through periods of being girls only but boys finally arrived to stay in 1995. Boys use the reception building as their form base while girls have one of the houses. Classrooms are hidden away up twisting staircases, the art room (very bright and modern when you get there) is perched in the attic and the much-used library takes up most of the main ground floor.

Pastoral care and discipline: Firm guidelines, but this is a happy and friendly school. A parent who accompanied a football tour commented on how considerate the children are to each other and how well mannered. Smart uniform with neat, trimmed blazers, pink gingham shirts (no ties) for girls and pink and

M

navy ties for boys; girls obviously like their scarlet games kit. Tinies – known as Cygnets, Swans and Kestrels – have practical all-in-one overalls for their weekly outings.

A sense of security is key. Asked what they value about the school, one parent told us: 'It's how they make my children feel.' Good behaviour is taken for granted and underlined by the notices about respect, consideration etc that appear at strategic points all over the school. Parents we spoke to said bullying is seldom a problem here, rules are very clear and the school gives very good guidance and education on issues such as the internet. They added that nothing is too much trouble and teachers always get back to them when they ring.

Pupils and parents: Most pupils are local, though the minibus routes include the Isle of Wight and Hayling ferry terminals. Down-to-earth, unsnobby PTA.

Entrance: No academic hurdle, just an interview. They recruit for balance, so where SENs are concerned they do turn away 'the one too many.' Dyslexia, dyspraxia, mild ADHD and ASD no problem, equally physical disabilities, but no emotional and behavioural disorders. 'There's only so much we can do.'

Exit: Havant and South Downs colleges popular, plus Peter Symonds College in Winchester. Some go to local sixth form colleges and academic independent sixth forms and a few straight on to BTECs etc. Lots of pupils progress to university afterwards.

Money matters: Fees are modest for what is provided and parents say it's well worth overtime and sacrifices. After-school care (tea included) is extra. Academic, creative arts and sports scholarships worth 50 per cent of fees. Some means-tested bursaries of up to 100 per cent.

Remarks: A real find for parents with children who need a little extra support. Friendly, business-like and affordable, it provides a wraparound care that identifies and develops children's individual talents. Whatever they are good at – academic, sporting or unusual skills like fire-eating or juggling – the school will find it and showcase.

McLaren High School

Mollands Road, Callander, FK17 8JH

• Pupils: 615 boys and girls • Ages: 11–18 • Non-denom • State

Tel: 01877 330156
Email: mclarenhs@stirling.gov.uk
Website: www.mclarenhigh.co.uk

Rector: Since 2004, Mr Peter Martin MA, who joined McLaren in 1990 as assistant head and was depute from 1996. A geographer, he loves the school and 'feels a strong responsibility to the area', though he actually lives in Bearsden (posh Glasgow). He sees McLaren as a community school, small but truly comprehensive both in ability range and socio-economic terms, serving families in all types of employment including some with none. His huge catchment includes the whole Loch Lomond and Trossachs national park, and his passion for outdoor education as a vehicle for learning draws inspiration from this area of stunning mountains and lakes. Involved with outdoor pursuits and the national implementation group for outdoor education, he believes it 'benefits all aspects of the development of the whole child'. Equally dedicated to quality 'improvement' (rather than 'assurance'), he proudly reports that Stirling Council (2011) was deeply impressed by McLaren's ethos and commitment to improvement. He encourages his staff, by example, to be as fully participative as possible in the many ski and other outdoor trips, which are 'a real learning experience of pupils and adults alike'.

Academic matters: Follows Scottish system with all mainstream subjects and a fair selection of practical courses (rural skills etc, though design technology is still at development stage). Could not provide subject specific exam results, but overall figures compare well with Scottish and Stirling figures and have moved pretty steadily upwards over the last few years: 68 per cent of pupils got the equivalent of five or more GCSE passes in 2012; 33 per cent got five or more Highers, 48 per cent three or more and 71 per cent at least one. Outstanding history, spurred on by lots of enthusiastic but rigorous teaching. Tellingly, demand for places on the battlefields trip exceeds demand for the Disneyland Paris trip!

Careful setting, max class size 30, with no more than 20 for practical subjects. French at all levels, some Spanish, business management up to Higher, also admin. Pupils work in flexible ability groups – 'individual timetables' and varying amounts of work experience where necessary. They are encouraged 'to aim for the best', 'take as many (exams) as you can'. Support, both academic and pastoral, is for everyone, the gifted as well as pupils with additional needs – good rooms available for individual counselling etc.

Labs, classrooms etc are all spanking new and up to date and lots of practical work (we met two pale girls retreating from dissection of a kidney – the rest clearly revelling in it). IT well equipped, interactive whiteboards in most classes. Lower school pupils clearly engaged in lessons while exam candidates had special revision classes available. Pupils trapped at home over snowy winter increasingly have access to course information via the internet. McLaren has embraced the spirit of the Scottish curriculum for excellence. S1 and 2 have a weekly 'Ace Challenge', which brings in outside experts and allows pupils and teachers to gain from methods of, for instance, professional artists. Mr Martin's conviction that outdoor experience is paramount is underlined by the large section on the website on role of outdoor experience in all subjects.

Special needs coordinated via the pupil support system, which assigns a teacher to each year group so as to have an overview of pupils' needs as they progress through their school career. Lots of individual help, from within school and Stirling specialist departments, and comprehensive learning resource centre (library in everyday speak) with help on hand and supervision for extra study/ homework etc. All achievement (academic or other) recognised.

Games, options, the arts: Given the time restrictions of a huge catchment requiring multiple coach runs, McLaren manages to pack in a lot: clubs and activities in the lunch hour and after school. Choirs, jazz, swing, guitar ensembles, string groups, lots of Scottish trad (pupils shine at the Mod). Stirling provides plentiful musical tuition in spite of other cutbacks, and even the most remote families manage to stay for after-school practices etc, thanks to supportive parents. Stirling's largest school orchestra in its smallest high school. In-school music festival with outside adjudicators – over a hundred pupils compete, with the non-musical pupils as supportive audiences. Impressive stage with professional-looking lighting for the annual musical – no one seemed quite sure whether it really was Guys and Dolls but everyone enthused.

The reinstated Dux Ludorum, ie the head of games, dating from 1904, is now awarded as a medal to the top boy and girl athlete. The on-site McLaren leisure centre is used for PE and fitness sessions, but gym and smashing dance areas in school. Rugby, for all levels and both sexes, tennis, cross-country etc supplemented by all sorts of other activities – canoeing, skiing, dance etc etc. All first year pupils do a residential outdoor activities course, as do fourth years, with other chances of outdoor pursuits – Duke of Edinburgh and its junior counterpart, the John Muir awards. Lots of excursions – skiing popular, with regular trips to France and Austria. Boundless trips and visits, from theatres, authors and artist field days et al – in line with the 'outdoor learning' ethos.

Background and atmosphere: McLaren High, established in 1892, grew from Free Church School in Callander, endowed in 1849 by Donald McLaren, a banker from the Strathearn area, who provided a 'salary of sufficient amount to induce men of superior talents and acquirements to become and continue to be teachers in the said school'. 'His daughter, Mary McLaren, ensured that the McLaren educational trust endowments were used for the benefit of the children throughout West Perthshire, including Balquhidder, without distinction of income or class.' The Clan McLaren's interest in the school is reciprocated and past pupils' networks are particularly strong. One member even attends annual reunions from New Zealand and several staff are past pupils. Pupils and parents see the school as a key element in the Trossachs community, with lots of links between local drama, jazz and traditional music, shared sports facilities and a section of the school available for community education. Pupil representatives are involved on local civic panel and are members of Stirling Council's student forum and of the School Improvement Planning Team.

Stunning site, on the edge of the river just south of Callander, with breathtaking views of Ben Ledi. A comprehensive refurbishment has provided a handsome, modern-looking school fit for the 21st century – 'like getting a new school but better because it keeps some of the character'. Central part of the school imaginatively retains the old school hall with flexible, Japanese-style, pale wood partitions cunningly placed to make a variety of spaces, including a modern cafeteria, much coveted for dances and ceilidhs. Buildings have been reorientated into a clean calm school, surprisingly bare, with restful eau de nil downstairs, but masses of pupil work in classroom area. Sculpted grass banks create an outside theatre space (in Scotland?) and pretty round columns with circular seats make a pleasant gathering space from a junction between old and new buildings.

The canteen is attractive and popular, with high take up meals prepared under the new 'Hungry for Success' healthy eating campaign. Cashless canteen system in operation, but could not cope with 100 percent take up, thus no worries about the 'healthy eaters' who choose the brisk walk into Callandar! Pupils drifting back for afternoon lessons, largely coatless in the Scottish drizzle, are informal but friendly.

Visits from the local Presbyterian, Church of Scotland, Roman Catholic and the Episcopalian Church in Scotland, but other communities are not forgotten by religious and moral education classes, which recently enacted a seriously researched Muslim wedding ceremony, despite the almost entirely Scottish UK ethnic profile of the school.

Pastoral care and discipline: Powerful team of three deputes run a well-organised pastoral structure in which any disciplinary action required is delivered with 'warmth and, when necessary, with steeliness'. It certainly seems to work because the school is immaculate, bar a couple of flaky paint patches in stairways – almost no litter and certainly no graffiti.

'ORCA' (order, respect, care, achievement) makes an easy mantra which pupils really do seem to remember and value, prompted by various pictures of a whale placed in strategic places. Time keeping is emphasized; good community policing. Very high profile prefects with gold edged blazers (basic uniform is minimal black trousers/skirts, jerseys and white shirts, deliberately kept as cheap as possible). Sinners get letters to parents and 'withdrawal of privileges'. The head of each year group is tutor to it throughout, managing general pastoral care as well as pupil support.

Masses of student involvement: student forum includes the top team of the head boy and girl, plus deputies. Active pupil council of all ages meets regularly to discuss specific concerns. First year pupils have a 'buddying system' (the McMentor system) to ease their transition into the senior school.

Pupils and parents: Very strong PTA currently campaigning for new Astroturf funds. All sorts, from a 600 square mile catchment area – tourism, farming, home-workers, Stirling University.

Entrance: By registration: automatic, places for all. Top year juniors have an induction day sampling things they can do when they get to McLaren. Innovative transition project, in which feeder primaries send their top year for a day out with McLaren's first year, with lots of resulting creative work and accolades from Learning Teaching Scotland, was a great success.

Exit: Nearly all go through to sixth form; of those, some 40 per cent to university, mostly Scottish ones.

Money matters: Original McLaren foundation (tiny as far as income goes) but school is well supported by local businesses, which can and will provide extra funds for excursions etc.

Remarks: Comprehensive indeed and a much-admired school. In its idyllic situation, a close-knit community in the heart of romantic landscape, the 'very positive ethos of the school based on its core values and high quality relationships between staff and pupils' (HMI) seems hardly surprising. It is, however, a tough, well-organised and self-critical school, as well as warm-hearted, doing a sound job for a very diverse population.

Merchant Taylors' Boys' School

Linked schools: Merchant Taylors' Girls' School; Merchant Taylors' Girls' Junior and Mixed Infants School

186 Liverpool Road, Crosby, Liverpool, L23 0QP

• Pupils: 595 boys • Ages: 11–18 • Non-denom • Fees: Juniors £7,566; Seniors £10,119 pa • Independent

Tel: 01519 499333
Email: infomtbs@merchanttaylors.com
Website: www.merchanttaylors.com

Headmaster: Since 2005, Mr David Cook (early forties); read history at Birkbeck College, London, taught at Caterham, housemaster and head of history at Giggleswick, deputy head at QEH, Bristol. Held short service commission in Cheshires. Sharp, decisive and energetic, mind clearly spilling over with ideas for school. Good listener, not without gravitas. Son in school and daughter in sister establishment.

Academic matters: Traditional curriculum, including German, Spanish, Latin, Greek; separate sciences. GCSE results 57 per cent A*/A in 2013. Relatively few go on to arts subjects at A level, where science and maths rule. Things may change after current radical curriculum review (head has some interesting ideas about early GCSEs) but few stronger science departments in the north. A level overall 80 per cent at A*/B and 51 per cent A*/A in 2013. Recent innovation is system of one-to-one back-up clinics for pupils having academic or organisational difficulties. SEN overseen by head of learning support. Teaching staff

M

experienced and effective. Big staff turnover, due to retirement, over past few years – big opportunity then.

Games, options, the arts: Only room for a few pitches on site, but main fields within walking distance. All the usual sports, taken seriously, plus strong rowing on Southport Marina. Plenty of representation at regional and national levels. Enormous and vigorous CCF (all three services), shared with sister school (250 in all). Plenty of expeditions and trips. Good art and lively drama: several shared productions with girls' school, plus usual in-house plays. About 25 per cent learn an instrument; annual family carol service in Philharmonic Hall raises money for Merseyside charities. Joint debating society with girls is over 100 years old.

Background and atmosphere: Founded in 1620 by London Merchant Taylor, John Harrison, moved to present agreeable site in 1878, in respectable suburb – handsome Victorian main building. New £5.5 million sports centre on site of Boys' School but available for use by all Merchant Taylors' Schools.

Special emphasis on ICT: latest software as teaching tool, and though a day school, every boy has email address and access to many campus computer sites. New school council seems to be more than a talking shop, if pupils' recent victory in matter of toilets is anything to go by.

Atmosphere decidedly northern ex-direct grant grammar school. Academic work a serious priority, more important perhaps than glitzy facilities – some classrooms are on the shabby side but serious refurbishments and new builds in progress.

Pastoral care and discipline: A small school, so it's claimed every boy is known. Usual day school network of form teacher/ year head/pastoral deputy head means no-one is overlooked. Chaplain also available to talk through problems and independent counsellor drops in once a week for chats in total confidence. Personal health taken seriously. As in all good schools, aim is to develop self-discipline. Drug dealers face the sack.

Pupils and parents: Families from all over Merseyside area. Professional, business, etc, only two to three per cent ethnic minorities, but broad range of social background – 'We are academically, not socially, selective'. Fourteen buses operate daily from as far away as Wigan, South Liverpool, Southport and Warrington; convenient suburban rail link as well. Boys cheery, frank, polite, academically ambitious, a mixture not always understood by southern incomers. Probably a greater community of interest between school and parents than in similar conurbations. Old Boys include Nigel Rees and ex-England rugby international Ben Kay.

Entrance: Academically selective and oversubscribed at 11+. Best chance is via infants and junior boys' school, which makes up 40 per cent of entry; any boy not likely to make it to seniors is flagged up well before exam time and discussed with parents. Ten to 15 lost every year to sixth form colleges (some then want to come back), numbers made up by sixth form entry (six Bs required at GCSE).

Exit: A handful leave after GCSEs. Sixth form leavers nearly all to Russell Group universities eg Manchester, Liverpool, UCL, Newcastle, to read traditional subjects (engineering, science, economics, medicine); three to Oxbridge in 2013.

Money matters: Probably the cheapest HMC day school in the country – a huge selling point. 'Considerable numbers' on sliding scale in own assisted places scheme. Some merit scholarships.

Remarks: Good, solid, dedicated former grammar school in northern mould, where nearly all work hard in and out of classroom. Now in the process of a 21st century update, but not likely to lose its traditional ethos of commitment and emphasis on the daily transaction of the classroom.

Merchant Taylors' Girls' School

Linked schools: Merchant Taylors' Boys' School; Merchant Taylors' Girls' Junior and Mixed Infants School

80 Liverpool Road, Crosby, Liverpool, L23 5SP

- Pupils: 845 girls • Ages: 4-18 • Non-denominational Christian
- Fees: £7,566–£10,119 pa • Independent

Tel: 01519 243140
Email: infomtgs@merchanttaylors.com
Website: www.merchanttaylors.com

Headmistress: Since 2006, Mrs Louise Robinson BA MEd NPQH (early fifties). Taught ICT and maths at Bolton School Girls' Division, rising to head of ICT and senior mistress; deputy head Manchester High School for Girls; principal Howell's School, Denbigh. Chair of GSA 2012. Teaches maths and supports ICT – enjoys having contact with the girls, whom she appreciates ('very engaging and forthcoming', 'We have some very feisty individuals'), accompanied school Ecuador trip. Elegant, astute, with strong opinions, seen as 'a very good manager' by parents but 'very busy' and 'a bit distant' by some. Wants the school to be 'the best at everything', provide 'the best education for life', give opportunities to the 'leaders of the future' to excel and develop all their talents – 'Why wouldn't you?' something of a catch phrase. Husband a retired headteacher; one grown up son; enjoys skiing, gardening and reading.

Academic matters: Excellent results: 2013 A level more than 78 per cent A*/B (nearly 52 per cent A*/A); especially strong maths, physics, art and design, French, economics, geography and psychology. Also offers business studies, ICT, government and politics, theatre studies, AQA Bacc, home economics; biology, chemistry and English very popular and good numbers for classical civilisation. Almost all subjects very strong at GCSE – more than 68 per cent A*/A 2013; astronomy possible through club. Some parents would like early entry maths and some more stimulation for top set girls.

Good spread of languages, including Greek, Latin and Mandarin – particularly impressive classics department: we would have liked a go at the interactive Latin course we saw in action. Setting for maths, languages and science. Average class sizes – 20 key stage 3, 14 key stage 4; 10 for sixth form; 24 max; buzzing, focused girls at work; lots of PCs.

Thoroughgoing tracking and monitoring. Success in national/regional science, maths, classics, poetry and politics competitions; STEM subjects and participation in external courses encouraged. Stable staff – 'hugely experienced and talented' (head); girls spoke warmly and appreciatively of their teachers, feeling lessons are fun and varied and they are well taught and supported if having difficulties. Parents very pleased – 'They've brought her out academically...She's really bloomed and exceeded our expectations'.

Well-designed gifted and talented provision for selected members of years 7-10 (the Harrison Group); lectures for sixth form Harrison scholars open to all; lots of support for Oxbridge, law, modern languages and medical school applicants.

Thoughtful and comprehensive provision for special needs: individual sessions, IEPs with detailed suggestions for teaching strategies, specialist science support teacher; co-ordinator

M

feels she can cover all needs. Grateful praise for the way her daughter's needs have been met from a parent. General initial screening for dyslexia with checks again at end of years 9 and 11; individual EAL support available.

Games, options, the arts: Own courts and use of recently constructed sports centre shared by all four Merchant Taylor senior and junior schools. Usual sports plus badminton, lacrosse, dance (some would like more of this), trampolining, rowing, golf, scuba diving, pilates and step aerobics, so plenty for the less sporty. Local, county, regional and some national level success for hockey, netball, athletics, tennis, cross country, badminton, swimming; two young national biathlon competitors; runs A and B teams.

Thriving music ('wonderful teachers... one of the greatest strengths of the school' – parent): three orchestras, four choirs, ensembles; choir performs at classy events – Royal Navy, cathedrals, Lord Mayor of London and his High Sheriffs' dinner; film/show music as well as classical; tours to Belgium, Germany, Holland; individuals attend Royal Northern College of Music and Chethams' summer school; annual music comp; piano master class by Richard Meyrick; Saturday morning co-ed music school, Crescendo!, open to all schools, seven to 18 year olds.

Two joint senior school drama productions annually, one musical, one play, at both schools, eg Calamity Jane, Les Mis, Daisy Pulls It Off, Shakespeare. Drama festival for years 8 and 9 – plays written, directed and organised by sixth formers, who also run drama club; arts award. Lively, well-designed magazine, Calliope; visits from writers.

Truly stunning art – painting, 3D, multi-media; excellent exam results (2012 accolade for 'exemplary practice' from AQA); GCSE art looks up to A Level standard. Inspiring, vibrant art studio. Several fascinating creative partnerships with John Moores University School of Art, Aintree and the Royal Liverpool Hospitals, eg a series of works based on treatment of blood disorders. Own art gallery, The Vitreum, hosts exhibitions by leading regional, national and international contemporary artists and designers. Visiting printmakers work with students, thanks to school's own etching press (also has an Albion letterpress, rescued from a barn in France by the dynamic art director) and stone lithography facility.

As well as key stage 3 textiles and home economics, girls take a technology course including mechanisms and computer programming; the STEM club is designing and building a solar powered car – so these girls will have no problem with changing a plug whilst knocking up a soufflé (and translating a Virgil Eclogue to boot, no doubt).

CCF – with the boys' school (all three services) – very big; much D of E; all sixth formers do community service. Debating, Model United Nations comp, European Youth Parliament and business enterprise/investment comps. School council, lots of charity fund raising (run by sixth form committee), fortnightly fair trade stall, Eco schools' Green Flag status – to be featured on Eco Schools' website as case study of good practice. Joint schools' youth club for years 7-9.

Trips to France, Italy (skiing), China, Australia, Greece, Iceland, World Challenge to Equador, culture trip to New York; linked schools in Sierra Leone; year 11 jolly at Alton Tours before GCSE exam leave starts.

Very good careers programme – breakfast events (with boys) for upper sixth give opportunity to meet reps from companies/business people plus joint working lunches and dinners with guest speakers from various fields; work experience in year 11 and through sixth form, in Merseyside and sometimes beyond; Merchants' community network used; annual joint careers fair.

Background and atmosphere: A hotch-potch architecturally – the original house (the Merchant Taylors' Schools were founded in 1620 by John Harrison of the London Merchant Taylors' Livery Company) is juxtaposed with a 1960s concrete monstrosity, 1980s red brick extensions and modern reception area plus the generous gallery space. Harmonised décor within – lemon walls and blue carpets and chairs. Classrooms look nondescript but attractive displays cover all walls around the school. The sixth form library in the old house is furnished with traditional wooden book cases, tables and chairs; the ground floor section is enticingly stocked with varied fiction. Much promotion of reading and general knowledge – book lists and shadow competition judging, visits from writers, house quizzes. Lawns (one with benches for alfresco lunches), an eco garden and inspiring modern sculpture of a girl reaching for success.

Much focus on the latter but, we were assured by girls, not in an oppressive way – 'Teachers will help you find out what you're good at', so you 'find your niche'; 'There's something for all aspects of your personality'; 'If you want the best, it's there for you'; 'You can be accepted for what you want to be – so long as you work for it'. 'Healthy competition', but girls don't feel pressured and support each other, said a parent. 'A unique combination of high expectations in a non-threatening environment,' said another. No opportunities wasted for improvement – including literary extracts on the loo doors! Public speaking encouraged to develop confidence; scholars hone their social skills at a formal dinner with governors.

School council chose names of the four houses – Minerva, Thalia, Gaia, Selene. Smart uniforms – navy blue jackets and skirts, light blue, striped blouses. Food well thought of – plenty of choice; sixth can go out in lunch hour but some choose to stay in. Three full school assemblies/week with religious elements.

Pastoral care and discipline: Very reasonable behaviour policy, elegantly headed 'concordia parvae res crescunt' (small things grow in harmony). Girls' happiness seen as integral to achievement – pupils see the school as very friendly and feel well supported, with plenty of people to turn to if they have problems, which will get sorted out. Sixth form mentors provide a listening service, plus access to two trained counsellors every lunch time. Well planned transition to year 7 including summer holiday scheme – state school children integrate quickly. Focus more on rewards than sanctions – merits for exceptional helpfulness, showing initiative, outstanding effort; 'honours' and prizes.

Pupils and parents: Most from prep. Catchment area from South Liverpool to Bootle and Crosby, north and east beyond Southport, as far as Warrington, Wigan and St Helens. Wide socio economic range – 20-25 per cent have financial support. Ethnically mixed. Open, confident, articulate and thoughtful girls who enjoy all aspects of school life. Good links with parents, who feel involved and that concerns are responded to swiftly and patiently – website, newsletters, handbook.

Famous OGs: arts/media types such as Beryl Bainbridge, Jane Garvey and Kelly Dalglish (Woman's Hour/Sky Sports presenters); Professor Janet Finch, vice-chancellor Keele University; Winifred Lambert – distinguished social worker, promoting housing for families and disabled, and lifelong member of the Communist party; Jane Greenwood, Tony award-winning fashion designer; Joy Swift MBE, creator of the original murder mystery weekends.

Entrance: Year 7 – tests in English, maths, online reasoning plus report from current school, late January/early February (register before December of year 6).

Years 8-10 – tests in English, maths and reasoning; some spoken and written questions in languages and sciences.

Sixth form entry: at least seven GCSEs at B with A/A* in would be A level subjects; open evening to discuss subject choices; interviews held before Easter holidays.

Exit: Some 15-20 per cent leave at end of year 11 for local sixth form colleges, for financial or travel reasons or to take less traditional subjects.

2013 Manchester, Durham, Leeds, Liverpool and Newcastle popular. Most to Russell Group (the odd Oxbridge place – one in 2013). Most favoured subjects: psychology, medicine and classical civilisation; otherwise more do various kinds of science than arts; the odd girl to drama degree, some art and design.

Money matters: Year 7 entry – discretionary award varying in amount (short term, linked to academic merit); scholarships for academic, sporting and musical prowess; five or six school assisted places awarded on academic merit, means tested, up to full fees (home visits to assess financial need). Sixth form – Harrison scholarships (more kudos than dosh) and some bursaries available. Ten per cent discount for siblings.

Remarks: Very successful, happy mixture of the traditional and 21st century education. High achieving girls who don't feel hot-housed. Outstanding art evidence that creativity and individuality are prized too. Excelsior!

Merchant Taylors' School

Sandy Lodge, Northwood, HA6 2HT

• Pupils: 890 boys; all day • Ages: 11–18 • A multi-faith school rooted in Anglican values and traditions • Fees: £17,325 pa • Independent

Tel: 01923 845514
Email: admissions@mtsn.org.uk
Website: www.mtsn.org.uk

Head Master: Since 2013, Mr Simon Everson (late forties). Previously head of Skinners' School in Tunbridge Wells. Studied at Cambridge and Nottingham, has masters' degrees in English and philosophy and has taught at state and independent schools and a school in Japan. Married to Ginny, a psychotherapist who specialises in treating victims of domestic violence and supporting children in foster homes. His outside interests include prehistory, philosophy, running and travel.

Academic matters: Ideal for the curious free-thinker with a deal of self-motivation. A rare breed, an academic school with a wonderfully cool feel; understands there is more to academic excellence than great exam results but achieves top notch performances anyway. No specialism, just try to do everything to a high standard and adamant they are not an exam factory or hot-house. 'There is so much else to do, we're more rarefied'. Boys take a number of IGCSEs (English, science and maths) and go beyond the syllabus but head cautions, 'We're in a market, we might not do January retakes but the boys do.' Consistently outstanding results: nearly 40 per cent of A levels at A*, more than 74 per cent A*/A and 94 per cent A*/B in 2013. At GCSE 90 per cent A* or A. No weak subjects. All boys study French and Latin in years 7 and 8 and begin either German, Italian, Spanish or classical Greek in year 9. French, German, Spanish offered at AS and A. English offered as three different A levels (lang, lit, and lang and lit). Maths and further maths popular at A level, geography increasingly so. Biology very good, and new head of physics upping the ante by introducing dynamic elements such as electronics and robotics. Bright bunch, a number take the sought-after extended project qualification (EPQ) though head confessed, 'I get the ones who teach me. It stretches them but they rise gloriously to the challenge.' Recent introduction of drama A level and GCSE illustrative of way school listens, 'They consult with us and very much run the school for us, which is a real honour.' Drama A level may seem incongruous in such an academic setting, but one recent alumnus who gained a place at Imperial to read medicine, in part because, in addition to starry science, panel impressed with his A level drama.

Emphasis on encouragement and inspiration not pressure and perspiration. 'You go to the gym to work out, and to school to work yourself out,' say staff. Introduced hour-long lessons to ensure sufficient time to explore, pause and reflect. 'Just when a lesson might be getting difficult or dull, teachers have the knack of lighting the touch paper and bringing back to life. They work us hard but they care and make learning exciting. They're always happy to help, whenever and however.' Parents equally enthused: 'My boys buzz with enthusiasm when they come home from school. The teachers understand boys and know how to structure lessons to suit inquisitive boys.'

Learning support not a traditional métier but, says school, 'We're getting better, fast.' Asks parents to be up front about learning difficulties: 'If we don't know, we don't know what we are dealing with and precious time may be lost'. One parent felt support was in danger of becoming too thinly stretched, another that school is not always swift at detecting difficulties, but praised the way they meet the needs of both child and family once they're apparent. 'As soon as I met the head and staff I realised they would go the extra mile to help my son.' Views every teacher as a teacher of specific learning difficulties with support available to anyone. Caters for boys with physical difficulties, including wheelchairs. Those with identified needs are monitored and helped; one off or regular, but strictly no withdrawal. Work towards self-help; one boy heading to uni requested a book on Asperger's to better understand his condition and how to explain it to others. Extra time and use of laptop not unusual, but here, even lowest maths sets pursue maths A level and are oft rewarded with top grades. Enrichment for Oxbridge (around 18 successful applicants per year) focusses on feeding a passion, not spoon feeding.

Games, options, the arts: Boys enjoy rough and tumble, 'They are like puppies, they need to be let out for a good run around', say staff, and run around they do. Not a macho rugby school, boys confessed, 'Often we seem to be half the size of our competitors but we still try to give them a good run for their money.' Hockey big and getting bigger, thanks in no small part to charismatic England coach on the staff. Keen to find something for everyone – both on and off the sports pitches. Tries to ease boys out of their comfort zone: 'Sometimes they simply lack confidence.' Range of sports extends beyond cricket, basketball, athletics, swimming, tennis, soccer, badminton, croquet, cross-country, golf and shooting. Super facilities include sports hall, cricket nets, heated indoor pool, all-weather hockey pitches, athletics track, lakes for sailing and windsurfing, tennis courts, squash, handball fives courts, assault course and fencing Salle. Director of sport as pleased with a good, gutsy performance from E team as those in top squads achieving national recognition. Pros coach all teams. Believe most important thing is taking part and having a good time but enjoy winning too! Moral attitude to sport, no truck with swearing or arguing with the ref, and unbending insistence that, win or lose, they do so with grace.

Serious charity work, includes long-term, on-going, outstanding work with Phab – residential Care Week held annually and funds raised throughout the year. Head openly enthused and inspired by boys' enterprising and benevolent spirit and visibly glowed as he recounted numerous anecdotes of their generosity, including recent competition win (first prize in Bank of England competition) and their insistence that the cash prize be donated to one of their charities. Myriad of community activities, links with Harefield Academy plus weekly sports sessions and reading with youngsters from local state primary school; 'We shared an end of term concert: that really cemented the relationship between the schools.' Excellent music with orchestras, swing band, jazz bands and every kind of ensemble. Concerts throughout the year with recitals galore and performing opportunities for all. Plenty of drama; technical side revered, 'Productions are amazing; expect fireworks, bangs, flames and fun,' said one boy; another commented, 'There is so much humour, not just in the plays but in the school, perhaps that's what sets it apart', though added hurriedly, 'We're serious when we have to be or when it is inappropriate not to be.' DT popular, with good and imaginative teaching; boys involved in design of new DT building, art equally impressive. Merchant Taylors' Diploma being introduced: will provide formal recognition of co-curricular activities.

Background and atmosphere: Founded in the City of London in 1561 by the Worshipful Company of Merchant Taylors and Linen Armourers, it was then the largest school in the country. Moved in 1933 to current impressive 250-acre green belt site, with exquisite formal gardens and spectacular protected area for wildlife, including a lake that is home to herons, swans, moorhens plus countless interloping fowls. Feels like a cross between a boarding school (which it once was) and an Oxbridge college: unhurried calm, timeless beauty but oozing with purpose and discovery. Lush, manicured playing fields outside, plus core of (listed) buildings, with a dominant Deco angularity, pay homage to superb facilities inside, including newish library and information centre, politics and economics centre, entrance hall and sixth form common-room. Boys confided, 'Sometimes we wander round the grounds and just explore the school; it's an exciting place with nooks and crannies.'

Pastoral care and discipline: Criticisms few and far between: 'We live in a perfect bubble. They set you up for uni and are so caring and supportive we worry we might not be equipped for the bad things life might throw at us.' Vertical tutor system popular with most staff, who enjoy getting to know a mixed bag of boys well, but mixed reports from parents, boys and moles. 'Not all teachers are born tutors, some are naturals, others take time to grow into the role but when they get it right, the tutor is almost an extension of your family, wonderful.' Christian services held in the chapel, but other faiths welcome with a Muslim prayer room, Jewish society, Christian discussion group and three much-praised whole school assemblies. Lunch important – head insists all boys dine together; no packed lunches but all reasonable dietary requests catered for. Expulsions rare, school is good at giving second chances but not at any price: 'Sometimes it becomes clear that we simply are not the right place for a child.'

Pupils and parents: Unlock your daughters, these are the good guys, charming, amusing, entertaining and self-effacing; the ideal dinner guests. Lots of social entrepreneurs who take moral responsibility seriously, are quietly competitive but will ask 'How can I help you?' not 'What will you do for me?' Boys are acutely aware of their privileged education and humbled by it saying, 'You won't find any pomp, plums or fat-cats wearing silly hats.' We certainly loved their sense of fun and the gallant way they responded to gentle teasing; no airs or graces, 'School doesn't try to mould us, they find out what's best for us, they adjust. I guess we do too, because we want to. Importantly they don't try to make us tick boxes.' Parents say boys are 'down to earth, grounded with a healthy degree of humility and tolerance.' Staff agree, adding, 'They respect others, sometimes they lack edge and aren't good at pushing themselves forward.' Others comment on the friendly rivalry, with each boy wanting to be just a little better, achieve a little more, than his friends.

Broad appeal to Bucks, Herts and London sets but with a touch of Goldilocks – Bucks think school rather urban, London a bit in the sticks and Herts just right. Ethnic mix reflects the area, roughly 35 per cent Asian, 65 per cent white, many faiths including Christian, Muslim and Jewish. Increasing numbers from London for the ethos, lakes and space, including first time buyers and dual income families. Parents say school is wonderfully inclusive: 'We have friends of all races and faiths and our boys do too.'. Another volunteered their enthusiasm for the carol service: 'It is a Christian service but boys of all faiths take an active part and parents and siblings join in'. Parents very involved with school and encouraged to attend events and take part in committees, which, according to our moles, eliminates parents' moans and whinges. Revered old boys' network. 'I love the fact that my friends all do very different things to each other and to me,' said one OMT. Famous alumni include Sir Edmund Spenser, Clive of India, Titus Oates, Samuel Palmer plus, more recently, Reginald Maudling, Lord Coggan (Archbishop of Canterbury), Nobel prize-winning medic Sir John Sulston, the sculptor Lynn Chadwick (whose work graces one of the many manicured lawns), comedian Michael McIntyre (who left when his family fell on hard times and could no longer afford the fees) and Conn Iggulden (author of Dangerous Book for Boys).

Entrance: Competitive, good mix at 11 between state and independent schools including from Radlett Prep and Reddiford. Odd state school refugee at 13 but vast majority from independent schools: St John's, St Martin's, Northwood Prep, Durston House, Orley Farm, York House, Gayhurst, Chesham Prep and Davenies, Trevor-Roberts, Devonshire House, Lyndhurst and others. Buses from everywhere. Huge surge in demand for year 7 entry, year 9 constant. Average IQ of 121 (equates to pass mark for Bucks grammar schools) but accepts those as low as 105 and does a great job with them. Adamant they are not seeking statistics or grade point averages; want boys with an interest or passion, whose presence in the school will help others get a good deal out of it. For 11+ entry, register by November 30 preceding the January exams in English, maths and verbal reasoning. Boys who do well are asked to return for interview. At 13 need to be registered by June a year in advance, with interviews in autumn preceding entry. School's own exam in all CE subjects with scholarships divined from outstanding performances. Scholarship candidates who do well are invited back for further interviews. Sixth form places by examination in March – candidates must register by December 31 and will be tested in the subjects they wish to study, followed by interviews. 'My child loved the interview, that's when he decided he really wanted to go to MT'. Uses interview to gauge level of interest and engagement, get boys off script, attempt to delve under the skin of those who have been tutored to the hilt, see what lies beneath; can they cope with the unfamiliar, do they have a passion, are they enthusiastic?

Exit: Virtually all stay on to sixth form. In 2013, 16 to Oxbridge, rest to a broad range of academic subjects at Russell group and other top universities – lots to London unis, others to Nottingham, Warwick, Birmingham, Durham and Bristol. University and careers advice a strength with each sixth former assigned to a senior head of department who acts as his university adviser. Work experience – some of which can be done abroad – is highly developed and includes a companies link.

Money matters: Keen to attract parents from all walks of life whose son's life would be enriched by attending MT. Honorary academic scholarships as per Oxbridge (20 at 13 and 10 at 11); scholars receive status plus enriched programme. A clutch of music, sports and all-rounder scholarships at 11, 13 and 16. Music scholarships include two up to 25 per cent of fees and up to two music exhibitions (worth up to one tenth of the fee.) Additional music awards, covering the cost of tuition of up to two instruments, also available. Hope to fulfil school founders' dream whereby up to 200 boys receive some sort of means-tested financial assistance up to 100 per cent of the fees; used the 450th anniversary to launch 'Forward to our Roots' appeal.

Remarks: A premier league school of quiet confidence and substance with room for the erudite but not for ego. Produces bright, happy, savvy boys with a caring and compassionate outlook. Provides a truly rounded, high-octane education in a friendly, unstuffy, and surprisingly stress-free environment. Allegro not andante, hits the high notes with ease, in a lively-paced, vibrant setting; tingling with team-spirit, sparkling with wit, infused with emotional intelligence.

Merchiston Castle School

Linked school: Merchiston Juniors (aka Pringle)

294 Colinton Road, Edinburgh, EH13 0PU

- Pupils: 470 boys (330 full boarders, 15 flexi boarders and 125 day pupils) • Ages: 8-18 • Non-denom • Fees: Day £12,522-£20,190; Boarding £17,595-£27,465 pa • Independent

Tel: 01313 122200
Email: Admissions@merchiston.co.uk
Website: www.merchiston.co.uk

Headmaster: Since 1998, Mr Andrew Hunter BA PGCE, educated at Aldenham and Manchester University, where he read combined studies: English, theology and biblical studies. Came to Merchiston after eight years at Bradfield, where he ended as housemaster of Army House and, before that, eight years at Worksop, housemaster of Pelham House. Trails of glory on games fields: ex-county hockey, squash and tennis player (school has tennis academy in partnership with Tennis Scotland). An expat, he was brought up on a Kenyan coffee farm and started school at Kenton College, Nairobi. Married to the glamorous Barbara, who teaches art and design. Three children – one son a Merchistonian now at university, one son at college and a daughter also now at university. Keen on the arts, theatre, wine tasting.

He goes from strength to strength – spot of tinkering with the syllabus, trawling all over the UK, Europe, and the world on behalf of school, plus a dabble into building. A purpose-built sixth form house opened after an £8 million fund-raiser. Excellent Hunter-inspired 45 page information booklet that is undoubtedly the best guide to any school we have ever seen, plus a really comprehensive leaflet on exam results, including a rather complicated value-added section – other schools please note.

Academic matters: School continues to ply the mainly English system, though a few sit a combination of AS and Scottish Highers over two years. In 2013, 51 per cent A*/A grades at A level; 59 per cent A*/A grades at GCSE. All boys must do two separate sciences at GCSE and a large proportion go on to study science at A level. Maths, English and science results very good; humanities good, too, and increasingly popular. A level critical thinking, economics and classical civilisation and junior school Mandarin added recently. Excellent showing in out-of-school activities, maths, physics and chemistry Olympiads and the like.

Recent investments include Mount Olympus – a suite of classrooms for classics, economics and geography, and the Masterchef kitchen, in which senior pupils complete a practical course and gain knowledge of nutrition, food hygiene and healthy eating. The Balfour Paul science laboratory was opened by Air Marshal Sir John Baird, Merchistonian (1951-55), primarily for use by junior pupils. The labs have all been refurbished – interesting design, repeated throughout

the school: a mixture of trad tables and octagonal plinths. Interactive white boards and projectors in many classrooms – increasing use of computers as teaching tools; pupils from age 12 upwards are required to have their own laptop. Also a good IT suite plus more computers in the magical, double-decker Spawforth Library, but prep is not necessarily done online.

The modern and well-equipped new Pringle teaching centre provides a teaching block for eight to 10 year olds – we enjoyed a treatise on tropical fish from the youngest year group; computers in every classroom and a bank of laptops for class use. Pupils must score 100 in IQ assessments to follow main curriculum and do the standard eight or nine GCSEs.

Learning support teacher dedicated to the juniors. No pupil taken who can't 'access mainstream education'. She heads a team of one full-timer (dedicated to junior school) and roughly three part-timers. All pupils are assessed on entry on a whole year group basis for their reading, writing and maths. Support is specially geared for each pupil – all have individually tailored profiles. Timetabled support varies from year to year, with small groups for foreign languages and Latin, as much to get boys up to speed as for actual diagnosable problems. In-class support too, plus 'concentrated units' for spelling, reading and individual subjects. Maths on the whole catered for by the maths department, whilst the SEN specialists provide support lower down the school – sometimes via withdrawal, sometimes in class. Complex problems need more info and background than she feels the SEN department can give. Support for the gifted too. Mrs Stewart appears to be a one woman, 24 hour, referral unit – boys can and do come at all times.

All the dys-stream catered for, plus two or three currently with 'mild Asperger's' diagnosed in-school; ADHD not a problem, physical disability not 'a real problem': classes are re-located if access complicated; profoundly deaf boy recently went through the school with a (free) monitor paid for by West Lothian authority – wow! Can scribe in exams and pupils get extra time both in school and public exams. Really quite a large number of boys 'in the system'. Laptops not provided by the school, but masses in the special needs department, all on the school network, and parents often buy their own.

Games, options, the arts: Rugby popular, cricket, athletics, curling back in favour, hockey growing, skiing, sailing. Well-used sports hall, very well used swimming pool, weights room replaced by fitness centre. New Gold Academy launched in 2011 led by Alan Murdoch FPGA BSc, based both at the school's 100 acre campus in Colinton, Edinburgh and nearby Kings Acre golf club. Tennis academy run jointly with St George's and Tennis Scotland – serious ambitions.

Wide variety of activities and successes in many areas. Popular CCF – community service and work in special schools a viable alternative, rifle range built into school wall. The head and the dean of sixth form extremely keen on outreach, so the latest initiative is a group of lower sixth formers mentoring in several Edinburgh primary schools. Masses of trips all over the place in every discipline.

Fantastic pipe band, sounding good during our visit, with some of the smallest pipers looking like embryo masons, lugging their oblong bagpipe cases with grave determination. Strong choral tradition, including close harmony group, and a number of orchestras and bands. Super art department, with terrific paintings both in the department and displayed all over the school. DT uses Cad Cam – good juxtaposition with computer suite and music hall, open till late.

Background and atmosphere: Founded in 1833 by scientist Charles Chalmers, moved from Merchiston Castle (now owned by Napier University) to the rather gaunt, purpose-built Colinton House in 1930 (ruins of Colinton Castle in grounds). Set in 100 acres of park-like playing fields, with stunning views to the north.

Pringle House, for junior boarders (aged eight to 12 or 13), recently much extended, yet enclosed in its own private (secret) garden; own houseparents. Boys can climb the tree as far as the white mark and generally allowed to be their own age without being pressurised 'to join the grown-ups'. Book inspired dayroom, plus obligatory television and rather complicated game of Diplomacy up on the wall. School in good heart, well used, nothing flash here but no signs of real distress either. Huge amount of cash recently spent on revamping loos and individual showers and refurbishing various boarding houses. Step-up boarding popular with the juniors as an introduction to boarding.

Boys work in their dorm space and day boys have desks in the same area – superb posters. Sixth formers are billeted to each house for the year to act as monitors and have attractive kitchens to make their tasks less onerous. Cooking the flavour of the month, both in Pringle and, certainly, in Chalmers West – stunning pupil inspired kitchens. 'Steaks would be good,' said our guide and housemaster. Impressive sixth form boarding house, Laidlaw House – 126 ensuite bedrooms, modern kitchens, a café area, multi-gym and open plan social spaces with stunning views of Edinburgh.

Sick bay with visiting sports physiotherapists, own ultrasound machine and a delightful bubblegum pink isolation room (which would put any self-respecting boy off thoughts of malingering). Dining hall with servery and buffet service. Food very good – soup, meat and veg, acres of bread and rice pudding when we visited, impressive salad bar for a boys' school too. Boys praise the new arrangement: 'The food is still good at the end of term' – when the budget is low.

First floor Memorial Hall doubles as a chapel (service inter-denominational) and dance hall and boasts Cameron tartan cushions on removable pews, with an impressive tartan stair carpet up to the entrance. Girls are regularly corralled in from (primarily) St George's, but also Kilgraston and St Margaret's, for reel parties, with lots of practice before the real thing – Merchiston boys are regularly voted the best dancing partners in Scotland. Visiting girls 'not a problem' – they come and go at weekends and can join the boys in the sixth form club. Vast number of trips and options for boarders – day pupils can join if space available.

Pastoral care and discipline: Good rapport between pupils and staff. The horizontal house system is said to have made bullying practically 'non-existent' and 'Anyway, physical bullying has been superseded by text bullying from mobile phones'. Head will and has asked pupils to leave. Believes in tough love, though a couple of prefects to whom we spoke obviously hadn't needed to hear the phrase before. Mr Hunter is keen on parent/pupil/school partnership; will take in boys who have been excluded elsewhere – both boy and parent sign a contract and the boy will be subject to very stringent and regular drugs testing routine. Expect to be drugs tested if either caught or suspected of dealing or dabbling, followed by (but nothing in black and white) temporary or permanent exclusion.

Ordinary misdemeanours (alcohol, smoking etc) are treated on their own demerits. No longer cool to smoke. Discipline seminars. Jolly school policies booklet, re-printed every year, of which head is justifiably proud, lists all the dos and don'ts of the place. Purchase of cigarettes or alcohol on or off the campus and dealings with betting shops are no-go areas. Betting is a new one to the GSG, but perhaps other schools aren't as clear-cut in their expectations.

Pupils and parents: 'A down to earth school, rooted in values,' says the head. The only all-boys boarding school in Scotland. Strong middle class ethos, good values – no change here. Record number of pupils in the school. Sixteen per cent from abroad, of whom about five per cent are expats. Real foreigners come from all over – Japan, Hong Kong and mainland China as well

as the States, Mexico, plus a number from Europe, usually for the sixth form. Germany popular at present. Head keen not to lose the boarding ethos and littlies at Pringle are encouraged to flexi-board. Day officially ends at 4.10pm, but pupils can stay till after supper if they want to – must be the cheapest babysitting service in the country. Senior boys can flexi-board too, at the housemaster's discretion and dependent on availability, without charge if they are about official business – 'debates, plays and the like', or for £45 a night if for 'parental convenience'. Boys open, friendly and well-mannered.

Entrance: At eight, 10, 11, 12, 13 and 16, always via exams; 55 per cent pass mark at CE; boys come from prep schools all over Scotland and the north of England. Entry to sixth form automatic from inside school, others need a satisfactory report from previous school.

Exit: Refer again to the useful little booklet for details of the favoured universities – six to Oxbridge in 2013 and nearly two-thirds to Russell Group universities. Durham, Bristol, London, Newcastle, Edinburgh, Glasgow, St Andrew's, Aberdeen all popular. Science, engineering, economics, management/business and languages/classics/English the favoured subjects. Pupils go on to be fully paid up members of the Edinburgh mafia – law lords etc.

Money matters: Myriads of scholarships and bursaries for almost everything but all are now means-tested – scholarships awarded for the honour alone. Sibling discounts with Kilgraston, Casterton and Queen Margaret's York. New Laidlaw scholarships donated by Merchistonian to pay full fees for several boys each year – targeting 'talented individuals whose financial circumstances would not otherwise allow them to attend Merchiston'.

Remarks: No change. Still the top boys' school in Scotland (indeed, the only boys-only boarding school north of the Home Counties, which extraordinary position achieved through defection to co-education by the rest) and on the way up anyway, as named Scottish Independent Secondary School of the Year a few years back by The Sunday Times. Charismatic head; boys are encouraged to 'try their hardest, make the most of their talents and look after each other'. 'No thoughts of going co-ed,' say head, staff and boys – the latter positively shuddered at the idea.

Michael Hall School

Linked school: Michael Hall School (Lower)

Kidbrooke Park, Forest Row, East Sussex, RH18 5JA

• Pupils: 540 pupils (280 girls, 260 boys); up to 20 can board with local families • Ages: 0–19 • Non-denom: Member of Steiner Waldorf Schools Fellowship • Fees: Day £8,250–£11,750 pa, Boarding + £6,300–£7,340 pa • Independent

Tel: 01342 822275
Email: adele.yeoman@michaelhall.co.uk
Website: www.michaelhall.co.uk

Chairperson of the College of Teachers: No head – instead a chairperson of the College of Teachers appointed annually, along with chairs of faculties (early years, lower and upper school). The school is a charity, with its only trustee a company called Michael Hall School Ltd. The trustees and directors of this company (council of management) are evenly split between parents, teachers and independents – all elected by members of

The Michael Hall Association. The system is designed to avoid hierarchy and promote the transfer of skilful teachers into managerial positions.

Some parents find the lack of direct accountability disturbing, especially when faced with the substitution of specialist staff and/or the management of high-spirited children. Ideally the 45 members of the College of Teachers will together know all the children and the school will develop organically through their growing knowledge and experience, rather than sudden changes of direction when a new head takes over.

Academic matters: Kindergarten feels like a farmhouse kitchen, homey and calm. Earthy rather than bright colours are used in the decoration, pictures are wiped clean or taken home rather than being put up on the walls – children are encouraged to find their own level of creative play and imitate the adults with plenty of repetition and ritual. Each of the four classes (age range three to six and a half) has access to its own garden, where apples are peeled, crushed and juiced in the autumn – a strong seasonal rhythm.

In the lower and middle school ideally one class teacher from seven until 14, some specialist teachers for maths, English and languages from 12. The classroom layout is traditional, with a rolling blackboard, games and music used in lessons. Children are taught to write before they read (seven or eight – usual in mainland Europe, startling in the UK); they learn manually and are encouraged to do before they understand.

Range of ability is huge – one parent complains that the classes (of 25) are all taught at the pace of the slowest pupil, resulting in bored bright ones, while another delights that her bi-lingual children get to expand their language skills creatively while less fluent children are coached. This variety of experience must stem from the skill of the teacher, which used to be a bit of a lottery, less so nowadays with tighter appraisals and continuous training. The mnemonic power of free-ranging discussions and holistic links cannot be underestimated – caesarean sections while talking about Rome. The purpose-built library is well stocked with old Steiner favourites and eight computers available for project work, the ICT department has 20, the labs and learning support department three each (and alpha smarts).

Kindergarten and the lower school teachers keep records as well as planning their lessons – but no external targets or tests until mock GCSEs. The classes are regularly screened by the learning support department (two full-time and two part-time staff). End of year reports are ramped up to come out twice a year in the upper school. This organic schooling relies on a three-way partnership between the child, the teacher and the parent – communication between these is vital for success. Some parents have been frustrated during parents' meetings (once a term) by the lack of focus on individual children – a separate meeting must be set up for that type of discussion. Lower school teachers frequently do home visits to enable a good dialogue to take place between parents and teacher about the child.

A level choices in upper school (14-19) mean more select groups, even though the main lessons can be in a community of around 30. These operate concurrently with A level choices – each one lasts a shorter time than they did in the lower school, but the curriculum still covers a huge range of topics (eg ecology, meteorology, economics, gym, drama). Subject cross-pollination is ubiquitous. In a maths main lesson golden geometry leads to an exhibition at a London gallery and pupils compose a haiku. In a science main lesson, children cling to each other in threes mimicking atoms combined together to make a molecule of water. A recent student initiative resulted in a handbound book of work in the upper school, a beautiful record of an individual education. This breadth of education is really appreciated by the upper school – they feel it is one of Michael Hall's USPs. A relatively traditional range of A level

choices on offer and some courses are validated by the Open College Network (OCN). Exams certainly not the be-all-and-end-all but in 2013 78 per cent of pupils got 5+ A*-C grades at GCSE including English and maths; more than 40 per cent of grades were A*/A. At A level, 84 per cent A*/C grades and 48 per cent A*/A grades.

Games, options, the arts: Balance between practical and academic disciplines is the aim: each class of 11-12 year olds has a chance to cultivate a bed in the two and a half acre walled bio-dynamic garden. The seasons run through the timetable too: whole school assemblies mark natural festivals as well as the end of term – Michaelmas, Advent. Poems learned by rote and recited, costumes, lighting and sets designed for productions in the theatre. Learning games involve singing and later the playing of wooden flutes. Other instruments and the reading of music are introduced from eight.

And Eurhythmy – described by Rudolf Steiner as 'visible speech and music'. At first glance it looks like a bunch of kids clanking metal pipes to the accompaniment of a piano, kept in check by a softly spoken lady. However, no denying that it aids the development of rhythm, teamwork and coordination – and it's fun: an upper schooler admitted he had spent a while wishing they could learn dance instead, but now he was right back into it.

Everyone learns woodwork as well as to knit and sew, moving from a case for their flute to their own shirt. In art, colour is the essence of the work until the age of 15, when a period when only black and white is used – to link in with the 'I love this, I hate this' period of development. Drawing is also integrated into all topics – eg, while studying the Renaissance, everyone will draw a room with perspective.

The multi-purpose gym is used by children in the lower school and above, with lots of imaginary narratives to link different disciplines together – balancing, climbing, skipping, trampolining, trapezing. No organised games until middle school and then only ones that use the hands, eg basketball, netball, tennis – but no football (Waldorf Steiner development philosophy encourages upright throwing of a ball rather than kicking and heading) – some parents miss the kick-around in break as a traditional way of burning off their sons' energy. The year after they enter the lower school, everyone takes part in the Olympic Games (this coincides with the study of ancient civilisations in the curriculum). Steiner schools from all over the UK come and camp and compete – but with enough categories to ensure everyone receives a medal.

Background and atmosphere: In 1919 the Austrian philosopher and scientist, Rudolf Steiner, began a school in Stuttgart for children of the workers at the Waldorf-Astoria cigarette factory, using a curriculum based on nurturing emotional and cognitive intelligence. Today 958 schools and 1,600 early years centres in over 60 countries now use this holistic approach, making it the fastest growing independent education system in the world. Their curriculum is unique and, in the lower school, all teaching is done 'through the teacher and not via text books'. Michael Hall, founded in 1925, is the longest established of the 34 English Steiner schools to offer national curriculum exams.

Many families move to Forest Row so their children can attend, as local estate agents well know. This makes for a community feel – 'You can drop your homework round to a teacher if it's late'. Some school buses to Tunbridge Wells, Lewes, and Brighton and East Grinstead train station, allowing children to come from far and wide – you can walk down the hill (the estate consists of 60 acres of park land) from the A22, along the Cow Path, to the main building (Georgian listed). An ongoing plan for site development. However, many of the buildings are modern and distinctive, eg the kindergarten (Hobbitshire-like – the Waldorf Steiner font on all signage begs more Elvish references), the gym, the theatre. Pupils build climbing frames, edge a path (both class building projects in summer before GCSEs start) and help to maintain the bio dynamic garden – this produces food for the kitchens, sells to the community and feeds a compost dragon each year.

The site and school do feel magical and slightly removed from reality – a huge spider's web woven onto a tree is a legacy of a middle school project – but reassuringly, still some sulky-looking teenagers milling around. The school council is very strong – they recently managed to get student cards issued to enable discounts: children are clear-thinking and effective. This school is a beacon of professionalism among the Steiners in the UK – inter-school appraisals and assessments are vital to the self-regulation of this strand of education.

Pastoral care and discipline: The class teacher is the first point of contact in the concerns procedure, followed by the chair of faculty. Each upper school child also has a tutor – he or she can request a particular teacher for this rôle, choosing one to suit a particular subject choice or emotional support. Ideally the one class teacher for eight years in the lower school should be a constant, could well see you through your parents' divorce, puberty, your gran's death. Obviously character clashes – children go through love and hatred of parents and class teachers – and this system teaches you to confront the things you don't like, instead of turning away from them. If open and honest conversation fails, the child may move into the parallel class (in the lower school) or leave. However some parents hold back from complaining for fear of jeopardising their child's relationship with the teacher and instead resort to out-of-school tutors.

Pedagogical stories are used a lot in the younger years – remarkably effective (obviously this does not work so well in mid-teens). A points system in upper school for behavioural, alcohol or drug incidents – resulting in anything from detention through a behavioural contract and finally to exclusion.

Pupils and parents: Practically all local families – some as far as Lewes, Tunbridge Wells, Nutley and London. Twenty-five per cent non-UK born. Lots of small to medium sized business owners – natural risk-takers, musicians, architects, lawyers, teachers. Can be roughly divided into three groups – the New Age-ers (instinctively want their children to have as much of a childhood as possible before being forced into tests), the Anthropops (done a lot of reading on the Waldorf Steiner philosophy) and the cosmopolitans (moved from Holland, Germany or a Scandinavian country where their children attended a state-funded Steiner school). Lots of Steiner pupils send their children to a Steiner school and many return to teach or volunteer.

Coffee and tea are served in the canteen each morning (a cheerful yellow hut) by parents and staff for parents and staff. Those parents who are frustrated with the unconventional way the school is run are those who are least involved. The community surrounding this school looks after its own – but the outside world can be a bit of a shock for some pupils. A girl who left to go to Lewes Sixth Form College wanted to return after three weeks – no exercise, she missed mixing with a wide peer age-group and she didn't like the regimented way subjects were taught.

Past pupils: Oliver Tobias, Sean Yates (international cyclist), Bella Freud, Esther Freud, Marty Boysens (mountaineer), Prof John Pearce (author and professor of child psychiatry at Nottingham University), Stuart Korth (osteopathy centre for children).

Entrance: At no specific age – 'the younger the better'; natural breaks in the Steiner curriculum occur at six and 14 years old. Non-selective in academic sense, although much effort to ensure class communities mesh. Mild dyslexia and dyspraxia fine (often diagnosed and always supported by learning support

department) – more severe conditions sometimes OK as long as children are in system from kindergarten and their needs do not detract from quality of whole class education. Class teacher will interview potential parents/pupils – previous experience of French or German and music an advantage. Brighton Steiner and Steiner School of south west London are main feeders at age 14. Sixth form entry by interview.

Exit: Up to 15 per cent leave at age of 12/13 to enter public schools. Fifty per cent after GCSE for sixth form college in order to take more vocational A levels. Sixty per cent of upper schoolers go on to degree courses at eg Cambridge, York and Bath; many European universities take Steiner pupils without external qualification. Subjects include architecture, history, psychology, drama and art foundation. Some take gap years to improve language skills and cultural appreciation.

Money matters: School runs a bursary scheme through which families on lower incomes are able to pay lower tuition charges. To qualify, a detailed statement of income has to be provided to the school. Discounts on fees for siblings.

Remarks: A gentle school which aims to keep children from rushing into adulthood before they're ready (school says, ' Children are taught in an age appropriate way'). This education may not work for every child, nor every parent – both would need to be tremendously involved in the educative process. Very difficult to explain a Steiner school without direct experience or attending an open morning – hippy stereotypes abound – yet the children who emerge are confident, articulate, international, open-minded and grounded. Lucky them.

Mill Hill County High School

Worcester Crescent, London, NW7 4LL

- Pupils: 1,720; 55 per cent boys and 45 per cent girls; all day
- Ages: 11–19 • Non–denom • State

Tel: 0844 477 2424
Email: admin@mhchs.org.uk
Website: www.mhchs.org.uk

Headteacher: Since 2004, Geoffrey Thompson MA MBA (Ed) FCMI (fifties). Formerly head of Duchess's Community High School in Alnwick, Northumberland. Educated at Campbell College, Belfast, then at St Catharine's College, Cambridge, where he read music. Started his teaching career at Langley Park School for Boys in Bromley, where he worked for 18 years, before moving to Norfolk as deputy head, then on to Northumberland. Though Mill Hill County has always been a school with high standards, his decade in charge has improved it significantly. 'Having a vision and a blueprint is not my way,' he says. 'You have a set of principles and good judgement, you make decisions with other people and the place grows organically.'

A dapper soul, whose own tie is always immaculately knotted, he has a dry sense of humour and a delightfully precise command of the English language. Married to a teacher (who also works in the school), he has two daughters and a son. Out of hours, he enjoys reading, particularly modern history, travelling and music.

Academic matters: Mill Hill County is one of the country's highest performing comprehensives. With 70 per cent A*/B at A level in 2013 and 79 per cent A*-C at GCSE (including English and maths), this is a school which believes in an academic focus. Apart from a handful of vocational qualifications in ICT and media, the curriculum is traditional, with a good range of modern languages (Spanish, French, German, Latin) and a quarter of pupils taking all three sciences at GCSE. In the sixth form – the largest in the borough – the 33 subjects on offer include sociology, psychology, economics and dance. Maths and science, however, are the most popular options (with 10 groups for maths). Most sixth formers take four AS levels ('a few do five, but we don't encourage it,' says the head).

Teaching strong throughout (with regular awards for science, geography and maths) and most subjects provide plenty of enrichment. In English, for example, there are Shakespeare and poetry workshops, in DT, direct links with industry. An undoubted strength of the school is the focused attention it offers for all. 'Every child is taught to their own individual abilities,' commented one parent. For those at the top of the spectrum, there are two members of staff to encourage A level students to aim for A*s and Russell Group universities, while those who struggle to make the A*-C benchmark at GCSE are offered a one-year course in which to resit. At this juncture too, the school participates in a Barnet-wide scheme which sandwiches vocational college training with English, maths and employment skills. Largest number of SEN pupils in Barnet with a department reflective of their very varied needs (including provision for the blind). A raft of teaching assistants provides in-class aid and specialist staff oversee classes and support students beyond. 'It's quite an operation,' says the head.

Games, options, the arts: The school prides itself on its extra-curricular offering, but there's little doubt that music is the jewel in the crown. 'There are few local schools that can hold a candle to us,' says the head with legitimate pride. He himself rehearses all year 7s to appear in the Christmas concert and from time to time plays the piano at assembly or a duet alongside a visiting professional. Standards throughout are exceptionally high. Recently, for the fourth year in a row, the orchestra is performing a joint concert with the Royal Philharmonic ('you have to be quite good for the RPO to come and play with you,' says the head). Meanwhile the school band will feature alongside that of the Royal Air Force at the Watford Colosseum. Regular lunchtime concerts, major concerts twice a term, large-scale musical in the Easter term, plus an annual European tour for concert and jazz bands. A full range of other sounds, including gospel, African drum and steel drum. Boys participate as enthusiastically as girls – 'unheard of,' says the head – and one talented former pupil performs regularly at Ronnie Scott's.

In sport too, the school has become a 'force to be reckoned with,' particularly in boys' football and girls' netball. Basketball and rugby also on offer and table tennis played enthusiastically by all. Excellent facilities for sport include a range of pitches, three playgrounds, gym, sports hall and in summer, six-lane track and three tennis courts. Art thriving, with a weekly art club and life drawing workshop run by the Royal Academy for A level pupils. Numerous guest speakers and in-demand trips (languages to Barcelona and Normandy, politics to the US, annual ski trip) to inspire and raise aspirations. Good range of clubs run early morning and after school (which can be difficult for those who live at a distance), plus D of E, World Challenge and CCF (shared with nearby independent Mill Hill).

Background and atmosphere: Originally opened in 1931 as Orange Hill Boys' Grammar School, which then combined with matching girls' grammar in the 1970s. Merged again with Moat Mount School in 1984 to create Mill Hill County High School. The school, fringed by a good expanse of playing fields and forest, now sits on a hilly site with panoramic London views. There, however, the picturesque ends, with well-used buildings crammed together in an intricate hotchpotch to accommodate more students than ever. 'It is overcrowded,' said one parent. 'They're the victims of their own success.' Older parts of the fabric include some fairly basic Portakabins (which house dance and drama), but recent additions have provided modern labs, a sixth form centre, computer suites and an air-conditioned assembly hall. Seven new classrooms are currently under construction.

The lack of elbow room doesn't seem to detract from the upbeat mood, with friendly and positive staff (on the day the guide visited a member of the office team was ringing up a local primary school to ensure a forgotten jumper was returned to its owner) and parents praise the general sense of wellbeing. 'The school is very good at communicating,' said one. 'They keep us informed and I have the email addresses of all my child's teachers.' Another was grateful for the empathy shown at a difficult time. 'They were understanding and supportive when we had family problems.'

Not the easiest school to get to. No tube nearby, which contributes to the mood of semi-rural calm, but can be difficult for those wanting to arrive early or stay late for clubs or games. Mill Hill became an academy in 2011, but still works closely with Barnet Council, particularly in its responsibilities for Oak Hill, a successful facility for 32 emotionally and behaviourally disturbed children, four and a half miles away.

Pastoral care and discipline: One of the first things parents tend to mention is the uniform policy. 'They're very strict on uniform,' said one. 'Everyone looks very smart.' The head sees uniform as a means of setting the expectation bar. 'We're very clear about what we say and insist that what we say is done. We aren't repressive, but you'd be unlikely to see anyone with their shirt tails not tucked in or their ties not tied.'

The head also spends one lesson a week making surprise visits to a range of classrooms. 'That way, you see what's happening. You chat to the children, look at their books. It's a co-operative relationship, but you could potentially see those same children in another context behaving badly.' The insistent focus on behaviour, attitude and good manners undoubtedly pays off. 'Most people who come across our students have positive things to say.'

Pupils and parents: About half the school's intake comes from the leafy and prosperous suburb of Mill Hill, with its high concentration of professionals and business families, but the intake is certainly not uniform. 'There are quite a lot of deprived children and the ethnic mix is huge,' says the head. It includes significant numbers of families who originate from the Indian sub-continent, Asia and Africa. Only a few, however, 'don't speak excellent English.'

Entrance: Mill Hill has entrance criteria guaranteed to drive north London parents into a neurotic frenzy, with 240 places at 11 sliced up into small print sub-sections. Lucky locals can benefit from one of the 90 guaranteed 'geography' places. But distance from the gates is frighteningly close (0.8 miles in 2012). Siblings, too, are ensured a desk. After that the 60 places awarded on aptitude are split into: 24 for technology, 24 for music and 12 for dance. Technology is tested in two stages – a reasoning test in the summer term of year 5 whittles down about 1500 to 240, the second round (in abstract reasoning and maths) held in September cherry picks the rest ('it's harder than getting into Oxford,' jokes the head). Music equally competitive, with 389 auditioning last year. 'You can, however, play a snappy piece on the classroom xylophone and come out higher than a carefully coached grade 4 violinist.' Dance candidates are selected by audition.

The large (and heavily over-subscribed) sixth form admits a further 40 to 60 pupils out of 600 applicants, with minimum entry requirements of six grade Bs at GCSE, including English and maths. Those wishing to study science and maths need As in their chosen subjects though, and most come garlanded with a string of A*s and As.

Exit: No one is ever asked to leave (except for disciplinary matters), but a fair few move on after GCSE to local sixth form colleges, independent and grammar schools. More than 70 per cent to university, the majority to Russell Group (the school has one of the highest representations here of any comprehensive in the UK). Nine to Oxbridge last year. Quite a number to drama and art-related degrees. A consistent trickle to the US.

Money matters: The transformation to academy status has released additional funds and these are now being used for building projects. Otherwise not rich, but not poor either.

Remarks: A cheerful, well-run school producing highly motivated, high achieving students. Exceptional music.

Mill Hill School

Linked schools: Belmont Mill Hill Preparatory School; Grimsdell, Mill Hill Pre-Preparatory School

The Ridgeway, London, NW7 1QS

• Pupils: 650; two-thirds boys, one-third girls • Ages: 13–18
• Non-denom • Fees: Boarding £23,964–£28,194; Day £17,844 pa
• Independent

Tel: 020 8959 1176
Email: registrations@millhill.org.uk
Website: www.millhill.org.uk

Headmaster: Since 2007, Dr Dominic Luckett BA DPhil FRSA (forties). Educated at the University of Leicester and Magdalen College, Oxford, where he did his doctorate in Tudor history. Taught at Harrow, where he became both head of history and an assistant housemaster, then at Worth, where he was deputy head. He is a serving inspector with the ISI and on the council of the University of Leicester. Attracted to Mill Hill because it mixes day with boarding and because of its location in north London. Married to Cara, a barrister, and has two young daughters.

A tall, softly spoken and sincere man who pauses before giving a considered response – a likeable head. 'He's very focused,' one parent said. He is under no illusion that the school still has a way to go academically before it can pit itself against other north London rivals, but says the foundations are there to make it a truly 'phenomenal school.' 'My job is to realise some of the potential this school has,' he told us. 'And I think we're getting there – we've already achieved the best A level results we've ever had this year. We're never going to be the most massively selective school, but we pride ourselves on having students with really lovely values, who may bring other things to the table.' That's why, he says, they interview potential candidates before seeing their exam results. 'If someone comes along for an interview and demonstrates they have extra strings to their bow – great at sport or drama for example, we may be a bit more lenient if they're borderline in their CE exam.'

The head's main objective is that each of his pupils feel really proud about being a Millhillian, and that he steers away from the school's reputation of being the 'back-up' school because they didn't get into UCS or Highgate. Says he would have given his right arm to have attended a school like this, having come from a non-privileged background with parents who had low academic aspirations. 'I know the difference a good education can make. I'm only where I am today because I got into the local grammar school, otherwise I could easily be working in the local Sainsbury's.'

Academic matters: Record A level results in 2013, with more than 82 per cent A*/B grades. A third of the 127-strong cohort achieved AAB or better, with 44 per cent of grades being A*/A. More than 14 per cent of grades were A* – twice the national average. GCSE results showed a dip from last year with 51 per cent A*/A and 80 per cent A*/B but the head is not disheartened. 'We've made a very great deal of progress in this area in the last few years and 51 per cent is unusual in the pattern of recent results.' School's aim is to achieve each child's full potential while working in a way that makes them feel comfortable – 'for some, three Bs at A level is a real achievement, but others here get three, four or five As,' he says. Some children, too, require a lot of pressure to achieve and others buckle under pressure.

Twenty-four subjects on offer at A level, including Chinese, business studies and government and politics. One parent criticised the subjects on offer as limiting compared to other schools. 'My friend removed her child from the school to go to another sixth form as they didn't offer psychology as an A Level,' she told us. Good spread of languages offered at GCSE: French, Spanish, German, Greek and Latin, plus Portuguese and Chinese as extras.

Two of the learning resources on the campus are worth noting. The library (an 'innovative conversion' of the school squash courts) is a two-tiered, large, bright space, incredibly well stocked with books and a gallery for magnificent artwork by students. The stunning and contemporary Favell building has a glass atrium – providing a light and airy home for seven departments, including modern languages, history and geography. Also used for exhibitions and entertainment. Startlingly quiet classrooms (we had to check to see if there were students inside) surround the atrium on three floors. Well presented but scant student displays and artwork adorn the walls, encased in glass frames.

New science block is underway to replace the rather old-fashioned labs where Nobel-winning scientist Francis Crick once studied. (This doesn't seem to hold pupils back since Imperial College is a popular university destination).

Mill Hill takes in a reasonably broad spread of academic ability and aims to get the best out of each child by helping them to learn effectively. 'We're not a hot house,' says the head. 'We're never going to be the top academic school in the country, but we want to make teaching accessible and enjoyable and give children high expectations.' That said, we have some very bright children. It's a question of identifying what each child is capable of and providing what each child needs.

The school has limited facilities for SEN. Head is sympathetic but pragmatic. 'We have facilities in place to deal with mild to moderate dyslexia, but for anything more severe, we just don't have the resources in place.' All new entrants are screened for dyslexia and dyspraxia and are given extra time in the CE exam. One parent whose child is moderately dyslexic said the school was 'helpful to a point,' but she had to fight for most things.

Games, options, the arts: Sport, sport, sport. A clincher for pupils and parents alike when choosing this school over others. Competitive and recreational sport has always played a big role at Mill Hill and with its expansive site, it's easy to see why. Rugby and cricket are the two biggies here. As one parent told us: 'My son only agreed to come here because of the rugby.' The school established a reputation as a rugby playing school from the outset, and has produced a large number of international rugby players. Great facilities in which to play.

The school's cricket arena has been called 'one of the most beautiful grounds to play cricket in the London area.' To add to this, they have the services of a professional coach. Players are regularly selected to represent Middlesex and Hertfordshire and occasionally England. Girls too have done exceptionally well, representing both school (playing as part of the boys' team) and country.

M

Golf is another major sport here and is even incorporated into the timetable. They are the only school in London to boast a golf academy, (although ironically no golf course – pupils play at nearby Hendon). One girl has just been selected for the England U16 girls' golf team. Tennis is very strong – one of the strongest schools in the south east.

Soccer, netball, hockey, cross country and swimming (the school boasts a beautiful, new 25m pool) on offer. More adventurous pupils can try their hand at sailing, skiing/snowboarding, riding, clay pigeon shooting and Taekwondo (these incur extra cost). Mill Hill is also one of the few remaining independent schools to have an Eton Fives court. The shape of the court is modelled on the chapel at Eton (we thought it looked like a Roman gladiator chamber).

For non-sporty types (and they are seemingly few and far between), drama is very popular and taken by many at both GCSE and A level. With drama studio, theatre and large school stage, it is rare for a production not to be in rehearsal. House arts festival takes place every two years (alternating with a house music competition), with ten plays performed over three nights. Many ex-students have become thesps of stage and screen. Art is strong and some of the art displayed around the school is amongst the best we've seen. This year saw the first inflatable sculpture floating around the studios. Good music facilities (specialised equipment for composition and recording) and in addition to curricular music, lots of opportunities to participate in a wide range of musical activities (chapel choir, string orchestra, jazz band and chamber music). Well-equipped on the DT side with 30 top-end computers and industry standard 3D printers.

A series of monthly lectures on a variety of topics – from classical history to journalism and politics (presenters include Jonathan Dimbleby and Terry Jones) are a popular and successful addition to the already crammed Mill Hill diary.

Thriving charitable work and partnership trips every summer; lower sixth form pupils have the opportunity to work for two to three weeks in a variety of educational projects with partners in Zambia, India and Nicaragua. Those taking part often talk about them being a 'life-changing experience.' As one parent told us: 'The school does exactly what it says on the box – there's something there for everyone.'

Background and atmosphere: Founded in 1807 by a group of non-conformist Christian ministers and city merchants, who placed their school outside London because of the 'dangers, both physical and moral, awaiting youth while passing through the streets of a large, crowded city.' Once peaceful and rural, The Ridgeway, where the school is situated, has become a busy and frustrating road (to be avoided like the plague at school pick-up). Nonetheless, it is still a very pretty part of the old Mill Hill village, laced with ponds and rambling cottages.

The school itself doesn't disappoint, with its handsome, neoclassical, pillared façade (BBC News website often uses a picture of Mill Hill School for articles about boarding schools). This is more like a stately home than a school, with pale yellow walls, marbled floors, pillars, plaques and elaborately framed portraits (most notably that of Mill Hill's former member of staff, James Murray, the third editor of the Oxford English Dictionary).

Our tour began at the top terrace, with sweeping views across parkland (undoubtedly the school's selling point) and 120 acres of green belt. The panorama is one of immaculately kept lawns, gravelled walkways, ponds and a smorgasbord of varying architecture which marry beautifully from arts and crafts buildings to the glass exterior of the new Favell building. The previous head, we are told, wanted to 'massively transform' the school for its bicentenary. We poked our heads into the beautiful, basilica-style chapel, designed by architect Basil Champney (best known for his work at Oxford and Winchester College). For students it means a compulsory weekly chapel visit, although the school is officially a non-conformist foundation.

Very much a campus school with little access to urban reality, some distance from the gates. It's a vast space for seemingly few pupils (nearly 650 in total) and indeed the walk to the furthest boarding house is so far that we were going to suggest adding nordic walking to the syllabus. Around a quarter board, many on a weekly basis. No longer has Saturday morning school – 'the best thing the school could have done,' a parent told us, and a major factor in her deciding to send her son there. Another parent disagreed and says it gave her son structure and all he'll do now is just 'watch TV.' Day pupils stay onsite during the academic day and are members of one of seven day houses. Pupils can hang out in their houses between classes.

Boarders are allowed out after lessons to the local (limited) high street. Those who opt for full boarding are offered a Saturday morning programme of academic workshops and other activities. One boarder told us: 'I have been offered so much help with filling out my UCAS form, which is something those with parents around may take for granted.' Boarding house we saw was slightly tired looking – in need of updating.

Although a fully co-ed school since 1997, it is still very male-centric – around 70 per cent boys and 30 per cent girls. This has put some prospective parents off sending their daughters there. One parent told us: 'Any school which is not balanced worries me slightly. You wonder if it is as well geared around girls as it so clearly is for boys.' However, a girl we spoke to disagreed. 'The diversity here makes it a really unique place where everyone is accepted,' she said. Indeed the girls we met on our tour didn't appear to be the shy, retiring types who would worry about being outnumbered. Pupils generally seemed a happy and spirited bunch. Merging with The Mount School in September 2014, which should increase the ratio of girls.

Pastoral care and discipline: Uniform is their thing – 'extremely strict,' one parent told us, and the deputy head is often seen reprimanding students for this reason outside the school gates. The result is an extremely well turned out (and good-looking), bunch of teenagers in traditional dark blazers adorned with the school motto and a myriad of ties denoting their houses. Sixth formers wear their own suits.

Housemasters and housesmistresses are the first point of contact for students or parents with concerns. A full-time boarder told us: 'They have become like a surrogate family to me. I came over from Africa when I was 13 without anyone to look after me. My housemaster and my teachers made me feel so welcome and went step by step through everything. The pastoral care is great.' Another said: 'It can be quite a daunting school to come to and I kept getting lost, but I had an excellent mentor and settled in quickly.'

Considered to be a kind and gentle school, consistently praised by parents and officials for its outstanding pastoral care – 'very good at giving children their freedom,' one parent told us. Another parent said you can spot a Mill Hill child in a crowd. 'They always seem to be the most social and well rounded.' One pupil told us: 'It's like being part of a big family.' His only criticism was that 'you can't do an extra year.' This 'freedom' has led some parents to feel that the school is fairly slack in some areas though. One criticised the fact that pupils get the same detention for smoking behind the bikeshed as for chewing gum. She added that the head has improved the standard of the school greatly and praises him for not having double standards or being swayed by money or influence. She said: 'It seems to have been a problem with heads before, that it was one rule for one, and another if you had money.'

Formal exclusions are few and far between. Unlike some other schools, with their zero policy on drugs, this head is realistic, but not lax. 'If you are found with drugs once, it's a suspension, twice, you're out.' He says it nearly 'broke his heart' to permanently exclude a very bright and promising student for bringing drugs onto the premises. But 'you can't start making exceptions,' he told us. 'It blurs the line.'

Pupils and parents: No typical Mill Hill pupil. Quite a lot live locally, even boarders, though in the sixth form there's a significant influx from China, Africa, Germany, France and Russia. Diverse ethnic and religious mix – Catholic, Jewish and Greek possibly the most prominent. Strong entrepreneurial element and urban professionals among the parents, together with 'the seriously rich.' The odd celebrity parent has also been known to grace the hallowed halls. Former pupils include Richard Dimbleby, Francis Crick, Simon Jenkins, Timothy Mo, Denis Thatcher, Katharine Whitehorn and Norman Hartnell.

Entrance: Total of 140 places in year 9, with about 70 or 80 going to pupils from the junior school (Belmont) and a handful of other feeder schools. No place is guaranteed though – 'the school will politely tell you if they don't think your child is up to it.' Approx 20 places reserved for boarders. Sets its own exams in January before entrance in English, maths, French and science and uses the CE pass mark for setting. Oversubscribed, so 'we want to know what a child will bring. It's partly personality, and partly other factors like sport, music or drama.'

Entry to the sixth form requires two As and three Bs at GCSE, a requirement that applies both externally and internally. These requirements have not always been strictly adhered to, but one of the head's first acts was to enforce it, involving about 15 pupils leaving. 'We've always had a minimum grade requirement, now we're insisting it's met,' he said. One parent grumbled: 'The school is always moving the bar. It used to be automatic entrance into the sixth form.'

Exit: Most leavers progress to Russell Group universities. In 2013 the most popular destinations were Nottingham, Bristol, Birmingham, Bath and Leeds. Five to Oxbridge.

Money matters: Middle to higher end of fee-paying schools in London. A selection of scholarships in academic subjects, the arts and sports. Fully-funded bursaries awarded each year and a range of other bursaries up to 90 per cent of the fees, on a carefully graded system of finance. The head's intention is that by 2020 20 students a year will be offered full bursaries.

Remarks: Suits a busy, engaged child happy to try out a wide range of activities and use all the facilities and range of a boarding school, while still being able to go home at night (unless, of course, they board). A well-balanced school, with a head determined to put the academic underpinning firmly in place.

Millfield School

Linked school: Millfield Preparatory School

Butleigh Road, Street, Somerset, BA16 0YD

- Pupils: 1,260; 770 boys/490 girls; 930 boarders • Ages: 13–18
- Inter-denominational • Fees: Boarding £32,385; Day £21,810 pa
- Independent

Tel: 01458 442291
Email: admissions@millfieldschool.com
Website: www.millfieldschool.com

Head Master: Since 2008, Mr Craig Considine MA (fiftyish). Degree in applied science in human movement (Australian version of sports science) from Royal Melbourne Institute of Technology; diploma and master's in education from Melbourne and Charles Stuart Universities. Was headmaster of Wanganui Collegiate School, New Zealand (Prince Edward worked there for two terms in his gap year). Before that taught at Geelong Grammar School, where he was much involved in the school's five week Timbertop programme in 'Alpine wilderness' (Victorian Alps, in case you're imagining St Bernards and yodelling). Would like to increase this kind of 'experiential education' at Millfield (it's said to develop life skills, values, independence, teamwork, leadership ... Has no one told them about the Duke of Edinburgh Award?). A large bear of a man – represented Australia in the Commonwealth Games (decathlon) and played professional Aussie rules football. Quieter, less flashy than his predecessors. Thought, by parents and pupils, to be steering the school towards greater emphasis on academics and generally tightening up rules and behaviour – not to everyone's approval. Keen on more structure; would like more staff living on site; wants year 9 pupils tended more carefully; more opportunities for 'middle ability' games players. Aims for nothing less than the school being known as the 'best boarding school in the country'. Some parents (and staff) concerned this means turning Millfield into a run-of-the-mill boarding school by diluting the quirks and sports obsession that make it special, and some resistance.

Married to Penny, who has much experience working in boarding houses (BA in youth work). Four children – twins at Millfield, an older teenager boarding back at Geelong High, and one on a gap year.

Academic matters: Breathtakingly broad ability range – one of the few big, famous public schools that remains proudly non-selective academically. Exam results close to the national average for A levels. Usually comfortably above average for GCSEs – in 2013, 87 per cent of pupils earned the equivalent of five or more GCSE grade C or above including English and maths and 37 per cent of grades were A*/A. School results highlight 100 top scores rather than dwell on the huge spread that reflects the ability range. In 2013, over 54 per cent of A level grades A*/B and 28 per cent A*/A. The bright end is clever indeed – four to Oxbridge in 2012 – and the dimmer end stretches out eternally to the distant horizon. So setting is important here: 'There's setting for everything – even art!' a pupil told us. Twenty-eight pupils took BTEC examinations in 2013 – everything from art and design to business, music technology and sport.

Pupils say the head wants to beef up academics and cite as evidence the move to longer lessons (from 35 minutes to 50 – head says it was planned before he arrived; helps the organisationally challenged). But academics will never be the point of Millfield – parents choose the school for the full Monty: the 'Millfield mix'. Enormous range of A level subjects, from Latin to media studies. 'World development' available as an AS – not sure where else you'd find this. Has dipped toe into the medicinal baths of the Pre-U by offering it for History instead of A level. Has introduced Extended Project Qualification and CISI Securities and Investment course. Vocational BTECs in art and design and in sport; a double A level award in leisure studies also popular. One girl said to be doing ancient Greek. Well-stocked library open from 8.30am Monday to Saturday.

Millfield is dauntingly large, yet classes are pocket-sized (maximum 15, usually much smaller) and the staff:pupil ratio an extraordinary 1:6.5. With nearly 200 academic and coaching staff, Millfield boasts the largest common-room of any school in the UK. Prep in house for an hour and a half each week night. Lots of support and empathy for overstretched sportsmen and women. 'They understand how time-consuming sport is and help you to work around it,' said a cricketer. Busy pupils can take fewer GCSEs. 400+ pupils with SEN 'from mild to quite severe'. Millfield's expertise in specific learning difficulties goes back a long way: Jack Meyer was summoned to London in 1941 to discuss the possibility of Attlee's 'word blind' son entering Millfield. He passed his exams to enter the School of Navigation at Southampton 18 months later and Millfield's reputation for helping dyslexics was made. Support delivered by school's SEN unit mainly in small groups rather than one-to-one. Bright

M

dyslexics may 'drop in' to work with SEN specialist teacher – no shame in visiting the unit. Others will be timetabled to be there, usually in place of a foreign language – there is an entire English class in each year who are taught English in the SEN dept. 'Language development' lessons help pupils struggling with writing to structure essays – helps them across the board. Maths dept runs dyscalculia workshop in lunch breaks. Dyslexics, dyspraxics, Mild Asperger's, autism, ADHD all assisted – some come with statements of needs and ed psyche reports, others are identified during their school career. Five full-time staff and two part-timers, all qualified teachers and either dyslexia qualified or with loads of experience. NB: No extra fee for SEN. Some 100 international pupils take advantage of the very good EAL provision.

Games, options, the arts: Seen by many as a specialist sports school, and it would certainly qualify – if it wasn't so maddeningly good at everything else. Sports teams habitually bring their opposition to its knees, so much so that they have been known to dispatch their B team to play the A team of some quite famous schools. The high standard can be a shock to some pupils who played on their prep school A team and now find themselves demoted to the bottom of the Cs. Rugby, hockey, cricket, swimming top the fixture list. Rugby players won all the levels they entered in the huge 2010 National Schools Sevens Competition (prep, U16 and Open).

Fabulous cricket pavilion, the glass walls etched in cricket balls (this editor thought they were coffee beans until put right), 50m swimming pool one of the best in Britain and used for Olympic training, nine-hole golf course with indoor tuition centre (Independent Schools Golf Association winners in 2009 and team and individual boys and girls World Schools Challenge Champions in 2011.) Golfers have a winter top up session in the Desert Springs resort, Almanzora, Spain, indoor tennis centre (plus lots of all-weather courts), running track, shooting range, three Astro hockey pitches, acres of playing fields, dedicated fencing salle and judo room, high power ski team. Equestrian centre has indoor and outdoor arenas, X-C schooling fields, Derby course and stabling for 53 horses including facilities for pupils' own horses. Pupils can study for their British Horse Society Preliminary Instructor's Certificate as a timetabled subject. Own polo pitch and won the National Schools' Polo Championships in 2010 and 2011. Lots of overseas tours.

Minor sports not given as much peer approval, say some pupils. Sports scholars tell us that serious sportsmen and women need to hunker down and concentrate on excellence in their chosen sport – not the place for all rounders if you're playing at the highest levels: 'It's very full time'. Some specialist treatment – sports nutrition, sports psychology and physiotherapy – available to these top athletes. Fifteen Old Millfieldians competed in the 2010 Commonwealth Games (mostly rugby, swimming and hockey) and six took part in the 2012 Olympics, including Helen Glover who won gold for Team GB in the women's pair rowing. Well-staffed physiotherapy department and weights rooms. Ten Tors for those wanting a physical challenge that does not involve bat or ball.

Two main school productions each year (in school's 500 seat theatre), with large casts, but still plenty of disappointed would-be thespians in a school of this size. GCSE and A level pupils have smaller coursework shows and years 9 and 10 take part in the house drama competition. Dance – all kinds – big here, especially for a co-ed school. Elite 'Bazique' programme for the school's top nine or 10 dancers. Debate society going strong, with pupils taking part in the European Youth Parliament.

Art extraordinary with fabulous facilities and space, space, space. BTEC art pupils mount a fashion show each year. Music surprisingly good and housed in splendid newish building with acoustically perfect concert hall. Awash with pianos, top of the line Macs, beauteous music lockers, recording studio, drum kits and lovely practice rooms – nothing is wanting. 'Tea and music'

informal concerts provide lots of performance opportunities. Quality, at the high end, is impressive, with Millfield pupils in the National Youth Orchestra every year and moving on to music conservatoires.

MAP – the school's activities programme – offers a virtually unlimited range, from dissection to chunky knitting to Caterham car club to jewellery making – year 9, 10 and 12 pupils must take part in one each week. D of E involvement strong. Impressive food technology dept under Leith's aegis popular. 'It used to be that sport was everything here,' a pupil told us, 'but not so much now.'

So what does Millfield not do? No gymnastics, trampolining, diving. So it's all here, but be warned – the emphasis is on choosing what you want to be good at and going for it rather than dabbling across the myriad spheres: 'Otherwise you will be left behind'.

Background and atmosphere: If you're seeking ivy-clad spires or comically antiquated uniforms, look away now. Feels exactly like a small American university campus, beautifully tended with walkways, sculpture and a mishmash of building styles. Over 300 acres of grounds: large, non-traditional, and slightly impersonal by UK private school standards – 'You don't know everyone in your year,' a boy told us. Top heavy, numbers-wise, with enormous sixth form somewhat dominating the feel of the place.

Founded in 1935 by Jack Meyer with seven Indian pupils, of whom six were princes, and swiftly adopted the Robin Hood principle – squeezing money from the exceedingly rich to subsidise the needy, talented poor. From day one, in a large, rented Somerset house, he set about promoting individual ability, in whatever sphere. Proud of having been built up from nothing and owing nothing. Used to paying its way – hosts range of Easter revision courses and summer English language courses as well as conferences.

A large dining hall, notable for its finer than average fare, sits at the heart of the campus and is given a universal thumbs up by pupils, even the vegetarians.

Pastoral care and discipline: Always a challenge at a co-ed school with so many pupils of such diversity. Drugs and alcohol bound to enter the frame, but head maintains that Millfield's policy is 'tight compared to other schools'. Five boys suspended in autumn 2010 for use of cannabis. Transgressions always helpfully flagged up by The Daily Mail. Pupils noticeably more streetwise than at many private schools, and not a school you'd choose if you're looking for mollycoddling. Sixth formers given much freedom to come and go on weekends. Girls' skirts shortish, though not horrendous. Keeps going throughout the term with activities for those who live abroad (though guardians etc pick up during half term). Chaplaincy centre a haven for exam-stressed pupils, plus other counsellors in the place, dedicated prayer room for Muslims. Strong community service locally.

Fine boarding houses – pupils mainly in double rooms, then singles in sixth form. House identity not the huge deal it can be at other schools (school allocates houses – we hear Orchards is good at cricket, Keen's Elm swimming, the day houses academics). Three boys' boarding houses off campus (boys bused in and out), all other boarding on site, including 'day centres' for day pupils – two for girls, two for boys – to base themselves. The girls' day house moved in 2012 and now boasts enhanced facilities including dedicated areas for prep and relaxation, with WiFi throughout. The new on-site boarding houses particularly impressive with smashing kitchens, Sky and huge common-rooms.

Pupils and parents: Varied – first school that has ever answered our question about geographical range of intake with 'the world' (63 countries). Some 22 per cent international pupils, six per cent expats – 'We see ourselves as an international school – we want that diversity,' explains the head. Majority of pupils come from Surrey, followed by Glos and Sussex. (Boy/girl ratio is 60/40). Immense range of family backgrounds, from the dyslexic sent by a local authority in north Wales to the one-armed swimmer from Essex to a Middle Eastern prince wallowing in cash – makes for some challenges. 'Not the place to send your son if you want him to learn to speak like a gentleman,' one overseas father murmured. 'My son left Millfield far better prepared to deal with the real world than if he'd been cocooned at one of the traditional public schools,' said a mum.

The school sent us a five page, small font, narrow spaced, alphabetised list of noteworthy former pupils: John Sergeant, Max Mosley, cricketers Ian Ward and Ben Hollioake, British Lions and Wales rugby international Gareth Edwards, DJ Tony Blackburn, Diana's special friend James Hewitt, film producer Jeremy Thomas (The Last Emperor), chief executive of the Royal Aeronautical Society Simon Luxmoore, Nicolette Sheridan (Edie in Desperate Housewives), Sophie Dahl (expelled), Steward Copeland (of The Police) and lots of Olympic swimmers are the tip of an eclectic iceberg.

Entrance: At least 210 enter at year 9, 30+ at year 10 and 130+ at sixth form. Interview and previous head's report the usual route in, with CE used to determine set for core subjects – 'We have 16 maths sets in year 9'. No written test required for overseas applicants – a huge selling point for many. Anything up to 80 feeder schools, but by far the largest day number come from its own prep school (see separate entry). Pupils enter and exit at odd times including mid-year and, at least once, we hear, departing in the middle of the night (money problems; overseas pupil).

Exit: Most to university, the full range with over 60 UK universities and colleges listed and a large slice to overseas universities, especially in the States and including Harvard.

Money matters: Over £3.5 million worth of 'fee concessions' each year, and the Millfield Foundation (former pupils) is beavering away to swell the pot. Scholarships for all-rounders, sportspeople (was the first school to offer these), academics, musicians (instrumental and choral) artists, actors and even chess players – they're worth no more than 15 per cent of fees, but can be topped up with means-tested bursaries. Also a limited number of Headmaster's Awards of up to 50 per cent. Sixth form scholarships said to be more plentiful than 13+ (fewer years for the school to shell out, and helps cherry-pick 16 year olds).

Around 35 per cent get some form of award, so a couple of pupils mentioned tensions between 'rich kids' and 'scholarship kids'. Famously muddy fee structure has finally shaken the habit of three-quarters of a century and is now 'crystal clear'. No longer a separate fee bracket for 'international' students.

Remarks: One of the few schools that really is all things to all pupils (almost). But less and less a school for all rounders than for passionate specialists. Undergoing a slight, but seismic, culture shift. SEN still excels.

Milton Abbey School

Milton Abbas, Blandford Forum, Dorset, DT11 0BZ

- Pupils: 220; 185 boys/35 girls; 210 full boarders/10 day pupils
- Ages: 13–19 • C of E • Fees: Boarding £31,200; Day £23,400 pa
- Independent

Tel: 01258 880484
Email: admissions@miltonabbey.co.uk
Website: www.miltonabbey.co.uk

Headmaster: Since January 2014, Magnus Bashaarat, previously deputy head of Stowe. Studied English at Edinburgh, then worked as a journalist before training as a teacher at King's College London. Started teaching at Sherborne; 15 years at Eton before joining Stowe. Passionate about theatre and likes to run, row and cycle 'when time and the weather allow'. Married to Camilla; three children.

Academic matters: Milton Abbey's strengths lie in its value-added, rather than the barren tale told by league tables, it says. However, it refuses to supply us with 2013 exam results or information on where its leavers went, so we must take its word for this. More than half its pupils are assessed as having SEN on entry, and it accommodates a far wider range of difficulties (such as hearing, emotional difficulties and mild Aspergers) than dyslexia, though this is the commonest, at around a third of pupils. It's a very broad and tolerant church indeed, but resolutely mainstream. A great deal of support both practical and moral from its accredited CreSTeD unit results in commendable grades for pupils: 'Confused chemists can expect a C at GCSE, rather than an E or U', said one happy mum. English, maths and a language are compulsory at this level, PE, PHSE and religious studies too, but unexamined; sciences taken as options with a good take-up in applied science.

An average in past years of 50 per cent of the cohort achieved five or more GCSE passes. Class sizes of between 10-15 must help, much smaller in the sixth form, where BTECs in hospitality, equine studies, sport and countryside management sit comfortably alongside A levels, gaining strong results, particularly in countryside management and hospitality. A level results have been creditable, rather than stellar, as one might expect. Interestingly, upper sixth is known as middle sixth, to reflect that extra seventh term for Oxbridge (or possibly to nail elusive A levels); certainly it is not unusual to find leavers aged 19 or nearly with no ridicule attached.

Progress report every three weeks; this is in part diagnostic, commenting on organisation and punctuality as well as grades, and setting 'challenge grades', which we were assured are not dry predictions – and by raising academic sights. 'We're not changing our entry levels and will never do so.'

What distinguishes the academic offering from any other school this editor had visited is that the SEN provision complements academic life seamlessly and totally without stigma. The unit has a permanently open door, and offers support not only to those currently on its books, but to anyone wanting the odd tip for effective revision or essay planning, for example. Special mention must also be given to the librarian, who has made a fabulously welcoming and accessible resource designed to appeal to the most reluctant bookworm. One sixth former however intimated that, in its missionary zeal for supporting SEN pupils, the school could be guilty of neglecting those needing the routine kind of boost to morale or tlc that ordinary, adequately performing mortals should expect. Take note.

M

Games, options, the arts: Sport is taken pretty seriously, but not at the cost of enjoyment: so much is on offer that even the most ball-shy find something to do. Rugby, hockey, cricket and football predominate, but golf – handy to have a course in the grounds – sailing and polo also strong. The fixtures list and results suggest a school that punches above its weight – perhaps as a consequence of the annual tug of war, sometimes won by the girls. The girls' small numbers mean everyone has a chance to represent the school at hockey, netball and lacrosse during the winter and at tennis and rounders in the summer.

The possibility of combining a boarding education with a burgeoning equestrian career really marks out this school: it has paddocks, stabling, even a horse-walker for those times when young riders simply can't evade the classroom. Pupils bring their own steeds, terrifying nervous parents having to tow horse-boxes down the narrow lanes leading to the school. At least one professional polo player and point-to-point rider are in the slips and hunting is perfectly OK, of a winter Saturday.

Activities are legion, and take full advantage of the school's bucolic setting deep in the Dorset countryside – fishing, ferreting, shooting (clays, hapless game-birds and targets with rifles), beagling and mountain biking allow all to have a heavenly outdoor existence. But there's serious countryside management going on here too: 'All pupils leave with a working knowledge of vegetable and stock cycles, as well as the pitfalls of sex, drugs and rock and roll', and there's no room for the squeamish, with three shoots a year, where the boys beat and the parents are the guns. One lad has a gundog at school for training, and ferrets have to come home for the holidays. (This editor was asked to billet one – readers, she declined).

The more cerebral are also accommodated with (recently much improved) music, drama (a musical and junior play most years) and wonderful art and photography. The first artist in residence has been appointed, suitably eccentric with a fine collection of music on vinyl, and a composer and poet are to follow. Music ranges from the singing of Compline once a week in the abbey itself, to Funkchestra – make of that what you will – and there's some collaboration with other schools for bigger choral works. 'We hope there'll be more on show than the carol service' said one musician's mother.

Background and atmosphere: Very very rural. It would be impossible not to be seduced by the enchanting setting of the ancient abbey nestling in a Dorset valley, though the school was founded only in the 1950s and occupies the converted monastery buildings, plus several additions of varying degrees of beauty. The abbey itself still belongs to the diocese of Salisbury, but the school has full use of it. The pupils realise they are lucky to live in these idyllic surroundings, yet a proper but unpretentious air of country house grandeur prevails and the school wants them to enjoy its glories, for example there are black tie dinners with decent wine – in moderation – for senior pupils and parents in the Kings Room. Every pupil we talked to raved about the, in our view, isolated country setting, and was quite uncomplaining about the lack of mobile signal except by perilous hanging out of top floor windows. 'Stems the flow of unhelpful communications from one's teenagers,' remarked one relieved mother.

Unquestionably a proper boarding school, with pupils from all over the UK and beyond, and therefore arrangements for exeats tailored to suit them, such as three day weekends to allow for longer journeys home. A full fixture and activity list, socials with other schools to balance out the lack of girls below sixth form, sung eucharist on Sunday mornings and animal husbandry responsibilities mean busy and purposeful weekends.

A breathtakingly ambitious building programme has seen three fully refurbished and two new boarding houses – one for girls – with facilities for resident staff and the development of a new learning resource centre. Girls now welcomed into third form (year 9) as well as sixth form since 2012. Now a Round Square school, a global network of 60 or so, where 'beyond academic merit, commitment is shared to personal growth, and responsibility through service, challenge, adventure and international understanding', worthy aspirations developed by Kurt Hahn, founder of Gordonstoun. Quite possibly cold showers as well, then.

Still feels like a boys' school with girls though: the resident boys hang out of windows to inspect the new third and sixth form fillies as they arrive, shaking their lustrous manes.

An air of benign neglect, even anarchy, which characterised a previous régime has been replaced by something much more vigilant; the school 'has not been been helped by rumours' – too right: we heard of pizza delivery men bringing in alcoholic contraband, but now it seems the deputy head is not above patrolling the grounds in a golf buggy to catch the unwary smoker or drinker. Several parents we spoke to acknowledged that recent events have been difficult for older pupils, used to much more latitude.

Pastoral care and discipline: Much improved, following a huge recent shake-up in the last year. The school has made determined efforts to stamp out not only bullying, but also initiation rites and the more ridiculous or dangerous high-jinks in dorms. The role of housemaster has been redefined, house staff are now expected to be resident and to crack the whip where necessary; parents view this with relief. The emphasis now seems to be more on sanctions rather than reward or recognition, though we were hastily assured that plaudits are alive and well: all praiseworthy endeavours are given an award.

High praise for the enduring family feel of the place, and the sheer niceness of the staff, from the cleaners upwards. Excellent medical care too, including a collaborative approach to food allergies and dietary quirks. In fact quirks of all kinds accepted, even encouraged here (too unkind to describe them as basket cases, as one father did!), which makes for an endearing feel to the place.

Pupils and parents: Despite such privileged surroundings, noticeably down to earth, unsnobby, tolerant and likeable, with a real love of the countryside – but wealthy (you'd have to be). Parents mention 'cracking friends', 10 per cent of pupils from overseas, a few Brit expats, but several from Spain and a sprinkling from elsewhere. Socially narrow, we suspect, and content with a very rural existence. It would be hard to find a nicer bunch, when they could have been so obnoxiously huntin', shootin' & fishin'. School engenders fierce loyalty amongst its alumni, the most notable of whom are in the film industry or representing England at rugby.

Entrance: CE at 13 where an average of 50 per cent is expected; that said, 'we want potential and reckon we can spot it', so there's some flex there. Enthusiasms and passions important too. School sets own exams for foreigners and those not from prep schools, and pupils come from a variety, with no particular feeders. At sixth form, five GCSEs at a C or above, plus interview and literacy test at an assessment morning. Learning support unit may recommend support sessions on entry, in which case this becomes a condition of entry. Good variety of scholarships, including sailing and equine, offered at both points of entry.

Exit: To a variety of destinations: parents like the school's acceptance of the fact that there's more to life than university and that it supports those who want to go straight into occupations which don't require higher education as much as those who do. Land-based careers an obvious path, plus professional sport and the occasional iconoclast to the city. University choices notably focused on The Royal Agricultural College, Newcastle, Oxford Brookes and UWE.

M

Money matters: Boarding and day fees in line with comparable schools, nominal scholarships worth no more than 10 per cent of fees. 'very splendid' top-up bursaries are means-tested. Learning support is all chargeable.

Remarks: A truly country (not county) school and a first rate choice for young people who have got something which does not make formal education easy for them, yet emphatically not a 'special' school. Its space, freedom, countryside expertise and traditions give opportunities to shine outside the classroom, and provide a refuge from glitzier, more competitive environments. Tweedy, but definitely not stuffy; possibly the prettiest school in Christendom – where you can also have your own ferret. Its move towards full co-education will be watched with interest.

The Moat School

Bishops Avenue, London, SW6 6EG

• Pupils: 70 boys, 20 girls • Ages: 11–16 • Fees: £25,845 pa
• Independent

Tel: 020 7610 9018
Email: office@moatschool.org.uk
Website: www.moatschool.org.uk

Headteacher: Since February 2013, Miss Clare King (late thirties). Has only taught at The Moat, where she started as an NQT and received accelerated promotion. Previously director of studies and deputy head.

Academic matters: Small classes (approx ten) and a Learning Support Assistant ensure each child is given attention, especially during the first three years of secondary school. Education is broad – pupils taught lots of communication and study skills alongside literacy and maths. They are weaned off the extra help during the two year GCSE syllabus but by then class sizes get even smaller. Each pupil is issued with a laptop and helped to manage this responsibility by having convenient lockers to store them in between lessons (an example of the practical solutions to problems of organisation for dyslexics). '

'A good range of subjects,' according to pupils, who all aim to leave with at least five GCSEs, though no language or classics teaching. All sit maths, English and science (many sitting additional science), but creativity high on school's and pupils' agenda since popular subjects are business communication, design technology, drama and media studies. The year groups and classes are small and so results vary each year, but of the 20 children in the GCSE year, 20 per cent or more leave with at least 5 graded A*-C GCSEs. Considering almost every child ends up with access arrangements that often include a scribe or a reader, this is no mean feat, but clearly The Moat is not a school for those primarily seeking academic results. Everything taught as kinaesthetically as possible – we saw a paper ball being thrown from teacher to pupil and back while being questioned – to help keep focus, keep energy levels high and pupils on their toes. Media studies and business studies are popular GCSE subjects – partly because they are ideal for visual learners with plenty of ICT input, but also because of 'brilliant' teachers. Teachers clearly working together – staff meetings, socialising, eating together, extra training – all evidence of a good staff team. Specialist subject teachers are trained in Specific Learning Difficulties and share good practice via cross curricular learning. For example, vocabulary is extended with a 'word of the week' programme that is used in all lessons. Concentration problems associated with learning difficulties eased by having regular break times rather than endless and confusing lesson changes. With many practical solutions to pupils' learning difficulties, stress is removed from the equation allowing for calm, purposeful teaching.

Because all pupils have specific learning difficulties and all teachers are trained in special needs, individual pupils are not withdrawn from lessons for extra literacy but instead an integrated Skills for Learning programme takes the form of small, cross-age range groups, who are mentored in literacy skills three times a week throughout their school life, working on specific areas of weakness. Occupational therapist available and two speech therapists work with individual children but also teach language and communication skills throughout year 7. Speech therapists run 'Talk About' sessions in small groups to discuss how to speak in public, how to present oneself, how we make other people feel; these culminate in an outing to practise skills in public. Pupils particularly appreciated 'the chance to go out' and the female students especially liked their separate sessions and, 'having time to talk about girl things'.

Games, options, the arts: Practical subjects predictably popular – science, media studies, music, art, PE. Drama a large part of the school curriculum with all children taking part in productions in one form or another. School achievements include productions in West End theatres as part of competitions (including Shakespeare for Schools). Sport encouraged but it is definitely not a competitive school and sport is 'more about keeping fit than winning'. Usual range of sport takes place in the playground – no large playing fields, though some rowing and yoga too, and tennis courts across the road. Music for GCSE but also plenty of individual music lessons – drums, saxophone, guitar, piano etc. Facilities for composition as part of music technology in GSCE. Gorgeous art all over the school includes collaborative and fine art (and lots of visits to galleries) but also wider design technology and resistant materials, and even film making. On our visit we saw very practical wood turning and food technology lessons – skill-based practical activities that suit pupils who have lots to offer, allowing for achievement outside the strictly academic spheres. Extracurricular activities are not an after school option but each day ends with an hour of a chosen extension activity such as quilting, drama, cricket, debate, sport. DofE and residential school trips each year, as well as much loved day trips related to school studies (theatre, galleries, museums etc).

Background and atmosphere: Food is cooked on the premises and staff join students for lunch with vegetarian option and salad bar (only used by teachers according to one pupil!), though predictable complaints by pupils about food – not enough, not enough choice, too many vegetables! Pupils and staff may eat together but the fact that no first names are used for teachers is indicative of clear boundaries and rules which include zero tolerance of bad behaviour. This helps keep the school calm and 'stress free', critical for many academically fragile pupils. Many choose to stay inside and read magazines at break rather than play football. Not really enough 'chilling' space according to pupils and especially for the girls who are in the minority anyway and who want to be outside but not standing around avoiding footballs.

The building is practical but dull, some areas clearly in need of a refit. This fits with the ethos of the school somehow – practical solutions and purpose more important than image. Even the terminology used is unambiguous – each morning starts with a 'gathering', Friday's gathering is for giving merits to pupils and sharing successes. The year book is called 'The Keep' as pupils hold on to these at the end as a memory of their school life. Pupils say they are 'respected for who we are, not how we look'. 'It is what's inside that counts', and what is inside the school is respected and respectful pupils and staff, working together to achieve.

M

Pastoral care and discipline: Behaviour and control are evidently an important part of what is taught and learned at the Moat School. Clear boundaries and sanctions intended to assist with the teenage problem of organisation and lost property that is exacerbated by dyslexia and dyspraxia. Friday litter detention for loss or carelessness with laptops. After three warnings for misbehaviour students are sent to the Referral Room, a reflection sheet is completed together with staff following the misdemeanour to work out what happened, why and whether an apology or other action needed. A serious offence (physical violence, swearing) or three referrals leads to consequences that range from weekend detention to temporary exclusion. Pupils need to be, 'persuaded to behave appropriately', but if not, then it is not the right school for them. Pupils we spoke to found sanctions fair but explained that, 'it didn't happen much'. Understanding their own thinking and learning styles and self-reflection are encouraged and a school counsellor is available for children who are referred or who ask for time to talk.

Pupils and parents: Pupils come from far and near making socialising outside school tricky. Eighty per cent have statements and are paid for by Local Authorities from all over London. They are all dyslexic but come from a wide range of backgrounds and there's no one type – sporty, academic, shy, drama queens – all sorts sharing a common tolerance. They need to be bright enough to manage the expectation that they attempt GCSEs but academic achievement is not the only goal. Parents say there is plenty of communication and regular reviews, with open access to teachers – many of whom assist parents by emailing homework or notes directly if pupils can't organise their homework alone. All parents we spoke to raved about the teachers. Concerns by parents over lack of consistency in homework being dealt with by a review of the entire homework policy and strategy – showing some openness to criticism – and parents felt that their suggestions were acted upon. The school council is active and pupils use this as a conduit for change. Students say, 'teachers come to you if they see you are struggling and don't wait for you to ask or put your hand up'. Many famous patrons act as role models of achievement, including Richard Rogers, Jeremy Irons, Ruby Wax.

Entrance: Entrance by way of careful review of a pupil's reports. The head will also take a view when the child comes in for an 'acquaint' day and if the school feels they can support the child they will take them in even if reports are poor. Primarily a school for a child with dyslexia or dyspraxia, many also have expressive language difficulties. Many more interviewed than taken on because a good match needed in such small classes. From mainstream primary schools but we also met several from Blossom House and Fairley House in year 9, though late entry to the school a real disadvantage since the preparatory learning that takes place from year 7 all builds towards good learning skills for GCSE.

Exit: The school ends at GCSE; some parents and pupils expressed the desire for the school to continue to sixth form, but at present 75 per cent of pupils go into mainstream sixth form colleges or schools rather than supported placements and so the need is not there for this provision. It's a credit to the school that they are able to wean the pupils off special support. No data re where every child goes after further education but school suggests that about a third go on to higher education.

Money matters: The Constable Educational Trust set up the school in 1997 and continues to run it (one remaining founder Governor). They are about to open two new primary free schools which, while not for dyslexic children specifically, will work towards early identification of learning difficulties. This is evidently not a wealthy school, it relies on charitable donations and fundraising efforts. Money used for education rather than capital projects – no stinting on school trips and outings or staff pupil ratios. All credit to a school that spends money on pupils rather than buildings – though the buildings are ready for some input too.

Remarks: This special school is remarkably conventional in many ways – discipline, high behavioural expectations, solid learning leading to GCSEs in usual range of subjects. What is unusual is such innovative and integrated teaching. This Good Schools Guide reviewer found it a joy to see alternative ways of learning and teaching employed to such good effect.

Moira House Girls School, Eastbourne

Linked school: Moira House Junior School

Upper Carlisle Road, Eastbourne, BN20 7TE

- Pupils: 230 girls (including 101 full time boarders) • Ages: 11–18
- C of E • Fees: Day £13,050–£15,030; boarding £23,820–£27,615 pa
- Independent

Tel: 01323 644144
Email: info@moirahouse.co.uk
Website: www.moirahouse.co.uk

Principal: Since 2013, James Sheridan BSc MA. Grew up in Scotland and read mathematical sciences at university, followed by teacher training, postgraduate certificate in school leadership and MA in education. Taught in both day and boarding schools and spent more than 10 years teaching in the Middle East. Also an ISI Inspector.

Academic matters: A broad church here, with non-selective entry and a good reputation for value added. In 2013, 35 per cent A*/A at A level. Maths and the sciences popular, followed by business studies and psychology. Inspirational science teaching; trips all over the world including one to NASA. Indeed, our strong impression is that the general standard of teaching here is good. The science labs are well equipped but quite small so girls taught in very small groups.

Drama, PE and photography offered. Mandarin and Japanese as extra-curricular subjects. GCSEs: 49 per cent A*/As with IGCSEs in English, maths and science. Over 20 subjects to choose from including ICT, PE, German and Spanish. Separate sciences available. Year 7 and 8 girls are introduced to five languages within the curriculum – French, Latin, Spanish, German and Mandarin, with numerous trips and exchanges arranged.

Results generally pretty good for non-selective entry and all girls are allowed to sit exams irrespective of ability – no one is turned away because they are not expected to get the 'right' grades.

The learning support department consists of one full time SENCo, mainly for mild dyslexia and dyspraxia. All those from overseas with English as a second language are given a language assessment on arrival and, if necessary, have to complete a one year foundation course in intensive English and are expected to take the English IGCSE.

Good careers advice. Girls encouraged to think about their long term future from early on, and careers interviews start in year 9. Compulsory Friday afternoon lectures for sixth form – former students often come back to talk about life at university and beyond.

Welcoming, well-used library with enthusiastic librarian, assisted by student librarians. Girls encouraged to read books for pleasure and then discuss them at the MoHo Bookworms book club and book chat groups. Lots of trips and visits to bring the subjects to life – Hampton Court Palace, Imperial War Museum etc. French exchange programme, annual Spanish trip and Latin trip to Bath, St Alban's and Fishbourne.

Games, options, the arts: Vibrant music department with various ensembles, a chamber choir – 38 girls recently went to Barcelona to sing at Montserrat. Newly refurbished music studio and a recording studio. The school will go to great lengths to make it possible for a girl to learn any instrument. Drama productions every term for the senior, middle and junior schools. Biennial performing arts tour: music and drama productions at link schools around the world. In recent years they have performed in St Petersburg, San Francisco, Hong Kong and Dubai. Despite this, not heavy on or particularly successful at arts-based exams.

The usual sports – hockey, netball etc and also cricket, which is on the curriculum from year 7 – Moira House was one of the first girls' schools to introduce cricket and have several county players. Everyone does a bit of everything each week up until year 10 and tend to keep going – it is considered quite cool to continue with sport. Extraordinary variety of minor sports, including sailing, windsurfing and canoeing in the sea. The school is very flexible about outside events eg training for an international eventer in the U21 Italian team. A number of keen and highly competent golfers, a GB archer, some county level athletes and particularly strong swimmers – currently U14 national champions in relay. Very fortunate to have their own playing fields across the road.

The principal is keen that girls are involved at a local level and that the school works with the local community. The sports hall and swimming pool are used by pupils at neighbouring schools, and they also come in for Mandarin lessons and masterclasses as well as dance and drama. Moira House girls take part in the Eastbourne Festival of Music and Drama every February. Girls and staff play in the local netball league and girls also play in the Eastbourne Hockey Club teams. The older girls visit local old people's homes and the disabled and get involved with local charities.

Background and atmosphere: Founded in 1875 by Charles Ingham and Mona Swann – pioneers of female education who were determined to give girls the chance of a good start in life. Charles Ingham's philosophy of 'respect for self and for others and a sense of duty and responsibility' lives on in the school today.

A step back in time, at least for Londoners. A jumbled, flamboyant late Victorian house complete with turrets and towers in the semi-rural outskirts of Eastbourne. Comfortably scruffy in places with a welcoming and homely atmosphere. The two head girls are known as Knights and the prefects as Standard Bearers, others with positions of responsibility are called Pages and Squires.

Much of the teaching in 1960s blocks in the garden – not architecturally inspiring, to speak unreasonably kindly of them, but no one seems to mind. The grounds open directly onto the South Downs and there are views of the sea from the upstairs windows.

Pastoral care and discipline: A few weekly and flexi-boarders, but mostly from overseas, from year 7 up. About 45 in the lower years and 60 in sixth form. No Saturday school but plenty of matches – never a problem getting girls to come in for these.

Always something going on for the boarders at weekends– visits to art galleries, ancient buildings, bowling, ice skating, cinema etc. Boston House for the sixth form serves as a bridge between school and university; girls are given increasing independence and are expected to manage their own time. Tutorial-based lessons with tutors acting as mentors and guides. Good relationships with teachers – very natural and relaxed. As one girl put it, the MoHo spirit is 'about respect and

friendship with teachers when you are lower down the school, and the other way round when you are in the sixth form'. 'A very nurturing school – not just of the girls but the parents as well,' says one happy mother.

Pupils and parents: Boarders from a huge range of countries (27 different nationalities), the biggest proportion coming from Asia – plenty of cross-pollination between cultures. Locals generally down-to-earth business people who like the small classes and the all girls environment. 'Popular with parents who want a bit more than the state can offer,' according to one mother. Most of the day children live within a 20 mile radius, with a fleet of nine minibuses bringing them in from as far away as Hastings, Battle and Brighton. The two groups of children get on well, and parents are clearly very happy with the school.

Pupils thoroughly nice, charming in fact. Welcoming. Entrepreneurial. Old Girls include Prunella Scales, Susannah Corbett (actor Harry's daughter), author Rumer Godden, explorer Virginia Fiennes, whistleblower Katharine Gunn who founded the Truth Telling Commission. Katie Gibbons was the first girl to win the Top Gun award at NASA and was awarded an airforce flying scholarship – she flew jets for the RAF and is now a pilot with Cathay Pacific. She first discovered her love of flying whilst on a school trip to NASA.

If we were to single out one quality of this school it would be the calm, not at all brassy, self-confidence of the older girls: 'I can do it', 'I'll give it a go'. Unusual, and most heart-warming to see.

Entrance: Students can and do join every term as long as there are spaces – some international students come on a short stay for perhaps a week, a term or a year – very flexible. Lots of Spanish in the autumn term and French, Germans and Italians in the summer – all integrated within their year group. Accept girls with a wide range of abilities, but they must be able to follow the GCSE course. No entrance tests – really non-selective – everyone comes for a taster day and those coming in at 11+ are assessed by interview and on their school reports. Those coming from the junior school just move on up, but can apply for academic scholarships and art, music and drama awards. Girls also come from local primaries and prep schools.

Exit: A few leave after GCSE – tend to go to sixth form colleges for more vocational courses. To a variety of universities, some to Russell Group, art foundation courses. Some to former polys to read everything from veterinary science and law, politics and history and biomedicine to product design and fashion photography. Very few take a gap year.

Money matters: Two academic scholarships worth up to 35 per cent of fees are awarded each year. Can be topped up by means tested bursaries. Exhibitions up to 10 to 20 per cent of fees in drama, music, art and sport, can also be topped up with a bursary.

Remarks: A traditional English girls' school with a 'cosmopolitan and international flavour and a global perspective'. Does not look for UK pupils beyond its local catchment, but for the right girl will be the perfect school wherever she comes from.

M

Monkton Senior School

Linked school: Monkton Preparatory School, BA2 7HG

Church Lane, Monkton Combe, Bath

• Pupils: 400 boys and girls (including 240 boarders) • Ages: 11–19 • Church of England, evangelical • Fees: Day £15,288–£18,564; Boarding £21,825–£29,328 pa • Independent

Tel: 01225 721102
Email: admissions@monkton.org.uk
Website: www.monktoncombeschool.com

Principal: Since 2005, Mr Richard Backhouse (forties). Educated at Marlborough and Selwyn College, Cambridge, where he read economics, was vice captain of boat and ran the college Christian Union. The roles equipped him well for Monkton – a school where pupils speak enthusiastically about having Wednesday afternoons off for CU, with an inspiring range of speakers visiting. Previously at Oundle and Bradfield, where he was a housemaster.

Has achieved all 35 or so targets he originally had for the school but in so doing has identified and is eagerly embarking upon at least as many more. Staff describe him as visionary, strategically astute, constantly aspiring to do better and a joy to work with. Likeable and humorous, but not to be underestimated. His single-minded determination that every improvement should directly benefit pupils has produced spectacular results, including some stunning new buildings and an unpretentious workaday practicality evident in the neatness and efficiency of even the least spectacular areas of the school – loos, offices, dorms and classrooms.

A stickler for tidiness – 'it gives children instinctive standards' – so Monkton is about as tidy as a school gets. He is also acutely aware of his accountability to parents, listening to them systematically. Not into micro management because he has highly motivated staff but has an eye for detail ('are we using the right sort of light bulbs?') Nothing is too much trouble if it contributes to pupils' potential for self-development. Says he tends to be either working flat out or at a full stop but personal interests that survive include golf and Southampton FC. While his Christianity informs his thinking about education he is open-minded and focused on helping his pupils to understand that though achievement is important, who they are and how they live matters most. He describes the Christian nurturing of Monkton as a kind of unruffled eddy in a millpond in which young people can grow their own strengths and vision un-coerced by cultural or psychological pressure.

Married to Debbie, with a son and daughter at the school.

Academic matters: Several years of best-ever results (43 per cent A*/A grades at A level in 2013 and more than 60 per cent A*/A grades at GCSE).

At the lower end everyone with at least 5 A*-C grades and less than 10 per cent below grade C at A level. For a 'not particularly selective' school which has 'a default position of supporting a pupil's ambitions, even if they are a long shot' this is pretty respectable. Pupils say they enjoy lessons, work hard and get lots of encouragement. Exams still feel on the tough side to them, so those we met were proud of their results and parents gave across-the-board thumbs up – 'the brightest are definitely stretched.' School is currently upping its academic image. Though intake at year 9 'gets a gentle ride' (gives them a chance to settle between CE and the start of GCSE syllabus) bright children are taught 'up to their level.' Class sizes 18 to 20 up to GCSE, smaller thereafter.

Safe curriculum for GCSE, with few soft options. Mandarin now available at KS3. Increasing number of subjects going to IGCSE. One or two languages for all except extra English candidates at GCSE. Latin but no Greek. In science top set do three separate sciences and the rest dual award. A level courses include photography, theatre studies, sports studies, DT, critical thinking and psychology. Some smashing maths results – shiny new £4 million maths and science centre may have helped, plus programme of university links enabling sixth formers to get placements in science research departments. Smartly refurbished arts and crafts library, now renamed learning resource centre.

The learning support unit is sound but the school is no longer registered CreSTed as Monkton provides only for minor difficulties. Nonetheless it is inclusive and copes well with unusual children and physical problems. Students get up to 45 minutes a week one-to-one and teachers are tuned into special needs and work with the learning support unit. Study skills on offer too.

Games, options, the arts: Strong for a smallish school, with the expected trio of rugby, hockey and cricket for boys and hockey, netball and tennis for girls. Male and female tennis players sponsored by LTA via the University of Bath. Rowing's the in thing – perhaps not surprising with a new Olympian rowing coach Matt Well (won bronze at Beijing). Several former pupils have achieved national and international rowing success, including Steve Williams (who won Olympic golds in 2004 and 2008) and Alex Partridge (who won silver in 2008). Pupils don't have to be sporty – but the surroundings encourage them, as do the facilities – new Astro surfaces, good sports hall, picturesque cricket.

Music has had a huge boost with new £3.2 million music school (opened by Felicity Lott and Richard Stilgoe) complete with magnificent wood-lined auditorium, multitudinous teaching and practice rooms and larger rehearsal rooms, all the electronic 'mod cons' of recording and manipulating music. Some pretty impressive piano playing doing justice to the brand new Steinway during our visit. List of successful ex-Monkton musicians is growing. Every sort of music, including lively jazz, professional sounding big band and rock bands (always the sign of a truly musical environment).

Art room bursting at the seams (too small and no kiln) – overripe for expected new development but has smashing little studio spaces for A level artists who rival mathematicians in the success rates. Lots of exciting stuff – sculpture, photography and first-rate painting. Lashings of drama, with ambitious productions (Shakespeare and Dickens as well as more contemporary shows) and good enough facilities, though they are in the list for development. Visiting artists and workshops, links with local galleries and University of Bath. Art trips abroad every other year, plus exchanges, music trips et al.

CCF is an attractive if compulsory option. School building up community service. D of E on the up. Other activities include poetry, creative writing and Dearlove Society (focuses on European intellectual life – Camus, St Augustine, the influences of Classical Greece – and ends the year with a frisbee competition in Greek robes).

Background and atmosphere: Campus still has a whiff of the school's clerical foundation. Founded in 1868 by the evangelical Revd Francis Pocock, school started with five pupils. School is still popular with clergymen and missionaries. Since merging in 1992 with girls' school next door it's been fully co-ed, with a prep and a pre-prep. The setting at the bottom of a deep-cleft valley is ravishing – sufficiently isolated to feel safe to parents but handily near Bath for weekend shopping and other forays say pupils.

The school is centred on its strong Christian tradition. This is embodied in the attitude of staff to children and symbolised by such groups as the International School Society and array of social projects it initiates at home and in far-flung places. Pupils definitely buy into respect for each other's needs and

M

personalities. A parent reports a commendable understanding of the occasional oddball. The vibrant Christian Union is run entirely by the students and around a third attend every week. No Sunday service but a large number go into Bath or to local services (often those aimed at university students) of their choice.

Pastoral care and discipline: 'Pastorally brilliant,' say parents, many of whom add that this was their reason for choosing Monkton. The house system (mixed ages but single sex) involves boarders and day pupils alike and husband and wife houseparent teams include both in their care. Day pupils can sleep over if necessary and most go home so late it hardly seems worth it. One boarder said it didn't matter if his friends were day boys because he had so little time when they weren't there and anyway he got on with everyone. Houses are run like families, with pupils learning to take responsibility. The number of day pupils who come in at weekends is good measure of how much there is to do.

Academic tutors attached to houses, though in the sixth form pupils choose their own tutors, The system aims to support inspire and encourage good working habits and is part of the network of personal support which characterises Monkton. Induction for prefects teaches them to be kind, not martinets. Definitely no sense of parading prefect privilege, though they are proud of their level of responsibility.

The trust between pupils of all ages and pupils and staff is very evident, for instance in the dining hall where the interchange is informal and considerate. Statistics show no bullying. 'We pick it up before it's a problem,' said one tutor. 'If you know a child you can see when something is wrong.' One might wonder if this is a little too trusting? One parent definitely felt that cooping up large number of teenagers in a small valley brings its own problems and that pastoral staff have sometimes been a bit naïve, though principal is tougher than his charm suggests. Problems are tackled and for teenagers this is a safe place where they can be themselves and there is unfailing support for the troubled.

Pupils and parents: Popular, of course, with evangelical Christians and those who want the values, but plenty of non-subscribers too. Seven-day boarding week is good for the many Forces' families. Wide geographical range, including 10 to 15 per cent international students (20-plus nationalities). International tradition strong and long established. Some need ESL support, but all are tested in English before arrival and many go straight into mainstream English classes. Cultural acclimatisation is thoughtfully addressed too.

School is handy for both ends of the M4, so London and Wales mix harmoniously. Children seem friendly, unpretentious and modestly confident.

School's church connections only account for part of the exalted list of past pupils promoted to glory on earth – former spymaster Sir Richard Dearlove, songwriter and humourist Richard Stilgoe, blockbuster novelist Bernard Cornwell, Piers Forster (who shared a Nobel prize for climate change). The development department is doing a professional and very enterprising job keeping the school in touch with old Monktonians in the worlds of business and arts.

Entrance: Monkton looks for 50 per cent plus at CE. Standard rising. Special needs evaluated to make sure a pupil will cope comfortably with what has become a slightly more academic curriculum. 'Definitely pulling out of their less able image,' a parent commented, but parents of 'strugglers' are delighted with unexpected A*s and As. Pupils come from Monkton Prep, St Andrew's School (Turi, Kenya), Castle Court, Mount House, Rose Hill, All Hallows and Summer Fields.

Exit: About 80 per cent go through to sixth form. Up to 10 Oxbridge applications per year – though only a smidgeon get

in. A tranche to good solid courses and good solid unis and plenty to useful-looking vocational courses, not on the whole the whacky sort. Plus some to US and other countries.

Money matters: Bursaries on offer to children of missionaries and clergy – means-tested. A clutch of academic, art, drama, music and sport scholarships on entry to years 7, 9 and 12. Has secured a £2 million donation for the school and is embarking on a £35 million development programme – seriously confident in straitened times.

Remarks: A school that sees itself as on the up, its image polished by a super efficient development department busy developing everything in sight. Governors clearly have no fears for the future. Despite the ongoing makeover, its Christian ethos shines out in the unforced friendliness and directness of its pupils and through the disciplined but loving care of its staff. Service to others comes first, but confidence and academic achievement are treasured as the means of achieving it. One parent said 'I thank my lucky stars every day that I found Monkton.' These boys and girls go on to do well and to do good.

Monmouth School

Linked schools: The Grange, Monmouth Preparatory School; Haberdashers' Agincourt School

Almshouse Street, Monmouth, NP25 3XP

- Pupils: 575 boys (including 160 boarders) • Ages: 11–18
- Anglican • Fees: Day £9,660–£13,773; Boarding £18,171–£26,460 pa • Independent

Tel: 01600 713143
Email: admissions@monmouthschool.org
Website: www.habs-monmouth.org

Headmaster: Since 2005, Dr Steven Connors (mid forties). Came from Christ's Hospital where he was deputy head for five years. Read English at Swansea University – PhD was on the poetry of William Wordsworth. Started teaching at Denstone College, followed by head of English posts at Queen's College, Taunton and Sevenoaks, where he was also head of boarding and housemaster of the sixth form international centre. His wife is a specialist in the education of high functioning autistic (Asperger syndrome) children and her professional knowledge and contacts have given an edge to his own concern for provision of specialist help to both ends of the special needs spectrum. They have two sons, one at university and one studying drama.

He has spearheaded major development at Monmouth, including the fantastically lavish sports pavilion where parents can sip coffee in warmth and comfort or bask on the sunny veranda 'while their offspring suffer on the pitches,' as a sixth-former puts it. A stickler for civilised and sportsmanlike good behaviour for his successful teams, and their supporters, he has given parents every reason to enjoy sport in the most luxurious surroundings. Pristine new prep school, The Grange, allowed him to give its old building (Buchanan House) a makeover to include 40 up-market sixth form en-suite bedrooms, with a comprehensive range of sparkling but slightly stark leisure areas. When we visited the development of a huge teaching area for maths, English and humanities as well as admin areas for the head and others was underway. The Heart of Monmouth project is in celebration of the school's 400th anniversary, with further phases including new dining and more teaching areas.

Head talks inspiringly of the accessibility of his school (it offers its own assisted places) and its potential to 'transform lives by enabling pupils to see and strive for higher academic and personal standards.' He regrets calls on his time that have reduced his pupil contact, which included teaching English and coaching rugby. An easy unpretentious manner and gentle humour disguises an eagle eye and strong organisation skills so the school he leads is tidy and purposeful without being over-regimented. His relaxation activities include walking, reading, occasional surfing and skiing and playing the guitar.

Academic matters: Good performance at both GCSE and A level over the last five years, with consistently impressive grades for high fliers – though whole year averages fluctuate a bit. Best case 60 per cent A*/A grades at A level and at worst 40 per cent. More telling is that between 20 and 35 out of around 85 candidates regularly get three or more A*As. There is a small tail of C, D, E grades which probably reflects the school policy of allowing enthusiastic hard workers to 'have a go' (they only need five B grades at GCSE to join sixth form).

At GCSE results are consistent, with 95 per cent or more grades at C and above and more than 50 per cent at A*/A. English, maths and science (now IGCSE 'because it's more rigorous') have a pretty impressive clutch of top grades and minimal below C. All take core subjects of English, maths, three separate sciences (a few do double award) plus a modern language (French, Spanish, German, Russian and Mandarin – Welsh can be arranged as an extra). Latin (good take-up) and Greek (a few) right up to A Level. Lots of A level choice – around 30 options in conjunction with Haberdashers' Monmouth School for Girls. Arrangement gives flexibility amounting to virtual freedom of choice as well as spin-off benefits of mixing with girls for curricular and extra-curricular stuff.

The Monmouth Science Initiative gives boys the chance to work alongside scientific development at Cardiff University and is extended not only to the girls' school but also to local state schools, with clear feedback that it is making a significant difference to potential science highfliers.

Learning support on an individual/shared basis from qualified staff, although additional charges apply for numeracy and literacy support.

Parents say individual teaching staff are exceptionally encouraging to enthusiastic pupils, though one commented that you have to push quite hard to do more than the statutory ten GCSEs. 'The school could vaunt its academic image more but likes to be seen as inclusive,' said another. Lessons in study skills for all and the sixth form are encouraged to tailor choice towards career. Class sizes – maximum 22 but can be under ten in sixth form. Lots of additional help from local experts in minority subjects.

Games, options, the arts: Sport is tip-top here and Monmouth (comparatively small) has consistently challenged the giants of school sport in rugby, rowing, soccer and cricket. Rugby is top dog though parents say other sports have had more of a look in recently. Not content with schoolboy competition, pupils have played for the Newport Gwent Dragons, Junior Welsh and other professional and semi professional teams. Recent head boy is combining medicine at Cardiff with his professional Welsh Rugby commitments. This and the fact that former Wales and Lions player John Bevan is a teacher first and rugby coach second typifies the school's approach to sport as something to be done alongside life rather than an end in itself, though it doesn't stop them taking some significant trophies. As well as coaching the 1st XV he takes the younger boys on tours to Blackpool, Ireland and Italy.

Rowing, not surprisingly as the Wye surges right past the games pitches, has a strong though small take-up. It's in the tent-and-sandwiches league rather than turreted-pavilion-and-champagne at the posh school competitions but still manages to sweep the board. Tennis, cross-country, squash, golf and sailing all flourish. Several teams in each year group – gives more boys a chance to represent the school and helps identify potential.

A bewildering range of activities available – artistic, intellectual, sporting, and practical. Juniors (11 to 13-year-olds) must do two a week and everyone does either CCF or some form of community service. In A-Z terms astronomy to water polo (no zoology) gives a flavour of what's on and its good to see literature and poetry enjoyed by boys (something the head sees as too easily excluded by sex stereotyping in co-ed schools).

Perhaps the music school looks a little elderly in comparison with the jazzier modern developments but it is comprehensive and bursting with energetic activity. Around 40 per cent play instruments and enjoy a plethora of groups, choirs, bands and orchestras. A recent deputation from the Haberdashers' Company was staggered to find themselves entertained by a full scale performance of Carmina Burana, involving the second year en masse. A good record of music college entry (recent leaver offered four scholarships to different academies) and parents feel the school gives boys a musical resource for life. The usual gamut of school visits, choir trips and exchanges.

Drama studio and new 500-seat theatre (as well as being used by the school it hosts a programme of public performance art, including ballet and world cinema). Quality art – the venerable but well-equipped art block full of boys working in a wide range of media.

Background and atmosphere: Founded in 1614 as a local 'fre scole' by William Jones, a member of the Haberdashers' Company (one of the oldest Livery Companies in London), it became a 'public' school in the 19th Century to expand its boarding beyond the locality and was a direct grant school until 1975. Part of the Haberdashers' family of Monmouth schools, which includes Agincourt (pre-prep), the Grange (boys' prep) Inglefield (girls' prep) and Haberdashers' Monmouth Girls'.

Rebuilt in the 1880s, with a magnificent Jacobean style main building, it occupies and gives character to a significant part of Monmouth. Sensitive restorations, acquisitions such as the lovely mansion and gardens of Chapel House, bursting with happy junior boarders, the ex-pub housing the maths department and rows of almshouses (now staff offices) complement the new buildings that house the prep school and swimming pool. The William Jones building, well on its way to completion, will provide new classrooms, meeting space and admin centre. Meanwhile the temporary prefabs for the history department are, says a sixth former, 'the nicest classrooms in the school.' Pleasant grassy areas break up the hotchpotch of main buildings but it's something of a maze and not worth even trying to park in the centre until the builders leave. Gorgeous playing fields bordering the Wye are reached by a pedestrian tunnel under the busy A40.

Over a quarter of the senior school board or flexi-board (60:40 day to boarding in the sixth form). Still has Saturday morning school for all but the sixth form – not universally popular with parents, but how else would the school have time to run all those activities? Plans afoot to increase boarding capacity. Five boarding houses have sensible rather than luxurious accommodation for boarders though the old Grange (prep school) buildings make a shamelessly luxurious sixth form house. Uniform is plain navy blazer and grey trousers, replaced in the sixth form by a 'smart' business dress code. Food, boys say, is pretty good at lunchtime and OK-ish in the evening.

A huge jamboree is planned to mark the 40th anniversary of all the Haberdashers' schools in Monmouth in 2014, including thanksgiving celebration at St Paul's.

Pastoral care and discipline: Tutors are the focal point for monitoring academic performance, while housemasters look after pastoral wellbeing. One parent commented that no trouble is spared to find specialist help where needed and to support boys in difficulties. School rules are sensible and concentrate on the standard of behaviour expected, rather than a prescriptive list of dos and don'ts. Relations between staff and boys appear relaxed, but are formal enough to engender respect. Clear policies on drinking, smoking and drugs – not considered a problem, but boys are made aware of the damage they could do to themselves.

Pupils and parents: School attracts boys from south west England and south Wales, plus a few from Hong Kong etc, but is spreading the net wider and is popular with Forces' families and ex-pats. Definitely unstuffy and produces confident but considerate young men who are open and independent. Notable old boys include Christopher Herbert, the Bishop of St Albans, David Broome, Eddie Butler, Major Dick Hern, Lord Moynihan, Lord Ezra, Steve James, Keith Jarrett, Tony Jordan, Victor Spinetti and recent silver medallist Olympic rower Tom Lucy.

Entrance: Three-form entry at 11, from its own prep department and local primary schools. Both groups sit the school's own entrance exam, with scholarships awarded on that performance alone – no supplementary papers. Headmaster at pains to stress that there is no pass mark, but looking for potential – great store put on interviews. A further one-form entry at 13 from a growing list of prep schools – based on CE. Foundation scholarship exam or an entrance exam for those at state schools.

Exit: A dribble post GCSE. Majority to sound universities – Bristol, Cardiff, Exeter, Swansea etc. Regular ten or so to Oxbridge and masses to medicine.

Money matters: About a third of the government assisted places now replaced by the school's own scheme and this offers a number of scholarships and bursaries. One in three get means-tested help with fees in the senior school. Day fees about what you'd expect from similar schools but boarding is exceptionally good value.

Remarks: A school that sets out to serve its community and has now been discovered by the wider world, with high quality education and a real flair for sport and the more aesthetic life skills.

More House School (Farnham)

Linked school: Stanbridge Earls School

Moons Hill, Frensham, Farnham, Surrey, GU10 3APw

• Pupils: 440 boys (including 100 boarders) • Ages: 8–18 • RC foundation but all welcome • Fees: Day £11,757–£16,470; Boarding £21,060–£25,635 pa • Independent

Tel: 01252 792303
Email: schooloffice@morehouseschool.co.uk
Website: www.morehouseschool.co.uk

Headmaster: Since 1993, Mr Barry Huggett, worked in the City and scientific research before moving into education. Pleasant, polite and formal, married to Geraldine, the school's admissions tutor, two grown-up children (a doctor and a headmistress). Lives on site, runs a tight ship and is not only incredibly hard working but also always readily available to pupils, parents and staff.

Academic matters: An exceptional, specialist school; the caring and supportive ethos shines brightly. Every boy has an ILP

monitored regularly to check progress, with detailed annual reviews for all. Classes are small and carefully structured to take into account everybody's different learning needs. Literacy and numeracy embedded into all subject areas across the curriculum. Most boys receive some individual or small group teaching by specialist literacy teachers and/or speech therapist. Very wide curriculum; all boys take eight or nine GCSEs.

Impressive science teaching and achievement; three sciences are offered at GCSE and A level. Winners for two years running of the Surrey Scientific Problem-Solving Challenge – no mean feat, especially considering stiff competition from neighbouring, highly selective grammar and public schools. Good choice of GCSEs, BTECs and A levels. Results continue to move upwards and remain considerably above national averages.

Boys are encouraged to, and do, engage with their learning, developing awareness of their own styles and preferences. 'Understanding how you learn best and succeeding is a great motivator and confidence booster,' said a parent, 'particularly as a number of boys arriving here have not always been successful or comfortable in previous schools.' Teachers, speech therapists, occupational therapists and a small army of literary support specialists ensure academic and creative success. Compulsory training every four months keeps staff on their toes – those wishing to do further qualifications for SEN are funded by the school. Recently invested £1.6m in a training school, as many courses are run for visiting professionals.

Games, options, the arts: Boys enjoy and excel in many creative areas – performing arts, stage-craft, design. Good facilities including theatre, dedicated music building with a concert hall, heated outdoor pool and specialist rooms. Art continues to flourish – broad range of media: painting, sculpture, ceramics, DT, photography and computer animation. Drama for all to year 9 and ever-popular at GCSE – boys are regulars on stage, whether their own or further afield at the Chichester Festival or National Theatre. Instrumental tuition can be arranged and boys are encouraged to join the various jazz bands, steel band and choirs. Music is offered at A level.

Fabulous opportunities for outdoor pursuits enthusiasts: mountain biking, orienteering, rock climbing, high ropes tree walk, together with the more traditional rugby, football, cricket, athletics and D of E. Actively twinned with a school in Tanzania – has a number of joint projects and some staff exchange positions. Sixth formers visit Africa and is currently sponsoring a student from Tanzania through medical school.

Background and atmosphere: Founded in 1939 by a forward-thinking, somewhat eccentric monk, Joseph Gardner, for boys who were not thriving in mainstream schools. The original curriculum included circus skills, with the school successfully running its own travelling circus throughout the 1940s.

Delightful wooded site, some of the modern additions are built into the hillside creating unique spaces to observe plants and wildlife. Sixth formers have study cabins in the woods. Boarding accommodation recently refurbished; younger boys share dorms, older boys double, with oldest graduating to single study bedrooms. Rooms are adequate and immaculate. Sixth form facilities being extended and work is now complete on new school of engineering.

Parents are genuinely pleased with the school – often they and their children have received appalling treatment elsewhere and are delighted that their children can finally make friends in a friendly and safe environment. Atmosphere is genuinely calm and cool, with both pupils and staff palpably proud of the positive ethos, something that didn't go unnoticed when Ofsted inspected.

Pastoral care and discipline: Parents appreciative that boys are taught to understand why good behaviour for learning is essential and that poor behaviour can lead to negative consequences, both for themselves and for others. Good staff-pupil relationships are a high priority. Speech therapists double as class tutors for daily support and each boy has a weekly meeting with his mentor; plenty of anticipatory tactics in place to help with planning and organisational skills.

Pupils and parents: Specialist provision and excellent reputation mean boys come from all over the UK, with a few expats and Forces families. Always a waiting list for boarding places and day parents organise car pools. School bus meets morning and evening trains from the local station. Parents are encouraged to communicate with each other and some parents have formed Friends of More House, which raises funds by organising events such as the Christmas Fair.

Entrance: Some children are severely dyslexic, often with dyspraxia/ADD, others have autistic/Asperger's traits. Those with base IQ of less than 100 and/or with behavioural difficulties are unlikely to be offered a place. As a first step, parents talk to the admissions tutor and send in any medical and psychological reports for consideration. If it appears that the school can support the student, the parents are invited to meet the headmaster and view the school. Following this, the student will spend an assessment day and an overnight stay, if applying for a boarding place. The main purpose is to see how the child fits into the school environment and to ensure all his needs can be met by the school.

Exit: Around half stay on and study in the sixth form. Nineteen different A levels or BTECs are offered. Most go to university or art college; in 2012, universities included Southampton Solent, Gloucestershire, Bath Spa, Kent, St Mary's Twickenham, Nottingham Trent, York and Brighton. Wide enrichment programme to 'plug gaps' and enable students to move comfortably into adult life and careers.

Money matters: Different pupils have different needs, so three bands of fees, as some individual specialist help has to be charged for at an extra cost. Fees are kept as competitive as possible – will try to help in cases of financial crisis. Fees for the sixth form are discounted between 10 and 50 per cent, depending on how long a boy has been in the school.

Remarks: 'An answer to our prayers,' said a parent. A truly good place for boys with learning differences.

More House School (London)

22-24 Pont Street, London, SW1X 0AA

• Pupils: Around 200 girls, all day • Ages: 11–18 • RC, but others welcome • Fees: £15,900 pa • Independent

Tel: 020 7235 2855
Email: office@morehouse.org.uk
Website: www.morehouse.org.uk

Headmaster: Since 2007, Mr Robert Carlysle BA MBA AKC PGCE Cert Dysl & Lit MCoLP (fifties). He was founding head of the Moat School in Fulham, a specialist school for children with dyslexia, and has also taught at two independent girls' schools and a co-ed state grammar school. A historian, he is also a keen girls' hockey coach and a qualified leader for the D of E award – both are activities which have developed greatly at More House since his arrival. He teaches IT, English, history, philosophy and ethics.

A comfortable and compassionate man, wearing Bart Simpson socks with his suit, and a committed Catholic, who sees this as vital to the school's ethos – 'It is built on the Catholic notion of worth – that everybody matters. It is part of our ethos to care. It is the head's job to believe in the girls – they need to know that they matter to me'. Parents comment, 'He is very thorough, very kind, very concerned to do the best for the girls. You feel he knows exactly who your child is and how she is doing.' Particularly effective one-to-one, he makes a good team with the deputies, who tend to present the more public face of the school. Retiring in April 2014. His successor will be Amanda Leach, currently deputy head.

Academic matters: A broad spectrum of ability here, including many girls who would sink without trace in larger, more ruthless environments. 'I'd never passed a maths exam before I came here,' said a dyslexic sixth former, who now has a clutch of top GCSEs and the offer of a good university place. With such a small year group (usually fewer than 30), GCSE results variable. Twenty-six per cent A*-A grades in 2013.

Everyone learns French, German and Latin in year 7, and can take up Spanish in year 8 or 9. 'We chose German because it's good to have a language that most come to fresh. They often find it easier than French and the year 7 activities week in Germany gives them a substantial immersion in German language and culture.' Everyone studies RS to GCSE, but no obligation to adopt a Catholic viewpoint – 'My daughter's an atheist and really enjoys RS. She doesn't have to pretend to have particular beliefs'. Three ability groups for maths, English and languages from year 7.

A level subject groups are often tiny, always fewer than 10 and sometimes one-to-one – 'We have a moral obligation to run a subject if a girl wants to do it. We're about encouraging them to find out what they want to do with the rest of their lives, so we won't tell them they can't study geography, for example, because they're the only one signed up'. The subject range is necessarily narrower than in larger establishments but encompasses five languages, including Latin and Arabic, RS (very popular), drama and textiles. In 2013, 14 per cent A*/A grades at A level and 37 per cent A*/B.

Well set up to help those with special needs – 'We're successful because they're not regarded as the mad relative to lock away – staff are well aware of their needs. A school like ours resolves these issues easily because once we have taken them on, we see it as our job to educate all our pupils to the highest level irrespective of their needs – it's our ethos to care for all of them'. As well as individual help for those with learning difficulties and ESOL lessons for girls whose English is not colloquially fluent, the school now offers weekly lessons with a visiting speech and language specialist.

Games, options, the arts: 'We've always had a massively strong tradition in the creative and performing arts.' Art is conspicuously successful; all three art teachers are also professional artists. Artwork of great quality, from life drawings to an intricate ballgown, lines the corridors. The sixth form has its own art and textile room on the top floor, complete with skeleton, and quite a few go on top art and design schools, eg St Martin's, London College of Fashion.

Music is also very strong. The school is too small to field a full orchestra, but girls from year 7 learn composition from a visiting specialist teacher. They play in ensembles and perform in the many school concerts each year, such as a 'fabulous' performance of Mozart's Requiem at the Cadogan Hall. The school is known particularly for its choirs, with an annual international singing tour – 'They rehearse really hard. It is clearly a professional music tour rather than a school trip with a bit of singing'. A sixth former described her tours as 'the best memories I'll take away from More House'.

Drama is increasing in profile, with a whole school play each year alternating between straight play and musical, eg Twelfth Night and Pirates of Penzance. 'We have so much fun,' said a pupil. School hall used as theatre, dining room, assembly hall and space for house competitions; also a dance/drama studio.

Pupils are unlikely to choose the school for its sport, but the head has introduced PE GCSE and A level, 'as well as the concept of exercise being a part of healthy living'. School fields a hockey squad for the London Youth Games, running is popular, girls visit Hyde Park and Cadogan Gardens for lessons and play in inter-school competitions. 'We don't work on an élite squad approach to anything – we encourage everyone to take part.' Fencing and dance are optional extras.

Activities week every year, which can be D of E, and school trips to, eg, Russia – 'We went on the Trans-Siberia overnight. It was eye-opening'. Sixth formers enthuse about the 'great fun' they have at the Berkeley Dress Show, traditionally the inaugural event of the London Season. The only outside space is a small courtyard but activities abound at lunchtimes, eg cooking, keep fit, arts and crafts and movie club, as well as sports clubs. 'You're always so busy,' say students.

Background and atmosphere: Named for the Tudor sage and saint, Sir Thomas More, the school opened in 1953 at the request of a group of Catholic parents. It moved to its present site in two adjoining red-brick panelled houses a few streets south of Harrods in 1971. Around 50 per cent of the girls are Catholics and mass is held in the school chapel and in the church of Our Lady of Victories down the road – 'But our Catholicism is about service – about how we treat people. We don't see ourselves as an evangelical outpost of the Vatican'.

Small, cosy and friendly, the school suits girls who value its nurturing atmosphere rather than those seeking the bracing winds of competition – 'London girls' day schools can have a reputation for ruthlessness and I came here expecting it to be like a scene from Mean Girls. But I found a family atmosphere – the girls have time for one another and so do the staff'.

House system is now a central part of school life, with all the staff below deputy head level attached to houses, which field teams in competitions – sport, drama, art, music and even English and maths. 'It gives you a sense of identity in the school,' said a pupil.

Pastoral care and discipline: Described by parents as 'a very caring school' – 'The girls really are treated as individuals, with things tailored to their own needs'. Minor skirmishes about skirt lengths, with girls being told to wear trousers if their skirt is too short – 'the war of the skirt,' as one parent described it – irritate some, who feel that discipline on such subjects has got stricter. But most girls, says the head, want staff approval. 'Catholics do guilt well. We always distinguish between the behaviour and the person.' He is on door duty every day as the girls arrive – 'It is easy to drop into the conversation that I've heard something good about them. By investing in their self-esteem, you get girls who like themselves'.

Active leadership programme for the lower sixth, who act as mentors for year 7s and run the lunchtime activities programme alongside staff members. They also have their own private penthouse area with two cosy common-rooms, kitchen with coffee machine ('our favourite toy – it was a present from Mr Carlysle'), IT suite, textile studio and other specialist teaching rooms.

Pupils and parents: A diverse lot, more international than Sloane. Many European and diplomatic families, with Catholicism as the draw, alongside London girls travelling in from Hammersmith and Hampstead.

Entrance: Part of the North London Consortium, with common maths and English exams. Interviews everyone in groups before the exams, including a series of lessons to give them a feel for the small school environment – 'I'm interested in what they find interesting, what they find difficult. We begin to build up a picture of their strengths and weaknesses before the exam, and we're very interested in potential as well as performance'. A large number of feeder prep and primary schools, including Hill House, Thomas's, Finton House, Our Lady of Victories and the Oratory primary. Worth trying for places higher up, as international families come and go.

Sixth form entrants are interviewed and expected to have at least five A*–C grades at GCSE, with B or above in their AS subjects.

Exit: About 20 per cent leave after GCSE, to co-ed schools or abroad. After A levels, to a broad range of universities to do a broad range of courses and destinations ranging from Bristol to Chelsea College of Art to London Met. 'We don't see any one destination as better than another. We try to encourage girls to recognise that it is their life and think deeply about where will suit them best'.

Money matters: Various academic scholarships, some aimed specifically at Catholic girls, and exhibitions for prowess at art, drama, music or PE, which can be topped up by means-tested bursaries.

Remarks: Small and nurturing school with strong Catholic caring ethos, that does well by girls of a wide ability range. Ideal for those of a creative bent who do not feel the need to compete in the more ruthless worlds of many larger London day schools. 'It is a lovely school,' said a parent. 'My daughter is so happy there.'

Moreton Hall School

Linked school: Moreton First

Weston Rhyn, Oswestry, SY11 3EW

• Pupils: 315 girls (boys in junior school); 190 boarders and 125 day pupils • Ages: Girls aged 3–18 and boys aged 3–11 • Non denom • Fees: Boarding £27,630–£29,220; Day £22,260–£24,090 pa • Independent

Tel: 01691 773671
Email: registrar@moretonhall.com
Website: www.moretonhall.org

Principal: Since 1992, Mr Jonathan Forster, BA, PGCE (mid-fifties). Educated Shrewsbury School and Leeds University. Girls' housemaster at Strathallan before coming to Moreton in firefighter role: rescued the school from outrageous misfortune. Says he has no plans to move on – they all say that, but we believe him: his achievement is massive, financially and educationally, though he won't tell you this, and he wants to be around for exciting developments coming up next – 'I enjoy being part of a success story'.

Exudes capability and good humour. None of the exquisite oratorical strokeplay of so many heads – no boasting nor reposing on self-congratulatory laurels, only ever forward looking – 'You've got to push on': that's what he's all about. Alert to shifting winds in education and his market, he trims this school constantly to get optimal performance – 'We never forget we are competing, so league tables are important and we've got to win our matches and we've got to hit our targets'. Married to Paula, who helps in the superbly resourced library and teaches English. Two daughters, both ex-Moreton.

Academic matters: Results matter like mad here, but they are wholly averse to flogging girls to death in pursuit of them, so how do they do it? Inspiring teachers, 30 of whom live on the campus, almost half of whom are male; masses of support and a far from joyless work ethic – it's a great team, no doubt about it. They describe their entry policy as 'not frightfully selective' and do a very good job with those who come, with a clutch every year to Oxbridge. In 2013, 65 per cent A*/A grades at GCSE and 62 per cent A*/A at A level. Proper curriculum – no silly soft subjects, invidious to name the best. Seriously strong maths and science, excellent English, business studies and geography very fondly spoken of by the girls. Most important of all, no weak links. Plenty of IT – internet connections everywhere.

A unique enrichment programme and good, specialist supplementary support for gifted and talented, dyslexia, dyscalculia and EFL (roughly 70-80 girls with special needs) – holistic, all-staff approach and – you don't often see this – no extra charge for it. Meticulous university preparation, accelerated Oxbridge programme and sound careers advice.

Games, options, the arts: In all things, punches above its weight. Lacrosse is the sport of sports here and they travel far and wide in search of worthy foes. Splendid sports hall plus fitness suite, all-weather surface, brand new indoor pool – something for everybody.

Much, much music: masses of ensembles – instrumental and choral – and a heartening number of brass players. Eighteen visiting teachers from conservatoires, successful auditioners for National Youth Choir and Youth Orchestra, a musical a year and biennial tours abroad. Brilliant art – real art taught by real artists, can do it as a subject or for art's sake. Plucky, plentiful drama – always difficult in a single-sex school.

And then their extraordinary entrepreneurial initiative, Moreton Enterprises. All first year sixth girls take on executive rôles in running businesses – shops mostly and a branch of Barclays. They do the lot – the degree of independence is astonishing. Enterprise girls have just raised funds and built a new shopping mall. Yes, really! The aim is to give girls a taste of real life but, of course, it's a proving ground for those with a taste for it, as former pupils testify. Good range of out of school activities plus D of E. Strong social links with Shrewsbury School.

Background and atmosphere: Founded in 1913 by Mrs Lloyd-Williams for her own daughters and those of local friends. A homely place – 'We never lose sight of that,' says Mr Forster. Seventeenth century hall fronted by a comely ha ha and the customary hotch-potch of buildings behind it, including an extraordinary sixties creation, all roof, dubbed The Toblerone, which now houses Moreton First. All new building is high spec (including new Centenary Science Centre) and all parents praise the excellent facilities. They've spent an unleveraged £3 and a half million in the last five years, all of it raised from income – a separate study centre for overseas students, multi-activity holidays and conferences; new science building with medical science faculty next on the list. 'We never close' – so they never stop earning. Older girls live in hotel-style accommodation, which may just make going to university a bit of a comedown. Boys' boarding now offered in years 3 to 6. Fine, spreading grounds across which girls scoot to the petrol station just outside, where they can stock up on comestibles. A rural location but quickly reached by fast roads from every direction.

Pastoral care and discipline: Rigour and seriousness underpin all things here, but they don't manifest as furrow-browed Puritanism. Quite the contrary – it's the rigour and seriousness that make the liberal ethos work. A notably unstuffy, completely unsnobby place, relaxed and friendly, an easy place to be whoever you are. Ninety per cent board at 11+, but it's not bang-up boarding – it's responsive-to-the-individual boarding ('We go home when we need but there's so much going on'), and that's why most day girls spend between one and four nights at school and why the school is 80-90 per cent full at weekends. Much stress is laid on being nice to one another, living together

among friends – 'We're not just a school, more of a family'. This is a corny thing to say perhaps but it's the literal truth, so not corny. The girls are unspoilt, unaffected. 'You don't feel under pressure to be anyone or do anything,' they say, but they're all jolly nice, and don't they do a lot? Close monitoring, academic and pastoral, but it's not smothering – it's kind. Girls are genuinely appreciative of the way they are looked after. Induction programme for new pupils praised by parents.

Pupils and parents: Most live within an hour and a half's distance. From Cheshire, the West Midlands, Wales and, since the Malverns merged, a greater flow from the south. Single sex is a major choice factor – those few single sex schools that have survived have done so because they are the fittest (stats show still an academic advantage). Parents can drop in whenever they want, unannounced. They like to muck in and join trips to the theatre, skiing holidays, even meals, and also like the way they can see the principal whenever required, and that he never seems to need briefing first. Good communications, frequent updates. Informative, vibrant website. Very supportive former pupils; stalwart, canny governors.

Entrance: At three from Moreton First, at 11 from primaries and at 13 from preps. Test, interview and head's report to make sure can cope. Entry into sixth form, too. Taster visits popular. Superb retention after GCSE – a hallmark of quality. Once in, you're safe: 'If we take them on, we have a responsibility to make a proper job of them'. Lists pretty full, oversubscribed at sixth form. Five per cent from overseas, capped.

Exit: Nearly all go through to sixth form and on to university. Bristol, Durham, Imperial College, Leeds, Birmingham, Newcastle all popular; three to Oxbridge in 2013.

Money matters: Some scholarships and bursaries. The astute use of the school in holiday time makes the most of your fees.

Remarks: A school attuned to its market – highly responsive to the needs and aspirations of its parents, constantly evolving. Well worth the hike for parents turned off by perceived la-di-da pretentiousness in rival schools. Moreton girls take their place in life after school without adjustment.

Morrison's Academy

Linked school: Morrison's Academy Junior School

Ferntower Road, Crieff, PH7 3AN

- Pupils: 265 girls and 275 boys • Ages: 3–18 • Inter–demon
- Fees: £10,839 pa • Independent

Tel: 01764 653885
Email: principal@morrisonsacademy.org
Website: www.morrisonsacademy.org

Rector and Principal: Since 2004, Mr Simon Pengelley BA PGCE (fifties), historian, educated at Repton, followed by Bristol University and PGCE in London. He has taught up and down the country: Abingdon, Strathallan (head of history), Rossall and now Morrisons, where he has overseen a huge sea change. Boarding numbers had been dwindling for some time and the final boarding house closed a few years ago. Former boarding houses are about to go on the market ('Silly them – they missed the moment' critique) and 'all sorts of plans are in the pipeline' – though we couldn't find them on the web.

Our visit came just after an exhausting HMIE inspection: everyone appeared quietly confident (from the nursery up). The rector's vision (his word) is to make Morrisons the top academic school in the 'locality'. Independent rivals include Glenalmond, Strathallan, Dollar Academy and – the one they really have to beat – The High School of Dundee. This editor was surprised not to be shown ambitious plans for future building, and, with the rector having stabilised the school (it was in dire straits – both numerically and emotionally – when he arrived), by closing the remaining boarding houses while greatly increasing pupil numbers (no mean achievement), wondered whether the M6 wasn't beckoning again. Their three sons are now all at university, but he and his wife, Louise, 'love Scotland and have loads of friends in the area' – so that's all right, then.

Academic matters: School follows Scottish curriculum: good takeup for Advanced Highers and remarkably good results all round (46 per cent A*/A grades in 2013). Outstanding results in Highers across the board (45 per cent A*/A grades in 2013). The traditional bias towards science is slightly fading in favour of arts-based courses. Intermediate 2 more or less across the board: 17 Highers, with photography for media at sixth form only on offer. Sciences perform consistently well, also maths; English Highers impressive last year, ditto accountancy, goodish art and design, not really much language take up, humanities OK. No obvious terminal cases; human biology popular at Higher level and results indicate that it is obviously either better taught or more interesting than its bog standard twin. Inspirational English department produces plays 'every other year' as part of the syllabus (alternate years = musicals).

Fantastic flat screen computers all over the place – pupils can take their European Computer Driving Licence, though no-one was quite sure whether the head of the computer department still built his own. Can cope with special needs and programmes much used. Dyslexia, dyspraxia and mild Asperger's not a problem – no extra charge. (Junior school has 1.6 remedial teachers and this continues all the way up.)

Games, options, the arts: Masses of pitches at Dallerie, a ten minute walk from the main buildings, and school plays all the standard games. Good rugby. Swimming pool on site, still labelled Baths (bless). Stronger pipe band than ever, with Scots reclaiming it as their own; parents seem to think that this eruption of interest in piping and drumming is a direct consequence of closing the boarding houses, as the pipe band was previously once almost run as a private fiefdom with Chinese (who made up the majority of boarders) students playing a mega part – made for interesting photographs. Band plays at Murrayfield rugby internationals as part of massed bands. Huge CCF, D of E strong (straight to silver if part of the CCF) – almost all get bronze, lots of silver and gold. Forty five extra-curricular activities in total.

Enthusiastic art department in inspired converted attics – terrific fabrics, which were exhibited at The Scottish Parliament, but still no CAD. Music and drama strong (and based in what was once the girls' loos – check out the plumbing in the store cupboard); not totally soundproof practice rooms: 'We can hear what they are working at,' said the head of music. Stunning girls' chamber choir which plays regularly to local acclaim.

Background and atmosphere: Built in 1859, this Scottish baronial-styled building with its crow stepped gables was described thus at the time: 'Its healthful locality and commanding view of extensive and beautifully romantic scenery cannot be surpassed, if at all equalled, by any such public building in Scotland'. The gift of Thomas Mor(r)ison, who lived in the neighbouring village of Muthill and made his fortune as a master builder in Edinburgh (constructed its new town). He instructed his trustees to erect an institution carrying his name 'to promote the interests of mankind, having a particular regard to the education of youth and the diffusion of useful knowledge'.

Always independent, at one stage did have grant-aided pupils, but this finished in the late 1970s. Fabulous buildings revamped following the sale of underused outlying houses. The impressive original school building, with its large open corridors, works well today, though some of the more recent constructions are less inspiring. The glorious first floor hall, much used for theatricals and the like, doubles for daily assemblies and socials, boasts a new organ and a 'recently restored' floor. Recording studios on the wish list. Re-development of the library, the installation of an artificial hockey pitch and increased ICT in classrooms are all planned for the coming year. A magnificent newer build for maths and jolly attic transformation into a vast art complex. Dining refectory off campus – rector lunches with heads of houses on Tuesdays, food said to be 'OK', though our guide and most of her peers preferred to eat at The Tuckie across the (not very busy) road.

New purpose-built nursery just opened on campus.

Pastoral care and discipline: Excellent pastoral care. Head quite tough on sin, though pupils on the whole 'quite docile' – 'Tobacco could get you suspended', regular boozing could ultimately result in expulsion and use of drugs means that 'you should expect to be expelled'. Not really a street-wise school.

Pupils and parents: Pupils from all over the middle belt – Falkirk, Stirling, Dunblane, Comrie, Perth (masses), Auchterarder – are bused to school (no trains since Beeching). Catchment area extends to south of Stirling and north: past the House of Bruar and Crianlarich. Not really a toffs' school.

Entrance: Children can and do arrive at any time – during the term and at the start of any term. Interview and testing for nursery and junior school and more or less automatic entrance into senior school from the junior. Some join the senior school at 11 from the state sector or from local prep schools such as Ardvreck or Craigclowan – interview and exam. Sixth form entrants are assessed on their potential, taking into account their grades at Standard Grade or GCSE.

Exit: Three or four off to (usually) Scottish independent schools at either 11 or 13. Otherwise a dribble occasionally to Oxbridge, one to Cambridge last year, plus four to London – Imperial and King's. Regular mini stream usually to engineering or allied science at Imperial or Manchester, Newcastle, Leeds. Most stay in Scotland with law, computing, business and sciences prevailing, though sports science and sports medicine in the ribbons.

Money matters: Discounts for siblings, one or two means-tested bursaries, scholarships for the final year.

Remarks: A good proud school which does well by its pupils.

Mossbourne Community Academy

100 Downs Park Road, London, E5 8JY

• Pupils: 1,300 boys and girls • Ages: 11–18 • Non-denominational • State

Tel: 020 8525 5200
Email: enquiries@mossbourne.hackney.sch.uk
Website: www.mossbourne.hackney.sch.uk/

Principal: Since 2012, Mr Peter Hughes (thirties), who took over when founding principal Sir Michael Wilshaw left to lead

Ofsted. An Australian, he came to Mossbourne as part of the future Leaders programme, which identifies, supports and trains potential head teachers. He has taught at Pimlico and Highgate Wood, and was an advanced skills teacher. He can be seen out running at 6am with rowers (the school has a liaison with London Youth Rowers and is close to the River Lee).

Academic matters: Truly outstanding results: in 2013, 82 per cent of pupils got 5+ A*-C grades at GCSE including maths and English. Forty-seven A*/A grades. At A level, 70 per cent of grades were A*/B and 89 per cent A*/C. Not only are these some of the best state school results in the capital, they are also all the more extraordinary, given the fact that a significant proportion of the pupils arrive in year 7 hardly able to read.

The country's highest ranking school for 'value added' – how is it done? Well, a formula that bears no relationship to wishy-washy liberalism – a tough-love approach with a strict uniform policy, ferocious discipline, meticulous monitoring with weekly target setting and a 'can-do' culture. Young and enthusiastic teaching staff (who receive performance-related bonuses) have no official office hours and parents universally praise their dedication. 'My kids never complain about their teachers,' said one mother. 'They seem to be in school at seven every morning. They recognise that not everyone is going to be a rocket scientist, but still manage to make every child feel relevant, included and loved.'

The banded intake is set on entry in all the main curriculum subjects (English, maths, science, humanities, ICT and modern languages), though considerable movement between sets. Music, drama, dance, PE, art and design technology are not setted. Three languages on offer at GCSE – French, German, Spanish – as part of the core curriculum, but students also have the opportunity to take public exams in Turkish, Latin, Bengali, Swedish and Italian. Both vocational and academic exams on offer post GCSE (though considerably more academic than vocational), with a BTEC in business studies and level 3 ICT. Homework is set in abundance. Two specialities: ICT and RATL (raising achievement, transforming learning). ICT facilities are therefore state of the art, with interactive whiteboards in all classrooms and all students offered access to the internet and laptops. What really makes the school excel academically, however, is the minutely monitored assessment – the 'personalised learning agenda' is certainly not just government jargon at this school.

The SEN provision is particularly remarkable, with its own well-resourced teaching centre and well-qualified specialists who cope with the full range of difficulties from autistic spectrum to dyslexia. All pupils with academic, social, emotional or behavioural difficulties have a learning mentor and those who require learning support work with a teaching assistant (in class or outside), receive specialist teaching and the support of external specialists if required. Handwriting club and homework club. Additional English classes, too, for non-native speakers on Saturday mornings. Strategies to suit all, including the brightest. The head quickly followed up on one parent's suggestion that Latin might be a desirable addition and equally quickly found himself with 30 students, who went on to take GCSE.

Games, options, the arts: Extra-curricular here is part of the curriculum, with an additional, compulsory, off-piste period every afternoon from 3.10 to 4.10pm. This time is used to help strugglers, and also to broaden horizons, with more than 70 activities on offer. All pupils required to take a minimum of two extension classes, which include everything from journalism to marathon running. Saturday morning school provides a safe place to have fun and weekend activities include the City explorers club, to discover the joys of London. Sports include football, netball, basketball, cricket and even rowing, and 'best in Hackney' for athletics. Wonderful head of sport, reports

one mother – 'My son had no problem getting up at 6am three mornings a week to be at cricket practice at 7'. Clearly buzzing on all fronts – annual junior concert, dance and drama production; trips to Edinburgh, Belgium, the Isle of Wight, language trips to Spain and Germany; Spanish play, poetry competition, debating, links with London College of Fashion.

Background and atmosphere: Founded on the site of Hackney Downs School, once a successful local grammar school, whose alumnae include Sir Michael Caine and Harold Pinter. By the 1990s, however, it had become notorious as 'the worst in Britain' and was eventually demolished. Mossbourne was rebuilt on the same site, a tricky triangle bounded on two sides by railway lines. Founding principal Sir Michael Wilshaw worked alongside architects, Richard Rogers and Partners, to design a school (costing £325 million) which met his requirements. Now one of the largest wooden structures in England, it was created in a V shape, which holds in its arms a triangular social area. Wilshaw believed that pupils need to be kept under constant observation, so the head's office and the classrooms all overlook the grounds. No corridors – hotspots for bullying – and no staffroom, since Wilshaw felt teachers need to be involved at break times and after school, when most trouble occurs. Indoors, the triple-height space is light and airy and learning takes place in 'learning areas'. Sparkling new sixth form centre added in 2009.

Pupils' aspirations always focused upwards. Rather than the Lord's Prayer, students recite the Mossbourne reflection: 'Throughout this lesson I aspire to maintain an inquiring mind, a calm disposition and an attentive ear, so that in this class and in all classes I can fulfil my true potential'. Parents without hesitation describe the school as 'absolutely amazing' – 'The kids are plainly very well cared for, polite, helpful and considerate. You feel that they are looked after and they are looking out for each other'. An incredible loyalty between kids from completely different ethnic and social backgrounds. Perhaps the greatest compliment any parent can pay is: 'You walk into the school during the day and there is an air of studiousness and control. I don't think about it any more – I know the teachers are in charge'.

Pastoral care and discipline: As celebrated for its discipline as for its academic success – little opportunity to slip up here. Particularly in the early years, pupils are drilled in army-like expectations. Detentions commonplace – for lost homework, left-at-home games kit, being more than 10 seconds late when the morning whistles goes at 8.40am – and students stand when a teacher enters the room. Wherever the potential for rule breaking, staff are on hand – stairwells manned between lessons and students monitored after school. Pre-GCSE pupils wear smart grey and red school blazers and neatly knotted ties, sixth formers graduate to business-like suits and skirts (at or below the knee). No piercings allowed, except for ears, hair must be kept to an acceptable norm (those indulging in the shaven look work in isolation until locks re-grow). Mobiles banned and students not allowed to enter shops on their way home or loiter outside the gates in groups. 'Structure sets a child free,' says the head. And it certainly seems to – a 96 per cent attendance rate.

Pastoral care is as strong as the discipline – few personal problems go unnoticed, whether bullying or self-harm. At the first sign, parents are invited to come and speak to the staff. One grateful mother has nothing but praise for their intervention – 'They made it very easy for my children speak to a counsellor. Mossbourne is a place where you can talk and get support when you can't always get that at home'. Food healthy and delicious.

Pupils and parents: A large percentage of the intake comes from the adjacent Pembury estate, an urban sprawl which tends to hit the headlines for its shootings and drugs rather than its high educational aspirations. Four-fifths of pupils are from minority ethnic groups (many Turkish Kurds), two-fifths speak English as a second language, fifty per cent are on free school meals. But also a fair number of clued-up, middle-class parents – the kind who used to go private or bus their children out of the borough – who fight from a great distance to get their children the superb education the school offers.

Entrance: Two hundred places – now one of the country's most over-subscribed schools. The head is looking for a balanced intake: 'We want a comprehensive – we don't want a secondary modern'. Applicants sit reasoning tests to divide into four equal ability bands. 60 per cent of places in each band are given to whose who live within the inner zone (now less than 500 metres from the gates); 40 per cent of places go to those outside the zone. For those inside the zone, priority is given to those in public care and statemented children, then siblings, then distance from the gates. For those outside the zone, the order is the same, though the final criteria is not distance from the gates but distance from the home address to a co-ed, non-selective comprehensive. Those who live furthest from that type of school are given priority at Mossbourne. Introducing a lottery system from 2014.

The lower sixth form has only 125 places and priority is given to those who have come up through the school. Most places are filled automatically, though pupils looking for academic courses need to meet the demanding criteria of seven A*-C GCSEs, including English and maths; those wanting vocational courses need four A*-C. A few candidates come in at this stage from other Hackney comprehensives.

Exit: Most proceed to the sixth form. Three to Oxbridge and two medics in 2013. Many others to Russell Group and other top unis.

Money matters: Money is not a problem at this well-resourced school – everything from the buildings to the technology is of the highest standard and whatever the head wants to get done he has the means to achieve.

Remarks: Proof that with sufficient resources and the right direction, the kids who life intended to fail can succeed. Parents rightly fight to get into its safe, inspiring and eco-friendly classrooms.

The Mount School

Linked school: The Mount Junior School

Dalton Terrace, York, Perthshire, YO24 4DD

- Pupils: 235 girls; 60 boarders, 175 day • Ages: 11–18 • Quaker
- Fees: Day £7,140–£16,065; Boarding £17,700–£26,385 pa
- Independent

Tel: 01904 667500
Email: registrar@mountschoolyork.co.uk
Website: www.mountschoolyork.co.uk

Principal: Since 2009, Ms Julie Lodrick BA music and related arts (University College, Chichester), PGCE (Kingston University), MA education, leadership and management (OU), professional practice certificate in boarding (BSA), national professional qualification for headship (NCSL) (late thirties). Wide experience in educational management; deputy head of Farlington School, West Sussex for four years. Also a tutor and lecturer for the Boarding Schools Association. Previously housemistress at Queenswood School, Hatfield, Hertfordshire, for five years; head of music at St Margaret's Senior School, West Sussex, for five years.

Academic matters: Strong A level results – 82 per cent A*-B in 2013. At GCSE, 52 per cent A*/A. Maths setted in year 7 onwards, English in year 9 onwards. A strong set of traditional A levels on offer with PE, theatre studies, psychology and business studies added due to demand. EPQ and AQA Baccalaureate offered with strong takeup. Good IT provision – interactive whiteboards in most classrooms and two state-of-the-art computer suites; qualifications including OCR National taken in middle school and sixth form. Attractive and well-designed new sixth form study centre has revitalised the top end of the school, giving private study areas as well as allowing extra activities such as cookery and social gatherings. York used for local cross-curricular and thinking skills work via 'Investigating York' in year 7; archaeology is part of history lower down the school; links with university. Does well with all abilities including EAL – support available; also specialist learning support teaching. Girls enjoy lessons and have good relationships with friendly, cheerful and enthusiastic staff. Very good careers education with work experience.

Games, options, the arts: Beautifully kept grounds with numerous tennis courts, sports fields for hockey and athletics, an indoor pool and sports hall including a fitness suite. Successful at traditional team games as well as fencing and orienteering. Current players at county and country level in netball, cross-country, biathlon and hockey. Very strong and varied musical life, from classical to rock; all abilities participate in Christmas concert; regular concerts with other Quaker schools. About one-third learn instruments at school; regular speech and drama successes. Huge range of after-school activities, eg jewellery making, photography – all take part. Very impressive artwork throughout the school, especially 3D work. Creative writing competition successes. Duke of Edinburgh popular – strong tradition of community involvement. An understanding of the wider world is important – currently enjoying involvement with Peace Jam and electronic links to Quaker schools in Palestine and Lebanon.

Background and atmosphere: Origins go back to 18th century; present building, close to the centre of York, has a very fine 1857 façade with modern additions. Classrooms are a mix of old and new, very traditional library, which the girls enjoy, and a delightfully modern dining room. Set in 16 acres of gardens and green fields – girls make the most of the outdoor space, practising their tennis strokes, others deep in conversation and even 12 year olds are not too cool to race to the garden swing at break times. Though only a small percentage of staff and girls are Quakers, the ethos is central, manifest in respect for everyone in the community, a high degree of tolerance of differences, caring for others and democratic practices like the school council, which discusses internal affairs and, unlike most, really does have a voice. Morning Meetings include a period of silent reflection. Widespread involvement rather than bald achievement is regarded highly and girls view additional activities, such as lectures from visiting speakers, as 'opportunities not to be missed'.

Pastoral care and discipline: Considered very important – girls feel they receive a lot of individual attention. Four sixth form girls to a tutor group. Non-confrontational approach to discipline; exclusion only for persistent offences or major breach of rules (eg alcohol abuse) – huge amount of trust around the place, which girls appreciate with a typical common sense approach – 'If you mess up, you mess it up for everyone'. Plenty of contact with parents – school website, weekly newsletter.

M

Pupils and parents: Not just those with Quaker connection (it's the only all-girls Quaker school in England) – large number of local parents, often without an independent school background; not a county set school. Wide range of religions or none. Several boarders from Pacific Rim, South America, USA and Europe and others from a variety of other countries, though 'not too many from any one language group', plus overseas British. Girls wear white shirt, tartan skirt and blue jumper; no uniform for sixth form – 'relaxed' dress code. Famous Old Girls include Dame Judi Dench, Margaret Drabble, Antonia Byatt, Mary Ure, Kate Bellingham, Laura Sayers.

Entrance: Assessments for years 7-10 entry in English, maths and verbal reasoning plus interview with head, who looks for 'spark – interesting girls with wide interests'. School report also important. Average and above average abilities catered for. Six GCSEs A*-C and interview for sixth form.

Exit: A very small number leave post-GCSE, most for local sixth form college. Otherwise to a variety of universities, old and new, a few to Oxbridge, most to their first choice; a wide range of subjects studied; some take a gap year.

Money matters: Year 7 academic and music scholarships; year 9 academic, art and design, sport, music and drama; lower sixth (College) academic, art, sport, drama and music – all give five per cent remission of fees, to which a means-tested bursary of up to 100 per cent can be added. Music and drama scholars get free lessons. Separate bursary fund for Quaker children.

Remarks: Well-established Quaker girls' school – multi-faith and with an international student body. Lively, creative, warm atmosphere in a framework of orderly calm – mature, articulate and magnanimous sixth formers setting high standards for younger girls. Girls are highly motivated self-starters – collaborative rather than competitive, as you would expect in a Quaker school, nevertheless driven by a determination to do well.

Newstead Wood School for Girls

Avebury Road, Orpington, Kent, BR6 9SA

• Pupils: 1,045 students; years 7 to 11 – girls; sixth form – mixed; all day • Ages: 11-18 • Non-denom • State

Tel: 01689 853626
Email: office@newsteadwood.bromley.sch.uk
Website: www.newsteadwood.bromley.sch.uk

Headteacher: Since 2001, Mrs Elizabeth Allen BA MA FRSA (early sixties). Previously head of Altwood (mixed) Comprehensive in Maidenhead. Currently teaches critical thinking to the sixth form but previously taught RS, English and drama to advanced level. She impresses with her understanding of what works best for bright girls and the educational scene and is immensely proud of what the pupils and staff achieve. Credited for being business-like with clear vision and having the school's best interests at heart. While parents lower down the school have limited contact and pupils tend to be somewhat in awe of her, sixth formers call her inspirational and parents say she is very focused on the job at hand.

Academic matters: Not so much an academic hothouse as the sort of place where, if you don't work reasonably hard, you're the odd one out. The head places great emphasis on staff and pupils 'co-constructing' the learning experience and on staff leadership and development – they should be critical questioners and facilitate, rather than direct, learning. An active school parliament and students lead the review and revision of the school's mission statement. In addition to termly reports and annual parent teacher meetings, an academic tutoring day each term includes individual interviews to discuss achievements and set targets for improving learning.

Building learning and thinking skills starts early. Year 7's 'Journeys of a Lifetime' programme encourages pupils to articulate how they learn and where they need to focus and is allied to lots of opportunities to expand and get beneath curriculum subjects. Further up the school, the engineering diploma (years 10-13), IB and extended project in the sixth form are designed to promote independent study and breadth of learning. Exam results are consistently impressive, with popular subjects being biology, chemistry, maths, English lit and psychology. In 2013, 75 per cent A*/A grades at GCSE. A level results no less creditable: 81 per cent A*/B grades and 49 per cent A*/A grades.

Strong enrichment programme – the usual timetable is effectively suspended for three weeks each year. Specialist engineering and languages status provides opportunities to extend the scope of study (eg engineering diploma and Mandarin Chinese and Japanese from year 8). Also a designated gifted and talented lead school – these pupils aren't noticeably singled out for special treatment but staff ensure lots to stimulate and push them. Dyspraxic and dyslexic pupils' coping strategies often uncovered during GCSEs. Individual education plans then agreed between pupils, parents and staff to overcome any difficulties.

Games, options, the arts: 'Whatever they do, they do well,' says one parent and the evidence seems to support this. Good performances in hockey, netball and gymnastics and, though the school has no pool, it tops the results tables in national and county swimming events. Older girls help the youngsters.

The year 7 and 8 vocal ensemble was conceived and is run by sixth formers, one of several choirs and orchestras which perform regularly. Music is a real strength and taken seriously and at tempo here (better make sure you rehearse!). Vox CC, its senior choir, has performed at the Royal Albert Hall and in Prague. Drama is popular; 20+ student societies in anything from debating, politics, history, the environment, medicine to law, all run by year 12 pupils. Leadership and participation is very much what this school is all about and it's rare to find a sixth former who doesn't voluntarily take on extra responsibilities. For others, too, judging by the somewhat overwhelming stream of calendar reminders on the electronic board in reception, little excuse to be idle. Lots of after school and lunchtime activities, as well as positions as sports ambassadors, Arkwright scholars to promote engineering in schools, language teaching in local primary schools, maths and debating competitions, Dragon's Den workshops and charity events – plenty going on.

Background and atmosphere: Set in a quiet residential area, has wonderful views across the playing fields towards the Downs, but the school buildings, though quite spacious, are unremarkable and jumbled – the 1950s, when it was established, not perhaps the best architectural era. Inside, the walls are brightened with artwork and a lick of paint from the girls over the holidays. Recently added a new suite of maths rooms and a new sixth form block. Alongside these additional classrooms, upgrades to staff areas and lab refurbishment. Already has wonderful indoor tennis courts open to the public.

Pastoral care and discipline: Ongoing and slightly half-hearted battles regarding sixth form dress code but, in the head's view, it's churlish to make too big a fuss when most girls behave and perform well. In an all-female environment they are generally not interested in acting beyond their years and the school encourages them to assess for themselves what's appropriate in different circumstances. More commonly issues arise through poor organisation or conflicting priorities, typical, the head says, amongst bright, enthusiastic pupils.

As long as you are willing to work with the school, issues are normally swiftly resolved in liaison with staff, the emphasis being very much on motivation rather than chastisement. Parents cite examples of a generally good response to concerns voiced, whether individual (friendship) or more general (chain emails). The school is also alert to mixed expectations relating to academic and home life. In such cases, a counsellor and family worker are available to provide guidance and support. A strong PSHE programme, which, eg, incorporates financial literacy, in which pupils can gain accreditation. Careers support very good with lots of individual advice, a calendar of related events, a well-stocked library and lots of exposure to different areas of work through placements and contact with professionals.

Occasional incidents of bullying are addressed, with the girls themselves tending to side with the victim. Informal vertical contact is encouraged through extra-curricular clubs and older pupils acting as mentors. The travel buddy scheme is a nice example, combining as it does environmental targets to reduce car use with accompanying year 7 pupils on public transport their first few weeks. Occasionally girls are to be seen eating and smoking outside the school grounds, but few complaints from local businesses and residents, who seem grateful to have such a well-thought of school in their midst – 'We'd all like our kids to go there'.

Pupils and parents: Says one parent, 'If they're really not up to and up for it, they won't enjoy it' – ie you need to be self-motivated rather than coached to get here. From a range of socio-economic and ethnic backgrounds. 'They stand out for being bright, self-confident and just getting on with it,' says one business regularly offering work experience to pupils from local schools. PA is active and effective, holding a variety of social and fund-raising events over the year, as well as organising regular fairs through its careers sub-committee. Notable former pupils include Christine Hancock, Barbara Harriss-White, Emma Johnson (clarinettist who came back to hold a masterclass at the school), Susan Tebby, Josie Long and Kim Medcalf.

Entrance: Most from local state primary schools. For year 7, entrance tests in verbal and non-verbal reasoning in November. Standards high, but the test experience 'more friendly' than for other local schools. Around 650-700 applications for 130 places. When, very occasionally, places come available further up the school, those on the waiting list are invited to take an age-appropriate test and the highest scorers offered a place. Additional places are available for sixth form entry – including boys. A minimum of six GCSE grades A*-C with A* or A in the subjects for further study needed.

Exit: The head makes it clear that those entering at 11 are expected to stay the course and only a few leave at 16, mostly to pursue specialist studies, eg performing arts or media studies. In 2013, six to Oxbridge. Other popular destinations London, Leeds, Nottingham, Bristol, Birmingham, Exeter, York and Durham as well as art, drama, music, veterinary and medical colleges.

Money matters: Dedicated and enthusiastic PTA raises £30,000-50,000 annually, which funds the artists in residence each year and extra teaching resources. A covenant scheme and continuous fund-raising events and activities to support the ongoing developments. Girls raise money for charities during house charity week.

Remarks: Capable and committed girls do really well here, most setting out on their future studies and careers well-qualified and equipped for the challenges ahead.

Nonsuch High School for Girls

Ewell Road, Cheam, Sutton, Surrey, SM3 8AB

- Pupils: 1,240 girls, all day • Ages: 11–18 • Non–denom • State

Tel: 020 8394 1308
Email: office@nonsuch.sutton.sch.uk
Website: www.nonsuchhigh.co.uk

Headteacher: Since 2013, Mr Peter Gale BA MA, previously deputy head of Rosebery School in Epsom, and the school's first male head.

Academic matters: Anything these girls do, they do not just well, but very well indeed. Exam results (79 per cent A*/A grades at GCSE and 51 per cent A*/A at A level) put them towards the top end of grammar school performance and well into the rarified heights of super-boffin territory. A small number of children (just over one per cent) have learning difficulties, currently spanning physical disabilities and mild dyslexia.

There's some setting (maths from year 8, for example) but many subjects are tutor group based up to the start of GCSEs (girls take a minimum of 10.5). A generous handful will get 12 or 13 straight A*s, many going on to five AS and four A-levels. Some complete GCSE maths in year 10.

A science and languages specialist, the school does both proud. Demanding GCSE triple science is taken by all, taught in 11 well-equipped labs with adjacent prep rooms, and vast numbers carry on to A-level, 100 doing physics alone. Girls study two languages from the off, choosing from French, German, Spanish or Latin and, from year 10, GCSE ancient Greek. There's even Mandarin, run as an after-school club for the linguistically adventurous. Lessons can be good fun – European Day of Languages was marked in year 7 by a Eurovision-style contest including 'Baby, hit me one more time' in German – and there are extensive study/work experience opportunities, currently European-based but no reason why, thanks to Skype and well-equipped language labs, girls shouldn't soon be at least chatting on-line to peers in China and elsewhere, believes the school. Arts are also on the up, with drama GCSE performances singled out for praise by exam board.

It's good to see a range of less traditional GCSEs on offer, photography among them (some stunning images in school magazine) and, unusually, astronomy – school has its very own dome, open to local societies, in a secure, passworded building, where budding Sir Patrick Moores troop for their own Sky at Night sessions, though not all the girls are alive to the magic of the constellations. 'It's just a telescope in a white dome,' said one, prosaically, when asked if a tour could be arranged.

Inevitably, pupils with a broad range of interests have to make tough decisions at A level, especially would-be scientists and medics. At A level critical thinking and the EPQ are offered.

Judged solely by the results, the teaching clearly delivers the goods, and, for sixth formers especially, can be inspirational. 'You really see the passion in the teachers, you've got a different relationship… (The teachers) leave you to do the mundane stuff on your own, then use the lessons to explore the subject,' says one. Staff regularly go on to greater things elsewhere – one of deputy heads promoted to headship at Wallington High School, for example. However, the school is also committed to developing wider skills and is beginning to introduce a curriculum which develops independent learning, teamwork, communications skills and resilience. The culture of the school is shifting to encourage risk taking and to ensure students are prepared for the test of life rather than a life of tests.

Games, options, the arts: Monthly school newsletters invariably feature pupil sporting successes in school and out and there's huge enthusiasm for fiercely-contested inter-house competitions and even (a surprise) a burgeoning cheerleading team. Clubs abound; some, like judo, pilates and aerobics, run by outside firms and paid for, others, like lunchtime cycle club, exploring Nonsuch Park grounds, run by motivated staff (average age early 40s, 65 women, 19 men) and all done for love.

Facilities, including tennis/netball courts, playing fields, 400m grass track and floodlit artificial turf pitch, are good, while a deal with a private fitness firm has also added a cavernous sports hall, small(ish) changing rooms and, in some parents' eyes, rather limited access (morning lesson time only) to a jewel of an indoor pool. Parents, though realistic about inevitable bias towards academics, feel sport becomes somewhat perfunctory higher up the school. 'If you have a very sporty child, you end up getting your fix elsewhere,' says one, though school fields respectable number of sports alumni.

Arts, meanwhile, are buzzing (possibly humming, too), with several children selected for national drama and music groups and so many learning instruments (650 and rising) in and out of school that you could staff a symphony orchestra several times over, with spares. With lots of highly regarded productions, recently My Fair Lady and Lawfully (sic) Blonde, house talent shows and a range of ensembles – some, like the flourishing Indian music group, are set up by the pupils – all nine practice rooms are usually busy at break time (forward booking, somewhat inevitably in these highly organised surroundings, is essential).

Add an excellent range of trips to Sorrento, Large Hadron Collider at CERN, China and Costa Rica together with extensive community service options and it's almost impossible not to acquire a CV bulging with career-enhancing goodies. Even year 7s compete to design and sell their own fundraising product, while sixth formers run a huge range of clubs and societies in school and at local primaries. CCF is optional for year nines upwards) and DE (all levels) is run in conjuction with local authority.

Background and atmosphere: So quiet that the only thing a visitor hears is the clicking of the friendly PA's heels as she escorts you down grey corridors offset with lots of colourful photography and artwork to the staff loos (and waits outside to escort you back again).

The red brick buildings, mainly three-storey and geometrically straightforward (though feeling anything but to the first-time visitor) date back to 1938, when the school, named for the next door palace built by Henry VIII, first opened. They're in generally good shape with lots of nice, bright rooms, many refurbished – art is especially appealing with vibrant-looking masks and wire sculptures.

From the plasma TVs giving regular updates on school events to smart card technology allowing girls timed access to buildings and fingerprint payment for meals, everything resonates with efficiency, though the motion-detecting lights which can take a while to come on give winter evening forays up dark staircases a certain adventurous quality. Even the loos have useful notices on the inside of the doors – 'I suppose it gives us something to read,' says a pupil.

Pastoral care and discipline: Behaviour is generally excellent – lapses are so rare that there's a pause while girls struggle to remember what happens, the only recent incident of note being a brief on-line teacher-baiting episode in 2010, swiftly sorted with suspensions and detentions, and reinforced by new cyber mentors – girls, not robots – trained by CEOP, the on-line protection body, to keep everyone on the straight and narrow virtual road.

As for the rare underachiever – a relative term as they'd be a big success anywhere else – there's lots of help. Form tutors are the first point of contact for most issues and keep a watching brief on academic performance, working with the child and parents to resolve any underlying problems and organise a bit of extra support if required.

Most importantly, girls are extremely supportive of each other, often working and revising together informally, with younger pupils readily approaching older ones for assistance through the house system.

'There's the feeling that everyone wants to help,' says one girl, who agreed, as did others, that knowing their friends were looking out for them takes the edge off the anxiety that all accept as an inevitable, if occasional, fact of life. '"Love God and be cheerful" is our school motto,' points out a sixth former, 'and that is our ethos.'

Pupils and parents: Parents 'very supportive', thinks school. Come across as a hard to impress bunch – 'Ambitious, focused and driven families pushing to get their children in there,' says one mother – who expect the school to deliver against stiff competition from neighbouring girls' grammars, Tiffin Girls in next door Kingston in particular, and are quick to note any slippage in results. Does it matter? To this bunch, very much indeed. Having delivered their side of the bargain – producing bright, motivated daughters – it's up to the school to ensure they fly through exams and straight into Russell Group universities. Some have Oxbridge in their sights when their daughters first arrive. Not that they necessarily leave it up to the school, and novices assuming tutor traumas are behind them once their daughters start here are in for a shock. What one mother describes as a 'significant percentage' carry on having them tutored all the way through, not because they're struggling but to keep them at the top.

The girls, meanwhile, are a nice, modest bunch – braggadocio must be one of the least-used words in extensive vocabulary – and have a genuine and touching pride in each other's achievements. They're delightfully enthusiastic, too, writing reviews in the school newsletter that describe everything from competing in the local music festival and even 'a short geography trip in Cheam Village' as 'exciting' 'great' and 'fantastic'.

And while they may be lacking in spontaneity, perhaps it's no bad thing, given their likely careers, madcap impetuosity being low on the list of desirable qualities for any budding brain surgeon or atom-splitting scientist.

Ex-pupil Joanna Rowsell won gold in the track cycling in the 2012 Olympics.

Entrance: One hundred and eighty places in year 7 through September 11+ exam – two papers (VR and comprehension). Hugely over-subscribed (around 1,650 sit the exam) and highly competitive – numerous on-line/local press tutor ads say it all. Early deadlines, so essential to keep track – Nonsuch Supplementary Form, from school, must be in by early Sep; Common Application Form (CAF) – from candidate's LA – submitted Oct (both can be completed online). Pass/fail results in October, but as more candidates pass than there are places, agony continues till March when offer letters sent out. Top 80 awarded places regardless of location (unless a tie for final place, when proximity is the deciding factor): remaining 100 places go to top-scoring local candidates within catchment area. No sibling priority. Waiting list for runners up runs to December 31, then deleted unless parents advise otherwise; very occasional vacancies in other years determined by science, English and maths exams – unsuccessful 11 plus candidates won't be considered again until sixth form, though.

Limited intake in sixth form (minimum 10 places but can be slightly more) – requires minimum GCSE average points score of 50, places offered on the basis of predicted grades.

Exit: Around 95 per cent to higher education; sends more girls off to read science subjects than almost any other school in the country. Seven to Oxbridge in 2013, lots of medics, vets

N

and linguists, plus a broad range elsewhere, from psychology, sociology and economics to editorial photography, management and art foundation, and one off to start a brand new degree course in paramedic practice.

Remarks: Does well by its seriously bright, highly motivated and caring girls – 'Unus pro omnibus, omnes pro uno' could be its alternative motto. While not necessarily a natural home for the seriously zany, its strengths in performing arts add a welcome swirl of colour to its more sober, science-based accomplishments. There's no getting away from it, however. Elsewhere, girls may just wanna have fun. Here, first and foremost, they wanna do well.

North Berwick High School

Grange Road, North Berwick, EH39 4QS

- Pupils: 955; 480 boys/475 girls • Ages: 11–18 • Non-denom
- State

Tel: 01620 894661
Email: northberwick.hs@northberwickhigh.elcschool.org.uk
Website: www.northberwickhigh.net

Head Teacher: Since 2013, Mrs Lauren Rodger MA PGCE. A former pupil of North Berwick High, she studied English at Aberdeen University, then did PGCE at Manchester. Head of English at St Margaret's School in Edinburgh for eight years and was chair of the SCIS English professional development group. Achieved the Scottish Qualification for Headship in 2006 and was depute head teacher at North Berwick High for seven years. Occasionally teaches English and regularly takes a leadership class for senior pupils. Runs the school with three depute head teachers and a business manager. Her three children were educated at the school.

Academic matters: North Berwick High follows the Scottish system: National Qualifications followed by Intermediates and Highers and then Advanced Highers. Six parallel classes at S1 and S2, with pupils set for maths in S1 and S2. Thereafter, six parallel classes, taking into account option choices, when specialist subject teaching kicks in – deliberately made broad to ensure that pupils' needs and interests are met within the national framework. Maximum class size 25 (a few exceptions), 18/20 for practical subjects.

Consistently turns in best results in East Lothian – always in what Scottish figures describe as the first decile (top tenth) overall in Scotland for S4 results and better than that for Highers. HMIe calls exam performance 'outstanding'. At S4 level, all three sciences, English and maths, history, modern studies, and PE stand out as really solid and taken by a majority of pupils, while achievement and take-up in French is notable. Spanish has become an increasingly popular choice, with pupils sitting up to Higher level.

Higher level sciences, English and maths, geography, (among best in Scotland) modern studies and PE are very strong and this trend continues on the whole to Advanced Higher with physics and history outstanding. In 2013 69 per cent of Advanced Highers were A/B grades and 47 per cent A grades. The adventurous range of Higher subjects includes graphic communications, philosophy, psychology, technological studies, product design and information systems.

Good remedial back-up means children with records of needs are not a problem, nor those with ADHD; double teaching in class, laptops as needed, plus extra time in exams and for those with learning needs which cannot be tackled in the classroom, workshops on basic processes, individual educational programmes and individual tutorials. Reading Recovery programme, plus educational psychologists, outreach teachers et al. Support for learning for the most able as well. The school takes and is well-equipped for the quite severely disabled and works successfully to integrate all into mainstream lessons. Vocationally orientated courses on offer from Prince's Trust, hospitality at Intermediate level, and lots of enterprising opportunities. The hairdressing salon, offering Intermediate qualifications, is open to local people (a really good community service). The school aims to meet the needs of all pupils, not just the top section, and recent emphasis has been on enhancing this 'but not taking the eye off the academic ball'.

The integrated pupil support faculty includes a pupil support base in which the most vulnerable pupils have a 'sanctuary' with additional needs met in various ways: in class by teachers, auxiliaries and S6 pupil helpers. Some are extracted to work on particular areas in the support base, or on a well-established programme of paired reading. Alphasmart and laptop computers in use where required. Individual education programmes in place.

All classrooms have interactive whiteboards and multimedia systems, allowing interactive learning and teaching in all areas, plus dozens of wireless laptops.

Games, options, the arts: Has an enviable collection of games pitches with the local sports centre and swimming pool next door – they have partnership with local users. Astroturf, two gyms in school, plus dance studio with mirrors, of course. Strong rugby and getting stronger with some real successes and girls' basketball under 14 and boys under 14 and under 18 teams reaching Scottish Cup finals. Huge hockey fixture list for girls, plus volleyball, football, cross-country, and clubs for badminton, netball, sailing, swimming. Local authority development officers on hand for coaching. D of E very popular. Trillions of clubs for everything including the latest success story, bee-keeping, and lots of things for the non-sporty. More than 40 different choices, many on offer to several different age groups. Drama, D of E, debating etc as expected plus science and language clubs, eco (with coveted Green Flag award) and fair trade groups, chess, newspaper, scripture union etc. Sports activities coordinator, an ex-pupil, has got even more involved. Plenty of serious fun fundraising for carefully planned range of charities with almost everything linking with the efforts of the local community, which has school at its heart.

Music exceptional, though no pipe band of their own – pupils (of both sexes) play with the town band. Bands, orchestras, masses of instrumental: wind, jazz, brass, piano etc. Senior and junior choirs (some really outstanding singers) and a popular staff/seniors choir – carols sung outside the church for charity at Christmas. Musicians have played with the Scottish National Orchestra in the Usher Hall. Scottish country dancing popular, as are regular ceilidhs. A group even taught highland dancing to a school in Malawi on their trip there.

Recording studio; huge assembly hall used for school drama (very good) and by the locals – for partying as well as plays. Deaf loop in operation. Rows of keyboards, computers and highly decorative guitars stored on walls in music room are all in regular use. Oodles of practice rooms. Creative chaos reigns in the art department, crammed with fabulous work: ceramics, amazing sandblasted glass, block printed fabrics to die for, fantastic costume design with beautiful embroidery and even architectural layouts. Swathes of young artists go on to art schools all over the country. Huge art library and darkroom are supplemented by CAD, Macs and computer links to art department. DT is impressive though mainly in wood. Home economics (cookery) now refurbished with good take up from both sexes and fashion now attracts a few boys. Impressive computer suites and everything technological imaginable can be taken for granted.

Lots of trips, Italy, Belgium, Washington, China, Ardeche, London and to crown it all, visits to partner school in Malawi.

Background and atmosphere: Founded in 1893 with 13 pupils. Originally North Berwick boasted a Parish School (which started in 1661) and the Burgh School; these amalgamated in 1868 and joined forces with the High School in 1931. The current buildings date from 1940s, and very impressive they are too. Refurbishments in 1990s and more recently an interior revamp have created a school which still looks and feels like a real Scottish Academy but is absolutely up to date in every detail. The intriguing café space has been brilliantly constructed surrounding the old central courtyard so that it forms a circular 'high street' right round a charming herb garden, mercifully sheltered from the fierce coastal winds. It is the venue for the Christmas fair, which is a highlight of town life in North Berwick and makes healthy sums for charity.

Light and airy classrooms, which must have some of the best views in Britain, cheek by jowl with the pyramidal Berwick Law on one side and in sight of the Bass Rock and spectacular coastline on the other. Strong links with the spectacular Scottish Seabird Centre, which is used for regular study, as well as providing summer and weekend jobs for impoverished pupils. Loads of participation in town life, concerts for the elderly, tree planting, riding for the disabled. Pupils have contributed entertainment, singing, dance and the like further afield, including Edinburgh.

The huge library is subdivided into little seminar areas and crannies for private study. A tidy school, and pretty well maintained, with lots of eau de nil paint (a favourite with Scottish schools) giving a clean calm feel, though the unwise choice of white painted breezeblock does not respond well to regular wiping down. Walls full of pupil work on display everywhere.

Pastoral care and discipline: Good PSE and strong anti-bullying programmes backed up by a restorative positive behaviour policy and behaviour codes. Pastoral care is delivered via the four houses each managed by a member of the guidance team. Pastoral staff co-ordinate with the deputes, who function as year heads, and an extensive support and counselling team. Working with parents is a key factor. Embedded in a geographically self-sufficient community, the school has taken on a role in community welfare and co-operates with initiatives such as the Youth Project to help keep young people safe and well-balanced out of school as well as in.

Pupils take real responsibility in school, as heads of school, and of houses, as prefects, as mentors for younger pupils and as representatives to the community. Head boy/girl elected annually by pretty stringent process. An onerous task – they have to do the Burns' Night supper at the local Marine Hotel, which brushes up their public speaking. The head boy and girl are principal speakers for S1/2/3 prize-giving at the traditional time in June, and then for the senior prizegiving in mid-September, which is followed by soft drinks, wine for the adults and nibbles in the Dining Hall; very popular.

Four chaplains visit, three Church of Scotland and one Episcopalian, who help to tackle moral issues and teach pupils to listen and be open to the views of others.

Pupils and parents: North Berwick has its share of Edinburgh commuters, bankers and businesspeople from England etc but also an indigenous farming and services community, so intake is pretty mixed. Not quite exclusively Scottish middle class, though only a minuscule element of ethnic diversity. Incredibly supportive parents – usually over 95 per cent turn up for parents' evenings and a very strong PTA, wizards at fund-raising. Parent-led parent council drawn from parents, staff and a couple of members of the local community.

Uniform is kept as simple as possible: white shirts with black and red ties and sweatshirt plus blazers for top years. Pupils encouraged to stay in school at lunchtime. Cafeteria is well used for informal relaxation and they can bring packed lunch or eat in the sports centre. Closes at lunchtime on Fridays for staff training, which may not be over-convenient for working parents. School buses for all outlying districts.

Entrance: Effective programme of visits to feeder primaries, mainly Law Primary (700) which shares the site but also drawing in the scattered small schools in Aberlady, Athelstaneford, Dirleton, Gullane and Law. Head meets parents, and children have a two-day induction programme followed by another parent meeting. Entry automatic if parents live in catchment.

Exit: Two departure dates a year, one at Christmas, the other at the conventional end of school year. Over 90 per cent stay on for fifth year and only few go before sixth. Some leave to go into further education, some work, 50 per cent to university – quite a mix: medics, law, business administration, economics, English, maths, education. Primarily to Scottish universities but a regular and quite impressive trickle to Oxbridge annually (one in 2013).

Money matters: No child disadvantaged – good backup from the local LA, as well as parent-inspired foundation.

Remarks: A real thriving local school, doing well by everybody. About as good as it gets.

North Bridge House Senior School

Linked schools: North Bridge House Junior School; North Bridge House Preparatory School; Royal School Hampstead

65 Rosslyn Hill, London, NW3 5UD

- Pupils: 290 boys and girls • Ages: 11–16 • Non-denom
- Fees: £14,340 pa • Independent

Tel: 020 7267 6266
Email: seniorschool@northbridgehouse.com
Website: www.nbhseniorschool.co.uk

Head: Since 2013, Georgina Masefield. An English graduate from University College London, she was previous head of English at North Bridge House Senior School before leaving to become education officer for Cognita in 2010.

Academic matters: The senior school is a small school and most of the intake is made up of those children who would not aim for the academic powerhouses of north London. No sixth form, with the sense of impending adulthood and university that tends to lend a school; nonetheless, in the last few years, all leavers have gone on to sixth forms elsewhere and thence to university. The academics are gently flourishing here and 2013 saw excellent GCSE results – 89 per cent A*/A grades. Everyone learns French in year 7 and then Spanish in years 8 and 9. Surprisingly wide range of GCSE options for so small a school includes photography and media.

Year 7 taught English, maths and history by class teacher to homogenise all-comers and weld disparate intake into cohesive group. Everyone assessed on entry and SEN specialist supports those deemed to need it – sometimes with up to three withdrawals per week. Some places conditional on parents agreeing to such support. Help given mostly to those with mild dyslexia and dyspraxia.

Games, options, the arts: A seriously arty school, partly because of the backgrounds of the children but also through some inspired teaching. Art and photography impress in particular – both in terms of the work and in the excellent results. Art is taught in a real studio with good light and large windows – evidence of sound teaching of basic skills and results to boast about. Attractive collage work and good textiles along with the exemplary photography. Lively drama in basement room and several productions annually. Lots of visits and outside speakers – including cast of actors and artists among parents, who give generously of time and support. Sports in Regent's Park, the Talacre and Swiss Cottage centres. New sports centre underway and despite small pupil numbers, school performs remarkably well in competitive sports, with wins in all usual team games. Main sports are football, netball, rounders, athletics and tennis. Lots of clubs including dance, drama, football, table tennis, cricket at Lords, cookery, choir, touch typing, Amnesty International, science and French culture.

Background and atmosphere: The amalgamation with the Royal School in Hampstead in 2012 has seen the senior school move to the Royal's central Hampstead site. Much building work over the past year has resulted in a drama and media suite, science, music and DT rooms and refurbished classrooms. The school is owned by Cognita, chaired by former chief inspector of schools, Chris Woodhead, which has provided funds for the work.

Pastoral care and discipline: Pupils are open, enthusiastic and quite palpably happy. They pay tribute to their teachers who 'are always there to help us and treat us as individuals. They want us to be happy'. One refugee from a less congenial school said, 'I always wanted to look forward to coming to school and I do here.'

Pupils and parents: Very mixed north London intake ensures no typical pupil. School so small that everyone knows everyone.

Entrance: Around 70 per cent from state sector – frequently parents who had found decent junior schools but are less gruntled by what the state offers at secondary level. Some from preps that end at 11 and the rest from the North Bridge House Prep School. 'We fill a niche – we're not an academic hothouse,' says head. Pupils invited to admissions day and tested in maths, English, vocabulary, comprehension, verbal reasoning and non-verbal reasoning. A reference from the current school is also necessary.

Exit: Many to Camden Girls' (state comprehensive) sixth form or, occasionally, to Fortismere – a mixed comprehensive. Many to Highgate. Some to sixth form colleges, some to independent day schools, eg Channing and UCS, and some to independent boarding schools, eg Rugby, Bedales or even Westminster.

Money matters: Some academic and music scholarships.

Remarks: A gentle school. Could be the answer for your shyer or less robust son or daughter, who will flourish given the opportunities and security available in this close-knit, nurturing nook, particularly now it has moved to the Royal School's more commodious Hampstead site. We hope the new head will bring some stability after a year unsettled by an acting head in charge of two schools, over-running building work on the new site and staff changes.

North London Collegiate School

Linked school: North London Collegiate School Junior School

Canons, Canons Drive, Edgware, Middlesex, HA8 7RT

• Pupils: 770 girls; all day • Ages: 11–18 • Christian foundation, but all faiths welcomed • Fees: £16,629 pa • Independent

Tel: 020 8952 0912
Email: office@nlcs.org.uk
Website: www.nlcs.org.uk

Headmistress: Since 1997, Mrs Bernice McCabe BA MBA PGCE, (a glamorous mid-fifties). Had exemplary, if not wholly predictable, credentials for this top job in girls' independent education. An English graduate, she spent 23 years teaching in the state sector and was appointed to her first deputy headship in 1986 at Heathlands School, Hounslow. Her various responsibilities there helped her gain the expertise needed for the effective running of a modern school and she took her MBA during her first headship at Chelmsford County High (qv), which, under her seven year tenure, became one of the country's leading state schools.

She teaches all year 7 – an excellent principle and one that all heads should practise, in our view. She is not interested in drilling or ranking girls, 'We have no class positions, no prize-giving except when they leave... I want the staff to find out what the girls are good at and develop their potential, not just teach them to jump through hoops'. She lunches with her Big Six – the committee of sixth form girls who act as a conduit between her and the school community. She fosters a democratic community, which is generally appreciated and comfortably taken for granted now.

Clever, charismatic and good company. Also stunningly pretty and elegant – clearly a rôle model in all ways for her girls, who appear to adore her: her dark red nail varnish is imitated by half her sixth form. She is relaxed, dedicated to education in its truest sense and committed to sharing what she and her school has with the wider world, notably with those who teach or learn in the state sector. Hence her directorship of The Prince's Teaching Institute, a high calibre residential project to reinvigorate subject teaching in schools and re-inspire the teachers. At NLCS she is, clearly, very much in charge and the régime is benign, respected and popular. It is also now a long-standing one. 'She is simply wonderful,' say parents in unison.

Academic matters: Second to none and, as with all truly top schools, it is achieved through a preparedness to teach beyond the curriculum and celebrate the pleasures of learning for its own sake. Offers the IB in tandem with A levels and an increasing number of Pre-Us; the IB is now taken by up to a third of the year. The IB points score is 'phenomenally high' – an average of more than 40 points per pupil, something achieved by only three per cent of students worldwide, and two students in 2012 achieved the maximum 45 points. Top IB school in the UK for last five years. A level results are as good – over 82 per cent of subject grades A*/A and 98 per cent A*/B in 2013. The curriculum has no surprises, though it is good to see a healthy Greek contingent at A level and five modern langs too – French, German, Russian, Spanish and Italian. Mandarin now an option for the sixth. RS is popular, as are biology and chemistry, but maths and English are way ahead of the rest in terms of take-up. Now teaches triple award science IGCSE alongside maths and music. I/GCSE results impressive – 97 per cent A*/A in 2013.

Long-serving, sensible, deputy head is i/c SEN. No current statements and a very few with special needs. Of those, most are mild dyspraxics and some use laptops and have extra time in exams. No withdrawal from classes or in-class support. SEN

N

here mostly means even more gifted and talented than the rest, and the latest inspection report paid tribute to the individual help given to these, as well as to dyspraxics and the use of IEPs where appropriate. School's philosophy was articulated by past head – 'Everyone matters' – and now, in Mrs McCabe's words, 'I try to do everything I can to put them in charge of their own destiny'.

Games, options, the arts: The endless playing fields and superb facilities – with which no other London girls' school can compete – inspire sporting enthusiasm and prowess. Options abound – even, now, riding, scuba and golf along with the trad games. Lacrosse especially successful (school has players in national squads) but cross country thrives too. Art practised joyfully by many – as the super paintings and other exhibits round and about demonstrate: witty, fluid in style and imaginative. Music is celebrated and many play to top standards. Good music tech. Very good music hall with gallery – light and inviting. Grand pianos seem to breed here. Numerous ensembles, choirs, tours and concerts and much success in major musical competitions, festivals etc – as you'd expect from girls with this amount of creativity, energy, opportunity and encouragement.

The performing arts centre (PAC) is a superb facility. Its auditorium seats 350, with a removable floor over an orchestra pit and, helpfully, it is connected by corridor to the music school. Drama, always good here, has now a tremendous buzz – everyone can take part on or backstage and productions are numerous and exciting. Good drama studio in use for smaller productions, exam work, lessons etc. The PAC has a café/bar which the girls talk about almost more than anything else – a smart meeting place with coffee and snacks, patronised by sixth form and staff – all very cool and chic: 'It's like going out of school with a friend'. The roof terrace, with benches and view over the whole estate, is another great place for coffee and chat and the sixth form love it.

Vast programme of complementary activities. Parents pay tribute to the imaginative and high-calibre opportunities and the girls look almost bewildered by the range on offer – 'You have to prioritise – there's too much to do; you just can't do everything'. Debating especially popular – we enjoyed ads for forthcoming meetings, eg 'This house would die young', 'This house would be a boy', 'This house would ban violence in entertainment' etc – many of them pinned onto noticeboards which line the rather stark staircases, reminiscent of a students' union in which everyone has opinions. Charity work a priority, though we aren't sure when they find time to do it and so much of it.

Background and atmosphere: Venerable and unique – no other school in the history of girls' education in the UK has such significance. It was founded by Frances Mary Buss in 1850 in Camden and set the standard for ambitious, forward-looking education for girls on a par with the best of that offered to boys. In 1939 – remarkable foresight or luck? – the school moved to Edgware. It acquired the former estate of the Dukes of Chandos – of Handelian fame – then comprising a splendid, late 18th century house, now the school's central building (recently refurbished), and 30 acres overlooking formal gardens and down to Canons Park. The original ducal palace – Canons – was demolished in the 1740s after the financial collapse of the first Duke. Perhaps, in his distress, he would have been glad to know what an excellent site for a girls' school his domain would become.

The main building – housing the offices, sixth form centre and some teaching – is elegant outside and impressive inside – wood panelling, grand portraits of former heads, some of them the prime movers in girls' education in their day, archival photographs, stucco and cornicing. Later built additions range from functional and boring – eg the main teaching block – to inspired and enlightened. This last is especially so of the library – a fine building full of light and cleverly constructed on four storeys. It is also as well-stocked and managed as you'd expect here. About to start building a large indoor extra-curricular space and an extension to house extra classrooms and labs.

You reach the school either via a walk from the tube across the park or by a meander down Canon's Drive – all large detached houses, much mock Tudor and with more than a whiff of Wisteria Lane. The road goes only to the school or the park so a sense of entering a wonderfully secluded world. And secluded, safe and stimulating it is, though what is provided here hardly excludes the outside world – true partnerships with schools elsewhere (notably in Zambia and in Dagenham): reciprocal visits, educational collaboration, mutually informative and enlightening both ways. And Mrs McCabe's Prince's Teaching Institute also informs the school's ethos and daily life. Outsiders, though, must goggle at the lime tree avenue, the grand aged cedar tree, the sizable reedy pond, formal gardens and sheer glorious green space, overlooked by the very pretty main house.

Food served in huge lunch room is clearly terrifically good – girls don't usually worry about ODing on school food but it's clearly a temptation here: masses of choice and high, high quality. The atmosphere overall is collaborative, enthusiastic and relaxed. Lots of male staff – many of them young – and the average age of staff here is only 32. Old Girls will raise several eyebrows at all this! We can't recall visiting another all-girls' school and finding quite this kind of relaxed self-confidence – normal in the best boys' and co-ed schools. 'My fundamental belief,' says head, 'is that anything is possible for the girls – it's about stretching, enrichment, passion.'

Pastoral care and discipline: Classes are uniformly orderly, relaxed and full of concentrating faces. Relations between staff and girls are clearly warm, especially so in the sixth form, and girls pay tribute to the time and individual care their teachers give them. A noticeable cachet to sixth form life here – the girls move into the upper rooms of the charming old main house, they don't wear uniform and they chat on easy terms with staff. They are also given responsibilities for younger girls, often running clubs for them – this fosters a healthy bonding between the years and probably contributes to the tiny number of leavers post-GCSE. Strong tutor system throughout. No major problems within last five years: 'They're very sensible,' says head. Lots of collaboration with boys' schools – Eton, Harrow, Winchester and Whitgift – socially and in extra-curricular activities. Occasional bullying dealt with firmly and parents are 'pleased with the approach'. 'The girls know where they stand,' says Mrs McCabe.

Pupils and parents: Multi-ethnic, multi-faith, multi-brains – we spoke to no two pupils from the same ethnic or geographic origins. In common is a desire to learn and share the fun of doing it here – along with a fair bit of cash, though bursaries help (see below). Notable Old Girls' list is uniquely long and impressive – see Wikipedia – but, for starters: Barbara Amiel, Alice Beer, Eleanor Bron, Tanya Byron, Gillian Cross, Fenella Fielding, Margaret Fingerhut, Helen Gardner, Stella Gibbons, Susie Orbach (expelled), Myfanwy Piper, Anna Popplewell, Stevie Smith, Marie Stopes, Judith Weir, Rachel Weisz and Anna Wintour, along with a great many useful types – doctors, civil servants, scientists, artists and academics.

Entrance: At 11+ by exam in maths and English and interview. Forty-four come up from the junior school and a further 60 places for the 550 who apply. Don't despair – someone has to get them. Junior school children are not in competition for their places – they take the exam like everyone else and, if a chance of them not thriving in the senior school, they will have been warned and helped well in advance. At 16+ by exam in their A level subjects and by interview – around 80 applicants for 25 places.

Exit: Most go through to the sixth form and Mrs McCabe stresses, 'No-one is ever prevented from going into the sixth form. Once the girls are here we never write anyone off'. Later, Oxbridge is the norm (33 in 2013) – along with UCL, Bristol, LSE and the best of the rest, including quite a few at Ivy Leagues, notably Harvard. They do solid subjects – lots of medics – at the top places and, unsurprisingly, do well.

Money matters: Lowish, we feel, for what is offered here and a generous number of valuable bursaries available. Means-tested but offering between 10 and 100 per cent of fees. Scholarships up to 50 per cent and can be held along with a bursary. Music schols too.

Remarks: Possibly the best advertisement for girls-only education in the country.

Northampton High School

Linked school: Northampton High Junior School

Newport Pagnell Road, Hardingstone, Northampton, NN4 6UU

• Pupils: 660 girls; all day • Ages: 11–18 • C of E foundation
• Fees: £9,297–£12,348 pa • Independent

Tel: 01604 765765
Email: nhsadmin@nhs.gdst.net
Website: www.northamptonhigh.gdst.net

Headmistress: Since 2007, Mrs Sarah Dixon BA PGCE (fifties). Educated at Belvedere School, Liverpool (another GDST school), then joined HM Customs and Excise straight after A levels. Left at 24 to go to Warwick University, where achieved first in English, followed by PGCE. First teaching post at Stamford High School, then moved to Bedford School, where she was head of PSHE and year 11. Became head of Peterborough High School in 1999 before taking reins at Northampton High eight years later when school became part of GDST. 'I felt as if I was coming home when I arrived here,' she says. Warm, inspiring and hugely experienced, teaches year 7 girls for one period a week – 'It means I get to know all of them'. Also sees every girl for a one-to-one meeting each year. 'Mrs Dixon takes a real interest and always follows up on stuff,' one sixth former told us. 'My mum thinks she's awesome.' Firm advocate of single-sex education for girls – 'If you've been at an all-girls' school you find it easy to set your own goals and pursue them with confidence'. Has been ISI inspector for 18 years. Husband Mark is chair of science at exam board OCR. Two grown-up daughters.

Academic matters: Head says girls 'mean business' and recent results prove her point. ISI report in 2011 praised 'The quality of the pupils' learning, attitudes and basic skills is excellent,' and noted girls' focus, concentration and progress. These comments are borne out by 2013 A level results – 72 per cent A*/B, 41 per cent A*/A. Sixty-six per cent of GCSEs A*/A. Most take at least nine GCSEs. Dual award science available or three separate sciences. At A level girls can choose from 28 subjects – all the traditional ones, plus classical civilisation, critical thinking (AS), economics, food, nutrition and health, government and politics, PE and psychology. Four girls recently piloted AQA's Extended Project Qualification and more will follow suit in coming years. Curriculum based on national curriculum guidelines. In addition, Latin taught from year 7 and German and Spanish from year 8.

Staff very keen on preparing pupils not just for university, but also for workplace beyond – from skills days for all to work experience placements for sixth formers. A year 12 keen on studying veterinary science, for example, spends part of Friday afternoons working for a local vet, while in recent years several have won paid internships at HSBC.

Believes in being as inclusive as possible – full-time SENCo gives one-to-one support and in groups, as well as to gifted and talented.

Two-thirds of teachers are women, a third men. Clear policy on homework – year 7s, for instance, get nearly seven hours' worth a week. Laptops given to all from year 11 up – cost incorporated in fees and school gets them back when girls leave. Classroom teaching supplemented by specialist speakers, theatre visits, lectures and trips abroad (including annual expedition to Normandy each year for year 8s).

Games, options, the arts: Prides itself on its sporting achievements. As head says: 'We have élite teams but believe in fitness and enjoyment for all.' Girls do netball, hockey, swimming, squash, tennis, badminton, rounders, cross-country, athletics etc. Sports hall, dance studio, Astroturf, netball and tennis courts, plus three hockey pitches and 25m five-lane swimming pool.

The music department is located at the heart of the school and boasts everything from an orchestra, choir and jazz band to a strings group that played at the Royal Albert Hall a few years ago. More than 160 girls have individual music lessons in school. Drama is very popular too, and girls take it at both GCSE and A level. Annual school production (from Charlie and the Chocolate Factory to Hamlet) performed in main hall, which seats 650.

Art really has the wow factor. Department gets outstanding results and many go on to do art, architecture, graphic design and fashion later on. Head of art believes in encouraging pupils to expand their ideas and creativity and her approach pays dividends. When we visited, just ahead of the school's annual arts festival, the walls were a feast for the eyes – from a dress made entirely of bottle-tops by a GCSE student to etchings, screen prints, oils and collages.

Other activities include community service, Young Enterprise and D of E, as well as voluntary lunchtime clubs like printmaking, ceramics, public speaking, book group and eco-team. Resourceful group of year 10 and 11s produces their own online school magazine, complete with 'what's hot, what's not,' fiction, poetry, recipes and even an agony aunt.

Background and atmosphere: Founded in 1878 by committee of local church people. Moved from historic Rennie Mackintosh building in centre of Northampton to purpose-built, two-storey building on the outskirts of town in 1992. Envious visiting heads frequently comment on 'intelligent and very civilised' design. Set in 24 acres so plenty of space to run off steam. Main building is designed in a figure of eight, with two pretty courtyards in the middle. Corridors decked out in school's trademark blue with a few bright pink IKEA sofas dotted around to provide light relief. While some schools appear noisy and hectic, this one is refreshingly calm and orderly. All girls encouraged to use well-equipped library, which boasts 12,500 books. Full-time librarian on hand to help them develop their research skills – no relying on Wikipedia here.

Pastoral care and discipline: Girls say it's a friendly and welcoming place, with approachable teachers who 'really care'. Very good at settling new girls in, with induction days the term before they start and imaginative new Big Sister, Little Sister initiative, where sixth-formers keep an eye on new year 7s. School council, with reps from each year group, and new house system in place. Girls belong to one of four houses – Hestia, Selene, Artemis or Demeter. Lots of house competitions, from drama and singing to sports and film-making. Head girl is voted in by girls and teaching staff, along with leadership team

N

consisting of deputy head girl and two more deputies for social services and charity.

Rules on drugs, alcohol, smoking and bullying all clearly stated, but girls and staff say these aren't issues here. One sixth former told us: 'It's just not what we do.' Another joked: 'No one would even dare.' If concerns about work or behaviour do arise, letters sent home to parents. Saturday detentions imposed if eight work or behaviour reports in one term are sent out, but no one can remember it ever happening.

Stylish new uniform recently introduced for 11 to 16 year olds – blazers, crisp navy and white blouses, navy skirts. Sixth-formers wear own clothes but must look smart – no strappy tops, short skirts, hoodies, jeans or trainers. Oldest girls have their own common-room, café and study room. School lunches are wholesome and served up in three light, airy canteens. Lots of choice – hot meals, salads, vegetarian options, dessert, fruit and yoghurt. Recent school dinner competition asked girls to design their own meal, and as a result obliging catering staff served up couscous, tacos and even square-shaped chips! Some girls bring packed lunches from home. Very working-parent friendly, offering early supervision and breakfast from 8am, supervised prep sessions till 5pm and after-school club till 6pm.

Pupils and parents: Head reckons typical Northampton High girl is 'outgoing, articulate, hard-working and caring', while head girl says approvingly, 'You are allowed to be yourself here'. Pupils from a mix of rural and urban backgrounds. Many live in Northampton and surrounding villages, but some travel in (by school minibus) from as far afield as Brackley, Daventry, Wellingborough, Milton Keynes and Bedford. Parents, a mix of professional types, county set and self-employed, very supportive of school. 'It has a real buzz about it,' one mother told us, while another said: 'The school seems to embrace everything and everybody. When we go to a concert or play the pupils do everything, whether they're conducting the orchestra or doing the lights. I really feel the girls are being prepared for the outside world.' Eclectic list of old girls includes former MI5 boss Baroness Eliza Manningham-Buller, novelist Anne Fine and Olympic swimmer Caitlin McClatchey.

Entrance: Main entry points are at 11, 13 and 16. Girls sit school's own entrance exam (English, maths and verbal reasoning) in January prior to entry. Half arrive from own junior school, while rest come from wide range of local primaries. A dozen or so enter the school at 13, mostly from preps like Spratton Hall, Winchester House and Beachborough. Up to 10 new girls join sixth form each year. All need minimum of five GCSEs at A*-C, including English and maths, but school likes to see at least Bs in proposed A level subjects.

Exit: About a third leave after GCSEs, mainly heading to co-ed schools like Northampton School for Boys. Virtually all sixth form leavers to higher education. One to Oxbridge in 2013. Average of five per cent opt for deferred university entry and take gap years between school and university. Good spread of degree subjects, but physics, biomedical sciences, medicine and classics lead the pack. Popular university destinations currently include UCL, Nottingham, Birmingham and other Russell Group luminaries.

Money matters: Several scholarships on offer at 11, 13 and sixth-form level – academic, arts and sports. A number of means-tested bursaries available too.

Remarks: A happy and high-achieving school that nurtures and educates girls throughout those all-important teenage years. School prospectus says, 'Kindness, courtesy, service and fun go hand in hand with striving for academic success,' and pupils certainly bear this out. With its increasingly sparkling achievements, a school on the up.

Northease Manor School

Rodmell, Lewes, East Sussex, BN7 3EY

- Pupils: 110 boys and girls (65 day, 45 boarding) • Ages: 10–17 • Inter-denom • Fees: Day £20,151; Boarding £27,423 pa • Independent

Tel: 01273 472915
Email: pa2headteacher@northease.co.uk
Website: www.northease.co.uk

Headteacher: Since 2007, Mrs Carmen Harvey-Browne, BA Hons PGCE NPQH. Early fifties. Previously deputy head at More House, Farnham (qv) which (as here) has pepped up academic aspirations.

Trim-looking, unflamboyant and reassuring, she's an example of that increasingly rare breed, the reluctant head. Took heavyweight prompting from well-wishers before she applied for post, fearing it was a step too far, both literally – it's a longish commute to Surrey – and emotionally, given seven day a week commitment, though sometimes 'let off home for good behaviour' midweek. Saw school on drive-by with knowledgeable husband, a surveyor for an education firm – she also has three grown up children – and 'the emotional link was there from the start.'

English (her degree subject at Reading, followed by teaching qualification at Avery Hill) is her thing, communications too, coupled with a burning desire to foster similar skills in everyone from young corporate guns to educational underdogs. Initially vacillated between commerce and education, starting as a PA at London Business School, then to Guildford College, guiding lecturers (bunches of florists; clutches of driving instructors) through their PGCEs as well as teaching functional English.

Dipped into commerce again as a management trainer before permanent move as an English specialist at Guildford/Godalming schools, secondary and primary, drawn inexorably to pupils with learning difficulties, reading problems in particular. Brief and 'upsetting' post at an EBD school was followed by more conducive surroundings of More House where, initially as head of lower school, she shone at helping pupils nail GCSEs in English 'even though they weren't meant to' and did her head-in-waiting training.

Sensitively (and sensibly) she trod warily on arrival here. 'You go into a school with its own culture and history and you [can] feel you're walking in on someone's territory'. Though a passionate advocate, with even her open day speeches a must hear, say parents (unusually), has only recently felt that 'it's my school.'

Pupils, who have specific learning difficulties (dyslexia, dyscalculia and dyspraxia, also ADD and social/communication difficulties) find her approachable and straightforward. Non-readers who can 'articulate their thoughts and feelings can succeed,' she says. Bar may be set high but it's about reaching for the stars rather than taking leaps in the dark.

Academic matters: Pupils line up to tell you that school 'is the best in the world' and praise kind teachers and small classes (eight maximum, often far fewer). Palpable relief at contrast with previous miseries. 'At my old school, I didn't know how to tell the time. How can I tell the time when nobody will help me?' says one boy.

Here, assistance is in seemingly limitless supply; academic achievement against the odds the goal. While there are bright pupils here – and must be of average ability or above – complexity of needs makes acquisition of decent GCSE grades a real achievement, and the (occasional) A*/A very special indeed.

Trend-crunching, given small size of cohort, is predictably tricky, with considerable year to year variation in results which span gamut from A star to G. Everyone takes core subjects of science (GCSE only), maths and English (also taken as less demanding Entry Level Certificates). Most secure at least one decent GCSE pass – 100 per cent A*/C grades in art in 2013, three quarters A*/Cs in drama and two-thirds A*/Cs in additional science.

Head's influence isn't hard to discern. 'When I first came here, the seniors absolutely refused to pick up a book,' she says. No longer is it a reading (or writing) averse culture, confirm parents, with one pupil accelerating from two lines on arrival to five pages now. Initiatives come thick and fast, including done-in-a-day newspaper and text-to-test reading scheme, with fun quizzes working out if material has sunk in (with depth readings), and Dr Frankenstein-themed shoebox displays (complete with lovingly added trailing wires) bringing Mary Shelley's text to sizzling life for year eight pupils.

Success had seemed to be at the expense of maths, results tumbling from 66 per cent at C and above in 2007 to one third in 2010/2011. Reversed in 20121, now closing in on fifty per cent and even desperate cases waving, not drowning. 'If they can't do multiplication, it doesn't mean that they can't do shapes or geometry. It's about giving them coping strategies,' says maths teacher.

Plenty of justifiable pride elsewhere, too, with 100 per cent passes in option subjects including geography and history GCSEs and flourishing BTEC courses including home economics (on-site) and horticulture (with Plumpton College). Most attract tiny numbers, art excepted (and exceptional) and taken by half year group – 14 entrants in 2012, 92 per cent achieving A*-C grades (100 per cent in 2010/2011). Seemingly loved by all – 'It makes me feel happy,' explained year seven pupil.

Other GCSE subjects wax and wane, with school playing to pupils' strengths with such virtuosity that may have learned from nearby Glyndebourne (within a soubrette's warble when there's a prevailing wind). RE has made its entrance – a big exam hit in 2009 'because we had a cohort who were interested,' says the head – and bowed itself out again. Music and media studies, both recent introductions, could be added to (or conceivably replaced) if pupils show a yen for something completely different. Only no go area is a language (modern or otherwise). Though predictable given pupil makeup it's of slight regret, you feel, to the head, putting new EBacc forever out of reach.

Getting there is down to sensible ways of working (maximum of two homework subjects a night), good structure (teaching and learning and behaviour and safety teams have each acquired a new assistant head) coupled with patience and imagination.'They really understand you if you have problems,' says a year ten pupil. 'They go at your pace with all the subjects.' 'I like how they make the lessons exciting. They do experiments, lots of practical things,' confirmed year eleven boy. 'We filled a balloon with hydrogen and oxygen and lit it – you felt a shock wave in your chest.'

Effective esteem and motivation boosting as well as gap plugging is helped by close liaison between much praised therapy and academic teams. Though one teacher mourned decline of daily note-swapping staff meeting 'our water cooler moment', well-thumbed pupil log book, updated by all, does a good job of keeping everyone in the loop.

Staff morale extremely good, with sizeable proportion recruited from mainstream environment and all displaying bucket loads of the 'intuitive understanding of our children,' highlighted by head as recruitment must-have. (So many first timers in need of specialist training that 'if you can't beat them' approach has seen school become Spld qualification training centre). 'I've never had so much fun,' says science teacher, herself dyslexic. Her lab, in well tended and appealing block that also houses DT, is crammed with shark-themed ephemera (her passion). 'I have to visualise things myself so it informs my teaching style.'

Fun, while a big feature of the school (DT room's anti-stress device, a circle labelled 'bang head here' a case in point) doesn't swamp determination to help children succeed. 'The culture of the school is about fighting every child's corner for them,' says head. Daunting for some – pupils may grumble that a teacher has 'got it in for them and nags them to death,' says head until persuaded that 'it's the member of staff who believes in you so much that they won't let you not achieve'. 'I was a little bit scared of one teacher but she was firm and fair and fantastic with my son,' confirms mother.

It works. One unwell child begged to go to school so didn't miss GCSE mocks. 'Most kids would say, "I'll shirk school today," but he obviously enjoys it,' says father.

Games, options, the arts: 'All sorts' on offer, feel parents, with decent after hours range from Eco Warriers to pottery (slightly more of a fuss made of boarders – flexi and weekly – who have first dibs on activities. And why not?).

Hands-on experience a speciality, including fire lighting by youngest pupils as part of forest skills course (to the slight disappointment of the oldest), vast saws in DT handled with insouciance by year sevens up (apart from the year ten girl we encountered who had sensibly delegated her share to enthusiast).

There's a sense of letting go, of a deliberate blurring at the edges. Though sports leader course, as well as recently introduced D of E, gives older pupils a taste for helping others (work experience is also proving a huge hit – with employers as well as pupils), they aren't dragooned but almost, in quite adult way, encouraged to see gaps and fill them, reaching out for life skills rather than having carefully prepared menu finely cut up for them.

One year seven boy, for example, had recently set personal goal of raising £1,000 for charity – and achieved it, too – while Year 11 pupils have recently taken on DJ-ing at school disco, teaching themselves how to operate the sound system in the process. 'We had to Google how to do it.' says one (better equipment is top of their wants list).

In the background there's an unstinting use of time, resources and support to turn everyone into little train that could with lots of input from OT team, which works miracles with beanbags for pupils who arrive with so little spatial awareness that 'if you get them to shut their eyes and spin round, they think it's the door that has moved.' says teacher.

Sports facilities include swimming pool and super gym, we're told – it was, as they say, 'just glimpsed' – with strugglers and stragglers encouraged to try their hand (and feet) at sporting pick and mix selection that boasts tennis, badminton and the like, as well as American football in addition to an elegant sufficiency of the ordinary sort.

High levels of creativity are particularly well catered for in this seriously arty school – stunning examples on website well worth a look, with turned wood creations (DT) oozing tactile charms. Some former pupils go on to further study and even those lacking bubbling well of natural creative juices have an oeuvre to warm the cockles of their parents' hearts.

Extends to music, in similar schools sometimes of the teacher's quirk variety, lasting only as long as they do. Here, however, definitely on the up(beat) with decent dedicated area including all comers practice room presided over by amiable custodian, with drums, guitar and piano lessons on offer, plans for a parents' choir and excellent links with Glyndebourne too.

Drama, in contrast, is a long-term big favourite, strength unimpaired by departure of highly rated teacher (seems anecdotally to be a fairly regular staff turnover, though head has a good eye for picking replacements and 'new teacher is just as good as old one,' says budding thespian). Lots on the go, from large scale productions held in knockout beamed hall (available for wedding hire, too), to recent live local youth radio broadcast, with pupils overcoming nerves – 'I just cowered right in' and acquitting themselves with credit – all proud of representing only non-mainstream establishment to take part.

Background and atmosphere: Succession of solemn-faced pupils sporting assorted ornate headgear adorns the website, it seems that dressing up (for events) is something of school speciality (this reviewer was one of the very few not sporting at least one Santa accessory on pre-Christmas visit). Everyday wear, in contrast, is of the relaxed variety (sweatshirt/trousers favoured by all) and well worn, too, judging by the odd trailing shirt tail. While the easy informality may not appeal to all, it certainly isn't attracting complaints from parents, instead setting the scene for a place that emphatically doesn't judge by appearances. Aesthetically minded in any case able to cop an eyeful thanks to location – period house and buildings in picturesque courtyard setting, including a few traces of what was possibly a medieval chapel. ('Some old men remember pieces of carved wainscot,' says 1940s account).

Décor generally doesn't let the side down either. Boarding accommodation rates an 'OK' from one pupil. Two dorms for boys, older in upper floor of science/DT block, not viewed by this reviewer (we weren't alone: 'I've never seen it,' said one member of staff, when quizzed) but apparently Mrs Rochester-free. Junior boys' due for rejigging. Though adequate (star feature is much-coveted corner bath), outflanked by girls' accommodation, attractive two-bed rooms, made more so, in one case, by swags of home made paper bunting. Gives 'a homely feeling and an atmosphere of love,' writes pupil in newsletter (we agree). There's also a delightful common room with microwave, toaster and instant boiling water tap instead of kettle.

For the most part, thoroughly pleasant environment. A tad confusing for first timers with some subjects housed together, others not, though mix as well as match approach to layout has benefits, points out a teacher, as 'makes us talk to each other' while potential pupil confusion is averted because 'they'll always have the same room and the same teacher.' Some teachers as keen on personalising space as pupils, one maths room a riot of handwritten numbers to take the fear factor out.

Few quibbles apart from looming classroom presence of computers – might be better 'hidden from view' to break their hypnotically distracting spell, felt one insider. Otherwise, good looks marred only by almost obligatory temporary-turned-semi-permanent classroom sprawl behind the main building, about to be done away with now funding boat has come in. Once joined by planning permission, replacement by new middle school block should make school a lovesome thing all round.

That aside, radiates strong sense of 'community' (so regularly mentioned by parents and staff that at a pound a go you'd quickly cover a year's fees) and kicking in, we're told, on arrival, where to take a seat is to invite cheery greetings.

Pastoral care and discipline: Aim is light support rather than marshmallow pillow, though this is a natural stamping (or clucking) ground for mother hen types whose unobtrusive lunchtime presence (required for fair few who require encouragement here, as in other areas) can translate to rapid response where necessary. This reviewer was gently guided away from table when one child was distracted by conversation. 'Can't eat and talk at the same time,' we were told.

Parents all spoke (some with almost tearful relief) of the easy acquisition of friendships, that precious social lifeline often lacking in previous schools. 'For the first time in his life he has genuine friends he cares about and who care about him,' says one.

Mentors are appointed (or you can pick your own) with year ten guide quickly able to cite two members of staff she'd be comfortable (and obviously relaxed about) talking to, though aim of reintroducing pupils into the tougher outside world means a fine balance has to be struck.

A first step in acquisition of fledging independent living skills, boarding is felt to be well handled, from reassurance

of visual timetables to readiness of houseparents to dispense mobile numbers to parents and witching hours tea and sympathy to pupils when first (or second) night wobbles strike. 'We had a blip with boarding. My child woke up the housemaster at two in the morning and he spent time chatting. Now he goes back on a Sunday rather than a Monday which he's quite happy to do,' says a father. One pupil described it as 'a big sleepover'. Watching another delightedly announcing that 'I'm boarding tomorrow,' proved the point.

Though nurturing, school's expectations are clearly set out, with A to E grades handed out at the end of lessons, points for C and above and prizes every half term for top achievers, and tricky situations managed, from what we saw, with good humour and absence of confrontation. At end of day registration, one boy, lying prone across the desk, was calmly asked to sit down on a chair.

While there had been some recent (anonymous) reports of bullying, all the parents we spoke to stressed that this was a fester-free zone. When problems occur – as they will, in every school – swift action follows, in line with anti-bullying policy (a jargon-free model of its kind). The most serious incident (a pupil having head pushed under water) resulted in threat of no swimming for those responsible, and stopped. For minor misdemeanours (smuggling of Christmas tree into dorm) pupils may be asked to do a spot of community/school work.

Occasionally, badinage tips over into disruption lite – head had recently sat in on some science lessons to quell excess noise – 'nipped in the bud,' we were told by parent. Our only reservation was that there were a few odd corners of time twixt end of lessons/beginning of activities when potential slippage round the edges seemed possible: three out of seven no-shows for tutor group end of day sign-out (one represented only by handbag), a child whizzing round on mini scooter in the dark by concrete slipway.

Parents, however, felt occasional niggles were inevitable and praised generally excellent staff/pupil relationships, with well-handled home/school communications ensuring that 'I feel I'm in the loop' says one.

Pupils and parents: The inevitable weighting towards boys isn't a problem for the minority who aren't. Girls, says head, are brilliant at detecting anxieties in others and will 'scoop them up and look after them.'

Other sterling qualities span the gender gap, with delightful pupils, many funny, charming and polite – 'thank you for interviewing me,' says year six boy – and as confident as you'd hope for. 'You're speaking to a good reader, a good writer and a good chef; three combined into one,' says one, with huge pride.

Many parents are very hands-on, active friends' association ensuring they 'are involved as much as they want to be.' Lots of activities – some, like decorating the school hall and making Christmas hampers, inevitably easier for those who live locally.

Friendships between families can develop – one mother was particularly keen to emphasise the joys of apology and tension-free socialising compared with previous mainstream school where even in these more enlightened times there's 'still a feeling of "that family's got a bit of leprosy, we won't get too close to them because we don't quite understand it."'

Entrance: Families often look at two or three schools – Frewen (qv) often makes the shortlist, a minority paying for places themselves, around 80 per cent funded by 17 LEAs, some local (including East Sussex, West Sussex and Brighton and Hove), others a fair distance away, with predictable par for the course rhyme nor reason battles over funding (school provides helpful list of tribunal experts).

Word 'sheltered' crops up frequently – this is school as a place of healing and it doesn't always suit those from mainstream backgrounds who either 'find it amazing or feel

"I'm way beyond this ethos and family community" in which case it's not going to work,' says head.

Most round pegs will be screened out at paperwork stage. Where it's not clear cut (learning difficulties may tell one story; IQ results another and 'a lot of our children have spiky profiles') parents of borderline cases may be invited in for an interview.

Numbers wax, most years starting in the 90s and finishing 20 or so up, including occasional castaway from similar school in need of a fresh start (sympathetic reception a speciality).

Exit: Parents are, in the main, a realistic bunch and need to be – 'Some expect the school to be a magic bullet, that their child is going to be a vet and it's not going to happen,' says one mother. Nevertheless anecdote (no figures) suggests growing numbers make it into higher education.

Improved links with local sixth form colleges both big and small (Sussex Downs, Varndean, Ringmer, Plumpton) help, though results, say parents, can be variable. Teachers, however, are fabulous pupil advocates, one blagging talented artist on to advanced course, overturning initial rejection.

No plans for extreme growth or an add-on sixth form, though transition class offering more vulnerable pupils support in first year at college is planned. For parents, departure can feel like exile from Neverland but pupils 'grow out of us' as they must, thinks head.

Money matters: Unusually, offers bursaries for years nine to 11 to join Tall Ships crew (courtesy of previous headmaster). Otherwise, it's the standard means tested bursaries for landlubbers.

Remarks: Sheltered environment that gives children back confidence and lets them experience joys of academic and social success. One parent (speaking for all the others we talked to) said, 'My son had been in a mainstream school with one-to-one support. After his trial day at Northease he said, "Mum, that's the happiest day of my school life," and we felt we had found our school.'

Northwood College

Linked school: Northwood College Junior School

Maxwell Road, Northwood, HA6 2YE

- Pupils: 400 girls; all day • Ages: 3–18 • Non-denom
- Fees: Seniors £14,250 pa • Independent

Tel: 01923 825446
Email: admissions@northwoodcollege.co.uk
Website: www.northwoodcollege.co.uk

Head Mistress: Since January 2009, Miss Jacqualyn Pain MA MA MBA PGCE NPQH (fiftyish), a theology and philosophy graduate and a most experienced head. Two previous headships, both impressive – Henrietta Barnet 2000-2005, St Albans High 2005-2008 – prior to which she'd been deputy head at Northwood. She'd had no intention of leaving St Albans until Mrs Ruth Mercer, her predecessor at Northwood College, was appointed to the headship of Godolphin and Latymer (qv). Miss Pain, who believed 'so strongly in the ethos of the school – that it does so well by every kind of girl' – couldn't resist coming back and is a round peg in a spherical hole, if ever we saw one. 'The school has changed, of course,' she admits cheerfully, 'because schools must move on, but the underlying principles are the same and I passionately believe in them.' Highly competent, understated, relaxed, elegant and popular, she is quietly but enthusiastically building on the energetic modernisation initiated by Mrs

Mercer. She likes cats and chocolate. Northwood College, too long the unsung school in this well provided for part of the world, is lucky to have her back.

Academic matters: Takes a spread of ability – but well above the national average. Value-added very strong here so you should achieve your potential, whatever it is, and not feel pressured while you do it. Your 10 A*s pupil happily coexists with your artsy, mathematical struggler and both feel good about themselves. This is very much the Northwood ethos and the one Miss Pain was keen to come back to and strengthen.

At GCSE, all take two Englishes, maths, a language, three sciences; options include art, classical civilisation, drama, Latin and Greek, home economics, RE and textiles. RE is the star subject – taken by most with exemplary results; maths (IGCSE) and English pretty good too. 2013 results saw 75 per cent of subjects taken achieve A*/A. At A level, maths, economics and RE impress. Maths, the sciences and psychology are popular. Tiny numbers for history and English (though good results), reflecting the science orientation and aspirations of the school's current core constituency. The same is true for languages, but scope for new-ish HoD (a French and Mandarin specialist) to boost numbers and broaden curriculum. Much to be done here, especially in increasing the uptake at A level of a broader range of subjects – parents as well as girls will need to be convinced – and the school, in fact, offers an admirable range. In 2013, 79 per cent A*/B grades and 49 per cent A*/A.

Most mild SENs managed in lessons with occasional extra temporary support and withdrawals. Can cope with mild ADHD and Asperger's along with dyses. Older parts of site not really set up to accommodate serious motor difficulties, though will adapt where possible.

School is pioneering 'thinking skills' and they approach this seriously from nursery to sixth form via 'cognitive development programme', plus f/t director to coordinate it. We were seriously impressed – junior school pupils feel empowered and the results are tangible. School held a recent Dragons' Den event – with high profile 'dragons' – and even juniors' projects were taken seriously – to the extent of possible commissions from the commercial world outside. Clever stuff, integral to the overall ethos of the place and a real selling point.

Games, options, the arts: It's got the lot – in miniature, in some cases. Yer actual sports hall, of course, plus 25m pool –and everyone swims all year. Pitches and courts abut the main campus and most girls are keen. Some parental feeling that more effort is needed and girls should be pushed harder. Performing arts centre cleverly shoehorned in, and now providing good drama studio, range of music teaching/ practice rooms and much-used recital room. No room here for grand theatre or concert hall, but assembly hall does as well and, though hardly glitzy, has all a good school needs. Art is enthusiastic – painting, modelling, textiles, principally. Music likewise, enthusiastic – 50-strong orchestra, jazz bands and lots of fun had in staging productions – more Oliver! than Othello. Forty-nine page booklet details all the extra-curricular activities from the physical (trampolining, badminton etc) to the cerebral (think club, puzzle club, chess) to the fun (book club, bridge, life drawing etc etc) – good stuff. 'Fabulous' trips – 'We went to Brazil for a month on World Challenge' – and closer to home, eg Regent's Park theatre, and good in-school events, eg African drumming evening.

Background and atmosphere: Founded in 1878 in Endsleigh Gardens, Bloomsbury, with around 25 boarders and a few day girls. Headmistress, Miss Buchan-Smith, who had modern ideas about the importance of the extra-curricular as well as the curricular, and was concerned about the unsavoury influence of the Euston area on her girls, moved the school to Northwood in 1893. Interestingly, this area – now leafy, prosperous and safe as £1m+ houses can be – was, in 1871, described as 'a destitute district near Moor Park'. But the coming of the tube, a few years later, changed all that and made Northwood a jolly useful commutable suburb, which it remains. In 1893, the present, late arts 'n' crafts red-brick with leaded lights building was opened for 20 boarders and two day girls; the next door Briary accommodated little boys. Boys long since gone, but touching tribute paid to their presence – especially to those who went on to fight and fall in the two wars: school still lays an annual wreath at Ypres.

More land has been acquired, more buildings built and the school is now a nest of attractive, disparate edifices, centred on a couple of tennis courts, which make a kind of quad. To the side of the school are the pitches and playing fields – the overall feeling is one of a slightly crowded campus made up of pleasant, purpose-built or acquired blocks forming a cosy community. Despite the somewhat cramped feeling, it is a surprise, in a quiet residential street, to find it there at all. The latest additions – the early years centre and the performing arts block – are notable assets, in terms both of their additional provision and imaginative design – which cannot, here as elsewhere, be said for the few, lesser, 1960s architectural indiscretions.

Cosy, civilised library in old, converted, vaulted gym. Excellent string of sixth form studies – each shared by five/six girls – for private work in free periods (boarding ended in 1990). Exemplary displays everywhere. Good dining room, cafeteria system, food exceptional – home-made soups and yoghurts, lots of fresh everything; everyone above nursery eats school lunch, which is included in the fee. A formal partnership with the nearby John Lyon Boys' School (qv) enables collaboration on curricular and extra-curricular matters, to the considerable benefit of both communities – a sensible and enlightened move begun by Mrs Mercer and Kevin Riley, former head of John Lyon, and continued by its new head, Katherine Haynes.

Junior school in three buildings on site. The early years centre, home to 80 nursery and reception children, is a super building, sensitively conceived and completed. Sensory garden, excellent playground, and lots of lovely touches and thoughtful additions – wellies for rainy days, masses of well-integrated IT, colourful toys, space, cookery, a beautiful library. We loved the collage on the life cycle of a hen and the display about the Philosophy Bear who 'likes to look at things carefully and ask questions'. Years 1 and 2 in Vincent House, 3 and 4 in junior school – both attractive, small scale houses. All safe, well-maintained, full of impeccable and attractive displays. Parents are thrilled – 'My daughter was so shy – they've really brought her out...They're so caring and nurturing'; 'They take the child and encourage her to be the best she can, but according to their own character – they don't have to fit a mould'.

Part of the Girls' Day School Trust (GDST) from November 2013 and combining with Heathfield School for Girls from September 2014. A most unusual move – it is rare for schools to join the GDST family, although Heathfield was acquired by the Trust in 1987. The school will continue with the same head on the same site and all Heathfield girls have been promised places. This will require ingenuity and creativity as the Northwood College site is not generously endowed with space. But we are promised exciting and imaginative developments and will watch with interest.

Pastoral care and discipline: Year heads and form tutors handle most pastoral matters. Tutor changes annually. Discipline seldom a problem here – one minor recent drugs incident. Girls feel involved in decisions – 'Miss Pain really wants to hear from us – our ideas about what can be improved,' we heard. 'The girls do as well as they do here because of the way we nurture them,' says Miss Pain, and parents concur. Overall sense of a relaxed, orderly community in which little disturbs and everything encourages.

Pupils and parents: As you'd expect in this cosmopolitan, well-heeled suburb: majority are British Asians – mostly Hindus – and Christians and sprinklings of everyone else. Little need for EAL. Contingent from local NATO base makes for movement in and out and enriches the mix. Five extensive coach routes bring in girls from Ealing, Edgware, Kenton, Gerrards Cross and Radlett. Proximity to the Metropolitan line makes tubing it easy. Sense of community, and devoted parents from all backgrounds pitching in to support. Former notable pupils include Dame Margaret Booth – a judge – and actress Sue Holderness.

Entrance: At 3+ into the nursery via observation and little tasks, ditto at 4+ into reception. Forty-eight places at this stage. At seven, via maths, English, reasoning and interview – up to 10 new places at this stage. At 11, via the exams set by the North London Consortium, to which the school belongs, plus online test and group interview – 30 places. One out of three girls who apply usually gains a place, many off the waiting list.

At 16, conditional on GCSE results, plus online test and interview – 20 places. Occasional places do occur in other years – particularly on account of NATO personnel coming and going – so always worth a call. 'We're looking for girls who will fit into the school,' says Miss Pain. 'We're academically selective but not narrowly exclusive – we want people who will benefit from an all-round, holistic education.'

Exit: Nearly all stay on to sixth form. Majority go to a range of Russell Group and newer universities; a few to Oxbridge. School produces an extraordinary number of pharmacists and a good number of dentists; otherwise anything from art to retail, English to – well, pharmacy.

Money matters: A few means-tested bursaries – up to full fees. Also scholarships for academics, art, music and sport.

Remarks: The parents have it: 'My daughter has been given opportunities and she's flourishing'; 'Northwood has given my daughters so many opportunities'; 'It was the best decision we ever made'.

N

Norwich High School for Girls

Linked school: Norwich High School – Junior School

Eaton Grove, 95 Newmarket Road, Norwich, NR2 2HU

• Pupils: 520 girls; all day • Ages: 11–18 • Non-denom
• Fees: £11,691 pa • Independent

Tel: 01603 453265
Email: admissions@nor.gdst.net
Website: www.norwichhigh.gdst.net

Headmaster: Since 2010, Mr Jason Morrow MA, an Oxford historian and modern linguist, originally from Belfast (fortyish). Previously, deputy head at North London Collegiate School and at Sevenoaks School, prior to which he was head of sixth at NLCS, having begun his career teaching in a London sixth form college. Mr Morrow teaches the A level historians and some languages lower down the school – we approve. He started making changes at once – can be risky but we met no-one with qualms. Imaginative early 'shadowing' of pupils by senior teachers to see school life from the girls' point of view resulted in much sensible and practical innovation.

Mr Morrow is a man of varied enthusiasms and a great sense of fun. He is good to talk with – a real, but gentle and humorous, communicator – serious about his charges and the excellence he wants for them but also warmly appreciative of all that goes on in his newly invigorated school. A modern and modernising head with a palpably human heart. 'The most important thing,' he told us, 'is to keep the sense of warmth, fun and enjoyment that characterises the school while making sure we are sufficiently ambitious for the girls and have a fizzing intellectual life in the school.' He has brought unshowy energy, a sensitive approach and a big smile to Norfolk.

Academic matters: 'They encourage a work ethic,' a parent told us. Small classes – few are taught in groups of more than 20, 12 in the sixth form. Results impress across the board and Mr Morrow's initiatives support enriched learning – not just hoop jumping. New head of co-curricular developing lots of different courses as 'a break from the purely academic'. At A level, Eng Lit, maths, chemistry and biology top the faves – maths being notably successful. Fewer language takers hitherto – though results are good – but this now on the rise. Art, history and geography also shine. At GCSE, history and geography the most popular options but results in art, classical civilisation, languages and music are startlingly good. Englishes and maths show more of a spread but all get A*-C with a high proportion at the upper end. In 2013, 68 per cent A*/A grades overall at GCSE and 57 per cent at A level.

Emphasis – especially in sixth form – on independent learning – hence many areas for quiet study. Lots of short term individual support for those struggling with individual subjects. 'If you're stuck you can go to a teacher – you're never made to feel embarrassed. They encourage you to come.' And sixth form helpers for younger girls struggling with a subject – good both ways, we feel. Everyone screened in year 9; much praise for special needs teacher. At the time of our visit, 21 pupils in the senior school and 38 in the juniors were receiving some form of extra support in their learning – timetabled additional help – mostly one-to-one, support within the classroom and a variety of other specialist interventions by internal or external staff – depending on need.

Good library with 'our lovely librarian'... 'the best of the changes'. 'Drop Everything And Read' scheme = 15 minutes of 'out' time, a new idea. Gorgeous fiction library and good programme of visiting authors.

Games, options, the arts: Excellent sports provision and we were inspired – coming as we did in summertime – by the six grass courts spread around the gardens – what a treat! Universal approval of the new games afternoon which makes for more time on pitches and courts and better squad development. Improved performance as a result and general praise for new head of sport and the introduction of teams for those not destined for sporting stardom. Sports hall and 25m pool.

The arts thrive and design, in particular, is celebrated here. Lively art and textiles – an innovation much appreciated – girls enthuse about their teachers and we loved the wittily designed, cleverly made bags and shorts. 'The fashion show is one of the really good changes Mr Morrow has made,' the girls told us – note the 'one of'. Good drama, now with fab new drama studio and well-equipped tech gallery overlooking the hall. Dance a Morrow innovation, again much enjoyed. Much success in arts and sports – everything done with huge energy and drive.

Despite neglected accommodation – major refurbishment underway at time of our visit – music is a glory with acclaimed head of dept: 'Fantastic, amazing music teacher who really pushes our talents'... 'she gets everyone involved'... 'she's taught me that it doesn't matter if you're not specially talented – she got me playing the glockenspiel and ocarina and now I'm taking grade 3 piano!' And much more of the same. Around a third learn an instrument in school and more outside. In 2012 the Chamber Choir won Barnardos' Choir of the Year at the Royal Festival Hall (resulting in concerts at the Royal Albert Hall, St John's Smith Square, Barbican etc and other 'professional' engagements). Annual music tours – an astounding 79 girls

went to Tuscany in 2012. Previously sung in St Marks, Venice; Salzburg Cathedral; St Thomas', Leipzig; St Nicolas, Prague. Regular concerts and service in the Norwich Anglican Cathedral and occasional appearances at the RC one too. Not just classical – popular and musicals done with pzazz.

Background and atmosphere: The first senior school opened outside London by The (then) Girls' Public Day School Company, now the Girls' Day School Trust (GDST). So, a notable and venerable institution with nearly 140 years of excellence to celebrate. Housed, principally, in a delicious 1820 residence on the generously proportioned, tree-lined Newmarket Road – one of the main roads connecting the city with the country. The school has been sensitively extended over the decades and there is much, internally, to delight the eye – splendid cornices, ceilings, plaster friezes, galleried atrium and sumptuous stained glass. Preserves former conservatory as part of the staff-room and The Gadesden Room – elegant with splendid cornice and ceiling rose plus super long table for small scale events. No harm done to young minds to be educated surrounded by such architectural felicities. Attractive garden with lofty trees and grateful bird life contribute to sense of overall harmony here. 'Forest school' for the younger pupils – laid out on logs under trees used as classroom area and also chat space – very relaxing.

Modernisation has brought high tech facilities in the hall, drama studio, lang labs etc and in 'the portal' – efficient school/home intranet used by all to access assignments and staff email. Much of school now trim and polished though here and there a dab of Polyfilla and a splosh or two of emulsion needed.

Very stable staff – almost half have been at the school for 10 or more years and the numerous new appointments since Mr Morrow's arrival seen as adding strength and breadth to the provision. Parents nod wisely – 'he's rising to the challenge and has clearly got The Trust behind him. It's much more open and welcoming now.' Most staff seen as very efficient, though we picked up that a few could be better at home/school communication.

Pastoral care and discipline: Year 7s into The Churchman Centre – a gentle transition from wherever they've come from into senior school with adored head of year – 'any time you want to talk to her, she's always there'. Sixth form centre in old Lanchester House plus excellent new extension with study areas, small teaching rooms, huge careers room – 'we get lots of help with uni choice' – lecture theatre and super-cool café. Good food – special praise for 'Nick the Chef' who will do special diets if needed without fuss. Girls in six 'companies' – houses to you and me – and, again, Morrow innovation has strengthened these, to general approval. Likewise with longer break times – 'so we're not late for classes any more,' and more comfortable uniform. New emphasis on communication and sharing responsibility. 'He wants to hear our ideas. We have a "Moot" meeting when you can suggest things and lots of good changes are coming out of that.' No prefects – all sixth form girls have responsibilities – taken seriously by most. Parents are warm in their approbation – 'The teachers are good at seeing the girls' point of view.' Mr Morrow evinces a rare sensitivity that trickles down – 'we need to get the vocabulary right, not "you've done well – for you", but "you can do better than that"'. Minimal discipline problems sorted out by pastoral staff – if it gets that far.

Pupils and parents: Among the most articulate, courteous, thoughtful and quietly assured girls we have met anywhere. Families from Norfolk and North Suffolk – not much competition in the area if you want a top quality academic girls' school. Buses run from Dereham, and North Norfolk and more are planned. Mostly, local professional, business, academic, medical and farming families with a tiny number for whom English is their second language. Celebrated Old Girls include athletes Anna Bentley (fencing), Emma Pooley (cycling); authors Rafaella Barker, Pat Barr, Jane Hissey, Stella Tillyard and Anne Weale; sopranos Jane Manning and Elizabeth Watts; composer Diana Burrell, up-and-coming theatre director Genevieve Raghu, dress designer Ann Tyrell, scientist Jennifer Moyle and a nurse called Edith Cavell.

Entrance: Over 20 local schools regularly send pupils to NHS. Not, currently, wildly oversubscribed at any level other than at 16+. But when reputation catches up with reality here, what with the newly energised staff and the effect on both results and general satisfaction, that is unlikely to remain the case. Get in while you can. At sixth form, the word is already out. Far fewer now leave after GCSE and, of course, lots want to come – from local state schools and even the odd local independent. Not hard to see why.

Exit: Few now leave after GCSE – for the local boys' school, recently turned co-ed – or anywhere else. Post A level, most to sensible courses at good universities – mix of the soundly academic eg history at York or chemistry at Birmingham to the soundly vocational eg aerospace engineering at Leicester or retail management at Surrey. Two to Oxbridge in 2013. Altogether, a sense that people go where they should.

Money matters: The GDST isn't a rich organisation but under its current management much energy is going into upping the bursary provision. Academic and music scholarships at 11+. Academic, music, drama, sport and art scholarships at 16+. Bursaries at 11+, 13+ and 16+ on a means-tested basis. Over 50 students in receipt of bursary assistance in the senior school at time of our visit

Remarks: Best summed up by pupils: 'I've been here since reception and the school has just got better and better.' 'You're allowed to develop in your own way – there's no limit to what you can do.' And parents: 'I wish I could put my sons in dresses and send them there.' Now, there's a thought...

Norwich School

Linked school: Norwich School Lower School

70 The Close, Norwich, NR1 4DD

- Pupils: 850 pupils; 560 boys/290 girls • Ages: 11–18 • Christian
- Fees: £13,167 pa • Independent

Tel: 01603 728449
Email: admissions@norwich-school.org.uk
Website: www.norwich-school.org.uk

Head Master: Since 2011, Mr Steffan Griffiths MA (Oxon) Classics BA (Open University) English literature (forties). Educated at Whitgift School, where his father was headmaster, and had a spell at Timbertop School in Australia as a 'rentapom', before Oxford. Taught classics and games at Tonbridge School, then Eton (also deputy housemaster) before returning to Oxford for appointment as usher (deputy head) of Magdalen College School. Has made a confident start at Norwich, where his relaxed, low-key style has been welcomed all round. 'He seems right for the school now,' commented pupils, though a mother we spoke to said, 'I am not sure I would recognise him in the street.'

Acknowledges and defends the rapid expansion of the school in recent years to admit girls throughout; proportion now roughly 70:30, aiming at 60:40. No dramatic changes planned, and says he is 'very impressed by what I find here.' Has chosen to teach his own subjects (Latin and Greek) at GCSE and A level. He is married to Harriet, who teaches at another school, and they have three children, two at the lower school.

Academic matters: The bar is set high by a committed and enthusiastic staff of over 100. Parents and pupils acknowledge the outstanding quality of the teachers – many are leading lights in their own disciplines and write the textbooks. A father spoke of 'highly intelligent, motivated teaching – the pupils are lucky'. 'My favourites are fun, as well as making us work,' said one boy, and a sixth former praised 'the way we are made to think – it blows your mind at times!' Academic pressure is there, 'but it's more self-imposed; we are under pressure from ourselves', said a girl. 'It's hugely competitive, but most of us like that'. The head is frank – 'those who struggle to keep up just wouldn't be happy here' – and parents agree that 'scraping in and not thriving is worse than not getting in, in the first place.'

Examination results excellent; A*/A grades par for the course at GCSE (81 per cent A*/A in 2013), notably in English, French, history and the sciences. Options with a high take-up include Spanish, photography and 2D design. Latin, perhaps surprisingly, is not popular and Greek even less so. A levels again mainly sciences, maths and history, though music and philosophy are both popular. The art and design department has national recognition. Over 65 per cent A*/A grades in 2013. School provides plenty of help with university applications – 'we received emails about courses our son might be interested in nearly every week', one mother told us, preparation begins early. Some resentment about the dominance of Oxbridge in all this – master-classes and interview advice for suitable pupils can irritate. 'It really bugs me – one teacher kept saying, "you'll need this for your Oxbridge entrance", when only two in the group were doing it.'

The school provides plenty of support for study skills and revision. Though there is limited SEN provision a new post has been created to provide specialist learning support. They will organise extra time in exams for dyslexics and help is available after school (either from school staff or outside specialists) but pupils must be able to follow the whole curriculum.

Games, options, the arts: The message is 'get involved'; enormous variety of clubs, sports, musical activities and drama productions. Pupils are 'very diverse, nerdy, sporty and cool types', said one mother.

Sport is compulsory throughout. The greatest importance is attached to the competitive team sports – rugby, cricket, hockey, netball – and the best are creamed off into the coveted A and B teams in each year. 'The boys can be cocky if they are in the teams,' said one girl, and the star status of the first XV is evident, though the girls' success in hockey and netball is giving the boys a run for their money. Playing fields a bus ride away. Those who don't catch the selector's eye do Potted Sports, having a go each term at different activities – mostly rowing, fencing, and non-team games.

Music is taken seriously and at least 70 per cent of pupils are involved in some kind of instrumental group, band or choral society. The school educates the cathedral choristers but also has its own chapel choir, which leads school worship and performs at concerts. Over half the school learn an instrument and there are regular music competitions including House Shout, in which everyone takes part. 'Music is cool,' said everyone we spoke to. Each year the school stages a major musical production – eg Guys and Dolls and most recently Les Miserables, involving at least 50 pupils. The school has no hall, studio or dedicated space for performances but has successfully used local theatres – 'one of the great advantages of being so central,' says the head, making a virtue of necessity. The school runs a popular sea scout troop (own boathouse on the river), which is one of the largest in the country.

Background and atmosphere: The cathedral close setting gives school bags of style and the blessing (or curse) of a number of medieval buildings to occupy, mainly clustered to the north of the cathedral. 'The site has to be negotiated,' says the head, and though the city location has great benefits, the drawbacks are lack of space and privacy. 'We have to remember we are on view all the time,' said a pupil; another commented, 'There is nowhere to spread out and play football at breaks'. 'The cathedral is in all we do and is a huge strength,' says the head, conjuring up visions of pupils strolling through cloisters or popping in to say prayers, but in reality it is, understandably, out of bounds after the daily assembly each morning and used on an ad hoc basis for special events, services and concerts. As a tenant of the dean and chapter and occupying many listed buildings, the school is limited (some would say, mercifully) in what alterations they can make. Elsewhere in the Close they have converted a 60s office block into science labs. Pupils wander calmly around; 'promenade' time is built into the timetable, no rushing or bells. School is stuck, it seems, with the unlovely canteen built circa 1970, but pupils don't seem bothered – the bag racks area next door appears to be the hub of the school, with pupils clustered there continually.

'It's a happy school, non-fussy, non-pernickety – no waving fingers for the wrong sports kit', said a mother, though uniform is worn throughout – bright blue blazers exchanged for black suits in the sixth form. Badges – house, prefect and sporting – are worn by many. Pupils look cheerful and friendly, though we did not see much in the way of door holding. Their confidence is promoted and achievement applauded in all areas. 'It can be rather, "look at me",' said a mother, and a father summed up, 'Success really matters and the going is hard if you're not a high flier at something'.

Pastoral care and discipline: For a school where expectations of pupils (and parents) are high, getting the pastoral bit right is the key. Pupils stay with the same tutor up the school and houses are important for sport, music and drama. Staff are quick to respond to parental worries (via email or phone); there is a counsellor that pupils (or parents) can see confidentially (many do), and a much-liked chaplain – also a member of the staff. Prefects are a select group with privileges and are chosen via what sounds like a terrifying process of written application, weeding out by housemaster, interview, final choice. Pupils agree with the sense behind most rules, though a mother said, 'The bright boys who want to buck the system...get detention after detention, report cards, things can escalate.' Not a school for the non-conformist.

Pupils and parents: The great majority from within 20 miles and from professional, business and academic backgrounds; very few ethnic minorities (a reflection of East Anglia). Parents are aware of, and in the main regret, the school's aura of privilege. 'It is not a good social mix. My father and grandfather came to this school from a council estate in the 1930s when it was direct grant. It is much more bourgeois today'. There is wide support for means–tested bursaries and one father suggested, 'Put the fees up and offer far more bursaries to widen the social catchment'. 'We do what we can, and wish it could be more', acknowledges the head.

Entrance: Main entry points 11+ and 13+. Of the 90 places available at 11, half go to pupils from the lower school (unsuitables warned and weeded out in good time) and the rest take an entrance exam – maths, English NVR, plus a morning of assessment and a private interview with a staff member. Another 30 places available at 13 (exam again or CE, plus interview) and a further 30 at sixth form stage (minimum six Bs at GCSE plus interview). 'We are looking for a base line of academic ability; this is a pastoral imperative', says the head.

Competition varies year by year, but roughly two-thirds of applicants successful.

Exit: Top drawer universities in the main with a good bunch to Oxbridge (17 in 2013). Heavyweight subjects, mathematics, sciences, engineering, law and medicine, all popular. Around 15 per cent take a gap year.

Money matters: Fifty per cent off for cathedral choristers and staff children. Variety of scholarships for academic, music, art, and sporting prowess, usually 10 per cent, though a few 100 per cent awards for sixth formers joining from the state sector. Limited means-tested bursaries.

Remarks: The grammar school style makes it an excellent choice for the bright, motivated boy or girl who will benefit from all the school offers. Not a school for natural non-conformers or those who need to challenge authority.

Notre Dame Senior School

Linked school: Notre Dame Preparatory School

Burwood House, Convent Lane, Cobham, Surrey, KT11 1HA

- Pupils: 360 pupils • Ages: 11–18 • RC • Fees: £14,025 pa
- Independent

Tel: 01932 869990
Email: registrar@notredame.co.uk
Website: www.notredame.co.uk

Principal: Since April 2013, David Plummer BEd Dip.HE FRSA, previously long-term head of the prep school, has been principal of the prep and senior schools. We said of him as the prep school head, 'A self-assured and likeable Welshman, he's hard to miss as he proceeds around school dispensing bonhomie to girls, staff and parents alike...Does not sit still, yet pays great attention to detail...He's approachable, enthusiastic and super-committed.'

His wife teaches at the school and both daughters were educated there.

Vice principal and head of the senior school is Mrs Anna King MA (Cantab) MEd PGCE, previously deputy head.

Academic matters: On the up with good value added. At GCSE more than 60 per cent at A*/A grades. Theology – not religious studies mark you – is compulsory and most pass with A*-A grades. Latin is an option but only a handful take it. Similarly lowish take up of music and drama, despite lots of girls involved in this in extra-curricular time. Art and design preferred and done well – 100 per cent passed GCSE with A*-A grades. History another popular and successful subject.

At A level, 54 per cent A*/A grades and 70 per cent A*/B. Five new subjects are offered for 16+ students – psychology, sociology, business studies, classical civilisation and economics – and there is now a group taking AS drama. Low sixth form numbers mean just a handful in many classes. Most popular subjects are biology, chemistry, history, maths – only one physicist of late.

Average class size is between 12-14. Fairly hefty amounts of homework – two hours a night ('More than my friends at Tiffin,' said one girl) and parents feel their daughters are pushed. Holiday homework not routine, but was set this summer for girls staying at the sixth form. 'Nothing too onerous, but kept her brain in gear', said one mother. 'I really feel they have got all the basics covered,' said another mother.

School has put a strong focus on science recently and beat 1,300 other entrants to win the School's Chemistry Challenge final at Imperial College – 'I jumped out of my seat,' said the delighted previous head. 'It was the result of years of hard work and investment'. The school's 10-year development programme included investment in science and there are now plans to put the same effort into raising the profile of maths.

Parental praise for teaching staff who 'go the extra mile', although we did encounter one parent who felt strongly that some areas could be tightened up – 'Her [daughter's] class barely finished the syllabus in time.' In an otherwise wholly positive interim report, ISI did recommend more consistent monitoring of teaching quality and use of pupil progress data. Worth asking a question when you look around.

Some seriously impressive facilities include the learning resources and sixth form study centre – a shame that more students don't stay on to take advantage of it. 'I'm very impressed by the sixth form', said one mother. 'They get so much more out of it than purely their A levels, with masses of opportunity to get involved throughout the school, mentoring and helping younger girls with their sport and studies. And career suggestions have come flying thick and fast.' School says average size of sixth form fluctuates, but is usually between 50-55, although only 37 currently.

In year 7 the girls are taught in three groups, apart from maths where they are set in four. Then from year 8 they are set in all subjects apart from PE, technology and art. They can take up to 11 GCSEs; most take nine or 10.

Parents feel it's a plus that a straight A* daughter and her significantly less academic sibling could both thrive in the same school – there's a good mix of girls of differing abilities. School has around 80 pupils with learning difficulties or disabilities, of whom 40 receive specialist support, and 30 with EAL requirements, although most are actually fluent in English.

Games, options, the arts: Some great provision for sport, which is popular here. Top notch swimming and netball. There are compulsory swimming lessons for years 7 and 8 in on-site indoor heated swimming pool (recently retiled and refurbished) resulting in competition success. For netball, there are 14 teams so that 120 girls represent the school at various competitions from U12 to U16 and older girls head to Tobago for a tour. Cross-country success at county and national level, also plenty of gymnastics, badminton and even football and a little lacrosse. But several parents mention that, given the seductive grounds the school enjoys, there is potential for further development of sporting facilities. Biggest bugbear is that there is no hockey – 'A big omission', said one mother, mystified as to why there is no all-weather hockey pitch and peeved to hear that the school's new Montaigne theatre was a £3 million plus project. 'Why not have spent some of that on sport?' she said. (It's next on the list, says school).

But that said, what a bonus – a 370 seat Elizabethan-style theatre, nonagon shaped, best for acoustics so picks up even the tiniest voice from a nervous performer. Its first production, the musical history of St Jeanne's life and her Order, was streamed live across the world to the Company of Mary Our Lady schools, colleges and convents. Parents have come to expect polished productions from Notre Dame, where drama and music are very popular – 38 per cent take external LAMDA exams and 33 per cent take extra-curricular music lessons, and merits and distinctions abound.

Standout GCSE results in art and design, with all students gaining A*. Students work displayed around the school includes mosaics, sculpture and paintings.

Background and atmosphere: Opened on its present 17 acre site just outside Cobham in 1937, the school is part of the Company of Mary our Lady, a worldwide educational foundation and the oldest recognised order for teaching girls in the world. It was founded in Bordeaux in 1607 and current pupils, staff and governors still pilgrimage there today. The vision of the order's founder, Saint Jeanne de Lestonnac, is embodied in the school's mission statement – you will be in no doubt that your daughter is at a Catholic school.

Set in parkland on the banks of the River Mole, the school buildings comprise the rather splendid Georgian Burwood House, home to the prep (qv) with a maze of modern buildings running off it. All is tidy, well-maintained and resourced with plenty of space. An air of calm pervades.

Transport has to be a consideration as the school is tucked away at the end of a long narrow lane with access by car or school coach only. Rapped knuckles for parents attempting to drop their daughters off to take a walk or cycle up to school – deemed unsafe. There is a mini bus to take sixth formers into the town at lunchtime. But generally day to day, girls have to rely on coaches or lifts from parents; 'Doesn't do much to foster their independence,' laughed one rueful mother/chauffeur. And those at after-school clubs miss the last coach and have to be collected.

But this slightly out of the way location is actually very appealing to some parents, especially those with daughters joining at 11 and looking for a nice transition from a protected primary school environment. The school feels safe, with its pretty setting, away from it all. And the strong Catholic ethos furthers the nurturing feel of the place. Even though a significant percentage of families are not actually Catholic, they sign up for the school as if they were – accepting that the belief system is very much part of the set-up here. Parents need to feel comfortable about their daughters attending masses, studying theology and undertaking days of reflection. On the school's 'reflection day', pupils and staff take a break from 'hectic and eventful lives'. It includes bible discussions, prayers and meditation, with soft melodic music playing in the background. 'Pupils and staff come back to work with a fresh mind. Young people don't generally have enough proper quiet time – there's always a red light bleeping at them from a phone or computer even as they go to sleep'.

No plans for expansion. 'I know there's a tendency to think bigger is better, but if you get too big I don't think your young people can still feel as special and important,' said the previous head.

Pastoral care and discipline: Girls are well looked after – this place is very strong pastorally with gospel values at its core – 'respect, honesty, forgiveness, kindness, patience,' says school. Lots of peer mentoring and 'big sister' schemes, while praise and reminders about 'desirable behaviour' are drip fed by staff. 'My daughter feels valued and recognised; she is not a number,' says one parent. There's a 'telling' culture and school says any necessary action will be swift. 'I think of the school as a loving envelope around our girls,' said the previous head.

Tradition of pupils helping with a pilgrimage for sick people to Lourdes and sixth formers working in a local home for the elderly and contributing to a project for disadvantaged students in Albania. Even girls with no Catholic belief get involved with this. There are still a few nuns with a pastoral role at the school. 'I think Notre Dame is very good at sorting out girls who don't fit into a standard mould,' said a long-standing parent. 'It's not a very big school, so nobody gets lost and issues get picked up'. Another parent felt that the school was well organised so that the girls all got to know each other and were 'well aired – they are in different groups, for registration, sets, teaching groups and houses so that they are not continually with the same group of girls. I think that helps avoid a lot of issues'.

It's not an intense place and generally speaking parents feel the girls get on well. 'My daughter and her friends all feel happy and valued,' said one. 'So I think bullying and bitching are less likely to happen then. And I feel confident the school would deal with it if I ever went in with an issue.'

Pupils and parents: A supportive bunch of largely local professional and business families, including a scattering of celebrities among the parents and actress Ruth Wilson and hairdresser Sacha Mascolo-Tarbuck among the Old Girls.

Girls we saw were a neat and tidy bunch – it's hard to roll up a kilt. Sixth formers in business wear. Some grumbles that day to day communication with the school is a bit hit and miss and could be better for the everyday enquiry and message. 'I don't get the speed of response I'd like,' said one parent. Parents' association, Friends of Notre Dame, is busy and well supported, organising plenty of events – all the usual from quiz nights to golf days.

Entrance: At 11, entrance assessment in English, maths and non-verbal reasoning. 'It's all humane and not hard-edged like some of the London schools we considered', said one mother. School says it is looking for talents that already exist that they can foster. Fifty per cent of places go to girls moving up from the prep school. The rest from all over, including St Charles Borromeo, Weybridge; Cardinal Newman, Hersham; Our Lady of Lourdes, Thames Ditton; Rowan, Claygate; Rydes Hill, Guildford; Halstead, Woking; Holy Cross, Kingston; Westwood, Walton on Thames; and Greenfield, Woking. Dedicated to Catholic faith, but welcomes those from other faiths or none provided they are 'sympathetic' to the school's ethos. 'Not all Catholic by any means, judging by the numbers taking communion,' said one mother. 'But Catholicism clearly underpins life here'.

Exit: At 18+ most to first choice universities, over 80 per cent to Russell Group and always a few to Oxbridge. School stresses that admission tutors report back that the quality of the students' personal and school statements is frequently the deciding factor for choosing a Notre Dame student over another.

Money matters: Bursaries and scholarships for year 7 and the sixth form. Parents warn of a few extras to include when budgeting – 'There are always trips to pay for, plus lunches and the coaches are quite expensive'.

Remarks: Solid, good all-round, ecumenical. 'My only gripe would be that Notre Dame does not sell itself,' said one. 'While some come from out of London, it's not on the radar at all from Guildford, where no-one seems to have heard of it – it's a hidden gem'. Does a good job of keeping its girls busy and focused.

Notting Hill and Ealing High School

Linked school: Notting Hill and Ealing High School Junior School

2 Cleveland Road, London, W13 8AX

- Pupils: 580 girls, all day • Ages: 11–18 • Non-denom
- Fees: £14,982 pa • Independent

Tel: 020 8799 8400
Email: enquiries@nhehs.gdst.net
Website: www.nhehs.gdst.net

Head: Since 2008, Ms Lucinda Hunt BSc ARCS PGCE (Oxon) (late forties). Formerly deputy head at St Paul's Girls, read physics at Imperial. Striking, clear-sighted and determined, enjoying a meteoric career in education with a year's secondment at Goldman Sachs to boot. Working in a bank reinforced her appetite for teaching – 'When profit is the motivator the bottom line is that it's dull'. In the early years of her career she taught science, maths and geology in Australia and France. Well versed in the ethos of GDST (and very happy with it) – a period

at Putney High and eight years at Wimbledon High, where she rose to head of sixth form.

'I'm not afraid to rock the boat if it needs rocking,' declares Ms Hunt, but adds that she is no Hazel Blears, and will only make changes that are needed. Quick as a flash, she has fearlessly cut swathes through the existing management structure. At the same time she is well tuned to the relatively gentle spirit of the place – 'that indefinable quality that makes a school different from the others, despite the fact that we all say the same sort of things,' she explains. One of her aims is to open up the windows and doors – 'At the moment not enough people know what we're about'. Parents agree and some comment on poor communication about the day to day. She starts with her own door which, unlike that of her predecessor, is always open to staff and pupils alike. The best thing about the job is the 'wry, intelligent' girls she says, despite the fact that she doesn't teach any. The energy that she brings to the place is tangible. Here's someone whose influence is restoring the school to its former status as one of the best girls' schools in west London.

Academic matters: 2013 results were league-table topping and, for the first time, the school outperformed the most traditionally academic of its GDST sisters. At A Level 92 per cent of entries were awarded A*/A/B and 70 per cent of all results were A*/A. This is a very high level of achievement indeed. Subjects taught are wide ranging, including philosophy of religion and ethics, and psychology. Maths and geography strong. Chemistry and biology also popular as well as drama, history and English. Year 12s choose a general studies option, can range from jewellery making or music technology to Russian, Mandarin or Ancient Greek. Mandarin compulsory in year 7, which they learn alongside a European language. Class sizes large for an independent school – maximum 30 in years 7-9, average 22 in years 10-11. A lot of young teaching blood – Ms Hunt asserts the usual turnover you would expect in every London school. Twenty per cent have been at the school for more than 10 years, one third men. Pupils speak of the commitment of the staff and generally feel well supported.

Ms Hunt reluctant to be drawn into specific learning difficulties – wary of labelling she explains – but five to 10 per cent of children are eligible to have extra time in exams and school is becoming more adept at identifying who should be screened. The SEN teacher will go into lessons to work with individuals. No extra charge for any extra support. School proud of its success with one girl with serious visual impairment who went on to read English at Durham University. 'The term "gifted and talented" could describe almost every girl in the school,' says Ms Hunt. These are catered for with the various activities that take place during the school week including whole school assemblies. Parents praise an inclusive approach to academics – girls in lower sets are not ignored as 'dunces'.

Games, options, the arts: As with most suburban schools, space has always been at a premium, and this school now has little outside space. In September 2013, however, it unveiled a massive and beautiful new building at its heart which includes a huge, subterranean sports hall, big hall for assemblies and concerts, good-sized studio theatre and large dance studio. Four Astroturf pitches, swimming pool and tennis and netball courts also on site.

For hockey, rounders and athletics girls can run or be bused to nearby sports grounds. Not known, hitherto, for its sporting achievements – 'but girls get plenty of physical activity,' one parent told us and the new build looks set to transform opportunities. Mutterings among some that if their daughter is not in the tennis team they are left to play among themselves. Ms Hunt keen to introduce some less conventional individual sports for which you 'don't have to get undressed (so many girls just prefer not to)' – fencing currently riding a wave of enthusiasm; other innovations may follow.

Drama jolly good fun. Music well provided for – orchestras, choirs and ensemble groups, with about half the school playing a musical instrument; school will accommodate the few who want to do it at A level. The choir has performed in Tuscany and in Venice and planning is now under way for a tour to New York. Plenty of trips abroad for the non-musical too – recent trips have included a classics expedition to Rome, an art history trip to the museums and galleries of New York, geographers to Barcelona and Iceland, history trips to Russia, Germany and the battlefields of northern France, physicists to CERN and a sixth form trip to China led by the economics department. French students go to Paris and Spanish ones to Andalucia. Lots of enthusiasm for debating – whether it be competing against other schools in debating competitions or Model United Nations events. Duke of Edinburgh awards – most girls take bronze, over a third take silver and a thriving gold award group in the sixth.

Background and atmosphere: Founded in 1873 – the oldest of the Girls' Day School Trust schools. Moved from Notting Hill to its present site in a large house (grand entrance with columns) in a broad Ealing residential avenue in 1931 and a number of features of the original building moved with it.

People we spoke to commented, rather blandly, on the warmth and friendliness of the school: Ms Hunt attributes this partly to the intimacy created by the leafy central quadrangle that connects the old with the new – lots of meeting and greeting as girls pass each other on stairs. Refurbished and much extended dining room with a bright, airy feel and plenty of space.

Newish sixth form centre in a separate building on the south west corner of the main site – a listed modernist building that had been a children's home, lying empty since 2006. It was gutted and converted into a bright, modern, airy building with seminar rooms, common room (with the obligatory leather sofas), multigym, café and outside terrace.

Strong community sense around this school – current pupils often the daughters or granddaughters of Old Girls and their annual OG bash always a sell-out.

Pastoral care and discipline: Girls are noticeably well behaved around the school – some of the quietest entrances in and out of assembly that we have seen anywhere. Head acknowledges instances of bullying (a good sign – it's the ones who deny any at all that one has to look out for). New area of concern – not just here – is the opportunity for students to use cyber space to make each others' lives difficult. Ms Hunt well aware of this and ready to take on the challenge. With her modern, forward-thinking approach, if anyone born in the early '60s can meet that challenge, she is your woman. A few worrying reports from parents about having nobody to go to talk to about pastoral issues ('Don't want to be nuisance and worry the head – she's got enough on her plate'), but encouraging signs that school is onto this and attempts are being made to plug the gap.

Pupils and parents: Families more modest than you would find at most London independent schools – typical GDST parents: professional, ambitious, looking for value for money but not prepared to compromise on their daughters' education. It's a local school – but some come from as far as Richmond, Perivale, Harrow and Greenford to the west and Notting Hill to the east. Cosmopolitan (particularly Asian), community – reflective of the local area. Lots of doctors and dentists, chartered surveyors, but creative types too – record producers, fashion journalists, business consultants. A wide range – ethnically, culturally and economically.

Girls here are focused but enjoying life. Not so pressured as their contemporaries in more central schools – they can work hard without being cowed by expectation and league tables. We saw lots of initiative – girls writing scores for musicals, scripts for witty renditions of the Theseus and Ariadne myth and choreographing amusing Michael Jackson dance routines for mythical monsters. They emerge articulate and confident, full of west London sophistication, but without the trendy, street-wise demeanour characteristic of their peers in more high profile schools in west London. OGs include Angela Rumbold, writer and TV presenter, Bettany Hughes, BBC children's presenter Angellica Bell and Blue Peter's Konnie Huq.

Entrance: Competitive consortium examination in maths and English plus interview. About half come up from the junior school, the rest from west London state and independent schools. Most go on to the sixth form. External sixth form applicants have interviews in their potential A level subjects and sit a general paper; They are expected to have obtained A*/A grades in their chosen A Level subjects, with A or above in the majority of their other GCSEs. For the occasional place in the senior school girls are tested according to their age and stage.

Exit: Now losing far fewer after GCSE. Why go elsewhere with these results and facilities? Each year a number of girls go to Oxbridge (nine in 2012), some win scholarships. A lot read sciences – and not just medicine (five medics in 2012). History, politics and English are also popular. Bristol, Manchester and Nottingham favourites at the moment.

Remarks: A well run, efficient GDST school that does exactly what it says on the tin. Your daughter will get a very good, balanced education here. Oversubscribed, and no longer in the shade of other schools of its kind. The dynamic Ms Hunt has been busily making the school her own – without altering the relatively relaxed, down to earth friendliness of the place.

Nottingham Girls' High School

Linked school: Nottingham Girls' High School Junior School

9 Arboretum Street, Nottingham, NG1 4JB

• Pupils: 730 in senior school • Ages: 11–18 • Non-denom
• Fees: £11,235 pa • Independent

Tel: 01159 417663
Email: enquiries@not.gdst.net
Website: www.nottinghamgirlshigh.gdst.net

Head: Since 2006, Mrs Sue Gorham BA MA (mid-fifties). Educated Manchester University (French) and Open University (education management). Widowed, three adult children. Hers was a wind of change appointment – she came from Burgess Hill with a reputation as a tightener, a tweaker, a freshener-up. Not that NGHS had become the dowdy Duchess of Arboretum Street, far from it, but the time was right just the same. With cheerful courage and steady nerve she ruffled feathers at the outset but in short order won over the glum, the cross and the doubtful. She's here not to build a reputation but to lead from the front and get it right. A moderniser for sure, up to speed with latest thinking and practice, but does not rate processes higher than people. Inspires affection and approval in all constituencies – girls really like her: she is approachable, she wants to know. One parent says, 'You don't just get the party line, she listens to you, really listens.' An admirable, kind and likeable head with a notable achievement so far – a gentle revolutionary.

Academic matters: In 2013, nearly 36 per cent A*/A grades at GCSE and 70 per cent A*/A at A level. Traditionally strong in maths and the sciences and once arguably over-focused on them, it has enjoyed an academic culture change and now attaches equal value to all subjects – girls are encouraged to go for what they do best. A culture change in delivery, too. Teachers as a breed don't do change with anything approaching alacrity – they get terribly upset by it, so we can only conjecture what their response must have been when Mrs Gorham, on arrival, had windows put in all classroom doors, opening them to the gaze of those outside, then threw them open to a new way of doing things. Modern teaching methods, best practice sharing and inter-disciplinary team working are how they go about it now.

Lots of brand new IT in sparklingly refurbed classrooms. Watching them at it is to observe lit-up students and animated teachers – we wondered if some weren't perhaps having too much fun. The proof of the pudding is in the exam results – they march from strength to strength, with value-added scores to match. Some resultant staff turnover and some bright young things brought in. Most girls here like most of their teachers a lot; one mum added, 'Do they ever go home?' – the work ethic is shared.

Nottinghamians generally do not – you'll notice this if you're moving here – buy into the intense pressure ethic evident in other big city top schools. They work jolly hard, though. Parents and girls talk of workloads that keep them up o' nights and of teachers who insist it is done on time. This is a school for achievers all right, one of those that cannot accommodate daffiness and unfulfilled promise – simply can't afford to. Actually they did indulge a bit of that recently and it skewed the results. They've bounced back with attitude since. If your daughter has problems with deadlines, think again. If she doesn't, she may occasionally utter words like 'unremitting', but never 'crushing'. Yes, exam stats matter, that's the way of things, but they really do educate the whole girl here – they care about their well-being and about character, life outside the classroom and life after school. SENs, mild to moderate at most, are supported in the classroom, not one-to-one.

Subjects studied are all gold standard, no sillies, and the full range, of course. Sciences remain especially strong, maths and economics mind-blowingly good, and no weaknesses, though art is notably undersubscribed. All year 9s do a classy three modern languages. Sixth formers can learn Mandarin. Partnerships with local universities have added inspiration and grown-up perspectives, with PhD students coming in to talk about their research. Green chemistry is big in this eco-aware school.

Games, options, the arts: An impressive range of enrichment activities available but, here's the striking thing, they're not there as ornamental window dressing – they make time for them, they actually really matter. This is a school with a joy ethic, for sure, underlying which is a deadly serious belief that personal qualities and social values count as highly as working hard and keeping up, so character-building pursuits are central. D of E and Young Enterprise buoyant. Plenty of music, resurgent under its new choir director. Boys imported from over the road as and when, particularly for drama. Sport is cramped by the school's location and lack of space, but they do well with the facilities they've got. Compulsory up to year 12. Everyone has a go at a wide range, from netball, hockey etc, to kick-boxing and self-defence. Swimming in the boys' pool. In spite of the lack of rolling acres of freshly-mown greensward, the school boasts a pretty impressive roll of sporting success.

Background and atmosphere: A Girls' Day School Trust school. Sound a bit corporate? Collaborative would be a better word; localism is favoured. Check it out at gdst.net. NGHS was founded in 1875, situated just north of the city centre in an area which has been described as insalubrious – as indeed it until recently was. Nearby Victorian townhouses which had seen better tenants are now being bought by Nottingham Trent University. The area is perfectly safe – charming, actually, with the Arboretum next door. The school is bisected by Arboretum Street and occupies a small site where new buildings jostle old.

There are competitor schools which offer more elbow room and more eye-catching facilities. How does the school answer them? By focusing instead on the human scale and the quality of relationships. Among teachers and students a strong feeling of shared purpose. This is a warm, kind and purposeful place, neither snazzy nor haughty – and perhaps all the more impressive for that. Much recent refurbing has brightened and improved what there is. Splendid new sixth form centre with its own garden – an essential recruiting tool for itchy year 11s on the lookout for greener grass. What the school now needs more than merely urgently is a decent performing arts centre.

Pastoral care and discipline: This being a school where teachers and students look out for each other as a matter of course, pastoral care really is as good as it gets. We were as much impressed by the shining dedication of those charged with it as we were by the endorsement of students and parents. Problems are addressed speedily. For wide-eyed and apprehensive new girls a fun, bonding weekend when they arrive. Food, another important quality of life issue, is very good. Snacks and meals throughout the day and breakfast for students and parents.

Pupils and parents: Socially mixed they say, and true up to a point – pupils come from up to 30 miles away. Active parent-teacher association. The head welcomes parent involvement – all part of the team working. You find the sort of relaxed social atmosphere you expect in a single-sex school, decidedly affectionate. Males are never too far away: good relations and joint enterprises with the boys' school over the road. Eminent alumni include Stella Rimmington, head spy; Helen Creswell and Julie Myerson, authors; Parosha Chandran, human rights lawyer; Jane Smit, England cricketer; Clare Hammond, fiery pianist.

Entrance: At 11 by test (English, maths and verbal reasoning) plus interview. On the lookout more for potential than what a girl actually knows. At any age, 'if we think they'll benefit' – in other words, if they think your girl is bright enough. At sixth form, average B in best eight GCSEs. Any who leave after GCSE and undergo second thoughts, as they do, admitted to sixth form if possible.

Exit: A declining number leave after GCSE, despite some superb free competitors, notably Bilborough. Sixth formers go on to good universities (Leeds, Nottingham, York, Durham, Manchester and Newcastle all popular) and a decent wodge to Oxbridge (ten in 2013).

Money matters: Scholarships and means-tested bursaries available – the bursaries very much targeted on those who would not otherwise be able to afford the fees. The full fee offers good value for money.

Remarks: A school not without strong competitors, especially to the south. Though lacking glitzy, soaring bricks and mortar, NGHS more than makes up for it with a most engaging and carefully wrought quality of humanity. Hardware's all well and good, but it's software that matters most, and this is a school with an impressive operating system.

Nottingham High School

Linked schools: Lovell House Infant School; Nottingham High Infant and Junior School

Waverley Mount, Nottingham, NG7 4ED

- Pupils: 740 boys; all day • Ages: 11–18 • Fees: £12,291 pa
- Independent

Tel: 01158 452232
Email: enquiries@nottinghamhigh.co.uk
Website: www.nottinghamhigh.co.uk

Headmaster: Since 2007, Mr Kevin Fear BA PGCE (mid forties), educated at Douai and Southampton University. Taught at The King's School, Chester, from 1986, joined Nottingham High, 2000, as senior teacher, 2004 deputy head with academic and marketing responsibilities. Married to Denise; two children: girl at the Girls' High and boy at the junior school.

Approachable, open, modest, has overseen considerable building development and improved staff conditions since his appointment. Very focused on communication with parents via surveys, also his blog (worth a read) and is one of only a few HMC heads on Twitter. Keen to maintain the school's high standards in all areas and continue to produce well-rounded boys who enjoy school life, don't feel pressured to achieve and would perform well at interviews. Interested in IT and sport, especially football.

Academic matters: Very strong and consistent all round, with maths, all three sciences, economics (all very popular), history, politics and government and English lit particularly successful at A level. Other choices include music technology, philosophy, psychology, Spanish; 65 per cent A*/A grades in 2013. All do AS general studies and some do the Extended Project Qualification and AQA Bacc; small numbers for languages, DT and art; will run subjects for only two students (if staffing allows). GCSE 2013: 72 per cent A*/A – most get 10, high numbers with all A*/A; two languages common.

Also does very well in all three science and maths Olympiads, sometimes attaining international level. National successes at chess (very popular, international level too), DT and finance competitions; boys attend chemistry and physics camps/competitions at universities and achieve well in regional Latin and Greek reading competitions. Max class sizes: 24 for years 7-11, 16 for year 12, 12 for year 13, but often less; teachers enthusiastic and dedicated and have friendly, good-humoured relationships with the boys.

The large library is managed by enthusiastic professional librarian with a generous budget – lots of current fiction, DVDs, full range of broadsheets, including French and Spanish newspapers, and magazines; reading widely popular and encouraged, eg through a cleverly designed inter-form competition for year 7s based around certificates, chocolates and publicly posted charts (this is a school that understands how to motivate boys). Twelve good-sized science rooms, including five very modern, half lecture hall style, half lab; well-equipped language classrooms; masses of tip top computers and electronic whiteboards everywhere.

Learning support department, headed by a full-time qualified coordinator, covers mild learning difficulties and disabilities (the dys-range), ADHD, Asperger's, and would try to accommodate physical problems – provided the required academic promise is present. She advises subject staff and provides (free) individual or small group support outside the class, eg with spelling – a year 8 boy spoke very appreciatively of his dramatic improvement in this since joining the school.

The gifted and talented are identified and receive plenty of extension opportunities inside and outside the classroom.

Games, options, the arts: Very good playing fields a short bus ride away – on site: a large, well-equipped modern sports hall with a fitness suite and climbing wall, full-size indoor hockey pitch, cricket machines; indoor swimming pool with canoes.

Outstanding achievements nationally and internationally in orienteering (very popular), rugby, squash, swimming, but not dominated by sport – other spheres well regarded too; plenty of opportunities to be in school teams. Also successful at bridge, badminton, chess (lots involved); hockey, archery, tennis, cross-country, golf, athletics and cricket (Barbados tour) on offer too.

Very strong and diverse music – orchestras, ensembles, bands, choirs, a recording studio; success in national competitions; tours to Barcelona, Venice and New York; boys in national and Nottingham orchestras and choirs; very attractive recital hall with drum kit, small organ and Steinway, used for concerts and master classes with professional musicians. Joint musical events with Nottingham Girls', eg Carmina Burana, Pirates of Penzance, Guys and Dolls and a chamber music festival. Curriculum drama coming soon but no purpose-built theatre nor studio – conventional Founder Hall used for performances, eg Latin comedies – impressive choice.

Good art – varied media: painting (regular life drawing class), print making (three presses – two old, one modern), ceramics, sculpture (we saw some very inventive masks, created with a visiting sculptor), pottery; talks from visiting artists; local trips plus weekend residential in York or Leeds and visits to London, Edinburgh, Liverpool for sixth. A very large, well-equipped DT room with two ICT suites.

Parents value the 'wealth of experiences' on offer: several lunch time clubs, which boys help run – reading, arts, politics, debating, philosophy, community action; CCF with all three services, D of E, scouts; house choral verse speaking competition (organised by sixth formers – a challenging task); external general knowledge and spelling competitions; various house charities; year group councils. Masses of trips – World Challenge to Siberia, New York/Washington, Hadrian's Wall, Rome, Sorrento. Unusually, year 11 and 13 boys are trained in how to deliver language lessons to reception and year 4 classes.

Background and atmosphere: Founded 1513 by Dame Agnes Mellers in memory of her husband – originally situated in the Lace Market; moved 1868 to present site. Attractive mock Gothic façade with two quads; later expanded by opening up the cellars to create a third floor, plus externally featureless 1970/80s additions. A lot of dreary carpeting and a few corridor walls in need of brightening, though often improved by displays of boys' art work, big colour photos of boys engaged in various activities and educational posters. Maintains contact with its early 20th century past, eg the large portrait of the spectacularly heroic Rev Hardy VC, accompanied by a case of his medals. The White House, a freshly decorated separate building formed from two Regency villas, is aptly used for sixth form politics and economics classes and also contains a small kitchen for the cookery club.

The most remarkable modern addition is the recent atrium style sixth form centre on two levels – the Brasserie is a space for snacks and relaxation; the colourful, circular Pod contains one large-screen television, two Playstations, a music centre and pool table; at the top is a large light area for private study, chilling (we saw two boys playing shove ha'penny and were pleased that at least some low tech games survive) and discussion work. On the ground floor is the spacious dining hall used by the rest of the school – good choice of hot, cold, snacks and veggie.

Parents (and Mr Fear) say it is a happy place where boys of all kinds are accepted. The younger boys we spoke to had found it easy to settle in and thought people friendly and the teachers helpful.

N

Pastoral care and discipline: The main focus is the vertical tutor groups of 24 where boys remain throughout their time at the school, staffed by two teachers – parents praised this. It encourages the helping of younger boys by older ones that is a feature of the school, eg prefects work with younger boys in form groups; sixth formers help with lunch time maths workshops. Thoughtful transition arrangements for the new year 7 boys, including no homework for the first month. Parents say any issues are dealt with well and quickly, although one felt boys could receive some more praise – 'a bit more carrot than stick' (school points out the head and deputy see boys with distinctions regularly).

A sensible, comprehensive anti-bullying policy – the boys we spoke to didn't see bullying as a problem – and a strict drugs policy: out for supplying and almost always for possession/using. Boys apply to become prefects; house and school captains are chosen with input from boys and staff.

Pupils and parents: About 40 per cent from the junior school, the rest from various independent and local state primaries. Most from the city and its suburbs plus others from as far afield as Chesterfield, Grantham, West Hallam, Matlock, Lichfield. Predominantly white British with a substantial Asian contingent and several parents who make sacrifices to send their sons to the school – down to earth boys who are neither arrogant nor snobbish, take academic achievement as a given and are very interested in the other activities too. Plenty of communication with parents – two detailed colour newsletters (Connect) a year and fortnightly electronic newsletters.

Old Boys cover a wide political spectrum including Ken Clarke (Conservative), Ed Balls and Geoff Hoon (Labour), Ed Davey (Lib Dem); also DH Lawrence, Geoffrey Trease (author); Gordon Richardson (ex governor of the Bank of England), Jesse Boot (founder of Boots the Chemist's), Jonathan Charles (BBC news presenter); Andrew Turner (international athlete), Henry Nwume (Olympic bobsleigh team).

Entrance: For year 7, exams in English, maths and reasoning plus interview for all non junior school candidates – looking for above average ability with some extra spark. About 70 places available for outside candidates: about 100 interviewed after exams have been marked. Can take up to 120 but won't lower standards to maintain numbers. A few places available for years 8-10 by academic and general interviews.

Six to 12 boys join the sixth from outside: interview plus Bs at GCSE in AS/related subjects and C or better in others.

Exit: Almost all to a broad range of universities – majority to Russell Group and other top universities, for a wide variety of courses (medicine, vet science and dentistry popular); a respectable number to Oxbridge (more Cambridge than Oxford) and the best London universities, mostly for maths, sciences and business management/economics.

Only a few leave after GCSE for sixth form colleges, often to do courses not on offer at the school or for financial reasons.

Money matters: Part scholarships not related to parental incomes; means-tested bursaries from year 7 (up to full fees) awarded on basis of entrance exams and interviews; music scholarships (auditions in June); bursary support for foreign trips. The bursary fund is due to be developed as part of the forthcoming 500th anniversary celebrations.

Sixth form: Ogden Trust science scholarships up to full fees; school bursaries up to full fees.

Remarks: A very strong all-round school, achieving academic and extra-curricular excellence while keen to avoid being a hothouse. As one parent put it, 'They know boys – they work them hard, feed them well and give them lots of exercise.'

Nunnykirk Centre for Dyslexia

Netherwitton, Morpeth, Northumberland, NE61 4PB

• Pupils: 30, including 15 weekly boarders; 25 boys, 5 girls • Ages: 9–18 • Non-denom • Fees: Please apply to school • Independent

Tel: 01670 772685
Email: secretary@nunnykirk.co.uk
Website: www.nunnykirk.co.uk

Head Teacher: Since 2008, Mrs Carol Hodgson BA PGCE NPQH ACFPS(SpLD/Dyslexia) BDA-Approved-Teacher. Been here since 1986, formerly as SENCo and deputy head; her husband also teaches at the school. Mrs Hodgson is in 'her dream job' because, despite the frustrations of having to watch and wait as parents and children jump through far too many hoops to gain a supported place here, she remains steadfast in her belief that it is 'a privilege just to be here – every teacher wants to make a difference, but here it's so marked'.

Academic matters: This is a CreSTeD SP school specialising in dyslexia and all the associated info-processing quirks that huddle under that umbrella term. With the right intervention, children improve quickly here. Ofsted were uncharacteristically charmed by what they saw but couldn't put their finger on how they did it. Cast aside all objective criteria, stop ticking boxes and switch to subjective mode – a good school is an affair of the heart. It's the individual focus, the being known and liked, that enables these children to achieve so far beyond expectation, above and beyond the application of any modish methodology. Two former pupils recently received first class honours degrees at a good university and have both been asked by the university to stay on to study for a PhD. The school wants pupils to feel comfortable in telling people they are dyslexic and that requires confidence. No lack of academic rigour, plenty of challenge and achievements are both recognised and celebrated. Tiny classes, most four to five, max eight, one-to-one as necessary. Results put this school in the top five per cent of the value added tables – says it all.

National curriculum, all go for GCSEs, most tackle five to eight, and entry levels for those who need longer. English and maths, good IT, and options spanning history and geography through photography to rural science. No modern languages – 'They can do them later if they want'. Vocational subjects also popular. Big hands-on element in all things. Sixth form options vary from year to year – the school works with the pupils' choices and tries to accommodate all, including a range of academic and vocational qualifications. AS and A2 photography and art available. Classrooms are basic but certainly adequate; a science lab (home to corn snakes), art room, library and various multi-use spaces for music, drama, assemblies and group teaching. The cellars no longer store wine but provide an atmospheric gallery space to display high quality artwork.

Games, options, the arts: The extracurricular programme is an essential element of the rescue remedy, not only because achievements in other areas cross-fertilise performance in the classroom, but also because parts of the academic curriculum are embedded within it. Much of what they do is vigorous. Sport, given the numbers, is not competitive at school level, but they play the customary ball games and athletics; plenty of playing fields and outdoor areas for sitting, thinking and playing. Floodlit courts for tennis, basketball and five-a-side. The gym, with weights, punchbag and array of exercise machines, is popular. Swimming and the use of the sports hall in Alnwick, and sailing (RYA quals) at Amble. Annual endurance race for

N

all, summer sports day with bbq, former pupils often returning to join in.

Plenty of art, well done – photography especially good. Music brave and enthusiastic, if not symphonic. Lots of plays. D of E, of course, and scouts, karting, mountain biking, canoeing, bird watching, cross-stitching, egg painting – all tastes catered for. Rural studies is the big thing – a number of pupils go on to qualify and earn their living in the field, literally.

Background and atmosphere: Founded in 1977 with just two boys and one girl, essentially for children not at home in the hurly-burly of bigger schools. Studies of pigs show that, though they like toys and nice buildings, they'd much rather have a good relationship with humans – children are no different. It's a tiny staff and all are encouraged to develop their own approaches and run hobbies: 'This is no place for anyone wanting to work 9-4'. Informal and shirt-sleeves-y. Stability and routine are the foundations of this notably calm, notably busy school. Most teaching is done in the manor house, though a couple of wooden outbuildings provide much-needed additional space. The gardens are very attractive, with a river running by, perfect for fishing, rafting and dam-building – it's the only school we've visited with a dedicated wellie shed. Fruit and veg grown in the walled garden – 'We eat what we produce' – and a menagerie of pigs, ducks, geese and turkeys (on the menu at Christmas – it might be remote but they don't run away from the real world here) all in the care of pupils. Bothy in the grounds, home to go-carts – hands-on mechanics all part of the learning curve: 'If you drive it and you break it, then you fix it' – fair enough.

You know you're remote when a sign on the school drive asks you to 'slow down for red squirrels'. And if you see a teenager reaching out of a window, standing on one leg with an arm in the air, it's only because they are trying to get a mobile phone signal. Set in the midst of Northumbrian loveliness, a few miles from Morpeth, this Greek revival John Dobson manor house is home to a hugely impressive hive of activity. Admittedly it could do with an injection of funds (where is Richard Branson when they need him?) but you cannot fault the quality of educational provision. These children enjoy a wealth of all that is good in education: highly committed and knowledgeable teachers, a curriculum that works for and with them rather than against them, and all the individual care and support they need. Staff here not only teach but also mentor and support in an old-fashioned but much-missed approach as role models, showing how to work and live alongside each other in a civilised society. A climate of mutual respect where independence and taking responsibility are not only encouraged but expected.

Pastoral care and discipline: Well looked after children greet visitors with unfussed naturalness, and these do – no reservations on that score: they are happy to chat and to talk about their work. Standards are high – important for those rougher diamonds when they first arrive. Manners are excellent, discipline not an issue, and they all know exactly where the line is. Smoking? Not a blind eye in the house. It's a big deal – parents instantly informed. Drugs? Out.

Weekly boarders come from as far south as Birmingham and as far north as Edinburgh. No more than two to a room in the warren upstairs. It may look well worn, but they don't mind this a bit – it's fun. Supervision levels are high, older ones guide the younger ones with a warm welcome for new arrivals. So much goes on in the evening, no time for telly, and it's not missed. Day pupils welcome to stay on for activities. Plenty of computer use, but Facebook not allowed – 'They can do that at home'. Former pupils have set up their own Nunnykirk website for networking.

Food is good, the pupils reckon – high praise. They're not mad, all of them, including parents, about the gluten-free diet, and some pounce on the toaster when they get home. Additives are out, sugar rare, fish oils in, fruit abounds. The head is certain this makes a difference, keeps them calmer and more focused. A written record is kept of what each child eats. Healthy living tuck shop.

Student council and an anonymous pupil voice box, though most happy just to chat with the head about any concerns. Efforts are made to mix with the local community despite location – excellent work experience for years 10 and 11 with local businesses. Trips to the cinema and theatre and overseas visits for sixth formers.

Pupils and parents: Pupils a mixed bunch socio-economically, spanning the 50 per cent funded by their LA to the scions of stately homes. More girls needed. Because this is the only school of its type between Oxford and John O'Groats, a big geographic mix (they offer weekly boarding). For many parents this is not at all what they wanted, so the school goes to great lengths to allay fears and thereafter keep in touch – parents united in grateful applause. Day children from 45-minute radius.

Big expectations made of parents – 'If work is sent home, we expect it to be done – and we expect parents to help' – though many parents are grateful for the offer of teacher-supported prep in school. It's all about partnership, which means 'parents have got to make an effort, too'. One parent described it as 'feeling part of a large happy family', crediting not just the teaching staff but also cooks, cleaners, gardeners, matron – everybody – for their work in creating such a special atmosphere. Another parent told us that she had 'gone from constantly worrying about her child's future to being confident in his development,' since moving him here from a mainstream school where his learning difficulties were 'neither identified nor managed'. A training day for parents where you can find out what they do, how they do it, how you can help. If your child thrives remarkably, they won't hang on – but many opt to stay nevertheless – they reckon they'll do even better. Informative website.

Entrance: Careful selection process. All the usual reports, but the (long) interview's the thing. Boys and girls here are refugees from mainstream schools with, most of them, anything from an antipathy to a horror of being educated, plus a history of being teased or bullied. Repairs to damaged self esteem are all part of the package, but no entrenched EBDs of any sort – they're outside their specialism: 'If we feel we can't help there's no point'. IQs reckoned from 95 up. Formal acceptance after a trial half term when, if a child has settled, an IEP is drawn up.

Entrance to sixth form is not automatic. Year 11 students follow an interview process and their best interests are discussed with parents and staff.

Exit: Careful advice precedes post-16 decision making, finding the right course at the right college. It's a huge leap, obviously, reliant on the self belief they've acquired. They go on to the full rainbow – degree courses to clock making. Decided bias in favour of hands on, fresh air careers.

Money matters: Some bursaries for private feepayers. For parents seeking to persuade their LA to apply the statement, the news is that, sadly, although the needs haven't changed, the funding has, and it's getting harder.

Remarks: Parents describe it as 'a little dyslexic oasis'.

Oakham School

Chapel Close, Oakham, Rutland, LE15 6DT

- Pupils: 895 (450 boys/445 girls); 415 full boarders • Ages: 10–18
- C of E • Fees: Day £15,615–£17,625; Boarding £23,955–£29,355 pa
- Independent

Tel: 01572 758758
Email: admissions@oakham.rutland.sch.uk
Website: www.oakham.rutland.sch.uk

Headmaster: Since 2009, Mr Nigel Lashbrook BA (late forties). Educated at King's Heath Boys' Technical School (he was one of the last grammar school intake) and Hertford College, Oxford, where he read chemistry, played in the university's 2nd cricket XI and captained his college rugby side. Stayed on at Oxford to train as a teacher and began teaching career at Manchester Grammar School, where he taught science and coached rugby and cricket teams. After eight years moved south to Tonbridge School as head of science and chemistry. Later became a housemaster and, at the age of 40, second master. Jumped at the opportunity to become acting head for a term while head was on sabbatical – he did so well that returning head predicted, 'I don't think you'll be here for long'. Sure enough, he was appointed head of King's Bruton soon after and spent five years at the helm there before moving to Oakham.

Approachable, affable and ambitious, he took to Oakham like a duck to water. Married to Jill, a geography and economics teacher. They live on site and have two grown up sons and daughter at Oakham.

A firm believer in education not just being about what happens in the classroom, he is proud of the fact that Oakham manages to be a 'happy and successful' school 'without being a hothouse in any shape or form'. He's determined, too, to open Oakham's doors to pupils who would thrive at the school but whose parents can't afford to send them and is busy developing stronger links with local state schools, especially the 11-16 Academy. Proud of Oakham's sense of community – the school has a lively volunteering programme and the school's musicians give free (and very well attended) concerts for the town at All Saints' Church every Wednesday.

Academic matters: Results get better and better. In 2013, 50 per cent of grades were A*/A grades whilst 85 per cent were A*/B. Twenty-six subjects on offer at AS/A2 – all the usual ones, plus business studies, classical civilisation, economics, PE and sport studies and politics. Prides itself on being an innovative school and has offered the IB since 2000. In 2013 average IB points score was 36, with nearly 42 per cent scoring 38 or more points. School helps pupils decide between IB and A levels. Deputy head reckons it's a myth that the IB is only for the brightest – 'It depends on the breadth of pupils' academic interest,' he says, 'but it's quite transformative in developing a much broader approach to their work'.

At GCSE, 61 per cent of grades were A*/A in 2013. All core subjects (maths, English, modern languages and the sciences) are now examined through the more academically rigorous IGCSE. Unlike some comparable schools, Oakham still submits its results for listing in the league tables. 'But,' says the head, 'it's just a snapshot. There is far more to what we offer than the league tables show.'

Impressive computerised language labs where pupils learn French from year 7. German and Spanish on offer from year 8. Everyone takes at least one language at GCSE, but most take two. Setting for all in maths, French and science from year 9. Up until GCSE, maximum class size is 24, though often much smaller, whilst A level and IB classes tend to have ten pupils or fewer. SEN supported by team of four learning support teachers. School prefers to give in-class support rather than take pupils out of class – no charge made for this.

Games, options, the arts: School talks a lot about the 'total curriculum' and the importance of pupils achieving their full potential in every sense. With this in mind, opportunities galore in sport and the arts. By any measure, a very sporty school – independent school of the year in the Daily Telegraph Sport Matters Awards a few years ago, 1st XV rugby side reached the final of the Daily Mail U19 national schools' rugby cup in 2011. Loads of top sportsmen and women started at Oakham – GB Olympic bronze hockey medallist Crista Cullen, cricketer Stuart Broad and rugby internationals, Lewis Moody, Alex Goode and Tom Croft, to name a few. School has more than 40 acres of games pitches (pretty much the summer home of ECB age group county cricket), sports centre, 25m indoor pool, two all-weather pitches, squash courts and a fitness centre. Around 30 sports on offer, including cycling, golf and sailing (on nearby Rutland Water), but main sports are rugby, hockey, cricket and athletics for boys and hockey, netball, tennis and athletics for girls. Seven hundred pupils take part in competitive sport, from 1st XV rugby to polo. Some weekends the school fields six rugby or hockey teams per year group. Over 60 staff involved in sports coaching – 12 full-timers, 20 visiting coaches and some 30 teachers from the common-room.

Drama is an integral part of the school. Two hundred and fifty-seat Queen Elizabeth Theatre hosts four main school productions a year (rehearsals for Little Shop of Horrors in full swing when we visited), along with shows by touring companies. Each house competes for the MacFadyen Shield, given to the school by Pride and Prejudice actor Matthew MacFadyen, a former pupil. Music just keeps expanding, with 600 instrumental lessons a week (some of the instrumental teachers travel from as far afield as London and Manchester). Around 80 concerts a year. A quarter of pupils sing in a choir and for the past four years pupils have won the competition to compose a fanfare for the Royal Opera House. The go-ahead music department is the first in the school to offer the subject as a Cambridge Pre-U qualification (alternative to A level.)

Art is amazing – everything from life drawing, abstracts and sculpture to textiles and jewellery. Has been offering critical and contextual studies (a modern form of art history) at A level for three years and has won The Good Schools Guide's award for the best results by independent school girls in the subject two years running. DT department rightfully proud of the brand new Jerwoods School of Design, which cost £2m and is equipped with state-of-the-art technology. Third formers (year 8s) get off to a productive start by making their own USB sticks, whilst an enterprising former pupil recently set up his own business selling the gun box he designed for his DT A level.

On two afternoons a week everyone does activities, trying their hand at everything from aerobics and film production to stone carving and yoga. From year 10 onwards pupils can opt for Duke of Edinburgh Award scheme (school was first to achieve 1,000 D of E golds), CCF or community service.

Background and atmosphere: Founded in 1584, sits in the centre of the prosperous market town of Oakham, surrounded by the rolling Rutland countryside. The main parts have the feel of a Cambridge college – quiet quads, old stone buildings overlooking immaculate lawns and flower beds. Much is owed to pioneering former head, John Buchanan, whose tenure from 1958 to 1977 oversaw the school's move to full independence and co-education, as well as the landscaped garden feel of the whole site.

No weekly boarding – very much a full boarding school, with so much going on at weekends that day pupils often pitch up to join in activities on Sundays. Day boarding, ie boarding three or four nights during the week, is a popular option. More flexible

0

boarding is available in the lower school (Jerwoods), where 10-13 year olds can opt for full or transitional boarding. The latter is a great way for youngsters to try boarding life (signing up for two to four nights a week) and see if they like it. As well as half-term, two 'leave-out' weekends every term when boarders can go home.

Lessons take place in two to four-storey purpose-built blocks. Superb Smallbone Library is a match for public library standards – spacious, well-stocked, computerised, it boasts a careers room, first floor for silent individual study and is open every day. New science faculty (opened in 2013) brings biology, chemistry, physics and sports science under one roof and there's a new auditorium that provides much-needed lecture space. Chapel twice a week and all meals eaten in school's light, airy dining hall.

Pastoral care and discipline: Sixteen houses, scattered across the large campus: four junior houses (two day and two boarding), 10 houses for 13-17 year olds (five for boys and five for girls) and two upper sixth houses (one for boys, one for girls). Comfortable, well-kept houses are run by staff, who have teaching responsibilities too. Useful 'settling in' guide for new pupils, with wise advice from prefects, like 'Don't be shy or afraid to get involved' and 'Give everything a go'. Houses all have common-rooms, quiet rooms and games rooms. One housemaster, aware that it would be all too easy for boarders to live in 'this little Oakham bubble', gets his GCSE boys to lead a debate every week – everything discussed, from politics to the Pope's visit to ideas for house trips. Sixth formers get rooms of their own, with younger years usually two, three or four to a room. Parents can express preferences for boarding houses but school has final say.

Rules clearly spelled out in Oakham's 'red book'. Anyone who tests positive for drugs or admits to drug misuse faces suspension or expulsion. Any pupil who supplies or brings drugs into the school is out straight away. One youngster expelled for drugs in last five years. Rules on alcohol and smoking crystal clear too. Head boy and head girl appointed every year, along with 22 school prefects (known as The Decem, because used to be 10 of them).

Plenty of sympathetic ears for pupils in need of advice and help – housemasters/mistresses, tutors, matrons, chaplains, medical centre and school counsellor. New pupils given mentors to guide them through their early weeks. Uniform is compulsory and pupils look well turned out as they hurry between lessons. Business suits for sixth formers, while boys wear blazers and ties and girls are clad in black and white tartan skirts and blazers. 'We want them to look smart,' says head. 'They are ambassadors for the school.'

Pupils and parents: Outgoing, enthusiastic bunch, determined to make the most of every second at Oakham. 'It's hard to stereotype an Oakhamian,' the head boy told us. 'There is so much on offer here for everyone and it's given me the chance to have a go at so many new things.' Most come from one to three hours' drive away. Around 10 per cent from overseas. Past pupils (known as OOs) are an eclectic lot – they include actors Matthew MacFadyen and Greg Hicks, director Katie Mitchell and international sports stars Lewis Moody, Stuart Broad, Lucy Pearson and Crista Cullen. Parents are a supportive crew – director of sport reckons 60 per cent regularly turn out to cheer teams on.

Entrance: More and more competitive to get in, with 2014 list almost full and filling up for subsequent years. Pupils come from all over the shop – 30+ different preps. At 11, intake is mostly youngsters from local primary schools and preps, while 13+ entrants tend to be mostly boarders. Entrance exams at 11+ in maths, English and verbal reasoning. At 13+ CE mark of 55 per cent needed or, for those coming from schools which

don't do CE, school's own exams in English, maths, French and science. Lower school pupils don't need to take exam to progress into middle school. Around 40 to 50 new pupils enter the sixth form each year – they need seven Bs at GCSE, with a minimum of Bs in the subjects to be studied in the sixth form.

Exit: A handful (seven per cent in 2013) leave after GCSEs, mainly to take vocational courses or subjects Oakham doesn't offer (like law, psychology or the dreaded media studies). At 18 virtually all progress to higher education – six Oxbridge places in 2013. The top universities are Leeds, Edinburgh, Durham, Newcastle, Exeter, King's College London and UCL, with the most popular courses including business management, economics, the sciences, engineering, maths, medicine, art and history.

Money matters: Variety of scholarships on offer – academic and music at 11, academic, music, art, DT, sport and all-rounder at 13. More available at 16, including the recent introduction of science and engineering scholarships for pupils to join the sixth form from a state school. Oakham scholarships offer five to 10 per cent off the fees, but the school says greater financial assistance may be available (in cases of proven need, this can be up to 100 per cent).

Remarks: A friendly, unpretentious and forward-thinking school that achieves impressive academic results. Far from being an academic hothouse, has high expectations and achievements across the board. For all-rounders who like rolling their sleeves up and throwing themselves into a staggering range of activities it's a very exciting place to be.

Oban High School

Soroba Road, Oban, Argyll, PA34 4JB

- Pupils: 1,040 boys and girls (capacity 1,300); 55 boarders • Ages: 11–18 • Non-denom • State

Tel: 01631 564231
Email: enquiries@obanhigh.argyll-bute.sch.uk
Website: www.obanhigh.argyll-bute.sch.uk

Head Teacher: Since August 2008, Mr Peter Bain MA MSc PGCE, who was educated at Musselburgh Grammar and read history at Edinburgh University, where he did his masters in the science of historical research, followed by PGCE at Jordanhill plus courses on headship and leadership. Started life in the civil service, which gives him the strategies to deal with the vagaries of Argyll and Bute Council education service. Six schools under his belt, from the depths of Fife to quite grand Trinity in Edinburgh: he comes from Eyemouth High School, Berwickshire, where he was depute head, and runs Oban High with four deputes.

Bouncy, caring and fun, he is married, with two children currently in the next door primary, and potty about surfing and snowboarding (neither of which spring to mind as usual Oban activities), waxes lyrical about drama. Runs a complex and complicated ship with children ranging from bright middle class, some with a fairly lively hippy ancestry, to offspring of local farmers and fisherfolk, and, following the closure of Drumore Special Unit, has a dedicated unit for autistic children with severe and complex needs (some of whom need two carers). We high-fived one young man several times during our tour. A fulfilling and challenging job, and one he relishes. 'My vision for the future of Oban High School is to work in partnership with pupils, parents and the local community to ensure that every single pupil becomes a successful learner by developing their knowledge and their talents to the best of their ability. We will endeavour to provide an enriched and broad experience beyond the academic, thus ensuring that they become confident individuals and effective contributors within society.' This is what he said, and he seems to be getting there (and how). Last year he commissioned a professional assessment from Investors in People which came out with flying colours.

Academic matters: Full range of subjects offered at Standard grade, Highers and Advanced Higher, including Gaelic (both for native Gaelic speakers and for learners – amongst whom the head counts himself, as do many of his staff) plus politics and sociology. Business studies popular and good success here. Results significantly above average for Scottish state schools in most subjects. Good emphasis on the academic. Advanced Higher mathematicians have mind-blowing residential weekends, maths challenge popular. Scientists work alongside the Scottish Association for Marine Science. Exciting new laser cutter (£10k) in design and tech department. ICT is taught in five well-equipped rooms but other departments have good access to the school's many computer facilities.

Effective learning support operates for those with specific learning difficulties. Class sizes generally smaller than in most state schools – average 23 for academic and 20 for practical subjects. SQA certificate an option. Home economics superb, master classes from chef of the Isle of Eriska Hotel (five star, two rosette restaurant – that sort of thing) and prize winners in national competitions. Subject choices (choose one subject from each column) include the Prince's Trust and skills for work, plus uniformed emergency services (fire brigade), land management, make up, hairdressing and hospitality. Pathways – a structured 24 week timetabled semi-secondment – allows pupils in S4 to try out various (more or less) service activities: the fire brigade were recruiting during our visit and the police expected to come on board shortly. Work experience too with the Northern Lighthouse Board – 12 would-be engineers learn how to make buoys. About 90 per cent stay on post Standard grades and a further 70 per cent for Advanced Highers.

No real problem getting staff – head has strategies to uncover Argyllshire wannabes, and is contemptuous of applicants who haven't done their homework before interview. School has silver award from Inverstors in People (the only one in Scotland). 'very good' HMIe reports.

Games, options, the arts: Large games/assembly hall, well-equipped dance/fitness studio, two gyms; wide range of sports available including sailing, climbing, basketball, rugby (uses Oban Rugby club as well as their own; currently a Scottish Rugby Union School of Rugby where those seeking to play for their country can get an early start), grass pitch with flood-lighting, footie (girls very strong) and badminton plus shinty, basketball, sailing, boxing, dance and cheer-leading. Cross-country running, athletics, hill-walking, climbing, canoeing and gorge-walking are timetabled in PE curriculum from S3 upwards, as is D of E. Number of golds. Serious and successful swimming (off campus).

Impressive wind-band, strings section, plus 75 strong prize-winning pipe band (world champions last year), samba band, choir and Gaelic choir (which competes successfully in the Royal National Mod). From 2013 will become a School of Traditional Music, offering specialist programmes in pipes, clarsach, accordion, voice, piano, guitar and fiddle for those aiming at conservatoire level. Music and drama have merged and all S1 and S2 learn keyboards. Dance, in conjunction with Taynuilt based Balletwest (who also use the hall for their outreach classes), is amazing – we could have been watching any professional troupe, anywhere. Scottish country dancing (hall – splendidly sprung – also used by locals). Fantastic art and really inspiring fabric and design, school took part in Homecoming

'09. Air-training corps, Scout troop, sea cadets. Plenty of other extra-curricular activities on offer – difficulties because of long distances and buses are generally overcome. Variety of trips in most disciplines, free for those on free school meals – no one is excluded.

Background and atmosphere: Smart looking façade conceals a mass of serious re-build, but the old school is still there. War memorials and jolly photographs. Dining hall is cashless and parents' handbook publishes list of food available with prices. S1 not allowed to leave school grounds during their first half term. Loads of displays throughout the school including an imaginative art gallery exhibiting students' creations.

Uniform is largely adhered to, with individual styling by some and a constant battle with girls and ties. Hostel for islanders and those who live afar, recently beset with problems but with a new manager at the helm it is up to scratch. Spare space available for the new S1s to stay and spend a couple of days in the school before their arrival in August.

Pastoral care and discipline: All year groups are divided into tutor groups of 20 pupils or fewer. Each has its own tutor and sixth year prefect buddies. Year groups are managed by a head of year and school depute. School boasts an attendance officer, health worker and social worker. 'Good discipline prevails with effective sanctions for those who don't conform' – often involving local social workers. All staff trained in assertive discipline. Successful Truancy Watch scheme operates in conjunction with the local community. Lots of certificates and awards. Local ministries (all 10 of them) support a chaplaincy centre H20, which in turn supports an array of local services via The Well and two and a half workers who – along with pupils – organise activities for pensioners and the disadvantaged. Huge charity input.

Pupils and parents: The lot, including incomers, but not many ethnic minorities. Majority Scottish, many travelling long distances from North Argyll and the Islands. Famous Old Boys/Girls: Iain Crichton-Smith (writer), Kirsten Campbell (BBC political correspondent) and Maureen Scanlon (MSP), Shona and Mairi Crawford (British Ladies' ski team) and Lorne McIntyre (author and journalist).

Entrance: Catchment area plus placing requests. Twenty plus feeder primary schools – some are tiny, with perhaps eight or nine pupils in total. Six are on the islands – this involves 'hopping on a plane or a ferry to visit those who will transfer to Oban that year; takes a whole day, rather than popping round the corner for a couple of hours'. Enormous care taken to ensure S1s are not swamped on arrival. Head visits all primary schools, as do the support for learning staff (if necessary) plus new form teachers; pupils and their parents visit the school.

Exit: Automatic jobs for all at the end of the summer term: Oban is a popular tourist destination. Come September/October, some may have gone off to university (mostly Scottish, very occasional Oxbridge), some to further education, training schemes or family firms (fishing, farming) and some may sneak back to school for a bash at further qualifications.

Remarks: Wow. Has to be one of the most challenging and inclusive schools in the United Kingdom. Brilliant – really holds the community together.

Old Palace of John Whitgift School

Linked school: Old Palace of John Whitgift Preparatory School

Old Palace Road, Croydon, CR0 1AX

• Pupils: 870 girls (550 seniors and 320 juniors) • Ages: 4–18
• C of E • Fees: £9,228–£12,480 pa • Independent

Tel: 020 8688 2027
Email: admissions@oldpalace.croydon.sch.uk
Website: www.oldpalace.croydon.sch.uk

Headmistress: Since 2011, Mrs Carol Jewell, MA PGCE DipEd NPQH CSBM, fifties. Preceded by a brief spell as acting head and a longish one as deputy, a role she took on in 2005, having originally joined the school in 1997 as director of music. Before that, had assorted teaching roles in a 'tiny' London sixth form college, a Banbury comprehensive and then (after a spell in Wales) at top-rated St George's School back home in Edinburgh (she's Scottish born and bred) where she achieved first senior management role, before heading south again. Rambling cross-country route (even Virgin Trains would shun the franchise) was dictated by husband's burgeoning career, first in further education, then IT. 'I was always following on – it's one of those inevitable things,' she says, matter of factly.

Though a musician by training (at St Andrew's, where she studied with Cedric Thorpe Davie), a head by inclination and posture. Nobody with such an immaculately straight back could, you feel, be anything else. Melodious voice helps, and is also useful cover for wry wit that's probably kept largely under wraps in school hours.

Her office, formal but friendly, sets her off to a T. Only drawback is its slightly thin, no doubt listed, walls that render conversations in adjoining office intermittently audible, though visitors distracted by delightful outlook from study windows – delightful medieval garden with (in season) suitably onomatopoeic bees – may not notice. (General gorgeousness means ever-present danger of 'oohs' and 'ahs' overload).

Her appointment follows a turbulent time for the school, which in 2008 acquired nearby Croham Hurst, a failing and less academic secondary. Parents on both sides greeted the news with fury, while damning comments in local press and (anonymously) online fuelled the flames.

Matters weren't helped by parental concerns about Dr Judith Harris, Mrs Jewell's predecessor. Though well-intentioned, she was felt to be dangerously progressive, taking Old Palace away from its academic roots and into territory few were comfortable with. 'She tried to make the school more like a comprehensive,' says one mother. 'The girls liked her but the discipline wasn't very good, or the finances,' says another.

School has something of a reputation for easing out heads who don't quite fit and announcement from parent body, the Whitgift Foundation, is a masterpiece of the genre, Dr Harris having apparently agreed that 'the situation presented her with a unique opportunity to pursue her career aspirations in education.' Yes, indeedy.

Mrs Jewell, who radiates copious amounts of 'all's well' reassurance, appears to share this consummate corporate nous. A safe pair of hands (expressive, too, says one old girl, with a conducting technique 'a bit like Sian Lloyd doing the weather forecast' – in a good way) she's definitely the von Karajan of the show, in overall charge of the whole kit and caboodle, prep and nursery too, with section leaders responsible for the day-to-day nitty gritty. School is now, think most, back to the road more travelled, bounded by the familiar trappings and traditions that were its pre-Dr Harris hallmark. 'very committed to the school,'

says one. 'She's bringing up the standards, getting it back to what it was. It had lost its way.'

Liked by many. 'Gorgeous,' was one verdict. Her emphasis on courtesy and manners – 'important because they are... everything to do with sensitivity' – she believes is just the sort of thing parents want to hear. Naturally good, you feel, at rising above problems, though not remote, thanks to a strong dose of gentle self-deprecation. 'As a Scot, I probably have some very traditional and quaint ideas,' she says. Parents, confounded by her suggestion for rustic game at school fair – 'It wasn't turnip throwing, but it was close,' says one – wouldn't disagree. Phrasing, too, can be a charming blast from the past. 'We don't need to have a fit of the vapours because we're expected to put out cups and saucers,' she says, explaining importance of hands-on rôle.

She's out and about a lot, running regular surgeries for parents, taking weekly assemblies at the prep school ('She's joyful,' was one pupil's verdict – no raffia work prizes, though) and, thanks to marvels of rigorous Scottish four year degree, also teaches Latin to pupils in years 7 and 9.

Though parents understand her need to stick to the official script, some feel she can over-adhere to the party line, giving impression that their concerns aren't being registered. One mother felt she was treated as 'a child [rather than] an intelligent professional'.

'I've always thought of her as a softish music mistress and very quiet, but I think behind the façade is a robust personality,' says an insider. With some aftershocks from the merger still to be negotiated, it's probably just as well.

Academic matters: Some schools would have merged and purged. Not this one, where decision was made to keep both sets of subject teachers for existing GCSE and A level students to minimise stress. Never any doubt that was a temporary measure, though, and around 15 jobs were shed (not all, as hoped, through voluntary redundancies) in 2011.

The long-drawn out nature of the affair, with juniors and some staff settling into Croham Hurst site in South Croydon (everyone was previously at Old Palace) perhaps accounts for varying shades of parental opinion that cover the pantone range.

'A Marmite school,' says one old girl of her time here, and little seems to have changed, with everything from effusion – 'I wanted the best education [my daughter] could get and I've been really pleased,' says one, to praise with reservations. 'I have mixed views,' says another.

Specific concerns include quality of maths teaching, felt to be variable, while loss of other talented specialists, notably art teacher, was also keenly felt. However, there's a sense that – finally – the worst is past. 'They've sorted the problems of transferring staff and children and it seems to have settled down now.'

Results bear this out, ranging from good to vintage: in 2013, A*/A grades were achieved in 58 per cent of GCSEs and 55 per cent at A level, where 79 per cent were A*/B. Plenty of choice post-16, with a good range of two-year AS subjects (including dance, critical thinking – one of school's Big Things – as well as DT, philosophy and PE) plus normal A2 selection (nice to see both Latin and Greek offered).

Given aspirations of pupils and parents, you'd expect maths and sciences to lead the popularity pack, as indeed they do, with twice as many taking biology and chemistry as physics (and psychology). Predictably good showing for English literature (less rigorous English language not offered), French and RS, with history the aberration, numbers plummeting to just two at A2 in 2012.

Good range of languages offered, modern and otherwise, with GCSE French (taught in sets, as is maths) way ahead on numbers, as is Latin. Some pupils also take Gujarati (Chinese and modern Greek pop up in other years) while Russian is available as a sixth form option.

Parents who, like particularly discriminating sundials, tend only to record the top results are, in general, satisfied with how their 'good, good girls who want to please their parents,' as one puts it, are doing. Mention of occasional 'over-exuberant' behaviour in recent inspection report causes head to bristle slightly – it's not a picture she recognises and tour of school elicits absolutely no signs of roaring, gorging or indeed anything untoward.

Not that we were encouraged to get too close. One drama teacher was notably un-keen on our presence. Elsewhere, we were ushered away from classroom doors if heads started to turn, for fear (presumably) of providing an alternative source of interest. Entertainment value (much appreciated in sea of tranquility) came in the form of really lively A level biology lesson led by an amiable teacher and involving a great deal of yeast. 'Smell this!' said animated student, thrusting a steaming, strongly scented beaker in our direction.

The overwhelming impression, based on brief glimpses of heads bent conscientiously over books, was of orderly, efficient learning in classes that average around 20 up to GCSE, dropping to far fewer at A level (three isn't uncommon) and where motivated, bright girls do their utmost to get their grades. Learning support, as with the juniors, is in place, with range of needs catered for, says Mrs Jewell, including ADHD, though emphasis on pace and focus would indicate compatibility with mild difficulties only (and 'we're not equipped to take on children with serious SpLds.') With parents' experience in some cases at odds with official line, dyslexia in particular, it would be worth, if possible, asking to speak to parents who know the ropes.

In contrast, there's excellent joined up academic support. Stunning library, far more than a pretty face, features syllabus-linked book displays helping the focused to plan their own 'now read on' programmes: one conscientious modern language specialist was ploughing her way through Gabriel García Márquez's oeuvre to complement modern language studies. Key subjects also have timetabled clinics run by staff and older pupils, more informal help on tap, willingly given by tutors. 'You don't feel as if it's a hassle,' says pupil. 'They'll say "Come and find me".'

School is currently trying to up parental involvement, which doesn't come naturally to all. Website goes back to basics, highlighting (startlingly for some) importance of eye contact, praise and even turning up at child's concerts. Message reinforced in workshops. Mrs Jewell herself addresses parents on need to 'read aloud to your child every night, ideally into their early teens,' getting a fair few abashed looks in the process. 'I said "Come now, there's no need to look down and be apologetic",' she says.

A few idiosyncrasies to get used to, headed by two-weekly timetable – a breeze once acclimatised, apparently, allowing longer, more productive lessons – and separate though apart presence of year 6s. From the security of own 'little empire' as head puts it (two bright classrooms and pleasant courtyard garden), they make controlled forays into main school, while imaginative 'expanding horizons' curriculum knits humanities together, with Victorian life and times, for example, covered by church visit (RS) and river trip (geography). It all adds a dash of va va voom to what can, post 11 plus, be a fallow year.

As to the future? You could be picky and argue that an all girls' selective school should regularly trounce the equivalent boys' version. No chance thus far, with Whitgift the outlier, streets ahead especially at A levels. Trinity (co-ed at sixth form) does better too.

There is, though, potential to be stronger still after 2013, when the last batch of merged school intake complete their GCSEs (2015 for A levels), especially given head's uncompromising focus on quality over quantity. Though school isn't at capacity (it's down 20 in current year 7) she won't 'bring in girls to be miserable' to make up numbers. 'We allow a bit of scope but it's an academic setting.'

Games, options, the arts: Hockey sticks not really jolly, with parent mood neutral to apathetic. 'She doesn't like group sport,' says one father, while another confirmed that 'If your girl's sporty, you're not going to go to Old Palace.' Prospectus, by way of corroboration, doesn't go a bundle on action shots (girls raising hands in class is about as energetic as it gets) though fab new pool (devoid of pupils) does feature and is extremely popular, with plans to increase squad training for the best and lunchtime clubs for the rest soon. Recent introduction of football could also prove a popular move, bumping up the number of sports, dance and fitness-related extra-curricular activities – which also includes Duke of Edinburgh – to a round half dozen.

Arts and DT include lively pieces, nicely displayed. Biggest buzz, however, comes from performance side, admirably embracing school's history and culture. Drama department plans to 'develop work that explores the theme of pilgrimage to Canterbury' (school was on the route). For the musically inclined, the take is topical rather than Chaucerian. While three smaller music rooms are used for teaching (with as much fabulous classic choral singing as you'd hope for, including monthly evensong in the Minster), biggest is dominated by thriving steel bands, one per year group, with many pupils playing in highly-regarded external ensembles like Croydon steel orchestra and heading off to Notting Hill Carnival.

Background and atmosphere: Some of the oldest buildings in use as a school within the M25. Site of Croydon Minster, dating back to the ninth century and long-time summer palace for assorted Archbishops of Canterbury, who abandoned it in the 18th century for a drier new build. Somehow escaped demolition, though endured a century's rough treatment as, amongst other things, a calico bleaching factory, before being given to the Sisters of the Church, who founded a school here in 1899. Visitors flock (by pre-arrangement) to gawp at early brick guardroom (now library), medieval great hall (one of south England's finest) and 15th century chapel.

The site, in current scholastic incarnation, works perhaps unexpectedly well, though with some of the more idiosyncratic uses of space, such as IT support housed in gallery pew off the chapel, an effort of will can be required to banish Hogwarts-related thoughts.

Though there's a bit of a sub fusc feel on the cathedral side – and little in the way of outside space – the school modernises where it can (there's an exceedingly nice, recently refurbished, year 7 science lab, for example). However, those in search of light-flooded rooms are best served by the attractive Shah building across the road.

Housing a large sports hall, attractive language and performing arts rooms together with super dining hall, where girls linger at the long, attractive dining tables complete with fresh flowers (a major disaster if they fall over), it is also home to comfortable sixth form common-room. 'They know how to live,' says teacher, surveying end of day overflowing bins.

With such an array of goodies to enjoy, it's unsurprisingly easy to forget the contemporary world outside, though total escape from Croydon's signature tower blocks is impossible – a prize-winning specimen rears up, Tripod-like, across the road.

Contemporary life does have its uses, however, what with the handy tram stop located a stone's throw away from the front door, though many parents prefer to drive. You sense slight disapproval from Mrs Jewell, who feels parents worry unnecessarily about the area. Even the 2011 riots, though not exactly the publicity you'd seek, left the school completely untouched. '[Parents] are more edgy. The girls are fine,' she says.

However, while we're told that for hungry sixth formers, the main city centre feature of note is the nearby McDonalds' lunch menu, location is an issue for a minority of families. 'Mrs Jewell won't have it but the middle of Croydon isn't what it used to be,' says a grandparent. 'If the girls are coming out of school late, you have to pick them up.'

For majority of parents, though, the charm of the school trumps the area. Variations of 'girls are so privileged to be here and they just don't appreciate it,' were heard more than once.

Pastoral care and discipline: These are, you feel, girls with high energy levels, carefully checked by fairly heavy staff presence in the corridors and on surging staircases: one pupil departs for the day trailing slipstream of bubbles aft, wand and detergent to the fore. Ban on mobile phones up to sixth form helps create calm atmosphere, thinks head, though wonders how long technological tide can be resisted. Outside, there's the wonderful Michael who mans the street crossing and is renowned for impeccably good humoured early morning banter and 100 per cent recall of every pupil, parent and sibling.

House system is the glue that creates the unifying bond between youngest and oldest pupils. Even year 6s elect officers, take an active part in meetings and 'may find themselves planning and speaking in assembly,' says head. Strong ceremonial aspect includes regular house assemblies in the delightful chapel as well as an end of term church service, with bannered-up procession down the aisle.

Pupils praise what one describes as a 'big support network with a form tutor and deputy form tutor'. Essential for girls expected to care for younger children where, says Mrs Jewell, 'life is not always easy,' and also the key to swift resolution of bullying ('friendship issues' as ever the biggest cause) 'My daughter had a problem with a friend but the class teacher called us and it was quickly sorted out,' says father.

Pupils and parents: Splendidly multi-cultural, spanning the gamut of faiths, cultures and backgrounds and seemingly an accurate reflection of the local area rather than gated ghetto for privileged Caucasians. Old Girls (strong, loyal network – hugely active) approve. 'I go down for founders' day and it's lovely to see the church full of every colour and race under the sun, all wearing the Old Palace uniform. Very moving,' says one.

Whitgift Foundation does what it says in the prospectus – some families suffer real hardship after losing jobs (and in case of one parent we spoke to, home as well) yet manage to keep daughters at the school, thanks to the near 100 per cent bursaries it can provide.

Families praise the sense of community while not necessarily playing much part in it. While there's equal involvement of both parents in their daughters' education (and fathers dominate at drop off and pick up), interest tails off when it comes to socialising with other parents, and the PTA survives, but sometimes only by a thread. 'It's something I can take or leave,' said one mother we spoke to. She wasn't alone. 'A very mixed crowd,' said another parent. '[Some] are lovely individuals, trying to work very hard to pay the fees and keep their jobs..so they genuinely can't get involved. With others, the idea of paying [for] an event is ridiculous because what are the fees for?'

Entrance: 11 plus for all, including current year 6s, with mixture of written and online tests in maths, English and reasoning, together with observation of social skills and interviews for candidates and parents. Those who need it will be allowed extra time (this wasn't, thought parents, the case until very recently).

Slightly pared down version at 10 plus. Occasional places on offer up to year 10 – same subjects again but minus social interaction, plus satisfactory school report. School reporting some readmissions when girls who secure grammar school place find it not to their liking. 'We don't crow,' says head. 'It takes courage to retrace your steps.'

Catchment area largely but not exclusively local, with increasing levels of interest from Wandsworth and Clapham fringes as London day school bunfight for places continues to superheat.

At sixth form level, you're not left in any doubt as to what the school wants. 'Is Old Palace right for your daughter?' thunders large font heading, warning of the dangers of poor choices that could leave students to 'flounder' and feel 'unstretched..lost and overwhelmed.' The bottom line: don't leave home without a goodly number of B grades at GCSE as bottom line minimum and preferably better.

Exit: Almost everyone to well regarded universities. Five to Oxbridge in 2013. Others to top universities including Imperial, Warwick and Durham. Favourites are headed by science, chemistry and biomedics in particular. Law also popular, ditto psychology, otherwise broad range of subjects and destinations.

Money matters: Whitgift Foundation does what it says in the prospectus – some families suffer real hardship after losing jobs (and in case of one parent we spoke to, home as well) yet manage to keep daughters at the school, thanks to the near 100 per cent bursaries it can provide. Scholarships for academics, music and sport.

Remarks: It's a question of Annie, get your grades. Having had a period of thinking outside the box, this school seems to have hopped back in to give parents what they want – a decent, solid education in beautiful surroundings with few surprises. Message to outside world is just what you'd want to hear (unless sports success is the deal breaker). How well it matches up to the reality of life on the inside remains an evolving story.

The Oratory School

Linked school: Oratory Preparatory School

Woodcote, Nr Reading, RG8 0PJ

• Pupils: 430 boys – 240 board, 190 day • Ages: 11–18 • RC foundation but all faiths welcome • Fees: Day £15,435–£21,390; Boarding £20,715–£29,535 pa • Independent

Tel: 01491 683500
Email: enquiries@oratory.co.uk
Website: www.oratory.co.uk

Head Master: Since 2000, Mr Clive Dytor MC KHS MA (Cantab) MA (Oxon), (fifties). Attended Christ College, Brecon thence to Cambridge to read Oriental Studies (speaks Arabic). Joined Royal Marines, serving in Belfast and the Falklands (where he earned that MC). Back to university, Oxford this time, to read theology and then church work and first teaching post at Tonbridge. It was the writings of Cardinal Newman that set in motion his conversion to Catholicism and, via a housemaster post at St Edward's, Oxford, brought him to the school the Cardinal founded. In our previous review Mr Dytor was described as 'towards the top of the strictness scale', so imagine the intake of breath when we spied two swishy bamboo canes on the bookcase. They are for historic reference only, the one with a broken handle being a gift from a former pupil. Ouch. In fact, as parents predicted, we found Mr Dytor charming: owlish, dapper, academic but not aloof, he is robust in his commitment to The Oratory's founding principles and reassuringly 'old school' in his values (although, interestingly, he sets high value on emotional intelligence). He wants Oratory boys to be 'the kind who would gladden any parent's heart were they to be brought home by a daughter' (or even a son, we hope). Oratory boys we spoke to said he was 'amazing, he doesn't just know our names, he really knows us.' Parents concur, 'he is a very good communicator,' and, 'he genuinely cares for the boys.' Named Tatler Head Master of the Year in 2013.

In just over a decade Mr Dytor has reversed the school's fortunes: finances are healthy, places full, significant capital projects completed. He describes his headship as a vocation and is still fired up with enthusiasm and energy for future plans including a new swimming pool and theatre to be completed in 2013/14, and wireless IT in all teaching areas. Mr Dytor's wife, Sarah, is a musician and they have two adult children.

Academic matters: Mr Dytor describes academic results as, 'inching up' although this is perhaps a little too incremental for some parents. Relatively non-selective intake yields solid results at GCSE (IGSEs now in English language and literature, French, Spanish, three sciences). Majority achieving A/B at GCSE with improving numbers of A* in English, maths, sciences (nearly 34 per cent A*/A grades overall in 2013). Wide choice of subjects at A level and school will accommodate single students who wish to study, for instance, Dutch, Latin, Italian. All take RS GCSE (Catholic syllabus) and subject remains compulsory in the sixth form, although it is not a public examination subject. As for A level results, leaving aside art (see below), majority achieve A to C but there's clearly still work to do on the A* front (nearly 29 per cent A*/A grades in 2013). Time spent talking to the director of studies about the school's 'value added' results will add some colour and detail to the statistics. Academic high flyers certainly not held back as Russell Group and Oxbridge success attests. Sixth form are encouraged to do the Extended Project Qualification and have tackled subjects as diverse as military law, hotel management, and Greek tragedy. There's a new head of SEN and for boys who need it there is the option of taking nine, rather than 10, GCSEs, the remaining timetable being reserved for curriculum support – thus improving final outcomes. A system of mini reports ('fortnightlies') means that any academic problems/homework issues are not allowed to slide too far. Parents we spoke to were on the whole pretty positive about this provision and felt that it would be hard for a boy to fall down any cracks. 'Our son feels secure, that the school is on his side.'

Lessons we observed were in good order: challenging, information-rich chalk and talk in A2 classical civilisation, sparky and good humoured quick-fire thinking challenges in first year English. Science labs have been refurbed but we were delighted to find boys and Bunsen burners at the original wooden benches with old burns and battle scars still visible beneath the new varnish. Usual technology seemed to be present but not dominant in labs and classrooms; library peacefully free from such modern menaces but is, apparently, soon to be networked into the 21st century.

The area is hardly undersupplied with high-achieving academic schools but these are not for everyone. Parents we spoke to had chosen The Oratory because it offered their boys an academic environment that is individually challenging without being overly competitive – along with lashings of unashamedly competitive sport. School acknowledges that the timetable might seem a little old fashioned and some parents observed that there is a certain amount of 'wasted time' post games that could be put to more profitable use. Dr GSG tentatively wonders if shaving just one or two hours a week from the time spent on corpore sano might not improve the mens sana still further.

Games, options, the arts: Let there be no mistake, this is not a school for boys who don't enjoy running around or those who raise a cynical eyebrow at competitive sport (such boys do exist). Sport is big here, pitches seemingly endless and there's nowhere to hide. Cricket is played on a glorious sward with views over the Chilterns and Thames valley and, apparently, 'the best match teas.' Morning lessons and lunch are followed by two and a half hours of rugby, football, cricket, rowing, real tennis, shooting, swimming, golf, polo and the rest (delete as appropriate according to preference/season). Sport happens every day, apart from Thursdays when it's CCF, compulsory until fifth year after which the less military minded can take part in conservation work or community service. No wonder The Oratory was crowned Sports School of the Year in the 2011 Education Business Awards (this in addition to similar accolades in previous years). The yellow and black-hooped Oratorian rugby players are formidable foes for many opposing teams drawn from larger schools. Celebrations for the school's 150th anniversary were heightened by the 1st XV declaring an unbeaten season, as did the junior colts A and B teams. No sloping off for sixth formers either. Sport may be big, but it's also inclusive and everyone gets to play in matches whether representing school or house. We asked a number of boys what they thought about this during our visit but were met with rather blank responses. 'If you don't like rugby you can do shooting.' And boys who don't want to do rugby or shooting? 'It's probably not the right school for them,' we were told but got the impression that such boys were beyond the imagination of Oratory chaps.

And so to art. Some schools have art rooms, others may boast art departments; the Oratory says it has an art department but what it really has is a kingdom. Results in art and design subjects, both at GCSE, A level, Pre-U and foundation (yes, foundation) are in a league of their own. School has won GSG top boys' school for A level art award an unprecedented six times in the last eight years. The head of art (who lives on site in the cottage where J R R Tolkein wrote several of his books) may look the part with his paint spattered tie and avuncular twinkle but while one hand urges the boys forward to explore their own and others' creativity, the other has a death grip on the specification details of the syllabus. It's clearly a winning combination. Wonderful facilities (printmaking, etching, ceramics, DT, sculpture) arranged around a gallery corridor with tomes on plinths open at pertinent pages. A professional painter gives drawing lessons or, as he describes it, 'lessons in how to look,' and boys work standing (no chairs allowed) at easels. There's a dark room too; in these days of ubiquitous cameras and instant images, all boys learn the ancient art of developing photographic prints.

Culture more than holds its own alongside sport. Plenty of music, Schola Cantorum sings at masses, vespers and school functions and there's a variety of bands, orchestras and ensembles. Popular programme of visiting speakers. The Hopkins society (named after poet Gerard Manley Hopkins who was a master at The Oratory School under Cardinal Newman in the 1860s) oversees cultural activities such as trips to the theatre and also runs a bookshop. Sixth formers debate and deliver papers on a range of topics at Windhover Society meetings (named after Hopkins' poem – nice to see the old chap getting a double look in). Drama is a popular after school option, girls are borrowed from nearby Our Lady's Abingdon or St Anne's Caversham, but as an academic subject it is perhaps more Cinderella than Fame. The soon to be finished 200 seat theatre complete with the latest sound and lighting technology may inspire future thespians.

Background and atmosphere: The Oratory School was founded in 1859 by Cardinal John Henry Newman. Newman, who was beatified in 2010, was a Christian thinker and educational pioneer and the school was intended as a boarding school along the lines of the English public schools ('Eton minus its wickedness') serving England's Catholic community. Newman's personal motto is also the school's: 'Cor ad cor loquitur' (Heart speaking to heart). While it remains a proudly Catholic institution the school welcomes boys of all faiths and none; the doctrine of valuing the special gifts of every individual makes The Oratory an accepting and welcoming community.

The school may be only 20 minutes' drive from Reading but enjoys, to quote Hopkins out of context (but not out of county), a 'sweet especial rural scene.' Visitors ascend a drive flanked by red maples and velvety playing fields leading to the Queen Anne style manor house, home to the school since its move from Birmingham in 1942. Grounds, all 400 acres of them, are immaculately maintained. Front of house is impressive with echoing marble foyer and arresting 'black room' (black and gold are Papal colours) used for concerts and teas. Business areas the usual confusion of scuffed corridors and unremarkable teaching rooms. Pace art department, school not lavishly decorated with boys' efforts, rather restrained, formal atmosphere prevails – but our visit was at the start of term.

Pastoral care and discipline: Boarding houses we saw were in pretty good nick, there are two brand new and three refurbished. Seniors have single study bedrooms, younger boys are four to a room and occupants are mixed up every half term. St Philip house is for junior boys (11-13) and they have separate recreation, social and teaching areas as well as their own sports teams and clubs. Day boys have a locker room (and we do mean just lockers, nary a chair or poster) in each house but perhaps they are not intended to linger here. Resident house parents, live-in tutors plus a day house mother and gappies oversee proceedings. In senior houses boys are responsible for washing and ironing their own clothes – with some assistance at first; great training for future domestic harmony we thought but limited evidence of ironing (although the Spanish boys are apparently exemplary at this task). Sensible rules re use of laptops, mobiles, social networking sites. Junior chapel is in a rather charming former tithe barn, senior chapel is a slightly less inspiring modernish building. Daily prayers in houses, weekly assembly for all; Sunday evening Mass for all boarders, optional for day boys. Non-Catholic parents we spoke to seemed to have different perceptions of the religion's role in school life. One thought it was a dominant (dominating) feature; another didn't think it impinged too much on their boy's school day. All participate in the spiritual life of the school and Catholic and non-Catholic boys serve at Mass.

Not much in the way of transgression: one imagines exhaustion may be a contributory factor (the head's mantra is 'a busy boy is a happy boy'); three hours of games every day plus weekend matches and evening activities such as circuit training must take the edge off boyish over-exuberance. In those cases where it doesn't, standard regime of detentions is called into play. After matches on Saturday boarders can go into Reading; some parents felt older boys left a little too much to their own devices on these trips. Houses have cinema and steak nights, pool competitions etc and there are socials with girls from Queen Anne's Caversham and St George's Ascot as well as ballroom dancing for the lower sixth – culminating in a ball held at Queen Anne's. Our guides thought the food was 'excellent'. 'There's loads of it. It's boy food,' they said. So, anyone for seconds of slugs, snails and puppy dogs' tails? Breakfasts came in for especial praise: 'you can have cereal and then the works, every day'. Boarders can supplement with toast, pot noodles etc from the kitchens on each floor. Newly formed food council has managed to get Cocoa Pops onto the breakfast menu but on the whole one feels that the school is closer to benign dictatorship than democracy. The school day officially ends at 7pm after prep but day boys may question the logic of going home; some live up to an hour's drive away and there's no bus service. Parents advise packing provisions for pick up at 7pm because supper is not provided for day boys (although those staying on for other activities get supper and it's not billed). Boys can stay overnight if they are involved in evening activities but we have also heard that some GCSE options necessitate staying in school until 9pm. Boarding numbers certainly increase in the upper years, pragmatism triumphing over home comforts perhaps.

Pupils and parents: The old fashioned certainties are all present and correct here. Boys are confident, smart, polite and look you in the eye. RC and non-RC – all religions welcome. Day and flexi-boarding pupils come from Reading and South Oxfordshire villages. Boarding is a cosmopolitan mix of UK boys, those from European Catholic families (Spain in particular, some for just one year) and Russians; fewer Chinese boys than at other places. No parents' association (Mr D seemed to be allergic) but plenty of opportunities for fraternisation at matches etc.

Entrance: Numbers from nearby Oratory Prep (co-ed up to 13) or on-site junior house. For entry at 13, CE pass at around 55 per cent required plus head's report from previous school and interview. Special consideration will be given to brothers of boys already in school and the sons of Old Boys. Five C grades at GCSE minimum entry to sixth form.

Exit: Respectable universities and proper subjects – from criminology at Aberystwyth to PPE at York, plus one, or sometimes two, to Oxbridge and a couple to study art and music. A few embark on military careers.

Money matters: Scholarships and exhibitions up to half fees available: academic, art, music, sport and all-rounder. Generous bursaries. Extra charges for specialist sports coaching eg golf, real tennis, books, trips, laundry and haircuts.

Remarks: One of a kind. Go and explore, meet Mr Dytor, chat to the boys – we doubt you will be undecided by the end of your visit. If you have an exuberant energetic boy with an artistic bent this could be the perfect match.

Oundle School

Linked school: Laxton Junior School

Great Hall, New Street, Oundle, Northamptonshire, PE8 4GH

- Pupils: 650 boys, 450 girls; 865 full board, 245 day • Ages: 11-19
- C of E • Fees: Day £14, 970-£19,695; Boarding £23,355-£30,705 pa • Independent

Tel: 01832 277125
Email: admissions@oundleschool.org.uk
Website: www.oundleschool.org.uk

Headmaster: Since 2005, Mr Charles (Charlie) Bush MA (sixties). Previously head of Eastbourne College. Says he is '100 per cent head' in term time (watches up to 48 fixtures per week), but enjoys a round or two of golf and family time when opportunities present. Married with children (flown the nest), according to parents Mrs B is a wonderful asset, 'she looks at things from our perspective and understands our anxieties'. Head says he feels privileged to work in an environment where youngsters are optimistic that life is going to be good for them but isn't afraid to push, 'It is sometimes necessary to be outside one's comfort zone to achieve'. Mr Bush is assured, business-like, old-school – we couldn't suppress a wry smile when he suggested we wouldn't understand their system of offering a mix of A levels and Pre Us. Parents say he is intelligent, confident, talks a good story, presents well and commands his audience, though confess they have few dealings with him outside formal occasions.

Academic matters: Possibly the most academically selective of all the co-ed full-boarding schools. Results are good – 86 per cent A/A* at GCSE/IGCSE and 66 per cent A*/A at A level in 2013. Many end up with a mix of qualifications, depending on the subjects taken: Pre U (linear, no modules), a more rigorous alternative to A level, is the only option in seven subjects including English lit, history, German and government and politics. Students taking economics, physics and chemistry can choose between Pre U and A level, most of rest – including art, French, biology and maths – are offered only at A level. No weak spots but Latin and chemistry perceived to be especially strong. Staff teach beyond the curriculum, investigate, explore and extend. All sixth-formers follow a non-examined general studies course which includes weekly lectures, discussions, debate and more.

It's not only cool to work but to do so with pace and purpose. Staff say pupils are a delight, 'Teaching is a serious business but students help make it fun, they have a good sense of humour, you can let your guard down a bit.' Not all are angels all of the time, 'My child had a problem concentrating and was allowed to change groups to get away from another child who was messing around'. We dropped in on a couple of lessons to find pupils engaged and on task, aided by some inspirational teaching. Parents happy with school but not gushingly so, they choose Oundle because their baseline is excellence and, for almost all, Oundle delivers. Very few parental moans: ad-hoc report times irritate some; girls, top students and strugglers (ie borderline B/C grade at A level) do well but feel some middling boys could do better; parent portal on wish list, but appreciative of extensive use of email.

School will support and encourage those with mild SEN, mainly specific learning difficulties but Aspergers and other SEN considered, so long as child is good university fodder. Parents say approach is matter of fact, no pandering: 'This is what we have, this is what we will do.' Help given with study skills plus whatever is identified in Ed Psych report. Minimal one-to-one help available but support for all (SEN or not) from individual departments. Pacey, demanding curriculum means EAL students need excellent English prior to arrival.

Good and ever improving facilities; latest jewel is the SciTec block with 16 well-designed labs. New languages block opened in 2013. The super 20,000 volume library opens late and offers a book-ordering service. Flagship, innovative DT (BBC B computer started life here) – a veritable hive of activity and inspiration when we visited – continues to thrive. Industrious atmosphere, wonderful, woody workshops with casting, lasers, wind tunnels, micro-electronics and CAD all adding to the scintillating sensory experience. Mr Bean's car may have vamoosed but others remain, in various glorious states of build and disrepair.

Games, options, the arts: All major sports pursued including rugby, football, hockey, netball, squash, fives, water polo, rowing, athletics, aerobics, cross country, golf. Recently became a Marylebone Cricket Club Foundation Hub, working to improve coaching for local state school children. Good facilities include a multi-sports complex with sports shop, pool, an outdoor synthetic athletics track, rifle range etc. Generally hold their own, win some, lose some, with a few key successes along the way including notable individual honours and national team selection – not bad considering sports schols only recently introduced. Parents say, 'Not all coaches are equally capable and enthusiastic; lower teams very much at mercy of master in charge but genuine sport for all – if they can put a team out, they will'.

For the stage-struck the charming Stahl Theatre, enjoyed by school and locals alike, provides a professional venue for touring companies as well as for esteemed pupil productions. Busy music department has recently formed a partnership with the Royal College of Music, a huge nod to the very high standard of musicianship. Two thirds learn an instrument though far fewer perform. Music and drama lean towards the exclusive, pupils and parents grumble that those whose trumpet blowing is enthusiastic rather than virtuoso, or who hide their dramatic light under a bushel, are unlikely to be placed centre-stage or even on-stage, making it difficult for late developers to get a look in.

Art popular and prolific. We saw superb sculptures and castings, plus exquisite fine art. Yarrow Gallery regularly hosts visiting exhibitions as well as pupils' own masterpieces. Millennium marked by pupil-design inspired, vibrantly coloured stained-glass windows made for the school chapel, a lively foil to John Piper's sedately beautiful east windows.

Field trips, exchanges, tours and expeditions galore to the near, the exotic and the remote. Extraordinarily varied list of activities known as 'voluntaries' are, paradoxically, compulsory for younger students; courses range from knitting, bee-keeping and bridge through to junior economics, dance and DT. Virtually all do DofE. CCF compulsory in the fourth form, remains a popular choice thereafter. Optional fifth and sixth form community action programme recognised as a class-leader, not just holding hands with the elderly or cleaning out chicken sheds but tough stuff too, including street sleeping to help understand the harsher side of life and instil a 'give-back' culture. A busy school with little let-up, though all get chance to let their hair-down via active social programme now enhanced by transformation of old fives courts into social centres.

Background and atmosphere: Situated in the delightful market town of Oundle, with its gentle, honey-toned Cotswold stone, the school was founded in 1556 as the local grammar. In 1876 the school split into Laxton, for the sons of tradesmen and local farmers, and Oundle for the sons of gentlemen. Full co-education came in the early 1990s and Laxton was brought back into the fold as a day house in 2000. Today it's hard to distinguish the extensive school campus and its 1100 pupils from the eponymous town. Size matters and head says when he arrived the school resembled a well-equipped ocean liner, large but lacking a whole-school feel. Has worked to engender school spirit – a tricky business. Fortunately house loyalty endures, with pupils theorising that house popularity is positively correlated with length of tenure of HM. The thirteen self-contained, well-maintained boarding houses have unique personalities; according to 'Oundelian', the school's own rather chic publication, Sanderson is 'intimidating', Laundimer 'friendly'. In reality school mixes pupils to ensure no cliques, or types ('the Scottish house' notwithstanding) – apply early if you yearn for a particular house. Compulsory chapel on Sunday plus two other weekly slots.

Pastoral care and discipline: No time for prolonged hand holding – pupils heed the emphasis on self-reliance – but HMs and personal tutors help and support, 'Most youngsters get something wrong at some point. We keep our ear to the ground and lines of communication open. We watch them try and sometimes fail, try again. We pick them up, dust them down, help them move on.' Parents say some HMs are excellent, stress there are no weak ones, but caution that HMs vary in outlook, attitude, expectations and communications. All dine in-house which means a careful eye can be kept on eating issues, friendships et al. Odd comment from parents of girls that house system is more geared-up for boys, citing fewer events with parents, and more fall-outs between girls (no more than anywhere else we suspect), certainly the girls we met were friendly, articulate and clearly had a sense of community. Parents of boys praise the range of house activities, camaraderie, and parental involvement, 'We appreciate the even-handedness of staff in dealing with issues'. Parents who live afar are especially praiseworthy of helpful, prompt and detailed home-school comms and of school's honesty about 'incidents'.

All incidences of bullying taken seriously, work done with victims and perpetrators. On the very rare occasion when things don't work-out, students may be sent home to rethink, or supported in their quest to find something that suits better.

'Sometimes a fresh start elsewhere is all that is needed. All will make fantastic adults, we simply have to help them through the stupidity of adolescence.' Pupils at ease with each other and with staff, though some older students confess to feeling a little stifled by rules and ready for the freedom of life after school. Rules are fair and the head, perceived to be 'very, very strict', upholds the policy re drugs and sex – instant out. Those aged 18 allowed controlled access to pub and alcohol (understandably strict – in 2009 a former student tried unsuccessfully to sue school after a drunken fall in 2005 left her permanently disabled). Hot on electronic footprint, work hard to ensure youngsters understand cyber dangers.

Pupils and parents: From all over UK, including strong Scottish contingent, currently over 120 prep schools represented. Close family ties, some 12 percent are off-spring of OOs. Twelve per cent from continental Europe or the Pacific Rim. Parents range from the professional to farming folk – open minded, ambitious. Not an obvious choice for first-time buyers but those who opt-in are justifiably proud of their acquisition. Head says London parents are the trickiest, 'They want the Oundle experience but on weekly boarding terms' – little chance of that we suspect. Social credentials abound but social club this isn't, some parents keen to be more involved and for greater social interaction and parental events but a tricky feat for what is a genuine boarding school with a global community. Exeats a rarity; officially one per annum but flexibility when essential.

Pupils are bright, friendly, articulate and courteous. Uniform adhered to, girls look glam in their swishing culottes, boys business-like in dark suit and tie. OOs include Arthur Marshall, Cecil Lewis (aviator), Peter Scott (ornithologist), A Alvarez, Anthony Holden (royal biographer), Richard Dawkins, Professor Sir Alan Budd, Charles Crichton (film director), Bruce Dickinson (lead singer of Iron Maiden – allegedly expelled following a rock-star style prank).

Entrance: Rigorous at 11+, 13+ and 16+. Waiting list (up to two years) with sibling preference (a third have a brother or sister in the school). Feeder schools are well primed and start preparation early. The registrar makes it his business to ensure only those who will succeed are entered. Minimum CE requirement of 55 per cent in English, maths, French and sciences but in reality those accepted typically average 70 per cent (scholars do even better). Officially no pre-testing but run practice CE day in November, 'to avoid disappointment', those not following CE are weeded out early via assortment of assessments and tests. Sixth form entry requires minimum three As and three Bs in GCSEs but competition for handful of places at 16+ means successful external applicants typically have fistfuls of A and A* grades. As with many popular, larger schools, when visiting you are unlikely to meet with the head (unless specifically requested); potential Oundelians are left in the very capable hands of trusty registrar, Gary Phillips.

Exit: Nearly all move on to the sixth form and thence to university. Mainly traditional courses at traditional universities with Newcastle, Bristol, Exeter and Edinburgh favoured destinations. Forty per cent take arts degrees with the rest split between social sciences and sciences; history, economics and engineering the most popular subjects. Plenty of extra help for those wishing to apply to Oxbridge – 14 successful candidates in 2013, though school says it is sometimes surprised by who is accepted and saddened that some outstanding students are turned away. Increasing numbers head across the pond thanks, in part, to well-versed influence of US staff.

Money matters: Range of scholarships awarded at 11+, 13+ and 16+ most limited to 10 per cent of fees. Bursaries, as high as 100 per cent available in cases of proven need; apply at least two years prior to entry for help, expect to fill in extensive forms designed to unearth every last sou. No automatic sibling or Forces discounts but Old Oundelian bursaries for the sons and daughters of Oos.

Remarks: A very busy school, ideal for the resilient, confident, energetic, academic child, who thrives in a large, pacey setting, rejoices in a heavy, focused work-load and delights in an abundance of extra-curricular activities. Average all-rounders should head elsewhere, stragglers will struggle, strugglers will likely be lost in the milieu. For those who can, Oundle does. Anyone considering a full-boarding education for their motivated, able off-spring should short-list Oundle.

Our Lady's Abingdon

Linked school: Our Lady's Junior School Abingdon

Radley Road, Abingdon, OX14 3PS

- Pupils: 470 boys and girls • Ages: 11–18 • Roman Catholic
- Fees: £12,399 pa • Independent

Tel: 01235 524658
Email: office@olab.org.uk
Website: www.olab.org.uk

Principal: Since 2012, Mr Stephen Oliver (late forties), previously deputy head of St Benedict's, Ealing. He was educated at the universities of Birmingham, Cambridge and St Andrews and has taught at Stonyhurst, The Royal Grammar School, Guildford, Uppingham and Haberdashers' Aske's School. Has taught classics and RE, coached cricket and been a CCF officer for 20 years.

Married to Caroline; three young children, two at the junior school. Has bought a house across the road to make family involvement in school life easy.

Was a novice monk at Downside Abbey for a year and a half in his 30s and remains attracted to Benedictine spirituality. Enjoys cricket, jazz and writing – has published Smoke in the Sanctuary, a comic novel set in a Catholic parish in the west of England.

Academic matters: Perhaps unfairly, the school's reputation has been somewhat overshadowed by the stellar achievements of the girls from nearby School of St Helen and St Katharine, but results here are still good, with average of 10 GCSEs taken; 49 per cent A*/A grades in 2013. No IGCSEs as yet but these are 'under consideration'. Separate sciences taught by subject specialist teachers throughout but dual award science GCSE only. Apparently the subjects are taken 'beyond' the GCSE curriculum and over 50 per cent go on to study science at AS/A level, where all three subjects are taught. Fairly traditional range of GCSE subjects with business studies and psychology on offer too.

At A level 22 per cent A*/A grades in 2013 (percentages affected by some small class sizes). The benefit of those small classes is that all pupils get individual attention – lots of active questioning and free discussion in the lessons we observed. Latin offered up to A level, Greek too, although this is an extra (lessons in the lunch hour and after school). Technology has now been added to the list of subjects, prompted by change to co-ed.

Good mix of male and female staff, many have been with the school for more than ten years. Learning support described by one parent with dyslexic daughter as 'excellent', one-to-one and paired extra lessons offered, and pupils also benefit from the small classes in lower sets.

Games, options, the arts: Head stresses the importance of extra-curricular interests. Buses leave at 5pm three days a week to allow time for participation in a varied timetable of after school clubs including astronomy, synchronised swimming and 'Uganda Team', where pupils take part in regular email and webcam communication with their partner school. The indoor swimming pool, right at the heart of the school, means that kayaking, scuba diving and snorkelling are all on offer too. Recent expedition destinations include Everest Base Camp and trekking in South America. A junior and senior choir trip to France, including a performance at Disneyland Paris, is planned to celebrate the school's 150th anniversary. Proud of its strong links with Maryhill High School in Uganda (see above) and regular visits and energetic fund-raising activities to support this.

The library is modern and well stocked with separate sixth form study area; helpful librarian who organizes reading challenges and inter-school literary activities. The dedicated computer suite next door does much to maintain bookish quiet. The standard of work in the art department is particularly impressive, much of it is also beautifully displayed throughout the school. New director of music has extended the range of ensembles and enlivened what had been a very traditional department. Two choirs, a wind band, chamber groups and an orchestra perform at two concerts a year. A whole school drama production in the winter term and frequent smaller productions (usually for GCSE and A level drama).

Multi-use games area built during the 2012 summer holidays to accommodate extra sports, and for use during the lunch times.

Background and atmosphere: The school was founded in 1860 by Sister Clare Moore, a nun from the order of the Sisters of Mercy who worked closely with Florence Nightingale in the Crimean War. It was originally co-ed, but then became girls only until 2009, when the governors decided to accept boys once again. Numbers increasing and there are now boys right the way through the school, apart from year 11.

Tucked away in a residential area of Abingdon in a mixture of old and modern buildings. The older parts were once the convent – the junior school has a marvellous door with sliding grill through which the nuns would speak to strangers. Newer buildings include a spacious entrance hall with versatile open plan space (on the other side of a glass divide is the swimming pool – an unusual centrepiece), an assembly hall which doubles as a theatre space and light and modern sixth form centre, all pale wood and big windows. The newer parts of the school are distinguished by extremely effective use of natural light; by contrast, the older classrooms and corridors seem dingy, although these, like the rest of the school, are much enlivened by displays of the pupils' work. The let down is the dining room, where the low ceiling and awkward layout give a subterranean feel, but plans to improve this. Science rooms are well-equipped, dedicated art, textiles and home economics spaces are light and spacious and music practice rooms and a keyboard room. New DT block opened in 2013.

Sizeable outside space for an urban site, large playing field just across the road and the school uses nearby Astroturf facilities (as do other Abingdon schools). The atmosphere is calm, efficient and relaxed and genuine rapport between staff and pupils was notable in the lessons we observed.

Pastoral care and discipline: The motto is 'Age quod agis' (Whatever you do, do well) and its influence is palpable throughout the school, undoubtedly helped by an average class size of 14 (max 22), much smaller in lower ability sets. Pupils have half an hour of tutor time/assemblies per day, split between the start and the end of lessons. Although only around a third of the intake is Roman Catholic and no longer any teaching nuns, the school's religious ethos is strongly in evidence – crucifixes

in every room, frequent masses and a clear emphasis on service both local and international: on Wednesday afternoons sixth form pupils do voluntary work with the elderly, the local hospital and other community projects.

The head is proud of the enrichment programme (year 12), intended to 'prepare pupils for life after school', offering tuition in a range of skills such as financial management, car maintenance and cookery, as well as courses exploring ethics and morality. Standard house system headed by sixth formers with emphasis on sharing responsibilities and tasks throughout age groups. Sensible uniform will appeal to parents; possibly unpopular (nearby girls' school abandons uniform after GCSEs) sixth form dress code allows pupils to choose, as long as it is smart and monochrome.

Catholic and non-Catholic parents are attracted by school's strong moral and pastoral reputation and parents we spoke to were full of praise for staff/pupil relations and the ways in which each child's individual abilities are developed. When questioned about bullying (in relation both to school policy and specific incidents), the head pronounced confidently that the school is a 'telling school' where pupils are encouraged, for example in PSHE and whole school assemblies, to report incidents. Any problems are dealt with sensitively and all concerned followed up for some time afterwards.

Pupils and parents: Predominantly white, from a wide catchment area extending to Berkshire and Gloucestershire, the school's religious character appeals to those who want an unashamedly Christian education for their children. Apparently it was pressure from those with boys in the junior section of school that was partly instrumental in the decision to become co-ed. Unusually for a secondary school, the head actively encourages parental involvement, helping with trips etc. Most recent Christmas Fair raised an impressive £7,000 for charity. Parents we spoke to were fiercely loyal – 'a gem,' said one; others praise the school's 'family' atmosphere and the way in which their children are treated as individuals rather than league table fodder. All parents commented on how pleased they were with home-school communication. It's still fairly early days for co-ed integration; sixth formers say that boys have 'not changed the school as much as they thought they would'. We saw year 7 boys absolutely engrossed in cutting patterns for Mondrian-inspired cushion covers in the textile department. It's cookery for them next term, and that can only be a good thing.

Entrance: Interview and assessment for junior school. Examination in years 6 and 8 for entry to years 7 and 9. Sixth form: interview and minimum of five GCSE passes at B or above, grade A or B for subjects to be studied at A level.

Exit: Approximately two-thirds stay on for the sixth form and are joined by students from maintained and non-maintained sector. Careers teacher is sixth form tutor and has an office near the common-room and study areas; these are at the top of the school, spacious and well-designed – usual common-room mess but an air of serious study too. The size of the school means that A level students benefit from very small classes with plenty of individual attention and advice. Majority of leavers go on to first choice, mainly Russell Group universities (one or two to Oxbridge).

Money matters: Fees are on a par with the other local independents. Lunches are extra. Bursaries and academic awards that account for up to seven per cent of the annual fee turnover; a number of these give up to 100 per cent remission on fees. Several bursaries funded by The Sisters of Mercy are available for Catholic children.

Remarks: A happy, well-resourced school with a secure moral and pastoral ethos and the feel of a thriving community. Great plans afoot for expansion, both architecturally and in pupil numbers.

0

If your child thrills to the competitive pressure of an academic powerhouse, two of these nearby whose reputations have, in the past, partly eclipsed Our Lady's. But perhaps you want something slightly different. If so, take a closer look: this school is strong in all areas with exam results and facilities to match and prides itself on 'revealing the special talent of each individual child'. The brave new world of co-ed status means it is now a much more clearly distinguished part of the Abingdon triumvirate.

Oxford High School GDST

Linked school: Oxford High School GDST Junior School

Belbroughton Road, Oxford, OX2 6XA

• Pupils: 605 girls; all day • Ages: 11–18 • Non-denom
• Fees: Junior £8,976; Senior £12,288 pa • Independent

Tel: 01865 559888
Email: oxfordhigh@oxf.gdst.net
Website: www.oxfordhigh.gdst.net

Head: Since 2010, Mrs Judith Carlisle BA (early fifties). Educated in a 'small Kent convent.' Studied English and drama at Bristol then worked in theatre in education for a few years followed by a PGCE at Goldsmiths. Previously deputy head at King Edward VII School, Norfolk and then head of Dover Girls' Grammar. Oxford High is her first post in the independent sector but so far she has found that the similarities between the grammar and independents more than outweigh any differences – committed pupils and parents with high expectations in both. She says that working in the state sector has given her a 'sense of perspective, the ability to see the whole picture of education and where our young people sit.' Very friendly, genuine and refreshingly informal; her style is smart Bohemian – good camouflage for forays into Summertown and beyond.

Oxford High's previous head, Felicity Lusk, left things pretty ship-shape when she decamped to Abingdon, so 'what next?' we asked Mrs Carlisle. 'OHS doesn't need fixing, it's a fabulous school. Part of my task is to make sure that we respond to what girls need, running with change but standing firm with the school's values and ethos.' Her plans are for increasing bursary provision and developing community links, including possibly becoming educational partners with a free school in East Oxford. She is also keen to help the girls develop what she calls 'good habits', such as 'steadiness and thoughtfulness.' 'We want girls to have strong core values, to value relationships as well as careers.' Mrs Carlisle has no truck with the 'factory model' of education and believes that 'the added twinkle in OHS results comes from pleasure, from very bright girls being encouraged to go one step further.'

Mrs Carlisle's husband also works in education and both enjoy outdoor pursuits, especially walking, cycling and cross-country skiing – Norfolk is a favourite destination. She recently went trekking in Nepal with some of her pupils. 'I'm so glad I went, mountains make you feel small and that's a good corrective for a head!'

Academic matters: All you could wish. Girls study for 10 GCSEs (none taken early) and in 2013 an impressive 92 per cent of grades were A*/A. Dual award science, but subjects are taught separately and enhanced with a tailored science enrichment course that is, apparently, 'better preparation for A level.' IGCSEs currently in maths, modern foreign languages, English language and literature, science. Decisions on syllabus are devolved to department heads and 'always under review.' Responsive and flexible when it comes to A level choices; girls choose from 26 subjects and staff timetable around them, running courses even

for three or four only (including Greek, Latin, Mandarin and Russian). School say that most take three A2s and a few do four. One girl we met was doing five and she probably wasn't unique. In 2013 75 per cent of grades at A level were A*/A. Very strong science, plenty go on to study medicine and up to 30 per cent in any year head for Oxbridge.

Teaching is taken 'beyond the curriculum' and staff enjoy the opportunity to lead (or possibly follow) girls off piste academically. All sixth formers do critical thinking as part of their general studies programme and many opt to take this as an AS level. Also available is the extended project qualification (EPQ) and ACPA baccalaureate. No Pre-U as yet but it's not ruled out for the future. Lessons we saw were a teacher's dream – bright, curious girls excited by their subjects and full of questions and ideas. And what of the perennial problem, girls' reluctance to take risks and get things wrong; how does the school encourage courage? Mrs Carlisle is on the case. 'We want to help girls develop a core, an inner strength, a sense of self.' She speaks of a drive to foster bravery, of setting the bar higher and higher, either literally in PE, or metaphorically. 'We get girls to talk about the fear, to confront the worst that could happen.'

Games, options, the arts: We were astonished by the ambition and quality of the pieces made in what used to be called woodwork but is now known as resistant materials. A wonderful chicken coop (it was, in fact, a chicken gypsy caravan) with heart-shaped shutters; a beautifully designed desk; an elegant console table. Impressive welding too. DT facilities are extensive, more like a small industrial unit, and girls can come and work on projects outside timetabled lessons. In years 7 to 9 girls sample creative subjects such as textiles, DT, ceramics etc via a 'circus' system that gives them a term of each. Inspiringly messy art room with very high quality work on display, likewise textile creations of an impressive standard – OHS girls have gone on to the Ruskin and the Royal Academy. Sixth formers can opt to take an AS in art or textiles over two years as an extra subject; this creative outlet is apparently popular with girls intending to study medicine. How do they fit it all in? Staff say that girls enjoy being able to draw on their other subjects such as psychology and history to inform their art. We're sure they do but it still doesn't quite answer our question!

Masses of musicians, as one might expect, with choirs, orchestras, ensembles and bands for all levels of ability. Girls benefit from Oxford's cultural venues and OHS performs in the Sheldonian and various college chapels. Music and drama enthusiastically and successfully pursued as extra-curricular subjects but penny numbers taking them at GCSE and A level – not quite academic enough, perhaps.

Clubs are, with exceptions such as bridge, CCF and knitting, subject or sport based. Thus: engineering club, dissection club(!), biomedical club – all serving to extend studies beyond the syllabus. But lest you think OHS girls are living up to the school's bluestocking reputation by being worthy but dull, take a look at the school magazine: it's one of the most witty, affectionate yet wickedly irreverent we've read (and we've read a few...). The rules from 'Top ten secret tips for writing articles about school trips' should be carved into the desks of all school magazine editors: 'Thou shalt not murder... us with boredom,' being the first.

We have heard mixed reports about sport, some feeling that it doesn't quite match up to the standard of academics (rather a tall order) but girls have represented their county and country in a range of events, notably hockey – under 16 and 18 county champions – swimming and cross-country. Indeed, swimmers from OHS were selected for British Olympic and Paralympic trials. Girls pursing individual sports at national and international level are fully supported eg exam timetables adjusted to avoid clashes. Sixth formers may take a sports leadership course. Super swimming pool, standard issue sports hall, but on a 10 acre town site space is pretty limited – use is made of the playing fields at the nearby Dragon School (although this is not mentioned in the prospectus). Partnership with Oxford Hawks hockey club means girls get specialist coaching and use of their pitches. Fair to say, we think, that sport gets A-, rather than an A*.

Background and atmosphere: Tucked away unexpectedly behind dons' grand Victorian villas (school is somewhat at odds with local vernacular), the site has undergone considerable renovation to the tune of £9,000,000 and now almost works as a coherent, if constrained, campus. Bold metal sunflower centrepiece outside reception is an effective focal point and is illuminated at night, thus delivering school's motto 'Ad lucem' (To the light) at all times. Founded in 1895 with just 29 pupils, the school has moved between various North Oxford venues and settled in Betjeman's 'bonny Belbroughton Road' in 1957. Reception and year 1 are in Woodstock Road and years 2-6 at Bardwell Road – both within walking distance of big sister. Was a direct grant school and head is committed to continuing the meritocratic tradition by beefing up bursary coffers.

Inevitably, given its central Oxford location, OHS has a reputation for being the bluestocking school. And what's wrong with that? It's hardly an insult to be linked to a movement that championed women's education and no one could accuse OHS girls of being dull or frumpy. The uniform is comfortable and low key with sunflower logos on navy blue sweatshirts. Sixth formers wear their own clothes and do not, thank goodness, have to adhere to the style black hole that is 'business dress.' No token nod to democracy here: the OHS school council is an effective and well-supported body that has a real influence over school policy – part of what the head refers to as the school's 'yes culture.'

Pastoral care and discipline: The new dining hall is a bright and welcoming space with glass walls overlooking outdoor space for al fresco lunch, but with its determinedly jolly coloured plastic chairs looks as though it was designed by adults to be 'down with the kids'. Ditto the reception area in grey and lime green: it's smart now but we hope it will stand the test of time and not look dated in a few years. Sixth form cyber café with laptops open all day. Girls say that the food has improved and all usual options – baked potatoes, pasta, salad bar, etc served up. We were surprised to see beanbags lining the walls of the corridor outside the dining room. 'What are these for?' we asked, imagining perhaps wearyingly long queues for baked potatoes. They are, apparently, a relaxation area for sixth formers, rather popular and thus much hijacked by other years. Since we were not invited into their common-room – it was 'undergoing renovation', and 'not even the teachers want to go in there,' one can only hope that conditions will become a little more salubrious. School says that sixth formers are project managing the revamp, including the budget, themselves so the end result should meet their needs.

There doesn't seem to be an OHS 'type'; several parents told us they were surprised to find 'a real mixed bunch.' Mrs Carlisle says that it is important for OHS not to have a 'house style'; she wants all pupils to find someone to whom they can relate and we can report that the phrase most often used to describe the girls is 'really friendly'.

Parents praise the way in which staff treat pupils as individuals, giving positive encouragement to the less confident and helping to bring out the best in every girl. Particularly important at a school where there is bound to be a vocal 'hands up' team in every class. Discipline low key, bullying or other friendship group problems headed off at pass or dealt with promptly. Usual range of sanctions for smoking, alcohol (short-term exclusion), drugs (exclusion).

Pupils and parents: Broad international mix of cultures, especially for a day school; some families are connected to Oxford University or the nearby hospitals. Not snobby; Mrs

Carlisle is keenly aware that parents make significant sacrifices to send their daughters here. They've probably seen the list of former pupils. Deep breath: Dame Maggie Smith (actress); Sian Edwards (conductor); Elizabeth Jennings (poet); Emma Bridgewater (potter); Ursula Buchan (journalist); Sophie Grigson (cookery TV/writer); Louise Williams (violinist); Dame Josephine Barnes (first woman President BMA); Miriam Margolyes (actress); Dame Rose Macaulay (novelist); Anne Pasternak-Slater (academic); Julia Hollander (director); Harriet Hunt (international chess Grand Master); Joanne van Heningen (architect); Cressida Dick (Metropolitan Police); Martha Lane Fox (lastminute.com). OHS girls are most definitely not highly-strung thoroughbreds – these tend to be stabled elsewhere.

Entrance: Main entry at 11 and 16. Year 7: own assessments in maths, English, reasoning and interview. Parents say that the entrance test is a good filter and doesn't disadvantage bright girls from state primaries, but don't imagine that these children aren't given a little coaching. For sixth form entry, admissions interviews and at least grade A in most GCSEs, and certainly for chosen subjects. Academic potential and ability looked for. Only occasional leavers across all years; most juniors transfer to senior school.

Exit: All to higher education; 28 per cent to Oxbridge in 2013, a few to US universities and vast majority of remainder to Russell Group. Ten to 15 per cent decamp elsewhere (local co-eds) post-GCSE.

Money matters: As other GDST schools, regarded as good value for money. Fees include day trips and ISCO test in year 10 (many other schools charge this as an extra). Variable number of scholarships worth 10 per cent of fees awarded at 11 (academic, music and head's scholarship). Scholarships (worth 15 per cent of fees) also awarded at 16 (academic, head's, art, sport, music and drama). Bursaries, up to 100 per cent of fees (based on financial need), available at age 11 and 16.

Remarks: Oxford High manages the seemingly impossible task of turning out confident girls with exemplary academic results without turning up the pressure. Serious matters are certainly taken seriously but there seems to be time for plenty of fun. As Mrs Carlisle says, 'When the time comes we want them to be ready to burst out of the doors but we want them to look back with a tear in their eye.'

Palmers Green High School

Linked school: Palmers Green Lower School

104 Hoppers Road, London, N21 3LJ

- Pupils: 120 girls, all day • Ages: 11–16 • Non-denom
- Fees: £8,895–£12,750 pa • Independent

Tel: 020 8886 1135
Email: office@palmersgreen.enfield.sch.uk
Website: www.pghs.co.uk

Headmistress: Since 2002, Mrs Christine Edmundson BMus MBA LRAM ARCM PGCE (Cantab) (early fifties). Came to London from the Isle of Man to study music at Royal Holloway, University of London, where she was a choral scholar undergraduate and a postgraduate, and entered teaching after a bizarre twist of events. 'Someone from New Zealand working at the British Museum had published his doctoral thesis on my unpublished manuscript, so I changed course.' This launched her teaching career at a day school for girls in Warwick, which, with its link to a local boys' school 'was great for co-educational productions'.

P

She went on to become director of music at a co-educational day and boarding school in Ascot and then deputy head at a girls' day and boarding school in Bath.

She is a chirpy and warm character with a great sense of humour, a sort of mother figure, which fits well in a school where the atmosphere is like one big family. Parents say she is 'approachable, you can talk to her,' and that 'it's good to see her at the gates in the mornings rather than like some [heads] tucked up in the office'. Interestingly, in the head's view, her presence helps to see off 'parents who are naughty and park on the zigzag lines'. She is known for getting to the bottom of things when parents complain but is no pushover for those who try to pull the wool over her eyes and ask for things like days off to 'go to a family wedding in Scotland'.

She has been here long enough to see a whole generation of children come through, which is 'nice... just one or two left that weren't my generation'. She still teaches, not music but ICT, RE, and general studies. 'I don't get involved in music except through general studies or for Founder's Day and the carol service.' She is vocal about changes in education, and because she talks about these issues during general studies, the girls are also clued up on current debates – 'Oh good,' she says, 'general studies is working'. She says her speeches at the annual prize giving ceremony are not the norm – she uses them to remind parents of changes afoot in education, eg the debacle around GCSE exams and competition for university places.

Academic matters: Consistently high GCSE results: 73 per cent A*/A grades in 2013. Relationships between pupils and teachers are strong; class sizes are small, between 10 and 16. 'That's why we chose this school,' said a parent. 'It was pretty tough to see how overstretched the teachers were at our previous state primary school.' With a teacher pupil ratio of 1:9, 'we get the attention we need', say pupils.

The school offers IGCSE French and Spanish. French currently compulsory to IGCSE, with Spanish as an additional extra; from 2014 girls will be able to choose either or both. A few girls study additional maths; firm favourites when choosing options are history, geography and ICT. Parents will be pleased to know, however, that the school is flexible towards subject choice catering to, for example, those who study a language outside school or who have taken a GCSE/IGCSE early (frequently in a modern foreign language spoken at home), allowing them to continue to study the subject at school.

Head believes in teaching 'children to work smart and play to strengths'. She sees the school as moving more toward IGCSE because GCSE 'doesn't stretch the brightest of students'. Parents agree: 'Ms Edmundson made no bones about the school being selective,' said a parent. 'I wanted my daughter to be in that environment.'

Majority of pupils do D of E bronze level and the UK Maths Challenge. There are visiting teachers, educational trips and residential stays to enhance learning – eg year 8 geography trip to Dorset to prepare pupils for their GCSE fieldwork, trips to Poland and Berlin for GCSE history and to the Isle of Wight where pupils study the impact of the festival. 'We've just returned from a trip to Spain,' said a pupil. 'Every morning we had Spanish lessons with a native speaker; even if we asked what a word meant they would explain it in Spanish.'

Pupils say the trips aid what they learn in the classroom: 'it's so amazing to go and see everything expanded... it is all very well learning from a text book...' They particularly look forward to the annual year 9 visit to the Guardian newspaper office as part of the English curriculum, where 'you get to see how everything is put into action, you choose the stories, you choose a name and print the papers'. They bring the papers back to school and stick the front pages up on the walls.

School introduces specialist teaching in subjects like Latin and DT much earlier than most (in the junior school) and this clearly benefits pupils in the senior school. Older students are able to access AS level course material – this is mainly in modern foreign languages and for those who have already successfully attained an A* in year 9 and year 10. 'The main purpose is to enrich and extend language skills in preparation for taking A levels.' Head says pupils often surprise others with their knowledge due to their early access to specialist teaching or advanced materials: one went for a sixth form interview 'and the interviewer said, "How did you know that? You shouldn't know that at your stage".' However, one parent said that highly able students could be better challenged: 'There have been several instances where the homework has been so basic that my daughter has become demotivated.'

Teachers generally described as friendly; head of history praised by pupils for making the subject one of the most popular. Head of maths also praised: 'In year 7 I didn't like maths and now I'm doing additional maths. They made me enjoy it and that's really good as it's so important. I know that's the case for lots of people in the class.'

No children at present who do not speak fluent English but EAL support can be provided. Around 20 to 25 girls are identified with SEN, mostly dyslexia, and a few pupils have autistic spectrum disorders (ASDs). They can have support in lessons and there is some help for the ASDs in social skills arranged by the individual needs coordinator, who can involve outside agencies if necessary. Extra classes before and after school and one-to-one tuition are also available at an extra charge.

The school helps prepare the girls for moving on to a sixth form elsewhere – 'We want to make sure they have lots of opportunities when they leave because of the opportunities they have had here,' says the head. 'It doesn't matter if they are not strong academically as they will have other strengths which may help them to get a sixth form place somewhere.'

Games, options, the arts: Although the school no longer offers PE as a short course at GCSE, the opportunity and enthusiasm for sport across the years is evident. This is commendable given the shortage of sporting facilities at the school. Until 2012, the main hall was the only space available for assemblies, gymnastics, drama and exams. The newly built Elizabeth Smith Hall now provides a multi-purpose space for all these activities and leaves the main hall free during exams.

Not much of a playground, just a small yard used by junior pupils, and there are no fields. Girls travel 10 minutes by coach to nearby Walker Grounds for outdoor games and to Southgate for swimming lessons. Year 10 and 11 travel to Southbury Leisure Centre for a range of sports. Still, nothing is lost and time is well managed so that, for example, pupils receive pre lesson instruction in transit, 'with the added advantage that they don't stand freezing listening' on the fields. Parents certainly don't view this as a problem, since 'it's not that far and they are not in the bus for half an hour'. Another said 'My daughter isn't particular sporty but we go and support netball matches.'

Dance and gymnastics are taught on half term rotation, and netball is popular. They have won the Barnet Netball League for four years consecutively, 'playing bigger schools', adds the head, 'who have 200-odd in each year group, where we have only 30 girls to choose from.' She puts it all down to the fact that this is a small school where the girls 'know each other incredibly well', something parents attest to.

Around half choose art and design at GCSE and the self-portraits mounted in the art corridor show there is plenty of talent here, as do pupils' willingness to talk thoughtfully about their work. Classrooms are well equipped with colour wheels for guidance and artefacts for inspiration, 'to help you make a decision about what you are trying to express through colours, shapes, textures, perspectives... which is helpful if you are not too familiar with art,' said one pupil. Another commented: 'We did 3D art and I found that is my niche'. She showed us the model of a figure drowning in money, explaining that it was to show 'how greed can take over... how too much money is never enough for some people. People always want just a little bit more.' The remedy? 'It depends on the sort of person you are,' she said.

Around a third of the girls choose drama at GCSE. It is also popular as an extracurricular activity, as is dance: pupils have performed in the Nutcracker ballet at the Bloomsbury Theatre in Euston. Not many take music at GCSE (15 per cent). At the time of our visit, there was only one girl studying music in year 11 and five in year 10. The music department offers timetabled lessons in different instruments: sax, trumpet, singing – but pupils say that if you want to learn an instrument not offered, the school will get a teacher in. Around 80 girls across the whole school take lessons inside school and many more take lessons outside school hours. Their music skills range from beginners to above grade 8. There is an open door culture in the music department where 'you can come during break if you want to practice your instrument'. There is a senior school orchestra and and two choirs, plus other instrumental groups.

Plenty on offer in terms of extracurricular clubs, though, again, some (particularly working parents) say they would like to see more after school provision. The school currently offers netball, choir, music, knitting, drama, debating, swimming and a Christian union, and tries to ensure everyone gets involved in something. As well as lunchtime and after school activities, there's a gym club at 8am and weekend cross-country competitions, D of E expeditions and training. They also take part in eg inter-school debating competitions.

There is a 'very competitive' annual house choral competition. Pupils describe it as a 'bit like a musical but not'. The girls choose songs on some pretty powerful themes – 'about war, politics, women in power, the economy, green issues'. 'People sing, play instruments, costumes get dragged into that... but most important, you don't want your competitor to know what you're doing so it's very secretive, all covered up.' 'Green house won last year,' another butted in, 'yellow house won year before, and we won the year before that. So far we're equal... but we're worried about what will happen this year [after we leave] so we will have to come back and see how they get on without us.' The audience for the house choral competition always includes some recent leavers.

Background and atmosphere: Founded in 1905 by a Christian Quaker called Alice Hum whose motto, 'By Love, Serve One Another', still guides the ethos here. The building was originally located in nearby Osborne Road and opened with 12 pupils. It had grown to 300 when it moved to its present location in Hoppers Road in 1918. The original and main building, Avondale Hall, is still the heart of the school. Classrooms and a dining room were added between the 1960s and 1990s. Over the next decade a new office block was built and more recently the new Elizabeth Smith Hall (with a couple of one bed flats above – which the school says will suit student teachers) and a medical room. The school could do with more space but as the site is on a residential street, neatly tucked between houses, expansion is difficult.

Despite its age, the school has a modern feel. The building is intimate and compact yet the rooms, hallway and stairwells are airy and bright. Most spaces, including the head's office, double up for other uses, and there are well thought out rotas for use of the hall and library resource centre to accommodate the needs of both the junior and senior pupils. The prep department shares the same building, and the linked pre-school (Alice Nursery) is about a mile and half away.

Whatever the school lacks in space it greatly makes up for it in friendliness: if there were a prize for the most welcoming atmosphere this school would be in the running. Teachers invited us into lessons, and pupils showed impeccable manners. A science class in the middle of an experiment gladly redid the combustion exercise just for our visit – or so they claimed. Pupils are keen to talk about their work displayed on classroom walls, like the 'wonder posters' they created about different countries that took part in the Olympics.

Pastoral care and discipline: As a relatively small school contained in one building, it would be hard for any child's problem or unhappiness to go unnoticed – 'It is quite common for a member of staff to take a girl aside if she seems troubled in any way'. Very good staff-parent relations as all share the ethos of: work hard and your reward will be a good career.

Pupils told us that settling into the school was easy. 'If teachers can see you are struggling they introduce you to someone'. Pupils have two induction days before they start plus a three-day team building residential trip within the first few weeks of September, 'so we made friends straight away'.

Small group sizes here mean no-one gets lost. 'We have an open door policy so we can talk to any teacher and get help if we need to,' as 'you can feel closer to one particular teacher'. In such a small school teachers 'can spot if something is wrong', and pupils develop good relationships with their form tutors – two to a form – who sometimes stay with the groups as they move up.

The house system also helps them know and support each other well across the school: during the fire drill 'one older girl must each grab a younger child and walk them to the meeting place'. Parents mentioned this 'nurturing environment' with girls 'across different year groups interacting and playing with each other' as one of the appealing characteristics of the school. Senior pupils mentor younger pupils and take up roles as head girls, house captains, form and other types of prefects. Prep prefects help out in the prep school, form prefects help year 7s to settle in and career and public relations prefects help out in their relevant areas. Sometimes they double up on roles to share duties.

This culture of active citizenship means that the girls are consulted on lots of important decisions. They formed a committee to help choose a new catering company for the school – the winner was not only chosen because of its great home made yoghurt (which has gone on to become a favourite), but also because it creates menus linked to the curriculum. Pupils also formed a panel to choose a new uniform to mark the school's centenary – they hated the old green one, says the head. We walked into a geography lesson where the girls were being consulted on what colour book to use for a new GCSE unit. They went for green.

Behaviour is good and incidences of bullying are rare: 'I've never had a problem... you would know about it,' said a pupil. 'I've been here since reception and never heard of anything.' Another said, 'The worst is you have an argument with your friend but that happens anywhere.' PSHE includes lessons in study and life skills and careers guidance.

Encouragement to work hard includes a star chart, embraced by even the most senior pupils, with stars awarded for high results in the weekly French and Spanish vocab tests – 'if you get 10 out of 10 you get a star, it's a good way to ensure you learn the vocabulary'. Parents praise the commendation system because it means their daughters are 'stretched in individual subjects... achievement and effort even within the subject gives more to aim for'. Notices on classroom walls include injunctions to 'turn up on time', 'help friends', 'have a good attitude', 'show respect'.

Pupils and parents: Parents are mostly professionals and come from a mixture of cultures and backgrounds. There are no parent governors: 'it avoids problems if there are financial difficulties', says the head. However, the parents' association organises events like theatre trips, quiz nights, the summer fair and other fundraising events and has raised money for benches for the grounds, an audio system for the hall and the school mini bus. It also helps new families settle in, 'especially if you have moved to London from outside,' said a parent who moved from Cardiff.

Notable past pupils include Marion Tait OBE, CBE, Prima Ballerina and assistant director of the Birmingham Royal Ballet.

Entrance: Girls joining at 11 sit English, maths, science and reasoning tests, with those who show promise invited for interview. However, the vast majority come up from the lower school.

Exit: 'I always say we have the largest sixth form in London. It just happens to be located in all my colleagues' schools,' says the head. Many move on to selective state sixth forms eg Latymer, Dame Alice Owen's and St Michael's. A few to Woodhouse College; others to independents eg City of London School for Girls, Haberdashers' Aske's School for Girls, Highgate, North London Collegiate, St Albans High School for Girls and St Paul's Girls'.

Money matters: Academic scholarships, music awards and means-tested bursaries are available to cover up to 100 per cent of fees at 11+. There are also other internal awards related to progress within the school.

Remarks: A small, cosy and nurturing school which prepares girls well to move on to a wider world at 16.

Pangbourne College

Pangbourne, Reading, RG8 8LA

• Pupils: 400 boys and girls • Ages: 11–18 • C of E • Fees: Day £14,880–£20,970; Boarding £20,955–£29,655 pa • Independent

Tel: 01189 842101
Email: registrar@pangcoll.co.uk
Website: www.pangbournecollege.com

Headmaster: Since 2005, Mr Thomas Garnier BSc PGCE (forties). Educated at Sandroyd and Radley, read physics at Bristol and was a seaman officer in the Royal Navy for seven years. He left the Navy 'for love' after meeting his wife Alexandra and trained as a teacher. Did PGCE at Oxford, followed by first teaching job at King Alfred's, high performing state school in Wantage, Oxfordshire. Spent 10 years at Abingdon School, where he progressed to housemaster and then head of boarding.

Dedicated, energetic and keen to listen to pupils' views, he still manages to fit in some physics teaching and runs the naval section of Pangbourne's CCF. He describes Pangbourne pupils as 'good, solid citizens who are prepared to work hard and willing to participate.' Makes a point of being out and about in school and meets the two chief cadet captains (head boy and head girl) for 10 minutes every morning. 'We suit active children who like being busy,' he says.

Head's wife is very involved in school life and they have two sons. They live in a house attached to the main school building, with panoramic views stretching 20 miles across the Berkshire countryside. In his spare time (not that there's much of it) he enjoys rowing, running and music. A firm believer in 'lifelong learning,' he recently took up the flute again after a 25 year gap, passed his grade 8 with ease and plays in the school orchestra. He is keen to start piano lessons too, 'someone said to me "you can always find 15 minutes a day and if you do that it adds up to 90 hours a year".'

Academic matters: School takes children across a broad range of ability. Head agrees that Pangbourne is sometimes perceived as being 'for the less able' but says they do a very good job for academic children (there's a gifted and talented programme for the most able). In 2013, 50 per cent of A level grades were A*/B

and 24 per cent A*/A. The school told us: 'While the top students gained their straight A grades, some of the most heartening performances were to be found in the middle ground, among those who worked tremendously hard to secure Bs and Cs. We take real pride in these.' Some sixth formers, particularly those considering careers in the Services, take public service BTEC as well as their A levels.

Most pupils take 11 GCSEs, including IGSE English and maths. French, German and Spanish taught and music, art, DT, drama, business studies and PE on offer at GCSE. In 2013, 43 per cent A*/A and 71 per cent A*-B grades. New timetable has introduced one-hour lessons. Pupils are setted for maths, English, science and languages – four sets in years 9 and 10 and five sets in year 11.

Teaching staff (two-thirds male and a third female) are a healthy mix of experienced and newly qualified teachers (school has links with teacher training departments at universities of Buckingham, Reading and Oxford Brookes). Half the teachers live on site. Staff hold regular academic clinics for youngsters who need help (pupils can also email their teachers). Learning support available for pupils with minor learning difficulties – individual lessons on offer at £40. Tutor system – in senior school pupils stay with same tutor for year 9, then change for years 10 and 11 and again for the sixth form.

The youngest pupils (years 7 and 8) are housed in Dunbar, a detached red-brick house with its own garden (loads of space to play football, jump about on the trampoline and catch up with friends). Lower school lessons take place in the main school but the rest of the time pupils trot back to the cosy environs of Dunbar. Dynamic housemaster of Dunbar ('he's strict, but huge fun,' one parent told us) also teaches DT and memorably described his subject as 'making a noise and making a mess.' Dunbar pupils have their own head boy and head girl and all pupils are divided into four 'watches,' (Port, Starboard, Forward and Aft), each with their own 'watch captains.' Currently more boys than girls in this age group, but numbers vary from year to year.

Games, options, the arts: A very sporty school. Teachers and pupils alike told us that 'Pangbourne punches above its weight' when it comes to sport, and its impressive results bear this out. School regularly beats far larger schools, particularly at rugby and rowing. Pangbourne boathouse is a mile from the school, on the scenic banks of the Thames, and school has won the Princess Elizabeth Challenge Cup at Henley four times.

Unlike some schools, where pupils drop sport in the sixth form, everyone does sport here. School's size means that virtually all get the chance to represent Pangbourne. Main boys' sports are rugby, hockey, rowing and cricket while girls do netball, hockey, rugby, rowing and tennis. Open-air pool (keen swimmers get bussed to indoor pools at Bradfield, Reading and Newbury). Lots of equestrian enthusiasts – riding and polo are popular.

Stunning new music school houses recital hall, recording suite and 10 practice and teaching rooms, as well as four prized Steinway grand pianos. Around a third of pupils take individual music lessons, with brass, drums, guitar and singing leading the pack. Loads of musical groups to join, including orchestra, jazz band, choirs and a marching band. Art and DT departments thriving, with healthy numbers taking subjects at GCSE and A level. Performing arts are on the up with a variety of college productions, theatre trips and drama workshops. Three drama studios and pupils encouraged to take LAMDA exams. Everyone does CCF for at least a year and D of E is compulsory in year 9.

Background and atmosphere: School is set in 230 acres, in an area of outstanding natural beauty. Founded in 1917, Pangbourne's aim was to prepare boys for service in the Merchant Navy and Royal Navy. In 1969, however, the school was established as a charity, with a similar curriculum to other schools, and these days only two or three leavers a year join the forces. Even so, Pangbourne prides itself on maintaining many of its original traditions and is the only school in the UK where pupils wear Royal Navy officer cadet uniform every day.

Pupils parade in their number one (ceremonial) uniforms every third Sunday. Uniforms have to be immaculate and shoes polished. A guest of honour inspects the whole school on the vast parade ground and takes the salute as pupils march past. Head says Pangbourne's parades are an integral part of school life and help to develop self-discipline (pupils have to stand still for 15 to 20 minutes, often with a biting wind whistling across the parade ground), confidence, teamwork, leadership and a community spirit as well as attention to detail. When we visited pupils told us that the parades 'bring us together' as a school, while parents are hugely supportive (many turn up to watch every parade). 'It is very impressive,' a mother told us. 'It seems to give them great pride in what they do.' But despite the emphasis on teamwork, the school encourages youngsters to be individuals. 'We certainly aren't trying to put everyone in a mould,' one teacher told us.

Pangbourne has its own distinctive vocabulary, much of it nautical. Study bedrooms are cabins, house common rooms are gunrooms, the dining hall is the mess hall and casual clothes are always referred to as scruff. When the head arrived he introduced 'flag values' – kindness, integrity, industry, moral courage, selflessness, resilience and initiative. He sees these as the school's core values and pupils are urged to display them throughout their time at the school. Firm Christian ethos. Chapel is a key part of Pangbourne life, from 'congers' (congregational practice) to Saturday evensong for boarders. Many services are held in the Falkland Islands Memorial Chapel, opened by the Queen in 2000.

School has been fully co-ed since 1996 (it's now two-thirds boys and a third girls). Four boys' houses and two (ultra-modern) girls' houses. Just over half of the pupils board – more than 100 are full boarders while the others board four nights a week (Monday, Tuesday, Thursday and Friday). Boarding grows in popularity as the pupils move up the school – by sixth form 75 per cent are boarders. 'We don't actively push boarding,' one teacher told us. 'It's a natural phenomenon.' No flexi-boarding, although school offers parents chance to buy 15 extra boarding nights a year per pupil. Girls' houses are stylish and bright – 'I want to make it like home from home,' a housemistress told us. Pupils eat breakfast, lunch and supper in the central mess hall.

School is keen on student voice and pupils sit on food committee and pastoral welfare committee. Very inclusive 'Team Pangbourne' feel to the place and pupils are fiercely loyal to their school. Sixth formers can apply to train as peer mentors, helping others to cope with everything from time management and exam preparation to friendship issues and internet safety. Raft of prefects – called cadet captains – chosen by head and senior staff. Lower sixth pupils take leadership course in readiness for their responsibilities in the upper sixth and head reckons this has reaped dividends.

Pastoral care and discipline: Head says school's policies on drugs, alcohol, cigarettes and knives are 'crystal clear.' Any pupil caught using, selling or possessing drugs 'can expect to be expelled,' he says, though 'every case is treated on its merits.' School devotes a lot of time to PHSE and is strict about boy-girl relationships – PDAs banned. Sixth formers have their own bar (Medway), which is open for soft drinks on Thursday evenings and pizzas and beer/lager (strictly limited) on Saturday nights. Pupils are allowed mobile phones but firm rules on when they can be used. If phones go off in lessons, for instance, they get confiscated for 24 hours.

Staff believe that the school's strict uniform policy is a 'great leveller.' Pupils must need hefty trunks to pack all their kit though – list includes number one uniform (jacket, trousers and cap with badge for Sundays and ceremonies), number two

uniform for everyday (trousers, navy jersey, epaulettes, beret and Dr Martens shoes), and recreational rig (known as 'rec rig') for social occasions and away matches. And that's before they even think of throwing in games kit and weekend clothes.

Pupils say that Pangbourne is 'a caring, friendly school' and that it's easy to settle in. One boy told us that wearing the distinctive uniform had given him 'a sense of discipline' and that most pupils see it as 'really cool.' Asked whether it's a snooty school, sixth formers said 'definitely not.' Other pupil comments during our visit included 'people come out of their shells here,' 'it makes you really independent' and 'it prepares you for life outside.'

Pupils and parents: Fleet of minibuses brings day pupils in from as far afield as Basingstoke, Newbury and Highclere. Majority of boarders live within an hour's drive. Around eight per cent from overseas (including the Far East, Kenya and Germany). Despite school's naval associations, only 20 youngsters from Services families. Former pupils include the late film director Ken Russell, Olympic gold and silver medallist sailor Andrew (Bart) Simpson, motorcycle racer Mike Hailwood, hedge fund founder David Harding, former Second Sea Lord Admiral Sir Michael Layard and Dazed & Confused founder and journalist Jefferson Hack.

Pangbourne prides itself on taking pupils 'from a broad spectrum of ability.' A parent told us: 'Pangbourne isn't known for being an academic school but the opportunities are there for academic children and they do really well. At the same time the school brings out the best in those for whom studying isn't so easy. Every child seems to have their chance in the sun.' School says it selects as much on character and suitability as academic criteria and is looking for youngsters who will throw themselves into Pangbourne life and make a difference. The only children the school might turn away, says the head, are those whose learning difficulties are 'too profound for us to cope with' or youngsters with 'behaviour issues.'

Entrance: Pupils come from a host of state and prep schools, including Brockhurst, Moulsford, Thorngrove, St Andrew's, Pangbourne and many more. Main entry points are at 11, 13 and 16. At 11 and 13, admission is by school's own entrance exam or CE (interview and head's report taken into account too). Pupils joining sixth form (up to 20 a year) must have at least five GCSE passes, including English and maths.

Exit: A few leave after GCSEs, mainly to do subjects not offered by Pangbourne, or as one pupil told us wryly, 'because they want more free time.' Around 90 per cent to university (in 2013, 40 per cent to Russell Group, highest ever) and usually one or two a year to Oxbridge. The rest start full-time work (one boy recently went straight to aviation college to do his commercial pilot's training), with a handful going into the Services.

Money matters: 'We're not a rich school,' the bursar told us, although with its centenary coming up in 2017 the school is busy upgrading many buildings. Means-tested bursaries available (from 10 per cent to 100 per cent) and a variety of scholarships (including academic, music and sport) at each entry point.

Remarks: A small and distinctive school that puts huge emphasis on self-discipline, teamwork and leadership. Caring and supportive, Pangbourne buzzes with activity and encourages every pupil to have a go and get involved.

P

Parkstone Grammar School

Sopers Lane, Poole, BH17 7EP

• Pupils: 1,230 girls; all day • Ages: 11–18 • Non–denom • State

Tel: 01202 605605
Email: enquiries@parkstone.poole.sch.uk
Website: www.parkstone.poole.sch.uk

Headteacher: Since 2013, Mrs Tracy Harris. Was previously deputy headteacher at South Wilts Grammar School for Girls and has a strong track record in selective single sex education. Educated in the south west and studied history at Exeter University. Her husband Ian is also a teacher and she plays in a brass band in her spare time.

Academic matters: Results at GCSE and A level live up to its local reputation for excellence. Almost all do three sciences at GCSE, with pretty spectacular results. In 2013, 65 per cent A*/A grades across all subjects. At A level, maths, English, biology and chemistry have a high take up rate and pretty impressive results. In 2013, 79 per cent A*/B grades at A level, making it the most successful sixth form in Dorset and Hampshire.

This is a maths, science and modern languages academy with a wide choice of other subjects: drama, electronics, textiles in addition to usual GCSEs; plus computing, food, media studies, graphics, geology and politics at AS and most of these at A Level.

Girls learn French, German and Spanish in year 8 and choose between German and Spanish in year 9. Most (85-90 per cent) continue with at least one language to GCSE, and girls can do up to three. No Latin, Greek or eastern languages at present, though Italian is now on stream. Girls are absolutely confident that the school would support anything they really wanted to do.

Sixth forms are sufficiently coordinated for girls to be able to slot into all-boys Poole Grammar School courses if Parkstone can't offer the combination they want and vice versa. Further maths, computing, geology and graphics A level courses available at Poole Grammar; the boys come to Parkstone for sociology, theatre studies and politics.

Large classes of up to 30 plus in lower school but very good monitoring. Subject prefects are good at providing help schemes and revision clubs with lots of encouragement from staff. Exceptionally good staff-pupil relationships with girls declaring, 'at risk of sounding cheesy, our staff are amazing, inspiring, working really hard to give us good lessons and ready to do anything to help.' SEN help available and an atmosphere of trust makes emotional, organisational etc support easily available. A small percentage with SENs including physical/medical and emotional difficulties and school can support those with mobility problems. Almost no EFL needed.

Homely library, evidently much used for borrowing, as well as study in the sixth form computer section. Help on hand and girls encouraged to read anything they fancy.

Games, options, the arts: Well-known in Poole for their lavish joint musical productions with Poole Grammar, but these are led by Parkstone. Lots of smaller drama things going on, often with Poole via theatre studies; art gets a smaller take up. Music is important and has the most attractive building on site, purpose-built and homely in brick complex shared by sixth formers who use it as a class base. Orchestras and groups (string, saxophone, choir etc) abound.

All girls do PE to the end of year 13, and rugby, cricket and football are popular. Netball and cricket strong – national finalists in 2013; but sport cannot be underestimated in a school boasting three Olympic athletes (sailing, volleyball and beach volleyball) amongst its recent past pupils. There's a fantastic sports hall with stunning beechwood sprung floor, masses of tennis courts and room for everything else, but sixth formers can do their own thing off-site in local clubs etc.

Extra-curricular options extensive and adventurous; some shared with Poole Grammar. Twenty or so clubs include, of course, debating, books, films and drama etc but also some further educational opportunities: Japanese at several levels, Mandarin Chinese, Russian plus engineering and robotics. Parkstone girls have built three racing cars from scratch – as opposed to one from a kit at Poole – and raced them nationally, winning commendations for their exceptional teamwork. As a team, the school has been totally behind a member of staff walking 630 miles of the south coast path to raise funds for several charities, plus a bit for the school's technology department. Parkstone has a British Council award for its links and work with other countries – Zambia and Kenya particularly. Trips on offer for languages, skiing etc, with Poole Grammar providing geology and other exciting options. Concert band and choirs recently did open air concerts in Rome and performed in Barcelona. Girls say that financial help is available and they can spread the cost – and regard trips as unprecedented opportunities.

Background and atmosphere: The school started as co-educational in Parkstone and has been at its current site since 1961. Its 20 acres abut residential lanes of bungalows and industrial areas – the derelict Poole pottery is just up the road. The nearby sewage works, which occasionally make their presence felt, were not detectable on the GSG visit. The buildings reflect their surroundings and even the bandbox-new £6 million technology, maths and art block could be mistaken for a factory, though the long wide interior corridor with its distant glass wall opening on to silver birches is a felicitous piece of design. This was funded to provide the extra facilities needed when the Poole schools, hitherto starting in year 8, begin to admit year 7 pupils in 2013.

As well as a common-room in the music block, sixth formers have access to the new spacious and welcoming dining area at all times, and find it a good place to work. Early risers can use its café at 8am. Food, say the girls is really good, with plenty of choice and cheap too. 'You can order an omelette and have it made in front of your eyes!'

The language block, dating from 1995 but looking curiously like a 70's product, is well-equipped, and a deceptively large new lecture theatre, full of girls being given some gruesomely graphic anti-drugs education on our visit, has been squeezed in between buildings.

Pastoral care and discipline: Big tutor groups, with the same tutor for the first four years, get an hour's tutor time/PSHE each fortnight. Mentoring schemes help new girls fit in and are continued for those who need it. All staff take a positive role in pastoral care – the school stresses, and the girls confirm, that any member of staff can help any girl, not just their allocated charges. Uniform quite stylish and, surprisingly, girls like pale yellow shirts, grey v necks with striped edges and crested and multi-pocketed black blazers. Expensive-ish, 'but cheaper than us having to provide constant fashion updates.' Sixth formers value an own-clothes-but-suitable-for-work dress code.

School has few rules about jewellery etc and girls do not take advantage of this. Few problems, but girls say they make their own pressures and find the staff are good at recognising the signs and helping them to cope with stress. Girls' trust in staff and respect for the amount of trouble they take to support them is impressive.

Pupils and parents: Poole has a largely white Anglo-Saxon population with both some very affluent and some very underprivileged areas, and families come from all over. Parkstone's reputation is good enough to attract those who could afford independent education and the school is keen to make sure those who most need Parkstone find it accessible. Sixty-five per cent come from Poole, the rest from up to an hour away. Around 40 per cent of girls come to school by bus – local bus company, city bus or via private arrangements made by parents. One of the nicest things about the girls is their awareness that not all their primary school friends get the opportunities that they do – which both motivates them to make best use of their chances and to want to make things better. Parent-staff association raises lots of funds for extras like minibuses and special equipment.

Entrance: Poole changed from a three-tier (junior, middle and senior) to a two-tier system in 2013. So in September 2013 only, the school had entries at 11 (year 7) and 12 (year 8); in subsequent years entry will be at age 11 into Year 7 only.

There are between two and three applicants for each of the 180 places in a year group. All girls now have the right to take the Parkstone test (late September – register by mid-September – exact dates etc available from the school) before they commit themselves to choosing which schools to apply for. Previously, successful Poole applicants automatically got places, and those outside the town were allocated the remaining spaces in rank order of score. The new admissions code now allows pupils to take the test before applying. They will be told their test score and whether or not this meets the required standard (but not whether they have got a place) before the deadline for applications. Once they have applied, they will be ranked according to results, but further candidates not yet tested will also go into the pecking order, so things are not clear cut. Best advice is probably to take the test at first opportunity, though it may mean a bit of a wait to know if you have gained a place. An independent admissions appeals panel can and does allocate further places – occasionally up to about 40 as parents are very well aware of the excellent education on offer here. It's confusing – especially in the first year of change – but after that the school will have a clearer view of how it works in practice.

Girls come from all over Poole, but some schools are better than others at raising awareness: Broadstone Middle School, Baden Powell and St Peter's School, Canford Heath Middle School, Oakdale Middle School and independent preps like Buckholme Towers, The Yarrells and Castle Court in Corfe Mullen.

Can take up to 50 girls at sixth form – currently, the school requires a bare minimum of six GCSEs at A*-C, with at least a B in subjects to be studied at A level; specific entry requirements for each subject can be found in the sixth form prospectus/website.

Exit: A few go after GCSE (17 per cent in 2013) – either to good local sixth forms or occasionally to independents; others join from elsewhere. At 18, nearly all to uni. South west ones to the fore, eg Southampton, Bournemouth and Portsmouth, though a sprinkling everywhere, with a high proportion to the older, well-established universities. Law popular, masses of scientific courses and a very wide spread of other subjects. Three to Oxbridge in 2013.

Remarks: A hive of clever, purposeful girls, who nevertheless have wide interests. Unpretentious but high powered, Parkstone gives girls an exceptional level of support and a rich experience. The enthusiasm of the girls speaks for itself.

Parliament Hill School

Linked school: LaSwap Sixth Form Consortium

Highgate Road, London, NW5 1RL

• Pupils: 900 girls, all day plus 300 in sixth form • Ages: 11–19
• Non-denom • State

Tel: 020 7485 7077
Email: headteacher@parliamenthill.camden.sch.uk
Website: www.parliamenthill.camden.sch.uk

Headteacher: Since 2005, Ms Susan Higgins MA (Cantab) MA (Ed) (fifties), previously head of Brentford School for Girls for five years. She studied English at New Hall (now Murray Edwards) College, Cambridge, after a peripatetic school career, as her family moved around the country. The first Oxbridge student from her Bradford comprehensive, she was enthused by 'an inspirational English teacher'. She was head of English at Walthamstow School for Girls for much of her career, taking time out to become deputy head at Skinners' Company's School for Girls in Hackney and spending time as a school-based PGCE tutor for the Institute of Education before returning to Walthamstow as deputy head. She has two children.

A strong and capable leader with a good back-up team. Parents say: 'I'm very impressed by her.… She's personable and engaging, with great people skills. She has a firm grasp of what needs to be done.…The girls love hearing about her experience of going to Cambridge as a working class girl…She's a great role model for them.'

Academic matters: A huge ability range here, with lots of bright girls and also plenty in need of extra support, whether educational or emotional. Accordingly, the school offers a range of options. Everyone studies for a core of GCSE subjects which includes maths, English, core science, RE, and short courses in PE and citizenship. They can add on more GCSE subjects, or choose a vocational BTEC from a range that includes business, art and design, ICT and health and social care, or go for a young apprenticeship. Most of the latter two options are taught elsewhere in Camden. Everyone is allocated to either French or Spanish classes for the first three years, and can start the other language in year 9; about a third take a modern language GCSE. Other popular options at KS4 include additional AS maths and triple science; ICT AS and photography GCSE are taught after school as twilight classes.

In 2013, 69 per cent of girls got 5+ A*-C grades including English and maths at GCSE. English has been very strong, maths and science historically rather weaker. However, maths now taught in ability sets from the second term in year 7, and the curriculum has been redesigned substantially. The latest Ofsted report judged the school as outstanding, and commented: 'recent improvements in maths have been striking'. Girls arrive at the school with, on average, much higher verbal than non-verbal aptitude scores – 'But as a technology college we focus on building up their confidence and aptitude in maths and science'. The science department has appointed some very highly qualified teachers over the last few years. Triple science courses very popular, with excellent results. 'They're very good at assessing strengths and weaknesses,' said a parent, 'and throwing lots of energy at weaknesses.'

The head is reviewing all the schemes of work in key stage 3, including building in greater differentiation for ranges of ability – 'In a comprehensive you have to keep revisiting this and doing it better'. Homework and marking – aspects raised by parents as sometimes inconsistent – are other key priorities – 'Every department has produced its own guidelines with clear expectations. Parents need to know these'.

P

SEN provision has been 'transformed', with an assistant head leading the way on SEN and inclusion. Consultants brought in recently to review the provision were 'very positive'. Few state schools feel that they have sufficient funds to provide all the help every child needs, but 'We feel we've made substantial progress'. The Extra Mile project targets under-achieving year 10 girls, who are mostly from white low-income families.

Gifted and talented provision focuses on what goes on in lessons – 'In a comprehensive you've got to make sure you're providing stretch in the classroom. We get professionals in to make sure we're getting it right'. Also masterclasses and mentoring, and year 7 girls recently visited Murray Edwards College, Cambridge, to meet undergraduates and visit the zoology department – 'Many of our girls wouldn't naturally consider applying to a university like this. It's essential they have their aspirations raised'.

Joint sixth form with next-door William Ellis School, with co-ed tutor groups. It is also part of La Swap, which includes La Sainte Union and Acland Burghley schools. Each school teaches the core sixth form subjects, but students visit other schools in the group for more minority subjects eg film studies and further maths. The ability range encompasses those aspiring to read medicine at Cambridge and those working for an introductory BTEC diploma in health and social care, with appropriate entry requirements. A scheme in conjunction with La Sainte Union targets very able scientists, who study together and take part in organised work experience and masterclasses. English is the most popular A level subject at Parliament Hill, with psychology second. In 2013, 51 per cent A*/B grades and 22 per cent A*/A overall.

Games, options, the arts: Everyone takes DT GCSE, with a choice of four options – year 7s were busy cooking muffins during our visit. The single storey DT block was built to an environmentally-friendly design with a green roof, and forms the fourth side of a grassy courtyard, twisting up to meet the original Edwardian building. On another corner of the building is the performing arts block, clad in green glass, which provides music rooms and dance and drama studios. The top floor corridors are lined with expressive GCSE and A level photography and artwork, and textile designs hang in the stairwells.

Music probably not the highest profile subject here, but many girls have instrumental lessons and play in the orchestra or in the jazz, string or brass ensembles, or sing in the choir. Those on free school meals get free music lessons. Two hours' timetabled PE a week for everyone. Two tennis/netball courts at the front of the school and a grassy area at the back where the football teams practise, plus a rather ageing hall for gym and badminton with a fitness suite. On the wish-list is a new sports hall. All year 7s learn to swim at Swiss Cottage baths and the head hopes in future to make more use of the Lido, which is more or less next door. Sports teams play successful matches against other Camden schools.

A breakfast club every morning at 8am and plenty more activities ranging from Italian and chess clubs to basketball and rounders. Girls perform in musicals such as the 'excellent and ambitious' production of The Wiz, run round Parliament Hill in fancy dress to raise funds for Sports Relief, visit China and go on physics trips to Switzerland.

Background and atmosphere: Opened in 1906, has an idyllic site on the edge of Hampstead Heath. Plenty of grassy space, including a sculpture park and kick-around area. Buildings range from solid Edwardiana to the 21st century award-winning DT and performing arts blocks. Is at last – hurray – in receipt of £19.2 million to rebuild the well-past-its-sell-by-date Heath Building ('we're all going to lean against it until it falls over,' promised head when we visited) which houses maths, English, science, canteen and library.

Harmonious atmosphere. Despite the huge range of pupils, both ethnically and socially, girls tend to get on well together, with few reports of bullying. Recently one of six in the country to win a Diamond quality mark for cultural diversity. 'They manage the mix very well,' said a parent.

Pastoral care and discipline: Many vulnerable pupils here, including refugees and those with learning difficulties, who get 'excellent' support, says Ofsted. Liaises with its feeder primary school to identify girls likely to be in need of extra help with making the transition to senior school. It works with outside agencies that provide therapy or counselling to those in need. It also runs many programmes to motivate disaffected pupils, stretch the aspirations of bright girls and ensure everyone gets a chance to broaden their horizons. Assertive classroom management keeps most lessons running without disruptions.

Older girls are allowed to go out onto Hampstead Heath at lunchtimes, together with pupils from nearby schools, William Ellis and La Sainte Union, and locals have complained about litter problems – 'We're very concerned. The girls regard the Heath as very special to them, and we're doing work on social responsibility to educate them that it's for everyone in the community'.

Pastoral care is very good, report parents. 'I've always felt they know my daughter very well,' said one. 'They've contacted me whenever they've had concerns, and they've dealt with any problems quickly and well.'

Pupils and parents: 'Amazingly diverse' student population speaks some 50 different languages at home, though few are at early stages of learning English. Over 200 refugees. Nearly half of the girls are on free school meals, but also good support from some local middle-class families. OGs include actress Katrin Cartlidge, BBC journalist Laura Trevelyan and Lola Young, Baroness Young of Hornsey.

Entrance: Takes 180 girls into year 7, with admissions organised by the LA. Priority for particular SEN, siblings, children in care and those with exceptional social needs. Then by distance – generally within a mile and a half. Those joining La Swap sixth form to do A levels must have at least eight GCSE passes including three C and two B grades; various vocational courses available for those with lower grades.

Exit: Between two-thirds and three-quarters of pupils join La Swap sixth form. Some move on to other sixth forms, eg Camden School for Girls or Woodhouse College, others to colleges such as City and Islington or Westminster Kingsway to do vocational courses.

One or two a year to Oxbridge; one student off to read maths at Cambridge with a full scholarship in 2012. Many others reading sciences eg biomedical science, pharmacy and physics. London universities popular – King's College, UCL and Queen Mary recently. Sussex, Nottingham and Leeds popular for a range of subjects – languages, history, English, architecture and psychology. Quite a few to art foundation courses.

Remarks: Popular girls' comprehensive in idyllic situation on the borders of Hampstead Heath, with a diverse but harmonious student population and an 'outstanding' Ofsted rating. Strong, popular head who is a driving force in building on strengths and tackling weaknesses. 'My daughter has been so happy there that she has become an ambassador for her school,' said a parent.

Parmiter's School

High Elms Lane, Garston, Watford Hertfordshire, WD25 0UU

- Pupils: 1,365 boys and girls all day • Ages: 11–18 • No-denom
- State

Tel: 01923 671424
Email: admin@parmiters.herts.sch.uk
Website: www.parmiters.herts.sch.uk

Headmaster: Since 2010, Mr Nick Daymond MA Cantab PGCE NPQH (forties), previously head of Roundwood Park School in Harpenden. He went from St Paul's School to Queens' College, Cambridge to read modern languages, but changed to theology in his third year. He did a PGCE out of pragmatism rather than vocation, but had an 'inspirational' PGCE language tutor, and found Goffs School, where he had a placement, 'a stimulating place to be'.

Married with two children, he is popular with parents and pupils, who comment that he is 'very approachable' and 'always around at school events, often with his family'. They are appreciative that he did not leap in to make immediate changes 'just to make his mark', and that he evidently values the traditions of the school.

Academic matters: The ability range is undoubtedly skewed towards the more able, with 25 per cent chosen by academic ability, and 10 per cent for musical aptitude – 'Musicians tend to be good at maths and languages too'. Plus their siblings, of course. However, says the head, 'It's more mixed than you would imagine.' Everyone is in all ability form groups for the first three years, with setting and a variety of other groupings in subjects such as maths, science, languages and music. 'It seems to work really well,' said a parent. 'My son really likes working with people at the same level as him.' The school has specialisms in technology, music and languages, and everyone takes a language to GCSE, starting French in year 7 and taking up Spanish or German in year 8.

Maths, English and sciences are much the most popular A level subjects, but most other A level subjects are well supported too. Nearly everyone gets 5+ A*-C GCSE grades, including maths and English, with 51 per cent of these grades being A*/A in 2013; 75 per cent of A level grades were A*/B in 2013 and 48 per cent A*/A. Very high value added scores.

The school works with Villiers Park Educational Trust to develop independent learning in sixth formers and encourage high aspirations. 'I want to ensure that we're not just an exam factory, but end up with well-rounded students.' Groups of teachers and year 12 pupils have jointly explored how they can improve teaching and learning and research skills. 'It's very powerful having students talk to you about what works and what doesn't work.'

Games, options, the arts: The 60 rolling acres of playing fields have a public school feel. Also an Astroturf, sports hall with fitness suite and dance studio plus floodlit tennis and netball courts. Plenty of inter-school matches and tournaments in all the usual sports, including boys' rugby and basketball and girls' football, with teams often reaching county finals. 'It's good that there are B and C teams too,' said a pupil, 'so everyone can have a go.' PE popular at GCSE and A level. Music places given for aptitude rather than ability, so not all recipients are hugely experienced, but plenty going on, with many instrumental and choral groups performing in 'fabulous' concerts and going on European tours. Lavish school productions of, eg, Jesus Christ Superstar, featuring actors and musicians. DT and art both popular and high quality – a high proportion of 2012 GCSE art entrants got an A*. Vibrant art studios jammed with photographs, ceramics and silk screen printing as well as interesting paintings.

Lots of language exchanges, as one would expect, plus physics trips to Switzerland, geography trips to Iceland, history trips to the Somme. Refreshingly, the visits are designed to be affordable – eg Normandy rather than Quebec – though students spend a long time raising funds for the sixth form trip to Tanzania, 'the experience of a lifetime'. Huge numbers take part in D of E.

House system provides lots of opportunities for competing in, eg the golf tournament, short story competition, ironman challenge and ICT design competition. Colours awarded for dedication to and achievement in extra-curricular activities.

Raises large amounts for charity – 'I've been very struck by the amount of charity work we do. So many students are actively involved outside school as well as inside, and it is a good opportunity for them to initiate things'.

Background and atmosphere: Founded in 1681 in Bethnal Green with funds left by wealthy East London silk merchant Thomas Parmiter in his will. Became a boys' grammar school, but turned comprehensive and co-ed when it moved to Hertfordshire in 1977. Still has links with Bethnal Green: the Old Parmiterians' Society, with many members from the East End grammar school, is very active, and each year some 60 or 70 East London pensioners travel up for lunch and entertainments. The head is educational adviser to the Bethnal Green Educational Fund – 'It is a very important part of the school and brings a different dimension to our lives'.

The school looks like a classic '70s comprehensive from the outside, but has a traditional grammar school feel on the inside, with portraits of former head teachers and honours boards. Parents and staff evidently value the combination of traditional values and progressive outlook and the head comments: 'It was the traditions and ethos that appealed to me'.

Pastoral care and discipline: 'I've had very little to do in terms of behaviour,' says the head. Most upsets are related to 'the usual bits of nastiness, such as friendship issues and routine run-of-the-mill problems, such as late homework'. A parent commented that staff are 'very supportive, really approachable. They have been fantastic in helping with the settling in issues we've had (and these have been very few).' Another said, 'I always find the children well-behaved, walking along after school chatting and smiling in friendly groups.'

Pupils and parents: It may be 'more mixed than you would imagine', but pupils are largely from nice Hertfordshire families from the surrounding postcodes. Runs buses from Shenley, St Albans, Bushey, Harrow, Radlett and Hemel Hempstead. Former pupils include ambassadors Sir Terence Clarke, Emrys Davies and Alper Mehmet, Nick Leeson of Barings Bank fame, footballer Jordan Parkes and TV gardener Tommy Walsh.

Entrance: Looked after children get first priority; then 10 per cent of places to those living closest; then siblings; then compelling medical reasons; then 25 per cent academic, via verbal reasoning and maths tests; then 10 per cent musical aptitude (test and audition); then remaining places by proximity (generally not much further than a kilometre). Nearly all the medical, academic and music places are allocated to children from surrounding WD, AL and HP post codes; however, 'Applications will be welcomed from the Ancient Parish of St Matthew, Bethnal Green'. Consistently the most over-subscribed school in Hertfordshire, with more than seven applicants for each place.

Students going into the sixth form – internally or externally – need at least six GCSEs with mostly B grades or above.

P

Exit: Between 10 and 20 per cent leave after GCSEs, mostly for FE colleges. Nearly all sixth formers go to university, studying anything from medicine at Imperial College to biblical studies at Sheffield. Eleven to Oxbridge in 2013.

Money matters: Parents' Association very active and raises large sums from, eg Three Peaks' Challenge, craft fair and Bollywood evening. Also gets funds from the Parmiter's Foundation charity, which has helped with considerable redevelopment: new languages, music, sixth form and drama centres have been built over the past few years and a new maths block is at planning stage.

Remarks: Extremely successful, semi-selective state school with public school facilities and grammar school traditions, in enviable green surroundings.

Pate's Grammar School

Princess Elizabeth Way, Cheltenham, GL51 0HG

- Pupils: 1030 pupils; 440 boys/590 girls; All day • Ages: 11–18
- Non-denom • State

Tel: 01242 523169
Email: office@pates.gloucs.sch.uk
Website: www.pates.gloucs.sch.uk

Headmaster: Since 2012, Mr Russel Ellicott BA. Read history at Royal Holloway and then completed his PGCE, became a teacher of history and PE first at The Crypt School in Gloucester, then at Marling School in Stroud before moving to Pates in 2007 as deputy head. Married with two children. Teaches GCSE history. Passionate about cricket – and had carefully selected his headmaster's XI for the Cricket Festival in the week that we were visiting.

Friendly, direct and effective. Doesn't appear to be a man to thrust himself into the limelight – a careful, analytical listener who interrogates assumptions. Enthusiastic, organised and strategic. Keen to turn the school more 'outward', to be a 'magpie' of best practice in other schools and to go 'beyond outstanding'.

Says pastoral care and creating a happy school are 'what we are here for', not just for pupils but for staff – 'there must be a work life balance'. Passionate about developing and distributing leadership within the pupil and staff bodies (large numbers of staff involved in leadership projects and research into learning strategies). Staff say he is 'warm, open, supportive', 'won't make false promises' and 'will give anyone an opportunity to do anything'. Parents say he is 'wonderful with the children, quiet and calm, completely engages them'.

Academic matters: Extremely impressive results: strong across the board. In 2013, 91 per cent A*/A at GCSE. All take triple award science, maths, English language and literature. The vast majority also take a modern language (French, German, Spanish, Mandarin). Lots of other options including Latin, DT, PE, RS and drama. There are five one hour periods a day and the GCSE syllabus, as with some other academies, is taught from year 9 so options have to be chosen in year 8 – parents say there is lots of help and information with this. However, the longer lesson times and three year curriculum leave masses of time for enrichment and mean that Tuesday afternoons are generally free for extracurricular activities, most of which are sixth form led.

Intranet and VLE are fully integrated into teaching and learning. Well organised use of a good library, a good supply of laptops and networked computers, and very good technical support.

Results at A Level are excellent: 72 per cent A*/A in 2013, with sciences particularly strong – maths, physics, chemistry and biology are the most popular subjects here. However, you would have to search long and hard for a weak area. A good range of subjects too – including Arabic, Latin, politics, psychology, theatre studies.

Pupils remark on the helpfulness and availability of staff, and staff speak very well of the students – but no-one comes to Pates without an enthusiasm for learning. For those on the SEN spectrum (about 15-20 in the school at any one time – mostly high functioning Aspergers/ADHD) there is careful, tailored support.

Games, options, the arts: All the usual sports; athletics and cricket are particularly strong. A large and well maintained sports hall, fitness suite and climbing wall. Less gifted sportspeople get a chance to compete in inter-house competitions, and a large number of students take PE at GCSE, some at A Level too.

Large CCF, an active Duke of Edinburgh programme, outdoor pursuits most weekends. Very good art facilities with lovely light studios and art rooms, and a rather charming gallery which has risen out of the shell of the old school kitchen. Lots of student work on display around the school and very good GCSE and A level art results.

Music at the school is very strong – good exam results, as well as plenty of opportunities to perform: lots of ensembles, choirs, charity concerts and recitals. There are orchestras as well as composition classes, a good range of school instruments available to those wishing to learn and good practice rooms. Music is strongly linked with drama and dance, also popular. There is a small performing arts space for those productions not suited to the full 'school hall' experience.

Debating, film, Latin, 'wearable art', kayaking clubs – lots to do. Sixth formers organise many of the activities, part of a school-wide policy of sharing and encouraging leadership. Parents say 'there is something for everyone'. In addition, many students are involved in charitable fundraising, and the school has a very popular charities committee with a 'keenly contested' application process. As many pupils have a long commute, the majority of extracurricular activities are scheduled for lunchtimes and Tuesday afternoons.

Background and atmosphere: The school was founded over 400 years ago by a local – the eponymous Richard Pate. It was a free grammar school for boys until 1904, when a girl's school was added, the two merging about 20 years ago. It has recently been substantially rebuilt, and has added a lovely new refectory and IT suite. Pate's is not exactly set in rolling parkland – it's at the less glamorous end of Cheltenham, and perimeter fences make the initial impression somewhat forbidding. However, the school buildings are uniformly well designed, and based round a large quad which gives a sense of openness. There are good sized playing fields to the back alongside a very well set up sports hall, and generally the school is well maintained and well equipped. Food, according to the pupils, is good, varied and healthy. The atmosphere is one of confidence, aspiration and determination – the pupils and staff seem comfortable, confident and happy.

Pastoral care and discipline: Pastoral care, which has long been a high priority for the school, has been re-organised: alongside the tutor groups and house system (four houses from Y7 up) there are now individual year heads for every age group plus a personal development lead tutor (focussing on co-ordinating the usual PSHE stuff plus financial and economic know how, personal resilience etc). A school counsellor comes in twice a week and a SENCo acts as lead for pastoral interventions in the case of illness, eating disorders or similar. We sense that pastoral care is highly tuned here and co-ordinated well with outside agencies where appropriate.

The school takes the opinions of its students seriously – members of the student council sit as associate governors of the school and their input is described by the chair as 'exceptional'. We have a strong impression that students are treated with great respect and care by governors and staff, a respect which is appreciated and reciprocated. Parents say discipline is 'quiet, never heavy handed'; and that the the interest in looking after every child is 'heartfelt'.

All Y7 children get birthday cards from the head, and small groups of Y8s get birthday cake in the head's office. Little in the way of a formal disciplinary system in evidence – although there are occasional withdrawals from lessons for an afternoon for those who overstep the mark.

Pupils and parents: Pupils are largely from around Cheltenham but they also come from further corners of Gloucestershire, and even Worcestershire, West Oxfordshire and Herefordshire. Most parents are middle class and aspirational, with many coaching their children very determinedly to get a place, but the school is also very keen to encourage entrance for those from less advantaged backgrounds and to make it 'a school for everyone'. There is an active PTA and communications between parents and school are generally very good, with good turnouts to parents' evenings and positive responses to reports. The pupils themselves are friendly, confident and happy. They say they chose the school because they 'want to learn', that 'teachers don't talk down to you' and that the best thing about the school is the 'incredibly kind' people in it. Parents with children who have been through Pate's and gone on to university say they feel 'they have been better prepared for further study than their peers'.

Entrance: Highly over subscribed – about 10 candidates per place for year 7. Two opportunities for entrance: at year 7 and again in the sixth form where there are an extra 50-60 places available. At year 7, selection is via the LA but based on the school's own verbal reasoning entrance test (you have to register with both the school and the LA) and places are offered strictly to the 120 top scorers. Applicants will already have self-selected to some extent as the school is known for its very high academic standards. Practice papers are available to prospective pupils. The competition is quite tough – not for the faint-hearted. Work is ongoing to make the tests less coachable, so that the school is accessible to 'anyone who is bright enough to be here'. Registration for the test is in the September prior to entry, with the test itself in October, and places offered (or not) by the beginning of March.

External candidates for the sixth form are expected to have As, preferably A*s, predicted in the subjects chosen for A level study, and strong results are expected across the board. Internal candidates have to meet the same criteria as external candidates. Places for the sixth form are offered by the end of April (apply by February).

Exit: Very few leavers after GCSE. All sixth formers to university – 28 to Oxbridge in 2013. Exeter, Cardiff, Bristol, Nottingham all popular; a trickle abroad (Princeton, Milan). All sorts of subjects – lots into sciences, but also business, languages, law etc. Lots of support and help in choosing courses and putting UCAS forms together, say parents. Developing contacts with alumni.

Money matters: Financial assistance to help ensure that no-one is excluded from wealth of extracurricular bits and pieces, trips abroad, skiing expeditions etc. Gets funds from the Pate's Foundation.

Remarks: Continues to be really outstanding academically and pastorally, with no sense of slowing its pace. Pate's offers a great combination of academic excellence and extracurricular enrichment. A very strong sense of kindness and community, but still committed to the individual. For those who seriously aspire to excel intellectually and personally, this is a fantastic place to be.

The Perse Upper School

Linked school: The Perse Preparatory School

Hills Road, Cambridge, CB2 8QF

• Pupils: 1,060; 711 boys and 349 girls • Ages: 11-18 • Non-denom
• Fees: £14,451 pa • Independent

Tel: 01223 403800
Email: admissions@perse.co.uk
Website: www.perse.co.uk

Head: Since 2008, Mr Edward Elliott (early forties), who has been at the school since 1997. Educated at The Royal Grammar School, Worcester, then St Anne's College, Oxford, where he got a first in geography. Tried commerce (a graduate trainee at De La Rue) but quickly moved to teaching at the Whitgift School in Surrey. Married to Sue, a paediatrician, with two daughters and a son of Pelican and Prep age. Certainly a finger very firmly on the pulse at The Perse as well as in the wider education community, though 'not swayed by current trends in education to make knee-jerk reactions' surmises a parent.

Academic matters: Brainpower is not thin on the ground in Cambridge and the Perse aims, and achieves, high academically to meet its market. Even given the genes, results are impressive across the board – 95 per cent A*-B at A level and 80 per cent A*/A in 2013. Pre-U and International A level are offered alongside A levels. Three-quarters IGCSE and the other quarter GCSE, with 90 per cent of grades A*/A in 2013. Heads of department have the freedom to choose the exam they feel offers the most rigour and currency. Results are of course stellar in maths and science, yet history, geography and languages are also among the popular sixth form options – a hint to the breadth of education on offer here. The Perse has developed its own course in engineering technology and makes innovative use of IT. 'Global studies' in year 7 offers a taster of a range of languages – Mandarin, Japanese, Arabic, Portuguese and Italian. All labs recently refitted to highest standard and computer science now lauded as 'the fourth science'. More than 60 students each year involved in the Higher Project Qualification (HPQ) – 'intellectually liberating' says head – and the sixth form equivalent, the Extended Project Qualification (EPQ)is also popular.

SEN provision is excellent, although head prefers the term 'learning maximisation'. All pupils are screened on entry, with the result that 120 pupils are supported, including those perhaps running at 80 per cent capacity who would not be spotted elsewhere. On-site SEN teacher plus liaison with educational psychologists, who all feed through to director of teaching in a concerted effort to work around the barriers. 'The school's reputation for only concentrating on high flyers is not borne out by the extra sessions, reviews and learning aids that have been provided for my child,' says a parent.

A few parental rumblings about the school's commitment to nurturing young teachers, some of whom don't come up to scratch straightaway. The school points to its significant new teacher induction and continuous professional development programme, with mentoring from more experienced staff.

Games, options, the arts: Surprisingly for a day school, manages to keep two or three sessions a week for games and other extra-curricular activities right through the school – 'almost too many to choose from' say pupils. This is, in the main, a very popular

P

policy and pupils relish the opportunities to develop sporting, musical or dramatic skills, and various adventurous options on offer – notably CCF (RAF only, unusually, and a popular choice for many girls). There's also the Perse Exploration Society, which runs trips in the UK for younger pupils, as far afield as Vietnam and the Himalayas for the eldest. Excellent sports hall block includes squash court, weights room and a large and well-appointed fitness suite; school employs a fitness coach who provides guidance and fitness programmes for students and staff. Much effort has gone in to providing a wide choice of sports and fitness opportunities for girls, who show their appreciation by their enthusiasm.

Art is rich and colourful, evidence of inspirational teaching, and includes ceramics and printing. Local artists exhibit in The Pelican Gallery within the teaching space. Impressive lecture theatre doubles as drama studio seating 180 – productions have really grown in recent years. New (very neat) music building – an extension to existing block – provides plenty of teaching/practice rooms, as well as space for larger ensembles and rehearsal hall to accommodate full-scale symphony orchestra with chorus. This doubles as a concert hall and is made available to the local community. About two-fifths learn at least one instrument and musical activities of all types flourish – baroque string ensembles, jazz, brass, wind and chamber groups, choirs and music technology. The school's musical excellence now seen by parents as a principal reason to apply and attracting correspondingly good budding musicians. A new performing arts centre is on the wish list for the 400th anniversary fundraising pot in 2015-16.

Background and atmosphere: The school's history – nearly 400 years of it – is chequered and includes embezzlement in the 18th century, an assault on the head in the 19th and an incendiary bomb hitting it in 1941. Since 1960 it has occupied award-winning, purpose-built accommodation on a 28-acre site. Buildings are low, few higher than two storeys as is customary in this part of the world, but although not imposing, they are inviting and well integrated into the site. Hall doubles up as dining room, necessitating daily quick setting out and packing away of tables. Meals taken by staff and pupils together perhaps explaining the unusually orderly atmosphere. Two Astroturf pitches, very attractive, tree-lined playing fields, real feeling of space. A new outdoor pursuits centre and an additional full size all weather pitch have just been completed and construction of a second new teaching block (complete with lifts) is underway. Good careers room and resources in sixth form centre, which also has a well-used common room area, expanded to provide a separate work area.

Pastoral care and discipline: Interestingly, the house system was dusted off a few years ago to fill a gap in pupils' enthusiasm for extra-curricular activities. Re-introduced as eight houses for pupils in years 7 to 11, leadership opportunities are appreciated by those lower down the school.

International links are being forged 'to prepare students for a world where employment will be global' explains head. Exchanges to Spain, France and Germany as well as Sewickley, near Pittsburgh. Member of SAGE – Strategic Alliance of Global Educators – consortium of ten schools from around the world (UK, US, Australia, Singapore, Hong Kong, China...) who share best practice and work together on a range of projects. Also involved in Christel House charitable foundation to establish first class schools in the most deprived areas of the world – Perse staff have been seconded to Bangalore and Cape Town.

Parents appreciate the school's meticulous planning and communication, making life easier particularly for those juggling several offspring – all information is provided well in advance and with great attention to detail. Emails from pupils and parents are responded to swiftly, 'even on a Sunday night' marvels a parent.

Although common sense prevails in all corners of the school and its operation, there is room here too for eccentrics, who only add to the increasing richness of Perse life.

Pupils and parents: A school for the 'intellectually curious' says head, although fees prohibit mass takeover by bright children of poorly-paid Cambridge academics. There's a healthy mix of modest and affluent backgrounds, rare in independent schools – a 'cosmopolitan meritocracy' says head, who values it for its contribution to the development of all pupils' emotional intelligence, preparing them well for life in the real world.

School ceased taking boarders in 1993, two years before girls arrived in the sixth form. Most girls blossom here, with opportunities and resources few girls' schools can offer. Pupils are relaxed, unpretentious and natural – many come for the science but find they relish the sporting and artistic possibilities they discover. Majority live close by, though some from as far as Ely, Saffron Walden, Newmarket, Royston and elsewhere. Annually, a very few from abroad, under special guardianship scheme, seen as bringing new and refreshing dimension to school life. Distinguished list of Old Boys includes Sir Peter Hall, Rev Dr John Polkinghorne, David Tang, Dave Gilmour, Pete Atkin, Sir Mark Potter.

Entrance: Competition for places at The Perse is not as fierce as the rumour would have it and pales into insignificance next to London's bunfight. At 11, roughly two and a half applicants for each place – 60 come up from the Perse Prep and another 50 from local juniors and preps. Sixty more are added at 13 (largely from King's College, St John's College, St Faith's). Entry is by tests in English and maths and verbal reasoning, as well as an interview and report from the previous school.

Entry to sixth form is by interview and a subject test for scholarships, with all offers conditional on GCSE performance – usually above 70 points required, with A*/A in A level subjects. Most joiners come from local girls' independent schools (Stephen Perse, St Mary's) and the maintained sector. Around twenty leave The Perse after GCSE, choosing Hills Road Sixth Form College in the main.

Exit: Medicine hugely popular and many depart for top medical schools. Thirty to Oxbridge in 2013, rest to wide spread of other universities. Engineering, medical and natural sciences preferred subjects, but history also recurring.

Money matters: Scholarships are mostly five per cent, occasionally ten per cent. Determined to maintain its direct grant tradition and increase the amount of means-tested financial support available to bursary applicants. In 2013 spent over £1million on fees assistance for families who could not otherwise afford a Perse education.

Remarks: Now a fully co-ed academic school and a 'cosmopolitan meritocracy' which prepares students well for the real world, not just intellectually but also emotionally.

Perth Grammar School

Gowans Terrace, Perth, PH1 5AZ

• Pupils: 1,100; co-ed • Ages: 12–18 • Non denom • State

Tel: 01738 472800
Email: perthgrammar@pkc.gov.uk
Website: www.perthgrammar.pkc.sch.uk

Head: Head since 2007, John Low BEd (fifties), brought in at a week's notice from the highly sought after Breadalbane

Academy as a temporary secondment to sort out the school. After the 2008 inspection showed considerable improvement, he was enjoying the challenge so much that he accepted the headship as a permanent post. 'The school, like a super-tanker, took several miles to turn', but in 12 months he had changed it from a school with 'weak academics, poor behaviour, staff and pupils with low morale', losing lots of its rural catchment pupils to Breadalbane, into one which won £80k in The People's Millions TV show, is attracting pupils back and has had to cap its annual intake at 220, having previously averaged about 170. (Mr Low would like eventually to see 1400-1500, but that would need some more building.) Above all, pupils and staff have gained confidence, which he sees as the key factor.

Confidence has been created by bringing in international coaches, Eilidh Child European 400 metre silver medallist, Scottish basketball coach Russell Kesson, creating a sports trust to give them charitable status for fund-raising, making the letters of Perth Grammar larger than the signage of any other Perth school, winning the £80k and using it to revamp the theatre, upgrade all pupil toilets and improve the grounds. He looked for 'plus factors', such as first whole school photo, courses for mums and child minders, state-of-art playground complete with wendy house and little wicker dens for nursery, linking in with childcare course, forging links with China, France and Germany, taking ski trips, winning the Scottish education award for ambition. More recent developments are sports and health, with the school now shortlisted for the Scottish Education award for 'Getting Scotland Active', plus very high profile expressive arts, with a musical production in the pipe line.

Academic matters: Since the catchment area covers both inner city areas of Perth and part of county Perthshire, courses provide for academic high fliers and direct entry to employment. Initially all classes are mixed ability, but some subjects are set for ability during the course of S1 and S2: maths and French from S1, English, Spanish and German from S3. All do S grades (or Int I /II) or vocational courses – hairdressing, construction, horticulture (new poly-tunnel), engineering, childcare, sport and recreation (all joint with Perth College etc) – and technical – technical studies, graphic communications, home ec, admin, craft/design etc, as well as a solid set of academic possibilities.

S5/6 offers fullish range of Academic Highers and Ad Highers, kept under review according to the needs of each year group. Results and takeup both improving steadily. Courses in hairdressing (a non-examined level 6 Higher equivalent) and beauty (with Perth College, which has massage beds etc), Professional Development Award in General Insurance (now Aviva is a major Perth employer) etc are tailored by Mr L to fit up-and-coming employment opportunities.

Learning support department of 22 (teachers and support staff) led by Bill Colley, who used to be head of New Butterstone. Children who came in as non-copers are now making out in mainstream. Lots of initiatives: C 20 group with a pre level A life-skills programme – 'Super soups' enterprise group making profits for charity, equalities programme. School now a magnet school for special needs. New 'assertive tutoring' guidance programme gives one-to-one support to keep up motivation and work output when necessary.

Games, options, the arts: One of the few assets Mr Low inherited is a sports stadium with a proper grandstand and a good running track. This is used by Perth clubs for evening training and Mr Low's team of Scottish national level coaches (G McIntosh – hockey, S Cameron – football, K Munro – netball et al) can make after school practices join up with evening club times. This facility is shared by the St John's RC School, recently opened on other side of the site. Perth Grammar is a step ahead, already offering sports training to its feeder primaries. Usual range of soccer, netball, hockey, athletics etc. Forty-five per cent

of year 1 took up sports clubs last year, 75 per cent this year. The 'Sustrans' sport health initiative has provided oodles of bike lockers, which are dotted colourfully all over the grounds, and a flash of inspiration provided girls arriving dishevelled from their bike helmets with free access to the hairdressing department for half an hour before school.

Lots of outdoor activities, climbing wall at planning stage and plentiful trips, sporting and other, abroad: ski trip, Rome, Boston and New York, China and Barcelona. Music and drama now getting a turn with a summer musical production in the recently equipped hall. A few competitive activities are adding to the feel-good factor: a girls' team won the under 15 Girls' Final of the SSFA; gardening (Perth in Bloom trophy); science (Perth and Kinross Schools science quiz); architecture (a team designing school leisure space won the Dundee College Creative Space competition). Lots of effective fund-raising: over £22,000 for Rachel House children's hospice (£22,000 in total raised in the last two years) and other projects, such as a very active link with a school in Bangladesh and more planned with Poland and Spain. All these are beginning to open the doors to the world beyond both downtown Perth and rural Perthshire.

Background and atmosphere: Perhaps the most unpromising school buildings ever devised. Gaining admission via an unanswered buzzer, and finding the school office, curiously located on the upper floor some way from the entrance, were only possible because both staff and pupils were so friendly and helpful. Narrow corridors, pretty clean considering, though all still in garish colours, inevitably noisy and battered with the regular passage of 1100 children. Mr Low has prioritised his maintenance budget on classrooms and equipment, often stretching it by buying second hand, with impressive results such as the home ec room, enthusiastically in use by both boys and girls alike.

The extensive suite of art rooms is filled with masses of creative squalor and pupils working with enthusiasm. Sad to see the old tennis courts now used as car parks. The school suffers from its setting, sandwiched between two council housing estates in a semi-industrial part of Perth, though this may improve with the extensive, though not universally attractive, new-build round about. The school hall, once the library, is far too small, but has been opened up and given a large screen wall for wet day amusement etc, while Mr Low rents empty industrial space locally as exam halls away from school noise, thus freeing the school from a month of break times spent whispering in corridors. A school canteen serving sensible fare using 'cashless catering', the card system Scottish schools use to avoid having cash in school, but it also supplies a perky kiosk, The House of Munch, by the hairdressing Portacabin, with baguettes, hot drinks etc, in an effort to tempt pupil customers from the rather too local McDonald's.

However the shortcomings of buildings and general ambiance are more than made up for by the friendly, welcoming and extremely smart staff, which to a certain extent seems to have brushed off on the pupils, who look on the whole happy and purposeful. No mean achievement in that part of Perth.

Pastoral care and discipline: Mr Low's two-pronged approach has been, first, his code of 'pride, respect and ambition', implemented by the second, a team of deputies, three heading the houses, Almond, Earn and Lomond, and the fourth dedicated to support for staff and pupils, with the aim of further raising standards. Another full time member of staff heads the attendance project. Parents are involved at every stage communicated through Group Call, which texts parents both with general school information and, if necessary, about problems, parents' evenings reminders, homework, absence etc. Formal reports covering progress and social issues are only once a year, but the school stresses that parents can make contact at any time, not just at parents' meetings.

P

Social education is managed by the guidance department and includes programmes on bullying etc. Any instance of bullying is dealt with quickly and rules (on website) are simple and practical, including those on mobile phones and Mp3 players. Sanctions are mainly detention and withdrawal from class (into supervised alternative), though exclusion is the last resort. Tutor system based on houses is well enough staffed to allow individual monitoring/support where needed.

Pupils and parents: The catchment includes the least salubrious parts of Perth and a chunk of 'county' Perthshire, spreading north to Dunkeld and east almost to Crieff. Previously this meant that Breadalbane Academy creamed off the rural bits, but this trend has now reversed, which must make for a dynamic mixture. The Perth sector features alarmingly in Scotland's deprivation stats. Dress code (more PC than uniform) is black blazers, skirts/trousers, school tie, white shirt, and the usual means-tested uniform allowance is available. Mr Low is looking for sponsorship for some smart sportswear and casual coats to enhance general attitude to dress. Perth LA does not give breakdowns on ethnic mix – but then Perth is pretty Scottish, anyway.

Entrance: To year 1 from designated primaries, with a few moving into the area.

Exit: Two thirds stay on for S5 and about half to S6. Approximately 30 per cent to university and a good chunk to all sorts of vocational course, with an increasing swing to apprenticeship type employment. Very few unplaced.

Remarks: Certainly not the Eton of the north, but a school in which every single statistic that should be climbing is doing so, some slowly (academic averages) but all surely, and some exponentially – minor successes, teams and competitions. A long way to go, but everyone and everything seem to be growing on the journey. Nice to see the leafy glens knowing a good bit of Scottish education when they see it.

Peter Symonds College

Owens Road, Winchester, SO22 6RX

- Pupils: 3,265 boys and girls; most day, 80 board • Ages: 16–18
- Non-denom but with strong links to C of E • Fees: Boarding £11,370–£12,204 pa • State

Tel: 01962 852764
Email: psc@psc.ac.uk
Website: www.psc.ac.uk

Principal: Since 2013, Mr Stephen Carville. Joined Peter Symonds in 2002 as assistant principal and was promoted to vice principal two years later. Prior to joining Symonds he was an HMI inspector for Ofsted, leading college and area inspections nationally and before that, worked at Barton Peveril College as curriculum manager for business, economics and modern languages. He has been a manager and teacher in other sixth form, tertiary and general FE colleges.

Academic matters: Everything is here, both in terms of subject matter and the full range of human ability, from the star student who became head of the Cambridge Union last year to those who bump along at the bottom with a string of Ds and Es. A level performance on a mega-roll, improving year after year. Exam results outshine many independent schools – 'And we send more students to Oxbridge!' In 2013, 62 per cent A*/B grades and 34 per cent A*/As. The usual wide array of courses one finds

at sixth form colleges, includes, eg, photography, film studies and environmental science. Everyone takes general studies ('It strengthens university applications') and quite a few go for other non-subjects like critical thinking (very good results) and citizenship. A few subjects beam particularly brightly: maths, art, textiles, music, media studies. Some courses are 'victims of their own success' and students have reported that they could not study their first choices. Candidates may have to audition for dance or performing arts.

Numbers are huge – 21 sets for biology. No streaming. Largish class sizes with 15-19 average – sounds overwhelming in theory but seems to work in practice. Less academic students (about 100 of the total) can pursue vocational courses – level 2 BTECs or OCR Nationals in, eg, health and social care or business and finance: 'Much more useful than re-sitting GCSEs and struggling with A levels'. A few GCSEs on offer for retakes, and good linguists may pick up Italian or Spanish from scratch, taking GCSE on the way to A level in just two years. In 2012, 20 per cent A*/As for GCSEs. Those aiming for Oxbridge or competitive courses such as medicine or vet science get additional guidance (with governors roped in to provide interview practice).

Fifteen per cent benefit from some form of learning support including essay planning and self-organisation. Wheelchair access to much of the site ('We don't do badly for a sloping site'). Corridor to learning support centre lined with pictures of successful and famous dyslexics. Lunchtime workshops for those needing extra tuition – at both the top and the bottom ends of the achievement spectrum. Students report all the help they need if they ask for it – but they have to ask for it. Organisational ability is important here – 'It's like going to uni,' said a girl – and indeed PS has now been authorised to offer university courses for those who cannot tear themselves away from the place.

Latest Ofsted report gushingly rated Symonds 'outstanding' across the board.

Games, options, the arts: Strong teams because of its size. Sports hall funded by 'Mercers' money' (loosely part of the Mercers 'cluster' alongside, eg, St Paul's and Abingdon). Lots of grass about the place but the principal dreams of an Astro; however, new sports pavilion now open. Drama strong and an A level in performing arts is offered. A performing arts centre also on the principal's wish list. Brilliant results in art – course said to be very broad: 'almost like a foundation course'. Former fives court enjoying a second life as a photo studio. DT wedged into one large workshop. Students take part in an extra-curricular programme (two hours a week) with activities chosen from long list (50+) ranging from Amnesty International to creating the high quality American-style yearbook; knitting particularly hot at the mo. Some of these are accredited, such as the Community Sports Leader award and the Duke of Edinburgh award. Lots of fund-raising and local community work.

Fabulous, unique Hampshire specialist music course curiously low profile. Around 12 students a year are selected and study two instruments (free of charge) to a high standard, alongside academic music and two or three further A levels. 'Costs a fortune – we spend three times as much on the music specialists as we do on the other students,' says Mr Hopkins. The course gives the college a solid core of talent, but music spills out over its edges:140 students are studying music and/or music technology A level. Other music students receive free tuition on their main instrument and can play in a variety of bands, orchestras and choirs.

Background and atmosphere: Peter Symonds founded Christes Hospital (no relation to the Horsham school – it was a 'trendy name' at the time) in the 17th century to look after aged brethren, assist two divinity students and educate four poor boys. Sale of land during the expansion of the railways enabled a boys' grammar school to be built on the current site in

1897, operating first as a boys' independent, then a grammar and finally becoming a co-ed sixth form college in the early seventies. Heads arrive and proceed to make the place their life's work: only six since 1897.

An intense conurbation perched on a hilly spot overlooking the suburbs of Winchester. Original late Victorian building now completely surrounded by dedicated buildings purpose-built in the last 10 years, including newish cavernous learning and resources centre (library plus). Everything being used to full capacity – jam-packed with strapping youths. Students socialise in giant departure lounge style common-room and sunbathe like seals on Hopkin's Hump, a little knoll named after the head. Large canteen plus satellites provide cheap and plentiful food. No uniform (style leans to grungy rather than trendy), teachers called by their first names, 55 minute lessons, no bells: really a halfway house between school and university.

Two boarding houses (girls one floor, boys the other, electric door between). School House is a handsome Victorian building in which students share two to four bedded rooms. Falkland Lodge was opened in 1998: single or twin rooms, all en suite, but it costs more. Feel almost, but not quite, like university halls of residence, with an air of independence, eg boarders do their own laundry, aside from bedding. Boarding inspection reports rated it 'outstanding'.

Pastoral care and discipline: Sanctions minimal, although a zero tolerance policy on drugs and alcohol on site and smoking is not permitted except in one small fenced off area outdoors. 'Six or seven' students expelled most years – more common for them to leave 'by mutual consent'. Most common reason is 'laziness'; the occasional drugs bust. Full time counsellors available for personal matters.

Pupils and parents: Fifty per cent from the three Winchester 11-16 schools – Kings, Westgate and Henry Beaufort. Perins in Alresford top the long list of other feeder schools. A further 15-20 per cent from independent schools and the rest from far and wide – Reading, Salisbury and the Isle of Wight included. Student social profile directly reflects Winchester skew towards ambitious middle classes – one teacher remarked, 'Nothing as formidable as a Winchester mother protecting her young'. Former pupils include comedian Jack Dee, Olympic gold medallists Ben Ainslie and Iain Percy, Coldplay drummer William Champion, 'Page 3 girl' Lucy Pinder.

Entrance: 1600 pupils pile into the school at 16. Deadline for application is December. Non-selective, but requirement for A level courses is at least five grade Cs at GCSE level, 'ideally' including maths and English. Maths and science are exceptions – you need a B. Every applicant is interviewed. Vastly oversubscribed – local pupils automatically get in; beyond that pupils are accepted geographically in concentric circles radiating out from Winchester. Exceptions made for musicians, boarders and students from a windswept corner of the South Atlantic (has the honour of being the official sixth form of the Falkland Islands – construction of Falkland Lodge boarding house was partly funded by the Falklands government). Candidates for the Hampshire specialist music course audition in February/March on two instruments, one of which should be at grade 7/8 standard.

Exit: Some 85 per cent to universities of all descriptions. Forty-eight to Oxbridge in 2013 and 535 to Russell Group. Students on the music course frequently move on to the top music colleges.

Invited by Cambridge University to act as a regional hub as part of its HE + initiative. This will involve providing extension classes for its own and other local sixth formers and helping with applications to the most selective universities.

Money matters: Sixth form colleges receive less money per pupil than normal schools so the management employs meticulous budgeting, plus a dash of sorcery, to keep the whole shebang on the road. Hardship fund available. Students compete for several bursaries each year for gap year projects.

Remarks: A huge, friendly metropolis which falls neatly between school and university in approach. Most people would be happy here, but not those who need spoon-feeding.

Plymouth College

Linked school: Plymouth College Preparatory School

Ford Park, Plymouth, PL4 6RN

• Pupils: 325 boys (80 boarders), 220 girls (75 boarders) • Ages: 11-18 • C of E • Fees: Day £12,510–£14,040; Boarding £24,855–£26,880 pa • Independent

Tel: 01752 505100
Email: mail@plymouthcollege.com or admissions@ plymouthcollege.com
Website: www.plymouthcollege.com

Headmaster: Since 2006, Dr Simon Wormleighton BEd PhD. Educated at Rendcomb College and Exeter University, where he obtained first class honours in English and education. Doctoral thesis was on First World War poetry. A talented schoolboy cricketer, he began his career teaching English and was an assistant housemaster at Langley School, Norfolk before 12-year stint at Cheltenham College where he was a housemaster. Head of Grenville College, Bideford ('a steep learning curve'), before taking up present post. Personable and energetic, with an entrepreneurial feel for what will be successful.

Parents we spoke to rate him as 'a capable headmaster' – decisive yet sensitive to children's needs and 'approachable' for parents. Proud of pupils' achievements and quick to trumpet their successes on behalf of the school. Active recruiter abroad – had just returned from mainland China when we visited. Lives on site during term time with wife Sandy (manager at Plymouth's Theatre Royal) and their two daughters (one at the school, the other at university). Has lifted boarding numbers from 60 when he joined to current healthy level and sees strong boarding as vital for the future.

Academic matters: Outperforms itself academically given wide range of ability in intake. Increasing number of students doing IGCSE (92 per cent pass rate in 2013). Fifty-eight per cent A*/B grades at A level in 2013. Strong art, economics, chemistry and engineering students. IB cohort averaged 32.5 points each. Outstanding national success in business competitions spearheaded by head of sixth form and IB co-ordinator, who was a finalist in 2010 national teaching awards.

Year 7 pupils remain largely in mixed ability groups with setting in core subjects and French from year 8 upwards. RE compulsory to end of year 9 and thereafter optional RS at GCSE and A level. We watched several lessons including a lower English set in year 10 fairly buzzing with its creative writing task and sixth form geographers making shoreline models out of Play Doh. Sixth form business studies/economics students were thrashing out how to survive a 'fire in the warehouse' of their imagined company in realistic fashion. Students can choose Latin, German, Spanish or classical civilisation in year 8. Small classes: five to ten students common at AS and A levels, with average of 16 in younger years. Sports and adventure baccalaureate for those wanting a hands-on as opposed to academic route in sixth form.

P

Staff tend to stay here but we noted how younger staff take initiative when it comes to giving workshops on new approaches to learning. 'very inspiring,' said one old hand. Excellent library open daily for homework and research until 5.30pm, linked cultural activities such as Andrew Motion poetry workshop and enrichment days.

Effort put into making transition from own prep and other feeders as smooth as possible. Contact with future pupils can start as early as year 4 and parents praised sensitivity of head of year 7 and the 'comfortable feeling in school' for new arrivals.

Comprehensive learning support based in suite of three rooms at top of Victorian turret, with spectacular view over Plymouth Sound. More than 100 students receive help with specialist staff able to tackle SpLD and a variety of other needs. Individual and drop in sessions before school, at lunchtime and after school. SEN co-ordinator worked previously at Plymouth state school and offers counselling alongside learning support. Key information shared securely online with staff. All pupils screened for dyslexia in year 7 and classroom assistants employed with statemented pupils if appropriate. One mother praised how her son's memory had been boosted by use of innovative resources. Separate EAL unit for overseas pupils.

Games, options, the arts: On-site sporting facilities include 25 metre heated indoor pool (low chlorine content helps those who spend hours in it every day), sports hall complex with two squash courts, original school playing field with 1st X1 cricket square and now an adjacent mini all-weather pitch. Delganey is eight-acre site, with own changing facilities for rugby etc including 1st XV; slightly nearer is new Olympic standard Astroturf (owned and shared with Marjon College). Plymouth Life Centre (on doorstep) is now 'icing on the cake,' providing Olympic standard pool complex.

Sporting reputation on international footing thanks to highly successful partnership with Plymouth Leander swimming club: four swimming scholarship pupils competed in the London 2012 Olympics, including gold medallist Ruta Meilutyte, who powered her way to a shock win in the 100m breaststroke and bronze medallist diver Tom Daley. Host of accolades for school's top stars who achieve unparalleled national and world class success. Impressive rugby results: Devon Cup champions in each year group and senior player in U18 England rugby team. Representative colours for rugby at U20 level for England, Irish Exiles and the South West. Modern pentathlon and fencing academy with national athletes and full-time coach. Year 7 girl is double British fencing champion. Other recent successes include a sixth former making top ten in world clay pigeon shooting rankings, horse riding and triathlon. County successes in netball, hockey, athletics, cricket and tennis. Squash and basketball academies (latter with Plymouth Raiders).

House system fosters community spirit and inter-house competition: many events held at lunchtime. Activities fair organised in September for younger pupils to choose from extensive lunchtime and after school menu; seniors have Friday afternoon activities programme which includes CCF, D of E, art and junior sports leader award.

Flourishing outdoor education department has specialist vehicle, fleets of mountain bikes and kayaks and makes frequent use of Whiteworks (school's own outdoor residential centre on Dartmoor for up to 20 pupils). CCF had been in decline but has been revived under ex-regular CO. Contingent is made up of both Plymouth College pupils and those from a neighbouring comprehensive: 'a good experience for both lots,' we were told. Shooting range can be modified for either cadets or pentathletes. School enters 35, 45 and 55 mile Ten Tors teams, with serious overnight training on Dartmoor beforehand. Recent sixth form expedition to Annapurna in Nepal involved survival at high altitude. Ecovation (college's young enterprise business) won national honours and even sold one of the company's bird

feeders to cabinet minister Vince Cable. Visits pile up on each other and range from scuba diving off Gozo to helping to build accommodation at a Gambian school. Annual activities week for years 7 to 10. Careers programme includes introduction to workaday world in year 8 through 'The Real Game' and work experience in lower sixth.

Plenty of practice and performance rooms for music. Over a quarter of pupils take instrumental or singing lessons; chamber orchestra and wind band brass group both strong. Chamber choir had successful music tour to Prague, lower school and year 7 choirs meet at lunchtimes. Two boys in national youth choir. In-school concerts often fund raisers for charity eg £900 towards educating orphans in Gambia. Annual remembrance service draws congregation of more than 1,000 in St Andrew's, Plymouth. Recording studio and performance hall with professional audio and lighting equipment. Music scholars showcase talents at evening concerts and there's a creative arts week at end of school year.

Separate art house displays fantastic artwork. Recent Good Schools Guide winners in art and design A level categories. More than 40 take art in sixth form (emphasis on fine art) and photography and digital graphics especially popular. We enjoyed seeing a year 9 class making face masks using strips of gummed tissue paper as part of their work on the human body. 'Inspired' drama department. Studio space (in former squash court) for GCSE and A level work plus large stage in main auditorium for major productions.

Background and atmosphere: Founded in 1877, Plymouth College has sprawled towards nearby Mutley Plain (in contrasting architectural styles) from the castellated, granite fortress that formed the original school. Embraces a number of Victorian villas and houses that provide mainly boarding and office accommodation. Reception area lined with photos of medal-bearing Plymothians, leaving no doubt about school's strengths. A myriad of corridors and doors make for a quiet and peaceful atmosphere, though must be somewhat daunting for newcomers.

A Christian foundation, but neither chapel nor daily service. Assemblies held separately for different years in 1970s auditorium. Staff applications are high volume: a dream for any committed teacher. American style yearbook provides a glossy annual overview (we particularly liked the inclusion of cleaners and catering staff).

Pastoral care and discipline: Experienced married couple run joint boarding house on main site: boys are accommodated in three houses to one side of the houseparents' flat and girls in three on the other. Room for more girls when we visited. Firm, parental type discipline based on reward and praise. Mainly shared study bedrooms with modern facilities and 'lashings of hot water for showers etc' say pupils. Common rooms and kitchens are well used. Occasional boarding offered to day pupils (up to 14 nights per term).

Separate sixth form house, plus newly converted accommodation with single rooms for sixth formers opened over past few years. Distinct international flavour in boarding houses – all get along and one English boy told us 'it's better than being at home.' Captain's house exclusively for élite swimmers has clinched this option for serious minded athletes who rise at 5.30am. Activities at weekends range from bowling to surfing, with more relaxed régime generally. No moans about food: modern cafeteria style dining area and portions to match the consumer. Bacon baguettes in sixth form centre from 8am, with snacks and coffee available through the day.

Pupils and parents: Very international: 27 nationalities currently on roll. Largest contingents of overseas boarders from Germany and Spain, but plenty from China, Africa and Americas as well as Eastern Europe. Introduction of IB and the high profile sports

P

programmes account for the growing international interest. Well-presented and polite mixture though different cultural mores sometimes call for careful management. 'Elite swimmers in top ten per cent academically,' we were told and staff see these athletes as role models for others. Parents we spoke to had 'no axes to grind' and subscribed to a 'healthy body, healthy mind' philosophy.

Sixth form senior prefects adorned with graduate-style gowns when accompanying visitors or on special days. Day pupils from varied social and professional backgrounds. Red piping on blazers for main school and double breasted blazers or charcoal grey suits for sixth form boys and girls respectively. Lessons finish at 3.30pm but most are on site until 5.15pm, when coaches leave. Future Council looks after sustainability and green issues generally whilst active school council voices pupil concerns. Recent charity fund-raising included leg waxing for year 11 boys and a staff v pupils swimming gala. Active parents' association organises social events, helps at key functions and raises funds for school's wish list.

Former pupils include David King (developer of the CT scanner), former Labour leader Michael Foot, landscape painter Gerry Hillman, Welsh rugby player William James and comedienne Dawn French to name but a few from an impressively long list.

Entrance: Wide range of ability on entry. Some 50 per cent enter from own prep, with remainder from mix of local primaries and some independent. Day catchment area extends from Fowey in Cornwall to Exeter in Devon. Often lower ability than neighbouring grammars on 11+ entry, but GCSE and A level results compare favourably. Six GCSE passes, including maths and English and a minimum of three B grades to enter the sixth form.

Exit: Higher than usual percentage take a gap year. About half head for traditional courses and universities, with remainder covering everything imaginable. Oxbridge entrants few and far between. Increasing number look for sports scholarships at American universities and IB also opens up wider possibilities, especially for Europeans.

Money matters: Year 7 academic scholarships available (up to half tuition fee). Similar year 9 plus awards worth up to one third remission for art, music and sports. Sixth form academic scholarships worth up to one third remission for outstanding candidates. Rugby, golf and swimming scholarships plus other sports awards. Also a limited bursary fund. Modern pentathlon and fencing programme with scholarships on offer for this discipline.

Remarks: Plymouth College has bucked the boarding trend and reinvented itself as a thriving international campus – to the benefit of locals. Combines a sense of tradition with an unapologetic commitment to excel at what they do best.

Plymstock School

Church Road, Plymstock, Plymouth, PL9 9AZ

• Pupils: 1,565 boys and girls, all day • Ages: 11–18 • State

Tel: 01752 402679
Email: info@plymstockschool.org.uk
Website: www.plymstockschool.org.uk

Headteacher: Since 2007, Mr David Farmer, former head of Torpoint Community College.

Academic matters: Seventy per cent 5+ A*-C grades including English and maths at GCSE in 2013. Offers 25+ A level courses, besides good GNVQ, NVQ, RSA opportunities via a training consortium. Lots of awards. Enhanced specialist provision – centre for communication difficulties and intensive numeracy and literacy programme for SEN in years 7 and 8. Good extension studies for gifted/talented students through faster moving classes, earlier entry into subjects; supportive services include reading and homework club.

Games, options, the arts: Excellent reputation for county, national and international sporting achievements – hence has specialist sports college status. Enviably large, outdoor floodlit sporting area with flat grass track and netball/tennis courts. Newly completed third generation artificial football pitch and very large sports hall. Parents believe separating boys' and girls' groups for PE works. The less academic will not fade here and budding actors still have a chance with drama and performing arts A level. Growing percentage of students do PE, dance and sport studies. The art adorning the corridors shouts high quality. Parents impressed with varied range of musical and dramatic performances from Shakespeare to rock and roll. Work experience in Germany popular for A level German students – a big confidence booster.

Background and atmosphere: Very attractive school with garden courtyards. Teachers, students and parents work well together. Quiet and hard-working atmosphere of which it is proud. Recent investment of £5m has replaced temporary classrooms with well-resourced dance and drama, modern languages, mathematics, pottery and sport areas. Science, technology and humanities refurbished. Keeps up with leading edge ICT development – electronic whiteboards in every department, digital music recording. Wheelchair friendly.

Pastoral care and discipline: Bullying or behavioural problems are dealt with quickly. It's 'cool to be clever at Plymstock' so ridiculing high achievers – 'boffs' – is out. 'Unreserved support' for any necessary punishment is expected from parents.

Pupils and parents: Mixed social backgrounds, although Plymstock is more affluent than many parts of Plymouth. Parents are 'proud' to send their children here – 'It really encourages individuals to celebrate their talents'. Students believe they achieve because the teaching is good. Olympic swimmer and gold medalist Sharron Davies came here before winning a scholarship to Kelly College.

Entrance: Pupils from eight feeder schools: Oreston, Elburton, Hooe, Dunstone, Pomphlett, Goosewell, Downham, Wembury – belonging to the Plymstock (Plymouth) area Academic Council. This family of schools communicates well. One per cent choose Plymouth grammar schools instead.

Exit: Approximately 75 per cent of year 11 students progress to sixth form, others head for the local college of further education, the College of Art and Design, employment based training and other schools. Regularly sends students to top universities, including Oxbridge.

Remarks: Highly successful and good all-round comprehensive in a pleasant suburb of Plymouth.

P

Polam Hall School

Linked school: Polam Hall Junior School

Grange Road, Darlington, DL1 5PA

- Pupils: 146 pupils (75 girls/31 boys in senior school and 40 in sixth form). 40 full boarders, 5 weekly boarders. • Ages: 11–18 • Quaker origins • Fees: Day £12,210; Boarding £23,445 pa • Independent

---

Tel: 01325 463383
Email: information@polamhall.net
Website: www.polamhall.com

Headmaster: Since 2011, Mr J R Moreland MA (Oxon) PGCE NPQH (mid fifties). Educated at Huddersfield New College (then grammar school) and then modern history degree from St Edmund Hall, Oxford. Previously headmaster of Bury Lawn School, Milton Keynes; housemaster, head of history and assistant head Rugby School; taught history at Epsom College, started teaching life with history, geography and politics at Watford Boys' Grammar.

Played rugby, basketball and athletics at school and university (a double Oxford Blue). Holds Northern Ireland record for the discus and now competes in Masters championships, currently British champion. Teaches history, coaches and huge supporter of school sport. Believes in leading by example – for Sport Relief competed against a relay of pupils running a mile by throwing a combo of discus and wellies the equivalent distance – and won! Fifty-one times in 4 minutes 10 seconds – for the record.

Wife, teacher Alison and adult son, privately educated. Enjoys walking, reading, cinema. Keen to see 'pupils add to their skills and competencies, build on their talents and exploit opportunities in preparation for careers that currently do not exist'. Introducing challenge-based learning experiences; problem solving in teams to find collaborative learning solutions. A brave new world for the seniors.

Also developing ICT in the school – encouraging pupils to use Web 2.0 applications and make the most of personally owned smart phones and other mobile devices. Seeking to increase the number of boys and widen the international flavour in boarding as school grows to fully co-educational model – 'a 10 year plan'.

Academic matters: Non-selective intake – diagnostic tests to assess level of attainment for setting purposes only. Some 20 per cent of pupils on SEN register. In that context A level and GCSE results good, with nearly 28 per cent A*/A at A level in 2013, and 35 per cent A*/A at GCSE.

Pupils expected to work hard, with non-high flyers achieving beyond expectations in all areas; art, music and drama vibrant and popular; physics and chemistry labs fully refurbished; ICT much in evidence; comprehensive range of A level subjects for size of school.

Broad curriculum with French from year 7 and opportunities for German and Spanish from year 8. Sciences taught separately and with specialists from year 9. Mathematics and French set from year 7, science and English from year 10. IGCSE English introduced in 2012. Small groups at A level, average five per subject; some one-to-one, thus losing group dynamic.

New emphasis on developing pupils' skills and competencies needed 'to think outside the box'. Introducing 'Kangaroo Days' of problem solving, team building and challenge-based learning. Big push with ICT, embracing mobile technology and encouraging pupils to use free online software to hone their research and presentation skills. Students incentivised by collaborative learning competition which involves whole school community, pupils, staff and parents, in professionally-run training sessions.

Very modest about their SEN provision, saying, 'We strive to support effectively our pupils with special needs, but we do not wish to present ourselves as experts in the field'. Difficulties range from dyslexia, dyspraxia and dysgraphia to Asperger's and autism. Support is provided using a range of educational programmes, one-to-one teaching, assistants to support in class, reduced timetables, focused study support, mentoring, differentiation in class and bringing in outside specialists.

Games, options, the arts: Netball, swimming, cross-country, tennis, athletics all popular. Cricket, football and rugby (emerging) for the boys and mixed hockey. Fixtures against local schools and independent schools further afield. Good level of sports for the boys but would suggest not enough yet for those sports-driven and hyper-competitive.

Attractive playing fields, courts, new dance studio and sports hall on school premises; range of indoor sports activities and clubs; a national swimmer and a member of the England equestrian team. Recent major sports tours to Canada and Gibraltar.

Music through to A level; 30 per cent play a musical instrument; plenty of opportunities to perform from termly music concerts; intimate 'coffee' concerts held in the music centre to showcase developing talent. Purpose-built theatre with big summer production, West Side Story this year. Curriculum drama through to A level.

Duke of Edinburgh Award operating with sustained success at all levels. Fledgling CCF – in early stages. Extended view of the world encouraged with inspirational speakers, annual overseas visits, World Challenge to Malawi. Orienteering – pre-drive schemes and Young Enterprise for sixth formers.

Background and atmosphere: Founded in 1848 by Quakers sisters for young Quaker ladies paying 50 guineas a year. In 1854 school moved to Polam Hall, a Georgian mansion set in 19 acres of parkland, close to the town centre, with a history of sharing its grounds with the people of Darlington. Descendants of founding families still represented on governing body and school remains true to its Quaker roots. The sense of a shared, warm, caring community is evident throughout the school.

Tight, cohesive site including main school, junior school and boarding houses, with a number of newer additions to original school house. Residential on three sides, attractive open parkland adjoining school grounds on other side lends a feeling of open space.

Recent changes to main entrance hall replaced museum pieces of school history with brightly lit display cabinets of pupils' work and an arresting contemporary wall hanging above the main staircase, symbolising changes afoot at this school.

Boys in school since 2010 with closure of boys' school Hurworth House. Brief flirtation with diamond model but since 2012 fully co-educational. Parents we spoke to were fully supportive of the change and 'feel the school is moving in the right direction' though some have been lured by all girls' offering in Durham or good, local state co-educational.

Core of long-established, experienced teachers with more recent injection of new blood; average age 48. Mutually supportive, spirit of goodwill – 'working together for the good of the whole' encouraged by collaborative leadership style.

Boarding facilities upgraded a few years ago. Accommodation homely, clean and comfortable with three and four bedded rooms the norm and shared rooms even in sixth form. Warm and caring house staff; boarders have freedom of grounds for relaxation with limited access off-site (depending on age), logging themselves in and out. Regular organised activities at weekends.

Boarders elect a leadership team of head boarder, assistant head boarder(s) and two heads of house who work closely with the staff to ensure the smooth running of the boarding community. Good preparation for life after school. The boarding council has representatives of all age groups and meets regularly. An Independent Listener is available to all boarding students.

Pastoral care and discipline: Few formal rules but very clear guidelines to sanctions; high standards of courtesy and behaviour expected and delivered, based on respect for self and others. Strong anti-bullying policy; serious misconduct extremely rare. Head says, 'staff care about school' and 'work closely with pupils to provide support for them'. Peer mentoring recently introduced though size of school enables friendships across age groups.

Regular assemblies ('readings') reflecting Quaker foundations; awareness of the wider world and strong spirit of generosity. Successful and enthusiastic fund-raising for charities, in conjunction with Interact, Junior Rotary. Active school council produces manifestos and contributes to relevant decision-making throughout school.

Pupils willing to take responsibility as form representatives or house captains. House system with inter-house competition in music, drama, sport and orienteering. Before and after school care, and homework clubs. Pupils can arrive at school at 8am, breakfast in the dining room and stay up to 7pm in the evening, with tea.

Pupils and parents: A broad cross-section of abilities, backgrounds and cultures here in a community that welcomes diversity. A changing profile with 25 per cent (and increasing) of pupils from overseas, mainly from year 10 onwards. A number of armed forces' boarders too. Pupils are friendly, remarkably modest about their achievements and down to earth, reflecting the honest, unpretentious character of this northern school.

Parents a mixture of urban and rural, first-time buyers and second and third generation Polamites. Strong Parents' Association organising free events for parent body. Parents' focus group presents views/perspectives to head.

Notable old girls Nadine Bell, NASA scientist, Ruth Gemmell, actress.

Entrance: From junior school and state and independent schools from a wide geographical area: Durham, Middlesbrough, Bedale and Barnard Castle. International students from Hong Kong, mainland China, Thailand, Nepal and Russia.

For entry at 11, non-verbal reasoning papers for diagnostic purposes. At 13 English and mathematics papers and personal profile. At 16, candidates for the sixth form sit general studies and critical thinking papers and complete a personal profile. All EAL students complete mathematics and EFL papers. All candidates have interview with head.

Occasional placement by local authority of pupils on autistic spectrum (Asperger's).

Exit: Varying numbers depart post-GCSE – to local sixth form college or co-ed boarding schools. Students go on to a wide range of universities and courses, including a small number of Oxbridge candidates. Destinations in 2013 included Aberystwyth, Bristol, Edinburgh, Leeds, Liverpool, St Andrews, Teesside, York, Bath Spa, Chinese University of Hong Kong (CUHK), De Montfort, East Anglia, Essex, Harper Adams, Huddersfield.

Money matters: Academic, sport and music scholarships available for entry at years 7, 9 and sixth form. Means-tested bursaries available.

Remarks: Warm, welcoming atmosphere emanates from busy pupils at work and play, supported and encouraged to do well by their teachers. After introduction of boys in 2010 and brief fling as diamond model school, now embedding co-education and widening international boarding. Intent on providing pupils with skills, competencies and technological knowledge to 'future proof' them for life in 21st century. Winds of change blowing over Polam Hall but still remaining true to its Quaker roots.

Poole Grammar School

Gravel Hill, Poole, BH17 9JU

• Pupils: 1210 boys; all day • Ages: 11–18 • Non-denom • State

Tel: 01202 692132
Email: office@poolegrammar.com
Website: www.poolegrammar.com

Headmaster: Since 2004, Ian Carter BSc PGCE NPQH FRSA (fifties). Member of the Institute of Biology, chartered biologist and one of a small group of state school heads who are HMC additional members. Educated at Worthing Sixth Form College and Durham University, where he read zoology, then PGCE at Pembroke College, Cambridge and Farmington Fellow of Harris Manchester College, Oxford. Previously senior deputy head at The Perse in Cambridge and before that taught at University College School, London (a seminal point in developing his educational philosophy), Cranbrook Grammar School, Monkton Combe and Woodbridge School.

Charming and easy to talk to, he believes that policy of giving priority to Poole residents makes for a more cohesive, community school. Values the 'calm' of a single sex school and sees pastoral care as key to getting good results. Head is also keen to focus on the psychological pressures on young people and sees early intervention as vital – hence the school's fully qualified and in-house counselling service.

Head makes himself available to parents without an appointment and greets boys on their birthdays (chance for informal chat about well-being, concerns etc). His wife works as an interpreter for the Border Agency and they have two children, one at Oxford, one who works locally in the caring professions. He's also a keen occasional cricketer and a board member of Bournemouth University.

Academic matters: Specialises in maths, computing and cognition, so it's no surprise that maths is top of the pops at A level, closely followed by physics, which everyone does at GCSE. Mostly separate sciences with some dual award at GCSE when boys can also take a few curiosities like astronomy, human health, food (no textiles) and French, Spanish or German, though no classics or eastern languages. Fantastic results in maths and chemistry but also, impressively, in English, RE, geography and history. Exciting ICT with everyone doing the short course ICT GCSE at the end of year 9. In 2013, 60 per cent of GCSE grades A*/A and 38 per cent of A levels.

Boys take five or six subjects at AS and narrow down to four for A level. About 30 subjects to choose from. Joint sixth form teaching in many subjects with Parkstone Grammar School (girls) means almost any combination of subjects can be timetabled. Lots of enrichment choices in AS levels and a few unexpected AS subjects, including archaeology, critical thinking, theatre studies and media studies. English language is a popular A level, plus computing, the inevitable sciences and above all maths, while most boys take general studies. Masses of add-ons: boys can take the AQA Baccalaureate virtually in their stride if they do the right mixture of subjects. Accelerated courses in maths etc supplemented by school extension courses, mainly in form of IGCSE in preparation for A level. Poole has Cisco and Microsoft Academy status and students can earn the CCNA networking qualification in the sixth form.

Setting only in maths, as head believes it's a bit divisive in modern languages (all the ex-prep school boys in one set) and bright boys learn from each other. Careers guidance includes a week on university choices etc (head is particularly well up on Oxbridge access) and all pupils do two weeks' work experience in year 11. Class sizes not more than 30 and some much smaller groups in sixth form.

Less of an academic sausage machine than you might expect. Surprisingly for a grammar, SEN is one of school's specialisms – head sees it as truly cross curricular and serving the needs of the most able, gifted and talented, as well as those with identified academic difficulties. Excellent results for disabled pupils and those coping with profound deafness and other personal challenges. One former pupil with severe cerebral palsy has just finished a computer science degree at university, with outstanding results. A five-strong department recognises that almost everyone has some sort of need, hand-in-hand with the belief that supporting pupils through any kind difficulty will be beneficial to their academic performance.

Games, options, the arts: Boys are adamant that music, art and the humanities are important to the school. Exam take-up in art and music belies this, but the life-like and often enormous paintings and drawings in the art department and the impressive new music department, with its record of concerts, musical and drama productions (often with Parkstone Grammar), all justify their pride. A completely pupil-led play – written, performed, produced, managed by pupils – is on the bill. Popular orchestra and huge year 8 choir etc.

This is a pretty sporty school. Head believes the largely Poole-based population makes for a sense of identity and commitment to teams. Sport is compulsory for all and a good tranche of boys are in teams. Football is the most popular sport, but rugby, cricket (on 'the best cricket square in Poole') and athletics are probably more successful. Sports hall rather outmoded now, ditto the fitness room, but good new outdoor facilities. No pool but pupils use nearby Dolphin pool, which currently occupies the school's original site. Distinguished past and current athletes have trained through local clubs as well as in school. Inevitably there is sailing (at Hamworthy), plus squash, outdoor education etc. off the premises. Parents say sport is good but that school also encourages pupils to use excellent local facilities and clubs, where specialists can (and do) excel in minority pursuits like trampolining.

Bags of clubs at lunchtime and after school. These include philosophy, debating, classics... and lots of subject specific extras. Enterprise and languages well catered for as well as Formula 24 Greenpower car club, aero modelling et al. Big theatrical productions on alternate years, with smaller studio plays in between and some boys opt into Parkstone Grammar's big musicals. Terrific range of DT rooms, including a brand new food lab complete with rhubarb growing by the front door. Masses of trips – language visits, expeditions to Second World War sites and popular geography beano to Iceland post-GCSE.

Background and atmosphere: Poole bucked the usual trend and the school started as a co-ed in downtown Poole in 1904, before splitting into boys' and girls' grammars in the 30s. Present site in Gravel Hill, a nondescript wooded artery into Poole famed for its speed traps, has acres of well-groomed space, including good pitches and athletics space. The original redbrick sixties blocks marry well with the square glass and brick modern extensions, giving a pleasant though unremarkable whole. Inside the new bit, with libraries (always manned), state-of-the-art music and drama and some pretty smart classrooms, is bright, light and user friendly. Boys keen on the little work carrels tucked in at the top of the stairs. Reception area bristles with achievement certificates (over 40 of them) and trophies, plus huge historical photos of the school. Main dining hall serves locally sourced largely organic food ('delicious,' according to one pupil we spoke to) and certainly a majority of pupils and staff vote with their stomachs. A silver Food for Life award earned partly for

the supply of fresh fruit and vegetables planted in the school grounds and partly for the school spreading its culinary largess to a swathe of Poole middle schools using their catering – a nice income for the school. Chef recently presented with catering worker of the year award at 10 Downing Street.

School has academy status so has more freedom in what and how it offers. Part of the South West Academic Trust, (consisting of several grammar schools and Exeter University), it takes a lead in local academic matters and is formally linked with several primary and special schools. Head is proud of its lead in staff training – all in-house by his own staff – and of the links forged with schools in Europe and further afield. There are nearly as many female as male staff – possibly why the atmosphere is so normal – though heads of department are mostly men.

School has now expanded to include year 7 and has a remarkably calm feel for what is essentially a hothouse for more than 1,200 teenage boys. Humanities and enterprise flourish, lessons evidently absorb attention and boys are enthusiastic about all aspects of school. Adding 'cognition' to the potentially 'nerdy' specialisms of maths and computing allows the staff to boost their care of individual boys, whatever their needs.

Pastoral care and discipline: Heads of year take responsibility for all boys in the year. Head of year 7 makes sure the little lambs settle and takes them into year 8. There's a remixing of forms in year 9 which then remain static through to year 11. Uniform requirement relaxes over the years – from blazer and tie for years 7 and 8 to jumper and tie for years 9,10 and 11, to ties only (not literally) in sixth form. Out (either temporarily or permanently) for bringing drugs on site. Bullying could result in exclusion – either entirely for a time or in school's exclusion room, though there are few reported incidents. Strong mentoring of year 7 and 8s by senior boys is valued by both. Prefects are a very select few elected by senior boys and staff. Parents praise the discipline here and the rapt and concentrating faces in lessons certainly bore this out. Social events arranged with Parkstone Grammar for all year groups and older boys take lessons in both schools.

Pupils and parents: Head says has a particularly wide social mix because it positively seeks to provide first and foremost for the bright boys of Poole – so is less open to 'advantaged' children from further afield. Small but varied ethnic minorities – 19 languages spoken other than English and bilingual boys increasingly encouraged to do GCSE in their mother tongue. Ability range broader than you might expect, perhaps because of Bournemouth School just down the road, some very good local comprehensives and also because entrance policy favours local pupils above potentially brighter but more distant applicants.

Entrance: Complex and intensely controversial. School admits pupils who have passed the test and who live in Poole, irrespective of where they go to primary school. Takes some pupils from outside the borough. In 2013, for the first time, most (but not all) of Poole senior schools had their main intake into year 7 rather than year 8. In 2013, for one year only, Poole Grammar admitted 168 boys into each of year 7 and year 8 (year 7 only after that). Applications by late October but if you want to do the test in advance of applying (to see if it's worth the try), apply by mid-September. Tests are in maths, English and verbal and non-verbal reasoning. Main feeder schools include Broadstone, Oakdale and Canford Heath Middle Schools and Dumpton Prep.

Sixth form entry is much less competitive – surprising that more people haven't caught on. Applications depend on 'satisfactory achievement' at GCSE.

Exit: Occasionally boys defect after year 8, in search of small classes at local independent schools. Some 13 per cent leave after GCSEs for vocational courses, apprenticeships or sixth form college. Three sixth form leavers to Oxford in 2013, others to universities like Durham, Exeter, Southampton, Bath, Bristol, Imperial, UCL, Kings, Warwick and Nottingham. Bournemouth popular for media programmes.

Remarks: A high achieving school for the bright boys of Poole.

Portland Place School

56–58 Portland Place, London, W1B 1NJ

- Pupils: 375 (285 boys, 90 girls); all day • Ages: 9–18 • Non denom • Fees: £17,250 pa • Independent

Tel: 020 7307 8700
Email: admin@portland-place.co.uk
Website: www.portland-place.co.uk

Headmaster: Since 2011, Timothy Cook BA (fifties). Educated at Chislehurst and Sidcup Grammar School in Kent and Leeds University (first in modern languages). Previously head of middle school and head of upper school at Dulwich College, London (where he spent 14 years), then deputy head at St Dunstan's College, London.

Wife Karin – senior post in financial services industry; son at Dulwich College, daughter at Nottingham University. Parents describe him as 'very professional and an excellent communicator.' With two teenage children of his own, he understands the challenges of these years and brings a human touch to the job as well as aeons of professional experience. So hands on that he is known to respond immediately to emails sent at the crack of dawn in the morning (he cycles in, rain or shine, from south east London and is at his desk by 7am). He may well be the one to answer the phone in the middle of the afternoon and will be in a position to reassure an anxious mother by personally confirming the exact whereabouts of her child. The door to his study is always open and he sees most children at some point during the day. This is a man who when he says he enjoys knowing every pupil, means it. 'It's the joy of running a relatively small school,' he says with a humility, which, one suspects, is typical of him.

While learning to adapt to a more informal approach than he has been used to, he embraces the founder and former head's legacy of a small, nurturing environment that can genuinely meet the needs of every individual and bring out the best in them – in terms of their wider interests, academic and social. 'Boys and girls at Portland Place gain a sense of self-worth from being valued for who they are and what they can contribute. This in turn instils a sense of self-belief, which is the platform for both academic achievement and success in later life.'

Thorough, earnest, completely without affectation and as straight as a rod, he is a head you feel you can trust but 'not the type that wants to be your best friend.' remarked one parent with relief.

Academic matters: A broader band of ability than in most of the fiercely competitive London day schools – something the school takes pride in and, together with its small class sizes, sees as a 'unique selling point.' Only 12 in a class in years 5 and 6, an average of 15 in years 7 to 11 (we saw several smaller ones) and smaller still in the sixth form means that attention can be given to each child – you can be sure that there will be both stretching and confidence building. A godsend for the discerning parent who can see through the merry-go-round nature of 11+ and wants to ensure their child is educated rather than exam-processed. Hence the increasing demand for places lower down the school; there is now one class in year 5 as well as two in year 6. Piles on the value added – 'We're always near the top of the value added tables' is the boast.

No Latin or Greek at GCSE ('there isn't the demand from our parents,' we were told). Economics, computing, sport studies and media are offered, along with the traditional subjects. All pupils take at least one of French, Italian or Spanish, not much enthusiasm for taking up a second modern language. If your daughter speaks Italian at home, she is encouraged to do Spanish as her GCSE option. If you want your child to take a GCSE in, for example, Arabic, the school will facilitate it within the timetable, but the onus of paying and finding the teacher is on you.

At GCSE, 85 per cent achieved five or more A*-C, 33 per cent of grades A*/A in 2013. Some subjects achieve 100 per cent A*-C – these include the sciences, music, art and media. The value added shows at A level, where the results are more impressive, most being in the B-D bracket, with a decent sprinkling of As (23 per cent A*/A grades and 52 per cent A*/B in 2013). We saw small tutor groups of as few as five – notably these were in science subjects. Clever ones, with offers from Oxbridge as well other Russell Group universities. Arts subjects tend to be busier (up to 15 in a group). Library manned by full-time librarian and a nice place to sit and read. Lots of fiction, used for competitions, book club and quiet study. As an academic resource it is risible (school prefers 'needs developing' and reminds us that the individual heads of departments keep library resources in their offices). Good IT suites and resources for the popular media and film options.

Setting in maths, science and English from year 7. Plenty of movement between sets we were assured. Sizeable number of mild dyslexics but no additional support in lessons apart from general support from class teacher. Staunch policy of no withdrawals from classes (except once weekly for children who have EAL). School employs four specialist learning support teachers who will arrange to see children outside lesson time in groups of two or three to devise strategies to help them access the mainstream curriculum. No screening on admission. However SENCo oversees general provision and monitoring – 80 to 90 children perceived as having some kind of mild learning disability or difficulty and some have IEPs. Most with more than the mildest difficulties seek support outside school. Inside school, the attitude is healthy – 'I'm not treated as if dyslexia is a crime – unlike at my last school,' we were told. Two of the three buildings have lifts but school will be helpful if someone breaks a leg and move lessons to the ground floor.

Games, options, the arts: Well known for sporting prowess despite there being virtually no facilities on site. Pupils are bussed or walk everywhere – mostly to Regent's Park, with pitches and courts of all kinds, Seymour Place for swimming – and the results and achievements, given the conditions, are impressive. Years 7 to 9 have sport timetabled four times a week (one of the advantages of no canteen and shorter lunch breaks, time can be reallocated to sport). Football and netball tours of Barbados, swimming teams win competitions (Westminster champions five years in a row), masses of medals in cross-country and local honours in athletics and team sports. Pervasive pride in school sports, helped, no doubt, by classy Olympians on staff. However most really keen sportsmen and women do their serious sport outside school – girls' football a particular highpoint. Sport now compulsory to year 12 – one afternoon a week minimum of netball or football. Music and drama similarly 'massive.' Music mostly means pop and jazz (we saw lots of ukulele enthusiasts). There are also a few violinists and woodwinders amongst the jazz pianists, guitarists, drummers and bassists who predominate, but eclectic range of music taken seriously. We were shown round by a budding actor in year 10 who enthused about the opportunities he has been given to develop his talent. Wholehearted, whole school productions annually – West Side Story, Singin' in the Rain, The Producers and Annie are recent offerings; not on site as no

P

suitable space but venues include The RADA Studios in WC1. Upper school recently performed a resoundingly successful Richard III – which was then a sell-out at the Edinburgh Fringe. Lower school (up to year 9) most recently performed Skellig as their annual production. Good-sized on site drama studio can accommodate smaller productions (we were impressed with the assortment of costumes and props).

Art in the lower school is lively and inventive. We saw ink portraits in the style of Peter Howson, as well as Pop Art-style Creme Eggs. Fewer than 10 do art A level – facilities limited, though there is a textiles room and school excels in photography. DT similarly energetic – resistant materials, pewter casting, CAD and CAM, though all in rather small and poky rooms in basement. Lots of extracurricular stuff – when we visited a stress management workshop was being delivered to all GCSE students. Trips galore – we have seldom seen such a full programme. Much use made of London's galleries, museums and exhibitions, plus the nearby wider world and the opportunities it offers for field, sporting and other educational exercises, both here and abroad.

Background and atmosphere: This is a young school, founded only 20 or so years ago by the visionary head of science at St Paul's Girls, Richard Walker (Tim Cook's predecessor). His aim was to create a smaller independent co-ed senior school that wasn't super selective. Part of the Alpha Plus group, it forms one of their 19 UK schools and colleges, bringing the advantages of the economies of scale. Portland Place – the road – is a broad, straight thoroughfare in the heart of regency London, two minutes from Oxford Circus to the south, two minutes to Regent's Park to the north. It is lined by august embassies (China, Kenya, Poland, Portugal) and the HQs of royal and learned institutions (architects, physicists, radiologists, anaesthetists). The main school building – Portland Place – identifies itself with a modest brass plate and is elegantly splendid. It is rare for us to compliment a school on its decor but a pleasure to do so here. Eye-catching blue carpet up and down the stairs (not just on the ground floor for show as elsewhere), magnificent ceilings, cornices, columns, capitals and fireplaces: nowhere more so than in the old ballroom, rescued from its carapace of false ceiling and fluorescent tubes and very much in use. All in tip-top nick. This building houses the lower years, the hall (used for gym and dance) and the top floors (formerly the servants' quarters) accommodate music and languages.

A second building in Great Portland Street, five minutes away, houses the upper years and has a breathtaking eyeball-to-eyeball view of the BT Tower, seemingly within grabbing distance. Harford House, also in Great Portland Street and with a facade resembling that of a corporate HQ, is home to art, drama and science. It's a logistical nightmare – five or seven storeys to be up and down all day, three buildings and it all has to be timetabled, supervised and navigated. We suppose everyone to be very fit – a real bonus for children who need lots of movement and exercise if they are to perform well mentally.

No school kitchen. Pupils bring packed lunches or order in from local cafes (which deliver dozens of paninis etc in little brown carriers). Years 10 and 11 and the sixth hang out in the many cafes in or around Great Portland Street and just love the privilege of this kind of freedom.

Pastoral care and discipline: Definitely an informal feel to the place. Although not quite on first name terms with teachers, one can sense an equality in the relationships not seen in more traditional establishments. Good use of sixth form mentors for years 7 and 8 – really fosters inter-age group understanding and friendships, especially helpful in so small a school. Solidly structured pastoral care hierarchy picks up and deals with problems, but there's a pervasive sense of everyone looking out for everyone else. People seem to know each other's little brothers and sisters here. Parents praise the home-school communications and especially the termly parents' evenings. 'The teachers are mostly young and energetic,' enthused a parent, 'and you really get to know them.'

Pupils and parents: More boys than girls (about 60:40 in lower years) – simply because there are so many more girls' and co-ed schools in London. Mixed, as befits its location – trad, moneyed independent education veterans alongside newbies and newcomers from here, there and everywhere, blended with those who couldn't get into the 'academic' schools and for whom PP has been a jolly lucky find. From the whole urban sprawl – no longer just the north and west but around 30 per cent from east and south too. Mostly UK born and based but also from pretty much the rest of the globe, solar system and beyond, in a great undivided family. Brains? Yes, though common denominator more palpably pleasure, pride and enthusiasm for the place.

Entrance: There are now 9+ and 10+ intakes – partly to steal a march on the competition and partly to meet the needs of those who dread the 11+ circus and will do anything to avoid it (wise move). 'Informal tests' in English and maths with deputy/head of year. Year 7 has tests in English and maths and a chat with a teacher. For places at 12+, 13+ and 14+ – same format plus additional test in science. School keen to dispel image that it's the go-to place for a child on the dys-strata. Child has to be able to cope and pupils who can't will be turned down. A few join at year 12, on flexible terms. They come, at 11, from a large number of schools – state and independent.

Exit: Wide range of post-A level destinations and courses, including applied sound, sports and exercise science, mechanical engineering and forensic investigations at the newer universities. The odd one to study music and to art college, as well as maths, philosophy and English at Sussex and Italian at Bristol. About 30 per cent leaving after GCSE (mostly to non-fee paying sixth form colleges).

Money matters: Five scholarships for academic, music, drama, sports and art. All worth 25 per cent of fees. No bursaries.

Remarks: Small, nurturing and refreshingly relaxed. A haven of creativity in the pushy academically competitive world of London day schools. A place for engaged, lively, normal kids – privileged, yes, but Sloanes, no. Becoming ever more popular as more and more people discover it. The challenge will be to maintain its ethos of 'broader academic intake' in the face of increasing demand.

The Portsmouth Grammar School

Linked school: The Portsmouth Grammar Junior School

High Street, Portsmouth, PO1 2LN

- Pupils: 1100 co-ed • Ages: 11–18 • Christian non-denom
- Fees: £13,173 pa • Independent

Tel: 023 9236 0036
Email: admissions@pgs.org.uk
Website: www.pgs.org.uk

Headmaster: Since 2008, Mr James Priory MA (late thirties), previously the school's assistant head and head of sixth. An Oxford graduate (got a first) in English, Mr Priory was educated at King Edward's School, Birmingham, and Taunton School, where he became head boy and a hotshot debater, winning the World Public Speaking and Debating Championships. His first teaching post was at Bradford Grammar School where he became head of year 7, introducing the first girls into the school. Arrived at PGS as head of English in 2000, later assistant head in charge of sixth form.

Became PGS's first internally appointed head in 200 years when he took over the reins from Tim Hands (now at Magdalen College). After the promotion, was permitted an enlightening sabbatical term shadowing heads and scrutinising IB schools all over the UK, USA and Canada – as a precursor to PGS gearing up for the IB programme. Interested in Portsmouth history and culture and teaches a course about Arthur Conan Doyle (who had his first medical practice in Portsmouth) and his links with PGS (one of Conan Doyle's brothers is an OB; a PGS maths teacher, Alfred Wood, was the model for Dr Watson). Has replaced Hands as chairman of the Portsmouth Festivities, a city-wide celebration of young people and the arts held each June. Teaches songwriting as a sixth form general studies option and is known for 'getting the guitar out, David Brent style'. Writes and performs songs for leavers' occasions and the like. A stickler for detail, he sent us back our draft of this write-up covered in red ink. Married to another English teacher and they have three young children, all at PGS.

Academic matters: Takes its academics seriously – A level results rock solid, with little movement up or down, year after year. Radical approach: all pupils do four A levels; exam-free lower sixth – AS modules not taken till January of upper sixth, 'So pupils are taking the exams at their most mature,' explains the head. In 2013, 84 per cent A*-B, 53 per cent A*/A at A level. Similar strategy for GCSEs – none taken early except maths in the top two sets, and then only by a few months, still firmly within year 11. Results impressive across the board: 73 per cent A*/A in 2013. Two modern languages plus Latin compulsory in years 7 and 8. A levels lean towards the geeky – maths the most popular A level by a long chalk; sciences also up there with almost as many pupils taking physics as biology or chemistry. English also successful, along with most other subjects really, modern languages excepted perhaps. IB introduced in 2009 with 35 sixth formers – 25 from PGS and ten joining from other schools; expects half the sixth form to opt for the programme eventually. 2013 saw average point score of 37, with six students getting 40 or more points out of 45.

Setting in maths and science. Average class size 24 in years 7-11; down to eight (and often fewer) in the sixth form. Head recollects that he was in charge of SEN when he was head of English years ago; things have moved on – now a learning support department with three dedicated staff for the senior school alone, plus other members of staff with SEN training. Extra support delivered through individual lessons before school, at lunch or in small timetabled groups – pupils not taken out of lessons. Year 8 pupils may have extra help instead of a second foreign language, 'But they still do Latin and one modern language'. Not a school to seek out specially for SEN – Mayfield School down the road has cornered that particular market. Brilliant list of sixth form general studies options includes songwriting (with the headmaster), car maintenance, introduction to medicine and philosophy through film.

Games, options, the arts: Extra-curricular activities now have their own deputy head, whose job is to make sure all pupils are squeezing in as much as possible outside the classroom – but not too much. Strong, competitive sport, with many county successes. Placed in the top three independent schools for sport for several years running in the Daily Telegraph. The usual games are played one afternoon a week. Has been keen to improve girls' sport, which some felt was the unfortunate stepsister of the boys' programme – netball, athletics and hockey particularly stand out. Cricket is the most popular and successful boys' sport. Sports hall on site, with three squash

courts, fitness suite and aerobics/dance studio. No playing fields on site but owns 18 acres at Hilsea, a couple of miles away, complete with all-weather hockey pitch – pupils are bused there for games and matches. Sailing on the doorstep, though mainly pursued outside school. Swimming not a particular strength, but junior school has small covered pool; the senior school uses nearby naval facilities.

Uniquely, a non-denominational cathedral school and member of the Choir Schools' Association. Parents rave about the music, taught in its own building with loads of practice rooms, recording studio and lovely rotunda for concerts. Partnership with the London Mozart Players and promotes new classical music through annual commissions from leading composers for Remembrance Sunday. 'It's very inspiring for young people to be involved with a leading international composer and it brings prestige and a sense of history,' notes the head. Numerous ensembles including a swing band and African drumming group.

School drama energetic and popular – LAMDA exams taken and loads of performances, including a major musical production every year in a Portsmouth theatre and an annual open air Shakespeare production. A school production taken to the Edinburgh Fringe was singled out by the Guardian as the best show produced by children. Art still lower profile than music and drama, but exam results very good. Masses of overseas trips and exchanges, eg a trip to Argentina to work on several charitable projects aimed at helping children. D of E now involves over half of year 10. CCF attracts 200 pupils. Debating has risen from ground zero and now has a weekly Model United Nations club – its own conference each March is now a firm fixture on the MUN circuit. Big on fundraising for charities: its campaign to raise funds to build a school in northern Cambodia won PGS the Best School award in the community awards run by the Portsmouth News.

Background and atmosphere: Founded 1732 as the dying wish of Dr William Smith, Mayor of Portsmouth and physician to its garrison (mayor of Portsmouth remains a governor). Went independent in 1976 and fully co-ed in 1995. Faint lingering scent of regimented past in the air, mostly owing to the stern, brick, listed architecture, remorseless view of tarmac, brisk sea air and urban setting. Re-development in 2005 produced a new dining and theatre complex, a new library and state-of-the-art science laboratories. Mega science centre opened 2010 a wonder of the Hampshire world and connected to the already swish 2005 labs. New sixth form centre under construction. Straightforwardly academic feel (a strong 'culture of aspiration', prefers the head). Cheery year 6-11 library; another grander one for the sixth form. Sixth form centre with little café a nice touch, as are the house 'bases', with table football, lockers and study areas. Head says Portsmouth has become increasingly international and outward-looking, reflected in the ethos of the school (perhaps more inspirationally than actually, thus far). Numbers have steadily increased to almost 1200 in the senior school – presents a challenge for inclusion in school plays and sports teams.

Pastoral care and discipline: Four houses, each divided into mixed-age tutor groups, meet three times a week. Tutor stays with same group for two or three years and is the pastoral care lynchpin. Buddying system for year 7 and 8 pupils to guard against bullying. Sixth formers may go home for the day at 12:50pm if they have no afternoon lessons, but no others allowed off campus. Piles of off-putting marketing bumf heavy on fashion-shoot style photos of pupils – not sure why such a fine school has invested so heavily in such froth. An exception is the sixth form handbook – a model student-friendly publication with useful email addresses, times when staff are available to students (including the head, who has a 10 minute slot every morning when pupils can drop in) and revision advice. Very occasionally a pupil is asked to leave, usually owing to laziness or 'behaviour'. Head vigilant on cyber bullying and has embraced new technology as a means of combating it. After much consultation decided to allow Facebook on school computers: 'You need to get behind the digital bikeshed'. Staff encouraged to join Facebook; pupils are taught the importance of protecting their identity.

Pupils and parents: Some travel from as far as Southampton, Winchester, Petersfield and Isle of Wight (and beyond). Six parent-organised coaches bring in the hordes and others take public transport. Pupils not polished but generally diligent and polite. Parents work for IBM, the navy, professions. Not posh; informal – boys' shirts cheerfully hang out of trousers. Feels a bit like a boys' state grammar or a London day school – 'Feels just like Latymer,' said a teacher. Girls look much more at home than when we visited before; un-tarty. Old Portsmouthians include lots of rear admirals and other military leaders, but also some colourful surprises, eg Paul Jones (lead singer of Manfred Mann on their hits Do Wah Diddy Diddy and Pretty Flamingo), James Clavell (bestselling author of Shôgun and director of To Sir With Love), and Ian Osterloh (inventor of viagra).

Entrance: January entrance tests for 11+ (160 places, but half filled by junior school children) in maths (no calculators), English and verbal reasoning, plus interview. For pupils coming from prep school, CE usually replaces school's own test at 11 and 13. Families frequently transfer in and out of Portsmouth, so places open up in most years at odd times – always worth inquiring. Entry to sixth form requires seven GCSE passes at B or above, with A or A* grades recommended in four subjects to be studied at A level or IB. School's own pupils who fall significantly short may be encouraged to look elsewhere. Minimum requirement to join IB programme at sixth form: four As in GCSE subjects to be continued to IB, Bs in other subjects.

Exit: Around 15-20 pupils leave after GCSEs, some for a wider curriculum, others because their GCSEs are not up to scratch. Almost all those who stay on depart to universities far and wide, with sciences the most popular degrees. Bucking the national trend of increased competition for medicine by producing several vets and medics. Around seven per cent to Oxbridge.

Money matters: Fees kept low; no lunches included; no sibling discounts. Range of academic scholarships at range of ages bring more status than cash. Bursaries also mostly small, but can run to full fees. Only academic and all rounder awards at 11+, same plus music at 13+. At sixth form also awards for sport, leadership potential and the Peter Ogden sixth form science bursaries for pupils from state schools.

Remarks: Ambitious, frankly academic grammar providing a top quality, seamless education for robust children, from toddler to adult.

Portsmouth High School

Linked school: Portsmouth High Junior School

25 Kent Road, Southsea, PO5 3EQ

• Pupils: 350 girls; all day • Ages: 2–18 • Non-denom
• Fees: £11,685 pa • Independent

Tel: 023 9282 6714
Email: admissions@por.gdst.net
Website: www.portsmouthhigh.co.uk

Headmistress: Since 2011, Mrs Jane Prescott BSc PGCE NPQH. Was deputy head of Leicester High School, then deputy head of Loughborough High School, with a background in the army. Energetic and engaging, she is liked and admired by parents and pupils alike. Very focused on the well-being of her charges (she feels that the girls' well-being is the most accurate indicator of the school's success).

She is 'very hands on', one parent told us, and has open door to pupils, staff and parents (apparently fully used). 'She is very approachable and comes to everything,' said one pupil approvingly.

A devoted advocate for single sex education, she sent her two sons and daughter to single sex schools. 'Boys shuffle for the top of the pack while girls tend to take a back seat', she told us. 'Girls feel the benefit here – there is no subject stereotyping'. Her aim is for her pupils to emerge as confident learners and resilient young women who will rise to the challenges of the world of work.

Academic matters: Results are very good. At A level, 56 per cent A*/A grades in 2013 while at IGCSE, 59 per cent A*/A. Overall IGCSE results from 2007 to 2010 showed a steady decline, but soared when the current head arrived. Head says the school was on a complacent 'OK plateau'. The girls were very well behaved and the focus was purely academic (ironically, given the falling results), which was 'just not good enough'. 'Pastoral care was nowhere', she told us. 'I switched it around'. Invigorated staff and pupils now aim for outstanding, and the school's results reflect this.

Pupils report a surprising lack of pressure to get those A*s. 'It's very caring', said one girl. 'I got a D in my mocks, and they said, "let's work out what went wrong". I got an A in the actual exam – but there wasn't pressure to get an A'. Parents talk of nurture and 'support without pressure'. One said that a D grade would be celebrated as much as an A grade if that was the best a girl could achieve. 'The competition is for the girl, not the school'. Parents say the school is less fiercely competitive than the nearby grammar and that there's no pressure here to retake disappointing grades to tweak those league tables. 'Move on', says the head firmly. 'All things are explainable'. (Even if the explanation might be laziness and recent reformation of character).

A smaller selection of subjects on offer than at larger schools, but staff will do their best to accommodate a girl's urge to learn something in particular. A parent whose daughter spoke good French asked if she could learn Spanish instead. The school did better than that, and she now learns Spanish as well as having a weekly one-to-one French session. Most girls take a language up to GCSE, but a few struggling with the basics can drop their language to focus on maths instead. School offers French, Spanish, Latin, Mandarin and Russian. Pupils who arrive with little English are supported to learn the language – only a basic ability in English required before joining the school.

More than half of pupils take maths at A level – lack of stereotyping means girls don't avoid maths and sciences. Subjects offered at A level include government and politics, drama, psychology and Latin (provision shared with St John's College in Portsmouth).

RS is popular – we observed a lively IGCSE class doing some bartering (a slight relief to hear the noise after the sheer concentrated effort of most classes observed). The topic was economic trading with ethical dimensions. 'They are trying to solve world poverty', explained the teacher. 'They haven't done it yet,' she added dryly.

Spacious labs, which after the imminent £1.2 million refurbishment will (amongst other things) allow pupils to use the data feed from solar panels on roof. When we visited, upper sixth pupils were just off to hear Lord Winston speak. 'We try to give the girls all the opportunities we can – as much extra curricular as possible to make science relevant to the rest of life', says the school. No more ICT – computer science has taken over. Bookable sets of iPads for pupils, particularly used for language lessons. Much focus on trying to encourage independent thought. Analytical, philosophical, ethical and political skills lessons launched in 2013, with the aim of diffusing these skills through the curriculum.

Constant data collection on performance, so those falling behind are quickly spotted. Immediate redress, starting with a chat to pupil and parents. Annual parents' evening, half-termly report cards and one full report a year.

All pupils are screened for SEN, but just a handful with special needs. SENCo for the whole school and special individual and group sessions where necessary. One pupil has been given an iPad of her own to assist her learning.

Games, options, the arts: Sport taken seriously and despite small urban site, school offers almost everything. If there is a criticism from the girls, it is that they don't get enough games lessons (although most years have five sessions a week). Sport England standard sports hall and school uses fleet of minibuses to reach the naval sports ground and pool and Portsmouth University's multi-use games area and synthetic turf pitch (co-owned with the school). Nearby common is used for rounders and tennis. Games range from pop lacrosse to Pilates, with everything in-between (including football and tag rugby – no sex discrimination here). Sports trips for netball and hockey.

Wide enrichment programme offered. Before-school trampolining is popular, as is sailing club, cookery club, chess, debating, pupil-led Christian society, and Amnesty group. Girl-led initiatives are encouraged. Big take-up for D of E.

Strong music department, with individual instruments encouraged from year 7. Plenty of public performance, overseas tours, recent choral performance at Royal Festival Hall. Big musical every other year. Drama studio, plus larger stage in the hall next door. Girls have performed at Portsmouth's Theatre Royal, and Edinburgh Festival.

Lovely art space – central atrium flooded with light from glass ceiling. Art courses cover ceramics, textiles, photography and fine art, with girls dictating the content as they get older. DT room packed with exciting equipment and a Tiggerish devotee of DT for a teacher. Rows of tiny models lined the shelves when we visited – a mini-me project for year 7s. DT lunchtime club very popular too.

Background and atmosphere: School buildings are a hodge-podge of styles. Old buildings are lovely, particularly the sixth form house, though some of the new buildings look a bit like Tesco. Interior is mostly well cared for. New catering manager has improved food dramatically. Eating in the dining room compulsory for year 7 (tables laid and waiting), but optional from year 8 onwards, so many opt for the school café. Parents astonished that their daughters choose to sit next to a teacher and chat at lunch time.

'You are known for who you are here', said one girl, adding that she felt 'anonymous' at the local grammar. Class sizes of around 20 for years 7 and 8, 15 to 20 at GCSE. A level classes vary in size. Parents feel that school's small size is its strength – girls can't get lost, literally or otherwise. Numbers on school roll are down – head reckons this reflects economic climate but bewildered parents suggest more marketing might work. School wouldn't want to be larger than 500 though, says the head. Small numbers mean staff and girls know each other well, and the curriculum can be tailored to individuals.

School is calm – difficult to imagine extremes of behaviour here. The pupils are confident and friendly. One parent told us that girls have 'confidence without cockiness', while another commented that her shy daughter was transformed after a couple of years here.

'It's nicer without boys – boys are disruptive', said a year 8 girl firmly. This seemed to be the prevailing view of pupils, and the school attracts a few disillusioned escapees from the local grammar. One parent who worried about single-sex education before she sent her daughter here said: 'I thought they would

be, you know, bitchy, but they are almost too nice to each other. They are very caring.' With two boys' schools nearby, girls have plenty of opportunity to socialise on the way to and from school and during activities like the cathedral choir. Sixth formers share a few lessons with boys from St John's too. Parents happy with communication – email update every week and email queries to school get prompt response.

The sixth form centre is part of the school, but sixth form girls get far more independence. Head girl and senior prefects (elected by peers) have lots of responsibility. School has tried to create a college atmosphere for the sixth form, and succeeded. Sixth formers attend house meetings and assemblies first thing, then come and go as they please. If they abuse the system, they have to stay in school, but this is very rare. No uniform, but smart dress with the silver Portsmouth High badge – no jeans. They are self assured, polite and friendly. The sixth form house has a white seating area, very tidy kitchen (with its own dishwasher) peaceful study rooms, small library, computer room and conservatory. 'When things are stressful at home, I just want to get to school and be in the sixth form centre', a sixth former said.

Officially it's a non-denominational school but in practice it's mildly Christian. Morality is a general approach, not religion-led. Lots of community activities too. Girls contribute to local charities, volunteer at the local food bank and at beach clean ups and are part of the British Council's Connecting Classrooms project.

Pupils travel in by school minibus, public transport, hovercraft from the Isle of Wight, by bike and on foot. Day ends at 3.40pm but pupils can stay until 6pm and use the library, which is well-stocked with books, online periodicals, computers and iPads.

Pastoral care and discipline: New emphasis on pastoral care under current head. Girls feel that they can talk to the head, that they will be listened to and that their efforts are appreciated. 'You get a handwritten card the day after you are in something – a proper one, not just one of those ink print things'. If something is wrong, the girls had no doubt to whom they would turn – 'the deputy head ... she's like a mother hen'. School also has a welfare officer.

Bullying very rare. Girls supported through any friendship problems by deputy head. Pupils can become peer supporters in year 9 and receive training in confidentiality. 'You have to fill out a proper application, like a job', a pupil gravely assured us. Great care taken in smoothing the transition from junior to senior school for year 7s. Girls appear to have good relations with teachers – 'not invasive, but caring', said a sixth former. Another girl told us: 'If you are struggling (with work), it's caring... how can we work together, how can we sort this out?' This is certainly not a rap over the knuckles, must do better, sort of place. Head is a firm believer in pupil voice and school has a code of conduct that all are expected to maintain.

Pupils and parents: Famous old girls include Dame Mary Donaldson, the first woman Lord Mayor of London, Dr Jane Collins, chief executive of Marie Curie Cancer Care, author and broadcaster Jane Hill, MP Meg Hillier, TV presenter Charlotte Jackson, Dr Katharine Vincent, an expert on sustainability and climate change, and actress Denise Black.

Parents are a broad church. 'I thought it would be all Boden mums, but it really isn't', one mother told us. Parents say it's for those who value education and are prepared to invest. 'We don't go on holiday much,' said another.

Entrance: Most girls start in year 7, but pupils can join in any year. Standard entrance exam in English and maths. Seven or eight pupils join at sixth form level.

Exit: Around 25 per cent leave after GCSE, many going to local sixth form colleges. Most sixth form leavers to top universities (including four to Oxbridge in 2013).

Money matters: Much cheaper than most schools of its ilk – great value for money. A number of small scholarships and bursaries (a couple of which pay the fees in full).

Remarks: A super no-frills choice. School is big enough to appeal to almost any girl, but not at the expense of the personal touch. Pupils and parents agree that all girls would thrive here and that it's a place where shrinking violets will flourish. Prestigious local reputation and a member of the GDST sisterhood.

Prior Park College

Linked schools: The Paragon School; Prior Park Preparatory School

Ralph Allen Drive, Combe Down, Bath, BA2 5AH

• Pupils: 570 pupils (310 boys/260 girls); includes 90 full boarders and 50 weekly boarders • Ages: 11–18 • RC • Fees: Boarding £22,635–£26,625; Day £13,035–£14,385 pa • Independent

Tel: 01225 831000
Email: admissions@priorpark.co.uk
Website: www.thepriorfoundation.com

Head Master: Since 2009, Mr James Murphy-O'Connor MA PGCE (early forties). Educated at St Benedict's, Ealing, before reading history at Greyfriars Hall, Oxford, and then PGCE at Peterhouse, Cambridge. Began career at Stamford where he taught history, thence to Sherborne, where he was a housemaster before appointment to headship of brand new Sherfield in Hampshire. Father, Jim, played rugby for Ireland and was eldest of five brothers who attended Prior – most illustrious of them being (Cardinal) Cormac. Previous career experience was commendably outside the Catholic fold.

He is fourth lay head since Christian Brothers left in early '80s. Married to Ali, they have four children (two at senior school and two at The Paragon). 'Has worked really hard to get to know everyone,' say parents, who find him 'extremely easy to communicate with'. Acknowledges pupils' achievements in all areas (writes them personal, handwritten letters) and has won their respect. Parents like the way 'he looks you in the eye' and are impressed by how quickly he learns names. Has built up the boarding side, gone for a sports hall and moved the school forwards with IT. Makes no excuse for pushing sport, particularly rugby, but is also keen on the arts: fan of F Scott Fitzgerald and Thomas Hardy plus Picasso's 1920s' art. Enjoys mountain climbing and surfing when able to get to family house at Mayo in Ireland. Intuitive understanding of Prior's mission; loads of energy, a firm faith and refreshingly open-minded.

Academic matters: In 2013, 78 per cent A*/B grades at A level. Mathematics currently outshines sciences at this level, philosophy is outstanding but humanities and modern languages more than hold their own. Strength in depth and wide choice of subjects on offer are healthy signs. Head keen to consider new sixth form curricula but disinclined to embrace IB. We witnessed a lively A level philosophy session based on Nietzsche's ideas on property. Theology is compulsory throughout. Well established PSE programme also reflects Catholic thinking and the resident school chaplain ('He's fab,' said one non-Catholic mum) plays a central rôle.

At GCSE in 2013, more than 50 per cent A*/A grades and more than 80 per cent A*/B. Vast majority take separate sciences. Smartboards commonplace and some innovative

teaching: we also watched an interactive year 8 maths class (pupils all had separate white boards to work out their answers) with a teacher (ex-PWC accountant) who was more hip than his pupils, with cool lines such as, 'I'm loving that answer – it's beautiful', to encourage even the most innumerate. Now teaches IGCSE maths. DT suite works well with lively staff: textiles area alongside well-resourced workshop and classroom areas. Maximum class size 20 in years 7 and 8; 24 in year 9. Staff to pupil ratio is 1:10 overall, with a good balance between experienced long servers and high octane younger blood.

Highly experienced learning support team (one full-time and two part-time teachers) – heavily oversubscribed area (accounts for around seven per cent of 11+ entry each year). Applicants need psychological report; school now includes non-verbal test in entrance exam; thorough screening of all entrants for SpLD. Learning support situated alongside library and sixth form centre (some seniors help with paired reading). Open door policy; main emphasis on dyslexia and supporting literacy, but copes with range of specific learning difficulties including dyspraxia and mild Asperger's. Sixty-five pupils currently have individual learning plans. EAL is provided by two members of staff to overseas pupils – one of whom won last year's English essay prize: enough said.

Games, options, the arts: Sport, music and drama all impressive. Sport, though strong, doesn't dominate and achievement in the arts is equally recognised. Younger pupils get plenty of exercise (timetabled PE and games) and a good tradition of seniors helping to coach juniors. Recent appointments include top rugby coach from head's alma mater. More flexibility with sports options from year 10 upwards. Extensive playing fields plus Astroturf are all within jogging distance from the main school buildings. Strong fixture lists in all sports with plenty of local rivalry. Basketball players use military facility at Colerne. Lots of representative athletes from district to national level. Sports tours are affordable – rugby tour to France latest venture. Major sports field 10 teams weekly; host of 'activity sports' plus Ten Tors, ski trips and D of E activities. Dance (offered to A level) has been a great hit: popular annual show features both sexes. Traditional Fisher Road Relay involving staff and pupils winds up Lent term enthusiastically.

New sports hall (due for completion in 2014) will plug a gap in sports provision, though carpeted gym fulfils need meantime and recently completed Mackintosh dance studio is up to professional standards. Planners prevented extension of indoor pool from its present, quirky 19 metres to 25, but it provides a well-used space. Old fives courts another area ripe for imaginative conversion (planners willing).

We discovered some keen sixth form artists (they enjoyed showing off their eye-catching folders) in suitably bohemian, basement studios, working on a variety of approaches under inspired direction. Not huge numbers for A level but plenty of passion and variety of work on display around the school.

Cracking music department fields three teachers with well-established director, Roland Robertson, whose reputation goes before him. Over half the pupils take instrumental lessons and standards vary from grade 1 to diploma level. Aim is to 'take pupils musically where their interests (and talent) lead them' – seems to bear fruit. Exquisite John Wood chapel provides venue for lots of concerts – we attended an informal ('get up and have a go') lunch-time one, following on from a junior brass practice which belted out a recognisable James Bond theme inter alia. Music to suit all tastes: high level of participation with several choirs, bands and orchestras. Opera every other year, annual musicals and a choral society which includes staff and parents – recent performances include Handel's Messiah and Verdi's Requiem. Many pupils participate in Mid-Somerset Festival. We liked the whole ambience of the music department (once we had panted up seemingly endless flights of stairs to reach it) – recording studio, class and individual practice rooms plus split

P

level area for music technology (limited numbers who take it seriously at AS and A level here) taught by a muso housemaster. African drumming group especially popular with international pupils. Over 50 per cent of chapel choir are day pupils – incredible, given requirement to turn out every Sunday.

The Julian Slade Theatre provides a small but cutting edge theatrical environment. Three drama teachers and one theatre technician all have a professional background and it shows: no end to the number of productions (well, 23 actually in current year) from musicals (head of science directs these) to Ibsen and Beckett. Recent production of The Crucible got rave reviews. Parents 'brilliantly supportive' when it comes to meeting late night returns from theatre trips to Bristol etc.

Has gone overboard when it comes to activities: over 60 on offer each week with main slots on Saturday mornings (140 boarders and day pupils turn up for this) and Tuesday afternoons. Activities range from a Leith's cookery course to Padi scuba diving. Prior Concern for those in sixth wishing to get involved in community service. We saw one sixth former going through a tai chi form as his alternative to the prescribed Tuesday choices – 'Quite acceptable here,' confided an assistant head.

Majority join CCF at start of year 10 in either naval or army sections; well-organised alternative programme caters for the non-combatants. Compulsory residential course early in year 7 and team building day for year 8 pupils make for better relationships from the junior end upwards. Lots of educational visits including history trips, school exchanges with France and Germany, plus study visits to Spain. Recent pupil exploits include participation on polar and Uganda expeditions and national youth choir member.

Background and atmosphere: Founded in 1830 and run by the Christian Brothers until 1981, now the largest independent co-educational, Catholic day and boarding school in the UK. This position owes much to the successes of the three previous headmasters, who guided the school into the modern educational age. With about one third boarding and 30 per cent practising Catholics, it does not feel like yet another largely day school with token boarders or nominal religious affiliation. Seven senior houses (three mix day pupils and boarders and four have day pupils only). Unmistakably co-educational, with fairly even numbers of boys and girls throughout. Magnificent Georgian architecture of the 'mansion' provides backdrop for an unsurpassed vista over the grounds (much of which are now National Trust property, including the famous Palladian Bridge) and Bath beyond.

Imposing chapel accommodates whole school for weekly assemblies (impressive level of pupil and staff involvement). Mass for whole school roughly once each half term plus particular feast days. Compulsory mass on Sunday mornings for boarders.

New ICT centre and is networked throughout school; well-organised library has 20 laptops which can be signed in and out. Pupils' use of fiction, reference and study areas speaks volumes for the self-regulating approach here. Day pupils have nominal workspaces in their rather crowded house accommodation, where prep is supervised between 4.50 and 5.50pm. Junior pupils split into small vertical groups, which counters the risk of year 8s dominating within Baines House (recently upgraded) where juniors are registered.

Roche and Allen are relatively civilised boarding houses for boys on the upper floors of the mansion, whilst girls are accommodated in enviable surroundings in St Mary's House, which occupies the nearby 'Priory'. Some day pupils opt to be in boarding houses because they prefer the ethos; weekly boarding is popular. Sixth form centre (located above theatre which is used for assemblies) comprises classrooms, a large common-room and well-resourced careers suite.

Pastoral care and discipline: Catholic approach 'looks at whole child,' insists head. Lots of help and advice from all

quarters: 'Staff at Prior (compared with her son's previous school in Bath) are superb at following things up,' we were told by one mother, whose son transferred at lower sixth level. Reward system (head's distinctions doled out for all kinds of worthy endeavours) breeds a positive approach. No evidence of a punishment culture. Pupils are generally well turned out without being ostentatious. Strong counter-bullying policy and all sixth forms shoulder some responsibility through a variety of committees; pupil hierarchy survives in terms of a head boy and head girl together with heads of house. Pupils are 'at ease with the staff,' say parents.

Half-terms are of sensible length (10 days in Michaelmas term) and don't exploit guardianship arrangements. Central but not overly accessible medical centre. Suite of dining areas copes with peak periods and provides good choice of menus to suit most tastes.

Pupils and parents: Most from within an hour's drive. Half of the leavers from own boarding prep school at Cricklade transfer to Prior at 13. Nearby Paragon (acquired relatively recently) provides good co-ed intake at 11. Six daily mini-bus and coach routes transport day pupils from a 30 mile plus radius. Boarders generally come from further afield, including a mix of overseas boarders (most of whom are Catholics). Good environment for language learning, insisted our Chinese guide, who spoke impeccable English. Former pupils and current parents are very supportive, with a range of fund-raising and social events and pages on the school website.

Majority of pupils are non Catholics. Religion is packaged sensitively for all persuasions. Former pupils have gained selection for England and Scotland under 21 rugby teams; others on master's degrees at Royal Academy of Music (choral and composition). Famous Old Boys include Cardinal Cormac Murphy-O'Connor (see above), former archbishop of Westminster, famous musical producer, Sir Cameron Mackintosh, international rugby player Damian Cronin and television presenter Hugh Scully.

Sense of mutual respect between pupils and staff: 'No horrible teachers,' confided pupils. 'A school you have to immerse yourself in,' explained one new parent. Sixth formers have a particularly open and relaxed manner without being laid back. Pupil mentoring now under way. We liked the idea of information evenings for parents prior to each term's personal development programme (for pupils in years 7-11), which includes topics such as 'sex and responsibility' and 'respect for life'.

Long-term link with Catholic archdiocese of Songia, Tanzania, where gap year students spend five months teaching in local schools. Student-run charities committee raised over £11k last year through all kinds of activities (main focus is annual charities week – former head's performance of Show Me the Way to Amirillo, dressed as Elvis, at the Staff in Your Eyes show apparently 'brought the house down'); worthy causes range from Searight Hospital to Aid for Albania. Parents join Saturday activities (eg Leith's cookery class). Active parents' group hosts range of events (eg annual quiz served with curry and pud).

Entrance: Register at least 18 months before entrance. January entrance tests for 11+ with majority of entrants coming from own 3-11 prep and about 20 per cent from state primaries. Non-verbal reasoning score used as baseline for assessment. Lists close at least a year in advance for LDP (see above) applicants. About 40 pupils join at 13+, with about half of them from the junior school at Cricklade, Wiltshire. November interviews for entrants into lower sixth, who need a satisfactory reference and a minimum of six A*-C grades at GCSE with higher grades in chosen AS subjects.

Exit: Very small numbers leave after year 11. Almost all to universities (lots take a gap year) with Durham, Cardiff and Swansea recent popular choices, plus art and music courses. Regular successes at Oxbridge entry – two in 2013.

P

Money matters: Extensive range of scholarships (academic, art, music, all-rounder and sport) and bursaries, with good academic scholars typically gaining 30 per cent remission of fees. Services bursaries. Currently around 150 award holders (normal range between 5-50 per cent). Drama awards at 13 and 16. Some continuity scholarships from preparatory school. Discounts for siblings. Bus services charged monthly and quite pricey. Music tuition fees represent excellent value for money.

Remarks: Full school which suits parents looking for deeper values and an ethos which 'enables rather than prescribes'. Unusually successful at nurturing, encouraging and stimulating its pupils. Gentle Catholicism in the broadest sense within an inspiring setting and atmosphere.

Prior's Field

Priorsfield Road, Godalming, GU7 2RH

• Pupils: 450 girls; 45 full boarders, 50 weekly boarders, 120 flexi boarders, rest day • Ages: 11–18 • Non-denom • Fees: Day £15,855; Boarding £25,575 pa • Independent

Tel: 01483 810551
Email: registrar@priorsfieldschool.com
Website: www.priorsfieldschool.com

Head: Since 2006, Mrs Julie Roseblade MA (late forties). Educated at Pate's Grammar School followed by York and London Universities. Taught English and drama in a variety of schools, in the UK and overseas, before becoming deputy head of St Helen's, Northwood and then headmistress here. Other experience includes being an ISI inspector and a prep school governor. Calm and businesslike, says she has no plans to move on yet. Parents certainly feel that she is doing an excellent job and managing to keep the school on an even keel; top class teaching but no hothousing. She has brought in more male members of staff (a big tick from us), says the teaching age range is now more balanced and feels that her team is one of the huge strengths of the school. Parents agree and add 'communication is good too'. She feels strongly that, because it is a single sex school, girls can make choices and follow paths they might not be able to do were boys in the equation. Certainly the sixth form girls we talked to were perfectly happy with the status quo. Believes strength is breadth, that a child solely focused on academics would not fit in the school, that 'value added is the key'. Said 'All girls are individuals and we encourage them to respect each other's differences. They don't need unnecessary pressures' and that it is the happiest school she has worked in.

Academic matters: Not the top academic school in the county but possibly the most rounded and least competitive. The school does not totally agree with this, saying it's more that 'Prior's Field girls are not unhealthily competitive. They can be when they need to be, as in sport and when winning the Surrey Schools' Problem Solving Competition in 2013'. Head says they are now attracting more girls at the top end of the ability range and parents are confident that they are capable of dealing with all sorts. Certainly their results are more than acceptable, and the fact that it 'does not feel like a pressure cooker' enables girls to learn and develop at their own speed. Set in maths, English, languages and the sciences from day one, but this is flexible and not definitive. In 2013, 40 per cent A*/A grades at A level and over half A*/A at GCSE

High quality teaching with average age of staff at 42, around a quarter of whom have been at the school for over 10 years. Average class size 15, never more than 22. Pupil:teacher ratio

approximately 8:1. A parent said 'their main strength is that they focus on an all round education'. That is certainly born out by the range of subjects they can study, plenty of extras and a huge variety of clubs and activities. Just reading the possibilities is mind boggling – especially in such a relatively small school.

Each girl is treated as an individual and, because the school is not overly selective, the focus is not solely on her intellectual achievement but also on finding the best path for her to follow to develop her personality and confidence. This also encourages most of them to stay on for sixth form, where a girl can pursue pretty well any course or combination of courses that she likes. We met one, on her own, doing AS level food technology, thrilled at the individual help she was being given. Versatility definitely reflected in their results: in 2013, 36 girls went to 32 different universities.

Flexible and inclusive approach to SEN. Anything beyond mild unlikely to be catered for. Prefer to do as much as possible within the classroom situation; anything more may involve individual or group support lessons, charged for as an extra. G and T also treated within the classroom, with an extension programme for scholars. EAL tuition also available.

Games, options, the arts: Good space within the school grounds and sports hall for all the usual activities, especially since recent addition of large all weather pitch. Only small covered swimming pool, so girls taken to Surrey Sports Park for lessons. About 45 per cent take part in some type of competitive sport during the year – either extracurricular or inter-house matches. Some 35 winter and 21 summer teams compete locally and regionally against other schools. Several pupils also reach national level, or higher – one of their tennis players reached number 90 in the under 14 English ranking and others have represented their country in riding, kayaking and skiing. The seniors can choose their own sports, whether they be competitively physical or more along the yoga/pilates line.

Wonderful art on display, the standard appearing exceptionally high. Plenty of opportunities to follow various courses and techniques. Talent abounds; several go on to do degree courses using their well nurtured creative ability. When we visited the textiles department, some sixth form girls were creating extraordinarily complicated designs for an A level millinery project. It really would seem that this school is able to cater for anything anyone wants to learn.

Music also important. Around half of the girls play, ranging from grade 1 to diploma level, on a variety of instruments. They can try orchestral, pop and rock music and learn music theory. Singing also important, with several choirs.

And, of course, there is drama: a whole school production – usually a musical – each year and a lower school play. Everyone is involved in something – on or off stage. Other smaller plays and productions as time and curriculum dictate. Several girls follow the LAMDA courses, and RADA lessons are also offered. Some even go on to drama school and a stage career.

Plenty of outings and expeditions, and after-school clubs cover a wide range of interests. D of E programme which included a trip to Norway for the gold in 2013, and some girls also follow the national Sports Leaders programme. Then there are trips to France, Spain and further afield. Lucky were those who went to Malaysia as part of the World Challenge in 2013.

Background and atmosphere: Founded in 1902 by Julia Huxley, the granddaughter of Thomas Arnold of Rugby and mother of Aldous, the only boy ever to have attended the school. The main school building was designed by Charles Voysey and, externally, provides an interesting contrast to the extremely modern, state of the art facilities that have been created inside over the last 10 years. All very well done, his oak hall and staircase remain, as well as his quirky motifs, and the Gertrude Jekyll rose garden is still there for the girls to run round.

The first stop on our tour of the school was the main hall, where all the juniors were seated on the ground in circles drawing small falcons perched amongst them. We had arrived on a cross-curricular day involving problem-solving in mathematics, feathers, flying and sketching, encouraging enthusiasm and the desire to find out and discover. This appeared to typify the general adventurousness of the school, the imagination brought to engaging the pupils and the importance they put on cross-curricular learning.

The sixth form building was our next port of call. Very grown up. Their own café and common room, and self-decorated, individual bedrooms for all. The overseas pupils get slightly bigger ones – 'they have more stuff to store'. All looked great fun. No uniform; supposedly some limitations but looked pretty relaxed to us. Black suits and jackets for formal occasions. Open, relaxed pupils perfectly happy with the all girls' situation. They said they have 'good relationship with teachers'. Small classes, average eight, some just two to four pupils.

Same buzzy atmosphere throughout the rest of the school. State-of-the-art facilities everywhere. High tech science wing housing six laboratories. New creative arts section, everything to stretch imaginations. Music corridor including composition room full of computers. Everything bright and airy. Incredible DT room, where one pupil was working on her GCSE project – a very modern-looking circular rocking chair. Some other wonderful small creations, and the beginning of an idea for a hovercraft – 'that will take at least two years to put together'. Their last such major engineering project, a solar powered car, has qualified for the national final at Goodwood each year since. Here was a teacher positively brimming with enthusiasm. The old biology lab, now relocated to the science wing, has become a food technology room suitable for MasterChef. And the library, possibly the lightest one we've seen in many trips round schools, is well equipped and resourced. School is acceptably proud of it.

Good boarding facilities for 11-15s. The younger children share double rooms, the older ones have single rooms but can choose to share if they prefer. Bathrooms look a bit shabby but, we gathered, there are refurbishment plans. A couple of common rooms for them to relax in after school is over. Happiness is paramount.

Pastoral care and discipline: Sympathetic, positive head of sixth has been there for seven years and never had a problem with drugs, drink or smokers. Says girls give each other lots of support and the vibrant PSHE programme really does seem to work. Appears to be true throughout the whole school, where it is incorporated into daily routine. Sixth form have one-to-one sessions with their tutor each week, and form tutors meet all girls regularly. We were told 'there is a real yes culture', 'staff do seem to care about their students'. Small school, so really does become 'one big community' where every one cares for everyone else. Nobody should slip through the net.

Pupils and parents: Wide range, local and further afield; day girls, weekly, flexi and full time boarders. Not so much social Surrey, more those looking for value, but not a hothouse. All wanting an all-round education and an unthreatening atmosphere for their daughters, that, even so, pushes them to their full potential. Generally a friendly, relaxed lot. Approximately 10 per cent from overseas, four per cent Oriental, the rest from all over. Good bus service for day girls. Interesting former pupils: Sam Cam's great grandmother, author of National Velvet, Enid Bagnold; Baroness Mary Warnock, educationalist and philosopher; Lily James, actress; and senior style editor for Vogue China, Grace Lamb.

Entrance: Now this is different: all those registered for 11+ are assessed in the November prior to entry. They sit maths, English and verbal reasoning papers, have a group interview with a member of staff followed by lunch and an afternoon trying their hands at circus skills. Parents get feed back from the school and girls return in January to take more maths and English exams. Places then offered to approximately one in three.

Exit: All over. Some leave at 16+ on the hunt for mixed sixth forms but the majority stay on and leave after A level for an exceptionally wide range of higher education establishments – 36 girls to 32 different destinations in 2013 (one to Oxford), all to their first choice.

Money matters: Several scholarships available at all entry points, worth up to 20 per cent of fees; exhibitions worth 10 per cent. Quite a few bursaries which could be worth 100 per cent. Some means-tested sixth form bursaries for locals who will need top GCSE grades in chosen subjects. Services children eligible for 20 per cent discount and daughters of old girls get 10 per cent. A school, ready and willing to help.

Remarks: If you are looking for a school that will provide a broad education, excellent facilities and get the best out of your daughter in an unpressurised environment, then this could be it. In this high flying, girls'-school-rich corner of Surrey, it provides a refreshing change, nurturing rather than hothousing, unearthing each girl's strengths and teaching her to use them.

The Purcell School

Linked school: Purcell School Junior Department

Aldenham Road, Bushey, WD23 2TS

• Pupils: 185 boys and girls (60 per cent girls). Three-quarters board. • Ages: 8–18 • Non-denom • Fees: Day £24,777; Boarding £31,686 pa • Independent

Tel: 01923 331100
Email: info@purcell-school.org
Website: www.purcell-school.org

Headmaster: Since September 2012, Mr David Thomas (late forties). A chorister at Magdalen College School (where he boarded from the age of 8) and an organ scholar at Oxford. Director of music at Fettes College and deputy head of Trinity, Croydon. Brings with him 11 years of headmasterly experience at solidly-high-achieving, feet-on-ground Reigate Grammar. Keen singer, teaches A level music and conducts the chamber choir. Married to Andrea, a PhD historian, who writes books on Scottish history. No children.

Was brought in to steady the vessel after a few years of choppy waters which culminated in the previous head resigning in the middle of the Christmas term 2011. With its gifted pupils, uniquely talented staff, and parents who have notched up many years of sacrifice supporting their children's abilities, the good ship Purcell is not an easy one to steer. Governors have appointed headmasters from well-respected, mainstream independent schools that would be good leaders of just about any other school in the country – but are they right for a school like this? It may be that no one, short of Daniel Barenboim or Lang Lang, could lead this school to reach the excellence of which it is capable. The baton is with Mr Thomas, and we wish him well.

Academic matters: Academic results have collapsed in recent years. In 2013 A level results improved 18 per cent over the previous year, nonetheless three quarters of A level maths results were Ds or Es. Physics results consisted of one C and one U; no sixth form students were examined in biology or chemistry. Music A levels good, but not dazzling. All of this is a sharp change from the fairly recent past when the school routinely featured high in the independent school A level league tables. The head is working hard to 'sort out the academic side', has appointed two deputy heads to help, and green shoots are already appearing. GCSE results much more promising: in 2013, 95 per cent of GCSE grades were A*-C (65 per cent A*/A).

Years 5 and 6 taught as one group; thereafter pupils taught within their year groups. Setting for maths starts in year 9. Everyone in the GCSE years takes music, maths, English lang and science but generally take no more than seven or eight subjects. Small classes for everything. New music library and IT has been upgraded throughout. Much individual help and support, especially for musical prodigies who arrive playing perfect Paganini but with little English. SEN well supported.

Games, options, the arts: Sport surprisingly good for a school that doesn't really offer any. 'My son never liked sport until he came here,' enthused one mum who reeled off the games he was now involved in: badminton, volleyball, football. One competitive football match each year against fellow music geeks at the Yehudi Menuhin School. Currently one PE lesson per week; plans perpetually afoot to offer more physical activity. Lots of ad hoc activity, from kicking a ball about the enormous playing fields to a bit of netball and off-site swimming. Art and drama enthusiastically pursued, and drama has recently been formally added to the curriculum (art already there).

Music provision is, of course, superb. The musical day begins at 7.20 with pre-breakfast morning practice and continues, interspersed through the day, until bedtime. Practice supervisors support the under-13s. Choir compulsory for all – though resented by some as an intrusion into their practice time. That said, the senior chamber choir was described by a parent at 'simply the finest and most exciting youth choir I have EVER heard'. Most of the staff teach at the RCM or RAM and all are of that professional standard – they have to be. Professional accompanists work with the pupils – a real and special privilege. No shortage of performing opportunities. Last year there were 71 public concerts, 15 'outreach' concerts and upwards of 150 lunchtime concerts. Composing very strong and one girl was one of five winners of the BBC Young Composers' Competition last year.

The mint green music centre features a stunning recital room, teaching rooms, a recording studio, dozens of practice rooms, from which concert quality playing seeps, and nice little architectural touches everywhere. Music tech covers all aspects of creative studio work including multi-track recording, electro-acoustic music, arranging, studio engineering, producing and composition for film. A large new percussion suite opened 2013. The multi-purpose school hall is still used for most concerts.

Background and atmosphere: An interesting history. Founded as recently as 1962 by Rosemary Rapaport and Irene Forster – but nonetheless the UK's oldest specialist music school. It began life as The Central Tutorial School for Young Musicians, at Conway Hall, then resided for a while in Morley College, from where it moved to Hampstead. In 1973, it was renamed The Purcell School – perhaps reflecting the new enthusiasm for 'earlyish' British music and, in 1998, relocated to the site of the former Royal Caledonian School in fairly dismal Bushey, Hertfordshire. The main building is an attractive low-rise Edwardian pile with wide corridors, good-sized concert hall, assorted classrooms, smartened up canteen (food now provided by outside caterers and has improved no end) and new girls' boarding accommodation.

Staff and pupil morale knocked in the spring of 2013 by the redundancy of the school's well-liked head of music who conducted the school orchestra. Redundancy, after 25 years at the school, left bad feeling, with pupils melodramatically

taking to wearing green ribbons to protest his removal. 'It makes us feel like music is less important now,' said one pupil. 'It's like the nerve centre has been ripped from the school', said another. School governors have had a much-needed shake-out and the average age has plummeted by around 20 years. All the specialist music schools are going through a period of introspection and Purcell is no exception.

Pastoral care and discipline: Boarding accommodation, formerly poor, now tickety-boo. Sunley House, upstairs in the main school building, provides accommodation for 50 girls plus resident staff. New co-ed boarding house very popular – with a boys' wing and a, larger, girls' wing. The recently refurbished junior boarding house makes a cheerful home to around 20 (mostly) girls and (a few) boys ages 8-12, all in double rooms (a few singles), though with such small numbers friendships can be hard to form. Sixth form pianists have a piano in their rooms!

Pupils enthuse about their fantastic camaraderie – 'We all encourage each other – everyone is so supportive of everyone else,' and you feel this as you see them greet each other in the corridors. A few girls mentioned feeling (geographically) divided by the current split of girl boarders between Sunley, in the main school, and the new co-ed boarding house. Would make more sense to put all the girls in the new house and whack the boys into Sunley. Most boarders go home on Friday nights and return 48 hours later, but there are always around 50 in on weekends, many from abroad.

Pupils given more leeway than at most schools and chafe when their freedoms are reigned in. Much friction over rules eg about when children are allowed out to visit shops and which shops they may visit. A few expulsions for use of alcohol or cannabis.

Pupils and parents: 'A school of individuals' says the head with admirable understatement. All sorts, from every economic, academic, national and social background, all united by a love of music. 70 per cent 'British' (many dual nationals), nine per cent Korean, five per cent Singaporean and rest from all over. No quotas or limits on nationalities joining. A healthy slab of local children make up the day contingent who lead a very different existence to the boarders. Children can attend from age 8, though numbers are so low at that end of the school that we can't recommend boarding here quite that young. Big intake of (mainly) boarders at sixth form. Former pupils include Oliver Knussen (composer and conductor), Nicholas Daniel (oboist and first winner of the BBC Young Musician competition), Catrin Finch (former harpist to the Prince of Wales), Lara Melda (winner of 2010 BBC Young Musician), Janice Graham (leader, ENO Orchestra), and Yiruma (Korean pianist and composer).

Entrance: Pupils are selected by musical audition, supported by interviews and reasoning test. Auditions take place every week from September to March. Children come for a preliminary audition and then a majority return for a more thorough going over. Musical standard for admission is very high but not ridiculous. No academic threshold, but school must be 'able to cater for them'. No set numbers for entry at any particular age, and more coming and going here than at most schools. About 20 musicians enter at sixth form.

Exit: Mostly to The Royal Academy of Music, The Royal College of Music, The Guildhall and Royal Northern College of Music. The rest mostly to other music courses hither and yon; a few to university to read other subjects. Most pupils end up with careers in music – whether teaching, production, business or performing.

Money matters: Fees have been frozen for four years. Which cannot be said of any other independent school in the United Kingdom. Indeed, fees now significantly less than many public schools, if you factor in the cost of music lessons which are included here.

Meanwhile, most pupils receive some kind of financial support – under the government's music and dance assisted places scheme, school bursary or scholarship. An amazing opportunity for the brilliant but broke – many pay nothing.

Remarks: Buffeted, but not bowed – still providing a unique education to some of the world's most talented youngsters.

Putney High School

Linked school: Putney High Junior School

35 Putney Hill, London, SW15 6BH

• Pupils: 560 girls • Ages: 11–18 • Non-denom • Fees: £14,958 pa (Senior School) • Independent

Tel: 020 8788 4886
Email: putneyhigh@put.gdst.net
Website: www.putneyhigh.gdst.net

Headmistress: Since 2002, Dr Denise V Lodge (fifties). She has an absolute army of impressive letters after her name, too many to list – obviously a very learned soul. Previously headmistress at Sydenham High School (also in the Girls' Day Schools Trust stable), deputy head at Sheffield High, and before that head of curriculum, sixth form and chemistry at Sir Roger Manwood's School, Kent. Former finalist in Salters' Prize chemistry teacher of the year. Is definitely not one of the touchy feely, we must bond sort of heads. 'She's not a PR person,' says one mother. 'Better one-to-one than with big groups.' She may not talk the talk, but on the plus side she is credited with being quite progressive, promoting a fantastic breadth of opportunity for the girls and injecting a real international feel to the place by introducing exchange scheme programmes with schools in China and India. Seen to prefer the older girls, with whom she enjoys discussing current affairs and how events may impact on them and their chosen careers. Married with a son and a daughter, both late 20s. In her spare time enjoys jazz, theatre and the gym, and by all accounts is a mean cook.

Academic matters: Very academic place – some seriously bright girls here, working very hard, but not too pressured. Excellent results – at GCSE in 2013, an impressive 88 per cent A*/A grades. Good performances in sciences, history, music and art. At A level 70 per cent A*/A grades. Fantastic to see in a girls' school that maths is the most popular choice at A level – by a long way. Parents happy school holds its own against St Paul's and Godolphin and Latymer, though the feeling on the outside is that St Paul's is still a jump ahead.

In year 7, when girls are mainly taught in form groups, they average (a large) 28. School is quick to defend the numbers – 'One third of lessons in year 7 are taught in groups of 21/22 – maths, art and science. Furthermore, DT/ textiles is taught in half classes of 14. By year 9 only PHSE (life skills) is taught as a group of 28'. For sixth formers, the average class size is eight.

Good to see that girls are not over-burdened with lots of homework – theory is that they work hard enough during school day. No setting in year 7, but in year 8 they are set for maths. It's more a matter of pace than ability – all can still aim for A grades by the end. Studies all based around a considerably developed national curriculum which is pleasingly broad and flexible. Sciences all taught separately from year 8, when Latin also makes an appearance. Nice to see Mandarin on the list of modern foreign languages – now available as a GCSE and A level subject, with all A*s at GCSE again in 2012. School happily retains minority subjects.

No testing for SEN, but specialists on the staff, though the impression from the school is that it is not a huge specialist area, so not a first choice school for a girl with SEN problems. Extra-curricular activities for the exceptionally gifted and talented.

Games, options, the arts: A great place for all-rounders as games and music are very well done here. 'Would be a shame to come here as a pure academic – you would miss out on so much,' sums up one parent. Storming sports results lately – school has produced GDST champions in netball, lacrosse and tennis. Playing fields are off site (but close by) – the downside of London location.

Great music – choir tours are legendary and colossal, orchestras and ensembles abound. 'I just cannot get over the music here,' says one mother to a chorus of agreement. A mixture of planning and fortune has seen the music department refurbished, with all the toys necessary for GCSE and A level composition. Lovely to see 16 girls a year take music GCSE – higher than the average elsewhere. Art also very good – average of 20 go on to A level, with eight or nine then to art school. Tons of extra-curricular stuff on offer – too numerous to mention (includes life drawing and medical society). Almost everyone does Duke of Edinburgh.

Background and atmosphere: Set up in 1893 with 54 pupils in five scattered houses, coming together as one on its present site in 1918. Typically of London schools, the site is relatively small, but it really makes the most of what it has, with some beautiful gardens, and is something of an oasis off uninspiring Putney Hill. Just a few steps from this busy London road and you are in a far more rarefied atmosphere – parallels with Narnia and Mr Benn abound. And of course the upside to this urban location is fab transport links – short walk from tube and BR trains and streams of buses stop right outside.

Inside some super-smart facilities – spectacular library, swish new drama studio and language lab, but overall facilities won't blow you away with glitz and glamour. Doesn't matter, though, as everything underpinned with great teaching and wide-ranging opportunities. State-of-the-art new sixth form centre opened 2011; performing arts centre set to open in 2014.

Pastoral care and discipline: Parental praise for pastoral care – knows the girls well and understands all the ages and stages they go through. Worthwhile life skills programme is used to discuss bullying, eating disorders et al. 'We pride ourselves on spotting problems early on,' says Dr Lodge. 'Obviously there are occasional issues, but we address them fast and in a supportive way.' Happy, well-motivated girls with things to do and places to go to are unlikely to spend much time in detention. The usual system of praise and punishment in place as and when necessary – house points, detentions, that sort of thing – but overall a happy ship. Good teacher/pupil relationships make formal sanction the exception rather than the rule. 'When a school is working well like this you can afford to be a bit relaxed,' says Dr Lodge.

Tough rather than tender, no nonsense rather than nurturing – but the bright and robust will thrive. Can be rather rigid about rules and regulations – parents complain about a lack of a personal touch with standardised responses to their queries and of secretarial/admin staff at times not being as helpful as parents would wish.

Pupils and parents: The hard-working middle classes abound and are really supportive of the school. Perhaps not surprisingly, as they are discussing their own daughters and her friends, most parents describe the girls as 'down to earth' and the place as 'not snobby or élitist'. Pupils are largely a full-on bunch, full of attitude and ideas – and might overwhelm those who don't shine in anything in particular, so not the obvious place for the shy or unconfident. School is proud of its girls and their 'can do' attitude – when confronted with a minor inconvenience, they

P

just get on with it. Pupils are a reasonably smart, normal bunch with no wacky hairstyles, jewellery etc.

Parents very welcome to contribute – preferably via parents' association – rather than helping within the school itself: 'They prefer to keep us out of the way a bit,' says one mother. The parents' association is thriving, seemingly a great place for a night out and one of the few we've come across who make special mention of welcoming single parents who might otherwise find some school events a little daunting. Newcomers will be swept up and supported. Generally the school is big on fundraising.

Old Girls bear witness to the wide range of talents encouraged at the school, eg newsreader Sophie Raworth, fashion designer Edina Ronay, gardening broadcaster Pippa Greenwood, author Sophie Kinsella, politicians Virginia Bottomley and Baroness Elizabeth Symons, journalist Melanie Phillips, sculptor Emily Young and entrepreneur Calypso Rose, a London young business person of the year.

Entrance: Selective, at 11+, described by the school as 'by competitive examination (papers in English and maths, each one hour 15 minutes) and friendly interview'. If an average selective school is looking for the top 25 per cent, Putney is after the top 10. Don't struggle and coach to get your daughter here – school knows exactly the girls it wants and you either fit or you don't. 'They'll need to have been well-taught,' is the only hint we could glean for you. Competitive, lots of interest – 2000+ at open day, 400 will sit entrance exam, and bear in mind that every other year almost 50 per cent of the places will go to the about 44 possible arrivals from linked juniors (less than a handful of the junior school brigade won't qualify). The school alternates between a three and four-form entry. In September 2014, it will take four forms into year 7 (about 110 girls). Register by November the year before admission. Lots of locals, but as girls are older and travel independently, net cast slightly wider than for juniors.

At 16+, girls need six GCSEs at A*/A, with A*/As in subjects they want to study at A level. Used to have a reputation for weeding out at this stage, ie booting out those of their own who do not make the grades, but Dr Lodge insists this is no more – a major relief for parents. Newcomers will need references and informal interviews with Putney staff.

Exit: Majority move up to the sixth form, though some head off to co-ed or boarding elsewhere. At 18+ most to redbrick universities of their choice, eg Bristol, Leeds, Imperial College UCL; about 10 per cent to Oxbridge. In 2013, three to Cambridge, three to Oxford, one to study economics at the LSE, two to the US, four to study medicine, two to veterinary medicine and one to arts foundation courses.

Money matters: Academic scholarships awarded on merit – all 11+ candidates automatically considered. Music scholarships via audition. At 16+, academic, music, art, drama, design and sport scholarships. Travel scholarships in modern languages and science for internal candidates only. Means-tested bursaries available.

Remarks: Super school best for very bright and diligent all-rounders who enjoy a busy life. An impressive and substantial offering.

Queen Anne's School

6 Henley Road, Caversham, Reading, Berkshire, RG4 6DX

- Pupils: 440 girls (50/50 day and boarding). • Ages: 11–18 • C of E
- Fees: Boarding £28,845; Day £19,575 pa • Independent

Tel: 01189 187300
Email: admissions@qas.org.uk
Website: www.qas.org.uk

Headmistress: Since 2006, Mrs Julia Harrington BA NPQ (fifties). Previously deputy head at Prior's Field School, Godalming, a school with a similar feel to this one. She was educated at Lydney Grammar School and read history and politics at Exeter. In the 1980s she joined the Independent Television Companies Association, the trades association which represented the interests of the, then, 16 independent television companies. Buckets of enthusiasm, much of it directed towards getting the girls to aim high and believe in their ability to make a difference – was saying, 'Yes, we can!' years before anyone had heard of Barack Obama. Married to an IT director; her two daughters are studying at Oxford and her son at Durham.

Academic matters: It's all about personal best here. Not a hothouse, not part of the academic super-élite, but does well by the girls, whatever their ability. In 2013, 50 per cent of A level grades were A*/A. At GCSE, 60 per cent A*/A grades overall.

Impressive octagonal two-tier library well-stocked and constantly updated with hardbacks, softbacks and software. Two dedicated IT rooms fully equipped with latest technology. Small classes for all – standard size 16-18. Swish £3million science block, modern languages block and performing arts centre opened in 2006. Mild dyslexics catered for – no specialist teacher. Prep sessions scheduled during the day help procrastinators to stay on track. We're told Saturday morning lessons have been replaced with an 'optional programme of exciting activities' including sports, drama and music and creative options.

Games, options, the arts: Focus of huge investment in recent years. Superb sports centre opened in 2000 by Princess Royal. Multi-functional hall (international competition standard) plus squash courts, dance studio, a climbing wall, 25-metre indoor pool and a gym. Great reputation on lax field (arch rivals: Downe House) – current student is one of the youngest players ever to be selected for the senior England lacrosse team. Tennis, rowing and golf have all celebrated recent success. Netball, athletics, squash and swimming also hotly contested; riding, gym and dance. No hockey ('But no one minds,' said our guide, 'because lacrosse is so much better!').

Art and design studio opened by old girl Posy Simmonds – lots of space and light and the school is experimenting with an artist in residence; girls' work has been displayed in professional galleries. Drama a particular strength – the purpose-built performing arts centre, incorporating fabulous 250-seater theatre plus music practice rooms, is well used (three full dramatic productions a year). One QAS girl played a role in Sky One's drama series Hex, another in the film remake of St Trinians. Public speaking a serious extra-curricular and QAS has hosted the International Independent Schools' Public Speaking Championship. Music getting a lot of attention lately: the deputy head is deputy chief examiner for the IB music course and the school offers IGCSE music. The music department runs a series of subscription concerts and workshops as well as informal/formal concerts and choir tours; recent performance at Westminster Abbey. D of E, Young Enterprise, Team Challenge etc. Lovely room for cookery lessons. Fund-raising for numerous charities.

Background and atmosphere: Dates back to 1698 when the Grey Coat Hospital was founded for children of Westminster. In 1706 Queen Anne granted it a charter and the governors decided to use part of the endowment to found a country boarding school, ultimately creating QAS in Caversham in 1894. The school still has Queen Anne's favourite flower, a deep red rose, as its emblem. Girls' traditional capes (now only used for special occasions and the triennial service at Westminster Abbey) are also red, while their more up-to-date replacement, the humble fleece, is navy. Set in charming red-brick assortment of original and modern buildings up hill from the Thames in 35 acres. Grey Coat Hospital (girls' state comprehensive in Westminster) remains a sister school.

Reading is a tricky market for a school of this kind, with so many other good girls-only options just down the road, including state ones. But QAS is something special. Drive through the school gates and you forget the busy roads and parking hassles: you could be at any rural girls' boarding school. Indeed, the boarding is an important ingredient of the ethos here and the school gets it just right. Girls sorted into houses on arrival – two for boarders, three for day girls and two for sixth form. Super dorms (largest sleep five), with attention to things like showers that matter to girls. Lots of space, but never feels like too few girls knocking around in too much room.

Sixth form accommodation especially fab, with boarders sharing rooms with day girls. Upper sixth house has wall of lacrosse sticks parked on hooks outside the entrance – says so much about the school – and its own car park. These oldest girls eat supper in their house – Wednesday night is wok night. Loads of space, sofas, sitting rooms ('sits') – luxury. Male guests allowed. Café 6 is the funky purple and green sixth form snack bar/café/games room created out of the old school gym; school socials with Shiplake, Oratory and others.

Some lovely, feminine touches, eg tea which rotates between bread and jam (Mon and Wed), cakes (Tues and Fri) and choc spread (Thurs). Home economics and ballroom dancing sit comfortably alongside chemistry and further maths. While girls more likely to be found poring over their personal statements for university applications than sewing machines, the sewing machines still get some use (as the brilliantly beaded and coloured cushions scattered around registrar's office amply demonstrate).

Pastoral care and discipline: Twenty minute worship every morning (female chaplain) in charming chapel. We didn't see much makeup being worn – what's the point when no boys around? Girls allowed (in groups) into Caversham, where the Waitrose is about the height of excitement, on Wednesday afternoons. Older girls can go into Reading – 'We give the sixth formers quite a lot of freedom – this is not a cotton wool school'. No alcohol to be consumed at school, except for a few sixth form events. No permanent exclusions since the current head arrived. Drug offences warrant immediate expulsion. Sliding scale of punishments for smoking.

The head is keenly interested in the differences between how girls' and boys' brains work, reads widely in the field, trained as a psycho-dynamic counsellor and referred knowledgeably to assorted experts (none of whom this poor ignorant editor had heard of) throughout our conversation. In short, she knows a thing or two about the cliques, friendship group nightmares etc that frequently bedevil girls-only schools and takes care that the school avoids the situations from which such tensions spring, eg girls are not allowed to 'save seats'.

Pupils and parents: Bright eyed, well-spoken girls. Sixth formers allowed to wear home clothes for lessons but must look businesslike when acting as ambassadors. Uniform, compulsory for everyone else, comprises red and white striped shirt with navy skirt and jumper sporting red band on cuff. Mixed family backgrounds, we were assured – does not have quite the cachet of some of the more famous girls' schools, so does not attract the flashest of parents. Broadly middle class, professional and well-heeled, from within an hour and a half radius. About 15 per cent from overseas (China, Hong Kong, Spain and Nigeria top the list, but quite a lot of exotics including two Mongolians and a Kazakh) – almost too many, but not quite. Plus large handful of expats (FCO, Services etc). Famous Old Girls include Posy Simmonds, Jenny Seagrove, artist Brenda Rawnsley, T S Eliot's second wife Valerie Fletcher (not the crazy one) and Joan Hunter Dunn – John Betjeman's 'muse and fantasy love'.

Entrance: Assessment days are held in November for 11 plus entrants. They sit pre-entry exams in English, maths and verbal reasoning, followed by 11 plus Common Entrance in January. 13 plus entrance exams take place in January. Papers in English, maths, science and humanities (either geography, history or RE) and a choice of French, Spanish, German, Latin or Greek. Sixth form entry: minimum of five GCSEs at grade C or above and Bs for subjects to be studied at A level. Applications require English and maths entrance exams and predicted grades. Long list of feeder schools includes preps and state primaries.

Exit: Some (18 per cent in 2013) lost to sixth form colleges, art colleges or mixed independents after GCSEs. The rest to good universities absolutely everywhere; six per cent to Oxbridge. Lots to business/marketing/management courses, also sciences/medicine and three girls recently to read international relations, underlining Mrs Harrington's claim that the girls are developing a political consciousness. Few gap years.

Money matters: Academic, drama, music, art, sports and all-rounder scholarships at 11+, 13+ and sixth form. Help on hand in cases of hardship.

Remarks: A super little school, within easy reach of London, that deserves to be better known. Suits girls who might wither under the remorseless pressure of some of the better known girls' boarding schools. A feel-good school which keeps its eye on the future without losing sight of the past. Don't let its proximity to Reading put you off!

Queen Elizabeth Grammar School (Penrith)

Ullswater Road, Penrith, CA11 7EG

- Pupils: 840 boys and girls; all day • Ages: 11–18 • Non-denom
- State

Tel: 01768 864621
Email: secretary@qegs.cumbria.sch.uk
Website: www.qegs.cumbria.sch.uk

Headmaster: Since 2004, Mr Christopher Kirkup BA PGCE NPQH (late forties). Read history at Queen Mary College, University of London. Taught at Torpoint School, Cornwall; Bourne Grammar School Lincolnshire; deputy head at Devonport High School for Girls, Plymouth. A serious, approachable, focused man, ambitious for the school; has pushed its maths/IT specialist status – with spectacular results in classroom provision – but has also improved status of performing arts (he directs the annual stage show). Committed to high academic standards.

Academic matters: Results at GCSE and AS/A2 are very good and, in view of the school's ability range at entry ('wider than most other 163 UK grammar schools'), they are remarkable.

Expectations are high and targets consistently challenge pupils; they seem happy with this and a real sense of academic purpose about the place. Average class size up to GCSE is 28, without noticeably damaging effects on achievement (independent schools take note). Broad banding and setting in English, maths and science at KS3, minimum nine subjects per student at GCSE. All do French and German to year 8, then can drop one for ICT. All students must take a language at GCSE. Spanish is an option alternate years. No classics. Over 80 per cent do separate sciences. Sciences achieve most A* grades at GCSE. In 2013, 48 per cent of grades A*/A overall. Usual prescription of four AS plus general studies in year 12, then three A levels. A level results excellent: 68 per cent A*/B in 2013 and 37 per cent A*/A. No big takeup for modern languages (seven from year group in 2012) but good geography, history, economics, English and maths (half sixth form do maths in one form or another). Extra lessons for Oxbridge. School has dropped special maths and computing science status preferring to promote its focus on an overall academic curriculum. SEN catered for in-house, works in partnership with outside agencies.

Teaching is broadly traditional without being rigid. Well qualified and very experienced staff – they tend to stay, Cumbrian quality of life being very attractive. Well-developed programme sharing expertise with feeder schools; evening classes in maths for local year 6 too.

Games, options, the arts: Good range of team games for boys and girls; cross-country (both) and rugby (boys) particularly strong: about 200 runners in Junior Great North Run every year, organised by charismatic head of geography. Playing fields on site and now vast sports hall extends games options. They breed them hardy up here, but boys sing in the choir too as well as having their own all-boys choir. Instrumental music and drama strong (students in National Youth Orchestra and Theatre). Dance outstanding. All year 8 have a 'residential experience' in the Lake District Borrowdale valley. Otherwise the usual run of clubs and societies, trips abroad and theatre visits – the school is a long way from most urban centres and knows it has to work at this. Much fund-raising by students (especially green/Fairtrade variety). Young Enterprise popular.

Background and atmosphere: Founded by Royal Charter in 1564, moved to present site in 1915, changed from 13-18 comprehensive to 11-18 selective grammar in 1993; now an academy, which means that governors have control over finance and buildings. Games pitches on site, plenty of grassy areas and some wonderful trees. Not an architecturally striking school, some rooms in the main building a touch cramped, but school works hard at upkeep. A continuous building programme has provided fine IT, technology and science facilities, classrooms for the English department and an impressive sports hall.

What sells the place is the pupils' demeanour – cheerful, confident, purposeful and courteous; they are happy to be here and show it. Last Ofsted report justly drew attention to behaviour and development of social conscience and rated school as outstanding in all categories. Sixth form centre in refurbished former primary school across road from main site; students treated as if at college (no uniform, but 'smart and appropriate' formal dress) and live up to responsibility.

Pastoral care and discipline: Pastoral unit is form-based up to year 11, then tutor groups. Parents generally happy with school's attitude; minor incidents quickly and effectively dealt with. Big city wickedness (drugs, alcohol etc) not really an issue, says head; in many ways, the North really is a different country. Small-town life may lack urban buzz, but a lot to be said for old-fashioned virtues and a strong school/home common interest.

Pupils and parents: Enormous catchment area of 400 square miles – half of pupils live in Penrith, half in surrounding country.

Twenty-eight buses a day carry them in and out. Whole range of wealth and status, quite a few from low-income families. Most are white British, reflecting local population. Parents very supportive; still a strong desire for self-improvement, especially in rural areas.

Entrance: Almost entirely from primary schools, by September entrance test – usually about 260 candidates for 120 places. Five GCSE A*-C qualification for sixth form entry – high grade (A*-B) expected for all subjects at A level.

Exit: About eight per cent leave after year 11, more than balanced by sixth form joiners. Well over 90 per cent post-A level to higher education, a few to college diploma courses. Steady trickle to Oxbridge every year (four in 2013), otherwise to predominantly northern universities. A few take gap years.

Money matters: Voluntary school fund payment of £15 per year helps buy a few extra luxuries for all pupils to enjoy.

Remarks: The only selective grammar school in Cumbria and proud of it, but it works hard at self-awareness and outward vision (eg cooperation with primary schools and neighbouring comprehensive). Remarkably successful at sustaining academic ethos and responsibility to local community. Pleasant location, happy and business-like students. World-weary parents moving from the south will appreciate its uncomplicated sense of purpose – if their children can get in, that is.

Queen Elizabeth Grammar School (Wakefield)

Linked school: Queen Elizabeth Grammar Junior School (Wakefield)

154 Northgate, Wakefield, WF1 3QX

- Pupils: 745 boys • Ages: 11–18 • Inter-denom • Fees: £10,755 pa
- Independent

Tel: 01924 373943
Email: admissions@qegsss.org.uk
Website: www.wgsf.org.uk

Headmaster: Since 2010, Mr David Craig MA MEd (forties). PGCE at Birmingham University and MEd in educational leadership with the Open University. Previous head of department posts at Edgbaston High, Birmingham and Wolverhampton Grammar School and deputy head at Merchant Taylors' School, Crosby. He aims 'to cement QEGS as one of the best boys' schools in the north of England.' His outside interests include cricket, rugby, choral music and Derby County FC. Married with two children.

Academic matters: High standards – 79 per cent A*/B at A level, 56 per cent at A*/A in 2013. At GCSE, 69 per cent at A*/A. IGCSE in maths, English and now sciences. 'Boys come here knowing that academic expectation is placed upon them.' Not tempted to push students into different subjects just to help the results tables – 'We have worked hard to improve our academic standards, but some of the results that give me most satisfaction are those achieved by boys who you might not have expected to shine so well at a particular subject,' said the head.

A parent told us, 'At QEGS nothing is looked at as impossible. You might not become the best but if you put in the effort, push yourself, you can succeed.' Strong across the board, especially maths, sciences, English and humanities. French and German on offer to all, plus Spanish, business French and Latin. Business studies and some languages, drama, studied with the Girls' High across the road.

Max 24 per class, 10/12 in sixth form. Work clinics available at lunchtime. No streaming. Conscious of rising expectation. Not convinced by International Baccalaureate but embracing A* grade at A level – 'It is getting harder to get into the best universities and we have to be aware of that and prepare our boys accordingly'.

Computers throughout and interactive whiteboards. Good remedial help on hand for mild dyslexia and the like, can 'cope' with mild Asperger's. Children are automatically screened and additional help can be organised, usually at lunchtime, laptops allowed. Recent improvements include new learning resource centre, 240 seat theatre, library, sixth form centre and English department.

Games, options, the arts: Emphasis on sport, music, drama, with Duke of Edinburgh (300 take), chess, bridge and trips/expeditions favoured. Art is very strong, aided by art department in the top of the school with masses of light. Screen printing, photography, etchings. Great music – regular scholarships to the Royal College of Music, finalists in the National Festival of Music; Outstanding Performers at National Festival for Youth Music. Brass section wins prizes, over 300 individual players, swing band (played in front of the Queen during her Jubilee) and junior swing bands (available for hire). Concerts often held in Wakefield Cathedral, where the junior boys provide choristers, joined by girls from the High. Music and drama often joint with High girls, eg Grease, Guys and Dolls. Regularly places students on best drama courses. 'My son had never picked up a musical instrument until he went to QEGS – now his life seems to revolve around music,' said a parent.

Use of over 27 acres of playing fields, pavilion and sports hall with special 'resilient' flooring hired out to locals. Training pool for junior school only, seniors use the pool in town. Proud of its sporting heritage, especially rugby – including old boy Mike Tindall. Produced England U19 cricket captain, England U18 rugby cap etc. Masses of sporting trips to South Africa, Namibia, South America, Australia, Canada, West Indies, plus cultural tours and exchanges to France, Germany, USA and expeditions to Costa Rica, Madagascar and Tanzania.

Background and atmosphere: Founded by Royal Charter in 1591 and moved to present site in 1854. From 1944-76 it was a direct grant school and reverted to fee-paying in 1976. Imposing Victorian Gothic façade hides mish mash of good, bad and ugly extensions. Junior school also on site – they play games on the grass in front of the school. Boys all smart in grey uniforms (think boy band in blazers). Modernisation is removing any sense of stuffy grammar school and proud of friendly, all-inclusive atmosphere. Impressive new entrance is very grand. Motto is 'turpe nescire' – 'It is a disgrace to be ignorant': fat chance of that here. Ethos of boys 'doing their best and fulfilling potential'. Inspection speaks of 'dedication and humanity' of staff. Great sixth form centre with popular café. Sixth formers drop uniform in favour of a smart suit (think boy band in suit and tie).

Pastoral care and discipline: Tutor-led pastoral system with boys encouraged to treat each other with respect. PHSE and pastoral care fosters good behaviour by encouraging informed choice by the boys – 'To try to pretend society is not as it is would be wrong. Different challenges face the boys – drugs, sex etc. Through PSE, our pastoral care, assembly and careers education we educate them, give them advice and guidance and help them arrive at their own choices and pathways'. Seems to work – parents report good relationships, camaraderie and 'help each other along' attitude.

Record book incorporates the school rules, inspected by staff and must be signed by parents at preordained levels.

Punishments include detentions and suspensions for most serious misdemeanours. Drug possession gets automatic expulsion. Smoking equals detention, three detentions equals suspension. Suspensions and exclusions for bullying, vandalism and aggressive behaviour. Poor academic performance can also find you shown the door.

Pupils and parents: Great motorway and rail links give it a wide catchment area and it is seen as the only acceptable alternative to the state system for miles around. Boys come with strong work ethic and parents and pupils must make a 'positive choice' to come here. Fair assortment from ethnic minorities, 'a broad, UK social mix'. None with EAL requirements. Good breeding ground for bishops – Lincoln and York – plus John Scott, former director of music at St Paul's, latterly at the prestigious Saint Thomas Church NYC, and a tranche of internationalists.

Great links between home and school – parents are enthusiastic in their praise: 'We have found even the slightest issue or concern we have had is resolved within 48 hours'; 'QEGS gives the boys the tools but also gives them the blueprint and the instructions to follow – other schools just provide the tools'.

Entrance: Most (60 per cent) from QEGS junior, if their results are up to scratch (only two or three a year aren't). Others from Sandal Endowed and Willthorpe feeders. Entrance exam and interview required. Latest inspection said school's induction process was 'excellent'. Always oversubscribed and academic achievement is obligatory – baseline qualifications for entry at sixth form are six GCSEs (but most come with seven or eight) with at least two As in subjects to be taken at AS/A level. Occasional boy comes into the school at other times, subject to academic OK and space.

Exit: A few leave to art courses or employment post GCSE. Most destined for A levels and heading to good university – a handful to Oxbridge (seven in 2013), Manchester, Northumbria, Warwick, Sheffield and King's College London. Medicine (seven in 2013), law and business related degrees popular.

Money matters: Ogden Trust can get the lucky few a 100 per cent bursary. Must be key stage 2 shiner and parental income of less than £40,000 per annum. Sprinkling of other scholarships and bursaries (which are awarded post exam and reviewed annually) plus music and sixth form schols. Bursaries for choristers in junior school, paid 50/50 by school and cathedral, but only whilst boy is in the choir. Ogden Trust sixth form science scholarships available (worth up to 100 per cent of fees) each year for a student wishing to study maths/science at A level. Parent told us: 'It is a fee paying school and of course you cannot help but think of the other things you could have used the money for – but it is the best investment a parent could ever make.'

Remarks: Great results and great facilities but not a sweatshop. Very traditional feel and loved for it, but very aware of changing society and ensuring boys are ready for those changes. Downside? Tough to get in – expectations high.

Queen Elizabeth High School

Whetstone Bridge Road, Hexham, NE46 3JB

• Pupils: 1230 pupils (615 boys/615 girls) • Ages: 13–18 • Non-denom • State

Tel: 01434 610300
Email: admin@queenelizabeth.northumberland.sch.uk
Website: www.qehs.net

Headteacher: Since 2008, Mr Neil Morrison (fifties), a former rugby player and Cambridge economics graduate, commands a powerful figure. He is now federation headteacher for Hexham Middle School and QEHS. A new leadership structure and new teams focussing on pastoral and curriculum issues are ensuring that the school keeps raising achievement year on year.

Academic matters: Most start with good results, which continues to sixth form. In 2013, 69 per cent five or more A*-C GCSEs including English and maths; 32 per cent of all entries were A*/A's. At A level, 54 per cent of A levels A*/B in 2013 and 24 per cent A*/A.

Full GCSE and A level curriculum, including five languages, four sciences, three art courses and a range of humanities, social sciences and performing arts courses up to A level, vocational courses and some BTECs.

Games, options, the arts: Wide choice of extra-curricular activities – everything from music and theatre to popular and active Fair Trade club. Strong links with overseas institutions including a Tibetan monastery and school in India. Good range of sports for all abilities – particularly strong on rowing.

Background and atmosphere: The Hydro Building is an impressive Victorian building. The building and impressive grounds make for a pleasant working environment. The year 9 social and dining area is housed in a Victorian glass winter garden, which is also hired out for weddings and private functions. A magical walled garden is manned by green-fingered staff and students. Co-operative and friendly atmosphere all around the school. Good but respectful relations between teachers and pupils. New dining and study facilities for sixth form students make this an excellent place to work and learn.

Pastoral care and discipline: An on-site student services group is tucked away just outside the walled garden, lending a college air to the place. A new student support office in the main building contains academic staff, heads of year, and non-teaching learning mentors who provide pastoral care and support to all students. Mr Morrison has been responsible for the school's policy of allowing parents access to their child's records. This, he says, has created much better channels of communication between school and home. It also encourages praise and reward among the critical mass of students who are neither high-achievers nor special needs and often feel sidelined.

Pupils and parents: Popular and oversubscribed. Intake from Blanchland in the south to Wark in the north but mainly from the surrounding mainly affluent, mainly white British villages. Small number with special needs (20 statemented). Average class size 21 (maximum 34). Many move to the area specifically to send their children to the school.

Entrance: Based on LA catchment criteria. Three feeder middle schools: St Joseph's, Hexham and Corbridge. Retention into sixth form extremely high and pulls in around 30 a year extra from elsewhere.

Exit: A third left after GCSEs in 2013. Majority of students go on to higher education with a clutch to Oxbridge each year. Rest go into higher education, training, apprenticeships or work. (But Mr Morrison says, 'Our role is also to give them the skills and personal qualities that they need in life.') Over the past few years many to leading conservatoires and drama schools thanks, in part, to specialist staff from Artsmark Gold.

Remarks: "The thing is, most kids are nice," says Neil Morrison as he strides purposefully down the steps. As his students cheerfully call out to him or grin on passing, it's easy to see the effect such a philosophy has on a school's atmosphere. But the kids aren't just nice at QEHS, they are also high-achievers.

Set in a leafy suburb of the Northumberland town, QEHS is a specialist performing arts and science academy with a reputation exceeding its catchment area and encouraging applicants from far and wide.

The 1290-strong school is housed over two sites, in a late 19th-century former hotel (the Hydro Building) and a more modern secondary school building. The Hydro Building sits in considerable grounds and has behind it a walled garden which is maintained by the staff and students and which provides some produce for the school's on-site restaurant, The Charter.

Queen Elizabeth's Girls' School

High Street, Barnet, Hetfordshire, EN5 5RR

• Pupils: 1,165 girls; all day • Ages: 11–18 • Non-denom • State

Tel: 020 8449 2984
Email: office@qegschool.org.uk
Website: www.qegschool.org.uk

Headteacher: Since 2001, Mrs Kate Webster BA PGCE MA (education management) (fifties). Studied geography at Sheffield University and taught at Furze Platt School in Maidenhead and Herschel Grammar School in Slough, before joining Henrietta Barnett as deputy head. No children; likes walking, music, theatre and art. Amiable, competent and straightforward; excellent manager. Teaches (where needed) geography, RE and PHSE.

Academic matters: Some at the top end are creamed off by Barnet's selective and semi-selective schools, but this is a comprehensive with a full ability range, achieving commendable results because of good teaching and high expectations from the start. In 2013 74 per cent 5+ A*-C grades; 39 per cent A*/A grades). Geography, history, maths, RS, media studies, psychology and sociology are all popular and successful A level choices, alongside English and biology. The 20 subjects available include vocational courses in ICT and business studies. In 2013, 53 per cent A*/B and 26 per cent A*/A grades at A level.

The school's media arts specialism means a focus on English, drama, art and media studies – 'It's about teaching and learning styles which use IT and the media as much as possible. But this does not deflect us from a broad and balanced curriculum and we don't allow over-specialisation'. A good selection of computers around the building – 'Though you are always running to catch up with IT – it's a priority to keep updating our provision'.

Setting for maths from year 7; all pupils now study French and Spanish in years 7-9, with setting from year 8. All other subjects are taught in mixed ability groups – 'We tried setting for science but the results didn't improve'. Ofsted comments that most teaching caters well for the whole range of abilities. Maths has, historically, been one of the weaker subjects, 'But we've made lots of progress at key stage 3 and the school now

Q

has a high performing specialist school second specialism in mathematics and computing'. This has allowed increased investment and focus on maths, producing strong results at GCSE and A level.

Good SEN support, mostly within the classroom. Split-level site unsuitable for children with physical disabilities, but around 10 per cent of pupils have special educational needs, including specific learning difficulties, dyslexia and dyspraxia. The gifted and talented co-ordinator identifies very able girls, who are encouraged to take on extension research projects – 'But we don't want to be exclusive, and others can join in too'. Masterclasses in, eg, music and history. Good careers advice – has Investors in Careers status, recently renewed. Latest Ofsted judged school to be 'outstanding'.

Games, options, the arts: As befits its media arts specialism, drama GCSE is very popular, involving regular show-cases to parents. Two drama studios, media editing suites. Music is also strong, though relatively few take it to GCSE or A level, where it is available through Barnet Music Centre. Senior and junior orchestras, a jazz band and various ensembles depending on the strengths and numbers of musicians. Links with the ENO, Wigmore Hall and various orchestras. Several art studios and plenty of innovative art on display. Good sports facilities – a refurbished swimming pool, sports hall, gym and several tennis/netball courts; girls compete in county football and cross-country tournaments. Girls doing PE GCSE often organise dance and games tournaments for local primary schools. Trips abroad include skiing in the Alps, watersports trip to France, language trips, art/drama trips to New York and history trips to the battlefields of France.

Background and atmosphere: Opened in 1888 as a grammar school; has been comprehensive since the 1970s. Hilly site on the edge of London's green belt. Buildings range from Victorian to 1960s. Looks rather tatty round the edges and could do with a major influx of cash for refurbishment. The loos, however, were revamped at a cost of £150,000 at the request of the school council when the head first joined – 'We've done what we can in terms of improving the environment, but we have no space to rebuild'. Relaxed atmosphere with confident, articulate girls, used to speaking up in public.

Pastoral care and discipline: Renowned for making new girls feel at home quickly. The dedicated head of year 7 'puts lots of time and effort going to feeder schools and getting information on the girls who will be joining us'. High expectations of good behaviour and discipline do not appear to be problematical – only two permanent exclusions in the last four years. Clear policies on drugs and bullying – 'Obviously girls are exposed to drugs outside, but inside it is not an issue. Our PHSE programme is very good and we put a lot of effort into equipping girls to make informed decisions on all aspects of life. The form tutor or head of year is the first port of call if a girl is troubled, but they are not fazed about coming to find me if they feel strongly about something'.

Pupils and parents: Not a purely middle-class school – higher than average percentage of girls on free school meals. But neither is it a gritty inner-London comprehensive – plenty of nice, confident Barnet girls. Old Girls: Elaine Paige, actress and singer, and Stephanie Beacham, actress.

Entrance: Generally around three applicants for every place. First in line are girls with a statement of social or medical needs specifying the school; then siblings; then those living closest – which in practice tends to mean within about two miles. Girls entering the sixth form – about 18 do so each year – are asked to have five grade Cs or above at GCSE, though many A level courses specify a B grade in the A level subject.

Exit: About a third leave after GCSEs, with some high achievers moving on to selective sixth forms, some to co-ed sixth form colleges, others to FE colleges to pursue vocational courses. Some return when the grass elsewhere proves to be less green than it had appeared. Most sixth form leavers go on to higher education, to do courses ranging from medicine to audio-visual production at old and new universities, including one or two a year to Oxbridge.

Money matters: Not a rich school – low down in the queue for government cash for refurbishment, but does its best with available funds. Loyal parent body works hard at raising money.

Remarks: A successful comprehensive with high expectations that caters well for all abilities and produces self-assured girls used to discussion and debate.

Queen Elizabeth's Grammar School

Linked school: Queen Elizabeth's Grammar Junior School

West Park Road, Blackburn, BB2 6DF

- Pupils: 700 pupils (including 205 girls) • Ages: 11–18 plus junior school (see below) • Inter-denom on C of E Foundation
- Fees: £5,967–£10,485 pa. Plans to be free from 2014
- Independent

Tel: 01254 686300
Email: admissions@qegsblackburn.com
Website: www.qegsblackburn.com

Headmaster: Since September 2007, Mr Simon Corns MA. Read modern languages at Gonville and Caius, Cambridge. Sharp-suited, twinkly-eyed and old-school without being stuffy, Mr Corns has been behind several measures to take the school back to its roots by strengthening links with the cathedral and introducing a Founders' Day. He is married, with two school age sons.

Academic matters: 'All our heads of departments are accountable,' says the head. To this end, marking is closely monitored and there are regular meetings with staff. Science is the school's trump card but other areas such as art also delivering creditable results. He has instigated a renewed focus on results: 'it was considered a mucky area before', 'If we don't do that we are letting our pupils down.' However, is hampered by falling rolls and a consequent loss of specialist teachers and is applying for free school status from 2014.

Exam results reasonable: 61 per cent A*/B grades at A level in 2012 and nearly 35 per cent A*/A; at GCSE, nearly 10 per cent A*/A. Class sizes of around 20-25 in main school and 8-10 for A levels. Students take 10 GCSEs, including English, maths, at least one modern foreign language (French, German or Spanish), a combination of sciences (core plus additional award or separate sciences on offer – IGCSE courses now being taken) and a short course in ethics and philosophy. Latin and Greek available too.

Facilities are good with four networked IT suites and state-of-the-art science and language labs as well as a dedicated learning support department. The average age of the staff is 42 and the staff room chat shows a dedicated and enthusiastic ethos.

Games, options, the arts: Excellent reputation for games. Three-time Sportsmark Gold award-winners and voted the local Sports School of the Year 2010-11 by Blackburn and Darwen Sports

Q

Council. QEGS has also won the Independent Schools FA Cup three times (the first school to win the cup more than once) and has very strong links with local club Blackburn Rovers. Rugby, cricket, swimming, athletics, golf and cross-country are all strong and there's a new impressive pool facility with an electronic timing system, which is open to locals outside school hours.

There's a very strong musical life at the school and all students are required to take part in productions (even if it's for one night). Art provision and facility is bewilderingly good, with one pupil recently selected for the Royal Academy's A level online exhibition. A new art block (opened by former pupil Wayne Hemingway) showcases the extremely impressive talent on offer.

Background and atmosphere: School founded in 1509 by the second Earl of Derby, granted Royal Charter by Queen Elizabeth I in 1567. Moved to present site in leafy Blackburn suburb in 1884. Went direct grant in 1944 and returned to private sector in 1976. Girls have been admitted throughout since 2001 and well integrated, but they are still a tiny minority and the school is keen to change this. Original school building, with stunning stained-glass windows, known as Big School and used as school dining hall. Portraits of previous heads, school silver, team photographs and press cuttings proudly on show.

Large impressive campus boasting five acres (excluding playing fields) and numerous buildings. There are games fields and sports hall 20 minutes away at Lammack, to which the pupils travel by minibus. Light, airy library with panoramic views. The dedicated sixth form common-room Singleton House has its own cafe, careers suite and private study room.

Is suffering from a shortfall in pupils as local families experiencing hard times opt for state schools in increasing numbers, with several popular faith schools in the area, and a local girls' school recently turned co-ed.

Pastoral care and discipline: There's a mentoring system in place to support struggling pupils and a peer mentoring scheme (fourth years looking after first years). The prefect system for both junior and senior school to enable pupils to develop leadership skills, a sense of community and responsibility from a young age. Former pupils' association sees individual former pupils lend their expertise in talks, career advice and work placements.

Long-standing partnership with the Good Samaritan School in Uganda. Biennially, a party of sixth form students travel to the school and help with practical projects to enhance the school (preceding the visit the whole school is involved in fund-raising for the project).

Pupils and parents: The pupils come from very mixed backgrounds (from wealthy Ribble Valley families to those on bursaries). Around one quarter Asian heritage. Catchment is roughly a 20 mile radius of the school. Some pupils are very local and walk to school but there is an extensive bus service covering the whole catchment area. Former pupils include film director Michael Winterbottom, designer Wayne Hemingway, Ivor Bolton Chief Conductor of the Mozarteum Orchestra and Sir Netar Mallick, Professor Emeritus of Renal Medicine in Manchester.

Entrance: Main point of entry is 11+. Enthusiasm and interest is gauged both in written examinations (English, Maths and VR) and an interview. Pupils are above average ability nationally but the school is not ferociously selective and is suffering from a shortfall in applicants. Sixth form entrants need minimum of five Bs at GCSE.

Exit: Proportion leave after GCSE (50 per cent in 2013), mostly for local FE colleges offering subjects like law and media studies that are not available at QEGS. With very few exceptions, all pupils go on to university – Blackburn, Leeds, Surrey, Loughborough and Leeds College of Music popular. One to Oxbridge in 2013.

Money matters: There are more than 20 main school and sixth form bursaries (typically up to one third of fees), two Ogden scholarships and two means-tested Blakey Scholarships (one in languages and one in science) courtesy of a local businessman and former pupil. Head says, 'The school is proud of its traditional social mix, which is maintained by a generous provision of bursary support, despite the demise of the assisted places scheme.'

Remarks: The school is efficient, friendly and impressive with a warm atmosphere and respectful students. Students are evidently proud of their school and full of praise for its artistic and sporting endeavours. Extra-curricular sports are encouraged and this is reflected in the diverse career ambitions of several students canvassed (politician, professional footballer and biologist) and the support offered to them in these careers by the head and his staff. Unfortunately suffering from hard times like many in the North (and elsewhere).

Queen Elizabeth's Hospital

Linked school: Queen Elizabeth's Hospital Juniors

Berkeley Place, Clifton, Bristol, BS8 1JX

• Pupils: 570 boys • Ages: 11–18 • Non-denom • Fees: £12,234 pa • Independent

Tel: 01179 303040
Email: headmaster@qehbristol.co.uk
Website: www.qehbristol.co.uk

Headmaster: Since 2000, Mr Stephen Holliday MA (forties), educated at Batley Grammar School, Yorkshire, then Jesus College, Cambridge (where he obtained 1st class honours in history). Spent two years with British Rail before shunting himself to Dean Close, Cheltenham, for six years (including three as housemaster), followed by four years at Giggleswick as head of history before deputy headship at Queen Elizabeth's Grammar School, Blackburn. Wife is head of geography at Colston's Girls'; has two 'sporty' sons at QEH. Teaches PSHE to all of year 7 and GCSE history. Methodist lay preacher but 'doesn't wear religion on his sleeve,' say staff. A 'straightforward man', welcoming and a good listener – 'What you see is what you get,' say parents. Loves QEH and likely to stay a while. Aware of the political and other pressures in the city but confident that QEH will hold its own in face of massive investment in local state provision. Strong business streak – currently savouring success of joint development with Bristol City FC on Failand sports field. He enjoys skiing and 'escaping' in holidays.

Academic matters: Results consistently outstanding: in 2013, 86 per cent A*/B grades at A level (63 per cent A*/A) and 69 per cent A*/A at GCSE (harder IGCSE for English and maths included). Emphasis on quality rather than quantity – maximum nine subjects sat at GCSE and generally three at A level (though 'one boy asked for five A grades to read economics at UCL,' we were told). Sciences and maths very strong; drama and theatre studies outstanding; Spanish appears most successful foreign language. Popularity of government and politics doesn't seem to have detracted from success in history. Large numbers also take geography. Design and technology is only taught to GCSE. Success in Latin and economics point to school's academic breadth. Individual achievements recognised and valued across all year groups. Regular target setting for boys and frequent reporting to parents leave little scope for backsliding. All do three sciences to end of year 9 and after that choose dual or triple award at GCSE. GCSE options include Latin (compulsory in years 7 and 8), drama, art, ceramics, Greek and Spanish. Lots of ICT. General studies programme in sixth covers topics such as finance at university. Boys generally rate their teachers highly – 'especially some of the younger ones'.

Learning support seen as increasingly important in this selective school as well as gifted and talented. NFER screening for SpLD. A few overseas boys have ESL support; other special needs include hearing impairments, several ADD, mild cerebral palsy and Asperger's.

Games, options, the arts: Very sporty. Main off site activity at Failand – QEH sports field with changing and pavilion some 10 minutes away (depending on time of day) by coach. Enviable facilities developing apace in partnership with Bristol FC. Autumn term rugby, spring term football. All boys play rugby to end of year 9. Diversification of sports as boys move up school. A2 boys not forced to continue games but most do. Cricket and athletics strongest options in summer. Lots selected for Bristol rugby and/or Gloucestershire cricket teams with some rugby players competing nationally at U16 and U18 levels and footballers playing at club level including Bristol City. Swimming and tennis have to be played for time being at outside facilities. Plans for new sports hall and swimming pool on site of present gym complex, currently used for PE, basketball and badminton plus squash (two courts), fitness and weights.

Wide range of extra-curricular activities and clubs at lunchtime and after school. Boys not discouraged from pursuing own outside interests (eg pistol shooting, cycling, rowing etc). Impressive programme of visits abroad, from visiting Roman Pompeii to the choir in the United States and rugby players just about anywhere you'll find an oval ball. Outdoor pursuits a special strength: D of E popular – 150 boys involved, three teams in Ten Tors. Hugely successful at local and national debating and public speaking competitions. Flourishing Young Enterprise teams and past winners of European Youth Parliament competition. Strong links with local community enhance work experience scheme.

Music is important: many boys playing instruments (a lot also have lessons outside school). Suite of practice rooms and three classrooms including music technology; largest space used for informal (eg jazz and acoustic) concerts. School rated locally for its contribution to choral music (several boys in national youth orchestra and choir); regular slot in Lord Mayor's chapel; sell-out events in Bristol and Clifton cathedrals; regular overseas tours with Red Maids. Trickle of boys to music at universities,

Drama is hugely popular – productions of all kinds throughout year. On-site theatre ('the most vibrant in the west') seats 220 – heavily used by school and touring companies. New drama teaching space in main building. We visited during reading week – homework for younger boys is suspended in favour of literature with follow-up activities. Good library, and adjacent careers room is well maintained. Art department housed in former gym: lofty main studio; separate ceramics area. Applemacs and digital photography replacing older dark room; sixth form achieving high standards – plenty of art displayed around school.

Background and atmosphere: Only all boys' independent school left in Bristol. Motto: 'Dum tempus habemus operemus bonum' ('Whilst we have time let us do good'). School charter and grant of arms given by Elizabeth I. Enviable tradition of scholarship established over four centuries. Strong competitive edge – Crispin Shield for sport most coveted trophy, according to boys we met. Main building (grade II listed) towers (literally) on slope below posh Clifton and close to university. Sense of foreboding on approach – boys love the 'Hogwarts' feel of the place. Within, an impressive stone staircase rises to 'headmaster's landing' – huge flagstones and ubiquitous archive material. Original 'schoolroom' little changed from 1840s and used for supervised study periods through day. Scary, until you talk to friendly boys and staff. School has thankfully moved with times (the

'dungeons' now house refurbished classrooms including ICT). Plasma screens linked to school intranet brought us abruptly back to 21st century. Smartboards everywhere.

New sixth form centre (modern space to work, relax and eat plus discrete IT facility) an obvious privilege for older boys. Purposeful atmosphere created by boys themselves; comfortable relationships built on mutual respect; lots of younger staff – about 40 per cent are female. Exciting plans for redeveloping site including science as part of new complex to match wow factor of school's theatre.

Traditional bluecoat uniform now limited to choir members. Blazers and school tie up to year 11 and suits thereafter. Firm guidelines on appearance (no long hair, jewellery etc) and staff chivvy where necessary. Active school council meets regularly. Plenty of joint activities with girls' schools – especially Red Maids and Redland High. Most boys dig into honest grub (good choices and boy sized portions) at lunch-time in baronial hall (includes gallery and organ loft) with house shields and honours boards; doubles up for whole school assemblies twice weekly. Theatre used for sixth form assembly. Knockabout area in centre of school known a 'the yard' where boys can let off steam. Generous lot – raised over £10K in a year for various charities.

Pastoral care and discipline: Pastoral care underpinned by tried and tested tutorial system. Part-time school counsellor very involved and offers 35 minute slots during day or an hour after school in homely sanctuary. Separate room for highly valued peer support and mentoring schemes (overseen by a sixth form tutor and counsellor). 'Drop in' arrangement every day after school manned by selected seniors – ideas 'have evolved from boys' own suggestions' and so are accepted. Sixth formers are trained and take work seriously – involvement 'makes them good at listening to others when they reach university,' claims counsellor. E-buddying and timetabled group activities also form part of scheme. PSHE (one lesson a week) covers issues such as binge drinking and drug awareness. Induction for new boys includes enjoyable residential expedition.

Parents impressed by way school responds quickly to any problem they raise – 'Staff always have time for me,' said one mum. Sanctions, when imposed, are seen as fair. School rules are few and straightforward. No expulsions in recent times. Long-serving staff help to uphold ethos whilst younger ones give lots of energy. Inspired multi-faith 'quiet room' recently installed for those who need 'time out' for reflection.

Pupils and parents: Academically selective but not socially exclusive – very mixed bunch. Parents more affluent than in past but many choose QEH to 'steer sons away from more socially exclusive places' and feel it is 'a better preparation for the real world'. Parents 'delighted' with relatively small size – 'Teachers really know the boys,' they report. Close involvement of parents is encouraged and 'Friends' association raises money for small improvements – currently 'greening' a hitherto neglected part of school site. Termly newsletters and school intranet help keep parents informed. Unpretentious boys – friendly, open and polite. Thriving Old Boys society; former pupils include film star Hugo Weaving; BBC soccer commentator Jonathan Pearce; Ashley Pharoah – writer and creator of TV's Life on Mars series; William Friese-Greene – pioneer in cinema, portrait photographer and inventor; Mike Smith – director of Columbia records.

Entrance: Selective – exam taken in January for entry to years 7 and 9 (about 15 enter at latter stage – mainly from prep schools). Two applicants for every place at 11 and draws from about 40 schools across Bristol area. Popularity soared after decision taken to dispense with Saturday lessons. Red Maids' and Redland High siblings tend to favour QEH.

Exam comprises VR test (multiple choice) – 50 minutes; 50 minutes non-verbal reasoning test (multiple choice); 30 minutes maths; 30 minutes creative writing exercise; 20+ minutes interview. Nice of them to let one know – many don't. Entry to sixth form – at least six grade Bs at GCSE plus headteacher's reference. Picks up increasing numbers from comprehensives and academies at this stage.

Exit: Some 95 per cent of year 11 pupils go into sixth form (a few leave for financial reasons) and most go on to higher education (largely Russell Group). Eight pupils got into Oxbridge in 2013 and plenty to medical schools.

Money matters: In a city which had the highest takeup of the former government assisted places scheme, QEH has always sought to help the less fortunate. About 15 per cent of boys benefit from school's own (means tested annually) assisted places scheme. A very few receive 100 per cent support. Academic (six) and music (four) scholarships awarded at 11 and 13. Ogden sixth form scholarships. Historically, frugal when it comes to spending, but new development plans already in place and buildings have recently been substantially upgraded.

Remarks: An academic school with 'plenty of heart'. 'Open, honest boys who work and play hard,' say staff. Atmosphere reminded us of bygone days, though school has moved with the times. Teachers 'go the extra mile' in terms of extra curricular involvement. The importance given to boys' welfare strikes us as exceptional and parents we spoke to had 'no regrets' about choosing QEH.

Queen Elizabeth's School, Barnet

Queen's Road, Barnet, EN5 4DQ

• Pupils: 1,180 boys • Ages: 11–18 • Non-denom • State

Tel: 020 8441 4646
Email: hmoffice@qebarnet.co.uk
Website: www.qebarnet.co.uk

Headmaster: Since 2011, Neil Enright, MA (Oxon) MBA NPQH FRSA (mid 30s). Educated at St. John's College, Oxford, and has worked at Queen Elizabeth's School, Barnet, since 2002, rising to become head of department (humanities – a geographer), head of year, deputy head. MBA in 2010 from the University of London, Institute of Education, which focused on aspects of leadership, management and systems of effective learning.

Sees himself as 'an experienced educational leader committed to safeguarding the academic, pastoral and spiritual interests of able boys, irrespective of their ethnic, religious or socio-economic background'. Aim is to preserve and build upon the reputation of Queen Elizabeth's as a school where able boys who have entered on academic merit will become well-rounded and responsible young men with unbounded opportunities to succeed at university and their chosen careers beyond.

Academic matters: Consistently top of the academic league tables, rivalling most schools, independent or state, in its exam results. Definitely not a school for slackers. You work hard here and you work consistently hard, which can be stressful for some, particularly in the early years. Testing is very much part of the modus operandi. Base-line assessment in year 7, then setting in all subjects, with half-termly tests thereafter. 'It's quite nerve-racking at the beginning,' says one sixth former, 'but it does mean by the time we get to GCSEs we don't find exams a problem.' Certainly not. A*s the norm at GCSE (average 10 A*s). In 2013, 92 per cent A*/A grades. All take French and Latin from year 7 and German from year 8, continuing at least one to GCSE, with Mandarin and Spanish offered as extras. A level choices are decided by tests in years 10 and 11 designed 'to tease out' aptitude. 'GCSE grades are not a good indicator,' says the head. 'Of 180 boys here, 165 will get A*s in maths, but not all will be good enough to do maths.' Seventy per cent of boys do four A levels, most get four A*/A grades (87 per cent of grades were A*/A in 2013); 60 per cent take maths, two-thirds some science, many do a mix. No fluffy options whatsoever. 'We don't want to dilute the curriculum,' say the head.

Most departments and most teaching is very strong – 'so many departments get all A*/As'. Boys enthuse particularly about geography and history. Homework load is strenuous (one and a half hours in year 7, one hour per subject per night at A level), but few problems with hungry dogs here. 'We don't need to whine and cajole, it's a culture of achievement.' The school has recently extended its extra-curricular enrichment with the Williams Society's weekly tutorials in informal logic, literary theory and analysis of concepts. 'We talk to them about the social sciences and concepts such as liberty,' no doubt helping to up the school's Oxbridge success rate to an all-time high last year.

Class sizes, 30 in year 9, 18-23 in year 10, 17 at A level. All the latest gewgaws throughout with up-to-the minute ICT and all labs refurbished in the last 10 years. 'Special needs' at this school tends to be on the gifted-and-talented end of the spectrum, but every department runs a clinic to support the struggling and challenge the most able. School says it can accommodate mild autism, Asperger's and dyslexia.

Games, options, the arts: This is a school where competing is important and a big part of the competition takes places on the sports field. All play rugby in year 7. 'Rugby serves boys so well,' says the head. 'It has a gentlemanly ethos, of which I enormously approve.' England under-16 head coach coaches the rugby squad and the school fields up to D teams on a regular basis. (Sport, however, is setted from year 7, and it can be difficult to move up the scrum, according to one pupil). Swimming, water polo, Eton Fives, tennis, cross-country and fencing also popular. Plenty of county and national representation in sport, bridge, chess. (Old Boy Tom Aggar recently won a gold medal for rowing in the Paralympics.) Eight-lane swimming pool, all-weather tennis courts, multi-gym and plenty of neatly trimmed green fields for team sports.

School has three full-time music teachers, 12 peripatetic teachers and a music suite where boys can study A level music technology with all the latest recording equipment. Big band, jazz quartet, north and south Indian collection ensemble. 'We are in the vanguard of international music development. It epitomises a strength of the world, the dialectic between different cultures. It's beautiful to listen to a group which includes the sitar, the sax and the violin.' Visual arts take place in open-plan, light-filled art rooms but plenty going on elsewhere, with a daily art club held in the lunch hour, an exhibition space for displays of work and field trips to arty destinations like St Ives and Paris for A level candidates. Growing national reputation for chess. Outside the classroom, the school has invested heavily in infrastructure. In recent years, the school has seen the launch of a dramatic, architect-designed new hall, which, as well as drama productions and debating competitions, will host recording sessions for professional orchestras. New food technology facility; DT also focuses on product design and ICT.

As one might expect, careers advice taken very seriously. From year 7, pupils have half-termly meeting on their future. 'We want them to ask early on: What do I want to do in life? After the age of 14, they won't do it for their parents or teachers; they do it because they believe it themselves.' Decision making is aided by extensive work experience from year 10. Loyal old boys, too, come back for an organised meeting with sixth formers to chat about university and subject choice. Some act as Oxbridge buddies for the next generation. Boys also do voluntary work related to their career aspirations.

Background and atmosphere: Founded in 1573 by Robert, Earl of Leicester, with a charter from Elizabeth 1, the school was rebuilt in 1931-32 by Hertfordshire County Council in a noble civic style with terrazzo flooring, parquet and panelling, all kept in spick-and-span condition. Still relatively well endowed with land held in perpetuity and its own Foundation Trustees, QE went comprehensive in the '60s, reverted to grant-maintained status in 1989 and became a grammar school once more in 1994. Difficult to imagine a more orderly and focused environment. Even in traditional chatty art, boys work with heads down, quiet as mice. Significant increases in responsibility from year 11, when own suits are allowed. Ninety prefects voted for by staff and students, monitor lunch (fresh food produced daily), playgrounds and classrooms. 'They lead the school in so many ways.' School captain and house captains appointed from on high.

Pastoral care and discipline: Boys motivated by reward and praise with loads of 'celebratory occasions'. (Homework diaries with merit stickers for every subject in the early years; hand-written notes home later on.) Certainly not a school where misbehaviour is the norm. 'I will expel a boy for violence on the premises aimed at staff, consciously creating racial disharmony or bringing drugs into school, but no boy has been expelled in over fourteen years,' says the head. Occasional fixed-term exclusions, however, for persistent 'failure to carry out school protocols' or misbehaving in lessons. Registration twice a day and homework diaries are also monitored for extra-curricular activities. 'If a boy is not sufficiently engaged in extra-curricular activities, that's often the first warning sign.' If concern is felt, the year head will be involved, then, depending on the issues, parents, special needs or an ed psych.

Pupils and parents: Defies the traditional middle class grammar school profile in its diverse student body. Over eighty per cent of boys come from ethnic minorities, predominantly Asian. Most are first generation, most speak English as a second language. 'Our boys come from very ordinary backgrounds,' says the head. 'In our last Oxbridge intake, many boys had parents who hadn't gone to university, and in recent years one was a refugee from Rwanda.' The head feels the school 'contributes massively to social mobility and social cohesion. Here, they have to interact across the divides, whether they're scrumming down on the rugger field or playing chess.'

Entrance: More than 2,000 boys apply for 180 places. Tests now take place in September, and boys are told whether or not they have met the 'standard required' before they have to make their choice of schools, so they have nothing to lose by taking the test. NB Meeting the 'standard required' does not guarantee a place. Pupils come from around 90 primary schools, but the ability range is narrow, most are in the top 10 per cent nationally. Head is against the 'industry of preparation' that leaves children trembling in the exam queue. 'It's a waste of time stressing children out.' Parents, however, wouldn't necessarily agree. Occasional vacancies between years 7 and 10, offered to those on the waiting list. No sixth form entry for external candidates. 'This is a seven-year education and I don't want to tread on any of my colleagues' toes.' Automatic transfer to sixth form for virtually all but pupils have to be recommended for individual subjects. Further maths is particularly hard to gain access to.

Exit: Some boys leave after GCSE (14 per cent in 2013). Some prefer mixed sixth forms, are looking for subjects the school doesn't teach (law, psychology, media studies), or are not offered the subjects they want to take. Some win scholarships to independent schools. Other just prefer a more relaxed environment. Others don't make the grade. Virtually all who stay go on to top universities. In 2012, 26 Oxbridge offers. Otherwise primarily to Nottingham, Imperial, UCL and Warwick. Economics most popular degree, 20 plus to medicine and medical-related degrees. History and law also popular. The school gives excellent UCAS guidance.

Money matters: State aid is minimal and the head has to put up with the fact he gets less money than many local comps. Gaps are filled with funds from the Foundation and with carefully husbanded donations from parents, old boys and friends, which underwrite school trips and new buildings. Most parents contribute £60 a month, though this is entirely voluntary. 'We say to them, if you want to have a sound education and provide the polish for boys to go to the best universities, you can't do it on state funding.' The head has managed to raise £10m during his time at the school. His next large-scale project is a new library (due to open in September 2013).

Remarks: An extraordinary school that offers the able, the diligent and the aspiring, whatever their social or ethnic origins, an education hard to rival in the state or private sector. You do, however, have to be the right boy. Not a good option for those who would struggle with the workload, rebel against the discipline or dislike competition.

Queen Ethelburga's College

Linked schools: The Faculty of Queen Ethelburga's; House Preparatory School; King's Magna Middle School

Thorpe Underwood Hall, Ouseburn, York, YO26 9SS

• Pupils: 365 pupils (310 board co-ed) • Ages: 3-20 • Inter-denominational • Fees: Day £12,585; Boarding £30,825-£32,325 pa; International Boarding £37,785-£39,885 pa • Independent

Tel: 01423 333330
Email: info@qe.org
Website: www.qe.org

Principal: Since 2006, Mr Steven Jandrell BA (early fifties), married to Margaret, with a young son at home. Warm, friendly, genuine and approachable, he understands education and enjoys discussing it. Well-respected and liked by staff and pupils, he's part of the furniture, having been here for many years as head of music and deputy head. Long-standing parents describe him as 'the best head so far'; 'He's a good listener who doesn't bat you away with standard answers'. A successor to more commercial heads here, he's a breath of fresh air.

Academic matters: Small classes, unashamedly setted, with regular testing for all – pupils say 'it's good for us'. Sixteen maximum per class for A levels. Choice of 20 A levels, with BTECs for those with less academic bent. French from nine, Spanish and German for all at 12, Russian and Chinese all on offer. No classics. Single science available – and fab modern labs with spectacular views. High percentage of overseas students means that science and maths are a strength. In 2013 48 per cent A*/A grades at GCSE. Nearly 81 per cent A*/A grades at A level and average IB score of 40.5.

Dyslexia help available. All children tested on arrival in the prep school during the first half term, ed psych's report if necessary, usually individual lessons for free once a week, if more needed then extra charge. Dual teaching at the bottom end with two and a half dedicated accredited British Dyslexia Association staff on site, ie SENCo plus. EFL free throughout the school.

Q

Very happy to be judged by its positioning within school league tables. However, this is achieved largely by separating off the less-academic children from year 10 upwards into the Faculty, a school-within-a-school which offers more vocational courses and serious mentoring. Although this is on the same site and with the same uniform, its results are supplied – and judged – separately. About 60 per cent of Faculty students are from abroad. NB overseas parents in particular should note that the fees – including the astonishingly high international ones – are the same for both schools, and ensure they know which they are paying for.

Games, options, the arts: Horses are an important part of QE: clearly, in Yorkshire, where there's (horse) muck there's definitely brass – large numbers are accommodated in the new outdoor equestrian centre. Impressive outdoor manège and masses of pony paddocks available – pupils may (and do) bring their own animals. Pupils get up to muck out at 7.30am but full livery is available at £3,105 per term, indulgent fathers please note. QE horses are available to borrow free of charge.

Music (for all) on the up under 'fantastic' head of music, with frequent opportunities for performance. The old refectory (now the Phoenix Centre) contains no fewer than four practice drama and dance studios – though the pupils tell us they would 'really like a dedicated theatre, please'; school tells us it's on the cards. Art good and strong, with sewing machines in the art department. Enthusiastic home economics and Leith's food and wine course for sixth formers (no more than two sets of eight per year group), with the smashing kitchen used for grown-up classes in the holidays.

Ten acres of floodlit pitches for hockey, soccer, rugby, high jump, volleyball etc and brand new Astroturf. CCF popular, clubs for IT, archery, fencing, golf. A new swimming pool has just opened as part of the giant sports centre. D of E with plenty of gold participants. Lots of extra-curricular activities – the list is (almost) endless, but some are costly.

Background and atmosphere: Founded in 1912, was the intellectual doyenne of the Northern Circuit, rivalled only by St Leonard's in Scotland. However falling numbers and threatened closure precipitated the move to Thorpe Underwood, conveniently situated 25 minutes from York and Harrogate and a 10 minute drive from the A1. Owned by the Martin family (who still live on site), Thorpe Underwood dates back to the Domesday Book, where it is described as Chirchie, Usebrana and Useburn, before becoming part of the monastery of Fountains Abbey in 1292. (The stew pond used by the monks to supply food for the passing travellers has been meticulously restored, though it now boasts a fountain, which might surprise earlier travellers, and has been reinforced with trim stones round the edges.) The hall itself was rebuilt in 1902 in best Edwardian Tudor style and the extensions have been sympathetically carried out with leaded paned windows to match the original. The place is a complex mix of old and new – in style and attitude – and full of surprises. Modern facilities sit comfortably alongside a trad country house setting, and modern teaching sits (less comfortably) alongside old-fashioned notions of a 'no trousers' policy for female students and staff.

Impressive newer office facilities include a vast dining room (The Undercroft) that doubles as an assembly hall – though the acoustics are pretty grim and mealtimes can be a deafening experience, say some staff. Huge solid oak tables fill the room with comfortable seating on the balcony above, alongside exciting sculptures courtesy of Mr Martin's brother. Fruit available at all times with good salad bar, home-cooked food with a veggie option, all served on monogrammed crockery. Self-service queuing system moves around barriers like a busy post office. A lift has been installed for wheelchair users, a stair lift is also available. Very popular internet café sits alongside the dining room.

The original Hall – previously the home of the Martin family – houses a traditional library and the Phoenix Centre. Some

of the classrooms and corridors are a tad surprising, not to mention the excess of taxidermy and hunting trophies around the place – look out for the crouching tigers, which might upset small children or anyone sensitively – or PC – inclined, though they remain one of the most photographed parts of the school.

Modern boarding accommodation consists of smart and well-equipped bedrooms, the majority now with private bathrooms, all with flat screen TVs (in fact two TVs in some twin rooms – just in case these lucky pupils wish to watch different programmes...), DVD players, telephones with voice mail, fridges, electric kettles, microwaves, air conditioning, trouser presses, room safes and ice-makers – pretty much everything except a mini-bar in fact. Great attention to detail and, it would appear, no expense spared – new boarding houses have fantastic limed oak doors, skirting boards et al. A classy medical centre that resembles a private hospital and oodles of huge common-rooms – all with leather sofas, toasters and TVs. Houses for the younger ones surrounded by squidgy playgrounds filled with serious kit. Boys' and girls' accommodation is separate. Day pupil centre for day children plus B & B available if needed. Pay phones on almost every corner, mobile signal dodgy but improving.

Leased for a peppercorn from a charitable foundation (originally the brain child of Brian Martin), has benefited from millions of pounds' worth of investment. Good, if not lavishly stocked, library, banks of computers, teletext business info displayed around the school, free internet available to all boarding houses, with wifi covering the whole 100 acre estate as well. Regular formal dinner parties with silver service and speaker for sixth form 'to give them practice in the real world'. Almost 50/50 boy/girl mix, boarding numbers up, though still relying heavily on the overseas market (55 different countries represented here), and a clever move some years ago in reducing day fees has brought a considerable rise in day pupils too.

A car park for which most schools (and parents) would give their right arm, an apparently endless building programme and growing numbers – all in a quiet little backwater between York and Harrogate. Describes itself as a 'broad church' – and it's certainly that, though all faiths and none are welcome. In fact anyone who can afford it (with or without a horse) is welcome really – with little academic selection and a determination to meet all needs, the place could be in danger of becoming a jack of all trades, but its current level of success in doubling pupil numbers in six years is due, they say, to 'painstaking and careful design' and they are enormously proud of their 'very real and rapid progress'.

Pastoral care and discipline: According to one parent, the pastoral care here is really good – 'Can't plug it enough'. Tutorial system – tutors change yearly, no more than 20 tutees to each. Discipline is described as 'sensible' – exclusion for violence and selling drugs, possibly also for taking drugs, 'depending on what it is'. Reserves the right to search boarders' rooms and to test for drugs and alcohol – and does. Bullies are confronted head on and the bully box, where notes, either signed or not, can be deposited for scrutiny by the head or his deputy, is rarely used. Charming 'leavers' letter' inviting any former pupil (until they 'leave university, or their 21st birthday, whichever is the later') to contact the college or Mr Martin – reverse charge – at any time, if they have got into a scrape and need help or (free) legal advice (a GSG first). 'One or two take up the offer,' says Mr Jandrell.

Houseparents occasionally express concern that individual facilities are so good that pupils, particularly senior (Chinese) boys, are loath to leave their bed/study rooms and join in communal activities. No Saturday school, but full range of activities on offer during weekends – trips to Whitby, the latest cinema preview. After their first term sixth formers can nip into York or Leeds on a Saturday night, but must meet the pickup by 10pm at the local station (or be in by 10.30pm if they miss the train).

Q

Pupils and parents: No longer so fiercely middle class – lots of first time buyers, pupils come to board from all over: Scotland, Wales as well as East Anglia and locally on daily basis. Expect a mass of regional accents, as well as students from abroad – Chinese, Germans, Russians, Scandinavians, with a number just coming for the sixth form. Eight buses collect day pupils from all over Yorkshire (not cheap – one parent said it was less expensive to call a cab), buses collect from local station. Parents talk of 'exponential growth' at the school with a mix of pride and delight at being part of that success and the improved facilities, and some regret at both the loss of the small-time old school and the change in student profile.

Entrance: Many via Chapter House, but generally aged 11; As and Bs at GCSE for potential A level candidates at sixth form. External candidates come from other independents, local state schools or out of the area. Pupils below year 10 accepted at any time during the school year 'if places available'. Promotes itself heavily locally, nationally and internationally – regular pop-outs from Good Housekeeping, Horse and Hound and the like. Informative DVD which plays in Chinese Simplified and Traditional, English, German, Japanese and Russian. The heaviest prospectus bundle that we have ever encountered, though fear not, it is fairly repetitive. Entry to College sixth form requires at least six B grades at GCSE; entry to The Faculty is four C grade GCSEs – more a matter of state of mind and wallet than qualifications.

Exit: A quarter of pupils left after GCSEs in 2013. About two-thirds to university, mostly traditional eg Edinburgh, Durham, Liverpool, London and Nottingham, with a steady four or five a year to Oxbridge.

Money matters: Provost Brian Martin FCMI, FFA, FinstD, executive trustee of the QE Charitable Foundation, hasn't lost his Midas touch. A true businessman, he masterminds the marketing of the school and drives the development of the site. The school is well underpinned financially but quite expensive and 'you pay for absolutely everything,' say parents. Countered a little by masses of scholarships, plenty of awards, 30 per cent corporate body awards (boarding fees only), rebate if you move to QE from another independent school; 20 per cent discount for Services, diplomats and professional bodies. Add to that list sports, art and music scholarships and many, many more. 'You can also pay by Barclaycard or Amex' – but it costs extra to spread the payment over several months. Very streetwise management and 'all awards granted will be repayable in full, if the school fees bill is not paid seven days prior to the commencement of each term, and, or, if a pupil does not complete their education with us for any reason, regardless of commencement age, until the completion of the end of year 13...' etc etc. Read the small print – very carefully.

Remarks: Has come a long way, not just in its facilities but also in its academic provision, and is quietly and deservedly gaining more respect amongst its competitors.

Queen Margaret's School

Escrick Park, York, YO19 6EU

• Pupils: 375 girls; 85 per cent are full boarders • Ages: 11–18
• C of E • Fees: Day £17,631; Boarding £27,825 pa • Independent

Tel: 01904 727600
Email: admissions@queenmargarets.com
Website: www.queenmargarets.com

Head Master: Since 2009, Dr Paul Silverwood MA PhD (late thirties). Educated at Queen Elizabeth Grammar School, Wakefield and read natural sciences at Cambridge followed by a PhD in nuclear chemistry at Manchester. Initially worked in industry but then landed a teaching post at North London Collegiate School, followed by head of chemistry at St Edward's School, Oxford. Prior to this he was assistant head and director of studies at Benenden. Married to Rebecca, two young daughters. Teaches critical thinking and biology and leads The King Society for scholars – 45 girls who meet weekly to discuss recent news and events from around the world.

A quiet, unassuming mover and shaker, with a can-do philosophy and a refreshingly unstuffy approach, he is making seemingly subtle changes to the feel of the school whilst having a greater impact on the bigger picture. Academic extension's the thing – politics, personal finance, philosophy, philanthropy, current affairs – opening hearts and minds alongside a lecture series with external speakers to bring the wider world into school. Girls appreciative of the changes, being given more independence, greater opportunity for self-reliance and space to breathe. Parents seem happy – he's doing 'a sterling job,' one parent tells us, and even old guard staff are shifting his way.

Academic matters: Although entry is not particularly selective, academic success matters. Fine GCSE results: 60 per cent A*/A grades in 2013. At A level, mathematics, English, physics, chemistry, geography, art and French popular, but no weaknesses. Overall performance very good – 55 per cent A*/A grades in 2013. Pupil support department (three full-time) and two teachers for EFL.

Games, options, the arts: Lots of healthy outdoor life – an hour a day of sport for all. Highly successful sports department with games keenly played in glorious surroundings and stunning facilities: nine-hole golf course, lacrosse (long journeys for fixtures), hockey (floodlit all-weather pitch), two swimming pools (one indoor, one outdoor), sports hall, tennis courts, dance studio etc – hard to find something they don't have. Riding popular (private riding school on campus); some girls bring ponies, school keeps 15. Good art, but not an 'arty' school. Home economics for all. Strong choral music, and lots of drama in wonderful theatre. Stunning modern chapel, Catholics go to nearby Thicket Priory for Mass; half-termly Vigil Masses in school; annual Anglican and RC confirmations. Extra-curricular activities too numerous to mention but include clay pigeon shooting, driving remote control cars and climbing walls.

Background and atmosphere: Founded in Scarborough in 1901, moved to this fine Palladian house (by John Carr), with later 'rustic timber' purpose-built classrooms, in 1949. Glorious sweeping drive, set amongst 60 plus acres of North Yorkshire loveliness, the flag is flying proudly from the rooftop. A school where girls have big hair and even bigger ideas – aspirations and expectations, of self and others, are high. Confident yet not brash, articulate and considered, girls are fiercely loyal, hard working and committed. New social areas where girls of all ages meet together and the use of in-school mentors have

Q

brought increased opportunities for greater independence and responsibility. Girls now feel they have a voice and, being girls, they use it. The school earns many approving noises from parents as well as envious glances over the wall from its competitors, with good reason.

It's been top notch academically for quite a while now, but is cultivating a purposeful nurturing side without losing any of its academic rigour. Has a large yet tight and cohesive campus with a number of Victorian additions, clever conversions, award-winning centenary theatre, chapel and indoor swimming pool. Superb library – wood panelling everywhere, open fire, huge windows looking out on to lawns – but not too precious to be used, the range of reference books is impressive; also smaller but well-stocked fiction library with the relaxed feel of a welcoming bookshop.

Circular dining hall (once an indoor lunging school), with somewhat noisy acoustics. Food much improved in recent years, say parents and girls, with school rarities such as a cappuccino machine and balsamic vinegar; younger girls envious of the privilege of pain au chocolat delivered to sixth form houses for breakfast, all very civilised. Breaktime snacks provided, excellent cakes and fruit, girls on school council keep a watchful eye over food provision and choice.

Welcoming, homey boarding house for 11 year olds with a Cath Kidston inspired kitchen for tea, toast and home comforts around the Aga. Girls live in year groups all the way through – 'Prevents them from growing up too fast,' observed one pleased parent. School claims the strong vertical house system, house supper nights on Fridays and an assortment of trips and visits encourage girls of different ages to mix, new social mixing areas encouraging and supporting this. Year 5 have a boarding house named after old girl, Winifred Holtby; lower sixth boarders are housed nearby and enjoy sitting and walking on the Cloisters lawn – they do because they can. Upper sixth form have increased independence in attractively converted cottages on site; head girl has the first pick of houses; all have large kitchens 'great for entertaining' and communal sitting rooms; cottage life has the feel of a college campus.

Recent changes include an alteration to prep time; once timetabled and closely monitored – now girls choose where and when they do their prep, and, if need be, learn by getting it wrong. All part of the independence = taking responsibility philosophy. And it's working. However girls are kept 'pretty busy' all the time – new girls are monitored to check they aren't overdoing it and taking on too much in the early days. Uniform is an attractive tartan and charcoal; own clothes worn after tea – don't provide anything that you wouldn't want boil-washed. Smart dress code rather than uniform for sixth form, jackets required.

Pastoral care and discipline: The pace of life in this rural idyll is anything but slow and a noticeable air of protectiveness towards the girls. 'There are no silly rules,' say parents and girls, but it is by no means light on discipline – 'We are pretty old fashioned about smoking and drinking'. Parents speak with great enthusiasm about the life skills provided by being part of a boarding community, citing 'independence, knowing how to get on with people, young and old, and standing up and being counted' as so very important. All girls have a personal tutor, around eight girls per staff member (including the head), and run on a three year cycle. Add to this a mentor for sixth formers who acts as a guide in their subject of choice to provide extra reading, advice and support university applications.

A café, assortment of TV rooms with games (including Wii), a room for Skype-ing home (priority given to overseas boarders) and new ICT rooms have really given the place a lift and provided the girls with much-needed places to go. Quiet work rooms for those who need or want it, and other rooms where girls can work or chat, computers arranged in pods and some even blissfully Facebook-free for those serious about working. Sixth formers also have their own socialising area known as the 'cellars' – once used for keeping wine cool, now a cool place for maturing girls to hang out with friends before, during and after school and to bring guests (boys even) at weekends.

Apart from school, not a great deal to do around here, so a trip to the village shop is an exciting treat – a shock for girls with serious shopping habits. Sixth formers can go into York during free time on Wednesdays and Saturdays; they are usually careful not to abuse this freedom.

Pupils and parents: Friendly pupils, happy to chat and proud of their school, clearly enjoying the many benefits of living and learning in such a lovely environment. No lack of ambition – even younger girls talk about going to university as though it is a self-evident truth: 'You'd be hard-pressed to find someone who is not heading for uni,' they tell us. Parents mainly upper and middle class: landowners, farmers, professionals; boarders span 13 nations and four continents, many from Scotland ('It's the first real boarding school you hit driving south'), Cumbria, East Anglia, and of course Yorkshire. Essentially the main catchment is the east coast train line. OGs include Winifred Holtby (author), Ann Jellicoe (playwright), Sarah Connolly (opera singer), Dame Justice Eleanor King (High Court judge).

Entrance: Own exam at 11, 12 and 13. Additional intake into sixth form: minimum eight GCSEs, including English, mathematics and a science, with at least two As and three Bs.

Exit: Virtually all go on to higher education nationwide, five to 10 per cent to Oxbridge. Small trickle post-16 to co-ed sixth form, a few girls becoming restless each year, though many go and look elsewhere before then deciding to stay put.

Money matters: Scholarships at 11, 12, 13 and sixth form; Academic, art, choral, dance, drama, music and sport scholarships. Means-tested bursaries.

Remarks: According to one parent, with three daughters at the school, 'Whether your daughter is tall or short, academic or sporty, shy or confident, it works for them all – and that's the beauty of it'.

Queen Mary's School

Linked school: Queen Mary's School

Baldersby Park, Topcliffe, Thirsks, North Yorkshire, YO7 3BZ

- Pupils: 135 girls (including 23 full boarders, 38 weekly boarders and 60 flexi boarders) • Ages: 3–16 • C of E (Woodard school)
- Fees: Day £13,485–£15,120; Boarding £17,940–£19,950 pa
- Independent

Tel: 01845 575000
Email: admin@queenmarys.org
Website: www.queenmarys.org

Headmistress: Since 2011, Mrs Sandra Lewis-Beckett BSc PGDip, PGCE (forties) previously senior mistress at Downe House. Worked in retail and international banking before training as a teacher. Married to Kevin, a classical musician; three children. Called Mrs LB by the girls.

Academic matters: No sixth form and therefore no A level stream, though some girls are venturing into AS levels a year early. A very mixed ability school – all take English, maths and the sciences, nearly all take French as well; French starts early; email exchange with school set up by previous French assistant. 'It is good because you can practise your grammar. It makes it a lot easier in exams,' seems to be the general opinion of the pupils. Excellent showing across the board at GCSE, with a pleasing number of As and A*s – 40 per cent in 2013. Classics on offer at 11. German and music results consistently good and the humanities well represented.

Streaming and setting, tiny classes. Good and sensitive dyslexia help. Buzzy library with sagbags. Classrooms in the main building and converted outhouses, plus attractive new build for tinies. Science department boasts a greenhouse and freshwater pond for hands-on experience. A goodly supply of computers throughout, plus dedicated IT rooms, many of the girls also have their own laptops; internet OK, but girls not allowed to use chatrooms. Senior girls do coursework online. Tinies have computers too and good basic three Rs in the lower school. Thirty-five staff on hand plus 12 part-timers. School never closes and girls can be found wandering around in the Easter holidays having been 'doing extra workshops' with dedicated staff, who never seem to take holidays either.

Games, options, the arts: Music is very important and the place hums with junior and senior choirs and delicious concerts open to the general public as well as for inmates – impressive for a school of this size. Chapel choristers wear much-coveted green sweatshirts and give regular performances both home and away. Stunning art in the attics including creative textiles and ceramics, sewing machines in the DT room. Home-grown art all over the place. Drama good and popular, cooking timetabled and enjoyed by all.

Trad sports, with lacrosse, athletics and tennis teams all doing well, own tennis courts and all-weather pitches. Superb equestrian facilities, children can and do bring their own ponies and ride daily, girls enjoy mucking in – and out – in the stables at weekends, after lessons and occasionally before breakfast. Outdoor manege of Olympian size, as well as rides across the local landowner's fields, school in constant negotiation with neighbours to increase riders' scope, cross-country course on site. Tadcaster polo club is nearby and looks like becoming the next horsy activity. Small indoor swimming pool and the adjacent River Swale is popular for canoeing and the occasional swim (hardy girls up north). Climbing frames. Superb selection of expeditions for all, plus D of E.

Background and atmosphere: Baldersby Park is a grand Palladian mansion (Colen Campbell 1721, Jacobethanised following a fire in 1902) and was converted into residential flats in a previous existence, so the girls have a rash of good-sized dorms with private bathrooms, all incredibly tidy and well-organised and with great views all round, mostly well-furnished with just a few old Victorian lunatic asylum beds remaining. Glorious main hall used for daily service, with the girls sitting on the carpet, Mrs Lewis-Beckett sitting in front of the stairs, the choir ranged behind her in serried ranks. When it is not being used for formal occasions, girls can be seen walking the trapeze from balcony to balcony high above the main hall, wisely harnessed; it's not compulsory but, as with most things here, girls encouraged to 'have a go'. School uniform evolves over the years with girls graduating from beige to green jerseys and royal hunting Stewart tartan kilts, slight pressure currently to change the uniform but neither the LBs nor the girls can see the point. School food is good quality wholesome home cooking and girls generally approve though 'would enjoy a visit from Jamie Oliver' to liven things up.

Staff and girls are happy with the relaxed atmosphere – like an extended family (all ages mix) with a mass of sisterly teasing. Younger girls like to play and build dens in the woods, 'benign supervision' allowing a sense of freedom with a nod to health and safety. Charming chapel, a peaceful haven for all, school has its own chaplain; Mrs Lewis-Beckett is keen that religion should be 'part of the school routine' but not rammed down the throat. The early assumption of seniority (at 16 rather than 18) gives girls confidence and maturity – a great balance with the younger girls happily staying young and the older girls demonstrating early maturity and grace. All pupils have to play some part in keeping the school neat, clean and tidy.

Pastoral care and discipline: Like home. No petty rules and others which are bendable, but an underlying sense of organisation. Parents' requests granted when reasonable. Not a sophisticated place, no obvious sin, just an occasional ticking off for a girl wearing makeup, but it's few and far between and an acknowledgement that 'girls like to rebel – and better makeup than vodka'.

Pupils and parents: Local as opposed to county school – combination of first time buyers, local farmers, landowners and professionals – 'not as Tatler and Vogue as some of its competitors'. Relaxed 7.30am drop off time for working parents. Quite a lot of army families – Catterick is just up the road – some of whom pop their daughters into the school 'whilst they are based in Yorkshire' and are so pleased with the place that they leave their daughters there, younger sisters often joining them, when they are posted elsewhere. Plenty of flexi-boarding, with some full-time boarders living closer than some of the day girls, ditto the flexi-boarders – 'Girls come to escape'. If girls regularly stay three nights a week they get their own permanent space; no charge for extra meals, only for bed. Boarding mainly from 11, and day girls often opt to stay at least on a weekly basis. Parents and pupils can use school facilities in the holidays. No real overseas presence, one or two expats, but boarding is now pretty full and no wish to change its nature by overloading. Parents run a website and are delighted to answer any queries.

Entrance: At any time, middle of term if needed. At all ages. Entry test but, places permitting, only those with special needs beyond the school's capability are liable to be turned away.

Exit: At all ages. Some take common entrance at 11, and a small number at 13. Girls have previously mainly gone to Queen Margaret's Eskrick, with one or two to Tudor Hall, Heathfield or co-eds, Uppingham, Millfield, Rugby. Senior girls go on to do A levels at Ampleforth, St Aidan's, Ripon Grammar, Oundle, Queen Margaret's Eskrick, St Peter's, Uppingham etc etc. Good collection of scholarships – music predominates, plus academic and sports.

Money matters: Not a rich school and not endowed, though has benefited recently from generous donations. Scholarships for academics, music and art plus bursaries for clergy daughters, sisters and Services discount.

Remarks: Useful, popular, small, girls' – predominantly weekly – boarding school without a sixth form. Fierce competition locally, but has no intention of being 'the one to fall off the edge' and the recent increase in numbers would suggest it is in safe hands. A home from home, with muddy wellies on the doorstep, smiling cheery girls and a predominance of four-wheeled drives in the car park, it provides a good solid education focusing on creating girls with a 'have a go' mentality. It's possibly too cosy for those at the sharp end – but exactly what many need and the girls say they 'wouldn't change a thing'.

Queen Victoria School

Dunblane, Perthshire, FK15 0JY

- Pupils: 265; boys: 135; girls: 130 – all children of Services personnel • Ages: 10–18 • Church of Scotland • Fees: Funded by the MOD but a parental contribution is expected for some expenses. • Independent

Tel: 01786 822288
Email: enquiries@qvs.org.uk
Website: www.qvs.org.uk

Head: Since 2007, Mrs Wendy Bellars MA PGCE (late forties), born and educated in Glasgow. With an English mother and Scottish father, holidays with relatives in Somerset and Thurso were the norm, so it was only when she moved to England (for work) and north Wales (to live) in 1988 that the real cultural differences dawned on her.

She taught English in Renfrew High School for two years, then moved to Gordonstoun. Since then she has taught in virtually every type of school – day, boarding, independent, state, mixed and single sex (both girls and boys) in a variety of roles, including a spell as head of St Leonard's in Fife when it was undergoing cataclysmic change and as a housemistress at Cheltenham Ladies' College. She returned to Scotland in 2004/5 and worked for the Open University, developing the then new to Scotland OU PGCE etc.

She has been involved with ATC and CCF cadets and held a 10-year Volunteer Reserve Commission in the Royal Air Force. Theatre, reading and walking two large pupil-friendly dogs – sweeping long-skirted with an elegant greyhound reminiscent of 19th century paintings – occupy her leisure. As an enthusiast for both playing and listening to music, one of her dreams for the school is to extend its fantastic tradition in military music to a wider field and to establish a full orchestra. She and QV seem to be on duck and water terms: she exudes deep and knowledgeable concern about the minutest aspect of school life, bringing a wealth of relevant and well-balanced experience.

Academic matters: A very firmly Scottish school using only the Scottish curriculum. Services children often find themselves moving from school to school – the known record is 11 and the average four or five – so P7 (approximately half way between top primary and first year secondary in English terms) is used to assess and consolidate. The very occasional pupil may have to repeat a year at this stage. After the entry year spent consolidating in three streams (red, green and blue) carefully not labeled by ability, pupils are setted (by ability) for maths, English and sciences. Curriculum is trad but flexible, classes not more than 20. Down to earth labs (new ones on the way as part of a complete classroom rebuild planned by the MoD for the middle term future) and lots of computers in class and available in houses at night, including impressive Macs for the enterprising art department (better for photography and image manipulation).

Learning support flexible and pupils say 'really supportive', with in-class help, withdrawal, extra tuition in groups or one-to-one etc as appropriate. Good rapport between SEN and teachers. School prides itself on 'holistic' education. Results pretty good – 48 per cent of S5 cohort achieved three or more Higher passes in 2013, school's best result for at least six years. Though wholly MoD funded, QV competes and compares with independent rather than state schools in style (both academic and pastoral).

Games, options, the arts: Games staff assert proudly that as a small school QV 'punches above its weight' in both girls' and boys' sports. Football, rugby, hockey, netball and athletics strong, tennis less so. Spacious terraced pitches, huge multi-purpose sports hall with free access to smashing fitness training for older pupils and ancient but serviceable swimming pool often on loan to neighbouring primaries.

Military music is king of the activities curriculum. The pipe band has played for every home rugby international since 1922, until last year's ban on health and safety grounds! QV pipes, drums and dancers (PDD) are renowned throughout Scotland and perform in the Edinburgh military tattoo and all over the world. Every pupil must learn one PDD skill. Marching is also compulsory and during our visit pupils joining after S2 (year 10) were doing daily catch up marching practice. The head girl reckoned that her brother's role of drum major was as iconic as her own. Pupils said that almost everyone enjoyed and felt a sense of pride in the military identity the school gives them. Masses of tours abroad, mainly with band but also recently to Malawi on a school building project.

Pupils choose own charities and recently raised £1,700 for Help for Heroes, as well as doing a sponsored walk to help themselves (the school development fund). About 80 clubs in all, ranging from skiing to jewellery making and some participation is compulsory. CCF plays a strong part with units for all three services – myriad activities extending into holiday time and D of E is much in evidence. The friendly dogginess of school, spearheaded by Mrs Bellars' Dash and Ginger, is highlighted by girls doing D of E service at a stray dogs' home and completed by Molly, the IT department dog.

Background and atmosphere: With a mission 'to provide stable and uninterrupted education for the children of Scottish service personnel', has to balance an imposing site steeped in military history with the need for a 'home from home' environment for children with parents on inaccessible active service. Founded by public subscription as a memorial to Scots who fell in the South African wars, has been co-ed since 1996. The magnificent chapel is dedicated to Queen Victoria and its splendour, enhanced by modern audiovisual equipment and comfy seats, typifies emphasis placed on service to Queen and country. Pupils confirmed that this gives most of them a sense of purpose and identity. The school chaplain cares for all denominations though children can go to Dunblane for mass etc.

The granite cliff of a main building, opened by Edward VII in 1908, is maintained, like everything else on site, by the MoD – hence the brilliantly polished but battered floors, doors etc. Public gifts from, for example the MacRobert Trust, have provided a smashing and recently refurbished, up to date and very fully used library, plus (much earlier) pool and sports hall. The accretion of buildings, each in the style of the current MoD (War Office), has made a hotch potch of buildings over the years, but the more recent boarding accommodation is well thought out and comfortable. A particularly telling touch in Trenchard (junior house) – the common-room with clocks showing the time in Afghanistan and Iraq. Older pupils volunteer to spend a term or so in Trenchard to act as mentors for new arrivals.

The development fund has taken over from the centenary appeal. Its planned new theatre/auditorium had to be abandoned because MoD requirements were escalating the expense. Priority is now a major upgrade of the existing theatre, still hidden under wraps/tin hats.

The san, shiny with new pastel paint and a 'chill out area' complete with relaxation tapes, candles and every kind of health information leaflet, retains its 'hospital ward' since QV, unlike other boarding schools, cannot ship pupils home at the first sign of an epidemic. Efficient looking bedsteads sport teddies and pretty bedspreads. Someone was in for a bit of space and motherly care on the day we visited.

One of the few schools where pupils really do look smart and seem to enjoy it. Formal dress is real military red, high collared jackets, with hunting Stewart kilts and Lovat tweed for everyday, plus some fantastic ceremonial gear – nylon bearskins and the like. MoD supplies, so cost not a problem.

Food looks good; no one complained though not all were entirely complimentary.

Pastoral care and discipline: Full boarding, seven days a week for all, though weekend leave is allowed, except for parade days. Sixteen and over can visit cinemas etc in relatively sleepy Dunblane. Not many real problems bar the occasional smoker and, 'surprisingly', no drugs. Very structured disciplinary system including categories of offences, a behaviour management group and punishments such as litter picking days or clearing tables. Strong PSHE and careful discussion of problems – medical services much involved here. Observable loving attention to the real underlying needs of children away from home underpins pastoral care – impressive. Pupils claimed to like the training of a military style discipline ('teaches you how to manage your things') but evidently also enjoyed a bit of teenage squalor in their bedrooms without undue interference.

Pupils and parents: By definition, parents are serving members of Scottish Forces or are/have been stationed in Scotland (eg Ghurkas in Glasgow). Founded for NCOs, but officers' children are eligible, so a real mixed bag. Oddly the MoD don't fund a past pupils' database but voluntary help is starting this – with a huge reservoir of Scottish history to tap. Strong parent network and generations of same families. Liaison group welcomes new families and supports children. No guardian system needed because most have relatives or close colleagues ready to help.

Entrance: Applications deadline 15th January and admissions board sits in Feb/March. School is full but tries to keep a few places for emergency postings/compassionate need etc. Purpose is to take orphans and needy (in that order) and parents meet the high powered, but 'not too scary', admissions panel, while children are assessed for academic and emotional suitability. Mrs Bellars wonders if info on the school actually reaches those who most need it.

Exit: Increasing percentage to university (now about 50 per cent) though still low in view of its academic record. A few go straight into the forces. Others to local colleges or nursing. Most have a gap year. No notice required since MoD posts are instantaneous.

Money matters: Places are funded by the MOD if you meet the eligibility criteria, but a 'parental contribution' is expected (to cover cost of travel, activities etc). Details of the parental contribution are available from the admissions secretary.

Remarks: Thriving – an amazing opportunity for those who qualify.

Queen's College (Taunton)

Linked school: Queen's College Junior School

Trull Road, Taunton, TA1 4QS

• Pupils: 380 boys and girls (including 215 boarders) • Ages: 11–18
• Methodist foundation • Fees: Day £5,840–£15,540; Boarding £11,790–£28,950 pa • Independent

---

Tel: 01823 340830
Email: admissions@queenscollege.org.uk
Website: www.queenscollege.org.uk

Head Master: Since 2001, Mr Christopher J Alcock BSc FRSG (late forties). Graduate of Durham University (geography and anthropology). Taught at Stamford School, where he was boarding housemaster and rugby coach, before going on to be deputy head at St Edward's, Witley.

Friendly, approachable, amusing and deeply committed to his charges. Not a pin-striped suited, jargon-spouting managerial head but a get-in-among-the-troops-and-love-them head. Study is full of 'significant' photographs. He singled out one in particular, a boy who had written to thank him for his time at Queen's – 'No one else would take me, but you did and now I'm at university'. 'Lowly grades, but he really fought for them', added the head. 'That's what I delight in. Literally and metaphorically the winning pass in a fourth XV match is as important as anything in the first XV.' That's not empty rhetoric – he really believes it, always looking out for opportunities to praise and encourage all round efforts. Waxes lyrical about holistic all round education. His monthly letters to parents are not couched in flowery prose but, for the most part, lists of individual achievements. Parents love that. 'If I had a son of school age,' said a successful prep school head, 'I would send him to Alcock, whatever the distance.' Evidence that others are doing just that – numbers have increased by over 100 since his arrival. Wife, Linda, teaches French in the junior school and they have two sons at Queen's.

Academic matters: 'What I really love about Queen's,' a mother told us, 'is that they go for potential rather than force-feeding. If your child is A grade material, that's what he will achieve; if he's D grade, he won't be made to feel stupid. He'll be congratulated on his achievement and made to feel good about it.' GCSE results are excellent with good performances from the brighter pupils and gutsy performances from the less able. In 2013, 47 per cent A*/A grades. Twenty-three subjects to choose from at A level – 40 per cent A*/A grades and 71 per cent A*/B. But this is not a school overly bothered with statistics – go back to good teaching and potential.

Wonderful support from the SEN department with super-caring staff. The designated area is presided over by a brilliant lady who combines compassion with common sense and expertise. Careful screening and individual follow up for the 10 per cent who are dyslexic, help and encouragement for those with ADHD – 'They often make good rock climbers or swimmers. The important thing is to find something which will engage their interest'. Not just a learning support area – an overall support area: 'My daughter's not bad at maths, but she goes for individual help because it increases her confidence'; 'I love coming here -' said a bright and engaging girl, 'it's a comfort zone'.

Has invested in computers in a big way and pupils are very proud of their proliferation. They are skilfully woven into lessons, much clever use of interactive white boards. Classrooms are functional with a good but not outstanding library – very helpful librarian, though. No lessons on Saturday mornings – not just the inspectors who have noted an improvement in academics since that decision was taken. 'It's a question of charging batteries,' says the head. 'They really do arrive fresher on Monday mornings after a break.' No lessons does not mean that nothing happens – three hour rehearsals for plays, expeditions out into the country, hobbies and activities abound.

Games, options, the arts: Sport is compulsory up to year 10, but most continue beyond that because this is not just a first and second team school. Everyone has a chance to play in a team – up to four in each sport. Beautiful cricket and rugby grounds and masses of floodlit, all-weather pitches and tennis courts. Brand new hockey academy opened September 2012 with Olympic coach. Good swimming pool with notable successes (Matt Clay, near Olympic swimmer, is an old boy) and shoals of pupils representing the county and beyond. National and international successes at rugby, cricket, swimming, cycling, athletics and fencing. Talented games players thrive; less talented have a go and love it. 'Everyone finds an activity they can enjoy,' said a charming girl who had experienced

Q

six schools. Some 50 per cent of the pupils play a musical instrument and the facilities are encouraging, with bright airy practice rooms in the theatre complex. When we were there, pupils were queuing up to practise. Bags of opportunities for playing in orchestras and ensembles and indulging in various sorts of music.

Large and well-equipped theatre doubles up as an assembly hall and chapel. Drama of all kinds is very popular with pupils and parents and eagerly looked forward to. School reviews have been known to include a memorable performance on the spoons by the head and the four notes he can play on the sax. 'Was it as many as four?' asked a boy. Wonderful and sympathetically designed art school overlooks the cricket pitch (how suitable it should have been opened by Jack Russell) and is full of exciting work. Every year an arts festival where artists visit and exhibit, evidence of which can be found in the beautiful stag and imposing giraffe which guard the buildings to the front. Much emphasis is placed on inculcating leadership (the head does not have a senior management team; instead he has a leadership group – a subtle and genuine difference). Lots of D of E with rock climbing and expeditions, to say nothing of community service. The cross-curricular approach encourages self-esteem and confidence as well as a strong sense of community

Background and atmosphere: Founded in 1843, the first independent school in Taunton, one of nine schools owned by the Methodist Church. The main building, fine educational Gothic, is impressive without being threatening – as you look at it you're surprised you haven't approached it by a long tree-lined drive. Instead you slip in off a pleasant leafy suburb. New buildings crowd around the back – and they do crowd – before giving way to acres of beautifully mown playing fields. 'This is a Christian name school,' said the head groundsman – groundsmen are always a useful indicator of school's morale. 'It's very, very friendly.'

Indeed that is the over-riding atmosphere of the school. The pupils we met were marvellously forthcoming and fun and clearly used to chatting with alleged adults. 'We're suave, sophisticated bachelors,' said one boy. The last word is probably true; the other two, mercifully, not. In more measured tones, the inspectors commented on the pupils as 'open, tolerant, friendly and self disciplined'. Boarding houses have been, and are being, refurbished, and are brightly coloured and comfortable. We were interested to see pin ups of handsome RC priests in a girls' house. Lovely, ebullient house staff, including matrons who care.

The sixth form centre is 'a school within a school', housed in its own building with restricted access to ensure greater privacy; new centre opened in September 2013 and stays open every evening and at weekends. An impressive learning resource centre with banks of computers and shelves of books. Downstairs are good chilling out facilities, including television and music systems, and a snack bar. Boys and girls were very enthusiastic about it and seemed to enjoy the monthly meetings of the sixth form society, when a variety of guest speakers come and entertain and opportunity for discussion. It certainly acts as a good bridge between school and university.

Pastoral care and discipline: Thanks to the excellent parents' handbook, which tells them everything they need to know, and thanks to the very detailed but not overly fussy school rules, clear courts are laid out within which pupils know where they stand and are the happier for it. Reins are held lightly but never dropped. Prefects are selected through sixth form ballot and consultation with staff – ongoing training with opportunities to discuss their responsibilities and any problems they may encounter. Parents we spoke to described the pastoral care as 'brilliant'.

The house system is the spring of tutoring and sets the tone. Each pupil is assigned a tutor with whom they have regular meetings. Clear guidelines on drugs (zero tolerance), and

bullying is swiftly confronted, though 'very little of that'. A calm, peaceful atmosphere permeating the busy bustling, an indication that pupils are happy, know where they stand and appreciate the genuine interest shown in them. All schools are very fond of trumpeting 'family atmosphere/values and a sense of community'. It isn't always easy to detect that on a visit – here those qualities are obvious.

Pupils and parents: Parents come from a cross-section of society, a number making considerable financial sacrifices to send their children. Boarders are drawn from the Forces, particularly the navy and the marines; others from abroad. A feature of the school is the loyalty and involvement of parents.

Entrance: Seventy per cent come from the prep school. Others from local preps and a few from state schools. Entrance requirements are broad and generous. Pupils at 11, 12 and 13 sit school's entrance papers in English, maths and verbal reasoning or common entrance. 'I find it very hard to refuse anyone,' said the head, 'though, very occasionally, I am forced to conclude this is not the right school for an applicant.'

Exit: Around 30 per cent move on after GCSEs. Regular handful to Oxbridge (five in 2012); otherwise to a wide range of universities. Difficult to detect any pattern in subjects read, but as wide a range as you would expect from such a school.

Money matters: Scholarships for the usual things and discounts offered to Forces parents.

Remarks: Not a swaggering school nor a showing off one. Nor does the apparent happiness disguise anything – it enlivens and invigorates a wholly unpretentious school.

Queen's College London

Linked school: Queen's College Prep School

43–49 Harley Street, London, W1G 8BT

• Pupils: 340 girls, all day • Ages: 11–18 • C of E • Fees: £15,915 pa
• Independent

Tel: 020 7291 7000
Email: admissions@qcl.org.uk
Website: www.qcl.org.uk

Principal: Since 2009, Dr Frances Ramsey MA DPhil (Oxon) (forties). Completed doctorate in medieval history before starting teaching. Taught at Westminster School, where she was head of history and director of studies. Discovered the importance of the pastoral side when she became Master of the Queen's Scholars. Cerebral and professional, she is determined to lead the school onwards and upwards. Says it has the same feel and ethos as Westminster and parents and staff feel familiar. All the latter have full lives beyond day-to-day teaching, which she thinks is important. Very much likes the all girl set up – 'no distraction in the classroom'.

'The school has a certain quirkiness and it is important that this is not ironed out,' say parents. They are impressed with 'the buzz of the school and the direction it is going in'. There were mixed reactions from parents to the introduction of uniform for years 7 to 9, mainly because they didn't want general informality of the school to change. But, as Dr Ramsey is a firm believer in 'evolution not revolution', we don't feel they need to worry and the change was enthusiastically welcomed by prospective parents. She misses having the time to teach but makes sure that she is as visible as possible, taking assembly twice a week, having coffee/tea meetings with the senior girls and congratulating younger ones who bring her their 'show principal' reward cards. Is also seen at all school performances. She interviews all the parents of new applicants and the school maintains a continuous open door policy (parents tell us that they can go in and go anywhere any time they like), so she is not inaccessible.

Married to an Oxford academic, with two children in central London schools. We think that Queen's College is lucky to have her.

Academic matters: Excellent results across the board, with a curriculum that covers a broad range of subjects and is as strong on the creative side as the academic. Parents say, 'Well structured, but girls don't feel it is rigid and therefore thrive on it'; 'Art is taken as seriously as maths.' Dr Ramsey has upped the academic ante, increasing the number of subjects taken as IGCSE and bringing in triple science for the top set. She says, despite the school not being super selective, the girls are all able and ambitious. In 2013, 68 per cent of GCSE grades were A*/A. Parents say the school 'embraces a girl's whole brain'; is 'sympathetic, understanding and supportive'. All agree that the school is not a hothouse, the atmosphere is relaxed, yet it manages to bring out the potential in all girls, academic or artistic.

Teachers praised for their dedication and support. The new director of studies, one of the good proportion of males on the staff, is bright and approachable, and was appointed to oversee academic developments. Appears to cater well for different types of children guiding them towards opportunities. No EFL tuition but will give support for EAL if necessary. Small classes in the sixth form (average eight) are, a parent said, 'the jewel in the crown'. A huge range of subjects available to be studied, including several languages. Maths, English literature, history and biology seem the most popular. In 2013, 72 per cent A*/A grades at A level.

Popular, fully trained and experienced SENCo four days a week. Can cope with the milder end of the spectrum. All children assessed in year 7 and extra tuition given where necessary. Deputy head says head of English superb at finding any problems – in fact, all teachers good at spotting and communicating concerns: 'Nobody gets through the net'. Classroom assistants not needed as class sizes small (15-20 in years 7-11) and varied. Parents kept fully in the picture – communication lines are good.

Games, options, the arts: As in many town schools, physical activity an ongoing problem, but one they do seem to have cracked here. Head of PE has completely re-organised the system and all girls have at least one sport-type session four days a week. Could be gymnastics, in a beautifully re-furbished, fully-equipped hall, ballet, seasonal games in Regent's Park, swimming or anything else that demands physical activity. In fact, when we were discussing the school uniform issue, one parent suggested that they didn't really need to bother as 'my daughter seems to wear her sports kit most days!' Lots of matches played against other schools and the Duke of Edinburgh award is a popular option. Senior girls can go to the University of Westminster gym for exercise or pilates and yoga type classes. Very grown-up.

Wonderful pictures on display everywhere. Well-equipped art room up in the eaves (north lit, of course), showing coverage of all aspects of the subject. We were fascinated by a huge sculpture made of wire coat hangers. Talented head of art develops ability and encourages imagination, as is evidenced by their results. Music from beginner to grade 8. About 50 per cent learn an individual instrument or have voice tuition. Several concerts, formal and informal, and musical ensembles each year, as well as musical theatre productions and opera. Enthusiastic head of drama finds many different ways to stimulate and stretch her students such as The Crucible being performed in the round – an exciting first. This school is not scared of experiment or innovation.

Clubs abound and take place in the middle of the day as well as at the end. Each day is jam-packed with activity. Lots of girs stay late on Tuesdays to attend the thriving running club. No excuse for any girl ever to sit twiddling her thumbs. Plenty of outings making use of all London has to offer. Regular trips home and abroad, both educational and social. Lots of charitable involvement and fund-raising activities.

Background and atmosphere: Founded in 1848 and given a royal charter in 1853, a pioneer in education for women, this was the first institution in Great Britain to give academic qualifications to girls. Still on its original site in four elegant, well-proportioned Georgian houses, internally it has often been altered through the years in order to provide the best modern education possible. Wouldn't those early Victorian students be amazed to see the state-of-the-art glass computer room, 'the goldfish bowl', so cleverly integrated, science and language laboratories beyond their imaginations, the wonderful libraries and the great hall, where modern lighting and sound equipment helps to enhance perhaps almost recognizable costume dramas? They would certainly enjoy the more relaxed atmosphere and the idea of learning through discovery rather than rote. Teachers that really care and want to help their pupils to learn and discover in an informal way. A happy atmosphere in the school today that gives girls confidence and helps them find their own way to go forward.

Two of the earliest students, Miss Buss and Miss Beale, went on to found the North London Collegiate School and Camden School for Girls, and St Hilda's College Oxford, respectively. Katherine Mansfield and Jacqueline du Pre also stand amongst the long list of distinguished old girls as well as, more recently, Daisy Goodwin and Imogen Lloyd Webber. A distinguished tradition and history in the making.

Pastoral care and discipline: Dr Ramsey has added a layer of pastoral staff giving, she believes, better co-ordination and consistency. Girls have a year tutor as well as a form tutor, so should always have someone to talk to if necessary and should not slip through the net if difficulties arise. Has also introduced midterm mini reports in every subject, 'a quick reality check', as she calls them, which should help highlight potential academic problems. Apparently the girls have responded well to this idea. Strong anti-bullying policy – would not hesitate to exclude an offender.

Pupils and parents: The usual cosmopolitan London mix of nationalities and backgrounds. About 10 per cent don't speak English at home.

Entrance: Mainly at 11+ via the North London consortium exam. Must also have reference from previous school and be interviewed by the principal or a senior member of staff. A good percentage from Queen's College Prep, about 25 per cent from local state primaries, the rest from other private preps. Another intake at 16+ subject to GCSE results and letters of recommendation from their previous schools. All prospective entrants at this level interviewed by the head of sixth form.

Exit: Mostly after A levels to top universities, to study everything from art and design to science subjects. A few each year to Oxbridge and the London colleges, the rest all over. Bristol, UCL and Nottingham popular in the last couple of years.

Money matters: Several means-tested bursaries available at 11+ and 16+, funded by the Old Queen's bursary trust fund. Academic, music and art scholarships, for up to 25 per cent of fees, for both internal and external candidates. Would hope always to be able to find a way of keeping a pupil in need.

Remarks: A happy, rounded school where girls are encouraged to be individuals in an informal, unstressful environment; where nurturing teachers bring out the best in them and help them to find their own paths; where they develop confidence and a desire to succeed. Where being yourself is respected and really matters.

Queen's Gate School

Linked school: Queen's Gate Junior School

---

133 Queen's Gate, London, SW7 5LE

- Pupils: 350 girls; all day • Ages: 11–18 • Non-denom
- Fees: £16,695 pa • Independent

Tel: 020 7589 3587
Email: registrar@queensgate.org.uk
Website: www.queensgate.org.uk

Principal: Since 2006, Mrs Rosalynd Kamaryc BA MSc PGCE (late forties). Born and brought up in Ballymena, Northern Ireland, won a first in maths at Queen's University, Belfast, before sailing seamlessly through schools in the British Isles. Her first teaching post was in Scotland (St Leonard's), then London (Forest School), on to Suffolk (Woodbridge School, where she was deputy head and then acting head), then Hampshire (Wykeham House School in Fareham, where she was head for 10 years), before returning to London as principal of Queen's Gate. Married to an engineer who works for Thomson Reuters, she now commutes each day from Guildford, 'I can be home each night by 10'. A keen sportswoman (tennis, skiing, hockey and horse riding) she is also highly intelligent, organised and feminine. Her lilting Northern Irish (or is it Scottish?) accent can be hard to keep up with.

Whereas her predecessor, we were told, 'could silence a room on entering it,' Mrs Kamaryc adopts a more gentle, (perhaps modern?) tactic. Extremely approachable, she is respected by her girls but not feared. She teaches maths to the GCSE year (the lowest set, as it happens). She also has frequent visits from the girls (they can book an appointment or simply knock on the door of her comfortable and pretty study). It might be because they need the go ahead for a junior disco they've organised (to raise money for one of their many charitable causes, you understand) or simply because they want to air a grievance.

Academic matters: In 2013, 60 per cent A*/A grades at A level and 70 per cent A*/A at GCSE. Maximum class sizes 26 (A level classes vary between one and 10). Streaming in maths, English and science as well as some in languages. Half-termly tests, girls move up and down. Pupil:staff ratio of 7:1 – impressive.

Fair number of teaching chaps in evidence. Sciences 'strengthening all the time,' says principal. The junior school's move down the road has allowed for three more shiny labs in the new building. Three separate sciences taught from 11. Geography, biology and art popular. French, German, Italian and Spanish offered, all taught by native speakers, with masses of hands-on and trips abroad. European section fast tracks French native speakers and many girls take modern languages early at GCSE; AS and A2 Ancient Greek as well as Latin. Regular maths clinic. Interesting collection of specialisms: sociology, graphic communication/products and information studies, as well as psychology and philosophy.

Interactive whiteboards and computers in most classrooms, serious computer suites and wireless network. VDI allows girls and staff to enjoy all the school's software packages at home. All learn word processing and do touch-typing in the junior school. Girls screened after entry into senior school. Dedicated head of learning support for those who have learning difficulties ('nothing terribly serious' – dyslexia, and mild cases of dyspraxia). Help given (including EAL) as required before and after school, during lunch as well as during some lessons. Challenge and enrichment programme.

Games, options, the arts: Sport has really taken off in the last few years with Mrs Kamaryc's appointment of a dynamic head of PE, a former Great Britain pentathlete. Girls from 4-18 now enjoy their sport and are involved in an ever-increasing range of activities. Early morning clubs at 7am for climbing, running, ball skills, yoga, swimming and dance attract around 400 girls each week – breakfast is then served in school at 8am. Girls compete successfully in all their sports, including biathlon, triathlon and aquathon. Fencing with a Great Britain coach and also rowing introduced. Running very popular – girls have won the Kensington and Chelsea trophy for the mini-marathon for nine years in a row. Individual successes too with girls competing at the World Biathlon Championships.

Plenty of enthusiastic noises also about art, drama and music. Fantastic roof conversion for art suite, with fabric design, screen printing, CAD-CAM and a clever vinyl cutting machine, lots of real hands-on stuff. Good strong work on show, much of it research based. Good use made of local museums, art galleries and theatres.

Drama vibrant. The girls do everything – play every part and design the sets. Regular end of term house plays in impressive hall. Most take the LAMDA exams in acting and the speaking of verse and prose, with a good number obtaining gold medals each year. Terrific music, chamber choir, individual lessons and popular singing; girls join the W11 choir and take part in West End musicals, as well as frequently visiting there for opera and musicals. Clubs for almost everything at lunchtime – girls must go to two a week. The range is huge, everything from debating, yoga, aerobics and jewellery making to Japanese and Queen's Gate Chambers. Hot on charity, with regular fund-raising events, and particularly keen on cancer research – sponsored readathons, spellathons and fashion shows.

Background and atmosphere: Founded in 1891, the school is housed in three large Victorian mansions in South Ken. Civilised and elegant with considerably more room now the junior school has relocated. An extensive refurbishment programme has resulted in music practice rooms, a drama studio, and LAMDA room as well as a comfy sixth form centre, complete with plush leather sofas, study, and dining areas. These buildings underwent an extensive further refurbishment in 2011. The school spreads into the mews behind and all but one of the rooms have at least two fire exits – some of them about five feet high. New pupils should probably be issued with a map, compass and bits of chalk for orienteering practice in their first few weeks.

New junior school library and new librarian – another of Mrs Kamaryc's appointments – has breathed life and dynamicism into the senior school library. Well-used careers library. Lots of the old features still remain – imposing marble fireplaces, ornate cornices and fire doors make curious companions. Walls filled with photographs, children's work and noticeboards, and a sense of calm prevails.

Girls remarkably well behaved, stand up when the principal enters. Sadly, they no longer curtsey or wear white gloves (haven't for years) but instead are colourfully and casually dressed. No uniform – 'How can you say you encourage individuality when you make them wear the same thing?' is the oft quoted line of the founder of the school. Expressions of individuality do not stretch to facial or body piercing, however.

Food excellent. Mrs Kamaryc working her innovative magic here too. More girls opting for school lunch since her arrival but they may bring packed lunches which they eat in their classrooms, otherwise the whole school eats in two sessions in

Q

either the white (glammed up since our last visit) or the black (still the grander) dining room. In the summer, the younger seniors go on picnics or lunch on the roof garden.

Pastoral care and discipline: Mrs Kamaryc has been busy setting up new 'firm but fair' systems to tackle discipline. Section heads and the director of pastoral care have recently been exercising a policy of zero tolerance. Detentions given for almost everything ('after verbal reminders, order and conduct marks,' school asks us to add). When the girls were coming in for Saturday detention they started to get the message. Section heads will stop girls from dressing inappropriately with the ignominy of being forced to wear a 'granny skirt' instead (we saw one or two skimpily clad unfortunates being taken aside in assembly).

On the more nurturing side, two sixth form girls are attached to each of the younger forms as 'sisters' – 'Often easier to confide in than a member of staff – after all, they leave,' said our informant. We were also told by one of the girls of the unique trusting relationships that are frequently formed between staff and pupils. In a small school that can happen. Not many rules. Three roll calls daily, in the morning, after lunch and before they go home, 'We are in loco parentis'. Tutor system for all (they meet twice a term). Good PSHE system in place – outside counsellor, health adviser, vigilant for anorexia.

Pupils and parents: We would stick with our previous comment, 'pretty upper class' – from a range of ethnic backgrounds, though principally of Sloane extraction. We were regaled by a number of accounts of 'Camilla's' visit to open the new building. The principal's angle was that the girls just carried on afterwards as if nothing out of the ordinary had happened, 'I suspect a number of them knew her socially'. Pupils, parents and staff all frightfully discreet and unassuming, 'Everyone welcome'. Girls are fiercely loyal, delightfully mannered and very pretty. Ol Girls: HRH the Duchess of Cornwall, Redgraves, Sieffs, Guinnesses, Amanda de Souza, Jane Martineau, Nigella Lawson, Lucinda Lambton, Tracey Boyd, Aurelia Cecil, Trinny Woodall and Imogen Poots. The former head of MI5, Eliza Manningham Buller, used to be on the staff.

Entrance: From junior school – at least three-quarters of junior girls come on to the senior school – and a huge variety of other schools; confirm entry for the January exams the November before you want to come. New arrivals throughout the year, but preferably in September, though pupils who have left and have then been unhappy at their new school often re-join again mid-term, if a place. School holds four open evenings for potential parents during the autumn term and it is not unusual to have 800 parents attend. Girls take the North London Independent Girls' Schools' Consortium exam for entry at 11 plus interview, assessment and test for entry at other times.

For sixth form entry, at least six As at GCSE, subject tests and interview. Usually over-subscribed, but, because of the volatile nature of London, places do occur, but are quickly filled

Exit: Some to Oxbridge (four in 2013); eight to US/Canadian universities in 2013; some take a gap year, otherwise to various universities – Durham and Leeds popular; some to art school. Small leakage after GCSE to (mainly) boarding schools, normally because they have been at Queen's Gate since they were five and want a change.

Money matters: Four internal scholarships for sixth form entry. Two academic scholarships at 11+ with means-tested bursaries available for entry to other years in the senior school.

Remarks: Plus ça change. Charming popular school, with a mixed intake, which does jolly well by its girls. Touch of the Miss Jean Brodies. Brings out the best in girls who enjoy the intimacy and security of a small school where they are encouraged to think for themselves. Mrs Kamaryc is breathing fresh life and ideas into the place, guiding it gently but firmly into the 21st century.

The Queen's School

Linked school: The Queen's Lower School

City Walls Road, Chester, CH1 2NN

- Pupils: 390 girls; all day • Ages: 11–19 • Non-denom
- Fees: £11,400 pa • Independent

Tel: 01244 312078
Email: secretary@queens.cheshire.sch.uk
Website: www.queens.cheshire.sch.uk

Head: Since 2010, Mrs Sarah Clark MA (early forties). Read history and classics at Newnham College, Cambridge. Previously deputy head at Wellingborough School in Northamptonshire. Married to a history lecturer, with two teenage children. Avid supporter of Chelsea FC and loves to cycle, paint and write fiction. Active and breezy, she spoke to us exuberantly about working in single sex education. 'Girls can really be who they want to be here. They don't hold back because they don't feel they need to be cool in the same way they would if there were boys around.' Girls describe her as 'chatty and down to earth,' and say 'she's really in touch with people our age. She even takes part in the sixth form panto.' She is also a bell ringer for the local church.

Academic matters: An academic school; 53 per cent A*/A grades at A level and 73 per cent at GCSE in 2013. Language provision is worth noting. All year 7 girls study Mandarin, with the option of continuing it in year 8 right up to A level if they wish. A trip to China is run every other year, subsidised by the Chinese Government's department of education. Main European language is Spanish, with Latin also taught. School has introduced the Pre-U in art after teachers became frustrated with the subjectivity of examiners at A level. We saw some breathtaking artwork in the bright, airy studios in the school eaves.

Sixth formers study four AS levels, then drop down to three subjects at A2s. Critical thinking in year 12 for everyone. One girl we spoke to felt exam results could feel 'like the be all and end all at times here,' but others felt that the pressure was manageable. Part time SENCo can offer one-to-one support if needed a broad spectrum of SEN, although girls must be able to keep up with the fast pace of work. Widely stocked library, spanning many rooms, with plenty of workspace, but some girls say its relatively early closing time of 4.15pm can be inconvenient.

Games, options, the arts: New sports pavilion with changing rooms, spectator space and kitchen opened by Olympic bronze medallist gymnast and old girl Beth Tweddle. Girls complain about the lack of sporting space but the school achieves success in both team and individual events. New fitness suite, tennis courts and Astroturf have been resurfaced and the school has recently introduced rowing and sailing.

Music and drama both popular. All year 7 girls encouraged to try different instruments and around two-thirds take individual tuition. Wide range of extra-curricular clubs and activities, including podcasting and riding.

Background and atmosphere: Founded in 1878 by the Dean of Chester to educate 'the daughters of the middle class.' Moved to its present location (once the site of the city gaol and house of correction) in 1882, a short distance from Chester racecourse. The school has expanded over the years as neighbouring houses and a hotel were bought. However, space is limited and any changes

Q

are encumbered by the need for archaeologists to hunt down Roman remains. Sixth form areas could do with a make over.

Up until year 9, girls wear pale blue shirts and fuchsia jumpers, changing to navy for years 10 and 11 and smart workwear for the sixth form.

Pastoral care and discipline: All new girls teamed with a peer buddy. Older pupils mentor younger ones. Sixth formers have the liberty of being able to pop into town for lunch. Pupils told us they feel comfortable talking to their tutor or head of year about any problems. A number of pupils we spoke to reported incidents of bullying via Facebook, mobiles and emails and some felt that the school didn't do enough to combat this. The school, however, feels it deals with such episodes firmly and this is backed up by the ISI inspection.

Pupils and parents: Mostly white and middle class, with a small percentage of British born minorities. Some foreign families brought to the UK by work. Most pupils live in Chester, but a good bus network brings pupils in from other parts of Cheshire, the Wirral and 20 per cent from North Wales. Notable old girls include Vivienne Faull, the first woman to become Dean of an English cathedral, and Olympic gymnast Beth Tweddle.

Entrance: Around 40 per cent from The Queen's Lower School, the rest from other preps and state primaries. Girls take 11+ exam in English, maths and verbal reasoning. Written reports from current schools are important and all candidates are interviewed.

Exit: Queens girls are very successful academically, with most making it to redbrick universities. Handful to Oxbridge every year and around 10 per cent to medicine. Steady trickle at 16 to sixth form colleges or boarding.

Money matters: Small number of honorary scholarships are awarded to girls who perform exceptionally well in school's entrance exam. One Hastings bursary awarded every year and one Owen Jones bursary, with preference given to freemen of the City of Chester. Aside from this, the school has a small bursary fund, although when asked the head refused to reveal how much this was worth.

Remarks: Elegant campus within the city walls for girls who aspire both academically and personally. Those who might struggle with the high expectations may be happier elsewhere. One girl told us: 'It's not good here to be able to spell anything with your exam results.'

Queenswood

Shepherd's Way, Brookmans Park, Hatfield, Hertfordshire, AL9 6NS

- Pupils: 405 girls; 205 boarders, 200 day pupils • Ages: 11–18
- Christian/non-denom • Fees: Day £20,070–£23,670; Boarding £28,170–£31,170 pa • Independent

Tel: 01707 602500
Email: admissions@queenswood.org
Website: www.queenswood.org

Principal: Since 2006, Mrs Pauline Edgar BA PGCE (early fifties). Educated at Dudley Girls' High School, then read history at London University. Previously head of sixth form, teaching and learning co-ordinator and head of history and politics at Francis Holland School. Married to Hamish, a maritime lawyer, with two sons and a daughter.

Only the seventh head in the history of Q, as it is affectionately known. A petite, elegant, well-spoken, cheerful principal. Passionate about history, politics and music, enjoys running, swimming and sailing holidays, but acknowledges she hardly has a life outside Queenswood. 'This is not just another school,' she explains. Has added even greater depth at Queenswood in recent years with innovations in the curriculum and organisational structure and opportunities for girls to be 'open-hearted.' Has an easy way with pupils and they appreciate her 'genuine interest.'

Academic matters: A level/Pre-U results very strong. In 2013, 84 per cent A*/B grades and 56 per cent A*/A. At GCSE, 69 per cent A*/A grades. Broad intake, coupled with commendable performance, places school at pinnacle of Hertfordshire's value-added tables. Languages are hot here, with most girls taking two at GCSE and one to A level. Japanese really gaining momentum from year 8 up, thanks to enthusiastic teaching and a cultural visit to Japan (alternative for those staying at home is a week of Japanese visitors and activities). Latin from year 7 and the recommendation is that pupils either continue with it or switch to classical civilisation from year 8. Italian and Spanish also on the menu and girls encouraged to continue studies in their own native languages.

No one is refused a go at a GCSE – 'they're keen to push the academic students as much as possible, but are also prepared to coach and encourage those who are less academic and need a different approach,' notes a parent. Teaching is mainly traditional with ICT increasingly used by all – every girl has a laptop. Sets for maths, French, English and science; class sizes not larger than 24, many smaller (DT scheduled against ICT in year 7 and textiles in year 8 to allow for smaller groups, for example). Pre-U English and history of art going great guns and EPQ alongside A levels (no IB here and no plans). RE growing in popularity with a dozen taking A level and one or two per year to study theology or philosophy at uni (often Cambridge). Government and politics a popular newcomer. Academic scholars have a staff mentor.

About 15 per cent have EAL needs. Support available for those with moderate dyslexia or other, mild SEN. Some 90 on register, many monitored and some receive one-to-one (max two lessons a week) from helpful and enthusiastic learning support co-ordinator. Most have SpLD type difficulties but a few with mild ADD, ADHD or ASD. School earnestly insists that parents matter. 'They're the ones who know the girls, what makes them tick, what causes them to crumble, so we're always keen to discuss issues, strategies and ways forward.'

Games, options, the arts: A school for budding international sports stars – 'I love watching sports and it's a joy to be part of a school that wins,' says principal. Lots of successes at regional and national finals. National hockey players include members of the England junior squad and one recent leaver is now a promising player on the international tennis circuit, another a world-class rower. School is a national LTA clay court centre and hosts the annual national schools' championships. School's tennis team were silver medallists at the 2013 World Schools Tennis Championships and the Lawn Tennis Association recommends it for would-be tennis stars. With 27 courts in all – 12 clay, 13 all-weather and two indoors – 'you can play tennis at any level,' and at almost any time. Budding stars in all disciplines are carefully mentored – help given with diet, fitness (fitness coach onsite who devises individual programmes), training, fixtures etc. Masses of inter-school competitions ensure sport for all. Facilities include large, modern indoor swimming pool, Astroturf hockey pitch, fully equipped fitness suite, aerobics room, professional dance studio and huge sports hall.

More than half learn a musical instrument and many at least two. Ensembles for everything and very enthusiastic teaching – a lively percussion session was in full swing when we visited.

School rock band. Meanwhile drama thrives with half taking LAMDA lessons and awards for actors and public speakers. Lower and upper school productions every year, plus one for GCSE and A level students and scholar plays in between. Rehearsals for Sweeney Todd in the rehearsal space when we visited – great gusto on display. Dramatists visit Edinburgh Fringe.

Thriving 3D art department with its own kiln. Around 10 a year continue to A level (upper sixth students have individual atelier workspaces) and a few move on to art school, while architecture is also popular. Artists are inspired on trips to Milan and Florence.

One of only 20 schools to run the elite Leith's cookery course in preference to food tech – taught right from the beginning (even including lessons on choosing the right wine to accompany). When we visited girls were whipping up macaroni cheese or rack of lamb with a herb crust, depending on ability. Timetabled lessons for years 7 and 8 and a club thereafter. Each student issued with her own set of Sabatier knives, uniform and Leith's 'bible' to keep. Leith's teacher was formerly a chef in the school's own kitchens.

Dance unsurprisingly popular and the school has its own dance team (puts on an annual spectacular and contributes to other school shows too). Model United Nations, Young Enterprise, debating society, plus charity works. Thriving D of E – 25 working on gold, 45 recently achieved bronze. School awarded silver level eco-school status.

Trips galore, especially with London on the doorstep (museums, galleries, Wimbledon etc). Year 9 girls have the opportunity to study for a term overseas, usually Australia or New Zealand. Language visits to Spain and Japan. Sports teams tour all over the world – all 'help the girls to develop independence, work as a team and cope when things don't go right,' says principal. Acknowledgement of the global community though exchange schools in Australia, New Zealand, South Africa, Canada, Japan. Girls work on education projects with schools in Malawi and Zambia. Closer to home, community work in local primary schools and with the elderly – developing 'generosity of spirit and the importance of giving, to counteract the materialism communicated by the media,' principal explains.

Background and atmosphere: Founded in Clapham Park in 1894 and moved to purpose-built neo-Tudor building in 1925 (masses of later additions). Splendid grounds – glorious gardens open to the public at end of May and 120 acres of sports fields and woodland. Two miles from the M25, a 'commutable hour' from London. First-rate Audrey Butler Centre (aka the ABC) houses lecture theatre, language labs and masses of classrooms. Impressive new theatre and associated facilities a jewel in the crown. Science labs recently refurbed. Principal is leading the school in 'quietly fundraising' for a Queenswood Hall to seat the school as an alternative to chapel.

Sixth formers have their own comfortable pad – known as the Pizza Hut, originally thanks to its reminiscent shape and roof, but latterly more for the number of Domino's orders. Beautifully decorated common room – very girl suitable, with squishy leather sofas, large flat-screen TV, chic bar tables and stools and pool tables. Quiet area equipped with computers for studiers, plus kitchen corner for break-time snacks.

Cosy houses with contemporary interior design to please even the pickiest of teenage girls integrate day and boarding pupils – one for years 7 and 8, four for years 9, 10 and 11, plus sixth form houses. Day girls have the flexibility to board when they wish if a bed is free and this is encouraged. Some fixed 'in school' and 'home weekends,' otherwise boarders can spend full weekend at home with choice of Sunday evening or Monday morning return. A few traditionalists would prefer a return to full boarding, but most appreciate this is a move to meet 21st century family needs and preserve the boarding ethos. Girls are smart in grey and purple – 'unfussy and not ridiculously expensive,' approves a parent – with sixth formers in office-style apparel.

Pastoral care and discipline: There is a Queenswood way of doing things, which begins with the principal and 'permeates its way through the rest of the school,' comments a perspicacious parent. Certainly the school day reflects the level-headedness that typifies the school's approach to everything. The day starts with boarders' breakfast at 7.30am, then chapel (school is Methodist foundation but services are non-denom) twice a week at 8.15 and lessons from 8.45 until lunch, with a mid-morning break. Year 7s have a study hour incorporated in their day and all girls participate in their chosen activities – crafts, sport and other clubs – after formal lessons finish at 4.20. 'Balance is key,' says the school.

School's approach is to encourage girls to adapt and assimilate change – 'we applaud having a go,' says the principal. 'We tell them that failure is a part of learning and challenging themselves.' A secure support and pastoral network through housemistresses, tutors and friendly faces. The overwhelmed or anxious are free to confide in any member of staff with whom they feel comfortable. All keep an eye out in particular for girls who are stretching themselves thinly to take advantage of all Queenswood has to offer.

Houses are run by teaching housemistresses, with assistants and a team of academic tutors (around 10 tutees each). Pupil-teacher and parent-teacher relationships relaxed but respectful – 'we work in partnership with parents; we want them to take an active interest in the school and their daughter's education.' Now a large prefect team with specialist responsibilities. Girls who put themselves forward for head girl must present on stage to the whole school and everyone votes for the speech they found most compelling. Principal's choice from then on.

Range of visiting speakers use personal experiences to raise awareness of hard-hitting issues such as drugs, sex, HIV and alcoholism. Girls taking drugs 'lose their right to be a member of the school.' Rewards and sanctions system aims to reward girls for contributions to school life and help them overcome any problems they may have with that. Postcards of praise, gold badges and stars reward pupils; demerits and detentions aim to deter miscreants. Parents involved at early stages.

Food is 'delicious,' enthuses a self-confessed foodie year 8. Serving area a top hotel would crow about, even with its own showcase area where food is cooked to order. Option of outdoor eating in new picnic/BBQ area when weather permits.

Perhaps acknowledging the reason some girls opt to leave for sixth form, school now hosts joint projects with Bedford and Radley but principal says Q girls never have a problem integrating in a mixed environment when they go to university – 'that's just a myth.'

Pupils and parents: 'The girls are self-confident, not arrogant, and very resourceful,' says principal, though adds that there's no particular type. 'They're real individuals, not moulded.' Fifty per cent boarders and 50 per cent day girls. Twenty per cent from abroad – fair proportion from Hong Kong and mainland China, with some expats. All continents represented. EAL taken seriously. Scholars are well recognised around the school – 'there's no envy,' said our eloquent sixth former guide. 'Everyone is inspired by them and shares in their success.'

Very much a 'sleeves rolled up' school for community-minded doers who are happy to get stuck in. Refreshing to find pre-teen girls as excited by camping out and playing hide and seek as they are by beauty and make-up sessions. Sixth formers articulate, poised, feisty but sensible.

Lots of first-time buyers, with both partners working. Masses from London. Drawn by Q's 'warmth and positive energy,' explains one. Strong parents' association much involved with social activities throughout the year and generous contributions to school development projects.

Old Queenswoodians' Association is arguably one of the largest, with more than 4,000 members and branches around the world, ready to befriend and advance Queenswood girls in all sorts of careers and all sorts of places. OQs include Sky Sports presenter Georgie Thompson, actress Helen McCrory, Professor Dame Alison Richard (former vice-chancellor of Cambridge University), journalist Carol Thatcher, tennis player Naomi Cavaday and GB athlete Jodie Williams.

Entrance: Early registration advised, but entry into most years if vacancies permit, either by CE or own entrance exam. Visits welcome by appointment, pupils act as tour guides. Broad ability intake but should be capable of gaining good grades at GCSE. Strong sixth form intake – candidates must get six GCSEs at B or above, with As in the subjects they want to study at A level. Pupils join from a number of schools, including Stormont, St Mary's (NW3), Lyonsdown, Beechwood Park, St Hilda's (Harpenden), Heath Mount, Maltman's Green, Duncombe, Edge Grove and Palmers Green High.

Exit: Ten per cent leave at 16, usually lured by co-ed. Some come back. At 18 majority to wide range of universities eg London unis and Bristol, three to Cambridge in 2013. Many gap years – school offers support with planning.

Money matters: Majority of scholarships are honorary, bringing glory and support rather than cash, though bursaries available in cases of need. Very much looking at what they can offer that will foster girls' talents rather than offering financial sweetener. Music (including organ scholarship), drama, art, tennis and sport scholarships. Occasional bursaries – means-tested. Discount for forces families.

Remarks: A modern girls' school to which others should aspire. A winning combination of traditional values with a broad, forward-looking education to equip bright young women with the integrity and self-belief to make a difference in the world of the future.

Radley College

Radley, Abingdon, OX14 2HR

• Pupils: 685 boys; all board • Ages: 13–18 • C of E • Fees: £32,100 pa • Independent

Tel: 01235 543000
Email: admissions@radley.org.uk
Website: www.radley.org.uk

Warden: Since 2000, Mr Angus McPhail MA (fifties), educated at Radley's local rival Abingdon School and read PPE at University College, Oxford. Previously head of Strathallan School in Perthshire and started life as a banker before switching to teaching ('far more satisfying'). He taught first at Glenalmond, followed by Sedbergh, where he was housemaster. A delightful man with ease of manner, many talents and interests. Someone to whom you could feel entirely confident entrusting your rosy cheeked 13 year old son for the next five years. Years ago we called him a keen cricketer and all-round sportsman; with the passing of time, he now suggests 'active golfer and occasional cricketer'. The years have been kinder to his musical talents. The warden has reunited with the members of his university rock band and, although not ready to give up the day job, they perform '60s, '70s, '80s covers (they 'try to cover five decades'). Wife, Elizabeth, and three children; he's fond of children – 'You can't be a good teacher unless you like children – and I've met lots of people in the profession who don't like them'.

Retiring in July 2014. His successor will be John Moule, currently head of Bedford School. A historian with a first from Oxford, he has also taught at Dean Close School and Stowe and is married with three children.

Academic matters: If it ain't broke, don't fix it. Not a school constantly striving to reinvent itself or pilot the latest educational strategies (sat tight while the IB and Pre-U were adopted at similar schools). But in its rigour, it has become something of a maverick. Teachers under pressure to deliver and results are frankly astonishing, given the entrance criteria. All A levels – AS and A2 – are sat at the end of upper sixth. Hadn't realised this policy would mark them out as different from almost every school in the UK. Their reasoning? 'We're boys only,' says the warden with a dismissive gesture, referring to the masculine gender's late development, 'and it frees up weeks of time in the lower sixth that would have to be used for revision.' The school's outstanding A level results – nearly 70 per cent A*/A grades in 2012 – indicate they're getting it right. Virtually all boys sit four full A levels, with the fourth in a contrasting subject. One reason for not adopting the Pre-U is the school's reluctance to go back to only three subjects in upper sixth: 'We get boys who choose three sciences and history ... and then go on to read history at university. And our experience is that their ability to get a university offer is enhanced by doing four subjects.' More than half of sixth formers take the Extended Project Qualification – a 6000 word essay.

Languages outstanding, no mean achievement at a boys' school. First years do French, Latin and a choice of Spanish, German or Greek. Russian also available 'if you're good at languages,' said a pupil. A locum comes in to teach some Mandarin. Up to 50 boys take Latin for GCSE plus a healthy handful of Greek – with exceptional results. French (and maths) IGCSE can be taken a year early, with boys then sweeping straight on to AS. No separate sciences at GCSE, but a good enough foundation for outstanding A level results and a steady stream of successful natural scientists at Cambridge. History enormously popular – almost every boy chooses to do it for GCSE. In 2012, 91 per cent A*/A GCSE grades overall. History and maths the two most popular A levels with super results year in, year out. Politics and economics also draw A level crowds. Sciences less so.

Not SEN pioneers, but learning support department (SENCo plus several part-timers) provides help for 120 'able boys whose progress may be held back by a learning difficulty'. Heart-warming praise from parents about the careful and unobtrusive support dyslexic sons are given. A school where things like beautiful handwriting still matter – if your son's fingertips are soldered to his laptop, you may wish to look elsewhere (boys not allowed to bring own laptops to school during their first year).

Games, options, the arts: A vigorous dollop of games a key ingredient in the Radley recipe. Rugby, hockey, cricket and rowing soar over all lesser games. Also hot on racquet sports: tennis (boys say the coaching is 'now' very good), squash, racquets, fives, badminton and 'real tennis'. Thursdays set aside for these and other minor sports including golf, cross-country, polo, swimming, basketball and (limited) football. Immaculate playing fields and generally wondrous sports facilities including five star sports pavilion with 360 degree view, nine hole golf course, superb track. Boys explained earnestly that the rugby posts are the tallest in England – they aren't, but please don't tell them. Rowing taken very seriously with amazing new rowing machine, like a Torchwood facility out of Dr Who, housed in its own building. Rowers consistently among the top British schools VIIIs at Henley and in the National Schools' Regatta over the past five years.

Beautiful theatre and Silk Hall recital room (formerly the main theatre). Music tech room and plenty of practice spaces. A level musicians thin on the ground but their results (including music tech) are first rate. Radley's legendary Piano Extravaganza involves more than 50 boys of all musical abilities. Twenty-one pianists play on seven pianos in a sort of piano orchestra – the school commissions special music for it each year. Fabulous art exhibited far and wide throughout the school, though the art rooms themselves strangely tidy and almost bare. Parents gush over the quality of the dramatic productions. 'Central Hour', 1.30-2.30pm, daily set aside for 'music, culture and creative activities', ie orchestra, choir, drama rehearsals, music lessons, but also sailing, sub-aqua, debating.

As we so often find in boys' only schools, chaps dip their toes into streams they wouldn't touch with a bargepole at a co-ed establishment. So here we find first year pupils taking French cookery and pilates as part of their Wednesday afternoon carousel of activities. Lots of grand visiting speakers; one parent mentioned her son's creative writing being reviewed by OR Andrew Motion and later Carol Ann Duffy. Annual expeditions to help children in Romania and build homes in Southern India. D of E – goes without saying. CCF compulsory in year 10, to most boys' regret.

Background and atmosphere: Boys only, all boarding, traditional – but half as many boys as you'll find at Eton, so a very different product. Understated rather than flash – a fine wine rather than overpriced bubbly. Navigation tricky for new boys, with the mixture of old and new, eg The Donut – a futuristic round structure (handsome, useful – and at odds with the rest of the architecture); new building housing history and politics classrooms and exhibition space completed in 2013.

Tucked safely up a drive on the suburban outskirts of Abingdon, 'away from temptation – a bit like a prep school,' said a mum. The serenity can be an irritant to some sixth formers, but permission to go into Oxford helps satisfy their urges to slay dragons (and meet up with Downe House girls). Featureless entrance drive (school disagrees: 'The avenue of horse chestnut trees lining the front drive is much admired by visitors') reminiscent of the dismal approach to Disneyworld before you reach the Magic Kingdom. Emerge through the castle-like entrance archway, though, and a hidden world is revealed. Swathes of mellow red brick (1720) and Victorian Gothic overlook 800 acres of prime Oxfordshire, totally self-contained and away from the rest of the world.

School founded in 1847 by the Revs William Sewell (don at Exeter College) and Robert Congleton Singleton on Oxford college model – with cloisters, quads and dons (teachers). Boys look like mini-undergraduates circa 1962 in their black gowns. The gowns, much like burkhas, are 'weird at first, but then you hardly notice them'. Individuality and status marked by style of school tie – about 80 of them. School tuckshop where pupils have their own 'jam account' – also sells uniform and other necessities.

Pastoral care and discipline: Much emphasis on 'character', values, decency, leadership – and it's not just talk. Boys live in one of 10 Socials (from Latin socius, meaning companion, since you asked) inventively named by the letters of the alphabet, so we have A, B, C, D, E, F, G, H, and two newer ones – J and K (what's wrong with 'I'?). Shells (first years) in cubicles, but single rooms with hotel-style safes (and fridges in upper sixth!) from then onward. We hear that G is currently 'sporty' and H 'academic'. 'Cocoa' is both a drink and a formal part of the Radley timetable – all boys in the house gather at 9pm 'to gel' over the warm bevie. Privis (exeats) each half term, but boys can go out any Sunday after chapel. Saturday nights made special by socials with pizza etc. Youngest boys kept very busy on weekends, older boys given more rope. Whole school squeezes into lovely chapel four evenings a week at 7pm: 'Chapel was quite important to my son,' a parent told us – 'never a nuisance'. Vast majority of staff live on campus in school accommodation – helps attract the best and brightest.

Junior Common Room (school bar) serves limited alcohol with a meal for 17 and 18 year olds, and housemasters may share a beer from time to time with their sixth formers. Abuse of these privileges leads to punishments ranging from £30

fine plus four hours' 'labour' (hit them where it hurts) up to losing some holiday time. Boys adamant that drugs not a problem here, and Mr McPhail agrees – 'More difficult is the boy who repeatedly offends in small ways'. School works hard to encourage boys to be nice to one another: 'It's not easy!' Parent after parent praised this aspect of the school ('110 per cent brilliant,' said one). Two boys expelled for bullying not long ago, according to our guides: 'It's treated more seriously than ... than ... anything,' they told us, with a touch of awe. Much care taken with youngest boys. Boys in lower sixth are mentors (previously 'nannies') for two or three 13 year olds – old and young both benefit.

Pupils and parents: Mostly British 'because of the entrance system,' says the Warden (foreigners come along too late) and because it flies under much of the overseas market's radar. Wealthy but unpretentious: reverse snobbery more than a small part of many parents' choosing this school. ORs include Andrew Motion, Lord (Richard) Wilson of Dinton (former Cabinet Secretary), Lord Scarman, Lord Craig of Radley, Lt Col Rupert Thorneloe, Clive Stafford Smith, Ted Dexter, former world rackets champion James Male, England captain Andrew Strauss, chairman of John Lewis Charlie Mayfield, chief executive of Next Simon Wolfson and Sandy Nairne, director of the National Portrait Gallery.

Entrance: Names down at birth still the wisest £100 you'll ever spend. One of the few remaining first come, first served schools where it really does make sense to phone the school from the delivery ward. When your son is 10 you'll be asked to cough up an acceptance fee (£700 at the mo) if you really want the place (55 per cent pass required at CE, though some flexibility in individual subjects). 20 to 25 latecomers are cherry picked from the Warden's List. The bar is higher for these laggards, with the school looking for clever all-rounders – 'go-gettery, make-the-most-of-the-school types,' specifies the Warden, whose talents are established via a 20 minute interview; no exams ('We do give them an aptitude test to keep them occupied on the day, but it's not that important – the recommendation from the prep counts for more').

No 11+ exam ('A lot of boys haven't got going yet at 11 – or even at 13!') or pre-testing annoyances. No open days – senior staff meet parents all year. Boys applying from state schools sit Radley's own entrance papers instead of CE. More places available at sixth form than in past – now up to around eight boys join at 16+, including one via the HMC's scheme for pupils from Eastern Europe.

Exit: Lost only one boy after GCSEs in 2013. At 18 a minority of boys go straight to university. More take a gap year, with or without resits. Leeds the most popular destination (why?) followed by Bristol, Exeter, Edinburgh and Newcastle. Fifteen to 18 to Oxbridge most years.

Money matters: Mainly honorific scholarships (up to 10 per cent, but often less) awarded each year at 13+ for academics (10 years of past papers cheerfully supplied on the Radley website), art, drama, music and sport prowess. Can be topped up by means-tested bursaries. Foundation awards of up to full fees available for a few extremely gifted boys of modest means. Academic, music and organ scholarships available for boys joining at 16. In the process of raising a new fund focused on the children of those killed or wounded on active service: up to full fees, will educate younger children at preps and girls at Downe House or St Mary's Calne.

Remarks: The most traditional of schools, but also intimate, academic, robust, kind. The connoisseur's choice saunters into another decade riding high.

R

Reading Blue Coat School

Holme Park, Sonning Lane, Sonning on Thames, Berkshire, RG4 6SU

• Pupils: 740 pupils (650 boys plus 90 girls in sixth form) • Ages: 11-18 boys; 16-18 girls • C of E • Fees: £14,010 pa • Independent

Tel: 01189 441005
Email: admissions@rbcs.org.uk
Website: www.rbcs.org.uk

Headmaster: Since 2008, Mr Michael Windsor BA (forties). Read modern languages at Durham, trifled with publishing and then, accompanied by his double bass, taught English in Italy, where he found his vocation. Returned to England, took a PGCE at the Institute of Education, London and, after a deputy headship at Royal Grammar School, Guildford, is enjoying riverside life in Sonning with his wife Shanti and their two daughters. He is open and charmingly unstuffy and speaks modishly of powers devolved to subject leaders in matters such as choice of GCSE or IGCSE, yet one is in no doubt that his clear vision for Blue Coat is a driving force. The double bass that stands in the corner of Mr Windsor's huge study, somewhat distressed from its travels in Europe, is not for show – the head plays in the school orchestras and a jazz quartet. As the bulldozers rumbled outside he explained that from the building site, formerly 1950s classrooms too far gone to save, would rise a new teaching block (now open). New classrooms notwithstanding, no plans to increase pupil numbers or go fully co-ed; the aim is to provide the 'very best' for the school's existing population of around 700.

Mr Windsor speaks with quiet passion about the importance of Blue Coat 'staying true to its founding principles' and although the boys who enter at 11 are not, for the most part, 'indigent', the school offers up to six 100 per cent bursaries – impressive for a foundation without significant endowments. The chair of governors benefited from the bursary scheme as a 'foundationer' at the school and much work goes into encouraging candidates to apply. Links with local primaries and (since the economic demographic of Sonning may not be fertile ground) outreach work in central Reading schools are pursued with genuine purpose.

Academic matters: All the usual subjects plus a few unusual are taught here with results that are going from strength to strength. In 2013, 70 per cent A*/A grades at I/GCSE. Currently IGCSEs in maths and English, but geography is next and science set to follow. Sciences, maths and economics most popular A2 choices and leaver destinations reflect this, but the takers of English, art, history of art and languages are equally successful, though fewer in number. In 2013, 70 per cent A*/B and nearly 43 per cent A*/A grades at A level. Enrichment opportunities in the sixth form include Mandarin, visiting speakers and the school's own PLUS course, which covers giving a presentation, writing an extended essay and effective note-taking as well as careers, personal statements, finance etc. Lessons are a boy-friendly 35 minutes, Latin is compulsory until year 9 and all take RS and IT short courses. We were delighted to open a door off the library (very quietly) and see a whole class of boys relaxed on beanbags reading. Once a week for the first two years all boys read books of their choice in these peaceful surroundings.

The world of geology has much to thank Reading Blue Coat for – the serendipitous result of a former teacher's passion for rocks is a dedicated lab full of fascinating specimens. Boys take a taster course in year 9 and many go on to study geology (via a Welsh exam board) for GCSE and beyond. Variations on the usual theme in the sixth form are classical civilisation, DT, government and politics, performance studies, sports and physical education and psychology.

The beautifully produced 'creative arts' publication, The Whetstone, is a delight to read and contains writing and art of exceptional quality. In fact pupils' artistic endeavours are on display all over the school – a particular talent for portraiture, with over-sized faces to be seen everywhere. The huge canvases that decorate the dining room are really impressive and a wonderful papier-mâché giant's head greets visitors in reception.

All are screened at 11 and 16, learning support department provides assistance for those with mild SEN (dyslexia mainly) and pupils who require it are given extra time in the entrance exam.

Games, options, the arts: Given its wonderful Thames-side location and fine new boathouse, one might expect trophy cabinets bursting with rowing glory but, so far, Abingdon and Eton are beating them to it. Instead Reading Blue Coat's sporting successes take place on the soccer, rugby, hockey and cricket fields with a number of boys also playing at county and national level. Oh, and the synchronised swimming – a sixth form girl is in the UK squad, but while the school gives her every support and is proud of her success, it's not on the sporting timetable (although photos of the squad of sixth form boys she trained to perform for a charity fund-raiser were rather fetching).

CCF is very strong here and popular with boys and girls – much orderly drilling was taking place outside during our visit and cadets have represented the whole movement at national remembrance events. Impressive public speaking record – junior and senior teams have orated their way to become local, national and world champions in recent years. Music is at the heart of the school – all boys are auditioned for the choir and learn a musical instrument for the first two years. Musicians perform at the popular 'Swing into Summertime' concert for parents who picnic on the lawns and listen to the latest talent; also a chance for school bands to play, 'if they're good enough'. Riding, shooting, archery, politics, Young Enterprise, D of E, fencing, scuba diving, creative writing, journalism and technology are on offer alongside drama productions and sports activities. Sixth formers help in local primary schools and with sports coaching as part of the Sports Leadership Award. As the head put it, 'We want every pupil to find their niche'; as a pupil put it, 'There's a ridiculous amount of things to do here'.

Background and atmosphere: 're'ading' may be in the name, but put whatever mental picture it engenders aside and think instead of Wind in the Willows or Three Men in a Boat. Better now? Reading Blue Coat is in the delightful riparian village of Sonning-on-Thames – ancient bridges, half-timbered and thatched houses, tea shops and, at certain times of the day, gridlock in its narrow roads. Founded in 1646 by local merchant Richard Aldworth to offer education for the poor children of Reading, the school moved to its current site 300 years later. The traditional uniform of long blue coat (hence the school's name), breeches, yellow stockings and buckled shoes is now only worn on high days by prefects – girls and boys.

The school sits amid cricket and rugby pitches (yet more across the road), and wooded grounds roll down to the Thames and the new boathouse. The classical proportions of the Regency mansion that once stood here (a picture in the head's study) fell victim to a serious case of Victorian mock Gothicism and sprouted towers and mullions. Not at all sinister on a bright spring day but could be rather a brooding presence on a winter's afternoon. Nevertheless a striking building, and the brick and flint exterior is more in keeping with the local vernacular. In the entrance hall polished panelling, huge display of fresh flowers and honours boards full of names, just as one would expect. The charming 'buttery', formerly the boarders' dining room, overlooks the gardens and is the venue for many musical events including jazz concerts featuring (among others) Mr Windsor

R

and his trusty double bass. Above is a confusion of back staircases and half landings, and every so often a delightful teaching room complete with oversized stone fireplace and arched windows framing ancient trees. A slightly makeshift feel to this part of the school, not surprising as a number of departments are camping here as building works progress.

Considerable effort (signs indicating a one-way system?) has been made to achieve what interior designers call 'flow' – but as the bell went during our visit it was more of a tidal surge, as busy boys channelled to their next lesson. Staff and pupils stoic about this – the new building, now open, worth the temporary disruption. It has 23 new classrooms for several departments and a middle school common-room.

Two separate receptions (one for visitors, one for pupils) and a scattering of rather functional teaching blocks must make the first few weeks rather confusing for new boys (and girls). 'I couldn't understand how everyone got to the lessons before me,' said our guide, 'until I discovered the short cuts.'

Pastoral care and discipline: The recent ISI report is enthusiastic in its praise for pastoral care, an opinion endorsed by parents and the pupils we spoke to. The school has active and well thought through policies to foster vertical as well as horizontal bonding and pupils were keen to endorse the fact that these work in practice as well as in theory – 'You don't feel so small as a first year,' one said. Four houses, named after the school's founders and benefactors, are the focus for competitive sport, music – house singing – and charity fund-raising. Tutor groups comprise two years so, for instance, new boys mix with those from the year above. One guide, who had come to RBC from a local primary, remembers how thrilled he was to receive a letter from his future tutor group in the term before he joined. Girls coming into the sixth form have at least three taster days and get to meet their subject teachers and fellow pupils. Our guide felt that the school had made every effort to ease her transition from a small girls' independent and relations between sixth form boys and their new classmates seem mature and appreciative.

Pupils and parents: From roughly a 30 mile radius, taking in Reading, Maidenhead, Wokingham, Camberley, Wallingford, Fleet, Twyford and villages between. A fair few first-time buyers. The split of boys coming in from state primaries and local preps, such as Crosfields and St Edwards (Reading) and Holme Grange (Wokingham), is pretty equal and bodes well for balanced, un-cliquey year groups. Girls come from schools with no sixth form such as Cranford or for a change from single sex education. Fees roughly a couple of thousand per annum lower than local competition but this is regarded as a nice bonus rather than a deciding factor for most parents. Former pupils (Old Blues) include television presenters Jeremy Kyle and Matt Allwright (Rogue Traders), Reading West MP Alok Sharma, round-the-world yachtsman Mike Golding OBE and the actress Natalie Dormer (Casanova, The Tudors).

Entrance: Just under three applicants for every place at 11 and two at 16. Interview with headmaster or senior colleague, entrance examination in January comprising English, maths and verbal reasoning plus reference from current school. A further competitive intake at 16+: around 30 girls and five boys enter the lower sixth each year. Entry at this age requires verbal and non-verbal reasoning tests plus a minimum of seven GCSEs grade C and above, with at least Bs in the subjects to be studied at A level.

Exit: About 85 per cent go through to sixth form. Nearly all to first choice university (Bath, Birmingham, Bristol, Cardiff, Exeter, Leeds, Loughborough, Nottingham...), four to Oxbridge in 2013 and most, but not all, to study heavy duty subjects such as aeronautical engineering, medicine, maths and physics. Sports science and, not surprisingly, geology also popular.

Money matters: Cheap-ish, as Basil Fawlty would say – fees lower than at a few prep schools in the area. Scholarships for art, music, academics – up to 25 per cent of fees – and a number of means-tested bursaries of up to 100 per cent. Two foundation scholarships awarded annually on merit and means-tested (up to 100 per cent of fees).

Remarks: No shortage of other good schools to choose from in this area, state and independent, so why do parents opt for Reading Blue Coat? 'It's down to earth', 'friendly and approachable', 'genuinely interested in developing my son's talents'. Maybe small is beautiful or perhaps it's the civilising influence of the sixth form girls, but this school is not inclined to spar with the big beasts in the Berks/Oxon independent jungle. Yet Reading Blue Coat wears its laurels lightly and remains true to its founding principles; it continues to put all its efforts into providing a first class all-round education for the boys and girls fortunate enough to go there.

The Red Maids' School

Westbury Road, Westbury-on-Trym, Bristol, BS9 3AW

- Pupils: 490 girls, all day • Ages: 11–18 • Not denominational
- Fees: £11,700 pa • Independent

Tel: 01179 622641
Email: admin@redmaids.bristol.sch.uk
Website: www.redmaids.co.uk

Headmistress: Since 2001, Mrs Isabel Tobias BA PGCE (50). Read English at New Hall, Cambridge and started work in publishing. Began teaching at Henrietta Barnett, London from where she moved to Royal High School, Bath as head of English then deputy head before taking up headship at Red Maids'. Keen to be forward-looking and modernise, she nevertheless really listens to her girls and respects their sense of tradition. Keeps the school's original red capes and bonnets for a coveted few to wear in the annual founder's day procession through Bristol.

Her own children being largely off her hands (a daughter, who went to UCL to study biology from Red Maids' and a son doing A levels at Queen Elizabeth Hospital), she has a bit more time to enjoy Bristol's theatre and do more walking and reading. Deeply involved in all that goes on in school, she is obviously proud of the girls' achievements in all fields.

Terrific new sixth form house has materialised under her management as well as numerous exciting projects, such as a joint observation of cosmic rays with Bristol Uni using equipment on Red Maids' roof, funded jointly by school and parents, with year 12 physicists processing and interpreting data. She was also responsible for introducing the IB, which now has a take up of about a quarter of sixth formers. South west chair of the Girls' Schools Association and an ISI inspector.

Academic matters: The only Bristol independent offering A levels and IB; some A level girls also enter for the Extended Project Qualification with distinguished results. Choice of languages includes French, German, Spanish and Russian with everyone doing at least one to GCSE. Psychology, English and history consistently popular A level subjects alongside maths, biology and chemistry, with a proportion of girls moving on to medical school every year. Latin but no Greek. All girls take either three separate sciences or do the dual award science plus additional science.

Some pretty impressive GCSE results recently with 43 per cent at A*, 70 per cent A/A*, putting the school in the top 100 nationally in 2013. English, maths and science all done as

R

IGSCEs 'because they are more academically demanding', with English thus avoiding the recent mess up on grades and doing exceptionally well into the bargain. Splitting the sixth form between IB and A level means groups are really too small to identify trends, but results have gone steadily upwards over the last few years. Average 38 points in IB in 2013; 58 per cent A*/A grades at A level.

Choices at both are wide enough for most needs with lots of creative stuff. Shiny new food technology kitchen installed in summer 2012. Resistant materials (the tough stereotypically male bit of technology, harder for schools to do as it's expensive) is incorporated into textiles, which may look more girly but is certainly not sidelined. Surprisingly for a 'not religious' school, a goodish take up of philosophy and ethics. Spirituality and 'thoughtfulness' definitely encouraged. Even its small group of IB students earn it a 'top IB school' status.

A small proportion of SEN but the school is 'accessible' and has one partially sighted pupil, supplying every required facility and the few dyslexics are well and considerately catered for. Almost no need for EAL but there is a Talented and Gifted programme targeted to stretch the brightest. The weekly sixth form Academic Symposium is part of this, presented alternately by girls and academic outsiders on topics such as stem cell issues. Similar initiatives in place for younger groups too.

Games, options, the arts: Enormous sports hall with dance studio and fitness centre upstairs for 'unsporty' sixth formers as well as acres of Astroturf. Endless teams for hockey, netball, etc plus football and some high flying tennis stars. Options include fencing, basketball, and gymnastics. Staff are very hot on encouraging girls to join local sports clubs as well. Strong music department includes iMacs (Sibelius and recently Logik, ie music writing and multitrack recording programmes) for composition. Over half the girls learn a musical instrument (including singing at a very high standard with choir, chamber choir and barber shop group). Three orchestras, ensembles etc and frequent musical productions on stage, though girls looked a little surprised when asked about pop groups. Absolutely fabulous art department, and that's saying something in Bristol, where the competition at school level is strong. Some delectable fashion design too; dresses made from sweet wrappers are popular say sweet-toothed girls.

It was interesting to see several girls sporting neat black moustaches in preparation for the evening performance of Twelfth Night at the new Bristol Tobacco Factory Theatre. Big adaptable performance space in the 300 building (named for school's 300th birthday) with an energetic new American head of drama who is galvanizing the school's already enthusiastic performances. Quite a high proportion of male staff, giving plenty of good role models. A well-tried programme of annual concerts, joint productions with QEH and an annual whole school festival alternating between drama and dance allows girls at all stages to perform at progressive levels without missing out on games.

Working library stocked with books, rather than computers and gadgets (plentiful DVDs too) with some working space for after-school homework, supervised at all times. Masses of clubs – a whole wallful of club posters in the dining room and trips of every sort both educational (exchanges or China with QEH boys) and philanthropic, and some impressive international links: Emma Willard School in USA and Pymble Ladies' College in Melbourne, Australia. They really did build a small school in Cambodia and start a charity for Moldovan children. They do pretty well in all the school speaking, debating and the like competitions and have all sorts of whizzy projects such as a link with local GKN Aerospace where there's an ex Red Maid 'young engineering ambassador'. Career advice includes the gamut of conferences and top local speakers from all disciplines. Special conference on medical and engineering careers open to all SW schools now and annual event.

Background and atmosphere: The original 'red Maids' benefited in1634 from the generosity of Bristol mayor and MP, John Whitson, who having been widowed thee times and lost a daughter from each marriage, died, leaving no heirs but bequeathed £90 per year to provide a dwelling house for 'one grave, painful woman and modest woman' and 'forty poor women children' who would be taught to support themselves. As, amongst other things, he imported red dye, they were to 'go apparelled in red cloth.' It is the oldest surviving girls' school in the country and moved from inner Bristol at beginning of the 20th century to its present 12 acre site. Wide lawns and green Astroturf shaded by a winding avenue of lime trees are edged by an array of purpose-built school buildings centring on the pillared mansion bought with the site. An impressive array including the huge 1930s '300' building housing much of the teaching areas, the 1950s Denmark Hall and airy 2011 sixth form centre complete with teaching and recreation areas, cafeteria, 'film theatre', as the girls call a resources room, and careers library. Sixth formers have special electronic passes so that it really is their exclusive domain. WW2 air raid shelter is hidden under a bank in the grounds, complete with anti Nazi graffiti – a popular attraction for local primary schools.

While valuing its purely altruistic beginnings, the school is forward thinking in all respects and firmly 'not' rather than 'non'-denominational with assemblies covering all kinds of issues, though the head is supportive of individual religious observance.

Girls were quite enthusiastic about the food: much healthier than it used to be and things like Caesar salad made specially for you as well as masses of pasta etc. Breakfast club runs from 7.45am.

Pastoral care and discipline: Houses are named after John Whitson's merchant ships but main pastoral care is through form teachers who meet girls twice daily. Excellent 'big girl/little girl' buddying system – Mrs Tobias was persuaded to let them keep the name – for new arrivals. 'Big girls' meet their new girls on induction day and write to them in the summer holidays as well as shepherding them through their first term. It's all part of the culture of respect for each other's feelings that she sees as instrumental with dealing with bullying. 'Of course girls are sometimes unkind and sometimes upset', but staff talk to all concerned as long as they know about it and it's tackled along with other life skills in PHSE. The girls we met say bullying doesn't happen! Head of year 7 oversees transition from wide range of state and independent feeder schools; pastoral evenings in autumn term for years 7, 8, 9 and 10. The senior tutor is in charge of pastoral for whole senior school including sixth form. Plenty of chances to 'develop leadership potential' as girls can be appointed to positions in houses, school clubs and tutor groups as well as head girls, head almoners, games captains and house captains. Sanctions include detentions or at worst suspension or expulsion, but the school favours a positive behaviour code and encouragement. A clear list of policies and appeals procedure on the website means it's easy to know where you are with things.

Pupils and parents: Friendly, open girls from a wide social and ethnic background, though the majority look distinctly English. Though sounding quite sophisticated, and some very academic, girls on the whole look natural and not artificially grown up.

Girls look neat, wear simple red jumpers over a white blouse with red skirts for ages 11-16, not expensive though there were some crumpled pleats and current jumper goes out of shape easily according to one parent. Sensibly interpreted dress code for sixth formers. Parental discussion group meets regularly with head. Former pupils include novelists Susan Lewis and Kate Sedley, TV anthropologist and presenter of Coast Dr Alice Roberts, Helen Marsden, winner of 2004 WISE (Women into

R

Science and Engineering) excellence award, and Executive Editor of the Daily Express Tina Moran.

Entrance: Year 7 intake has increased recently to around 75 per annum. Candidates (including those at junior school) sit entrance exams in January in English, maths, verbal and non-verbal reasoning. Brief interview with headmistress for all including short presentation on subject of girls' choosing. For sixth form entry, minimum six grade B GCSEs with A*/Bs in chosen IB or AS level subjects plus interview with director of sixth form.

Exit: Some leave after year 11 for colleges or co-ed or maintained sixth forms but majority stay despite the advent of academies and free schools in Bristol. All sixth formers go to uni with a regular flow to medical schools and around five per cent annually to Oxbridge.

Money matters: One of the very few girls' school with a good scholarship and bursary programme, thanks to the founder; all development is paid for, not funded by loans, so it's really financially stable. Two major awards of up to 100 per cent, plus two music and one sports scholarship awarded at 11+. Entrance scholarships at year 9 (13+) and sixth form (year 12) for external candidates. A number of bursaries available.

Remarks: Far from a stuffy school, despite its historical cachet and strong academic record. 'Staff care hugely' and 'girls are genuinely proud of their school,' say parents. It feels like a school on the up. Head definitely has her eye on the future of her girls.

Redland High School

Linked school: Redland High Junior School, BS6 7EF

Redland Court, Redland Court Road, Bristol

- Pupils: 450 girls; all day • Ages: 11–18 • Non–denom
- Fees: £11,085 pa • Independent

Tel: 01179 245796
Email: admissions@redlandhigh.com
Website: www.redlandhigh.com

Headmistress: Since 2006, Mrs Caroline Bateson BA MA PGCE (early fifties), a historian. Previously deputy head down the road at Badminton, where she rose from her post as head of history. She is also an independent inspector. Her husband being deputy head at Queen Elizabeth's Hospital (all boys) down the road means the schools have strong links, with plenty of activities such as debating and a very grand annual joint ball, generally in one of Bristol's most expensive hotels. One duaghter at university. She still manages to teach a bit of history, including A Level. After seven years at Redland, she has no current plans to move.

Academic matters: For a small school there's pretty impressive choice, with 27 subjects at A Level and 25 at GCSE. Parents see the school as definitely having an academic bias but insist it's not a hothouse. As a small school in a volatile market, Redland necessarily takes quite a wide range of abilities and does extremely well for them. Staff are hot at spotting a high flier resting on laurels and issuing a challenge. Stimulus for small groups at A level comes from having several different teachers per subject, nearly all of them inspiring, as well as from the peer group.

They cunningly avoided the 2012 debacle in English grades by moving to IGCSE in which girls did 'even better than expected'. There's talk of moving to IGCSE in ICT and maths, though coming national changes mean the exam future is a bit of a mystery. Some pretty spectacular individual results at GCSE with six or so getting more than 10 A*s; girls do between nine and 12 subjects. Everyone does at least one modern lang and some do two as well as Latin. Greek available when needed. Overall, 65 per cent of I/GCSE grades A*/A in 2013.

Redland will put on an A level for only one or two candidates. Particularly spectacular results in fine art and French A level (masses of trips and exchanges help, as do things like debating in French with other schools) and a fairish sprinkling of A/A* (35 per cent in 2013). A clever girl can do really well here. Lots of stimulating stuff via the gifted and talented co-ordinator, though Mrs Bateson stresses no one is excluded from things targeting the top layer.

Lots of take up for minority subjects – Latin, music, HE and textiles, ICT etc though they sometimes don't always get much of a look in at A Level. Surprisingly, religion and drama are more popular than physics and ICT. Native speakers can take exams in their own language.

SEN help for those identified when everyone is tested in year 7 mostly delivered in small group work. Individual programme for dyslexic pupils is coordinated by SENCo, who is also junior school deputy head.

Games, options, the arts: Music reigns supreme! Friends of the school recently commissioned a well-known composer, who is a school governor, to write the anthem for their 130th celebrations ('absolutely beautiful,' according to one aspiring girl composer who had been lucky enough to have a few lessons from him.) Choirs sing all over – Paris, Bristol Cathedral, Wembley – were finalists at the Barbican for the school choir of the year and are in for the BBC Songs of Praise trophy. Eleven different ensemble groups include a gospel choir. The music school (a three-floored house down the road) bursts with practice rooms, instruments and IT, though large performance space is the school hall or gym. Huge take-up of instrumental teaching results partly from masses of introductory lessons in the junior school and year 7. Big groups for music GCSE though A level tends to be only for the few really dedicated musicians.

Drama really flourishes. A new take on Romeo and Juliet played the Edinburgh fringe with lots of home-grown music. Masses of GCSE and A level candidates too. The art department, now under new leadership, is exceptional. In three floors of its own imaginatively converted house, every scrap of space is crammed with activity, pictures and installations. Girls gain proper drawing and painting skills with life classes etc but also branch into sculpture, printing and some remarkable portraiture. It's like a mini art college.

Public speaking, debating and Model UN etc encouraged. Half year 12 get involved in Young Enterprise scheme, which lets loose hitherto untapped entrepreneurial skills and D of E, orienteering et al on offer. No sports hall but a big old-fashioned multi-purpose gym, which serves drama and music as well, with an extremely popular climbing wall. Most clubs are in lunch hour but rehearsals and some sports happen at any time at weekends and evening as the school has full-time caretaking and is always available. Seven hockey and eight netball teams benefiting from having good playing fields at Golden Hill with Astroturf, proper changing rooms, and a classroom. Quite a few county etc players and even one national player – for Poland in squash! Sport doesn't get quite as high a profile as music and drama but bookish sixth formers are now encouraged to use their own fitness centre. Dance is popular too.

Background and atmosphere: Founded in 1882 and moved in 1885 to Redland Court, a striking 18th century mansion, now full of bright girls, perched on a terraced hilltop in the second leafiest of Bristol's leafy suburbs. Its city location has dictated a cunning jigsaw of unobtrusive facilities. Apart from the rooms in Redland

R

Court and the Hall, sixth form house and art, even the stunning library is shoehorned into a classical shell. The school has also taken over about six of the rather grand family homes around to house art, sixth form and junior music. It's managed over the years to insinuate a fair amount of purpose-built extensions (all the classrooms and labs built between 1930s and 1950s) while retaining the sweeping terraces and gardens as netball and tennis courts plus a few corners of formal garden and secluded arbour. The school hall looks like a chapel, though it was really a very upmarket stable and has kept the slim metal pillars originally at the end of each stall. It serves as dining room as well as everything else and has a streamlined server area adjoining with plentiful school food, the puddings particularly appealing. The main door has 'So hateth she derknesse' above it, – a reference to the daisy or 'day's eye'. A daisy seems a curious choice of school emblem, but 'day's eyes' according to Chaucer, seek the sun – current girls seem unlikely to shrink from limelight.

Space being at a premium, has produced some interesting solutions: a sunken but definitely up-to-date IT centre, open from 8am so girls can start early. Classrooms, including labs (looking quite old fashioned but bristling with equipment and busy girls) are piled up behind the hall. The sixth form house, across a quiet suburban back road, feels more like student centre than a school. Lots of casual lounging areas, kitchen, 'deli' where meals can be ordered and coffee etc on tap pretty well all day, and flexible small teaching areas. Sixth formers wear what they like 'within reason'. 'reason' in this case is broad-minded and not averse to heavyish make-up, but staff assert that they look fantastically smart when called upon to officiate at concerts etc.

The magnificent iron gate below the flight of terraces in front of the main house is open morning and afternoon for pupils and staff and at times for junior pupils. There are two other entrances, but the only one we could find lurks half way up a precipitous hill climb with (thank goodness) a miniscule parking area inside, but this is a free parking area of Bristol so quite a few parents drop off by car and then bus themselves into the city for work

The library is the star of the show, perhaps the nicest school library this GSG reviewer has yet seen. Open until 5.30pm with cosy quiet areas for swotting, separate computer suites, help on hand and a comfy-looking carpeted story area round a giant rocking chair for junior visitors. Careers clearly taken seriously, well resourced and posters everywhere advertising information sessions on UCAS, entry to medical school etc.

Pastoral care and discipline: Lack of space means classrooms double up as social areas at all levels. Pupils actually have trad desks in their class bases but lunch times are too busy for them to spend much time there. Parents stress the extremely good pastoral care and thought that any issues (bullying, drugs et al) were well and quickly dealt with before they became problems. A girl might be expelled for taking drugs but only as a last resort if she couldn't be helped. Pastoral care is through form mistresses, and school houses are mainly competitive with a plethora of fund-raising activities – all really worth the effort according to the girls. Uniform of blazer, kilt, V-neck jumper and open shirt worn smartly by most. Good second hand shop.

Pupils and parents: Girls come from every background and ethnic group. Redland is an upmarket area but the catchment extends all over Bristol and as far as Weston-super-Mare one way and up to Chipping Sodbury in the other, hence travel needs can inhibit evening and weekend activity (Bristol schools are tending towards weekday matches these days).

The city environment with the largest concentration of schools outside London means girls get plenty of mixed social life. Even shrinking violets make friends with boys via joint sixth form academic events – French debates and so on with Queen Elizabeth's Hospital. Girls see the school as academic and

supportive, have an easy rapport with staff and are friendly and natural with visitors. Bustling, purposeful atmosphere with no danger of remoteness in this multi-cultural and commercial city.

Famous old girls include Dame Elizabeth Hoodless, chairman of CSV, and Geraldine Peacock, charity commissioner. More recently actresses Lucy Biggs-Owen (now RSC and generous with time for advising current pupils) and Lynn Farleigh.

Entrance: Exam and through individual interview at 11 with about one third coming from junior school (qv). Remainder mainly from Bristol state primaries. More applicants than places and consideration given to ability to fit into a purposeful girls' environment as well as to academic standard.

Exit: A few defect post GCSE, some for mixed sixth forms and some for money reasons. Some Bristol independent schools have just become academies, free, but as yet retaining their 'privileged' feel. A new sixth form college almost next door and a temporary dip in teenage population have nibbled at sixth form numbers for a year or two. This is unlikely to continue as the nursery/junior population is growing.

Virtually all sixth formers to uni with a few Oxbridge places and plenty to medicine, law and mainline subjects at established unis. Increasing numbers to drama and even dance schools.

Money matters: Scholarships at 11, 13 and 16 include academic, art, sport and music. Means-tested bursaries available for entry into all years from year 5 upwards.

Remarks: Priorities are academic but this hasn't inhibited some outstanding music, drama and art. Sport is now benefiting from good off-site facilities. A smashing school, working hard to maintain its academic sixth form. It also has to fight against quite erroneous impression of being a little old fashioned, given by its historic building. Girls here appreciate the good teaching, work hard, support one another and take full advantage of what's on offer outside the classroom.

Reeds School

Sandy Lane, Cobham, KT11 2ES

• Pupils: 645 (including girls in sixth form); 85 boarders, rest day • Ages: 11–18 • C of E but all denominations and faiths are welcome. • Fees: Day £16,905–£21,135; Boarding £22,530–£27,960 pa • Independent

Tel: 01932 869001
Email: admissions@reeds.surrey.sch.uk
Website: www.reeds.surrey.sch.uk

Head: Since 1997, David W Jarrett MA (sixtyish), read classics at Oxford, followed by PGCE at Cambridge. Governor at several schools, married with two grown-up children. Passionate about sport (cricket and hockey blue) and delighted that every youngster, regardless of sporting prowess, gets a chance to play for a school team. Sabbatical in 2010, trotted off to the USA; visited 25 schools and universities on fund-raising fact-finding sortie. Says aside of his sojourn he is very much tied to the office, no time to teach, less time to interact with pupils but sees all on their birthdays, which pupils say they appreciate. Head is fiercely proud of the school and keen to maintain the hallmark family feel. Pupils clearly very fond, but respectful, of the head. 'He takes a great interest in all that we do and knows all of us by name. He has a great memory and is very fair; he will always try to look at things from our point of view and tries to give us chances if we get things wrong.'

Retiring in July 2014. His successor will be Mark Hoskins, currently senior deputy head of RGS Guildford.

Academic matters: The once gentle, nurturing Reed's that welcomed all-comers, fed, watered and nourished them, fortified their self-esteem but languished near the foot of league tables, has galloped into the first division. In 2013, 51 per cent A*/A at A level and 55 per cent at GCSE; though parents caution that not all leave with glittering grades. Maths, English, economics, biology and geography top the A level popularity polls. No consistently weak subjects, variation in numbers achieving good grades, in minority subjects, probably a reflection of pupil aptitude rather than teaching quality. School say the modular approach to exams, with its bite-sized learning and ample resit opportunities, suits their youngsters, but they haven't shied away from challenging and stretch, 'We've just sweated them a bit more'. IGCSE sciences introduced to help bridge gulf between GCSE and A level. Latin offered, Greek an extra, good range of MFL with plethora of trips and activities to bring lingo to life.

A welcoming place for youngsters with mild to moderate specific learning difficulties. They keep a watchful eye on assessment grades of all pupils to nab those who may have slipped through the net. Some 140+ 'on the list' with 50 per cent of those receiving additional support; 'We are keenly aware that a dyslexic pupil is dyslexic in every lesson. Fortunately we have very good relations with teachers and support staff and all work to best support the child.' Have a fully-equipped English language support centre which uses a structured, individualised, multi-sensory approach – otherwise minimal withdrawal.

Bright, modern classrooms but numbers can creep beyond the 20s and we sense there is little room for further expansion. Good facilities including wondrous new DT building with gadgets, gizmos, CAD/CAM and lego-technic. We watched in awe at the ease with which plastics were moulded and were lucidly educated on the differences between injection and vacuum moulding but, just as we were about to roll up our sleeves and get stuck in, we were dispatched to science. Chemistry did not disappoint; smells, smoke and spectrum colours galore tickled our senses, as a range of substances were toasted in bunsen burner heaven.

Games, options, the arts: Premier league sport: tennis takes centre court, golf up to scratch, skiing traverses the two with wild cards of swimming and hockey completing the elite. Twice won the world school championships for tennis, currently a top five UK school for golf and Britain's number one ski school. Some 90 pupils play at county level or above with 15 internationals among their number including Junior Wimbledon and Junior Davies Cup competitors. Timetable flexes for elite squad members. School has a charismatic, full-time strength and conditioning coach who works with a range of children, not just the elite. Does a lot to help children with dyspraxia or other physical difficulties and parents are free to refer their tubby teens: 'We don't make a distinction so some kids think they are being honed for bigger things rather than a smaller self.' All usual sports and many additions offered. Play as many squads as they have boys willing to give it a go.

Parents of sporty boys think non-sporty struggle, but parents of non-sporty boys insist their children get a good deal and have fun. 'My son is quite able and very into drama. He loves anything cerebral or dramatic and Reeds offers him a multitude of opportunities in a friendly, non-judgmental environment.' Superb facilities: tennis academy, lots of indoor and outdoor tennis courts, squash courts, 25 metre indoor pool, shooting range, fencing Salle, climbing wall – and just for good measure 100 per cent A*/A pass rate for A level PE. Music a strength, more than a third learn an instrument; we listened

to the tuneful orchestra marching through tunes with flourish and flare. Termly concerts plus musicals play to critical acclaim and enthusiastic audiences. Consort Choir sings annually at St Paul's Cathedral. Director of drama ensures delivery of innovative productions such as 'Socialism is Great'. Fine art adorns corridors, walls and any unsuspecting space. Great range of extras including LAMDA, cooking, environmental club, photography, car maintenance and film-making. Outdoor pursuits scheme for third form a precursor to fourth form D of E or CCF; can join the Coldstream Guard cadets or reach for the sky with the RAF.

Background and atmosphere: A warm, family friendly school with great spirit and a history of caring for, and nurturing, those who need help. Founded in 1813 to educate children whose fathers had died, the school still takes pupils on foundation awards – if they have lost one or both parents, if their parents are separated or divorced, if they come from a single parent family, or, if for some special reason their home life has been unhappy or unsatisfactory. Approximately 10 per cent are Foundationers, benefiting from up to 100 per cent fees remission; seeks out those who will benefit from their time at Reeds.

Set on a sprawling 40 acre site, the main Edwardian building sits adjacent to the brand new purpose-built elegant DT building. An assortment of other additions date back to the sixties. Most corners, nooks and crannies now full. Three well-kept boarding houses all clean, tidy, spacious and inviting. Dorms sleep up to six in younger years, with single man rooms from fifth form. Youngest have super social centre/ games room with pool tables, table football machines and more. Older ones have computer suite, seminar room, common-rooms with sofas and TVs but tend to gravitate to their 'party kitchen', a super-sized room with cookers and toasters. Thursday coffee mornings very much a middle school highlight: 'We gather for hot chocolate, cakes and chat. It is something we all really look forward to,' say pupils. Smart uniform, strictly enforced. Sixth formers dress in 'office wear'. Tasty food, excellent variety: salad bar, veggie meals, pasta – with food clearly marked with nutritional and dietary information. House system with range of competitive activities – arts, chess, music, singing – engenders fierce loyalty. Much support from housemasters and tutors, prep in house, with buses leaving at 5.30pm for day children, ensuring sufficient after-school time for activities or work.

Pastoral care and discipline: Pupils expect to get Gs and Bs for good work and behaviour with Ms and Ws for misbehaviour and unacceptable work. Rewards for the former, sanctions for the latter, though pupils assure us, 'We get lots of help and support with our work, teachers will explain something in different ways until you understand it.' Parents commend good, structured discipline. Few expulsions in recent years but odd one 'asked to leave', though school does give second chances and will support a child even after they have shown them the door. Pupils say stealing and bullying are no-nos. Will test for drugs if suspicions raised, no problem in school but can't counter what happens outside. School outgrown chapel so visits are limited to three or four times a week and by year groups.

Pupils and parents: 'We admit a range, some are solid all-rounders, others mono-focused'; this includes 10 percent Foundationers and 10 per cent sporting supremos. Attracts a number of Dutch children – historically a separate Dutch school shared the campus but closed some years ago – a dozen come for half a term to improve their English. 'Our child floundered at prep school but has shone at Reeds; we don't understand how they do it but they really do get the best out of them.' Fee-paying parents perceive that youngsters from poorer backgrounds 'bring down school averages', but school adamant this is completely untrue, saying Foundationers generally outperform the rest (a need for better parental PR perhaps?). Foundationers ensure pupils have a balanced outlook, and staff say drive, determination and diligence of the very sporty rubs off on other students. Sixty girls in sixth-form – tend to be skewed towards the more able, reflecting the gentle competition for places. Many girls come because of reputation for sports, the great facilities and the friendly ambiance. 'My previous school was very pressured, I felt the focus was on the academic with everything else a poor second. Here you are encouraged to play sport, be in the orchestra and have interests. I don't do any less work here, I just have a better outlook, and attitude.' Parents find the lack of cliques among the girls refreshing: 'There isn't the same angst, or bitchiness; the girls all seem to get on.' Parents from all walks of life, the very wealthy, celebs, professional and entrepreneurial families, where typically both parents work, plus a chunk of Foundationers on up to 100 per cent fees. School buses serve a wide area of Surrey.

Entrance: At 11+ tests in English, maths, VR and NVR in January, interview and report from current school. 13+ via pre-test, CE and prep school report. Sixth-form admits 30 girls and a dozen or so boys (depends how many places freed by those who flee at 16-30 per cent in 2012). Get odd state school refugee at other times. From a range of schools, at 11, Surbiton Prep, Donhead, Westward and local state schools; at 13, Parkside, Feltonfleet, Danes Hill, Shrewsbury House, Ripley Court, Cranmore, Hoe Bridge, St Andrew's, Rokeby and Lanesborough.

A first choice school for tennis and skiing – a good option for golfers and swimmers (though school insists it won't be pitching up poolside to fish winners from the water or stand, flag aloft, on the 18th). Has a wealth of experience in flexing to meet the training/ performing demands of sportsmen, music maestros and other prodigies and tailor the academic programme accordingly. Official CE passmark is 55 per cent but may flex for spiky IQs. Has introduced pre-testing at 11; some harrumphing from local parents who feel this is contrary to the school's ethos of taking a broad church rather than creaming off the top, but unlikely to change as school insists it is no longer one that will consider taking those pupils who might struggle to get in elsewhere.

Exit: Most to university including a number (mainly the sporty) to unis in the USA. In 2013, one to Oxford, most of rest to a range of universities; popular destinations include Exeter, Nottingham, Bath, Loughborough and Durham. Many to art college or design-based courses; some take gap year to consider their options.

Money matters: Have held an annual appeal for funds (to support needy children) since 1815 and about to raise the stakes. Expect between 20 and 50 per cent for an academic scholarship (based on how well your child performs, not how thin your wallet) with additional awards for music, sports, drama, art and DT.

Remarks: A school where once upon a time pupils rattled around, with more slips and slides than Bambi, is now something of a gazelle, still smaller than some rivals but with a speed and grace many can only dream of emulating. While the trophy cabinet overfloweth with sporting regalia, we suspect academic awards are in sight. 'A rounded school,' say pupils. 'Not for the posh or cliquey but where if you have dreams the school will do all they can to help you achieve them'. In a populous and popular area of Surrey, Reeds is riding on a tide; we just hope that it keeps its balance and vision and remains true to its soul.

Reigate Grammar School

Linked school: Reigate St Mary's Preparatory and Choir School

Reigate Road, Reigate, RH2 0QS

- Pupils: 860 boys and girls (just under half are girls); all day
- Ages: 11–18 • Non-denom • Fees: £15,480 pa • Independent

Tel: 01737 222231
Email: info@reigategrammar.org
Website: www.reigategrammar.org

Headmaster: Since 2012, Mr Shaun Fenton MA PGCE Med NPQH (forties). Formerly head of Pate's and founded and chaired National Grammar Schools Association. Educated at Haberdashers' Aske's, then PPE at Oxford. Started and ditched City career for education, first in west London comprehensive until drawn by challenge of The Ridings School in Halifax, labelled worst in Britain in TV documentary. Exhilarated by challenge of working with one of the first superheads, who achieved rags to riches magic, forged in hotbed of innovation. 'If something worked here, would work anywhere.'

Much in demand to repeat the process, quickly promoted to first deputy headship in Hertfordshire, followed by spell as troubleshooter injecting aspiration into other troubled schools that had shed senior management following inspection failures.

Tough, energetic, enthusiastic and 'comes up with about 1,000 ideas a week,' said member of staff. 'A very nice young chap,' reckoned a paternalistic local.

His arrival has had a mixed reaction from parents, who seem to be holding back while they gauge the measure of the man. They love his God particle-like ability to be in several places at once (one had recently come across him at a hockey umpiring class – his latest qualification) and the way he's handed out his email address and positively implored parents to get in touch – no issue too small. 'I love to hear from them,' he says (he also likes to use them to gauge temperature of public feeling – the words 'focus group' crop up, in other contexts, more than once).

Particularly good at unpicking existing school practices and refashioning with more stuffing. Sixth form mentors don't just talk to pupils but are also charged with speaking to their families. Scholars are challenged from day one, with a programme designed to shape talents into Oxbridge-friendly material if academic and all-weather leadership fabric (sport) with captaincy a managed exercise in building relationships, helping develop struggling teams and nurturing individuals. 'No point just getting them to play matches – it's about the psychology.' Lots of praise, too, for innovations to date, notably reintroduction of house system.

Parents worry that new system of offers to some prep pupils as early as year 5 could reduce numbers making it through to senior school. But though one parent felt it had 'put the cat among the pigeons' head was clear that 'it means offers for the vast majority of Reigate St Mary students and not just the high performers. Overall, 'admission at age 11 is approximately half from excellent local state primary schools and half from prep schools.'

Conundrum for some might be why, with solid A* career he has opted for first time move into independent sector instead of carrying on down the path to government darling roles as a super head's super head, advising the great, good and better on how to do it. But it's simple. As at Pate's, he can educate society's leaders himself and cut out the middleman. As to why here – it 'was the only school that stood out for its ambition to make a real difference.'

Nervous to start with (he says), he certainly isn't now. Has been charged by the governors with providing education 'the way it should be, with no short cuts.' Slow cook approach lets top grades rise from teaching that lets pupils live their subjects – converting hall into mini Parliament to explore legislative process, for example. 'This could not be further away from a hot-house approach but can deliver stunning, authentic learning,' says head.

Wants to make school one 'you drive past others to come to' – and there is an extensive coach service. And, yes, he does want to get results up, though refused to be drawn on any specific targets, or schools he'd measure himself against (Caterham is the long term rival at the moment). He also wants staff asking 'what excellence looks like... what are the best teachers and schools in the world doing? What does it mean to us?' Too many schools coast, he thinks, relying on showy but shallow academic gimmicks, where pupils, drilled to the test, fetch up as 'charlatans, not historians.' As to 'outstanding' inspection ratings, pretty much waved aside as something that for any really good school is the starting point.

Will know is hitting the sweet spot when shared language of excellence permeates the building and crosses the departments. No wonder 'some staff feel have been hit by a tsunami – need to hold on tight,' thought insider.

Pupils, meanwhile, see a lot of him as he beams out from airy office overlooking playground. He somehow manages to pack in a bit of teaching, too. An RE teacher originally, he takes 1675 (school's foundation date) as starting point for philosophical debate about pupils' place in the world. Lively charm makes him a winner. Jolly, determined and, through previous posts, has seen it, done it and got the results to prove it, you're left in no doubt that this head will leave his mark on every area of the school without, despite recent appearance in full Darth Vader regalia, necessitating a walk on the dark side.

Married – wife Anna works part time at the school – with two sons at linked prep.

Academic matters: 'Not a hothouse, but academic,' is the view of one prospective parent who, like others, reckons head has been charged with ramping up results. Sciences and maths top the popularity chart, history close runner up, geography, government and politics and RS leading second wave, while marginals include music and Latin (13 taking music A level a couple of years ago was 'exceptional' says department director, who is happy with small exam numbers and big involvement).

Much that's good, little bad and nothing ugly, with GCSE and AS grades both 'at record levels in summer 2013,' says school. Expect it to manifest itself in next batch of A level results, which have shown slight drift in the last three years with A*/B grades down from just about 85 per cent in 2011 to just over 81 per cent in 2013. Chemistry, school's single biggest subject, was main offender, with seven unfortunates failing to secure Cs. Down to staff changes and acclimatisation, says Mr Fenton – and thus a one-off. Pupil comments bear him out. 'I love chemistry – teaching is brilliant,' said Oxbridge hopeful.

Expect best feet to be put forward and pips squeaked, all however, without imposing undue stress. Meanwhile, direction of travel is already gladdening new head's heart – more than 74 per cent of GCSEs graded A*/A in 2013, up on previous two years. Lots of glorious individual results – drama and computing amongst stand-out successes.

Ten subjects taken by most, with IGCSEs for sciences, Eng lang and maths, where very able whizz through a year early. Maths is only formally set subject apart from languages, grouped to allow later starters (often from state primaries) to catch up with early adopters.

Following tried and tested approach at Pate's, where A* grades shot up from the merely very, very good to the stratospheric, head is rethinking time taken to cover GCSE ground, covering foundation stage in two years, then taking three years (years 9 to 11) to cover the rest.

Teaching of a fairly formal nature (and some classrooms plain rather than purl when it came to display) but judging by interest levels – front-facing, engaged pupils clearly absorbed in subjects – it's quality stuff. 'Not every single teacher is brilliant,' felt parent, though praised the many who were. 'There's lots of laughter and interaction.' And while teenagers 'might moan, they do get on with lessons.' Plenty of oohs and ahs in year 8 chemistry class, as teacher created solid. Computing another winner – first year pupils animatedly creating crests and GCSE candidates' amazing robotic creations proudly on show (A*s the norm).

Relaxed pupils clearly weren't feeling the strain. Big benefit – plenty of time for non-examined goodies on offer during the normally exam-dominated GCSE years of fourth and fifth form as electives ensure there's no lull in the pace of learning. Result is sense of open house, with teachers welcoming followers in and out of lesson time, subject loyalties very keenly felt and endearingly expressed. 'It's my third home,' says year 9 enthusiast of computing. 'Music's my second.'

Games, options, the arts: Something for everyone, even down to flourishing forensic club (DNA testing one of covetable skills covered) with music, drama and sport taking joint curtain call in neatly blended annual summer festival featuring show-stopping goodies like fashion catwalk, school v MCC match and assorted productions and concerts.

Extracurricular, indeed, is 'the heartbeat of the school,' says head (who should know, what with taking games lessons on a Wednesday afternoon and being brains of the enterprise). D of E, CCF and many, many trips – 'more than we need' thought one parent (but in a good way). Clubs and activities get a brochure of their own, writers' enthusiasms waxing and waning. Much made of indulging pupils' 'love of numbers' and 'passion for writing' in writing/maths clubs – trickling down to lower key 'interest' in arts clubs, while medical discussion club can muster only the quiet decorum of 'relevance.'

Sport big but not bloated, (offers 'the opportunity to play both winter sports simultaneously' – now that's what we call co-ordination) and gets unusually modest showing in school literature. Success, though substantial (fourth form rugby team stuffed with county players) isn't a front, back and middle pages splash.

The talented are well catered for, girls too (their sixth form rugby team 'popular,' reckon pupils), as well as enthusiastic triers. 'My son had a fixture practically every Saturday, daughter hardly at all,' thought parent – now approaching equality for both. Particularly strong in athletics (dogged too – one national biathlon finalist swam and ran in below zero temperatures) as well as cricket (impressive wins against strong schools).

On site facilities stretch not just to sports hall but very snazzy swimming pool (open to parents every Sunday). Focus for games is 32-acre site (stonking but chilly 'about four degrees colder than everywhere else,' thought staff member), just 'five to ten' minutes away (15 in rush hour – we tried it) and worth a Saturday visit for the bacon butties alone.

Arts, performing and visual, cast equally long shadow. Supercharged head of drama reaches across age and interest range. Pulsating productions including puppet play, Animal Farm and A Winter's Tale complete with revolving clock – 'bonkers but really good' thought pupil. Breathtaking in both scope and ambition, with talented individuals scoring places in national youth ensembles of every type (including largely undergraduate-level festival).

With strong singing (many prep choristers move up to senior school), you'd expect super music and you get it. 'Jaw-dropping,' says parent. Around 50 per cent have individual music lessons, some reaching diploma standard. Once a year giant orchestra (participants numerous rather than Goliath-proportioned) scoops up local junior school performers. Normal sized version for daily use plus concert band, intermediate versions too, for those en route to grade greatness but not there yet. Add free

R

theory/aural classes, five choirs, most audition-free, one open to staff and parents, new house music competition and evening soirees in head's garden, and it's a wonder the director of music isn't fraying at the edges. 'Music is so relaxing,' he says, however, smilingly picking way round percussion break-out sessions in attractive (and tactically soundproofed) building.

Background and atmosphere: Despite 17th century foundations, it's the 19th century that dominates, with up to the minute additions nicely accommodated (delivered via smart new Ballance building with change in floor covering only hint to seamless welding to existing block).

Close to centre of Reigate, market town made good thanks to commuter-friendly train connections (and very slow level crossing). Canny land acquisition almost allows stroll into town to be accomplished entirely on school land. School has personable, unintimidating, family-centric feel. Its two sites are mere yards apart, quickest walk along the front restricted to sixth formers because of thunder and fury of non-stop A25 traffic (teachers stand guard by pedestrian crossing at end of school day to block off-piste excursions). Other ranks, like earlier generations, commute between buildings along peaceful path behind the school that runs along perimeter of St Mary's Churchyard (venue for year group assemblies, four times a year whole school get-togethers in extendable concert hall).

Atmosphere nicely inclusive, and not just for pupils – support and academic teachers, who share common room, all muck in, clearly feeling both wanted and involved. They include head of IT, former City type, running lunchtime talk on morality of banking and head of catering heavily involved in ICT. Until recently, 'was nice but a bit sleepy,' thought school insider. 'Not any more – there's something new happening every week.'

Pastoral care and discipline: Pupil happiness and pastoral care is the priority and carries all before it, says head. Get it right and you 'can light the touch paper of success in all other areas of their life.' Parents confirm school's fleet-footedness in troubleshooting and what mother described as 'open door feeling' to problems. One girl's friendship issues reported to teacher who 'sorted it' effectively. 'Unique' staff lend an ear with problems, with form tutors (who move up with pupils) as well as sixth form mentors and listening service run by chaplaincy.

Poor behaviour a minority interest, serious problems almost unknown, reckoned pupils we talked to. Detentions 'for cheekiness' and late work, rewards via on-line credit system.

Pupils and parents: Mixes 'indigenous Surrey with incomers,' says local. Lots from south west London. Some grew up here, went off to work and then came back, says local estate agent. 'I know lots of families.' As to children? 'A credit to the town,' he reckoned. Most famous old boy is David Walliams, who was recently doing a spot of filming at the school.

Entrance: School proud of flexible approach, despite applications at record levels since arrival of new head. For the right candidate, computer doesn't invariably say no, even out of season. 'Come and talk to me,' says head.

Entrance isn't 'just about testing and measuring,' he adds. Teacher feedback and reports count too. He's after children 'who will make the world a better place,' especially when 'parents would want them to be their child's best friend.' Choristers, though welcome, subject to same criteria as the rest.

For sixth form, A grades at GCSE in subjects to be studied at A level and an overall tally of at least four As, four Bs and no grades lower than a C. Some parents worried that entry requirements were being toughened up but school again works on case by case basis resulting in 'a number without the full requirement coming back,' says head. 'I see any individual leaving because they are without the grades or even grades close enough as really sad,' – and where possible, 'will waive the requirements'. If it isn't possible, 'they are a very, very small minority.'

Also notably brilliant at resolving AS nightmares. Head 'hugely supportive' when things go wrong, agreed parents and pupils, moving mountains to keep pupils at the school, sometimes repeating year or dropping a subject.

Exit: Head's Oxbridge focus paying off – offers up from six to 14 between 2012 and 2013. Highly rated for quality of HE destinations by Sutton Trust which placed school in top two per cent of all UK co-eds. Saturday morning help sessions for leavers needing help with deferred entry post A level a real boon.

Money matters: A scholarship programme (about 150 awards across the school), with awards of 30 per cent, potentially 'significantly more' at head's discretion. Also head's scholarship – for children bringing a je ne sais quoi activity or interest which offers 'value to the school community – scholars are expected to give back.' And, a nice touch, all those with straight A*s at GCSE automatically get £1,000 off the sixth form fees (parent to child bribe chats, you'd imagine, are rife as a result).

Remarks: Hothouse ethos not on the agenda but, given the head's success at Pate's, where similar approach had transformational approach on results, we'd predict similar marvels here. Definitely one to watch.

Rendcomb College

Linked school: Rendcomb College Junior School

Rendcomb, Cirencester, GL7 7HA

- Pupils: 255; 55 boys board, 80 day boys; 45 girls board, 75 day girls • Ages: 11–18 • C of E • Fees: Day £14,580–£20,025; Boarding £20,835–£27,555 pa • Independent

Tel: 01285 831213
Email: admissions@rendcomb.gloucs.sch.uk
Website: www.rendcombcollege.org.uk

Headmaster: Since 2011, Mr Roland J Martin BA (forties) – scholar at Rendcomb College, read English and related literature at York, recently completed National College leadership pathways programme. Taught English, ran general studies, directed plays, coached sport and involved in marketing at Newcastle-under-Lyme School (six years); Eton (13 years) – English, drama, head of year 11, housemaster. Married to Kerri, former head of English – active in school life; two children. Interests include travel, theatre, music, sport.

Believes education should be 'inclusive, broad-ranging and centred on learning', wants school to 'continue to produce well-nurtured, rounded and modestly confident young people who have a strong set of values based on their experiences of our community here'.

Academic matters: Consistent if not trail blazing results in recent years. Small numbers overall but 26 per cent A*-A at GCSE and 37 per cent grades A*/A at A level still creditable. May not match high flyers in Cheltenham, but delivers as much if not more than Rendcomb parents generally expect. Small groups at GCSE a definite advantage; some tiny ones at A level may be viewed differently by some. Wide range of subjects made possible by part-timers offering psychology, business studies etc alongside traditional subjects. Art shines at both GSCE and A level with a regular crop of top results. A third of each year group takes double science instead of single GCSEs. Versatile DT department is drawing more pupils into its stimulating environment. We witnessed some effective lessons in English, maths and theatre studies: lively discussion in sixth form groups and hands up everywhere in lower years. Sixth formers can now take Extended Project Qualification. Pupils assessed for effort and achievement every three weeks. Library a good place to work (complete silence when we visited) but looking a bit tired, we felt.

Support for mild dyslexia and a range of other mild specific learning disabilities: all pupils screened after entry and help offered either on one-to-one or one-to-two basis. Pupils needing support are generally withdrawn from tutorial lessons rather than main curriculum. Director of studies looks after most able with encouragement to participate in maths Olympiad, other similar national competitions, as well as relevant talks, visits etc. Parents say that school is good at celebrating any success (single or multiple) achieved by pupils. Two EFL teachers support regular batch of overseas students, including five annual Japanese students. End of the school day is blurred, making it easy for day pupils to slide into prep alongside the boarders.

Games, options, the arts: School is six days a week – long days too; some potential parents may be put off, but for others it's just what they want. Fifty or so, mainly sporting, extra-curricular activities on offer – most take three or four but two is the minimum. Sport is a big deal, enthusiastically supported by staff and pupils alike. School teams generally play 'one down' when they face numerically larger schools but otherwise punch above their weight. Facilities are excellent, with grass pitches and Astroturf, squash and badminton courts, a heated outdoor swimming pool and a large sports hall. Team competition only on sports day, though 'this might be extended,' we were told. Individuals regularly make it to the county teams. Offers traditional country pursuits of clay pigeon shooting (highly successful to national level), riding and polo. Four hole golf course on site, while the nearby Cotswold Water Park hosts windsurfing and fishing. National small schools' lacrosse champions. New outdoor education initiative for seniors; trip to Everest base camp in July 2013.

Very popular art run by extremely enthusiastic head of department. Most play a part in annual fashion shows, almost all at least embark on individual music lessons and the choir is highly rated. Ambitious productions in the school's theatre, once the orangery of the Victorian main house, include large scale musicals – most recent was We Will Rock You. Lower School pupils recently staged The Demon Headmaster, also regular performances by GCSE and A level drama students. MAD (music, art and drama) festival at end of summer term includes professionals and a whole range of activities ranging from circus skills to mosaics. Music department is very strong: 18 peripatetics, one girl currently in national youth choir and five students working beyond grade 8. Variety of ensembles and choirs as well as rock and contemporary music group (whose recent concert featured John Cage's Water Music). School hosts popular world music day for local junior and prep school pupils. 'Performing arts centre is top of my wish list,' says head. Recent visits have included art students going to Barcelona, geographers to Iceland, a battlefields trip and regular local trips by minibus.

Background and atmosphere: Founded in 1920 when a member of local, land-owning (fags-to-riches) Wills family bought this vast Italianate pile after the First World War from its previous Jewish owners, whose legacy (a rather large and incongruous statue of Saul) greets visitors on arrival. Impressive parquet flooring in main house and gracious 'reading room' provides an elegant backdrop for many a function. Noel Wills was inspired by the notion that 'the only aristocracy is the aristocracy of brains and character', offering an antidote to traditional public schools of the time (a wreath laid annually on founder's grave in Miserden churchyard honours his memory). School has kept aspects of its original philosophy, though current market forces operate here at least as much as anywhere else. Committed itself to building a one-school ethos since the opening of the junior school. 'Facilities generally not very swish but natural setting provides wow factor,' explained one mother. No CCF and a lack of strong inter-house rivalry hark back to the idealism of the founder. School council has increasingly given pupils a greater say in decision making and is listened to by head.

If ever a 'school with a view' this is it: looks out over rolling greenery in all directions. Victorian main house sits cheek by jowl with the junior school, enabling lots of interaction both formally and informally. Sixth form and other boarding houses are separate, as is the stable block, which has been modified to provide a range of laboratories and classrooms. Shared bedrooms of younger boarders have refreshing air of light and space, while seniors' rooms are bright, compact and practical. High standard of cleanliness and orderliness reflect well on pupils and boarding/domestic staff.

The grounds spill seamlessly into the village of Rendcomb – the village post office (school was at forefront recently of saving this threatened local facility) doubles as the school tuck shop; village church and its incumbent also double up, though post was vacant when we visited. Old Rectory provides great boarding house for boys in years 7 and 8. Large, well-equipped games room can transform into cinema with projector and screen for favourite movies. Girls' equivalent (Godman) has a pink, fluffy common-room complete with disco lights. Friday night challenges (eg building the tallest paper tower with help from sellotape) popular with 11-13 year olds. Events for this age group have included a 22 mile cycle tour, a big sister evening and an adventure weekend – a tremendous programme rolls out week after week.

Boarders move on at 13 to more senior accommodation. Boys' and girls' common-room is a refurbished stable (named The Barn) – just right for this age group. All sixth formers have their own study bedrooms in dated but flexible co-ed house. Takeaways are restricted during the week; seniors make good use of own kitchen facilities, especially after prep. At weekends, boarders can taste town life in Cirencester, provided they are back on time. Flexi-boarding popular with day pupils, who like best of both worlds.

Pastoral care and discipline: School succeeds at being inclusive. All staff appear in school photo – from the head to the maintenance team (who run some sports activities as well as keeping the grounds beautiful). Real sense of caring abounds, with a quarter of staff living on site. Seasoned house parents on hand for support as well as medical staff and part-time counsellor. 'Any instances of bullying are dealt with impeccably,' said one parent. Achievement, whether good results or a small kindness, rewarded by praise in assembly or commendation from the head. Rules enforced vigorously by deputy head. Smoking is forbidden, but treated more as a problem than a crime. Sixth form 'cellar' club operates within law and serves food plus alcohol carefully regulated by senior staff. Experiment with independent living – via sixth form house in village where a single sex group of pupils lives for a week, manages a budget, cooks meals etc – has drawn national media interest.

Pupils and parents: Low density of pupils of all ages on such a vast site makes for an unusually civilised atmosphere for a school. Pupils grow to be all-rounders; family feel (enhanced by growth of junior school) attractive to prospective parents. New uniform and sixth form dress code 'will smarten pupils up,' we were told. Not too much, we hoped. Most boarders as well as day pupils come from within a 30 mile radius. Unexpected contingent (20+) of Americans from Fairford now part of special link with US defence department. Not swamped by overseas pupils: a few Chinese and German pupils and its annual quota of Japanese in third form only. Children are smiley, polite and quiet. Staff skilled at 'raising the bar' in all areas to avoid excessive cosiness. 'rendcomb has found my daughter,' said one satisfied mother, who was not at all put off by higher proportion of boys – 'relationships tend to be fraternal,' she concluded. Formerly a secluded bastion for farmers' sons and Forces' children, now many more first-time buyers discovering the school via much improved road link between Gloucester and Swindon. 'Many parents sacrifice holidays abroad to send their children here,' says school.

Meaningful and well-established link with Lords Meade Vocational College in Uganda: school has been helped with whole range of projects with visits by ORs etc – opening privileged eyes to need in developing countries. Lively, glossy magazine splurges pupils' doings in colour photos across its 100 or so pages. Pupils really committed to greening the school across the board from recycling to tree planting. Not many big names amongst alumni – jockey Richard Dunwoody is best known.

Entrance: Selection by own examination at 11 and/or common entrance at 13. Interview, report and GCSE grades at 16. Majority from own junior school, though good numbers from Prior Park and other local preps at 13. School considers each application on individual basis. Not solely concerned with exam aptitude but also ability to try hard and function as part of a team.

Exit: Around 30 per cent move on after GCSEs. Most sixth formers get into university of choice across HE spectrum – art, acting as well as academic subjects. Generally one a year to Oxbridge; about 60 per cent to traditional universities.

Money matters: Good value, particularly boarding. Almost everything included in price. Individual music tuition extra but ensemble lessons free. EFL teaching and learning support are charged to parents. Generous academic, choral, music and art scholarships on offer. Bursaries supported by Wills family and Dulverton Trust, plus Noel Wills full bursary annually to one local state primary pupil.

Remarks: Developing the junior school has brought real benefits – numbers have risen overall and the interaction between older and younger pupils seals the family atmosphere. Never an academic hothouse – offers a complete education whilst ensuring that pupils achieve their best academically. A good place to make friends for life.

Repton School

Linked school: Foremarke Hall (Repton Preparatory School)

Repton, Derby, DE65 6FH

- Pupils: 670 (370 boys, 300 girls); 450 boarders, 220 day pupils.
- Ages: 13–18 • C of E (other faiths welcome) • Fees: Boarding £30,438; Day £22,584 pa • Independent

Tel: 01283 559222
Email: registrar@repton.org.uk
Website: www.repton.org.uk

Headmaster: Since 2003, Mr Robert Holroyd MA (late forties). Educated at Birkenhead School and Christ Church, Oxford, where took first in modern languages. Began teaching career at Oakham School, where met wife Penny. A teacher, she's fully involved in the school community and chairs the school's annual sale of work, which raises thousands for charity.

Head says he believes in 'standards without pretension' and that it's crucial that youngsters 'keep their feet on the ground and guard against the trappings of privilege'. Reckons

Reptonians come across as 'natural' and 'aren't too pleased with themselves'. Very keen on getting pupils to have a global perspective too, rather than looking inwards. Greets pupils by famous arch every morning and emphasises the importance of school, home and community all working together.

Unlike many heads today, he fits in as much teaching as his schedule permits. He teaches Oxbridge candidates French and Spanish and sometimes offers to step in and take sets lower down the school. 'I haven't been turned down yet,' he says drily. He and his wife know virtually all pupils by name. They make a point of inviting those celebrating birthdays down to The Hall, where they live, in groups of 12 to 15 for 'birthday drinks' – usually lemonade, sandwiches and cake.

During his headship, he's also seen the launch of partner school Repton School, Dubai, opened in 2007. Although Repton didn't provide any of the capital investment, it helped to design the buildings and create the curriculum. Year 10 pupils from Repton have done two-week exchange trips to Dubai and school hopes this will become a regular event.

Academic matters: In the past Repton produced sound but unexceptional exam grades, but these have been well and truly been put in the shade by recent results. In 2013 nearly 53 per cent A*/A grades at A level and nearly 80 per cent A*/B grades. GCSEs strong too – 66 per cent A*/A grades. Lots of maths and French GCSEs taken a year early. Most subjects setted according to ability. Traditional teaching methods, with all pupils allocated an academic tutor to monitor progress. Year groups of 110-120 in years 9, 10 and 11 (or B block, A block and O block, as they're known here) and up to 150 in both lower sixth and upper sixth. Class sizes are 15 on average.

Wide choice of subjects on offer, including business studies, PE, drama and politics. Everyone does French, and keen linguists can take Spanish or German from year 9 too. Youngest also take either Latin or classical civilisation. Pupils very much encouraged to read for pleasure. Year 9s have graded reading scheme, with target to read three books of a certain level every term. Appointment of academic 'tsar' has seen more outside involvement in school curriculum, with well-known names invited to lecture students. Recent guests include BBC foreign correspondent David Loyn, Holocaust survivor Freddie Knoller and diplomat and environmentalist Sir Crispin Tickell. Academic deputy has also introduced electronic reporting on pupils' progress. Teachers' reports on academic work (effort and achievement) emailed to parents every four or five weeks, plus usual end-of-term reports too.

Learning support available in small groups or one-to-one and individual education plans for each pupil to monitor progress. Relevant information and strategies passed to subject teachers to ensure support continues in class. Head full of praise for his team and pupils agree that teachers go the extra mile to help them. Teachers we met seemed to have boundless energy and enthusiasm. Prep from 7 to 9pm on weekday nights (all day pupils stay till 9pm too). Youngest supervised, the rest work independently in their houses.

Games, options, the arts: Sport goes from strength to strength. Boys play football, hockey and cricket, girls hockey, netball, tennis. At the time of our visit the boys had recently won the national U18 hockey championships for the first time, whilst the girls had clinched the national U18 title for the sixth year in a row. Not only that, a trio of old girls are in the current England ladies' hockey squad. Football is pretty impressive too – indeed a sixth form boy already has four full Northern Ireland caps to his name. Cricket, tennis, athletics, fencing report similar triumphs. Clutch of county and test cricketers regularly produced. When it comes to principal sports, school regularly fields three teams per year group, sometimes five. Impressive sports facilities, including sports complex, large indoor pool, water-based and sand-based Astroturfs, 16 outdoor tennis courts, two indoor tennis courts, squash and fives courts. CCF compulsory for youngest pupils and then can opt to continue or choose D of E or community service.

Unusually for a school, has three art galleries in the village, exhibiting the work of pupils as well as resident and visiting artists. Artwork on display everywhere throughout school – a huge abstract painted by former pupil Matthew Drage hangs in pride of place in the headmaster's hall and particularly caught our eye. Money made from hiring out school artwork to local businesses goes into pot to fund foreign trips for art students – very entrepreneurial.

Music is huge, with around 250 individual instrument lessons a week. Stunning newly refurbished music school in former san, with 200-seat recital hall, recording studio, 16 practice rooms. Vast array of orchestras, choirs, jazz bands, string quartets etc, annual musician of the year prize and RockIt competition for budding young rock bands. Series of subscription concerts held throughout year for school and community attracts musicians of international renown. Everyone does term of drama in year 9 and some go on to take it at GCSE and A level. Plethora of productions, will now take place in the newly renovated auditorium, throughout school year, including house plays, lower school production and charity cabaret.

Background and atmosphere: On the banks of the River Trent (the head's study is in a free standing medieval tower overlooking the river), the school is absorbed into the village of Repton rather than dominating it. Pupils are kept fit as they hurry between boarding houses up leafy lanes and classrooms, sports centre, games pitches etc. With a busy B road running through the village, Repton is by no means a sleepy idyll, but the school lends the place a certain vitality. The central part of the school is based around a 12th century Augustan priory. School founded under the will of Sir John Port, who died in 1557. It celebrated 450th anniversary of its creation in 2007 with a son et lumière production.

Good blend of ancient and modern architecture. Two-floor library in old priory building is breathtaking. National Literacy Trust has recently published report saying a third of today's students don't use their school library, but this isn't the case here. When we visited a happy group of year 9s were reading (everything from Bill Bryson to Conan Doyle) in comfy leather armchairs. Library criticised by inspectors in past but latest inspection said situation had been 'amply addressed,' with first-ever full-time librarian brought in and million-pound make-over. Recent building developments include 400 theatre (opened in 2011) as well as the spectacular multi-million pound Science Priory, complete with animal centre, observatory and ecological research centre (opened in 2013).

Once boys only but fully co-ed since 1991 – boy/girl ratio roughly 55/45. Head reckons school is big enough to create a 'buzz' and maintain standards of real quality but is small enough for everyone to know each other. Pupils and parents say it's a very friendly place and the latest ISI report specifically commented on the school's 'sense of community'.

The house system is integral to the school. Each house (four girls' and six boys') has resident houseparent and prides itself on having 'family atmosphere'. All pupils eat breakfast, lunch and supper in their houses. Food cooked in-house and every pupil we talked to claimed the food in their house was the best. We were invited to lunch in a girls' house and it was one of the most delicious school lunches we've had in a long time – chicken pasta, homemade focaccia and excellent chocolate brownies. Vegetarian and gluten-free options always available too. Lunch is the most formal meal of the day, often attended by guests from within school and outside, and students are encouraged to chat and be sociable. Mealtimes also give houseparents the chance to keep an eye on whether pupils are eating enough. Youngest pupils tend to be in dorms of four, sixth formers have their own study bedrooms with wash basins. Houses also have quiet rooms for working, kitchens to make toast and pasta and mixed-age common-rooms, where pupils from other houses can visit at specified times.

Pastoral care and discipline: House system underpins everything at Repton. As one housemistress says: 'We are here 24/7 and I see each one of my girls every day.' Plenty of people for pupils to talk to if they need a sympathetic ear – including house prefects, matrons, houseparents, house tutors, school counsellor and chaplain. Head boy and girl plus heads of houses and raft of prefects. New pupils given a mentor, someone who has been at school for at least a year, to guide them through the early weeks. Mobile phones allowed but only at certain times of day and youngest must hand them in to prefects at night. All pupils attend chapel twice a week. School prides itself on being a 'seven-days-a-week boarding school' – no exeats, but each pupil allowed three Saturday nights of own choice a term at home ('privilege weekends'). This helps to ensure that the school 'doesn't empty at weekends,' says a member of staff. Weekend activities on offer, or SLOPs as they are known (Sunday leisure options) include cycling in the Peak District, paintballing, trips to Clothes Show Live etc.

Clear school rules, with written tasks for minor breaches and detentions for more serious lapses. Meanwhile policies on drugs, drink and smoking are unambiguous. Zero tolerance on drugs – as deputy head for pastoral side of school says, 'repton isn't a second-chance school'. Drinking and smoking both yellow-card offences. Sixth formers allowed two alcoholic drinks with a meal at JCR on Saturday nights. Smoking is a 'minimal' problem, but if pupils are found smoking they incur loss of privileges (or 'lopping', as it's known in Reptonese).

Uniform is compulsory and looks very smart. Dark suits for sixth formers, while boys wear blazers and ties and girls are clad in grey skirts, blazers and a V neck jumper of their own choice in a 'quiet' tone – pale pink, mauve and grey from Zara seem to be the current favourites. No nail varnish and minimum make-up.

Pupils and parents: A very down-to-earth, straightforward lot – polite, ultra-proud of their school and appreciative of the opportunities it gives them. Pupils come from all over – north, south and everywhere in between. Around eight per cent from overseas. Past pupils of school include writers Christopher Isherwood and Roald Dahl and Top Gear supremo Jeremy Clarkson.

Entrance: Students arrive at Repton from a large number of schools. Roughly half from Repton's own prep up the road, Foremarke Hall, other half from prep schools like S. Anselm's, Terra Nova, Terrington Hall, Malsis, Orwell Park and Swanbourne House. Not overly selective – director of admissions says the school doesn't state common entrance pass mark required, but in previous years it has been 50 per cent. About 30 new teenagers into sixth form each year – they need minimum of five Bs at GCSE, but preferably As in chosen A level subjects. School takes pupils with special educational needs who can cope with the curriculum – every case considered on individual merit.

Exit: About 85 per cent go through to sixth form. Nearly all sixth formers to top universities, including around 10 a year to Oxbridge.

Money matters: Range of scholarships on offer – academic, music, art, DT, drama, ICT, sport and all-rounder. Also Foremarke scholarships, given to children who want to transfer to Foremarke Hall for years 7 and 8 and then on to Repton.

Remarks: Repton is definitely on a roll. A happy school that offers an all-round education in the wilds of Derbyshire. It gives students time to be themselves, whilst opening their minds and nurturing their interests and enthusiasms. As the head girl told us: 'I'll be very sad to leave here. It's a special place.'

RGS Worcester

Linked schools: RGS The Grange; RGS Springfield

Upper Tything, Worcester, WR1 1HP

- Pupils: 755 pupils; mixed • Ages: 11–18 • Non-denom
- Fees: £10,404 pa • Independent

Tel: 01905 613391
Email: office@rgsw.org.uk
Website: www.rgsw.org.uk

Headmaster: Since 2005, Mr Andrew Rattue MA PGCE (fifties). Educated at Bishop Wordsworth's Grammar School and Brasenose College, Oxford, (English). Taught at Mill Hill School and Haberdashers' Aske's School, Elstree, head of English at Highgate School in the early 1990s and then second master at RGS Guildford. Also taught in Thailand and the USA. Dynamic, friendly, cheerful, determined, unstuffy. Says that aside from academics the school offers 'common sense, sanity, good humour and a strong sense of social responsibility'. Still teaches as one of the English staff. Married with four children. Keen on sports, American culture, France, the Victorians, hill walking and cooking.

Off to head King's College Madrid in 2014.

Academic matters: Doing well alongside other local schools- King's Worcester, Malvern College, Bromsgrove School etc. Fully co-ed following its merger with Alice Ottley in 2007 – about 60 per cent boys in the sixth form but more or less equal numbers for GCSE.

Academically very sound across the board, with 71 per cent A*/A grades at GCSE in 2013, and at A level, 38 per cent A*/A grades. About 70 per cent of pupils take triple award science at GCSE. Has a particular reputation for its science, engineering/design and maths teaching, and though quite boy heavy in these subjects, the girls also make a good showing. Lots of Arkwright scholarships, three different DT subjects taught at GCSE, and strong in art and textiles as well, giving a creative edge to technical subjects. Impressive labs and well lit, well-equipped classrooms. Good use of electronic whiteboards – and the hint that fairly soon all pupils may move onto tablet technology, enabling easier access to learning resources. Introducing a new computing GCSE and A level option (from 2014 and 2016 respectively).

Economics, politics and business studies are popular choices at A level too. All study a modern language in year 7 and take on a second, plus Latin or classics, in year 8. All take a modern language at GCSE (French, German or Spanish), though not especially popular at A level – a fair number take French but few go on to study German or Spanish.

Attainment and attitude are graded every half term, with pupils given specific objectives. Most GCSE classes are small - under 20. Private reading is timetabled for lower school pupils and takes place in a well-resourced and attractive library, with lots of guidance and monitoring of who is reading what. Well-equipped language lab with stacks of Macs, which doubles as an ICT suite.

Staff are very enthusiastic about the school, positive about the pupils and parents, and say that the school management is also very supportive in promoting the personal and professional development of its teaching body.

Games, options, the arts: Very busy! Lots of sport (rugby, soccer and cricket for boys, netball for girls, rowing, hockey, athletics for both). Rugby and cricket are regarded as particularly strong. Rowing is increasingly successful with a number of RGS rowers attending GB trials. Regular Saturday fixtures, though no formal Saturday school. Fitness suite, two sports halls, all weather pitch

and lots of space on playing fields at RGS The Grange just north of the City Centre. CCF and Duke of Edinburgh awards are popular.

Masses of clubs (literature, debating, model making, dance, chess, choirs etc) and lots of school trips - staff say they have trouble fitting them all in. Lots of music - 14 ensembles including three jazz bands, a gospel choir, junior and senior choirs, chamber choir etc. About 15 peripatetic instrumental teachers, 10 practice rooms. About a third of pupils are taught an instrument through school. The principal teaching areas for music are being improved, with soundproof recording areas and new lighting and seating in the pipeline. Nice theatre with full lighting box - and drama is quite popular at GCSE. Lots of pupils also take LAMDA exams and school plays attract large numbers of eager participants.

Parents and staff love the range of activities but also say this can be very demanding - the phrase 'trying to fit a boarding school offering into a day school timetable' has been used. The head is aware of the potential for a rich variety to become unmanageable and has recently appointed a head of co-curricular activities to co-ordinate and manage this aspect of school life.

Background and atmosphere: A very ancient school, dating back to the seventh century. At the Northern end of central Worcester, and benefitting from very large playing fields at its junior school (RGS The Grange, which is just outside the city). Mostly Georgian and Victorian buildings, well maintained and with a nice balance between preserving the character of the architecture and functioning fully in a 21st century market. The library is a good example of this. Generally well-maintained and pleasant - there are enough open spaces and gardens to give a sense of light and movement and there are pleasing displays of the pupils' work throughout the school.

Facilities are very good - from the DT workshops to the sports fields - and there is no sense at all of resting on laurels. The management of the school is being reorganised to put all teaching on a faculty-based foundation, a move designed to improve coherence and depth across the board, and there is a sense both of excitement and determination amongst staff to keep pushing at the edges of what can be achieved.

Parents describe it as 'a school that wants to win' and say their children 'can't wait to get here'. All seem to feel that the merger with Alice Ottley has been a happy marriage which has produced a school offering more than the sum of its parts. There is an atmosphere of steady attention and diligence about the place, and staff are fully engaged with what seem to be quite radical curricular and management changes. One of a number of strong schools in Worcester- a very positive place with a great deal to recommend it.

Pastoral care and discipline: EA strong ethos of 'right, wrong and good manners'. Pastoral support is provided both by prefects and by form tutors and year heads. There is a strong 'family feel' and pupils emphasise that pastoral support is everyone's responsibility. Staff are 'always there if you need help'. The school's anti bullying policy has been reviewed recently and is strong. Parents say, 'the school was already getting it right'. A CEOPS programme on internet use is offered annually to parents and pupils. Very few disciplinary glitches in terms of drugs or alcohol. Students, parents and staff speak highly of levels of care and speed of response in the event of any issues arising.

Pupils and parents: Retains something of its original grammar school flavour. Parents like the friendliness, open door feel and academic breadth of the school. Many pupils from the north of Worcestershire - Kidderminster, Droitwich, Birmingham. Parents engaged in commerce, medicine, law etc. A lot of 'ordinary people who work hard to pay the fees'. Wide catchment and just a few minutes walk from the station at Worcester Foregate– transport links to Malvern, Evesham,

Tenbury Wells, Bromsgrove etc. Pupils seem calm, purposeful, polite and friendly.

Entrance: In year 7 about 50-60 per cent come from the school's junior feeders - RGS The Grange and RGS Springfield. Others from Abberley Hall, Winterfold House, Dodderhill and other local prep schools. Some others join at 13 via CE, and others again post-GCSE (entrance requirement of six Bs at GCSE for sixth form). A handful from feeder schools are 'counselled out' in years 5 and 6. Of external candidates at 11, around 75 per cent offered a place.

Exit: About 10 per cent leave after GCSEs. Of those, most will go to local sixth form colleges. Post sixth form the great majority go on to university. Five or six to Oxbridge, and lots to Russell Group – UCL, Cardiff and Nottingham are popular. Lots of engineers off to Bath, ICL and Loughborough. The popularity of engineering, product design and technology-based degree subjects reflects the school's strength in DT and sciences, but others go on to study music, art etc. Many alumni also go into business, one currently managing the Poole Lifeboat service - quite a few out of the normal boxes.

Money matters: Some scholarships at 11+,13+ and 16+ worth up to 33 per cent of fees - awarded for academics, sport, music and art. Bursaries of up to 100 per cent. Some packages of support are also put together with organisations such as The Ogden Trust and The Rank Foundation. Keen to improve access for children from poorer backgrounds and not to leave them feeling marginalised or 'sweaty palmed'.

Remarks: A friendly, grounded school with its sights set high. Suitable both for the very bright and those whose potential is yet to be unleashed. Strong academics across the board and managed with a real vision for excellence. Good value for money.

The Ridings Federation Winterbourne International Academy

High Street, Winterbourne, Bristol, BS36 1JL

• Pupils: 1,880 boys and girls • Ages: 11–19 • Non-denom • State

Tel: 01454 252000
Email: office@trfwia.org.uk
Website: www.trfwia.org.uk

Principal: Since 2009, Mr Rob Evans (fifties), who should know the school better than anyone – he has never taught anywhere else. A former geography and economics teacher, he was promoted to the top job after being acting principal since February that year. 'Hands-on and business-like', affirm both staff and parents. Long attachment to the school doesn't seem to have stopped him being keen to implement big changes.

Academic matters: Parents enthuse, 'They're not shy of trying new things'. First in the region to offer the International Baccalaureate, and relaunched as an academy (2009), with a federated sixth form with the nearby Yate International Academy, offering a wide range of academic and vocational course at Levels 2 and 3.

About 10 to 20 per cent of sixth formers take the IB, including six subjects, a compulsory foreign language, community work, and an extended essay. In one recent year, two leavers went on to study veterinary science at Bristol, one with A levels, one with IB. Some of the 'extra bits' of the IB curriculum now standard

for all sixth formers, including the creativity, action, service section, and the school has also introduced critical thinking to A level students.

Academy status has given the school freedom to pursue the IB Middle Years curriculum in lower years. Languages a priority, in keeping with international school status – nearly everyone takes at least one language at GCSE, but only small numbers at A level. Most popular A levels – general studies, psychology, biology and maths. At least one non-European language, most likely Mandarin, on the menu soon.

Classes are setted by ability in some subjects from year 7 onwards. All types of SEN are catered for, but the numbers are fairly low – 20 or so with SEN statements in the whole school, with another hundred or so getting some support from the SEN team and teaching assistants. Only a handful of EAL students.

Specialist technology school status has now been dropped, but the high-spec DT and ICT suites remain, along with links with industry, notably Airbus (nearby at Filton) and CISCO.

Results above average for a non-selective school: around four-fiths make it over the crucial benchmark of five A* to C grades including English and maths at GCSE (67 per cent in 2013), and the overall pass rate is around 90 per cent. At A level, 75 per cent A*-C grades, 48 per cent A*-B.

Games, options, the arts: A very sporty place, especially since the opening of the shiny new sports 'village' (2010), including new sports hall, all-weather pitch and refurbished swimming pool. Some of the gym rooms not yet fully equipped, but the main sports hall is a vast improvement. Full-size pool popular with pupils, their families and locals, who can use it out of school hours.

Rugby is the biggest thing here, and not just due to the Welsh head's influence. The 'rugby academy' offers training to all, and produces strong players for the school teams and beyond: one former pupil has been selected for the England rugby squad. Other sports are not neglected: several footballers are training with professional teams, and school teams for just about everything do well in local leagues.

Drama, music and debating standards are high – the academy gives the local independents a good run for their money in regional competitions, and often comes out on top. Art and drama have plenty of space and enthusiasm – lots of school productions, and some impressive art displays around the school. Library disappointingly small for the size of school, but at least they still have one.

Overseas trips limited, as not everyone can afford to go, but video conferences with an imaginative range of partners (from astronauts to school children in Afghanistan) help make up for it. The international outlook pays off for some students with gap year plans – the school has had five leavers over several years picked for the Prime Minister's Global Fellowship, which awards funds for work in developing countries.

Background and atmosphere: Formerly known as The Ridings High School, the school shook off local authority control in 2009 and became Winterbourne International Academy, part of a new Ridings Federation with the smaller Yate International Academy. Not many visible signs of change, apart from the appointment of the head, and smart new blazers and ties on years 7 to 11 (sixth formers must dress as 'young professionals' – open to quite broad interpretation, but most seem to have got the idea that it is not jeans and hoodies). The former head, Dr Rob Gibson, is chief executive principal of the federation.

The modern red-brick office-style building at the entrance to the school campus hides the rather dilapidated core of 1950s classroom buildings lurking behind it. The Academy will benefit from a £19.3m capital investment programme which will provide a twenty-first century Learning Environment. Construction started in August 2012 with the final phase due for completion in December 2014.

International status seen as a big positive by some parents, others not bothered about the languages and extra bits but like the good results and the sports.

Pastoral care and discipline: A big school (intake is 302 a year), and possibly a bit daunting for the younger ones. To ease the newbies in, year 7 tutors start visiting feeder primaries from year 5 onwards to get to know the likely applicants. Year 6s come to school taster days and even the annual panto.

A part-time in-school counsellor is on hand, and other referrals can be arranged. House system introduced from 2010, but most pastoral care organised via tutor groups. Vulnerable students have older students assigned as peer supporters, and sixth formers are attached to each year group to provide more general support.

Behaviour expectations clearly laid out in personal planners, and parents and pupils have to sign a home/school agreement. Principal says exclusions are down since the school became an academy, and there is low tolerance for disruptive behaviour. Disciplinary measures include detentions and referral to an in-school behaviour unit. The pupils working at desks outside the principal's office on our visit didn't look pleased to be there, but they were quiet and getting on with their work.

Repeat offenders get referred to the Behaviour for Learning Centre – an alternative to exclusions, with specialist staff, where troubled and troublesome pupils follow the same curriculum as their classmates as far as possible. The aim is to reduce outright exclusions and eventually reintegrate pupils into the rest of the school.

Pupils and parents: Cover the whole range from well-off families in commuter villages to those getting the bus in from some more deprived areas on the fringes of Bristol. Comprehensive intake, but on the bright side. Not many non-native English speakers, and the few there are tend to catch up quickly. An international touch comes from engineering staff at nearby aerospace companies, which have strong French links and some overseas workers.

Entrance: There are good reasons why so many Bristol families move to the other side of the M4 when their children are nearing double figures. Many Bristolians would love to get their children into this place, but if you don't live in a small corner of South Gloucestershire – namely, Winterbourne, Frampton Cotterell, Coalpit Heath, Frenchay and Hambrook and consortium area of prime responsibility – you are most likely out of luck (unless you have a sibling already there or a special educational need). The academy is heavily oversubscribed, and catchment-area based admission rules haven't changed with the shift to academy status. No entry tests for banding as used by other local academies. Applications through South Gloucestershire council in October before year of entry.

For the sixth form, minimum B grades at GCSE expected in A level subject picks.

Exit: Growing numbers in the sixth form – well over half stay on, but some leave at 16 for work, training or more vocational courses at local colleges. Sixth form leavers go anywhere and everywhere, the majority to some form of higher education, including Oxbridge and Russell Group universities, but a few straight to employment or training.

Money matters: New freedom from local authority control means the academy now manages its own budgets and can shop around for better-value outside services. Parents' association has active fundraising programme – lotteries, quiz nights etc – and partners in industry have helped out with equipment and some funds in the past.

Remarks: Deservedly popular commuter-belt comprehensive turned academy, with big ideas and an eye on the wider world.

Good results and a strong sporting tradition keep its feet on the ground.

Ripon Grammar School

Clotherholme Road, Ripon, HG4 2DG

- Pupils: 860 boys and girls; 795 day/65 boarding • Ages: 11–18
- Non-denom • Fees: Boarding £8,100–£10,875 pa. Day-free
- State

Tel: 01765 602647
Email: admin@ripongrammar.co.uk
Website: www.ripongrammar.co.uk

Headmaster: Since 2004, Mr Martin Pearman (pronounced Pierman) MA (early fifties). Read chemistry at Oxford, taught previously at Bristol GS, Stamford and Woodhouse Grove, where he was deputy head. Three sons, one still at his school. Staff positive about their head and his method of gradual, thoughtful change. 'It's the atmosphere in this school which sets it apart', he told us. 'The quality of relationships between staff and students is better than in any school I've worked in'.

Engineering specialism has attracted significant funding. A very approachable, unpretentious man, who brings a wide experience of schools and a clear vision of his school's purpose, which is 'to serve the local community with a high quality education, increasing the life chances of ordinary boys and girls'.

Academic matters: Exam results consistently very good – 79 per cent A*-B at A level in 2013, including over 51 per cent A*/A grades. Sixty-one per cent A/A* at GCSE. Engineering specialism has brought astronomy, statistics and product design into the GCSE curriculum. A level science and maths unsurprisingly strong – roughly equal numbers of girls and boys take chemistry and maths, though physics remains a male stronghold. Complete lab refurbishment recently. Elsewhere some evidence of 'girls' subjects' – for example in English literature and French (compulsory at GCSE). Latin, classics, psychology (popular), theatre studies, PE also available. German (declining in many schools) still on offer, and Latin, originally started as a twilight subject, appearing by popular demand at GCSE. Ancient Greek offered as an extra curricular subject.

Does a very fine job over value-added; near the top of the tree nationally. This is all the more remarkable, given that RGS is not as highly selective as some grammar schools in, for instance, Kent and Essex, being unable to draw pupils in great numbers from outside its defined catchment area. SEN support very good – SENCO oversees provision for, eg, visual and hearing impairment and a range of special needs.

Games, options, the arts: Over 90 different clubs and activities, ranging from the Greenpower electric car to dancing – something for even the most reluctant sportsman or woman to get involved in. Compulsory sport: rugby and cricket mainstay for boys, hockey for girls. Football popular for both sexes (girls were Yorkshire junior champions), also mixed hockey, badminton, rock climbing, dance, swimming (in newly refurbished swimming pool). New sports hall paid for by independent fund-raising campaign, available for local use too. New Astroturf.

Music block plus performing arts facility in the new sixth form centre. Funding for new classroom block secured which should be ready for September 2014. Lots of enthusiastic musicians – big band performs frequently in Ripon Cathedral, even entertained the Queen. Vocalists encouraged to join one of the two choirs. Superb art on display.

R

Background and atmosphere: School originally housed in Ripon Cathedral, granted a royal charter by Queen Mary in 1555. Moved to present green and pleasant 23-acre site in 1874. Original Victorian buildings added to over the years, not always sympathetically, and sports hall, sixth form centre, maths and engineering block, state-of-the-art music block, observatory and girls' boarding house have more of the dignity one expects in a school of this kind.

Boys' boarding house (School) is integral, girls' (Johnson) stands on its own. Boarding facilities were recently fully refurbished, which has met with considerable approval by boarders.

Weekly boarding popular; pupils come from North Yorkshire and beyond, some from Europe, North Africa, Dubai and Hong Kong. Boarders (room for 100 out of 800+) do well academically and the few in residence over the weekends are well catered for. Demand for boarding places (14 available a year) outstrips supply, especially post-GCSE, where demand for girls' boarding is particularly popular.

New sixth form block serves both RGS and the community. Around 140 applicants for the first 25 places for students from other schools (mainly state and local independents) post-16. Numbers applying on an upward trajectory.

Pastoral care and discipline: Good pastoral system in operation; in addition pupils look after each other, sixth formers are trained as peer listeners and teams of form tutors ably support heads of school. School says students interact well and both poor behaviour and exclusions are rare. Genuinely good relations between staff and students throughout the school; friendly and compassionate house staff create a relaxed boarding environment. House system in the day school involves all students in sport, debating, Masterchef, University Challenge and house drama competition.

Pupils and parents: Boarders from abroad, Yorkshire Dales and London, some from Forces, day pupils from Ripon and around. Wide range of parental backgrounds and wealth (or lack of it). Pupils a friendly, courteous, grounded bunch of individuals, proud and privileged to be at the school – little sign of the pushiness and fake sophistication often found further south. Former pupils include fashion designer Bruce Oldfield, rugby international Peter Squires, William Hague MP, David Curry MP, Guardian journalist Katharine Viner, TV presenter Richard Hammond.

Entrance: Mainly from local primaries but a smattering from prep schools. Heavily oversubscribed at 11+. Selection by verbal and non-verbal reasoning tests administered by local authority; school takes top 28 per cent of cohort. Sixth form requires minimum six B grades at GCSE but vast majority comfortably exceed this, achieving mainly A*/A grades at GCSE. Increasing number from local independents highlights excellent cost-free A level education.

Exit: Very few leavers at 16+. At 18 most progress to university – many to Russell Group or 1994 and some to Oxbridge (nine in 2013). Medicine, law, sciences, engineering popular, also art and psychology. University destinations include Newcastle, Manchester, Edinburgh, Sheffield, Imperial and Bristol. Excellent careers advice has meant apprenticeships at Barclays, Deloitte and Armstrong Watson for students considering alternatives to university.

Money matters: Yorkshire's only state boarding school, free for day pupils, boarders charged on a sliding scale, but still much cheaper than independent alternatives.

Remarks: An unashamedly academic school, exemplifying much of the traditional English grammar school tradition, though certainly not an exam factory; even so, those with an IQ of lower than 120 could eventually find the pace too hot. A school that gives the impression of being happy with itself and its aims, sitting comfortably in its community – clearly wanted by the people of Ripon.

Robert Clack School

Gosfield Road, Dagenham, RM8 1JU

• Pupils: 1,965 boys and girls • Ages: 11–18 • non-denom • State

Tel: 020 8270 4200
Email: office@robert-clack.bardaglea.org.uk
Website: www.robertclack.co.uk

Headteacher: Since 1997, Sir Paul Grant MA PGCE (sixties), famously promoted from head of humanities when the school was at its lowest ebb, and who has since transformed it into an outstanding success story. He is the eldest of seven children from a working-class Liverpudlian family. A keen football fan, he once hoped to turn professional. He went to the Salesian Grammar School in Bootle, where an influential teacher inspired him to study history at Hull University. He completed a PGCE at Durham and an MA at London University, and taught in North Yorkshire, Australia and Newham before joining Robert Clack in 1990.

At this point the school was sliding downhill. Weak leadership meant a lack of support for those teachers who did try to keep order and behaviour was deteriorating rapidly. There was a serious gang culture, children smoked in the corridors and caused chaos in the community at lunchtime. Pupils rode bicycles inside and it was commonplace to set off fireworks indoors. In 1996, only 17 per cent of pupils gained five or more A–C grades at GCSE and the school was on the verge of special measures. The humanities department, however, was going from strength to strength. Sir Paul was appointed headteacher with an emergency plan of action which included a tough, transparent code for bad behaviour and a new system of rewards. He suspended 300 troublemakers in his first week.

'He led by example,' says a deputy, who had then just left the school as a pupil. 'I saw him stopping a bus outside the school and talking to passengers about how the school was going to change and inviting them to phone the school if they had any problems with Robert Clack pupils.' Most teachers were delighted by the new regime but some parents were outraged. Sir Paul insisted on meeting every one and gradually won them round. Changing behaviour was a gradual process which included driving around picking up truants and talking to local shopkeepers, local councillors, council employees such as housing officers, and police.

Sir Paul was knighted in 2009 for services to education, a few weeks after the school received an Evening Standard award for excellence in challenging circumstances. Larger than life in build and character, and described by Ofsted as 'tireless', he is married with three daughters. The school has been his life's work, he says. 'I wanted to prove that the children in this school could be excellent and my colleagues could be excellent. I'm incredibly proud of the children, parents and staff.'

Pupils are proud too. 'He always works hard to make us succeed in life.' 'He's strict but fair. You know not to get on his wrong side but he always congratulates you when you do well.'

Academic matters: The school is one of 12 outstanding secondary schools feted by Ofsted for excelling against the odds. Some 40 per cent of pupils are on the special needs register and 40 per cent have free schools meals, but results have improved steadily from the 1996 nadir: in 2013, 68 per cent of pupils got five or more good GCSEs including maths and English. At A level, 80 per cent A*/C and 21 per cent A*/A grades.

R

Alongside a strict disciplinary procedure, high quality teaching from a mostly young staff has helped the school achieve outstanding status. The 'Robert Clack good lesson' is a template devised by staff which involves explaining to pupils the objective, content and process of each lesson. We met one teacher who was off to Suffolk, appointed to help a school there achieve 'outstanding' status by using his experience at Robert Clack.

The school is a specialist science, maths and computing college and has recently added a modern languages specialism – a bold move in a strongly working-class school. Although everyone takes French and Spanish for the first three years, at present only 15-20 per cent continue to GCSE. However, the department plans to increase this considerably over the next few years and hopes to introduce Spanish A level alongside the new French course. Everyone takes double science, with some opting for the vocational applied science option and 100 or so taking three separate sciences. Other vocational options include health and social care, business studies, catering, beauty and ICT.

'We have got where we are because all the children feel there is a pathway for them. They're not finding themselves stranded in set 11 for everything.' The school sets right from the start for English, maths, science and languages – 'We're auditing progress all the time, and a significant number have worked their way right up through the sets'. Other subjects, such as history, geography and RE, are taught in mixed ability groups from year 10 onwards. The ability range is massive, from those aiming at A*s to those who joined the school with a reading age of five or six – 'Teaching a huge range is possible if the behaviour is excellent and class sizes are small, so we make sure that they are'.

Learning support and mentor rooms where children can come to catch up on literacy and numeracy, perhaps because they have had time off sick or are middle of the road and tend to be overlooked in class. Or they may come here because they are upset because of family problems and can't cope amongst their peers – 'If children are in the wrong place they will disrupt the lesson. We want to be proactive and avoid problems if possible'. But the 40 per cent on the SEN register – including partially sighted and deaf children – are mostly integrated into the classrooms. We saw a boy with cerebral palsy putting his views across forcefully to the class, despite speech problems – 'The children are very protective of each other'.

The sixth form is part of the North East Consortium with three other local schools, offering over 40 courses at different levels. Over 800 sixth formers in the consortium, including some 450 at Robert Clack. No minimum entry requirements, as courses range from a certificate in motor vehicle servicing to further maths, though students who want to take A levels must have at least five grades Cs at GCSE – 'Many of these students are the first in their families to stay on at school after 16. We don't want to set the benchmark too high – despite the risk of being marked down by Ofsted – because we want to give these children a chance'. Media studies and general studies are the most popular A level courses; maths, further maths, physics and chemistry the most successful. BTECs in business, IT and sport are popular too, as is beauty therapy, taught in a state-of-the-art on-site beauty salon – 'We give everyone the opportunity to be successful here'.

Games, options, the arts: Sport is hugely important here and the school is frequently borough champion at athletics, swimming, rugby and cross-country. It has also been county champion at rugby and netball, a huge achievement against the Essex selective schools. A rugby academy attracts talented players to the sixth form. Pupils have competed nationally at sports ranging from netball to ski-ing, and their team shirts are displayed proudly alongside photos and trophies. 'If you're good at something we'll encourage you and give you recognition,' said a deputy. 'Paul is very good at reinforcing our successes and using them to motivate pupils.'

A plush leisure centre includes a sports hall and fitness suite, open to the local community outside school hours. There are also tennis and netball courts and a large playing field which includes an all-weather pitch. Numerous sports clubs before, during and after school, and even on Saturday mornings, range from hockey to dance to girls' boxing.

The girls' and boys' choirs performed movingly in assembly during our visit, the boys' choir was recently voted best in the borough, and one pupil has starred in a West End musical. Instrumental lessons are free, and there's an orchestra and a jazz group. Sixty pupils are studying for music GCSE, and a few each year move on to music technology A level. The school puts on major performances of eg Oliver! and High School Musical. Plenty of high-quality art displayed around the school, and DT is another popular option at GCSE. The school debating team recently won 'best delegation' at a Model UN conference.

School trips range from French exchanges to sports trips to Canada and Barbados and a conservation expedition to Egypt. Few parents could afford to pay for these trips, so the school raises funds from eg the Worshipful Company of Chartered Surveyors, and children fund-raise enthusiastically too. 'We believe these trips are vitally important to our children's development, and our wonderful staff will always go the extra mile to make sure they happen.'

Background and atmosphere: This is a huge, split-site school, named after local legend Bob Clack, who was mayor from 1940 to 1942. The lower school site, which houses years 7 and 8 and most of year 9, opened in 1935, the upper school buildings – half a mile away – in 1953. The tower blocks of the Becontree Estate – one of the largest in England – bear down on the school like a fortress. It is one of the most deprived areas of the country, and has been a BNP stronghold. Staff and pupils alike express delight that the BNP was routed in the last election, and credit the school with considerable influence. 'The school is the centre of the community.' 'You can't be racist here.'

The buildings range from shabby prefabs put up 'temporarily' in the '40s to the bright new science block and the media block with facilities for drama, music and media studies, as well as the pristine beauty salon. There are plentiful computers and whiteboards, but the planned rebuild now seems to be receding into the far distance as government funds are cut. However, a £3 million expansion of the lower school site has seen 18 new state-of-the-art classrooms.

The school was the highest placed education establishment in the 2010 Sunday Times Best Hundred Companies to Work For list, and winner in the medium-sized company section. It also came first for the quality of its leadership, for personal growth and for its employees' pride in working there.

Pastoral care and discipline: This is one of the smartest and most ordered schools we have ever visited. Children are immaculate in blazers and ties, orderly in corridors and attentive in lessons. 'People know not to mess about,' say pupils. 'But it's all fair – punishments are fair. The rules are good ones.' The school works on a combination of iron discipline and plenty of praise. There are colours for sport, music and performing arts. During the assembly we attended large numbers of children lined up to receive merit awards. They approve of their uniform. 'It makes you feel proud to wear our uniform, when you see pupils from other schools prancing around in polo shirts and trainers.'

Children feel very safe here. 'If something happens here they get straight on top of it. This school really does hate bullying – they don't tolerate it.' There's a close bond between pupils and teachers. 'They're always really cheerful. They'll make a joke out of things if they can. And they treat us like grown-ups. They respect our feelings.' Staff are stationed in corridors between lessons and outside the school when pupils leave at the end of the day. No-one below sixth form is allowed out at lunchtime. Sir Paul tours classrooms daily, greeting pupils with words of praise or good-natured censure.

The pupil referral unit handles children who have disrupted lessons, breached the uniform code, started a fight or played truant. 'We get in quickly – we're proactive – and so we've only had two permanent exclusions in the last 10 years.'

Pupils and parents: Largely from the surrounding estates, though proximity to the school puts a premium on the prices of the few houses for sale in the area. Large numbers of single parent families and those with several generations of unemployment. The school employs a parental adviser who visits families under stress and helps with housing, clothing and food allowances. Around 20 per cent Afro-Caribbean families, the rest mostly white working class: Robert Clack was the only London school on Ofsted's 'excelling against the odds' list with a preponderance of children from such typically under-achieving backgrounds

Entrance: Takes 300 children into year 7 but there are over 200 appeals every year, so the intake invariably increases. Looked after children get priority, as do those with special educational needs, then by distance from the upper school site – generally within a mile or so. Some 2000 applications for the 300 places. Large numbers from other schools join the sixth form.

Exit: About 70 per cent of pupils move up to the sixth form, up from around 20 per cent ten years ago. Two students off with scholarships to study for A levels at Eton recently. Excellent careers advice and encouragement to aim high. The school has links with Oxford, Cambridge, Essex, York and East London universities, with visiting speakers, university visits and summer schools.

Remarks: Outstandingly successful comprehensive in one of the most deprived areas of the country. Excellent leadership by a tireless head has transformed a failing school into one that is a source of pride for staff, parents and pupils. 'This school gets you ready for the future,' said a pupil.

Robert Gordon's College

Linked school: Robert Gordon's College Junior School

Schoolhill, Aberdeen, AB10 1FE

• Pupils: 1,115 pupils (615 boys/500 girls) • Ages: 11–18 • Inter-denom • Fees: £11,185 pa • Independent

Tel: 01224 646346
Email: enquiries@rgc.aberdeen.sch.uk
Website: www.rgc.aberdeen.sch.uk

Head of College: Since 2004, Mr Hugh Ouston MA (Oxon) DipEd (sixty). Educated at Glenalmond, he read history at Christ Church, Oxford, DipEd from Aberdeen. Previously deputy head of George Watson's, and before that taught in the state sector. Has the SQH headship qualification. He runs the school with a powerful management team: Jenny Montgomery is head of senior school (her post is currently being advertised), with four deputy heads; and Mrs Mollie Mennie head of junior school, with two deputy heads. Ailsa Reid is in charge of the nursery.

Ouston 'would love to teach,' but, 'impossible – not fair to the children'; however he (and some of his senior staff) make a point of watching every member of staff take an entire lesson, 'a good insurance policy'.

A wandering head, 'though I am liable to get to the end of the corridor and then be called back'. Says 'I inherited a tightly-run school, superb'; enjoys the tremendous academic achievements of his pupils (still) – 'Tops in everything – it's all down to picking

the best possible staff'. 'The greatest strengths of the school are its co-educational and cosmopolitan community, the work ethic of its pupils and the fact that 20 per cent of senior school pupils are on bursaries.' Vast number of new staff; 'over 80 since I came here'. Good jazzy mixture of old and young – the highly popular classics master sported a splendid pony tail – and 'is really good on expeditions', (said our guides) he does a regular 'Richard and Judy' book recommendation – currently anything by Dickens. Spent four months in 2012 on a job swap with the principal of Scotch College in Adelaide.

Head's own four children Gordon's educated, three now at university, one still in the school. His wife (whom we met on our rounds) 'terribly happy here', she teaches music in the junior school and comes from Aberdeen; her mother lives close by. The Oustons have bought a farm house 10 miles north of Aberdeen. He is relaxed, confident and outgoing, very much in control, he blogs (does he twitter?) and is still riding on a serious high.

Retiring in July 2014. His successor will be Simon Mills, currently head of Lomond School, Helensburg. A Cambridge geographer, he worked in the oil industry before taking up teaching. Has worked at various day and boarding schools, including Portsmouth Grammar.

Academic matters: Unashamedly academic – 'Top passes per pupil, top passes per candidate'. Follows the Scottish system, hot on maths and sciences, 'Science strong – exceptionally large number of excellent results – and consistently good on languages,' which more-or-less echoes the majority of parental careers (oil, business). School thrilled to have pupils achieving top marks in Scotland in advanced higher science subjects over past few years (we said this last time too). Five highers the norm in fifth year (lower sixth); in 2013, 42 per cent A*/As at advanced highers and 54 per cent A*/As at highers. Huge choice of subjects – 30 on offer and masses of add-ons: philosophy, psychology, cooking (head demurred at this point, but it is still there), plus pre-med courses, Scots law course, university skills, Chinese (Japanese no longer). Business management and economics come as a Pre-U, which counts as a higher.

Good ICT – internet connection sourced through the university (ie free), computers throughout, from nursery up. Email for all. Computer-based projectors in every room, interactive whiteboards throughout – though often backed up with the old fashioned sort; some teachers prefer 'em. Head said he thought 'he was the only member of staff who is not good with them...' but we met other elephants.

Eight or 10 parallel classes throughout, max 22, two classes of 'mixed ability' (from an indisputably high base) in each of the four houses, French for all, Latin for all, Greek for the bright (up to advanced higher), Mandarin Chinese for the ambitious. Some setting for maths in P4, otherwise not till S1, S2: English and maths 'continuous assessment' thereafter. German popular, ditto Italian and Spanish – the latter to advanced higher level. Tuition to advanced level in 'many pupils' native tongues'.

Support for learning department straddles junior and senior school and is linked into guidance. Actual hands-on assistance plus dual teaching in class, mainly from specialists. School doesn't really do dyslexia per se; 'a few of the most able have support to overcome ADD, dyslexia'. One or two on the Aspergal spectrum. Any pupil who hits 'either a temporary or a permanent barrier' will be given as 'much help as is necessary'. 'Learning and support for learning definitely comes into that'. But no drop-in centre, though we were assured by our guides that the 'staff are fantastic and will give you all the help you need. Whenever you need it.'

Games, options, the arts: Art school at the top of one of the wings – variety of disciplines, keen on photography; graphic communication now on stream. Architecture taught both in the art and the ICT department, ditto design. Drama timetabled throughout junior and senior to higher level, good and thriving,

R

with three new staff and ditto studios. Theatre set design has a good following.

Music department recently refurbished (we said this last time, but they've gone and done it again) and flourishing, new practice rooms – masses of instruments on offer, trips all over the place: Barcelona, Italy, the recent trip to USA was a tour de force. Enormous (brass) oompah band, pipe band part of the CCF (army and RAF sections only). Hugely popular D of E – 'biggest in Scotland,' says the head, with oodles of bronze, plus silver and golds galore. Zillions of clubs and societies.

Magnificent 45-acre sports ground at Countesswells with artificial pitches for tennis/hockey et al is bisected by mega pylons ('you don't notice them after a while'); an amazing water-based hockey pitch – remember Cyril Lawn? (gets hosed down at half-time to keep it super smooth) is used by the international squad. (The grounds at Countesswells are comandeered during the hols both for junior sports camps and international hockey practice.) Historically, school has fielded strong rugby, but also hockey, cricket and golf. Internationalists in all disciplines and trips abroad for fun as well as for rugby (Canada, Italy, Australia), hockey (Prague, Ireland), skiing (USA). Powerful swimming team 'narrowly beaten for Bath Cup in last two years and regularly among the best in Britain,' adds the head. Well-used swimming pool due for a revamp (water polo, canoeing) on site. Tennis coaching trips on cards to Portugal and Spain, said our guides, head not quite so sure. 'Sadly not, I think'. Two gyms; new games hall on the cards in place of the particularly nasty 60s science block.

Expeditions in every discipline: Malaysia (scuba diving aka biology) Iceland (geography), Australia (sports).

Background and atmosphere: 'Robert Gordon was born in Aberdeen in 1668; he spent most of his life as a merchant in the Baltic ports, building a significant fortune in the process. He always had the idea of building a Hospital for maintenance, aliment, entertainment and education of young boys and, when he died in 1731, that was his legacy.' Magnificent 'Old Hoose' by William Adam in the centre of Aberdeen; the Governor's Room is splendidly evocative: complete with models of early pupils in uniform.

Originally occupied by Hanoverian troops under the Duke of Cumberland on their way to Culloden; the first 14 boys did not take up residence until 1750. The Hospital changed its name to Robert Gordon's College in 1881, went co-ed in 1989 and added a nursery unit in 1993 (popular after-school club for nursery and junior pupils until 5.30pm each day, where they can either play or do supervised homework).

Until recently, the school only occupied the northern side of the extended quadrangle, having gifted the lion's share to The Robert Gordon University in 1909 ('for the enhancement of adult education'). But the university is amalgamating its entire campus down by the riverside at Garthdee and RG governors agreed to buy it back for £10.4 million (out of 'housekeeping' – no special fund needed – we understand that the dosh was paid up front, and skool gets back buildings piecemeal as uni abandons them). The Blackfriars Building and former engineering workshop are now a stonking modern junior school with glass walls and specialist rooms for anything you can imagine, from art and music to languages and video conferencing, plus various 'relocated and refurbished departments', including English, maths, technology and drama, from the senior school. The move has reduced class sizes, adding an extra class in each junior school year group as well as extra sets in the senior school. Though to be honest, our guides found the new lay-out a tad confusing: 'How do we get to the lecture theatre'? (I suggested a Hansel and Gretel approach....)

Enchanting nursery department with cunning horse-shoe shaped desks (junior school has them too, but with longer legs) in a 360 degree configuration.

The final tranche falls in (technology building and total control of the quad) between 2013 and 2015, when the school will be able to spread back into its wings, demolish the excessively nasty 'temporary' buildings which were going up in the playground during our last visit and equip itself for the 21st century including new science and technology centre with 35 new labs and workshops. This is exciting stuff – few inner city schools get such an opportunity, though some of the plans are so grandiose that it will be a challenge to fit them into the current footprint, 'but we will manage,' said the head. School has no thought of expanding its actual roll.

Sixth formers who help with school meals are spared paying for lunch, though from 14 onwards they can (and most do) go into the town for food. The (upmarket) Olive Garden is stowed out at lunch time (Scots vernacular for crowded). 'Food fantastic,' said the head; the weekly menu for breakfast and lunch is published on line (so the poor darlings don't get macaroni cheese twice in one day). Girls wear rather jolly Dress Gordon kilted skirts. The whole school processes behind the pipe band down the streets of Aberdeen to St Nicholas Church on Founder's Day – 'My favourite day of the whole year,' said the head. The head boy and girl carry the standards behind a somewhat futuristic school mace, which is borne ('very proudly') by the head janitor (and I was presented with a paper knife more or less in the same mould – we love being bribed).

Pastoral care and discipline: House system recently reinforced, with class captains at all levels plus sixth form assistants at 11 to help those newly arrived in the senior school feel more at home. Guidance system in operation – tutors – as well as good PSHE. Fairly sin-free school – pupils allowed out for lunch and 'no bad reports'. No smoking on the premises (campus too small), one expelled for drugs during head's reign. Strong anti-bullying programme, would be suspended for booze, which is a bit obvious out of school; ditto smoking. Heads of school hot on discipline and when, during our wander, we came across some rather boisterous junior chaps practising drop shots (with the nursery dept balls) they were summoned to order by the head boy with the word 'Gents'...

Pupils and parents: This is the school in Aberdeen. Lots of university parents (easy to drop off), oodles of professional and oil-related ditto, plus farmers etc. Day starts early at 8.30am and children often come from as far away as Montrose, ie 35/40 miles. Parking at drop-off and collection times hideous. Vast and increasing number of first time buyers consistent with the vagaries of the oil industry, and strong global ethnic mix. Good Quadrangle newsletter bi-monthly and parental involvement. Parents love the school so much that often, having spent years in the oily wilderness, they buy a proper house and, at the next placement, Maw and the wains stay behind, leaving Paw to travel the world alone.

Entrance: Interview for nursery and five-year-olds entering junior school; test for those over nine and exam for senior school. Fewer leave post Highers than arrive: usual strictures for entry plus test. Pupils either come up from primary school or from local state schools, hugely oversubscribed – particularly for the junior school and S1, but Aberdeen has a fluid population and it is worth applying at any time: school can cope with a short period of 'overlap' if they know a family is about to be re-located. Rather jolly in-house instruction manual for S1s (ie first year senior school). Official open day second Saturday in November.

Exit: Coming and going with relocation, otherwise (95 per cent) to universities all over, the odd gap year. 'Few don't go to university.' Still fairly conservative in choice – more than 50 per cent to Aberdeen, Edinburgh, Glasgow or Robert Gordon University. Around 10 per cent down south, eg Bristol, Durham, Manchester, Newcastle, Warwick and Oxbridge. A few to eg

Canada or Australia. Medics, lawyers and would-be scientists, engineers and economists top the wish-list, almost all getting into their first choice – 'But then we have no delusions,' said the head.

Money matters: Fees range from £4,305 for half day nursery (including lunch) to a whopping £10,705 (no lunch) for sixth formers. Unusually, monies are paid 40 per cent autumn term, 35 per cent spring term and 25 per cent summer term; two per cent extra if parents pay either by 10 monthly direct debits or credit cards. From August 2012 sibling discount reduced to zero for second child in the school, and 30 per cent thereafter – though pre-existing (more generous) arrangements will stand until child leaves.

Huge number of endowments – Robert Gordon's expectation being that 'those who came to the Hospital and did well in later life would plough back some of their gains'. In 1816, 'A generous bequest by Alexander Simpson of Collyhill made it possible to extend the accommodation', and Gordonians and FPs have continued to do so ever since.

Some 185 children on some form of bursary, with 100 per cent help available to those in real need with bright children. The Aberdeen Educational Endowment provides extra bursaries. Around 20 means-tested free places in S1 each year. A mega appeal for more dosh (as ever) and an appeal to help convert the newly re-acquired bits of quad running concurrently as we write.

Remarks: Strong co-ed day school with a far-sighted head who is relishing the challenge of re-absorbing The Robert Gordon University (two sides of the not-quite original quad; but see Background) back into the school proper. If you want to keep the little darlings at home, and live near enough, you couldn't do better. Not a school for social climbers and probably rather intimidating for gentle souls. (Head has added that the 'emphasis on happiness makes the school seem smaller than it really is'). In reality, each age group is fairly tightly timetabled and logistically compartmentalised, so there's not really a lot of overlap on any space; crocodiles of tablier-ed tinies line up for the dining room as pre-teens kick around a ball (which was rapidly confiscated).

The Rochester Grammar School

Maidstone Road, Rochester, ME1 3BY

• Pupils: 1150 girls (boys in sixth form) • Ages: 11–18 • Non-denominational • State

Tel: 01634 843049
Email: office@rochestergrammar.medway.sch.uk
Website: www.rochestergrammar.medway.sch.uk

Principal: Since 2010, Stuart Gardner, who joined the school in 2006 and worked his way up through assistant head and deputy head. Read history at Bristol University and began his career as a history teacher at King Edward VI Chelmsford, followed by a head of history post at Borden Grammar, Sittingbourne, then director of studies at St Catherine's in Twickenham.

Privately educated himself (St George's College, Weybridge), he says he didn't plan to teach in the state sector, but is now evangelical about grammars. 'I love that you can take a child from any economic or social background and transform their life chances', he says. He's also passionate about getting women into the top jobs. 'Gender equality is one of the great lies of the 20th century. I consciously make sure I'm addressing the issues and I do a lot of work on inspiring pupils to see what women can achieve.'

'very approachable' parents report. No mud on him – students and parents all seem to like him – and if you get irritated by heads who seem to be not quite in the real world and can't contemplate a better way of doing things, you're going to like it here. He's business-like in his approach, from firing underperforming staff, to changing methods which aren't working, and ensuring the girls understand the meaning of a return on their investment when considering where to spend their tuition fees.

Two small children and a teenage stepdaughter, plus working on an MSc in professional practice, leaves little room for hobbies but time off finds Gardner on road trips – recently driving 3,000 miles from southern Portugal to the Hook of Holland.

Great GCSE results have resulted in 'a few unsolicited emails' but Gardner says he sees himself in post for at least another five years – 'this is a difficult place to leave' he says.

Ms Denise Shepherd oversees this school as executive principal, as well as its role as a National Support School to other schools.

Academic matters: In 2013, 68 per cent of GCSE entries were graded A*/A (99 per cent of students got five A-Cs including English and maths). At A level, 85 per cent of grades were A* to B, and at IB the average total point score was 37. The school has specialist status for maths, ICT and music; history, English and science are all strong departments. Modern foreign languages haven't matched up so Mr Gardner has replaced the department head and is introducing new language teaching methods from September 2013. Students in years 7 and 8 will learn languages through drama workshops and role play and no written work, with the aim to build their vocabulary and confidence before moving to the next level. 'The brain is wired to learn languages orally first. The worst that will happen is that students will get Bs, but they will be able to order sandwiches confidently and catch a train using that language', he says. 'Language teaching hasn't worked for so long. I have watched children dumbstruck in France and Germany, asking "do you speak English?" in English. If I see a problem I get to the bottom of it and I'm prepared to take a bold step to make a difference.' The school also offers Latin, which unusually is oversubscribed. One parent explains why her daughter loves it: 'They also cover the civilisation, history and literature. It's a good option if you're not a good linguist'.

As we walk the corridors there's a hubbub coming from all the classrooms. Pupils are animated, some half on their feet. Tables aren't arranged in serried ranks, but in blocks or U-shapes and there's much collaborative work and discussion going on. 'There's lots of guided discovery. We are told a limited amount, and we are supposed to find out the rest, we're not spoon-fed', say the girls. Thinking and memory skills are big buzzwords in the school, or as the students explained it to us, 'We focus on how to learn, not just what to learn'. They all know what type of learner they are, and how they work best. 'I'm a logical thinker', says one. 'I can't understand diagrams', says another, 'so the teacher gives me an explanation in words'.

Sixth formers speak of an individualism in teaching styles that makes lessons lively and interesting. 'History and politics are fantastic, the grades are consistently amazing and the teacher has such a passion for the subject he turns bright red when we're having a debate', says one. Another, who transferred from a different school says the gap in expectations between the two is huge. 'It's very demanding, the school expects you to be on top of your game'.

Mr Gardner will not tolerate any slack in teaching. 'If a member of staff, after appropriate support, is unable to demonstrate an ability to improve, they move on. It's the same with supply teachers covering sickness absence, we might have two or three supply teachers in quick succession which concerns parents, but it's important to get the right one.' You can't argue with the success of this strategy.

One parent calls the school 'a jewel in Rochester'. But the other side of the coin is that the pace is fast and your daughter will have to be prepared to work hard. The school follows a two year compressed KS3 to enable some accelerated students to sit English, maths and science GCSEs in year 10 and AS courses in year 11. One parent relates that when her child took three GCSEs in year nine, 'She got three As which she wasn't happy with, so she retook them to get A*s'. The pace and quantity of work can impact on family life too, as one parent explains: 'Some parents find it quite hard to accept the amount of work their child has got to do'. Her daughter worked a couple of hours a night in year 7/8, and all evening in year 9, but willingly she says. The school expects around 14 hours of homework per week to be completed in the sixth form, but many students go beyond this of their own volition. Parents report one or two girls who have left because this environment didn't suit them. But they stress that children are not left to flounder. 'There are lots of support clubs, they don't just write them off,' says one.

Speaking to sixth formers, it's apparent that the vast majority develop a self-belief that they are capable of anything, rather than being flattened by the expectations. 'It does get to the stage that you think a B is not good enough. But that's how life is', one told us. 'When I got a B in a mock I was distraught, I didn't deserve a B. Then I think, if they're getting A, why can't I? If she can do it, I can, and I ask other students how they are doing it.' Another girl told us, 'I don't want to go to Cambridge, but I know that if I did, the school would enable me to get there.'

Games, options, the arts: Lack of green fields equals lack of serious sporting provision. Football and athletics are the school's main areas of competitive success. An old girl made the GB synchronised swimming squad, another's an international skier.

The school has the largest girls' D of E centre in the country and opportunities include a three week trek in China. Takes part in the Comenius project, promoting European culture. Individual trips encouraged to develop the girls' personal interests and career intentions. One girl is going to the student UN in Geneva, with the school matching her fundraising, another has been to CERN for an extended project.

'Join the choir, see the world', they say – anyone can be in the choir, which has taken them to the Vatican City and the USA. Music concerts on a termly basis, international musicians brought in to perform in the school's Thorndike Arts Centre. Two governors' places for musicians – students get bursaries to spend on music lessons, in return they give back to the whole school by running extra-curricular activities – one girl runs two choirs, another a quartet.

Language exchanges to France, Germany, and Spain. 'I believe in exchanges and immersion, spending a week with a host family, I do not believe in day trips,' says Gardner.

Background and atmosphere: No dreaming spires, it's a functional building, but it's modern and in a good state of repair by the standards of state grammars. 'A bit soulless' says a parent.

The school moved to this new building in 1990, having opened in 1888 with a then progressive aim to educate young ladies. Became an 'academy of excellence' in 2011. The school is a combined mathematics/ICT and music specialist school, a Thinking Foundation school, and the first 'Memory' school accredited by Exeter University – teaching students how to learn and memorise is a priority.

It's a powerhouse for women. Houses are named after an eclectic group of women such as Jane Tomlinson, Eva Cassidy, Ella Fitzgerald, and Hildegard (of Bingen). Corridors are lined with posters detailing the most powerful women in the UK today, as well as the illustrations of ex-pupil Evelyn Dunbar, held up as a beacon for forging her way into the entirely male dominated theatre of war when she became the only female commissioned war artist during World War II.

Work is underway on developing an old girls' network. 'In public schools the former students associations can be very powerful, I want to give our students that same advantage. There are still some industries where it matters who you know, and I would like our young ladies to look after each other,' says Mr Gardner. Its young alumni group, now 100 strong and growing, brings back former pupils to help current students see themselves five years down the line, and to give them contacts to go to for advice.

Everything reinforces a message to be the best, which concerns one parent, who said: 'One thing I didn't like when we looked around, there were so many lovely displays and all the work was excellent; other schools had things up which weren't quite as good, but where people had done their best. I wondered, if you weren't quite up there, how would you feel?'

Pastoral care and discipline: Discipline? There's quite a pause before the sixth formers respond, 'People don't really go out of line here'. It usually only comes into play for uniform infringements, for which the girls have to do community service, helping out the teachers.

Pastoral care thrives on teachers knowing their pupils very well indeed. Girls have the same head of house and the same form tutor for six years, which means problems are spotted and interventions organised early. There are vertical form groups, with years 7 to 12 mixed together, and family groups of five or six within each form. Younger girls like this because they can ask senior students for help with their homework, or advice on which options to choose, and it means they don't find the big girls so intimidating. All new girls are mentored by a girl a year older. For year 13 they are put in subject specialism forms – those headed for medicine in one, musicians in another, for example.

Parents speak highly of the school's rapid identification of and solutions for any learning difficulties. One recalls: 'Soon after she started the school, her CAT tests showed a big discrepancy. The school arranged further testing and we found she was dyslexic with processing difficulties. I was astonished because this had never been suspected before. They've given her a range of strategies to help her cope, and it's not holding her back in any way.' 'I'm very proud of the special educational needs provision at this school, we find a lot of students have SEN which wasn't identified before,' Mr Gardner says.

To deal with the pressures they are under, the school has introduced a Sumo initiative, to develop 'bounce-back ability' as Mr Gardner dubs it. 'It's about developing their resilience to take the knocks when they occur', he says. It takes students through a series of responses, such as: How can I change this situation? What can I learn from it? Is there anything positive about it? Am I responding appropriately? and how important will this be in six months' time?

Pupils and parents: Gardner's social engineering wish is working, no question about the added value here. From a school community where just 25 per cent of parents are graduates, it delivers one in three pupils to a top ten university.

The pupil body is a true social mix. Some parents are not working and are in difficult circumstances, some are doctors and lawyers. Some children live in public housing, around 10 per cent were privately educated at primary school. One in ten pupils are from non-white backgrounds. What they have in common, say pupils, is that, 'everyone really wants to do well'.

The pupils feel it's an extremely supportive community. 'There isn't a person who won't help you', says one. Another says she has experienced 'overwhelming kindness' from fellow students. A third needed to raise funds for a work experience placement at the United Nations and was humbled that with fellow pupils' help, she managed this in one week.

Entrance: There's no catchment – entry is entirely based on scores in the local 11+, the Medway test. The pass mark for this fluctuates around 509 and last year students needed 514 or higher for a place at Rochester Grammar. There are two music

R

scholarships and five places are held for appeals. 'Some of our greatest successes didn't pass the test,' Gardner says.

Around 30-40 places become available in the sixth form, when entry also opens up to boys. Gardner says that 12-18 boys join the sixth form each year as the school achieves better results than any other in the area. Minimum entry requirements are 5+ A*-C grades at GCSE, with B grades in all courses to be studied at A level or IB except maths and the sciences which require an A grade.

Exit: Around 80 to 90 per cent stay on into the sixth form when they can opt to take either A levels or the IB. There's a tailored programme for students wishing to apply for medical school or Oxbridge. All are expected to go on to university and the school does a great deal of work on guiding pupils' choices, many of them will be the first in their family to take a degree. A virtual university week is held in year 12, when pupils are taught in university format and given advice on UCAS applications and accessing bursaries.

Pupils looking at wackier courses are likely to be discouraged. Gardner says, 'We engage in a lot of research with the students, looking at where that course is likely to take them, and the value of investing in their education. A student might say "I want to do X course at Y university, I like the tutor, and the facilities are really nice," We unpick that. Where do people from that course go to post-university? What percentage gets full-time employment at a certain level of money? We make them understand, it's not just the next three years, make the wrong choice now and you play catch up for the rest of your life.'

The result is that one-third of pupils go to a top 10 university, one-half to a top 20, and all to a top 40. The most popular destinations last year were UCL, Kent, Southampton, Exeter and Manchester, with history, medicine, biochemistry and English literature being the top degree choices.

Remarks: The poise, focus and articulacy of sixth formers here is incredible – it's like talking to young graduate professionals rather than a bunch of schoolgirls. So is their work ethic. 'I want to stay in and study on Friday nights, I'm not forced to,' says one, as the others nod in agreement. The head is determined that his girls will make the best use of their intelligence and take their rightful place at the high table of professional life. You'll be hard pressed to find a school more likely to steer your daughter on to great things. But you need to be sure she'll cope with the pressure.

Rochester Independent College

Star Hill, Rochester, ME1 1XF

• Pupils: 280 boys and girls • Ages: 11–19 • Non-denominational
• Fees: Tuition £9,900–£16,000 pa; Boarding + £7,875–£12,258 pa
• Independent

Tel: 01634 828115
Email: admissions@rochester-college.org
Website: www.rochester-college.org

Co-principals: There are three co-principals: Brian (Pain), Alistair (Brownlow), and Pauline (Bailey) – it's all first names here. The three heads say they work in a collegiate way, sharing responsibilities. The kids tell you Brian is the big chief, and the one they're a bit scared of. Brian is as far from a typical public school head as you can imagine. He has a passion for sailing barges, and he walks into the meeting as if he has just stepped off one – clad in a T-shirt, hair looking like it's been in a force eight, and hands he needs to wash before shaking

as he's just been scrubbing blackboards. He tells it like it is, including telling kids who aren't putting in any effort that they are not staying to waste their parents' money. Alistair's the great communicator, bouncing with enthusiasm like Tigger, and expressing the school's beliefs and methods with an articulacy which backs up his reputation as an ace English teacher. Pauline has a background in management and is the one who ensures they are meeting regulations and dotting the 'I's. She oversees all boarders and the year 7-10s.

It's a stable ship – Brian set up the school with a co-founder in 1984; Alistair joined as a new graduate in 1997, while Pauline was once a pupil here, joined the staff in 1989, and has sent her own two children here. All three still teach, 'so we don't lose sight of what we're here for'. There's no board of governors – the three run it as a plc, and are the only shareholders. It started as an A level college, and extended to take pupils from year 7 in 2007.

Academic matters: There's no uniform or dress code, and the teachers are just as likely as pupils to be wearing a hoody. Everyone goes by their first name. So far so hippy – until you walk around the building during lessons. Hush has descended, and opening a classroom door reveals silent pupils, and desks in rows. Alistair says: 'People try to place us in the progressive/ alternative mould, but we're not. It's common sense; small classes, good teaching, and an informal but ordered and respectful atmosphere.'

The next surprise comes in the teaching methods. 'We teach-test-teach-test,' says Alistair. The idea that testing thwarts children gets short shrift here. 'A lot of schools don't do enough regular testing. At A level we do a test every week in each subject. If we're going to put something right we need a rigorous diagnosis of what is wrong,' Alistair says.

There's no objection to this degree of testing from pupils – in fact the students seem to welcome it. 'Testing means you can't get delusions, you really know where you are at any point,' said one. Another, who was told by her grammar school that she needed to 'lower her sights' said: 'The teaching style is completely different, we are tested all the time and my grades have gone up consistently.'

There is a firm concentration on exam technique, but still the school isn't seen as an exam factory. One sixth form pupil said: 'The focus is on exams, but it is still enriching. We get a two hour lesson for everything which means the teachers can drift off topic which helps a lot with general knowledge and essay subjects.'

Teachers are 'very passionate about their subjects,' say parents, and another pupil comparing the teaching to that at his former grammar school said: 'The teaching is of a better quality and the teachers know their subject to a greater depth.'

And a pupil at the lower end of the school said: 'You don't get to the end of one lesson without doing something fun.'

Many students transfer here after poor progress at AS or A level and the effect can be dramatic. One pupil told us he was predicted to get Ds and Es at AS; he moved from his grammar to the college in February, and in July he achieved three As at AS and an A at A level. Another student moved after getting a U at AS, and she says, 'In my first two weeks here I learned more than I had in the whole previous year.'

There are three pathways through the sixth form, mainly set in different teaching groups. There are those doing a two year A level course through the school; students who have transferred here for year 13 after disappointing AS grades; and those who have done two years elsewhere and are doing retakes. The A level programme is flexible with no option blocks, and students can do speed courses in a new subject to complement retakes. Results for 2013 A levels show nearly 27 per cent of entries achieving A*/A (62 per cent A*-B, 83 per cent A*-C).

Maths is the biggest A level subject. English Literature and film studies are also strong departments, both having received Good Schools Guide awards in recent years.

At GCSE, biology, chemistry and physics are taught at GCSE level for those aiming to study sciences at A level, and students also take the IGCSE in English and English literature. Languages on offer include German, French and Spanish, but it is not compulsory to take a language. Pupils can also take subjects such as astronomy, film studies and photography at GCSE.

And it would be hard to find better provision for an artist. GCSEs are offered in six disciplines – fine art, graphics, photography, textiles, ceramics and 3D. Some students take three of these to A level, which enables them to bypass a foundation year. There is terrific work on display. Two students have won places on the prestigious fine art degree course at UCL's The Slade School. Dominik Klimowski, former BBC online picture editor, teaches photography, and local artist Billy Childish is a visiting lecturer.

GCSE results for 2013 show 75 per cent of pupils got five A* to Cs including English and Maths, and 14 per cent of entries gained an A*/A. The intake means that for some, passing five at grade C level represents an enormous achievement; others achieve a string of A*s.

Parents especially appreciate the efforts made to ensure each pupil gains the best possible grade. One said: 'There are a lot of extra lessons before exams, in the holidays and so on. They will do as much as they can if they think you can improve your grade.'

Another praised the fact that they don't charge for extra tuition in the evenings and holidays, adding: 'I was concerned about my son's maths and suggested getting him some tuition. They said it was their responsibility, and I should not be looking for tutors. They did some extra work with him and he got an A, so I was ecstatic.'

But there is some dissent among parents about the college's policy of sitting AS levels alongside A levels in year 13, as one parent said: 'I would prefer them to be done in year 12, I think it puts too much pressure on to revise two years' worth in one go.' The principals' view is that students inevitably perform better at the end of a two year course, and that this policy in no way prejudices students' chances of receiving offers. Students are only likely to sit them in year 12 if they are expected to get an A, and the pupils say it is an advantage to go to university interviews talking about your predicted grades, rather than possibly some poorer grades from the year before.

Classrooms are named after Brian's beloved Thames sailing barges; 2014 will see this interest taken a step further, with the introduction of an apprenticeship course in boatbuilding, enabling students to gain City and Guilds qualifications up to NVQ level 3.

Games, options, the arts: Sport is growing, but the school doesn't have the infrastructure to provide serious provision. There's a newly created rugby team for year 11 to 13s, which uses the facilities of a local rugby club and is coached by a player from England's women's team. It also supports those playing at higher levels – one sixth former is training with a London football club, and the school enables him to fit lessons around his sporting commitments. Another sixth former is hoping to compete as a sprinter in the next Paralympics. But as one student points out, it is not the type of school which tends to attract the sporty, and so PE provision tends to be more activity based, like ice skating, sailing, self-defence and climbing.

Lower down the school the students play in mixed teams, so boys say games have to be less rough.

There's a rich cultural programme – a drama theatre hosts visiting theatre companies and art shows, and the school's on-site cinema regularly hosts the National Schools' Film week.

Background and atmosphere: The campus is as unique as the school. It started as one terraced house, but as the school expanded, it gradually bought up 13 properties in adjoining roads, including a Georgian terrace which houses the boarding accommodation. What would once have been the back gardens to these houses now form the grounds with ancient apple trees and wild garden areas, paths to secret nooks and crannies, a viewing platform to climb – and an oversized garden shed where Brian likes to hold his maths classes. Students work on garden projects such as the allotment as part of their D of E award, and the gardens have won a Kent Wildlife Trust Gold Award.

Mid-career, Brian took time out of teaching to become an architect, and the campus reflects this interest. The theatre in the grounds is known as the Womble building – the theatre space is under ground, whilst over the top there's an outdoor seating area which can be used as an open-air auditorium.

Work is underway on an igloo-like structure in the garden, which will be used as an outdoor classroom, shelter, and quiet space. Intended to inspire and motivate, it will have a central roof opening for cloud watching.

And the school is awaiting delivery of some steel sculptural musical gates – an art installation created by Henry Dagg, who plays with Icelandic pop star Bjork, and has transformed his garden fence into a glockenspiel. You will be able to play three octaves on these gates, sufficient to pass your music A level, according to Brian. Reflecting on the £100,000 price tag of these gates, Brian says, 'I'm committed to culture'.

Pastoral care and discipline: A level students have one-to-one meetings with a personal tutor every couple of weeks, more frequently if they wish, and pupils lower down the school have individual meetings every half term.

Parents receive formal reports once a month, which are 'meaningful, not full of euphemisms, and not from a software package'. Younger pupils have a parents' evening, but in the sixth form tutors deal directly with the students as young adults, and reports only go home which they have seen first. 'We promise there will be no surprises through that feedback,' says Alistair.

A number of the pupils have been labelled as bad apples or having limited prospects in previous settings, but have quickly turned things around at the college, where they are free from discipline based on minutiae. One such pupil, previously at a girls' independent, says: 'I was constantly getting picked on by teachers and getting detentions for stupid things, like going to the toilet'.

The principals say they are strict about homework and behaviour, but removing petty rules means the rapport between pupils and teachers is much better. Or, as one pupil put it, 'The only thing to rebel against here is education itself'.

Other pupils have come from grammars where they felt under too much pressure, or from large schools where they felt overwhelmed, and all say they are learning better and enjoying school more here. 'I worried a lot at my old school, here it's a better environment,' said one. 'At my old school if you improved, they didn't notice,' said another.

Parents all speak highly of the pastoral care, and the growth in confidence they have witnessed in their children. One has three children at the school and she says: 'They are all very different but they are spot on about all of their weaknesses and strengths.'

Boarding is only available to students of 16+. Virtually all students have single rooms. Some have a very small 'pod' ensuite, otherwise it's shared bathrooms. Furnishings are basic but the Georgian high ceilings and big windows add light and space, and all rooms have a phone and internet point. There's a big common room with a pool table and comfy chairs, and a study for quiet work.

Currently 60 out of 280 students are boarders – 40 per cent of these are from the UK, 11 per cent from Europe, and the remainder from countries including Canada, USA, Thailand, China, Russia, Nigeria, and South Africa.

Pupils and parents: Local pupils form 70 per cent of the cohort and come from a wide catchment – there are minibuses from towns including Tonbridge, Tunbridge Wells, Maidstone, Ashford and Sevenoaks, and the train station opposite brings pupils from Bromley and London. A further 15 per cent come from elsewhere in the UK, and 15 per cent from overseas, including Thai government scholars.

Numbers lower down the school are small. It starts with around 10 pupils in year 7, who have deliberately opted for a small and different type of school. These are added to over the years, generally by pupils who have been disaffected or haven't thrived in other schools, to numbers in the mid-20s for GCSE years. By sixth form it grows to 50 in year 12, and 130 in Year 13/14. This is something to consider in the younger year groups, especially as currently two girls are both the only girl in their years. The flipside is it makes for more natural relationships between the boys and girls and less of the gender division that you see in big schools – they are clearly relaxed in each other's company. None of the pupils or parents we spoke to see the small year groups as a problem – there's much more mixing between years, and pupils keep up with other friends in their neighbourhood – and many see this as a plus.

The students are a strikingly nice bunch. It's a place for individuals, and there's a lovely air of tolerance and warmth between the pupils – many of whom seem relieved to have found a home among other square pegs. 'They look after each other, and if someone does well they are pleased about this,' says a parent. Those whose strengths lie outside the traditionally alpha areas of academic or sporting have their own kudos. 'There is a lot more respect for art and creativity,' said one pupil.

Students say it is not competitive, and that there's a huge range in academic ability and ambition. 'If you work your hardest and get an E that's fine,' said one. 'Stronger people help the weaker people, no-one's struggling because everyone helps each other,' said another.

Parents love the lack of school gate competitiveness: 'That playground talk, everyone wanting their child to be in the top set, you don't have that here,' said one relieved mother.

About 50 per cent of pupils have been previously in the independent sector, but a lot of pupils come from families with no tradition of private education.

Entrance: It's non-selective in that there's no entrance exam for children joining at 11 or 13, and there's no minimum GCSE grade requirements for sixth form entry. But every prospective student is interviewed, and the principals say they do turn some away.

Direct entry into any year group at any point in the academic year is possible, and places can be secured in the short gap between exam results and the start of a new term. Around 60 students join each year, either to retake their A levels having completed two years of A levels elsewhere, or directly into year 13 after disappointing AS results in year 12 elsewhere.

Exit: The top five student destinations in the last eight years are Leeds, Nottingham, Sussex, Cambridge and Imperial.

The courses students go on to reflect the broad range of abilities and interests catered for: some go on to read law, maths, medicine or classics; others have taken up courses in animal behaviour, film studies, marketing, photography or midwifery.

Money matters: Around £100,000 per year goes into means-tested bursaries, which are awarded not on academic ability, but 'if we think they'll make a good contribution'. Scholarships include the Ralph Steadman Art Scholarship, which offers a two year full scholarship for A levels.

The school has a policy to keep extras to the minimum – music lessons, buses and exam fees are extra, but extracurricular trips are kept deliberately modest. 'We don't take for granted that parents have bottomless pits of money,' says Alistair.

Remarks: This won't be one that sits on your shortlist and you can't make up your mind about. You'll either love or hate this place. Your money won't buy the trappings of a public school – no mahogany-rich headmaster's study, certainly no suave head in a handmade suit. No pupils with collars and lips firmly buttoned. No PTA committees or fundraising balls. For some that will be a blessed relief.

You'll get that warm buzz in your heart when you recognise your kid in the personalities here – or not. That might be one of several types we saw – the quirky one, condemned to be picked on in an average school; the fiercely intelligent, who has rubbed teachers up the wrong way by being too smart for his own good in other settings; the kid whose education gets derailed by too much focus on petty rules and discipline.

It won't suit sporting jocks – facilities are meagre, and there are rarely enough pupils of the right age and inclination to make a team.

But it's a great option for the cash-strapped; many parents with only enough gold in the pot to fund a couple of years in the independent sector buy in for the last year of GCSEs, for the A level course, or for retakes. And it's a sound investment – 21 per cent of all students got AAB in facilitating subjects last year, and among the retakers, all got into university, and three-quarters won Russell Group places.

Roedean School

Roedean Way, Brighton, BN2 5RQ

• Pupils: 380 girls; 110 day pupils, 240 full boarders, 10 flexi boarders, 20 weekly boarders • Ages: 11–18 • C of E, but all faiths are welcome • Fees: Boarding £25,452–£32,610; Day £16,380–£18,900 pa • Independent

Tel: 01273 667500
Email: info@roedean.co.uk
Website: www.roedean.co.uk

Headmaster: Since 2013, Mr Oliver Blond, previously head of Henrietta Barnett School in Hampstead Garden Suburb. He gained his teaching qualifications at Cambridge and London, was previously deputy head of North London Collegiate School and is married to Helen, a teacher and author. They have two young children.

Academic matters: At A level, a maths and science powerhouse – partly due to the intake of girls from the Far East at the upper end of the school. On the other hand, fewer for languages but school says 'it's an area of development.' Economics a popular option. Overall, in 2013, 56 per cent A*/A grades.

At GCSE, 69 per cent A*/A grades in 2013. Now taking IGCSE in maths and science; physics dept has opted for the more demanding AQA syllabus. School plans to expand the academic opportunities – 'We now have philosophy and ethics. I'm determined to bring in an ethical dimension to science'. This is Roedean, but not as we know it. IT whiteboards etc all much more in evidence now, plasma screens with latest news, good school intranet.

EAL taken by many, although a good level of English is a pre-requisite for all candidates for places here – around 100 have one-to-one language/learning tuition, which includes good support for a wide range of mild SENs. Group lessons to prepare for the IELTS exam. School's location and sloping site make wheelchair access virtually impossible, though a range of other physical disabilities, eg mild visual or hearing impairments, catered for. Of 105 on current SEN register, two-thirds are dyslexic to some degree. School copes well with dys's, Asperger's, ADHD etc. IEPS

R

where needed. Small group and one-to-one help (extra charge) but no withdrawal from curriculum subjects. Gifted and talented stretched as befits need. Good careers centre and library with first-rate full time staff.

Games, options, the arts: Around 30 sports available here including riding at Ditchling riding school and very active polo club, popular with girls from all types of backgrounds. Multi-purpose sports hall and additional fitness suite for older girls, inviting indoor pool and plenty of outdoor space – fields rolling seawards and robust attitude to go with it – 'We don't stop because it's raining a bit,' we were told. Girls return from matches envying the Astroturfs on offer elsewhere and school currently managing doughtily without, though, 'In due course there will probably be one', and they do borrow a couple at nearby sports centre. Everyone takes dance for the first two years and many thereafter. Successes in many sports, notably netball. Yoga, zumba and scuba diving now offered. Lovely adventure playground for younger girls (money raised by parents) and a great attraction to visiting prospective pupils.

Arts flourish, though in rooms of varying sizes – much work in many media delights the eye: super textiles, ceramics and very lively DT – all witness to clever and inspirational teaching, as are excellent results. Music is strong in good-size class teaching room and many smaller spaces. Music tech 'there if you want to', but, as yet, not many do, though fab new music tech room in the ensemble room should change all that. Concerts in the wonderfully atmospheric Edwardo-Romanesque chapel, the hall or theatre – an exceptional asset with wholly flexible staging, allowing for theatre-in-the-round or an orchestra pit and seating 320. 'Team' plays, one senior and two junior productions a year. All looks professional, well-supported and enjoyed with no hint of flashiness. D of E, Young Enterprise and masses of highly enjoyable and very effective charity work. Each year thousands of squids raised for various charities. More extra-curricular opportunities than you can fit into your week.

Background and atmosphere: You drive out of Brighton heading east, the huge marina clinking below between you and the open sea and there, in front, bolted to the hillside and above the cliffs, you see a vast, twin turreted, red-roofed pile and, if you don't know, you wonder what on earth it could be. This is Roedean of unique (and largely outdated) reputation, but no longer with the stern aspect of yore. Its recent makeover with six washes of honey limewash has restored it to the hue of its youth. Now, most attractively, it changes colour according to the light and time of day and no longer looks determined to outface invaders and marauders, especially those of the opposing sex. The school was designed in 1898 by the architect of the former Wembley stadium – hence the trademark twin turrets – Sir John Simpson. The sign says, 'Welcome' – and welcome you feel in this relaxed, orderly, spacious and warm – in all senses – school. Signage overall, however, needs improvement – it is perfectly possible to drive out of Brighton with Roedean on the cliff above and get lost trying to reach it.

Having begun at the end of the 19th century as a school with 10 pupils and three mistresses, 10 minutes away in Lewes Crescent, the school rapidly expanded and the present building bears witness to the confidence, solidity and durability its redoubtable founders felt about girls' education. It has a medieval baronial feel with huge high windows, vast tiled fireplaces and many pretty massive rooms – one feels the place could take twice the number of pupils and be far from crowded. Corridors and many other areas are cheerily decorated in a bright primrose yellow and smart new blue carpets giving a fresh, warm feel. Clearly it's a nightmare to keep up and the battering of the elements is visible not just outside, as patches of bubbly damp on many walls, but the place is attractively and not skimpily furnished and feels like home. A few atmospheric, rather Gothic corridors and staircases and a lovely cloister area

on the way to the chapel – for quiet and repose. Girls in French navy uniforms seem relaxed and friendly and keen to give of their best.

Pastoral care and discipline: Discipline is never a problem. No drugs or similarly serious incidents in recent times, but 'there would be no alternative to exclusion' if anyone were endangering herself or another member of the community. Integration of overseas pupils is more successful here than in many comparable schools – far less struggle in getting everyone to join in after the first few weeks.

Strong pastoral system and all staff on the alert for a long face or other signs of unhappiness or disturbance. All girls have open and wholly confidential (except in cases of actual danger) access to a counsellor. Active peer-listening scheme. Pride taken in caring for each other and family atmosphere. 'My daughter finds it a very nurturing environment,' said one parent, 'and she's very happy there.' All female teachers are called 'Madam', but this does not imply a stilted formality in the relationship. 'The pastoral care is amazing,' a sixth former enthused. 'If you ever need to you can chat to anyone. They really want you to do well. Because they live here, they're with you all the time – you become really comfortable with them. You know there's a line you don't step over, but we are really relaxed with them.'

Boarding accommodation undergoing rolling programme – phase one completed, phase two due to be finished in 2014. Best upper school rooms now quite large and with en-suite bathrooms. We saw some much improved since our last visit. Younger girls share in rooms of two to four but all have space and all rooms are quite cosy. All upper sixth in Keswick House in single rooms with proper sized beds, good kitchen and common-room. Nice touches like hot choc and coffee on tap all day. Food, in general, excellent, complete with dietary warnings/info where necessary and special needs catered for. Special help given on occasions like Ramadan fasting. Boarders come on a full, weekly or flexi basis. Currently 240 girls in school over weekends. More helpful than many schools when it comes to booking travel arrangements etc.

Excellent main hall in the sixth form house used for outside speakers, careers talks, house meeting etc. Sixth form girls do their own laundry – good practice! Other houses linked by 'bunnyruns' so you don't have to go outside from one to the other. Good support for overseas boarders includes escorted service to/from Victoria and taxis to airports; some belongings can stay at school over hols. A café for visiting parents, girls and staff – Horizons – incorporates excellent shop, which sells everything including uniform. Everyone has email and wireless internet throughout the campus. Help for day pupils includes buses which take girls away from school late into the evening, after the extra-curricular activities no-one wants to miss.

Pupils and parents: From 30+ countries and every continent. Some 55 per cent from UK. Chinese, but also Thai, Russian, Korean, African and Europeans of all sorts. Also more than half British, most from the south of England – school busy recruiting in this area. Clientele not the stiff upper class and diplomatic types of yester-year but everyone – it's hard to imagine a girl who would not feel welcome here. Happy parents in an interview said that they saw their daughters as 'children of the world'. Lots of famous ORs include Baroness Chalker, Verity Lambert, Sally Oppenheimer, Jill Balcon, Katherine Whitehorn, Adele Geras, Tanya Streeter, Honeysuckle Weeks, Rebecca Hall, Philippa Tattersall and Dame Cicely Saunders of blessed memory.

Entrance: Entry at 11, 13 and 16 is via Common Entrance, scholarship or the school's own entrance exam. Entrants are normally required to visit the school for interview and may spend a couple of days at the school prior to joining. Not oversubscribed, but register in good time.

Exit: Very few leave before 16; several do go, post-16, to local sixth form colleges. Some – as elsewhere – return, gratefully, after a few weeks outside. Recent leavers in large numbers to the London universities; others, mostly, to Bristol, Nottingham, Warwick, Edinburgh and Durham. Courses in everything from cosmetic science to veterinary medicine, German to law. One in five pupils to universities abroad.

Money matters: Lots of scholarships – academic, music, sport, art or performing art – competed for at 11, 12, 13 and 16 by exam and audition, worth up to 20 per cent fees, with additional bursaries if necessary. Sixth form scholarships also by exam in A level subjects and a general paper. Three 100 per cent bursaries, the Brighthelm Awards, are available for entry into year 7, with the next place becoming available in September 2014. This should increase awareness of the school amongst potential day pupils of high ability. These fully funded places are means-tested and cover the day fees for the duration of the student's stay at Roedean. Has also taken over St Mary's Hall's historic commitment to provide generous bursaries for the daughters of clergy – this should be better known.

Remarks: School has a healthy spirit and much to offer. The failure of the St Mary's Hall venture is a disappointment but the school is relaxed and says 'confidence is strengthening.' Bin your old prejudices about the place – go and look.

Rossall School

Linked school: Rossall Junior School

Broadway, Fleetwood, Lancashire, FY7 8JW

• Pupils: 647 pupils (270 girls/380 boys); includes 320 full and weekly boarders • Ages: 11–18 • C of E • Fees: Day £7,410–£11,940; Boarding £11,880–£32,940 pa • Independent

Tel: 01253 774201
Email: enquiries@rossall.org.uk
Website: www.rossallschool.org.uk

Head: Since September 2013, Ms Elaine Purves, previously head of Ipswich High School for Girls. Read languages at Hull; has also been deputy head of Royal High School Bath, so the move into co-education is new for her. Married with two young children.

Academic matters: Acceptable and improving results given the range of pupil intake: 'Rossall is a broad church'. In 2013, average of 31 points at IB, 61 per cent of A level grades were A*/B and 35 per cent A*/A. Forty-eight per cent of GCSE grades were A*/A. Improvement underpinned by much more support from EAL department. Widening subject choice at A level, though increasing number of overseas sixth formers looking for IB.

Excellent art facilities and outstanding DT workshop and design room. Recent investment in IT infrastructure and evidence of new hardware (with more to come). Outdated science laboratories and some tired classrooms and public areas tell of recent difficult times. Science laboratories recently updated and redecorated.

International study centre (ISC) for students from over 30 countries: China, Hong Kong, Korea, Taiwan, Thailand, Vietnam, Germany, Poland, Spain, Turkey, Switzerland and Dubai. Intensive English language courses lead to International GCSE or a transfer to main school (about 30 a year).

Transition to senior school is through middle school (years 7 and 8), newly heralded as Dragon, and housed in a stand-alone building at the front of the school. Pastoral continuity assured through oversight of junior school head, whilst academics come under senior school auspices.

Games, options, the arts: Traditional team sports of rugby, hockey and cricket for the boys, with regional and national competition success. Hockey and netball for the girls. Floodlit Astroturf makes a statement. Swimming pool, fives, eight courts recently renovated by the Rossall Foundation and basketball in gym, makeover recently completed – popular additions. Recent staff appointments strengthen specialist coaching available but sport optional from year 10.

Famous for Rossall ('Ross') hockey, played on the beach, tides permitting, and very popular – invented in 1860s, with esoteric rules, providing fierce inter-house competition. Keen CCF (all three arms); leads to BTEC in year 11. School has its own outward bound award – Lake District and Yorkshire Dales used.

Plenty of opportunity to make music, in individual tuition or joining choirs and ensembles. Full music, dance and drama programme from weekly informal performances to overseas summer tour. New sports centre and performing arts centre planned.

Background and atmosphere: Founded in 1844 on the windswept north Fylde coast overlooking the Irish Sea, an easy tram ride from Blackpool. Unprepossessing entrance to the campus eclipsed by the Oxford-type quad which opens up with mellow red-brick buildings and a handsome chapel to one side. Healthy sea air, pretty brisk in winter and, according to Dr Winkley, 'The sea air banishes asthma and eczema and hay fever and promotes complexions of which French beauticians would be envious'. However, not so kind to window frames – an overdue programme of refurbishment is under way.

The ISC obviously looms pretty large – an influencing factor in the surge in recruitment of international boarding students? Redressing the balance of overseas to UK students and ratio of girls to boys, particularly for sixth form, is high on the school's agenda. Senior houses mix day and boarding students (boarding houses recently refurbished) to encourage friendship, respect and understanding of different cultures. The success of this is evidenced in social groups seen around the campus – 'I've had the opportunity to make friends from across the world and I am sure I will stay in touch with them when we leave here,' said one sixth former.

Church of England foundation, whole school chapel every Friday morning. Large dining hall, seating at traditional long tables and benches, informal seating with staff and pupils happily sharing tables. In-house catering, cafeteria style service – dining hall and kitchens recently refurbished and new menus are now hugely enjoyed by pupils and staff. A full programme of events, activities and field trips runs each weekend.

Pastoral care and discipline: Strong anti-bullying ethos – 'Spotted quickly and dealt with quietly and effectively,' said one sixth form prefect. Not a druggy school. Blackpool a temptation, but head says whole-school vigilance pays off. Overseas pupils 'often set our boys and girls very fine examples'. Discipline set on positive values. Expectations of a high standard of pupil behaviour are seldom disappointed. Excellent staff/pupil relationship.

Pupils and parents: UK pupils from local catchment area, predominantly day, though with some flexi-boarding. Parents are mainly business people, often first time buyers with little or no understanding of boarding. Growing number of Forces children amongst the boarders, though 80 per cent from overseas.

Socially at ease, confident without arrogance, courteous students, happy to be at Rossall. Lots of smiles, eye contact and deference at doors as you walk around. Cultural breadth encourages tolerance and respect, making it easier for pupils 'to be themselves'.

R

Entrance: Entrance exams at 11+, 13+ and 16+. Otherwise two latest school reports and reference from head.

Exit: Majority of students to UK universities in 2013 (nearly half to Russell Group), with a further nine per cent choosing to study abroad.

Money matters: Twenty academic, music, sports and all-round scholarships awarded annually.

Remarks: A happy co-educational school with a successful international study centre providing a cosmopolitan experience in north west Lancashire. Sweeping reforms at a critical time now bearing fruit with improving academic results and a surge of overseas students. Restoring the balance of pupils, particularly in the sixth form, may prove a more difficult matter.

Rougemont School

Linked school: Rougemont Preparatory School

Llantarnam Hall, Malpas Road, Newport, Gwent, NP20 6QB

- Pupils: 380 boys and girls (including sixth from) • Ages: 3–18
- Non-denom • Fees: £10,200–£11,460 pa • Independent

Tel: 01633 820800
Email: registrar@rsch.co.uk
Website: www.rougemontschool.co.uk

Headmaster: Since 2002, Dr Jonathan Tribbick (fifties), a classicist, arrived from a deputy head position at the more traditional Newcastle-under-Lyme school. Made an unusual – though brief – mid-career foray into tax inspection before deciding that teaching was indeed his thing. He says his first impression of Rougemont was the 'happiest and friendliest' school he had been to, and sees his brief as keeping that feeling while pushing ahead with academic performance and extra-curricular activities.

Academic matters: Not an academic hothouse by any means, but the school produces good results for its intake. Value-added scores are high, and exam results very respectable: 54 per cent of GCSEs at A*/A in 2013 and 42 per cent at A level. Refreshing (relative) lack of concern for league tables means that pupils are encouraged to have a go at subjects they are interested in, even if they are unlikely to get the top grades.

Science is a strong point, and sciences are taught separately from year 7. French is the main foreign language, while German is being phased out and replaced by Spanish as an optional second language from year 9. All but a handful take a language GCSE. French and maths are setted from part-way through year 7, English from year 9. Most take nine or 10 GCSEs. The head – predictably, given his subject – reintroduced Latin for all in year 7 (optional from year 9), and offers Greek lessons after school on Friday evenings. A surprising number take him up on it.

Maths and science are the biggest focus at A-level – around half to two-thirds take maths, and a third take physics. Mainly traditional subjects on offer – economics rather than business studies, for example, though the latter is available at GCSE – but a few takers for media, sports and theatre studies. Art is a growing strength – the displays of coursework during our visit were outstanding, and last year's A level results were all A*-B grades.

Wide range of gifted provision, from fiction writing and code breaking in the juniors to maths challenges, reading groups and extended projects in engineering, media and music for seniors. Open university courses are a possibility for sixth formers. The main SEN provision is for dyslexia – a team of four

specialist staff teach juniors and seniors individually or in pairs. No current demand for EAL support, since a nearby Korean-owned plant shut down, but can be called on if necessary.

Games, options, the arts: Junior-level sports are very successful, particularly hockey and rugby, with lots of local and regional trophies in the cabinet. At upper school levels, the school's teams are still 'developing'. Some strong individual players, including county and national level team members, but finding enough good players to make up a winning rugby or netball team in a smallish co-ed school can be hard. At least the on-site sports facilities make it easy to get plenty of practice. Regular international sports tours and other overseas trips (skiing and so on).

Drama popular as an activity, less so as an exam subject. Lots of in-house performances, but also some for wider public, such as an annual link with Gwent police to put on an anti-drugs play, Wings to Fly, with audiences drawn from other local schools. Still lacks a really good large performance space – next on the development list. Full range of music going on, with two orchestras (training and main), brass, wind and jazz bands, and school choirs. Full school concerts twice a year, as well as house music and smaller shows.

Young Engineers scheme, for sixth formers studying physics, gives an opportunity to work with local companies on real-life problems, and compete with other schools across Wales – has won prizes most years. An Exxon Mobil subsidary in Newport offers work experience to one budding chemical engineer every year. Also young enterprise scheme, Duke of Edinburgh award, public speaking, chess and so on – 'We try to find something for everyone,' says the head.

Background and atmosphere: Has evolved from a small junior school focused on prepping for local grammar schools to an all-through independent. The original owners sold up in the 1970s, the first A levels were taken in the 1980s and it moved to its present site in 1995. Currently running at a little below maximum capacity of around 750 in the whole school.

The site is huge and green, with playgrounds, gardens, sports fields, and even woodland areas to learn and play in. Juniors look sweet in their red-trimmed grey blazers, seniors more business-like in their black uniforms. The low-slung, purpose-built blocks (apart from the Victorian mansion which now houses the juniors) could be mistaken for a state school, but the academic gown hanging in the head's study is a reminder that this has been an HMC school since 2000 – gowns are worn for formal assemblies and major school events. New science and technology building; sixth formers have refurbished block with new café.

Almost the only clue that the school is in Wales is the names of the houses: Caradog, Dyfrig and Gwynog, named after Welsh saints. The Welsh language is not formally taught, but some staff are fluent, a Welsh club and the chance to participate in regional eisteddfods.

Pastoral care and discipline: Pupils seem relaxed with teachers, confident with visitors, and at home in their environment. They like the heavy teacher involvement in the PTA and in extra-curricular activities and trips, which give them a chance to get to know teachers on a more personal level. Also good for inter-year friendships and support.

The school's policy on welcoming children who have been bullied elsewhere means that any hint of bullying is not tolerated. In the younger years, problems are dealt with in circle time; later on, always someone, whether a staff member or another pupil, to talk to informally if you have a problem, the children report. Rarely a need to escalate to formal measures.

Expulsions are extremely rare, and discipline issues tend to be minor. The head says he had to suspend two pupils (briefly) last year: one for a driving offence outside school and the other for bringing a penknife to school – with no ill-intent, but rules are rules.

Pupils and parents: No one would call this a posh school – 'We are not – and do not want to be – socially exclusive,' says the head. The typical parent, he says, would be a doctor or local small-business owner, but you find all sorts here.

Broad intake geographically as well as socially. The only independent secondary in Newport, but also serves the surrounding area: school minibuses bring pupils in from a 25-mile radius, with an extra coach from Chepstow. Fewer come from the direction of Cardiff, as more independent competition over there.

The head says the main aim of the PTA (recently renamed from the 'parents' association' to make a point of teacher involvement) is to have fun and socialise, rather than raise funds. The school does have ambitious plans for a new dining/performance block as the final element in the development of the new site, but the £2m projected budget means it is still a few years off and may require outside financing.

Entrance: Selective, but not excessively so – 'I think we can offer something to a wide range of abilities,' says the headmaster.

Most arrive at the upper school by way of the junior school, where entry is virtually non-selective, but around a third are new in year 7, mostly from local state primaries, and small numbers join in years 8 and 9. About five to 10 newcomers in the sixth form each year. Potential newbies are encouraged to come and spend a day – or even two or three – in the school to get a feel for it before making up their minds.

Progress from juniors to seniors is almost automatic – no need to sit a test unless trying for a scholarship – but the school reserves the right (very rarely exercised, though) to advise parents their children are not suited to the upper school. Outside candidates take a test for entry to year 7 and up.

At least five Cs at GCSE required to join the sixth form for both internal and external entrants, though most have much better results under their belts.

Exit: About 85 per cent move through to sixth form. Lots stay in Wales for university – the financial incentives to do so are strong – but of those who venture further afield, popular destinations include Bath, Kings College, UCL, Imperial College, Durham, Liverpool, Exeter and Bristol. A few make it to Oxbridge (one in 2013). Largest numbers go into engineering and medicine. 'One or two a year' who don't go on to university.

Money matters: A newish school so no endowment fund to fall back on, but roughly five per cent of fees are allocated to bursaries and further funds to scholarships. Bursaries for deserving newcomers, including some who have struggled with bullying or other issues at previous schools, or existing pupils who might otherwise have to leave the school in exam years due to financial difficulties. Six year 7 scholarships of 25 per cent awarded every year. Sixth form bursaries depend on academic ability as well as financial need.

Remarks: Relaxed and friendly school with an inclusive approach, aiming to give everyone a chance – or even a second chance – to do well at something. Academic standards are high, but not the be-all and end-all.

Royal Grammar School (Guildford)

Linked school: Lanesborough School

High Street, Guildford, GU1 3BB

- Pupils: 900 boys; all day • Ages: 11–18 • Non-denom
- Fees: £14,670–£14,955 pa • Independent

Tel: 01483 880600
Email: admissions@rgs-guildford.co.uk
Website: www.rgs-guildford.co.uk

Headmaster: Since 2007, Dr Jon Cox BSc PhD (forties). Educated at St Mary's College, Southampton, then studied physiology and bio-chemistry at Southampton University. Postgrad course at Royal College of Music (French horn is his instrument) and toyed with becoming a professional musician before deciding on a career in teaching. Joined Whitgift School in Croydon as a biology teacher in 1992 and stayed for 14 years, rising through the ranks to become deputy head before his appointment to the RGS in 2005 as headmaster in waiting.

Hasn't frightened the horses with wholesale changes to what was already a very successful operation, but neither has he rested on the school's considerable laurels. He began with a long 'to-do' list, which he still runs today. 'Every time I cross off a job done, I add something new to the bottom. It's just like a house, something always needs doing,' he says, brandishing another long list of 40+ points he's jotted down to mention during our interview. It covers all sorts – everything from academic innovations, creation of new staff roles, building programmes, community links; the list literally goes on – he's a man on a mission.

Affable, down to earth, buzzing, you sense his delight at having what he calls 'the best job in the country – fantastic boys, inspirational staff, parents on side and appreciative'.

RGS is very much his show and he's great at managing parents – they don't run this school. 'He's very much in control and you don't get the impression he would welcome a waste of his time,' said one mother. 'But equally he's approachable and I wouldn't hesitate to speak to him if necessary'. 'He's very at ease in his role and really cares about the school,' said another. 'A fabulous figurehead for RGS,' agreed a third. 'I've heard him talk to prospective and current parents many times and he's a good speaker, witty and easy to listen to, he handles all that side of things very well'.

Pupils like and respect him – 'he's a nice guy' and 'smart' they say – and seems to know what they are about; writes a comment on every boy's report. 'He never talks down to them,' said one parent.

While absolutely mindful of his school's many strengths, not least its academic prowess, Dr Cox says he takes most pride in the fact that RGS is 'a wonderful community. Mostly you'll ask your son if he has had a good day, not for details about his maths test,' he says. 'There's a great, supportive atmosphere here that really enriches the boys in all aspects of their lives'.

With his own son having recently joined the school, he understands the anxiety parents feel around the admissions process. 'I was out of school when my son did his test and interview, but it was agony nevertheless, so I do empathise with parents. I know that for lots of them, it's this school or a state school.'

He's working hard to overcome the school's elitist tag and dispel two main myths about RGS – that it's a hothouse and not for the sporty; 'Neither are remotely true,' he says. 'I want people to recognise that we are a school for bright children, irrespective of their backgrounds'. To this end the school entertains children from local primary schools every Monday to do Tudor project work (buildings reflect school's Tudor origins and Dr Cox's office includes a Chained Library) and runs Saturday master classes and a summer school. Service to the local community is a big theme at RGS.

He is married with three children, still plays the French horn and is a keen amateur magician. Also a governor of a school in Watford.

Academic matters: Outstanding in all respects and very much the academic school for boys in the area. RGS features in top 10 or 20 of league tables of all variety. Pupils are selected from the top ability band, working far above the national average. Maths and science very popular and two-thirds take maths a year early. Maths is also the most popular option at A and AS level, followed by physics, economics and chemistry. Pre-U offered in chemistry and the school has great success with this subject – at the 2012 Chemistry Olympiad RGS achieved five gold, 10 silver and seven bronze awards. English and humanities give equally good accounts of themselves – around a third of A and AS students continue with English literature to A level. Modern languages (French or Spanish from 11+ or German at 13+) compulsory to GCSE. Arabic, Chinese, Russian and Japanese also available. Latin a popular option and Greek also on offer. Positively dizzying success in exams overall – in 2013 93.6 per cent of grades at GCSE were A*/A while at A level 80.4 per cent of grades were A*/A.

Dr Cox has conducted an enormous push on teaching and learning, including lowering the pupil/staff ratio. We've heard nothing but huge parental praise for 'exceptionally good' teaching staff. 'Teaching is inspirational – absolutely no dead wood,' they say. The boys are encouraged to be self-motivated, independent learners, and the lessons are intensive and conducted at a brisk pace. It's cool to be bright at the RGS and the boys set themselves high standards as they jostle for position. 'My son was surprised to find himself towards the bottom of the class having been top dog at his old school,' said one parent. 'I really wouldn't coach a boy to come here as it would be no fun if you were struggling', said another, more seasoned parent. 'These boys are a competitive bunch and frankly anything less than an A* is a disaster for them. But that's really not because it's a hothouse – it isn't – it's simply that they do so well on their own abilities'.

It's a can-do culture – the school talks of 'strengths' and 'development areas' rather than 'weaknesses'. Extra work on offer to help anyone falling behind. 'I know they keep a watch on grades and are absolutely on top of everything,' said one mother whose son had slipped a little. 'He got all the help he needed to get back on track'.

On average two to three homework assignments an evening of around 30 minutes each – 'nothing too onerous,' parents feel. Support available for the handful of boys with a learning difficulty or disability.

Games, options, the arts: A broad and balanced offering. Popular option choices include RE (for which read philosophy and ethics) and design and technology (a pupil proudly showed us a 3D laser cutter). No PE or drama taken at GCSE (though a handful take theatre studies at AS and Dr Cox is now promoting drama lower down the school). Not huge numbers doing art either, but what there is is remarkably good and again 100 per cent A*/A grade work.

Most sport is off site at Bradstone Brook, the school's 20-acre playing field and pavilion a few miles away. School rails against its reputation for being less sporty than some of its heavyweight public school neighbours in the area and can in fact hold its own. Rugby, hockey and cricket on offer, but football is lacking. 'Such a shame good footballers cannot represent the school,' moaned one miffed mother. But lots do play at break on the Astroturf and Dr Cox points out that, 'We do run football very successfully in the sixth form with A to D teams'. Shooting

range is popular. Facilities not whizzy – no swimming pool for example, so boys troop down to the local Spectrum swimming pool (a bit down market for some!) and to Guildford Lido for the annual gala. 'Actually the boys love getting off site for this,' said a mother. 'It's only 10 minutes away and the walk warms them up – plus they get to run past Guildford High (School for Girls)!'

Music now has the space it deserves –a fab new music centre, including a recording studio and rehearsal space.

There's an extensive timetabled programme of extracurricular activities, known as Period 8, which includes all sorts of clubs and societies, house competitions in an array of sports, plays and musical performances, CCF, D of E and even a scout group. It's a school where things happen, lots going on, often until about 7pm.

Background and atmosphere: Historically a grammar school and still a grammar school at heart. The school was founded in 1509 under the will of Robert Beckingham, and became 'Royal' in 1552 by charter of King Edward VI. Was run as a state school for 30 years after the war, but returned to the independent sector in 1977 rather than become non-selective. Charming tall, white 450 year old building on one side of Guildford High Street (includes Chained Library and various public rooms) while on the other side of the street the school buildings date mostly from the 20th century, although pleasing facades mean there's no horrid 60s look to them. The site is a little cramped, but fortunately RGS boys have manners and respect, otherwise it could be mayhem. Pupils are respectful of staff, hold doors open for each other and parents say they relish knowing where the boundaries are and settle into what is expected of them. 'The school understands them, how they learn and gets through to them in a way that switches them on and makes them responsible for their own studies,' said one parent. 'They really play to their strengths.

Pastoral care and discipline: Although a non-denominational school, its ethos is firmly based on sound Christian principles. Parents describe the school as very supportive. Senior staff operate a pastoral data base and a 'care list' of boys to keep a special eye on. Parents feel their sons form good relationships with each other and across the year groups. 'They bond really well', one parent told us. 'And it's a joy to see'.

Dr Cox claims to have improved the behaviour of many a 'scallywag' – 'I'll give them some responsibility, that generally turns them around'. In the grand scheme of things any bad behaviour is of the mild variety. These are regular boys, school appears very on top of things and is quick to clamp down on anything untoward with the occasional incident of the argy bargy variety firmly and quickly stamped on. Nothing serious enough to warrant exclusion in the last few years. A benevolent atmosphere, with no hint of a heavy hand. 'I think we do a good job of selecting them in first place and sussing out their attitude to work', said Dr Cox, who for all his bonhomie, is no soft touch – 'They really don't want to come to me for a telling off,' he acknowledges. 'But I think they know I am basically on their side. These are impressionable young men, finding their feet in the world. I see our job as being to correct their behaviour. I'd rather they made their mistakes here, before going off into the world'.

Pupils and parents: School's town centre, close-to-station, location means it attracts families from some distance away, involving a few quite complicated train journeys. Some parents are really discerning (there are plenty of good independent schools in the area, although no other single sex boys' day schools). For others RGS is their only independent option and if their sons don't pass the exam, they will stay in the state system.

Latest parental survey attests to parents being happy with their choice. 'There's a pretty good mix of boys here, with the extremes probably drawn to the centre by the camaraderie and sense of "we are grammar school boys with a shared identity",' said a long-standing parent. 'No outlandish types among boys or parents' – although some quite quirky, dare we say eccentric, boys find a happy home at RGS. Generally a nice broad spectrum of society, all bright, but a mix quite reflective of life generally. 'The longer he's there the more I am happy,' a parent told us. 'The school seems to have had a very insidious effect that has turned him into a lovely young man. They're not swotty and snobby, but a down-to-earth, nice group of lads'. Boys we came across were very courteous, not super smart, just regular teenage types, but seemed friendly and happy as they milled around.

Parents pleased that they don't have to crack the whip at home; it seems that the school sorts their sons out to be completely self-sufficient. 'These boys are the real thing from an academic point of view – they are not arrogant and don't grow up believing the world owes them a living,' says Dr Cox.

Entrance: Tough – has one of the highest academic hurdles in Surrey. On average there are 350-400 applications from boys from almost 100 local schools for 140 places. All sit exams in English, maths and verbal reasoning plus an interview 'We're looking for potential,' school says. Advice from everyone we spoke to is 'don't coach, other than a little exam practice'. 'You'd be miserable here if you'd just scraped in,' summed up one parent, speaking for many. 'Even a bright boy who was absolutely top dog at his old school might well find himself 25th in the class here'.

By and large the school is happy that they get admissions 'spot on'. Dr Cox can only recall one or two boys who subsequently couldn't cope with the academic rigour of the place. At age 11 the majority come from the state sector, reflecting the relationships built up with local schools. Then at 13+ another 45/50 boys join from prep schools, with Lanesborough the major feeder school, sending around 30 boys a year.

Don't expect red carpet treatment when you visit. 'Everyone is very nice and it's well-organised, but they don't have to try very hard', one mother said. 'We visited other schools where we got more special treatment because they really need to fight to get families to choose them – RGS are in a strong position because they don't have local competition.' Dr Cox sees all prospective parents himself – can be 20 or so a week –and unsurprisingly he has a great conversion rate. NB After an interregnum of a couple of years when no sports scholarships were awarded, RGS is introducing scholarships for sport from September 2014.

Exit: Almost all to their first choice of university. Thirty-one boys to Oxbridge in 2013. Many to Imperial and Durham (which can be harder, Dr Cox points out) and the rest as you would expect to other Russell Group heavyweights including notably Exeter, Nottingham, Bristol, Bath and Warwick.

Money matters: Lower than average fees, with the school working to keep them low. Appeals to parents who don't have the funds for more expensive schools. 'Proper' bursaries include money for uniform, sports kit and books, 'There's no point otherwise,' says Dr Cox. A few years ago RGS could not give bursary money away, but now there's a good take up following the establishment of better links with other schools.

Remarks: One of Surrey's most highly regarded and sought after schools. Cutting edge and working hard to keep its top spot as the best school for boys in the area. It's an environment where boys spark off each other and learn at a fast pace, so it's not for a worrier or a 'scraper-in'. A school for bright boys, who don't have to have been overly prepped or privately educated at primary level.

Royal Grammar School (Newcastle)

Linked school: Royal Grammar School Junior School (Newcastle)

Eskdale Terrace, Newcastle upon Tyne, NE2 4DX

- Pupils: 1,250 pupils in junior and senior schools; 25 per cent girls. All day • Ages: 11–18, juniors 7–10 • Non-denom
- Fees: £9,024–£10,710 pa • Independent

Tel: 01912 815711
Email: admissions@rgs.newcastle.sch.uk
Website: www.rgs.newcastle.sch.uk

Headmaster: Since 2008, Dr Bernard Trafford MA PhD (in educational management), early fifties; previously head of Wolverhampton Grammar School from 1990. Married to Katherine, two daughters post-university. Educated at Downside and St Edmund Hall, Oxford, taught briefly at RGS High Wycombe, went to Wolverhampton in 1981 as head of music, then head of sixth form, finally head. A former chairman of HMC. Has a fine voice, noted for organising a choir at HMC conferences; has been known to sing and blow his trumpet in public at RGS Newcastle. Has particular interests in inclusion and accountability and has written widely on democratic school management.

An urbane, approachable and talented man, with an avuncular air that somehow calls Stephen Fry to mind. No dilettante, though: he led WGS from the front through stormy waters during the end of assisted places and the advent of co-education, and knows what he wants for a school; very clear-sighted and experienced. Has his own website, where you can read all about his jazz band and compositions. Left our meeting (by pre-arrangement) to go and read Humpty Dumpty to a junior form.

Academic matters: Impressive – outstanding results, always up there with the best. All take three sciences at GCSE; 10 subjects the norm, seven core plus three options, ranging from Latin and Greek to music. Enormous enthusiasm for economics, history and politics at A level; in 2013, more than 71 per cent A*/A grades, 87 per cent A*/B at A level: 82 per cent A*/A at GCSE. Wide choice of subjects at A level. Sciences particularly strong, boosted by impressive science and technology block with state-of-the-art labs running off wide corridors filled with home-grown art.

Keen on local partnerships and runs practical courses on Saturdays and in the summer with local comprehensives on genetics and the like (the Newcastle science enrichment programme). Computers everywhere, email for all, but 'ICT not currently offered as an exam subject'. Computer-based language lab and grand new modern languages suite; Spanish and German on offer – plenty of takers at GCSE but few at A level. Mandarin Chinese non-exam course in sixth form. School does well by SEN pupils it takes, but head observes they could do better – they now have a member of staff in charge of learning support.

Games, options, the arts: Rugby unbelievably strong, beating all contenders, with regular trips abroad – runners up in the national Daily Mail cup in 2010. Vast array of sport on offer – football, cricket, athletics and gymnastics (currently national champions at two out of the three age groups) plus hockey, netball (reached national finals), basketball, swimming, tennis and squash. Girls do well; new director of sport is a woman (also – relax, chaps – a male head of rugby). Enviable new sports hall and new pool, all-weather pitch, aerobics room and fitness suite underway. Own rugby pitch on site, and outfields rented

R

nearby, much use made of local facilities for minority and individual sports. Fifty-year lease on magnificent Newcastle County Cricket Ground, five minutes' walk from school.

Huge variety of clubs – chess meets three times a week and bridge is popular. Outstanding debating – regular prize-winners. Technology club equally successful. CCF for both boys and girls as well as involvement with local community – the inner city partnership, where pupils work with deprived children on a one-to-one basis. Strong charity commitment. D of E flourishing.

Music does very well, not unexpectedly – £10 million development includes performing arts centre with 300-seat auditorium, recording studio, recital room, drama/dance studio, 10 rehearsal rooms and percussion studio. Masses of orchestras, bands and ensembles. Regular concerts – most recent ones well attended, encouraged no doubt by swish new accommodation. Choir recently sang mass in St Mark's basilica and other cathedrals throughout Europe. Drama important here – performance studies and film studies established at A level. Masses of take up in all disciplines of art, eg screen printing and 3D, plus frequent trips abroad; pupils' work exhibited in local galleries. Trips to battlefields for historians, to Greece and Italy for classicists, as well as World Challenge (recently to Kyrgyzstan, Argentina, Peru).

Background and atmosphere: Foundation dates back over 450 years, current buildings much revamped with stylish glazed arches linking the main buildings and making the whole place look more put together and elegant. Red-brick 1906 Queen Anne style frontage conceals a mass of add-ons round the impressively large, five-acre sports grounds (remember this is a city centre school); more new build planned. Surrounded by inner ring road motorways and 100 metres from Jesmond metro station, used by vast majority of pupils. Well-used handsome old hall, with organ. Lecture theatre with fine stained-glass windows. Sixth form centre flourishing. Libraries recently upgraded and a certain amount of re-jigging in the classroom area. Junior school extended and refurbished in recent years. Performing arts centre, languages suite, junior school extension

A buzzy, busy place; sets high expectations in and out of the classroom: 'Students' natural curiosity means they constantly surprise themselves – and their teachers – with how much they can do and achieve, being willing to try out new ideas without fear of ridicule even when they get things wrong'. Plenty of North Eastern can-do in evidence. Success in just about anything celebrated and applauded in assemblies.

No specific provision for G and T (many will fall anyway into this ill-defined category), but school willing to 'make space', eg with special programmes, for the very clever. Value-added statistics treated as amber light, especially for lower middle group as they approach GCSE. Girls admitted to sixth in 2001 – school completely co-educational since 2006 but girls still small minority.

Pastoral care and discipline: Pupils are allocated a personal tutor who stays with them throughout – weekly meetings. Vigorous anti-bullying policy; PSHE for all. 'Tackled bullying head on,' says school, with loads of help from prefects: 'On the whole it appeared to be careless insensitivity rather than malicious bullying'. Out for violence and drugs. Smoking not tolerated and no particular problems with drinking or smoking off-site. Crack cocaine now appearing in certain parts of the north east and head and staff are constantly vigilant.

Pupils and parents: First choice for clever and lively-minded boys and girls from every corner (inner and outer) of Newcastle and Sunderland, Durham and County Durham, and also from far-flung rural corners, eg Berwick, Wooler, Alnwick. Broad social mix; new uniform and stricter enforcement has minimised previous scruffiness. Popular with local bigwigs in industry, the professions, academics from the universities. Fifteen per cent from ethnic minorities. Closer relations with parents now fostered. Pupils keen to succeed and 'don't feel life owes them a living,' observed a master with memories of working in a famous public school further south. Old boys include England winger David Rees, Lord Taylor, Brian Redhead, composer and saxophonist John Harle.

Entrance: Tough and competitive via the school's own entrance exam at 11. About 75 from the junior school, as long as their work is up to scratch. Very healthy entry post-GCSE, far outweighing 16+ leavers – minimum six GCSEs at A/B required plus report from former school. Entry from over 80 different schools throughout North East.

Exit: Recent average of 20 or so a year to Oxbridge, otherwise to Newcastle, Leeds, Edinburgh, Manchester, Nottingham and London, mainly to read hard traditional subjects. Small coterie to art or music colleges, though the latter are more likely to read music at university and then go on to conservatoires. Two recent professional footballers (how they need them at St James's Park!). A few leave after GCSEs, either for financial reasons 'or because the RGS sixth form is inappropriate for them'. Gap year gaining in popularity.

Money matters: Four bursaries available under aegis of the Ogden Trust for 'above average children with limited or no parental means from a state primary school'. Big current drive to raise cash for bursaries (since 2002 a bursary campaign has raised in excess of £4 million) – school keen not to be seen as socially divisive; around 90 pupils helped financially, 50 of them at a level of 90 per cent of fees or above. All bursaries means-tested, ie no traditional scholarships. Some new sixth form subject-specific awards.

Remarks: Powerful traditional grammar school, with high morale under dynamic and civilized head, and an obvious choice for ambitious locals. Not a results factory: pupils avid for – and get – all-round opportunities.

The Royal Grammar School, High Wycombe

Amersham Road, High Wycombe, Bucks, HP13 6QT

- Pupils: 1,370 boys (including up to 70 boarders) • Ages: 11–18 • Christian foundation but inter–denominational
- Fees: Boarding £11,561–£13,036; Day £3,780 pa • State

Tel: 01494 524955
Email: admin@rgshw.com
Website: www.rgshw.com

Headmaster: Since 2006, Mr Roy Page BSc PGCE NPHQ (sixties). Has been with RGS since before some of his pupils' parents were born – he started his training there in 1972 and stayed. Rose through the ranks via second in maths, boarding housemaster, head of sixth and deputy head. Chairman of the State Boarding Schools' Association and a classic car enthusiast (visitors, note the pristine MGB GT in the head's parking space). He was once a keen cricketer and hockey player but now sticks to golf and early morning lengths in the school's sunny pool.

'Extremely approachable' according to parents, and 'goes to absolutely everything'. Passionate about community and adamant that the school should continue to serve its local catchment, despite recent academy status enabling grammars to set their own selection criteria. Considers parents to be a key part of school community and is trialling day boarding, largely

R

to ease the pressure on dual income families commuting to London, so boys can stay at school until 9pm for about a third of weekly boarding costs.

Believes school is head and shoulders above the competition when it comes to enrichment ('no school in this area can compete with the extracurricular offering at RGS') and is proud of the school's ability to 'instil a love of learning' in its boys, saying the loyalty and donations from the extremely active OB network is testament to the school's supportive culture.

Married with two adult children, one of whom is an RGS old boy and Cambridge graduate, the other an academic at Leeds University.

Academic matters: Consistently delivers a good showing in national league tables for academics, although still snaps at the heels of the area's top performing grammar when it comes to hard exam data. Local competition is very stiff but school proves itself a real all-rounder at GCSE with 72 per cent of GCSEs graded A/A* in 2013. Eighty-one per cent of A levels achieved grades A*-B in 2013 with particularly strong results in English lit, geography, history, modern languages, maths and further maths.

Boys take an average of 10 or 11 GCSEs, with about 60 per cent taking four subjects at A2 level. Brainboxes can take more (one boy took seven in 2012, achieving A* in all of them) but the school only encourages this in exceptional circumstances. Good range of subjects on offer at GCSE, including Latin and Greek, with French compulsory and a large take-up of geography, history, Spanish and German. Sciences, economics and maths highly popular at A level. Languages 'really excellent' according to pupils and parents, with Italian, Mandarin and Japanese all available either on or off curriculum.

Six classes of 32 in each year group with setting in maths and French starting from year 9. School 'goes in heavy with homework from the word go', according to parents, with at least three thirty minute pieces per night, but boys seem to take this in their stride – as they do the rigorous tests they take after every topic. The minority of pupils joining from prep schools (about 25 per cent) 'can coast a bit' in year 7 say parents, and the uplift in recent years in children from non-English speaking homes presents some challenges for teachers initially, but by the time the heat is turned up in year 10 things are reportedly pretty equal across the board.

Cutting edge technology not widely used across the board of subjects, although iPads are starting to creep in, but parents say the VLE is 'great – and genuinely useful', particularly when it comes to revision. Geography department is trialling virtual lessons to be taken at home over the VLE then followed up with practical discussion and development in class.

Games, options, the arts: Sport, sport and more sport for those so inclined, with rugby leading the charge as a year-round occupation. When the rugby league season finishes, top players continue to play rugby union – and to a very high standard, with the 2013 under 12 rugby league team going to Wembley to compete in the finals of the 2013 Carnegie Champion Schools tournament. No football ('we get used to it quickly', say boys), but hockey and cricket are main sports and taught to a high standard by the 'inspirational' games teachers, although a few parents grumble they don't get the same quality fixtures or kudos as the rugby teams. Sighs of relief from some non-rugby parents though as it's a 'major commitment' with training five times a week and fixtures most weekends in season.

A-D teams in junior school take on – and frequently beat – schools such as Wellington, Marlborough and Harrow as well as their local grammar peers and recently vanquished Charterhouse at Eton fives, despite only having played the sport for two years. Although parents consistently equate sports here with rugby, there really is something for everyone, whether it's rowing, fencing, swimming or tennis. Just don't expect the same hero status in the playground.

Thursday afternoon activities (TAA) allow boys to choose from a vast array of sporting or academic enrichment activities ranging from Japanese or Mandarin to eco army. This is in addition to after school activities and indulges boys' passions for more marginal activities like climbing (the school boasts an impressive 40 ft climbing wall in main sports hall) and astronomy or endeavours like the 'Caterham project' which sees year 13s building a car from scratch. CCF is also extremely popular from year 10 and 'offers huge leadership opportunities', says head.

Music 'really, really strong', according to parents. A quarter of boys learn one or more instruments – 'they all play about three these days', according to head – and about 180 turning up on a weekly basis to participate in various choirs, bands and orchestras. The school's big band is currently run by the BBC big band leader and the director of music is 'highly charismatic', say parents. The performing arts community is also thriving with high quality productions put on annually, most recently a 'stunning' performance of Les Miserables in conjunction with local girls' schools. Check it out on YouTube for instant goosebumps. Plenty of opportunities to get involved for non-performers too, with the school's stage lighting and sound team proving hugely popular.

Trips, tours and exchanges galore. World Challenge scheme starts in year 7 then branches out globally higher up the school, with destinations in recent years including China, Vietnam and Belize. Lots of other opportunities for boys to get out and about to enhance the curriculum, enrich their cultural experience or just for fun.

Background and atmosphere: Founded in the 12th century and given a royal charter in 1562. Centred round an attractive red brick Queen Anne style building, with the usual ubiquitous additions bolted on from the Sixties onwards. An interesting mix of ancient (the oldest classrooms are just approaching their 100th birthdays) and modern, the school has recently been the beneficiary of large grants from the Academies Capital Maintenance Fund and now boasts gleaming new facilities including a bright, modern canteen, cookery suite (all boys do one term of cooking 'to prepare them for real life'), multi gym plus outdoor terrace with panoramic views of the sports fields and new changing facilities for the sports hall and swimming pool. There's also a lovely pool with retractable roof which, despite its 40-year vintage, still knocks spots of many we've seen, three lofty art rooms displaying an array of boys' superb work (pity some of this hasn't made its way into the rest of the school though) and a large, airy library with plenty of space for quiet study. Sixth formers lack a common room, although measures in place to fundraise for one, but do have two study mezzanines to cram for those all-important exams in free periods. Size of the vast music block gives away the school's collective passion for music, driven by the 'inspirational' director of music, and is home to a drumming suite ('as far away from head's office as possible', say staff) and a music technology centre.

Overall vibe of the school is traditional with a modern, multi-cultural twist. Despite its mixed socio-demographic and ethnic profile, with its boarding house, chaplain and expectation for formal manners (all staff are 'sir' or 'ma'am' to boys) place feels like a 'natural step from prep school' and, say parents, 'offers the roundedness of public school'. The majority join from state primaries, however, and all are polite, fun and talk with genuine enthusiasm about their school. A true camaraderie between year groups is immediately visible in the playground and boarding house.

The bright, modern boarding house (1999) sits in the heart of the school campus and is home to just 70 boarders, albeit 'an important 70,' insists head. Boarding offers great value for money, with full boarding costing less than most day school fees. Boarders say they 'feel really at home' and the boarding house has a relaxed, happy feel, partly dictated by the energetic and approachable head of boarding who seems almost like one of the boys, and partly by the way older boys mentor the younger ones. Each academic subject has a pupil champion that younger boys can approach if they need guidance with any part of their studies and the pupil food and boarding council electorate voices collective opinions about how the boarding house is run.

Younger boys are housed in spacious four-man dorms, decorated with personal effects to varying degrees. Years 12 and 13 are in cabin-like single rooms with en-suite shower rooms and the communal areas are peppered with boy toys like pool tables, table tennis and air hockey tables and flat screen TVs. No wonder most years are oversubscribed.

Boys return to the boarding house after school to get the blood sugar levels back up with a snack then participate in organised group activities on two or three afternoons a week. All meals are taken in the boarders' own canteen ('better food than in the main school', agree pupils) and prep takes place after supper from 7.30 to 9pm. Major advantages according to boarders' parents are that 'masters are on tap' to help with tricky homework and they have the 'luxury of not wasting time commuting to school', instead playing touch rugby or football with friends while others sit on the bus for up to 45 minutes each way.

The majority go home at weekends, with around 20 – mainly international pupils – staying. The schedule at the weekend is 'pretty relaxed' and boys are allowed into town in groups of two or three. There is a major trip organised every half term – paintballing and Thorpe Park recent highlights. Mobile phones are allowed until bedtime when prefects collect them from the younger boys. Older boarders are given lots of responsibility to mentor and guide their younger housemates, with one describing the self-discipline and independence he has gained during his time at the school as 'great preparation for uni'.

Pastoral care and discipline: School 'doesn't put up with any rubbish' according to parents and pulls boys back into line quick smart if they step out. Few major disciplinary issues, but severe punishments administered for smoking, although 'apparently all the sixth form do,' sighed one parent. Boys dismissive of bullying question and it's clearly not a regular feature of school life here, with reports of just occasional issues in the Twittersphere. School is active in social media and carries out periodic checks to ensure no pupils are breaching the online code of conduct – acting swiftly if they do. Full care for boarders from matron, housemasters and tutors.

Pupils and parents: Diversity at its best with all-comers ranging from those hailing from leafy south Bucks villages to boys from the less affluent local towns. Ethnic mix changing rapidly and school is now about 30 per cent non-Caucasian (higher in lower years), reflecting the local community. Intellect is the common denominator and head sees social mix as 'one of our great strengths', adding, 'if we're preparing future leaders of the world, we have to be fully appreciative of other backgrounds and races'. Parents of boarders lean towards the middle classes, often professional dual income families, and internationals. About half a dozen girls join for specific lessons (Greek, classics) in year 13.

A plethora of high profile alumni from the sporting, political and showbiz worlds England rugby players Matt Dawson, Nick Beal and Tom Rees; GB hockey captain and Olympian Jonathan Wyatt; professional golfer Luke Donald and, representing the artsy crowd, pop stars Howard Jones and the late Ian Dury and comedian Jimmy Carr.

Entrance: Ferocious competition for places. Selection subject to success at 11+ exam and Buckinghamshire criteria, including the ever-moveable feast of catchment. School's own procedure adopted as and when places become available higher up the school. Some places available in year 10 when a few boys each year choose to move, largely to independent schools, and again in year 12 when around 25 new places are up for grabs, about half of these in the boarding house.

Worth considering boarding at 11 if a day place looks unlikely and candidate has a high 11+ score. Forces families and boys in care are prioritised and these are mixed with some overseas pupils (although they must have a British passport) and locals keen for the boarding experience.

Exit: Majority straight into higher education with between 10 and 20 into Oxbridge most years (slight dip in 2013, down to six) and strong numbers to other top universities – Bristol, Birmingham, Durham, Nottingham and Warwick perennially popular. Good university advisory provision in place, with specialist support for those hoping for entry to international universities.

Money matters: Rolling renovation plan funded by a number of external sources. Ongoing fundraising by highly active parents' association who run well-attended events, including family quiz nights, wine-tasting (parents only!) and good old-fashioned school discos. Old boys also generous donors and current parents are asked to make annual voluntary contributions to be channelled towards music, transport, the school as a whole or all of the above – and many do.

Remarks: Don't believe the hype pitching The Royal Grammar School as a hotbed of rugger boys. Yes, they play rugby (and 18 other sports from Eton fives and racketball to fencing) to an exceptionally high level, but there's also outstanding music, drama and academics all wrapped up in a supportive, friendly package. Parents at other local grammars might consider it 'a bit God and country' but the traditional values that have the school competing ably with its independent and state maintained neighbours – and thrashing many top public schools on the sports field – mean boys (and their parents) benefit from a private school ethos without the hefty price tag.

The Royal High School (Edinburgh)

East Barnton Avenue, Edinburgh, EH4 6JP

- Pupils: 1,250; 625 boys and 625 girls, all day • Ages: 11–18
- Non-denom • State

Tel: 01313 362261
Email: admin@royalhigh.edin.sch.uk
Website: www.royalhigh.edin.sch.uk

Rector: Since 2009, Mrs Jane Frith BA (Dunelm), PGCE. Previously acting depute rector.

Academic matters: Max class size 30, going down to 20 for practical subjects and much less in higher years. Regular turnover of staff, with younger and more numerous common room. Usual subject suspects: maths, English and modern languages set in S1/S2, other subjects set in S3 where necessary. Strong on humanities; modern studies popular. Least hot on geography and biology but other sciences holding up well. As ever, nigh on impossible to get detailed marks by subject for national exams but according to their website 22 per cent of S5 pupils attained five highers; 45 per cent of S6 pupils left with at least five passes at higher in 2013. At advanced higher level in 2013, 35 per cent of S6 pupils achieved at least one advanced higher and 19 pupils achieved at least three. Ofsted report varies from above average to consistently above average...which isn't too helpful. Academic dux each year. Few take Advanced higher languages though drama and history said to be popular, with oversubscribed library lunch-time history club (library lunch-time clubs generally oversubscribed anyway). Careers advice on Tuesday in the library. Clubs for almost everything, often curriculum related: maths, chess etc plus Tai Chi or Japanese. Pupils wanting to follow more esoteric subjects can often be accommodated in other Edinburgh schools ('we go by taxi'). Good take up in national competitions, with gratifying numbers in ribbons: in every discipline.

Computers everywhere. Number of pupils with 'record of needs': variety of strategies available: one-to-one, plus support teaching, (and, a first as far as we know) a family support group for those with special needs. Head of learning support, plus two trained staff plus two assistants on hand; strategies in place, too, for the brighter pupil. Curricular support for the staff; advice on how to differentiate work sheets and the like (aka staff training). Sixth form involved in mass of extra-curricular activity ranging from paired reading for younger members, plus befriending and 'helping in subject departments across the school' (slavery perhaps?). Recognised fast track for primary pupils, who may combine studies in both places. French and German, plus optional Spanish, with Urdu on the side. Masses of trips abroad in every discipline. Year tutor stays with that class for their time at school. Classrooms and facilities used by adults and locals out of hours – this is a community school in all but name.

Games, options, the arts: House system (nations) in place for pastoral care, inter-house competitions and assemblies, as well as games. Terrific new games set up with games hall, fitness room, swimming pool and gym, much used, and former pupils (who have a rather posh sports pavilion on campus) use all the sporting facilities (car parking a bit tight). Myriad of rugby/football pitches, including bright green Astroturf; the school does well on the games front with masses of individual and team activities; athletics, badminton, cross-country, fencing and curling, sailing and water sports. Rugby and football for both boys and girls, plus basketball. As ever, problems with those who think it cool not to play the game (any game).

Exotic trips abroad: skiing in the States, rugby to Barbados to name a couple, and participants run a daily blog home to keep parents and class mates in touch; the battlefields of France proved very popular. Music strong. Long-established pairing arrangement with Munich and Italy where school orchestras perform in each others' home towns in alternate years; outstandingly popular concert, choral and orchestra, which used to be in the Usher Hall. Jazz, woodwind, but no pipe band. Mass of choices. The Keith Thompson 'KT' singers are much in demand and contribute a sizable amount to the Sir Malcolm Sargent Fund for Children at Christmas each year. Drama on the up, strong links with the Edinburgh Festival fringe. School entered a musical show in the Edinburgh Festival Fringe – first school to do so, followed up by another the following year. Lottery funding. Dance in all its disciplines. Art dept perched on top floor: imaginative stuff, flat plus ceramics, but gosh it must be tough to be creative in a blue box. Home economics popular but apparently not that good (according to Ofsted – our guides disagreed), fabric plus design technology (computer linked with state-of-the-art engineering software).

Background and atmosphere: Unique history: dates from 1128, the school 'provided education for 60 boys'; the site most people associate with the school is on Calton Hill, a site much loved by the telly news cameras (think overnight vigils, think home rule for Scotland). Girls admitted in 1974. Established on the current site in 1968 (were it not for the name, we could have been looking at Davidson Mains or Cramond High), the school buildings have been revamped (50 per cent refurb, 50 per cent new build) over last five years. Holding up well, we noticed one tiny square of scuffed carpet in the library and one bit of missing trim, but still incredibly uninspired: three storeys (plus basement where sixth form study area was locked) of blue covered passages with assorted square class rooms interspersed

with prep rooms round under-used (ie not) courtyards. Not nearly enuff public space, break was a logistical nightmare – with a disused adjacent courtyard unavailable to the milling masses – why not a temporary roof – or parasols? One constant, however, is the memorial door, out of which each graduating student steps, to be greeted on the other side by the president of the FPs' club. The huge marble door is a memorial to those who died in the First World War and the west-facing stained-glass windows to FPs who fell in the second. 'Significant prize-giving.' Highly vaunted end-of-school leavers' dance, often held in Edinburgh City Chambers, strong charity commitment.

Uniform worn by all, though you might not recognise it as such; current craze is leggings and the shortest of skirts – pupils can be sent home for inappropriate dress. We bounced through the door of a dedicated SEN room hoping to quiz with the nattily-clad occupier of the teacher's chair, only to find a fully made-up Barbie-doll who was obviously about to go on a photo shoot, until she confessed she would 'rather be in class' and it was 'too difficult to go home'. Quite. Variety of sports and club ties, 'they work their way up towards the neck as the owner goes through the school'; our charming guides had ties about three inches below their top shirt buttons, whereas some of the youngest members wore theirs at tummy button level. 'Bonding' week during the first year, when the whole class plus class teachers take off during November/December for a week's residential at an outdoor pursuits centre.

Pastoral care and discipline: Regular assemblies, good, strong PSE programme, school has to follow City of Edinburgh 'guidelines', so difficult to exclude, but will do so in the case of drugs, bullying, physical or otherwise, and abuse. Strong prefectural presence. Very few 'refusers'. 'Civilised guidance strategies in place'. Regular school assemblies. Pupils who misbehave in class are sent out of the room; we found two or three all looking fairly sheepish. Counsellor on site.

Pupils and parents: Strong PTA and parent council organisation (this is a new name following change in legislation in Scotland), basically 'affluent middle class, but a very wide intake – with a whole range of social and ethnic backgrounds'; the catchment area covers Davidsons Mains, Clermiston, Blackhall and Cramond. The school is capped at a 220 pupil intake and there is always a waiting list. Range of grub available; school has its nutrition group, SNAG.

Entrance: Automatic but see above. Some join the school from other state schools post standard grades, otherwise, penny numbers arrive on a re-location basis.

Exit: Over 90 per cent of all pupils generally stay for fifth year (ie Highers) and some 75 per cent for sixth year. Trickle to Oxbridge, masses to the Scottish universities (financially it makes sense for Scots go free in Scotland) or tertiary education. Bias towards engineering, architecture, creative design courses. FPs include Sir Walter Scott, Alexander Graham Bell, Lord Cockburn, Ronnie Corbett, Sarah Boyack (MSP) and the principal of St Andrew's University, Fraser Docherty (aka Superjam).

Money matters: Current building has been revamped under the aegis of the PPP. Regular PTA fund-raising including discos and jumble sales, tranche of endowments (including Mary, Queen of Scots) provide tiny scholarships for pupils who have done well at the school; not a lot, 'just a nice wee extra'. Below average number of free school meals: social profile of school rising.

Remarks: This is a high school in the old-fashioned sense – strong discipline and work code, good results, masses of extra-curricular activities – which also doubles as a local centre with adult learning classes and much use of the sports facilities. You can't get much better for nowt.

Royal High School, Bath GDST

Linked school: Royal High School, Bath, Junior School GDST

Lansdown Road, Bath, BA1 5SZ

- Pupils: 370 girls (105 boarding) • Ages: 11–18 • Non-denom
- Fees: Boarding £20,796–£24,285; Day £11,193–£11,409 pa
- Independent

Tel: 01225 313877
Email: royalhigh@bat.gdst.net
Website: www.royalhighbath.gdst.net

Head: Since 2010, Mrs Rebecca Dougall, internally promoted from deputy head and director of the sixth form college – an English specialist. She started her teaching career at Wycombe Abbey. Much as she adores her subject, she realised early on in the course of a year spent in library services at the Bodleian that there wasn't much of a living to be made from it. She nailed her teaching qualification via the graduate training programme the day before she became deputy head at Oxford High (GDST).

Mrs Dougall is chic, sparky and dynamic – just the sort of woman most would like their daughters to emulate – yet she is still compared unfavourably by some (pupils and parents) to her charismatic male predecessor. She manages not to be one whit defensive about this, claiming to be 'continuing the strategic direction started by James Graham-Brown' and to have restored 'a woman's touch' to the place, to boot; if that's what results in a front hall smelling of lilies and floor polish, then we'd agree. The same attention to detail has meant a crack-down on uniform and scuffed paintwork, which needs to extend to loos and clocks. Parents think she has still to make the school her own, others that she has made it a business rather too quickly. We think she's livened it up a bit – the new school mag 'Aquae Schoolis' which she instituted is some of the jolliest school writing and vibrant production values we've seen in a while. A product of a similar education herself, Mrs Dougall remains passionate about single sex schools: a placement in a boys' school during her teacher training 'confirmed my desire to teach girls', and this is now the way forward for the school, with the sixth form college focusing only on educating girls.

Her husband teaches history at Bristol Grammar; he possibly sees less of her than their West Highland terrier, Gertie, who is to be found in her study. Extra-curricular interests include medieval literature, design, property, travel and absorbing other cultures – in style. Material aspirations? A string of National Hunt race horses.

Academic matters: In 2013, 62 per cent A*/A grades at GCSE and 59 per cent A*/A at A level. Pupils taking IB achieved average of 38 points. Wide choice of subjects plus IB must make the 15 per cent exodus of girls after GCSE particularly galling, but we imagine that's not really about options. Relatively small classes where active participation is encouraged makes for a happy flock. A level classes run for sole takers, on occasion.

Achievements recognised both inside and outside GDST, with successes in Maths Challenges/Olympiad, Nuffield Bursaries, Nomura Scholarship and Young Science Writer prize recently awarded; one parent, however, had reservations about the quality of advice offered for Oxbridge during UCAS. But all three IB Oxbridge applicants plus three others were offered places in 2012. The school's recent ISI report judged its academic offering to be 'excellent' and its value-added scores are high. That same report also sounded a cautionary note that GCSE pupils should be allowed to lift their nose from the grindstone from time to time....

SEN gets a thumbs-up from parents. Early identification of problems in the junior school means the senior school is well-equipped to deal with their own new intake. Parents cite a supportive culture with no stigma and teachers who employ a variety of techniques to help, not just with the three Rs but also with organisation, presentation and strategies for revision. 'Concentration on their performance skills builds their confidence enormously,' remarked one father, a leadership expert. Extra help is paid for.

Games, options, the arts: Lots on offer from Dance Storm to D of E. All the games and sports you would expect are played on the school's own facilities: Astro, tennis courts and sports hall on campus, larger grass pitches and athletics a short drive to more level but windswept terrain on top of Lansdown. Swimming in the outdoor pool in summer or at the university across the city – the facilities and coaching are worth the drive. Hockey and netball particularly strong and the school puts on a good showing locally and nationally. One girl, whose sister left in search of springier pastures after GCSE, said she couldn't possibly think of leaving because of the sport. Sporting interests which fall outside the curriculum well catered for too, eg judo, fencing and aerobics, and individual talents encouraged, not just amongst the pupils: a teacher is a serious Olympic prospect in archery. A full voluntary activity programme is offered on Saturday mornings, but members of school teams are expected to commit at least some of their weekend to their sport – maybe going on tour to Barbados compensates. It is, however, quite possible to blag your way out of sport completely in the sixth form, it seems.

Wonderful art emanates from the fantastic new art school, where light airy studios with panoramic views give students every opportunity not only to create masterpieces but to exhibit them as well. All you could wish for, including ceramics, textiles, sculpture and photography. RHS has long been known for its music and drama; these remain strengths, though one parent reckons that music has perhaps lost a little of its sheen in an attempt to 'become more democratic', as she put it; 10 ensembles seem to us to be a sign of a healthy musical life and a recent choral scholarship to Cambridge, soloists in Bath Abbey and the current leader of the county orchestra suggest that music produces the goods. Associated Board results confirm this, with most entrants getting merits or distinctions.

The jewel in the crown is drama: loads of plaudits from the Mid Somerset Festival and LAMDA. Single sex schools do of course demand versatility on the stage from their pupils, though boys are imported from local boys' comp, Beechen Cliff (qv), to form Bathos (!) theatre troupe, and no poverty of dramatic ambition: recent productions include The Crucible and musicals and Gilbert and Sullivan are staged to general acclaim. Strong support given to girls keen on the tech side too with the opening of an new media centre offering activities from sound recording to green screen CGI filming. The chapel, which is now known as The Sophie Cameron Performing Arts Centre, named in honour of a former head girl, hosts key cultural events throughout the year.

Background and atmosphere: Victorian stone monolith stands back from the road up a drive through an off-puttingly narrow archway. First impressions of austerity are dispelled by the warmth and courtesy of staff and pupils and by more natural light at the back of the main building – the library is lovely, though other parts the head hasn't spotted could use a lick of paint here and there. It all feels rather traditional, despite mod cons, and the girls fit in. Edgy it isn't, despite valiant new initiatives such as the sixth form college (with its brief introduction of boys) and IB. The Royal High has blazed something of a trail within GDST as its only school to offer boarding (a legacy from the amalgamation between Bath High and the Royal School in 1998). The school draws a distinction between the experience of the first five years and the last two, by housing the sixth form college in a separate block with teaching space for small groups, space to chill for larger ones and a café,

R

in a genuine attempt to address the gap between school and university. Each sixth former is issued with a bright red laptop, all wired up to the school intranet and ready to go, a move universally welcomed, coming as it does with full technical support. Further down the school, it feels reassuring – a place where girls can be girls and pursue trad 'male' subjects without distraction or fear of censure: the shortish school day (finishing at 4pm but with an option to stay till 6pm) and proximity to town mean plenty of opportunity to socialise after school.

Parents report a happy school with an inclusive culture, where results aren't everything, and achievement of all kinds is celebrated. Social awareness is also inculcated and a sense of the world beyond school, with a good current affairs programme, Model UN and a partnership with a Kenyan school, as well as the 20 or so foreign pupils. Most, whose daughters have come up from the junior school, look nowhere else.

Pastoral care and discipline: Girls are well looked after and look after each other. The detailed PHSE programme ensures they are as savvy as the school can make them about the pitfalls and downsides of teenage life – and sanctions for those who transgress. Anyone caught smoking, drinking or with drugs can expect the heave-ho or suspension for shop-lifting. Sixth formers lead discussions about aspects of contemporary life with the younger ones; sessions have included celebrity culture and Fairtrade. Conduct within school, and occasionally beyond, is governed by a system of merits, commendations and debits – the emphasis, according to the school, very much on praise rather than blame, although we picked up the odd gripe from parents about heavy-handedness over petty things. Support structures and expertise in the problems besetting teenage girls, eg eating disorders, definitely in place, though.

Pupils and parents: 'Hard to generalise,' said the head, but went on to talk about the values which RHS girls share, namely open-mindedness, respect, courtesy and a sense of their own individuality. We found them polite, articulate – and perhaps a touch inhibited by the presence of a senior teacher over lunch, for reasons of safeguarding, note. A good cross-section of parents – most professions and some media types represented, plus humbler occupations. Not a snobby school – girls come from anything up to 20 miles away by bus or train; the school runs a minibus from the station and, as well as its own, two buses run in collaboration with King Edward's across the city.

Famous old girls include Mary Berry, Baroness Elspeth Howe and the last head of Queen Anne's Caversham (qv).

Entrance: Seventy-five girls arrive in year 7, having passed examinations in English, maths and verbal reasoning the previous January, plus interviews with the head and year 7 co-ordinator. The main route in is its own junior school, but girls come from local independents and primaries too across Wiltshire, South Gloucestershire, Somerset and Dorset as well as from overseas. More will arrive in year 9 after entrance exams in English, maths and science and the offer of scholarships at this entry level, then another intake in lower sixth, where six GCSEs, with A grades for AS subjects, are required. Transition arrangements come in for particular praise at year 7.

Exit: Five per cent left after GCSEs in 2013 to go to local co-eds, state and independent. After A levels or IB, pretty well everyone makes their first choice destinations, embracing a range of courses from the vocational to the theoretical. Nottingham, Cardiff, Exeter and Birmingham currently the most popular destinations. Half a dozen or so to Oxbridge most years (five in 2013), despite some caution on the school's part about putting pupils forward. Gap years the exception rather than the norm. GDST girls become members of GDST Alumnae, the Trust-wide network for communication and support amongst former pupils, which offers the inside track on various universities and professions.

Money matters: Remarkably good value for money – unusually, exam fees, books and insurance are included, though most extras and lunch are paid separately. Forces' offspring get a 10 per cent discount. Boarding fees are significantly cheaper than any boarding establishment we know of – how do they do it? Thrift extends to sensible and well priced uniform. Scholarships and bursaries offered for academics, art, music, drama and sport; bursaries for bright girls whose parents could not otherwise afford it also available, as is short term assistance for temporary hardship cases.

Remarks: Consistently good girls' day school, as befits the GDST, with some interesting departures – boarding, a collegiate sixth form offering A levels and the IB. A safe bet which should fulfil almost any girl, but not perhaps for the rebel.

The Royal Hospital School

Holbrook, Ipswich, IP9 2RX

- Pupils: 700; 420 boys, 280 girls; 550 board • Ages: 11–18
- C of E • Fees: Boarding £20,595–£25,437 Day £12,394–£16,770 pa
- Independent

Tel: 01473 326200
Email: admissions@royalhospitalschool.org
Website: www.royalhospitalschool.org

Headmaster: Since September 2012, Mr James Lockwood MA BEd (late thirties), previously deputy head. Educated at Manchester and Surrey universities; taught at Exeter School and St John's Leatherhead, where he was also housemaster and in charge of cricket and rugby, before joining the Royal Hospital School in 2009. Avid sports enthusiast and accomplished cricketer, rugby player and golfer. Married with two young children.

Academic matters: Not known to be an overly pressured, academic hothouse – parents talk about staff who are always available for extra help if it's sought and children going at their own pace. But change is in the air – the head has made it 'his personal priority to raise the school's academic profile' and said pupils are to be 'stretched as much possible in the classroom'. No empty words these – according to our guides, raised expectations have hit the chalk face. Year 7s learn French and sample Spanish, German and Latin before selecting one to be their second language. Streaming with ability sets for maths, English, languages and science plus monthly assessments which keep parents up to speed re academic progress. Standard GCSE choices including dual award/separate sciences, PE and drama. Average class sizes pre-sixth: 18. At GCSE: 89 per cent with 5 A*- Cs, 43 per cent A*/A in 2013. Twenty-five subjects at A level, including drama and theatre, media studies, PE, psychology and politics. Sixth have to follow an enrichment programme which, amongst the usual cooking on a budget/managing your workload, offers more heady stuff for boffs – AS law, GCSE Russian or Greek. Steady improvement in results: 58 per cent A*-B in 2013.

Regarding curriculum support, school says it has 'high academic standards' – translate this to mean they only accommodate mild needs. All entrants are screened (be sure to let RHS know about any educational needs or learning difficulties, including those of other family members: parents may be asked to withdraw their child if information is withheld). Low key department with one full-timer plus head of department, who's a dyslexia specialist. One-to-one remedial help (extra charge) normally two periods a week – some Forces children experience disjointed schooling and need a boost. Small groups for learning support (no charge) – pupils usually drop a second language and have help with spelling, maths, handwriting and organisational skills. Overseas centre with three full-timers plus one part timer for EFL students – 20 per cent in the sixth; they need to have a reasonable grasp of English.

Games, options, the arts: Sport is popular and, according to a dad, 'There's plenty of it – helps keep them on an even keel'. You're not going to find earth shattering results – however the 'breadth of opportunity' is a big plus. Cavernous sports hall, 96 acres of playing fields, wide range of individual sports including golf (proudly told by our guides that 'we have a nine hole golf course'), squash and swimming (slightly tired but perfectly adequate large indoor pool). But ask anyone about RHS and they'll say, 'Oh, the place where they sail' – seafaring is one of its defining features. A recognised RYA training centre with a varied collection of dinghies and, for pootling along the coast at the weekends, a fleet of Cornish shrimpers. Nearby Alton Water reservoir is a perfect venue – all year 7s go through an intensive introductory course. Sailing lessons, canoeing and windsurfing on offer for those who take to the spray.

Mouth-watering new music school, with its acoustically top notch recital hall, was opened by John Rutter. School choir so impressed him that he invited them to join the Royal Philharmonic Orchestra at his Albert Hall Christmas celebration – something worth trumpeting. Voices of the whole school plus beast of an organ (largest in Europe – so much here seems to be enormous) help create the mythical 'Holbrook sound'. Fifty per cent learn an instrument – according to a parent, teachers are inspirational and pupils are encouraged to be part of a band or group. (Marching band accompanies 'divisions' – see under Atmosphere – and band members get free music tuition.) Large, permanent display area for art work. Lively photographic images – photography seems to be the hot thing and department has recently purchased 21 mini Macs. DT with its tremendous workshop full of metallic 'dinosaurs' is a Mecca for older pupils.

Spare time is filled with a host of activities – according to an insider always something to do, and one parent said their daughter 'always seemed too busy to talk on the phone'. The CCF is big – one of the biggest contingents in the country with four sections: royal marines, naval, army and RAF – and all year 9/10 pupils have to take part, often opting to continue through to the end of their school career – 'It really helps us develop leadership skills'. Large numbers involved in D of E with a goodly clutch getting gold. Extensive list of clubs and societies. Something for every taste – under 'D' you'll find dance, drama, dry skiing, debating.

Background and atmosphere: Primarily a co-ed boarding school – the largest in East Anglia – it was founded in the early 18th century to educate boys for service in the Royal Navy. The building which now houses the National Maritime Museum was its original home – the move to the present 200 acre, 'beautiful in the summer', but in the middle of nowhere, Holbrook site came in the 1930s.

Changes had to be made in 2005 when the Admiralty Board made substantial funding cuts – RHS was no longer the 'navy's cradle'. Seriously tarry icons were jettisoned, day pupils were introduced and the proportion of full fee payers and/or those who don't have a naval connection increased. The head has worked hard to broaden the school's appeal without losing its unique character – a precarious balancing act. An armoury remains centre stage on a large parade ground overlooking the wide Stour estuary, staff might be seen wearing fatigues, houses are named after famous seamen and every pupil is supplied with a naval uniform for formal parades and 'divisions', when the whole school marches in time to music. Pupils are proud of the tradition and don't seem to mind ironing their kit and polishing their shoes – 'Gives them a bit of discipline,' said a parent. Morning 'skirmishes' and 'stations' keep everything spic and span.

Spacious, regimented environment with few frills. Buildings are reassuringly solid and on a large scale – it's a windy kilometre from one end of the campus to the other. But the place doesn't seem intimidating – 'It's really friendly for its size'. An £18 million parting sweetener from the Admiralty Board funded the music school, generous refurbs of the houses and an upgrading of the pleasantly calm, large library – wide stock includes copies of The Times, Telegraph – and Guardian.

Pastoral care and discipline: This is where eulogies flow fast: 'absolutely fabulous'; 'I know the children are in safe hands'; 'Pastoral care is one of the greatest things about the school'. Anti-bullying counsellors, stand-alone medical centre with a doctor, dentist/orthodontist, 26 beds and six full-time staff, including a counsellor who can be seen totally confidentially. Plenty of sensible advice from house and teaching staff plus good liaison with parents through email and phone contact.

Majority of pupils board and purpose-built houses with comfortably furnished central forums are warm and welcoming. Juniors have their own house – 'Our housemistress is like a second mother and the matron a second granny' – as do the sixth (day pupils are mixed in where appropriate). No official exeats but two 'quiet weekends' a term (not compulsory), with activities for those who stay behind – sleepovers, shopping trips etc. Seriously good food. Bread is made on site and ingredients sourced locally, with Sunday brunch of 'waffles, pancakes and lots and lots of orange juice' a favourite. For the odd hungry moment generous bowls of fruit in the houses (what a good idea!).

Older ones are allowed into Ipswich at the weekend (they have to order a taxi and pay for the five mile journey) but discos, themed evenings and The Nelson Arm, a supervised bar where a quota of drink tokens can be exchanged, seem a popular alternative. We hear the régime is 'fair', with clear boundaries. Zero tolerance re banned substances and inappropriate fraternisation, but pragmatic approach to sixth formers caught smoking – they're sent to the health centre for 'health training'.

Pupils and parents: Local (bus services from nearby towns), out of county, Forces (25 per cent) and overseas (10 per cent) – all walks of life. Difficult for many parents to be involved but a PTA for those who live nearby. According to a mum, 'an eclectic mix of pupils who seem to get on with each other even across age ranges'. Pupils come across as confidently polite, unaffected and well-behaved. Admiral Arthur Philip, founder of Australia, was a past pupil.

Entrance: Not hugely difficult – entrants need to be scoring no lower than the national average. Contact made with the headteacher of a candidate's current school for a reference. Candidates also have an interview with the head; 'This is not a bit part boarding school' – they're looking for children who will happily adapt to the school's structured ethos, including divisions etc. At 11+ entrance tests in maths, English, verbal reasoning. At 13+ satisfactory performance in CE. For the sixth they say average 5.5 at GCSE (C=5, B=6) including C in English – but depending on AS choices this can be higher.

Exit: A fifth leave after GCSE, mostly to sixth form colleges. Nearly all to higher education – great variety of institutions and courses, from sports and exercise science to biotechnology and civil engineering. Two or three a year to Oxbridge.

Money matters: For exceptional candidates a limited number of scholarships (lower school/sixth form: academic, music, art, sport, sailing). A scholarship cannot be combined with any other award. Number of means-tested sea-faring bursaries and discounts on boarding places available to those with parents or grandparents who have served for more than three years in the navy, Royal Marines, Royal Fleet Auxiliary or merchant navy. Forces families eligible for Continuity of Education Allowance (formerly Boarding Schools Allowance) receive a discount on the normal fee.

Remarks: Privilege and public with a small 'p'. A secure environment for the outdoorsy type who's happy to conform and buy into a naval heritage. Excellent full boarding provision – particularly for parents overseas.

Royal Masonic School for Girls

Linked school: Royal Masonic School for Girls Cadogan House Prep & Pre-prep

Rickmansworth Park, Chorleywood Road, Rickmansworth Hertfordshire, WD3 4HF

• Pupils: 650 girls, including 140 full/weekly boarders • Ages: 11–18 • Non denom • Fees: Boarding £16,050–£25,050; Day £9,000–£14,700 pa • Independent

Tel: 01923 773168
Email: enquiries@royalmasonic.herts.sch.uk
Website: www.royalmasonic.herts.sch.uk

Headmistress: Since 2002, Mrs Diana Rose MA (mid fifties). Educated at Channing School, London before becoming one of the first women to attend King's College, Cambridge, where she read history and social and political sciences. Knows her market inside out having spent over a decade in Buckinghamshire grammar schools and six years as head of sixth at St Helen's Northwood, before becoming deputy head at Oxford High. Also a governor at Wycombe Abbey school, and has been on the education panel of the Wolfson Foundation for twenty years. One half of a local educational super-couple, she is married to Stephen Nokes, head of John Hampden Grammar, High Wycombe. Her two sons, schooled at Berkhamsted and the Royal Grammar School, High Wycombe, have flown the family nest, freeing her up to study for GCSE Italian and indulge passions for cookery, theatre and the ballet.

Proud of the school offering, 'a unique ethos in the area.' Wedged between academic hot-houses on the edge of London and uber-competitive South Bucks and Herts grammar schools (says school is not a 'tough environment' like they are), she is clear that, 'no RMS girl is ever told she's not good enough to continue with us', as illustrated by the fact that there is no entry requirement for sixth form for existing pupils. Expects girls to form good work habits but says she does not nurture 'a perfectionist culture', understanding the harm that such pressure can do to young minds. The antithesis to local grammars striving for A grades at any cost, she takes her girls on a 'calm and broad journey' where they are not pressured to give up extras in favour of academic cramming, even in exam years.

Walks her dogs (as do many parents) around the school grounds daily and keeps fit by cycling which, coupled with a natty wardrobe and stylish shoe collection, all contributes to the fact that she looks a good ten years younger than she actually is. Has an easy smile and sharp sense of humour. Girls say she is 'very approachable' and love the fact that she knows them all well – not just by name but what they are studying and all their interests too. Passionate about educating pupils to be independent learners and claims that despite the idyllic cosseted campus feel of the school, 'they all thrive at uni'.

Academic matters: Turning formerly dismissive heads and winning more and more parental votes with persistently improving results. In 2013 50 per cent A*/A grades at A level and nearly 57 per cent at GCSE. Small class sizes (maximum 20) across the board and setting from year 7 in maths and French, with fewer than 10 in some lower sets. More setting (English, science) from year 9 but these are totally flexible, with one parent delighted that her child moved from the bottom to top of six sets for maths in the space of a year. Must be the 'outstanding teaching' that the head is so proud of. Teachers 'go the extra mile', say parents and pupils, and are happy to tutor any stragglers in their free time. Enrichment programmes and extra work for the gifted and lots of clinics to make sure nobody slips through the gaps.

Parents say it's a 'good all round school' where their children can have a go at 'absolutely anything'. They like the fact that the brightest children are made to feel so in this mixed ability environment rather than bumping along feeling average in a class packed with boffins as they might in more selective schools. Geography and history most popular subjects at GCSE with sciences and maths coming to the fore at A level.

Both highly academic parents with children to match and those with less intellectual offspring feel that the school has the 'right balance' regarding achievement. Girls can choose to do between nine and eleven GCSEs depending on ability and those staying on in the sixth form to take two A levels in photography or art are treated with as much care as mathematicians and scientists taking four. To keep everyone happy, academic girls wishing to take arty subjects can take A2 exams in these in year 12, freeing them up to concentrate on their academic subjects thereafter. EPQ results are also impressive, with 25 per cent choosing to enter and all of these achieving grades A*-B. Strong languages on offer, with girls able to choose two plus Latin at GCSE if they are that way inclined and mandarin on offer for the most gifted linguists from year 8.

Girls put on a 'carousel' of arty subjects in years 8 and 9 to eke out talents and preferences. Dipping into subjects from ceramics and 3D design to home economics and DT, all taught by specialists in purpose designed (albeit a bit tired) facilities, helps guide them in the right direction when it comes to choosing GCSEs.

Good SEN, with individual lessons on offer to girls needing support. All pupils screened to detect literacy or numeracy difficulties on entry. Specialist EAL teaching for overseas pupils, charged as extra.

Games, options, the arts: Impressive sports facilities. Gymnastics, trampolining, dance et al take place in a jawdropping new purpose built double sports hall that would give most public sports centres a run for their money. Four squash courts and a multi-gym, available for the girls' use whenever they wish, also housed in the complex. Swimming pool is poor relation to the rest, functional at best. Acres of playing fields, great for cross country and adventure training, but no floodlights or Astro.

Lots of competitive sport with trophies galore of late – the school recently claimed the independent girls' schools golf championship title and the gymnastics team has just been placed nationally. Occasional grumbles from parents, however, that the school needs to work harder to engage more of the less obviously sporty girls in physical activities that are in tune with their lifestyles, claiming that some older girls get away with doing, 'hardly any or no sport at all', although head disagrees: 'they have all sorts of options from year 10 including Zumba, pilates and yoga.' Recent injection of young sports teachers has opened up more opportunities, including football and rugby.

School has strong artsy feel, offering a well used photography studio and dark room, drama studio and 'loads and loads' of musical and theatrical productions throughout the year, according to girls. Music 'improving all the time', say parents, with 300 girls learning an instrument and plenty of opportunities to show their skills in concerts and shows.

Trips and tours of all sorts, for sports teams, choirs, curriculum and just for the fun of it. Vast array of extra-curricular activities including very popular D of E and cadets means the school continues to buzz after lessons are over. Girls enthuse over chess and Chinese clubs as much as astronomy (in school's own planetarium) and taekwondo. Plenty of charitable works too, with prefects nominating a charity for the school to support each year. Others such as the Royal Hospital in Chelsea and schools in far flung places (Ghana, Japan) also benefit from visits and performances.

Background and atmosphere: Founded in 1788 to educate the children of masons who had fallen on hard times, the current 150 acre site, built in the 1930s, is the school's fourth home. A vast campus (NB visiting parents – wear flat shoes, if not trainers, for your tour), more akin to a red brick university than a suburban girls' school, with smart, identikit buildings surrounding two quadrangles ('teeming with girls chatting in the summer term' said one), and the longest teaching corridor in Britain. Became an independent school, open to all, in 1978 while continuing to fulfil its charitable obligation and still offering full bursaries to some 50 children in need of financial support at any time, although most staff don't know who they are.

Spanking new sixth form centre opened in 2012 where all year 12 and 13 girls take the majority of their lessons. Fabulous common room, interior designed by pupils, complete with hot pink walls and matching sofas. All whistles and bells, with girls able to borrow laptops from the library, or bring their own, and log onto the centre's wifi network. A senior team of twenty drawn from year 13, plus a head girl and eight deputies, elected by girls and teachers. Girls describe guidance at this stage of their education as 'excellent', with teachers giving up free time to help with personal statements and a dedicated Oxbridge co-ordinator on hand for brainboxes.

Lovely rotunda library, one of the nicest we've seen, with state of the art fingerprint withdrawal technology giving girls freedom to borrow and return books with ease, and plenty of space for quiet study.

Around 140 boarders in the senior school live in three boarding houses. Boarding most popular in years 10 to 12 with a mix of weekly, flexi and full time girls from across Europe, the Far East and, increasingly, Russia. Traditionally very popular with forces families but this is in decline due to MOD cuts. Boarders are treated to an outing every Saturday (bowling, cinema, theatre, London attractions). Older girls allowed to London in groups for shopping and lunch and in years 12 and 13 to the cinema in the evenings. A renovation programme of boarding houses is underway. We visited the most newly refurbished which, like the rest of the school, was extremely spacious, clean and well-equipped with a pool table, DVDs and Wii in its large common room. Not as cosy and homely as many boarding houses we've seen but certainly not lacking in mod cons. Light, bright and modern dining room, where boarders and day girls take all their meals feels like a hub of chatter at lunch time, with girls seated at sociably round tables, enjoying freshly cooked meals which are, by all accounts, 'outstanding'.

Parents say the school is 'very into tradition' and this feeling permeates its very fabric. RMS is the only school in the country still to do 'drill': a spectacle of pinafored girls with pinned back hair performing something akin to synchronised swimming but without the water. Places in the squad are highly sought after, with dozens volunteering even for the reserves.

Pastoral care and discipline: Head is 'anti-clique' and works hard to minimise the inevitable girly issues. Sixth formers are trained as peer mentors by the school counsellor, with year 9 girls taking on 'big sister' roles to new year 7s when they join the school.

Serious disciplinary problems are few but parents say head has never been afraid to 'take a hard line' when necessary and has even been known to call in police to educate girls on the outcomes of certain scenarios if they rear their ugly heads. Head claims alcohol is 'not an issue' and persistent bullying is dealt with by permanent exclusion. In a recent Ofsted boarding inspection 92 per cent of girls interviewed said they had never seen or experienced bullying; 'an exceptional figure', says head, compared to most boarding environments. Year 13 girls are well prepared for the real world with a range of seminars offering advice on subjects from budgeting at uni and car maintenance, to getting the most out of gap years.

Parents can email head direct with issues or queries. Boarders know that she works with her office door open on Sunday mornings and often pop in to share news or discuss problems. Year 7 pupils love the fact that she has frequent 'birthday parties' in her office with lashings of chocolate cake for the month's birthday girls. Often takes 'refugees' from high pressure schools and is proud to welcome them into her community where there is a 'real tolerance of difference'.

Chapel once a week, plus Sundays for boarders, taken by the school's full time chaplain. Boarders of other faiths do not have to attend Sunday communion, although many choose to. The whole school crams into this impressive space at Christmas for the traditional carol service.

Pupils and parents: Unlock your sons. RMS girls seem much younger and fresher than their more streetwise grammar peers and are just the kind you would love your boys to bring home for dinner. Confident and articulate without arrogance, they seem a genuinely grounded bunch. Good ethnic mix, reflecting the school's position on the London borders, with the vast majority taking full advantage of all the extras the school has to offer, 'Lots of bat mitzvahs to go to at weekends', said one parent.

Parents from all walks of life from the well-heeled to hard working, dual income, first time buyers. Some expats and international parents, largely of overseas boarders. Many from across the Chilterns and Hertfordshire, with an increasing North London crowd. The school provides an excellent coach service from all these areas, with the London brigade able to take advantage of the shuttle bus from the tube station. Parents of girls at smaller prep schools reported a bit of a culture shock when their daughters joined this vast establishment, but added that they felt totally at home 'after just a few weeks'.

Entrance: Increasingly selective, now parents are seeing RMS as a desirable option in an area of excellent independent and maintained schools. Majority join at 11+ but some places are also available for girls to join up to 14+. Candidates spend a full day during which they take the University of Durham online test to assess skills in English, maths and reasoning. The test is designed to accurately gauge girls' natural ability and – pushy parents be warned – cannot be tutored for. There's also a creative writing exercise, group activity and group interview. Head is keen to find space for girls with 'something else to offer' and looks closely at report from current school as well as test results. Candidates for entry in later years sit tests in English, maths and non-verbal reasoning.

Around 170 girls compete for approximately 40 places with successful ones, about half from state primaries, guaranteed a place in all future stages. Good sibling policy too, a relief if younger ones aren't as starry as big sister. Approximately 50 per cent join from the school's own prep, Cadogan House (these girls are guaranteed entry, making for a mixed bag academically). Around 25 new places are available in year 12, with girls being selected on GCSE results and extra-curricular achievements.

In line with its charitable ethos, school has an ongoing social mission to offer a limited number of assisted boarding places to disadvantaged children from London boroughs of Hillingdon and Tower Hamlets, and Norfolk. Head says that integration of these girls, and that of the mainly international boarders, is 'fantastic'.

Exit: Majority to Russell Group universities, with one to Oxbridge in 2013. Durham, Exeter, Leeds, Nottingham,

Birmingham, Southampton, Warwick and Loughborough all popular. Worth bearing in mind that as school's academic reputation continues to improve, this is likely to increase as fresh talent filters through. A small exodus at 16 recently to local grammar schools; perhaps girls wanting a somewhat more worldly environment, although head says all were for financial reasons.

Money matters: Capital expenditure is underpinned by an endowment set up by the Masons and the school is a tenant of the site. Multitude of scholarships and exhibitions available at 11+ (academic, all-rounder, art, music and sport), and sixth form (adding performing arts to the list) offering a maximum 25 per cent discount on fees. Five per cent discount for siblings and 10 per cent for forces families. Means tested bursaries available.

Remarks: A school where girls can be girls and sing, act and run their way to well-roundedness in a safe and nurturing environment. Happy to take 'refugees' from other schools and gently lick them into shape. Steadily improving academics over a number of years mean RMS has now secured its position as a serious contender in the competitive local market, and first class facilities help turn out real all-rounders.

A school that aims to draw the best out of everyone, whatever their abilities and turns out confident, rounded young ladies. Parents 'never mind writing the cheque to RMS', according to one. Egg heads and pushy parents might prefer some of the surrounding competition though.

Royal Russell School

Linked school: Royal Russell Junior School

Coombe Lane, Croydon, CR9 5BX

• Pupils: 600 boys and girls • Ages: 11–18 • Christian • Fees: Day £15,285; Boarding £30,240 pa • Independent

Tel: 020 8657 4433
Email: admissions@royalrussell.co.uk
Website: www.royalrussell.co.uk

Headmaster: Since September 2011, Mr Christopher Hutchinson BMet Sheffield, PGCE Cambridge FRSA (mid-forties). He started his teaching career at Clifton College in Bristol, where he was head of physics and a housemaster. Thence to Wellington College as head of science and assistant director of studies, before taking over the headship of Newcastle School for Boys. Married to Alex, a fellow science teacher, he enjoys singing, sports – particularly squash – tennis and gardening. Committed to providing a stimulating classroom education alongside a robust co-curricular programme. He has been officer commanding the CCF and also master in charge of rowing.

Academic matters: Exam pass rates have been climbing steadily – 35 per cent A*/A grades at A level and 36 per cent A*/A at GCSE in 2013. Mathematics is one of the school's strengths with a number of pupils taking GCSE a year early and AS in year 11, carrying on to A level and further mathematics and the sixth form. A flexible approach is taken to setting; most classes are mixed ability and pupils move into sets for maths, English, science, and modern languages for GCSE. Good choice of GCSEs offered. Pupils can study dual award or three separate sciences, although only two languages – French and Spanish – available.

Recently been upgraded ICT – everything is interactive with a parent/pupil portal which enables school computer system to be accessed from home. According to parents, good team of male and female teachers from the more mature to young sporty and

artistic types. Healthy turnover sees new blood and new ideas coming in each year. Refreshingly unfazed by the league tables, staff are committed to ensuring every pupil reaches their potential. Whilst the school is academically rigorous, a focus on producing broad, well rounded young people.

ESOL tuition is included in the fees and is available for pupils whose first language is not English. Strong learning support department, a charge is made for one-to-one lessons. All departments run lunchtime and after school clinics offering additional support to those who require it. Beautiful library and sixth form centre with small classes and individual attention. Added value is outstanding; sixth formers feed back very positively.

Games, options, the arts: Arts strong all round. Flourishing music department has earned an international reputation, orchestras and choirs travel far and wide to perform. Over 200 ABRSM exams taken by pupils each year – needless to say, pass rate is 100 per cent. Musical experiences are enhanced by workshops, excursions and working with professional musicians. Enviable suite of rooms, including a recording studio, lovely light practice rooms and a 200 seat concert venue.

Lively drama department teaches all age groups, giving pupils the opportunity to try their hand at acting, directing and being light and sound technicians, whilst developing public speaking skills and learning to work cooperatively. Theatre history is also taught and pupils can become involved in helping to make costumes and set designing. Theatre groups visit the school to perform and run workshops, also after-school drama classes and trips to local and West End performances. Pupils benefitting from the recently opened superb performing arts centre. Martin Clunes and Naoko Mori are old boys. Inspiring light airy art studios where students benefit from expert teaching and a great range of resources.

Just about everything is on offer from traditional sports to archery and windsurfing. Eager representatives at local, regional and national level sports teams and events, school and house matches – being physically active and enjoying sport considered part of pupil well-being. Lots of fun and successes – teams are coached by outside specialists as well as in-house PE teachers. Extensive playing fields and courts of every shape and size, cross-country course through their own woodland, indoor swimming pool and sports complex. All sporting facilities are well utilised and operate as a local sports centre for the public, parents and local clubs, adding to the community feel of the school. Community link with Coloma Convent for CCF. The range of clubs, societies and activities is almost unlimited. Large number of senior pupils participate in the Modern United Nations programme and the school hosts one of the biggest UK conferences.

Background and atmosphere: Hidden from the public eye beyond a long driveway lies a great school for the 21st century offering a remarkable number of opportunities for all tastes and talents. Once thought rather down in the doldrums, now offers stiff competition to other South London and Surrey schools. Open-minded and flexible in its general approach, the atmosphere is vibrant and purposeful, a very busy place. The senior management are thought to be caring and in touch with the requirements of today's parents and pupils. An optional extended school day.

Established in 1853 at New Cross for the sons and daughters of textile workers – one of the earliest co-ed schools. In 1924 purchased the Ballard's estate, an extensive, wooded, 110 acre site, which now houses both the junior and senior schools. Long history of royal patronage – the present Queen has visited the school four times since the 1950s and Edward, Earl of Wessex, opened the performing arts centre. Lots of new buildings have popped up recently: a rolling rebuilding programme to upgrade and redevelop is underway and some rather unattractive 1960s

R

buildings have been pulled down and replaced. Christian based, now multi faith and boasts its own recently restored chapel – much of the original stonework carved by Eric Gill in the 1920s.

Pastoral care and discipline: House system, nine houses, three of which are boarding houses. Approximately 130 pupils board, boarding houses have been refurbished and a full programme of activities runs at weekends. Day pupils enjoy the luxury of having their own houses, with the sitting rooms for each year group to relax and socialise in during breaktimes and after school. Supervised homework sessions run each evening and day pupils can stay at school until 9pm – evening meals are included in the fees. Prefect system with head and deputy head boy and girl; each house has its own head of house and sports captains, so a large number of pupils are involved with aiding the day to day running and school functions.

Pastoral staff pride themselves on their knowledge of the needs of young people and understanding the whole child. Housemasters and mistresses together with the chaplain are always available to talk, pupils are treated as individuals and staff go out of their way to help sort out any problems. Small tutor groups also ensure parents and pupils are kept well informed about academic and personal development. School rules regularly reviewed, predominantly in place for everybody's security and safety. Quite strict uniform code and tip top behaviour expected at all times. Pupils tell us the food is delicious, plenty of choices and everybody eats together – the sizable dining hall provides the perfect place to enjoy the company of others.

Pupils and parents: From around 20 mile radius between Clapham Junction and the M25, Bromley, Dulwich, Wimbledon and Croydon. Fortuitously, the tramstop is opposite the entrance, making it an easy journey for many. Folk from all walks of life – many different types and characters, first-time buyers to children of old Russellians. Interesting mix of nationalities, the sixth form being particularly popular with foreign students. Very active PTA helps organise the numerous social activities, car boot sales and fund-raising for charity.

Entrance: At 11+: exam (English, maths and computer based verbal reasoning or cognitive abilities test), interview and reference from previous school. Small number of places are usually available at 13+ and 16+ for sixth form.

Exit: At 16+, a few to local colleges to study vocational courses. At 18+, all to university or art colleges, an increasing number of students choosing law, economics and veterinary sciences; Royal Holloway, Brighton, Durham, Exeter, Kent and Leicester popular in 2013, plus one to LSE to study law and three to Central St Martins to do art and design.

Money matters: All applicants for year 7 and year 9 are considered for academic scholarships via their performance in the entrance exam. Further scholarships are available for year 12 on the basis of GCSE results. Also junior, senior and sixth form art, music and drama scholarships. A limited number of means-tested bursaries. Five per cent discount for siblings.

Remarks: Confident and socially accomplished pupils, proud of their increasing successes across the curriculum. Solid reputation for producing cheerful young people, well-prepared for successful futures at university and in the workplace.

Rudolf Steiner School (Kings Langley)

Linked school: Rudolf Steiner Junior School (Kings Langley)

Langley Hill, Kings Langley, Hertfordshire, WD4 9HG

- Pupils: 410 girls and boys • Ages: 3 –19 • Fees: £6,245–£8,945 pa
- Independent

Tel: 01923 262505
Email: info@rsskl.org
Website: www.rsskl.org

College of Teachers: Like all Steiner schools, does not have a headteacher but is run on a non-hierarchical basis by a College of Teachers, which also forms smaller committees called mandate groups to advise on different matters such as staffing and finance. The main initial point of contact for parents is the admissions secretary.

Academic matters: One of the few Steiner schools in the country that goes right through from three to 19, covering GCSEs and A levels – albeit a year later than most mainstream schools. But exam results are far from being the school's raison d'etre. It shares a common curriculum with some 900 Steiner Waldorf schools worldwide, aiming 'to nourish each child's innate curiosity and love of learning'. The curriculum is organised according to the Steiner philosophy of three phases of child development.

In the kindergarten, the children learn 'through activity and through interpreting impressions'. Three to six year olds play together, making boats or shops or houses from chairs and tables, baking and modelling, dressing up and listening to stories. They spend lots of time outside, and all their playthings are of natural materials – wood, cotton, silk. Reading and writing are not on the agenda at this stage but rhythm and repetition are important.

At the age of six they move up to the lower school, where they meet the class teacher who will, ideally, remain with them for the next eight years. At this stage, in Steiner philosophy, they learn through feelings and memory. They begin to learn the alphabet through stories and pictures and come to reading through writing. They learn poems and recite times tables. Each morning they have a two-hour main lesson, studying a particular topic in depth for three weeks. Art, craft and drama are all important. French and German, taught by specialists, are also on the curriculum. No computers in the lower school – 'All learning takes place by human contact and artistic activity'.

At 14, in Steiner philosophy, they move into the 'thinking' phase of learning. At their most questioning and critical, they have specialist teachers for each subject and begin to prepare for GCSEs, but cramming is not on the agenda. GCSE results – from a limited selection of subjects that includes German, history and drama but not at present geography – are creditable, particularly when one considers that these are the first exams Steiner children have experienced. Sixty-seven per cent of candidates got five or more A*-C grades in 2013, with 43 per cent of grades A*/A. At A level the subject range is still more limited: maths, biology, chemistry, French, German, drama, English literature, history, history of art, art and photography; 52 per cent A*/A grades in 2013. Plenty of class trips to galleries, museums, concerts and theatres. Residential trips have included a class 9 journey to create a forest pathway in Switzerland and a class 6 visit to Hadrian's Wall.

Children with special education needs who are not coping at conventional schools often gravitate towards a Steiner education, with its emphasis on the practical and creative

R

and on learning through experience. The school can cope with dyslexia, dyspraxia and dyscalculia, but not behavioural difficulties – 'Unless the bad behaviour stems from frustration with academic work, when we will consider it'. Since Steiner children do not begin to learn to read and write until they are six, most can cope in the mainstream class until they are nine or so. They may have one lesson a week with learning support, and the movement and co-ordination work often helps them academically. But since the classes have around 30 pupils, teachers cannot give individual children large amounts of one-to-one attention.

In 2005 the school opened the Tobias class as a pilot project for 9 and 10 year olds who need specific extra help. The plan is for them to spend up from a few terms to a few years in the class, then integrate or reintegrate into the appropriate mainstream form, preferably before the start of the upper school at 14, so it is not suitable for children with severe difficulties. In this class, run by a trained dyslexia specialist, the emphasis is as much on bodily co-ordination as on academic skills. The children do plenty of maths and English, but also learn circus skills, have massage therapy and curative eurythmy – a harmonious dance therapy that is believed to help with learning and co-ordination. They also go riding, and join in gym, gardening and music with mainstream classes. 'Their progress has been phenomenal,' says their teacher, 'Not only academically, but also in their whole beings. They are much happier and more confident.' 'It's been fantastic for my daughter,' said a parent. 'She has improved so much.'

It is not suitable for children on the autistic spectrum. 'They like to know exactly what is going to happen next, but we are creative and unpredictable. I have no assistant, so I can't spend my time dealing with one child's behaviour.'

Games, options, the arts: Arts and crafts are an integral part of Steiner education. The walls are lined with paintings in the classic 'wet on wet' Steiner technique. Separate studios for fine arts, woodwork, metalwork, pottery and modelling and photography. Pupils bake bread, tend their allotments. Everyone does art to GCSE and art and history of art are the most popular A level subjects.

Music and drama also play a large role. Everyone plays the recorder and has singing lessons, can try playing the violin in class 3 and continue if it suits them, many learn other instruments. Class, middle and upper school orchestras. Every year the orchestras from the Steiner schools in Kings Langley and in Ottersberg, Germany, exchange places to perform a prepared programme in the other school, which means, on alternate years, students from Kings Langley stay with local Ottersberg Steiner families. A major upper school musical every other year and many other productions by different classes. The theatre, equipped with fly-tower and full lighting, seats 450 and hosts cabarets and concerts as well as plays – 'Our children are used to appearing in public from an early age'.

Gym/sports hall and extensive playing fields. But while the older children play inter-school volleyball and basketball matches (with considerable success), competitive sport is peripheral to the Steiner curriculum. Eurythmic dance and outdoor activities in general are integral, however. The younger children play non-competitive, co-operative games, go for nature walks, garden. They plant Christmas trees, cut willow for lime kilns, dig clay to make tablets. Class 5 visits the Michael Hall School in Sussex together with class 5 students from all the other UK Steiner schools to recreate the Ancient Greek Olympics.

Background and atmosphere: Opened in 1949 in 10 acres of grounds on the site of a 13th century royal palace. Peaceful, harmonious atmosphere with trees and grass, climbing frames and tree houses. Parental involvement vital – parents run the school shop and cafe, which also provides simple school lunches. They help to run the huge fund-raising event, the Advent Fair, which has approximately 3,000 visitors, the midsummer

market and the fireworks and bonfire night display. They share their expert knowledge – of architecture or embryology or philosophy – with pupils, can apply for an allotment in the school grounds, decorate classrooms, make curtains and help with camping trips and class outings.

Pastoral care and discipline: Rewards more important here than punishments, but this is not a free-for-all – the atmosphere is quiet and ordered. Misbehaving youngsters are given warnings, then moved to a seat close to the teacher, then sent to the staffroom to get on with some work. Detentions in the upper school. Strong sanctions against those found smoking or using drugs or alcohol, 'But we are very unwilling to expel unless absolutely necessary'. Great attention to individual needs – 'The level of pastoral care is exceptional,' said a parent.

Pupils and parents: Many families have moved to King's Langley to be part of the school community. Others come from a wide catchment area, including a number by school bus from north London. These are not, on the whole, carefully mannered, diligent, respectful, public school children – they are lively, questioning, active. 'They can be a wild bunch,' said a parent. Quite a few have failed to thrive at more conventional schools. The school limits the number of SEN pupils it accepts in order to keep a balance of abilities within each class.

Entrance: Families who want their child to attend the kindergarten are encouraged to go to the pre-school parent and child group. These get more or less automatic entry; next in line are siblings, those from another Steiner kindergarten and local families. Applicants are interviewed by two kindergarten teachers.

For entry into class 1 and above, children are asked to bring a copy of a report from their previous school and some examples of their maths, writing and drawing. They will have an interview with the class teacher for an hour or so, but no formal test.

Exit: Around half the class generally moves on after GCSEs – they may have had enough of long journeys to school or want to study subjects the school doesn't offer. A few join the sixth form, mostly from other Steiner schools. Most of those leaving after A levels go to university or art college, some directly into usually craft-related professions.

Money matters: Has appointed a bursar and handed over school fee collection to an agency, to combat a tendency amongst some parents to view fee-paying as voluntary. Fees are in any case very low by independent school standards, and many parents benefit from reduced fees. These factors have led to a lack of funds for capital expenditure. Embarking on a tightening up of financial matters, including a major fund-raising drive.

Remarks: Friendly, caring school in idyllic surroundings with a focus firmly on the needs of the child, which nevertheless produces creditable exam results. A haven for some children with specific special needs and for refugees from the exam-driven culture of most mainstream schools.

Rugby School

Lawrence Sheriff Street, Rugby, CV22 5EH

• Pupils: 805 pupils; 655 boarders, 150 day pupils. 450 boys, 355 girls • Ages: 11–18 (day pupils only at 11 and 12) • C of E
• Fees: Boarding £31,245; Day £19,605 pa • Independent

Tel: 01788 556274
Email: admissions@rugbyschool.net
Website: www.rugbyschool.net

Headmaster: Since 2001, Mr Patrick Derham MA (late forties). At 11 was sent to live and study on the naval training ship, Arethusa, run by the children's charity, Shaftesbury Homes, to prepare young men for the navy. His potential was spotted and he was transferred to Pangbourne College, where he eventually became head of school. Read history at Pembroke College, Cambridge, and began his teaching career at Cheam School. Moved to Radley, where he was head of history and a housemaster, and joined Solihull as headmaster in 1996. Says he was 'bowled over by the atmosphere' at Rugby when he visited for the first time. Still teaches four periods a week of A level history. 'It's terribly important,' he says. 'It's what I came into the job to do.' The week we visited he'd switched an A level lesson about William Pitt the Younger's rise to power to a Sunday evening to fit it into his busy schedule. Dynamic, level-headed and caring. Very popular with parents. Says it is 'a huge privilege' to be head of a school that 'strives for excellence in everything we do' and is 'so unpretentious, friendly, busy and purposeful'. He lunches with pupils in different houses each day, goes to as many matches as possible and loves watching 'really skilled classroom practitioners' in action. 'It's nice for pupils to see you taking an interest and you can always do your paperwork at night,' he declares.

Delights in the fact that he's sitting in Thomas Arnold's study – complete with a portrait of the great man, Arnold's own (surprisingly small) desk and the spiral staircase in the corner where pupils could come and go if they wanted to see him privately. Their modern-day counterparts still use it before chapel to show good work to present head and pass on the school's latest sports results.

This isn't a highly-selective boarding school but a broad church where everyone is encouraged to achieve their full potential. Head rightfully proud of Arnold Foundation which he set up in 2003 to provide fully-funded boarding places (plus uniform, essential books and trips) for talented youngsters whose parents could not afford to send them to the school. 'Rugby has always provided bursaries for day pupils and I wanted to replicate those opportunities for boarders,' he says. School aims to increase number of funded pupils to 10 per cent of the school – figure currently stands at 8.5 per cent (boarders and day pupils) – and recently launched a £30 million fund-raising campaign. 'One of the problems for all boarding schools is their increasing social exclusivity,' he adds. 'Something like this helps to make the school more diverse and representative of society.' In 2012 school signed a memorandum of understanding with the Coventry Diocesan Board of Education (CDBE) – the first agreement of its kind and intended to promote opportunities and raise aspirations across the schools which make up the CDBE. Around 100 year 11 to 13 students mentor pupils in four local primary schools.

Married to Alison, who is head of learning support at Bilton Grange, the prep school down the road. They live in a house in the grounds (head cycles virtually everywhere) and have two grown up children – a son and a daughter, both of whom were pupils at Rugby.

Moving onwards and upwards in September 2014 to take up the headship of Westminster School. His successor will be Peter Green, currently head of Ardingly College. Began at Strathallan School before moving to Uppingham, where he served first as head of geography and then as boarding housemaster. From 2002, second master of Ampleforth. A rugby-keen Scot, he is married Brenda and they have a teenage son and daughter.

Academic matters: Rugby has always prided itself on its pioneering approach to the curriculum – it was, for instance, the first school in the country to teach science as part of the formal school curriculum in the 1850s – and this continues apace. Now offers IGCSE in seven subjects, plus the Cambridge Pre-U, an 'academically more rigorous' alternative to A levels where pupils write traditional, essay length answers. Meanwhile has piloted and developed perspectives in science (now accredited by Edexcel). Led by Dr John Taylor, formerly head of physics and now director of critical skills, this is a new course in the philosophy and ethics of science and helps pupils develop high-level research skills. Over one or two years, sixth form pupils (around 95 this year) produce a 6,000 to 7,000-word research project on a topic of their choice – everything from quantum mechanics and black holes to animal welfare and witch hunts so far. One Rugby pupil called it 'a refreshing break from the narrow confines of the A level syllabus,' while another said it was 'an amazing course, not just for learning about what you're interested in, but also for transferable research and writing skills'. The quality of work produced played a key role in encouraging the QCA (Qualifications and Curriculum Authority) to promote the development of extended projects, now available to all schools as qualifications equivalent to A level.

In 2013 79 per cent A*/A grades at IGCSE and GCSE and over 55 per cent A*/A grades at A level/Pre U (nearly 79 per cent A*/B). Wide range of languages on offer – French, German, Spanish, Russian, Japanese, Chinese and Italian. Lots of exchange trips – to Paris, Vienna, Madrid. New state of the art language labs, with computers and software in every language. Pupils are setted for all subjects from day one. Three separate sciences at GCSE for top five out of seven sets – others take double award. Class sizes max 24 or less. Stunning 'science schools' about to be opened by Earl of Wessex when we visited – Victorian building imaginatively refurbished to provide lecture theatre, seminar rooms and labs. Learning development department (with five-strong staff) offers support to those who need it, on regular or more informal basis. Caters for pupils with mild to moderate learning difficulties. EFL programme in situ. Enrichment programme for academic scholars (110 currently). All pupils have their own laptops – supplied by school and charged to parents. Virtually all classrooms have interactive whiteboards.

Games, options, the arts: Huge investment in sports facilities in recent years. Boasts the only listed gym in the world. And, of course, the famous Close, where William Webb Ellis first ran with the ball in 1823 (the first XV very proud to play on it, along with leading players and teams who visit from all over the world). Immaculately-maintained playing fields – with 12 rugby pitches and five cricket squares. Locals use school's Astroturfs, tennis courts, 25-metre indoor pool etc. New sports centre, with squash courts, polo pitches and fitness centre. Boys play rugby, hockey, soccer, cricket, tennis and athletics while girls get hockey, netball, tennis, rounders and athletics. Lots of other sports on offer too – from golf to polo.

Art flourishing and photography too. When we visited, pupils were busy building pushcarts in school's design centre – ready for a hotly-contested pushcart race round the Close that weekend. Lewis Gallery a light, airy space cleverly converted from old squash courts, with programme of exhibitions by pupils and outside artists. Drama very popular – all singing and dancing Macready Theatre. Pupils stage major school play and a musical every year, along with a house drama season and

R

Arts Festival too. Recent school productions include Stoppard's Arcadia and Pirates of Penzance.

Fabulous media studio with all the gear for pupils to practise making videos, CDs etc. Music is magical: masses of orchestras, choirs, ensembles, rock bands – everything you would expect from a school of this size and importance. Keen voluntary CCF, D of E, Young Enterprise and lots of community service and other charity input.

Background and atmosphere: Founded as a grammar school in 1567 by Lawrence Sheriff, purveyor of spices to Elizabeth I, it moved to its present site 200 years later. Home of the famous Dr Arnold of Tom Brown's Schooldays. School situated on imposing site in centre of Rugby. Feels rather like north Oxford, with school houses scattered all over the place. Glorious Victorian library, the Temple Reading Room, has had facelift and provides quiet, inspiring place to work. Total of 37,000 resources – books, DVDs, periodicals etc. New modern languages building with individual conversation rooms and impeccable eco-credentials eg solar shades that move with the sun, windows controlled by CO_2 sensors.

Pupils attend chapel at 8.25am three mornings a week and on Sundays. Chapel – Thomas Arnold is buried beneath chancel steps – is breathtaking. Walls boast tablets in memory of famous Rugbeian writers like Lewis Carroll and Rupert Brooke. Whole school sings heart out – upper chapel choir runners-up in Songs of Praise School Choirs of the Year competition several years running.

Weekend leave-outs every three weeks or so. But school buzzes at weekends – buzzes all the time, really. More than 30 societies – law, medical, philosophy, debating, science forum – and everyone seems to be involved in masses of things. In one of the girls' houses helpful sixth formers had posted useful tips for new pupils on unmissable events. School went fully co-ed in 1993. Boy/girl ratio is now 55/45, with eight houses for boys and seven for girls. All eat in their own houses – despite cost head 'wouldn't dream of changing it': it encourages 'real family community,' one parent told us. 'Social' eating in each other's houses by invitation. Girls' houses very civilised – rooms vary from singles for sixth formers to dorms of four to six for younger pupils. Housemasters and housemistresses all live in (many with their own families) and see pupils as they come and go during the day. Youngest have to be back in houses by 9.30pm (lights out half an hour later), while sixth formers return by 10.15pm (don't have to be in their rooms till 11pm, though.) Boys' houses less ritzy in past but huge amount of dosh put into upgrading them. Two day houses.

All wear smart uniform for lessons. Girls sport distinctive ankle-length grey skirts, now redesigned so they can run in them, say they really like them – you can wear woolly tights and leggings underneath to keep warm in winter, they told us. Prefects – or levée in Rugby-speak – get to wear different ties and gold buttons on dark blazers: four buttons for heads of school (boy and girl), three for head of house and two for school prefects.

Pastoral care and discipline: Forget the fagging of Tom Brown's Schooldays – has put enormous amount of time and effort into its pastoral care. PHSE programme tackles issues like bullying, relationships, even safe driving. Each pupil is given a copy of the school's Guidelines for Life, which details everything from bedtimes to fast-food carry-outs. The standards expected are made very clear. If you are caught dealing or with drugs in your possession you are out. If name comes up in an investigation, then random drugs testing for duration of time at school. No smoking at any time – counselling for smokers. Boozing in school hours has a variety of sanctions – four sins and pupils are out. At Saturday evening Crescent Club, sixth formers are allowed maximum of two drinks (wine or beer) with food.

Public displays of affection (PDA) between pupils banned – anything that might cause embarrassment to others, says school. New pupils mentored by older pupils and the levée are assigned to look after each year group.

Pupils and parents: Pupils come from all over, from Orkney down to Cornwall. Lots from London, Oxford or locations within two hours' driving distance. Around 10 per cent from overseas – France, Germany, Russia, US, Hong Kong, mainland China, Taiwan etc. Some expats too. Wide social range but pupils say school isn't 'snobby'. Many are sons and daughters of ORs – nearly 16 per cent at last count. Parents very supportive of school and say a real sense of community – 'I just don't know of anywhere else I'd want to send my child,' said one. Illustrious former pupils include Rupert Brooke (who has girls' house named after him), Lewis Carroll, Robert Hardy, Tom King, Salman Rushdie, Anthony Horowitz – and of course Harry Flashman and Tom Brown.

Entrance: Oversubscribed. Admission at 11 is open only to day pupils from local state schools or independent schools finishing at 11. All join Marshall House, a small day house for year 7s and 8s. Entrance exam consists of computerised test, interview and report from current school. Pupils starting at 13 are interviewed four to five terms before entrance. CE pass mark 55 per cent. Boys and girls come from more than 300 feeder schools across the country, including The Dragon, Bilton Grange, Packwood Haugh and St Anselm's.

Around 40 new pupils (mostly girls, but some boys) join in the sixth form. UK candidates need six Bs (existing Rugbeians pupils need the same). They sit two academic tests in subjects of their choice and have a house interview too. Potential scholars are invited back at a later date for scholarship interviews. Keen competition for sixth form places – three applicants for every place.

Exit: Nearly all stay on to the sixth form. Thirteen to Oxbridge in 2013; Edinburgh, UCL, Manchester, Bristol, Newcastle and Durham popular too. Good spread of subjects.

Money matters: Huge numbers of scholarships (academic, music, art, design and sport) and bursaries on offer. No limit on number of scholarships. 'We make awards to all those who show the requisite skills and potential,' explains school. Led the way by limiting scholarships to 10 per cent of the school fees – although this can be augmented to 100 per cent if family need can be shown through a means test. 'It was the obvious and right thing to do,' says head.

Remarks: Famous public school that continues to go from strength to strength. Prides itself on treating everyone as an individual, with boys and girls encouraged to develop their talents and initiative and make the most of their time at the school. One of the most popular co-ed boarding schools in the country, and deservedly so. Just as we said last time round, it is friendly, hard-working and fun. Genuinely innovative too – both on the academic front and with the launch of the Arnold Foundation.

R

Ryde School with Upper Chine

Linked school: Ryde School with Upper Chine, Junior School

Queen's Road, Ryde, Isle pf Wight, PO33 3BE

- Pupils: 515 boys and girls, 60 board (mostly weekly), rest day
- Ages: 11–18 • C of E • Fees: Day £10,875; Boarding £21,000–£22,440 pa • Independent

Tel: 01983 562229
Email: admissions@rydeschool.org.uk
Website: www.rydeschool.org.uk

Headmaster: Since 2013, Mr Mark Waldron MA. A historian with a first from Cambridge, he was previously head of The English College in Prague. He has also been a deputy head of Sherborne School and worked at The Leys School and Radley College. Has been a principal examiner in US history and enjoys drama, debating and sports coaching.

Academic matters: A non-selective school – 'Our profile is about half-way between a typical state comprehensive and a selective independent'. Some very high-flyers – 'It is as good as any mainland public school at the top end,' said a parent of one – and about 15 per cent receiving learning support (mainly dyslexics but a couple of children with Asperger's), plus the whole spectrum of ability. In 2013, 44 per cent A*/A grades at GCSE. Twenty-four A level subjects, including government and politics, psychology and theatre studies. 'The school is very flexible about A level choices,' said a parent. 'If you let them know your options in time, they will do their best to accommodate them.' Seventy-four per cent of A level grades A*/B and 44 per cent A*/A in 2013. School also offers IB.

Class size is around 15 or 16, divided into four streams for most subjects. Two ICT rooms, plus a trolley with 20 laptops; all classrooms have powerpoint and most interactive whiteboards. In 1997, Ryde took over Bembridge School, which specialised in learning support. As a result that department is particularly strong, housed in its own unit with pictures of famous dyslexics (eg Einstein) on the wall alongside photos of its own pupils and their achievements. But the head emphasises that, while he wants the school to cater for any Island children with special needs – though not behavioural problems – who want an independent school education, he does not intend to expand the department. 'We have a good balance of children and I do not want to upset that.' High calibre, committed staff. 'Hard work is rewarded and respected,' said a parent. 'The children are motivated and set their sights high.'

Games, options, the arts: Excellent music, with four choirs, an orchestra and a jazz combo (and good exam results, with virtually all candidates getting A and B grades at GCSE). 'The standard is higher than I would have thought possible,' said a parent. Music tours abroad every year to, eg, Barcelona and Verona. The annual school musical, performed in Ryde Theatre to an audience of paying public as well as parents, 'is reckoned to be the best amateur dramatics on the island,' says the head; parents agree. Recently they performed the musicals, Thoroughly Modern Millie and Cabaret, while plays have included With a Pinch of Salt, Our Country's Good and a modern adaption of Romeo and Juliet. Has taken part in Global Rock – understandably, a pupil-led undertaking – and did extremely well, with African Sanctus a big hit. The art department produces excellent work in limited space and regularly exhibits at public galleries on the island. DT also popular and imaginative, with pupils working in any medium from stained glass to concrete.

A variety of sports played on the school's 17 acres of playing fields with a rifle range, tennis courts and a sports hall on site, plus an Astroturf hockey pitch a mile away. Teams play Island state schools and mainland independent schools; the girls' hockey and netball teams are particularly successful. Swimming at the public pool down the road – 'It's far cheaper and easier to use someone else's pool'.

Four houses, mostly for sporting and other competitions – 'The younger ones are very competitive over the citizenship cup'. CCF is available in year 10 for one afternoon a week, with air force or navy options. 'My children loved it for the sailing,' said a parent. 'They didn't take the parading terribly seriously, but there were lots of opportunities to go on exciting camps for amazingly low prices.' Reports of these camps fill several pages of the school magazine. One pupil at 15 became the youngest person to sail across the Atlantic (and has now made it round the world) – 'His parents asked if it would disrupt his GCSEs. I said of course it will, but it will look very good on his CV'. D of E popular.

Background and atmosphere: Founded in 1921 and moved to its present site in 1928; in 1995 it merged with Upper Chine girls' boarding school and, in 1997, took over Bembridge School, which had a large number of overseas pupils. The Bembridge site, some six miles away, houses Ryde School's boarding department in a companionable house atmosphere, and a combination of school transport and the occasional taxi ferry the boarders backwards and forwards. The boarding house is highly distinctive and spacious and the site still has all the old Bembridge facilities (100 acres of playing fields and woodland) and is right on the cliff edge, which is tremendous for the boarders. Friendly houseparents oversee – the only slight fly in the ointment is the sharing of the very large site with a holiday club company.

Now more or less the only independent school on the island. Atmosphere is ordered but relaxed, with a considerable stated emphasis on pupil initiative and on their growing up in an environment which lacks, because of its island situation, some of the pressures of teenage life on the mainland. Head stresses this factor and relishes the lack of sophisticated worldliness of many of his pupils. Pleasant situation at the top end of Ryde, a 10 minute walk from the esplanade, where hovercrafts and Seacats dock; several families commute from Portsmouth every day. Buildings range from the Georgian admin and sixth form block to the light, galleried library block, and the new Bembridge building with IT, art and DT rooms and a dining hall. Modern language and English blocks newly refurbished; the head has hopes for a cantilevered gallery addition to the 200-seater theatre.

The junior school has been expanded and is housed in pleasant half new/half old buildings, with a sympathetic and child-centred headmaster. Much evidence of purposeful and creative activity in a structured environment which does not weigh heavily on the pupils' shoulders. Parents were unstinting in their praise. Most go on to the senior school at 11+. Five Ways, where the nursery to year 2 pupils are taught, is a delightful place with new buildings, excellent facilities and a great head.

Pastoral care and discipline: 'I was impressed that the head wanted to show us round at breaktime,' said a parent. 'That's when a lot of heads want to keep you clear. But the children were very courteous.' Discipline firm but low key – 'We don't have institutionalised bullying – we do have personality differences. We use a no-blame policy and we tend to be successful by sorting it out without making it a huge deal. Calling in the parents is usually enough'. Very few pupils have been expelled in recent years, but head reserves the right to do so over serious issues such as drugs or theft. 'PHSE is superbly taught,' said a parent. 'It addresses real issues.'

Pupils and parents: About half of the boarders are from Portsmouth naval families; a few full boarders from overseas. The day pupils, from a wide cross-section of families, come from all round the Island, with one or two from the mainland. The school runs buses from different points of the Island. Some parents agonise over the lack of choice of independent schools, which means that Ryde School's fortunes are linked to those of the local state schools rather than other independents. But all we spoke to were impressed by its standards. They liked the staff and found them approachable (reports every half term), innovative and interesting, on the whole, although a few worries about the possibility of difficulties in recruiting staff to the island backwater. These were rejected by the school, which maintains that the pleasant environment and the affordability of housing ensures that it holds its own in competition for good teachers.

Entrance: Non-selective but all are interviewed by the head, do some maths and English and an IQ test – 'We want to ensure that they're of a standard to fit into the school. The tests are to look for discrepancies between their IQ and their maths and English standards'. Five Bs 'represents a sensible starting point for A level', but occasionally those on lower grades will start AS courses if parents and the school think that they can succeed. Three or four a year turned away, mostly for misbehaviour. Most go through to the sixth form. The school has open days, but prospective parents can make an appointment to look round at any time.

Exit: About 90 per cent to university, mostly redbrick. Around half to humanities/social science courses, 20 per cent scientists and engineers, a few medics, dentists and vets or artists. Trickle to Oxbridge.

Money matters: Some means-tested assisted places, plus a few external scholarships worth 10 per cent of fees, which can be added to an assisted place. The senior school's main intakes are into years 5, 7, 9 and 12, and its awards are available at all these times.

Remarks: A mixed, non-selective, school that aims to cater for any island child that wants an independent education, plus a few mainland boarders and a few foreigners. Academic strengths and a strong commitment to all round education both in the classroom and outside it. Character and initiative come strongly to the fore as priorities for the development of pupils. 'My daughter has been very well taught and has developed a real love for nearly all of her subjects,' said a satisfied parent. Numbers on the up.

Rye St Antony School

Linked school: Rye St Antony Junior School

Pullen's Lane, Oxford, OX3 0BY

• Pupils: 360 girls; 80 boarders. A few places for boys aged 3–8 • Ages: 3–18 • Roman Catholic • Fees: Day £8,655–£13,170; Boarding £17,310–£21,420 pa • Independent

Tel: 01865 762802
Email: info@ryestantony.co.uk
Website: www.ryestantony.co.uk

Headmistress: Since 1990, Miss Alison Jones BA. Miss Jones studied English literature at York University and did her PGCE at Oxford. She spent 14 years at St Mary's School, Cambridge as an English teacher, head of English and head of sixth form.

Only the fourth headmistress since Rye's foundation in 1930, she is poised, calm and immaculate, self-possessed but not aloof and utterly dedicated to her school. 'My heart is here', she says. Apparently she was 'born wanting to be a headmistress' and never considered any other path. Miss Jones knows all the pupils and their families by name and, although she no longer teaches regular lessons, she works with girls at lunchtime and visits classes. She is herself taking lessons in how to use her Blackberry – from a first year. She lives on site, as did her predecessors, and shares their belief that her work is 'faith in action'. Does she get lonely in the school holidays? Not at all. Her four nephews love coming to stay and old girls are in the habit of dropping in unannounced; they are always made welcome. She loves the poetry of Eliot and Hopkins, both wrestlers with faith, and her desert island novel is Middlemarch. Indeed, perhaps Miss Jones shares some of Dorothea Brooke's more admirable qualities – a sense of higher purpose, the desire to serve.

Academic matters: Rye is not a league table school, nor does it seek to be. In a city like Oxford you have to be pretty steadfast not to be sucked into the slipstream of academic competition, to steer a different course. Miss Jones is indeed steadfast; she is concerned about the pressure to win that comes from society and girls themselves, 'They can become like racehorses,' she warns. Rye is an inclusive school with a 'wide focus'; the school's aim is for every girl to achieve her full potential. The school's public exam results endorse the soundness of the Rye approach; in 2013 36 per cent A*/A grades at GCSE; 89 per cent of girls got 5+ A*-C grades including maths and English. At A level, 70 per cent A*/B grades and nearly 48 per cent A*/A. Rye may be a small school but this in no way limits the subject choices available at GCSE and A level. The school can support individuals who wish to take GCSEs in subjects such as classical Greek, Chinese and Russian and also offers the additional maths and science. Girls may choose from 22 subjects at AS/A level including theatre studies, textiles, Latin, Japanese and Spanish.

The average class size is 16 and the pupil to teacher ratio is 1.5, so no chance for a pupil who may be struggling to slip under the radar. EAL specialist teachers support up to 25 pupils and learning support tuition is available to any pupil, whether for help in a specific area or with wider study skills needs. The curriculum is extended with, for example, a science fair when girls present research projects. In 2011 Rye fielded the only all girls' team in the Annual International Space Settlement Design Competition and won through to the finals of this prestigious and demanding event held at Imperial College.

Games, options, the arts: The director of studies referred tellingly to the 'arms race' to provide bigger and better facilities in independent schools. This is a race Rye doesn't need to enter, partly because its residential location limits expansion and further building but also because Rye pupils are already well catered for.

Staff and pupils run a large programme of more than 30 lunch time and after-school clubs from photography to juggling, pottery, dance and debating. Service and charitable activities are enthusiastically undertaken and girls volunteer and fund-raise for local and international causes, including on-going support for street children in Calcutta.

The library is large and very well stocked; displays change frequently as the librarian guides and challenges readers to try books from outside their comfort zones. The librarian also organises creative writing workshops led by authors, literary quizzes and book groups. Sixth formers have a separate study area and loans are made using a fingerprint system. The art facilities are generous and AS/A level artists have spaces to leave work out; the displays of pupils' work all over the school were inspiring – wonderful textiles, paintings, still life drawings and collages with all year groups and abilities represented. According to the head, 'all girls participate in the musical life of the school'; this must be so with five choirs, an orchestra, two jazz bands, chamber groups and various instrumental and voice ensembles. Choral groups compete in local and national competitions and recent choir tours have performed in Paris, Spain and Italy. Plenty of practice rooms and a full range of instrumental tuition including the harp. The acquisition of a set of Jamaican steel pans and an Indonesian gamelan reflect the head of department's enthusiasm for world music.

Beyond the tennis courts a curving path winds through trees to the sports centre – its wooded exterior blends perfectly with the surroundings. Inside is a very large multi-purpose space with a well-equipped gym on the first floor. On the day we visited it was hosting an inter-form debating competition; subjects under discussion included 'This house believes that Barbie is a positive role-model for young girls' and 'This house believes that vampires are cooler than werewolves'. The motions were extremely well argued and backed up with creditable research including the possible medical origins of vampires and werewolves and references to their first cinematic appearances. The audience listened intently and asked challenging questions, but we left before the vote so cannot reveal which mythical creatures won.

Sports teams participate in fixtures against much larger schools with success across the board, notably in netball, tennis, hockey and cross-country. Sports options and clubs include all the usual ones plus volleyball, football, rowing, sailing, boxercise and a rock climbing course at Oxford Brookes for sixth formers. An outdoor heated swimming pool for summer term use.

Background and atmosphere: More than one parent described Rye as 'a hidden gem' and never is this truer than on one's first visit. The entrance is via electric gates in a quiet residential cul-de-sac just off Headington Road in central Oxford; a small car park and cluster of modernish additions give a less than imposing first impression, but don't rush to judgement. The extremely helpful staff in the school office must have one of the best views in town, pace nearby dreaming spires – beautifully tended gardens, rolling lawns, huge ancient trees and, instead of traffic, birdsong. Pretty much everything is on a charming domestic scale, but we are talking wealthy late-Victorian domestic. New buildings such as the sports hall, sixth form centre and library have been skilfully designed to provide ample modern space without jarring or dominating the original architecture. Can't be many city schools where children can run off at break time and play in a 'jungle' of trees rather than concrete.

It's hard to describe the very special atmosphere at Rye without making it seem like an anachronism (it's not at all), but something of the pioneering spirit of its founders, Elizabeth Rendall and Ivy King, lives on. On the wall in Miss Jones' bay-fronted study is the most wonderfully evocative black and white photo of Miss Rendall, the school's first headmistress, sitting thoughtfully at her desk, cigarette in hand. Miss Rendall and Miss King started the school in a house on the Woodstock Road in 1930; rising pupil numbers prompted a move to the current site, a house formerly owned by Arthur Balfour, curator of the Pitt Rivers, in 1939. (The beautiful Japanese screen in the dining room was bought for £5 with the house.) King's mother and sister, Gwen, moved into the new school and adults and children saw out the war here – growing vegetables and fruit in the gardens and taking fire warden duties at night. Girls learnt to scull on the Cherwell and swimming lessons were at Dame's Delight (ladies' counterpart to Parson's Pleasure). On Miss Rendall's retirement, Miss King became headmistress. Her successor was Miss Sumpter, from whom Miss Jones took over in 1990. What inspiring role models are these redoubtable women, who were as capable of fixing the electrics as teaching Latin; who did the maintenance and the gardening as well as persuading parents to allow their daughters go to university. No wonder the school has such a devoted band of 'Old Ryes'.

Pastoral care and discipline: Rye is a lay Catholic school. What this means in practice is that while Catholicism is integral to its ethos, the school is inclusive and outward looking, welcoming girls of all faiths and none. Where other schools have rules, Rye requires its pupils to understand and observe principles – these are intended to develop habits of tolerance, consideration and service that characterise the school community and will benefit the wider world.

Each new pupil is allocated a housemother (a year 6 pupil in the junior school; a sixth former in the senior school); her role is to help with adapting to school life, someone to turn to for all those questions or worries that a new girl might not feel able to ask an adult. Responsibility for organising this system lies with the Patricians, senior prefects who also help staff and governors and are involved in management and policy making. Girls are expected to participate at all levels of school governance, not just the school council, and are represented on all committees. They are appointed to roles such as prep, ICT and library supervisors, minute secretaries, food committee and care of the environment. This is not tokenism, nor is it a crafty way of getting jobs done (although this must be a side-benefit!). Miss Jones calls it 'learning to lead'; positions have proper job descriptions and are intended to develop workplace skills such as negotiation, organisation, problem solving, planning, public speaking and communication.

No more than 65 girls boarding at any one time and the school is flexible, able to offer accommodation for a single night or short-term response to a family crisis. An Australian gappie showed us round The Croft, a large late Victorian house where younger boarders (years 5-10) live, its former grandeur somewhat compromised by the necessity of fire doors and generations of feet and bags. Notice boards and walls rather bare, but then our visit was near the end of term; shared bedrooms full of photos and stuff from home. Older girls have lovely rooms in the eaves, endless stairs more than made up for by character and privacy. Saturdays are for organised activities with trips to London, street dance workshops, ice-skating in Oxford and the like. Also organised socials with Magdalen and Abingdon boys' schools. Year 10 girls can go into Oxford in groups on Sunday afternoons. Years 11-13 live in The Cottage, a low-rise building arranged around a peaceful courtyard garden. Each boarder has her own small study bedroom, good preparation for university. The sixth form centre is here also, beautifully designed in wood and glass with a cafe (hot food and salad bar) and socialising area on the ground floor and IT, study and teaching rooms above. We chatted with a group of girls who thought that the school has the balance between freedom and supervision just right in the sixth form – 'Staff have lots of time for you, but they also chase up work if it's late'. They loved the fact that they knew practically everyone in the school by name and they felt that their opinions counted – ' If you aren't happy, they listen to you and try to change things'.

Takes a whole-school preventative approach to bullying – tolerance and respect for others are central to the school's principles and these values are integrated into the curriculum. Housemistresses, form tutors, the school nurses and chaplain are the foundation of pastoral care and pupils may be referred to external counsellors if necessary. Senior pupils are trained as peer counsellors and anti-cyber bullying mentors. Distinctive red uniform until year 11, thereafter own clothes.

Pupils and parents: Cosmopolitan mix of local and international pupils. Only around a third of the school population is Catholic, others are attracted by Rye's principles and inclusivity. Parents include medics from the nearby John Radcliffe hospital, resident and visiting academics. Longstanding links with families in France, Spain, Italy and Germany bring visiting pupils for the last half of the summer term.

R

Entrance: Prior to examination, 11+ entrants spend an 'ordinary' year 6 day at the school and meet the headmistress. The school sets its own examination papers in English and maths. Boarding applicants combine the day visit with an overnight stay. Girls wishing to enter the sixth form are interviewed and must have a minimum of five GCSE passes with grade B or above in subjects to be studied.

Exit: A quarter left after GCSEs in 2013. One sixth former told us that she had left, only to return a short time later, having found that the grass wasn't greener. With such a small cohort of leavers each year no significant subject bias or trend in university destinations, although Bath, Birmingham, Bristol, Leeds and London all popular. Fifteen per cent to Oxbridge in 2013.

Money matters: Up to five scholarships at 11+, 13+ and 16+ and some means-tested bursaries. Girls can apply for a King Award while at the school, a sum of money (usually between £100 and £300) that enables them to further an interest or learn a skill, for instance music lessons, scuba diving, riding, dancing, or fees for a short course.

Remarks: Miss Rendall and Miss King founded Rye as a school where 'academic potential' would not be the sole deciding factor for entry. They believed that both sides of the personality should be allowed to 'grow together'. Eighty years later this principle still holds true. While Richard Dawkins might not approve, Rye's inclusive and humane approach to education has an appeal that is catholic as well as Catholic.

Ryedale School

Gale Lane, Nawton, North Yorkshire, YO62 7SL

• Pupils: 590 pupils; 295 boys/295 girls • Ages: 11–16 • No religious affiliation • State

Tel: 01439 771665
Email: admin@ryedale.n-yorks.sch.uk
Website: www.ryedaleschool.org

Acting headteacher: Since 2013, Mark McCandless, until a permanent head is appointed for September 2014.

Academic matters: High in ranking of North Yorkshire state schools – 65 per cent 5+ A*-C including English (before re-marks) and maths at GCSE in 2013; 29 per cent A*/A grades. Specialisms in performing arts and science with maths, leading edge status. Mainly academic subjects at key stage 4 – options include Latin (will run it for three students), particularly successful separate sciences, German (big numbers), art and design, dance, drama, music, PE. Good range of vocational BTECs.

Established partnerships with other local schools for sixth form – now developing own with Malton School: offers history, English lit, theatre studies, music, music technology. Starting with 35 students, who attend two days a week – likely to grow; purpose-built common-room attractively decorated and furnished.

Thorough-going tracking and monitoring, stable staff who know pupils very well and set high expectations; developing use of ICT in teaching and learning, eg VLE. Average class size 21 but we saw quite a few smaller ones; high quality, attractive displays in all classrooms. Setting for academic subjects from start of year 7 (flexible approach, smaller groups for lower ability), mixed ability for practical subjects. Very good and improving key stage 3 attainment; year 8s do dance, drama, music, art and food tech (boys too – modern man in the making); ICT GCSE in year 9. We saw lots of well-behaved, focused pupils and lively,

pacy teaching; intelligent arguing and independent learning encouraged – pupils feel their views are sought and listened to with respect. Gifted and talented students identified and monitored; senior management team mentor low achieving year 11s, teaching assistants do lower school.

Excellent, warm, very thoughtful SENCo greatly valued by parents ('amazingly wonderful'). Covers broad spectrum of needs – strong on dyslexia awareness and support. Works with external agencies, trains other teachers, who can access subject specialist advice through school's Moodle online learning management system – other schools please emulate. Year 7s with low literacy and numeracy levels supported individually and with paired reading – year 10 and 11 'buddies' do some and mentor them in other ways. Well resourced – 11 teaching assistants and 'The Cottage', base for more intensive support, providing a refuge for children who find the breaks difficult.

Games, options, the arts: Great range of sports – all the usual ones plus ultimate frisbee and indoor rowing – and sports leadership qual. Smallish sports hall also used for assemblies, good-size fitness suite, netball/tennis courts, several playing fields (Astro on pupils' wish list) and year 11s use Ampleforth College facilities for two hours a week. Impressive success for its size at district, county and national level in various games – some international sportspeople.

Well-resourced performing arts building with drama/dance studio – high standard performances involving large numbers of pupils, eg Guys and Dolls, Dracula, Shakespeare Schools Festival Playhouse; links with Helmsley Arts Centre. High percentage A*/A in drama and music GCSE.

Huge music room with lots of computers, recording studio – various singing and instrumental groups (a quarter of school learn an instrument – very good exam results, singing too), girls' chamber choir, jazz band, rock groups, a few pupils in National Youth Choir/ Orchestra, one in Rotary Young Musician of the Year North of England final, music tour to Paris, visiting choirs from Uganda and New Zealand.

Splendid art room and excellent art much in evidence throughout the school, brightening up what would otherwise be rather drab corridors. Well-equipped DT and (bright green) food tech rooms – has produced a Rotary Club young chef of the year.

Over 80 clubs per week – arts award, chess, Latin, Italian, D of E popular; end of summer term enrichment activities, eg history trip to Berlin, outdoor activities in France; ongoing trip to Camp Kenya. The less academic may do a day a week work experience, rest of key stage 4 have career days.

Background and atmosphere: Built in 1953 in rural location half an hour away from Malton in North Yorkshire – soothing views of fields and trees. Used to have own railway stop till Beecham got busy with his axe – hence all the clubs, as all stay on site during the lunch hour (so no town-school-type mischief). Pleasant, unfussy architecture – yellow brickwork with blue and white paintwork and sloping roofs, much less bleak than some of the '60s concrete we have seen. Very well stocked and laid out library – lots of enticing fiction, modern and classics, good selection of books on art and music, plus factual books geared towards the interests of reluctant boy readers. Light cafeteria with bright orange chairs – fish fingers and chips as well as virtuous choices (has healthy school status), a lively buzz that never felt unruly.

A mixture of the traditional – school motto is the rather Edwardian sounding 'aspire and achieve', prefects, ties groaning with badges for positions and achievements – and what head calls 'cutting edge', eg use of latest technology (science refurbishment planned) and teaching and learning research. House system central – lots of competitions organised by students.

General consensus that school is very friendly, pupils and teachers, with a strong community spirit, closely related to its small size. Active school council that feels its views are regarded

– head boy and girl plus deputies attend some governing body meetings regularly.

Pastoral care and discipline: Parents – really – say no real discipline probs ('They all know where the boundaries are and are very polite,' according to my taxi driver, who turned out to be a very enthusiastic parent-governor – I don't think he was a plant) and no bullying – 'very tight at the first whiff of it,' said another parent. Praise from Ofsted for 'excellent attitudes and relationships' – we found it so quiet in the corridors during our tour we began to wonder if there were any pupils present.

Great care taken with transition starting from end of year 5, when children and parents can attend an open evening at the school. In year 6 teachers give presentations at feeder schools, assisted by year 7s, and children have a taster day during which they are allocated to their houses so they can start to pal up. Older pupils take care of younger ones, a long-standing tradition (as some may come solo from their primary school).

We were told of exceptional efforts made for SEN children by very grateful parents – a day at school just for them and their parents before starting; reorganising the rooming for a pupil with cerebral palsy, to the extent of moving the library to the ground floor ('He was enabled to be equal with all the others'); a child shown around several times before the year began, to alleviate his anxieties about finding his way about, and action plans for any possible future problems created with his parents ('We were blown away by all the care our son was given'); an autistic pupil subject to daily epileptic seizures who has managed to make 'amazing progress' socially and academically – 'They formed a friendship club for her so she would never be on her own during the breaks'.

Pupils and parents: Mainly from Helmsley and Kirkbymoorside, also from village primary schools in a large area of the North Yorks Moors National Park and surrounding countryside. Up to 20 per cent from outside catchment area, such is its reputation. Mainly white middle class – very few ethnic minority, EAL or FSM. The pupils we met were a delight – intelligent, articulate, thoughtful, clearly enjoying their school experience and making the most of their opportunities. We were very impressed on arrival by a conscientious young citizen who diverted from his business to inform my taxi driver in an extremely polite way that his rear number plate was obscured by mud. Notable old pupils: England cricketer Daniel Broadbent and the band, One Night Only.

Active PTA; parents full of praise for school, particularly for SEN, pastoral care, speedy resolution of problems, ease of communication, discipline and mentoring – main wish is for a full range of A levels on site as they feel Ryedale is so much better than the other state schools in the area; only niggle re need for more lockers.

Entrance: Standard admissions process through county authority.

Exit: Most to further education, eg sixth forms at Ryedale, Malton and Lady Lumley Schools plus Norton College; a few straight into employment.

Remarks: A little gem in an appealing rural setting – it was a pleasure to see and talk to happy pupils engrossed in learning and hear the appreciative comments made by parents: 'They go well beyond the call of duty'; 'a fantastic school'. House prices in the area reflect its standing – some parents choose it in preference to a private school.

Sacred Heart Catholic High School

Fenham Hall Drive, Fenham, Newcastle upon Tyne, NE4 9YH

• Pupils: 1,410 girls • Ages: 11 to 19 • Roman Catholic • State

Tel: 01912 747373
Email: enquiries@shhs.org.uk
Website: www.sacredheart-high.org

Headteacher: Since September 2013, Anita Bath, who was previously deputy head St Thomas More Catholic School in Blaydon.

Academic matters: For results at GCSE and value added, best state school in Newcastle and one of the best at A level for last six years. Newcastle's centre of excellence for music and the city's 'music hub'. At GCSE 75 per cent of pupils got 5+ A*-C grades including English and maths in 2013. At A level, 27 per cent A*/A grades. All from non-selective intake. Science strong at key stage 3, GCSE and A level. Single sex 'avoids stereotypes coming to the fore. So here science and mathematics are more popular than they are in mixed schools because traditionally boys dominate in those subjects,' says head. Eight form entry at year 7, children tested and placed in ability groups in four tiers, two classes in each. Class size up to 32 (average 26) except tier 4 when number drops to 20. Average of 20 at KS4 and 16 in sixth form.

Broad curriculum, including one modern foreign language (possibility of second from year 8) taught at KS3 with flexibility to meet individual girl's needs. English, mathematics, science, technology and religious education are core – science stays right up to 16 'to give the girls a balanced diet'. 'We tailor the curriculum to the gifts of each child. Option blocks follow the child rather than the other way round,' says head.

All-encompassing bespoke progress monitoring and review system for each child, also foundation of teacher performance management, developed in school. DfE suitably impressed, considering rolling it out nationally. Baseline assessment on entry in year 7 predicts GCSE grades and reviews each half term academic targets, behaviour and attendance. As the assistant head data controller put it, 'We build a culture of accountability – there's nowhere to hide!' Individual tailored support provided where needed – highly valued by parents we spoke to. Secure parent platform allows parents online reporting and encourages email contact with teachers. In fact web-based virtual teaching environment provides staff, parents, students, partner schools and organisations with a phalanx of school information – statistics, curriculum, performance, preparation material, email, library system, management information etc.

Desire to see girls achieve excellence in subjects they take rather than push for huge lists of GCSE attempts – 'We give them the time to excel in what they are studying'. Pupils appreciate teachers giving up time to provide extra help: 'They put in a lot of extra effort at lunchtimes and it is great that it is there if you want or need it'.

BTEC, City and Guilds and applied A levels on offer in sixth form. Head wants to extend these to provide much greater range: 'We pride ourselves on excellence across the curriculum because students have a right to expect that'. Art and design, dance, drama and ICT available to A2 as might be expected considering school specialisms. Collaboration with Catholic boys' school St Cuthbert's for study there where timetabled subjects clash.

Great store placed on developing and acknowledging staff achievement too: 'I want fresh and energetic teachers'. Sharing of skills/ideas is key. Teachers have visits home and abroad to learn and develop new ideas. School's success is recognised by the National College of School Leadership, which has licensed it to deliver leadership development, one of only 26 providers across the UK.

Games, options, the arts: Full range of sports available from the usual – football, hockey, netball, badminton, trampolining etc – to the unusual – judo, tag rugby and rowing. Something for everyone and willing to add to the list if sufficient support and interest.

Specialist technology and performing arts status – great opportunities for the musically interested and gifted, from rock to string bands and more. Music fund purchases instruments for use by those unable to afford to purchase their own. Drama encouraged (core curriculum in KS3) with lots of performance opportunities and joint productions with St Cuthbert's, most recently Kiss Me Kate. New dance studio opened December 2012 – lots of links to Newcastle community dance groups.

Extensive art facilities in spacious, light and airy facilities offering all disciplines from ceramics to sculpture. Separate art room for sixth form. GCSE and A level textile students have the opportunity to strut their stuff in annual fashion show.

Exhaustive extra-curricular programme – every faculty has something to offer from mathematics' cipher club to physical education's zumba. Educational visits include theatre, lectures, concerts, museums and holidays/exchanges to France, Germany, ski trips, exchange trips to other Sacred Heart schools. D of E, enterprise days and sports leadership awards.

Girls encouraged to pursue charitable work – each tutor group raises funds for their chosen project. On-going support for visiting, renovating and providing scholarships to Ugandan school – advertising for fund-raiser Teachers' Got Talent when we visited.

Background and atmosphere: Sisters of the Society of the Sacred Heart founded a small, private secondary school in Fenham Hall for girls in 1905. From 1920 scholarships were provided, and by 1945 virtually all girls were scholarship students educated at either the grammar or secondary school on the Fenham campus. Became comprehensive in 1977 and granted academy status in 2011. The head sees this as an opportunity as 'Being an academy provides our governors with the freedom and independence which we believe best suits the interests of our school'.

Prior to 2005 on two sites, but £10m spent on the school in past few years: £1.3m on sixth form study centre; £8.7m on new build and re-modelling to bring everyone on to one site. New building is in keeping with old. Plans to create vocational studies centre to extend current provision, and enlarge sixth form. Parents told us that 'the school keeps moving forward, offering new opportunities for our children and doing that little bit extra'.

Great pride in being 'a Sacred Heart girl': one sixth former told us, 'At the open day mass you meet people who had been to the school in the past and get the feeling you are part of something special. There is a real sense of community'. Catholic faith and Sacred Heart ethos are important – prayer and worship integral part of school life and each day begins with morning prayer. Group of Sisters live nearby, one is a governor. Religion not forced upon pupils: 'It is a personal thing and everyone takes from it what they want'. There is a residential retreat at the Youth Village in County Durham each year.

Pastoral care and discipline: Pastoral care is spearheaded by assistant head, year heads and personal tutors. Each girl will have the same year head and personal tutor from year 7 to year 11 to provide continuity – a real strength. Buddying system teams up trained sixth formers with year 7, 8 and 9 pupils to provide a listening ear. Peer mentoring gives year 10 and 11 pupils regular access to sixth formers for advice. Well-resourced pastoral team with full-time counsellor and parent support

adviser, while school chaplain is faith presence in school, providing support to students, staff and parents.

Up to sixth form, rewards system recognises effort and achievement across the spectrum by merits and star awards for specific achievements. These build to bronze, silver and gold awards. Warnings and ample opportunity to correct poor behaviour precede any detention or exclusions. Total exclusions are rare – the last was more than three years ago: 'Exclusion goes against our ethos of welcoming each child and taking them through the ups and downs of school life'.

In a school of this size there is little opportunity for building links between year groups. Assemblies cater for just two year groups together and inter-house competition restricted to sports; clubs and out-of-school activities are seen as ways of bridge-building.

A representative student council has a voice in school whilst leadership opportunities are provided for the two head girls and prefects chosen by their peers and staff. Rules are clear and strictly enforced; unequivocal enforcement of strict uniform code and mobile phones confiscated if seen or heard, released only to a parent on Fridays.

Pupils and parents: A total of 30 different feeder schools but bulk from 13 Catholic schools in north and west of Newcastle. A third come from further afield – Newcastle, Northumberland, Durham. A breadth of social and academic backgrounds with 20 per cent of pupils with English as a second language and 12 SEN statemented children. Former pupils: Newcastle North MP Catherine McKinnell and TV presenter Donna Air.

Entrance: Over-subscribed, at least two applications for each place. Catholic applicants have priority, followed by other faiths. Seventy per cent are baptised Catholics and nearly 20 per cent of Muslim background. No academic selection though 10 per cent of places awarded on aptitude and ability in performing arts.

Exit: Usually 70-80 per cent stay to sixth form. After sixth form, three-quarters to university, rest to foundation courses, employment or gap year. Excellent at making sure girls make the right choice after sixth form.

Remarks: A school that is moving 'onwards and upwards'. Never content to rest on its laurels for its pupils, deserving of its award of outstanding in all categories in the last three Ofsted inspections. Continuity provided by pastoral system is outstanding. Inspired and inspiring teaching observed, stimulating lessons whilst harnessing the latest technology. What really sets the school apart is its development of teaching and teachers who go that extra mile to set girls on course to make the right choices after Sacred Heart. Every child really does matter here. Advice to lapsed Catholics, baptise your children, attend Sunday worship and move into the catchment area.

Sacred Heart High School (Hammersmith)

212 Hammersmith Road, London, W6 7DG

• Pupils: 820 girls; all day • Ages: 11–18 • RC • State

Tel: 020 8748 7600
Email: info@sacredh.lbhf.sch.uk
Website: www.sacredhearthighschoolhammersmith.org.uk

Headteacher: Since 1992 Dr Christine Carpenter BA PhD FRSA (early sixties). A formidable and much admired head, the girls speak of her with a mixture of awe and fear. 'She's scary,' said one. We attempted a formal visit but were rebuffed – no reasons given. This report is therefore based on our own research and a tour of the school on one of the official open days.

The head clearly has a strong work ethic and devotes herself to her job with tireless energy. She held the chapel filled with more than 500 hopeful parents in the palm of her hand. Her blistering authority is in no way diminished by her short frame, sensible hair, modest suit and shoes. A hint of her background can be discerned from what she wrote when campaigning to encourage more families to sign up for free school meals. Some families, she said, don't apply for free school meals because of the stigma attached to it. 'You should know that I, too, had free school meals because of my family circumstances,' she wrote. 'I don't believe this made me less successful or less socially adept – indeed, quite the contrary.'

Girls commented on the quips Dr Carpenter has been heard to make when she sees a particularly short skirt: 'Does your skirt need an absence note, or is that a belt?' she has been known to remark, with some humour. She regards all her girls as 'the leaders of tomorrow' and so makes the nurturing of leadership qualities a priority. Leaders clearly don't wear short skirts.

Academic matters: Sacred Heart has been a specialist school in maths and ICT since 2005. New sixth form opened in September 2013 for 80 of school's own pupils moving up from year 11. School will admit up to 30 external pupils to sixth form from 2014.

Academic results are impressive, even for the upmarket intake. Dr Carpenter proudly explained that the school had outperformed the Oratory, equalled Cardinal Vaughan and come within the top 25 per cent nationally. In 2013 91 per cent achieved five or more A*-C passes at GCSE including maths and English. Forty-nine per cent A*/A grades.

We were told that science and geography were school's strong subjects. Girls can either do the more simple core science and additional science or opt for three separate science modules. Pupils perform exceptionally well in RE, as you might expect (the data shows that history and RE are the school's 'popular and strong' subjects). French also stands out, as well as maths and English. Spanish is on offer but no German or Mandarin. Latin by invitation only. A teacher is supplied by a charity, the Iris Project, and comes in once or twice a week to teach a handful of keen and lucky girls. Plans afoot to offer an exam in Latin in partnership with Latymer Upper. All credit to Dr Carpenter that she facilitates this – apparently she is a classicist herself. Good DT facilities, but sadly no cooking. Girls praised the music tuition and music is offered as GCSE subject.

Setting from year 7. The girls we observed in a history lesson were attentive but the class size – even once setted – approached 40. Most teachers are Catholic but many are not.

One person responsible for SEN. It wasn't clear how effective the provision is but it would appear from the prospectus that differentiation in lessons – what one would hope for in any event – is the main kind of support available. Bearing in mind the large class sizes, a parent might be forgiven in worrying that her mildly dyslexic daughter could become 'lost.'

Games, options, the arts: Facilities not bad for an inner city state school, with four tennis/netball courts on-site (they can double up as rounders pitches too). School has a gym and dance studio as well as the use of Hammersmith and Fulham Health and Fitness Centre. Softball, basketball and volleyball on offer. Girls are kept active with at least two hours of PE per week and PE can be chosen as a GCSE subject. School has had some success in the borough in netball, hockey, rounders and athletics. After-school clubs include street dance, yoga, cheerleading, fencing, trampolining and football. There are inter-house competitions, the highlight of which is the annual sports day held at local playing fields.

The usual musicals take place annually – Little Shop of Horrors, My Fair Lady, West Side Story etc. Debating and public speaking (getting girls ready to lead) takes place after school, as well as sports and AS courses to stretch the brightest. A number of girls play musical instruments and there is a school choir and orchestra.

Busy art studio. 'Everyone loves art,' enthused one girl. We saw lots of pop art style self portraits, plastic neon jewellery and key rings crafted in DT. Plenty of opportunities to get involved with charitable work, such as raising money to support an orphanage in Zimbabwe.

Background and atmosphere: The school, or 'convent of the Sacred Heart,' is built on a site steeped in Catholic history dating back to the early 17th century. Four different orders of nuns have taught girls here for more than 300 years. The current Tudor styled buildings were built in the late 19th century. Sacred Heart was a secondary grammar school until 1976 when it received its first comprehensive intake. Since 2012 it has been an academy. To the uninitiated it looks rather forbidding, not helped by the fact that the impressive gates on Hammersmith Road do not yield to entrants, nor is there any sign to explain where the main entrance is. A number of prospective parents we spoke to were baffled at the lack of help in finding how to get in.

Once you do arrive within the red brick walls (the entrance is on Bute Gardens by the way) there is a wonderful calm and peace, wholly unlike your typical state school, let alone your inner London state comprehensive. The site is leafy and well-kept and it's hard to believe that seconds before you were pounding round the hectic Hammersmith roundabout. You won't think for one moment, however, that you are anywhere other than a Catholic establishment. As soon as you go through the door you are faced with a huge mural of the crucifixion. The wide spacious corridors of the cloisters are similarly adorned with religious paintings and look out over a beautiful garden (only for year 11s and up). The chapel is simple and peaceful and the library well-stocked and imaginatively designed, with a 'traffic light system' to denote how quiet you need to be in different areas. The nuns have recently vacated, which has made room for the new sixth form intake. The school is currently busily spending an £8 million grant on a new building development to house science and sports over three storeys.

There's a canteen where girls can buy hot food and cold lunches are also on sale. Civilised place to eat, talk and relax.

Pastoral care and discipline: This is without question a strict school. From appearance (short skirts are not just the subject of corridor quips, but regularly feature in the head's letter) through to punctuality (your daughter will be in detention at lunchtime if she is even one minute late) and general behaviour, Dr Carpenter rules with a very tight rein. The good thing, we were told by one girl, is that pupils don't just get put 'on report' for bad behaviour, they might be required to see a member of staff regularly because they are feeling overwhelmed with work or struggling in some other way.

A peer mentoring scheme between year 7s and year 11s encourages the older girls to take a leadership role and also fosters good relationships between all years. Inevitably we heard tales of 'bitchy' behaviour, often a feature of all girls' schools, but obviously not tolerated by the conscientious and vigilant Dr Carpenter and her team.

Pupils and parents: To adhere to the strict admissions procedure, jump through the various hoops and keep within the tight deadlines, parents here have one thing in common. They are committed, determined and quite often strategic. It is the state school of choice for many families, not only in west London, but even as far as Islington (Tony Blair's daughter being the obvious example). Despite its 'non selective, fully comprehensive' label, girls here are overwhelmingly middle class (for an inner London comprehensive), white and with English as a first language. Far fewer children on free school meals than is usual in this part of London (fourth on the Fair Admissions Campaign list of the most socially selective state schools in the country). Reassuring for many parents – as one said to us, 'I feel happy to be part of a club of like-minded people who share the same values as me.' Old girls include Kathryn Blair, Pauline Collins, Patricia Hayes, June Flewett, and Mel Martin.

Entrance: If you ain't Catholic then don't even think about it. Even if you are, start to sweat if you haven't had your child baptised before she is six months old and you can't produce the baptism certificate of at least one parent. Make sure your daughter attends an RC primary and then you might want to think about how close to the school you live. Applicants are banded – to ensure a 'comprehensive' intake – and sit a reasoning test as part of the admissions process. There have been instances of siblings failing to get in.

Exit: Vast majority go on to do A levels. For the first year of sixth form, 80 out of of 164 stayed on at Sacred Heart. Traditionally quite high numbers go to either Cardinal Vaughan or The London Oratory as well as Twyford C of E. The odd one to the independent sector including UCS, St Benedict's and Latymer Upper.

Remarks: An excellent, smaller than average, state school in the heart of London, if you are after a traditional education, are lucky enough to qualify and prepared to toe the very tight line, this may be the school for your daughter.

Saffron Walden County High School

Audley End Road, Saffron Walden, CB11 4UH

- Pupils: 2,085 (50 per cent boys, 50 per cent girls). All day.
- Ages: 11–18 • Non–denom • State

Tel: 01799 513030
Email: info@swchs.net
Website: www.swchs.net

Headteacher: Since 2004, Mr John Hartley MA PGCE (fifties). Educated at Oundle and St Catharine's College, Cambridge, where he read engineering. At university he volunteered for the charity Children's Relief International, helping to run holidays for children from disadvantaged backgrounds, and became committed to comprehensive education. Trained as a teacher, then taught physics at schools in Aylesbury, Crawley and Swindon before moving to Moulsham High School in Chelmsford as deputy head. Became head of Notley High School in Braintree in 1997 and took reins at Saffron Walden County High seven years later. He's also a National Leader of Education, one of the outstanding heads appointed to provide leadership to schools in difficulty. Firmly believes comprehensive schools work best when a traditional approach to rules, behaviour and uniform is combined with a contemporary, progressive approach to teaching and learning. Adamant that this doesn't mean mixed ability classes, but 'engaged, exciting, stimulating teaching that draws students into learning and helps them fulfil their potential.' Focused, unflappable and determined to set high standards. Wife is a teacher and they have three grown-up children.

Academic matters: School sets 'pretty rigorously' across all core subjects. Ten sets per year group. Pupils set for maths and English from year 7, for languages (all study French and German at key stage 3) from year 8 and for sciences from year 9. School is excellent at tracking pupils' progress throughout, so no one slips through the net. One of the advantages of large

school, says head, is the 'breadth of opportunity' it can offer across the curriculum. Spanish from year 9 and, unusually for a state school, County High (as everyone calls it) offers Latin to more able linguists at GCSE as well A level. Pupils choose GCSE options in year 8 and then start their GCSE courses in year 9, rather than the usual year 10. Most take eight or nine GCSEs, some a year early – head reckons giving able youngsters the opportunity to take a limited number early has 'a powerful impact in providing additional challenge and curricular breadth.' Dual award science available or three separate sciences. GCSE results good. In 2013, 75 per cent got at least five A*-C grades including maths and English; 36 per cent A*/A grades. A few take BTECs in vocational subjects, like construction, hospitality, car mechanics and small animal care – but, says head, 'as part of a balanced academic curriculum.'

Sixth formers follow one of three routes – one for the most academically able and requiring at least five GCSEs at A*-B (including maths and English) and at least Bs in chosen A level subjects, another for those with five GCSEs at A*-C and a third for those with five GCSEs at D or above. At A level, pupils can choose from a vast array of subjects – all the traditional ones, plus classical civilisation, media studies, philosophy, PE, psychology and sociology. A level results impressive, with 37 per cent A*/A grades and 72 per cent A*/B grades in 2013. Sixth form was recently named as the top performing in the country for A level value-added performance (ie progress made from GCSE to A level).

SEN team of 24 offers one-to-one support and in groups to pupils needing extra help. Additional challenges provided for gifted and talented. Teaching staff of 140. Good mix of ages. Strong links with Cambridge University's education faculty, and every subject department has at least one trainee teacher. Head has encouraged culture of professional development and staff are keen to enhance their skills, with many taking education masters degrees in their spare time. Teachers a particularly dedicated bunch – maths department holds maths surgeries for all twice a week during lunch breaks, while many staff lead D of E expeditions at weekends. Each year group divided into 10 tutor groups and children stay with the same tutor up to GCSEs. Communication with parents is good – via email, student planners, yearly reports and parent evenings. 'I call it a tripod of support,' says the head. 'Each part – children, parents and school – needs to be working well.'

Games, options, the arts: School very proud of its sporting achievements (an impressive array of silverware on display in the sports hall). Everyone plays sport up to 16 (rugby, hockey, netball, cricket, tennis and more) while sixth formers can choose from range of activities, from competitive sports to paragliding and rock climbing. Art is particularly strong. Everything from giant murals to ceramic teapots displayed along school corridors and a large proportion of the students who take A level art gain A*s.

The music department is right at the heart of the school and boasts two orchestras, a concert band, jazz band and a myriad of choirs and ensembles. More than 400 pupils have individual music lessons in school. In 2014 school is launching a post-16 music academy, with the aim of becoming a regional centre of excellence for music education.

Drama is popular, and can be taken at both GCSE and A level. Film studies available at A level, and school runs the Gordos, an annual short film competition for budding Steven Spielbergs. Lots of clubs at lunchtime and after school, and trips galore. The day we visited, one of the two deputy heads was preparing to take more than 80 youngsters on a cultural trip to China. Strong emphasis on green issues and charity work. Sixth formers run annual charities week every December, raising money for global, national and local causes.

Background and atmosphere: Located on the edge of the pretty market town of Saffron Walden, in north-east Essex.

Extensive grounds, including a grass cricket square, pavilion, tennis courts, Astroturf and own farm with cattle and sheep. In springtime pupils can see lambs gambolling in the paddock from the rugby and hockey pitches. Main building dates back to the 1950s and while no one could claim it's an architectural gem, the site is well-kept, with modern classrooms, plenty of trees, a state-of-the-art sports centre and a multi-purpose hall that doubles as the town's cinema. Pupils fiercely proud of the school, and of Saffron Hall, its new, multi-million pound auditorium for music and drama. The bulk of the money has been donated by an anonymous local donor and it's set to be a world-class venue for the area.

Pupils wear uniform – blazers, black trousers and ties for boys and blazers and tartan kilts for girls – up to the age of 16. Sixth formers can wear what they like, within reason, and get their own block, with study centre (silence during lessons) and common-room. More than a quarter of the pupils have school dinners (there's a cashless cafeteria – pupils' accounts are charged via biometric reading of their fingerprints) while the rest bring in packed lunches. Head says 'children don't learn well unless they are happy' – and everyone we spoke to described it as a happy place, apart from the odd gripe about having to wear uniform. Parents agree. 'It's done my children proud,' one mother told us. 'We count ourselves lucky to have such an excellent school on our doorstep and the sixth form is exceptional. The only issue I have is with some children taking GCSEs early – I'd rather they waited till year 11.'

Pupils are generally happy with the school with few gripes apart from the usual – too much work and the uniform policy is too strict.

Pastoral care and discipline: Relatively few formal rules but pupils are expected to exercise self-discipline. Few permanent exclusions, though no hesitation in taking this step if required. Head takes 'very strict line' on drugs and says anyone bringing drugs on-site would be permanently excluded. Smoking has 'almost disappeared as an issue,' while alcohol problems rare. Instead of having a head boy and head girl, County High has a team of 10 head students. Year 11s are appointed prefects and encouraged to mentor year 7s and 8s. Head is very keen on 'student voice' and pupils come up with plenty of their own ideas. Recent innovations include solar panels on the roof of the technology centre and a stunning mural along one of the main corridors. Lots of support for children who need it. As well as their tutors and heads of year, children can talk to the school's full-time counsellor or nurse, or a worker from Relateen, Relate's counselling service for young people, who comes in once a week. There's a student information point run by year 11s and pupils get a personalised daily bulletin emailed to them giving details of events that day. Parents told us the size of the school is well managed, while children reckon it's easy to settle in – thanks to a special induction programme for new pupils, maps and mentoring from older students. 'They really do understand every child,' a mother with two sons at County High said. 'Despite its size I feel the teachers know and understand my children and I love the way the school celebrates excellence and is proud of it.'

Pupils and parents: Pupils come from a mix of rural and urban backgrounds. Many walk or bike in from Saffron Walden, while others travel by bus from surrounding villages. Despite the town's middle-class appearance, a number of pupils are from disadvantaged families. Ex-pupil Ben Maher was part of the gold medal winning GB show jumping team in the 2012 Olympics.

Entrance: Heavily over-subscribed. There are 290 year 7 places and siblings get priority, followed by residents of 12 listed parishes. Further three criteria, but the vast majority of places are offered on the first two. 'To be sure of getting a place here, you do need to live in the catchment area,' says the head. Most come from County High's nine feeder primary schools. More than three-quarters stay on for sixth form, when they are joined by 80 to 90 newcomers a year. Places at this stage are very keenly sought-after.

Exit: Around 80 per cent of students go on to higher education. Twelve to Oxbridge in 2013, 95 to Russell Group universities and four to study medicine. Students get loads of one-to-one help to guide them through the complex UCAS maze. One sixth former told us: 'I'm sad about leaving. The school has supported me so much. I feel I've really been stretched and grown as a character.'

Remarks: A local school of exceptional quality. It buzzes with activity from dawn till dusk – ideal for children who want to work hard and play hard. Even though it's a big place, pupils are very well supported and thrive in a vibrant, fast-moving school that prides itself on knowing every child as an individual.

St Aidan's Church of England High School

Linked school: St Aidan's and St John Fisher Associated Sixth Form

Oatlands Drive, Harrogate, HG2 8JR

• Pupils: 1,935 boys and girls • Ages: 11–18 • C of E but welcomes children from all Christian traditions • State

Tel: 01423 885814
Email: admin@st-aidans.co.uk
Website: www.st-aidans.n-yorks.sch.uk

Headteacher: Since 2012, Mr John Wood BA PGCE (late fifties). First joined St Aidan's as a religious studies teacher in 1977 and has held various positions within the school until his appointment as head.

Met his wife, Lynn, at St Aidan's; they have two children (both teachers!).

Very involved in local church community, and Chair of Harrogate International Youth Music Festival. Keen on cricket, music and walking in the Yorkshire Dales and Lake District.

Head says he regards his appointment 'as a great honour and privilege.' He is 'passionate about the role of a church school in today's society and will seek ways of ensuring that the students within the school are provided with an all round education that enables them to move on to higher education and into society where they can make a significant impact.'

Academic matters: Students' attainment at entry is well above average and the school has been judged 'outstanding' (in all respects) in three Ofsteds. Average class size well below average (23 in years 7-9, 20 in years 10-11). Relationships between students and teachers are excellent – students spoke appreciatively of how helpful their teachers are, to the extent of coming into school on a bank holiday before public exams. It has science and maths plus modern languages specialisms, with high uptake and achievement in these areas. Members of the science department produce textbooks and CD roms and students are successful in national competitions; French, Spanish, German, Mandarin Chinese, Arabic and Italian are available, with very effective use of video conferencing; every year has eight annual language trips, eg week-long visits to language schools in Spain and Germany and work experience in France.

Key stage 3 results are very good, especially maths, science and art. Year 7s start with one modern foreign language (MFL) and several take a second in year 8. Year 9s do separate sciences.

S

At key stage 4 all take a MFL and RS (Islam is an option). The very bright can sit maths and French early and then AS.

GCSE results are amongst the best nationally, with a steady improvement in the level of grades obtained over most of the the last few years: 41 per cent A/A* and 71 per cent A*/B in 2013; almost all students obtain five A*-Cs at GCSE or equivalents (83 per cent including maths and English). All three sciences, RS (notably starry), Spanish, music and food technology stand out.

The associated sixth form with St John Fisher RC High School, the largest school-based sixth form nationally, offers a ecumenical environment, each preserving its own identity via separate pastoral systems; a small number join from other schools. High praise in the most recent Ofsted report: 'terrific' progress, 'superb' attitudes to learning, 'exceptionally high quality' teaching, 'excellent relationships...founded on mutual respect and trust', 'a family feel'. Fifty-nine per cent at A*/B grades at A level in 2013; in 2011 one student gained a stunning seven A*/A grades and three more gained five. Forty-three subjects offered: sciences (very popular), maths, history, ancient history, English lit, German, Spanish, psychology, government and politics, RS, art, design and technology, drama and theatre studies and performing arts particularly successful. Students benefit from links with three Yorkshire universities' RS and science departments. Other less usual subjects include dance, engineering, law, geology, plus vocational courses, eg health and social care, travel and tourism, music technology. All do RS – very successfully – as part of the AS general studies programme (Buddhism as well as Christianity studied), then non-examined RS in year 13. The AQA baccalaureate is being piloted – A levels plus extended project and community service. Advanced extension awards for the most able. Also a one year intermediate course – IT, leisure and tourism, maths, English and a certificate in career planning.

SEN and disaffected students progress well too. The latter can do the ASDAN vocational course and a diploma in digital applications; they may follow individualised workplace and further education college related programmes. The independent learning centre, with walls covered with motivational quotes, provides a safe space with one-to-one support. Provision is made for school refusers outside school in a local church. The very well resourced learning support department, deliberately placed by previous head at the heart of the school and given an excellent ranking by the education service for inclusion and dyslexia, has a highly qualified, flexible, very thoughtful and innovative head. All are tested on entry – in years 7 and 8 statemented students receive individual or small group support outside the classroom. Other children needing support are also placed in small teaching groups for a number of subjects, for as long as seems necessary. Inside class support is provided too, in a sensitive way, and teachers have a lot of communication with the department. Parents of dyslexic students are given training so they can do reading work with their children at home.

A small, purpose-built, fitted kitchen helps autistic students to develop life skills; a lunchtime games club enables them to develop social skills and provides a refuge at a time of the day they find stressful (a shed with a model railway layout developed by an autistic boy is another refuge for vulnerable students); a special rest area has been created for three Down's syndrome children who are worn out by 2 pm. We have heard reports of a few past parents feeling the school was unwelcoming to new dyslexic students, perhaps a result of its renown proving a drain on restricted resources, but current SEN ones speak with great appreciation of the school's attention to individual needs and quick response to their concerns: 'You can't fault the support... the school is very flexible and innovative'; 'prepared to do everything to meet his needs'; 'A city wide autism specialist (contacted by the school) came to our house for tea and got him back on track'; 'a very open door policy'; 'The teachers provided fantastic extra backup on all his expeditions'. A parent support group meets regularly for information sessions.

Games, options, the arts: Described as a 'sports mad school' – indeed the day we visited all outdoor facilities were in use after the end of school. All the main sports plus basketball, cycling and equestrian clubs, aerobics, rowing, tag rugby, dance, fitness and weight training. Lots of success in regional and national competitions plus some outstanding individuals, eg martial arts, gymnastics, an international fencer ('Teachers are very supportive about helping me catch up with work I've missed for competitions'). Football tour to Holland, leadership awards, every school year from year 8 has an outdoor education residential, including a winter mountaineering weekend.

'The school fizzes with music, sport and drama' (Ofsted) – unsurprisingly, has Artsmark Gold. Stunning music in huge quantities, with a high regional and national reputation – 12 ensembles, including the wittily named brass quintet, No Strings Attached, and various choirs; lots of public performances, eg at the Labour party conference, the Birmingham Symphony Hall, the Albert Hall, and regular 'outstanding' awards in regional and national festivals; ambitious programmes, eg Karl Jenkins' The Armed Man; concert tours to Canada and Europe. The big sixth form chamber choir (50 per cent male) has been in all possible finals of the BBC's Songs of Praise School Choir of the Year competition (the only choir to have done this) and can often be heard on Radio 4's daily service. The world music group gives African drumming workshops in local primary schools (using their own set of African drums); the worship band, Aidan's Flame, is much in demand for local services.

Drama also of a high standard and ambitious – History of Tom Jones, West Side Story, 1950s rock and roll version of Twelfth Night, their version of The Comedy of Errors was one of only three chosen for The Royal Shakespeare Company's schools festival; regular successful applicants to the National Youth Theatre; tours, theatre trips, workshops, drama clubs, plays produced by sixth formers; a community theatre project takes workshops and performances to local primary schools. A considerable amount of framed, excellent, very original art by present and past students on display throughout the school – fine art, graphics and photography on offer; art trip to Paris.

Students very enthusiastic about the huge range of extra-curricular opportunities (some run by older students), with high uptake – eco club, chess, organic gardening, signing, enterprise clubs for all ages, debating (the mock election was won handsomely by the Lib Dems – 83 per cent turnout), science and technology competitions (regional and national successes), D of E (several golds), cooking events and competitions. Lots of new fiction in the well-resourced library – reading very popular with boys as well as girls, says the librarian ('I can't keep up with the demand!'); authors visit during the annual Book Week; creative writing workshops with writers and a residential course in Wales. Has international school status – links with schools in Morocco, China, Uganda, Tanzania, Sri Lanka, Australia (year 9s do a six week exchange), Canada, France, Germany. Impressive sums raised for a great range of charities (£56,000 one year); several students do third world voluntary work in their gap year. Year 12s do a leadership course and modern language students teach local primary school children at an annual languages day.

Background and atmosphere: Founded in 1968 on a large greenfield site bordering the Harrogate Stray. Pleasant modern front, only two or three levels high. Very thoughtfully and attractively designed throughout, eg a cafeteria with a low ceiling to absorb noise, a convivially arranged staff room. Well maintained throughout (no graffiti), steady programme of development – recent new classrooms, dance studio, second chapel with lovely stained glass windows, deli bar for sixth, careers area and learning resource centre.

The Christian ethos is central, expressed in the thorough going concern for individual needs and tolerance of difference, and assemblies play a big rôle, but sixth formers say it isn't 'very churchy'. Newcomers (some have moved from schools where they haven't been happy) feel welcomed. Academic success is not embarrassing, but neither is it seen as an all consuming goal, we were told – an attitude of 'everyone is good at something' is supported by the wealth of extra-curricular activities. A senate of ten elected sixth formers makes suggestions the school responds to – 'It's always trying to improve what's on offer'.

Recently awarded The Times Educational Supplement award for the best school dinners in England. Everyone enthuses about the – decidedly upmarket – food: a sixth form boy (sixth form has deli bar plus separate cafeteria, year 7s have one and years 8-11 another) declared, 'The food is fantastic – I could sit here and eat all day!' Parents come in to sample the lunches and praise the 'lovely, varied menu', 'The children get to try new food', 'I don't need to cook a main meal in the evening'; an amazingly cheap (50p) healthy breakfast on offer for early arrivals.

Pastoral care and discipline: Parents (and Ofsted) talk glowingly about the 'caring ethos' and attention to the individual needs of students of all abilities and needs – 'The pastoral care is second to none; all staff are extremely approachable and any problems are dealt with straight away with kindness and consideration' (usual structure of form tutors and heads of year, plus a 'very supportive' school nurse). Thoughtful transition arrangements – all (65-70) feeder schools are visited in year 6. The behaviour policy shows understanding of the need for a flexible approach to discipline, taking developmental stages into account – behaviour rated 'excellent' by Ofsted. Rewards policy includes badges for 'being special', award evenings, postcards to parents.

Pupils and parents: Mostly white middle class parents, reflecting Harrogate's social composition – only a few ethnic minority, EAL and looked after students. Pupils present as open, articulate, thoughtful and happy, valuing what the school provides.

Entrance: After SEN and children in care, takes local children, extending out to the whole archdeaconry. A big waiting list decided on by an elaborate points system based on regular church attendance by children and parents, siblings at the school and service to the church (or faith equivalent). About 200 from other schools join the sixth form – five A*-Cs needed.

Exit: Very few leave at 16 – almost all to further education college for a course not offered by the school. Most sixth formers proceed to a great range of universities, including several top ones, eg Oxbridge (10 in 2013) and the best London University colleges. Several do foundation art courses and degrees; medicine popular.

Two dedicated careers officers give one to one advice; year 12s attend a three day careers conference after their AS exams – 'An amazing careers department,' enthused a sixth form student.

Remarks: Regularly ranked in the top 12 comprehensives nationally and always striving to improve – 'Children can grow in every direction', 'a fantastic school', 'everything we hoped it would be'.

St Albans Girls' School

Sandridgebury Lane, St Albans, Hetfordshire, AL3 6DB

- Pupils: 1,165 girls; all day; boys in the sixth form since 2007
- Ages: 11–18 • Non-denom • State

Tel: 01727 853134
Email: admin@stags.herts.sch.uk
Website: www.stags.herts.sch.uk

Headteacher: Since 2010, Mrs Margaret Chapman BSc, NPQH (forties). Educated at the University of Wales, Aberystwyth before teaching geography, geology and ICT and ultimately becoming deputy head at Mill Hill County High School. Moved as deputy head to The Priory School, Hitchin. Parents say she's 'business like, but with a sense of humour,' pupils 'strict, but in a good way,' and staff describe her as 'highly driven,' saying she has infected them with her determination to 'never stand still.' A definite contender for hardest working head award, should one exist, she can often be tracked down to her office at 9pm. Lives locally with husband and teenage children, a daughter at Leeds University and a son at St Columba's School. A geologist at heart, is the proud owner of a large rock collection and loves the outdoors, particularly the sea.

Indefatigable on the subject of STAGS, brimming with opinions on all things educational and extremely proud of the changes she has made since her appointment. Sets high standards of behaviour and work for staff and pupils alike: 'if you follow it through and keep on message you get the right result.' Believes in teaching staff taking ownership of student pastoral care rather than just academic success and has aimed to empower all members of the school community – including support staff – to create a dynamic, democratic environment. 'Highly energetic,' according to parents, holds a monthly surgery for them to keep channels of communication open on subjects from academic progress to frustrating behaviour at home. Keeps her hand in teaching A level economics and geography to year 8. Focused on turning out 'articulate and confident women who are ready for society and the world of work.'

Academic matters: Robust results, particularly given school's non-selective intake and broad range of abilities. In 2013 91 per cent of GCSE pupils achieved five or more at grades A*-C, with a quarter of girls achieving straight A*/A grades; 72 per cent of A levels graded A*-B. Smallish take-up (14 in 2012) of EPQ but half of those taking it achieved an A* grade.

Form groups of 28-29 girls, with some GCSE classes as small as 15 and up to six sets for most popular A levels to keep groups as tight as possible. Girls benefit from a bespoke learning progamme, enabling them to take between eight and 13 GCSEs depending on ability. For those who struggle with the challenges of academia, the school offers specialised programmes to help with life skills and build self-esteem and confidence. Consortium arrangement with other local schools and colleges enables a few girls to take vocational courses such as hair and beauty from year 10 during school hours.

Quality not quantity is the order of the day in languages, with just French and Spanish on offer from year 7. Languages and history popular at GCSE with a good showing in sciences and maths for A level. Dance, media studies, food technology and textiles available for those looking for diversity in their GCSE choices. Some 'ologies' very popular at A level, as are government and politics, media studies and English lit. Setting from year 7 in maths and languages, with sciences and English streamed from year 9 and languages from year 10.

VLE offering expanded from a formerly piecemeal approach to having a whole school focus, 'aiming to create a seamless

S

link between home and school learning,' says head. School keen to use it to encourage greater parent engagement too and 'flipped' lessons being trialled, where pupils take online lesson at home, followed by discussion in classroom time.

SEN all in a day's work for the 12 per cent of school requiring additional help, with policy of 'inclusion' into classrooms. Four full-time SENCo teaching assistants cover one to one classroom support – head considers this 'an area of outstanding provision.' School well equipped to deal with its significant proportion (19 per cent) of EAL requirements – the product of a 'huge array of backgrounds' from around 60 feeder primary schools and ensure that it remains a language issue rather than a barrier to academic achievement. Strong gifted and talented programme touches 22 per cent of pupils, with all staff now required to plan enrichment exercises into lessons to benefit everyone, encouraging them to think creatively and lead, preventing a 'more of the same' approach for bright sparks. Mutterings from parents that reporting system is 'a bit impersonal,' but most concede that it is 'getting better.'

Games, options, the arts: Head adamant that pupils 'don't miss opportunities to develop talent and roundedness,' and school is well equipped for sporting excellence, with nine tennis courts, three hockey pitches, a cricket square, athletics track, outdoor pool (heated to tropical temperature) and purpose built sports hall (2006) complete with multi-gym for staff and pupil use. STAGS families can buy summer membership to use pool in evenings and weekends for the princely sum of £40 and many do, although the odd parent grumbles it's not used enough for timetabled swimming lessons.

Teams successful at district, national and county level (packed trophy cabinets adorn the school entrance), although we only noticed fixture lists for A and B teams. Particular strengths in swimming and athletics, with year 7 recently being crowned district football champions and the addition of a new Astroturf bound to help secure this specialism. Girls' accolades out of school also celebrated, with press coverage of Olympian alumni and a current national judo champion proudly festooning the reception area.

Dance and gymnastics very popular and school has recently renovated a mobile unit to accommodate enthusiasts in these areas. Not the most appealing dance studio we've seen but head says girls 'really appreciate it' and the quality of the biennial production, part choreographed by the girls, is 'exceptional,' say parents. School is 'a hotbed of creativity,' according to staff, with drama and music both 'excellent' and around 16 per cent of girls taking individual music lessons in school. Two well-used (and rather well-worn) drama studios, with girls constantly preparing for performances, often transporting their talents to competitions and events such as the Shakespeare Schools Festival. Large, inspiring art department with an impressive and diverse array of work on show, to a notably high standard, throughout the school.

Good range of extra-curricular from year 7 up, ranging from the intriguingly named Spitfire and Battle of Britain club, to more predictable drama, textiles and sports activities, with girls rewarded for regular attendance and parents happy that they are 'actively encouraged to do at least one.' After school academic support in the form of spelling, reading and English clubs for younger girls, with the likes of history 'stretch those brains' seminars for A level students. D of E taken very seriously as a means of gearing up to higher education and broadening horizons. Trips and tours galore, from London Fashion Week to the Himalayas. Charity work is 'an enormous focus' for the girls, says the school; 'they really get their teeth into it,' raising on average £18,000 each year for their selected chosen charities.

Background and atmosphere: Founded in 1920 as a girls' grammar, STAGS shrugged off its selective mantle some time ago in favour of status as a business and enterprise college.

Occupying a ubiquitous low level 1960s warren of buildings in the north of the city, the uninspiring fabric of the school belies the fact that behind its façade lies a buzzing hub of enthusiastic, independent learners turning out commendable academic results. These, by the way, are consistently on the up with girls also benefiting from a culture which helps them develop employment skills through its 'leadership passport', a bespoke programme that from year 7 instils in them the skills they need to be successful in the world of work.

Few whistles and bells where facilities are concerned but those that matter are functional and well-equipped. Sixth form centre is a star attraction, with a bright (and unusually tidy) common room and two large study rooms; one unsupervised (chatting allowed) and one for silent study with a member of staff on duty. The well-stocked, fully computerised library provides more space for quiet study and handy types should be impressed by the superbly equipped DT lab. Seven purpose built ICT suites benefit from a rolling renewal programme, with wifi across the school.

A rolling technology upgrade programme has heralded the arrival of iPads and iMacs in the new Innovation Centre to allow girls to access high level technology, not just in the context of ICT but across all subjects. This is all part of the school's reshaping of its strategic vision – to bring a 21st century learning experience to its pupils, not just through IT but also through awareness of relevant developments in the employment market. With its state maintained budgets, the school has to 'tread carefully' with expenditure and technological improvements must 'enhance learning rather than distract pupils,' says head.

Grounds and buildings generally in fine fettle (staff are militant about tidiness and order), with thoughtful touches such as covered picnic areas and plenty of outdoor seating, to ensure the girls have somewhere to 'loll' during break times. Dining room spotless and ruthlessly efficient, with fingerprint technology payment scheme, and a 'snack shack' for those preferring to grab something on the hoof.

Staff 'not allowed to sit still,' according to one. Strong measures in place to ensure a 'critical mass of outstanding teaching,' ranging from staff 'coaching triads', enabling teachers to share good practice, to personal development programmes including staff book groups. About 20 per cent of teachers are male, lending a healthy dose of testosterone to the school.

Pastoral care and discipline: Directors of learning for each year group ensure that girls are kept on track academically, socially and emotionally. Hugely successful house system, with seven houses named after influential women. Good work and behaviour rewarded with house points, with girls working hard to keep 'consequences' (that's minus marks in old money) to a minimum for the greater good of their housemates. Heaps of events to build house spirit, from competitions, plays and challenges to a plethora of fund raising efforts, with each house choosing its own charity – almost daily cake sales attack the staff's waistlines with ruthless efficiency. Leadership is a 'big deal' here, says head, with girls offered opportunities to show their metal at all stages; there are two heads of house per year group from year 7, captains of everything, from games to charities and over one hundred year 10s working towards their bronze Duke of Edinburgh award.

A team of empathetic year 12 and 13 girls run a 'hear 4 u' group to mentor younger pupils through school related personal or academic problems, an initiative that won the school a Diana anti-bullying award. Trained by the school counsellor, they run frequent drop-in clinics and have a dedicated email address for those too shy to approach them directly. Anti-bullying ambassadors in each year group to keep awareness up: 'the more you know about it, the more resilient you become,' says head. Alcohol, drugs and smoking are 'not an issue', with staff describing the girls' behaviour as 'generally immaculate'. Exclusions extremely rare but staff ensure an 'on the table' conversation before offenders return, offering them holistic support and guidance to make sure they feel part of the school community again.

Pupils and parents: Fresh faced, pony-tailed and immaculately turned out pupils more akin to convent girls than those from a large comprehensive move calmly around the corridors. School in general has the feel of a traditional grammar about it, perhaps a legacy of its history, more likely rigorous standards put in place by current head. New deputy head says he has 'never come across a more focused cohort of students'. A few boys filter into year 12, looking for 'an enhanced educational offering', and integrate well with the girls according to staff.

Majority from St Albans and surrounding towns, with just a few from further afield. Broad socio-demographic, ranging from affluent families choosing STAGS over fee-paying alternatives to less well-off but aspirational families, seeking a traditional yet forward thinking education for their girls. Head says she is happy – and has been known – to knock on doors to engage the few parents who are 'scared to aspire.' About eight per cent qualify for free school meals but staff say they are 'hard to spot' even in this middle class setting. STAGS girls are described by teachers as 'well presented, serious about their studies and very pro school.' About 27 per cent from ethnic minorities.

Regular PTA meetings with the school's senior team ensure parental voices are heard and that, in line with the ethos of the school, things keep moving forward. This is replicated by the 'vociferous' pupils via the student leadership team ('the student voice is huge,' say staff), giving the impression of real partnership between school and its community.

Entrance: Parents 'move heaven and earth' (not to mention house) to get into STAGS and despite the school's academy status, it remains non selective, with admissions still administered by the local authority and no plans to change this. Majority join at 11 from a wide range of local primary schools, although some from as far afield as Borehamwood and Hitchin. Any admissions post year 7 are dealt with by lottery if there is more than one applicant for the place. Extra places available in year 12, with applicants required to achieve a minimum of 5 grades A-C at GCSE and B grades or higher in their chose A level subjects.

Exit: Around 40 per cent leave at 16 as mixed gender environments beckon, or to pursue more vocational courses, with the odd one seeking out subjects, such as classics, not on offer at STAGS. Majority (about 80 per cent) leaving at the end of year 13 go straight on to higher education, with around 30 per cent winning places in Russell Group universities and an impressive Oxbridge record (11 girls from the class of 2012 heading off to study either medicine or veterinary studies). Huge amount of advice given to guide girls down right paths right from year 7, from frequent work experience opportunities to Oxbridge days in year 10. Parents say school 'has got it all covered.'

Money matters: State maintained. PTA is 'very involved – and then some', says head, raising around £40,000 a year for the school with various events. Funds have significantly enhanced the sixth form centre, dining hall and the next target for these formidable parents is the library. Around 10 per cent of parents make a voluntary contribution to bolster coffers towards rolling improvement programme.

Remarks: Whether your daughter wants to sing, dance or swot her way through school, there's something for everyone from the top of the academic pile down. In the words of the head, 'everyone can shine at STAGS.'

St Albans High School for Girls

Linked school: St Albans High School for Girls – Preparatory School

Townsend Avenue, St Albans, Hetfordshire, AL1 3SJ

• Pupils: 660 girls; all day • Ages: 11–18 • Affiliated to the Church of England • Fees: £13,680 pa • Independent

Tel: 01727 853800
Email: admissions@stalbans-high.herts.sch.uk
Website: www.stahs.org.uk

Headmistress: Since 2009, Mrs Rosemary Martin MEd NPQH FRSA (sixties). Educated at Halesowen Grammar School, Liverpool University and the University of London. Previously head of the girls' school at Forest School for seven years and head of Combe Bank School in Sevenoaks for eight years.

A fervent believer in single sex education, she says girls flourish in girls' schools and that along with its excellent exam results St Albans High offers girls friendship and support. 'It is about the girls developing a sense of responsibility to themselves and to others and ensuring that they are well prepared for the next stage in their lives,' she says.

Head is married with two sons. She is an ISI inspector and a member of the Girls' Schools Association's development committee. As well as spending time with her family, she enjoys travelling, skiing and reading. She is retiring in August 2014.

Academic matters: School prides itself on achieving stellar results in 'a very caring environment.' Results are certainly impressive. Eighty-two per cent A*/A grades at A level in 2013. Twenty-two subjects on offer at A level – all the usual, plus others like classical civilisation, drama and theatre studies, economics, food technology, government and politics, PE and product design.

GCSE results the best ever in 2013 – nearly 60 per cent A* and 18 girls achieving straight A*s. Two thirds take 10 GCSEs, the rest do either nine or 11. Double and triple science on offer and all girls take at least one language (French, German or Spanish). IGCSEs taken in all core subjects, as well as in history and modern foreign languages. No early exams these days – 'we want the girls to have time to extend and enrich themselves,' says the deputy head. Most pupils take a creative GCSE, whether it's textiles, art, DT, drama or music.

All girls are screened for literacy difficulties at the start of year 7. One-to-one 'additional curricular education' lessons (ACE for short) for specific learning needs like dyslexia and dyspraxia available at an additional charge. Currently 46 girls with SEND. Class sizes of up to 24 in years 7 to 9, average of 18 in years 10 and 11 and maximum of 16 in sixth form, though in practice often smaller.

Lots of guidance given when it comes to university choices, UCAS forms, personal statements and work placements. Girls are encouraged to use the careers room (which has a vivid pink wall and scores of university guides and resources) from an early age.

School recently introduced a two-week timetable (five one-hour lessons a day) and girls get five minutes to move from one lesson to the next. The teaching we saw was engaging and interactive, from a year 11 Spanish class on pronouns to a year 8 geography class where the girls had written and recorded their own songs about global warming. 'We try and be as innovative as we can,' the enthusiastic head of geography told us. Girls say that the teaching is top notch and teachers are hugely supportive. 'If I hadn't been at this school I would never have come out with A*s and As at GCSE,' a sixth former told us. 'This school makes you want to do well. You learn how to revise and you feel really well prepared.'

S

Games, options, the arts: Even though the games pitches are a five to ten-minute walk away, sport is big here, with six PE staff and teams trailing clouds of glory in netball, lacrosse, swimming, gym – the whole gamut really. Dynamic head of PE and sport says that in a highly academic environment 'it's important for the girls to let off a bit of steam' and girls jump at the chance to take part in every sport under the sun. Facilities also include new sports pavilion, dance studio, netball courts, lacrosse pitches and 25m swimming pool. Unlike some schools, sixth formers carry on with sport, though they can opt for activities like keep fit and yoga instead of traditional sports if they prefer. 'We try and get girls to find something they like,' says head of PE. 'It's brilliant to see them enjoying sport so much.' Matches (often four teams per year group) virtually every night of the week, plus Saturdays too. Sports hall boasts cabinets bulging with silverware and wall of fame highlighting girls' very varied sporting triumphs. When we visited these included an England U19 netball and lacrosse player, a British dressage rider and a national level Irish dancer.

Drama is a key activity, whether it's year 13s studying political theatre in an A level class or everyone throwing themselves into the annual house drama competition. The houses are given a theme (last year's was 'horrors' so Sweeney Todd and Dracula featured heavily) and girls must choose a play, adapt it, choose a cast and direct it. Jubilee Hall, the school's new theatre space, can accommodate 350 and is used for shows, concerts and public exams (it has retractable seating). Music impressive, with around 520 instrumental lessons a week across the prep and senior schools. A host of choirs (chamber to gospel), bands and four orchestras. Light and airy art studios (one specifically for A level students, with electric windows, northern light and huge ceilings). Lots of work on display, including a set of acrylic sheets sculpted into flowers by a former A level art student and worthy of a top London gallery. 'She was so prolific that she worked her way along the corridor, filling up every inch of space,' the girls told us.

Sixth formers get the chance to do Young Enterprise, D of E and Model United Nations and also have an enrichment programme – including AS critical thinking, GCSE Italian or astronomy and the Extended Project Qualification (EPQ). Recent trips to China, Nepal, Iceland and Washington.

Background and atmosphere: Founded in 1889, the school moved from its original location to its current site half a mile from the city centre in 1908. It maintains close links with the diocese of St Albans through the bishop and the dean. Locals call it the High School to distinguish it from St Albans Girls' School.

School entrance looks traditional, with wooden floors and long corridors, but behind the front façade tradition gives way to modernity, with new performing arts centre and swish art and technology block. Staff and pupils set great store by the three Cs – challenge, creativity, community – which underpin the school's vision and ethos. Girls attend assemblies four times a week.

Pupils aged 11 to 16 wear smart uniform of striped navy blazers, skirts and blouses. Sixth formers are allowed to wear their own clothes, just so long as they are 'appropriate.' Jeans allowed but 'no shoulders, no shorts,' no wildly coloured hair and no heavy make-up. On formal occasions, such as for the carol service and founder's day (when girls walk through St Albans to the abbey), sixth formers wear 'official navy' – smart blouse, skirt and school blazer. Sixth form block accommodates 170 year 12 and 13 girls and has its own library, with copies of all A level books, newspapers and an eclectic selection of magazines (everything from History Today to Marie Claire), plus kitchen and common room. When we visited during morning break the place was festooned with balloons, party poppers and birthday cake. 'We go overboard for 18th birthdays,' laughed our sixth form guide. She also confided that 'I'm dreading leaving. I'm going to miss my teachers.' Praise indeed.

Main school library has more than 16,000 resources and is well used. Librarian has introduced the 'whole school read,' which involves buying more than 600 copies of the same book, asking the girls to read it and then posting their reviews on the school's VLE. The most recent choice, Wonder by RJ Palacio, got the firm thumbs-up.

Most girls have school dinners (a specially-themed pirate menu on the day we visited) and tuck shop serves up flapjacks, sandwiches and cheese on toast at break. The school even has its own Starbucks (sixth formers can use it any time, year 11 at specified times and anyone after school).

Pastoral care and discipline: 'The girls have an inbuilt sense of how to behave towards each other,' says the deputy head and pupils have written their own eight-point code of conduct, including tenets like treating others 'as we would like to be treated ourselves' and giving 'encouragement and support in times of success and disappointment.'

Atmosphere is focused and busy, with many commenting on the good rapport between staff and pupils. 'The school is very upbeat,' a mother told us. 'They encourage the girls to work hard and they are brilliant at developing the girls' self confidence.' House system is integral to the school. All girls belong to one of four houses – Julian, Mandeville, Paris or Verulam – and housemistresses play key role in pastoral care. Raft of school officers and house officers all voted in by girls and staff (including head girl, three deputies and games captain). School takes a lot of care in settling new year 7s in. No homework for first two weeks and year 8 pupils act as buddies to new girls, writing them a letter of welcome in the summer holidays before they start.

Sixth formers get more freedom. They still have to be in school first thing, even if they have don't have a lesson during first period, but are allowed to go home once they have finished in the afternoons.

Pupils and parents: Many girls live in St Albans but others travel from as far afield as Luton and Potters Bar to London suburbs like Winchmore Hill and Mill Hill. Parents admire the school's ethos. 'The teachers are very good at instilling the importance of learning and of the girls getting their heads down and getting on with it,' one mother told us. 'But it's not all about results. There are so many extracurricular activities, for girls of all abilities too.' Well-known old girls include the late Dame Anna Neagle, TV weather presenter Isobel Lang and Selfridges MD Anne Pitcher.

Entrance: Heavily oversubscribed (up to 300 applicants for the 96 year 7 places available each year). Girls selected by means of assessment, group interview and school report. Up to half the year 7 entry comes from school's own prep, four miles down the road at Wheathampstead. Others arrive from local state primaries and preps. Sixth form entrants need at least five A*/A at GCSE (regardless of whether they are already at the school or not).

Exit: A handful leave at 16, primarily for boarding, co-ed schools or simply a change of scene. At 18 all progress to higher education. Eight to Oxbridge in 2013, with other popular destinations including Birmingham, Bristol, Durham, Edinburgh, Exeter, Imperial, Leeds, Nottingham, St Andrews, UCL and York.

Money matters: School offers a number of means-tested bursaries (up to 100 per cent). There are also academic and music scholarships from year 7 and academic, art/DT, PE and drama scholarships for sixth formers.

Remarks: A happy and high achieving school that turns out confident, down-to-earth pupils who feel nurtured, supported and well prepared for university and beyond. For girls with ambition it could be just the ticket.

St Albans School

Abbey Gateway, St Albans, Hetfordshire, AL3 4HB

• Pupils: 830, all boys except for 75 girls in the sixth form • Ages: 11-19 • Multi-faith • Fees: £15,294 pa • Independent

Tel: 01727 855521
Email: hm@st-albans-school.org.uk
Website: www.st-albans.herts.sch.uk

Headmaster: Since 1993, Mr Andrew Grant MA PGCE FRSA, late fifties (looks much younger), a Cambridge English graduate who recently served as chair of HMC. Married with two adult sons, both former pupils. A keen and serious club cyclist (covers around 5,000 miles a year), he also enjoys theatre and reading, especially Shakespeare. Smart, professional, shrewd, renowned for his attention to detail and as a task-master who demands high standards from staff and pupils. 'He is friendly, intelligent, commands respect and wants us to succeed. We see him cheering us on the touch line, he comes to all the plays and productions, has a wonderful way with words and really cares about us.' Staff and parents agree, adding, 'He is an impressive leader who is in touch, measured and helpful.'

Retiring in July 2014. His successor will be Jonathan Gillespie, currently head of Lancing College. Read modern and medieval languages and did a PGCE at Cambridge; taught at Highgate School and Fettes College before joining Lancing. Keen sports coach – especially hockey (he umpires at national level), and has been involved in CCF. Likes hill walking and golf, and celebrates family's Scottish roots by playing the highland bagpipes. Married to Caroline; they have two teenage sons.

Academic matters: Typically circa 85 per cent of all GCSE grades are A*/A (80 per cent in 2013), placing the school in upper echelons of league tables with no weaknesses at either GCSE or A level. Homegrown sixth formers average an impressive points score equivalent of 10 A*s at GCSE. Top performing subjects are art, maths, geography, RS, DT, science and classics. IGCSEs in maths, sciences, languages and English. More than 67 per cent of A levels were graded A*/A in 2013, with 93 per cent A*-B. Maths popular, with strong showings in all sciences, art, classics, geography, economics, DT, RS, history, ancient history and English. Languages less popular but interest increasing. French, German and Latin are on an equal footing in year 7; top sets take French in year 10 and AS in year 11. Modular A levels – resits the norm, not just to get higher grades but to get a more secure grade if borderline. Many take an extended project qualification (EPQ) which facilitates independent study and research. Recent titles include 'Is the creation of Chimeras ethical?' and 'Was Cicero as influential an orator as he thought?' Well-stocked main and junior libraries, packed to the rafters with hard-working, motivated students when we visited. No room for complacency or coasting: 'You have to want to be pushed and like learning, but teachers are helpful and approachable.' Parents agree, saying, 'Staff are extremely committed and work exceedingly hard but the average, borderline or overly tutored pupil would flounder.' Lessons taught traditionally but with much discourse and many interesting twists. One younger pupil told how biology revision involved wearing an apron, drawing on body parts and organs and naming them, and we observed a drama lesson where youngsters enthusiastically and earnestly discussed different ways of creating tension.

Not the place for heavyweight SEN but good, competent staff, cheerfully and successfully handle the bright child with processing or other difficulties. 'A school that says it does not have any youngsters with special needs is fooling itself,' says head, who takes a keen, informed interest in all. Learning

Support is positioned centre school and regularly accessed by a handful of pupils; 'We offer mentoring and support for youngsters with social or friendship issues as well as those with learning needs'. Only a handful enter school diagnosed with an SpLD but all are tested and monitored so the one or two per cent swell to four or five per cent by third form. Lots of mentoring to ensure those with spiky IQs achieve top grades. 'Most have managed in primary or prep school but may struggle when the text becomes dense. Cracks appear and we have to be there to support.' Help is centred around relieving stress and facilitating study skills. Speak of the 'gift of dyslexia' and how it enables the world to be seen in a different way.

Good, professional, helpful careers guidance starts in fourth form, reaching a crescendo in sixth. Any youngster aiming for Oxbridge or any of medicine, dentistry or veterinary science will be given abundant, specific, detailed assistance. 'My son was well prepared for his interview at Cambridge, they helped him prepare his personal statement and spent a long time covering all the bases so he knew what to expect: the types of questions, interview style, approach and technique.' Some parents would like to see greater focus on, and help with, work experience. 'It's fine for those who know what they want to do but can be tricky for those who aren't so sure.'

Games, options, the arts: All major games on offer plus sailing, squash, badminton, aerobics, golf, cross-country, athletics and table tennis. School owns a 400 acre farm – 'Woollams' – with 75 acres dedicated to first-rate pitches and courts plus two elegant and impressive pavilions, one 'boy-proof' and the other belonging to the energetic Old Albanians. Outstanding outdoor facilities are complemented by a state-of-the-art sports centre with good-sized climbing wall, fitness centre, dance studio, sports hall, swimming pool and even an endless pool with motion-capture technology to analyse style, strength, conditioning etc. Sport strong and plentiful with excellent coaching, and national and international sporting honours, plus numerous school representatives in county teams, across many sports. In the English Schools AA national cross-country championships, half the county senior team come from St Albans and the intermediate team are current national champions. School are 10 times winners of the King Henry VIII relays and recently notched up fourth place in the world cross-country championships. 'Coming here meant I could concentrate on my cricket as well as my academic studies.' Don't win all their matches (apparently head skims over defeats in assembly, while lauding wins) but school quick to drop schools they thrash, 'We want a good match, not a whitewash.' Some parents and pupils believe the sporting ethos dominates everything. 'It is hard for the younger lads who don't make top teams. It can be quite a challenging time for them and could be handled better.' School run C and even D teams but say there comes a point where some degree of competence is a necessity. Parents of the sporty say, 'Boys can feel under a lot of pressure to win yet they seem to cope'; those of sixth form girls say they are very much encouraged to have a go and try new things, take part.

Drama improving thanks to recent appointments bringing life, vitality and variation. Twice-weekly school service in the cathedral showcases excellent choral work which oft provides solace for the not-so-sporty. Music good and set to get better; a number play instruments to a high standard and school recently became a Steinway school. Creativity to the fore via DT (delivered in first-rate robotic suite) and impressive, creative art. Outdoor spirit and team-work fostered through robust and popular CCF and D of E; 'We offer activities to both groups,' say the leaders who work in a spirit of camaraderie and cooperation not competition. Army and air options available, though parents say RAF wing plays second fiddle to Coldstream Guards – despite the former offering opportunities to take off and fly! Boys kept busy with lunchtime clubs, games afternoons and training, yet younger, less sporty pupils say they'd like more – school insists there is plenty on offer for all. Trips for everything, to everywhere, including to Pen Arthur, a rugged farmhouse in rural Wales (owned by the school) and used for multifarious activities and field work, and triennial charity visits to an orphanage in Tanzania (one of many charitable ventures).

Background and atmosphere: A friendly, county school, rooted in the heart of a small city with a big village feel. The school was founded in 948, making it one of the oldest extant schools in the country, so ancient the first pupils did not speak English. Adjacent to the cathedral, school (but not The Cathedral School) has inherited many of the foundation's buildings plus some extraordinary rooms and nooks with Gothic windows and yard-thick walls. One such is home to the school's small museum. Busts and memorials to the school's venerable history abound and sit comfortably with all the accoutrements of a thoroughly modern educational environment. Fortuitous acquisition of Aquis Court building, (former home to KPMG) has allowed school to unzip and exhale. This light, well-kept, modern building provides much-needed space for art, with five studios including ceramics and kiln, sixth form centre with private study area and classrooms with other buildings nestling amid beautifully-kept gardens. Parents hope the expansion won't impact on the school's uniqueness; 'I love the fact older pupils can go into town for lunch, it is part of the community, doesn't feel remote and elite'. School may have a somewhat rarefied approach to academia, but they are passionate about enabling children from poorer backgrounds to share in the advantages of an independent school education, whether through programmes with primary schools, sport, masterclasses, inviting youngsters from local senior schools to join societies and talks or via bursaries and scholarships. Maintain strong links with local state schools; sixth formers mentor primary school children, with masterclasses in maths, sciences and drama just some of the outreach offerings.

Boarding went in the 1950s, direct grant in the 1970s – girls arrived in the sixth in 1991. Very much consensus that girly-girls might struggle amid the trail of testosterone. Parents say it is important to look at the character of your daughter, 'Will she enjoy being a girl in a boys' school?' Those who cross the threshold, (mainly from STAGS, the local state girls' school or local independent schools), love the competitive air and friendly disposition of the natives. Boys say, 'Presence of girls makes us mature fast!' but some girls not quite so magnanimous, 'Boys' banter can get irritating but we have our own space to retreat to should we wish.' Most staff work hard to ensure girls are fully integrated and involved, though parents say there remain some staff who don't quite get the nuances of teaching girls.

Pastoral care and discipline: Carefully structured horizontal tutorial system plus prefects, a full-time school nurse and two heads of sixth-form reflect the importance given to pupil support. 'The school nurtures your talent, they sow seeds, feed and water, enabling it to flourish but if you don't have a strength you may struggle,' say boys. Parents say care has softened in recent years but discipline and boundaries still to the fore, 'They go out of their way to help boys get things right. School is a safe environment to make mistakes and to learn from them – as long as incidents aren't too serious or frequent.' Random drugs testing used 'on good grounds' and in coordination with home. Head has expelled for drugs and stealing and would again. School is disciplined and orderly, with clear boundaries. We witnessed usual boisterous, boyish behaviour at break – messing in corridors, pushing and shoving but school hope a new common room for juniors will improve things. Sixth-formers treated with respect and the grown-up facilities, including an on-site Starbucks complete with cappuccino, frappuccino or whatever froth you fancy, the envy of staff, many of whom drop by for coffee – civilised indeed!

Pupils and parents: Pupil body representative of the 'catchment area', over 70 per cent per cent from local Herts area and about half of those from St Albans itself. The rest, including a good number of Jewish pupils, from north London, mostly from Enfield. A smaller number from other ethnic minorities or families where the first lang is not English. School works hard to integrate girls but it remains steadfastly a male environment, attracting the capable, robust, feisty female into the sixth form. Ambitious children, ambitious parents, 'Though elbows not quite as sharp as at some schools within the M25,' says head. Parents mostly professional, business, cultural with many first-time buyers of independent education plus a handful on income support or whose children would otherwise qualify for free school meals. Social balance is largely unchanged from the direct grant days, but typically parents place high-value on a good education. Very strong Old Albanians, many of whom send their sons here and, later, their daughters. Only 13 schools have produced more Fellows of the British Academy and Royal Society. Notable former pupils go back to the year dot but recent ones include Sir Tim Rice, archaeologist Lord Renfrew, film producer Mike Newell, General Sir Richard Lawson and Prof Stephen Hawking.

Entrance: A seriously oversubscribed school for high flyers. IQ of 125+ at 11+ and 127+ at 13+ (say discrepancy is due to tutoring, not innate ability). At 11, tests in English, maths and VR and interviews, all on the same day. At 13, apply early, conditional offers made following psychometric assessment in Y7; late-comers compete for the few remaining places. Tests as at 11+: three interviews and entry dependent on CE results. Around 90 applicants for 40+ places at 16 – with minimum grade A required in A level subjects.

Exit: A commendable 88 per cent take up places at their first choice university. Impressive list of subjects and destinations, large numbers read philosophy, economics or history at top universities such as Exeter, Nottingham, Warwick, York; equally large numbers read maths, engineering, sciences at Bristol, Durham, Imperial, Leeds, UCL, et al. Up to a dozen medics, with 15 or so to Oxbridge, in a spread of disciplines – all testament to a broad and serious education.

Money matters: Scholarships, for absolute excellence, worth 10-20 per cent of fees awarded on the basis of performance in the entrance tests at 11 and by separate exam at 13 and 16. Choral scholarships by audition at 11+. Bursaries for instrumental tuition from 11 and for art. Currently 125 bursaries, 24 full-fees remission. Bursary funds equivalent to five full fees pa allocated by combination of need and merit so if top three pupils require 100 per cent bursary there will be little left for anyone else, but school usually manages to offer something to almost all who need it.

Remarks: Work hard, play hard, very much academia first, sport a close second. A serious school with strong, confident leadership, structured discipline and a can-do, will-do attitude; unwavering in its demands for high standards from all. A good alternative to pressured London day schools (20 minutes from St Pancras) but only for the genuinely very able.

S

St Aloysius' College

Linked school: St Aloysius' College Junior School

---

45 Hill Street, Garnethill, Glasgow, G3 6RJ

• Pupils: 830 boys and girls in senior school, all day; roughly 50/50 boys/girls • Ages: 11–18 • RC • Fees: £7,200–£9,648 pa • Independent

---

Tel: 01413 323190
Email: admissions@staloysius.org
Website: www.staloysius.org

Head Master: Since September 2013 Mr John Browne, previously deputy head of Ampleforth College. He has also been head of Westminster Cathedral School and director/assistant director of music at Berkhamsted School and The Latymer School. He is married to Marie and they have one son.

Academic matters: The Jesuit approach to education is summed up as 'improvement in living and learning to the greater glory of God and the common good'. In practice this means educational rigour. Breadth in S1 and 2 includes French and Latin for all as well as three separate sciences fitted in by having a term of each. S3 and 4 offer Intermediate II in core subjects with everyone taking a language and a science (no general science but biology most popular by a small margin and a reasonable take up of more than the minimum of one). Italian and Spanish, no German but product design, economics. Music, PE, econ and business studies all available at Higher and Advanced Higher as well as the usual suspects. Some pretty spectacular Int II results recently in English and maths, also the sciences and art. French and art shine at Higher and chemistry and biology most popular at Advanced Higher. St Aloysius, being independent, is able to hang on to Intermediate II for the present despite SQA's changes. (Previously St Aloysius simply omitted S grades leaving the vital Highers as pupils' first exam experience.)

State-of-the-art labs with lofty urban views in the award-winning but controversial Clavius building, which also has extensive IT suites. Despite their streamlined design they look lived in, and staff are enthusiastic and friendly. Clavius, named after a 15th century Jesuit astronomer, typifies St Aloysius' approach: up to date technology and teaching imbued with an aura of history and the sacred. Staff report an increased interest in science and maths courses at uni. Economics and business studies are also popular, and a sixth former reported attending a conference of Jesuit school formers on Catholic social teaching had been useful for both subjects.

SEN is taken very seriously for an essentially academic school with a team of four specialist teachers and several classroom assistants. Lots of expertise and knowledgeable innovation is lavished in this area using Glasgow's pool of experience, as well as technology and personal mentoring.

Games, options, the arts: A rugby school, though, like any team it has its ups and downs, at best being up among the top schools. Girls enthusiastic about hockey and cross-country. Large multi-purpose gym in former convent building with serious-looking fitness equipment used for training teams. Not much space on site though three playgrounds are jigsawed in among the streets and buildings which cling to the top of a fearsome hill. Extensive rugby pitches are a longish bus ride away in the direction of Stirling, hockey pitches have been added and Astroturf is on its way.

Exceptionally good art department in the old 'Mount' building – particularly striking was a very sophisticated architecture project for a hospital physio department with rib-like supports based on the 'simple and effective' human framework. Plenty of Macs – a whole room of them for design work. Oodles of boys (few girls) working at product design in their lunch hour, which is used for a plentiful choice of activities: chess, debating etc together with the usual field for a school with academic ambition, but also a few oddballs such as Manga cartoon creation (on computers), girls' football and heraldry. Lots of sport after school and matches at weekends. Skiing trips evidently very popular but equally a full range of exchanges, cultural trips etc. D of E and outdoor education in plenty with John Muir activities (mini D of E) for younger children

Music shares the Mount with art and drama. Choirs and orchestra expect 90 per cent attendance and are flourishing. Instrumental teaching rooms sport a huge range of music computers for seniors as well as music teaching centre for the junior school.

As might be expected the school is very charity conscious, with pupils helping on Lourdes pilgrimages for the sick and handicapped, working with disabled children and supporting local initiatives. During our visit a scrumptious-looking cake sale in aid of Salt and Light, a Glasgow non-conformist charity, was in enthusiastic progress. The school's ethos encourages helping with Jesuit and other initiatives abroad, both as gap years and in later life.

Background and atmosphere: From 1859-2004 the school was run and mainly staffed by the Jesuits, who still live next door and are visibly around in school. A gradual transition to lay staff was completed by the appointment of the first lay head in 2004, but all the key posts in school are still held by practising Catholics. The adjoining St Ignatius church is used for full school masses, though there is a smaller chapel with daily mass before school, attended by a few pupils normally and quite full in Lent. Crucifixes in every classroom, frequent reminders in form of saintly statues or portraits in almost every stair turn and corner, plus the requirement to write AMDG (Latin initials 'for the greater glory of God') on every piece of work presented, means pupils are constantly reminded of their faith.

The main building in Garnethill, a once particularly insalubrious sector of Glasgow, was the original Jesuit house. A handsome stone mansion perched on a precipitous hill. Inside it is opulent but institutional, with a wide square stairwell under a lofty atrium surrounded by black and while paved landings. Solid oak doors lead to the series of small libraries, the head's office and sixth form workrooms, which once accommodated the brothers. In the neighbouring teaching space, polished red lino and dark wood reinforces the institutional feel, which pervades most of the more modern, well-equipped but definitely functional teaching spaces. It's pretty spick and span, despite acres of book-strewn bright blue lockers everywhere. The rear half of the newest Clavius building has a multi-purpose hall for extra dining space, lectures and the occasional class mass. Open at one side to an outdoor seating area, this is several stories high but not quite big enough to make the building feel spacious. It seems a curious use of space, as the two stairways are so narrow that a one way up, the other down, system operates. The startling Clavius and the slightly older junior school building are still seen as 'sore thumbs' in an area graced by a Rennie McIntosh Art School and other gracious piles.

Strict uniform rules are adhered to – not a tie sagging or shirt untucked! Very dark green blazers and grey trousers or below the knee box-pleated grey skirts, 'pretty comfortable', for the girls. S6 are distinguished by smart ribbon trim and special jerseys while games colours etc are edgings on the embroidered pockets.

Pastoral care and discipline: The change from a house pastoral system to year heads and form tutors has not been uniformly popular, though our S6 guide thought it worked. Discipline is strict. Expulsion has been used, though 'only as last resort'. No in-school problems with drugs, and out of school, 'it's the parents responsibility, though we try to give every possible support'.

Mobiles taken for granted as necessary and not a problem in school, though dangers of Facebook bullying etc are to the fore in the social programme provided. The school community 'forms a safe haven in which pupils take their teachers' concern for granted and know their mistakes mean trouble but not rejection'. Huge emphasis on weighing the evidence before making moral or other decisions, supplemented by plentiful talks on current issues – devolution, gay marriage etc always presenting all points of view. Questioned on the sensitive issue of child abuse in Catholic schools, head was certain that there had been no instance in the rememberable past.

Pupils say the canteen food is good, and S6 who are allowed out into the city prefer cheaper school food and a chat in the common-room. They can come into school from crack of dawn and the canteen is open, though not after school when clubs, extra tuition and homework clubs run until 6pm.

Pupils and parents: Some 95 per cent are Catholic, the highest in any UK independent school, and the remainder, Greek or Russian orthodox, Episcopalian or Muslim, the only proviso being that they accept the school pattern of Catholic activities. Being dead centre in the city gives better access to Catholics from all round (Glaswegians don't cross the city) and also to some who come from Edinburgh on the train to Queen's Street, a quick walk or taxi ride away.

Lots of loyal alumni keeping in touch. Parents exceptionally supportive of school ethos.

Entrance: School claims 'to admit pupils in the top half of the general population. Seventy-five per cent of our pupils come from the top quarter of the population' – we are talking academically here. Priority given to practising Catholics and those who 'share the aims and values of Jesuit education'. More-or-less automatic transfer from the junior school. Active sibling policy. Assessment by tests but previous school reports, school reference (and preferably one from the parish priest) are all taken into account. If pupils transfer from another independent school, St Aloysius checks that there are no outstanding fees as well as getting a reference!

Exit: Fewer now leave after Highers (S5) as uni entry on Highers alone is getting tougher – though 25 per cent still go straight on to uni from S5. The vast majority to Scottish unis with Newcastle and Oxbridge – a few each year – being the only real alternatives.

Lots do work experience and good works abroad in gap years.

Money matters: The school receives no state funding – not even, apparently, for classroom assistants for those with a record of needs, which is odd. The original Jesuit concept was that their role was to educate free and the school has a certain amount of funding available. Parents are asked whether they need bursarial help at the time of application, almost automatic for families on income support, plus family discounts, but no named or dedicated bursaries. School does what it can to help. Will also try and help out if family hits financial crisis but with the usual strictures – parents must be upfront about the extent of their problems.

Remarks: A quintessentially Catholic school, with a strong academic tradition still closely attached to its Jesuit roots. St Aloysius is not afraid to combine modern thinking and technology with the best of old fashioned Catholic values. It's out on a limb from the rest of Scottish education, but dedicated to giving a rigorous academic, personal and spiritual grounding to its pupils.

St Ambrose College

Hale Road, Hale Barns, Altrincham, Cheshire, WA15 0HE

• Pupils: 940 boys; • Ages: 11–18; • Roman Catholic; • State

Tel: 01619 802711
Email: office@st-ambrosecollege.org.uk
Website: www.st-ambrosecollege.org.uk

Headmaster: Since 2000, Michael D Thompson, MA (Keele), FRSA, Cert Ed (London), NPQH. Married, son in sixth form. Widely experienced, from inner-city comprehensives ('needed to experience the deep end') to all girls' grammar school run by nuns, he's done it all. Mathematics and theology are his thing, but also keen on sport, especially climbing. Yorkshire born, straightforward, unfailingly modest, quietly spoken, a rare mix of commercial acumen and sound, spiritual heart – honest to his core, and highly respected and adored by the boys in equal measure; they describe him as 'inspirational'.

Academic matters: Selective on intake, boys are able, highly motivated and supported by parents with high aspirations for their sons. Consistently high-achieving school, value-added especially good. In 2013, 71 per cent A*-A grades at A level; at GCSE 98 per cent A*-C, 48 per cent A*/A. Sciences, maths and ICT especially strong, unsurprisingly, and English/English Lit flying high also at GCSE. Sets for maths and science. Average class size 28, pupil:teacher ratio 20:1.

Decidedly and unashamedly traditional and academic, no vocational subjects here and no media studies. All boys take a minimum of nine GCSEs at the end of the fifth year. Boy-friendly infrastructure and teaching styles. High in value-added across the board, academically and socially. Way ahead of most schools in use of technology, scrapped whiteboards in favour of graphics tablets and podcasting. Teachers offer on-line support as needed after hours.

Multi-media language labs for French, Spanish and Latin, Italian society also available. Enriching language trips overseas – Le Mans 24 hour race track especially popular. Overseas work experience also on offer for sixth formers. New building widening curriculum opportunities for expanding technology, drama and cooking.

Distance learning with universities an option to challenge the most able, online tutorials changing, revitalising and transferring knowledge through a wide range of opportunities.

Very small number of statemented boys, one member of staff assigned to support SEN.

Games, options, the arts: 'Competitive, testosterone-fuelled house events,' say the boys, whilst adding the party line that 'it's not the winning but the taking part that counts'. Lots of sport and big rivalry in rugby, cricket and athletics, especially if opponents are in Liverpool. Athletics under-15 side are Trafford champions; under-15 rugby side reached quarter finals of Daily Mail Vase; under-16s county rugby union winners; two pupils playing rugby for national under-16 and under-18 sides. Wow-factor facilities in the new building include superb sports hall and pool and there is no shortage of outdoor space – boys kicking, throwing, passing balls everywhere, and staff joining in. Soccer, cross-country, basketball, table tennis, badminton also available. Sports teams tour widely – Barbados, Vancouver, South Africa, Italy, Holland, Australia, South America, New Zealand, Fiji, Hong Kong and USA.

Music suite and well-stocked library; the school is generously resourced, hard to think of something they don't have. Plenty of extra-curricular activities on offer; D of E strong.

Boys are actively involved in the liturgical life of the school: assemblies, prayer groups and Holy Mass are regularly celebrated.

Background and atmosphere: Christian Brothers' Roman Catholic boys' grammar school with selective intake. Founded by the De La Salle Brothers in 1940, after evacuating Guernsey, taken over by the Irish Christian Brothers in 1946; Blessed Edmund Ignatius Rice still at its core. Awarded maths and computing specialist college status in 2005; rated outstanding by both Ofsted and the Catholic Diocese of Shrewsbury in recent inspections. Long-standing traditions and high aspirations, both academically and spiritually, all housed in newly built (2012) state-of-the-art facilities.

No official catchment area; boys come from a 30 mile radius and full range of social spread of intake, right across the board, and proudly so. Boys from Moss Side rub shoulders with sons of multi-millionaires, but nobody really cares too much. Much opportunity for reflection away from the college: annual trip to sister college in Sierre Leone, much hard work and fund-raising involved, including work in slums and on rubbish tips, this is no holiday; first year boys enjoy a retreat at St Cassians during their first few weeks; older students head to Myddleton Grange and provide regular assistance at Cornerstone, the Christian Brothers' project to help disadvantaged and vulnerable homeless people. Sixth formers join Old Boys on visits to Lourdes, a profoundly deep and lasting experience for all involved. Looking after the margins of society deemed important: strong links with Revive, a refuge for asylum seekers in Salford – 'in some cases silence is dangerous', Saint Ambrose. Very clear on the reason why: 'it's not about you feeling better, it's about someone else feeling better because of what you have done,' says the head. And they live out that message here.

Four college houses led by student house captains.

Pastoral care and discipline: Consciences worked on rather than harsh restrictions imposed, underpinned by Christian values. Emphasis on self-discipline and taking responsibility for your own actions. Rewards are age-appropriate and poor behaviour is quickly checked and fairly and duly punished. House points can be won for academic excellence and any activity which can be defined as service.

School community takes its model from the family, and rewards and disciplines accordingly, 'fairly' say the boys – 'behave yourself, work hard and wear your uniform, everything else is negotiable'. An all-boys' school that speaks comfortably about the importance of valuing people and relationships is a breath of fresh air – here are articulate young men who genuinely value being 'a part of something' – they live it, they breathe it, they feel it, happy to quote rugby statistics one minute and the words of St Ambrose the next. They smile when referring to 'their Holy Trinity' – food/rugby/chapel (though not necessarily in that order).

Pupils and parents: Parents and boys are from a wide range of backgrounds, professional/local business/self-starters/trades. Current parents appreciate 'the high morale and catholic standards which it upholds and works into daily activities' and the fact that the 'sporting facilities are second to none and allow boys to excel in their chosen sporting activity'. The 'caring and compassionate approach' is also of high value to boys and their parents as delivered by 'highly qualified, committed, caring teachers and staff, as well as high standards of discipline'.

The new building has taken longer than expected to complete, and whilst some parents bemoan that fact as their sons are at the tail end of their academic career now, they are immensely proud of the school's advancement from tired old premises and know that their boys have 'had a great time and done extremely well' regardless. 'Classrooms do not maketh the man' apparently – though the stunning new buildings will have quite an impact, not only award-winning architecturally but also in bringing the school's hopes, dreams and aspirations together.

Former pupils include king of skiffle Lonnie Donegan MBE, graphic designers Peter Saville and Malcolm Garrett, Damien Hinds MP, Paul Maynard MP, Greg Mulholland MP, Keith Breeden Royal Society of Portrait Painters, Martin Baker organist and master of music at Westminster Cathedral, Dr Kieran Moriarty CBE consultant gastroenterologist.

Long established Old Ambrosians and Parents' Association.

Entrance: Most enter at 11 via competitive entrance exam comprising verbal reasoning, English and maths tests, taking top 30 per cent of ability range. Admissions policy includes lengthy and detailed over-subscription criteria as demand for places is high and school is invariably over-subscribed. Boys come from a plethora of schools, most notably its own – St Ambrose Prep School.

Exit: About two-thirds stay on into sixth form; new boys join and add to the numbers. Pupils are well-taught and well-advised and most proceed to good universities, a number to Oxbridge each year (one in 2013).

Money matters: Some funds available for uniforms, lunches, transport as necessary.

Remarks: First and foremost a Catholic school with a Catholic ethos, strong and clear convictions that sing through the hearts and minds of both staff and boys.

St Bede's College

Linked school: St Bede's College Prep School

Alexandra Park, Manchester, M16 8HX

- Pupils: 825 co-ed • Ages: 11-19 • RC • Fees: £6,360-£9,450 pa
- Independent

Tel: 01612 263323
Email: enquiries@stbedescollege.co.uk
Website: www.stbedescollege.co.uk

Headmaster: Since 2011, Mr Daniel Kearney BA, following the abrupt and somewhat mysterious departure of Mr Michael Barber who was head from 2008. Mr Kearney joined St Bede's as head of religion in 2001 and became deputy head in 2008. Has also taught at Portsmouth Grammar and the King's School, Macclesfield. Focus on a 'return to traditional behaviour' and discipline.

Academic matters: Strong academic results; pupils are expected to work hard. Class size 26 maximum with an average of 20, smaller in the sixth form. Setting in maths and statistics to stretch the more able (with IGCSE introduced in 2010). Broad range of subjects includes classics, politics and business studies; religious education is compulsory throughout the school though, in the sixth form, the approach is less formal and pupils enjoy discussion groups. In 2013, 70 per cent A*-B grades at A level. A healthy age and gender mix of staff.

DT (the proud recipient of many awards) and art have excellent facilities and display impressive creations. Science labs are being gradually updated and nevertheless produce robust results. The multimedia language lab is impressive and fully computerised. IT facilities good, computers abound, linked to the school's intranet. Impressive, newly refurbished, Maher library with approachable and knowledgeable librarian. Open after school and during the holidays in the run up to exams.

Games, options, the arts: Games compulsory throughout the school. Football achieves notable success, being previous finalists in the Boodle and Dunthorne Independent Schools' Football Association Cup and Greater Manchester county champions. Netball is strong but rugby, hockey, cricket, athletics and tennis are also offered. Floodlit all-weather surface.

S

Plenty of extra-curricular activities from chess to robotics. Sports and studies are enhanced by foreign tours, field trips, pilgrimage to Lourdes etc. Less than expected uptake of individual music tuition possibly due to costs involved for many. Nonetheless there's an orchestra, a concert band and choirs.

Background and atmosphere: Founded in 1875 by Cardinal Vaughan, the school moved to its present site in 1877, taking over the buildings of the Manchester Aquarium, and has since expanded onto an adjoining site separated by a quiet road. Originally a boys' Catholic grammar school, it became direct grant but reverted to independence in 1976. Girls were admitted from 1984. Traditionally, the school served the local inner city area but now draws pupils from a 25 mile radius encompassing a wide social spectrum. The Christian spirit is omnipresent but not, according to pupils, repressive; there's an atmosphere of mutual respect and warmth with excellent pupil-teacher interaction.

Pastoral care and discipline: Pupils comment on the excellent provision of pastoral care. All pupils have a member of staff to whom they can turn and peer support is available, though this is not formalised. Clear moral framework; pupil behaviour is good with very little bullying, theft etc.

Pupils and parents: Majority white British or Irish with a number of first and second generation African children who have settled in Manchester. The social mix is broad, in line with the school's ethos. Pupils are courteous to each other and staff, polite and hard working. Uniform is worn throughout the school, with 'office wear' in the sixth form.

Entrance: 11+ selection is by examination and interview. The interview is of particular importance for those children from inner city state schools who have not been 'prepped' for the entrance exam and is aimed to spot potential. Sixth form admission requires seven GCSEs.

Exit: On average eight per year to Oxbridge. Other top redbrick universities are the most popular for the remainder, to follow a broad spectrum of courses.

Money matters: One third of pupils receiving financial assistance from the bursary fund.

Remarks: An excellent choice for committed Catholics seeking an academic education within a Christian environment. 'I cannot recommend St Bede's too highly,' comments one such parent. A fantastic opportunity for bright young Catholics from underprivileged homes.

St Bees School

Linked school: St Bees School Prep Department

S

St Bees, Cumbria, CA27 0DS

• Pupils: 345 boys and girls; 100 boarders, the rest day • Ages: 11–18 • C of E • Fees: Day £12,315–£15,885; Boarding £12,315–£29,995 pa • Independent

Tel: 01946 828010
Email: admissions@st-bees-school.co.uk
Website: www.st-bees-school.org

Headmaster: Since September 2012, Mr James Davies BMus(Hons), ACertCM, LGSM, FASC, PGCE. Joined St Bees from Kings' School in Tynemouth where he was deputy head.

Academic matters: Broad range, from special learning unit to top scores at A level. Purposely not a hothouse; small class sizes, individual attention, staff on hand for additional reinforcement. Much satisfaction over Ds and Es turned into Cs and above. 'Each pupil is given every opportunity to do their best,' says one satisfied parent, whose boy and girl have blossomed in confidence with support, positive encouragement and by being treated as individuals. GCSE – generally over 40 per cent at A and A* (43 per cent in 2013) with Latin and statistics offered and IT, French and Spanish taught in innovative Management Centre (see below). In 2013 43 per cent gained A*/A at A level. Usual small school constraints on A level choices but mathematics and sciences very popular, a number go on to science and engineering related degrees.

Pupils assessed prior to or on arrival by Learning Support Unit (LSU) which is CReSTeD registered and staffed with equivalent of 1.5 full-time teachers. Any individual support identified is provided in LSU by qualified staff at an additional charge.

International Centre offers specialist EFL plus general courses for one year for 26 overseas students aged 11-16 – doubtless a necessary boost to boarding numbers. Many now from mainland China but work in progress to widen intake. Most join St Bees after basic course though some return home or transfer to other UK schools. All international pupils integrated into existing boarding houses and add a new dimension to the local community. Cumbria goes global!

Games, options, the arts: Space is not a restriction as games fields abound everywhere in stunning 150-acre site. Rugby strong, particularly sevens, with competitions and fixtures against north west independent and state schools. Recent success coming second in group stages of the National Schools Sevens tournament, the world's biggest sevens competition. Girls' sport also good, hockey played off campus on local Astroturf pitch. Large sports hall, squash and fives courts. Much PE teaching mixed. Golf academy with smart technology and newly laid putting green. School owns 60-acre nine-hole golf course on headland, shared with locals. Czech Republic athletics star got pupils up and running for track and field success. Traditional swimming pool available to all pupils. 'Everyone is encouraged to give sport a go,' said one parent 'and many who do not consider themselves sporty are surprised to find an activity they enjoy.'

Bracing sea air and proximity to unspoiled part of Lake District mean outdoor activities are taken seriously. Adventure training much enjoyed part of curriculum for first two years of senior school. CCF for all aged 13-15; hosts annual weekend known as Bega Banga, military skills competition for all north west CCF/ACFcontingents. D of E greatly encouraged, considered to have 'international currency'.

Artwork displays everywhere; sixth form follow a broad syllabus allowing them to focus on their particular genre, working in a mezzanine garret, authentic except for the lack of good, natural light. Drama lively with productions in dated school hall, music fizzing; refurbished music centre with soundproof hi-tech recording studio in basement – many instrumental groups, choir sings in chapel and village priory church. Outreach to local primary schools through musical roadshows.

Library – a quiet haven in the heart of the school complete with small IT area. More integration with curriculum would increase use as a learning resource centre and bring a buzz to what should be a focal point in the school.

Background and atmosphere: Founded as a grammar school in 1583; original schoolroom now a dining hall with past pupils' names carved on wall panels. Handsome Victorian additions in local sandstone spread over fine site 'between the sea and the sheep'.

Well integrated with St Bees village, where pupils wander freely but need to be on their mettle when crossing the road from the school to the music house – though traffic calming measures are on the way. Thanks to Sellafield, there is still a regular train service used by some day pupils, though an extensive school bus service covers a 15 mile radius.

Girls admitted since 1976, so a proper co-educational school. Girls' houses in attractive terrace on the far side of useful local railway (footbridge), senior boys in two houses, one in the same building as the head's residence. Accommodation homely, clean and comfortable with shared rooms in the junior houses, pairing weekly and full boarders where possible. Warm and caring house parents, the majority with an academic role as well. Prep completed in house and report 'effort grades' determine whether a pupil is supervised or allowed to study independently. Real family feel with sixth formers having a role in the junior houses and all day pupils being assigned to a house – all the benefits of vertical integration. Small year group of boys – 'it's not a problem,' said one day boy, 'I'm just friendly with the boys in the year above'. All new staff have boarding house duties.

The Management Centre, an unusual and successful joint venture – in demand commercially as a conference centre in the week (primarily nuclear and related industries) and by the school at evenings and weekends. One mum commented that her son was thriving in the environment and said that, "he would have sunk without trace in the local comprehensive'.

There's a general air about the school of unhurried but purposeful activity. Pupils are encouraged to try everything, the size of school makes that possible and instils a real 'can do' philosophy. The aim is for pupils to leave 'well balanced, with a sense of purpose and know how to occupy their time'. Various efforts to overcome inescapable sense of isolation and expose pupils to more urban ways eg trips abroad, visits to Stratford, Chester and Edinburgh, lecture programme, Oxbridge taster visit. Leavers' Christmas Sixth Form Ball a high point of social calendar.

Pastoral care and discipline: Housemaster/housemistress plus tutorial system. Day pupils affiliated to appropriate boarding house, helps integration, particularly with International Centre pupils. Flexi-boarding encouraged.

Twenty-three male, 21 female staff, though senior management skewed to male. Discipline not really an issue here – claim that in a small 'family' school no one slips through the net seems reasonable. Backed up by 'on the ball' auxillary staff eg kitchen staff notice if someone isn't eating properly.

'Centralised matrons', male and female GP team, counsellor on call. Not much real naughtiness in this quiet backwater; guidelines are clear, pupils seem content with traditional discipline. Drug supplying or sex mean the sack.

Pupils and parents: Many local, increasingly as day pupils due to downturn in Lakes tourist industry; foreign nationals more in evidence further up the school, majority Chinese. Extensive private bus system ferries day pupils to and from distances up to 45 minutes drive away; boarders picked up at nearest airports.

Pupils refreshingly open, perhaps a touch unsophisticated – most well turned out in formal uniform, frank and unaffected in manner, earnest to give a positive account of their school experience. Many boys and girls attracted to St Bees because of greater chance of representing school in multifarious activities. Swamped in a large state school, easy to make a fresh start here.

School forum where parents, staff and governors exchange views, held twice yearly and well attended by parents from all parts of the school. Very active parents' association – events like Proms on the Crease, musical finale to speech day. Parents very supportive (some allow their names to be used in prospectus for potential parents to telephone – what a good idea); Cumbrian farmers and professionals, local industrialists (Sellafield with related business infrastructure, still provides huge employment). Rowan Atkinson a former pupil.

Entrance: Not selective – entrance examination up for review, main purpose to determine scholarships. SEN assessed, IQ rating needs to be average or above and International Centre students have to show realistic level of competence. Two-form entry, mainly from state schools (no local independent school competition) and preparatory department, topped up at 13 and 16. Prep department augments numbers.

Exit: Nearly all to higher education (little fall-out after GCSE); a sprinkling to Oxbridge (one in 2013), mainly to a wide range of old and new universities usually out of north west as pupils keen to spread their wings. Leavers' list shows a broad balance between arts and science subjects, with an increasing number of engineers.

Money matters: Bursaries ranging from £500 per annum to 100 per cent of fees awarded on a means-tested basis to over 30 per cent of pupils currently. Academic scholarships range similarly, available at 11+ and 13+. Music scholarships awarded at 11+, 13+ and 16+, art and sports awards post-16 for exceptional ability.

Remarks: Size does matter and everyone here does too; endless care taken over individuals. Good school with strong reputation locally. Palpable atmosphere of security and friendliness in beautiful surroundings. Facing 21st century by introducing change whilst maintaining traditional values and cherishing ethos.

St Benedict's School

Linked school: St Benedict's Junior School

54 Eaton Rise, London, W5 2ES

- Pupils: 770 pupils, all day. Fully co-ed since 2008 • Ages: 11–18
- RC • Fees: £13,350 pa • Independent

Tel: 020 8862 2254
Email: enquiries@stbenedicts.org.uk
Website: www.stbenedicts.org.uk

Headmaster: Since 2002, Mr Christopher Cleugh (rhymes with rough) BSc MSc (late fifties). Read chemistry at Hull. Resonant Liverpool accent ('I prefer Everton' he says), he grew up and taught on Merseyside until he came here. Educated at St Mary's Crosby where he returned as a teacher for 17 years (by the time he left he was deputy head). Went on to become head of St Anselm's in Birkenhead for eight years, before moving south to run St Benedict's, which felt fated: 'I remember the day I saw the advert,' he says. Married with two sons and two daughters – his wife is head of a Catholic primary school in Acton, his first grandchild is a pupil in the junior school here. Utterly unpretentious and forthright, Mr Cleugh is a keen sports fan and loves his cricket and football. Warm and humorous, one nevertheless detects steel beneath the avuncular surface.

Only the second lay headmaster since the school was founded, Mr Cleugh is a practising Catholic and a firm believer in co-education – 'in the modern world it's the right way forward. It's a co-ed world out there and this is the natural preamble to it,' he says, adding that there's 'all sorts of nonsense about which environment produces the best academic performance, but at the end of the day it's nothing to do with single sex or co-education – it's the way they're taught and how you instil confidence and self discipline.'

You know where you are with this head, who is not afraid to risk unpopularity for the good of the community, and is a man of quiet but total conviction. Knows, and knows about, all his pupils, and has a sensitive understanding of their concerns.

S

Much loved by parents and pupils alike – 'he's always around'; 'easy to talk to'; 'makes time for everyone'; ' you can talk to him about anything – he never makes you feel uncomfortable' is the resounding message. Mr Cleugh unequivocal too about his favourite thing about the job – the children.

Academic matters: Respectable results, especially bearing in mind the school is not highly selective academically. Seventy-three per cent A*/B grades at A level in 2013, 44 per cent A*/A. However, a starry place in league tables is not what they're about, Mr Cleugh is keen to point out, and what he cares most about is that each child fulfils his or her potential. Among the 73 per cent who got A*s, As and Bs there would have been a number who would have fallen by the wayside in a more pressured environment. A good range of GCSE subjects on offer with everyone taking RS. RS curriculum largely RC in content and other faiths learned about in PSHE. History, maths and chemistry most popular subjects at A level. Record GCSE results in 2011 with 57 per cent A* or A grades, down to 53 per cent in 2013. Modern languages reasonably popular and take place in swanky new language labs in the new £6.2 million development.

Wheelchair access throughout the school (lifts and ramps) means they have been able to accommodate a number of children with severe physical disabilities. Three children in the school currently have statements, including one with cerebral palsy and one paraplegic. 'As long as I feel they would be happy I will take them,' says head, who is keen to emphasise his inclusive approach. Full time SENCo who occasionally withdraws pupils from lessons but prefers to provide in-class support as well and extra time pre- and post-school. Lots of support given to children with their organisational skills and the SEN room provides a useful base for children who need more help. Very positive noises from parents about the caring and supportive approach of the school to a whole range of special needs. At the other end of the spectrum, a Gifted and Talented Coordinator runs a programme through the curriculum, but also does a lot outside.

Excellent ICT facilities. The subject is well taught and IT skills used extensively in other areas including art and music.

Games, options, the arts: Rugby is huge here. It's the main winter sport (they don't play football, nor do they row, and it's not the place for your son if he's mad about ballet) and school recently ranked the top rugby school in the country (currently slipped to fourth but we suspect not for long). Tours to Dubai, Japan and New Zealand. Girls as keen to perform as well as the boys. Netball tours to Sri Lanka and Barbados. Full size Astroturf pitch completed in 2011. Cricket, athletics, rounders and tennis in the summer. School uses 14 acres of playing fields in Perivale about a mile away and plays hard, winning more than losing. Games staff everywhere – proper professionals in their matching coaching kit.

Onsite sports hall, sparkling multi-gym and fitness centre as well as fencing salle and dance studio. Fencing a major sports option with regular fixtures against other schools. Basketball, volleyball and yoga are also offered.

Less than world-class pupils appreciate the school's attitude to sports – 'everyone's given a chance,' said one in heartfelt tones, having experienced the 'if you're not in the first team you're nobody' syndrome elsewhere.

Music strong and there's a huge variety – a symphony orchestra, lots of singing – four choirs (strongly influenced by the Abbey choir), jazz band, big band, swing band, string ensembles and brass groups. (Almost) everyone gets involved at some stage and one parent remarked on how well talent is spotted and nurtured. Excellent facilities, three grand pianos and lots of uprights in tip top condition. An IT lab is dedicated to music, posters of Led Zeppelin and the Beatles decorate the walls, lots of computers equipped with piano keyboards.

Exciting art. Intensely imaginative, disciplined and creative sculptures are dotted around the school and spectacular oil paintings adorn the reception area. IT facilities dedicated to art in the attractive one-storey modern art/DT block. Before – and after – school study supervision in the library on offer, and over 80 clubs which include karate, history society, CCF, D of E, Saint Vincent de Paul charity fund-raising, debating and current affairs. One boy keen to point out that if you want to do something new, school will make it happen.

Background and atmosphere: Founded in 1902 by the monks of Downside Abbey, St Benedict's is the only Benedictine day school in the country. Its sister schools are Worth, Downside and Ampleforth which, like St Benedict's, have all recently started to take girls all the way through. (There have been girls in the sixth form here since the 1970s, from year 7 since 2008). The Roman Catholic faith is evident in every aspect of the atmosphere and the environment of the school, its publications, its ethos, yet almost half the pupils in the senior school are not Catholic. Eighty-five-ish per cent are Christian including those from other denominations, and you will find Muslims, Sikhs, Hindus, and Jews. The only condition is that they must respect the Catholic faith and take part in the regular masses that take place throughout the school year.

The buildings are a mix of un-gloomy Victorian red-brick and various 20th century extensions, additions and blocks – some of which are wearing better than others. The Cloisters, a stunning development costing £6.2 million, is the first thing you come to as you enter the school and has the same contemporary feel as some of the underground stations on the Jubilee line. Smooth concrete walls, aesthetic balconies, quadrangles and colonnades, an imaginative foil to the glorious abbey, which is situated across the playground and adjacent to the junior school. Whole school mass is said in the warm and totally unforbidding abbey, but smaller class mass is said in the intimate chapel in the modern Cloisters development – stunningly light and bright with a large window in the shape of a cross taking up most of the ceiling.

A generation of trust in the Benedictine ethos of respect for each other, and an unquestioned local reputation for quite exceptional pastoral care, have been battered by a storm of revelations, the most recent relating to 2007. See the website for the report of an inquiry, commissioned by the school's trustees and conducted by Lord Carlile (who we rate as unquestionably independent). The school tells us that it has fully implemented his recommendations. It is now fully independent of the Abbey Trust; the governing body has a lay majority and a lay chair, whilst three members of the monastic community are governors and another three work at the school. It regularly reviews its safeguarding and child protection policies.

Against that background, parents and pupils pay tribute to the trouble taken over the smallest worry, and pupils feel supported and secure. Advent of girls throughout has also contributed to modernisation and a sense of opening up.

Pastoral care and discipline: Very strict – until the sixth form all children carry around a yellow card – reminiscent of the traditional satis cards (short for satisfecit – has he done enough?) in order that their behaviour – good and bad – can be constantly monitored. Parents are kept in the loop, they sign it each week and house points are affected. However, it's not inflexibly strict – 'first and foremost I'm a parent – I know children can get it wrong sometimes,' is Mr Cleugh's humane approach. Regular parent forums on, eg the dangers of ICT at home, 'I would ban Facebook if I had my way,' Mr Cleugh exclaims. He likes to keep the sixth form in at lunch time (though they can go out). There is so much to do here,' he says, 'plus there are a few too many muggings in Ealing'.

Pupils and parents: 'Pupils in state schools think we're posh but Latymer kids think we're common,' a sixth former told us. You don't get many posey trust fund kids here. Solidly middle class but a genuinely wide range of parents, a number of single mothers and families who have made huge sacrifices to get a good education for their children. A number of parents talked of how supportive the school was – not just of their child but of the family as a whole. One boy commented on how no one is arrogant about money – the influence of the abbey means that everyone feels welcome. Mostly local. Some come from as far afield as Barnes or Holland Park. Just over 50 per cent are Catholic.

One girl we spoke to was keen to mention that girls are not treated as second class citizens, attributing it to the fact that there have been girls in the sixth form for over 30 years. There are good inter-year relationships. Mentoring schemes where the older ones help out with the juniors and whole school involvement in drama and music. Pupils here are extremely courteous and mature. Old Priorians (the official title for former St Benedict's pupils) include Julian Clary, Lord (Chris) Patten (who also sits as an advisor on the governing board), Peter Ackroyd, Declan Donnellan, Andy Serkis, Professor Denis MacShane MP and poet/songwriter Labi Siffre, as well as plenty of rugby players, including Hugo Ellis and Joe Simpson of Wasps.

Entrance: (Practically) all start at 11 – though school will still take the occasional few at 13. Ninety-six places, 40 of which go to the children coming up from the junior school (almost all transfer automatically). Entrance exams in maths, English and verbal reasoning. Most interviewed. Looking to discover what the child will give back to the school. Sixth form requirements – a minimum of six GCSEs at B or above and Bs in A level subjects. A number of people join in the sixth form from local girls' schools looking for a more inclusive approach.

It's no longer true that if you don't get in anywhere else you will get a place at St Benedict's. Although Mr Cleugh is keen not to be too selective, as numbers rise priority will have to be given to Catholics and siblings.

Exit: Virtually all to good universities and to an impressive range of courses – no stereotypes here. Three Oxbridge offers in 2013. A tiny few leave after GCSE to go to eg Latymer Upper, Catholic state schools or sixth form colleges.

Money matters: About half a dozen on 100 per cent bursaries, lots of others get help. 'Once a child is in if a parent falls on hard times we will do our best to help them,' says Mr Cleugh.

Limited number of academic scholarships at 11+ and at sixth form – up to 50 per cent fees and can be augmented by bursaries.

Bursary Appeal Fund launched in 2010.

Remarks: We said, 'A wholly unpretentious, good solid school with sound values that is never going to squash your child into a box. Exactly the school for your brightish but quietish child who would sink in a larger, or tougher, environment. An honest, hard-working place with a gentle and loving approach', and we still think that that is a fair description. Although there are still occasional ripples from its troubled past, the school is now a very different place.

St Brendan's Sixth Form College

Broomhill Road, Brislington, Bristol, BS4 5QR

• Pupils: 1,700 boys and girls • Ages: 16–19+ • Catholic • State

Tel: 01179 777766
Email: info@stbrn.ac.uk
Website: www.stbrn.ac.uk

Principal: Since 2012, Mr Michael Jaffrain. Originally from France and worked as a bank cashier in Paris, before moving to England to become a language assistant at South Cheshire College followed by a post at Shrewsbury Sixth Form College. Appointed assistant principal at St Brendan's in 2010. Aims to 'develop concrete, working partnerships with other educational establishments, be a leader of innovation and change, have close ties with business and become an international college.' Huge rugby fan.

Academic matters: College offers three levels of post-16 study: as well as level 3 (A levels), a small number of level 1 courses caters for the most educationally disadvantaged; 15 level two courses in a wide range of subjects provide the equivalent to four GCSEs at grades A*-C. The City and Guild CAD course provides a back-up for A level design students whilst other level 2 courses include level 2 BTECs in art and design, business, health and social care, media, music technology, public services.

Much wider range of AS and A2 courses (currently approaching 50) than you would find in a school sixth form, with every opportunity to mix and match. Principal commented on how even medical schools now appreciate entrants with unusual subjects alongside the expected ones. A and AS results above national average with growing number achieving four or more A grades. Some 40 per cent A*-B grades overall in 2013. Good A*/B percentages for science and maths (over half A*/A grades in chemistry, biology and maths) and in German and Spanish too.

The International Baccalaureate introduced in 2010 provides an opportunity for students in the state sector to study this well-regarded qualification with one student already heading to Oxford. Average IB score in 2013 was 30.5.

Annual visit to 'Your Future in Europe' conference in Paris for honours students who are expected to study a minimum of four AS and A2 subjects and take AS critical thinking as an additional AS level.

Being taught the 'spiritual journey' and 'preparation for working life' aspects of the core programme in 'honours' groups is making a marked difference to student performances and aspirations, claim staff.

Growing learning support team helps in or outside classroom and includes 18 LSAs. All students have access to learning support and almost half of the student population take up the opportunity in some way. Two hundred of these students have regular support or exam entitlements. All areas of the college are accessible to wheelchair users. High percentage achieve better grades than predicted. Students praised support they've received – one African girl we met explained how she is now able to progress properly after getting extra English through the ESOL programme.

Games, options, the arts: The football and rugby pitches in front of the college may hark back to former days but college still fields strong teams in football and rugby. A new building containing sports hall, fitness suite and dance studio provides modern facilities where participation in health and fitness is encouraged.

Lots of demand for creative courses such as photography, fashion and textiles with some stunning displays. Lots of studio space for art and design with more excellent work, and a newly-refurbished design and technology suite has extensive computerised facilities. State-of-art music department caters for all styles and levels as well as production and studio engineering. Drama students were fully involved when we visited and share studio space with dance. Lots of dynamic overlap, especially for productions. Film students very innovative and even have their own Oscars evening at college.

Activities, visits and sports rely heavily on student organisational input. Surprisingly varied programme given the logistical difficulties of getting people together outside lesson time. What runs is well-supported but students here also get to enjoy hanging out with peers. Atmosphere encourages making new and lasting friends – more like what students will experience at university. Active student union organises parties and charity fund-raising and has a voice on the college's governing body.

Background and atmosphere: Founded in 1890 as a boys' independent school run by the Christian Brothers, it later achieved direct grant status before emerging as a co-educational, Catholic sixth form college in 1979. Currently a hodgepodge of buildings – some date back many years (about to be demolished) others (such as social sciences and creative studies) already state-of-art, purpose-built facilities. Building programme 'will lend a new coherence,' says principal, and reconstruction was planned not to impede the working life of the college.

First names used throughout college; dress varies widely but errs on side of comfortable. We were impressed by the self-imposed silence in library area, which includes a lot of computer spaces and remains open until 5pm. There is an internet café/IT work area adjacent to student canteen where a staff member is on hand whenever there is a need; other ICT suites around college. Increased numbers are placing a heavy demand upon these work stations. Flexible auditorium with raked seating for about 200 provides performance and lecture space. Assemblies held here to celebrate Christian festivals with extra masses in chapel for Catholic students.

Pastoral care and discipline: Parents rate highly pastoral system which keeps a tight rein on attendance and progress. Role of student support managers is pivotal: each has five tutorial groups (about 150 students) whom they see for three 45 minute periods a week. In cases of poor work or behaviour students can be placed 'on contract'. Retention over year is 94 per cent, which is high compared with FE institutions. All follow core programmes in life skills and a 'spiritual journey' course (non-sectarian and popular with students as an opportunity to explore their values and beliefs). Careers form important part with a rolling programme of fairs, visits, speakers etc as well as HE advice and an excellent resource base. Qualified counsellors also on hand to meet both referred and self-referred students. Catholic chaplain's role is separate from spiritual journey course; chapel is used for a wide variety of purposes.

Airy student canteen spoilt by failure of majority to clear up after themselves. Healthy options available but no salad bar yet and many go for greasy spoon choices it seems.

Pupils and parents: Only about 30 per cent are Catholics but college is favoured choice of a number of other Christian churches in Bristol. Fifteen per cent ethnic minorities ('more Muslim girls would come if there were a direct bus,' says principal). Being part of Bristol's south east area partnership alongside City of Bristol (FE) College has opened the doors to many more non-Catholics. Usual choice for Catholics from Bristol and Bath Catholic collegiate for whom it is the only denominational post-16 option. Increasing uptake from ex-independent school pupils. Decision by First Bus to offer a student ticket which can be used for any journey in city has proved extremely popular.

Entrance: Impressive, university-style prospectus makes task of selecting courses much easier. About 27 per cent of entrants come from Catholic collegiate schools, where they are interviewed prior to admission and meet student ambassadors from St Brendan's. Parents generally like to attend these meetings and are welcomed. Remainder are interviewed at college. Over 70 feeder independent and state schools covering area between West Wiltshire and North Somerset.

Exit: Majority proceed to wide range of degree courses including several to Oxbridge. Many to vocational and arts-related courses. Some into employment.

Remarks: Welcome to the real student world! More of Bristol's young adults see this as the right compromise between school and university or work. Staff strike us as in tune with this age group and whole place buzzes. A great place to make friends and learn independent study skills. University would be less of a cultural shock after two years here.

St Catherine's School

Linked school: St Catherine's Preparatory School

Station Road, Bramley, Guildford, Surrey, GU5 0DF

- Pupils: 800 girls; 165 boarders, rest day; • Ages: 11–18; • C of E;
- Fees: Boarding £26,550; Day £7,920–£16,125 pa; • Independent

Tel: 01483 899609
Email: admissions@stcatherines.info
Website: www.stcatherines.info

Headmistress: Since 2000, Mrs Alice Phillips MA Cantab (early fifties). First teaching post was at the Royal Masonic School, Rickmansworth where she rose to being head of English. Thence to deputy headship at Tormead in 1993. Mrs Philips is Chairman of the Girls' Schools' Association's Professional Development Committee, Chairman of the GSA South Central Region and is a member of GSA Council. She impresses at once as being full of brisk common sense, good humour and get-up-and go. But she is also super-bright, super-articulate and super-focused on the highest of standards for her staff, her charges and herself. 'She is utterly determined for her girls,' one mother told us. And this blazes forth in her dedication to the job of equipping girls for the future – 'girls need to be in an environment which demonstrates that there's nothing you can't do'.

Mrs Phillips relishes the process of turning her 'rough-cut GCSE diamonds into highly polished gems' – and the process needs the St Cat's sixth form to be complete. 'We hit the wall of hormones together,' she says, 'I love the wall of hormones,' which she sees as an essential stage in becoming an adult. And she is not interested in turning out demure young ladies. 'We teach them to challenge every darn thing.' Neither is she a petty disciplinarian, 'you pick your fights with teenage girls. If you pick on something trivial and make a fuss about it they will hate you forever.' Parents are universally impressed – 'her speeches are very entertaining and she devotes her whole life to the school.' 'She is very fair and very good at sorting things out.' A few parents – and girls – can find the intensity of her commitment 'scary', but one's impression is that her uncompromising concern is for the 'whole' of each girl. When her pastoral care is praised, she responds, 'but we do also seek to get the girls into the best possible universities and to do that you have to get them to aim high and target improvements all the time'. One awe-struck mother summed her up – 'She is amazing.'

Academic matters: IGCSEs in almost all subjects now. No plans to move to the Pre-U or IB – Mrs Phillips is that rare thing – a fan of the AS year. Success relies on traditional good teaching alongside the best that modern IT can offer – and keen to keep abreast of all that is innovative and helpful. 'The apps for learning languages are fantastic,' enthuses Mrs Phillips, who tells us that her classics department have always led the way when it comes to embracing good new IT. So ipods/ipads allowed in class with an emphasis on 'learning to discriminate' between reliable web info and the rest – we applaud. We saw nothing but quiet and attentive classes and teachers who kept order by being interesting rather than via sanctions. Results excellent across the board – no weak areas. Ninety per cent of subjects taken at A level in 2013 were graded A*-B. Good to see Greek and German surviving alongside business, economics, history of art and photography. At IGCSE in 2013, 83 per cent achieved A*/A, 97 per cent getting A*/B. It cometh not much better than this. Lots of options, lots of opportunities – real education takes place here.

Disquiet among some parents and girls on the subject of 'SCAGS' (St Catherine's Assessment Grades) – the St Cat's method of assessing and tracking progress. It's designed to support girls in the pursuit of improvement in their different subjects but some are confused or unconvinced. Mrs Phillips – an ardent believer – concedes, 'we are mindful that it is complex and try to inform parents as best we can.' She is lightning quick to react when we report concerns raised with us – 'it is not the St Catherine's way not to listen to parents – we will expand the explanation and make it more user friendly for parent use.' And latest results support school's contention that the scheme works – the first group of girls brought up this way achieved 17 per cent more A* grades than their predecessors.

Library open all hours and well-stocked – the only one we have so far seen with a section on 'feminism'. Sensible system of sixth form subject mentors – you're twelve and struggling with physics? – find the sixth former who understands! Overall, the best of trad with the slickest of innovative in matters academic.

Girls with only mild dyses likely to be able to stand the heat. 'We pride ourselves on our tracking system,' says head, 'and on spotting any late-emerging problems' and monitoring, academic mentoring and clinics are more the way here than a busy special needs set-up.

Games, options, the arts: Lively art in many media – photography especially strong but ceramics, DT, life-drawing – all thrive and all run clubs for those who aren't taking them as curricular subjects. A sense of vibrant life and colour about the studios. 'The drama in the senior school is really good,' we were told and the new building has given drama and the technical side of production an immense boost. Music also lively and productive – just as you'd expect with this calibre of girls and encouragement.

Excellent sports facilities and sport now seen as more inclusive – lots of opportunities for those less than Olympian in their prowess. 'My daughter is in C and D teams', said one mother, 'and she has lots of matches.' The Olympians regularly reach the heights – county and national finals places in several sports and stellar showings in swimming, lacrosse and tennis. Range of sports on offer. Riding club run by parents. Duke of Edinburgh thrives and everyone is productively busy all the time. Excellent outside speaker programme, sixth form lectures – and PTA lectures – and lots of stimulating trips.

Background and atmosphere: Established in 1885, this is a school with a proud tradition and, unusually, has grown and developed all on the one site. Located ten minutes south of Guildford in a quiet leafy village, it is unremarkable architecturally apart from its striking conference room plus Arts 'n' Crafts fireplace, its memorable Gothic style chapel – splendid stained glass windows celebrating notable female saints, fabulous rose window and Willis organ. Now boasts a 'fantastic' £15 million complex – the '125th Anniversary Halls' arts and sports building with an unrivalled auditorium (seats 300 and has 'better acoustics than the Barbican') plus other studios and backed by the sports hall, gyms, dance studios etc. All carefully, thoughtfully and skilfully integrated and an exceptional new resource with which the girls are clearly thrilled. School buildings mostly abut big central area used for car parking though pitches and courts stretch away on the perimeter. Latest addition is 'university style' sixth form study centre, designed with input from the girls.

Boarding and most of the school areas are functional, a little tired in places, with the emphasis on workfulness rather than opulence. Useful 'chat-rooms' for one to-one sessions – a good idea but the one we nosed into was freezing! Bedrooms and dorms are spacious enough, welcoming and homely. Most in two-bedders, often with a third bed for flexi-boarders. Even sixth formers mostly share – they in their own separate and much-appreciated block with common rooms – possibly the messiest we have seen – most refreshing! – workrooms etc. Everywhere is now internetted. Around half sixth formers board but designated working spaces for day girls. Many sixth formers drive to school in their own cars. Most full boarders – normally between 50 and 70 girls – remain in school each weekend and are offered a 'full and varied programme of activities'.

Immensely strong house system – everything done in the six houses to which loyalty is unflinching – underpins virtually all school activities. Strong ethical dimension to energetic charity work – extends to water vending machine which supports pumping system in Africa. Food seen as improved – salads particularly praised – though 'it can get a bit monotonous for boarders,' we were told. The day we visited the choices included 'deep fried battered pangasius' and 'oven roasted pangasius'. (We had to look it up too – it's a type of catfish.)

Pastoral care and discipline: 'Lovely dedicated staff,' universally praised. A sense that all girls can fit in and do well here – whatever their aptitudes, enthusiasms, personality – something to which all parents we spoke to attested. 'It can be a bit full-on for some of them,' one parent admitted – and others agreed –'the girls themselves push themselves to the limit – the atmosphere makes them want to be the best of the best.' 'They do the best they can,' another said, 'but they do it while looking after each other.' 'They are very supportive of each other's differences,' another agreed. School divides the girls into houses, sets, classes – lots of mixing up to encourage friendship and to discourage cliqueyness – and it works.

Serious misdemeanours off the radar. Preventative and common sense approach. 'We do some very robust woman-to-woman talking with the girls about our expectations and what is and is not acceptable,' says Mrs Phillips and a sense of friendliness, mutual support is tangible. Some of the most approachable staff we know.

Pupils and parents: St Cat's 'Association' founded in 2004 – now a 3000 strong membership of alumnae, parents, former staff – make a real community of the school, past and present. Head's PA one of around a dozen alumnae now on the staff. Lots of parental involvement and unquenchable enthusiasm. Mostly local-ish families. Lots of Old Girls' daughters. Middle class and comfortable backgrounds, in the main. Notable Old Girls include Francine Stock, Juliet Stevenson Elizabeth Beresford, Zena Skinner, Davina McCall, Fay Maschler, Joan Greenwood, UA Fanthorpe, Dorothy Tutin, Elinor Goodman, two ambassadors and legions of academics and other high flyers.

Entrance: Entry by academic selection, using St Catherine's own assessment. 11+ candidates take papers in English, maths, science and verbal reasoning. Few places at 12+ – 14+ – papers in English, maths and reasoning. Reports from existing schools.

Sixth form general paper, verbal reasoning and predicted GCSE grades – As expected in A level subjects. Interview for potential sixth formers. Roughly 1.3 applicants for each 11+ place – so not too daunting for a bright girl; for those who try for places in higher years, date of registration is important so register as early as you can. Around 70 apply for the 10 or so annual places in the sixth – they can afford to be very choosy. School flexible and helpful – happy to interview via Skype if you're abroad. Locals come from everywhere but mostly the school's own prep and from Haslemere, Midhurst, Farnham, Guildford, Godalming, Cranleigh, Woking, Esher, Oxshott, SW London. Overseas pupils predominantly English with some EU nationals. Full boarders from Turkey, Moldova, Nigeria, Japan, Hong Kong, Russia, Ukraine, Malaysia, Korea and Singapore. Not a school for anyone with less than fluent English.

Exit: Handful leaves after GCSEs – mostly to board, to co-ed sixths or to have a change. Sixth form leavers to top unis – 10 to Oxbridge in 2013. Lots to Edinburgh, Exeter, Imperial, Leeds and UCL. Unusual number of geographers. Good number of medics. All do proper subjects.

Money matters: Small number of scholarships – some open and some internal – most worth up to 20 per cent of fees. Music and art awards. Bursaries for the bright broke at 7+, 11+ and sixth. Usual means-testing and disclosures required but up to 100 per cent of fees on offer.

Remarks: If you want convincing that girls only education is the right and modern way for your bright and motivated daughter, go and look. This is as good as it gets.

St Charles Catholic Sixth Form College

74 St Charles Square, London, W10 6EY

• Pupils: 1,200 boys and girls • Ages: 16–19 • RC, but other faiths welcome • State

Tel: 020 8968 7755
Email: admissions@stcharles.ac.uk
Website: www.stcharles.ac.uk

Principal: Since 2002 Mr Paul O'Shea BA, PGCE (fifties). Educated at a Kent grammar school, scholarship to read history at St John's Oxford, he went on to study at St Mary's Strawberry Hill for his PGCE. Started as a history teacher, later becoming head of department at Woodhouse School which is now Woodhouse College. In 1994 he joined St Charles as vice principal. Cool, calm and collected, he is extremely well thought of by both staff and pupils, and encourages the whole school community to get along and work in partnership with each other. He leads a highly successful and inclusive college, with Catholic values at its heart. All other faiths are welcome who are happy to fit in with the Catholic identity of the college. Mr O'Shea still teaches citizenship and is chairman of the London Citizens. He lives in North London and is married with two grown-up children, now at university.

Academic matters: Whilst around three-quarters of the students follow traditional A-level courses, St Charles also offers BTEC firsts, certificates and diplomas, vocational courses and foundation skills in English and mathematics. The college also offers GCSE retakes for those wanting to improve their grades. More able students can take the Extended Project Qualification. Students are all taught to plan and develop their work alongside

how best to manage their time. Being a rounded thinking individual is part of the college's mission: everyone follows the compulsory general RE programme, which involves much critical discussion around the purpose and meaning of life through theology and philosophy. Students who are successful in completing the course gain the nationally recognised Certificate in Religious Investigation and Moral Reasoning. The school is well-known for added value, with around a third of A level grades A*- B (69 per cent A*-C in 2013); this is no mean achievement for a mixed ability college. Spread across two floors, the library provides quiet areas for working and a good range of books, multimedia, newspapers and periodicals. Active and well-resourced learning support department provides assistance to students with a range of specific needs. The building is now fully wheelchair accessible. Intensive courses for students with English as an additional language are organised for small groups to ensure much personal attention.

Games, options, the arts: Impressive and modern sports facilities; sports block also incorporates new IT suites. Huge sports hall, four new indoor courts and their own fitness suite; students can also use the Birkbeck College sports ground for football and rugby. Basketball team have won the London Pioneers for three out of the last four years. Very strong art and design department puts on well-attended exhibitions, and a number of students go on to foundation courses at top London art schools. Drama and music are also popular and the school produces plays and musicals, with auditions open to all students. Film and media students are involved with projects run by the British Film Institute, enabling them to show and discuss their creative work with film and television professionals. Very enthusiastic and successful young enterprise team recently won Best Overall Company for North Central London. The college links up with other organisations to provide community out-reach opportunities, be it helping older people gain ICT skills or mentoring other young people. Students can also become involved in the CitySafe initiative run by London Citizens, an organisation committed to improving young people's lives and skills and combating street violence.

Background and atmosphere: As you walk into the entrance hall, a peaceful and positive atmosphere is immediately apparent, the most inspiring design taken from Milan cathedral. Everywhere is spotlessly clean, and well cared for corridors positively shine. The college is named after St Charles Borromeo, a 16th century Italian archbishop who believed strongly in the redeeming powers of education. Founded by Basil Hume in 1990, it continues to go from strength to strength. Quite overwhelming feedback from staff that St Charles is a breath of fresh air, organised, and with a positive attitude across all disciplines really matter. The college is conveniently located in St Charles's Square, often referred to as 'The Little Vatican', due to the neighbouring Catholic primary and secondary schools, St Pius Church and a Carmelite monastery. Much about the college is designed around hope and inspiration, and a large amount of wall space is dedicated to portraits of students with accompanying testimonials and histories of their educational and career development. Interestingly, quite a few ex-students return to work at the college in both academic and non-academic posts.

Pastoral care and discipline: St Charles's continues to work very hard to ensure the best possible pastoral care and that every student feels part of the community. Everyone has a group tutor group under one of the pastoral managers which looks after their progress and well-being. There is a referral system for students with academic and/or personal problems. An outside agency provides both male and female counsellors who visit the school on a weekly basis. The full-time chaplain looks after the small but beautiful chapel, where daily morning prayers are said and a mass every Friday lunchtime. The chaplain is available to students on a drop-in basis. Whilst supporting students, he also organises voluntary work experience and charity work. Students are provided with a Code of Conduct, so everyone knows exactly what is expected of them in all aspects of college life and behaviour. Zero tolerance towards smoking, alcohol and drugs, all banned from the site.

Pupils and parents: Very diverse 21st-century London group of students, from all over the world, Portuguese, Filipino, Hispanic, Afro-Caribbean and Eastern European. About 80 per cent from ethnic minorities, many of whom are the first members of their family to have the opportunity to attend an A level college and go on to university.

Entrance: First priority goes to those with specific needs, then to students applying from four partner Catholic secondary schools, which makes up about 20 per cent of the intake. Other than that, fairly open access; students come from around 150 feeder schools. Everyone applying on time will be offered an interview to discuss their application and suitable course.

Exit: Approximately 75 per cent go on to university, others to art colleges or FE colleges to follow vocational training courses or apprenticeships.

Money matters: College raises some funds by hiring out the excellent facilities including the large hall, indoor and outdoor sports areas and equipment, and spacious restaurant and catering area. The student bursary scheme provides grants for those in financial hardship while studying full-time.

Remarks: Some remarkable achievements happen here. Great place for motivated and hard-working young people from all walks of life who want to move on, regardless of previous achievements or background.

St Christopher School

Linked school: St Christopher School Junior School

Barrington Road, Letchworth Garden City, SG6 3JZ

• Pupils: 345 boys and girls in senior school, including 32 boarders • Ages: 11–18 • Non-denom • Fees: Day £9,780–£16,200; Boarding £17,700–£28,650 pa • Independent

Tel: 01462 650850
Email: admissions@stchris.co.uk
Website: www.stchris.co.uk

Head: Since 2006, Mr Richard Palmer BEd (Nottingham Trent), FRSA. Mr Palmer has deep roots at St Christopher. First came in his gap year, then did his teaching practice here. After a mild flirtation with the idea of going into PR, took a job setting up the IT system and teaching DT and science. Became resident tutor in a boarding house, then, after meeting his wife, Jenny, warden of the sixth form boarding house, moved to St John's College School, Cambridge, as a housemaster. Spent six years there as deputy head, before returning to St Christopher in 2004 as head of the junior school. Took over as acting head during a troubled period and was eventually asked to fill the job permanently. When the news was announced the children cheered. Jovial, energetic and warm, Mr Palmer knows even the tiniest nursery child by name. Feels school should be fun – 'examinations are important but not mutually exclusive from enjoying yourself.' Despite the first-name, own-clothes regime, Mr Palmer wears a suit and tie and is clearly capable of setting boundaries. 'Sometimes it's important to say I'm the head and

we're doing it this way.' Has a son and daughter at the school. Enjoys travel, music and cooking.

Academic matters: The academic range is quite broad – 'average and above' – but this is no longer a school for all comers. It now carefully edits out those who won't fit in, though every effort is made to ensure the right children pass through the admissions net. 'When my son sat his entrance test he came out after five minutes in tears,' recalls one mother. 'The school just led him into another room and gave him one-to-one support throughout.' There is a definite St Christopher's type. 'If you're "not bothered",' says the head, 'it would be dishonest to offer you a place.' If you are, the school will go the extra mile. Don't, however, expect your child to be militarily drilled into As and A*s. 'If they want to do it, they can do it here,' says one parent, 'but if they don't want to work, the school is not going to make them.' Generally strong teaching (though some recent parental concerns about curriculum monitoring, particularly in IT, now, according to head, 'resolved'). About 25 per cent of the intake has some kind of learning difficulty and receive excellent support from a specialist team. Copes well with dyslexia and dyspraxia at mild to medium levels and operates a counselling service. Some pupils have one-to-one tuition (at extra cost); others are helped by a learning support assistant. Everyone takes nine GCSEs but with a wide choice and only five compulsory subjects (two English, double science and maths). Generally good results, considering the intake. In 2013, 70 per cent A*/B at GCSE, about 70 per cent A*-B at A level. Twenty-five per cent achieved straight A*/A. Small classes – 13-20 up to GCSE, 5-7 in the sixth form – mean every pupil gets plenty of attention. Curriculum, too, is unusually tailor-made with almost any mixture of subjects accommodated. 'If you want to study art, drama and photography, we'll create a timetable for you if we can,' says the head, 'though we'll make it clear it may limit your options later on.'

Games, options, the arts: Strong and vibrant art department offering pottery, ceramics and photography. DT also important with much emphasis on craftsmanship. Decidedly buzzy atmosphere, with energetic teaching and energetic work. Possibly not the most aggressively sporty school but growing reputation for and commitment to team sports (football, rugby and cricket) and much has been done to expand the range of available games and fixtures list. Wonderful climbing wall, skateboard park and outdoor pursuits club, which has weekends of surfing, climbing, potholing, white water rafting, etc. Good facilities – extensive playing fields, sports hall, indoor pool and plenty of enthusiasts. Philosophy, team spirit, but also high-level representation in basketball and rugby. Letchworth tennis club next door.

Plenty of performance opportunities from major school musicals to orchestral concerts and fashion shows, jazz, a capella choir. Unusual for a co-ed school, too, there is an all-boys singing group. 'They appreciate others taking risks.' Drama, too, highly thought of. Community service plays a major role and pupils have the opportunity to work on an international project working with an NGO in India and/or Kosova visiting schools and development projects with which the school has had considerable involvement over the years. Excellent range of extra-curricular activities, with 'Thursday afternoon' options – 'everything from archery to jewellery' – as part of the curriculum.

Background and atmosphere: Set up by Theosophists in the middle of the WWI, the school was then at the extreme end of radical – a co-ed boarding school, with no uniform, no prescribed discipline, teachers called by their first names and sofas in the back of the classroom for any exhausted pupils. 'Essentially, the founders were New Age forward thinkers,' says the head. Though the sofas have been excised from the classrooms, the underlying liberal, family-based roots still permeate the school like writing in rock. Nowadays, it's not the first-name terms or own clothes that strike you but the fact that pupils are genuinely treated with respect, not merely as exam statistics. 'People can voice an opinion,' says one boy who moved here from a comprehensive. 'You can be who you want to be; you're not just put into a box.' There is more than lip service, too, paid to the notion of community and caring for others. One sixth former, showing me round, pointed out the work of a fellow pupil, not because he was the star in the class but because he'd had the courage to start art A level from scratch and was doing well.

The school still welcomes all faiths and none, still calls for Quaker silence in morning assembly and lunch hours and there is still a very strong family feel – 'I sometimes think it is an extension of my family,' said one mother. 'I can ring up and interrupt the head when he is eating dinner to find out where my son is.' A small school, just 150 from reception to year 6, 350 in the senior school, everyone knows everyone well. Founded in a beautiful purpose-built building in the same Arts & Crafts style as the surrounding garden suburb, all the later additions – including a RIBA-award winning IT and English block and a sensitively updated Montessori nursery (the childhood home of Sir Laurence Olivier) – have the immaculately swept and polished appeal of a private home. The manicured flower-filled grounds are another glory, plus allotments for pupils and staff. Food is vegetarian, freshly cooked in the morning and enthusiastically consumed at lunch time.

Small boarding element – 32 throughout the school, 13 in the sixth form – is cared for by residential tutors and supervised by an academic tutor.

Pastoral care and discipline: 'We have the usual problems with young people who make mistakes,' says the head. 'We exclude for damaging the school, supplying drugs or persistently disrupting lessons.' 'About six children have been excluded over the time my son has been here,' said one mother. 'But they do it in the best way possible. They always try and help find another school and don't blacken the child's reputation.' Huge amounts of discussion and debate when get things go wrong and individually tailored punishment. 'We may ask a child, "is this the best you can do?"' says the head. 'Since children are inherently honest, they often say no and decide to try again. It's much better than a detention.' Pupils are expected to get involved; recognise what they are not good at and do something about what they're not, have fun and enjoy themselves. A strong sense of discipline coming from within. A bell is struck for silence at lunch and immediately there is not a whisper. Some issues that would be disciplinary matters at another school are school-wide issues here. One boy, for example, accessorised with an empty cartridge belt, found himself the centre of a whole-school debate. The head will intervene when lines are crossed. 'One day, we just got fed up with 'sagging' and told everyone they had to pull their trousers up. They haven't slipped yet.'

Teacher-pupil relationships are notably good, eased by the informality of first-name terms and teachers here are very willing to go the extra mile. 'Classes are so small that you can go and get help from a teacher that you are not assigned to,' said one sixth former. Plenty of opportunities to take responsibility. Head boy and girl, plus eight major offices. Lively school council.

Pupils and parents: You won't find many bankers or those whose idea of discipline is short back and sides here. (Indeed pupils picketed the poor army officer who tried to come and talk to them about military life.) Parents are mainly liberal media and professionals – 'who are genuinely interested in their children's development,' says the head. Americans, too, tend to identify themselves with the lack of uniform and strong student voice; one or two overseas students from Hong Kong, some Europeans. The students are articulate and responsible

and unusually supportive of each other. Pupils are given a clear sense of the harsh reality of the world outside the gates, leaving with a higher than average sense of social and political idealism. Quite a large contingent (about 25 per cent of the senior school) commute from north London, the rest are mainly from local Hertfordshire towns and villages. School bus operates from the station and from north London, including a late run at 5.30.

Entrance: Entrance is by a test of cognitive ability and an extended piece of writing. Head then interviews the parents and the deputy interviews the children. They also talk to the head of the child's current school. Parental interviews are as important as those of the children. 'We will take someone if we feel we can support their needs, they can access all parts of the curriculum and won't be a detrimental force or unbalance a class or year group,' says the head. 'This is a particular style of school, however. We want to ensure parents understand what we're about and not suddenly come in and decide they want blazers and boaters.' With rare exceptions, all the junior school transfer to the senior. Generally five Bs minimum for entry to sixth, though reasonably flexible. 'We'd pause if it was all Cs and Ds.' Capacity for about 50 boarders full boarding throughout, including in the sixth form, though the majority are weekly boarders.

Exit: About 50 per cent leave post-GCSE, mainly to the state sector. 'A lot of parents here are not particularly rich,' said one mother. 'They've made sacrifices to give their children the kind of education St Christopher offers and I think a lot of children, too, who need the kind of environment the school offers are better able to cope by the time they reach the sixth form.' To a wide range of universities. One or so a year to Oxbridge.

Money matters: Scholarship and bursaries out of school income. Separate bursary fund in the sixth form with two bursaries a years on reasonably complex means-tested basis. Ten per cent discount for siblings.

Remarks: A very unusual school which still works largely against the grain of our current obsession with exam statistics, and you certainly have to be both the right child and the right parent to be able to make the most of the school's philosophy. 'It can be a difficult school in which to hold your nerve if you have a child who'd prefer to play video games, but it does produce profoundly – not merely superficially – confident young adults with a genuine concern for others and for the community in which they live.' For those who want this type of education, it also makes most children very happy. 'Neither of my children has ever said they don't want to go to school. They love it.'

St Clare's, Oxford

139 Banbury Road, Oxford, OX2 7AL

- Pupils: 230 boarders, 30 day students, mixed • Ages: 15–19
- Non-denom • Fees: Boarding £32,476; Day £15,843 pa
- Independent

Tel: 01865 552031
Email: admissions@stclares.ac.uk
Website: www.stclares.ac.uk/ib

Principal: Since 2005, Ms Paula Holloway MSc PGCE. Educated at Cowbridge High School for Girls in Glamorgan and the LSE, where she read geography. She began her career in banking but started teaching when she moved to Hong Kong and has never looked back, 'I just knew I had found what I wanted to do for the rest of my life', she recalls. On her return to the UK did an

MSc in Educational Studies by research at Jesus College, Oxford, and became deputy and then head of Latifa School for Girls in Dubai. Head of Ashford School in Kent from 2000 to 2004. Married to management consultant and lives close to college. Astute and professional but friendly with it, described herself as, 'not a soft touch but not unapproachable'. Efficiently runs an international staff with no clerical tier; slightly surprised at the school's continued success, 'I don't know quite how we do it' though it is apparent she and her 'wonderful senior management team' set the standards high, 'we are very good at modelling what we expect'.

Academic matters: They come from the four corners of the globe to study here for the two-year IB Diploma. The school was a proud pioneer in offering the IB, now has over 35 years' experience, and achieves consistently high results. IB is no walk in the park, six subjects: three at standard level, three at higher, including home language and English, a humanities subject, science, and maths, not forgetting the compulsory theory of knowledge course; extended essay and community, action and service (CAS) programme. Principal describes it as an, 'outstanding qualification in terms of the breadth and depth it offers'. Parents happy with the diversity of subjects, 'my daughter had no clear idea of what to do, therefore keeping it broad in range of topics rather than specialising too early was one of the things that attracted us to the IB'. Others with children who had attended a range of different schools abroad felt the IB was the only option, 'it would have been difficult for him to settle into a traditional English school, with uniform and rules'. St Clare's has the edge over other IB schools, claims the Principal, in that it doesn't attempt to teach A levels at the same time. Recent leavers' results of ninety-nine per cent pass rate, including a perfect score of forty five points for several years on the trot, put St Clare's regularly top of the Oxfordshire sixth form tables. Average score of 37 in 2013.

Students too young to sit the IB course or whose English needs practise, take the Pre-IB course. This is flexible in length (up to one year) and can be joined at any time, to prepare English and core subjects for Diploma level.

All tuition is in English and class sizes average nine, some even smaller. All students study the literature of their home language so individual tutors are often recruited from the university for more exotic tongues, anything from Ukrainian to Farsi. Classrooms, in a number of nearby houses, are abuzz with IT equipment – students encouraged to bring their own laptops. Informal teaching style from a multi-lingual staff, 'if you can't enjoy teaching at St Clare's, I don't know where you will enjoy teaching', says the Principal. Parents impressed by calibre of staff, 'They simply ooze experience' said one, 'None of this fluffy "your son is such a nice boy" stuff'. A new teaching block, with four new science labs and classrooms co-ordinates with local architecture. Cosmopolitan lab technicians and librarians can juggle Dostoyevsky in English or Harry Potter in Cyrillic. Art takes place in a charming converted chapel, where the high ceilings and gallery provide a serene light for painting. There's a dark room, complete with leering skeleton, for photography.

Apart from the display of retro propaganda posters from various nations, the classroom was more like a modern boardroom, throbbing with discussion about European current affairs, 'it brings history and economics to life' said a student. Watching these 16 year olds unpick global economics certainly gave us hope for the Euro crisis.

There is no SEN department. Profound learning difficulties are not provided for, but the college has had students with dyxlexia, ADHD, or hearing impairment.

Games, options, the arts: As a mandatory part of the IB programme, students take CAS (Creativity, Action and Service) over the two years to develop personal skills of planning, team work and conscientious thinking. A minimum number of points is needed in these areas, preventing any of the students becoming too bookish. In reality the plethora of activities from art to zumba make up the social life of the school and run into the weekends and evenings. A mass of notices about clubs, classes and overseas projects draw students to the 'covered way' a busy corridor between classes and café. One family chose the school for the efforts it made to accommodate their son's ice hockey talents, 'I didn't want to go to a school where everybody rowed or played rugby'. The creative part involves a wide range of arts, music, writing, debating, Model United Nations, dance and drama. Behind the guitars, drums and piano in the music room is a full-time music teacher and Sibelius music software is available for the budding composer. Concerts take place throughout the year, but the hot ticket is the international day concert in which students and some staff stage their own gig, with singing, dancing and jokes. Theatre productions by each year group were remembered fondly by senior staff, even if they had a senior moment remembering the titles.

The school has no playing fields. All students are given membership of the local sports centre and swimming pool; other facilities are a short minibus ride away at local schools or at Oxford Brookes' University. Football and rugby teams use Astroturf pitches at Oxford City grounds. Parents forgive the lack of facilities, 'St Clare's do a great deal with very little'. Girls' volleyball is a particular strength. The CAS programme also involves community service (not the punitive kind), which takes the form of charity work in local shops, visiting the elderly or helping at local schools. A personal tutor is on hand every week to monitor progress and offer advice. The programme is open to Pre-IB and IB students and changes every term.

Background and atmosphere: The school motto, 'To advance international education and understanding' stems from the principles of the visionary founder, Anne Dreydel, who despite being confined to a wheelchair by a bomb during the blitz, established exchange programmes for German students in her drawing room. Rightly recognised with an OBE and the German equivalent, her cultural olive branch towards international peace has grown into a thriving sixth form for 260 students. A collection of fine Victorian villas (twenty-seven buildings in total) along the cherry blossomed streets of genteel north Oxford provides boarding accommodation and classrooms. 'The buildings do not look as smart and luxurious as those of most boarding schools', commented one parent. To the rear, gardens dotted with the quirky addition of red telephone boxes have been joined and landscaped to allow the students some green space to eat, work or chill but no loud music, smoking or ball games.

St Clare's Boarding houses are in discreetly converted neighbouring houses, all within a five-minute stroll. First years share rooms with someone of a different nationality, 'arguments are rare' we are told, and language learning rapid. 'Suddenly she had a massive range of friends from other backgrounds' chimed a dad. Second years can have a single room or join with a friend in a double. All are comfortably furnished, most with own shower, hairdryer, strongbox and wifi. Fraternising takes place in the common room, over the TV and kitchen area. A warden, in loco-parentis, handles general wellbeing of the youngsters and counts them all in before the strict curfew. Day students are allocated a house and can stop over one night a week. Our impression when stepping out into the raked gravel drive was less of having visited a typical teenager's bedroom and more of a comfortable hotel.

Students can take three meals a day in the canteen, which serves up a suitably international menu. Predictably, none of the students rated the dish from their own country but were positive about the others. Stylish refectory tables encourage mingling and English chat out of the classroom. The Sugar House (refreshingly un-pc name) offering a continuous temptation of snacks, pizzas and lattes, was doing good business when we visited.

Students make full use of the cultural life of Oxford University, as well as the local shops and cafes of nearby Summertown. There are organised excursions to places of interest in half terms, plus D of E field trips. Students are encouraged to go home in the holidays to recharge, but foreign excursions and tours to more remote parts of the British Isles are arranged for those who want them. Each year's leavers celebrate by cruising on the Thames in a party boat.

Pastoral care and discipline: With so many youngsters far away from home discipline could be a problem, but isn't, thanks to the school's clear code of actions and 'consequences' – a portentous term that is famously effective at deflecting trouble, we are told. A strict curfew is respected, eleven during the week, midnight at weekends. Alcohol is not tolerated, drugs result in an immediate suspension and we couldn't see any bike sheds for the usual teenage experiments: smoking and sex. The system works on trust, 'it's a very powerful glue' says the Principal. The students are given a reasonable degree of freedom in return for responsible behaviour. 'When my son transgressed (in a very minor fashion), they were immediately on to him', said a parent. Lateness or poor behaviour results in loss of free time, confinement to the library or the house for varying spells, at worst for a term. 'It's rare someone will transgress twice', smiles the Vice Principal, eloquently.

A weekly session with a personal tutor, on first name terms, covers pastoral and academic issues. Rather than homesickness, the students complained that home life now seemed quiet, 'I miss people around me'. Student council, elected democratically, is first experience of democracy for some of these youngsters. Councillors hold office from January to December so as not to interfere with serious study and meet with senior staff once a week to pow-wow: coffee machines, laundry problems and swivel chairs were the order of the day when we visited. 'It's easier to deal with a small problem than let it grow', says the Principal pragmatically. Parents have email addresses of teachers and tutors as well as official parents' days at the beginning and end of terms. 'There isn't the tradition of parents' evenings as in a normal school', said a parent, but in practice, there is an open invitation to visit whenever in the UK. Reports and test results can be viewed electronically via the parent portal, explained a parent, and 'we can see when he's been late!'

The students grow noticeably in confidence over the first term, and parents report that after seven weeks a different person has come home, 'the levels of motivation are astonishing'; confident in English and more self-reliant. 'At the start of the year people looked for comfort in their own national group, but not now', chorused a bunch of students, 'the more you get to know about each other, the more relaxed you are'. Despite the school's name, there was no sight of any religious bias, rather an emphasis on internationalism, learning about culture and diversity from each other, 'people think differently here...you learn a lot of stuff about the world. It's eye-opening', said one student, 'Awesome' said another.

Pupils and parents: Forty-six different nationalities with almost as many different languages; biggest groups are German and Italian, but Russian is also common. Students criticised the size of some of the national groups. Eight per cent are British, who join from international schools abroad or are UK youngsters with an interest in the IB. Ten per cent are day children, with parents working in Oxford at the University, BMW or similar businesses. Round a table, they are an impressively mature, articulate and dynamic bunch, redolent of a UN delegation. Principal says, 'students bring each other on'. Perhaps they were hiding the mumbling moody teenagers but we didn't meet any. Instead, the break time discussion was open-minded and lively, peppered with a dose of multi-cultural joshing. Hugely purposeful about the work, 'studying in the UK gives international prestige and broadens your interests', said one

girl. The standard of English was astounding – rivalling many native schools, and the dress sense a positive improvement.

Entrance: Students are drawn to St Clare's by word of mouth or siblings' experience. No entrance test, but highly dependent on two years of reports and references from previous school. The 'personal and intense' selection process won over one family who had initially looked for a public school. Interview in UK is compulsory, at which students are sized up for their enthusiasm for the IB programme, 'this is not a place for people to try to escape from their existing school', said the Principal. Her instincts must be good as St Clare's is full to capacity. Test for maths at interview determines which IB maths course students can tackle. There is a four day induction programme for newcomers, supported by senior students.

Exit: Majority go to university, 75 per cent to UK (LSE and UCL are recurring choices) some to US or European universities and business schools. Three to Oxbridge in 2013. Popular courses are engineering; medicine; law; economics and, not surprisingly, international relations. Principal is proud that St Clare's has equipped them well for it, 'our students do not drop out of University'. An award-winning careers advisor offers 1:1 advice on applications and c.v. with seminars to prepare for UK and USA applications in the final year. 'Within a month...he was suddenly seriously considering his future and deciding what he should do', revealed a shocked mum. An education day of visiting speakers from business was underway when we visited, with groups of students carrying out Alan Sugar-style challenges, the kind of thing most of us first experienced at job interviews. These global citizens are ahead of the game, 'they are more willing to look abroad for opportunities in education and for work', says the careers advisor.

Money matters: Fifteen students each year receive scholarships or means-tested bursaries; February deadline. Registrar called the fees, 'reassuringly expensive, good value for Oxford'.

Remarks: Academically and pastorally midway between school and university or, as Principal said, 'University life with safety nets'. St Clare's attracts ambitious students from around the world, with an eye to a global career via a UK university. 'In some ways St Clare's is not a boarding school', said one mum, 'but rather a pre-university college'. The diverse student population is savvy; already aware that the world is a shrinking place and that the motivation to do well comes from within. Restores your faith in world peace.

St Columba's School

Linked school: St Columba's Junior School

Duchal Road, Kilmacolm, Inverclyde, PA13 4AU

• Pupils: 735 boys and girls; all day • Ages: 11–18 • Non-denom
• Fees: £3,295–£10,120 pa • Independent

Tel: 01505 872238
Email: secretary@st-columbas.org
Website: www.st-columbas.org

Rector: Since 2002, Mr David Girdwood DL BSc PGCE MEd SQH (fifties); educated at Alva Academy followed by St Andrews, Jordanhill, Stirling and Edinburgh universities; previously 'taught chemistry for 15 years' at Stewarts Melville, now a governor. His solicitor wife works in Glasgow, elder daughter at Cambridge while younger is in sixth form. The rector first visited St Columba's as part of an HMI team and was 'enchanted

S

that pupils gathered for assembly should be so numerous that Transitus sat on the stage in front of the rector'. Not so the boss of the HMI team and, as we reported previously, the Transitus 11-12 year old class is now banished (apart from forays to the, science, art and music blocks) to the (admittedly all singing and dancing) junior dept (but the new new build – planning permission notwithstanding – aims to bring them back into the senior fold).

School recently bought a couple of Victorian villas adjoining school on Gryffe Road, with the intention of building a mega new class room block in what was, basically three adjoining plots (much needed – particularly in the science departments). Alas, the planners were agin it, as were the neighbours; a gentler scheme is now in place, and, with luck, the proposed one story extensions with grassed over roofs may yet come to completion. The neighbours appear to have been – more or less – won over. Basically a political hiccup; Kilmacolm has been arbitrarily transferred out of quiescent Renfrewshire into educationally militant Inverclyde.

Several staff were surprised at the rector's modus vivendi in his first couple of years. Staff appraisal weekends, committees to develop anti-bullying policy, child-protection, and health and safety guide lines were unknown to the stalwarts of St Columba's academe. Twelve years on, Girdwood, still keen to include governors, management and staff in decision making, announced that 'there is yet another (very important) questionnaire doing the parental rounds', to ascertain parents' and pupils views. Trad vocal local parents, who felt that participation at various seminars seemed (often inconveniently) mandatory, were somewhat underwhelmed at the prospect of yet another school gathering or three, whilst first time buyers were enchanted at another opportunity to network. Gossip is a wicked medium!

Also a 'proper' questionnaire, to help children find their chosen career, designed by an outside company, Futurewise, and sponsored by ISCO. Pupils age 14, 15 and 16 complete a combo aptitude/ability test and interest questionnaire with follow up discussion evenings at school (a strategy this editor never found particularly useful where her own brood were concerned: just expensive, though in this case included in fees).

Academic matters: Little change. Scottish curriculum on offer – highly structured learning with masses of parental encouragement.

The new Scottish kids on the block this year (2013), National 4s and 5s, replace standard grades. Most schools, as here, seem to be 'doing' national 5s over a two or year period St Columba's has joined the pack.

French, Spanish and German on offer; all three available at Higher level 'but not simultaneously' – head of lang dept writes text books. German 'holding its own remarkably well' – some native speakers. Latin for all, currently 12 enthusiastic Latinists, no Greek scholars and minimal take-up for the former at sixth form.

Higher results: 65.6 per cent As and 95.5 per cent pass rate. Advanced Higher: 59.2 per cent As and 96.9 per cent pass. Results 'fantastic' and St Columba's is consistently in top six of the Scottish league. English, modern studies, music, Spanish and the sciences particularly strong.

Support for learning important with two dedicated staff (including the head of guidance) covering both the senior and junior schools; help on hand for dyslexics (15-20 pupils have IEPs) and for those who find some subjects particularly difficult (one-to-one if necessary – costs extra). 'Can cope' with ADHD and Ritalin. No problem with pupils with disabilities (but no lifts in the classroom block). Comprehensive measures to check that St C's is doing well by its pupils, including testing which picks up problems as well as monitoring progress. ICT strong with pupils 'taught on computers rather than taught computing'; trolleyloads of laptops rolled round each floor of the labs (also liftless).

School complained that labs were delapidated, and so they were – not the ground floor chemistry and first floor physics labs, with their sturdy 30 year old wooden tables which have withstood the test of time, but the more recently made-over physics and biology labs with their chipped formica-holed benches (view from the bilge lab a stunner). Teachers make a school, not facilities – though the latter may improve a learning experience. There was no reason, except idleness, for the brown venetian blinds in the chemistry lab to be wonky and at half mast. Any competent caretaker (or staff member come to that) could/should have been able to cure the problem in minutes. This is housekeeping at a fairly low ebb, and could be the reason that the fabric in the top two labs resembled an abandoned squat. (OTT, comments school.)

Class size 20, three classes per year, and pupils setted from 12 (SI) for English, French, and maths; larger numbers have allowed a fourth set which is often a small group that helps strugglers. The science block obscures the fab view once enjoyed by those in the library above former gym; old library now a business study centre. Pupils can work in the library in their free time.

Staff common room younger after 'lots of retirements' with recent head of department posts in maths and physics 'attracting high calibre from good schools', though, according to the rector, 'it rather depends on timing': ads in September are not good, March is magic'. Interestingly, there was a knitting lesson in the staff room when we visited. Stunning new head of humanities.

Games, options, the arts: School is sportier than it looks. Good and enthusiastic rugby team reached the final of the Scottish rugby plate twice in the recent past; hockey team has won the South West Cup (again!) Regular rugby and hockey tours to Canada, Barcelona, Italy etc. Astroturf pitch near senior school for hockey and tennis, though most rugby games are played on local park opposite the junior school, which has a vast games hall, tactfully curtained off for little ones so they're not overwhelmed, and a fearsome-looking fitness room. Loos and showers in new primary building are next to the sports hall and the boys' showers have the controls outside, which could – but doesn't – cause hours of entertainment. Tennis is at the Kilmacolm tennis club adjoining Shallot (as the junior school, previously the girls' boarding house, is known), but on an individual basis, rather than available to the whole school. Why? Variety of pupils compete at national or UK level in seven or so different sports. D of E hugely popular. Extra tennis courts and smallish Astroturf on t'other side of the not very busy Gryffe Road.

Impressive art and music (fabric design to die for) in the Cargill Centre, opened by the Princess Royal in 1998 and now a tad jaded. No pottery or sculpture noticed. Rather unexpected Victorian chaise longue on the top floor. Mass of sound-proof practice rooms, huge number of instruments on offer and equally large number of peripatic staff. Music and pipe band popular (terrific trip to New York recently), for girls as well as boys, as is choir (lots of travel), NYC tartan week last year, jazz band, art, photography. Biennial exhibitions with real artists as well as pupils, parents and local art club.

The self-contained ground floor houses a technology department with serious equipment but fun teaching and some rather strange offerings. Home economics for 11s, 12s and the usual pre-uni stuff for sixth form; head girl busy sifting flour during our visit.

Exchanges going out of fashion (inhibited by health and safety); recent links with St Petersburg and a one-way Russian exchange. Debating a real wow with victories in Scottish and international competitions – school has had its first ever member of the Scottish debating team (rector's daughter!)

Regular revision classes, weekends, evenings, and classes for all locals, from 7 to 70-year olds, everything from computers, to languages, to bridge. Very popular and good for the community, classes run from September to May, now back on form, for a couple of years no one came!

Background and atmosphere: Originally part of the Girls' School Company, the school was founded in 1897; the junior school went co-ed in the face of falling numbers in 1978; and all the way in 1981. Junior school is a long half mile from the senior school. Healthy amount of walking as juniors visit senior school for music, art, IT, home economics and the sciences, but Shallot (the former boarding house, boarding finished in 1970s) is home to the junior school, games hall, weights room and gym, but otherwise self-contained. Certain amount of shuffling round of classes: Transitus, the youngest class in the senior school, is based in the junior school.

Fair amount of tinkering with senior school fabric under the previous (impressive) incarnation, but whilst the original red-brick building is still 'just' recognisable, it seems to have a lot of space dedicated to cloakrooms and passages; the dining hall doubles as assembly, with fold up stool/tables that stack in a cupboard.

Imaginative architectural overview badly needed here since 'planning blight' is definitely in evidence in the older spaces. Both lab building and the original school are groaning under the impact of modern equipment, school bags, most St Columba's green, hockey et al, litter the passages, water bottles everywhere and, suprisingly, a water fountain (what's wrong with the latter?). The senior school campus is pretty cramped, with little play space, mostly rather dreary tarmac.

Pastoral care and discipline: Four houses (sibling and FP tradition) and inter-house everything. Zero tolerance – drugs/theft means out. 'No significant problems with bullying,' said the rector. Juniors address potential bullying via a week of stories and activities in assembly, six 'golden rules', all 'dos' not 'don'ts'.

'Don't do bullying,' said the rector, small school so probably not.

Pupils and parents: Pupils come from a 30km radius, very much a Renfrewshire school, with about 70 per cent from within 8km, regular bus comes from north Ayrshire, and a small nucleus from Dunoon 'across the watter'. Pupils catch the 7.30am boat and join up with the Greenock/Port Glasgow bus. Juniors and seniors can stay in school until 6pm. Kilmacolm, a popular sprawling suburban village, once served by the railway, is booming: first time buyers, a tiny wide ethnic base as well as the traditional Kilmacomics (sic). FPs Lord (Ian) Lang, and Eleanor Laing MP. Don't get it wrong, this is not a toffs' school by any means, just good and sensible; pupils 'are not terribly street-wise'.

Entrance: Own test and interview to Transitus and senior school. 'People fail it,' rector says, though not perhaps, now, as rigorously as previously, ditto siblings/FPs' children, but automatic entry from junior school. Certain amount of sixth form entry. No waiting lists at the moment.

Exit: Small trickle (very small trickle) leave to go to trad prep schools at eight or public schools at 13, plus occasionally after they have got university entrance qualifications – ie first year sixth transfer (latest wheeze is to opt for the local state school and apply to Oxbridge – or Bristol – from there) or even for a final year toughening up in a boarding school. Otherwise approx 97 per cent to university, usually in Scotland, two or three to Oxbridge on occasion, one or two to art school.

Money matters: Means-tested bursaries, more now than previously: OSCR threatens and school is madly doing homework and risks losing charitable status if it can't make its fees more accessible for lower income families. The school can be hit hard when one of the local companies goes down (and

suffered badly on the demise of the local sugar company). Fees remarkably reasonable, but all parents must cough up £350 for a debenture when their child is accepted; this is returned at the end of the child's time at school (without interest or increase in value). There is a 50 per cent penalty if a place is accepted and not taken up. Discount of 25 per cent for the third and subsequent children. Blazers (about £80 depending on size) and summer/winter uniforms for all girls. Juniors have waterproof jackets (£40); little ones wear fetching green overalls for lunch.

Remarks: Thoroughly sound, rather than setting the world alight. 'Still a local school' with local middle class and aspiring attitudes. Tiny ethnic mix. Victorian values, popular, the reason that houses in boring Kilmacolm (and this editor once lived there) change hands at a premium, and, to quote an incredulous local landowner (who has done quite well out of the school), 'they actually move into the village because of the school'.

St David's College

Llandudno, Conwy, LL30 1RD

- Pupils: 245 pupils, 176 boys/68 girls (115 boarders) • Ages: 9–19
- Christian (all denominations welcome) • Fees: Day £8,700–£14,940; Boarding £18,360–£27,700; SEN Day £11,700–£18,060; SEN Boarding £21,460–£30,810 • Independent

Tel: 01492 875974
Email: hmsec@stdavidscollege.co.uk
Website: www.stdavidscollege.co.uk

Headmaster: Since 2008, Mr Stuart Hay, BEng PGCE (late thirties). Mr Hay joined St David's as deputy head from Warminster School, where he was head of electronics and product design. After gaining his electronic engineering degree and PGCE at Bath University, he taught in both the independent and maintained sectors; he is married to Lucy and they have two children, Ben and Milly. Mr Hay's main interests are mountaineering, road cycling, mountain biking and racquet sports.

Academic matters: Academic results are significantly above the national average but the emphasis is not solely on classroom work and, in terms of added value, achievements are spectacular. The school was one of the first schools to implement a multi-sensory teaching policy. Support programme enables some pupils to have individual lessons at the Cadogan Centre, a specialised unit within the campus. These pupils have an individual learning plan appropriate to their needs.

IT provision is first class. The school offers NVQs in CAD and technology. We were shown some space age designs that were both impressive and practical. Pupil:staff ratio is less than five to one.

Games, options, the arts: The school believes that outdoor activities can build both teamwork and individual confidence. What is available would challenge Indiana Jones. Sailing, climbing, fell running and kite-buggying are among the large range of activities on offer. The pupils have pride in the skills they have acquired and are determined to continue these activities when they leave school.

Art is popular. We viewed some photographic projects which caught the beauty of the surrounding countryside. About three-quarters of the pupils learn a musical instrument and there is ample practice space.

Background and atmosphere: Founded in 1965 by John Mayor. He felt that there was a need for a school that could help those

S

who might sink in the mainstream system. A late medieval mansion with 39 acres was leased on the outskirts of Llandudno, near the Snowdonia National Park. The oak-panelled rooms are still used and fireplaces provide a cheering blaze. Additions have been made over the years, including new boarding houses. The head would like to see a further new boarding house when funds allow. While some of the buildings could benefit from some TLC, they are welcoming and well used. Staff and pupils seem at ease with each other, a feature that is mentioned in the latest CSSIW visit.

Pastoral care and discipline: Housemasters, tutors and other staff are available to support pupils. Open door policy. During our visit to the chaplain a number of pupils came in and were given space to take time out. Sixth form boarders were housed separately but they have since been reintegrated into the boarding houses. This move has been welcomed by house staff.

Pupils and parents: From a wide range of primary and prep schools. Day pupils from across the whole of North Wales. Boarders from all over the UK, a small number from overseas. Inclusive entry helped by quite a number of pupils being funded by their local education authorities. Apart from those with special educational needs, many parents choose the school because of its broad all-round education and its small class sizes.

Entrance: The majority enter at 10. Selection by interview and school report.

Exit: A few leave at 16. The majority moves on to university, with technical subjects being most popular. Pupils are usually successful in being accepted to their further educational establishment of choice.

Money matters: Given the staff:pupil ratio the fees represent good value.

Remarks: A school that transforms the lives of young people who, when they enter, have both low expectations and low self-esteem. The all-round support gives them the skills and confidence to achieve and move forward.

St Dominic's Sixth Form College

Mount Park Avenue, Harrow on the Hill, HA1 3HX

• Pupils: 1020; just over half are girls • Ages: 16–19 • RC but other faiths accepted • State

Tel: 020 8422 8084
Email: registrar@stdoms.ac.uk
Website: www.stdoms.ac.uk

Principal: Since 2013, Andrew Parkin. Educated at St John's RC Comprehensive School and Queen Elizabeth Sixth Form College in Darlington. Studied music at Durham and Cambridge and started his professional career in London at The St Marylebone Girls' School. Went on to be deputy head teacher at Sion Manning Girls' School in Kensington and then St Augustine's High School in Westminster. Mr Parkin is a keen amateur musician and is chairman of the BBC Symphony Chorus.

Academic matters: Very wide range of courses – some 30 subjects available in more-or-less any combination. Maths much the most popular subject, with chemistry, biology and economics close behind. Impressive results: 70 per cent A*-B grades in 2013. Option to change subjects in the first week or two if you really

loath psychology or have just developed a passionate interest in Italian. A level 3 BTEC in business studies is the only vocational course on offer, but those of a less academic bent can take a BTEC in travel and tourism or engineering, or a lower level business studies BTEC, at the Sacred Heart and Salvatorian sixth form centre down the road.

Nearly everyone does an extended project. 'They have a free choice of subject, but it makes sense to relate it to a subject they may do at university, and gives something to talk about at interview.' Large numbers of aspiring medics, so the college runs a programme of BMAT preparation and mock interviews. Excellent university and careers advice. 'We're realistic and honest, and allow no poverty of aspiration.'

The Study Plus learning support centre is staffed by a manager and three assistants. Some drop in from time to time, whilst others, often identified at initial interviews, are assigned one-to-one help. 'Some resent it at first but soon don't want to be taken off the list.' Student mentors train to offer help with specific subjects eg chemistry and maths.

Games, options, the arts: Sports hall completed in 2010 includes a multi-gym and hall for badminton, table tennis, five-a-side football, with its use juggled between A level PE students and general recreation. Sport is not compulsory, but the new hall 'has increased motivation and attendance. We've been pleasantly surprised that participation rates have been very high.' On the morning of our visit the multi-gym was full of (mostly) young men working out – many of whom, we were told, would not normally have come to college so early. The only outdoor space is a five-a-side football/netball court, but the college fields football (girls' and boys'), rugby, netball and cricket teams. It also offers opportunities for cheer leading and street dance for those less competitively inclined.

Small numbers do music A level, but many keep up their instrumental skills, and play in the termly concerts. Top floor studios showcase sophisticated artwork and fashion creations, and several each year go on to art and design courses. No college drama productions, but theatre studies students showcase their devised pieces.

Volunteering and fund-raising are important parts of the ethos. 'Charity efforts spring up out of nowhere.' Students do sponsored walks and sleep outs, work in soup kitchens, volunteer on a Catholic farm, go off to work in a school in Uganda, join a pilgrimage to Lourdes. 'There's an ethos of respecting other people and helping the wider community,' said a teacher.

Background and atmosphere: Opened in 1979 in what had been St Dominic's Independent Grammar School for Girls, run by Dominican nuns. Sits on a hill above a leafy, gated estate of substantial houses with large gardens that could have strayed from the Chilterns, with views across the west London fringes to Ealing. By the entrance to the site is the chapel, a peaceful and atmospheric building with lovely stained glass, 'the heart of the college'. Assemblies and introductory talks take place here, as well as morning masses, and Muslim students use a side room for prayer.

Planning permission is not easy to come by here – it can take up to seven years – but the college has gradually developed most of its open space and is well off for indoor facilities (remodelled library, ICT suite, music and art rooms) if not outdoor. No common room, but students gather in the canteen, and can work in the library, which has a mezzanine floor with a row of computers.

Faith is a major part of the deal here. Mass is held every week, tutor groups take it in turns to choose readings, everyone studies RE. 'We want our students to develop on an academic, moral and spiritual level. We want them to critically examine their faith, to mix with people from other faiths and hear why it is important to them. It makes a tremendous difference to what we can offer and how they develop in later life.'

About 50 per cent of the staff is Catholic, but all teach RE and buy into the ethos. 'It's a very happy place to work,' said one. Prayers are said each morning and each tutor period. 'It is a moment for thinking outside oneself – a lovely sharing moment.' Very good relationships amongst staff and between staff and pupils. A student commented: 'The staff are so committed and positive.'

Pastoral care and discipline: The atmosphere may be relaxed, with staff and students on first name terms, but students are under tight control. Electronic registration for every lesson means that everyone is accounted for: the pastoral team phones parent and student if the student is not in by 10am. Effort and achievement grades given every six weeks. 'Our monitoring is much more frequent than they have time to do in schools. All our staff are focused on the sixth form – not on settling in year 7s or helping year 9s choose GCSE subjects – and we're very good at it.'

Zero tolerance for drugs or violence. No drugs problems for many years – 'why would they do it here?' The rare offenders usually withdraw, 'and we support them to move on elsewhere'.

Pupils and parents: About 50 per cent Catholic, most of the rest Hindu or Muslim. Homogenous in that all take their religious faith seriously and may talk about it at interview. Also tend to be serious about academic life, since the college offers virtually no vocational courses and there is a high level of competition for places amongst non-Catholics in particular. Mostly from Harrow, but some from further afield from a wide range of schools.

Entrance: About 30 per cent from the two partner schools, Salvatorian College and Sacred Heart Language College. Students from these schools are guaranteed a place providing they get at least five A*-C GCSE grades including English Language (applicants from elsewhere must get at least seven) and meet the individual subject requirements. These range from a C in English for religious studies to an A in maths for further maths. Priority to Catholics, then other practising Christians, then other faiths: applicants other than those from the partner schools must provide a reference from their priest/imam/rabbi, and fill in a form about their own religious commitment. Successful non-Catholic applicants are those with the highest predicted grades. Everyone is interviewed, mostly to check that their chosen subjects correlate with their future ambitions.

Exit: Around 90 per cent to higher education. University of Hertfordshire very popular, as are many of the London universities, Nottingham and Warwick. Law and medical/biomedical subjects tend to top the tables. Fewer Oxbridge applicants than one might expect given the calibre of students (six offers in 2013), largely because so many are prospective medics aiming at the London teaching hospitals.

Money matters: Free if you're under 19. Excellent and enlightened system of bursaries for students and staff to fund specific projects and trips.

Remarks: Greatly sought-after college in pleasant leafy location with high academic standards and a strong Catholic ethos of care for each other. 'A lovely place to work and study,' say staff and students.

St Dunstan's College

Linked school: St Dunstan's College Junior School

Stanstead Road, London, SE6 4TY

• Pupils: 850, 50/50 girls/boys, all day • Ages: 11–18 • Anglican foundation; • Fees: £14,622 pa • Independent

Tel: 020 8516 7200
Email: Info@sdmail.org.uk
Website: www.stdunstans.org.uk

Headmistress: Since 2005, Mrs Jane Davies BSc mathematics London (early fifties), married with one grown-up daughter. An enthusiastic maths teacher with many years' experience under her belt, her career started in state secondary schools before moving on to be head of maths at Trinity, Croydon. In 2000, she arrived at St Dunstan's, initially as deputy head, a few years later taking over as headmistress. Takes a special interest in the Duke of Edinburgh awards, and as a lover of hillwalking she joins some of the trips and has even been known to enjoy a weekend camping in Snowdonia. Good results are a must, but not enough: pupils must be fitted to do well in life.

Not easy (we failed) to find a parent with reservations about her. Personally very pleasant. Easy to get to see. Easy to talk to when you are there. Ambitious for the school.

Academic matters: Not the top of the South London heap, but ability to breathe no longer the only entry criterion. Mrs Davies's leadership has made the school more sought-after, and she has taken the opportunity to up the bar. This is a perennial affliction of good heads – comes from them having been academic successes themselves, we feel – but we think that Mrs Davies is a broad enough personality, and enough of a realist, not to take this too far. The proportion of SEN children has fallen, but the school cherishes those that remain, and the old, good habits that came from a focus on SEN – teachers taking an interest in individuals, picking up problems fast – are still encouraged.

Splendid results considering the still broad intake. At GCSE, 55 per cent A*/A grades, 85 per cent A*- B grades at A level and an average points score of 37 for IB students in 2013. Class sizes average around 20 dropping to 14 or so at GCSE.

An arty school in overall feel, but maths is a strong subject (good results in competitions and in exams at all levels – 74 per cent A*/A at A level) and, with the more academic intake, the sciences have been given a boost. Available as three separate subjects, though most do dual award, and much lab refurbishment. French, Spanish and Latin at year 7-9 with older pupils being offered German and Italian. Classics Department continues to thrive with around a third of pupils taking Latin GCSE; ancient Greek is offered as a club.

Lively sixth form, the only one in south-east London to offer the choice of A levels or IB. Offered as a free choice after good consultation – whichever suits the individual best.

Pupils setted for most subjects. All screened for specific learning difficulties in year 7, those identified given an individual Pupil Profile which sets out strategies and support needed. SENCo works with teachers to assist them in developing inclusive and multisensory teaching within the classrooms. Extension classes are run for more able pupils in a range of subjects and those who are ready can sit maths, languages or science GCSEs early.

Friendly staff work hard to make their teaching exciting and inspirational, healthy mix of gender and ages. Lots of creative activities in all the academic subjects; trips, workshops and competitions back up solid teaching.

S

Games, options, the arts: Sporty school with great on-site facilities considering its inner city location. Everyone, including the juniors, has a full afternoon's sport each week – part of the 'fitted to do well in life' business.

All trad sports on offer, plus Rugby fives, golf and sailing. Very active D of E and CCF, which is increasingly popular and operates in partnership with St Matthew's Academy. Links with the Worshipful Company of Marketors, who installed Mrs Davies on a float for the Lord Mayor's show.

Drama and music very strong, again with a wide range of opportunities. Drama department puts on several performances each year from traditional Shakespearean plays to modern musicals. For those not so keen on acting there are many other technical and design areas to be involved in. Choirs, bands, orchestras and ensembles of almost every style run with the options growing each year depending on pupil's interests and talents.

Two lovely light art studios, where a very high standard of work is produced, 90 per cent of GCSE pupils achieved A*or A grades in 2013. Countless clubs and societies at lunchtime and after school. Hamster club is popular with younger pupils who learn how to look after small animals whilst making new friends. Interhouse mastermind and drama competitions run alongside electronics, modern language society, drawing, sewing and debating. In conjunction with all the sports, arts and clubs are a fabulous selection of annual expeditions to join from singing in Estonia to diving in Egypt.

Background and atmosphere: Busy inner-city site next to a road junction is not enviable, nor is tangling with the South Circular a joyful way to spend your mornings. The original school was a 15th century foundation in the City of London; hence the continuing links with livery companies. St Dunstan's was refounded and relocated in the 1880s to the current site in Catford.

Striking in appearance – some would say ugly – the main Victorian buildings are aptly described by the children as 'very Hogwarts'. The interior is a warren of corridors, lunatic-asylum style, but with some effective efforts to soften the look and an attractive enclosed garden. Great Hall for assemblies, performances and other gatherings, recently restored Victorian stained-glass windows tells the story of the school.

Dining room, purpose-built in the '50s, has plate glass windows with a curved roof (like a Pringle crisp) and no pillars – an amazing space. Doubles up as the ideal spot for school discos and other social events.

Pastoral care and discipline: Pastoral care excellent, continues to be hymned by parents. Pupils, parents and staff encouraged to contact each other whenever they need. The school expects everyone to be supportive and helpful to each other; relationships between sexes are exactly what you would hope for from a co-educational school – realistic and not primarily hormone fuelled. House and prefect system. Bullying is not tolerated and is dealt with swiftly when it occurs. A strong and successful drugs education policy – the school takes a harder line than the rest of society on misdemeanours.

Pupils and parents: Largish multicultural mix reflecting the local area. Hard-working and aspirational parents, many of whom are first-time buyers in the independent sector. Mostly professional, down-to-earth types, who might consider the Dulwich foundation schools rather too pushy or even aloof. Huge catchment area from Kent and all over South East and South West London, coaches run from Blackheath, New Cross, Clapham, Streatham, Farnborough and Bromley. Catford stations are a few minutes' walk away bringing children from central London. The continuing success of the IB attracts new groups of parents and young people to the school each year. Notably enthusiastic and active 'family society' run fetes, social and fundraising events throughout the year.

A friendly school that appeals to, and produces, interesting people across the disciplines. Old Dunstonians are musicians, politicians, businessmen, sportsmen and scientists. Martin Evans, Nobel Prize winner for genetics, the very Rev Dr John Hall, Dean of Westminster, and Michael Grade, executive chairman of ITV are amongst them.

Entrance: Harder than it was, but gentle by London standards. 11+ competitive entrance exam with papers in maths, English and reasoning. Children registered to sit the exam can opt to attend 11+ preparation classes held shortly before. Fifty percent of the intake comes from the prep school. Common entrance at 13+, entry to the sixth form at least seven GCSEs grade B and above with A grades in the subjects to be studied at AS or higher-level IB.

Exit: University, and a good one, is the object of most – ambitions have risen along with the entry hurdle. Between five and ten to medical schools, veterinary colleges and Oxbridge each year (four to Oxbridge in 2013). At 16+ a few leave for local sixth form colleges or specialist arts courses.

Money matters: Full fees bursaries from age 11. Art and design, music, drama, sports and academic scholarships at 11, and for sixth formers at the discretion of the head.

Remarks: A place with a good strong heartbeat taking care of individuals and considering what is best for each. Turns out well-prepared, mindful citizens.

St Edmund's College

Linked school: St Edmund's Prep

Old Hall Green, Ware, SG11 1DS

• Pupils: 630 boys and girls of whom roughly 130 board, full, weekly, occasional • Ages: 11-19 • Roman Catholic but all faiths welcome • Fees: Day £8,484–£15,405; Boarding £20,424–£25,989 pa • Independent

Tel: 01920 824247
Email: admissions@stedmundscollege.org
Website: www.stedmundscollege.org

Headmaster: Since 2012, Mr Paulo Durán BA MA (London). Educated at the London Oratory, King's College London, and Heythrop College. Married to Alice, a teacher, with one daughter about to start at St Edmund's. After spells at South Hampstead and Alleyn's, he took up a post as head of modern languages at Mill Hill School where he stayed for six years, before moving to St Edmund's as deputy head in 2009. After three years he was offered the headship, and, he says, would like to stop here. Parents hope so too. 'A very warm, very charismatic man and a very strong leader,' said one mother. 'Please don't leave!'

Academic matters: Generally a sound performance with top grades consistently accounting for around two fifths of results. 2013 figures, for instance were 42 per cent A*-A at GCSE and almost 40 per cent A*-A at A level, which percentages are broadly on a par with the previous two years. 'results are very good, and I want them to improve,' says head, but aims to achieve same 'without changing the children or the school. It's about moving up those league tables the hard way.' One big change is coming, however. From September 2014, the school will offer the IB alongside A levels. This is in response to parental demand, says school, as well as to a growing awareness that, as an international school, it's the right route to take. 'Catholic means universal, so we're already part of an international network.'

Broad curriculum comprises all the usual arts, humanities and sciences, with maths being a particular favourite. 'I like maths, purely for the fact that the teachers are so willing to help you,' said one boy, and his friends agreed. French (compulsory), Spanish, German and Latin on offer, and all students learn at least two of these, with Italian offered to the particularly able linguists in year 9. As you'd expect in a school of this ethos, religious education has a high profile, and RE is compulsory up to and including GCSE. The pupils aren't bothered by this, because 'the RE teachers are really good!' Bang-up-to-date ICT suites, and well-resourced classrooms and science labs. Food tech a popular option, and the children were proud of their achievements in the school bake-off. Lots of good quality work on the wall displays, and we were pleased with the standard of writing and spelling. The handsome library is surprisingly small for a school this size, but was lively and welcoming and regularly hosts visits from the likes of Kevin Crossley-Holland and Dave Cousins.

Our young tour guides were upbeat about lessons and about the amount of individual attention they got from teachers; the average class size is 21 (14 in sixth form). Parents described the teaching staff as 'really fantastic' and 'always there for the pupils', and praised the unwearying help given, in any subject, to students who needed it. 'If you're in the top set, you're pushed just as hard as you would be in a top academic school,' commented one sixth former. But a broad range of abilities is catered for here. The school currently has 105 children on its Learning Difficulties and Disabilities register, and pupils with SEN requirements are well-supported, both in class and at homework club, which happens four afternoons a week. EAL is also important here, because of the school's international intake. IGCSE second language English is offered to overseas students where appropriate.

The intake is only gently selective, which may account for the odd unexpected hiccup in student knowledge here and there. Talking to us about the school's history, a year 9 pupil told me, 'France wasn't Catholic back then, which is why the school moved here.' But the school's history is quite long and involved, and we were impressed by the pride with which the children talked about it. Everyone we spoke to was adamant that the school fostered a strong work ethic and helped all students to achieve their best.

Games, options, the arts: One happy parent, a musician herself, described the music as 'fantastic', and we certainly liked what we saw. The school's top choir, Schola Cantorum, regularly gigs at the likes of Canterbury and Westminster Cathedrals; chapel choir sings on Sundays during term time, and the chamber choir is much in demand for more secular school functions, such as weddings and dances. Lots of ensembles including an orchestra and jazz band, ably supported by a 21-strong team of peripatetic music teachers who get the children up to scratch on voice, strings, brass, woodwind, percussion, piano, guitar, harpsichord and organ (there's a magnificent organ in the school chapel). The school is particularly keen to build on choral scholarships 'and to see where that takes us.' There's a musical production every year; Our House by Madness is a recent example, and the curtain will shortly rise on Half A Sixpence at the nearby Broxbourne Civic Hall. 'They're a lot of work and a big commitment but they're absolutely wonderful!' enthused one student. Drama is also popular, with lots taking LAMDA exams, and student-directed productions such as – amazingly – One Man, Two Guvnors.

The last period of every school day (which finishes at 4.30pm) is given over to extracurricular activities, so all pupils participate in something. An extremely wide range of arts, crafts and other interests are offered, including CCF, D of E and Model United Nations. There are also some pretty special opportunities for travel. 'The trip to Thailand was one of the most amazing things

I've ever done,' said one girl, and other pupils were starry-eyed about their experiences in India, America and Barcelona.

Wonderfully spacious campus means lots of playing fields plus tennis courts and Astro. Girls' sport, including football, is strong and successful, but the boys' provision for traditional team games appears to be something of an issue. 'I'd like to see more organised compulsory training for the top teams,' said one boy, diplomatically. Parents (eager in their praise of all other areas of the school) were more forthright, criticising what they claimed was a 'lazy' lack of coaching for school teams who then had to 'go out and get slaughtered every week against better-trained sides.' Students confirmed that rugby/football practices were sometimes scheduled after the school buses had left, so that pupils, who travel in from an unusually wide geographical area, had no choice but to miss the sessions if they wanted to get home. The school counters by saying that the late afternoon practices were scheduled at the request of parents, who had seemed happy to collect their children themselves. The less traditional sports – table tennis, golf, badminton, aerobics – are all flourishing, and there can't be many schools which can offer their students fishing (in the school pond) as an option.

Background and atmosphere: Founded in France in 1568 as a seminary for English Catholics when the Reformation's prohibition of Catholic education forced Cardinal William Allen to decamp to Douai in Flanders. A couple of hundred years later in 1793, the French Revolution had professors and scholars packing their bags once again and moving to the village of Old Hall Green just north of Ware, where a small (and very secret) Catholic school had formerly acted as a 'feeder' for the Douai seminary. On the 16th November 1793 – the feast of St Edmund – the school was created. It weathered various changes of fortune during the 19th century, but celebrated its quarter centenary in 1968, admitted girls to the sixth form in 1974 and has been fully co-educational since 1986. The school lists 20 canonised saints and 133 martyrs amongst its alumni, and is proud of its history, which it commemorates throughout the building in drawings, paintings and artefacts. Now occupying the whole of the village of Old Hall Green, the site is spacious (440 acres), wooded, and stunningly beautiful.

If Catholic iconography makes you uneasy, this ain't the place for you. Pictures of popes, archbishops, cardinals and saints are everywhere, along with statues, shrines, relics, holy paintings, and even a graveyard, containing, said an earnest pupil, 'people who died for the school'. Although not Catholic ourselves, we rather loved it. It was something to see students lining up, in their own free time at their own volition, to use the Scofield Chantry for a few moments of candle-lit private prayer. The prevailing mood throughout the school, even at its liveliest times, was one of calm benevolence and order. 'We pride ourselves on the way we talk to our students and the way they talk to each other,' said the head, and all the young people we spoke to were in agreement. 'Everybody is nice, everybody respects each other,' 'I love it here, all my friends are nice,' 'The atmosphere is lovely,' were typical comments. Prayers are said before every lesson, 'And some of the prayers are really nice!' cried a pupil, who then recited one for me with great affection, adding 'You don't have to join in, but everyone respects it.' The school's Pugin chapel is lofty and awe-inspiring, and is used for weddings, funerals and baptisms as well as for school services. It's flanked by the smaller shrine chapel, built to hold St Edmund's left fibula that was presented by Cardinal Wiseman in 1863.

The college is overseen not by a specific order but by the Archdiocese of Westminster and the Roman Catholic ethos is completely central to the life of the school. Even the year groups are named after Catholic principles: Elements, Rudiments, Grammar, Syntax, Poetry, Rhetoric I and Rhetoric II. 'We're proudly and unashamedly Catholic,' as the head put it, but added, 'We're also proud of being inclusive.'

For many decades the school's resident priest was the much-loved Father Pinot de Moira, who came to St Edmund's over sixty years ago as a boy. His recent death has left the school in mourning but, says head, 'he'd be furious if he thought we were just going to roll over.' A new chaplain will be appointed in due course.

Pastoral care and discipline: Everyone we spoke to was especially warm in their praise of this aspect of the school. 'It's really good, very strong,' 'The school is very nurturing,' 'A very, very welcoming place, my child settled in straight away,' were some of the comments, and the last ISI inspection report praised the pupils' spiritual and personal development as outstanding. The house system is the main source of pastoral care with each pupil having a tutor and head of house. Boarders are very well looked after, with lots of staff living on site, and the school counsellor is always on hand. 'Bullying here is mercifully rare, and we set the bar low,' said head, firmly.

A number of pupils and parents commented on the lunch queues, which, they alleged, were not always well-managed. Some children spoke of having to miss lunch if they needed to attend clubs, or even if the queue just was too long. 'She loves the meals, but doesn't always get to eat them!' said one mother, 'I can't understand why they haven't nailed that problem.' (School admits that the situation needs addressing, and says it is working on ways to improve things.) On the plus side, the boarding means that all pupils can stay for supper at the school when they need to – when there are concerts or parents' evenings, for instance – and generally students seemed cared for and contented, moving with calm purpose about the school; uniform was worn tidily and behaviour everywhere was good. The spacious, well-kept and eye-pleasing buildings themselves seemed to help create a relaxed and happy community of individuals, quirky and otherwise, with a refreshing range of life-aspirations: one student hopes to set up a museum dedicated to vacuum cleaner parts.

Pupils and parents: Day pupils make up the majority of students, and are bused in from all over Hertfordshire and beyond via a network of 16 different routes. Excellent scholarships and bursaries ensure wide social diversity. Significant community of international students, many of them from eastern Europe, Africa and Asia. About 40 per cent of pupils are from Catholic families. The rest are from other Christian denominations, and from 'all other faiths and from none'. ('We have a fantastic Diwali celebration every year,' the head told me.) Notable alumni include William Scholl the sandal designer, perfumiers James and Robert Floris, and Ralph Richardson.

Entrance: About 20 a year from St Edmund's Prep, for whom entry to the senior school is automatic, provided they joined in year 4 or below. The rest, who come from a wide range of preps and primaries, sit entrance exams in maths, English and non-verbal reasoning. However, the report from the child's previous school is just as important, along with the St Edmund's interview. 'We interview everyone for at least 30 minutes, and for as long as it takes, really,' says head, who puts great emphasis on getting to know what the children are like. The school's popularity continues to rise and they are now oversubscribed, with around 270 applicants for the 80 available places. Small additional intake at 13+. Some join the school at 16+, for which they need five A*-B grades at GCSE with at least B in their chosen A level subjects.

Exit: At 16+, around 30 per cent to state sixth form colleges, or, very occasionally, to other independents (one boy found he'd grown away from the Catholic ethos and wanted a change). The rest stay on for sixth form here. At 18+ mostly to university, with 'good numbers' to Russell Group institutions, and 2 or 3 to Oxbridge.

Money matters: Academic scholarships at 11+ and 13+, awarded on performance in the entrance exam. Music, art, sport and all-rounder scholarships also available, often in combination with academic awards. Total awards can be extremely generous – we heard from one parent whose child's scholarship was worth 90 per cent of the annual fees. A few sixth form scholarships. Limited number of means tested bursaries, covering up to full fees.

Remarks: A successful, flourishing, dependable school with real spiritual heart. Well worth considering.

St Edmund's School

Linked school: St Edmund's Junior School

St Thomas Hill, Canterbury, CT2 8HU

- Pupils: 175 boys, 105 girls; 80 board. • Ages: 13–18. • Christian foundation but all faiths welcome. • Fees: Day £18,054; Boarding £26,190–£28,095 pa • Independent

Tel: 01227 475600
Email: admissions@stedmunds.org.uk
Website: www.stedmunds.org.uk

Head: Since 2011, Mrs Louise Moelwyn-Hughes BA MA MEd, previously senior deputy head of The Perse in Cambridge. Educated at the Methodist College, Belfast, where she also studied at the City of Belfast School of Music and played a variety of sports at county level. Studied classics at Cambridge, then spent 13 years at Marlborough College in a variety of roles. She hopes 'to further strengthen the already successful academic profile of St Edmund's and to encourage each pupil to discover and pursue their talents by way of the rich extracurricular programme which the school offers.'

Academic matters: Recent introduction of IGCSE in maths and separate sciences at GCSE. Introduction of AQA English Baccalaureate has brought new challenge to able sixth formers by adding a unit of critical thinking to A levels and a research project in their last year and includes a service element. Wide range of A levels offered including psychology, Spanish, music technology, PE, photography and theatre and film studies. Food technology a popular option for boys as well as girls at GCSE. Native speakers able to take GCSEs in their own languages eg Chinese, Russian and Polish. Little difference between performance of boys and girls in national exams. At A level in 2013, 34 per cent A*/A and at GCSE, 37 per cent A*/A.

Wide ability range – 'a private comprehensive,' as one parent put it. About 65 with some form of SEN mostly mild dyslexia, dyspraxia, Asperger's and ADHD. Good one-to-one support. One statemented pupil funded by Medway. Around 50 pupils have English as an additional language, most of whom receive help.

Good communication on curriculum matters between junior and senior schools – some teachers work across both sites. Average class size 12 with a max of 18 and smaller class sizes in lower sets. Very dedicated team of teachers. A number of staff have retired recently and new young teachers have reinvigorated the common room. PSHE includes careers' guidance as well as sex and relationships education.

Games, options, the arts: The usual mix of sports – football, hockey, cricket, netball etc. Rugby recently introduced as an option. Team games compulsory until GCSEs. More flexible in sixth form but all continue with sport. Small numbers mean that everyone has a chance to play in a team. Under-19 Kent County Cricket Lemon Cup winners recently. County and national representation in sports ranging from hockey and cricket to martial arts and Ultimate Frisbee.

Lots of trips and outings – New York for drama, Paris for French and art, exchanges with a Polish school and visit to Auschwitz-Birkenau. Annual Middle Fifth Afloat, a four-day sailing trip to the Solent – effective team-building and bonding exercise always great fun, even for those who thought they hated sailing. Work experience compulsory at end of year 11.

Purpose-built music school with practice rooms, a Steinway grand piano and well-equipped recording studio. About 40 per cent of pupils play an instrument. New director of music has brought a new vitality to department – very persuasive and encouraging. One or two recent pupils to Oxbridge to read music. Five or six pupils attend Royal Academy lessons in London and several pupils selected for National Youth Theatre and National Youth Choir. More than 12 grade 8 students per year, six or more at diploma standard. Invite primary school children into school to take part in East Kent Youth Orchestra. Lots going on – a major concert each term and one in the cathedral once a year, plus lunchtime concerts and smaller chamber concerts and an active choir and jazz choir.

Large well-equipped 450 seat theatre – apparently the largest in East Kent. One major play every year and plays every term. Senior school pupils gain valuable technical experience by helping behind the scenes at junior plays. Occasionally St Edmund's productions have transferred to the Marlowe Theatre in Canterbury and to the Edinburgh Festival.

They have a lot of fun as well eg St Edmund's Got Talent. Most boys and girls do CCF because it's fun – compulsory for Middle 5th (year 10). Strong art department – plenty on offer, ceramics particularly impressive.

Background and atmosphere: Established in Yorkshire in 1749 as the Clergy Orphan School, school moved to Canterbury via London and settled in its present location in 1855. Centred on school house, an impressive ecclesiastical high Victorian building with chapel attached, set in 50 acres on St Thomas Hill overlooking the cathedral. Most of the classrooms are in separate blocks around the campus – some quite scruffy and shabby, although plans are afoot to refurbish them – but that is not what the school is all about.

Great emphasis on good works and the wider community and St Ed's has picked up Kent awards for service to the community eg the school has its own Rotary Interact Group with a pupil president who coordinates all fund raising and charity work and fosters international links. St Ed's pupils have helped paint a local primary school and have dug two ponds for Kent Wildlife Trust. They have also set up a one-to-one reading support scheme with a local primary school, and adopted a beach on the Kent coast and taken responsibility for keeping it clean, as well as fundraising for charities in Tanzania and Eastern Europe.

Pastoral care and discipline: Tight-knit community with a nurturing ethos and emphasis on developing individual talents and interests, and with the aim of making education fun. One parent said, 'the school has transformed my son's life and has made him feel good about himself for the first time in his life'. The division of pupils into four houses means that everyone has a sense of belonging and children integrate well and get to know other year groups. Small classes and tutor groups mean that pupils and staff get to know each other well and even the most retiring have the chance to have their voice heard. The boarding houses are very comfortable and the lucky ones have a fine hilltop view over the city to Canterbury cathedral. Girls all have single or twin rooms with en-suite bathrooms. Younger boys are housed in dorms, older ones in single or twins with en-suite bathrooms. New common rooms with Sky TV and pool tables where they can make toast and tea and where girls and boys can meet in the early evenings. Saturday school for the moment but might well be phased out within the next few years. Weekend activities organised but pupils often happy just being at school. Whole school meets in the chapel three times a week.

Pupils and parents: Local professional families, lots of first time buyers who are prepared to make sacrifices to send their children here – discerning parents who are interested in education but not looking for status. Very supportive bunch – good relationship with school and staff. Head takes a lot of trouble to maintain good relations with parents and have them on side – plenty of feedback about the school's work and children's progress. Various handbooks plus comprehensive website – 'Parents' Zone' – keeps everyone up to date. Foreign nationals – 40 per cent of boarders, from a range of countries – integrate well. Regular parents' mingling events – coffee mornings and Saturday breakfasts. Old Boys include actor Orlando Bloom, writer Lawrence Durrell, pianist Freddy Kempf and ex-England cricketer Robin Jackman.

Entrance: Accepts a broad range – not really selective in terms of ability but keen to take pupils who will thrive, and school takes trouble to get this right. Every child interviewed and personality and character considered very important. Most children come up from the junior school but also from local prep schools – Northbourne Park, Junior King's, increasingly from Wellesley House, Marlborough House, St Ronan's and Dulwich Prep at Cranbrook. Those from local primaries will spend two years in the prep school before transferring at 13+. About 20 a year join in sixth form, some from the grammars and some from overseas – all seem to settle in well. Sixth form entrants need six A*-Cs at GCSE and Bs in the subjects they wish to study at A level.

Exit: About 10 per cent of a year group of 65 leave after GCSEs, mainly to grammars or sixth form colleges – mainly for financial reasons. High proportion to university or further education – a couple to Oxbridge every year plus Russell Group, former polys, art foundation courses, drama school, music conservatoires – the whole spectrum.

Money matters: Many give up a lot to send their children here. Significant numbers receive help through bursaries and scholarships. Not a rich school – bursaries out of fee income and help is given to see children through to next set of exams. Means-tested fee concessions can be provided for children of the clergy, Forces, diplomatic service and the third and subsequent children of the same family in the school at the same time. A foundation has recently been set up to secure scholarship and bursary funding and to fund future developments.

Remarks: Warm welcoming, nurturing school, feels like one big family where everyone has a strong sense of belonging – and not doing badly on the academic side either.

St Edward's Oxford

Woodstock Road, Oxford, OX2 7NN

• Pupils: 680; 410 boys, 270 girls. 80 per cent board, 20 per cent day • Ages: 13–18 • C of E • Fees: Boarding £32,082; Day £25,671 pa • Independent

Tel: 01865 319200
Email: registrar@stedwardsoxford.org
Website: www.stedwardsoxford.org

Warden: Since September 2011, Mr Stephen Jones MSc MLitt (fifties), previously head of Dover College. Educated at both Hurstpierpoint and Lord Wandsworth Colleges. Erudite, a man of many degrees, went to Durham to read maths and physics but graduated with a rare first in philosophy, then read maths before embarking on research in philosophy of maths. Was an assistant housemaster at Cheltenham College, head of maths at Berkhamsted School and a social tutor at Radley before his appointment at Dover. Married to the delightful Katie who has her own successful career in the church – no mean feat alongside being a headmaster's wife. They have three children, two flown the nest, one not yet at senior school.

We're told he is a good sportsman, keen on staying in shape, enjoys fives and sailing and has a keen sense of humour, 'His student house was dubbed Front, so he could talk about going back to Front'. An accomplished mathematician he loves poring over the figures and has a brain that specialises in pure logic, in whatever discipline. Parents say, 'Youngsters respect him, he is easy to talk to.' When we meet he is chatty, relaxed, enthusiastic – 'I don't have all the answers, what head does?' – but stresses that 'I want to engender a culture of academic excitement, sharpen things, raise expectations tempered with understanding of what the world is really like'. He is realistic too and under no illusion that keeping St Edward's on top of its game and rubbing shoulders with competitors will demand toughness and vision.

Academic matters: Most take nine or 10 subjects at IGCSE/GCSE, all the usual plus Latin or classical civilisation and Greek alongside PE, DT and drama. In 2013 59 per cent of GCSE papers were graded A*/A. Philosophy/ethics/political literacy courses for lower school pupils and all sixth formers study for an EPQ or equivalent: 'Great preparation for independent study at university and beyond,' says warden. In 2013, 74 per cent of A level grades were A*/B (50 per cent A*/A) and the IB average was a solid rather than starry 35.9. Scholars' societies – OX2 for lower school and The Woodstock Group for seniors – stretch the able. Parents say science teaching is variable: 'Joint offering of IB and A level has resulted in good teachers being stretched too thinly' – school aware and say they are working hard to redress. At A level biology and art and design popular and successful.

Good for self-esteem, those who can will, those who can't will be helped to. Currently 15 per cent of pupils receive learning support, mainly for mild dyslexia – timetabled and free: 'We are an inclusive school so subject support is offered'. Learning support concentrates on strategies, including use of smart phone and ICT. 'If they are disaffected we look closely at what is going on. They can't hide here.'

Has a reputation for being gentler on the old grey matter – both entry and exit – than many of its near competitors yet, in these league table propelled days, parents may seek a school that is 'forgiving' on entry but don't want an apology on exit – nor do they get one. Teddies (as it is affectionately known) has been shimmying up the league tables: not via hothousing – 'There are enough schools in the locality doing that,' says school – nor by upping the entry ante (though scholarships have been expanded and a new girls' house, Jubilee, helpfully nudges boy-girl ratio close to 3-2); rather the main thrust has been to eke more out of everyone, think good breezy airing, rather than squeezed through the wringer. Pupils write A* and keep in their pockets; IGCSEs introduced; IB has been extended ('Oversold' say parents, school says not the case, but don't deny its enthusiasm for it, adding 'Pupils are choosing it in increasing numbers'). A levels remain – mix linear and modular to suit subject, though no Pre-U, the tougher alternative to A levels, 'Not really the thing for our cohort', said warden. However the biggest buzz (and buzz-word) is meta cognition ('know about knowing' said our young informant). Warden wanted children to develop intellect, to reason, question and enquire. 'Some children arrive brow-beaten through CE; we have to rebuild their confidence, inspire and invigorate them'. Working on the youngsters meant developing staff. 'I appointed a new academic director who encourages staff to share good practice,

go off-piste, explore and enjoy their subject,' says warden. A move that appears to be working: 'Teachers love the curve ball question but some had lost their nerve, teaching only to pass an exam rather than exploring their subject,' says academic director. 'That is changing'. Dead Poets Society this isn't, there is still a generous nod to the syllabus and ticking boxes – plenty of routine revision, past papers, chalk and talk during our spring visit but our guides said they're treated to discussion-based, interactive, active lessons. Parents approve: 'It's a happy, friendly common room with a great vibe that rubs off on kids'. Academic push still a work in progress but generally all things learned are looking up and bucking up.

Games, options, the arts: Fabulous facilities – 100 acres of prime north Oxford – outdoor courts, cricket pitches, a new cricket pavilion (Gloucestershire Cricket Club runs a satellite academy at the school for pupils and local juniors), a nine hole golf course, boat house. Indoors there is a superbly equipped, sparkly leisure centre – the hub of middle class Oxford mummies working off their lunches – shared with, and leased from, the school, providing a fantastic gym, indoor and outdoor pools, indoor tennis courts and fitness and dance studios. Pupils win accolades – cricket team undefeated, have their fastest first eight ever, runners up at National Schools' and Henley; several GB junior oarsmen and county cricketers; girls' senior hockey team have been county champions seven years in a row – currently county champions at U14, U16 and U18. Rugby less robust,: 'We take a few hits,' confess boys, though school hopeful tide turning. New director of sport is working hard to tempt talent of tomorrow to Teddies – with an array of special events. Not that those who wince at the thought of catching a ball should worry: 'They will find a sport, you can not only do but do so proficiently; it's all about building confidence. Staff get involved too – it's lovely to see their commitment – it rubs off on the youngsters.' Only moan is expense of sports kit: 'Always something else on the bill; they must be in-league with the supplier,' joked one parent.

Art good with results to match, especially at A level with facilities for jewellery making, ceramics, sculpture and large fine art displays. The North Wall Arts Centre (enjoyed by the local community – hosts visiting artists and theatre groups) boasts exhibition galleries, drama studios and a cosy 250 seat theatre. Parents say dance has come on in 'leaps and bounds' and music is on the up, with something for everyone regardless of where you sit in the talent pool. 'Kids try hard, there's a huge number of bands, plus excellent choirs including one for parents and the community.' Excellent extracurricular provision including ever popular Duke of Edinburgh and CCF.

Background and atmosphere: Situated in leafy north Oxford, the setting is privileged indeed. Much akin to an Oxford college, the main buildings surround a lawned quad. Recent additions include an eco-inspired life sciences building – solar powered with 'more technology than you could wish for'. School isn't the grandest we've seen, it may lack the edge of some of its established upper-crusty rivals, but it has enough of everything, is polished and looks good. Simple peaceful chapel, compulsory on Sundays for boarders, C of E but all faiths welcome. Boarding houses have own identity – Quad or Field side – choose quad for a disorganised child, field for those who relish open space. New girls' house, Jubilee, is, according to warden, 'more like an upmarket hotel than a traditional school house!' For most of the rest, including odd Cinderella house ('about to improve' say school) it is standard, homely rooms – shared save for the older years, with an assortment of communal facilities. Day pupils stay until 9pm (ad hoc early finish at 6pm on request), all can have a bed in the boarding houses and sleep over if they're too spent to go home.

Pastoral care and discipline: Parents say pastoral care is excellent, only caveat, 'We'd love our child to have the same tutor throughout, someone who can help and support when pressure builds or child overloaded, overwhelmed or overwrought'; school counters 'structured tutor system for continuity of tutoring in lower school and in sixth form is ideal for a boarding school'. Cohesive boarding houses provide welcome support and foster inter-year friendships. Good food, all dine centrally, pupils say it's fun to mix with friends from other houses, parents rue table manners, 'They're noticeably very much "bolt-food" variety.' Safari suppers, ice-skating and discos are a sample of the many weekend jollies. Still has its fair share of rich kids, some with arguably too much pocket money at their disposal. Tough on drugs, warden says, 'If we suspect, we test; if positive, save the most exceptional circumstances and I can't think of any of those, they're out.' Punishments for smoking, parents say booze handled brilliantly for the child. 'Quite a number drink and smoke in younger years (same everywhere?), they push boundaries but school pushes back.' Local pubs policed, those aged 18 get a pub pass but other savvy sixth formers sneak off to Summertown for their Saturday night tipple. 'If they get caught they get bust but it doesn't stop them,' said our mole, adding, 'You must be able to say a lucid goodnight to your HM, otherwise it's a night in the san and the ignominy of being woken every 30 minutes.' School adds, 'All have cheese and biscuits and spend an hour with HM when they return, its great fun for HM and means we get to keep a friendly eye.' Despite tolerance, some parents feel school needs to be more trusting, offer more privileges to older ones, with a long rein tugged hard for those who rail against.

Pupils and parents: Parents a mix of academics, professionals and business. Twelve per cent overseas from a huge variety of countries. Most of rest from Oxford or the Home Counties. 'Lots of boarders go home on Sunday after chapel, leaving school feeling somewhat empty and unloved for those forced to stay in,' said one parent, but another added, 'I like that they can come home on Sundays, we relish the family time.' Has a local reputation of privilege and at times pushing the boundaries – Teddies' girls in particular – yet the pupils we met were grounded, down to earth and friendly, a view shared by others we spoke to. 'They're clubbable, they've had to live with people in close confinement, they learn how to get the most out of others,' says warden, with a student adding, 'My parents gave me The Good Schools Guide and I chose Teddies, it has lived up to all in the review but especially on the friendship and friendliness front.' Notable former pupils include Kenneth Grahame, Laurence Olivier, Douglas Bader, Guy Gibson, Jon Snow and Sam Waley-Cohen.

Entrance: From a range of prep schools, majority of day from Dragon. Skype interviews possible for those based overseas. Gently academic 55 per cent at CE, non CE candidates take the school's own exam. A handful sit an exam at 11+ to guarantee a place. Runs an academic challenge day for local year 6 pupils, with diet of philosophy, Arabic, economics, architecture and politics, to spot scholarship potential and encourage applications.

Exit: Handful leave post 16 to pursue courses not offered here or to save on fees (10 per cent in 2013). Three to Oxbridge in 2013, most of rest to Russell Group. Favoured destinations: London, Newcastle, Leeds. Popular subjects include geography, biomedical sciences, engineering, maths, modern languages and history. Inspiringly, St Edward's doesn't view the path to university as job well done: 'We look to the bigger picture, the young employable 25-year-old making strides in business, commerce, enterprise and academia. Understanding the cut and thrust of the world beyond university is paramount.'

Money matters: New scholarships introduced – academic, music, sport and all-rounder can be means tested to a maximum of 100 per cent. Sizeable number on bursaries: 'Often the most able,' says warden. 'Attracting bright pupils is good for the school, good for the teachers and good for results.' All are considered annually for an honorary scholarship. Minor scholarships available for drama, art and dance.

Remarks: For those uncomfortable with ultra prestige, the trappings of the old and bold, or the sheen of highly-polished academia, St Edward's offers an established, acceptable, dependable alternative. Those who seek out Teddies will either be judging it against day school rivals or other co-ed boarding schools; it doesn't sit at the top of either pile but it holds its own, taps on elbows and keeps them on their toes. All-round broad education with plenty of nurturing, perceptibly raising expectations and results while maintaining its discernible cheer and friendliness. A busy school with a rosy outlook, ideal for the average to above average child, the late bloomer, the all-rounder and the high-flyer who doesn't wish to be a mere pebble, fighting for survival, in the tidal wave of Oxford's academic powerhouses.

Saint Felix School

Linked school: Saint Felix School Pre-Prep and Prep Departments

Halesworth Road, Reydon, Southwold, Suffolk, IP18 6SD

• Pupils: 385 boys and girls; 95 boarders • Ages: 11–18 • Non-denom • Fees: Day £13,980; Boarding £19,590–£24,420 pa • Independent

Tel: 01502 722175
Email: schooladmin@stfelix.co.uk
Website: www.stfelix.co.uk

Head: Since September 2013, Fran D'Alcorn, previously long-serving deputy head.

Academic matters: Mixed ability intake and dedicated staff who encourage rather than wield the stick. Small, teaching groups (especially in the sixth) and above average value-added. Three separate sciences for the more able and alongside French and Spanish the option of taking Latin. Most study languages up to year 11 either in conversation (three native speakers on the staff) or for GCSE. In 2013, 41 per cent A*/A grades at GCSE and 42 per cent at A level. No Saturday school but lessons finish at 5pm every day except Friday (4pm).

For those who find the going tough, good support from the maths department. SENCo full time and qualified (dyslexia specific). Learning support is now delivered in a number of key ways: advice and planning with class/subject teachers, teaching assistance within the mainstream classroom, small group teaching and one-to-one individual lessons. 'Parents are fully consulted and are often involved in helping to set out individual education plans for their child.' SENCo charged with getting the staff up to speed on anything needs-related; she works with three part-time classroom assistants.

Games, options, the arts: All appreciate the sporting provision. Weekday fixtures give pupils the chance to play for local clubs at the weekend. No hockey for the boys but all the other majors, with a wider range of options for the sixth. Generous modern sports hall, swimming pool, fitness suite and squash courts – also used by parents and the local community. Swimming is a big thing – 'Our son hated the water but they taught him to swim and laugh,' enthused a mum. Two coaches (one GB) work with élite, youth, junior and development squads, which include children from other schools, state and private. Swimmers take part in county and national championships and hold a number of county and national times. Pupils can train as life guards and if they wish work for the school – 'a good way to earn a bit of pocket money, especially if they're boarders'. Extra-curricular activities cater for a variety of tastes – sailing, canoeing, climbing wall (very popular), CCF, D of E, sewing, cookery.

Displays of interesting photographic images and cheerful artwork (created in the north-lit, spacious studio) are everywhere – stuck to corridor walls or perched on ledges. Popular drama department puts on at least one good, serious play or musical a year. Inclusive approach gets almost all involved – if not in the limelight, back stage or making props. 'Caring' head of music. Just under half the pupils learn an instrument. Oodles of practice rooms.

Background and atmosphere: Queen Anne-style purpose-built red-brick buildings dating from 1897 plus well-crafted modern additions are set in a breezily expansive site a brisk walk away from the quaintly old fashioned seaside town of Southwold. Originally a school for genteel girls. Come the late 1990s, a new direction was needed – now fully co-ed. Pleasant, positive atmosphere. Essentially a day school with a growing dollop of flexi and full time boarders – the majority of whom are in the sixth. Politeness and courtesy are encouraged – the head believes manners and academia go hand in hand. Girls are well turned out and charmingly friendly – as yet boys aren't as polished, but the girls appreciate their sense of fun.

Classrooms are a trifle lacklustre but the Scandinavian-style wood-clad dining hall, which offers standard fare plus chirpy bonhomie, is inviting. The library has been given a preliminary facelift with the introduction of squishy sofas and the removal of tired tomes. A new fiction library has been established and the Gardiner Hall has been totally refurbished as a sixth form study area.

Pastoral care and discipline: Everyone knows everyone and the school really scores when it comes to confidence-building. Consideration for others is encouraged and problems are dealt with promptly and sympathetically. Kindly house mistress keeps a weather eye on sixth form boarders.

Pupils and parents: Active PTA and supportive parent body. All sorts from entrepreneurs to old brigade who remember when cucumber sandwiches had no crusts. Largely from north Suffolk, south Norfolk and the A12 corridor. School has organised an impressively comprehensive bus service to cover the wide catchment area. Significant number of overseas students (mainly from the Pacific Rim) in the sixth form.

Entrance: At all ages. Two day entrance procedure for outside applicants – behaviour and academic ability are assessed. For the sixth, five A*-Cs with B or above in subjects taken at A level. Interviews for outside applicants.

Exit: Variety of courses with a focus on the courses at top universities and art colleges.

Money matters: For entrants 11-16 academic, performing arts, music, tennis and swimming scholarships (up to 50 per cent) and exhibitions (up to 25 per cent). For sixth form entrants academic, music, sport, art and drama scholarships. Bursaries in cases of need. Forces discount.

Remarks: Friendly, not overly pushy place giving an all round education – suitable for those who might flounder in a larger pond. We look forward to seeing what direction the school will take under its new head.

St George's College, Weybridge

Linked school: St George's Junior School

Weybridge Road, Addlestone, Surry, KT15 2QS

• Pupils: 935 all day • Ages: 11-18 • RC (Josephite) • Fees: £14,190–£16,140 pa • Independent

Tel: 01932 839300
Email: contact@stgeorgesweybridge.com
Website: www.stgeorgesweybridge.com

Headmaster: Since 1995, Mr Joe Peake MA (Oxon) in chemistry, PGCE (aka Le Directeur, El Director, Der Direktor, Magister Princeps according to language week special pinned to office door). Age: 'a young' (advises school info sheet) upper end fifties. You sense he's not one for impetuous career moves, what with previous decade-long role as head of chemistry and director of curriculum at Millfield School preceded by a solid five years at The Manchester Grammar School, though cut teaching milk teeth as a VSO recruit in Ghana. Also in demand as chair of prestigious independent schools' bodies; has been a top A level chemistry examiner too.

Married to high-powered biochemist (they met at Oxford) and has three grown up children, a doctor, astrophysicist and food science expert who all went through the school. Lives on site 'somewhere' say pupils vaguely gesturing into the middle distance (privacy issues clearly not too much of a problem) and so much part of the warp and weft of the school that you can virtually feel his DNA running through the brickwork.

Firm handshake, excellent eye contact and scintillates in the US trick of frequent conversational name repetitions (a technique shared with junior school colleagues – perhaps it's covered in training days). Happiest when he's out and about and confesses occasionally to being on walkabout when he should be exuding gravitas round a boardroom table.

As to character, 'well, he's just Mr Peake, what can you say?' muse parents. When pressed, they highlight his charisma and relish for the up-front, showman's role, ably supported by deputy who, says one, tends to be the details man. One to one, he's 'very compassionate and supportive' if a family crisis strikes, says a mother with first-hand experience. 'An extremely nice man,' confirms another, though he is also reckoned to have a good line in gentle intimidation, assisted by mastery of the bland-sounding enquiry and tactical conversational pause which must serve him extremely well when it comes to eliciting information.

To pupils he's a benevolent, Dumbledorean presence – 'wise and quite personable' says one – well-liked and 'increasingly respected as you go up the school' and rated brilliant at pupil recognition thanks, he says, to the wonders of technology, allowing him to spend quality computer time before start of each academic year matching faces and names though he says it's trickier when pupils hit adolescence and acquire 'spots and facial hair'.

While he exudes charm, isn't for turning. Has all the assurance you'd expect from someone who has steered a large school from ho-hum average to increasingly successful and over-subscribed, with an instinct for being bang on trend – was a co-ed pioneer, for example, admitting girls from 11 as early as 1998 (even earlier in the sixth form). Has his views and you either go with them or go elsewhere. Given strength of the school under his leadership, you can't really blame him.

Academic matters: Like head, school radiates confidence. There's a sense of having arrived and pausing to take stock. Yes, pupil numbers have doubled and standards have risen steadily but though there's natural enthusiasm for further upwards striving, head isn't, 'remorselessly trying to make this more and more academic.' Parents back this up. 'It's not force feeding,' says one.

Results consistently good, some very good – lots of A*-A grades at GCSE (71 per cent in 2013). Similar story for A levels with 83 per cent A*-B and half graded A*-A in 2013. something that puts them amongst area's stronger performers (and local competition, state and private, is fierce).

How's it done? Head's long service means that by now, around half of the nearly 100-strong teaching staff (average age 41), like choice crops, have been hand-picked by Mr Peake. Enthusiasm comes as standard with teachers not just on emergency call out in exam season but still working to timetable when pupils are on study leave (though they request emails to avoid teaching to empty rooms). Attitude filters down – year two pupil, unprompted, rushes over to visitors during drama class to extoll delights of rehearsing 'Pardoner's Tale' for performance. 'A head girl in the making,' says the incumbent.

Overall, there's sense of constant nudging to bring everything on that bit quicker and better, less hothouse, though, than prize winning allotment (all quality produce – think asparagus rather than bog standard giant marrows).

You see it in imaginative projects for gifted and talented cohort (year four poets clad scale models of London landmarks with photographs and words) and English language IGCSE taken a year early by everyone, sensible as capitalises on three years of timetabled library sessions where 'we can direct pupils' reading' says head of English, who's clearly good at inspiring a love of books further up the school. 'reading is all I do in my spare time,' says sixth form boy.

Unusually, no fast track maths (top number crunchers take additional maths GCSE by way of compensation) though a flair for languages can find pupils sailing through AS exam before they reach sixth form (here as elsewhere, language take up falls off sharply post GCSE, something school is keen to reverse).

Don't, however, expect subject choices to extend beyond tried and tested varieties. Unlike Maureen Lipman of BT ad fame, Mr Peake is not a fan of the 'ologies' (technology is the exception) feeling that A level psychology and sociology don't carry the same clout as what he describes as traditional 'hard currency' subjects. Budding girl rocket scientists should also consider the gender fault line that runs through the school at A-level – and elsewhere, of course – with biology a largely xx chromosome subject and chemistry and, overwhelmingly, physics dominated by the xy brigade. 'It just tends to be a boy's science' says pupil. Mr Peake, too, sees it more as an unwinnable nature versus nurture issue (girls' only schools, however, would almost certainly not agree).

When things go wrong, school does best to help. Policy is emphatically not to throw weakest to the wolves but catch problems early. May be the option to repeat a year. First port of call is often the academic support unit which also helps those with specific learning difficulties (dyslexia, affecting 50 or pupils by far the most common, handful of pupils have ADHD, ADD and ASD, only two statemented; around twenty with English as an additional language). Attendance at its supervised study periods, used to hone study rather than subject skills, is very strongly hinted at, though not compulsory, and parents are kept in the loop. 'It's not a draconian approach, more "if we don't feel that you're achieving this ... we'll all get together and try to work it out,"' says a mother. 'You're not allowed to slip but it's not done in an unpleasant way.'

Games, options, the arts: Would be criminal if games results didn't live up to glorious facilities (so many pitches, courts and nets that you could play somewhere different just about every week of the academic year). Fortunately they do, successfully, with whacking great double-fronted trophy cabinet stuffed with silverware – a challenge to even a posse of cat burglars – as proof.

It's all set in 100 acres, vast for home counties, let alone within M25 – property developers must salivate every time they drive past – and comes with a delightful 19th century cricket pavilion, a boathouse on the Thames and even a brace of rivers running through the grounds (why stop at one?).

Natty ultra traditional cricket and rowing blazers confer huge cachet on wearers, though the new is also embraced with basketball, currently being beta tested with series of successful friendlies and just about to go live. Overall, lots to cheer on and about with rugby a particular star and many other teams regularly reaching national finals. A few heroic near misses, too. 'The boys' first XI only lost three matches [...] unfortunately two were in the semi-finals...' begins wry hockey report in school mag.

Triple-colour awards are a regular phenomenon, as are small but steady numbers of rowers, cricketers and netball players cherry picked for regional and national squads. Keenness as well as talent is rewarded – turn up to under 12 boys' hockey training and you're guaranteed at least one go in school team.

The only fly in ointment is felt to be strength of mind required for those joining at 13 where 'it's a hard effort to get included in teams,' says parent. Not deliberate, she adds, 'it's just human nature'. 'Of course it's going to be tough,' adds another, more forthright mother, 'but there again it depends on how determined you are.' With school offering 100 timetabled activities every week, vast majority included in fees, no shortage of opportunities to find your inner sporting hero – or indeed cook, artist or musician. Volunteering ethos very strong and often with religious dimension. Highlight for many is over-subscribed week in Lourdes where lower sixth volunteers become full-time carers for disabled children – 'life-changing' says one. Standard fare of D of E and slightly more glamorous International Challenge also on offer.

Feel, though not macho, is equally far from precious. Music, highly successful (school won prestigious BBC Songs of Praise Senior School Choir of the Year in 2012 – the first time it had entered) balances highly selective with audition-free: whole school choir, open to all comers, tackles demanding choral works with panache. Energetic department director is unfussed by smallish numbers taking GCSE or A-level music, refreshing in an age when there's increasing sense that if you can't measure it in exam results it's scarcely worth doing. 'I'd rather have a full orchestra and big choirs than massive exam sets,' she says. She also relishes large amount of informal music making that goes on out of hours in first come first served practice rooms. Sound of pupil playing the grand piano in the chapel, not for an audience but just, apparently, for the pleasure of it, underpins her words.

Background and atmosphere: 'You won't see a macho school,' says the head. Instead, you'll hear a good deal of the phrase 'politesse and douceur'. Hard to pin down but think Arthurian knightly values (the good ones) given a 21st century co-educational makeover and you're probably not far off.

May sound a bit highfalutin but clearly goes in: pupils don't just behave exceptionally well in school (doors routinely held open a good forty feet in advance in longest of corridors) but out of it, too – a test with far higher ecological validity. Watching small group of unsupervised 11-year old boys in local country club restaurant eating and chatting quietly 'ignited the spark' for parent who hadn't previously considered the school for her children and ended up sending both there.

Ethos stems from Josephites, a small Belgian Catholic order dating from early 19th century who founded school in 1869. Though declining in Europe, order is vibrant in the Congo and blessedly scandal-free everywhere (only hint of controversy is at US school run by similarly named though unrelated order which is fighting, with strong parental backing, to retain corporal punishment).

As the UK mother house, the school is home to elderly priests who, like everyone else, must relish the space at their disposal. For vista-starved visitors from London it's a breath of fresh air (quite literally) with many pretty buildings, some Victorian, others a slight mish mash of periods and the widespread use of gorgeous unifying and beautifully tended greenery to bind everything together.

There's a green and pleasant quad for the youngest pupils accessorised with what sounds like the loudest blackbird in Surrey (possibly also hand-picked by Mr Peake) and, amongst many other areas, a sixth form garden – though if the school put its mind to it, pupils could all have their own plot and you'd scarcely notice.

Many of the classrooms have been refurbished and with the exception of the occasional beige carpet tile moment, overall effect is smart and welcoming – music floor with cream and blue walls is particularly inviting as is dining hall, all light wood and toning shades of school burgundy. (Well trained guides dutifully intone virtues of appealing and varied meals though there's widespread ditching once they cease to be compulsory.)

Tradition looms large, from new stained glass chapel windows, some inspired by words from school prayer to an almost subliminal appearance of the school crest all over the place, etched into windows, in undertones on walls and even face-painted on to pupils featured in the magazine. Corridors, too, pack a momento mori frisson. One is adorned with team photos, many pre-dating the Great War, with fresh-faced youths staring, unknowing, into the camera ('We sometimes try to work out which of us they look like,' says sixth former); the next stuffed with GCSE and A level artworks, all thoroughly of the moment, though, reassuringly, prevalence of tortured-looking figures tearing at faces signals response to exam themes rather than profound inner torment, say pupils.

Recently completed Henderson Centre, however, is very much of the moment. All soft curve loveliness, it's the best incentive for staying on at a school post GCSE that this reviewer has so far encountered. Sixth formers delight in café-style common room complete with balcony, mood lighting and instant boiling water (kettles – so old hat). Keep out signs warn off incursions by younger pupils – 'they get "The Stare" if they come in' says prefect. Also home to sixth-form only subjects like economics, plus humanities (geography and history, previously housed in less than glamorous huts, got first dibs on best seats in the house by way of compensation).

Pastoral care and discipline: 'A very nurturing school,' say parents. Four-house system provides the focus for inter-school competitions but caring role is down to much praised heads of year. They win accolades for their light touch but effective approach to bullying – 'once I'd pinpointed it, they were quick to make sure it was not going to happen again and didn't involve the children so they never knew anything about it,' says a mother – and in theory stay with a year group as they move up through school. It's not bombproof and promotion or maternity leave are, as elsewhere, the enemies of continuity, though in in the (rare) event that you don't get on, 'it can be a good idea to have a change because then you've only got to tolerate it for one year,' says a parent.

For minor misdemeanours, there's 'lots of nipping in the bud' says school, with parents called in for meetings. Next come Friday detentions followed by suspension for repeated offences. Removal or expulsion 'a very rare occurrence' ('school doesn't like to wash its dirty linen in public so it's hard to know how many,' says parent) but would normally be automatic for drugs. Drink possibly ditto, though at head's discretion might be commuted to a warning or suspension instead.

Any bad or even slightly dubious lots would have to undergo a very public Damascene-type conversion to be considered as prefects. Informal talent spotting starts well down the school though, 'people think the head sits in his office drinking gin and tonic and making the decision,' says Mr Peake. Once appointed (towards end of lower sixth), powers include the ability to impose instant detentions on everyone, theoretically extending to year above 'though staff and pupils counsel against it,' says one (wisely so, it's reckoned, to avoid detention at dawn showdowns).

Would-be head boys and girls, meanwhile, put their names forward, deliver make or break 'I could be so good for you,' speeches, followed by a one pupil one teacher vote and 'almost perfect concordance' on the winners, says head. Judging by bonhomie in the corridors they're liked, not feared, by younger pupils, something that should stand current head girl in good stead if plans to introduce informal 'doctor is in' drop in sessions for the troubled and needy come to fruition.

Pupils and parents: Sensible and cheerful children with exquisite manners with more socialising and less friendship exclusivity the higher up the school you go. Families cover more of a social mix than the area might suggest, with a predictable number of marble hall dwellers but plenty who don't need to plug in Satnav to borrow cup of sugar from neighbours. Anecdotally reckoned that there's a growing number of families where both parents work. Though parents, like children, can find it hard to fit in if they join the school after common entrance, everyone rubs along. Lots of social events help (even second hand uniform shop has termly coffee morning). 'I just think it's got a good balance of people, there are some very wealthy, there are some not very wealthy, but you don't feel it too much,' says mother.

Entrance: Junior and senior school combined dominate independent education locally, with 90 per cent coming from within ten miles radius, subsidised coach services doubling the distance for remainder (school open to suggestions for new routes if there's sufficient demand) and convenient rail links making commuting a doddle.

Large numbers of places – 110 on offer at 11+ – sounds good on paper but at least half (and rising) are collared by own junior school pupils – standard scholarships with some, like art and drama, available only at 13 + and in sixth form.

Additional 44 places at 13+ are in equally hot demand, especially since schools like Kingston Grammar, one of the few other selective co-eds in the area, ditched common entrance. School has no plans to follow suit. 'I could scrap [it] and fill those 44 places at eleven but what would it give me?' asks head. Money, perhaps? That's not why he's in the business, he says, austerely. It's about giving the children who wouldn't be ready for school at 11 an extra two years to mature, though they will need to sit 11+ or, if unsuccessful, 12+ pre-test to stand chance of a place. Parents and teachers in school's 30 or so feeder preps, Bishopsgate, Cranmore, Feltonfleet, Hall Grove and Hoebridge among them, others as far away as Kingston/Twickenham and southern side of Guildford, can breathe a sigh of relief.

Decent GCSEs needed to join at A level – entry 'dependent on maturity and academic profile' says school. Further down the school exam success is just one of the factors, 'We want the vast majority of our junior school children to get through so we take in children who academically will not be as strong as the others,' says head. Siblings, too, will be accommodated wherever possible. For aspiring newcomers, demonstrating strength of commitment is advisable – high profile attendance at open days and strongly articulated desire to be part of school community won't go amiss.

Exit: Having taken in some borderline candidates at the start, school does spit out a few along the way, some post GCSE, a very few at the end of first year of sixth form, though only D or E grades at AS level are currently required to carry on. It's 'tragic' if it happens and 'extremely rare', stresses head, compared with a few years ago when veteran parents talk of small scale but regular culls as school fought its way to better grades. 'I couldn't understand how it squared with the Josephite ethos,' says one. However, while the order may have coined its own version of 'every child matters' philosophy well over a century before UK government advisors saw the light, they were always clear about where to draw the line. 'It is always better that one be abandoned rather than the good of several be destroyed,' said 19th century founder, firmly.

For the vast majority who make it through, university places are the norm. Steady numbers to Oxbridge (usually half a dozen or so make the grade – seven in 2013 – sprinkling of choral scholarships too and lots of support) and close to three quarters secure Russell Group places (up from just under half only a few years ago). Range of subjects, geography and history well represented but almost everything from law and medicine to architecture featuring somewhere; psychology too. Careers followed later are just as diverse – apart from respectable numbers of first grade sports stars amongst the Old Boys and Girls, impressive list also numbers Sir Clive Sinclair and Lisa Tarbuck.

Money matters: Scholarships, capped at 25 per cent of the fees, won't do much to plug financial gaps but there are also assisted places and some nifty behind the scenes footwork to help struggling families in 'torrid times'.

Remarks: Unlike some other confident schools, avoids tipping over into either arrogance or complacency, instead exuding bonhomie and a sense of being happy in its own skin, something that it transmits successfully to bright, motivated pupils (the few slackers who fail to get the message may not necessarily stay the course). Add nurturing atmosphere and wraparound pastoral care and it's no wonder it can be a hard place to leave. 'I've never been outside the St George's bubble,' says one sixth former. You have to hope it doesn't come as too much of a shock when they do.

St George's School (Ascot)

Wells Lane, Ascot, SL5 7DZ

• Pupils: 270 girls • Ages: 11–18 • C of E • Fees: Day £19,575; Boarding £28,260–£30,060 pa • Independent

Tel: 01344 629900
Email: rlloyd@stgeorges–ascot.org.uk
Website: www.stgeorges–ascot.org.uk

Headmistress: Since 2011, Mrs Rachel Owens MA PGCE NPQH, previously vice principal of New Hall School, Chelmsford. Educated at a convent school in Bolton, she read modern history at Oxford, and has taught in a range of schools, state and independent. While at Oxford she represented Somerville within the University Student Union, and played netball and rowed for her college.

Academic matters: In 2013, 75 per cent A*-B grades at A level and 59 per cent A*/A at GCSE. Single sciences for those who are capable but double for the weaker brethren. Maths 'surprisingly good,' said the last head, 'and popular'. Various languages on offer and school helps foreign nationals take exams in their own language which boosts results of course!

Personal laptops can be connected to the system. Keyboarding skills are important here and girls get CLAIT and RSA qualifications. EFL and good dyslexia/dyspraxia cover plus study skills for all, provided by the Helen Arkell Centre.

Games, options, the arts: Art, textile and design strong as ever. Super art and textiles work (rather natty corsets) on show throughout the school. Fabulous music, joined-up concerts with Eton (popular), lots of own CDs, masses of instruments – and lessons can be arranged for any instrument. Drama and

public speaking popular with regular awards for the former, LAMDA exams.

30-acre campus, multi-purpose building – very versatile – the hall can be used as a lecture theatre, auditorium, dance floor and for exams. Stunning sports hall, with enviable dance and fitness centre (new art block is next on the agenda). Games important here, especially lacrosse and tennis. A new post of director of sport has been created with a particular focus of improving B and C team fixtures; every girl in the first and second year has competed for St George's in a team sport (and so far the netball teams are undefeated!).

Background and atmosphere: Founded in 1877 as a boys' prep school and converted to girls at the turn of the century. This is rhodie-land. Mega rebuild with purpose-built dorms, and classrooms – incredibly narrow claustrophobic staircases and passages everywhere.

There is a certain amount of B&B (currently £55 per night) and flexi-boarding on offer. Tailored boarding launched in September 2012 allows girls to board 4, 5, 6, or 7 days a week. Day boarders often move to becoming real boarders further up the school. Boarders move from dorms of six/four to dorms of one or two (always called dorms even if it's only one). Common rooms, pay phones (mobiles OK but not in lesson time) and kitchens for each year group. Sixth formers can take driving lessons and go out one night a week. Increased privileges come with age, no uniform in sixth – though our guides were wearing very smart black suits (skirt or trousers à choix), plus trips to Windsor (Eton next door) etc. Cookery club popular and sixth formers often cook their own supper. Living in the self-contained penthouse gives U6 a taste of university life.

No timetabled lessons on Saturdays, but all girls start with an hour's prep, then matches, riding, and afternoon activities. With the exception of four closed weekends a term, can go out from lunch time on Saturday till Sunday evening. Complaints that there was 'not enough to do' at weekends were refuted by our guides who said there was masses to do, lots of activities organised by the staff throughout the week as well as at the weekends.

Pastoral care and discipline: Good pastoral care via house and prefectorial system; sixth form day girls are assigned to boarding houses where they have work stations cocooned off from each other with gloomy grey screens. Shadows for all new pupils, form deputies and year tutors for all; all girls have a personal tutor and the sixth formers choose a director of studies. School operates school code, enforced on the seven deadly sins – 'girls are in big trouble' if they get involved with drugs, sex, alcohol, cigarettes, bullying, going out without permission, or theft. 'Straight out' for drugs; cigarettes and alcohol = suspension; strong anti-bullying policy and 'quick follow-up'.

Pupils and parents: From the south, increasing number from London (new weekly bus from West London picking up from South Kensington on Sunday evening and dropping off on Friday night has apparently been very popular) and masses from further afield, around eight or nine per cent foreigners. Some first time buyers.

Entrance: From lots of different schools – basically the toffs' prep schools: Coworth-Flexlands, Upton House, Windsor, Maltman's, Garden House, Pembridge Hall, Thomas's etc plus local primary schools. CE at 11 and 13, pass mark 50/55 per cent plus previous head's report. Plus interview. Sixth form entry, standard six GCSEs at A*-C. B or above recommended for A level subjects.

Exit: A few do leave after GCSE, going to Wellington, Stowe, Bradfield or sixth form colleges, otherwise 98 per cent to tertiary education. Small tranche to Oxbridge (one in 2013). Guides said careers advice and university suggestions tiptop.

Money matters: Academic, art and music scholarships on offer at 11; academic, art, drama, music and sport at 13 and 16; which can be further means-tested, plus bursarial help (means-tested annually) for those already in the school. Scholarships to sixth form have recently been opened up to external applicants.

Remarks: School increasingly popular locally (ie day boarders), good for the less academic, with impressive results. Arguably, still a bit Sloane.

St George's School (Edinburgh)

Linked school: St George's Junior School

Garscube Terrace, Edinburgh, EH12 6BG

- Pupils: 790 day, 60 boarding • Ages: 2-18 • Non-denom
- Fees: Day £7,260-£11,805; Boarding £21,885-£24,315 pa
- Independent

Tel: 01313 118000
Email: admissions@st-georges.edin.sch.uk
Website: www.st-georges.edin.sch.uk

Head: Since 2010, Mrs Anne Everest BA, (fifties). A classicist, Yorkshire born and bred, who has lived in Scotland for 30 years. Formerly deputy head of Robert Gordon's College, Aberdeen (qv) and head of St Margaret's School, Aberdeen (qv). Educated at St Mary's Grammar School and Hull uni. Everest taught classics and ancient history, lectured in ancient history, Latin and New Testament Greek at her alma mater. Married 'very early' to an oily husband she, 'had three babies instead of finishing her PhD', resuming her career in 1991 when she was appointed acting head of classics at St Margaret's, Aberdeen and, subsequently, head. Oily wives must follow the drum. The head runs the school with a senior management team, including the heads of both junior and lower school, and a clutch of deputies.

Everest lives in Edinburgh with her (now retired) husband, is about to sell up in Aberdeen, and regularly hosts visits from foreign academics, head teachers, and probationers. No mega staff changes, 'teachers replaced as retirement happened'. A delegator, when this editor asked for detailed exam results, and offered her card, she was told to 'email the request, and she would pass it on'. (We might have delegated someone to remove the security fencing). Interestingly, during our 25+ years with the GSG, we have seen many heads pick up detritus in the school grounds and drop it in the nearest bin; encountering a pair of socks by the side of the path, Everest merely kicked one to the side and continued talking to the new Mandarin teacher (it was left to my companion to collect them both).

Academic matters: School no longer narrowly academic; girls follow English or Scottish system as best fits the bill. League tables are meaningless in this school, given that two systems are followed. Current exam boards' status on either side of the border is nothing short of chaotic, St G's timetabling both systems must be a nightmare. 'Absolutely no thought of moving to the IB'. Some impressive results in both disciplines, though rather more glitches than we have seen previously, and quite a number of soft subjects: early education and childcare (three takers, one F), media studies (two takers one D, one F), travel and tourism (1 taker: C), all at higher level. We have no difficulty with penny numbers doing langs, but to have one each taking graphic communication, information systems and computing, and two doing modern studies cannot make economic sense. Results include those from the Royal Environmental Health Institute of Scotland: number of pupils have achieved introductory (two hour course) or elementary certificates in food hygiene (six hour course) though we couldn't find any hospitality exams higher than intermediate 2.

Possibly more followers of the Scottish system, physics and geography strong (oil?). As ever the English system popular for art and design, religious moral and philosophical studies, hefty showing in highers. 'Lots of flexibility' in course selection (this editor reckons too much; but no doubt horses for courses). School employs VLE – Virtual Learning Environment – students can access/collect coursework, or refer to staff notes online. Claims to be the, 'top school in Scotland for A levels and advanced highers'. As do many others, though perhaps not both at the same time. In 2013, 90 per cent of advanced higher entries were awarded A or B. No particular bias: English, maths, langs; French (from big nursery age 3-4), German, Spanish, Latin and classical Greek. Latin for all in L4 (top end of the junior school), thereafter girls must choose from a 'revolving carousel' of double period tasters in Spanish, German, Mandarin. The latter popular with both pupils and parents in the school's Chinese centre. Thirty-six native speakers in school, many pupils host sessions in their native languages: Russian, Chinese, Gaelic; and can study for individual A levels (or whatever) in those langs. School will arrange specialist tutors. Rate my teachers makes interesting reading, the head does not feature. Four or five parallel classes in the upper school, max class size 21 and down.

Much toing and froing with local unis, pupils and staff combine on various projects, 'and take part in an impressive outreach programme which encompasses both the academic and the appreciation of the wider world'. 'Joint seminars in a plethora of subjects with an eclectic collection of schools, the state sector as well as other independents (in all disciplines: sport and music as well as academia)', according to the school. Good general studies, curriculum choice support and careers advice (careers breakfasts), 500 options in careers dept.

Comprehensive learning support, pick up early, can deal with most of the dys-strata and ADHD; lap tops encouraged. SENCo on site, four specialist teachers plus rash of assistants. Small ESOL department to help non-nationals (charge). Drop-in centre for instant problem solving, 'weekly support sessions in every subject, plus subject clinics at lunch time, in break, before school or by email in the evening', (so presumably pupils have access to staff emails). This is what we like to hear. Buddy system: older girls help tinies with reading and much else besides.

School split into three distinct departments – junior, which encompasses the nursery, lower and upper (senior in GSG speak). Everest has offices in both lower and upper. School not totally wheelchair friendly but will make allowances and change classrooms if necessary (lift in junior school new build), chair lift in the main building; no problem with boarding houses. Hearing loops.

Games, options, the arts: Fabulous centenary sports hall with viewing area over hall and squash courts; much-used lacrosse pitches, floodlit all-weather pitch. Trad games played with a vengeance: lacrosse tours, hockey tours, swimming, judo, cycling. Local sports clubs use facilities: Grange Junior Hockey Club et al. Robertson Music Centre houses untold numbers of choirs, ensembles, three orchestras, over 600 musicians (can be hired for functions, popular with Alex McCall Smith's Really Terrible Orchestra, as well as National Youth Choir of Scotland, Edinburgh Youth Orchestra and Waddell School of Music). Impressive collection of music results. Vibrant art department, pottery, textiles, sculpture et al. Drama and theatre good, timetabled, not much pursued at higher level.

Oodles of D of E, dozens of bronze but tails off somewhat as girls grow older. CCF, Outreach outdoor education from age 10. Sixth formers join forces with Merchiston for dances, sport, art, music, drama etc. Zillions of after-school clubs that offer everything from keyboarding to extra IT. Hot on exchanges: girls as young as 12 whizz off to spend a month or so in Canada, Hong Kong, Australasia, Chile, wherever.

Background and atmosphere: St George's High School for Girls, a member of the Girls School Association, founded in 1886 as a training school for women teachers, transmogrified into St G's in 1888. The purpose-built, colonial neo-Georgian 1914 complex by A F Balfour-Paul is pure Jean Brodie, and sits uneasily with inspiring new additions. Lower school in converted former boarding house (plus ugly add-on); magical extension for junior school, complete with dance studio (that hall again) and dedicated nursery area has a cantilevered first floor over a bungee surface popular with senior pupils as well as a strategic undercover play area for tinies.

Stunning dining hall (exit bridge known as Bridget), entertainment area below has released valuable space for extra libraries and study. Parents can (and do) use the dining centre as a coffee shop.

New uniform introduced 2011, compulsory for all within the year, certain leeway in upper sixth. Kilts for all from lower sixth down, in St G's ancient red millennium tartan, with optional trimmed fitted jackets, 'kilts not more than six cm above the knee,' (most appeared much longer). Otherwise pretty standard, check dresses, blue gym tunics, navy tights, red or blue wellies. No problems with headscarves (number of Muslims in the school), presumably like the hair bands they will need to be in school colours. Sibling led house system.

Boarders live in a couple of converted Edwardian villas behind the tennis courts in an uninspiring road full of equally dreary (if upwardly mobile) villas. Hardly swinging Edinburgh. Purpose-built bungalow for sixth formers, singles or twins, all very jolly, lots of extra activities, but perhaps not very stimulating. Serious revamp last year; re-wired, new heating. Mixture of real foreigners and long distance Scots who can have friends to stay (charge). Flexi and weekly boarding option. Long-running romance with the Edinburgh Academy fractured by E A's decision to go co-ed, though they still share the same bus routes. St Gs tell us that links with Merchiston Castle are very much alive, the Edinburgh rumour mill, not to mention the local education rumour mill, assured this editor that St Gs had made an approach to Merchiston to link up on a more formal footing some time ago. Everest dissed this as a canard, but numbers are less buoyant than previously, particularly lower down the school (despite St Margaret's untimely demise).

Student council includes both juniors and seniors, terrific charity input/output, latest wheeze was to approach posh Edinburgh restaurants for their chef's fav recipes, publish them in a book and charge the restaurants to advertise. Help with City Mission. YPI with the (oily Sir Ian) Wood Foundation gives girls practice in marshalling arguments and persuading fund to dosh out for good causes. God followed broadly via Christian principles, regular assemblies, PSE cross year on Fridays, business on Mondays, year groups Thursdays and Fridays. Local minister for high days and holidays. Loads of staff jollies: keep fit, choir, and dedicated welfare programme.

IT (mostly wireless) and for tinies and in the boarding houses. School website dominated by down-market woman's magazine type romantic fuzzy pic of Balfour-Paul's garden side. Website should be a window into the school, St G's is full of head's previous speeches but pretty low on content: collection of badly written (and often incomprehensible) mission statements but no staff list with email addresses, list of governors, senior management team – info that could be useful. For an academic school to live or die by something out of People's Friend is incomprehensible.

Pastoral care and discipline: Miscreants are given heavy hints that they should, 'move elsewhere' (and sometimes they do). 'No need to break out, this is a liberal environment.' 'No sniff of drugs.' Good PSE, positive behaviour policy which incorporates 'the best of human rights legislation'.

Pupils and parents: The Edinbourgeousie: middle class Scots, professionals, incomers, wannabes and first time buyers. Boarders from the Highlands and Islands, the Borders and the Scottish diaspora abroad (alma mater stuff). Handful of real foreigners. Skype useful. Global links and exchanges. Trad. Lots of parent/pupil forums on every subject under the sun; Friends of St George's for social events. Quick poll round parents (in address book) produced no surprises: non-stimulated girls were bored at the top end, parents were fed up at having to buy a new uniform for such a short time (not in second hand shop yet), sixth formers seemed to be working (and playing) hard. Particularly the latter. School shouldn't be so petty about make up. Not really a sophisticated bunch, and probably not yummy mummy's school of choice.

Entrance: 'Unashamedly academic in outlook', was how we previously described this school, indeed there was a time when wannabe parents coached their five year olds pre school interview. Everest maintains, 'not so strict an entrance test; important that we can meet a child's needs'. Will welcome a girl who is able to keep up with the pace of academic life but who seems set for Bs and Cs rather than A*s. Interview via nursery and elsewhere at four and a half. Otherwise, assessment, school report and interview. Entry to sixth form is more or less automatic for home-grown pupils; external pupils by interview and school report. Demands for sixth form places heavy. 'Skype handy for interviewing girls from abroad'.

Exit: Rare trickle to trad independents at eight and 13, some leave after GCSE/Standard grade to go co-ed; otherwise gap, uni, and higher education of all sorts – Scots law popular, as are the sciences and medicine. Around 50 per cent opt for Scottish universities, Aberdeen, St Andrew's, Edinburgh and Glasgow. Surprisingly, more girls went south (Bristol, Durham, Newcastle) in 2010 than stayed to reap the financial incentives to stay in Scotland. Irregular Oxbridge trickle; 98 per cent go to their first choice uni.

Money matters: Means-tested bursary scheme now replaces assisted places; 'mustn't let the really bright down'. Full bursaries available plus help with school uniform. Will keep child if parents fall on hard times, as long as bursar is kept in the loop. Sibling discounts. Joint discount with Merchiston Castle School. Has been given 18 months by the Scottish Charity Regulator to make the fees more affordable for lower income families or will risk losing charitable status.

Remarks: The top girls' school in Scotland (pace chaps in nursery); more liberal than previously. Tatler calls it the 'St Paul's of the north', but with only four girls' schools in Scotland (two of which are overgrown dame schools and one of which takes boarders and ponies, there's not much competition). We were refused entry by new head last year because 'they were building a hall' in the junior school, and very nice it is too but somehow, after all the palaver, this editor had expected to see a HALL, rather than an overgrown dance studio/gym with a pristine sprung floor. We were also surprised to find the school drive blocked off at the end with security fencing and wonder whether there is another development in hand to which we are not privy.

At regular intervals this editor is asked for advice by parents who have had their little darlings at St George's since they were in nappies and are looking for a change of scene in sixth form (teenagers being what they are and Edinburgh being what it is). We have to say that, in all honesty, if it is a challenge they need then they must go South, for there is nowhere in Scotland that can hold a candle to St George's, be it in the realm of academe or of global awareness.

S

St George's School (Harpenden)

Sun Lane, Harpenden, AL5 4EY

- Pupils: 1,327 boys and girls (including 125 boarders) • Ages: 11–18
- Non–denom Christian • Fees: Boarding £10,401 pa; Day – free
- State

Tel: 01582 765477
Email: admin@stgeorges.herts.sch.uk
Website: www.stgeorges.herts.sch.uk

Headmaster: Since 2013, Mr Raymond McGovern MA, formerly head of Sexey's School, Somerset.

Academic matters: As a high-performing, yet totally non-selective, comprehensive school, value-added is the watchword at St George's. Whatever their merits on arrival, some 93 per cent of St George's students leave with five A*-Cs at GCSE, over 43 per cent of GCSE grades were A*/A in 2013, and up to 90 per cent leave with a clutch of top-grade A levels opening the door to university (68 per cent A*/B grades in 2013). 'It's hard to exceed that because after all we are an all-ability school,' said the previous head, but he put this success down to 'dynamic teaching staff who want to teach, and children who want to learn', backed up by a supportive faith-based family environment arranged in houses, which are 'schools within a school'.

A marked absence of pressure, so no early GCSE or AS entry. 'School should be a fulfilling experience, not a race for examination results,' said previous head, who eschewed students collecting exam passes 'like postage stamps' and instead recommended whole-hearted participation in sport, drama and art and time spent on charity and community work.

Ofsted inspectors judged the school 'outstanding' in all categories and, in key stages 3 and 4, students from every level of prior attainment – including both genders, all ethnic groups, day students, and boarders – now exceed the result expected of similar students nationally. Year 7 is taught in mixed ability groups, although setting kicks in after the first three months. French is taught from year 7 with German offered the following year. English and history are both successful options at A level and the vast majority of maths takers come out with an A or a B.

Careful analysis of children's needs and strategies to help, even if only short term. Learning support ranges from extra spellings to a tailor-made timetable. Christian ethos means 'there's no stigma to having a learning challenge here; everyone is valuable'. More than a quarter of pupils are identified as gifted and talented and they are extended both inside and outside the curriculum with Science Olympiads and Maths Challenges, for example, and the school's re-designation as a Technology College and the award of a second specialism in languages has meant more support for pupils completing controlled assessment and preparing for exams. Parents impressed by the teachers' extra revision sessions and their capacity to mark as much extra work as the students can churn out.

The International School status – thanks to pioneering cultural and educational exchanges with China – develops pupils' cultural awareness and their Mandarin.

Games, options, the arts: Rugby is the main sport for boys and lacrosse for girls – this is the only maintained school in the south of England to play lacrosse so all fixtures are against independent girls' schools – and St George's has turned out some fine lacrosse teachers. Cricket, netball, rounders, basketball, tennis and athletics are popular and, in common with the many other activities on offer – such as cross-country, football, chess, art, drama, music, dance and sailing – there is some healthy competition between the school's long-established houses.

The annual inter-house music competition shows off the best musical talent and there is a range of choirs, orchestra, jazz and wind bands. A major drama production every year and smaller events. 100+ clubs and societies and more for boarders. CCF is well attended. World Challenge Expeditions to Madagascar, Argentina, India and Mongolia and the connection between St George's and Gansu Province, China, has seen exchange trips and a visit by a small team led by the head to lecture at the University of Beijing.

Background and atmosphere: 'St George's is like an orange. The school is in segments, and the skin holding it all together is our Christian foundation. We do all we can to keep that interior together.' Founded in 1907 by Rev Cecil Grant, St George's is a non-denominational Christian foundation with its own Anglican chaplain and Sunday chapel taking place every week – all pupils, day and boarding, must attend at least three a term as an requirement of being awarded a place. Many come as families to swell congregations to a maximum of 400. It is one of the longest-established fully co-educational independent boarding schools in England and, in 1965, it became voluntary aided. The school has retained many historic connections and traditions, and, while some may see them as idiosyncratic in the modern age of state schooling, pupils at St George's genuinely love them. They revel in the house competitions, the formality of chapel, speech days, commendations, and all the different ties awarded. We try to encourage individuality, which is part of our ethos and Christian belief.'

The original buildings, in a leafy lane on the edge of the modern commuter town of Harpenden, date back to the 1880s and are in the Victorian Gothic style, but there have been various extensions and additions, particularly over the past decade or so, and with the recently completed £7.5m refurbishment programme. 'It's a constant battle to maintain the site and attract support for the school, which is still short of adequate specialist accommodation.' As a voluntary aided school, St George's buildings are owned by the school's Foundation, which has to find 10 per cent of the cost of all capital projects and on-going building maintenance from very limited funds. 'There is a lot of do-it-yourself work here'; school enlists the assistance of parents, who give willingly of their time, skills and knowledge – and also cash.

State-of-the-art technology centre, drama studio and several computer suites around the campus, and those top-notch facilities have recently been joined by a new languages block and sports hall. Work is underway on the refurbishment of the science labs. A new music department and sixth form computer study area opened in 2010 with parents' fund-raising and support from the Foundation. Despite the necessity of this upgrading, the landscape at St George's is very peaceful and welcoming. Pupils are credited with the widespread flower planting and the thriving vegetable garden – a gardening club is run by a parent with a passion. 'Quality of life here is important. Children feel safe and valued, and they have fun.'

Pastoral care and discipline: Parents choose St George's for its 'traditional values and caring Christian ethos' and the school is built on a system of praise and reward that recognises students who demonstrate the school's core values of courtesy, integrity, manners and good discipline. Parents support these values wholeheartedly, along with the discipline policy for those who transgress on rare occasions. The four houses give the school its shape and these are presided over by a head of house, assistant and a team of tutors for a close-knit family feel. Tutor groups arranged in lower, middle and upper school groups give students time to develop a rapport with the member of staff responsible for them. Such close attention leaves very little room for bad behaviour, and a well-supervised site means truanting is extremely difficult to pull off.

Pupils and parents: Harpenden and environs provides the majority of St George's day pupils, with the addition of boarders mainly from overseas. According to the school, any child of a Christian faith who is prepared to try hard and be fully involved in the St George's lifestyle will thrive there. The previous head described the parent body as 'articulate', which sounds like a euphemism, and certainly there is a definite parental contact procedure to prevent the teaching staff from being inundated. Parents demonstrate their loyalty to the school at fund-raising times and it is not unusual to see over 100 parents on the touch-line at sporting events. Sunday services are very well attended by families, as is the termly Catholic mass held by the local monsignor, who brings his parish to join with those of other faiths at the school. Parents from different Christian churches also preach at family services. Families are kept informed thanks to regular contact from staff and the head's traditional end-of-term letter, originally aimed at boarders' families, which has grown into a substantial magazine and now goes out to all. Ex-pupils include Kenneth Horne, Patrick Heron, Michael Oakeshott, Sir Maurice Drake, Andrew Hunter, Rex Warner, Laura Haddock and Owen Farrell.

Entrance: There's no academic selection and the school is still oversubscribed. Admission is by a complicated system of priorities, but those with siblings and or living locally and attending a recognised church for at least two years (a minister's letter is required) are most likely to be successful. Parents have been known to resort to underhand methods to get their offspring in – but be aware that the school is wise to this. Boarders are totally integrated into the school and potential candidates need to provide a good reference from their previous school and apply at least a year in advance to be in with a shout. A state grant for new accommodation – a sixth form house with en-suite rooms – has recently boosted boarder places to 135.

Exit: Some 80 to 90 per cent to university – impressively high for a comprehensive. Small number of gap years.

Remarks: One of the most successful non-selective schools in the country, welcoming students into a secure, Christian community where academic achievement and altruism are encouraged in equal measure.

Saint Gregory's Catholic College

Combe Hay Lane, Bath, BA2 8PA

• Pupils: 875 girls and boys; all day • Ages: 11–18 • Catholic • State

Tel: 01225 832873
Email: stgregorys_sec@bathnes.gov.uk
Website: www.st-gregorys.bathnes.sch.uk

Executive Headteacher: Since 2004, Mr Raymond Friel MA NPQH (mid-forties). Born and raised on the west coast of Scotland, with a first in English from Glasgow and a PGCE from Aberystwyth, he has always taught English in Catholic secondary schools, starting in west London (St Charles Catholic Sixth Form College qv) where he met his wife – a primary teacher; they have three teenage sons. Thence to St Augustine's Trowbridge, then via the headship of St Joseph's Salisbury (to which he administered the kiss of life) to St Gregory's just two years later. It was, he says, an unmissable opportunity. Since, under his leadership, the school has gained and kept a grading of 'outstanding' from Ofsted, the school surely grabbed an unmissable opportunity in appointing him.

A committed Catholic, he ensures that its values course through the school's veins – and parents, Catholic and non-Catholic alike, love pretty well everything this calm, twinkly Scotsman does. Cerebral, devout and doubtless scary enough when the occasion demands it, he seems universally respected. In fact, he takes no prisoners, according to one dad.

In 2011, Mr Friel took on St Mark's, a small comprehensive on the other side of Bath, so he is now executive head of both schools, dividing his time almost equally between them. Mrs Anne Barrett (head of school) holds the reins day to day, an experienced pair of hands, with stints as an acting head and current Ofsted inspector to her name. Parents have accepted this with equanimity, though some commented on the inevitable loss of the head's visibility. This development does mean though that a joint sixth form – both schools formerly ceased at GCSE – opened in September 2013.

If Mr Friel ever has a spare moment, he might (occasionally) be found in the gym, but is more likely to be striding through the countryside with family, friends and golden doodle Mabel (Labrador/poodle cross, not poultry). Reading material tends towards the spiritual; he is also a published poet – latest collection entitled Stations of the Heart.

Academic matters: Excellent results, particularly for a non-selective school. Performance at GCSE has shown steady and sustained improvement; in 2013, 65 per cent of pupils achieved five A*-C grades including English and maths and 28 per cent of grades were A*/A. Interestingly, the school has kept figures on the English Baccalaureate (five traditional academic GCSEs in maths, English, a science, a language and history or geography) long before Mr Gove deemed it desirable. The data impresses: against a national average of 15 per cent, St Greg's generally achieves well over 50 per cent (41 per cent in 2013), but lower results in maths take a bit of the shine away. Nevertheless, some parents grumble about the amount of homework – too much of it, material not previously covered in class, too many negative comments – this last remarked upon in a recent interim inspection.

School has specialist language status; Spanish is particularly strong, but we were also impressed by the lively German class we popped into, where pupils were speaking unselfconsciously in a supportive environment. Polish and Italian were also put on last year; Japanese on demand.

All new pupils in year 7 are streamed according to ability, with some adjustments made for English and maths; at the start of GCSE courses, they are assigned different pathways (fittingly and tactfully named Canterbury, Glastonbury and Walsingham) designed for a range of abilities, and incorporating some vocational courses at Bath College to be taken alongside fewer GCSEs. Parents reckon their offspring have a clear idea of their individual targets and next steps; they like the culture of endeavour. 'My daughter wants to be a medic, and the school's right behind her,' said one mother.

But we did pick up some dissatisfaction with the maths teaching – when tackled about it, the head said that 'the results and final outcomes were very good and well above national averages' – when in fact maths has the lowest pass rate of any subject at GCSE of 72 per cent – and 'that some variation in 50 teachers was inevitable'. Granted... but at least one mother reckons that private tuition 'which nice middle class parents resort to' masks true results. That said, there are plenty of maths clinics, one entitled 'revision to ensure that grade C'.

Around seven per cent of St Gregs' pupils have some special educational need – all are screened using NFER on entry, which tests numeracy, verbal and non-verbal reasoning. Dyslexia expert on staff, and TA dedicated to children whose first language is not English. Ofsted praised support given to pupils with learning difficulties, disabilities or any other kind of vulnerability.

S

Games, options, the arts: Designated Specialist College of Performing Arts, and strong local reputation. Recent production of The King and I was 'fabulous', according to one mother, who chose the school on the strength of its drama; 'very good and lots of it,' said another. Gilchrist Studio is a dedicated performance space and the school has actively sought grants to refurbish its art and music facilities to good effect. The (small) choir sang beautifully at the assembly we went to; music is well-resourced and prominent, and dance enjoys a good following.

Opinions divide on the question of sport, however. Ask the school, and you will be told about the Olympic swimmer (currently seventh best in the world), three England athletes, two cross-country runners and a rugby player, a Royal Ballet pupil (who spends half her week in London) and an impressive list of county players – plus the 1st XV who had just thrashed arch rivals Beechen Cliff (qv). All this is quite remarkable – but pupils and parents find attitudes to sport inconsistent and facilities just about adequate.

The jocks complain that the top brass prioritise academic performance over everything else, and that tutors don't cut them enough slack, or give them enough credit for the glory they bring the school. A home pitch, team shirts and fixtures with local independents in this rugby-mad city are on their wish list. One parent reckoned that there were not enough matches for girls, and that team practices were stymied by bus departure times – the school's response was that parents are in fact quick to co-ordinate lifts. Some anxiety was also voiced that, in his zeal to create the new sixth form block, the head would sell off the school's sports pitches (grass and Astro) to the neighbouring housing development. 'I'd be interested to know where that came from; certainly not from me!' said he in riposte.

Good range of trips offered to complement most subjects and interests, eg China, New York, ski-ing. D of E recently introduced (what took them so long?) and in 2012, an adventure trek to Namibia, for which pupils were expected to raise sizeable funds.

Background and atmosphere: Founded and built in the late 70s (in buildings less grim and better preserved than you might think) by Clifton Diocese, to make a logical progression from the eight local-ish Catholic primary schools which feed it. Since 2011, all nine schools have become the South Clifton Catholic Federation 'to provide an even better Catholic education for young people in the area' and to show solidarity in the face of the 'significant lobbies (...) who argue for an end to faith schools'.

That describes St Greg's: from the huge banner which dominates reception 'In Christ we flourish' to the creed written by the pupils, this school proudly wears its Catholic heart on its sleeve – but it's a big and inclusive heart. Everyone, nay everyone we spoke to mentioned the strong family atmosphere and the forces for good which prevail in the school, which embraces the handful of non-Catholics who attend and where 'bullying is jumped on'. A sense of religious observance was palpable, and pupils accept large doses of spiritual input (and revival of old edict of no meat on Fridays) along with the three R's. 'Our kids are taught not to be embarrassed about their faith', says the head. At a time when Catholic education is in paroxysms of guilt about the dodgier aspects of its past, such pride in its best manifestations is cheering. 'My children don't know who is Catholic and who isn't – all are blessed,' one mum commented: says it all, really.

School sits just inside the city boundary on top of one of Bath's seven hills (like Rome, but greyer) and overlooks sweeping countryside to the south. Green belt concerns over sixth form block will be addressed, parents hope. Piazza with picnic tables and chairs, recently created at centre of school at pupils' request, enhances break times, and year 7s have a designated area to call their own.

All are assigned to a house on entry (named suitably after popes) and within that, tutor groups. Transition arrangements from primary schools are good, though some parents would rather newbies from the same school weren't always put together.

Opened a sixth form in 2013.

Pastoral care and discipline: Pupils feel exceptionally well looked after by their tutors and appreciate the high standards of behaviour, which make life bearable for all. Bus monitors, selected from senior pupils, oversee any over-exuberance on the way to and from school, even on public buses. Bad behaviour inside or outside school is counselled in the first instance, rather than censured.

But once sanctions apply, they appear pointless to some, eg writing out 'Your parents are very disappointed in you' X times, or an excuse to escape going outside in winter. A compulsory session or two at the after-school homework club might meet the case better, say pupils, who also mentioned some inconsistency from teachers. Understandable disquiet at the introduction of CCTV in the loos (not in cubicles, we were assured) as a deterrent to vandals. No complaints from parents, however, in this climate of guidance and gentle correction, rather than brute force.

Pupils and parents: Some 75 per cent Catholic, socially mixed but sharing the same values in education. 'Most of our children come with the right expectations – we encourage debate but ask for respect for what the school stands for,' says the head. When pressed, he conceded that a young person who had 'turned his or her face against religious expression' might not thrive at his school. We found his flock thoughtful and grounded, with a refreshing lack of cynicism. Notable alumni? School is on the young side to have produced anyone with a long and distinguished career, but observers of the current music scene should watch out for Hannah Collins' début album.

Entrance: Intake of 160 into year 7. Governing body responsible for admissions, although applications are made through normal LA channels. Vast majority of pupils come from Catholic primary schools as far away as Wells and Chippenham. A sprinkling from others – some parents are reckoned to have dredged up any vestige of Catholicism to get them in. Some tactics – such as strategic late baptisms – frowned upon by other parents. 'Catholic children are admitted by baptismal certificate, not by how their parents practise,' states the school. Oversubscribed – and the criteria are applied in strict sequence, so that even sibling cases have gone to appeal.

Exit: Most to Catholic sixth form college, St Brendan's (qv), on eastern edge of Bristol. Others to mix of local sixth forms, state and independent, to vocational options at Bath College and a few into work. Scattering to top flight independents eg Sherborne, Millfield on sports scholarships. All change now it has its own sixth form.

Money matters: Catholic education is not fully funded by government, so schools have to find 10 per cent of capital expenditure; for St Greg's some £10,000. Parents are asked to contribute and gift-aid any donation they care to give; requests go out every autumn. Active parents' association funds extras and all Name and Praise book tokens (given out in assembly for commendable work or behaviour) – it does well, raising around £7,000 per year.

Remarks: Top choice non-fee paying Catholic secondary in the area, in our view. Long journey times from huge catchment area and hotly contested places are testament to the thirst for this kind of spiritually-led education, which turns out great results and thoroughly nice kids. We will watch the development of the new joint sixth form with interest.

S

St Helen and St Katharine

Linked school: St Helen and St Katharine Junior School

Faringdon Road, Abingdon, OX14 1BE

- Pupils: 700 girls; all day • Ages: 9–18 • Anglican foundation
- Fees: £13,020pa • Independent

Tel: 01235 520173
Email: info@shsk.org.uk
Website: www.shsk.org.uk

Headmistress: Since 2008, Miss Rowan Edbrooke (forties) BEd in PE from Bedford College of Higher Education. Formerly head of St Margaret's School, Exeter and deputy head of Haberdashers' Aske's School for Girls, Elstree. Elegant and rather reserved, girls and parents admire her and many commented on her devoted attendance at matches (not just the A teams), concerts and events large and small. She coaches year seven girls in netball, which she says helps her get to know them individually and to observe year group dynamics. Passionate about sport, she plays tennis and has taken up golf and sailing; opera and theatre are her other interests. Favourite book? Middlemarch.

Moving on in July 2014.

Academic matters: Takes no prisoners. In 2013, 92 per cent gained A* or A in all subjects at IGCSE/GCSE and while it is not quite a truth universally acknowledged that 'St Helen's girls don't get Bs', this perfectly respectable grade is looking as endangered as the eponymous insects. Most girls do ten subjects and choices include DT, drama, Latin, Greek and home economics. In addition to French, language options are, in order of preference, Spanish, Italian and German. Take up for separate and dual award sciences roughly equal. A level results also inevitably lofty (80 per cent A* or A grades in 2013) with sciences, maths and English the most popular choices closely followed by French, psychology, history, geography and religious studies. Some subjects (government and politics and history of art) are taught jointly with Abingdon boys, thus extending sixth form options and, no doubt, enlivening debate; teaching of theatre studies is fully shared between the schools.

The head's vision is for girls to develop as 'active, independent learners, able to think for themselves and prepared to take risks.' She wants to ensure that girls take a 'broad and balanced approach' to their education, a nod perhaps to criticism that the focus is too exam orientated. Lessons we observed were challenging and interactive, girls were buzzing with questions, determined to work things out, certainly no sign of young brains being crammed with facts by latter-day Gradgrinds. Teaching in the sixth form often extends beyond syllabus requirements providing the extra breadth and depth that can make all the difference. Some parents commented that the first term or so can be pretty steep for those arriving from primary school what with French, Latin, homework and competitive sport, but most acclimatise quickly. Learning support available for those few girls with mild dyslexia/dyspraxia.

So where did it all go right? St Helen's Olympian heights of exam success are achieved via the reassuringly traditional recipe of good teaching, hard work and high expectations. Staff are dedicated, girls are able and keen to learn and, thanks to a very generous private donor, study facilities are superb. While a nostalgic few may sigh at the passing of the old library in its awkward rickety eyrie, on the top floor of the old building, the library in the Jean Duffield building (opened 2010) is quite stunning. No narrow ranks of shelves, bookcases are curved and arranged spaciously in circular sections – the only straight lines here are in the books themselves. Glass walls, comfortable seating, silent study areas, banks of computers, natural light amplified by central well, Farrow & Ball toned walls. The overall effect reminds one of shopping at John Lewis but in the best possible way. Dedicated archive area with displays that change regularly is a particularly nice feature, popular for history lessons. On the ground floor are a university style lecture theatre and a fair trade coffee shop with opening hours to cater for early birds or girls staying on for the numerous clubs and after school activities.

Games, options, the arts: Art, design & technology and ceramics are little worlds of their own – the former has sky-lighted atelier-like studios in the old building, the two latter are housed in separate not entirely permanent looking structures. The creative results from these are displayed everywhere and A2 art of a very high standard was being exhibited in the 'old hall' when we visited. Ambitious music and drama productions are staged, often in conjunction with the Abingdon thespians; Dido and Aeneas is the next blockbuster with all singers and orchestral support drawn from the combined, deep talent pool of both schools. Performance spaces are the intimate studio theatre, a larger stage in YPH and Abingdon School's Amey Theatre. The practice rooms in the music department are in constant use for singing and instrumental lessons (450 per week) and, unsurprisingly, school musicians win prizes at local and national competitions. There are four orchestras, four choirs and any number of ensembles, a string quartet recently reached the finals of the National Chamber Music competition. Large and successful uptake for D of E, World Challenge and Young Enterprise.

As with academic subjects so it is with sport; a recurring grumble is that less attention is paid to the B and C teams and girls who start school keen to have a go at lacrosse or play in netball matches feel sidelined if they don't make the As. The head is alert to parental concerns and change is underway in the PE department. On our visit the most eye-catching display on the under used notice boards in the sports hall was robustly headed 'Most Able' – cultural change clearly still lagging behind in the C team. Among the less predictable activities on offer in lessons or as after-school or lunch clubs are football, rugby, sailing and golf so there ought to be something for everyone. An extra twelve acres of sports fields (just across the road) has been acquired and this should go some way to widen fixture lists.

A joint bus service with Abingdon delivers from as far as Reading, Oxford, Thame and Faringdon in the morning. Separate ride home at 4.10 unless detained by activities in which case it's back on the bus with the boys at 5.20pm.

Background and atmosphere: Distinctive red brick building is original to the school's 1903 foundation by nuns of the Community of St Mary the Virgin who wished to provide a 'liberal and advanced' education to the young ladies of Abingdon. Approach to the main door is via a path bordered with wonderful lavender bushes (perhaps that's where the bees go) and the herb's soothing properties must permeate the walls because inside the atmosphere is equally calm and controlled until the bell goes for break or lunch when it's as noisy and excited as one would expect. Behind reception is a central atrium used as a dining room but also offering small group teaching space and a venue for functions such as parents' evenings. Enhanced and extended kitchen and dining facilities due to open as we go to press. A light glass gallery corridor where art and design work is beautifully displayed skirts the main hall/theatre. Since the completion of the library the school's old and new buildings form a quadrangle enclosing a garden with old fruit trees which leads out onto further green space and the sixth form centre. Work due to start on a new 12 lab science facility in 2013, due for completion in September 2014. There are playing fields beyond the large modern sports centre and additional acres close by.

Uniform was a rather confusing wardrobe worn according to year group but a new 'all through' kit of grey skirt and burgundy jumper (plus tartan kilt for games) has been in use for the past year. Preferred outfitters to the sixth form are Messrs Ugg and Jack Wills; long hair not compulsory despite appearances.

Pastoral care and discipline: Parents we spoke to were full of praise for form tutors who are vigilant and proactive when it comes to defusing inevitable friendship group tensions. The school's founding Christian values remain central to its ethos and girls are enthusiastic and aware charity fundraisers busy with lunchtime cake sales and other enterprises; many serve in the school chapel as sacristans, readers or choristers. There is a full-time chaplain and nurse plus a doctor and counsellor as necessary.

There is a persistent whisper that the house of St Helen and St Katharine is a just a little too hot and the recent ISI report recommended a broadening of focus in some lessons. One feels some sympathy for Miss Edbrooke having to defend what is quite clearly a very happy school with results most heads can only dream of. When asked what sort of girl would suit their school our sparky year ten guides replied as one, 'you've got to be able to handle pressure'. This was candidly declared as a badge of pride rather than a criticism, they simply meant that while they thrived some might wilt. We agree.

Pupils and parents: Bright ambitious girls. Ditto parents. About half come from local primaries and the rest from feeder preps. A few from the school's own small junior department (years 5 and 6 only). Former pupils include Samantha Cameron and her sister, Deputy Editor of Vogue, Emily Sheffield (both of whom decamped to sixth form boarding at Marlborough), Alice Thomson (leader writer the Times), Belinda Bucknall QC.

Entrance: Entry at 9, 10, 11, 13 and 16 though the majority come in at 11. Exam at 11 (maths and English) plus observed 'taster days' and informal interview with head, roughly three candidates for every place. Existing pupils gain entry to sixth form even if they have wobbled at GCSE – there's no weeding out to 'bump up' A level results (not that this seems necessary); candidates from other schools need good GCSEs (A or A* in subjects to be studied) and a positive reference.

Exit: Around a fifth leave post GCSE but most stay on – no uniform and shared teaching with Abingdon boys has worked wonders for retention. Over the past three years 43 Oxbridge places have been offered (14 in 2013), the rest mainly to first choice Russell group institutions, Bristol, Exeter and Warwick being favourites. No significant subject bias, we can look forward to Helkat doctors, lawyers, engineers, vets, musicians and psychologists in years to come.

Money matters: Fees comparatively low but watch out, extras (including lunch at £190 per term) can soon mount up. A small number of academic scholarships are awarded according to performance in entrance exam. Music scholarships (free tuition on one or two instruments) offered on basis of audition. A few means-tested bursaries of up to 100 per cent are also available.

Remarks: Encourages girls to aim high. The pupils we spoke to were spirited, funny and articulate; all were fiercely proud of their school and keenly aware of how fortunate they were. Parents pay tribute to the dedication of staff and value the way the school has 'stretched' their daughter. If your daughter is bright, confident and ambitious (or just in need of a bit of a stretch) then this school could be the golden ticket to Oxbridge and beyond.

St Helen's School

Linked schools: Little St Helen's and St Helen's Junior school

Eastbury Road, Northwood, HA6 3AS

• Pupils: 1,120 including junior school and Little St Helen's; all girls • Ages: 3–18 • C of E but all faiths welcome • Fees: £9,888–£14,370 pa • Independent

Tel: 01923 843210
Email: admissions@sthn.co.uk
Website: www.sthn.co.uk

Headmistress: Since 2011, Dr Mary Short BA PGCE PhD (early fifties) – did her PhD, in the politics of budget-setting in the 1920s, at Cambridge. Has taught undergraduates at Cambridge and pupils at independent schools including St Paul's Girls, City of London Boys and Haberdashers' Aske's Girls (deputy head). She has teaching in her blood and is married to a fellow teacher. Apart from history, likes walking, bread-making and travel. Aims to up the academic performance, partly by 'reviewing the admissions process to more accurately identify academic potential' but more by curriculum reviews, consistency of aims, better monitoring of performance, peer review of teachers, that sort of thing. Good relationship with her top-notch governors.

A smile of measured mischief, and a fascination with bringing the best out of each pupil. Her eyes light up when describing how the school is going about sorting out one of her more troublesome charges. 'Is quietly powerful', says a parent, 'I really, really like her, and so do the girls.'

Academic matters: Not the top of the highly competitive North London academic tree, but no slouch. Lots of male teachers, lots of teachers who have had other professional lives before or even during teaching. Every pupil we talked to had at least one teacher they found truly inspiring. Pupils describe the atmosphere as 'competitive but collaborative': in maths, for instance, where randomly chosen pairs of girls help each other to tackle problems and be the best pair in the class.

In 2013, 65 per cent A*/A at A level, 86 per cent A* or A at GCSE. Good range of subjects in the sixth. The overwhelmingly popular subjects at this level are the sciences, maths, economics and history, with maths results particularly strong. Physics as ever with girls the slightly weaker relation, but school working hard to encourage and take-up is growing – the Heath Robinson Club is clearly popular and interest in engineering is strong. The cuttings that adorn the corridor walls in the science department are totally fascinating, and would repay an hour's dawdling.

Way ahead of the Government on the EBac: have been doing it for years, with a strong emphasis on having a second language. Tendency to do art and/or drama as the 'free' choices. Highly IT literate: great facilities and teachers who know how to use them. Students are able to: complement their A level programme with the 'St Helen's Portfolio' which comprises additional qualifications such as the European Computer Driving Licence; take up modules offered by the Open University; continue with languages they have studied to GCSE or acquire additional languages or study Further Mathematics; also recognises CCF, DofE, other clubs and societies

Thoroughly sympathetic to SEN, from the headmistress down. Everyone is screened at seven and 11 for potential educational difficulties. 'We then discuss with parents how we can make it better.' One teacher qualified to support pupils diagnosed as dyslexic and school is planning to appoint a head of learning support in the coming year. School can and does support autistic spectrum difficulties, mild dyslexia and dyspraxia, mild speech difficulties and children with hearing impairments. Currently focusing on better provision for those who struggle with numbers – some children have extra help with maths. 'All take IGCSE maths – we have no intention of becoming a specialist centre for dyscalculics, but do want to become much more effective at picking up those who struggle with number work before they become paralysed by algebra!' Support, but not separate teaching, for those who have English as an additional language. Some 100+ children currently identified as Gifted and Talented and supported with 'differentiated work schemes and activities'.

Games, options, the arts: The huge surprise for anyone visiting St Helen's and who, perhaps, has only seen it behind its sedate hedges and modest perimeter walls, is the unbelievable amount of space it has. Acres of playing fields, courts and pitches extend in all directions and you begin to realise that most of this end of Northwood is St Helen's! A vast new sports complex and superb, seemingly endless pool, in a stunning new building, already in enthusiastic use. Lacrosse, netball, tennis, athletics, badminton and rounders all popular and many other games and activities available including pilates, aerobics, fencing and trampolining. Lots of success – representation in lacrosse, swimming, cross-country and netball county teams and much success for school teams in all these sports plus athletics and rounders at impressive levels. Supports those who excel (and need time off for national teams) and has no beef with those who prefer music (but still have to do games).

Art, DT and drama housed in the June Leader building, named after school's outstanding, and aptly named, head of 20 years (1966-1986), the great builder of the school, both in physical terms and in terms of the quality of education and values promulgated here under her uniquely humane regime. First rate art – teachers are real artists, teaching combines strong basic skills such as life drawing with experimentation, breadth and understanding. DT bubbling and well taught if not as jazzily equipped as some (though there is CAD and a 3D printer is on the way). Dance and drama (some joint with Merchant Taylors') much enjoyed, especially in the context of the annual House Arts festival. It is good to see the arts so strong in a school whose spirit is essentially academic. The Centre, a new multi-purpose space for the performing arts and sport (converted from the existing Gym) set to open in spring 2014.

Music – with real musicians with flourishing musical careers as teachers – going from strength to strength with numerous orchestras, choirs and, bands. The jazz band has made a CD, the huge choir tours abroad annually, there are many and varied opportunities for performance in school and the wider community, including regular concerts at St John's, Smith Square, London. The majority of girls play at least one instrument.

Collaboration with Merchant Taylors' also in CCF. D of E and Young Enterprise also popular. Visits from profs, writers and theatre companies. Successes in debating, Maths and Physics Olympiads, technology competitions. Lots of trips – Madrid, Kobe, Ypres, Berlin, Cern, Kew, Rome, House of Commons, Paris, British Museum, galleries.

Underlying ethos of opportunity, progression and support. Hundreds of things for pupils to try and, when they latch on to one, the school will find ways of allowing it to be taken further – as far, indeed, as the girl can go.

Background and atmosphere: Founded at the end of the 19th century with a vision of education for the whole child to which it still holds dear. A spacious school, trim and imaginative grounds, relaxed, not at all authoritarian. Dark green uniform up to 16; conservative freedom in the sixth.

Strong Indian, Tamil and Jewish (a strong JSoc and well-established links with the local synagogue) contingents, but absolutely no sign of segmentation or separation among the pupils, and parents report that it's like that with the ones they bring home too. Watch them swirl around you at break time and wish the world could be like that. Strong relationship with Merchant Taylors', already noted, supplies all the male element the girls want, and no more.

Notable absence of the unhealthily thin. Eating is a social rite here – you stumble across snacking groups all the time. School encourages this with decent breaks, delicious cookies and time enough for lunch.

The junior school is an integral part of the whole. Situated centrally, it is natural for girls here to stay the course – now from three to 18 – and continue to feel that it's all in the family. Longworthe, one of the former boarding houses, is now used for before and after school care in which pupils with busy parents can spend a long day – breakfast and tea included and quiet places for prep and recreation. Nicely decorated rooms for sixth form relaxation and study (much studiousness observed).

Pastoral care and discipline: Each individual teacher is expected to notice and to care how their charges are, and to react supportively and promptly to any sign of trouble. As a result, while teachers talk of all the usual friendship and family problems, the girls seem hardly aware of them, and prefects do not see dealing with social ills as a significant part of their remit. Relationships within houses, year groups and tutor groups all seem close, giving girls a variety of communities to turn to.

Staff/student relationships palpably cordial. 'A lot of our teachers are role models,' said one sixth former. 'They are so kind and helpful and it doesn't just stop in the classroom. They will keep helping you achieve what you want to achieve.' A younger pupil agreed, 'and', she added, 'you just have to be friendly here because everyone is. The teachers are so sweet – they really look after you – there's always someone to talk to and problems are sorted out really quickly.' 'Never a door closed, they always have time for you'. The same applies to the San, with its welcoming Sister, and the two school counsellors (called Confidential Listeners).

Clear sanctions policy. System of warning and detention cards. MP3s/mobiles illegal in schooltime. No drugs incidents in living memory. The occasional foolish misdemeanour is dealt with individually but 'sanely. It's never public, it's not about humiliation – ever.' You're allowed to slip here.

Pupils and parents: Resilient, personable, happy, chatty girls who 'know who we are and why we are here', and whose attitude to problems is to 'tackle not buckle'. Alongside that is, a deep-rooted conservatism: wary of the poetry shelves in the library and reluctant to take gap years (although the pupil we talked to whose ambition was to be an inventor was thought eccentric, she was still very much one of the girls). The head 'hopes to encourage greater risk-taking'.

Northwood is prosperous, with lots of large detached houses. Girls come from wide area – good coach service covers Beaconsfield, Elstree, Barnet, Amersham, Ealing, Hemel Hempstead and points between.

Old Girls' network huge and devoted. St Helen's inspires great loyalty. Alumnae include Patricia Hodge, a great supporter, Vanessa Lawrence (director general Ordnance Survey), Lady Lowry, Luisa Baldini, Penny Marshall and Maria Djurkovic.

Entrance: School part of North London Consortium which shares tests at 11. First point of entry is at three into Little St Helen's. At 11, exams in English and maths around 300 apply for 50 places – not too terrifying as lots apply elsewhere but school is increasingly candidates' first choice. Junior school girls have to sit the exam too, but none have failed in recent years.

Interview and reference from current school as important as scores. 'Aim is to explore potential and to ensure that girls will be able to take full advantage of the curriculum and wider opportunities the school has to offer,' says the school. As ever true but never spelt out, parents should remember that they are on show too.

At sixth form, 'places are available for girls who the school considers will benefit by the educational programme offered and who will enjoy becoming members of the school community. We don't fix the number of places.' You need seven plus GCSEs at B+. Some leave along the way – around 10 leave at 11 for state system, boarding or (few) other local independents. A few leave after GCSEs.

Exit: Everyone to higher education. Handful to Oxbridge annually (three in 2013), otherwise a wide spread of universities and courses with about a third science related: strong bias to medical, biological and engineering courses. Careers advice considered by the girls to be top notch, and in general they have a much clearer idea than usual of what courses they would like and what careers they might pursue afterwards.

Money matters: Range of scholarships and means-tested bursaries. Bursaries awarded annually and are either awarded to girls whose parents could not otherwise meet fees or to girls whose families are experiencing temporary difficulties.

Remarks: Thoroughly impressive. Not in hock to the league tables, but plenty of ambition for its pupils, academically and otherwise.

St James Senior Boys' School

Linked schools: St James Senior Girls' School; St James Junior School

Church Road, Ashford, TW15 3DZ

• Pupils: 365 boys, all day except for 20 weekly boarders • Ages: 11–18 • Inter–denom (but see below) • Fees: Day £14,400; Weekly boarding £20,550 pa • Independent

Tel: 01784 266930
Email: admissions@stjamesboys.co.uk
Website: www.stjamesboys.co.uk

Headmaster: Since September 2013, Mr David Brazier BA, PGCE. Mr Brazier studied English and American literature at the University of Kent and has an MSc from Reading University. He joins St James from six years as head of Long Close School, Slough. Prior to this he was head of English and drama at Crosfields School in Reading and assistant headmaster at Davenies in Beaconsfield, Bucks.

Mr Brazier is passionate about cricket, having played for Berkshire Schools and Hurst in the Thames Valley League and is a qualified cricket coach. He also has an abiding love of Shakespeare and the performing arts and has written three plays that have been performed in schools.

Academic matters: Academically selective, but academic promise is not everything – see below. In 2013, nearly 45 per cent A*/A grades at GCSE; 37 per cent at A level. School propounds the sensible view that nine GCSEs is ample for anyone and these are taken early where possible to 'allow space for a proper education'. Parents say that St James is not a school to push your child to his absolute academic limits – too committed to breadth and character.

All subject teaching is underpinned by the philosophical principles espoused by the school and the ethos is inescapable throughout curricular and extra-curricular life. It influences, among other things, the subjects offered and their popularity with pupils. Allows pupils to specialise early, following their individual bents. Science, logic and ancient history the best performers, while subjects that are usually popular in boys'

schools like maths, economics and business, take a back seat. Sanskrit – the Indo-Germanic language pre-dating even Greek and Latin – is introduced to all year 7 entrants and continues for those who can manage it until year 9, becoming an option thereafter. It is heartening to see Greek and Latin as relatively popular GCSE options, though few continue classical or any other language to A level. DT, introduced with encouragement from the inspectorate, not yet well resourced but proving popular and on the school's list of areas to upgrade. Good IT kit and ICT training, but not much real computing. Business studies BTEC since 2012.

Nothing trendy about the approach to education: King James bible, whole Shakespeare plays, proper languages. Boys' choice of adjective to describe teachers in general: 'enthusiastic'. Some stars, many good, in boys' and parents' opinions. Chimes with what we saw of the staff. 'Mrs' and 'Sir', but without the feeling of distance that accompanies that in some other schools. Help instantly and easily available – email teachers when on study leave, or come in for support. They respond readily to parental emails too.

SENs numerous and well supported. Use interesting innovative techniques such as The Art of Science – a way of making difficult scientific concepts visually accessible. School will take pupils with a range of special needs including ADHD and, as far as possible, support them in class: usually takes a couple at the heavy end of the spectrum. All pupils are allowed four 'units' of support free of charge – the value of a unit depends on whether it is individual or group support, but anyone who has more than four has to pay extra.

Games, options, the arts: Edexcel on track to accredit a St James Baccalaureate, recognising the breadth of education as well as academic success. Not intended to be a shoe-in: will take commitment to achieve.

Music traditionally the strongest of the arts subjects, though 'boys give up their instruments so quickly unless you keep them at it', says a parent. School is especially keen on singing, which 'is part of our philosophical approach, opening hearts and minds and hearing the sound of one's own voice.' Major, serious music and drama productions in collaboration with the girls' school in Olympia, and everyone makes light of the considerable amount of inter-school ferrying this involves.

School lays much emphasis on its extra-curricular programme of activities. They are able to do kayaking on the school lake (head determined to get them swimming there too) and sailing on the nearby reservoirs and further afield. They go climbing and love it, and around a quarter enthusiastically take up the cadet force and do all the adventurous things that that offers. A popular D of E scheme attracts others. Around three-quarters of the school take up one or other of these outdoor options. Some charitable and social activity, but less than we had expected to find.

Drama much appreciated, centred round the studio called The Empty Space after Peter Brooke gave his support for it (a deliberately minimalistic rendering of 'creative space'). Performance is important, as is speech itself. 'If you have not mastered speech by the time you leave here, then those who have will master you,' is a maxim quoted at the boys. 'Makes them talk and engage in conversations' say parents. Art is no great shakes.

The school now has all major sports facilities, such as rugby, hockey, football and cricket, within its grounds but there are lots of minor sports and opportunities for even the least sporty to find something to do. Boys like to win, and are increasingly doing so, but 'not at all costs' as a parent put it.

The idealistic leadership programme in Lucca, Italy, presents an unusual and scenic opportunity to all boys twice in their school career to develop all kinds of personal skills. At home there are guest speakers and sixth form dinners hosted at home by the head – a broadening and inspirational programme.

Twice-yearly lectures at the RSA given by everyone from eminent physicians to ambassadors. Also, the Ficino Society – a programme of academic talks designed to foster and care for potential Oxbridge candidates, which adds to the intellectual life of the school and thus meets its requirement to nurture the gifted and talented.

Quiet time for all is a major feature at the beginning and end of every day. Silent pauses before and after lessons with benedictions, grace before meals and expressions of thanks in Sanskrit are embedded in the daily life of all pupils.

Background and atmosphere: Rooted in the ethos of the School of Economic Science, founded in 1937, which aims to explore through the study of the world's great religions and philosophies what it is to be fully human in a spiritual way and, in so doing, what goes to make a spiritually healthy and prosperous community. The school was founded in the 1970s, when the SES flame burned high, but has now become 'a philosophically inspired school whose roots are in the SES, but which has grown and evolved, with the philosophy and ethos made available to all.' Only a few members of staff and even fewer parents are active members of the SES; only a couple of SES families are young enough to have pupils to send.

The school now occupies a fine site in the West London Lake District, in buildings erected by The Society of Ancient Britons in 1857 to house the Welsh Girls' School. They have been well renovated to make a spacious and light environment, its coherence regularly shattered by the most unpleasing klaxon that signals the end of each lesson. Facilities not as glossy as at some neighbouring schools, but serviceable.

Pastoral care and discipline: The pervasive philosophical ethos of the school is its principal defence against misbehaviour and anti-social behaviour of all kinds. 'A school where children have no problem in admitting their vulnerability', said a parent. Little bullying, no serious drugs incidents (crisp and clear policies), and all other problems dealt with through talk and parental involvement on an individual basis. Boys not prepared to toe the line have a tough time of it – most come round in the end. The prefect system, class representation on the school council and the form masters pick up the rest. 'Manhood', 'character' and 'character-building' are terms much in evidence here. 'Gets teenage boys, all noise and go and fast paced, to meditate in silence.'

School food is vegetarian and organic and is largely composed of fresh and dried fruit, nuts, cheese, home-cooked soups, pasta and rice dishes and quiches. 'Excellent', 'Doesn't weigh you down and make you sleepy after lunch', 'I get all the meat I want at home' typical boy comments. Parents say 'he never comes home hungry'. Not canteen: laid out on tables, staff and pupils eat together

Boarding is weekly only. All junior boarders in two five-bed dorms, all older boys, ie from year 8 upwards, in pairs or singles. Common-room with sofas, kitchen area and TV and, in the evenings, the boys have the school's other facilities to themselves.

Pupils and parents: All but one pupil came West when the school moved, and the catchment area still stretches way to the East, if that's a reasonable description of Twickenham. School runs buses to keep it that way. Ethnic and social mix is typical of the area. Lots of different faiths, notably those (Hinduism, Buddhism) on which the SES drew heavily. Some SES initiates among the parents, some out and out sceptics, most in-between: no pressure to join.

Aims for boys imbued with kindness, generosity and determination. 'He has blossomed. No more hunched shoulders. He walks square'. More about looking up to Nelson Mandela than Richard Branson. Lively, creative, sparky boys. 'Emerge as young men not youths,' say parents. 'There are so many events that parents are involved in that you really get to see the way the boys relate to each other. They are such good friends, so supportive of each other'. 'Know who they are, and what is important.'

Entrance: Selection is on the basis of entrance tests in English, maths and verbal reasoning plus interview with the prospective pupil and his parents. Interview can outweigh the entrance test if it is felt the boy has 'character' or other gifts which the school feels would benefit from its distinctive educational approach – we have heard some most cheering stories from parents of such boys. Entry into the sixth form depends on a minimum of six B grades at GCSE plus interview with the head of sixth form and headmaster. This requirement extends to the boys already in the school and some are encouraged to look elsewhere or helped into more vocational areas if the school feels that A levels are not appropriate.

Exit: A wide range of universities and courses, with a particular interest in history. A few to Cambridge (not so much Oxford); Durham, SOAS, Southampton, Warwick, Kent and Canterbury popular: a broad spread beyond that. Some leave after GCSE for a clutch of comfortable reasons – access to the IB, wanting more practical courses, or just having been there since age four.

Money matters: Not a rich school; the fees are lower than average and the pot for scholarships and bursaries is correspondingly small. School aims to support with means-tested bursaries those who could otherwise not come or who have financial problems once accepted.

Remarks: Distinctive, different and, in many ways, special and valuable. Not for those committed to one religion to the exclusion of others (or none) nor those for whom a liberal creative freedom is everything. Acquaint yourself thoroughly with the ethos.

St James Senior Girls' School

Linked school: St James Senior Boys' School; St James Junior School

Earsby Street, London, W14 8SH

- Pupils: 385 girls • Ages: 10–18 • Non denom • Fees: £15,150 pa
- Independent

Tel: 020 7348 1777
Email: admissions@sjsg.org.uk
Website: www.stjamesgirls.co.uk

Headmistress: Since 1995, Mrs Laura Hyde Cert Ed MEd (fifties). Mrs Hyde trained as a primary school teacher and taught at two London schools before joining the St James Junior School (qv). She became PA to the founder of the St James schools and of the School of Economic Science (see below). After some years at home bringing up her children, she became assistant head at the St James Senior Girls' School in 1994, assuming the headship a year later.

None of which prepares you for the charm of the woman herself. Quietly spoken, measured and exuding calm, Mrs Hyde exemplifies the qualities she hopes to develop in the young women she sees into the world. She answers questions thoughtfully and frankly in her cheerful, elegantly-furnished study and inspires trust. A subtle, gentle moderniser, she has, while maintaining the core ethos and traditions of the St James family of schools, done much to bring her branch into the 21st century. Parents enthuse – 'she's fantastic – she's my current heroine – she has created a gentle, loving, caring atmosphere.'

Mrs Hyde's already lengthy tenure has given the school the stability and confidence it needed. Retiring in July 2014.

Academic matters: Girls take the IGCSE in maths and all three sciences – for greater rigour. At GCSE, 68 per cent A*/A grades in 2013. Stunning success in physics, history and English and at least respectable everywhere else. At A level the 20 subject options now include theatre studies, Spanish and art history. Results creditable in most subjects – few grades below B – and English and maths impressive. In 2013, 79 per cent of A level entries were graded A*-B (56 per cent A*/A). School also offers EPQ to give students the opportunity to get deeply involved in a subject that interests them, to pull together learning from other subjects and to develop extended research and writing skills – all of which are hugely valuable preparations for university study.

But this is not a school to think of solely in these terms. The school's culture largely determines the extended curriculum. Sanskrit is continued for those who join from the junior school (introductory course offered to those joining in Year 7) and available as an option at GCSE. Singing, dance and philosophy are taken by all and everything is taught from the philosophical perspective which underpins the St James schools' ethos. Philosophy is taught all through the school; Mrs Hyde teaches years 6-7 and 11-13. This approach extends to the LDD provision which is managed on the basis of an individual's needs, although the hope is that most pupils can work independently by the end of year 8. Thereafter, the SENCo sees girls individually or in small groups according to need – no withdrawal from academic lessons. The staff monitor progress with care. Strong gifted and talented provision.

Games, options, the arts: This is a compact city site so anything involving running takes place at the Chiswick playing grounds, a bus ride away. On site, they cram in netball, aerobics, gymnastics, health-related fitness and dance etc and off site lacrosse, netball, athletics, rounders and tennis are the main sports. They have their own adventure club – the St James Challengers – and D of E. Two good art rooms in which, largely, the trad skills are taught by much-admired staff. Visiting instructors add to the core curriculum and the school now has a kiln but no dark room. And no DT. One of the best schools we know at actually displaying its own pupils' art – everywhere and with style. Music is big here – again under charismatic leadership – everyone sings – we heard it everywhere – the whole school sings together twice weekly. Music seen as part of the spiritual education provided. Lots of individual lessons and good collaboration on concerts and productions with the boys' school – despite the distance. Drama popular and lively. The 'art of hospitality' is taught to years six and seven – cookery but not as you might have known it elsewhere – the thrust here is on sharing food and using it as a way of nurturing relationships. The sixth form cook for each other, have formal dinners with high profile guests etc. In year 10, all go on a residential week which focuses on 'becoming an adult' – life skills, presenting oneself at interview and being a responsible citizen etc. Much emphasis on community service.

Background and atmosphere: Founded, along with its sibling junior school and senior boys' school, in 1975 by the School of Economic Science (see the review of the senior boys' school for background and history), the girls' school and junior school moved to their impressive modern accommodation in 2001. The outside is daunting. The main gate, within sight of Olympia down a quiet side road, is encased in uniquely secure architecture – grilles, grids, gratings and entry phone. If you happen to be a billionaire or high profile political refugee, you will deposit your daughter here in the mornings, confident that the bad world will be kept firmly outside.

The two schools co-exist happily and it is rather nice – if surprising – to come across classrooms full of six-year-olds as you cruise around the corridors. Nonetheless, the schools are finding, as was inevitable, that both need more elbow room. New building started in 2010 with a balcony in the assembly room and further extensions including a new sixth form centre will be built over the next few years. The place is in good nick – lots of white-painted corridors, blue carpets, good wall displays and useful noticeboards. The sixth form have privileges – eating in the staff dining room, for one – and responsibilities which are taken seriously.

Classrooms, while not quite providing the 'beautiful environment' aimed at, are orderly and well-kept and all now have whiteboards and projectors. The library is clearly too small and a new library is part of the building plan. Outside space is limited though care has been taken to provide little trellised alcoves for quiet chat around the tarmac playground. A sense of cheery collaborativeness abounds – girls look relaxed and happy and appreciate their unusual school. Staff, according to parents, 'always smile and are friendly'. 'Silence, stillness and meditation' are important – everyone has a few moments for these at the start and finish of each lesson. The food is vegetarian and the tables are laid invitingly – hot home-cooked food plus fresh fruit, salad, bread and cheese.

The boys' school move to Ashford provides much-needed expansion space in a very attractive position. But while the arrangement presents opportunities for the St James schools, there may well be difficulties now that the family of schools is spread over a wider geographic area. How families wanting the St James brand of education for their boys, girls, juniors and seniors will adapt remains to be seen. Nevertheless, we hear that so far the majority of the junior boys are still transferring to the senior boys' school. Senior boys and girls also enjoy a good number of extra-curricular activities together.

Pastoral care and discipline: Highly praised. Pupils like the mentoring system and the 'strong bond' they feel to many teachers. Younger pupils are assigned sixth form prefects as mentors, sixth formers have form tutors. 'Your mentor is your friend – they always give you someone who doesn't teach you – you go to her with any problems – not just academic ones.' Head relies on the 'very strong programme of education' to guard against the usual teenage problems. 'We emphasise strengthening a girl's social conscience and confidence...if you present with difficulties we will help you so long as you are not harming the rest of the community.' On bullying, 'we keep working at it... stressing the importance of unity and not harming each other.'

The school's strong spiritual ethos underpins the disciplinary side but girls don't feel it's thrust down their throats. A parent expressed the general view – 'we like the way they approach education – they believe strongly in the spiritual side of it – it doesn't invade life but they look at the whole development of the girl and believe that the academics will follow.' A sixth former confided, 'Mrs Hyde wants us to be great women – she doesn't want us just to stay at home.' She herself says, 'my emphasis is on creating responsible citizens.' Who wouldn't fit in? 'Someone who is only out for themselves wouldn't find themselves in their natural environment...our girls are gentle on the outside but inwardly strong and independent – they are women of some integrity.'

Pupils and parents: Mixed as befits its west London location. Unsurprisingly, given the influence of 'the wisdom traditions of east and west', the school has an appeal to families with Asian backgrounds who make up around a fifth. Some of the staff are members of the School of Economic Science, some are ex-pupils, but a large majority of the pupils are now from families who have no direct connection with the SES. Pupils come from great distances – at least for the first five years – though most are relatively local. Former pupils include actresses Emily Watson and Sasha Behar and novelist Laura Wilson.

Entrance: St James Junior pupils move seamlessly through – NB at year 6 – and, at present, given that they share the site, this is much easier for girls than for boys, who head off to Ashford. Main feeders are Pembridge Hall, Orchard House, Chiswick and Bedford Park, Glendower, Ravenscourt Park Prep, St Nicholas Prep, The Falcons School, Bute House, Garden House, Kew Green Prep, Thomas' Battersea and Thomas' Kensington. A few join at year 6 but main intake into year 7 when around 175 apply for around 25 places. School is part of the North London Consortium so tests in maths and English. School's own reasoning test day also includes activities in baking, art, drama, dance and chemistry. A few come in at year 12. NB how small the school is. Head says, 'I'm looking at the character of the girls and whether what the school is about resonates with her and her family.'

Exit: Currently a fifth leave after GCSEs; some to co-eds, often to colleges, occasionally to board or to nearer home. A pity as the sixth form classes are small – one-to-one in some cases – the teaching is good and nothing beats the continuity of staying where you are known. This foolish fashion of moving for doubtful gains is on the wane, one hopes. Some gap years. Thereafter, many to the south of England Russell Group or the 1994 group and new unis. An increasing number are pursuing science degrees and over the last three years a third have left to study science of some kind. Many pursue careers in which they contribute to the community. Two to Oxbridge in 2013.

Money matters: The school operates a means-tested bursary scheme. All current and future parents may apply. Future parents need to be registered with the school. This is not a rich school so don't look for masses of help.

Remarks: If the high moral tone appeals and you enjoy the repetition of words such as 'fine' 'wise' and 'beautiful' you have achieved Nirvana here. A tiny, peaceful school offering what many parents dream of.

St John Fisher Catholic High School

Linked school: St Aidan's and St John Fisher Associated Sixth Form

Hookstone Drive, Harrogate, HG2 8PT

• Pupils: 675 boys, 740 girls; Sixth form: 1100 (in association with St Aidan's C of E High School) • Ages: 11–18 • Roman Catholic • State

Tel: 01423 887254
Email: office@sjfchs.org.uk
Website: www.sjfchs.org.uk

Headteacher: Since 2001, Mr Paul Jackson MA (late-fifties). Educated at St Bonadventure's School (where he taught initially), then read natural sciences at Cambridge. Also taught at The Campion School, Hornchurch and All Saints Catholic School, Dagenham, first headship at St Mary's Catholic School, Bishop Stortford. Dynamic, cheerful, relaxed – seen as 'very approachable and friendly' by pupils and parents, and very 'can do'. Astute and realistic – comfortable with the demands of the post, which he enjoys and handles in a very balanced way, eg lets the heads of departments make their own decisions in their subject areas. Strong commitment to the school's Catholic ethos and spiritual life, but not in a narrow fashion. Teaches science to year 7s and RE to the sixth form, for two to three hours a week, and 'writes a number of sentences on every pupil's report,' enthused a parent. Married with two adult children; enjoys walking and travelling in his spare time.

Academic matters: Has humanities and performing arts specialist status, so these subjects are especially carefully monitored and the latter used to develop creativity across the curriculum. Constantly striving to improve its very good results by systematic target setting and use of data. Calm, purposeful atmosphere in classrooms. Lots of computers regularly upgraded; all classes have electronic whiteboards and all teachers laptops. Pupils and parents see the teachers as helpful and generous with their support at exam time. A parent described the teaching as 'dynamic' – 'The children have a lot of fun along with learning'.

The Associated Sixth Form with St Aidan's C of E High School offers an ecumenical environment and each preserves its own identity via separate pastoral systems; over 150 students join from other schools. High praise from the most recent Ofsted report: 'terrific' progress, 'superb' attitudes to learning, 'exceptionally high quality' teaching, 'excellent' relationships. Steady 60 per cent A*-B at A level, 59 per cent in 2013. Ninety-five per cent of students achieved first choice destinations. Offers 43 subjects: sciences (very popular), history, ancient history, English lit, German, art, maths, psychology, government and politics, RS, design and technology, drama and theatre studies and performing arts particularly successful. Others include photography, dance, engineering, Spanish, law, geology, sociology, plus vocational courses, eg health and social care, travel and tourism, music technology. All do RS as part of the AS general studies programme, then non-examined RS in year 13. AQA baccalaureate is now established – A levels plus extended project and community service. One year intermediate programmes are tailored to meet individual needs and include maths, English and career planning.

Very strong GCSE results – 90 per cent 5+ A*-C including English and maths, 47 per cent English Baccalaureate and 40 per cent A/A* grades in 2013 – reflecting a steady and consistent rise over the last decade. Art, English, sciences, geography, history, drama and music do particularly well. Wide range of subjects with over 80 per cent students following traditional GCSE courses leading to the English Baccalaureate: all kinds of science – separate, combined or applied for the less able; the biology lab houses two live snakes – which we declined to view. Has a developed citizenship programme leading to GCSE and all students now do a GCSE in applied ICT. Also does very well by the less able/academic or disaffected students, who can take a wide range of practical qualifications more commonly offered by further education colleges, eg BTEC business, BTEC engineering, digital applications (ICT), health and social care, music technology and performing arts, even if the take up is small. Personalised work-related learning with college courses are available for the small number who require such provision.

In 2008, the school moved to a GCSE course starting in year 9 'to avoid the year 8 dip, offer challenge and enhance the curriculum,' said Mr Jackson. This enables teachers to go beyond the curriculum (hurrah!), has improved behaviour and is popular with teachers, parents and pupils. Strong KS3 results obtained at the end of year 8. English and maths now setted in year 7, then English, French and maths in year 8.

Very enlightened and thorough-going SEN provision: the department has its own IT suite and provides in and outside class support. Weak year 8s are given one-to-one tuition in English and maths, SEN and reluctant learners have individual programmes – they can chose vocational courses at college and/or work experience. Learning mentors and good EAL support. Performing arts used to promote inclusion, eg of less academic KS4 students.

S

The gifted and talented can do additional GCSEs via independent learning (with an e-tutor), eg the Cambridge school Latin project in years 8-10; separate sciences and additional maths.

Games, options, the arts: Three soccer and one rugby pitches, four tennis/netball courts, an oldish gym and more modern sports hall, plus a big field with lots of trees. Also offers cross-country, cricket, golf at a local course, cheerleading and hoop fusion for girls, self-defence, junior sports leader award, leadership academy. Success in regional, county and national (athletics, football and cross country) competitions; strong tennis.

Big focus on the performing arts: has Artsmark Gold and a modern performing arts area; plays tend to be musicals, eg Phantom of the Opera, Sound of Music, Wizard of Oz (seniors) and Mulan, Beauty and the Beast (juniors, with partner primary schools); theatre trips to Leeds and London. Very strong and diverse music includes jazz orchestra, steel pans, strings, Dixie band and a full set of African djembes (drums) shared with the community; the concert band, jazz band and choir all reached the finals of the National Festival of Music for Youth; students who opt for performing arts GCSE get a free term of music instruction. Also music technology equipment – a recording studio, video editing suite, lots of computers. Dance is a special feature: links with the Ballet Rambert, eg a master class workshop from its artistic director; students belong to the North Yorkshire Dance Company; a twilight dance GCSE class for year 9 gifted and talented boys (urban funk favoured).

Offers a huge range of activities with over 40 clubs and societies including D of E, a winter mountaineering course, fundraising for, eg, CAFOD; aiming for Fairtrade school status. Sixth formers help the staff run activities and with lessons, as well as managing their own facilities via elected committees. York University lecturers and students work with history and politics A level students and debating is strong: the school belongs to a local league and has taken part in an Oxford-based competition. A representative selection of politicians gave talks before the last general election – in the school's mock version, the Lib Dems won by a large majority, with a strong showing by the Greens. International trips to France; Greece and New York (performing arts); Barcelona (art); Germany (history). All year 8 students have an opportunity to do a team-building outdoor activity at the end of the summer term. As an extended school it offers sport and community based activities in the evenings and at the weekends, including an arts programme.

Background and atmosphere: Voluntary aided; situated on the outskirts of Harrogate – originally a convent school built in 1904, with an attractive 1970s sandstone extension supplemented by seven recent mobiles. The main problem is lack of space – some of the passageways are narrow, which can cause shoving, but students soon adapt, according to a parent; year 7 classrooms, which have largest numbers, seem cramped and some areas need decorating (we would have liked to see more artwork displayed). A small cafeteria for years 7-10 has now been refurbished through a national project initiated by year 8 students – conventional hot food, sandwiches and fruit or a packed lunch for, eg, those who want to eat on the large front lawn; the school has healthy school status. Also a huge plasma screen for menus, school and national news – a number of these in entrance halls. Years 11-13 share a modern, larger and lighter space with a small work area equipped with a few computers; the sixth form common room, painted each year by the students, is rather functional and well worn. Quite a good size library with a wide selection of newspapers and excellent stock of modern teenage fiction, but small adult fiction section.

The traditional chapel plays a central part in the school's spiritual life: one chapel assembly a week for separate year groups, to which various teachers contribute – the one we visited

was lively and the students seemed engaged. Each year goes on a retreat, either one day or residential (year 10s visit Lourdes) and year 8s have trips to non-Christian places of worship.

Pupils have a say on school life and learning via the school council and surveys, and participate in lesson observations to identify the best teaching and learning practice. Individuality is allowed: girls wear some of the shortest (plaid) skirts we have ever seen (but Mr Jackson says they have worked on uniform over the last year and skirts are longer) or trousers, with blue shirts, ties and jackets; boys wear blue shirts, now tucked into black trousers – and some of the shortest ties we have ever seen.

Pastoral care and discipline: Very thoughtful and comprehensive policies, eg the sensible advice issued to pupils on how to cope with bullying, including cyber-bullying. The focus is more on rewards than sanctions. Planners are used by form tutors and parents to get problems resolved quickly and effectively. Year 7s are looked after very well, said a parent: they are encouraged to join clubs, take responsibility and belong to the school community – 'It's a happy, friendly and embracing place that develops confidence'; 'There's an ethos of mutual respect and lots of individual care,' said others.

A very up-to-date electronic system records data – attendance in all lessons, behaviour, academic progress – which teachers, form tutors and parents can access on-line, and enables tracking and monitoring to identify vulnerable students and children with emotional difficulties. Pupils who need support or time out can visit a reflection area in a secluded part of school with a space for prayer, The Oratory; a quiet room with a snooker table and access to an approachable, young lay chaplain. Year 13s and adults provide mentoring and the learning support centre is open at lunchtimes. The number of exclusions is going down, but zero tolerance of 'inappropriate language to staff' and abuse of illegal substances prevails.

Pupils and parents: The majority are practising Catholics – white, middle class professionals from Harrogate and Wetherby and the surrounding district. However, school has greatest ethnic diversity in North Yorkshire with significant numbers of Polish and Phillipino students. Pupils are lively, outgoing and enthusiastic about the school. Parents are kept well informed via two-weekly e-bulletins, termly newsletters and a parent focus group reviews new systems.

Entrance: Over subscribed: 335 applicants for 196 places. Has its own complicated admissions system – baptised Catholics get preference. Sixth formers: up to 30 from outside the two main schools; five A*-Cs with at least one B needed. Deadline for applications: mid-March.

Exit: The great majority continue into the Associated Sixth Form (90 per cent in 2013). The school is justifiably proud that scarcely any students become NEETS (not in education, employment or training). Most sixth formers proceed to university – a great range, including several top ones, eg Oxbridge and the best London University colleges. In 2013, over 90 per cent achieved first or second choice destination.

Money matters: The Hayra Educational Trust provides a fund for help with extra-curricular activities, including gap year projects, for sixth formers.

Remarks: A deeply impressive school in all respects, apart from the limitations of its accommodation – deservedly researched by Ofsted for a report on the features of outstanding state schools.

S

St John's School (Leatherhead)

Epsom Road, Leatherhead, Surrey, KT22 8SP

• Pupils: 625: 445 boys (347 day + 98 boarders) 180 girls (128 day + 52 boarders) • Ages: 13–18 • C of E but other denominations accepted • Fees: Day £20,880; Boarding £26,370 pa • Independent

Tel: 01372 373000
Email: admissions@stjohns.surrey.sch.uk
Website: www.stjohnsleatherhead.co.uk

Headmaster: Since September 2011 Martin Collier MA (Oxon), married with three older children. He read modern history at St John's College Oxford, followed by PGCE from London University. His first 10 years of teaching were in the maintained sector, at the 'fantastic' Thomas Tallis in south London and the 'tough' Weavers School in Wellingborough. Fifteen years ago he moved into the independent sector and Oundle School, where he worked through roles of head of history, director of studies and second master. He also has many years' experience as an examiner with different boards, has been involved with the Qualifications and Curriculum Development Agency and has appeared as an examinations expert before the House of Commons Select Committee on Education. In short, he has a broad experience and detailed knowledge of all things educational. We found him to be a quiet, almost unassuming man, a strategic thinker who is looking five years ahead in planning for St John's and has launched some very major changes at the school in September 2012.

In addition to his responsibilities for the school's strategic management and teaching standards, Mr Collier also covers the outward facing aspects of St John's, which includes meeting all prospective parents and visiting local prep schools. He has delegated much of the day to day nitty-gritty running of the school to his deputy Mark Mortimer who, as the first port of call for many pupils and parents, is the one they seem to know best. Even after a year in post Mr Collier is still rather an unknown to some parents, although they are aware that he has been hard at work behind the scenes developing the significant and progressive changes now taking shape at St John's. We hope his softly, softly approach works.

Academic matters: St John's has been gradually on the up academically over the last few years and is aiming still higher. Exam results in 2012 were GCSEs 62 per cent at A*/A with at 19 per cent at A*, and for A levels 46 per cent at A*/A, seven per cent at A*. It has been considered as a school which provides a good education but not a high pressure one – a suitable place for a child who would not be happy or comfortable in an academically high-flying school. Parents here certainly want their children to do as well as they can academically, but are also looking for an all-round education including social values and leadership.

Mr Collier believes improving academic results goes hand in hand with improving pastoral care and, unsurprisingly, higher levels of academic selection at entry. It's not rocket science, and the effects of changes taking place now should be seen over the next few years. There has been somewhat of a range of teaching styles and standards at the school including one or two described by parents as 'rather unimpressive', but they are reassured by the new broom and improving exam results. The head tells us he has made important new appointments to improve the quality of teaching, introduced new staff performance assessment and a new management structure with a focus on academia – he's obviously on the case and wants to 'increase fizz in the classroom'.

This big academic push has still to filter through to all pupils; parents tell us that hard work and academic success is not universally seen as cool. Although pupils do work hard and want success, sometimes they keep it rather quiet. Mr Collier notes that girls' academic work and success help to pull the boys along, although by the sixth form they are equal. In his extensive experience, he has found that boys and girls have different needs and pace at different ages, their operation and processing is different, girls gain confidence and maturity earlier than boys. The range of academic ability is catered for by setting in all subjects based on the pace at which pupils learn.

All pupils are tested on entry to identify their 'learning profile', which also identifies any SEN. School tells us that learning support is available to all pupils at all ages, ranging from study skills and time management to specialist tuition for specific learning difficulties. Around 10 per cent of pupils currently have SEN and they are catered for by staff in the classroom, by extra small group sessions and, where necessary, by individual one-to-one support. Parents praise the 'excellent' SENCo'. The small number of pupils with EAL have flexible, small group provision alongside support from tutors.

Games, options, the arts: All extras and additions to the academic curriculum are taken very seriously at St John's. They are well taught and valued by pupils and their families; deputy head Mark Mortimer is very keen on leadership development and believes that sport, drama and music are of equal value to academics in developing a rounded and balanced individual.

Sport is pretty well at the centre of life at St John's and is compulsory, daily and at all ages. There are lots of options and the facilities are very good, with spacious pitches and sports centre. Essentially boys play rugby and football, girls play netball and rounders and both boys and girls play hockey, cricket, tennis and do athletics, cross-country and swimming. There's also a whole array of less usual sports and activities available. Saturdays are match days and older pupils tell us they watch and support their school teams. Rugby is at the top of the sports pecking order; the girls' housemistress is a top women's player and she referees matches – much to the surprise of visiting teams.

All this sporting activity brings a deal of success: in rugby St John's boys are currently Surrey U16 county VIIs champions and in football they won the national independent schools league in 2011. The girls have recently won an U16 county hockey trophy and, over the last two years, have been runners up in the county netball championships.

Music is another big part of St John's life, a third of pupils learn an instrument (up to diploma standard) and choral singing is also very strong – pupils win choral awards to universities and are involved in the National Youth Choir and other top external choral groups.

Drama is well represented with lots of opportunities for aspiring actors in many and varied school productions. St John's recently won a number of awards at the local Leatherhead Drama Festival.

Art and DT facilities are superb, housed in a gleaming new classroom block and equipped with everything the most dedicated artists and design technology students could want. The standard of work is correspondingly high, with displays of impressive and inspiring art and functional DT projects. The brainy (and charming) sixth former who showed us round was combining maths, physics and DT at A level and heading confidently towards an engineering degree.

Other activities include CCF (compulsory for four terms), community service and D of E, all involving challenging activities and trips. There are also lots of school activities going on in the evenings: concerts, plays, rehearsals and talks, all of which pupils are routinely involved in. It can be very demanding of pupils' time, particularly if they are not boarders, but it suits families who are busy and those who like their children to be fully occupied with school activities.

S

Background and atmosphere: St John's is very much a local school – most pupils come from within a 15 mile radius – with a strong sense of its own community. Essentially it's a traditional environment providing a 'values based education'; deputy head tells us that parents here are interested in much more than academics, they want a well rounded, emotionally intelligent education for their children so they leave school able to interact well with others.

However, there is no doubt at all that St John's is currently going through some major changes, as previously mentioned regarding academic matters. These changes are also apparent in other areas and are leading to something of a culture shift, from an ultra-trad boys boarding school into something much more 21st century, whilst still holding on to the values of an all-round schooling which are popular with parents. September 2012 saw the first year with girls throughout the school, albeit in the minority, Saturday lessons disappeared a couple of years ago with the arrival of the younger girls, though St John's is very definitely a six day a week school. Boarding is 'family-friendly' and flexible; no full time, seven days a week any more. New buildings have popped up to accommodate the 50 per cent-ish increase in pupil numbers over the last few years, entry requirements have just been hiked to a new high, lesson lengths and timetable arrangements have all been changed and a new tutor system introduced. It's not exactly a case of being dragged kicking and screaming but there's a lot happening and there may well be die-hards who need to be convinced. All this change has been brought about by a consultative process, Mr Collier reassures that 'everyone has had their say' – but it's early days and, like everyone else, we can only wait and see.

Some things remain the same – notably the school's structure around houses, 'important in engendering loyalty and belonging in pupils'. School life revolves around pupils' houses, the day starts and ends there, their tutor is to be found there, studying and socialising takes place there. The culture of each house differs depending on the master, but they are not quirky.

The look of the place reflects its character. It comprises a splendid Victorian building with cloisters running around a central quad and an imposing panelled dining room used by everyone for all meals (and once rumoured to be a potential set for Hogwarts). Just beyond the quad are other newer buildings including the terrific classroom, art and DT block opened in 2010 and a very attractive modern new boys' house opened in 2012.

On one side of the quad is the modern chapel which is a crucially important part of the school. St John's has a Christian foundation which forms the basis of daily life. Pupils are required to attend daily chapel as well as Sunday evening services with their house around once a month. Parents also attend these house services and go on to drinks in the houses.

Pastoral care and discipline: Pastoral care is yet another aspect undergoing a revamp at St John's. The tutor system has been reorganised from September 2012 so that every staff member is a tutor to a small group of pupils and every pupil has their own tutor for support and monitoring. Mr Collier describes the tutor as 'the pupil's champion and mentor'; deputy head, Mr Mortimer, who is head of pastoral care, explains the tutor's role as the point of reference for those pupils under their care and the individual who oversees all aspects of a pupil's school life. An ex-army officer and successful transatlantic rower, he is confident and upfront and is an advocate of the value of modern boarding.

Discipline is much in evidence; bad behaviour in class is not tolerated with detentions for minor infringements. There are clear punishments for drinking and smoking, fines and detentions – it does happen; the housemistress pointed out that pupils are easy to spot around town and do get pulled up. Mr Collier expressed his zero tolerance policy towards drugs – any offence and a pupil would be 'straight out'; he feels education of pupils and parents is the key and more is on the cards.

The majority attend as day pupils although boarding is flourishing. Parents say flexi-boarding, two or three nights a week, has been a real winner and many pupils love it. Mr Collier has further long term plans for boarding: he describes it as 'currently in the foothills of change; it needs to lose its old-fashioned connotations and become fluid, social and involve parents in order to thrive'.

Care in the boarding houses is practical and pragmatic, although the nail polish remover in the entrance hall of a girl's house had obviously been ignored by one young lady we spotted unashamedly sporting fushia nails. The accommodation itself varies from neat, modern twin rooms with small en suite loo and shower to somewhat institutional six or eight person dorms with loos down a chilly corridor.

Pupils and parents: Deputy head says the differing styles of boys and girls are beginning to rub off on each other; he tells us that most girls here are 'outgoing and get stuck in', he describes St John's as providing 'a values-based education, for privileged children who learn the responsibility of service'. Families here are well-heeled, middle class professionals but less flashy and more down to earth than many other parents at Surrey boarding schools.

Pupils who enjoy St John's are those who can cope with the pace – academic plus everything else, who want to get involved in school life and enjoy the long day. This all-encompassing style of full-on days, Saturday sport and Sunday chapel would be a godsend for families with two working parents who need their children to be kept busy. However, pupils wanting to run a social or sporting life outside school may find the time commitments of school demanding.

We found the pupils to be sparky, friendly, chatty and well-mannered. On the sports field boys are competitive but very decent; rugby is their number one sport and many display its characteristic discipline alongside fun laddishness. Girls are mostly boisterous, sporty, outgoing and comfortable with the boys' banter. On our visit a group of girls were snuggled up chatting on the sofas in their house, while another group in a different house were catching up on work together. Much time is spent in pupils' single sex houses, whether day or boarding, and pupils mainly socialise with others in their own house, so boys and girls tend to socialise separately; a recently opened mixed common-room may help them all normalise a bit more in each other's company.

Notable OJs include the architect Lord Richard Rogers and the BBC's Europe Editor Gavin Hewitt.

Entrance: St John's is a popular local option and has around three applicants for each place. Selection is on the basis of pupil's current head's recommendation and a pre-assessment taken in the January of year 6; parents report that lately some applicants are being turned away at this stage. The common entrance entry standard is now 55 per cent across the board and Mr Collier feels 'maths is the key to selection'. St John's has its own entrance assessment in maths and English for any applicants who are not taking CE. Consideration of the pupil's strengths in sport, music or drama is also important. At 13 most pupils come from a range of local preps, particularly Danes Hill and Downsend.

For entry to the sixth form, applicants sit an assessment and interview in November of year 11, places are confirmed by GCSE results. At 16 lots of girls come from nearby Manor House, and a few boys wanting a change from local state schools or other independents.

Currently the gender mix is around two-thirds boys to one third girls, but the school is aiming for a 50:50 mix.

Exit: Pupils exit to a huge range of universities, no clear favourites due to the broad academic range here. One or two a year to Oxbridge. Parental and pupils expectation is certainly for university and hopes are pinned on places at the Russell Group.

Careers and university guidance is built into the curriculum from the lower fifth (year 10) onwards and there is regular contact with army, navy and RAF careers officers.

Money matters: Scholarships available in music, drama, art, design and technology, sport, academic and all-rounder, at both 13+ and sixth form entry, worth up to 25 per cent. Means-tested bursaries and grants available, including up to 100 per cent of fees for children of Anglican clergy – Foundationers, reflecting the school's foundation. Also two free places available per year – Albany Awards for children from disadvantaged backgrounds. Discounts for siblings are 10 per cent and for children of Old Johnians are five per cent.

Remarks: A local, newly fully co-ed school currently undergoing quite a lot of change. Excellent facilities and a well-deserved reputation for an all-round education. Straightforward middle class pupils and parents enjoying a busy school with days full of activity.

St Laurence School

Ashley Road, Bradford-on-Avon, BA15 1DZ

• Pupils: 1,170 boys and girls • Ages: 11–18 • C of E • State

Tel: 01225 309500
Email: jane.rodway@st-laurence.wilts.sch.uk
Website: www.st-laurence.wilts.sch.uk

Headteacher: Since January 2013, Mr Fergus Stewart (early fifties), previously deputy head at Nova Hreod School, Swindon.

Academic matters: Academic strengths across the board with science and modern languages strong. Provision for exceptionally able. A levels 57 per cent A*-B grades in 2013. At GCSE, 62 per cent achieved five A*-C grades including maths and English, and 23 per cent achieved five A*-C in their E-Bac. Setting progressively from year 7. 'Oxbridge awareness programme' in sixth form.

Games, options, the arts: Grass athletics track; playing fields provide enough space for cricket, tennis, hockey, rugby and football. Some athletes at county and national level. A Sportsmark School. Riding once a week for SEN students. A hits-you-between-the-eyes art department where dynamic and dedicated team nurtures each pupil to locate the ceramicist, sculptor, textural artist, colourist or draughtsman they didn't know they were. Strong on drama, dance and music – close links with Theatre Royal in Bath. One in five take an instrument. Two choirs – linked to a school in Japan, several string groups, two jazz bands and an orchestra. An Artsmark Gold school. Foreign exchanges to Sully (France) and Norden (Germany), and recent sixth form trips to Paris, Berlin, Romania, Gambia and Kenya. Participated in Model United Nations. A DfE International School. Each year timetable is collapsed for a week of special projects/outward bound/challenge programmes for all years. Drama and dance trips aplenty.

Background and atmosphere: The prosperous Italianate town of Bradford-on-Avon spawned rich merchants in the wool trade. In 1860, a free-thinking philanthropist, Lord Fitzmaurice, set up a technical school with the radical aim of educating young people for the 19th century. In 2002, archaeologists unearthed a vast Roman Villa on the playing field and uncovered a rare mosaic in almost perfect condition. Fitzmaurice Grammar merged in 1980 with 250 year old Trinity Secondary Modern on a site above the picturesque town. The marriage was St Laurence, blessed with enough land to offer a slice for the Wiltshire Music Centre, opened in 1998 with £2.8 million lottery and local sponsorship. Although independent, the 300-seat auditorium, recording studio, music technology suite and nine workshop spaces are used for pupils as well as by 2,000 visitors a week for concerts/jazz and voice workshops/dance/lectures/filming. The Schubert Ensemble, The Orchestra of the Age of Enlightenment, Howard Skempton, Jason Rebello, Pee Wee Ellis hold workshops for the school. This fairy godmother has done much to glamorise the image of St Laurence's fast improving environment. Enthusiasm from staff is infectious. Rock star Midge Ure recently visited – 'I wish I'd been to a school like this!' 250 seater restaurant serves healthy options and gives the kind of lift to the place that the head is keen to see generally. 120 seat lecture theatre and plans for a new Independent Learning Centre (library).

Pastoral care and discipline: No rebels given reins here. Discipline achieved through reward and sanction system. Hot on parent-staff rapport. Inter-personal skills highly valued – sixth formers taking part in two different mentor schemes and getting certificate of recognition as part of record of achievement. School counsellor and nurse on staff. Tutors and year heads provide continuity of care from year 7. Clear behaviour management policy including response to bullying. Clear policy on dealing with drugs and other substances, parents are involved and they work in close co-operation with police and other agencies. Tries to lure students into dining room with imaginative sandwiches. Also – excellent idea – breakfast from 8 to 8.45am. Why, oh why, cry pupils, do only year 7s and sixth formers get lockers, forcing the rest to troll around with books, PE kits, props for drama and kitchen sink from class to class?

Pupils and parents: Large contingent from affluent villages of Freshford, Westwood, Winsley, Limpley Stoke. Most from middle class catchment area. Professors/teachers/county hall bods/self-employed media/musicians/actors/architects. 'All our teachers send their children here, which is a good sign,' says old-timer. Students willingly swap from private schools like Sherborne to endure the mundane uniform of navy sweatshirt with logo, navy trousers/skirt. Body piercing or dyed hair is out. For sixth form, nets are cast wider than catchment, and casual dress allowed. Parent who dumped a 100 per cent bursary from a private school in Bath to send girl here instead say, 'Every child in private education needs to come to a place like this to get ready for the real world'. Former pupils include recent stars of small screen Charlotte Long, Emma Pierson, Michael Rouse, singer Mike Edwards, Joe England (Royal Shakespeare Company).

Entrance: Over 200 places at year 7 but anyone in catchment area automatically gets in. (The school's cachet has driven up house prices by 10 per cent.) Induction days for sixth form in June and September.

Exit: Just over two thirds stay on for sixth form and most of these progress to higher education eg Cardiff, Nottingham, Liverpool, Sheffield, London. Several a year to Oxbridge. Small tranche to art/photography colleges.

Remarks: Stimulating environment which can take just about anybody and get magnificent results. Good relationships between teacher and parent; teamwork and creativity to the fore, putting St Laurence back where it was in terms of local reputation.

S

St Lawrence College

Linked school: St Lawrence College Junior School

College Road, Ramsgate, CT11 7AE

• Pupils: 360; 215 boys,145 girls; 190 boarding, 170 day • Ages: 11–18 • C of E/Christian • Fees: Day £6,516–£16,437; Boarding £21,648–£28,803 pa • Independent

Tel: 01843 572931
Email: ah@slcuk.com
Website: www.slcuk.com

Principal: Since 2013, Mr Anthony Spencer, MA (Oxon). Educated at Chesterfield Boys' School, read PPE at Oxford, played hockey for the university and continues to play, coach and umpire today. Qualified as a chartered accountant with Ernst and Young, worked in finance for eight years. First teaching post at Eastbourne College where he taught business studies and economics; thence to Denstone College as director of studies. Deputy head at Clifton College for five years. Married to Suzanne, a history teacher. Four children, all at St Lawrence.

Academic matters: In 2013, 78 per cent achieved five A*-C including English and maths at GCSE (30 per cent A*/A) and 24 per cent A*/A at A Level – good results for an unselective school. As well as the usual subjects, psychology, music technology, drama and theatre studies and PE offered at A level.

Sixty pupils with EAL requirements; strong emphasis on integration from the word go and sixth form intake must have adequate English to be allowed to join. Lots of support individually tailored to needs and will run an intensive course for those who need it, but reluctant to separate them from the mainstream as keen to build an integrated community. Class sizes start at 20, reducing as you go up the school.

Forty need some sort of AEN (SEN) support, mainly for mild dyslexia and there is one statemented child. Two specialist teachers. Children withdrawn from class where necessary, usually from Latin or French. Specialist SENCo.

Games, options, the arts: Boys play rugby, hockey and cricket and girls play netball and hockey. Tennis a major feature. Good balance between desire to win and inclusion of all. The major sports are compulsory until sixth form when pupils may give up organised games but are encouraged to take some sort of exercise eg aerobics in fitness suite, basketball etc or swimming. Astroturf, all weather tennis courts, indoor swimming pool etc.

Community service encouraged and aimed to give pupils a sense of social responsibility – service being very much part of the ethos of the school. Kent Institute of Art and Young Enterprise provide pupils with contact with the realities of life in the big wide world. The Chapel band visits local churches and the award-winning Chemical Magic show is enthusiastically received in nearby primary schools. Trips to Calais and Boulogne plus foreign sports tours. CCF popular with boys and girls, Duke of Edinburgh popular – several children attain their gold award each year – impressive in so small a school.

Music compulsory for years 7 and 8. School has its own recording studio. Choirs, orchestra, jazz club musicals, concerts, visiting professional musicians. Annual Arts Week with a play, poetry readings, a book fair etc. House plays and singing competitions. Drama not timetabled until sixth form. Various societies eg maths and creative writing – debating society recently set up.

New multi-use theatre opened 2012, with large theatre, classrooms and boardroom.

Background and atmosphere: Founded in 1879 as a boys' boarding school to provide a first-class education based upon sound Christian teaching, it went fully co-ed 1983. As you drive through the arch and enter a 150 acre oasis in the middle of Ramsgate – a remnant of high Victorian muscular Christianity with imposing Virginia creeper clad buildings dominated by the chapel – it is easy to imagine the sons of the Empire going forth from here to all corners of the world. The calm, slightly other-worldly feel belies a thoroughly modern and creative approach to education.

The school sold a plot of land to fund building programme: new ultra-modern middle school building opened in 2007 and most classrooms, boarding houses and the sixth form centre have been refurbished. There are two specialist computer suites and plenty of networked computers throughout the school and in the boarding houses. New girls' boarding house – all en-suite bedrooms and a lovely central atrium.

Pastoral care and discipline: The strong evangelical tradition of the school underpins its religious and spiritual life. Daily chapel and Sunday services for boarders are based on a strong Christian ethos, but an open-minded approach is encouraged, and alternative provision is made for those who do not want to attend eg Jewish pupils can attend the synagogue in Ramsgate and Muslim pupils observe Ramadan. Good interaction between the year groups and international pupils well integrated (the Chinese, as always, find this more difficult than most) – the recent appointment of a director of international students has helped this process. Multi-ethnic nature of the boarding community helps pupils understand the needs and aspirations of others. Strong sense of community and personal responsibility. Pupils have clear sense of right and wrong and moral issues are discussed in lessons eg world health and poverty in geography and fair play in sport. Great emphasis on teamwork.

Very low staff turnover – 24 have been in the school for over ten years and a number have children in the school.

Pupils and parents: Day children from Thanet and East Kent – the school is on the wrong side of the Pfizer site from the traffic point of view, so catchment is limited. Boarders from around the world. Lots from Europe, about 14 per cent Hong Kong Chinese. Sixth form popular with the Germans. The pupils we met were spontaneously friendly and helpful and unassumingly self-confident. Parents encouraged to participate in school activities and all parents are invited to a dinner in the autumn term. Well-known old boys include General Sir Richard Dannatt, Sir John Stevens, McDonald's chief executive Peter Beresford and Gordon Edington.

Entrance: Most children join at 11 and entry is through an interview and testing (not too strenuous) where appropriate. Entry at 13+ is via CE. About half come up from the junior school, the rest from small independent schools and primary schools – the inevitable fallout from the Kent Test. 15-20 pupils join in the sixth form – they are assessed on GCSE performance (normally five passes) and an English test for those from abroad.

Exit: To a wide spread of universities old and new, plus a few to art school and a trickle to Oxbridge (none in 2013). A few leave after GCSEs, some to go to the grammars and others to vocational courses.

Money matters: Academic, music, sports and all-rounder scholarships offered at 11+, 13+ and 16+ plus various bursaries.

Remarks: A charming and warm school, openly Christian but open to all. Coming out of a long period in the doldrums (as an 'all right' school for those missing out on grammars or more selective independents).

S

St Leonards School

Linked school: St Leonards Junior School

South Street, St Andrews, KY16 9QJ

• Pupils: 550 boys and girls (roughly 50/50) of whom 165 are in St Leonards-New Park, the preparatory school of St Leonards. 119 boarders. • Ages: 16-19 sixth form (145) 12-16 senior school (240), 4-12 junior school (165) • Non-denom • Fees: Day £8,589–£11,730; Boarding £28,200 pa • Independent

Tel: 01334 472126
Email: info@stleonards-fife.org
Website: www.stleonards-fife.org

Headmaster: Since 2008, Dr Michael Carslaw BSc MBA PhD (early fifties). Glaswegian by birth, is 'still delighted to be part of such a vibrant school community with so much going on.' After some pretty cataclysmic changes and a period of consolidation under previous head, Dr Carslaw feels 'that the reeling stage is past now, as exemplified by the strong growth of the last two/three years.' He is 'now looking very much to the future' with extra classes in years 8, 9 and 10; roll is at a record high. He adds, 'the students are very lucky to be part of such a historic yet vibrant and forward-looking school and I am enjoying sharing the experience with them.'

He attributes quick recent growth in numbers to the huge positive impact of introducing the IB (International Baccalaureate – not to be confused with the more watered-down new Scottish Baccalaureate) 'as well as the positive buzz about the school as St Leonards re-emerges into the mainstream of Scottish education. Co-ed' he says 'is fully bedded in' (!) with 50/50 all through. Dr Carslaw feels that the long-established status which St Leonards enjoyed as Scotland's most academic girls-only school should now be equalled by its distinction as a co-ed IB school. Sensibly, realising that the sixth form college image is a mixed blessing, he is working to bring the three sections of the school together, giving the juniors in St Leonards Junior School (formed following the merger with local prep school, New Park in 2005) the bonus of lots of help from sixth formers required to do 50 hours of 'service' as part of the IB.

Academic matters: School prides itself on 'high quality education right from the preparatory school through to the senior school.' Scotland's only all-IB sixth form – focuses 100 per cent on the IB. 'We haven't taken any half measures with the qualification by offering alternative post 16 options, we have dedicated ourselves to it and we believe that's to the great benefit of our students.'

In 2013, IB Diploma candidates scored an average of 33 points, equivalent to 457 UCAS points, and more than the worldwide average of 29 points. As a result, more than 80 per cent of them have gained their first choice university places and, impressively, more than 20 per cent of the 52-strong cohort achieved the minimum entrance requirement for Oxford University of 38 points. Almost one third of the group also gained Bilingual Diplomas, indicating fluency in at least two languages.

Thirty-four percent of 2013 GCSE grades were A* or A. Head says 'the IB is probably the least tinkered about with qualification in the world – its basic philosophy of keeping a breadth of subjects going into the sixth form but also studying three to a level comparable to Advanced Higher or A level has remained.' 'Native lang' for IB may be English, Russian, German, French, Mandarin (currently on offer) or whatever, while Latin qualifies as a foreign language, as well as French, Spanish, German, Italian (from scratch). UCAS is now giving points for individual subjects studied under the IB system which means that non-linguists/ mathematicians etc, previously disadvantaged in the overall IB grading, can now get full credit for their strong subjects. Most study two or three langs with all doing French from year 1 and Spanish and /or German from year 5. Latin flourishes. Head of dept was named German Teacher of the Year by the German Embassy in 2011.

Max class size 20. Links with St Andrew's Uni are still strong and progressing, Dr Carslaw assures us. School now appoints a St Leonards Associate Researcher, a research student at St Andrews who acts as a point of contact for St Leonards pupils as well as helping them to develop an appreciation and knowledge of research. St Leonards students have access to the university library and regularly attend special lectures. (Lots of profs' children and consequently no dearth of academic governors or visiting speakers.)

Dyslexia/dyspraxia support – 'no statemented pupils accepted' – mostly provided for 'a small proportion of pupils' in mainstream teaching but a good programme with some withdrawal for learning support and, more prominently, for EAL (English as an Additional Language). About one fifth of non-English (native) speakers need it to start with; all the overseas IB pupils have to pass an English assessment and they don't need any EAL support. Good IT but rather in the wings (still).

Games, options, the arts: Full range of sporting options – chaps' sports fixtures have taken off in recent years. First ever home rugby matches in school's history last year with rugby pitches on the main school site and a growing fixture list for all ages, and increasing number of football fixtures. Girls' sports still strong, with usual mass of international lax players. Rugby good at junior level (parents agree!) and head has high hopes for senior school. Otherwise loads of individual sports: judo, trampoline, skiing, badminton, swimming – university uses pool for water polo – rock-climbing, snow boarding and surfing; occasional rock-climbing expeditions to the Alps. Skiing trips now an annual occurrence.

It being St Andrews, golf reigns supreme with about a third of the school playing; all lucky boarders can and do become youth members of the St Andrews Links Trust (as residents in St Andrews) so they can play the Old Course. Great new all-weather pitch, despite prolonged problems with Historic Scotland about floodlights. Sports hall probably on the wish list, though school has quite a lot of spare cash after some judicious sell-offs, but talk of lottery funding and community-type use. Grass sports field is extensive and in the past has attracted Everton FC and Bradford City FC for pre-season training.

Outstanding art department, attracting pupils outside normal lessons as well as curricular – huge range of alternative media, dark rooms etc. Gigantic sculptures much in evidence in dining room and about school. Spectacular 'body casts' making Gormley-style figures. Artists in residence doing printmaking etc. School hosts two public art shows every year. School pupils have won prestigious local photography prize – the Kodak Cup – four years in a row. Music strong in fabulous Bob Steedman (husband of four heads ago) designed centre. St Leonards Junior School pupils sang in front of the cameras at the televised St Andrews Royal Wedding Breakfast celebrations. Drama on the up; school performs twice a year in the revamped nearby Byre theatre in St Andrews (this is popular with both school and public) plus D of E etc. etc. Trips (one per subject per year) with major ones like a drama visit to New York planned on a two-year cycle.

Background and atmosphere: A curious mixture of gracious living, with house drawing rooms reminiscent of Country Life plus lawned courts nestling among old stone building in dreaming spires style combined with faintly scruffy corridors, classrooms, common rooms etc with a distinctly old fashioned (and none the worse for that), schooly feel. Founded and purpose built in 1877, St Leonards inhabits a notoriously windswept corner of Fife, on the sea, bracing air, bone chilling easterly gales, track suits popular for games. Golf, riding and the beach all great draws, as well as trips up town and forays to the surrounding countryside. Castle and cathedral a two minute walk away. Mega library and selection of 'Maryana' in Queen Mary's House (oddly flanked by a boys' loo). Mary Queen of Scots and King Charles II were both reckoned to have stayed at Queen Mary's Library when it was a private house. Individual research emphasis in IB has made library a popular place again with a really helpful new librarian thrown in.

School praised for high standard of pastoral care for boarders by the Care Commission. Weekly and termly boarding but the emphasis is now more on day; numbers have risen since day fees were reduced by 25 per cent to align more with local day schools than with higher day fees for full boarding schools. Boarders have comprehensive facilities, mostly single rooms and down-time freedom appropriate for 21st century to visit the town, dress informally and decorate (or litter) their own living space. Day pupils in the sixth form included in house system with 'day rooms' in boarding houses. Central dining room recently given an overhaul.

Buses for day pupils: Dundee, Kirkcaldy, Auchtermuchty, Perthshire. Juniors can be dropped off early (8am) and collected late (5.30). This represents a reduced school day but incorporates time for activities, which has 'settled down well and parents appreciate it.' Sixth formers now wear suits during the working day. The few boys visible during an exam time visit looked suave and sophisticated young professionals; the girls less so. Trad but machine washable blazers (£80) and blue tartan kilts for girls are senior school uniform. There is a second hand shop run by the 'bullish' PA which also organises family fun tennis etc.

Pastoral care and discipline: School rules feature punctuality, security and civilised behaviour; the student handbook has a rash of rules, most of which are sheer common sense: L-drivers may not drive other pupils and the like. But members of the sixth form have a mass of privileges – can visit some (some definitely out of bounds) local pubs, smoke off-campus ('but not if I feel they are bringing the school into disrepute and are identifiable as St Leonards pupils,' says head) and are generally expected to behave like grown-ups. No smoking on campus, no under-age drinking and absolute zero tolerance of drugs. Parents like the drugs policy – random drugs testing and testing on suspicion, out for pushing, forfeit right to remain in school for using – depends on individual and other factors and for how long, and pupils may be allowed back under fairly arduous conditions – and the like. Suspension for continued failure to observe the booze rules. Police are called for theft. No chaplain but team of local ministers who regularly preach. Plenty of fund raising for good causes.

Pupils and parents: No boarding in junior school, hence strong Scots contingent up to senior school; small number of UK boarders but most from abroad, particularly at sixth form level, when incomers swell the ranks to follow the IB course – this is encouraged, as the internationalism of the college is seen as one of its strengths. School is proud of its Scottish heritage and tradition – Burns Day celebrated and Scottish Country Dancing taught. Still a few nobs but huge mix of foreign and first time buyers. Fifers beginning to see school as a good option again. St Leonards has a strong Old Girls' network and many at the school are offspring or grand offspring of seniors. Some concern recently among seniors about school's new direction though others welcome its possible new impetus. Famous seniors include Betty Harvey Anderson, Dame Kathleen Ollerenshaw, the previous President of St Leonards, Gillian Glover of the Scotsman (who didn't last the course), Stella Tennant (ditto), Baroness Byford (current President) and Anji Hunter.

Entrance: Accept CE, but usually own entrance assessment (English and maths) or scholarship exam. Six GCSEs or equivalent for sixth with As and Bs in subjects to be studied at higher level in the IB. 'We usually pick up 30/40 at sixth from entry' for IB.

Exit: 'Minimum' drop out at transition from St Leonards Junior School to seniors and some (40 per cent in 2013) depart post-GCSE (only accept good English speakers to sixth form). Around 90 per cent to universities – a regular 8-10 per cent to Oxbridge. Destinations in 2013 included St Andrews, Edinburgh, Queens Belfast and Essex as well as a number of overseas universities. Many do a gap year, armed with addresses of welcoming seniors throughout the world (a boon for worried parents).

Money matters: A means-tested, Assisted Places scheme in operation; open to application from existing parents in financial difficulties. Currently restructuring scholarships (all means-tested) and bursaries to satisfy Scottish charitable status requirements. Serious – though only of nominal monetary value – collection of scholarships, ranging from academic through music, drama and sport – golf scholarships very popular (as you might imagine).

Remarks: St Leonard's hit back at the spate of Scottish elite 'public' schools going co-ed to fill up the gaps in their budgets and academic records with clever girls by going co-ed itself. Dr Carslaw is determined to make St Leonards a cohesive and mutually supportive school community rather than three separate parts. Some revolutionary upheavals in style and leaderships have produced (three heads later) a school that is just beginning to gel into a whole with the potential to become greater than the sums of its parts. Seizing the IB niche gives it an academic edge with an international flavour – visionary, certainly, but not for the fainthearted!

St Leonards-Mayfield School

The Old Palace, High Street, Mayfield East, Sussex, TN20 6PH

• Pupils: 400 girls; about 200 board/flexiboard • Ages: 11–18 • RC (but non-RCs welcome) • Fees: Day £17,925; Boarding £28,650 pa • Independent

Tel: 01435 874600
Email: admissions@mayfieldgirls.org
Website: www.mayfieldgirls.org

Headmistress: Since 2008, Miss Antonia Beary (late thirties). Read English at Trinity College, Cambridge, and has an MPhil in Catholic Education. Two years at The Leys, Cambridge where she became assistant housemistress of the sixth form house, followed by six years at Ampleforth where she started as an English teacher and ended up in charge of the first girls' sixth form house. Two years as head of sixth form at New Hall before joining Mayfield in 2006 as pastoral deputy. Thoughtful, approachable, charming. Likes to help girls develop a sense of perspective and the confidence to make the right decisions. Humphrey the spaniel, always by her side, offers a comforting paw to any nervous juniors who need a cuddle.

Academic matters: A level results good – 56 per cent A*/A grades in 2013, and at GCSE 67 per cent A*/A grades. Average class size 14 for GCSE and about 10 for A level. Good mix of teaching staff: some NQTs, some more venerable. Everyone has a laptop connected to school intranet – some financial assistance where necessary. Twenty-four girls currently doing City & Guilds GCSE in cooking, a practical, hands-on course taught in a big, light, airy kitchen – leads to Diploma. A level home economics available. Cooking clubs and Saturday workshops well attended.

Library a bit dated but a popular, quiet place to work. Plenty of help with personal statements and UCAS forms.

Learning support department very much in the centre of the school, where girls can go for help and reassurance: 'a real haven,' as one dyslexic girl put it. One full-time and two part- time teachers. Some 10-15 per cent need some sort of extra help, mainly for mild dyslexia – girls given coping strategies and learning support closely linked with teaching (first six 35 min lessons free; subsequently charged at £18 per lesson). All girls do baseline tests on arrival and staff quick to pick up any problems. Good ESOL department – eight periods a week – girls taken out of English and PE. Generally high scores on IELTS (average of 7.5 over the past four years) very good reputation with universities.

Games, options, the arts: Spectacular ceramics department. We were there when the GCSE and A level exhibits were on show in the cloister and it was like walking through a museum – we would have happily bought the lot. Enthusiastic and inspired art and textiles teacher. Lots of flexibility for girls to do what they want at after-school workshops four nights a week. Life drawing studio, jewellery, silversmith plus resins and plastics.

The usual sports but no lacrosse. Plenty of sporting opportunities for those who want. Riding a major feature – have won the National Schools Championships for the past three years and have a current show jumping hopeful. A recent leaver a Badminton regular. Girls can keep their own ponies at a nearby farm. Outdoor sand school and cross-country course within the school grounds; small indoor sand school available locally. Strong fencing; many girls represent their county and some have represented England at rounders. About 10 girls do Duke of Edinburgh gold each year. School very supportive of what the girls do outside school. Sport seems to tail off a bit in sixth from with a focus on top teams but school is trying to engage other girls in different sports eg sailing. PE offered at GCSE and A level (100 per cent and 33 per cent A*/A respectively).

Strong and very experienced music department. Singing particularly good – school's premier choir, the Schola Cantorum, recently performed evening mass in the Basilica di San Marco in Venice. Chapel choir often asked to sing at weddings. Good orchestra plus classical, musical theatre and rock band. Supervised practice after school. GCSE and A levels offered in music. Two or three drama productions per year – girls get involved in all aspects of production, direction, lighting and textiles department make the costumes in-house. A group of girls took a production up to the Edinburgh Fringe Festival. All performed in wonderful concert hall as are fashion shows and various musical events. Theatre studies taught at A level and drama at GCSE. Annual inter-house performing arts festival – sixth form write, choreograph and produce a range of pieces and hone their people management skills. Dance is compulsory for years 7- 9 and is a popular option further up the school, with ballet and salsa being taught by qualified visiting teachers.

Background and atmosphere: Founded in 1846 by Cornelia Connelly, foundress of the religious congregation for the education of Catholic girls, the Society of the Holy Child Jesus; a woman ahead of her time. In 1872 it moved into the The Old Palace of the Archbishop of Canterbury. Stunning medieval chapel which is central to school life and can seat every pupil and where The Live Crib is performed each Christmas with a real donkey and real baby. All classrooms and facilities on one site; four boarding houses split by age. Lower school have their own separate building and their own dining room in the main school. Three separate dining rooms – sixth form eat with staff. Girls in years 11-13 have study bedrooms and can opt for single rooms. Approximately half of pupils board (including weekly and flexi-boarding) and there is no school on Saturday. Strong Catholic ethos but over half now non-Catholic. Chapel is very important and central to school life. Everyone has to go and

girls organise some of the liturgies. Encouraged to question everything and not take anything for granted.

New £1m sixth form centre to open in September 2013. Will house a lecture room, digital learning suite, small-group seminar rooms, independent study chambers and an exhibition foyer.

Pastoral care and discipline: The first lay head was appointed in 2000. Nuns are still involved in pastoral care and are active in school community. Very supportive school – both girls and staff. 'Be yourself but be aware that you are part of a community.' Actions not Words programme takes girls outside the classroom to serve others and raise their awareness both of the needs of others and of ways in which they can all make a difference. A school of individuals – girls are encouraged to think independently and develop a strong moral awareness and sense of perspective. Not a hothouse. Compulsory mass on Sunday mornings and compulsory liturgy during the week for all year groups as well as occasional whole school masses throughout the term. Christianity rather than Catholicism at the centre of school. A lady chaplain recently joined the school and has livened up the weekly liturgies.

Pupils and parents: Mostly local, London and south east. Eclectic bunch from a wide range of prep and primary schools – currently working on building relationships with local and London primary schools. Hold masterclasses to bring in prep and primary school children for art and music taster days. Up to 10 per cent foreign nationals: a number of Hong Kong Chinese, Spanish and Mexicans but no one group dominates. School maintains good links with parents. Strong old girl network – Holy Child link helps. Old girls include dress designer Lindka Cierach, journalist Dame Ann Leslie, author Maeve Haran, French actress Anouk Aimee, screenplay writer Olivia Hetreed and immeasurable numbers of barristers, physicians, etc.

Entrance: Two-thirds take school's own exam at 11+ and one third take 13+ common entrance. Entrance exams double as academic scholarship exams at 11+ and 16+; at 13+ there is a separate academic scholarship route. Entrance in other years by school's own exam. Not highly selective but do not want someone to struggle academically, as they would not have time to join in other things and have fun. Look for potential. 10-12 per year come in sixth form, often from schools which finish at 16. Tend to settle in well – tutor groups mixed at this stage which helps. Looking for girls who will be open to opportunities and engaged with the ethos of the school.

Exit: Some leave after GCSEs to go to co-ed schools. Many find this quite a culture shock and some even come back – the door is always left open for anyone who changes their mind. Most girls go on to a wide range of universities to read a huge variety of subjects – several to read medicine. A few to Oxbridge each year. One girl had to choose between Trinity College, Cambridge and Harvard – poor love!

Money matters: Means-tested bursaries for up to full fees. Awards made at three stages – for year 7, year 9 and year 12 and means-tested every year. Academic and gifted and talented scholarships (creative art, drama and physical theatre, music and sport) – max award is 20 per cent of day or boarding fees.

Remarks: A cosy, happy, caring school with something for everyone. Some can find this cosiness a bit limiting and leave for the co-eds after GCSE. Produces well-rounded girls who are expected to roll up their sleeves, get on with it: 'sew on a button, bake a cake and change a fuse', as one mother put it.

St Margaret's School (London)

Linked school: St Margaret's Junior School (London)

18 Kidderpore Gardens, London, NW3 7SR

• Pupils: 155 girls • Ages: 4–16 • C of E foundation; all faiths and none welcome • Fees: £10,011–£11,538 pa • Independent

Tel: 020 7435 2439
Email: enquiry@st-margarets.co.uk
Website: www.st-margarets.co.uk

Principal: Since 2008, Mr Mark Webster BSc (mid-forties). Educated at Highgate School and University College, London (where he read psychology), PGCE at Cambridge. Spent 15 years at the Royal School, Hampstead (first in primary, then IT, psychology and maths, before becoming deputy and acting head). Never planned to become a teacher – 'If you'd asked me early on what job I wanted to do, I'd have said teaching was 999th out of 1000'. A chance encounter changed his mind. 'I was working in publishing, when I met someone who said their job in teaching was fantastic. I'd never met anyone who felt that way about work.' Now equally enthusiastic about his chosen profession, Mr Webster continues to be hands on in his approach, teaching mathematics and '125' (see below). Particularly positive about working in a small school – 'I like the proximity and enjoy seeing the children grow up. You feel you can make a significant difference'. Operates an open-door policy and is constantly updating and improving what's on offer. Fundamental to his approach is the view that education is about instilling a sense of curiosity – 'Qualifications are a passport to the next stage, but if you remain curious you will never be bored'. He himself retains a passionate interest in art, history and reading. Also plays football for Highgate Old Boys. A tactful, sympathetic enthusiast, Webster is a good fit for this family-like school. 'It's unusual to have a man,' said one mother, 'but I think he really cares.' Married to a teacher with two young sons.

Academic matters: In the juniors, all pupils follow the national curriculum (with the addition of French) from reception. GCSE options include Spanish, French, psychology, drama and music. An unusual addition is the head's own invention, '125' – a tribute to the school's 125th anniversary – which provides pupils with a list of activities to attempt at some point in their schooldays. 'There are, in fact, 158 options, so they do have some choice.' The range includes the practical, the cultural and the altruistic ('Do a nice thing for someone who can do nothing in return'). In years 7, 8 and 9, 125 is a designated lesson. In 2013, 31 per cent of GCSEs graded A*. The majority take additional science (taught in a compact, but efficient, lab), enabling them to go on to science A levels, the most popular A level choice. A modern language is compulsory (enthusiastic chatter about letters from French pen pals on the day we visited).

The school is relatively non-selective and the ability range always includes the very able and those with more modest aspirations, such that in mathematics in year 11 there will be at least one girl taking the Foundation paper, whilst an A* at 'A' level is achieved by another. The plus side of a small school is class size (between 11-15 in the junior school, 11-19 thereafter) and personal attention – 'You don't get excellent results without teachers having spare time to help'. Setting introduced when necessary but, with limited space, teaching is usually differentiated rather than physically separated. Outsiders have been known to view the school as a haven for the struggling, but it is only the right school for those with up to moderate special needs. 'We don't have the depth of resources for learning support that a larger school would have,' says the head. SENCo,

plus a couple of teachers trained in dyslexia and dyscalculia, but the main support comes from classroom teachers. All abilities equally well catered for – 'We aren't results-driven and we exhaust every avenue'.

Games, options, the arts: The head's view is that education is a 'can-do', 'must try' matter and – inspired by the celebrated art historian Sir Ernst Gombrich's attitude – 'You don't have to like it, but it's important to understand why other people do...We compel them to try lots of things. They may moan, but we make them give it a go'. Drama is taken seriously. Performance is compulsory – 'We don't do Hamlet and let some people end up as third tree on the left. We make them write their own script and perform on a series of nights'. Music, too, is important – 'We have a super-motivated music teacher' – with a variety of traditional and less traditional extra-lesson options ('Handbells are very popular'). A number of choirs, plus a junior school orchestra. Some 80 per cent of girls have private instrument lessons at the school. Art immensely popular, with excellent results at GCSE: two studios, one reasonably spacious, the other definitely petite. Outside space, too, is relatively restricted, with a largish garden transformed into an Astroturf playground. A local hall is used for gym and the school now has a sports area for netball, tennis and other sports two minutes' walk away. Mini-bus takes girls to Hampstead Heath for rounders or running, to Hendon Leisure Centre for aerobics, rock climbing and badminton and the Welsh Harp for rowing. In David and Goliath mode the school is unafraid to compete with much larger north London schools like Highgate and Channing – 'We often lose' – but succeed when more evenly matched. Plenty of clubs (fencing, theatre, cookery, bicycle maintenance, knitting, philosophy, book club, tennis) and trips, local and international, from walks on Hampstead Heath to Spain and Iceland.

Background and atmosphere: Founded in 1884, it moved to its present site in a quiet, suburban Hampstead road in 1943. Senior and junior schools both occupy the same building and have the same head, with different uniforms but little separation between them. The school has three houses, where pupils of all ages work together to raise funds for charities of their own choice and compete at sports. It is small, cosy and friendly; a parent commented: 'It allows the girls to achieve whatever they can – but in a safe, non-confrontational environment'. Red and white uniform in the junior school, black and white in the senior. 'The head has changed the uniform and it's much more flattering,' said one mother. 'These things matter to teenage girls.'

Pastoral care and discipline: Discipline not a significant issue. Though head insists this is not the garden of Eden, disciplinary issues tend to be confined to infringements of uniform – 'We can live with earrings if there's no drink or drugs'. Bullying – 'We get a case every year' – is dealt with promptly. 'Parents tend to be very supportive. They come to this school for its caring environment and they're quick to back us up.' Parents couldn't agree more – 'You get ups and downs with some of the girls, but if you ever get a problem it's dealt with straight away,' said one. Most parents feel one of the school's greatest strengths is its pastoral side, allowing girls to fulfil their potential and know exactly who they are. 'It's too small a school not to be a community. Girls, for example, will discuss a problem on Facebook and say, let's resolve this.' The school has its own head of pastoral care but also relies on a school counsellor when needed and pro-actively encourages 'bonding' with a variety of trips. 'The girls mix across the years and are often close to girls in the year above and below,' said a parent.

Pupils and parents: Nice, well-behaved, confident girls from a cosmopolitan range of backgrounds reflecting the school's north London location. A sizeable chunk come from within walking distance, then in an arc stretching from Wembley to

Islington (school minibus on offer for those who require it). Very much a family school in every sense – 45 per cent of pupils are sisters or relatives of current or ex-pupils. 'A lot of people like the sense of support and nurturing.' Most newcomers hear about the school by word of mouth, though the internet (and recent accolades in The Sunday Times) have slightly altered the traditional intake. Those relocating can find it a particularly valuable resource. 'I like it because there is more of a mix than usual in north London,' said one mother.

Entrance: Benign selection at 4. 'We're primarily looking to see if they're school ready,' says the head. Guaranteed transition from within at 11. 'Once we've made the commitment, unless there are particular special needs we can't support, we stick to it.' At other points, assessment varies according to age. From reception to year 3, girls come in for the day to spend time with other girls and 'encounter some maths and English'. From year 4 more formal testing, with year 6 applicants given 'a booklet of exercises'.

Exit: School has no intention of opening a sixth form despite parental requests. 'By then it really is time to move on.' About 30 per cent leave at 11, usually to the most academic schools in the state or private sector, such as Henrietta Barnett or North London Collegiate. Notably successful with applications at 16. Most popular choices at that point are local co-ed sixth forms like Highgate and UCS, and similar atmosphere girls' schools like Channing. A reasonable number to the state sector (St Marylebone particularly popular). Good guidance on offer at both 11 and 16 – 'It's really important to make an informed choice. Not every school will suit every girl and they are used to being supported here'. School also works with them on interview practice and personal statements. Girls generally get their first-choice sixth form – 'My daughter got in everywhere she applied,' said one parent.

Money matters: Not an expensive school by any means, but not much scope for additional funding. One 50 per cent scholarship at 11, about five per cent get some sort of bursary.

Remarks: A gentle, nurturing school with a strong and secure family atmosphere providing a stimulating, tailor-made education. 'A little gem,' to quote one parent, though possibly not the ideal venue for the child that needs plenty of space to run around or one who requires the challenge of a big stage at 11.

St Margaret's School for Girls (Aberdeen)

Linked school: St Margaret's School for Girls Junior Department (Aberdeen)

17 Albyn Place, Aberdeen, AB10 1RU

• Pupils: 390 girls, all day • Ages: 3–18 • Non-denom
• Fees: £10,824 pa • Independent

Tel: 01224 584466
Email: info@st-margaret.aberdeen.sch.uk
Website: www.st-margaret.aberdeen.sch.uk

Headmistress: Since 2010, Dr Julie Land (fifties) BSc, PGCE, EdD. Educated at Dame Allan's Girls' School, read maths at Manchester, PGCE in Newcastle, whence she returned for her Doctorate; but not really a Northern lass. Taught maths for nine years before 10 year 'family sabbatical' when she did most of her doctoral research. Returned to teaching in 2000, came to St

Margaret's in 2003, deputy head in 2004. Currently involved with the curriculum area review group (which must be a nightmare).

'Intends to lead and support staff through a period of educational change and oversee new buildings such as a new school hall and classrooms, together with improvement of games facilities.' Quite.

Married to a (global) oily husband who rides a Harley Davidson and 'feeds her' (can we all have one like that please?). St M's is about to visit Prague and Land admitted that she had been there last summer – on the back of the Harley. Now that's a sporting woman. Her daughter, who was at St Megs, recently graduated from Newcastle (biochemistry); son at uni. Entertaining, chic and fun, she bubbles with enthusiasm, yomps and 'gardens' – 'well I select the plants and do scaled drawings' (which seems a sensible way to garden) and, having been 'an accomplished table tennis player in her youth', has resurrected a table tennis club for twelve year olds and plays occasionally, 'though I am not a qualified coach'. She teaches maths three periods a week, to 13 and 16-year-olds.

School appears enormously fecund, with a couple of pregnancies in the biology department as well as the head of junior school. Maternity cover sought for all appointments. Land has appointed a new head of ICT as well as a couple of new form takers (there have been six retirals and six re-locations – oily town remember – in the past year). No problem with probationers (newly qualified teachers).

Academic matters: Academically strong across the board. The lovely exam website to which we were directed by the school only gives percentages and our request for results by subject by grade hiccupped with the head saying that she 'can't disclose this information due to our exam results being small and the risk of pupils being identified'. Nevertheless, 92 per cent pass rate at higher level and 98 per cent at standard grade in 2013. Stonking 17 subjects offered at higher level. Previous head tweaked the curriculum, dropping admin and adding economics and PE in sixth form, together with crash courses in Italian and higher philosophy. Sixth formers can do modules from the Open University: astronomy, molecules, medicine and nutrition. All setted for maths, English for first two years, but classes fluid, lots of movement.

French (from five), Latin, compulsory for one year from age 11, German and Spanish option age 13. NB before the school trip to China last year trippers were given Mandarin lessons: the girls had a happy time communicating, but the accompanying staff 'remained stumm'. Head keen that girls should have the advantage of 'learning independently' and enjoy their lessons (not quite sure how the living independently lessons fit in). Three ICT suites, all intranetted, plus personal laptops/ipads.

Programmed support for learning throughout the school with help for the gifted as well as the underperformer. Dyslexia, dyspraxia, ADHD and mild Asperger's: individual, clusters, plus support in class if needed. No automatic testing on entrance for additional needs but 'everyone has a spelling assessment which is a good indicator.' Departments keep detailed notes of problems that might be 'just around the corner.' Support available from form teachers, and dedicated head of guidance, and they can go 'to anyone if in difficulties', though not, apparently, instantaneously, 'make an appointment with the maths base' says Land, 'or come to me'. (We at the GSG quite like individual departments to staff a drop-in centre at lunch/ break/post school – to pick up instant problems). Paired reading initiative, senior girls 'trained in specific reading techniques' work with younger pupils in their free time. Apart from 'fostering community spirit', senior readers get brownie points through 'certification from the Institute of Management'; ie it looks good on the UCAS personal statement.

Games, options, the arts: Impressive netball and tennis teams. School keen on team games, especially hockey (reams of

Scotland reps) but loads of individual sports too; swimming important, (current county reps) all juniors have regular dips in local pool. Trad athletics, tennis, rounders; snow boarding/skiing by Garth Dee on dry slope, and the real thing, both in Scotland and abroad. Huge take up. Skool competes regionally. Curling is the new kid on the block, ten year olds up ('well we had to do something during the last two awful winters'), curling rink about five miles north of school. Individual representative in the Olympic dressage. Impressive, but not really a feather in the school's personal cap.

Art and design department is 'fantastic', with a stunning panorama of urban Aberdeenshire providing part of the flexible natural lighting. Art dept recently produced a mural 'to brighten a dingy corner of the playground'; used to provide scenery for school plays, but these are now performed in the local art centre, and sadly the art dept have lost a potential stimulator for those – possibly non-academic girls – who might want to follow a career in scenery design. Shame. Trad disciplines plus ceramics, printmaking, metal jewellery-making (sold via YE, mass on show outside head's office), sculpture ('small sculpture because there is no room for storage'). Book binding on the cards (but probably as a club). St M's keen not to have a 'precious' image, so food technology only up to second year, but it reappears as preparation for living in sixth. But why no hospitality training?

Art and music taken to Advanced Higher level. Lively drama, Sound of Music next performance (pace Julie Andrews) three major musical productions regularly, it's hardly surprising that there is a 'resurgence of drama as an academic subject'. Music vibrant. Collection of orchestras: string, chamber, jazz plus outstanding 'travelling' choir with regular trips (Prague next, but no Harleys?). Number of current pupils and FPs in the national youth orchestra, and the (proper as opposed to pop) proms. St Margaret's schools worldwide band together for choir tours, heads chit-chat electronically. 'Gives the school a global dimension,' (though didn't stop the one in Edinburgh going belly up).

Masses of activities: 20+ clubs and classes include ballet, highland dancing, eco, wildlife, film, choi kwangdo, tennis, French, dance, chess and very strong debating/public speaking. St M's ain't that brave and usually compete in the North East region of Scotland, though a starring 15 year old did well representing Scotland at the Euro-Parliament competition at Brussels, not so long ago.

Prioritising arts/music/games a problem of huge take-up overall in a small school. Staff need to be flexible and not squabble over musical games players. ('Can be a problem', said the head.) Strong D of E, regular golds. YE 'made fudge last year, not good for diets'. Masses of charity input, particularly with the YPI (Youth Philanthropy Institute) and (oily Sir Ian) Wood Family Foundation where 16 year olds find and adopt a charity, do detailed research and then give a presentation to trustees. Reward: £3,000 per charity. Good global awareness from international pupil mix; school has achieved its first Green Flag award (loads of oily children, this must be either a wake up call, or a feather in the collective cap). Comprehensive careers department. Week's work experience for all age 15 (we wonder whether – as in the South, parents have to ante up?).

Background and atmosphere: Founded in 1846, St Margaret's is the only all girls' school in the north of Scotland. Based in a hotchpotch conversion of Victorian merchants' houses (Albyn Place and the adjacent Queens Road in Aberdeen are home to some six or seven various schools). The gardens at the back are filled with fairly uninspiring new-builds, recently refurbished art studio and resources centre. But alas, though the flat roofed new classroom block looks ripe for development, the architects have been rather economical with concrete. Expansion can only be achieved by demolition and re-build, which may in fact be a cheaper option: currently new builds are exempt from VAT.

Plans in pipe dream for new hall with classrooms above. But perhaps not quite yet.

Charming well-equipped library. Corridors everywhere: walls drip with bright artwork, photos of pupils, productions, school trips, expeditions, press cuttings etc – friendly and buzzing. Wizard adventure playground on refurbished lawn, slightly squiffy globe on tarmac, with detailed maps fixed to nearby tables. Couple of trees removed ('ealth and safety) have been recycled as table and chair, to a design by pupil for her higher art work.

Cooked lunch available, with girls ordering main dishes in advance, in a pretty cramped room in the basement which doubles as after-school club for tinies, adjacent to the revamped dead posh loos. Girls eat by class, own sandwiches. School not wheelchair friendly (no classrooms on ground floor). Early drop off from 8am, pupils can stay till 5.30, clubs etc after school. Senior blazers (expensive: £130) are worn only on the way to/from school. Grey kilts or straight skirts. Special braid on blazers for sixth form, more braid for prefects, some of whom end up looking like Christmas trees. Good second-hand shop (well, this is Aberdeen) run by parents and one enterprising parent has found a cheaper supplier and started a shop within the school to sell uniform for about two thirds of regular shop price (there are provisions for really cheap kit for those on 100 per cent bursaries).

Pastoral care and discipline: Strong moral background with joint PSE and RME syllabus. Some Muslims in the school, headscarves and longer skirts OK; pupils made to feel inclusive with Ramadan respected, special prayer room available. Ecumenical assemblies. All join in the Easter service and Christmas concert and the whole school troops off to the cathedral for St Margaret's Day when the smallest have to be restrained from trying to find St Margaret's shield on the roof and falling over in the process.

Worry boxes for juniors; dedicated junior guidance counsellor and buddy system. Strong anti-bullying programme. Head of guidance an experienced 'resolver', each case 'resolved on merit'. 'Both the bullied and the bullyer need support'. Detention for the few and far between 'naughty girls' replaced by a pc 'extra learning opportunity to brush up their skills' (sometimes after school). Whole school assembly most Fridays, pupil council and charity reps meetings include juniors and seniors. With 30 school prefects plus form prefects, sport and activity captains etc, most pupils get a chance to lead. Social life is active with PTA dances and discos and a friendly eye kept that 'someone's brother will arrange partners.'

A change of emphasis in sixth form; new sixth form head, and realistically tidy sixth form flat. The sixth formers prepare for the world beyond Aberdeen with their own out-of-school conference: annual theme this year (as last, and the one before) 'Being the Best You Can Be', led by past pupils and specialists: speakers include FPs who have become CEOs in their fields of expertise.

Pupils and parents: Large number of first time buyers, large number of non-Brits, strong parent association. And very strong FP links. Charming. Polite and well-mannered. Tessa Jowell is an old girl. Girls come from surrounding areas and the city itself. Dedicated buses.

Entrance: Assessments for all, mini test for tinies where they play in groups and are surreptitiously assessed by experts. Siblings not usually turned away. Young coming up through the nursery/junior school will have been quietly assessed throughout their time, and if wobbles are detected, the school will have a 'discreet word' with the parents. No surprises then. Girls can (and do) come at any time if space available. Currently waiting list for year 1.

Exit: Odd one to Oxbridge, most to Scots unis after sixth form, though just occasionally some opt for Scottish universities immediately after Highers. Inevitable before a four-year degree. This year's sixth seem to be aiming at medicine and vet-med.

Money matters: Means-tested bursaries up to 100 per cent, plus help with books and uniform. School has sinking fund to cover impoverished lead soprano singing in Vienna, but does not cover jollies. Will keep a child to next public exam if parents have problems but with the usual caveat about parents being upfront and realistic.

Remarks: Jolly nice, old-fashioned school with proper values and the best of modern teaching methods. School seems merrier under present regime. Numbers a tad down but financial climate not helpful. Certain amount of recent fabric titivation and exciting wish list for the future. If single sex education is what you want, St Margaret's is a school which does its girls exceeding well.

St Mary Redcliffe and Temple School

Somerset Square, Redcliffe, Bristol, BS1 6RT

• Pupils: 1,590 boys and girls • Ages: 11–18 • C of E • State

Tel: 01173 772100
Email: enquiries@smrt.bristol.sch.uk
Website: www.smrt.bristol.sch.uk

Headteacher: Since 2005, Mrs Elisabeth Gilpin, formerly head of St Augustine's RC/CofE Upper School in Oxford. Appointed a National Leader of Education in July 2013.

Academic matters: Exam results well above national average for GCSE (72 per cent achieved 5 A*-C including maths and English in 2013) and in line with it at A level (60 per cent A*-B). Pupils' individual achievements recognised and valued. Curriculum balance carefully maintained and complemented throughout by a wide-ranging enrichment programme. Special needs resourcing 'adequate but not generous'. Many departments involved with visits, exchanges and links abroad. Has specialised status in humanities, training school status and designated a school of excellence for gifted and talented as a result of its position as a High Performing Specialist School since 2009.

Games, options, the arts: On-site facilities for games surprisingly good given city-centre location, with courts, an all-weather pitch ('the arena'), gym, sports hall and indoor pool. Further sports facilities locally. Many pupils compete at local, county and national levels in a wide range of team sports (rugby, football, hockey, netball, basketball and others) and individual activities such as athletics, judo and aerobics. The list is long. Music vibrant and encouraged. Orchestral and choral concerts held in adjacent and outstandingly beautiful church of St Mary Redcliffe, a superb historic setting, very inspiring, which also serves as school 'chapel'. Drama offered as a GCSE option, and regular ambitious productions involving large numbers of pupils.

Background and atmosphere: The school moved into new buildings in 2010, with state-of-the-art science, art, music, PE, DT, library, maths and English facilities. Parents kept up to date about all aspects of the school's life via the monthly newsletter.

The close relationship with parents and their underpinning of the school's Christian ethos create positive attitudes to the development of each pupil's potential.

Pastoral care and discipline: Impressive system of mixed-age tutor groups reflects the powerful ethos of the extended Christian family. Warmly appreciated – 'a strength' – by parents and former pupils. Enables older students to know and mentor younger ones. Year 7 spend a year in separate house to establish their own year-group relationships before moving into the senior houses; These provide the cornerstones of very good discipline, based on exceptionally effective tutoring. Problems, academic or other, generally detected at an early stage. Parents involved and feel confident about it.

Pupils and parents: Pupils come from all areas of Bristol and beyond as this is the only C of E VA school in the diocese. The educational provision is explicitly Christian with daily worship, much of it pupil-led, a distinctive feature at its core. The broad social and cultural mix is absorbed comfortably and the close involvement of parents is encouraged, including in worship. Attendance well above national average. Pupils friendly and open. A new uniform in place with both girls and boys in shirt, tie and blazer since 2011. Pupils as cheerful as they ever are about school meals.

Entrance: Comprehensive intake, admissions policy based on family church attendance history and other priorities (siblings, residence). Some pupils of other faiths admitted. Oversubscribed. Applications for year 7 must also be made to the Local Authority. Sixth form admission based on academic performance at GCSE and 'agreement to respect the faith of others'.

Exit: Nearly all year 11 pupils go into the sixth form. 75 per cent go on to universities or other higher education institutions – a few to Oxbridge (five in 2013). Some gap year students go abroad on scholarships and as community service volunteers.

Money matters: Generous enabling fund supports those from disadvantaged background for school visits etc.

Remarks: 'If only we had qualified... ' the cri de coeur of many parents in Bristol and the surrounding area. This is a school born of faith and led with conviction. Its atmosphere is purposeful but also welcoming and considerate. Parents and staff did not need Ofsted to tell them that the school is 'Good with outstanding features'. Not over-focused on league tables, but undoubtedly able to hold its own, academically.

The St Marylebone C of E School

64 Marylebone High Street, London, W1U 5BA

• Pupils: 785 • Ages: 11–18 • C of E • State

Tel: 020 7935 4704
Email: info@stmaryleboneschool.com
Website: www.stmaryleboneschool.com

Headteacher: From January 2014, Kathryn Pugh, previously assistant head. A Cambridge graduate with first class honours in English, she joined St Marylebone in 2005 as English teacher and learning co-ordinator, and became assistant head in 2008. She has experience in business and the developing world as well as teaching.

Academic matters: St Marylebone's offers a lot of subject options – 'an amazing variety,' enthused one parent. Dance, health and social care, Latin and business studies canter alongside the front runners at GCSE and all are in the ribbons. Ninety-two per cent 5+ A*-C grades in 2013 including maths

S

and English with some outstanding performances (51 per cent A*/A). RS results are knockout and the curriculum is praised for its earnest inclusiveness. The Englishes are good, so are the single sciences though most take the double award. Maths more than respectable. Good to see German holding its own but no other lang apart from French, which does pretty well too. Art and history strong and popular. School has policy of taking some subjects – langs, ICT, RS – early to excellent effect. RS and German especially successful.

At A level, 73 per cent A*-B with 14 per cent A* in 2013. English by far the most popular. Psychology, sociology and economics among the options – the first much the favourite with a spread of results. Low take up for German and French – more support for modern langs seems needed here. Some parents wonder how the results are achieved with so little homework. Relatively good teacher:pupil ratio and school spends money on retaining good staff.

Gifted and talented programme. School caters for a range of SENs, has a SENCo, a full time SEN teacher, learning support assistants and specialist centres for students with learning difficulties. It is a centre of excellence for severe emotional and behavioural difficulties and can provide for ASD, ADD and Down's – if not severe. Can provide for moderate physical difficulties too.

Games, options, the arts: By all accounts it's the arts that flourish here and sports come a very poor second. 'Sports are useless,' said a parent, 'they just don't bother apart from the regulation double period.' 'You can do it if you feel like it,' said a pupil. 'We get our fitness from dance and drama. There are after-school clubs for people who are good' – open to all, says school. And there are – netball, football, trampolining, rugby and tennis as well as before school sessions in fitness, running etc. Underground sports hall – more than many so urban a school could muster. Nonetheless, St M's is a performing arts college and this is evident whomever you speak to. Dance and music are outstanding and production values are high. 'The girls take huge pride in their performances,' we were told, 'even if not everyone can take part. It is inspirational.' The inspiration is further fuelled by the long-awaited £6m performing arts centre. This makes a huge difference – not least to the amount of space it frees for other curricular activities. In all respects the arts reign here. You can make everything from jewellery to ceramics and print your own photos. Debating, dance and musical performance of all kinds thrive.

To an extent these options are only available for the brightest and best. Parents who rave about the musical standards – 'the concerts just blow you away – it's like going to a serious musical event' – acknowledge that only the best will get in on the act. Opportunities like GCSE photography work in the highly professional Metro Studios only available to the three or four girls whose applications to take the course are considered sufficiently impressive. This is the reality of a state-funded school but it must be trying for the also-rans and would-bes.

Background and atmosphere: Unique city setting – off Marylebone High Street with Regent's Park over the (horribly busy) road. Victoriana with some attractive features – high ceilings, gothic windows and plenty of light. Radical building plans now completed. Cramped and crammed – though the performing arts building makes a big difference, as does the new sixth form centre on Blandford Street; every nook has something educational squashed into it. No space for lockers so girls are adept at carting their lives around with them and being organised about what they need for each lesson. Lunch is eaten in form rooms, though year 10 examinees and upwards are mercifully allowed out to settle in the numerous cafes round about at lunchtime.

The admissions policy (see below) dictates that active membership of the C of E is the main criterion for entry and this also influences the ethos. Parents are, in general, impressed. 'I trust it,' said one, 'to give my daughter a good education.' 'It's highly organised,' said another. 'very efficient, there's plenty of notice about everything. They're very attentive to detail.' Far better equipped and resourced than most such schools largely due to the head's incessant and skilful fundraising and the band of supportive parents.

Has just opened The St Marylebone Bridge School, a co-education free special school for children with statements for speech, language and communication, which will share some governors and teachers with the main school.

Pastoral care and discipline: Discipline reportedly 'fearsome' and 'slightly on the petty side' but generally felt to be effective and well understood by pupils. Not a whisper of drugs or even smoking being 'issues'. Links with home are excellent, say parents – and not only when there are problems. 'They write and tell us if our daughter has improved at something or just made a big effort,' nodded a parent. Much appreciated are the proper, old-fashioned termly reports which don't just parrot at you what the class has done but actually talk about your own daughter. Good, realistic and collaborative target-setting also works. House system. Pastoral care and support seen as very good overall on both academic and personal matters and many teachers seen as good and dedicated – but a few glaring exceptions and some just felt to be uninspiring.

Pupils and parents: About 65 per cent from ethnic minority backgrounds and from 90 different countries. Over 50 per cent of pupils are bilingual. More than 60 languages spoken at home. Sixty per cent C of E members; the largest second religious group is Muslim. Some feeling among parents that little is done to encourage friendships between the different ethnic and religious groups. Others reported that, 'The school is big enough for girls to make real choices about friendships and there's a very open environment.' School clearly tries hard – has an annual World Culture Day among many other initiatives – and attracts fierce loyalty. Active parents' group works hard though has problems involving all but the usual – mostly white, middle class – suspects.

Entrance: Absurdly and maddeningly oversubscribed – something like 1,000 applicants for 125 places. School no longer allowed to interview applicants – 'they hate that,' said a sympathetic parent. Admissions criteria are primarily that you have to be C of E – 60 per cent are – though looked after children and those with statements have priority. Thirty per cent of places are 'open', with distance the only criteria. Twelve places annually given to those with outstanding aptitude in an aspect of performing arts. Selection also on basis of ability – school takes 25 per cent from top ability range, 50 per cent from average band and 25 per cent from the below average band. Tie breaker of how near to the school you live. 275 places in the sixth – priority to existing students though they have to fulfil requirements (minimum of five A*-C GCSEs). Boys are taken into the sixth and, again, more apply than there are places for. School receives five applications a week for occasional places.

Exit: One-quarter leave after GCSE and go to sixth form colleges, the independents, eg Latymer Upper, or other state schools, eg Camden, largely for a greater range of A level subjects or for boys. Most stay though entrance to the school's own sixth form is not a given, even for their own. Sixth form leavers to good universities and a range of courses – six to Oxbridge in 2013.

Money matters: National funding programmes such as Excellence in Cities ended several years ago so bidding for extra money from various sources takes up a lot of time. The result, however, is a school that is well-staffed and well-equipped, if not to lavish private school standards.

S

Remarks: Exceptional, successful inner-city school serving a diverse community with a strong middle class core. Combines best traditional values with best modern practice. New head will undoubtedly take some time to make the school her own after her predecessor's 20 year reign.

St Mary's Calne

Linked school: St Margaret's Prep School

Curzon Street, Calne, SN11 0DF

- Pupils: 335 girls; over three-quarters board • Ages: 11–18 • C of E
- Fees: Day £24,150; Boarding £32,751 pa • Independent

Tel: 01249 857200
Email: admissions@stmaryscalne.org
Website: www.stmaryscalne.org

Headmistress: Since January 2013, Dr Felicia Kirk. Previously head of sixth form at Ipswich High and director of higher education at Wycombe Abbey. An American citizen, she studied French and Latin at the University of Maryland, has an MA and a PhD from Brown University, and also studied at the Ecole Normale Supérieure in Paris. She is married to John, a chartered accountant, is a keen event rider and keeps her horse at livery nearby.

Academic matters: Sees itself as distinctly academic – though girls clearly take academic success in their stride, rather than seeing it as the only objective of education. The impressive results at GCSE and A level – called 'sensational' in one starry-eyed school guide – scarcely do the girls justice, as the many subjects taken early at both levels do not actually appear in the league tables.

Girls appear to work very hard and to enjoy doing so, yet the atmosphere at exam time (which coincided with the GSG visit) was definitely more of excited anticipation than of exam nerves. At A level in 2013, 68 per cent per cent grades at A*/A. GCSE results remarkable as well (77 per cent A*/A in 2013), with ten or eleven for most with compulsory RE (taken seriously, to judge by the results). Most girls take triple science and a modern language. In the first three years, girls are mainly taught in form groups but setted in maths and French. German, Spanish, Latin, Classical Greek and Japanese on offer; Chinese and Russian on demand. Everyone does two lessons of Chinese in first year. Latin compulsory up to 14 and some hang in till A level, while Greek A level scholars enthusiastically promote it to younger girls. The school encourages girls to 'find their own path' through exams, allowing them to take subjects early (maths GCSE, drama A level etc) thus freeing up the curriculum for real preferences as well as necessities.

Sixth form lecture programme much enjoyed – politicians, poets, pop promoters et al. The school has good links in every field. Three libraries: senior fiction (rather quaintly called the Oratory), junior fiction and reference. State-of-art IT taken for granted though no Apple Macs. Not the ideal place for severe dyslexics but does have a learning support department for mild dyslexics etc. Everyone does Critical Thinking. Key to education at St Mary's are the enrichment weeks – when in-depth non-curricular study ranging from a week in the Belize rainforest to philosophy workshops or 'Shakespeare from scratch' allow girls to immerse themselves in a topic or project.

Games, options, the arts: Sport not just about winning, though school has a star-spangled record. Multiple teams in all main sports – 'everyone should have a chance' – with masses of success including numerous county players; girls go on to play for university etc teams. Riding (local stables) increasingly popular; a current pupil's clear round recently ensured a win for Great Britain's John Whitaker International Pony Team. Super indoor pool with fitness suite upstairs much used by staff, pupils and the people of Calne. D of E flourishing with nearly 60 going for gold this year.

Truly amazing drama in purpose-built theatre putting on one annual, grand, all-embracing production, often a musical, which has transferred to the London stage (Royal Hunt of the Sun) through RADA connections. RADA lays on 'Speak Out', an advanced 20-week communications and skills course, unique in the school world, covering presentation techniques for business, finance, media, politics etc. Sir Tim Rice (former parent) regularly visits. LAMDA and drama A level very popular and St Mary's regularly takes productions to the Edinburgh Fringe.

Stunning music building and numerous music groups, including the chamber choir (which produced a first class recording of David Bednall's new Requiem, played on BBC radio). Tons of concerts and tours (Tuscany, New York). Fourth form music competition a fun event 'even if you're no good', said a girl. Music exam results for singing are outstanding. Girls clearly love singing and say that they will join choirs at uni and later.

Chaotically creative art department, (with artist in residence) happily producing a spectacular range of sculpture, textiles, paintings. We saw a particularly striking series of clever political cartoons done for A level. (Both art and art history get smashing results). Weekend and other activities range from practical: cookery club (plus occasional sessions with a Michelin starred chef), wine club, dance club, gardening, Alexander technique, fitness, first aid, Young Enterprise etc, to spiritual: the Alpha course started by a sixth former; and intellectual: debating, young medics etc. Weekends are pretty full but girls say there is time for just chilling out with friends.

Background and atmosphere: Functional, practical, purpose-built rather than gracious, St Mary's was founded 1873 by Canon Duncan (Vicar of St Mary's Church, Calne) in 25 acres of central Calne, a pleasant but undistinguished little Wiltshire market town. Buildings have been added haphazardly forming a mishmash of styles divided by prettily planted and grassed areas. Spectacular new sixth form centre with ensuite study bedrooms and a disconcertingly bouncy rubber path leading to it across the grass playing field. Uncluttered, refurbished minimalist chapel and curious octagonal glass fishbowl reception area. Everything spacious, light and scrupulously clean with girls' bedrooms stuffed with personal icons and surprisingly tidy for teenagers. Each year group has its own house called after women (saints etc); pupils move each year while remaining throughout in multi-age 'companies', called after English bishops, which accumulate 'red points' for good deeds, including tidiness! Inter-company competition in drama, music, sport, general excellence etc and each company has an annual black-tie dinner. Pets' corner, said to house a menagerie of animals from guinea pigs to ducks, was almost deserted on our visit, though the newly-hatched chickens, Buff Orpingtons etc, were much cooed-over. Charitable fundraising – good fun which brings in respectable sums for organisations chosen by the girls – is on both a house (year group) and a company basis. The school takes its religious foundation seriously with attendance at chapel or local Catholic church compulsory on Sunday (with twice termly visits to the parish church) and sees religious education as an integral part each girl's journey towards a confident personal world view.

Pastoral care and discipline: Plenty of sensible adults around. A housemistress and day housemistress plus a team of five house tutors for each year group, so every girl can have a personal tutor. Staff keep a careful watch – 'we are well aware of social pressures' – for anorexia, friendship wrangles and other teenage pitfalls. Letter home and serious talking-to for smoking, suspensions (occasional) for alcohol and straight out for drugs. Dorms (first two years) recently refurbished and futons introduced in all the houses for the day girls to sleep over. All girls from age 14 up have their own study bedroom – even day girls have two-girl study rooms. Girls seem well aware of and responsive to the facilities and care given and say proudly that this school does not have cliques or exclusive 'in' groups: 'Everyone knows everyone'. Nice touch – making individual named cake for each of a very big confirmation group. Girl-friendly food, delicious with really good salads and plenty of choice – for supper sixth formers can eat in their new dining room or in the main refectory or cook for themselves.

Social Services praised the school's 'self-harm policy' which takes a firm line with behavioural issues while seeking to resolve any underlying crises. Quite strict on mobile phone use, though some wiseacres try to outwit system by bringing two. Systems and polices up and running for bullying/cyber bullying, complaints etc but girls say that the supportive atmosphere with teachers and older girls mentoring and caring for each other means these policies are seldom used in anger. Girls at all levels take an integral share in the daily running of the school with all sixth formers having a particular responsibility. They feel involved in school decisions and 'almost on equal terms' with the staff. No sixth form uniform but smart black suits 'for formal' with some fabulous footwear! No make-up and only one stud per ear allowed but girls pretty elegantly turned out.

Pupils and parents: Largely establishment intelligentsia, in strong C of E ethos. Many girls from Wilts, Hants and Glos (within hour and a half drive) plus London. 12-14 per cent overseas pupils – must have fluent English when they arrive. Dedicated travel office – its necessity emphasized by the recurring volcanic ash cloud. Medical centre (will do travel jabs) has 24 hour health cover, three beds, a counselling service and two weekly surgeries. Amazing network of celebrity past pupils and parents extremely well used by the school. Parents tend to know each other. Past pupils include David Cameron's sister Clare, Dame Suzi Leather, Jade Jagger and Laura Bechtolsheimer, part of the gold medal winning dressage team in the London Olympics.

Entrance: At 11, 12 or 13 plus a few at sixth form. Visit (an absolute requirement), then register. Before entry, girls attend Taster Day. Assessments take place on Entrance Day and these together with references from current school and discussions with parents and heads are designed to let St Mary's give a firm indication of whether the school will suit, subject to CE or entrance test performance. Many pupils from the cream of London preps and also from Farleigh, Daneshill, Leaden Hall, Beaudesert and St Francis Pewsey plus some local primaries. Usually a largish bunch from own prep, St Margaret's (which shares site, governors and lots of the facilities but is co-ed, sending boys on all over the place and girls mostly but not exclusively to St Mary's). Siblings encouraged. Sixth form entry (very few places) more straightforward and based on good GCSEs.

Exit: Tiniest trickle post-GCSE; a strong sixth form. Lots make blue chip unis – Bristol, Edinburgh, Durham etc with a handful to Oxbridge (eight in 2013) thanks to tiptop preparation. Music, art etc popular. Sprinkling of gap years (some really philanthropic) and post-A level applications.

Money matters: Selection of academic, art, choral, drama, music, sport and all-rounder scholarships at 11 and 13. At sixth form, three academic, one art, one drama, one music and one sport scholarship. Academic scholarships (can be up to 40 per cent) and academic exhibitions (may be awarded up to 10 per cent) are means-tested and only the first five per cent is automatic – parents are invited to apply for the remainder of the award.

Music scholars offered free tuition in two instruments; choral scholars offered free vocal tuition. Art, drama and sports scholarships are honorary awards, for which the recipient will receive £1000 per annum. Foundation scholarships, one at 11, one sixth form, which could be full fees, for a highly gifted girl from the state sector who couldn't otherwise come.

Remarks: Certainly cutting edge among the small, rural, academic girls' boarding schools, but also very homely. Long seen as a good place for well-bred brains to mix with their own kind, but it's a bit more than that – truly educative on every level.

St Mary's Catholic School

Windhill, Bishop's Stortford, CM23 2NQ

• Pupils: 940 boys and girls, all day • Ages: 11–18 • RC • State

Tel: 01279 654901
Email: info@stmarys.net
Website: www.stmarys.net

Headteacher: Since 2001, Mr Anthony Sharpe BA MMus NPQH MBA. Educated at Cardinal Langley High School in Greater Manchester and University of Liverpool, where he studied music and divinity. Taught music and RE in Liverpool before taking up post of deputy head at Loreto RC Girls' School in St Albans. Music is a passion – his liturgical compositions have been published and broadcast; recently demonstrated a lighter side by playing guitar in a school rock band. Married with three children. Is very involved in parish life, 'faith is very important and permeates through all we do.' Staff welcome changes introduced by the head which have upped the pace and expectations.

Academic matters: Pupils are taught in mixed ability groups in year 7, with setting only for maths, additional setting later. GCSE results are good with year on year improvements; 75 per cent gained five A*-C including maths and English in 2013. At A level, 30 per cent A*/A grades; sociology, film studies and English literature popular options. Alternatives to traditional A levels include applied courses, BTEC performing arts and NVQ business.

SEN well looked after with successes celebrated via a 'caring to achieve' board. Nine children have statements, plus others on SEN register. Range of SENs catered for including children with ASD, SpLD, medical needs, MLD and VI; have technicians and support staff to help as required. Work on self-esteem through circle of support programme etc. Some grumbles from pupils that they don't always get individual attention, particularly in larger classes. School says, 'In part, our drive to increase standards has raised the demands and aspirations of our pupils, but as 90 per cent gain five good GCSEs and all pupils leave with at least five qualifications we feel we meet all needs'. Sixth formers happy – 'we have small teaching groups, it makes a real difference, you get to know the staff really well and they, you.'

Games, options, the arts: Plenty of trips to theatres, exhibitions and places of interest and opportunities for travel abroad including rugby to Italy and netball to Jersey. Wide-ranging extra-curricular activities include D of E and plenty of sport. Regular music and drama performances involving large numbers of pupils in everything from Cabaret to Coldplay liturgies. Have jazz band, choir, orchestra, brass group etc. First class new sports centre complete with under floor heating, cricket nets, climbing wall, brand new kit etc. GCSE dance group works in partnership with nearby St Elizabeth's special school. Pupils are encouraged to help in the community through various activities, head stresses importance of interacting with the community, including non-faith.

Background and atmosphere: Established by an order of nuns in 1896 as a girls' convent but co-ed since 1976. Situated near the centre of Bishop's Stortford on a large and pleasant site. Near to bus routes but about a 15-minute walk from the rail station. A mixture of old and new. The new include a modern library and sports hall plus recently built sixth form centre offering plenty of space for both study and relaxation. The old is scruffy and past its use by date; there is a big current building/refurb programme, aiming for first class facilities, but not there yet.

Pastoral care and discipline: Praise from all quarters. Pupils say school is incredibly caring and any problems are swiftly and effectively dealt with. Discipline straightforward, firm. Staff have high expectations; recognise they have a duty to educate pupils to be the citizens of tomorrow. Work hard to keep and support students but not afraid to exclude temporarily or permanently when needs must. Recent innovations include peer mentors trained by Childline and an inclusion unit to prevent exclusion. Prospective sixth-formers have a team building/induction week with taster lessons at end of year 11. Very strong Catholic ethos. There are regular lunch-time masses and residential retreats; chapel always open, chaplain visits frequently.

Pupils and parents: Predominantly white Catholic families. St Mary's serves the Lea Valley Deanery, which stretches from Bishop's Stortford to Hoddesdon, Cheshunt and Waltham Cross and many pupils travel significant distances across Hertfordshire and Essex. Unlike some local schools, St Mary's does not practise backdoor selection so has, the head stresses, a truly comprehensive intake. Serves a fairly affluent area so pupils tend to have relatively few social problems. Very enthusiastic support and fund-raising from parents through the PTA.

Entrance: Has expanded to five form entry. Heavily oversubscribed – even practising Catholics may miss out on a place. First priority goes to Catholic children with a brother or sister in the school. Next in line are Catholic applicants with no sibling connection. Places are awarded according to where applicants live, with 40 per cent going to children in Bishop's Stortford and Sawbridgeworth, 40 per cent going to children in other parts of the Lea Valley Deanery and 20 per cent to those living in another five surrounding Essex parishes. Next come any other Catholic applicants who don't fit the above criteria. Criterion four offers places to those with a non-Catholic sibling in the school. Contact the school for full admissions information.

Entrance to sixth form is dependent on GCSE grades. 'If students are not able to sustain the level, we ensure that they leave that course and take up alternative provision.'

Exit: A few pupils leave after GCSEs to move to other sixth forms in the area, a few go straight to work. The majority of those leaving the sixth form go on to further education, with a quarter going directly to employment. One or two most years head for Oxbridge (one in 2013), but the head hopes to see this figure increase with the introduction of a new year 12 extension studies programme.

Remarks: Aims to produce well-rounded youngsters with values they can defend. Ideal for Catholic parents who are keen to have their children educated in their faith, in a happy and academically successful environment.

St Mary's School (Gerrards Cross)

Linked school: St Mary's School (Gerrards Cross) Preparatory Department

Packhorse Road, Gerrards Cross, Buckinghamshire, SL9 8JQ

• Pupils: 325; 220 in senior department • Ages: 3–18 • Non-denominational • Fees: £3,855–£13,956 pa • Independent

Tel: 01753 883370
Email: registrar@st-marys.bucks.sch.uk
Website: www.stmarysschool.co.uk

Head: Since 2010, Mrs Jean Ross BA (French, Manchester) NPQH. Previously deputy head at St Albans High School. Her educational philosophy is one of identifying the individual talents of each and every child and giving them the tools and motivation to reach beyond their best.

Academic matters: Good results, given broadish church, thanks to good value-added across all subjects. In 2013, 80 per cent of GCSE entries were graded A*-B; 41 per cent awarded A/A* – commendable. All usual subjects offered at A level, plus theatre studies, PE, media studies and health and social care. In 2013, 42 per cent A*/A at A level. Lots of loyal, long-serving staff; head comments, 'they're not stick-in-the-mud; they're very proactive, keen to stay ahead of the game'.

Fifty girls benefit from learning support with 10 or so receiving ESL help. The team copes with a range of mild SEN – mainly mild/moderate dyslexia and some medical/sensory needs. Focus is very much on the individual, regardless of where they are on the learning spectrum. Small classes and attention to learning styles and individual needs ensure all have the opportunity to achieve. Has various events for gifted and talented plus French verse speaking competition open to all. Some of the brighter girls do the 11 plus but it isn't their raison d'être – 'we encourage enjoyment of education, not the confines of cramming'.

Games, options, the arts: Girls enjoy their sports – plenty of netball and tennis plus football, cricket, gymnastics etc. Success on the sports pitches doesn't feature as regularly as hoped for but they don't get hung up on 'the games that got away'. Flexibility and support offered, plus allowances made, for those with talents such as ice dancing, horse riding etc, which require time out of school. Musicians entertain via school band and orchestra; lots of singing with recognised success for some choirs. Plenty of trips and tours, near and far. A number of girls are D of E Award holders. More dance was the only thing on wishlist of girls and their parents, and they're hopeful that will come with the new, state-of-the-art sports hall, a welcome addition to a good range of outdoor sports facilities.

Background and atmosphere: Originally an Elizabethan manor house, the estate has shrunk over the years but number of buildings has grown. Founded in Paddington in 1872 as a school for girls, run by Anglican nuns, it moved to its current premises in 1938. Very much a school where girls are known to each other and to staff. There's a real sense of community, a feeling that everyone matters, 'people don't get left out; it isn't cliquey,' insisted senior pupils, adding, 'there's a real big sister, little sister feel'. Facilities wouldn't win prizes; all are well kept but they're more Hennes than Harrods, though there is a decent smattering of gadgets, including whiteboards, laptops, data-logging kit etc. Purpose-built labs and specialist tech areas, two functional libraries (we like the 'donate a book on your birthday' idea), a multi-purpose hall, small teaching classrooms and clinical corridors.

S

Pastoral care and discipline: The school sits just outside the M25 but is a refreshing contrast to many within the zone. Nurturing not pushy, nor highly pressurised; believes the best way to get the most out of the girls is via gentle encouragement, unstinting support and a bit of oomph. Indeed, the school's reputation for caring about the girls and the way the girls care for each other have tempted many a parent through its doors. Drink, drugs and other unhealthy options seem to bypass these savvy girls. A strong house system ensures girls, and their work and efforts, are valued and rewarded. Good careers preparation – work experience in year 11, community service in year 12 plus self-evaluation and mock interviews etc.

Pupils and parents: A broad(ish) social mix – some struggle to meet the fees, others very affluent. This may be 'des-res' land but it's not 'debs' res'. Girls are confident and caring but unfazed by brands and labels. Odd moan – middle school would like an indoor breaktime area, some older children would like a more varied lunch menu (though parents say it is improving) and some grumbles, not about quantity of homework but spasmodic way in which it's sometimes set. Parents would like to see improved facilities for sixth form, citing current Portakabins as less than ideal. Active school council has negotiated recent changes to uniform and additional subjects at A level. Parents kept informed via parent-mail and active parents' association welcomes anyone who wants to get involved.

Entrance: Majority from Gerrards Cross and environs; not league table driven but keeps a canny eye on performance and improvement. Getting harder to get into but, if there's space, girls are welcome and welcomed at any time. Takes all-comers at three, many stay for the duration; odd one or two who won't make the grade asked to leave prior to 11. In junior school, some come with an eye on a grammar school place at 11, others because they want an all-through school. Selective entry at 11, ideally seeking a VR score of 110+ but does have a number of average children who will benefit from all the school has to offer. Many feeder schools including Maltman's Green, Chalfont St Peter's and High March.

Exit: One or two leave post-GCSE but most stay on into the sixth form (varies year on year); a few enter the grammars or opt for co-ed boarding or local sixth forms. However, as sixth form numbers are small (usually five or fewer girls per subject) they get lots of individual attention. All move on to university, range of courses, occasional one to Oxbridge (two in 2013).

Money matters: Not a rich school but academic scholarships available at seven, 11 and 16, plus a music scholarship at 11. Offers a small number of means-tested bursaries to those in need.

Remarks: One contented youngster remarked, 'I think this school is wonderful, every single bit of it.' A good choice if you want a school that will nurture, add academic value and care as much about your daughter as you do.

St Mary's School (Shaftesbury)

Donhead St. Mary, Shaftesbury, Dorset, SP7 9LP

- Pupils: 300 girls; 200 board, rest day • Ages: 11–18 • RC
- Fees: Boarding £23,166–£25,980; Day £15,885–£17,856 pa
- Independent

Tel: 01747 852416
Email: admin@st-marys-shaftesbury.co.uk
Website: www.st-marys-shaftesbury.co.uk

Headmaster: Since 2006, Mr Richard James (forties). Educated at Kirkley High School in Lowestoft before training as a musician at the Royal College of Music (piano, violin and conducting). Was director of music at Cottesmore Prep for ten years before moving to St Mary's Ascot, where he became a head of house with his wife Becca, who taught art; later director of music. Composed choral music, mostly for the Campion Singers (chapel choir). Arrived as deputy head at St Mary's Shaftesbury in 2005. Became acting head (six months before an ISI inspection!) and then head. First male head of any Congregation of Jesus (CJ) school. Teaches composition and jazz history at A level; pursues his love of music when time permits. Very down to earth, easy to talk to, clearly loves the place. Three children – two older sons and a young daughter at St Mary's.

Academic matters: Results outstanding for mixed ability intake. A recent ISI report stated: 'Progress at A level is exceptional'. Almost half the girls do A level English; RS, French and art/history of art popular too; very large up-take of sciences for a girls' school. In 2013 43 per cent of A levels graded A*/A. Separate sciences for all at GCSE and rather whizzy science labs with just the whiff of Dr Strangelove about them, GCSE results also very impressive (56 per cent A*/A in 2013). Language exams usually taken by native speakers, otherwise Spanish, German and French. A level options broadening with recent introduction of AS photography, economics, further maths and PE. Trained staff stretch the most able 'through our gifted and talented programme'. 'Girls being pushed more and harder these days'. Good calibre of staff and increasing numbers of them. 'We won't give in over little things' – homework must not be late, poor work is not accepted. Strong learning support department; good links with prep schools.

Games, options, the arts: Strong on netball, tennis and hockey; Astroturf, 25m indoor pool, polo popular. New art department on the way – expect it in 2014. Old art rooms burgeoning – lots of textiles. Stunning music dept, with practice rooms and concert hall. Jazz, rock, orchestras, choirs, trips abroad. Envy-making. Keen drama, LAMDA. Fab drama studio with seating for 130. Strong on extra-curricular activities – self-defence, modern dance, masses of clubs for just about everything and stunning cooking facilities. Duke of Edinburgh Award taken to gold level. Retreats, expeditions to India and Rwanda and pilgrimage to Lourdes.

Background and atmosphere: Sister school to St Mary's Ascot and St Mary's Cambridge, founded by IBVM (now CJ) in 1945. School tucked down wooded drive; hidden among the moss and pines, it feels almost like one is arriving at the Beast's enchanted palace. Charming converted late Victorian house with hotch potch of architectural mismatches. Fifty-five acres of rolling grounds, wonderful views and – for the boarders – a strong sense of 'being out in the sticks', but girls can walk into Shaftesbury. Recent building includes an extension to the upper sixth boarding house, a new academic teaching building and art department extension (to be completed September 2014).

Boarding throughout whole school. Boarders graduate from larger bedrooms (never dorms) to individual bedrooms – upper sixth house gives girls much independence and is a significant factor in sixth form retention. Day girls may go home at 4:45pm but most stay later for activities, study and supper. Long flowing wrap-around kilts for all and full length for the sixth form: quite a sight. Strong community happy-family feel. Masterful prospectus.

Pastoral care and discipline: All newcomers (even the head) have a mentor for the first term and welcome cards abound. Pastoral care improved and improving with increased numbers of staff per house; pupils meet with their tutor each morning. Palpable RC ethos throughout: 'It underpins everything we do', says the head, 'and that will not change'. Quite a number of C of E girls, Anglican priest comes once a week and celebrates Eucharist in the chapel every few weeks. Head notes the girls are given a bit of freedom. Thirteen-year-olds can walk into Shaftesbury, two miles away, in groups of three; older girls can visit Salisbury and sixth formers may stay out till 10pm at weekends. Weekend activities considerably boosted in the last few years. Girls allowed cars in the sixth form. Fierce anti-smoking policy – fine and letter – suspended – expelled. The odd suspension for overindulging in alcohol.

Pupils and parents: Only 10 per cent first time buyers. More local than in past: 75 per cent live within an hour of the school. Good mix from overseas (but not more than 10 per cent non-nationals) – Mexico, Spain, Hong Kong. Unspoilt, jolly nice, articulate, uninhibited girls – and relatively unsophisticated. About 50 per cent RC. Quite a few refugees from the hurly burly of London.

Entrance: At 11, 13 and into sixth form. Scholarships in all disciplines, music, art and sport as well as academic with the option of bursarial top-up. The school is currently full with registrations rising fast.

Exit: Small trickle post-GCSE to sixth forms elsewhere, often co-ed. Of those who remain, almost all to university, including Oxbridge candidates (head sez: 'special Oxbridge preparation classes. Each year we have at least two Oxbridge offers' – three in 2013), loads to various art courses – foundation or history of art plus medics and chemical engineers.

Money matters: Not a rich school but does its housekeeping well. Bursar an acknowledged genius.

Remarks: Jolly nice girls' Catholic boarding school, from the same stable as St Mary's Ascot, unpretentious and good at bringing out the best. A safe harbour.

St Mary's School Ascot

St Mary's Road, Ascot, Berkshire, SL5 9JF

• Pupils: 380 girls; 370 board (full boarding only), 10 day
• Ages: 11–18 • RC • Fees: Boarding £31,440; Day £22,380 pa
• Independent

Tel: 01344 623721
Email: admissions@st-marys-ascot.co.uk
Website: www.st-marys-ascot.co.uk

Headmistress: Since 1999, Mrs Mary Breen BSc MSc (forties). Married, no children. Previously spent seven-year stint at Eton, where she ended up as head of physics. Before that, taught science at The Abbey School Reading.

Her career was kick-started by head at Wellington who having appointed her husband to a teaching post saw Mrs Breen's useful physics degree lying fallow and suggested putting it to practical use. 'A few months later, my first class was 22 Wellingtonians. I discovered I could do it and loved it,' she says. The rest, as they say, is history or in her case, science.

The school's first lay head, she has commendably piloted St Mary's through the choppy waters of changing educational fashions without once changing course. The result is a school that has remained totally true to itself – and unapologetically so. 'We're not trying to be all things to all people,' she says, 'but we've got a coherence that works.'

Smart, with a hint of va va voom (and no doubt requiring every ounce of it at times), she relishes the job and is reassuringly in control without anything of the martinet about her. Her genuine and purposeful charm is particularly effective when directed at parents. 'I say "we're Catholic. We're all girls. We're full boarding. We're a good medium size, with just under 400 and no plans to get any bigger or smaller. And we're very proud of is our academic reputation. If that's a match for your daughters, let's take it further".' Most do.

Head is no slouch when it comes to heading off potential defection higher up the school. 'Having seen them grow up as teenagers, you want them as your gorgeous sixth form', she says. Plenty of official endorsement too. School recently breezed through visits from Ofsted and ISI (who decided to pop in at the same time) and scored glowing reviews from both.

Parents are universally full of praise, highlighting head's professionalism and nous. One father told us she should have a sainthood. 'All you could ask for in a head', said another parent. 'She's the right person at the top to build the right team round her'. 'Admiration,' extends to 'excellent' communication following a one-off resignation of a member of staff found with inappropriate images on computer in an incident which was, the head is at pains to point out, 'unrelated to school'. Equal enthusiasm from pupils. 'She knows everyone's name and is personable, efficient and approachable', said one. Felt to be particularly good with family-related issues requiring delicate handling.

Wears regular questions about whether she's thinking of moving on with slight (and understandable) weariness. Her answer? Until she wakes up thinking she doesn't want to do this job, she has no intention of moving on, though she wouldn't be averse to a bit of industry-spokesperson duties on the side were the opportunities to come her way. Our advice to suitable bodies? Snap her up while stocks last. A natural in front of a crowd, she'd be jolly good at it too.

Academic matters: 2013: GCSE – 95% A*/A, 99.8% A*-C

All round excellence, helped by well-stocked staff room (overall pupil-teacher ratio of six to one). Class sizes average 16 up to year 9, 15 for GCSE years and seven at A level. Three in a class not uncommon for more rarefied subjects such as further maths.

At A level, over 94 per cent A*/B grades in 2013. Though slightly lower than previous two years, percentage at A* has shot up from just under 21 per cent in 2010 to 37 per cent in 2012 (30 per cent in 2013), helped by outstanding individual subject results, including English literature (65 per cent at A*) and history (over half at A*).

GCSE results similarly classy. In 2013, 93 per cent A*/A grades.

Head is keen to dispel the suggestion that results are easily come by or a foregone conclusion. While they may suggest highly academic intake at 11+, with the vast majority at the top end of spectrum, behind the scenes number crunching (school uses MIDYIS) tells a very different story. Pupils span just about everything from the mid-range and below to the giddy super-bright heights.

A well-managed process steers a careful line between encouragement and pressure. The universally cheerful and confident demeanour of sixth formers about to enter final preparation for A2 exams indicated that it was working. Pupils rated supportive ethos – 'It's cool to work,' said one – and extensive out of hours access to staff. 'So many of the teachers stay late that it's easy to meet up with them', confirmed another. Well-structured lessons where peers, as well as staff, assist with problem areas are a boon, too, say pupils.

Transformation of geese to high-flying swans isn't lost on parents, who talk of being 'staggered' by strings of GCSE top grades achieved. It's something that the head, to her credit, doesn't care to over-stress, given that it's unlikely to do much in the way of improving pupil confidence.

Subject range, though not vast, is well chosen and augmented only after considerable deliberation. Religious studies a non-negotiable core subject at GCSE. Latin (taught like French from year 7) taken by around half the year group at GCSE, well ahead of Spanish, German, Italian (added year 8) and Greek (year 9).

Three cheers for science, a particular strength, with five well equipped labs and surging physics numbers post 16 (head takes some classes) on a par with biology and chemistry. Around ten (not far short of 20 per cent) take it to A level and the numbers are about to double as a particularly science-oriented group works its way through the school.

Maths also has consistent numbers of fans, though broad sweep of subject popularity (English literature, politics and French all make an appearance in the top five most years) means most tastes are well catered for. 'There's no subject that's a no-go area. When people ask me, I'm really proud to say what I'm doing,' says a further maths and science star.

Games, options, the arts: 'We're academic but with lots of extra-curricular activities,' a pupil told us. 'The school encourages you to thrive'. And how. Being not just good but 'brilliant' at everything, including sport, drama and music, is the goal, though not easy in such a small school, stresses the head. If anything holds them back, it won't be resources, with sports facilities positively glistening with new honed and toned additions. In addition to swimming pool, the Orchard Centre has a big sports hall, two squash courts and a dance studio. Will soon be one of few girls' schools to have own 400-metre running track, green instead of customary red. Polo available, courtesy of local stables.

While there's a steady crop of outstanding individuals and teams at county level and above (tennis a particular strength), any lingering perception that the keen but hopeless are left to languish is out of date, says the head. All shall have matches (if not prizes). Team sport ceases to be compulsory post 16 but there's enough to inspire even the most sedentary-minded to stay happily active. Body conditioning, universally (though to official disapproval) known by girls as LBT (legs, bums and tums) particularly popular.

As with sport, the arts boast range of spaces that would be outstanding in a school with double the numbers. With its studio, full-size theatre, enormous green room (partitioned for girl/boy casts) bar and extensive costume room, the Rose Theatre is a budding thespian's dream.

Many work towards LAMDA exams, gaining the full set by the time they leave. Productions every term, some girls-only, others involving other schools. Production of The History Boys featured an all-girl cast, apart from the French mistress, who was played by an Etonian. A sixth form group took their own play to Edinburgh Festival, gaining good reviews into the bargain.

Art, housed with textiles (DT, though not a GCSE option, is taught as a carousel subject in years 8 and 9) is terrific. In some schools, head of department's hand often all too visible in strikingly similar interpretations of GCSE/A level coursework theme: here, variety (including burqa-clad, slogan adorned figures in entrance) suggests pupils really do think for themselves. Quality is so impressive that you almost forget where you are and start peering for red spots. Portraiture

wonderful – not surprising as school, in one of many go-ahead moments, offers life drawing. Here as elsewhere, school's decision to go its own way has left it ahead of the game. 'We stick to traditions worth sticking to,' a senior teacher told us.

Music is a high-profile affair. Well equipped recital room, numerous practice rooms (including one, doubly soundproofed, for drums), concerts also in the chapel to capitalise on 'wonderful' acoustics. New head of music who grows her own compositions is now inundated with requests for new works following première of spine-tingling Easter Story and also plans to up numbers taking subject at GCSE and A level (scant handful currently).

Activities provide outlet for girl power in every form. For younger pupils, few delights trump pet club housed in mish-mash of cages and runs. Hamsters and rabbits dominate. with talent shows featuring animals in natty little homemade outfits. Animal friendliness is a big thing generally and mercy dashes aren't unknown. 'Only this school would put a damaged pigeon in a taxi and send it to the only vet open on a Sunday,' said a member of staff.

Wide range of clubs and societies, from the mind-expanding (human rights, music appreciation, current affairs) to D of E, London theatre trips and upscale wine-tasting (upper sixth only). Born movers and shakers (and there are many) can hone their organising skills in assorted forums, from influential school council ('what we recommend gets done,' say girls) to range of committees. Old girls regularly pop up to widen careers horizons as part of a programme that kicks in from year 9.

Background and atmosphere: School was founded in 1885 by the Institute of the Blessed Virgin Mary (IBVM), a religious order begun by Mary Ward (1585-1645). Her dreams of founding a Jesuit-inspired apostolic women's order (she even crossed the Alps on foot to put her case to the Pope) came to nothing in her lifetime. Undaunted, followers continued to plead her cause, though it was 2009 before her 'heroic virtue' was recognised by Rome.

Catholicism defines the school, sweeping in the committed and the less so. Morning chapel compulsory for all while regular weekday masses are optional, attracting anything from a dozen to 60 just before exams. Houses take it in turns to organise mass and pick the hymns, the more rousing the better. Recent election of Pontiff greeted with huge excitement. 'Someone started screaming "white smoke!" – I had coursework to do but the Pope comes first', a sixth former told us.

School makes the most of its 55-acre site. Main buildings, some on Gothic revival lines, go up rather than out, with long but not unfriendly corridors, helped by warm terracotta and mosaic tiles and a riot of gleaming staircases (some now adorned with essential if unattractive anti-slip edging).

We were the first outsiders to experience the gorgeousness of school's former concert hall, now transformed into a terrific new senior library (juniors separately and snazzily catered for). Nicer than many universities, say pupils. No wonder, with its curvy window seats, acres of bookcases and wonderful first floor curved ceiling. Café, complete with morning papers, coming soon. No learning resource centre faffage here. Pupils can take in iPads and laptops but the printed word is definitely the star of the show. 'Books betoken silence,' says head firmly.

Modernising elsewhere in the school has seen large-scale abolition of big dorms (mostly no more than five to a room). Top favourite, however, was blast from the past curtain-partitioned 'cubies' in year 8 dorm, voted the best fun, with last night of term midnight feasts.

Sixth form privileges include no uniform (pupils were delighted by this, some parents less so), permission to queue barge at meal times and annual ball. Biggest perk is separate living quarters, away from main school hurly burly, circle of little homes corralled around own courtyard. Decent kitchens are well used (fruit and veg high on request list, adding to menu staples of toast, pasta – and chocolate crispie cakes). Entertaining is encouraged, with guests treated to more elaborate fare (visiting Etonians haven't thus far reciprocated in kind. 'They don't have the same facilities,' say the girls).

Pastoral care and discipline: A little light rule-bending aside, few serious offences on this head's watch. Sanctions, when they do occur, are now consistent from house to house (just about the only minor imperfection found after recent inspections). Internet misuse would lead to merit-cancelling red ticket. Drink and smoking, almost unheard of, would result in suspension and 'you'd be out' for drugs.

Day to day, six heads of house have the biggest pastoral responsibility. They're considered mainly excellent. Praise too, for boarding. Inevitable beginner homesickness well handled with the help of older buddies and kindly boarding staff, vast majority of whom don't teach. 'They're lovely and very sympathetic if you say you have too much work,' says sixth former. Residential chaplain is mentioned by almost everyone as inspirational force for good and a multi-tasker to boot.

Multitude of house-organised weekend activities also helps to dispel boarding blues. Staples include mass pizza ordering as well as rare forays into deepest girly territory (nail decoration a favourite) and specials like St Patrick's Day marked with cookery (Irish potato scones) and crafts (shamrock felt jewellery).

Day to day, there's a fair bit of moving around which stems from a sensible desire to head off anything that could lead to cliques forming. Sleeping arrangements changed at least once a term and occasionally twice to mix and match the personalities. As a result, happiness tends to rule, and on the rare occasions it doesn't, there's a swift resolution of problems. Sixth form exceptionally strong, with friendships that often endure for life.

Pupils and parents: Around a third from London, a third within an hour's travel, a fifth from overseas (half non British) and the remainder from elsewhere in the UK.

Before head's arrival, vibe was a bit 'Frost in May', with slight sense that the very grandest of old Catholic families had a more exalted cachet than others. Now, though they're still represented, and anyone paying full fees needs to be 'mega rich' to afford them, there's a more egalitarian spirit abroad.

Increasing numbers are funded by bursaries, and though there's lots of emphasis on socialising with other top notch schools (Eton the top favourite) there's careful control of the trappings of excess. Nickames, amongst them Biggles, Squeaky and Booey, are plentiful and once bestowed are generally there for life.

Parents are a happy bunch. Not hard to see why, given the St Mary's effect, resulting in girls who emerge ready to subdue the world with charm, intelligence, confidence and poise. 'I think anyone in my year could stand up quite happily in front of 500 people and speak,' one former pupil told us.

Entrance: Selective but not awesomely so. Siblings, while favourably viewed, need good dose of what it takes to secure a place. School gives preference to girls who are Roman Catholic (98 per cent of pupils are Roman Catholic). Many from bilingual backgrounds, though no formal support offered. Learning support geared towards those with 'generally mild' dyslexia and dyspraxia, with weekly, external support from Dyslexia Action.

Main entrance points are 11 (English, maths and general knowledge/intelligence tests) and 13 (English, maths, science, religious studies, history or geography, MFL, Latin). Feeder schools many and various (300 preps and maintained primaries); so oversubscribed that process can be 'an exercise in disappointment' says head.

For the unsuccessful, there's another chance in the sixth form (test in proposed A level subjects plus general paper).

Chances of success are diminutive though. The maximum new intake is just five, though in reality often fewer.

Exit: A solid percentage to Oxbridge each year – 20 per cent in 2013. Bristol and Edinburgh also popular. Subjects range from sciences to languages, law to art. Numbers going into performing arts are increasing – one old girl is currently working with Steven Spielberg.

Money matters: Standard range of scholarships at 11, 13 and 16 on offer (five per cent reduction on the fees). Music scholarships include free tuition on up to two instruments.

Remarks: Catholic education at its best. So popular that when it comes to getting a place, faith may not be enough.

St Mary's School, Cambridge

Linked school: St Mary's Junior School (Cambridge)

Bateman Street, Cambridge, CB2 1LY

- Pupils: 505 girls including 90 boarders (full time and weekly)
- Ages: 11–18 • RC but all faiths welcome • Fees: Day £8,445–£13,521; Boarding £25,074–£29,124 pa • Independent

Tel: 01223 353253
Email: admissions@stmaryscambridge.co.uk
Website: www.stmaryscambridge.co.uk

Headmistress: Since 2007, Ms Charlotte Avery (late thirties) BA MA PGCE. Read English at St Anne's Oxford. Began teaching in South Africa at a politically tense time when some of the older boys carried AK-47s to school. Back in the UK and several professional moves later – two via GDST schools – became deputy head at Highgate, where she met her French husband, now a teacher at Sevenoaks School. (Pupils may only address her as Madame Pillet as long as their pronunciation is correct).

A palpably determined bundle of energy and breathless, almost unstoppable, advocate of St Mary's, with ambitious plans to squeeze more space out of a cramped site. Equally passionate about Lourdes – where 'our girls rose to the challenge in true St Mary's spirit' – and food. 'Dining is an important experience and I'm enjoying eating my way socially through each year group.' Everyone's pleased she's taken on board requests to learn cookery and that a perfectly formed, albeit compact, cookery suite has been installed. Pupils appreciate her up-to-date approach and, as a committed communicant member of the C of E, she wholeheartedly supports the ethos and values of St Mary's. An arty background makes visits to a gallery or the opera a must, whilst membership of the Ministry of Defence Ethics Committee ticks the public duty box and 'provides a chance to inject some common sense into proceedings.'

Academic matters: Not fantastically pushy but competitive in a 'nice way'. Considering the broad intake, good results at GCSE – 73 per cent A/A* in 2013 with hardly any slippage below C. Abundant encouragement plus drop-in surgeries for girls who need help – school says there's value-added across the board in spadefuls. Relaxed dialogue and mutually respectful relationships between staff and pupils. Parents are full of praise for the teachers and are convinced the bright do as well here as they would at the stratospherically academic institution round the corner. Recently introduced two-week timetable seems to be working well – head has her finger on the pulse in case tweaks are needed. French plus Latin in year 7 with German and Spanish in years 8 and 9. At GCSE, option of dual award or individual sciences but full RE course for all – the RE teachers are an 'incredibly sane and dynamic lot', according to the sixth, who love the discussions on every sort of issue.

Strong support network in the sixth. Reasonable spread of A level subjects has been maintained because school offers subjects to groups as small as one or two. High A*/A rate – around 65 per cent – with results getting a big boost from impressive performances in maths and the proportionally high number of Chinese nationals, not surprisingly, getting A*/As in their own language.

All year 7 pupils are assessed on entry in English, maths and reasoning. Needs, including those of the gifted and talented, are monitored and sensibly handled – ethos that all have something to offer isn't just prospectus speak. School reckons it's 'dyslexia friendly' but not CReSTed or likely to be despite appointment of experienced head of individual needs/language/ learning who has an MA in specific learning difficulties. Three part-timers to hand, access to ed psych and EFL teaching for international students. Differentiated activities enable most to stay in class but, if necessary, withdrawal during a second foreign language lesson. Usually groups of four. One-to-one tuition outside the normal timetable incurs an additional charge. Small teaching space, laptops as teaching aids.

Games, options, the arts: No practices at dawn but the sporty aren't held back – a number of girls play for the county. Enthusiastic staff and older girls happy with the range of options including rowing, touch rugby, yoga and kali – a seemingly ache-making series of movements with long sticks. Limited space so only two netball/tennis courts and smallish first floor gym on site. Hockey pitches a short minibus ride away. Hired pool and Astro nearby.

Drama and music (just over a third learn an instrument) are in fine fettle – conventional orchestras for instrumentalists and samba band for those who fancy something more lively.

Slightly cramped art department but the personal 2D and 3D work is liberally displayed and sixth formers have their own space. For the creation of something more practical there's D and T textiles with its large bright classroom filled with sewing machines.

School is hot on events for charity and, amazingly, given the number of pupils, raises around £25,000 every year. In the summer hols sixth formers join the popular pilgrimage to Lourdes, where they help the needy.

Two-weekly timetable has freed more time for extra-curricular activities, and an Arts Council sponsored award scheme (includes journalism, dance, digital film work, music and drama) is taking root with awards beginning to roll in. D of E is hugely popular and an impressive percentage get gold every year.

Background and atmosphere: This former convent – the nuns moved out in 1989 – is sandwiched between terraced houses and an edge of the Botanic Gardens. Although there's nothing remarkable, apart from the maze of corridors and staircases, in the diverse collection of dull buildings from the '60s, '70s and '90s which have been tacked on to an early Victorian structure, a sense of safety and warmth pervades this well-loved, tidy place. Sizeable classrooms and science labs. Standard gadgetry. Full library plus good range of newspapers and magazines (a sixth former has been appointed as newspaper scanner and daily poster of interesting articles on a corridor noticeboard) and fresh librarian who looks set to shift some of the dustier tomes. Sixth have a separate house where they can browse in the careers library or escape to a somewhat lacklustre common room – as one of the girls put it, 'not the tidiest in tidyville … but it's ours.' Noisy bonhomie in the spacious dining room, which doubles as part of the hall. Consultant has transformed the lunches and, much to everyone's relief, there's a wide choice of tasty dishes and tropical rainforest of a fruit bar.

Virtually all boarders from abroad. Ordered, typically personalised accommodation is neatly housed on the upper floors – single rooms for all the sixth and some GCSE students. Common rooms are welcoming, with the slightly quirky junior one being especially homely. Likeable and eminently sensible house-staff set great store on trust – sixth are allowed out by arrangement until 10pm on Fridays and Saturdays as long as they let the school know where they are – which, by all accounts, gets the hoped for response from the girls.

Pastoral care and discipline: Catholicism with a small c but charitable Christian Ethos in capitals – there's an understanding that all belong to a wider community and behaviour is expected to be, and is, supportive. At the heart of the school is the universally popular chaplain, who's often found sitting on the radiator at the foot of the main stairs. Parents say he's a gem. He knows everybody and is a source of comfort and solace.

Open, unspoilt girls at ease in this secure environment. They're allowed to develop at their own pace and 'aren't pushed or shoved into a box.' New pupils settle quickly – parents appreciate promptly established lines of communication by phone or email and the way staff are on the ball with problems including difficulties at home. (Some moans though about the patchy website and we agree it's not the best advert for the place – school says it's going to be given a facelift.)

Pretty well behaved lot – the pragmatic policy re banned substances is rarely implemented. 'We need to think about the wider community so out for dealing. In cases of possession we look at circumstances.'

Pupils and parents: Day pupils are very local whilst others commute by car (absolutely no parking in the vicinity) or train (station is a healthy 10 minute walk away). All sorts – about a third are Catholic – make up the loyal and supportive parent body. Majority of boarders are from overseas – international spread with a fair number from the Pacific rim.

Entrance: Mostly at 11 from own prep or local schools. Small number after GCSE. Informal chat with the headmistress then an application when she ascertains whether child is of 'sufficient calibre to benefit from a St Mary's education' – not hugely difficult as school draws from '60 per cent of the ability range' – bit ambiguous but we think we know what they mean. 'Bottom line is girls need to be enthusiastic about learning and committed to the wider community.' No surprise policy and basic expectation that those from the prep will join the seniors. Any not up to the mark can repeat year 6 (fine if the child stays in the private sector but problematic if, pre 16, there's a transfer to state education where child must be in the correct age banding and may have to 'jump' a year).

Exit: After GCSE many of the locals to Hills Road. As a strand to its career guidance, school has produced a collation of career stories from alumnae – oodles of advice and thoughts including the balance between work and family. Good stuff. Sixth move on to a broad range of courses and unis. Respectable number to Oxbridge and the heavyweights.

Money matters: Academic, music, art, textiles, drama, performing arts and sports scholarships at 11, 13 and 16. Mary Ward scholarships for those in years 8 and 10 who make a positive contribution to the school and wider community. Small number of 100 per cent bursaries for year 7 and sixth form entry. Possibility of help, usually to the next public exam, for those who fall on hard times.

Remarks: Energetic head and loyal staff with a positive outlook. Level of pastoral care and awareness of social responsibility give this place something extra special.

S

St Michael's Catholic Grammar School

Nether Street, London, N12 7NJ

• Pupils: 760 girls, all day. Boys admitted into sixth form • Ages: 11–18 • RC • State

Tel: 020 8446 2256
Email: office@st-michaels.barnet.sch.uk
Website: www.st-michaels.barnet.sch.uk

Headmaster: Since 2012, Julian Ward, BA, PGCE, MBA, fifties. Born in Lancashire and educated at the Pilgrim School, Bedford, and Manchester University, where he read modern history and economics. Then went on to study for an MBA at Bradford, before deciding that 'business was not my cup of tea' and training to be a teacher at Christ's College, Liverpool. ('I enjoyed every minute.') Has spent his entire professional career in London, where he started out teaching economics in 'front-line' local authority schools (Bishop Challoner in Tower Hamlets, John Paul II in Wandsworth, Sir John Cass's Foundation and Redcoat in Stepney), before moving to St Michael's in 1988.

Became sole deputy head in 1995, and his close working relationship with his predecessor, Ursula Morrisey, means he sees his current role more as evolution than revolution. Throughout his time at the school, has been a driving force in setting the highest academic targets, helping move the school from a middle-of-the road grammar to one that consistently sits at the top of the league tables. Since becoming head, has put particular emphasis on improving the percentage of A*s at A level, developing the gifted-and-talented programme and improving the school-parent partnership. A measured presence with a firm vision of what the school is about. 'Girls like him,' said one mother. 'They think he's strict, but fair.' 'very dedicated,' said another. Married with three adult children, he continues to teach citizenship and RE.

Academic matters: St Michael's has won numerous awards for providing an outstanding education and is now one of the country's leading secondary schools, always sitting within the top 20 grammar schools (often in the top 10) nationally at A level, usually in the top five at GCSE. 2013 saw its best ever A Level performance with over 91 per cent of A*-B grades, 60 per cent A*/A. At GCSE, an equally impressive 87 per cent plus A*/A. Teaching is undoubtedly a strength ('There are very clever teachers who provide very good teaching,' said one parent) and the school works hard to maximize both pupils' and parents' aspirations. 'We give a great deal of time to thinking about it,' says the head.

All the girls accepted here are bright, but St Michael's still offers significant added value, with a packed, fast-paced curriculum ('You need to enjoy academic work and want to find out about things,' says the head). Almost all take 11 GCSEs, including a large compulsory core, which includes English, maths, history and/or geography, RS, a science (about a third take all three) and a modern foreign language (large numbers take two). Language offering particularly vibrant, with French, German, Spanish, Latin, classical Greek and Italian all on the timetable, and Japanese and Mandarin offered outside it. Italian and Spanish particularly popular A Levels (as well as psychology, RS and maths). Sixth form has its own building ('St Michael's is really two schools, with two distinct regimes,' says the head, 'a girls'-only school from Year 7-11, and a co-ed sixth-form college.') Only small numbers with special needs, but 'strugglers' are kept back at the end of lessons for help. Homework is pushed hard. 'If you're ill you have to catch up on what you've missed,' said one mother.

Games, options, the arts: No playing fields and only a handful of courts, so team games not a forte (no hockey, for example), but a spacious four year old sports hall (the largest school gym in Barnet) is used to the full to deliver high standards in athletics, netball, volleyball, gymnastics, table tennis and badminton. Professional basketball and netball coaches bring out the best in nascent stars and the school is successful at local and regional level in a number of sports.

Academic music is excellent, with dedicated practice rooms and a recording suite, though the head is pushing for higher standards of extracurricular involvement. 'Lots of girls participate in choir and orchestra, but I would like us to have a greater opportunity for high quality performance.' Large, well-equipped art and DT studio (offering material technology, food technology and graphics) with plenty of enthusiastic participants.

Good range of clubs (mainly in the lunch hour rather than after school as many pupils live far away) and trips (including skiing, modern languages and faith-centred activities, such as retreats and a visit to Lourdes).

Background and atmosphere: Founded by the Congregation of the Sisters of the Poor Child Jesus in 1908 as a prep school in the grounds of its convent. In 1958, a girls' grammar school was launched to share the site and eventually the prep school was closed to allow the grammar school to expand.

Still quite a compact school housed in a motley collection of periods and styles. The Grange, which now accommodates the sixth form, was once a 19th century private house, and has the elegant proportions reflective of this history. The main school was built in the 1950s and comes with large windows and bright views. Modernisation is a constant theme (and drain on finances), but recent additions include an air-conditioned media suite and sixth form study centre. Classrooms remain a mix of old and new, but all are equipped with interactive whiteboards. Attractive gardens, once the convent orchard, are graced by a monkey puzzle tree, large redwood and shrine to the Virgin Mary.

The school, which is voluntary aided, is conducted by its governing body as part of the Catholic Church and the Catholic ethos remains fundamental. Prayers are said daily and every pupil attends a weekly religious assembly, as well as mass on Feast days. But this is contemporary Catholicism. 'They go to mass, but they don't expect them to be cleaning the vestry floors,' said one parent. Attractive chapel with superior stained glass windows by Patrick Reyntiens, a master craftsman whose work also features at Liverpool and Coventry Cathedral. Girls put their faith into practice with charity work, helping in the community and giving food to homeless. Generally, the atmosphere is kind, warm and supportive. 'Academically, they push them to their limits, but they do look after them,' said one parent. 'There's a very nice feeling to the school.' 'No one gets lost,' says another. 'It feels very safe.'

Pastoral care and discipline: The primary aim here is the formation of responsible and committed Catholic citizens. 'We try and create a relaxed and happy atmosphere,' says the head, 'but we expect high standards of behaviour, self-discipline and responsibility.' Those from bohemian families are advised to think carefully about their choice. Even those who aren't acknowledge the regime is firm. 'There is very strong discipline, which can irritate the girls,' says a parent. 'They will stamp on anything – possibly too hard.'

The pre-GCSE years have a slightly old-fashioned air. 'There's no talk of drugs,' said one mother. 'They do go to parties, but there's no big modern teenage culture.' Girls leap to attention if Mr Ward is spotted in the corridor and pupil pressure as much as teacher pressure patrols the classroom. 'My daughter said to me in astonishment, "a new girl in the school keeps answering the teacher back. Nobody will be friends with her. We like our teachers. They're on our side; we're on theirs".'

In the pre-GCSE years, uniform strictly enforced, with purple skirts at the knee or close to it, no jewellery or makeup. In the sixth form, mufti is permitted and the dress code becomes 'decency'.

Pupils remain accountable for what happens outside of the gates if in uniform. Few problems, however. 'Most people who come here are impressed by the behaviour and friendliness of the pupils.'

Pupils and parents: Cradle Catholics from all over London and the world, with increasing numbers of Eastern Europeans, particularly Poles. Not as skewed to the professional middle classes as some other grammar schools, with more new immigrants (33 per cent speak another language as their first language at home).

Entrance: Not perhaps as tricky to get into academically as some of the other North London grammar schools (390 apply for 96 places), simply because of its single-sex faith criteria. That said, the Catholic hurdle is not for slackers. Applicants at 11 plus must provide proof of baptism and First Holy Communion and at least one parent must also be a Catholic with a written reference from their parish priest stating they attend Mass on Sunday with the applicant. There is no catchment ('you can come from Sheffield if you want') but only girls who meet the religious criteria are allowed to sit the admissions tests (in verbal and non-verbal reasoning, English and maths). Sixth-form applicants are not required to be Catholic (about 20 per cent come from other faiths) but 'must subscribe to the Catholic ethos'. At this stage, there are a further 60 places (open to boys and girls with at least six GCSE passes at *A to A, with at least an A in the subjects they wish to study and no lower than a B in English and maths). Boys in this relatively large sixth form remain in the minority, with about 30 a year. 'The boys have to be quite brave,' said one parent.

Exit: About 14 or 15 girls leave post GCSE, to nearby sixth-form colleges, like Woodhouse, or larger co-ed selective schools. Most sixth formers go onto the older universities. A handful each year (six in 2013), to Oxbridge, guided by the school's own Oxbridge specialist.

Money matters: St Michael's is a voluntary-aided school and parents are expected to contribute towards the cost of the buildings and facilities. 'The school would fall down otherwise,' says the head. An annual contribution of £275 a year is asked for and 90 per cent of parents contribute something. 'We don't go chasing the other 10 per cent.'

Remarks: A happy school, with firm discipline, high expectations and outstanding results.

St Ninian's High School

Eastwood Park, Rouken Glen Road, Giffnock East Renfrewshire, G46 6UG

• Pupils: 1750 Co-ed • Ages: 12–18 • RC • State

Tel: 01415 772000
Email: headteacher@st-ninians.e-renfrew.sch.uk
Website: www.ea.e-renfrew.sch.uk/stninians

Headteacher: Since 2005, Mr John Docherty (early fifties), who spent much of his early teaching career at St Ninian's (and his daughter was a pupil), later becoming assistant headteacher.

He was then appointed head of St Andrews, Clydebank, where he 'served his apprenticeship' as a head, 'learning that what goes into making a good school is, above all, not being a one-man band'. On moving back to St Ninian's he felt that, despite its good reputation, standards could be better; the school had reached a plateau and both senior pupils and departments needed to be given more opportunities to take responsibility and initiative. His watchword is teamwork and parents are part of his team. As a result, reports are issued termly, parents are invited in to discuss education, 'not just be told about it'. In a radical approach to parents' evenings, one teacher collates information on a particular pupil and then spends a useful amount of time in discussion with parents ('not the usual two minute slot').

Mr Docherty, meticulous in attention to detail, is highly critical of the standards everywhere, from mealtimes to maintenance. If his super modern halls and wide corridors look miles better than most school buildings, it was only achieved 'through constant nagging'. Similarly, every aspect of school information is at his fingertips to the extent that he appeared to know the name and current concerns of each of his 1750 pupils that we met during our visit.

Academic matters: East Renfrewshire schools have such good academic results that families are queuing up for places and in 2013 St Ninian's was top of the board once again with more than half of fifth years achieving five or more higher grades. (St Ninian's is so popular that East Renfrew Council are running a consultation into the places problem.)

All pupils take a full range of subjects including French and Spanish but (unlike most schools) select their subject choices for Int I or II (rather than Standard Grade) before entering S2. 'This focuses them on the subject area where pupils are strongest and most interested, cuts time wasted in subjects which pupils do not wish to study and avoids timetable pressures and subject rotations.' Emphasis on modern langs with some distinguished results. French, Spanish, German and Italian on offer together with Mandarin – open to all year groups with a real Chinese teacher. Amidst great flourishes of Chinese dragons, the school has just been inaugurated as a Confucius Hub – the initiative for Mandarin Chinese in Scotland. No Latin or Greek but an impressively high uptake of English, maths and sciences at Higher and a swathe of technical/admin/business subjects. Learning support has five teachers and St Ninian's can and does provide for profoundly disabled pupils. Easter holiday revision courses to the fore as well as Mass for exam candidates just before Easter (belt and braces?).

Vocational options not forgotten with access to courses in sport, engineering, beauty, cookery, childcare, fashion, nautical etc some with Glasgow Caledonian or other higher/FE colleges, including some courses leading to possible full-time employment.

Games, options, the arts: Sport provided for within the curriculum though 'there is never enough room for everything', so bags of it as extra-curricular. St Ninian's has no all-weather facilities for rugby or football. The depressingly muddy sand pitch is frankly uninviting in a Scottish climate and badly needs updating. Football strong (girls and boys), rugby less so, hampered by rain and mud. Netball, tennis, badminton and athletics all boast school teams and have access to local clubs, but hockey 'has not really taken off'. A few 'talented athletes' excel in golf, football, karate etc. Activities are available in school until 6pm run by the school or East Renfrewshire but after that the buildings are open for public activities.

Drama, art and music feature strongly in the academic curriculum with all three getting sound grades up to Higher. The school benefits from a site which includes the Eastwood Park Theatre and Sports Centre, as well as having its own drama studio and sports hall. Did The Crucible recently. Art

S

seems popular with lots using the department after school. The Eastwood Park Centre recently displayed a fantastic life-size and life-like sculpture (paper pasted over a cane frame) of a rhinoceros made by St Ninian's pupils for their performance of Ionescu's Rhinocèros helped by county visual arts co-ordinator who also had taken pupils to be part of the Streetwise exhibition and the Burrell Collection. Masses of music, typified by the 60 strong and jolly tuneful string orchestra rehearsing at the GSG visit. Pupils get into Scottish national youth orchestra etc. Endless after-school clubs: ceilidh bands, public speaking, language clubs, string quartets, choirs, fashion etc and lots of outdoor education though not D of E.

Oodles of holiday activity (something of a crusade in East Renfrewshire) and term time outings and projects: London, Kitzbuhel (skiing), Ardêche, Alton Towers, Wimbledon, law courts, lots of theatre etc plus a good smattering of pilgrimages and a pretty sophisticated scheme of retreats and spiritual experiences (moral theology, medical ethics etc); for this is a Catholic school through and through.

Background and atmosphere: Founded and built in 1984, St Ninian's is part of a civic complex of council offices, arts and sports centre surrounded by grassy banks and urban forest. Huge and spectacular '90s additions by Jarvis cunningly provide an all-purpose, open-plan dining and performance area – a lofty central space set between three wings with acres of wall space. Potentially a bit bleak but light, airy and full of activity. This is tacked onto the back of the original school, joined seamlessly to the now dwarfed original octagonal hall (rather elegant ceiling) which opens into the newly-refurbished library. Further extensions house large well-equipped classrooms, (interactive whiteboards and computer projection now goes without saying) and some state-of-the-art new labs (and some less so – teachers have to work hard – and do so – to keep them up to scratch). The various extensions enclose a large oblong of 'patio' pregnant with as yet undeveloped possibilities. Catholic ethos much in evidence, not just in a rather startling Lenten display but also in the strong sense of the Catholic community. Not exclusively Catholic with quite a few headscarves in evidence though Mr Docherty reports no withdrawal from religious activities. Pupils polite but no tidier than most, ('It's a challenge to raise dress standards'), majority look pleased to get to the end of the school day, though one or two incredibly dapper prefects set a high tone in their maroon blazers and sharply knotted ties.

Pastoral care and discipline: All round care of pupils is managed in 'families' (rather than houses) by eight 'pastoral' teams, 'pastoral' being more Catholic terminology than the usual Scottish 'guidance'. These have 'a strong handle' on issues like bullying. Apart from accessible policies, such problems are dealt with, when necessary, by the 'focus for the week' which has included topics like 'mobile phone bullying', 'anti-racism', and the more mundane 'using your planning diary', 'lost property' or 'Advent charities'. The pastoral team also manages personal and social education in the curriculum and provides individual supervision which Mr Docherty would like to systematise further. Lots of parental contact and a view that, the better the school does things, the more supportive parents will become. The programme for careers and life skills uses speakers and visits covering every aspect from 'modesty is elegance' to 'gap year projects' and 'world development'. Responsibility for the state of the world is encouraged by fundraising and awareness raising for both international and local charities.

Sanctions mainly as a last resort (because the chief weapon is 'high expectations') but include exclusion. Mobile phones switched off inside the building. Intranet bullying – 'dealt with immediately and not really an issue'.

Pupils and parents: Supportive PSA (Parents Staff Association) does massive fundraising and entertainment for school.

Parents work in groups based on the pastoral 'families'. Pupils use public bus service.

Entrance: School is inundated with demand for places and the catchment includes parts of Glasgow as well as East Renfrewshire. This may change, as limiting the catchment may be a means of keeping numbers at manageable level.

Exit: 90 per cent stay on to S5 and of those 85 per cent stay for S6. 70 per cent to uni, mostly Scottish/Glasgow but a smattering to Oxbridge. Nobody in 'negative destination' (unemployed or not in a training, further ed or somewhere useful). Some gap year uptake. Ranked sixth in Sutton Trust list of UK comprehensives most successful at getting pupils into 30 most highly selective UK universities; comes second for exam points per pupil.

Remarks: Very big, but after negotiating the usual palaver of entryphones, locked doors and office corridors, does not feel impersonal. Clearly a dynamic school with a dynamic head and a consequently dynamic team of teachers and parents. Aims for 'all pupils to aspire to university and college without becoming singularly focused on academic results'. They achieve their aspirations and also focus on fun.

St Olave's Grammar School

Goddington Lane, Orpington, Kent, BR6 9SH

• Pupils: 860 boys, plus 105 girls in the sixth form, all day • Ages: 11–18 • C of E • State

Tel: 01689 820101
Email: office@saintolaves.net
Website: www.saintolaves.net

Headmaster: Since September 2010 Mr Adyin Onac (fifties) B Mus, BSc ARCM FRSA, originally from Derbyshire; his father was Turkish, hence the name. He studied music under Cyril Smith at the Royal College and later mathematics at University College, London. With two first-class degrees under his belt he decided on a teaching career, starting as a mathematics teacher, moving on to be head of Tewkesbury school, Gloucestershire and Fortismere in North London. Whilst being a talented mathematician and musician, he also has great interest in sports, particularly climbing, mountaineering, and rugby having once played for the North of England. Divorced, he has two grown-up children: a son who is also a mathematician and now works in the City, and a daughter who is a GP. His ambitions and energy are boundless: he hopes to take St Olave's to even higher levels, write a piano concerto, learn to speak Turkish properly and possibly even do another degree. He recently featured in the Times Educational Supplement in an article about how to combine a career as a headmaster and be a concert pianist at the same time.

Academic matters: An outstanding grammar school by any standards, over-subscribed and hugely sought after – 'a traditional education for the academically able'. All pupils assessed on entry, thereafter school's own Individual Pupil Monitoring Scheme ensures every pupil has their own challenge grades set. Broad range of subjects taught, with all the traditional bases well covered. Languages include French, Spanish and Latin. No one here just teaches the syllabus, pupils actively encouraged to think for themselves. Forward-thinking homework policy – one subject per night, a godsend to the 47 per cent of pupils who live more than half an hour away, leaving them more time to pursue the mind-boggling range of extra-curricular activities – 'crucial for extending students' confidence and knowledge,' says head.

S

Pupils confirm that the workload is 'just right'. Academic results are outstanding: 100 per cent A*-C, 87 per cent A*/A at GCSE in 2013. At A level 93 per cent of results were A*-B grades and 74 per cent were A*-A, placing school in the top ten state schools nationally.

Excellent facilities in every department – beautiful libraries, a brand new sports/drama hall, state-of-the-art computing suite, airy and spacious classrooms. High calibre, lively staff, and pupils enjoy lessons – 'even the subjects you don't like are interesting,' enthused one year 8 boy. 'They teach you above and beyond the curriculum,' added a confident and well-spoken sixth former. The girls who join the school in year 12 are equally positive – 'coming here was the best decision I've ever made,' 'I've gained so much confidence,' 'everyone's been really friendly,' were the verdicts of a group of girls' school refugees. Small number of SEN pupils are well supported by the SENCo, with individual assistants for statemented pupils.

Games, options, the arts: Strong and diverse, with outstanding tuition and facilities available – the only state school to play Eton Fives at national level. A few lament the lack of football below year 12, but rugby is extremely popular, with opportunities for all boys to play, and top players going on to local and national success. 'Our son loves cricket and rugby here, he's incredibly happy,' reported one parent. Sixth form netball also strong; girls have been selected to play for the Kent Netball Academy and the London and South East Region. New multi-purpose sports and drama hall opened in autumn 2010, which should up the game even more. Music equally strong – large number of orchestras and ensembles, and tuition available on any instrument. Pupils can learn blues and African drumming as well as the more classical repertoire – even organ is taught, on the magnificent instrument in the main school hall. School provides choristers for the Queen's Chapel of Savoy, and it's not uncommon for pupils to win choral and organ scholarships to Oxbridge. Theatre studies AS recently introduced but we reported that drama for the younger years was somewhat lacking. School says that this is now offered as part of the KS3 curriculum with three annual productions drawing casts from all age groups. Art and design are well represented, with lots of excellent work on display around the school.

Background and atmosphere: Originally located in Southwark, St Olave's received its Royal Charter in 1571. Forward-looking school with a strong sense of history – reception area contains a magnificent watercolour of 'St Olave's Grammar School, Tooley Street' hanging alongside a thoroughly modern Infoscreen, which pairing seems to sum the place up. School moved to its present green field site in 1968, in quest of more space and its own playing fields – also, perhaps, to get away from ILEA and the threat of being turned comprehensive. School buildings are lightsome and airy, combining the best of 1960s architecture with postmodern additions – lots of gardens, sloping roofs and quadrangles. Pupils and staff move about the site with calm determination and seem courteous and respectful.

Pastoral care and discipline: Praised by parents and pupils alike, a 'do as you would be done by' approach. Heads of year and their tutor teams oversee the pastoral system, and form tutors stay with the pupils throughout each key stage. Ofsted commented on the 'particularly good' staff/pupil relationships' and pupils' comments bear this out. 'I really felt looked after,' one said to us. 'Looking back, you appreciate all the care you had,' said another. Older students very much involved with younger ones, running clubs, arranging outings, helping with tutor groups. School has refused to expand beyond the point where the whole community can fit into the hall for assembly, and we were struck by its friendly family atmosphere.

Pupils and parents: All boys come from families where education matters, otherwise very diverse both socially and culturally – gilded youth and council estate boys all in the scrum together. 'There's a real mix of people here,' observed one sixth former. School's catchment area is massive, but applications particularly encouraged from its original boroughs of Southwark and Lambeth.

Entrance: At 11 by competitive exams in November. Hundreds apply for the 112 places, which are awarded, without interview, to the highest achieving. For sixth form, competitive exams plus at least eight Bs at GCSE. Well over 400 girls and boys apply for around 70 external places.

Exit: At 16+, almost all boys stay on to the sixth form and of these all progress to higher education. In 2013 24 were offered places at Oxbridge and almost everyone gained a place at their first choice university. Strong contingent to all the top places – Oxbridge, Bristol, Durham, Imperial, UCL etc. Consistently high numbers take medicine, law and engineering.

Money matters: The whole outstanding package is free, thanks to its grammar school status. State funding supplemented by its own foundation, which ensures funds for new buildings and additional teaching staff. Very active PTA raises money for all kinds of projects, while sixth form runs a charity week and raises an impressive amount for various good causes. OBs include John Harvard, Abba Eban, Lawrence Durrell, Wing Commander Andy Green, Baron Hill of Luton, Roy Marsden, Sir Roger Sims, Sir John Smith.

Remarks: One of the finest schools in the country, and a testament to the grammar school system. A superb, inspirational place. As one parent put it, 'All of our expectations have been not just met, but exceeded.'

St Paul's Girls' School

Brook Green, London, W6 7BS

- Pupils: 730 girls, all day • Ages: 11–18 • Anglican foundation
- Fees: £19,692–£21,168 pa • Independent

Tel: 020 7603 2288
Email: admissions@spgs.org
Website: www.spgs.org

High Mistress: Since 2006, Ms Clarissa Farr MA PGCE, (fifties), who previously spent 14 years at Queenswood, the last 10 as head. She has also taught English in Hong Kong, in a Bristol comprehensive and in a sixth form college in Farnborough. She is married to a sports journalist and has two teenage children.

As the established incumbent of one of the most exposed headships in the land, she exudes an elegant, intellectual confidence that could intimidate nervous potential parents and pupils. 'She seemed aloof initially,' said a mother, 'but she's much warmer when you get to meet her.' As a parent commented, 'You could easily get the wrong impression of her – she seems like a cut-glass ladies' college type – but my daughter really likes her.' 'Mine is really scared of her,' admitted another, 'but I noticed that the head girl and her team are all very relaxed with her, and they all clearly value each other's opinions.' Another added, 'She's always around, she knows them all by name. And my daughter says she'll sometimes give her particular look that makes you feel very important – as if you're the one person who matters.' By all accounts always present at school events, 'even the little drama club productions'.

Academic matters: Pretty close to unbeatable. School can afford a lofty disdain for league tables as it is always at or near number one (over 40 per cent A*s at A level, and over 92 per cent A*/A grades in 2013; over 90 per cent A*s at GCSE, negligible (0.6 per cent) B grades). The common claim to prioritise a broad education is undoubtedly justified here: many parents chose the school amidst a plethora of offers from other London powerhouses for this very reason. 'It really does feed a broader intellectual curiosity,' said one. Another commented: 'The teaching is second to none – exciting and stimulating. The teachers really get the children and make the most of them.'

Those few with special education needs often have coping strategies in place before they arrive, but the school is well set up to help. 'They've been astonishingly good at responding to my daughter's needs, and put in plenty of support for her,' said a parent, 'so it hasn't been too much of an issue. But they have made it clear that she is expected to meet the standards of the school.'

Tight group of almost entirely academic subjects at GCSE and A level, which includes Italian, Chinese and Russian in the wide range of languages, though with relatively few takers at A level, and the recently added government and politics and theatre studies A level. Maths is by far the most popular A level subject, as one would expect, with a fairly even spread between the runners up – biology, chemistry, English and history.

The school considered offering the IB but decided against it. 'We decided that A levels are a more flexible instrument – you have time to do things outside the curriculum that are not measured, and you can be a specialist or a generalist. It also gives more time for the bespoke Paulina unique co-curricular opportunities.' These include the Senior Scholarship project, which sees girls between years 12 and 13 carrying out projects with titles ranging from 'Is There Beauty in Chaos?' to 'Visualising Polytopes in 4 Dimensions'; and the Friday lectures from luminaries such as Shami Chakrabarti from Liberty and documentary maker Michael Cockerell on his latest work, The Life of Boris Johnston.

Games, options, the arts: With a legacy of Gustav Holst as first director of music and in-house composer, music has always been exceptional. Indeed, the recently renovated music department and singing hall – 'where Holst and Miss Gray [the then high mistress] listened to girls singing' – are an important nerve centre of the school. There are orchestras, music ensembles and choirs open to all, but the symphony orchestra and senior choirs are by audition only and perform at astonishingly high levels.

Art, too, is high profile. When we visited, the impressive coursework for the school-directed art GCSE course was on display in the hall. 'Art here is very special,' commented a student. The top floor art rooms include a terrace with a panorama of the London skyline where girls learn about architecture. There are spaces for digital art, animation, ceramics, sculpture and print-making as well as painting and drawing. DT is a GCSE option only as part of art and design (a school-designed course), but an example of the talent was an impressive pupil-designed bus shelter that adorned the entrance drive when we visited.

Drama has perhaps been a poorer relation in the past. 'Music and art have always been great strengths,' says Ms Farr, 'but theatre studies is my second subject, and it struck me that drama had not developed to the same level, so we have evolved a separate drama department.' The A level theatre studies students in 2013 all got A*/A grades, and it is a thriving GCSE option (though a mother commented that she was unusual in encouraging her daughter to take two arts subjects at GCSE: 'Lots of parents only want their daughters to do academic subjects'.) The purpose-built Celia Johnson Theatre hosts several annual school plays, with smaller scale productions in the drama studio. Students devise and direct their own plays, including the year 12 Colet Play, which has been performed at the Edinburgh Fringe on several occasions. Girls also join in St Paul's Boys' School productions.

Lacrosse is the main sport, with 7.30am practices for team players ('they all love it, so it's fine', commented a less devoted pupil), international tours and players often making county and area squads. The school also competes successfully at sports including netball, basketball, rowing, cross county, fencing and swimming. However, there are opportunities for the less talented too, with teams down to D and E in the lower years. 'My younger daughter is in a team even though she's rubbish,' said a parent honestly.

One parent commented: 'It's very inclusive. There's choirs and orchestras anyone can be in, and the same from drama and sport.' Amidst so many very talented girls, however, some of the younger ones in particular can take time to gain confidence and find their niche. 'My daughter plays an instrument but hasn't been asked to take part in anything so far. She and her friends like singing, but they found the choir too highbrow. And they were very disheartened when none of them got through to the second round of auditions for the school musical.' Another parent said, 'There are huge opportunities, but it's up to them to make the most of it.'

Huge numbers of clubs, seminars and trips: writing courses, physics and maths competitions, conferences in Paris, museum visits in St Petersburg, dance shows and debating competitions. 'The girls get caught up in the energy of the place,' says Ms Farr, and a parent commented, 'My daughter always comes home having done amazing things.'

Background and atmosphere: Some 400 years after John Colet founded St Paul's School 'for the children [not girls, naturally] of all nations and countries', the Mercers' livery company, guardians of his estate, decided girls were also worthy of an education and set up SPGS. Its red-brick main house, designed by Gerald Horsley, with marble-floored corridors, and panelled and galleried great hall, has a gracious, traditional and peaceful feel. 'But if you go in at break time it's very buzzy,' said a parent. 'They're all running round the hall, there's music blaring out.' Lack of uniform gives an informal air, with most girls dressed in ubiquitous jeans or shorts and tee shirts.

Ms Farr recognises that the school has an undeserved reputation for being 'very formal, starchy, cold, highly competitive, ruthless and unforgiving'. But once families join, she says, 'they find it's much friendlier than expected, and more informal. We like to do things in a friendly, collegiate way.' Parents agree: 'It's a much more normal place than you'd think from its image. It's much nicer from the inside than from the outside.' 'They really care about the individual.'

Impressive admin: 'It's really well run, which means a lot to us,' said a mother. 'Induction week in particular is brilliantly organised. They told the girls what would happen, and it did. They're very accommodating and very professional.' Another said, 'Unlike at my son's school, I don't feel I have to stress about homework and deadlines. I leave it to them.'

Pressure to achieve tends to come from highly-ambitious girls and their families rather than from the school. However, some feel that the school could do more to mitigate anxieties. 'Success is taken so seriously that it sends out a message of pressure,' said a parent. 'Lots of girls really worry about how they are going to do in school exams. You can feel very unsuccessful if you aren't brilliant.' Some parents of younger girls feel the homework can be overwhelming. 'It tends to take much longer than intended because they're perfectionists,' said a year 7 parent. 'She and her friends take all evening doing homework.' 'I don't know how they cope if they miss anything, because lessons move at such a fast pace,' said another.

'We had the preconception that you had to be pretty, funny and clever to fit in here,' said a mother. 'But my retiring daughter has come home beaming from day one.' Another said that her daughter has found it tough: 'It took her a while to make friends.

Coming from a state primary was particularly hard from a social point of view. But she's already gaining in confidence. They make the girls feel really proud of being there.'

Girls are encouraged to take the initiative. 'If you come up with an idea, the school will back you up and support you all the way,' said a sixth former, citing the in-house second-hand clothes shop, housed in a restored Victorian coal cellar that previously acted as a junk room, set up and run by students to raise money for local charities.

Pastoral care and discipline: 'I like to think it is a kinder school than it was,' says Ms Farr, who has increased the emphasis on the pastoral side. 'We have clear boundaries but lots of room for independent expression. We treat the girls like adults as soon as possible.' 'There's a marked lack of rules,' agrees a parent. 'There's a respect and a feeling of equality between teachers and girls.'

Some of these highly-ambitious girls do succumb to eating disorders or other expressions of teenage angst, but the school is very conscious of the problem and encourages a relaxed approach to eating. The dining room has recently been refurbished and the food, said a pupil, is 'amazing. I feel as if I am eating in a restaurant every day. Food is important to Paulinas.'

Small tutor groups of 12 girls keep the same tutor for two years in the lower school and three in the middle school. The sixth form has a vertical system to enable those in different forms to share experiences. The sister scheme sees girls from the middle and upper schools help new girls settle in, and two year 13 girls are attached to each lower year group, available for mentoring and encouragement. 'The sixth form isn't hived off in its own area but is very much part of the school. The girls are role models and figures to look up to for the younger ones.' 'very approachable' school nurse.

Pupils and parents: Intellectual, ambitious, often multi-national families. 'I sometimes feel that my daughter's in a minority having two English parents. Lots of girls speak a second language fluently.' From a range of backgrounds – journalists and artists, academics and scientists, with a large proportion of bankers and lawyers ('You can spot those with bursaries,' said a parent wryly, 'because their dads aren't bankers.') Largest single cohort from Bute House, which regularly sends up to 20 or so girls here; the rest from a wide range of preps and primaries across London and beyond.

'There is a view that you must be super-confident to succeed here,' says Ms Farr, 'but girls vary here as much as anywhere. We do have a place for sensitive, quieter girls, and we enjoy the challenge of bringing them out. However, some parents still don't feel that their daughter is tough enough.' Parents agree that eccentricities are well tolerated. 'Of course the top dogs are the cool girls,' said one, 'but you can be a total geek and it's not a problem.'

Old Paulinas include (amongst many) Harriet Harman, Shirley Williams, Carol Thatcher, Stephanie Flanders, Rosalind Franklin, Rachel Weisz, Imogen Stubbs, Marghanita Lanski, Dodie Smith and Rachel Johnson.

Entrance: A computer-based test in November, aimed to be tutor proof and to identify 'girls with intellectual potential', deselects around 20 per cent of applicants. 'There's a vast industry preparing girls for St Paul's, and we don't want to miss bright sparks who haven't been tutored.' The rest take maths, English and comprehension exams in January, with those short-listed invited back for interviews. 'Our admissions process is a very careful, solemn business. We try to make it humane as well as thoughtful, and we discuss every candidate in detail.' The school optimistically asks parents to state if their daughter has been tutored, 'though we know they will answer what they think we want to hear'. They are trying to increase the proportion of successful state school applicants (currently around 15-25 per cent), and run a series of enrichment days for gifted and talented year 4 and 5 girls from local state primaries. Parents are given information about bursaries and encouraged to attend an open evening. 'We don't positively discriminate, but we do try to see through disadvantage.' The school is clear that it is looking for a particular type of girl. 'Our girls devour intellectual material very quickly. Those who want to work at a slower pace will be happier elsewhere.'

Exit: No-one is asked to leave because of poor academic performance (though they might reconsider someone who showed a lack of interest in learning). 'We make an undertaking to see them through, and every year we take through one or two girls whose GCSE performance is less than starry.' A few girls are tempted off to co-ed sixth forms, particularly Westminster, but the vast majority stay the course, and move on to do mostly solidly academic subjects at a very narrow range of top universities. Around half get Oxbridge offers (35 in 2013); seven or eight a year go off to study liberal arts at Yale, Harvard and other Ivy League universities; virtually all the rest to Durham, Edinburgh, Bristol and the London universities. The school is investigating European destinations, but no-one has been tempted across the Channel as yet.

Money matters: Four music (£100 a year and free music tuition) and four academic (£250 a year) scholarships at 11+; various art, music and academic scholarships at 16+, all worth £250 a year. The school aims to fund 20 per cent of girls through its means-tested bursary programme – 'we would like to feel that any girl from any setting could plot her way here' – and staff visit likely families at home to ensure they are not running a fleet of Ferraris from a multi-million pound mansion. Those on 100 per cent bursaries also receive a grant towards music or PE lessons, school trips, textbooks and travel.

Remarks: Unmatched environment for girls who thrive on hard work and have an appetite for intellectual experiences. 'What is on offer is exceptional. They have so many wonderful opportunities.'

St Paul's School

Linked school: Colet Court

Lonsdale Road, London, SW13 9JT

• Pupils: 933 boys, majority day; one boarding house • Ages: 13–18 • C of E • Fees: Day £20,853; Boarding £31,233 pa • Independent

Tel: 020 8748 9162
Email: admissions@stpaulsschool.org.uk
Website: www.stpaulsschool.org.uk

High Master: Since 2011, Professor Mark Bailey (early fifties). Married to a HR consultant, and with a teenage son and daughter. Career has comprehended both academia and education: former head of The Grammar School Leeds, he has also been a fellow at Cambridge and at All Souls, and professor of late medieval history at the University of East Anglia, with whom he continues to be involved. Found time to be a rugby international (1984 to 1990) and is now president of the Cambridge University Rugby Club. A thoroughly engaging, astute, relaxed and kindly man, the complete reverse of what one might expect of the High Master of such a venerable institution as St Paul's. We meet many head teachers who are fonder of their school than of the pupils in it. Professor Bailey, extremely clever himself, still cherishes the achievements of others. A people-person through and through, who likes 'reading, walking and the wines of the Rhone Valley'. Talks with a refreshing lack of jargon.

Self-imposed mandate, on coming to St Paul's, was, 'Not to meddle with what this school does outstandingly well; leadership of exceptional institutions is as much about stewardship as change.' That said, he is skilfully overseeing a vast programme of refurbishment that is transforming the 1960s site into a school for the 21st century, and steering both school and students towards greater meritocracy and social responsibility.

Academic matters: The St Paul's recipe for academic stardom remains the same: cream off the very brightest, recruit the very best, light the blue touch paper and stand clear. The resulting sparks illuminate the sky. As one boy put it, 'The real pleasure about being here is going off-piste academically.' Another said, 'The quality of the teaching is beyond compare. It really pushes you further.' Parents agree. 'The teachers are brilliant at their subjects'; 'They're highly skilled at imparting their knowledge'; 'The teaching is simply superb'. A recent inspection report summed it up: 'The effectiveness of questioning in lessons, both from pupils and teachers, is outstanding.'

Broad and challenging curriculum includes ancient history, engineering and technology, and an excellent range of languages, Italian, Russian and Greek among them. Exam success is seen as a by-product of the boys' broader intellectual development, but it ain't a bad by-product: nearly 96 per cent A*/A at GCSE in 2013 (78 per cent A* grades), and 86 A*/A at A Level (nearly 45 per cent A* grades). Amazing new science building now offers 18 state-of-the-art laboratories, but such is the subject's popularity that, according to staff, 'space is still tight'. Beautiful library, silent and inviting, and facilities everywhere are excellent, although we were amused to see far fewer interactive whiteboards in the classrooms than we'd seen in a state primary school the week before. Interactivity here is still verbal and cerebral perhaps, rather than fibre-optical. Huzza! But we applauded the really intelligent decision to install air-conditioning in all teaching rooms, ensuring that minds stay alert in the muggiest of weather. (How many times have we seen pupils wilting in the heat of south-facing temporary classrooms?) Specialist support is given to those few students identified as having special needs, but this isn't the place for anything more than mild cases.

There are no plans to introduce the IB, which the High Master describes as 'enforced breadth', adding that the Cambridge Pre-U is 'chunky and prescriptive'. A levels are preferred here, because 'they're the easiest of the post-16 qualifications; they enable the boys to matriculate, and this then leaves time to pursue other areas.'

You can feel the thinking going on here. Academically, a very special place.

Games, options, the arts: Superb facilities include six rugby pitches, six football pitches, five cricket pitches, swimming pool, courts for rackets, squash and fives, and its own boathouse stuffed with state-of-the-art rowing craft. The students wax lyrical about the sport on offer here – 'Sport for me has been the highlight here'; 'There is so much!'; 'It's a big part of my life at St Paul's'; 'Most of my friends have been the ones I play sport with' – and we saw dozens of boys throwing themselves about the playing fields in organised and impromptu games of just about everything. Music and drama are both extremely strong; concerts are held in the world-class Wathen Hall, and the already-good theatre is about to be replaced with something even better. Art is taught in a magnificent suite of rooms, and the engineering and technology room is surely every young boy's dream. Clubs cater for every taste, although oddly enough we didn't see any, despite having arrived at lunchtime;

even the four lads we finally came across in the 3D Art room turned out to be revising their French ('I don't know why they're doing it here,' mused the art teacher). But the student-produced magazines we read were testament to the vibrancy of this community of thinkers: page after page of exceptionally mature, sparkily written articles on cinema, sport, current events, modern architecture... a real treasure trove of ideas.

Background and atmosphere: Founded in 1509 by Dean John Colet, and moved four times before arriving in 1968 at its present riverside home in leafy (and very wealthy) suburbia. A £77 million redevelopment began in 2011, and has already transformed much of the site. Visitors now are presented with an exceptionally elegant, blond, modern school campus; an architectural version of the Paulines we met, really, and with the same air of informality and purpose.

Having survived the Great Plague, the Fire of London, the Civil War and the twentieth century, St Paul's can afford to relax and enjoy its own success. 'Academic rigour and loose ties' was how one parent described St Paul's today, and this was echoed by the High Master: 'It has the feel of an über-grammar school. It's more like a university than any other school I've known.'

St Paul's is a day school – one of only two to be included in the Clarendon Commission's 'nine great public schools of England' – but it does have a very small community of boarders as well, many of them from overseas, who seem to exist to justify the superb round-the-clock catering which all the boys, day and boarding alike, can access if they need to. Boarding facilities have been recently upgraded, and the boarding provision was praised in a recent ISI report.

It's cool to be clever here, and so, inevitably, there is peer pressure to do well. This is mostly positive, say boys and parents, and drives everyone on, although one parent added, 'If you were at the bottom of the class, SPS would be a horrible place.' But High Master denies this emphatically: 'More time than ever has been put into teaching underachieving boys and providing better support.' And another parent observed, 'The bottom of this particular pile still represents an extremely high level of achievement.' We saw boys working with good humoured focus for an eccentric and witty geographer who was padding around in Muppet-motif socks, interspersing teaching points with cheerful insults which the boys lapped up and batted back, in time-honoured boys' school way. (But there was a detailed scheme of work on the board that accorded with modern practice, demonstrating that old and new styles of education can be blended successfully.)

Indeed, SPS remains an extremely masculine community, where the testosterone coming out of the circuit-gym knocks you over at 20 paces; and perhaps this shows most in the school's being unaware of just how masculine it is. The Sur Master insisted that there was much 'mutuality' between the Boys' School and the Girls' School, but this was flatly contradicted by the Paulines we spoke to, and by one mother who felt that the school could do much more in this regard. We were ourselves surprised to find a large-scale female nude looking breastily down on us as we ascended the art department stairs, and more surprised to find another one as we went down a different way. There were no male nudes on display, and we couldn't help wondering why, out of all the subject matter that might have been on show, the school had chosen these particular canvasses. There are 'no plans whatsoever to admit girls at any stage of the school; no parents, boys or staff have ever suggested it' (High Master). Which, if they want to go all Rubens-y about the stairwells, may be a good thing. But the Paulines we met were very personable young men, and the same mother who wanted more contact with SPGS also affirmed, 'Paulines are lovely, decent boys, really articulate, fun, clever and very nice.'

Pastoral care and discipline: Vertical tutoring system, ie mixing the ages of form groups so that younger and older boys are together. The concept is simple: boys will listen to their peers sooner than their parents, so utilise the more experienced boys for pastoral care and to lead extracurricular activities. It's been in place for over 10 years, and is clearly popular. As one parent commented, 'From the moment they arrive, the 13 year olds meet boys in every other year and get a sense of what they might do.' Tutors stay with the boys throughout their time at the school, and often become family friends. The nature of this hand-picked community means that bad behaviour is rare: 'There's an intuitive understanding of where the boundaries are,' says High Master. 'I've never seen any evidence of bullying here,' was a typical student comment, and Sur Master concurs: 'We have very, very few boys that would do what could be called bullying more than once, and if they do, we apply school sanctions quickly.'

Pupils and parents: One of the most expensive day schools in the UK, and compared with similar institutions, financial support for poorer families is small – see Money Matters. The result is a community which is highly diverse religiously and culturally, but not socially. Parents mostly ambitious and successful professionals with sons to match, hard-working and free-thinking. Old boys list reads like a Who's Who of Influential Britons: a sample includes John Milton, Samuel Pepys, Field Marshal Montgomery, Isaiah Berlin, Oliver Sacks, George Osborne, Rory Kinnear – and Nicholas Parsons.

Entrance: State-educated parents who are starry-eyed for their children but don't know the entrance procedure should start reading it now. SPS takes about 180 13-year-old boys each year, but it's impossible to go there directly from a state school. 13+ candidates apply either from Colet Court, whose 80-90 boys nearly all go on to the senior school, or from any other prep school – usually those in the London area. Colet Court has its own admission procedures at 7+, 8+ and 11+; see our separate entry under Junior schools, and don't leave it any later than September of your child's year 6 (be grateful, it used to be year 5). Prospective Paulines sit an online common entrance pre-test at their prep school, on the strength of which about 350 are invited for interview. The school then makes conditional offers: boys have to get at least 70 per cent at common entrance. The school is looking for 'intellectual curiosity and embracing of novelty'. About 20 more boys also join in the sixth form, which at SPS is called the Eighth.

Exit: Around a third to Oxbridge, the rest to Bristol, Durham, Imperial, Edinburgh, UCL and other top quality universities. An increasing number leave for USA Ivy League giants such as Harvard, Yale and Princeton.

Money matters: Only five per cent of students receive any form of means-tested bursary assistance (although for those few the assistance can be up to 100 per cent of the fees) and scholarships are honorifics only – £60 pa and a silver fish in memory of John Colet. Some remission for families who send three or more children to the school. High Master's vision is to increase the amount of bursaries available, so that the school can become genuinely needs-blind.

Remarks: For very bright, confident, motivated boys who like to think for themselves, St Paul's provides a truly unrivalled education. A unique start in life.

St Peter's School, York

Linked schools: St Olave's School; Clifton Pre-Preparatory School

Clifton, York, YO30 6AB

• Pupils: 560–140 boarders, 420 day • Ages: 13–18 (Pre prep and Junior school 3–13) • C of E (but other faiths welcome) • Fees: Day £15,390; Boarding £25,185 pa • Independent

Tel: 01904 527300
Email: admissions@st-peters.york.sch.uk
Website: www.st-peters.york.sch.uk

Head Master: Since 2010, Mr Leo Winkley MA MEd (forties), previously managing head at Bedales. Read theology at Lady Margaret Hall, Oxford. Taught at Ardingly College and The Cheltenham Ladies' College as head of religious studies. Still teaches religious studies and contributes to the global perspectives programme for sixth form, and enjoys teaching – 'it keeps you honest'. A keen runner and follower of sport. Married to medical oncologist Jules, they have three young children. Committed to the breadth and all-round nature of independent education as lessons for life – says 'school should be serious fun', currently encouraging all parties to 'think big'. Pupils tell us he has 'smartened things up a bit and increased pupil involvement', parents say he is a 'fine chap' and has 'got the bit between his teeth'. You get a very warm welcome from this clear-sighted, ambitious strategist; he was born into the world of independent education, son of a headmaster so knows the perils, pitfalls and joys, though it is different up north and it will be interesting to see how the school develops under his leadership.

Academic matters: Consistent achiever, sets the bar high in a robust local market. Strong work ethos with plenty of stretch and challenge, normal to try hard but fine-tuning from the top is pushing to 'broaden the pupil experience' ie accumulation of exam certificates is great but balance is also important.

Take the academic rigour for granted, bright pupils will always do well, but hard workers also do well here, hence the very positive value-added. Believe good results are down to having really good teachers as well as selective but not highly selective intake; no weak subject areas; staff know what is expected and are multi-talented and self-driven. 'Learn Something New' is a St Peter's initiative that persuades staff to share interests and learn from each other with a range of activities across the school(s) encouraging staff to try out and learn new skills – 'learning teachers teach better' is the head's strapline.

Class size averages 18, in the middle school (maximum 24) and 12 in the sixth form. The occasional D or E grade creeps in, but all pupils pass at least six GCSEs at grades A* to C with 67 per cent of passes A/A* in 2013. IGCSEs being taken in maths, science and languages. Equally impressive performance at A level where 56 per cent of grades were A*/A and a very commendable 83 per cent of all entries graded A*-B.

Some support for the handful with mild dyslexia – must be bright and able to cope. Part-time dyslexia specialist. Approximately 10 per cent have an ed psych report; five per cent qualify for extra time in exams. Third modern language replaced by extra English and study skills for some. Gifted and talented programme in place but don't target top ten per cent. 'All the children here are bright, it would be wrong to concentrate on a handful.' Olympiads and similar challenges stretch those with real talent. Global Perspectives an additional course for sixth form with Horizons introduced for middle school. Does not allow students to take GCSE early and moving towards more challenging IGCSEs.

S

Careers advice and support flagged up by parents as something to be worked on and improved, especially important for boarders whose parents are not around to have those all-important conversations. They are getting pupils into good and great universities but what next? Both pupils and parents feel they would like more guidance and direction as life beyond university becomes tougher and more competitive. The school has responded swiftly by bringing in a second careers advisor and opening up careers events, visits, conferences plus 'exploration week' for the lower sixth – 'life after St Peter's' is a drum they will keep on banging.

Games, options, the arts: A surprising amount of outdoor space, you'd never guess it so close to the city. Nearest to the school is the hallowed ground of the first XV rugby pitch, but there are plenty of others beyond. Sport is compulsory for all. Facilities include two sports centres, one with super climbing wall, multi-surface pitch, fitness centre, indoor swimming pool, extensive well-kept playing fields, boathouse and tennis and squash courts. Rugby popular and strong, rowing crews regularly pick up national honours and awards, boast 20 international rowers in the last eight years. Hockey, rowing and netball are the most popular girls' sports but tennis, athletics, squash, swimming and usual suspects on offer for all. Generally put best coaches with best teams but playing opportunities for all via B teams and house competitions. Competitiveness and fair play are a prominent feature of the school and success is universally applauded at weekly assembly. Duke of Edinburgh and CCF flourishing. Plenty of trips including expeditions to Morocco, sports tours to New Zealand and South Africa, language holidays and music tours to the USA, Prague, Italy as well as singing in York Minster.

Very good art facilities, including super gallery. Art department appears in the Guinness Book of Records for a remarkable 100 per cent A*/A grade pass rate achieved four years running, though recent years have seen lower grades creep in – 'we were pleased, it took the pressure off, allowed the pupils to experiment, be more creative rather than formulaic,' said one art master. Many learn a musical instrument or two, 300 individual lessons each week with professional specialist music staff, 160-strong choir and plenty of opportunities to perform; director of music described as 'inspirational'. Each boarding house has a practice room with piano. Over 100 pupils involved with Community Action projects and all participate in charity fundraising.

Background and atmosphere: The school was founded in 627 AD by Paulinus, first Archbishop of York, and is one of the world's oldest schools, 'only two older' we are told. In 1844 it was established on its present, impressive, green, grade two-listed site in Clifton, with 47 acres, river access and all within walking distance of York Minster, the city centre and station.

Beyond the imposing main building, others are a mix of ancient and modern. Some classrooms and corridors are a bit tatty round the edges, get the sense that it's not a priority; it's a workhorse not a show pony. Good range of facilities, with all angles covered though pupils tell us they are pestering the head for a new sports hall, 'it could be so much better' – it's one of the head boy's pet projects though not on the agenda (yet), might have to settle for a new boathouse instead. Pupils rave about the new swimming pool, with the added excitement (for the girls) of it being opened by Olympic diver Tom Daley. Other recent additions include four bright biology labs, a sixth form microbiology lab, chemistry lab and design and technology room with Cad Cam technology. Three computer rooms are complemented by clusters of computers throughout the school and houses – virtual learning environment with WiFi throughout the campus.

Pastoral care and discipline: Pupils are members of one of the six day or four boarding houses. Boarding received an Outstanding rating in last Ofsted inspection. Boarding houses are well equipped with a selection of common rooms, games rooms and a kitchen for snacks (all eat in school dining hall). Pupils and staff strike a good balance between amity and mutual respect. Houses are headed by husband and wife teams and supported by resident and non-resident assistants. Good pastoral care, 'just wonderful,' say parents. They describe house parents as, 'something out of the ordinary' creating boarding houses that are 'home from home' with all the care and support that may be needed and equally 'a kick up the jacksy as required'. Staff vigilant – invariably have one or two they're watching for eating problems etc. Advice, help and support may be sought from tutors, house staff, resident health centre staff or the school chaplain. Pupils tell us that the unforgivables are drugs and bullying, if caught smoking it's three strikes and you're out.

Pupils are allowed to visit town twice a week (more in older years) and for younger ones a timetable of supervised events is on offer. All eat in the modern dining hall. Menus offer a wide choice with mixture of typical school meal fare, continental options, salad bar, sandwiches, fruit and healthy eating options. Pupils say food is 'great', with 'boy-sized portions'; Sunday brunch is legendary.

Strong Christian ethos, pupils meet thrice weekly for collective act of worship in school chapel – the new chaplain has 'livened things up a bit,' pupils tell us with a grin; assemblies at other times.

Pupils and parents: Day pupils mainly from North Yorkshire, Harrogate, Leeds conurbation, York, and surrounding villages. Majority of boarders live within an hour's drive but others from wide area in the UK. Parents in business and the professions, a popular choice for Forces families, small minority from overseas – 'it's a world view we need to develop,' says the head. Mix of Hong Kong, China, Russia, one or two others – just eight per cent overall.

'Parents,' say school, 'are interested – but not helicopters', ambitious and driven; quite a few first time buyers here but also dynasties with names all over the honours boards.

Pupil voice has grown and developed through a pupil symposium. Head's question time is chaired by the head boy or girl – 'direct government-type stuff' – raising all kinds of ideas and questions from the downright silly to the well-considered and serious.

Middle school uniform uninspiring, disliked, yet (bizarrely) defended, by pupils – when push comes to shove there's nothing more conservative or radically opposed to change than your average fifteen year old: brown blazer, grey trousers for boys, and brown checked skirt for girls, apparently the current line is 'brown is good'. Sixth form (boys and girls) wear dark business suits. Old boys (Old Peterites), include Guy Fawkes, Alcuin (eighth century scholar), Greg Wise, John Barry, Laurence Eusden (poet laureate), Harry Gration (journalist, TV presenter), C Northcote Parkinson (inventor of Parkinson's Law) and Clare Wise (director of the British Film Commission).

Entrance: Automatic entry from Clifton Pre-prep to St Olave's (St Peter's junior school) and then from St Olave's to St Peter's. Seventy per cent follow this route, rest by CE and school's own entrance test at any age including 13 or 16 (minimum six GCSE grade B passes). Assessment and filtering does take place in prep and pre-prep to weed out those who won't cope with the demands of St Peter's, but it is rare. Generally entry to St Olave's requires a child to have a reading age at least a year ahead of chronological age (sympathetic to siblings). Will take pupils who pass exam at any time provided a place is available. Other main feeder schools: Terrington Hall, Cundall Manor and Aysgarth, some state schools also.

Exit: Three or four pupils (ten per cent) leave at the end of year 11. Of those leaving after A levels, 95 per cent go directly to university, vast majority selecting Russell Group, seven or eight to Oxbridge (though UCL and Imperial favoured mostly for high fliers); some to overseas, including USA (Harvard and UCLA) and Germany; roughly seven per cent take a gap year, a few to employment.

Money matters: Not a rich school but has increased bursary funding considerably since 2012. Means-tested bursaries available at 11, 13 and at sixth form regardless of previous school. Qualification criteria for bursaries on a sliding scale from ten to a hundred per cent based on need and typically if household income is less than £45,000. Honorary (ie no dosh) subject scholarships are awarded; music awards, including fee remission, available for tuition and instruments.

Remarks: Very much the big brother of the 3-18 triumvirate of St Peter's schools encompassing Clifton Pre-Prep and St Olave's junior school ('continuity, but difference' is the mantra here) and you get the impression that this is where it all becomes rather serious. If it were a car, we'd probably describe it as a Volvo, albeit a top of the range high performance 4WD version with sporty extras such as a ski rack and maybe a tow bar. It can accommodate the whole family and you can't doubt the quality, reliability and solidity of the product, it delivers, pretty much unfailingly, in all areas. There has been a change in the driving seat and that has brought about some interesting and enriching tweaks to the latest model, but at heart it remains essentially a Volvo – recognised as a pretty much faultless brand with a wide and fiercely loyal fan base.

St Swithun's School

Linked school: St Swithun's Junior School

Alresford Road, Winchester, Hampshire, SO21 1HA

- Pupils: 485 girls; 270 day, 115 weekly board, 100 full boarding
- Ages: 11–18 • C of E • Fees: Day £17,655; Boarding £28,290 pa
- Independent

Tel: 01962 835700
Email: admissions@stswithuns.com
Website: www.stswithuns.com

Headmistress: Since 2010, Ms Jane Gandee MA (forties). Read French and Spanish at Girton College, Cambridge. Had a brief spell as an accountant before moving into teaching. Has taught in a number of schools and was previously director of studies at the City of London School for Girls (qv).

A keen sportswoman, she represented Cambridge at athletics and cross-country and captained the university's women's football team. Married with three children. She intends 'to continue to build on extremely sound foundations and to listen to, and learn from, all members of the school community.'

Academic matters: Incredible exam results, up in the dizzying thin air at the top of the league tables. How a relatively unselective school like this one manages it is mysterious and must drive the London hothouses – with their exacting entry testing of pupils from the age of four – around the bend. Famed for its hotshot sciences (especially chemistry) and maths – so much so that some parents of bookworms have been hesitant to send their girls here. No need to worry, given that English is just as impressive, even if pursued by fewer girls. In this heartland of blue stocking education, it is nice to find lady-like subjects like food tech and art history offered at A level (though take-

up is low – cookery not seen as a golden ticket into Oxbridge). Compulsory GCSE subjects are English language and maths plus a foreign language and a science. Setting in maths and modern languages. French and German both studied to the end of year 9 when Spanish enters as an option. All take (only) nine GCSEs and no-one takes any early – a strategy that produces hardly any results below a B. In 2013, 82 per cent A*/A grades at GCSE. At A level, 94 per cent A*-B, 81 per cent A*/A.

Boarders have 6-8pm study period, with social time afterwards. The learning support department gives one-to-one help to some 50 girls who may have dyslexia or dyspraxia or just need help with planning their work. Hillcroft, the newest boarding house, is wheelchair accessible, as is most of the school (one girl currently uses a wheelchair).

2012 saw the launch of Stretch, a weekly academic enrichment programme for the entire school. Girls in L4-L5 follow a compulsory programme of activities such as astronomy, thinking skills, experimental art, discovering the news and the great egg challenge while the older girls will have a choice of courses including ethics and science, Socratic discussion and UK political issues.

Games, options, the arts: Plenty of lacrosse fields, tennis and netball courts, 25m swimming pool 'with Olympic springboard standard facilities' and a newly enlarged sports hall with gym upstairs. Currently extending the sports facilities to provide a dedicated grass athletics track and associated all-weather throwing and jumping areas, due for completion summer 2013. Hot on lacrosse – often dispatching arch rivals Downe House and Godolphin – and swimming and netball strong, but no hockey. Games follow a compulsory rota until GCSE years when choice kicks in including judo, fencing, and volleyball. Music high profile and high quality, with a range of orchestras, choirs, bands and ensembles. Over 70 per cent of pupils learn a musical instrument and 170 candidates are entered for external music exams each year. Senior choir sings evensong each term in the cathedral and tours overseas every other year. The performing arts centre provides a wonderful hub for music and drama in the school (and doubles as the venue for morning assembly). Drama studio backs on to the main stage and is used for lessons. Annual mega musical – much excitement on the day we visited as the watertight news embargo on choice of musical for the forthcoming year was lifted – not even the head knew!

Art very popular at GCSE, less so at A level, but fab results all round. Textiles (part of art and design) involved in a project with high street shop Accessorize. Brill cookery room – everyone does food tech for the first three years. There are also after-school clubs and a food hygiene certificate course, in addition to A level and GCSE work. DT – splendidly housed – holds its own at GCSE but only one girl did it for A level, two the year before. Our guides made a point of detouring to proudly point out the laser cutter. Overseas trips – Borneo was a destination last year plus skiing and battlefields trips to France, lacrosse players to Prague (!), classicists to Germany (!!). Eleven rather earnest sixth form societies, all with some fund-raising element, from Amnesty International to debating to Young Enterprise. Almost 150 girls take part in D of E. Extra-curricular clubs recently beefed up – now in excess of 50 different activities to all girls including debating, polo, karate and ballroom dancing to name but a few.

Background and atmosphere: Founded as Winchester High School in 1884 by Anna Bramston, daughter of the Dean of Winchester, who remained as school secretary for over 40 years. Changed its name to St Swithun's in 1927 and moved to the present 45 acre site in 1931. Vast, intimidating, red brick, Queen Anne style building with polished wood, long corridors and large windows – sends some parents off screaming before they even make it up the drive. Those who persevere will find smiling faces and some wonderful teaching beyond the imposing exterior. An 'intense footprint' said a teacher, describing the school's impressive buildings, all bunched in a cluster while the glassy games fields and grounds radiate outward, unbesmirched.

Has always been a 'local' school and weekly boarding for girls whose homes are within an hour's radius is where it really shines (St Swithun's started as a day school and only later tacked on boarding). 'It's so nice not to have guys around during the week – you can get on with your work and meet up at the weekends,' said one studious sixth former. 'I didn't want an isolated convent – I like it that our daughter could get into town, use her mobile phone and come home on weekends,' her mum concurred. Full boarders herded together in one house – mainly from overseas ('and one from Scotland,' explained our meticulous guide). Boarding houses we visited were very high quality and well kitted out with loos, showers and common rooms. But younger girls had curtains instead of doors (noisy?!) and there was an impersonal feeling, a bit like a Travelodge.

Pastoral care and discipline: Alcohol more of a problem than drugs (despite Winchester being the drugs capital of Wessex). It is allowed only at a few senior bashes, otherwise, 'if they are caught drinking in school I will send them home.' Not hugely pioneering when it comes to managing friendship group problems and other irritants of all-girl communities. However, its 'cluster groups' have been held up as a model by the Boarding Schools Association – small vertical groups of boarders representing the full age span who meet for suppers once a month. They plan the menu to a budget, do the shopping, cooking and eating, all with the eldest girls as the leaders. Girls do their own washing and mending – good preparation for life we think, although a few parents grumbled that boys are not expected to do the same at their schools.

Girls kept busy on weekdays. Lessons finish at 4.10pm with sport and activities thereafter, then prep. Sixth formers allowed into town two afternoons plus on weekends. Younger girls have more restricted access. In common with every other girls' school in the south-west of England, St Swithun's speaks of its 'links' with Winchester College (though St Swithun's definitely 'out-links' its rivals). The two schools work together on occasional plays, societies and musical endeavours, along with more informal social interaction. Activities at weekends tend to be sporadic – or as school prefers, 'specific to their needs'. All meals taken in the dining hall and girls report good food.

Pupils and parents: Not a place oozing with social cachet. Middle class, middle-of-the-road, Wessex girls with mostly professional parents. 'Our girls are not natural rebels or rule breakers.' Any of these will tend to leave after GCSEs for more free-spirited establishments. Girls not swamped by make up, Jack Wills or Ugg boots (though all are here).

Entrance: Entry at 11 and 13. Everyone must pass CE (whether from state, private, or school's own junior school) and produce a report from their previous head. Taster day in September or October where applicants take a one hour 'computer generated pre-test'. Staff repeatedly stress that the entrance requirements are not high. A few join the sixth form, generally with A grades in their chosen A level subjects.

Exit: About a quarter leave after GCSEs, bound for the local sixth form college or for other co-ed sixth forms. Almost all the others go on to university, mostly the old-established ones, with Oxbridge (eight in 2013), Bristol, Edinburgh, Durham and Exeter being the top destinations (in that order) over the past five years. Sciences unsurprisingly popular, but also classics.

Money matters: About one in five pupils has a bursary, an academic scholarship, sports scholarship or a music award (available at 11, 13 and 16). All scholarships are for up to 20 per cent of fees. Academic scholarships are based on the calibre of the applicant, rather than need. Music awards include free music lessons. School working to plump up a bursary fund to fight off Charity Commission bullies.

Remarks: Academic powerhouse taking in a relatively wide range of abilities, working its magic, and producing a shimmering set of academic results year after year. Not as scary as it looks, but still not the place for rebels or slackers. Change may be brewing with leadership in new hands. Weekly boarding specialists.

St Teresa's Effingham Senior School

Linked school: St Teresa's Effingham Nursery and Preparatory School

Effingham, Surrey, RH5 6ST

• Pupils: 310 girls, including 85 boarders • Ages: 11–18 • Roman Catholic but all faiths welcome • Fees: Day £14,685–£14,985; Boarding £23,715–£26,085 pa • Independent

Tel: 01372 452037
Email: a.charles@st-teresas.com
Website: www.st-teresas.com

Headmaster: Since 2012, Mr Michael Farmer, formerly head of Kilgraston School, Perthshire. His teaching career started at Godolphin School, Salisbury, progressing to assistant head at Headington School, Oxford in 1997 and appointed in 2003 as head of Kilgraston School which, in 2011, was named the UK Independent School of the Year. Married to Mary-Ann with two grown up children. Delighted to be appointed and looking forward to the challenge of leading 'a wonderful school in a beautiful location'.

Academic matters: The school is selective but not hugely so, priding itself on developing the whole girl. Girls of all academic abilities. Good and improved results from such a cross section: 74 per cent of A level grades A*-B, and 74 per cent A*-B at GCSE. Languages are strong – French, Latin, German, Spanish, Italian on offer and Japanese as an extra. Unanimous thumbs up from parents for the language teaching – 'a huge asset to the school'. Girls are setted in maths, French, science and humanities. Computers and interactive facilities used in the classroom in all subjects. Classrooms are large and colourful and the library offers a very wide range of books and resources. There is a cross-section of ages amongst the teaching staff. One SEN teacher on site full-time and one part-time. The girls are regularly assessed – parents have to pay extra for SEN support.

Games, options, the arts: Sports facilities aplenty. An indoor heated swimming pool complex and all-weather hockey pitch, hard tennis courts and a multi-purpose sports hall means that the girls are spoilt for choice. Strong in netball and hockey, says a mother. At least 50 per cent play an instrument and the school choirs beaver away preparing for a main concert every term with lots of other musical events, both informal and formal. There are 22 opportunities in the year for girls to perform musically and professional musicians are invited to perform to the music society. An impressive performing arts theatre hall – fully equipped with a 750 seat theatre, sound recording studio, two large interconnecting drama studios, dressing rooms and two music teaching rooms as well as five music practice suites. 'Much needed,' according to a satisfied mum. Photography, art and textiles are impressive. 'The girls produce work of

S

professional standard,' commented one enthusiastic mother and the artwork we saw was of gallery standard. Textiles, photography and small metals classes are popular – taught in a relaxed atmosphere with the radio playing in the background – you feel as if you are walking into a gallery or a workshop rather than a classroom. 'I can't even sew a button, my daughter can make dresses!' says a parent. School is constantly buzzing – 'there's always something going on' – with lots of clubs; even the astronomy and lifesaving clubs are popular.

Background and atmosphere: St Teresa's was founded in 1928 by the Religious Order of Christian Instruction on what was originally part of a manor site recorded in the Domesday Book. The present house, dating from 1799, is the centre of the senior school set in 48 acres of parkland – the small buildings where the classrooms are located and the gravelled walkways give the feeling of a small, self-contained town. Boarding girls comment that it is like 'a home away from home.' (Girls have the option to full board, weekly board or simply stay one night a week – useful for the odd nights when parents are short of baby-sitters). Full boarders are taken out to London, nearby Kingston or Guildford at the weekend. They certainly seem to enjoy their time. Boarding girls are very down to earth – older girls do a great job taking care of the younger ones. Boarding facilities are very clean, spacious and recently refurbished. A nice touch for those who board occasionally (eg once a week) – they get the same beds and do not have to play musical beds changing every time. Non-boarders say that 'sometimes we wish we were boarding' – day girls can be left till six or seven in the evening. The school has a pleasing, almost family atmosphere and environment. As one parent says, 'it has a feeling of old-style establishments.' Many new refurbishment projects and living accommodation is smarter, but it will always be a homely school rather than grand. And everyone is very approachable and friendly. 'Focused and happy' is the general feeling amongst parents.

Pastoral care and discipline: As one ex-pupil with a daughter at the school said, good pastoral care is one of the main reasons for choosing the school. Strong RC ethos based on 'the unique value of the individual,' but girls from all faiths are welcomed. Teaching staff are respected and liked. Discipline well-managed, structured, strict but fair. Drugs have not surfaced and the few smoking and bullying incidents are swiftly sorted. Parents are kept in close contact generally, and are encouraged to approach staff with any concerns.

Pupils and parents: A noteworthy number of pupils are daughters or even grand-daughters of ex-pupils: 'I went there, my mother went there, my daughter is there and hopefully, one day, her daughter will too.' Also popular with the Far Eastern community, and 15 per cent of the girls are from overseas. Pupils are smart, skirt lengths are decent, one or two unnatural blondes in the school but not enough to call the highlight brigade! Some experiment with fashionable hair styles and makeup in the sixth form but nothing too worrying. Local parents are a mixed bunch – professional mums and dads as well as first time buyers. The school seems sheltered from the growing 'Surrey Mums' syndrome – the atmosphere at sports days and school events is still quite relaxed with no obvious competition between the mothers.

Entrance: Many enter via the junior school after sitting the entrance examination in year 6, but a large number also come from other schools including Hoe Bridge, Halstead, Danes Hill, Downsend, Feltonfleet and Rowan, and from local state primaries. Tested in English, maths, science and VR – not too onerous. Increasing numbers of girls join at 16 for the sixth form. Special exam for entry from overseas.

Exit: Fewer, we're assured, now leave at 16 to sample co-ed independent schools, sixth forms or specialist colleges. Others finish their A levels and head for a variety of universities which include Bristol, LSE, York, Birmingham, Leeds, Warwick, Bath, Durham and one or two to Oxbridge. Girls are regularly offered unconditional places to Central St Martin's, Chelsea, Camberwell and all other colleges which make up the University of the Arts, London.

Money matters: Academic, music, sport, drama and art scholarships are available and can amount to 50 per cent of the fees. Good to see that tuition fees include lunch and before- and after-school care facilities.

Remarks: An ordered, friendly, all-round school with strong religious ethos and good pastoral care.

St Thomas More Catholic School

Croftdale Road, Blaydon-on-Tyne, Tyne and Wear, NE21 4BQ

• Pupils: 1,550; boys 740, girls 810 • Ages: 11–19 • Catholic • State

Tel: 01914 990111
Email: pellis@stthomasmore.org.uk
Website: www.stthomasmore.org.uk

Head Teacher: Since 2005, Mr Jonathan Parkinson (late forties) BSc physics (Leeds University) PGCE. Previously deputy head, assistant head, head of science, head of physics, all at St Thomas More. Previous schools: Carre's Grammar School, Sleaford; All Saints High School, Huddersfield. Positive, energetic and witty with easy but respectful relationship with pupils. Still makes time to teach, last year physics to year 11; this year sixth form psychology. Gets a buzz from 'seeing the lightbulbs go on in little brains, watching children grow and go out into the world as young adults and to know you have had an impact on them.'

Places emphasis on development of staff, looks for innovation and sees 'the teacher in the classroom as absolutely key' to pupil progress and keeping the school moving forward. Not driven by results. 'We do things here for the right reasons – the needs and abilities of the pupils, and our results grow from that', underpinned by 'great emphasis on creating a strong Christian nurturing environment.'

Regular early morning fitness regime in privately operated fitness suite in school; away from school a keen, but slow, runner. Loves Bach; grade 8 flautist but will re-take as he 'only scraped through'; runs own ceildh band.

Academic matters: In past awarded Technology College status (first in north east); Leading Edge School. One of first tranche of Teaching Schools, joined with Cardinal Hume Catholic School, St Mary's Catholic School and Newcastle University to form Northern Lights Teaching School Alliance with mission to, 'Illuminate, Innovate and Inspire'. Converted to Academy in February 2012.

Full A level and GCSE curriculum, along with GNVQ and BTECs offered and matched to pupil's ability. In 2013, over 60 per cent of A level grades were A*-B (a third A*/A) and large numbers of students following vocational courses attained distinction and merit grades. At GCSE or equivalent qualifications in 2013, 83 per cent 5+ A*-C grades including English and maths and 40 per cent of papers graded A*/A. Compared with national expectations, pupils leave the school achieving significantly higher grades than their levels of attainment on entry would suggest.

Eight form entry in year 7 offered a broad curriculum and pupils are set by ability in maths and English. Regarded as 'diagnostic year' with scope to alter through year as abilities change. From year 8 setting extended to science, humanities, technology and modern foreign languages. Tests every ten weeks throughout KS3; reports with grading on attainment and effort, targets set by pupils. A choice of route A, vocational, or route B, academic at KS4 and again in the sixth form. English Bacc recently introduced needing little change to curriculum since approx one-third of students achieve this qualification. Mathematics GCSE started in year 9.

Unusual timetable: two week rota with three lessons of one hundred minutes per day.This provides technology and science with required time and is seemingly popular with pupils though contrary to some contemporary research on effective learning.

Good careers advice and visiting professors from nearby university provide mock interviews for university entrants. Visits to colleges organised for Oxbridge students.

Games, options, the arts: Growing reputation for music, drama and dance. Abundance of bands, choirs, orchestras stems from compulsory instrument tuition from year 7. Pupils are allocated instruments – can cause some resentment because there's no choice. Team sports abound, with a list of county and national sporting honours. Cricket a strength, led by enthusiastic coach, indoor nets in sports hall which also offers usual range of indoor sports plus climbing wall. Playing fields but all-weather surface on wish list. Wide selection of clubs and societies – from sports to chess, Scrabble and hoola hooping; enjoys exchange/educational visits to French/German-speaking countries and outward bound-type weekends. Big school production annually: We Will Rock You last year, Grease this. In a school of this size pupils find participation, 'a good way to get to know others out of your year'.

Background and atmosphere: Catholic faith is strong in school, evidenced in worship, teaching of mutual respect and in charitable works. Head believes that Christian ethos binds children and staff and encourages all to give of their best. 'This feels like a community; happiness emanates from the classrooms, we have high standards and expectations of everyone, value manners, show respect and expect exemplary discipline'.

Situated in Blaydon, a former industrial area currently undergoing significant housing regeneration. Opened in 1967 as co-educational secondary modern, became comprehensive in 1987 and has doubled in size along the way to current roll. Buildings chart the school's history and growth spanning four decades with uninspiring frontage and narrow corridors of the early build necessitating rigorously enforced traffic movement between lessons. Sport England helped fund the sports hall/fitness room and library. Newly opened, self-financed humanities and English block is jewel in the crown for both staff and pupils. Airy, light classrooms with interactive whiteboard walls provide good teaching environment and wide corridors link all parts of the school.

Pastoral care and discipline: Pastoral system is bedrock of school. Pupils allocated to one of four houses in year 7 (following elder siblings) and each year group comprises two forms for each house, developing allegiance and competitive spirit. Competition ranges from sports to chess and the TV classic 'Countdown'. Houses mixed on gender and academic ability. Tutor groups stay the same until year 11 for continuity.

Pastoral system dedicated to ensuring each child feels secure, confident and valued. Programme ensures tutors look after social, emotional and academic needs. 'It is important that children enjoy school and our pastoral system helps ensure they do', says head. Target setting, supported by pastoral mentors, assists development. Strong on discipline and maintaining standards eg inflexible uniform policy, litter-picking duties. Good behaviour, manners and attitude to work are paramount. Merit system based on both academic and social achievement and contribution to the life of their house and the school. Certificates/head's commendation much sought after by pupils. Pupils look up to sixth formers and aspire to be one. Competition for head boy and head girl posts is stiff. Pupils taught respect for others and their school environment.

A school marches on its stomach so it's disappointing to hear that quality, portion size and price of food in the dining room seem to be a universal disappointment.

Pupils and parents: Bulk of children come from nine Catholic feeder schools, mainly in West Gateshead. Predominantly British white with some from other backgrounds. Comprehensive intake, above average KS2 results. Pupil/staff ratio 15:1. Seventy per cent stay for sixth form. 'Everyone here gets on really well and there are opportunities to get involved in everything, and we are encouraged to do so. I never thought I would say that I love coming to school, but I do.'

Entrance: Oversubscribed. Priority to Roman Catholic children from feeder schools, then those with siblings already at school; other Roman Catholics; other faiths. 'People come here partly because of our results but a lot is down to our reputation for setting high standards of work and behaviour.'

Exit: Majority of A level students go to university. Three to Oxbridge in 2013.

Remarks: A school true to its Christian foundation, pupils leave well prepared for life outside the schools gates and flourish in an environment that promotes mutual respect, high expectation and strong citizenship. Great emphasis on teaching the teachers pays dividends. Consistently good academic results though these are not the driver here. Pupils work hard, play hard and are clearly very proud of their school. Advice to lapsed Catholics: baptise your children, attend Sunday worship and move into the catchment area.

Sale Grammar School

Marsland Road, Sale, Cheshire, M33 3NH

• Pupils: 1250, boys and girls, including 350 in sixth form • Ages: 11-18 mixed • Non-denominational • State

Tel: 01619 733217
Email: office@salegrammar.co.uk
Website: www.salegrammar.co.uk

Headteacher: Since 2010, Mr Mark Smallwood BEd MA PGDip NPQH (early 50s). Studied at Manchester and Lancaster Universities (physics), taught in a number of state schools in the North West and for three years in the Bahamas; previously head of Fearns Community Sports College in Lancs. Teaches one lesson a week (IT, general studies). Married to a primary school teacher; three children – two at university, one in year 6. A Manchester United supporter and plays the tuba in a community wind band. Approachable, balanced, good sense of humour, well liked by children and parents, 'He's pragmatic, listens well, is fair and firm when necessary', relates in a natural, easy way with pupils, very visible around school.

Academic matters: High performing specialist school in visual art, science and maths. Consistently strong A level results: 2013 91 per cent A*-B, 55 per cent A*/A – no marked gender divide. Twenty-four subjects including philosophy, psychology, sociology, business studies, economics, politics, PE, performing arts, AQA Bacc, EPQ (perspectives on science), but no ICT; will run courses for very small numbers. Particularly successful geography, maths, physics, art, business studies, sociology; big numbers for separate sciences, English, maths, history, psychology.

Generally strong at GCSE – 55 per cent A*/A in 2013 – especially separate sciences, French, geography, art, expressive arts. Spanish and French IGCSE, plus possibility of psychology; most achieve eight/nine at C or above; girls do better at very top grades. All do ECDL computer qualification in year 9; ASDAN (personal and social skills for life) taken via PSHE – good idea to give an extra qualification for what is usually an unexamined course.

Classes 20-30 at Key Stage 4, 5 -16 at A level. Lots of extension activities by all departments and pupils encouraged to go beyond syllabus in homework (called 'extension studies' to promote this). Active learning week at end of summer term for year 7s (arts), 8s (humanities), 9s (camping), 10s (work experience), 12s (eg more work experience). Many opportunities for the most able students, eg university language enrichment course, poetry slam competition. Teachers praised by pupils we met as always ready to help – individual or revision sessions outside the classroom. Tiptop ICT facilities – home access to school network, masses of PCs and laptops, much use of electronic white boards, by staff and students.

Can accommodate all SENs provided entrance exam passed – in-class support if needed, outside for, eg spelling; SENco qualified to test for special exam considerations.

Games, options, the arts: Trad gym, good size sports hall with climbing wall, own Astro, uses off-site facilities for swimming and hockey. Usual sports including rugby, plus (successful) girls' football, lacrosse, indoor rowing, table tennis, trampolining, taekwondo; national and county players. Sports leadership qualification; sports tours to Cape Town, Malta.

Various ensembles, choirs and bands – wide range of instruments taught and music played; all year 7s take part in Christmas concert, spread over two nights. Annual school play is a big musical, eg Oliver! (girl Mr Bumble), West Side Story. Limited facilities, new performing arts centre on wish list. Plays performed in school hall; the drama studio lacks stage lighting and rehearsal space doubles as sixth form relaxation area (furnished, oddly, with a complete set of Hansards 1970-2000 donated by local MP). Also dance (boys too) and LAMDA. New music and PE facilities.

Outstanding visual art – excellent work in various media on display around school (year 12 artists successful in national competition). Input from professional artists and latest technology (iPads); ceramics area – own kiln. Interesting community projects, eg providing installations for Manchester hospitals. All take GCSE technology – choice of resistant materials, electronics, textiles (particularly strong results), food tech and graphics: not too influenced by gender (though we did see only one girl in an otherwise all male electronics class).

Good range of extra curricular clubs – debating, media team (produces high quality newsletter and monthly bulletins), science: medical/engineering/astronomy, chess, Spanish film, YE, expressive arts; community involvement as part of enrichment programme for sixth. International school status – works with twinned schools in South Africa; World Challenge to South America and Namibia; cultural exchanges with South Africa; annual trips to Spain and France. Plenty of careers advice.

Background and atmosphere: Pleasant red brick original building with interestingly designed, spacious, modern additions. Light, wide corridors, spiral staircases and brightly coloured, fresh decoration – all well maintained. Much purple (school colour) throughout – fetching silver and purple ties, screensavers, sofas, pale purple brickwork... Attractive LRC primarily for sixth but shared with other years – lots of PCs but not many reference books: sign of these digital days. Sixth form

also housed in Claremont Centre in town, 15-20 minute walk away (shuttlebus service), where some subjects are taught and assemblies held – new sixth form centre under construction. Cheerful, light, modern canteen – pupils speak well of food. We liked the Key Stage 3 quad with four wooden shelters and metal benches for packed lunch eaters. Lack of room for expansion is the main problem – existing space, eg a car park, has to be used cannily for any new build.

Formed from amalgamation of Sale Girls' and Boys' Grammar Schools 25 years ago. Outstanding last full Ofsted, 2006, endorsed by 2010 interim assessment. An academy trust grammar – partnerships with University Hospital South Manchester, LIME (arts in health charity), Findel plc, Manchester Metropolitan University, the Manchester Museum of Science and Industry. These provide expertise and resources used in educational and community projects (community engagement award for primary school and family learning work) and activities, as well as work experience opportunities for pupils and professional development for teachers.

Atmosphere is orderly and purposeful – a quiet hum and sensible movement between lessons. Head boy and girl elected by pupils – no prefects. Four houses (called Halls) with officers; activities led by sixth formers. Each house has own council, occasionally assembling for whole school council – seen as effective. House points for achievements, including community contributions and charity activities – end of year 'thank you days' for pupils who've accumulated the most points feature fun activities such as BMX riding, laser tag, cupcake decorating. 'Strong community spirit', praised a parent, which is developed in children 'as soon as they arrive'.

Pastoral care and discipline: Pastoral care a strength – traditional structure with form tutors, heads of progress and learning (ie heads of year) and key stage managers. Separate student services reception desk; counselling provided by professionals plus mentoring of younger pupils by years 11-13. Year 7s settle in easily, thanks to general friendliness and three day outward bound residential in their first term. Bullying very rare and would be dealt with effectively. 'Sensible, responsible and respectful' behaviour code; strict on not using mobiles in school; exclusions very unusual.

Pupils and parents: Pupils from over 50 feeder schools, mostly Trafford. Middle class, but not all well off; 70 per cent white British; lively, involved in lessons, happy with school, especially sporting and extra curricular activities. Regular communication with parents via newsletters, emails, questionnaires; lots of parental support. School and public buses plus Brooklands Metro station a short walk away.

Entrance: Takes around 180 for year 7 – top 40 per cent of ability range; over subscribed – 1600 for 180 places. Tests early October of year 6 in VR, NVR and maths; apply to school from mid April of year 5 to take exam; also have to complete Trafford LA common application form. Over subscription criteria: looked after children; priority postcodes (may use proximity to school measured by straight line); then for those from outside this area rank order in tests, again possibly using proximity.

Sixth form: five GCSEs including two As, three Bs, at least C in English and maths; takes 40 external candidates (always over subscribed).

Exit: Post GCSE 10-15 per cent leave for FE colleges for non traditional subjects. Eighty to 90 per cent of year 13s to university, mainly in the north west, high proportion of Russell Group – Manchester, Sheffield, Leeds, Durham popular, one to five to Oxbridge; others to jobs, eg Royal Bank of Scotland apprentices.

Remarks: High achieving without being highly pressurised, with learning opportunities going beyond exam syllabuses. Aims to provide a blend of tradition –academic rigour and high expectations, with innovation – up to date technology and opportunities for the development of the whole child – and makes a very good job of it.

Seaford College

Linked school: Seaford College Prep School, Wilberforce House

Lavington Park, Petworth, West Sussex, GU28 0NB

- Pupils: 610 boys and girls; 143 boarders and 468 day pupils
- Ages: 7–18 • C of E • Fees: Juniors £8,505– £18,900; Seniors £17,850–£27,900 pa • Independent

Tel: 01798 867392
Email: jmackay@seaford.org
Website: www.seaford.org

Headmaster: Since September 2013, John Green (forties). Previously the school's deputy. Educated at Campion School in Hornchurch, Essex, then studied sports science at Cardiff, followed by a master's business and sports science, plus advanced diploma in economics from the OU. A first class rugby player, he played rugby for the England U16s, U19s and U23s and captained England students for three years before playing professionally for the Saracens for five years.

Was director of sport at Barry Boys' School, then moved to Ardingly College, where he was deputy head of the prep and director of sport and PE. After two years as director of sport at Seaford College, he became head of the upper sixth and a housemaster at Hurstpierpoint, progressing to deputy head. He and his wife Sian have three children.

Academic matters: Non-selective, with 40 per cent SEN, but still a mainstream school – one which does dyslexia teaching better than others. No longer seen as 'a collecting house for kids who couldn't get in elsewhere'. GCSE A*/A 24 per cent and 33 per cent at A*/A at A level, but school's ethos is definitely not about being top of the league tables – 'That's like measuring driving ability by the power of the car: the driver of a Ferrari may do no better job that than of a family saloon – he just gets more attention!'

Campus is arranged by subject area marked with smart blue and gold signs. Wireless network throughout means everyone's laptop can be online everywhere – Skyping home especially useful for international boarders; also two ICT suites with 20 desktops. History has a passionate and very popular HoD, maths and science taught in beautiful new labs/classrooms with interactive whiteboards and scope for exciting experiments. Bright murals painted on the walls of the language department and popular school trips.

Sixth form size is creeping up to full capacity; entrance guidelines are 45 points at GCSE but no stipulation as to whether any need to be C or above – this means places for all who work hard. Crafty three for two offer on GCSE retakes encourages application for A levels.

Learning support unit housed in a central flint cottage which it shares with careers – definitely not a broom cupboard under the stairs. Eight staff deal with mainly dyslexics and dyspraxics on a release basis – pupils are never taken out of core subjects or ones they particularly enjoy. One-to-one class each week and each teacher has been trained to deal with dyslexics within class and invites comments from LSU on improving delivery.

Games, options, the arts: The waving golf flags mark this out as a sporty school from the moment you drive in the gates. Hockey (the head often umpires) is the top game, but rugby, golf, tennis, cricket, squash, athletics and swimming are all popular and successful. External membership of the Golf Academy; the rugby coach, an ex-Scottish International, has excellent contacts with inspiring guest speakers/coaches; and the football coach is an Aston Villa scout as well as a classicist! The small outdoor swimming pool is due to be replaced by a new complex. Competitors whose chosen sports can't be practised on campus are encouraged, with recent success stories in riding, sailing, polo, judo and skiing – some representing England at a school level.

Woodwork, DT, ceramics, textiles, photography and fine art are all taught in the purpose-built arts faculty around a central gallery used for temporary exhibitions – plenty to encourage individual talent and the evidence is on display. Art trips to London galleries and to foundation exhibitions in the summer.

Graphics (now with 20 new machines) is the only option currently not available up to AS, Inventor software has been introduced recently. Electric cars have been in the Greenpower races at Goodwood for the past three years, with steadily increasing handicaps to keep Seaford's success in check. Pupils' imaginations caught by this competition and even those not directly involved in construction pop in for an update from the DT department.

The music rooms are based around a courtyard set apart from the main school – this is covered over for events such as the sixth form prom. The choir practises for its performances (Eaton Square, Chichester Cathedral, St Mary's Shoreham etc) both here and in chapel. House music encourages competition for excellence internally and inspiring organ teachers have groomed at least two pupils for scholarships at Oxford.

School production, Seaford Stock (like Woodstock...) and a sixth form play each year (the hall has a stage at one end and floor to ceiling windows on either side), with the Festival Theatre in nearby Chichester providing inspiration.

Background and atmosphere: Main building is a gracious Georgian house set in 400 acres with stunning views of the South Downs – if you arrive on a sunny afternoon you'll definitely want your child to grow up here. A campus feel because of distinct departments and boarding houses, but the local flint has been re-used in some of the new buildings so much is in keeping. The chapel was mentioned in the Doomsday Book but, more recently, assemblies held there at least twice a week, as well as regular eucharists and evensongs. In the summer everyone is outside (football on the terrace behind the Mansion) as much as possible, but big common rooms for each year provide table football and tennis, pool and lounging space when the clocks go back.

Wilberforce, the junior school, has its own dorms (10-15 per cent weekly boarding), classrooms, library and a different sitting for mealtimes to avoid the little ones being intimidated. Gap students help look after the dorms and preps here and the house parents are sensible and experienced. The children seem happy, busy and communicative. Pupils and parents appreciate the enthusiasm and support provided by the staff – 60 per cent of them live on site and a fair few have children in the school, many of whom have held positions of responsibility recently.

Younger girls sleep upstairs in the Mansion House – as ever, their rooms are more personal than those of the boys, the new furniture with lockable drawers is particularly welcome. The '60s boys' boarding houses are functional; a new one is under construction. Most popular feature is the upper sixth's common-room with its bar (home brewed beer is planned...) and full size snooker table. The boys' houses appear to run on well-founded trust in the pupils, which makes for a happy environment. Girls need permission to relax next to the fireplace in the lower sixth boys' area, but boys are not allowed vice versa. Everyone now flexi or weekly boards, except those in the sixth who have the option to full board.

Pastoral care and discipline: Each child changes tutor every year (15-20 per group) until they share a personal mentor in the upper sixth with just five others. Prep sessions are less supervised the further up the school they rise. Good manners and consideration for others expected – very much three strikes and you're out. Bullying – letters home, warning of suspension next time around. Out for serial wickedness – drugs usually equals out. Beautiful grounds for hiding behind a bush and smoking, but apparently mostly the foreign students who do this. Science department is using a new breathalyser to demonstrate the levels of carbon monoxide in a smoker's exhalation, hoping education 'will hammer home the message better than short-term disciplinary action'.

Pupils and parents: Lots of local farming families and those who have created their own businesses, a few lawyers, doctors and dentists. Many choose to send all their children here, confident that the school will educate a wide range of academic abilities. Fund-raising support for the school through tables at the summer ball etc. Most boarders are weekly, a handful of full from Asia and Eastern Europe, a few British expats. Old boys include a more recent winner of the same Daily Mail award as Dyson, music scholars to Oxford and the de Haan brothers.

Entrance: After trial day and ability tests. Lots from Haslemere schools, also a handful of preps – Windlesham, Amesbury, Prebendal, Westbourne House, Dorset House, Great Ballard. About 30 per cent internally from Wilberforce. New entries at sixth form are often hard workers who were strained out of other sixth forms because of range of GCSE grades.

Exit: Around half leave after GCSEs, some to take more vocational courses at sixth form college. Practically everyone who goes through sixth form goes on to university, two or three to Oxbridge (good links with Jesus, Oxford, through music), also Exeter, Bristol, Warwick, Loughborough, Durham, UCL and Imperial. Good relationship with selection boards – since this is a non-selective school, if the children get great grades, they've done so through hard work.

Money matters: Small scholarships (maximum discount £500 per annum) at 11+ – choral and music only. At 13+ and 16+ in art, music, sport, academic and DT. Bursaries available through means-testing.

Remarks: The happiness of the children is this school's greatest strength – they're great fun to be around; academic successes are celebrated but certainly not the only ones. The staff are really approachable – parents say, 'A visit to the school can feel like a social event!' Everyone seems to be appreciative of opportunities it affords and snob value is not an issue.

Sedbergh School

Linked school: Casterton, Sedbergh Preparatory School

Malim Lodge, Sedbergh, Cumbria, LA10 5HG

- Pupils: 500 pupils (315 boys and 185 girls) • Ages: 13–18 • C of E
- Fees: Day £21,519; Boarding £29,202 pa • Independent

Tel: 01539 620535
Email: enquiries@sedberghschool.org
Website: www.sedberghschool.org

Head Master: Since 2010, Mr Andrew Fleck MA (late forties), educated at Marlborough College, read geology at Nottingham and has an MA in education from Sussex. Member of HMC Professional Development Committee, a governor of Westville House Preparatory School and a Fellow of the Royal Geographical Society.

Urbane, charming and appears, as one parent put it, 'very comfortable in his own skin'. Seems to be going down well with parents although a very different personality to predecessor, cricket aficionado 'King Chris' Hirst (as he was affectionately known), who reigned for the previous 15 years. Committed to the Sedbergh values of a 'properly balanced education', providing pupils with the 'vision, aspirations and leadership skills to succeed in a global labour market' and determined to dispel the public perception that only sports rule here.

Married to Anne, who runs a software development company working primarily in agro-technology and with whom he cycled the deserts of central Iceland and the northern Sahara on a tandem! Interests include sailing, canoeing and cycling – canoed around Ireland, Newfoundland, Japan and Arctic Norway to the Russian border and cycled the east/west European border. Has twin daughters, both at Sedbergh.

Academic matters: In 2013, nearly 30 per cent A*/A grades at A level and nearly 20 per cent A* grades at GCSE. Not bad for a school with a comprehensive intake, that welcomes all to stay for sixth form and a policy of entering all pupils for exams; very good value-added. Average class size 15 with a ceiling of 24. Pupils and parents speak of 'caring, dedicated and helpful staff, committed to the children'. Gifted and talented are stretched and learning support (primarily for dyslexia) is provided in the classroom or by individual tuition in a separate building known as The Shack. Head admits more to do in this provision and it is 'work in progress'.

Broad curriculum, French plus German or Spanish on offer for year 9 (overseas visits but no exchange programme). Drama recently introduced at GCSE and jewellery design at GCSE and AS level. Many classrooms, language labs and laboratories have been given a face lift, extensive art facilities and good DT workshops, embracing new IT investment. Investment and drive to upgrade IT and integrate it fully throughout the curriculum apparent. Well-stocked departmental libraries and shelves of fiction in the boarding houses – does this deter pupils from making the main library a centre of learning and research? Housed in a super conversion of Georgian building on the site of Lupton's original school, the library has been revamped recently, but its primary use seems as a venue for debate, lectures and academic house competitions.

Games, options, the arts: Although renowned for its sporting prowess (34 sporting activities on offer) with many pupils winning representative honours, especially in rugby and shooting, a lot more on offer here. However sport is timetabled five times a week, adjusted winter and summer to make best use of daylight. All you would expect in facilities and more (even a heated cricket square) set in idyllic surroundings. Also famous for its Wilson Run – a 10-mile fell race open to ages 16+. All pupils participate in CCF in year 9 but involvement is optional after that, though many continue.

The hills here are certainly alive with the sound of music! Some 350 pupils take individual lessons up to grade 8 and diploma, with representation in national ensembles. Fizzing director has developed choral singing to a crescendo, together with classic chamber groups and orchestra, swing, jazz, rock and CCF bands. Excellent, spacious and recently updated music school with state-of-the-art composing and recording facilities, plus the Thornely Studio, a £1 million performance hall with sprung floors.

Lots of performance opportunities for music and drama at home and away with regular trips and tours abroad. Range of clubs and societies available, from mountain biking to debating and specialist lectures in science, medicine and music. Flourishing D of E award scheme.

Background and atmosphere: Founded in 1525 by Roger Lupton, a provost of Eton. School lies in the centre of a small, picturesque town surrounded by magnificent fells, in the heart of the splendid (if often wet and cold) Yorkshire Dales National Park but only a short drive from the M6. Departments housed in a number of well-spaced, separate buildings, the eight boarding houses widely dispersed through campus and town, giving pupils plenty of daily exercise as they move through the school day. No wonder a bicycle for transit around campus is a prefect privilege.

Pivotal to the success of the school are the keen house loyalty (quickly assumed by new entrants) and the level of care pupils receive there. Each pupil is assigned to a house where they live, eat all meals, including lunch, collectively, when manners and conversation are nurtured. Excellent food, lots of choice, special diets catered for. Girls' boarding houses are bright, modern and well furnished; all the boys' boarding houses have been refurbished in recent years. One parent commented that her son 'enjoys it so much he never wants to come home'.

Girls arrived in 2001 and with the opening of a third girls' boarding house in 2013 they now account for nearly 40 per cent of the school population. They have made their mark as a significant, vibrant and impressive part of the school. Few shrinking violets here, matching the boys for healthy inter-house rivalry, success in extra-curricular, whilst helping the academic results along the way. Make sure to check out The Sedberghian, the school magazine, for information on every facet of the place and the pupils who populate it.

Sedburgh merged with Casterton School in 2013. The merged junior school has moved to the Casterton site (and is now known as Casterton, Sedbergh Preparatory School), whilst the merged senior school, named Sedbergh School, remains on this site.

Pastoral care and discipline: Very effective house system with strong, popular and caring housemasters and mistresses heading up dedicated teams who have good relationships with the pupils. Rules recognised by pupils and parents as firm but fair, well thought out and communicated clearly. Structured and well-thought-out sanctions and rewards system. Bullying is rare – the ethos in houses militates against it.

Pupils given freedom around town, a safe bet when you consider you're never far from someone connected to the school. Bar available at weekends to sixth formers, school encourages a sensible attitude to alcohol. Controlled access between boys' and girls' houses but over-familiar relationships between boys and girls discouraged.

Pupils and parents: A complete mix – mostly northern professionals but increasingly from Scotland and the South. Traditionally a school for land-owners, industrialists and farmers' sons (Wordsworth was a parent), but now an eclectic mix including Forces, expats and a few foreigners. Pupils are confident, sparky and generally, though not universally, sporty, very grounded, have a practical approach and are not afraid to get their hands dirty. They might call a spade a spade, but willingness to help others, loyalty and compassion are values universally to the fore. A very happy school – lots of laughter in and out of lessons. Still not a place for the timid or loner but anyone else, especially those who appreciate the fantastic surroundings and teamwork, will love it here.

Old boys include Simon Beaufoy (Full Monty), Wills Carling and Greenwood, Lord Bingham (Lord Chief Justice), James Wilby, Sir Jock Slater (First Sea Lord) Sir Christopher Bland (chairman BT), Robert Napier (chief exec of Met Office, ex chief exec WWF and chairman of governors).

Entrance: For most, CE is the normal route, others applying in years 9-11 sit exams in English and maths. A current school report is required. Sixth form requires a minimum of five GCSEs at C or above. Main feeder is Casterton, Sedbergh Preparatory School, but significant proportion come from prep schools across the north of England and beyond.

Exit: Mostly to university, northern popular, a number of Scottish; degree choice spread across science, business and arts. Steady trickle to Oxbridge (traditionally strong links with Cambridge). Several opt for a gap year having secured their university place. Handful embark on vocational courses or careers at 18, trickle leave at 16.

Money matters: A number of scholarships for entry at years 9, 10 and 12: academic, all-round, art, DT, music sport and drama. Awards vary but may be up to half fees. Index-linked major scholarships – in exceptional circumstances. Exhibitions and bursaries also available.

Remarks: Has retained its traditional values and ethos (and market) whilst responding to the demands of the 21st century. Renowned as a formidable force on the sports field, it seeks to embed that gold standard throughout the school. Pupils, whether sporty, academic, musical or arty, are well catered for and seem to love it, although a love of fresh air and the great outdoors is a distinct advantage. Opportunities are provided in a happy and caring environment to create a 'can do' philosophy in pupils. Numbers suggest that pupils and their parents very much approve. We will watch with interest the results of its merger with Casterton School.

Seven Kings High School

Ley Street, Ilford, Essex, IG2 7BT

- Pupils: 1,400 boys and girls, all day • Ages: 11–18 • Non–denom
- State

Tel: 020 8554 8935
Email: enquiries@skhs.net
Website: www.skhs.net

Head Teacher: Since 2008, Ms Tracy Smith BA PGCE (forties). Educated at St Martin's School, Brentwood. Read history and sociology at Warwick, PGCE at Goldsmith's College, London, then taught at Barking Abbey School for seven years. Moved to Seven Kings as head of sixth form in 1995, then deputy to former head Sir Alan Steer, and a key player in the team which transformed this east London school into one of the country's most successful comprehensives. Before taking over the headship, she led a project on Assessment for Learning carried out by King's College, Cambridge and the Institute of Education, and continues to sit on a number of influential committees, including the SSAT London Headteachers' Steering Group. Energetic, level-headed and good-humoured, she's undoubtedly a safe pair of hands to keep this school top of the form. Married (to the vice principal of an FE College), with two teenage children. A keen West Ham supporter, she spends down time watching football, going to the theatre, hill walking and travelling.

Academic matters: If academic matters are uppermost in your schooling choice, then you have very little to fret about at Seven Kings. Despite its 'very average' intake, Seven Kings seems to sail effortlessly to the top of the league tables. Eighty-three per cent of GCSE candidates in 2013 achieved 5+ A*-C grades including English and maths. The hugely oversubscribed sixth form produced equally dazzling results – 64 per cent A*/B grades and 32 per cent A*/A. Teaching is vibrant and committed – 'the quality of the teaching manages to challenge every student,'

S

said one parent – and teacher-pupils relationships are strong. 'Teachers know you well and know how you are feeling,' said one boy. 'You can ask them anything.'

Success is down to monitoring, tracking and a can-do approach, and certainly no one here gets lost at the back. 'You won't find a pupil we haven't spoken to in the past three weeks about their learning,' says the head. 'They don't give us grades, they give us comments,' said one student. 'They tell you what you can do to improve and what you've already done well. They know what you need to do to get better.' Every student is also given two one-to-one interviews about academic progress. 'We track, interview and talk.' 'This isn't an exam factory,' says the head, 'but we do know the syllabus and the exam requirements.' And not only can they distinguish their Pre-Us from their A levels, they know how to prioritise a UCAS form, with a large chunk of the high-powered sixth form going on to all the country's top universities.

Three languages on offer – French, Spanish and Mandarin – with well over half the students studying at least one language to GCSE. Science newly energised by a 'skills-based' approach, and bangs and smells part of the fabric of school life. 'Students now say science is their favourite subject,' says the head. 'There are about 50 experiments going a day.' After-school clubs include the academic as well as the just for fun, providing support with homework and coursework.

Games, options, the arts: Art, DT and PE all highly valued and popular. 'Our kids do two hours PE a week and even on days when they don't have sport, we make sure they get off their bottoms,' says the deputy. Football, cricket, netball, rugby, running and athletics all core to the curriculum. Rugby. One basketball superstar recently won a scholarship to a top US university. Music and drama are popular options with plenty on offer for aspiring performers. Plenty of other extra-curricular activities are available for spiritual, social and cultural nourishment such as Amnesty International, chess, model airplanes, astronomy and a film club.

Background and atmosphere: The school began life as a girls' grammar in the 1930s, and some remaining original features give a feel of the inter-war years, with an expansive spread of low rise brick buildings and a Betjemanesque assembly hall ideal for listening to the clock ticking away the exam minutes. Inside the tall-windowed classrooms, the focus is on learning, helped by full range of thoroughly modern additions, from a new lecture theatre and a spacious, glass entrance hall to a wheelchair park and interactive whiteboards. The motto is 'friendship, excellence, opportunity' which most pupils and parents believe the school more than delivers.'The kids know we really care about them,' says the head. Seven Kings is particularly noted for its SEN provision and has a national reputation as a centre of excellence for disabled children. As well as the specially adapted entrance and well-equipped medical centre, classrooms are accessible by wheelchair and there is well-staffed, highly-skilled SEN department.

Pastoral care and discipline: Seven Kings serves a neighbourhood that is certainly on the less affluent side of the rich-poor divide, with the social problems and deprivation typical of many parts of urban London. But despite its relatively stark surrounding streets, the school itself is a haven of purposeful calm. Discipline is assumed, corridors are quiet, classes orderly. That's not to say, of course, that every child's an angel. 'We have 1500 hormonal kids,' says the head. 'Of course we have discipline problems.' But few that aren't sorted out rapidly. 'We haven't excluded anyone permanently since I've been head.' Short sharp shocks for fighting or cheeking the teacher. 'Expectations are very clear, as are sanctions, but we try and apply them sensitively. This isn't a zero-tolerance environment.' Positive peer pressure is a definite help keeping potential bad boys on the straight

and narrow. 'Some kids are definitely from challenging homes and we do our best to keep them going.' No-one from years 7-11 let off site at breaks or lunchtimes. Proactive pastoral and timetabling used constructively. 'How you timetable the school day has a massive impact on behaviour,' says the deputy.

Pupils and parents: This is a neighbourhood comprehensive and more than three-quarters of the pupils come from Indian, Pakistani or Bangladeshi backgrounds. Parents here want their children to do well and give their full backing to the education on offer, with nearly all seats filled at parents' evenings. They aren't, however, a cake-baking, raffle-holding crowd and the school has no PTA. The kids themselves support their parents' aspirations, work hard and behave well. 'The kids are bright and ambitious,' says the head.

Entrance: The school is extremely popular and over-subscribed with 1800 eager candidates queuing for the 180 year 7 places with a waiting list well into the hundreds. 'Fortunately, that's all done by the local authority,' says the head. Strict catchment rules apply, though those with statements automatically go to the top of the admissions ladder. Around 80 per cent go through to the sixth form, which attracts a massive number of outside applications every year – those successful have predicted GCSE grades that meet the entrance criteria for their chosen A level subjects.

Exit: Around half to Russell Group universities; rest to other good universities or destinations such as internships in the City.

Remarks: An inspiring place, where any parent could feel confident their child's needs will be met and where every child will reach or exceed expectations.

Sevenoaks School

High Street, Sevenoaks, Kent, TN13 1HU

- Pupils: 1,025 boys and girls, including 345 boarders • Ages: 11–18
- Non-denom • Fees: Day £19,287–£21,897; Boarding £30,798–£33,408 pa • Independent

Tel: 01732 455133
Email: regist@sevenoaksschool.org
Website: www.sevenoaksschool.org

Head: Since 2002, Mrs Katy Ricks MA (fiftyish). Educated at Camden School for Girls (to which she attributes her feistiness) and Balliol, where she took a first in English. Taught at Latymer Upper, King Edward's Birmingham and St Paul's Girls, was head of English at St Edward's Oxford and deputy head of Highgate. An impeccable, co-educational, academic and quality school cv and one which made her, possibly, uniquely qualified for this job. And that's just what's on paper. Vivacious, articulate, deliciously enthusiastic and hugely appreciative of her luck in having charge of such a school, her pleasure in it all is palpable and infectious. We canvassed masses of parents and heard not a word against her. 'My children think she is wonderful'…'she comes to everything'…'she speaks brilliantly'…'she's a brilliant ambassador for the school'… 'she's very thoughtful'. 'She's an outstanding head,' an old hand claimed, 'and in a different league.' She, likewise, pays tribute to her staff and her pupils. 'People here think all the time about what they are doing. I have an incredibly clever staff – both in their intellectual expertise and passion for their subject and in their relationship skills. They talk to pupils and parents like proper people – which, of course, they are!' We know what she means. Wisely, she sees the recruitment of top-notch staff as her main responsibility and she pays great attention to the 'feel' of the school. 'I do really believe very strongly that environment shapes character.' The school feels smiley – and she is a very smiley head. Her pride and excitement in the school permeates the place. We felt it in everyone we met.

Academic matters: Sevenoaks is best known for pioneering the IB and for being a strongly international school – not just in its intake but in its outlook. All take IGCSEs in many subjects though GCSE survives in Ancient Greek, Russian and some arts subjects. Everyone does a MFL, everyone takes all three separate sciences. And, in the sixth form, when everyone takes the IB, the language options are exceptional – seven are on offer as part of the IB curriculum and tuition is available in at least eight more for native speakers and others. Greek and Latin thrive, economics, psychology, philosophy, history – med and mod – it's all here. The results are terrific – in 2013, the average point score per student was more than 39 points. At (I)GCSE in 2013, 22 pupils gained 10+ subjects with all A* grades. Over 85 per cent of exams taken got A*/A. That is pretty amazing. You won't find Sevenoaks in league tables – the IB/IGCSE combination make them meaningless. Virtually all teaching praised, virtually universally. Staff seen as assiduous – 'they're concerned, caring, tough'. A seriously impressive library – would grace an Oxford college – 30,000 books and 70+ periodicals – good blend, here as everywhere, of old and new – the august portraits of Edwardian and Victorian headmasters overlooking the gallery of PCs. Up to 10 per cent on Learning Support register with, mostly mild, dyslexia/dyspraxia/dysgraphia. Some with ADHD and visual impairment. Wheelchairs not a problem. Everyone has to have excellent English though school will support EAL if necessary but with no more than one weekly lesson.

Games, options, the arts: Huge amounts of space, all the impressive facilities you'd expect including sports hall, pool, dance studio, indoor climbing wall et al. The usual sports are compulsory but range of super options includes trampolining, judo, yoga and fencing. Regarded as the top sailing school in the country and outstanding success in both tennis and shooting. And both sexes play football. Sport no longer the Sevenoaks Cinderella – impressive wins in athletics, hockey and rugby and numerous individual successes and county colours.

2010 performing arts centre surely unrivalled in its Pamoja (Swahili for 'togetherness') Hall which seats 450. Built according to sustainable principles from locally sourced wood, matched by the pale gold fabric seats and heated via solar panels, with water from a bore hole, it is vast, light and provides a venue of international quality. The stage can accommodate a full orchestra and the two grand pianos we spotted there looked, from the back of the auditorium, like dolls' house instruments. Building also full of practice rooms, a recital room, recording studios, theatre – you name it – and it feels good. And productions to match – arts, visual arts, theatre and musical events to high standards. Virtually all involved in something arty – a large number learn at least one instrument and ensembles for everything. Not too much pupil art on display as you go round – could do with more, perhaps, though head's extraordinary minimalist study has a vast, meticulous, charcoal representation of the huge tree outside her vast window. Stunning range of awards and prizes in arts, public speaking and representation in National Youth Orch/Theatre etc. They pop up everywhere there's a competition in which to shine and it's their intellectual and expressive skills which most impress. 'Fantastic' outside speakers who are 'really inspiring – especially when they are Old Sennockians'. Internationalism translates into trips abroad – less of the glam skiing and snorkeling and more of the DT trip to Toyota's assembly line in Japan and Model United nations in The Hague.

Background and atmosphere: You'd pass it without noticing as you drive out of sleepy Sevenoaks on the road to Tonbridge.

You might notice the sign to Knole (think Sackvilles, Sackville-West and sofas) on your left but you wouldn't realise that the path to Knole bisects the 70 acre site of Sevenoaks School and that the glories of that Jacobean pile and park abut the playing fields and are a considerable resource to the school. The school's foundation is almost as old as that of its illustrious neighbour. And in some respects it eclipses it. Sevenoaks (1432) is the oldest lay school in the UK and this liberal, unallied ethos underpins the exuberance of its intellectual and social life today. There is no one imposing main school house but a collection of 33 buildings from the last 250-odd years – the old and new all generously conceived, stylish and attractive in their own ways and somehow blending to make a welcoming gesamtwerk. The ambience is much assisted by the ubiquitous greenery – gardens, imaginative planting and the disposition of the houses hither and yon. The head's house – perhaps the least inspired architecturally – is plumb centre and reflects the current incumbent's involvement in everything.

A proper co-educational school. Boarding provision is good everywhere and exceptional in the sixth – the international students are housed in separate buildings – the boys in a state-of-the-art building – a stunning design with views and provision to match – and the girls in a Queen Anne period house with comparable facilities. We were struck by the zest with which pupils from everywhere share information about their homes and countries – a true global community, literally in the making. Years 7 and 8 housed in Lambardes – much-loved, as is the current housemaster – 'he's ex-army – excellent fun but he knows how to keep discipline,' a parent enthused. 'Even at this stage, there are enough boarders for you to find a friend. We have a battle to get our children to come home at weekends, though; sometimes it's so full-on at school they like to just flop.' Much praise, too, for the way younger and older pupils mix and collaborate. Some houses eg Park Grange a delight and with a big and enviable, communal kitchen in which 'everyone gets to know everyone'. This school understands about sofas, carpets and big TVs. Huge dining room with vast choice of truly tempting food. One pupil who vouchsafed little in answer to our questions, broke out with, 'I'm so pleased I came here – the food is so good!'

Pastoral care and discipline: Few problems here. No house system. Sound and well-established pastoral system in years and boarding houses. You stay in the same boarding house from 13-18. No drugs incidents in recent years, no exclusions, few minor misdemeanours mostly sorted by detentions. No-one wants to be kicked out of this place. No drinking allowed anywhere and boarders under 16 not allowed to go to day pupils' parties if alcohol is offered. Nonetheless, lots of integration of day and boarding pupils and those who can bear to forgo all the weekend activities often invited home by locals. Universal feeling among parents that you are expected to be independent, take responsibility for yourself and if you forget something or don't do your homework, no-one will cosset, prompt or mollycoddle you. 'It's a very grown-up school – it expects you to be grown-up,' we were told. 'Sometimes,' another parent felt, 'the boarders are just left to get on with it.' But this seen, again, as part of the self-reliance the school builds and not as a deterrent. 'Strongly secular' ethos, as one parent described it, 'very hands-off, no spoon-feeding.' However, one international sixth former, clearly ecstatic at his good fortune, breathed, 'it's the support – it's flawless – after two years I still haven't found anything wrong'.

Pupils and parents: A truly – and uniquely – global clientele. Possibly nowhere other than our elite universities accommodates such an international crème de la intellectual crème, blending them so successfully, and creating such a rich and enriching mix of cultures. Around a quarter from overseas – but from a bigger range of home countries than any other school – 35 or so – no cliques or sects here, though Germans and Italians are relatively numerous. The majority of overseas students join for the sixth form and are given an unbeatable education in the roundest and broadest sense. The rest from the UK – and two-thirds are day pupils, reflecting the strong local commitment to the school, despite strong competition from Kent grammars. And local can mean right up into London and into Surrey. Pupils are open, unpretentious, clever, thoughtful and hugely appreciative of their luck in being here. Parents describe them as independent, confident but not arrogant. Also as individuals, 'they don't go into tweed jackets and stay in them for the rest of their lives'. Parents likewise, and mostly just grateful for their children's chances here. Some feel that home-school communication could be better but this, as everywhere, varies from house to house and teacher to teacher.

Entrance: Around 190 apply for the 65 places in year 7. Candidates sit the school's own exam, are interviewed and prep/primary reports are considered. The odds against getting a place are not as high as they look as there is strong competition at this stage from the Kent grammars, and many who get places here will opt for the state sector. At 13+, around 180 apply for 80 places – again exam – or CE – interview and report. Lots of feeders including Holmewood House, New Beacon, Hazelwood, Windlesham, Dulwich Prep. Stronger competition for the sixth form which really is an elite institution. 400 apply for 80 places. Required with the application are a personal statement, three exams in their likely 'higher' level subjects and school references. All must have taken the school's pre-test/interview – this can, if needed, in some cases, be conducted in the applicant's home country or on Skype. 'We want people with above average academic ability, strong co-curricular interests and an enquiring spirit,' says head, 'someone who will enjoy their time here.'

Exit: A trickle leave after GCSEs, mostly for overseas schools or those offering A levels. Truly impressive in the quality and diversity of the post-A level courses and institutions. 2013 saw 31 to Oxbridge. Large numbers to Bath, Bristol, UCL, Durham and the LSE. Many overseas, including Ivy Leagues or close to. And studying everything from aeronautics to zoology. Notable alumni include musicians Emma Johnson, Mathew Best; journos and writers Plum Sykes, Olivia Cole; academics Francis Everitt, Jonathan Bate, Oliver Taplin; sportsmen Chris Tavare, Anthony Roques, Dan Caprice; and in the arts Daniel Day Lewis, Charlie Higson, Simon Starling, Paul Greengrass, Geoffrey Streatfeild, Emma Hope; also spook Jonathan Evans (DG of M15). To say nothing of William Caxton.

Money matters: Not a rich school but offers bursaries up to 100 per cent of the day fee following means-testing. Scholarships worth up to 20 per cent of day fee awarded for excellence in academics, sport, music, art and drama. One big sports scholarship on offer.

Remarks: Tough for any university not to be an anti-climax after Sevenoaks. Hard to imagine a Sennockian not being an asset to any uni they grace. 'It feels,' one sixth former confided, 'as if I'm an apprentice and the whole school is one big teacher.'

Sexey's School – A Church of England Academy

Cole Road, Bruton, Somerset, BA10 0DF

• Pupils: 480 boys and girls; 215 boarders (majority board in years 7–11) • Ages: 11–18 • C of E • Fees: Boarding £8,700 pa; Day free • State

Tel: 01749 813393
Email: admissions@sexeys.somerset.sch.uk
Website: www.sexeys.somerset.sch.uk

Headmaster: Since 2013, Irfan Latif (forties). Previously deputy head (academic) at Bedford School. Educated at Emanuel School, then King's College, London, where he read chemistry. Started his teaching career at Haberdashers' Aske's School for Boys and then moved to Whitgift School, where he was senior housemaster. Became director of science at St Benedict's School, where he continued his love of rowing on the Thames.

Regularly lectures at the Royal Institution of Great Britain, is a fellow of the Royal Society of Chemistry and also a magistrate. He is a sports enthusiast and keen traveller and adventurer – he recently led expeditions to the Everest base camp, Venezuela and the Red Sea. His wife Jocelyn is a biology teacher and they have two young daughters.

Academic matters: Consistently good A level (62 per cent A*/B grades and nearly 29 per cent A*/A grades in 2013) and GCSE results (nearly 70 per cent of pupils got 5+ A*-C grades including English and maths; 25 per cent of grades A*/A in 2013). Amongst best value-added results in Somerset. 25 subjects on offer at AS, slightly fewer at A2. Specialist humanities college (quite a battle to gain this status) with new facilities and initiatives in these subject areas. Recent results indicate strengths in art, DT, maths, sciences, sociology and business studies. Outstanding GCSE results in history may presage things to come. Head keen on AQA baccalaureate (extended sixth form project) involving two hours a week spent outside main taught curriculum. Buzz word is 'personalisation' – means taking time from year 7 upwards to consider each pupil's needs. Relatively small classes helps and fortnightly timetable with five hour-long lessons per day (doubles where required for science etc) reduces chaotic lesson changes. Flexibility offered in DT choices and we were pleased to see food technology carried through to AS level. Religious studies and citizenship figure at both GCSE and AS level. Good level of ICT with smartboards throughout school; many students use own laptops.

Clued-up learning support provided for around 10 per cent of pupils. Improved base also acts as sanctuary for more vulnerable. Expanded team with four LSAs and teaching assistants attached to specific pupils. Sexey's claims for special needs funding are probably hampered because of its relatively affluent social profile but SENCo maintains system is fair. Pupils screened (CATs) on entry; voluntary support given to pupils until 5.00pm. Some pupils receive three or four hour-long sessions a fortnight. Lots of computer games (eg Number/Word shark) to help. 'It helps being such a happy school,' we were told. Less able placed on IFP (individual flexiblility programme): involves small number who spend time at FE college in years 10 and 11. Assistant head very focused on getting gifted pupils in all year groups onto relevant extra courses and activities – about half are on school's NAGTY register. School also benefits from being link school for Exeter university teacher training programme.

Games, options, the arts: Promotes sport (house rivalry includes sport, music and drama); enthusiastic participation in main games and teams with fixtures against state and independent schools and success in various inter-school competitions. Representation at county level in cricket, rugby, athletics and badminton. Karting team have reached national finals two years running; equestrian team now competing in inter-school events. Ideal terrain for cross-country; heated indoor swimming pool; good pitches, no Astroturf but easy access to Bruton girls' facility; sports hall and four hard tennis courts which double up for netball.

Strong on drama: 'new HoD has done wonders,' say parents. Good studio space for smaller productions plus traditional hall for bigger performances. Music department has come on 'by leaps and bounds' also under new HoD – 130 pupils currently play instruments; boys have joined school choir (featured recently in BBC 2 series) – who has transposed concerts into a jazz café format – 'goes down well,' we were told. Former head's house provides a good atmosphere for music-making: large classroom, recording studio and individual practice rooms on three floors. Good uptake at GCSE but small numbers to A level. Performance groups include choir, wind band and soul band. Separate, cramped two storey art department (new dual purpose art/DT area in new building will alleviate this) achieves success at all levels in a suitably bohemian ambience.

Wide range of extra-curricular activities and after-school learning. Range of visits abroad: Paris, Berlin and Egypt plus trips to plays, House of Commons etc to broaden horizons. Established link with German school through annual exchange – with visitors dividing time between boarding houses and host families. Public speaking, Ten Tors challenge and D of E (four currently doing gold) all well supported. Some 20-30 pupils participate as cadets in ACF from 13 onwards. Eco School bronze award. Good level of charity fund-raising through variety of student-led initiatives.

Background and atmosphere: Named after Hugh Sexey, who rose to become auditor to Elizabeth 1 and James 1. He established Sexey's Hospital, which still provides care in Bruton for 30 elderly people. In 1889, trustees founded a trade school under guidance of Hon Henry Hobhouse, who drafted the 1902 Education Act. Unremarkable original buildings stand behind an attractive small garden; front entrance leads into a pleasantly modernised reception area. Sexey's has metamorphosed through boys' grammar, voluntary controlled, grant maintained (when school became cash-rich and improved facilities) to voluntary aided. Went co-ed in early 80s, took its first 30 day pupils into year 7 in 2003. We encountered a lingering resentment from some Bruton villagers that day places remain so difficult to obtain, but head is walking this political tightrope with some skill. No day versus boarding issue as far as pupils we spoke to were concerned. School is a 'victim of its own success locally,' said one mother.

Expansion over years has resulted in a mishmash of architectural styles squeezed into narrow site between main road and cliff edge, but the glorious countryside that bounds up on three sides makes up for its shortcomings. Some overdue developments – eg junior science labs and smart design/ humanities centre spelled end of shabby huts and mobile classrooms: a vast improvement all round. Head aims to create a new social area for lower school pupils on site of former DT workshop.

One-way system through buildings helps ease congestion at lesson changes. Relatively small but workmanlike library with study carrels on mezzanine floor for independent learners. Sixth formers 'feel comfortable' wearing their own clothes and mostly heed dress code. 'Some stuffiness over dress rules for younger pupils,' thought one mother, who then endorsed the school's insistence on good manners. Attractive, purpose-built sixth form centre provides necessary social focus for Sexey's large body of 16-18 year olds – includes small IT suite plus tutorial offices (eg for careers/HE advice); plenty of space to relax and snack bar facilities available throughout day.

Pastoral care and discipline: Emphasis on boarding ethos influences whole school; vertical tutor groups (20 minutes' tutorial time each morning) led by heads of houses plus head of lower school responsible for years 7-11. Head keen to participate in Pathfinder scheme to offer boarding places to children in care of social services, but little uptake by latter to date. Code of conduct set out in school diary exhorts courtesy and consideration. Pupils generally understand school's uncompromising line – few need to be hauled over the coals it seems. Staff trained in restorative justice – provides forum for all parties to explain their feelings and to express regret. Only sixth formers allowed mobile phones during school day but not in lessons. Girl we spoke to had lost her father whilst on tour of duty in Iraq: she could not praise the school enough for the consideration and support she had received through a difficult and upsetting time of her life.

Chapel part of new building; school pays more than lip service to its Christian foundation – witness appointment of a lively Christian youth worker to raise profile of this side of school life. Some lovely houseparents and assistants (strengthened by post A level Aussie gappers and two foreign language assistants) help to make boarding at Sexey's highly enjoyable. Minimum of four staff resident every night. Boarding houses vary in layout, tidiness and social provision; we were impressed by fantastic set-up for years 11-13: range of facilities allowing students to socialise or retreat as required. Young staff (average age is 35) though 19 teachers have served over 10 years. Some sixth form prefects attached to each of lower school houses plus peer mentoring scheme – younger pupils really appreciate this. Students' common-room also put to good effect during day as a lecture hall. Good medical arrangements with 24 hour cover by qualified staff and adequate sick bay. Head aims to add to staff accommodation and to rationalise boarding for younger pupils so they no longer have to come and go beside busy Wincanton road.

Traditional approach – leaders (head prefers this term to prefects) first chosen from year 11 pupils and then responsibilities shared higher up. Head boy and girl plus heads of house retain importance. School has 'healthy plus' status; meal arrangements work well in modern dining area and 'food has improved,' say pupils. We saw good choices on offer at lunch: salads as well as hot veggie and meat dishes. Sittings at supper work on house basis; day pupils can also sign up for tea.

Pupils and parents: Generally bright eyed, cooperative and well turned out – blazers and ties in lower school for first two terms then polo shirts in summer. Sixth formers provide leadership and want to do well; organise own social programme. Easy relationships between staff and students as well as between year groups. Active school council and environment committee. More boys than girls but not patriarchal. Annual meeting (two in year 10) with parents before exeats; loads of email contact at all levels between staff and parents. Former pupils include Alex Tew (creator of the Million Dollar website; BBC wildlife film maker, James Brickell, John Bryant – consultant editor of The Daily Mail – and broadcaster, the late Ned Sherrin.

Entrance: Parents can visit year round – usually on Tuesdays. Separate interviews with head and head of boarding. Head will ask if child wants to board and refuse a place if they don't – he places priority on child's welfare and happiness. Not much hope of a day place at 11+ if you live more than a mile away – blame Somerset CC not the school. Some further afield may qualify on church or sibling grounds. Popular choice for boarding within county – can usually accommodate more boy boarders at 11+ than apply; some girls usually turned away – plans to increase accommodation for them. Good number of army families and navy from RNAS base at Yeovilton. Large transfer from other Somerset comps for sixth form plus some from independents. Minimum GCSE requirements spelled out in prospectus. Interviews for all applicants. School operates two

S

minibuses to pick up students in addition to those who come by other means.

Exit: Small number leave at 16+ to vocational courses; one of the broadest portfolios of university destinations we've seen in terms of spread of courses and variety of institutions. Leavers destinations in 2013 included King's College, Birmingham, Cardiff, Manchester, Durham, Bristol, Plymouth, Oxford Brookes and the Royal Veterinary College. One or two a year to Oxbridge.

Money matters: Boarding fees only for British passport holders and EU citizens.

Remarks: Look no further for value for money: all the advantages of boarding in a small school without the enormous price tag or social pretentiousness. Since admitting day pupils from year 7 has tidied itself up and broadened its appeal. Perennially popular at sixth form level. Lots of good teaching here and a genuine sense of community.

Shapwick School

Linked school: Shapwick Prep School

Shapwick Manor, Shapwick, Bridgwater, Somerset, TA7 9NJ

• Pupils: 105; 80 boys and 25 girls; including 75 boarders • Ages: 8–19 • Non-denom • Fees: Day £14,406–£17,028; Boarding £21,123–£24,468 pa • Independent

Tel: 01458 210384
Email: office@shapwickschool.com
Website: www.shapwickschool.com

Headmaster: Since 2013, Martin Lee BA PGCE. Head of the senior school as well as the prep. 'The school has over many years succeeded in delivering the national curriculum to students who might otherwise fail in a mainstream setting,' he told us. 'I believe my main role is creating a safe supportive teaching and learning environment, where our students respond with creativity and hard work.' Sees the key elements at Shapwick as 'strong values, highly skilled, experienced teachers, an embedded therapeutic programme, excellent teacher/student relationships, motivated students and supportive parents' and says he sees his job as 'more climate control and less command and control.'

Academic matters: Percentage of pupils achieving five or more GCSEs at grade C or above has risen from 40 to 69 per cent over last four years and was 60 per cent in 2012. A tremendous achievement with so many statemented SpLD pupils – eight per cent above the national average. Figures including maths and English are less impressive and have actually worsened over the same period, though pupils are entered in years 9 or 10 for maths if they are ready to achieve grade C or better. GCSE English remains the battleground for these pupils, and recent reductions in proportion of coursework in the syllabus (with a corresponding increase in functional skills and technical accuracy) have made things even more difficult for dyslexics. A good reason for staying here beyond 16 is to have a second or third crack at GCSE English – with some success, it seems. No setting in English throughout school ensures mixed literary abilities though 'word attack' (spelling) groups are set. CReSTeD Category A (the highest level of provision) for the last ten years.

Many pupils receive occupational and speech and language therapy. 'Parents are glad when they hear that there is something we can fix,' explained guardian angel and senior therapist, Cynthia. Health Professions Council (subsumed RCSLT with whom Shapwick was only UK school to have accreditation) 'has already praised school's degree of ownership of language problems,' she adds. Tip top therapy centre is very much at core of school's success: three speech and language plus three occupational therapists. THRASS picture chart used throughout the school to reinforce spelling. Lots of cross-curricular work and encouragement of joined-up thinking. SCAEP (social competence enhancement) introduces pupils to problem-solving and negotiating skills. Emphasis given to improving short-term memory. Tremendous range of help in public examinations: pupils often able to request amanuensis they know and virtually all receive extra help of some kind.

Pupils take core science in year 10 and additional science in year 11. Most take four of five optional GCSE subjects: resistant materials technology combines with product design and engineering to provide two GCSEs. Surprisingly, no food technology, but geography, drama, photography and art all do exceedingly well with 80 per cent of grades at B or above. Lots of ICT and most pupils have own laptops provided by LAs. Maths taken 18 months early – 50 per cent achieve grade C or above. Traditional boarding timetable: nine 35 minute lessons per weekday, two supervised preps and no escape from lessons on Saturday mornings.

Until 20 years ago, post-16 students simply stayed on for re-takes or moved away to sixth form colleges. Without continued specialist support, even those who had done brilliantly at GCSE floundered or panicked and fled – 'crash and burn' in SEN-speak. Scheme between Bridgwater College and Shapwick has created a dyslexia-friendly sixth form, which enables pupils to have all the advantages of the wide choices offered for A level and GNVQ by a large college without losing the multi-sensory teaching and speech and language therapy back at their familiar base where they still spend two days a week. Learning to get the correct bus and find their way round Bridgwater prepares them for life in the world outside Shapwick.

Games, options, the arts: Sport compulsory for all until sixth form. County level players in badminton, athletics and rugby. Semi-finalists at ISA rugby sevens tournament. Walled garden has been converted to provide floodlit, all-weather surface. More than adequate sports hall is well used with extra facilities (including swimming) available at Strode College in nearby Street. Teams play state and private schools. D of E generates much enthusiasm and bronze awards. Annual ski trip to France combines junior and senior schools; improves co-ordination, listening, confidence, high level organisation while they learn to bum-board, snow board and ski. Recent art trips have included to Egypt and Normandy.

Stunningly lively art studio run by charismatic HoD who masterminds summer arts festival – local artists workshopping tapestry, painting, willow-weaving etc. Pottery and photography particularly strong. Drum, guitar and keyboard taught to a handful but no music classes in senior school as 1:1 tuition has been found to work better. Pupils showcase talent at end of year concert. Loads of activities (from potholing to go-karting) everyday after lessons. Ten Tors challenge and D of E ever popular. Fleet of five minibuses to shuttle pupils between outlying houses and Manor. Year 10 have work experience at end of year; good careers database and links; mock employment interviews for year 11.

Background and atmosphere: School motto 'The same road by different steps' says it all. The sense of relief at having gained a place here amongst these dyslexic pupils is almost palpable – 'I have to pinch myself to be sure I'm here,' said one. One teacher said pupils 'were a pleasure to be with and a pleasure to teach.' Staff are hugely experienced and many come from state sector.

Shapwick Manor, previously owned by Lord Vestey, is the hub of the school and dates from 16th century. Fifteenth

S

century dovecote sits rotundly on front lawn. Tuscan-style stables have been converted into therapy centre but retain their unique external appearance. Shared foundation with Millfield – remained in ownership of Atkinson family until 2008 when it passed to Kedleston UK, who currently own four specialist schools in UK. No town distractions here to distract pupils from work – school sits comfortably in this quiet, pretty village. Has retained former Millfield model of outlying boarding houses including The Lakes (currently houses 24 boys) in Meare and sixth formers on prep school site in Burtle. Originally a boys' prep school, has grown into a co-ed senior with an expanding sixth form (about 50 per cent stay beyond 16). Classrooms and laboratories (biology was the largest and pleasantest we saw) are scattered around split site with DT centre in old village school. Pleasant dining area: food given thumbs up by pupils.

Pastoral care and discipline: Tutor groups based on three houses. Mentoring system for incoming year nine pupils works well. School council meets regularly with senior management. Small boarding houses run by houseparents (some even cook for pupils at weekends). Games room beside sports hall provides on-site space for relaxation with pool tables and easy chairs. Some year 11 pupils act as prefects and have separate room in the Manor. Staff bring a new meaning to the word dedication – many have family members and children who have suffered with dyslexia or dyspraxia, so their compassion and zeal does not stop when the bell goes. School offers parents opportunity of up to 12 meetings a year with staff and 'we can ring any member of staff at any time,' said one mother. Strong parental involvement contributes to its success. Discipline is firm but fair with well-established procedures for bullying (virtually none here) or drugs which rarely have to be activated.

Pupils and parents: All pupils are dyslexic/dyspraxic – come from all over UK and a few overseas. Many arrive feeling crushed but soon begin to flourish. Uniform and the routine of boarding come as a shock for many – 'none of our pupils are natural boarders,' says Jon Whittock, 'but they generally cope better with boarding than their parents.' Percentage of girls has crept up and they seem to fit in well. School prides itself on close contact with parents. Summer Diary has replaced newsletter and is published annually to illustrate breadth of activity. One mother told us, 'the difference it makes to our whole family's life is incredible.' For day pupils, another parent said, 'it's no problem now getting them to school.'

Entrance: One third of younger pupils either have or are in process of seeking LA financial support. Process usually takes up to 18 months; nearly all applications from state schools pupils go to tribunal and can involve costs up to £10K (though occasionally more). About one half of pupils are privately funded. School offers 'taster' days or even 'taster weeks'. Open days generally spread over Friday and Saturday and include opportunity for applicants to be assessed to ascertain level of need. No admissions, apart from lower sixth, allowed after first term of year 10.

Exit: About 50 per cent stay into sixth; remainder go mainly to variety of FE colleges.

Money matters: Parents pay for trips and uniform but everything else is included in fees.

Remarks: Parents full of praise: 'Staff are miracle workers,' says one. 'Our son is a different child,' confirms another. No doubting benefit for dyslexic boys and girls whose self-confidence grows by leaps and bounds here. We encountered a staggering volume of positive testimonials from parents past and present who had given up hope for their children until they discovered Shapwick.

Sheffield High School

Linked school: Sheffield High Junior School

10 Rutland Park, Sheffield, South Yorkshire, S10 2PE

• Pupils: 780 girls; all day • Ages: 4–18 • Non-denom
• Fees: £10,926 pa • Independent

Tel: 01142 660324
Email: enquiries@she.gdst.net
Website: www.sheffieldhighschool.org.uk

Headmistress: Since 2004, Mrs Valerie Dunsford BA PGCE NPQH (fiftyish), educated at Huddersfield High School and Manchester University (French and Italian). Previously taught at Ryburn Valley High School, Benfield School, Newcastle, and Durham High School for Girls (deputy head). Husband, Stephen, is a teacher; two adult daughters, who both attended Sheffield High. Approachable and unassuming; very committed to developing extensive partnership projects with local primary and secondary maintained schools – the school recently received an Independent Schools Award, for the third time, for the best independent/maintained school collaboration in recognition of years of innovative work; ISI inspector; adept at raising bursary funds from various educational trusts; emotionally astute – 'our girls need educating in how to cope with failure'. Soon gets to know girls individually when they enter the school.

Academic matters: Consistently very strong – its value added score is in the top five per cent nationally. At A level 76 per cent A*/B, 53 per cent all A/A* in 2013. Wide range of options including geology; maths and sciences very popular; especially good results in art and design, sciences, maths, English and geography; will run subjects for just one or two girls. AQA Bacc well established; links with the two Sheffield universities; successful in various academic competitions to national level.

GCSE also very strong and consistent across the board: 97 per cent A*-C; 67 per cent A*/A in 2013. Languages are a particular feature of the school, which offers Russian (A-level only) and Greek and can also provide teaching in Chinese, Persian, Arabic and Italian. At key stage 3 all do three separate sciences, two modern foreign languages (German and Spanish as well as French) and Latin; ethics lessons for year 9. Average class sizes: 22 for years 7-9, 18 for years 10-11 and eight in the sixth.

Very well resourced: has Becta ICT mark and ICT Quality Mark – plenty of well-designed IT suites; one class of year 7s is trialling use of iPod Touches in lessons; extensive VLE, which proved its worth when the school was closed for three days owing to snow. The last ISI report praised the standard of teaching, development of independent learning and positive relationships between girls and between girls and teachers; regular subject clinics for extra informal support; several girls and parents expressed appreciation of how helpful the teachers are; regular subject clinics for extra informal support. A more thorough policy for the gifted and talented now – year 10s onwards have an extension work booklet; classwork has been developed and an option of doing an extended project at the end of year 9.

Very good learning support, under the leadership of the qualified, warm head of pastoral care – all girls are screened for dyslexia in year 7 and again in year 9 (a charge for individual lessons from an outside specialist, but this will become free soon); mild autism, ADHD and other learning difficulties can be managed; they would do their best to accommodate physical disabilities, but much of the school isn't 'wheelchair friendly' – though the sixth form block is fully equipped for the disabled. Girls who would struggle with the standard ten GCSEs do fewer, allowing time for extra individual or small group support; EAL support also available.

Games, options, the arts: As befits the first girls' school in the country to have its own gym, sports are outstanding, recognised in a 2011 trophy for outstanding sporting success (having eight teams in national finals for five sports and being national champions in three) and the Daily Telegraph/School Sport Matters award for the best independent school in the UK for sport; tours to New Zealand, Fiji, China, Barbados, Dubai; sports leadership award popular. PE Quality Mark with distinction awarded in 2013.

Has Artsmark Gold. Much music: performances in the community and more trips abroad; joint sixth form choir with a local, mainly boys independent school; a parent thought the standard of the classical music ensembles could be improved (the school demurs) but praised the concert band. Now has its own stage, in a hall, though not a purpose built theatre – standard choice of plays and musicals but, unusually, year 13s direct and design year 7 and 8 productions; LAMDA exams and dance popular. Some stunning art in a wide range of media – has received a Good Schools Guide award for the top AS results for art and design nationally and enjoyed success in national competitions. Technology has advanced: lots of imaginative key stage 3 work on display; year 9s have a half day session on cookery at the Sheffield College of FE and the sixth get one, to prepare for university (girls would like food technology to be available at the school). Interesting creative writing in the school magazine, High Times, with some well-written, unusually long articles on activities.

Over 50 clubs – even knitting; success in business enterprise, debating, film making and poetry competitions; Go4it award for 'the encouragement of positive risk-taking, enterprise, initiative and a can-do attitude'; off timetable days for years 7-9 to develop problem-solving, teamwork and leadership skills; D of E popular. Year councils and a school council – seen as an effective vehicle for changes; the Kitchen Cabinet meets with the catering manager. Much eco activity – all forms have an eco representative, various eco awards. Large sums of money are raised for a wide range of charities – a school in Bangladesh is supported and old textiles and computers are given to schools in Kenya. Many other academic and cultural links with schools in Africa, India, China and the USA as well as Europe, and an exotic range of trips including a summer school at a university in China, Peru, the Galapagos Islands, Iceland – recent British Council international school award.

Several opportunities for the sixth to take on responsibilities (all year 12s become prefects) by running clubs for the younger girls; working with staff to improve subject teaching; training as peer educators in sex and relationship issues for years 5 and 8, in conjunction with a local state school and Sheffield University; helping in local state primaries or the school's own junior section; running conversation classes for asylum seekers and refugees in the community. Strong careers education – links with local industry and commerce provide a broad range of work experience opportunities.

Background and atmosphere: Founded in 1878 by the Girls' Day School Trust, in Broomhill, Sheffield, near to the university. The original Victorian building dates from 1884 – most of the mansions in the road have since been acquired and the modern additions blend in well, apart from the 1960/70s ones. The extremely well-stocked and attractive library also houses an ICT and careers area; art, technology and science areas have recently been extended, and the much-improved sixth form accommodation – small, intimate classrooms looking out onto part of the gardens, lots of modern pine furniture – is a great draw. We were very taken with the two common rooms, decorated according to the girls' specifications in various shades of red, pink and purple, with glamorous large light shades, and the Pink Room, for study/relaxation, with pink and chrome bar stools and tables and cooking facilities (sixth formers can also go out of school for lunch). New year 11 social area too with common room and kitchen facilities.

The latest ISI report praises the 'warm, stimulating and happy environment', supported by the girls we spoke to: 'The people are lovely; coming here [for year 12] is the best thing I've ever done – it's like a second home', 'It's easy to make friends if you're new', 'There's a strong community spirit', 'You're free to be yourself'. The uniform is green or navy plaid skirts and blue jumpers – home clothes for the sixth.

School won the Independent School Award in both 2010 and 2011 for the Best Independent-Maintained Schools Collaboration. In 2012 they received their third Independent School Award in succession – the only school to achieve this – for community links.

Pastoral care and discipline: Good policies for behaviour (referring to staff as well as girls) and bullying (not seen as a problem). The school is well aware of the kind of emotional difficulties very able and ambitious girls can suffer from and provides a full-time nurse plus a counsellor, who comes in one day a week, as well as liaising with external support services and holding evenings on teen issues for parents. Also a regular happiness questionnaire with input from the school council, now online, enabling identification of girls with problems. Parents and girls feel concerns are handled promptly and well. Year 7s have most of their lessons in rooms on one corridor, to help them adjust gradually to the school's size; sixth form prefects assist with years 7-8 and the house system allows younger girls to get support from older ones. Sixth form tutor groups formed by combining self-selecting friendship groups.

Pupils and parents: Ethnically (15 per cent EAL, with 40 languages spoken at home), socially and economically diverse – a large number of professional/self-employed. From Sheffield, South Yorkshire, North Nottinghamshire, North Derbyshire; half from the junior school, half from state primary and other prep schools. About 15 join the sixth from outside. Girls present as articulate, confident, grounded, ambitious and appreciative of what the school offers them.

Parents find the staff approachable and accessible and the school responsive to concerns and suggestions – regular contact via newsletters, forums and a very informative website. Girls have lifelong access to the 50,000 strong GDST alumnae network, which helps them with work experience, careers advice and gap year funding.

Old pupils: AS Byatt, Margaret Drabble, Angela Knight (CEO Energy UK), Deborah Ann Barham (comedienne).

Entrance: Year 7: test in English and maths similar to KS2 Sats, taken by all; year 8-11: age-appropriate tests in maths and English; well above average ability standard needed. Sixth form: seven GCSEs A*-C with at least a B in subjects to be taken at A level.

Exit: About 20 per cent leave post-GCSE for boarding schools, coeducational state and independent schools or Sheffield College for practical courses.

Sixth form leavers depart for a wide range of universities (two to Oxbridge in 2013) and subjects, particularly medicine, dentistry, veterinary sciences, science; also politics, economics, law, psychology, art and design and performing arts.

Money matters: About 15-20 per cent have means-tested bursaries or academic scholarships. Year 7 scholarships awarded on basis of entrance exam; bursaries for girls in the top 50 per cent, up to full fees; HSBC scholarship for children from a state primary. Sixth form scholarships awarded in individual subjects; Ogden Trust scholarship for state school students taking science and maths A levels and physics at university – up to full fees. Four HSBC scholarships awarded annually.

Fifteen per cent discount for third and fourth children at the school; ten per cent loyalty discount for sixth form girls if they have been at the school for ten years.

Remarks: The only all-through independent school for girls in Sheffield, offering exceptionally high levels of academic and extra-curricular opportunities in a very supportive and responsive environment – perhaps not so suitable for the less ambitious and conformist, though.

Sherborne Girls School

Bradford Road, Sherborne, Dorset, DT9 3QN

- Pupils: 440 girls; most board, 30 day • Ages: 11–18 • C of E
- Fees: Boarding £24,150–£29,940; Day £17,685–£21,750 pa
- Independent

Tel: 01935 812245
Email: enquiry@sherborne.com
Website: www.sherborne.com

Headmistress: Since 2006, Mrs Jenny Dwyer BEd (late forties) formerly head of Prior's Field. Educated at Bradford Girls' Grammar and then read maths at Homerton College, Cambridge. First job at Benenden (teaching/housemistress), then went on to Queen Anne's School, Caversham, where she was deputy head responsible for pastoral care. 'Glad to be back in full boarding', she asserts that 'all girls, not only the very brightest, should have a chance of a seriously good education'. Boarding numbers are up by more that 20 per cent since her arrival and the school is nearing completion of a huge development programme of new buildings and thorough refurbishment of old.

Married to a 'very supportive man', they have two sons (educated at Charterhouse and Milton Abbey). Keen on maths, hockey and dinghy sailing at her home on the Norfolk coast. Pastoral care is her particular passion. Vivacious and easy to talk to she appears full of creative energy and very stylish. Her most obvious attribute, apart from the ability to negotiate stairs and rough ground at speed on needle thin three-inch heels, is the ability to get people talking freely and confidently. She also listens to what they say.

Academic matters: The number of girls taking IB has grown. Sherborne Girls' now offers it as the boys' school dropped it from their curriculum (boys can still do IB with the girls). Mrs Dwyer says girls thrive on its rigour and staff return from IB training courses full of enthusiasm which filters down to everyone. Evidently it's horses for courses as one girl said she had started it but found she preferred A levels. Results were pretty impressive with 55 per cent of subject grades at 7 and 6 (equivalent of A level A*/A). Average points score was 34 with one girl scoring 44 (out of 45) putting her in the top one per cent globally.

At A level greatest uptake is maths with strong results – exceptional in further maths – followed by art and art history (also impressive) and religious studies. Wide range, including Russian, Japanese, theatre studies and DT reflects broad curriculum. In 2013, 81 per cent of A level entries were graded A*-B (54 per cent A*/A). IGCSE now used for sciences, maths, and English. These core subjects and modern languages are really star-studded at GCSE, as are art and food technology. In 2013, 76 per cent of GCSE papers were graded A*/A. One parent commended the school for being hot on picking up and remedying any weakness in the curriculum.

Brand new labs, each with practical and teaching areas, don't even smell of chemicals and announce their purpose to the world via curious sundial on the squat turret. Adjoining is the bright refurbished language department with lots of lovely language IT. When Sherborne refurbishes it's root and branch, not just a lick of paint! French, German, Spanish (plus Latin) on offer and native speakers of other languages can study them to GCSE. New languages, including Russian, introduced in second year – they also get a Prue Leith Cookery School course (the sixth form can brush up with Prue Leith too!)

There is flexibility to take subjects jointly with Sherborne Boys' at A level and IB (which the girls' school now runs). Theatre is the genuinely a joint enterprise but has quite a small take-up.

Much setting and streaming from age 13. No form tutors, girls meet individually with personal tutors moving to a new one approximately every two years. The Junior Diploma is an initiative to keep girls consciously reflecting on their own competencies in the foundation areas of knowledge, learning skills, personal attributes and contribution to the curriculum. About 20 per cent of pupils have mild special needs. Any extra lessons are at a time agreed: girls are not withdrawn from lessons or key activities.

Games, options, the arts: Sport has a high-ish profile now at Sherborne and girls' teams are definitely up with the best in Dorset. They are old hands at the increasingly popular lacrosse and have hosted ELA lacrosse finals for 1st and U15 teams throughout UK. The girls are proud of their record and Sherborne holds pop lacrosse tournaments for prep and primary schools. Even the less sporty get encouragement.

Hockey (county champions and have provided England team members) and netball seriously competitive! All levels of players have access to good coaching. L4 and U4 have sport every day, L5 to U5 have at least three sessions per week, plus activities. The Oxley Sports Centre, with indoor pool, fitness suite, gym, dance studio plus floodlit Astro is getting a facelift, and offers first class facilities to girls and to the town in a smooth-running shared arrangement. Plenty of grass pitches and 27 tennis courts (eight floodlit), mostly artificial.

Bags of other sporty things. Riding team does well in National Schools' Show Jumping at Hickstead, polo, ski trips, various martial arts, dance etc and opportunities via Sherborne Boys' for things like rifle shooting as well as everything (almost) put on for the town in the Oxley Centre.

Art block with libraries, photography and printmaking, has cunning wooden bars across the wide stairwell and entry, allowing for effective display of textiles etc. There are ambitious plans to link this with a new performance centre in the next development phase. Masses of accomplished architectural studies all over the school as well as a few landscapes that might be mistaken for one of the modern masters! Head of art is an inspirational teacher. Good studio space for A level candidates who appear virtually to live here. Weekend workshops offered on juicy topics eg book-binding, stained glass, paper or jewellery making. Overseas trips made jointly with history of art dept. Computer-aided design and manufacture suite.

The lovely singing from above when we arrived was Friday choir practice. Several choirs sing in the Abbey and even Salisbury Cathedral and benefit from having accessible boys' choirs. Sherborne Choral Society runs jointly with boys' school, one area in which their proximity really enables girls to keep up in an area notoriously hard for girls' schools to build a good tradition. Sherborne Schools' Symphony Orchestra skims off the cream of musicians from Sherborne Girls, Sherborne Boys and nearby Leweston to produce two joint orchestras. Singing, chamber orchestra, jazz band, senior choir, elite madrigal choir etc etc. Girls enjoy music and even take up instruments when previous experience has been off-putting. Current music building bursting out of its breezeblocks into huts alongside, so the new performing arts centre is eagerly awaited. Joint musical theatrical productions with Sherborne School and some separate drama.

S

'A plethora' of societies and clubs for intellectuals (from astronomy to current affairs), the arty crafty (life class – gardening), domestic goddesses (cookery – all sorts) or sporty types (ballet – yoga). D of E gets about 150 and 40 plus go on to gold.

Lots of charitable activities including a lovely project for the juniors in the New Aldhelmsted West (just say West) with past pupil Camila Batmanghelidjh CBE, who opened the house, hosting children from her Kids' Company charity. Trip to Nepal exploring and helping in an orphanage – plus all the usual exchanges and field trips such as sea kayaking and trekking in the Spanish Picos. School exchange links with Toronto and Tasmania.

Background and atmosphere: Founded in 1899 by the Wingfield Digby family – local bigwigs owning Sherborne Castle – the main building is a rambling Victorian warren in the pretty local hamstone. Meticulous planting makes an attractive site with the main boarding houses and teaching facilities forming a crescent round a green expanse of playing fields and lawn on the edge of the town. Still a few 'huts' for drama and music but the 5 year development plan is already nearing completion after only four years, making way for the next performing arts phase.

Recently completed Aldhelmsted West is a fabulous environment for the first two years with sunny dining room, laid out for birthday tea on our visit, work rooms for homework, lots of comfortable play space and room for music practice. Parents get involved in sports as West positively encourages them to get to know one another. Several live-in staff and a housemistress' house attached with openings onto all three floors. Good big bedrooms, mostly for four, with loo and shower en suite.

The undoubted advantage of an all boys' school in the same small market town means the girls can share entertainment and have sensible and reasonably safe access to town life, a situation envied by similar girls-only schools in the area. Younger girls can go into town at weekends. Lower sixth can go as far as Yeovil, Exeter, Salisbury. Upper sixth girls allowed into the sixth form bar at Sherborne Boys. Common features include coordinated term dates, some A level courses, IB social events, two joint plays, the Academic society and Epicurean society as well as music. Sherborne is one of the few true boarding schools remaining with only about 30 day girls (seven per cent). Day girls are allocated to boarding houses and given their own space (some even their own bed) there. They can stay for the occasional night. No flexi-boarding and there is Saturday school. The majority want to be in on the weekend ativities. Ideal for expat parents! Day girls allowed home at 6pm but some stay to do prep until 8pm.

Pastoral care and discipline: School rules are straightforward, based on 'keep safe and consider others'. Exclusion for dealing drugs; experimenters can 'expect' to go but 'touch wood no issues' and smoking not really a problem. 'Robust' attitude to alcohol, shared by boys' school, includes possibility of breathalysing. Daily living still done the old school way with all meals in houses with their own separate kitchens and dining rooms. Formal lunches (sixth form do table plans, staff at each table), but cafeteria-style suppers. Hot drinks machines for girls to entertain friends, male and female, in the downstairs areas. Afternoon tea at five and supper at 7.30 means sensible pre and post supper time for supervised prep and activities. Girls say food's pretty ok.

Resident housemistresses, some with families and pets (one house is pet free for allergy sufferers), run the houses like homes with minor medical help and a friendly ear available during the day. Proper school san. The popular school chaplain teaches, offers confirmation etc and keeps an eye open so all denominations get spiritual support. Has the right balance of welcome and warmth with respect for girls' views, say parents. Teams of house tutors give personal and academic

support on an individual basis. Issues (homesickness, cliques, etc) do crop up but they are very well resolved said one parent. Massive refurbishment of boarding houses means all have pleasant meeting, working, library and dining areas plus 'drawing rooms', for entertaining or watching Downton Abbey. Some girls sleep in cubicles (partitioned compartments in a dormitory – they claim not to make a habit of vaulting the partitions!) but most in double or single rooms. Upper sixth girls move into Mulliner with individual study bedrooms and bit of independence. After February of their final year they are allowed into Sherborne pubs.

Pupils and parents: Still lots of old west country families but also forces families, diplomats, Londoners with south west connections (Sherborne is on the main line to Waterloo). About 10 per cent come from Hong Kong and elsewhere: Dubai, Nigeria etc plus Europe since IB was introduced. Around 25 need EAL support of one lesson per week. Recently awarded the DfE International School Award in recognition of the international dimension being a key part of school ethos. Sixth form are let out of uniform but have regulation black tailored suit (with a quite skimpy skirt!) worn with their own accessories.

Old girls – Camila Batmanghelidjh (founder of Kids Co and 2006 Woman of the Year), soprano Dame Emma Kirkby, violinist Ruth Rogers, writers Sophie Kinsella, Santa Sebag Montefiore, Dames Deirdre Hutton of the Trading Standards Institute and Juliet Wheldon who was legal advisor to the Bank of England. Sherborne old girls are exceptionally efficient: organised into regional circles they support all sorts of school initiatives, their own charitable causes and a careers information network. Such benevolent networking may lie behind the remarkable collections of speakers who visit Sherborne – AC Grayling on the day of our visit, Germaine Greer, recently, Becky Anderson of CNN, Matthew Pinsent ...

Entrance: Visit, registration, 'at work days', taster weekends, deposit paid, then scholarship exams, common entrance papers or own entrance exams in maths, English and reasoning plus an interview. One form enters at 11, a few girls join at 12 but the majority (three forms) enter at 13. Mainly from Hanford, Port Regis, Hazlegrove, Knighton House, Sherborne Prep, Leaden Hall, Perrott Hill, Cheam, Bute House, Newland, Thomas's, Mount House Farleigh, Forres Sandle Manor, Twyford and Sunninghill. About 20 join for sixth form – at least five grade B or above GCSEs required for A level or IB.

Exit: A few leave after GCSEs, mainly to sixth form colleges. After A levels, practically all go on to university to read a wide variety of courses (modern languages, theology, lots of sciency things including medicine). Bristol, Durham, Edinburgh, Exeter, Newcastle, Oxford Brookes and London LSE imperial and UCL currently leading the pack. A few to Oxbridge most years and several to art schools, academic art history.

Money matters: Boarding fees about what you would expect, on a par with co-ed fees for boarders though less than the boys. Day girls on the expensive side, not really surprising since they are in school nearly twice as long as a day school!

Scholarships generous for a girls' school. Academic, art and music awards pay up to quarter of fees, plus bursaries based on need. Music scholars get up to three lessons per week – more than at most schools. Nearly 100 girls are receiving some sort of award or bursary. Currently appealing for bursary fund!

Remarks: No longer the stuffy warhorse of girls' education, though its academic standards are undiminished! Parents appreciate that its good teaching avoids hot housing and encourages a balance of activities. A real gem amongst the girls' – only full-boarding schools with all the advantages of its symbiotic proximity to Sherborne boys'.

Sherborne International College

Newell Grange, Sherborne, Dorset, DT9 4EZ

- Pupils: 150 pupils: 95 boys, 55 girls. All board. • Ages: 11–17
- Non-denom • Fees: £36,225 pa • Independent

Tel: 01935 814743
Email: reception@sherborne-ic.net
Website: www.sherborne-ic.net

Principal: Since September 2013, Mrs Mary Arnal MSc, PGCE, FRSA, formerly head of the prep school at St Teresa's, Effingham. Mrs Arnal has a background in university lecturing and teaching in the UK and overseas. Her specialist subjects are English language and philosophy and she has experience teaching the IB in Spain, where she was Director of Studies at a school in Madrid. She has also taught and lived in Peru.

Mary is married to mathematical analyst, Antonio Arnal; her younger son attends Sherborne School while her eldest is completing his postgraduate law degree.

Academic matters: Very close academic supervision with mini-reports on each pupil every three weeks, though some feel the supervision is rather inflexible and not tailored to the individual. Excellent teachers all trained in EFL as well as their subject of instruction. Pupils come from over 30 countries and most stay for one year, preparing for CE, GCSEs or IGCSEs, but the college offers a two-year GCSE course (along with a more demanding 'express' course – essentially a one-year crammer for older children, some of whom may have covered much of the material already and just need to nail down some exams and spruce up their English). Unsurprisingly, the subjects studied lean towards maths and sciences, where language ability is less crucial. Class sizes tiny: six to eight usually for the main academic subjects and for options like art or IT. In 2013 over 87 per cent A*-C grades at GCSE – a super achievement considering the linguistic hurdles.

Little in the way of SEN provision – these kids have enough on their plate without adding learning disabilities to the mix – though currently one pupil with mild dyslexia.

Games, options, the arts: Plenty of sport available using Sherborne's superb facilities (but no rugby) and a surprising number of matches are organised against other schools. Music particularly well provided for with concerts and good tuition. The most talented can join the main Sherborne School orchestra.

Background and atmosphere: The original and the best. Founded in 1977, the college was the brainchild of Robert Macnaghten, then head of Sherborne School, who was frustrated with having to turn down applications from non-English-speaking boys. A mixture of handsome stone farm dwellings and sympathetically designed purpose-built school blocks close to the centre of town and Sherborne School. Strong feeling of industry and purpose – parents are not coughing up this kind of money for their children to have a holiday. Twenty-five small classrooms, a small library, computer room, eight science labs, playing fields and basketball courts. A large new all purpose hall opens in January 2014.

Friendly atmosphere, with boys playing basketball in the sun and girls chatting in small groups when we arrived at break time. Technically, pupils allowed to speak in their home language only after prep in the evenings and at the weekends, but this is impossible to enforce. Boarding facilities much better than at most boarding schools. Older boys live on site in single or double rooms. Girls, and younger boys, board a three-minute minibus journey away in the very lovely Westcott House, a converted Georgian residence (they are bussed to and from school). Eleven to 13 year old boys live in their own wing of the house. Lovely canteen with piles of fresh fruit, plus evening snacks available in the boarding houses. Pupils aged 13 and over are allowed to wander freely in town (must sign out) and can be found hovering in newsagents and over the sushi display in Sainsbury's. An education in itself, and lovely Sherborne is an ideal town in which to wander. Much emphasis on instilling British manners, culture etc alongside learning the language.

Pastoral care and discipline: Pastoral care is very strong as evidenced by recent ISI boarding Inspection. Ratio of two staff to one student means little can escape the notice of teachers and houseparents. Discipline is tight as it has to be. There is little time to inculcate manners and rules of behaviour so students need to learn fast. Induction includes road safety, British etiquette and manners, drugs awareness and internet safety and use. Sanctions apply if house or school rules are broken and parents are informed immediately. The ultimate sanction is to be sent home.

Pupils and parents: The school has a diverse parental group from international aristocracy to farmers and entrepreneurs and the national origins of the student body have always reflected international economic and political trends. Started off with three Iranian boys – a sign of the times in the late '70s. Later became dominated by pupils from the Far East. Now numbers from the former Soviet Union have rocketed: pupils not only from Russia, but also from Ukraine, Azerbaijan, Georgia, Uzbekistan, Kazakhstan – the school could host its own Eurovision Song Contest. Indeed, the biggest change in the school since we last visited is the increased number of nationalities represented. The college keeps a low profile in the UK, but is promoted by 250 agents overseas, plus plenty of personal recommendations.

Former pupils: King Mswati III of Swaziland, Crown Prince Tamin of Qatar, Princess Marie-Gabrielle of Luxembourg.

Entrance: At ages 11 through 17. First come first served. No entry test but (translated) school reports checked to screen out bad apples. Pupils' academic abilities and knowledge of the English language vary widely. Students entering the one-year intensive GCSE programme need to have at least Lower Intermediate Level English (equivalent to IELTS score of 4+). It may well be that those coming with minimal English are better suited to the programmes here than those whose English is fairly sophisticated. School also runs a highly successful and flexible summer (and Easter) course that caters for some 300 pupils.

Exit: Pupils go on to study A levels at Sherborne School and Sherborne Girls as well as Winchester, Charterhouse and a plethora of other independent schools – an impressive list, given the broad intake. The 'future schooling adviser' is devoted to slotting pupils into good schools when they leave International College – each pupil visits up to three schools, which some feel is too few, and is groomed for interviews.

Money matters: Not cheap: £36,000+ for one year – costs more than a year at Harvard. Terms and conditions mirror those of Sherborne School.

Remarks: You do get what you pay for, but don't expect the college to turn your disaffected son into a scholar. Schools that have accepted International College pupils tell us that they find their levels of English and general academic ability vary widely. The college follows the pupils' fortunes after leaving and while many go on to earn three A*s at A level or stellar IB scores, some are earning mostly Cs and Ds.

Sherborne School

Abbey Road, Sherborne, Dorset, DT9 3AP

- Pupils: 600 boys; all but 55 board • Ages: 13 –19 • C of E
- Fees: Day £25,635, Boarding £31,665 pa • Independent

Tel: 01935 812249
Email: registrar@sherborne.org
Website: www.sherborne.org

Headmaster: Since 2010, Mr Christopher Davis MA (fiftyish), the son of a schoolmaster, educated at Eton, where he was a clarinettist in the National Youth Orchestra and played cricket for the first XI. Read English literature at Cambridge, also a Manners Scholar. A brief flirtation with teaching preceded his joining the Bank of England's International Division, then seconded to the Cabinet Office for two years during the first Gulf War, before returning to the Bank to write and manage some of its most influential publications. In 1994, it was back to teaching and to Eton, joining the English department where he also did stacks of other things, for boys (nine years as a housemaster and various societies) and indeed for staff, chairing the Staff Remuneration and Conditions of Service Committee. Married to Innes, a highly regarded teacher of Latin, with two daughters at Leweston.

Tall, affable and very chatty with a shock of grey hair ('Won't be bothering us much' quips local barber), Mr Davis comes to Sherborne as a complete apologist for single sex education from 12-16: 'Boys do so much better on their own,' he states, citing plenty of evidence to back this up. That, coupled with the fact that he 'didn't want a campus school', meant not many headships remained attractive to him. However, some parents (and boys) resent the many references to Eton, and any whiff of Sherborne being second best: he might do well to tone it down a bit. Parental opinion as yet sharply divided on Mr Davis: to some, he is warm and engaging, to others aloof and remote, particularly from the lower school – parents perhaps, rather than boys. He has, though made real efforts to get to know all the boys, by a series of informal suppers in his home. Interests include reading poetry, watching sport and the odd political mini-series.

Clearly ambitious for the school, he has shone a bright light into the dustier corners of academe and the pastoral system – and has found them, well, dusty. 'The boys just don't work hard enough,' he says and, as well as reshaping the school day so that there is more supervised hall [prep] time, he has overhauled a pastoral system which had been graded 'outstanding' by Ofsted. Both previous deputy heads, academic and pastoral, have moved on and gained headships since he arrived. Will Sherborne change the man as much as the man changes Sherborne?

Academic matters: New academic deputy, David Smith, has gone down well both with boys and parents and is busy delivering the head's wish that academic life is 'at the centre of the wheel, with everything else forming the spokes', as he put it. Boys encouraged 'to become much more independent about their learning', and at the same time they are incentivised to do well by the payment of £10 per 10 commendations! Nine or 10 GCSEs is the norm out of the 20 subjects on offer; virtually all do separate sciences (all science is at IGCSE), and at least one language and one humanity, from a list including Latin/Greek, is compulsory. Results are good, rather than stellar, with A*/A grades awarded to 61 per cent of entries in 2013. Individual subject stars tend to be art, all three sciences, history, RS and German. A*-B grades awarded for more than 75 per cent of A levels taken in 2013. No plans to raise the bar at entry, but the head means business: those who did not achieve their target GCSE grade in the exams

held in the last week of the Michaelmas term were required to come back a day early in January to resit them. Teaching is praised by boys and parents alike: stimulating, with levels of banter which do not overstep the mark (mostly). 'They teach the subject, not just to pass exams,' said one mother, approvingly. Learning Support, housed in the top corner of the beautiful science block, was pointed out with the wave of the hand by our guide, whose own needs, hitherto unrealised by him, had been identified and acted upon by its staff. 'Sensationally good, and I still pop in there for extra help,' he said, unprompted. All boys are screened on arrival, and sessions on learning styles and study skills are timetabled, as are revision classes as GCSEs loom. Subject teachers work closely with learning support staff in individual cases – all quite unobtrusive, but clearly effective.

Games, options, the arts: Gosh, where to start! Sherborne does everything rather well in the sporting line except rowing, and it's an important part of life here. Acres of verdant pitches (including the hallowed turf of the Upper, a piece of which went to Rwanda as part of a cricket pitch the boys constructed in 2008), tennis courts, Astro, the school has in abundance. Twenty-six sports on offer – including fives, polo and real tennis outside the mainstream; clubs and/or trips cater for minority tastes like surfing, canoeing and skiing. Simply masses of fixtures for all standards and tours (recently Australia and Dubai) for top teams. Main sporting rival is Marlborough. Boys get to try most things out in their first year. Pool and fitness suite on site used by local community, and school has sports physio on the staff. Prominence in the regional or national arena actively promoted by director of sport, who says 'I don't want us to produce good players on an ad hoc basis'. Strong tradition of CCF, Ten Tors and D of E too, actively supported by boys and staff alike.

Arts too are tops here. Strong drama emanates from Powell theatre and Victorian Big School Room, neither one ideal performance spaces on grounds of size or original purpose. Lots of productions on school and house level, plus lavish musicals with other schools, Sherborne Girls particularly, but also Leweston and local comprehensive, The Gryphon (all GSG schools). School has produced several notable thespians: John le Mesurier, Jeremy Irons, Hugh Bonneville and rising star Charlie Cox, the latter two posh chaps in Downton Abbey, and Charles Collingwood, womanising landowner Brian Aldridge in The Archers. Foreign language plays too, and productions to Edinburgh Fringe.

Music has been re-housed in a splendid new facility since 2010, a contemporary yet sympathetic addition to Sherborne's fine buildings. All is state-of-the-art here, so that rock bands (v big here, at least 10 in school) and string quartets can rehearse in neighbouring rooms without conflict. Gorgeous 120 seat recital hall graced with one of several concert grand pianos, all bought new. Technically top notch recording and music tech facilities too; provision, teaching and charismatic head of music, who has returned to teach at his alma mater, all combine to produce some outstanding musicians of all timbres. Practice time protected in an hour after lunch (Q time). Music is a much-loved part of Sherborne for many boys, past and present: 'My son isn't particularly musical, but still plays the piano,' said a parent. Singing, whether in the sublime setting of the abbey twice a week, chanting on the Upper or in the revived house song (banned for a few years for being too rude), matters a lot. Hymns for Sunday services are practised with gusto at Congo and everyone knows the school song, with its rousing chorus of 'Vivat ! Vivat ! Vivat !' How sad that limited space in the abbey constrains some lower school parents from attending the carol service, an exposition of the finest English choral tradition.

Visual arts have super, dedicated block and permanent exhibition space, where teachers' art is displayed alongside pupils'. Scope for fine art, digital media and DT enormous and very well resourced. Boys love weekend availability, when dabblers seeking light relief are as welcome as fevered public

S

exam candidates hard up against a project deadline. Artworks shown all around the school, which also collaborates with local galleries to put on exhibitions and shows in the town. Impressive results at all levels – 100 per cent A* at GCSE in 2013.

Background and atmosphere: Beautiful school forming a substantial part of a charming and well-heeled Dorset market town, fashioned from gloriously golden hamstone. Founded as a grammar school by Edward VI in 1550 (and still using some of those ancient buildings), yet tracing its origins back to the eighth century, it travelled a somewhat rocky road until a period of mass expansion and financial bolstering up in the mid years of the 19th century. Boarding houses all over the town – some in existing buildings (Wallace and the Digby used to be hotels), some purpose-built (Lyon). School's heart is in the Courts, surrounded by the most historic of its mostly exquisite architecture, boasting two cloistered walls and sharing one with the abbey, and main school facilities, including the dining hall are centrally located. Additions sensitively designed so that they blend well – Pilkington science block an outstanding example. Boys walk through the town on their way to and from lessons. 'I can't believe the freedom, Mum', marvelled one new boy on arrival.

Atmosphere is one of entitlement – to fabulous surroundings, facilities and opportunities – yet it does not feel horribly posh: no anachronistic uniform here, but supremely practical navy blue shirts and jumpers, which don't show the dirt. Suits and ties at sixth form. Definite masculine and work-a-day feel to the place – boarding houses comfortable but certainly not luxurious, and female staff in an obvious minority. 'Sherborne remains a place where boys will be boys – and girls are welcome,' says the school. Tremendous house loyalty and fierce though good-natured competition between them. Much made of the ideal combination of single sex education provision within the same town, with plenty of opportunities for socialising. Boys in their first year have tended to be housed in one enormous dorm, with individual sleeping compartments for a modicum of privacy, though school tells us they are now mostly in smaller units; thereafter twin rooms and, finally, single rooms at sixth form, sometimes before.

Pastoral care and discipline: Our previous write-up alluded to the 'occasional Sherborne refugee [from bullying] at other schools', something the head is determined to strike out. To that end, he has completely overhauled the pastoral guidelines (which have long included an entire section on culture shock for international boys). His mission is to change the culture in boarding houses, where, to an extent, house custom and practice was down to the senior boys; in some, 'chores' (younger boys might nip down to the chippy on behalf of sixth formers, for example) still persisted. No longer. Senior boys are now heavily involved in the pastoral education (not 'care', note) of the younger boys – and assertive, not aggressive or submissive, is what they should all strive to be. Head is keen on the idea of value-based leadership promoted by the Bloxham project; school chaplain Lindsay Collins (a senior female appointment which raised a few eyebrows) is a trustee.

A close eye is kept on all boys by their tutors, who meet them at least once a fortnight and who oversee their well-being in and out of the classroom, and by the house staff, particularly matrons, whose status has definitely been raised. It would be difficult for anyone to go on being unhappy for long without someone noticing, according to the pastoral deputy. Bullying swiftly jumped on, school claims, and 'I'd be disappointed if a delicate flower or a quirky chap couldn't survive', the head told us. We will see – Sherborne's reputation for a robust environment (robust, mind, not tyrannical) will take some dismantling, even if it no longer reflects the place.

Sanctions have been simplified and far more rigorously enforced too, to some dismay among boys who have been there

longer than the head. 'Heavy-handed,' said one, with numerous house gatings on a Saturday evening being handed out for academic shortcomings, as well as the ever-present smoking and drinking offences. 'OTT!' said another, outraged at being gated for being 'one minute late'. 'Clarity of expectations', says school, which, in the head's first term, suspended 30 boys for different things; suspensions rarer now boundaries are better defined.

Pupils and parents: Varies from long-established families to first time buyers, but we nearly laughed when the head talked about 'a wide economic mix' – with fees touching £30k per annum. Catchment tends to be London extending westwards and eastwards from Devon and Cornwall but not much further afield. Members of all professions, the Forces and local gentry send their sons. Turns out confident (perhaps not confident enough, says head – but he is an Etonian) and likeable boys, who form many enduring friendships at school. So many people we spoke to remarked that they 'had never met a Shirburnian they didn't like'. Sprinkling of foreigners who enhance the place. Limited opportunities to meet parents from other houses socially is a pity, say some; school does put on fantastic events such as Commem (Speech Day), but jollifications are organised within houses, as are refreshments at parents' evenings and the carol service – if you can squeeze in. Parents report improved communications from school, especially by means of the parent portal, where every aspect of their son's school life can be viewed.

Notable old boys include Sir Alastair Pilkington, John le Carré, Chris Martin (Coldplay), Gulf War commander Major General Sir Patrick Cordingley DSO, political commentators Peter Oborne, Tom Bradby, newsreaders Chris Vacher, Simon McCoy, in addition to many others who have reached the top of the tree in the diplomatic service, academia, the church or the sporting arena.

Entrance: At 13, by entrance exam – either CE, scholarship papers or school's own papers. Average of 55 per cent expected at CE. Process starts a minimum of three years in advance by registering and paying a non-refundable fee, currently £100. Parents wanting a particular house advised to say so and register early. They may not then know who will be housemaster when little Johnny goes – housemasters remain in post for 10 years, with a further two by mutual agreement. Boys spend a day at school two years before they start. Final confirmation (subject to meeting entrance requirements) plus hefty but refundable deposit 18 months before entry. At sixth form, entry requirements are 5 GCSEs at grade C or above, with AS subjects at grade B or higher. School not shy to suggest to weaker candidates that they look elsewhere for sixth form. Handful of newcomers join, often to do IB. Houses sometimes enlivened by one or two able foreign students entering lower sixth.

Exit: Almost all to higher education and university of first choice. Inordinate care taken over UCAS advice and applications. Exceptionally well researched and well resourced programme, which extends to boys who defer or redo UCAS after they have left. Surprisingly small numbers to Oxbridge, which the head is determined to address. Top choices are Newcastle, Durham and other northern universities, old and new. A dozen or so to London, Cardiff and Oxford Brookes also popular. Wide range of degree courses taken.

Money matters: Six scholarships of up to 20 per cent and six exhibitions of up to 10 per cent of fees offered at 13+, on basis of 'academic potential and proficiency'. One closed exhibition to 10 per cent of fees offered to sons of the military. Academic scholarships also offered at sixth form, plus awards for artistic, sporting, musical and practical abilities at both entry points. A third of boys receive some financial assistance. Sherborne

S

Foundation supports occasional exceptionally deserving cases, as well as helping the school's wish list to become reality. Expect extras on the bill for trips, all learning support, plus of course the siren call of the school shop.

Remarks: First class boys' boarding in spectacular golden setting, which succeeds in combining the best of ancient and modern without diminishing either. Sharpening up of the academics will secure its place in the galaxy of the greatest English public schools.

Shiplake College

Shiplake Court, Shiplake, Henley-on-Thames, Oxfordshire, RG9 4BW

• Pupils: 410 pupils, mostly boys (30 girls in sixth form). 200 boarders • Ages: 11–18 • C of E • Fees: Day £14,925–£18,630; Boarding £27,615 pa • Independent

Tel: 01189 402455
Email: registrar@shiplake.org.uk
Website: www.shiplake.org.uk

Headmaster: Since 2004, Mr Gregg Davies BSc Cert Mgmt (forties), an ISI inspector, married to Alison (teaches in the learning development department); one teenage daughter. Tall, athletic, follicly challenged, he has something of the tri-nations about him – Welsh birth, Scottish heritage, English country life and a northern lilt that blends the three. He greeted us in his trademark, Davies-tartan trews but later switched to his second uniform, smart sports kit. Describes his hobbies as loud singing (runs head's choir for non-singers) and log-chopping; he harbours a desire to branch-out, climb to the top of the tree and claim the crown – as a Tree Surgeon!

A talented sportsman, equally at home kicking or running with the ball, his own Shrewsbury school days were spent on field, not river. That changed when, aged 18, he discovered his sea legs, and crossed The Pond to Connecticut. In a country where football is characterised by shoulder pads and 'Giants', he wisely swapped balls for oars, garnering gold in the Stotesbury Cup and New England Championships. St Andrew's student life saw him switch sculls for scrums, a move that eventually paved the way to international honours (as a referee).

Began his career at Haberdashers' but disliked the dearth of teaching challenge, 'They didn't need me, just my university notes.' Next stop Fettes. At a time when rot had set in, he not only learned about school as a business but spent glorious days in various remits. His favourite being housemaster, which he says is 'the best job in the world, so long as your wife agrees and those who inspect understand the job, its demands and the decisions you take.' Talks not of potential but of targets and stretching – finger-tip stuff, climbing mountains, appreciating the journey – recognising that sometimes it's not a higher peak but new direction and challenge that are needed.

Described by the boys as approachable, caring, funny, inspirational and charismatic, they say he sets very clear boundaries but does help you when you get things wrong. Praised by parents too, who say he is pivotal to the character and strength of the school. Mr Davies says he's not a typical head, we disagree: he may not be stereo-typical but headly characteristics such as tradition, stature, moral code, strong leadership skills and a love of learning are evident. Passionate about (good) teaching, learning, biology and statistics. Not afraid to upset the apple-cart: on arrival head fired strutting-peacocks, expelled the errant and swept dead-wood from the staff. The result is a school that has recently crossed the divide (just) from recruiting to selecting.

Academic matters: Beefed-up academics, including monitoring and expectations. Introduced IGCSE maths for most able and single sciences for all; Y9 have learning to learn (study skills, organisation, planning, revision techniques etc) but no happiness lessons – that's a given here. School channels youngsters towards courses and colleges that will work; as much about stretching ambition as curtailing misplaced enthusiasm. Good post-16 choice of A levels (including further maths and recent addition of economics) for the erudite, plus generous smattering of 'studies' (PE, media, drama) and, for those with a practical bias, BTECs in music, business, travel and tourism – hands-on, modular, 100 per cent coursework. Politics and photography on pupil wish list, no guarantees of the former, photography currently offered as an art module.

Nine GCSEs the max here, allowing time to concentrate on English, maths, sciences. Eighty-three per cent got five or more GCSEs at grades A*-C including maths and English in 2013, 21 per cent of exams at A*/A. Fifty-one per cent A*-B at A level in 2013. Headline results seem pretty ordinary until you dig out the value-added (very positive for almost all) and see that kids perform beyond predictions. Director of studies moved from reactive pursuit of academic rigour to proactive; differentiated work and low-key scholars programme aims to stretch the able. Still some grumblings from parents, who feel talented children aren't as challenged as they might be elsewhere – others say 'shouldn't mistake kindness for weakness, standards are high, school very on the ball and incredibly quick to get in touch if child appears to even think about slipping.'

Pupils say they enjoy most lessons (though harrumphed about hour long sessions) and appreciate continual help and support of staff. Art & design, history and geography front-runners in the popularity (and performance) stakes (with good showing for girls taking biology); physics and French less so, English on the up. Teaching good and improving; lots of young blood with imagination, ideas and energy, honing their craft alongside the experienced and in some cases, inspirational. We saw traditional, teacher led-sessions but alas didn't witness any of the pizazz that head recounted: biology lessons exploring pond life and the yelps of delight when pupils realised the muddy water houses whole colonies of creatures; or the history lesson where boys not only built trenches, complete with sandbags and duck-boards but spent a miserable 15 minutes up to their knees in cold, damp and dank conditions. A fleeting glimpse of trench life but a life-long appreciation of the horrors of WW1 and the need to 'remember them.'

Lots of support for the 25+ per cent identified with SEN and a deservedly excellent reputation for learning development. There isn't a pill for dyslexia et al but the recommended strategies – small classes, careful monitoring, addressing dominant learning styles and a whole school approach are among the viable antidotes offered here.

Still no proper library (a big black mark in our book), only small, under-utilised department libraries. Even the paltry shelves in the lower school were too high for most boys to peruse. We left our guides with the task of finding somewhere to position Horowitz, Shan, Ransom et al; hopefully they'll be well-thumbed, scanned, and savoured when we return.

Games, options, the arts: A school for doers; dirty knees okay, wellies obligatory, though we are less sure about the rainy day 'smell like wet dogs' description of the boys that staff shared! Rugby, rowing, hockey, cricket athletics and netball plus good smattering of minor sports and house fixtures, important, improving, inclusive and competitive (notable successes against much bigger rivals). In line with school spirit, fixture boards welcome the opposition and wish them luck. Good facilities, plenty of pitches, Astroturf, tennis, gym (with squash courts), sports hall, heated outdoor pool used by hardy souls well into the bowels of November. Piece de resistance is a wonderful bend in the river, below school's terrace and grassy slope, with boathouse and island for adventure/rafting/camping exercises. Enthusiastic and popular D of E, community service and CCF.

Art much improved and displayed school-wide. Drama edgy, believe in pushing boundaries (ask about the camel, sand and theatre in the round). Lovely studio theatre in old tithe barn, scented with woody smells. Music something of an unfinished symphony; working towards music for all – sixth form girls must join school choir – no sing, no entry and all in lower school play either brass or strings. We listened to the whole (lower) school orchestra rendition of Fanfare; more cacophony than flourish but we'd blow a raspberry at anyone who knocked their heart, hale and effort; a sound all the sweeter when you realise that just two months prior many couldn't even name their instrument, let alone play it.

Background and atmosphere: Stunning middle-England setting, overlooking the Thames; manicured, groomed, Wind In The Willows idyll. Just five minutes from Henley, Shiplake Court was built in 1895 as a family home and farm; today, characterful, adapted red-brick barns and buildings dot the site along with (mainly) attractive newer buildings, boarding houses and subject blocks.

Houses allocated according to boarding status: day, full or weekly boarder. Boarding flexible – a boon to busy parents though some full-boarders rue increasing numbers of part-timers. Boarding accommodation varies – some younger boys in rooms of up to five, older pupils in singles, mainly functional and reassuringly untidy. Good provision of games rooms, kitchens, common rooms etc plus tuck and endless bread supplies. Food tasty: fruit and salad offered alongside hot; dietary needs catered for, all served in gothic Great Hall.

School-home communication, covering everyone (from receptionists to head) and everything from drug awareness, through disciplinary matters and very regular academic feedback with associated praise, rewards and merits, is outstanding, frequent, inclusive and inescapable. Not a school for a fire-and-forget parent.

Pastoral care and discipline: Available, alert and approachable, the support team, from nurses and The Rev through caterers, cleaners, matrons, masters and mentors make it their business to look out for problems; eating, depression, self-harm just some of the sensitively handled issues. Parents love the fact that girls will always be picked up for high-heels, tight skirts or a blush too far on the make-up front.

Whole school assemblies important – indeed this is one of the few schools where pupils (and parents) have spoken about the inspirational assemblies led by the head – not only do they not nod-off but it seems they duly act on the pearls cast. Head speaks oft to boys about 'choice, risk and consequences'; so we were most impressed when one of our guides cited this – but slightly less so, when head admitted candidly that this probably had more to do with a recent 'scrape' involving sibling of said guide.

Big on building confidence, esteem and self-belief, work to generate a can-do attitude but with consideration and respect for others. Said one parent, 'My son is able but a complete softie; he's beginning to toughen up though, and school always keep in touch and deal with sensitive issues speedily.' Kids are genuinely caring and nice (in the best, not boring, sense of the word). Indeed when we asked a group of strapping 16-year-olds what they would change if they were head, the second most popular answer (after abolish Saturday lessons) was 'make more of the mentoring'. Every Y9 boy is allocated a sixth-former who befriends and advises. Those who benefitted from its introduction are keen to expand the remit, with a desire to add socials and structure, to maximise benefit. Older pupils feel they should be given more slack – allowed out at weekends (or perhaps a student bar / dining club, now drink alone is verboten). Somehow we doubt they'll get the town pass – shenanigan's of

Shiplake boys (in mid noughties) not totally erased from long-memories of locals. Cleaned its act on the drugs front – a zero-tolerance approach sent shock-waves then, but appears to be paying dividends now (though never say never, whatever the school) – smoking still a burning issue.

Pupils and parents: Parents pretty grounded for this part of the world but demanding and discerning never the less. Not a smart or fashionable school, with parents citing manners, etiquette and old-fashioned courtesy as some of the things they love about the school. Few Forces children, fewer yet from overseas; majority from local schools some relieved to no longer be in pressure-pot environment of local preps that push hard for places at nearby grammars.

Very much a school for children who enjoy challenges and stretch. 'Kids are privileged yet earnest; no tribes, no real cliques ' said one parent, another added, 'My son has a dimmer switch, sometimes it's turned down low but since he's been at Shiplake the bulb is burning brighter for longer.' Notable former pupils (aka Old Vikings for most implausible reasons) include Sydney gold medallist Ben Hunt-Davies and Starbucks UK CEO Phil Broad.

Entrance: Getting more picky but not academically so. At 11 and 13 selection takes place during taster day which includes an interview, discussion groups, outdoor activities and short tests in English and maths, not as a pass/fail exercise but to inform. Girls from 16. Incomers require 5+ GCSEs (with English and maths at C or higher) 'though they make exceptions' for those they feel will fit in. 'We will let our own boys stay on if we can find something useful and enjoyable for them to do.' Rescue those burnt-out from (or shot-out of) Thames Valley swot-houses.

Some 25 per cent have a learning difficulty or difference. The dys-strata and ADD account for most, plus a sprinkle of ADHD and Aspergers and a handful with EAL needs. Trying to attract more scholars and all-rounders.

Exit: Outcomes divergent; everything from the Oxbridge/ Harvard student (two of each in recent times) to those who pursue art and the vocational. Around 80 per cent to degree courses with new universities Bournemouth, Southampton Solent etc outweighing trad – Leeds, Newcastle et al. Handful to vocational further education courses, rest into interesting gap year activities or employment.

Money matters: Art, music and sports scholarships awarded but more for prestige than pounds. Sixth form schols depend on general aptitude test, plus test results in two subjects to be studied at A level. Means-tested bursaries awarded at the school's discretion with small pot to assist existing pupils, should financial hiccups occur.

Remarks: A good school on an upward curve, with a charismatic, no-nonsense, forward looking head (complete with iPad and tweets) plus dedicated team in an enchanting location; especially suited to the reserved or those with bruised esteem. IQs cross many centiles but Shiplake is unlikely to suit the struggling child with little to offer, nor the multi-talented, über-confident, high-flying know-it-all. For everyone else, including abler, gentle souls, sporty or not, there may well be a fit. Send for the prospectus (we love the student one), visit and see if life by the river will float your child's boat.

Shrewsbury High School

Linked school: Shrewsbury High Prep School

32 Town Walls, Shrewsbury, Shropshire, SY1 1TN

- Pupils: 650 girls, 75 boys • Ages: 3-18 • Non-denominational
- Fees: £11,652 pa • Independent

Tel: 01743 494000
Email: admissions@shr.gdst.net
Website: www.shrewsburyhigh.gdst.net

Head: Since 2012, Mr Michael Getty, previously deputy head of Hill House in Doncaster which, shortly after he left, won the Independent School of the Year Award. Schooled in Liverpool, he went north in search of university, heading to Newcastle to read economics. Began his teaching career at Durham High School for Girls as head of economics, and remained there for nine years, during which time he became head of sixth form. He also spent time teaching overseas at the New English School in Amman, Jordan, and for three years was assistant head at Sheffield High School, another GDST school, before going to Hill House. He is Shrewsbury High School's first headmaster. Married to an Ofsted inspector; they have two young children, both of whom are destined shortly to join the ranks of the prep school.

Mr Getty showed no signs of fatigue when we met him towards the end of his first year at the helm. He appeared irrepressible, and as we listened to ideas tumbling out, he looked just like a boy who has found himself in a sweet shop with the freedom to buy whatever takes his fancy. He simply could not stop smiling. He has reason to smile: he has great financial support from the GDST and has already added to the buildings and facilities he inherited. Many of the girls talk of innovative ideas, the head's willingness to listen and see how their ideas can be initiated. 'I really think he puts the girls first,' said one girl. 'Phew!' was the response of the head, 'job done.' Not quite yet. Many of the parents appreciate Mr Getty's innovations and changes; others remain to be convinced though, as he pointed out, interest in the school has increased dramatically.

Academic matters: Shrewsbury High School has always prided itself on its success in A levels and GCSEs and recent results have not bucked the trend. Statistics are readily available on the website and in the prospectus (over 60 per cent A*/A grades at GCSE and 82 per cent A*-B at A level in 2013), where the blurb says that 'we are the best performing school in Shropshire.' Statisticians and grade junkies could have a lot of fun following that one up. The head has trenchant views on girls' education and the direction in which it is moving. As a result, two houses have recently been bought backing on to the secret garden of the school and complementing the delightful collection of buildings clustered around. One is destined to be the Business School, the place for business studies, economics, for manufacturing and selling, for enterprise. The other is already an amazingly swish sixth form centre with an eye on university-style living.

The head was characteristically enthusiastic about it when he showed us round the day before the keys were due to be handed over. 'Here, through technology linking up with the outside world and the main school network, girls will be able to research, explore, experiment. Independent learning, as the girls prepare for university study. As well as banks of iPads and laptops, the girls are also able to connect their own mobile devices, such as tablets and phones, to our own network. This is a great symbol of how we are trying to combine an awareness of the girls' lifestyles with a forward-looking take on independent study in preparation for college.'

Well, not many universities have computer rooms hung with chandeliers (sic), cooking facilities with granite work surfaces, common rooms with chandeliers (encore), leather sofas, arm chairs and side tables, a patio for elegant luncheons overlooking the gardens and a gym next door. For some schools, doing your own washing and being allowed a glass of cider in the school bar is the only preparation for university. Mr Getty says schools should be preparing girls for the sort of careers they will be following after university, such as management, architecture, engineering, running businesses, leadership and much else. But the school needs to be more than academic. That's why in addition to academic awards the school has introduced scholarships for sport, art, drama, music and all-round promise. There is more than one of each available if the standard merits.

Despite this new sixth form centre represents a preparation for university and life beyond, though some may gasp at a charitable institution spending £1m so luxuriously. Chandeliers, forsooth! Instead, the 'SHS has been shortlisted in the UK Independent School of the Year Awards, 2013. In this case The High School has been listed for the Outstanding Strategic Initiative Award in recognition of the school's highly ambitious recent development.' Some might say it can afford to be ambitious.

The school is alert to the fact that the sciences are becoming increasingly popular in girls' only schools and, in the case of Shrewsbury High, even physics. So how can the school increase the momentum and raise the interest in physics? Enter them for the competition to design an electric car in the national Greenpower electric racing car competition involving 400 schools. Rumour has it that the girls have been drawn to race Shrewsbury boys at Brands Hatch next year. Watch this space. Buy a crash helmet.

All this is trendy, ground-churning stuff, but what of the old fashioned virtues? Well, there's a delightful library with decent books – oddly enough, that's not always the case with schools these days. We saw some inspirational teaching in the arts and in the superbly equipped IT facilities and science labs, and in the magical cottage which houses the very lively and successful music department. We saw an excellent art exhibition and met talented, enthusiastic and happy artists. Drama is extremely active and popular with a recent performance of Noye's Fludde taking Shrewsbury by storm and involving a number of schools around the town. There's no doubt there's a lot of lively creativity about.

Games, options, the arts: A fabulous sports centre in part of the main complex offers a tremendous variety of sports; the river nearby beckons oarsgirls; tennis courts, lacrosse, hockey: they're all available; and recently the school enjoyed county championship successes in athletics, netball, rounders, hockey and cross country. All this without seeming at all hearty. Optional activities abound and the range of possibilities listed in the enrichment programme is endless, from jazz ensemble to Duke of Edinburgh, from helping in primary schools to yoga.

Background and atmosphere: A GDST school which, since its foundation in 1885, has been a distinguished feature of Shropshire education. The bridge which separated it from Shrewsbury school for boys – the Santa Trinità Bridge of the West Midlands – witnessed much to-ing and fro-ing, both in terms of shared activities and social encounters. When Shrewsbury School decided to take girls, following a brief period of girls only in the sixth form, shock waves permeated throughout the county, rendering life difficult, challenging and unsettling for, in particular, the High School. Initially, girls flocked to Shrewsbury School sixth form, and Mr Getty's predecessor was understandably upset. Mr Getty says he is very calm about it all. 'To be honest, we don't notice,' he says. 'We are full for year 7 and numbers in the sixth form have increased by 25 per cent.

We're busier than ever.' Girls only versus coeducation. Game on. You pays your money......

Wandering around the school, lost in the warren of buildings – some old and institutional; others plate glassed and modern – the visitor must be struck by the open friendliness of the girls, the smiling faces, the courteous offers of help. This feels like happiness and those to whom we spoke did not deny it. 'It's good fun here. The days are packed.'

Pastoral care and discipline: There seems to be a happy relationship between staff and pupils, and the provision for pastoral care, support and help over academic matters and guidance over more personal issues is well in place, and much appreciated by those to whom we spoke. Rules are clearly delineated, and on the whole the existence of those recognisably blue uniformed girls in town is a welcome addition to the social mix. All girls have personal tutors and form teachers, and parents are invited to discuss worries and concerns. This is, after all, a day school. One of the most appreciated aspects of care is the help and advice given not only with choice of GSCEs/A levels but with university and what to read there. We spoke to a mother whose daughter had benefited enormously from the various layers of academic support. She is delighted with the outcome.

Pupils and parents: Yes, SHS girls appear confident, outgoing, friendly and stylish. Not really a school exclusively for toffs. Nor plebs. Most parents come from the professional classes, with some farmers and a hint of county. A good Shropshire mix. The catchment area is large and the new head has introduced an extraordinary bus service from Church Stretton, Ludlow, Oswestry, Bridgnorth, Ellesmere, Welshpool. All about an hour away and most passing by or close to other girls' schools. SHS is no shrinking violet, any more than the girls themselves, let alone the marketing department.

Entrance: Entrance at 11+ is by examination in verbal reasoning, non-verbal reasoning and quantitative skills. Intake is not overly selective and staff are good at helping those with learning difficulties, including dyslexia. As for girls who wish to enrol in the sixth form, they are expected to achieve 'a minimum of six A*-B grades at GCSE with at least Bs in those subjects they wish to take on to AS... Movement onto the A2 course is dependent on satisfactory progress at AS level'. That quotation from the website reveals more honesty than many schools offer, but it still hints at a self-conscious approach to those ghastly league tables. When challenged, Mr Getty said that no girl would be asked to leave purely on the strength of her grades in AS, 'though clearly new strategies might have to be drawn up in the best interests of the pupil.' It is always worth asking that question when visiting schools. You won't always get a straight answer: more and more schools are weeding in the interest of league tables.

Exit: A few leave for sixth form elsewhere – for coeducation, boarding, a change – but on the whole the majority stay. The most recent band of leavers did not include any Oxbridge, but a very good range of universities from all over the country. Modern languages were the most popular subject.

Remarks: The school is not in the middle of town as has been suggested: it is actually on the site of the old mediaeval town walls overlooking the river and Kingsland. The school has recently taken out an 80 year lease on the only remaining wall tower. Close to the sixth form centre, it will be used as a museum, curated by interested girls. It's another example of the zany, the original, the questing way in which the school is seeking to extend horizons, to encourage research and inquisitiveness: to enliven. New Headmaster, new buildings, new equipment, new facilities, new money pumped in. There's a fresh approach

and much excitement and buzz. But, of course, none of this is of any use unless there is a reason, a plan. The thought behind the action is as important as the action itself. What lies behind all this is new stuff is how the years ahead are perceived. Will it be chandeliers?

The main theme seems to be preparation. That's, after all, what schools are for. This is a school well worth visiting if you live within an hour's drive. Do check it out.

Shrewsbury School

The Schools, Shrewsbury, Shropshire, SY3 7BA

• Pupils: 750 pupils; 570 boarding, 180 day. 100 girls in sixth form. • Ages: 13–18 • C of E • Fees: Boarding £30,420; Day £21,300 pa • Independent

Tel: 01743 280552
Email: registrar@shrewsbury.org.uk
Website: www.shrewsbury.org.uk

Headmaster: Since 2010, Mr Mark Turner MA PGCE (fiftyish). Educated at Rossall School where he was head boy, followed by Mansfield College, Oxford where he was an army scholar and read geography. Served with the Royal Artillery for four years before completing a PGCE at Cambridge. Housemaster at Oundle and then headmaster at Kelly College (age 32), followed by Abingdon for 8 years. Married to Elizabeth, also an Oxford graduate, who teaches religious studies; they have two sons. Spends spare time in Devon where he can indulge his twin passions of bass fishing and lobster potting.

A 'crisp and keen administrator' who wants to 'retain the best of the past with the cutting edge technology of the future' and to up the academic ante. Having a close look at teaching styles and practice and work ethic, but does not want the school to become overly selective – believing in rigour rather than elitism. Cuts a slightly remote figure; parents and boys still feel that they hardly know him. Abingdon parents felt that Mr Turner's military demeanour and focused approach was just what that school needed – and we agree – but while many Shrewsbury parents feel that discipline did need tightening up, some are concerned that he is bearing down on eccentricities and traditions, and is too pernickety and keen on process. Capable and ambitious: rumour has it that he has his eye on the headship of Eton when that position becomes available in a few years' time.

Academic matters: In 2013 83 per cent A*/B at A level/Pre-U but also a few lower grades – a comforting indication that this is a school that does not chuck out kids at 16. Particularly good showing at maths and further maths. Sixty-five per cent A*/A in IGCSE (most subjects) and GCSE in 2013. Wide choice at A level/Pre-U – usual academic subjects plus ceramics, photography, computing, design, theatre studies, PE and most combinations can be accommodated. 'Clinics' offer support for anyone who is struggling. Vibrant academic life outside main curriculum – Voluntary Complementary Study Programme in sixth form, some examined and some not eg global perspectives Pre-U, BTEC in public services, extended project, sports leadership programme, Russian, Arabic, law and book keeping for beginners as well as debating societies and Model United Nations. Range of academic societies with presentations by pupils and visitors. School sent a team to the International Young Physicists tournament in Germany (and will play host to the competition in 2014) and received a gold medal in the British Biology Olympiad.

S

About 130 pupils with SEN – mainly mild dyslexia. One full- and five part-time members of staff provide support. EAL offered but pupils must be able to follow the curriculum. Plenty of careers and university advice includes help finding work experience and talks on what employers are looking for. The school offers tuition for SATs (American University Entrance exams) and is a registered SAT centre. Lectures from universities, agricultural and art colleges and the world of work plus lower sixth talks on interview technique and an interview coaching course (charged for).

Low turnover of staff – loyal band, some were at Shrewsbury themselves. Increasing number of NQTs but most changes come from retirements – two women teachers on the Senior Leadership Team. Hugely supportive staff who 'bring out the best in everyone and take children as far as they want to go academically'. One parent told us, 'The school has brought out things in my son that none of us knew he had'.

Games, options, the arts: Sport taken seriously here both at house and school level but still with an emphasis on 'fun, friendship and fitness', as the school puts it. Wide range of sports; big on rowing, girls are now also afloat in numbers – lots of national competitions, significant presence at Henley and many Shrewsbury boys have represented their country on the water. Newly opened (2012) Yale boathouse with training room and indoor rowing tank. New head of rowing is from Abingdon – so interesting times ahead on the river. The elite can take it as a major sport for all three terms, the rest compete at house level. A leading Fives school (Eton variety) with 14 courts – a recent pupil was one of the first girls to be awarded a half blue at Oxford.

Venerable cross country running club known as 'The Hunt' is prominent on national circuit. Stunning cricket pitches described by Sir Neville Cardus as 'the most beautiful playing fields in the world'. Top class indoor cricket centre also used by local and regional clubs, funded by the Foundation. Recent winners of the national boys cricket 20:20 championships.

Masses of non-team sports including canoeing, kayaking, climbing, mountain biking, and sub aqua club. Outward bound and hill walking weekends to 'Tally' the school's own cottage in Snowdonia, with the aim of having 'serious fun'. Thriving CCF and Duke of Edinburgh up to Gold.

Rich and impressive musical tradition with numerous ensembles and choirs (places in the chapel choir particularly sought after), annual house singing competition. Pupils often take productions to the Edinburgh Fringe and perform concerts in London and Birmingham. All new pupils offered a free lesson on an instrument of their choice and there are several Steinways and an organ to practice on. Two major drama productions a year a well as house plays.

Buzzing art department with Mezzanine art gallery where upper sixth students can hold solo art exhibitions – particularly strong ceramics. A number go on to art school each year.

Dozens of societies, both academic and not so academic, from millinery and wine tasting to bee keeping and the green power electric car racing team. Witty and irreverent school magazine follows in the satirical tradition of the Old Salopian founders of Private Eye.

Community Service popular, but not compulsory, involves work in old people's homes, schools, charity shops etc – oh, and a trip to Malawi. School has close links with Shrewsbury House community centre in Liverpool, known as The Shewsy, sixth formers can spend a week there and see another side of life and children come back for a return match to Shrewsbury.

Background and atmosphere: Founded in 1552 by Edward VI, the school throve, faltered and then revived in 1882 when it moved across the river into the old workhouse-cum-lunatic asylum. It was named as one of the 'Great' public schools by the Clarendon Commission in 1886 along with Eton, Harrow et al.

Set in 100 acres high above the river Severn with distant views to the Malvern hills. Sir Arthur Blomfield's chapel was one of the first buildings to be built and is very much the centre of the community with its vibrant red and blue interior, striking modern ceramics and pew runners representing the River Severn. Not everyone can fit in the chapel so houses take it in turns to have a Sunday lie-in.

Elegant Edwardian houses cluster round the cricket pitch connected by immaculate lawns and fine avenues of trees. Programme of refurbishment underway and new buildings (more to come) blend into the landscape overseen by imposing statues of famous old boys Charles Darwin and the warrior poet Sir Philip Sydney.

The ancient Chained Library, open on Sunday mornings, contains some remarkable books including John Gower's 'Confessio Amantis' printed by Caxton in 1483 and Newton's 'Principia' which the school bought on publication in 1687, as well as books, manuscripts and letters of Charles Darwin.

The first girls joined sixth form in 2008 and school is going fully co-ed in 2014 aiming for 65:35 ratio with scope for numbers to increase to 780. Parents divided on this change between the huffers & puffers and those who felt it was a bit of a pity but probably inevitable. The blow softened by the evident high quality of the current sixth form girls, and the long lead time that means that all who joined for a boys' school with girls in the sixth will get just that. In our view Shrewsbury boys will adapt well to co-ed – a civilised and courteous lot.

Pastoral care and discipline: Strong sense of community and a family atmosphere with many staff living on site. 'Staff totally committed and often find it difficult to leave' but still a healthy number of young teachers. Comfortable relationships between staff and pupils who are still expected to call teachers 'Sir'. Eight boys' boarding houses, of about 60, two day houses and two purpose-built sixth form girls' houses – mixed day and boarding, with a third opening in 2014. Housemaster or mistress, matron and team of four or five tutors in each house. Boys' houses scruffy and comfortable – girls' houses newly built or refurbished with en suite bathrooms – some harrumphing from the boys about this but their houses next on the list for refurbishment. Boys start off in dorms and then graduate to study bedrooms as they move up the school.

The house system 'preserves the innocence of school days but makes sure children are ready for the next stage' says one happy mother. Children not allowed out on Saturday night without good reason (granny's birthday dinner likely to be as exciting as it gets) and they mostly keep to their side of the river anyway. It is too far away to, 'bunk off to the King's Road on a Saturday night', says another. Strong house loyalty with lots of inter-house competitions in music, drama and sport. Enormous dining room where everyone can eat together – pupils sit in house groups with tutors. Food much improved in recent years – lots of choice, praised by children.

Sixth form common room, known as Quod (no one knows why) with separate social and study areas and a shop is run by a committee of sixth formers who organise talks, lectures, film nights and socials. Sixth formers choose their own tutor and anyone who wants to be a prefect, known as a praeposter, has to write a letter of application to the headmaster.

The chapel is central to school life but Catholics can attend services at the cathedral across the river and other faiths are accommodated. Whole school policy on bullying is underpinned by extreme vigilance from housemasters (a comfortable and friendly crew): none of the parents we talked to mentioned bullying as a concern, and we heard no grisly stories from the boys either. If there is clear evidence of drug taking a pupil will be asked to leave, if it is unclear they have to comply with a testing regime. When asked about drinking, children said there was 'no point as you would only get caught', and there is no doubt in their minds as to how Mr T would react.

Pupils and parents: An eclectic mix of landed gentry, City money, local farmers and intellectuals, all happy to keep their children away from the rat race of the South East. From all over the country including London but most live within a couple of hours of the school. About ten per cent from overseas. Fleet of coaches ferries children home for exeats – as one father said, 'the school has something special and it is worth the long journey'. Lots of children of Old Salopians, sometimes fourth or fifth generation.

A school with a genuine sense of individuality, 'where you can really be yourself and where everyone's personality has a place' according to one sixth form girl. Described by a parent as 'interesting, interested and able to get on with people from all backgrounds'. Lovely quirky Salopian sense of humour can be seen in the Blue Chair Charity set up some years ago to raise money for Leukaemia research. Old Salopians take two blue chairs with them on their gap year and photograph them in unusual places – they have been spotted outside the Blue Mosque in Istanbul, at the Taj Mahal – one fell down a ravine and had to be rescued and another is being held hostage on the Somali border and an £8,000 ransom has been demanded! The 8,000 members of the old Salopian Club have a great bond and sense of community. Most famous old Salopian of all is Charles Darwin, who was at the school from 1818-1825. Others include Sir Martin Rees, President of the Royal Society and Astronomer Royal, Richard Ingrams, Willie Rushton and Christopher Booker who cut their satirical teeth on the school magazine The Public Nose and went on to found Private Eye, and Paul Foot who was a major contributor; also Michaels Palin and Heseltine.

Entrance: Fairly broad church and also looking for potential. Most come from about 12 preps within about two hours of the school. Entry mainly via CE (55 per cent required) or academic scholarship (held in the May before entry). School's own tests in English and maths for those at non-CE schools. A few join in the fourth form (Year 10) if things have not worked out elsewhere but must be able to 'hit the ground running', 25 boys and 50 girls join for sixth form – a number of boys come from local state schools.

At sixth form entry they are looking for candidates who will make a contribution to school life – sport music academic, drama. Assessment weekend in Nov prior to entry – candidates can choose three or four subjects in which to be assessed, plus a reference from current school, interview and personal statement.

Exit: About 50 per cent take a gap year – Shrewsbury International School in Bangkok useful source of employment for gappies – travel scholarships available for interesting and challenging gap years. About 98 per cent to university, 13 in 2013 to Oxbridge otherwise mainly Russell Group – Bristol, Newcastle, Leeds, Edinburgh. Anyone who does not achieve at least five Bs at GCSE will be asked to leave – parents get plenty of warning if this is likely to happen and headmaster has said that he will stick to this policy.

Money matters: Scholarships and bursaries a tradition since the school was founded. Not a rich school but very supportive Old Salopians and parents put their hands in their pockets for the annual Foundation appeal, a telephone campaign staffed by sixth formers and recent leavers. Range of Foundation awards and scholarships worth up to 50 per cent can be topped up with a bursary – testing, interviews and consultation with prep schools (and some primary schools) for talented children who can't afford fees. Academic, sports, all rounder, music and arts awards offered. Cassidy Sports Scholarship worth up to full fees for a boy entering sixth form from a state school and Alex Wilson day boy scholarship also worth up to full fees.

Remarks: A school where individuals and individual talent are truly celebrated and where there is a 'breadth of opportunity without pressure cooker atmosphere' Produces people with a wonderful and quirky sense of humour who are not afraid to be different.

Sibford School

Linked school: Sibford Junior School

Sibford Ferris, Banbury, Oxfordshire, OX15 5QL

- Pupils: 420 boys and girls; 60 board, the rest day • Ages: 3 –18
- Quaker • Fees: Boarding £15,555–£24,195; Day £7,758–£12,453 pa
- Independent

Tel: 01295 781200
Email: admissions@sibfordschool.co.uk
Website: www.sibford.oxon.sch.uk

Head: Since 2004, Michael Goodwin BA PGCE. Educated at Bury Grammar School, read history at the University of Nottingham. Previously head of Sheringham High School, Norfolk. Married to Veronika; they have four children, three flown the nest, youngest about to. Spends spare time with family, walking the dogs, going to theatre or travelling overseas; used to live in Spain and likes to return whenever possible.

Chatty, confident open, with a good sense of humour, parents say he is energetic, personable and friendly. 'I'd only ever encountered formal heads before so it was a shock to call him Michael but that is the Quaker way'. 'The more I get to know him, the more I think he is superb. He interviews all potential pupils and is excellent at putting them at their ease and making them feel special. Importantly the children respect him, he listens.' Liked and respected by pupils, but praise from some peppered with criticism – 'He can drone on in morning meetings, he talks a lot about his family and tries to be funny and tell jokes but doesn't always succeed' – though they unanimously add, 'He really cares about us, wants us to do well. We know if we have a problem we can always talk to him and is genuinely interested in us.'

Academic matters: Generally good facilities, including a smart, bright, well-stocked senior school library with plans afoot to upgrade those few areas in need of TLC. Classes are small and set independently, so it's possible to be in high group for maths, middle for science, low set for English etc – whatever works for the child. A third take triple science, usually those thinking of studying science at A level, with rest taking 21st century science. 'The course applies science to everyday life which stimulates interest in a subject when otherwise it might not have been there,' say science staff. Enlightened approach to English setting, look at the whole child and at their ability to understand, analyse and interpret English. 'We have children in top sets who use Dragon software. Sometimes the mechanics of reading or spelling may not be there but they may be incredibly insightful with a high verbal IQ. We have to stretch them, not constantly criticise every spelling mistake or punctuation error.' In 2013 88 per cent of pupils gained five GCSEs at A*-C.

Range of activities for those identified as gifted, talented or able (which includes some 40 per cent also identified as dyslexic). Sixth form pupils make guided subject choices. 'I like the freedom within subjects, the support from teachers when you need it and small classes mean lots of attention.' For the 20 per cent or so who need additional support, learning is tailored to the individual. 'We wanted a school where our son mattered as a person. He slipped under the radar in his previous school. He deserved more, so we looked for a school that would make

S

him feel special and found that in abundance at Sibford.' Full support consists of five 35 minute lessons per week plus in-class support if needed, and consists of any combination of literacy, numeracy, fine motor and speech and language input. Super revision library display board sets the tone, with handy hints such as 'use a timetable', 'record questions and quotations onto your iPod' etc. Lunch time activities include popular trampoline and swim sessions for those with gross motor difficulties. Regular internal audit process includes pupil interviews to ensure staff are supporting youngsters in a helpful and constructive way so they can learn to articulate their difficulties and accept that it is permissible to be dyslexic. Parents say support is impressive. 'There is no stigma, my child's self-esteem has rocketed; I cannot believe how chatty and confident he is; Sibford has transformed him.' Not a school that worries about league tables, stands by and encourages pupils.

Music/music technology and textiles currently in vogue, with girls generally performing better than boys, especially in the sciences and maths. Good value added though typically fewer than 50 per cent score A*-B grades at A-level (49 per cent in 2013); grades must be seen in context of intake and school's policy of allowing pupils to pursue subjects that interest them, not what shows the school in the best light. As pleased with a child who struggles and achieves four or five GCSEs at grade C as they are with the most able who achieve their fistfuls of A stars. 'We take great store by the journey to get there and the effort a child makes.' Wonderful collegiate approach means if a child hasn't understood something with one teacher, it is fine to seek extra help later, either from their teacher or from a different one. If a strength is identified, or child has a passion, staff will do all they can to encourage that. Working to embed independent learning allows youngsters to fail then succeed. Striving for excellence, candid about where they are, 'We've climbed the mountain and can see the summit, but like a diet, it's the last push that is the hardest to achieve.'

Games, options, the arts: Something for everyone: proud of music facilities, practice rooms, recording studio, music tech and bright, light ensemble room. Plenty of bands, orchestras and ensembles – with opportunity to perform publicly, regardless of grade. Super art with atmospheric lessons; we dropped in on an introduction to pop-art via the psychedelia of Sgt Pepper tracks – fun, and saw impressive displays of pottery, textiles and sculpture. All usual sports: rugby, football, cricket, hockey, netball, rounders plus squash (own courts), riding at local stables and swimming in own swish, 25-metre pool, with rowing and a multi-gym on wish list. Clubs galore with youngest expected to participate in at least three lunch offerings; huge variety: knitting, science awards, board games, origami and more. Range of inter-house challenges include musicals for the creative, quiz nights for the cerebral and construction challenges for the practical.

Pièce de résistance, guided by enterprising head of environmental science and horticulture, is outdoor education; whether through science, history, gardening club or just as a hobby. Lessons stretch beyond those of ecology, horticulture and the environment, to the economic, with plants marketed and sold to fund future ventures. The fantastic themed beds, ranging from sensory and historical (world war two utility garden and rotating allotment) to a sprinkling of the whacky and experimental, sit alongside a sturdy reconstruction of a Celtic roundhouse and wattle fence. We admired the student-designed prototype greenhouse built from recycled plastic bottles; very much epitomises the school's approach to learning: expect pupils to think up ideas, create designs, lay foundations, construct, kit-out, appraise, refine and improve. About to embark on BTEC Countryside Management and animal husbandry: expect to see pigs, sheep and cows among the throng.

Background and atmosphere: Sibford Ferris isn't a manicured Cotswold weekend retreat for city slickers playing at country life but a pretty, homely, much-loved village and community, with the school central to that. Sibford was founded as a co-ed boarding school by the Quakers in 1842. Originally housed in a splendid Cotswold stone manor house, in the 1930s it expanded into a hotchpotch of buildings known as 'The Hill'. In recent times, the manor was sold and the proceeds astutely ploughed back into purpose-built music and art blocks, with new sixth form centre following a couple of years later. Extensive, idyllic, 50-acre grounds, include an orchard, woodland, pond and even picnic benches for students. All new year 7 pupils (and new staff) mark their arrival at the school by planting either a tree or bush.

A school with a family feel, attention to detail and few places to hide, it was a heartbeat from failing when Michael arrived. 'I could see the potential but lots had to change. The location is wonderful, I pinch myself that I am here, but the school was looking unloved and uncared for.' He wasted no time appointing a financial director and together they worked out an investment/development plan. Resuscitation was needed, but recognising it is all too easy to pour money into schools, then watch them haemorrhage, they went for the full face lift, rather than sticking plaster approach. Tough decisions were taken. School changed from boarding to a day school with boarding; a sustained and sustainable refurbishment programme began in earnest and some staff departed, not all wholly voluntarily. 'We had become the school of second choice, but thanks to our development programme and marketing initiatives we are now a conscious first choice. People understand what we are about; we focus on the child, take them as our starting point, and that is what our families buy into. The school has a wonderful local feel so we consciously restrict international boarding to 10 per cent. We'd like a few more boarders but not at any cost'. Three boarding houses at varying stages of refurbishment: boys' is newly decorated with laundry, games tables and new TV; girls and sixth formers bemoan dearth of power to showers, problems with heating, lack of laundry facilities, depressing paint colours, broken piano and tiny kitchen but praise the atmosphere, camaraderie and care.

Pastoral care and discipline: Excellent pastoral care is a given. 'It is crucial we consider long term mental health, so we start with values and relationships, not academic excellence.' Aim to develop emotional fortitude so pupils leave with emotional robustness. 'We help them balance social life and work so they don't burn out.' Daily staff briefing ensures all aware of potential pupil issues. Parents say pastoral staff never leave problems until the following day, 'They spend an inordinate amount of time dealing with issues, nip things in the bud, give time to parents, explore avenues and work out how to proceed; with child's interests at heart.' Has a deserved reputation for being nurturing and is very much the place where 'if dyslexic you go', but the perception that it is just for dyslexics no longer holds, 'They really do find the best in every single child,' say parents, adding, 'To feel special and to be good at something is incredibly important for self-esteem; our children go from strength to strength. It isn't an easy or soft option, they just have the knack of getting all children to really want to do well.'

Only a handful of full boarders (do check age and gender mix) so weekends operate on a cosy, home from home basis with brunch rather than breakfast, a trip out, 'Trips are great fun, they encourage you to mix across the years', and emphasis on relaxation and rest – no Saturday school or matches. Food much improved but not yet cordon bleu and surprisingly, no-one objects to technology/gadget free lunchtimes. House parents mainly get huge thumbs up, 'They listen, are fun and there for us.'

Pupils and parents: Not a 'stand aside, call me Sir' school; equitable outlook extends beyond the classroom, so expect to find staff queuing and eating with children. 'Can do, will do' attitude means there's never a lack of volunteers, even if they're not quite sure what they are volunteering for! Happy to get their hands dirty and rise to any challenge. Emphasis on team work. Lack of overt competitive edge means some parents feel it isn't a great place for those aiming for top tier sport, but conversely believe it is ideal for the bright boffin who may either struggle to fit in elsewhere or who finds the social aspects of school life a challenge. Huge praise from parents. 'It's a fantastic school. If I had known how good it was I would have sent all my children here, safe in the knowledge that all would have done extremely well. Teachers have time for individual pupils so different characters can grow and flourish.' No typical pupils but tolerance is in the blood. 'My child has a huge variety of amazing friends, some slightly weird, some terribly normal.' Few families (or staff) are practising Quakers but all buy into the ethos, with tolerance to the fore. 'My child is geeky but he fits in and is accepted.' Go beyond the bounds to support and encourage ambition; expect to find budding artists, thespians, entrepreneurs, eco-warriers et al. A school where tomorrow's doctor will be helped and encouraged, not just to gain a place at medical school but to think fully about career paths – surgery, Africa, professorship, though always with emphasis on the importance of all team contributors, whether cleaner, technician or top-dog.

Parents from a wide range of backgrounds and income brackets, including a number of first time buyers; many very involved in school. Not a school for the pushy brigade; most choose Sibford precisely because they do want their children to achieve and do well, but that means prioritising mental health and well-being above exams and grades. Notable old Sibfordians include the late Paul Eddington, Guy Ritchie and Charlie Boorman.

Entrance: Into senior school at 11 and 13 with entry at other times if places are available. Pretty broad brush intake: 10 per cent gifted, 10 per cent who might struggle at hotter-houses. Look for youngsters who want to be at the school and will benefit from their time there. Good at second chances and helping those who have struggled elsewhere; Sibford picks up the pieces, stands by its brood, when other schools surrender. Often second choice school but not second best; it isn't unusual for parents to visit just to tick the boxes, then become enamoured. 'They think they want fancy facilities, labels or names but end up buying into the Quaker values and ethos; those of respect, nurturing, care and quiet ambition.'

Exit: Up to 25 leave after GCSE, mostly for further education colleges, independent schools offering different subjects at A level, apprenticeships or training. Majority to university but school conscious that uni is not right for everyone. Some to Russell Group universities including Leeds and Southampton, occasional one to Oxbridge, but most to newer universities including UWE, Bournemouth, Westminster and Bangor.

Money matters: Not a rich school but offers a number of academic, music and art scholarships, plus means-tested bursaries to both Quaker and non-Quaker families. Sound financial management means the school continues to improve buildings and facilities.

Remarks: In the words of one youngster, 'It just gels; they make you feel important, believe in yourself and want to do well.' No boxes or moulds. A school with a comprehensive intake, universal outlook and concentration on the individual; not fine or fanciful but fun and fair with a flair for finding, and focusing on, talents.

Sidcot School

Linked school: Sidcot Junior School

Oakridge Lane, Winscombe, North Somerset, BS25 1PD

• Pupils: 400 • Ages: 11-18 • Quaker • Fees: Day £13,770–£15,150; Boarding £22,740–£29,520 pa • Independent

Tel: 01934 843102
Email: admissions@sidcot.org.uk
Website: www.sidcot.org.uk

Head: Since September 2012, Mr Iain Kilpatrick BA MEd FRSA PGCE (mid-forties), previously head of Beaconhurst School at Bridge of Allan. He worked in banking before doing a degree in English and teaching qualifications and became resident tutor at Strathallan, near Perth. Joined Beaconhurst as housemaster and head of expressive arts/English before being appointed head.

Married, his wife is a pharmacist who has always taken an active part in school life, both during his time as a head and when he was a housemaster. Two children who both attend the school. Outside interests include theatre, reading, hill walking and golf.

He hopes to bring his prior experience of boarding and day provision to bear in strengthening the school's existing offer.

Academic matters: Traditionally holistic but academic results have improved greatly in recent years – maths and science strong with 92 per cent A*/B at maths A level and 79 per cent in science. Won Good Schools Guide Award for the best further mathematics A level results for boys in the country for three years in a row. School has made strong play for overseas students whose work ethic has had positive influence overall. Staff:pupil ratio of 1:7 in sixth form and 1:15 lower down. Head doesn't like AS exams at end of lower sixth and has offered IB ('breadth with depth') alternative since 2007, alongside A levels. 2012 IB entrants averaged 32 points. In 2013 47 per cent of A levels graded A*/A. At GCSE in 2013 96 per cent 5+ A* to C grades (over half A*/A)) which, given significant number of dyslexic pupils, suggests any pupil can fulfil his or her potential here. Sats have also gone – head wants pupils to 'like thinking about things' and prefers them to be 'happy and creative' away from the constant exam treadmill. Pupils with special needs are well catered for by specialist staff. Dyslexics especially well supported. Not unusual for dyslexics to get top GCSE grades.

Light, airy classrooms with well-equipped practical areas; lots of ICT, interactive whiteboards with LCD projectors etc but not techno crazy. Some dedicated and charismatic teaching. Seemed appropriate that RS group we saw was learning about Gandhi. Pupils enthused about DT which also covers product design (quite a few choose this at uni, having enjoyed it here), fashion, textiles and food. Head working hard to persuade more day pupils to stay for sixth rather than get a free 16+ education nearby. GCSE choices include Latin; able mathematicians add statistics. New arrangement for science taken at end of year 10 with additional science a year later. Boys do as well as girls at GCSE here – attributed to lack of peer pressure problems. Day pupils can stay for supervised early prep (5-6pm) but no Saturday lessons.

Academic English School accommodates about 20 overseas entrants in refurbished and discrete area of school with fast-track and one-year induction programmes. IGCSE, plus three levels of Cambridge English and mother tongue exams with visiting Chinese teacher to support A level candidates. ICT and GCSE subjects also offered; lots of cultural visits and full use of Sidcot facilities, though some resistance towards early and full social integration, say indigenous sixth formers.

S

Games, options, the arts: Quaker emphasis on involvement before competition or compulsion; sport is 'not a vigorous and pump thing' in the sixth form according to some students. However, there are three houses for internal competition and school produces winning teams in traditional sports plus representation at all levels. Cullis Centre (named after OB donor) boasts large sports hall plus awesome 25-metre swimming pool, now properly managed by sports graduate to give pupils plenty of access outside lesson time. Sixth formers were eyeing squash court as a possible disco venue when we visited. Sports choices include lively table-tennis tournaments, Octopush, canoeing, fencing, riding, dry slope skiing and golf. Three short tennis/netball courts close to school; 20 acres of playing fields (reached safely via bridge over A38) for hockey, rounders, rugby, football and cricket.

Huge range of mainly weekday activities caters for all tastes and interests from aerobics to pottery; chess to guitar construction. How many other schools make life drawing an 'open' activity from year 7? 'Younger pupils can really get into the drawing once they get used to the idea,' commented a committed sixth form artist. Public speaking and UN club encourage pupils to engage with peace issues whilst environmental action group is also 'up for it' and plans to 'green' areas of the school. Lots of D of E to encourage self-motivation, with community service, overnight expeditions on Quantocks etc. Cultural/educational trips; visits abroad include skiing and to USA; non-Quakers can join annual Quaker schools' pilgrimage (affectionately known as 'Foxtrot') to Pendle Hill in the Lake District.

Arts centre officially opened in 2009. Successful art department (check out their on-line gallery) is well-resourced and includes animation and computer graphics as well as facilities for ceramics and sculpture, screen printing, painting and drawing. Lunchtime concerts for parents and locals feature choirs, jazz group and band. DJ academy run by a peripatetic has led to home-grown, student-run discos. Music technology has expanded with new facilities and a new drama studio means that drama will no longer have to cope with the acoustic nightmare of acting under a tin roof. Full orchestra and over one-third of school play an instrument, with many reaching diploma level.

School has own horses plus limited stabling for mainly boarders' horses; working livery arrangements; preparation for British Horse Society certificates; hacking in local countryside. Great for boarders who can't bear term-time separation or any who want to learn to ride.

Background and atmosphere: Founded in 1699 by tolerant Quakers in West of England to spread a liberal educational ideology, but still not well known. Equality of sexes and critical enquiry valued from year dot and the 10 per cent of pupils with SEN issues have high self-esteem, know they can achieve and that they are valued. Meeting hall used for daily assemblies and weekly 'meeting for worship' run by two sixth form 'elders', Sidcot's serene 150 acre location close to Cheddar Gorge is just off busy A38 and near Bristol airport. Onside parents commented, 'the Quaker atmosphere hit us immediately we entered,' but for most of us it would take a little longer, especially as there are few overt Quaker symbols. Smaller than most independent schools with no far-flung boarding houses, and its teaching accommodation all within close proximity. Parents have kept faith with school despite some upsetting media allegations regarding a teacher no longer on the staff.

Environmentally aware. Catering mantra is '25 per cent organic, 25 per cent locally produced and 50 per cent unprocessed,' but there wasn't a carrot or apple to be seen at the tuck shop. Superb, light dining area with great veggie options, salad and pasta bars; breakfast club free to early comers. Mounting pupil pressure for outside play areas likely to upset erstwhile 'peaceful' atmosphere of school's well-kept gardens.

Inside, stunning library on two floors with stained glass cupola based on pupils' own designs. Well-appointed sixth form centre with networked study spaces, careers and conference facilities. Corridors displaying pupils' art work well and also highlight contemporary issues.

Five sensitively-run, if largely forgettable boarding houses vary a lot in lay-out and accommodation. Personal expression extends to students choosing furnishings in common rooms and cooking own meals; local Chinese take-away predictably faring much better than its Italian predecessor. Generally alcohol free; health education an initial response to illicit smoking. Lesson-free weekends allow day leaves to Bristol giving plenty of freedom to boarders, but many stay on site. As you'd expect, lots of fund-raising through year for worthy causes with famine lunches etc.

Pastoral care and discipline: Pupils care for each other with uncommon empathy in this 'community of individuals'. Vertical grouping in boarding houses encourages everyone to mix easily and juniors are in and out of senior school during day. Strong sense of fairness and honouring individual differences; recognises a child with a prestigious talent may not be straight down the line, won't fit in neatly or think as majority do but will make own way with help, support and guidance. Believes some aspects of SpLDs are an advantage – help a child think outside the box. Won't write children off, use role models where they can, including parents. Bullying an anathema here. College of Teachers confers on important decisions. Twenty sixth formers called 'office holders' organise various events. Female pastoral deputy co-ordinates all aspects of discipline with horizontal year heads and houseparents in the front line. Usual mix of sanctions and rewards, but you'd need to be beyond the pale to get expelled. Most problems sorted out with gentle rather than authoritarian response from staff.

Pupils and parents: Only 10 per cent Quakers; most day pupils come from affluent local area, for whom Sidcot is seen as socially preferable (at least to 16+) plus progeny of Bristol's more liberal illuminati, who are transported to and from the city by coach; weekly boarders from M4/M5 corridor; international students currently represent 23 countries with strong oriental contingent. 'Could fill a second school with special needs children,' remarked one teacher, so school selects those 'who'll give something back'. One-third board with over half from overseas (more in sixth). Quaker attitudes seem to rub off on those who stay into sixth; pupils described by teacher as 'predominantly justice seekers.' Pretty scatty lot (to judge from volume of lost property waiting to be claimed in sports centre) but it's 'safe to leave stuff lying around,' insisted pupils we met.

Smartly uniformed pupils up to 16 in blue and white striped shirts, ties (for boys), neat hair etc, whilst sixth formers wear what they like within reason. Sixth formers dress smartly, however, for weekly meeting for worship, which mystifies Quaker old hands for whom it's not important.

Week's pow-wow for former pupils every Easter when pupils put on concerts/theatricals/art exhibitions. Old Scholars include Sir George Trevelyan, Robert Shackleton, George Palmer (Huntley & Palmer), historian Edmund Ashby, Justin Webb and some of the younger Dimbleby clan, Zoe Wanamaker, Tim Bevan, Deborah Warner (RSC director) et al.

Entrance: Automatic entry from junior school. Entrance test at nine and 13 can be taken at applicant's present school. Common entrance a possible alternative to school's own entrance exam in February. An overnight taster day can be arranged. Entry to sixth form requires minimum six C grades at GCSE or equivalent. EAS students accepted at any time of the year. A genuinely mixed-ability school but not usually for severe SEN cases, though everyone is given a fair chance. Handful of students have a range of special needs: exceptionally bright, gifted and talented, dyslexia, dyspraxia, dyscalculia, Asperger's, ADD, ADHD and physical disabilities (improved wheelchair access on cards). Looks at every single child, takes those who'll benefit from school and give a bit back; only has room for occasional child requiring a learning support assistant.

Exit: After GCSE some join local sixth forms or college in Bristol etc but majority stay. Geared to finding right course at right institution, however talented a student. Recently helped a very bright dyslexic student who wanted to study medicine find a course with a practical bias (a great comfort to those of us who'd rather be opened up by a surgeon with a steady hand and good eye than a whizz at spelling!). At 18, 70 per cent proceed to wide range of universities and degree courses. Significant number take a gap year. Twenty per cent to art foundation/art colleges; some to drama colleges; usually one or two to Royal Academy of Music; a couple to Oxbridge.

Money matters: Day fee higher than QEH and Bristol Grammar but compares favourably with other independents in area. Means-tested bursary support is available and non-financial scholarships are awarded in academic and non-academic subjects. With six other Quaker schools in UK, offers up to 100 per cent remission of fees for Quaker families.

Remarks: A school which serves a wide constituency, both locally and internationally; draws strength from its Quaker foundation and generally walks its talk. Singularity of style lays it open to misinterpretation but pupils become its best ambassadors. A rare breed of school which values individual worth above corporate success.

Sir John Cass Foundation and Redcoat Church of England Secondary School

Stepney Way, London, E1 0RH

- Pupils: 1600 girls and boys (including post 16) • Ages: 11–19
- C of E foundation • State

Tel: 020 7790 6712
Email: sirjohncass@sjcr.net
Website: www.sjcr.net

Head: Since 1995, Mr Haydn Evans (sixties), who arrived in Stepney after deputy headships in Tonbridge and, briefly, at a large rural comprehensive in Bridgend. His then school-age children failed to settle in Wales, and he returned happily to commute in from Kent to the headship of this inner-city church school. Praised as a strong, determined, strategic thinker and very successful head ('exemplary', said Ofsted), he has overseen the opening of the sixth form and the upward trajectory of the whole school, transforming it from an under-subscribed comprehensive with exam results on the minimal side to one with over 1,200 applicants for 180 places. The Building Schools for the Future programme has now extended the school buildings to give it increased accommodation and capacity.

A hands-on head, he teaches chemistry to A level and is frequently out and about in the school with other senior managers, helping to police the comings and goings between lessons as 1,600 pupils move round a school built for 800. 'We act as an unobtrusive presence – we rarely have to say or do anything.'

Academic matters: Consistently near the top of the value-added tables and has three times been ranked the most improved school in the country. Most pupils come in with lower than average achievement, but around 80 per cent (82 per cent in 2013) get at least five A*-C grades at GCSE or equivalent. This falls to about half if you include maths and English, unsurprisingly since English is a second language for around 80 per cent of the pupils. They come from a huge range of primaries and many have difficult home lives. 'Our first focus is on behaviour, on creating a climate for learning. Then we engage them with exciting teaching.'

The latest Ofsted report, which rated the school 'outstanding', praised its very high expectations of all pupils. New year 7s are tested and placed in sets for maths, English, science and RE. These are fluid and there's plenty of scope to move up as one's English improves or down should the maths start to prove tricky. There are vocational as well as academic courses at KS4, for example in science and IT. The school keeps a close eye on pupils' progress, targeting those who need extra help to ensure that everyone gets the grades they need to move on to the next stage. 'They have very high aspirations for my daughter,' said a parent. 'They push the children very hard to succeed.'

It is a specialist language college and everyone studies two languages for the first three years, from a choice of French, Spanish and Bengali, continuing at least one to GCSE. There is also a choice of 11 languages in twilight classes (for parents as well as pupils), and many pupils take a GCSE in their own native language before year 11. Many go on French or Spanish exchanges. The school has links an instituto in rural Spain, and children who had rarely left the East End of London have found themselves travelling to school by horse and cart.

It also has a business and enterprise specialism and good links with Canary Wharf and City firms, with some offering work placements, scholarships to cover university fees and jobs after graduation to talented students. Sixth form business studies students can have mentoring from business partners, visits and seminars, lectures and summer internships. One pupil recently spent the summer in America, having won a coveted place on a Student Leadership programme.

The large sixth form, with some 600 pupils, has its own new centre, including a library, IT suite, mixed and girls' only common rooms (the latter with pink net curtains) and a popular café. It offers a variety of vocational courses alongside A levels and GCSE retakes, and is piloting the new IT diploma, with business and finance and society, health and development diplomas to follow. Many students come in from elsewhere to join those moving up, and quite a few have relatively low qualifications. Some start with intermediate level courses then move up to higher levels en route to university. Science and maths A levels are particularly popular and successful, alongside psychology, RE and sociology.

About ten per cent of pupils have some kind of special need. 'We have an elaborate academic support team. The governors have decided to invest heavily in this and it is a very worthwhile investment.' Gifted and talented pupils are also identified for extra support. Learning mentors and assistants work through teachers and directly with pupils, helping to track their progress and ensure they know what they need to do to improve. There are regular extension and catch-up classes. Staff recruitment is not a problem, with over 60 applicants for a recent RE vacancy. 'We have a high profile and we attract high quality applicants.'

Games, options, the arts: Sports facilities include a swimming pool (everyone learns to swim by the end of their first term) and a sports hall with space for basketball, badminton, football and cricket. Football and basketball teams play enthusiastic and successful matches against other schools. Table tennis, boxing and fencing are also on the agenda. A level sports science students coach younger pupils. Girls and boys have separate PE and sports lessons, as well as separate entrances and playgrounds – an innovation that is very popular with pupils and parents.

Actors perform at the Mile End Theatre and the steel band has played at the Albert Hall. Guitar club and a gospel choir, and many pupils have individual music lessons. Trips to operas and musicals. A school ski trip in the Easter holidays, D of E, ice skating, rock climbing and canoeing trips. Sixth formers organise societies, including Christian Union and Muslim Students' Society.

Background and atmosphere: Formed in 1964 by the governing body of Red Coat School (established in 1714 for boys born within Mile End Old Town) and the governors of the Sir John Cass Foundation (a charity set up in 1710 by Sir John Cass for poor children in the East End of London). The school is owned by the Foundation, one of London's oldest educational charities, and Founder's Day in St Botolph-without-Aldgate church is one of the highlights of the school year. Its present site, with its pleasant red-brick buildings, dates from 1965. It is right in the middle of the East End but in a deceptively rural-seeming setting with a city farm opposite, a park next door and the school church and its tranquil graveyard beyond.

The school has been refurbished to include up-to-date science labs and learning centres stocked with computers. These are open before and after school and on Saturday mornings, with learning mentors around to help. Many pupils have no computer at home, nor quiet space in which to do homework. The great hall with stage and balcony doubles as a lecture theatre and can accommodate the entire school for assemblies. 'These are important for setting the behaviour tone for the school.' Lower school pupils wear a traditional uniform including a blazer, which becomes more informal higher up the school. Honours boards line the reception area. Although this is a C of E school, the vast majority of pupils are Muslims and they have their own prayer room.

Pastoral care and discipline: An orderly atmosphere is central to the ethos of the school. 'Security and mutual respect are very high priority. First of all we make them feel secure and safe, then we start to cultivate respect for all. A feeder primary school may be less traditional than we are but we're confident that when they come here we'll get them into our ethos by the end of the first half term.' The atmosphere is indeed calm and orderly, with some exuberance in the corridors between lessons but quiet concentration in the classrooms. There are CCTV cameras throughout, which, say staff, discourage vandalism and add to students' sense of security. Staff check on the destinations of those wandering the corridors between lessons.

By all accounts very little racial tension and very few exclusions. 'We do very occasionally have some challenging behaviour but it does not threaten the learning environment. We try hard not to exclude if we can possibly avoid it.' Two qualified counsellors on the staff. 'It's a very happy school,' said a parent, 'but the kids are expected to knuckle down and achieve.'

Pupils and parents: About two-thirds of the pupils are Bangladeshi, the rest from a variety of ethnic minorities, including many Somali refugees. Parents mostly very supportive of the school and its high expectations for their children. They join in maths workshops and twilight language classes and become involved in the numerous community projects. Pupils form strong peer groups. 'There's a very strong ethos of care for one another,' said a parent.

Entrance: Some 1,200 applicants for 180 places. Everyone is placed in one of four ability bands, assessed by the standard Tower Hamlets primary school test, with equal numbers of places offered from each band. This is a C of E school, so it does allocate a minority of places to committed Christians. Thirty-six places go to worshippers in a recognised Christian church, with looked-after children, social and medical needs, living in one

of the listed parishes and then siblings in order of priority. The other 144 places have a similar priority order, but 20 are offered to first-born children. Families in the area tend to be large and siblings would otherwise monopolise the intake. Distance from the school is the tie-break.

The sixth form is also highly over-subscribed, with over 1,000 applicants for 300 outside places. Most advanced level courses require five or more A*-C grades at GCSE including English and maths, with some higher stipulations eg an A in maths for maths or further maths A level. But those with lesser qualifications can take lower level courses, and the majority of pupils from year 11 go through to the sixth form.

Exit: Those who leave after GCSEs – about 10 per cent of year 11s – mostly go on to another sixth form or straight into a job. All year 13 leavers for the past three years – and some of these may have spent several years in the sixth form improving their qualifications – have gone straight to university. For social and cultural reasons, the vast majority choose London universities, but some venture further afield. The first successful Oxbridge applicant started classics at Cambridge in 2008 and three had offers in 2009. Two further students were accepted at Cambridge and began their courses in 2011 and 2012. 'I am confident that once they start coming back to tell our students about it we'll have more applicants.' Some students return to the school as teachers or learning mentors.

Remarks: A beacon of excellence in a deprived area of London, which takes in students with low levels of attainment and sends the majority off to university with commendable exam results. A strong head and committed staff insist on good behaviour, provide expert teaching and inspire high aspirations. 'It's gone from strength to strength,' said a parent. 'It's a great school.'

Sir Roger Manwood's School

Manwood Road, Sandwich, Kent, CT13 9JX

- Pupils: 910 boys and girls, of which 55 board • Ages: 11–18
- None • Fees: Boarding £9,300 pa; Day-Free • State

Tel: 01304 613286
Email: info@srms.kent.sch.uk
Website: www.srms.kent.sch.uk

Headteacher: Since September 2013, Mr Lee Hunter, previously deputy head of Tiffin Girls' Grammar School in Surrey. A biochemist (read natural sciences at Cambridge), he first joined Tiffin Girls' as head of science in 1997. His career also includes stints as a science teacher at the Royal Grammar School in High Wycombe, the Sir James Henderson British School of Milan and Framwellgate Moor School in Durham.

Some of Mr Hunter's proudest school moments have included leading expeditions to the Indian Himalayas and introducing the Duke of Edinburgh award. Moving to the Kent coast will enable him to enjoy his hobbies of running, walking and cycling, as well as travelling frequently to France.

Academic matters: In 2013 70 per cent A* to B at A level and 48 per cent A/A* at GCSE. A quarter take history to A level. Maths is also a popular choice with more than a third of students taking A level and others taking further maths. The school has a resident maths genius who competed last year in the International Mathematics Olympiad and was placed 30th out of 548 of the world's best mathematicians. All three sciences also strongly represented at A level. The school is designated a High Performing Language College, and languages offered include French, German, Spanish and Mandarin Chinese, plus Italian as a sixth form option.

If there's a weak department, it would appear to be ICT. Given that the school has computing as a specialism, it's surprising that only five candidates took the A level in 2012, and none took it in 2013. 'It's the way the lessons are taught, it needs changing,' complain sixth-formers. This cohort were among the first to take a compulsory GCSE in business and communications systems which has appeared to turn many off computing (although it may well be a qualification they appreciate more when they are drawing up CVs). There are plans to introduce ICT courses which students will find more stimulating and relevant, following a government review of the ICT curriculum. Student requests led to A levels being introduced in film studies, psychology and sports studies, although head says that some universities' preference for traditional academic subjects seems to be turning the tide away from these newcomers.

Pupils feel they are largely taught well, 'There are one or two teachers I wouldn't employ myself, but many are the best you could get,' says one student. It's a competitive environment, but not harshly so. 'People who arrive here for the sixth form say they are pushed harder here than at other schools, but teachers work with you, they help people who are not doing so well,' one student says.

In the sixth form group, the brainy boy off to do medicine at Cambridge comes in for as much gentle joshing as the one who has found the going harder and will be reading sports sciences. 'I was one of the people who got extra help, but it didn't make me feel that everyone else was better than me,' says the latter. Another relates how effective the teaching support was. 'It was spotted that I was weak at French and I got extra help. Well then I got an A* in my French GCSE,' he says.

Games, options, the arts: Sporting whizzes will be right at home here. The head reels off a long list of current and former pupils who are competing at the highest levels. 'We're very good at tennis, we've got the under-14 number two in the country. We've allowed him to reduce his timetable and take time off school. One girl is representing the country in the under-19 MCC ladies' cricket team. Two girls represent England in the ISF World Cross Country Under-18 championship. One girl competed in the National Youth Swimming championships, and the school has produced an international hockey player who has represented GB at two Olympic games, and a member of the England ladies' cricket team.' Such high levels of sporting success gave one parent of a boy out of this league cause for concern, but she says, 'He is not sporty and I worried about him fitting in, but he quickly found friends through the CCF and music groups.'

About 120 pupils get involved with the CCF, going on annual camps, shooting days and field weekends, and D of E awards are also popular. One parent wishes there were more kudos for the musicians. 'Music is tiny within the life of the school, sports and languages get much more attention,' she says. However the school counters that music has a very high profile with lots of students learning to play an instrument, and many opportunities to play music in the orchestra, various bands, choirs and concerts. Orchestral tours have recently taken pupils to Sicily and Istanbul, and the school is 'very good for musicals' according to the sixth formers. The annual big production is open to all. 'Obviously some singers are better than others, but you can still get a part if you're mediocre,' says a student.

An internationalist approach is a big part of the school's ethos, and this sees children offered exchange visits to China, India and Germany. There are language tours to Barcelona, Madrid, Paris and Berlin, a politics trip to Washington, and a visit to the Gambia every Easter, where sixth formers work at the village school.

Background and atmosphere: Tucked down a quiet and leafy residential street, the school is an appealing jumble of historic buildings with modern day additions such as an IT resource centre, science blocks and Astroturf. It was founded 450 years ago by Sir Roger Manwood to bring learning to the townspeople of Sandwich.

Academy status, granted in 2011, has given the school more autonomy and extra funding which has so far financed building refurbishments and an extension to the sixth form common room.

It's a spacious campus with lots of green space and the two boarding houses are a stone's throw from the teaching blocks. Boys have the grander accommodation with oak floors, ornate staircases and mullioned windows. The girls' house is nondescript but cosy. All but two bedrooms are shared. Rooms have high sleepers with desks underneath and look like every teenage girls' bedroom with mates' pictures on the walls and hair straighteners lying across the beds. The housemates are 'like a family', says a boarder. The menu pinned up features school meal standards – the food is 'bad', laments a boarder, although the school argues that it has been rated good by Ofsted.

Boarders' weekends are filled with a mixture of organised outings and pursuing individual interests – students can, for example, take riding lessons or go for sleepovers at friends' houses.

Pastoral care and discipline: Asked who is most approachable on the staff, the students rattle off a long list of names – clearly it's the majority rather than the odd one. Relationships with the staff seem unusually warm. 'The teachers are friendly, they really care and they know you on a personal level,' says one pupil. 'They care about us so much, and help us so much,' echoes another. And it would seem that treating students with kindness and respect filters down through the school. The sixth formers look genuinely surprised when we ask about any tendency for the big kids to put the younger ones in their place, and say that would never happen. A parent concurs, 'There is no rough and tumble, there's no bullying, our child has been happy all the way through'. Another parent was worried about her child making the transition from a small independent school, but she says: 'He fitted into a family incredibly quickly.'

SEN department caters for students with dyspraxia, dyslexia and autism and provides individual support for a pupil with visual impairment.

Pupils and parents: There's an uncommon gentleness about the school, which makes it an absolute find for parents who are concerned about how their child will deal with the hurly-burly of secondary school. A few minutes in the company of these young people is all it takes for pro-single sex school arguments to crumble. There's a warmth and naturalness between the students – no macho posturing from the boys or cliquey ring-fencing from the girls. 'Our year gets on really well,' the year 13s agree.

Sandwich regarded as posher than many of its neighbouring towns on the depressed East Kent coast and free school meal numbers lower than at nearby schools. Recently the town has been hit hard by the withdrawal of pharmaceutical giant Pfizer and the loss of 2,500 jobs, although the local council is offering enticements to businesses with the aim of creating a life sciences hub on the site. The commute to London is a slow trundle stopping at all stations; parents tend to be employed locally or stay in town for the working week.

Boarders from Nigeria, Nepal, Hong Kong, Estonia and Germany bring a healthy melee of cultures and backgrounds to the pupil mix.

Entrance: Pupils must pass the local 11+, the Kent test. Children with British or EU passports are entitled to a free education here. Out of 120 places in year 7, six are reserved for boarders. The boarding places are not usually over-subscribed, but day places are. Each year around 30 cases go to appeal, with around a further six places being awarded after appeals.

Pupils come from more than 30 feeder primary schools and the catchment is just below five miles, with the majority of pupils living in Deal, Walmer and Sandwich.

Entrance from year 8 onwards via a test administered by the school. Vast majority stay on for the sixth form, new pupils need six GCSEs at A* to C, and at least a B grade in chosen subjects.

Exit: Six to Oxbridge in 2013, others to the old guard of Imperial, UCL, Durham and Bristol. Creative types headed for courses in advertising, footwear design, sports journalism, dance, and musical theatre. Each year a few go on to study medicine, encouraged by the Claringbold scholarship from an old Manwoodian which provides an income of £1,000 per year during their studies.

Remarks: If you're seeking a school to move house for, this should be on your list. With a full hand of grade ones from Ofsted it's unquestionably a good school, and the town of Sandwich offers a gorgeous beach, a golf course which regularly plays host to the Open Championship, creekside walks, and some of the best preserved mediaeval architecture in the country. Plus, unusually, it's a mixed sex grammar, so you can educate sons and daughters together.

If you don't want to move house, there's also the option of boarding at state school prices. Parents fighting whitened tooth and manicured nail over places in the West Kent grammars may be missing a trick here. You can get a top flight education paying only the boarding fee, a snip compared to independent day school prices in the south east.

Sir William Borlase's Grammar School

West Street, Marlow, Buckinghamshire, SL7 2BR

- Pupils: 1,000 boys and girls; all day • Ages: 11–18 • Inter–denom
- State

Tel: 01628 816500
Email: enquiries@swbgs.com
Website: www.swbgs.com

Headteacher: Since 1997, Dr Peter Holding MA BA MA(Ed) (late fifties), studied both in the United States and back in United Kingdom. Married with no children. Approachable – his dog certainly is – although some parents say he can appear a little distant. Sits on various educational committees and praised for implementing the latest thinking at a good pace and with a firm grip. Values international experience. Seizes on opportunities to enhance individual achievement and develop young people in the wider community. Few successes seem to pass him by or go uncelebrated.

Academic matters: Selective intake and consistent performance well above average, with parents and pupils loath to pinpoint particular areas of strength or weakness. Some references to truly fabulous teaching and one or two to weaker staff members, most of whom appear to move on of their own accord. Cross-disciplinary collaboration an increasing focus. 'We want creative physicists and mathematicians.' Lauded for wider personal and leadership development.

No-one rests on their laurels, the school included. It is seeking specialist status in additional subjects, subscribes to a commercial IT-enabled virtual learning environment, reports to parents online and allocates learning mentors from amongst staff and sixth formers to ensure all on track and sufficiently challenged. Not considered overly pushy – but could some lower down the school be pushed more? Some think so, but a very minor criticism and one which the school seems to be addressing. Recently it has introduced an accelerated two-year key stage 3 programme to create opportunities for extended project work, independent thinking and wider spread of subject areas. Most pupils take 12 GCSEs and in 2013 99 per cent gained A*-C, with 73 per cent achieving A*-B. At A level in 2013 81 per cent of candidates gained A*-B. Very few SEN pupils but when problems emerge responsive to parental concerns and, of late, general agreement that getting better in dealing with them effectively.

Games, options, the arts: Croquet matches in progress in the quad at lunch time, with aspiring players waiting patiently in the wings, but the school offers much more than that on the sporting front. Around 20 at any one time form the Borlase Elite Sports Team (BEST). Strongest are rowing and hockey with two full international girl rowers, and 40-50 county hockey players. Through the School Sport Partnership pupils flex their leadership and other muscles, organising extra clubs and competitions in cheerleading, dance, table-tennis and girls' rugby, to name but a few.

The school's specialist performing arts status is well-deserved. Ex-pupil Ben Smith who appears in Disney Channel UK's comedy sketch show Life Bites is a source of considerable pride in the community. Another sixth form student popularised dance at the school through hip-hop. There is little resistance to it being compulsory from year 7 to 9. The hugely impressive technology and performing arts centre hosts regular productions involving pupils from all years, again with an eye to reinforcing different aspects of the curriculum and individual achievement. There is even an annual 'Boscars' complete with red carpet and bronze statuettes. Marvel at the recording studio and equipment and huge range of musical talent. Musicals, hip-hop, jazz, rock, choral performances – talent abounds and gets due recognition within the school and local press. Varied activity weeks and excursions organised throughout the year and fantastic opportunities to prepare for life beyond school including the Engineering Education and Young Enterprise Schemes, foreign language exchanges and fund-raising for a month-long World Challenge over the summer for 20 plus students in years 11 and 12.

Background and atmosphere: Founded as a boys' school in 1624 by Sir William Borlase in memory of his son. Some of the original flint and brick buildings are still in use, alongside modern additions housing up-to-date facilities more in line with today's less austere and expanded education system. Great café and outdoor areas populated by relaxed and happy-looking pupils with lots of socialising outside school too. Ample opportunities for parents to get involved but virtually non-existent parking must be a disincentive at this main street site. On track to provide full disability access throughout the school.

Pastoral care and discipline: 'Your skirts are much too short for our school,' read the headline in the local paper. Staff do not shy away from reminding parents and pupils of the perils of showing too much leg. Walking around there is an honest, ordered and respectful attitude in evidence. Rooms containing expensive equipment left open and five pound note found outside a classroom handed in promptly. Extensive PSHCE could well be a contributory factor to low levels of bullying and other troubles at the school, but also strong is its commitment to developing pupil voice, leadership and team skills, particularly amongst prefects. They speak highly of mentor training and encouragement to take on real responsibility.

Pupils and parents: A moneyed and ambitious parent body and children with aspirations to match. Suits doers, the enthusiastic and keen. Unsolicited testimony from member of the public regarding good behaviour during a London theatre trip pinned in reception and general reputation for being pleasant and positive members of the community.

Entrance: Catchment area shrunk in recent years but still heavily over-subscribed at 11+ with entrance by county exam. Forty-five enter sixth form from outside, both from within Bucks and further afield, selected on GCSE results and school's assessment of their general enthusiasm and commitment to chosen field of study.

Exit: A week-long masterclass in year 12 exposes pupils to a wide range of professions and careers through presentations and workshops, and helps them build their leadership skills and prepare for the university application process. Some pupils groan about leadership overkill but some parents certainly see its value. Whatever, many go on to top level universities and colleges, Oxford and Cambridge amongst them. Popular destinations are Birmingham, Exeter, Nottingham, Oxford Brookes and Warwick. Wide range of disciplines chosen from science, business, ICT, management and sport.

Money matters: 'Build a Better Borlase' highly successful in mobilising financial and other support for the school from current and past parents and pupils, resulting in outstanding facilities. Voluntary contributions invited to make school funds go further and few miss out on broad range of activities offered.

Remarks: Strong focus on creating and celebrating confident and responsible individuals who will do well in their chosen fields. Far from detached from the outside world and yet there's a feeling of being an oasis from many of the worries and problems that typically beset teenagers. Deep sense of appreciation amongst pupils and parents alike.

Sir William Perkins's School

Guildford Road, Chertsey, Surrey, KT16 9BN

- Pupils: 570 girls, all day • Ages: 11–18 • Non–denom
- Fees: £13,293 pa • Independent

Tel: 01932 574900
Email: office@swps.org.uk
Website: www.swps.org.uk

Head: Since 2007, Mrs Del Cooke BSc MBA NPQH (early fifties) married with three sons. Maths graduate with MBA in educational management. Her broad experience covers the comprehensive system, sixth form college, adult education and boarding at Cranleigh, where she was head of maths, housemistress and finally deputy head. A very likeable, relaxed lady, her mathematical bent fell into conversation a couple of times – obviously an analytical soul. She had almost lost her voice the day we visited; however she was very willing to talk even though it was in a whisper! Parents describe her as approachable – which we would echo. She is a great advocate for the school's ethos of a caring and supportive community, and plans to build on these strengths. Interested in music, she plays a number of instruments, including self-taught bassoon – not many heads can boast that accomplishment.

Off to head Henrietta Barnett School in North London in September 2014.

Academic matters: Academic standards are consistently good; Mrs Cooke describes the flavour of the school as 'highly academic but not a hothouse' and 'full of motivated, busy, happy girls.' Parents very much agree – 'academically rigorous – they expect success and help you achieve,' and 'a well-rounded school,' are among the typical parental comments. Most girls gain a string of A grades – 71 per cent A*/A grades at A level, 77 per cent A*/A at GCSE in 2013 – but the aim is to receive a balanced education, developing their personal and leadership skills. Popular subjects at GCSE include English, sciences, maths, foreign languages and history. Maths is particularly strong, results very impressive (a refreshing change for a girls' school). Critical thinking is now a regular part of sixth form studies.

Form sizes below the sixth form average 21 but can get up to 24; teaching group average is smaller. In the sixth form, class sizes of eight. An individual education plan (IEP) is drawn up for each pupil with any special educational need in consultation with the special needs coordinator, the pupil and the parents, and these are reviewed regularly. Strategies are agreed to help each pupil and the information is circulated to all the relevant teachers who then take steps to support the pupils as appropriate. About four per cent of pupils have IEPs. 'A lot of pupils have one-to-one help from teachers for a period at one time or another but no pupils are withdrawn from lessons,' says Mrs Cooke. She is refreshingly open about SEN at the school. 'We are delighted to take any pupil who will thrive at the school and this includes pupils with quite a diverse range of special educational needs. If pupils need specialist SEN teaching then they are referred externally to experts.' A large number of pupils are gifted and talented and 'there is endless provision for high achievers both within lessons and outside lessons in our extensive extra-curricular programme.'

Facilities are good, notably the language and science labs, and the design and technology facilities are out of this world – another unexpected delight in a girls' school. The ground floor houses loads of machine tools for wood, metal and acrylic work and the first floor has a laser cutter, drawing tables and computers dedicated to CADCAM work. Parents comment that the 3-dimensional work the girls produce is 'fantastic'. The clean and modern home economics room was recently refurbed. There are two air-conditioned IT suites – modern and airy and all pupils have their own email accounts.

Games, options, the arts: A great selection of sports on offer, from netball, hockey and rowing to orienteering, football, volleyball, fencing etc etc. A new extension to the sports department completed 2011 including dance studio and rowing gallery. Some rowers represented GB in the summer and team won Women's Henley. Clubs after school and at lunchtime. 'Girls have a go and enjoy most things and get included in matches, even if they're not very good,' say parents. Really strong D of E – usually 50 per cent of the sixth form do gold award and the scheme has its own training room and office.

Drama prominent; the performance hall has been impressively refurbished to include electrically operated, retractable seating and smoke machines (much to the delight of the drama students). Also a large drama room. The performing arts centre has good acoustics, a private drama room and seven music practice rooms, all with pianos. Music very strong, loads of after school groups (swing band popular). Artwork is bold, bright and creative and very much reflects the girls' own characters. There are three lovely, big, bright and airy art rooms, a kiln, and printmaking facilities with a resident printmaking artist. Head of art encourages lots of different types of media.

Background and atmosphere: Founded in 1725 by Sir William Perkins, a wealthy Chertsey merchant. Started with 25 boys but a decade later added 25 girls. Moved to present site in 1819. Twelve acres of gardens and playing fields. Original 1905 redbrick building imaginatively extended to form a figure of eight of interlocking buildings with two pleasant courtyards – a tranquil oasis in the red brick.

Lots of energy and enthusiasm about the place. Mrs Cooke says, 'we try to ensure that girls achieve academically but not in an environment that makes them think that only academia is valued.' Very friendly school with good teacher/pupil relationships – 'The teachers are always willing to help; they're concerned, friendly and very welcoming.'

Pastoral care and discipline: Head places strong emphasis on pastoral care with rigorous policies, which parents like. No problem is ignored and staff deal with issues quickly and sympathetically. Fully accessible to physically disabled pupils – stairlifts on all short flights of stairs where a lift is not available.

Discipline is good. Girls comment that you could get a detention if uniform rules are not adhered to, but there's still the odd ladder in tights, scruffy shoes and skirts rolled up. No summer dress – the girls lobbied for this through the school council and also agreed that the uniform should be updated: out with ties and white shirts and in with striped open neck blouses.

Pupils and parents: Large school bus network. Girls are lively, fairly boisterous, individuals, down-to-earth, friendly and enthusiastic. They like to 'get involved'. Parents are a cross section – as one commented, 'There's a good mix of cars in the car park. It's not all Porsches and Mercedeses. Some parents are obviously making sacrifices.'

Entrance: Forty per cent come from surrounding state schools, the rest from a wide range of independents. Lots of care is taken over the selection process. (A pat on the back for the school as it will accept girls who are out of year.) Parents need to register their interest in the October before the pupil is admitted. Entrance exam is based on key stage 2. Maths and English tested, backed up by report from current school. Girls need to be academically inclined – it is not for the non-motivated. Entrance for sixth form needs at least five GCSEs at grade B or above including English language and maths, and interview.

Exit: A few want the experience of mixed schooling after GCSEs but most stay on to sixth form. Majority then leave for top of the range universities where maths, science and languages are popular choices. Around 10 per cent to Oxbridge.

Money matters: Fees 'good value for money'. Means-tested bursaries available to deal with personal hardship are re-evaluated each year. Two Perkins bursaries available each year up to 100 per cent of fees for local girls who would otherwise be unable to come here. Some scholarships – academic, art and musical.

Remarks: A friendly school with very good academic standards – ideal for unstuffy girls who enjoy healthy competition and getting stuck into what is on offer. Not for hooray Henriettas, who would stick out like a sore thumb.

Skipton Girls' High School

Gargrave Road, Skipton, North Yorkshire, BD23 1QL

• Pupils: 799 girls, all day • Ages: 11-18 • Non-denom • State

Tel: 01756 707600
Email: sghs@sghs.org.uk
Website: www.sghs.org.uk

Headteacher: Since 2002, Mrs Janet Renou BA PGCE NPQH (mid fifties). Educated at Cleveland Grammar for Girls, followed by art and design degree at Loughborough. Taught technology at three Midlands schools, rising to vice principal. As a national educational leader she has to be away from school for increasing amounts of time to mentor other heads. Friendly, approachable and enthusiastic, she has pioneered some remarkable, very creative and successful innovations involving significant contributions from girls, including popular netbook leasing scheme. Main wish is for a re-build, to provide girls with space and facilities to develop their talents even further, but admits ruefully that a highly academically successful school comes low on the priority list. Husband is educational consultant. Two adult daughters. Enjoys music, gardening, walking.

Academic matters: Very strong A level results. In 2013, 75 per cent of entries graded A*/A and school is consistently in top 50 state schools nationally. In top 10 per cent for value added over last three years. Classes rarely over 20. Options include engineering. Also PE, taken at nearby, very good Ermysted's Grammar School for boys, some of whom take subjects at Skipton Girls' High. 'Boys have a more challenging, risk taking approach, which benefits the girls,' says head. Biology, maths, Eng lit, history, government and politics all strong. Psychology very popular, small numbers for mod langs. All do AS general studies and can choose the A level. Also AS critical thinking.

Very good value added and consistently impressive results at key stage 4 – very high ranking nationally. In 2013, 62 per cent A/A* grades at GCSE. Key stage 4 starts in year 9: girls can take maths in year 9 or 10 and begin AS in year 10/11. All take RE in year 10. Choice of engineering (two groups), systems and control or food tech, also media studies, but only French and German (Spanish also on offer at two-year key stage 3).

Thorough going monitoring and tracking. Lots of differentiation in lessons and choice of learning approaches; teachers seen as very helpful. Several modern ICT suites (two just for sixth form). Netbook lease scheme (paid for over three years) allows complete integration of ICT with learning – girls with netbooks to be seen all over the school. These have a good range of programmes installed (but no Facebook or Hotmail et al) and provide access to the highly developed virtual learning environment (VLE) in and out of class. Sixth form have two year laptop/netbook version with Toshiba, including insurance and on site warranty. This hugely increases the amount and sophistication of work that can be achieved in each lesson.

Another very impressive innovation is a project where girls collaborate with teachers to design course content and approaches, making lessons and homework far more interactive and engaging and developing a deep understanding of learning processes. These girls have a grasp of and fluency in educational terminology that you would expect from recently trained teachers (they are used to presenting the project to outside adults, as well as delivering professional development sessions to their own teachers after school). Consequently lessons may be like tutorials – teachers not seen as 'the sage on the stage' says deputy head. They can choose their 'individual pathway,' leading to higher motivation and results, with more independence, opportunity to pursue their

S

intellectual curiosity and freedom from the constraints of the national curriculum. The only drawback is that they may start university ready for the second year – we felt quite envious of teachers working in this buzzing environment. An additional outstanding venture is the e-mentoring by sixth formers, who offer help to students at home in the evening via the VLE and by text – with clear bonuses for both parties.

Thoughtful, sensitive special educational needs co-ordinator. Confident she can handle full range of disabilities (no moderate or severe learning ones present, though, owing to the admission tests) and will offer whatever support needed, even if no statement, including one to one in class. She matches her variously qualified assistants to individual students, to enhance relationships. All screened for dyslexia on entry. School is (deservedly) regional centre for gifted and talented students.

Games, options, the arts: The downside of the size restrictions is the lack of a decent sports hall (just a small gym, plus well used mini fitness suite and several netball/tennis courts). School uses nearby, very good sports centre. Usual sports, plus football, rugby (competes), gymnastics. Extra curricular Zumba, Kangoo, non contact boxing and Thai kick boxing. National achievements in fencing, golf and fell running, as well as an elite gymnast and ladies' mountain boarding champ – happy to buy in top level coaching.

Music flourishes – a large number learn instruments and professional orchestra in residence, various ensembles, informal teatime and other concerts. Drama (supported by Judi Dench and Celia Imrie – classy) takes place in trad school hall or big Judi Dench Studio, with fetching purple curtains, also used for dance (modern rather than ballet – no barre). Year 11 students can do drama focused EPQ – recent very successful production of Twelfth Night with Ermysted's boys.

Outstanding engineering opportunities – has national reputation for science, technology, engineering and maths (STEM) teaching and works with local schools to promote it. Strong links with industry, eg Bentley, Silver Cross. Girls made winning go-kart out of a 1970s Silver Cross pram for James May's My Sisters' Top Toys TV programme, beating Ermysted's as well as James May, whose entry was purpose-built by the company – yay! Rolls Royce is a sponsor – sixth formers are racing and working on Ford Greenpower electric car, along with RR apprentices, engineers and managers. Two teams working with local companies on real science, engineering and technological problems, including residential at Liverpool University.

Sizeable art room – very good work, especially 3D, displayed around school, though more could be used to brighten up the original building. Annual exhibition of art and engineering projects and products.

Masses of activities – over 80 in a term. Projects with schools in Morocco, Jordan, Germany and trips to places like Iceland, EuroDisney, German exchange. Extended day (7.45am-5.15pm) four days a week – breakfast club, after school support and enrichment.

Excellent sixth form enrichment programme includes counselling, team leading (business management), debating (a strength), new languages (e.g. Mandarin), engineering education scheme, AQA Bacc, L2 BTEC iMedia. All do peer mentoring training, some do academic mentoring of younger students or organise activities for them. Work experience/shadowing encouraged – mod lang students can go to Germany or France. Annual higher education day attended by university admissions tutors and university taster courses.

Background and atmosphere: Old building has mostly trad classrooms and science labs, with some drab and poky walls and staircases, but girls like its quirkiness and sense of history and say it's homely. Standard multi-use hall, well stocked library (full of girls during the lunch break). Pleasant, yellow brick modern extension, plus several chocolate coloured Portakabins, euphemistically called 'chalets,' with darkish classrooms (apparently lighter in summer). Small porch and lawn with picnic benches for munching packed lunches. Woods at back of school. Westbank, sixth form centre in Edwardian house, has IT room, bistro and relaxation area with bar stools – girls wear business dress.

Now an academy, school has had two outstanding Ofsteds in 2008 and 2011. Involved in research promoting gender equality in schools and has worked with local universities on the health and welfare of girls.

Much scope for influencing decisions and exercising leadership (the girls we met were given this report to check). School council, executive body of students from across year groups involved in three major projects to enhance school, house captain and head girl teams (houses are called Bronte, Curie, Johnson and Franklin). Girls feel they are encouraged to aim high, but not in competition with each other, that their teachers know them well and can judge how much pressure to achieve is appropriate for them individually.

Pastoral care and discipline: Unusually, has vertical tutor groups of about 22 – two or three from each of years 7-11, plus three or four from years 12-13, whose ability to mentor younger girls frees tutors to concentrate on individuals. This produces a supportive atmosphere ('people get on'), friendships across year groups, easier transition for new year 7s and 12s and improved behaviour. The much valued and used, centrally located student progress centre – 'there's always a friendly face you can talk to if you are feeling down or confused,' according to one of my guides – provides academic and careers advice plus Relate counselling and access to other external health agencies. The school nurse can be accessed by text (very modern). As you would by now expect, discipline is personalised rather than rule bound.

Pupils and parents: Feeder primaries in Skipton and surrounding area – about a quarter from outside catchment area. Skipton is fairly privileged, but pupils come from a range of backgrounds, with quite a few ethnic minority. Confident, friendly, articulate and enthusiastic girls. Notable old girls include opera singer Elizabeth Harwood and Ruzwana Bashir, chair of Oxford Union in 2004. Parents are very happy with school ('absolutely fantastic,' one told us), especially with speedy, two-way e-communication via SimplyClick. Key stage 3 parents and daughters meet tutor at mutually convenient time of day to review and set targets rather than conventional parents' evening.

Entrance: Governors are responsible for admissions. For entry at 11 girls take tests in maths, English and verbal reasoning in September of year 6 (112 places a year). In-catchment or looked after pupils have priority, then girls with a sister in the school, then distance from home. If spare places are available in years 8 to 11, applicants take school's English, maths and science tests. For entry to sixth form, girls need five GCSEs at C or above including English and maths, usually with a B in A level subjects. Maximum of 20 from outside at this stage, plus replacements for girls who leave – increasing demand.

Exit: Virtually all stay on post-GCSE. Maximum of 10 leave at at the end of year 11, often to specialise in sport or art at FE colleges or to take up music scholarships at Giggleswick School (though they often ask to return). At 18, vast majority to university, including Oxbridge and other top ones, to do a variety of courses. Engineering features, but the most popular subject recently is psychology.

Remarks: Reminiscent of the Tardis – the unexceptional exterior is the entry to an excitingly futuristic learning world. You sense that these are girls who will not be limited by glass ceilings. Watch out for flying shards!

Slindon College

Slindon, Arundel, West Sussex, BN18 0RH

- Pupils: 100, all boys, about 70 per cent board • Ages: 8–16/18
- non-denom • Fees: Boarding £27,240; Day £16,590–£17,010 pa
- Independent

Tel: 01243 814320
Email: registrar@slindoncollege.co.uk
Website: www.slindoncollege.co.uk

Headmaster: Since 1999, Mr Ian Graham MA BEd Cert Ed, early sixties and no sign of him stopping – not by a long chalk! 'I can't retire – it's just so fascinating and brilliant running a little school like this!' His long tenure has borne rich fruit in recent years and, since our previous visit, the school has noticeably grown in confidence – a natural result of its many achievements and successes under Mr Graham. Prior to Slindon, Mr Graham taught history and PE for 25 years at Rugby School, where he tended to take on the boys with problems or who were struggling. He has a natural touch, together with the required toughness when appropriate, for this, perhaps, not-so-very-different milieu.

What comes across is energy and zip – physical and intellectual. He plays squash and racketball at national and international levels – was the over-60s national champion at the time of our last visit. He is voluble and canny – 'Being the son of a Yorkshire shopkeeper, I know how to keep things going on a shoestring.' Slindon, under his chivvying and nurturing regime, is achieving remarkable things for his pupils and everyone goes that extra mile – though not all can go as fast as the head! Mr Graham is married and bought a house on the coast to retire to – he doesn't see it much. 'When I wake up the first thing I want to do is get to school.'

Academic matters: Small classes – none bigger than 12 – allow for lots of differentiated teaching and plenty of 1:1 where needed. Most aim for GCSEs and BTECs and school is inventive and imaginative at finding out who can do what and tailoring the curriculum to suit. Everyone is pushed to achieve their potential – whatever it might be, so all take core subjects of English lang and lit, maths, science (single or double) and IT. Then most take four from an excellent list of options which includes DT, graphics, art, history and geography and a BTEC in food skills. Two outstanding areas are photography – to professional standards – and the BTEC in horticulture, pioneered here with the sensible and sane aim of equipping boys for employment in eg garden centres. French, German and Spanish all available though mostly taken by native speakers. 'Farm tech' latest innovation. Supervised prep is done each morning – another clever move as no-one feels much like it after classes when there are donkeys to visit and vegetables to tend, to say nothing of the superb work being done in the graphics/photography studios. GCSE results are the mix you'd expect but all get something – ranging from a string of As, Bs and Cs to hard won and triumphant Es and Fs. Photography and graphic results astonish.

'Primary' takes from year 4 and school accepts boarders from year 6. Lowest form has room for nine boys and two who come for taster days – lots of these. Excellent room – highly structured yet welcoming – big sofa, reading area, PCs, 'small animal' nook and plenty of stimulating equipment. Each day begins with a work-out – motor skills and hand-eye coordination stuff. 'Enrichment' classes for years 10 and 11 to plug gaps and provide 1:1; staff good at buttonholing those who would benefit. School has own assessment system which takes in more than the academic – all testament to the terrific

Value-Added embedded here. Accreditation by the National Autistic Society in process at time of our visit arising from the increased numbers of boys on the ASD spectrum now being admitted. All the usual aids are employed – Pecs, Teacch, Makaton – but those are seen as less important than the smaller classes and individual attention in which the school specialises. Kinaesthetic learning, lots of structuring, scaffolding and other support to motivate, encourage and support. Speech and language therapy threaded through the entire curriculum – body language, social interaction, communication skills seen as core to all. OT similar. School has invested in more LSAs in recent years. Lifeskills and PSHE loom large on the timetable. Brain Train works to activate a larger percentage of the brain and much emphasis on 'visual learning' for those who benefit. New sensory room. Good library – books are colour coded to guide readers to their own levels.

Sixth form offers various options including a one-year course to prepare leavers for college, BTECs in eg food tech and animal care – school houses two donkeys, Loopy and Norman, a red-bearded dragon, a Mongolian gerbil and a corn snake. A levels in art, science, DT. A counselling course. Only six students at time of our visit so high level of individual provision.

Games, options, the arts: Photography, graphics and arts impress – new iMacs, four professional quality printers and a policy of constantly being ahead of the game. This dept is at the heart of the school. 'We have a very good budget – what we want we get. We build the self-confidence in here that feeds other subjects, we have a huge impact on confidence.' Textiles are witty and fun – we enjoyed the imaginative ties with their fish, Mondrian, guitar and cupcake motifs. Lively tie-dye T-shirts, cushion covers on a graffiti theme. Fabulous extravagant costumes. No concessions here to 'special needs', 'we push the boundaries'. DT is strong – clever, practical chairs made from simple designs and painted in primary colours. Long tradition of building 'green power' electric cars. Drama and music potter along – lots of enthusiasm and musicians take grade exams and achieve well.

Huge, super fields on which football and rugby are played, a floodlit court, purpose-built squash courts, archery, golf, tai kwondo, basketball, tennis, mountain biking, cross country, skateboarding etc dependent upon interest. Outdoor heated pool is open from Easter to late October No shortage of things to do even though there is, as yet, no sports hall. Some worthy achievements here – especially in cross country. Excellent bunch of extra-curricular activities – something for all. Stage lighting, cookery, shooting, chess and masses more – especially outdoorsy stuff, including D of E. Boarders have range of trips at weekends – matches, theme parks, museums, bowling, films, shopping.

Background and atmosphere: The site and buildings are owned by the National Trust. The impressive main school house is a sturdy and robust, three-storey pile in Sussex flint on top of a superb site overlooking the south Sussex landscape. On a clear day you can see over to the sea and the Isle of Wight. Nice Hogwarty features like a lodge with real crenellations and little gothic porches and leaded lights must make a pretty enticing first impression on unsure potential pupils and their parents.

Internally – and it must be a nightmare to keep up – it could do with patching and painting here and there but much refurbing in process, especially in older boys' study bedrooms with desks, comfy chairs and proper carpet. Strip lighting and tired lino depress the adult visitor somewhat but the boys don't care. Most rooms, including dorms, have stunning views.

Pastoral care and discipline: Joint heads of boarding have nearly twenty years experience between them. Bernie used to run a residential home for Met police cadets and Daniel is a PE teacher. Bernie is also a counsellor and anger management expert – very confidence-inspiring. Hands-on – in all senses – no politically correct squeamishness about grabbing a lad to haul him off for extra support or an arm round the shoulders if he's upset. Boarding staff a laudable mix of tough and tender – seen as mentors and vital recourse in wobbly moments – 'once they're in the boarding house they're home', says Bernie. 'It's highly disciplined,' a parent said, 'without going over the top. My son takes responsibility for himself because they empower him to do so.' Sensitivities are understood – in a small school all the compulsions and obsessions are OK – 'we have lots of places to go to if you need to get away.' Catering staff know the boys and their dietary needs and 'everyone knows what to do if somebody freaks,' we were assured. 'Everyone's allowed to be the person they want to be as long as they're not upsetting others.' Parents enthuse: 'We were dreading private school but it was like a home-from-home, loving and so warm. It changed our lives.'

Boarders in rooms of four at lower end to singles and doubles at the top. Rooms are a good size. Inviting 'family room' for everyone – staff and boys – in the evenings, with sofas, TV, board games and someone's dog. Here the residents learn about social interaction, taking turns, winning and losing and coping with either. Games room has table football, snooker etc – cash prizes funded by tuck shop takings. Day boys allowed to board eg for a birthday sleepover or to give parents a break. Sensible system of 'boxes' in all classrooms so that pupils can keep relevant books and materials where they will need them rather than tote them around and forget them. This way they always have Sanctions, yes, but success of system depends on rewards – 'lots of carrots and very little stick', says Mr Graham. 'If you breathe', we were told, 'you get a trophy – perhaps just for being Mr Nice Guy!' Everything here is designed to be real and realistic – 'I'm not going to allow our boys to be set up for failure – it's a hard world out there and they're going to have to deal with it,' says Mr Graham. 'My son feels respected,' one mother told us.

Parents are warmly appreciative, 'It turned my son around,' one mother told us, 'they've listened and given him time. They work at his pace, push him at the subjects he's good at and support him where he needs it.' Another told us, 'Nothing seems to be too much trouble for them.' Another said, 'If my son is anxious the head always calls me himself.'

Pupils and parents: ADHD/ASD spectrum. Serious behavioural problems not accommodated here. Around 15 boys' families are from overseas so very sensible policy of taking them out 'to stop them getting institutionalised'. Most locals come from Hants and Sussex; boarders from everywhere. Few with EAL needs.

Entrance: Immense care taken over entry – can take up to a week to assess. Ed psych reports, statements, interview, trial period etc etc. Sensible, direct and straightforward approach.

Exit: Most leave after Year 11 though new sixth form means more now stay on. All leavers go on to some kind of further education. School has own horticultural apprenticeship scheme to enable the boys and their parents to set up little businesses to give them a future. They bring in driving instructors and do all they can to prepare for The Big Out There.

Money matters: Virtually all additional therapeutic input covered by fees. Few means-tested bursaries. 10 per cent reduction for siblings and for the children of HM Forces personnel.

Remarks: A sixth former told us what he felt: 'What I like is the opportunities and that they're keeping it a small school. The facilities are great and the food is excellent – I always look forward to my croissant on Thursdays and we have barbeques in the summer. I think Slindon has moved me on as a person and I've matured here. If there's a problem, there's always someone there.'

South Devon Steiner School

Linked school: South Devon Steiner School; Early Childhood Dept

Hood Manor, Dartington, Totnes, Devon, TQ9 6AB

• Pupils: 300 boys and girls • Ages: 7-16 • Christian foundation; non-denom • Fees: £2,775-£8,100 pa • Independent

Tel: 01803 897377
Email: admissions@steiner-south-devon.org
Website: www.steiner-south-devon.org

Head: None. Steiner schools don't have them and it's one of their distinguishing features. At SDSS monthly 'mandate circles' provide a first level of discussion for teachers, key admin staff and parents. Teaching vision, strategy and direction arise from the weekly 'collegiate' and departmental meetings. Principle is that fuller discussion leads to better long term outcomes. Prospective parents are advised to do their homework beforehand if new to structure of Steiner schools.

Academic matters: From class 1 (six year olds) each day begins with a two hour 'main lesson' on themes which follow Steiner curriculum but which allow for individual interpretation by class teachers. Main lesson in classes 9 and 10 (years 10 and 11) are taken by specialists. Lower and main school class teachers follow same children through four or eight year cycle – often broken for a variety of reasons but concept of keeping same class teacher is central to Steiner philosophy – when it happens, results can be astounding. Everything is done to encourage self-directed learning so tiniest sparks of interest are fanned into passionate flames of enthusiasm. Class themes run for three weeks and cover topics such as Norse myths, house construction or geology. When we visited, class 2 girls were all dressed as native American Indians whilst class 3 were starting to look after animals, grow their own food and learn about forestry. School uses unconventional approaches eg class 6 pupils get to understand principles of levers by making baseball bats. You won't fall over computers and tellies here and books only make a gradual appearance. Writing and 'feeling' shape and sound of letters precede reading. Main lesson (exercise) books provide record of what has been learned with standard of presentation all important, as is ability to recall earlier topics. We saw class 4 enjoying story time (Little Grey Men) while class 5 were building model Trojan towers out of clay to 'storm' later. Creative writing is encouraged at all levels.

Children get engrossed in whatever they are doing and there is a productive buzz wherever you go. Artistic learning is central to what happens – children learn colour blending (using a palette of primary colours) in classes 1-3 then appreciation of form grows out of that. Class 9's 'science of agriculture' lesson included learning about medicinal herbs then finding and drawing them on site; felt work, growing crops (school has an area marked out for larger scale agriculture) and investigation work in small but adequate laboratory. Science of lime cycle involves constructing, firing and manufacturing from a lime kiln.

No Sats here and senior pupils only take four GCSEs – English language and literature plus maths and a foreign language. Academic results (around the national average) not seen as be all and end all by parents; staff seek to instill genuine thirst for knowledge. German (chosen for its sound quality and closer relationship to English) is introduced from class 1 with French as an optional extra in classes 7-10. Self-assessment is seen as important though teachers do grade older pupils for content, presentation and effort. New wooden hall (previous one burnt down whilst parents were rehearsing Macbeth) is a

S

fine structure comprising five classrooms plus specialist music and handwork rooms.

SENCo has brought valuable experience from state sector and benefits from help of two LSAs. Learning support with groups of two or three pupils covers range of needs from SpLD to Asperger's. SENCo says that Steiner approach offers those with learning difficulties many more opportunities to work from gross to finer motor skills and 'keeps children in touch with their bodies', preventing them from being 'sensory deprived'.

Games, options, the arts: The 'new' concept of the 'outside classroom' is old hat here. Much of the land is given over to growing produce and keeping animals. Pupils literally 'make hay' here plus logging and other outdoor skills. We watched class 6 harvesting organic produce to sell at their weekly food stall. Class 10 students had just returned from two week ecology trip (staying with staff at Trevose Head near Padstow, Cornwall) and had put on an exhibition for parents in the marquee (used for games, wet breaks etc). One boy had whittled a fishing rod out of driftwood and another had created a human shaped sculpture out of garbage collected on the beach. Parents clearly appreciated how the sculpture 'said it all' about human impact on the environment. We caught up with class 10 in the garden caravan (another of the 'temporary' structures) as they returned in full protective gear from a bee keeping session. Earlier we had watched weekly class 9 music class (singing challenging Georgian song Batone Bo in four-part harmony). Impressive for 15 year olds, but we were told that the same group had produced an opera based on life of St Francis (written by a teacher at Wynstones in Stroud) whilst in class 7.

Main hall also serves for assemblies and eurythmy (origins of this dance-like form lie in Greek temples – movement is related to specific sounds and is central to Steiner education). There is a specialist music room in same building plus individual practice rooms for lessons with peripatetic music staff – some pupils graduate to Torbay youth orchestra. Class 7 have formed own orchestra thanks to parents who include several professional musicians. Hall had just witnessed a class 9 production of Romeo and Juliet (school stages a Shakespearean play every year and most productions run for three nights). Emphasis is upon a combined effort rather breeding prima donnas. Class 10 complete their time here with a major production. Moving on, we saw some of class 8 doing 'handwork' – natural fibres (wool comes from school's own sheep) and dyes are de rigueur and manual dexterity ranks high in the Steiner taxonomy of skills. Boys and girls were equally engrossed in making hats and hand puppets. Across the site another part of class 8 was carving heads for the puppets in the small but perfectly adequate woodworking hut. There is also a forge where a local blacksmith comes to lead practical sessions. The upper school art rooms (one is a uniquely shaped wooden structure) are immersed in creativity and show what pupils achieve artistically. In other, less impressive huts we discovered a dark room for photography, a pottery and (well hidden) a small ICT base.

Competitive sports not a big deal here though class 6 pupils recently won a regional gymnastics tournament. Sports include hockey for boys and rugby for girls. After school clubs include basketball and volleyball. Older pupils go to sports facilities at Dartington College and Ivybridge but own sports hall is on wish list. Cycling is a structured activity from class 5 upwards; there is a cycle path from Totnes to the school.

Trips away from school are vitally important – these grow in duration and scope as children get older so that, by class 7, pupils are canoeing and exploring down the Wye and in class 8 they go abroad for three weeks. Recent destinations have included Hungary, Romania and Portugal. Foreign cycling trips have included Brittany, Holland and Germany. Class 9 have a term of intensive outward bound activities and begin with a fortnight on a working farm in Scotland. Class 10 trips includes surveying on Dartmoor and art history in Germany.

Background and atmosphere: School founded by local parents as a kindergarten in 1979 before moving to present idyllic eight acre site between Totnes and Dartington. Main school (classes 1-8) divided between Hood Manor (formerly the dowager house on Dartington estate) and the new hall and classroom block opened in 2007 – classrooms have colour washed walls and enjoy plenty of natural light. Senior school (classes 9 and 10) housed in disparate, idiosyncratic collection of temporary classrooms, huts and shacks whilst Early Childhood Department enjoys a discrete, purpose-built area. Classes 1 and 2 also have a separate play area at front of Hood Manor.

School retains an 'alternative' feel but an extremely safe one – a gentle approach to all that happens – and it is reassuring to see so much mutual respect. Steiner educational movement has worldwide influence but has only recently (2008) achieved final state recognition in UK with granting of academy status to a hitherto independent Steiner school in Hereford. Plans are afoot at SDSS to add a sixth form to the senior school and planning permission has been granted for the necessary extension as well as a sports hall. Now it is simply a matter of raising huge amounts of money. Parents are amazed though at how successful school has become at fund-raising.

'Outside classroom' is of prime importance here as well as the creative life. School day starts at 8.30am for all ages and ends at 3.00pm or 4.00pm for main and upper schools respectively. Staff:pupil ratio is 1:12 but with LSAs and other adults on site this ratio is often much less. When we visited children were dancing around the maypole which had been erected for May Day – one of the festivals celebrated annually. Relationships between pupils and staff are quite different from most schools – first names are used throughout and there is an obvious two-way feeling of trust. We also liked the balance of ages and gender amongst the staff.

Pastoral care and discipline: From the outset, children learn tolerance, respect and reverence. There is never a sense of pupils being talked down to and they are really 'heard' by staff. Anti-social behaviour or bullying would be anathema to pupils as much as teachers here. Each new class 1 is adopted by class 8 pupils. Pretty basic veggie catering; parents make pizzas and pasties on Wednesdays (half day for lower and main school pupils) otherwise food taken round to classrooms. Majority bring own lunch. Nothing is swept under the carpet and emphasis always on getting the emotional, physical and spiritual balance right in each individual. School comes down heavily on smoking; possession of alcohol or drugs can lead to immediate expulsion.

Pupils and parents: Mostly local. Some pupils cycle to and from school (new cycle path between Totnes and Buckfastleigh facilitates this). Strictly for parents who are prepared to get involved and kids who want to discover and express all aspects of themselves. Some escapees from state sector but most home grown. Few schools involve parents as much as SDSS – parents attracted (about 75 per cent have relocated) by what school provides. Relatively few parents are anthroposophists, however majority find Steiner philosophy fits their value system – especially how it develops creativity alongside ecological and spiritual awareness. We met one parent mandate holder who explained how parents have a real say (they even have own room, used for study, school shop, tea breaks, meetings etc). Parents volunteer in all kinds of ways: hearing readers, gardening, serving food and cleaning classrooms on a rota basis. Parents' evenings are not at all conventional but still provide for one-to-one chats as well as group interaction. You notice a difference right away – children are focused and involved in a freer, warmer environment than in mainstream education.

Quite a lot of giving to charity – eg class 8 made and sold toys for school in South America. Always some European students who attend upper school for one or two years and who are found host families in area. Oldest former pupils barely 30 years old but are beginning to send second generation to SDSS. Many have achieved academically as well as in arts and drama.

Entrance: Most children enter through oversubscribed Early Years Department but gaps appear infrequently further up school. Three day visits for older children ensure they and parents know what school is about before signing up. Class teachers have an eye on dynamics of whole group which can have positive or negative consequences for individual applicants. Parents of children with special needs must produce educational psychologist's report. Lots come through attending an event at school – a play, concert or perhaps one of two main annual public functions – Christmas indoor market and summer fair. At end of year 9 parents and pupils have to recommit to upper school (years 10 and 11) which involves an interview and review of work.

Exit: School's local reputation and reference enables students to move from year 11 to join 16+ colleges in Totnes, Plymouth or Exeter for A levels or appropriate vocational training.

Money matters: Parents don't pay fees – they make 'contributions'. Discounts for siblings and bursaries for needy cases. Like most Steiner schools, SDSS started out trying to be wholly inclusive but financial realities soon began to bite. Still comparatively affordable though parents we spoke to would love school to become an academy or free school to remove financial burden.

Remarks: Just brilliant. 'A lovely environment where emphasis is not on cramming knowledge,' say parents. Stands educational claptrap on its head, defies conventional wisdom and produces confident, creative and genuinely independent thinkers. Not for bookworms, perhaps, but a wonderful antidote to left brain overload we find elsewhere.

South Hampstead High School

Linked school: South Hampstead High School Junior Department

3 Maresfield Gardens, London, NW3 5SS

- Pupils: 640 girls, all day • Ages: 11–18 • Non-denom
- Fees: £14,499 pa • Independent

Tel: 020 7435 2899
Email: senior@shhs.gdst.net
Website: www.shhs.gdst.net

Headmistress: Since September 2013, Miss Helen Pike MA (Oxon) (early forties), previously director of studies at the Royal Grammar School, Guildford. An Oxford history graduate, she studied for a Master's in modern history in the States, has an MA in fiction from Birkbeck and a PGCE from the OU. Miss Pike, who is working on her second novel, has so far taught entirely at top boys' schools – Westminster, City of London and St Paul's as well as RGS. Married to an Oxford don, she has an adult step-daughter and two school-age step-sons – and she is, judging from first impressions, exactly what this flagship school has needed for some time.

Very striking, tall, with evident sparkle and style, she has the personality, wit and flair to give this school the blast of energy and confidence it deserves. She is overseeing the extraordinary rebuild opening in 2014 which will, in many ways, be a new school. Hampstead and its clever, creative girls will doubtless rise to meet the challenges set by their new clever, and creative head. Another good GDST appointment.

Academic matters: A super-star in the exam league tables (though lower this year than usual). In 2013, over 84 per cent of GCSEs were A*/A and nearly 95 per cent of A levels were marked A*-B, 64 per cent A*/A. Particularly impressive, however, is the percentage of A*s at A level, with 22 per cent of exams taken last year receiving the top grade (national average eight per cent). Though one of the previous head's ambitions was to make the school 'fly' academically, teaching to the tests is not part of the school's agenda. Girls here are provided with significantly more substantial nourishment than mark schemes to feed their intellects. 'They're very creative and individual, they need a challenging environment.' All years do a beyond-the-curriculum themed project (Year 8, for example, focused on murder mystery, Year 10 created a language), and sixth formers undertake the school's own (unexamined) extended essay. 'They have the old public-school ideal of the whole person,' said one parent, 'You feel they're confident about getting the results, so can afford to be less obsessed by exams than elsewhere.' A good balance between arts and science. Six compulsory subjects at GCSE, plus ten options (including Latin and Greek). Over 20 subjects, including art history, philosophy and economics, in the sixth form, with maths, economics, chemistry and English amongst the most popular. Very strong emphasis on teaching and learning and plenty of lunchtime clubs to clear up difficulties. Form tutors provide one-to-one chats every half term and girls rate teacher support highly: 'They really want to help you rather than just seeing you as someone who will produce good results,' said one A level student. Special needs here primarily mild dyslexia and dyspraxia, though some experience, too, of autism. About 10 per cent get help. 'We give them the support they need, whether that's improving study skills or using a word processor in every lesson.'

Games, options, the arts: Music exceptional (with generous scholarships at 11 and 16). Fourteen instruments taught, numerous ensembles, bands and orchestras, as well as two junior and four senior choirs. High rate of finalists at national music competitions; and a school radio station to rival Radio 3. The visual arts equally vibrant, with healthy numbers going on to art school and plenty of enthusiastic part-timers, who pursue it alongside more traditional academic disciplines. (One recent leaver studied art foundation before reading politics at Cambridge.) Sport, compulsory throughout, is taken seriously by the school, with four acres of playing field a five-minute coach drive away and a games staff ornamented by high-flying internationals. That said, for the majority, traditional team games are perhaps not top of everyone's to-do list. 'It varies from year to year,' said one keen athlete. 'It's there if you want it.' Fifty-plus clubs, from Mandarin to trampolining, and plenty of trips abroad (classics to Sicily, geography to Iceland, World Challenge to Peru). Regular guest speakers and active participation in out-of-school activities, from Young Inventors to the Arvon writing course. 'The extra-curricular is very good and the girls really participate,' said a parent of two.

Background and atmosphere: Set up in the 1870s on enlightened principles, South Hampstead was one of the founding members – and is now one the flagships of – the Girls' Day School Trust, typical of its approach in prioritising fine teaching rather than frills. Until the previous head's arrival the school buildings were perhaps a bit too unfrilly. 'They were no longer fit for purpose,' she said decidedly. 'The girls deserve a beautiful environment.' Persistent lobbying has finally resulted in a state-of-the-art schoolhouse designed by world-renowned firm Hopkins Architects (designers of the Olympic velodrome), which is due to open in 2014. The sleek glass-and-steel tour de force will include ultra-modern facilities for art, DT and music, as well as a new library, classrooms and sports courts. 'The school has been really let down by the restrictions of the site,' said one parent, 'this will be a huge improvement.' The 20th-century science

S

block and elegantly refurbished Arts and Crafts Oakwood House remain. In the meantime, pupils are based for four days a week in temporary classrooms at the sports ground in West Hampstead.

Pastoral care and discipline: Girls are taught meditation, 'mindfulness' and 'keeping it real' by two designated members of staff. 'Clever girls will always think, if, but, what... We want to keep them grounded in the now.' 'Nurture week' encourages thinking, too, about others. The previous head re-introduced the house system which allows girls to get to know each other across the year groups, with annual competitions in dance, drama and music. Plenty of leadership opportunities too, with both house captains and elected school prefects. Navy and yellow uniform in the lower school; sixth formers wear their own clothes – mainly tidy jeans.

Pupils and parents: About 60 per cent of girls live locally, the rest come from as far afield as Notting Hill and Brixton. Parents are cosmopolitan, often professional, with a high proportion of foreign nationals. Financially the range extends from bus drivers to hedge-fund managers and, though some parents see the latter in the ascendant, South Hampstead is generally considered considerably less flashy than some of its local counterparts. 'There are all types of parents,' said one. 'It's like a breath of fresh air.' Girls are enthusiastic, hardworking (very), and sensible (this is not a school where being 'cool' is considered 'cool'). 'It's more real, more honest than some other schools,' said one girl, 'and it's not as cliquey.' Parents care about achieving the best possible education for their bright daughters. 'All the girls here are motivated and have very high standards. I tell them, "You're diamonds, go out and sparkle".' Old girls include Helena Bonham-Carter, Rabbi Julia Neuberger, Fay Weldon.

Entrance: About 40 come up from the junior school, the rest sit the North London Girls' Schools' Consortium joint 11-plus exam. Competition is fierce, with as many as six applicants per place. Occasional vacancies are filled from the waiting list. Sixth-form entrance tests include data analysis and an essay and, if relevant, subject tests. Offers are made on the basis of results and interviews. At all levels the school is looking for the intellectually engaged. 'They've got to be up to it academically,' says the school. 'We won't take someone who won't thrive here intellectually.'

Exit: Used to be a reasonable exodus post GCSE to co-ed independents, particularly Westminster, but the flood has slowed to a trickle. No doubt the introduction of a stunning sixth-form centre – which looks like a boutique hotel – is part of the magic potion. One or two to state schools at 16 (Camden, La Swap). At 18, about 25-30 per cent to Oxbridge, a handful to medical school, three or four to art school or music colleges, the rest to Russell Group universities, with Durham, Warwick, Bristol, Birmingham and Nottingham the most popular.

Money matters: Fees, in keeping with the Girls' Day School Trust philosophy of a value-for-money education, are generally competitive. Five per cent of annual income is spent on scholarships and means-tested bursaries (with increasing emphasis given to the latter) at 11 and 16. New applicants are automatically entered for scholarships; those moving up the school need to sit the entrance exam to qualify. Excellent music scholarships (up to 50 per cent off the fees), with grade VI generally required for auditions at 11.

Remarks: A school once considered all work and no play. Now better results than ever achieved with a broader education and vastly improved pastoral care. Will shine even more brightly under sparky new head.

South Wilts Grammar School for Girls

Stratford Road, Salisbury, Wiltshire, SP1 3JJ

• Pupils: 1020 girls, all day • Ages: 11–18 • Non–denom • State

Tel: 01722 323326
Email: head@swgs.wilts.sch.uk
Website: www.swgs.wilts.sch.uk

Headteacher: Since 2011, Michele Chilcott BSc PGCE NPQH (mid forties). An environmental geographer with a degree from Wye College (now Imperial) and a PGCE from Oxford, Mrs Chilcott taught in a range of secondary schools in southern England before coming to South Wilts as assistant head in 2004. Clearly still enthusiastic about her subject, she teaches all of year 7, partly as a means to get to know them all, lives on the coast (well away from school) and is a keen and adventurous traveller: 'I don't want to visit the same place twice,' she says. She's also very pro single sex education: 'Coming here means girls can still be girls at 11,' she says 'before going on to excel in traditionally male subjects like maths and sciences.' Highly regarded by her girls and their parents, if not terribly visible ('Superb', said one father simply, and 'She knows where she's going and is really hot on recognition – and not just for academics', according to one girl), we found her understandably keen to talk about the school, but somewhat guarded as a person.

Academic matters: An outstandingly academic school and makes no bones about it. Highly selective at entry, with three bright girls trying for every place at 11+, its results jolly well ought to be good – and they are. In 2013, 89 per cent A/A* grades at GCSE and 44 per cent at A level, results which places South Wilts among the top performing schools in the country. Preparation for such stellar performance starts early: these girls work hard from day 1, with an amount of homework which is sometimes baulked at, even by parents, but 'when my daughter said she was jealous of the little homework her friends at the local comprehensive got, I just said that's the deal at South Wilts', said one. Teaching appears traditional; everyone was sitting at desks facing the front in the lessons we saw. Subject choices are wide – most girls take 11 or 12 at GCSE (some at IGCSE) and 33 subjects are offered at A level in conjunction with neighbouring and similarly excellent boys' grammar Bishop Wordsworth (qv). This year AS Latin is on offer for the first time, but there is neither photography nor media studies – though communication studies is included. The top five per cent of this exceedingly bright bunch are tracked and encouraged to enter national competitions, such as maths Olympiads etc, though this is open to all, and specific support is laid on for any girl considering Oxbridge (about 10 get in each year), medical or veterinary school. Progress is closely monitored: parents appreciate the frequency (three per year) and quality of reports, but one mother described parents' evenings as 'a time-wasting scrum', which would be better replaced with exception reporting if things go awry.

All girls are CAT tested on entry, and school employs a dyslexia expert. Extra time can be given for 11+ exams, where girls come with a recommendation from primary school; South Wilts is keen to open access to very able girls with SEN. Once in situ, there is help available for spelling, handwriting and organisation, such as scheduling work and completing exams. An assembly at the start of sixth form deals expressly with barriers to learning and where to seek help for them.

Games, options, the arts: Plenty of all these on offer – this school is not just about what goes on in the classroom. Extensive grounds (for a city school) include tennis and netball courts, hockey pitches and – jewel in the crown – an all-weather athletics track. Sport of some kind is compulsory up to the end of year 11; school has Healthy School award. For a school which has neither a pool nor horses, its success at swimming and riding is commendable, and it brings back quite a bit of silverware from local-ish state and independent schools and from regional contests; national badminton player a current pupil too. Minority choices include trampolining and tap-dancing – plus some alternative sports (ultimate Frisbee and American football inter alia) laid on by a sixth former as part of the Sky Sports Living Programme.

Arts scene also strong, as befits a school which holds the Gold Artsmark award. Masses of music (a third of girls take music lessons) for all standards: three orchestras, wind band and guitar group, plus three choirs, one of which is good enough to sing at weddings and at evensong at Queen's College Oxford, where three of the 18 choral scholars are ex-South Wilts. School takes full part in the musical life of this cathedral city. Recent drama productions include Grease, A Midsummer Night's Dream and Animal Farm, the latter in collaboration with Bishop Wordsworth; there's also an annual Oscars ceremony. Visual arts are clearly a strength too and on display all over school. In 2013 the Arts Award was run for the first time; two lower sixth girls gained their gold straight off. Packed schedule of clubs at lunchtime, some just for fun, some with more serious intent, such as the pond club, which helped the school gain its green Eco Flag; good take-up for DofE too. A wide range of trips and jaunts – most are educational for linguists, historians and geographers – but also ski-ing just for fun. School proud of its international links with schools in France, Germany, India and China and has sent staff and pupils on exchanges to all those countries.

Background and atmosphere: Four-square brick buildings in a leafy suburban street dating from 1927 when the school was founded convey the impression of no-nonsense academic seriousness we imagine the school would wish for. The usual collection of 'temporary' buildings providing extra space do not encroach too much on to the grassy grounds where girls were relaxing at lunchtime in sizzling sunshine the day we visited. Bits of the school could do with a coat of paint, but we loved the new learning resources centre (aka library) with its sofas and beanbags, and super new sixth form block, complete with lounging Bishops' boys, sofas, toasters and kettles. Canteen kitted out with garish chairs seems small for the number of girls passing through it at lunchtime; much of the sixth form prefer nearby Waitrose. Practical and good value uniform (kilts, polo shirts, sweaters in navy and bottle green) in keeping, and sixth formers tidier than many we have seen. Fearsome reputation for academic rigour borne out by a sense of intellectual endeavour we could almost smell: 'I was bullied for being clever at my last school,' one girl admitted, 'so I wanted to come to South Wilts because everyone would be a boffin'. All this is not at the expense of fun, however: 'The girls have rather a jolly time while learning really quite a lot,' as one mother put it. Local opinion that the school might be 'boring' is stoutly denied by the girls, who appear to enjoy the fact that they can pursue whatever subject takes their fancy without fear of ridicule, 'though having boys here would mean fewer arguments', said one. It seems a happy place for staff too: one father commented on the positive relationships between staff, their commitment to the place and the rapport between them and the girls.

Pastoral care and discipline: Gets the thumbs up from parents, as does the school counsellor from the girls, though this is not a touchy-feely school. Parental concerns are dealt with swiftly and effectively; the only real gripe we heard, and which is common to most state schools, was the lack of medical facilities (eg sick room) and trained staff. Sanctions mostly handed out for poor behaviour, and certainly for late work, and take the form of detentions at break, lunchtime or in the most serious cases, Friday afternoon. 'We're generally pretty well-behaved,' said our sixth form guide, 'but the school would certainly act if something outside school like drink or drugs was affecting academic performance' – we did not feel anyone was much troubled by this

Pupils and parents: Girls unpretentious, bright and not afraid to admit it. Refreshing lack of preoccupation with personal appearance: hardly any make-up, micro-minis, body art or piercing – no boys to impress, see. Parents clearly relieved their daughters got in and grateful for all the school offers; there's an active PTA, raising about £10K per year which has a 'symbiotic relationship' with the school, said one dad. All seem remarkably content with their lot; the only things on the wish list might be a proper sports hall and better lights at the entrance. 'Not a hotbed of ethnic diversity' our last write-up noted, and little has changed.

Entrance: By way of the 11+ exam in VR, maths and English in the previous September; passing the exam does not guarantee a place at the school, to which applications are made through the LA once results are known. Coaching for the exam is endemic – 'You play the game, because everyone does it,' according to one parent, 'but it's not the place for someone who has been coached to the max just to get in'. Girls come from 58(!) local primary schools and several prep schools; those who don't make it often to go to independent schools.

At sixth form, about 80 girls arrive with a minimum of six GCSEs above a C, with at least a B in any subject to be taken at AS/A2 and Bs in maths, English and the sciences. In our view, this is quite a low hurdle for a school of this calibre, and a few newcomers find the academic pace daunting initially, though the school does its best to integrate them on arrival.

Exit: About 10 per cent leave after GCSE, mostly to local sixth form college – more choice and greater freedom. Those who stay get into top universities – a good handful to Oxbridge (11 in 2012, seven in 2013), the rest to worthy runners-up in the south, such as Bristol and Exeter. Most popular subjects biased towards sciences but also law, English and music. Careers revealed at a recent reunion included an architect, doctor, opera singer and controlled risk consultant.

Remarks: Unapologetically academic no-nonsense girls' education. Certainly not no-frills though: this school has a range of activities to nurture all talents – and none. When we put it to the head that her school was so good it could be independent, her face gave her away: 'We're a state school and the only form of élitism we go in for is academic. We're here to serve the community'. Sums it up, really.

Southbank International School – Westminster

Linked schools: Southbank International School – Kensington; Southbank International School – Hampstead

63-65 Portland Place, London, W1B 1QR

• Pupils: 350 boys and girls; all day • Ages: 11-19 • Non-denom
• Fees: £23,130-£25,230 pa • Independent

Tel: 020 7243 3803
Email: admissions@southbank.org
Website: www.southbank.org

Executive Principal: Since 2013, Dr Chris Greenhalgh. Born in Manchester, worked in Italy and Athens for five years and

S

returned to UK to complete PhD on the American poet, Frank O'Hara. He has since been head of English and academic deputy head at Sevenoaks School and is currently a governor of Campion School in Athens. Author of three books of poetry and two novels, including Seducing Ingrid Bergman, published by Penguin last year. He wrote the screenplay for the movies Coco Chanel and Igor Stravinsky. Married to Ruth, they have two children.

Academic matters: Southbank Westminster follows the IB Middle Years Programme (11-16 year olds) and IB diploma (sixth formers). The Middle Years Programme (MYP) covers a broad curriculum, including PSE, with links between different subjects. It culminates in the MYP Personal Project, which is a major research exercise that can take the form of text, videos, plays, music, models: whatever the kids think works for them.

The IB diploma includes six subjects, plus an extended essay, a theory of knowledge course and a creativity, action and service section. In 2013, scores averaged over 36 points; 20 per cent of students scored 40+ points and 20 per cent were awarded bilingual diplomas, which involve taking language and literature courses designed for native speakers of those languages in addition to English.

Classes are small, never more than 18; good feedback on pupil progress via pupil-led conferences in November and May as well as written reports. A recent decision to administer tests (externally designed and marked) in the middle school is not popular with some parents and pupils, who question its compatibility with the MYP approach to assessment and evaluation; others are in favour of these 'quality assurance measures'. Twice-yearly school reports; incidental ones sent out if areas of concern arise, or to highlight praiseworthy achievements. Pupils completing four years of high school are awarded 24 credits and given a Southbank high school honours diploma in the US tradition in recognition of their IB coursework. School offers PSAT and SAT examinations for American university admissions.

Languages are important. Middle schoolers choose between Spanish (also taught at the primary campuses) and French. They must choose one, then stick with it. Non-English native speakers are encouraged to continue to learn their mother tongue. There are 17 languages taught as mother tongue or second languages with others available on request (generally incurs additional fees). Some language-related residential trips.

Teachers dedicated and enthusiastic; staff turnover was decreasing, partly a result of recent enhancements in salary packages. However, a series in changes in the leadership and management seems to have impacted teacher morale, and there are those with serious reservations about the planned introduction of merit pay. The pupil-teacher ratio is eight to one.

Full-time SENCo provides support for mild learning problems, but if it becomes clear that Southbank cannot support a pupil adequately, then the school and parents work together to find alternative solutions. EAL lessons are part of the standard programme.

Games, options, the arts: Art, including pupils' coursework, is on display in the library. The sixth form art studio at the Conway Street building exhibits a bit less of the 'creatively chaotic environment' found at Portland Place; music practice rooms crammed full of enthusiastic pupils when we dropped in. Buses wait to take kids off to PE at off-campus facilities (no space at the Westminster campus). Although Southbank bought a newly-refurbished sports facility in Kilburn in 2012 to serve all three Southbank campuses, the Westminster PE teachers seem for the most part to be sticking to the established facilities closer by. Recreational sports take place after school; some competitive fixtures, culminating in the ISSA (International School Sports Association) tournaments which are hosted by schools in locations such as Madrid and Cairo.

Westminster has a small theatre for drama classes and activities, and pupils participate regularly in the International Schools' Theatre Association (ISTA), attending festivals abroad. Film studies is a popular IB subject, perhaps inspired by a Southbank alumnus whose movie, starring a fellow graduate, has been nominated for international film awards in six countries, including the BAFTA. Some who learned violin through the compulsory Suzuki programme in the Southbank primaries continue this at Westminster on an optional basis after school. Music carries through to the diploma level (though it is not at present on offer as an IB course) with choirs, rock bands and other small musical ensembles.

Clubs include newspaper and yearbook, creative writing, maths support and maths enrichment, and a range of individual and team sports at various levels. Model United Nations and the newer Global Issues Network prepare pupils for international conferences.

Everyone in the middle school goes on two five-day adventure Discovery Week trips somewhere in Britain as team building exercises. While this urban school lacks the space of the suburban international school campuses, it has the advantage of the city on its doorstep and there are plenty of visits around town. 'London as a classroom' is, after all, the school mantra. Some say it is hard to keep track of all the classes that are visiting museums, galleries or learning events around the capital at any one time. Previous GSG concerns about inconsistencies in trips between year groups had died down, but a decision to reduce the number of residential trips has not been popular with some students and families.

Led by the secondary at Westminster, all three Southbank schools, with enthusiastic backing from the PTAs, have had a long-standing commitment to supporting the Marweni School for blind pupils in Tanzania, raising substantial funds for building facilities, sending teachers and grade 11 volunteers to help build, install IT equipment and teach. However, some members of the community are concerned about the future of this programme following the recent departure of the coordinator who spearheaded the school's relationship with the Marweni School. Parents report there is 'misinformation and ambiguity' coming from the administration about the state of this relationship – raising concerns from some members of the community as hundreds of Southbank alumni of all ages share a legacy in the Marweni project. Another African-based school now appears to be the focus of the school's overseas community service activity, though confirmation has been slow in coming and there is lack of clarity on the state of the annual grade 11 trip. Closer to home, volunteer projects range from teaching in children's centres to a programme where Southbankers teach pensioners about computers and how to use IT, something that is equally popular with the pupils as with their budding silver-surfers. The Milton Toubkin Community and Service Award honours pupils who demonstrate genuine service that has made a difference to others.

The Janet Kuehn Travel Award gives £1500 annually to a pupil nominated by the community on the basis of qualities that emulate the award's namesake, a founding teacher who died of cancer, for a dynamic educationally-sound (and safe) travel proposal that ensures the recipient brings the learning back to the school.

Background and atmosphere: The school opened its doors in 1979 on the South Bank of the Thames, an idealistic concept of the South African Founder, Milton Toubkin, inspired by (Englishman) John Bremer's 'school without walls' Philadelphia Parkway Program. Following some growing pains and moves, established campuses now include the primary campuses at Kensington and Hampstead, and the Westminster Portland Place (middle and high school) with the addition in 2007 of the IB centre on nearby Conway Street off Fitzroy Square. Shuttle service and door-to-door bus service (at extra cost) between the campuses, though most pupils are soon ready for the freedom of using public transport.

Westminster Southbank is a grade 2 listed Regency building, described by parents as 'beautiful', refurbished with classrooms and modern science, ICT and DT labs. The library, with its big windows and high ceilings, is a welcoming and inspiring setting for research and reading and the library staff are knowledgeable and helpful and well versed with the curriculum. The canteen in the basement is open throughout the school day. It seems small for the number of kids at school and can feel a bit claustrophobic, but many have off-campus lunch privileges so they seem to make it work. The alluring aroma of pain au chocolat and other pastries filled the air just before morning break during our visit, though the catering manager assured us that healthy snacks are also on offer.

A drawback cited by some families is the lack of outside space where energetic adolescents can let off steam, though they do get exercise climbing stairs between the five floors. Middle school pupils get some fresh air and exercise during breaks at nearby Regents Park.

The Conway Street sixth form IB diploma annex, with its own classrooms, a library and labs, has a feel of serious and purposeful study where pupils can focus undistracted on their important final years. The silence was deafening when we visited, and the atmosphere of studiousness was tangible. Many of the IB teachers have offices in this building, so are easily accessible to pupils needing tutorial support or general bucking up during the rigorous final IB year. Diploma pupils have some classes in the Portland Place building, an eight minute walk away, not popular with some, particularly on cold or rainy days.

Southbank was purchased from the founders in 2007 by Cognita Schools. Chaired by former UK chief inspector of schools Sir Chris Woodhead, who in the early days worked regularly at Southbank Westminster, it is one of about 40 UK schools owned by Cognita. At the time of purchase, Cognita assured parents and staff that they would let the current administration run the school to 'preserve [its] established ethos'. By 2012, all three campus principals had resigned, ending all ties at that level with the founders. An education board created in 2007 was replaced in 2012 with a management team consisting of the new executive principal (who also served as principal of the Westminster campus), the primary school principals, and two other operations managers. A series of advisory school board models have been tried since 2007. The latest change to re-constitute its membership by replacing school staff positions with appointed parent positions (chosen and invited by the executive principal in consultation with Cognita) raised more than a few eyebrows, although there are three positions for elected parents from each campus as well.

During the 2012-13 academic year there were a few unusual mid-year teacher resignations at Westminster; the Kensington principal was replaced by an interim who, according to parents, has no previous IB experience, while at Westminster four senior leaders (the IBMYP and IBDP coordinators, the deputy head responsible for pastoral care, and the community and service coordinator) left due to a re-structuring of the organisation. Executive principal Graham Lacey now has oversight of the three Southbank schools and the implementation of a new strategic plan, with responsibility for Westminster turned over to the newly-appointment principal, Chris Greenhalgh. Parents question the relative lack of IB experience of some of those appointed to the new leadership positions created at Westminster to manage the responsibilities previously held by the four departed staff members.

This series of changes in leadership, management, and the role of the school board continue to cause jitters throughout the community. Speculation about Cognita's commitment to the three IB programmes and about the game plan of Brega, the private equity company that owns Cognita Schools, is an on-going topic of discussion amongst those who believe that Southbank is the company's biggest profit-maker, as it continues its global expansion purchasing schools worldwide. The school's strong IB results in 2013 have given some comfort, though parents credit the previous administration with much of this success, and wait to see whether the new team, and what appears to be a strategy to create a different learning environment, will sustain these outcomes. Parents who have been there for a longer period of time lament what they perceive to be a shift away from a school culture that was based on the ethos and values of the school's founder.

Pastoral care and discipline: The pastoral approach at Southbank has undergoing change under the new administration. Previously there were no onerous school rules – zero tolerance for drugs, alcohol and chewing gum and staff trained to recognise the signs of substance abuse. There had been no problems reported for the past several years so parents have been somewhat surprised to receive notification that the school is introducing drugs testing. Smoking was more of a concern, addressed through PSE classes; now smoking off campus (previously allowed with parental permission) is banned. The oldest IB students who have been allowed in the past to leave campus when they did not have a scheduled class are upset at the loss of this privilege. While some welcome this new disciplinary regime, some parents feel this diminishes the development of personal responsibility for independent learning that has historically characterised the 'social contract' between students and their teachers, and that many perceived was an authentic application of the IB learner profile.

Bullying is not an issue as everyone is so different; in fact the school celebrates difference. Students are expected to work hard and get results. Each pupil has an advisor who they see daily, who monitors their overall progress and who is the first line of communication. Further up there are deputy principals for middle and high school and a personal counsellor, so lots of support in place.

Pupils and parents: Many Southbank pupils are expats, children of diplomats, corporates, journalists and the occasional artist or entertainer. The school has a lower turnover than many international schools (a little over 20 per cent per year) and this partly because expats are opting to remain in London, making it their permanent home. Local parents at the school say that worries that friends will move away are exaggerated, that the old boy and old girl network is still there – it's just a global one. This on-going network appears to be informally driven by former pupils (and families) of all ages, owing more to Facebook than any formal programme managed by the school.

There are just under 60 nationalities represented, including many dual nationals. Some 15 per cent US Americans and 10 per cent Brits; the school is truly internationally diverse with no dominant nationality. It seems to appeal to families who have one British parent with a foreign national spouse, where being bilingual or multilingual is the norm, and where being in a globally-minded community is seen as an advantage. There are no uniforms and a relaxed dress code prevails. Pupils are sharp, friendly and self-confident, forming strong bonds of friendship. Classroom exchanges are lively yet respectful.

There is an active parent teacher organisation (PTA), though parents say there is no real pressure to participate. The PTA coffee mornings organised by each year group help parents to get to know each other and find out who their children's friends are. The three Southbank PTAs occasionally meet together, and a tri-campus bi-annual Winter Benefit raises serious money for the PTA-sponsored charities. Ex-Southbank parents are known to have reunions, maintaining long-distance friendships and gathering in London, New York or other exotic places.

Entrance: Open mornings and IB information sessions for local families during autumn and spring terms. Inbound

S

expats on 'look-see' trips may book appointments with the admissions department. Candidates must be above average, and able to cope with the demands of the IB. Transcripts, teacher recommendations, a statement from parents and a profile written by the pupil are considered. The school is no longer offering its intensive English as a second language classes; students must now demonstrate an intermediate level of fluency to manage the programme. Testing not required unless reports seem insufficient to assess their English language fluency or readiness for the IB. Applications are accepted all year and usually considered in date order. Waiting lists depend on the class but there is some turnover, and an additional class at IB1 level accommodates pupils joining after GCSEs. The admissions process states that applications are not actually reviewed until they know they have a vacancy available, which is a bit awkward when families want to know where they stand. If you are accepted, be prepared to pay the deposit and full first term's fees to secure the place, both non-refundable if you change your mind, with a few exceptions. Read the small print.

Parents of Southbank Kensington and Hampstead pupils who transfer to the Westminster secondary speak highly of the advisory system that helps new pupils to organise themselves and manage the additional rigours of the IB Middle Years Programme. However, parents at the two Southbank primary schools have been advised that admission to the secondary school will no longer be automatic, and there will be some screening of the records.

Southbank is an international school that understands the problems of these secondary school pre-adolescents and teens (and families) who have moved frequently, and they know how to make them welcome. The PTA is active, with welcome and orientation activities, so there is scope for a newly-arrived parent to get involved.

Exit: The guidance department has two advisers: one for North American universities and one for universities in the UK and the rest of the world. A careers survey is taken by all pupils in grade 10 and a university course survey in grade 11. Information evenings for parents who might be unfamiliar with the application process and careers days for all pupils.

All go on to university – sometimes preceded by a gap year or compulsory military service – mostly in the UK, but the number heading to the US has been creeping up each year. Popular destinations include UCL, Imperial, Warwick, Edinburgh in the UK, Stanford, Columbia, Cornell in the US and McGill in Canada.

Southbank's IB programme makes it easy for mobile families to find a common curriculum worldwide. Transfers during the two year IB diploma programme are not encouraged, and may even require starting the programme over again rather than picking up half way through. However, Southbank tries very hard to make transitions work.

Money matters: Some bursarial help is available for existing Southbank families suddenly in reduced circumstances. The Milton Toubkin Scholarship awards one scholarship per year to an outstanding, motivated pupil at the diploma level.

There have been rumblings from some parents in recent years about the level of the fees and the supposed profits going to Cognita, but others say the school offers value for money. With the recent improvement in teacher salaries, the provision of a long-awaited sports facility, and the arrival of the new executive principal, a 'wait and see' posture is in order.

Remarks: Good family-orientated urban school with international flavour. Well geared for smart, curious, self-motivated and internationally-minded pupils. As the first UK school authorised to offer all three IB programmes, Southbank has solid international school cred, though some parents now say that it is more of a 'British school with an IB programme',

dubbing it 'Sevenoaks in the City' in reference to the previous experience of the executive principal and Westminster principal. Six years after the sale of the school by its founders to Cognita, the wariness of the community continues, particularly amongst the families who joined the school before the change in management. The new executive principal and Cognita will no doubt continue efforts to win over the hearts and minds of the stakeholders of the school they claim as their international flagship.

Stamford High School

Linked schools: Stamford School; Stamford Junior School

St Martin's, Stamford, Lincolnshire, PE9 2LL

- Pupils: 630 girls; 65 board, rest day • Ages: 11–18 • C of E
- Fees: Day £13,029; Boarding £18,147–£23,949 pa • Independent

Tel: 01780 484200
Email: headshs@ses.lincs.sch.uk
Website: www.ses.lincs.sch.uk

Head: Since 2003, Mrs Dyl Powell BEd NPQH (fiftyish), a PE and maths specialist, and a football enthusiast who supports Barcelona but likes 'good football' whoever plays it – including her own girls. Mrs Powell came from The King's School in Peterborough where she'd been deputy head for nine years. Sensible, practical and down-to-earth, Mrs Powell is clearly a 'doer' rather than an administrator or ivory tower-dweller. 'Involved' – ie she involves herself – is the word most often used of her. She teaches, she sings in the chapel choir, she is a member of the schools' CCF, she is a hockey umpire and, working comfortably with the other two heads of the Stamford Endowed Schools (SES) and the principal, she has been busily changing, renewing, updating. 'Our school song begins, "Within these walls of grey..." and that's exactly what they were,' she admits. 'I set myself to lighten the atmosphere – new colours, refurbishment, signage, plasma screens, redecoration of the hall, an honours board, a new house system and, well, it seems to have worked.' Parents agree and all talk of the friendliness in the school and its new sense of confidence. Something good is happening here and Mrs Powell is at the heart of it.

Principal: The three schools in the Stamford Endowed Schools foundation are overseen by the Principal, Mr Stephen Roberts, who arrived in September 2008 from Felsted School of which he had been head for 15 years – a safe pair of hands then. This was a clever appointment and Mr Roberts sees eye to eye with the three heads of the individual schools over the aims – near and far – of the foundation. 'He comes to all events,' we were told.

Academic matters: Given that the school has a pretty comprehensive intake, the curriculum and the results are impressive and value-added in particular is notable. In 2013, at GCSE, 100 per cent of girls gained at least five A*-C grades and a remarkable 67 per cent of grades were A*/As. Particularly successful were DT, drama, RS and music. At A level – which is taught co-educationally with the boys of Stamford School – 28 subjects are offered (63 per cent A*-B grades, 35 per cent A*/A). Most popular are biology, business, chemistry, Eng lit, geog, history, RS, business studies and maths. Exceptional maths and RS results. At Stamford School languages are popular – good to see French, German, Russian and Spanish on offer, though numbers not huge. Chemistry is very popular, with the number of girls taking science bucking the national trend. GCSE French is fast-tracked for top two sets and taken early. Setting in English, maths, langs and science to GCSE.

Good learning support dept for those with SEN. LSAs in class, individual help given in lunch and morning breaks and no withdrawal from lessons. School eager to support all-comers – 'we look at the individual'. Wheelchairs users would have difficulties because of the site – and its spread over the town – and especially in the main high school building which is listed so modifications are a problem. But head says, 'we look creatively at what we can do within the internal structure.' A positive attitude overall. Head has inspirational new initiative – RiFTT – 'reaching for the Top' – which aims to encourage girls 'to think outside the syllabus and expand their horizons' – especially important for the G and T and those who might take Oxbridge. Currently 14 need EAL but no-one accepted who can't deal with the curriculum. Weekly EAL lessons for those who need it, mostly one-to-one, sometimes in groups of two or three. The EAL teacher liaises with subject staff. More support given in boarding houses. Sixth form EAL students sit IELTS examination.

Games, options, the arts: One parent summed up what everyone told us, 'There is a good balance between the importance the school gives to academic achievement and the rounding the girls get from doing other things.' There are lots of other things but sport and music, perhaps, stand out most. Excellent sports facilities – all three schools benefit from excellent spread of shared facilities and no big posh independent school can offer more. New sports centre with state of the art fitness suite, gym and 25m pool. Much success – girls often unbeaten in badminton and equally successful across the range. 'You can pick what you enjoy,' we were told – if only it had been like that we were at school, we mused. Masses of after-school activities – too much to choose from for many. CCF is especially popular.

Music is 'really big' and is mostly in collaboration with the boys' school – the same head of dept oversees all three schools which makes sense but must be a huge job. The dept occupies an ancient building opposite the High School. There is every kind of ensemble – orchestras, choirs of various types and sizes, bands and chamber groups – among the most energetic music set-ups we have met anywhere. Girls pay tribute to their teachers – 'you can learn any instrument you like – they'll always find you a teacher'... 'there's so much music on offer here'. Even the non-musical feel the effects and walls we passed trembled with drum-beats, piano rhapsodies and brass clarions. Music tech popular but more so with the boys, we were told. Lovely art – precise and imaginative – excellent DT and clever textiles – a sense of enjoyment pervades all. Speech and drama also 'big' and successful with girls carrying off prizes at local and national events. New performing arts centre under construction.

Background and atmosphere: Though less venerable than the boys' school, the High School is no Joanna-Come-Lately and it occupies a stunning Georgian building on a broad and elegant street in this stunning Georgian town. Stamford, for those who think they don't know it, will be familiar to all as the ready-made backdrop to most of the 18th century costume dramas you've drooled over – not least Pride and Prejudice – yes, that version. It is simply delicious – especially out of traffic-snarly periods – and one can understand an occasional gentle smugness and unwillingness-to-look-outside quality in its denizens. The High School occupies a fine position next to Burghley House and its estate, a splendid Elizabethan pile built by Elizabeth's Lord Burghley and helped along in the following century by Capability Brown who didn't half get about. A useful resource to have next door.

And the new has most definitely arrived here too. Whiteboards everywhere, IT bristles around the place, plasma screens hither and yon announcing the events of the day – both internal and external. New lang labs – school very proud. New and excellent dance/drama studio and another drama studio – well-equipped

– elsewhere. New spectroscopy suite – this was explained to us and we left feeling erudite and impressed. Nice to see Rosalind Franklin honoured in its naming. The arts rooms have recently been refurbished, creating a hub of artistic endeavours and beautiful, spacious studios. In other ways, it still feels very much like a trad girls' school – narrowish corridors, smallish classrooms and a bit of a rabbit warren ('they give you maps when you arrive,' we were told) full of happy bunnies in long skirts. Two good sized rooms for home economics – which is very popular. Excellent library – especially well stocked in English. Good displays everywhere and they have much that merits it.

The SES was formed in 1997 and now works well – all the administration managed centrally and overseen by the principal. The co-ed sixth form is a popular and unqualified success and works well on academic, social and economic grounds. In effect, rather than the sexes being entirely mixed in the sixth form classrooms, timetabling more frequently results in the pupils of each school sharing their teachers. This is partly because there's a ten minute walk between the two schools and you can't have the pupils belting across the town and back all day. Parents applaud the single sex tuition in years 7-11 and the co-ed sixth with all the shared opportunities it brings. Girls clearly approve, 'it's great being all girls until you're 16 but it's also great being mixed in the sixth form,' said one. There is every sense that the three heads and principal like each other and collaborate fruitfully, though communication between the two senior schools and the staff – and opportunities for co-operation – still need work, as many acknowledge. There is the potential for a constant stimulating dialogue and sharing here – it's not fully realised yet.

Pastoral care and discipline: Friends in Stamford High School – 'FISH' – is school's mentoring system in which year 10 girls keep an eye on year 7s – around 80 per cent of the older girls take part. Form tutors pick up most other problems and parents enthuse about the pastoral side. 'It's one massive big tick,' a current dad assured us, 'they are very good at handling the business of being a young kid in a community'. Surprisingly, to this addled urban writer, all the High School girls, including the sixth, wear uniform and an eccentric one it is – the younger girls wearing long – ankle-length in some cases – skirts. 'We love it,' we were assured and it is attractive in an Edwardian kind of way.

House system ensures vertical mixing and is popular and it makes the girls very competitive. Over-competitiveness and cliqueyness were the only two common grouses we heard – but we did hear them quite a lot. On the other hand, everyone told us, 'it's very friendly – the teachers help you a lot – all my teachers have different teaching styles – they're all great characters.' Boarding in big old house – used to be the junior school – girls in years 7-11 in twos, threes or fours and sixth formers in en-suite ones and twos in a separate building. Boarding is cosy and small and, unlike in so many other places, rather on the increase here – mostly due to the school's wonderfully flexible policy about girls staying for a bunch of nights as and when. Boarding rated as 'outstanding' in latest Ofsted report.

Pupils and parents: Mostly local though some day pupils from up to an hour away. Some few parents commute the hour's train journey to London – well worth a ponder if this is the sort of school you want. Useful school bus system. Most boarders are from Forces families though a few come from overseas and are helped with EAL if needed, though their English must be good enough for them to cope with the academic demands. The County Scholarships have long ensured a good social mix – within the meaning of that in rural Lincs/Rutland – but in truth, this is a pretty homogeneous, and exceptionally pretty, we thought, bunch of girls. They were also open, unpretentious, highly articulate and warm – of great credit to the school. Lively and supportive PA but some complain – of all three schools – that they need to be more ambitious and promote the foundation more vigorously. The principal and his dept will probably address this – early days yet – but it is interesting that the Stamford parents, conscious of what a treasure they share, feel that the wider world could – and should – take note. Lots of famous Old Girls eg Eleanor Turner, Sarah Outen, Sara Cawood, Bishop Maureen Jones, Lucy Cohu, Daphne Ledward-Hands and Susannah Ivens – 1998 Dressmaker of the Year for wedding dresses!

Entrance: Most come in from the junior school. 125 sit exam for the school's 90-odd places – quite good odds overall, given that many will have also applied elsewhere. They come from Copthill Prep, Malcolm Sargent, St Gilbert's, St Georges, Uffington, St Augustines, Bluecoat. At 13, applicants from Orton Wistow, Laxton Junior, Brooke Priory, The Bythams, Ketton and Witham Hall. Sixty candidates for the 12 coveted County Scholarships (see below). Entrance to the sixth form requires five B+s at GCSE and school advises with candour and compassion those few of their own who are unlikely to cope to look elsewhere. Twenty or more come into the sixth from all over – some from quite far afield – and all are quickly integrated.

Exit: The move to a co-ed sixth stopped the outflow after GCSE and only a few go now – far fewer than hitherto to the local independents. Those who do leave after GCSE go mostly to the local sixth form colleges. The vast majority at 18 to further/higher education – a good spread of mostly Russell Group universities – Birmingham, Sheffield and Leeds currently the faves. Impressive range of subjects too – no pigeon holing here. No Oxbridge in 2007, 2008 – are these bright, delightful girls selling themselves short? But school assures us that six went to Oxbridge in 2010 and three in 2013.

Money matters: Both SES senior schools supply their own means-tested bursaries and scholarships programme. Much highly successful fund-raising among alumnae.

Remarks: This school and the foundation of which it is a part offer rare opportunities and at a more than competitive fee. In the words of one sixth former, 'the teachers put so much into helping us – there's nothing they wouldn't do,' and a fifth former, 'it's a school for anybody. I don't know anyone who doesn't enjoy it.'

Stamford School

Linked schools: Stamford High School; Stamford Junior School

Southfields House, St Paul's Street, Stamford, Lincolnshire, PE9 2BQ

- Pupils: 900 boys, 95 board • Ages: 11–18 • C of E • Fees: Day £13,029; Boarding £18,147–£23,949 pa • Independent

Tel: 01780 750300
Email: headss@ses.lincs.sch.uk
Website: www.ses.lincs.sch.uk

Head: Since 2011, Mr William Phelan MA (early forties), previously deputy head of Warwick School. He was educated at Queen Elizabeth's Hospital School in Bristol and went on to study medieval and modern history at Royal Holloway in London. After teaching history at the Royal Grammar School in High Wycombe – also coaching the rugby and cricket teams – he completed a MBA at Leicester University and became the head of sixth form at Abingdon School in Oxfordshire before joining Warwick School. He is married to Lorna with two young daughters, Penny and Posy.

Mr Phelan is working closely with the principal and heads of the other two schools in the Endowed Schools family. He joined at a time of great change for the schools, as they completed the multi-million pound swimming pool and sports complex and turn their attention to a new performance arts centre. "There has been a clear evolution in everything the schools are doing and my role is to continue that."

Principal: The three schools in the Stamford Endowed Schools foundation are overseen by the principal, Mr Stephen Roberts, who arrived in 2008 from Felsted School of which he had been head for fifteen years – a safe pair of hands then. This was a clever appointment and Mr Roberts sees eye to eye with the three heads of the individual schools over the aims – near and far – of the foundation. 'He comes to all events,' we were told.

Academic matters: More than respectable results. In 2013, 50 per cent of subjects taken at GCSE achieved A*/A. Exceptional showings in all three sciences, maths and RS. RS seems to be exceptionally taught across the three schools. Popular options at this level are geog, hist, PE and DT. At A level – taught co-educationally with Stamford High School – 63 per cent A*-B grades in 2013. Of the mainstream subjects, languages, maths and history achieve most highly with exceptional results in maths. Unlike in so many boys' schools, languages are properly supported and successful – hooray!

School good at liaising with junior/primary schools over pupils with SEN and also good at picking up those who arrive without a diagnosis but who need support. Learning support dept helps with weekly and drop-in classes and works closely with teachers to develop strategies tailored to individual needs. 'We really support those with physical disabilities,' says Mr Phelan. 'They need looking after and special attention but fundamentally they just need stretching rather than being hived off.' A sense of care and attention to individuals here.

Good provision with new developments currently underway. The new Research and Learning Centre integrates 10,000 books with an 'online learning suite'. This facility places a modern, spacious and well-equipped study and research centre at the heart of the school and is well-used by students. We do wonder why the word 'library' is verbum non gratum anywhere these days! A new sports centre with fitness suite and swimming pool opened in 2012, and the new performance arts centre will be the next major development.

Games, options, the arts: 'Sport has come on hugely,' everyone told us, because of the new director, an ex-London Irish player. Cricket has been given a boost with the recent addition of Dean Headley – the former England international cricketer – to the coaching rostrum as well as new facilities. Some of the most stunning playing fields we've seen anywhere. Good Astro provision and the sharing of facilities across the three schools makes every kind of sense. Good open air pool – used by boarders whenever – and the new sports centre, which houses a brand new 25m pool. CCF is huge here – the indoor shooting range supports highly successful shooting team which wins everything going. School sports generally very good – opportunities and successes and something for everyone.

Art impresses wherever you go. Excellent displays of boys' work; we rejoiced to see evidence of the trad skills – eg painting and drawing, to a high level as well as applied work of various kinds. Fine portrait work here and good use of small art library though art history not offered. We loved the DT and craft work eg clay profiteroles (looked scrummy) and a pizza which we nearly took away. We admired the exam work – the wine rack, the shoe locker – simple, imaginative and deft work. Music – here as in all three schools – exemplary – rich, various and dazzling. Music not for the geeks but an integral part of life and overseen by the same head of dept for all three schools. Pupils positively fizz when they talk about the sheer fun of all

S

the opportunities they have, ensembles, tours etc – and doing much in collaboration with the girls clearly doesn't hurt. Music tech is big news here too. Good, lively drama – again popular, especially when the two schools work together. Work will soon begin on a performing arts centre so that more parents and people from the town will be able to enjoy the large-scale productions.

Background and atmosphere: Stamford is an 18th century aficionado's bit of heaven and any such visitor will virtually know their way around as so much of the town has been used in costume dramas over the years. This is Georgian, honey-coloured elegance not yet ruined by constant traffic – though they're working on it.

In 1997, the governors of Stamford School and Stamford High School decided that 'the two schools should work more harmoniously together' and brought in new structure overseen by a new principal of all three schools, including the junior school. The idea was that the three schools should 'maintain their individual character but that the foundation which would then comprise all three schools would be able to educate the school population from 4-18, girls and boys, day pupils and boarders'. 'It's been huge for the schools,' says Mr Phelan. 'The co-ed sixth form has been, perhaps, the most profound change – it's like a mini university,' he says and it does have a flavour of that. In effect, rather than the sexes being entirely mixed in the sixth form classrooms, timetabling more frequently results in the pupils of each school sharing their teachers. This is partly because there's a ten minute walk between the two schools and you can't have the pupils belting across the town and back all day. Parents applaud the single sex tuition in years 7-11 and the co-ed sixth with all the shared opportunities it brings.

There is a substantial programme of renewal going on. As so often happened, 20th century architects here clearly felt under no obligation to design in sympathy with the existing glorious school buildings and Stamford is saddled with a number of edifices from Grimsville, notably the old gym, the bridge – clearly inspired by Motorway chic – and the central quad – but the well-funded and sensitive renewal programme is doing its best to conceal or enhance where they can. The old gym will face considerable regeneration to house the performance arts centre, which in turn will mean a revamp of the quad outside it. This, along with the recently completed glass atrium, will mean the aesthetics of the heart of the school will be much improved.

Boys and parents alike feel that, not just in the sixth form, the 'merging' of the school with the girls' school has 'really raised our game' However, some boys' school parents also feel that the school could be better organised and there is a palpable difference between the efficiency of the girls' school in this regard and the boys' – as several parents of children at both confirmed. 'The girls' school staff are always quick to get back to us – sometimes you never hear back from the boys' school.' Other parents, however, express themselves happy with both schools in this respect. School comments that recent parental survey rated communication in both schools as very good or good in nearly 90 per cent of cases, with less than five per cent rating it negatively. Some parental feeling that the SES schools don't 'court' the locals enough. 'Oundle, Uppingham and Oakham really promote themselves – in the local preps and so on – the SES should do far more,' we were told.

Despite its laudable upgrading and new sense of pride, the SES is not at pains to 'up the academics' (ie position in the league tables) which would result in doing itself out of much of its loyal traditional market. Nonetheless, the schools deserve to be far better known and appreciated. This writer can see little reason why some locals might choose the big three, relatively close-by, independents given all on offer here. The principal, Mr Roberts is affable, forward looking and a true educationalist. It is, in part, his job to up the school's confidence, boost the cooperation between the schools and to bruit abroad the excellence of his foundation. Stamford's pride should be more than just a smug local secret.

Pastoral care and discipline: Parents praise the pastoral care – 'they are extraordinarily nurturing,' we were told, 'and boys with problems get wonderful support'. Mentoring of the young by the older and 'we don't accept bullying,' said previous head, 'we go straight at it – we work with parents, we don't wait for it to sort itself out.' Yes! In general, the pupils – especially in the sixth form when, of necessity, they have to be able to move around the town unsupervised, are trusted to behave and they do. 'We live or die by our reputation in this town,' said previous head. Few major incidents – no physical contact allowed (a 'six inch rule' obtains, we were informed) between sixth formers, and misdemeanours of the drink/smoke/drugs nature are mostly few and petty.

Slight sense among some parents that the 'shut-up-and-get-on-with-it' boy can get overlooked. However, others told us that the school's students are 'not just cardboard cut outs' and very much seen as individuals. Some parental feeling that the discipline 'could be better' and that there is rather too much variation in behaviour deemed acceptable by different members of staff. 'Sports stars seem to get away with stuff others never would', we also heard – but there may be a tinge of jealousy here? And school strenuously refutes the idea. Most parents feel the school has a 'very good atmosphere' and that the boys are prepared to 'be able to mix with anyone'. There is a 'lot of banter and lots of respect – a balance that wins boys' interest. But they know there is a line.' 'The good education gives them choices but they also learn the life skills to work with others and motivate themselves and other people.'

Boarding is tiny – in relation to the overall numbers – and cosy – surprisingly good for so few and rated as 'outstanding' in the recent Ofsted inspection. Four resident tutors and two matrons in houses, all sixth formers in single rooms – mostly en suite – year 11s in singles/twins and younger boys in twins. Around 15 per cent from overseas – Hong Kong, China, Russia etc. Excellent common rooms and facilities, good kitchens in boarding houses, WiFi all over, rooms small but sensible. Good healthy food eaten by all.

Pupils and parents: From a good 30 miles around – sometimes more in the sixth. Families mostly local and professional and as you'd expect – people who value the education, location, good social mix and very reasonable fees more than the name of a glitzy, famous public school. It's only one hour by train to King's Cross – some parents commute and you can see why. Boarders often from RAF families with a sprinkling from overseas. The boys we met were some of the most unpretentiously impressive and charming we have met anywhere. This particular writer has visited over 150 schools for The GSG and cannot remember more open, articulate, and delightful boys anywhere. They do the school great credit. Famous OBs include the Lord Burghley and various later ones, Alfred Harmsworth (Viscount Northcliffe), also musical knights Malcolm Sargent and Michael Tippett, various literati including Colin Dexter and his most famous creation, numerous military men including Sir Michael Jackson, many divines, industrialists and sportsmen of note.

Entrance: 130 external applicants for 60 places at 11+ – tests in English, maths and reasoning – junior school pupils transfer more or less automatically. Also from Copthill Prep, Witham Prep and local primaries. Five or more B+s required at GCSE for entrance to the sixth. Not huge hurdles. Perhaps seemingly too easy? If they made it harder, maybe people would value more what is on their doorstep?

Exit: Penny numbers each year to Oxbridge (three in 2013), clutch of medics, chemists, engineers. Popular in the large mix of destinations are London University colleges, Newcastle,

S

Leeds, Loughborough and many of the newer universities. Impossible to select favourites from the vast range of subjects undertaken. Clearly no sausage-making going on here.

Money matters: School offers numerous academic, music and art awards at 11,13 and 16. A special scholarship fund for Poles – result of strong local Polish community from WW11. Also means-tested bursaries for the bright broke.

Remarks: Impressive on all fronts. A privileged – but not spoiling – start in life for all but snobs. Why pay more?

Stephen Perse Foundation

Linked schools: Dame Bradbury's School; Stephen Perse Foundation Junior School; The Stephen Perse Sixth Form College; Stephen Perse Pre-Prep

Union Road, Cambridge, CB2 1HF

• Pupils: 440 (all girls until 16 but changing from 2014), all day • Ages: 11-18 • Non-denom • Fees: £10,200-£14,985 pa; • Independent

Tel: 01223 454700
Email: office@stephenperse.com
Website: www.stephenperse.com

Principal: Since 2001, Ms Patricia Kelleher MA (late forties), read history at LMH Oxford, followed by MA at Sussex. Taught at Haberdashers then Brighton and Hove GDST before deputy headship at Brentwood School. Absolutely perfect in her role as the 'face of the Stephen Perse Foundation' (rebranded, discrete educational entities comprising the Stephen Perse junior and senior schools and the Stephen Perse Sixth Form College) – an engagingly sagacious, forward-thinking principal who readily thinks outside the box. Actively promotes add-ons to the traditionally strong academic provision – says a pupil. 'Discovering an inner ability' is the most rewarding aspect of her job. Much time is spent charming potential punters and managing the foundation (areas needing development or fine tuning are collaboratively resolved) so day-to-day headmistressy business in the senior school is handled by the approachable Dr Stringer – fantastic and clearly visible, according to parents.

Academic matters: How is it done? Ninety-four per cent A/A* in 2013 with the vast majority taking 11 GCSEs and some even managing 12. And about a third play an instrument. Answer – very able pupils plus a combination of high quality teaching ('we appreciate just how bright our teachers are'), an examy environment, excellent reporting ('they really know and understand the girls'), maximum class size of 24, plenty of homework ('we're all geeks – we work so hard') and expectations. The latter is all-pervading – from home ('it's the Cambridge mentality,' mused one pupil), school and, most importantly, the girls themselves. Arty or sciency pigeon-holing is minimal and all areas shine, from single sciences to languages – a goodly clutch including Greek and Latin. Fine facilities; a recently-refurbed 'designer' library where books can be ordered or computers accessed, science labs aplenty and a funky, circular IT suite with two spotlit computer-topped concentric work stations – the 'mother ship' according to our guides. No EFL or SEN unit in the school – only the mildest of learning difficulties are manageable in this environment.

Sixth: from 2008 marketed as the co-ed Stephen Perse Sixth Form College. Slightly out on limb – a mile away from the senior school – but shuttle buses are provided for those who need to be there for lessons. Laptops for all, with class sizes no more than 14, although this is likely to increase if college grows as intended. Seventy-five per cent A*/A at A level in 2013 with IB now on offer (average, highest in the UK, of 41.2 points in 2013). Haemorrhaging after GCSE not nearly so acute (50 per cent left after GCSEs in 2013), as this clever move provides something previously unavailable in the city. Fresh-faced head of college 'wants to encourage thinking' and is tremendously enthusiastic about compulsory TOK (theory of knowledge programme) – much discussion and blogging of ideas – he says unis approve.

Games, options, the arts: Over the years, netball and hockey teams have enjoyed county successes – but some parental wizzles re games; from the sportier girls too. It's not a lack of staff, facilities or choice; it's time. For younger ones it's reasonable but, once GCSE courses start, something has to give. Of course, the less sporty are perfectly happy with the 80 minutes a week (minus 10 mins there and 10 mins back from the Astroturfed sports field) – and there is plenty of support for those who want more and can shoehorn a practice or club (dance, basketball, football, badminton, rowing or anything else the girls can initiate) during the lunchbreak or after school. Sixth have access to nearby sports/fitness centres.

Music flourishes – three orchestras, bands, choirs, chamber groups and concerts abroad. Broad choice of instrumental tuition and plenty of practice rooms. Well-endowed visual arts centre. Tidy general studio with trendy back-lit lettering proclaiming 'ARTS' in 'post-feminist pink' (q. the principal), a print room and huge atelier for sixth formers. Not much work on show round the school, but what we saw was carefully considered, with some interesting use of materials in textiles. Annual drama production for every year group plus speech and drama lessons in preparation for LAMDA examinations.

No shortage of extra-curricular activities – some before school. Recently reintroduced gold and silver D of E and annual trip to the Gambia for sixth formers who can find the air fare – they take money raised for projects and give help. Long list of foreign visits and collaborative ventures – school has an EU Comenius award in recognition of international activities.

Background and atmosphere: Founded in 1881 as a sister school to the much older Perse Boys. Association now firmly at an end – the boys have gone co-ed and the SP foundation is taking boys in the sixth and pre-prep. Main school tucks into narrow streets near the centre of Cambridge and is a 10 minute walk from the station. Understated dark blue front door in a characterless brick wall belies what's beyond – much money spent coupled with bold design statements has made a warm, comfortably stimulating place of learning (same goes for the sixth form centre even though it's in a bland ex-office block). Sparkle comes from the brightly lit and imaginatively designed dining-cum-common room, which pleasantly buzzes as girls happily spend time together, and a courtyard area where there's a large flower power mural created by pupils and a local graffiti artist. A secure, well ordered environment filled with conscientious pupils who have a clear sense of direction – greater freedom in the sixth form centre produces more of a bustle.

Pre-preps at Madingley and adjacent to the junior school are already co-ed. The Madingley Pre-prep has Forest School designation (since 2013). School has announced that it will take boys in the juniors from 2014 and in the senior school from 2018, teaching most subjects separately from 10-16 years.

Pastoral care and discipline: Ethos which builds self esteem – 'they're good at making the girls feel good about themselves,' said a parent. Steady encouragement to be independent and give reasoned opinions – 'they're not "yes women" – but that does make for an interesting time at home.' Pupils speak of positive relationships with staff – for help or advice it's the year head or form tutor. If that doesn't suit there's a choice of school nurses – for the sixth an off-site counsellor.

S

School lunch for all except year 11, who are allowed out twice a week. Ample choice with lasagne a firm favourite. Apparently, girls now spend longer in the dining area where the relaxed atmosphere has led to a healthier relationship with food – an unexpected and positive spin-off from the refurbishment. Light snacks are available for the sixth, who are allowed to do their own thing.

Biddable, well-behaved lot so no real discipline issues – but just in case, there's a code of conduct which has been drawn up by the student forum. Year 11 take on roles of responsibility and, after the autumn term, are allowed to wear their own clothes – greatly appreciated. Competition between the six 'houses' (house talent contest is highly popular) but form loyalties are the strongest.

Pupils and parents: Pupils mostly local. Articulate and mature. Loyal parent body – quite a few academics who come for a year and a high proportion of working mums. Old girls include author Phillippa Pearce, archaeologist Jacquetta Hawkes, broadcaster Bridget Kendall and Olympic gold medalist Stephanie Cook.

Entrance: Exam and interview at 11 – latter is the clincher. About half from Stephen Perse Junior – entry is more or less automatic. Rest from local prep and primaries (according to one mum 'a great deal of testing with no let-up with the teaching' can be a shock for those used to a state school regime). A number also join in year 9. For the sixth, A grades in subjects to be studied at AS/A or IB. 'We like international diversity but not dominance,' so cap of 10-15 per cent on students from abroad. 'We're looking for the brightest and they must have at least an IELTS (International English Language Testing System) score of 6.5 in writing ... 7.5 to 8.5 is typical.' Universities want 7.5 so Stephen Perse is being pretty picky.

Exit: Number staying on for the sixth on the up (approximately half) but Hills Road SFC remains a popular alternative. Impressive list of university destinations – around a third to Oxbridge. Good showing for medicine and other heavyweight subjects.

Money matters: Wide range of scholarships at KS3 and for the sixth (up to 20 per cent). Means-tested bursaries. Nuffield bursaries awarded annually for science.

Remarks: First-rate selective school with a forward-thinking head who is working hard to make it much more than an academic hot-house.

The Stephen Perse Sixth Form College

Linked schools: Stephen Perse Foundation; Dame Bradbury's School; Stephen Perse Foundation Junior School; Stephen Perse Pre-Prep

Fitzwilliam Building, Shaftesbury Road, Cambridge, CB2 8AA

• Fees: £14,100 pa • Independent

Tel: 01223 488430
Email: admissions@stephenperse.com
Website: www.stephenperse.com

Head of sixth form: Mr S Armitage BA Hons Oxon (Geography) MPhil Cantab (Environment and Development).

Principal: Miss P Kelleher – see Perse Girls/Stephen Perse Foundation.

Remarks: See full entry for Perse Girls/Stephen Perse foundation.

Stewart's Melville College

Linked schools: ESMS (Erskine Stewart's Melville School); The Mary Erskine School

Queensferry Road, Edinburgh, EH4 3EZ

• Pupils: 745 boys • Ages: 11–18. (Separate entry for junior school)
• Non-denom • Fees: Day £9,726; Boarding £19,023–£19,512 pa
• Independent

Tel: 01313 111000
Email: admissions@esmgc.com
Website: www.esms.edin.sch.uk

Principal: Since 2000, Mr David Gray BA PGCE (fifties), who was educated at Fettes, read English at Bristol, where he did his PGCE. Taught English in a Bristol comprehensive, before moving to a language school in Greece, then taught English and modern Greek at Dulwich and was head of English at Leeds Grammar, before heading Pocklington School in East Yorkshire for eight years. Since the Stewart's Melville vast conglomerate forms the largest independent school in Europe, it is not surprising he feels he is in a position here 'to give something back to Scotland having been away for almost a quarter of a century'. Brought up in Inverness, he is proud of his Scottish roots and sees himself and Stewart's Melville/Mary Erskine as at the 'most exciting cutting-edge of Scottish education' and stresses that he's the first overall principal who is actually Scottish. Mr Gray spends part of the week in each school. We visited him at his base in Mary Erskine, where he was busily involved in compiling a history of the school for his teaching contact with the girls.

Very much a hands-on head, the principal reckons to keep sane (and fit) by swimming and jogging at 7am each morning, and is a familiar sight as he cycles between the two campuses. He also 'works the room' quite beautifully, 'we all think we know him well and that he knows our children almost as well as we do,' said one father (a gift no doubt inherited from his politician father?). Keen on promoting self-confidence in his pupils, he sees himself as an 'educator', and teaches English and coaches cricket at Stewart's Melville. He feels pleased that the school has 'become a gentler place' and that the 'children are wedded to our ethos of reasonable, sensible behaviour'. No need for draconian action on the discipline side recently and, when there is silliness, 'the student body can be very conservative on behaviour,' while parents 'don't want to be ashamed of the school.'

Mr Gray runs the twin senior schools with two deputy heads, and the head of the co-ed junior school, Bryan Lewis, who is also vice principal. Mrs Linda Moule took over as deputy head of The Mary Erskine School in August 2009; she was previously vice principal of New Hall School in Chelmsford. Mr Neal Clark, depute head of Stewart's Melville for the last 10 years describes himself as a 'grammar school boy, in tune with Scottish social culture.' All school facilities have been upgraded in the last 10 years 'so future plans are for maintenance rather than development.'

Academic matters: The principal and three heads have agonised together over the pros and cons of single-sex v co-ed. All four speak with the same passion – and often the same phrasing – of their 'best of both worlds' system. Boys and girls educated

S

together at junior school, separately from age 12-17 – gains for girls (being able to get on with learning) and boys (feeling free to talk about poetry etc) – then the social etc plus factors of co-ed for sixth year and all activities. 'Not a highly selective school,' however, described by an educationalist as a 'grade one academic machine.' Classes of up to 25 (20 for practical classes) setted, with groups subdivided to extend the most able. School has embraced the new Advanced Higher in depth – greater analysis, independent study, projects and dissertation. Recent results show a pleasing number of As and Bs across the board (43 per cent of entries graded A in 2013) in both schools, with some outstanding successes in history, sciences and maths. Higher results impressive (84 per cent A-B, 63 per cent A in 2013), particularly at MES 'on the languages front' and for SMC in history and geography. French, German, Spanish and Latin on offer to Advanced Higher Grade.

Since 2002, Standard Grades phased out (except drama) in favour of Intermediate 2 (which is based on the same assessment pattern as Highers). Results pretty impressive here too!

Very good links (still) with the Merchant Company which does masses of business breakfasts and links with professional firms around Edinburgh. Single IT network across all three schools with 'massive schools' intranet', interactive whiteboards galore and close on 1000 computers. Biology dept links with the horticultural dept of the world-famous Edinburgh Botanic Gardens. Impressive careers structure across both schools and excellent library facilities. Pupils can sign in for private study.

Schools combine for sixth form, most extras, and pastoral structure. In the interests of integration sixth formers have to take academic courses from both schools – a feat resulting in limitless (almost) variety of course permutations, miraculous timetabling and quite a few bus journeys. Outstanding back-up for those with learning difficulties; school has its own educational psychologist; 'some on Ritalin'; 'will never abandon anyone.'

Games, options, the arts: Big is beautiful; providing a list of over 75 different clubs for all – from goldsmithing to Greek, costume design to curling and cross-country – lunch time and post school. Popular. Major sports have separate clubs for ages/stages and 27 rugby teams. Good at football too! Girls prefer hockey and basketball, still better at shooting than boys and both sexes join the voluntary CCF (trillions of girls, over 400 members in all). A second super new floodlit Astroturf at MES, 'so everyone gets a chance,' dramatic wavy roofed swimming pool (at Stewart's Melville) with co-ed sixth form slump-out room adjacent, new gym (at MES), cricket pavilion (MES again). FPs and current pupils share sporting facilities at MES; extra games pitches at Inverleith. Needle matches in almost all disciplines, with FPs representing both county and country across the board. Smart dining room complex serves all juniors and 80 per cent seniors opt in. Sixth form coffee bars with stunning overview of school and pitches.

Incredibly strong drama – regular performances at the Edinburgh Festival and throughout the year at the Playhouse etc. Masses of every sort of orchestras. Pupils can learn to fly, ski (Hillend and the real thing, the Alps, Canada); brilliant debating team (regularly the Scottish Debating Champions, European Youth Parliament finalists) and SMC has represented Great Britain abroad all over the shop. Good home economics. Arts spectacular. Dramatic art room atop MES (with adjoining pottery and greenhouse). £3.5m performing arts centre's opening splash was Snowman composer, Howard Blake and Scottish Chamber Orchestra. Centre took 12 years in the planning – seats 800 with a retractable stage and dividing walls, replacing the old assembly hall – which was huge and impressive – and jolly nice in its way.

Background and atmosphere: Stewart's Melville campus is based round the magnificent David Rhind-designed Daniel Stewart's Hospital which opened in 1885 and merged with Melville College in 1972. Fairy-tale Victorian Gothic with a cluster of necessary modern additions surrounded by ever-decreasing games pitches and car parks. The old chapel is now a library complete with organ and stained glass windows. Stewart's Melville is also home to the senior department of the junior school – see separate entry.

Mary Erskine was founded in 1694, as the Merchant Maiden Hospital, moved to Ravelston in 1966, changing its name to The Mary Erskine School, and amalgamated with the boys' school in 1978. (Girls wear charming Mary Erskine tartan kilts.) MES clusters in decidedly 1960s architecture with, now, quite a lot of more modern extensions, round the pretty but sadly overwhelmed Ravelston House (1791): swimming pool, tennis courts, games pitches, Astroturfs etc. The last much used by FPs. The nursery department and the youngest classes of the junior school are also based here – see separate entry.

Two boarding houses, Dean Park House and Erskine House, furnished like large (and very well-equipped) family houses and based on the edge of the Stewart's Melville campus. Tremendous family feel, boarders are encouraged to invite friends home, caring house parents and only 60 boarding places.

Regular buses from East and West Lothian and Fife service both schools, which operate as one, under the auspices of Erskine Stewart's Melville Governing Council. Each school, though, is fiercely proud of its individual heritage.

Pastoral care and discipline: Both schools have a tutorial system for the first year, followed by house system in Upper Schools. Houses are common to both schools and house competitions have mixed sex teams. Good links with parents. Brief is that 'all children have a right to be happy here.' Code of conduct established by consulting pupils so 'they know exactly where they stand.' Excellent anti-bullying policy: wary pastoral staff and peer-support group 'with professional training' stop 'children slipping through the net.' Sophisticated PSE programme right up the school, including study skills. Buddy system for those coming up from junior schools. Automatic expulsion, 'zero-tolerance,' for those bringing in illicit substances – 'those on the periphery of the same incident will not necessarily be excluded but can come back in as long as they agree to random testing'. Fags 'unacceptable and pupils suspended'. Booze 'not an issue in school'.

Pupils and parents: Edinburgh hotch-potch of New Town and suburbs, with many first-time buyers and lots up from England. Siblings and FPs' children. Taking over a third of Edinburgh's independent secondary pupils, it's less elitist and perhaps less dusty than some city schools. Children living far out can spend the night when doing evening activities. Parent-teacher group ('the red socks brigade') slightly better organised into a Friends of the School group, fund-raising, ceilidhs, 'good cash cow.'

Entrance: At 11,12, 13 or sixth form – otherwise 'by default.' Automatic from junior school. Entrance assessments held in January but can be arranged at any time. Waiting lists for some stages but just go on trying. Entrance to upper school is by interview, plus school report plus GCSEs/Standard grades (five credit passes for S5 entry.) Numbers up overall.

Exit: Minimal leakage pre Highers, most sixth year (96 per cent) go on to university (gap years growing in popularity, especially for girls), most opt for Scottish unis but a few Oxbridge, London, Bristol etc. SATS (for American Colleges) not a problem. Art college, music/drama are popular alternatives.

Money matters: Scholarships/bursaries available, some linked to the Merchant Company, others sibling directed. 'No child will be left wanting in a (financial) crisis.'

Remarks: A glance at the school mags, Merchant Maiden and The Collegian, sums it up: bags of boys' poetry, multiple hockey, rugby and cricket teams, nine Oxbridge places, fabulous art, photos and writing plus fascinating glimpses from boys and girls reporting on the same activities with subtly different views.

An outstanding school; happy pupils, happy staff – focused on self-development with impressive results!

Stockport Grammar School

Linked school: Stockport Grammar School Junior School

Buxton Road, Stockport, Cheshire, SK2 7AF

- Pupils: 1,030, all day, 50/50 boys and girls • Ages: 11–18
- Secular • Fees: £9,981 pa • Independent

Tel: 01614 569000
Email: sgs@stockportgrammar.co.uk
Website: www.stockportgrammar.co.uk

Headmaster: Since 2005, Mr Andrew Chicken BA (London) MEd FRSA (early fifties), came from head of Colfes (qv), temporary headship of Stockport's closest rival Cheadle Hulme (qv) and, before that, teaching at Manchester Grammar. A passionate historian, teaching, leading history trips and waxing lyrical about the school's heritage and founder. Married to a former Withington Girls' (qv) languages teacher, no children, loves walking and the Derbyshire hills. He's a straight-talking northerner with transient traces of a Geordie accent, a 'nice guy' say staff, 'he's really nice' echo pupils. Beyond academic education, he describes the 'real guts of this school' as being 'in the children's personal development, encouraging children to think for themselves and of other people'.

Academic matters: Ambitious for results and consistently strong. In 2013, 71 per cent of GCSEs were A*s and As, 98 per cent gained five A*-C grades including English and maths. At A level over half score A* and A (56 per cent in 2013). 2011's ISI inspection described the overall achievement of pupils as excellent. Five one hour periods a day over a two week timetable leading to ten GCSEs. Lots of Challenge and Olympiad successes. Latin and PE taken right through to A level and the food tech room is gleaming stainless steel. Only the art department feels under-loved up a dank stairwell on the far reaches of the campus, although one recent leaver went on to take fine art, and art trips feature in the glossy school newsletter, Taking Stock. Maximum form size 25 but many senior classes are half that. All subjects offer additional teaching for Oxbridge candidates and in sixth form. Three or four hours weekly homework per subject is expected. Thirty or so children with extra needs, one statement in 2011, and a SENCo organises a variety of extra learning support; little mention of gifted and talented; perhaps because most here are. Pupils can run a bookshop account or bring cash and the bright library has periodicals and foreign language dvds. Pupils speak of enjoying outside visiting speakers.

Games, options, the arts: Sport taken seriously and Stockport make formidable opponents. County, regional and a few national players, but the house system aims to make sure all play, not just the first XI. Sports hall to rival any with super 25m pool, cafe mezzanine level with table tennis, multi-gym, squash courts and permanent climbing wall. Apart from acres of grass there's an all weather pitch as well.

'The music here is second to none with the philosophy to get as many involved as possible,' one parent told us, and indeed the music department boasts three professional musicians and 20 visiting instrument teachers including organ and singing. Lots

of choirs, orchestras, bands, performances at The Royal Northern College of Music. Three school drama productions a year.

The long list of extra-curricular happenings includes Model United Nations, Mock Trial, French Cine Club, Young Enterprise and most notably D of E. School is a D of E centre itself with a 21 year history and over 1,000 awards gained. Dozens of clubs and societies including a stage lighting group, creative cuisine and mountain activities – one teacher told us 'there's extra-curricular for all tastes, it's amazing if a child's not involved' and pupils agree, 'there's something for everyone here; well, except cross-country'. Plenty of leadership opportunities with prefect system, house captains and community service including running maths competitions for local junior schools. Links with India and Sierra Leone.

Background and atmosphere: Founded in 1487, admitted girls in 1980 and with recent new library and physics labs there's no stagnation here. An arts block for English and drama is under construction and head believes in a balance between top notch facilities and altruistic bursary provision. The founder Sir Edmond Shaa left the Pennine foothills to become Lord Mayor of London and remain Court Jeweller to three kings of England, attracting the current head's admiration for his spirit and wits. To this day close links are maintained with patrons The Worshipful Company of Goldsmiths.

Some glorious buildings, two lovely quads in the old bit but overall campus-like, with an open air walk, or dash in the rain, to some departments past acres of pitches, with signposts pointing the way. All bordered by Bramhall homes with a Derbyshire Peak District backdrop. The only blot on the landscape is a Kwik Fit tyre fitters in the school's parking area, slap bang in-between two exits onto the A6 out of Stockport. A friendly place from the cheery porter in his lodge at the entrance gate, and all hemmed in by secure fencing. Head's and caretaker's houses on site. The character of the pupils here does not conform to their uniform colours in nature's warning livery of black and yellow.

Pastoral care and discipline: School administered in lower, upper and sixth form divisions with form tutors, heads of year and then division, and a full time school nurse. Sixth formers volunteer to be 'first form friends' to help little ones settle in and find their way around in the early days. Pupils say any bullying, 'there's not much', is dealt with quickly but that the cardinal sin here is chewing gum, 'that's really a detention', says one, 'but it is unhygienic,' counters another. Inappropriate use of phones seems the next blacklisted thing.

School open from 8am, the library until 5.30. Three digital screens convey news and messages to pupils and there's a newspaper clippings board. Colours assemblies with awards for sport, music, drama, clubs and activities. House system for competition in sport, chess and a yearly talent show.

Pupils and parents: Culturally fairly diverse, mainly from south and east Manchester, east Cheshire and Derbyshire; on bus routes from Glossop, Middleton and Buxton. Well served by other private bus routes, public bus and train services. Broadly Christian, links with two local churches for Founders and carol services, separate Jewish, Hindu and Muslim assemblies. Half intake from own juniors, the rest a mix of prep and state primary children.

'My child's here for everything the school offers, the approach, the choices, the extra-curricular, the site and history, it's a beautiful place,' one dad, an Old Stopfordian himself, told us. 'It's about all the opportunities I had and want to offer my child, about buying ourselves out of behavioural issues in the state system, about the links and university expectations'.

Other Old Stopfordians include NEA and England basketball champion John Amaechi OBE, Professor Sir Freddie Williams (inventor of the first stored programme computer), the controversial Sir Victor Blank (chair of The Mirror Group and Lloyds TSB during the recent banking crisis), Gordon Marsden, Labour MP for Blackpool South, Harvey Locke (President of the British Veterinary Association), Geoffrey Downs (of the band Yes) and Alex Denman (RHS manager of the Chelsea Flower Show).

Entrance: By full day examination in January with maths, verbal reasoning, English and comprehension papers. Followed by 'informal' interviews with pupil and parents. Local state schools stop at 16 with sixth form colleges so Stockport Grammar gains a few more bright ones then.

Exit: Some depart post-GCSE (19 per cent in 2013). Those who stay go on to their first choice of university; lots to Nottingham, Leeds and Lancaster, a handful, six in 2013, to Oxbridge. One parent told us, 'The overall product of the school is amazing, young people with fantastic presence and confidence, even those who might initially have been intimidated by their peers'.

Money matters: Pupils keen to point out that overdue library books attract fines of 2p a day, dvds a daily 10p. Parents might be more interested in two 25 per cent music scholarships available each year and a range of bursaries including an Ogden Trust sixth form science scholarship that could yield 100 per cent of fees. Lunches compulsory at c£160 a term.

Remarks: Solid northern grammar with excellent all-round education, great facilities and bags of opportunity for all. Yes independent, but not la-di-da.

Stonar

Linked school: Stonar Preparatory School

Cottles Park, Atworth Wiltshire, SN12 8NT

• Pupils: 165, 75 board • Ages: 11 –18 • Non-denom
• Fees: Boarding £25,965; Day £13,320–£14,385 pa • Independent

Tel: 01225 701741
Email: admissions@stonarschool.com
Website: www.stonarschool.com

Head: Since January 2013, the very switched-on, Mr Toby Nutt, previously deputy head, and appointed without outside advertising. A geneticist by training, but a pretty competent musician too, Mr Nutt spent some years in marketing 'before every day became the same' and he broke free to do his PGCE at Reading. A spell at Reading Blue Coats encompassed the roles of housemaster, head of biology and of sixth form, before an unmissable opportunity to create a British sixth form at Tanglin Trust School in Singapore was offered him. He and his young family returned to the UK in 2006 in time for the run-up to his eldest's CE, on appointment to his current post. Parents are glad of the continuity Mr Nutt will bring the school; all the girls we spoke to delighted. No-one the slightest bit concerned by a chap heading up a girls' school: 'role models are not gender-specific', said he, faintly narked. Let's hope Mr Nutt will stay in the saddle longer than his two predecessors.

Academic matters: Completely non-selective, and does well by its girls. Sound teaching, a staff to pupil ratio of 1:6 and rigorous tracking using all the gismos at the school's disposal (CAT, ALIS, YELLIS) have been put in place to squeeze every drop of potential out of them. 'We want the best academic development for every child – but not at the expense of everything else'; we should think so too.

School's results shine more brightly when looked at in relative rather than absolute terms: value-added scores compare well with competitors, and both GCSE and A level grades are anything up to 30 per cent better than the national average (47 per cent A*/A grades at GCSE in 2013 and 16 per cent at A level, down from 57 per cent in 2012). That said, clever girls also get results which stand up anywhere: 13 GCSEs at A*, as one recent brainbox achieved, ain't bad, alongside a number of offers from Russell Group universities and in 2012 a scholarship to Royal Holloway, but 'Not the school to choose if you want your daughter to go to Oxbridge,' opined one mother. That said, recent A level results stand up very well against all the Bath independents; star subjects currently maths and geography. Good single science results at GCSE, but more effort perhaps needed for weaker scientists, where not everyone manages a C even in core and additional syllabuses. Spanish far and away the most popular modern language at GCSE; a two year certificated classics course including basic Latin in years 8 and 9. Twenty-six subjects on offer at GCSE but a mere 15 at A level (18 on demand, says school); mention must be made, though, of the vocational options up for grabs in sixth form such as the British Horse Society Assistant Instructor qualification, Leith's Basic Certificate in Food and Wine and ECDL. Parents appreciate these alternatives and the clear indication given by the school when their daughters are not A level material.

SEN well catered for: about a third of girls have some kind of identified need, mainly dyslexia, but visual and hearing impairments as well as ASD also accommodated.

Games, options, the arts: A horsewoman's heaven. The celebrated cross-country courses and show-jumping arena border the drive and lift any rider's heart (this editor's included) and provide a permanent home for the Inter-Schools One Day Event, ISODE. The equestrian facilities (an indoor and outdoor floodlit school, stabling and grazing for 65 horses) and resources thrown at it deserve their reputation, further burnished by the arrival in 2011 of a new director of riding, Darrell Scaife, an international event rider of some repute in his first role of this sort. His aim is to produce horsewomen, rather than solely competition riders, and he starts with the building blocks to successful riding: position, anatomy and movement. He's also much interested in learning styles and in equipping his riders to bring on young horses; in fact he has persuaded the school to purchase, with help from sixth form fund-raisers, a youngster for his riders to develop. It may all sound rather high-flown, but Mr Scaife has come from Brixton where he is still involved with Ebony Horse Club, which gives inner-city troubled youngsters the chance to ride, and has arranged a highly successful exchange – an eye-opener for all concerned. 'No glamour and plenty of muck', he says and the busy girls, who do everything for their steeds, whether owned or loaned, bear this out. Clinics from visiting luminaries like Mary King, competitions and trips to national shows and events, plus an exchange with an equestrian boarding school in Virginia, give riders lots to aim for.

But the riding is prominent, not dominant. About a third of the girls ride, but those who don't are in no sense second class citizens – and they don't have to get up early to muck out. All usual sports on offer for them (hockey, netball etc but also full contact rugby coached by a Welsh rugby international, no less) and parents like the fact that small numbers mean players of modest ability get to represent the school. Tennis courts grace the front of the main house, and usual independent school provision of floodlit Astro, sports hall, fitness suite and squash courts, 'but the swimming pool is tired', said one parent. Recently upgraded, says school. D of E and lots of trips – to Cornwall for the artists, to Le Touquet as a combined offering for the modern languages and food tech departments, plus skiing and Challenge Romania, where girls build a home for a destitute family in the course of one formative week, preceded by raising the funds for the opportunity to go. Back at school,

S

there are allotments and chickens to be tended – and their produce to be enjoyed. Goats and pigs to follow.

Better known for its drama than its music, perhaps. Vibrant drama dept puts on (amongst other things) a Shakespeare play every year to great acclaim – and not just the easy ones either: Othello was a recent choice. Tons of silverware comes home from the Mid-Somerset Festival and is displayed in the front hall. Small class sizes mean all hopefuls get to star – in a performance space which is functional rather than flashy. About a third of girls take music lessons up to grade 8, but lots of scope too for the more technically inclined, with a well-equipped recording and music tech studio. Concerts at notable Wiltshire Music Centre in nearby Bradford-on-Avon as well as local venues and in school. No singing at assembly though when we visited, but a certain amount of bopping and lip-synch-ing in seats, as Aretha Franklin's Respect launched the (entirely secular) topic for the day.

Visual arts housed up stairs in a series of studios; we were lucky enough to see the end of year exhibition hung the height of an airy staircase. The huge dark-room, kilns and Macs ensure all types of artists are well provided for.

Background and atmosphere: Looks and feels like a slightly run down country house. The school moved to its present home in 1939: it was evacuated from Sandwich and never returned from the Grade 2 listed Cottles Park, a very pretty Strawberry Hill Gothic mansion sitting elegantly in acres of rural Wiltshire about eight miles from Bath. 'No muddy boots!' on every outside door – we'd never seen so any pairs of Hunters and Du Barrys gathered in one place. Gracious panelled hall and head's office soon give way to unfortunate, though doubtless durable, red lino corridors, along which purposeful girls scurry, sometimes in regulation navy jodhpurs and fleeces. Again, functional but not flashy: in fact parts of the school could do with a make-over, such as the science labs and much of the junior boarding, a view strongly endorsed by most of the parents we spoke to. Upper sixth boarding much more like it, with individual study/bedrooms and lots of communal space in purpose-built York House.

Less pretty additions hidden behind the main house, as are all the stabling and manèges, and all that green space and lack of traffic – barring a few landrovers and horseboxes – is beguiling. But it is very rural, with intermittent mobile signal – 'definitely not for metropolitan types,' say parents, which is perhaps why they chose it, and for the fact that girls can be girls without having to keep up appearances (we saw no make-up, jewellery, tattoos or short skirts) or grow up too fast. The girls like that too.

'At least they're not hanging about on street corners' said one mother. Super homely feel, particularly from house staff and nursing sister; tasty food also an important morale-booster with such limited opportunities for shopping. Enough male staff ensure it does not feel like a nunnery, including the male head, though some parents feel there could be more.

Pastoral care and discipline: Highly praised. Girls and parents love the sense of family and the house staff seem nothing short of cuddly. Communication between home and school on the boarding side is reported as good, issues raised are dealt with: 'We've found the school open and accommodating,' one mother confirmed, and girls have opportunities to ask for help with any aspect of their school life.

Discipline was hardly mentioned, but sins listed include lateness, untidiness and lack of co-operation. Drink and drugs in school will usually result in suspension, or the boot, depending on the severity of the incident, as will persistent smoking. School anxious to stress that such issues are extremely rare: 'but we've got the policies'. Sanctions start with a green slip progressing to detentions, 'internal exclusion' before sending hard-core miscreants off site on a temporary or permanent

basis (not many of those). What did impress, though, was the self-discipline of riders, who need to be up at seven and to fit all the care and exercise of their mounts in and around the school day.

Pupils and parents: Day girls come from about a 35 mile radius, but boarders from much further eg London and home counties; around a quarter from overseas, predominantly SE Asia. 'I was so shy when I came here', said one charming, bright Hong Kong Chinese, misty-eyed at the thought of leaving 10 days later, but destined for Imperial. Girls and parents refreshingly down-to-earth, and free from the hoof-mark of arrogance and pretention which sometimes brands the horse world. Seemingly more than content with their rural lot, and unencumbered by pressures from boys/mobiles/Facebook, none of which function reliably at Stonar. 'Sparky, energetic, quirky but not cliquey,' according to the head. Parents speak well of school events, such as firework night and the end-of-year ball, a splendid affair, judging by the billowing expanse of marquee we saw when we visited. Friendly integration between nationalities and year groups appears to be standard, but more between day girls and boarders would be welcome; particularly marked at sixth form, where day girls are allowed into the upper sixth boarding house only by invitation. 'But they can all use the sixth form centre', says school, with justification.

Entrance: Non-selective, but girls do sit an entrance exam in January, preceded by a taster day in November, for setting purposes once they arrive in year 7. Scholarships are offered for academic ability, drama, music, sport and riding.

For sixth form, admission depends on an interview and report from current school; same range of scholarships on offer, plus all-rounder. Figures from the school suggest quite a few comings-and-goings in most years.

Exit: Quite a few peel off after GCSE, in search of brighter lights, boys and wider A level choices in Bath or Chippenham; some parents reckon it's all a bit sheltered and quiet for sixth form, and not a realistic preparation for life beyond Stonar's Cotswold stone walls. Of those who stay, the majority head straight off to further education, in many – but not all (eg Sandhurst) – cases to university. Degree courses include medicine and veterinary science at institutions all over the country. Distinguished old girls include big names in riding such as Junior and Young Rider gold medallist Georgie Spence and twice Olympic short-lister Lucy Weigersma; actor Romola Garai and controversial author Gitta Sereny.

Money matters: Fees cheaper than many competitors, which is commendable, given the high staff:pupil ratio. Extras on the bill, as expected, but riding good value at about £300 a term. Scholarships to a maximum of 15 per cent of fees, even if more than one awarded; Forces and sibling discounts. Bursaries means tested to, in exceptional cases, 100 per cent.

Remarks: Stonar's reputation as being a place for the dim and horsy is undeserved and out of date. Not a hot-house, but the distinction between exhorting girls to do their best and exerting too much pressure is well made. Hunter wellies essential, ability to drive or at least negotiate an oncoming horse-box highly desirable.

S

Stonyhurst College

Linked school: St Mary's Hall

Stonyhurst, Clitheroe, Lancashire, BB7 9PZ

- Pupils: 470: 280 boys, 190 girls; 305 boarders • Ages: 13 –18
- RC but enquiries welcome from all Christian denominations
- Fees: Boarding £29,439; Day £16,392 pa • Independent

Tel: 01254 827073
Email: admissions@stonyhurst.ac.uk
Website: www.stonyhurst.ac.uk

Headmaster: Since 2006, Mr Andrew Johnson BA, (early forties) former deputy head of Birkdale School. Previously at Winchester College for 10 years, head of modern languages for final four years. Educated at the Skinners' School, Tunbridge Wells, read French and Spanish at Bristol University, followed by postgraduate diploma in Education Management from Portsmouth University. Catholic, clear sighted, energetic, confident yet approachable; married to Dawn, sixth form tutor, member of the marketing team and musician who teaches piano, with two sons approaching GCSEs – all at the college; quite a family affair. Interests are walking, cinema, music and drama – when time allows. Loves his job '90 per cent of the time' and sees his role to develop young people 'to be as good as they can be in the areas where they have talents' and 'to be comfortable in their own skins'.

Academic matters: Good value-added, especially at GCSE; in 2013, 48 per cent of all passes were A/A*. Sixty-eight per cent of A level passes were graded A*-B, 43 per cent A*/A. Maths consistently popular at A level, achieving good results. Introducing International Baccalaureate from 2013, 'fits approach to learning in a Jesuit school,' says the head, who believes success in IB lies in being 'organised, hard-working, academically able but not necessarily super bright'.

Broad curriculum including French, Spanish and German, together with Greek and Latin. Average class size 18, 10 in the sixth form. Compulsory RE to GCSE, non-examined theology/ethics in sixth form. Four classes set according to ability at entrance. In recent years influx of new teaching staff who 'provide a good balance'; much investment in sharing good practice, training and development. Head sees his appointment 'to focus on academics' – and he has.

Pupils are assigned a personal tutor whom they meet weekly to discuss all-round progress. Stays with them through their school career, just one aspect of the Jesuit ethos of individual care. Broad ability intake and thus not the academic powerhouse of city day schools. Genuine desire for each pupil to fulfill their potential – many pupils exceed this and very able pupils do particularly well.

Twenty per cent of pupils have EAL support provided in discrete lessons and within mainstream lessons. Special needs (mainly dyslexic and dyspraxic) similarly provided under supervision of specialist SEN teacher. Learning mentor helps with organisation and study skills.

Plenty of computers around linked up to the school's intranet and all pupils have their own email address. Pupils timetabled IT to year 9, then GCSE option. Laptop internet connections in sixth form study bedrooms; PCs at study work places for younger pupils.

Games, options, the arts: A 'sport for all' policy encompasses both pupils and wealth of activities on offer. Compulsory sport throughout the school, achieving notable success in rugby, golf, hockey and netball. Super indoor swimming pool and all-weather pitch.

Music is highly valued; extensive music department in the basement complete with high tech soundproof pods for practice and lessons. The proud owner of three grand pianos, a Steinway, a Bosendorfer and a Bechstein. College's orchestras, ensembles and choirs thrive – pupils win places with regional orchestras too. Opportunities near and far – most recently the Big Band Belgian Tour.

Good DT department with plenty of scope for those artistically inclined. Strong drama – recent big musical productions emulate West End success in Les Mis, Sweeney Todd and the Sound of Music. Excellent performance space provided by newly upgraded Academy Room. With 'horizontal boarding' pupils divided vertically into four 'lines' for competitions, aka inter-line. More recent emphasis with appointment of a master in charge – now compete across sporting disciplines, and interestingly, share dealing.

Body of prefects called Committee, selected through interview process and votes from staff and lower sixth. Duties include affiliation to a particular playroom. Girl and boy head of Committee chosen from the group of 13.

Outdoor pursuits in abundance – fishing, canoeing, sailing, fell walking and clay pigeon shooting. Hugely proud of VCs awarded to seven OS, not surprising CCF (compulsory in year 10) thriving. Further afield pupils participate in world challenge trips, pilgrimages to Lourdes, D of E expeditions, to name but a few.

Service to the community and charity – writ large. Arrupe Programme – sixth form pupils give a period of voluntary service each week in the local community, sixth form holiday week for disabled children and a mentor scheme and swap visits with Catholic primary in Liverpool plus support for partner school in Zimbabwe.

Background and atmosphere: Founded by the Jesuits at St Omer, in what is now northern France, for English families forced to pursue a Catholic education abroad. After a succession of moves the school was given refuge at its present site in the Catholic part of Lancashire by Thomas Weld, who later donated the property to the school. The buildings are magnificent, though perhaps don't quite live up to the idyllic photography in the glossy marketing materials. No doubting the majesty of the architecture, and with its own observatory and nine hole golf course, set in a 2,500-acre estate, most of which is farmed. 'I arrive each morning and cannot believe that this is my school,' comments one pupil.

Much of the school is truly splendid; huge staircases, wood panelling, polished stone, works of art, brimming with history and tradition. Some formerly hidden treasures and the Waterton Collection are now exhibited in the Long Gallery for all to enjoy. The Collections Group, under the auspices of the curator, is allowed access to the treasures in the Square Library.

Recent developments include a sympathetically refurbished and equipped library and study centre in the heart of the school – a wonderful environment for independent study, a view shared by the pupils by the number we saw there. New sixth form boarding house with en-suite facilities, raising the standard of accommodation up a notch. Future plans include a new refectory and further refurbishment of boys' boarding accommodation.

Be prepared to learn a whole new vocabulary to enter the world of a Jesuit school. For starters 'lines' are school houses, 'playrooms' are year groups, 'playroom masters' are housemasters and as for the school year groups – Lower Grammar, Grammar, Syntax, Poetry and Rhetoric.

Boarding accommodation mostly situated in the upper reaches of the historic buildings. Boys board in playrooms but there is separate accommodation for the girls, in two linked houses, one for sixth form. Each playroom has its own common room and boarding facilities, cared for by a married couple; girls are looked after by a housemistress. On entry it's four or five to a room but this reduces, so by the sixth form single study/bedrooms are the norm. Well-presented, spacious with adequate storage, the standard of facilities is only surpassed by the care each pupil receives, rated outstanding in all respects by a recent Ofsted inspection.

This is essentially a full-time boarding school, 'no mass exodus at weekends', but exeats are readily approved, according to pupils. Long and busy school day, Sunday afternoon appreciated by some as their only free time to do as they please. Much of the weekend is consumed by prep, sports, excursions and church though activities available on a Sunday afternoon should the pupil choose. Religion is taken seriously but is not oppressive. Co-ed for more than 10 years, feels as if it has always been so. Girls 'have improved communication at all levels'.

Though 2009 was an annus horribilis, when Stonyhurst hit the tabloids twice, parents we spoke to showed overwhelming support for the way the issues were dealt with. 'Open and honest communication, the school showed compassion while taking a firm line': one parent's word encapsulated the opinion of others.

Pastoral care and discipline: Spirituality is at the heart of the school, promoting a 'caring, supportive and prayerful community', providing a safe environment that allows 'pupils to feel safe in doing their own thing without fear of ridicule'. Tolerance and respect of each other's differences, collaboration when working together. Demonstrated by the non-sporty keen photographer, whose talents were spotted, and is now the official chronicler for the first XV rugby team, accompanying them on tours and at matches.

Pupils 'are given quite a lot of freedom based on the mutual confidence and trust that exists between pupils and staff' according to one parent. A Family Handbook sets out clear expectations of conduct and behaviour; rules are few, clear and enforced; 'we expect them to get it right,' says the head. A review of sanctions has introduced a more incremental scale of chastisement. Rewards success celebrated through playroom and headmaster award ceremonies. A 'line' card accumulates debits and credits for academic and social performance which then contribute to the relevant 'line' grand total.

Cases of bullying are rare, dealt with by playroom staff and the pupil-run playroom committees. A few suspensions in the past for soft drug offences, but not a drugs school and no regular random testing. Alcohol restricted to one drink on a Saturday evening under supervision for year 12. Saturday evening access allowed to village pub for year 13 until 10.15pm. Suspension for those bringing alcohol on the premises. Discipline not a big issue here.

Pupils and parents: Diverse – more socially mixed than equivalent schools, with 65 per cent Catholic faith. Southern parents like school's lack of consumerism and social competitiveness. Rich mix of accents – regional and international, 25 per cent pupils are non-Brits, with small numbers from 28 nations, predominantly Spanish and Mexican, but with a league of nations from Nigeria to Korea. International links are highly valued and there has 'never been a problem with racism'.

Confident, articulate and mature pupils praise the community feel of the school and are rightfully proud of its heritage. Day pupils are encouraged to stay after school for studies and activities – a facility valued by parents – and may feel left out if they choose not to do so.

Alumni include 12 martyrs, seven VCs, also Arthur Conan Doyle, Charles Laughton, General Walters, Paul Johnson, Peter Moorhouse, Bishop Hollis, Bishop Hines, Charles Sturridge, Hugh Woolridge, Jonathon Plowright, Bill Cash MP, Bruce Kent, Mark Thompson, Lords Chitnis and Talbot, Kyran Bracken and Robert Brinkley.

Entrance: Day pupils from local Lancashire schools, day and boarding from own prep (St Mary's Hall), boarding from St John's

Beaumont and a variety of other schools, both here and abroad. Particularly strong links with Spain. Broad ability intake – 'for some, six GCSEs will be an achievement'. Academic entrance exam but other factors taken into account, particularly family connections with the school. Five GCSE passes at C and above, plus interview, for entry into sixth form though many AS subject choices require a minimum grade B. Those unable to attend for interview eg overseas pupils, write a 500 word essay explaining why they wish to come to Stonyhurst.

Exit: Wide range of English universities, Russell Group and redbrick, London popular, and Edinburgh. Numbers vary to Oxbridge, but average 5-10 per cent over recent years (five places in 2013 – and one to Harvard). Breadth of degree courses from medical to media arts, engineering to economics with 'ologies' as well. Plenty of international links and scope for travel through the Jesuit community with many students taking a gap year.

Money matters: A variety of scholarships awarded at 13+ and sixth form; academic, music and art and design, as well as all-rounder awards, ranging from 10 per cent to a maximum of 50 per cent of fees. St Francis Xavier awards of 20 per cent of fees are also available to those who 'are most likely to benefit from and contribute to life as full boarders in a Catholic boarding school'. All can be topped up with a means-tested bursary.

Remarks: Jesuit values permeate every aspect of this distinguished boarding school, steeped in history and set in beautiful surroundings. A genuine concern for the individual ensures that each pupil is given every opportunity to fulfill the school motto 'Quant Je Pius' – all that I can.

Stover School

Linked school: Stover Preparatory School

Stover, Newton Abbot, Devon, TQ12 6QG

• Pupils: 475 girls–180 boys • Ages: 3–18 • Christian • Fees: Day £7,800–£11,640; Boarding £17,670– £23,820 pa • Independent

Tel: 01626 354505
Email: registrar@stover.co.uk
Website: www.stover.co.uk

Principal: Since 2005, Mrs Sue Bradley BSc CBiol MI Biol PGCE (early fifties). No stranger to Stover, Mrs Bradley and her husband, a senior lecturer in micro-biology at Plymouth University, arrived from teaching in London in 1986. Quickly worked her way through the ranks via head of science, director of studies and deputy head. A restructuring of the hierarchy saw her emerge as principal. Approachable and reassuring, she enjoys good relationships with staff and pupils, and clearly loves the set-up. Realistic about the school's position in the market-place. Conversation enlivened with bursts of common sense. Thoughtful and compassionate. 'If the boys and girls are happy, they'll thrive.' A safe pair of hands with a clear eye on future developments.

Academic matters: At GCSE in 2013, 32 per cent A*/A grades, a strike rate that compares very favourably with local schools with bigger names. A level results are good, 82 per cent A*-C, (33 percent A*-A) in 2013. Bright pupils achieve very good results and the less bright also achieve their potential; given the non-selective intake this is impressive. 'Children enjoy their lessons and like their teachers,' said a mother. 'Nobody is made to feel a failure.' 'We are guided by a programme of assessment for learning rather than of learning,' says the principal. 'It's important that pupils are at ease with themselves and realistic about their abilities.' As far as is possible the school builds timetables around the pupil's choice of subject. Daily help is available for children with special needs.

Games, options, the arts: Good facilities in the beautiful and extensive grounds with six all-weather floodlit tennis courts, football, rugby, netball, tennis, hockey and cricket pitches. Good record at county level. 'Everyone finds a sport they can enjoy,' says a happy girl. Cross-curricular activities are important to the school. 'We are looking to educate the whole person.' Astronomy and public speaking, home economics, and riding. Busy music centre with about 200 learning musical instruments. Wide variety of concerts; choral, orchestral, jazz, ensemble, given all over the county. Duke of Edinburgh and Ten Tors Competition on Dartmoor. Lots of good art, photography and media studies in the attractively designed Millennium Building, opened by HRH The Princess Royal. Charismatic art master, also head of sixth form, believes strongly that the beautiful surroundings encourage creativity.

Background and atmosphere: Lovely entrance through Arcadian fields brings you to a great fist of a house built of granite ashlar, with an incongruously huge portico with double flight of balustraded stairs. Inside, beautiful plasterwork and elegant fireplaces. The school looks after the building well and pupils commented on how proud they felt to live in such surroundings. The refurbished boarding accommodation retains interesting features which contribute to the homely feel. Intimate rather than dominating. Boarding is much appreciated, and boarders often opt to stay on over weekends. Indeed, we met one girl in the sixth form delighted by the prospect of staying on for another year.

Founded in the grounds of Stover Estate by two sisters in 1932, the object was to help pupils lead independent lives. Boys and girls have been in the prep school since it started in 1996. From 2005 they have continued into the senior school. The sixth form building is a homely study centre where pupils talk of knowing the staff well and discourse openly and naturally about the pleasure of being at Stover. 'I know it sounds a bit cheesy,' said one elegantly attired girl, (uniform in the sixth form is 'smart for work') but it's the feeling of living in a community which makes it all such fun.' A number of pupils like it so much that they can't leave; instead they come back for a gap year to help out with the younger pupils. It's a school for friendships.

Pastoral care and discipline: Courtesy and common sense seem to be the watch words, and with the genuinely good relations that exist between staff and pupils, and boys and girls, there aren't many discipline problems. 'Surely, you must get up to some mischief?' we asked. 'We have a lot of fun,' replied a girl enigmatically. House parents, school nurse, tutors are all involved in keeping an eye on the pupils and overseas pupils are made to feel at home with, for example, Stover's special Chinese mid-autumn festival and the American fourth of July celebrations. The school appears open and honest.

Pupils and parents: Day pupils from Newton Abbot, Exeter, Woodbury, South Hams, Torbay, Bovey Tracey, Plymouth. Boarders from as far as Aberdeen, or overseas. Parents are mostly in professional occupations.

Entrance: By examination in English, mathematics and non-verbal reasoning, together with school report and interviews.

Exit: Some 75 per cent stay on for sixth form, the others move on to non fee-paying alternatives. Popular university choices are Bath, Sheffield, Warwick, Cardiff, Exeter, York. All sixth formers who stay go on to university.

Money matters: Academic, music, art and sport scholarships available at most ages up to 25 per cent of day fees, a small number of bursaries for existing pupils. Stover has introduced two means-tested scholarships at year 10 and sixth form entry, the Maurice Key and Laurus Scholarships offering up to 100 per cent of day fees.

Remarks: An attractive, well-run school embarking on new challenges with justifiable confidence.

Stowe School

Stowe, Buckingham, MK18 5EH

- Pupils: 770; 500 boys, 270 girls • Ages: 13–18 • C of E
- Fees: Boarding £30,975; Day £22,500 pa • Independent

Tel: 01280 818323
Email: admissions@stowe.co.uk
Website: www.stowe.co.uk

Headmaster: Since 2003, Dr Anthony Wallersteiner MA PhD (late forties), Cambridge history scholar and art historian, married to Valerie, three children. Previous two posts were at the academic powerhouses of St Paul's and Tonbridge, but in Stowe he has discovered his nirvana. Charming, impressive, a maverick with a keen sense of fun; on arrival we said, 'Think sired by Stephen Fry out of Nelson's Column with a trace of HRH the P of W and Boris Johnson somewhere under the blanket. He is frank, relaxed, confident, charming and unstoppably chatty.' Plus ça change plus c'est la même chose. 'He is inspirational, lacks ego, delegates,' say staff; pupils add, 'Dr Wallersteiner is friendly, funny and fun; he gets involved, chats to us, knows our results and how we are doing but doesn't pigeon-hole.' Parents equally enamoured: 'Simply magnificent. Not an intellectual snob: he just gets the best out of all in the most charming way.'

Dr Wallersteiner's appointment was no accident. Stowe was in the doldrums, needed lifeblood and direction but, with a dictum of academic excellence, nervous onlookers twitched; would this erudite polymath try to morph Stowe into another A* and Oxbridge hothouse with selection limited to the bright and bookish? Or, would his vision be the panacea? 'I wanted to return Stowe to the glory days, to its founding principles, but with a 21st century twist. We used to stand shoulder to shoulder with the great public schools: Eton, Rugby, Harrow; Stowe was renowned for being idiosyncratic, for looking after the individual, encouraging them to pursue interests with enthusiasm, allowing characters to emerge – Leonard Cheshire, David Niven – Stoics with an innate sense of confidence. Branson in the 60s probably typifies what it is to be a Stoic and that's what I wanted to inject into the place. Old Stoics have set the world alight; I want that to continue'.

A perfect fit for the school, precisely because he didn't always fit at school: a boy whose prep school reports tell only of a time waster, a lazy boy who would never amount to anything. Yet his final school report dazzled; a cerebral scholar heading for Cambridge. Inspirational teachers unlocked both talent and a desire to learn; masters lit the flame, he uncovered a universe. 'You can't underestimate the power of a teacher in transforming lives. I want the pupils to find their passion and drive, to be inspired and to inspire, to love learning, to appreciate the beauty of life, to be creative, to find their Utopia. You have to be so careful with children: they remember the time they were told they were thick or stupid, it sticks. If you say they will never amount to anything that one line can define their experiences, motivation and determination. A teacher should stand up,

S

perform and remember that the hundredth time for them is still the first time for a child.'

Academic matters: Buildings have had almost as many facelifts as Anne Robinson, so few blots remain. We were in awe of the library with its magnificent ceiling (part of an £8.8m restoration) but less enamoured by the 1960s science block and so keen to view from the inside. In one lesson children were eagerly examining the effects of emulsifiers on oil and water and in another teams were collectively working out how to construct model DNA. Dr Wallersteiner has moved academic rigour centre stage: 'I didn't want people to apologise for coming to Stowe'. Pupils are motivated to achieve, some aiming for traditional paths, medicine, economics, others for courses we had never heard of – lots keen on the environment with study to match. Head passionately believes if one path is blocked others should be tried, so good teaching and openness to new ideas, delivered in a supportive environment, are the priority. 'I watch some staff teach and feel so humble: many are masters of their craft, they are inspiring and motivating.' He pleads the fifth amendment when we quiz him about weaker departments and staff, but concedes not all are centres of excellence, though says the pockets are getting bigger. Drive to improve teaching and learning has included time spent looking at how all individuals learn, not just those with a recognised need. Teaching has new blood, greater monitoring and evening clinics for everything; if you don't get it first time round, there is always a second chance: 'A child's brain has to be unblocked with sympathy and care'. We met dyslexics who enthused about help not just from support staff but across the board. Value added is excellent and confidence high; results fine given the comprehensive intake. A level results on the up (38 per cent A*/A in 2013), and approx 46 per cent A*/A at GCSE in 2013. Latin and Greek remain, chemistry and religious studies popular options, DT – the Cinderella when it comes to provision – as favoured and successful as ever. Head wants the school to embrace the estate and hopes to offer farm-orientated courses in the future.

Games, options, the arts: Heart and soul spring to mind – whether trout fishing or trotting, beagling or bugling, singing or shooting, running or reading. All do CCF or D of E with push towards community work. Sport strong, with national representation in rowing, cricket, rugby, lacrosse, golf, fencing and equestrian events. Teams draped in accolades too – top the National Schools' League Table for cricket, first division lacrosse champions, with similar levels of success for polo, hockey and rugby. Superb facilities: playing fields, assault course, a new golf course, courts, sports hall, climbing wall, fencing salle, fives courts, and pool. Latest offerings include a scrambling track (shiny motor bikes) and brand new equestrian centre with 20 stables. Bring your own horse or ride one of the rescue ones. Key winter sports of rugby, hockey and lacrosse cede to summer offerings of leather on willow, athletics and tennis, with polo, rowing, sailing, clay pigeon shooting and golf just some of the country-club offerings.

Strong art and arts – several to art school – annual arts festival encompasses science, sport, dance, music, art, drama. Music popular, plentiful, oft polished with weekly, summer al-fresco performances the perfect backdrop for picnicking parents. School boasts its own radio station with resident DJs plus weekend nightclub (kitted out from the remnants of Crazy Larry's in London) hosting high-octane party nights, ranging from themed skiing to bungee runs and magic.

Background and atmosphere: Breathtaking, such stuff as dreams are made on; so resplendent that romance, not tragedy, be inspired; imagine Isolde sailing into the sunset with Tristan, Anthony falling not on his sword but into the arms of Cleopatra, Romeo living happily ever after with Juliet. Youngsters adore the place: 'Once you get here you never want to leave; when it snows, it looks more magical than Narnia.' The 750 acres of parkland and sublime landscape gardens are widely regarded as most significant in Europe and the embodiment of 18th century enlightenment. They include exquisite woods and waters, temples and gardens. The school campus is surprisingly compact with boarding houses, courts and other facilities nestled cosily in sylvan wilderness. The main building – 'the mansion' – is a splendid, neo-classical palace, largely modelled by Robert Adam in the mid-18th century and benefiting from the respective geniuses of Sir Johns Vanbrugh and Soane, William Kent and Capability Brown among others, and became a school only in 1923. In 1989 house and gardens passed to the National Trust and opened to visitors – much restored, Plug Street, named after the village of Ploegsteert south of Ypres, at the southern end of a famous series of long tunnels, is home to the school's nerve centre. This stone-flagged, below-stairs administrative centre includes the head's breathtaking study – 'Sir John Soane in gothic fantasy mode' – a mini replica of Henry VII's chapel in Westminster Abbey with fabulous fan vaulting, lead canopies, brass screens and tracery. Grandeur yes, but if London and the bustle of the city set your child's heart racing or, when visiting, they see fields not dreams, Stowe may be a county too far. 'It is a tight-knit place, but can be too claustrophobic for some,' say pupils.

Pastoral care and discipline: Care is delivered in abundance with everyone from cleaners and caretakers, housemistresses and academic staff on hand to help, plus close liaison with parents, as befits a proper full boarding school. Twelve boarding houses in total, all comfortable with kitchens and communal rooms. Boys envious of newish, purpose-built accommodation for the girls (en-suite rooms) which boasts in-house gym, pool room etc. All eat together in super dining hall overlooked by three Knellers. 'Food is simple but tasty with plenty of variety,' say pupils. Head sees every child on their birthday. 'It's a good opportunity to chat to them, find out what works, what doesn't.' We quizzed the pupils on vices and sins: drink and drugs? 'Compulsory and random testing. Second chances may be possible but never a given'. Bar for sixth form but random breathalyser catches those who transgress. Eating disorders? 'Careful monitoring and being there for friends,' with a comforting 'putting friend before confidentiality and informing staff', if things look serious. Cyber bullying? 'Fairly recent exclusions, discussed openly and frankly in both assemblies and pastoral time so all informed and understood.' Not that there are many transgressions these days, but the press hounds round at the merest whiff of a wrongdoing. Google the craft knife incident if you must but remember virtually all schools have skeletons somewhere; Stowe's are in the open not the closet.

Pupils and parents: Eclectic accepting place where cultures and languages mix. Attracts the solid and the decent plus odd balls and those who might be overlooked elsewhere. Blend of high flyers and spiky IQs: 'We like those', confided the head. Pupils, formal in approach, are polite, grounded and know how to behave and interact. 'They are confident and entertaining, the sort of person you want to sit next to at a dinner party,' say staff. Parents a mix of entrepreneurs, academics, old money (lots), new money (handful), country, creative and celebrity. 'Stowe may look posh but most of us aren't,' say pupils; parents add, 'A few are from wealthy backgrounds but equally some live in modest semis with parents who struggle to find the fees'.

Entrance: Handful from state schools, rest from a range of preps, including Winchester House, The Dragon, Summer Fields, Ashdown House, Papplewick, Sunningdale and Windlesham. School is no longer the 'back-up plan' but a conscious first choice. Looking for 50 per cent plus at CE and happy to take a chrysalis and nurture until a butterfly emerges. 'When I interview prospective pupils it is not high grades that are

S

important, though they are welcome, but there must be a spark, something we can ignite. I look for success – however small. Plane spotters, stamp collectors, ferreters, budding astronauts, entrepreneurs, the imagined destination less important than the drive and journey.'

Exit: Majority to a broad spread of universities, usually a couple to Oxbridge (four per cent in 2013). Business-related courses popular. A considerable number to good art schools, with some going to highly-acclaimed music or drama schools.

Money matters: Range of means-tested scholarships (more about honour than finance). Means-tested bursaries available, a small number of fully-funded places for exceptional candidates with proven financial need. Additionally, Roxburgh schols (named after Stowe's revered founding headmaster) awarded to outstanding all-rounders nominated by the heads of their previous schools. Stephan schols available for bright day pupils from the state sector – worth up to 25 per cent of fees, with further support from bursaries as with other scholarships.

Remarks: 'My son loves it, there is so much to do, he is flourishing, has great friends – boys and girls – like a huge extended family.' Captivating from first glimpse to last breath, something for everyone. Mixes the erudite with the sporty and studious, with space reserved for the eclectic and maverick. Ideal for those keen to learn within, and beyond, the bounds of the classroom; but if your sights are firmly set on bright lights, league tables and brags about academia, Stowe is ready for you but you're probably not yet ready for Stowe.

Stratford Girls' Grammar School

Shottery Manor, Shottery, Stratford-upon-Avon, Warwickshire, CV37 9HA

• Pupils: 595 girls (all day) • Ages: 11–18 • Non-denom • State

Tel: 01789 293759
Email: info@sggs.org.uk
Website: www.sggs.org.uk

Headteacher: Since 2005, Ms Kate Barnett BA MA (fifties). Educated at Pate's Grammar School in Cheltenham. The first of her family to go to university, she read English language and literature at Birmingham, where she achieved a first. Stayed on to do an MA in old Icelandic, followed by a PGCE. First teaching post was at boys' independent King Edward's School, Birmingham, then moved to King Edward VI Camp Hill School for Girls, where she progressed from head of English to assistant head. Spent four years as deputy head at Edgbaston High School for Girls before being appointed to current post. Taught up until three years ago, but still keeps her hand in by taking cover lessons for the English department.

Dedicated, energetic and a passionate advocate of girls' schools (she's spent her entire career in single sex schools). 'It frees girls up to be whatever they want to be,' she says. 'Girls learn differently to boys. They can be themselves here and do the subjects they want to do without fearing ridicule or being put down by boys.' Very efficient and knows her school like the back of her hand. When we emailed a list of questions on the morning of our visit she powered through them in the blink of an eye. Describes her pupils as all-rounders who have boundless energy and are 'willing to have a go at things.' 'The head lives and breathes the school,' a parent told us. During the week we visited she'd shaken the hand of every incoming year 7 pupil at their induction day and shaken the hand of every leaver at the year 13 garden party.

Husband worked in publishing and academia and they have two grown-up children, a son who works in the theatre and a daughter at university. Enjoys walking, sailing and, not surprisingly, with the RSC just down the road, the theatre.

Academic matters: Everyone is 'pretty bright' here, says the head – and exam results bear her out. School was ranked the 45th state secondary in the country for A level results in 2013. Fifty-three per cent A*/A grades at A level. Not only that, 80 per cent of pupils took the EPQ and more than half achieved A*/A. Twenty-five subjects on offer at A level – all the usual, plus classical civilisation, DT, ethics, food technology, photography, PE, psychology and theatre studies. Maths, then sciences the most popular subject choices at A level.

GCSE performance good too, with 78 per cent A*/A grades in 2013. All pupils take three sciences at GCSE (slightly old-fashioned science labs, but they definitely do the job). Unlike some schools, languages are flourishing. Everyone does a language at GCSE and more than half take a second language too. French and Latin from year 7, and German or Spanish on offer from year 8. Thanks to 'charismatic' German teacher, German is bucking the national trend and growing in popularity. Girls take their GCSEs in year 11 although performing arts, graphics communication and geology GCSEs can be taken earlier as after-school 'twilight courses.' 'We don't routinely accelerate,' says the head. 'I don't believe in jumping through hoops just for the sake of it. We want the girls to enjoy their learning.'

School doesn't go in for setting, apart from maths and French from year 9 (usually a top group and two parallel second groups). Very few pupils on the SEN register – around one per cent, mostly physical or visual disability or autistic spectrum. Parents we spoke to were delighted with the school's results. 'It is very good academically and sets very high standards for the girls,' a mother told us. 'The teachers are very focused on them getting the grades they need.'

Games, options, the arts: Lots of keen sportswomen. School is strong on traditional sports – hockey, netball, athletics – but rowing and tennis are thriving too. A current pupil is in the British archery team while another is a champion clay pigeon shooter.

Flourishing music department housed in a new building called Stratford Academy of Music (SAM for short – school loves acronyms), with practice rooms, classrooms and a recording studio. Orchestras (main orchestra has strong links with Stratford's Orchestra of the Swan), string quartet, choirs and jazz band. More than a third of pupils take instrumental lessons in school – wide range of peripatetic teachers visit each week. Drama in performing arts studio (PAS for short), which boasts a wall of fame detailing previous sixth formers' successes. Annual musical and play and senior girls run drama productions for juniors. Art and DT both popular – the girls are 'really innovative,' said the head of DT, proceeding to tell us about a girl who'd designed a mini pinball machine made entirely of chocolate. Perfect for party bags – you play the game, then eat it afterwards.

Loads of other activities, including D of E, Young Enterprise, Engineering Education Scheme and community service. Trips galore – Costa Rica scientific research tour and creative writing expedition to Himalayas particularly caught our eye.

Background and atmosphere: School was founded in 1958 by a far-sighted lady mayor. Site is now a mix of old and new buildings but the heart of the school is Shottery Manor, a 15th century manor house steeped in Shakespearean history. The Bard is said to have proposed to Anne Hathaway in the manor's former chapel (now a sixth form study room) and the wooden balcony is thought to have inspired the balcony scene

S

in Romeo and Juliet. More recently an enterprising group of sixth formers, all clad in red, used the balcony to lead the whole school in a dance in support of the One Billion Rising campaign to end violence against women. We reckon Shakespeare would have been enthralled.

The manor is home to the sixth form centre and admin offices, and every morning two pupils take charge of signing visitors in and out. Building boasts lots of wood panelling, a priest hole and traditional sloping school desks (sadly about to be replaced by modern tables). There's apparently a ghost – 'but it's a friendly presence,' a member of staff assured us. Pretty sixth-form garden next to the manor (perfect for building a 'snow family' last winter, said a sixth former).

Some of the classrooms look a bit dated but lots of building work going on. New library a hive of activity – the girls read widely and librarian buys 2,000 new fiction titles every year. Everything from Hilary Mantel to Stephenie Meyer. Impressive IT suite, with computers that rise up from the centre of the desk at the flick of a switch. 'All we need is dry ice,' grinned the head of IT, confessing that the school pinched the idea from Coventry University. Girls take IT in years 7 to 9 and are whizzes at designing apps. A year 9 group recently won a national competition for their nifty Pitch Pals app (it helps musicians of all abilities tune their instruments).

Pastoral care and discipline: 'We don't bang the table about school rules, but expectations are very clear,' says the head firmly. Parents agree, although one told us that the school is 'a bit rule-ridden.' No alcohol problems in last five years and no drug problems in last eight (countywide protocol states that drug-taking would result in permanent exclusion). Head reckons that 'any school that says there is no bullying isn't telling the truth' and like most girls' schools occasional 'friendship issues' crop up. PSHE sessions and vertical tutor groups (each tutor has between three and five girls from each year in their tutor group and the groups meet once a day) are effective in sorting problems out. 'The tutor groups are like a family,' says the head. 'For the younger girls it's like having big sisters.' Sixth formers can train as peer mentors (they wear blue badges so girls know who they are).

Senior student leadership team of 14 (including head girl, two deputies and three house captains), plus 50 prefects and mentors. Girls write letters of application for posts, then head, senior staff and outgoing team interview them, staff throw in their views and candidates attend hustings assembly in spring term. House system – Cygnus, Orion and Ursa – with house assemblies, concerts, drama and sport.

Year 7 to 11 girls wear black blazers and skirts and pale blue blouses (far more chic than the purple macs and boaters of yesteryear). 'We have quite a few dress down days,' says the head, 'but having a uniform equals everything out. The girls don't have to fret about labels or what to wear each day.' Sixth formers wear business suits (any colour). Very jazzy new games kit in purple, navy and yellow – you can certainly spot a Stratford Girls' Grammar pupil at 50 paces.

Canteen is slightly retro, but girls say there's enough choice, with salad bar and hot food on offer. Sixth-formers can sign out at lunchtime and walk into town. Year 11s granted this privilege on Fridays.

Pupils and parents: Pupils come from a host of state primaries and prep schools, including The Croft, Warwick Prep and The Kingsley School in Leamington Spa. Around 20 per cent live in Stratford-upon-Avon but others travel in by bus from up to an hour and a quarter away – from as far afield as Birmingham and Solihull to the north, Banbury to the south, Evesham to the west and Kenilworth to the east. Around three per cent of girls in years 7 to 11 have EAL requirements.

Entrance: Very competitive indeed, with four or five applicants for every year 7 place. Prospective pupils must register by July the previous year and take 11+ entrance test in September (for a place the following year). Priority given to girls living within a 17-mile radius of Stratford-upon-Avon. School is expanding – four forms of 28 girls in year 7 from September 2013 (previously three forms of 28).

Pupils joining in 240-strong sixth form need at least four A grades, two Bs and two Cs at GCSE, including As in the subjects they are taking at AS and at least Bs in English and maths.

Exit: Around five a year leave after GCSEs, mainly to go to music or performing arts colleges or to do subjects not offered by the grammar. King Edward VI School (KES) in Stratford-upon-Avon admitting girls from September 2013 but at the time of our visit only one Stratford Grammar girl had confirmed a move to KES.

Virtually all year 13 leavers head to university – six to Oxbridge in 2013 and 84 per cent to Russell Group. A plethora of subjects, but medicine and law lead the pack.

Money matters: A handful of girls are eligible for free school meals. School runs a hardship fund so no one misses out on school trips because of financial problems. Parents apply to head 'in confidence.'

Remarks: A friendly, purposeful school that prides itself on educating 'the whole girl.' Unpretentious, sparky and high achieving, these girls will go far.

Strathallan School

Forgandenny, Perth, PH2 9EG

• Pupils: 550 pupils; 347 boarders; 203 day pupils; 87 in Riley (the junior house) • Ages: 9–18 • Non-denominational • Fees: Day £12 495–£19 044; Boarding £20,019–£28,065 pa • Independent

Tel: 01738 812546
Email: admissions@strathallan.co.uk
Website: www.strathallan.co.uk

Headmaster: Since 2000, Mr Bruce Thompson MA (forties), educated at Newcastle High, thence New College where he read literae humaniores (classics to the rest of us) and came to Strathallan via Cheltenham College, where he was head of classics, and Dollar Academy – he wanted to 'try the Scottish system'. 'Loves Scotland, and loves Strathallan,' as does his wife, Fabienne, (French, teaches at a local prep school, worked in travel and tourism, expert skier – coaches it and most likely to be found whizzing round the campus on her bike). The Thompsons have two young daughters (in the school, they were 'desperate to come') and were delighted to find young staff with similar aged children on their arrival. No change here. Head teaches classics and coaches rugby; the pupils enjoy finding him practising weights alongside them (and he takes the odd coaching session on Mondays and Thursdays). He has a reputation for calling into houses – unannounced as far as pupils are concerned – for the odd chat on their own ground and has lots of informal brain-storming sessions in the evenings. ('Great fun, got to kick 'em out'.) Though, alas, the increasing burden of headmastering (HMC Sports Committee, Scottish Rugby Council – busy boy!) 'gets harder and harder as one gets more involved in things' means that he has less time for the 'pupil stimulation' he so enjoys.

Academic matters: Not tremendously academic (school says 'strong academic record') – but you can reach the heights from here. School reports it has been top co-ed Scottish A level school

S

from 2009 onwards 2013 with 47 per cent A*/A grades and 100 per cent pass rate. Twenty-three A levels currently on offer, pleasing number of As and Bs in science based subjects, ditto maths, with a couple of glitches in further maths. School plays the system, both Scottish and A levels. Seventy-five per cent take A levels, the others opt for Highers (over two years). School tries to please parents but the choice between A level and Highers is always a contentious one.

Around three-quarters take single sciences now, rest do double award science at GCSE. No subject much stronger than others and exam grades are generally good across the board (48 per cent A*/A in 2013). DT continues to be excellent. Sophisticated computer design equipment, pupils work here in spare time. Intranet access all over. Four separate computer rooms and a £1 million ICT Centre (known as the Royal Bank – it is all steel and glass). We met 'a lesser member of the team' with one of his labradors in situ: 'if you've met one, you've met all three,' said our guide. Mixed age common room: discrimination 'even to raise the subject of age.'

School has always had a welcome reputation for supporting weaker brethren and has a small but effective learning support system which had a smashing HMI report with talk of 'systematic identification', 'sensitive support', 'informative advice' (yawn yawn). All pupils screened on entry with ed psychs brought in where necessary. One-to-one, small groups, plus after-school clinics in various disciplines which act as drop-in centres. Two full-time trained staff, plus three others, and a dedicated full-timer for 9-13-year-olds in Riley who has strong links with the senior school. Extra time for exams. Regular assessment orders for all – ie reports (these are becoming more commonplace). 'Rarely costs extra.' School can cope with mild Asperger's/autism and the dys-stream, physical infirmity not a problem, most classrooms on ground floor.

Games, options, the arts: Fantastic state-of-the-art art school over three floors with marvellous light and inspired work; very much in use, a rather cumbersome painting was screwed onto the window sill of the top floor blocking a fair amount of light from the north when we visited. Art/history combined field trips to Venice etc graphics, camera and screen printing. Good music (Copeman Hart manual organ) including keen traditional Scottish music group. Popular pipe band plus jazz and choirs and cathedral choir in St Ninians, Perth (choir gets paid by cathedral), plus concert in Perth Concert Hall which holds a thousand and has always been full (freebie) aka Headmaster's Music. Lots of drama and small theatre, a clever conversion of a former dining hall, the insides cleverly scooped out (theatre doubles as an examination hall).

Swimming pool revamped with the swimming team developing under new outside coach – has two national champions, a national record holder and one of the top teams in the country. Sport taken seriously, two synthetic pitches, rugby, football, cricket, hockey, netball, own golf course, skiing, CCF (boys and girls, voluntary), flying, sailing. Shooting, clay and small bore. Sports hall with climbing wall and old fashioned gym. School has 18 national champions and 12 national representatives. Former member of SRU also qualified in weights takes classes in either general fitness or elite sport. Some rather unhappy girls were about to go for a serious run in the rain during our visit. Masses of charity work: grannie bashing now more likely to involve teaching them computing than listening; help in charity shop. D of E.

Background and atmosphere: School founded in 1913 by Harry Riley, based in 19th century red sandstone country house with masses of sympathetic additions, set in 150 acres. Two fantastic double-deck libraries, one with the carpet reflecting the plaster work in the ceiling; adjacent media rooms – cosy and useful. Fairly utilitarian chapel (children quite rude about it) and refurbished dining room, million quid – ceiling dropped,

new floor – though not sure it is that good for dancing. Main classrooms 150 yards away beyond the old stable building which has been converted into a splendidly cosy junior house, Riley, boasting a most amazing atrium plus library and music practice rooms etc. Classroom blocks undergoing programme of refurbishment, latest improvements including three new state-of-the-art chemistry labs. Houses new and newish, boys and girls have own study bedrooms for their last four years, lots of kitchens and common room area on each floor. New girls' house now completed and as a consequence there has been an increase in girls. Much general to-ing and fro-ing, but co-ed works well here; girls' houses out of bounds to boys on Sunday mornings so that girls 'can laze around in their dressing gowns if they want.' School facilities much used by groups during holiday period. Over 70 staff live on site in school houses, lots of young and good family feel – 'nice place for a family – a complete way of life.' All the houses are quite close together – with the new girls' house being perhaps the furthest away, which gives a cosy air of friendliness. Not an overwhelming school. School council operates under aegis of head girl and boy.

Pastoral care and discipline: Houseparents live on site with two staff on duty in each house every night. Academic tutor attached to each pupil and tutorial team in every house. Tutors often using the time available for informal chats. Mr Thompson 'aware that things happen' and talks of rustication and drugs testing 'in case of suspicion'. Will suspend; automatically out for drugs and contact police. Head works hard on bullying awareness, lots of briefing – expectations, ownership, relationships, 'be reasonable'. 'Like running a huge great family,' with a 'good cross age group.' Boy/girl relationship 'works well'. Punishment system for misdemeanours of 'fatigues' – jobs around the buildings and grounds – 'no shortage of them'!

Pupils and parents: A quarter of the pupils from overseas, mostly ex-pats, plus 50-odd foreign pupils from Spain, Russia, Africa, China, Eastern Europe, Hong Kong, Germany et al. School is popular with Scots (regional accents of all kinds), well-placed, an hour from both Edinburgh and Glasgow, plus a small contingent from south of the border. (School claims it is 'two hours from London': three from Heathrow or Gatwick more like). Day pupils allocated to one of the houses; daily buses to and from Perth, Kinross, Auchterarder, Stirling, Crieff and Dundee. FPs Dominic Diamond (computer games whizzo), Colin Montgomerie (golfer), Sir Jack Shaw, (Bank of Scotland), John Gray (former chairman of the Hong Kong and Shanghai Bank). Not a toffs' school, despite brief showing in the fashion stakes when David Pighills took the school co-ed. 'very good relationship with parents,' says the head.

Entrance: At 9, 10, 11 or 12 for the junior house (entry day and aptitude report/tests) then automatic entry, otherwise by CE. Not a high hurdle but popular. Later entry by report and interview if space available. Excellent route map for parents unfamiliar with public school entry procedures – complete with CD which is currently jammed in this editor's lap top.

Exit: More than 95 per cent to an enormous range of universities (Glasgow, Aberdeen and Edinburgh are popular). Trickle to Oxbridge, ('where they often get firsts'). Forces popular.

Money matters: School financially strong. All the recent revamping and building has been done without appeal or fundraising – impressive. Junior scholarships, open scholarships and sixth form scholarship plus academic, all-rounder, sport, music, cathedral and art scholarships. Parents can also apply for means-tested help with fees – 'moving towards bursaries' for all.

Remarks: Outstanding head – tops in Scotland. The school is in fantastic heart and at ease in the local community.

Streatham and Clapham High School GDST

Linked school: Streatham & Clapham High Junior School

42 Abbotswood Road, London, SW16 1AW

• Pupils: 390, all girls • Non-denominational • Fees: £11,130–£14,325 pa • Independent

Tel: 020 8677 8400
Email: enquiry@shc.gdst.net
Website: www.schs.gdst.net

Head Master: Since 2012, Dr Millan Sachania MA (Cantab) MPhil PhD (early forties). Former comprehensive student who gained a double first and a doctorate in musicology at Cambridge and then stayed on as a music tutor for five years. After (shock, horror) reading an undergraduate's paper on Beethoven's 'Nineth' Symphony, he decided to train as a schoolteacher and acquired a PGCE at Kingston University. Was impressed with GDST experience at Croydon High while following the course and after stints as head of music at a girls' school in Windsor and deputy head at a co-ed HMC school in north London was delighted to accept this post. 'Are you married?' we asked. 'Yes, to my piano'.

Parents praise his 'phenomenal attention to detail'. One told us he was 'not an obvious choice, but perfect', while another reckoned 'we are lucky to have him'. Other parental comments include, 'definitely an individual', 'quirky', 'incomparable' and 'probably just what we needed but not everyone's cup of tea'. The girls seem to love him – 'even though he uses words we've never heard before'. Has a 'rescued' Bechstein grand piano in his study, which they are definitely allowed to tinker on.

Dr Sachania is amazed by the energy of both the school and the girls, which he feels derives from their cultural diversity. Impressed with their intelligence and really wants them to broaden their horizons and achieve beyond their potential 'across the width of endeavour'. Says he has an holistic approach and doesn't believe that pupils should obsess about being competitive with each other. He wants each girl to find her own forte and achieve her own personal best.

Has already made a few changes – some popular, some less so – and there are more to come. Lessons have been shortened. Head says that 'shorter equals sharper and if necessary lessons can become double'. The sixth form, which is in a separate building, now has its own popular café area while a small lecture theatre is used for a variety of activities, from musical recitals to the once-a-week head master's lecture period.

Academic matters: 'The school has really pulled its socks up' – that's the view of one parent we talked to. It offers a broad curriculum covering all the core subjects, and a wide variety of co-curricular activities to ensure pupils can learn and discover in depth. Economics A level and English IGCSE (to replace GCSE) recently introduced. In 2013, more than 89 per cent A*/B grades and 60 per cent A*/A at A level while more than 60 per cent grades at GCSE were A*/A. Setting in maths, sciences, modern languages and, occasionally, English. Class sizes are maximum of 26, many groups in the sixth form in single figures. Teacher/pupil ratio is approximately 1:12, slightly smaller in sixth form. All staff friendly and enthusiastic – average age 42. About a quarter have been at the school for more than 10 years, giving stability and a sense of continuity to a school that is growing and changing. Plenty of men on the team as well – four out of five of the senior leadership team are male. All pupils are expected to take four additional subjects alongside the core at GCSE; a selection of 12 on offer to which they can add ancient Greek and astronomy if they wish. Parents say science and humanities are now particularly strong. Head master sees each year 11 girl individually with her parents to discuss A level choices.

One of the first things the head master did was to introduce Kinza, a compulsory enrichment programme offering a range of over 30 topics which the girls study one afternoon each week in the Michaelmas and Lent terms. Staff run courses in subjects they don't teach (including forensic science, beekeeping and Arabic) and mixed age groups work together. He says the course is 'emblematic of my educational philosophy'. His aim is to create 'civilised human beings equipped with a philosophy for living'.

Bubbly and enthusiastic head of learning support in school three and a half days each week. School has inclusive policy, as long as girl passes entrance test. Statemented children have individual teaching assistants who produce strategies to help them deal with problems. Otherwise school provides help in small groups for 20 minutes once a fortnight from year 7 to year 9, and before school, after school or at lunchtime for years 10 and 11. One-to-one help has to be resourced externally.

Games, options, the arts: Surprising to find a girls' school in a leafy London suburb with its own sports grounds and an enormous, all singing, all dancing sports hall, plus a dance studio and fitness centre. Plenty of cups to indicate sporting success. Football, hockey, tennis, athletics and lots of indoor sports – something for everybody. National gymnastic champions in 2012 and notable successes in acrobatics, fencing competition, tennis and netball. The only criticisms from parents are that the school 'needs to offer more for C teams to improve their skills' and 'the sports department needs better organisation and more staff'. Needless to say, this is being addressed. One mother told us: 'The school is truly inclusive – my non-sporty child loves sport'.

Music strong (as you would expect with a musically talented head master), with lessons compulsory up to GCSE. Several choirs, orchestras and ensembles. Roomful of keyboards specifically for compositions. Parents say art facilities are 'brilliant' and we were impressed too. Large art room, smaller one specifically for the sixth form and separate pottery room with its own kiln. Drama also right up to standard. When we visited the whole school was involved in A Midsummer Night's Dream, with non-performers making costumes and painting scenery.

D of E taken pretty seriously – girls go trekking in Morocco's Atlas Mountains and have reached base camp of Everest. Most participants reach at least silver level.

Background and atmosphere: School was founded as Brixton Hill High School for Girls in 1887 and was one of the earliest GDST member schools. It later became Streatham Hill High School, housed in the building now occupied by the junior school. Current building was originally Battersea Grammar School. This merged with Rosa Bassett School to form a comprehensive in Tooting, allowing Streatham & Clapham High School to move to bigger premises in 1993. Large, light classrooms are a good legacy and the new buildings have created a spacious, well-equipped school, with facilities suitable for the 21st century. The four and a half acres of ground they stand in are miraculous in this busy area of London.

School dining hall has relaxed atmosphere and offers reasonable selection of different food, which girls said was always pretty good. Plenty of staff around to make sure everyone eating properly. School lunches are compulsory up until year 11. New sixth form café is popular and older girls like having their own area to meet and chat.

Pupils' general feeling is that this is a happy, focused school. Parents say the support given to pupils is second to none. Although the school says the expectations are definitely there for girls to achieve and do their best, parents are adamant

S

that it's 'not a hothouse'. Comments included 'there's no excessive pressure', 'they are allowed to be individuals and gain confidence', 'they mix across the year groups and get to know each other better that way'. One told us: 'At parents' evenings, they really do seem to know and understand our two very different daughters'. Another, with an exceptionally bright daughter, said that the way classes are divided, sometimes by ability, sometimes mixed, works a treat. 'My daughter is never bored', she said. 'The expectations of each girl are relevant to the goals she has been set'.

Pastoral care and discipline: Deputy Head Mistress is in overall charge of pastoral care and system is in force for identifying problems early. Parents say communication is exceptional – emails are answered immediately and problems dealt with sympathetically. A parent told us of 'some unpleasantness... handled and dealt with properly and quickly'. Another talked about 'problematic disorder' in a particular class, which was 'completely sorted out by the head of department within a week'.

House system ensures girls work together as teams, across year groups, competing to gain house points at all levels. Each form has a representative on the school council, alongside form captain, so ample chances to raise welfare problems. PSHCE programme deals with topics such as relationships, moral issues and citizenship in a sensitive and informed way.

Deputy Head Mistress says that school aims to deal with problems promptly. It acts positively in rare bullying-type incidents, normally resolving quickly and amicably. Sixth form mentor teams are invaluable – girls often prefer to talk to them rather than a member of staff. Year 9 form mentors help girls transferring from the junior school.

Pupils and parents: Mainly from the surrounding areas of south London and from variety of backgrounds – moneyed professional classes and entrepreneurs to local shopkeepers. Typical GDST range of ethnic and racial diversity.

Around 85 per cent arrive from the junior school and others join from state and private schools. Parents of girls in state primaries said they like the smaller size classes, which gives all girls a chance to be involved. Ex-pupils include June Whitfield, Angela Carter, broadcasters Maryam and Nazanine Moshiri, soprano Elizabeth Llewellyn and V&A curator Susannah Brown.

Entrance: Competitive – interview and exam at 11+ and 13+. Those coming up from the junior school at 11 have to pass a test in year 5 and also sit the 11+ exam. Prospective pupils are interviewed in groups at 11+ and individually at 13+. At 16+ minimum of six GCSEs required, with A*/A grades in subjects to be studied at AS level, letter from previous head and interview with SCHS head master and sixth form head. Early registration for all levels suggested as waiting list is limited. Occasional places crop up at other stages, subject to relevant testing.

Exit: Some leave at 16 for local comps, sixth form colleges or boarding but this is decreasing, with most opting to stay on. Majority progress to Russell Group universities.

Money matters: Typical GDST school fees, so more reasonable than elsewhere. Several non-means tested academic scholarships available and number of means tested, subject-based scholarships/bursaries at 11+ and 16+. All curriculum-related non-residential trips included in fees.

Remarks: Streatham & Clapham High is on the up. Take one new Head Master, add a good handful of enthusiasm, pep up the curriculum, add ambition and belief, introduce Kinza, tune a grand piano and – eureka – numbers rise. It would certainly appear that something is working. There is now a consistent waiting list for places and numbers staying on for A levels have rocketed from 36 per cent to over 60 per cent. As one parent told us, 'the new head master is having an amazing effect'.

Stroud High School

Beards Lane, Cainscross Road, Stroud, Gloucestershire, GL5 4HF

• Pupils: 900 all day girls • Ages: 11–18 • Non-denom • State

Tel: 01453 764441
Email: admin@stroudhigh.gloucs.sch.uk
Website: www.stroudhigh.gloucs.sch.uk

Interim headteacher: Since January 2014, Mark McShane, previously deputy head of Gloucester High School for Girls.

Academic matters: Selects bright girls at entry and does well by them. Results are excellent, despite staff's constant refrain, 'We're not an exam factory.' Pupils take 10 compulsory GCSEs from a range of some 30 subjects. Less mainstream subjects include astronomy and photography. The school has a long history of outstanding academic achievement; in 2013, all students achieved five A*-C grades at GCSE with 70 per cent at A*/A. Seventy-three per cent of A level grades were A*-B. Everyone takes a science subject and some 20 per cent of leavers go on to study a variety of science subjects. Modern foreign languages specialist status: good recent A level results for French, Spanish, Russian, more mixed at GCSE for German and Spanish. Staff go to great lengths to offer flexibility. 'The more unusual the subject combinations, the better I like it,' says one pupil. 'We don't do columns of subjects here.'

The school forms part of the Stroud District Partnership, a collection of nine local secondary schools and Stroud College that between them offer a wide range of subjects and diploma courses, though in practice just a handful of students seem to cross over. Specialist science and maths status, which has helped provide funding for an army of interactive whiteboards, and opened up new initiatives: a recent project involved building a plane from scratch. English, maths and psychology are currently the most popular subjects in sixth form, with very good results. Joint sixth form teaching with the boys has not affected girls' results, and the verdict seems largely positive. 'It has made things more chilled and sociable, in and outside school' says one sixth former. 'The boys bring a lot of fun to everything.' Another confides: 'At first, we all mill round the new sixth form block being social, then gradually – usually after the boys have a bit of a shock with their ASs – everyone gravitates upstairs to study.'

Very dedicated staff: about half are early 40s and under. 'Staff don't just go that extra mile, but two or three,' remarks a parent. Year 7 is taught in four tutor groups of around 32. Year 8 onwards divides into smaller groups of about 25, up to sixth form. You can hear a pin drop, walking round during lessons. 'My brothers teased me I was off to school with the nerds,' says one girl, 'but everyone just wants you to do your best – it doesn't matter what sets you're in.' 'No stigma' for the school's 20 or so pupils on the SEN register. SENCo works alongside all members of staff. Pupils can have one-to-one mentoring. Some who find coping with a whole school day difficult due to their medical conditions are on reduced timetables. Other SEN students say they feel so supported by their peers and teachers they cope without teaching assistants. A few use laptops in lessons and examinations.

Games, options, the arts: Lots of sports on offer, from netball, athletics, hockey, rounders, tennis to football and basketball. Large, well-equipped sports hall and newly renovated gym. Girls compete at national level in athletics (including one tipped for potential Olympic stardom); cross-country, rounders and swimming. Recent overhaul of the tennis courts seems to have paid off, with the school reaching national finals of the prestigious Aberdare Cup for past two years running. School represented at regional level in netball and hockey, plus county level. 'There are lots of fun sports as well as team sports,' says one girl. Recent attempts to boost numbers for fun sport clubs.

Around one-third of girls take a musical instrument, with singing lessons very popular. Regular school concerts open to all ability and a range of choirs, orchestras, ensembles and groups. Gospel choir performed recently with Mica Paris, the senior choir sings at Cheltenham Festival. Wide range of clubs available within school day: popular ones include badminton, street and contemporary dance. Notices are posted on in-house plasma screens dotted around school, in assemblies and the fortnightly newsletter. Art and drama good and very popular. Terrific – and well-used – photography room.

Success in national competitions – Investment Challenge, Young Consumer of the Year – and local ones: the High School Food Team won at an enterprise day at Calcot Manor. Lots of trips, plus visits, exchanges and work experience in France, Germany and Spain. Foreign trips seem to be expanding: recent destinations include New York, St Petersburg and China. (One girl quick to point out: 'Not everyone has the money to do things but there's enough going on that you don't feel you miss out'). Very strong ICT department, which permeates all levels: as a tool for staff to track pupils' progress, and giving girls excellent access to computers, plus a range of music technology and software and state-of-the-art multi media equipment. 'Nothing's ever locked up and we have no vandalism,' says a teacher.

Background and atmosphere: The school was started in 1904 by far-sighted local dignitaries to give girls an education similar to that enjoyed by boys at Marling School. In 1911 the school moved to its present site beside Marling, set just off the main road into town (mayhem at drop-off/pick-up). The school's first fourth generation pupil started recently, and the School Birthday and prize giving remains the celebratory highpoint of the school year, with cake for all. The original red-brick, creeper-clad main building can feel cramped inside, but is sunny, both in aspect and atmosphere. Some old pre-fabs remain, and the school remains divided from its former junior school site by a car-crammed residential street, but there has been a feverish programme of building and refurbishment over the past few years, and the school is justly proud of the smart new sixth form block.

'The school's come rocketing into the 21st century,' says one parent, and there is a real sense of a good school sharpening up still further. This shows in various ways, from a smart new uniform, introducing burgundy jackets –'not "blazers",' the girls explain – although pupils voted to keep their distinctive candy-striped shirts; to an overhaul of the way the school tracks and monitors pupils' and teachers' progress throughout school, to the building programme, and removal – both physical and psychological – of walls between the girls' and boys' schools.

Pastoral care and discipline: Lots of support systems in place. Girls struggling, for whatever reason, are mentored by designated staff, whom they can choose. Girls think buddying system and peer mentoring work well. Active whole school council, with all senior pupils eligible to be termly prefects. Separate sixth form council. 'We're encouraged to be independent in improving the school,' says one girl, eg some Year 11s set up their own informal homework club, The Space (known as 'the Biscuit Club'), which has become a focal point for other year groups too.

'I like to think we're nurturing the next generation of eccentrics,' says one teacher. 'The girls are very eco-minded, always checking my recycling bins,' says another. Stroud High girls are continually described as 'quirky', 'original', 'vocal' and 'feisty' by parents and staff alike, and so they are, although not dauntingly or overwhelmingly so. This is Stroud, after all, and the school reflects the town's liberal-minded, arty/artisan ethos – what one teacher calls 'the Stroud effect'.

Which is not to say discipline is airy-fairy. 'It's about recognising things can go wrong and positive behaviour management,' says Mrs Pride. School adopts a graded approach to discipline, starting with a warning, then room detention. The ratio of praise to sanctions is about 6.1. It's not about hanging people out to dry.'

Pupils and parents: Interesting, fun and fair-minded girls have a touching sense of their good fortune, and a strong sense of the world around them. They raise huge amounts for charity, and are 'always coming in with fund-raising ideas.' Some pupils travel from as far afield as Ross-on Wye, Malmesbury, and the fringes of Bristol, but majority are from Stroud and surrounding area. Energetic Parent-Staff Association and strong governing team.

Entrance: Approximately three applicants for every place. School has own exam, two verbal reasoning tests, usually in October. Pupils come in from over 50 partner schools which vary from year to year. Additional places at sixth form, with minimum requirement of five A*-B at GCSE.

Exit: The majority of students achieve their first choice university destination. Six to Oxbridge in 2013. Students are given careful careers advice, including opportunities for higher apprenticeships and management training schemes.

Remarks: Really warm, vibrant school that offers bright, sparky girls a combination of single-sex education and co-ed. Girls go it alone up to sixth form, then join forces with the neighbouring boys' grammar to form the Marling School and Stroud High School sixth form.

Summerhill School

Linked school: Summerhill School (Junior)

Westward Ho, Leiston, Suffolk, IP16 4HY

• Pupils: Around 95; roughly half girls, half boys; majority board but also a small number of day pupils • Ages: 5–18 • Fees: Day £4,116–£9,846; Boarding £9,444–£16,416 pa • Independent

Tel: 01728 830540
Email: office@summerhillschool.co.uk
Website: www.summerhillschool.co.uk

Principal: Since 1985, Zoe Readhead (a very youthful late-ish sixties) – proprietor, keeper of the ethos and daughter of school's founder AS Neill. Literally born, bred and educated at Summerhill. Has been a staunch guardian of school's core values when lesser mortals would have wavered. Inspiring, uncompromising, down to earth rather than airy-fairy (is a qualified riding instructor), does not mince words. Married to Tony, a farmer, with four grown-up children all educated at Summerhill. In many ways a traditional family business: son Henry presides over the music studio; son William is deputy head and expected to take over running the school whenever Zoe retires.

Academic matters: Of secondary importance here. Summerhill is a 'free' school run on the principle that children have the same rights as adults and should be able to choose their own educational goals unfettered by the interference of anxious parents. Lessons are optional – some children will not attend a single lesson for a number of years, if ever. As the parents' handbook emphasises, 'remember, at Summerhill your kid could theoretically NEVER go to a lesson – they have that right. Staff members are not going to persuade, cajole or bully your child about lessons.' Play is considered as valid a part of a child's development as formal teaching: 'Many kids just need to play until they are ready to learn.'

That said, most pupils end up taking at least a few GCSEs, some take five or more. Results all over the shop from A* to G. 'My daughter might have got better exam marks at a different school,' a parent told us, 'but she got the grades she needed for the next step she was planning to take which is what mattered!' Prime emphasis is put on reading and writing, much of it delivered via one-to-one teaching. We observed a physics lesson which consisted of one seated pupil soberly facing a whiteboard where the teacher was instructing – curiously alternative and traditional all at once. A great environment for independent learners – the school brings this out in many of its pupils – but less ideal for those who thrive on a collegiate buzz and constructive competition from like-minded pupils. Nine full-time, live-in teachers, plus peripatetics, offer normal range of subjects plus environmental management, specialist music lessons, sound recording, drama, catering, psychology, French, German, Chinese and Japanese – staff try to accommodate kids' interests. Pupils are entered for Cambridge International O levels for some subjects rather than GCSEs.

One senses kid gloves in Ofsted's almost comically gushing most recent report (how times have changed from 1999 when it recommended the school be shut down): 'An outstanding feature is the way in which learning is closely tailored to match individual pupil's needs, including those with special educational needs and/or disabilities. A fundamental aspect of the school's curriculum is that learning takes place out of lessons as well as in them.'

'Special needs' not recognised here. Pupils labelled ADHD elsewhere are taken off the Ritalin and dispatched to play in the woods until they feel ready to learn. 'We take a rather old fashioned attitude to things like ADHD,' says Zoe. 'You've got to get on with it. Everyone is treated an individual here and there's so much one-to-one teaching.' However, school does apply for pupils to be given extra time in exams if they're eligible.

Games, options, the arts: Sports not high on the agenda and, despite its rather windswept tennis court, Summerhill is not likely to produce the next Andy Murray. Various games played, including Summerhill's own 'tork'. Swimming for the bold in unheated outdoor pool and for the meek at the Leiston Leisure Centre. Dance is an option and performance of all kinds is valued here. Music important with some excellent teaching and good facilities for music technology and studio recording. Similarly, drama is big among these arty kids and the school has a small theatre. Woodwork taken seriously, operating on same footing as English or maths – except it is probably more popular. Other activities include metalwork, Japanese, Chinese, gardening, photography, calligraphy, film-making, crafts, riding, cooking in the café, camping in the grounds, making tree forts etc. But no one is coaxed into any of this: at Summerhill boredom is considered an important ingredient of education. Children become practical, hands on – can light a fire, cook, run a meeting.

Background and atmosphere: Founded in 1921 by AS Neill near Dresden, Germany; settled in Leiston in 1927, where it became one of the most famous and controversial schools in the world. The school has been threatened with closure on several occasions, most recently in 1999 after a damning Ofsted report that called the pupils 'foulmouthed' and accused the school of failing the children educationally. Summerhill contested the notice of closure in court and four days into the hearing – in the face of enormous protest from current and former parents and pupils – the government's case collapsed.

Rough and tumble 11-acre setting includes large Victorian house, many single-storey additions, staff accommodation (some in basic, hippy-style caravans – you've got to see it

to believe it), wooded grounds. Spectacular beech tree for climbing, rope-swings and general play – a 'Summerhill thing', the pupils told us. Felt less full than on our last visit but school says its numbers wax and wane over the course of the year. Long holidays – five weeks at Christmas, five weeks in the spring and nine weeks each summer, but no half-terms or bank holidays – works well for overseas pupils. Annual festival-style camp for parents and former teachers over a summer term weekend.

Pastoral care and discipline: Far from being a place where you can do anything you like, Summerhill has more rules than any school we have ever visited. However, there are few fixed rules (other than the laws of the land). Everything is voted on at 'the Meeting', held twice a week. All children, from age five upward, have an equal vote, as do the teachers. No special authority invested in adults, indeed quite the contrary as they are vastly outnumbered! The Meeting is chaired by pupils and will sometimes make outlandish decisions eg to banish bed-times (sooner or later a glassy-eyed pupil will suggest they be reinstated). Misdemeanours are 'brought up' at the Meeting and an appropriate 'fine' is decided upon. Meeting proceedings surprisingly formal, with older pupils chairing on a rotating basis after first attending training sessions – lots of juicy educational stuff going on here. Pupils not afraid to voice complaints about their peers; bullying usually dealt with calmly and swiftly. As a former pupil told us, 'what Summerhill does give you is an ability to communicate with people, and it teaches you to just be nice.'

The school makes much of its claim that it allows kids to be kids. To us, however, at times it felt that it allows kids to be adults. Summerhill's freedom and democracy can extend into unsettling areas. The Meeting decides how to filter internet access and DVD/ video restrictions. Sex is not officially sanctioned, but boys and girls allowed in each others' rooms and there is no effort made to discourage it. The school will assist pupils with contraception 'when it is thought necessary' and parents will not be informed unless the child requests it. Smoking allowed over age 14 but pupils must announce that they are smokers at the Meeting and sit through an anti-smoking information DVD. Smoking rather more prevalent than last time we visited. Drug taking or drinking will get a pupil sent home for four to eight weeks, but a child would only be asked to leave if they consistently made clear they could not fit in eg for extremely disturbed behaviour or consistently failing to follow the community's rules. A young boy we saw walking through the school with an open evil-looking folding knife was chastised by an older pupil.

Not a hippy wilderness – TVs and X-boxes in some of the dorms. Girls' rooms generally nicer than the boys' and fewer girls to a room. Pupils allowed out to Leiston town – a quiet backwater roughly 10 minutes' walk away. No Saturday activities or lessons – 'we just live' – but kids can ask for a lesson if desired. Everyone up by 8am on week days. At lesson times teachers await pupils for 10 minutes, then depart if no-show. Student investigation committee deals with any reported thefts. Food a bit basic, portions smallish, vegetarian option – can be a challenge for hearty or picky eaters, but toast and fruit always available. 'Poc' – weekly pocket money – handed out by age. £3 for under eight year olds up to £10 for the eldest. The school recommends children not bring in extra money (though some do).

Pupils and parents: An international community. The school is well known abroad and almost two-thirds of children come from overseas: Japan, Korea, Holland, China, Germany, France, Poland, Russia ... the nationalities wax and wane over the years. Around half of pupils are receiving some sort of EFL help (if they choose to turn up). Recent drop in Japanese pupils (recession) – made up for by upsurge in Chinese. Hodgepodge of languages can be heard as one meanders through the school.

Like home schoolers, parents at Summerhill tend to be ardent advocates of the school, born, no doubt, of having continually to justify their choice of this kind of education. 'A profound place,' said a parent, 'Love creeps up through the floorboards'. Parents here have taken the decision to 'let go' for the benefit of their children; keeping parents at arm's length so that the children can develop free of parental anxiety and interference is a key tenet. There are no school reports and parents will not be informed if their child transgresses. The school's literature says, 'what happens at school is usually considered to be the kid's own business, not necessarily to be shared by parents. Accepting this is part of learning to accept your new independent, free child.' Some children were previously home schooled or attended other alternative schools, though lots come straight from mainstream education. 'Many of us didn't get on in normal schools,' a pupil told us.

Entrance: 'Selection is based on whether we feel the child is suitable for Summerhill and vice-versa – the parents also need to understand and support the ethos of the school.' Takes children up to age 11 – older kids enrolled relatively infrequently. There are day places, but it is basically a boarding school with children going home twice a term for weekends (although they can ask at the Meeting and usually get away more frequently if they want to). Weekly boarding is an option for the youngest children or as a settling stage for pupils who will become full boarders later. Pupils may enter the school at the start of any term and, as they seldom start with a cohort, it is common for them to take several terms to fully integrate. Interested parents are encouraged to read about the school, and then to visit.

Exit: A few leave at 14 to attend a more traditional GCSE course elsewhere; most leave at 16/17; a small number stay on until 18. Majority go on to some kind of further education. Many proceed to sixth form colleges (and then university) although entering a normal school can be a jolt. Some end up working in skilled craft jobs. Children's writer John Burningham (The Snowman) attended the school, as did several successful actors, musicians, dancers, artists and scientists – others are off making tepees in the Welsh hills.

Money matters: Mega-cheap, but then they do not have the overheads of keeping up historical buildings, state-of-the-art sports centres, interactive whiteboards etc etc. Whole place runs on a shoestring with an air of frugality. Teachers' salaries lowish. Ten per cent fee discount, or more, for children of ex-Summerhillians. Some subjects – like Chinese, riding, dancing and music lessons – charged as extras. School squirreling away funds for the AS Neill Summerhill Trust, which will eventually be able to provide limited bursaries for existing pupils.

Remarks: You know tiger parenting? Well this is the opposite. A living, breathing St Trinians of a school, and we mean that in the best possible way (indeed, its 1999 battle with Ofsted was made into a CBBC TV series). Other schools seek to incorporate watered-down elements of the Summerhill philosophy, but none provides such an uncompromising, full-on, 'free' education – accepting the good (enlightenment) and the bad (illiteracy) that may result. Thank goodness something like this still exists in 21st century Britain where exams and paper qualifications are almost a religion. Educational philosophies and government initiatives may come and go, but Summerhill glides serenely on.

Sunnydown School

Portley House, 152 Whyteleafe Road, Caterham, Surrey, CR3 5ED

• Pupils: 80 boys; 35 weekly boarders • Ages: 11–16 • non-denom • State

Tel: 01883 342281
Email: office@sunnydown.surrey.sch.uk
Website: www.sunnydown.surrey.sch.uk

Head Teacher: Since 1982, Mr Moore Armstrong. His wife Jill also teaches history at the school – 'I did not appoint her!' Smiley, caring and respected – fierce when necessary, obviously loves coming to work. 'I could be accused of failing in ambition in not moving to another job but this is a very interesting place … ' Not complacent, yet shows endless delight in boys' achievements.

Academic matters: All the boys have very severe dyslexia and arrive at the school streetwise – albeit with behavioural and communication difficulties – but with their only academic experience one of failure (eg 11 years old with a reading age of 5). Immediate assessments of reading, comprehension and spelling set challenging targets for each boy, which are achieved and rewarded with the focus and encouragement of form teachers and learning support staff. About 8 boys and two adults in each class; outgoing yet disciplined behaviour with laughter, practical examples of subjects and peer evaluation holding the kids' attention. Mainstream curriculum from year 7, good range of GCSEs; mainly focused on work-related skills. Entry Level Certificates mean everyone leaves with a qualification. Effective and well-used IT room, ditto library. An excellent working environment where fear of failure does not exist; 'if they don't make it here, they won't make it anywhere.'

Games, options, the arts: Games and outdoor activities recognised as immensely important for 11-16 year old boys. Lunchbreak lasts an unfashionable 80 minutes, giving everyone time to let off steam before more lessons – the basketball court is very popular, the London Towers professional team come and coach 24 boys each week. Swimming takes place in the pool at the neighbouring mainstream state school – and snowball fights between the two when the weather is right! Astroturf area enables all-weather football. Sunnydown competes with the 70 other members of Surrey Special Schools Sports Association – trophies displayed in the school hall. Duke of Edinburgh Award Scheme, Ocean Youth Trust South, Army, Sea Cadets, St John's Ambulance – the biggest problem is not enough days for all the available options. Many of the activities stem from pupils' suggestion books. Music is part of the curriculum but there is also an opera workshop each week. Art is of a mainstream standard – pupils recently took part in a national sculpture competition and were ranked by the V&A as one of the top ten schools in the county.

Background and atmosphere: Friendly atmosphere as soon as you enter and are given a bright visitor's badge. Each individual's needs are known without looking them up in a file. Boarders love it here – not just because of the range of evening activities – rooms are clean, bright and there are obviously no problems with stealing, since I saw mobile phones lying around and a dorm's safe box wide open. Zero tolerance to bullying means that everything is reported – including complaints such as 'so and so is not talking to me' – if that is seen as bullying then communication has to be pretty important here! The care staff is dedicated and perceptive, six and half in total; one of the two men is an ex-pupil. Couple of whole school assemblies each week; no group religion outside RE syllabus. Two dogs (pets of care staff) and a part-time cat (belonging to head's daughter). Form tutor and care staff are the first points of contact for concerned parents yet head operates open (truly) door policy. Written report at Christmas and in July, three parents' meetings a term and pupils' statements are reviewed every year.

Pupils and parents: From all over Surrey (weekly board available for those with long commute) and families have moved into the county to attend.

Entrance: Surrey LEA SEN panel meets each November and examines statements – the youngest with the most severe SEN come to Sunnydown. School does not really want to dilute effective size but may stretch to 80 pupils with extra facilities in the future. Open mornings for parents alone.

Exit: 95 per cent stay in education, mostly to local colleges for vocational GNVQs.

Money matters: State financed, parents and friends contribute to extra fund-raising; a few eyebrows were raised at letter proposing a collection for Guinness – the name of the often sick – now deceased – school cat!

Remarks: A remarkable school with a family feel, effective and inspiring for the visitor and obviously for the pupils too – old boys return to visit, normally around lunchtime... Sunnydown builds boys' self-esteem fast; one applied for a job as a apprentice at a hairdresser's and ended up cutting hair on national TV.

Surbiton High School

Linked schools: Surbiton High Junior Girls' School; Surbiton High Boys' Preparatory School

Surbiton Crescent, Kingston Upon Thames, Surrey, KT1 2JT

• Pupils: 875 girls; all day • Ages: 11–18 • Christian ethos (but all denominations accepted) • Fees: £8,601–£14,103 pa
• Independent

Tel: 020 8439 1309
Email: surbiton.high@surbitonhigh.com
Website: www.surbitonhigh.com

Principal: Since 2008, Ms Ann Haydon BSc (Hons) (early forties). Arrived with an excellent reputation from Guildford High (Surbiton's sister school) where she spent five years as deputy headmistress and was therefore already au fait with school's owners UCST. Previously she was at Sutton High for seven years, having joined as youngest-ever head of department (geography), and before that she was at Putney High.

Was quick to make her mark on the place, showing dynamism and commitment to change, but without making great waves. Homed in on music and sport – which our previous review identified as in need of some oomph – significantly raising the profile of both. Has also expanded the extra-curricular side. Girls like her, parents seem pleased and consensus is that she is good for the school. 'Supremely professional,' says one parent. 'She's very charming,' says another, 'Personable, but formal,' declares a third. Always around and has made great efforts to get to know the girls – teaches year 7 geography, holds form captain lunches, sees girls with especially good reports – which helps her put names to faces. She describes herself as 'passionate about the whole child – it may be a cliché but there really are only visible children as far as I'm concerned.' Hobbies include sport, theatre and music, while her real love is to travel – especially to Africa where she has set up, and continues to run, a children's charity.

Academic matters: Though not the crème de la crème, the girls are generally above average on entry and the school does well by them, delivering solid results with very good value-added. More nurturing than a power house. High quality teaching and learning – girls are pushed to their ability in appropriate sets for core subjects. In 2013 at GCSE (girls generally take nine or ten) nearly 70 per cent of results were A* or A grades, and over 90 per cent were A*-B. Good place for linguists – wide breadth on offer at key stage 3 including French, Spanish, German and Latin – even Mandarin available through enrichment programme. Also separate sciences at KS3. At A level, 50 per cent of girls achieve grade A or A*; 84 per cent A*-B. Less common offerings include Italian and Russian. Critical thinking and further maths also available. Average UCAS points 400 and most students get places at universities of their choice including six to Oxbridge in 2012. Ms Haydon is keen to improve on this and has appointed a coordinator to promote the idea to the girls a bit more, with potential candidates identified in year 10 and supported with special lessons and master classes. Parental perception that Oxbridge places are coveted above all others has put a few noses out of joint.

Lessons are pacey, taking account of different learning styles, and the girls are well challenged. Excellent monitoring systems in place. Nice emphasis on encouraging pupils to organise themselves – good note-taking skills drilled into them from the off, so that by year 10 it is automatic. Well-resourced, the school makes excellent use of technology all round – one neat example is via Active Expression handsets, linked to software and interactive whiteboards, which the girls use to answer questions during lessons. Means that no-one can be anonymous and teachers can analyse the information later to identify anyone in need of support. The technology moves lessons along more quickly and is proving a powerful tool.

Healthy mix of male/female, young/older teachers and pleasingly not much use of supply staff. No SEN screening on entry but screening for literacy difficulties in year 7. Supported learning section provides individual and small group tuition as needed, literacy booster groups if required and EAL. Parents pay extra towards SEN but cost is subsidised by school – currently eight per cent of the girls receive such help. There is gifted and talented programme for the most academically able girls, involving master classes, mentoring and a range of challenging learning opportunities.

Games, options, the arts: Great tradition of high quality art – school won 17 top candidate awards at GCSE – with girls flourishing in gorgeous open plan art studio. The artwork on display in reception is so good that a visitor might think it was professional. Budding thespians be aware that drama could be stronger – it's there but not as high profile as some places. Music is emerging from a bit of a dip and has been reinvigorated by a new director of music ('he's outstanding,' say parents). Although there appears to be lots going on and school points to a number of individual stand-out performances, parents generally don't recommend the place for a very sporty daughter. All could be about to change as Ms Haydon is determined to turn this around and wants all girls to have more opportunities to participate and perform. Initiatives include overseas hockey and netball tours, tennis development programme and a fitness suite for sixth form. In any event it's not at all bad – outstanding skiing (school produces champions on plastic and snow) with strong rowing and gymnastics (one selected to compete at London 2012) and there's an existing gifted and talented programme for sport. School has also recently announced plans for a new sports hall with badminton and netball facilities. Strong emphasis on extra-curricular clubs since current head arrived. There are over 70 options, from Bollywood films to word games – new ones include riding and astronomy – and breadth of interest is encouraged; girls are not encouraged to specialise academically or otherwise. Numerous examples of individual successes with girls winning places and competitions in all sorts of areas from music to design to literacy. Put some money aside for some enviable overseas trips – recently France, Spain, USA and Iceland.

Background and atmosphere: School celebrated its 125th anniversary in 2009 – it opened at the same address in a large Victorian house in 1884. Still owned by the United Church Schools Trust, an independent Christian educational charity. But few other clues to such heritage these days. Newcomers searching for the place would easily mistake it for a corporate headquarters. School fills one suburban block, 10 minutes walk from main shops of suburban Surbiton, and is surrounded by assorted housing stock and wide, but car-choked, avenues. Recent years have seen tremendous investment and expansion – all good, but new buildings and layout involve girls in a fair bit of walking to different sites for different lessons – including crossing a main road, albeit with a permanent crossing warden. Refreshing exercise on a summer's day, more miserable in the winter, and it does put a few families off.

Classrooms are light and bright, and facilities first class. Only real minus is a lack of outdoor space on site. (Off site there are extensive sports grounds at Hinchley Wood.) Sixth form has its own building with good IT and private study facilities and a common room. Overall a purposeful, business-like atmosphere with pupils and parents alike raving about how friendly the school is. 'There's a lovely feel to the place,' sums up one.

Pastoral care and discipline: High praise for pastoral care. When talking to one prospective family visiting with their (generally) sweet 11 year old, school staff assured them that, 'we'll still like her when she is 15!' 'And they do,' says that mother; 'the pastoral care is really very good.' Most parents report an immediate and effective response to any issues. Generally a well-behaved bunch – largely complying with the zero tolerance policy on drugs, drink and cigarettes. Smokers hauled before Ms Haydon even if they were caught out of school hours and uniform. School nurse on site, doctor available weekly. Good induction routines for year 7s, followed up with 'big sister' mentoring programme. Healthy culture of 'telling' about problems and school quick to support anyone in difficulty and any of their friends who may have been involved. Not a bitch-fest – girls say their classmates are supportive of them. Parents pleased that school somehow manages to keep cliques and queen bees under control.

Pupils and parents: Townie mix – English middle-class predominate. Some families pay the fees without a thought, while other families work extra shifts to afford the place. 'We're a fairly down-to-earth bunch,' says one. Parents delighted when their unconfident 11 year olds emerge five years later completely self-assured. Several mention how their daughters have blossomed under the Surbiton High watch. Not the smartest set of girls and several parents said they'd like to see tighter monitoring and control of standards – usual problem of creeping hemlines. Sixth formers wear their own clothes – no 'business-dress' requirement. Street-wise, the girls are by and large dedicated and hardworking and can't get away with coasting as involved parents and caring school marshal them in an effective pincer movement.

Entrance: New initiative allows 'natural progression' from the junior to the senior school. 'We know our girls well and there is no need for them to have the stress of an exam,' says Ms Haydon. The 'handful' who may not make the grade are given fair (year 5) warning. Newcomers are assessed in English and maths and will write a personal statement which they are encouraged to consider beforehand. Word on the street is that the exams are not as hard as others taken on the entry exam round. The school says that 'interest in the school is such that we have become increasingly selective.' Six forms of 24 – though occasional one-off years of seven form entry (eg 2009). There are isolated parental moans that the school and classes are too big with such a substantial

new intake every year – it is a large school so make sure your shrinking violet would not feel lost in the crowd. Head says there is no such thing as a 'Surbiton girl,' but they are all 'interesting girls'. Intake from south-west London and north-east Surrey. Main feeder schools are Fern Hill Primary, Holy Cross Prep, Rowan Prep, St Michael's C of E, St Paul's C of E, Thames Ditton Junior and Twickenham Prep. For sixth form entry, offers are based on interview and GCSE predictions.

Exit: Some fall out at 16, mainly to co-ed sixth forms (there's a good mixed state sixth form nearby). From sixth form most to good universities of their choice – new emphasis on Oxbridge (see above).

Money matters: Parents happy they get value for money – it's not the dearest in the area. Some recent parental disquiet over reports that fees go towards subsidising other schools in UCST group – but the school says there is absolutely no truth in this statement. Help with fees available three ways: from scholarships – academic, music, art, sports; Church Schools Foundation Assisted places (dependent on family income) and bursaries for 'daughters of the clergy'.

Remarks: A large school with a good local reputation – it is not elitist nor a school that treats you as if you are lucky to be there. Head is forward-thinking and full of plans. Parents recommend heartily. Friendly place with happy girls who are achieving academically and progressing personally.

Sutton Grammar School

Manor Lane, Sutton, Surrey, SM1 4AS

• Pupils: 840 boys, all day • Ages: 11–18 • Non-denom • State

Tel: 020 8642 3821
Email: sgs@suttonlea.org
Website: www.suttongrammar.sutton.sch.uk

Headmaster: Since 1990, Mr Gordon Ironside MA PGCE (fifties). Read physics at Cambridge, then taught maths at Alleyn's and Sutton Grammar before becoming deputy head in 1987. Married to a fellow teacher, he has three grown-up children who all attended Sutton grammar schools. One son continues what has become a bit of a family tradition and teaches in a local grammar school. Head is involved in a lot of charity work; he is a governor of the local hospital school and adult education college. Affable, hard working and thoroughly dedicated to education all round. Parents say he is always on hand and has the confidence to allow his staff to run their own departments. They appreciate his experience and all the guidance he offers their sons. Head has many interests in the arts, sports and enjoys the occasional round of golf.

Academic matters: Highly selective and always in the top ten per cent of the highest achieving schools. Needless to say, it delivers mostly excellent results: in 2013 73 per cent of papers were graded A*/A at GCSE; 53 per cent A*/A at A level. The school specialism is science – all three sciences are very strong and many pupils opt for the science and maths route at GCSE and A level. Very inspiring large and light labs, greenhouse on the roof and boys breed trout and salmon to release into the River Wandle. Two physics teachers run electronics project clubs and boys have won UK Engineer of the Year and Intech science awards.

Top performing pupils also excel in maths and physics Olympiads. Sixth formers help to teach science in primary schools, while some local schools visit Sutton Grammar to experience working in a lab. Early work experience is arranged in hospitals for those considering careers in medicine. Head stresses that staff work hard to make sure the curriculum is balanced with arts and humanities. Parents say the fairly dynamic English department really stretches boys, as well as organising fun activities with plays and poetry. No classics, modern languages only. Boys can choose from French, Spanish and German. Rigorous computing skills are taught – AIDA qualifications in year 9, leading to GCSE and A level computing. Good mix of male and female staff, most of them long serving. One boy told us it's great that the teachers guide the whole way through school.

SENCo oversees SEN provision throughout the school for a small number of pupils with statements, SpLDs, sensory impairments or high functioning ASD. Refreshingly honest approach from head, who says this is not school's area of expertise and stresses that pupils have to be able to cope and enjoy the fast moving and competitive environment.

Games, options, the arts: A fabulous 27-acre sports ground in Cheam, utilised by pupils, old boys and Surrey football clubs. PE staff make a tremendous effort to help boys find sporting pursuits they enjoy, from table tennis to county league cricket. Around 12 football teams and three rugby sides compete in fixtures list, along with a host of house sports competitions. The school also boasts its own largish heated open-air swimming pool. Standard D of E programme and well established CCF (run with Nonsuch Girls School). Parents say the sporting opportunities for all are a great credit to the school.

Some impressive art displays around the school, although only a small number choose to take GCSE and A level art. Many more opt for the design and technology path, either in graphics or electronics.

Chamber groups, orchestras and choirs engage in a range of musical pursuits, including a cappella singing. Tuition on any instrument of a boy's choice can be arranged. Composer in residence runs an annual composition festival. Music and drama departments team up with Sutton High School (neighbouring girls' school) for concerts and plays, including a biannual musical production. Both schools and parents pull together to produce fabulous productions. Drama on the curriculum – a reasonable number of boys go on to take GCSE and A level theatre studies. LAMDA courses and exams on offer too. The old gym has been converted into a drama studio (for which a talented pupil has designed a lighting system).

During the summer term there is an annual activities week; trips include foreign travel, adventure sports camps and a year 9 visit to the First World War battlefields. Others attend first aid training courses and some older pupils try their hand at teaching in local primary schools.

Background and atmosphere: The school has always been single sex. It opened as Sutton County Grammar in 1899, charging fees of two pounds and ten shillings per term. More or less everything you could want is on site, so it's all fairly compact. Remodelling and new buildings are constantly popping up (the latest addition is a two-storey maths block).

Playground areas are small. Boys from year 10 upwards are allowed to go off site during the lunch hour. Sandwich bar in the playground (known as the Snack Shack) helps to relieve the lunchtime crush. Stylish but small newly designed canteen serves hot meals. Everything runs like clockwork on the whole in this traditional focused grammar school. Boys are well-behaved, motivated and articulate.

Pastoral care and discipline: Traditional house system and year group tutors look after pupils' welfare. One parent told us she felt confident that problems were dealt with 'very swiftly.' Boys taught to respect others and take responsibility for all aspects of the school and themselves. Everyone is expected to follow a strict but fair code on behaviour, hair and uniform.

The school has a no-nonsense approach to discipline and stresses to pupils that silly behaviour wastes valuable time. Parents' information evenings and discussion groups run on a wide range of topics, often led by outside speakers. Parents are canvassed on subjects they'd like to know more about each term and pupils are welcome to attend too if they wish.

Pupils and parents: Parents are mostly professionals from all kinds of backgrounds – wealthy Surrey and south Londoners along with those from less affluent areas. Great mix of brains from all over the world, 30 to 40 per cent of the boys are from other cultures. PTA is an impressive group, raising around £60,000 each year for the benefit of pupils and for school developments.

School runs mock test days for around 2,000 children each year wanting to prepare for 11+ entry into selective grammar schools. A recent application for a government grant to convert classrooms into a science lab was unsuccessful, so PTA stepped in to help with the cost. The Suttonians have a very active old boys network and a large number of them remain involved with the school. Famous alumni include Brian Paddick, Christopher Bigsby, David Bellamy and David Farrar.

Entrance: Places are highly sought after, with around 1,500 boys competing for 120 places at 11+ every year. School sets its own exam, reasoning paper, English and maths. Currently no catchment area, so highest scorers win the places. At 16+, approximately five competitive entry places are available for newcomers to the sixth form.

Exit: Almost all to university, although the occasional pupil takes up a specialist apprenticeship in the workplace. Up to 15 to Oxbridge every year and 15 to veterinary sciences and medicine. Others to a range of top universities, with London colleges particularly popular at the moment.

Remarks: School offers fantastic opportunities for those who make the grade. A must for academically able and enthusiastic young men.

Sutton High School

Linked school: Sutton High Junior School

55 Cheam Road, Sutton, Surrey, SM1 2AX

- Pupils: 720 girls, all day • Ages: 11–18 • Non-denom
- Fees: £8,343–£14,085 pa • Independent

Tel: 020 8642 0594
Email: n.new@sut.gdst.net
Website: www.suttonhigh.gdst.net

Headmistress: Since 2012, Mrs Katharine Crouch BSc NPQH. Joined Sutton High School in 2003 and has held many roles including head of biology, head of pastoral and deputy head.

Academic matters: Solid results across the board in academics and the arts; 65 per cent A*/A at GCSE and 46 per cent at A level in 2013. School is very aware that today's young people need a range of skills and accomplishments to succeed in the competitive 21st century world; provision throughout the school is being reviewed and updated. Teachers are currently trialling the best way to maximise each individual's potential; consequently, girls are set according to ability and their strongest learning style. School appreciates the importance of ICT skills, offering DIDA and GCSE qualifications and an ICT club. Separate or dual award science. Maths fairly strong

S

all round, although some parents feel that less confident mathematicians should be identified and assisted much earlier. Good, practical help is also available: everyone is taught about budgeting and money management. Very impressive results for Latin (91 per cent A*/A at GCSE); French, Spanish, German and Latin are offered throughout the school, with Greek run as an after-school class. Decent number of trips both here and abroad. Lots of girl-power on the staff – female majority – who are all committed to ensuring there are no ceilings or barriers for any pupil. Small number of pupils with mild dyslexia are monitored and supported by the SENCo; provision for EAL.

Sixth formers undertake the Extended Project Qualification to help prepare them for university. Girls say it's quite a lot of extra work alongside A levels, but they generally consider it a good thing to do. Enrichment course enables sixth formers to look at a wider range of topics and skills from cookery to philosophy. Friday afternoons are set aside for community service and fund-raising activities. Girls collaborate with Sutton Grammar boys for a number of activities, including the Challenge of Management conference, giving them the opportunity to gain an insight into the business world. Bi-annual careers fair invites representatives from many companies into the school to pitch career paths and ideas to the girls.

Games, options, the arts: Fab facilities and very active and successful sports department. Enormous gym and 25m indoor pool, which is open to pupils and their families at weekends and in the holidays. Gymnastics is popular and there is a beautiful new dance hall for budding ballerinas and dancing divas. Sporty girls compete in house and in local competitions, and do particularly well in county athletics and cross country championships. Assortment of sports tours organised annually to all parts of the globe.

The arts fare well across the school, particularly music: dedicated music teachers, lots of practice rooms and music technology suite. Different choirs to choose from, traditional to gospel, depending on the girls' interests. Fine groups of young instrumentalists play in a range of ensembles; tuition can be arranged for any instrument, subsequently, dynamic and well-thought-of orchestras. All this considered, rather a low take-up of GCSE and A level music. In-house and joint music concerts and drama productions with Sutton Grammar. Largish hall for drama, department always welcomes volunteers who'd like to help with staging or learn to use lighting equipment. Girls also have the opportunity to take the LAMDA acting and speaking exams.

Light, airy art rooms and a separate sculpture hut for pottery, an area where girls are particularly successful. Artistic types are offered the full range of art and design courses through to A level, being able to choose from painting and pottery, textiles, and resistant materials. More inventing and designing for all age groups goes on through the Young Enterprise Scheme. Some lovely creations, textiles, paintings and sculptures, are displayed around the school. Lunchtime and after-school clubs, for which an additional charge is made, offer further opportunities for sports and music. Most subject teachers run drop-in clinics to provide extra support for individuals and extension work.

Background and atmosphere: Founded in 1884 with just a handful of pupils. Over the years, as pupil numbers have grown, neighbouring buildings have been purchased alongside a rolling building programme to keep pace with modern demands. Latest additions include the sixth form centre and sports complex.

In the midst of all the buildings, well-maintained gardens and sports areas create a cloistered look. Busy pupils move round the site in an orderly way. Girls have a good local reputation and the school is always interested in setting up community links, the most well known being their work and artistic pursuits

with Sutton Boys Grammar. Old Girls Association has a reunion at school every year.

Pastoral care and discipline: The headmistress is very keen to review and develop the pastoral care, so that she can build on the good foundations. All new entrants are allocated a buddy to chat to and to help them overcome any small problems. Professional counsellor visits weekly and there is also a school nurse. Head is clued up about the emotional needs and external pressures that affect young people. Form tutors and heads of year monitor academic progress, personal welfare and development. Student council helps compile the Code of Conduct in partnership with staff, giving everybody a chance to have their say.

Pupils and parents: Good mix, socially and ethnically; lots of local business families and city types. Others travel from the edges of south-west London and various parts of Surrey; school is conveniently located close to Sutton station so attracts a wide catchment. School bus services from Wimbledon and Croydon areas. The Parent Staff Association works together to arrange social events and to further sporting opportunities through the parent-run clubs Otter and Centipede. Staff and parents organise an annual multicultural evening. Interesting group of old girls include Dora Black (Lady Russell), Susan Howatch, novelist, and BBC correspondent Sue Littlemore.

Entrance: At 11+ examination in maths, English and verbal reasoning plus an interview with a senior member of staff. At 16+ entrance test consisting of general papers, verbal reasoning and interview with the head of sixth form. At least eight GCSEs, grade A or above in subjects chosen for A level.

Exit: At 16+ some move to coed or grammar school sixth forms. 18+ more or less everybody goes to a wide variety of mostly top universities or art colleges. Small handful to Oxbridge each year (two in 2013).

Money matters: Academic scholarships at 11+ and 16+ based on top performance in entrance or public exams. Other small scholarships awarded for art, music, drama and PE. Means-tested GDST bursaries are also available.

Remarks: Would suit those who want a single sex education in a calm environment. Parents and friends are looking forward to the head bringing all the school's strengths out into the light. A school to watch?

Sutton Valence School

Linked school: Sutton Valence Preparatory School

North Street, Sutton Valence, Kent, ME17 3HL

- Pupils: 500; 330 boys, 170 girls. 160 boarders, 340 day; • Ages: 11–18; • C of E; • Fees: Day £14,295–£18,645; Boarding £19,050–£28,410 pa; • Independent

Tel: 01622 845200
Email: enquiries@svs.org.uk
Website: www.svs.org.uk

Headmaster: Since 2009, Mr Bruce Grindlay MA Cantab (organ scholar) MusB FRCO. Mid-forties, he came from Christ's Hospital School, Horsham where he was director of music for eight years. Previously boarding housemaster and head of chapel music at Bedford School. Came in with desire to up the ante on discipline and academics and has succeeded in taking pupils and parents with him. Parents find him calm, personable and articulate with his nose to the ground and swift to take action when needed. Pupils frequently pop by his office for advice or to tell of an achievement. Expectations are set high and all are challenged to do their best. 'I'm not slow to remind pupils, or staff for that matter, that family fees are the cost of a small Caribbean holiday.' His wife teaches English in the sixth form and is completing a PhD. Two children, one here, the other a chorister at Westminster Abbey Choir School.

Academic matters: Parents bridle slightly at the notion that it's a school for the less academic. 'The strong ethos that there's a lot more to school life than exam results in no way means the bright aren't stretched.' The head highlights solid value-added scores; school has moved into the top 15 per cent nationally for adding value at A Level this year, equating to half to one grade better for each child than initial predictions, per subject. He emphasises that a pupil moving a D to a C is every bit as significant as another getting an A* and that its main focus is on producing confident all-rounders. Small class sizes and a caring, individual approach draw many. ESL and other learning support staff commended for their kindness, patience and dedication with highly-rated SEN support in lessons and, by arrangement, during extra sessions, at times in place of non-core subjects. 'Staff always happy to go the extra mile to help my son and, with such a broad intake, he's never felt different or out of place.' Popular subjects include geography, maths, business studies, art and design. In 2013, 86 per cent gained five A*-C including English and maths, 45 per cent A*/A at GCSE and 58 per cent A*-B (34 per cent A*/A) at A level. A few grumbles that problem areas, either in relation to particular subjects or pupils, come to light slowly, but once issues are identified, most agree action is swift and effective. The e-newsletter, information evenings and other recent initiatives are welcomed. 'More of the same please. It's great to now know when and what homework is being set and to be able to get more involved.'

Games, options, the arts: It's easy to see why sport forms a major part of life at Sutton Valence. Playing fields stretch as far as the eye can see, there's a track used by Olympic athletes, Astroturf hockey pitch, sports hall and hugely inviting indoor pool. The socialising that goes on around regular after-school practices and fixtures also tempt even the least sporty to have a go. The school fields several teams in hockey, cricket, netball and rugby. Some parents comment that inclusion comes at the expense of developing real excellence and that pupils would benefit from more specialist coaches, but several pupils play at county level and above in hockey, rugby and cricket and the website is brimming with team sport successes. Pupils excel in more unusual endeavours too – roller dance, small bore shooting, ballroom dancing, fly fishing and race walking being just some examples.

So much part of life here are CCF and D of E that there's no great fanfare when pupils routinely go onto the higher levels, though their contribution to individual development and community spirit is emphasised. With his musical background, the head was always sure to encourage that side of things, though music has long been considered strong. Noticeboards are crammed with news of rehearsals and performances and the schedule of clubs and, along with, we're told, truly excellent drama productions in the plush Baughan Theatre, you're left wondering how pupils, parents and staff fit everything in. Little wonder flexi-boarding is such a popular option.

Background and atmosphere: At the core of a small village in Kent, in beautifully kept grounds, gracious old buildings house pleasant and at times grand communal areas and well-equipped classrooms. On a clear day, though, there's a danger it's all overshadowed by the breathtaking view of the Weald to the south. Main site separated by a short distance from the prep

school (and junior mixed boarding house). Most staff live on site or nearby. 'A happy and relaxed local community – what better place for my child to learn and grow?'

Perhaps that accounts for its longevity. It's one of the country's oldest established schools, founded by William Lambe in 1576. In 2010 over 1000 attended a ceremony in Westminster Abbey, a fitting location given the school's strong Christian ethos, to mark the centenary of becoming part of the United Westminster Schools Foundation.

Pastoral care and discipline: One of the boarding house matrons in no way resembles the dragon poster she pins on boys' dorms to remind them to tidy up. Not sure that a dragon would have such a keen interest in every child's welfare either. Lots of space, friendly faces and homely touches. 'Often think my children would prefer to live there and on the various occasions when it suits us too the school has always done its best to accommodate.' Day, full, flexi or occasional boarders, it's clear staff keep tabs on pupils and do their best to develop a joint approach to overcome homesickness or other issues, most of which are minor. Visits to local preps to put future pupils' fears at bay are also not unknown.

Head has impressive recall of pupil names and goings-on and has got the prefects, parents and pupils almost universally on side in introducing somewhat tougher discipline. Nothing too draconian, 'tough love' is its basis. Correct uniform, orderly lunchtime queuing/clearing up and, at the prefects' initiative, the use of pleases and thank yous are all in hand. Head also sweetened pupils up with a fresh system of rewards to acknowledge even small individual contributions and achievements.

Pupils and parents: Other than real non-conformists, most likely to feel at home here. 'No one thing defines you. I'm not a bit like my siblings but we've all found things to get our teeth into here.' Pupils are described as nice, normal and confident without arrogance. Many parents both work and are a mix of local businessmen/entrepreneurs, farmers and city workers. Foreign students – mostly from Germany and Asia – do not exceed nine per cent of the total and on the whole settle in well, though for some life in rural England is somewhat of a culture shock. Head would like to see a more vibrant PA but, even though most UK families are based in the south east, he may face an uphill battle as many travel quite a distance to get to the school. This can be an issue, especially in bad weather, and makes flexi and occasional boarding popular options (which younger full-time boarders can find unsettling). The school runs buses and some sixth formers drive – some in rather flash cars.

Famous alumni include journalists Robert Fisk and Ben Brown, Ashley Jackson, GB hockey player, Kathryn Choonara of Scottish National Opera and Sir Rustam Feroze, gynaecologist.

Entrance: Most come up from the prep school and an assortment of other local preps and primary schools. At 11 the school sets its own entrance exam. There's usually a waiting list but a number drop off having secured places at local grammars. Smaller intake at 13 when a CE mark of approximately 55 per cent is required. State school applicants must pass the school's exam. The 25 or so students entering sixth form from outside need at least five GCSE passes at B grade or above. Most international students come in the sixth form and also sit a language exam.

Exit: About 20 per cent leave after GCSEs, most going to local grammars. Almost all sixth formers go on to further education and each year a number (40 per cent in 2013) gain places at Russell Group universities. Loughborough, Bournemouth and Bath are other popular destinations. One to Oxbridge in 2013.

Money matters: Academic (11+ and 13+), art, DT, music, sports and drama (at 11+, 13+ and 16+) scholarships and the

Westminster scholarship (to those obtaining five GCSEs at A*) available. Worth up to a maximum of 20 per cent of either boarding or day fees. Also offers bursaries and reductions for Forces families.

Remarks: Friendly and relaxed atmosphere and solid all-round confidence-building credentials. Its idyllic setting and enviable sports and other facilities make it a popular alternative to more academically demanding senior schools in the south east. Can suffer perhaps from being labelled the non-academic alternative. 'That old chestnut,' says one parent. 'Obviously needs to market itself better. Put all your kids there. It's got lots to offer any child.'

Sydenham High School GDST

Linked school: Sydenham High Junior School GDST

19 Westwood Hill, London, SE26 6BL

• Pupils: 475, all day • Ages: 11–18 • Fees: £10,920–£13,899 pa
• Independent

Tel: 020 8557 7000
Email: info@syd.gdst.net
Website: www.sydenhamhighschool.gdst.net

Headteacher: Since 2002, Mrs Kathryn Pullen BA MA PGCE (mid-fifties). Studied English and American Studies at Warwick, later completing a PGCE in drama. Began her teaching career as head of English at St Saviours and St Olave's before moving on for a brief period at Glenthorne High School. Despite more than 20 years at Sydenham, first as deputy head, she shows no signs of getting stale. Quite the reverse. She oozes enthusiasm for the girls and clearly works hard at creating a dynamic environment to match their diverse backgrounds and interests. She counts amongst her main achievements giving them a voice in shaping the school and building a senior management team excited by and responsive to change. 'I've got no magic wand and this is no place for prissy princesses, but the eager and intellectually curious will find plenty to stimulate them here.'

Academic matters: Of course the school has an eye to results and, given its broad intake, achieves well. In 2013, 70 per cent A*/A at GCSE and 78 per cent A*-B (35 per cent A*/A) at A level. But it hasn't lost sight of the need to relieve the pressure and inject fun into, in particular, years 9-11.

Many activities designed to develop personal learning and thinking skills and break the routine. A parent attendee at the year 7 study skills workshop throws up her arms: 'Why oh why didn't schools teach me good habits so early on?' Year 12 has a busy schedule of outside speakers to help pupils make decisions about their future. In younger years an annual off-timetable day encourages them to reflect on themselves as learners using anything from Dragon's Den workshops to mixed discussion groups.

Staff clearly also recognise technology's potential to engage pupils. In its first year, the maths blog with lesson podcasts received over 37,000 hits in the run-up to GCSE, indicating the high standard of teaching in this area. Other web-based tools are available and staff welcome email contact, particularly during study leave and from parents with concerns. Pupils can take some GCSEs early to free up time for other interests and areas of study. Science is an area of strength – two year 10 and sixth form pupils recently won national awards and another sixth former a Nuffield bursary to study cancer treatments at King's College. Getting science GCSE out of the way in year 10 doesn't deter pupils from taking it up again in sixth form and beyond. Care is taken to highlight the relevance to different careers, leading to a high proportion taking science-based degree subjects. Their flying in the face of gender stereotyping is a source of great pride at the school.

Moving around the school, there's a real feeling that pupils and staff feed off each other's enthusiasm. The teacher looking on almost smugly, they positively fall over themselves to show off their geography presentations. The GDST network also provides a wider forum for experience and idea exchange, impressing many parents. 'Staff are endlessly inventive and flexible in meeting different pupils' needs.' It helps being relatively small. 'Many pupils leaving after GCSEs are surprised how much they miss being known to staff and the reassurance that familiarity provides' says one parent and, as many others, identifies it as a real asset which the school often doesn't do enough to promote. SEN pupils are well-catered for too. There is dyslexia screening and other testing in year 7 and the Learning Strategy Team provides by all accounts excellent tailored support with a clear focus on inclusivity. Says the head, 'We know girls don't want to feel different and if printing exam papers on yellow paper helps some of them, then why not do it for all?'

Games, options, the arts: Stalwart and welcome efforts from newer staff to raise interest and standards in sports are reaping rewards. Regular netball and hockey clubs are well-attended and successes against local schools are notching up. Rugby, football and cricket also have a keen following – they are not girly-girls. Trampolining is popular and, to encourage the less sporty, the school has recently introduced fencing, golf and scuba diving. Even so, most parents agree that this is not the best place for the more competitive, 'never happier than when on a games pitch' girl. The separation by a short bus ride of the main school site from the major eight-acre sporting facilities is probably a deterrent but also the distraction of other strong departments, most notably music and drama.

Supervised and informal music and drama rehearsals are very much in evidence around the school with girls so absorbed that they barely seem to register your passing. Even those not opting to take exams get involved and opportunities abound. In addition to two junior and two senior drama productions each year, a variety of choirs and orchestras, ranging from wind, guitar, string and jazz, perform regularly with an expanded schedule of diverse concerts in the school's new 90-seater recital hall, complete with music technology department. A number of girls have auditioned successfully to appear in West End shows and the school choir has been invited back time and again to appear at the Royal Albert Hall at Christmas. Standards are high but above all girls seem to relish the freedom of being able to join up with friends and enjoy themselves. The slightly chaotic art room is overflowing with talent and more and more are going on to study art-related subjects at university. Usual range of extra-curricular clubs, including D of E and some, such as ICT, maths and DT, designed to bolster academic progress. More unusual tastes – code-breaking, Japanese and fashion – are catered for too.

Background and atmosphere: The original Victorian buildings where the school opened in 1887 are across the road. In 1934 the school transferred to its current main building which is slightly set back and surrounded by a jumble of more recent additions, most prominently the music block and sports hall. While they provide welcome facilities they, and the sixth form block, rather detract from its overall elegance. Behind and away from the busy road and buses struggling up the hill, you can well imagine girls sunning themselves on the terrace overlooking the large Astroturf pitch bordered by mature trees. Inside, a relaxed, friendly and purposeful air with girls unselfconsciously running from one lesson to the next. 'So nice that they don't seem to feel the need to have the latest phone or bag.' Intimate feel in the sixth form block. 'Some felt uncomfortable being in a small independent girls' school but those of us left behind really appreciate it.'

Pastoral care and discipline: Parents praise staff for understanding girls' different character traits and identifying individual strengths, focusing on those in order to develop all-round confidence. Nice touches such as cards of congratulation posted home and the odd hug in the younger years. They also sense a 'spirit of sisterhood' and 'moral strength' amongst the girls, which prompts them to be mutually supportive and keep each other in line, generally without disciplinary measures from staff. The school prides itself on understanding girls, and the needs of each year group are carefully considered and programmes developed to support them. A full-day of PSHCE each term often involves outside speakers and is designed to engage pupils fully. There is a clear underlying message. If they are to succeed, they must take the initiative and think for themselves.

Pupils and parents: Tends to attract creative parents – less from established professions – of varied social, cultural and racial backgrounds who don't feel their girls would completely fit the mould elsewhere. They and staff tend to think of the girls as 'edgy, quirky and boundary-pushers' though they don't overtly appear so (little evidence of uniform rules being stretched). They want their uniqueness to be celebrated and for them to have the freedom to be themselves. For most it is a careful investment calculated to bring maximum return – many first time buyers. Old girls include actress Margaret Lockwood, Philippa Darbre (scientist), Sophie McKenzie (author), Sandy Powell (Oscar winning costume designer), Claire Bennett (fencing champion), Winifred Gerin (writer) and Elizabeth Anstruther (philosopher).

Entrance: Of around 200 applicants, 40-50 girls join the 30-plus coming up from the junior school. Most are from local preps and state primaries, although also from Wandsworth, Bromley and, since the opening of the East London overground, from north of the river. Many have brothers at Dulwich College. The head and senior teaching staff interview all girls, inviting them to talk about something they are proud of. They also take an entrance exam in English and maths in which they are expected to attain equivalent to level 4 or 5 in national curriculum KS2. Occasionally places come up in other year groups and the school is keen to expand its sixth form. Overall there's been a drop in numbers in recent years, which the head attributes to the effects of the economic downturn and more boys' schools opening up to girls, but numbers increased for the 2013/14 academic year.

Exit: After GCSEs some feel they have outgrown the school. Cost-saving and convenience are also factors and about 30 per cent leave to go to local state schools and some to board outside London. Of those who stay, usually one or two get Oxbridge places (none in 2013) with others going to, in particular, London colleges, but also further afield to both the more established and newer universities.

Remarks: The school doesn't have an instant wow factor but there's a palpable, almost defiant, energy running through the place. It seems to say, 'I will be who I want to be'. Girls emerge independent thinkers and confident communicators. All credit can go to the school that they become so in a happy, mostly settled environment.

Sylvia Young Theatre School

1 Nutford Place, London, W1H 5YZ

- Pupils: 85 boys and 155 girls; 27 board, rest day • Ages: 10–16
- Fees: £9,135–£12,540 pa • Independent

Tel: 020 7258 2330
Email: info@sylviayoungtheatreschool.co.uk
Website: www.syts.co.uk

Headteacher: Since 1981, Sylvia Young OBE (seventies). The founding principal, she is something of a legend in London's theatreland and has been supplying junior talent to the West End stage for over 30 years. With some early training, she decided 'performance was not for me', but soon realised she had a knack for spotting and inspiring talent in others. She started on a small scale, working with local children at a youth club in east London, then launched a full-time school at the suggestion of one of the parents. The school is her passion and she now lives on the site with her husband. Two grown-up daughters have both entered the profession, one (Frances Ruffelle) as a Tony-winning actress and singer, the other (Alison) as a theatrical agent. Her granddaughter is the pop singer Eliza Doolittle. Sylvia Young is a sympathetic soul, whose persistence and drive has developed the school from a walk-on role to full stardom. 'It's the Oxbridge of theatre schools', said one parent. She was appointed OBE in 2005 for services to the arts.

Since 2005, Ms Frances Chave BSc PGCE (forties) has been the academic and pastoral head. Ms Chave read maths at Exeter University, followed by a PGCE at Southampton, then taught at two large comprehensives (Cranford Community College and Feltham Community College), before helping to set up a third, Overton Grange School in Sutton, where she was deputy head. 'When I decided to move on, I wanted something completely different', she says. Sylvia Young is about as different as it gets and Ms Chave has steadily improved the academic offering, particularly on the science side. A strong and sensible presence, she enjoys theatre, 'but only as a spectator', and in her spare time plays golf and other sports.

Academic matters: Sylvia Young Theatre School has long been known for the high standard of tuition in the performing arts, and has put increasing emphasis on the more academic side of the curriculum. 'We decided early on we didn't want our pupils to lose out by coming to a theatre school', says the founder. The school is unusual in that it hives off academic lessons into three hard-working days on Mondays, Tuesdays and Wednesdays, leaving Thursdays and Fridays free for professional studies. The subdivision is reasonably demanding. 'Both staff and students have to be very focused,' says Ms Chave. Unsurprisingly, the academic curriculum is more compact than you'd find in a mainstream school – so no PE (no need with all that dancing), geography or DT – and the emphasis is definitely on the arts. All pupils study English lang and lit, maths, science (core and additional), expressive arts and drama to GCSE, when other options include music, art, media studies, history and Spanish. English, drama and theatre studies are the most successful GCSEs, but the head has worked hard to bring up attainment in science and maths (both of which are set). Results are very respectable. In 2013, 70 per cent achieved five or more GCSEs at A*-C, including English and maths, with 33 per cent of grades A*/A. 'Most of our pupils do better than expected', says Ms Chave. 'If you're somewhere you really want to be, it does have a knock-on effect'. Parents agree: 'My daughter was at a mainstream academic school before. Here she's achieved because she wants to, not because she's being pushed'.

The school, which is non-selective academically, tests all pupils for learning difficulties on entry and copes well with moderate problems, from dyslexia to Asperger's. 'We have two children here on the autistic spectrum, one's a great dancer, the other a great actor'. Well-qualified SENCo oversees help in class and out, with teachers kept well in the loop. Inevitably, lessons here are interrupted by professional work, but no one is allowed to lag behind. 'We have very good systems in place to catch up,' says Ms Chave. 'Every week staff write out what has been covered in class and what has been set for homework and everyone gets a copy'. Students are expected to make up what they've missed in their own time. 'They're amazingly adaptable, they just fit straight back in'. When a professional engagement is protracted, staff liaise directly with on-set tutors.

Games, options, the arts: The performing arts are of course the raison d'etre of this all-singing, all-dancing institution and Thursdays and Fridays are devoted to the training needs of aspiring stars. Many of the performing arts staff are themselves working professionals and don't spare their students from the profession's harder knocks. (At one lesson the Guide attended, the class was asked to vote on the best singer.) Students are set by ability across the age range in all the performing disciplines – so, for example, a talented year 7 may be in the same ballet class as a less nimble year 11. Everyone studies all aspects of drama, music and dance, with classes ranging from voice production to recording technique, and all take annual LAMDA exams in speech and drama. All pupils, too, are represented by the in-house Sylvia Young Agency and put forward for professional work, ranging from West End musicals (the school regularly supplies cast members for Matilda, Oliver! and Billy Elliot) to advertising voice-overs and language tapes. 'You have to understand what a real performance is like', says Sylvia Young, 'and you have to learn that you may not get picked because you're not right for the part, no matter how talented you are. It's part of the training'. The school takes care, however, to ensure work doesn't interfere with academic priorities. 'My daughter has GCSEs coming up and they don't allow her to go off every five minutes', said one parent. 'School work comes first'.

Background and atmosphere: The school started out by running part-time classes in the 1970s, then opened full-time in Drury Lane in 1981. In 1983 it moved to Marylebone and in 2010 transferred into spacious premises in a converted Christian Science church just behind Marble Arch. The newly refurbished building provides excellent facilities for both the vocational and academic, with 10 purpose-built studios, two computer rooms, two science labs, two bright art rooms and a small library (mainly used for catching up with homework). Priorities, now as always, remain the family atmosphere and care and attention of children, whether they're constantly in work or destined for a civilian career ('we do sometimes have to tell parents a child doesn't have what it takes for performance'). Regardless of the eventual outcome, all are equipped with valuable 'transferable skills' – confidence and the ability to communicate well and work with adults: 'The aim is to ensure they're secure in themselves', says Sylvia Young. Parents say pupils take on board the virtue of industry. 'They know the world they're contemplating is fiercely competitive', said one mother, 'and it's not going to be an easy ride. They learn a very strong work ethic'. Though clearly those who've gotta dance or act or sing (or all three) are ideally served here, the school works equally well for those who might want to enter the profession in more self-effacing roles. 'They teach you about every aspect from choreography to TV'. Twenty or so pupils board with London host families (generally present or past parents), often in groups of two or three. 'The woman my son boards with is marvellous', says one mother. 'She picks him up from the theatre at night, makes sure he does his homework, and arranges fun evenings of singing or games'.

Pastoral care and discipline: This is a school which is essentially about self-discipline, and disciplinary problems of the mainstream sort are rare. 'We don't have bullying', says Sylvia Young firmly, 'just children being silly sometimes'. The school monitors each child carefully, with an individual log kept on each. 'The children know they can come to us and we'll listen'. Parents feel confident their children are happy. 'My son feels so lucky. He is doing what he want to do every day and there aren't many adults who can say that'. The school has a strong disciplinary structure. 'We're very firm about the basics,' says Ms Young. Rules are clearly spelled out – no make-up, no micro skirts, no uploading of photographs onto the internet (a serious danger in a school where celebrity is a daily fact of life) – and consistently enforced. 'Other schools have these rules, but at Sylvia Young they really impose them', said one parent. 'It's quite old fashioned'. Two uniforms, one for academic work (white shirts, blazers, jumpers and ties), another for vocational days (tracksuits and unitards). Both are neatly worn.

Pupils and parents: Parents cover the full range. 'They're not pushy stage-school parents at all', says Ms Young. 'They're a very normal group, from all backgrounds'. Though certainly some are affluent, many really struggle to send their children here and travel considerable distances to do so. The children, of course, are as diverse as the parents, but significantly more talented than the average. They're all here because they really want to be. One parent told us: 'My son, who'd been at a local primary school, said when he first saw Sylvia Young, "Mum, it's amazing. I just fit in there".' Other who fitted in equally well include Billie Piper, Denise van Outen, former Spice Girl Emma Bunton, Jade Ewen from The Sugababes, Nathan Sykes of The Wanted and, the late Amy Winehouse, whose father has recently set up a scholarship in her memory.

Entrance: The first entry point is year 6. 'Year 6 is a good time to come', says Sylvia Young, 'because either pupils can continue into year 7 or they have time to go elsewhere. A few decide it's not what they want'. Most enter at year 7, with the occasional place at other times. At all ages, the audition is the most important part of the process. The school offers a preliminary audition, with low-key workshops. Those with most potential are invited back to perform two drama pieces (one from Shakespeare and a modern work), a song and a dance. Candidates also sit academic tests in English and maths. 'But we're not a grammar school. We just need to feel happy they'll cope with the pace and be able to get done in three days what most do in five'. That said, the stronger an applicant is on the professional side, the more leeway is given academically. Motivation, too, is carefully examined. 'There's a lot of discussion about what the child wants and what the parents are looking for'. The school sees up to 500 applicants for 40 places at 11.

Exit: Pupils are assessed at the end of years 8 and 9, which provides an opportunity for families to reassess their child's career path. Currently all move on at 16 (though the school is contemplating a sixth form). About half (mainly dancers) go on to specialist colleges, the rest to traditional academic sixth forms to do A Levels and then frequently to study drama at university. Close links with all the central London tutorial colleges (Lansdowne, Ashbourne, Duff Miller, DLD etc) and quite a number of pupils proceed to these with scholarships.

Money matters: Three official scholarships (one full and two half), and many more get some sort of help. Quite a number put their theatrical earnings towards the fees.

Remarks: A school which combines a sound academic background with outstanding vocational training and professional opportunity Hard work, but hard work undertaken with purposeful pleasure.

S

Talbot Heath School

Linked school: Talbot Heath Junior School

Rothesay Road, Bournemouth, Dorset, BH4 9NJ

- Pupils: 345 girls in the senior school. Mainly day, with 37 Boarders from age 11. 215 in the junior school. • Ages: 11–18
- C of E • Fees: Day £5,340–£11,646; Boarding £19,662–£20,631 pa
- Independent

Tel: 01202 761881
Email: irichards@talbotheath.org
Website: www.talbotheath.org

Head: Since 2010, Mrs Angharad Holloway MA (forties), previously director of International Baccalaureate programme at Royal High School, Bath (qv). She read German and Italian at St Anne's College, Oxford, and has also taught at Sir William Perkins's School and Clifton High. She is married with two small daughters.

Academic matters: Traditional teaching + high standards = fabulous results – much better than the relatively broad intake might lead one to expect. In 2013, 82 per cent A*-B grades at A level. Maths and science very popular – all take dual award GCSE science and a number go on to study medicine and veterinary science at university. Setting by ability for French and maths the term after 11 year olds start – 'we give them time to get settled,' says head – and for science at GCSE level. In 2013, 69 per cent A*/A GCSE grades.

Plenty of computers. Staff tend to put down roots – 29 members of staff have been here for more than 10 years. One teacher who did move on is local Liberal Democrat MP Annette Brooke who taught economics here. Class sizes range from 20 at lower end of school to 15 at GCSE stage. School has EAL teacher and caters for those with dyslexia, dyspraxia and ADHD. 25 girls currently receive some help for SEN – the school is quite meticulous about this and girls can be given a reduced schedule if necessary. Still, this is first and foremost an academic school and, helpful as staff may be, probably not one to seek out for a child with anything more than mild learning difficulties.

Games, options, the arts: Gym, dance, hockey, netball, swimming, tennis, rounders and athletics, plus lacrosse, volleyball and badminton from year 9 on, and even more choice as girls move up the school, including golf. The school now offers a Tennis Academy – a joint venture with the West Hants tennis club – providing full-on tennis coaching alongside a specially designed academic curriculum. Not cheap, incidentally, but less costly than moving to Florida. Talbot Heath was named Dorset Tennis School of the Year by the LTA. Many individual sporting and team successes nationally and even internationally (these are competitive girls). Heated outdoor swimming pool used from May till October for lessons and lunchtime clubs. Large sports hall (check out the lovely wooden ceiling), playing fields across road, netball and tennis courts, new Astro. Almost three hours a week of sport in year 7 decreases to an hour and 25 minutes in year 11, an hour in lower sixth, and sport can be dropped altogether in the final two terms. Not enough activity for several parents we spoke to – 'it's a shame they don't do more, given the wonderful facilities they have. It's all available but there's no one pushing you to find your sporting niche.' Won national junior and senior tennis championships in 2010 and were national finalists in 10 sports.

Music is a particular strength – cellist Natalie Clein, a former Young Musician of the Year, is an old girl as is soprano Kate Royal, winner of the 2004 Kathleen Ferrier Award (interestingly both of these students left the school briefly but came back!).

Some 250 girls have instrumental lessons in the well-appointed music school and there are loads of choirs, ensembles and orchestras to join. Bournemouth Symphony Orchestra's education department works from an office here and the BSO's contemporary music group, Kokoro, rehearses in the music school. Drama also gets a big tick. Between ages of 11 and 14 every form produces a play for the annual drama festival – 'every girl takes part, even if it's just pulling the curtain.' Two drama studios, loads of LAMDA exams and some girls go on to take theatre studies at AS and A level. Art impressive, though elbow space in the department is limited. Domestic science room a 1980s marvel but does a great job with lots of space and cookers.

Background and atmosphere: Founded as Bournemouth High School in 1886, its first head, Mary Broad, believed girls should have same opportunities in education as boys and shocked locals by teaching her pupils cricket and gymnastics. School moved to eerie 24-acre purpose-built site in Talbot Woods in 1935, when it became known as Talbot Heath – school birthday is still celebrated every May. Senior school is built round two dated quads which have been vastly added to over the years. Not a school that bowls you over with charisma, the words 'forbidding' and 'drab' (as well as 'charming' and 'efficient') came up several times among the parents we spoke to – all of whom were fans of the school. 'The first time I came up the drive and saw the windswept pines, I almost put the car in reverse,' said a mum who sent both her daughters to Talbot Heath and never looked back.

Girls wear navy blazer, skirt, blouse and tie; sixth form girls given more freedom – no uniform (but no slobs), more free periods, and sixth form common room. Many take part in Duke of Edinburgh Award scheme and Young Enterprise. Local employers have praised Talbot Heath girls on work experience post-GCSE for being reliable, competent, able to shoulder responsibility and work as a team. School monitors the girls' extra-curricular commitments – including those outside of school – to check they are not taking on too much (or too little?)

Pastoral care and discipline: School has system of sanctions – order marks, detentions etc – for unsatisfactory work or behaviour. Parents always informed. Each form has two form leaders, voted for by peers each term, and there are two head girls, two deputies and a raft of prefects. Assemblies, often with outside speakers, every day but Thursday. Like any girls-only school, friendship group problems surface but the younger girls say they can talk to the older prefects about any problems. In severe flare-ups the head has been known to interview every single girl in a class individually to get to the core of the problem. 'I'm not saying I've never had a complaint,' said a parent we spoke to, 'but when I have, it's been resolved quickly.'

Small number of boarders enjoy loads of flexibility at St Mary's boarding house, a short walk from main school building. Dormitories for younger girls and cubicles for older ones. Full-time housemistress (not a teacher). Boarding judged outstanding by Ofsted (2008).

Pupils and parents: Girls come from enormous catchment area – some cycle in from close by while others travel from as far afield as Beaulieu to the east and Weymouth and Portland to the west (good train service and the school runs several buses and minibuses). Wide range of backgrounds, including people who never expected to be paying for private education. Most, but not all, boarders come from overseas, particularly Forces families. Sixteen overseas pupils when we visited, mainly from Hong Kong and Korea. Not a snobby school – very down-to-earth. Notable old girls include Dame Shirley Williams, Caroline Gledhill (first woman to receive Young Engineer of the Year award), Frances Ashcroft (first woman to receive Fellow of Royal Society award), Natalie Clein and Kate Royal (see above).

T

Entrance: Senior school holds entrance exam in January for the following September. Most Talbot Heath juniors progress through to senior school but all must pass exam. At 11 girls sit papers in English, maths and verbal reasoning and at 12, 13 and 14 there is a French exam too. Not too horrific a hurdle: despite its reputation as 'academic', the ability range is wide. Girls come from local preps The Park, Castle Court, Dumpton, Talbot House and Durlston Court, or from 'local church primaries'. Entry at sixth form requires a minimum of five A*-C grades at GCSE and at least Bs in subjects to be studied at A level. Entrance to the tennis academy is highly selective.

Exit: Three-quarters of girls stay on for sixth form – those who don't tend to move on to Brockenhurst Sixth Form College or the Bournemouth or Poole grammars, often to do subjects not on offer here. Virtually all sixth form go to university – Exeter, Birmingham, Bristol, Bath currently popular choices. Few gap years (three last year).

Money matters: Academic, all-rounder, music and sport scholarships available at 11+, 12+, 13+ and sixth form, plus bursaries (currently received by 23 per cent of girls in the senior school) including one fee-free place each year. Discounts for Forces children and clergy.

Remarks: With two girls-only state grammar schools within 20 minutes' drive, Talbot Heath needs to offer something above and beyond. And it does: a wholesome and sheltered environment, academic rigour, musical excellence, reasonable fees, and a safe landing pad for girls who didn't quite make the grammar school cut. Lots of good things going on here.

TASIS – The American School in England

Linked school: TASIS – The American School in England (Lower School)

Coldharbour Lane, Thorpe, Surrey, TW20 8TE

• Pupils: 750 boys and girls • Ages: 3–19 • Non–denom • Fees: Day £9,880–£20,600; Boarding £35,110 pa • Independent

Tel: 01932 582316
Email: ukadmissions@tasisengland.org
Website: www.tasisengland.org

Headmaster: Since 2010, Mr Michael McBrien BA (counselling, psychology, and communication), MA (education), previously in US as head of Baylor School, other teaching and leadership posts at the University of California, Berkeley, Babson College, and Frontier Academy. Three years after a series of successive heads, he's brought some welcome stability and is spearheading a TASIS community-wide strategic planning process, and review of the entire curriculum.

Mr McBrien stays connected to students by hosting, with his wife Betsy, 'Taco Tuesday', which grew from when his own son was at TASIS inviting his classmates over for supper, and has become a regular event for day and boarding students; with fiestas for younger ones. With an extended contract and no plans to move on, Mr McBrien appears confident, parents find him approachable, and he comes across as excited by what he's doing. Parents commenting on recent turnover in school leadership seem to feel that things are on an even keel under his stewardship. One parent was impressed that after meeting him briefly (with many others) at orientation, when they passed on campus a few weeks later, Mr McBrien stopped to chat and ask how the family was settling. Has two grown daughters and two sons – the youngest a TASIS graduate.

Academic matters: The primary programme (ages 3-9) is based on a 'Core Knowledge' curriculum – with specialist teachers for music, art, PE, with lessons in technology and library skills. Parents like the approach to homework, saying TASIS teachers are 'very forgiving and highly supportive' teaching children in a 'more academic' learning environment. The littlest ones from nursery (half day) through pre-k have a gentle introduction to school described by one enthusiastic parent as the 'best kept secret, with its multicultural aspect; lots of learning taking place and investigation through play providing an unbelievable foundation year'.

Middle school (ages 10-13) emphasises independent study using the house system, peer leaders, and advisory system. Besides the usual subjects, middle school electives include Latin, photography, yearbook, journalism and broadcast journalism. One parent, a zealous convert from British key stage 1 describes the primary programme as 'holistic and inter-disciplinary', nice foreign language element, comprehensive content yet fun and flexible that inspires a love of learning and promotes 'self-learning' versus 'memorisation rote teaching'.

Upper school is designed to prepare students for university entry and features US Advanced Placement or IB Diploma courses (taught separately, with the exception of a few language classes). The TASIS High School Diploma follows the US curriculum, but is designed to accommodate second language English speakers, or may suit short-term students who come for a semester.

Spanish introduced in primary, and while parents like this, some (non-English speakers or from bilingual families) feel the language provision could be stronger for the international children and lament the discontinuation of a native-Spanish programme, apparently a result of a drop in mother tongue speakers in the lower school. Students choose between French or Spanish in middle school with an optional school language trip to Spain and France. IB diploma Italian, Russian, English, Spanish, and German are offered as mother tongue, another dozen are available as self-taught, and Spanish and French are offered as a second language. EAL is in place throughout the school.

Mostly good and some outstanding exam scores. In 2013, mid-range SAT scores were: math 560-680, critical reading 490-660, and writing 540-660 (32 per cent were ESL). The mid-range composite score achieved by those taking the ACT (9 percent ESL) was 23-29. Over the past three years, IB average was 33 points, with a 98 per cent pass rate. Nineteen AP subjects offered in 2013; all achieved three or more points in art history, French, Spanish, music theory, calculus BC, and physics C – mechanics; computer science A was less impressive, at low end with 57 per cent achieving three or more.

Average class size is 15, maximum about 18; teacher to student ratio is 1:6 Average age of teachers is upper forties, over half at TASIS for over 10 years, with retirement of long termers contributing to recent staff turnover.

For an additional charge, learning support available up to three lessons per week for children with diagnosed mild learning differences. Some language requirements may be deferred for students with special educational needs.

Games, options, the arts: Varsity sports include basketball, cross-country, dance, golf, lacrosse, soccer, tennis, and volleyball as well as boys' teams in rugby and baseball and girls' teams in cheering and softball.

TASIS is known for its strong music, art and drama programmes, but Mr. McBrien feels this needs a fresh look to see if there are any tweaks that can be made to upper school academic workloads and timetables to make it easier for all students to take advantage of these great activities.

T

Loads of school trips have always been a part of TASIS: all boarders go somewhere during the October half term for a week (meaning they don't have to travel home), mostly to European destinations. These trips are optional for day students but many choose to take part. The humanities trip, related to ancient civilisations, to places like Greece or Florence and Rome is recommended for all seniors and IB students.

Big emphasis on community service. Students travel regularly to volunteer for Romania-based projects; raise money for a charity helping children born with cleft palate; volunteer to help local elderly and disabled children.

Plenty of after-school activities daily but also on Saturdays with a range of team sports organised by the school with lots of parent involvement. Parents say that there are so many older day students on campus doing this and that, it's hard to distinguish which ones are boarding and which are not.

Background and atmosphere: TASIS England was founded in 1976, a sister school to TASIS in Switzerland, by Mary Crist Fleming, and is controlled by the TASIS Foundation, a Swiss, independent, not-for-profit foundation. The School's board of directors oversees governance, policies and strategies, and finances.

The campus is located in the village of Thorpe, close to Virginia Water and Ascot and handy for Heathrow and Gatwick. TASIS sprawls over two adjoining estates, each with its own Georgian manor houses and assorted listed centuries-old out-buildings – looking like something from a National Trust calendar. TASIS seems pretty connected to the village, not always the case with international schools.

Thorpe Place, the main building, looks out over an expansive lawn and lake with sports fields and a baseball diamond beyond, and contains the large dining room, a smaller canteen with Starbucks coffee bar, offices and beautiful rooms for high school seminars or parent coffees. Upper floors have newly-refurbished dorm rooms, many overlooking the lake. Other cottages contain student rooms, lounges with microwaves, fridges, and laundry.

The library is in the former splendidly converted chapel with leather sofas creating a comfortable reading nook at one end. A new dorm is under construction (the plan is to have all the boarding on one side of the campus). Another project is the labour of love of a recently-retired history teacher – the restoration of a hidden walled garden and greenhouse, shared by villagers who have allotments there. Students grow fruit and veg which they harvest, cook and eat in the dining hall, or use to make jams for fundraising projects. The wildlife pond is used to learn about creepy crawlies, the bee hive produces honey. The star attraction is the Beatrix Potter garden complete with play house and Peter Rabbit for the youngest children who regularly visit.

The other side of the campus centers around Thorpe House, where the primary school is located with its own library; a modern addition accommodates classrooms, lunchroom and offices, with more classrooms in the converted coach house. Pretty incredible facilities generally, in fact, including new buildings with science and technology labs, purpose-designed music and practice rooms, a great theatre that gets lots of use, an art gallery, studios, dark room etc. all full of students' work. There's also a large gym with dance studio, exercise rooms, and changing rooms conveniently located for the additional sports fields beyond.

The youngest children are in a self-contained chalet, 'Frog Hollow', on the edge of a grove of trees, with access to their own playground.

With boarders, food service is 24/7, and compulsory unless there are dietary restrictions. Upper school eat in the dining room overlooking the grounds, tables spill out onto the terrace for al fresco eating in the nicer weather. Middle school uses the primary lunchroom. Food is healthy, balanced, and varied, but not much to rave about and a bit too 'English school meal' for international tastes ('You can always order pizza delivery!'). An advantage to the boarding dimension is that day students staying late or coming to study can have breakfast or dinner there.

Pastoral care and discipline: Tutor groups meet daily for 30 minutes for problem solving, brainstorming and relaxed chat with peers and teacher or doing homework. Tutors serve as advisors, the first port of call for families with concerns, and the student stays with the same tutor through to graduation. Parents like the simplicity of this, knowing that there is someone on the inside who really knows their kids. Boarding and day student prefects provide peer support for students.

The boarding programme is supervised by a long-serving teacher. Live-in teachers (some couples) serve as boarding house parents, with other teachers living on campus or locally doing their bit during evenings and weekends. Students who speak different languages are well mixed in to speed up their English acquisition and confidence. Boarders are well-supervised, and say 'it's becoming more strict, but it's open-minded'; parents say 'it's more carrot than stick'. Boarders are required to stay on campus Friday nights, no one is allowed to go off to visit people who are under 25 (no overnights with cousins or older siblings in uni). Day families invite boarders for dinner, to work on school projects or to stay overnight, which makes for a nice change, and there is a good system in place to keep track of the comings and goings.

'Safe Hands' is a life-skills programme designed with boarders in mind. The school will try to make things work, but if students repeatedly offend, they're out. A parent saw even during the first visit that, 'Students were presentable, polite and respectful yet friendly. The school culture was tangible and appealing.' The only co-ed international school in London with uniforms, parents appreciate that 'there is no thought to the fashion stakes and who's wearing what label this week.'

Pupils and parents: Two thirds are American but community includes numerous other nationalities of expat families – German, Spanish, Canadian, Russian, Italian, Japanese, Chinese, and Brazilian – on assignment in the UK.

Parents love the PIRC (Parents Information Resource Committee) with its own library and speakers who advise on successfully raising a globe-trotting expat family and which even maintains a list of baby sitters. The TPA (TASIS Parent Association) always have something on the go; during the summer they work with admissions to match new families through the Buddy Family Program. 'They connected and we Skyped before we arrived; shared some family pub lunches after we got here'.

Boarders who arrive with lower-level English speak of a different experience; the first weeks are challenging and it's hard to assimilate, but once they adjust they are happy. A new scheme to assign freshman (9th grade) boarders to a buddy family has started to address this.

A TPA boarding coordinator liaises with boarding parents by sending regular emails so they know what's going on, helping to explain college counselling, fundraising initiatives. New families' picnics coincide with boarder drop off weekend. TASIS parents have plenty to do... there's even a group for 'non-working accompanying dads' called 'Trophy Husbands Club'.

The bus service extends to Camberley in the southwest, Beaconsfield in the northwest, into Richmond and Kingston in the East, and Woking and Weybridge in the south... which lets you know the social network is spread across the map. Parents, be ready to drive.

Entrance: Early application recommended; students must be re-invited yearly. Admissions based on previous reports, references, student questionnaire, parent statement. English testing if deemed necessary. The school tries to be sensitive to the sibling issue.

Exit: College counsellors work with students starting in grade 9 helping with course selection, development of a student portfolio of work, and management of university applications.

Over half of the graduates head to North America, many stay in the UK, or head to Europe and beyond. Recent university destinations include: American U, George Washington, MIT, NYU, Notre Dame, Queens, Penn State, Princeton, MIT, Vanderbilt; in Canada, U of British Columbia; in the UK, Bath, Edinburgh, King's College, Royal Holloway, Oxford Brookes; others: Keio University (Japan), IE University (Spain), Bocconi University (Italy).

Money matters: No endowment; financial aid available on the basis of merit, need, and available funds (approximately £150,000–£200,000 given annually in financial aid).

Some fundraising initiatives by the Parents Association and the School, but parents say they are not 'bombarded'.

Remarks: Parents say it's a fantastic school, the ethos and the character values they develop are what make it special. A critical mass of international boarders add an interesting flavour to this sound American school in the Surrey countryside.

Taunton School

Linked school: Taunton Preparatory School & Pre Prep and Nursery

Staplegrove Road, Taunton, Somerset, TA2 6AD

• Pupils: 565 pupils; 255 boarders. 320 boys; 245 girls • Ages: 13–18 • Inter-denom • Fees: Boarding £12,030–£30,840; Day £6,195–£16,485 pa • Independent

Tel: 01823 703700
Email: registrar@tauntonschool.co.uk
Website: www.tauntonschool.co.uk

Headmaster: Since 2005, Dr John Newton MA, PhD, FCollP and DipMS (late 40s). Educated at Manchester Grammar School and typical of that breed of classy northerners, thence to Merton College Oxford before doing his doctorate in 'organisational culture in independent schools'. There can't be many of those around. His own track record speaks volumes: a working-class lad from Denton in Greater Manchester, he wears his provincial heart on his sleeve, is passionate about Manchester City Football Club and has 'Meritocrat' imprinted on his forehead. And, my goodness, he talks a good fight! He has four young children, all at Taunton; his wife, Catherine, is a qualified primary school teacher and musician.

Dr Newton served a worthy apprenticeship as Director of Studies and a housemaster at Eastbourne College and Head of Modern Languages at Bradfield College. He is also something of a Renaissance man, fluent in Russian and French, plays the tuba, sings in the school choirs has been heavily involved in the CCF, and coaching rugby, hockey, cricket, fives, rowing and football. He is an accomplished public speaker and educational evangelist. He took great pride in telling us that when he played host to Michael Gove on a visit to Taunton, he managed to get him alone in a taxi for ten minutes and offered the Secretary of State his views on current educational policy. No doubt Mr Gove was all ears.

As befits his meritocratic principles, Dr Newton is a powerful advocate of development of opportunities for girls in all walks of life and the promotion of a global view of the future, especially with respect to development and resource issues and new areas of growth like Asia and Africa. Above all, he espouses a burning desire to see Taunton School flourish.

John Newton may be a formidable presence, but he is not an ogre. Parents and pupils respect him immensely, his rhetoric inspires them and they are in awe of his work-rate and commitment to their future. Pupils also relish the pizza lunches to which he regularly treats them, in the certain knowledge that a school marches on its stomach.

Academic matters: Results pretty sound considering the non-selective intake: 61 per cent A*-B at A level and over 40 per cent A*/A at GCSE. The IB Diploma points average is 34 (world average is 30 out of a total of 45).

Alongside the IB, Taunton maintains a broad curriculum culminating in 23 subjects at A level, including photography, music technology and critical thinking (a school passion and something of a hallmark). Mandarin and Chinese literature are offered as part of the IB syllabus.

Taunton's goal seems to be to produce young people from John Newton's mould: highly motivated, fully developed and ready to meet the challenges of the 21st century. Taunton may not be a strongly religious school, but there is whiff of Victorian 'muscular Christianity' in its ether: 'we believe we should prepare pupils for the next 50 years of their lives, not just for the next five. Our job is to equip them with values and experiences for a future anywhere in the world.' Dr Newton echoes this evolutionary zeal, 'I am not interested in producing children who are clones of their parents; I want them to be themselves.'

In keeping with its commitment to being prepared for change, Taunton is planning a radical overhaul of teaching in science and technology. New facilities for departments of engineering and life sciences will be created to make the academic structure more relevant to new technology and contemporary employment prospects. Scheduled to begin in 2014, it is an absorbing venture. New courses will include: robotics, electronics and computer programming plus co-curricular projects like biochemistry and green power. Courses in food and nutrition are also planned as is the possible transfer of psychology from humanities to the sciences. So far, so impressive, but for any readers who struggled with O level physics it may present a daunting picture of the modern world.

Games, options, the arts: If the headmaster is an inspiring example of a successful all-rounder, the heads of art, music and drama are also role models for their pupils. They spoke with passion about the importance of their departments and the value of their subjects to the youngsters. We were treated to Bach on the chapel organ (a spontaneous moment, not a pre-arranged performance), a drama rehearsal by a group of boys who all seemed to be in touch with their inner Kenneth Branagh and witnessed myriad examples of paintings, sculptures, installations and photography.

The design technology department is a delight, with tools and machines from modern digital gizmos to old fashioned benches, vices and even a huge anvil a traditional blacksmith would be proud of. It is also the proud manufacturer of a 'Greenpower' car. When we asked about the teaching of craft skills, the answer was short and sweet, 'The pupils confront the task, work out what skills they need to meet it and then acquire them; they could involve a laser or a carpenter's mallet and chisel.'

Sport and exercise are high priority for staff as well as pupils: the registrar is an ultra-runner and the head of classics, in addition to a PhD in classical literature, has the muscles of a body-builder! When he's not describing the deeds of the heroes of the Trojan War, he can be found pumping iron in the school's new fitness centre, an amazing facility that looks like a private members' gym and which earns outside revenue for the school.

There is an abundance of more traditional fields of play, including 20 tennis courts, three gymnasiums, two swimming pools and a pair of Astroturf pitches. Competitive sport thrives

T

at all levels and county-level participation is given precedence over school fixtures. As a consequence, results are excellent and individual achievements impressive.

The range of extra-curricular options at Taunton is fascinating. Radio astronomy, greenpower, rifle shooting, Warhammer and vocal funk are just a few of the more unusual on offer. There's also healthy uptake for D of E and CCF and we were assured that the senior wind band was an ensemble of musicians, not a nickname for the staff common room.

Background and atmosphere: Taunton's grand Neo-Gothic Victorian exterior conforms to the popular image of a traditional independent school. The tall clock tower and spire overlooking immaculate lawns and flowerbeds is archetypal, likewise the long corridor of gothic arches and wood panelling. But don't be fooled, this school is far from being educationally conservative, declaring, '...we have little time for social pretence,' and the headmaster is proud that it is a school that has 'no snobs and no yobs'. Typically, a recent trip to China was subsidised at a fixed price of £200 per head to ensure that as many children as possible had the chance to go.

Established in 1847 as an inter-denominational foundation for the sons of non-conformists and co-ed since 1973, Taunton still has a radical feel. Overtly non-selective, the banner headline for its very glossy, highly professional marketing literature (also emblazoned on its huge fleet of buses) is: 'Offering More'. For that, read 'more' than a narrow commitment to academic success; 'more' than sport; 'more' than a single focus on a particular kind of education. Taunton's goal seems to be to produce young people from John Newton's mould: highly motivated, fully developed people ready to meet the challenges of the 21st century.

Staff, parents and pupils alike claimed that, despite its strong work ethic and drive to succeed, Taunton is a very friendly and relaxed place to live and work. Our experience, from two nourishing visits to the dining hall and a parents' evening, where we were left to roam and natter to our hearts' content, suggest that Taunton has got the balance exactly right. The staff mingled jovially, the parents smiled appreciatively and the youngsters behaved like responsible young adults.

Our charming 'minder' was a model English gentleman, except that he was Bulgarian, a product of the school's strong international perspective. Taunton International School, a 9 to 17 adjunct to the main school, serves as a proving ground for foreign students preparing to join the English system, and runs a programme for Taunton youngsters hoping to go to university in America.

Pastoral care and discipline: The core of the pastoral system at Taunton is the five boarding houses and six day houses. Each housemaster/mistress is responsible for each pupil's well-being and progress and is the first point of contact for parents. They are supported by a house assistant and a team of house tutors. There is a chaplain, a health centre and school prefects. Peer monitoring is encouraged and an 'independent listener' is available by phone.

Boarders represent 45 per cent of the school population, most stay at weekends when there is a rota of activities which includes: conservation projects, clay pigeon shooting, cycle trips along the local canal, house cookery, fishing, house outings to theme parks and castle visits and picnics. All very jolly.

School is savvy enough to realise that society's ills lurk everywhere and that to keep them at the gates takes constant vigilance. Dr Newton believes that experienced house staff are vital. They must be able to 'read the tea leaves' and sniff and smell for problems when they are brewing, not when it is too late. Reassuringly, he does not pretend that Taunton is free of the problems that afflict us all, but is confident that most are nipped in the bud, or, on the occasions when they become more serious, are dealt with quickly and appropriately. Parents concurred with this, 'The school is relaxed, but the children know where the boundaries are'. The young people we spoke to agreed, 'The senior staff set a good example, they're easy to talk to, but you respect them because we all know how much they do for us'. 'Most problems are dealt with in our houses, even if they've come in from outside. It's very unusual for anyone to be unhappy here'.

Pupils and parents: Taunton is a modern school for modern times. We met confident, articulate young people and grateful and contented parents. The staff were evangelists for their subjects and it was easy to imagine the positive impact they have on their students.

Parents are a cross-section of society from a huge catchment area; bus routes run from as far away as Bristol, Exeter, Yeovil and Minehead. We met farmers, teachers, nurses, small business owners, civil servants and military personnel; all were gushing in their praise: 'lovely school', 'good kids', 'the head's a star, the staff are great'. Several parents praised the school's inclusivity, 'Even though we live on Exmoor, we thought it was worth the effort. Both our boys have flourished, especially one of them who had dyslexia, he's flying now.'

John Newton feels his mission has reached its first set of goals. He has achieved long-term financial stability and built a business that makes a surplus (not a profit) for further investment. The next stage will see the school take an imaginative leap into the future of the sort typified by his engineering/natural sciences initiative. This he sees as exciting, but also daunting.

Entrance: Seventy per cent of Taunton's intake comes from its own preparatory school at 13. External entrants take Common Entrance but school insists that the interview is more critical, as is the report from the child's previous head.

Entry at 16+ normally conditional on a minimum of five GCSEs at grade A* to C, but, again, the interview is also important.

Exit: Up to a quarter of students leave after GCSE. Taunton does not offer vocational courses so it believes most leavers at this stage have reached their academic ceiling and need to go elsewhere to continue their education or vocation. Post A level, 96 per cent of leavers go to universities or colleges (UK and abroad). One or two to Oxbridge.

Money matters: There are scholarships at 11, 13 and 16 for academic, music, art, sport and for all-rounders.

Remarks: Our view is that prospective parents can be confident that whatever the future holds, John Newton and his team at Taunton School will give your children the best possible chance of meeting its challenges.

Teesside High School

Linked school: Teesside High School – Preparatory Department

The Avenue, Eaglescliffe, Stockton-on-Tees, Cleveland, TS16 9AT

- Pupils: 120 girls, 80 boys • Ages: 11–18 • Non-denom
- Fees: £3,300–£11,955 pa • Independent

Tel: 01642 782095
Email: info@teessidehigh.co.uk
Website: www.teessidehigh.co.uk

Head Teacher: Since 2012, Ms Deborah Duncan, previously head of the English School in Cyprus. Read French and Spanish at Durham, PGCE at York and masters in educational management. Does consultancy work for the Association of School and College Leaders (ASCL published her book, Work-Life Balance: Myth or Possibility). As if to prove the fact, she enjoys music and is a member of the local operatic society. Has a daughter in the prep school.

Since day one she has focused her attention on running a tight ship, bringing greater rigour, strategies for stretching, peer observation and collaborative coaching to raise the game. She knows pupils and parents well and school remains hot on pastoral care under her strong but sound leadership. Teaches French in senior school and prep. Pupils describe her as a 'hands-on head', approachable yet commanding respect. Grateful parents say she is 'moving the school in the right direction'.

Academic matters: Good. In 2013 86 per cent of pupils achieved five or more A*-C grades including maths and English at GCSE (40 per cent A*/A). At A level, 50 per cent grades A*-B. Traditional academic curriculum. Option of three separate sciences at GCSE or dual award science course. All 11 to 13 year olds take separate sciences, three languages (French, German and Latin – Spanish also available as an extra), RE, music, food and nutrition, economics and IT.

Free access to IT suite during school hours and each pupil has own email address at school. Staff using iPads to enrich and challenge – homework may occasionally come straight to mobiles via an app. And just to show that they are covering both the ancient and modern here, gifted and talented pupils enjoy Ancient Greek in readiness for performing a Greek tragedy in the school grounds.

Small classes, some very small at sixth form. Average class size 14. Experienced staff – over half have ten or more years experience with the school. Very low turnover. Some mixed ability teaching for 11-year-olds but from year 8 pupils are set for maths, science and languages.

Homework ranges from 90 minutes a night for 11-year olds to three hours a night for sixth form. Pupils get report of some kind every term, with full report sent out at end of year. Special needs co-ordinator – support for dyslexia and dyspraxia.

Games, options, the arts: Sport is strong and compulsory for all – several county standard players and a silver equestrian medal for a former pupil at London 2012. Sports include athletics, tennis, football, hockey, rugby, badminton, cricket and canoeing. Superb fitness suite for those less inclined to team sports.

All take part in wide range of activities – including origami, golf, bridge and many more besides. These are sensibly accommodated in an extra long lunchtime break, which allows pupils to eat and enjoy enrichment activities too. All-weather sports pitch and sports hall used throughout the day for teaching and at lunchtime for extra activities. Most year 10 pupils take D of E awards.

Music and drama very strong. Well-equipped room with plenty of keyboards, instruments and computers for budding composers and a new drama and dance studio. Many play a musical instrument and there is a choir, orchestra and jazz band. Large number take speech and drama awards. Art is very popular, paintings and sculpture on show everywhere. House competitions fiercely fought in a wide range of disciplines, including singing, sport, photography and Masterchef.

Background and atmosphere: Teesside High was founded as a girls' school in 1970 when Queen Victoria High School and Cleveland School amalgamated. School follows the 'diamond' model of education where boys and girls are educated together up to year 5 in the prep school and in the sixth form, and separately in between. Slightly more girls than boys – 60/40 – but no one seems to mind and therefore it doesn't seem to matter. We met plenty of bright, articulate boys able to hold

their own and not looking or feeling like a minority. Plenty of success in boys' sports underpins this. Non-selective intake (and proud of it) yet still punching well above its weight in a number of areas.

Set in 19 acres bordering the River Tees, with stunning views of the Cleveland Hills and a stone's throw from the delightfully tempting shops and coffee emporiums of picturesque Yarm. School is hidden from sight, tucked away down The Avenue, an approach road bordered by private houses and a retirement home. Main buildings sit neatly in well-kept grounds. Brightly coloured picket fence surrounds the prep school. Lovely grounds, with river frontage, large pond and newly created woodland school used for outdoor teaching in wide range of 'low-risk' activities for pupils of all ages. Recently unearthed air raid bunker in the grounds is being refurbished to bring history lessons to life.

Classrooms and corridors have an air of calm, unusually clean and tidy, lots of good work on display. Food is 'better than good', say pupils. Dining room operates on a cafeteria system, with bright blue tables and murals painted by pupils and choice of hot and cold meals. Halal food on menu and even though this is a day school, breakfast and tea are available too.

Sixth formers have their own car park and there is a real buzz of anticipation about their new sixth form building, which will include teaching rooms, private study areas, common room and conference facilities. Due for completion 2014.

Pastoral care and discipline: The school prides itself on being 'a community in which everyone is treated with respect and understanding and where all talents and gifts are nurtured and valued.' Form tutors play key role in guiding pupils. School is multi-faith and there is a small prayer room.

School sets store by community projects – Christmas parties for OAPs, charity quizzes and visits to local hospice. Dialogue and discussion are strongly encouraged. Head pupil and deputy head pupil run school council – each year group has three reps and recent innovations include chilled water supply and napkins in dining room. Buddy system introduced to encourage older pupils to befriend and help younger pupils. Open forum for parents to raise issues once a term. Behaviour is good – no vandalism, graffiti or discipline problems, says head, just occasional high spirits in corridors. School has introduced extended day to help working parents – now open from 7.45am till 6pm. Also runs popular holiday clubs for three to 13-year-olds during school holidays.

Pupils and parents: Parents are mostly medics, accountants, lawyers and local business people. Lots of first-time buyers, though a scattering of alumni offspring too. A small number of overseas pupils live with local families. We spoke to several parents who had moved their children from the maintained sector and were 'delighted' at their children's 'increased levels of interest and achievement'. Parents spoke about the very positive care given to children and the 'individualised' education, enthusing that 'there is so much to offer beyond the curriculum'. Pupils travel in by bus (organised in-house) from 25-mile radius, from as far afield as south Durham and north Yorkshire. Former pupils include broadcasters Shiulie Ghosh (formerly of ITV News) and Pam Royle (Tyne Tees and Border TV).

Entrance: At 11, all pupils (including those from the prep) sit verbal reasoning paper and emotional intelligence questionnaire. Two-thirds entering senior school come from prep, a third from primary schools. Pupils entering sixth form need at least six GCSE passes (preferably grade B and above).

Exit: About ten per cent leave post-GCSE. Almost all sixth form leavers go to university. York, Sheffield and Leeds are currently popular choices.

Money matters: School offers means-tested bursaries each year on a first come, first served basis. Scholarships and exhibitions available for academic ability, music (and sport in sixth form and prep).

Remarks: 'Everything is possible' is the school motto and the school certainly feels that way. Staff and pupils at this unpretentious, hardworking school exude a very special charm with a refreshing lack of arrogance.

Thames Christian College

Wye Street, London, SW11 2HB

- Pupils: 120, 60/40 boys/girls • Ages: 11–16 • Fees: £11,700 pa
- Independent

Tel: 020 7228 3933
Email: info@thameschristiancollege.org.uk
Website: www.thameschristiancollege.org.uk

Executive Head: Since September 2006, Stephen Holsgrove (early fifties) PhD. Studied engineering and ICT; before setting up Thames Christian College he worked as a development director of a software engineering company. Married to Catherine, three daughters, who all attended the school, two are now pursuing their own careers, the youngest is studying performing arts. Catherine is the school registrar and runs all the administration. Head and governors are all committed to making a difference to future generation's education and lives. It is hoped that in the future Thames will be a model for further similar establishments.

Academic matters: A non-selective school doing extremely well by its pupils, who mostly outperform their predicted grades. In 2013, 36 per cent of GCSE grades A*/A. The school commits to ensuring that, wherever possible, everyone achieves at least a C grade in English and maths. The ethos is to bring out the best in each individual and encourage pupils to find and develop their strengths. All pupils are monitored, small classes, setting for some subjects, as well as small group teaching for those who need it. Head of English is a bestselling author of English curriculum materials for 11 to 16-year-olds, so ideally placed to help everybody achieve the highest results. Good range of GCSE and IGCSEs subjects to choose from; the options are tailored to each year group's preferences. Alongside maths, all study personal finance to prepare for running their own budgets, be it financing university or setting up a business. Everyone studies Spanish and there is an annual trip to Spain for a mixture of sightseeing and intensive Spanish lessons. Lunchtime and after-school enrichment classes offer the opportunity to study in more depth. Ideal for those who need stretching. The school strives to broaden young minds with a variety of cross-curricular activities, eg medieval murder mysteries to solve, design a Tudor king's football kit and film making. Thames is building its reputation for understanding how different types of pupils learn best. Whilst doing very well for its brightest pupils, it is also able to bring on pupils with specific learning differences: dyslexia, dyspraxia, mild Aspergers and those who have not fared well in much larger establishments. CreSTeD listed, the school has a dedicated team of learning support teachers. It prides itself on attracting well-qualified teachers, some of whom also work in their own industries, giving pupils an insight into the world of work and how certain skills and qualifications can translate into careers. Parents feel they are prepared to go the extra mile to assist pupils in their learning.

Games, options, the arts: Excellent art department nurtures much budding talent and achieves outstanding results. Art curriculum has recently been redesigned to give pupils the option of taking two art GCSEs, graphic communications and fine art. The graphics element includes a brief designed by a creative director of an advertising agency, who is a visiting lecturer at the school. Part of this course involves pupils having to pitch their ideas for client presentations. Design and technology curriculum introduces pupils to ceramics, woodwork, sculpture and textiles. PE teacher and various specialist coaches offer a range of different sporting activities and team games. The school uses local sports centre facilities and the various courts and pitches at Wandsworth common. Strong drama, led by a working actress; pupils study the LAMDA Bronze Certificate and other LAMDA qualifications. New keyboards and mixing desks are part of the update to the music department, there is a band and choir, and two professional singers are amongst the staff. Tuition on any instrument can be arranged and many pupils choose to have individual instrumental lessons. The school has links with a primary school to give pupils the opportunity to work with children in the community. Community projects involve drama, music, art, sewing and a mentoring scheme. Friday afternoons are dedicated to clubs. Each term a selection of clubs and societies: eg inventions club, textiles, debating, current affairs and creative writing.

Background and atmosphere: Founded by Dr Stephen Holsgrove and his wife Catherine, Thames Christian College opened its doors just over a decade ago in 2000 with 12 pupils; today it accommodates around 120. Having viewed secondary school choices in London for their own children, the Holsgroves decided there was room for something a little different, and decided to set up their own school. The underlying principles of the school involve individuals and values alongside top service delivery. Their aim to provide suitable education in a safe environment has paid off: the school expands year-on-year. The main premises are a converted library, and they have leased additional neighbouring buildings. Exterior of the premises is utilitarian in appearance; the interior has been sympathetically adapted into bright and welcoming classrooms. The atmosphere is about hard work and caring for each other rather than flashy facilities.

Pastoral care and discipline: As a Christian foundation, the schools ethos centres on mutual respect, Christian values and understanding others' opinions. Pupils of all faiths and backgrounds who share these values are welcome. School rules are very clear and non-negotiable, expectations are high: behave sensibly, work to the best of your ability and be considerate to others at all times. Teachers need to be able to channel their energies into teaching rather than having to deal with discipline issues. 'We do have strict rules here,' say pupils, 'and things like bullying or any type of unkindness are not tolerated.' Lunches are a treat as the caterer is their well-known neighbour Levi Roots, creator of Reggae Reggae sauces.

Pupils and parents: Wide catchment area: families come from all over London and Surrey – the school is located a few minutes' walk from Clapham Junction. Pupils come from a variety of backgrounds; ethnic and social mix typical of the surrounding areas. Parents are encouraged to be involved and work collaboratively with the school, particularly with fund-raising and religious festivals and celebrations. Thought to be a committed bunch, with shared values and hopes for their children's futures.

Entrance: 11+ test to assess potential and ability. Non-selective.

Exit: At 16+ most continue to A-level or IB at London day schools eg JAGS, Kings Wimbledon, Emanuel, Esher College, Richmond

T

College or popular state schools Tiffin's, Greycoat Hospital and Graveney. Some go on to study vocational qualifications at the Brit school and the Performance Preparation Academy. Odd one to boarding school.

Money matters: A not-for-profit organisation; fees are inclusive making them very competitive in comparison with other independent schools. Small number of bursaries available at the head's discretion

Remarks: Small is beautiful. A unique school set up to meet the needs of individuals. Able children are stretched, and for those who find school more of a challenge there is plenty of support

The Thomas Hardye School

Queen's Avenue, Dorchester, Dorset, DT1 2ET

• Pupils: 2,300 boys and girls, all day • Ages: 13–18 • Non–denom
• State

Tel: 01305 266064
Email: admin@thomas-hardye.dorset.sch.uk
Website: www.thomas-hardye.dorset.sch.uk

Headteacher: Since 2011, Mr Michael Foley BA MEd (late forties), previously head of Great Cornard Upper School in Suffolk. He was educated at St Mary's College, University of London and at the University of Cambridge. He is a very keen sports enthusiast, especially enjoying skiing and football, and is also a Crystal Palace fan. He is married with four children.

Academic matters: Creditable results here with 33 per cent A*/A, 64 per cent A*-B grades at A level, and 69 per cent getting 5+ A*-C grades at GCSE, including maths and English, in 2013. IB students averaged 33 points. Maths particularly strong and far and away the most popular A level subject here. School points out that there are more pupils doing A level maths here than in all the schools in the rest of the county combined. Science popular but results a little disappointing for a school that became a science college in 2002, although school remarks that science results have improved significantly and the school has the 2010 UK Young Scientist of the Year. It is now a High Performing Specialist School and has two other specialisms – humanities and SEN. Ofsted report so over the top with gushing praise that it makes embarrassing reading. Has been given every award going: Charter Mark, Schools Curriculum Award, Investor in People, Arts Mark Gold, Leading Edge School, Education Extra Award, School Achievement Awards ... you get the picture.

Being so large allows the school to provide some unusual subjects, including Latin and dance at GCSE, and sociology, dance, electronics, food technology, travel & tourism and accounting at A level. Also offers the CACHE diploma in nursery nursing. On top of all this, Hardye's is a teaching training school, working in partnership with Exeter and other universities. IT a sore point for some pupils: though well-equipped with swarms of new boxes, monitors, interactive whiteboards etc, pupils speak of perpetual printer problems down on the shop floor – while the head's printer purrs like a dream ...'we believe that our printer options have improved significantly – much now centrally linked – and my printer is very old!'

Some 180 pupils take advantage of SEN provision here, ranging from moderate learning difficulties (the majority) to a handful of pupils in wheelchairs. The school has a physiotherapy room, a unit for the hearing impaired, two large SEN rooms and several specialist SEN staff. And for pupils who just need a boost,

there are after-school homework help sessions – well attended 'and no stigma attached,' said a pupil. A few parents of kids with minor problems (eg poor handwriting, organisational issues) felt the school could do more.

Games, options, the arts: Super sports facilities – floodlit Astro, sports hall with climbing wall, fitness suite, verdant playing fields, plus use of the facilities at the Dorchester Rugby Club and neighbouring leisure centre (two swimming pools). New swimming pool complex for dual use between the school and community. Rugby keenly played, along with football (boys and girls), cross-country, netball, athletics, traditional cricket and swimming. Vast numbers of pupils to choose from means the school's 'won' column contentedly exceeds its 'lost'. A good range of minor sports eg water polo and kayaking, plus outward bound activities. Drama, music, art and dance are all buzzing. Music department stands out, with recording studio and music tech room. Music tours, two orchestras, school music festival, lots of rock bands, annual joint concert with Imperial College, steel band, chapel choir – 'you name a cathedral, they've sung in it!' says the head. Drama in own theatre, RSC visits every second year. Small museum area displays some excellent artwork. THTV, the school's in-house television channel, shows pupil-produced programmes on a plasma-screen TV in the heart of the school, known as the Spine. Lots of charity do-gooding and recycling.

Background and atmosphere: Thomas Hardye founded the first free school in Dorchester in 1569 (the school has nothing to do with Dorset novelist Thomas Hardy who confusingly attended school in Dorchester in the 1850s, in case you were wondering). Doubled in size in 1992 when amalgamated with local girls' school. Is now enormous, heaving, multi-layered campus. Feels more like a small university than a comprehensive – owing partly to the absence of 11 and 12 year-olds, a key element of Hardye's uniqueness. Sixth form immense. 'We think it is the largest of any comprehensive in the country,' says the head, which gives you some idea. Just in case any other school is plotting to eclipse them, Hardye's is in the process of expanding its sixth form further still, until they will be the ... SUPREME ... MASTERS ... OF ... THE ... UNIVERSE. A gigantic sixth form means better funding which 'percolates down through the rest of the school.' It also allows them to offer their good range of A level courses.

School's swish office and reception area immediately radiates a school that has its act together. Lots of new building including £2.7 million English and modern languages block with central glassed-in atrium housing 50 computers. A new learning centre, nursery and sports hall. Beauteous sixth form centre, with own mini-canteen, well appreciated by the students. Class sizes pushing the boundaries in the sixth form.

Pastoral care and discipline: The few local parents who do not choose the school mainly cite pastoral matters (will my child be lost in the vastness? Will he suffer peer pressure?). But parents who have taken the plunge are almost all happy here. The school points out that, by breaking the school down by year group, they have created five manageable-sized groups of children. Pupils coming into year 9 keep the same tutor for three years – helps enormously. Appearance a constant source of skirmishes, with the pupils' guerrilla tactics usually overpowering the administration. Barber shop visits have not greatly troubled the boys. However, the school outflanked the pupils in the battle of the neckwear, introducing clip-on ties for new pupils in 2005.

Behaviour otherwise OK, if informal. No uniform in sixth form. Out if caught in possession of drugs but there have been no permanent exclusions in the past eight years – 'easily the lowest temporary exclusions in Dorset.' Area where sixth form pupils store their bags is guarded by CCTV (a good idea). Library well used and quiet – a sea of heads earnestly down. Bullying low on list of concerns – 'it's uncool to fight here,' said a pupil.

T

Pupils and parents: School is the pinnacle of Dorchester's Schools Partnership, a cohesive 4-19 educational pyramid. Hardye's has traditionally been able to count on this mainly homogeneous, middle income, non-urban catchment to provide reasonably wholesome kids with a good work ethic. Sadly, some negative aspects of youth culture are reaching even here, and Hardye pupils are not quite the bushy-tailed, fresh-faced youngsters they used to be. Negligible sprinkling of ethnic diversity – most with English as their home language.

Entrance: 475 pupils at 13+ mainly from Dorchester's three middle schools. Some 50 pupils come from outside the area, from as far away as Sherborne and Blandford. Handful from local prep, Sunninghill, settle in just fine. Number seeking entry roughly matches places available, although this is changing. All candidates for entry to the sixth form are interviewed, including the school's own pupils. 180 new pupils enter at that stage, a few from Poole and Bournemouth's grammars, attracted here by wide range of A levels, less authoritarian sixth form and lure of the opposite sex.

Exit: At least 85 per cent to higher education. One-third leave after GCSEs, most of these to further education elsewhere. School says that none are pushed out, but that the less able tend to leave, some looking for more vocational courses. UCAS a Herculean labour here. Half a dozen pupils to Oxbridge most years – sometimes more – but also students to UCL, RVC and LSE (48 per cent to Russell Group, 2012). IB element of the sixth form continues to grow – it was the first (and only) school to introduce the qualification in Dorset.

Remarks: Bulging metropolis, humming purposefully. Exactly what educationalists had in mind when comprehensives were first invented and going from strength to strength. Head's job is to help it carry on surging forward.

Thomas Mills High School

Saxtead Road, Framlingham, Woodbridge, Suffolk , IP13 9HE

- Pupils: 525 boys, 605 girls. All day • Ages: 11–18 • Non-denom
- State

Tel: 01728 723493
Email: inmail@thomasmills.suffolk.sch.uk
Website: www.thomasmills.suffolk.sch.uk

Headteacher: Since January 2013, Mr Philip Hurst, who came from a deputy headship at The Philip Morant School and College in Colchester.

Academic matters: Impressive results across the board at both GCSE and A level and superb value-added scores. A specialist school for technology since 1996 – the then new head used the funds to improve provision for science, maths (a whole new block) and IT, which is impressive in every area. A language and arts college too. Express streams in maths and science take GSCE in year 10, and there is setting in maths, science and languages at KS3/4. Developing opportunities for able students to take AS qualifications in Year 11. 'Key players' used to teach the, mainly male, middle sets – aims to bring boys' performance more in line with girls'. 2012 A level results showed 50 per cent A*-B grades. Very few linguists at this level. At GCSE in 2013, 83 per cent got 5+ A*-C including English and maths. Around half A* grades for each single science. Latin taken by a handful in year 10 though none take it further.

Humanities and arts subjects also do very well. A language is compulsory at GCSE and all pupils do French and German at KS3. Latin is taught as an optional extra-curricular subject and is increasing in popularity. Some 26 subjects at A level – take-up is variable so some, like languages, have small groups, whereas maths and biology nets 50 or so at A level. Not that results seem adversely affected by group size. Provision for learning support is excellent, and the department has its own cheerful area.

Games, options, the arts: Bought back a lost games field, so facilities are good and shared by the public after hours. A thriving house system, dating from grammar school days, means that large numbers are involved in competitive sport, much encouraged as part of the school ethos. On Sports Day, there is an 'open mile', in which around 300 children take part.

Art department a haven of creative chaos, producing bold, quite avant-garde results. Music is superb. Orchestras, choirs and instrumental groups abound, catering for all tastes and providing frequent concerts. Drama is on the curriculum in years 7/8, and the new performing arts studio with its dramatically sweeping black curtains is every young thespian's dream environment. Every member of staff is involved in one or more of the wide range of extra-curricular activities, visits and foreign exchanges.

Background and atmosphere: This is one of the 18th century Mills schools, a grammar school from 1902 to 1979. The campus is large, in a semi-rural setting on the outskirts of Framlingham, and consists of a hotch-potch of buildings. The main block is a bit battered-looking, with rather oppressive long corridors, but new building in the last ten years lifts the spirits. A much needed new canteen was recently completed, as was a new gymnasium. There are some nice touches; two air-raid shelters preserved on site provide a WW II museum and an experience of the blitz, complete with terrifying sound effects. The general atmosphere is exceptionally studious and disciplined. In the large, well-appointed and modernised library, even when it is full, you could hear a pin drop. Pupils are relaxed, courteous and well behaved. The head is keen to promote a sense of pride and the site is peppered with plaques celebrating this or that achievement or new development.

Pastoral care and discipline: System of form tutors appears to work well, with sixth formers involved in befriending and counselling younger pupils and also helping those with reading problems. Traditional values and individual responsibility. A real feeling that the highest of standards of behaviour and effort are expected. The house system, which permeates many areas of school life and is entirely run by the sixth form, promotes a strong sense of pride and belonging.

With so many pupils on a crowded site, noise levels are surprisingly low and unauthorised absences are well below national average, although this is probably to be expected in a school with an essentially problem-free intake and few inherent issues with discipline.

Pupils and parents: Pupils are all from the surrounding region and from a broad spectrum of social backgrounds but there is very little ethnic diversity. Both pupils and parents are highly complimentary about the school and tend to express only minor complaints about, for example, the untrendy design of the girls' trouser option (you have to look hard to see any girls in trousers!). Parents are very supportive and everyone seems extremely proud of the school's outstanding achievements.

Entrance: About 70 per cent come from the catchment area of surrounding villages, plus 30 per cent from out of catchment (quite a few more apply in this category than can be accommodated). There is an influx of 25-30 per cent into the sixth form, from other high schools and even from independent schools.

Exit: Vast majority go on to higher education and a wide range of courses, including a good number to top universities. Seven to Oxbridge in 2012. A few to vocational training or directly into employment.

Remarks: One of the best comprehensive schools in the country; a real community school. Judged by Ofsted to be 'outstanding' in recent years. Has now become an academy.

Thomas Telford School

Old Park, Telford, Shropshire, TF3 4NW

• Pupils: 1,330 boys and girls, all day • Ages: 11–18 • Non-denom • State

Tel: 01952 200000
Email: admissions@ttsonline.net
Website: www.ttsonline.net

Headmaster: Since the creation of the school in 1991, Sir Kevin Satchwell BA, OU education degree plus a diploma in educational management. Taught PE, ran his department in two schools, then deputy head in Kirkby and head of Moseley Park in Wolverhampton, before being appointed as TTS's founding head, with the brief 'to raise educational standards in Telford and Wolverhampton'. Softly spoken, direct, utterly committed to engaging the children, 'the child comes first, always'. Says there is nothing better, than being in the company of his pupils, 'it's uplifting'. Uncompromising about the delivery of exceptional outcomes; thinks nothing of overturning conventions (eg the school has two three-hour learning sessions a day) and sees teachers not as imparting knowledge but as catalysts in the process of enabling children to become autonomous learners, 'it's not about being the fount of all knowledge'. Gives the children real responsibilities: 'We gave them the choice between outdoor learning areas and a swimming pool. They chose the pool'. 'Sir Kev' remains part of the personal tutor team, holds regular working lunches with students of all ages, and runs one of the school football teams. An exceptional man adored by his pupils; 'When he talks you feel he talks directly to you'.

Academic matters: The academic standards are at the heart of the school, and 97 per cent get five GCSEs at A*-C including maths and English with 54 per cent A*/A grades in 2013. For a school that takes children from the full spectrum of ability this is an extraordinary result. With its unusual timetabling (two three-hour sessions a day) and longer working week (each child has about 30 hours of lessons a week compared to a state school average of 24), each pupil has simply more time to get to grips with the curriculum. What's more, GCSEs are taught over three years so students have an extra year of 30 hour weeks to get up to speed. It works. The whole year's curriculum is prepared the previous summer and is available to the students online at any time. Teachers are there to 'facilitate, share and excite,' but all teach the same lessons, planned centrally in advance. At A level, 21 courses are offered, plus BTECs in hospitality, performing arts and sports. Results are strong – 47 per cent A*-B, especially in sciences, business and art.

Reports are sent to parents every four weeks, to be signed, commented upon and returned, very tight oversight of academic work. In addition to the normal compulsory curriculum, everyone takes business GCSE and a modern language. Geography and history provide the springboard for lots of trips abroad – Belgium, Spain, Italy. Help is available to those who might not be able to afford such trips without

assistance. As a technology college, sciences, maths and business make a particularly strong showing, but vocational courses are also very popular – a lot of performing arts courses available in the sixth form as well as sports studies, hospitality and health & social care. Modern language dept is described as a 'small but strong' department and offers a choice of Spanish, French and German.

Learning facilities are impressive throughout – stacks of networked computers, well-equipped labs, DT rooms and workshops. Learning spaces are large, well lit and well maintained. Strong careers advice too, with a walk-in service for sixth form students, lots of support and ideas posted through the school website. Good support for those with special educational needs and the buildings are readily accessible to those with physical disabilities.

Games, options, the arts: Excellent sports facilities including a fabulous gym, floodlit pitches, Astroturf and a massive swimming pool. Lots of cricket, hockey, athletics, football, recently rugby as well. Sportsmark. Strong student representation at district and county level. Many students also involved in D of E, and over 100 taking individual music lessons. Performing arts are very strong with many opportunities to play in the school bands, sing in the choir, etc. A great theatre which is used to stage some stunning productions – good dance too. In addition public speaking, Young Enterprise and a host of placements available to gain work experience with local industry and business. This interaction is a feature of the school which is clearly valued both by pupils and parents.

Background and atmosphere: The school buildings themselves are kept to an extremely high standard – no loose plaster on the walls, no dirty floors or damp smelling corridors. No bells ringing, no mess anywhere. The work of the students is displayed proudly, and the school media team produces weekly videos of the pupil of the week, and the school news, uploaded onto the school website. Students say, 'it's hard work,' but 'you get out what you put in', and, 'we work as a team'. Staff remark on the respectful, collaborative relationships with children and the unequivocal support from parents. Pupils, parents and staff all remark on high levels of expectation, courtesy and co-operation.

The school is housed in an attractive purpose-built campus; plenty of open spaces, including open areas where two or three classes are taught simultaneously. The 'work hard, play hard' ethos seems to permeate. Everything, from the toilets upwards, is built, maintained and presented beautifully. Uniform is worn neatly, top buttons done up – older pupils say, 'it matters because the little things lead to big things'. It's a pretty secular place – with a multicultural catchment area, it has all the standard RE and PSHE, and plenty of information about the diversity of life – but not much in the way of formal religious content of any sort, if that's your bag.

An 'incredibly supportive governing body' (the principal sponsors of the school are Tarmac and the Mercer's company) has enabled ongoing enhancement of the school's resources in IT, sports facilities etc.

Pastoral care and discipline: The school takes great care of its pupils – not least in facilitating access to what's on offer: it runs coaches to and from Wolverhampton – all of which are stewarded, and later coaches also run to enable all to participate in extracurricular activities. There is daily time in tutor groups, which run 'vertically' through the school – this seems to work very well, giving older pupils responsibility and younger pupils role models. Zero tolerance of bullying and a strong sense of mutual respect between pupils. In a large school, which appears to run on rails and might tend towards the overwhelming, pupils say that tutors work hard at nurturing diffident pupils and unearthing their talents.

T

Pupils and parents: The students are remarkable – speaking passionately about the self discipline and sense of aspiration the school has fired in them, confident, articulate, polite, focused, and open. Parents, like their children, come from the full spectrum of Wolverhampton and Telford – single parents struggling to make ends meet alongside the businessmen and women of the area. They wax lyrical about the school, feel, 'part of the team', and are very positive about the monthly reports home. They speak highly of the pastoral care and the 'family feel' created by the tutor groups; saying any disciplinary issues are dealt with quickly and fairly, 'every child in the school is a credit to the school'. They also love the values the children absorb, 'respect, discipline, courtesy'.

Entrance: Massively oversubscribed (1300 applicants for 180 places in year 7). Applications are accepted so as to reflect the whole of the national 'curve', so being outstandingly bright is not necessarily an advantage. There is no sibling policy either, a factor to consider if you have more than one child.

The catchment area is basically Wolverhampton (around 40 per cent of places) and Telford Town (60 per cent) in accordance with 'the criteria embodied in the funding agreement between the school and the Education Secretary', when the school was founded. Granted the competition for places it is well worth checking the details of the process early with the school's admissions office – generally applications close in mid-September of the year prior to admission.

As a City Technology College, the school does prioritise offers of places for children whom it feels will have particular 'competence in technology, science and mathematics,' and those, 'who have the strongest motivation to succeed'. In other words if your child has no passion for these subjects, or little aptitude for them, you may be better off looking elsewhere. Parents get an opportunity to look round the school whilst the assessment of candidates is taking place, but there is no opportunity for individual visits. Some places available after GCSE – especially popular for those wanting to pursue the BTECs in performing arts and sports. Applications close in the October prior to admission.

Exit: Well over 90 per cent stay on for the sixth form and of those a large number go on to university – over 25 per cent to Russell Group and a handful to Oxbridge as well. Sheffield, Nottingham, Manchester, Liverpool and Birmingham are popular destinations. As might be expected, sciences and business are particularly strong, but there is also good representation of humanities, languages and performing arts.

Remarks: This school is exceptional whichever way you look at it, with some approaches radically different from those of conventional comprehensives. Led by an innovative and uncompromising head, who is unapologetic about a relentless drive for academic excellence, it caters for the whole spectrum of ability and background. A culture of very high expectation produces appreciative, confident and capable pupils who are delighted to be at school. No wonder that it's so heavily oversubscribed.

Thurston Community College

Norton Road, Thurston, Bury St Edmunds, Suffolk, IP13 3PB

- Pupils: 1,435 boys and girls, all day • Ages: 13–18 • Non-denom
- State

Tel: 01359 230885
Email: admin@thurstoncollege.suffolk.sch.uk
Website: www.thurstoncollege.org

Principal: Since 2005, Miss Helen Wilson BSc MBA NPQH (forties). Studied applied physics with chemistry at Durham, followed by a PGCE in science and PE at Bristol. Previously assistant principal at Comberton Village College and vice principal at Thurston. A dynamic, clear thinker whose enthusiasm is palpable, as is her fervent support of the comprehensive system – she means it when she says she's not just interested in exam results. Despite managerial load is still 'passionate about teaching' and lessons with year 9 provide some of her happiest moments. Definitely a team player who works hard to make staff and pupils feel valued – Ofsted says her management and leadership are outstanding. Sport offers a safety valve and way to maintain a 'healthy work-life balance'. Captains a local hockey team. Also enjoys skiing and wind surfing.

Academic matters: Approachable staff who're always there to help. Some 'outstanding' teaching – to address inconsistencies the principal has instigated a collaborative learning scheme for staff. Wide range of subjects at GCSE including separate sciences, business studies, engineering and dance. Above average value-added with 64 per cent getting five or more A*-C grades, including maths and English in 2013. Sixth form caters for a broad spectrum of abilities with BTEC courses in sport, hospitality and catering. A level results have steadily improved with 82 per cent scoring A*-C, 30 per cent A*/A in 2013. Fair amount of prodding in the main school but, once in the sixth, according to one of the students, 'it's your responsibility to get the work done'.

Most of the time those with SEN are supported in class by one of the large team of teaching assistants. There's also a 3+2 scheme – two days in school, three days working on vocational courses at the local college. No fast tracking for the extra bright – 'we extend rather than accelerate'.

Games, options, the arts: Strong emphasis on taking part with most club activities at lunchtime (four out of five pupils come to school by bus or coach). Not overly competitive but sporting achievement is recognised and there's friendly inter-house rivalry on the games field. Success in sport with numerous teams and individuals participating at local, county and regional level.

Individual music lessons and selection of musical activities – 'They really go to town on the annual productions,' said a parent. Large, recently refurbished art and design studios. Textiles is popular and the unusually sophisticated work well worth a look.

Sixth formers are encouraged to get involved with extra-curricular activities – at the last count 16 were going for gold D of E. Lots of fund-raising and committees who organise anything from social events to the installation and management of recycling boxes in every classroom.

Background and atmosphere: Airy, pleasant setting in dormitory village on the outskirts of Bury St Edmunds. Spacious, 70s single storey main school with interconnecting pods – has something of the hospital about it – and newer, self-contained sixth form centre. All softened with attractive landscaping and colourful planting. Good IT provision, two libraries – one is used by the local community – and large playing fields at the back of the site. Smiley, exuberant crowds of pupils (no smaller ones to dilute the considerable physical presence of year niners and their elders) teem in the corridors, but once in class attentive calm appears to be the norm. For many the positive relations with staff and a friendly atmosphere are the best things about the place.

Pastoral care and discipline: Because of its huge size the school is divided into four houses, each with a team of tutors. High priority is given to welfare and support – ranked as outstanding by Ofsted. Good lines of communication with parents and, according to a pupil, 'always someone who looks out for you'. Sixth form mentors, who are given specialist training before working with year 9s/10s, plus an effective inclusion policy which identifies and supports kids who are in danger of exclusion (one-to-one or small group teaching in a dedicated area) helps keep almost all in main stream education.

Ethos which rewards rather than chastises. All sorts of endeavour (academic, sporting, good deeds etc) are rewarded through the hugely popular points system. Points mean prizes – a few points will earn a non uniform pass but serious savers can aim for goodies like a Top Shop voucher, a day at Alton Towers or a DVD player. How things have changed. Head is refreshingly firm but fair and, on the odd occasion when it's necessary, will stand her ground on permanent exclusions.

Pupils and parents: Largely from surrounding rural area, predominantly middle class with a tiny number from ethnic minorities. Informal uniform (pale blue polo shirt, navy sweat shirt and black trousers – girls rarely wear skirts) is strictly adhered to in lessons but customisation seems to be fair game at break and lunchtime.

Entrance: Heavily oversubscribed. Catchment rules are stringent and at times oversubscription criteria may have to be applied. Important to check out the county council admissions policy for Suffolk maintained schools. School will move from three tier system, to two tier in September 2014 ie from an upper school to a secondary school taking pupils from year 7.

Exit: Fifty-ish per cent stay on to the sixth and a good proportion go on to higher education. Around 40 per cent to Russell Group universities, one or two to Oxbridge.

Remarks: Large rural comprehensive where all are valued. Forward-thinking head who looks set to take this lively school to the top of the ladder.

The Tiffin Girls' School

Richmond Road, Kingston Upon Thames, Surrey, KT2 5PL

• Pupils: 930 girls; all day • Ages: 11–18 • Non–denom • State

Tel: 020 8546 0773
Email: contact@tiffingirls.rbksch.org
Website: www.tiffingirls.kingston.sch.uk

Head Teacher: Since 2010, Mrs Vanessa Ward MA PGCE NPQH (late forties), a qualified solicitor who specialised in media law for five years before seeing the pedagogic light and taking a PGCE in 1998. She taught English at Nonsuch High for three years, thence, briefly, to Wilson's before moving to St Philomena's Catholic High School in Surrey where she was, successively, head of English, assistant head, and then deputy head. Such a rapid rise to the headship of one of the most successful grammars in the country suggests uncommon abilities.

She is highly professional but warm with it – not too common a mix. Parents enthuse: 'She is very caring...' 'She took the trouble to write individually to girls after the GCSEs.' 'She has authority but she can talk to the girls at their level.' Mrs Ward stresses her school's commitment to 'the quality of learning' – her measured delivery acquires a sudden catch in the throat born of her commitment to this ideal. And she is not pressure cooking her girls either – 'We are academically ambitious but we're not a hothouse.' She is smart, svelte and assured – the perfect role model and a square peg in the right hole, her own sons having been educated at Tiffin Boys. A clever appointment.

Academic matters: Outstanding results, of course, but how could they not be? If you get in here, you will be super-bright, be stimulated by your peers and superlatively taught and you will get the level of results that is normal and expected here. 2013 results saw 91 per cent of GCSE grades at A*/A and at A level 95 per cent at A*-B. Recent results placed the school as the fourth highest state school in the country in the Sunday Times Schools' Guide 2011, up from 7th place in 2010. Few GCSEs gain anything lower than B grades and one 2011 league table ranked Tiffin's GCSEs as the best of all girls' state schools in the country. Of the mainstream subjects, only the Englishes, physics and statistics get a fair sprinkling of Bs – all the rest are largely A*/A.

Sciences are popular, languages less so. Latin survives and does well. Drama and art excel at GCSE. At A level, nineteen subjects available plus General Studies and Enrichment Programme – taken with Tiffin Boys. Maths has by far the most takers with the majority achieving A*/A. Also popular are biology and chemistry, English and psychology. French and Spanish the only languages. Latin jointly with the boys' school and tiny numbers take music; few but increasing takers for D and T. Lots of Oxbridge graduates on the staff and we heard nothing but praise for the teaching.

The stringently applied entrance criteria mean that few with learning difficulties clear the hurdle. Only 22 on School Action or School Action Plus when we visited. However, the school is very accessible and would be a good option for your bright daughter with mobility or other physical difficulties.

Tiffin Girls' gained academy status early in 2011 – the first in the borough – this seen as enabling the school to continue what it does so well with less outside interference rather than as a major landmark.

Games, options, the arts: Rowing an increasing strength – very rare and pretty special for a girls' state school and it's now on the KS3 carousel of sports – the J15 squad won gold at the Kingston Small Boats Head in 2011; cross country and volleyball similarly impressive and the school boasts a number of individual stars in various sports. Most games played on site though school also uses the Hawker Centre, a minute or two down the road. Six netball/tennis courts, small Astro for hockey, one field in front of school used when not muddy. Two adjoining gyms plus one small multi-gym. Sixth form required to do one hour's sport a week – but many do more outside school. Most take the CSLA award. Flourishing Duke of Edinburgh. Lots of trips – sensible, subject-based and not too exotic for most wallets though the US ski trip option seen as prohibitively expensive by many.

Art – judging from the massed and massive canvases that grace the corridor walls – is quite exceptional – figurative and topographical paintings which you want on your walls – brilliant use of mixed media and collage. The same applies to the ceramics and textiles. We loved the highly glazed ceramic shoes along one walkway – and art, though taken at A level by far fewer than the talent would suggest – is a key strength here. Music seen as very good if somewhat exclusive – this despite school's strenuous efforts to involve everyone – witness the carousel in year 7 in which everyone has a chance to try out instruments with the encouragement to learn one and every girl in year 7 sings in the year 7 concert after which many join whole school choir for which there is no audition. In this, as in some other respects, the school's reputation seems to be lagging behind the reality. Drama clearly a major school occupation and great gusto expended on productions. Good programme of outside speakers and visits to museums etc. A great sense of the girls themselves using initiative to up their overall experience.

Background and atmosphere: In 1638, Thomas Tiffin, a prosperous brewer, left £50 so that the town clerk could choose a boy 'from ten years of Age, or there abouts' and educate him so that he might gain an apprenticeship and 'git his living'. His brother John left a further £100. There were further benefactors – eg Elizabeth Brown who wanted 'the Children of the poor inhabitants of the Town of Kingston,... to read the English Tongue and learn some Godly Catechisme...' and Edward Belitha who, in 1717, left money specifically, and to his eternal credit, for the education of 'twenty poor Persons' Daughters'. However, no actual school was founded until two hundred and fifty years later, after decades of local wrangling, when two 'lower middle class' schools – one for each sex – were established in the 1870s and named after the Tiffin brothers.

Initially, the boys and girls shared a school building – girls upstairs – the fees were modest and scholarships were offered. The schools blossomed and, in 1899, the girls moved to splendid new accommodation in St James's Road where they remained until a second move in 1937. Further expansion led to a further move to a former boys' secondary modern school building between Kingston and Ham. All went fine until 2003 when a ferocious fire demolished most of the teaching block and a lot of coursework. They talk of it still, down Kingston way. The final result of the fire was a terrific new building, at the centre of the present school, and which rescues the site from being sadly undistinguished to having a centre full of light and a sense of generous spaciousness.

The wide new corridors are hung with impressive canvases mentioned above and, in fact, the framing, glazing and hanging of the girls' art makes a major impression on any visitor. The hang is rejigged three or four times a year – we applaud. No classrooms seem crowded and we enjoyed the mix of layout – some are eyes forward to the teacher behind her desk, others are arranged in tables for four and a wandering teacher. Whiteboards are everywhere and used imaginatively. Large school hall but also good drama studio with clever retractable seating. Good facilities for music, music tech and applied arts. Big project to refurbish and re-site the sixth form centre and the library completed in 2012 – the girls involved in all aspects of the design. The result has been to put the sixth form back at the heart of the school and to give the library and other resources a new home. Girls greatly appreciate sensible central siting of all four IT rooms in the new main building – no hunting around for a free PC. New science labs and art room, plus refurb for Astroturf and netball courts. Security has been upgraded with keypad entry for students. Site is litter-free and functional and mostly in pretty fair nick though some careful planting could humanise it considerably. Good food – really good – and on a cashless system.

Pastoral care and discipline: Some of the best-presented girls we've seen. Uniform was being reconsidered when we visited but all the girls we saw looked comfortable and tidy in mid-blue jumpers, knee-length grey skirts and, seemingly compulsory, long hair. Sixth form just have to look respectable and they all do. Excellent new system of two head girls and seven deputies introduced by Mrs Ward. The deputies each have a 'job': environment, learning, integration, well-being, creativity, community, enterprise – and work to develop their area within

the school. All girls in a house 'family' – one from each year – which strengthens relationships between the year groups and is a very good idea. The girls we met were adamant about not missing boys during their seven years. 'We see the Tiffin boys all the time,' we were told. All those we asked said they would send their daughters to a girls' only school.

Praise for the head of pastoral care. The usual problems of highly motivated, clever girls though no more here than anywhere. Some sense among some parents that not all staff have pastoral care as a priority. Mrs Ward stresses how much is done discreetly and behind the scenes and certainly we liked what we saw of girl-teacher relationships. Few transgressions of the drugs/drink/smokes kind.

We have never met a more articulate, intelligent and thoughtful bunch of girls. They credit the school for giving them the confidence to hold their own in any context: 'They make you take an active role.... Everyone has to take an assembly at least once a year... You get very used to doing PowerPoint presentations, debating and we have masses of practice at presenting ourselves.' A quite extraordinary sense of pride in the school pervades the place: 'We love singing the school song... I wish we saw more of our Old Girls... we could learn so much from them.'

Pupils and parents: Pupils are the very bright daughters of highly organised and ambitious parents – increasingly not local and there is some resentment amongst those who do live locally that this, the pre-eminent academic state school, does not serve their community. A knock-on is that, although tight friendship groups are formed inside the school, the demographic and logistics mean that socialising outside the school and in leisure time is less easy and some pupils and parents are saddened by the fact that girls live too far away or social life is not valued at home. One mother told us that only one girl in her daughter's class lived within walking distance and others told us that developing a social life did not rank high in the priorities of many of the parents. This is something Mrs Ward and her team are very aware of and much effort is made to build a school community – clever ideas like getting year 10 parents to talk to the parents of girls in the year below and share experiences, parents' evenings of all kinds – but there is a sense among some that once the big push to get a place at the school has been achieved, too many parents sit back and don't involve themselves as they could. Most parents voluble in their appreciation: 'they strive to bring out the best in the girls'... if ever we have a problem you can always talk to someone – they are good at getting back to you.' 'They are hot on time-keeping... and academically amazing'. Some parental scepticism too: 'it suits the academic, the focused, the conscientious. It wouldn't suit the erratic, the eccentric, those who are academically one-sided.' School strenuously refutes this and it is true that the range of opportunities and activities is impressive and the list of leavers' destinations is as varied as you could hope to find. It may just be that a some pupils choose not to take advantage of them and just work.

Notable former pupils include Ritz muralist Helen McKie, actresses Jill Gascoigne and Katherine Parkinson, Lynne (Shoots and Leaves) Truss, Michaela Strachan and Olympian sculler, Sarah Winckless.

Entrance: This is probably the paragraph you are reading first. 1600 applicants for the 120 available places. One successful appeal out of 32 in 2011. Worth noting is the fact that the selection dates are constantly changing and parents are advised to keep up to date with the school's website. Currently, registration closes in late July. Now two stages of selection tests: first stage, age-weighted verbal and non-verbal reasoning as before, takes place in late September. The top 450 or so performers are invited back for the second stage (and the rest can apply elsewhere without using up one of their applications on Tiffin). Second stage, in early December, is maths and literacy tests – ie maths, comprehension and essay much as everywhere else. Places offered to the 150 girls who do best and distance between school and home used as a tie-breaker. A waiting list then operates and, again, distance is the deciding factor if test results are tied but the school must have been your first choice. Waiting list for entry to year 7 stays live to end of year 7 and then only those on it who have above the cut off score are eligible to apply for testing for entry to year 8. They would be the girls who have scored higher than the cut off score ie lowest in year 7, but who put a different school as their number 1 on their form. Got that? In reality, the tests are sat by some of the brightest girls in the south east and applicants come from a very wide radius – and 82 primaries and preps – although the school tries to discourage this. Practice in reasoning tests – the kind you can buy from WH Smith or Galore Park – helps you prepare, although the school commissions its own tests and you can't buy these. A healthy tutoring industry thrives in the local boroughs and Saturday schools, which will be greatly boosted by introduction of maths and literacy tests. This should make for a more realistic and manageable – and, probably, in the end, fairer system. Although great disappointment, of course, for those who make the 450 but not the final 150! When the results come out you can hear the whoops and wails from Mitcham to Marylebone.

300 apply for roughly 20 places at 16+. 8 GCSE passes including 4 As and 2Bs is minimum requirement. Applicants send their year 10 report and may be invited for a future pathways discussion.

Exit: Very few, if any, depart after GCSE. Thereafter Tiffin girls leave for good courses everywhere. In 2013 25 to Oxbridge and 60 per cent to Russell Group. Medicine and engineering, history and English predominate but really there's nothing they don't do – and do well.

Money matters: All families asked for £30 per month to contribute to school funds.

Remarks: Don't apply if you live more than 45 minutes away or if your daughter is only average at school. If she is super-bright, loves to learn, to think and take part in everything, you could find no better school – anywhere.

Tiffin School

Queen Elizabeth Road, Kingston Upon Thames, Surrey, KT2 6RL

• Pupils: 1,100 boys; all day • Ages: 11–18 • Broadly C of E, all faiths admitted • State

Tel: 020 8546 4638
Email: admissions@tiffin.kingston.sch.uk
Website: www.tiffin.kingston.sch.uk

Headteacher: Since 2009, Miss Hilda Clarke BA PGCE (fifties), a historian originally from Hull, and there is a fleeting touch of the Yorkshire still in her vigorous loquacity. The first woman to head this most successful of boys' grammar schools, Miss Clarke is impressive, and anyone who doubted the appointment at its announcement, couldn't have doubted long. Her career has been spent in the state system – beginning in a large comp in Cheshire, thereafter to Tiffin Girls as deputy head and thence to head Langley Grammar in Slough, where she made an outstanding contribution to the school in all areas – notably academically and in its building programme. Not, unlike some we have met in comparable posts, in any way an apparatchik

or admin freak – her talk is refreshingly free of edujargon – she is smiley, bustling, open, authoritative and clearly full of enthusiasm for what education should be. 'Our job is to educate the whole child...we should top league tables because we have a very select group of boys, but we want them to be socially successful as well. If they can't talk to people and work independently we will have failed them.' Parents are largely delighted – 'someone you'd want batting on your side', 'on top of things, 'very good on money', 'exactly right'.

Academic matters: Always among the highest performing grammars in the country. Results uniformly outstanding. Trad range of subjects – no business or psychology here – Latin sails on and the boys can take Greek. Other collaboration with Tiffin Girls'. Maths popular as are the individual sciences followed by English, history and economics. Eighty-eight per cent of all A level results in 2013 achieved A*-B. Fabuloso. GCSEs similarly – compulsory religion and philosophy much enjoyed and achieves sky-high results – in 2013, 77 per cent got A*/A. In maths – wait for it – 99 per cent got A*/A. A staggering 81 per cent of all subjects taken achieved A*/A. Langs – never the top take in a boys' school – relatively strong and well-supported with visits and exchanges. Great common sense in allowing boys to take double or triple sciences – no regimentation means that natural artists or linguists do not feel squeezed out as in many more blinkered places.

It's not just results. Parents – and boys praise the intellectually stimulating and challenging teaching styles – 'it's traditional and it's excellent,' we were told. 'The teachers don't feel they have to dumb down for these boys.' IT taught as a discrete subject up to year 9 and all are 'encouraged' to take the EDL thereafter. Learning platform – the VLE – enables rich interaction online between home and school.

Small number have SEN – mostly mild dyses – a few statemented pupils on the ASD spectrum ('we're used to dealing with bright Asperger's boys,' says Miss Clarke) and school accommodates with ease. Full-time SENCo plus full-time LSA and one part-time learning support teacher are 'there to support any boys with problems'.

Games, options, the arts: Huge sports hall incorporating dance studio on far side of field (very muddy when we visited) However, new all-weather pitch and cricket nets completed in 2011. Most practices held 15 minutes' bus ride away on their extensive playing fields near Hampton Court. Sports engaged in as intensely as everything here and with proportionate results. Good showings in cross country, badminton, sailing, tennis, rugby, cricket and rowing etc etc. For a school described by some as 'very male', the place has a tangible feminine side. A quarter of the staff are women and the arts life is remarkable in all areas. Music is massive. Around a quarter learn at least one instrument in school – many more learn outside. Deliciously refreshing to come to a school where music isn't all about 'tech' these days – blissfully, no music tech within these portals but real orchestras, choirs and bands and stunningly good performance values. Older boys tell us, 'it's brilliant if you hit the ground running but they won't give you the basics and help you up if you haven't,' – to which school's retort is a robust, 'the music staff is always on the look-out for potential' and, apparently, 'music is compulsory and every boy in years 7 and 8 performs at evening musical events'. And you can't quibble with the results and reputation – regular Oxbridge choral scholarships, legendary concerts – especially choral – and overall standard is outstanding.

Dance – uniquely in an all-boys' school? – is hugely popular and seen as 'cool' by the coolest boys. Combining the physical with the aesthetic, it is compulsory for first three years under clearly terrific teacher and taken right through to GCSE, after which many boys continue to perform. Collaboration with Ballet Rambert. Good little drama studio but most productions take place in school hall – often including Tiffin Girls' girls who don't, seemingly, return the compliment. Great fun and energetic shows, we gather. Art is a delight. Three studios in various states of joyous, creative chaos full of things you want to stop and look, laugh and wonder at. We loved the tiles depicting the Gujerati alphabet all made from lentils, the glorious fish mobiles, the totem poles made from 'kebabed' Greek pots, the witty, colourful textiles and the sense of discovery in boys who are allowed to explore rather than told what to do. Not that the basic skills are in any way neglected. Creativity notably encouraged in music, art and drama – but in writing? Some feeling that this is a relatively neglected area. Number of extra-curricular opportunities support Miss Clarke's contention that it doesn't do to apply if you live too far away – you'd only go home to sleep. Masses of achievements in every field. In 2010, a 15-year-old Tiffinian won Countdown! Boys regularly sing in the chorus at The Royal Opera House and one had just sung a solo the week before our visit. Several boys play games at national level.

Background and atmosphere: One of the few schools set up to educate the deserving – rather than the rich – which still fulfils its brief. Two local brewers, John and Thomas Tiffin, in 1638 left money to educate 'honest poor men's sons'. A convoluted history involving various other donors and institutions ultimately resulted in two new Tiffin schools in 1874 – one for boys, one for girls – this coinciding with the great surge in the movement to educate women. The boys' school moved to its present site in 1929, became a grammar in 1943, is currently voluntary aided and, in 2010, applied for academy status. 'Tradition and heritage is at the centre of school life for us,' an earnest sixth former confided. Tiffin has two official specialisms – in performing arts and languages – but it is hard to see that they excel any less in eg maths and the sciences.

The main building is attractive – especially the frontage which faces away from the street. Small, wonderfully old-fashioned school hall with glittery honours boards and stone tablets commemorating the dead of both wars. The additional buildings include Elmfield, a rather splendid, if somewhat obscured, building from the 1750s used as a classroom block but which also houses the school archives. Ghastly prefab houses the canteen which serves exemplary food – scrummy marinated pork ribs plus trimmings for £1.20 and no junk on offer – and the neat sixth form café. Newer blocks – easier on the eye than many school buildings – include the library, engagingly modelled on the British Museum Reading Room's wheel and spokes design – not that the pupils seem to know this – and it is well-used, well-stocked and cleverly enhanced with a circular gallery accommodating PCs. Super lecture theatre in which speakers – both teachers and external – give fortnightly lectures. It is only in the general internal maintenance of the buildings and, to some extent, the site as a whole that one is aware that this is not a privileged private school. The state of decoration could be better but boys couldn't care less, for the most part, and why should they?

Pastoral care and discipline: Six houses of huge importance to the ethos, competitive spirit and much fun. Also good for mixing up the year groups – a real and valued feature here. System of prefects, head and deputy head boys with varying responsibilities greatly valued, especially on account of some of the choice in election being given to senior boys. 'It's a big honour,' said one modest – but ennobled – lad, 'I've been surprised by how non-corrupt it is.' Discipline, we're told, is 'firm but fair' – all concur. 'You don't accept a lack of respect or toleration,' affirms Miss Clarke and no incidents of onsite smoking, drinking, drugs in her first 18 months. One exclusion for unacceptable behaviour. We saw only quiet, attentive classes. Few incidents of bullying, dealt with robustly, parents agree. Lots of rewards – merits and demerits which matter. Uniform which is really rather nice – stripey red and blue

blazers for the younger boys and dark suits for the older ones with numerous different ties depending on your abilities and proclivities – is worn with more attention to smartness than we've seen in comparable schools. Blazer felt by some to incite aggression in local youths – 'this is not a fair statement on neighbouring young people in Kingston,' protests Miss Clarke – but accepted as an inevitable price for the privilege it brings. Remarkable latitude accorded to length and style of hair does much to soften any sense of over-uniformity.

Pupils and parents: Brains and aspiration the only common denominators. Most from local areas – 80 per cent come on public transport – though they commute from up to an hour away – into Surrey, up to Ealing, over to Wimbledon. School discourages longer journeys for good commonsensical reasons. Some parental feeling that school-home communication could be better now countered by 'Parentmail' – all can now email any teacher and response, in general, is good. Huge outreach programme and evening events. Parents and locals come in for everything from language classes to concerts to lectures. Miss Clarke upping the school's local inter-activity on all fronts. Ethnically as mixed as you'd expect – large Asian contingent from all over – most of the rest UK/European. And in the smart uniform they blend and mix perfectly. Around 30 per cent speak a language other than English at home though few require additional help. Socially equally diverse – plenty in this well-heeled area could afford to pay for education and a very few of those offered places here still opt to shell out elsewhere. Hard to understand why. Others can't afford occasional extras – trips, music etc – and school fund helps out. This is privileged education – available to all with the requisite brainpower, whatever their background – a great leveller. Great for all who are open and eager to learn. Who would it not suit? Perhaps, say some, not so good for the shy and withdrawn – but school disagrees.

Entrance: You may not want to read any further. 140 places in year 7. 1500 applicants for these in 2012. No worries about where you live but don't bother to tutor your brightish lad. Testing is done purely via verbal and non-verbal reasoning tests and the only thing that will help you there is practice and building up speed. If your lad is young for the year, you may cheer up a bit – the tests are weighted so as not to disadvantage younger candidates. Looked after children take precedence – so long as they make the grade. And there's no point in applying at all if you don't put them first choice. Very occasional places thereafter – apply to the local authority. For the sixth form, you will need at least 4 As and 2 Bs at GCSE and As in your A level choices – achieved with ease by most. NB The same criteria, in fact, are applied to internal candidates ie you don't progress to the sixth form if your GCSEs aren't good enough. 25 per cent of sixth form do enter at this level.

Exit: As impressive as you'd expect. Most popular university destinations Oxbridge – school averages 19 places annually (20 in 2013), followed by Durham, the London colleges and Warwick. Subjects taken cover the range though science and related courses predominate. Famous OBs include Jonny Lee Miller, Alec Stewart, John Bratby ARA

Money matters: School asks for a contribution – £530 pa – and around 55 per cent of families give some or all of this. Funds used to widen opportunities for all, subsidise trips, IT or music equipment and help towards new facilities such as the all-weather pitch and cricket nets..

Remarks: If all state schools were as good as this the independent sector would die – fast.

Tonbridge Grammar School

Deakin Leas, Tonbridge, Kent, TN9 2JR

• Pupils: 1060 pupils; all day • Ages: 11–18 • Non-denom • State

Tel: 01732 365125
Email: office@tgs.kent.sch.uk
Website: www.tgs.kent.sch.uk

Head Teacher: Since April 2005, Mrs Rosemary Joyce BA (Hons), MA, PGCE, NPQH (forties). Read religious studies and history at Stirling, followed by a PGCE and MA at London. Previously deputy head of Nonsuch High School for Girls, Cheam; senior teacher at Clarendon School, Trowbridge; head of religious studies at Aylesbury High. A highly effective administrator who managed to get funding and organise the rebuilding of large parts of the school in record time. She is charming and businesslike and considers her role to be a privilege rather than a job, saying that, 'education should be about transforming people's lives'. Teaches philosophy to the sixth form and takes assemblies but some pupils and parents feel she cuts a slightly remote figure and they don't really know her. She has twin daughters in the school.

Academic matters: High achieving selective grammar with academy status and specialisms in maths, computing and languages. Has received the British Council's award for internationalism each year since the introduction of the IB in 2004 and has been top IB state school in the UK for five consecutive years. Ran IB and A levels side by side for a number of years and exclusively the IB from 2012 – caused a bit of a fuss at the time as some families felt they had not been given any choice. However, this has settled down and school and teachers are fully committed to the IB; students who want to do A levels move elsewhere after GCSEs. The head stresses that the IB has not meant a change in direction and the ethos of the school remains the same; Academy status means the school is free from the constraints of the national curriculum, 'we are now in charge of our own destiny'. Average points for the IB over the last few years has been 37, about ten per cent get 40 points or more and usually a couple a year get the maximum 45 points. Languages and sciences particularly strong with German, French, Italian and Spanish offered and regular foreign exchanges. Latin also offered. Wide choice of subjects maintained under IB but sometimes a subject doesn't run if not enough takers. 'Natural sciences a more natural fit than than sports science' but film and theatre studies popular.

At GCSE over 80 per cent A*/A, with 94 per cent A/A* in maths and 15 per cent of pupils achieving ten or more A*s. School works within the principles of the IB Middle Years Programme (MYP) but is not accredited and will continue with IGCSEs and GCSEs.

Co-ed sixth form since 2000 with about 20 boys in each year who appear to integrate well and 'add a new energy to the classroom'. Good support for Oxbridge and more pupils being encouraged to apply – help with choice of college and preparation for tests, Oxbridge tutors invited to talk to students. Reciprocal arrangements with local schools for interview practice. Medical and vet students come back to talk about the application process.

Good balance and age range of staff (respectable number of male teachers), from very experienced to newly qualified – extraordinarily dedicated team who give up their time to run clubs and sporting fixtures. Maths and chemistry teachers are old girls of the school. Class sizes no more than 30 or 25 for practical subjects with setting from year 8 for maths and French and ICT integrated into every subject. Ofsted consider the teaching to be 'outstanding'. Study skills programme and regular assessments through practical projects, online assessments and presentations. Progress reports sent to parents and pupils are 'given the freedom to learn from their mistakes'. Form time every day and sixth form have daily contact with their learning mentor – three tutor reviews with learning mentor per year to review progress and set targets. House points awarded for good work.

Curriculum designed to stretch the gifted and talented – maths challenge in Holland and a national level language olympiad held at school. Enrichment programmes include debating society and subject-led clinics at lunchtimes to stretch and support pupils. School sends a team to the Model United Nations and recent study trips to Iceland, Singapore and Swaziland. Good SEN support, mainly for mild dyslexia, either individual or small groups. Everyone screened on arrival and new entrants to sixth form also screened; teachers alert for other difficulties. About one per cent need some sort of EAL help – families who speak another language at home or those who move into the area to join school for IB in sixth form. Increasing number from abroad who stay with local families.

Games, options, the arts: Music particularly strong and caters for all ages and levels of talent. About 300 pupils learn at least one musical instrument. Masses of group music and individuals can shine at house musical events. Three formal concerts a year, array of ensembles, swing bands and orchestras, often student run eg the ukelele orchestra. Three choirs, classical and contemporary – Motet choir won Barnardo's National Choir competition which led to an invitation to sing at the Royal Albert Hall, and were runners up in Songs of Praise Choir of the Year competition. Concerts at St John's Smith Square and at the Cadogan Hall with London Chamber Orchestra. Over 90 per cent of papers graded A/A* in music GCSE and music offered as a Higher in the IB.

Active drama department with lunchtime and after school clubs and drama is part of the curriculum in the lower school. Whole school production every other year with annual smaller productions as well as some joint drama with Tonbridge School. Theatre studies is offered as part of the IB. New drama and dance studios. Creativity encouraged at all levels. Vibrant art displayed around the school taught by 'enthusiastic and friendly teachers'. Art taken early with excellent results – textiles popular.

Team sport compulsory until sixth form and many continue as it forms part of the CAS element of the IB, but can be 'a bit patchy' according to the girls. 'There are not enough matches and sporty girls join outside clubs' says one. Netball, tennis and hockey are the main sports; some hockey coaching on site and at Tonbridge School. Basketball popular with boys and girls in sixth form and boys have their own football team and many play for local clubs. School's own pool has seen better days and swimming now done elsewhere but school says plans are afoot for 'an exciting new development project' on the site. Fab new sports hall and netball/tennis courts recently resurfaced. Clubs and activities at lunchtime and 'Action!' on Wednesday afternoons for years 7 and 8 – something for everyone – anything from sports, first aid and glass painting to Indian head massage but clubs 'peter out further up the school' according to some pupils. Some run by sixth form as part of the CAS element of the IB. School also take part in the Young Enterprise scheme and run their own radio station, Radio TGS. Pupils also take part in a community project in Africa – recently a group of about 20 raised money and built a library for a school in Swaziland – 'they lived in fairly basic conditions and it was a life changing experience for my daughter' says one mother.

Background and atmosphere: Founded in 1905 on the top floor of Tonbridge Library with 19 girls and the motto 'Courage and Honour'. Moved to current site in 1913 when it outgrew the library, 14 acres on a hill in south Tonbridge with great views in all directions. £10 million Hands Building opened in late 2009 with a large glass atrium and 43 new classrooms – some with moveable walls, a drama and dance studio and sports hall. £850,000 raised from loyal band of parents and former pupils and helped by a land exchange with a house builder. Science labs refurbished with help from a grant from the Wolfson Foundation in 2012.

Strong sense of community with compulsory service activity once a week – younger children do something within the school, older pupils might help in a primary school or volunteer in an old people's home and sixth form do community service as part of the IB. 'We like to take pupils out of their comfort zone where they flourish and it helps them see themselves as part of a broader picture', says the head. In a recent project some senior pupils worked with children from a pupil referral unit using the photography and IT facilities at the school.

Pastoral care and discipline: Pastoral care seen as a whole school responsibility, 'we want to get the support right so pupils can be as successful as they can be' says head. Programme of monitoring, tracking, support and interventions. Learning and peer mentors offer support to girls at form time and, 'there is always someone to talk to and the school want us to be happy' says one pupil. Dedicated student manager oversees the transition from primary school and provides a crucial link between home and school; children are put into forms with similar postcodes so they can make friends with girls who live near them. Years 7, 8 and 9 have registration together so they can get to know other year groups and sixth form have mixed year tutor groups. Year 7 have a Bushcraft camping week in nearby woods and new sixth formers invited for a bonding weekend at the University of East Anglia in the summer before they join. The sixth form have their own café and supervised study area.

Pupils and parents: A fairly middle class group whose parents take an interest in their education – only 14 children on free school meals. Loyal alumni who come back and speak to pupils and often send their daughters here. 'Well rounded, grounded children who are highly motivated with a good work ethic – we cannot believe our luck' said one delighted mother. 'Our daughter is interested and happy and loving every minute'. 'The school has high expectations and the children have so many experiences and opportunities' The pupils have a 'privileged education but are not necessarily privileged, they push themselves in all areas and have a strong sense of being part of the wider community' says the head.

Attractive uniform with blue jerseys and straight check skirts and dress code for sixth form of dark matching suits with skirts as short as they can get away with. Alumni include Victoria Hislop (novelist and travel writer); Rebecca Stephens MBE (first British woman to climb Everest and the seven summits); Lynn Wallis (Artistic Director of the Royal Academy of Dance); Angie Sage (author of Septimus Heap series); Felicity Aston and Jo Vellino (polar explorers). Active and committed PTA involved with fundraising and social events.

Entrance: Entrance via the Kent Test at 11+ in verbal, non-verbal reasoning and maths administered by Kent County Council and places are hard fought. No allowance made for siblings. No catchment area but most fairly local and proximity to the school taken into account where there are two girls of equal ability. A minimum of 35 'Governors' places' reserved for able pupils from outside the area but same criteria apply as for Kent selection. Sixth form entry based solely on academic results with a minimum of 3As and 3Bs at GCSE or equivalent and guidance meetings offered at the school to discuss subject choices. Mainly from other grammars for the IB and East Sussex

schools which finish at 16+. Occasionally spaces in other years – entry via school's own test.

Exit: Historically very few left after GCSEs but numbers have increased as those wishing to do A levels move elsewhere. Over 95 per cent to higher education and a huge range of universities, the most popular being Exeter, Loughborough, Southampton, Manchester and Leeds. About 10 a year to Oxbridge (we are surprised there are not more).

Money matters: Music bursaries available and awards in sixth form. Tradition of helping families where money is tight. Pitchford Fund set up by PTA in 1950s and enables those in immediate financial need to take part in activities.

Remarks: A remarkable school and anyone who gets in here is very fortunate. Considered to be one of the most academic schools in the area but pupils wear their learning lightly and have time for so much else. Everyone we met was self-confident and ambitious but down to earth and very much aware of the wider world beyond the school gates.

Tonbridge School

High Street, Tonbridge, Kent, TN9 1JP

- Pupils: 770 boys; 460 board, 325 day • Ages: 13–18 • C of E
- Fees: Boarding £34,137; Day £25,062 pa • Independent

Tel: 01732 365555
Email: hmsec@tonbridge-school.org
Website: www.tonbridge-school.co.uk

Headmaster: Since 2005, Mr THP (Tim) Haynes BA PGCE (early fifties), a historian, married with two school-age boys. After a post-university stab at stockbroking, Mr Haynes sensibly moved into teaching, beginning with QEGS (qv), Hampton (qv) and then a 13 year spell at St Paul's (qv), where he rose to be surmaster. Ten years as head of Monmouth (qv) gave him lots of experience for this higher profile job in which he followed the 15 year tenure of the much-respected Martin Hammond. So not a school which needed pulling up by boot-straps. 'I came here and found a fantastic school so I don't wish to turn the place upside down,' he acknowledged. 'I want to build on the strengths my predecessor developed, particularly its balance and breadth.' It's almost a pity so much had already been done here, as the man has abundant nervous energy and dashes about all over the place, involving himself in a way everyone appreciates. 'He's very willing to chat,' say boys, 'he wants to get people's opinions about things – to hear it directly from them.' Parents are generally enthusiastic – 'he's approachable, a good communicator,' we are told. He's certainly smiley, rangy, open, chatty and immensely proud of his school, its staff and boys. A sound man for a blue chip school.

Academic matters: Truly excellent. In 2013, at A level 77 per cent of results were A*/A and 94 per cent A*-B. Modern language results especially pleasing – unusually so in a boys' school. Whizzy multi-media centre for langs surely helps. Everyone starts the first year taking two langs and they must do at least one to GCSE. In 2013, 91 per cent A*/A at GCSE. Mandarin now a curricular option and can be taken to A level. Sixty-one per cent who took French got A* and most of the rest got A. All 20 of the Italian takers got A*/A and German also holds up well here. Most popular A levels are maths, economics, physics and history. Results pretty breathtaking – 100 per cent A in Greek and as near dammit in Latin, art, and English – (astounding, given the numbers). No weak areas. Languages notably popular and successful. Subject choices are trad rather than trendy – no psychology or tourism at Tonbridge.

Mild dyslexia and dyspraxia the likeliest SENs here and boys may be withdrawn once weekly by top-notch SENCo for one-to-one help in developing strategies for self-reliance later on. A few with controlled ADHD or mild ASD might make it through the entry procedure – 'mild' being the key word here. No specific G and T programme but masses of enrichment and stretching across the curriculum and the extra-curricular activities – along with setting and streaming in the younger years – will challenge your nascent Isaac Newton.

Staff universally praised, and what struck us when we barged into lessons was the sheer enthusiasm of the teaching. Good library with quiet, workful atmosphere and good stock of books – older and newer – though most boys were typing away rather than turning pages. School up-to-the minute in home-school intra-netting and work, tutors, news all accessible from home PCs or terminals in boarders' rooms, houses etc. Large screens about the school also update everyone on news and activities.

Games, options, the arts: If you don't love games before you come here, you will after a week or two: or if you really really won't this is probably not the right school for you. A vast choice of sports. Miles of fabulous pitches tempt the most firmly-couched potato – and various county teams who practise here – and the wonderful sports centre has every imaginable facility – you'd happily pay a couple of grand a year for membership if it was in London. School's new water-based Astroturf used as an Olympic training venue. School offers 20+ sports – lots of choice. The most popular are cricket, rugby, hockey, soccer, tennis and athletics. Teams at all levels means that if your idea of rugger is a gentle chat during a slow canter you won't feel threatened. They don't win everything but they compete fiercely and give their all. Several individual stars in rugby, fencing, athletics and cricket. CCF is big and there are gentler alternatives – community service being especially strong, popular and useful locally. Boys feel encouraged to use their own initiative to start pet projects and many do.

Famous for music – excellent facilities include two impressive recital rooms and seriously good staff. Art and DT are lively though it would have been nice to see more boy-work around the place. Indeed there is no guiding sense of beauty about the place: each department does its own thing, from history's inspiration to science's expiration. Masses of applied arts and crafts. A knock-out theatre – perhaps the best we've seen – seats 375 and would grace any lively provincial town – a real privilege in a school. Lively music, theatre and arts programmes involve girls from two local schools. Week-long annual arts festival brings in professional companies and artists but also a staff play and school-run productions, exhibitions and concerts.

Tonbridge reaps benefit of being only 35 minutes from Charing Cross yet in unsophisticated setting in which there is an appreciative buzz at so many good things. Outstanding programme of visiting speakers – as good as anything a top London school could lay on – lectures, debates and discussions – to stimulate, challenge and involve.

Background and atmosphere: Founded in 1553, school moved to its present privileged site in the mid-19th century and the main buildings are splendid, but not opulent, Victorian gothic. School's chapel burnt down in 1988 and its replacement, rededicated in 1995, is huge, simple and dignified. We thought it a great waste of money at the time – cost about £10 million – but it is a place of great beauty and calm, and beyond price. Its massive organ was a vast investment and, on its own, would justify the school's pride in this confident and determined rebuild. Chapel accommodates the whole school three days a week and boys value opportunities to read and speak in such a place. Later school buildings are imaginative and represent the better aspects of 20th century architecture. Short-term

expediency has not dictated building here. DT and the arts especially imaginatively housed in 1996 building. Excellent lecture theatre.

Boarding mostly in solid Victorian houses abutting the playing fields. Younger boys in functional four-bed dorms, older ones in one or two-bed rooms. Nice touches like little TV rooms with tiered carpeted stair-seating and dozens of cushions – great for communal heckling during football matches etc. Healthy eating has taken off in the last two years and food is substantial but sensible – fizzy drinks etc off the menu. Boarders eat in houses – relaxed and homely atmosphere. Fierce house loyalty in general. 'It's an incredibly happy school,' a grateful parent of three happy boys told us.

On a 150 acre site adjacent to Tonbridge's main street, this is an ideal position – private, secluded and in the middle of things at the same time, and boys are sensibly allowed into town, so no monastic seclusion found elsewhere. The site is beautifully maintained – though some of the boarding still to benefit from the rolling refurbing and we saw some fairly scary carpets and wall-peel here and there. It's all very boy-friendly though and the boys themselves were about as well-turned out as anywhere – in nice grey jackets for the first three years and inoffensive suits for the sixth. A sense of order without repression prevails – evident in a fairly relaxed range of hair-styles but no eyesores or nose-rings. Boys happy with things as they are – don't miss girls as lots of interaction in co-productions etc. 'It's a real boy atmosphere – I just love it,' one alpha male sixth former told us, rather sweetly.

Pastoral care and discipline: Little to worry about – the school's culture simply doesn't encourage transgressing. Successful house system seen as crucial to overall care and watchfulness. Lots of male and female staff in each house, close relationships between tutors (half a dozen attached to each house) and tutees, well-structured prefect system and a clear policy on disciplinary matters. Head will test on suspicion of drug misuse but no incidents in recent memory. Boys really value what they have here – 'we don't really like the idea of smoking or drugs,' said one, 'it's something to do with the sports culture and people know it's incredibly bad for you.' Over-18s allowed into pubs for a drink or two but no drink in school. Nowhere is immune to temptations, especially where cash abounds, but it's hard to imagine real problems here. Likewise, little talk of bullying – a sense that boys 'look out for each other' and a real trust in the pastoral system. Especially in the houses. 'The pastoral care is there when you need it but not in your face,' a parent felt. Likewise the disciplinary side – 'it's firm but fair – they're tough when they have to be.'

Perhaps not the best school for boarders from over-the-hills-and-far-away or overseas who want the full-on 100 per cent boarding school experience – and particularly so if they are not dedicated sportsmen. Even loyal parents admit that 'not enough goes on at weekends' and one complained that his boy 'rattles around in the house on Sundays with no-one to talk to – not even the housemaster'. However, school now upping weekend activity programme but makes no claim to provide what, say, Harrow would. 'We're not a weekly boarding school – the culture here is boarding,' says head, 'but with so few boys (around a third of boarders) here over the weekends we can't offer what a school with 100 per cent boarding could.'

Pupils and parents: Ninety per cent from the UK. Most – day and boarding pupils – live up to one and a half hours away – this is a very south-east England school. However, some from up north and lots of boarders from overseas – popular in Hong Kong though not yet in Russia. Around ten per cent speak English as a second language – most are fluent. School sensibly separates entrants from the same prep schools into different houses so everyone has to make new friends. Usual problem of sixth form entrants from HK who come to work and can be a bit cliquey –

though perhaps less so here than elsewhere. A Tonbridge boy is unpretentious, un-ostentatiously 'can-do' and a thoroughly good chap – often not from a traditional boarding family. Parents are sensible, supportive, appreciative and increasingly now involved – unobtrusively rather than bawling from the touchline. Have their own flourishing arts club. High-achieving Old Boys include Colin Cowdrey, E M Forster, Derek Barton, Frederick Forsyth, Sir Patrick Mayhew, Dr William Rivers (he of WWI fame), Vikram Seth, Sidney Keyes and 'Keane'. A touching plaque commemorates George Austen – Jane's pa – who was second master here.

Entrance: Oversubscribed three to one. Applicants register at start of year 6 and school report is sought. All candidates seen for non VR-type test – so don't bother with coaching – it won't help. It does, however, mean that applicants from state primaries are not disadvantaged. Conditional offers made thereafter and an acceptance allows you to express a preference for a house. Head reserves a few places for special circumstances or late-comers. Academic scholarship exam happens one month before CE – your bright son's best bet for a means-tested bursary – see below. Recent scare stories about soaring CE required grades are rubbished by head. 'Aim for 65 per cent'. Applicants with possible SENs seen at early stage by school's SENCo to aid assessment and develop strategy. Around 15 taken into the sixth – minimum of six Bs at GCSE required but 'minimum' means you'd be better off with a clutch of As.

Exit: Virtually no-one leaves after GCSE. Twenty-five to Oxbridge in 2013 – around double that apply. In fact, in The Sutton Trust's ranking – based on five years' worth – Tonbridge ranked third best boys' boarding school nationally and the best in the South East at getting pupils into the top two. One to Harvard on a scholarship. The rest to good universities – Exeter, Durham, Bristol, Nottingham – to read solid subjects – medicine, engineering, accounting, and proper arts/humanities. They go on to be sound citizens who contribute.

Money matters: Exceptionally well-endowed. Twenty-two academic schols awarded to new entrants – 10 per cent but top-uppable on a means-tested basis. Up to 100 per cent remission schols/bursaries – academic or musical – for the deserving but impoverished. 220 boys on some kind of fee remission – 30 have over 80 per cent remission and 15 have 100 per cent remission. Take a careful, serious look.

Remarks: 'It's like a beautifully made watch,' a delighted parent enthused, 'it just works.'

Tormead School

Linked school: Tormead School Junior School

27 Cranley Road, Guildford, Surrey, GU1 2JD

• Pupils: 565 girls, all day • Ages: 11–18 • Interdenom
• Fees: £6,720–£13,140 pa • Independent

Tel: 01483 575101
Email: registrar@tormeadschool.org.uk
Website: www.tormeadschool.org.uk

Head: Since 2010, Mrs Christina Foord MA MPhil PGCE, forties, previously deputy head and head of boarding at St Catherine's, Bramley. Prior to this she taught English and history in a number of schools including The Queen's School, Chester. A passionate choral singer, she takes a keen interest in music of all sorts and is eager to provide her girls with opportunities to showcase their talents. Known throughout the school as being 'up for a challenge', she recently abseiled down the tower of Guildford Cathedral in aid of charity. Married, with two senior-school aged children and two dogs. Staff remark in admiration that she's ready to get 'stuck in', and when the new climbing wall was inaugurated this September, she was one of the first to scale it.

Academic matters: One of the high fliers in Surrey (and way beyond). Excellent academic results across a wide range of subjects – 2013 GCSE results were 77 per cent at A*/A; A-level results were 63 per cent A*/A and 86 per cent A*-B, with particularly good performances in maths, English, sciences and languages (mostly As). 'Does really well even by less academic students,' says a parent. Plenty of scope for choice in languages at GCSE and A levels including Spanish, German, and Greek.

Ten GCSEs is usually the maximum allowed. Refreshing to see that risk-talking is also encouraged – pupils who are keen to pursue a subject which may not be their academic forte are still encouraged to follow their dreams. Pupils do not feel unduly under pressure academically ('not as pushy as other schools,' says a parent), and any worries about exams are sensitively handled by the school. Grade sheet system introduced where pupils are marked for effort as well as attainment throughout the school year, so the less academic still get plenty of credit for trying hard and 'you feel on top of how your daughter is really doing,' says a parent.

SEN provision recently upgraded from peripatetic support to a full-blown department, offering not only dyslexia support but also study skills, maths clinics and acknowledgement of different learning styles. 'Brilliant,' say pupils, 'Extremely good at helping you out,' and no stigma here for anyone having extra help. Personal attention pays off. Pupils with dyslexia credit their teachers with helping them flourish – dyslexic pupils have achieved A*s and served as head girl.

Games, options, the arts: A school known for its gymnasts ('we're hot on gymnastics here,' says one pupil, proudly); there's an excellent complex with sports hall, specialist gymnasts' training hall with sprung floor, strategy area with teachers' rooms leading off and viewing gallery. All sport is played keenly and to a high standard – including hockey, netball, rounders, swimming and tennis. Enthusiastic uptake of a new system of 'development squads' for the keen but less naturally able players. Increased number of fixtures for the B and C teams after parental complaints that the A teams were stealing the show.

It's a small campus and space is at a premium, but on-site facilities are supplemented by use of formidable local ones, such as the Surrey Sports Park at the University of Surrey – the school has an agreement that lets the hockey team use it as their home pitch, allowing the introduction of junior hockey; other sports include spinning, zumba, a climbing wall and squash. Tennis is on two on-site all-weather tennis courts. Tormead has sporting success at county level and nationally, especially in swimming, gymnastics, biathlon and sports acrobatics – a lack of on-site facilities isn't holding them back.

Music strong but school is looking to improve. Mandatory until year 9, enthusiastic participation afterwards. Some 275 individual music lessons a week, plus two senior school orchestras, a jazz band (which tours Europe biennially), numerous ensembles and choirs. School actively seeking to develop performance opportunities for budding musicians, including lunchtime concerts on campus and in town. A programme of events throughout the year, including the inter-house music competition in which every girl takes part. The performing arts centre provides a modern and vibrant venue, with a proscenium stage and professional lighting and sound. Drama teacher described by pupils as excellent – nearly 100 per cent of GCSE students attained A*/A. LAMDA speech and drama awards are a popular extra-curricular option and several girls each year get gold medals. Art is exceptionally strong here – wonderful examples are on display around the school.

Much buzz around other extra-curriculars, including additional sporting, language, film, art and craft activities, plus fencing, movie club, cake decorating, origami and debating (another school success story). Sports and music clubs can be selective, but there is something for everyone and there is a definite 'have a go' attitude. Students regularly achieve recognition in D of E Award Scheme (multiple gold awards achieved each year), the Wings of Hope Achievement Awards, and others. School is one of only a handful nationally to have been awarded Star status by the British Schools Exploring Society. Pupils also participate in the World Challenge expeditions; past destinations have included Costa Rica, Bolivia, China, and most recently, Vietnam.

Background and atmosphere: Founded in 1905, the school has made do in the past with a hodge-podge of classrooms and Hogwarts-style corridors tacked onto the original Victorian building ('Frankenstein's building,' quips Foord), but is now launching an ambitious building project to modernize existing facilities, expand classrooms and exhibition space, enlarge the dining hall (allowing longer lunches and mid-day activities), and create a drop-off zone to ease congestion on the residential street in front of the school. Goal is not to increase size of the student body, but to 'improve the experience of those already there.' Grounds are relatively small, befitting Tormead's practically urban status within Guildford. It feels quite intimate and is divided into four sections, each with its own head reporting to Mrs Foord – junior, lower, upper and sixth form; parents comment on how 'sensible' this arrangement is.

Numerous and well-equipped science labs (sciences very strong here), plus a dedicated sixth form physics room with a white board, computers, etc. Super textiles room (inspiring stuff going on in there), plus the impressive art department and design and technology room. Two libraries, one small and snuggly, the other larger and brighter, used for lessons, quiet research, etc. Library resources accessible from home. The dining hall is used by both the senior school and the junior school across the road, so the crush is considerable, but the new facilities should solve the congestion problem. Food described as 'pretty good for school food,' with an array of hot and cold selections – salad and pasta bar, jacket potatoes, etc. Increasing uptake of the early morning breakfast club, which starts at 7:50. IT provision good, with plenty of computers and internet connections, wi-fi soon available to the whole school, but closely monitored, as school is still considering how to integrate technology into school life without opening the floodgates to Facebook and Twitter on campus.

The sixth formers have their own department (revered and envied by the younger girls), no uniform, and recently refurbished lair complete with kitchen facilities, groovy furniture and a clock designed by the DT teacher. Sixth form girls love their freedom and love being treated as equals, compliment the school on letting them organize charity events, discos, etc themselves. They are visibly proud of their achievements in maths and science and comment on how much extra time teachers will spend to help students understand the material. Popular socials with local boys' schools – RGS, Lanesboro, Cranmore – plus quite the social life with other Guildford schools via the daily train journeys.

Pastoral care and discipline: A strength of the school is its nurturing environment. Various problem-solving options that start with the form tutor. A trained counsellor on hand. System of 'aunts' whereby every new girl has another girl assigned to her to help through the first few weeks. New full-time staff member for university counselling and professional development, keen to refocus pupils not only on university entrance but also 'what they will be like when they're 35 and beyond.' 'Oxbridge teas' to link past and present pupils, higher education evening for lower sixth, even support for SAT tests for those pupils considering university in the US.

Pastoral care programme unanimously praised by parents as superb, for some the deciding factor in choosing the school. 'My daughter comes off the bus happy all the time. Nothing seems to overwhelm her,' says one parent. Another notes, 'Mine doesn't compare herself to others, but she used to in her old school. Academics used to be very hard, now she just takes it in her stride.' Less confident girls benefit from the caring and positive ethos; girls leave the school with self-confidence, good social skills and a dash of worldliness.

Parents 'have no hesitation' in getting in touch with the school. Any issues are dealt with promptly. PSHE lessons start in the junior school and extend, by the time they reach the sixth form, to discussions about substance abuse, personal safety, relationships and childcare. Assembly an important beginning to the school day, emphasis on care, respect and highlighting the six 'core values' of the school, which cover topics such as respect, academic excellence, a varied curriculum, and bringing out the best in the girls in preparation for life beyond school. Tough line on all transgressions – drugs possession a cause for instant expulsion, similar stance on persistent smoking or misbehavior. Both pupils and parents say bullying is confronted openly and with great success.

Pupils and parents: Pupils are bubbly and enthusiastic, self-confident and friendly. They appreciate their all-girl campus ('You can come to school ugly!') and have a strong sense of their good fortune in being there. Neatly dressed in blue blazers (with new rules for wearing them), no ties, with the occasional personalized uniform in evidence. Happy chatter in the hallways between classes.

Parents mostly English or foreign nationals raised in the area, with a mixture of backgrounds – old girls, professionals, London-bound commuters, first-time buyers. Excellent bus service extends all the way to Esher and Haslemere (and beyond); parents and offspring alike sing its praises. Old girls include comedian Sandy Toksvig and Claudia Parsons, the first woman to circumnavigate the world by car.

Entrance: Entrance exam at 11, with pupils selected for academic potential (reasoning, maths and English), extra-curricular interests and current school reference. No interview. At least 95 per cent of Tormead Junior School girls make the transfer to the senior school, and the remaining places are hotly contested. Top students from feeder schools including Rydes Hill, Rowan, St Hilary's Godalming and Halstead. Some 25 to 30 per cent from state schools. Sixth form entrance requirements include seven GCSEs, A*-C, with a minimum of four Bs in the subjects to be studied (Tormead students usually far exceed these requirements). Girls entering sixth form from other schools will be interviewed.

Exit: Most stay on for sixth form – about 25 per cent go elsewhere. About ten per cent each year go on to Oxbridge (three in 2013), otherwise a wide array of destinations: Birmingham, Bristol, Cardiff, Durham, Exeter, Imperial, King's, Leeds, Nottingham, Southampton, St. Andrews. Medicine, engineering and art strongly represented.

Money matters: Parents remark on the 'good value' represented by the school. At 11+, five academic, three music and three art scholarships, worth up to 25 per cent of tuition fees. For sixth form, five academic, two music, and two art scholarships, plus two internal sport scholarships. Full bursaries available at 11+ and 16+ on a case-by-case basis.

Remarks: A nurturing, buzzy school with a tradition of high academic standards that is not content to rest on its laurels. Ambitious plans for facilities should bring it in line with its aspirations. Opportunities for pupils to find their niche, whether in art, sport, drama or music, while still encouraging experimentation and maintaining an all-round approach.

Torquay Boys' Grammar School

Shiphay Manor Drive, Torquay, Devon, TQ2 7EL

• Pupils: 1,050 boys • Ages: 11–18 • Non-denom • State

Tel: 01803 615501
Email: enquiries@tbgs.torbay.sch.uk
Website: www.tbgs.co.uk

Head: Previous head Roy Pike retired in December 2013.

Deputy head Peter Lawrence will be acting head while a successor is appointed.

Academic matters: Eighty-one per cent A*-B grades and 52 per cent A*/A at A level, and 60 per cent A*/A at GCSE in 2013. Maths, English and science have all scored extremely well. Interesting choices abound at A level. 22 subjects on offer including some taught to mixed classes with girls from neighbouring Torquay Grammar School for Girls – optimises available resources and a good way of mixing. Fortnightly timetable gives more flexibility and allows for one hour lessons. Boys encouraged to take AS critical thinking; A level RE is also popular across the board (course focuses on philosophy and ethics). History is rated highly by parents. Number of further mathematicians indicates strength of the subject – 'fabulous' teaching said one parent – noteworthy successes in national maths challenge (made top one per cent and has represented UK internationally). IT suites in each department and no shortage of interactive smartboards. Aspiring medics given lessons looking at ethical issues. Also offers IB.

At a time when MFL are suffering a decline nationally TBGS is offering Spanish, French, German, Japanese and Chinese. Spanish and Chinese are emerging as front runners; designated as a Confucius school, committed to helping other schools improve their Chinese provision. Amazing range of exchanges, visits, links (including one with Jiaxing university in China), work experience abroad etc. Joint winners of Spanish embassy's school of the year award. Spanish head of department is taking Chinese herself and reported that it is 'very challenging' but that 'boys are picking it up remarkably well'. Business and enterprise specialism, sponsored by HSBC. Boys meet for lessons in 'wow factor' boardroom atmosphere with 25 computers with dual flat screens 'churning out economic information'. Reuters link enables boys to simulate city financial dealing. Boys in year 9 get an introductory lesson per week.

As school has increased in size, has created two new houses enabling class sizes to be reduced to 25 in lower school. Library is well stocked: a good place for boys to work during free periods.

Panel for individual needs for pupils who are dyslexic or have problems with numeracy etc. Opportunities galore for gifted and able.

Games, options, the arts: Dedicated staff, talented athletes and good facilities provide recipe for success. Boys all get two hours of games and one hour of PE each week. Matches are generally played on Wednesday afternoons or after school. Reputed to be a football school but also has strong tradition in swimming and water-polo. Rugby, cross-country, hockey, athletics, cricket and tennis (full time coach). Every sport has regional or county championship teams and all four Torbay Hockey Club teams are stuffed with students from here. When we visited, U16 team had just become national football champions – no mean feat. Fifty boys in year 10 take sports leaders award. Astroturf shared with TGGS next door plus half-size one. Sports hall large enough for three basketball courts. Boys pay £10 a year to enjoy benefits of heavily-used fitness suite. Ten Tors (school holds 45 mile record time) and D of E Gold Award plus demanding Three Peaks Challenge. All students are treated to potholing, canoeing, rock-climbing, orienteering plus special rates with local sailing club for all.

Lots of visits further afield: economics conference in Paris, 27 art students going to Barcelona and A level biologists spending 10 days in Costa Rica. Strong house system includes novel ways of charity fundraising. Music is especially strong with whole range of activities from trad to modern. New block includes five individual practice rooms. Over 30 boys play in wind band and a dozen or so in strings orchestra. Twenty-strong jazz band recently played at Montreux Jazz Festival. Director of music forms ad hoc orchestra for one-off events. School choir for all ages plus full scale musical each year at end of spring term. Individual successes include national youth choir and distinctions in grade 8 music exams. Boys often make Devon orchestra.

Drama has benefited from new theatre in addition to well-equipped studio. Number of productions has increased with new theatre; GCSE well established and A level in pipeline; lots of co-operation with TGGS. Lively media studies department – film-making, local radio, podcasts, blogs etc; excellent school intranet is kept up to date by students. Innovative art department involves upward of 30 boys in each sixth form year – includes digital design and sculpture work. Benefited from relocation to Manor. DT staff also enthusiastic and workshop area well resourced with CADCAM suite and latest production software to capitalise on boys' creative designs and ideas.

Whole range of clubs and activities at lunchtimes and after school; local ATC has HQ on site – some boys belong to this or in larger numbers to school's own scout troop. Some 250 participate in house chess championship and top players go on to win at national and international level. School has a 19-inch Newtonian telescope, one of the largest in the south west; members of the after-school astronomy club undertake deep sky photography and video imaging of the moon and planets. Not surprisingly, the school's patron was famous astronomer, Sir Patrick Moore, and Chris Lintott, Sky at Night presenter, is a past pupil. Dartmoor society extremely active. List is endless.

Background and atmosphere: A fine site of 40 acres situated 15 minutes above Torquay town centre. School benefited from former grant maintained status and continues to be successful at attracting investment. Sixty-five classrooms well arranged in different subject areas. Entrance foyer juxtaposes past glories and present day achievements. Purposeful atmosphere and dedicated teachers (parents testify to this). Works closely with neighbouring Torquay Community College to help raise standards and academic aspiration of pupils. Refurbishment of the Manor as an art centre allowed further expansion of science laboratories and a resource area for maths. Head believes that keeping things constantly on the move raises morale generally.

Pupils rave about the food. School's nutrition action group (including community dietician, school nurse, parents and pupils) recently won award for promotion of healthy eating; 'boys only get chips once a year,' said chef, but at least one mum thought boys should still be allowed doughnuts 'which they loved' as an occasional treat. Good value. Newly branded 'bistro' operates in former school hall. In 2012, school became a multi-academy Trust incorporating Torquay Academy, a neighbouring non-selective school.

T

Pastoral care and discipline: Evident respect between pupils and teachers. Consultative approach to rules. Participatory and co-operative culture among pupils. Bullying dealt with sensitively – where possible would try to turn the bully around; instant punishment is not preferred route. Strong house system through school with seniors encouraged to take leadership roles. Year 13 boys mentor years 7-9. Active school council: junior and senior sections meet regularly to voice boys' ideas – recent successes have included the new Astroturf. Parents approve of school's hard line on drugs etc and praise work of heads of houses. Appearance is mainly tidy without being rigid. Uniform cards operate if things get too sloppy. No stone left unturned.

Pupils and parents: Parents come from a large area stretching from Plymouth across to Exeter; many move to be near school. Recent establishment of Metereological Office in Exeter has brought fresh influx of professional families. Notable past pupils too numerous to mention but include Chris Read (Nottinghamshire captain and former England wicket keeper), former Wimbledon tennis player Mike Sangster, newspaper mogul Sir Ray Tindle, Marcus Bateman (world champion rower) and six times British swimming champion Malcolm Windeatt; Professors Simon Whittaker (St John's, Oxford), Ian Diamond (Vice Chancellor, Aberdeen University) and David Southwood, Director of Science at the European Space Agency. One former languages graduate, Marcus Richardson, now fluent in Serbo-Croat, became interpreter at the War Crimes Tribunal at The Hague, and Tom Ewing is one of the UK's top fund managers. Chris Lintott, old boy and Cambridge astronomer, worked alongside Patrick Moore.

Not much ethnic diversity but school has grown links with a school in London through the Beacon initiative. As long as they have the ability, all types of boys excel here, from slightly-built budding masterminds to burly rugby types. Student of the week award recognises every conceivable kind of achievement. Younger pupils seem relaxed and happy, while older ones are extremely polite and incredibly mature. All seem modestly proud to be here. 'Phenomenal,' say parents. One father had turned down a job elsewhere to keep his son at TBGS. No regrets.

Entrance: 'Not super selective.' Takes from up to 70 primary schools, with some coming in at 13 and some at sixth form. Exam includes NFER verbal reasoning, plus maths and English set by the school. Candidates have to pass at least two of the three elements. Numbers have risen from 750 to 1,000+ in last five years; head trying to resist further expansion. Boys not admitted to sixth form with fewer than six GCSE successes at B or above.

Exit: More than 95 per cent to university including Oxbridge. Other preferences are Cardiff, Bristol, Bath, Southampton. Medicine is popular as is science, followed by maths, law, business and sports studies. Various scholarships and awards.

Remarks: Achieves fantastic results compared with far more selective schools. Produces career-driven, well-presented boys who work hard and play hard. Amazing that Torquay should be able to boast a school of this calibre.

Torquay Girls' Grammar School

30 Shiphay Lane, Torquay, Devon, TQ2 7DY

• Pupils: 890 girls • Ages: 11–18 • Non–denom • State

Tel: 01803 613215
Email: admin@tggsacademy.org
Website: www.tggs.torbay.sch.uk

Headteacher: Dr Nick Smith MB BS PGCE NPQH, a pragmatic, determined man in his late 40s, has been in the hot seat at TGGS since 2007. A qualified scientist who practised medicine for a couple of years, and, yes, he did work at London Zoo looking after the penguins, he has brought the clear thinking of a trained empiricist to his task at TGGS.

Dapper, self-effacing and charming, he has brought vision and vigour to an old-fashioned grammar school. 'He knows what he wants and is relentless in achieving it' was typical of the comments we heard from parents. But we got the distinct impression within the school that the culture was not just geared towards better and better results. 'Caring for others' and 'working in a happy and caring environment' were the kind of phrases mentioned often and there was much evidence that these were not just platitudes.

Universally admired by pupils, parents and teachers alike, Dr Smith could deservedly rest on his laurels at his home on Bodmin Moor, where he lives with his wife (and fellow-teacher) and two children, and from where he yomps across the Cornish wilderness (he's a former marathon runner), but he is not finished yet.

Although his justifiable claim that TGGS is very successful in 'adding value' to his incoming cohort, he wants to do much more, especially in terms of enhancing the aspirations and ambitions of his female pupils. Of course, phrases like these are often spoken by headteachers, but this man has a gleam in his eye when he uses them that is very convincing.

Ideally suited to lead an academy school, he relishes the independence it gives him and is not daunted by the chief executive challenges that come with the autonomy; in fact, he relishes them.

Academic matters: TGGS is, first and foremost, a school that sees the achievement of outstanding academic results as its primary responsibility. The girls are encouraged to work hard and aim high. There is an aura of quiet industry about the place. In fact, we heard neither shrieks nor screams. There was an absence of the more typical mayhem of narrow corridors channelling too many youngsters to the next lesson and of doors being slammed with teachers bellowing orders over the din.

But the girls do not learn by rote, nor do they learn just to pass examinations. Here are the school's 'Four Common Teaching Elements', a praiseworthy benchmark for the staff:
1. Are the girls told why they are doing this work?
2. Are the girls made to think?
3. Does the lesson maintain the girls' focus?
4. Are the girls shown how to improve?

Results continue to progress in a steady climb and the school has the graphs to prove it. Recent A level figures include an A*-B success rate of 78 per cent across 24 subjects (including a few subjects shared with Torquay Boys' Grammar School), up from 73 per cent previously. This improvement moves the school into the top 20 nationally (among girls' state schools). GCSE results show a similarly strong improvement, meeting the school's latest target of 72 per cent of grades A*/A.

The curriculum is described in great detail in a lengthy booklet, part of an elaborate set of marketing brochures (although they would all benefit from some diligent proofreading) which are not unlike the glossy sales material of a private school. There is plenty of detail for each department, a 'Careers' box, which lists the likely employment destinations in that subject area, and useful lists of 'Students will need to:', which itemise 'compulsory' and 'optional' study requirements. At 40 pages of A4 in a small font size, it is a heavy read, but a good one.

The school is proud of its membership of the South West Academic Trust, an elite 'Russell Group' of nine Wessex schools in association with the University of Exeter, which brings shared values and commitment to excellence.

Although TGGS is a humanities specialist school, with geography being particularly strong, it has strengths across the curriculum, including good biology, maths and art departments. It also offers the AQA Baccalaureate in the sixth form and has introduced innovations like academic mentoring, where older girls support younger ones in a Big Red Bus bought specifically to provide a novel environment for the initiative. Although it is something of an endearing gimmick, it works; the girls cherish it – 'It's our space, we love it' – and Dr Smith readily embraces gimmicks that produce results.

The school has kept pace with technological change and many teaching spaces bristle with digital gizmos of all kinds. Those of us in the older echelons of the population might be daunted by it all, but we were impressed that both teachers and staff talked about learning together through the internet and that whiteboards, YouTube and social media outlets are as much part of the teaching fabric as blackboard and chalk were in the past.

Another important didactic tool is the list of learning skills, which gives 16 semantic anchor points for the school's aspirations. Key words like Concentration, Resilience, Collaboration and Creativity are recited like a catechism throughout the school by both staff and pupils. It is a somewhat clichéd mechanism, but again, it works and focuses everyone on the school's aspirations.

There is an admirable procedure to support those girls who find the rarefied intellectual atmosphere difficult. The incoming intake is assessed by the MidYIS cognitive test and all the girls are then colour-coded on a huge display board in the staffroom. This then becomes the touchstone for the girls' progress throughout their school careers. Significantly, there are clear strategies for girls who are at the bottom of the league and those who start to slip downwards. In some years it can be as many as 15 (slightly more than 10 per cent of the intake), in other years it can be as few as five.

Driven by its own imperative of ensuring that all girls achieve a minimum of five A*/As at GCSE, underperforming girls are supported by a study programme in the school's Study Centre, run by two full-time members of staff. Girls can be taken off timetable, or subjects dropped, to create more time to concentrate on other priorities.

Each of the senior staff, including the head, 'adopts' up to five girls in this category and becomes their mentors through this remedial programme. All the while, the objective, in a telling phrase, is the desire 'to get them through', a worthy sentiment that is mirrored in the school's approach to any girls who may be having emotional or behavioural problems, or issues at home. At examination time they can engage in a study programme which provides breakfast, keynote sessions and revision in the library.

Games, options, the arts: There is a wide range of sports on offer, both within the curriculum and as out-of-school activities, some more esoteric than others. They include aerobics, cricket, fitball, boxercise, hockey, netball, tennis, badminton, rounders, swimming, outdoor pursuits, athletics and football. There are also options offered externally in scuba diving, mountain biking, dry-slope skiing, squash, horse riding, sailing and windsurfing. Fixtures are frequent and at all levels and there is success at local, county and national level.

It is a huge list; but is sport a major priority at the school? It appeared to us to be more about 'rounding' the girls, and an opportunity for them to let off steam, than central to school life.

Facilities are good and improving, including an Astroturf, plus a second one shared with their neighbours (Torquay Boys'), and a brand new sports hall, replacing the antiquated, yet evocative, previous hall, which had the wooden wall bars and climbing ropes many of us remember from our own school days – ah, happy memories!

There is a very strong art department with commendable results and its impressive work is on display around the school. The music, media and drama suites are modern and there is a range of drama productions and performances from the orchestra, choir, flute group and jazz band.

There is a somewhat whimsical House Culture Calendar, which includes several Dr Smith 'traditions' designed to bring the school its own idiosyncratic identity. They include the 'House Shout', where the girls and the staff in each house sing a song of their choice at the end of term assembly, and the formal handover ceremony of the head girl's jacket – as at the Augusta Masters' golf tournament.

These 'Smith traditions' are a consequence of something he was told when he arrived at the school in 2007: that the school was proud of its long-standing traditions. But when he asked what they were, he found that nothing of substance was forthcoming, other than that the school had been around for a while! Thus, his innovations: the Culture Calendar, Big Red Bus, 'Shouts' and other clever mechanisms designed to bring an old-fashioned school into the 21st century.

The list of clubs, trips and activities is exceptional. Not surprisingly, given the school's proximity to the marvels of Dartmoor, The Duke of Edinburgh Award is prominent, as is the Ten Tors Challenge. The school owns a residence in Brittany, to which all pupils will go twice in their school career, while the current rota of trips includes: China, Cuba, Iceland, Mongolia, Nicaragua, Croatia (to study Adriatic dolphins) and Kenya, where TGGS supports a local school. Interestingly, when we questioned the unusual choice of Mongolia, the answer came back quickly, 'Because that's where the girls wanted to go.'

Background and atmosphere: 'Never judge a book by its cover'; this aphorism sits well with TGGS. Its central building is a 1939 structure with an unconvincing claim to be Art Deco; it is better described as Pre-War Drab. It is the school's least endearing feature, although new buildings, including a new dining hall and sixth form centre, help alleviate the dour central block.

Not surprisingly in this jaunty institution, nobody within the school seems to bemoan their dreary abode. In fact, they tend to nurture it like an aging relative: 'Yes, it's a bit cold in the corridors and some of the rooms are cramped, but we love it; it's our home.'

The central reception area is a motif of the school in miniature. Compact and brightly decorated, four black and white portraits of former headmistresses hark back to the old days. But everything else reflects the new TGGS. No photographs of the staff in their austere academic robes here, rather a collection of pen pictures of smiling faces, including all the non-academic staff.

Pastoral care and discipline: The school boasts, legitimately, much pastoral care and little need for discipline. Of course, bright girls are not without problems, both behavioural and social, and TGGS has a strong pastoral care regime led by the heads of year. Inevitably, the school has 'problem' pupils like any other, but places a strong emphasis on human relationships and core values.

There is strict code on bullying; a phenomenon that pupils and parents are unanimous in reporting is almost non-existent. They are equally adamant that ill-discipline is a rarity. In an affirmation of this, the girls we spoke to were at pains to explain that they felt it is their responsibility to deal with most issues and that they hope members of staff would only need to become involved on rare occasions.

Problems are dealt with according to very clearly defined procedures. The school is proud of the commendable belief that the first line of defence in dealing with issues is the girls themselves and that it promotes an ethos of support and mutual care between them, an article of faith that was confirmed by the girls we spoke to.

Further bulwarks are the class tutors, year heads (who follow their year group up through the school), the school's own dedicated personal counsellor, a part-share of careers adviser and a visiting nurse. Finally, Dr Smith's three deputies oversee the heads of year.

When we pressed Dr Smith about where his threshold on behaviour was fixed, it was clear that he would have no hesitation in excluding a girl whose behaviour was unacceptable. Reassuringly, we were left in no doubt that he meant what he said.

Wholesome food is a top priority and a recent innovation is a cashless service (operated biometrically by thumb print) which allows parents to monitor exactly what their daughters are eating. Indeed, the entire school is cashless and every parent has an online account. The new kitchen and servery gleam and are staffed by a very cheerful group of dinner ladies.

Pupils and parents: There is a strong consensus in this focused and happy school between parents and pupils about its ambitions and ethos. 'The school punches well above its weight', 'There is a strong emphasis on decency and human values', 'The rapport between the girls and their teachers is remarkable', were a few of the positive comments from parents.

Pupils were equally voluble with their positive comments: 'It's like nowhere else', 'The staff are always there to help', 'We want to do well for them'. When asked about the school, the word 'pride' came up repeatedly from the girls. They also stressed that the pejorative terms, 'nerd' or 'boffin', sadly so common in the adolescent vocabulary, are not in the lexicon at TGGS. 'We are admired for being clever here', 'it is easier to succeed here than at schools our friends go to'.

School uniform is an uncomplicated navy blue for the main school and a black and white ensemble for sixth formers. However, the current vogue of pulling skirts up as high as they will go is a blight at TGGS, just as it is in so many schools.

Famous alumni are impressive, as they should be of course, and include leading academics, people in the media, lawyers and doctors. But Dr Smith is very committed to new employment opportunities for his girls. Because women remain underrepresented at the highest levels in many areas of employment, he feels his continuing mission is to expand the personal development of his charges, while maintaining the school's lofty academic standards. 'Encouraging future leaders in industry, finance and commerce' is his avowed cause.

Entrance: TGGS is over-subscribed and admission is based solely on ability. There are 120 places available at 11+. Selection is determined by verbal reasoning, maths and English examinations in two sessions and the intake represents the top 25 per cent on the academic scale.

About 60 girls join the sixth form from other state schools. The entry requirements are: seven GCSE A*-B, plus some subject-specific requirements set out in the school's sixth form prospectus.

Exit: Some 95 per cent of girls stay on for the sixth form. Almost 90 per cent to their first-choice university, around three-quarters to Russell Group institutions; five Oxbridge offers in 2103. There is a broad range of future careers for TGGS girls. A recent cohort produced eight doctors, four vets, two physiotherapists and several dentists and pharmacists and there was a typical spread of lawyers, teachers and jobs in other public sectors.

Remarks: 'Definitely one to watch' was a key phrase in our previous report. We also proffered the thought that it was time for the school to claim a 'bigger share of the limelight'. Sharp eyes would now readily attest that TGGS has indeed moved directly into the bright glare of the academic elite of the South West.

Not for nothing has the school been awarded an 'Outstanding' accolade by Ofsted. If you are looking for a single-sex haven for your daughter, which places great emphasis on intellectual gifts and the future employment prospects of its girls, this is the school for you.

It does not disregard those towards the lower end of its academic intake, indeed it offers them great support and encouragement, however, it is unashamedly about nurturing excellence for as many girls as possible.

It firmly believes in creating a cheerful and caring environment and in producing rounded individuals, but is candid in stating that its primary concern is academic success.

Tring Park School for the Performing Arts

Linked school: Tring Park School for the Performing Arts Preparatory School

Tring Park, Tring, Hertfordshire, HP23 5LX

• Pupils: 320; 230 girls, 90 boys. Three quarters board. • Ages: 8-19 • Non-denom, but traditionally Christian • Fees: Day £19,050-£20,700; Boarding £28,950-£30,990 pa • Independent

Tel: 01442 824255
Email: info@tringpark.com
Website: www.tringpark.com

Principal: Since 2002, Mr Stefan Anderson MA BMus ARCM ARCT (fiftyish). Attended Carleton University, Ottawa, the Royal College of Music and Emmanuel College, Cambridge. Previously director of music at King's Canterbury for seven years and prior to that assistant director of music and organist at Wellington College. The first man – and, we assume, the first Canadian – to be principal of Tring Park. For someone with a background in the most traditional of traditional public schools, he brings a surprisingly light touch, a dash of eccentricity and buckets of enthusiasm to this very special job. 'He's got exactly the right balance,' one parent told us, 'between holding the line on discipline and gaining the trust of the children.' The trad background probably helps keep feet on the ground, order intact and the mundanity of things like GCSE revision cracking on, in a place where the airy fairy is always whispering temptingly from the wings.

Academic matters: Academic work takes up half of each day and 'vocational' work, ie dance, drama, music theatre and music, takes up the other half. Given that, and the fact that pupils are selected only for their performing abilities, the academic results are more than creditable. In 2013, 90 per cent A*-C at GCSE and 74 per cent A*-B at A level. A smaller number of subjects available here than elsewhere – 17 A level options (and several of those are 'vocational' eg dance, theatre studies and film studies) and BTEC National Diploma in performing arts. Popular subjects are all the vocational ones plus art and design. Few other subjects get more than a handful of takers at A level. This makes for small classes and a range of decent results mostly in the A-C bracket. French and German on offer but only one can be taken at GCSE. Newish science labs. SEN is big here – a quarter of pupils are dyslexic – something to do with

T

people with aptitudes in drama and musical theatre having a tendency in this direction, apparently. No statemented kids when we visited but 56 at School Action Plus and 34 at School Action. One or two full time equivalent learning support staff. No Saturday lessons per se but some extras are bunged onto this spare day, eg preparation for RADA exams and Spanish classes.

Games, options, the arts: Well, that's what this place is all about – minus the games. We have previously said that 'you simply wouldn't come here if sport matters much to you,' but sport is keenly missed by many, especially by the younger pupils ('but if they have the time or the energy to do sport, after everything the school throws at them, then they're not working hard enough!' a parent insisted.) Of course dancers can't afford sports injuries and everyone expends huge energy and develops high-level fitness with the rigours of dance training. Everyone dances, including drama students who may never have done a step before coming here. 'Dance' covers classical ballet, contemporary, tap, jazz, musical theatre, notation and choreography, dance medicine, dance journalism etc etc. The top dancers are a joy to behold. A former pupil, now in Matthew Bourne's Company, was making a film involving 11 Tring students on the day we visited. Lots of rigour, but perhaps not with the hardcore, blood-on-the-toe shoes ferocity you find in the specialist ballet schools? Musical theatre students study acting, voice and speech, singing – and dance. Drama students do all the above plus more extensive theatre training in many technical areas. Energy levels are dizzying – no shrinking or self-consciousness here – everyone gives their all.

There is some confusion over the role of music in the school: while this is a musical place – with over 200 individual music lessons a week and much emphasis on singing and choral music – music in not offered as a specialism in the way it is at the specialist music schools (despite what some school literature suggests). There is no school orchestra (at the moment) and, aside from singing, the standard of music is no higher than at other mainstream independent schools. Everyone takes art to GCSE and a good range of media available. Super, purposeful art studios – not too tidy. Classes in film take in camera technique, story-boarding etc – all very practical and seriously undertaken. Debating society competes against other schools.

Background and atmosphere: Founded as the Arts Educational School in 1919 in London, Tring Park was bought from the Rothschild family in 1945 to be used as a second location overseen by the same principal. Over the years, the two locations grew apart and in 1994 formally separated. In 2008 the school decided to change its name to Tring Park School for the Performing Arts: a mouthful, but a more accurate and better name. The director of dance, who has been at the school for 25 years, wrote a brilliant article in recent school magazine describing the school when she first arrived: 'Tring was rather like a parallel universe where the strange 'matrons' in white coats ruled the school, and the dormitories were so cold that the girls (we did not have boys until 1992) used to wear all their home clothes over their PJs to keep warm and scrape ice off the inside of the windows to see outside ...and 'hairwashing' featured on the timetable...'.

The main building is as knock-out and as OTT as its denizens. Few schools can boast an atrium, staircase, wallpapers and ceilings of this quality. We peered through 'the biggest piece of glass in the world' to watch the girls-only chamber choir sing like angels. All this said, the school is in need of more teaching space and a variety of upgrades. The Markova Theatre, seating 170 and built in 1990 when the school was still girls only, would be brilliant in a normal school but feels a bit pokey here. Tring has already received a grant from the DfE towards an ambitious development plan and the school has planning permission for a three-phase development including studios, a new art block and sixth form study centre and finally a new theatre. Phase I

of this programme is now complete. The Park Studios consist of five state-of-the-art performance studios which are used for dance and musical theatre.

Music and movement resounds from room after room. Costumes for the English National Ballet's Nutcracker slumber in the hallways, waiting to be unleashed each winter when pupils from the school take part. Only the quiet corridors where the academic lessons take place, the newly expanded library and the conventional uniforms, strictly regulated eg no trainers, remind a visitor that this is a real school where coursework, prep and curriculum successfully co-exist with everything else. 'Below stairs' – mostly white-tiled and with narrower corridors – as much in use as the grander areas – for classes, dining, everything. 17 acres of super grounds in which the buildings sit comfortably and lots of huge mature trees make for a very pleasant, established feel. Reach4Dance, the school's outreach programme, offers dance workshops to primary schools in the area, a boys' coaching scheme and other projects.

Pastoral care and discipline: You might think that with this amount of general artiness and hyper-activity, discipline would be a real problem here – but it isn't. A sense of self-discipline is palpable as you go around. Everyone seems to understand that, as the head says, 'they can't mess themselves up,' without risking everything they work so hard for. So only a few incidents of smoking and drinking and three exclusions for drugs since Mr Anderson's arrival.

Boarding accommodation variable but some in splendid grand rooms and all is homely and cosy. Upper sixth girls live in Victorian houses down the road – much appreciated until you're ill and have to trek up to the san (bus whisks girls from the house at 7.15am for breakfast in school at 7.30). Upper sixth boys live a short walk from school. San a large, important hub – counselling available as well as a breathing space and a quiet moment for television-assisted recovery. The school feels like a healthful place – very good salad bar, fresh fruit everywhere. If pupils get below a certain weight, they are taken off dance; if they get thinner, they are sent home.

Pupils and parents: From everywhere. Forty from overseas – in ones and twos, and from some pretty unusual places eg Mexico, Egypt, Cayman Islands, UAE and Ukraine. Ten get EAL help. Otherwise from North Yorks to Cornwall. High proportion, of course, from Herts, Bucks and Beds. Girls outnumber boys throughout – 2.6 to 1 – but boys are an important ingredient in the mix and the school is a haven for some boy dancers who may not have met another boy who danced before they came here. Diversity of backgrounds – many first time boarding families, some experienced public schoolers, some new to the whole thing, on full bursaries. Around a fifth from some kind of performing background. What unites these disparate spirits is the common purpose, the commitment and the energy. Eyes sparkle everywhere and everyone smiles. Ex-pupils include Jane Seymour, Thandie Newton, Caroline Quentin, ballet dancer Tyrone Singleton, Amy Nuttall (Emmerdale) and Anna Carteret. Current pupils are performing in the West End's Sound of Music and Oliver, Inherit the Wind and Angelina Ballerina with the English National Ballet.

Entrance: By audition in your chosen specialism and, for under 16s, a 'very straightforward academic test' used for setting only. Entrants up to age 13 opt for either dance or theatre arts specialisms. In sixth form, theatre arts pupils must choose between musical theatre or drama.

Exit: Recent past students have done everything from read physics at Imperial College to study film at NYU in the States. A few stars straight into major companies eg English National Ballet. Three former pupils in ITV's Downton Abbey; 3 starred in Mamma Mia in the West End; a current pupil playing "Billy" in Billy Elliot and another who's in the Live Finals of ITV's X Factor. Some to university courses in anything from drama to physics. Many to drama or dance schools eg Laine Theatre Arts, The Place and the Bristol Old Vic. Some gap years, some to employment. The school is not particularly rigorous about cataloguing leavers' destinations. Tring has recently introduced a 'third year' sixth form, so far only available for dance, but may extend to musical theatre. The programme includes a 6-performance tour to the Midlands and Wales. Straight-talking career guidance ('we're gently realistic with them') and several pupils mentioned that they saw coming here as a 'low risk option': they could pursue their love of performing without jeopardising their academic opportunities.

Money matters: One third are on 'funding of some kind', but it is a complex mosaic. Forty-one dancers, who enter at 11, 12 or 13, are funded through the government's means-tested Music and Dance Scheme (NB if you are aiming for this pot of funding, it's probably easiest to win for entry at age 11). Thirty-seven dancers enter at age 16 on non means-tested DADA scholarships. Some 20 musical theatre and drama pupils received means-tested scholarships given by the school itself. One of the increasing number of schools to charge a higher fee to pupils who enter in the sixth form.

Remarks: No sacrifice on the academic front if you send your young dancer or actor here – they'll get a pretty balanced regime but masses of what they love best.

Trinity School

Shirley Park, Croydon, Surrey, CR9 7AT

- Pupils: 960; all day; co-educational sixth form • Ages: 11–18 • Christian (respectful of other faiths) • Fees: £13,716 pa • Independent

Tel: 020 8656 9541
Email: admissions@trinity.croydon.sch.uk
Website: www.trinity–school.org

Headmaster: Since 2006, Mr Mark Bishop (forties). Educated Charterhouse and St Edmund Hall, Oxford, PPE moving to theology. Previously deputy and acting headmaster for a term at Caterham School. Brisk, frank, easy to talk to and very determined. Parents and prep heads agree that he is friendly, welcoming, knowledgeable about individuals and focused on getting his school right. Took time out to work in business (as a headhunter for senior leaders; good training, he says) before coming to Trinity, and has an MBA from Henley Business School. This background shows in much of what he has done at Trinity, and he has a vigorous, business-like approach. The organisation of his impressively thought-through three year development plan is stiff with mission statements, key objectives, detailed plans and mild management jargon – and none the worse for that. Performance management and staff development is the key, he believes, to moving the school forward. He thinks that schools and businesses have much in common in management terms, provided one remembers that 'schools are ultimately about children and not the bottom line'. Trinity, he says, was a good school before he arrived, but he is keen to make his mark and says that the place lacked sufficient ambition. This he is anxious to instil in teachers and in pupils. He wants staff to share good practice, to reflect on what they do, and to have feedback, including from the students if they are happy to do so. The school councils (pupils) have discussed both teaching

and learning and he has offered to video teachers teaching. All this could be quite alarming for those in a comfort zone and anxious to remain there, but one gathers that the staff are enjoying the new wind of change blowing through the place, and squaring their shoulders for the advance into the middle of the 21st century.

But Mark Bishop is not a business automaton. His theological degree led him to prioritise pastoral care in his career and he spent a year in Australia and New Zealand on a Churchill Fellowship studying their approach to pastoral care and moral development. Well, people do say that the moral tone of Neighbours is second-to-none. He has spoken at numerous conferences on pastoral care, and now his mission statement at Trinity is 'the rigorous pursuit of excellence balanced by compassionate concern for individuals'. He wants to achieve 'real balance' for his pupils, academic ambition coupled with all-round and varied extra-curricular experience. Parents all mention how good Trinity is at bringing out individual aptitudes and talents, and every parent surveyed said how happy their children were at the school. Brothers and sisters with very different interests have thrived and, for a day school, the list of clubs and societies, the activities on offer and the opportunities available are impressive.

Academic matters: Trinity's results rank highly in the very competitive atmosphere of south London. Mr Bishop is insistent that Trinity is, and will remain, an all-round school with strong extracurricular emphasis, but this is not to be at the expense of academic excellence. In 2013, 85 per cent A*/A at GCSE and 59 per cent A*/A at A Level, 89 per cent A*-B, but Bishop still has some particular departmental targets. He has brought in outside inspection, new teachers, and individual development plans to liven up departments. This brisk approach should pay dividends and results will be worth watching in the next few years.

The subjects offered are on the conservative side – a solid sciences/humanities/modern languages mix. But Mandarin and electronics spice up the curriculum to GCSE and A level respectively. Three boys took Chinese at university in recent years and there is a Chinese exchange programme. Impressive photographic successes and facilities enrich a more traditional approach to art and a local artist has taken up residence. Electronics is on offer at A level and modern foreign languages have received a boost with an influx of new blood recently. Theatre studies and classics have enthusiastic followings with Latin taken to A level by a few, and others taking it in addition to their GCSE loading lower down the school. Greek, government and politics and psychology have recently been introduced to the curriculum.

Most staff teach with their doors open, which is a good sign of their confidence. Their average age is 40 and they are a relatively stable group with 41 having been in the school for more than 10 years. Older classrooms are traditional in layout and in their wood finishes, but the new classroom wing is impressive and airy. Class size averages 22 in the first three years, descending to 10 in the sixth form, but pressure on numbers is pushing this a little higher (see Entrance below). Electronic whiteboards abound and ICT facilities, language technology and equipment generally are impressive. IT is taught in 'chunky' sessions outside the timetable, to allow for the introduction and practice of new software techniques in sustained session. Pupils conduct virtual operations and dissections in the biology labs, and lessons seen were lively and full of interchange between students and staff. Parents and children say that relations between pupils and their teachers are respectful but very friendly, with appropriate familiarity as the students become more mature in the sixth form. Many departments lead days out and trips to support the curriculum, including a recent physics trip to CERN in Geneva (but see the school magazine for the good times had by all). There are a good few women in evidence, although it would be good to see more in management and a few more on the governing body (the Whitgift Foundation with a Trinity Committee).

Special needs are handled sensitively with a new SEN head in place but Trinity is not the school for any other than those with mild difficulties. Lunchtime clubs support both the less able and the gifted.

Games, options, the arts: One of Trinity's greatest strengths is the music. The website and school magazine are stuffed with references to wonderful musical events, such as professional appearances at the Royal Opera House, Garsington, the Coliseum and Glyndebourne as well as television appearances at the Royal Variety Performance, the Pride of Britain Awards and the One Show, to name but a few. Instrumentalists have performed at both Wigmore and Cadogan Halls. There are numerous orchestras, ensembles and choirs. Pupils confirm that it is really cool to be a musician at the school. But it is not just for the specialists; music involves all the new boys when they first arrive and one parent commented how impressed he was that his son took up singing as a result of the encouragement he gained from the junior choir at Trinity, when he had only mimed at his previous school. The music school is a modern, dedicated space. Some have ambitions to continue with musical careers, others see it as a fund for enjoyment in their future lives. Over 500 individual music lessons take place weekly, carefully organised not to impact on academic studies too much. Trinity became London's first All-Steinway secondary school in 2012 (meaning that every piano in the school is a Steinway, including 3 grand pianos).

Trinity has numerous theatres and halls, of varying sizes and architectural impact, and drama benefits accordingly. Drama productions at all levels abound, from the junior self-produced efforts to the high standards of the boys and girls of the sixth form. Examples recently include Great Expectations, Lord of the Flies, Animal Farm and involvement in professional productions. There is an impressive TV/video mixing production facility, partly run by an enthusiastic old boy now working in TV in London. PSE is taught through drama, which must be more effective than a classroom approach to bullying, relationships and the other pitfalls of adolescent life that form the curriculum.

Art has a fairly new, purpose-built building in which to spread itself, with exhibition space and generous classroom facilities. Light floods in to some areas but it is disturbingly gloomy in others. Traditional photography produces pupils who understand about dark rooms and chemicals and computers are plentiful. The design department has CAD facilities and their stylish work is evident from the school's magazine. Trinity students are pretty vocationally focused (see below Exit) and this may be why art does not seem to attract the numbers one might see elsewhere, although one parent specifically cited the art dept as the reason her son had chosen Trinity above other local schools. Conversely perhaps, design has a considerable fan club, and extra-curricularly extraordinary Greenpower F-24 cars take their designers and drivers (junior boys who weigh less) to the finals of competitions in this esoteric field of motor racing.

Sport has received a boost through the recruitment of a number of international sportsmen to the staff and there is clearly the intention to raise Trinity's sporting profile amongst the pupils and the local opposition. Parents have noticed a considerable increase in expectations of staff in this area since the arrival of the head, and all the senior managers take games sessions. The standard school sports, rugby, hockey (boys and girls), netball and cricket, are augmented by an interesting and wide array of alternatives, including soccer, sailing, and sub-aqua, and water polo in the school's newly-refurbished swimming pool in which pupils reach top levels nationally.

In addition to these three main areas, there is a host of clubs, societies and activities in which to get involved: Duke of Edinburgh Award, CCF, community service (ecstatic great-grannies at the Christmas party), mountaineering, electronics, dalek building, journalism, the Hard Sums Club, to name but a few.

The extra-curricular provision at Trinity is overseen by a recently appointed director whose function it is, amongst others, to reconcile conflicting demands of the timetable for individuals.

Background and atmosphere: Trinity School was founded by John Whitgift at the end of the 16th century, as the middle school for Whitgift School. It has branched out on its own now, and occupies a large site in Croydon with generous playing fields augmented by extra pitches half a mile down the road. There is a grass running track, four tennis courts, two Astroturfs and a cricket pitch, delightfully positioned outside the school's windows, with a pavilion. The buildings are perhaps not the school's greatest asset but, in fact, the white concrete materials, the wide corridors and delightful fountained courtyard are all rather appealing. It is certainly functional rather than beautiful, but plenty of green around – grass, trees, shrubs and climbers. Students opt for the light and airiness of most of Trinity over the more hallowed buildings of other local rivals. A new sixth form centre opened in 2011.

Pastoral care and discipline: One of Trinity's main selling points, often reiterated, is its emphasis on pastoral care. Parents make frequent references on how good the school is at responding to individuals. The main emphasis for tutors is individual academic monitoring and pupils commend the friendliness of staff and the generally happy atmosphere in the school. One parent commented on how the children from diverse backgrounds 'all come together; all are equally valued'.

Discipline is firm but explained rather than simply enforced, and the impression is of pupils being allowed to mature into responsibility rather than of a straightjacket. Uniform is mostly neatly worn on the school campus – black with white shirts and school ties and smart business attire for sixth formers. Attitudes to bullying are clear in the PSE programme and the excellent parents' handbook, and the rule on drugs is that anyone who brings them into the school will be asked to leave.

Pupils and parents: Trinity School 'never forgets you have a choice', and parents have many schools within reach to choose from, some independent, some good state. The chief reasons for choosing Trinity are its lack of stuffiness ('Trinity is not precious, it does not have delusions of grandeur,' said a parent), its happy atmosphere, its relatively wide cultural and social mix, its academic record, its music, its activities ('there is something for everyone, it is very diverse,' another parent). The teachers are praised for their care of individuals and their quality of teaching, and their encouragement of weaker brethren. One parent whose son had previously been at a state primary school thought the day was overlong, including activities, with homework on top, but others were delighted that their children were being challenged (which is a word Mr Bishop uses a good deal too) and broadened. Many parents comment on the good friends their children have made at the school.

Entrance: Entrance exams in verbal reasoning, English and maths, and an interview by which the school sets considerable store, particularly for boys not coming from prep schools. Boys need to be at about level 5 in Sats in most subjects to be sure of a place. They come from local prep and state schools and those who do well in entrance tests are automatically assessed for an academic scholarship. Sixth form scholarships are awarded on the basis of entrance exam and interview (honorary ones for those already in the school are awarded for excellent GCSE performance). While children are being examined the parents have the opportunity to meet the headmaster individually. Boys can come at 10+, 11+ (the majority) and 13+, and boys and girls at 16+.

Exit: Most students go on to university, usually without taking a gap year. They choose vocationally-orientated subjects in the main, rather than the humanities or modern languages, such as engineering, accountancy and medicine, maths and law. They choose all the universities one might expect, 50 per cent Russell Group; 10 per cent to Oxbridge.

Money matters: Generous bursary fund where help with fees is awarded to parents on a sliding scale. Will always try to help pupils on bursaries and scholarships when it comes to expensive trips which augment the curriculum or the extracurriculum, and they are often free. Scholarships awarded for academic performance, music, sport, drama, art and design technology.

Remarks: Definitely one to watch if you want a forward-looking, diverse community which puts individuals and their needs first and offers a sufficiently wide range of opportunities to be able to do so. The staff now need to match their pastoral focus to the academic élan to get the school to where Mark Bishop wants it to be.

Truro and Penwith College

College Road, Truro, Cornwall, TR1 3XX

• Pupils: 5000 full time • Ages: 14 upwards • State

Tel: 01872 267000
Email: enquiry@truro-penwith.ac.uk
Website: www.truro-penwith.ac.uk

Principal: Since 2010, Mr David Walrond MA MBA PGCE. Previously worked at the college for seven years as director of curriculum and quality. Has worked in further education institutions in London, Hampshire and Cheshire and has been an associate Ofsted inspector. Early on in his career he lived and worked in Italy where his work ranged from driving a fork lift truck in a scaffolding warehouse to lecturing in English and linguistics at Padua University, and believes that living and working abroad provide invaluable experiences. Introduced the Academic Academy, which offers additional sporting and academic programmes for talented students. He is a passionate follower of cricket and has a keen interest in classical music and literature.

Mr Walrond believes that the college has a reputation for innovation and initiating change rather than just responding to it. 'Above all we focus on giving students the best possible deal. That has to be the pattern for the future and I'm looking forward to working with all staff and students to take forward the remarkable success story of this college.'

Academic matters: You can research courses on the college's excellent website, written in admirably plain English. International Baccalaureate on offer and 36 (out of a possible 45) was the average score in 2013. Fifty AS/A2s to pick from and you can do them in any combination. 'We are always trying new things. With this range of courses you can definitely find the right ones for you.' At A level in 2013, 83 per cent of papers were graded between A* and C. Class size 17, though this is likely to be exceeded in faddy subjects like psychology. No small classes in the interest of efficiency and good educational experience. Twenty-two level 3 extended diplomas on offer, 16 sporting academies and one academic academy. Re-takes in maths and English. Determinedly not de-selective at any stage,

they say, but the proof of the pudding lies in what they call internal progression – the numbers allowed to stay on from year to year. Figures show that the college does not protect its results by deft weeding. You can fail your AS and still go on to do A2 so long as you failed for a good reason. Considering the amount of roguish stats-mongering that goes on in this sector, the college performance in the Department for Education Attainment tables, which puts it in the top 10 per cent of all providers nationally for value added is all the more admirable, on this count at least, and testifies to its loyalty to the needs of the people of Cornwall.

Wonderfully resourced at every turn, this is the sort of place that would tempt any fee-paying parent to toss their chequebook gratefully aside. Quite simply, state-of-the-art everything down to the underground soundproofed bunker in which rock musicians thrash their stuff. Quiet study rooms liberally scattered where you can hunker down or have an impromptu tutorial with your lecturer.

Close relationships with all local schools so as to manage the transition to this big and potentially (initially) bewildering campus. On starting, they'll set you minimum target grades based on your GCSE results, after which regular monitoring won't let you forget them. National stats show good value-added in A level performance. Special needs provision a matter of pride. In this notably adult environment where students must take responsibility for their own learning, many who chafed in what they felt to be a pestering school setting take wings and fly.

Games, options, the arts: Sport a matter of excellence here because of the strength of the sports academies, most of which welcome participation by the student body. 'You'll find the most able sports people in Cornwall here.' What they call Study Plus is your way in to all manner of sporting, creative and recreational activities, some 50 of them. It's a Wednesday afternoon thing and it looks good on your cv. Some courses carry accreditation. Art, music and drama all seriously top notch.

Background and atmosphere: Architecturally stunning but also humane. Ever-expanding (fast but sustained) as HE takes off. Truro College stands in the western suburbs, well served by buses from everywhere which arrive in wave upon wave. The newly redeveloped £30 million Penwith campus based in Penzance significantly adds to the college's provision. The inspired quality of the building makes sense of the college's mission statement in a way that other colleges' retail park architecture dully doesn't. The White Building, a three storey art facility and the Seaton Building for automotive, engineering and construction with classrooms, vehicle bays, workshops and a covered construction area opened in 2012. The feel is that of a university campus (which it now partly is), decidedly adult and also conspicuously friendly. Not a place where you'll feel lost – plasma screens in every building carrying latest info and what's on. It's a buzzy place, everyone looks happy to be here. Ne'er a graffito to be seen – that's what they think of it. Broad range of students of all sorts and ages from the PMLD (profound multiple learning difficulties) group to the growing band of HE students (this is a Plymouth University satellite), bright young things and a sprinkling of grizzled codgers gearing up for a career change. Almost all daytime students are 16-18 year olds. Student satisfaction surveys posted visibly and you can see why. There's less close monitoring than you get in some schools, of course, but doing your A levels here has to make the transition to university easier. Parents universally report satisfaction with the way their sons and daughters were looked after but there's a caveat: only if you can hack this level of responsibility.

Pastoral care and discipline: Your little world within the big world is your 15 strong tutor group; your tutor is someone who teaches you. Parents' evenings, termly report, instant tip-off in case of bunking off. Student services help-desks where you can bring worries about everything from a lost bus pass to HE guidance. Counselling for graver problems. 'If you need help at any time,' says a student, 'they're really open and I've found they really put themselves out for you. As far as the work goes, I think they've been quite strict at keeping me on track.'

Pupils and parents: They come from all over the county. Not ethnically mixed, as isn't Cornwall. Just a few from abroad.

Entrance: Interview at which you get to discuss and choose courses best suited to you. For A levels you'll need five GCSEs at C to get in; for the IB, As or Bs for those areas you want to study.

Exit: Between a dozen and 20 a year to Oxbridge, over 100 to Russell group universities every year and over 1,000 to other universities. Or you can stay on here and do an honours degree (small selection) or one of a growing number of vocational foundation degrees.

Money matters: Pay for your meals and transport. Tuition and textbooks are free.

Remarks: A really inclusive place where you can come with nothing and leave with a degree. Wonderful opportunities in all zones. A level and IB students the majority. People here are more important than glittering statistics – hence, probably, the glittering statistics. That's a win-win.

Truro High School

Linked school: Truro High School Preparatory Department

Falmouth Road, Truro, Cornwall, TR1 2HU

• Pupils: 410 girls (40 board) • Ages: 11–19 • C of E • Fees: Day £11,217; Boarding £21,075–£21,624 pa • Independent

Tel: 01872 272830
Email: admin@trurohigh.co.uk
Website: www.trurohigh.co.uk

Headmistress: Since 2009, Mrs Caroline Pascoe BSc MSc PGCE NPQH (forties). Educated at Tiverton Grammar before reading microbiology at Bristol then opted for a PGCE in physics and science at Roehampton. Completed her MSc in educational leadership at Leicester and followed this with study for a doctorate in education at Exeter. Has also fitted in useful qualifications in youth training and mountain leadership. Began career teaching physics at a Twickenham girls' secondary school before moving to Elliot School, Putney as HoD (whilst there she rowed for GB at the Barcelona Olympics – a finalist in the women's VIIIs). A spell as head of science at Ibstock Place School was followed by six years running her own trekking and climbing business in India: founded Burua School for poor 'hill' children (now 140 strong) and climbed three unnamed peaks in Ladakh. Came to Truro from Wellington School in Somerset, where she had been a successful deputy for five years.

Mrs Pascoe whirled into Truro High not a moment too soon. Girls think she's great and it's clear that she means to carry on as she's started: leading from the front. Married to Brian whose work commitments now limit his involvement in the boarding house. Son, Kiran, is at Truro School. A boarding dad said that his daughters 'like seeing the head in a family mode away from her office responsibilities'. Extra-curricular opportunities for boarders 'have increased greatly,' he added. In addition to headship duties and running boarding (numbers at long last on the up), Mrs Pascoe teaches science to two out of three year 7 groups and recently led expedition from school to climb in the Himalayas and help at Burua. Rowed Cornish gigs across to the mainland from the Scillies as a fund-raiser in summer 2011. Loves what she's doing, exudes purposefulness and trumpets girls' achievements.

Off in April 2014 to head Haberdashers' Monmouth School for Girls.

Academic matters: Recent results show 77 per cent A*-B at A level and 49 per cent A*/A at GCSE in 2013. Head believes in value of the A2 extended project which now overlaps lower and upper sixth years thus avoiding clash with summer AS papers. Twenty-one subjects on offer in the sixth: maths and physics very strong (all girls take separate sciences at GCSE plus a large number take additional maths). English consistently good at both A level and GCSE. Latin holds up very well at GCSE and is still there at A level. Difficult to make direct comparisons with competitors when class sizes are so small but the 'long tail' in a number of A level subjects suggests that some girls are pushing the limits of their academic comfort zone.

Teachers are committed to getting the best out of every pupil – and the small class sizes allow miracles to happen. We noticed how the girls don't hold back in giving their views: no fear of censure by male peers here. We enjoyed watching a year 10 group locked in discussion in their religious philosophy and ethics lesson (compulsory to GCSE with great results). The teaching we saw was enthusiastically delivered and thorough.

Classroom accommodation is generally refurbished, some smartboards and sufficient computers without being a cyberdrome. Some exteriors are short on aesthetic appeal but generally the site works well; juniors, boarders and sports facilities all within easy reach. We were particularly impressed at sixth form level where the atmosphere was relaxed but academically rigorous. Some groups would be considered unviable elsewhere but girls see the sometimes 1:1 ratio in the sixth as a big plus. Just one girl was taking A2 textiles but she certainly wasn't complaining and her work was top standard (as was the teaching room). Parents think their daughters have improved academically by leaps and bounds since joining the school.

Learning support is free on a one-to-one basis for an hour weekly in any girl's first two years. Experienced and well qualified staff; friendly ed psych called in to observe and test as required. Roughly 30 girls currently require support. Sessions are timetabled carefully to minimise losing ground in key subjects; extra help before and after school as well as at lunchtimes. EAL help as required for overseas pupils. Staff have been made increasingly aware of special needs issues. Over 60 enrichment activities – from study trips through digital animation competitions to work experience and a chemistry camp.

Games, options, the arts: School punches above its weight in most sports. Staff include top flight hockey and netball players, school is rightly proud of its reputation for sporting success (two year 11 girls representing England – netball and high jump plus Welsh fencer and two top national pentathletes). School defended seven county team titles in recent years, 25 girls represent county and nine play either hockey or netball for West of England. Increasingly popular girls' football and tag rugby now included in broader sports spectrum. Around 50 per cent of years 7-9 attend extra-curricular sports practices, fewer in higher years. A 25 metre heated indoor swimming pool is well used (open some evenings for boarders). Full sized Astroturf, extensive playing field and two good netball/three tennis courts provide ample outdoor sports facilities. Head's current wish list is topped by sports hall to transform indoor PE provision. Double award GCSE on offer for top athletes.

Music is joint top dog here with loads playing instruments and singing – we watched a lunchtime choir rehearsal with 140+ girls. Carried off main choral accolade at recent Cornish music festival. School orchestra is 50 strong and rehearses after school. School acts as centre for its own diploma candidates, many play in Cornwall youth orchestra. A few have played in national groups and some proceed to music colleges. Director of music regularly leads tours abroad with girls, staff and parents – Belgium and Hong Kong. She is a tower of strength and encourages budding talent where she sees it – even writes parts for beginners to be able to play in the orchestra.

Not much in the way of co-ed collaboration apart from annual concert bash with Truro School. Performing arts centre provides an alternative indoor space to the main hall. Sixth form lesson we saw in Agutter drama studio was quite edgy: 'helps girls to find themselves,' said talented HoD. Lots of performances including major annual production. Strong art department sends plenty of girls to prestigious Falmouth foundation course; experienced, male HoD predates school's ownership of the studios; Kensey group formed to provide exhibition opportunities for former students; technician a well-qualified illustrator. Charity fashion show organised by girls who also went to the NEC for Clothes Show Live. Seventy girls involved in D of E – 16 at gold level. Recent trip to India included community project at Burua school and 12 day trek in the Himalayas (including 5000 metre Bhaba pass) plus some sightseeing. School's first ever team in 2010 Ten Tors challenge on Dartmoor – third fastest all-girl team in 2013. Foreign exchanges, work experience for AS French students as 'mini assistantes', choir trips and loads of excursions at all levels to broaden horizons beyond the peninsular (recent destinations include The Scillies, Malta and Greece). Girls are keen on debating and participate in competitions organised by the ESU and the Cambridge Union. Large numbers take LAMDA qualifications and take part in Rotary public speaking competitions.

Background and atmosphere: Founded in 1880 by Bishop (later Archbishop) Benson (first Master of Wellington College) who built Truro cathedral and gave Henry James the idea for The Turn of the Screw. School motto: Luce Magistra (With light as my teacher) has been stridently transposed into 'Girls First' as its modern logo. Not very churchy despite its origins and we couldn't see why girls who love music wouldn't want to sing hymns in their assemblies. Friendliness between staff and pupils is tangible though school's earlier grammar school incarnation haunts corridors and honours boards. Original school building is relatively small and lies closer to the city centre than its main competitor. From the befittingly Cornish granite (partly castellated) entrance we proceeded towards what is otherwise a hodge podge of buildings stretching back and across a deceptively large site (which includes the useful, if somewhat tired, remnants of a former girls' secondary school) and up the hill to sports pitches. Cross-country can be fitted in without leaving the site we were told. Some building replacement has already happened and super new modern languages suite has shown what can be realised on this site. Ten year development plan to rationalise the rest.

Highly experienced staff includes significant male teachers and some young blood but high property prices 'make it difficult to recruit newly qualified teachers,' says head. Main hall doubles as a gym space but not used for dining (there's a pleasant and spacious refectory which provides yummy lunches for day girls plus breakfast and supper for boarders). Well-stocked library (33,000 volumes plus networked pcs) at heart of school is a welcome haven for private research and study – one girl we spoke to with three noisy siblings at home said she preferred to work there after school. Recent authors visiting have included Cornish children's novelist, Ann Kelley.

Sixth formers have their own recessed study area in addition to individual carrels in their own centre: not ritzy but sensibly planned to allow for leisure or study. Separate boarding houses: Dalvenie for girls in the prep through to year 8 and Rashleigh for girls in year 9-13. Links with Scillies now include offering boarding accommodation to islanders studying at Truro College – 'great PR and a valuable service,' said one islander we spoke to. Both houses offer refurbished accommodation with loads of ensuites plus comfy sitting rooms with all the gizmos. They also interconnect with the dining room so no getting wet on the way to brekky. Actually, there is no brekky on Sundays – girls have opted for lie-ins and inhouse brunch instead. Yawn.

Pastoral care and discipline: Relatively small numbers mean that pastoral deputy has direct leadership of the form tutors who move up with their groups within an overall 'care plan' approach: tutors deliver the PSHE scheme of work and combine pastoral and disciplinarian rôles. Robust anti-bullying policy operates at all levels. Sixth formers (allocated to girls in years 7-9) receiving mentoring training for scheme they call CHAT from Red Cross and the Samaritans. School has been at forefront of National Healthy School Programme with fresh air, healthy food, PSHE and general well-being championed alongside well-honed substance education policy. 'Bonding' residential weekend held at beginning of year 7 for staff and girls at the Penzance or Fowey youth hostel. Everyone here is very accommodating and friendly so individuality can blossom. Discipline problems are rare. Mobile phones were banned under a previous head and no-one seems to mind.

Pupils and parents: Girls we met were fun and loyal: 'every teacher knows who we are,' they beamed. Self confident girls who communicated with us readily and happily. Appearance (Balmoral tartan skirts and green pullovers up to year 11) is neat but not in a stiff and starchy way. Sixth formers take the dress code sensibly and are somewhat difficult to differentiate from staff. Middle-of-the-roaders do particularly well here. The hoped for increase in sixth form numbers would help lift things even more. Head is working at bringing parents and old girls into closer working partnership to support school. Old girls include Dame Lynne Brindley (CEO of British Library), TV presenter Hannah Sandling and mezzo soprano Anna Burford.

Entrance: Mainly from own prep plus Polwhele House, Roselyon, St Piran's, Bolitho and Truro prep. Good sprinkling from state primaries – particularly in Truro. Boarding numbers are finally on increase: majority from UK (some come from Scillies), 15 currently from overseas. Good rail link to Paddington and air (from Newquay) to Gatwick. Applicants for senior school invited to spend a day with appropriate year group then usual round of exam and interview before admission. For sixth form entry, GCSE grade A*/A looked for in proposed A level choices plus interviews for UK candidates (test papers and school assessments for overseas).

Exit: Some (probably too many in recent years) leave at 16 to go to (free) Truro College up the road, Truro School or co-ed boarding elsewhere. Those who leave appear to do so as a change from what they've known since they can remember, rather than as a negative reaction. Art foundation at Falmouth, medicine at Bristol and Cardiff plus wide range of other courses and destinations beyond the Tamar (including two on average each year to Oxbridge).

Money matters: Full range of scholarships (academic, music, sports, art) and means-tested bursaries at year 7 entry and into sixth form. Boarding (all-rounders') scholarships at 13. Extra bursaries occasionally for those suffering from special or temporary pecuniary hardship. Maximum 50 per cent remission of fees.

Remarks: Flying the flag for girls' education in Cornwall. Look beyond the exterior for a Cornish treasure that performs beyond expectations. Under its inspiring head looks set to raise its game across the board. 'Small, family school with lovely relationships,' say parents. A 'must visit' for those seeking an academically challenging yet emotionally nurturing environment for their daughters.

T

Truro School

Linked school: Truro School Prep

Trennick Lane, Truro, Cornwall, TR1 1TH

- Pupils: 965 boys and girls • Ages: 11–18 • Methodist foundation
- Fees: Day £11,865–£12,210; Boarding £20,055–£22,680 pa
- Independent

Tel: 01872 272763
Email: jeg@truroschool.com
Website: www.truroschool.com

Headmaster: Since January 2013, Andrew Gordon-Brown B Com MSc QTS, who comes from a deputy headship at Stonyhurst College in Lancashire; has previously taught at Radley College in Abingdon. He graduated from the University of Cape Town, and qualified as a chartered accountant in South Africa. He then completed an MSc in agricultural economics at Keble College, Oxford, before achieving his QTS via the University of Gloucestershire. Prior to teaching, he spent a dozen years in the financial services industry. He is a keen sportsman, having rowed for South Africa in the 1992 Olympic Games, and for Oxford University in 1994 Boat Race, and sings whenever he gets the chance. Married to Harriet with three young children who are at Truro Prep School.

Academic matters: The previous head's description of the school as 'Cornwall's grammar school' accurately describes the down to earth, meritocratic feel of the place. It's cool to work hard, it's a busy little campus and you can easily see that there's a whole lot of achieving going on. If you haven't done your homework, your fellows will ask you disdainfully, 'Oh? Why not?' For most parents, results are not at all the be all and end all – you don't live in Cornwall to adopt an exclusive focus unless it's for surfing or painting. They want good stats, oh sure, but they also want everything else, all the extra-curricular stuff. The word most apply to the desired end product is 'rounded' by which they mean enriched rather than supersized.

But, yes, results are good across the board. In 2013, 45 per cent A*/A grades at A level and 57 per cent at GCSE. We could find no weak areas, just the odd misfiring teacher (well, everywhere has some of those). Science and maths, though, are particularly strong and popular, with a good many going on to be medics, engineers and – a quirk of this school – geologists (it's an old tin mining thing). Pupils speak very approvingly of the staff and a notable feature is the collaborative way teachers work with the boys and girls – you can watch for yourself as you go around. Relationships are informal, personal and mutually respectful, you can see how it brings out the best, which is why one pupil told us 'no way do they let you get away with being cheeky.' It's all rather grown-up, even more so in the sixth form where uniform yields to smart business suits, a move which has goaded some of the tattier teachers hurriedly to get their sartorial act together.

The curriculum is recognisable to any parent of a certain age – bog or gold standard, whichever you will – the core academic subjects unleavened by anything faddish or vocational. There's theatre studies, a strong department, and art, of course, superbly taught. And there's design technology taught in a proper workshop by proper teachers with oil under their fingernails and machines that make proper things out of proper materials. You get the feeling you could knock up a pretty handy railway carriage in a month of lunchtime sessions. This being Cornwall, they like to make (you guessed it) boats, but they've built an aeroplane – oh, and flown it, too.

Special needs catered for only if your reading is good enough to pass the entry exam – which doesn't leave a lot of room for special needs. A lesson a week for those who need tweaking but, understandably, there's not a lot of call. Gifted and talented programme for the 25 per cent who need it. For sixth formers needing to be taken through a puzzling topic once more, there are drop-in clinics offered by all departments on Wednesday afternoons. Critical Thinking and EPQ also on offer.

It's a buyer's market down here, with the superb FE college up the road offering unbelievable facilities, all the courses you could ever want in any combination and, above all, that chimerical thing they call freedurm. The temptation to take a two-year fees holiday post-GCSE and put together a stash for university must be strong but parents and pupils stay loyal to the school in droves (37 per cent left after GCSE in 2013). Great effort has been made to make the sixth form different, interesting and fun. There are enrichment activities you'd expect, like Young Enterprise, and there's a local initiative, ACHE (advice, care, help and empathy), which trains pupils as listeners (think Samaritans), who then make themselves available to their younger fellows. Very nice café where they can buy healthy snacks and natter and a refurbished sixth form centre. New dining room, with a separate staff and sixth form seating area which has transformed the old heart of the school.

Games, options, the arts: Sport is important and, Cornwall being a county where cauliflower ears are more numerous than cauliflowers, rugby is king. The top players are looked after by the England Under-18 coach and Bill Shankly would approve of the spirit in which they set about it. A new football coach, who is also very involved with the local City team, has now also been appointed. Non-combatants have to do rugby up to GCSE but not in a bloodletting way. Girls' sports growing in stature as numbers rise and the hockey and netball teams now accompany the 1st XV on tours abroad – major, let us tell you, highlights of the school year. Sailing strong, of course, Optimists the boats of choice. Annual inter-house surfing competition. Indoor swimming pool, sports hall and all-weather pitches. Regional and national representation not at all unusual, testifying to good coaching – 'we tend to monopolise the county in terms of excellence.' Brand new Sir Ben Ainslie Sports Centre with an eight court multi-use sports hall, two county standard glass-backed squash courts with viewing gallery, large fitness suite, multi-purpose dance and exercise studio with a sprung wooden floor, five changing rooms and conference facilities.

Art is superb, local artists drop in and do masterclasses, and the school has an excellent gallery of work by local luminaries, Terry Frost et al. Drama top notch, marvellous theatre, highly professional direction. Lots of top class music of all sorts, and they embrace the Cornish wind band tradition. 60-piece orchestra and jazz band. The choir sings at St Paul's and has sung at Festival Mass in St Mark's, Venice. Whatever they do at this school, they like to get out and about and do it.

They like lungfuls of fresh air, too. D of E Award exceedingly strong – 40 going for Gold this year says it all. Ten Tors expedition team places are hotly contested at all three levels. There's an outdoor centre on Bodmin moor where the youngest go and get back to muddy basics.

Wednesday afternoons are for clubs and activities – they operate in lunchtimes, too. There are plenty to choose from. Chess strong, as is fencing. Parents say there's so much to do they have to curb their children's enthusiasm or risk watching them frazzle.

Background and atmosphere: Gloriously situated looking over the River Truro and down onto the cathedral. A Methodist school founded in 1880 and Methodist values infuse the ethos. Original Gothic building in local stone much added to behind making it, in the words of a parent, 'a bit of a warren'. Co-ed since 1990 and feels co-ed for all that many locals still reckon it to be essentially boyish. The only HMC school in Cornwall.

Pastoral care and discipline: Expectations are clear and personal. Nothing heavy-handed and prefects are trained to fill a big brother/sister role vis a vis the younger ones. Yes, some uniforms can look a little louche but we're hardly talking about the dressiest county in the UK. Parents express themselves perfectly happy and rejoice in the way the school really does address itself to the individuality of each and seek to discover peculiar talents. 'He/she just loves going to school,' is something of a refrain. The school motto encourages pupils 'to be rather than to seem to be' and when you've worked out what that means it has to be said that the school remains absolutely true to this.

There's a house system, but it's not characterised by strong local patriotism. Your tutor is your first port of call and your significant other. Parents say they can ring teachers at home in the evening and encounter no terseness – 'the staff really put themselves out'. The chaplain gets rave reviews. Food is cooked by a chef lured from a local hotel. Uptake for lunch has soared from 35 per cent to 80.

Around 70 board, boys and girls, separate houses for each. They're a minority but they don't feel like one – this is definitely not one of those schools where the tide goes out leaving you beached and mateless. There is much praise for houseparents, for close family feel and for ease of contact. Parents with daughters absolutely feel they're safe, we checked this carefully. A good deal for parents living in further flung parts of the county.

Pupils and parents: Parents from all over Cornwall, some from the Scillies, professional folk and a growing number of incomers who've turned their back on serious rat racing to work in the knowledge economy. Prosperity levels are rising fast hereabouts. Very nice, unaggressive lot and it shows in their children. Nothing flash or lah-di-dah here.

Distinguished alumni include former chair of M&S Paul Myners, actors Robert Shaw, John Rhys Davies and Nigel Terry, baritones Benjamin Luxon and Alan Opie, quadruple Olympic Gold sailor Ben Ainslie, chess grandmaster Michael Adams and Queen drummer Roger Taylor.

Entrance: At 11, 13 and 16. For 11 and 13-year-olds exam in Jan in English, maths and verbal reasoning or, where appropriate, CE performance. Around 160 compete for 120 places. At 16, predicted GCSE grades plus school report plus interview. Prep pupils make up about 40 per cent of the entry. Up to 25 per cent of sixth form newcomers.

Exit: Good universities, mostly not too far up-country. Six to Oxbridge in 2013. Exeter, Bristol, Cardiff especially popular. Falmouth College of Art, too.

Money matters: Decidedly good value for money. True to itself, the school has its own Assisted Places scheme for the deserving indigent, means tested and up to full fees. Not a rich school – no endowments – so must rely on prudent husbandry. Strives to be as inclusive as it can afford to be.

Remarks: Not at all the sort of school that looks over its shoulder but operates according to its own dynamic, its own values. Makes the most of all sorts and everyone seems to find their own niche.

Tudor Hall School

Wykham Park, Banbury, Oxfordshire, OX16 9UR

• Pupils: 335 girls; 250 boarding, 85 day • Ages: 11–18 • Anglican but makes provision for RCs • Fees: Boarding £29,190; Day £18,606 pa • Independent

Tel: 01295 263434
Email: admissions@tudorhallschool.com
Website: www.tudorhallschool.com

Headmistress: Since 2004, Miss Wendy Griffith, BSc PGCE (early fifties). Educated at Queen Elizabeth Grammar School, Carmarthen and the University of Wales where she read zoology. Previously head of sixth form, Tormead School, then director of studies, St Catherine's, Bramley. This is her first headship. Married to a history teacher, they have a daughter.

Parents speak of her 'can do' attitude – 'an excellent role model for the girls' – bold, bubbly, attractive and driven – you get the sense there is nothing Miss Griffiths won't tackle. Large, warm green eyes – a compassionate head as well as a 'savvy' one (her word). Clear sighted and thoroughly committed to her staff, her girls, her school as well as her profession. She inspects other schools and networks like mad – knows everyone in the industry, but marketing has to be done in the 'Tudor Hall style – with subtlety and discretion'. Still finds time to teach biology several times a week – 'it's my treat,' she says, 'a good lesson can turn your day around'. Knows every girl by name and is prepared to run with any ambition the girls might have – whether it's to be a national shot putter or an Oxbridge candidate (with less than perfect credentials). 'What matters most, whatever the outcome – is that they try and we nurture their confidence. Too few women appreciate what they are capable of,' she says.

Academic matters: Once known as the school for toffs' daughters without academic aspirations, but this is not the case now. Performs well in value-added terms and Miss Griffiths is firmly focused on the academics. Respectable results – in 2013, 98 per cent achieving five A*-C grades at GCSE with girls taking an average of nine subjects and 77 per cent A*-B at A level. 20 subjects offered at A level. Still a strong preference for arts subjects – particularly English, history and French – but enthusiasm for sciences from the top is filtering down and more girls are choosing biology. Junior and senior science clubs, science festivals and field trips including a physics trip to European Centre for Nuclear Research, and the lure of eminent scientists (recently Professor Jocelyn Bell Burnell) as well as Etonians at the joint Eton and Tudor Hall science lectures.

Small number receives help with eg mild dyslexia or learning difficulties. Withdrawn from prep periods and given one-to-one help – for a fee. School has SENCo as well as a Gifted and Talented co-ordinator to stretch the brightest.

Inspiring library, well-used and brimming with books and computers as well as comfy bean bags and sofas. Devoted librarian forever changing attractive displays, entering school into book-judging competitions and promoting unusual reading material. Current favourites (among these girls and practically every other of this age) Twilight series and Marjorie Blackman.

Lots of fresh blood among the staff as well as a few devoted and long serving. Average age 36. Average class size is 16, maximum 20.

Games, options, the arts: Sports strong – significantly improved since the arrival of Miss Griffiths, say parents. Lots of fixtures in hockey, lacrosse, rounders, tennis and netball. Girls exude fresh-faced enthusiasm in their tartan games skirts and cheery red socks. Stunning green house-style swimming pool – the

T

walls can be removed in summer. In sport, as in everything else, if you show signs of talent you run (or jump) with it – currently one national high jumper. Sports day happens at Radley; 'it's so much more convenient,' gushes one girl, without making it clear precisely why – as you would expect, playing fields stretch away into the distance here.

Textiles department fizzes with talent and originality. Poky but busy design tech dept where we saw girls designing model radio-controlled cars to enter the Formula Schools' Racing at Silverstone (a far cry from the flower arranging of an earlier era!) and a beautiful oak folding dining table – 'the kind of thing my parents would buy,' said one.

Relaxed art room where senior girls listen to the radio as they work on perspective – the fresh Oxfordshire air pouring through the double doors from the balcony. Energetic cookery department with excellent kitchen – large, bright and squeaky clean. Full of eager girls in blue aprons, hair tied back, assiduously making pastry.

Vibrant music – good quality pianos in every music room – and people playing them. 85 girls play at least one instrument; choirs, orchestras and bands perform concerts throughout the year. Pupils frequently win festivals and occasionally local musician of the year comp. Dance strong – you can choose dance as a GCSE – lots of enthusiastic noises from parents. New drama studio and sports complex under construction.

Strong debating and public speaking tradition, with girls taking part in Model United Nations. Lots of trips – gritty as well as glamorous – to Auschwitz and the WWI battlefields as well as to schools in India and Canada.

Background and atmosphere: An imposing, beautiful and immaculately-kept school, Tudor Hall presides over the 48 acres of Wykham Park where it's been since 1946. Founded as an Anglican girls' school in 1850 by the Reverend and Mrs John Todd, it's one of the oldest girls' school in the country. You sense the tradition from the moment you enter the large iron gates, negotiate your way past sheep along the long drive and arrive at the fine former manor house in honey-coloured stone, smelling of freshly polished wood floors.

An abundance of discreet (and uniformed) staff industriously tend fine gardens, clean well-equipped and comfortable boarding houses, and maintain solid Cotswold buildings old and new. A lucky few of them live in the grounds. A magical walled garden – with a mass of purple wisteria when we saw it – surrounds tennis and netball courts. An enchanting place to watch your daughter in her matches.

A mix of buildings. Some more tasteful than others. From the inappropriately named cowshed (it couldn't look less like one though, legend relates, this charming boarding house once housed cattle) to the exciting circular dining room with floor to ceiling glass known as the spaceship, and the delightful cottage where the first year (Todds) live. Here the young ones can enjoy an (even more) sheltered existence. A short walk away from the main buildings, girls breakfast in the cosy dining room and at the end of the day can play on the swings or tend their own patch of garden. It's as if you had sent your daughter to stay with a friend in the country rather than to boarding school.

Each year group lives in a separate building which, we were told, makes for strong, lasting friendships. Cheerful dormitories splashed with colourful Cath Kidston duvet covers and walls of photos of parties and holidays. Upper sixth girls have rooms of their own, many with fabulous views. 2012 saw the completion of a major rebuild of the sixth form boarding houses.

Civilised behaviour and values permeate the place. Girls can help themselves from a large choice of food ('the fewer issues that surround food the better at this age,' remarks the head, sagely). Flowers on individual tables in the dining room and no benches. A sober uniform (no hoisted up skirts here) until they reach 15 when it's gradually dispensed with as the girls earn their 'privileges'. By the sixth form no one wears a uniform but

girls look a lot neater here than in many other places we've seen with more unforgiving dress codes.

Quirky traditions befitting of such a small community. The whole school departs on a jolly (eg to Stratford-upon-Avon, The Globe, Kew or World Music) to celebrate the school's birthday. Lots of weekend activities and trips to Oxford, London etc. This is a full boarding school; until the sixth form they are here to stay – with two organised exeats twice a term.

Pastoral care and discipline: Tudor Hall's forte. Praised by all – girls, their parents and the official reports. Firm line taken on smoking (drugs and drink are off the radar – fingers crossed) – the aim is to educate rather than punish but if you're caught red-handed then you go home, with all the ignominy that entails.

School's motto is habeo ut dem – I have that I may give. Strong emphasis on courtesy, manners meetings held twice a term where each girl is awarded marks for conduct, kindness, helpfulness etc. Grade A denotes 'an outstanding member of the community' whereas grade E is 'unacceptable behaviour'.

Head girl 'rotates' every term – chosen from upper sixth for one term and then lower sixth for next two terms. Lots of other highly-regarded positions of responsibility – eg Music Prefect, Public Relations Prefect. Group prefects for each of the year groups. Privilege system provides incentives to encourage good behaviour – girls earn the right to dispense with uniform or to go into Banbury. Strong, positive relationships between girls and the staff that last well beyond their school days.

Pupils and parents: Thoroughly well-bred girls, polite, courteous and discreet. They know how to behave and seem to be in control – assured and confident – whilst being natural and open. An apparent sensitive awareness of their privileges. Recent project to raise money for a local homeless project involved a few girls sleeping in cardboard boxes in various sheltered spots around the school. Even with the hot chocolate and biscuits brought to them by Miss Griffiths in the middle of the night, they said how much it reinforced the horror of being without a roof over one's head.

Largely rural families from all over the UK. A few from London who want their daughters to experience the freedom of the countryside and enjoy being young for longer. Not many from abroad, but nor are there large numbers from down the road. Some come from as far as Scotland. High proportion of mothers are Old Tudorians. Notable old girls include Artist Tessa Campbell, Financier Nicola Odey, Sculpter Candida Bond, Serpentine Gallery director Julia Payton-Jones.

Entrance: Register early. Entry at 11 and 13. Selection process includes school report, common entrance and interview with the head who looks for that 'special spark'. Occasional vacancy in the sixth form – minimum of seven GCSEs with grades A*-C in subjects to be studied at A level.

Exit: Some to art college, a tiny few to Royal Agricultural College or Cirencester (no longer a popular destination for Tudor girls), most to university – popular destinations are Leeds and Bristol where they read combinations of philosophy, politics, languages or other arts subjects. Head points out that more are choosing medicine and veterinary science than ever before. Occasional one or two to Oxbridge (none in 2013).

Money matters: Scholarships for excellence in anything (academic, music, art, dance, drama and sport) but you won't get a huge amount of money. Bursaries available but this is not a particularly rich school, despite an impressive building programme funded from income.

Remarks: No longer the automatic fall-back for your less bright child but still a safe and beautiful place for young girls to grow up away from the pressures of the real world, where they can discover the important things in life and build strong friendships. The wide range of opportunities, high level of support, and small size means your daughter will always feel special and, whatever her strengths, is unlikely to be lost in the crowd.

Twyford Church of England High School

Twyford Crescent, Acton, London, W3 9PP

• Pupils: 1,400 boys and girls • Ages: 11–18 • C of E • State

Tel: 020 8752 0141
Email: lwelch@twyford.ealing.sch.uk
Website: www.twyford.ealing.sch.uk

Executive Head Teacher: Since 2002, Ms Alice Hudson MA (Oxon), (late-forties) educated at Slough Girls' High and Leighton Park, then St Hilda's, Oxford, where she read English. Previously deputy head at Brentside HS, also in Ealing, and prior to that taught at Central Foundation Boys', Islington and Maria Fidelis, Euston. Joined Twyford in 2000, first as deputy, then acting head and appointed head in September 2002. Married to Michael Lyon. He works for the Bank of England ('more public servant than banker,' she says). He is Roman Catholic, she and their four children are Anglican. Her eldest daughter was given a place at Oxford to read modern languages having completed the sixth form here, her son also attends the school.

'The first five years were Herculean,' she says, 'cleaning out the stables'. (She comes from a family of classicists and her conversation is littered with references to the ancient world.) There was the thorny issue of a divided community: the haves and have-nots. The crude observer would put it in plain black and white terms – the churchgoing but poorer and underachieving black community as opposed to the playing-by-the-book, aspirational and privileged white community. Ms Hudson takes a more sophisticated approach. 'The cultural capitalisers and disenfranchised,' she elegantly puts it, 'overlaid with typical inner London underachievement issues connected to socio-economic disadvantage, race and gender'. Whichever description you prefer Ms Hudson was determined to 'harness the diversity of the student/parent body'. 'Exclusions were high,' she continues, 'and I didn't want to exclude, but to sustain a positive culture.' She proudly announces that she has now achieved three of her original goals: fixed behaviour and attainment, fixed cohesion, fixed aspiration. An intelligent and sensitive woman, she explains she learnt from watching the children, 'you have to read your institution,' she says.

During her tenure she has introduced a public school style house system (there are seven houses named after cathedrals, including Truro, York and Canterbury), a process of electing head boy and girl, the new post of school chaplain (allowing her to employ high calibre teaching staff who are not necessarily practising Christians), Latin and geology. Ms Hudson is a team player and her team consists of all the staff, all the students and all the parents.

Refreshing to see the head of a challenging, big state comprehensive not just running a business but also a passionate educator, lover of youth, life and learning. Not always the case in this inspection and results driven age. Parents and pupils admire her quiet authority (you could hear a pin drop in the assembly she took when she stopped mid-flow to say, 'distressed to hear three people talking', looking directly at them across the packed school hall). This, combined with more than a superficial knowledge of all the pupils as well as their parents, her infectious enthusiasm, disarming modesty, and striking physical presence – 'Miss Hudson is everywhere,' says one

admiring fifteen year old – and her sensitive awareness of every nuance, all contribute to making her an outstanding head. Lucky school. The only flicker of concern is whether her eye be taken off the ball as she works to open a new Free School in North Greenford. Due to open in September 2013, the school (to be named William Perkin Church of England Academy after a local chemist and industrial entrepreneur) will have a Christian ethos but will be a local school for local people with science and languages as its specialisms. The plan is that operations at both schools will be 'directed strategically from the centre'. Alice Hudson will become Executive Headteacher, and there will be an Associate Head of Twyford and an Associate Head of William Perkin. Ofsted, reporting in May 2012 – (unsurprisingly, rating the school 'outstanding' in all categories), also picked up on this concern among parents. Ms Hudson is channelling an enormous amount of energy into the project but if there is anyone who has more passion to spare and who has the team building skills to pull off her vision, she is your woman. Again, unsurprisingly, Ofsted agree.

Academic matters: Results just get better and better in this, academically, non-selective school. Three Bs average at A level – 67 per cent A*-B in 2012; school particularly pleased with 79 A* grades. Nineteen top ability students completed extended project – mostly with A*s. Maths results exceptional. Choices include economics, music tech, photography (very successful), psychology, sociology. Biggest improvement is in sixth form – head's especial baby – 'it's a reliable place for your high-achieving child ... we chase them much more in the sixth form', but the less academic well supported too. In 2012 GCSE results saw 67 per cent of students achieve five plus passes at C or above (including English and maths). Overall 36 per cent A/ A*grades. ICT (we saw loads of computers) a developing area though head refreshingly cheery when asked about the poor showing of interactive whiteboards, 'the most important interactive resource in the classroom is the teacher', she observes. Head sees wisdom in steering the less academic to the practical and creative which 'can be studied alongside A level', so double AVCE in ICT popular along with other more vocational subjects. Visual arts are a considerable strength of the school with significant numbers of students going on to art colleges.

Twelve per cent have SLD or SEN ('disproportionately high number of children with statements,' remarks Ms Hudson, 'skewed towards the severe end'). About five per cent of these including those with autism (across the spectrum) and Down's syndrome. All pupils are well supported, either by regular staff or from outside. 'They will be valued and survive here,' says head, 'and parents are also given support – we have very good home-school links.' Although 280 pupils have EAL – first languages in this very ethnically mixed area Gujurati, Punjabi, Arabic and Urdu – no one needs additional help in English.

Since she arrived there has been a tremendous push on languages and it became a specialisation (along with music) several years ago. 'We identify potential linguists in year 7, accelerate them in French and, in year 8, give them a choice of German and Spanish.' The person responsible for the language programme 'is a zealot' she says. All children have to learn speaking the language, not just from text books, and there are numerous exchanges, to China as well as to the obvious European destinations. In 2009 she introduced Latin which is taught once a fortnight and pupils can also choose to do it after school. It's not just a hobby, but also a GCSE option. One girl we met who moved here from the Middle East has recently achieved an A* in GCSE Arabic at the end of Year 9. If there is a demand or a talent, the school will make it possible to follow that talent and achieve the potential. Other GCSE options include food technology and electronics but DT has been temporarily paused. Setting in most subjects (including science, maths and languages from Year 7, English and the humanities from Year 9). From year 9 boys and girls are separated in the top two sets

T

in English. There are at least eight sets straddling seven forms plus a tiny nurture group for the extreme special needs. Parents remark on the fluidity of movement between sets, 'you don't just get labelled as 'D' set.' Pupils can sit the more rigorous IGCSE in maths and science (Harrow school provides support with this). RE very much a feature of everyday school life and supported in the sixth form by two conferences each year, often with outside speakers on moral or spiritual topics. Curriculum taught on an alternating two-week cycle which some find confusing at first but they get used to it.

We heard some mutterings about the SEN department not always picking up strugglers (without statements) as fast as it should nor providing the continuous support needed. We wonder whether the major advances at the upper end of the ability range are sufficiently matched by rigorous attention to those who are finding work hard. There is no doubt that the formidable Ms Hudson, with her passionate eye for detail, would not like to give less than her full attention to everything but it's a question of priorities. Expectations are undoubtedly high. Referring to one boy, who happens to be of African/ Caribbean descent, who recently achieved eight A* in his mock GCSEs, Ms Hudson says, 'unless he achieves ten A* when he sits the exams, we will have failed him.' When it comes to academic achievement, Ms Hudson comments, 'the big issue is that although we are doing well as a comprehensive state school, an independent school would be expecting those results. We need to push beyond.'

Games, options, the arts: Remarkable playing fields (albeit rented, not owned), well-concealed along this urban high street site. Netball especially strong here but you can choose to play hockey, tennis, football, cricket, and basketball too. Inter-form competitions are a major event. Everyone stays to watch the big matches. Another one of Ms Hudson's effective community-knitting devices. Dance and athletics popular. Rugby coached by pros from London Wasps. Consistent successes in many sporting areas and representation in borough and regional levels. Thriving art, and stunning music (some parents confessed they wished sport was given as much emphasis as music). The church influence from gospel to choral filters through at every level. A main orchestra plus smaller groups and ensembles present opportunities for lots of live performing. At every assembly there will be live music. When we visited we witnessed a potential Rumer, singing from the heart as she accompanied herself on the piano. Music and music tech facilities impressive and well-used (including the state-of-the-art audio-visual recording studio). Drama is popular and lively and as well as smaller studio performances throughout the year the main event is the massive whole school production that takes place in February. The King and I and Oliver! have recently been performed and one parent commented on the enthusiasm and commitment of her usually shy and recalcitrant daughter while acting as one of the boys in Oliver!

There is a good work placement programme though we heard some talk of the aspiring white middle classes with lots of contacts in the world of media and law etc getting plum placements while the less advantaged among the black community ended up working in the charity shop in Shepherd's Bush. School keen to point out that there is support (large data base with useful leads, past placements etc, plus an 'Aspirations' conference run annually which invites successful black professionals and entrepreneurs to speak about their work), but the students have to take initiative to tap into that support. The pushy ones are sorted by the end of Lent term, the more lackadaisical are scrabbling around for something a week before they have to start towards the end of the summer term. You can take a horse to water and all that. Pupils enthuse about the number and quality of trips and expeditions – everywhere from St Petersburg to the New Forest for every activity imaginable – photography to water skiing. Lots of charity work.

Background and atmosphere: School tucked behind rare bit of green along the Uxbridge Road. Main building, grade 2 listed The Elms, an elegant, early Georgian house, built 1735, well-preserved and sensibly painted in blues, houses the admin and offices side of things. A diverse mixture of less distinguished and pretty scruffy later blocks, A, B, unaccountably then D and M, house rest of school. Rather alarmingly nick-named 'the Cage' is the large central piece of tarmac surrounded by fencing where six hundred and fifty pupils line up in alphabetical order each morning. A logistical challenge in a disciplined corporate environment, at Twyford C of E high school it's like sliding a knife through butter. Some attractive modern buildings have organically emerged, including a wonderfully peaceful chapel, a contemporary and refreshingly un-institutional cafeteria (more Café Nero than trad school cafeteria), state-of-the-art performance centre, creative media suite with radio station and refurbished music areas.

Black uniform with white shirts creates somewhat sombre impression but most pupils look tidy (head strides around, not averse to pointing out, amicably, 'shirt!' to any wearer of stray shirt tails) and overall impression is of a good-humoured, confident, mix of the boisterous and the purposeful. No uniform for the sixth. Huge ethnic diversity – 52 per cent from non-white British backgrounds, of whom the largest number from Afro-Caribbean families; Asians make up next biggest group. Christian principles in practice evident in staff's approach to all aspects of this richly diverse community. While Anglicanism predominates, all churches and faiths are celebrated and explored here and everyone feels part of the school. Two minutes' daily silent reflection before lessons – 'everyone is quiet', said a sixth former. 'Faith has a big profile here', says head, 'we place a high premium on formal acts of worship.' Everyone attends a termly communion service and there is a weekly voluntary one. Assemblies are inclusive but have an unashamed Christian bias. 'The key to inter-faith issues,' believes head, 'is to be clear about what one's standpoint is.' She talks of the validity of each individual's own 'faith journey'. 'Spiritual matters are neither embarrassing nor taboo here' – a big claim but it feels legitimate. Pupils, though seldom deferential, respect teachers – there is a good working relationship between staff and pupils at all levels. 'They stretch you as far as you can go – but not beyond what you can do,' reflected one sixth former.

Pastoral care and discipline: Well-established system of form tutors first resort though pupils able to talk to whichever member of staff they choose. Heads of year back up the tutors and pupils have regular meetings to check on targets, progress, happiness. Chaplaincy team also available. Interaction between ages encouraged – actively by sixth form mentoring of younger pupils and system of form reps. School recently mixed up tutor groups in the sixth form to avoid tutors having particularly strong bonds with the 'homegrown' students and less good ties with the newcomers. School Council much appreciated – 'it has a lot of power over changes and we can meet the governors,' we were told. Few serious problems – most pupils feeling that offending in school time and on school property 'not worth it' and seemingly a bit immature, though usual crop of minor misdemeanours.

Pupils and parents: As above, huge ethnic mix, Christianity being the unifying principle though thirty places reserved each year for those from 'other world faiths', and Christianity itself taking in Russian/Serbian/Eastern Orthodox along with other denominations. Pupils come from wide geographic area – Brent, Hounslow, all over Ealing and further into town. Most, though, from Christchurch junior school, half a mile away, and nearly fifty other primaries. More boys than girls though this not generally perceptible. Princes and paupers here – all social strata represented and cheerfully interrelate.

Entrance: Now here's the rub. To get in you not only have to be practising a religious faith but have all the badges and medals to show it too. As the school becomes ever more oversubscribed an increasingly complex pecking order is developing based on family's attendance at and commitment to church (you can't just turn up and be counted, we're talking about assisting with Sunday school, running the church fete etc), along with home's distance from school. Worth checking this out in detail before losing your heart to the place. No-one is fooled by rapid conversion when your child is in year 6 – though it is still – widely and unsuccessfully – tried. Thirty places for pupils from other world faiths where the family is committed to the idea and principles in practice of 'faith'. Sixth form, hitherto less stringent, now oversubscribed 11:1. They must be getting something right. For external places in the sixth form students must meet individual entry criteria for courses as set out in the sixth form prospectus (minimum usually a B with one or two exceptions) and must be in sympathy with aims and objectives of a C of E school.

Exit: Vast and creditable range of courses and universities. They break a new record for Oxbridge offers each year. Ten offers in 2012, including a couple to read modern languages and theology, one to read law, one medicine, and one natural sciences. Five other offers to read medicine elsewhere. The increasing uptake of the extended project has resulted in glowing feedback of pupils' performance in interview and an increasing offer of scholarships.

Remarks: This is an outstanding school. Don't make the mistake of thinking it's anything other than a highly successful inner London comprehensive, however, with all the challenges that entails.

University College School

Linked school: Phoenix School Linked school: University College School Junior School

Frognal, Hampstead, London, NW3 6XH

• Pupils: 790 boys, plus 65 girls in the sixth form; all day • Ages: 11–18 • Non-denom • Fees: £17,160 pa • Independent

Tel: 020 7435 2215
Email: ssadmissions@ucs.org.uk
Website: www.ucs.org.uk

Headmaster: Since September 2013, Mr Mark Beard (early forties). Formerly deputy head of Brighton College. Studied chemistry at Oxford and has a master's in education management from King's College London. Taught at King Edward's Birmingham and St Paul's before joining Brighton College. He is married with two young children, lives in North London and enjoys squash, reading and ancient history.

Academic matters: Says it does not measure success by exam league tables – can afford not to, with an impressive 87 per cent of GCSE grades A or A* and 89 per cent of A levels graded A*-B. An unusually wide GCSE choice – two English, maths, a science and a modern language are compulsory but boys have a free choice of their other five subjects. 'The kids do the subjects they enjoy and we achieve good results in every subject.' There is guidance to ensure that, for example, someone with an inclination toward medicine does not end up doing only one science.

But the numerical bias is undoubtedly towards the social sciences – economics, government and politics and history are particularly popular A levels and around a third of leavers go on to do social sciences at university. 'This says more about the families; the boys are encouraged to talk and discuss and think a lot from a young age, so they tend towards the discursive, argumentative subjects.' Having said that, plenty take maths A level and the sciences have a good minority showing.

Everyone is assessed when they enter the school and those in need can get extra help outside the classroom and can eg use laptops. 'But they must be bright enough to cope with the classroom work.' At this liberal school the emphasis is on self-motivation, and some north London parents find it insufficiently pushy. It is stricter, say pupils, in the early years. 'As the workload increases you develop an instinct for getting on and doing it.' Undoubtedly, some develop more of an instinct than others, but there are safety nets. 'We have huge rafts of processes in place to help them develop their own motivation. But we want to get them off those systems as soon as possible and get them self-supporting.'

Teaching styles vary from the military to the liberal but tend toward the latter. 'The relationship between teachers and pupils here is very individual,' said a sixth former. 'You can disagree and question their views. But it is disciplined in the classroom because we respect the teachers. If someone you respect is talking you'll listen to them.'

Games, options, the arts: The swish Sir Roger Bannister sports complex includes a swimming pool, sports hall, multi-gym and dance studio – and a Costa Coffee bar. Small Astroturf pitch on site and sports fields a couple of miles away in West Hampstead. New pavilion and renovations to playing fields underway. Most people play twice a week and sports include hockey and basketball as well as rugby, soccer and cricket. The teams win reasonably often but it is fair to say that macho ultra-competitiveness is not a UCS characteristic, and the captain of rugby is equally at home giving a camp starring performance in the school play. 'We're not triumphalist. We like to do things for the hell of it.'

A range of orchestras, choirs and ensembles, including a joint symphony orchestra with South Hampstead High School. Plenty of concerts including a lunchtime classical series in the great hall and jazz evenings in the Lund Theatre. But UCS is best known locally for its rock groups, including Bombay Bicycle Club and Cajun Dance Party, formed to play in assembly and now signed up for the Reading Festival. The annual Battle of the Bands showcases talents like these to a boisterous audience of north London teenagers. Revamped lecture theatre can now be used as a flexible rehearsal and performance space for music and drama departments.

Excellent art, DT and modern language facilities are housed in the recently-completed Jeremy Bentham Building, providing fully-equipped studios, workshops, classroom and two language laboratories. Drama strong too, with a large variety of plays from West Side Story to Macbeth, including some joint performances with South Hampstead High School. Plenty of opportunities for those with a technical bent to get involved backstage.

Numerous extra-curricular activities: Ten Tors challenge, skiing in Colorado, cricket in Florida, language trip to Hamburg. Raises £20,000–£30,000 a year for charities, some of which goes to linked schools overseas – one in Uganda, run by an OG (Old Gower), schools in India and Sri Lanka and an orphanage in Romania. Pupils go out to work there during holidays and gap years and many find it a life-changing experience.

Background and atmosphere: Founded in 1830 by the University of London as the 'Godless College' of Gower Street, it was one of the first schools to teach modern languages and sciences, and one of the first to abolish corporal punishment. It moved to Hampstead in 1907 and maintained its liberal and secular outlook. There are no school bells, no religious observance and technically no religious education – though a few boys each

U

year, nonetheless, do take RS at GCSE. 'It develops free-thinking, self-assured and entrepreneurial boys,' said a parent. 'It fosters independent thinking and makes the boys feel that they are very clever.'

The main building – including the panelled great hall with organ – is a notable example of Edwardian architecture. Recent developments include a sports centre, art, DT and modern languages block, and refurbishment of classrooms, administration area and play spaces.

The Independent Schools Inspectorate commented on a 'lack of clarity about the required standards of dress and appearance', and there is certainly a feeling that uniform is a somewhat voluntary matter. 'They're intelligent young men, and they understand what the school's priorities are. If they've worked hard and are getting on well but don't tuck their shirts in, we know what is most important.'

Pastoral care and discipline: Renowned for its friendly atmosphere and caring attitude. The Lower School, years 7 and 8, is organised largely apart from the rest of the school, with its own building and pastoral staff. In year 9 boys join one of five Demes – roughly like houses – and are looked after by Deme wardens and form tutors.

Boys report that bullying is virtually non-existent. The tolerant and open-minded atmosphere reaps good relationships between pupils and between staff and pupils. 'There's no set code of conduct except that you behave responsibly,' said a sixth-former. Boys feel that it is very hard to get punished: 'The gardener is the only one who's strict when it comes to discipline. You don't mess with his flower beds.'

'Boys do get punished,' says the school, 'but we don't have a tariff of offences. We try to treat each offence and each pupil as an individual. So some kids spend a lot of time talking to teachers about what's going wrong. Most north London boys like talking about themselves, so they don't see it as a big deal.'

Pupils and parents: Mostly wealthy families from a relatively small area. The school does not record the ethnic or religious background of its pupils but they mirror fairly accurately the inhabitants of the Hampstead/Garden Suburb/Hendon/Finchley catchment area, with around half Jewish and a good sprinkling from various ethnic minorities.

Pupils tend to be confident and self-opinionated. 'They go through an arrogant phase,' said a parent, though the school feels that most teenagers do so, and prefers to say, 'we at UCS are quite good at developing assurance rather than arrogance.' Another parent commented, 'You need to be the life and soul – to throw yourself into things. It's probably not ideal for a quiet, bookish boy. They like you to get involved.' Students say, 'You have to be open-minded and accept other people and their views. And it helps if you have an in-built inclination to do well. There's space for all here – but the UCS type does tend to be out-going.'

OGs include Sir Chris Bonington, Sir Roger Bannister, Sir Dirk Bogarde, Alex Garland and – yes! – the Hampstead-liberal-hating Daily Mail editor, Paul Dacre.

Entrance: About two thirds of 11-year-olds come from the junior school in Holly Hill. They move up without needing to take an entrance exam. Another 30 or so come from outside – mostly local state primaries. About 200 applicants take maths, English and non-verbal reasoning tests, and about half are called back for group activities and interview. Another 30 come in at 13, mostly from local preps. They are assessed during the summer term of year 7 in maths, English and non-verbal reasoning, with half invited back for interviews, with offers conditional on common entrance.

A few boys and some 30 girls join the sixth form. The school sets its own assessment test, which is not subject-specific but measures thinking skills, problem-solving, interpretation of data. It takes GCSE forecasts into consideration but offers are not conditional on achieving particular results.

Exit: Nearly all end up at university, around half after a gap year. UCL and Bristol popular with 20 to Oxbridge in 2013. Social sciences, as mentioned, particularly popular, alongside humanities and languages.

Money matters: The school has successfully met its target to double the amount of means-tested fee assistance available and provides over 50 bursaries per year. There are also various scholarships, though the school regards these as 'basically pat-on-the-back awards', feeling that they should be means-tested rather than handed out to those who can well afford the fees.

Remarks: Achieves impressive exam results with a relaxed atmosphere. An ex-pupil insists that we describe it as 'the top liberal public school' and says, 'I look on my time at UCS as a golden age.' Certainly parents and pupils are uniformly happy – 'My son is having a fantastic time. If you're enthusiastic, there's so much scope to do what you want to do.'

Uppingham Community College

London Road, Uppingham, Rutland, LE15 9TJ

• Pupils: 850 boys and girls, roughly split 50:50; all day • Ages: 11–16 • Non-denom • State

Tel: 01572 823631
Email: principal@ucc.rutland.sch.uk
Website: www.ucc.rutland.sch.uk

Principal: Since 2007, Mrs Jan Turner MA Cert Ed (fifties). Mrs Turner began her teaching career in schools in Lancs and N Yorks, then moved to the East Midlands, becoming head of dept, pastoral head, assistant head, deputy principal and, briefly, acting head all at Robert Smyth School in Market Harborough where she stayed for 20 years. So she knows the territory from the bottom up and she knows UCC of old as her own daughters were pupils. Svelte, pretty, relaxed and on the ball, Mrs Turner is popular with everyone. 'She gets things done,' we were told. 'She responds promptly to questions and she makes sure the staff do too.' 'She's smartened up the children – the new blazers were a good idea.' We found her delightfully disarming. 'I've never done this before,' she twinkled when we sat down to grill her. Her office is light but stark – nothing here to distract the eye or mind. One reason, perhaps, why this clear-sighted, articulate principal seems so naturally and deftly in charge.

Academic matters: UCC is a Technology College, specialising in DT, maths and science. It works in a collegiate system with two other local schools that have Business and Enterprise and Visual Arts specialisms. Lots of ICT integrated into and underpinning the curriculum includes four banks of laptops and a proper home/school communication system. Everyone takes a core of nine subjects at KS4 and they then have a choice of three 'pathways' from which to choose one. Blue is a diploma course in either ICT or creative media, red is trad GCSEs of which they take four, and green is vocational courses in eg motor vehicle mechanics, hairdressing or construction. Also young apprenticeships in eg catering. A true 'comprehensive' mix on offer, then.

While most (especially girls) opt for red, the vocational and diploma courses are popular and successful. Much praise for day release sessions in Stamford and Melton – felt to be valuable and well-organised. In 2013, 66 per cent achieved 5+ A*-C including English and maths (23 per cent A*/A). Geography more than usually popular among the options and DT notably successful. Much praise for head of mod langs, the lang exchanges and the recent introduction of Spanish. More boys than girls opt for the green pathway but this does not disguise the fact that girls seem significantly to outperform boys in their GCSEs here though, interestingly, the value added tables tell a different story. Head expresses interest in the IB – could be significant developments then – watch out.

School is especially well-supplied with teaching assistants who play a number of important supporting roles, especially on the pastoral side. They are essential to the progress of pupils with SEN – more than 10 per cent of the school population. Twenty-one statemented pupils at the time of our visit plus 120 on School Action or SA Plus. In-class support, withdrawal for individuals or small group help. Sensibly, the SENCo liaises with all the main feeder primaries so that all children with identified SEN are known before they arrive, and everyone is screened on arrival anyway. Good team of specialist teachers. G&T pupils under the care of the impressive head of DT dept who sends them on courses, works with the other two schools in their local 'family' who offer art and enterprise courses and special awaydays. But parents of the super-bright feel the work needs to be more challenging on occasions. Also some feeling that 'it's the middling pupils who don't get all the attention they need'. Much parental concern about the irregularity of homework setting, especially in the first three years.

Games, options, the arts: Lots of space outside but limited inside. One largish sports hall but not enough for a school this size, especially when there is no separate hall or assembly space. A timetabling nightmare, one imagines but a new second sports hall is anticipated within a year. Good Astroturf a real asset. 'Session 6' allows pupils to stay for an extra hour after the school day, which otherwise ends at 3.00pm, and choose activities eg Chinese, cooking and badminton. Parents, while praising Session 6 as an idea, complain that not all staff take it seriously and that the popular options eg sport get oversubscribed too fast. This is a general complaint – not enough sport. Swimming is a session 6 option – otherwise, there is no swimming. However, we gather that changes are afoot and the school reports that they now have an Academy of Sport. Existing sports do well – a good range of games played here including athletics – school has numerous county winners. Equestrian team competes around the country and there are hopes to extend access to this to those who can't provide their own mounts. Lots of outward bound and subject-based trips. 'My Berlin history trip? – loved it! Brilliant.' Popular Don Bosco sporting exchange to Belgium.

Good-sized drama studio but this is the only sizeable space other than the sports hall and it is very well used, including for lunch when music is played. Drama and music both popular minority pursuits – no orchestra yet, though a good concert band and a new choir under teacher from outside. School hosts annual music festival for local primaries. Art and DT are exceptional – we were knocked out by the skill and craft of the pottery, the individuality of the work and the professionalism of the approach. A choice at GCSE between product design – taken by most of the year – textiles, graphics, ceramics, wood, metal, plastics, art, electronics on offer – or food tech, taken very enthusiastically by those who do. 'They're making things of marketable quality,' we were told. Yes. A real school triumph.

Background and atmosphere: A mile south of the sleepy little town of Uppingham, high on a hill overlooking classic British countryside, sits UCC, a medley of less than stunning buildings dreamed up in the 1960s and 1970s, not exactly the Golden Age of school architecture. It is surrounded by space and, apart from the lamentable lack of a hall, feels pretty spacious inside too. (There had been a hall but it became the dining room with fixed seating – not a good idea!) One's first impression is of open skies,

one's second is of dull buildings and one's third is of smiley faces. This is one of the smiliest schools we have visited. Classes are orderly and quiet, we saw no litter and the place is kept in good nick. Pupils are taught to look after their surroundings and they appear to do so. Nice features include a gallery space with glass cases in which DT work is properly displayed – though we felt the exhibits could be changed more frequently. Outside there are several good places to sit, picnic and chat – little courtyards and gardens – someone has thought about this and, inside, the buildings are airier and more congenial than their outsides suggest. Nice library with 17 PCs but, except in fiction, pitifully small stock for a school of this size. Library used for socialising in break.

Three screens around the place announce the notices and events of the day and pupils look purposeful and focused. Mrs Turner has initiatives to make them more involved in school decisions – despite their youth and the lack of a sixth form – and this is yielding good – and appreciated – results. For example, she allots them a 'bursary' with a choice of what to spend it on – they chose between a rock climbing wall and more staging for the drama studio – sensible, mature choices. Nonetheless, uniform is an issue and staff swoop, hawklike, onto infringements. Most pupils looked pretty orderly to us, though we are told of staff who keep make-up and nail varnish remover in their desks. What we felt, though, was summed up by a party of school nurses who were just leaving as we arrived. 'It's been a lovely atmosphere,' they said which, considering they'd been administering jabs, is pretty good. And everyone smiled at us.

Pastoral care and discipline: Good relations between staff and pupils. School tries to keep classes with same form teacher for the five years. Year 11 mentoring scheme with younger pupils. 'If you do something well the teachers really appreciate it,' a year 10 girl told us. 'They stay after to school to help you if you need it.' Disruptives are put on report or sent to cool off to the Remove Room where staff sort out the problems. The rest report that the system works well. 'In years 10 and 11, you're not kids any more. It's your learning and the teachers say they'll help you in every way but if you're here just to be disruptive they don't want you here – you're not going to ruin the learning of others.' Atmosphere generally healthy – includes eating – good food – though only eaten by around half the school, and three vending machines selling only healthy drinks. Little serious sinning.

Pupils and parents: Most pupils from seven local primaries but also increasingly out of catchment as reputation grows. Seen as an alternative by some to Oakham School (qv) which is 50:50 day:boarding – but not so much to near neighbour Uppingham School (qv) which is virtually all boarding and which, while more or less occupying the town of Uppingham itself, seems a little reserved in terms of finding opportunities to collaborate with its sparky neighbour. Many rural families, some from local regiment at Edith Weston, and head says that some Forces families now apply to that regiment on account of UCC. Some from Corby, Market Harborough, Melton. Real social mix from the area.

Entrance: Oversubscribed but not vastly so. Well worth applying even from out of catchment and recent record of won appeals too.

Exit: Few to employment but vast majority to sixth forms, sixth form colleges or to FE. Quite a choice available – in Stamford, Peterborough, into Leicestershire or local colleges. School cries out for its own sixth form though practical matters make this a non-starter. However, with collaboration, investment and an imaginative strategy? Some each year to Oakham School for the sixth and UCC has a stunning recent record of providing Oakham Oxbridge successes. More mileage for the sixth form idea?

Remarks: A well-run, friendly school, doing well and set to do better under excellent leadership.

Uppingham School

High Street West, Uppingham, Rutland, LE15 9QE

• Pupils: 790; 455 boys, 330 girls. Virtually all boarding, apart from 18 day pupils • Ages: 13–18 • C of E • Fees: Boarding £31,569; Day £22,098 pa • Independent

Tel: 01572 822216
Email: admissions@uppingham.co.uk
Website: www.uppingham.co.uk

Headmaster: Since 2006, Mr Richard Harman, MA PGCE. Uppingham's 31st headmaster. Educated at The King's School, Worcester (he was a King's Scholar), followed by Trinity College, Cambridge, where he read English. Spent two years working in sales and marketing for academic publisher Harcourt Brace Jovanovich, then 'literally woke up one morning and realised that I ought to be teaching at a school.' He was offered a job at Marlborough and taught English and drama there for five years (with a sabbatical half way through to do a PGCE at Exeter University). Spent 12 years at Eastbourne College, progressing from head of English to housemaster of sixth form girls' house to member of the senior management team. Then became head of Aldenham, where he oversaw major expansion in both pupil numbers and facilities.

Energetic, approachable and charming (also slightly bashful at previous edition of The Guide referring to his 'film star looks'). Says being headmaster of 'such a wonderful school is an amazing privilege.' Firm believer in benefits of co-education. Taught English AS level during his first year at Uppingham (most of his students got As) and now teaches drama to new 13 year olds. 'It's great because drama is an "on your feet" subject and it means I get to know them all very early on,' he says. Married to American wife Karin. They met at Marlborough – she was a teaching fellow from the University of Virginia and he was assigned to be her mentor. They live in a house on the school site and have a grown-up daughter.

Academic matters: Not an academic hothouse but results are good and teachers confident they deliver the best for the individual. School says curriculum is, 'sufficiently challenging for us to need to insist on a certain level of academic ability in the pupils we take, but the emphasis is upon identifying and bringing out the strengths of all pupils – in whichever field they may shine.' In 2013, 80 per cent A*-B at A level (54 per cent A*/A). Twenty-eight subjects on offer at A level, with maths and history currently the most popular subject, closely followed by RS, business studies, geography, art and politics. Refreshingly un-hung up about league tables but 62 per cent A* and A grades at GCSE and 98 per cent of pupils attained 5+ A*-C grades in 2013. Most take 10 or 11 GCSEs. Triple and dual award science on offer, plus French, Spanish, Italian and German. Beginners and intermediate classes have recently commenced in Mandarin. IT lessons for all. Average class sizes of 16, and nine in sixth form. Learning support department for pupils with mild learning difficulties offers help 'according to individual needs'.

Games, options, the arts: All very strong. Music as superb as ever. School was first in the country to appoint a director of music – in 1865! – and still leads the way. Music groups galore, including two orchestras, chamber groups, jazz, wind and swing bands, chapel choir, chamber and close harmony choirs etc. Around two-thirds of pupils learn an instrument and there

are more than 60 music scholars and exhibitionists. Chapel choir is much in demand and has performed all over the place, from St Paul's Cathedral to Hong Kong and China. Third music school opened in 2006, with 100-seat recital room and recording studios. Total of 80 practice rooms in school. Lots of lunchtime concerts, annual music festivals and breathtaking carol service.

Stunning glass-fronted art block designed by old boy Piers Gough. Walls hung with vibrant artwork and there's also a photo lab (complete with 3D printing). Pupils encouraged to try their hand at everything from fine art and ceramics to photography. Drama very popular. Two venues – 300-seat main theatre and smaller drama studio with foyer, two drama classrooms, workshop space etc. Major school production every year, ranging from Sweeney Todd to Pygmalion, along with sixth form and lower school productions, junior drama club and performances by visiting professional companies.

Sport very good. 'Our teams do pretty well but you don't have to be brilliant,' say pupils. Sixty-five acres of playing fields (apparently the largest in England) and a fabulous new sports centre opened in 2010 (with large six court sports hall, six-lane 25m swimming pool, 50 station fitness studio, gymnasium and dance studios), three Astroturf hockey pitches, a separate all-weather pitch, plus reams of tennis and netball courts, squash courts, fives courts, a shooting range and a climbing room. Vast range of sports on offer. Rugby, hockey, cricket for boys and hockey, lacrosse, netball for girls – along with tennis, athletics, squash, badminton, swimming, basketball, cross-country, shooting, fencing, dance, aerobics, golf and sailing (on nearby Rutland Water). Rugby excellent. Links with Leicester Tigers and Northampton Saints RFCs. Lots of pupils play county sport, and some regional and national. D of E popular. CCF or community service (visiting the elderly, helping in primary schools, working for Riding for the Disabled) for fifth and sixth formers.

Background and atmosphere: Founded in 1584 by Archdeacon Robert Johnson. The school's handsome, honey-coloured buildings are dotted throughout the pretty market town of Uppingham. Pupils are much in evidence scurrying along picturesque streets but some places are out of bounds and only prefects (or 'pollies,' as they are known in Uppingham-speak) are allowed in tearooms like the popular Baines' Cafe.

Work underway on the construction of a new science centre which is being built on the footprint of the old sports centre. The facility will include a research centre, 17 labs (including an environmental studies lab and a project room), lecture theatre, departmental offices and meeting rooms. This development takes the school a further step nearer the completion of the Western Quad (the first stage of the Western Quad development was the construction of the new sports centre).

There are 15 boarding houses on the school's 120-acre site, six for girls and nine for boys. All have their own character and ethos. According to their location, they are 'town,' 'country' or 'hill' houses. Boys' house, Brooklands, for instance, is situated up the hill in a rambling Victorian mansion, complete with its own swimming pool and flood-lit tennis court. The downside is that it's about ten minutes' walk from lessons – 'but it keeps us fit,' one 14-year-old told us enthusiastically. Meanwhile Samworths' is a modern, purpose-built house (also created by Piers Gough) for 60 girls aged 13 to 18.

Around 40 new girls enter the sixth form each year and they are assigned to the one sixth form girls' houses – The Lodge – or to the existing 13-18 girls' houses. New fourth formers (year 9s) are mainly in dormitories (they have individual partitions, known as 'tishes', to give them privacy), with separate cabin-like studies, while sixth formers (and many upper fifth) get bedsits. All pupils have their own school-provided desktop computer in their study or bedsit. Parents and prospective pupils are encouraged to look around the houses and make their own choice, though some have waiting lists. Pupils eat breakfast, lunch and supper in their houses – 'not the most economic way to do it,' says school, 'but it

U

encourages friendship within a family setting.' One parent told us, 'it makes for a real home-from-home atmosphere – none of this awful going into a main hall and worrying whether you will have anyone to sit with.' Visitors are frequently invited to lunch in houses and youngsters take a pride in looking after their guests.

Pupils attend morning chapel five times a week. Atmosphere everywhere is busy and purposeful. Girls very well integrated – have been here since 1975 and school went fully co-ed in 2001. There's a tuck shop (known as the buttery) selling fruit, sweets, yoghurt and drinks, and a club for upper sixth pupils (tightly-restricted hours/consumption of drinks). Grey/black/claret school uniform for all till 6.20pm most days. Some parents grumble about pupils' 'scruffiness' but no sign of this when we visited. Loads of different house and prefect ties. So many, in fact, that a new pupils' handbook features a tie spotting guide! It also includes a list of dos ('when emailing a teacher make sure the email is polite') and don'ts ('don't use your mobile phone or iPod in the street'). Two school captains (boy and girl) and raft of prefects.

Pastoral care and discipline: School prides itself on its pastoral care. Most boarding houses are run by husband and wife team (often with own family) who live in. There is also a pastoral matron in each house. At one house girls regularly troop into the housemistress's drawing room to play the piano while at another the housemistress's two black labradors are an integral part of pupils' lives. Lights out for youngest at 9.45pm while sixth form have to be in their rooms by 11pm. All boys and girls have a house tutor whom they meet once a week to discuss academic progress. New pupils get slightly older mentor to help them settle in and there is a wide choice of possible confidantes for youngsters – housemaster/housemistress, chaplain, matron, tutor, independent school counsellor etc. All pupils have life skills lessons – covering sex education, personal relationships etc. Rules are crystal-clear and outlined in the school's invaluable 'white list,' a prep diary containing maps, house lists and details of everything from uniform to exam timetables. Everyone gets a copy. Head takes firm line on drugs (expulsion), drink and smoking but says he can count the number of pupils he's asked to leave 'on the fingers of one hand'. Pupils told us school is 'strict but fair'. Detention system mainly for academic matters but also used for cutting a lesson or inappropriate behaviour. No exeats but parents welcome to visit and, by arrangement, take their children out on Saturday afternoon or Sunday (provided they have no school commitments). School passionately anti-bullying – 'persistent bullies must expect to be required to leave,' say rules.

Pupils and parents: Pupils come from far and wide – Scotland down to Kent and Sussex, but many live within two hours' drive. Around 100 feeder prep schools but regular arrivals from Maidwell Hall, Old Buckenham Hall, Winchester House etc. Around twelve per cent from overseas but some children of Brits working for multinationals abroad. Around ten per cent are children of former pupils. Old Uppinghamians an eclectic lot – including Rick Stein, Stephen Fry, Carphone Warehouse founders Charlie Dunstone and David Ross, former health secretary Stephen Dorrell, Jonathan Agnew, Johnny Vaughan and John Suchet. A smattering of musicians too – Andrew Kennedy (Tenor), Charlie Simpson (ex-Busted) and Harry Judd (McFly).

Very friendly, well-mannered pupils who are outgoing and confident but not arrogant. Most throw themselves into the myriad different activities on offer, from beekeeping and cookery to dance and building go-karts. As one girl told us, 'it's cool to be involved'.

Entrance: Apply at any time from birth – but ideally more than three years before proposed entry. Head says lists looks 'pretty full' for next couple of years but it is always worth talking to the school. Pre-assessment and interview when prospective pupils are 11, plus report from present school. Provisional offers are made at this stage and deposits taken but youngsters still have to sit CE at 13 (head has upped baseline CE mark to 55 per cent), scholarship exams or tests/reports for those who haven't been prepared for CE. All pupils, whether they've been at Uppingham since 13 or are new at 16, must get six Bs at GCSE to progress into sixth form.

Excellent information pack for prospective parents, stuffed with detail. Information even includes contact details of parents of current and former pupils who are happy to talk about the school. High contentment rating among those we spoke to.

Exit: Virtually all to higher education – a number to Oxbridge each year (13 in 2013), with Bristol, Newcastle, Edinburgh, Oxford Brookes, Exeter, Leeds, Manchester and Durham popular. A few to Harper Adams and one or two to US universities. Around a third of leavers take gap years.

Money matters: A wide range of academic, music, sport, art, design and technology and all-round scholarships (known as Thring scholarships after 19th century headmaster Edward Thring, who transformed Uppingham from a small grammar into a large public school) awarded at 13. Some at 16 too (but not all-rounder); science scholarship recently launched to reflect investment in new science facility. Means-tested bursaries scheme for able children whose parents might not otherwise be able to afford it (up to 95 per cent of the full fee and much of this financed by former pupils).

Remarks: A wholesome, positive, happy place – both traditional and forward-thinking. Benefits from being a real seven-day a week boarding school, with lots to do at weekends. Pupils, whether they're academic or sporty, musical or artistic, seem to love it and results are good too. The previous head told us that children 'aren't "sent" to boarding school any more – they come because they wish to'. It's still very much the case here.

Upton Court Grammar School

Lascelles Road, Slough, Berkshire, SL3 7PR

- Pupils: 1,240; mixed, all day • Ages: 11 to 18 • non-denom
- State

Tel: 01753 522892
Email: office@uptoncourtgrammar.org.uk
Website: www.uptoncourtgrammar.org.uk

Principal: Since 2010, Mrs Mercedes Hernandez Estrada, BA, MA (forties). Previously deputy head teacher at Tonbridge Grammar School for Girls, Kent and, before that, assistant headteacher at Regent's Park School in Southampton, preceded by three year spell leading curriculum design for schools 'from Plymouth to Kent' says website. Husband is a drama teacher, busman's trips to each other's school productions something of a feature of married life.

Petite and engaging, she's very much the clever, industrious little girl grown up (and fetchingly doing the full Downton Abbey in a long dress for World Book Day on morning of visit). She inspires praise for her poise, glamour (has a wonderful complexion, too) as well as achievements which are both formidable and, in the case of fund raising, essential, with school built for 500 and now housing more than double the number.

Former piecemeal make do and mend fudging has been replaced by master plan, well underway. Partly pre-fab snap together English block – 'like Lego; amazing,' says head – already in place; wonderful new building housing large scale café is taking shape and there's more in the pipeline.

Not desperately high profile at least to parents. 'I don't really get to see her,' said one father. Not that they appeared to mind, given faith in the school – 'The best!' says one – coupled with the knowledge that pupils approach her freely, once they get to know her. 'Because she's so polite and proper, she can be quite daunting but she genuinely does care about the students,' says one.

When it comes to the importance of education, she doesn't mince her words. It is 'the key to breaking social barriers. With it, you're powerful. Without it, you could be lucky, but I don't trust luck.'

No wonder, given her own experiences. Raised in industrial northern Spain, she was blessed with parents (steelworker and housewife) who saw education as 'the way you prepared your children to have a better future than you had yourself.' Encouraged by teachers, she was the first in her family to go to university, studying languages at Oviedo (speaks at least six, ancient and modern).

A thirst to communicate led her to travel but, in the event, no further than the UK where she met 'someone' during a year's Spanish teaching at Bath University and never left.

Her affinity is, she says, with 'people who have high expectations of themselves,' something she relishes both here and at earlier posts at non-selective state schools, locations, including Haringay and Swindon, to some extent influenced by partner's career moves. 'It's great to work with people who want their children to do well and children who want to push themselves,' she says.

Starts each day by walking her two dogs in local park (their toys adorn a chair in her office) and bringing them into school where they're collected later by dogsitter. Provides valuable breathing space where she often does her best thinking.

Just as well as there's plenty to mull over, in particularly the best way of helping education set her pupils free regardless of financial or family circumstances, as it did for her. 'A selective school is for a lot of people the step into a life of possibilities and if I can make that happen, I will.'

Academic matters: Despite super selectivity, feel is 'more laid back' than other local grammars, reckoned one mother, who counted it a benefit. Pupils agree. 'The teachers will say pick the subjects you enjoy, not the subjects you're being told to do, or the job that will offer you the most money,' says sixth former.

Similarly, while voracious appetite for learning is encouraged – some, who complete the European Computer Driving Licence in a term go on to take GCSE computing, for example – school doesn't go in for the M4 special executive exams lane, everyone sitting everything together.

Punches aren't, however, pulled. While 'sixth form is an exciting time, full of opportunities,' begins presentation, 'attendance is vital...AS and A levels are much more difficult than GCSEs and students must make good use of their time, inside and outside of (sic) lessons.'

That'll larn you... so how much excitement was that, exactly? Actually, given subject range, quite a bit. IB, though previously a big feature in wobbly A level years, is now, it appears, being sidelined as A levels, fortified with added Gove-inspired marking rigour, take centre stage, recent additions to the subject roster including media studies and photography, which 'you won't find at other grammars,' thinks head.

GCSE offering up as well – first cohort to take Chinese will be coming through soon, trialled initially as a club then, as numbers climbed, promoted to full curriculum status. Japanese, however, didn't take off in the same way, lacking superpower appeal and thus felt by students to be less useful, reckons head.

Progressive range of subjects isn't necessarily matched by enlightened attitudes to post-16 choices. 'Humanities are meant to be seen as more girly subjects just because boys are meant to be more mechanical,' said ... a girl. And while maths remains popular with all (and consistently the biggest A level subject), as elsewhere, physics is one for the boys. Sigh.

Having said that, chemistry in last three years has overtaken biology as top science (psychology, in 2010 attracting well over double the class sizes of physics, has retired for an early bath and in 2012 was only just ahead).

Results, as you'd expect, are terrific, though they do reflect school's determination not to make pyrotechnic stats its be all and end all, tending politely to let the other three local grammars nudge ahead. So while 56 per cent of A level entries were graded A*/B, that was 10 per cent behind Herschel Grammar. It's a similar story with GCSEs, with 43 per cent graded A*/A, compared with 55 per cent up the road.

As to reasons, there's a bit of blippage here and there: you could point the finger slightly at languages where results have slipped a bit, in numbers as well as results, with more D and (even, though occasionally) E grades probably representing a rather bigger wobble than school would like, feeding through into lower take up at A level (just one taker at A2 for French and Spanish in 2012).

But here, as in every other decent grammar school, you can end up picking holes in what is ultimately a high quality fabric, with parents giving thumbs up for most subjects (one queried A level physics, where numbers have dropped by over a third in the past two years) and, courtesy of the new head, a sense of a slight ramping up of academic focus,.

Quality staff are the key – and with an average class size of 24 and one to 16 teacher to staff ratio, they'd need to be. There was admiration for RS teacher who asked husband, a serving officer in Afghanistan, to field questions about the morality of war. 'A lot of teachers just wouldn't do that,' said pupil.

Mind you, with crème de la crème teaching school status, you'd hope for substantial out of the box approaches. If lesson with whizzy English teacher, coaxing bottom GCSE set into life, top responses rewarded by decorous whoops, even 'phone a friend' system to encourage the unsure to seek help, was anything to go by, there's plenty about. Sixth form lessons were also rated very highly. 'Sometimes we're doing notes, but discussions can be quite open ended,' says pupil, with others praising science lessons' high practical to theory ratio in nine well-equipped labs.

Support, too, is comprehensive and well organised. Back up extends from clubs to surgeries, revision sessions (notionally voluntary but attendance strongly recommended and absences logged) and after-hours homework club. Everything is run either by subject teachers or, increasingly, by older pupils. Initial one-to-one sessions for year 11s, run by sixth formers, so successful that sixth form prefects (every year group has its own) hope to extend so that pupils through the school can book themselves an Oxbridge style one-to-one tutorial with fifth or sixth formers.

Decent stack of resources, too, from the virtual, with super subject-by-subject overview in each key stage to the tangible. Library, on borrowed time, can't, like its stock, be renewed, but will instead move to fine new learning resource centre, leaving current premises, a nice old room with curved ceiling (not unlike cut and cover London Underground station). It's decorous – we'd have liked to see a few more agent provocateur type initiatives to encourage the less enthusiastic readers to buck the trend and pick up a book – though librarian, who bemoans decline in reading above year 8, does her best.

Book champions event recruits pupils to defend a chosen title against all comers (and hopes to do more) while staff undismayed by majority of pupils in home clothes ('We're muggles,') had enthusiastically embraced World Book Day. We particularly enjoyed sight of food technology department

U

dressed as fetching St Trinians girls complete with a 'Miss Naughty' flask, in the midst of their soberly-clad pupils.

It's not just gifted and talented who have a cracking programme – extension work embraces development of critical thinking and analysis (well-organised website is rich in detail) but those with learning needs, too. Unusual for an ultra-selective school, opts for full immersion rather than lip service, stressing importance of dignity and privacy, with warm, experienced team on hand to deliver the goods. Autism and dyslexia crop up with reasonable frequency, BSE too. As with wheelchair users ('we rearrange as many lessons as possible so they're on the ground floor,') team copes with equanimity and a fuss-free and inclusive approach, from OT to physiotherapy.

Games, options, the arts: School's sporting prowess is well camouflaged. Though in fact it has its own website, link, barely visible to the naked eye, gives initial impression that you'd need a largish microscope to discern activity (as well as a sense that school would probably prefer you to be more interested in the microscope).

In fact, sporting talent is considerable. As well as individual successes (badminton and rowing at county/national level) – a small number also take sport/PE at GCSE and A level – there is also a decent run of good team results – girls' rugby fast becoming a star turn.

Recent innovations include sixth form sports day featuring all the retro favourites, egg and spoon and sack race amongst them – brought back as centenary celebrations special and so popular it has become an annual fixture.

With plenty of non-team-based activities, timetabled and run as clubs, early morning kick boxing amongst them, recent converts praise choice and encouragement.'My primary teachers made me hate sports at primary: here I love it,' says one pupil. It could all be part of a cunning plan to confound opposition as pupils delight in deceptive appearances. 'They think that because we haven't got an Astroturf, we look like underdogs and then we play,' said burgeoning rugby star with considerable satisfaction.

Current facilities as they stand would undoubtedly lull opponents into false sense of security but burst with promise. Once wacking great field gets the makeover it's crying out for – and if proposed development deal goes through, will happen – Astroturf and a full monty sports hall likely to give opponents considerable pause for thought.

A similar story elsewhere, where pizzazz, though in abundant supply, has to be hunted out, with traditionally wacky areas such as textiles of a very decorous disposition, featuring neatly wall-mounted row of gorgeous if slightly chilling dolls and neat, criss-crossing lines of bunting) and art. Even the cupboard 'is jam-packed, but tidy,' said pupils.

Creativity, as witnessed by steady GCSE take up for fine art, continued though in small numbers post 16, is busting out all over on the approach to large art room, via staircase transformed by lovingly painted time line. Once inside there's – hurrah – a pile of satisfyingly authentic mess to one side (educational equivalent to shoving it all behind the sofa, perhaps?), cabinet of curiosities taking up almost an entire wall, composed of assorted, pupil-made and ever so slightly wonky wooden boxes, each about to be filled with special objects. Well-curated end products dot the school walls with self portraits, each a study in light and shadow that you feel Joseph Wright would have enjoyed.

Quality continued in DT room, now with fab new laser cutter, won with well-targeted bid for funds (hit rate increasingly impressive) was in midst of casting aluminium with hugely impressive results though 'terrible smell,' said teacher.

Drama splendidly high profile, with lively lessons (year 8s working in threes to create own walking, talking living dolls, two as puppet masters, third as puppet) setting the pace and productions a coming together of whole school talent, written by drama teacher and featuring enticing titles ('A stereotypical

musical set in a high school' was recent effort) with productions and involvement by many, on and off stage.

Though far more than a background noise, day to day musical presence tends to be via individual involvement, with talented soloists showcased regularly in assemblies. Tone is set by list of enrichment activities, featuring enticing-looking extras for science, maths and English, and 'choir, band' for music. As to orchestra? 'I don't know,' says senior teacher. No more questions, m'lud.

However, with its own nice suite and double handful of regular takers at GCSE music (though rarely beyond), plenty of potential and though just 75 pupils have individual music lessons in school, many more 'almost certainly' learn outside).

As to extracurricular, there's much on offer, from Children's University, for years 7 and 8 pupils, with credit for different activities leading to awards, to D of E. Much appreciated, as were outings generally – rare enough currently to have Christmas present feel to them (field trips were considered a huge treat) and just about the only thing pupils, very happy with school, would add to wish lists

Background and atmosphere: To the glens... announces sign on the main road close to the school. Wishful thinking, though you can see Windsor Castle from the road, we were told – and what better metaphor for aiming high?

Aspirations apart, it's been all change, several times over. Founded as a co-ed selective school in 1912, it split into separate boys' and girls' grammars in 1936, reforming as co-ed only in early 1980s on the current site, wheel coming full circle in 1993 when it regained its original name. Alumni, known since 1915 as Old Paludians (marsh, or slough in Latin) have had no such identity issues. Only downright loser is original school building, remains beneath Thames Valley University tower block.

Immediate surroundings cope without too much sense of strain, well managed given numbers packed into site that was intended to cater for many fewer. Getting better all the time, however, thanks to the fruits of head's fundraising efforts which are increasingly visible: gorgeous new English block (marred temporarily by mud carried in from rained-on rugby players and distributed generously round pale wood floors).

More coming very soon, in the form of 12 new classrooms, vast café area and gym, which could see the removal of asphalt-heavy areas round the back and Portakabins (those temporary cum permanent additions so many schools have and wish they didn't). In the meantime, there's plenty of corridor candy to brighten things up, well curated by art department (relative emptiness of art rooms explained by volume of works on display) mostly terrific, with the very minor exception of slightly out-of-date staff pics (a few had left) and the odd, unlaminated notice with curled up edges.

While surroundings might be ultra modern, what won't change is the delightful formality of staff titles. Male staff, conventionally enough, are 'sir'; females, endearingly, are 'ma'am' (to rhyme with 'harm'), which replaced 'miss', formerly in use, which was reviewed and found to be lacking gravitas. Applies to everyone: visitors and delightful admin staff as well as teachers, allowing many a personal Judi Dench/Skyfall moment and so ingrained that it's preserved in staff conversations, even when the pupils aren't around. 'It did strike me as different when I was called ma'am during my interview,' says head's PA.

Further proof of status accorded to backroom team is high profile website presence. School chef (pictured looking as if caught mid-soufflé crisis) is highly rated. With new canteen planned (much talked about, too – current one 'does its job,' say pupils, but that's about it) food is clearly a big thing and rightly so – we particularly liked the way that pupils are able to order giant celebration pizzas for friends' birthdays. Staff, too, are big on food, home baking a speciality – 'relieves the tension,' said one – end results regularly making it to the staff room as giveaways or charity fundraisers.

Respect, however, doesn't preclude humour. We enjoyed sixth former's description of a teacher's tireless promotion of clearly fab lecture on string theory as 'inspired and ever so slightly repetitive...' Always nice to find a school which doesn't take pupil jokes too seriously...

Pastoral care and discipline: Pupil support is commendably huge part of school's behind the scenes work and vital too, say warm team (separate director of student welfare as well as SENCo and three higher level TAs) who increasingly provide a drop-in shoulder to cry on service not just for children but 'sometimes staff, too'. Vital, as well, given that pupils, who may have only IQs in common, come from backgrounds that range from well to do to anything but, needing support that 'goes way beyond what we would class as the normal routine,' including, for example, pupils who are the main carers for family members with debilitating physical or mental health issues. Add in year in year out transition work (they run parenting sessions to ease fears, often linked to long distance commutes to school) and unsurprisingly, team reckon that they're busier than ever before.

No soft touch when it comes to boundaries, which are impressively clear cut, almost literally so in the case of the food line (two bins on either side of path) which mark start of food free zone).

No nonsense approach extends to instant fine of litter pick if you're caught dropping rubbish; in-class bans on mobile use – a phone in the hand during a lesson means instant confiscation for minimum of a week (some older pupils voluntarily turn them into form tutors for the day to reduce temptation). Uniform (worn by all, sixth form changing blazer colour but little else) is strictly enforced, breaches noted in homework book and, if repeated, on school record).

Goodness of all sorts is rewarded with house points leading to annual presentation of trophies, dominated by 'The Beast'. So big it looks as if it could eat tiddler cups for breakfast, it's awarded for academic success, a (perhaps) not so subliminal message about what really matters in life.

May sound punitive, but isn't. Pupils, who worked on revised behaviour policy with staff, were in no doubt about sanctions which were, they felt, simple to understand and, because consistently applied, rancour-free. They praise the way they're given a say. 'The teachers know we'll be adults so they treat us like it,' said one.

Pupils and parents: Widening diversity of backgrounds, with over 40 per cent Indian, followed by Sri Lankan Tamil and Pakistani and white English (accounting for under seven per cent of intake) is a source of pleasure to former pupils: 'exciting and stimulating when you go into the school,' says one. It's the geography that defeats many parents, wide radius (home counties and London fringes) making socialising a near impossibility.

Pupils, on the other hand, are an incredibly cohesive group, who think before they speak. Quiet confidence when they do, underpinned with a rich vein of understated humour, is well worth the wait.

Entrance: Much made, on website, of school's popularity – over 10 applicants per place (145 in year 7) though less scary than it sounds and places are actually offered to one in four applicants. As so often, essential to keep eye on ball, without blinking: first documents relating to entry are online almost 18 months before Sept of entry.

Whole competitive process, drawn out during the wait for results, is predictably 'a nightmare,' says mother, who didn't tutor 'but I think most do.' Families apply not just from surrounding boroughs, but, says admissions guru, as far away as Scotland and the EU, At least the tests, administered by Slough Consortium, take some of the pressure off pupils, who take just one batch of tests for four schools.

If unsuccessful at 11 plus, school remains off limits until sixth form entry when everyone, including school's own year 11 pupils, applies for places. Occasional places do occasionally crop up, however, and uniquely in the area, school hates to see a good candidate go to waste and may consider going over numbers (it's currently 60 above capacity) if there's a danger of genuine talent being missed.

Exit: A very few pupils leave after GCSEs, some to follow specialised courses, others because they want more freedom than school is prepared to offer (strict uniform policy sees sixth form wearing close to identical version of years 7 to 11 maroon, but in navy blue). A few take up apprenticeships; a very few drop out of education altogether. A shame? Head is forthright about reasons – often down to money – but crisply dismisses any thought of hand wringing about this or other inevitable disappointments. 'Life is not fair, we cannot pretend that we'll all be rewarded with what we deserve. However, if you cannot get what you want then maybe you need to be told to want what you get.'

For the most part, however, hard-working students and ambitions are well-matched. Oxbridge features on the list most years, as do other top tier universities, science and medicine-related amongst favoured courses, as you'd expect. The range of both, however, reflects school's admirable philosophy which trumps all. 'We encourage children to go to prestige universities but it's whatever is best for them,' says senior teacher.

Money matters: Government bursary fund to help 16-19 year olds who would find it hard to carry on education without financial assistance clearly flagged up on website.

Remarks: 'We try to allow students to develop themselves the way they want to be developed,' says senior teacher. Corridor with 'GCSE mocks star achievers' at one end and 'learn to knit' poster at the other just about sums it up.

UWC Atlantic College

St Donat's Castle, Llantwit Major, Vale of Glamorgan, CF61 1WF

- Pupils: 377 boys and girls; all board (full only) • Ages: 15–19
- Non-denom • Fees: £25,725 pa • Independent

Tel: 01446 799000
Email: jan.bishop@atlanticcollege.org
Website: www.atlanticcollege.org

Principal: Since 2011, Mr John Walmsley BSc PGCE (sixtyish). Previously head of Sidcot School, where he was assistant head. Before that, similar post at Simon Langton Girls' Grammar School in Canterbury, preceded by department head posts at Budmouth School in Weymouth, Greengates School in Mexico City and Churchill School in Somerset.

Educated at one of the first comprehensives in East Yorkshire, his first love and degree subject (at Leeds) was geology, though niche standing on the curriculum meant he tended to teach sciences and, at one point, geography. ICT also featured for years in his job title after IT course gave him sought-after expertise amongst schools desperate to get to grips with high tech delights coming their way.

Tall and engaging, with dry humour (Albariño, he thought, rather than amontillado, our suggestion) he has a committee-friendly voice – natural or honed by years of meetings it's hard to tell –betraying little in the way of emotion beyond occasional fleeting pained expression.

U

Headship at Sidcot, due to end when he reached 60 was, he'd thought, last hurrah before sashay into gentle retirement. Then came discreet call from headhunter and realisation that he wasn't yet ready to spend more quality time with his family (second wife Barbara is a former English teacher and burgeoning stonemason) and children (six in total aged mid thirties to early teens) or fishing boat in Ireland.

He's now completely hooked on what, if not the most interesting school leadership post in the country, must come close. Goals, structure and curriculum set it apart from just about everywhere else in the UK. Even hard bitten officials, including inspectors, get all shook up by philosophy that trains up pupils as emissaries for a better world – many, embedded in powerful institutions, endeavouring to inspire change from within.

Like many a minority movement not totally understood by outsiders, college radiates a certain cult-like fervour. Principal was slightly discombobulated by references to 'The Mission' when he first arrived. 'I thought, "Oh, no, what have I got myself into?"' Any resemblance to a niche religion is, however, entirely coincidental, with worshippers of every description catered for with multi-denominational prayer room as well as delightful church.

Considerable values overlap with Society of Friends makes this a sort of spiritual home from home, thinks principal. And though occupies its own quadrant in the educational universe, has kissing cousins, notably Gordonstoun (which shares the same founding father – German educationalist Kurt Hahn – as well as large chunks of the philosophy). Perhaps oddly, the two currently have no contact to speak of, something Mr Walmsley plans to rectify with a family get-together. How successful this is remains to be seen.

With everything else on his plate, retirement could be some way down the agenda. While many pupils come from settled homes round the globe, college is in effect an international rescue centre for others escaping conflict, poverty or the potentially life-threatening consequences of standing up to extremism, and requiring not just an education but a place of refuge. Often comes about following intervention of high profile celebrities and politicians – principal, a frequent flyer, meets the lot.

There's also a fair amount of missing organisational nuts and bolts business that needs sorting out. Sense of purpose might be rock solid, financial underpinning rather less so, spending having exceeded income for a number of years. Bureaucratic slippage meant that college wasn't even registered as a school and drifted off the inspection radar. First 'for about 20 years' happened in 2012, scoring, to principal's delight (and slight surprise), an all categories 'outstanding', despite unfenced swimming pool. 'I prepared them by saying the pool is unfenced – and so is the sea', he says.

Nuts and bolts paperwork was similarly lacking with few policies (now coming on stream). Tighter grip on the money side has resulted in a bit of natural wastage (departing staff weren't replaced) and temporary reduction on scholarships. Numbers now back in the black – essential when wooing potential sponsors (for donations) and bank manager (for loans).

Principal's first task on arrival was to write a formal strategic plan (and, no, there wasn't one of those, either). Biggest change will be addition of pre IB year for 25 students (probably in year 11 or 12) not yet ready for the full on two-year experience. They will lead largely separate lives, with own boarding house and co-curriculum, and the best will be invited to stay on. Many students aren't keen, seeing it as dilution, if not betrayal of the two-year education that they believe should define the UWC experience. Mr Walmsley, who is presumably getting used to having just about every decision challenged remains courteous but unmoved. 'It's controversial but unnecessarily so', he says. 'Some students think it will change everything. I don't think it will'.

On top of this, there are crumbling teaching blocks to be replaced and extras added, notably a big new sports hall. That, too, has been met with some opposition, this time from staff who see the mountains and sea as offering all the gym you'll ever need. Principal's view is that when there's a force nine blowing and it's dark, even the most rugged of spirits might prefer to commune with weights rather than nature in the raw.

Greatest ire has been reserved for alarms now fitted to dorm front doors. Though Ofsted and Welsh equivalent boarding school regulations non-negotiable, it's gone down extremely badly with anonymous notes, bannered-up protests and, months on, a still flickering flame of resentment amongst students.

Mr Walmsley is regarded as a slightly unknown quantity (discernible in pupils' quick, appraising glances when asked for their thoughts in his presence). Though does his bit with enthusiasm (was star turn at pupil fashion show, where his snappy outfit was so enthusiastically received 'that I couldn't hear the backing music') some would like more informal chatting time to share views.

When we visited a book of Quaker values had pride of place on his desk. Given fabulous but exhausting feistiness of colleagues and pupils, wouldn't be surprising if he opened the covers and inhaled a big lungful every morning, along with the bracing sea air. He must need every last drop he can get.

Academic matters: Education starts with the IB but, like the battery-powered toy bunnies in those long ago TV ads, keeps on going long after other schools have ground to a halt, courtesy of the Atlantic College Diploma, the compulsory, wrap-around co-curricular programme introduced in 2012.

Diploma extras take up a good 30 per cent of pupils' time 'and probably more' thinks principal, requiring the academic component of the IB (no picnic at the best of times) to be breezed through in just five mornings plus an afternoon in the classroom each week. Pupils choose one of four 'experiential' faculties, each big on the redemptive powers of active, selfless participation (very Kurt Hahn), that add to the IB's magnificent seven and tick off its creativity, action and service component en route.

There's outdoor (focus on those in peril on the seas – past pupil and teacher developed now best-selling RIB boat, then, combining brilliance and philanthropy in equal measure, selflessly donated patent to the RNLI); social justice (first hand encounters of a robust kind, including work with refugees and prisoners' families); global (everything from organising peace events to sharing a dorm with traditional enemies) and environmental, where commitment to sustainability is no light matter (students, who recycle everything, deeply miffed by college's failure to consult over green disposal of fittings following boarding house refurb).

It's education the immersive way, students picking a theme that interests them and following its thread through their studies – real world, practical applications dovetailing with academic side. Someone with an interest in Middle East might study Arabic, prepare an extended essay in world studies, help set up a project week in Jordan and, through this 'understand the UWC mission in the way they choose to develop their strengths,' says head of curriculum.

At its best (which is much of the time) diploma activities feed back into lessons, making for a buzzy classroom atmosphere where passionate debate is a way of life. There's nothing like hearing about refugees' experiences then discussing them back at base to add bite to economics or geography lessons, says principal. 'Makes it much more interesting and stimulating. I think it affects their exam grades, too'. Worked wonders on inspectors too, who assumed students leading lessons (spreading the word to peers in other diploma facilities is part of the syllabus) were teachers and had graded them outstanding before misunderstanding pointed out.

U

Structure won't be for everyone, particularly those with league-leaping performance as sole aspiration. Principal holds trenchant views on results which are 'meaningless after a few years. It's the outcome that is important. We measure the success in the effect our students have on the world'.

Despite this, college has earned itself plenty of bragging rights, with average IB scores of 37 in 2012, slightly up over previous years. If not at the very top of the tree, it's well ahead of the world average (around 30) and not to be sniffed at, particularly as for some students, who are selected on potential rather than educational back story, this may be their first ever brush with formal schooling.

Hot spots include spectacular languages (nine mother tongue or foreign options and a further 21, including Khmer, Mongolian and Welsh, as self-taught subjects). Maths and science are also very strong, say students – big clue to expectations the vast university physics textbook toted with pride by first year student.

With run of the mill IB students elsewhere already reckoned to be worked more intensively than A level counterparts, it's useful to arrive with work ethic fully formed and be good with stress, say students, who rapidly acquire super-efficient learning techniques.

In the main, it's attitude of mind that determines student suitability. 'Not for the weak-hearted,' thought one. Just as true for teachers, many with similar international background. Total conversion to college philosophy the norm and few moving back to conventional posts afterwards. Once recruited, becomes a forever post, others paling into comparison. 'You're spoiled for life', thought one, while college newsletter praised students' freedom to 'chase academic hares into the undergrowth of learning [...] keeping an eye on the syllabus and sometimes even a blind eye'.

Generous with their time (lots of impromptu one-to-one sessions were under way in final run up to IB exams), teachers praised for effective problem spotting system that kicks in early, tutors the first point of call, subject specialists alerted and involved as necessary.

Other areas (notably EAL, learning needs, gifted and talented), formerly a bit piecemeal but are having policies written and in some cases coordinators, including SENCo, appointed. Essential given some pupils' patchy educational history and/or imperfect grasp of English (no minimum language requirement for EU students). Lack of screening during committee-based recruitment system also means learning needs (mostly mild Asperger's SpLD and ADHD) will only be picked up on arrival, though good to see real commitment to disabled access. Wheelchair access determinedly provided wherever possible, whole classes relocated if necessary when it isn't.

Overall, exceptionally demanding curriculum covers emotional, intellectual and practical terrain that many adults would find hard going. Though something you'd hesitate to impose elsewhere, impressively mature bunch here take it in their stride. Only student doubt was perception that college is putting greater focus on IB scores. Principal is adamant this isn't the case. Teachers 'would not have the faintest idea' of college's ranking', he says. We assume he approves.

Games, options, the arts: Whichever diploma faculty they choose, students are unlikely to spend much time sitting on their hands, all areas being long on activity. Derring-do comes with the territory no matter what the gradient, acquisition of skills in graceful failure as important as trappings of success (fallibility reckoned by Kurt Hahn to be essential part of the learning process). As a result, there isn't much pupils here would say no to, from consorting with top scientists and politicians at climate change summit in Fiji to qualifying as a music therapist.

Outdoor faculty is the most obviously action packed of the bunch. Students join either aquatic water activities team (kayaking and surfing on offer but highlight lifeboat training at college's own RNLI station) or sign up to Terra Firma, which features mountain walking, navigation, emergency first aid and climbing (Brecon Beacons, a few miles inland, the venue for unlimited yomping).

While physical activity is compulsory, organised sport isn't. Stems from character building the Kurt Hahn way, which almost heretically relegates organised games to an 'important but not predominant' position in the hierarchy.

What happens and whether it happens at all is largely down to pupils. Though specialist coaches visit (pupils seemed slightly hazy about the details) there's no head of sport and activities vary from year to year depending on each cohort's enthusiasms. As a result, vast games field is intermittently used. Only sound on a fine spring afternoon was the bleating of newborn lambs from on-site farm. Anyone expecting pitches groaning with glory-seeking team endeavours may well be in for a bit of a shock.

Similarly, though IB studies are efficiently catered for with public showcases including drama reviews and weekly music recitals, there's not much in the way of large scale musical or dramatic endeavours.

Background and atmosphere: For mood and idealism, think educational version of Star Trek, the crew's goal less about finding 'strange new worlds' than improving the one they're in, one dilithium crystal at a time.

While hippies might give peace a chance by putting flowers in gun barrels, Hahn's solution to unify Cold War ridden world of the 1960s and ward off what he saw as the physical and moral decline of the young was to found a school (two if you count Gordonstoun, many more if you allow Round Square schools).

Here, the aim was to create a harmonious blend of nations and cultures, pairing opposites of every sort, oppressors and oppressed, poor and rich, who by living and studying together would develop shared outlook and common purpose (though took until 1967 before they got round to adding girls).

College remains a one-off in the UK and was the first of what is now 12-strong United World Colleges international movement. Its niche status and relatively low profile (even amongst heads, let alone the average parent) is, however, in inverse proportion to behind the scenes clout. Former students are embedded in some of the most powerful organisations and political administrations in the world, from the Chinese and US governments to top banks, providing under the radar alternative to conventional old boys' (and girls') network.

Setting – in 800-year-old castle by the sea – is out of this world and much appreciated by production companies (has featured in Dr Who). In addition to as many corkscrewing staircases as you can shake a medieval flail at, castle interior features terrific library, galleried and home to municipal quantities of books including Harry Potter (a college favourite) in assorted translations.

Appearances are slightly deceptive. Assorted chunks of apparently authentic gorgeousness such as stone entrance to dining hall pillaged wholesale from Boston Church in Lincolnshire by former owner, the newspaper magnate William Randolph Hearst. His salvage sweep also included the carved heads adorning the breakfast room ceiling – Lewis Carroll's inspiration, apparently, for Tweedledum and Tweedledee.

Lessons in many cases a perfect match for surroundings. History lessons complete with hard to improve vistas through arrow slits to wooded hill beyond, art and music located in nicely converted stable block. Other subjects are taught in three 1970s teaching blocks (science and maths, perhaps appropriately, in crumbliest and flakiest), all apparently constructed, together with admin centre, by embittered town planner having a bad day and featuring urban-style mini-underpass.

Seven boarding houses. Their distinctive characters, reflected in not always flattering secret student nicknames (we know what they are, too, but had to promise not to tell), are home to just under 50 pupils each. Pastoral care efficiently provided by brace of well-liked houseparents.

Facilities are 'simple', says college, and they're not wrong. Perfectly acceptable though, with extensive communal drying rooms and welly racks (essential given climate) and enough single showers to ensure sufficient privacy for those who find communal versions problematic.

There's the odd idiosyncrasy when it comes to equipment – irons are allowed in dorms, kettles are not (one boarding house has just been rebuilt following a fire). But this is outweighed by impressive, all-round sensitivity, subtle pooling of kitchen equipment in mixed common rooms avoiding distinctions between haves and have-nots, daily deliveries of communal food essentials.

With just one communal TV to its name, a climate that's far from tropical and the nearest cinema nine miles away by land (or 13 if teamed with a bracing swim across the Bristol Channel), this is a place that needs decent social events more than most. Until recently though, it wasn't getting them, felt pupil. Far better now, with weekly disco (noise levels bravely borne by principal, who lives opposite), boarding houses charged with weekend event organisation, and much more to do.

The sense of being a body apart is reinforced by two-term structure that follows the beat of the IB drum – with the result that pupils only have four days off between January and May and are then off on holiday until early August when second year pupils arrive back for a week's bonding before new intake turns up.

Physical apartness makes it something of unknown quantity within the local community. 'Out of my league,' thought one local. 'Feels exclusive – if you can afford for your kids to go there, you're doing well'. No wonder the principal is contemplating a hearts, minds and meters job to get locals, starting with taxi drivers, who are probably the college's most frequent visitors, onside.

Pastoral care and discipline: New arrivals are paired with 'excellent' buddies, big on tea and sympathy (favour returned when it comes to exam time). Their first task is probably to settle nerves after meeting and greeting ceremony where they're drummed in with chorus of pots and pans pillaged from common rooms by second years ('it leaves terrible dents', said one pupil who as kitchen monitor is charged with subsequent search and rescue mission).

With full boarding the only option (though parents can come and stay nearby at beginning and ends of term), inner core of steel probably helps, given policy of picking roommates for differences, the more apparently irreconcilable the better. 'We would always put Israelis and Palestinians together', says principal, who is currently spearheading drive to recruit Syrians from both sides of current conflict.

Pupils aren't just in favour of approach but drawn to college because of it. Beliefs that elsewhere would be on collision course (there's a strong GLBT movement, for example) spark enduring friendships and sometimes more, with potential for heartache when relationships breach cultural barriers.

Whether deliberately or by chance, student bonds are well and truly cemented by decision to involve them in the nuts and bolts of college operations. Open book policy on everything from finances to rebuilding ensures that student voice isn't merely heard but is a force to be reckoned with, from spontaneous orations in assembly on whatever issues take their fancy, college-related or otherwise (polemic following death of Mrs Thatcher made for edgy listening) to indignation over any perceived high-handedness. 'If they give us a voice, that's what they have to expect', said one.

Given disquiet over new pre-IB year, just as well college pre-empted decades of conflict by ditching uniform in the 1970s. 'Pupils fear change', thought principal. Might be right at that,

what with tolerance for far more obtrusive but longer-standing security measures such as airport-style library security gate and 11 separate entry codes (a school record, we reckon) covering everything from Mac lab to harp storage. No wonder one pupil adopts low-tech approach of banging on the window to attract attention instead.

Impressive maturity means that nobody sweats the small stuff. Courtesy on both sides is a given, teachers generally liked (only one got thumbs down) and while big issues go to the wire, there are minimal rules elsewhere, nous and good sense taken as read. 'We don't need a rule about using phones in lessons when it would clearly be rude', a pupil told us.

Pupils and parents: Easy to gush over pupils' self-assurance and intelligence which carries all before it (just one non-show in recent memory, pupil so overcome with nerves that unable to board the plane). A sassy bunch, it's no surprise that many have persuaded their parents that this is the place to be and in one case at least secured the sponsorship to pay the fees.

Though fees are 'low compared to other top boarding schools', says college, they are still high enough to skew social mix towards luxury ingredients rather than salt of the earth. Or in UWC words, 'similar people simply born in different places'. A pupil says that this 'isn't the place for the materialistic or those who believe the world can get better with money alone'. Parent philanthropy is a way of life, one family funding not only their own child but three others, too. Similar acts of generosity both widespread and long term.

Five-strong development department works with alumni who include King of the Netherlands, chairman of Shell and vice-president of European Bank to get that giving feeling early. And give they do. Vocal and passionate espousal of college and ideals often continues for life, endorsements from everyone from Nelson Mandela to Queen Noor of Jordan setting the tone. It's resulting in growing numbers from the poorest and most wartorn regions of earth.

Some local recruitment, extending to deprived Liverpool, Birmingham and Valleys schools, requires a bit of careful eggshell treading to avoid Orphan Annie connotations, college raising grateful poor to a life of privilege. So far so good.

Entrance: 'The world is our catchment area', says college. Makes a refreshing change from same old distance from home criteria, but downside is labyrinthine admissions process requiring minotaur-seeking levels of persistence (though no string).

Think Oxbridge inter-college pupil swapsies at admissions time, add international dimension requiring agreement between parents, students and UWC staff who may all be on different continents and it's not surprising that entrance process is officially badged as 'extremely complicated'.

On the surface it's highly competitive, too, with nearly 100 nations jostling for places, just 20 available for UK nationals and a further 17 places in other UWC colleges.

Would-be pupils submit applications either to one of 140 UWC national committees, often staffed by alumni, or direct to colleges –specific requirements as individual as they are. Though they can express college preferences, they're assumed to be signing up to UWC aims rather than a location, and so could end up being offered a place somewhere completely different.

Loving care is advised to ensure that focus on community work and support for UWC ideals shine through. Also useful to ensure academic endorsement (no GCSE minimum grades specified, every application considered on merit) is from teacher '... who supports the idea of you going to a UWC'. (Our tip: use the word 'mission' at least once).

Shortlisted UK candidates have an overnight stay at the castle, followed by informal 20-minute interview with committee members, alumni and, unusually, former rather than current teachers. Final decision communicated around three weeks later (though can take longer).

U

Whole process is an excellent Kurt Hahn-style challenge and, if you meet the age criteria (students normally start aged 16 or 17, though there's some flexibility), there's the chance to do it all over again the following year.

Exit: It's off to better things not just for pupils, but with 70 per cent ultimately ending up in humanitarian-linked careers, for the world as a whole. While US admissions tutors zoom in early, like dealers at a jumble sale before the doors open to the general punters, other top unis aren't far behind.

Oxbridge and Ivy League combined mopped up 15 per cent of the year group in 2012. US is the most popular university destination overall with close to 40 per cent of places, followed by UK (28 per cent – vast majority to Russell/1994 group members) and Canada (seven per cent).

Around 16 per cent take a gap year. Courses many and various. A pupil we we spoke to hoped to major in physics with laudable aim of investigating travel across vacuums in outer space.

Money matters: Admissions process supported by large fundraising and development department working overtime to bring in the dosh. Latest initiative themed to college's fiftieth anniversary (think of a number, any number, with a fifty in it and hand it over) is generating over £2 million a year, almost all used to fund scholarships. Other countries chip in, too (Norwegian government funds ten of its own students, for example).

Remarks: Once a glorious experiment, still out on a limb (and, we suspect, in no hurry to shed iconoclastic status), Atlantic College provides an education as remarkable as the feisty, impassioned students it attracts. The ticking of admin boxes may annoy but it's a necessary evil that parents will welcome. Its location may be isolated but its perspective, genuinely global, is anything but. Just don't expect a picnic by the sea.

Wakefield Girls' High School

Linked school: Wakefield Girls' High School Junior School

Wentworth Street, Wakefield, West Yorkshire, WF1 2QS

- Pupils: 730 girls, all day • Ages: 11–18 • Inter–denom
- Fees: £10,755 pa • Independent

Tel: 01924 372490
Email: admissions@wghsss.org.uk
Website: www.wgsf.org.uk

Headmistress: Since 2009, Mrs Gillian Wallwork BA (Manchester) English Language and Literature, previously deputy head of Cheadle Hulme School. Likes the theatre, a good book, the coast, family get-togethers, her spaniel, plants and Pre-Raphaelite art.

Academic matters: In 2013, 84 per cent A*-B at A level. Excellent results in all subjects and a wide range on offer, even if it means groups of only two or three at A level. Most take three A2s plus general studies. Art and design is very popular; the AQA external examiner the day we visited said that the work was the best he had ever seen. It's very well-resourced; girls are allowed a lot of freedom and respond with remarkable creativity, using a variety of media. Biology is popular too, and very strong, as is chemistry; maths, politics, psychology and Spanish also stand out. Boys from QEGS can join a number of subjects, eg theatre studies, ICT and RS. There are no hurdles for existing girls to enter the sixth form (but if it's clear a girl will struggle with the pace, she will be encouraged to go down a less academic route elsewhere) and no AS to A2 hurdles.

GCSE results are also consistently excellent, around 77 per cent A/A*; virtually 100 per cent A*-C in 2013. Large numbers do separate sciences; dual award also offered. Textiles are done by all in years 7-9 and girls make all the clothes for a fashion show. In design and technology the projects are tailored towards girls' interests and creativity, and product design is offered at GCSE. Lots of PCs and several interactive whiteboards; all girls do the ECDL in year 9 and learn keyboard skills in the junior school. Class sizes are around 24 for years 7-9, 5-25 at GCSE and 2-16 at A level. Setting for maths and French only from Years 8/9.

The well-staffed special needs unit, unusually, can be accessed easily by junior and senior girls, which reduces any sense of stigma. It's modern, bright and comfortable, catering for around 150 girls with eg dyslexia, dyscalculia, Asperger's – but not children with statements who, the school considers, would be better served in the state system. Support is given outside lesson time.

Games, options, the arts: The sports facilities are very good and exceptional results are achieved in local and national competitions in the usual range of sports as well as cross-country; netball and hockey are particularly strong, probably because they are started at the age of seven. Nearly half the school takes part in teams. Self-defence and various kinds of gymnastics are also available. Very good drama facilities – a drama studio and access to a purpose-built theatre at QEGS. Lots of productions – mainly conventional choices, apart from the drama comp for years 7-9 where girls write their own plays. Masses of music – a great range of choirs, some enjoying success in local competitions, and music groups for all ages, some in combination with QEGS, plus a wide choice of instrumental lessons (over half the girls learn) including jazz piano and bass guitar, with lots of very good exam results. Concerts, as well as plays, are put on with the boys' school (the Advent Carol Service is held in Wakefield Cathedral) and there is a recording studio funded by the PTA. Girls in years 7-9 create their own dance routines in an inter-form dance competition. The library is generously resourced and fiction reading actively encouraged at all ages; a major extension is being planned. Plenty of school trips, in England and abroad, eg a swing band tour of north Italy, a hockey and netball tour to Hong Kong, Australia and Singapore, visits to France, Spain, Rome. Year 7 girls have a residential at the start of their first term to help them make friends, which they greatly value. A very wide choice of clubs and societies, including hamster care, Fun with Food and a gardening club that cultivates a vegetable garden and has a wormery. Huge numbers achieve D of E awards.

Background and atmosphere: The school belongs to the Wakefield Grammar School Foundation, which offers 3-18 education to both sexes. It occupies a number of buildings in a conservation area near the centre of Wakefield, one-time town houses, the focal point being the original Georgian Wentworth House, with some attractive and thoughtfully-designed modern additions, though some areas are drab and in need of re-decoration. Subjects are located in zones, eg creative arts, embracing music/drama/English/textiles and food tech, with a common, well-equipped computer suite.

There is an immediate buzz as soon as you enter the school. Girls come across as well-mannered, happy, confident and eager to learn. They appreciate the understanding and support they are given by teachers if they have any difficulties, work hard and have fun, too, eg the sixth formers have a fancy dress day in their last week at school, and there is a Christmas review performed by girls with guest appearances by staff. Lots of marvellous artwork and photos of girls' activities on display. Girls' birthdays are highlighted on big TV screens in three locations and all are given a teddy both on entering the junior as well as leaving the senior school – the latter dressed in a

W

school hoodie! There is a strong sense of community, which the girls value; they see the school as friendly and safe.

Huge amounts of money raised for a broad range of charities, with the girls doing all the organisation, and there are links with a sister school in Tanzania, where girls teach on visits, as well as state school partnership events. The school council's views, eg on food, charities, etc are taken on board; its eco committee is aiming for the 'Green Flag Award'. The sixth form have their own building, an old house (due to be refurbished) with a café, kitchen and common room well supplied with battered sofas – the clutter is all very homely and they are allowed to entertain boys and enjoy a degree of independence there. There are three lovely memorials to old girls who have died young – a stained glass window depicting a rainbow, an indoor fountain and a small garden with wooden animal sculptures – that illustrate the school's humanity and thoughtfulness.

Pastoral care and discipline: Pastoral care is very good – girls are well known to staff, who soon spot signs of unhappiness. Girls see teachers as taking any upsets or arguments seriously and say there is no real bullying. The very good bullying policy was re-drafted by girls and there is a very sensible, realistic sixth form handbook. The transition from junior to senior school happens easily, as junior girls are able to use some of the senior school facilities. The girls are given freedom and clear limits (a code of conduct that 'gives guidelines for acceptable behaviour rather than rules') which they rarely breach, allowing a relatively relaxed atmosphere. A very strong line is taken with drugs and smoking.

Pupils and parents: Some wealthy parents but most are professional/middle class. This is not a prosperous area and about a fifth of the girls currently receive assistance with fees – 'No one knows who's on an award; money is not an issue'. The catchment area is extensive: Wakefield, Huddersfield, Barnsley, north Sheffield and south Leeds. Parents organise bus services to fill in any gaps left by public transport. Half of year 7 come from the junior school, the rest from local schools. Ethnically very mixed – one year had a Muslim head girl, 'clearly the best person for the job', so the school decided to adapt the post's duties to accommodate her religious beliefs.

Entrance: Eleven plus by exam in English and maths, with verbal and non-verbal reasoning (110 in verbal reasoning is the cut off point, as 'they must be able to cope with the work – it's an absolutely basic requirement') plus primary school report and reference. The school provides clear, detailed information on what needs to be covered. Almost all junior school girls continue but it's not automatic. Girls can join at other years (preferably not in the middle of exam courses, though). 20-30 leave after GCSE and up to 12 enter at year 12. These need a minimum of 440 points from their nine best GCSEs in a wide range of subjects and A/B in their proposed AS subjects.

Exit: To a wide range of universities – lots of Russell Group; steadily increasing numbers to Oxbridge; Leeds, Durham, Nottingham, Manchester, Newcastle and Sheffield popular; some to art/ veterinary college; almost all achieve their first choice. The most famous old girl is Barbara Hepworth (head's elegant study contains two of her sculptures, as well as an interesting collection of model owls); other Old Girls are writers Helen Fielding and Joanne Harris, and Katherine Kelly and Priya Kaur Jones from the media world – plus Claire Young, the runner up in the 2008 The Apprentice!

Money matters: Fees are all-inclusive – no extra charge for learning support or exam entries. There is a pot of money for means-tested Foundation Awards, from 25-90 per cent, where parental income is less than £35,000, which funds about 14 bursaries in each year group with additional ones available in the sixth form. Also a 100 per cent fees scholarship awarded at entry in year 7, with possibly another to come. There could be 100 girls on bursaries out of the 730 total. In addition, there is a 100 per cent Ogden award for the sixth form (reserved for state school applicants who want to take science/maths) and 12 other scholarships of 25/50/75 per cent.

Remarks: A very impressive and attractive school, offering a great range of opportunities for girls to develop talents and win respect for them, affording all the advantages of single sex education combined with plenty of interaction with nearby QEGS. It has the feel of a very stimulating, high achieving and caring family, where all the members are known and appreciated for who they are. Girls find it almost impossible to think of anything they would like to change – 'You just grow to love the school as it is,' said a year 12 girl. 'You're not judged on your cleverness; you're seen as an individual – everyone's got their own strengths,' said another. Also outstandingly creative – witness the school mag, packed with stunning art and very strong writing.

Waldegrave School

Fifth Cross Road, Twickenham, Middlesex, TW2 5LH

• Pupils: 1000 girls, all day • Ages: 11–16 • Non-denom • State

Tel: 020 8894 3244
Email: info@waldegrave.org.uk
Website: www.waldegrave.richmond.sch.uk

Headteacher: Since 2006, Mrs Philippa Nunn, BSc from UCL in Cell Biology, MA in Educational Management from Greenwich, PGCE and NPQH (late forties). Appointed a National Leader of Education in 2011. Married with two daughters at the local state schools. Was previously head of the Holt School in Berkshire, an all-girls 11-18 comprehensive. Started teaching science in 1987 and has only ever stopped for maternity leave; currently teaches ICT. Has a calm, measured and courteous manner, believes in stability, continuity and in taking the long view. Some staff have been at the school for more than 25 years, which 'adds strength to the ethos of the school'. Aims to develop the traditional curriculum by offering vocational qualifications. Introduced a house system (2009) to promote a greater sense of loyalty and belonging and to enhance student leadership opportunities.

Academic matters: Consistently achieves good results in English, maths and science GCSEs. French, history, art, drama, RE always good too. The success rate in A*-C grades is well above the regional and national average, 86 per cent 5+ A*-C grades including maths and English. EBac around 63 per cent and rising. A*/A 50 per cent in 2013. Mrs Nunn strives to give every pupil the widest possible access to a variety of subjects, as she is determined that they will leave the school intending to continue education. Virtually all do, so her determination is paying off. Quality of teaching is excellent. Teachers and support staff are committed to the school and urge the pupils to enjoy success and savour the rewards that accompany it. Achievements are recognised at assemblies throughout the year and at Celebration Afternoons at the end of the year. High academic standards are expected but provision is made within the curriculum for all abilities, and modest acts such as helpfulness to the school or to others are duly acknowledged and rewarded. Lessons are given in broad ability tutor groups initially but setting for maths, science and languages occurs early on in the first years. In subsequent years setting in other subjects if appropriate. All are entered for 6-10 GCSEs; some do

W

13 after discussion with parents and staff. Short course subjects such as ICT and PE well subscribed with good results.

Appointed as one of the first 100 Teaching Schools in 2011, and is also a National College for School Leaders National Support School. The specialist schools status provides extra funding for science and maths, including ICT suites installed in 2006. Designated area in an independent learning centre for gifted and talented girls and those with other special needs. With an incredible cultural diversity (43 different languages), EAL support is strong, even offering a lunchtime club for all age groups. On the subject of lunchtime, a great deal is compressed into a very short 35 minute break: careers advice, ICT, rehearsals for choirs and bands, puzzle club, homework clubs. Similarly, lots of before and after school activities. A breakfast club at 8.00am every morning with badminton on offer at the same time for the more energetic. After school up until 4.00pm – choice is much more varied with a high take-up rate.

School awarded Academy status in 2012 and plans to open a sixth form in September 2014.

Games, options, the arts: Good range of sports offered from the more traditional – rounders, tennis, volleyball, athletics – to the somewhat bizarre – Gaelic football. Classes in the fitness suite, cricket, rowing (linked in with Walbrook Rowing Club) and table-tennis. Hidden from view from the road is a huge outdoor green area with tennis courts and marked-out running track.

School regularly wins regional netball leagues and was recently the Middlesex hockey champion. Also borough winners at netball and rounders. Head positively oozes enthusiasm listing her school's sporting achievements. Another of her aims is to improve participation in sport. Gymnastics is strong – both a multi and traditional gym on site. A dance studio was funded through the national lottery. Extra opportunities include bridge, drama, study skills, chess, art, music theory, ICT, choirs, rock bands and full orchestra. Art and music are both strengths. Beautiful displays throughout the school testimony to the high standard of work. In year 11 the school offers a business mentoring system whereby girls are allocated someone from outside the school who comes in to see them on a regular basis over their last year. This is a forward-looking scheme, well-organised by welcoming staff, which helps develop their social and business skills and gives them a timely introduction to outside world experiences.

Background and atmosphere: Strange mix of building styles with the newer ones added on to the original (1930s) creating a bit of a hotch-potch. A 'temporary' cabin put up in 1948 still serves as the school canteen (due to be replaced by 2014). New caterers in 2011, with food freshly cooked on site, and a biometric system for payment. New science laboratories and English classroom added in 2011 along with remodelling of food and textiles rooms. Space is limited, and recent years have seen a new dance studio and fitness suite squeezed in. However, the major project completed September 2009 was the overhaul of the outside play area, transforming it into an outdoor theatre with landscaped surroundings. The money for this raised by the extremely supportive PTA. They also maintain three small internal quadrangles which echo different themes – pond area, bamboo garden and the vegetable patch. Touches such as these add an element of style to the otherwise uninspiring architecture.

The girls themselves give this school a buzzy atmosphere. A former pupil remarks that 'all girls is a positive rather than a negative.' Uniform is worn by all, albeit often customised as has ever been the case in girls' schools. The end result is not unpleasing to the eye.

Pastoral care and discipline: No real behavioural problems. Room 19a is their room 101, and no-one wants to go there. First

years are invited to spend a day in the school to find their way about and practise their journey to and fro – puts a stop to later excuses about buses being late. They also start the term a bit earlier before the older ones arrive. Prefects help out with the younger ones, organise charity events, welcome visitors and play an important leadership role in the school. Each tutor group elects a representative to attend the school council, which in turn represents the school at the Richmond School Student Council. All good training ground for debating and public speaking.

School is honest about bullying and admits that, like the poor, it is always with us. However, stringent efforts made to put an end to it. Girls, staff and parents exhorted to report any incident straight away and assured that something will be done.

Pupils and parents: Although the school has no religious affiliation, the majority of the pupils are Christian. More than 25 per cent are from an ethnic minority, and the school rules stipulate that whilst permissible to wear the hijab (for religious reasons) the niqab should not be worn to school. All come from the surrounding borough of Richmond, which is known nationally for its high level of professional parents. A local parent declares it to be the sort of school where 'decent folk will be prepared to break all sorts of rules to get their daughters in.' Its present lack of a sixth form does not deter as no state school in Richmond has one; a mixed sixth form will open in 2014. 'I had no problems undertaking coursework and I was taught how to take exams at Waldegrave, so I felt confident about my A levels and about my degree course,' is the view of a former pupil. They're an ambitious lot and they have a very strong PTA to back them up.

Entrance: Fully comprehensive intake. It is the only all girls' state school in Richmond so is always oversubscribed. Much to the head's relief, all admissions are dealt with by the local authority. Despite clear and rigid guidelines about admissions policies there are always appeals. Sibling policy includes stepsisters, half sisters and adopted sisters living in the same household. A percentage of their intake includes those with special needs and those in public care or who are deemed by the LA to have a particular need. Most girls will have attended local primary schools in the borough.

Exit: Students go to Richmond Sixth Form College, Esher College, Strodes College or to sixth forms of co-ed independent schools, day or boarding.

Remarks: A lively, happy school with pupils to match. Mrs Nunn strikes one as a slow burner who is moving this school forward. Her enthusiasm and her demand for high standards are reflected by the staff and students. A very good choice for those lucky enough to meet the entry criteria.

Wallace College

12 George IV Bridge, Edinburgh, EH1 1EE

• Pupils: 30 • Ages: 14–18 • Fees: Scottish Highers from £2,500 pa; A level from £2,700 pa • Independent

Tel: 0131 220 3634
Email: info@wallacecollege.co.uk
Website: www.wallacecollege.co.uk

Director of Studies: Since 1993, Lily Crawford MA (60s – you could knock 10 years off and still guess wrong); a Glasgow lass, who read English literature at Edinburgh and previously taught in the state system in Edinburgh and Falkirk. Slow speaking, deep thinking, she is point of contact for new students, passionate about keeping costs down and directing studies to be fit both for uni matriculation and future employment. Previously an examiner for AQA, SQA and the BAC, she has all the necessary know-how. Crawford leads students through the UCAS maze, helps with personal statements, engineers extra time (scribes if need be – but SQA must have proof positive of need). Very much hands on and, quite obviously, the glove fits.

Academic matters: Exam centre for AQA, Edexcel, OCR, CIE (for As or A2 in November): GCE, As, A2, GCSE and IGCSE; SQA: highers, advanced highers, intermediate 2 (death knell soundeth), national 4 and 5. One year three term courses start in September. Wallace prides itself on 'accelerated study programmes': super motivated can take a conventional two year course within the year; mega boost, too, in October and February with daily three hour concentrated blocks of lessons: five subjects each week. A two term IGCSE syllabus runs from January. Raft of options on offer; all tutors (of all ages: easy to find in Edinburgh) come with honours degrees, college will pull on extra lang tutors (usually native speaking) or just tutors for more esoteric requirements. Technical subjects cost more than a tad more – hiring lab time is expensive, though Wallace can often rustle up kit for physics experiments. All the usual suspects, plus philosophy, economics, accounting, computing and mod studies. Engineering not really feasible.

The flexi-study programme is geared to help 'students who wish to combine independent study with support from qualified tutors'; many of these are home schooled and just need pointers to keep them up to speed: 'read this chapter, forget that, this is really important' sort of thing. Usual course is two hours per subject a week for 10 weeks, but variations possible. No more than five independent learners per class, which may be timetabled to suit individual students: lessons in the afternoons to accommodate a morning job, five days' work reorganised into three for those who live further away. Back to the Crawford mantra – keep the cost down.

Max students at any one time 35, classes tiny, usually six or less, often one-to-one and never more than eight. Students come for regular sixth form studies, to improve GCSE/standard grades, As, AS, highers or advanced highers, or to expand their portfolio. No hard and fast rules. Emphasis on essay writing, good SEN help available. Three hours per subject per week, plus an hour's test with regular feedback, and detailed end of term report.

The acclaimed holiday revision courses, usually oversubscribed, are a haven for those still at school and overseas students, often in the independent sector, who find some of our educational lingo, particularly in exams, a tad quirky: 'if takes a man with a wheelbarrow ten hours to move 1000 kilos of sand one kilometre how long would it take three men with wheelbarrows?' And just what is a wheelbarrow? In a maths exam?

Games, options, the arts: No affiliations with sports clubs and the like, but director of studies can 'point in the right direction'. Theatre trips arranged if useful for course work (extra).

Background and atmosphere: Privately owned college, founded in 1972, incorporating English language school, variety of tutorial options, and a popular revision course (all disciplines except the BAC) during half terms and holidays. Tucked neatly away behind a (Georgian) red door above an unprepossessing row of shops on George IV Bridge, not quite within the sight of Edinburgh Castle, spectacular views from the west (castle et al). Very much into the 21st century, twitters away: 'GCSE results come out on August 22nd', happy tweets from students.

Pastoral care and discipline: Strong anti-drugs policy.
No parents evenings as such; parents 'welcome to pop in and see Crawford or individual tutors', otherwise most communication is by email.

Accommodation can be arranged, either through the EFL wing myriad of approved host families, or in university halls, assuming space available.

Pupils and parents: All sorts: aged 15+ to 19. Pupils come from all backgrounds for all reasons, including those who find that conventional school does not cater for their particular selection of subjects, those who have lived outside the trad school atmosphere, those who have been educated abroad, and those who have parted either willingly or unwillingly from their previous school.

Entrance: By interview with the director of studies.

Exit: College takes enormous trouble to launch students on the next step of their careers; matriculation the norm. Edinburgh uni popular, as with all the (free) Scottish universities.

Remarks: Good alternative for those who don't get on with traditional schools.

Wallington County Grammar School

Croydon Road, Wallington, SM6 7PH

- Pupils: 980 boys, all day. Girls in the sixth form • Ages: 11–18
- Non-denom • State

Tel: 020 8647 2235
Email: wcgs@suttonlea.org
Website: www.wcgs.org.uk

Headteacher: Since September 2013, Mr Jonathan Wilden (early forties). Educated at St Joseph's College, Ipswich; studied geography at University of Wales (Lampeter), postgraduate degree from Bath. Mr Wilden has taught in a number of south London boroughs and was formerly deputy head at Evelyn Grace Academy, Brixton. He joined Wallington as deputy headteacher in 2010.

Academic matters: You'd assume top grades in everything, all the time, and for the most part you'd be right, with results that make for the world's most boring game of Scrabble (depending on interest levels in vintage Swedish pop groups). In 2013, 71 per cent A*/A grades at GCSE, nine in 10 passing GCSEs with at least five A*-A grades. At A level, more of the same with 87 per cent of grades at A*/B, 60 per cent at A*/A.

Being bottom in a class of over-achievers can be a lonely place but here, stigma is neatly sidestepped – or at least addressed with humour. 'I know when x and y first met, but still I am in the bottom set,' says prizewinning poem in newsletter.

'I don't think you have to excel. They give their form order so everyone knows who's bottom but from what I can tell, nobody is given stick, or jeered or sneered at,' confirms one mother. All this despite the fact that the cleverest are 'ridiculously clever', say boys, citing a sixth former, nickname King Language, who taught himself Ancient Greek to A-level standard in three years.

While it would be awfully easy to ramp up the pressure – 'you can just push them, there's no limit to what you can get out of them,' says a teacher – the school knows where to exercise restraint. 'Extremely tedious' ICT GCSE was axed, leaving pupils free to concentrate on achieving 10 or 11 cracking GCSEs – eight core subjects, economics and business studies amongst the options – and up to four A levels, though 'they suggest only doing three so we get good grades,' confirms sixth former.

W

Around 80 per cent opt to keep going with a non-related but much-loved subject post-16 – one boy, hoping to study economics at university was sweetening the pill of straight sciences and maths with art – virtuoso timetable juggling ensuring that just about every sixth former, somewhat amazingly, is able to follow chosen subject blend.

Non-stop praise for staff, many seen as an inspirational force for good: '....the only reason my son wants to study classics at university,' says a parent. Another pupil, initially planning to be an architect, was ambushed by the fascination of psychology. 'It's the way it weaves its way through society.'

With everything from innovative blood points awarded in history and classics – the more the gore, the better the score (one boy even made a Medusa cake) – to year 9 English students filming themselves looking moody and disenfranchised in (sub) urban dystopia (a 'gritty portrayal of life' says one – or as close as you get in leafy Wallington) it's not hard to see why teachers and lessons are so highly rated.

Consistent overall quality makes the very occasional slippage round the edges that much more noticeable, with a few more C grades in A level biology and physics than you'd expect and a tiny number slipping into D and E hinterland. Home influence can be a factor, thought previous head. 'Though we have the conversation each year about how the subjects should be what the pupil wants to do, there is parental pressure to do the sciences even if they're not their best or favourite subjects.'

School, though, is far from passive. Flair-filled initiatives include book clubs and mini-libraries dotted around classrooms to get non-readers hooked (a surprising number see the printed word as a duty not a pleasure), while learning support for the 20 or so pupils with dyspraxia, dyslexia, ADD and ASD/Asperger's ranges from buddies to lend a hand with organisation to morale-boosting training as cyber mentors. Even parents are paired with others whose children have similar needs.

Add an extensive range catch up clubs and sixth form mentors who help year 7s in lessons and offer a listening ear outside and rigorous plotting of academic trajectories, and it's hard to slip through the cracks. 'We know pupils better than ever before,' says school.

Games, options, the arts: Sport is 'central to school life' says prospectus (music merely 'flourishes'). Lots of team finals (rugby particularly) and individual success (water polo gold at London Youth Games). Hockey is in decline; football, recently introduced to the relief of many, on the up – though relegated to the public park down the road. Only rugby and cricket grace the well-kept sports field.

While the talented are encourage to sign up, adulation for sporting legends is low key and there's plenty of kudos to spare if, as a fair few do, you direct your talents elsewhere.

Outside school, pupils regularly reach the finals of national maths, science and spelling. Inside, the arts are well represented with traditional ensembles and a popular Battle of the Bands, though eclipsed by 'Singstaff' – a teacher talent show. Drama bristles with high quality productions running the gamut from mainstream (including a well-reviewed Oliver!) to the quirky – sixth formers were 're-imagining' classics, 'the more eccentric the better,' said one, who planned a new take on the Odyssey. Art also has its idiosyncrasies, highlights including a jolly slimline Michelin man lookalike crafted from cling-film wrapped wire.

Lots of charitable activity with sixth form boys about to embark on moustache growth – 'few have the manliness,' says one – to raise awareness of testicular cancer, with Wednesday afternoons for years 11 upwards dedicated to enrichment activity (facial hair nurturing presumably being a 24/7 preoccupation) and science-based links with local primary schools a speciality, with would-be medics passing on resuscitation techniques and future scientists launching rockets on the playing field (arts types, meanwhile, prudently watched the fun from indoors).

Around 80 per cent of pupils, it's estimated, attend at least one of the 50 plus clubs that plug any gaps in the timetable, most with a strong academic raison d'être (physics geek club about as frivolous as it gets) though D of E is also on offer. There's even the Hutchins über-club, the society's society, that monitors the rest and 'aims to push the academic boundaries,' says a pupil, by ensuring other clubs are delivering suitably nourishing intellectual fare to their members.

Background and atmosphere: 'The deputy head told us to practise personal humility and professional will,' says sixth former. 'You never get too big for your boots but you're committed to doing well and going about it in a nice way.'

Judging by polite clouds of year 7s trailing grinning deputy school captain to plead for coveted school pins, awarded for participation, it's a lesson learned early on.

Not that an indomitable spirit is anything new, surfacing during world war II when the school, then fee paying (it became a grammar in 1944) stayed open during the Blitz, despite two direct hits and substantial damage, while others headed for the hills,

School's homely feel is 'such a cliché,' says pupil, rather crossly – but inescapable, while the presence of girls – first two joining in 2000 though one only lasted a fortnight, today making up a fifth of sixth form numbers – brings 'a different dimension,' says school.

Slightly battered charm, with some areas just for best (like green and pleasant quad) and lots of period details. Bath-sized hand basin in visitor's loo and vast original 1930s radiators – last chance to see as they're finally due for replacement – would probably make a fortune on EBay.

But behind all those curvy art deco brass-topped bannisters, the sixth form art room nicknamed Middle Earth (it's sandwiched between two others rather than home to a bunch of hobbits) and an abundance of gothic gilt lettering, there's a definite appetite for change.

Recent additions include funky new sports hall, twinkling away in on the far side of playing field with wow factors a-plenty (automatic doors, which have reset to manual, are the only feature not playing ball) which has allowed large scale musical classrooms elsewhere. Sixth form study area replaces the library, which has taken over the gym.

All eyes though are currently on big new food technology classroom featuring chairs in a zinging green that almost matches the walls and banks of ovens. Popular with everyone (there's already a school recipe book). Has also wrought miraculous reduction in queuing times at popular fund-raising lunchtime barbecues.

Only loser is the sixth form common room, now given over to classics, though pupils take this in good part – 'we've lost a common room but gained a subject' says one. A small patio constructed, by way of compensation, for their exclusive benefit, is little used, pupils congregating instead by the front entrance, as if waiting for a school bus that never arrives, while girls use their loos as a walk-in wardrobe, with a mish-mash of coats, books and makeup stashed under the washbasins. 'Surprising,' says sixth form boy, with masterly understatement.

Pastoral care and discipline: Things are back on an even keel after a period of what school terms 'low level misbehaviour' when pupil respect towards staff dipped. 'Towards the end, you felt [the previous head] was off the ball,' confirms a parent. 'I was surprised at the amount of latitude.'

No chance now, with a rigorously applied code of sanctions (with input from pupils) and (existing) practical measures including a separate, well-patrolled areas for each year group, (though sixth formers, rather hurt at implied lack of trust, would like more mixing of the age ranges).

Wonderfully waffle-free policies ('scorn cheating,' exhorts section on sporting aims in pleasingly Tom Brown tones) leave no doubts as to what will and won't be tolerated. Drugs

W

won't, though offenders expressing suitable contrition may get a second chance thanks to an informal 'you take ours, we'll take yours' agreement with Sutton Boys and Wilson's. (No guarantees, however).

Incentives to behave are thick on the ground, from the six houses which 'exert an emotional pull,' says a pupil (victors' flags in the hall provide at-a-glance summary of current success), to ties that bind, with a cornucopia of neckwear on offer for games, arts or brainpower-based accomplishments.

Family links have been strengthened, too, with work and well-being themed workshops for parents (who also get on-tap access to form tutors, front of house contacts for day to day issues), though attendance for those living or working some distance away can be tricky.

Proof that it's all working just fine is provided by parental endorsement and pupil approval of pastoral head – 'he's tops,' says one. Tiny numbers, usually three or four at most, stay after school for Friday detention. As to more serious Saturday version: 'we haven't had one all year,' says school.

Pupils and parents: Educationalist Chris Woodhead and Crimewatch's Nick Ross are best known Old Boys (Douglas Allen, later civil service chief Lord Croham, was debut pupil in 1927). Others include Surrey cricketers David Gibson and Arnold Long. List is currently all male – Old Girls are, presumably, still chipping away at the glass ceilings.

Pupils temper intelligence with humanity – a useful quality for tomorrow's top scientists, lawyers and medics. A trustworthy bunch, too – possessions can be left confidently in the open bag storage areas, widely used round the school instead of lockers, ditched after a pupil vote.

Sixty per cent come from ethnic minorities and approximately a quarter speak English as an additional language. 'Culturally very mixed, more so than a lot of schools, so that attracted me,' says a parent.

Entrance: In a civilising touch, current parents serve hot drinks and snacks to the 1,500 or so nervous candidates from a wide range of state and independent schools in south and west London (inevitably, there's a vast catchment area) who sit maths, English and verbal reasoning tests in mid-September. (Essential to note horribly early end of August/very early September deadline for completion of school's on-line application form). Results are out in October, giving parents of the 450 or so who have passed enough time to include school on the common application form used by all London boroughs.

Places are offered to the 120 top scorers in the spring of the following year, though there is a waiting list (automatic inclusion until 31 December of year of entry, when parents have to re-apply). Looked after children and those with statements who pass the exam take precedence, tie breaks determined by home to school distance – otherwise no geographical barriers.

For the many disappointed, appeals offer little hope (success rate in last four years is nil) though 15 further places are offered in year 9 and a minimum of 20 (in reality at least 30) in the sixth form, when girls join from a range of mainly local schools.

Exit: A few (18 in 2013) leave after GCSEs though for almost everyone else it's straight to university after A levels, with 70 per cent to Russell or 1994 group members and around eight or so off to study medicine, dentistry and veterinary science. Other popular subjects include maths (though numbers have declined over past four years), economics, history, engineering (all sorts), physics and biomedical science.

Recent dip in Oxbridge success rates seems to have been resolved and 13 boys achieved places in 2013. School has taken advice from big hitters in other top schools to ensure that only hopefuls with a realistic chance of success are put forward. Head also plans subject-specific clubs (medicine, law, architecture) run by sixth formers, with eminent Old Boys invited in to offer advice and set work.

Remarks: 'Wants the results but isn't pushy in the way another school might be,' says a parent. Cleverness, even brilliance, is there in force but never in your face and tempered with good manners and charm. No wonder pupils are attached to their school and 'boys cry more than the girls,' says a (male) sixth former when it's time to leave.

Wallington High School for Girls

Woodcote Road, Wallington, Surrey, SM6 0PH

• Pupils: 1,300 girls, all day • Ages: 11–18 • Non-denom • State

Tel: 020 8647 2380
Email: wallingtongirls@suttonlea.org
Website: www.wallingtongirls.sutton.sch.uk

Head: Since September 2012, Mrs Jane Burton BSc, 40s, previously deputy head of Nonsuch School (qv) just down the road in Cheam and one of the favoured destinations for area's bright girls. Has young son educated in Sutton and is currently going through purgatory of admissions system herself so has first hand empathy with parental anxiety levels (many can do fraught to off Richter within seconds).

Not wild on getting up close and personal with GSG reviewer without complete 'editorial control' afterwards so we had to be content with an encounter which, though delightful, was of a more distant variety – we ended up viewing her from the balcony of the school hall where, a well-manicured presence in corporate monochrome, she stepped up to the podium and, accessorised with a posse of head girls (well, two, anyway), delivered efficient speech with commendable energy (one of six appearances that afternoon), complete with matching body language – outwards-thrust arms emphasising key messages.

Mind you, you can't blame her for wanting to put a bit of blue water between her and the audience, some of the 1500 pantingly keen parents who would probably do anything (and that does, you'd imagine, mean anything) to obtain a place for their child in this thoroughly desirable establishment.

As a grammar school veteran, she runs her senior leadership team, you'd imagine, with a tight grip, though they appear to be thriving under her regime.

Littlies (year 7s) are a bit confused about what she does. They reckons she teaches (she doesn't, say older pupils) but no one has a bad word to say about her. Mind you, they don't have that many words full stop, largely down to the fact that with just a year under her belt, her presence was only just beginning to make itself felt. 'We don't really get to speak to her,' thought older pupil.

Parents likewise, particularly in younger years. 'Haven't seen her personally,' says one. Information, sparse though it is, was favourable, if largely because she appears to be employing an if it ain't broke, don't fix it approach. 'I've heard everything is quite positive,' thought a mum. 'Sometimes you see a big difference [when a head changes] but it's been a small transition.'

Making her mark felt, however. Since September 2013 sixth formers 'follow smart dress code' instead of home clothes. Second time lucky: Nonsuch girls appear to have fought off similar proposals under her watch, though appears to have fallen short of the mini me ideal she'd envisaged in initial consultation letter where 'business-like skirt[s], tailored trousers...and smart jacket[s]' were the goal.

Speech, shorn of corporate trimmings ('identity' 'mission statement' 'positive experience' tend to get fair share of the

W

word count) suggests heart is in the right place. Girls are 'proud of themselves,' school is proud of them (group hug, everyone) and it does, above all, superbly well, adding value to your child – 'sounds a bit clinical,' she apologised – as well as straight results which are, of course, superb.

Her aim is to turn out girls who will 'seize everything that life throws at them.' Vim and vigour of those we saw suggests they're up for it.

Academic matters: Expectations exactly as you'd expect and terrific results to match – almost 83 per cent of 2013 GCSE entries at A*/A, shade over (84.2) graded A*/B at A level (55 per cent A*/A). Head, however, reinforces message that it's 'not an exams factory' and there's no sense of undue pressure from girls we spoke to.

Subject choices surprisingly wide-ranging with media studies and DT four different ways at A level as well as a few GCSE rarities including photography (like Latin, offered as a twilight course) as well as business and psychology (rated by school for honing research skills).

Everyone must do separate sciences in decent, bright labs (juniors 'tend to have same teacher') and at least one language at GCSE (school specialism) and it's two for all from year 7, (choose from French, German and Spanish – school will do best to accommodate preferences though GCSE numbers roughly equal for all three).

Forms (each recruited en masse to one of seven houses) taught together in year seven so can stick together – almost literally as 'so big that for the first few weeks you just tend to follow each other round,' said year seven.

Minor criticism of maths is that with sets kicking in only at the end of year seven, can be a drag for most able first years, who have sometimes covered the ground already. One pupil, clearly at top end of ability range, felt it could be a bit 'boring if you knew the subject already.') 'At my daughter's primary school, they started doing some year seven work, so it depends if the teacher realises,' thought parent.

Current school preoccupation is need to upweight thinking skills. Manifested at GCSE in fusion of philosophy and ethics with RS (short course taken by most) and in the sixth form with philosophy of religion and ethics as one of go head A level options (school doesn't do the IB) as well as an extended essay project that encourages independent research.

Though there are masses of subject specific events, typical month including trips to Royal Observatory, Maritime Museum and War Horse for physics, history and drama students respectively, spanning the year groups and adding interest for all, teacher are real stars of the show.

Much praised by pupils brilliant at swapping round groups in years 7 and 8 – sensible 'as it means you meet new people', thought pupils, who have nothing but praise for staff, echoed by parents who praised staff emphasis on praise rather than pressure – slow boil rather than pressure cooker.

'You pick it up when you have parent evenings. Even subjects you think your daughter's not very strong in, the teachers are very encouraging,' says one.

Day to day, however, plenty of evidence of varied teaching styles that put a premium on initiative. Most recent inspection report was critical of over use of chalk and talk – now pared back to a minimum and group work something of a feature – 'we get 20 minutes to collaborate,' said year 7 pupil and choice offered wherever practical – menu of experiments adds interest to science.

'Couldn't be nicer,' thought one older pupil, though know when to get tough(ish). Lunch swipe card also acts as library ticket – food for the soul and stomach in one magnetic stripe –and everyone is instructed to have live book and not be scared to use it when reading is called for, which it often is – though all the girls we spoke to were enthusiastic readers, school diligent about keeping the light burning. If book is missing 'you'll be in

trouble,' said teacher, with ferocious smile – in practice, means 'you get moaned at,' said pupil.

Just about every core academic subject has own club, some involving older girls. Space also freed up wherever possible to assist with private study. Library open all hours (or a fair few of them) while sixth form have own small but nicely kitted out conference room which can be booked out for meetings, quiet work.

No doubt where interests lie, however, with massive 140 currently taking A level maths and sciences fab, too – 100 each for biology and chemistry and respectable 80 for physics. Head dismissive of any suggestions elsewhere that girls can't and won't do sciences as here they can and will – in their droves.

Their popularity, influenced by what can be 'lots' of parental pressure, thought teacher, inevitably puts many other departments in the shade, though 'we're winning' says English teacher, who has seen rising AS numbers for Eng lit (currently just over 50 in year 12) as well as Eng lang and combined.

It's helped, she thinks, by growing desire by would be employers to see evidence of broader spread of interests. Slightly disappointed by attrition rate into year 13, though in part, she reckoned, down to misapprehension that A level is a breeze – GCSE with a few more complicated bits – when 'it isn't.'

One parent felt that, in common with other local grammars, 'you can tell from the mixture of girls that with some, their English may not be very strong,' which she thought might affect the popularity of the subject.

That said, all-round enthusiasm is inescapable. What are school's biggest things? 'Everything here is a big thing,' said year 8 pupil with just a hint of reproof.

Games, options, the arts: Lots love sport, some don't and academic thrust can divert some who might otherwise be doing great things on the pitch, thought girls. While school scoops gold Artsmark award amongst others, sports equivalent is the conspicuous absentee on website roll of honour, with PE just about sole area not raved about by inspectors. Enjoyed by pupils, however. 'They have fun and that's part of it all,' thought mum.

Its standing on the website (lumped together with art and design, drama and music under 'expressive arts' with no accompanying blurb pretty much says it all, as does minimal timetable presence – two sports/PE lessons a week, dance and gym dominating in winter, great outdoors (including cricket, rounders and tennis) to the fore at other times.

However, produces small and hardy bunch who go on to take PE for A level (currently half a dozen) and winners, both team and individual, including two budding sixth form football stars, recently awarded vast sports scholarships by US universities. Add favourable feedback and rapidly improving facilities and will to ensure higher profile – and results – seems to be there.

Vast field, all weather pitches (no Astroturf as yet, though four new tennis and netball courts will be added to existing two by early 2014) joined last year by magnificent sports hall, a yodeller's paradise, mirrored dance studio on top just as nice and no gizmo spared, including retractable goals, dividing net allowing two classes to have simultaneous lessons.

Building, shaped like flat bottomed sausage roll with rounded corrugated metal top, so bizarre-looking that to start with, 'everyone was against it,' says sixth former. Now assorted delights are clear, 'we love it'. 'Amazing,' agreed parent. It's currently dwarfed by large crane as new mirror image teaching block extension, similar in format and planned for completion in 2014, takes shape.

Anything in danger of despoiling pristine floor such as trampolining is relegated to old gym which also incorporates very compact fitness suite, housed in section of main building beyond school hall and now largely disused or converted section (antediluvian-looking changing rooms now used for storage).

Art and drama very strong, quality excellent, visible manifestation of school's desire to encourage pupils 'to be who

W

you are.' All, from year 7 girls to sixth form, praised teachers' desire not to impose but to guide, with thorough briefing and lots of encouragement to personalise tasks en route to completion.

Thus masses of faces in art room (less scary that amazing but rather terrifying giant masks in school hall) are hugely different in style and design. (We also loved pictures of lamas bearing staff names and chosen to 'reflect personality'. One gorgeously cuddly example (creature, not teacher) with fetching crop of fleece was felt to be particularly accurate representation of staff member's 'wacky hair').

Painstaking creativity also a feature of relatively recent tech block, 'best in the country' thought pupil and, according to recent school survey, achieves some of highest pupil and parent happiness ratings around. Spreads the joy with lots of outreach to local primaries, separate building worth clocking for extraordinary through corridor, narrow but incredibly high, like passage way for emaciated, super tall giraffes.

Teachers diligent in 'explaining techniques' most projects starting with short list of designs and questionnaires designed to canvass friends' views ('You can ignore them but you have to explain why.') Projects included one of the most sensible we've ever seen – year sevens making covers for school planners – practical, fun and gorgeous (owners' had gone to town on personalisation – initials as well as frills and furbelows a real feature).

Those who stay the course end up with fab A level creations including terrific lamp complete with fronds of LEDs and mood lighting. 'Took three months to make.'

Lovely music – particularly strong on vocals, (recent finalist on TV 'The Voice' is former school pupil) with five choirs Glee and 60-strong Gospel choir both audition only (latter mostly seniors; year 7 girls delighted that one of their number had just won place), junior and senior versions open to all. Joint orchestra with Wilson's School down the road a happy union of brass and percussion (mainly boys) with strings (mostly girls). Enthusiastic teaching team feel GCSE numbers (currently around 17) could be higher. Though accept the necessity, slightly miffed that small number of A level students are currently having lessons at Wilson's and are fighting good fight to boost numbers so pupils can be brought back into the fold.

Background and atmosphere: Founded 125 year ago. About six minutes by bus from Wallington station, it's a fairly easy trek compared with boys' equivalents (detailed knowledge of public transport essential for first timers, emergency rations desirable) and presents unthreatening face to the world, brickwork, if not mellow, certainly not likely to frighten the horses (not that you'd see that many on these crowded streets).

Has embraced cultural diversity (and won an award for it, too) with gusto, recent events ranging from Japanese drumming to fab sounding international evening where girls and families ate, drank and danced way round the world, each table in school hall themed to a different country.

Lots of slightly faded warren of corridors, brightened wherever possible with rows of pictures, definitely showing its age, space at even more of a premium with additional year seven form (there are now seven feeding through). Generous sized lockers, dotted round the place, a well-used necessity. 'I could get winter coat, all books and full PE kit in mine,' reckoned pupil. New teaching block also on the way. In the meantime, subjects are ranged together wherever possible, occasionally dual use (modern languages lesson might take over English room 'though never a problem as teachers always bring all the resources with them,' says pupil).

Food was 'pretty good' except for the cheese, seemingly added to rather more dishes than you'd like. 'Texture a bit of a problem,' thought pupil. However, does offer much enjoyed freedom for dejeuner sur l'herbe, on outside tables and even in classrooms ('though not hot food,' thought year 7 pupils, as 'that would be a health and safety issue.'

Pastoral care and discipline: School excels here with common sense approach that starts with sensible line drawing with earlier start and finish (8.25am to 2.50pm) and prompt close on Friday afternoons, packed programme of after school clubs (sports, including badminton, football and hockey the most popular) mainly Mondays to Thursdays only, ensuring that everyone (including hard-pressed teachers) can start weekends promptly and with clean conscience, felt school.

In addition to form tutor and head of year, those with problems have access to what one girl described as 'superb' counsellor, accessible at all hours and 'like a second mum', as well as caring staff who have manifest understanding of pressures that go with life in top achieving school and go out of their way to deal with them.

Sports staff on hand for one pupil who 'went to them when feeling low just just to spend time there and kick a ball around.' A huge help, she reckoned. Younger girls seemed largely content with system and own company – they tend not to approach older girls who don't seem to have troubleshooting role and in any case could be 'hard to find' thought one.

As to bullying – incidents rare 'one a year, if that,' thought year seven pupil, while older girls, marvel at school's success in avoiding issues that friends and family elsewhere report as being routine. 'Younger sister has all sorts of problems at her school,' says sixth former. 'Here, even though it's such a big year group, there's not even one.'

School, also praised for approach to those at the bottom of the academic pecking order. 'teachers' policy is, sensibly, to compare the potentially down-hearted with the rest of the country. 'Don't remind us of our grades. We might be at the bottom here but for a lot of schools, that would be right at the very top,' said sixth former.

Others praised teachers' way of dealing with those struggling with the pace. 'Will go on to the next pupil but then come back to you and often see you in private to sort things out,' reckoned year eight pupil.

Though rule bending won't be allowed (range of sanctions in place, from confiscation of offending items to letters of apology through to exclusion), little more, though pupils, is usually needed than quiet chat. Behaviour policy states that 'staff are expected to use praise and appreciation many more times than they use sanctions.' Feedback suggest it's highly effective.

Pupils and parents: A super bunch – parents as well as pupils. No nonsense, lacking affectation, warm and, reckoned would-be mum 'not too up themselves.' Really appreciate school's many virtues – head girls who speak of seeking office 'because we want to give [something] back' coming across as genuine rather than CV glory chasers.

'I've seen a lot of friends and they're all very different. Some are laid back, some studious, some sporty. I think a mixture of girls seem to be able to fit in really well,' reckoned mum.

Arrogance definitely absent from this picture, good manners and charm still in evidence even under trying circumstances. On crowded open day when had been on duty for over four hours, enthusiastic escorts (guided by presumably exhausted staff, pleasant to the end) were tireless in efforts to ensure nobody missed a thing, even after end of official visiting time.

Entrance: Popularity not hard to fathom given the queues to hear the head's talk on open day. Not so much standing as queuing room only, despite promise that on-line version of talk would be posted the next day. Pill sweetened by red-robed gospel choir blasting the hordes with high quality, high energy numbers including (appropriately) 'Ain't no mountain high enough.'

Would that it were true. Even the best grappling irons in the business may not be enough to haul you up these particular slopes. Following early September deadline for applications, anything north of 1300 hopefuls sit mid-month VR and maths papers. The 700 or so who pass will hear in sufficient time to include school on CAF (common application form), though with only 210 year seven places to fill, majority will go away empty handed when formal offers are made in March.

Head, however, keen to inject a little hope into the process, points out that with sizeable numbers also doing the grammar school rounds (Nonsuch, Tiffin Girls and Bromley bunch) means that 'you could argue it's more like 1300 for a total of 400 [year 7] places,' says head. Lots of locals, open day blazer brands representing seemingly every primary and prep in the area, extending out to Croydon and Tooting. Distant reaches of London and Surrey not much represented – doesn't appear to have huge geographic catchment of, say Tiffin Girls' (though if results go up much further, it probably will).

Cleverness though essential, doesn't have to be extreme is head's message (though in many cases you'd imagine it is). 'Overwhelmingly, come with at least a level 5 in SATs and if likely to achieve this in year six, would be of similar ability to pupils at the school,' she says.

Where other heads have firmly set faces against tutors (Canute-like, you'd think, given overwhelming parental mood – pro or at least resigned to the inevitable) Mrs Burton is rather more pragmatic about the realities. Tests are designed 'to be accessible to all, whether tutored or not,' with exam content 'based on ground covered to end of year 5.' However, if content, particularly when it comes to VR, hasn't been covered, brief trip to WH Smiths or similar for a bit of mugging up can provide useful familiarisation.

Exit: Destinations ooze academic credibility though there's a decently mixed bag: one girl we talked to was part of a select group contemplating career in sport. Picky might hope for a few more to Oxbridge (single figures for last two years) but around a third make Russell Group, further 10 – 15 go to medical school each year with similar numbers off to art college. Around a fifth take a gap year.

Remarks: Thoroughly genuine. Schools speaks of warm, friendly and purposeful atmosphere. Yada, yada, we thought, another bland statement. Yet from the minute you meet teachers and staff, coping with crowds and doing with smiles what Jesus did with loaves and fishes, you have impression of a school that's genuinely living the mission statement. Though equally desirable, not all grammars are the same. We loved this one.

Walthamstow Hall

Linked school: Walthamstow Hall Junior

Hollybush Lane, Sevenoaks, Kent, TN13 3UL

• Pupils: 350 girls, all day • Ages: 11–18 • C of E • Fees: £16,410 pa
• Independent

Tel: 01732 451334
Email: registar@walthamstowhall.kent.sch.uk
Website: www.walthamstow-hall.co.uk

Headmistress: Since 2002, Mrs Jill Milner MA, PGCE (early fifties), educated at Maidstone Grammar School for Girls and St Anne's College, Oxford where she read English and took her PGCE. She took her finals at 20 and went straight into teaching, starting her career at St Helen's, Northwood where she taught English and drama. After a career break when her children were young she joined Headington School where she taught English and drama and was head of sixth form; moved on to Tonbridge Girls' Grammar as head of English and sixth form and acting deputy head in charge of curriculum development

and timetabling. A passionate believer in girls' education and the 'transformational and life changing potential of education'. She is an ISI inspector and serves on the GSA Membership Committee and is a governor at Holmewood House and The Schools at Somerhill. Married to Rupert, a retired teacher and businessman, whom she met at Oxford, they have two adult children and a daughter at the school. Her twin passions are reading and walking. Calm and relaxed but with a needle sharp intelligence. Easy and comfortable relationship with the girls who see her as approachable and her door is genuinely always open. Says she, 'feels truly privileged to have this job', and is passionate about the school and justifiably proud of the girls. Knows girls well and considers the finalising of the UCAS reference as one of the highlights of the job. Sees the school as her life's work and says that she could not imagine another school she would care more about.

Academic matters: At GCSE in 2013, 81 per cent of entries graded A*/A with particularly strong results in sciences, maths, history and English. Eighty-nine per cent A*-B or higher at A level and Pre-U (74 per cent A*/A) in 2013. Girls are helped to develop 'smart' study habits so they can take part in all aspects of school life – music, sport, drama, art etc and have an astonishing capacity for juggling time and taking things on. Curriculum and timetable very much set up for the girls and there is much discussion about teaching in the classroom and how to do it better. Girls take 17 subjects in first year including, Latin, French and design technology. Creative textiles and a second foreign language added in second year. Most do RE GCSE early at end of year 10 with the majority achieving an A*. IGCSE in about 80 per cent of subjects and Pre-U in history, English, maths. Particularly strong history department received Good Schools Guide Award for history teaching in the sixth form. Around 15 per cent of girls also take the GPR (Global Perspectives and Research project) Pre-U each year. Sciences taught separately from the beginning – top flight science teaching in modern labs part-funded by a grant from the Wolfson Foundation. Class sizes about 16 and not above 20 and much smaller in sixth form. Plenty of debate, discussion and interaction from early on – work in a team with teachers and lots of hands-on practical stuff. A 'stimulating, safe and challenging environment with high expectations for all,' according to one parent.

Most staff have been appointed within the last ten years and there is a good range of ages and an increasing number of male teachers. A few staff flats on site for new young teachers. Three part-time teachers offer SEN support where required mainly for mild dyslexics and dyspraxics. Extra help in maths and English offered in small groups to year 7.

In most cases girls can do the combination of subjects they want and 'twilight' GCSEs offered as extra subjects after school from 4.30-6pm for subjects that won't fit into the curriculum. Lots of help with UCAS forms from tutors and head of sixth form and sixth formers are taught in small seminar type groups similar to university. Extra clinics to help children with homework and make sure everyone is doing as well as they can. All year 7 have to do cooking as part of PSHE and it is offered as an optional subject in upper sixth. Well-stocked and well-used library with panoramic views.

Games, options, the arts: 'Girls get involved in everything,' said one happy parent. Inter-house music and drama festivals and inter-house sport – all girls take part. All girls in years 7 to 9 do music, drama and art and about half take Trinity Guildhall drama classes. Lots of plays every year and most girls involved in drama in some way, either on stage, backstage or with the music and lighting. Plenty of space for performances in The Ship Theatre and main hall as well as the new drama studio – drama is offered as an A level. According to one mother, 'Everyone is given a chance to get involved in a smaller and less pressured environment than many other local schools.'

W

Thriving art department, wonderful art and textiles rooms – both fine art and textiles can be taken at GCSE and A level. Music can be studied up to A level and is a big part of school life under inspirational new director of music. School has recently bought a harp.

Sport popular, many sixth formers continue with team games and there are a number of county netball, lacrosse and hockey players; the curling team are Kent champions. Girls usually find something they enjoy – gymnastics, fencing and judo are options for those who do not like team games and school has won the Judo National Congress two years running. Pilates, aquarobics and the fitness gym popular with the older girls. PE is offered as an A level.

Background and atmosphere: Affectionately and universally known as Wally Hall, it is one of the oldest girls' schools in the country. Founded in 1838 in Walthamstow as a school and home for the daughters of missionaries, it moved to its present Arts and Crafts building in Sevenoaks in 1882 – it was 'built on prayer with money raised from church collections', became the girls' grammar school under the direct grant system and is now a fully independent selective girls' school. The Junior school moved to its own building a couple of miles away in 1992 which allowed for the creation of a separate sixth form centre – the Emmeline Blackburn House, known as EBH. Girls have a self contained unit for most of their lessons and private study as well as two common rooms, a kitchen and an ICT room. Much building and refurbishment, mainly from fee income, in the last ten years, most recently Ship Theatre refurbished and new senior school sports hall under construction. The new entrance atrium (opened in 2012) has provided a modern, light and airy space and has linked the school together. Many parents attracted by the fact that this is a small school although as one observed, 'Girls do well here and get involved in everything, although a very ambitious girl might need a bigger environment'.

Pastoral care and discipline: School organised into three pastoral teams: sixth form, middle school (years 9-11) and lower school (years 7-8). There are six houses and this system means different year groups get to know each other. Competition between houses can get quite fierce (in the nicest possible way) eg sports competitions, inter-house performing arts festival, and each house chooses a charity to fund raise for. Members of the sixth form run the house events and organise rehearsals, costumes etc and all are expected to be leaders of some sort. Pastoral heads and form tutors provide guidance and mentor personal and academic wellbeing – girls review their own progress and set themselves targets and there is plenty of praise and recognition. There is good careers guidance and lots of time and care taken with UCAS forms and the school organises a programme of talks about university and beyond and also helps with work experience placements. Firm policies on bullying. Girls' views sought on whole school matters including food (which is extremely good) through school council and pupil/staff relations seem to be pretty good – they even invite their teachers to the leavers' ball. No Saturday school but girls often come in for matches, rehearsals, activities and Duke of Edinburgh. Assemblies three times a week not just a prayer and a hymn and everyone expected to participate in religious education and regular collective worship (parents of other faiths may withdraw their children from these).

Pupils and parents: Broad mix of parents from high flying City types, local business people, medics, members of the clergy and youth workers. Mainly local English girls. About 50 per cent of mothers work. When the school was set up it was serious about equipping girls to follow in their parents' footsteps and become missionaries, they needed to be adventurous, resourceful and brave and much of this spirit lives on in the present school. The school's emblem is a ship sailing on the high seas and at the end of their time at Wally Hall the girls take part in a special 'setting sail service' when they hand over their prefects badges to the year below. Girls tend to keep in touch and many old girls send their daughters here. 'Girls expect to do well and are not afraid to put themselves forward', they tend to be grounded with a strong sense of purpose and of community and want to make a difference. Almost all girls in sixth form take part in voluntary service – nothing compulsory – many help with reading in local primary schools, working in charity shops and riding for the disabled and help out at the local old people's home (which was founded and is run by old girls). Girls not frightened to succeed in front of each other. The school works closely with parents and there is an active group that organises social events and raise funds for bursaries and 'frills'. Some indomitable campaigners amongst the old girls who are often leaders in their field. Alumni include Beverley Hunt, Professor of Thrombosis and Haemostasis at King's College, London and founder of the charity Life Blood, playwright and triathlete; Janine Gibson, editor of Guardian online; actress Victoria Boreham and Rowan Pelling, newspaper columnist and broadcaster.

Entrance: At 11+, 13+ and 16+. Not super selective. Interview with headmistress and written papers in maths and English in the autumn term before entry. Girls who do particularly well are then invited to sit for a scholarship in January. Entry into sixth form via interview, school report and a minimum of seven GCSES at A*-C with A*-Bs in the subjects they wish to study. About 40 per cent come up from the junior school but have to pass the same test as everyone else. Otherwise from a range of state primaries and local prep schools, eg The Granville, Derwent Lodge, Hilden Grange. About ten girls join each year for the sixth form from other local girls' independent schools and grammars, often because of the wide combination of subjects available. Occasionally joiners into year 10 if things have not worked out at another school.

Exit: About five per cent leave after GCSE, some to co-ed boarding schools and some to the state sector. Only about ten per cent take a gap year, most straight to university to study subjects including medicine, maths, modern foreign languages and various sciences. Exeter, Nottingham, Loughborough, Manchester, Durham and York have been the most popular in recent years. Four to Oxbridge in 2013.

Money matters: About 16 per cent of girls on some sort of bursary. Various financial awards from the Founders Bursary which can cover nearly 100 per cent of fees plus scholarships in drama, music, art, and sport worth up to 50 per cent of fees. Help also available for current parents in financial straits. Sibling discount offered.

Remarks: Thriving girls' day school in leafy Sevenoaks. Produces quietly confident young women with a 'can do' attitude and an adventurous spirit. The strong academic results are a 'happy by-product' of all this.

Warwick School

Linked schools: King's High School; Warwick Junior School; Warwick Preparatory School

Myton Road, Warwick, CV34 6PP

- Pupils: Pupils 1220 boys, mostly day. Around 60 boarders.
- Ages: 11-18 • C of E • Fees: Day £8,505–£10,935 pa
- Independent

Tel: 01926 776400
Email: enquiries@warwickschool.org
Website: www.warwickschool.org

Head Master: Since September 2013, Mr Augustus (Gus) Lock, MA Oxon (late thirties). Educated at Haberdashers' Aske's School, Elstree, he read ancient and modern history at Oxford. First teaching post was at The Manchester Grammar School, thence to Merchant Taylors' School in Northwood where he became head of Middle School and met and married Alison (a French and Italian teacher). Mr Lock then moved to Warwick School, where he served as deputy head master under Mr Ed Halse until the latter's retirement. Gus and Alison have three young children, two of whom attend Warwick Prep School.

Academic matters: It is clear that academic work is a top priority and taken seriously by most of the boys. The pace is vigorous and demanding – for pupils and staff alike – and the overall results are impressive. When we asked if there was any truth in the rumour that Warwick was an exam factory, one boy replied, 'well, if it is, I haven't noticed it. There is lots of work but you expect that. You just get on with it.' One ex-teacher at Warwick confirmed that the pace was demanding. That word 'pace' crops up a lot – Warwick is a very busy school with lots to offer. It may be a day school but, in the words of another boy, 'it never seems to close. With all the extracurricular activities on offer, a twelve hour day starting at 7.30 am is not that unusual.' League table junkies can pore over the statistics, salivating at the various permutations but here's a quick fix: of the 26 subjects on offer for A level, maths, economics, physics, chemistry, biology and politics account for 242 entries; English, history, French and Spanish, 50. Just an observation but it does reveal the breadth of subjects on offer and the strengths of scientific subjects in the sixth form. How well they do overall is confirmed by the consistently high percentage of A* to B at A level (84 per cent in 2013). GCSE results from 28 subjects are impressive too. A*-B grades have not dropped below 91 per cent in the last seven years and in 2013 75 per cent of papers were graded A*/A. This is clearly not a school where boys spend time during their first few years 'settling down and making friends' before starting to work seriously.

The facilities for teaching and learning are impressive. Foremost is the new science building of which the school is justifiably proud. Like most of the new buildings at Warwick it is superbly designed, both aesthetically and functionally. From the moment you enter the large bright foyer, decorated with a fascinating creation stretching up through two floors like a curling spine, you are in a genuinely stimulating building. In this instance it is all about experiment, discovery and excitement. Each of the three floors is allocated to a science with spacious laboratories designed in consultation with the teachers themselves. All the latest gizmos and terrific teaching to go with. One huge laboratory is used for extended projects where budding Nobel laureates are joined by the no less budding girls from King's High and students from other local schools. Certainly no sign of science declining in popularity here – many boys go on to university to read science based subjects. How some of them must pine for the excellence of the facilities at Warwick. But it's not just the scientists who are well served; we hear many reports of excellent teaching in other subjects too. The delightfully designed lecture theatre hosts talks embracing all disciplines from within and beyond the curriculum.

If the heartbeat of real education is a library, Warwick is very healthy. The library is housed in The Masefield Centre, named after an old boy charmingly described to us by a current pupil as 'some kind of a poet, I believe.' A superb set-up with over 20,000 books it is an invaluable centre for reference resources and information files as well as CDs, DVDs and now e-books. The school even has e-readers to lend out. The wonderfully enthusiastic librarian told us that the issue of books had recently risen by 30 per cent and inviting pamphlets, one with an encouraging foreword from the Headmaster, explain and exhort. Those pupils we spoke to genuinely appreciated the facility.

Everyone entering the school is screened for dyslexia and those with learning difficulties receive help from the 'very good' learning support team. Currently about 27 pupils receive such help.

Games, options, the arts: This is a boys' school so naturally sport plays an important part. However this is not a hearty school where prizes and recognition are given only to games players. Colours are awarded for music and drama, for instance, and one boy we spoke to, a confessed non sportsman, said he didn't feel an outcast in any way. 'There are plenty of opportunities for taking exercise. In fact I'm almost spoilt for choice.' Nevertheless the ethos that permeates the school – 'if you're going to do something, do it to the best of your ability' – is much in evidence on the games field. In the winter term, for example, over 20 rugby teams could be turning out on a Saturday afternoon. The 1st XV has a very strong fixture list and is renowned for its prowess, but the great thing is that everyone who wants to has a good chance of playing in a team. However, 'it's not all about rugby,' as somebody once said. In addition there is hockey, cricket, swimming, tennis, cross country, athletics, rowing, canoeing, clay pigeon shooting: you name it. No wonder the boy who didn't like rugby didn't feel left out. Facilities are excellent with a top rate swimming pool (they have been national schools water polo champions more than once), squash courts, tennis courts, a superb sports hall, including an indoor hockey pitch, and games fields that seem to stretch on for ever. A recent cricket tour to Sri Lanka, golf to Spain and rugby to Ireland are just some of the opportunities to play abroad; boys who cannot afford to go are supported financially.

Music is excellent (ask for a copy of their DVD) and generally regarded as cool. Harmony maintained by a charismatic director with a wonderful team of teachers, most of whom are concert players themselves. In a recent and highly successful initiative, new boys were lent an instrument of their choice and given free tuition for a year; the enthusiastic take-up means the music department now has 720 lessons a week to organise. Five orchestras, three wind bands, three jazz bands, rock groups, quartets and much more. Huge programme of concerts and the chapel choir sings every Sunday morning during term; local parents, old boys, friends of the school and boarders attend. The musicians perform all over Europe (as with sports tours, financial support given if necessary) and in 2011 three bands were awarded platinum and two gold at the National Concert Band Finals. In 2013 The Little Big Band were awarded a Platinum Award for the third consecutive year and as a result were presented with a consistent achievement certificate.

Proximity to Stratford may account for the school's high achievements in drama. The superb Bridge House Theatre, overseen by a full-time theatre manager, is kitted out to professional standards with proper lighting and sound equipment, adjustable stage and seating arrangements for 300

W

people and musicians; it is used by community theatre groups as well as for school productions. A number of boys have taken small parts at the RSC, there are even two pupils currently in The Archers, and a few go on to take theatre studies at A level. One ecstatic mother told us of the huge encouragement given to her young son when he was given a demanding role. 'It boosted his confidence right across the board,' she said. Warwick productions have won awards at the National Student Drama Festival, the only school to have done so. There are large scale drama productions every term as well as pupil led plays, many shared with girls from King's High.

Art and DT very good. All pupils have a double period of art and design a week for their first three years and can then go on to GCSE and beyond.

Astonishing range of clubs and societies to try – cryptography, car mechanics, robotics (UK champions every year from 2009 to 2012). Boys can also sign up for D of E, Young Enterprise and CCF. Wonderful opportunities enthusiastically seized. Exam factory forsooth!

Background and atmosphere: The gates to the main entrance hint at the tradition of the school. In addition to the Tudor Rose and the school's coat of arms depicting, significantly, the Warwickshire bear without chains, you can read the dates 914,1545 and 1958. These refer to the traditional date for the founding of the school by Edward the Confessor, its reinstatement by Henry VIII and the visit of the Queen Mother when the school was once more in the ascendant after a period in the doldrums. From a succession of sites in the town the school moved out to its present position beside the Avon in 1879. The neo Tudor building with lovely oriel windows is typical of nineteenth century public school architecture, though to some, apparently, the colour of the brick is reminiscent of a hospital. A fascinating archive room with old photographs of school groups and haunting pictures of teams from 1914, testifies to the pride the school takes in its past. After all, isn't this one of the oldest boys' schools in the country, nay, the world? It is rumoured that a book is to be published in time to coincide with the school's millennium celebrations which will prove beyond doubt that this is the case.

The current site is a mixture of old and new buildings, increasingly dominated by the new, close but not jostling. Always an interesting insight into a school is to ask for directions and note the response; those boys we asked were uniformly helpful and charming, courtesy and good manners are the norm here. One new boy told us not to worry, 'Just ask,' he said, 'you can't go far wrong.' He spoke with feeling of the help he had received on arrival. All schools trumpet 'the excellent relationships between pupils and staff'; unobtrusively and naturally, this school demonstrates it. We witnessed a number of conversations between staff and boys and were struck by the obvious mutual respect and friendliness between them.

The school's aims may be serious and pursued with determination but there is an underlying sense of well-being and community which extends to the town; the civilised behaviour of the boys was acknowledged by the residents to whom we spoke. Sixth formers are allowed, with permission, to have lunch in town; so are senior girls from King's High. 'What we almost take for granted,' said one elderly resident, 'is that there is no arrogance about them. No swaggering and showing off. Not like those public school kids.' An interesting observation. Much is done for charity, an excellent way of combining community spirit and awareness of those less fortunate. Along with girls from King's High, teams swam the channel in 2009 and again in 2013. According to the records the boys' team was the 50th ever two-way swim; the 13th ever successful swim by any UK team and the first by a boys' school team.

Impressive chapel with college seating where services take place most days of the week. Upstairs in the old building is a little corner of Asia where the 50 plus Chinese boys in the sixth form live with the housemaster and his wife, a resident tutor and a matron. There are plans to expand this boarding accommodation in order to take more Chinese students. This is not a cynical attempt to swell numbers; Warwick has been taking Chinese students for many years now and those we chatted to seemed very happy and proud to be there.

Pastoral care and discipline: Typical of the caring efficiency of the school is the trouble it takes to welcome new boys and blend them in. There are unobtrusive but clearly delineated policies to ensure 'there is always have someone to pick us up' and the welcome package, written by young pupils, is helpful, informative and encouraging. The effortlessly friendly atmosphere that pervades is, perhaps, because boys know where they stand (a phrase oft repeated when we asked). Prefects, selected by peers and staff, regard it as one of their prime functions to ensure boys are happily integrated and that consideration for others is maintained. Rules and guidelines are clear and thorough, even down to expectations of behaviour in the classroom; uniforms are smartly worn, though not like guardsmen. One parent talking about a boy who had been expelled – a rare event by all accounts – spoke of the trouble the school had gone to ensure the boy was well established in his next school. 'They really do care about the individual but however friendly, they are strict about implementing the rules.' 'We know what is required of us. Mostly it's common sense,' a senior boy told us. 'Firm but fair.' No one – boys or staff – claimed that bullying could never happen here but parents we spoke to said it was quickly and sensitively dealt with. 'Staff are very approachable and understandable,' more than one boy told us.

Pupils and parents: Warwick has a large catchment area, a result not only of its excellent transport links but also the determination of parents and boys to make the effort. By bus, by train, by car, they come; from as far afield as Oxfordshire and Northamptonshire. Just under half the year's intake comes from the Junior School and others from local primary schools nearby prep schools. This is not a toff school, parents come from a broad cross-section of society, mostly professional middle classes, and thanks to the availability of bursaries many who might otherwise not be able to afford it do send their boys. The Head and governors plan to raise funds and offer more.

Eclectic is the word that springs to mind when considering notable old boys. Currently there are two MPs, Iain Pears the novelist; Marc Elliott of East Enders; Christian Horner, Red Bull motor racing; Michael Billington, theatre critic; an Italian rugby international, an Australian rugby international and, from the ranks of the departed, the poet John Masefield. More evidence of breadth.

Entrance: The school is selective: it is full with a long waiting list. The Head is anxious to avoid raising the bar because of that but inevitably competition is strong. It's not just the strongest academics who are awarded places, lively, quirky boys who can keep pace and bring with them especial talents will be given consideration. Entry points are 7, 11 and 13. Details of the examinations are on the website and follow the usual pattern. For entry to sixth form at least five B grades with A grades needed in some subjects to be studied at AS level.

Exit: Most boys stay on to do their A levels and nearly all go on to university. As well as purely academic subjects eg maths, classics, English, history, PPE, recent leavers have gone on to read marine vertebrate zoology, management with entrepreneurship, forensic science and architecture. On average 10-12 Oxbridge a year.

Money matters: The school is fortunate in benefiting from a number of ancient charities, some specifically aimed at boys living in the town of Warwick. Scholarships are offered in music and academics but not for sport. About a quarter of boys in the school are assisted financially.

Remarks: This is a winning school and achieves success right across the board. 'I don't know how we do it,' a boy told us in genuine amazement, 'there must be some reason for it.' There are plenty of reasons why this is such an excellent school although, like all good schools, it won't suit everyone. But for those seeking a day school that offers more excellent facilities and opportunities than many boarding schools; for those who are possessed of energy, stamina and self-discipline; above all, for those who can match the pace and plunge in, this might very well be the school. Not a school for drifting in, a school for striking out through the waves. Even across the Channel.

Watford Grammar School for Boys

Rickmansworth Road, Watford, Hertfordshire, WD18 7JF

• Pupils: 1,250 boys • Ages: 11–18 • Non-denom • State

Tel: 01923 208900
Email: brownc@watfordboys.herts.sch.uk
Website: www.watfordboys.org

Head: Since 2000, Mr Martin Post MA FRSA (early fifties). Former head prefect at WBGS in 1976. Started his career at King's, Rochester, moved to Mill Hill County High and then Richard Hale School in Hertford before joining WBGS as deputy head in 1995. Read English and related literature at the University of York. Teaches some English and PSHE. Married, with one son who, he hopes, will join the school when he is 11. Popular with parents – 'he has a strong presence. We think very well of him' – and Ofsted – '...outstanding leadership and management...' He says, 'I've got the best job in education'.

Academic matters: An unashamedly academic curriculum. Everyone tries three languages, and takes at least one to GCSE. Latin and classical civilisation are important departments. Separate sciences at IGCSE and many continue to A level. In 2013, 88 per cent of A level entries were graded A*-B; at GCSE it was 74 per cent A*/A. 'Outstanding' maths department, huge numbers take it at A level and most get A grades.

The only 'studies' on offer are religious and sports – the latter popular at A level as well as GCSE. The intake is undoubtedly skewed in favour of the top of the ability range, but since nearly everyone gets at least five good GCSEs, those who are less academic are evidently lifted by the same rising tide. 'There is plenty of mixed-ability teaching at KS3, so low-ability pupils are not ghettoized. They have their aspirations raised and it can be very liberating.' The school works with other providers where necessary – one boy learns basic skills at WBGS and construction elsewhere. 'You don't succeed with a broad range of students unless you are prepared to be flexible. We're very proud of the fact that boys with autism, dyslexia or dyspraxia succeed very well here. But they must want to work and to have their aspirations raised. With boys for whom this is not the appropriate school, we give them all the support and use our best influence to find the best place for them.'

Games, options, the arts: 'This is not an exam factory. It's about music and drama, sport and debating too.' Sports high profile here, particularly rugby, cricket and hockey. 'We're the best state school in the country for hockey. They can pick it up at 11 and take it to international level.' Football is not on the curriculum

– although, said our guide, 'it can be difficult to get from one end of the playground to the other because of footballs flying about.' More individual sports like cross-country, athletics and sailing also popular, and the school houses a table tennis academy.

Nineteen places a year are awarded for musical aptitude and there are lots of music groups and ensembles, including a joint orchestra with the girls' school. The stunning music centre has a 200 seat concert hall as well as many practice rooms, a recording studio and a music technology suite. Very few take art GCSE or A level, 'though it's interesting how many keep doing art even though they're not working for an exam.' Food, a new addition, 'has taken off hugely', and there is a sixth form survival cookery club.

Plenty of clubs – from chess to debating – and trips away: sports tours, World Challenge, language exchanges, field trips, creative writing courses. Lots of work with charities eg Mencap.

Background and atmosphere: Has its origins in the Watford Free School, founded in 1704 by Mrs Elizabeth Fuller, which split into separate boys' and girls' schools in 1884; these were renamed the boys' and girls' grammar schools in 1903. Has the feel of a '50s grammar school – and, indeed, The History Boys was filmed here and at the girls' grammar. Polished wood, cream panelling, stone stairs, honours boards, oil paintings of previous heads. The long neo-Georgian main block and adjacent Master's House are grade two listed buildings. The add-ons of various architectural pedigrees culminate in the award-winning Clarendon Muse music building on the front lawn, splendidly clad in blue/green glass, which is also used by the Watford Music Centre.

Pastoral care and discipline: Has a critical mass of pupils who want to work hard. 'It becomes a virtuous circle – our boys tend to want to succeed, so exceptions become isolated.' Boys say: 'They're strict when they need to be strict, but they try to make it as fun as possible.' One who had moved from an independent school was happy to find it freer and more relaxed than his previous school. There are around 10-15 short-term exclusions a year, but few of these become permanent. 'This is a very ordered environment. They take responsibility for themselves, and we can trust them to do so.'

Pupils and parents: Wide social and cultural mix; about a quarter have English as a second language. Those with specialist places come from up to five miles away, though the third or so who get in on distance usually live within about a kilometre. OBs include actor and comedian Terry Scott; publisher and chairman of West Ham United David Sullivan; England rugby international Josh Lewsey; poet Michael Rosen.

Entrance: Don't bother to apply for one of the 190 places unless you live in the right WD or HA postcode. Forty-five academic and 19 music places, 60 per cent allocated to those who live in the nearest Watford postcodes ('Watford Area') and 40 per cent to those in the 'rest of Admission Area'. Then 19 places to those who live nearest and haven't got a specialist place, then priority to siblings, including those with a sister at Watford Girls. After siblings, the remainder of the places are allocated by distance – usually less than a kilometre. NB Academic and aptitude tests now take place in September – sign up in May/June. A few students join the sixth form, with a minimum of six B grades at GCSE.

Exit: A few – usually less than 10 per cent – leave after GCSE, some because they didn't get the six grade Bs needed for sixth form study. 'It's rare for people to leave on bad terms. We tell everyone it's a seven year programme; the assumption is that everyone goes through to the sixth and everyone goes to university.' Medicine, economics and business all popular

W

courses, a large proportion at Russell group universities. Sixteen to Oxbridge in 2013.

Remarks: Very popular, high-performing, partially-selective school with a grammar school ethos. Boys work and play hard with results to match.

Watford Grammar School for Girls

Lady's Close, Watford, Hertfordshire, WD18 0AE

• Pupils: 1,320 girls; all day • Ages: 11–18 • Non-denom • State

Tel: 01923 223403
Email: admin@watfordgirls.herts.sch.uk
Website: www.watfordgrammarschoolforgirls.org.uk

Headmistress: Since 1987, Mrs Helen Hyde MA (early sixties, with no intention of retiring). Educated to degree level in South Africa; moved to the UK in 1970 and did a Masters at King's College London. She started her teaching career at Acland Burghley in Camden, then moved to Highgate Wood as curriculum deputy, before taking up the Watford headship. Married to a consultant paediatrician, she has two adult daughters, one of whom went right through the school during her headship. 'It was mind-blowing. I'd get the thumbs down during assembly if she didn't like what I was saying. We had girls from the school in and out of our house all the time, so I've got very close to them.' Has a South African lack of ceremony and breaks off our interview to go and hug one daughter, up at the school for a violin lesson. In the 2013 New Year's honours list she was honoured for services to education and her work as a holocaust trainer but still insists on being called 'Mrs Hyde' at school.

Her aims are to make Watford 'the best girls' school in the country' and to produce confident girls who are willing to take risks. 'Instead of "every child matters" I would say that "every teacher matters". If you make sure that your teachers feel confident to teach, they will make sure that every child learns.' The school motto, Sperate Parati – 'Go forth with preparation' – is translated by staff and girls as 'I can do it and I will do it'.

'I don't do hierarchy.' She views the school as a team effort, welcoming suggestions from governors – 'we come up with phenomenal ideas together' – and viewing teaching and non-teaching staff as all part of the team. Her PA is 'a proper partner', and the business manager – who spent most of his working life in Tenerife – assesses the Spanish level of applicants to cover a maternity vacancy in modern languages. 'They are all fully accountable. Trust goes all the way down. We work as a team to drive up academic standards.'

Her aunt and other family members were murdered in a death camp in Nazi-occupied Poland, and the school is a centre for Holocaust studies. 'If we don't look at the Holocaust in depth and find out how it came about, we won't be able to explain why Rwanda, Darfur and other tragedies happened.'

High praise from parents. 'She's a brilliant head...very strong, very dynamic...She wants girls to be aware of their wider moral responsibilities...She pushes everyone to do their bit for charity.' Indeed, she leads the way, climbing Ben Nevis in 2009 to raise money for the Anthony Nolan Trust, and cycling to Paris to raise funds for the new maths building.

Academic matters: Watford is one of only five UK training schools for De Bono thinking tools, and the head teaches all new staff and year 7 pupils to use these skills. 'I tell them that this is a no mistakes zone – that a mistake is just a little opportunity to try something else.' Staff and girls use these in conjunction with Mind Mapping. 'A combination of the two programmes makes them look at a subject from all angles.'

Certainly, it seems to pay dividends: well over 90 per cent of girls get 5+ A*-C grades at GCSE including maths and science, with 57 per cent of A level grades A or A*, 83 per cent A*-B in 2013. There is an expectation that everyone will work hard and do well, and most do, though some feel that the academic pressure can get too strong. Ofsted talks of 'an almost relentless drive to ensure that everyone achieves her very best'.

The school has two specialisms: visual arts, and maths and computing, which mirror its mix of academia and creativity, tradition and innovation. 'We teach the solid stuff – what history is, what geography is, French grammar – and then creativity.' The girls all study traditional subjects but they also do Young Enterprise, enter the Bank of England and the Times Interest Rate Challenge, win prizes in the Taylor Woodrow Art Competition.

Maths is a particular strength, with huge numbers taking it and further maths to A level. 'It's an amazing department,' says the head. About two-thirds do three separate sciences at GCSE, and biology and chemistry are consistently amongst the most popular A level choices. The head of physics fancied studying GCSE astronomy, so he enrolled a group of girls who learned alongside him. Now several take the GCSE each year, studying at lunchtime.

Everyone studies two languages – 'we teach them grammar, which is not part of the curriculum, but it helps them to speak better and write proper essays' – and takes at least one language to GCSE. 'As a linguist and a head I said no to allowing them to give up languages at 14.'

Offers the Extended Project Qualification in the sixth form, enabling girls to pursue an extended study of any subject that fascinates them. 'We get some weird and wonderful projects.'

There are a few girls with SEN statements, some with dyslexia or dyspraxia, and the school has accommodated special needs ranging from blindness to a girl with spina bifida. 'We're not wheelchair accessible, but she got on her crutches and made her way round the school.' Girls can get extra help within the classroom but no-one is withdrawn for special classes.

Games, options, the arts: Two playing fields, an indoor pool, tennis and netball courts, gym and sports hall including a fitness suite, dance studio and weights room, open to members of the public outside school hours. Teams play in galas and inter-school matches, and some make district and county level swimming, hockey and netball teams.

In keeping with the school's visual arts status and its Artsmark Gold, art in its different forms is high profile here. Highly original paintings, photos and textile designs line the corridors and a sculpture garden shows off sixth form work. 'My head of art is so original and so zany.' Fine art, 3D art, photography and graphics are all GCSE options, alongside graphic products and textiles. 'DT's great,' said a pupil. 'We're taught how the machines work then left to get on and use them.'

Large numbers have instrumental lessons, and there is a huge range of choirs, groups and ensembles, including a joint orchestra with the Boys' Grammar. Drama is important too – 'it's really good,' say girls – with some joint productions eg Wizard of Oz. Music and performing arts facilities are getting a 'major' makeover. Plenty of clubs – in year 7 girls are encouraged to try three, including one music and one sports. Lots of field trips, theatre and museum visits, ski-ing and sailing trips, expeditions abroad.

Background and atmosphere: Founded in 1704 by Mrs Elizabeth Fuller, the school originally taught girls to read, knit and sew, as well as recite the Church of England catechism. It moved to its present site – handily just down the road from Watford High

W

Street station – in 1907, and has been expanding ever since. The History Boys was filmed here and at its brother school, Watford Grammar School for Boys, and the original buildings have a traditional feel with polished wood floors and cream panelling. 'It's like a 1950s grammar school, in a good way,' commented a parent. Lessons are orderly, but pupils are encouraged to show their exuberance outside class. 'I like my girls to let off steam at lunch time.'

Recent additions include the bright and airy Food Factory (designed by one of the head's daughters) with its café-style tables – 'everyone loves it,' say girls – and the new Hyde House maths block – 'it's our pride and joy. We all worked hard to get it.' This was completed in double-quick time by a triumvirate of the head, business manager and site manager, who side-stepped the lumbering government Building Schools for the Future programme by raising their own funds and organising their own design and construction.

Year 7s have their base in Lady's Close House, reached by a bridge over a public footpath from the main part of the school, which originally housed the prep school until it closed in 1944. The latest fund-raising project aims to refurbish it into a vibrant teaching area for the English department.

Pastoral care and discipline: Firm and fair. 'I have some very naughty characters, but I won't allow a child to disrupt learning. If someone is seriously disruptive I will remove them.' No-one has been permanently excluded for many years, however. 'If you're very firm and everyone knows your expectations, most will live up to them.' Strong emphasis on building up girls' confidence and self-esteem. 'I believe passionately that the school is like a jewellery box. I tell the girls that they are my diamonds, and that we're going to polish and polish them. Alongside academia, we stand for respect, tolerance, caring and kindness.'

Pupils and parents: Good racial and social mix – bright, well-motivated girls make up a good proportion of pupils. 'There's a nice multi-cultural feel,' said a parent. Parents tend to be very supportive and join in the fashion shows, fairs, discos, indulgence evenings and aquathalons. Notable OGs: Geri Halliwell and EastEnders actress Rita Simons.

Entrance: Don't bother to apply for one of the 180 places unless you live in the right WD or HA postcode. Forty-five academic and 18 music places, 60 per cent allocated to those who live in the nearest Watford postcodes ('Watford Area') and 40 per cent to those in the 'rest of Admission Area'. Then 18 places to those who live nearest and haven't got a specialist place, then priority to siblings, including those with a brother at Watford Boys. After siblings, the remainder of the places are allocated by distance. NB Academic and aptitude tests held in September – sign up in May/June. Thirty or so join after GCSEs, bearing at least six good GCSEs, with A or B grades in their A level subjects. Those already at the school get first choice of subjects.

Exit: All GCSE students are advised to investigate alternative sixth forms in case they don't make the grade to stay on. Around 30 students a year leave after GCSEs, some because their results aren't up to it, others because they fancy a sixth form college experience. 'Brilliant' advice for sixth form leavers. 'The careers adviser knows everything there is to know about universities,' say sixth formers. Some to Oxbridge (16 places in 2013); a large proportion of the rest to Russell Group universities. Plenty of budding pharmacists, dentists and medics, and a good crop of engineers.

Remarks: Very popular semi-selective girls' school with a dynamic, determined head who ensures that it continues to go from strength to strength.

Wellington College

Linked school: Eagle House School

Duke's Ride, Crowthorne, Berkshire, RG45 7PU

• Pupils: 1050; including 415 girls. 220 day pupils, the rest board
• Ages: 13–18 • C of E • Fees: Day £24,330–£27,960; Boarding £32,940 pa • Independent

Tel: 01344 444013
Email: admissions@wellingtoncollege.org.uk
Website: www.wellingtoncollege.org.uk

Master: Since 2006, Dr Anthony Seldon MA PhD MBA FRSA FRHistSoc (sixties). Educated at Tonbridge School and Worcester College, Oxford. Was head of politics and sixth form at Whitgift School, head of history and general studies at Tonbridge and deputy headmaster of St. Dunstan's College before a nine year run as the transformational headmaster of Brighton College. So not a trembling novice when he blew into Wellington.

Intellectually curious, driven, ambitious for his school; mentioned Wellington's place in the A level league tables three times in our encounter 'not that we want to be competitive'. Wellington's canter up the league tables has been brisk since Dr Seldon's arrival. Has positioned Wellington as a 'world class' school and is as likely to take inspiration from top American schools as from British ones. Much focus on the 'Eight Aptitudes' (see below) and the now famous 'Happiness lessons'. 'Stillness' – a short weekly meditation period – on timetable for Years 9 and 10. Has introduced the Harkness Method, borrowed from US boarding schools, much centred on the pedagogical properties of a large oval table. Also from the States comes the 'Honour Code' (community rules which pupils themselves renew each year), a graduation ceremony, and the awarding of a leaver's diploma. One of the first independent schools to sponsor an academy – Wellington Academy in Wiltshire (dozens of joint projects including annual INSET day) – and is about to open a 'primary academy'. Has embarked on a series of international ventures spearheaded by Wellington College in Tianjin, China; others in the pipeline.

In neither personality nor appearance cut from standard headmaster cloth. Described by pupils as 'so cool' and by a parent as having 'the work ethic of Margaret Thatcher with the twinkle of Willy Wonka'. Mystifyingly hands on: directs a play most years, has an individual meeting with every student in the school, materialises at almost every school event and sports match ('there must be ten of him' said a mum) and he is working towards a GCSE in Mandarin. Every child in the school has lunch or dinner with him at the Lodge (that's 100 groups of ten to be entertained each academic year, but who's counting).

Author of many well-regarded books, including biographies of John Major, Tony Blair and Gordon Brown. Newest book, his first foray into the self-help market, is on Happiness. Ploughs profits from his books and speaking appearances back into education charities (at Brighton this allowed him to donate the tidy sum of £100,000 to a new performing arts centre). Writes thoughtfully about education in the national press, is a Radio 4 staple, has an innate gift for thinking in fully formed media packages, and is frequently quoted – not just in the press, but by his own staff. Several of his bon mots were recounted to us throughout the day, like sayings of the Dalai Lama. Wife, Joanna (Oxford double first and DPhil) teaches English and runs creative writing at Wellington; three children – the youngest attended Wellington and is now at the University of York.

Academic matters: Has leapt from genteel backwater to heavyweight. Over 70 per cent of A level results were A/A* in 2013, 92 per cent A*-B. Maths the most popular A level with biology not

W

far behind. Almost a third of pupils now opting for IB diploma instead of A levels, and the school is now fifth in IB league tables with 38.5 average in 2013, only its fourth year of running the qualification. Some overlap between the two programmes: unusually, the IB's Theory of Knowledge is taught to both. The impact of selection is unmistakable in GCSE results: 82 per cent were at A/ A* and 50 per cent at A* only in 2013. Boutique offerings include textiles, either via art or DT departments, and music technology (rarely offered as a GCSE). Wellington was the first independent school of its type to offer the IB's Middle Years Programme as an alternative to GCSEs. 40 per cent now opt for the MYP, though all pupils sit IGCSE maths and English language, and GCSE English lit. Quite a lot of attention given to languages in the impressive 'Modern Languages Institute' (swish languages block). It is here that one of the school's signature offerings – Mandarin – is taught, along with the usual range of languages ... and Hebrew! New Mandarin Centre now open – the country's first. A tiny clutch do Greek, more Latin. All sixth formers attend a series of lectures on astronomy, history of art and philosophy. 'Well-being' taught in years 10 and 11 – much rolling of eyes among the children on this one, but parents think it will serve them in years to come.

'The Eight Aptitudes' philosophy stands as the cornerstone of the school's twenty-first century reinvention – a reworking of Howard Gardner's theory of multiple intelligences. Staff encouraged to think across the aptitudes in order to develop the whole child. Hour long lessons; children kept busy. Their only real gripe to us was that they had too little time for lunch – a tiger parent's dream! 'Not a place to come if you don't have aspirations,' warned a parent, 'though the selection process helps to weed out those who don't tend to work.' 'You're in a bit of hot water if your effort grades slip', said another, 'but there's a good tutoring system to help bring you back up.' SEN provision not given the prominence it has at some similar schools (not mentioned in the school's prospectus) but around 90 pupils receive some learning support – department, and its head, commended by the children ('flamboyant' and 'enthusiastic'). The pupils' homespun advice was for children with learning needs to aim for one of the central boarding houses: 'they're very good if you're disorganised!'

Games, options, the arts: Sport 'diversifying away from rugby' – though all boys still start with a term of the game and last year the 1st VII won the National Schools 7's at Rosslyn Park after reaching the final for the fifth year in a row. Range of sports is vast, facilities impress eg two floodlit Astros, indoor and outdoor pool, dance studios, squash courts, shooting range, new sports pavilion. Nine-hole golf course still lovely (one of the top 18 courses every golfer should play before they die according to Country Life). Polo, skiing, shooting and rackets have had notable success of late. Football now firmly on the fixtures list. Chess going strong – another sign of the school's volte face since the days of Jonty Driver. Hospitality to visiting schools important, Dr Seldon told us, before describing in detail the chicken chasseur served at a recent match tea. Games seen as a reservoir of moral, social and creative aptitudes, not just physical! Nice to see the mad tradition of the 'Field Gun Run' (once described as trying to achieve an almost impossible task in a ridiculously short time with too few men on an unsuitable track) still going strong alongside the yoga and tree-hugging. And for the first time ever in the history of the country, there are girls in the field gun team. Girls' teams moving up the inter-schools ladder; hockey and netball well embedded with some girls competing at county and national level. Unusually for a co-ed school, lacrosse is played.

Art fizzing, housed in two spacious and airy buildings. School hosts a summer arts festival, most recently featuring an exhibition of Matisse lithographs in the student cafe! Textiles and ceramics both a strength – the quality of the textiles eloquent testimony to the authenticity of co-education here. Inroads being made into film and animation and there is

student TV company. Drama offerings rich and varied in the school's newly refurbished theatre. Dance a thriving GCSE and A level subject and soon to be offered as an IB option (popular outside the classroom as well). Music is becoming a major feature of the College – the a capella group are national champions and standards – particularly in the college orchestra and chapel choir – are high. An astonishing 40 pupils at grade 8 or beyond (scholars perform twice a year at St Martin-in-the-Fields), master classes, full range of ensembles including drum corp, jazz and two chapel choirs, weekly prize for the most diligent practiser. Impressive, student edited magazine; recent editions have featured interviews with Sebastian Faulks and Sir Michael Howard. A university style 'college carnival' at the start of each academic year allows clubs and societies to set out their wares. D of E. All fourth form take part in CCF and some carry on throughout their time at school.

Background and atmosphere: In 1852, when the Duke died, plans were in place to erect his statue in every town in England. Cooler heads prevailed and a school was reckoned to be a more fitting monument to Britain's most distinguished military leader. HM remains the school's official Visitor. So much has been written about the school, and all is in such fine fettle, that an arriving visitor feels as if he or she is entering the Emerald City wearing green-lensed spectacles. Immaculate, formal grounds reached via imposing avenue of oaks, Wellingtonias and Andean pines. Five lakes, endless lawns and abundant green space, three gardeners have been spotted simultaneously raking the gravel outside the Lodge. Beautiful chapel, tranches of memorials to the fallen now updated. With the opening of the £2.5m new E Learning Centre, a temple to iPads, Kindles and educational apps, the five year building cycle will be coming to a pause.

The changes have resulted in seventeen houses, each with 50-65 girls or boys, all of a good standard (in many houses only the youngest boarders share a room). Day pupils base themselves in one of the two day houses (the cheaper option) or are attached to a boarding house (an extra £1000 per term). Day pupils can leave at 6pm, though many stay much later. Splendid V&A social centre – feels like a cross between a hotel lobby and a Starbucks – is a pupil meeting place serving vaguely health conscious snacks, sandwiches, smoothies, coffee. Parent run charity tuck shop dishes up the pure refined stuff. The school raises loads for charity, presumably not all through the penny sweets priced, admirably, from 5p and up. A nice sideline in educational conferences – Wellington's are the best in the business.

Pastoral care and discipline: We're thrilled to bits to see the 'Basic Courtesies,' still published in school diaries – sets the high standard for behaviour (how many schools still have rules like, 'If you are wearing any kind of head-gear, you should raise it – or at least touch the brim – to all adults'? And, our favourite, 'In our culture, it is considered discourteous – and probably a sign of weak character – not to look directly into the eyes of the person who is talking to you'). Surprisingly fierce about drugs for such a caring sharing place: one whiff and you're out. 'Other schools say it, but here the pupils know they mean it', said a mum. Many new, mainly youngish, housemasters/housemistresses deeply beady eyed. Pupils can also be expelled for bullying, 'serious alcohol', theft, cheating or sex. Bullying carefully monitored via anonymous surveys which show that the school has fewer problems on this score than most, though it's never plain sailing. Facebook enabled on school filter 7-8am and 9-10pm. More than 60 Twitter accounts now operating out of the School.

Member of the Round Square since 1995 (international family of schools, associated in this country with Gordonstoun, Kurt Hahn and bracing fresh air and exercise). The organisation provides endless opportunities for fund-raising for impoverished schools in the southern hemisphere and ready-made destinations for school trips. Recently hosted the organisation's final conference ('it's grown too big for us all to meet'). A Service Learning Coordinator has recently been appointed to bring service into the heart of lessons via a 'connected curriculum'. Twenty minute chapel service once a week and a termly communion service on a Sunday evening; morality may be high on the agenda here, but this is not a churchy school. Girls wear rather shouty blue and lemon kilts in the lower years; all sixth formers in their own dark suits.

Pupils and parents: Vast number live quite close, spending most Saturday nights at home. Edging towards de facto weekly boarding, though boarders are required to stay in school with their year group one or two Saturday nights per term, so never an empty boarding house. 15 per cent foreign – 32 nationalities (no ESL tuition; the school requires very good English for entry). Still some Forces children, though numbers dwindling, and now only 2-3 per cent are from British families overseas. OBs include Sir Harold Nicolson, Robert Morley, Sebastian Faulkes, Rory Bremner, Peter Snow, Sir Nicholas Grimshaw (architect of Eden Project), Christopher Lee, Pop Idol winner Will Young and 15 winners of the VC.

Parents much involved at every turn. The school offers them outings, visiting speakers, concerts, happiness lessons, A level English and maths lessons, a book club – all reflecting the Master's view that schools work best when families are involved. Has cemented what was already 'a strong and loyal community', a parent told us, with OBs also integral as visiting speakers and sources of work experience or first jobs. Most parents cited 'innovation' as a reason they had chosen Wellington, particularly for sixth form. In a bizarre twist of fate the most traditional of public schools now finds itself the 'alternative' school of choice – viewed by some parents as an academically supercharged version of Bedales.

Entrance: Pre-testing and academic selection have reshaped the landscape. Academic ability may not be sole criterion – outstanding talent in music, sport or art can also gain you a golden ticket – but the broad ability range that characterised Wellington College for over 150 years is no more.

Three applicants for every place: 'We're inundated' the registrar told us. For 13+ register by December 31 of Year 6. Children then sit ISEB common pre-test around Easter time, either at their prep school or at Wellington. Strongest 300 or so are invited to assessment days during the first term of Year 7. These assessment days are based on Wellington's '8 aptitudes' and getting to know the whole child, rather than narrow academic criteria. Those offered places still required to sit CE (around 65 per cent mark), the school's own admissions test, or scholarship papers at age 13, although it is rare for an offer to be withdrawn at this stage. Main feeders: Broomwood Hall, Caldicott, Cheam, Crosfields, Danes Hill, Dragon, Eagle House (a mile away and owned by Wellington), Feltonfleet, Hall Grove, Highfield, Lambrook, Northcote Lodge, Papplewick, Shrewsbury House, St John's Beaumont, Thomas's Schools, Twyford, Westbourne House and Yateley Manor. A handful join at 14+. Forty enter at sixth form: 'academic bar rising' – most candidates have straight A/A*s at GCSE unless they are a star artist, musician or sportsman.

Exit: Largest numbers to Exeter, Bristol, Nottingham and Durham. Record number to Oxbridge in 2013. Many go on to art foundation and conservatoires. Up to 60 per cent to gap years. In 2013 20 students went to US, Canadian, Australasian and European universities. Increasing numbers applying to American unis: 'Oxbridge is looking for ego-driven monsters,' a member of staff said dryly. 'Some very bright kids just don't fit the mould.'

Money matters: Scholarships for academics, sports, music, arts at 13+ and 16+ now capped at 10 per cent, exhibitions five per cent, both with scope for bursarial top up. Means-tested foundation awards (up to full fees) available for children of members of the Forces, or other services eg the police, or for the children of civilians who 'have died in acts of selfless bravery'. Do pursue if you qualify and meet the school's academic requirements.

Remarks: Ignore the spin and the hype: this really is one of the most exciting and successful independent schools in the country.

Wellington School

Linked school: Wellington School Primary

Carleton Turrets, Craigweil Road, Ayr, KA7 2XH

• Pupils: 320 boys and girls in senior school • Ages: 3–18 • Non-denom • Fees: £4,129–£10,719 pa • Independent

Tel: 01292 269321
Email: info@wellingtonschool.org
Website: www.wellingtonschool.org

Headmaster: Since 2006, Mr Mark Parlour BSc BA PGCE MMBA FIAP FRSA (fifties) who has taken the school from strength to strength. Born in Calcutta, educated at the University of Wales, Trinity College Oxford and the Open University, with degrees in zoology, applied zoology, computing, maths and electronics. An IT whizz. Head of computing at Bloxham, Gordonstoun and Robert Gordon's College, with a short stint in the computing industry in between. He came to Wellington from The High School of Dundee, where he was a deputy head of the senior school. Married, with four grown up children, his wife is involved on the marketing side.

The Parlours live five miles out of Ayr and the head gets back late, having spent his 'whole life' helping children, he can't help popping into post-school clubs. In a previous life he was 'deeply involved with the boarding and the sports side' and before that was a serious rugby coach – was a rugby blue and had an oval ball balanced to the right of the fireplace in his study (most impressive, but alas 'ealth and safety made him put it on the shelf) – he also coached cricket, kayaking, scuba diving and swimming, played national league octopush and water polo, yomped over hills, and canoed. His knees now prevent him from such super activity, though he has 'cured them' by cycling. Quite a coup for sleepy Ayr to find such a star.

Since our last visit Parlour has combined the nursery and junior years under one head 'better accountability, much easier'. The nursery now has a popular outdoor wing when a dozen or so youngsters spend the entire day in the fresh air at Doonside, jolly pavilion and packed lunch: plus foxes, woods and adventure playground (come hell or high water, they wear specially designed dry suits). Parlour has continued improvements in the pupil welfare system, sixth form experience, curriculum balance, transition between nursery, primary and senior, extra-curricular involvement and learning and teaching, which is what we said last time. More staff employed – no apparent problems with getting staff, 'some even from Glasgow' (which he still pronounces with a short a). There were 130 applications recently for the post of bursar. New heads of departments appointed.

Enormous changes since his arrival, but still feels a tad Damey, particularly some of the more pernickety rules about uniform. Green hair bands and hair clasps?

Academic matters: Max 18 per class in primary, with slight expansion in size at age 10 and 11; two parallel classes throughout the prep and pre-prep; set from senior school with max class size of 20 (three or four classes per year group). Numbers capped 'naturally' – by building and room size. Head working on 'sixth year experience'; though most stay on after highers anyway. (Plans afoot and dosh apparently at the ready for new ICT and sixth form centre but... probably not enuff brown envelopes.) We saw nothing but Dell flat screens and interactive whiteboards in every classroom. Languages particularly strong, with Prestwick just down the road it's a natural; long-term exchanges with Germany and France; deeply involved with Comenius and regular exchanges with Europe including Slovenia and Hungary. New links with Jaipur. All do French from primary and can elect to do German at senior level but results not all singing and dancing at any level and minimal take-up at advanced higher level. Only two takers for French advanced higher last year (1 B, 1C) as opposed to 11 doing chemistry (9A, 2B). Slightly wider spread and success rate in highers, with geography and English popular, ditto maths and biology. Rather a challenge to make sense of results on website but according to school in 2013 Highers, 48 per cent 5+ A*-C including maths and English; 61 per cent A*/A. At Advanced Highers, 88 per cent A*-B, 60 per cent A*/A.

Four classicists, no Greek. Applied maths now offered at advanced higher level, but only one taker, 18 assorted highers subjects on offer, but penny numbers really, couple of Germanists. School might do better to abandon classical studies (1) admin (1) and concentrate on core subjects. Standard, intermediate I and II, higher and advanced highers all offered. (Scotland has a new exam: National 4 and 5, which comes into play next academic year although highers etc remain unchanged. We have yet to meet an enthusiastic head.)

Humanities strong, ditto sciences with well-equipped labs; few results of less than C (which in GSG parlance = fail). Media studies dropped recently in favour of proper academia. We hate league tables, preferring to see subject results, which we think more informative, but despite having a non-selective intake, Wellington has been consistently up there with the big boys. Native speakers can expect tutorial help to coach them through highers etc, in their native tongue; Hungarian, Serbian, Croatian whatever. EFL on tap to help newcomers get up to speed.

New phonetic reading programme should go some way to improving literacy; SENCo and a team of dedicated staff. Pupils assessed in primary, and individual lessons where necessary, will pull in ed psychs as needed. Drop in centres to hit problems on the head asap, auxiliary (ie dual teaching) in primary school, with perhaps 20 pupils receiving 'serious help' throughout the school.

Games, options, the arts: Twenty acre sports ground (a long) five mins away at Doonside in Alloway has pavilion, changing and reception facilities, Astroturf and floodlighting; parents use it for fund-raising events, as well as coaching and refereeing courses, barbeques (bouncy castles, good car parking) and the like. Locals use it too. Parlour, a sports guru, is sad that rugby, though strong, still doesn't have the numbers to thrash all comers. Terrific hockey, with hockey sticks kept in wheelie bins. Fair showing of Scottish caps; semi-finalists in the U14 tennis tournament working with the Prestwick tennis academy – both short and conventional. Swimming in the nearby Citadel pool in Ayr, head keen to use the sea more – it is, after all, quite literally on the doorstep. So expect kayaking, canoeing, (sailing?) – 'it takes time', but links on the horizon with local clubs. Skating, riding, golf growing in popularity, oodles of clubs in junior dept – (karate popular). Cycling plus lots of individual sports and head keen to build on the outdoor aspect; expect miracles shortly. New re-surfaced tarmac playground, and local (flat) beach much used for every conceivable activity. Alas some of the LEA cutbacks have affected local partnerships,

D of E and leadership expeditions (many of the specialist tutors also worked in the state sector) and Parlour doesn't reckon that Wellington can afford specialists on their own.

Spectacular music but space limited simply because of the number of simultaneous activities. Orchestra was practising in the dining room while the choir was in the music room when we visited. Mass of choirs, orchestras and school shows – down to P1. New music recording suite a couple of years back, loads of music technology. Jazz band. Can't fault it.

New head of art is into jewellery and art rooms a-buzz with pupils post-school. Fabric design and stunning silk screen printing, as well as conventional flat art and three dimensional stuff. Art & design results healthy but surprisingly few takers for music even at standard grade. Vast array of post-school clubs, with science on Wednesdays when the 'whole school hums'.

Background and atmosphere: Originally founded in Wellington Square in 1836 by the wife of an Ayr teacher for 12 young ladies (think dame school), the school moved to Carleton Turrets on the leafy outskirts of Ayr in 1923, dropping boarders and moving to co-ed 14 years ago. More or less 50/50 these days, though perhaps not enuff chaps to form proper teams. After a certain amount of logistical re-organisation, the senior school now occupies the Carleton Turrets, with the more recently acquired Craigweil House home to the music school, the lang dept and the dining room – the latter operates on a fairly tight timetable. The primary and nursery school are accommodated in Drumley, just across the road (they have their own dining facilities). A number bring packed lunches and it is a removable privilege to eat these in classrooms. Drumley has a bright and jolly extension in the nursery leading directly onto a dedicated play area for tinies. Nursery garden incredibly well used.

The three turreted Victorian grade B buildings (splendid stained glass windows) on the sea front have obvious limitations on expansion. The gym at Carleton Turrets doubles as assembly hall (new windows looking onto the playground) and a proper weights room is strategically placed to one side, but this editor was sad that offices still seemed to occupy so much space. New Alcatraz entry system to front/side door, not sure whether it is to keep the ungodly out or...

School looked in jolly good heart, though it still feels a bit dameish. Books in every classroom as well as on all the landings – with a shelf labelled 'for oversized books'. New, state of the art library, most of the classrooms on the top floors have whizzo views over to Arran and Goatfell, which must make concentration difficult. Fairly restricted play areas round the actual buildings but expansive (flat) links and beach opposite for informal footie and the like at break times.

Enthusiastic parental input, particularly at weekends. Ayr is proud of the school. Parents run second hand clothes shop.

Pastoral care and discipline: School works closely with parents. Efficient tutorial system throughout senior school, reports twice a term followed by parents' meeting to discuss the report. Strong inter-house competitions, siblings in same houses. Not a lot of sin, orange indiscipline slips for minor sin, three slips equals letter home, red slips for more serious sin, automatic letter home. All slips count against the pupil's house Conduct Shield. Weekly detention at lunchtime for repeated offenders or referral to behavioural timetable if pupil consistently sinful. Ultimate deterrent is expulsion. PSHE and anti-bullying strategies (anti-bullying email and strategically placed anti-bullying boxes), plus seminars on healthy eating et al. 'Occasional physical transgression', head keen on anti-bullying parent focus groups.

Detailed clothes list (down to hair clasps) and handy parental book of rules; actually handy books – both paper and on line – on almost every subject. Newly re-formed pupil-led school council. Recent HMI report thought more God would be good – 'I would hope our assemblies are meaningful,' 'huge moral

W

dimension,' muses head. No change here. Increasing number of pupil-led assemblies. Visiting chaplain. Active and helpful board of governors.

Pupils and parents: Not a Sloane school. Strongly middle class, parents (and grandparents) who may have gone to more trad schools elsewhere hold The Wellie in high regard; number of first time buyers, professionals, builders, company directors, refugees from 'London and Manchester'. Nice well-behaved pupils, not obviously that street-wise. Parent organised buses locally.

Entrance: Via nursery; P1 – P7 children spend a morning in school, thereafter school's own test in English and maths. Usual entry stage to senior school S1 but pupils accepted at any time if space available. Currently heavily oversubscribed for nursery, P1 and S1. Occasional entry post standard for highers or advanced highers.

Exit: Most stay the course; few leave after highers, some may go to state system post primary. Mainly to Scottish universities, vets, medics, biologists, mathematicians.

Money matters: Sibling discounts and bursaries available, both for external and internal candidates – but not enough, according to the Office of the Scottish Charity Regulator, which has warned that it risks losing its charitable status. Not a poor school. Fees from £1291 nursery to £3351 sixth form, sans lunch (fees deliberately being kept down).

Remarks: Smashing useful local school for Ayrshire, if limited in facilities by its site – sports/dining/assembly hall needed, a redundant church would be nice. No feel that it is still a girls' school with boys tacked on – it is properly co-ed throughout. Still (2012) not a member of the HMC – though exam results warrant inclusion. Ticks all the boxes.

Wellington School

Linked school: Wellington Junior School

South Street, Wellington, Somerset, TA21 8NT

• Pupils: Senior 580, 300 boys 280 girls. Day 450, boarders 130 • Ages: 3–18 • C of E • Fees: Day £11,754–£12,885; Boarding £19,395–£26,589 pa • Independent

Tel: 01823 668800
Email: admin@wellington-school.org.uk
Website: www.wellington-school.org.uk

Headmaster: Since 2006, Martin Reader (late forties), was educated at St Olave's, Orpington and read English, language and literature with Middle English and Old Norse at Oxford, and played rugby for the university. Deciding that he maybe hadn't the academic edge for a university career, he went to teach at St Edward's Oxford and from thence to Oundle, before becoming deputy at Reigate Grammar. His wife, also a teacher, runs the friends of the junior school and the second hand shop; like a large proportion of his staff, he has children in school, a girl in the senior, a son in juniors. He enjoys the very distinct ethos of Wellington rooted in the history of the school. It was the last direct grant grammar school and still has the purposeful feel of grammar school. 'Pupils', he says, 'are exceptionally "grounded", perhaps because this is a traditionally agricultural area and the majority of local families come from agriculture related backgrounds': – a trend substantiated by the number of boys choosing tractor design in the junior DT class we visited!

He would like pupils to be a bit more 'edgy'. He has delighted pupils and parents alike by abolishing Saturday school, supported staff in setting up the 'Aces' scheme to induce pupils to take responsibility for their own learning, and generally smartened up the school with some fantastic new facilities. In between, he loves sport and is an avid birdwatcher as well as a loyal supporter of his local church. He leaves in July 2014 to take over at Cranleigh. His successor, Henry Price, senior housemaster at Rugby, will have a lot to live up to. Parents say they will miss Mr Reader but trust the governors to 'pick another good one'!

Academic matters: Wellington sits comfortably between its local Taunton independent rivals in academic achievement and considerably higher than the nearest sixth form college. Over the past 10 or so years it has had pretty consistent sound results at GCSE and A level. It is rightly proud of 19 per cent A* at A level for the last two years (41 per cent A*/A in 2013), which is above local competitors. While it's not right at the top of the national league tables, recent scores in maths and science, both IGCSEs, are impressive. (In 2013, 49 per cent A*/A grades overall.) Classes average 22, but not larger than 25. All study French in the first three years and pick up either German or Spanish and Latin. All do RS, Eng lang and lit, maths (IGCSE), either three separate sciences (IGCSE) or dual award, and at least one language (if two taken one has to be French ie can't do Spanish and German). State of art language IT, in use on our visit. Outstanding classics department gives Latin an exceptionally high take up. Music and drama on offer in a basically standard selection, except for Greek, which has grown from a club started 10 years ago, is taught in spare time. The head's just taken it up! A level offers a free choice and generally manages to timetable it. Economics and classical subjects get a small take up as do all mod langs, with maths (plus further maths) and physics topping the bill, both with very good record of A/A*s. Plenty of options for less academic students, whose results are more than adequate. High fliers – quite a few of them – with some fast track arrangements when parents request it.

Extensive new labs are well designed (by teachers) with separate areas for study and practical work. Aristotle, the Axolotl (Mexican amphibian with external gills) is lovingly looked after by the physics technician, typifying the enterprising flexibility of the school. Though large and exceptionally well equipped, the labs are functional rather than spectacular, with lots of bare breeze block – reflecting the common sense economy which has allowed the school to undertake massive developments over the years. Spacious but understated new English teaching block also houses a comprehensive SEN department (SEN help offered at need on individual or group basis by qualified staff of three, though charges for Extra English for foreign students) and an enormous exam hall. It means other spaces don't get blocked at exam time and gives assembly and function space. One year GCSE programme for students from abroad allows them to get up to five basic subject passes in order to do A Levels in sixth form or IB elsewhere.

Games, options, the arts: Even those reluctant to exercise seem to get a look in. A parent commented that boys and girls alike are encouraged but not forced, and the truly non-sporty get support, a few concessions but enough exercise. Lots of teams for everything with girls' hockey and boys' cricket getting players to county level, while girls' netball is making a splash locally. There's definitely a rugby set, parents say, with 10 teams posting enthusiastic reports of results in the school mag. Most of the usual summer and winter sports (no soccer?) with athletics outstanding. Fantastic pale blue Princess Royal Sports Centre (she opened it) with its own department of sports medicine, huge adaptable sports hall with viewing and teaching spaces and fitness suite. Lovely dance studio is also home to fencing with a small but very distinguished take up reaching national level.

W

New music block is rather small, which belies the emphasis on music (apparently the first 'all Steinway school' in the country). Regular chapel sung services, lots of orchestras and small groups orchestral, choral, classic and pop, include 'Girlforce9' a self generated a-capella choir. 'Cushion concerts' in lunch hours for lower school as well as the usual full school ones and masses of encouragement for all types of music, such as the summer 'fretted strings' celebrations for guitarists. Drama uses the main school hall converted to a blacked-out all-singing-and-dancing venue, opened by past pupil David Suchet in 2011. A bit of a desecration of what must have been a gracious, light-filled school hall (not a permanent one, says school – curtains frequently drawn back for events), one of the few original buildings but allowing frequent huge musical productions which pupils clearly adore. There's serious stuff as well: The Crucible, Odysseus, Tristan and Isolde. Brilliant posters and some outstanding theatre photography attest to the quality achieved. Smashing photography in lots of the school's promotional bumf must emanate from the influence of the art department. Its policy is 'to encourage self expression' but the work on show in the cramped department bursts with exceptional observation and drawing as well as tremendous imaginative use of material, extending to 3D and photography. Some of the best school art around.

Prominent CCF means that school is full of service (all three) uniform every Friday and drilling seemed to occupy most of the afternoon we visited. Year 11 was embarking in huge numbers on a weekend camp. Air Force cadets get a flight before they leave sixth form, Navy actually get to sea plus plenty of free sail training etc and Army cadets were handling some alarmingly real guns!

'Almost too much to do' a parent commented. Twenty or so activities on offer, from semi academic to energetic, as well as all the sport/music/drama/CCF programmes. The usual exchanges and visits abound. A sample school mag reported 15, 10 of which were abroad – New York, South Africa, Greece and Alps for skiing etc – that was not counting CCF and D of E! – and Barbados, the Arctic Circle and Tunisia are in the pipeline. Occasional financial support for trips central to curriculum.

The recently devised 'Aces' scheme encourages pupils to take responsibility for their own development and learning. Pupils have a termly tutor interview to reflect on their underlying skills, based round competence in action, communication, exploration and self-development.

Background and atmosphere: Founded in 1837 as Benjamin Frost's Classical Mathematical and Commercial Academy, occupying the great hall, where all teaching took place, Wellington9 morphed into the West Somerset County School. In 1945, as Wellington School, it became the first direct grant school and became fully independent in the 1970s. Girls infiltrated it from 1972, and in 1997 it added Wellington Junior School, which will be called Wellington Prep from 2014. The current site straggles across a busy-ish road (no over- or underpass) in the little town of Wellington, birthplace of the Iron Duke. A mixture of Georgian-type houses converted into sixth form centre, head's house and san, and facilities purpose built or acquired over its 175 years rejoice in styles of these various times. A huge tree-lined green expanse edged by new labs, pool etc creates central campus. It softens the redbrick neoclassical great hall and gothic spikes of the chapel, built to commemorate the fallen of WW1, with a stunning blue star-studded ceiling, carved oak pews and angel decked organ. Used for daily assembly and masses of music it is, physically, the central point of Wellington.

Smart refurbished reception and head master's offices – definitely welcoming; comfortable library with terrific AV, friendly round tables for clean cafeteria style dining, serving a choice of Friday fish, on our visit, including popular but rather small portions of moules marinières. Lunch is extra but very few opt out.

Pastoral care and discipline: Top Juniors and first two years of senior have mixed boarding in Overside. Senior boarding boys have two houses, and one for senior girls. The vast majority of day pupils are split into three boys' and three girls' houses. Fairly basic accommodation in comparison the five star rooms of some schools, but boarders seem contented, and there are all the trimmings of common rooms, kitchens, showers etc and the odd bath for easing the rugby stiffness. Pastoral care is delivered via the houses, with each pupil allocated a tutor who takes pupils right through the school and is first point of call for parents. Problems are dealt with sensitively, say parents, and children given every support in settling and studying. No recent incidents calling for ultimate sanction of permanent exclusion. Parents agree that neither drugs nor drink are rife, and say pupils know where they stand on this (urine tests for suspects) and other matters of discipline. Plenty of responsibility for house and school captains, and for lower school prefects.

Pupils and parents: Definitely not a toff school but lots of Somerset families – inevitably farmers and businesses relating to farming. Professionals and families where both parents work to cover the fees. A few expats and a tranche of International boarders (about 20 per cent), some of whom come in via the school's one year GCSE programme. Huge majority of day pupils come in by bus from Exeter and Chard to the south, Minehead and Dulverton to the north west and beyond Bridgewater to the east.

Despite the usual reservations of some parents and pupils that kilted skirts don't suit all shapes and regulations are not always enforced, Wellington uniform of blue crested blazer (quite expensive), white shirt and grey trousers/skirt is worn with evident pride by pupils. Not a half-mast tie or dipping hemline in sight! Second hand shop run by head's wife.

Past pupils include David Suchet, Jeffrey Archer, the late Keith Floyd, actress Carly Bawden, ex Black Rod Sir Freddie Viggers, mathematician and author Simon Singh and marine biologist, Dr Jon Copley.

Entrance: Main entry at 11, with 30 per cent from junior school, then at 13 and to lower sixth. Pupils can enter for any year, but if it is half way through an exam course and the syllabus does not match, they may be advised to repeat a year. Broadly selective, tending to discourage potential non-copers. At 11 all, including juniors, take the school's own exam in January. At 13 from prep school, it is common entrance, or, as in all other years, by interview in maths, science and mod langs.

International pupils can enter via one year GCSE programme and pay a higher fee to cover any extra tuition needed.

Exit: Vast majority from upper sixth to uni, about half in mainstream subjects to established courses. A couple to Oxbridge, not many doctors but lots of mathematicians, linguists and classicists. Tiny trickle straight to Forces or training. Almost 20 per cent leave after GCSE, often to Taunton's Robert Huish College, which has a good reputation. The head points out that some parents make a strategic decision to fund years 7-11.

Money matters: Both boarding and day are pretty good value in comparison with similar schools.

Scholarships, both academic and talent related (music, drama, sport), between 10 and 50 per cent of fees awarded at years 7, 9 and 12 by examination audition etc. Scholarship holders can apply for means-tested bursaries of up to 100 per cent. The school spends cautiously, avoiding the flashily expensive, but has nevertheless achieved tremendously improved facilities over the last six or seven years.

Remarks: Can't think why Wellington hasn't featured in Good Schools' Guide before. Friendly, purposeful and busy, it is a solid, well-managed school, neat but not glossy, giving its pupils

W

a sound education and masses of high points in developmental experience. Its flexible and approachable style means happy pupils and happy parents.

Wells Cathedral School

Linked school: Wells Cathedral Junior School

The Liberty, Wells, Somerset, BA5 2ST

• Pupils: 530 in senior school; 250 boarders • Ages: Junior School: 3–11; Senior School: 11–18 • C of E • Fees: Boarding £26,658–£26,778; Day £15,387–£16,002 pa • Independent

---

Tel: 01749 834200
Email: admissions@wellscs.somerset.sch.uk
Website: www.wells-cathedral-school.com

Head: Since 2000, Mrs Elizabeth Cairncross (fifties), married with three children. Formerly deputy head of Christ's Hospital, Horsham, where she had been a mistress since 1986. The first female head in the history of the school, obviously delighted to be in such beautiful surroundings. 'Such a wealth of history and tradition that we can get on and do modern things.' Has a tough job, juggling a bewildering number of balls in the air while dropping none. Oversaw Wells' participation in the Channel 5 documentary 'How the Other Half Learns'. Three of her pupils swapped places with three kids from a sprawling Wembley comprehensive for two weeks – sensitively handled and a learning experience for all.

Academic matters: Flexibility without disorder. Maths the most popular subject, with brilliant results, especially among musicians. Began offering maths IGCSE in 2007 with able pupils taking it a year early. Sciences lacking quite the same pazazz (though A level marks in sciences consistently very good and many pupils go on to read medicine). Overall 56 per cent of GCSE entries graded A*/A in 2013. Broadish range of A level subjects including geology, Italian, Latin, psychology and politics. Law through video conferencing and distance learning, but not much take-up. in 2013, 67 per cent A*-B grades at A level (42 per cent A*/A). Leisure and tourism a GCSE option. Some hotshots take GCSE music two years early and power straight on to AS. Pupils we spoke to raved about the English teaching. Setting for French and maths from year 7. Specialist musicians throughout the school have adjusted timetables and curricula to integrate music and, especially, practice. They may take only two A levels, but most take three. Not a school where pupils are buckling under academic pressure – much emphasis on learning to work independently and be responsible for one's progress. Information on SEN provision not supplied.

Games, options, the arts: One of five independent schools in the UK with government-funded specialist music provision. So the music, of course, is fabulous. The prospectus lists over 50 music staff, with departments of strings, keyboard, woodwind, brass, percussion, vocal and choral studies, music technology and composition. Possibly a notch less hard-core and tunnel-visioned than the other specialist music schools. Lots of practice? Yes. At dawn? Probably not. Forty choristers (half boys, half girls, in separate choirs). Rehearsal five mornings a week before school and alternate Friday afternoons. They sing in the cathedral most Sundays during term time, plus evensong every day except one. Opportunities for music extend throughout the school and are not limited to the specialists.

A strong tradition of drama and fine art and, as would be expected in a school where performance is important, standards are high. The only specialist music school to allow its musicians to play in school games teams – in fact, the only specialist music school to have games full stop. Sport does not share the high profile of the arts but is well provided for – rugby, hockey, netball, cricket and tennis. Shooting triumphant at the moment: three members of the school's shooting team were recently selected for the Great Britain under 21 rifle and pistol squad. Newly renovated and now covered swimming pool. Newish dance studio used by all ages. D of E and CCF. Alexander Technique for the musicians (and others).

Background and atmosphere: Traditional on the outside, progressive on the inside. Celebrated its 1,100th birthday in 2009; Wells is one of the world's oldest schools, rambling through the ancient heart of one of England's loveliest towns. Buildings a mixture of the sublime (half-timber, cobblestones and mellow stonework) and the – less sublime – 'temporary' classrooms slated for extermination. The cobbled Vicar's Close, surely one of the loveliest lanes in England, is home to several school buildings. The lovely Stable Yard is home to a diminutive but homely library (a bit short on quiet space for work), sixth form centre and classrooms. The music department is centred on the medieval buildings down the road. Somewhat 'bitty' in feel: you need to negotiate a rather dicey roundabout to find the strings department and a boys' boarding house. A classroom building with dedicated space for maths teaching and providing a base for all year 7 opened 2010. Plans also for spectacular new music building, with architecture inspired by Elmhurst School for Dance and maximising opportunities for peer observation and learning (= glass walls). Junior and senior schools adjacent provides a family feel and also means that siblings can see each other in the day. Has not skimped on marketing – do bring along a wheelbarrow to carry the mountain of (beautifully produced) bumf with which you will emerge. School difficult to get through to by phone and can be hard to make an appointment to visit – perhaps marketing needs to shine its beam in this direction.

Pastoral care and discipline: The emphasis is on 'mutual consideration, respect and courtesy'. Drug testing 'on concern'. No school bar – never has been one. Drinking allowed at sixth form events where meal served and at certain pubs. Much emphasis on learning to support one another and biggest sanctions reserved for 'betraying trust within the community'. Head points out that it's easier to teach children to be independent when you have space and the safe rural environment of a town like Wells. More pupils per dorm than at most schools we see nowadays, with two or three sharing even in the upper sixth. No scheduled exeats after year 9 but school relaxed about pupils going home on weekends. Years 10-13 allowed into town after school day and on weekends. Day pupils assigned to boarding houses where they register, have lockers and flop. Schoolday formally ends at 4pm (4.30 on Wednesdays). Wells Cathedral involved in the governance of the school but keeps a light touch. The whole school gathers for a service there every Monday. Female chaplain was previously the British Army's first female chaplain and was stationed in Iraq for six months. Navy and grey uniform worn to age 16, with 'dark suits' acceptable thereafter.

Pupils and parents: Large local catchment area for day pupils, boarders from far and wide but mostly south west. Good balance of overseas pupils (about 10 per cent) – some for music, some not – enriches but does not swamp. EFL available and Chinese and Japanese feature in the A level results. Web of school bus routes includes villages towards Bristol and Bath. Pupils confident and articulate, interested in each other and in the community of the school, including the juniors. Old Wellensians (or Old Wellies even) include businessman Roger Saul (founder of Mulberry), opera singer Sarah Fryer, portrait painter Justin Mortimer, Bruce Parry of BBC2's Tribe, Olympic

W

gold medallist Danny Nightingale, and Glastonbury Festival founder Michael Eavis and his daughter, Emily.

Entrance: Formally at 11 and 13 (assessment tests are held at the school on a Saturday in late January), but 12 and 14 will also do nicely. Entry to sixth form is subject to interview and at least six grade C passes at GCSE, with grade B or better for subjects to be taken at AS level. Auditions for music places held in November, for sixth form, and January, for all age groups. A few prospective parents of musicians put off by the fixed date for auditions (the other music schools hold them on a rolling basis throughout the year).

Exit: Nearly all to higher education, most to Russell Group and other universities or musical conservatoires both in the UK and abroad, including the Juilliard School in New York. Four to Oxbridge in 2013.

Money matters: Not a school with a big endowment, so money is tight. 90 'specialist' musicians (72 government-aided music places – means-tested but can amount to full fees) plus 18 non-funded pupils (often from abroad). Seventy 'special provision' pupils take part in a programme similar to the specialists but – crucially – without funding; a moderately talented musician might do better financially, though probably not musically, to try for a music scholarship at a mainstream independent school. Choral scholarships, but NB boys are entitled to up to 25 per cent off fees and girls only 10 per cent off day fees. Means-tested academic, music and all-round scholarships available for entry to years 7, 9 and sixth form (worth a five per cent minimum). Sons and daughters of clergy and Forces may qualify for a 10 per cent bursary. Day fees a bargain, but watch out for annual music 'capitation fees' of £152.10 (or more), on top of music lessons charged at £40.45 per hour.

Remarks: Tranquil and cultured from afar but a bubbling cauldron once you get up close, with a very tasty stew sizzling within. Few schools – perhaps none – so successfully weave together so many strands: boys and girls, senior and junior (and nursery!), day and boarding, mainstream and music specialist, ecclesiastical and lay, old-fashioned and modern. If you have trouble making choices, you need look no further. But make sure to nail down funding questions in advance.

Wellsway School

Chandag Road, Keynsham, Bristol, BS31 1PH

• Pupils: 1,330 boys and girls • Ages: 11–18 • State

Tel: 01179 864751
Email: enquiries@wellswayschool.com
Website: www.wellswayschool.com

Headteacher: Since 2005, Mrs Andrea Arlidge BA (late forties). Previously head of St Katherine's School in North Somerset.

Academic matters: Specialist Sports and Science College. Fine results for a non-selective school in a not solely middle class area. In 2013, 95 per cent got five or more A*-C GCSE grades, 73 per cent including English and maths. Some 60-70 per cent stay on for sixth form – achieved 33 per cent A*/A grades in 2013. Sixth form study centre opened 2008 with computer suites and quiet study areas. Very strong departments led by specialist staff. Sound provision for statemented pupils.

Games, options, the arts: Heaps of teams in all sports. Artificial pitch. Annual French trip for year 7, ski trip, water sport trip.

World Challenge expeditions have been to Ecuador, South Africa and West Canada. Currently running 'Wellsway Challenge' introduced in 2004 to destinations in Europe.

Innovative and fabulous art department. Dedicated staff stay long after school hours to keep facilities open. Mad on musicals – staged Return to the Forbidden Planet, Barnum, Grease, Guys & Dolls, Billy, Cabaret, My Fair Lady, Animal Farm and Oliver!

Background and atmosphere: A once thriving market town between Bath and Bristol, Keynsham is a town of churches – five Anglican, one Baptist and one Methodist, denoting its past trade wealth. A spacious campus amongst green fields is cheek by jowl with Chandag Junior and Infant Schools. Highly motivated staff aged 22 to 60; seem far less frantic than most at large comprehensives. Many of them have own children here and the relationship between staff and pupils is that of a close-knit village school. Bulletin boards bursting with news or press cuttings of ex-pupils making local headlines.

Pastoral care and discipline: Policies on everything from asthma to child protection. School rules insist that anyone being bullied report it. Comes down ton-of-bricks on anti-social or violent behaviour and nips any incident in the bud by locating pupil's parent instantly. A counsellor is on staff. Sixth formers become 'buddies' to any year 7 who request one and may coach sports/share lunch and chat/solve bigger problems.

Pupils and parents: Local business folk, many Old Girls'/Boys' kids, every class and creed. Very loyal. A weekly newsletter keeps parents well-informed and asks parents to monitor homework and control absence. Excellent, informative website. Uniform of green blazer/black trousers/skirts. Strong on community service and raising funds for charities.

Entrance: Over-subscribed. Wellsway serves Keynsham (to the east of the River Chew), Chelwood Village, Compton Dando, Corston, Marksbury, Newton St Loe, Priston and Saltford. Children from within this area whose older sibling will be attending the school on the admission date come first, followed by other children from the area, then other siblings. Five Cs at GCSE preferred for sixth form entrance.

Exit: Around 60-70 per cent of GCSE pupils continue on to sixth form here, 20-30 per cent to education elsewhere. After A levels most go to universities eg Cardiff, West of England, Plymouth, Bristol, Exeter, Cheltenham, Birmingham, Leeds, Loughborough, Manchester, Nottingham, Oxbridge, Warwick. A few to a gap year or employment and a sprinkle to art foundation or drama school.

Remarks: Confident pupils with high expectations well prepared for life. Loveliest bunch of teachers in the county.

Westbourne School (Senior)

Linked school: Westbourne School (Junior)

60 Westbourne Road, Sheffield, South Yorkshire, S10 2QT

• Pupils: 340 (180 boys; 160 girls); all day • Ages: 11–16 • Non-denom • Fees: £11,190 pa • Independent

Tel: 01142 660374
Email: admin@westbourneschool.co.uk
Website: www.westbourneschool.co.uk

Headmaster: Since 2004, Mr John Hicks MEd (early 50s). Educated at a grammar school, then Exeter and Kingston

Universities; taught at schools in Weybridge, Cobham, London and an international school in Thailand. Teaches maths and sport; thoughtful and said by a parent to be 'very warm, when you get to know him, and parental with the children'. Three adult children; interests include travel, various sports, theatre and playing the guitar.

Academic matters: Overall GCSE results (five A*-C including English and maths) variable – 2013, 65 per cent. High achievement for top set (2013, 93 per cent A*-B, 64 per cent A*/A) and very good value added, especially with weaker pupils. Course starts in summer term of year 9, all do three separate sciences; options include Spanish, business communication systems, drama, ICT, media studies, sports science, home economics, electronics; after-school French and Spanish classes mainly for children wishing to take a second foreign language, plus (non-examined) Latin. Smaller scholarship set accelerated from year 7, take English language and science six months early and can choose to add an extra two subjects, further maths and astronomy.

Recent ISI inspection's outstanding judgement for teaching and learning endorsed by our very enthusiastic year 6 tour guides: 'Exceptional teaching – they're not like teachers, more like guides. They know you so well they know how to explain things in a way you can understand...They really care about us and find it rewarding to see us develop'. Thorough-going tracking and monitoring.

Classes average 14 but can be smaller for GCSE, eg eight. Setting for core subjects from year 7. Strong on differentiated learning in and out of the classroom – lots of stretch for able mathematicians; science university visits; lively approaches in French, notably a delightful room furnished with bar, bistro-style chairs, tables and stools (très authentique); Spanish room has cheerful yellow and red round table; small physics lab and large, modern biology one. Very good ICT facilities – four suites including Apple Macs, laptops, well developed VLE, much use of interactive whiteboards.

Top-notch SENCo keen to promote understanding of learning difficulties throughout the school – assemblies given by pupils and visiting speakers – and to support families: will link up parents. We liked the posters of several well known people with dyslexia, dyspraxia and ADHD on display. Mostly covers dyslexia (all screened on entry, in class support from TAs, individual lessons cost £40/hour), ADHD, mild autism; would assess other needs at a visit to judge if school could meet them – probably not severe behavioural difficulties. Has regular contact with parents and lots of resources, trains up other staff. Year 6 nurture group receives extra support, kept together in year 7 as long as required.

Games, options, the arts: Only has a small Astro and use of junior school hall but makes use of Sheffield's excellent sports facilities and offers a vast range – the usual ones plus basketball, lacrosse, water sports, girls' football, horse riding and aerobics with zumba, climbing, skiing, golf, tae kwon do, cycling, plus sports leader qual – and high level coaching; two games afternoons a week – no couch potatoes here. Inclusive approach to school teams – fields several. Cross-country strong at city, county and (a girl) national levels, strong netball, hockey, badminton, a Yorkshire squad cricketer, UK reps in swimming, diving, golf, motor racing. Trips to see international matches, annual sports tour to, eg, Lanzarote, Barcelona, Malta.

Music very strong – four choirs, orchestra, rock (annual Rockfest), brass and jazz bands, lots of formal (carol service at Sheffield Cathedral) and informal concerts, plays at local festivals, tours to Prague (years 6-11), Belgium, well-supplied with guitars, ukuleles (15, no less) and software; members of the Sheffield Schools' wind band and composition classes. Some take GCSE in year 9.

Big productions – Oliver!, Joseph and His Technicolour Dreamcoat, The Dracula Spectacular – put on in junior school hall or a local theatre; also uses outdoor natural amphitheatre, The Dell. Plays and workshops from visiting professionals, including Dominic West; street dance workshop; older pupils assist with technical aspects of junior school plays. Good, varied art on display around school, some at local exhibitions, success in city and Saatchi Gallery competitions.

Wide range of activities – baking (runs open Easter cookery course), chess, bridge, French cinema, eco, geocaching, D of E, business challenge, annual architectural workshop day, science week with parental input; year 7s did critical thinking course run by Oxford University; supports various charities, eg football boots for Africa; community work; pupils come off timetable for a week to study all faiths and cultures (parents contribute). Lots of local educational visits, year 7 residential in North Yorkshire, year 8 week in the Outer Hebrides developing survival skills, expedition to Kilimanjaro, ski trip to Alps. Improved post-16 advice; year 10s do two weeks' work experience at start of year (as better choice of jobs then – very canny), often organising it themselves. Good links with local business community – hosts business breakfast networking event.

Background and atmosphere: The only all-through to 16 co-ed independent school in Sheffield, which has remarkably few of them. Founded 1885 as a school for 'the education of the children of Sheffield Gentlemen', in a private house; 1888 moved to larger premises in Westbourne Road, 1997 became co-ed, 2001 new co-ed senior school opened, with 2007 extension.

Original building houses years 9-11: undistinguished exterior but attractive, large, light classrooms, mosaics on hall floor and stained glass windows. Surprisingly modest library – pupils consulted about fiction choices and how to spend allocation: trad books versus electronic resources. Gracious, more recently acquired mid-19th century house for years 7-8 (thankfully not modernised by previous occupants, Radio Sheffield) with smaller classrooms and some narrow corridors. Years 7-8 have a playground, years 9-11 enjoy access to a very pleasant garden.

Comfortable, relaxed atmosphere related to small classes and good humoured, friendly teachers – 'They know the children very well and appreciate them for who they are...The children feel confident about their core selves'; 'They're very motivated, energetic, enthusiastic, compassionate, tuned into children'; 'They're very good at getting the positives out of a child and finding their talents – they don't give up on them,' say parents.

Academic achievement respected, not a source of embarrassment. Lots of leadership opportunities – traditional posts plus enterprising charity committee; school council's suggestions regarded. Food is controversial (no packed lunches): school puts thought and care into it and provides a decent choice – hot and veggie option plus salad bar, trad pudding with fresh fruit and yoghurts – but not all children and parents happy (school argues you will never get total satisfaction with this) and some mentioned long queuing times, though attempts made to minimise this. Small dining hall – year 10 and 11s have own café and year 11s allowed out in lunch hour. Parking very difficult.

Pastoral care and discipline: Focus on praise and rewards for a wide range of achievements – central plasma screen displaying weekly commendations; child-friendly prizes and outings. Bullying not seen as a problem but would be dealt with firmly and effectively. Small, bleak sick room.

Pupils and parents: Mostly from Sheffield, Rotheram and Derbyshire; mainly professional or business backgrounds, ethnically mixed. Happy, confident, polite, well-behaved children – impeccably focused in all the classes we visited.

Parents very happy too: they like the family atmosphere – 'Everyone knows everyone and the children form friendships across years'; the extra support for the less able and stretch for the very bright; pastoral care; traditional values and a curriculum that combines studying with enjoyable activities every day. Several opportunities to get involved – active PTA, parent and staff choir. Plenty of contact – school magazine, newsletters, email, termly surgery with head.

Old Westbournians: actor Dominic West, various distinguished sports people, eg 2012 Olympics swimmer.

Entrance: Non-selective – taster day with tests; wide ability range – overall above national average. Will take children at various stages, even, unusually, mid year 10 – in 2010 accepted a number of year 11 girls from a local independent school that closed down very suddenly and provided teaching for any GCSE subjects not usually offered.

Exit: Most go on to do A levels at the city's top state comprehensives (mainly Tapton and Notre Dame) or Birkdale (nearby independent school – two scholarships recently); a few to further ed college.

Money matters: Six scholarships for internal and external pupils – academic, music, sport, all-rounder – worth 10 per cent of fees; more than five per cent of pupils have bursaries.

Remarks: Its mixed ability intake and attention to the individual differentiates it from the other, selective independent schools in Sheffield. Has a long-standing reputation for fostering children who need extra nurturing, and is now proving it can achieve very strong results for the very able as well. Its close integration with its thriving junior school is an added advantage.

Westminster School

17 Dean's Yard, London, SW1P 3PB

- Pupils: 615 boys; 125 girls all in sixth form; 465 day boys, 145 boy boarders; 95 day girls, 30 girl boarders • Ages: 13–18 (but a few Westminster Assisted Places from 11, see below) • C of E
- Fees: Day £22,500–£24,390; Boarding £32,490; Queen's Scholars £16,245 pa • Independent

Tel: 020 7963 1003
Email: registrar@westminster.org.uk
Website: www.westminster.org.uk

Head Master: Since 2005, Dr Stephen Spurr DPhil, an Oxford and Sydney classicist (late fifties), married, one son, one daughter. Dr Spurr was previously head of Clifton College for five years, prior to which he was at Eton for 16 years, successively as head of classics and as housemaster. Dr Spurr holds one of the most coveted posts in independent education, one regarded with awe, even wariness, by some. It can be a high profile job, but the elegant and quietly-spoken Dr Spurr has been assiduously keeping out of the press. His headship involves daily interaction with, possibly, the most erudite, stimulating, challenging and entertaining community of pupils, staff and parents in the business. In measured, almost laconic, tones, he speaks of the excitement he feels at doing the job. His thoughtful, understated manner of expression leads some to finding him 'inscrutable', even 'humourless' but the manner conceals a deeply-felt commitment and warmth of feeling. 'I feel more attuned here than anywhere I have been,' he asserts and, manifestly, the Westminster ethos of the pleasure and value of learning for learning's sake is safe in his hands. 'We will, whatever it takes, stick with the intrinsic good of the academic life'.

Since his appointment, Dr Spurr has set about streamlining and tidying, intending to sharpen, rather than dilate, its focus on the life of the mind. His is a scholarly and purposeful vision – 'we will continue to innovate, expand, look outwards – not withdraw into Fortress Westminster ... Westminster is on the crest of the wave and we all know what happens to waves.' There is the sunbeam flash of a rare smile. 'Our job is to prepare young people as well as possible so that they are flexible for an international future – to be individuals without being individualistic, yoking their high intelligence to social responsibility'.

Eight years into his tenure, Dr Spurr's assiduity and dedication continue to impress.

He is retiring in July 2014. His successor will be Patrick Derham, currently head of Rugby School. He read history at Cambridge and has also been head of Solihull School. Married to Alison, a teacher, with two grown up children.

Academic matters: Second to none. Always in the top five of any league table, but that is a by-product of what goes on here. Syllabuses can be almost incidental, to the extent that a check needs to be made near exam time to ensure that the actual requirements of the course have been attended to as so much else has. Teachers teach from immense depth and breadth of knowledge of their subjects and far beyond. Many are acknowledged experts in their fields. This enthusiasm is met by that of their pupils who may not all be boffins but who have lively, questioning minds, turned on by the general buzz of the intellectual life on offer.

If you want convincing, in 2013, at GCSE, 86 per cent of subjects taken got A*. In the previous 15 years, 100 per cent of subjects achieved A*-C in all but three years (it was 99 per cent in those). All GCSE subjects, and some others, can be taken to A level or Cambridge Pre-U and these results are equally impressive. In 2013, over 50 per cent of subjects taken achieved A* or the Pre-U equivalent (grades D1 and D2), close to 100 per cent getting A*-B (nearly all take four A levels or Pre-Us, and many five). Most popular are maths (massive), history (nearly so), sciences, English and economics. There are equal numbers of Latin and French takers and languages are always strong. German, so sadly moribund elsewhere, taught in part via poetry and song. Theatre studies, electronics, music and RE are taken by minorities as exam subjects but all have lively profiles on the extra-curricular side of life. Pupils sit the Pre-U in all classical and modern languages, English, art history and art. In all other subjects they sit A levels

Everyone does DT and electronics in year nine and school owns an electron microscope in its up-to-the-minute labs. Computerised projection system in all classrooms, whiteboards for mathematicians. Each dept has a supply of laptops available on demand. The library – in a stunning set of rooms – is open until 9.00pm and has its own much-praised website. Overall teacher:pupil ratio of one to eight. Recent injection of young teachers appreciated by Westminsters who also revere their sages. Some teachers seen as 'wacky and inspirational' rather than efficient but, of most, we are told, 'nothing is too much trouble'.

Dr Spurr looked bemused at the thought that anyone with the right kind of intellectual capacity might be denied a place because of an SEN eg mild or moderate dyspraxia – 'there's no problem'. Study skills coordinator sees all who need support, whether the super-bright but chaotic or those with a dys. All pupils provided for on a case by case basis. 'I believe that as you go through the academic life you move from one level of learning to another,' says the head. 'Our study skills co-coordinator helps everyone think about the skills needed to empower their learning at different stages.'

Games, options, the arts: The Westminster extra-curricular programme, extraordinary by universal consent, is impossible to encapsulate here and is much enhanced by the contribution of the academic staff who offer activities founded on their private enthusiasms. It is further embellished by a unique list of outside speakers. Recent visitors include Rowan Williams, Simon Singh, Martin Rees, Christopher Ricks, Colin Thubron, Tony Benn, David Ramsbottom, Margaret Hodge, Oliver Letwin, George Galloway, Robert Fisk, Jon Snow. There are evening concerts given by the like of Ian Bostridge, Imogen Cooper, Felicity Lott. If Westminster parents sometimes niggle that their children do not go out into London sufficiently that is because London comes to them. There are esoteric trips everywhere – to Iceland for plate tectonics, to New York for art, to the Crimea for rock climbing, Venice to row in the regatta and to Chios for classicists and on and on.

The arts are privileged and more so since the acquisition, in 2002, of the Millicent Fawcett Hall, now an excellent flexible studio theatre and, in 2005, the opening of the Manoukian Music Centre – an ex-army drill hall with recital room, teaching and practice rooms and recording studios. Outstanding music and drama and school mounts productions of eg Mozart and Weill operas to professional standards. Drama taught throughout school. Art, too, is breathtakingly good – four studio areas, a traditional printing press and much emphasis on the traditional skills – people can draw and paint here. Other options, reflecting the staff's eclecticism, include bookbinding, Warhammer, languages, board games, D of E, jazz, philosophy, carpentry, comic films etc. Debating is famously strong. PHAB, like other community service projects, gets enthusiastic participation.

Games (known as 'station') played vigorously and joyously and with stunning success in, particularly, rowing (winners of the Fawley Cup at Henley in 2009, runners up in 2010 and quarter-finalists in 2011), cricket (winning eight out of 13 matches in 2011) and cross country (London Schools champions). There have also been successes in football, fencing, netball and fives. Sporting opportunities are multifarious but no-one would claim world class sportiness for Westminster overall. Games mostly played on the surprisingly large playing fields in nearby Vincent Square and in 2012, the school acquired a large sports centre adjacent to these playing fields which used to be one of the Royal Horticultural Halls.

Background and atmosphere: The history of Westminster reads like the history of England and its list of Old Westminsters is a list of main players in that story. The thousands of tourists who tramp the precincts of Westminster Abbey must be startled to see knots of vaguely uniformed teenagers comfortably chatting round about Dean's Yard – the adjacent grassy square. They would need to peer through the inconspicuous archway that leads into Little Dean's Yard – the school's central quad – to find the hotch-potch of houses that form the nucleus of the school.

Westminster began in 1179 and has been in continuous existence since the fourteenth century. Elizabeth I bestowed royal patronage upon it in 1560 and is celebrated as the school's official foundress. The abbey is its chapel – an astonishing privilege in itself. Many meals are eaten in College Hall – a medieval room with coats of arms, portraits of former heads and wonderful painted corbels under a beamed ceiling – in which the abbots and monks gathered to eat in the early years of the abbey. It is an integral part of the deanery and adjacent to the Jerusalem Chamber. School has, of course, its own argot and it can be mystifying. Also its own traditions – ask about 'The Greaze'.

The school buildings have been built, acquired and developed over the centuries, most of them abutting Little Dean's Yard, the houses named after revered and redoubtable former housemasters and Old Boys. They include a series of rooms in the beautiful Ashburnham House which make up the library – a national monument in itself. The quiet streets round about provide outposts, all only minutes away. These include the girls' boarding house, in the Georgian silence of Barton Street (opposite T E Lawrence's former house), the Robert Hooke Science building on the far side of Smith Square, the theatre and music

centres and the Weston Building on Dean's Yard which provides airy, spacious new teaching rooms in a very Westminster mix of modern technology, cornicing, panelling and parquetry. The latest acquisition is a former monastery building in Tufton Street (next to the main site in Dean's Yard) which is now a house called Purcell's for boarding girls and day boys.

Girls arrived in the sixth form in 1973 and are much valued though there are no plans to include them lower down the school. Dr Spurr appreciates how a Westminster sixth form works for both sexes – 'the girls' results are the highest nationally, they thrive on our debating style of teaching and the boys pick up on their work ethic'. The Westminster sixth form life is relaxed and collaborative. A pupil told us, 'people make their own relationship with the school which the teachers respect... problems are worked out through a kind of bantering interaction with the teachers'.

Boarding recently upgraded. All rooms are now comfortable and most are well-appointed. Many are surprisingly spacious and, of course, have views over the abbey, school or college buildings and gardens. Younger boys in rooms of between two and eight and all pupils have their own rooms in the last three years. Thumb print recognition or key pad entry systems. Good kitchens, common rooms, games rooms and sensible, relaxed discipline maintained by resident housemasters (male or female are called this), many of whom have young families on site. All boarders in the lower school (up to the age of 16) go home every weekend. Some sixth form boarders stay at school at weekends but the school is very quiet on Saturday nights.

Overseas numbers remain small though Dr Spurr sees Westminster in a global context in interesting ways. 'We're not dragging in pupils from abroad but we need to see ourselves as a world-wide school competing with the best pupils from everywhere. I'm interested in links with the top academic schools worldwide and in learning what they do educationally. That's where our future competition for university places will increasingly come from – rather than from UK schools.'

Pastoral care and discipline: Famously relaxed and liberal as has been felt appropriate in a school which thrives on the individuality of its members. Dr Spurr has undertaken to smarten up his charges, much as he has restructured the school's top management – on similar principles – 'my belief is that there is some link between form and content... management should take care of things to allow housemasters and teachers to concentrate on their core activities... I like pupils to show a little more respect for school dress and I like them to look reasonably tidy in Abbey'. To our seasoned eye, however, Westminster pupils look much as they have ever done and shirts seem to not to stay tucked in for long. Girls have a dress code – plain colours, no denim, jackets rather than jumpers since '08, etc. Some staff grumbles about meetings and 'directives' and a less-than-accessible head. Times are clearly changing – our guess is for the better, overall.

No serious drugs-related disciplinary incidents in Dr Spurr's reign thus far. 'I'm probably more concerned with alcohol than drugs but I believe in taking a firm line.' The approach is very much to educate and to involve parents, establishing a collaborative and supportive home/school relationship. 'We have a disciplined system which, if it is to be fair, has to be consistent... you've got to keep talking to your young but, whereas we would look at infringements on a case by case basis, we can't be individualistic at the expense of the school community'.

Maybe not individualistic but individuals really count here and great efforts are made to support and nurture those taken into the school fold – sometimes at unconventional times in their careers. Pastoral care, not always the school's strength, now impressive and it's hard to fall through the net. Some parents feel that, for girls, the pastoral side 'has a bit of a hole in it'. One said, 'I don't think they really take on board that girls have certain issues', and some take longer to settle in than others, though the boarders have a cosy nest in their homely house. The tutor system, at its best, is supportive and comradely though 'some tutors are not really involved and are pretty useless,' we were told. 'People who are thought likely to get into trouble are allocated to really good tutors.'

Pupils and parents: 'We are more metropolitan and cosmopolitan than most public schools,' says Dr Spurr. Most pupils come from moneyed and clever families resident in London but originating everywhere, so many languages spoken at home. Only a quarter boards and most of those are Londoners with busy-busy families. Very few from really far away – Russia, China etc. Pupils are quirky, sparky, irreverent, natural sceptics, though seldom 'cynical' as reported in the rhapsodic 2006 ISI inspection report. They are articulate, endlessly intellectually curious, creative, individual, challenging in the best sense. Their parents, many of whom are active in supporting the school, know exactly what it is they are paying for and love it – 'it's fantastic'.

Former pupils (Old Westminsters) include some rotters, for example most of the officers in command during 'the disaster in the Crimea' such as Lord Lucan. Also Kim Philby. But then there are also Ben Jonson, George Herbert, John Dryden, John Locke, Christopher Wren, Robert Hooke, Henry Purcell, Charles Wesley, Earl Howe, Warren Hastings, Edward Gibbon, Jeremy Bentham, GA Henty, AA Milne (who vastly endowed the school), Adrian Boult, John Gielgud, Angus Wilson, Norman Parkinson, Andrew Huxley, Peter Ustinov, Flanders and Swann and, still with us, Tony Benn, Peter Brook, Nigel Lawson, Roger Norrington, Corin Redgrave, Andrew Lloyd Webber, Stephen Poliakoff, Helena Bonham-Carter, Ruth Kelly, Imogen Stubbs, Louis Theroux, Dido and Mika etc etc.

Entrance: Register your son by the end of year 5 for 13+ entry. He will be screened in the autumn of year 6 – ISEB computer tests in maths, English and VR and interview – places conditional on CE performance offered thereafter. At least 70 per cent expected. Further interview at 13 – 'we like it as it opens the teacher/pupil dialogue'. Alternative method of entry is the Challenge – a competitive exam for scholarship places. Those who don't win scholarships may be offered places with other financial help if they do well enough. Around 400 are seen at 11 when conditional offers for the 120 places are made. Boys and girls applying for 16+ places must register by the October before entry. Offers based on interview, tests and meeting GCSE requirements.

Exit: Some 45 per cent annually to Oxbridge and, now, about five per cent to Ivy League, though pupils stress, 'they make a big deal about not going to Oxbridge if it's not for you – they try to educate the parents that it's OK if we want to go somewhere else.' Most of the rest to Bristol, UCL, Imperial, LSE, Edinburgh, Warwick, Durham. Principal degree subjects history, economics, PPE, management, maths, languages, medicine. But they go everywhere and study everything to distinguished levels.

Money matters: Eight Queen's scholarships annually worth 50 per cent of the boarding fee and scholars must board. Music scholarship worth 25 per cent of the day or boarding fee at 13+. Means tested bursaries of up to 100 per cent of fees. Expensive trips highly subsidised by school when appropriate.

Remarks: For the right boy or girl, simply the best.

Westminster Tutors

Linked school: David Game College

86 Old Brompton Road, London, SW7 3LQ

- Pupils: 45 • Ages: 14–99 • Fees: £18,600–£21,600 pa
- Independent

Tel: 020 7584 1288
Email: info@westminstertutors.co.uk
Website: www.westminstertutors.co.uk

Head: Since 2007, Ms Virginia Maguire BA MLitt (early forties). Was previously director of studies at David Game College, and lectured at a Thai university for five years, publishing articles on sociolinguistics and aspects of Thai culture. She read English at UCL and gained distinction in her MLitt in English Studies from Strathclyde University. Her own mother took her A levels at Westminster Tutors. As well as running the college, she acts as SENCo, teaches English and delivers the PSHE programme.

Academic matters: This is a tiny organisation with some 50 pupils altogether, most of whom are taking or retaking A levels. The retakers – who may be there for a term or a year – are often high achievers who narrowly missed a place at a top university, and may be adding on another A level to improve their chances next time. Those who come for the full two year course tend to be attracted by the very individual attention. 'A lot of students who haven't coped well in a big school setting do well with us.' There is also a very small number – some five in all – taking or retaking GCSEs.

In spite of its size, the college offers a wide range of subjects, ranging from Greek to law to physics, by dint of having a large pool of freelance tutors it can call on, many of them Oxbridge graduates. These may be students working on PhDs, musicians, writers or experienced teachers moving towards retirement who want to keep their hand in. 'I will try to find someone to teach anything – I keep an eye out for what we are likely to need.' A large proportion of lessons are one-to-one, and each student has an individual timetable: drawing these up to suit teachers and students is a fiendishly complicated exercise.

Around a third of students have special needs of one sort or another, mostly dyslexia. The one-to-one system also copes admirably with, for example, the very bright girl with Asperger's who likes being immersed in two-hour-long lessons, and the boy with ADHD who works best in short bursts, including supervised homework sessions. 'It's like having one's own private tutor,' said the parent of a pupil who had floundered elsewhere, 'but in a friendly college setting.' 'My daughter's motivated at last,' said another. 'She's actually keen to go to school and to get on with her homework.' The school has links with an educational psychologist, and will adapt teaching according to her reports, but cannot cope with severe behavioural problems.

Exam results are highly creditable for such a mixed, totally non-selective intake. 2013 saw 40 per cent A*/A at GCSE and 81 per cent A*-B, 46 per cent A*/A at A level.

The college also offers private tuition for mature students who, for example, want to study medicine and need science A levels, helps with Common Entrance exams, and specialises in preparing outside students for Oxbridge, medical and law school applications. The head originally set up Uniprep as a separate company, but it is now merged with the college. She specialises in medicine and dentistry preparation plus LNAT, and her Oxbridge graduate tutors provide preparation for their respective degree courses. The college also runs half term and holiday revision courses. 'We work very well across the spectrum from special needs to very bright.'

W

Games, options, the arts: Art and photography are both A level options. Students visit the linked David Game College in Notting Hill to use their facilities, either joining an existing group there or forming their own. A 'wonderful art teacher' provides enrichment classes as well as taking history of art students for fortnightly gallery visits. The college is handy for the South Kensington museums and for theatre trips.

Sport is not a high priority, but the college does field a five-a-side football team, and weekly sport sessions are held at Chelsea Leisure Centre on the King's Road. One ping pong table – being used as a desk when we visited. Because of lack of space and facilities, the college cannot offer drama, dance, PE or media studies courses.

Background and atmosphere: The college was founded in 1934 and is one of the oldest tutorial colleges in the country. It is now one of the David Game group of colleges, which includes some 25 institutions in the UK and overseas.

It is based in two adjoining townhouses near South Kensington tube, and most of the space is decidedly compact. Staff and students share a common-room. 'We're really small so we all mix in together.' Library, IT room, physics room and biology practical room that decidedly resembles a small kitchen (chemistry students use the labs at David Game College in Notting Hill).

Pastoral care and discipline: All students have personal tutors – one of these 'is brilliant with wayward boys: we give him the younger ones who need to be constantly chivvied'. But the head is the personal tutor for the A2 students, supporting them through UCAS, as well as being the main point of contact for all parents. 'If parents have any concerns they always deal directly with me.'

Non-attendance at any lesson is swiftly followed by a phone call – first to the student then, if they don't reply, to a parent. But otherwise the atmosphere is informal: 'We're not oppressive about rules. It's easier to have a cooperative environment'. Students organise dinners or parties, with the head boy and girl in charge of younger pupils; only over-18s are allowed to drink alcohol. Bad behaviour unlikely to go further than a recent incident of older students placing bets for younger ones at a shop down the road. 'A warning is usually as bad as it gets. If I'm cross they know why.'

Pupils and parents: Eclectic mix of those with special needs and others who have not thrived in the rough-and-tumble of larger, more traditional establishments, combined with high achievers who come for the expert teaching.

Entrance: By interview with the head. 'We talk about what they are doing now, what they are hoping to do, their university goals. I look at their results so far and their school reports. But we're non-selective academically, and my main criteria are whether they are going to be happy, suit our way of teaching and fit into the college. We don't want to upset the harmonious atmosphere here.' She will not take students who have been expelled elsewhere for serious behavioural problems, drug or drinking offences, but will probably turn a blind eye to one-off misdemeanours, and rarely turns people down. 'But sometimes I can sense attitude problems, and I might not be so encouraging about them coming here.'

Exit: Over 95 per cent to higher education, ranging from anthropology at Durham to nuclear engineering at Birmingham and dentistry at King's College London. One to Oxbridge in 2013, 57 per cent to Russell Group universities. Advice is always geared towards find a course appropriate for the student. 'Some students are not suited to university, but I would always try to direct them to some sort of higher education. I try very hard to find a course that's right for them, which may have a very practical bent for someone with severe dyslexia.'

Money matters: As one would imagine, the one-to-one staff:student ratio does not come cheap. However, fees are comparable with other tutorial colleges that have much larger classes. Up to four A level scholarship places. A few statemented pupils funded by LAs.

Remarks: Has developed a niche providing one-to-one teaching for gifted students with special needs, and also helps prepare potential medics and Oxbridge candidates. The rest come because they are attracted to the cosy, friendly, supportive atmosphere, 'and you can be sure they getting the best chance to achieve,' commented a parent.

Westonbirt School

Linked school: Westonbirt Prep School

Westonbirt, Tetbury, Gloucestershire, GL8 8QG

- Pupils: 230 girls; 150 boarders, 80 day • Ages: 11–18 • C of E
- Fees: Day £16,950–£20,880; Boarding £25,305–£32,985 pa
- Independent

Tel: 01666 880333
Email: pstevenson@westonbirt.org
Website: www.westonbirt.org

Head: Since January 2013, Mrs Natasha Dangerfield BA (forties), previously deputy head and head of boarding at Harrogate Ladies' College. Studied PE and English at University of Brighton followed by a diploma in sports psychology at University of Newcastle. Prior to Harrogate Ladies' she taught at North Foreland Lodge, Downe House and was director of pastoral care at Gordonstoun School. During Mrs Dangerfield's time at Harrogate Ladies' College she oversaw significant developments in balancing the academic and pastoral needs of the school.

Outside school she is a county lacrosse coach and enjoys spending time with her family, keeping fit, walking, reading, travelling and cooking. She is married with three young children.

Academic matters: Rigour has taken hold across the curriculum but still lots of nurturing: plenty of 'late bloomers' thanks to small classes throughout and a 'tried and tested' learning support department. Inevitable seepage (for a variety of reasons) at 16 is more than counterbalanced by increasing numbers of girls arriving for sixth. Numbers opting for harder subjects have grown in recent years. Notwithstanding, the percentage of A*-B grades at A level has levelled out around a respectable 60-70 per cent (in 2013, 55 per cent A*/B and 36 per cent A*/A). Flexible timetable allows for unusual subject combinations. Sciences doing particularly well – biology and chemistry (75 per cent A grades) lead the way but English and maths more than hold their own. Art continues to flourish, Latin survives to GCSE with the occasional candidate at A level; languages have regained some popularity – year 9 girls recently wrote and performed their own French plays. A programme that is developed around an exciting 'Skills for Life' programme supports Saturday morning school and sixth form are given an optional independent study morning.

Most parents thrilled at daughters' progress. In past four years, the percentage of girls achieving five or more A*-C grades at GCSE (including English and maths) has increased from 71 per cent to almost 100 per cent – quite an achievement given the numbers receiving learning support. In 2013, 40 per cent A*/A grades at GCSE. We observed an English lesson with some strident year 11 girls who were articulate and mature in their analysis of each others' contributions to a commendably interactive lesson. Teachers appear 'on side' here, giving plenty of praise and encouragement. Displays are better than in many senior schools and help to create a positive learning environment. A level historians we observed looked set for good results and knew their stuff, as did the sixth form geographers we saw studying the effects of monsoon climate (except that the 'stuff' of geography is no longer about knowing where places are). By the time we reached the professional-looking chemists we were completely out of our league, so we didn't try our luck with questions there.

Twenty per cent receive some form of learning support. Close liaison with prep school SENCo. Initial screening to ensure none escape radar. Many come with psychological report and range from a very few 'almost non-readers' to girls needing relatively little individual help. Three in successful, caring department; dyslexia-trained staff deliver up to four 35 minute lessons a week according to need. Emphasis may be on reading, spelling, short-term recall etc. School can handle mild Aspergers or dyspraxia within limits. Girls are not taken out of mainstream lessons for learning support and therefore feel no stigma. All staff trained in differentiation, which includes stretching gifted and talented in all lessons.

Games, options, the arts: Highly successful in sport, especially lacrosse (coach is ex-international); all girls enjoy superb outdoor and indoor facilities. Early morning training demonstrates girls' great commitment. Triennial lacrosse tour to USA a highlight for many. All play lax to year 11 then around 50 seniors continue and generally reach national finals; similar numbers opt for tennis (year-round coaching available). Netball, rounders and hockey all get a look in. New tennis and golf academies. Own nine-hole golf course. Swanky new sports hall includes heated 25 metre pool and fitness/aerobics suites upstairs with viewing gallery – facility plays host to several hundred locals each week which helps to finance its high overheads (offered free of charge to local state primaries thereby earning charity status brownie points). No stabling for horses here but polo (girls play by arrangement with Beaufort Polo Club) and riding are particular favourites.

Art department boasts two large studios and makes its creative presence felt around the school. When we visited, year 10 were inspired by Van Gogh (having just visited the Royal Academy exhibition). Westonbirt was one of the first two schools to pioneer the Leith's Food and Wine course and its popularity is as great as ever – nearly all sixth formers participate over five terms to gain the coveted certificate, which provides access to jobs (particularly useful for gappers) on the Leith's list. Some outstanding musicians here and a really impressive programme of orchestral and choral concerts – 'it's cool to be in the choir now,' say girls. 'I never knew my daughter could sing,' crooned one mother. New music technology centre with keyboards, Apple hardware and a teaching station, a studio and an ensemble room. Drama also very strong. Lunch-time current affairs sessions for sixth formers help to broaden political horizons. D of E is popular and is offered at bronze and gold award levels.

Background and atmosphere: Few schools match the setting of Westonbirt: a magnificent neo-Renaissance pile built for ludicrously wealthy Holford family (who also founded nearby arboretum) at height of Victorian expansionism. Belongs to Allied Schools group (includes Stowe and Harrogate Ladies' amongst its five members). Girl guiding a strong influence in early years and some traditions survive: eg vespers sung whilst stood around edge of Great Hall. Christian life important but not dominant – Sunday chapel (on site) is still compulsory for boarders. Imbued with excellent taste, Robert Holford spared no expense here, and since the school opened in 1928 they have been worthy custodians of the grade 1 listed building and ornamental gardens, not to mention 250 acres of parkland.

Library has recently been renovated (thanks to deep pockets of some worthy old girls) with exquisite pelmets re-fashioned at Royal School of Needlework and wall fabric hand-dyed to match original colour. Adjacent reading room is next for the top drawer make-over. Some dorms are exquisite with plum billet in Lady Holford's boudoir: individual dressing tables here not just wardrobes. Girls' lasting memories tend to be of delightful gardens rather than of marble columns or frescoes. All sixth formers have personal study bedrooms, and their boarding provision has been much improved by a recent Cotswold stone fronted addition. Classrooms in the converted stables are in the process of receiving a much needed makeover; newer Francis Rawes building accommodates science, IT, art and DT not to mention the multi-use lecture room. Camelia House has been exquisitely refurbished (period drama producers please note) and provides a pre-Raphaelite backdrop for informal concerts.

Friendly atmosphere throughout; good balance of male and female teachers who put up with a cramped staff room – 'money goes to the children,' quipped one colleague over coffee. More girls studying in sixth has definitely improved the work ethic since we last visited. Lots of trips and activities for all ages with special events thick on the ground. Some girls would like more contact with boys' schools but sixth formers were preparing for a dinner debate with Abingdon when we visited and had just been to Eton for Scottish reels.

Pastoral care and discipline: Former is effective to a level where latter is now a rarity. Senior girls tend to defuse potential difficulties in many cases. Beaufort house provides haven for girls in year 7; three houses for 12-16 year olds with designated (mainly non-teaching) pastoral staff. Housemistresses often assigned other responsibilities, and parents praise 'mature approach' of house staff and say that moving girls around helps to ensure there are no major friendship issues. Academic tutor makes up trio of carers for each girl. Sixth form includes prefects ('Study One') who operate from summer term in year 12 until start of A levels. Counsellor comes regularly to lend confidential support; 'star' of a chaplain whom girls 'really trust'. Active approach to Christianity involves girls taking a lead but religion is not rammed down throats. Qualified nursing staff operate sanatorium 24/7. School likes ISCO careers support and believes in girls getting a wide range of work experience: '10 different sorts if possible,' said head of careers. Fines for rare instances of smoking (part of growing up); glass of wine permitted to sixth formers on special occasions but never spirits; tough on drugs. Night-time high jinks avoided by alarmed doors and night watchmen who patrol the grounds. Parents say that any problem is 'dealt with properly.'

Pupils and parents: 'Turns out polished and lovely girls,' beamed one parent. 'Not immaculate' and more down to earth than you'd expect – no riffraff but many families are making 'huge sacrifices'. Appeals to a broad cross-section of girls, mainly within a two hour travelling radius but increasing numbers of Londoners board here, and other enclaves of boarding families have sprung up in Cornwall and Wales; fewer overseas pupils these days (ceiling is now 25 per cent, we were told, which belied some parental observations but, says school, is absolutely true). Sociable, hearty girls in the main who enjoy the atmosphere and sporting opportunities. Some shrinking violets (present head girl admitted to having started in this category) who blossom over time. 'No naughtiness now,' claimed senior girls who 'get cross' if girls step out of line. Reading is part of the culture, as is throwing oneself into all aspects of school life. Percentage of boarders increases as girls move through school. Day girls can sleep over once a week for free and some buy extra nights to be with friends. Many 'convert' as a result of trying out boarding this way. Girls who leave at 16 sometimes live to regret their decision (and even return). Overseas pupils benefit from effective ELT teaching and bring an extra dimension; many short-term

W

German pupils want to stay longer if it can be arranged. Famous old girls include children's author Georgia Byng (Molly Moon series), TV's Hotel Inspector Ruth Watson, TV producer Patricia Llewellyn (Two Fat Ladies, Jamie Oliver), and socialites Lady Emily Compton, Lady Sybilla Hart and Lady Natasha Rufus-Isaacs.

Entrance: Common entrance at 11 and 13; own exam for those outside CE system and for sixth formers outside of GCSE system (otherwise minimum 5+ GCSEs at A*-C are needed). Most Westonbirt Prep girls proceed here at 11+; local primaries also provide some day girls. Beaudesert Park and St Margaret's, Calne have been favourites alongside Leaden Hall and Godstowe but net is being cast wider and wider it seems. Regular visits to Garden House to recruit from 'the smoke'. Daughters of clergy still receive a 30 per cent bursary. Educational psychologist's report if special needs – girls are only turned away if really unable to cope. Overseas pupils increasingly from Europe rather than Far East with German and Spanish girls coming for between one term and two years.

Exit: About half the sixth form leavers take a gap year. Most sixth formers proceed to reputable universities (for subjects including medicine and veterinary science) from Aberystwyth to Warwick and Winchester. Good HE advice ensures sixth formers make realistic choices and advice continues after they leave.

Money matters: Scholarships and exhibitions offered at 11, 13 and 16 include academic, art, drama, sport and music. Five per cent sibling reductions; more for Forces, diplomatic and clergy daughters. Extras include ballet, learning support and golf.

Remarks: Has got even better since our last visit with a more viable sixth form and greatly improved recreational facilities. 'If you want a small boarding school you can't beat it – miles ahead of others we looked at,' said satisfied parents of a year 8 boarder. 'My daughter has found it brilliant,' said another mother. A tight but happy ship and girls flourish in a setting which is second to none.

Whitgift School

Haling Park, South Croydon, Surrey, CR2 6YT

- Pupils: 1,373 boys; 69 boarders • Ages: 10–18 • Non-denom
- Fees: Day £16,356; Boarding £26,342–£31,500 pa • Independent

Tel: 020 8688 9222
Email: admissions@whitgift.co.uk
Website: www.whitgift.co.uk

Head: Since 1991, Dr Christopher A Barnett MA (Oxon) DPhil (Oxon) (late fifties), who has 'no intention of retiring at 60... take another generation of youngsters through... love it'. He runs the school with an eight-strong senior management team. A historian, he read modern history at Oriel, followed by a somewhat esoteric doctorate (also in history) whilst acting as research assistant for Nigel Fisher (then MP for Surbiton). By age 21, Dr Barnett was lecturing at Brunel University in economics, thence to teaching: nine years at Bradfield where he became head of history, followed by Dauntsey's as second master. He lives with his physiotherapist wife, who works at the nearby Mayday Hospital, in the grounds behind the Tudor wood. They have three sons, all educated at Whitgift, and one daughter.

Tall, commanding, full of initiative (addressing a complaint that 'he was often away,' he said he was 'pretty much ever present but sometimes away with large groups of Whitgift students'). He has both raised the intellectual bar and increased numbers in the school and his building/re-building programme is unlike any this editor has ever seen. New boarding house, new gym, new magical swimming pool, huge fencing salle, old gym has been turned into an impressive new Performing Arts Centre. The school hosted the Mary Rose exhibition in 2010 with over 32,000 visitors, and the car park was a bit muddly when we visited 'but (this was second week September – referring to the car park) all this will be changed next week'. Keen racing man (sticks and flat – often buys yearlings); his colours echo the school yellow and blue and nags are named Whitgift Rose, Whitgift Rock etc – has been known to bring Phar Too Gifted and Quick Whitted to school à la Red Rum. Charming, less extrovert than you might imagine, his educational vision should be cloned and marketed.

Academic matters: GCSE for all until first form sixth, when pupils opt for A levels (60 per cent of grades awarded in 2013 were A* or A), IB (straight or bilingual) or BTECh after mega consultation. Three sciences, maths, two English for all and two langs for most at GCSE: overall 44 per cent A*, with 72 boys gaining all A* or A grades in 2013. Occasional glitch in geography; French surprisingly underwhelming; classics (and to A level), Spanish, German, Italian, Arabic, Mandarin and 'the biggest Japanese dept in the country'. Russian on the cards. Bi-lingual programme – French, German and Spanish: Jstore and Factiva (French and Italian newsmags) available in the library plus on-line foreign lang news throughout). Foreign langs dept based in 'rue de Folkestone and Rheinstrasse'; native speakers, oodles of trips and exchanges. Enormous and vibrant science dept linked to DT and some rather trendy goodies on display – more Arkwright Design Technology Scholarships have been won by Whitgift than by any other school. Computer rooms all over, linked in every dimension and lap tops for all. IB results well above 'global average'; bold decision, seems to be working. Regular trickle doing PE at all standards.

Class sizes average 18 (10 in the sixth form) with 25 maximum, some setting in maths, science and langs. Staff mostly young(ish) – said to 'be under 30' – though not the ones we met, with 40 per cent women, 140 staff, plus 'peris' and 100 on the support side; heads of departments 'have a say in staff appointments'. School is serious about special needs, and particularly hot on dyslexia. SENCo, plus three assistants, either one-to-one or groups, well-used drop-in centre, with after-school clinics: 'teachers especially helpful during exam time,' said our guide. Help for the ablest as well as those with problems (no bored boys here). No charge. School has open access, currently none in wheelchairs; staff wear special mikes when they teach two deaf students (and head mutters darkly about the embarrassment of 'forgetting to take the mike off and discussing something scurrilous outside assembly').

Games, options, the arts: Sport exceptional: 27 rugby sides – including an E team – 20 cricket teams and 16 hockey teams. Win county and national competitions in rugby, cricket, hockey and fencing, and are local honchos in athletics, swimming and football. Cricket strong, with expert coaching, and possibly the longest nets in the country. Surrey CCC holds a Cricket Festival Week and four-day, first-class game at the school. Table tennis, golf, water polo and pentathlon all produce champions. Fabulous £9m sports complex – for many years a pipe dream – now open: 'one of the wonders of the educational world!' says head. Development includes indoor pool, four squash courts with moveable walls, fitness centre, conference room, kitchens, classrooms, plus vast sports hall (seating for 1600). Eton and Millfield eat your hearts out: this is truly international stuff and was used as a training facility during the Olympics – modern pentathlon, swimming, fencing. Astro pitch on site. Sports department open at 6.45 am (breakfast said to be worth it) and the list of sporting achievements legendary.

Exciting music with mass of orchestras, choirs, chamber groups, bands plus Whitgift's own Corps of Drums. No pipes. Free compulsory lessons for all their first term – no particular bias: 'if we need strings, they learn strings, if we are short on brass they learn brass'. Some amazing success stories. The gifted attend Saturday lessons at Trinity College of Music or the Royal Academy of Music and are members of the National Youth Orchestra. Whitgift hosts the Croydon Music Festival, the London Mozart Players are regulars: organising masterclasses, commissioning music and providing performance opportunities for pupils. Beauty and the Beast for all this year. Drama dept now re-located in old swimming pool – ginormous space (with massive storage underneath).

We were taken to task for admitting that we felt art was less 'in yer face' than we had expected – given the superlatives we use elsewhere – and indeed the art room had a strong and purposeful air, but stuff on show was more mundane than some we have seen – though it was the second week of term. History of art apparently not constrained by the nanny net (think Titian, think Botticelli). Pottery and photographic facilities are super, with textile design an add-on.

Regular Arts Festivals with an impressive collection of performers, plus political conferences; and, last year, a bilingual conference 'under the auspices of the French Presidency of the European Union and co-hosted by the French Ambassador'. Overseas expeditions for musicians, linguists, sportsmen and adventurers. CCF for all, outdoor pursuits and D of E on offer. Many and varied community service projects. Bonding trip for all lower firsts (ten-year-olds) for a week in Lake Garda which includes culture (Verona, Venice et al as well as mountain walking and sailing). Every three years 800 boys go to the French Alps, the Italian Lakes on an international study programme during term time. No charge.

Background and atmosphere: Founded 1596 by John Whitgift, Archbishop of Canterbury in the time of Queen Elizabeth I and endowed with, apparently, most of the land in the centre of Croydon (including the Whitgift Centre). The school has had a chequered career, changing name and location several times over the past 400 years before moving to Haling Park (one-time home of Lord Howard of Effingham, Lord High Admiral of the fleet sent against the Armada) in 1931. The immaculately-groomed 45 acre oasis is bordered by seriously posh pads on one side and gritty central Croydon thoroughfare on other. Glorious red brick (think Basil Spence) with panelled interiors and old masters and school photographs in almost equal measure. Grounds contain a three acre site of scientific interest.

Some eccentric touches. Prefects range around in royal purple gowns. Legendary central quad has topiary in shape of red squirrels (their furry counterparts are bred in cages here – they were due to be released into the wild in 2009, but the dreaded squirrel virus put paid to that scheme and more resilient Asian version is currently being bred) and rampaging peacocks (soothing to look at until they open their mouths: 'they can be a pain during exams,' said one boy: and one particularly vicious hen had a bash at this editor's face – glasses protected a full frontal assault). Fantastic new water gardens, replete with pink flamingos and exotic ducks, opened by Sir David Attenborough, two or three local junior schools visit each week for a touchy-feely experience. Junior section separated from main school buildings. Compact dining room serves the boys who eat in two shifts. Huge charitable commitment, including SNAP – in-house respite care – which operates at Whitgift during the summer holidays, plus charity comedy night and a musical extravaganza.

Boarding introduced in 2013 and proving popular with families from abroad.

Pastoral care and discipline: This is an Anglican Foundation, complete with in-house chaplain. The headmaster must be a confirmed member of the Church of England and the Archbishop of Canterbury is, ex officio, head of the Foundation, however all faiths welcome, with a 'bungalow' (aka the Spirituality Centre) set aside for prayers, no apparent lip service paid to other faiths' holy days. 'We are a light touch Anglican Foundation,' said the head. Zero tolerance of drugs. 'Head is big on discipline,' said the boys. Bullying, alcohol, dyed hair, 'excessive laziness' – all forbidden. Pro-active bullying strategy. Boys tend to arrive early (breakfast served from 7.30am) and leave at 3.45pm, unless they have sporting commitments at school, though the gates have been 'known to be open well after midnight'. Complicated house/tutorial system: eight senior houses and eight junior houses, tinies allocated a house on arrival, ditto a tutor, and there is a mentoring system. Heads of year cover two years, with assistant heads and tutors. Next intake doubles size of year, also allotted houses. Theft equals out.

Pupils and parents: Pretty good social mix thanks to bursary scheme but funds no longer doled out as liberally as they once were (see Money Matters). Around 25 per cent ethnic minorities; help with extra English. Most boys fall within the London day school species homo boffinus – this is not a hive of eccentric creative rebels – many are jolly grown up and focused. Astonishing geographical range for a day school – some from across the road, others via rail (South or East Croydon Station) from Surrey, Kent, West and East Sussex, north London. Nine school buses. Senior boys can drive to school, staff maintain that pupils' cars are smarter than theirs! Strong parents' association. OBs include cricketer Raman Subba Row, actor Martin Jarvis, Professor Sir Bernard Crick, WWII heroes Lord Tedder and 'Cats Eyes' Cunningham.

Entrance: Via report, interview and examination, with emphasis on the latter (taken in January in maths, English and verbal reasoning). Five applicants for each place. Commitment matters – places are most likely to go to persistent, keen, bushy-tailed families who make Whitgift their first choice. Takes up to 100 ten-year-olds and slightly more 11-year-olds. Another 30 boys cobbled on at age 13, and there is an intake at 16. Not on radar screens for many trad preps where all boys stay on to 13. Head not a fan of 13+ entrance, 'when they come at 11, they are a long way from public exams and have time to stretch themselves'. Half the pupils come from state primaries, half from preps. Main feeders are Elmhurst, Cumnor House (in Croydon, not the E Sussex prep), Downsend, Homefield, Oakhurst Grange and several strong local primaries. Dizzyingly large catchment area of more than 1,000 square miles.

Exit: 2013 was a particularly successful year in terms of university places, with two-thirds of boys securing admission to their first choice university; a greater proportion than ever before. Of those moving into higher education, 70 per cent gained places at Russell Group universities including Oxbridge (10 places, including one organ scholar, plus others to do eg PPE, engineering, maths, medicine and music).

Money matters: Once the primary beneficiary of the Whitgift Foundation's largesse, with up to 40 per cent of pupils receiving financial assistance, the school has had to share with nearby boys' school, Trinity and, more recently, with the girls at Old Palace. Bursaries now more competitive, but this is still the biggest bursary programme in the country, and thanks to the Whitgift Foundation, Croydon remains an excellent area in which to be clever but poor. Scholarships for candidates of outstanding merit also on offer for boys entering at 10, 11, 12, 13 or 16. All boys automatically entered for scholarship and bursary schemes when they sit entrance test. Awards also for music, drama, art, technology, sport and all-rounders. School does have 'particular' sponsors; Chelsea Football Club sponsored a boy here, and the social services occasionally suggest prospective pupils.

Remarks: Superb cosmopolitan boys' school, with outstanding facilities, reasonable prices and a strong academic reputation – an example of what education is really about.

Wigmore School

Ford Street, Wigmore, Leominster, Herefordshire, HR6 9UW

- Pupils: 470 boys and girls, all day • Ages: 4–16 • Non-denom
- State

Tel: 01568 770323
Email: admin@wigmore.hereford.sch.uk
Website: www.wigmore.hereford.sch.uk

Head Teacher: Since 2005, Mr Andrew Shaw BSc PGCE NPQH (forties). Married with two daughters. Previously worked in Worcester, Gloucester, Jersey and Staffordshire. Originally a PE teacher, he retains a strong interest in sports and maintaining health and exercise for children across the school. Courteous, friendly, effective. Passionate about improving standards not just in this school but further afield, he now supports four other schools and exports his staff as far afield as the South coast and Northumberland to share good practice. Still very stuck in 'at home' – visits every class every day. Hugely proud of the children in his care, 'they are beautiful children – kind, polite, community minded'. Has every plan, target, statistic and project at his fingertips. Pupils say 'he is just lovely'.

Academic matters: Now an academy, in federation with what was the neighbouring primary school. The school is a designated National Support School providing support and guidance to other schools and is recognised by Ofsted for its innovative and successful approaches to learning, leadership and quality assurance.

Very good GCSE results. Over 75 per cent five A* to C including English and maths. Apart from the normal SATs at the junior end of the school all children are tested at year 7 and there is setting for all core subjects in KS3 and KS4. Pupils have a good range of GCSE options to choose from – either dual award or (increasingly popular) triple award science, French or Spanish, and a dual award in IT, as well as geography, history, RS, drama, DT, art, music and PE.

All pupils benefit from a newly developed Student Support Centre, which comprises both learning support for those with specific learning needs, and careers guidance. In addition to two SENCos (one for the junior end of the school, one for the senior) the school, by using the income it gains from supporting other schools, funds a careers adviser and a counsellor – regarded as absolutely critical in the current harsh economic climate. The school was the first in the country to receive the IAG quality mark for its careers guidance. Work placements and university visits for all in year 11. Excellent IT facilities, well integrated into all areas of learning – lots of computers, iPods and video conferencing to enhance learning and enable some innovative projects.

Pupils are consistently encouraged to aim high. Reports to parents are sent every term with grades for progress, effort and behaviour. Staff are particularly aware of the potential for cultural isolation: ethnic minorities are practically non-existent in this corner of Herefordshire and great effort is made to ensure that the children are acquainted with the full spectrum of faiths and cultures, with visiting speakers, 'exchange' trips to Muslim schools in Birmingham etc. French trip every year for year 8, three-day trip to London for year 9, a high uptake of French exchanges and Spanish trips.

Games, options, the arts: Over 85 per cent of pupils participate in after-school sports activities – dedicated parents do a great deal of ferrying in this deeply rural area. Aerobics, Zumba and badminton, as well as rugby, cricket, netball, athletics. Circus skills for the juniors too. Games provision is impressive, with a huge sports hall, fitness room, cricket nets, 400m track and a large hard play area.

A high level of participation in all sports, and staff ensure that all who show enthusiasm get a chance to represent the school. This inclusive approach is no barrier to excellence. A number of children participate at county and national level (including netball and women's football). A great food technology room, buzzing with activity and enthusiastic chefs. Has Healthy Schools status, an award-winning kitchen manager, a choice of at least five main courses a day and 'no problems with obesity'. The school has also been awarded Artsmark Gold, a recognition of the very good work it does with sometimes limited facilities – there are some very interesting pieces on display in the hall and around the school. A lot of very good drama, inside and outside the classroom – Shakespeare to home-grown as well as a strong debating team.

A well-equipped music room, plenty of school bands and orchestras and a popular singing group as well as three choirs. Range of instruments taught by peripatetic staff directly contracted by the school ('we weren't happy with the county music service') – around 100 of the children take instrumental or singing lessons; some nice new practice rooms.

Background and atmosphere: In a pretty village in a rather remote corner of Herefordshire. Lots of fantastic outdoor spaces. The building itself is no architectural gem but is well maintained and there are some new classrooms as well as the new Student Support centre. A general sense of being well organised and tranquil. Children know what is expected of them.

The school is calm, happy, purposeful. 'Our environment, our atmosphere is of high standards, high expectations'. Despite high class numbers (we saw a couple of groups pushing 30) work is done with great concentration and care. There is no disruption and very little poor behaviour – 'the children won't have it,' says the head. Children are polite, focused, well turned out and very happy. Pupils appreciate the opportunities and care that they receive at Wigmore, 'Everyone is included, it's really friendly.' A huge emphasis on being part of the local community – the sports facilities are open to the public at weekends, the school runs wrap-around care for working parents, and in 2011 opened its nursery unit in response to local demand.

Pastoral care and discipline: A team of deputies head up the pastoral care system which is rooted in tutor groups. PSHE is known as life skills here, and carefully vetted outside agencies are used to support the resources and learning about sex/ drugs/ alcohol etc. Staff are aware that pupils from this corner of the world may find the city lights pretty overwhelming when they move on and are committed to equipping them with the information and maturity to cope as they do so. No exclusions in the last few years, very few disciplinary issues. Of greater concern pastorally is the increased pressure families face as the economic downturn continues to bite. A strong policy on bullying. The head says parents, 'want their children to be loved – and we do – we look after them with loving care'.

Pupils and parents: The catchment area is predominantly agricultural land and the pupils and parents are mainly of farming stock, although some from the professional classes and some from the much more deprived end of the social spectrum. Many parents attended the school themselves and are very supportive of the staff – they have to be if the extra-curricular sports offered after school are going to work. Staff say relationships are very positive with close to full attendance

W

at parents' evenings, 'parents recognise the quality of what we provide'. Parents say that communication from the school is excellent and that their children are well looked after, disciplined effectively, and happy.

Entrance: The school is a federation of Wigmore Primary and Wigmore Secondary, providing an all-through education since 2007. Those attending the primary are automatically entitled to a place in the secondary school, which also takes pupils from six other local feeder schools. It is wholly non-selective (about 20 per cent on school action plus of whom roughly a quarter have a statement). Accepts pupils on the traditional LA criteria of catchment area, siblings in school and so on. Oversubscribed, with a waiting list for each year group and a substantial number of disappointed parents on appeal to the LA. It is essential to be within the catchment area, but this is quite large (running north to Ludlow and west towards Presteigne) and, generally speaking, being in catchment gives a fairly good chance of a place.

Exit: Most go on to take A levels at Hereford Sixth Form College (very good academically) or Ludlow Sixth Form College. Others go on to local agricultural colleges such as Hartpury and Holme Lacy, with others heading for apprenticeships. The school estimates about 60 per cent end up at university though this percentage has fallen a little over the last two years due to difficult economic circumstances. The school positively encourages students to look at overseas opportunities (such as the Netherlands and the US) as alternatives to the UK for higher education.

Remarks: A delightful and extremely successful school. Relaxed, happy, community feel with very high expectations and a heartfelt concern for each individual. Children are encouraged not only to learn but also to take responsibility for themselves and one another. A quietly spoken, no-nonsense head who achieves results in a non-selective state school of which many selective independents would be proud.

William Ellis School

Linked school: LaSwap Sixth Form Consortium

Highgate Road, London, NW5 1RN

• Pupils: 870 boys, all day • Ages: 11–18 • Non-denom • State

Tel: 020 7267 9346
Email: info@williamellis.camden.sch.uk
Website: www.williamellis.camden.sch.uk

Head: Since 2011, Mr Sam White, chemistry graduate and previously deputy head of the London Oratory. He was appointed during the interim headship of Ms Jill Hislop after previous head, Mr Robbie Cathcart, left suddenly at the end of the summer term in 2010, after suffering prolonged ill-health. Mr Cathcart had joined the school in 2008 at a challenging time, with a half million pound deficit, a barely tepid Ofsted report and demoralised staff and pupils.

Fiona Millar, highly effective and outspoken chair of governors, commented, 'Sam White was an exceptional candidate, from an outstanding boys' comprehensive school. We feel that he will be able to build rapidly on the improvements made by our interim head, Jill Hislop, and that the school will go from strength to strength under his leadership'. Mrs Hislop maintains a link with the school as she has been appointed its professional partner.

Indeed, Ofsted visited in autumn 2012 and pronounced the school 'good', commenting, 'The school has improved a great deal in the last two years because leadership has been stable and effective. Parents and students are right to have confidence in its future.'

Academic matters: A huge ability range here, with large numbers at either end of the academic spectrum. William Ellis is a language college – the only boys' comprehensive with this specialism as far as we know. Everyone starts French in year 7 and adds German or Spanish in years 8 and 9, continuing at least one to GCSE – hurray – with the top set taking French in year 10. 'Fantastic' Mandarin club gives boys the opportunity to write and perform a Chinese play and visit Beijing. Evening language classes for parents; language staff teach at feeder primary schools. Science refreshingly available as three separate subjects (very popular), as well as a dual award and a single applied science.

Most lessons for the first two years are in mixed ability groups, with languages setted from year 8 and maths from year 9. It is fair to say that many boys find the school more convivial once they reach year 9 and join tutor groups organised largely by ability. 'We would like to set some subjects earlier, particularly maths, as we did at my previous school,' said the previous head. 'Being a small school makes it more difficult and more costly to organise, but we will look at it in the future.'

Only 45 per cent got 5+ A*-C grades at GCSE including English and maths in 2013, due to a dip in the English results. The previous head worked to regain parents' confidence in the school, beefing up the senior management team, with deputies who have responsibility for overseeing what is taught and how. 'We're focusing on making lessons more interesting across the board. Our big priority is raising standards and expectations.'

Parents have complained for some years about massive inconsistencies in teaching standards and expectations. Some still feel that whether homework is set, completed or marked can be somewhat random. Previous head commented: 'I have spoken to heads of year and told them that we have a homework policy and they must stick to it. The senior management team have done spot checks on homework planners to see what is being set. I'm acutely aware that parents want to support the school and I want to make sure we're meeting our side of the bargain. We have a new programme of teaching and learning development for all staff. It's about sharing good practice and making sure that every lesson is a good lesson.'

The school is looking at its KS3 curriculum and considering the Middle Years IB programme. 'From day one it encourages independent learners and global citizens. It makes us think about learning and about our place in the world.'

Bright boys do regularly achieve sheaves of A* grades. Gifted and talented year 7 and 8 boys are invited to a summer programme including trips and booster activities. 'My older son had a brilliant career at William Ellis,' said a parent, 'and his brother is having a great time there. He's enjoying the work and has a lovely tutor group – friendly, supportive and bright.' 'They get the measure of the boys,' said another. 'They don't underestimate the bright kids.'

The school runs a popular joint sixth form with Parliament Hill School, which is also part of La Swap consortium with Acland Burghley and La Sainte Union schools. This offers a huge range of courses including several vocational options at different levels. There tends to be a strong humanities bias with English, history and sociology much the most popular courses, and an average of around 20 per cent A grades at A level. It is discussing offering the IB, 'but there are lots of alternatives'.

The school has its fair share of boys with special educational needs and behavioural difficulties. It lost the dedicated learning support unit when government funding came to an end, coinciding with the budget deficit, 'but we're looking to put staff back, at least in reduced numbers'. The head of year 7

W

visits every feeder primary school and gets information about the boys about to join the school. Those who are likely to need extra support are invited to a summer school before they join, where they get help with literacy and with settling in to their new school. There is plenty of targeted support for those in need, though as with most comprehensives the SEN department is stretched thin. The building is mostly wheelchair accessible, with stairlifts giving access to the upper floors.

Games, options, the arts: Sport is improving. The sports hall includes basketball and badminton courts, and the school is enviably situated on the edge of Hampstead Heath, with running track, cricket nets and football pitches nearby. Football, basketball, cross-country, cricket and rugby teams compete against other schools and in borough events, 'though there's only one team for each year, and my son has never been picked,' said a parent sadly. Boys following the sports leadership qualification help to coach year 7 football teams.

Music is also on the up. There are 12 music places – now awarded for aptitude rather than ability, but have so far brought in talented musicians who play in the orchestra and ensembles. There are 'interesting concerts,' say parents, with 'flashes of brilliance'.

This is not a school that puts on large-scale school plays but it has excellent connections with hallowed establishments. Pupils might find themselves working on a version of the Magic Flute with staff from the Young Vic, or seeing their script performed at Hampstead Theatre.

The school owns The Mill residential field centre in Surrey. All year 7s have an outdoor pursuits week there at the end of the summer term. It is also used for master classes in music and drama, for study and revision weekends and for field trips. There are language trips to Europe and China, ski trips, field trips to Morocco and Spain, study tours to Russia and the USA.

Background and atmosphere: Founded in 1862 in Gospel Oak by businessman William Ellis, who wanted children to be taught 'useful' subjects like science instead of rote learning. In 1937 it moved to its present site on the edge of Hampstead Heath, as a voluntary aided grammar school. It became comprehensive in 1978.

Smallish but leafy site – many boys walk to school across the Heath – with buildings and facilities that are gradually being upgraded, including swish new sports hall and library, and a rather cramped tarmac playground. Planned major building works now kiboshed by Coalition cuts. Parliament Hill School is next door and La Sainte Union across the road, so lunch times and end of school can see a veritable swarm of pupils socialising.

Pastoral care and discipline: A robust school, with some low level disruption in class and a certain amount of jostling in corridors and playgrounds. Some boys take this in their stride; others find it more challenging. Simple measures have helped: the school has successfully reduced friction between lessons in its small building with narrow corridors by cutting down on the number of bells and giving more leeway at change-over times.

Previous head said: 'The biggest challenge any school faces is consistency of expectations. One of our priorities is behaviour for learning. We're focusing on consistent sanctions, so that boys know that if they do x the consequence is y. But we also know that one of the main ways of combating disruption is making lessons more interesting across the board and we're working on that.'

There are points and prizes for good referrals in the lower years as well as sanctions for bad ones. No head boys or prefects, but boys are encouraged to enter public speaking competitions, to become involved in the school council and outside organisations such as Camden Youth Council.

Exclusions are likely for dealing drugs, for extreme violence or for possessing offensive weapons. The school, like most others in Camden, has 'safer schools police officers' around most of the time. 'Part of their role is to educate children on what is the law so that they don't break it inadvertently. Far more actions are against the law now than there were 20 years ago – carrying a penknife, for example. Even a cricket bat could be classified as an offensive weapon. We don't want to criminalise behaviour unnecessarily, and we want to support students at risk to avoid them getting on the wrong side of the law.'

Pupils and parents: From a huge range of different countries, ranging from Kosovo to Somalia, from the council estates of Gospel Oak and the million pound houses of Dartmouth Park and Belsize Park. 'There are some really nice parents,' said a mother. 'Interesting, diverse and charming.' OBs include Len Deighton, Sean French, Richard Thompson, Toby Young, Andrew Sachs and Fred Titmus.

Entrance: Some 600 applicants for 123 places at 11. Admission criteria: (i) looked after children (ii) siblings (iii) 12 music places – now chosen for aptitude rather than ability, by aural tests rather than references from instrumental teachers (iv) location – in practice, up to about a mile and a half.

La Swap sixth form: About 200 new entrants join the 450 or so moving up from the four constituent schools. Applications by early February; most students who apply on time will be offered a place. Qualifications vary from D grades and below at GCSE for introductory diplomas, to at least eight GCSEs including two B and three C grades for A levels and advanced vocational courses.

Exit: About two-thirds of year 11 students move on to La Swap, the rest mostly to further education colleges or other local sixth forms eg Camden School for Girls. About 90 per cent of leavers with advanced qualifications go on to higher education, with about 20 per cent to Russell Group universities and several each year to Oxbridge (four in 2013).

Money matters: Voluntary aided by the William Ellis and Birkbeck Schools Trust, but otherwise is as hard up as most other state schools.

Remarks: Small boys' comprehensive which has had a rocky few years and now has its third new head in a short space of time. But parents are still optimistic. 'There are some really talented boys here,' said one. 'It has got massive potential.'

Wilson's School

Mollison Drive, Wallington, Surrey, SM6 9JW

- Pupils: 1065 boys, all day • Ages: 11–18 • C of E (but pupils of all denominations and none accepted on an equal basis). • State

Tel: 020 8773 2931
Email: office@wilsonsschool.sutton.sch.uk
Website: www.wilsonsschool.sutton.sch.uk

Head: Since 1999, Mr Damien Charnock. Tall, bespectacled and nicely accessorised (matching gold tie and watch for open day). Highly articulate – just as well, given verbal dexterity of pupils – with a twinkly sense of humour. Viewed and heard from a respectful distance, however, as he didn't care for previous GSG review and declined a face to face meeting (sigh).

Plenty of third person endorsement by way of compensation. While he remains a background figure for most parents it's for all the right reasons as he's the contact of last resort, most problems being efficiently sorted further down the food chain. He's rated a good all-rounder, with plenty of essential managerial savvy, who, 'runs a tight ship', comments one. Pupils like him. 'A normal person', says one, kindly.

His style, inspirational with a light touch rather than a heavy hand, presumably helps. Like every other head, he talks about the need to create whole, rounded people; unlike them, doesn't seem to have dragged prose wholesale from a bumper book of rhetoric beforehand. While he stresses the need to find your creative spark, either at school or later on, he also quotes Thoreau – 'the mass of men lead lives of quiet desperation' – to illustrate what happens if you don't, and with such conviction that you can't help wondering if he has someone specific in mind.

'Creativity is the secret of psychological health', he says. 'You have to dig a little, and often a lot, to find out what sparks a boy's creative spirit. Too many people who don't, endure their lives – a tragedy for society.'

Academic matters: One of a handful of grammars in the area, all high achieving (comparing their results is like differentiating between shiny, perfect apples from M&S and Waitrose: look hard enough and you might find the very occasional blemish but it's scarcely worth the effort), and the natural home of the innately clever child who's, 'looking at getting four A levels at A grade and going to a Russell Group university', says a mother.

It doesn't however, always do quite so well by the merely bright, not through neglect but because, 'only certain people can put up with being bottom of the pile', though that's a relative term. All achieve startlingly good results (so many finish with A*s in maths, taken in year ten by most able, that it's practically de rigueur). Setting is fairly extensive, starting with maths in year 8, followed by sciences, English and all languages except Latin in year 9. Eleven GCSEs are the norm – eight core, including separate sciences, and AS level ICT among the options for the remaining three. In 2013, 87 per cent A*/A at GCSE.

GCSEs followed by four AS and A levels plus critical thinking, compulsory for all in the lower sixth and extended project (EQP) which is voluntary. Modest menu of carefully chosen subjects – there's no psychology, for example (the demand isn't there, says school), though the numbers taking business studies are growing fast and economics is something of a star performer – bad financial news apparently does wonders for recruitment. Latin, though compulsory in year 7, doesn't have such an obvious current appeal higher up the school and is a 'marmite' subject, says a pupil – though the keen are very keen and currently 50 continue in year 9 when it becomes optional.

You're left in little doubt as to the big hitter subjects. Maths, daddy of them all, is taken by over two thirds of pupils at A level with 90 per cent of entries securing A*-A grades (how many other schools have to ponder the potential problem of overcrowding?). It accounts, together with the sciences and economics, for almost twice as many entries as all the remaining A level subjects put together. Boys work hard 'because they know they'll get good grades, they know it's useful and they enjoy it', says a maths teacher – and that seems to hold true across the range of subjects. Overall 93.8 per cent A*-B (72 per cent A*/A) at A level in 2013.

Like beady-eyed shoppers, pupils know how to choose a basket of carefully matched subject goodies and exactly what they're worth in enhancing career prospects. Teachers use this to their advantage. 'We tell them early on that if they want to work for companies like Siemens or Deutsche Bank, all the meetings are held in German', says one. Coincidentally, numbers taking German A level (in terminal decline elsewhere) have recently shot up from single figures to around 20.

Lots of help on offer, with an academic review day each year for boys to meet individual tutors and discuss progress, and valued catch up clubs in just about every core subject, introduced originally for GCSE pupils but now, by popular demand, run from year 7. Support also for those with learning difficulties – some

borderline Asperger's and dyslexia crop up now and then but you don't sense it's a big feature of school life. Generally, 'teachers know when to apply pressure and when to ease off – they're very good at reading the students', says one. Having said that, strength of character and robust self-confidence can be required if you're towards the bottom of the academic pack – occasional pupils suffering from sense of being 'at the bottom end of the academic scale' as one mother puts it, leave early, though it's felt that school is now far better at talent spotting and encouragement all the way down the school.

Atmosphere, however, is generally friendly and remarked on by visitors. One philosophy boffin, 'said he'd been to plenty of schools where it didn't happen,' says a teacher and indeed it's unmissable. 'Teachers are very open,' says year 7 boy. 'The head tells us to think of staff as your friends.' The trust between teachers and pupils, slightly jokey but respectful on both sides is evident and staff are missed when they go – one department head has recently been poached by private school for double the salary, it's said. Given head's emphasis in the prospectus on financial investment in top notch teachers, you have to hope that other even better funded institutions don't come to see staff list as akin to a particularly moreish educational tasting menu.

Games, options, the arts: Take a hobby or sport, preface with the words 'one of the top schools in...' and that's pretty much the gist. Head boasts that 'boys are never bored' though to be honest, even if it laid on nothing, they'd undoubtedly find ways of deriving nourishment from the most barren of intellectual landscapes. As it is, activities ooze from every pore – 'So many, it's silly' – says sixth former, with the usual suspects, including tip top CCF and D of E to gold award; some, like ecology, Freethinkers and even Rubik's Cube clubs, set up by boys themselves.

As a sports specialist, school excels here as elsewhere (though, 'we'd choose this school every time even if they didn't own a tennis ball between them,' says a parent). 'Paradise for the sporting boy', says head. Certainly true if you're fiercely competitive. 'There's a sort of elitism and you do have to be pretty good to get into teams,' confirms a mother. Lots of incentives, including medals for anyone taking three wickets out of five or scoring over 50 runs and a range of sports tours, some more enticing than others, with list offering cricket in Barbados and badminton in Bulgaria. 'I know which I'd choose', says would-be parent. To prove the point, reception area is stuffed with glossy photographs of sports champions, including Olympic hopefuls. Badminton and judo are among notable high points for individual players, though school is no slouch at team sports either, specialising in football while nearby Wallington County Grammar went the rugby route. Both now do the duo, ensuring double the competitive fun.

The un-keen and non-sporty get by, however. 'Nobody hates anyone who's bad at football', says one pupil, while from year 9, the timetable is compassionately arranged to allow students to choose how to fill two compulsory sports periods a week. 'My son isn't sporty and that's ok', says mother, whose child has opted for martial arts over team games.

While it's easy to define school in terms of conventional subjects you'd see as shorthand for academic excellence, that's not to underestimate success elsewhere. DT, for example, is a popular AS option not just because it's fun but because it's valued on 'serious' academic courses such as chemical engineering, 'admissions tutors say it's really useful because of all the planning and the way you have to take things apart and think them through', says successful student. Work on display routinely, as you'd expect, exceeds the brief (one particularly stunning electric guitar scored full marks at GCSE). School has also created a trio of hovercraft, as you do (though no plans as yet to bring back the much missed Folkestone/Bologne route).

Indeed, extension activity is way of life here. Students acquire European Computer Driving Licences – often a sixth form add on – in year 9, while ICT GCSE has been ditched as 'too boring' in favour of programming lessons (good news for Mr Gove). 'Celebrate your inner geek' cutting is pinned up on one of corridor walls.

Art, too, is excellent (staff blog, containing trenchant views on the Turner prize, amongst other topics, is well worth a read) and approached via snazzy light blue corridor and toning floor which serves as exhibition area. Unusually, life drawing classes are taken from GCSE up (and very good the results are, too).

Music, meanwhile, is one to watch, with a department head aged just 24 when appointed – very possibly, he thinks, the youngest in the country (this reviewer still not totally convinced it wasn't one of sixth formers putting on staff identity badge for a laugh). Big competitor is his equivalent at Tiffin, where choir regularly records, but, 'we haven't got the same choral tradition,' he says. Watch this space. With three orchestras and selective choirs already going great guns, plus open-to-all school productions – excellent Les Mis had cast of 200 – plus taster sessions for year 7s in trumpet, sax and trombone and plans for a parents' choir, you can't help feeling that school's professional debut is but a baton's downbeat away.

Background and atmosphere: 'Many grammars give the impression of being a throwback to the 1950s. This one doesn't – deliberately', says the head. Just as well it's not the look he's after, though he'd be perfectly justified in slipping into something a lot more traditional, what with the school's impeccable credentials: founded in the 17th century in Camberwell and, with the exception of a 38-year closure in the 19th century after a financial scandal, going strong ever since. In 1975, lured by the space and local council's pro-grammar stance, it moved to its current premises, once part of Croydon Airport, and commemorated in nearby street names like Dakota Close and Hurricane Road.

While it's not a looker from the outside, with square brown buildings set uncompromisingly in a large, plain playing field, like so many upturned cardboard boxes, the interiors aren't half bad. Corridors might be on the pre-loved side ('it's because the buildings have been here since 1666 that they want to keep the old look', says a pupil, with great presence of mind, if not architectural accuracy) but the classrooms, full of lovingly tended displays, more than make up for it. Science labs, too, slightly dishevelled from the outside, are a hive of well-resourced activity within.

No shortage of impressive large scale areas, either, including the traditional main hall which harks back to a glorious academic past (with still better to come, naturally) and a vast sports hall and gym (replacing expensive to maintain swimming pool and available for hire). But there are also more intimate and surprisingly luscious touches. The south canteen – as distinct from north canteen – (they don't go a bundle on fancy names; library has resolutely not morphed into a learning resource centre, for example) has cutting edge lighting, un-school-like black and orange walls and doubles as an attractive additional concert venue.

Pupils whizz purposefully round the site, assisted by traffic calming measures including one-way staircases (effective student council's recently implemented recommendation). Like the school itself, they look initially unremarkable (crests and striped ties are the only distinctive features). All in all, a lesson in not judging by appearances.

Pastoral care and discipline: Motto is 'Non sibi sed omnibus' (not for oneself but for all) and quite right too, given the huge emphasis on belonging, with forms recruited wholesale into one of five not overly competitive houses and, 'nobody a guest or merely tolerated,' says head. It's helped by approachable form tutors, first point of contact for pupils and parents, who stay with the same group for two to three years – 'easy to talk to when I had worries', says a parent. First class settling-in arrangements. Year 7s have their own common room (as do sixth formers) and also take precedence in the lunch queue during their first term, though after Christmas it's every boy for himself (works well, say pupils, with 'delicious' meals on tap even for latecomers).

When problems crop up they're 'churned through until they're resolved, no matter how long it takes,' says head. Anxiety can be a problem and school is doing its best to pinpoint early onset symptoms and treat them quickly. On-site counselling is available, together with a popular mentoring system which gives year 7s a sixth form buddy who reaches the worries that staff can't because they realise that, 'we're going through hormones and can relate to us', explains one.

School makes no bones about what constitutes unacceptable behaviour, though if there's bullying (it's rare, stressed one boy, who had suffered at his primary school) understanding of the bully as well as the victim is encouraged. 'They can't help it because they have issues, we do it in PSHE', says saintly year 7 pupil. One parent felt tolerance might occasionally err too much in the offender's favour, making recidivism a distinct possibility.

Detentions are widely used, or at least threatened (and immediate for unauthorised movement of instruments, thunders sign outside music room) though there's some wiggle room – it's three strikes and you're out when it comes to late homework, for example, and even the penalty is a starter detention lasting ten minutes. With plenty of chances to step back from the brink, pupils considered the system a fair one.

Pupils and parents: Pupils are an unbounded delight. Hugely focused (one 11-year old was busily teaching himself to multi-task, 'so I can be as good as my older sister – I don't like sexism') and, boy, do they talk, with an almost evangelical desire to draw you into their world, apparently without drawing breath, though the kinder ones do pause occasionally to allow dull-witted adults to catch up. Some have their lives sorted aged eleven – most lean towards the professions (research science, accountancy and law all featured on careers shopping list). Not too dissimilar, in fact, from many of the parents.

Head is proud of the school's diversity – families encompass every major culture and religion and, currently, speak 40 languages between them. As to parental involvement, the opportunities are there but, 'not handed to you on a plate. You have to search them out', says parent, who recommended a spell as a parent governor as the best way of seeing inside the works.

Entrance: 'Boys here are clever but not geniuses', says head, firmly. 'If they're doing very well at school, with level five A or B in English and maths key stage two tests in year 6, then they are clever enough to get in.' Ignore the horror headlines that tell of ten applicants per place, he stresses, as it's simply the same children sitting each exam and the reality is more like four to one. No advantage in having a brother here. 'That's now the law', says head, 'though I'm a bit sorry about it.'

Parents need to keep an eye on the calendar to avoid missing late August/early September deadline to register with the school for the entrance exams. There are two, English and maths, 'not Everest but Ben Nevis, with a brisk wind', says the head. Nothing is officially harder than key stage two work, though the word on the street is that final maths question can be a twister designed to give the most able chance to show the innermost workings of their minds. The English paper is based on comprehension, 'something every child is doing in primary school', though parents can help by building child's vocabulary and knowledge of literary techniques.

Head is grimly resigned to inevitability of widespread tutoring though he strongly disapproves. Has ditched verbal reasoning paper because 'we know it can be coached for'. For the same reason, doesn't make past papers available. Parents also urge caution. 'I really don't think you want to tutor your child and get them there under false pretences because they won't be happy', says one.

Pass/fail results in early October tell you if child is still in the running, giving enough time to include the school (essential that it's your top preference – non-selective backup choice should come further down to avoid missing a place says head) on council-wide school application form, with 150 places offered following March to highest placed candidates. Where there's a tie break, Sutton children have preference with distance to school the final deciding factor. Some join in the sixth form. Again over-subscribed, with offers based on current school's report and places awarded to top GCSE performers.

Consulting on expanding from five to six form entry and taking girls, initially in year 7 and sixth form, from September 2015.

Exit: Very few leave post GCSE. The rest – top subjects, top universities – all absolutely as you'd expect, and lots of it. A pretty heathy 24 in to Oxbridge in 2013 although one sixth former thought grammars, placed awkwardly between better funded, Oxbridge fixated independents and more socially acceptable comprehensives may be faring less well. It's the case especially with screening essays for subjects like humanities, here a by the book DIY effort, elsewhere, he reckoned, toned and honed with expert out of school help. 'We don't have the immense preparation independent schools get or the bias comprehensives enjoy.'

Money matters: 'We are very grateful for the voluntary funding we receive from parents, they are very generous', says Mr Charnock. 'May the money keep coming', adds a parent. 'We are in an area where it is needed.'

Remarks: Bright, clever and funny, and that's just the staff. Hard not to warm to a school where a pupil, asked what he likes best, says, 'everything's my favourite subject,' though wicked sense of humour ensures it remains a Paulyanna-free zone. A wonderful place if you're effortlessly clever, terrific for robust characters who need to work at it. Parents of bright but sensitive stragglers, however, may care to do a bit of soul-searching before calling in the tutors.

Wimbledon High School

Linked school: Wimbledon High School Junior School

Mansel Road, London, SW19 4AB

- Pupils: 585 girls • Ages: 11–18 • Non–denom • Fees: £15,024 pa
- Independent

Tel: 020 8971 0900
Email: info@wim.gdst.net
Website: www.wimbledonhigh.gdst.net

Headmistress: Since 2008, Mrs Heather Hanbury MA Edinburgh, MSc Cambridge in geography then land economy (late forties). A breath of fresh air with experience in the 'real world' prior to teaching – spent nine years working in various management consultancy roles in the City, then as a corporate fundraiser. She was always told she should teach ('and resisted it because I don't like to do the expected'), eventually had a change of heart and took a PGCE with the express ambition to become a head. 'I always wanted to run things,' says Mrs Hanbury. 'I like making organisations efficient, effective and happy.' Began her teaching career at Blackheath High School in 1996, quickly rising through the ranks to head of sixth form, before moving on to Haberdashers' Aske's School for Girls from 2000-03. Was deputy

head of Latymer Upper School from 2003-08. She hums with energy, is quick to smile and laugh and is intent on injecting some fun into this highly-academic school. 'This is a great school, but my first impression was that it needed to lighten up a bit to make sure the girls enjoy all that they do,' she says. Gets things done: persuades rather than dictates – but gets her way anyway. Has hit the ground running with three big projects already underway: a curriculum review, 'Six is the Best' – to make the sixth form the best in London – and Learning to Learn – aiming to foster courage and confidence in the classroom.

Warm and welcoming (makes her own tea for visitors), she's a bit of a dynamo, small and neat with auburn hair to match her Irish lilt. Really mucks in – she delighted the girls who had organised a pyjama day for Red Nose charity by joining them in assembly, barefoot and wearing pyjamas. Married. A keen ('but rubbish') bridge player, loves the theatre (hasn't missed an Edinburgh Festival in 20 years) and enjoys cooking ('entertaining friends and generally showing off!'). Huge hit with both pupils and parents. Parents are delighted that their daughters are so happy; she has made great efforts to know them all and turns up to watch teams and performances in the evenings and at weekends. 'My daughter absolutely loves her,' said one mother. Another said that her daughter described Mrs H as 'just the perfect head teacher.' Other compliments too numerous to mention.

Academic matters: An academic place – but not pressured. Each girl encouraged to reach her own potential, whatever her personal ambition. New curriculum and timetable introduced in 2011. Head encourages risk-taking in the classroom and ensures intellectual and emotional robustness. 'I can't bear to hear a girl say "do we need this for the exam",' says Mrs Hanbury. 'I want to make sure our girls are very good learners with wide interests.' Good scope for this via a broad curriculum including Latin and Greek, design technology and textiles. Popular options at GCSE are history, geography and French. Eighty-seven per cent A*/A grades, most girls get a full set of A*-B – a C grade is rare. At A2 high take-up of maths, biology and chemistry, results good across the board, 83 per cent A*-B grades (61 per cent A*/A) in 2013. Nice to see history of art option here. Good preparation for Oxbridge, but thankfully not a feeling that candidates are better than the rest.

Class sizes are initially large for a private school at an average 28 for years 7-9 (except for maths which is streamed, science, art and DT), but down to 22 for GCSE classes and 15 (or often fewer) at A level. In sixth form (years 12 and 13) pupils are in mixed tutor groups of about 14. Experienced staff have very high expectations. 'They are largely a most dedicated bunch,' said a parent. 'Great mentors'. All pupils are screened for SEN on entry and learning enrichment coordinator (SEN specialist) supports those with specified needs, advises girls and parents on study methods and offers timetabled 'Learning to Learn' lessons in year 7. Gifted children offered regular extension activities. New weekly enrichment afternoon for years 11, 12 and 13. School is active in London Challenge, bringing together the gifted and talented from neighbouring schools to participate in special projects.

Games, options, the arts: Lots going on both in the classroom and after hours. Doesn't attract the uber-sporty, one parent feeling strongly that expectations are not high enough in this area, but school has produced junior national representatives in skiing, three-day eventing and gymnastics. Usual compulsory sports and from year 10 upwards girls can also select from further offerings including aerobics, circuit training, squash, horse-riding, badminton, basketball. Wow-factor pool and sports hall on site. Girls go off-site to playing fields, games pitches and courts a few minutes walk away on the site of the original All England Lawn Tennis Club. Years 9 and 10 girls do duty as ball girls during Wimbledon tennis championships.

W

Drama and music strong and enhanced further by the opening of very impressive Rutherford Centre for the performing arts, which is now at the heart of all performance work. (It's named after old girl, actress Margaret Rutherford). About 80 per cent of the girls learn a musical instrument. Autumn and spring concerts are highlights – fathers and staff join as tenors and baritones, while at the informal summer soirée the girls' own compositions are showcased. Drama department stages many productions over the year, culminating in a summer musical.

Mrs Hanbury a strong believer that most pleasure in life comes from hobbies and passions – and so is keen for her girls to learn how to be passionate about something. 'They need to learn to use a hobby to help them to unwind and relax without resorting to blobbing in front of the TV. They need good habits for life,' she says. To this end girls take their pick from a pleasingly long and varied list of clubs, which as well as the usual offerings includes niche interests eg music for shy performers, 'knit and natter', mah jong and cryptic crosswords (solving and compiling). School's aim is for every girl to find her niche, however unusual or unlikely it may be. A new longer lunch break gives more time for clubs during the school day.

Background and atmosphere: Owned by the Girls' Day School Trust, the school celebrated its 130th birthday in 2010 – so great heritage and knows exactly what it's about. Like many London schools the site is relatively small; on the plus side its urban location has the benefit of excellent local transport links with tube, train, tram and bus terminals all within eight minutes' walk. Don't be put off by first impressions: Victorian red brick building fronts the place, surrounded by a rather grey site and unwelcoming (almost prison-like) entrance lobby – Mrs Hanbury has plans to remedy this and 'much else besides.' Inside there are some super-smart facilities, but these vie with some old-style labs, smallish classrooms, peeling radiators and a few grim corridors where a slick of gloss paint wouldn't go amiss. But more importantly the place is friendly, the girls very happy and free to play to their strengths. Sixth formers busy with 'Six is the Best' project, which includes new accommodation and furniture for their common room – working party of pupils was sent off to Ikea to choose it themselves.

Pastoral care and discipline: Happy, high achieving pupils in no great need of discipline, but for the five per cent or so who do require correction it is described as 'firm'. Teachers, though approachable, are strict and there is a head mistress detention every Friday. 'I am aware that parents are paying good money for a good education at this school and we do everything we can to provide it,' says Mrs Hanbury. Strong head of year system. Sixth formers very good at helping to run house system and peer counselling. From year 7, girls have 'behaving nicely' drummed into them, zero tolerance of bullying. Problems such as eating disorders taken very seriously. 'We don't hesitate or pussy-foot around,' says Ms Hanbury. 'We are straight in once we come across anything like this to support the girl involved and all her friends who undoubtedly will have been worrying themselves.' Less serious issues, eg uniform niggles, nicely handled – girls have worked with staff to draw up acceptable guidelines including deciding the maximum permitted distance above the knee for skirts!

Pupils and parents: Exuberant live wires and timid flowers will all find a happy home here – the school is very tolerant, even encouraging, of individual types and unusual characters. Good sense of community from a diverse bunch. English middle classes, mixed with Korean and East European families joining the longer-established Indian and Chinese communities. OGs include children's author Michelle Pavers, journalist Rosie Millard, investment banker turned Hollywood actor Amara Karan and Professor of Experimental Pathology, Harvard University, Lynne Reid. A chunk of parents from financial and legal worlds. Thriving parents' association.

Entrance: Selective at 11+ – tests verbal reasoning and non-verbal reasoning. Typically between 350-400 applications for 45 or so places, depending on exactly how many of the 48 possible arrive from juniors (only a handful don't make it). Extra form intake in year 7 every five years eg 2014. Register from Easter the year before entry, interview in autumn term and exams the following January. School references and interview notes decide borderline cases. Attracts families from Wimbledon and wide surrounding area. Feeder schools include The Study and Holy Cross Prep, with other applicants coming from various state and independent schools. At 16+ girls need GCSE grade A in subjects to be studied at AS level.

Exit: About 80 per cent move up to the sixth form and 15 per cent join from other schools. Mrs Hanbury will have to work hard to keep the percentage up – some pupils may be swayed as nearby King's College School for boys (qv) opened its doors to sixth form to girls in 2010. At 18+ most to good universities of their choice – mainly Russell Group; usually 5-8 to Oxbridge.

Money matters: Academic and music scholarships available at 11+ and academic, science, music, drama, art and PE scholarships at 16+. Hundred per cent bursaries on offer at 11+ and 16+.

Remarks: Terrifically purposeful place, with super head and tons going on – think Richard Scarry's Busy Town. Suits bright, hard-working girls prepared to muck in and have a go. All the activity is underpinned by hefty academic foundations, so a girl who would just scrape in or who doesn't like to knuckle down may want to look elsewhere.

Winchester College

College Street, Winchester, SO23 9NA

- Pupils: 690 boys; 685 boarding • Ages: 13–18 • C of E
- Fees: Boarding £33,750 pa • Independent

Tel: 01962 621247
Email: admissions@wincoll.ac.uk
Website: www.winchestercollege.org

Headman: Since 2005, Dr Ralph Townsend MA DPhil, an Australian with no trace of it in his voice (early sixties). Dr Townsend taught briefly at Dover College and Abingdon before proceeding to Oxford where he was first a senior scholar at Keble then a junior research fellow, tutor and dean of degrees at Lincoln, teaching theology. In 1985, he became head of English at Eton, leaving in 1989 to head Sydney Grammar School. Ten years later he returned to England to become head of Oundle – thus 16 years headmasterly experience before his arrival in Winchester. He is cerebral, direct, a bit intimidating, and the possessor of a very cool pair of circular tortoiseshell spectacles. Married to Cathy, a musicologist, who helps with visitors, staff and boys, and assists the music department during music scholarship awards and other periods of pandemonium. They have two adult children.

Intentionally avoids the media spotlight, oft frequented by the heads of similar schools. Mentioned 'league tables' with distaste. His commitment to the school's fundamental ethos, its unique traditions of scholarship and teaching through dialogue, is manifest and resolute. Described Winchester as the 'least conventional' of schools where the 'intellectual life' of pupils comes above all else. Some parents find him 'aloof', and certainly he has little to do with most boys' daily experience of the school which will be largely influenced by his housemaster and Div don.

W

Academic matters: In 2008, Winchester introduced Cambridge Pre-U examinations as a replacement for A levels in most subjects. The head takes a dim view of the latter, especially in modern languages which have been 'vandalised' ('you can now take an A level in French without reading a book!'). The Cambridge Pre-U has no coursework and opens up sixth form study as a serious two-year programme, studying three subjects in depth, with examinations at the end, much as A levels were before successive reforms of the last 25 years. Some mathematicians take four (or even five) Pre-U exams, sitting maths at the end of the lower sixth and further maths the following year.

Results always outstanding (79 per cent at D3 level or above in 2013 – equivalent to grade A at A level), and the school continues to offer the shortest list of exam subjects of any reputable sixth form in England. Forget film studies and froth – here you will not find examined drama, classical civilisation, politics, business studies, PE or psychology. Chemistry and physics the most popular Pre-U subjects, followed robustly by history and English lit. Philosophy and theology on a roll at the minute. All boys sit IGCSEs in three sciences, maths, English, Latin, and modern languages French, German, Russian, Spanish plus usually three other subjects.

'Div' is the unique and highly-prized complementary programme at the heart of the Winchester ethos. It aims to instil a knowledge and understanding of British, European and world history and culture and, as such, is a true, liberal education. 'The boys and dons love it,' says Dr Townsend, 'it's the one bit of this over-structured world in which they can pursue their own intellectual interests.' It's a holistic approach that we expect to find in Montessori education and schools on the alternative end of the spectrum. 'It means the staff have to be of the highest calibre so that they can lead this cross-subject, cross-cultural tutorial,' a parent explained. Average age of teachers has come down significantly in recent years, and is now a youthful 38.5.

IT not cutting any edges, reflecting an institutional reserve about the digital world. Little, if any, work done on computers in a boy's first year (or two) here. Offers learning support for around 100 boys, mainly for mild dyslexia, dyspraxia and information processing. One boy registered blind, one deaf.

Games, options, the arts: The sport is 'brilliantly flexible', a parent told us. Enthusiasts can play as much as they want. 'My son went from the 4th team at his prep school to the A team here', chuckled one mum. 'There's a great spirit in the school sport', another told us, 'very unpressurised.' 'If you are determined to do no games, it's possible', concedes the head (refreshing, and probably unique, to hear this said in a British public school). But some sort of physical exercise ('ekker') is compulsory. Main sports are soccer, Winchester College football (read the rules) and cricket (huge here – the cricket coach also runs the Hampshire U-16s) but these are supplemented by everything from aikido to water polo. Fabulous playing fields and sports facilities of all kinds. Recent national competition wins in rackets, fives, fencing and cross-country running.

Music very important, very strong and very classical. James Blunt, Genesis and Mumford and Sons may have attended public schools but they would not have been Wykehamists. Two-thirds of boys learn a musical instrument; many learn two or three, taught by a long list of specialist teachers. Pipe organ very strong here (one Winchester boy we know was making a tidy sum playing weddings while still in sixth form). Music school includes 50(!) practice rooms, a music tech classroom, recording studio and editing suite. Vast range of musical ensembles and performance opportunities – weekly Tuesday concert and many more throughout the year – many open to the public.

Art and drama lively and of quality, though they do not quite enjoy the accolade of music. CCF compulsory in year 10, after which it can be replaced with community service.

Background and atmosphere: Founded in the 14th century by William of Wykeham, Bishop of Winchester, Chancellor to Richard II, and the sage behind the school's motto: Manners makyth man. Began in 1387 with a Warden, 10 fellows, two schoolmasters three chaplains, 70 scholars and 16 quiristers – the Winchester version of choristers. The bishop also founded New College, Oxford, with which the college maintains strong links. The quiristers are now educated down the road at the Pilgrims' School but continue to board at Winchester College and sing in chapel. So this is a quiet land of flinty walls, leafy quads, a venerable chapel, many other buildings of ancient date and visible history (the school was used as Cosette's Paris convent in the film version of Les Mis). Later foundations, eg Eton College, seem like modern upstarts by comparison. Not that the college hasn't kept building and acquiring. There are 10 boarding houses in adjacent streets, and buildings for all major disciplines. The college is now building a new museum in a converted stable to display its trove of treasures – paintings, porcelain, silver, scientific instruments, books etc.

A boy's life here begins and ends with his house. Houses, while still more autonomous than at any other school in the UK, have been brought some distance into dreary conformity in this era of Health and Safety, school inspections and the like. There is now a lot more consistency of discipline, food (all meals are eaten in house) and day to day routine and less competition between houses (and housemasters). Current crop of housemasters praised by the parents we spoke to. Accommodation and food improving but still seen as of secondary importance, both to the school and to (British) parents.

The atmosphere is donnish – the masters are called dons here and the college has a language of its own (called Notions) for almost every aspect of daily life. The lack of girls, together with the school's academically elitist ethos, gives the boys the gift of unselfconsciousness, rarely seen elsewhere. The school considered admitting girls when Dr Townsend became head – 'I started off thinking we'd do it', he remembers. In the end, they decided against: 'Girls dominate academically, especially in the lower years. To introduce that here would change the intellectual ethos of the school. What we do is distinctive – we do not have a wide ability range. It is the high quality of the boys' ability at the 'bottom' that is key here.'

Surprisingly, the school has no formal relationship with Winchester Cathedral – who needs it when you've got such a superb school chapel (built 1392)? The cathedral is used for school choir concerts. 'It casts an ecclesiastical aura,' noted Dr Townsend. Saturdays consist of lessons until lunch, then sport, then reading, then prep. Most boys go out after chapel on Sundays – younger boys to lunch at home, older ones into town. The school's inflexible attitude towards Sunday boarding is a source of contention for a few boys who have to pass up outside sports fixtures. Has a 5+ year relationship with Midhurst Rother College (academy) and some pupils from the academy come to Winchester for a Saturday morning programme of classes.

Pastoral care and discipline: School rules cover 10 tightly spaced typed pages and make a terrifically good read. You will find a complex list of warnings for alcohol (depending whether wine, beer or spirits and where purchased) and learn that the possession of firearms or explosives is forbidden (with the exception of 'shotguns brought into school with parent permission'). Boys are also reminded not to wear 'T-shirts bearing slogans which are anagrammatical' (what harm is an anagram, we ask). No hats. And before you ask, no earrings.

All boys board. First year boys are generally in rooms of four. By IGCSEs they're in doubles. All sixth formers have single rooms, except the scholars. Mobiles allowed so long as they are 'inaudible and invisible'. School takes a hard line on drugs, but they remain a recurring nuisance. Unusually, for a school of this vintage, there is no sixth form bar. Housemasters run most

W

aspects of a boy's life – pastoral and academic – but serious matters end up with the head.

Pupils and parents: Some 87 per cent of boys come from the UK. All pupils speak English as it if were their first language; around 20 pupils are bilingual. Quite a lot of Hong Kong Chinese families – who tend to coalesce at the academic hothouses of this land. 'Russians haven't found us yet,' commented one of the admissions staff (more likely, they shun it because it's single sex). Boys come from a large assortment of preps mostly in the southern half of the UK, with Pilgrims' School, Horris Hill, Twyford, The Dragon, Summer Fields and Sussex House leading the field. The school does not break its back to court parents – neither current nor prospective: there is one rather low-key open day each year.

Parents we spoke to were keen to emphasise that though boys must be clever and academic to be happy here, they need not be geeks. There are some very studious individuals here – yes, but there are also normal, clever but lazy boys who like their sport and are not averse to sunshine.' Not the place for hovering parents – signing on here takes a leap of faith and the school is set in its ways ('clear about what it wants and expects,' says the school). List of well-known old boys is long, but curiously unexciting. Lots of politicians, academics, cricketers, journalists, pillars of The Establishment.... and Tim Brooke-Taylor.

Entrance: You'll need to be on your toes. The school asks parents to register their sons after they've turned 8 but 'well before the end of year 5'. No need for early registration for those attempting scholarships – winning an award carries with it the automatic right to a place. Admissions for 'Commoners' are via the housemasters who see 25 to 30 sets of parents when the boys are 10-11, interview and test them (a short verbal and numerical reasoning test), get reports from existing schools and offer places to around half. A deposit is then requested and the place is firm, barring (rare) failure of the college's entrance exam which is taken two years later in May of the year of entry in all usual CE subjects (with Greek and German as additional options, but not Spanish). It helps to have an idea of which houses you are interested in – parents may arrange meetings with up to three housemasters. 'If parents are still unsettled after seeing three houses, this may not be the school for them', said the admissions department with customary directness.

Scholars and Exhibitioners selected by exams in English, maths, science and a multiple choice 'General Reasoning' test. Candidates must also choose three optional papers from among: Latin, French, Classical Greek/German/Spanish, history, geography, maths II or general paper II. Scholars live in 'College' – a separate house pulsating with hyperactive brain cells. The life of a scholar here is not for all, and we know of families turning down an academic scholarship (especially now that they bring no automatic fee remission). A half dozen boys come fresh into the sixth form via exam and a minimum of six GCSE A/A* grades (ie mainly A*s but the odd A won't rule you out).

Exit: In 2013, 40 to Oxbridge. The rest to a predictable spread of the best redbricks. Increasing numbers (around 20 lately) to a distinguished list of top North American universities. Six As required at IGCSE to proceed to sixth form and, though this is a low hurdle for most boys here, the college is said to be 'ruthless' (school says 'firm') about enforcing this rule. A handful of unfortunate boys receive 'the letter' each year.

Money matters: Since 2011, all scholarships – given for academic and musical ability; no sports, art or drama frippery here (though candidates with those talents may bring along a portfolio of their work) – bring zero fee remittance. However means tested bursaries can be awarded up to 100 per cent of the fee where necessary. Music scholars, of which there are

10 (usually grade 8 by age 13), receive free tuition on up to two instruments and singing; music exhibitioners (closer to grade 6) get free tuition on one instrument. NB Charges an inexplicable £500 'entrance fee' (in addition to a registration fee and deposit).

Remarks: A very special place for intellectually curious boys and their teachers. Unique.

Windermere School

Linked school: Windermere Preparatory School

Browhead, Patterdale Road, Windermere, Cumbria, LA23 1NW

- Pupils: 255, even mix boys and girls, day and boarders with 25 per cent international • Ages: 11–18 • C of E, all faiths recognised
- Fees: Boarding £23,190–£27,900; Day £13,805–£15,580 pa
- Independent

Tel: 01539 446164
Email: ws@windermereschool.co.uk
Website: www.windermereschool.co.uk

Headmaster: Since 2009, Mr Ian Lavender. Has a strong background in independent secondary school education, boarding and the Round Square ethos, having been a housemaster at Gordonstoun School for 11 years, preceded by experience as a chemistry teacher at Cranleigh School and Eton College. In 2002 he gained the National Professional Qualification for Headship. Mr Lavender also has broad experience that extends well beyond teaching, including an early career in management consulting, service with the Territorial Army and a degree in chemistry from Oxford. His wife is a GP and they have three children.

Academic matters: Windermere pupils might not be dancing at the top of the league tables but they are hard-working and happy. Due in part to the broad intake, the results can't compete with selective schools so it focuses on its considerable international appeal. At GCSE 39 per cent A*/A. With small classes (around 12), teaching isn't frantic and time is given to each pupil.

An IB World School offering the IB Diploma for sixth form, the atmosphere is fresh and enthusiastic. Average IB score in 2013 was 32.8. A levels and BTECS are also offered. The core of the IB Diploma Programme encompasses many of the Round Square principles, making the curriculum ideal for Windermere School.

Students are given the opportunity to participate in worldwide exchanges by spending up to a term in another Round Square School. There are also annual language trips to France and Spain and Germany. The German exchange is organised through the Windermere and Diessen Twinning Association and students take a work placement during their visit.

Full-time head of learning support, dyslexia specialist and two part-time assistants. Parents are charged for the support according to whether it's in-class or on an individual basis.

Games, options, the arts: All students in years 7, 8 and 9 complete the Windermere Adventure Award. They also spend one morning a fortnight outside school doing anything from mountain biking to conservation and environmental work. In Year 10, students progress on to a service programme, linking the school to the wider community. A range of local and international service projects are offered along with a varied and community-based music programme with outside performances. The school sponsors the Mary Wakefield Festival and hosts the Lake District Summer Music Festival.

Major sports include hockey, netball, football, athletics and tennis but there's also rugby, cricket, cross-country, fell-running, table tennis and basketball. The school has its own jetty and boats on Windermere, competes at a high level in sailing.

Background and atmosphere: Founded in 1863 as St Anne's High for Girls the school moved to the Windermere site from Lytham in 1924. Called Windermere St Anne's thereafter and co-ed since 1999.

Nowadays there's a decent mix of boys and girls. The school undertook an extensive building programme in the '70s and '80s, producing a new arts centre, science block and sports hall. Newly refurbished girls' dorms and common rooms with some hotel-worthy views.

Upper and lower schools jostle along happily and there's a genuine family atmosphere, albeit one in which independence is strongly encouraged. The Round Square ethos is in evidence throughout with international flags displayed and a real multicultural feel to the teaching and friendships.

Pastoral care and discipline: Windermere pupils are encouraged to be self-disciplined. Sixth formers live in single-sex flats with their own bistro and it's clear from talking with staff members that any hint of out-of-control behaviour is dealt with very sternly. But, it seems this is rarely needed as older and younger students jog along happily in the knowledge that they want for nothing in their sprawling, healthy environment. Staff are no-nonsense but humane and the differences between efficiently run dorms and ordinary happy teenagers' bedrooms are subtle.

Pupils and parents: The largest proportion of students (approximately 74 per cent) are from the UK (mainly Cheshire, Yorkshire, North East Lincolnshire, London and Lancashire). A wide spread of students internationally (around 25 per cent) from China, Germany, Hong Kong, Lithuania, Poland, Romania, Ukraine, Spain and Russia. Pupils are hardy and parents those who want their offspring to enjoy the outdoors and learn some independence in a safe environment.

Entrance: Most pupils enter from school's own prep. The school likes to look for 'potential' rather than performance and 'well-rounded students with a genuine interest in education in the broadest sense of the word'. Candidates for entry (below 16+) sit papers in English, mathematics and non-verbal reasoning. Year 12 places conditional on a minimum of five GCSEs at grade C or above.

Exit: Most leavers continue in higher education home and overseas via gap years. In 2012, 19 different UK destinations plus universities in USA and Europe. A handful have gone on to key musical success. Notable former pupils include dressage Olympian, Emma Hindle and internationally respected soprano Claire Booth.

Money matters: Non means-tested scholarships are available in performing arts, visual arts, general academic subjects and sport. There are some means-tested bursaries available.

Remarks: Windermere is a school which revels in a hearty approach to everything from academia to friendships. It should appeal to parents wanting their offspring to end their days with rosy cheeks, air in their lungs and endless tales of the riverbank. Though the school doesn't top league tables, the introduction of the International Baccalaureate has encouraged a more diverse intake and pupils are introduced to a wide range of subjects with exceptional extra-curricular enhancements. It's not the ideal destination for the child without a kagoul but give even those a year or so and they'd be kayaking with the best of them.

Withington Girls' School

Linked school: Withington Girls' Junior School

Wellington Road, Fallowfield, Manchester, M14 6BL

- Pupils: 650 girls, all day • Ages: 7–18 • Non-denom
- Fees: Seniors £10,440; Juniors £7,710 pa • Independent

Tel: 01612 241077
Email: adsheada@withington.manchester.sch.uk
Website: www.withington.manchester.sch.uk

Headmistress: Since 2010, Mrs Sue Marks MA (early fifties). Moved from a nine year headship of Tormead School, Guildford (qv) where she also taught economics. Read PPE at Jesus, Oxford, bagging blues for rowing and athletics. Before teaching she had a career in banking in the City. She is treasurer of the Girls' Schools Association. No stranger to Manchester, her teenage years were spent in Wilmslow; she still has family nearby and of her move says 'it's bringing me home'. A mother of four, although her eldest daughter died suddenly in 2002 aged just 17. Her second daughter now teaches at Downe House School (qv) 'which gives me great pleasure and makes me enormously proud'; her younger two are at university and school. 'It's an extraordinary privilege to be given the chance to lead Withington, one of the very few schools in the country I'd have left Tormead for,' she says. A great believer in knowing every girl, probably through teaching from year 7, time permitting, and in 'educating the whole girl and not just the bit that sits exams and gets certificates.'

Academic matters: Off the scale, with almost all GCSEs awarded an A or A*: 96 per cent in 2013 (74 per cent A*), and at A level 38 per cent A*s, 80 per cent A*s or A grades, 94 per cent A* to B grades. It goes without saying that they're strong across the curriculum here and know how to advise girls to tackle exams, but a Withington education is so much more than that. At the entrance to the new sixth form centre an LCD notice board incorporates a BBC news feed. During our visit a sixth form girl exclaimed at the breaking news of Obama receiving the Nobel Peace Prize. The head of sixth came out of her office, girls gathered round, including several who uncurled themselves from the new cerise and burgundy sofas, and a discussion ensued about the merits and implications of this news. Beyond 'academic matters' for sure, but that's what it's like here. 'The teaching's fabulous, our daughter's completely engaged' parents tell us, 'it is a steep curve from a state primary but it's not the hothouse we expected.' Sunday Times Independent Secondary School of the Year 2009. Named again in 2012 as the 'Best Value Independent Day School' in the country by the Financial Times.

Classes aren't dramatically small, up to 28, although much less for many A level courses which will run for just a single keen student if need be. Very strong science, as stipulated by the founders, producing lots of medics and scientists. Links with university and lots of national academic Olympiad achievers, although there are no internal school prizes, in line with the founders' diktat of 'the pleasure of learning being its own reward'. Very strong foreign languages, very strong everything really. One teacher told us 'girls do work hard here, they get a lot of homework and the pace is very fast yet I still see them running around singing, and enjoying sport, music, drama and looking beautiful in the fashion show.' Drama recently introduced at GCSE as well as A level.

Games, options, the arts: Something for everyone and a can-do attitude to help girls with lots of interests fit everything in. Astroturf pitch for hockey, grass for lacrosse, county and country

W

players in both and county in netball. Strong lacrosse tradition, reaching national finals, also tennis. Community service in local nurseries, schools and residential homes for the elderly. Charity fundraising, links with schools and a hospital in Kenya and The Gambia. Recent trips to Uganda, Berlin, Mongolia, France and Wales. Over 70 D of E bronze each year and increasing numbers of silver and gold. Young Enterprise, Ogden Trust business game, public speaking competitions, strong Model United Nations and Mock Trials. Drama studio and hexagonal hall/theatre in the round for assemblies, concerts and drama, including some joint productions with Manchester Grammar (qv) boys, who also join girls for a combined Philsoc. Three orchestras, wind band, jazz group, several choirs. DfE-sponsored art and music partnerships with local state schools. Contemporary art collection initiated in 2006. Lots of other extra-curricular clubs including cheerleading and mosaic club. Girls look stunning in annual fashion show and are joined by boys from MGS, 'but,' they giggle, 'they're not usually very good'.

Background and atmosphere: Unprepossessing but neat and tidy site in suburban Withington south of Manchester with Tardis-like add-ons at the rear and compact playing fields, courts and an all-weather pitch behind these. Building projects in 2002, after a major fire in 2003, in 2005 and in 2009 mean most subjects now enjoy suites of classrooms round a departmental office. Carpets and blinds, Velux windows and open ceilings in the refectory, and in the sixth form centre huge windows, new sofas and lockers with cornices give the place a classy, comfortable but executive feel. Four houses carry the names of the founders who, back in the late 1800s, wanted the same educational opportunities for their daughters as for their sons. Girls seem naturally and spontaneously helpful to visitors and the mixed ages, from 7-18, mean it's a gentle place. Staff conversation buzzes over lunch with varied choices in their own dining room.

Pastoral care and discipline: The air is thin at these giddy academic heights so a main pastoral care issue here is helping those with a predicted B grade retain a 'global perspective and not lose their self-esteem ... to remember that low in the top five per cent is still high in the other 95 per cent.' Girls speak of 'phenomenal help from teachers in school' including a SENCo who's 'really great' and even helps over the summer, and whilst laziness is frowned on, both groups are adamant no-one's edged out for under-performance. One recent parent told us he felt the focus is on the brightest girls, but when asked how his daughter fared in the end, had sheepishly to admit, 'ah, she did rather well actually'. Otherwise the care structure is strong and includes an approachable full-time nurse in a super new sick bay. The last ISI inspection said 'the pastoral care of pupils is excellent across the school. Relationships between staff and pupils and amongst pupils are very warm and mutually respectful.' Older girls mentor younger girls and it's a small school with zero tolerance for bullying. Everybody knows everybody so the 'respecting other people and respecting self' guideline seems to be pretty much enough. Apart from no midriff on display and no shorts allowed, sixth form dress is 'up to us to act on our own responsibility, to bridge the gap between school uniform and uni.' Lower years are getting used to a blazer and a skirt designed so it can't be rolled over at the top.

Pupils and parents: You have only to look at the governors' page of the school website to see that the good and the great both use and support this school, but pupils aren't all super-wealthy by any means. Battered old family estate cars arrive alongside glitzy 4x4s, and one in five pupils receives some sort of means-tested bursary. It's a diverse community from varied ethnic and faith backgrounds, with opportunities for all groups to meet alone and together in assemblies, societies and with visiting speakers. 'The Christian Society comes and goes, it's pupil led,

but we do stand for mutual tolerance and understanding,' says head. Girls come from all points of the compass and often travel long distances on buses or with parents, some of whom therefore become long distance taxi drivers at weekends. Pupils describe a Withington girl as 'ambitious, determined, articulate, caring, well-mannered and intent upon an excellent career' and Withington as 'the Rolls Royce of schools'. Notable Old Girls include TV's Judith Chalmers OBE, opera star Christine Rice and pianist Katherine Stott.

Entrance: Head personally greets everyone arriving at and departing from January exams, two maths, two English, with drink and biscuit break. The standard is high, way beyond NFER 11+ tests, so a bit of extra prep is a good idea, using sample papers available from school. Two apply for each place and roughly a third of places will be filled by school's own juniors (who also have to sit exam), a third come from independent preps and a third from state primaries. Selection also depends on previous school report and a 15 minute interview, including a few minutes with parents. A 'spark' and potential are key and the amount of primary hothousing, or lack of it, is taken into consideration. Sixth form entry needs six A* or As at GCSE with A*s in chosen A level subjects and considers report from previous school and interview.

Exit: A few leave for sixth form elsewhere to join boys or for an end to fees, but there's always an influx too. All sixth form leave for university, mostly to top institutions on top courses. Some dozen to Oxbridge, ditto medicine. Head gives final individual supervisions before UCAS applications are sent and MGS and Withington swap teachers to make mock uni interviews more realistic. Gappers can apply for a £100 travel award on leaving.

Money matters: Cheap at the price for such excellence; you could pay a lot more for a lot less elsewhere. Almost a hundred girls on means tested bursary support. No scholarships. Termly £6 charge for insurance. Lunches £190 per term.

Remarks: Excellence on all fronts with very intelligent girls being very intelligently taught. Some might say it's a privileged and academic bubble – it's certainly a place where love of learning and avid interest in all things are inculcated and nurtured; and who'd prefer the 'real world' to that for their daughters' girlhoods?

Woldingham School

Marden Park, Woldingham, Surrey, CR3 7YA

- Pupils: 540 girls; 315 board, 225 day • Ages: 11–18 • Roman Catholic, but girls of all faiths welcome • Fees: Boarding £28,410–£30,945; Day £17,775–£19,365 pa • Independent

Tel: 01883 349431
Email: registrar@woldinghamschool.co.uk
Website: www.woldinghamschool.co.uk

Headmistress: Since 2007, Ms Jayne Triffitt, MA PGCE (early fifties). Educated at Truro High School, read chemistry at St Hilda's College, Oxford. A committed Catholic, most of her career has been spent in Catholic schools, 17 years in the state sector (La Sainte Union, Highgate, St Michael's Grammar School, North Finchley) before becoming head of the sixth at St Mary's, Ascot and then head of St Mary's, Cambridge.

A direct, pragmatic, highly-principled and serious soul, she can initially seem rather reserved but soon warms up. Even so, there is no spin and gloss to Mrs Triffitt. Her brief included tightening up the academics and bringing more structure and discipline to the timetable. This involved changing the structure of the day, raising expectations and introducing setting and banding into most subjects in years 7, 8 and 9 as well as setting tight boundaries. Like all good boundary markers, however, she also knows when to relax them. Her maternal commonsense won her the accolade of being the coolest headmistress, when she was witnessed giving two senior girls money for a cab back to school, rather than forcing them to leave a party early with her. Her motive for making any decision is a practical and principled conviction of what is the right thing to do. She does have a sensitive awareness of the feelings of the girls, but 'I am not a panderer,' she says.

Academic matters: Impressive, given relatively broad intake. A parent sums up the academic ethos, 'there is a clear understanding at the school that these girls will have to earn a living.' Setting in many subjects – from as early as 11. Average number of GCSEs is ten, with 100 per cent of grades C or higher – 69 per cent get A*/A in 2013. RS compulsory for GCSE, as are maths, English lang and lit. Geography popular and most take double award science. Currently in the top ten per cent in the country for value-added performance at A level; over 84 per cent of all grades at A*-B (38 per cent A*/A) in 2013. Courses available at AS and A2 include politics, textiles, design, music technology and psychology.

Handful of girls per year identified as having mild specific learning difficulties (dyslexia, dyspraxia, Asperger's) needing one-to-one attention. Full-time SENCo appointed by Mrs Triffitt. Extra support made available to everyone, not just those on the SEN register. One or two pupils with statements. Perception has always been that the school suits a wide range of ability from very bright downwards, but will this continue? As part of the drive for academic tightening, Mrs Triffitt is implementing a number of changes, including careful monitoring of special needs at entry to ensure the school can accommodate a girl's requirements. Although it would be very unusual to refuse to accept a sibling, 'we would do so if we couldn't offer the support they needed.' Gifted and talented provision includes an Oxbridge programme led by the head and a team of three other members of staff.

Games, options, the arts: Almost every parent we spoke to enthused about the attention given to renovation, innovation and refurbishment. Facilities 'truly excellent' ('for a girls' school') seems to be the general consensus and one of the reasons they chose Woldingham for their daughter. Sport, drama and music are rolled out in first class accommodation. Terrific grounds hold everything you would expect including a floodlit all-weather pitch. All major games played. Compulsory sport for all. One girl commented on the wide choice of sports available, 'you aren't forced to play netball if you can't stand it.' A tired acceptance among some parents (we hear this at virtually every school we visit) that their enthusiastic daughter never gets picked for matches – but 'that's just life'. Polo offered and body combat as well as dance club run by professional dancers. Three golf courses available nearby and riding at local stables, either with or without your own horse.

Saturday morning weekend programme (Saturday Active) – run by professionals to a very high standard – includes clay pigeon shooting, yoga and fencing. Drama happens in a splendid 600 seat auditorium, with a hydraulically raised orchestra pit no less, which would grace most towns, and studio theatre with computer-controlled sound and lighting system. Also dressing rooms and a costume workshop of a professional quality. Frequent theatre visits. Music teaching accommodation very high standard and senior choir go on frequent concert tours including performing mass at St Peter's in Rome. Annual musical hugely popular with girls and performed to an (almost) professional standard. Fifty per cent of the girls learn at least one musical instrument, but few take the subject for GCSE

or A level. Art strong, with art and history of art popular at A level – sixth form have their own desks in the art building, which also has a sculpture room, kiln and darkroom. Excellent careers programme mentioned by everyone – parents, girls and inspectors alike. Girls very well prepared and clued up about the opportunities available to them. Regular careers/university admissions sessions both for girls and parents. Girls can consult the careers officer at any time and regularly do.

Background and atmosphere: Idyllic rural setting in 700 acres in Area of Outstanding Natural Beauty, much of it let as agricultural land. As you approach the school after travelling up the long drive (10 minutes by car) it feels as if you have arrived on a BBC drama set. Mellow chateau-style house with wide sweeping balustraded steps to the front door. A statue of Christ stands on the perfectly manicured lawn opposite. Yet it is so close to London. Woldingham railway station is within the grounds and a free minibus shuttles girls to and fro – central London 35 minutes and East Croydon 15 minutes by train. The school has organised a bus from Keston, Hayes, Redhill, Nutfield and another from Sevenoaks and the Purley area.

Formerly a Convent of the Sacred Heart (has links with other Sacred Heart schools throughout the world and does a week's exchange if desired with some European ones). Overall impression is one of space, with some truly impressive modern building on site. Recently renovated chapel, suffused with the calming smell of incense and tranquil light from stunning stained glass windows. As well as compulsory Sunday mass, girls attend prayers here one night a week in their dressing gowns. Recently completed whole school dining area with state-of-the-art food preparation facilities and serveries, in addition to four new classrooms for history and politics. A new building in the pipeline – the Examination Centre. This will include spacious, contemporary testing rooms, individual examination suites and additional classroom space.

Boarding is structured according to year groups. Own room from year 10 onwards. Year 11 boarding area has been entirely refurbished to bring it up to date and in line with the newly redecorated and refurnished junior boarding house, Marden, for years 7 and 8. Girls delighted with separate new upper sixth form block, Shanley, or 'the Hilton'. Not only does it have university-style study bedrooms with ensuite bathrooms, but also a lift to get to the second floor. CCTV surveys the site and most buildings have linked TV screens displaying the day's activities, menus etc. Head of year is the equivalent of a housemistress and the first point of contact for parents. Some parents complain that they don't get the opportunity to build a long term relationship with one individual as they would do in a boarding house that operated on a vertical rather than horizontal system.

Saturday morning attendance compulsory for boarders (until the sixth form when things get more flexible) but they can then go home for weekends. Year 7s are allowed to go home on Fridays. Day girls can stay overnight, arrive early or stay late (a godsend for working parents who also want the occasional night away together), they can also come in on Saturday mornings and some Saturday attendance is compulsory for them. Typical weekend activities for the boarders as well as the usual visits to art galleries and museums are the (very popular) shopping excursions to London or Bluewater, Millennium Wheel, ice-skating, paintballing with Worth School and group treasure hunts around London with Worth. Socials at weekends with boys' schools for years 7-11.

The pupils seem a grounded bunch, their friendships relaxed and uncompetitive. Strangely, no pressure from sixth form to wear own clothes (wear black suits with their own pastel coloured shirts), apparently the absence of boys and any nearby town means that girls feel under no pressure to be mega-cool. Both RC and Anglican parents appear to feel comfortable with the religious ethos of the school – one Anglican mother said, 'we are not in any way made to feel second-class citizens.' Alternating C of E and RC confirmation years. Parents consistently praise the very happy atmosphere.

Pastoral care and discipline: Parent after parent comment that the pastoral care is the best aspect of the school – a feature highlighted by the latest inspection. Staff generally regarded to be 'a tremendous bunch of dedicated and caring professionals'. The same form tutor generally stays with the girls the whole way through from year 7 to year 11 and girls can in addition choose their own personal tutor. 'Buddy' scheme run by lower sixth girls to counsel years 7 and 8. Sixth formers can become Ribbons (prefects). Those who make it proudly wear their broad blue band across their black suits. They have special responsibility for the well-being of others and for promoting the spirit of the school – election is initially by democratic process. Parents praise the way the school introduces the girls to levels of responsibility, with lots of opportunities for leadership. The sixth form are given a good dose of independence during the week to counteract the effect of being cloistered in a valley, as well as leaving for the weekend on a Friday night (a sixth form privilege), back on Monday morning. A coffee bar, complete with comfy leather sofas and coffee machine, in one of the smart rooms in the main building, where the sixth form can mingle with staff, adds to a sense of privilege. Some girls remarked that the removal of their freedoms was a valuable disciplinary weapon – a sign of how much they value them. No make-up or nail varnish allowed, use of mobile phones permitted (Woldingham has its own mobile phone mast) but not during the school day.

Pupils and parents: Just over a third of pupils RC, equal percentage are Church of England, also several other non Christian religions, including Muslim, Hindu and Buddhist. Approximately, 25 per cent are foreign. Parents from professional backgrounds – bankers, company directors, Foreign and Commonwealth Office, lawyers, accountants. A number are undoubtedly posh (as are their offspring), but by no means all. Famous OGs include dress designer Caroline Charles, Caroline Wyatt (BBC defence correspondent), Clarissa Dickson-Wright, writer Victoria Mather and novelist and former MP Louise Mensch, Lady Isabella Hervey, Lady Caroline Waldegrave, actresses Dillie Keane and Carey Mulligan, Lady Marsha Ryecart, Princess Theodora of Greece and UK water-skiing champion Sarah Gatty-Saunt.

Entrance: Specialist Woldingham entrance exams taken in the December before entry at 13+and in the November before entry at 11+. Mrs Triffitt has ditched CE – 'I wanted to broaden the access and make it fairer for those schools who don't prepare for CE.' Candidates take papers in English, maths and science. The girls also see the head, or a senior member of staff, for a short chat. After the assessment day, school identifies any high-flyers to sit for the academic scholarship exam a few days later for sixth form entry and in January for 11+ and 13+. Girls come from a variety of schools in London and home counties. Also overseas pupils from the Far East, Spain, Africa and Mexico. Siblings (no longer quite so) automatically accepted – only if they can cope. About 15 taken into sixth form at 16. Applicants should pass at least eight GCSEs at grade B or above, including maths and English. Grade A or better is normally required in subjects chosen for AS and A2 Level. Applicants sit the school's own entrance exam.

Exit: Mostly to Russell Group universities, especially London, Newcastle, Nottingham, Manchester and Warwick. A fair number go onto the 'new' universities – Oxford Brookes, West of England and Manchester Metropolitan being the most popular. Wide variety of subjects – some go down the traditional path of medicine and law, a lot do business studies, also geography,

philosophy, politics and sociology, and economics. Drama courses and art school also popular. A few leave after GCSE, mostly unable to resist the lure of co-ed sixth forms at schools such as Charterhouse, Wellington, Worth and Hurtwood House – though girls we spoke to said they couldn't wait to get to the sixth form at Woldingham and all the privileges it held.

Money matters: Four academic scholarships at 11+, 13+ and 16+ to the value of 10-25 per cent of day tuition fees. Similarly drama, music, art sport and all-rounder scholarships. Music scholars receive free tuition on one instrument in addition. Science scholarship at 16+ to the value of 10-25 per cent of day tuition fees. In the case of need, means-tested fee remission may be available.

Remarks: Super-flexible in its approach to boarding – Woldingham provides best of both worlds for boarders and day pupils – and their parents. It turns out girls who are not prissy but resourceful and fun. Doesn't have the edginess of more City-type schools but, to compensate, there is a hugely supportive and cooperative atmosphere. A beautiful, safe environment for your young girl to grow up in away from home.

Wolverhampton Grammar School

Linked school: Wolverhampton Grammar Junior School

Compton Road, Wolverhampton, West Midlands, WV3 9RB

• Pupils: 675; 400 boys and 275 girls, all day • Ages: 7–18 • Non-denom • Fees: £11,955 pa • Independent

Tel: 01902 421326
Email: wgs@wgs.org.uk
Website: www.wgs.org.uk

Head: Since September 2013, Mrs Kathy Crewe-Read, previously deputy head of the King's School Chester, and the school's first female head in its 500 year history. She studied pure maths at Aberystwyth before gaining her teaching qualification at Durham University. She is married to Mark, deputy head at Manchester Grammar, and they have two children.

Academic matters: Not particularly selective but it is an academic school, producing good, solid results. GCSE and A level results have improved steadily over past five years. At GCSE in 2013, 66 per cent A*/A and at A level 4 per cent A*/A grades. Years 7-9 study Latin, French and German (with option of Italian in year 9) alongside usual subjects. Strong languages, maths, science (taught as three subjects), history. Recent improvements – more consistency in approach to marking, better co-operation between departments – seem to be paying dividends.

'We're not statistically driven. Weighing the pig doesn't make it any heavier. Youngsters are constantly measured and assessed, it's a harsh world for them. We're often asked "will it be in the test?" but we don't teach to tests. We have room to be experimental, go off at tangents, while being thorough and professional. We pick out initiatives that suit us. An issue for everyone now is the myriad of qualifications: IB, Cambridge, pre-U. We look at the best combination for us at that particular moment.'

WGS is aspirational and hard-working but not unduly pressured. 'Not a hothouse – they try hard to get a balance between work and life,' said a parent. 'It's very relaxed; they trust us to go and do the work,' says a sixth former. School at forefront of the OpAL programme (Opportunities through Assisted Learning) which started at WGS in 1998. A nationally

W

recognised model of support for academically gifted students with dyslexia, some 50 WGS pupils, supported by six teachers with one-on-one teaching; small groups, maybe doing nine, rather than usual 10, GCSEs. Cost is additional term's fees each year (usually reducing to 50 per cent after first three years). OpAL well supported throughout school by pupils and staff, who use OpAL inspired initiatives for all their pupils and has become school's academic Research and Development department. First OpAL pupils graduated recently, with range of good degrees from good universities, and are working in media, theatre design, teaching English and, most recently, winning a Saatchi apprenticeship over 10,000 other applicants.

Games, options, the arts: Football, rugby, cricket, tennis (a recent re-introduction) for the boys; hockey, netball, rounders, tennis for girls; mixed hockey, athletics and cross country for all. Strong football teams in a competitive region for football – first team acquit themselves well against bigger schools in independent schools cup, considered one of the toughest national trophies to win. WGS fortunate in its grounds, with pitches and Astroturf on-site. School big player in local, highly competitive games scene. For the adventurous, there is a popular climbing wall and the 24-hour Coast to Coast run. Year 10 pupils plus staff run in relay through the night across the country. Very popular, ambitious expeditions programme, from Duke of Edinburgh to climbing trips, Cotopaxi and Peru's remote Cordillera Blanca. Colourful photo-displays of pupils grinning in goggles and down jackets look like adventure travel company ad, an impression enhanced by particularly vibrant geography displays, with any available surface plastered with maps and quirky facts – feels a long way from Wolverhampton.

Pupils take part in range of local and national competitions, quizzes and debates. Drama popular, with whole-year productions in professional 200-seater theatre. Lovely, well-used library that would shame many public ones. Art strong: all WGS pupils have scored straight A*/As at art A level nine years running. More choirs, groups and ensembles throughout school than one might expect. Ambitious choral society programme – singing Shostakovich in Russian. Recital room (opened by local Led Zeppelin legend Robert Plant) and recording rooms particularly appreciated by band-nuts. Annual Jazz Spectacular is highlight for pupils and parents.

Background and atmosphere: School founded by the Merchant Taylors' Company in 1512. Moved to its present imposing building in smarter suburbs of Wolverhampton in 1875. Mellow red-brick towers and open green spaces, where pupils relax, gives school a collegiate feel. Buildings mix traditional and new – old-fashioned science labs crammed with specimens; snake skins (Monty the school python is a draw); smelly cockroach tanks and menagerie of creatures. School takes workmanlike approach: arts and drama complex was fashioned from a local car workshop; the old school gym is the new junior school's main hall. Big School – the school hall and heart of WGS – unveiled after a six figure refurbishment programme and phase one of the new sports pavilion development now open. WGS is a small oasis: 'we could feel rarefied', but whole atmosphere is unpretentious. Effort made to 'put the school back into Wolverhampton's life, in terms of its status and relationship with the town'.

Pastoral care and discipline: 'It's a cliché but there's a real warmth and community feel here. No school is perfect but we've found them quick to address concerns,' said one parent. Pupils say they feel 'listened to', and relations with staff notably respectful and friendly. Friendly air between year-groups: psychology A level pupils pounce on year 6s for experiments ('because they're so malleable at that age'). Pupils encouraged to take responsibility for themselves. Lively school parliament is consulted on whole range of issues although, in practice, not many pupils feel actively involved – something head is keen to change.

Pupils and parents: Pupils represent a fair cross-section, some travelling up to 20 miles to attend, including some from Birmingham, with its wealth of high-powered schools. One Shropshire based parent chose WGS above local schools because of its social/cultural mix. Not a 'smart' school, but friendly and confident, turning out good citizens (former Governor of the Bank of England, Mervyn King, is an Old Wulfrunian). Reporting on school netball tour, a pupil writes: 'Most young people will never get the chance to have a holiday in the Caribbean, let alone go there on sports tour with their friends'.

Pupils have more clear-eyed view of their futures than some – could hardly fail, given school's passionate belief they know about the world beyond school. Pupils are notably polite and orderly, though may partly be an effect of their very dark uniform which lends air of seriousness. (Splashes of scarlet have been added to lift the sombre black).

Entrance: Mostly from local primary schools and handful of prep schools, with around 30 coming in via the 'Big Six'. (Local primaries were not all thrilled by start-up of Big Six, nor WGS Junior School, but school has worked on relations, with WGS pupils volunteering in local primaries). Own entrance test at 11 and 13.

Exit: Ten per cent leave post-GCSE. Nearly all the remaining go to university, almost everyone to first choices in recent intakes. A few to Oxbridge (3 in 2012), a good proportion locally – Birmingham, Warwick, Nottingham – but also Durham, Leeds, Manchester, Exeter and many more.

Money matters: Social base may narrow with arrival of fee-paying junior school (many parents say they would have come to WGS earlier had there been a junior school) a matter school is aware of. Sense of not just paying lip-service but real commitment to school's original purpose, 'educating poor boys'. In that spirit a new Quincentenary scholarship programme has been launched which offers free places to the brightest performing students in the 11+ entrance test. Three further scholarships available – the Jenyns (an 'all rounder' scholarship awarded at Year 7); the Grove and the OW Sports Scholarship (both 16+). Fees are competitive.

Remarks: A fine school offering good education and value in highly competitive area. Particularly good for bright pupils with dyslexia.

Woodbridge School

Linked school: The Abbey

Burkitt Road, Woodbridge, Suffolk, IP12 4JH

• Pupils: 605 boys and girls, all day with some sixth form boarding • Ages: 11-18 • C of E • Fees: Boarding £26,700; Day £13,470–£14,400 pa • Independent

Tel: 01394 615000
Email: enquires@woodbridge.suffolk.sch.uk
Website: www.woodbridge.suffolk.sch.uk

Headmaster: Since 1994, Mr Stephen Cole MA, married with a grown up daughter. Previously taught at Wellington College and was head of science and housemaster at Merchant Taylors' School. He is an experienced schools' inspector and chairs the HMC (Headmasters' Conference) Inspection Committee. Despite tempting offers, he has chosen to remain at Woodbridge and his pride in the school is great.

Retiring in July 2014. His successor will be Neil Tetley, currently deputy head of Sevenoaks School.

Academic matters: Despite a keen eye for results, the school is not enamoured with league tables believing, as do many, that too much of a focus on the school's overall performance can lead to individual pupil's needs being ignored. Academically the right buttons are being pressed, in 2013, 72 per cent of A level entries were graded A*-B (46 per cent A*/A); maths, the sciences and performing arts are the strong suits. A similar story at GCSE, with 94 per cent of pupils achieving 5+ A*-C including maths and English in 2013, again maths, sciences and languages performing particularly well. Though less eye-catching, the middle range ability pupils' results reflect their solid achievement and success. Pupils are banded from year 7 and setted in certain subjects eg maths. Classes around 20. Everyone takes French in year 7, adding Latin and Spanish or German in year 8; at least one modern language to GCSE, with Mandarin and Japanese optional extras and Greek and Italian available in the sixth form. Around 60 pupils have mild learning difficulties; several full-time teachers offer support individually and in groups. The emphasis is on keeping pupils fully integrated into the mainstream classes. Strong EAL provision for overseas pupils. This is a school that works for all abilities.

Games, options, the arts: Impressive pitches and courts with the sports hall housed in the Eden project-style Dome, which provides room for several classes at a time. Sport is for all and everyone has the opportunity to play competitively in the school teams, often trouncing the opposition. The Sports Development Programme is devised to encourage the most talented pupils, many of whom catch the selector's eye at county and international levels. Swimming is for the hardy in an outdoor pool. Friday afternoon is time tabled for the Seckford Scheme, an extraordinary range of non-academic activities in which the whole school (staff included) joins. All interests and tastes are encouraged: eg sailing, cookery, chess (school has its own Grand Master), and CCF is a top draw for many. D of E is also popular. Music regarded as mainstream – no 'sporty' or 'aesthete', labels and half the school learn one or more instruments. It is 'cool to sing'. School has a close association with Aldeburgh and Snape with masterclasses, courses and recitals taking place regularly. Proliferation of choirs, ensembles, orchestras and bands. Drama also wildly popular with eight plays and shows performed annually in the impressive Seckford Theatre. Dance is increasingly popular and the head is keen to see new facilities. The school's international programme provides visits and exchanges throughout Europe, India, Australia, S Africa, China and the Oman. Pupils spend periods of up to 10 weeks at linked schools.

Background and atmosphere: Founded in the 17th century, the school is part of the Seckford Foundation and has occupied its present site in the town since the 19th century. It has been fully co-educational for 40 years. School stands on extensive grounds on a hilly plot with the various buildings dotted around, giving a campus atmosphere. The immediate approach to the school passes the slightly unprepossessing boarding house. However, the school buildings are a mix of styles from the Victorian to the contemporary, including the recently-built Seckford Theatre and sixth form centre. Atmosphere in classes, library and areas for independent working is palpably studious. Time-wasting is frowned on and most pupils spin from lessons to sport to activities non stop. One mother comments, 'pupils can have a crack at everything going – there is a niche for everyone'. Pupils themselves are friendly and polite; teachers, if anything, even more so. Unstuffy relations all round, and the staff give praiseworthy loyal service; most have been there 10 years or more.

Pastoral care and discipline: Enthusiastic endorsement by parents for vertical tutoring system, which operates from year 10 to 13. Younger pupils have the benefit of knowing older pupils well, and it provides leadership opportunities for sixth formers; 'most pupils know whom they would go to'. Boarders are fully integrated into the school, and as there are only 45 of them, they have a close relationship with the boarding house parents. Few discipline problems.

Pupils and parents: Pupils drawn largely from professional East Anglian families, many with a media background (Aldeburgh, BT close by). A fleet of buses brings pupils from as far afield as Norfolk, Felixstowe and Colchester. The school is very popular in the town and many parents have moved out from London to take advantage. Foreign students, many from the Far East, are encouraged to come for long or short periods, partly to ginger up what would otherwise be a very English school.

Entrance: Common entrance or test, together with a report from present school, and interview at 11 or 13. Two-thirds of intake at 11 transfer from the Abbey School, the prep department for Woodbridge, the rest from local state and private schools. About three-quarters of those tested are accepted. Entry to the sixth form is based on an interview and GCSE predicted grades.

Exit: Great majority leave sixth form for university. Leeds, Nottingham, Oxford Brookes and Manchester current favourites. Subjects include science, finance, economics, business and engineering. Four to Oxbridge in 2013.

Money matters: Academic scholarships worth up to 50 per cent of fees can be topped-up with means-tested bursaries. Music, sport and art scholarships are also available. Some sibling reductions.

Remarks: A good all-round 'country school in the town'. Lively, and although selective, would suit quite a wide ability range. Exceptional extra-curricular provision for what is, largely, a day school.

Woodford County High School

High Road, Woodford Green, Essex, IG8 9LA

• Pupils: 880 girls, all day • Ages: 11–18 • Non–denom • State

Tel: 020 8504 0611
Email: head.woodfordcountyhigh@redbridge.gov.uk
Website: www.woodford.redbridge.sch.uk

Headteacher: Since 2010, Ms Jo Pomeroy MA in English language and literature (St Andrews), BEd (Open), NPQH (forties). Spent two years in a comprehensive in rural Scotland before going to work in France at a mixed grammar school for three years. It was at this high achieving international school that she became aware of 'what can be achieved', 'what is possible' and 'what bright students are capable of if they are given enough challenge'. So the aim here 'is for students always to be working just beyond what they are comfortable with'. Back to the UK head spent another three years working in a comprehensive school with strong bias for European languages and at that point 'got interested in management, in getting into position where you could make a bigger change'. Sure enough, at her next appointment at a girls' grammar in Surrey, where she spent 16 years, she eventually became deputy head. 'There is enormous satisfaction in seeing incrementally what can be achieved in one place,' she says. Academic life at Woodford is very much influenced by this passion for great leadership as

W

well as head's English teaching background. 'What excites me the most is working from what you may be able to stimulate in your own life and career and then being able to share that with students so that they can enjoy challenges themselves.'

Academic matters: Best results in Redbridge. These are bright girls taught by committed teachers, a third of whom have been here for over ten years. Being a selective school they enter year 7 at above average ability (there are only four students with SEN) and the school has maintained an outstanding record of achievement with 79 per cent A*/A grades at GCSE in 2013 (99 per cent achieved five A*-C grades). And these stats despite most students – in fact well over half of the school population – speaking English as a second language. 'The joy of being in a school like this is that it is self-propagating, when students come in and they see other students valuing learning and success, and working hard on collaborative projects, it really affects everything else they do.'

This school models leadership extremely well. It has an impressive mentoring structure in place where older pupils mentor younger ones. There are literacy mentors who provide targeted additional support for year 7s where needed, and this 'sustained focus on academic literacy across the curriculum has been highly successful'. Head says, 'I have an interest in a great many subjects and I think the joy of English being my subject is that it takes you into everything, history, philosophy, art and music, and it is wonderful being able to investigate and enjoy literature and other languages as well.' These pupils have the opportunity to be mentored in other subjects as well, by sixth formers who relish the opportunity to 'give something back', though 'teachers still keep a close eye...'

In some classrooms desks are arranged to encourage interaction between students, not only with teachers. In the English department, year 7s are introduced to Shakespeare texts usually reserved for later years and invited to write an essay on what they have learnt. They also have lots of opportunity to visit theatres to support learning. Pupils take two languages from year 7 (French and either German or Latin). English, languages and science are all strong here and around 87 per cent of girls take triple science GCSE and 95 per cent study a humanities subject. Lots of information and support provided to both students and parents on choosing options.

In the sixth form, where roughly a quarter of students come from other schools, Woodford maintains good A level results with 81 per cent A*/B grades, 51 per cent A*/A, in 2013. Head says, 'If you are getting really outstanding results at GCSE you need to be seeing that followed through to A level.' The school has had some extraordinarily good A level results with students off to Oxford and Cambridge and on to medical careers. Academic mentoring and university preparation at sixth form, and guidance to final transition here is second to none, or in one parent's words, 'really very strong'. The school achieved the Investors in Careers Award in 2011.

Games, options, the arts: Head's commitment to leading a school that offers plenty of opportunity to be stretched is evident across the whole curriculum. Reasonable range of games on offer – badminton, athletics, netball, rounders, gymnastics and dance – and girls can pursue their interest in multi-cultural dance options such as Bhangra, African and street dance. Games either take place outside on the field and tennis courts or indoors in the newly built Lottery funded sports hall, which looks gorgeously fresh next to the main school building, already well over 100 years old when it opened as a school in 1919. Outdoor Greek theatre recently restored. The girls do well at games, they reached the UK badminton national finals in 2011, and they seem willing to try their best at everything, keen or not: 'Sport, I'm not good at, but it's a popular subject.'

Pupils speak highly of the sports leadership qualification offered in years 10 and 11: 'It gives you skills in being responsible, listening skills and classroom theory. We learn to create lesson plans.' Another said it 'opens us up to new areas; we realise there is more to our skill set and that motivates and opens us up to aim higher'. D of E also offered.

School does well at art and has had pupils featured in a Saatchi Exhibition. Major drama event each term as well as an annual musical (most recently, Oliver!) plus a summer production run by teachers and a spring production organised by students. A beautiful patchwork tapestry displayed under glass in the technology department harks back to the days when the school offered textiles. These days the girls focus their design skills in technology, where in 2011 they emerged winners of the National Technology Design Prize.

Instrumental and vocal lessons at all levels on offer but fewer than 11 per cent of students take these up although, in total, 'about 50 per cent of students in the main school have instrumental tuition either in or out of school, from beginners to diploma level'. Many others are involved in one of a large number of ensembles and clubs: guitar, singing, Carnatic music. There is a large junior choir and band, a folk group, a brass project, woodwind ensemble, and a staff choir too. Girls have also participated in Redbridge Choral Festival at the Royal Albert Hall.

Lots of trips to support lessons and extra-curricular activities, including eight expeditions since 2000 to eg Ghana, Morocco, Indonesia, China, Cambodia. Annual geography trip to Iceland.

Older students preside over all manner of different extra-curricular opportunities, such as talks, clubs and charity events, and there is a society for everything – even to discuss current affairs. 'We have house competitions and it is competitive,' head says. 'Sometimes there can be more drama off stage than on stage'. But because there is no adult intervention the girls learn to work together and develop great teamwork skills, 'that is a real success and selling point of the school.' It all comes good in the end, as evidenced by the year 11-led assembly held on the morning of our visit. In their well-structured presentation the girls demonstrated what they have learnt about self, learning and approaching life, showing extraordinary wisdom and the ability to work together. Head says, 'They listen to each other very well, and coming up the school younger students see this and that sets their aspirations.'

Background and atmosphere: Main building dates from 1768 when it was built as the country manor home of the Highams; school opened here in 1919. The house is old, although efforts have been made to brighten it up, and its venerable features lend an atmosphere of tradition – from the beautiful open air Greek theatre that stands in the grounds near to the tennis courts, to the hymnals still used in assemblies – 'I'm not a Christian but I enjoy it', a pupil remarked.

With its small classrooms, narrow stairwells and corridors, the school has an intimate feel. The lack of space noted at our last visit has been remedied by using Portakabins for some lessons. Population is not that large, with just 600 in the main school, but there is a larger than average sixth form of 277 students. Still, the girls lack nothing in terms of modern resources (thanks to a very active PFTA) and is well equipped with technologies such as interactive whiteboards and networked computers.

Pastoral care and discipline: Organised into form groups, they remain in these until the end of year 11. Pupils receive support from their form tutors and also have prefects to help school life run smoothly. Everything takes off from go with 'lots of homework straight away and a good diary and planner so you can organise yourself from the start'. Classes vary between 24 and 30 in the main school and average about 14 at sixth form, giving a teacher pupil ratio of 13:1. 'There is always contact with teachers, there is a friendship that is intimate; teachers are approachable, and there are smaller classes so you get to know everyone.'

Lots of careful thought has gone into ensuring peer support is strong. 'Our greatest glory is not in never failing but in rising up every time we fail' says a poster on the PSHCE board in the corridor. The board provides information about the peer support service run by older pupils so everyone can 'resolve and get to the bottom of issues,' said one pupil. 'So important,' said another, 'petty things getting out of hand is rare.' Pupils say they 'can't imagine peer support not being there. It's natural.' Also, 'Form prefects develop close relationships so you stay in contact even after leaving, like on Facebook.' House groups are active and help mobilise the girls to get involved in dramas and fund-raising events for the chosen recipient of charity week. Events like the five-penny race are popular and encourage heated competition: girls 'start saving as soon as September comes' and can raise as much £2000 in one hour.

As said, career support is good. There is a university success board to inspire the girls and year 11s have a review day including one-to-one meetings with teachers to 'help you identify what your strengths are'. Year 12s spend two hours per week in voluntary service, often working with children or the elderly or the disabled. 'It's a steep learning curve and you find yourself going back for several months.'

Sixth form here is very well managed and the academic mentoring and pastoral care is equally thorough. Girls joining at sixth form are integrated quickly, teachers observe where their knowledge 'differs from our own students, whether attendance is good and whether students are actively involving themselves in activities, which actually gives them the enthusiasm to get down to the nitty-gritty stuff'. All have a 15-minute interview with their tutor every fortnight and that keeps on top of any issues, 'as all these things play a part'.

Pupils and parents: As noted, the school has a large multi-ethnic population: over 40 languages are recorded as spoken here and there is a significant Tamil and Indian population. One parent said, 'My daughter benefits from being with children from many different ethnic backgrounds'. Overall, parents' opinions are positive and they support the PFTA as an opportunity to solve many of the school's cash problems. Many actively participate in the parents' and friends' association to raise funds for curriculum resources and other equipment (£25,000 digital language lab, a mini bus, external lighting) and parents also support school trips and attend recital evenings.

Parents are confident that the balance between pastoral support and academic challenge is just about right: 'I value the commitment of the school to ensure a balance of academic and extra-curricular activities that feed both mind and soul,' said one parent. 'Staff encourage and model positive approaches to both spheres and they note how sixth form girls exemplify leadership and citizenship in equal measures'.

When issues of bullying come up, 'once staff are aware of it the response is immediate and caring'. Every opportunity is made to 'help students to recognize that the things that they do in school, the challenges they take on, by juggling all sorts of interesting roles and responsibilities, set them up for the rest of their lives.' It all seems to pay off as the girls seem confident, resilient and creative. Former pupils here include Lucy Kirkwood, playwright (RSC, National Theatre), Sarah Winman, best-selling novelist (When God was a Rabbit) and Peggy Reynolds, Radio 4 broadcaster in the arts.

Entrance: Massively oversubscribed. Pupils must pass a verbal and non-verbal reasoning test in order to be considered for one of 120 places available and parents warned by the admissions authority (Redbridge) that 'the level of ability for entry is very high'. The test is written exclusively for the borough's only two grammar schools (the other being the brother school, Ilford County for Boys). Around 902 still apply. This is partly because of the vast number of feeder primaries (about 50) in both the maintained and the independent sector, partly because it is a high achieving school, and partly because it is one of just three all-girls schools in the area (the other two are independent and Catholic). Some areas in neighbouring boroughs (Waltham Forest and Hackney) are included in the catchment area, which is 'a circle drawn around mid-point between us and the boys' grammar school'. Selection tests are held in September of year 6 for transfer the following year and parents informed about a daughter's test performance prior to submitting the Common Application Form (and supplementary Grammar School Form) in late October. Children resident in the catchment area have priority. Offer of a place is based on aggregation of marks (the highest of girls around the same age). Head says the girls are tested on 'wit rather than what's been studied in the classroom'.

Nearly all girls stay on to the sixth form and are joined by another 25 per cent from other schools.

Exit: A few (14 per cent in 2013) leave post-GCSE but all that stay go on to university. Subject choices are academic but varied: physics, law, medicine, language (likely French), mathematics, geography, English or economics. A few go on to study business or architecture. Some success in applications to top universities and competitive courses with seven Oxbridge places and 11 medicine offers in 2013. Other destinations include UCL, Queen Mary's, Kent, King's College London, Birmingham, Nottingham.

Remarks: With the great pastoral and peer support in place and strong academic atmosphere there is no reason why a pupil should not do well here. The message from pupils to any year 6s considering the school is: 'If you love academic study, close relationships with teachers, clubs and societies, and you want to get involved, this is the place for you.'

Woodhouse College

Woodhouse Road, Finchley, London, N12 9EY

- Pupils: 1260 • Ages: 16–19 • Non–denom • State

Tel: 020 8445 1210
Email: enquiries@woodhouse.ac.uk
Website: www.woodhouse.ac.uk

Principal: From September 2013, John Rubinstein BSc (early fifties). Has been a teacher for over 25 years and still teaches A level maths, 'because it keeps me in touch with students, with the experience of colleagues, but most of all, because I love it.' His wife is also a teacher and they have three children, two of whom attended Woodhouse and are now at university. Mr Rubinstein is also a part-time Ofsted inspector. Enjoys running and takes part in 10K and half marathon races, 'four or five times a year.'

Academic matters: Woodhouse is one of the country's leading sixth-form colleges, always in the top five nationally, usually in the top three. This is essentially an academic place, whose main focus is on A-Levels. In 2013, over two thirds of entries were graded A*-B and 75 students gained straight A*/A in all their A level subjects.

Undoubtedly a key part of the success is enthusiastic, experienced and focused teaching. 'I've become much better at teaching A levels here,' said one department head. 'In the comprehensive I used to teach in before, I was always worried about my Year 9s.' Parents are very positive. 'Most of the teachers seem very, very good,' said one, whose son transferred from an independent school. 'They're excellent at monitoring and keep their finger on the pulse.' Results are certainly not achieved by hot housing or editing, and all students who pass AS Level can continue to A2s.

A wide range of options on offer, with 30 subjects in almost any combination. As well as two applied A Levels, there are also two BTECs in business and ICT ('We provide some vocational courses, primarily for students coming from our partner schools,' says the head.) Maths is the most popular A level choice (with 45 per cent taking it) and results are notably strong. One of London's largest providers of A level science with many going on to science-related degrees. Four languages, including Italian, and an abundance of 'ologies', from sociology to music technology. Critical thinking and the extended project also available (in 2013 over half of those who took the EPQ gained A*/A grades), as well as GCSEs in English and maths for those who require re-sits.

Though the majority at Woodhouse tend to favour professional courses at university, social science and arts-based studies are strong, with thriving theatre studies, economics, English literature and geography. 'Independent learning' is high on the agenda. 'We want students to prepare for lessons, so they can understand and interpret the information, using the teacher and their fellow students as a resource,' says the head. Motivated students respond well to this approach. 'Teachers assume if you're interested in your subjects, you will want to read around them,' said one. 'They don't force you to work, but they'll give you the resources and make themselves available to you,' said another.

All students, too, have access to two learning mentors – one for humanities, the other, science and maths – to sort out any day-to-day tangles. One full-time SENCo, plus two part-time specialists, providing individual support for those with dyslexia and dyspraxia, as well as study-skills aid for those who need it. The buildings are 99 per cent adapted for those with physical disabilities.

Games, options, the arts: Woodhouse prides itself on providing 'a broad and civilising education' and all are expected to participate in at least two six-week courses of 'enrichment', the majority of which take place on Wednesdays afternoons, when there are no lessons. Most relish the opportunities to develop new skills in everything from observational drawing to street dance. Duke of Edinburgh and Amnesty International also on offer.

Art and dance are strong curricular subjects here, with excellent A level results, and the college has a lovely bright dance studio and art department. Sports facilities, too, are good, with a new sports halls and floodlit all-weather pitch. Official team sports include football (girls' and boys'), netball and basketball, but individualists can also enjoy cross-country, squash, trampolining and kick boxing. 'If there isn't a club that you'd like to do,' said one student, 'the sports department are happy to try and set something up.'

Woodhouse students like to get involved and there's an active College Council, which has recently helped introduce a daily loan system for netbooks. Plenty of outside speakers and activities including art trips, foreign exchanges, a ski trip and the opportunity to undertake voluntary work abroad.

Background and atmosphere: Located in a pleasant leafy suburb, Woodhouse began it educational life as Woodhouse Secondary School in 1925, but became one of the capital's rare sixth-form colleges in the 1980s. Today all pupils are aged between 16 and 18 and all are studying A Levels. With 660 new pupils a year, the College is significantly larger than a traditional school sixth form, but smaller than a FE college.

The original stately Victorian façade (deriving from its former incarnation as the home of ornamental plasterer Thomas Collins) has now been joined by a motley timeline of newer buildings, leaving it today with well-equipped facilities. The state-of-the art 'Learning Zone' is one of the most recent innovations, offering space to work in solitary silence as well as in small groups, and supervised open-access IT. 'Quite a lot of students here can't work in silence at home and don't have the facility to do the "hard hours",' says the head. 'We wanted to create learners who can work on their own.'

Values here are traditional. 'We believe in honesty, hard work, mutual respect and taking responsibility for your own learning.' The atmosphere is generally enthusiastic, as much for work as for play. 'Here it's cool to work, cool to be involved,' says one student. 'The atmosphere is incredible,' says another. 'There's a massive sense of community. There are always things happening.'

Pastoral care and discipline: Not every 16-year-old is ideally suited to the self-motivation required by an academic sixth-form college, but here high expectations are supported by a well-thought-out tutorial system and plenty of individual guidance. Every student has their own tutor, 'My son sees a guy two or three times a week, whom he likes and respects,' said one mother. 'When he was having trouble at home, they really kept an eye on him.'

The college sees itself as a bridge between school and university, and new students are eased into this more adult world with an induction day in the summer before they start. The enrichment programme helps aid new friendships beyond the classroom. 'Everyone makes friends ridiculously fast because there are so many people in the same position,' said one boy. Boundaries are firm and there's zero tolerance on punctuality. 'It's an issue they have to grasp,' says the head. 'If they're not making the effort, why should other students suffer.'

In lessons, students are attentive. 'If a teacher leaves the room, people get on with their work,' says one boy, 'They want to do well.' One recent arrival, who'd left a successful local comprehensive, said, 'I came here because I felt I would be made to work. I've really grown up quickly into a different person. The change is on a biblical scale.' Few significant discipline problems. 'Issues found elsewhere are not even on the radar here,' notes the head gratefully. Standard formula of oral and written warnings, with a code of conduct signed by all parents and pupils, but exclusion is a rarity. 'We have pupils from quite challenged backgrounds, but I have thrown out just one student,' says the head. 'My predecessor excluded two.' Parents agree that discipline is firm but reasonable. 'They run quite a tight ship, but it makes them responsible,' said one father. 'When my son's attendance was only 90 per cent, he had to see the senior tutor every week. As his attendance improved, he went less frequently.' There's no dress code, but pupils don't push it. Relaxed but neat is the general rule.

Pupils and parents: An eclectic mix – 'some nerdy kids, some cool kids, all sorts, colours and creeds.' The core is probably typical of the reasonably prosperous 'squeezed middle' of north London, but with a far higher ethnic intake (Greeks, black and South Asians) than you'd assume from the location, and a far higher proportion of those who require some type of financial support. 'Last year, we did a survey and were surprised to find that over a third of pupils were on the full EMA [now abolished],' says the principal.

Parents tend to be involved and supportive, students upbeat, mature, outgoing and energetic. They clearly enjoy the school – more than half volunteered on the annual open day held on a Saturday. 'They want to do well and they want to enjoy themselves,' says the principal. 'They're trying to get the balance right of working hard and having a good social life.' A parent agrees: 'My son is so happy. He really appreciates the fact that people are there because they want to learn, not because their parents are pushing them. Most students here are trying to better themselves and work really, really hard.' Past students include journalist Johann Hari, comedian Michael McIntyre and actress Naomie Harris.

Entrance: Priority is given to two local secondary schools, Friern Barnet and The Compton. Students from these schools make up about 20 per of the intake. After that, it's predicted grades and/or interview. Competition is ferocious (about 4,500 apply for 660 places), particularly for in-demand subjects. 'We can afford to be choosy,' says the head, 'but we're looking for a range.' Those with high predicted grades, excellent references and a clear sense of direction (about 160 students) are invited to three 'direct offer' evenings for a talk. 'They have already demonstrated that they meet the requirements we would need to ask about at an interview.' The rest with minimum predicted grade requirements (evaluated on a point system, with specific grades for individual subjects) are given a 20-30 minute interview (with optional parental accompaniment) in the February/March prior to entry. 'We're looking for maturity,' said one teacher. 'We want them to demonstrate that they are committed to A levels and really want to work, but we also want people who will get involved on a wider basis.' The interview is frequently of as much benefit to the student as to the college. 'We often spend it giving careers advice,' says the head.

Travel time is also taken into consideration. 'We generally consider an hour and a quarter by bus the maximum desirable distance.' Applications available from the time of the open day in November until the closing deadline in January. All candidates require a confidential report from their current school and must be between 16 and 18 when starting at the College. The College operates a waiting list for the re-shuffle that often takes place after results day in August.

Exit: Over 95 per cent to university with the most popular destinations being Brunel, Queen Mary (London), Kent, Leeds, Manchester and Sussex. Most popular subject choices are economics, law, engineering, business and psychology. Twelve to Oxbridge, eight to medical school and 45 per cent to Russell Group universities in 2013. Good advice about careers and courses, including a full time careers co-ordinator. Regular tutorials on university admissions and interview practice for those who require it.

Money matters: Parents are asked for £100 contribution for the two-year stint, enabling the College to keep up to date with books and underwrite the enrichment programme and facilities. (Those who can't afford it, don't pay). A £50 refundable deposit also required for text books. The College has attempted to replace some money lost through EMA cuts with bursaries.

Remarks: An upbeat environment, with strong teaching and results. A firm stepping stone between school and university.

Worth School

Paddockhurst Road, Turners Hill, Crawley, West Sussex, RH10 4SD

- Pupils: 580; 435 boys/145 girls; around three quarters board (girls day only until year 9) • Ages: 11–18 • RC but others welcome
- Fees: Day £17,430–£20,940; Boarding £18,780–£28,950 pa
- Independent

Tel: 01342 710200
Email: registry@worth.org.uk
Website: www.worthschool.co.uk

Head Master: Since 2007, Mr Gino Carminati, BA MA. Early fifties. Third headship though his first in Catholic school – he was previously in the top seat at Methodist Kent College, Canterbury (similar ethos, different religious shading) and before that at Queen Elizabeth's Grammar School in Faversham.

Reckoned by parents to have been headhunted for current post, he's well into first decade there, firmly ensconced and loving the job.

A dapper and imposing presence, he's also a deft hand with a temperamental cafetière. Nice way with words, too, generating rolling sentences you could toboggan down.

A historian by training, Mr Carminati was tempted by law as career. 'Rumpole was one of my great heroes; I've always liked that type of semi-rebellious character but within the confines of justice,' he says (carefully, you feel, in order not to incite mass junketing in the ranks). And, like so many heads everywhere, 'I quite liked the idea of dressing up.'

Courts lost out on his sonorous voice when he opted for education instead, inspired by own experiences as a pupil at St Aloysius, an independent turned grammar turned comprehensive. Though perfectly adequate, it lacked the 'why' (rather than 'x') factor, he believes. 'I always felt I was being trained rather than educated, [to get] through the exam system.'

Like just about everyone here, big on quotes to make his point. 'I have a phrase, borrowed from Plutarch, that our pupils are not pitchers to fill but lanterns to light, although I always qualify that by saying you can't light a lantern unless you put some oil in it.'

Would have to be of the first pressing virgin oil variety to meet his goal, which is to produce people who are engaged rather than busy (a word he uses with caution because of frenzied hamster on treadmill connotations). Will also be rounded and (one of school's big buzz words) reflective, not to mention intelligent, intellectual and in touch with their emotions as well as their reasons, while 'not taking themselves too seriously.' Cripes.

With that lot to deal with, just as well he's a great believer in the importance of trying to get away from it all, mentally if not physically as 'it's very hard in a school like ours with full boarding,' Travelling, music and reading press his buttons – happily his shelf-lined, view-rich study was original library and very nice it is, too.

Balks slightly at anything that implies routine for the sake of it, like walking the school in a headmasterly fashion at set times. 'Sounds like duty,' he says, (though he does it – and now, with the exception of one boarding house with confusing back staircase, is expert on its nooks and crannies, of which there are many).

Under his watch, school numbers have risen from 420 to close to the 600 mark, most the result of move to full co-education. Some parents were initially dubious. 'We weren't mad about the idea because we thought it was a place for educating boys but it seems to have worked out all right,' says one. The school itself adapted easily, many women already on the staff, all but two teachers with previous experience of teaching girls.

Mark of success is that atmosphere hasn't changed, something head feels is down to the fact that 'we were never one of those macho schools in the first place.' Careful work to ensure that boys didn't feel they 'were being dislodged' has helped ensure that they have been 'really gracious in the way they welcomed the girls to the school.' Girls, meanwhile, 'were very willing to fit in and then quietly command, which is what they do.'

Make full generals, too, holding around half the prefect posts. However, says head, boys will continue in the majority as 'having only 300 boys would limit you with some of the sports.' Girl numbers are at Goldilocks levels, 40 per cent just enough to give them sense that 'they're a proper integrated cohort, not a token gesture.' (Girls agreed, apart from slight disappointment at tenterhook-light girls' house matches as 'with only two houses, result isn't much of a surprise.')

Balances the tricky dual strands of headship with panting anxiety of a parent (he has a son here) with minimum of angst on either side, achieved largely by ensuring that his wife Anne (who teaches EAL students at the school) attends the majority of consultation evenings. 'Difficult because as soon as I appear, I'm wearing two hats.' Is he intimidating? 'I hope not,' he says.

Not seen as such by parents though comes across as 'supremely self-confident ... very highly thought of,' thinks one. Reckoned to be something of a career head who is 'enormously in charge', which can occasionally prompt suspicion as to levels of sincerity, though tempered with acceptance that it's part of the inevitable corporate persona.

Not every head gets to run a school which comes with a monastery round the back. Best bit of the job, however, is seeing how the Benedictine values have stayed the course when former pupils come back to visit. What remains in place may not be what 'you choose yourself,' but seeing 'the things that remain ...and how they live life are fascinating.'

Academic matters: All about 'academic worth' says the relevant section on school's website and you really can't blame them for indulging in the occasional pun.

School has fair share of bright buttons. However, not all are 'are desperate high flyers,' thinks parent. More are having to gain altitude though, what with school upping the ante with six GCSE B grades or better required to make the cut for sixth form. Essential 'to stand realistic prospect of university success,' reckons school. 'Definitely becoming more academic,' agreed one mother, with slight regret.

Offers fully formed dual systems post-16, taught in class sizes averaging around nine (18 in the school as a whole). IB, currently taken by around a third of sixth form, pulls in some locals each year, drawn by rarity value and has strong European appeal (though formerly strong contingent from Germany has waned following changes to education system there).

Results, averaged 35 points in 2013, was 37 in 2012. Popularity may increase further now IB subject choices are a closer match with A level options (psychology is the latest to be added).

A levels, with 69 per cent of grades at A*/B in 2013 (75 per cent in 2011 is the goal to beat) continue to be exam of choice for the majority and a non-negotiable for some international students with specialisation already in their sights (maths and science for Chinese pupils, for example).

Sciences have been experiencing distinct off season, biology in particular, psychology broadly similar, with physics and chemistry probably not the best version of themselves, either. It's accounted for by status as third choice subject for many pupils, says the school, which stresses this is no longer the case and is also at pains to point out decent sprinkling of top grades including just over 55 per cent gaining A*/A in A level chemistry in 2013 (four candidates out of the nine that year).

However, plenty of strong subjects including history, art and religious studies, languages in general starting to pack in the boys 'like you wouldn't believe,' comments staff member. Some stunning results 2013 – 100 per cent A level French A*/B.

School doesn't shirk from shock of the new, or newish, with economics flourishing (felt to be good route to a crisis-defying well paid job) and government and politics A level on the way in. Unusually no DT, though with design element absorbed into art and successfully so, helping to spawn at least one budding architect in the process, doesn't need to be, thinks head. Ditto engineering which 'we incorporate into science and mathematics.' Lines on the sand are media and film studies. No snob factor involved. 'Just wouldn't be popular.'

GCSE results also very respectable in 2013, overall pass rate of 95 per cent.

Pedagogues span the age range, some so unnervingly youthful you want whatever they have sprinkled on their bedtime cocoa, others long haul troupers, including one who has featured 'in every school photograph for the last 40 years, even the faded ones,' says pupil.

Have fair share of idiosyncrasies, presentation-focused English teacher responsible for high density noticeboard achieving concours standard symmetry (writing quite literally on the wall), language specialist much admired for proselytising Spanish by highlighting party culture rather than demographics (yawn) as well as ways with vocab, word for 'potion' indelibly printed on IB student's memory following mime involving coffee granules and juice.

Overall, broadish palette of ability shades well catered for from the Oxbridge gang (about three or so a year) to the minority who don't have higher education in their sights, in line with one of the plentifully quoted St Benedict's dictums that the strong should have 'something to strive for,' the weak 'not be overburdened.'

Something school is definitely up for when it comes to support. International contingent are well served by EAL department which concentrates on weighting lessons towards nuance decoding – vital in science and maths exams where word games are all part of the fun (or perhaps not, judging by levels of concentration in EAL science class, ears almost audibly straining to grasp finer points of examiners' habits).

Learning support department doesn't venture much beyond 'dyses' in mild form, Asperger's ditto, as 'we don't have learning assistants in the classroom,' (screening for all in year 9). Individual or small group support by withdrawal (often replacing language).What it does do, it does well, though: parents speak of children 'transformed' by support.

Day to day helping hands plentifully outstretched, felt pupils, sixth form learning prefects who run sessions in range of subjects, including Latin are popular with younger gang as can have edge over teachers who 'don't have the experience of teaching themselves,' thought one.

More formally, anyone falling seriously behind will be supported through GCSEs with involvement of house tutors, learning support and addition of extra lessons in the hope, rarely unfulfilled, that galvanising effect will be sufficient to propel them into the sixth form. On rare occasions it doesn't, school will suggest search for suitable plan B school post 16.

Usually does the trick, think parents. 'Takes all comers, gets the best out of most children and they achieve their potential,' reckons one.

Games, options, the arts: Idleness, said St Benedict, is hostile to the soul, a message taken to heart here, particularly when it comes to sport. Website oozes Catholic take on muscular Christianity (a six pack, at least) featuring video that cuts away to reveal rugby team pitting strength against giant grass roller (and winning, naturally: it'll be a jumbo from nearby Gatwick Airport next). Deceptive, however, as you don't have to be terrifically sporty to enjoy it here, say pupils. Though football is finally acquiring the kudos supporters feel it deserves, rugby (which also musters six senior teams) continues to loom large on the sporting calendar.

School, thought one parent, is 'astute' at picking its opponents, middle rather than top rung, success consistent – with several unbeaten teams – if not always earth shattering, a few 'mixed' and 'disappointings' sprinkled through the end of school reviews (particularly good at quarter finals...). However, 'we're still really bad,' agreed group of pupils, cheerfully. On the plus side, there's no in or out crowd, change from days when rugby heroes were school idols (and life wasn't altogether plain sailing for less hearty). 'Completely gone, now,' says head. Pupils and parents agree. 'Friends can share emotional similarities even if interests are completely different,' thought articulate sixth former. Low stress environment allows sport and arts lovers to have their fill, others preferring not to do either with tolerance for all.

Attitudes haven't softened at the expense of choice. Plenty for die hard fanatics to get up to in the way of must-have team sports that tick all the participation boxes. While it's non-negotiable sport for all two afternoons each week and for Saturday fixtures 'not always popular with day pupils and weekly boarders,' most esprit de corps stuff is largely optional beyond year 9, 'though they like us to be in teams,' thought girl. Aerobics, fencing, golf and riding mop up those seeking a personal challenge, the perhaps slightly euphemistically entitled multi-sports catering for those who may not be. 'There's a lot of sport on offer but if you don't want to do it I don't think you have to,' thought parent.

Some sporty girls feel slightly short-changed as they're in a minority and therefore not stretched enough, thought a mum. Something school 'could do little about ... but will be rectified in the natural course of events as more girls come up through the school,' and benefit from 'excellent teaching.'

Gourmet facilities include assorted courts (smart Astroturf firmly padlocked, presumably against ovine marauders) which sprinkle the acres as well as eight hole golf course, nearby sports centre offering athletics tracks and splashtastic 50m pool (would be even better if school had its own, thought a parent). Access to pitches the other side of busy 'B' road is currently supervised, though a new bridge, completed now. Follows tragic death of a pupil there in 2011.

Two sports halls, smaller very slightly dingy; larger, approached through front door so heavy that even spectactors could end up with a decent six pack, kitted out with decent fitness suite. Somewhat off-message vending machine in foyer, stacked to the gunnels with confectionary and drinks and thoughtfully putting back the empty calories that exercise has taken out, is being restocked with healthier options. (A second, in sixth form house, will retain sugar as principal ingredient).

If sports don't trigger necessary inspiration, terrific array elsewhere (billed as − wait for it − 'Worth extra' − groan) should do the trick. Drama includes three plays for different age groups in the summer term with lots of Shakespeare (added treat is array of beautiful costumes, many borrowed from the National Theatre). Music also strong, helped by super recording studio and Mac-rich room to hone technical and composition skills as well as sensibly soundproofed rock room for band rehearsals. Forty per cent of pupils have individual instrumental or singing lessons, orchestra (quite audibly not an earsore) particularly praiseworthy for size and boy participation. Abbey Choir, which sings weekly mass (website features a nice bit of plainsong) ditto.

Midweek afternoon given over to colossal range of activities which range from chess, very successful with substantial input from keen father, to community service: 'pupils are taken to charity shops....' (to serve, not for sale) as well as 'invasion games' (you have been warned).

Some, such as choir and jazz club, are vetted with auditions; most are entrée libre, many designed for IB compatibility. D of E-worthy, too, driving lessons apparently counting as a credit-earning skill − who knew? − and school, as a licensed centre, able to run and approve awards, popular trips (South America a favourite haunt) adding an edge of glamour.

Sparky individual achievements, too: sixth form are 'influential role models', says prospectus. Not half, with posts including public relations prefects whose duties include scouting for pupils able to take visitors on guided tours. Further down the school, one year 9 pupil has self-published own fiction, originally prep that outgrew the exercise book/took on a life of its own.

Creativity a-plenty elsewhere, too, with two wonderfully big art rooms, generosity of seniors' space influencing scale of artwork − few miniatures here. 'Means you aren't compressed,' says pupil. By way of demonstration, there's vast, decorated tree trunk, donated to the school and apparently taking root in art room. Pupil creations, some selected for display at the Saatchi Gallery, include orchid-like shapes strung alone wires, while floor level delights include a sculpture with the precarious delicacy of a scaled up Jenga game and meticulous, technically brilliant paper and wood confections with concertina folds at crazy angles, like Escher on hallucinogens. Like pupils' poetry, seem to plumb otherwise hidden emotional depths.

Background and atmosphere: De haut en bas, literally so, with two main groups of buildings taking up 25 of the site's 500 acres and separated by hill steep enough for twice daily ascents, says head, half joking, to form basis of his daily fitness routine.

At the foot, approached by grand entrance (ornate electric gates, gryphon-topped portico, though you have to nip round the corner for commanding views over Downs) there's the stately pile originally built for Cowdray family and acquired by Benedictines, school's founding order, in the 1930s to mop up pupil overspill from Downside, becoming a separate school in the 1960s.

Teaching, meanwhile, goes on at the summit, school's very own mini Parnassus, with standalone main teaching block (a solid 1980s construction shortly to be extended) housing maths, humanities and languages together with serious looking learning resources centre (solid shelves and workaday displays suggest books as study essentials first, imagination firers second).

It's next to tranche of buildings, home to performing arts, science and the Pitstop, a small café-style eatery (main low-ceilinged refectory − slightly apologised for; 'it is what it is,' says member of staff; much improved by paint job, mint green replacing previous appetite suppressing mustard yellow − is down the hill). They're clustered in loose extended courtyard arrangement, centrepiece a clock tower so wantonly Disneyesque you half expect it to sprout features and break into song.

Dotted through the site, uphill, downhill and probably in my lady's chamber too, if such a thing existed, are the school houses, all nine of them, which come at you from every direction. Seen as hugely important centres of r and r for day as well as boarding pupils, they enable everyone to let off steam, enhancing sense of camaraderie as 'you spend a lot of time with your houses even if you're not boarding,' says pupil.

Communal rooms (too many to count − we did try) are swankiest for oldest, who also have study rooms, mainly shared if day, some solo if boarding, while younger day pupils stash stuff in lockers, tops cunningly (and frustratingly) sloped to prevent leaning towers of casually dumped textbooks.

While they take the same newspapers (in assorted shades of blue: Grauniad fans may pine) houses vary enormously in style, ranging from Rutherford House's touch of the Bridesheads (parquet and imposing marble fireplaces no whit disturbed by table football machine and mini bank of computers) to St Bedes's, the newest house, so far away from the main drag that only rooftop is visible on location map, which comes complete with soft furnishings co-ordinated in browns and greens (nicer than it sounds) and eco focus, much lauded though little understood. 'Didn't realise we even collected rainwater,' said pupil.

Boarders have well designed bedrooms, tidy but not unspeakably so − boys' gloriously free of après-trainer whiff − fours and fives to a room, dropping to two in year 13; star of the show the solo accommodation for year 13 boys in smart, self-contained Gervase House, the only one to blend day and boarding pupils, and amply conveying undergraduate feel (more upmarket than many a uni) complete with tiny but perfect en-suites.

St Mary's, sole girls' boarding house, is a delight with well thought out bedrooms, duvets adding flashes of pink to light wood sea, and a common room you actually want to spend time in, best feature 'the pit' − lowered hearth area used for house mass and picnic style meals but, alas, never warmed by roaring fire, vetoed by health and safety.

Parents hope houseparent, just leaving, will have successor equally rich in humour and discretion, from curtains ('you'd be surprised how many don't close them') to conversations (office, just off quiet room 'isn't very quiet' so hears 'everything − and amazing what you pick up.')

Thoughtful touches include washing machines for 'emergencies, delicates and underwear,' says school. Girls only, however, as no boys so far have expressed urge to do own washing

Pastoral care and discipline: Insulating tranquillity radiates both from surroundings and what one mother described as 'gentle, smiley' monks, though not a place to come for those with real issues with Catholicism or deep-rooted opposition to introspection.

Spiritual side is 'the heart of the school,' says one of many delightful pupils, impact felt most strongly in tolerance for others with soul-searching high up the agenda and a feature of student magazine which, like a thought for the day compilation, is jam-packed with worthy thoughts about happiness and love and, pick of the bunch, what nuns do all day (pray, apparently).

School temperament is accordingly mild. Even traditional post-exams photograph eschews standard shrieking, certicate-grasping, mid-air riot in favour of a nice, quiet group of girls and boys standing in semi-formal pose, looking slightly embarrassed at being singled out for glory.

Reflects notion of competition as being 'based on the idea of sharing excellence,' says head. Though a possible handicap if opponents' idea of competition is to slaughter the opposition (school team recently lost debating competition because it was 'too politically correct' says magazine report) seems to damp down house on house aggression despite ferocious-looking face paint applied, warrior fashion, before girls' matches. House music competition is the only event capable of triggering anything approaching blood lust 'because we organise it and it involves everyone,' felt pupil.

Pupils and staff spoke highly of events that blend spiritual with social rather than adversorial dimension in keeping with admirable Benedictine tradition of hospitality. 'Food is a very good reason to mix,' says housemistress. Civilised, too, with wine allowed for sixth formers on Feast of St Benedict 'but only with food,' and over 18s allowed to nip down to the local pub with permission (though hadn't been a single request when this reviewer arrived at the start of the summer term – unusual, thought member of staff). Many house parties, too, (not in the format most parents know and dread, we're assured) as well as 'young ladies' lunches' (young gents' versions, too) where pupils from same house or year group foregather in delightful panelled room to swap news and views in civilised surroundings.

Results in easy going, clique-free contact between year groups, think pupils. 'So refreshing compared with my previous school where the year 11s wouldn't talk to the year 10s. Here, everyone does,' says one recent arrival, who also praised unofficial problem sharing – girls' friendship issues the unsurprisingly regular hot topic.

Tutor groups, house linked except in sixth form, meet regularly; chaplains, one per house, are also useful listening ears. Pupils also felt that lectio devina – Benedictine tradition of reading sacred texts aloud and discussing themes raised – can be effective route in to problem sharing, akin to grown up circle time. 'You can raise worries – it's a personal thing,' felt one.

Head recently reported that behaviour had hit an all-time high, and pupils we talked to felt there was little in the way of badness beyond missed homework deadlines, with normal sanctions consisting of warnings and a series of ever-lengthening detentions or, in the case of 'rude or inappropriate' use of phones (a worry as 'can access everything' unlike computers where school wifi blocks undesirable sites, including Facebook) minimum 24-hour confiscation.

Not much obvious kicking over the traces in pupils we saw, who seemed born to walk rather than run (though sloping terrain is admittedly a fabulous natural deterrent), although some current models of decorum were, we were assured by pupils, former wild cards who have been 'subdued' as they come up through the school, ending up 'unrecognisably well-behaved.' Schools stays on top of things, confirmed parent. 'I don't get the impression that children drift off the radar. They're not allowed to misbehave or become lost sheep.'

Pupils and parents: Fair few Worthians wanting to spread educational joy to second generation, substantial overseas contingent, some from hyper-Catholic parts of the world. One Brit parent, while accepting school's need to get bums on seats, felt that 'you need to make sure that that percentage doesn't get out of hand.'

Riches represented amongst parents, rags less so, though neither end of the spectrum dominates. 'You'll see the odd Rolls Royce as well as the odd beaten-up car,' thought one mother.

Lots of parent socialising, from informal curry nights to large scale events including masked ball fab summer fair complete with fairground rides, jazz band and a profusion of strawberries. 'A very jolly scene,' thought one.

If all goes according to plan, pupils will emerge from the Worth experience 'wise [and] intellectually astute,' (according to prospectus, size defiantly non-standard and so glossy you could skate on it). They are, as well (so much so that it was a relief to hear off-duty younger girls described as 'very screamy' by sixth former). One parent, with ultra-serious child, felt distinctly frivolous in comparison.

Pupils take great pride in individuality and proclaim absence of a particular school type, backed by head who thinks school should 'allow people to grow into themselves – a pupil's inner talent could mean that you haven't mastered any one thing but are good at lots. We're 600 weird and wonderful individuals and we've got to learn to get on with each other.'

We admired fighting talk, though couldn't help but notice girls' near identical hairdos, most tumbling manes of mermaid-length tresses, varying in colour, finish as high gloss as prospectus.

Star former pupils include actor Robert Bathurst and publisher Sir David Bell, though sports dominated, from Tim Hutchings (athletics) to Tom Symonds (racing) and rugby (Nick Walshe). All admirable stuff. However, as Old Girls start to make their mark on the world aided by slickly run alumni society (which includes a 'Worthians in Property' group), we'd hope for more variety and quirkiness in years to come.

Entrance: Oversubscribed, says school, which advises registration two years in advance. Around 120 places a year, 40 in year 7, 60 in year 9 and 20 in year 12, occasionally in other years. Feeder schools many and various, majority independent, fair few Catholic (though not all) and also include local state primaries and secondaries, though with school bus network puts Tunbridge Wells, Haywards Heath and Horsham within reach.

Just shy of 20 per cent from overseas (Gatwick a 10 minute taxi ride away), some non-native English speakers, support offered though must be sufficiently fluency to cope with normal lessons.

Currently pushing convincing case for 11 plus entry by citing early leadership opportunities on offer to the brightest and best in years 7 and 8 when academic effort plus helpfulness and embodiment of Benedictine ethos can land a handful a place on school council or as prefects. Fine for boys, who can board from year 7 (with three nights a week flexi option), though it's day places only until year 9 for girls (might account for very low representation in current year 7 – just six out of 25-strong year group).

Exit: Around three or so to Oxbridge, wide range elsewhere recently including girl studying agriculture, boy doing fashion design. Economics, maths, business and management all popular, interesting combinations (history and theology, maths and philosophy) also a big feature. Sixth formers praised careers advice, helpful email updates arriving at least twice a week, approach informative but low pressure. Many (more than average, it seemed) were postponing university applications with official blessing, gap years viewed as logical make your mind up time.

Money matters: Fees about on a par with nearest competitors with good scholarships (music, academic and all-rounder) offering up to 40 per cent of fees (music also includes free instrumental tuition). Means tested bursaries are also available though total fees remission generally capped at 50 per cent. Local, bright Catholic children can also apply for St Benedict's Scholarships – fully funded day places, one in year 7, two in year 12.

Remarks: 'At some schools, it's all about how clever or hearty and sporty you are – not here,' thought one parent. Another, with experience of several other leading Catholic schools, had no doubts. 'It's the pick of the bunch.' Encourages reflection, not out to dazzle, producing thoughtful pupils, distinctly themselves and quite definitely Worth it.

Wren Academy

Hilton Avenue, London, N12 9HB

• Pupils: 1000 boys and girls • Ages: 11–18 • C of E but all faiths welcome • State

Tel: 020 8492 6000
Email: firstcontact@wrenacademy.org
Website: www.wrenacademy.org

Principal: Since June 2007, some 15 months before the academy opened, Mr Michael Whitworth (forties). Previously head of Kelmscott School in Walthamstow. Born and brought up in Northumberland, he graduated as a historian and has recently taught history and religious studies. After working in both private industry and the civil service, he entered teaching and has worked in schools in London, Hertfordshire and Essex. Excited by the 'unusual opportunity to create a brand new school from scratch', and has built up the school's reputation very rapidly. 'I think the governors recognised my capacity to stick to a task and see it through.' Understated but extremely caring, say parents, very driven and with sights set very high. Married with two young children.

Academic matters: This is a comprehensive, but the nature of the students in this leafy area means it is primarily an academic one. The biggest initial challenge was achieving a truly comprehensive intake: the previous school on the site had had a very poor reputation, and Barnet has a variety of popular state schools, including three grammar schools.

However, within a short space of time Ofsted stated that 'the teaching at Wren is stunning', and this is not something you read very often. 'As well as maximising achievement – because children need that currency to move on – we teach learning skills and aptitudes,' says the head. 'Children need the capacity to think for themselves. They are encouraged to seek out their own answers, to be flexible and take risks.' GCSE results in 2013 saw 78 per cent of pupils achieving five grades A*-C with 31 per cent A*/A.

Parents are enthusiastic. 'The teachers are very wisely chosen.' 'They're great at finding and encouraging talents.' 'They really encourage them to aim high.' Newsletters all include brainteasers for parents and pupils to solve, and articles on ways of building learning power.

English, maths and science are taught in single sex classes. 'This gives us opportunities to stretch children in gender-specific ways. For example, in English boys can look at their powers of reflectiveness and empathy, whilst in girls' maths classes we can encourage them to take risks and concentrate on answering quickly. It helps to broaden their skill sets, and they enjoy it.'

Research suggests that girls taught in single sex groups are more likely to continue with maths and science, and already a good percentage of girls is choosing single science GCSEs.

The school sets for English, maths, science and foreign languages from part of the way through year 7. 'We like to get data of our own rather than relying on Sats results.' Everyone studies a language (generally French, though some take Japanese or Spanish) and most are expected to take it to GCSE. Regular language days involve a range of linguistic activities. GCSE courses start in year 9.

The specialism of design and the built environment enhances rather than dominates the curriculum, says the head. 'It influences our culture and our ways of thinking about tasks. We have a high emphasis on creativity, and each task has a creative phase, a planning phase and an evaluation phase. But we also have the opportunity to plan projects in architecture and civil engineering.'

Those who need extra help are identified at the beginning of year 7 and follow a six week key skills programme to help bring them up to speed. There are also after-school support groups that help with spelling and comprehension. Although some get one-to-one help from teaching assistants, 'the aim is for everyone to be unsupported in lessons eventually. We do what helps them to access the curriculum in the appropriate lesson.'

Games, options, the arts: The school week includes three extended days, with compulsory enrichment activities from 3-4pm. These range from samba band, Latin and knitting to debating. Staff and students learn together and either can win Excellent Learner of the Week awards.

Houses – named for Wren churches – give the main opportunities for sporting rivalry, but football, netball, basketball, badminton and athletics teams also take part in borough and regional competitions with increasing success. There's a sports hall, netball courts and a football pitch. Opponents have commented on Wren teams' good sportsmanship. Pupils can take sports GCSE or BTEC, and enrichment options include rugby, trampolining and table tennis.

Art, design and technology very strong and creative – as one would expect in a school with a design specialism. Projects include designing sculptures of dream ice cream sundaes, creating a piece of artwork inspired by the River Thames and designing an Olympic stadium.

Music is keen – there's an orchestra, gospel choir, Indian drumming club – and increasing in quality as musicians move up the school and hone their skills. Drama also finding its feet; eagerly awaited annual school musical – eg Bugsy Malone and Hairspray. Wren's Got Talent showcases singers, magicians and musicians.

Background and atmosphere: Named for Sir Christopher Wren, designer of St Paul's Cathedral, which reflects its C of E status and specialism in design and the built environment. Opened in 2008 on the site of a failed school next door to Woodhouse College qv. Partly refurbished but mostly newly built, it has an open plan feel, with roof lights and large north windows, grey carpets and aluminium cladding. Steps leading down from the entrance hall to the library, 'the heart of the school', are lined by ledges where children can sit and chat, under treble-height rooflights, giving an amphitheatre-like atmosphere. There is a feeling of space and airiness throughout. Corridor walls are decorated with graphics of the footprint of St Paul's Cathedral, and with murals quoting inspiring biblical texts eg 'Be willing and available to provide support and guidance to others', from the Letter to the Thessalonians.

The school is sponsored by the London Diocesan Board for Schools, hence its Christian character, and by Berkhamsted School qv, which provides some of the governors. The schools work together on areas such as curriculum development, Wren students go over to Berkhamsted for activities, including a

W

year 7 residential retreat, and Berkhamsted sixth formers have visited Wren to give their views on appointing a new head of sixth form. 'It's a partnership, and we hope that both schools will get an equal amount from it.' Year 7s all travel to central London to visit St Paul's Cathedral and their house church during their first term at school.

Pastoral care and discipline: 'The teachers don't tolerate any bad behaviour,' say parents. 'It is a lovely, safe environment for learning'; and indeed the school had a supremely ordered feel during our visit. Three different breaks and lunchtimes help. So does the design of the building: staff and pupils share unisex toilets, and there is no staff room, so everyone socialises in the restaurant. 'It's a philosophy that when staff and students share the same space there is passive supervision, and students feel secure. They're encouraged to sit in here and chat – it's part of the curriculum.' Focus Days concentrate on matters ranging from sexual health to university choices.

Much emphasis on good manners and courtesy. Common sanctions include litter duty and community service. There's a Reflection Room for 'those who would benefit from time on their own to reflect'. Pupils get a high degree of autonomy, with plenty of opportunities to get involved in the way the school is run, from becoming prefects to interviewing potential teachers to taking part in curriculum reviews. 'In return, they generally play their part. There's a high level of buy-in.'

The chaplain, who plays a counsellor-like role, is generally considered a good egg. The only parental criticism is that some feel the school doesn't take their views on board. 'When you start a new school you have to put in place structures that will work. We opened with a very clear idea of what we wanted. We've always listened and explained to parents, but we haven't always amended our ways as a result.'

Pupils and parents: A diverse range, about 25 per cent white British, and characteristic of this leafy outer-London suburb; mostly 'ambitious people who want to do well'. Pupils have already taken GCSEs in 13 different home languages. Active PTA which organises quiz nights and festivals, organises second hand uniform sales and has raised funds for the gazebo, which offers a shady outdoor place to socialise

Entrance: Takes 180 into year 7, with 90 foundation (church) places and 90 community places. First priority for community places to looked after children, those with SEN statements or exceptional medical or social need. Points for having a sibling at the school and for attending a Barnet primary school, then by distance – generally within about half a mile. For foundation places, points for siblings and for regular church attendance, with distance as a tie-break. Has waiting lists for occasional places in other years. At least 25 external sixth form places will depend on GCSE results.

Exit: The school has already appointed a head of sixth form. Recently, 45 Wren students spent a day at Cambridge University to give them a feel for life at a university like this. In 2013 80 per cent of year 11s who achieved the entry requirements stayed on for sixth form.

Remarks: This young school has already established a reputation for high teaching standards, courteous students and excellent enrichment activities. Likely to go from strength to strength.

Wychwood School

74 Banbury Road, Oxford, OX2 6JR

• Pupils: 130 girls, of whom 40 are weekly or full boarders • Ages: 11–18 • Non-denom but Christian foundation • Fees: Day £13,200; Boarding £19,650–£20,610 pa • Independent

Tel: 01865 557976
Email: admissions@wychwoodschool.org
Website: www.wychwoodschool.org

Headmistress: Since 2012, Mrs Andrea Johnson BSc PGCE, previously assistant head at Tudor Hall School. Read chemistry at Durham and began her career as a chemistry teacher in a large comprehensive in Sunderland. From there she progressed to head of science and housemistress at Battle Abbey School, followed by head of physical sciences and housemistress at Tudor Hall.

Married with two children, she enjoys skiing, swimming, travelling, theatre and is a committed Christian.

She believes in the 'education of genuine girls, not imitation boys' and will do her utmost to 'ensure that the emphasis on the individual remains central to the school's ethos.'

Academic matters: Good range of subjects on offer considering the size of the school. Core subjects at GCSE include compulsory RS in addition to maths, English, one science, one humanity and a modern language for most (some dyslexic pupils and pupils where English is not their first lang are excused). IT facilities have improved – pupils taught in split year groups so each now has a computer terminal.

Not as academic as some of the Oxford schools, but given the ability intake the results are good. The ethos is non-competitive. English, maths and sciences are popular. In 2013, 96 per cent A*-C grades at GCSE with 48 per cent A*/A, 76 per cent A*-B at A level. Class sizes average 18 in the lower years with a max of 25, down to an average of 10 at GCSE and four at A level.

'Non-competitive,' say parent, 'but they get the results', with much tailoring of teaching to the individual by 'enormously dedicated staff' who are prepared to go the extra mile for the girls. Extra lessons are offered by teachers to those who need/ want it.

Good SEN policy. Girls are admitted with special needs as long as these are compatible with the education on offer. SEN are picked up through monitoring; all screened on entrance in year 7. Currently seven girls have ed psych's report, one girl is statemented and an additional six receive special support for which there is a fee. At any one time there may be additional girls being monitored for areas of concern. SENCo is the head of RS and PHSE. A number of girls (eight at present) have English as an additional language. These pupils have extra tuition according to individual need.

Games, options, the arts: All girls play sport, including the sixth form who have one timetabled lesson per week. Limited sports facilities due to the location. On site tennis/netball courts and a multipurpose school hall which doubles up ably as a gym. Further courts/pitches are a short walk away through leafy north Oxford and the school has use of the university swimming pool. Some difficulty with achieving success on the sports field – 'difficult to pick a good hockey team from only 15' – but not a problem in the higher years, say pupils, as you can choose from a wider age range.

Enthusiastic and thriving art department. Popular choice at GCSE and A level with the options of photography and textiles with very good results in the former. Older girls are able to

W

work in their own area dedicated to A level. A fair number go on to art foundation courses. No DT.

Half the school have individual voice or instrumental lessons and participate in the orchestras, jazz band, chamber choir etc. Chamber choir recently gained distinction in Oxford Music Festival. Multi-purpose school hall has tiered seating for concerts which concertinas against a wall when not in use.

Range of extra-curricular activities with almost all girls achieving Duke of Edinburgh bronze and many going on to do the silver award and a few to gold. Boarders in the lower years have organised weekend activities. Older boarders are free to choose their weekend activities. Fairly early curfews in the evening. 'If you want to go out clubbing, you stay with friends overnight.' Once a term there is a whole day out to London, Cadbury's world and the like to which day girls are also invited.

A sixth form extension course runs throughout the year for all pupils, including criticial thinking days, theatre trips, practical skills sessions, Bushcraft and other activities.

Day girls can stay for prep until 5.15 or 6.45 – great for working parents, at no extra cost.

Background and atmosphere: Founded in 1897 by Miss Lee, an Oxford academic who trumpeted the individual education of girls and individuality. Her legacy lives on. School housed in a large Victorian house on the main Banbury Rd; 'great location,' say girls who can walk into town very easily. Warren of staircases interlinking different parts of school. Gardens behind the school surround the courts and bridge to further school buildings and boarding facilities. Classrooms are small, ditto labs, reflecting the size of the school. Christian foundation with weekly religious assembly.

Cheerful, impressively tidy, boarding bedrooms, three or four to a room in lower years with individual study bedrooms in the sixth form. Mixed age groups in each bedroom with the oldest girl being head of bedroom – encourages peer support. Half the boarders are full boarders. Occasional boarding is possible. Help is given to parents in arranging transport, booking of flights etc. No resident matron but doctor's surgery nearby and a weekly visit to school by the doctor.

Pastoral care and discipline: Good. Very relaxed relationship between staff and pupils allowing good communication. Good peer support. Each new girl is allocated a house mother who is an older girl to whom she can turn. Later entrants are also allocated a house sister – a girl in the same year for support. Through this system girls say they can spot potential problems. Not a huge problem with discipline. Bullying stamped out early. Drugs have not been a problem nor alcohol but any case would be looked at individually. Elected school council of staff and pupil councillors has real clout, say parents. Pupils feel they are listened to.

Pupils and parents: Mix across the board from university dons to self-made men and first time buyers. Come from all over. Most within 20 miles. Choose school for small size. Just under half the boarders are from overseas. Pupils polite and relaxed and not overtly rebellious; notable lack of microskirts here. Notable alumnae include Vicky Jewson, film maker, and Joan Aiken, writer.

Entrance: Takes girls of average/above average ability but will consider every case on an individual basis and cites a girl who came in at level 3 maths and went on to win the maths challenge. Usual entry point at year 7 though entrance at other ages possible. Entrants come from local primary schools as well as prep/independent junior schools. Sixth form entrants need a minimum of six GCSE at C grade or above with the A*, A or B grade in the subjects to be studied.

All candidates interviewed by head – looks for their passion. Asks about reading matter, current events, what makes them tick. Tests in maths and English within a day's visit and participation. Entrants at later years tend to be those who are struggling ('looking for a change,' says school) at the more academic day schools in Oxford or those from the maintained sector.

Exit: Almost all to higher education. Some leave post GCSE, 'mainly to maintained sector,' says school, 'for boys,' say others. A few come in at A level. Sixth form leavers to a range of universities both new and established. Huge mix of subjects with art being a popular choice. Occasional Oxbridge entrant.

Money matters: Middle of the road fees plus usual extras. Three scholarships at 11+, three at 16+ of which one is for science. Music scholarships and creative art scholarships also available.

Remarks: Small, intimate, nurturing school where the individual is valued, within a highly supportive atmosphere. 'They never lost faith in me,' said one former pupil. 'Not a place for prima donnas,' says another. Look elsewhere for a high-tech, buzzing, competitive and highly academic atmosphere; this school promotes education in a relaxed, friendly environment and, according to parents, achieves results unachievable at other schools.

Wycliffe College

Linked school: Wycliffe Preparatory School

Bath Road, Stonehouse, Gloucestershire, GL10 2JQ

• Pupils: 420, two thirds boys, one third girls; two thirds board.
• Ages: 2–19 • Inter-denominational • Fees: Senior Day £16,050–£17,550; Boarding £27,240–£31,185 pa • Independent

Tel: 01453 822432
Email: senior@wycliffe.co.uk
Website: www.wycliffe.co.uk

Head: Since 2005, Margie Burnet Ward (early fifties). Invited initially to run the overseas development wing of the school and then became deputy head. She had been head of an international school which had without warning been sold off for development. 'I had to tour the country in a minibus full of overseas students, trying to find places for them. When I came to Wycliffe, they were by far the most helpful and sensitive school I had dealt with. Next day on my return I was telephoned and asked to join the staff.' Two years later through unexpected circumstances she was invited to become the first female head of Wycliffe. Universally popular – 'by far and away the best head since I've been here,' said a groundsman who has been trimming the lawns since the last century. 'The thing is, she's so incredibly fair,' a senior pupil told us. 'It isn't just that she knows the names of all of us – anyone can do that if they take the trouble to learn them – it's that she really understands us. She knows our hopes, our anxieties, our parents.' The latter is important to this universal mother, with two children of her own who experienced the Wycliffe adventure and who are now at university. 'You can't deal with a child without engaging with parents.' Conscious that many mothers of boarders are married to serving officers who are frequently away, she offers genuine friendship and support. Parents we spoke to were hugely appreciative – 'she absorbs everything at meetings and is warm, approachable and shrewd.' Doesn't play the grande dame, though she could; instead she is involved and active, bustling about reminding people to tuck in shirts (with lightness and humour), congratulating pupils on recent performances and engaging with sincerity and interest. She has restructured the senior management team who spoke of a 'real sense of leadership'. 'She's injected a new sense of purpose,' said a local head. No plans to go anywhere else – 'besides, no one else would want me. I'm not from the traditional background of heads. I've had an exciting life of travel and adventure and I love it here.' It shows.

Academic matters: Not a demanding school in terms of entrance requirements 'though absolutely not a dumping ground,' growls the head. GCSE and A level results are very respectable. In 2013, 91 per cent A*-C grades at GCSE with over a third of entries graded A*/A. At A level in 2013, 60 per cent A*-B grades (a third of these were A*/A). What the school really prides itself on is value-added. Last year's results put them in the top five per cent of all schools in terms of the government's contextual value added performance tables. There is a range of nearly 30 subjects at A level with seemingly no limit on the various permutations available. Plenty of guidance and advice on choosing the best options. 'We aim to find the right subjects for individuals, rather than shoe horn them into rigid blocks.' Japanese, for instance, is very popular and the school enjoys excellent relations with its sister school in Japan. Exchanges and visits abound. This school travels.

Supporting and encouraging individual and community progress is the compulsory life skills programme, a wider-ranging version of PHSE. Each year group is involved, the aim being to develop skills beyond the merely academic: thus there are courses on working as a team, problem solving, creativity and 'learning how to learn'. The pupils we asked were very appreciative of the programme. The school offers a Development (third) Year in the sixth form. Primarily designed for pupils from abroad (see Pupils and Parents) to get their English up to scratch for A levels but also used for pupils who will benefit from building deeper foundations. Pupils will only sit GCSEs and A levels when they are ready for them, not because they're the right age.

Very good remedial and special needs programme with lively, sensitive and fully qualified teachers who help and support. Pupils are automatically assessed on entry to the school. This is as much to identify Gifted and Talented (the school is the only independent school with an accreditation with NACE) as well as those with learning difficulties (the school is much praised by CReSTed).

Classrooms and laboratories have been revamped, repainted and in some cases redesigned. There is a light and spacious feel about it all. Computers are everywhere. They appear and disappear on the desks in the excellently laid out library which is also a fabulous multimedia resource centre, very popular with the pupils. In the delightful music department computers aid composition and musical appreciation; they appear alongside work benches in the DT department. Interactive whiteboards are in all the classrooms and are used to engage involvement and interest in ways which seem imaginative and effective. ICT is clearly very important at Wycliffe and the school has invested nearly a million pounds over the last few years.

Games, options, the arts: We hear mixed opinions on the standard of games at Wycliffe though clearly squash is good, with frequent tours to Europe and even as far as Peru. But there can be no doubting the excellent facilities. Floodlit Astroturf hockey pitch, an attractive cricket square, masses of squash courts with people queuing to play when we visited, an excellent sports hall: it's all here. Rowing, particularly sculling, is popular and successful as is girls' hockey and basketball. Not a hearty school but one where pupils are encouraged to participate and expected to take part in Saturday afternoon sporting commitments. Plenty of scope for outdoor activities with D of E and CCF along with plenty of opportunities for caving, climbing and adventure. An active, doing place. Music has always been important and the arrival of two new musical

whiz kids heading the department has seen a deepening and broadening of musical possibilities. A huge number learn instruments and both the house singing and drama competitions contests are tremendously popular. Interesting theatre. Theatre studies is very popular. Judging by the pupils' work on display all over the school, art flourishes. Indeed we had the feeling that this is a creative community. We heard much enthusiastic talk from pupils about debating and the Model UN with students going as far afield as Istanbul, Dublin and Chicago, where there's another sister school.

Background and atmosphere: A busy campus with friendly staff and pupils strolling purposefully around. Some interesting buildings, particularly the original listed building which now houses the head, admin staff and the advanced learning centre. Since the school's foundation in 1882 the powers that govern have chosen their architects with sensitivity and good sense, combining aesthetics with practicality and blending old and new into a pleasing and interesting whole. A feature of the overall layout of the place is the number of sofas and benches dotted around the buildings and grounds, inviting conversation with a sense of reasonable privacy. The dining room is delightfully airy – there's a lot of glass about at Wycliffe – and serves delicious food with a tantalising variety. Sunday brunches 'are to die for.' It's good to witness the easy relationships between cookers and eaters.

Accommodation has much improved. The mixed day house with generously broad corridors, brightly painted studies and common rooms with balconies overlooking the green sward is very pleasant and clearly much appreciated. 'We're like boarders who don't have bed and breakfast,' one told us. Flexi-boarding is a possibility. The new sixth form boarding house built round three sides of a quadrangle is miles better than much student accommodation. All rooms en suite and, we were assured, the boys have a sauna and Jacuzzi. The school has been fully co-educational for more than 30 years and feels absolutely right. There's a lovely atmosphere.

Pastoral care and discipline: The school revolves around the house system for day pupils and boarders, each presided over by a house master/mistress, supported by a matron, house staff and a team of house tutors. Prefects and responsible sixth formers provide invaluable back up and conduits. Those to whom we spoke impressed us with the seriousness of their approach and delighted us by their lack of pomposity. One told us that consideration for others is deeply ingrained. The pupils' handbook is admirably clear about the school's zero tolerance of bullying and via two splendid pieces of writing from the founder and a later headmaster, the current head establishes clearly the expectations and ethos of the school, while demonstrating that decency is timeless. There are clear guidelines to follow if any pupil feels aggrieved or threatened in any way. Pupils praised the (female) chaplain and appreciated the introduction of the school council. The head approves of pranks and high spirits (providing they are not unkind or thoughtless) and acknowledges that pupils will take risks and make mistakes. 'That's what they learn from.' All very civilised. Assemblies and church services in the delightful chapel, built in the 1950s by pupils and staff incorporating wood from a pier on the Isle of Wight and stone from a bombed church. All faiths are catered for, though many assemblies are forums for discussion rather than 'exclusively religious'.

Pupils and parents: Friendly, open, relaxed pupils who seem healthily proud of Wycliffe and grateful for the experience. We didn't encounter a whiff of arrogance or affectation: the pupils seemed secure in what they were doing and were uniformly and naturally polite. Parents to whom we spoke were pleased to feel included, and though there were some wrinkled brows over the question of extras, expressed satisfaction bordering

W

on affection for the school. A number told us that they enjoy the opportunities for involvement and appreciate the parents' council. A lot of pupils come from abroad, some 30 per cent from 27 different countries, so it's something of an international experience. That needs to be taken into consideration. As many from Europe as from the far east. Also a number of Forces children.

Entrance: The majority of pupils joining in year 9 come from the school's own prep school, though recently increasing numbers come from other prep schools as well. Pupils from the prep sit scholarship exams or the CE; pupils from outlying schools sit either CE, scholarships or tailor-made exams. Fifty per cent at common entrance is acceptable – or less, if there is clear evidence of specific strengths. (Remember their pride in value added). Entry into the sixth form usually requires at least five GCSEs at grade C or above but they do consider, more carefully than many, the question of potential.

Exit: Just over one-third leave post-GCSEs to vocational courses and sixth form colleges. Over 95 per cent of the sixth form go on to university with a few Oxbridge places. Nottingham, Cardiff, Birmingham and Bournemouth remain popular, as do Sussex, Kent and Exeter. Some art foundation courses and drama school, otherwise business related subjects and law are favourites.

Money matters: In terms of endowments, the school is not particularly wealthy though the head stresses that it is 'strong financially.' Scholarships are available at 13 and 16 for academic excellence, art, music, DT, ICT, drama and sport. Maximum value up to 50 per cent but in exceptional circumstances the school may make up the difference. Much depends on school reports and financial circumstances.

Remarks: Strong on breadth and individual tailoring. 'I have three very different children: very bright, very sporty and very dyslexic. Wycliffe was the only school which could cope with them all. It's been wonderful for all three,' said a mum. An Old Boy told us that a few years ago he had the impression that Wycliffe had become a bit dull and dry and 'lost its way. Now it's established its own identity again.' Fair comment.

Wycombe Abbey School

Abbey Way, High Wycombe, Buckinghamshire, HP11 1PE

• Pupils: 560 girls, all board except for 35 day girls • Ages: 11–18
• C of E • Fees: Day £24,977; Boarding £33,300 pa • Independent

Tel: 01494 520381
Email: registrar@wycombeabbey.com
Website: www.wycombeabbey.com

Headmistress: Since September 2013, Mrs Rhiannon Wilkinson MA (Oxon), MEd (Manchester), a historian (forties). Previously principal of Harrogate Ladies' College. Has also been director of pastoral system at Cheadle Hulme School, deputy principal at Jerudong International School, Brunei, and director of studies then senior mistress at Haileybury. Married to Donald Wilkinson, headmaster of Bearwood College; they have four children between them.

Academic matters: The school's raison d'être. Girls setted for most subjects 'but even the bottom sets get As in their exams,' a parent pointed out. In 2013 95 per cent A*/A at GCSE. All subjects superb but classics deserves special mention: 37 girls took GCSE Latin in 2013 – a massive number for a smallish school – and all but seven earned an A*. Four sat the Greek papers, and, you guessed it, all A*s. Maths the most popular A level, followed by history. Modern languages being beefed up under newish head of dept.

Generally small class sizes, and the teaching is superb: 'the girls buzz with it', a parent said, 'and they love bouncing ideas off one another.' Homework schedule 'mind boggling' according to parents. 'They work terribly hard but seem to thrive on it.' Prep hour each evening in each house's study area; other prep times individually timetabled. Girls normally do five AS exams including critical thinking (though nearly a third are currently taking six) and between three and five A levels. In 2013 86 per cent of A level exams were awarded A*/A (38 per cent A*). Nothing to speak of below a B. EPQ now also offered in sixth form.

Games, options, the arts: Music recital hall lovely with brill acoustics. Music very important here, though exam results – as in art, DT and drama – are a micron less phenomenal than in the straight up academic subjects. Brass and sax particularly hot according to girls (school says violin and piano are tops). Acres of practice and teaching rooms, though a few grumbles from girls that there is not enough space to practise in some of the houses. Something for everyone from the most able to the tonally challenged eg two orchestras, string, wind and brass ensembles, choral society and three choirs (chapel choir tours overseas every two years). Over three-quarters of girls play an instrument – there are lots of informal lunchtime concerts – but are never taken out of lessons for a music lesson. Three girls currently excused from Saturday school to attend London music colleges, part of the school's recognition that exceptional specimens may require external nurturing (a few hard feelings among their peers).

Drama taken seriously – they have a full-time theatre manager plus assistant, and a full-time wardrobe mistress. Very swish 430 seater proscenium arch theatre with alarmingly sloping seating – do bring your oxygen tank – staging 14 productions a year. About a third of girls do LAMDA exams and several each year get into the National Youth Theatre. Art receiving attention – it has 'become more important' and girls are able to work in the evenings and on weekends. Very high quality output on display, especially the textiles. School has set its sights, if not yet its pocket-book, on building a new DT and Art centre.

Fabulous sports centre with huge pool and brill gym, squash courts, climbing wall, sports hall, dance studio with sprung floor. Don't let these bluestockings fool you – this is a sporty school packed with girls who are used to winning. Lacrosse their 'signature' sport and the most important game here 'by far' (with some top coaching); Downe House the arch rivals. Netball also played hard, plus football, swimming, hockey, trampolining, gymnastics, fencing, golf, tennis, rowing, dance, skiing – you name it. Riding and polo for all age groups now including in Windsor Great Park on Sundays. Parents of un-sporty girls also commended the provision here: something for everyone. Debate unusually energised for a girls' school. Model United Nations, Young Enterprise, D of E – all here. And leave it to Wycombe Abbey to offer something truly unique: the Sir Adrian Swire Flying Scholarship offers 15 hours of flying instruction with the aim to going solo in a light aircraft.

Background and atmosphere: High voltage. Girls literally running from place to place like the female employees of a Japanese bank. Unlike most schools where we are shown around by pupils, the idea of girls missing lessons to guide us was dismissed out of hand. More international, outward-looking and cosmopolitan than most of the other academic girls' boarding schools – this is not middle England. Approached via an awkward sharp turning off a suburban roundabout near a Staples and collection of 60s architectural monstrosities. Main building a rather grey, grim Gothic structure – initially feels more like a London day school than a boarding idyll. But the school gates successfully shut out the sprawl, one feels safe and sheltered within the campus walls, and as one hesitantly ventures into 166 acres of exceedingly hilly, but pleasant, grounds, things start to look up. School founded in 1896 by Miss Dove, later Dame Frances Dove, whose aims to develop students' talents, foster awareness of God and understand others' needs are still upheld today.

No weekly boarding – for those thinking Wycombe Abbey is a halfway house between real boarding and a London day school, think again. Closed the first and last weekends of term. Other weekends girls can go home after morning chapel on Sundays, and every three weeks there is exeat or half term. Weekend activities 'improving' and you can never please everyone. Most girls potter into the Eden Centre in High Wycombe for a spot of shopping on Saturday afternoons. Girls attend short, simple service in school's rather austere chapel every morning, often led by the girls.

Pastoral care and discipline: Some boarding houses crammed to bursting. Eight girls in one dormitory may be fun for 11 year olds, but is unacceptable for 14 year olds working towards GCSEs. Yet this is the norm in the Abbey Houses – Pitt and Rubens. The junior house for 11 year olds, by all accounts a happy place where the youngest girls learn to organise themselves and make friends for life, has one room of 16 girls (with partitions), another of 12. Meanwhile, the three state-of-the-art Dawes Hill Houses ('the place to be,' say parents), already benefitting from the most spectacular facilities in the school, are expecting further renovation. Outhouses – Airlie, Barry, Butler and Campbell – vibrate to the hum of traffic noise but are otherwise very pleasant, with nice kitchens and lounges. The obvious discrepancies between the houses can spill over into status issues for some girls, according to parents, with girls in the Abbey Houses the lowest on the totem pole. School is aware of the discrepancies and is raising funds to eventually replace Pitt and Rubens. Houses also vary in terms of rules (eg on TV viewing).

Boarding is 'vertical' so girls sleep in rooms with the full age range from 12-16. Helps to build friendships across the years and punctures cliques. Lower sixth girls get smaller rooms of two or three (Abbey Houses) or singles (Dawes Hill). Bullying not a problem – 'they're kept too busy and there's a "we're all in this together" mentality,' a parent explained. No drugs. Occasional girl suspended for alcohol. Smoking punished by suspension. Housemistresses excellent, but as overworked as their charges. Much emphasis on 'work/life balance' – this is a school where girls frequently have to be leant on to work LESS hard. Clarence House for upper sixth designed as preparation for university. Wycombe parents ooh and aah over the single study bedrooms and adult ambience (own clothes, self-catering, fewer rules) but it's pretty standard girls' school upper sixth modern. Sixth formers allowed out Saturday nights until 11pm. Lots of socials, debates etc with Royal Grammar School High Wycombe (state grammar), Eton, Harrow, and the like. Food outstanding – huge variety – reflecting the school's international outlook.

Pupils and parents: Not for the faint hearted – stamina the number one requirement, even above brains. Introverted shrinking violets look elsewhere. Enormously popular with overseas families, especially from the Far East, who value its academic league table standing above all else (Wycombe Abbey always comes top of the boarding girls' schools). Proximity to London also a big tick. And the famous name seals the deal. Sixteen per cent of girls have non-UK main addresses. Lots of brothers at Eton but the schools bear no resemblance. Thirty day pupils – the number is capped by the governors. List of old girls contains surprisingly few recognisable names for a school of this age and pedigree – draw from that what you will. Includes judge (Baroness) Elizabeth Butler-Sloss and (Baroness)

Elspeth Howe, life peer and wife of Geoffrey, plus thespians Rachel Stirling, Naomi Frederick and Polly Stenham.

Entrance: 11+ and 13+ entry very different beasts. The former attracts mostly London parents who will also be applying to the top day schools. 'If they get a place at St Paul's,' says the old head, 'chances are they'll take it.' 13+ entry is smaller and candidates are coached to the teeth by prep schools, or are top brains applying from abroad. To be blunt: it's easier to get in at 11 ('we don't have to disappoint many girls at 11,' says the school), but not a doddle. Children wishing to enter at 11 are assessed at age 10 – an interview, a brief formal assessment and some mini lessons ('lots of puzzles', recalled a parent whose daughter was unsuccessful) – plus report from primary/prep. Provisional offers then made with CE merely a formality ('they never fail'). 13+ entry process similar but pre-tests more exacting.

Exit: Around 40 per cent of girls regularly head for Oxbridge (22 in 2013), most of the others to top universities like London, Edinburgh, Bristol, Durham and Warwick. Timetabled university entrance preparation sessions start at the beginning of lower sixth. An hour and a half of interview practice, entrance test practice, talks on the application process (from visiting university representatives) etc. Now we know what universities mean when they say applicants from top girls' schools are 'over-prepared'! Help for girls applying to US universities better than we've seen at any other school and the results speak for themselves with girls admitted not only to the usual suspects but to some real powerhouses less frequently chosen by UK applications (UC Berkeley, Stanford, University of Chicago) and to superb but lesser-known establishments. Specialist SAT tutoring is provided in school.

A fifth of year group leaves after GCSEs (5 per cent in 2013), some having chafed at the rules and regulations, others finding the work and pressure too much for them, a few simply seeking change. Replaced by chunk of overseas girls – only top brains need apply at this age.

Money matters: Scholarships at 11+ 13+ and 16+ for academic prowess though their financial value continues to decrease. Music awards available to girls under the age of 14 provide free music lessons, but nothing off the school fees. No awards currently for sports, drama or esoterics. School aims to target ££ toward those 'who really need it' so scholarships can be topped up with bursaries. Hoping to provide one full fees bursary, not necessarily to a scholar.

Remarks: A school for intellectually curious, outgoing, self-disciplined, ambitious girls. One parent summed it up: 'A tough school, and you have to work very, very hard, but the rewards are tremendous.' Select your house carefully (school says parents have no say in choosing a boarding house).

Wymondham College

Wymondham, Norfolk, NR18 9SZ

• Pupils: 1,325 boys and girls; about 50 per cent board (both sexes) • Ages: 11-18 • Non-denom • Fees: Boarding £8,643–£9,225 pa • State

Tel: 01953 609000
Email: admissions@wymondhamcollege.org
Website: www.wymondhamcollege.org

Principal: Since 2007, Mr Melvyn Roffe BA FRSA (mid forties). Read English at York, studied education at Durham. Previously

W

head of Old Swinford Hospital, another state-owned boarding school. Married with a son and daughter who are at the college.

Hints of public school, a residue of teaching and directorial stints at Oundle and Monmouth, are just the ticket for someone in charge of this state-owned but decidedly middle-class day and boarding hybrid. Personable, patient and calmly in control – one can't imagine him being in the least bit intimidating – he comes across as a clear thinker; also determined – a tightening of belts hasn't deflected efforts to raise money needed to upgrade the sports hall and previous antique language facilities – 'we now have a new modern foreign languages building'. Links and exchanges with far-flung schools in exotic places are pet projects – 'pupils need perspectives other than their own especially if they're in a field in Norfolk' – and he's well on the way to making them a college feature. (On the basis of interests or performance at the college, students are invited to join exchanges as 'ambassadors' and have most costs met by the college). Still manages to teach a little – English to the sixth – and has been chair of the Boarding Schools Association. Run of the mill interests apart from, as gamely admitted, a 'rather sad fascination with public transport.' Driving a decommissioned Routemaster bus from London to his old school fulfilled a boyhood dream.

Moving on in July 2014 to head George Watson's College. His successor will be Jonathan Taylor currently head of Torch Academy Gateway Trust.

Academic matters: Class sizes are on the large side but this doesn't seem to be a major issue; instead parents talk of the way effort and independent learning are encouraged and how, as one mum put it, children are 'nicely challenged'. School points out that class sizes are 21 per group in year 7 and 24 in years 8-11. There's a general sense that pupils are keen to do well and a recognition of the hard work put in by staff – 'teachers have a vested interest in us and will help us after school.' Given the comprehensive intake, good results and noteworthy value-added – 12th highest 'contextual value-added rating' (government speak) of any secondary in the country. In 2013 85 per cent 5+ A*-Cs including maths and English, 39 per cent A*/A. Definite academic slant in the sixth – only four vocational courses in the long list of subjects offered. Virtually all pass at A level with recent improvements at the top end – 62 per cent A*-B (35 per cent A*/A) in 2013.

Large SEN room with soft seating area and fair number of computers. Parental perceptions that this is a school for clever kids and that those with special needs would struggle to keep up go some way to explaining the relatively low number of statemented pupils or those needing additional help. Pragmatic approach ('I'm dyslexic so I'll have to develop strategies to cope and work harder') coupled with maintenance of self-esteem ('I'm clever because I'm at Wymondham College') seems to work. Paired reading with sixth form volunteers, SENCo and LSAs on hand at lunch time and for those with statements, withdrawal during second year (yr 8) language lessons. College has specialist language status and all have to take languages up to year 10 regardless of statements etc – powers that be won't budge on this. Also has a technology college status.

Co-ordinator to support the Gifted and Talented. Head isn't a fan of fast tracking but he has overseen the development of an interesting pilot scheme. Fifteen students, selected in year 10, spend two periods a week, plus their own time, on an extension programme comprising a research project (findings are presented in yr 11) and a course from one of the following – literature and ideas, space science, Russian, Latin, government and politics. Visiting staff from the UEA give 'additional academic clout'.

Games, options, the arts: All the mainstream, seasonally adjusted, team games plus wide choice of options for the sixth who are 'encouraged' to include some sport on their timetable. School has a couple of Sportsmark awards – also an Astroturf and vast

sports hall – and the sporty have plenty of opportunities to shine, especially if they make it to the first or second teams – parents say it's less zippy for those lower down the pile.

High standard of textiles and art (chunkily assured) produced in the spacious 'Tech Block' where large studios, IT suites and technology workshops radiate from an airy central atrium. Inclusive approach towards music with 30 per cent learning an instrument. There is a concert band, and the jazz band is excellent. In what is believed to be the first arrangement of its kind, the college has taken over the day-to-day running of Norfolk's D of E scheme whilst the county council provides funds and governance. According to the head, CCF has been 'revived and reinvigorated'.

Background and atmosphere: Founded in 1951, this state-maintained boarding school, the largest in Britain, is unusual in that it provides a good co-ed comprehensive education coupled with trad boarding provision – and they have a well-resourced sixth form centre. Generally, the tremendously tidy pupils and students come across as mini adults rather than revolting teens – as if they're preparing for the world of work. There's pride in the place and talk of a special sense of community amongst pupils and staff. Calm behaviour in and out of lessons and at lunchtime a cheerful buzz. Apparently food is getting better – 'we don't get awful meals any more.'

The 82 acre site – virtually in the middle of nowhere – has ample space between an assortment of disjointed blocks. The legacy of a US air force hospital is still just visible with a small memorial garden and one surviving Nissen hut – now listed – which, with its curving roof and well tended interior, makes for a surprisingly reassuring chapel. School officially non-denominational but chapel once a week with confirmations. Drably utilitarian boarding houses offset by good access for the disabled and newer builds eg new language block. The most recent, a state-of-the-art award winner, is a plush sixth form centre unfairly referred to by the students as the 'Travel Lodge'. Generous communal spaces and single, ensuite rooms for all upper sixth boarders – the move to university accommodation could come as a shock.

Pastoral care and discipline: House-based tutor groups with tutors overseeing academic and extra-curricular activities. Year 7 boarders and sixth are in age grouped accommodation. The rest in four mixed age houses – apparently some are more relaxed than others. Peel (year 7) is pretty strict – 'it gets you ready for when you move up' said one aficionado – and the adjustment to boarding can be hard, especially if the previous school was cosy. That said, when the chips are down, help is sensitively and readily given – but on a more day-to-day basis parents have sometimes felt sidelined. Head first to acknowledge that historically communication with parents hasn't always been good – 'it was dealt with as if we were simply a day school.' New parent support office – one mum said, 'it works like magic' – likely to put this bugbear to rest.

Two counsellors, recent appointment of a 'dean of students' whose role is 'to provide the support kids need to thrive here' and peer mentoring programme – children are encouraged to (and do) look after each other in a spirit of co-operation. Very little evidence of bad behaviour or bullying – sensibly, no complacency here, and the student council is working on a revised anti-bullying policy. Strict adherence to local authority code on banned substances.

Pupils and parents: Most are politely assured without the slightest whiff of arrogance. Value of education is clearly understood with Saturday school weeding out the less than serious punter. East Anglian/London bias – many from overseas. MOD presence (officers and ranks) has shrunk to 10 per cent and only a handful from ethnic minorities. Predominance of 'professional' backgrounds.

Entrance: Main intake at 11+, very few thereafter except for the sixth form. High pressure on day places – boarding increasingly oversubscribed. Applications need to be made a year in advance.

For day places: applications through the LEA. Admissions criteria in order of importance: looked after children, sibling, musical or sporting aptitude, distance from school – in one year once all the other categories were dealt with it was down to 0.6 of a mile. (Check carefully as this is a bit of a minefield). Approx five applicants for each place.

For boarding: applications through the LA and College. 100+ applicants for 81 places. Admissions criteria in order of importance: looked after children, boarding need, sibling, musical or sporting aptitude. Distance isn't a factor and at this point selection is 'random' – literally out of hat. NB potential boarders have an informal 10 minute 'interview' to see if they can cope with boarding.

Most stay for the sixth form, but with recent expansions in Year 12 and 13, there are just as many external candidates admitted. Minimum of four Cs and three Bs at GCSE doesn't seem to be much of a hurdle but, because of exponential growth of applicants, the final entry criteria after 'looked after children' etc has become rank order of GCSE results for day students from outside the college. Boarders' places are allocated randomly after priority criteria.

Exit: Majority on to higher education. Healthy mix of courses and institutions but lowish numbers to Oxbridge (six in 2013). The College employs a 'Lincoln Fellow'; a recent Oxbridge graduate, to help advise students through the university application process and to dispel the myths that exist around Oxbridge applications thereby encouraging potential candidates.

Money matters: College now an academy so centrally funded. Fees are only for the cost of full or day boarding provision – fantastically good value. Funds for large initiatives raised by letting buildings. Academic, sporting and music scholarships available in the both the lower school and the sixth form.

Remarks: A flagship school with the reputation it's long deserved. Positive vibes from local parents who see beyond the lack of frills and know a good thing when they find it – an alternative for those who'd like the benefits of a public school education but have a problem with the associated ethics or, perish the thought, cost.

Wymondham High School

Folly Road, Wymondham, Norfolk, NR18 0QT

• Pupils: 1635 boys and girls • Ages: 11–18 • Non-denom • State

Tel: 01953 602078
Email: office@wymondhamhigh.norfolk.sch.uk
Website: www.wymondhamhigh.co.uk

Principal: Since January 2013, Mr Russell Boulton, previously head of Flegg High, who took over after Victoria Musgrave was parachuted in to Abbot's Bromley School.

Academic matters: A true community school without hidden filters. At GCSE in 2013, 77 per cent 5+ A*-C (71 per cent 5+ including maths and English). Short course RE for all. Three sets, known as rivers, for academic subjects and fast track for those who shine in art, music and maths. Average class sizes are 25-26 although they sometimes creep up to 32. Parents speak of fantastically supportive, approachable teachers who go the extra mile – particularly in the maths department where 'they have a good way of getting kids on board.' Despite this, around

a quarter of maths results at AS level recently were graded as fails, although this reduced at A2 level. Governors provide late buses for pupils from outlying villages who want to stay for extended school activities or use after school 'helplines' – all subject areas provide a member of staff to give additional help at least one afternoon a week. Pretty pushy sixth form with strong academic bent – 'outstanding' says Ofsted. Every student takes five ASs and is interviewed after the first term in the sixth to see if they've done enough to come off probation. At A level in 2013, 78 per cent A*-C grades. No wandering off site in between lessons – 'they don't have free periods – they have study periods,' said the jolly but no-nonsense head of sixth. Virtually all stay for the full two years.

Support department for those with special needs and an enthusiastic assistant headteacher who's responsible for inclusion – she's overseeing a pilot scheme to give support through the family. Specialists based in the excellence centre (also caters for the gifted and talented and those who are falling by the wayside), differentiated work and classroom support given by assistants. Laptops and additional time in exams. In year 11, ten youngsters, the majority of whom are statemented, are given the opportunity to join a two year course – 'pathway two.' This involves spending a day at a local college, a day on work experience and three days in school where they are taught as a discrete group. As yet zero drop-outs – all credit to the school.

Games, options, the arts: Modern sports centre shared with the town and additional activities for the sporty – they've managed to spawn several English schools' athletics and judo champions. Designated a specialist school for the arts in 2004 – art, drama and music get an extra boost. In 2009, a science specialism was added, with new modern labs being created. Recording facilities, two orchestras, timetabled practice sessions and a small studio theatre which becomes a community arts venue in the evening. Recent rap workshop with an evening performance for parents 'went down a storm,' according to a participant. Productive art and DT departments where kids are happily engaged. After-school activities include Japanese club and African drumming – late buses every day so no one misses out.

Background and atmosphere: School is comfortably nested on the edge of Wymondham, a picturesque country town. Straightforward buildings, the majority of which hail from the 1950s onwards, are well maintained. Clutch of grim mobiles still in use but a recent extension has much improved the library and sixth form study area. Degree of separation between the main school and sixth who don't perform prefectorial duties (that happens in the fifth form) don't have to wear the uniform and are based around a generous quad to one side of the main school. Immaculately mown lawns – the school groundsman used to work at Royal Windsor polo club – and large playing fields provide ample space to spread wings and let off steam.

The 'snack shack' – a centrally plonked brown shed – is a popular way to beat the lunch queue. Serving jacket potatoes and soup, it's been so successful there's another in the pipeline. Sturdy picnic tables – supplied after a request from the school council – are dotted around for outside meets and eats.

Pastoral care and discipline: Good rapport between staff and kids plus vertical forms affiliated to one of four houses make this very large school a civilised place to be. Pupils settle quickly and support each other. Parents speak of an atmosphere of friendliness and well being – 'they're good at treating the kids as individuals rather than fitting them into a box.' Well structured school council gives a voice to all and encourages a sense of partnership. The school is focusing on dress and behaviour with a slightly modified uniform. The Head's Council, made of elected upper sixth students, meets weekly as does the Head's House Captains' Council.

Pupils and parents: Affluent Wymondham and surrounding villages are attractive to those who work in Norwich – easy commuting distance. Wide social mix with a high proportion living in the town – tiny number from ethnic minorities. Sixth formers come from an extensive catchment area including Norwich. Hugely supportive parents with high expectations and chirpy, good humoured pupils who enjoy being at school. Trad uniform until the sixth, who have to wear 'business dress'.

Entrance: Over-subscribed. Stringent catchment rules for yrs 7-11 (Wymondham and satellite villages). Check current precise locations with the LA advice centre – an absolute must). No preference for siblings. For the sixth, seven GCSEs (including English and maths) at C and above with no lower than a B for subjects to be studied at AS.

Exit: After GCSEs, those more suited to practical courses to local sixth form colleges. Post A level nearly all to university, one or two to Oxbridge.

Remarks: Popular, successful community comprehensive with a strong, academic sixth form.

Yarm School

Linked school: Yarm Preparatory School

The Friarage, Yarm, Stockton on Tees, TS15 9EJ

• Pupils: Senior school 740 • Ages: 11–18 • Multi–faith with a Christian tradition • Fees: £11,274 pa • Independent

---

Tel: 01642 786023
Email: dmd@yarmschool.org
Website: www.yarmschool.org

Headmaster: Since 1999, Mr David M Dunn BA PGCE (early fifties). Previously deputy head at Stewart's Melville College in Edinburgh; head of year 11 at Bolton School. Immensely cheerful, welcoming, energetic and forward-thinking, he is clearly and rightly proud of achievements here. Described by parents as 'courageous' and having done 'a fantastic job' in bringing hopes, dreams and new buildings to fruition. Only the second head in the school's history. Big on pastoral care – 'happy children have better self-esteem, learn better and have a go at anything. Treat every child as an individual and celebrate all their achievements.' Two daughters in school and wife is PE teacher with pastoral responsibility for the sixth form.

Academic matters: Pupils normally take 10 GCSE subjects but some more. Teaching begins straight away in the morning with assembly, less academic subjects (sports etc) kept for afternoons. 'It's great to get a crisp start in the mornings when we all learn at our best' affirms head.

Up with the very best, 70 per cent of GCSE entries graded A*/A in 2013. IGCSE in maths, English, physics, chemistry, biology and business studies. At A level in 2013, 84 per cent A*-B, 56 per cent A*/A. Top Teesside school. The recipe is simple: take cream of the local catchment area, add superb facilities and great, committed teachers and the results speak for themselves. Strong right across the curriculum and no lack of academic rigour, traditional academic curriculum, no vocational, though willingness to tailor courses to suit the individual. Pupils are in forms for first, second and third year but in ability sets for maths and modern languages from first year. More setting is introduced in the third year and by fourth year forms vanish.

Games, options, the arts: Yarm seems to excel at everything, from sport to music; the trophy cabinet is heaving. Next to River Tees so rowing is strong – former pupils now competing in Olympics, including 2012 gold medallist Katherine Copeland. Also strong in rugby, hockey (boys and girls), netball and tennis. Very inclusive and runs teams for all ages/skill levels to foster team spirit. Regularly provides sportsmen and women for county and country.

Lots of top grades in art, eye-catching DT and textiles very strong, as are engineering ('let's build a car..') and fine arts. Check out the hugely impressive design awards. Strong choral society and school choir sings Evensong in Durham and Ripon Cathedrals. Orchestra, jazz and funk band, concert band and various ensembles ensure widespread participation. Drama also a major strength across all ages and genres from classical Greek to Shakespeare and contemporary; very popular duologues competition also.

Breathtaking breadth of extra-curricular activities – the list is endless with every member of staff offering at least one. All the usual on offer such as debating and technology club but add to that rock-climbing, horse-riding, golf, strictly ballroom, circuit training, Ancient Greek, political journalism, stockbroker challenge, meditation and ultimate Frisbee and you're still not a quarter of the way through the list; you can even try your hand at silversmithing – a must-do for those aspiring to dentistry. Clubs and activities happen at lunchtime and after school and D of E is also thriving here.

Good opportunities for foreign travel: previous years have seen a summer trek through the mountains of North Eastern India and a winter trip to Cambodia. There are plenty of trips to Yarm's partner school in Werther, Germany each year, also long-standing annual exchanges to France and Spain. Typically trips to places like Holland (hockey), Northern Ireland (rugby), Cambodia (cultural), Berlin (languages), Austria (skiing), France (history and French), Barcelona (business studies), Italy (skiing) and Belgium (battlefields tour). Closer to home there is plenty of opportunity for outward bound/adventure trips (two full-time outdoor education teachers); this is a school that understands just how much can be learned outside the classroom.

Top London acousticians and Birmingham architects were employed to design the auditorium for performing arts and there isn't time or space here to eulogise enough about the 800 seat theatre with its 80 person orchestra pit, retractable seating, two (naturally) grand pianos, bespoke organ, touch-of-a-switch window blackouts, all stunningly housed in natural materials including Norwegian oak and Lake District slate. Has to be seen to be appreciated – you will forget you are in a school.

Background and atmosphere: Badge features a phoenix and the school has risen from nothing. Lacking a 'proper' grammar school for some years, executives at nearby ICI wanted a good school for their boys – so they started their own. They bought the old Yarm Grammar School building and started a new school with 50 boys in 1978. School bought the nearby Friarage (18th century stone-built mansion) in 1980, and by 1996 the whole of the senior school was based there, allowing prep school (opened in 1991) use of the old grammar school building. School has grown rapidly since. Girls joined in 2001, there is now a 50:50 boy/girl mix and the school has 'grown up'. Major £20 million redevelopment of facilities has taken place, including stunning classrooms with interactive whiteboards, widescreen 3D teaching televisions and state-of-the-art sound system; refurbished science labs; double-height dance studio; well-equipped gym and all-weather, floodlit netball and cricket facility.

From medieval buildings to modern sandstone developments, from the Friarage dovecote – 'probably the oldest building for miles around' – to the sixth form centre housed in the old stable block, the whole environment feels cared for and respected. Outdoor lockers, zoned in year group pods, ensure no tatty dark

Y

corridors inside school, which instead are proudly festooned with striking art and design technology work.

Parents say the school has 'character' – and they don't just mean the buildings, comparing to bigger purpose-built schools that are as 'soulless as Stevenage...' Here parents feel they know people, you can talk to them if there is a problem: 'They stamp on everything and do it well. Some of the boys might have their shirts hanging out but they get the important things right'. Good relationships with staff mean parents are happy to support school activities. Staff turnover here is low and although parents become slightly twitchy at any staff departures it would appear to be an unnecessary concern – 'a good one leaves but another equally good one comes along'.

Real sense of a working community, huge staff – '260 on the payroll'; teaching and non-teaching staff all play their part, 'it's like a village, there's nothing we can't do ourselves,' confirms the head. Chefs (not dinner ladies here), and an in-house team of electricians, joiners, painters, gardeners and general workers all kept busy taking good care of the place – evident sense of pride and belonging. Teaching staff are well-supported and valued with every department having its own well-equipped workbase. Intelligent management philosophy – 'set the bar high and people join in'. School recognises the needs of working parents and opens from 8.00 am to 5.00 pm with children old and young kept busy and supervised on campus.

Pastoral care and discipline: Majors in pastoral care. Each student is allocated a tutor who is key to their happiness and success at school. Programme of personal, social and health education is led by tutor and he/she is first point of contact with parents. Heads of year and head of sixth form co-ordinate work of tutors and monitor academic progress. Home-school links are strong, helped by regular reports, parents' evenings and a weekly newsletter. Tutor groups belong to one of four houses – Aidan, Bede, Cuthbert and Oswald – which promotes mixing of age groups for social, sporting and fund-raising events. Also peer support mentoring and sixth formers take a lead on some house activities to assist younger pupils.

Pupils and parents: You only have to spend half an hour window-shopping in Yarm High Street to realise that there is serious money in this town. Not everyone is local, however, and 12 private daily coaches bring children in from a wide catchment area beyond the town: Sunderland in the north, Thirsk in the south, Catterick in the west, Saltburn in the east. 90 per cent from white, middle to upper professional/management family background, remainder split Asian, American, African, preponderance of medics. Ten per cent helped by school bursary. Also Ogden Sixth Form Science Scholarships. Just one per cent have EAL requirement and eight per cent SEN – mostly mild dyslexia. Maximum class size in senior school is 22, sixth form just 16 (average is nine). Teacher/pupil ratio of one to ten.

Pupils are very comfortable to be around, and whilst they are aware of great opportunities offered here, they are careful not to abuse them. Parents closely involved and Yarm School Association well supported for social activities. Regular personal contact with parents allied to weekly newsletters, photo books, IT link-ups etc.

Entrance: For senior school, entrance exams in maths and English held January before September entry. Good school reports and interview also needed. Scholarships available and also possibility of a bursary.

Exit: Youngsters mostly head off to university with about 10 per cent a year to Oxbridge. Medicine very popular: 12-14 per cent most years. Several others to veterinary or dental courses. For the rest, northern universities – Durham, York, Leeds, Teesside, Newcastle, Northumbria – seem favourites, mostly to study traditional degree courses. Twenty per cent leave post-GCSE.

Money matters: Reliant on fee income. Invests mainly in staff, books, IT and recently, major school redevelopment.

Remarks: Pupils and staff are refreshingly unpretentious and hard working: no 'old school' complacency here, which can only be a good thing and adds to the charm. Very strong academically, excellent sporting achievements and more design awards than any other school in the country. There are wow factors throughout, not least the Princess Alexandra Performing Arts Centre, a real boon not only for the school but also a major asset for the region. The picture-perfect riverside classroom development is seriously high spec – and green too – heated by deep ground-source heat pumps and solar panels providing hot water. Add to that the views over the River Tees to farmland beyond, the riverside decking and Costa coffee bar franchise where teachers sit marking work in between lessons and pupils are deep in conversation whilst enjoying a skinny latte...it's a wonder anyone ever goes home.

Yehudi Menuhin School

Linked school: Yehudi Menuhin Junior School

Stoke d'Abernon, Cobham, Surrey, KT11 3QQ

• Pupils: 75 boys and girls; mostly boarders • Ages: 8–19 • Non-denom • Fees: Boarding £41,100 pa for those not on music and dance scheme. • Independent

Tel: 01932 864739
Email: admin@yehudimenuhinschool.co.uk
Website: www.yehudimenuhinschool.co.uk

Headmaster: Since 2010, Dr Richard Hillier MA PhD (fifties). Previously headmaster of The Oratory Preparatory School, in Oxfordshire and, before that, head of classics and housemaster at Repton. Not the obvious choice for the rôle, following Nicholas Chisholm's 22 years at the helm. Has taken quite a leap from head of a rural RC prep school to headmaster of an internationally renowned musical centre of excellence. A former chorister (at King's School Peterborough, then the only state cathedral school), he read classics at St John's Cambridge, where he sang in the choir, then teacher training and doctorate (on Arator: an obscure late Christian-Latin author) at Durham, where he was also a lay clerk in the cathedral choir. Still sings as a freelance baritone soloist (when asked!) and is involved in academic research. Married to Elaine: exams officer, school archivist and alumni contact. They have two grown-up sons – both attended Repton and went on to Cambridge – and a parson russell terrier. Day to day musical management in the hands of the school's head of music Malcolm Singer.

Academic matters: The most specialised of the country's specialist music schools, the Yehudi Menuhin School provides tuition on strings (violin, viola, cello, double bass, and guitar) and piano. 'We operate on a plane above the other music schools,' said one proud pupil. Half the school day is taken up by music (with practice on top) leaving a small but reasonable window for academic subjects. Most pupils take seven GCSEs (sometimes five if they come from abroad), three AS levels and two A2s. The range of subjects is small – English, modern languages, maths, science, music and history – as are class sizes: mixed age groups of between six and 12 pupils. Children in years 3-6 have all lessons with one teacher.

We sensed more emphasis on academics than on previous visits, when academic success was considered largely a matter of luck given the miniature year groups. Exam results certainly impressive when you consider that academic ability is not part

Y

of the admissions process. Chinese and maths (and of course music) GCSE results particularly stand out; one student from Hong Kong, one from mainland China and one from Taiwan. Small computer suite with Sibelius software for composition and other computers dotted around. Many pupils have own laptops. Music library stacked floor to ceiling with sheet music and CDs. Also traditional library for other subjects and fiction. Extra English tuition for 15 of the overseas pupils; three pupils with mild dyslexia.

Games, options, the arts: Music dominates both scheduled and free time, starting with a civilised hour of post-breakfast practice (rather than the dawn call we've seen at other music schools). Three or four more hours fitted in during the day (less for the younger children; more for the eldest). Two hour-long instrumental lessons a week on one's main instrument. All string players also learn the piano. Pianists may also learn a string instrument or harpsichord (no organ, but a new chamber organ delivered in May 2013 has opened up new possibilities). Lunch time concerts twice every week in the school's fabulous concert venue, The Menuhin Hall. Orchestra, soloists and chamber groups perform regularly in school, around the country and even abroad (school provided half the orchestra for the 2012 Menuhin violin competition in Beijing). Double bass players attend Royal College of Music junior department on Saturday mornings: 'It's important for group playing experience as they don't get as much as the other string players from chamber music here.'

Swimming now compulsory once a week (indoor pool opened in 2010). Table tennis, football, running, badminton, dance, yoga and tennis available, though not played against other schools. Sports that can cause hand injuries (eg basketball, volleyball) are abjured. A bit of Alexander Technique for all. Art part of the curriculum and of high quality; popular for evening relaxation after all that music. Drama also big here – these are not kids who shun the limelight. Growing take-up of D of E – from bronze to gold.

Background and atmosphere: Yehudi Menuhin founded the school in 1963, 'to create the ideal conditions in which musically gifted children might develop their potential to the full on stringed instruments and piano.' Five decades later, little has changed. While numbers have grown, the ethos remains the same, and the great man's posthumous presence seems to have grown. Buried in the leafy grounds of the Victorian Gothic 'Music House' (once owned by a member of the Hansard family), the school's music library contains much of Yehudi Menuhin's own collection. Pupils and some staff have started quoting Menuhin, in the manner of a spiritual guru, prefacing comments with 'Yehudi Menuhin believed ...' or 'As Menuhin said ...'

Dining room enlarged and refurbished since our last visit – offers good, healthy eating – and school continues to grow. Stood at a whopping 73 pupils when we visited. No noisy huddles of gossipy school-kids – even lunch was a relatively sober affair. Basically, they know why they're here, they want to be here, and if that means an amount of isolation to get in their two to six hours' practice, then so be it. Still using the same pictorial prospectus with a libellously unflattering shot of Nicola Benedetti on the cover – a new one is apparently in the works.

Pastoral care and discipline: Caring but relaxed. For a school that requires such rigorous self-discipline, YM gives its charges an unexpectedly loose rein. Teachers on first name basis. 'We're not a sanction-based school,' said the head. School day finishes at 6:30pm. Saturday morning school for all, except the 8-11 year olds. Behaviour not a big problem, though adolescence throws up the usual issues and the occasional pupil has been suspended. Fab boarding house for 11-19 year olds with a piano

in every room (most are doubles). Pupils live in 'pods' rather than along corridors. The youngest maestros live upstairs in the main house, over the dining hall. Teachers take pains to keep competition in check. It may come as a surprise to some that the effete world of classical music can be more brutally cut-throat than heavyweight boxing. School tempers this by eg rotating positions in the school orchestra (there is no one leader and even hotshots may have a turn at the back of the second violins). The pupils support one another and provide an enthusiastic audience. Still, for children who have been used to being big fish in less august ponds, the adjustment to a school where everyone is outstanding cannot always be easy.

Age is not the boundary that it is at most schools and YM prides itself on functioning like a family, with older pupils looking after the younger ones and all working and playing together. That said, uneven year groups can make boarding awkward in younger years. When we visited there were two children in year 5, two in year 6 and six in year 7. 'We take the children who NEED to be here', our guide told us. More mundane criteria, like keeping a balance of instruments and number of available boarding spaces, also come into the play. Increasing trend for 18 year olds to stay a further year to make the most of continued government funding (which carries on to 19). With no pesky national exams or academic lessons, this extra year can be fully devoted to music.

Pupils and parents: Totally non-denom, very broad mix of backgrounds (no parents pay full fees) and countries of origin. Equal mix of boys and girls in 2013/14. Roughly half are UK residents (though many of these were born abroad – overseas families often move to the UK lock, stock and barrel so their children can attend the school). Above all, this is a tiny school. Numbers in most year groups far too small to be true cohorts. Esteemed alumni include Tasmin Little (violin), Nigel Kennedy (violin), Nicola Benedetti (violin) and Paul Watkins (cello).

Entrance: Pupils can join at any age from eight to 16. Three stage application process ('long and drawn out,' said a pupil). Candidates first send a DVD to see if they 'are even in the ballpark'. If yes, they're then invited for an audition and interviews. The last hurdle involves spending three days living at the school. NB The middle stage is often omitted for overseas applicants. School says it is looking for potential rather than achievement but we suspect both come into play. 'We have applications from lots of well-drilled kids from the Far East but they're not always right for this school. Sometimes we suggest they come back to us in a couple of years. We're not just looking for ability, but something extra.' Also strives for a cultural and international mix. Lack of academic aptitude not an obstacle to entrance. Nor is eccentricity.

Exit: Vast majority to conservatories, either in the UK or abroad. Very few fail to make the grade and regular termly assessment quickly identifies pupils who are 'unsuitable or not interested'. Some pursue music courses at university if they plan to compose rather than perform.

Money matters: Fifty-two pupils qualify for an aided place under DfE Music and Dance Scheme (sliding scale according to parental income). School aims to provide bursary support for the rest on a means-tested basis until they qualify for the DfE scheme. Very few paying full whack. Launched fund-raising campaign Sept 2013 in concert (!) with the school's 50th anniversary. The aim is to be truly needs-blind (funds will also help build new music studios). Non-British EU pupils are eligible for sixth form funding only. 'Postgraduates' are funded in addition to the 52 government scholars – so staying on is a good deal for both them and the school.

Y

Remarks: This is no environment for the faint-hearted child or the over-ambitious parent. Don't be tempted unless this is something your child desperately wants – and then wait a year or two. Having said that, it's lovely, refined and nurturing within a harmonious conservatoire setting with a large dollop of eccentricity thrown into the mix.

Y

JUNIOR SCHOOLS

Abberley Hall

Worcester, WR6 6DD

• Pupils: 215; 135 boys/80 girls; full boarders 100; flexi boarders 30; day 85 • Ages: 8-13, pre-prep 2+ -8 • C of E • Fees: Boarding £19,935; Day £4,590-£15,885 pa • Independent

Tel: 01299 896275
Email: gill.portsmouth@abberleyhall.co.uk
Website: www.abberleyhall.co.uk

Headmaster: Since 1996, Mr John Walker BSc, educated at Bradfield and took his degree (in psychology from Surrey) on the wing. He went straight into teaching from school itself, with stints at West Hill Park, Edgeborough and Sunningdale, before going to Pembroke House in Kenya, where he became head of studies. He also spent four years at Bramcote. His wife, Janie, is 'fully involved with the school, particularly on the pastoral side'. He knows every child by name – and what their strengths and weaknesses are. A man on a mission 'to give each child confidence – to find something they can be proud of, whether it is academic, sporting, musical or artistic'. He teaches Latin and maths and also monitors the children's weekly effort cards, so that any incipient problems can be sorted out swiftly.

Retiring in July 2014. His successor will be Will Lockett, at present classics teacher, housemaster and school beekeeper at Bryanston. An Abberley old boy who spent several years in industry before becoming a teacher, he has also taught at Dauntsey's. He is married to Beth, a teacher, artist and fiddle player, and they have three children.

Entrance: Entrance is non selective and some financial assistance is available to those who might benefit from it – not based on scholastic potential but on need and as a partial reflection of the fact that 'we are an educational charity'. This is not a scholarship award and, as often as not, will go to a single parent. Main entry in September but can and will take at any time. Informal interview, no exam as such, but children are tested before their interview to give the school some idea of their strengths and weaknesses.

Exit: Popular co-ed schools include Cheltenham College, Gordonstoun, Malvern College, Marlborough, Millfield, Oundle, RGS (Worcester), St Edward's Oxford, Shrewsbury, Stowe and Uppingham. Boys also to Eton, Harrow, Old Swinford Hospital, Radley, Sherborne and Winchester; girls to Badminton, Cheltenham Ladies' College, Moreton Hall, Malvern St James, St Mary's Ascot, Tudor Hall and Westonbirt.

Remarks: Situated in verdant countryside just north of Worcester, in a rather impressive, listed Victorian pile, the school has a good range of modern blocks attached – a new classroom building, the Rhoddy Swire 'Palace', the renovated girls' boarding house and a very good sized school theatre/hall, the basement of which houses the music department.

The pupil body is almost exclusively English – with boarders from Warwickshire, Shropshire, Herefordshire, Gloucestershire, Staffordshire and Derbyshire. A number of Forces families and quite a number of very local children who come up from the nursery and pre-prep to board at the prep. A handful of Spanish pupils and one or two others from further afield.

Well integrated with the local community, the grounds provide a venue for local church events, and local schools and pre-school groups are also invited to make use of Abberley's facilities.

Considering its non-selective entry, the school has a strong academic focus and very high standards. Termly competitions improve fluency and confidence in prose, poetry and speech.

IT well used – though not as extensively as it might be for private study, 'as the abuse of it is difficult to prevent'. Lots of whiteboards used in class and plenty of access to computers in different parts of the school. Genuinely interactive learning – 'We have a troop of Viking re-enactors coming to camp in the grounds next week' – permeated by a sense of adventure.

All children learn French, Latin and Spanish, with those trying for scholarships at common entrance also learning Greek. The school owns a chalet in the French Alps and all pupils are shipped off for two three week stints in years 5 and 7, both to learn French and taste a different culture. The school day is demanding but plenty of help for those who need or want it – about 40 per cent of pupils have some additional help with everything from dyslexia to study skills (at an additional charge).

Great labs full of interest and set up on a semi-tutorial type plan, so that the most is made of the very small class sizes (10-12). A very good and well organized DT room open well into the evenings in which the children build everything and anything – including coracles – as well as a textiles room and ceramics studio where they learn enamelling.

Really well set up, light, inviting and well-stocked library and study areas (being redeveloped and improved when we visited) where individual pupils have their own little cubby holes – which they keep in slightly Molesworth-esque style. Dorms are well kept, welcoming, homely and cheerful, and lovely use made of the beautiful buildings which house many of the children.

Sport is central with an hour of games every day and all children from year 4 upwards given the opportunity to represent the school in matches if they wish. A tour of South Africa every two years with boys playing rugby and girls playing hockey. Tennis courts, cricket nets, Astroturf, a 25m indoor swimming pool, a climbing wall and a manège. Also a fishing lake and plenty of room to train up the cross country team. Set as it is in about 90 acres of parkland, room for everything and a tree house 'to sleep 25' under construction when we came by.

Most children also have individual music lessons – over 20 practice rooms (generous for a school with these pupil numbers) and a good range of peripatetic instrumental teachers as well as a gifted and enthusiastic head of music. The school concert we attended was awash with children clearly enjoying themselves and performing to a very high standard, all cheered on warmly by peers and parents.

A truly happy place – the children are confident, polite and enthusiastic, with just the convivial combination of opinions and manners you would hope for. Although plenty of pastoral support, with an overall staff:pupil ratio of about 1:7, 'you can go to any of the teachers, or to Mr Walker, if you have a problem' – pupils are expected to organise and discipline themselves to a considerable extent by the time they reach the upper years. When asked what the school has taught them they say, 'Honesty, co-operation with others, learning to be trusted, independence'.

Staff turnover is very low, with an emphasis on a good number of live-in staff and settled families providing the mainstay of pastoral support – it has a genuine family feel. Termly reports to parents – still handwritten to avoid them becoming formulaic – and children are free to call their parents as often as they like once lessons are over for the day.

If a niggle, it's the slightly overwhelmingly white, C of E flavour – it's far from culturally and socially diverse (although the pupil body does include a handful of Catholics and one or two Muslims), although granted its catchment area, this is pretty unsurprising. It is, however, certainly a place where any child would be made to feel welcome.

Bottom line: this is a place with a buzz of happiness and confidence and a very stable, settled core. It's in beautiful surroundings, a really nurturing place where your child will find their own voice, and its impressive academic results tell their own story.

The Abbey

Linked school: Woodbridge School

Church Street, Woodbridge, IP12 1DS

• Pupils: 155 pupils, 72 boys/83 girls • Ages: 7–11 • Fees: £11,889 pa
• Independent

Tel: 01394 382673
Email: office@theabbeyschool-suffolk.org.uk
Website: www.woodbridge.suffolk.sch.uk/theabbey

Master: Since 1997, Mr Nicholas Garrett, (late forties, formerly head of history and housemaster at St Andrews School, Eastbourne. He is married to Ruth, and they have grown up children at university. Tall, impressive appearance, with a quiet ease of manner, exceedingly approachable. During his time, all manner of developments have taken place: 'a pupil should arrive, books on back, carrying a hockey stick, violin, and with ballet shoes hanging off an arm'. He believes children should be given the chance to explore all possibilities during their junior years, and he has set his hand to that task impressively.

Entrance: About half of year 3 is made up from pupils progressing up from the pre-prep department, Queen's House, at seven; others join via test and interview from other local schools. Selective, but with scope for quite a range of ability, 'we are looking for those who can explore all that's on offer'. Places occasionally available in higher forms – always worth asking.

Exit: Vast majority make the seamless transfer to Woodbridge, the senior school. A few go to maintained schools in the area, or to board elsewhere. The parents of the occasional pupil that might struggle in the senior school will have been given advance warning, and advised to move elsewhere at 11. This is handled sensitively and is rare.

Remarks: This is a super school with many strengths and the widest and most varied curriculum possible. Main building is Tudor, lots of oak panelling, flagged floors, and even rumours of a ghost. Newer buildings for science, art and sport have been added, and the grounds are mature and delightful; 'this is a place for a sunlit childhood'. Pupils about the school are courteous, open doors and smile, but are intent on their own ploys and enjoyment. Small class sizes, around 20, gradually moving from class to subject based learning. Specialist teachers from the senior school teach science, languages and art to the higher forms. The Abbey language scheme gives all pupils a taste of four modern languages, Italian, Spanish, German, French, in consecutive years. The musical life of the school is outstanding. In year 4, all pupils learn a stringed instrument in school, with tuition in small groups, and as a result, a large number continue to play. The Abbey has four choirs, two string orchestras, and a variety of ensemble groups. Concerts and performances are regularly given. Drama and dance also strong. Ballet and tap are taught throughout the school with the emphasis on fun and a chance to perform. The summer play, performed in the Seckford Theatre, is a highlight for the town as well as the school. Sport is for all – the head is very pro everyone playing competitively and everyone has the opportunity to play in a match. Main sports for boys are soccer, rugby, hockey and cricket; for girls, netball, hockey and rounders. Swimming and tennis for all throughout the year, plus athletics in the summer, and cross-country in the Michaelmas and Lent terms: not a place for couch potatoes. Full time SEN teacher gives support throughout the school. There is setting for maths from year 3 and for English in year 6. Communication with parents is taken very seriously. As well as the usual parents' consultations, staff are available on a day-to-day basis via telephone or email and the head, incredibly, publishes his home telephone number for parents to use if they are worried over the weekends: 'I prefer a call at home than worries bottled up'. This care of the children is at the heart of such a happy school.

The Abbey Junior School

Linked school: The Abbey School Reading

30 Christchurch Road, Reading, RG2 7AR

• Pupils: 380 girls; all day • Ages: 3–11 • C of E • Fees: £8,790–£12,240 pa • Independent

Tel: 01189 872256
Email: schooloffice@theabbey.co.uk
Website: www.theabbey.co.uk

Head of Junior School: Since 2008, Mrs Carol Ryninks BA, HDE (Cape Town), MA(Ed) Warwick. Was deputy head at Kingsley School, Leamington Spa and before that taught at St Martin's School for Girls, Solihull and Sutton High. She is married with two daughters and describes how, despite her family being based in Warwick, she 'fell in love' with The Abbey. Extremely energetic and friendly, she radiates job satisfaction and is very proud of her school, her staff and the children.

Entrance: Informal play and assessment for youngest; tests plus interview for older girls.

Exit: Nearly all move up to the senior school unless gently redirected (in good time); some to nearby girls' grammar.

Remarks: Open the magnificent door to this grand Alfred Waterhouse villa in the university area of Reading and the tone is set by the welcoming and not at all grand front of house staff. Through the double doors the visitor is met with a wall of photographs, a foretaste of the wonderful displays that decorate every room and corridor. We arrived just after the start of a new school year; a few of the tiniest three-year-olds were still looking slightly dazed but most were having a whale of a time with paper, glue and plenty of glitter. Everything in the Early Years Centre is arranged on the scale of its small inhabitants with low-down smartboards, plenty of rugs, bean bags and exciting themed corners. Smallish outdoor space probably seems limitless to its pint-sized explorers. Each of the 60 three- and four-year-old girls has a pastoral carer and the emphasis is on learning to learn and focused play. Mrs Ryninks describes it as the 'early years curriculum plus plus', Ofsted describes it as 'outstanding'. In the 'role play room' the dressing up clothes were being enthusiastically plundered for anything pink, glittery or princessy. When we asked (as we must) about gender stereotypes we were told that 'there are police/fire uniforms in the box', but on the day of our visit that's where they were staying. At this stage the timetable is kept flexible, but in general, 'harder thinking stuff' takes place in the morning; the four-year-olds we saw having a 'magic carpet lesson' were just enjoying the moment. This gentle start is just the beginning of an educational journey that for most leads downhill (geographically, not metaphorically) to the senior school and beyond. The Abbey is developing a building and grounds close to the junior school. The result will be a new Early Years Centre with bright and airy classrooms and spacious grounds.

The junior school is a mix of Victorian and later additions – the upper years have a beautifully designed building with flexible performance space and music studio – great for all the singing, dancing, music and drama that goes on. Every year group has its own Christmas production – a great idea that gives all children a chance to shine and is less of a crush for the audience. Mrs Ryninks is particularly delighted with the central Astroturf lawn paid for by the PTA – apparently its natural predecessor was a sea of mud and limited outdoor play. Classes are 'muddled' every two years to promote year group bonding. Year 5 girls are trained to be 'playground buddies' and set up games, manage play equipment and mediate in squabbles. The miniature Victorian cottage garden and 'dig for victory' patch are great for hands-on history and the produce is cooked for lunch. A recent change was to the catering: food is now all cooked in-house and includes 'proper' puddings; water is provided in classrooms. Masses of day visits and excursions, all included in fees. The year 6 residential trip to Cornwall is a pre-senior school highlight, 'not a worksheet in sight', says Mrs Ryninks proudly.

Teaching in the upper years aims to develop independent learning; in a maths lesson girls displayed different coloured cups (red, orange, green) to indicate if they needed help – less obtrusive than a sea of hands. Requisite IT all present and correct but we liked the fact that classrooms are not dominated by computer screens. Specialist sports teachers are committed to finding every girl a sport they enjoy before senior school. The sports notice boards (which can so often undermine fine words about inclusivity) were excellent – full of fun and photos and instead of wall-to-wall winners a 'team of the month' feature. Apparently the main challenge to this enlightened approach can be parents who 'have to be educated to love mixed teams.' Specialist small group and individual support for mild SEN available. The head describes the ability range here as 'good average to very able' and believes that skilled teaching and careful monitoring produces better results than 'cramming'. While the school is, inevitably, a feeder for nearby Kendrick Grammar, girls who gain places at both often choose to stay on.

A confident and well-run school that knows exactly where it's going. Unusually strong parental involvement a great endorsement, not just fund-raising but social events and a programme of play dates to introduce girls to each other before starting. Happy girls who are stretched and challenged but not pressurised.

Abbey Lane Primary School

Abbey Lane, Sheffield, S8 0BN

- Pupils: 470 • Ages: 4–11 • Non-denom • State

Tel: 01142 745054
Email: enquiries@abbeylane.sheffield.sch.uk
Website: www.abbeylaneprimaryschool.co.uk

Headteacher: Mrs Maxine Stafford, previously deputy head.

Entrance: Non-selective and over-subscribed. Apply to Sheffield LA by end of February of the year due to start. Priority given to SEN, then catchment area children, then siblings. Most children come from the Beauchief and Abbey Lane area.

Exit: Most go to Meadowhead Comprehensive, a few to other state schools with sixth forms, eg Silverdale, High Storrs, All Saints.

Remarks: Very strong Sats results, especially at key stage 2; key stage 1 results are less exceptional but improving. Little gender difference in achievement. Thinking skills work done in small groups with four of the years, a particular strength of the school. An LA Foundation lead teacher has developed an individual approach to learning with reception children based on their interests, which encourages independence and allows very bright ones to be stretched, and now speaks on it

at conferences. Class sizes 28-30 but may go down in future. Strong on SEN support, especially for dyspraxia ('fantastic support staff'). A recently acquired computer suite with 20 computers plus one in each classroom, as well as eight interactive whiteboards. Staff 'very supportive of the children and the parents', dedicated and talented.

An unusually generous amount of outdoor space for a city school – small playground with a climbing wall and garden area plus very large playground facing onto a wood, allowing the older children plenty of room to play cricket and tennis and just run around. Good variety of clubs: choir, gardening, art, drama as well as cricket, football and athletics. The children run some of the extracurricular activities and have a well-established school council. A lot of emphasis on outdoor play: 'It's like a well-run nursery with academic development'. School food improvements are under way and mental health problems are addressed in collaboration with a child psychologist. Healthy child accreditation is a target.

The day we visited, the school was humming with creative activity, independent and adult-led, with elaborate, larger than life-size pinatas being completed in preparation for leading the Lord Mayor's parade that starts the annual Sheffield Children's Festival. The year 1s have a wedding each year, with a church service and reception at school, attended by parents in formal dress, as part of the RE curriculum. The school is light and bright, with walls covered with interesting displays and some excellent artwork, eg Tudor houses and robots, in the corridors, one of which has an interactive beach scene painted on it by a classroom assistant in her spare time. The main drawback is the lack of space inside the classrooms, especially in the top years.

Mainly home-owning/professional families; lower than average SEN, EAL and free school meals figures. Parents are very involved – they help inside the classroom, raise funds and cleared an orchard area, now sporting picnic tables and a nature trail. Polite, friendly and well-behaved children who get on well together and are very enthusiastic about their school; parents say their offspring are very happy here and enjoy learning. The chief motivation is by reward, eg certificates; Golden Time at the end of the week (half an hour's free choice of activities, forfeited for poor behaviour).

All together an impressive school that enjoys a strong reputation locally.

Aberlour House the Junior School at Gordonstoun

Linked school: Gordonstoun School

Gordonstoun School, Elgin, IV30 5RF

- Pupils: 100; 65 boys/35 girls, boarding 58 • Ages: 8–13
- Fees: Day £12,420; Boarding £20,199 pa • Independent

Tel: 01343 837829
Email: admissions@gordonstoun.org.uk
Website: www.gordonstoun.org.uk

Head of the Junior School: Mr Robert McVean, BSc (forties), taught science at Aberlour House from 2000, became head in 2003. Educated at Hurstpierpoint College, he read environmental biology at Swansea, thence five years in the state sector, followed by Edinburgh Academy. Married to Laura (bubbly and fun; she helps with SEN), two children in the school ('all been huge fun, wouldn't have changed a thing'). Looking down from our common room eyrie at children returning from games, this editor commented that a certain young man looked a tad sad – he was on his own, munching a fairy cake – 'he gets overwrought,' was the instant reply, 'he is just a little ADHD'). School wanted to remove this last comment, we prefer it remain to show just how on top of things the McVeans are.

Dedicated scholarships for juniors, who will lose them if they don't keep up to snuff.

Entrance: By assessment and interview plus report from previous school.

Exit: Nearly all to senior school.

Remarks: When we first visited this rather jolly purpose-built junior school in the grounds of Gordonstoun with self-contained classrooms and dorms all in the same building, the dorms, strategically placed on the second floor, with glorious views, were filled (and we mean over filled) with somewhat incongruous work-station type beds. The school opened two weeks late, all the young having been sent camping for a fortnight. The demand for places exceeded expectations and four young were farmed out. Aberlour has been a runaway success, an extension was built to cope with demand for boarding places, including extra classrooms, common rooms, a large assembly hall and houseparents' accommodation. The expanded boarding spaces are nearly full again – though in truth there is loads of room for extra beds.

Siblings of children already in the school are flocking in, often from abroad. EAL costs extra. Gordonstoun funds its own guardianship service. Parents appreciate the convenience of having all their young in the same place. Flexi and weekly boarding recently introduced. There are 100 pupils with an average of 35 or so in each weekend, which is jam-packed with activities. School day starts 8.20am, with brekky before that for day children if they turn up on time; ends at 5.35pm when day children can go home, having done their homework. Children use senior school facilities: fleet of mini buses to main school for music/drama/games/gym/pool, which is quite a hike for small legs. 'Lab in a Lorry' parked outside when we visited to stimulate would-be scientists.

Playing fields to the west (new all-weather playing field), protected by banking from north winds, provide a haven with child-inspired woods, and customised climbing frame (and another one beside the main games pitch further east).

Abingdon Preparatory School

Linked school: Abingdon School

Josca's House, Kingston Road, Frilford, OX13 5NX

- Pupils: 250 boys and girls; all day • Ages: Girls: 4-7; boys: 4-13.
- Christian • Fees: £9,600–£13,200 pa • Independent

Tel: 01865 391570
Email: registrar@abingdonprep.org.uk
Website: www.abingdon.org.uk/prep

Headmaster: Since 2011, Mr Crispin Hyde-Dunn MA (Oxon) PGCE MA(Ed) NPQH (thirties). Read history at Oxford. Previously deputy head of King's College School, Cambridge; was head of history at New College School in Oxford. He lives with his wife, Lucy, a medical research fellow at Oxford, in the school house just down the road.

Charmingly fogeyish in his immaculate pin-stripes, he presents a rather formal face to the world but has genuine rapport with the boys, all of whom he knows by name (they call him Crispin – more of that later). He is actively involved in teaching – takes the year 8 boys for PHSE every week and when we visited, just a few weeks before CE, PHSE was,

understandably, revision techniques for history. He ringfences slots in his diary for both reading with the pre-prep children and 'slipping in and out of lessons across ages and subjects – vitally important'. Also does a share of break duties, part of being a 'visible head'. Parents remarked how perceptive he is, 'really able to get to the nub of what makes a boy tick'. When asked about future developments, he reveals that the governors have agreed in principle to establishing a nursery and that plans are afoot for outdoor classrooms in the forest school tradition. And after that? Astroturf is top of his list.

Describes himself as a 'gentleman racer', his vehicle of choice being a Maserati. Favourite book? That perennial heads' author, George Eliot again, but this time it's not Middlemarch but Silas Marner, 'a story of humanity'.

Entrance: Co-ed up to age seven, boys 4-13 years. No formal academic testing for pre-prep, but children should be sufficiently mature to settle into a class. Thereafter testing in English, non-verbal reasoning and maths, but Mr Hyde-Dunn says that Abingdon Prep also looks for 'that spark', boys who 'would thrive', rather than relying wholly on test scores – this may include visiting a boy on his home turf.

Exit: Candidates for the prep's big brother (Abingdon) sit their pre-test in year 7 and then CE in the same way as those from other schools. Most (around three-quarters) go on to Abingdon; others to Magdalen College, Radley. School will have 'an early dialogue with parents' if they think it's best for a boy to depart at 11 (eg to Our Lady's, The Oratory, Bloxham, Cokethorpe).

Remarks: Our delightful guides were, if you will, two of Abingdon Prep's premier products – both had recently gained scholarships to the senior school. First stop on the tour was the wonderful mansard art studio, flooded with light and buzzing with creativity. Year 7 boys were briefing year 4 boys on the school's collaborative jubilee project – a splendid circular mosaic of the Queen. Every child and member of staff will have had a hand in it by the time it graces the front of the school – a cabochon jewel reserved for the headmaster to add the final touch of bling. Three very popular lunchtime art clubs each week.

Next was the best French lesson we've ever observed – a whole class of unselfconscious 13 year olds belting out their avoir and être verbs to (with true entente cordiale) God Save our Gracious Queen and the Marseillaise, followed by a brilliant rap complete with hand gestures. One feels this is French that will never be forgotten. The head says that the aim of his school is to provide a curriculum (academic and wider) 'that really inspires boys'; this certainly seems to be the case and all the teaching we observed was energetic, challenging and fun. Parents report that teachers are 'very approachable' and quick to respond to queries.

Subject specialist teachers from pre-prep onwards; languages are French plus Latin (taster Greek for the scholars). Years 7 and 8 learn programming in IT (batch of Raspberry Pies about to arrive at time of our visit) as well as touch-typing. Parents praise learning support – boys with dyslexia/dyspraxia or those who need help with core skills are boosted by small group work (usually instead of Latin) or one-to-one sessions.

Abingdon Prep is a leading light in synthetic phonics and has embraced this system with almost missionary zeal, believing it to be particularly suitable for engaging boys in reading and writing. The school has developed its own scheme that is now being taught in 12 other schools and disseminated via workshops etc. In the pre-prep classes we observed boys (grouped by ability, not age) were learning sounds using hand gestures, mime, raps, memory and active games, all kinds of kinaesthetic activities. Parents attend evening sessions to prepare them for what and how their children will be learning in reception. By year 3 teachers really notice the difference and the method is equally suitable for children with dyslexia, helping them develop coping skills.

An unusual feature is the tradition of pupils and teachers calling each other by first names. This practice stems from the establishment of the school in Oxford in 1956 when three of its first five pupils were the sons of the founder. It takes some getting used to at first if your ear is conditioned to the more formal practices of other schools and can, apparently, put some parents off. Mr Hyde-Dunn, though not an obvious candidate for such a Bohemian tradition, is a sincere champion – 'It's not a gimmick – it is the ebb and flow of natural respect and epitomises a sense of community'.

School occupies a large Victorian double-fronted country house just three miles from Abingdon, and the extensive grounds at the back merge into meadows, contented sheep adding to the pastoral charm. Generous running around space plus 'The Big Adventure', a huge rope and wood activity structure; quiet grassy quad too for reflective moments.

Practical mix of purpose-built additions provides light and functionality; we loved the colourful DT room with octagonal work benches – equipment here would not disgrace a small industrial unit. The head of DT is particularly proud of the pewter and acrylic moulding equipment. She (yes, she) told us plans too for a dedicated cookery room. The library, comfortably full with books and beanbags, is in a barn and staffed by parent librarians. The new drama studio space in another stone outbuilding was, perhaps, a little oversold – not a theatre (prep uses Abingdon's Amey theatre for their productions) but a series of rooms used for drama (taught from year 5) and after-school activities. Strong music with several choirs, an orchestra, a jazz band and chamber groups.

An impressive sporting programme and everyone gets a match, whether it's inter-house competitions or against other schools. In addition to the usual oval and round ball games (numerous rugby pitches across the road reached via a footbridge) boys can choose from activities such as fly fishing, sailing, water polo, judo, fencing and hockey. Like its big brother, the prep has a huge range of 'other half' activities including textiles, sculling, word games, films and chess. No lessons on Saturday (though year 8s get revision sessions in the run up to CE), but before booking that mini break parents should be aware that matches and other half activities fill the void.

Beyond weekend touchline duties an active parents' association that organises events including spectacular firework nights and the Christmas bazaar (bit of a local legend apparently). Home-school communication praised by all and what the head described as an 'open door' policy really does seem to be just that.

A thriving and deservedly popular prep school that more than acquits itself on the academic front without compromising on the broader curriculum. Parents like the fact that it's not 'super pushy' but will support or stretch as necessary. As the head observed, 'We like boys to leave the school well prepared, but not quite having grown out of it.'

The Academy School

3 Pilgrims Place, Rosslyn Hill, London, NW3 1NG

- Pupils: 70 boys and girls, all day • Ages: 6–13 • Fees: £16,230 pa
- Independent

Tel: 020 7435 6621
Email: office@academyhampstead.com
Website: www.academyschoolhampstead.com

Head: Mr Garth Evans (fifties), and Ms Chloe Sandars (forties), are joint principals of this small Hampstead school, which they founded in 1997. Ms Sandars studied at the Royal Academy of Music, followed by post-graduate work at Trinity College of Music, then played in a trio while teaching music part-time. Garth (as he is known to all), whose great-grandfather accompanied Captain Scott to the Antarctic, was educated at Falkner House, Westminster School and Queen Mary College, London, where he read English. He started tutoring privately at the age of 16 ('to fund my beer money') and went on to work at Trevor-Roberts', where he met Chloe. As private tutors, Garth and Chloe developed quite a following and parents encouraged them to start their own school. 'They liked the way we taught,' says Garth. 'Their children were inspired and given confidence.' The pair are an excellent foil to each other, she calm and organised, he a passionate and reassuring instructor. Chloe has two teenage daughters, both of whom attended the Academy, Garth a teenage son and daughter. Garth's wife Bea (who teaches geography and acts as the school nurse) and Chloe's husband, Andrew (ex-City, who runs the finances and also teaches history and maths) are very much part of the four-person 'leadership' team.

Entrance: Though they have occasionally taken a younger sibling, this is essentially a school which begins at 6, once children have learnt to read. 'We start with specialist subject teaching from the word go,' says Chloe. Pupils join at every stage thereafter, including mid year, if a place is available and the school feels it can meet the child's (and the parents') needs. Maximum of 90 pupils, however, and the school tends to be fullest in the summer. Pupils are assessed rather than tested, taking part in a class to see how they fit in. 'We're happy to work with the very strong and the very weak,' says Chloe. 'The questions we ask are: "Do we think we can do a good job?" "Do we like the family?"' Occasional year 7 places for boys after the 11-plus exodus of girls.

Exit: To a wide range of schools but most get their first choice. Girls to St Paul's, North London Collegiate, City of London, St Margaret's and St Christopher's, boys in significant numbers to local favourites UCS and Highgate, as well as to Westminster, City, Mill Hill, and boarding at Stowe and Bedales. 'Sometimes we have to work with parents to adjust their expectations, particularly if they've set their heart on a specific school from an early age, but most parents trust our judgement,' says Garth. Others are just grateful for the help given in pointing them in the right direction. 'My daughter is not at all academic,' said one mother, 'but they did everything to find a school that worked for her and she is now immensely happy.'

Remarks: The Academy is by no means a traditional school and its approach is perhaps defined by the backgrounds of its heads, who spent their early careers mopping up the fall-out from a traditional education elsewhere. The basis of their philosophy is that all learning stems from a happy child. 'It really is true,' says Chloe, 'if children are happy, everything follows from that.' Year groups here are soft-edged ('We're very flexible about birthdates') and so are classes. 'The whole school is planned round the individual and how best to work with their ability. If there's a problem we solve it.' Class sizes of about 14, but pupils are moved up a set in the middle of a term or taken out of a class to be given additional support. A significant part of the process is instilling the essentials. Teaching, particularly in the core subjects, is rock solid and maths and English are thoroughly engrained. Though most pupils can read fluently on arrival, they continue to read aloud two or three times a week. Older children read for 15 minutes at the end of every lunch hour and all have a reading list and a carefully monitored reading record. Maths is unusually strong. 'Children like being good at maths,' says Garth, who believes that any subject, no matter how complex, can be taught well if communication is clear. As proof, on the day the Guide visited, his class of 11-year-olds had clearly grasped logarithms, a topic normally reserved for sixth formers. The effect lingers into secondary school. 'My daughter has stayed in the top maths set at a competitive school,' said one parent, 'I feel that's down to the teaching at The Academy.'

The Academy started out with just seven children in the premises of a Unitarian Chapel in Hampstead village. 'I looked at every church in the area,' said Chloe. 'Then one snowy evening I knocked on the door here and the vicar said, "Step this way".' The lower years are now housed in two dainty white Georgian cottages, with room sizes that reflect the era, older pupils are taught in the chapel. Facilities are relatively restricted with only a small library and science taught on the move, but pupils are engaged and enthusiastic. 'They give us quite a lot of freedom,' said one, 'but work us very hard.'

The school day starts bright and early with the first lesson at 8. 'We always felt the best part of the day was lost if you started with assembly at 8.30,' says Chloe. There are no 'class' teachers (though the youngest do have one specifically devoted to their needs). The school believes that 'every child is special', but this is not a place that specialises in those with serious learning difficulties. It copes well, however, with those on the margins and a special-needs expert visits weekly. Whatever the child's ability, most parents agree every ounce of potential is fully exploited.

Games are certainly not the raison d'être here and if you had a madly sporty child, whose primary motivation was to be captain of this or that, The Academy would not be an obvious choice. PE is taught on site by a sports teacher and swimming at the nearby Royal Free Leisure Centre, but there's little in the way of team sports. This is more a place where the question is who would like to be in the team – if the answer's yes, you're in. There is, however, a recently established netball squad and matches have been played against other schools in cricket and football, as well as handball, badminton and netball. Music and art are more of a priority. Double art every week, with woodwork on offer and a separate pottery room with its own kiln. Music, too, is taken seriously. 'We do a lot of singing, since it's very inclusive,' says Chloe and the school has a violin teacher and a 19-piece orchestra. 'It's a pretty odd orchestra, with one person on brass and 11 violins, but it's fun and they learn what it's like playing together. Occasionally, an exceptional player will raise the bar for everyone.' The annual school musical, which involves the entire school, is the highlight of the summer term. School food is packed lunch.

Pastoral care is what this school is all about. 'Children are nurtured and encouraged and set very simple objectives,' says Garth. 'We then build it up little by little and make them believe in themselves.' The Academy is inspiration for all, but particularly so for those who've lost their way or lost confidence elsewhere. 'We're good at turning them round,' says Garth, and parents couldn't agree more. 'It's a bit of a cliché,' said one who'd sent two children from two different schools, 'but they do care passionately about the children. In the case of both my children, they were completely transformed both academically and emotionally.' The school has its own visiting counsellor, who teaches PSHE and is available for any pupil who wants to talk. 'They feel it's OK to cross a line with me,' she says. Boundaries here, however, are firm, just further back than might be the case elsewhere. 'We deal furiously with unkindness or making capital at someone else's expense,' says Garth. There is no expulsion. 'We never send them away, we just remove them from society from 8-3.30 unless they behave.' The school has a uniform – a navy sweat top with the school's logo – but it's not strictly imposed. 'We don't really mind as long as they're neat,' said Chloe.

Families are mainly Hampstead locals and the relationship with parents is fundamental. Garth gives out his mobile number and parents can ring whenever they feel the need, a privilege he say they don't abuse. The parents themselves are immensely grateful. 'This is the school we all wish we could have gone to,' said one.

ACS Cobham International School (Junior section)

Linked school: ACS Cobham International School

Heywood, Portsmouth Road, Cobham, Surrey, KT11 1BL

• Pupils: 695; 400 boys/295 girls • Ages: 2-11 • Fees: £6,860-£20,740 pa • Independent

Tel: 01932 867251
Email: cobhamadmissions@acs-schools.com
Website: www.acs-schools.com

Head of School: Mr A Eysele

Remarks: For further information, see senior school

ACS Egham International School (Junior section)

Linked school: ACS Egham International School

Woodlee, London Road, Egham, Surrey, TW20 0HS

• Pupils: 290; 135 girls/155 boys • Ages: 2-11 • Fees: £9,920-£19,540 pa • Independent

Tel: 01784 430611
Email: eghamadmissions@acs-england.co.uk
Website: www.acs-england.co.uk

Head of School: Mr Jeremy Lewis.
Lower school principal: Cindy Blanes

Exit: Most move on to senior school

Remarks: For further information, see the senior school.

ACS Hillingdon International School (Junior section)

Linked school: ACS Hillingdon International School

Hillingdon Court, 108 Vine Lane, Hillingdon, UB10 0BE

• Pupils: 215; 107 girls/108 boys, all day • Ages: 4-11
• Fees: £9,820-£19,420 pa • Independent

Tel: 01895 259771
Email: hillingdonadmissions@acs-england.co.uk
Website: www.acs-england.co.uk

Head of School: Since August 2012, Ms Linda Lapine.

Remarks: For further information, see senior school.

Akeley Wood Junior School

Linked school: Akeley Wood School

Wicken Park, Wicken, Buckinghamshire, MK19 6DA

- Pupils: 285; 175 boys/110 girls; all day • Ages: 12 months-11 years
- Fees: £8,415-£10,425 pa • Independent

Tel: 01908 571231
Email: enquiries@akeleywoodschool.co.uk
Website: www.akeleywoodschool.co.uk

Headmistress: Since 2008, Mrs Clare Page BEd (forties). Educated at Ancaster House in Bexhill, then Chelsea College, Eastbourne, where she did PE and science. First teaching job at Haberdashers' Aske's School for Girls in Elstree. Later moved to Akeley Wood senior school as head of girls' games and then to Beachborough School, a local prep. Returned to Akeley Wood Lower School in 2001, first as year 6 teacher, then as head of year 5. Smiley, energetic and enthusiastic. Teaches handwriting to year 5s and says that despite her head's workload, 'I wouldn't like not to teach'. Her door is almost always open and children pop in to chat. Husband Michael teaches PE and is head of year 11 at senior school, and they have two daughters – one a former head girl at Akeley Wood, the other in the sixth form there.

Entrance: Prospective pupils come for a low-key assessment day – looks for pupils who are 'well-behaved, well-mannered and enthusiastic'. Has a reputation for its special educational needs provision, which is widely praised. Head says school is happy to offer any child a place 'if we feel we can meet their educational needs and that they will be happy at the school'.

Exit: At 11, more than three-quarters go on to Akeley Wood's senior school. Others leave for local grammars – like The Royal Latin School in nearby Buckingham, Aylesbury High and Aylesbury Grammar.

Remarks: The junior school is housed in the Georgian-style Mansion School, set in a dozen acres of games fields and gardens – fantastic for running off steam at breaktime.

Subjects like science, French, IT, music and PE taught by subject specialists while all class teachers teach English and maths. Maths lessons start with quick-fire mental maths session. French taught from word go in year 5 and introductory Latin course offered to more able. Setting for maths and phonics. All children get a 35-minute library session each week, when they can choose what they want to read – Anthony Horowitz is a big favourite. IT suite of 12 computers (28 across whole school) – lots of cross-curricular work here and all lessons start with 10 minutes of touch-typing practice. IT club very popular – children make their own animated films and create stories. Teaching staff mostly women but two male year 5 teachers, plus a male PE specialist. Head says a wide spread of ability among pupils but the school is 'particularly good at finding children's strengths and nurturing what they are good at'. No Saturday school or late finishes. Head reckons that parents' lives are so busy these days that everyone 'values family time together in the evenings and at weekends'.

Four houses, like senior school: Hillcrest, Pilgrim, Stuart and Thompson. House captains showed us round when we visited and were very proud of their badges and smart ties. Housepoints awarded for good work and being helpful. Head also chooses a 'class star of the week' in each class and posts children's names on board outside her study. When we visited, results eagerly awaited by our guides. Pupils wear similar bottle-green uniforms to senior school but are distinguished with jaunty red and green tartan skirts. Self-service family-style eating with staff at end of each table and variety of appetising dishes, including yoghurt, fruit and vegetarian option. Manners important and children must show staff their plates (hopefully scraped clean) before they leave table.

Sport for all. Boys play rugby, football and cricket while girls get hockey, netball and rounders. Like its senior counterpart, lower school has its own equestrian team. Music is strong. Up to two-thirds of children learn an instrument – regular big productions, complete with brass, string ensembles and choir. 'They like jolly singing, with lots of actions,' the music teacher told us with a smile. Children very enthusiastic about art – everything from leaf prints to self-portraits when we visited. Lots of clubs – Warhammer, Mah-jong, Scrabble etc – and school trips to places such as the National History Museum, Northampton Museum. Annual ski trip and week-long expedition to Devon activity centre for year 6s.

Albyn Lower School

Linked school: Albyn School

17-23 Queen's Road, Aberdeen, AB15 4PB

- Pupils: 310; 150 boys/160 girls; 40 toddlers doing various sessions • Ages: 2-11 years • Fees: £6,990-£9,740 pa
- Independent

Tel: 01224 322408
Email: admissions@albynschool.co.uk
Website: www.albynschool.co.uk

Head: Mrs Karen Thomson

Exit: Majority to senior school.

Remarks: For further details, see senior school.

Aldenham Preparatory School

Linked school: Aldenham School

Elstree, Borehamwood, WD6 3AJ

- Pupils: 175; 106 boys/69 girls, 83 in prep, 59 in pre-prep plus 33 in nursery • Ages: nursery 3-4; pre-prep 5-7; prep 7-11 (boys and girls) • Fees: £8,121-£11,784 pa • Independent

Tel: 01923 851664
Email: prepschool@aldenham.com
Website: www.aldenham.com

Head: Since September 2011, Mrs Vicky Gocher BA PGCE (fortyish). Prior to Aldenham, deputy head of Caterham Prep School, having previously taught at Downsend School, Leatherhead.

Entrance: Two-form entry at 3 to nursery. Assessment-based one-form entry for places in reception at 4+, for which 50-60 apply. A few more at 7+, for which tests are set. Occasional places thereafter.

Exit: Natural progression is into the senior school, following assessment. Occasionally some transfer to local state selectives, Haberdashers' Boys' or Girls', Merchant Taylors', North London Collegiate etc.

Remarks: Two buildings house the 3-11 year olds. Woodrow House, a modern, low-rise building, is home to years 3-6. It has a large entrance atrium and a corridor off to the right with classrooms and further classrooms to the left. Rooms have an orderly feel but not too much – some reassuring blobs of clutter here and there. Very impressive IT suite. ICT taught as a subject in its own right but also used widely in the cross-curricular sense; masses of huge interactive whiteboards (clearly adored), nice little library and very good outside area – green space, Astro, own playing field, excellent play equipment, safe surface and a wonderfully safe-feeling leafy garden all round. Prep children can use the senior school's sports facilities and fields. Forest School lessons taught in the small wooded area at the back of the school. Good displays, eg The View From My Window, complete with framing curtains, and life-enhancing features like Mrs Gocher's Question of the Week, eg 'Who is your hero?' and 'What is mankind's greatest achievement?' – that is, questions that Google cannot answer for you. From year 3 everyone is in one of four houses – good preparation for the importance of houses in the senior school. Drama and music suite where all year 2s learn the recorder and all in year 3 learn the violin – excellent. Lots of small group work and clubs. Much to stretch the most able, not all of whom go on to the senior school – as seems to be generally accepted.

Pre-prep and nursery in Wilson House, an older building, a little like a cottage in the woods. Again, super outside area with wild space, Forest School in the woods, play area and bird boxes on trees. Good, lively orderly classes, a relaxed feel. In the nursery, all food is cooked on-site by chef using fresh ingredients. Nice touches like pretend doctor's surgery in reception. A sense of productive and comfortable activity. Parents enthuse, 'A very good school in terms of bringing them on', 'It's a happy school', 'A really good balance in terms of social interaction and academics', 'The teachers take no nonsense but they treat them with respect, even though they're children'. Parents of the super-bright seem, mostly, to look outside Aldenham for the next school, but most talk about 'the balance' wisely provided here. And it is for that that most decide to stay.

Alderley Edge School for Girls Junior School

Linked school: Alderley Edge School for Girls

Wilmslow Road, Alderley Edge, SK9 7QE

- Pupils: 150 girls • Ages: 2–11 • Ecumenical – Christian ethos
- Fees: £5,418–£7,827 pa • Independent

Tel: 01625 583028
Email: admissions@aesg.co.uk
Website: www.aesg.info/junior

Head of Junior School: Since April 2013, Bridget Howard BEd (fifty), previously deputy head. Educated at St Albans High, then Rolle College Exeter; returned to St Albans to teach in the prep, then a stint in Sydney, before coming back to teach at Manchester High Prep and Bolton School Girls Junior.

Entrance: No assessment for entry to nursery (now taking from 2 years, minimum two days or three half days from 3 plus) or infant school, nor any religious requirements bar sympathy with Christian ethos. Indeed a few Muslim and Hindu girls co-exist happily with Christian and non-church girls. Places in junior years offered after a taster day in school, not sitting papers as such but including some reading, writing and numeracy during a normal school day. Looking for 'behaviour,

attitude and a focused work ethic' from the bright to middle ability ranges, 'girls who're likely to get into the seniors', but keen to protect happy atmosphere – 'We have absolutely no disruptive elements in our classes'. Spaces in some years.

Exit: About half the top 20 senior school exam results are from prep girls, 'even though we don't cram for the exam'. Almost all move on up. A few move to high flying Manchester High, Withington or elsewhere.

Remarks: Happy eager girls cosseted in lower years, gradually blossoming and integrating with seniors for seamless integration at 11. Girls share senior hall, dining room, ICT suite, sports facilities and, as they advance up the years, a stairwell, the new dance studio and the senior library.

Large 'learning enhancement unit' with SENCo's office, mainly helping dyslexic pupils. Class size average is 15, maximum 22. Maths sets from year 4, reading age and spelling assessed yearly and summer tests.

Netball, hockey and cross-country popular, swimming at Wilmslow leisure centre. 'Best thing here is the after school clubs,' said one girl; lots of extracurricular including LAMDA exams and popular art club. Individual music lessons for many instruments and voice. Residential trips for top three years, lots of day trips. Library with pile of bean bags and huge armchair for newly introduced parent reading helpers.

Celebratory assembly gives out weekly star awards, certificates for successes outside school and presents chosen by captains from box in head's study for weekly house champions. Two reps from each class on council – only grumble is rickety loo locks. Every year 6 girl has a job.

From the 'golden rules' corridor girls selected 'Do be honest, do not cover up the truth' as most important. Friendship Council encourages girls to be friendly and work things through. 'It was the anti-bullying council, but there wasn't any bullying, so we didn't have anything to do and it was changed to the friendship council,' say girls, who describe the way they're treated as 'firm but fair' and say, 'It's a fun community'. Previous head added, 'No school can say they don't have bullying, but any problems are mainly about falling out with friends.' He introduced a mediator – 'a gentle, sensitive lady who gets all parties involved' – and found parents turning to her for other advice. School prayer, written by a pupil and said daily, ends with 'Dear Lord, help us in all we think, do and say'.

Weekly colour bulletin packed with info and news. Toast and milk free for early birds from 8am and a charged after school club runs until 5.45pm with extra levies for late collections.

Aldro

Lombard Street, Shackleford, Godalming, Surrey, GU8 6AS

- Pupils: 220 boys; 170 day, 50 board • Ages: 7–13 • C of E
- Fees: Day £14,985–£16,650; Boarding £19,755–£21,420 pa
- Independent

Tel: 01483 409020
Email: hmsec@aldro.org
Website: www.aldro.org

Headmaster: Since 2001, Mr David Aston, BA PGCE (fifties). Began his career teaching English at his old prep school, Monkton Combe, then was a geography teacher and housemaster at Shrewsbury.

A personable character, still full of enthusiasm for his role. Very involved in school life, he's like a favourite uncle around the place, joshing and chatting with pupils about everything from sport to their current reading matter, encouraging, calls them 'civilised animals' and genuinely enjoys their company. In fact he probably prefers them to their parents, who tell us that he is not a man to grasp a nettle and so will let things roll, rather than deal with a difficult pupil or situation. 'I think it's that he is trying to be Christian and understanding,' said one mother in his defence. 'He'll ask naughty boys to be nicer or more considerate rather than make them face actual consequences and it does upset people sometimes.'

Fans praise his leadership of the school – 'He's absolutely brought it into the 21st century,' said one – and describe him as 'morally and ethically honest,' 'a man of integrity and faith,' and 'kind and gentle'. 'I think he can be reticent about subjects that make him feel uncomfortable, but he has the best interests of the school and children at heart and loves them like a family,' said one parent. 'He's not especially tough, but then I wouldn't want my son under the direction of an autocrat,' said another. 'Sometimes boys need to sort themselves out'. For their part the boys like him; 'He's really friendly,' they told us.

He still does a little teaching, mainly RS to year 8 scholars – ethical issues and how to write discursive essays. Lives on site with his own family – two teenage children and wife Sue, who teaches Latin at the school. 'She wouldn't want any credit, but she's a huge asset and I don't think he could do the job without her,' said one mother. Their flat has a commanding view of the beautiful 30 acre school grounds in Surrey countryside, so Mr Aston is literally master of all he surveys. Outside school, hobbies include model railway, antiquarian books, and all sport, especially rowing – he's a retired coach.

'We love it here,' he says, describing the school as 'a boarding school where some boys go home to sleep at night'. Whole set up seems settled enough that he'll see it through to retirement.

Entrance: At 7+ a largely local intake. School is full and with a waiting list – boarding numbers are up since introduction of more flexible system, but generally more competition for day places than boarding. Two form entry. Exam, assessment and reports in January for the following September. Boys come from many different feeder schools – over 30 at the last count, but always a chunk from St Hilary's. A few substantial bursaries available through the Royal National Children's Foundation.

Exit: Expert and practised at feeding the public school system. Aldro boys hoover up scholarships and head off in their 10s to Charterhouse (five minutes away – Aldro seen as a feeder, but isn't officially) in handfuls to Eton and Wellington and ones and twos elsewhere – typically to around a dozen different destinations, including Sherborne, Radley, Winchester and recently the more local Royal Grammar School, Guildford and St John's Leatherhead.

Remarks: An old-fashioned, traditional school which sees itself as very much part of the 'establishment' of leading public schools. With academics at its core, be aware that the thrust of the place is to get the boys to major public boarding schools. 'It's an unspoken thing, but I very much got the feeling the school wondered why I would want to go anywhere other than those schools – that's the culture,' a parent told us.

Long school days with the youngest boys finishing at 5pm, older pupils going on past 6pm. Boys here are all of above average ability, but still divided on academic lines in year 7 into 'scholars' and 'others' (or 'brainy and thick,' as one son told his mother). School happy to support boys who may struggle in one area and will take those with mild dyslexia or dyspraxia. Around 10 per cent of pupils have some extra help from specialist SEN teachers. But it's probably not for a boy who may struggle across the board – he simply wouldn't get the best out of the place.

Each school day begins with short service in the beautiful chapel – whole school, two hymn and a reading and a few words from the head or senior staff. Then it's straight into lessons.

Prep is done at the end of the day, so no homework needs to go home with the day boys; 'wonderful,' chorus mothers, who don't have to chivvy.

It's a fairly challenging academic environment; Aldro boys are undoubtedly hard working, well monitored and generally encouraged to develop high levels of independence, self-motivation and organisation skills. Quite a few long-standing teachers doing what they've always done, with some young blood to leaven the mix. Higher than average numbers of husband and wife teaching combos. Particular parental mention for 'standout' science and 'superb' French. Although long-serving head of department has retired, two native French speaking staff are much praised – we spotted Monsieur teaching Pétanque during break and school has its own bouledrome. Pupils keen on history teacher operating out of distinctive classroom with mood-setting, old-fashioned fixtures and fittings, who organises chances to dress up and act out characters and events. Seventy per cent of full time teachers are male – great role models for the boys – 'lots of nice teachers,' they told us. Good manners abound – boys will sometimes say 'thank you' after a lesson and staff sometimes say it too, if boys have been particularly productive and engaged.

A pleasingly broad curriculum: boys say the best thing about this school is the variety of things they get to do – drama (in new studio), plenty of art and DT, including pottery, music (two-thirds of boys have an individual lesson every week and masses of practice rooms) and, of course, sport galore. Past feeling that less sporty boys get overlooked has changed as staff work hard to achieve 'sport for all'. 'I like the fact they go back to basics, including working on fitness levels that can be overlooked,' said one parent. Main sports are rugby, football, hockey, tennis, cricket and athletics. Aldro's 1st XV rugby team are national under-13 champions. Long-standing plans for a new sports centre still await planning permission. In the meantime, boys use outdoor swimming pool (bracing) and can hunt (for fossils), shoot (pistol and rifle) and fish. This place is also tremendously strong on chess and even a model railway – basically, if your son has an interest, this school will ensure he develops it.

Boys really can be boys here – blessed with seemingly boundless bosky grounds, bordered by woods where they make dens and play in the tree house, on the rope bridge and in the rowing lake. 'They have a lot of freedom outdoors and it can be quite a shock after their usually sheltered pre-prep experiences, where they are marshalled from pillar to post,' said one mother. 'It's simply idyllic,' said another. 'And because the boys are free to roam in the great outdoors they get great self-confidence, which has benefits in all sorts of areas.'

Indoors, the main building is arts and crafts, centred around an imported Jacobean staircase. Most of the classrooms are in a much newer 1990s block including the flashy IT stuff and a tip-top library. But generally the school is selected for its reputation, rather than swanky facilities. A glance around the car park on match days will confirm Aldro parents are generally a very well-heeled bunch; the majority are the married upper-middle classes.

Aldro has a distinct boarding school ethos, even though on bald numbers it has many more day pupils. DA is a huge fan of boarding – he did so himself as a child. While the school has the occasional boarder at 7 or 8 (these tend to be Forces families), more typically pupils board by 9 or 10 in readiness for their move to a senior boarding school. 'The whole boarding set up is brilliant and was just what we needed by year 7,' said one mother. 'The boys have supper and some time to relax and have fun, but are then brought back to task with prep and revision sessions – fantastic; I couldn't have done as well at home.'

'The boarding is great and be warned, your son will want to try it before he leaves,' counsels another mother. 'We live too close to make it viable, but my son would leave home for school tomorrow if I said the word.' About a dozen boys board full time, the rest part time, with an average of about 50 sleeping at school on any one night. In reality 'flexible' means 'pre-arranged part time', though of course the school will try to facilitate the odd night when required. But it takes its responsibility to the regular boarders seriously. 'A boy needs to feel settled and to know who'll be in the next bed on any given night,' says the boarding master, Nick Margesson. Certainly the current arrangements must work well, because since introducing this more flexible approach (in the past it was all or nothing) boarding has flourished here.

Boarders and hanger-on day boys have supper at six, after which the day boys leave and it's 'Mars time' for boarders – from the old advert 'work, rest and play'. But for 'work' school means 'do some', for a rest 'read your book' and 'play' means 'play your instrument'. At 7.15pm an activity, then 20 minutes or so access to phones/iPods before showers and bed (year 6 at 8.30pm). We spotted a Wii gathering dust in the corner of the common room – apparently it comes out in terrible weather – and a (thankfully more popular) pet hamster. Accommodation is typical of modern boarding facilities, functional and homely rather than luxurious, all supervised by young matrons in the 'big sister/concerned aunt' mould.

Parents find the school nicely sociable, usual set up of 'Friends', class reps and so on. Mothers enjoying a tennis morning when we were there. Not tons of extras to find. It's expensive, but that's it – you won't pay for much else. Lunch and books included in fees and not many outings or fancy trips. Thriving and established market in second hand blazers, so check that out before you buy a new one.

Overall a successful school with a real Christian ethos – no lip service here – and lots of traditional elements: high standards of work, play and simple manners. Good for active, go-getty characters. Not for the faint-hearted – academically or personality-wise. If your son needs brow-mopping and spoon-feeding, think again.

Aldwickbury School

Wheathampstead Road, Harpenden, AL5 1AD

• Pupils: 326 boys; 28 board • Ages: 4–13 • Fees: Day £11,175–£13,425 pa • Independent

Tel: 01582 713022
Email: registrar@aldwickbury.org.uk
Website: www.aldwickbury.org.uk

Headmaster: Since 2003 Mr Vernon Hales BEd (early fifties). Educated at Langley Park Grammar School and Exeter University, where his education degree majored in PE. After a year in the state system, he started his prep school career at Papplewick ('great fun') before heading off to New Zealand, becoming deputy head in its then largest boarding prep school. Returned as deputy head and boarding housemaster at Elstree School, then joined Aldwickbury as the school's fourth head. Partnered through entire professional journey by wife Claire, also a trained teacher and now head of marketing at school and 'traditional headmaster's wife'. Educated his two sons, now late teens, at Aldwickbury and The Leys, where they are full boarders.

Relaxed, warm and jovial with the boys, and 'very visible around the school', according to parents, he recently 'came out of retirement' to resurrect his passion for club cricket and harbours personal ambitions to become a good golfer (must be the stunning course surrounding the school grounds calling). Lives in the main school building and is proud of its unique local offering as a boys' (mainly) day school, based on a boarding school model. Recognises that although sport is very important to boys, he wants Aldwickbury to be an 'all round' school. He speaks with

conviction about understanding the distinctive needs of boys in their formative years, describing Aldwickbury as 'philosophically a boys school.' Would like to increase school numbers very slightly 'without losing our small school feel'.

Entrance: Non-selective at four, the school works with local feeder nurseries to ensure smooth transition for its youngest pupils as they join reception. Recently became three-form entry at the bottom of the school, with 15 to a class, due to increased demand for places. Maximum class size in pre-prep fixed at 18. Boys joining higher up the school are invited in for an informal session with their relevant year group head, where they are encouraged to talk about themselves and take tests in reading, maths and spelling to ensure they can access the curriculum. Means tested bursaries available.

Exit: Vast majority stay at Aldwickbury until the end of year 8. School loses just a few each year at the end of year 6 'for either financial or academic reasons', according to head. Feeds about half its boys into year 9 at St Albans School, 'a handful' each year with scholarships. About 30 per cent head off to board to schools like Haileybury, Bedford and The Leys, with one or two recently to Eton, Harrow and Shrewsbury and the remainder to other local independents. 'The key is getting parents to choose the right school for the boy', says head. Parents confirm that he gives them a strong steer in the right direction.

Remarks: Situated a stone's throw up the hill from Harpenden's second (less chi-chi) high street in Southdown. Aldwickbury Mansion, which dates back to 1871 and is full of Victorian character (albeit with a few tired corners), became home to the school in 1948. It makes excellent use of its leafy 20-acre site and has sympathetically incorporated a number of modern buildings to create an appealing and well-functioning school campus. Main school building sits atop grassy terraces and playing fields, affording the head and his boarders a panoramic view of the school grounds. A separate purpose-built pre-prep department was built in 2001, providing the school's youngest pupils with a bright and cheerful base, where they can ease their way into school life without the rough and tumble of bigger boys.

Reception has its own safe haven outside with a small adventure playground area, plus trikes, bikes and a sand table – 'very therapeutic if they've had a tricky morning in the classroom', says head of pre-prep. School places a large emphasis on outside learning at this stage – 'we're not a forest school but we do take on elements of that ethos'. On our visit, reception boys were enthusiastically doing Victorian-style laundry outside. The pre-prep building is festooned with topic-related art and written work and has its own hall for assemblies, activities and performances.

Junior department houses years 3 and 4, when the school starts to 'encourage independence in a gentle way', including the introduction of a more formal uniform. Even maths classrooms are creatively themed and staff overall exude energy and enthusiasm, reinforcing the school's ethos of 'really getting boys'. One year 1 teacher quietly plays classical music CDs when she wants her class to concentrate, and – try it at home – it seems to work. Boys in years 5 to 8 move around classrooms for specialist teaching to prepare them for senior school life.

Lovely heated indoor swimming pool – well used, with weekly lessons for all from reception, plus early morning and after-school swim clubs. The ever-popular DT workshop ('we really look forward to coming in here', say boys) has the shed-like feel of a real man space and industrious pupils turn out quality projects from wind chimes to fruit bowls. Art room on the basic side but a broad spectrum of work on display showcases the boys' enthusiasm. The gym is in dire need of some TLC but from spring 2014 the school will benefit from an 'all singing, all dancing' £3.2m hall and music department, with the development also incorporating several new classrooms 'to provide flexibility and accommodate growth'. The school also boasts a gleaming modernised dining hall (food to be recommended) and library.

Parents and pupils alike describe Aldwickbury as 'very friendly and welcoming', and the nurturing feel pervades the fabric of the school. 'Definitely not pushy', say parents uniformly, suggesting that league table watchers may want to look elsewhere. Boys have the knack of knowing when to be quiet (quite a feat in a dining hall of rumbling tummies waiting for someone to say grace) and when to let off steam. Confidence and manners, without arrogance, in evidence in all age groups.

A true 4 to 13 school. 'All year 8 boys have jobs' and are given responsibilities around the school, such as helping teachers get younger boys organised in the mornings and listening to year 5 boys read at lunchtimes. With around half the teachers male, the overall vibe is of a school where boys really can be boys. Year groups encouraged to mix at meal times, with lunch taken as 'sections,' (that's houses to the rest of us). Boys compete throughout the year for the section cup, not just in their academic lives and on the sports fields, but also with competitions and challenges, including section Scrabble and top autumn favourite, the 'conker-tition'.

Majority of pupils from the immediate environs, with 50 per cent 'sharing the AL5 postcode,' according to head. Remainder from surrounding towns and villages. Very few from further afield. Overwhelmingly Caucasian majority reflects the local community. Most parents in the professions, many dual income, but a by all accounts a pretty grounded bunch and a number 'stretching themselves' to pay school fees. A parents' association set up recently to bring together parents, staff and boys and foster the school/community relationship. Events so far have included discos with local girls' school, monthly tuck shops with home-baked cakes and a dads vs masters cricket match.

French with a specialist teacher from year 1, with Spanish and German added to the mix in year 5 and Latin from year 6. Specialist teaching from year 3 for ICT, art, music and drama. Mixed ability classes 'by ethos' to end of year 5, although head admits to some 'subtle setting' from year 3 and parents of able children report extra work being given to ensure the brightest are stretched. Classes mixed at end of years 2 and 4 which some parents grumble they find 'stressful', although they admit the school 'normally gets it right'. Streaming introduced from year 6, with two or three classes and a scholarship class in year 8. This, however, is not always uniform in its structure – head is determined to 'start from the point of what's best for the boys'. SEN all in a day's work and good provision in place to deal with minor blips rather than more serious problems.

Music taught by male teachers from pre-prep onwards, which really 'turns boys on to learning an instrument', according to head. Around 160 boys from year 1 upwards take music lessons in a wide range of instruments, with two music scholarships to St Albans School in 2012. Abundance of musical groups to join, from choir to guitar groups, including the popular Aldwickbury Strings group, a collaborative effort between staff (including the bursar, a talented violinist) and boys. Drama is 'really important', says head, with participation in plays compulsory up to year 5 to 'build confidence'. Main school play, most recently A Christmas Carol, performed in the round, is optional in years 7 and 8 but most choose to take part, if not onstage, then in lighting or costume, with the occasional rugby player taking charge of make-up.

Sport is the lifeblood of the school, with specialist teaching twice weekly from year 1 and boys from year 3 up having a daily games lesson. Competitive football, swimming and skiing are 'excellent', says head, and boys regularly compete at national level. Team fixtures for all from A-E teams, so everyone gets a ride on the school minibus and a shot at sporting glory. Colours awards on offer for stars of rugby, football cricket et al, but also for drama, music and citizenship, proving that heroes are not only found on the sports fields here. In the words of one boy, 'all things here are valued the same'.

Boarding almost exclusively flexi, with the occasional weekly boarder, but no provision for boys at weekends. The majority of those who board from year 6 are at their 'second home' (as they call it) two or three nights a week, with provision for 33 boarders at any one time. Once the plethora of after-school clubs has finished, there's more fun, with 'non-stop activities,' say boys, followed by weekly film nights in the cosy boarders' lounge and occasional events such as the popular 'chippy night' (one benefit of being so close to the high street). Functional dormitories sleep up to nine year 6 boys, with numbers dropping to four or five in the upper years. No phones with SIMs are allowed but, with all that's on offer, boys have got better things to do than phone home. With the majority of boys living so locally, most are here purely for the fun of it and speak wisely of their new found 'independence' and how boarding has changed them.

Day boys able to join boarders for breakfast from 7.40am and supper for a small cost – handy for commuting parents. All boys from year 5 up stay for prep until between 5.10 pm and 5.45 pm and there is an after-school club which can take pupils of any age up to supper time at 5.50pm.

Broad range of extra-curricular activities to cater for all tastes, from chess, Lego or general knowledge club for the cerebral crowd to skiing, fencing or martial arts for those wanting to try their hand at something more physical. Loads of opportunities to get out and about, with trips aplenty. School makes full use of being on the capital's doorstep, with trips to art galleries and theatres and also ventures further afield (expeditions to France, Iceland and the much anticipated leavers' trip to Dartmoor). A schedule of evening seminars on topics such as 'the history of the Ashes' ('much more interesting than it sounds', says head) is in place for older boys and their parents, and a number of external learning sources are brought in throughout the year. When we visited, boys were buzzing after a visit from a 'mathemagician,' part of the maths week itinerary.

Alleyn's Junior School

Linked school: Alleyn's School

Townley Road, London, SE22 8SU

• Pupils: 240; 50/50 boys and girls • Ages: 4–11 • Fees: £13,437–£13,995 pa • Independent

Tel: 020 8557 1519
Email: juniorschool@alleyns.org.uk
Website: www.alleyns.org.uk

Headmaster: Since 2003, Mr Mark O'Donnell BA PGD Des MSc (Arch) EdM ES (mid-forties). Previously deputy head of Thorpe House School, Gerrards Cross. Educated at Stonyhurst and St Ignatius College, New South Wales. Married with three school-age sons. Totally dedicated to his school, say parents, with finger on every pulse and an unusual degree of care for all the children.

Entrance: Tends to be very local – 'We try to be centred in the community'. At 4+, 18 places and some 220 applicants. No siblings policy – 'I could fill the place with siblings, and I like to encourage some diversity'. Intakes also at 7, 9 and 11 – 'If they don't get in the first time, I encourage them to see it as a postponement and to try again later'. Assessment 'looks for children who can participate in a very busy and structured timetable'. Allows for age: alongside raw scores, offers also made to those who come top in the month of their birth. Offers made to equal numbers of boys and girls. 'We try to take in children who have a lot to contribute. They may have lower academic scores but be brilliant at sport.'

Exit: Automatic transfer to senior school (one or two move elsewhere, often with scholarships), though everyone takes the 11+ exam and year 7 could be a probationary year for a child who is struggling to keep up. 'We value the real contribution of the child. A boy with dyslexia might have trouble with English but be brilliant at maths and go on to play for the school football team. We'd rather have a hard worker than someone who is bright but lazy.' The transfer exam 'is about celebrating hard work and achievement, not just about winning scholarships. Everyone gets a leaving certificate which includes details of what they have done for the life of the school.'

Remarks: A very busy, buzzy place tucked away in a quiet corner of the senior school site. Light, bright classrooms include a conservatory and a playground that doubles as an outdoor classroom. Magnificent IT suite; iPads integrated into lessons – 'We have embraced new technology'; giant iPad in art room. Science garden has wildlife pond, herb, flower and vegetable plots and ex-battery chickens.

English and maths taught in small groups from day one. Formal setting for maths from year 4 – 'For those in the B sets it's mostly about increasing their confidence and self-esteem'. Maths mentors come over from the senior school to help. Specialist teachers for French, music, art and PE from the beginning, and for every subject from year 4.

Support includes speech and language therapist, a literacy expert and learning support assistants – 'We've had children here with quite serious learning differences and we've done a great job with them. That's one of the things I'm most proud of about the school'. Pupils say: 'I like their attitude towards learning. The teachers help you to get better in a very calm way. The classes are very friendly.' Signs round the school during our visit proclaimed that it was anti-bullying week.

Excellent art in newly converted studio, set up to resemble a fish tank during our visit with strings of fish hanging down the windows. Pottery popular: 'Edward de Waal did a workshop recently and showed us how to make our own kiln and fire our own pottery'. Colourful artistic displays all round the school, and the Dulwich Picture Gallery is a regular destination.

Everyone learns a stringed instrument in years 2-4 and a brass or woodwind instrument in year 5, and many keep it up. Clubs include jazz band, choirs and L'Orchestre de la Grand Salle. Plenty of other music and drama – school tends to attract creative families so lots of talent/parental encouragement. The day of our visit was hip-hop day and year 6, in tee shirts they had designed themselves, were busy learning dance moves. Africa and India days also combine art, music and dance, and Alleyn's Junior Has Talent competition is a highlight of the year.

Sport particularly strong, with the enviable senior school facilities including rolling green acres just next door. Large numbers of sports clubs include ballet and tae-kwando; A, B and often C teams play against other schools in sports ranging from girls' football to biathlon. Pupils we met were very enthusiastic – 'I do seven clubs a week, nearly all sport'; 'There's something that suits everyone'; 'We're celebrating the Olympic year by making sure we have Olympic values such as determination and respect for each other'.

Congenial atmosphere. School aims to 'encourage respectfulness between adults and children. We're after more than good manners: we want our children to have the confidence to communicate with adults'. 'All the people here are very friendly,' say pupils. 'Even if you're not best friends with someone, you just get on with them.'

Allfarthing Primary School

St Ann's Crescent, London, SW18 2LR

• Pupils: 445 boys/girls • Ages: 3–11 • Non-denom • State

Tel: 020 8874 1301
Email: info@allfarthing.wandsworth.sch.uk
Website: www.allfarthing.wandsworth.sch.uk/

Headteacher: Since September 2012 Ali Silke BA (late forties) read geography at UCL. She started her career in publishing before deciding to train as a teacher. Married with two daughters at secondary school, she has been head of a beacon school in Tower Hamlets followed by Dulwich Village Infants, where she raised the Ofsted grading from good to outstanding. She has also spent time working as a trainer/consultant for the Ruth Miskin Literacy phonics programme, in primary, secondary and special schools. Fifth head in four years for Allfarthing, she assures us she is definitely staying put, much to parents' relief after an unsettled period. Committed and determined personality, always up with the larks; she is dedicated to pulling the school together and running the new expansion project to enable the school to be three class entry. Her interests include cinema, reading, theatre, running and travel.

Entrance: At 3+ into the nursery or 4+ into reception. Priority goes to siblings and then those living closest to the school. Attending the nursery does not guarantee a place in the Infant department. For occasional places in older age groups contact the school to check availability and put your name on their waiting list.

Exit: Popular state choices are Graveney, St Cecilia, Burntwood, Ricards Lodge, ARK Academy, odd one to Kingston or Surrey grammar schools. Around 30 percent to independents, Emanuel, Ibstock Place, Wimbledon High School, Trinity and Whitgift.

Remarks: Situated on rather a busy corner, the tall 1920s building offers large bright classrooms, eyes are immediately drawn to displays of children's work and art designed to capture imagination and interest. Standards are high and parents note a recent increase in monitoring and assessing progress across the age groups to ensure underachievement is picked up and addressed swiftly. Reception and nursery classes have indoor and outdoor classrooms, ample resources laid out thoughtfully. Early years classes follow the Read Write phonics programme offering a good grounding in literacy skills. Overall, school's results in English are impressive; lots of drama and speaking and listening activities are incorporated into the curriculum. Maths results not quite as high but catching up. Large inner-city mix around 24 languages spoken in the school; everyone learns Spanish from year 3. Parents report good traditional teaching with interesting history and geography projects alongside whizzy IT; all classes can access iPads, MacBooks and trolleys of laptops. Graded outstanding, the school does very well in national assessments and has an above-average added value score. Curriculum is further extended with masterclasses provided by special partnerships with Graveney for ICT, Burntwood for sciences and Southfields for PE. Mrs Silke feels SEN help should be delivered as required through small group or individual teaching, in addition to speech and occupational therapists visiting the school.

Two multi-purpose halls provide space for PE, assemblies and lunches cooked on site in the recently refurbished kitchens. On site sports include lacrosse, football and hockey and cricket; older pupils are bussed to Battersea Park School for swimming lessons. Sports days are held at Wimbledon Park where year 5 has a week of water sports, courtesy of the Friends Group.

Music features highly on the daily curriculum, super purpose-built accommodation with a dedicated music teacher. Opportunity for all from year 4 to learn an instrument, with many achieving grade 6 before moving to secondary school. Each child chooses a string or wind instrument for group lessons in year 3 and there is a budding choir that performs in the community. Parents say choir has really developed over the past year and are particularly impressed at the large number of boys who have joined in. Encouraging setting for musical families, currently something of a rarity for a state primary.

Remarkably good Friends of Allfarthing Group is an asset, raising money for all sorts of activities and equipment through traditional and creative ways. Friends contribute throughout the school, baking biscuits for meetings and fêtes and writing an introductory guide book for newcomers. Parent volunteers and staff recently collaborated to run a very successful lettuce planting project for the UNICEF day for change. Monthly book club lottery raises funds for the library and other book purchases. All tastes taken into consideration for after-school clubs, with parents and pupils suggesting some of the choices available.

Pupils are encouraged to voice their opinions through the school council and class reps, on school rules, sensible behaviour and other issues that benefit everyone's participation and enjoyment. A few rumbles from parents over staff changes and prospects of building works; most remain positive and feel the changes will be for the best. Overall a popular school, working hard to continually improve and develop provision, along with a number of little extras, or not so little, as the case may be.

Altrincham Preparatory School

Marlborough Road, Bowdon, Altrincham, Cheshire, WA14 2RR

- Pupils: 325 boys; all day • Ages: 3–11 • Non-denom
- Fees: £5,424–£7,428 pa • Independent

Tel: 01619 283366
Email: admin@altprep.co.uk
Website: www.altprep.co.uk

Head Master: Since 2000, Mr Andrew C Potts BSc PGCE (unbelievable early sixties), genial and prone to chuckle but serious about the ethics of education. Has steadily piloted school from former elitist, pressure cooker reputation to mellower, more caring times where SENCo is key. 'It's not just about academic success but also about that rounded young man who's polite, courteous, confident about talking to you, able to empathise with others and establish good relationships,' says head, 'because that, ultimately, is what'll make him happy.' Father of five, married to Marilyn, a modern language teacher at Chetham's School of Music, his youngest is on a music scholarship at Uppingham and another's still at university, so 'Retirement's a while off yet'. 'His assembly speeches are quite long,' say boys, 'but we like him – he can even make comprehension enjoyable.'

Entrance: 30 non-selective nursery places with a waiting list. Entry further up depends on assessment in school and parent interview with head; less about seeking geniuses, more about ensuring school can meet a boy's needs in a balanced year group.

Exit: Traditionally strong performances in 11+ entrance exams mean many can choose between Altrincham Boys' Grammar across the road and Manchester Grammar in town. Cheadle Hulme School and King's Macclesfield always feature on the leavers' list along with other local independent and state grammar schools. Head prides himself that 'all the boys go to the right school for them'.

Remarks: Welcoming boys' prep with sunny, open disposition where the strong chance of success at 11 is just a small part of the story. Articulate boys fall over themselves to share their school, telling of the lamb's heart they just dissected in science (year 5), and (year 6) how studying cartoons leaves them thinking they don't know much in French, 'But then the teacher asks a question and your hand automatically goes up, the answer pops out of your mouth and you find you do know it after all'. After our meeting they spontaneously tidy away the chairs, restoring order without prompting.

Maximum class size 24, smaller in lower years, with classes divided into smaller groups for much teaching. A full time SENCo, speech and language specialist and English as a second language specialist serve the 20 or so who need extra help. One has a statement of SEN, and eight have English as an additional language. 'We're very well qualified to help boys with difficulties and our ethos is that we help boys achieve their potential across the spectrum of levels,' says SENCo.

So it's no longer just rarefied academic air here, but the ample number of places bagged at top secondary schools suggest this doesn't hold the brightest back, partly thanks to gifted and talented co-ordinator. Homework rises each year – 'It's too much in year 6, even after the entrance exams, and they're pretty harsh if you don't do it – you have to miss playtime,' say boys, who do, however, reluctantly accept it might be good preparation for senior school. The latest ISI inspection (2010) called behaviour here 'exemplary', praising as excellent pupil-staff relationships, pastoral care, academic achievement – almost everything, in fact.

Specialist teachers for French, science, sport, art and tech (in a bright airy studio), plus music. Parents describe music teacher as 'amazing'; 'He encourages everyone,' boys say. 'Even if you're not very good you get a solo – he lets everyone have a go at everything.' Orchestra of 75, all boys sing, check the website videos.

Participation in sport isn't optional either, 'Every boy has to represent the school at sport even if he doesn't like it; we want the boys to feel valued but also to know they have a valuable contribution to make'. Both sports teachers came straight from college – one has been here for 30 years. Links with Bowdon Cricket and Hockey Club nearby and sessions in the grammar sports halls across the road enhance PE and provide facilities should ambitious proposed development of APS Marlborough Road site go ahead. If so, the junior school should then have an all-weather pitch of its own, bespoke music and ICT rooms, science and language labs and a modern kitchen and dining hall.

Hot meal at lunchtime compulsory – 'Wish they'd bring back curly fries'. Nursery at end of junior block with own playground. Infants in homely refurbished Victorian building a mile away. Has just bought an additional building for an early years centre. Car park chaos despite staggered finishing times. Lots of clubs, some after school. Active website with videos of recent events, up to the minute information for parents, even remote learning when school shut for snow one recent winter.

Boys compete for house points and merit badges – colours ties for special achievements worn with great pride. School council expected to bring ideas to the table and everyone in year 6 has a job. Links with an inner city mission and local residential care homes for charity and community work. Partnership with youth worker from nearby St Mary's. Trips to Lakes in year 5 and France for year 6. Uniforms and bags in burgundy and grey.

The American School in London Lower School

Linked school: The American School in London

1 Waverley Place, London, NW8 0NP

• Pupils: 423 girls and boys; all day • Ages: 4–10 • Fees: £21,050 pa • Independent

Tel: 020 7449 1200
Email: admissions@asl.org
Website: www.asl.org

Head: Coreen R Hester:

Remarks: For further information, see senior school.

Amesbury

Hazel Grove, Hindhead, GU26 6BL

• Pupils: 300 boys and girls, currently all day, weekly boarding being trialled since September 2013 • Ages: 2–13 • Christian non-denom • Fees: £8,820–£13,500 pa • Independent

Tel: 01428 604322
Email: l.Wright@amesburyschool.co.uk
Website: www.amesburyschool.co.uk

Headmaster: Since 1994, Mr Nigel Taylor BSc PGCE MA. Late fifties (looks younger). Previously deputy head, St Paul's School, São Paulo. Married to Caroline. Attractively self-deprecating with lashings of charm, used to devastating effect on prospective parents who may see the strings being pulled but succumb anyway. Sensibly takes most round himself. 'He was down on the carpet playing with my son,' says mother, who signed up on the strength of it, despite having previously registered elsewhere.

Charm is coupled with a keen intelligence. 'He's quite a political animal,' says a parent, 'but you can't be in that sort of position without some sort of astuteness.' However, he's anything but bland. Just glimpsed red socks are a subtle clue. For a whopping big one, try the mouse mat featuring him going the full Disney in the London Marathon dressed as a fetching Snow White, accessorised with wig, long dress, manly, hirsute arms and seven teachers as his dwarves.

Undoubtedly sincere, too. Read between the lines of the exceedingly well-written, occasionally poetic current prospectus (being revamped, so get in quick in case his sensitive prose is replaced by 50 shades of corporate beige) and you'll find clues to his own experiences.

Was described in previous GSG review as 'streetwise, not posh'. Spot on, he says. Though fits effortlessly into current surroundings (delightful room and study, complete with blazing wood fire of almost Narnian degree of cosiness; you expect Mr Tumnus to appear at any second bearing a plate of crumpets) upbringing took place against a very different backdrop.

An adopted child, he was raised on a tough Leicester council estate, attending 'appalling' primary school which told the most able they had 'finished reading' in year 4 and were cut free to fag for the head. Fairy godparent moment came via sympathetic teacher's subtle interview coaching which ensured he made it to grammar school and thence to bigger and better things.

Sport and writing were his first serious interests. Law, too (still indulges inner Perry Mason with occasional day off to watch Crown Court trials). Logical career choice, sports journalism, hit the buffers when political machinations saw him effectively ousted from postgrad scholarship course at Columbia University. Nothing daunted, he returned to the UK and was talent spotted while helping to run a holiday coaching course at Stowe School and that, in career choice terms, was that.

Clear sighted but unresentful about deficiencies in his own education (and, with an MA in educational management as well as hands on know-how, something of an expert on how it should be done) his pet hate is a system designed for the convenience of adults at the expense of children, public mortification all too often the unintended consequence. As a result, school teems with humane initiatives, including emailed exam results which are 'the business of the child, teacher and parents, that's all.' He wouldn't post details of staff performance in common room, he says – 'I'd have the unions in straight away' – so why should pupils endure it?

Also of note is emphasis on making everyone feel special. Mr Taylor decided early on that it was signally unfair for the most able to have unlimited extra attention to prepare for scholarships while parents whose children required learning support wilted under the extra charges. Now, unless parental requests would involve disproportionate time or funding, they're all included in headline fees. Similarly, subject teachers work with small groups in turn across the ability range so middle ranking as well as high and low achievers get the VIP treatment, initially in English and maths (both highly praised in most recent inspection). Undoubtedly successful and once the golden glow extends to other subjects, too, even more so.

Coming up for his 20th anniversary, Mr Taylor is open about having had a touch of the career fidgets 'a few years ago' (common knowledge to parents as well), but having looked round, has decided this is the place for him. He'd be missed if he went. To misquote: 'No head is a hero to his pupils'. Not that this one would want to be. 'My dad says you need adults to treat children as humans and he does,' says a pupil.

Entrance: Through registration plus visit – not a formal assessment but the opportunity for child and school to get acquainted, pupils accepted until spaces filled, numbers hovering around the 300 mark, 325 waterline avoided as feels too crowded for comfort.

Scholarships (academic, tennis and expressive arts) available years 3 to 7 for those 'head and shoulders above other very talented children' worth applying for, with awards worth up to 50 per cent of the fees.

Nursery flexibility a given, with full days for those who need them (complete with freshly cooked hot meals, served in nursery classrooms; reception eat in dining hall, served like year 1 and 2 pupils at the table) and though school will suggest at least two consecutive sessions a week, there's no minimum nursery stay, with staff on hand to plug gaps at relatively short notice if there's a sudden bulge in numbers, now recovering after a lean patch. Will not adopt government suggestions to ease staffing ratios but up entry qualifications by way of compensation. 'Stupid,' says nursery head. 'It doesn't matter how well qualified you are, you're still only one person.'

Exit: Fall out after year 6, formerly a bit of an issue for the school (as elsewhere), has been largely contained, ('resolved' – it has – year 7 next year back to where we were and ditto following year – more girls staying on than leaving) helped by head's decision to stem school gate chatter by bringing the debate back into school and proselytise the benefits of staying to the end. Pupils, in no doubt as to the benefits, all happily cited kudos-factor of being top in the pecking order. Wide range of destinations. Wellington College amongst parental favourites with an average of around 20 per cent gaining scholarships, a fair few (predictably) for arts.

Remarks: One of a cluster of preps in this well-to-do area of Surrey, now more primrose path than rat run following opening of Hindhead tunnel – 'Other schools build a new sports hall, we spend millions on an underpass,' jokes head – school is considered a breath of fresh air by its supporters, who extol approach as trad with a twist.

On the surface, it oozes convention, second occupants of Lutyens' only purpose-built school, having moved here in 1917 from Bickley in Kent (was originally founded in 1870 in Redhill) to swap air raids for fresh air. Designed like a scaled down Hollywood set, main building features windows at two-thirds height, with a baby grand entrance and chapel, added 1938, which potentially reduces a wrath-filled God to a Wendy house-sized deity – a much more comforting notion to the young. Even the reception signs, so tiny that this reviewer walked past them twice, may have been boil-washed one too many times.

Some areas, a bit factory second here and there on date of visit, have already been improved, with sagging maintenance shed in the grounds subsequently demolished and staff treated to what head terms a 'luxurious' common room. Coming soon (Sept 2014) is million pound centre for performing and visual arts.

There has also been considerable smartening up: blue-canopied entrances on more modern buildings including super performing arts centre, an attractive and well-equipped example of the genre, as well as impressive giant, echoing sports hall – a yodeller's dream – and general pepping up of floor surfaces and corridors.

Also notable for exceptional cleanliness. Wherever we went, a mop or broom was sure to be in attendance close by. Much appreciated cleaning team was particularly busy in recently (and handsomely) refurbished separate nursery/reception building – all whiteness and brightness, with space for big, pristine, set piece indoor toys, recently enhanced with modish freeflow into secure outside area (complete with inevitable freeflow mud), all presided over by caring, multi-tasking staff (capable of spotting child in need of TLC while extolling multiple uses of home-made Play-doh).

While parents appreciate surroundings, heading praise list (which is extensive) is school's philosophy – 'holistic' says one. 'They balance the academic side with lots of other things so that all the children can find a way of expressing themselves.'

Approach can manifest itself in an absence of surface polish: hair that little bit longer than the norm; uniform (traditional skirts for girls, boys in viyella shirts with dress down brown guernseys for all – 'only itchy with short sleeves' says plucky pupil) occasionally lacking in parade gloss finish; productions and matches feature all comers.

We'd written originally that these were in consequence 'a tad rougher round the edges' based on parent feedback. 'Inaccurate' says head. 'We are rougher round the edges on a day to day basis, hair is sometimes longer. However, we are neurotic about getting it absolutely right on match days.' Ditto chapel choir and school plays which are 'super professional.' The trick, he says, 'is to be more relaxed until the moment when it matters and then we are absolutely spot on.'

There's also convention where it matters – 'very strict on how they speak to the teachers, so not liberal in that respect,' says a parent and no shortage of competition. But while two houses, carefully matched for ability, are expected to slug it out for supremacy during the year, what shines through is wrap-round encouragement for everyone, not just the most able, with the slightest flicker of talent breathed into a living flame.

Upbeat approach embraces learning needs, catering for rather more than advertised. One parent who packed tissues before meeting teachers, expecting to discuss behaviour issues, ended up being overwhelmed by praise.

Dyslexia, official speciality, had own separate centre until around four years ago. A new head of learning support, also qualified to carry out assessments, has now been appointed and most support is now provided in class. Considerable flexibility, however. 'If pupils need somebody physically sitting alongside them in the lesson to support them, that's what we'll do – focus is not on one size fits all: it's the right programme for the right child,' says head of English.

Sets the tone for excellent pastoral care, in and out of lesson time, from twinkly matron, popular with the walking wounded and others – 'we have our regulars' – to staff mingling with pupils for 'usually good and never awful' lunches in delightful blue-painted dining hall, dominated by bison's head (which lends its name to major house trophy, though history and significance remain an apparent mystery to all).

Register ensures that everyone eats (older pupils can choose when) though latecomers have to negotiate bottlenecks either side of diddy double doors as two-way queues of well-nourished, 21st century children jostle for supremacy, accompanied by fairly vigorous shoving by all.

It's the only sign of anything other than cordial pupil relationships, with friendships, seen as a huge strength, crossing between year groups, welcome sense of 'freedom to talk,' says pupil and little in the way of conflict. One pupil who had experienced bullying in previous school felt 'there's just not the space for bullies. If you did it, you'd find yourself on your own.' Bonds strengthened by taster boarding week for everyone in years 6 to 8, groups of 10 boys or girls at a time – Mallory Towers lite, big on the hot chocolate with marshmallows element and so popular that, builders and space permitting, will be bringing in Monday to Friday version for 'a number' of years 7 and 8 pupils (they're not saying more...).

Academically, it's emphatically not a hot house, though parents feel that standards are rising across the board, helped by emphasis on focus group teaching and calm but engaging class lessons notable for levels of discussion (lots of confident participation through the age ranges, reception children working on 'ay' sounds as a group; year 3 children engaged in quick fire mental maths and a school-wide absence of furrowed brows).

English and maths are excellent, remaining subjects being brought into line, recent staff additions generally reckoned to be plugging previous gaps (Latin and French now much improved, felt one mother). Humanities, headed by hugely popular teacher, also has a starring role in whole school charity remake of Pixie Lott hit, well worth three minutes of anyone's time on Youtube, is very dashing, notable for dynamic text book light, tech-heavy approach to geography (we enjoyed contrast with low tech lunchtime message system – communicated in chalk, on a blackboard).

Plenty of extras on offer in the form of clubs, too, and if more pupils hadn't taken up Mandarin, it was only, they said, because there was so much else going on, with many ecstatic about performing arts, much open to all and sweeping plentiful numbers of boys as well as girls into their orbit.

Music embraces everything from formal chapel choir to semi-secret bands formed each year, strutting stuff at annual concert. There's plentiful dance and drama including ambitious takes on Shakespeare (a swinging sixties Comedy of Errors and 1920s gangland style Hamlet amongst them) while inaugural action-packed arts week in 2012, successful but so energy and resource sapping, hoovering up just about everyone, staff and pupils, into its maw, that likely to become every other year wonder.

While arts feature large in pupils' career horizons, sports were almost as popular with the pupils we talked to (and equally so in school as a whole, says head). Aspirations and confidence stem, think pupils, from school's desire to 'want you to like sport.'

Taken seriously ('steely' is head's description of sports teams in prospectus), as so it should be, with four grass pitches, one Astroturf and 'very fancy' sports hall, foyer decorated with motivational images of assorted sports, to do them in. No swimming pool and wouldn't be on pupils' wish list in any case. 'It would get cold and crowded and you'd want to get out,' says one, sensibly. Tennis, a big thing, is now offered from nursery, two ping pong tables installed primarily for year 7s and 8s 'and other years when they're away or not using them' also hitting the spot. But, just as school prizes aren't just awarded to 'the obvious people but the ones with the right attitude,' say pupils, team selection favours the also rans as well as the stars. It's a brave strategy, given level of local opposition, main rival prompting something close to pupil bloodlust when you quiz them.

All in all, adds up to an atmosphere that substantiates the blurb. Many a school may claim to be 'academically rigorous'. Not all would also make such a virtue out of also being 'relaxed' (Mr Taylor's prospectus wording). This one does. Parents in search of an education which will deliver confident children who see their futures in terms of unlimited options rather than curtailed ambitions – 'I'd like to be an international sportsman, I just don't know which sport yet,' says one – would be well advised to pay a visit.

Annemount School

18 Holne Chase, London, N2 0QN

• Pupils: 115; boys and girls • Ages: 2.75–7 years • Fees: £7,050–£13,500 pa • Independent

Tel: 020 8455 2132
Email: headteacher@annemount.co.uk
Website: www.annemount.co.uk

Headmistress: Since 1993, Ms Geraldine Maidment (fifties), previously head of Hilltop Nursery in Hampstead. First teaching experience was as an English teaching assistant in Vienna, during her University College London year abroad, whilst studying German and history of art. Worked at Sotheby's before teaching at Basset House School. A widely travelled linguist (she speaks five languages), she has visited and attended schools in many different countries. During a two-year sabbatical in Colorado, she did a master's in child and family studies at Denver University and joined a school board concerned with social and emotional issues of school age children. Has also been on UK local government committees related to early years and works as an educational consultant for pupils who need schooling advice at any stage.

Has two grown up daughters and five step-grandchildren, who have all attended Annemount. Parents say: 'she's very on the ball and intelligent.' 'she's not going to be your best friend,' commented one (another 'begged to differ, especially over a 2005 Lynch Bages'), 'but she's incredible with the children'; 'she's very strict, but in a good way'; 'she's very good at explaining what is going on and how we can help.'

Entrance: Main intakes into the nursery (2.75+ years), kindergarten (3+ years) and reception (4+ years). Two classes of 16 or so in each year group. Both parents are expected to come on the school tour: 'I tell them you're making the biggest decision of your life for your most precious possession. You both need to be involved'. More or less first come first served into the nursery classes, with preference for siblings. Assessments for kindergarten upwards: 'They must be able to fit in socially and behaviour-wise, and they must be able to cope. Our classes are very busy, and the children need energy and stamina'. Discourages applications from families who live further than about four miles away – 'Children shouldn't spend hours a day sitting in a car'.

Exit: Some move at four or five, but most at seven, to local independent schools, eg Habs' Boys' and Girls', Belmont, Highgate, Channing, South Hampstead High, St Margaret's, UCS, North London Collegiate and City of London Girls'. A few to local state primaries, eg Garden Suburb or Brookland.

Remarks: One of a quiet street of large, brick-built early 20th century houses in the midst of leafy and wealthy Hampstead Garden Suburb. The school, with small but bright and colourful classrooms, was built by grateful parents for the previous ex-governess owner, who was head until she died in 1993 at the age of 93. Large garden, divided into a nursery playground with Wendy house and grassy area and a playground for the older children with a climbing frame, sand table, sports equipment, planting areas and gazebo.

Inevitably, its ultimate raison d'être is to prepare the children for 7+ exams, but this does not overshadow school life – 'People feel we really understand children, their stages of development and their needs'. The early years concentrate on personal and emotional development: learning to listen, developing good social awareness and independent thinking skills – 'We encourage them to be well organised, plan ahead, problem solve'.

A broad curriculum with lots of practical emphasis. Cookery is used to learn maths, debating helps with language, chess with strategy and problem-solving, sports with coordination. Reception had just finished making its own playdough when we visited, another class had taken photos of the other houses in the road and made models of them, and in another were newly-hatched chicks. In year 2 children choose a project they present to the class – which can be on anything from Nelson Mandela to Arsenal. 'By the time they have heard about all the different projects, they know a lot about a lot of things.'

Children are assessed for developmental delays from an early stage and outside help may be recommended for anything from a lack of pencil control to poor social skills. 'We have a good bank of respected practitioners, and interventions work particularly well when they are very young. We recommend them to protect children's self-esteem and help them reach their potential.' Probably not ideal for a very boisterous child, or for one who cannot cope with change. 'We have had fantastic success with one or two Asperger's children, but this is not generally the place for them. We offer places if we feel we can fully meet the child's needs. It is most important that children's school experiences shouldn't be stressful.'

Teachers a mix of youth and old hands – 'some have worked with me for over 20 years, and we're like a family. We're more pedagogues than teachers'. Praise from parents: 'The children really love my daughter's teacher and want to please her'.

Children have plenty of opportunities for, and find great delight in, taking responsibility as head boy, head girl or a member of the school council, which has regular lunches with the head. Many performance opportunities too, in concerts, plays and poetry recitals – 'We like to celebrate the arts'.

Strong emphasis on all matters green: composting, reusing, exercise, healthy eating. Lunch boxes must contain 'real food': nothing processed or ready-wrapped. We saw children tucking into salmon risotto, sushi, tortillas and pasta salad. 'Seemed annoying at first,' said a parent, 'but my daughter is talking about why certain foods are good for you and why some are not, and how she feels when she eats something too sugary.'

Unusually wide range of extra-curricular activities for a pre-prep. Around a third of the children learn the violin at school – 'It gives them zillions of study skills, such as concentration and perseverance, and those who keep it up tend to do exceptionally well academically'. Everyone does dance and drama, gym and swimming, French and computing; also a very active and serious co-ed football team. 'When the children leave they have a whole breadth of experiences that stand them in very good stead later on.'

The head brought back with her from the States a belief in strong links with parents and the local community. Parents report lots of emphasis on getting together as families for meals and outdoor activities. The school runs parent education sessions, social events and plenty of whole school initiatives such as sponsored walks. Parents and grandparents come in to lead assemblies, help with topics, accompany school trips to anywhere from Hampstead Heath to the British Museum, talk about their jobs or hobbies. The PTA organises charity events, picnics and parties, and arranges school visits by theatre groups and farm animals.

'It's a very warm and friendly place,' said a parent. 'My daughter has thrived here and our experience has been brilliant. They do a nice mix of activities and she's really excited about learning.'

Appleford School

Elston Lane, Shrewton, Nr Salisbury, Wiltshire, SP3 4HL

- Pupils: 19 girls and 53 boys; 38 board (flexi/full) • Ages: 7–16
- Inter–denominational • Fees: Day £16,290; Boarding £25,002 pa
- Independent

Tel: 01980 621020
Email: secretary@appleford.wilts.sch.uk
Website: www.appleford.wilts.sch.uk

Headmaster: Since February 2012, Mr David King BEd (late forties). Previously head at Bishop Dustan School in Newton Abbot and before that at 24/7 College near Honiton, Devon, both special schools catering for children with emotional and behavioural difficulties. Married to Shelagh, a learning needs specialist, with grown up children and much-loved home in Devon (the reason why, like some of his pupils, he's a part time boarder with digs in the village, returning home at weekends).

Thrives on risk. Before entering teaching, he contemplated a career as a professional climber (we're talking Mont Blanc without the safety gear) until a serious fall coupled with parental pressure to 'make something of yourself, David' compelled him to choose a career.

Security and long holidays originally lured him into primary school teaching in assorted Somerset primaries in 1989. Becoming special needs coordinator (and maths specialist) followed by the realisation that he had an affinity with under-achieving children were what kept him there.

After securing pioneering dyslexia friendly status while at Wembdon St George's Primary School, Bridgwater, disenchantment set in with the growing pressure of Sats force-feeding. While dyslexic pupils 'might fleetingly have achieved level 4 in the test, they certainly weren't working to it.' In 2000, left to set up a family-run outdoor activity centre on Exmoor, gaining the management expertise and – thanks to an advantageous sale – financial freedom to pick and choose senior leadership posts, this time in the independent sector. While his two previous posts saw him transform underperforming schools into slickly run operations to a tight timescale, he decided he wanted a 'forever' school to keep him going until retirement. Saw Appleford and was hooked.

Wiry and immaculately dressed, he's a fizzing ball of energy barely contained (does 'occasional' triathlon – a necessity, you'd have thought, to avoid overload). Personal best for pupil annual review meetings is 23 minutes – 'don't do fripperies' – though he's a benevolent force. During our interview, several children erupted through his door, clearly confident of (and receiving) a sympathetic reception as long as they observed the basic courtesies (he's big on manners).

Clear on how he wants school to be seen. Not special (despite label) but 'just a school that teaches children in a specialist way'. His philosophy is 'you're dyslexic; get over it,' (pace Nelson Rockefeller) and by way of proof, he cites host of inspirational, high-achieving success stories (Zoe Wanamaker has recently become school patron).

Almost his first act as head was to extend the leaving age from 14 to 16. Wants a sixth form too – 'it's logical' – with woodland site earmarked for new building, planning permission permitting, though 100-120 would be maximum school size. 'We don't want to be a production line.'

Change is being implemented at an almost biblical rate. During the few hours of our visit, he had dreamed up and founded a business for year 9s from scratch as part of their work experience (selling hot drinks and snacks at local 'old dears' home coffee mornings).

One parent wondered if pace was a bit too fast and furious, but most are smitten, as are staff. 'I'm massively impressed,' was a typical comment. 'I'm blown away, he's amazing,' said one parent (echoed ad nauseam and unprompted). Pupils are impressed too. 'The candidates were taken round the school and he was the children's favourite," a mother told us. 'When I said, "you have a new head ... and it's David King," my son punched the air.'

You can't help wondering what will happen if his super-fast, risk-embracing management style finds him twiddling his fingers in four years or so when he's got the school where he wants it and is no longer living on the edge but a good bus ride from it. Officially, however, he's here for the duration.

Entrance: Parents meet head and provide ed psych report. Pupils are then assessed during two-day visit (and nights, if planning to board) before final decision is made.

Families apply from hither, thither and yon, with long-distance commutes common. Once they find the school, they will do anything, including moving home, to lick the logistics into shape (flexi-boarding can ease the pain). Statemented pupils (currently 18) face the customary battle with local authorities, though once admitted, head mounts a formidable defence to ensure they stay.

Pressing need to keep pupil numbers up and finances ticking over meant school slightly lost its way, unofficially broadening admissions criteria to include those with a primary diagnosis of ADHD. No longer, says head. Dyslexia must be the key issue, though 'if pupils have additional needs, as long as it doesn't impact on their learning or the learning of others, then that's fine.'

MOD funding possible for Forces families. School also offers eight bursaries worth up to 25 per cent. Sibling discounts range from five per cent for second child to ten per cent for fourth.

Exit: Up till 2012, pupils had to leave at 14, many miserably returning to mainstream education. Now they can stay till 16 (addition of sixth form is the next goal). Head would like leavers' destinations to be accurate reflection of underlying ability, so range is likely to cover everything from academic mainstream schools to more vocational further education colleges.

Remarks: Set in a compact and easy to navigate site in rural Wiltshire (Stonehenge a mere monolith's throw away). The school (Victorian gothic main building, ringed by additions of assorted styles and ages) exudes longevity (though actually founded only in the 1980s), together with an indefinable 'something' that frequently has potential parents hooked before they've even parked.

Head, hugely influenced by his Merseyside upbringing, saw his grammar school as an 'enclave of tradition in the sprawl of comprehensives and misery' and is a firm believer in the traditions that make schools work – honour boards, houses, prefects and juniors. Wants families to feel as proud of being here as they would 'at Eton or anywhere else,' staff too.

Underlying aim is to create a relaxed environment where children who arrive with their confidence in tatters can start to learn again. 'You want them to have lost that fear factor and that's what Appleford does,' says a parent.

It's achieved with sense and sensibility: small classes in reassuringly compact and well-equipped rooms, including decent science lab and art room with kiln and delightful solar powered planes, taken by exceptional, humorous teachers (puns a speciality). IEPs (individual education plans) that are formulaic elsewhere here are (almost) living breathing things, constantly referred to and updated.

Subjects are carefully thought through, with maths and English dominating the morning timetable. Humanities block-booked so pupils have eight weeks of geography or history rather than disorienting chopping and changing, and modern languages banished, allowing more focus on drama (one senior pupil, convincingly in character as a nervous flyer, was being gently manhandled on to a plane by energetic peers).

Therapists, who radiate enthusiasm, provide flexible support. Multi-sensory approaches abound, with a big emphasis on hands-on activity. We saw senior pupils, wielding enormous maps and rulers, tracking down six-figure grid references in geography while even 7 and 8 year olds use Bunsen burners and sometimes even make their own bonfire night fireworks.

However long it takes, the approach that yields the light-bulb moment will be found, without recourse to punitive and pointless fact repetition. 'There's no point saying the same thing over and over again,' says an English teacher.

Very occasionally a child will be removed by a parent desperate for signs of progress and disappointed by the deliberately gentle pace. 'You get the odd failure but they are much more to do with the parent than the child,' says a father. Head is aware of need for better expectations management. 'The reality is that you are always going to be dyslexic and there's the possibility that your academic progress will always lag behind,' he says. He is adamant, though, that dyslexia must never be used as an excuse. Whatever pupils are capable of achieving, from a decent bag of GCSEs to vocational awards, 'they are jolly well going to do it,' and with the certificates to prove it, too. He wants as many subjects as possible to lead to a tangible, confidence-boosting qualification, pre-GCSE entry level English for year 9s, for example, together with maths, science and ICT.

For pupils, the school's approach is a revelation. 'Teachers here never say "It's time to move on," when you're still trying to write something down from the board,' says a clearly relieved 11 year old. Good things tend to come to those who wait, agree old hands. 'The reading is coming on,' one mother told us. 'It's not brilliant but much, much improved. We've sort of got our little boy back again.'

Sport is helped along by high-powered sports team (world class Iron Man among them) and good facilities including two grass pitches and all-weather tennis courts. Though ostensible wow factor is provided by super new climbing wall in flash but hot sports hall (wonky surface 'bobbles if underfloor heating isn't on,' says one teacher), the ubiquitous presence of Mr King at matches ('he always watches' say pupils) osmosing energy from the sidelines, may well prove the greatest galvaniser of the lot.

'We used to lose all our matches,' a year 9 pupil told us, but embryonic winning streak has seen recent U13 rugby and hockey teams (both mixed, as is football, with star girl players) triumph over local mainstream schools. 'You'd have thought they were the special school, not us,' says the head, of one notable victory. Champions do emerge, such as a 2016 Olympic equestrian hopeful. School could do more to trumpet successes, feels head, pointing, by way of proof, to photograph of two England and Ireland rugby captains (both former pupils) relegated to shady spot under sports hall light switch.

While there's no pool, pupils all swim, while an equine therapy centre opposite the school, run by local GP and featuring five ponies from Balmoral donated by the Queen, can work wonders for pupils with complex needs. Boarders can also join local scouts and guides. With an ever-increasing sporting menu, most pupils find something they tolerate and are encouraged to come up with their own ideas. Pupil 'crushed when first arrived, didn't want to interact' had researched plan for birdwatching club and proudly showed off new badge.

Lots of outings, cultural and sporting – they range from visits to Hampton Court and National Army Museum to a team-building canoeing trip. Set to increase, as all year 9s will now work towards compulsory D of E bronze awards.

Chances to shine are many and various, with music and drama specialists working wonders. With recent production of Oliver coming in for lots of praise and 40 per cent of pupils learning instruments, emphasis is on encouraging even the most reluctant to try something new.

Head has overseen widespread sprucing up of buildings. Some, like new year 9 boys' quarters, done by pupils themselves as part of life skills programme ('no dungeons,' otherwise free choice of colourways).

Reception in original house is now very smart, staff and pupils, ditto. Former have been now kitted out in academic robes for speech day (qualifications are 'excellent,' says the head, 'so why not shout about them?'); latter in revamped uniforms: ties, blazers (head boy/girl has exclusive red-trimmed version) and trousers for boys (fiddly fastenings and dearth of larger sizes made them hard work for some) while girls have attractive pleated (and machine washable) kilts, handmade in Scotland. Three weeks into term, they weren't popular with all. ('It's horrible,' says one, quizzed by head).

New boarding and teaching block includes home economics room for upper school. But star of the show is undoubtedly the new dining hall masterminded by the bursar, who has Grand Design tendencies and, in a shock departure from the norm, 'loves spending money,' says head. Instead of the high, echo-ridden ceilings that bedevil many a sensitive child attempting to avoid sensory overload, its noise-cancelling panels make pupil voices round oval tables (shape is most conducive to conversation, apparently) a pleasure to hear.

Food is good, too, despite recent and much lamented departure of national prize-winning chef. Pupils choose between green and red apple menus in advance. They sit at correspondingly decorated tables, take turns to serve each other and also clear up and wipe tables. Grace is said and manners are a big thing. 'You could take any of our children to a top restaurant and they'd know exactly how to behave,' says head.

Homely feel is helped by cosy boarding houses. One apiece for boys and girls and completed (hurrah!) by that increasing rarity, the house dog (poodle in girls' boarding house, chows in the boys' house, all allergy friendly as they don't shed and very popular). Lots of boarding treats – including Christmas craft sessions and sewing, together with exclusive weekend access to the bath (part timers make do with a daily shower).

Huge amounts of positive reinforcement and bullying 'instantly jumped on,' says mother, whose child suffered some name calling. One parent said that the morale-boosting good behaviour certificates, previously doled out en masse for small achievements like helpfulness, were now harder to come by. However there is a celebration assembly every week. Particularly liked by one parent was post-match praise, where, regardless of the result, 'everybody in the team stood up in assembly and said something positive about another player.'

Head is especially proud that one child, asked who he could go to if he had a problem by inspectors said 'everybody' and that teamwork, that much over-used word, is much in evidence. In the run up to speech day, teachers shared out admin and catering tasks so support staff could be part of it rather than beavering away in the background. They're also kept in the loop about children's needs and it shows: one pupil, who had mistakenly ticked wrong lunch choice and was miserably regarding disliked meal was speedily offered alternative without comment or fuss.

Head has also cast his beady eye over behaviour and, predictably, revamped school policy. His predecessor, though lovely, was 'perhaps over-empathetic,' thinks an insider. Now, consequences for unacceptable behaviour are clear, with recently introduced four-colour traffic lights system. Sanctions range from warnings or break time detentions for minor infringements (bad manners or not doing as asked) to code red for leaving the school grounds without permission. Latter would will result in a fixed term exclusion (permanent if repeated in the same academic year). There had been an (unsuccessful) dash for freedom the week before our visit. Pupils were still rather vague about detail. 'Is swearing a yellow or amber light?' mused one.

There's also a 'black book' that lives in the staffroom and records, like St Peter, every detail of pupil goings-on (positive and negative). Purpose is less punitive than to provide hour-by-hour update on burgeoning pupil issues and tailor approach accordingly.

School has many more boys than girls. Big geographical range, with some coming from as far afield as Hong Kong, others from assorted southern counties, often some distance away. Flexi boarding eases pain of gruelling daily long distance round trip, though upping sticks to be closer isn't unheard of. As one father told us: 'I've had experience with all our children of state, private and now, I suppose, a special needs environment. It's without a shadow of a doubt the best school I've been to.'

Few non-white pupils. Relatively wide range of backgrounds from Forces to professions. Small minority (eight or nine) funded by local authorities, many families somehow scraping together money for the fees. Having found the school, articulate, friendly parents will do almost anything to keep their child here. Though geographic spread makes get-togethers tricky, parents work mini-miracles when it comes to fundraising.

Ardingly College Prep School

Linked school: Ardingly College

Haywards Heath, West Sussex, RH17 6SQ

- Pupils: 270 in prep school, 155 boys/115 girls; 110 in pre-prep
- Ages: 2½-7 in pre-prep and 7-13 in prep school • C of E
- Fees: Day £7,725-£13,950; Weekly Boarding +£4,005 pa
- Independent

Tel: 01444 893200
Email: registrar@ardingly.com
Website: www.ardingly.com

Headmaster: Since 2007, Mr Chris Calvey BEd (early forties), educated at Bearwood College, then (now defunct) Westminster College, Oxford. Comes from a family of teachers but initially worked in the world of finance. Housemaster at Feltonfleet School in Cobham, then deputy head at Bishopsgate Preparatory School, Englefield Green. Married to Nicola, who teaches English and French in the prep school. They have two young boys. Interests include running, squash, golf, photography, cooking and reading.

Head of pre-prep: since 2010, Mrs Hilary Nawrocka BSc MSc (late forties). Started her career as a radiographer and worked for many years in higher education as a university lecturer, before taking a PGCE in primary education. Taught in both the state and private sector before joining the pre-prep. Passionate reader and dog walker.

Entrance: Interview with the head and an assessment during a taster day.

Exit: All pupils sit common entrance in year 8. Nearly all proceed to the senior school.

Remarks: Lower school actually in two: pre-prep 'Farmhouse' in totally refurbished old farm buildings takes from 2+ to 7; prep school in wing of main building, from 7 to 13 – all integrated into one 'college'. Prep has excellent performing arts studio, strong music and much specialist subject teaching. Uses main school sports, music and other facilities but pretty self-contained otherwise. Weekly boarding and casual flexi-boarding available. Daily games, very secure site, parents met at end of day by head. Good, popular after-school activities, some until 7pm to help busy parents. 'My school,' announced, unprompted, an 11-year-old, 'is exceptional. They have helped me hugely even though I'm not sporty, and it's very good academically and musically too.' Parents agree, 'They produce all-round individuals rather than hothousing them.' This school is on the up.

Ardvreck School

Gwydyr Road, Crieff, PH7 4EX

- Pupils: 127; 74 boys / 53 girls; 71 board, 56 day. Full boarding (no weekly or flexi-boarding). • Ages: 3-13 (including Little Ardvreck)
- Inter-denom • Fees: Boarding £19,140; Day £5,871-£12,537 pa
- Independent

Tel: 01764 653112
Email: admissions@ardvreck.org.uk
Website: www.ardvreckschool.co.uk

Headmaster: Since 2011, Mr Richard Harvey MA, PGCE (thirties). Father part of Queen's clergy at St George's Windsor, hence educated at Windsor Grammar, thence to St Andrews where he read medieval history, philosophy and theology. After nine and a half years at St Mary's Melrose, he joined St Margaret's in Edinburgh two terms before it closed. Appointed as deputy head at Ardvreck, he had two months in the job before the departure of previous head mid term (GSG has chapter and verse on this, but sufficeth to say that the previous head is now chaplain at Loretto). Harvey then became acting head November 2011, and was appointed for real in April 2012. Unashamedly academic. His raison d'être is 'to ensure that each child achieves their academic potential as well as running the scholarship programme for 16 pupils, whilst mentoring and tutoring children on an individual basis', takes regular English and history classes and aims to be 'the best teacher in the sector'. Married to Susannah; two of their children are in the school, and the elder two at Glenalmond. Susannah supports children in the junior boarding house as well as welcoming guests for match teas. Outside of the school, she is the part-time legal director of an energy company.

Head runs an open door policy, 'if you haven't got the answer, come to me, and I will fix it'; and enjoys involving himself in many aspects of school life including helping with debating, playing blindfold chess (school now competes and in many cases has instigated chess marathons), coaching rugby, tutoring in the boarding houses and teaching English and religious studies. He emails every overseas parent every weekend with an update

Entrance: Via pre-prep but most come at eight. Boarding in the last year no longer compulsory but great majority do. Prospective pupils visit school, meet head and get a pupil tour, then spend a taster day in school (or overnight if boarding) wearing school uniform 'so they don't stick out'. Each child is issued with a 'school brother or sister'. They arrive at 10.30am and leave after lunch the following day. Head reports back to parents after feedback from staff.

Exit: Over the past five years senior school destinations have included Ampleforth, Bryanston, Eton, Fettes, Glenalmond, Gordonstoun, Harrow, Marlborough, Merchiston, Millfield, Oundle, Radley, Rugby, Sherborne, Stowe, St Mary's Calne, Strathallan and Uppingham.

Remarks: Jolly popular. School founded in 1883 by former housemaster from nearby Glenalmond. Purpose-built with swimming pool (rather grand but in a polythene tent nonetheless) and a fairly ad hoc collection of classrooms (some a lot better than others) perched on 42 hilly acres (woods etc) – we had 75 acres previously, wonder what happened to them? Littlest Ardvreckers all together at one end of the hog's back – rows of green wellies. Currently slightly boy heavy, not many in nursery (Morrisons down the road slightly cheaper) slightly down in boarding numbers – max 99, currently 75 – not bad all things considered.

Younger boarders live in main house (boys and girls on different floors) in a motley collection of cosy rooms; top two years live in his'n'hers chalets 'to prepare them for public school'. Common-rooms tarted up after our previous comments, selected television only, no Wiis for the younger boarders, whose mobiles are handed out when needed. Skype on offer. Older girls can do their own washing, stay abed late on Sundays – boys apparently watch Match of the Day at 8am... Dorms filled with climbing boots and rucksacks, school does three mini Barvicks (expeditions) each summer term. Fixed exeat every third weekend, Friday noon to 10.15am on Mondays now in summer term only, otherwise back to base by 6pm Sundays (but school 'not inflexible' to requests). Parents particularly pleased that this is a proper boarding school and not a day school with weekly sleepovers, consequently popular with the army and diplomatic corps as well as traditional parents. Day pupils stay till 6pm and usually try to board eventually (their choice). NB: School won The Tatler Award for Best School Food 2010 (signature dish homemade chicken pie).

Impressive weekend programme (parents and pupils confirm 'no time to get bored'); bonfire building practice the Sunday before our previous visit, which coincided with grandparent day (a tough, fairly toffish lot, some of whom fill in for expat parents). We spent 20 rainy minutes in mid-March hearing notices, observing the flag being raised and listening to the junior pipe band (senior boys on a rugby toot to Oundle) play Highland Cathedral followed by croissants, choccy spread and coffee. Pupils were in (their family) kilts and green jerseys. Not really a first-time buyer school, popular with quite grand Scots, many of whom aim to send their young South. Parents 'a close-knit group of families', with pupils 'tending to remain friends well into middle age' and beyond.

A splendid child-oriented school, though head would confess that the school is becoming 'seriously academic'. Class sizes 15/16, no streaming, but maths taught in sets. Two parallel CE classes in sixth, plus scholarship class (often taken by head, who also supervises prep). Lots of scholarships and awards, but no honours board ('The only honours board we have is our war memorial'). Percentage-wise, Ardvreck topped the Scottish League Table (not that we think there is such a thing) in scholarships last year with a whopping 18 to schools all over, in almost every discipline (three academic).

Head of learning support plus three pick up both the bright and those with dyslexia et al, three student teachers help in class. One hour at one-to-one, plus one hour group sessions are free, thereafter £20 per hour. All assessed on arrival for maths, English and spelling age. Handwriting important, and

lousy writers (like this editor) referred to handwriting clinic. Keyboarding skills important, computers much used for teaching maths and English as well as more trad stuff; French from four, lyrical art room (buzzy new art teacher). Latin with the legendary Mike Osborne, former head of Belhaven – he gets around, would that he could be cloned – and classical Greek (ditto). Two retirements shortly in the modern lang dept, replacements being actively sought; policy change in the offing: possibly more Spanish and a smattering of German. Watch this space. Revamp on the cards for the IT department. Head is active on all fronts.

'School has begun an enrichment programme in which leading educationalists are invited to the school in order to engage with the children about interesting topics' is how the school puts it, we say fantastic selection of really interesting speakers, with talks open both to day parents and local state children. Think International Relations, Young Engineers' Science Workshop, Expeditions in the Arctic or the History of the Plague (bubonic, pneumonic and septic emic) with pupils given envelopes containing their possible immortality. Magic. If not Faustian.

New expressive arts centre opened by Turner shortlisted Scottish artist Nathan Coley. Fab orchestra – 40 play at assembly each Friday – with trips both for the choir and the orchestras in the offing. Singing and drama outstanding – school regularly features in the ribbons at the Perth Festival, orchestra plays on Thursday assembly. Popular pipe band played at St Giles Cathedral for Prince William's inauguration as a Knight of the Thistle, at The Old Course, St Andrews, and St Ninian's Cathedral in Perth and on telly... trips too, to Edinburgh, the zoo, the botanic garden and Glasgow for the Burrell, as well as toots to Normandy, and Berlin (with pipes and drums).

Outstanding on the games front – all sports, all comers, though parents from other schools have been heard to mutter about trying too hard (still). Trips all over the shop, both sports and subject based.

New sports inclusion policy introduced and going down well – 'school continues to thrive on games field but not at the expense of sports for all'. Games pitches fairly well scattered on the flatter areas. New combo-hall, with carpentry below, all singing and dancing above, cunningly perched on really quite a steep slope. Four tennis courts, three netball courts, hockey pitch, Astroturf and shooting range. Serious rugby coaching camp during summer hols with top Scots and English players (Lewis Moody et al).

Arnold House School

1 Loudoun Road, London, NW8 0LH

- Pupils: 260 boys, all day • Ages: 5–13 • C of E, but all are welcome • Fees: £16,350 pa • Independent

Tel: 020 7266 4840
Email: registrar@arnoldhouse.co.uk
Website: www.arnoldhouse.co.uk

Headmaster: Since 2006, Vivien Thomas (fifties). A user-friendly, down-to-earth chap with an easy warmth and an unscholarly taste in garish ties (red flowers and giant yellow fish on the day we visited). Makes a point of being accessible on school gate duty at least twice a week and is generally popular with parents. 'Relaxed, confident, intelligent, and understands how parents feel about their children,' says one. However, according to another parent, 'he is better liked but lacks the authority of Mr Allen, the previous headmaster'. Educated at University College School, Hampstead, followed by St Luke's College, Exeter, where he studied PE and history. Had a trial for QPR aged 17 and dreamt of becoming a professional sportsman but, after failing to make the grade (at football, tennis and rugby), he turned his talents to education. Taught PE and maths at UCS, followed by a spell at an international school in Venezuela. He returned to London to become deputy head at Arnold House, then head of Keble Prep, Winchmore Hill, until 2006. Married to Rowena, he is a man of varied interests, who 'struggles with golf', enjoys travelling and takes guitar lessons with 'a madman in Dollis Hill who used to play with Ginger Baker of Cream'.

Entrance: Application form (plus the usual £100 fee) due before child's second birthday, followed by an open evening held in April/May approximately two and a half years before the intended entry date. Interested parents (roughly 170 families for 38 places) are then invited to meet the head for a 20 minute chat. As always, it is the parents who are being assessed as much as the child. Don't say, 'I need you to get my son into Westminster'. Do say, 'I'd like my child to be happy and enjoy an all-round education'. Prospective pupils then invited for an informal one-to-one assessment and places offered 15 months before entry date. 'I hate the idea that it'll be down to the little boy, that he might be "not good enough",' says the head. 'What I want to know is, will he be a nice little boy to teach? When you open a book is he able to be engaged? Or is he climbing the walls, unruly and impolite? I don't want it to be a skills-based test, and I find it astonishing that there are tutoring agencies for 3 and 4 year olds.'

Main entry-point is into year 1, with occasional ad-hoc places in other years. Younger siblings and sons of Old Boys looked on favourably. Partial and full means-tested bursaries are available in years 5, 6 and 7. Application via the school registrar.

Exit: Strongly 13-plus focused school. A wide intake means a broad exit, but high fliers get into all the top schools, often with scholarships to boot. Two-thirds go on to London day schools, with the remainder heading off to boarding school. Strong links with Westminster, St Paul's, City of London Boys, Highgate, UCS and Mill Hill. Boarders go to Eton, Harrow, Rugby, Marlborough, Winchester and Bradfield, amongst others. Over-ambitious parents are discouraged from entering their son for exams all over the place. 'After 12 years of headship I know the system inside out. I am very honest with parents. What may look like an opportunity to them is in reality a rejection letter on the mat. Granny's all keyed up, everyone is rooting for him, but I know it's just not going to happen. I'll say, "your son is moving along quite happily, do you really want him to get that knock back?"'

Roughly 25 out of 30 boys get their first choice school, the remaining five or six take a bit longer. 'When boys are on the waiting list it's my job to turn that into an offer. We have excellent relations with schools, and that's when the prep school head really earns his corn.'

The school offers excellent results with less of the stressful, hothouse hysteria that so often accompanies the 13-plus experience. 'I offer places to parents who understand the Arnold House ethos,' says the head. 'They should want their son to join knitting club, cooking club, play music and sport, and not be getting anxious if he doesn't get three hours homework a night. We are here for bigger things than getting into a top academic senior school.'

Remarks: While some sniff that it is old fashioned, for others the traditional values of Arnold House are its strongest selling point. 'It's just like the perfect country prep school, but in London,' sighs one happy parent.

In the stressful, results-oriented atmosphere of the London prep school system, Arnold House is an artfully constructed oasis where boys can still be boys. Pupils are even encouraged to have snowball fights and inter-house conker competitions (safely supervised, of course). Admission is non-selective and

the school frowns on hothousing, yet year after year leavers gain entry to the holy trinity of Eton, St Paul's and Westminster.

'These boys don't need to be pushed,' claims the head (rather airily). 'It's a question of 'nudging' and bringing a boy nicely, like a fine wine, to the point where he is ready.'

Arnold House was founded in 1905 with nine pupils by a Miss Hanson, who was keen to prove boys could be prepared for public school entrance by a woman. She was successful, and the school has now expanded to fill three adjoining houses in a quiet St John's Wood side-street. The buildings lack any particular architectural pizzazz, but inside it feels spacious and well laid out, and is probably one of the cleanest schools we've visited. Even the boys' loos were sparkling, and instead of the usual dank, unloved urinals we found modern boutique-style plumbing with glossy lime green and red cubicles.

Entrance is into year 1, with 38 places split into two classes, though classes are smaller at the top of the school due to natural shrinkage. They are mixed up every couple of years to ensure academic parity and 'social refreshment'. Setting begins in year 3 for maths and English, with subjects taught by specialists from year 5. French from year 1, Latin from year 5, and ancient Greek is an option in year 7. No separate scholarship class, but boys with scholarship potential are identified at the end of year 7 and invited to join specialist lessons.

Lots of examples of creative, value-added education. The Compass Course in years 5 and 6 aims to foster independent thinking, public speaking and IT skills. Pupils work collaboratively to design an EU leaflet, make an animated film, write a play and create a charity PowerPoint presentation. Instead of the bog-standard year 8 battlefields trip, pupils spend time researching Arnold House Old Boys killed in WW1 before visiting France and finding their graves in the war cemeteries to pay their respects. An inspired way to bring history off the page. There is an embarrassment of pre-school, after-school and break-time activities ranging from an 8am Quiz Club to Mad Scientist Club, Bug Club, darts, French Fun and Games plus all the usual sport, music and art activities.

Like many London schools has a shortage of outside space. There is an adequate playground, but boys must travel to the school's seven acre sports ground in Canons Park (35 minutes away) for games. The younger boys travel by coach, years 7 and 8 by public transport. ('You'd expect, with the fees we pay, that the boys wouldn't have to get there by tube', mutters one disgruntled parent.) Here there are classrooms, a theatre, tennis courts and pitches for football, cricket, hockey and rugby. Older boys play team games twice a week, younger boys once a week, and there are additional PE and sports sessions at local leisure centres. A busy fixtures list for A, right down to G teams, means that even the most athletically-challenged pupil has an opportunity to represent the school.

The music department is outstanding and has many scholarships under its belt. Some 85 per cent of pupils study at least one instrument and many learn two. Twenty different ensembles on offer, from flute group to jazz and African drums, with lots of opportunity to perform in concerts. Years 7 and 8 can use the whizzy i-music suite for production, recording and pod-casting.

Art is taught to a high standard and doesn't get quietly side-lined as exams loom for older pupils. No need to feign enthusiasm when pupils arrive home clutching yet another art project. We saw wonderful Cubist self-portraits from year 3 and some very accomplished papier-mâché shells that any parent would be proud to put on display.

SEN support is excellent and, with a year of free one-to-one sessions before charges kick in, is more generous than at many comparable schools. One permanent SEN qualified staff member is supported by three visiting specialists for dyspraxia, speech and language and occupational therapy. Pupils who need extra help are identified in years 1 and 2 and either given classroom support by the six teaching assistants, or allotted one-to-one sessions as necessary. Dyslexia screening for every pupil in year 4 as a 'final trawl' to identify those with SEN needs, which can often mean brighter pupils in which dyslexic tendencies are masked.

So what type of child does Arnold House suit? 'My son has been blissfully happy, but there is a certain rough and tumble that goes with a boys' school, and I think if they are very fragile they might find it easier at a co-ed. They don't have to be uber-sporty though, there's drama, singing, art, something for everybody.'

'We take the boys as they are' says the head. 'We have boys with IQs below 100 all the way up to 140. Once we take a boy on we're looking to be together as a team for eight years.' He admitted that, occasionally, if a boy looks like he is struggling by year 4 or 5 he will have a meeting with parents to decide 'whether or not this is looking like a good plan'.

Behaviour at the school is generally accepted to be good. 'We expect the boys to rise to a certain level of behaviour. I don't know if you can teach kindness, but you can certainly teach consideration,' says the head. There's the usual system of sanctions and rewards with Good Citizenship badges for 'being a good egg' and Industry badges for trying hard. Senior boys get ties for art, music, games and responsibility. 'I'm always pleased to hear how strict the school is,' says one parent. 'My son is well-behaved, but I occasionally hear of other boys being told off, and they are properly told off.'

Bullying is rare but, as in all schools, it happens. Usually nipped in the bud early by class teachers, but suspension has been used when necessary. 'In 7 years I've had only four situations where I've had to step in,' says the head. 'There isn't a parent I've met who thinks their son could actually be the bully, so it always has to be thoroughly investigated.' The head is very hot on cyber bullying. 'If a boy is being talked about in a derogatory way on Facebook on Sunday night, then it's going to cause problems at school on Monday morning. Even if it happens outside school, I will deal with it.' Only one parent we spoke to was unhappy, feeling that a situation had been dealt with 'too late'.

Parents are a mix of multi-national successful professionals, with 50 per cent close enough to walk to school (should they ever choose to leave the 4x4 behind) and others coming from further afield (Notting Hill, Islington, Highgate). Reputed to be a friendly, sociable parent body, though the higher-than-average fees mean there's a lot of wealth sloshing around. 'There are a few amazingly flash cars, but also plenty of beat-up cars like ours. It's an easy, mixed group and I've seen no snobbishness whatsoever.' This is not the place for wags, trophy wives or school gate show-offs. 'It's definitely not a "women who lunch" school,' said one mother. 'All the mothers have, or have had, interesting careers. At my son's nursery I was the only working mum and had nothing in common with anyone, so I find the professional ethos here a relief.'

School lunches would definitely win a triple gold star from Jamie Oliver. A very jolly cook was making roast beef, Yorkshire pud, parsnips and broccoli on the day we visited, and the gravy was even made with a dash of wine.

Ashdell Preparatory School

266 Fulwood Road, Sheffield, S10 3BL

• Pupils: Prep: 90 girls, all day; Snowdrops: 35 boys and girls
• Ages: Prep: 4-11; Snowdrops: 3-5 • C of E • Fees: £8,985-£9,600 pa • Independent

Tel: 01142 663835
Email: headteacher@ashdellprep.co.uk
Website: www.ashdellprep.co.uk

Headteacher: Since April 2008, Mrs Anne Camm (fifties), educated at Princess Gardens School, Belfast, Trent Park College of Education (now Middlesex University) and Bristol University. Taught at Kirkinriola Primary School, Co Antrim, class teacher and housemistress at Cabin Hill Prep School, Belfast and Edgarley Hall, Millfield Prep School, before becoming head of Birkdale School's pre-prep, Sheffield. Married to Peter, in property; two teenage daughters. Does some teaching.

Entrance: The school looks for confident, mature girls of at least above average IQ. Initial pre-prep entry by informal assessment; maths and English tests after that. Twelve per cent have bursaries.

Exit: Mostly to Sheffield High with a small number to local state schools.

Remarks: Attractively decorated Victorian houses with well-tended small scale gardens, including a lily pond, and thoughtfully designed asphalt play areas – pre-prep has three Wendy houses and prep a climbing wall. Classrooms spacious, bright, light and well-equipped, particularly for practical subjects; plenty of displays of good work and photographs of school activities in the corridors. Well-stocked library; all girls learn to touch type – 'Fabulous IT,' commented a parent.

Academic standards high, classes small (maximum 18, can be as low as 11); regular testing and an atmosphere of enthusiastic, disciplined learning in the classrooms; specialist teaching builds up over the years and offered throughout in ICT, sport and creative/practical subjects. The very able receive a separate stimulating programme delivered by staff specialists for half a term/year. Special needs girls receive extra support (no extra charges; all pre-prep children screened for dyslexia) and care taken to nurture every pupil's self esteem – emotional intelligence taken seriously, as are awareness of different learning styles, encouragement of creativity and independent learning and girls taking responsibility for enterprises. Woodwork, textiles and cookery timetabled. School dinners (made on premises) excellent.

Lots of music, in the lunch hour and after school (though girls mostly encouraged to use the lunch hour for outdoor play) – all learn the recorder and keyboard; orchestra for all plus choirs and instrumental groups. Other after-school clubs popular and plentiful. Girls compete against local schools in a variety of sports; everyone has a chance to play in a team.

Only a few obviously ethnic minority children but girls come from a mixture of cultures/countries and levels of incomes, three per cent having bursaries. Pupils confident, happy and enthusiastic. The uniform – dark red blazers, summer boaters and winter grey felt hats, and even red schoolbags – bespeaks the school's traditional leanings, but it has been brought tactfully into the 21st century. Teachers know the girls well and talk openly to parents.

A protected, very well-endowed little world for bright, responsive girls, but not so much for those of a less conventional or tractable turn of mind.

Ashdown House School

Forest Row, East Sussex, RH18 5JY

• Pupils: 125 pupils • Ages: 5–13 • C of E services but with wide ecumenical base • Fees: £16,200–£23,970 pa • Independent

Tel: 01342 822574
Email: secretary@ashdownhouse.com
Website: www.ashdownhouse.co.uk

Headmaster: Since January 2013, Haydon Moore B Th. (Oxon), previously deputy and acting head. A popular appointment: he 'understands the ethos of the school', say parents. Has worked in prep schools for most of his career; married to Annie.

Entrance: By informal assessment and a maths and writing test plus a report from the child's current school – the key criterion being that the child is going to be happy and won't struggle. The ultimate test is common entrance and they need to be up to this. Children can join at any time if there are spaces, and now takes year 1 and 2 pupils, but most start in years 3 and 4 (many as day children to start with) and a number of boarders join in the 3s (year 6) – just gives enough time for children to prepare for common entrance. About 30 per cent of children come from London day schools, some from local private and state schools and a number of ex-pats, many from Hong Kong, Singapore and the Caribbean.

A few start aged 7 as day children but are soon begging their parents to become boarders as feel they are missing out on all the fun. About 25 day children altogether – most end up boarding. Day children have to attend Saturday school and afternoon matches.

Exit: To the major national public schools: Benenden, Eton, Marlborough, Downe House, Harrow, Wycombe Abbey, Rugby, Radley, King's Canterbury, Bryanston, Stowe et al. Leaving at 11+ is not encouraged and virtually all stay on to 13. Good scholarship record.

Remarks: The school was founded in Brighton in 1843 and moved to its present site in 1886. The main house is neo classical in style and designed in 1793 by Benjamin Henry Latrobe, who later moved to the USA where he was responsible for the building of the Capitol and the White House. The original Tudor manor house, dating from 1575, forms one wing of the school. It is set in 40 acres of land, half a mile from the nearest road – many former pupils say that one of their lasting memories of Ashdown is the glorious setting. 20 minutes from Gatwick and one hour from central London.

Children streamed for the last three years but setted in maths from the 4s (year 5). Scholarship class for the last year. Average class size about 12, max 15. Latin for last three years and Greek for most for the last one or two years.

Ashdown recently became part of the Cothill Educational Trust and one of the many benefits is the use of Chateau de Sauveterre in the South of France. It is run as a separate French prep school with all lessons in French and the children learn French history, geography etc and includes a week's skiing in the Pyrenees for those going at the right time of year. All children in the 2s (year 7) spend one term here – a high point in their Ashdown careers and a real confidence builder. The younger children can spend a week at La Chaumiere, a farm on the estate.

Three well equipped science labs in the Jungle Block and there is a large pond for fishing for creepy crawlies. The Old Malt House, also part of the Cothill Educational Trust, is an ex-prep school on the Dorset coast which has been developed as a natural history centre staffed by experts from the Natural History Museum – the 2s (year 7) spend five days here studying real life science and geography and doing outward bound.

About 20 per cent of children need some sort of SEN support, mainly for mild dyslexia. One full time and two part time teachers based in the purpose built log cabin in the garden – individual or group tutoring for which parents are charged. Annual cognitive tests to ensure no one slips through the net. One EFL teacher for about 12 children – the school is careful that no one nationality dominates.

Sport every day – a day huge part of school life. The usual sports and enough teams for everyone to play in a match if they want to – give local preps a run for their money but all played with a balance of competitiveness and good humour. Particularly strong netball and recent SE England U13 football goalie. Cricket nets and football in the old barn – perfect for letting off steam on wet days.

Fab art and DT – pictures all over the dining room which doubles as an art gallery and the ultimate honour is to have a piece picked to hang in the headmaster's study. Art scholarships most years and brightly coloured totem poles dotted around the grounds. Chess also a big thing at Ashdown, on the curriculum for the juniors and many develop a lifelong love of the game here – lots of competitions and one girl recently picked for the U14 GB chess squad.

Lots of music – concerts, bands, etc under the direction of inspirational head of music and a dedicated team of visiting music staff – huge range of instruments played including the harp and electric guitar. Ten children performed in the children's chorus in Hansel and Gretel at Glyndebourne recently. Everyone is involved in the annual Choral Day – it is all about taking part, you don't have to be particularly good at singing. Music scholarships most years.

Series of lectures on Wednesday evenings teaches children to listen and ask spontaneous questions. Speakers have included cricketer, Henry Olonga, mountaineers and adventurers, a magician from the Magic Circle and the artist and conservationist David Shepherd.

Activities every Friday afternoon, anything from riding at the local riding school, martial arts, squash, water colours, gardening – the younger children love to grow their own vegetables – photography and ceramics. A huge range of clubs on Saturdays: nature watch, pottery, debating, cooking, film making. Staff do things they are passionate about and thus fire up the children's enthusiasm. Popular modelling area in the cellar and, of course, the Scalextric room where the headmaster still holds the record for the fastest lap.

Lots of plays – one for each age group every year and three for the top year. Super theatre with a big screen – useful for lectures. Lots of outdoor activities and trips all over the place, Dale Fort in Wales, Swallows and Amazons trip to the Lake District and the very popular three day bushcraft survival course when the children build their own shelters to sleep in and cook their meals over open fires.

Very much a full boarding school with day children in the lower years – no flexi or weekly boarding. Apart from the set exeats, children allowed out after chapel on four Sundays a term (although some seem to bend the rules a bit here). Everyone has to write a letter home on Sunday mornings – something particularly appreciated by the parents – a phone call is just not the same. Five landings divided between year groups, two for girls and three for boys, each with a houseparent, an assistant housemaster and gap student. Top year children act as dorm captains. School also vertically divided into four patrols: Hippos, Rhinos, Elephants and Kangs with two members of staff in charge of each patrol and with seniors looking out for the younger children. Church of England school but with an ecumenical approach. Chapel every Sunday, prayers in some assemblies and grace after lunch.

Warm and welcoming atmosphere. Top of the range facilities for the things that matter like science labs, ICT, interactive whiteboards (some masters still prefer chalk), art and music but other areas, like the dorms, reassuringly scruffy but that is the spirit of Ashdown – one cosy and happy home from home where everyone feels part of the family and the headmaster's door is always open. Family dogs wandering round the house – in fact one of them has its own blog – plus chickens, rabbits and guinea pigs in the garden. Golf clubs piled up in the front porch – the school has its own golf course. No one feels pushed or pressurised here but school still gets fantastic results and there is a spontaneous celebration in each other's achievements. Children are natural and confident and are happy to strike up a conversation with adults but can remain children for longer in these idyllic surroundings with lots of space and time to be free. They are allowed to climb trees and make dens in the jungle and there is plenty of time for just mucking about. An extraordinarily dedicated team of teachers, many of whom live on site, they run clubs at weekends and often build bonfires so the children can toast marshmallows and bake potatoes in the embers. Staff eat with children at lunchtimes – good food and plenty of choice and lots of barbecues during the summer.

Emphasis on kindness and consideration. Guidelines laid out at the back of the termly calendar: Be polite and smile, 'do not feel shy about using really good manners'. Stress on common courtesy and awareness of other people in the community. The school reinforces the simple message at the start of every term – Be Kind. Be Kind. Be Kind. Parents generally down to earth and unpretentious, some aspirational and a few first time buyers. About 30 per cent from London, others local or ex-pats. No parents' group but open house for matches, plays, concerts etc and always made to feel welcome.

Ex pupils include Boris Johnson, Rachel Johnson (The Lady), Damian Lewis, Nicholas Coleridge and Viscount Linley.

Ashfold School

Dorton House, Dorton, Aylesbury, Buckinghamshire, HP18 9NG

• Pupils: 270 pupils, 175 boys/95 girls; 5 weekly boarders but 80 per cent of 9-13 year olds board some nights every week • Ages: 3-13 • Christian • Fees: £3,600-£14,160; Weekly boarding £17,208 pa • Independent

Tel: 01844 238237
Email: katrina.hartley@ashfoldschool.co.uk
Website: www.ashfoldschool.co.uk

Headmaster: Since 1997, Mr Michael Chitty (fifties). Educated at Clifton College, Bristol then Exeter University where he read economics before following generations of forefathers to Sandhurst. First bitten by the teaching bug on his gap year in Kenya, where he was a student teacher at The Banda School and later, following an army career that saw him rise to the rank of Captain in the Queen's Royal Irish Hussars via Equerry to HRH Prince Philip, when he returned to Sandhurst as officer instructor.

Landed squarely on his feet in his first teaching position at Stowe School, where he taught economics, politics and European studies, always with an eye to his main ambition of becoming a prep school head. Given role of 'adjutant' to ease communications between the head's office, bursary and staff common room before being appointed housemaster of Grenville House (after which he later named one of his two black Labradors). Headhunted after six years to become head of Ashfold, which he transformed with his energy, enthusiasm and clear vision. No longer teaches, although he does share boarding duties, but parents say he is 'very hands on' and he still coaches rugby, hockey and cricket teams, as well as clay pigeon and .22 rifle shooting teams, sits with children at lunch times and is always visible at matches and other school events.

Prospective parents unlikely to meet many heads whose former jobs include 'deployment of the British army worldwide' and Chitty does not disappoint, with his overwhelmingly positive, driven – and some might say military – approach to managing his school. An animated and dynamic communicator, he likes to keep up to date with car park chit chat via parents. Says he is running a 'very together school,' and is now 'in a position to do some very exciting stuff.' Recent appointment (2013) of a female deputy aims to boost girls' numbers and bring fresh ideas, although head is realistic that the female intake will most likely remain mostly siblings and peak at about 45 per cent.

Lives in a house on site, as do around 15 staff, with wife Louise, a barrister. Two grown up children, now working, come back for regular visits and often join Chitty at his second home near Cirencester, where he enjoys spending weekends sailing, walking his dogs and occasionally indulging his passion for cricket.

Entrance: Non-selective, with the majority joining reception from the nursery. Prospective pupils for all year groups invited to spend a day in school for assessment only. Head likes children from state primaries to join by year 2 and will hold places for them to this point. From year 3, places are harder to come by, with waiting lists for most year groups.

Exit: Leavers to a wide variety of schools, with about 50 per cent heading off to board most years. Popular co-ed choices include St Edward's Oxford, Rugby and Stowe with Headington popular for girls and the most able boys opting for Abingdon or Magdalen College. Impressive scholarship record with a record year of 52 per cent of leavers winning scholarships in 2012 and 43 per cent in 2013. These range from art or DT to sport and academic. Head takes care to place less academic children in next schools where they can shine. Very few to state maintained grammars (just a couple each year), with head discouraging 11 plus examination entry unless for financial reasons.

Remarks: The cross country drive through rolling hills and farmland and rising fear that the satnav is playing tricks on you is well worth it for the first sight of Ashfold's stunning Jacobean mansion set in 33 acres of fields and woodland. Rugby pitches in the foreground give the impression of a traditional boys' prep but behind the magnificent building are three hard tennis courts, a well maintained, heated outdoor pool, full size Astroturf (2009), netball courts and a lovely adventure playground, proving that that the girls who make up roughly 35 per cent of the school population are well catered for and becoming more integral to the culture of the school.

Wood panelling, winding staircases and cobbled stable blocks bring Hogwarts to mind, and rosy cheeked, windswept and slightly dishevelled children litter the grassy play areas, giving an overall impression of an idyllic country school – worlds apart from the urban London schools many of its commuter families have left behind. Lacks some of the dazzling showcase facilities boasted by many preps, but every part of the campus is put to excellent use (and in the words of one parent: 'you're a bit restricted with a grade I listing') and the overall effect is of an inspiring, functional and nurturing environment, which, in the head's words, 'celebrates children.'

Purpose-built pre-prep building (2006) houses nursery to year 2 in a light, spacious and colourful setting with its own well equipped playground and large field, complete with bug hotel. Pre-prep children well integrated into the main school, sharing its assembly space (often the village church, situated on site), sports hall and playing fields. Junior department housed in main wing of house, while most senior lessons take place in recently renovated courtyard classrooms.

Largely rural catchment from surrounding villages, with majority of children from hard-working middle class families ('hardly any old money,' said one parent), who travel up to 30 minutes to school. Very few from non-Caucasian families. School keen to prove its country credentials with a flourishing veg patch tended by pupils and weekend challenges set for families, resulting in the presentation of the school's 'countryside certificate' on completion of all 30. Small number of scholarships, with the Stowe-Ashfold scholarship covering 100 per cent of fees and other awards up to 30 per cent, available for pupils 'who show outstanding academic, artistic, sporting, musical or all-round ability' for the last two years at the school.

Girls have been part of the furniture at Ashfold since the 1980s but are almost exclusively siblings of boys. Although they make up 35 per cent of the total cohort, numbers vary between year groups and are very small in some (as low as three in a class), which is 'a bit of a downside,' according to parents. In some year groups, however, girls actually outnumber boys and parents add that all children get the same opportunities, regardless of gender. School addressing gender balance with increased girl-focused activities such as dance, equestrian and girls' clubs, but head is realistic in his ambition to significantly grow numbers.

Whether arty, sporty, or musical, there's something for every child here ('they look at the child as an individual,' say parents) and academics are solid all round too. Class sizes average around 14 and are capped at 16 in the pre-prep and 18 in the prep. French with a specialist teacher from 7 and Latin from 9. Some mutterings from parents that they would like an earlier introduction to languages. No setting until last two years 'to allow for the genders' different rates of development,' according to head. Pupils entirely specialist taught from year 4 and move around the school for different subjects from thereon. All children screened for dyslexia aged 7 or whenever they join the school. Currently around 12 per cent of pupils under the SENCo for mild needs (SpLD, dyslexia or dyspraxia). In class support and small group work with a learning support assistant covered by fees. One-to-one lessons with the school's SEN specialist charged as extra.

Parents find channels of communication excellent and are able to email class teachers – who they describe as 'a really talented bunch' – directly with queries or issues. Recent introduction of i-learning online assessments for all children from year 3 up have 'really freed up teachers to focus on creative lesson planning,' says head.

High standard of art on show in and around a lovely bright art room; 'you can't usually see the ceiling for work,' said the head of department when we visited (it was the first week in September), although it would be nice to see a bit more of the pupils' work festooning the walls around the rest of the school. Plans afoot for a brand new £1m classroom block to include new art rooms and a food technology lab to be ready for joiners in 2015 which should further bolster this strength.

Almost 60 per cent of pupils learn a musical instrument peripatetically, inspired by the head of music (described by parents as 'magnificent'), a surprisingly young addition to the Ashfold team who doubles as a rugby coach and has 'changed the kids' perceptions of music,' say parents, by injecting the school with lively doses of musical theatre. He even had head singing 'greased lightning' (actions and all) in a staff and parents' choir recital. Waiting lists for all choirs underscore the school's renewed collective passion in this area and all pre-prep children learn the violin and recorder from year 1. Lots going on in the drama department too, with recent productions including Animal Farm and Charlie and the Chocolate Factory, and plans in the pipeline for more musical productions.

Once children reach the prep school they have an extended day, ending at either five or six o'clock, depending on age. This enables the curriculum to include daily sport for all, which although adored by most is 'a struggle' for some of the less sporty ones, according to parents. All the usual suspects played to a good level but head exceptionally proud of his U13 girls' hockey team which won the IAPS championship in 2013 and the clay shooting team which are also national champions after a few years as runners up. He puts this and other sporting successes down to a 'real focus on coaching' with specialist talent brought in to coach rugby, hockey, netball and football (with an ex-Oxford United coach). Gymnastics and indoor games take place in a good sized sports hall incorporating wonderful changing facilities – 'with hot showers,' the head assures. From year 6, those demonstrating talent in other areas are selected to join scholars' groups (academic, art, drama et al) in place of time allocated to games.

Boarding allowed from year 5, where children can stay for supper after games, then take part in one of a multitude of activities on offer (from rifle shooting or fishing to chess and cookery). Given that this takes them up to 8pm it's a bit of a no brainer for parents of children keen to sample boarding life and up to 30 children board on any given night. Dorms of up to seven beds have been recently revamped and provide spacious, comfortable accommodation in the mansion, girls at one end of the building, boys at the other. Head says, 'it's proper boarding, not a sleepover,' and boarders sleep in the same bed on their chosen boarding nights. Newly refurbed boarders' common rooms, complete with pool table, two flat screen TVs and comfy sofas provides a home from home feel and opens onto the house parents' accommodation. No mobile phones, iPods or other gadgets allowed with the exception of Kindles – a very popular move with parents. Lights out at 9.30pm and cooked breakfasts are a hit.

School has a Christian ethos but accepts other denominations. Rightfully proud of its pastoral care with parents reporting 'very clear lines of escalation' should things ever go wrong. Three houses (Gryphons, Lions and Dragons) compete in lots of eagerly contested competitions (parents describe the standard of work in the inter-house art competition as 'unbelievable') with the each term culminating in a house cup. Pre-prep pupils presented with star of the week awards for effort and attainment in weekly assemblies. Prefects appointed in year 8 with the head taking a steer from last year's crew on who should be considered then consulting with staff before making his new appointments. Head boy and girl chosen after October half term amid great excitement. Head clear that 'leadership is about serving others,' and says he won't have any arrogance in the school, on occasion passing over obvious macho choices for head boy for 'a lovely gentleman with outstanding manners.'

No school buses as head wants parents to bring children into school to keep lines of communication open: 'If a child has had a sleepless night, for example, we want to know about it,' he says.

Ashford Friars Preparatory School

Linked school: Ashford School

Great Chart, Ashford, TN23 3DJ

- Pupils: 350 boys and girls; roughly 50:50 • Ages: 3–11
- Christian, but all faiths welcome • Fees: £6,831–£11,997 pa
- Independent

Tel: 01233 620493
Email: ashfordfriars@ashfordschool.co.uk
Website: www.ashfordschool.co.uk

Headmaster: Since 2001 Mr Richard Yeates (fifties). Joined the senior school as deputy head in 2000 and became headmaster of the prep a year later. Educated at Exeter University and The Royal College of Music. Previously director of music at King's Hall, Taunton and housemaster at King's College, Taunton as well as being master in charge of the 1st XI cricket. He is also an ISI inspector. His wife is head of the nursery at Ashford, and they have three children who attended the senior school and are now at university or beyond. Mr Yeates is a good communicator and is popular and highly respected by parents and children alike. He believes that the breadth of education offered by his school 'unlocks ability' and enables children to flourish. The school is his home and visitors are welcomed into his house – all adds to the cosy family atmosphere. Music, golf, travel and fine wine are his extracurricular passions.

Entrance: Not overly selective. Majority join in the nursery and reception and there is also an entry point in year 3 but children can join at any time if there are spaces. At nursery stage children (and parents) meet headmaster and have a taster session. Older children have a taster day and literacy and numeracy tests. The latter are for setting purposes and the only occasion when a child will not be accepted is if it is felt that they would not be able to cope with the curriculum.

Exit: Two-thirds go on to the senior school, many with scholarships, others mainly to grammars including Judd and Skinners. Some to Benenden and occasionally to Wellesley House and other preps for last two years before common entrance. Will familiarise children with the Kent Test but no intensive coaching. Children's progress tracked via CAT tests so school aware of any weakness and can advise on appropriate next step. There is close liaison with parents and school is expert at managing expectations.

Remarks: There has been so much development since our last visit that the school is hardly recognisable. The Georgian house with Arts and Crafts additions remains the heart of the place, but now there is a fabulous glass atrium and classroom block with wide bright corridors, all sensitively blended with the original buildings.

Pupils set in maths and English from year 3 but plenty of movement between sets and scholarship children are taught within the class. Lessons seem to be enjoyable and interesting; our guide remarked, 'I have never been a fan of science but they make it such good fun'. Accelerated reading programme known as the Millionaire Club has been a great success for keen and reluctant readers alike. Children have to choose a book and do a quiz, and then their name is put on a board. Anyone who reads a million words gets a hoodie. Soundswrite, a first phonics programme, is used to teach reading and writing in the pre-prep. About 20 children have significant learning difficulties, one or two with mild Asperger's or dyslexia, and some who need help with organisational skills. There is one full-time SEN teacher plus several teaching assistants and a specialist dyslexia teacher. School very supportive of those who do not find academic work easy, so long as they are ultimately likely to be able to take GCSEs.

School sits in 25 acres of grounds and playing fields and offers the usual sports including lacrosse and Kwik cricket for the girls. Good results in biathlon, triathlon, cross-country and swimming and a number of children play hockey and rugby at county level. Strong cricketing tradition – England cricketer Richard Ellison is an old boy – there is a pitch on site plus school has use of Ashford Cricket Club for matches and borrows floodlit Astroturf from the senior school.

Plenty of concerts and musical events, about 65 per cent learn an instrument (school has recently become proud owner of a harp) and there is specialist music teaching from reception upwards. Year 3 pupils have free music lessons for two terms and the school is always on the look out for hidden talent. Good drama with something for everyone leads to blossoming self-confidence, most children are comfortable standing up in public and a 'have a go' mentality pervades. Two plays a year for years 6 and 2 and every class does annual mini production and entertainment.

Lots of healthy inter-house competition with weekly house points keenly contested – everything from academic, sporting and fundraising events, plus points also awarded for effort and progress. Over 30 clubs and activities to choose from including, sports, music, chess and even dry slope skiing. Saturday mornings are also for sports and activities but attendance is not compulsory. Cooking offered from nursery upwards and by the time they leave some pupils are quite proficient – we watched the construction of some beautiful gingerbread houses. Vibrant art department celebrating different styles: self-portraits, Venetian masks, pop art, funky landscapes and interpretations of Guernica. DT very popular and children often put in extra work on their projects in the lunch break. Numerous trips and visits all covered by fees, including the residential adventure training camp for leavers.

No boarding on the Ashford Friars site but children in year 6 can board on the main school campus and come over on the shuttle bus. Attracts children from a wide range of cultural and social backgrounds – lots of locals plus a number of European, Asian and Nigerian families who have relocated from London. Seven thousand houses are being built around Ashford and the high-speed rail link is changing the population of the area – it is now only 37 minutes into St Pancras. Some parents make huge sacrifices to send their children here and like to be actively involved. Flourishing PTA raises about £25,000-£30,000 a year and organises lots of social events. Generally a pretty happy bunch who 'like the way the teaching is adapted to suit the way the kids learn' and value the fact that their children are allowed 'the freedom to make mistakes'. Working parents appreciate the option of wrap around care from 7.30 in the morning until 6.30pm, not to mention holiday clubs.

Ashford Friars is a happy, caring school with a strong moral purpose. Appetite and enthusiasm for learning much in evidence but we detected no whiff of a pressurised atmosphere.

Ashville Junior School

Linked school: Ashville College

Green Lane, Harrogate, HG2 9JP

• Pupils: Prep: 155; 95 boys/60 girls (2 boarders); pre-prep 80 boys and girls • Ages: Pre-prep: 4-7; prep 7-11 • Methodist • Fees: Pre Prep £7,140; Prep £8,565-£10,365 pa • Independent

Tel: 01423 724800
Email: ashville@ashville.co.uk
Website: www.ashville.co.uk

Headteacher: Since 2008, Mr Jonathan Dolman BSc, PGCE (early forties), previously head of middle school for boys at New Hall School, Chelmsford. Prior appointment as senior boys' boarding housemaster at Worth School. A geographer, keen cricketer and rugby coach (Cambridge half blue) – all featured in early teaching appointments and well placed here in a school that values sporting achievement.

Energetic, enthusiastic and engaging, 'just right for the job,' say parents. Strengthened teaching and learning and added zest by appointment of young teachers. Values and promotes music and drama alongside wide range of activities and sports. Hot on manners and three Cs (care, concern and consideration of others), building on the foundations of the school's strong Methodist ethos.

Married to Clare, teacher of French and Spanish in the senior school; they have four daughters, all at Ashville. Interests: running, cycling, swimming – triathlete in the making? – and golf, together with music and art (watercolours). Has led expeditions to Morocco and Iceland and teaches geography and games across the school.

Head of Pre-Prep: Since 2008, Carol Berrie (fifties), formerly deputy for six years after teaching at primary school, Lady Elizabeth Hastings, Thorp Arch near Wetherby. Warm, capable and welcoming, sets high standards for both staff and pupils. Believes in the importance of listening skills in learning. Brimming with enthusiasm, she has great rapport with her pupils. Delightful to see how 'newly graduated' year 3s in the junior school vied for her attention to proudly show their descriptive writing. Has an open door and finds herself increasingly approached by parents for 'wise counselling'. Described by more than one as 'fantastic'.

Entrance: Entry to junior school is by mathematics and English tests and informal interview with the head of the school, usually as part of a 'taster' day. Entry to pre-prep is by informal assessment with head of pre-prep.

Exit: From junior school majority to Ashville College (about 90 per cent), some to local state schools, handful to other independent schools. All pre-prep usually transfer to junior school.

Remarks: Sited between senior school and pre-prep, the junior school presents a cheerful and pleasant environment, though feeling a little cramped with needed expansion planned to accommodate the recent resurgence in numbers and provide specialist teaching areas.

Academic focus continues in numeracy and literacy but broad curriculum with specialist teaching in Spanish, French, music, science and ICT. Pupils taught in form groups of maximum 20 children, two per year group in years 3 and 4, increasing to three forms in both year 5 and 6. Setting from year 3 in mathematics and English with gifted and talented programme in mathematics, literacy, music and art having a good impact on results. No complacency here – the competition from local state schools is fierce. Whiteboards in most classrooms, two pure ICT lessons timetabled per week and netbooks to be introduced in the near future. SEN children who need additional support are identified and are given one-to-one specialist teaching or in class support as needed.

Head's push on 'raising standards in academics, music and sport' so no surprise to find full use of the senior school music facilities by a 50 strong junior orchestra and 65 per cent of the school in the junior choir, winning their category in the recent Harrogate Festival. Performance by senior school and junior school musicians each week in assemblies and all year 4 pupils receive small group violin and cello tuition. Sixty children pay for speech and drama tuition (LAMDA); performance opportunity in annual school play – diverse offerings recently of Pirates of Penzance, Bugsy Malone, A Midsummer Night's Dream and Henry the Tudor Dude. Art strong, with well-equipped art studio and visiting specialist artist.

Sport always featured prominently at Ashville with its excellent facilities provided in sports centre with swimming pool (shared with paying public evenings and weekends) and extensive playing fields and courts. Recent addition all-weather Astroturf raising the profile of hockey in the list of traditional team sports available. Use of professional coaching raising standards demonstrated by recent success as national school competition finalists in swimming and cricket.

Head of junior school says that the Methodist ethos underpins the pastoral care and the school is committed to the development of the full potential of each individual. Parents praise excellent standard of care and say its what they like most about the school. Hot on manners and respect, 'instilling values and standards which are often overlooked in the 21st century'. Strong culture of inter-house competition between four houses, from poetry to public speaking; the prized Rigg Cup for sport. Unusually, continuity of house membership from pre-prep up – adds to house loyalty and vertical bonding.

Junior boarding in co-ed house, Greenholme, run by year 5 teacher and wife (ex Ashvillian). Nearly 20 full time boarders, year 5 upwards, with a number of weekly and flexi-boarders; consists 70 per cent boys and 30 per cent girls, mainly English ex-pat, Forces families. Seven or eight bedded in 'home from home' environment. Escorted visits to town alternate Saturdays, activities each weekend and some evenings, including geo-caching, extended to day pupils too. Integration further through memberships of local Scouts, football clubs and other groups. Daily tweet to parents keeps them involved and boarder-led newsletter when busy lives allow.

More than 30 clubs from art, gardening and chess to dancing, orienteering and karate – the majority provided free of charge. Year 6 have a mini-enterprise initiative, setting up and opening a Hollywood Café for two days when we visited. The school council meets every two weeks and gives children an opportunity to make decisions sensibly on behalf of their peers. Charity giving big, with traditional annual 20 mile walk on May Day, supporting Open Arms, a charity orphanage run in Malawi by a former teacher and local good causes.

Communications to parents good – extensive weekly newsletter valued by parents, celebrates success and achievement as well as notice/reminders of future events.

Pre-prep is accommodated in a bright, spacious and purpose-built school nestling in a quiet corner of the college's campus, adjacent to the sports facilities and a short distance from the junior school. The school is well resourced with a self-contained hall for assemblies, activities and dining; an open plan library; separate area for technology and baking and a 'quiet room' for individual or group work. Outside, a secure playground and learning environment have recently been enhanced by addition of new play equipment.

Curriculum focus on numeracy and literacy in maximum class sizes of 16 in reception and year 1, moving to 18 in year 2. Pupils 'eased' into more formal learning in year 1, building on early years' foundation stage. Rolling three year cross-curricula programme, though discrete science teaching. On the day we visited the school was a hive of activity with the happy buzz of quiet endeavour varying from a 'phonics sound search' in the garden to hands-on Mexican tortilla cooking and sampling in the Make and Bake Room.

Enthusiastic and committed teachers who 'know their pupils well,' say parents. In year 1 pupils screened through verbal and non-verbal reasoning tests to diagnose any learning support needs. One-to-one and small group tuition carried out in designated Quiet Room.

Lots of sports and music opportunities, from swimming in sports centre pool to singing in first choir. Bags of extracurricular choice: Whizz Bang Wallop! Science Club, WOW (Widening Our World) to ballet and Spanish at an additional charge.

Interaction with junior and senior school pupils through guest performances at weekly musical assemblies or sharing of success and good work. The special way each birthday is celebrated is evidence of the importance placed on each child feeling valued and part of the pre-prep community.

Aysgarth School

Newton-le-Willows, Bedale, DL8 1TF

• Pupils: 150 boys in the prep school, 60 boys and girls in pre-prep and nursery; 90 per cent plus board in the prep school.
• Ages: 3–13 • Christian • Fees: Boarding £20,970; Day £8,715–£16,110 pa • Independent

Tel: 01677 450240
Email: enquiries@aysgarthschool.co.uk
Website: www.aysgarthschool.com

Headmaster: Since 2002, Mr Anthony Goddard BA (fifties). Went from Cambridge to ICI and thence to Accenture. Successful manager and marketing expert; no teaching experience but was an Aysgarth governor for 10 years. So this was an imaginative appointment and numbers have risen by 20 per cent, while the boarding focus has been enhanced and teaching facilities have been developed and improved. Charming, friendly and approachable, he teaches geography and some games and is very involved on the pastoral side. His delightful wife, Caroline, is also busy on the pastoral side, where she is much appreciated, especially by new boys and mothers. She also teaches RS, craft and DT. They make a great team and, along with their dogs, are the lifeblood of the place.

Entrance: By interview and assessment to look for boys with a 'willingness to get stuck in'; no exam, 'We try not to turn anyone away'. A few scholarships and some bursary help. Siblings and Forces discounts.

Exit: Excellent record to public schools: Harrow, Eton, Ampleforth, Uppingham, Radley, Sedbergh, Shrewsbury, Stowe, Fettes and Winchester. Good sprinkling of academic and music scholarships: seven in 2013, including the Harrow Beckworth Scholarship.

Remarks: Grand, purpose-built, 19th century school, including splendid tower and gem of a chapel. Quiet, beautiful, rural setting with glorious views in 50 acres of parkland; feels remote but only a short drive from the A1. Described as 'a place where boys can be boys', though girls are welcomed into pre-prep. Very much focused on full boarding – in fact, north of Oxford, the only all boys' boarding prep in England and parents come from both north and south of the border and say, 'It's worth the journey'.

Day boys certainly in the minority and they follow the boarding routine. Traditional and demanding curriculum with streaming and setting and extraordinary continuity of tradition over the years in gaining places at top public schools. SEN provision improving all the time as the school becomes 'a broader and kinder place'.

Sports facilities to die for, especially cricket field and swimming pool. The Aysgarth game of COW – cricket off the wall – is a love of Aysgarthians old and new, the real challenge being to hit the ball from the playground into the head's garden. Sport is high profile and they play to win, whilst still managing a well done and a slap on the back for the chap who comes last. Rugby, football, shooting, fishing, sailing, riding, golf and climbing all on offer. After-hours activities for boarders include both pillow and water fights (though not at the same time) and it's fine to get down and dirty and build dens in the grounds as well as engaging in debating.

Art is strong and technology is popular in well-equipped rooms where the boys can get their hands on serious equipment and tools. Four recent classrooms which provide light, stimulating spaces for the first year of the prep school and

Latin. Music is outstanding and boys – both the very musical and the less so – can be seen enthusiastically practising their musical instruments in dorms and classrooms at break times. They can play anything here, including bagpipes if they so wish, and the choir is a joy to hear. Good to see boys enjoying reading sessions in the library after breakfast and lunch.

Many of the boys look as though they are about to take Eton in their stride – happy, confident and courteous, without being arrogant, they are both charming and endearing. They enjoy occasional socials with nearby girls' schools (though are coy about which schools/girls they prefer) but clearly relish this boy-friendly atmosphere where you can 'be your own man'.

Food is ample, prepared in-house using fresh ingredients and 'not bad for school food' (though the boys did say they would like a little more salmon and duck on the menu, please), served in a pleasant if slightly old fashioned Dotheboys Hall-style dining room with long tables and benches, where good old fashioned courtesy and table manners count.

Staff know the boys well and, although the phrase is often over used, really a 'family feel' about this place, thanks chiefly to great enthusiasm and care from the top. Boarding accommodation includes serried ranks of sinks, where boys have to be reminded to wash occasionally, and cheerful dorms where caring staff keep a close eye, tidying up after them and providing a homely feel.

Clientele mainly solid (upper) middle class from the North (including Scotland) and Midlands, and strong support from the Forces families at Catterick. Governors very active and close to headmaster, and a lively Old Aysgarthian association. Families are a mix of old school and new, many first time into boarding, including some who, interestingly, say they had previously neither considered boarding nor single sex. Whilst initially a little reluctant to let go, these parents place huge value on all that the school has to offer, both in and out of the classroom, the end result being that their sons are 'prepared, and then some' for the next school.

Badminton Junior School

Linked school: Badminton School

Westbury Road, Westbury-on-Trym, Bristol, BS9 3BA

• Pupils: 125 girls; boarding from year 5 (aged 9) and there are usually between 5–10 boarders in year 5 and 6 • Ages: 3–11
• Non-denominational • Fees: Boarding £20,190–£21,240; Day £8,040–£10,830 pa • Independent

Tel: 01179 055271
Email: admissions@badmintonschool.co.uk
Website: www.badmintonschool.co.uk

Headmistress: Since January 2010, Ms Emma Davies, previously deputy head of the Lower School of Bristol Grammar School.

Entrance: The school is very popular so early registration is recommended. Girls are invited for the day and observed by Mrs Davies and her staff. Of course they are looking for bright, inquisitive girls, but how they interact, how easily they become involved and caught up in it all is equally important – this is not a school for those who hang back. Girls applying aged 7, and older, are given tests in maths, English and non-verbal reasoning.

Exit: The expectation is that all girls will move automatically up into the senior school at 11, though all girls are examined in their last year to confirm potential. 'Moving up wasn't a problem at all,' a senior school girl told us. 'That's what I had been prepared for.' Boarding is available in years 5 and 6 for those who want it.

Remarks: Has recently enjoyed a complete makeover and the whole place is bright and welcoming. Downstairs is dedicated to the younger girls (known as Acorns, aged 3-6); the older girls go upstairs. Tremendous science room complete with a range of live exhibits for observation – science is taught properly – and all the apparatus. Homely and well stocked library, where budding young scholars snuggle into beanbags and devour books; airy rooms with small classes of girls who are monitored and encouraged by their form teachers. Tutor groups are structured vertically to break up cliques and broaden experience. An efficient-looking medical room.

All girls are encouraged to learn musical instruments and join in various musical groups and the choir. Outstanding musicians have the opportunity to join in music making with the senior school. In fact the proximity of the senior school is a great bonus: girls use the swimming pool, tennis courts, Astroturf, gymnasium and other sporting facilities; they become familiar with the senior school without losing their own safe identity and may attend concerts and plays. But for drama, it seems, nothing to beat the annual Acorn and junior productions, with every child involved. This really is a school for involvement: history days, for instance, are inclusive and fun, be it Agincourt, Roman, mediaeval, where clothing, appropriate food and language are explored with great gusto. Much is learned almost without them knowing. Visits are made to country houses and castles, museums and adventure parks.

Though the academic expectation and standards are high, not a hothouse school but one where learning and experience go hand in hand with having fun as well. Girls with special needs are helped at the nearby dyslexia unit. Family-style lunch lends itself to old fashioned courtesies gently instilled and the food is 'brilliant', 'scrumptious', 'really delicious'. Over a neat little bridge, spanning a sunken footpath, girls trip lightly on their way to an attractively laid out adventure playground. There's a mediator 'bus stop' and 'buddy bench', where girls can quietly signal that they could do with some extra friendship – staff are alert to that.

Financial assistance is available for daughters of parents in the Forces, siblings and those with demonstrable need. Foundation Awards worth up to 100 per cent off fees available for year 6. Arrangements can be made to arrive early (breakfast is an option) and post-school activities are available up to 5.45pm. Increasing junior boarding with very busy flexi-boarding.

A fizzing school where the girls are busy without being stressed, academic rigour is instilled, but not at the expense of fun and talents, and interests are nurtured. It encourages independent thought and individuality, ideal preparation for the excellent senior school, a confident stroll away.

Bancroft's Preparatory School

Linked school: Bancroft's School

611–627 High Road, Woodford Green, IG8 0RF

• Pupils: 260; 115 boys/145 girls, all day • Ages: 7–11 • C of E but other faiths welcomed • Fees: £11,505 pa • Independent

Tel: 020 8506 6751
Email: prep.office@bancrofts.org
Website: www.bancrofts.org

Headmaster: Since September 2012, Mr Joe Layburn MA, previously acting head. MA in German literature from University College London, followed by a 15 year career as investigative journalist and TV reporter, primarily for Channel 4. Retrained as a teacher and joined Bancroft's Prep in 2004. Author of a trilogy of children's books. Married with three sons, two at Bancroft's and one at a special needs school. Keen on running, cycling and West Ham United.

Entrance: At 7+ – over-subscribed by about 3:1. Testing in English – reading and writing – and maths for year 3 entry takes place on beanbags! Children seen (and offered doughnuts) in small groups with head and deputy – it's 'as informal and low key as possible'. Around 70-75 places offered – Bancroft's will be first choice for most applicants.

Exit: Nearly all to senior school; a few to local grammars.

Remarks: Two conjoined, inviting-looking, modern red-brick buildings at the lower right hand side of the main school playing fields – two-storeyed and with big windows. From the main school they appear small and modest; the main school, viewed from the prep, looks imposing and a little awe-inspiring, but the prep children spend time in the main school, and sensible links so that 'It's a bit scary as it's so big and the students are so big, but we had a meeting with Mrs Ireland so we know much more about it now and I'm not really scared any more'. Quite! And senior pupils trot over to visit their junior siblings in break too. However the prep is its own world and, as you descend the slope to its entrance, between the playing field and the tennis court, a gentleness and palpable sense of fun envelops you.

The prep has splendid new rooms which have greatly enhanced its overall space and provision. New science, drama, music and DT rooms, a good-sized hall with flexible seating – lots of IT and new laptops. Around 23 children in a class, but the rooms are big and airy enough not to feel crowded – we did not feel the need to open windows, as one so often does. The library is well-stocked and a good mix of fact and fiction. Outside space good and super all-weather surface for littlies with monster chess set and apparatus – not surprisingly, 'Everyone loves coming out here'.

Classrooms busy, not over-orderly and relaxed – we wanted to look at the displays, all of which seemed interesting and not as predictable as they so often are. We liked the alternatives to 'said' and loved the paper collages showing variations on the Arcimboldo fruity face and the glittery, sparkly, firework ones. We also approved some of the interesting work in progress, especially the lesson on moulds – 'We had to throw them away as they were beginning to smell,' was a rueful observation. Year 6 has critical thinking lessons – 'to expand our minds, to think out of the box, to widen our imagination,' we were told, earnestly. We were impressed by the sensible 'traffic light' system whereby pupils assess their grasp of what they have learnt and where they need help. All entrants assessed for SpLD at 7 and SENCo-led help laid on where needed – mostly mild dyslexia.

Exuberant sports, music and drama and lots of inspiring extracurricular stuff. Outgoing, relaxed and confident children from a vast range of local backgrounds, as you'd expect.

A true preparatory school in that what goes on here is sound, sensible and confidence-building for what is to follow. But is not just preparatory for senior school – four happy years here are a solid foundation for life. Apply early – and cross your fingers.

Barnardiston Hall Preparatory School

Barnardiston Hall, Nr Haverhill, CB9 7TG

• Pupils: 290; 160 boys/130 girls, (30 boys and girls board) • Ages: Nursery and pre-prep, 2–7; prep 7–13 • Non-denom • Fees: Day £7,200–£12,000; Boarding £16,599–£18,000 pa • Independent

Tel: 01440 786316
Email: registrar@barnardiston-hall.co.uk
Website: www.barnardiston-hall.co.uk

Headmaster: Since September 2012, Mr T Dodgson BA PGCE (Colonel Boulter has given day to day running of the school over to him). 1992 first joined school as a newly qualified teacher after London University and PGCE from Durham. Then Bedford Prep, before returning as head of history and pastoral care for five years. Deputy head and housemaster at Sedburgh before returning four years ago as deputy head. Very keen to bring history to life.

Principal (headmaster since 1990), Colonel Keith Boulter (late fifties), married with three grown-up children. Cambridge theology graduate, hockey blue and keen musician who joined the Royal Army Educational Corps in 1973 and administered five Gurkha schools in Hong Kong and Brunei.

Entrance: Children spend a day attending lessons and are observed and tested by subject teachers. Where appropriate the school's ed psych is used to assess a child's particular needs. Bursaries at the BSA rate for Forces personnel. Limited scholarships for Hong Kong based pupils.

Exit: Most to local independent schools of their first choice. Good smattering of scholarships. A few to local state schools.

Remarks: Firm belief that more to education than pushing to get through exams. Children quickly get involved in all sorts of activities. Sleep-overs start early, as do Enid Blytonesque night time expeditions; according to one mum, 'Barnardiston children are well-rounded and pretty resilient. You can throw anything at them and they can take it'. Traditional teaching styles and old-fashioned values – good manners, hard work and community spirit – plus spontaneous fun (staff appearing at the end of a school play with water rifles or dressed in tutus for the end of term netball match) and D of E-ish exploits make a 'school where life goes at 100 mph'.

Gently rural property, set in 35 acres, bought by the Colonel when he left the army in 1990 and now the core of a family business. His tremendously jolly sister teaches little ones whilst sunshiny daughter is head of the pre-prep. No board of governors but has senior management team. Also owns Riddlesworth Hall and Broadlands Hall (for autistic children), which is run by his son. Rambling main house is home to Boulters and boarders but the distinction between its comfy domesticity and the school is blurred – carefree children, smiley staff and two friendly retrievers mill between the two. Both are stuffed with an eclectic collection of objets trouvés, including full sets of armour and three half-scale wooden giraffes which Colonel Boulter couldn't resist – transportation from Cambridge with their necks protruding from car windows led to one acquiring a prominent bandage.

Initial 50 pupils (no boarders) have grown to 290 (30 boarders) and several major building projects have been completed – purpose-built pre-prep department, new prep extension with classrooms, language lab and well resourced SEN department. Plans are afoot for further developments – although nothing yet to replace the semi-permanent marquee, which is an adequate sports hall.

Broad intake. Those who might struggle in less accommodating institutions find areas where they can shine, and parents say the solid, not too hot-housey academic approach 'gets everyone to where they want to go'. Streaming starts early. French from the nursery and Latin from year 3. History continues to be a firm favourite – according to one insider 'because the gory bits aren't left out'. Good IT provision and a fully computerised weather station.

No academic elitism or stigmatisation here – school has a holistic approach and is very proud of those who, with the know-how of the friendly and highly-regarded support department (The Bridge), have 'been turned round'. Help, given to about a quarter of the school by up to 12 staff, including two fully-trained SEN teachers, is usually one-to-one or from classroom LSAs. Needs range from an extra boost to identifiable conditions (mild Asperger's/autism, Tourette's, dyslexia and dyspraxia. Won't take children they think they can't help, but a few have statements – fees are state-funded). Gifted children also attend the unit, as do those needing TEFL provision.

Parents are happy with art, drama and music (over 50 per cent learn an instrument) and chirpily, respectful children readily enthuse about school sport (national prep school orienteering champions from 2006 to date). They also enjoy letting off steam in the adventure playground or pedalling round the mini two-way road system with its roundabouts and T junctions. Long hoped for Astroturf (one in Haverhill is used at the moment) is due to be installed on a recently-acquired field, but date of materialisation not yet clear.

We've heard that over-anxious or inflexible parents won't last long, but those who can cope with the school's expectations and laudable desire to do what's best for the child are devoted to the place and often return long after their children have left. A school which isn't constrained by petty regulations – wonderfully happy and well worth consideration.

Beachborough School

Westbury, Brackley, Northamptonshire, NN13 5LB

• Pupils: 330 boys and girls; even split of boys and girls; 90 flexi boarders • Ages: 2½ –13 • C of E • Fees: Day £9,030–£14,190; Boarding £15,720–£16,890 (4 nights pw) pa • Independent

Tel: 01280 700071
Email: office@beachborough.com
Website: www.beachborough.com

Headmaster: Since September 2013, Mr Jeremy Banks BA MA (forties), previously deputy head for seven years. Educated at Warwick University (education studies and geography) and Buckingham (masters in educational leadership – distinction). Taught at Dulwich Prep London – director of studies and housemaster. Founder of local road cycling club, Freeman of the City of London and a Cutler (cutlery, swords and surgical instruments).

Married to Sophie, who is head of Beachborough's junior department, The Boardman. Also a Warwick graduate (education studies and music). They have three daughters, all at the school.

Entrance: Beachborough is non-selective. 'We're a broad church,' says head. Older children entering the school do cognitive ability tests when they visit prior to starting. Every year group has maximum of 36 (divided into two classes). Years 3, 5 and 7 are virtually full from September 2011 but it's always worth talking to the school. Numbers have remained buoyant throughout the recession and school says it tries hard to help parents in difficulty. Beachborough has some means-tested bursary provision.

Exit: One or two leave at 11 (for schools like Royal Latin, nearby grammar), but most stay till 13. Nearby Stowe and Bloxham the most popular, then places like Headington, Magdalen College School, Rye St Antony, Warwick and King's High, Warwick. Good smattering of scholarships over the years.

Remarks: Founded in Folkestone in 1910, the school later moved to Ewell, Purley and then Stockbridge. Since 1942 school has been housed in rambling country mansion (once owned by MP Sir Samuel Scott), three miles from Brackley. Total of 30 acres for pupils to enjoy – and they certainly do. We visited on a sunny June day and at break-time children were full of beans, running, jumping and playing on front lawn. On rainy days they all don boiler suits and wellies and still go outside to play. Many of 40-strong teaching staff live on site, including head, all three deputies (one for curriculum, one for pastoral and co-curricular and one for management) and head of boarding. School has its own farm – and sells its own sausages. Its entrepreneurial flair was recognised at the Independent School Awards in 2010 when it won the most outstanding financial/commercial initiative prize.

Beachborough wasn't regarded as highly academic in the past but that's all changed in recent years. Lessons up to year 6 are based on the national curriculum. In addition to core subjects of English, maths and science, all children learn history, geography, French (from age of four), religious studies, art, DT, music, ICT, drama, PE and games. Years 7 and 8 geared towards CE and scholarship exams. Subject specialists teach children from year 5 upwards, when they are set for English, maths, science, history and geography. Average class sizes of 14 to 18.

Those requiring learning support (dyslexia, dyspraxia) get extra help from four-strong 'Learning Zone' team, usually in small groups. No charge made for this (nor, incidentally for tea and after-school care). Good provision for gifted and talented via school's able child programme. Children from the nursery up to year 4 are based in the smart new Boardroom Building. Light and airy classrooms, all colourfully decorated and with their own outside space. Pre-prep also has own forest school in grounds.

Sport is highly competitive but school prides itself on involving everyone in team games. School motto is 'succeeding with every child' and staff place firm emphasis on inclusion. Head says 'the only area where we won't compromise is in the classroom.' Whatever their level of sports prowess children are keen to compete against other schools – and enjoy match teas and hearing their names read out in assembly along the way. School regularly puts out four or five sports teams to play against other schools. Rather than calling teams A to E head has introduced jaunty monickers like 'the Beachborough Wanderers' and 'the Beachborough Strollers.' Impressive new sports hall is underway and will open by March 2012. Old sports hall to be turned into school theatre. Girls play football and cricket too – a girl surprised the opposition by turning out for the first football squad and when we visited two girls had just been picked for the cricket team. Swimming lessons every week at pool in Buckingham, four miles away. Very wholesome changing rooms – school recently spent £30,000 on them.

Music is strong – staff reckon school's particular strengths are 'art and singing.' Two-thirds play an instrument and all year groups have weekly class music in delightful music department at the top of the school (with score of school song painted along the wall). Year 1s and 2s get the chance to try out the violin, recorder and percussion for 20 weeks before deciding if they want to have individual lessons. Two choirs – chamber choir and junior choir for all year 3 and 4 children. Lots of drama. Recent productions include a play to celebrate Beachborough's centenary in 2010 and Fiddler on the Roof with a cast of 120. Art is wonderful – and very imaginatively displayed throughout the school. Loads of other activities too – sculling at nearby Stowe, Brownies, Guides, cycling, clay pigeon shooting and croquet (front lawn makes the perfect setting).

School food gets the thumbs up, especially a pudding known as 'bird seed' – rice crispies coated in custard to the uninitiated. Children eat lunch at long wooden tables with teachers sitting at either end. All very calm. Grace said at start and finish and pupils take it in turns to clear away.

No Saturday school at Beachborough. School doesn't cater for full boarders, but flexi-boarding (up to four nights a week) is hugely popular with children and parents alike. Nearly half the children aged seven and up board at least one night a week. Lots of organised activities on offer for boarders (but no mobile phones, MP3 players, Facebook or Twitter). Bedtime for oldest pupils at 9.15pm. Boarding houses located on top floor of the main school building, girls on one side, boys on the other. Enterprising head persuaded senior schools to sponsor the decoration of the dorms – so boys' rooms are decked out in the colours of Bloxham, St Edward's and Shiplake while girls' rooms have Tudor Hall, Stowe and Malvern. Long-serving school matron is based in boarding house – 'she is the rock on which Beachborough is founded,' say staff.

School has very clear code of conduct, including advice like 'always do your best, whatever the challenge' and 'being friendly is easy and it can make the world of difference.' We agree. Pupils are very smiley, eager to help and hold doors open for visitors. One teacher told us: 'They are nice, all-round children who are keen to get involved.' Children are given credits for everything from academic work to being helpful and these are displayed on board in the main corridor. Bad behaviour is not an issue. As head says: 'Being good isn't uncool here.' House system in place, although Beachborough calls them 'clubs.' Four clubs named after former heads – Boardman, Carder, Chappell and Sprawson. School council, with reps from year 5 and above, comes up with host of ideas. When head suggested getting rid of ties for girls, the girls voted to keep them – so they did. Pastoral care excellent. Anti-bullying policy clearly stated in parents' handbook, which lists everything from school fire drill to morning and afternoon snacks (called 'ghab' at Beachborough, apparently the Indian word for 'snack.') Assemblies held several mornings a week, including Wednesday service at pretty parish church next door and Thursday hymn practice.

Children travel to Beachborough from all over but mostly from within a 20-mile radius and from as far afield as Towcester, Bicester, Banbury and Milton Keynes. School has strong links with RAF Croughton, US communications base seven miles away – 35 children from base are pupils at school. Parents include farmers, motor racing employees (Silverstone is on the doorstep) and hedge-fund managers. Asked whether Beachborough is a 'snobby' school, forthright head says 'too right it's not. I can't stand that sort of thing.'

Parents have high praise for the school. One mother told us: 'Beachborough has the most special atmosphere. It concentrates on all the essentials. It's caring, it gives the children individual attention and it has academic rigour.' Another says: 'It's good across the board. The children are stretched rather than pushed and leave here with an inner confidence.' Parents pleased with school's good communication links (including weekly newsletter emailed every Friday), buddy system for new pupils and the way their views are listened to. The school day ends at 3.30 up to year 2, 4.30 for years 3 and 4 and used to end at 6.45 for years 5 to 8. But when parents of year 5 to 8 children asked if the school day could end earlier, the school readily obliged. Parents now have the choice to collect their children at 4.30 or let them stay till 6.45, for activities, tea and prep (helpful for working parents). Lots of family events. The Beachborough Association puts on quiz nights, coffee stops, and even a family camp-out, where 70 families gamely pitched tents on the front lawn.

Beachborough fizzes with energy and enthusiasm. It's a school where children get the opportunity to learn, play and grow up in their own time. They are encouraged to have a go at the vast array of activities on offer, while being supported and nurtured throughout. As a year 8 girl about to head for senior school told us: 'It's like a family here. I don't want to leave.'

The Beacon School

Chesham Bois, Amersham, HP6 5PF

- Pupils: 470 boys including up to 24 in the nursery • Ages: 3–13
- Fees: £5,025–£14,625 pa • Independent

Tel: 01494 433654
Email: admissions@beaconschool.co.uk
Website: www.beaconschool.co.uk

Interim headmaster: Since September 2013, Mr Michael Spinney, who is a former Beacon School headmaster and takes up the reins again until a new head is appointed, after the departure of Paul Brewster to take up an international post at Repton School.

Entrance: Takes one class of 3-year-olds into the nursery, adds another in reception, and two more in year 3. Non-selective in the early years, mildly selective from year 3 upwards: 'We want to make sure that they're going to fit in with what we've got, and that we can deal with their needs'. Also takes some five to 10 boys into year 7, including boys from state primaries who have not got places in the local grammar schools, as well as 'those whose parents think they would benefit from two years at the top of a prep school rather than at the bottom of a secondary school'.

Exit: Between a third and half of the boys move on to the local grammar schools at 11 (some 60 per cent take the 11+ exam and around 70 per cent of those are generally offered places). Clear favourite is Dr Challoner's (the head is one of the Beacon governors), but the Royal Grammar School, High Wycombe, and one or two other schools, including Merchant Taylors' and Berkhamsted, also have candidates. Up to half of the 13-year-olds go to a range of boarding schools including Bradfield College, Wellington College, St Edward's Oxford, Rugby and Eton. A similar percentage generally go to Berkhamsted (local day options are limited), with a few to Merchant Taylors'. Record number of awards in 2013 (10), including academic, drama, music, art and sports scholarships

Remarks: This is a classic boys' prep, set on the edge of green Chiltern beech woods yet just down the road from the Metropolitan line. Many families moved out of London when they had children and quite a few fathers still commute to the City whilst mum stays at rural home: 'That supports well-mannered, disciplined children,' said the previous head. The school is based round what was once a Buckinghamshire farmstead, with brick and timber ex-barns and farmhouse now vaulted dining rooms and classrooms.

The nursery and pre-prep have their own separate building and playground, giving a cosy and secure start to school life in bright, colourful classrooms. The nursery has an academic basis, but with plenty of time for fun and creative activities.

Lively, interactive teaching. When we visited, year 3 were writing an adventure story they had spent several lessons planning, year 4 were learning about advertising and persuasion, and year 8 were doing a French crossword. We also saw boys painting intricate pictures of the insides of various types of fruit. Lots of trips to eg British Museum, Hampton Court, Bracknell Discover Centre and Apsley Paper Mill for hands-on learning.

Two libraries, one for the pre-prep and one for the prep. The main library is in the heart of the teaching area, complete with iPads, which are particularly popular with the boys, and, during our visit, a net containing chrysalises in the process of turning into butterflies. Two full-time librarians are part of the school team and help teachers enthuse boys about reading.

International Studies is an eight-term programme during years 2, 3 and 4, which introduces boys to the bare bones of a different major world language each term plus elements of that country's culture and geography. 'The purpose is to broaden their horizons, and to get them fired up and excited about learning languages.' They begin French during the final term in year 4, and start Latin in year 6. Some parents are very enthusiastic; others feel that children should learn a language from nursery upwards, 'but we think that inoculates them against fun and interest.'

Non-selective at pre-prep level, so a fair ability spread, though around half of pupils are in the top 10 per cent of the national ability range. Setting by ability in increasing numbers of subjects from year 3 upwards, with specialist teachers for most subjects. 'Fantastic' learning support department gives excellent help for eg dyslexia and dyspraxia with no stigma; plenty of differentiation in class ensures everyone achieves well. At least one boy in a wheelchair has gone happily through the school (his class organised a reunion at a bowling alley to ensure he could take part) with the help of lifts to upper floors.

The previous head pioneered the Beacon Certificate of Achievement (BCA) as an alternative to the narrowness of the common entrance format. Although it follows the same academic path, it also records achievements in sports and creative arts, and 'reflects the full range of prep school education'. It has cumulative and modular assessments as well as end of year exams. 'This suits most boys better, as they are working for immediate goals rather than just far-off exams, and it breeds better work habits.' Half of the boys who don't move at 11 to grammar schools are aiming at local day schools Berkhamsted or Merchant Taylors', which set their own entrance exams. All the other secondary destinations (apart from Eton and Radley, which insist on Common Entrance) are 'incredibly positive' about the BCA.

However, an exam set by only one school clearly has potential disadvantages with moderating standards, and the Beacon is one of six prep schools currently piloting the Prep School Baccalaureate in the hope that prep schools nationwide will adopt it as a common entrance alternative. It encompasses the same principles as the BCA, but with an added emphasis on skills such as critical thinking, independent learning and teamwork. 'It's rather exciting: we're involved in cutting edge stuff, leading the way in the curriculum.'

Sport very important, and not just for the stars: a parent reports that her 'geeky' son has greatly enjoyed playing for C teams. Sports hall, Astro pitch, outdoor pool and sports field round the back, with a cross-country course following footpaths across soft Chiltern hills. A climbing wall provides 'a diversion before going home'. Strong programme of matches, with football, hockey, rugby, cross-country, cricket, tennis and swimming teams competing with great success. Plenty of boys are successful at county and national level.

Drama is increasingly high profile. 'We're known to be strong at sport, but boys in particular can get really engaged in the performing arts, and we want to give them every opportunity.' There is a new studio theatre in the Old Barn, but at present the sports hall doubles up as the venue for large-scale performances. 'It is a very good sports hall but a less good theatre.' However, redevelopment plans are afoot which include a 300 seat theatre by 2014. But in the meantime boys perform enthusiastically in eg Joseph and the Amazing Technicolour Dreamcoat, and have great success in drama and public speaking exams.

'Superb' head of music encourages everyone to sing and many to play. The Beacon Young Musician of the Year competition is keenly contested, everyone composes and can record their own music; we heard an enthusiastic drumming class. Huge range of peripatetic teachers, many of them professional musicians. There are four choirs, an orchestra, a swing band and lots of ensembles.

Excellent, well-equipped DT department, and strong art with imaginative work displayed round the school. Food tech also popular – fab new Food Technology Centre – with some 40 boys competing in Beacon Mastercook 2013 (the winner cooked 'very tasty' coconut pancakes); other after-school clubs for different age groups range from rounders to warhammer.

'Lovely' teachers and a very caring feel, say parents. Newish director of pastoral care is overseeing a structured programme of PHSE lessons throughout the school. 'You can get exam results and win matches, but unless you help boys understand themselves and learn how to deal with pressure, you're not doing your job.' The new programme includes developing emotional intelligence and well-being, and talking honestly about issues.

Parents tend to be 'highly aspirational', and the previous head felt his job was to square the circle between their ambitions for their own sons and the needs of the whole school, 'to look after all the children's interests.' They also tend to get closely involved in events such as food and wine tasting evenings, cake sales and the summer ball, and most are hugely positive about the school. One parent expressed a general view: 'It's given my son an excellent start in life'.

Beaconhurst Junior School

Linked school: Beaconhurst

52 Kenilworth Road, Bridge of Allan, Stirling, FK9 4RR

• Pupils: 160 • Ages: 3–11 • Fees: £7,899–£10,626 pa • Independent

Tel: 01786 832146
Email: headmaster@beaconhurst.stirling.sch.uk
Website: www.beaconhurst.com

Exit: Most to senior school.

Remarks: See main school.

Beatrix Potter Primary School

Magdalen Road, London, SW18 3ER

• Pupils: 370 (but will be 400 soon); all day, 50/50 girls and boys • Ages: 3–11 • Non-denom • Fees: • State

Tel: 020 8874 1482
Email: Info@beatrixpotter.wandsworth.sch.uk
Website: www.beatrixpotterschool.com

Headteacher: Since 1988, Mr Stephen Neale MA DipEdTec (mid fifties). Popular, easy-going, very hands on, dedicated – attends every PTA event, takes charge of wall displays throughout the school, deals with all IT problems (a bit of a computer whizz). Has taken on the role of SENCo himself, with support from LSAs. Married to a Polish opera singer with one, now grown-up, son. Variously described as chaotic, friendly, relaxed, cynical – certainly a bit of a maverick.

Entrance: Strict admission policy, detailed in the school's joining letter. Those living closest and siblings are the first priority. Children who gain a place in the nursery are not guaranteed a place in the junior school. However, Wandsworth, like most London boroughs, does have a high mobility rate and parents moving to the area should always give it a whirl – 15 places per year come up on average in the different year groups. Perceived as a middle-class school, it is, in fact, totally non-selective and is merely defined by its location. Now in the third year of two-form entry, so a wider catchment area than before.

Exit: Some to private secondaries: Wimbledon High, Thomas's, Emmanuel, Dulwich, JAGS – but increasing number to state schools. Large numbers to St Cecilia's; Burntwood Secondary and Ernest Bevin (especially since the opening of their new sports centre) also popular. Other state secondaries are Wilson's, Southfields, Willington, Graveney and Wallington Girls'.

Remarks: Some schools just stand out when you visit them – like buying a house, you know immediately if you like it. Positively fizzes with energy and enjoyment. The corridors may be crammed with books and toys and apparatus, but they just add to the atmosphere of a place where children are encouraged to use every tool available to gain knowledge. Each pupil has their own individual computer housed in a separate IT suite. Not an effete centre of learning following government guidelines and ticking all the boxes all of the time – here the children's education comes first. An Ofsted inspection mildly baulked at some of the teachers' recording of pupils' progress but could not fault the behaviour, enthusiasm, personal development, enjoyment and positive attitude to learning which pupils display.

Sports coaches are brought in for lacrosse, cricket, netball, rugby and football. Dance lessons happen from year 1, music, singing and percussion all very popular, with drama classes every day. Large play area outside with a vegetable patch and pond to tend. Adjacent is a sports field belonging to Wandsworth, so available for the school's use. Also has links to schools in US through the Fulbright Project. Links to schools in Denmark, Germany, Holland and Poland are promoted by group projects using Skype and email. Each year the top two classes enjoy trips to Arran or Plas Menai, personally escorted by Mr Neale himself. Something for everyone at this school – 'It's a very happy place'.

Beaudesert Park School

Minchinhampton, Gloucestershire, GL6 9AF

• Pupils: 390; 200 boys, 175 girls, including 90 pre-prep. Up to 110 boarders – 90 flexi board, 20 weekly board • Ages: 4–13 • Mostly C of E • Fees: Day £7,500–£14,850; Boarding £19,355 pa • Independent

Tel: 01453 832072
Email: office@beaudesert.gloucs.sch.uk
Website: www.beaudesert.gloucs.sch.uk

Headmaster: Since 1997, Mr James Womersley BA PGCE (early fifties), educated at St Edward's and Durham where he read 'economics, history and rugby'. Previously at Eagle House, then Emanuel (London) before spending seven years at The Dragon School, Oxford, as a housemaster. Humorous, charming, straight-talking, eg 'Pre-testing for CE really screwed things up for everyone'. Teaches year 6 PHSE, referees and reads to pre-prep children (jumps onto piano at exciting points, to delight of little ones). 'I'd like to do more but, sadly, the days when the head took lessons, then whizzed round on the tractor mower have gone,' he confesses.

Beaudesert has nearly doubled in size during Mr Womersley's headship. 'He's raised the school's profile,' says one parent.

'Before, it was a local Gloucestershire school. Now people know of it in London.' Makes an impressive double-act with wife Fiona, who is right at the heart of Beaudesert. She comes from a prep school family – 'You either love it or resent it,' she says. 'I love it. Something makes you laugh every day.' 'They really complement each other,' adds a parent. 'She's brilliant on the pastoral side. You feel there's nothing they haven't seen before.' Three sons who all went through Beaudesert – eldest at Loughborough; middle just leaving and youngest still at St Edward's. Head's name cause of intense focus – 'It's very funny hearing the little ones trying to say it,' says his wife.

Entrance: Not selective. Fed by independent local nurseries; now has its own nursery. Children transfer from pre-prep automatically via basic assessment. Pupils come mainly from within 30 miles.

Exit: Despite strong connections with many senior schools, head is insistent that Beaudesert remains truly independent of any senior school and unbiased advice is given for the next stage of the children's education. Children currently move on to a wide spread of senior schools, though most go locally. Big clutches to Marlborough, Cheltenham College, Winchester, Eton, St Edward's, Cheltenham Ladies' and St Mary's Calne.

Remarks: School perches on top of Minchinhampton Common, overlooking one of Stroud's 'Golden Valleys'. Main building imposing mock-Tudor Victorian, with Cotswold stone wings. Mr Womersley has overseen a steady programme of building during his tenure, with clever use of space providing new classrooms, science labs, art and design studios.

Thirty acres of wooded grounds and grass terraces step down to games fields and Astroturf. Friendly, straightforward and happy children are an active, tree-climbing, den-building lot. (An onlooker at the Cheltenham Literary Festival complimented staff on their children looking 'so fit'.)

Three class groups per year, pupils setted for maths, English, languages (French, Latin from year 6) plus science in top forms. Approximately 60 children receive learning support, on withdrawal basis. Strong maths, Latin. 'A child in pre-prep who, we feel, would struggle with common entrance would find the prep stage difficult,' says Mr Womersley. 'It's a quite demanding curriculum.'

Smiley staff, average age of 40. Interactive whiteboards throughout and Apple Macs. Parents are invited for talks on cyber-bullying and internet safety. Great emphasis on effort and encouragement in all fields: Mr Womersley (who sets great store by people being 'purposeful') hands out weekly certificates. Prizes awarded for wide range of achievements besides academic. Parents get three-weekly reports on top of termly ones.

'Sport for everyone' taken very seriously – school regularly sends out 20 teams on match days. Children yomp over the airy common to rugger pitches ('You need an extra sweater watching matches here, but we never cancel fixtures,' says Mr Womersley). Sporting activities include golf, sailing, fly fishing and polo – school polo team particularly strong, thanks to keen polo-playing parents.

Strong music (senior choir recently sang Evensong at Worcester Cathedral.) Good art (lovely old-fashioned pottery room) and drama: 'My daughter, a real drama fiend, loves having plenty of opportunities to perform. The school seems to get particularly good LAMDA results, too,' says one parent.

School has very flexible approach to boarding – can do occasional nights, flexi or weekly. Virtually all children board before going on to senior school. Children, including weekly 'regulars', think flexi boarding works very well. 'It can mean the difference between having to employ a nanny or not,' says one parent. Boys' dormitories in particular pretty packed, but homely. Friday nights hugely popular for the football league:

children raise their own teams, the more wackily dressed the better. Wide range of activities for daychildren and boarders, from crochet to bushcraft skills (wildly popular). Recent innovation is the Beaudesert Badge, a programme of evening activities ranging from bread-making and shoe-polishing to pitching tents and moth-catching. 'It's not for every child, but those who do it love it,' says one parent. Food is good and plentiful. Dining room self-service, but with emphasis on manners – no eating off trays. An earlier Good Schools Guide report described Beaudesert children as 'not streetwise', which head takes as a compliment. 'We've found the school is approachable, and any problems are dealt with quickly,' says one parent.

Families comprise solid Gloucestershire and environs, with a mix of Bristol professionals and, recently, more Londoners relieved to find 'a country bolthole' for their children. A sociable place, for parents and children alike. Many families are related or know each other, and it really does arrange leaves around Badminton Horse Trials ('Only because many parents are involved'), though one parent comments, 'People joked we'd need ponies and labradors to come here, but we've found everyone to be very friendly.'

A happy, country prep school, where friendly, uncomplicated children enjoy being children.

Bede's Preparatory School

Linked school: Bede's Senior School

Duke's Drive, Eastbourne, BN20 7XL

• Pupils: 390 pupils, 250 boys/ 140 girls, 39 boarders • Ages: 3 months – 13 years • Inter-denominational • Fees: Day £8,895–£15,135; Boarding +£7,035 pa • Independent

Tel: 01323 734222
Email: prep.admissions@bedes.org
Website: www.bedes.org

Headmaster: Since September 2013, Mr Giles Entwisle, previously deputy head of Highfield School. Degree in French, politics and economics from Loughborough, PGCE from Bristol. Has worked entirely in prep schools, teaching modern languages at Cottesmore, Forres Sandle Manor and Holmewood House before joining Highfield. Married to Regina, with two daughters, he is probably the only prep school head who teaches juggling.

Entrance: No formal entrance exam – taster day at the school where staff can assess children's strengths and ensure any support needs can be met.

Exit: Most to Bede's Senior School eight miles away. Others to eg Eastbourne College, Ardingly, Brighton College, Lancing, Roedean and St Leonards-Mayfield.

Remarks: Situated at the end of Eastbourne seafront on the cliffs – wonderful sea views and a quick jaunt to the beach, but still sporting enough greenery for a rugby/football/cricket pitch. Years 6 – 8 also use the plethora of pitches at the senior school. Perched high on the cliff top is a large, architecturally-pleasing home where Mr Peter Pyemount, the founder of the now flourishing St Bede's Trust and head of history, lives. Tells pupils that the house was strategically placed so that he could keep a vigilant eye on their antics – so, of course, the pupils revel in recounting his more mischievous behaviour. He is apparently a 'thrilling and inspirational history teacher' given to the spontaneous acting out of battle scenes.

The school has sympathetically been extended to include large, light classrooms, ultra-modern dining hall, renovated boarding houses, large sports hall, swimming pool, pre-prep and nursery school, all with high spec fire and safety systems. Due to the trust's culture of inclusion for parents, staff, and pupils, everyone has similar to a coded Oyster card and is given clearance to suit their timetable.

Rather like the senior school, they have identified a particular cohort in the middle range of ability that were not reaching their full potential and are putting systems in place to address this. 'The ethos is about teaching children how to think, not to concentrate on tests and league tables which often neglect their thinking development. We are not concerned with spoon feeding or being academically the top dog.' Many children come here because they have floundered elsewhere, but, 'They really do cater to the individual; this is not mere lip service. I saw my child grow in confidence and it was uplifting seeing him succeed'.

Around a third have a special need of some description; strong learning support specialist team run by 'an amazing head of department' with a reputation for unlocking the potential of pupils, and many come through to study medicine, engineering, politics at prestigious universities. The head believes that if a child experiences success in one area, that often transfers to success in other areas. A gifted and talented coordinator; extension classes and master classes are given to the growing number of pupils spotted as very able.

All the heads of department speak with gusto about their subject. This sense of fun comes through when visiting the science department – live reptiles on display, a replica solar system (and tales of when the self-confessed Peter Pan head of science lit up the science room, which could be seen from the beach). The boarding houses are across the road from the seafront and children can board from year 5, although special circumstances will be considered.

Every year group does a dramatic production where everyone takes part. Lots of sport, serious and recreational, and the top teams can specialise five afternoons a week. Good to see girls' cricket at prep school level, plus the staff coach netball to local schools. Huge range of clubs and activities. Art is a strength – school exhibits at festivals. Annual year group concert plus all the usual choirs, orchestras, drummers and guitarists that compete for St Bede's Got Talent concerts.

An innovative school, not worried about ticking boxes. It is hard not to be impressed with the facilities and continuing success of the school obviously delivering on its promise of a good, all-round education for all abilities.

Bedford Girls' School Junior School

Linked school: Bedford Girls' School

Cardington Road, Bedford, MK42 0BX

- Pupils: 280 girls. All day • Ages: 7-11 • Fees: £8,145 pa
- Independent

Tel: 01234 361910
Email: juniorschool@bedfordgirlsschool.co.uk
Website: www.bedfordgirlsschool.co.uk

Head: Since September 2012, Mrs Carolyn Howe, previously deputy head and acting head of pre-prep at James Allen's Prep School in London.

Entrance: Prospective pupils attend an assessment day, where skills in writing, reading and maths are assessed. They also take part in art, science and a circle group discussion.

Exit: Virtually all transfer to the senior school across the road at the age of 11.

Remarks: The junior school is housed in a large Victorian house opposite the senior school, with delightful gardens and brightly decorated classrooms. Strong links with the senior school, with sixth formers popping over the road to help juniors with their reading. Parents we spoke to were full of praise for the way the transition from the junior to the senior school is handled. Year 6 girls go to the senior school for science lessons and take part in a host of activities there. 'It felt like a very natural transition,' one mother told us. 'There were no nerves on my daughter's part by the time she got to year 7. She was raring to start.'

Bedford Preparatory School

Linked school: Bedford School

De Parys Avenue, Bedford, MK40 2TU

- Pupils: 375 boys; 17 full boarders, 6 weekly/flexi boarders
- Ages: 7-13 • Fees: Day £10,806-£14,160; Boarding £18,330-£22,836 pa • Independent

Tel: 01234 362274
Email: prepinfo@bedfordschool.org.uk
Website: www.bedfordschool.org.uk

Headmaster: Since September 2013, Ian Silk, previously deputy head of Bishop Stortford's Junior School, and before that a housemaster at Ardingly College. An English and drama specialist, he is married to Sarah, and they have two sons.

Entrance: Mainly at 7, 8 and 11. Classroom visits in the Christmas term prior to entry, followed by assessment tests and an interview in January. If a place is not achieved in the first year, don't despair – could be one on the next time of trying.

Exit: Most move up to the senior school, via an internal test.

Remarks: Everything a small boy could possibly want, with academic excellence that more than satisfies his parents. Some specialised staff cross over with the senior school but predominantly a separate teaching team.

Situated in a southern corner of the campus, whilst it does share some facilities with the senior school, has its own entrance, own buildings and own all-weather games pitch. Good combination of old and new, the library and English and history classrooms being in the oldest building, the Inky – from 'incubator for fledgling Bedfordians'. Lots of light and space in the main Wells Building (mid 1990s), well-equipped science labs and great art facilities. Plenty on display everywhere. Music and sport mirror the senior school – excellent new music tech facilities including GarageBand composing/recording programme, and refurbed Astroturfs. Good pastoral care. Lovely and cosy for the first two years – own building, class teachers and library.

Modern purpose-built boarding house for 30. Foreign Office and overseas residents roughly 50 per cent. Homely, houseparents popular with boys and parents alike. Each boy has his own sleeping area for personalisation but is still in the security of a dorm.

A happy school full of cheerful, confident boys. A great place to start the serious educational years.

Beech House

Linked school: Bolton School Boys; Division

Chorley New Road, Bolton, BL1 4PA

• Pupils: 225 boys and girls, 50/50 split • Ages: 4–7 • Fees: £8,241 pa • Independent

Tel: 01204 434759
Email: info@boltonschool.org
Website: www.boltonschool.org

Headteacher: Since 2010, Mrs Deborah Northin, BEd, NPQH. Previously head of early years and infants at Westholme School, Blackburn. Married to a geography teacher, with two grown up daughters. Not much free time but enjoys walking with rescue dog Tessie. Forthright, but approachable, Mrs Northin has clear expectations of both staff and pupils. 'She does things her way,' states one mum, but admits, 'she's a fantastic leader'.

Entrance: Play-based, one-to-one assessment in the autumn of year prior to reception entry, with places offered in December. 'No formal skills in reading and maths required,' says head. 'We're looking for bright-eyed, curious children who ask questions'. If places become available in years 1 and 2 children are tested in reading, writing and numeracy.

Exit: In recent years virtually all children have gone to Bolton Schools junior departments, Hesketh House for girls and Park Road for boys. 'They're well on their way to being independent learners when they leave us,' says the head, 'and we never have to drill them'. Certainly parents enthuse that their children leave exceptionally well prepared for junior school

Remarks: Large, bustling infant school (three forms per year group, with 25 children in each form) housed in a beautiful, modern, architect-designed building. Bright, airy classrooms. Large outdoor spaces with plenty of colourful equipment; 'we have lessons out there in the real fresh air,' a year 2 girl tells us. Lots of computers (all classes have their own blog) and kindles for reading; iPads soon to be available for all. 'Parents are blown away by the facilities when they first come here,' says one parent. 'Mrs Northin seems to get whatever she asks for'. French taught from reception right through to year 2 by a native French speaker, and specialist teachers for music and PE also. Budding Beethovens can take piano lessons at extra cost in the school's own piano room. Fully trained SENCo, and school will assess its ability to cope with special needs on an individual basis in consultation with parents. Lift access to all floors.

'My sons are having the time of their lives here,' one parent told us, and this seemed to be the case in the oh, so cute reception ballet class we saw.

This is a smashing school, a welcoming place, where busy children can get on with learning in a happy and secure atmosphere, whilst having lots of fun to boot.

Beechwood Park School

Markyate, St Albans, AL3 8AW

• Pupils: 500 boys and girls, flexi-boarding and day • Ages: 2.5–13 • Inter-denom • Fees: Day £9,471–£13,539; Weekly boarding £16,764 pa • Independent

Tel: 01582 840333
Email: admissions@beechwoodpark.herts.sch.uk
Website: www.beechwoodpark.herts.sch.uk

Headmaster: Since 2002, Mr Patrick Atkinson BSc MIBiol PGCE (fifties). Deputy headmaster at New Beacon School, Sevenoaks, followed by 11 years as head of Lochinver House School. Talkative and affable, with an easy manner. Lives on site with wife Claire, an educational psychologist (doesn't work at the school herself, but is on hand to lend her support at school events). Their two children have now flown the nest after graduating from university.

Stresses the importance of a breadth of education – 'successful people have a balance in life', he says. Would love to see greater social mobility and less politicising of education. Ever the optimist, he (and the pupils) are eager to see more made of the woodland (is there a forest school in the making?) and would like a canopy for the outdoor swimming pool, but they battle against the trials and tribulations of planning legislation for Grade 1 listed buildings. 'We have to be creative thinkers,' he says, with slightly gritted teeth behind the smile.

Entrance: The school has a Montessori nursery on a separate site. All children are assessed prior to being accepted to the school (not applicable for the nursery). For reception children, expect informal assessment (school stresses this isn't ability testing, but assessing behaviour). Some year groups have waiting lists, so best to get in early.

Exit: The school is praised by parents for 'knowing the children', and parents and pupils alike are carefully navigated through the decision process. St Albans High School and Haberdashers' Aske's (Boys and Girls) are popular choices. Other contenders include local grammars, Berkhamsted and Haileybury. Respectable numbers of bursaries.

Remarks: Rural setting in west Hertfordshire, with far-reaching views over farms and woodland. That is, if you can find it. Our GPS took us down a muddy single track lane where we had to do a U-turn at a field entrance. According to school staff, this isn't uncommon, though they told us signage has now been greatly improved. The Grade 1 listed building and beautiful parkland have a rich history, playing home to barons, nuns and visits from royalty through the years. One effusive parent remarked it reminded him of Swallows and Amazons. We couldn't see any lakes, but we see what he means.

School caters for children up to year 8, with a separate (off-site) Montessori pre-school. Class sizes hover around 20. Setting begins in year 3, with a scholarship set in year 8. Pupils are prepared for 11+ and 13+ entry to senior schools. Parents we spoke to were happy with academics. 'The results speak for themselves', we were told. Boy to girl ratio is 60:40 up to the age of 11, when the majority of girls leave. A brave few stay on – 'I like to be different', said one. It is worth checking expected intakes for individual years as these ratios are not for everyone. Ethnic mix reflects the local demographic. Pupils commute from a 30-mile radius, many catching one of the school buses. There is a strong Christian ethos and assembly is held daily. Senior choirs sing at local churches once a term.

Around 10 per cent of pupils receive SEN support in school (principally for dyslexia, dyspraxia and Asperger's). No extra charge for this (three cheers), unless foreign language assistance is also required. Plenty of help offered in early years; children are weaned off one-to-one support by Key Stage 2. Staff promise the door is always open for children to return, although one mother has found this transition hard. 'It feels like my son gets less support now', she told us.

Classrooms vary from bright and modern in the junior school to more formal learning spaces for older children. Regency library was advertised as a wow factor by our young guides. Perhaps a little over-hyped (though we admired their enthusiasm) but it is well-stocked with antique books as well as a broad selection of children's literature. In the generous music block, we were treated to a recorder recital in one of the 15 practice rooms.

As you would expect with generous grounds, sport is important and the school has many successful teams, particularly in rugby and cross country, though we noticed that pictures of boys holding trophies dominated the news pages of the website. Pupils who don't make school teams are encouraged to develop as athletes with the aim that 'everyone can find something they are good at'. The 'sports for all' programme claims breadth, with sailing (for a select few), climbing and golf on offer alongside the more obvious, although this only truly kicks in from middle school.

Huge numbers of after-school activities – outdoor adventures to touch typing to Brazilian soccer – are a boon for working parents. Children are actively encouraged to take up an instrument and the head was keen to emphasise concerts and workshops. Five choirs, orchestra, drama, language clubs – 'my friend has really got into Greek this term' – and cookery are all on offer. Parents applaud the breadth. 'My seven-year-old does cello, football, cricket, drama and paper craft', said one. 'It is a well-rounded school'.

Pupils we spoke to were generally happy, apart from usual minor grumbles like 'too much homework' and 'food could be better'. We can't vouch for homework, but the lunch we sampled was adequate, if a little stodgy (schools says there are at least eight salads on the menu at each meal, sometimes more, food is generally considered excellent and menus are well-balanced). Parents are enthusiastic about the school too. We heard comments like 'the teachers know the kids well and have their eyes on the ball', 'it has met our expectations' and 'I wouldn't change a thing'.

Pastoral care is seen as a priority by the head. Pupils 'are aware of values' and enjoy a credit system awarded for good behaviour (our guide proudly showed us her badges and values booklet). School encourages good behaviour by 'supporting and challenging children so there is no time to be naughty'; the bad behaviour that does exist is managed with a debit system. Pupils we spoke to see it as a fair system. We heard no reports of bullying and while it was acknowledged that disagreements can break out, we were assured that teachers can be relied on to 'help them sort it out'. One parent (a former pupil himself) said that 'pastoral care was the key driver in choosing this school for my son', while another told us, 'I do have a few concerns sometimes, but I suppose it's hard to supervise that many children on the playground'.

Flexi-boarding is offered during the week (no boarding at weekends) in clean and modern dorms run by married houseparents. Roughly a third of all children in years 5 to 8 board, many staying a couple of nights each week: 'I'm not ready to board full time yet, so this is perfect for me', said one pupil. Boys and girls have separate dormitories, but share common rooms kitted out with air hockey, darts and Xbox. No mobile browsing allowed, but pupils can call home whenever they want.

Beeston Hall School

West Runton, Cromer, NR27 9NQ

- Pupils: 145; 85 boys/ 60 girls; 65 boarding • Ages: 7–13 • Mainly C of E, but provision made for RCs. • Fees: Boarding £17,220–£23,115; Day £10,761–£15,717 pa • Independent

Tel: 01263 837324
Email: office@beestonhall.co.uk
Website: www.beestonhall.co.uk

Headmaster: Since September 2009, Mr Robin Gainher BSc (mid forties). Read government at the LSE. Previously deputy head at Cranleigh Prep. Married to Ali, who assists in the learning support department, runs a popular cookery club and hosts a weekly 'come dine with us' competition with year 8 boarders. Two of their three daughters are at the school.

Breezy and affable. Parents view him as an 'educationalist' who is bringing the school up to date and is looking at things with a fresh eye. He says, 'We don't need more gadgets,' so the focus is on teaching and an open approach towards staff development – 'Teachers need to have time to think'. Enjoys being in the classroom whenever possible. Also clearly sensitive to pupils' emotional well being and keen that boarders should feel Beeston is home from home – dorms have been tastefully homeified and rules re mufti relaxed: an astute move.

Since his arrival several new appointments as the old brigade retire and a 'few formal edges knocked off' – but a traditional approach is still maintained when it comes to manners, meals, shoe cleaning and no to computers during break times (how sensible). Plays golf when he can and is passionate about family, food – and Leeds United football club.

Entrance: Informal assessment day. Relatively unselective but not a forgone conclusion. Mild to moderate dyslexia and dyspraxia can be accommodated – occasionally severe needs. 'Fun day' before entry with potential boarders getting a chance 'to try it out'.

Means-tested bursaries (general, academic, art, music, sport) plus in-house help for parents who fall on hard times. Sibling discounts if three or more children are at the school at the same time. Ten per cent discount for Forces families. Academic, music, art and sports scholarships now available for year 3 and year 7 entry.

Exit: 'super deputy who knows the ropes' and gives good advice. All get to where they want. Wide spread of schools and respectable clutch of scholarships (13 in 2013). High proportion board out of county. According to one father, 'Beeston plays on a national stage and sends kids anywhere. It's not parochial'. In 2013, pupils to Ampleforth, Eton, Gresham's, Harrow, Langley, Norwich School, Oakham, Oundle, Queen Margaret's, Repton, Tudor Hall and Uppingham.

Money matters: Means-tested bursaries (general, academic, art, music, sport) plus in-house help for parents who fall on hard times. Sibling discounts if three or more children are at the school at the same time.

Remarks: Most children become boarders before they leave, although the school says that day children play an important part in after-school life. High proportion of children come from county, boarding families so those who board are well primed and, with the help of 'brilliant' matrons, settle quickly. Everything about the place says boarding. Homely, well-ordered atmosphere with parents making positive noises about the level of pastoral care.

Children 'create a good impression' and seem happy, relatively unsophisticated and tremendously polite – door holding and standing up when adults enter a room are de rigueur. No PTA but parents kept in touch through email contact with their child's tutor, frequent newsletters and informal parent forums. Recently introduced clarion call texting service has seen the demise of days when parents forlornly appeared for a just cancelled match.

Teaching is traditional with children 'encouraged to succeed' by cheery staff, but new independent learning strategies and wider curriculum initiatives introduced. Sets from year 6 upwards: scholars, sets 1 and 2 (the latter for the less able). French from year 3 and Latin from year 5. Head says the breadth of 'the school suits a wide spectrum of abilities and, whilst it isn't an academic hothouse, kids do very well'. Some parents thought the super bright might not be stretched enough, but now a master of scholars has introduced a more defined and expanded scholars' programme. Learning support also given a boost with the appointment of an experienced, enthusiastic head of department (SpLD). She works with two part-timers and five teaching assistants, with support mainly in class – removal from lessons only when absolutely necessary. 'Link books' keep lines of communication open and parents can pop in for an informal chat after midweek matches.

Low key Sheringham is close by (older ones are allowed to venture out) and the setting is rural – National Trust woodland, heathland and the North Norfolk coast a stone's throw away. Plenty of space to run around and everything, everywhere immaculately maintained with the original core, a Regency house, carefully adapted and extended. Facilities, whilst not super glossy, are 'good for a country prep' – upgraded labs, library with sofas, spacious but acoustically challenging dining hall, Astro pitches, tennis courts and a recently completed large, heated outdoor pool.

Good, airy art department plus balcony for potential art scholars – achieves consistently scholarship-wise. Three drama productions a year – drama teacher from the Theatre Royal, Norwich. Cherry on the pie is the music school – more than generous, given the number of pupils. 'Music is "a cut above" – one of the school's great strengths,' according to parents. Over 80 per cent learn an instrument, including the harp and bagpipes. Plethora of music groups, choirs, ensembles and exam successes. Recently created ukulele band is brainchild of the infectiously bubbly head of department, who raves about the inclusivity of the instrument.

Parents feel that, for a small school, sport does well. All the usuals plus sailing on the Broads (school owns a fleet of Toppers which can be used in the hols) and shooting – extra special, as they've won the prep school league for seven consecutive years. Plenty to do out of hours – eclectic range of clubs: Japanese, origami, veg growing, 'shaking up Shakespeare', fencing, and numerous excursions and theme days, including Beeston's Got Talent. It's a Knockout on the beach plus twice-weekly visits from the ice cream van are firm favourites, whilst outside speakers, including a woman who rowed across the Indian Ocean, broaden minds.

Traditional boarding prep with a young at heart, ambitious head. Quietly confident, well-disciplined children who are 'expected to have a go'. It does well by its pupils and turns out friendly, eager, purposeful and confident children. Good foundation, particularly for those who move on to public school.

Belhaven Hill School

Dunbar, East Lothian, EH42 1NN

- Pupils: 65 boys, 55 girls; 105 board, 20 day • Ages: 8–13 • Non-denom • Fees: Day £13,785; Boarding £19,875 pa • Independent

Tel: 01368 862785
Email: headmaster@belhavenhill.com
Website: www.belhavenhill.com

Head: Since 2009, Mr Innes MacAskill BEd (fifties), who was previously head of Beeston Hall School, Norfolk, having spent 17 years at Caldicott, ultimately as deputy head. Educated at Bedford Modern (a Harpur Trust school) he specialised in history and sport and still – for his sins – runs the first XV. Married with three daughters, all now up and away, he is a hands-on head, and really enjoys knowing each child well and taking a fatherly interest in their concerns. Believes that school has to be 'homely and comfortable'. Popular; supported by wife, Sandy, lively and fun – this is a partnership. A fellow head says he 'has all the best bits of headmastering under his belt and actually likes the children' – not a universal characteristic.

Entrance: No test, but register as soon as possible. Children spend a day at Belhaven the term before they come. Informal test when they come in but no official screening.

Exit: About three a year to Eton, Ampleforth, Oundle and Queen Margaret's, York, otherwise to a wide range: Glenalmond, Harrow, Loretto, St Mary's Ascot, Downe House, Fettes, Radley, Rugby, Winchester, Sherborne, Shrewsbury, Strathallan, Uppingham, Marlborough, Benenden, Stowe, Bryanston.

Remarks: Numbers still as high as ever before and lists full for the next few years. 'Rash of new younger staff employed recently – they really care,' said one mother of three. School has 'a good combination of experience and enthusiasm' and 'brilliant house staff, matrons and learning support teacher'. Pupils not assessed on entry but glitches picked up early, tame ed psych, plus qualified SENCo, ditto assistant as well as two further assistants (one the husband of a housemistress in the midst of a career change who, as a trained engineer, is a whizzo at maths). The learning support base, The Hut, has now been fully revamped (to the envy of some non-learning support pupils). Withdrawn from class, one to one, small groups, dual teaching – all disciplines covered – at no extra cost; though if a child has severe and particular difficulties school is relaxed about parents employing additional help.

Scotland's school for toffs (head prefers 'traditional families': dearie me), which specialises in sending the little darlings to public school in the south. Dubbed Hogwarts for Muggles by Edinburgh Evening News. The school went co-ed in 1995. Boys based in late 18th century sandstone house (surprising long interlined flowery curtains in window seat in hall) with tower and imaginative additions; eight new classrooms, music school et al, but still a bit of a rabbit warren. Dorms recently revamped with carpets and pin boards, alas bunks now a thing of the past (and round the world ditto).

The snazzy girls' house has a spit new circular rumpus room, known as the Rosie room (after the much loved but probably only a distant memory for older members of staff, Rosie Conran Smith, who died – of cancer – at the school some 20 years ago) with a plasma television and plenty of brightly coloured beanbags to snuggle up in. More long double interlined rose patterned curtains. No books or newspapers spotted in either the boys' or the girls' common rooms, though head assured us there were libraries aplenty just steps away, but bored children are good at instant literary grazing.

All pupils online, two computer rooms. Own laptops not a problem. Pupils setted in core subjects – maths, English, science and langs for final three years, but lots of toing and froing. Tutors for top two years, otherwise classroom based, with form teachers and class sizes down to 10/14. No scholarship stream as such, but more a case 'of children extended through setting and provided with opportunities for further support in activities and prep' etc. Vast choice of extracurricular activities, bright creatures steered towards the more intellectually challenging.

Occasional Greek on offer (but not a lot recently, though all this may change as new classics enthusiast on staff), drama and dance increasingly popular; magnificent sports hall which adapts for school plays. Piping much encouraged and well taught with FPs the core of pipe bands in English public schools and much in demand at weddings and funerals; eight chaps and two chappesses were in Edinburgh playing for the Pope at the time of our visit (as was Mrs head, so we didn't meet). Manicured grounds including two cricket pitches, new cricket nets, six tennis courts, masses of Astroturf, a putting course and an 18-hole golf course 'over the wall'. Head plays too, though the clubs in his office belonged to one of the boys. Bracing sea air. Streams of unbeaten teams in almost every discipline. Regular trips to Hillend artificial ski slope. Young encouraged to have their own bit of garden in which they take great pride: current competition is for the biggest sunflower (school will be serving dried sunflower seeds next). One member of staff, along with the children, uses all the apples from the orchard to make one big brew of apple juice for the children and staff to drink (head suspects this has something to do with cider making) but expect home made apple pies, dumplings and crumbles. Grub for all in the dining room – benches and tables – with quartered oranges on offer during our visit.

Last HM Inspectors' reports could have been written by the previous headmaster himself, care commission expected, should be a shoo-in. Happy social parents and children, with masses of input from locals – tranches of farmers/Charlotte Rangers from East Lothian, plus the usual quota of quite grand children from the North and an increasing gang from south of the border, usually with Scottish connections. Girls fully absorbed. School is flourishing.

Belleville Primary School

Webbs Road, London, SW11 6PR

- Pupils: 800 boys and girls • Ages: 4–11 • Non-denominational
- Fees: • State

Tel: 020 7228 6727
Email: info@belleville.wandsworth.sch.uk
Website: www.belleville-school.org.uk

Headteacher: Since 2001, Mr John Grove (early fifties) BEd MA, previously head at West Hill Primary School in Wandsworth. Two children, both at university; partner also works in education. A man consumed by his job, who found Belleville failing in 2001 and has worked uncompromisingly to make it the most sought-after primary school in the area. In his rare moments off, admits to being a season ticket holder at Chelsea FC. A visionary, who still gets unexpected hugs from the youngest of his charges as he roams the corridors.

Entrance: At 4+, 120 places, in four forms of 30. Heavily over-subscribed. Usual local authority admissions criteria: special requirements, siblings and those living closest to the school (no more than 276 metres away for a first offer). Popular on-site nursery takes 52 children each year, but nursery place does not guarantee entry to reception in main school.

Exit: Since Bolingbroke Academy opened up the road in September 2012, approximately half to this brand-spanking-new non-selective school, which local residents campaigned for. Others to a range of local state and private schools, including Alleyn's, Dulwich, Whitgift and Emmanuel. A few sit successfully for Graveney School, Tooting, which has a grammar stream. A steady trickle to the Lycée Kensington and the German School Richmond, reflecting the number of European families in the locality.

Remarks: Already large, Belleville is set to get larger. Glossy new site at Meteor Street houses a reception and a year 1 class, and will become a one-form entry campus for the school's full age-range as time goes by, complementing the existing three-form entry at Webbs Road. Head admits intake will probably have to stop at 900, but clearly frustrated by lack of space in this cosmopolitan neighbourhood, where two-bed conversions with a view of the poor go for £700k. 'My dream is to take one of these nearby private schools, turn it into a state school and expand,' he told us, his eyes gleaming behind their gold-rimmed specs. 'Only one?' we asked. He smiled.

As well as a penchant for the state sequestration of private property, Mr Grove has a passion for doing things well. Housed in what was once a dark and gloomy Victorian maze, imaginative building work has turned Belleville into a really beautiful school, where old-time space and solidity meets modern light and technology. Walls have been knocked through, windows replaced, venetian blinds fitted in attractive colours, and everywhere painted to look bright and fresh. Intelligent, creative use of ICT is integrated into the fabric of the school and is awesomely good: iPads and tablets are mounted in every corridor, displaying slideshows of school events, offering information, etc. Classrooms have ICT projectors and interactive whiteboards, teachers use visualisers (for dinosaurs like this reviewer, that's a powerful digital camera that points downwards and projects onto the teacher's computer/projector screen, so that books, objects, etc can be magnified and displayed clearly to everyone in the room). We were gratified and impressed to see this head, at least, insisting that the children learn on both Macs and PCs, as well as on desktops, tablets, netbooks and smartphones, so that they can cope with whatever system a given environment has in place. But none of this has come at the price of old-fashioned excellence. Work on the walls showed both handwriting and content of a very high standard. Ofsted stated that 'pupils achieve exceptionally well', and everywhere we saw children working with a lively yet calm focus. 'The behaviour is excellent here,' asserts head, 'We have 800 children and I never have to raise my voice.' We believe him.

Specialist teachers are employed for art, music, PE, dance, French and computing, and the results are splendid. Wonderful artwork – inspired by, for instance, Van Gogh and Kandinsky – is everywhere, produced by the children from a modest-looking art room with love and skill. When we arrived, we were deafened by a terrific workshop on Sengalese drumming, which turned out to be a weekly event for all the classes. (One lad, so moved by the spirit that he couldn't sit still, suddenly left his djembe and did an impromptu breakdance, to fond applause). The children all learn French, and were keen to show us how much they knew.

SEN provision is strong and mostly integrated, with plenty of one-to-one support for individuals provided during regular lessons. 'We don't withdraw unless we have to,' confirms head. Parents report themselves satisfied: 'sEN support is really good'; 'The school's been brilliant both at pushing my abler child and supporting my younger one.'

Belleville is one of only five primary schools in London to be awarded the status of National Teaching School, and professional development is inescapably at the heart of everything it does. In each year group there are teachers whose core job is to improve pedagogy and teaching, and the children certainly seem to enjoy their lessons. 'The teachers are really nice'; 'The teachers are fair'; 'They really try and make the lessons fun and they do succeed'; 'The teachers are very good people,' were just a few of the comments we heard. Parents agree: 'We've been impressed with the enthusiasm of all the teachers'; 'The classroom assistants have been an invaluable resource'; 'The staff are brilliant and the academics are brilliant'; 'My children have always had fantastic teachers.' There was also praise for the many clubs on offer, both in and out of school, with parents particularly grateful for the breakfast and after school clubs: 'They cover long hours, which is very helpful for working parents, and have a wide range of activities.'

The school prides itself on its diverse community, although its location in the heart of Yummy Mummy Central (as Clapham Common is locally known) inevitably accounts for the very high proportion of articulate, well-mannered, middle-class children that we met there, most of them Caucasian. We heard murmurs from a few parents of different ethnic backgrounds, who, while remaining extremely positive about the school, felt that it could do more to acknowledge their children's needs. Belleville's motto, proclaimed in huge posters everywhere, is 'Relentless Drive For Excellence', and it's possible that this relentless drive has occasionally knocked a few obstacles out of its path. We couldn't help noticing the almost universal youth of the teaching staff, with its few older members hived off to the school's smaller Meteor Street site, where, presumably, fewer people could be offended by their wrinkles and grey hairs. (And in fact they too will soon be mostly replaced by younglings, head assures me, but will be redistributed at Webb's Road, where they can hide amongst the 20-somethings in plain sight.) But by any measurable standards, Belleville is an outstanding school. 'My children are thriving at Belleville, and are valued,' was a typical parental comment. 'My child has done as well as she could do,' was another. 'I can't imagine her doing better at a private school' . Which is just as well, really; if Belleville gets any more successful, there won't be any left.

Belmont House Junior School

Linked school: Belmont House School

Sandringham Avenue, Newton Mearns, Glasgow, G77 5DU

• Pupils: 100 boys and girls • Ages: 3–11 • Fees: £7,848–£10,308 pa • Independent

Tel: 01416 392922
Email: admin@belmontschool.co.uk
Website: www.belmontschool.co.uk

Head: Ms Linsay McDonald

Exit: Majority to senior school

Remarks: See senior school.

Belmont Mill Hill Preparatory School

Linked schools: Mill Hill School

The Ridgeway, London, NW7 4ED

• Pupils: 415: 40 per cent girls, 60 per cent boys • Ages: 7–13
• Fees: £15,276 pa • Independent

Tel: 020 8906 7270
Email: office@belmontschool.com
Website: www.belmontschool.com

Headmistress: Mrs Lynn Duncan

Entrance: By entrance test, reference and interview.

Exit: Nearly all go on to the senior school.

Remarks: Popular prep with few adverse comments.

Belmont Preparatory School (Dorking)

Feldemore, Holmbury St Mary, Dorking, Surrey, RH5 6LQ

• Pupils: 220; roughly 40/60 girls/boys; 40 weekly boarders; 180 day pupils. • Ages: 2–13 • C of E • Fees: Day £7,470–£12,780; Boarding + £2,700–£5,850 pa • Independent

Tel: 01306 730852
Email: schooloffice@belmont-school.org
Website: www.belmont-school.org

Headmistress: Since 2006, Mrs Helen Skrine, BA PGCE NPQH FRSA (forties). Educated at St Albans High School for Girls, Exeter and London Universities. Taught at Wrekin College, Greenacre School, Chinthurst Preparatory and Highfield School, Liphook, before taking up headship here. Met her husband, John, at university; they have two sons, Henry and Giles, one at university and the other at Marlborough. Enjoys watersports and and sailing (currently restoring a yacht) and has a passion for music; loves walking her dogs. Two were parked in the homely study (squidgy sofas) when we arrived. 'They're good for breaking the ice and excellent pastorally: children tell them their troubles,' ventured the head.

Children approve of the 'good-strict' head, saying she's brought a lot of new ideas, improved the school and can act too. Popular with staff and parents – 'she's tightened things up but kept the family feel that is so important to Belmont'. Shrewd and efficient but with a wonderful blend of care and compassion. We were about to meet with the head when a worried child came along: child was prioritised. We waited – would you have wanted it any other way? Teaches and feels it is essential to do so – 'That way I really get to know the children'.

Entrance: Main points of entry: 2+, 7+ and 11+. Broad range of ability and keen to maintain this. Pupils assessed during a whole day using verbal and non-verbal reasoning and time spent with appropriate teaching group (the two 'on trial' when we visited thought the place amazing). Two form entry from reception onwards with younger early years children in a purpose built building. Only one or two girls now leave at 11, with the majority staying till 13. 'I wanted my daughter to stay at Belmont until 13. Once a couple of us committed to staying here, others followed suit,' said a parent. Sibling policy, but no fee reduction until third child, and a good many travel long distances. Bursaries (up to 100 per cent) available from year 3.

Exit: Most to schools in south, eg Epsom College, St John's Leatherhead. Royal Grammar School Guildford, City of London Freemen's, Bedales, Brighton College, Reed's, Lancing, Reigate Grammar, Bradfield, Sherborne, Milfield and Hurstpierpoint. Approximately a quarter of pupils gain awards, mainly to local senior schools. One or two academic awards annually. Head a great fan of boarding and keen to encourage parents to look further afield at 13+ – some go as far as Gordonstoun. All Belmont pupils sit common entrance or scholarship in year 8

Remarks: Normal common entrance curriculum alongside key stage 2 and 3, to make sure those moving into state sector are catered for (no Latin). Two sets for maths, French and English in years 5-8 with general streaming for science and humanities. Smallish classes throughout, maximum 16. Science, history, geography, maths, English, French, games, PE, music, art and DT (called Studio 4) taught by specialist staff in specialist rooms. Bright and breezy pre-prep, good indoor and outdoor facilities. We discovered a class of wee ones delighting in the humour of Shampooed and Cinderburg, and others dressed as pirates, not for a special day but to help their stories come to life. Little Belmont 'a godsend,' added one parent. Recent inspections have been excellent.

Music not yet as head would like: three choirs and an orchestra but still room for growth. Sufficient keyboards for whole class teaching. Major musical production in spring term sees 80 children on stage and numerous eager hands helping with everything else. Recent major refurbishment of theatre including recording facilities. Christmas productions involve all; form assemblies turn into major events and it's okay for boys to dance – some even do tap. Fabulous drama produces young pros – one pupil acted with Derek Jacobi, another on the West End stage with the Von Trapps, and another with Johnny Depp. Sports teams compete against those from local schools; good offerings in art with art scholars most years.

Very good provision for dyslexics and other SpLD. Assessments carried out on anyone flagged up, at any time, either by parents or staff – so no worries if 5-year-old Freddie develops his dad's dyslexic traits. Youngsters can be supported in English and maths through Belmont's Learning Support Department or, in extreme cases, at Moon Hall – a separate but co-located school that utilises some of Belmont's facilities. Indeed we love the way the two schools play off each other's strengths: instant help for any child who may need significant support at whatever level is reciprocated via Moon Hall pupils using Belmont for lunches, PE, boarding and extracurricular activities. 'My daughter was bright but struggling with spellings. Help at Moon Hall put her back on track – a real bonus to be able to get timely specialist help for those odd hiccups.' (Note no link with Moon Hall's more distant offshoots, Moon Hall College and Burys Court.)

An idyllic setting. Bit of a sat nav nightmare to get to (seriously hairy roads), but 65 acres of woodland and outstanding natural beauty soften the blow. All-weather floodlit pitch, sports hall and outdoor heated pool (cover on the wish list), go-karting track, low-ropes, high wire and two adventure playgrounds keep youngsters busy in free time. Making Celtic round houses in Celtic style when we visited: 'Typical Belmont,' commented head. Sports fields rented from local country estate across road as school's 65 acre site is on a fairly steep hillside.

Variety of clubs. Boarding offers flexi and weekly options. Boarders stay in main house with separate wing for girls (currently 10). Parents a mix of first time buyers and old hands. A good number find fees from income. Headmistress is available at any time, except when teaching. Informal opportunity for all parents to talk to staff over tea on Friday when collecting pupils.

A refreshing honesty about the children: 'Oh, are you from the book?' one asked. On hearing the affirmative he ventured, 'And how many pages does it have?'

A secure, happy prep school experience lets children be just that. If the child's got it – the school will bring it out; if the child doesn't quite cut it, school will stand by and put everything in place until they do. Second chances not a problem here. On the up.

B

Belmont Primary School

Belmont Road, London, W4 5UL

• Pupils: 470; boys and girls • Ages: 3-11; • Non-denom; • State

Tel: 020 8994 7677
Email: office@belmont.hounslow.sch.uk
Website: www.belmontprimaryschool.org.uk

Head: Since 2010, Ms Verity Coates MA PGCE (late forties). She has been in various roles at Belmont since 1996, including deputy head from 2005. Ms Coates graduated with a degree in mathematics from Newnham College, Cambridge in 1987 and after a PGCE at York and a brief spell at a London primary school she worked abroad in Africa. On returning to England in the mid 90s, Ms Coates started as a class teacher and SEN coordinator at Belmont and is fiercely loyal to the school.

Keen to press her commitment to state education, she appeared anxious about Belmont being perceived as the middle class answer to independent schooling. Tight-lipped when challenged on the question of Sats results and the high numbers of pupils who have private tutoring – she is determined that her staff too get some credit. Quite right too.

Entrance: Preference given to siblings. Next in the pecking order are those who live within the Primary Admissions Area – 'catchment' to you and me. In recent years, even living in the catchment has not guaranteed a place at the school. Children in public care, those with medical/social needs come high up in the pecking order. After that – don't even try. Very over-subscribed. Parents are known to rent property within the area just to qualify, and then...? More hope from year 2 however as a steady trickle leave to go to prep school/move out of London. Places are snapped up though and school tends to be full all the way through to year 6.

Exit: About half to Chiswick School, although the numbers are decreasing with the advent of competition in the area. A clutch to West London Free School and Hammersmith Academy as well as the usual numbers to Twyford, Lady Margaret, Gunnersbury and the Green school. The rest (about 20 per cent) to local independents, including Godolphin and Latymer, Notting Hill and Ealing High, Latymer Upper, Hampton, Ibstock Place. The occasional one to Colet Court at 8 as well as at 11.

Ms Coates asks for a financial contribution for the school reports required for entry into such schools. Lots of outside coaching during years 5 and 6 to prepare for independent school entrance exams.

Remarks: The reluctance of the head and her staff to welcome us to look round this super oversubscribed, well-funded state primary (or indeed respond to our messages) bemused us – especially considering that Belmont is one of the most successful and popular state primaries in West London, with seven applications for each place.

The sunny, enthusiastic (and overwhelmingly white for this inner London area) pupils bubbled with enthusiasm and love for their school as they showed us round. An abundance of facilities – from musical instruments, playground play equipment, books and materials to the brand new stage for dramatic performances. Results are excellent, showing much higher than expected progress between key stages 1 and 2 and a quarter of pupils in their final year sitting the optional level 6 in reading and maths.

The school caters for an affluent corner of Chiswick and the catchment area is becoming ever tighter. Families from sumptuous houses in the Bedford Park area can no longer expect to get a place. Were it not for the council accommodation on the school's doorstep you might not get the social mix one would expect in an inner London state primary school at all. Head keen to give precise statistics: 52 per cent of pupils from minority ethnic groups. In any event a first impression of faces in the playground is that there is an unusually high proportion of white middle class kids. Those who would not come under the umbrella of middle class or British tend to come from Eastern Europe, a few affluent UK residents from say, Canada or Sweden. This ain't your typical London primary.

This big bustling school is housed in a large, three-storey brick building that benefits from the high ceilings, large windows, well proportioned rooms and wide corridors typical of Victorian buildings of its kind. A generous refurbishment programme has resulted in shiny polished floors and child-friendly primaries and pastels (plenty of aqua and primrose) painted on the walls – helping the building to fall firmly on the side of happy, cheerful school rather than gloomy Victorian mental institution.

Far from being the rabbit warren of most independent schools in the area, Belmont is beautifully mapped out, with two classes at either end of each spacious floor, each one charmingly named after fruit – apples, pears, cherries. The main hall in the middle space between classrooms is used for play (reception and year 1 – lots of dressing up and imaginary play goes on here), assemblies (years 2 and 3 on the middle floor) and drama and gym (years 5 and 6 on the top floor). As well as the classrooms on the fringes of the hall there are yet more rooms – housing musical instruments galore – drum kits, pianos, flutes, various percussion, two well stocked libraries, two ICT suites (the juniors have the luxury of one computer each, one between two for the infants) and dedicated SEN provision. Teaching up to the end of year 2 is mixed ability. Setting in maths and English arrives in year 3. Two sets – the higher being slightly the larger and, therefore, up to 32 children to the lower set's 28-ish. The upper set has just one teacher, no classroom assistant being needed with these children because, of course, they are motivated and keen to learn. We couldn't see much problem with the lower sets either.

About 20 per cent of children identified as having special educational needs but a very small proportion of these have statements (nine pupils). One of these on the autistic spectrum, no one currently in the school with Downs. School has coped in the past with more severe special needs, but children must be able to climb stairs.

About a quarter of pupils don't have English as a first language (about 43 different first languages other than English recorded) but no marked difference in the performance of these children – credit to the school. Dedicated part time EAL teacher as well as SEN coordinator with a team of teaching assistants give support in the classroom. Sats results in all subjects are at least 10 per cent above local and national averages and are far higher by year 6. Those with EAL needs are seen individually or in small groups for as long as necessary, until they are up to the general standard. Teaching assistants support individuals, pairs or groups under the supervision of the SENCo. A reading recovery teacher sees individuals who, by year 1, are falling behind – with 'fantastic' results. When we visited, there had been a relatively high turnover of staff (head assures us that this is a result of career progression, maternity – no reflection on the school). Five male teachers – always a bonus. Years 3 to 6 have 40 minutes of French weekly. Everyone has two hours of physical activity weekly.

All classes have class music lessons and learn singing with a specialist teacher. In addition to class music, many learn individually – often more than one instrument. Recorder is offered to the whole of year 3 and there is a choir. Swanky staging facilitates an annual production from year 6. Other year groups, sometimes working together, also put on shows each year. Photographs on display suggest a high level of dramatic productions, much supported by parents, many of whom are 'in the arts'.

Good sports provision. A school sports partnership linked to Chiswick School and an outsourced sports programme (football, netball and athletics) in addition to members of staff teaching sport. On Friday afternoons here there is 'enrichment time' when for 30 minutes children can choose from a wide variety of activities, from Glee Club to comic making. Strong after-school club provision. These include, as well as the sport and music, Big Bang Science and Doughlightful – a clay modelling activity.

The locality is certainly urban – school is on a crossroads with Sainsbury's and Starbucks opposite, lots of residential streets and light industry all around, near the tube and on a bus route. But once inside, the enormous playground creates a safe, comfortable and peaceful environment. The Belmont Home School Association – PTA to you and me – raises between £20,000 and £30,000 each year. This has helped make the playground ever more luxuriant, with designated spaces for quiet reflection, a wilderness garden, covered areas for performances with costume boxes, lots of bike sheds, a super climbing wall painted by parents and plenty of gardening boxes replete with flowers, herbs and plants. At playtime out come the toys (from hula hoops to skipping ropes, racquets and balls) and the place is filled with the sound of happy laughter.

The early years spill out beautifully into carefully designed outdoor play areas, secure from the rest of the large playground. The nursery is particularly roomy and attractive – 52 places with sessions of a maximum of 39 children, an a la carte choice of mornings or afternoons or a combination of whole days and half time sessions. Three large rooms, own toilet facilities and a large kitchen area ('mummy sometimes comes in to help us cook', said an excited three year old) as well as access to the hall and library. Few chic little independent nurseries provide as much as this. Everyone eats in the school canteen and the number of pupils having cooked lunches delivered by the borough increases all the time. The rest bring their own.

Ofsted hasn't done a full report since 2007, when school was judged 'outstanding'. Head is greatly aided by a posse of 'liberal middle class' parents only too eager to help in all areas of school life, including arranging fundraising events to enable disadvantaged pupils who might not otherwise be able to afford to take part in trips etc. She is aided, too, by an excellent governing body, as well as by a good relationship with her local authority. A very small number of exclusions in previous years, but none for some time. A proper and well-understood system of sanctions. Also an established homework system with extension work on the school website for those who want to push their offspring further – this school is working on all fronts.

Many parents commented that they were sometimes frustrated by the blank wall that meets their follow up questions on their child's progress and results. 'Teachers can be cagey', remarked one parent, 'which makes me nervous. I might be surprised'. If you can cope with this and a certain complacency ('we don't need publicity', remarked the head at one point), then this is a no brainer – an excellent state school with most of the advantages of an independent school without the fees.

Bentley Church of England Primary School

School Lane, Bentley, Farnham, Surrey , GU10 5JP

• Pupils: 105 boys and 105 girls, all day • Ages: 4-11 • C of E • State

Tel: 01420 525010
Email: admin.office@bentley.hants.sch.uk
Website: www.bentleyschool.co.uk

Headmistress: Since 2012, Mrs Katy Pinchess (forties); began her career as a buyer of children's books for Waterstones before settling on teaching (her mother was a head teacher, so it's in the blood). Experience includes setting up CET Primary School Westminster, a free school in central London. Returned to Hampshire and joined Bentley C of E after a stint as headmistress of Bordon Infants. Keen to build on 20-year legacy of previous head Phil Callaway, who transformed Bentley from two-room village school into highly sought-after primary through personal dedication and judicious financial management. Parents seem confident that she will step into his rather large shoes and say, 'Everyone's really pleased, she's a lovely person.' Energetic and hands on, she is married with two young children.

Entrance: Sought-after primary school and always over-subscribed. At the time of our visit almost all places were taken by children from the catchment area of Bentley and Froyle. Any remaining out of catchment places (very few) usually go to siblings of a child already in the school. Routinely has a waiting list for reception and years 1 and 2.

Exit: About two-thirds plump for Eggars School in Alton (local state secondary). One third chooses independent education; local private schools include Alton Convent, Churchers, Guildford Grammar and High Schools and Lord Wandsworth College.

Remarks: Founded in 1842 on land given by the Bishop of Winchester, Bentley C of E has been modernised and expanded several times since the turn of last century. Still sits in a pretty bucolic location more than 150 years later, next to a winding country lane surrounded by cottages, fields and hedgerows. It's very easy to imagine how this typical village school might have looked in Victorian times. Charming it may be, but any similarity to old fashioned education stops as soon as one crosses the threshold. Bentley is a vibrant, modern little primary school which punches well above its weight.

Eleven and 12-year-olds regularly achieve outstanding results in year 6 Sats tests (well above the national average). Some 97 per cent of students score level 4 or above in reading, writing, maths and science; the one or two that score below this, almost always have statements. Two or three manage a stratospheric level 6; 100 per cent pass rate in maths and English. With a full-time staff-to-pupil ratio of 1:20 and average class sizes of 30 children, we conclude that Bentley is fortunate to have some excellent teachers, ably supported by learning support assistants in each year group. 'Teachers are so enthusiastic and their energy reflects on the children.' Most unusually in a state school, everyone learns French. Rest of curriculum as expected; topic work links the disciplines, especially literacy, science, geography, ICT and history. Although classroom atmosphere is relaxed and very friendly, children appear busy, engaged and enthusiastic – even at the tail end of a science lesson just before the lunch bell. ICT provision is good; school has largely moved away from fixed terminals to laptops and tablets; contributions from very active Parent, Teacher and Friend Association (PTFA) keep these up-to-date. Wireless network throughout and interactive whiteboards are in every classroom (not always the case in village schools). Reporting system is fairly informal, via regular parents' evenings and written reports at year end. Head says, 'Meet and chat sessions for parents happen several times a year [for reading, maths and spelling].' Parents add, 'There is very much an open-door policy.' School looks after the gifted and talented as well as those with special needs. Deputy head works with the most able in small groups in years 5 and 6; special needs assistant in every class works with children requiring extra help (almost always classroom-based).

Naturally, Bentley isn't blessed with acres of playing fields like its independent cousins, but manages remarkably well with the resources it does have. Reception and years 1 and 2 have their own playground and equipment, fenced off from the 'big children'. Years 3 up use a separate courtyard playground at the front of the school. The 'back playground', a grass pitch at one side of the school, is marked out for games, eg football, cricket, tag rugby, athletics and rounders. Boys' teams drawn up from year 3 onwards – girls wait till year 5, and main focus is on boys' sport. Adjacent woodland area has a trim trail through the trees. School also enjoys the use of much larger, council-owned recreation ground for running and sports matches. The children showing us round said wistfully that they wished they had more access. Sighed the head, 'Health and safety doesn't allow us.' Swimming (at nearby Treloar School's pool) once a week for year 3; year 1 get a taste of tennis. Bentley has nonetheless notched up a respectable sporting record. Recent successes include: national six-a-side football championship runners-up, under-11 county football champions, Isle of Wight rugby champions, under-10 and under-11 country cricket champions (girls were Kwik Cricket county champions and came 4th in Southern National Championships in 2013) and area winners of national dance and basketball finals. Those with a talent for sport get extra coaching sessions from specialists on Friday afternoons. Clubs include netball, fencing and gym.

Music has a higher profile here than at most state primaries and Bentley has a dedicated, if cosy, music room. A big draw has to be Mr Hoare the piano teacher, who plays in a rock band and seriously looks the part. No surprise, then, that at least 50 children are learning the piano. A good handful each learns violin, clarinet, guitar and various brass instruments. Small school orchestra and choir perform from time to time (lots of keyboards and instruments stashed in a cupboard next to the dining hall). A local secondary offers extra coaching sessions to musicians with potential. Two Christmas plays, plus a fully-fledged drama production in year 6 (Bugsy Malone) make full use of school hall. No dedicated art room, but plenty of evidence of creativity on display, eg Giacometti-inspired figures from coat hangers made by year 6. School puts on as many educational visits as possible and firmly believes in residential trips for juniors from year 3 up, eg to Gordon Brown Centre (environmental studies) and Calshot (activities and watersports). 'They do a lot of off-site stuff and pull in experts regularly, such as sports coaches and authors,' said a parent.

Aims to promote a kind environment; regular anti-bullying days are reinforced by discussions in classroom circle time. School's close 'family' feel means that 'new children are treated like celebrities.' The Vicar of Bentley (also a school governor) leads assembly once a week. Teachers take the lead in pointing out unacceptable behaviour (we observed a reception teacher doing just that) but no child is ever made to feel the black sheep. Staff will always listen to parental concerns. Classroom assistants are usually parents themselves and are quick to pick up on any problems. 'There's always someone there to look out [for the children] on a motherly level.' Older children are encouraged to take responsibility for younger pupils, eg year 6 students read stories to reception. Good array of clubs on offer after school, from the musical (orchestra, choir, guitar, recorders) through sporting (judo, fencing, netball, gym, tennis, football, basketball) to ceramics and science clubs.

Keen swimmers in upper years can go to Treloar pool before school to train. School canteen provides hot meals to around three-quarters of children every weekday (food is fresh, varied and inexpensive). PTFA raises money for the school (typically £15,000 per annum) which helps to fund new building projects, purchase new books and technology, part-fund the very popular Bonfire Night and run one of the school's two minibuses. 'This means we can take an entire class out for a day trip.' Two class reps in each year group organise regular social events.

Located in rural Hampshire, the majority of families are inevitably white middle class, although we did spot the odd ethnic face here and there. Parents are very involved in the life of the school, helping out in the classroom, library, after school, on trips and during sporting events. 'A lot of people are prepared to give up time and money to make sure we continue to do what we do.' They stress, however, that Bentley isn't overflowing with pushy types. 'The children all see the school as an extension of their family ... it's more than just a school.' Anyone with young children living within the catchment area and willing to get stuck in to school life will be lucky if they gain a place.

Berkhamsted Preparatory School

Linked schools: Berkhamsted School

Kings Road, Berkhamsted, HP4 3YP

• Pupils: 370; 195 boys/175 girls • Ages: 3–11 • Christian
• Fees: £9,480–£12,660 pa • Independent

Tel: 01442 358201
Email: admissions@berkhamstedschool.org
Website: www.berkhamstedschool.org.uk

Headmaster: Since September 2013 Jamie Hornshaw BEd in Primary Education, NPQH, currently studying MEd (forties). Previously head of the British School in Paris Junior School; has also been deputy head of Brentwood Prep. Trained as a PE specialist and has been national level hockey umpire. Two daughters at the school; wife teaches elsewhere.

Entrance: Children observed by experienced teachers at play and undertaking fun activities to determine their readiness to enter pre-prep. Skills and abilities also tested at 5+. Interview with head/deputy at 7+ and 10+ along with English and maths tests linked to key stage 2 national curriculum. The main feeders are local primary schools including Christ Church C of E, Butlers Court Combined School, Bridgewater School and St Thomas More RC Primary School, though pupils also come from Francis House Prep School and a variety of other independent preps.

Exit: Vast majority – about 90 per cent – go on to senior school, where the boys and girls study separately from 11-16 – a major attraction for many parents. Very few do not gain entry – appropriate warning given to those who might not. Does not provide help for those seeking grammar school entry.

Remarks: Tucked away amidst leafy residential roads, a stone's throw from the high street, offers much in terms of convenience and happy seclusion. Opened in 1998 as a result of a merger of the former single sex boys' and girls' prep schools. It shares many of the facilities of the adjacent senior schools but retains a more playful atmosphere. Climbing frame and swings opposite the headmaster's office and a colourful dining room with encouragement to eat your greens and be healthy. The food gets high praise indeed from the pupils, but lots more they like. 'The school should open every day. I get so bored at the weekend,' laments one girl. Busy calendar of trips and activities

designed to drive greater independence and skills for life. The Skern Lodge residential trip in year 6 particularly popular, but on a more day-to-day basis much to keep the pupils at school and relieve pressure on working parents. The prep offers years 3 – 6 day boarding until 6pm Monday to Thursday and until 5pm on Friday, and a wide range of after-school clubs until 4.30pm, and for pre-prep until 4pm.

Suits the sporty with ample opportunities to take part in external and inter-house competitions. Further up the school grounding in cricket, football, rugby, hockey and lacrosse pays off with regular success at regional and even national level. Older pupils have PE lessons at Berkhamsted Girls' sports centre over the road. Music is encouraged with free lessons in groups of three to four in year 3 and lots of opportunities to perform in the orchestra and choirs.

Ofsted recently ranked the pre-prep outstanding. It provides a good basis for learning and being part of a community, as does the rest of the school. Pupils are proud of it and parents comment that its value system, and that of the linked senior school, is particularly strong, making for a caring environment and happy children. A lone boy was fair smothered with female concern during break. The school chapel hosts regular assemblies, services and concerts, which reinforce the sense of unity, allowing a wide range of children to perform and drawing in parents. They also enjoy regular communication with class representatives and invitations to participate from the Friends' Committee.

It caters for a wide range of abilities, with setting in maths from year 3 and specialist teaching in most subjects in top three years. Results at the end of key stage 2 place the school in the top five per cent nationally (ISI inspection report). Years 5 and 6 now study Spanish, food tech and drama. Parents are confident that all children are challenged and supported as appropriate. Report diaries are completed on a weekly basis and open lines of communications maintained between parents and staff. SEN provision exists but not fêted. Learning support team deals with all specific learning difficulties throughout the school. Children are assessed regularly with extra help provided where necessary. However some concern that class sizes have a tendency to creep up, diluting individual attention and making some classrooms cramped.

Bought Haresfoot School in 2012 and the infant classes gradually transferring there, leaving Berkhamsted Prep to concentrate on KS2 pupils.

BGS Infant and Juniors

Linked school: Bristol Grammar School

Elton Road, Bristol, BS8 1SR

• Pupils: 330; 230 boys/110 girls • Ages: 4–11 • Non-denom
• Fees: £6,825–£8,700 pa • Independent

Tel: 01179 736109
Email: recruitment@bgs.bristol.sch.uk
Website: www.bristolgrammarschool.co.uk

Head of Junior School: Since 2011, Mr Peter Huckle BA MEd PGCE. Educated at Monks Park School, Bristol, read geography at Birmingham University and obtained a master's degree at Bristol University. Previously deputy head at Bristol Grammar senior school, where he taught geography.

Entrance: Entry by informal assessment up to year 2. Entry to junior school – mostly into years 3 and 4 but also a year 6 entry for those aiming at the senior school – by reading, writing and reasoning tests.

Exit: Nearly all to senior school, now without exam.

Remarks: For further information, see senior school.

Bilton Grange School

Rugby Road, Dunchurch, Rugby, Warwickshire, CB22 6QU

• Pupils: 315 boys and girls including 135 in pre-prep (Homefield); 45 full/weekly boarders, lots of flexi. • Ages: 4–13 • C of E (all faiths welcome) • Fees: Day £8,910–£17,190; Boarding £21,540 pa • Independent

Tel: 01788 810217
Email: rlb@biltongrange.co.uk
Website: www.biltongrange.co.uk

Headmaster: Since September 2013, Mr Alex Osiatynski (thirties), previously director of music of the Loughborough Endowed Schools foundation. Educated at Dulwich College and Oxford; PGCE at Roehampton. Has also taught music at Gresham's, The British School in the Netherlands, Smithdon High and Oakham. Married to Freya, with two young sons.

Entrance: Non-selective but placement test and interview for candidates – academic potential looked for (aim is to find something at which each child can excel). When spaces available children can enter at any time. Typically two form entry in pre-prep and three forms in older years, roughly 60:40 boys to girls.

Exit: Majority to senior boarding schools. Popular destinations include: Rugby, Uppingham, Repton, Oakham, Princethorpe and Oundle, with typically 10 scholarships a year, including Foundation ones to nearby Rugby School. Odd grumble that school is not well disposed to those who flee Bilton at 11; school's defence is that early leavers miss out on scholarships, responsibilities and the excitement of the final year, including cementing life-long friendships. Plus side is that occasional places appear for those from schools that finish at 11.

Remarks: Main school, decorated and extended by Pugin in the 1840s, consists of an elegant mansion complete with grand entrance bordered on two sides by high red brick walls, stunning Pugin chapel used almost daily (all children, irrespective of faith, expected to attend) and superb, uninterrupted views across the Warwickshire countryside. Inside, the trappings of 21st century classrooms and teaching blend seamlessly with classic wood panelled halls (teeming at break-times with earnest youngsters playing chess and snooker), acres of windows, tiled floors and creaking floorboards.

Looks, feels and is a traditional 24/7 country prep, with good old-fashioned values, frequent assemblies and, in line with its boarding ethos, full Saturdays (from Y4). Pitches, playing fields, a nine-hole golf course, large sports hall and well-maintained swimming pool make this a haven for the sporty, yet even the most studious child would be hard-pressed to dismiss the Bilton outdoors. Intrepid explorers are free to investigate the 100 acres of grounds and woods, grow their own veg in the organic garden, participate in outdoor crafts or toast marshmallows on the fire pit – even an outdoor classroom complete with log benches and swings – all duly risk-assessed.

Sport and the open air are a major constituent of school life, but the arty are abundantly catered for. The director of music is boosting quality and quantity of music (most play at least one instrument but aim is to involve all) – choirs, concerts, bands and orchestras perform regularly; drama is consistently strong

and popular, with the creative arts and DT abiding favourites. Activity weeks are emphatic highlights of the school year; our guides jabbered enthusiastically about the posse of dare-devil activities – climbing, canoeing, 24-hour survival – and jolly japes: mud diving, arm jousting and mandatory dorm raids.

The work hard, play hard ethos is tangible, but pressure isn't. Even in the final year prep is completed in school, a conscious move by the school to keep a lid on what can be a difficult and demanding time. Small classes, some setting in prep and wide curriculum for all – even tinies are treated to drama, dance, ICT and French. All try Latin. No weak lessons. RE popular (do ask about WOW), maths divides, reading is ably supported by good teaching, knowledgeable librarian and well-stocked library. We were treated to two science lessons (loved the lively informative posters, the work of artistic scientists, adorning the modern labs), a lively whizz and bang session and a traditional chalk and talk, perhaps typifying the breadth of approaches and styles. Indeed, we were reliably informed, by our young tour guide, 'Teachers look at the type of learner you are such as audio [sic], visual etc and try to teach you in that way'.

No BG mould – former pupils include humorist Miles Kington, actor Alexander Hanson, composer Sir Arthur Bliss (organ on which he learned to play fully restored and in regular use) and film star Rupert Evans, but BG children are easily identified by their impeccable manners: they ask to be excused from the table, shake your hand, look you in the eye ('We practise that,' say staff), stand when an adult enters the room and speak with confidence, interest and knowledge but no tinge of arrogance. Universally good rapport between staff and pupils; school exudes warmth. It's a lovely, cosy environment to grow and be a child in and, 'regardless of ability, they get best out of them,' say parents.

Can cater for a range of needs, particularly the dys-strata and ADD, but nothing heavyweight – 'My child is dyslexic but I always felt they were delighted to have him, no sense they were doing us a favour'. Takes a genuinely broad church, celebrates diversity, welcomes and looks after all. 'Learning support staff are so fab, so lovely and so helpful,' said one delightful, delighted youngster, but odd parental mumble that knowledge of SEN across core teaching staff is patchy.

Parents praise pastoral care, 'staff are good at setting boundaries and stamping on transgressions before they become serious'. Boarding houses are light, bright and comfortable. Communal areas offer TV, gaming, board games and jigsaws. Facilities and rooms (up to nine per dorm) clean and cosy but not clinical (encourages youngsters to decorate with posters and teddies). Atmosphere in boys' a little formal, more relaxed in girls'. Mixed reports in recent times about both quantity and quality of girls' boarding (do ask how many full, 11+ girl boarders), but new housemistress a unanimous hit, 'she has transformed things for the girls. I try to persuade my daughter to come home during the week but she never does'.

Eclectic parent body – new money, old and those with very little who work long and hard to pay the fees. Plenty happening socially and just as friendly, inclusive and welcoming to parents as they are to pupils – even a Saturday parental networking breakfast complete with bacon butties and croissants.

Aims to offer a truly rounded education where all are encouraged to try out new things, have a go, take part. Staff say, 'We let children explore the ox-bow, not just row down the river. We want them to take a risk, make mistakes, work out the rules.' Parents agree, 'BG children are enthused by life and learning.' One added, 'Thanks to Bilton, my daughter has had two extra years of childhood and a relatively untroubled path to adolescence – that's worth thousands to us.'

A breath of fresh air – a welcoming prep that builds confidence in the shy, empowers the gifted and is equally ideal for the imaginative, rumbustious child who can turn a tree into their castle. A tad Boys' Own (precious children would hate it), but those who are happy to join in, with a little rough-and-tumble along the way, should have the time of their lives.

Birkdale School Preparatory School

Linked school: Birkdale School

Clarke House, Clarke Drive, Sheffield, S10 2NS

• Pupils: 235 boys; all day • Ages: 4–11 • Christian • Fees: £7,716–£9,216 pa • Independent

Tel: 01142 670407
Email: enquiries@birkdaleschool.org.uk
Website: www.birkdaleschool.org.uk

Head of Prep School: Since early 2009, Mr Christopher Burch BA PGCE (early 40s). Educated at The Skinners' School and Goldsmiths College, University of London. Taught at Prince's Mead in Winchester and The Minster School in York before joining the The New Beacon (Sevenoaks) as lay chaplain and head of RE. Deputy head at Great Walstead School, where he and his wife also ran the boarding house. Has always coached sports teams and is a member of the IAPS sports committee. Married to Pip (librarian and teaching assistant at Birkdale Prep). They have four boys, all at Birkdale, two in the prep and two in the senior school. A keen sportsman, especially cricket and golf.

A real prep school man who believes that boys learn best when they are happy and busy and keen to retain Birkdale's academic rigour whilst improving the breadth of opportunities available to the boys. He gets involved in every area of school life from playground cricket to Warhammer club.

Entrance: At 4, by interview and at 7, by interview and exam held at the start of the Easter term – English, maths and reasoning. Boys come both from the independent and maintained sectors and from as far away as Retford, Doncaster – huge catchment area.

Exit: All but a handful on to senior school, rest to other independents or into the state sector.

Remarks: Elegant, late-Georgian house, overlooking the Botanical Gardens and once home of the Osborn family, he a master cutler. School acquired building in 1988 and did a spot of adapting. Now works well – servants' quarters house the computer room. Hall was probably purpose-built when the buildings housed either the grammar school or the nurses' training establishment – some slightly surprising alterations giving rooms glass windows onto corridors. Gloriously cosy tinies' wing with sandpits and a dedicated play area. All immobile items labelled in large letters – door, printer, computer, desk.

Not a school with a nursery – academic, starting French at 4, science right through, specialist teachers from 7 when boys are setted in maths. Sets in English and science at 9. Strong learning support, both withdrawn and dual teaching in class, no problems with dyspraxia, ADHD, ADD, all boys screened. Good library – boys decide which books they would like to read. Christian foundation, act of worship four times a week; about 12 Muslims and Hindus, no-one feels indoctrinated – indeed, non-Christians prefer to be at a school with a 'living faith'. Appropriate religious texts all over. Lots of choice at lunchtime – 'We like kids to finish their veg but we don't insist'.

Loads of first-time buyers, not all middle class by any means – 'Parents beggar themselves to come here'. IT throughout, oodles of computers, ICT lessons from 7. Computer-linked piano, and masses of music and theory of music, drums and percussion and other instruments (everything except the harp). Good orchestra and choir. Drama vibrant.

Significant liaison between staff at senior and prep schools – older boys and girls come and help out on a one-to-one basis, and future plans for staff from the senior school to visit the term before boys move up and teach the relevant classes to ensure continuity. Uses sports pavilion and big school games field and cricket nets and shares the extensive playing fields 10 minutes from the campus. Hopes to develop building here, with enlarged classrooms, particularly in the pre-prep department. Masses of post-school clubs, late waiting till 5.30pm and children can be left at breakfast club at 7.45am. Jolly, academic prep school – zinging.

Birkenhead Prep School

Linked school: Birkenhead School

57 Shrewsbury Road, Oxton, Birkenhead , CH43 2JA

• Pupils: 249 boys (girls to age 4) • Ages: 3m–11 • Fees: £7,035–£10,320 pa • Independent

Tel: 01516 524114
Email: enquire@birkenheadschool.co.uk
Website: www.birkenheadschool.co.uk

Head: Since April 2013, Mr Harry FitzHerbert, previously head of King's College School in Madrid. Married to Joanne; their two children have joined the school.

Exit: Majority to senior school.

Remarks: See senior school review.

Bishop's Stortford College Prep School

Linked school: Bishop's Stortford College

Maze Green Road, Bishop's Stortford, CM23 2PH

• Pupils: 445: 255 boys, 190 girls; 45 boarders; plus up to 120 in pre-prep • Ages: 4–13 • Non-denominational • Fees: Day £7,554–£13,071; Boarding £16,440–£18,681 pa • Independent

Tel: 01279 838607
Email: psadmissions@bishopsstortfordcollege.org
Website: www.bishops-stortford-college.herts.sch.uk

Headmaster: Since September 2013, Bill Toleman BA MSc, FRGS, (forties), previously head of Yarm Prep School. Read geography at Nottingham University and has since added a master's in educational management and leadership. Previously deputy head at King's St Alban's, Worcester. Teaches games and enjoys surfing, cricket and rugby. Married, with three sons.

Entrance: Entrance to the pre-prep is by a day's assessment; for the prep school by entrance exam.

Exit: Over 90 per cent to senior school, Bishop's Stortford College, a few to local state schools; those unlikely to make the grade warned in good time.

Remarks: Co-located with the senior school; has its own well-furnished and equipped classrooms, kiln room, art facilities, science labs and outdoor space but also shares some of the senior school facilities. Academic streaming starts in year 4 plus setting for maths. All pupils study Latin from year 5; Saturday school for everyone above pre-prep. Common entrance not offered but does follow the CE syllabus.

Heads work closely together to promote the same work hard, play hard ethos. Sporting success aplenty: U13 national rugby champions (strong links with local rugby club), and boys' and girls' U11 and U13 teams are county hockey champions. House system popular: lots of competitions, challenges, high profile visiting speakers etc. Prep boarding house offers the same boarding options as the senior school, including weekly boarding. Plenty of good work on show – lively and interesting displays, changed frequently, ensures latest achievements celebrated. Tuesday and Thursday afternoons dedicated to wide-ranging activities, with all pupils sampling photography, bridge, origami, cooking, golf and a whole lot more. Oldest pupils spend the first week of the year under canvas, team-building and developing leadership skills; trips and tours for others.

A happy, lively school that encourages curiosity and creativity; ideal starting point for anyone intending to hotfoot across the tarmac to the senior school.

Blackheath High School (Junior Department)

Linked school: Blackheath High School GDST

Wemyss Road, London, SE3 0TF

- Pupils: 290 girls, nursery part time and all day, 4-11 all day
- Ages: 3-11 • Non-denominational • Fees: £8,586-£11,034 pa
- Independent

Tel: 020 8852 1537
Email: info@blj.gdst.net
Website: www.blackheathhighschool.gdst.net

Head of Juniors: Since January 2012, Mrs Sarah Skevington, previously head of the early years section at the school. A law graduate from Sheffield University, she worked as a solicitor for seven years before retraining as a teacher. She has taught in state and private primary schools and joined Blackheath High in 2007 as a class teacher.

Entrance: By interview prior to entry at nursery level. Individual assessment at other stages.

Exit: Fifty per cent of year 7 in senior school is from junior school. Some move into the state system or, occasionally, to other local schools.

Remarks: The original purpose-built structure, in which the whole school started in the 1800s, is now thoroughly refurbished but still retains a lot of charm. The parquet hall, with its classical subject frieze, busts, columns and elegant double staircase, is a delightful memento of days gone by. Yet the classrooms surrounding it are all large, light and airy and the specialist rooms – science, art, music, IT (several) – are all bang up to date. A great gym which is also used for class assemblies, a brand new drama studio and a friendly, welcoming library – everything a girl needs for a good broad start to her education can be found here.

The nursery and reception areas are big, bright and enticing, with their own well-equipped playground outside. The bigger girls' play section is divided into several areas where they can experience different sorts of fun, and an excellent buddy system so no-one ever feels left out. Lovely art displayed everywhere; computers and interactive whiteboards in every class; enthusiastic music – choral or instrumental; everyone gets to join in. French taught from nursery and Mandarin in year 6. Bi-weekly use of the sports ground and swimming lessons locally.

SEN policy the same as the senior school. Children are all carefully watched and potential problems quickly identified. Communication with parents good. An excellent SENCo and lots of classroom assistants ensure that children get the help that they need. Any possibly difficult issues are dealt with quickly and sensitively.

A house system that works, with house points available for everything, from being in a winning sports team to writing a good story to just being kind. A school council where girls have to apply for specific jobs provides them with a good feel of responsibility for others and a taste of things to come.

The two girls who took us round were relaxed, confident and enthusiastic – good ambassadors for their school, eager to explain everything that was going on. In fact, all the children we saw seemed well behaved and happy, attentive in class and chatting away 19 to the dozen outside.

Parents have nothing but praise for a school that they feel is a happy place with a sensible approach to work and play. Not a hothouse but somewhere with a strong work ethic – 'My daughter works hard on her Sats in the morning and then really enjoys the play rehearsals in the afternoon'. Another parent was keen to stress the ability to build up a child's confidence – 'The teachers were very responsive, flexible and willing to work with me'. 'The bottom line is: how is your child performing? Here they really do get the best out of them.'

The Blue Coat School

Somerset Road, Edgbaston, Birmingham, B17 0HR

- Pupils: 564 (including pre-prep), 290 boys/274 girls; all day;
- Ages: 2-11 • C of E, but respect shown to many other faiths
- Fees: £7,050-£10,845 pa • Independent

Tel: 01214 106800
Email: headssec@thebluecoatschool.com
Website: www.thebluecoatschool.com

Headmaster: Since 1998, Mr Alan Browning (mid-fifties). Married to Helen, who is very much involved in school life; three boys, one who has just left Cambridge, one at Durham, and one at King Edward's School, Birmingham. Educated Clifton, Trinity Cambridge and Oxford. A musician, started career as a lecturer at Leicester University, thence to Blue Coat as director of music in 1982 and then deputy head and director of studies in 1993. 'He is someone who has lived and breathed the school for most of his professional career,' remarks a parent. This is of course both a strength and a weakness. A devout evangelical Christian, sees his faith as central to his role as headmaster. A man who is deeply committed to the interests of the children. 'This is a school that really cares about its pupils,' says the parent – a reflection of the head's most important priority.

Entrance: Usually at two into pre-prep or seven into prep. Test and interview at seven. Most children sign up at or near birth. The vast majority of the pupils enter the nursery (Buttons), then move through the school. Head keen to ensure that the girl/boy balance is maintained. Some places (dependent on natural wastage) at all levels but especially at seven. The vast majority of the children are recruited from the local Edgbaston and Harborne areas but the school is expanding its catchment area.

Exit: Blue Coat copes well and in many ways prospers in the demanding educational environment of Birmingham. The aspiration of most parents is to get their child into one of the super-academic King Edward VI schools or one of the many fine selective maintained schools in the area. Bearing in mind that the intake is an academically wide one, the school does well to get the largest single group into the King Edward schools. Others to schools such as Solihull, Edgbaston High, St George's School and Bromsgrove.

Remarks: The school was founded in 1722 by the Reverend William Higgs as a co-educational charity school (making it one of the oldest co-ed schools in the country) and now occupies a truly beautiful site in 15 acres of playing fields and gardens. Moved here in 1930 and the buildings, nearly all of which were erected at that time, are clustered around well-manicured lawns, giving the impression of a cloistered antiquity that would not be out of place in a public school. This is a true oasis of peace and tranquillity just outside the bustling heart of inner city Birmingham.

One might suppose that the avowedly Anglican tone of the school might fit uneasily within the modern multi-ethnic West Midlands community. Yet it all seems to work remarkably well and the school has retained its Anglican tradition – with its own lay chaplain – and lovely collegiate-style school chapel. At the same time it has a school roll of which about 50 per cent are from an ethnic minority background, and only some of the rest are in any sense strictly Church of England. Whilst there is no doubt that the Anglican voice is the dominant one, the school has gone to great lengths to invite visiting speakers from other Christian denominations and to introduce discussion of the Muslim, Hindu and Sikh traditions. This is a school where tolerance and mutual respect are taken very seriously indeed.

It has an innovative approach to language teaching, with all the children having the opportunity to taste Spanish before focusing on the main language, French. Science and art both flourish conspicuously, helped by some quite outstanding facilities. The success of so many pupils in the demanding King Edward VI entrance examinations says much for the quality of the teaching of the core academic subjects. As you would expect with a musical headmaster, music is especially strong, and the school has well-established links with Birmingham Cathedral and Birmingham Conservatoire, no doubt one reason why Sir Simon Rattle sent his children here. Chapel choir and four other choirs, numerous orchestral ensembles and 235 children learning at least one musical instrument. A notable recent addition is a Steinway concert grand piano. Lots of wonderful concerts, most notably special events at Symphony Hall (conducted by Rattle), St Paul's, Hockley and the CBSO Centre.

Boarding a thing of the recent past. The house system, originally designed for a predominantly boarding population, has been imaginatively reorganised to meet the needs of a day environment. Every prep school child is designated a house, uses its commonroom facilities and is under the care of a particular houseparent. This ensures that pastoral support is especially strong and each child has a very intense sense of belonging to a small, intimate unit. It also means that the school is able to offer very effective and well organised out-of-school care until 5.45pm – a great boon for working parents. Happy, well-motivated children.

A great deal of emphasis is placed on a wide range of games, and the hugely impressive sports centre (incorporating a 25 metre pool) enhances this sporting tradition. The school organises its own sporting tournaments, which are enthusiastically attended by preparatory schools from far and wide.

Blue Coat's enormous strengths make it the natural choice for parents looking for a traditional preparatory school education within this city.

Blundell's Preparatory School

Linked school: Blundell's School

Milestones House, Blundell's Road, Tiverton, Devon, EX16 4NO

- Pupils: 210; 95 girls/115 boys • Ages: 2½-11 • Christian
- Fees: £5,820–£10,305 pa • Independent

Tel: 01884 252393
Email: prep@blundells.org
Website: www.blundells.org

Head: Since 2011, Mr Andrew Southgate BA Ed (mid thirties). Raised in Maidstone, but venturing westwards for his degree in physical education and history at St Luke's, Exeter, he then spent the first 13 years of his career at Moulsford Prep, ending up as deputy head. Impossibly youthful, he came bounding out of his office to meet us, and his enthusiasm for Blundell's, Devon, prep schools, children and life in general is infectious. Though he denies it – 'I talk quite a good game of rugby,' he says – he looks pretty fit: there is talk of introducing a veterans' rugby team for keen dads, and he still coaches and referees. Married to Sarah, and their two children are in the school

Entrance: Prospective pupils spend a taster day in school, during which an assessment in English and maths is carried out.

Exit: Some 90 per cent of pupils join Blundell's senior school; however children are prepared thoroughly to take entrance exams for the senior school of their choice.

Remarks: Sited next to Blundell's itself, so able to use some of its facilities, but separately run and administered. Attractive semi-rural setting in 12 acres on the edge of Tiverton, where plans to enhance outdoor learning with the development of a pond and wetland area are advancing. Old red brick house has been beautifully extended and adapted to create light and airy spaces, where art is effectively displayed. We particularly liked the science lab and the fabulous and well-equipped food technology room, where sessions for everyone are timetabled, and where keen young Blumenthals knock up delicious fare for parents and any other lucky diners. School lunch looked and smelt pretty good too.

'The children who come here are a broad church,' says Mr Southgate, 'and our challenge is to accommodate them all; we're not an academic hot house.' His watchword at this point in the school's life is differentiation; it is heartening to note that a teaching assistant is placed in some top sets to stretch the most able. SEN is good, but this too will be looked at to enhance provision still further.

School's location in Devon means all its glories are there for the taking – roughy-toughy stuff on Exmoor, derring-do on the coast, culture in Exeter or Taunton and so on. Much loved by local community. One commentator said faintly dismissively that Blundell's is the school for those who will never leave Devon – and refugees from the urban rat race – but it's a beguiling proposition for all takers.

Bolton School Boys' Division Junior School

Linked schools: Bolton School Boys' Division

Park Road, Bolton, BL1 4RD

- Pupils: 190 boys; all day • Ages: 7–11 • Fees: £8,241 pa
- Independent

Tel: 01204 434735
Email: juniorboys@boltonschool.org
Website: www.boltonschool.org/juniorboys

Head: Since September 2008, Mr Stephen Whittaker (fortyish), BEd from Chester College, part of Liverpool University, and an NPQH. Taught at St James' CE school in Lower Darwin for six years before becoming deputy head of St John's CE/Methodist Primary School in Brinscall, then head of St Peter's CE Primary, Chorley. Came to view job and school for a fresh challenge and something different – knew immediately from the welcome and life in the place that this was the school for him. Big fan of the 'tweak to transform' concept – taking something that's already good and making small changes to keep on improving it.

Married to an infant teacher, with two children settled in other schools. A vicar's son, he leads Leyland Methodist Church's music and drama group, co-writing and producing an annual musical involving over 80 youngsters in his spare time. Into music, he's a drummer in a band and has delighted boys, junior and senior, by enhancing school performances with his backing.

Entrance: Assessment by English, maths, VR and non-VR exams and interviews with head and deputy, looking at academic ability and extracurricular passions. Only slightly over-subscribed so bright applicants should bag a place; feedback given. Children from infants have rite of passage into juniors – they've already entered after assessment.

Exit: Junior boys have to sit same entry for seniors as outsiders but almost all pass, and in fact they tend to sit in the top quarter of the overall intake's ability. One or two to MGS instead and a few to state secondary schools.

Money matters: All junior places full fee-paying.

Remarks: Busy, bright boys bound along at speed here in super setting with great atmosphere. Two classes of 25 boys in each year in a spacious, three-storey, whitewashed building known as Park Road, newly extended and refurbished in a £1.5m project. It's just down the road from the senior schools and next to the infants' division in its own new, state-of-the-art Beech House.

Lessons are pacey, with specialist teachers and bespoke classrooms from the off; in some areas their work's a year ahead of other schools. All pupils soon to be given an iPad. No shortage of fun, though – during our visit one class was knee deep in a muddy flower bed planting bulbs, having learnt about sowing and reaping during harvest festival. Beyond them a full-size games pitch lies beside an adventure playground with a climbing wall. Head meets every class for a weekly session in the library, 'I'm a great believer in sharing stories'. A reading award scheme encourages even the reluctant to get reading for bronze to platinum-plus awards. Stick insects galore in the science lab, 'and sometimes out of it – just look at this spider plant, or what was this spider plant,' laughs head from the corridor. ICT lab, an exciting DT room buzzing with busyness, fabulous landscape paintings adorn the entrance hall and outside the music department (three practice rooms as well as two classrooms) lots of violins stand to attention in home-made racks. Older boys also stand to attention when head enters room, in preparation for senior school manners. A SENCo helps with minor learning difficulties.

Four houses mean boys can earn house merits, and dreaded demerits, where you lose 10 points just like that – after three demerits it's a report card, 'for bad behaviour, for, you know, whacking someone with a recorder or something'. Not much time for that sort of thing, though, with lunchtime and after-school clubs from jujitsu to brain games and play reading. Two representatives from each class take boys' ideas from the listening boxes to school council – a cookery club is starting as a result of this. The refurbished dining room is furnished with the same traditional refectory tables and benches as in senior school – 'Ah, no, we couldn't lose the benches' – and a further main hall for assemblies, concerts and indoor PE. Juniors share some senior facilities, most notably the swimming pool.

Bootham Junior School

Linked school: Bootham School

Rawcliffe Lane, York, YO30 6NP

- Pupils: 150 girls and boys • Ages: 3–11 • Fees: £6,390–£9,285 pa
- Independent

Tel: 01904 655021
Email: junior@boothamschool.com
Website: www.boothamschool.com

Head: Since September 2013, Mrs Helen Todd, previously deputy head at Edge Grove School and before that head of English and drama at Aysgarth School. Married with two young children.

Entrance: At any time from nursery to year 6, places permitting.

Exit: Most follow the natural progression to Bootham's senior school.

Remarks: Bootham School was founded in 1823 but the junior school is much younger. Opened in 1997 and moved to its present site in 2002. Lots of competition locally from good state schools and preps and it's simply a matter of horses for courses. Bootham Junior is smaller than most – only one form entry from nursery up to year 6 – but there is undoubtedly something special about a place for budding young learners run on sound Quaker principles. The principles are intuited rather than clearly visible; staff and children thrive in a warm, calm, happy and purposeful atmosphere – it doesn't leap out at you, it just 'is'.

National curriculum plus describes the curriculum – all the basics are soundly covered with extras such as Latin (years 5 and 6), French, German, Spanish (years 2 to 6) and the teaching of thinking skills, all adding to the width and depth. Smartboards in classrooms and extension opportunities for the more able, identified by regular assessment in all areas. Outdoor learning is taken to another level with the forest school in the grounds (racks of wellies in evidence) and yes, they go out in all weathers. All take part in a residential experience (right from reception, which is very rare). It's a gentle start with the youngest children pitching tents in the school hall for an overnight stay, complete with head-torches for a night walk and hot chocolate before bed. Staff and children sleep soundly, anxious parents less so – but the children love it.

Plenty of music for all, in and out of the curriculum, and a raft of other extra-curricular activity options, including Mandarin, horticulture, cultural dancing and coaching from staff at York City football club. Before-school care from 8am, after-school care till 6pm, so ample time for sampling the fun and games and homework can be done too (a boon for late pick-up parents). Annual school productions bring added life and colour, the oldest children performing at the senior school.

Classrooms are colourful and spacious. Dedicated ICT suite, shared area for art and music and delightful library. Large multi-purpose hall transforms from assembly area to dining room, to PE space and back, throughout the day (plenty of support staff on hand to make it happen). It tells you a lot about a place when you are introduced to the whole team, as we were. Chef was happy to chat about his healthy and child-friendly menu (including delicious homemade bread, cooked daily on the premises). An unprompted and enthusiastic 'really tasty' comment came directly from the children. Picky eaters and allergy sufferers are recognised and cheerfully accommodated. Nobody goes hungry and staff and children happily sit down to eat together.

Lovely outdoor spaces – soft play areas with tricycles, bicycles and toys galore for the youngest children, an adventure playground for the older ones and a vast green field for sport. Tennis and netball courts and the school minibus takes pupils to senior school for a weekly swim from year 2. Raised beds for growing vegetables and quiet sitting areas adjoin the playground, all reassuringly visible from the large plate glass windows of the staff room.

Children are bright, chatty and confident, but not obnoxiously so. They also have that rare but essential Quaker ability to maintain thoughtful reflection as necessary. Most are not Quakers (pupils from all backgrounds, all faiths and none), but the ethos pervades and all seem to benefit from this honest, open-minded and peaceful approach to life.

Bousfield Primary School

South Bolton Gardens, Old Brompton Road, London, SW5 0DJ

• Pupils: 430 boys and girls • Ages: 3–11 • Non–denom • State

Tel: 020 7373 6544
Email: info@bousfield.rbkc.sch.uk
Website: www.bousfieldprimaryschool.rbkc.sch.uk

Headteacher: Since 1998, Ms Connie Cooling MA DipEd. Previously deputy head of Sheringdale Primary. Purposeful, bright and approachable, with a good sense of humour. Loves her job, knows what she's doing and does it well.

Head believes that Bousfield is very good at offering a broad, rounded education but worries that today's urban children are 'programmed to the eyeballs' and under increasing pressure. Wants children to have time to skim stones and build dens too. Acknowledges this is not a tough school in terms of social deprivation, but notes there are other stresses on her staff, particularly the demands made by parents and meeting the needs of a wide attainment range. In her spare time, she enjoys the arts, travel and 'discovering good restaurants and the odd glass of wine.'

Entrance: Due to cuts in funding there are now 60 part-time places in the nursery on offer, rather than the previous 30 full-time places. Two parallel classes from reception to year 6, each with 30 pupils. Applications for the nursery are done through the school; applications to the main school are done via Royal Borough of Kensington and Chelsea.

No automatic transfer from the nursery to the main school – parents must reapply. Children who are in care or have an SEN statement are considered first, followed by siblings and then proximity to school (currently approximately 0.5 of a mile and shrinking). Distance measured as the crow flies. Places do become available further up the school, due to high mobility rates of pupils, so worth persevering. Hugely over-subscribed. As one current parent puts it: 'If you get offered a place here, you'd be mad to turn it down.'

Exit: Most popular secondary schools are Holland Park and Chelsea Academy. Over a third go on to independent senior schools, including Latymer, City of London, The Harrodian, Putney High and Christ's Hospital. No special preparation given for those doing 11+ exams. Head knows a large amount of tutoring probably goes on, though she says pupils get plenty of exam practice anyway. Much parental advice and support given when it comes to choosing next school.

Remarks: Strikingly international, with 41 different first languages currently spoken at home. Sixty per cent have English as an additional language. After English, the most prominent languages are French and Arabic. Head sees this cosmopolitan element as a real strength of the school and the high level of harmony being something to celebrate. A significant number arrive with very limited English. Head says it is 'sink or swim, but usually swim.' Much language teaching on offer, including Italian classes laid on by the Italian Consulate and French to all KS2 pupils. Bilingual pupils tend to outperform monolingual ones. Much coming and going due to large expat intake. Lots of French families have departed recently due to job losses in the City. Only about half the class in year 6 have been there from reception.

Superb academic results, particularly given the huge EAL contingent, though head says she is always looking to 'up the ante.' English, maths and science Sats results well above national average. There are plans afoot introduce some setting for maths and reading in year 6, though head regrets that lack of space means separating children into groups is a challenge. Pupils' progress is tracked carefully.

When we visited, children were beautifully behaved and all engaged. A sense of calm pervades the school. Manners and presentation clearly high on the agenda. No uniform. Packed lunch or school lunch. Fruit given to the younger years, funded by School Fruit and Vegetable Scheme.

One full-time teacher and one teaching assistant in each class, as well as extra support staff for pupils with statements and EAL pupils in the early stages of learning English. Head says she has a great team of dedicated staff, who 'put the hours in.' Many loyal, long-serving teachers (20 members of staff have been there more than 10 years), as well as newer ones. Head reckons they are a strong team – 'no prima donnas.'

Bright, vivid displays throughout the school. Some classrooms smallish; every iota of space used. School is a 1950s listed building which makes expansion and development problematic.

Arts are very strong in the school, though not at the expense of academics. Lots of music, dance and drama going on. Head believes performance helps to build children's self-esteem. Pupils are offered a rich curriculum, full of workshops, plays and concerts. More than 90 learn a musical instrument. Guitar and strings ensembles, two choirs but no orchestra. Parents attend practice workshops so they know what a good music practice at home should involve.

Plenty of sport – gym and games as well as after-school clubs offering tennis, football, cricket and even cheerleading. Swimming for years 3 and 4. Pupils take part in borough events (including athletics) in the summer term.

Quantity of homework has been reduced – parents were completing too much of the pupils' project work ('you can always spot the hand of a parent,' we were told) and copious amounts were being downloaded unthinkingly from the internet. Homework now more focused on the basics, with reading, spelling and maths given from early on.

Some children with SEN statements. More on the SEN register, receiving support of some kind. No specially trained teachers but head feels they have strategies and experience to help those in need. School has experience of pupils with Asperger syndrome, autism, ADHD, emotional/behavioural difficulties and moderate/severe learning difficulties, as well as dyslexia, dyspraxia and hearing and visual impairment. Head acknowledges school is not a centre of excellence for all of these – very occasionally pupils move to special schools, either when Bousfield can no longer adequately support them or when they move to secondary school. Staff say Bousfield is 'an inclusive school' that does its best to accommodate those with difficulties.

Strong parental involvement, with school questionnaires showing overwhelming parental support and high levels of satisfaction. Numerous opportunities for parents to attend curriculum workshops and 'book looks' (when they visit to look at children's books). Parents welcomed in at the beginning of the day.

Some wrap-around care available, albeit not all on-site. Breakfast club on offer and pupils can be escorted to a neighbouring school (with more provision) at the end of the day if required.

Bousfield has close connections with artist Quentin Blake, who attends prizegivings and pops in regularly. All leavers receive a prize at the final assembly and Blake says his spirits are raised as each leaver is celebrated. 'After the ceremony, I go away feeling that at this point in their lives perhaps they really have all won,' he adds.

A great sense of purpose permeates this thriving school, with pupils bright-eyed and focused. Head feels school has got the balance right and that pupils are offered a lively, dynamic and interesting education. As one satisfied parent lamented: 'I just wish it could go on into secondary school.'

Bow Durham School

Linked school: Durham School

South Road, Durham, DH1 3LS

• Pupils: 130 boys and girls • Ages: 3–11 • C of E but all faiths welcome • Fees: £6,225–£9,120 pa • Independent

Tel: 01913 848233
Email: e.cathrae@durhamschool.co.uk
Website: www.durhamschool.co.uk/prep-school.asp

Headmaster: Since 2000, Mr Nick Baird BA PGCE (mid fifties), educated at Fettes College, Edinburgh, Durham and Sunderland Universities (initially law, then history and English), taught history and sport at Foremarke Hall (Repton Prep), Gresham's Prep, Holt (head of history), head of Lisvane (Scarborough College junior school), head of St Petroc's School, Cornwall. Pleasant and thoughtful; wife teaches at school and supervises girls' pastoral care; two children at university and one at Durham School (as were the others); interested in sport, music, theatre, history and art.

Entrance: No exam – need a reference from current school/nursery.

Exit: Virtually all to senior school – no entrance exam unless applying for scholarship.

Remarks: Situated close to senior school and city centre, overlooking Durham Cathedral. Founded 1885 as an independent day school for boys 3-13 years, moved to present site 1888, incorporated into the Durham School Foundation 1976 and formally became the prep for Durham School. In 2006 went co ed – about a quarter girls, but proportion in a class can vary a lot (we saw one that was all boys).

Prep department (7-11 years) in the main building (1888), which overlooks the cricket square, with the cathedral in the background, views of trees. Red brick classroom block with later additions and upgrading; adventure playground.

Small classes – average 16; divided into two groups for core subjects, IT, art, swimming. Specialist teaching increasingly from year 3; setting for English and maths if considered appropriate; French starts in year 3, Latin in year 5; very good key stage 2 results. Networked IT suite but only two interactive whiteboards (all rooms have a computer and projector). The children we talked to enjoyed their lessons – 'Lots of fun activities' – and found the teachers helpful. Suggestion from a parent that more could be done for the academically gifted but others happy with teaching. Strong learning support department led by specialist – close monitoring, in class support where possible and some outside.

Netball/tennis court, big sports field and shares playing fields with the nearby Chorister School. Multi-purpose sports hall; also uses Astro and indoor swimming pool at senior school. Two one hour games sessions a week for 7 and 8 year olds, three for 9 year olds up. Music strong – well-resourced room, choir, jazz band, fiddle group. The Cottage, 250 years old and listed, originally a toll house, houses the art room – pottery and sculpture as well as drawing and painting. Two plays a year plus speech and drama after school. Wide choice of activities including fencing, judo, gymnastics, table tennis, karate; history visits, trip to Venice and Rome (links with a school there), ski trip to Italy.

Good pastoral care – all new pupils have a guide for the first two weeks; children feel happy and secure – 'People listen and understand if you've got a problem'; they use the senior school facilities often so find the transition smooth. Parents praised relationships with teachers – 'They're great with the kids'; 'The teachers and children respect each other'. The pupils we met were articulate, open and confident; praise from the last inspection report – 'well behaved, hard working and polite children'. All year 6s have a turn at being a monitor (prefect).

Pre-prep (5 – 7 years): core subjects plus French, history, geography, RE, IT, music and art; good results in key stage 1 tests; cheerful classrooms with good displays. Uses sports hall, IT suite and library in Bow; children swim all year round at Durham City Freemans Quay leisure centre or Chester le Street leisure centre. Concerts, nativity play, fundraising for charities, after-school clubs include fencing, judo, percussion, speech and drama. Prepares for transition to prep department through attending their assemblies, house competitions, some sport with older pupils and longer day in summer term.

Badger nursery (3 – 4 years) is on ground floor of Quarryheads House, a splendid, 100 year old, former family home (originally assigned to the head of Bow), next to main Bow buildings – white with big bay windows, a red slate roof and white chimney, resembling a children's storybook illustration. Reception has a terrific, large, open plan space with different learning sections (we particularly liked the play post office) and views of trees. Behind it is the Beaver transition area, for older children, a quirkily shaped room with several nooks and crannies, next to the pleasant welcome room for parents (haven't seen that before). Well equipped – interactive white board, large plasma screen; delightful outdoors play area. Small numbers; open 8am – 5.15pm. Enthusiastic parents: 'Excellent – very good attention from the teachers'.

Bradford Grammar Junior School (Clock House)

Linked school: Bradford Grammar School

Keighley Road, Bradford, BD9 4JP

• Pupils: 190; 100 boys/90 girls; all day • Ages: 6–11 • Fees: £8,985 pa • Independent

Tel: 01274 553742
Email: chsec@bradfordgrammar.com
Website: www.bradfordgrammar.com

Remarks: For further information, see the senior school.

Brambletye School

Lewes Road, East Grinstead, RH19 3PD

• Pupils: 275; 135 girls and 140 boys 60 full boarders and 10 flexi boarders • Ages: 2½–13 • Anglican • Fees: Boarding £22,220; Day £8,595–£18,600 pa • Independent

Tel: 01342 321004
Email: registrar@brambletye.com
Website: www.brambletye.co.uk

Headmaster: Since September 2012, Mr Nigel Westlake, previously head of Packwood Haugh prep school in Shropshire. Studied law and qualified as a solicitor before taking his PGCE at Exeter. We said of him there: finds his legal training 'comes in useful for dispelling myths about health and safety'. Taught at Sunningdale, The Old Malthouse (deputy head, head of English) and Aldro School, Surrey, before joining Packwood Haugh as deputy head in 1998. Married – Mrs Westlake was head of music before stepping down to look after two small sons. Dislikes 'pointless paperwork', likes 'getting out of the office as much as possible'.

Entrance: Non-selective into pre-prep. Nearly all go on seamlessly to prep school. No exam for prep school entry, but questionnaire with searching questions on literacy, numeracy and extra-curricular character to be filled out by current form teacher or head, 'To make sure our curriculum is suitable – we have a two-year CE syllabus'. If SEN concerns are raised, child will be invited down for informal assessment – mild dyslexia is fine. Fifty per cent from pre-prep, fifty per cent external, some entrance at 11. Majority local boarders (Oxted, Forest Row, East Grinstead, Turner's Hill), some from London (school coach at exeat weekend), ten per cent from abroad (Gatwick is very close) – USA, Spain, Thailand, India, Hong Kong, Russia, Ukraine. Has introduced more flexibility into boarding for younger years. London parents appreciate the growing local peer group – it 'keeps them from cruising King's Road for another couple of years!'

Exit: Not a feeder, instead to a range of about two dozen (mostly boarding) schools, most recently: Ardingly College, Benenden, Bradfield College, Brighton College, Bede's, Charterhouse, Cranleigh, King's Canterbury, Lancing College, Marlborough College, Stowe, Tonbridge, Wellington College, Winchester College and Worth School. The head visits at least four schools a term to maintain up-to-date contacts and information, also often invites a chaplain to preach at chapel on a Sunday and then stay for a coffee or a glass of wine in his study afterwards,

followed by a meal – a great opportunity for parents to do their own research. Scholarships (strong on art and music) awarded are listed in gold on a board in the old gymnasium hall. Old boys range from the actor Ben Cumberbatch to the current Admiral of the Fleet.

Remarks: Founded in 1919, moved from Sidcup to this old hunting lodge near Ashurst Wood in 1933; since then the rolling grounds have been semi-deforested and developed to make room for athletics, tennis, cricket, football and rugby pitches, modern sports hall, purpose-built pre-prep building and classroom block. Much of the main building is still panelled with dark oak, which makes for an atmospheric entrance hall (the boarders sit on the stairs and local oldies come in for carol singing, accompanied by the piano in the corner) and dining room (three sittings for lunch, led by the little pre-preppers).

Evidence of proud tradition faces you on the walls – not just oils of previous heads but the weighty house shield, the colourful houseboards (children are quick to explain their stereotypical characters by reference to Hogwarts' houses), the original PE lockers under the seats in the gymnasium hall where everyone lines up before chapel three times a week. The children look charming in their uniform (pink and grey, right down to the stripy socks), pay attention both during school notices and the lesson in chapel and greet teachers politely in the halls with a 'hello, sir' or 'miss'. Parents set store by these confident and respectful manners.

So much on offer here that the announcements of various auditions and rehearsals made in chapel call up are always prefaced by 'as long as you've got no clashes'. An emphasis on children managing their own time, and at least one teacher advises his pupils not to schedule anything on a Sunday so that they have some time for unstructured play. Despite all the amazing activities (every staff member offers something once a week, eg canoe polo, wildlife club, extra art or music, squash, trampolining), the children say that it is the summer term that makes day pupils want to board – after high tea at 6pm, no activities and most people just race outside and play until bedtime at 8pm (lights out at 9pm). An assault course with a climbing tower and balance pole (built by an ex-Royal Marine), plenty of trees, time to catch up on 'the goss' and the latest crazes (diabolos, remote control cars etc). Parents recognise the invaluable contribution that residential staff (several) make.

The girls' dormitories are warm and in a modern wing, while the boys have a better view (one is the old master bedroom of the hunting lodge) but are chillier. Dorm captains, Australian gappies and matrons form part of the pastoral team with Mrs Cocke. As ever, the girls are speedier at making their space homely, the boys are more likely to stick to a football club branded duvet set and then concentrate on working out the correct trajectory of a tennis ball to the next door dorm. Dorm raids are very popular but only happen at the very end of term – when the stars and minuses lists are closed. You get your post at lunchtime (and a chance to post it in a red pillar box donated by some old boys), payphones for calling home (no mobiles permitted), access to the ICT room for emailing directly after breakfast and parents can visit on a Wednesday or a Saturday to watch sports matches. If you're around at the weekend plenty laid on (10 pin bowling, campfires, Scottish dancing, trips to see club rugby matches, sailing, shooting) and local children go out to horse riding or Stagecoach schools.

One big school production each year (eg Oklahoma!) is staged in the multi-use theatre (art exhibitions and exams, when the orchestra pit is covered over) with jobs for everyone both on and backstage. The music department has well-used practice rooms and school instruments, with parents investing in their own when the children are definitely interested – the most talented musicians play in the Alpha Orchestra. They perform in concerts (some for charity, alternate years local and international ones) with renditions of modern classics such as

Spider Pig (from The Simpsons Movie – pupil suggestion) and other more conventional pieces.

The art department has moved to fresher premises with new site development and remains a hub of creativity (ceramics, drawing and painting, oils, an artist in residence) with external trips and full use of ICT. The summer holiday art course is so popular that children have begged their parents to shift their family trips abroad so as not to miss it.

Recent classroom block and two redeveloped science labs – inter-disciplinary competition rubrics include a croquet playing machine, parachuting eggs from the sports hall gallery, a soapbox derby. Practical learning is facilitated by destinations ranging from the Centre for Alternative Technology in Wales to Kenya.

Bullying and discipline are discussed in class and sometimes in assembly, ideally nipping issues in the bud through good communication. The form tutor is a kind of thermometer but the disciplinary system is heavily biased toward reward – 25,000 stars as opposed to 98 minuses given out per term. A pupil left recently after repeated breaking and stealing of other people's possessions – 'He used to get over-excited at competitions and kick out'. School works with two local educational psychologists, as well as the full-time learning development coordinator, who takes an English set as well as teaching one-to-one – 'If they struggle in the classroom they're sure to be doing well in other fields. Pastoral support is so good we can help those who are a little unusual'. Lots of happy siblings here; welcoming of differing levels of academic and sporting skills.

Tries to give each child the space for a simple childhood full of opportunities while avoiding becoming an anachronism. This popular aim, coupled with the school's proximity to central London and international airports, makes it a great choice for busy commuter and international parents looking for quality time with their children when they return.

Bramdean Preparatory School, Kindergarten and Pre-Prep

Linked school: Bramdean School

Richmond Lodge, Homefield Road, Exeter, Ex1 2QR

- Pupils: 115 boys and girls; all day • Ages: 3–11 • Inter-denom
- Fees: £5,250–£8,160 pa • Independent

Tel: 01392 273387
Email: info@bramdeanschool.co.uk
Website: www.bramdeanschool.com

Head: Mr D Connett

Entrance: Children are admitted to kindergarten at 3-5 years and pre-prep at 5-7 years.

Exit: Pupils usually move into the senior school subject to satisfactory common entrance results at 13.

Remarks: The transition through the school to full-day pre-prep after at least one or two terms of five mornings in the reception class is seamless. All parts of the school are close to each other, coming under the same Bramdean umbrella. Siblings are never far apart and by staggering the various activities, children are able to share the facilities; indeed, one of the bonuses for children in the junior school is being able to enjoy so many opportunities. Scholarships available for a variety of skills. Sibling discounts and a 15 per cent reduction for sons and daughters of clergy – do ask.

Busy, well-stocked classrooms with lots of bright pictures, posters and home-made creations. Well equipped. Several outstanding ratings in latest Ofsted report. 'It's brill and we have fun,' said a succinct tiny. Happy-looking children in smart uniforms. Lunch in the dining room at different times to the senior school. A school well worth a visit.

Brandeston Hall Preparatory School

Linked school: Framlingham College

Brandeston Hall, Brandeston, IP13 7AH

- Pupils: 280 boys and girls; 15 boarders • Ages: 2½–13 • C of E
- Fees: Day £12,721 pa; Boarding + £34–£37 per day • Independent

Tel: 01728 685331
Email: office@brandestonhall.co.uk
Website: www.brandestonhall.co.uk

Headmaster: Since 2007, Mr Martin Myers-Allen BSc PGCE (universities of Newcastle and Bath). A degree in marine biology. After a successful career in stockbroking and IT, Martin became a science teacher at Framlingham College and was enthusiastically involved with sport, D of E and CCF. A 'pied piper', constantly in the thick of activities with pupils, who say he is fun to be with and respected. He feels he 'understands the soul of the school,' and his knowledge of both Brandeston and its senior school, Framlingham College, has obvious advantages. A straightforward, sympathetic person who believes in, and fosters, the pupils' self confidence by discovering their individual interests and talents, in huge variety of areas 'not necessarily just in sport or music.' He is married to Helen, who teaches at Framlingham and they have three children, two of whom are now grown up.

Entrance: For entry to the nursery and pre-prep, pupils are invited to spend a day (or morning) for an informal assessment; same for year 3 upwards but their day includes an entrance test. Scholarships at 11+ for entrants to the senior school (Framlingham College) – academic, music and sport.

Exit: Everyone is prepared for common entrance. All but a handful transfer to Framlingham college (results help decide setting in year 9).

Remarks: Idyllic setting down the Suffolk lanes. The original manor house has been rebuilt and remodelled as a memorial to former pupils killed both World Wars. Remembrance is taken seriously and VC citations are proudly displayed in the panelled hall. This is a school for exploring and enjoying; massive oak staircases, terraces on which to play games or take off into the ravishing grounds. The country house atmosphere of the main building is complemented by a modern, multi-purpose hall used for concerts, assemblies and plays and well-designed buildings for DT and art, science and technology. Newish classroom block is reached via a covered passageway; spanking new dance and drama studio.

Nursery and pre-prep occupy their own purpose built accommodation and play areas, but are very much part of the same site. Notice boards with details of after school clubs, sport and music cover the walls including, one headed Celebration, and pupils proudly point out their names and faces. Boarding is on the top two floors of the original building with spectacular views from every window, redecorated dormitories(mostly four to six beds) and common rooms – no twangy-old sofas. Flexi-boarding very popular, 'The whole of year 7 and 8 seem to stay on Wednesday and Friday nights,' say pupils, partly no doubt, because there is Saturday morning school for these years.

Setting begins early for English and maths, and higher up for other subjects. French in pre-prep and Latin from year 7. Help for mild difficulties, notably dyslexia, but the curriculum is not geared for those who seriously struggle. Extension programmes are developed for 'exceptional students' (head prefers this to 'gifted and talented'). Pupils well-mannered and friendly, very at-ease in their school, 'Not precocious, but not scared of adults either,' is how the head puts it. This is a well-run, happy school with no problems recruiting. Would suit a wide range of keen, curious and enthusiastic pupils and is deservedly popular.

Bredon Junior School

Linked school: Bredon School

Pull Court, Bushley, Tewkesbury, Gloucestershire, GL20 6AH

• Pupils: 26 • Ages: 4–11 • Fees: Boarding £18,210–£18,690; Day £6,210–£8,850 pa • Independent

Tel: 01684 293156
Email: enquiries@bredonschool.co.uk
Website: www.bredonschool.org

Head: Since September 2013 Mr David Ward MA BEd. A former head of Skegness Grammar, he then headed St Felix School in Suffolk, moving from there to work for the David Ross Educational Trust, as an adviser to Skegness Grammar and its wider group of schools. A former rugby international, he is also a qualified canoeing coach and interested in swimming, sailing and riding.

Exit: Nearly all to senior school.

Remarks: See senior school review.

Brentwood Preparatory School

Linked school: Brentwood School

Middleton Hall, Middleton Hall Lane, Brentwood, CM15 8EQ

• Pupils: 405; 220 boys/1845 girls. All day • Ages: 3–11 • C of E
• Fees: £11,640 pa; Nursery £5,899 pa • Independent

Tel: 01277 243333
Email: prep@brentwood.essex.sch.uk
Website: www.brentwoodschool.co.uk

Headmaster: Since 2011, Jason Whiskerd BA PGCE (early forties). Attended an independent school in Wales, then university to study history and politics.

Entrance: Pre-prep takes two classes of 18, chosen after an informal assessment of child's language, dexterity and competence in a range of skills, 'and we meet the parents to ensure we are in tune with their expectations'. Pre-prep pupils must also pass the English, maths and verbal reasoning exams taken by outside applicants before they move up to the prep, which has three classes of around 21 pupils.

Exit: Large majority – around 75 per cent – goes on to the senior school but must pass the entrance exam. For those who aren't

going to make it, 'we flag up problems early and help the family look for alternatives'. A few move on to the local grammar schools.

Remarks: The prep and pre-prep – now amalgamated – have their own site, across the road from the main school, and use its facilities. The 1995 pre-prep building sits harmoniously alongside the gracious Middleton Hall, the heart of the prep school, with its stained and leaded glass and stucco ceilings. Art and science rooms in the old stable block, top floor drama suite also used for lectures and house meetings, lashings of computers. Bright and spacious classrooms in the pre-prep, which has its own walled garden area and playground with Wendy house, climbing frame and toys. Happy, busy children listen to story tapes, paint, use the interactive whiteboards.

Academic standards high and improving. Class average 20. French and drama both on the prep curriculum, taught by specialists, as are DT, science, art and music. Learning support for both ends of the spectrum. Thirteen different music groups, teams for 20 different sports, over 50 clubs including fencing, basketball, ballet, French and Spanish, trips abroad. Recent ISI inspection report praised 'caring ethos' that prevails throughout both schools and good relationships.

Brighton and Hove High Junior School

Linked school: Brighton and Hove High School

Radinden Manor Road, Hove, BN3 6NH

• Pupils: 225 girls, all day • Ages: 3–11 • Non-denom
• Fees: £5,985–£8,337 pa • Independent

Tel: 01273 505004
Email: enquiries@bhhs.gdst.net
Website: www.bhhs.gdst.net

Head of Junior School: Since 2011, Mrs Sian Cattaneo, formerly head of St Ives School, Haslemere.

Entrance: By varied tests and observation.

Exit: Around 80 per cent to senior school. Others to local state secondary schools and Brighton College.

Remarks: Situated further into the suburbs and half a mile away from the senior school, on a good-sized site with excellent facilities for a junior school – netball courts, full sized Astroturf and grassed areas for, amongst other things, tomato growing. Light rooms.

Two parallel forms in each year group, unstreamed and often brought together for social events, trips etc. The children are taught by their form teachers, who are specifically appointed for their all round strengths including music, art, drama – plenty of craft/art displayed around the whole school. Netball teams do well; PE and French specialists from senior school visit junior school.

The girls do Sats, and understandably shine. Numerous clubs. School menu looked appetising, all fresh produce cooked on the premises – salad bar, vegetarian option, very healthy eating. Parents remark how sociable the girls are.

Brighton College Prep and Pre-Prep School

Linked schools: Brighton College

Walpole Lodge, Walpole Road, Brighton, BN2 0EU

• Pupils: 300 in prep school (160 boys, 140 girls), 225 in pre-prep (125 boys, 100 girls) • Ages: 3-13 • C of E • Fees: £8,280-£16,350 pa • Independent

Tel: 01273 704222
Email: prepadmissions@brightoncollege.net
Website: www.brightoncollege.net

Head: Since Sept 2013, Harry Hastings (early forties), came from eight years at Cumnor House, where he was assistant head, head of history, director of sport and plays. Energetic, enthusiastic and entrepreneurial, in his last year there, he created Harry Hastings' History Heroes, a cross between Top Trumps and Trivial Pursuit, sparked by a quiz played to occupy kids on history trips. He's sold it now, relieved to be once more focused on his school full time – but it's a good example of his skill at coming up with creative solutions and ensuring they stick. His introduction to teaching was through gapping at his old prep, and his path to this first headship has led him through Exeter and Oxford Universities, a prep in Devon, Peponi House in Kenya and the Dragon School. Has a good support network of other teachers he's befriended along the way (now heads themselves) and has grounded himself with sport, both playing (Greyhounds at Oxford) and supporting. Passionate about rugby and athletics (always seen at the national championships with clipboard, stopwatch, radio and English Schools tie) and loves golf ('18 handicap ... in summer holidays').

Kate, his wife, is a consultant anaesthetist at the county hospital down the road, and they have three children, two at the pre-prep, one not yet. They commute in seven miles from near Lewes – at present by car, but he intends to cycle or run eventually. Is a great believer in finding space for peace and reflection in a busy life; one of his first actions as the new head of BCPS was to ensure the prep school kids are in silence as they snake in single file across the road to the main college. Initially, they thought they were being punished but the head feels being reflective is the unofficial 10th item in the BHPS code of conduct.

New in post, he feels very supported and privileged to be the headmaster of such 'extraordinary, brilliant and different children – beautifully mannered, fun, bright, interested and interesting, all wanting the best for each other.' They certainly greeted him charmingly and creatively; the responses to his request for a postcard over the summer are plastered over the hall walls, some in different languages, one with a 'postage stamp' made from a photo of the senior school's head. He knows all 300 children by name, greets them outside each morning, rain or shine, and teaches year 7 history, three times a week.

Pre-prep head since 2010 is Jo Williams, previously head of year 2 at Tanglin Trust School in Singapore. Alumni of University of Plymouth, head of early years foundation stage and then PE and girls' games at Oakwood School. Meets with head of prep weekly, phone calls and emails in between, he attends pre-prep open mornings and their staff share INSET days.

Entrance: Into pre-prep at 3+ (nursery) and 6+ (when third form is added, year 2 entry). Into prep by assessment in maths, English and verbal reasoning plus observation. Special arrangements for dyslexic pupils, with recent educational psychologist's report. There's a waiting list. Pupils come from the maintained sector and private schools (lots of the girls from single sex schools) and the staff also have experience of both. Some 98 per cent of those that leave the pre-prep school come through to the prep. Travel via the same buses that serve the senior school – a third of the prep school children live in town, a third from Hove and the rest come from Lewes, Worthing, Shoreham, Hassocks etc.

Exit: Some 95 per cent to Brighton College, although they have to take CE on a par with outsiders, with at present a pass mark of 55 per cent, to be raised to 60 per cent in 2015. The rest mostly to St Bede's, Roedean or Hurst. If your child seems like they're not going to make the CE pass mark for the senior school then form teachers/head may well encourage going for another school rather than taking a punt on good luck on the day – so as to avoid a feeling of failure. About four children each academic year leave early, 50 per cent financial reasons, 50 per cent deciding to settle into a school that is not so academically ambitious, with advice from BCPS.

Remarks: Compact busy campus, just one block to the east of the senior school and the two are very closely linked – the little ones walk across in reflective silence for lunch, chapel and games; both schools have the same shape of the day. The children are focused and engaged, polite and sparky – the eldest ones very aware of regular exams and what hangs on them. 'Why are we doing this when it has nothing to do with CE?' asked one, when being taught some tools for writing an essay. The head uses a metaphor for twice yearly exams as series of little hurdles rather than the Grand National. The achievement grades have been rejigged recently, aiming for more transparency in the comparison of these and common entrance percentages; it may feel a bit bumpy initially for the kids who are struggling to hit the marks necessary for entry to the senior school, but the new head is convinced of the importance of clear communication and welcomes meetings with parents as soon as they have any concerns.

They do have an enormous amount of fun too; the teaching is inspiring and embellished with plenty of non-curriculum activities – from sleeping overnight on the Golden Hinde II in London to dancing with Kenyan Massai. The children are taught by class teachers initially, working up to being setted in year 6. Three forms per year, each with 20-22 pupils – no physical room for any more. A buddy system makes for good cross-year peer support, also there are lots of siblings, reading groups with the pre-prep are about to start and the prefects cover wet break in classrooms for the little ones. Normally they are outside on two playgrounds, kicking balls and shrieking about – although lunches are also used to squeeze in a mime class (60 per cent of the school do LAMDA), or to catch up on some work in the ICT room.

Four houses compete in sport, drama, debating etc. Pastoral care is well organised, with spreadsheets covering achievements, pastoral concerns and public recognition, ensuring that every child gets an acknowledgement – whether it is the star of the week trophy for the little ones or a Headmaster's Show up in the Pelican Post weekly newsletter. Some parents feel the flip side of this effective documentation is a need to pigeon hole or label kids, whether as dyslexic, dyspraxic, having a processing problem or as a scholar. All of whom are well catered for here – there is a smaller dyslexia centre and two full time SENCos as well as strong connections to the main one in the senior school. A maximum of nine pulled out for each SEN group, with 12 or so students left in the English or French lesson in the 3rd set, so both clusters benefit from the more focused attention of the teacher. Humour is used to tackle awareness of dyslexia too eg a great assembly by a couple of older boys playing on hot grills/girls.

The children begin their days with assembly in the main hall four out of five mornings a week, sitting on the wooden parquet floor. It is also used for rehearsals, art displays and, when we visited, storing the Christmas shoeboxes for communities in

Eastern Europe as well as local hospices. Music is marvellous here – from the accomplished chamber choir rehearsal we heard in the main hall to the junior wind group squeaking their way through Jingle Bells. Recent choir trips were to Disneyland and Barcelona.

The very youngest children (3-7 year olds, at the pre-prep) have their own purpose designed building (ex-St Mary's Hall, ex-Roedean Junior). Gorgeous light classrooms, well-stocked library and IT room, a big playing field as well as a playground out the back and all look jolly in their sweatshirts for nursery, smart uniforms for reception and upwards. Specialist teaching includes music, PE, art, Mandarin and French. Weekly swimming after reception, competitive matches for the top year and a huge variety of clubs run by outside coaches and teachers. Among the school council's achievements has been the idea for three new after-school clubs (Horrible History, Singing, and Calligraphy) and adding chicken curry and treacle pudding to the lunch menu.

The little ones at the prep do projects every three weeks, getting passionate about making a video on volcanos erupting or designing a tooth hygiene poster. The library is a converted chapel, bright and well used, as an alternative ICT room and for English lessons, reading on the bean bags in the corner (as long as you write a book report...) The oldest years get to use email, only with their @brightoncollege.net address. One of the two science labs has a veritable menagerie of pets – from snakes to rabbits. The pet club love to take some home at the weekend and there are tablets for each child to use for individual research during science lessons.

There's a wonderful home economics room, with tasty ingredients laid out and recipes published in the weekly Pelican Post – as ever, the most popular is pizza. This is compulsory up until year 6 and then the separate sciences take over that slot in the timetable. Latin is done in year 7 and 8 for those in the first set in English.

The art and DT departments are also impressive, the shelves stacked with class projects and a couple of big ones like a clock for the playground and a sign for the revamped Brighton train station (the children wrote a letter and got shown around). There's a new head of art whose intention is to move away from what has been described in the past by parents as a contained feeling, as opposed to the freedom of creativity. The work produced looks fabulous and the kids seem to love it – they are aware they may get an art or DT scholarship if they put together a portfolio and hand it in.

There is a clear scale of minus and misconduct marks leading up to the normal worst case scenario, a headmaster's detention, for which the miscreant will have to fill out a TAL form (Trigger, Action, Learning) – head commented, 'children need to be taught the right, the wrong and the way to get it right'.

Sport is spread all over the town but minibuses nip back and forth and there is a huge range of team abilities – one main sport for boys and girls each term but always clubs on offer, with boys recently joining in with the girls playing hockey on the Astroturf. The director of sport organises several football tournaments and athletics matches each year for local primary schools including a separate girls' one. You couldn't possibly try everything that is available, since the buses leave at 4.45pm each day. Homework is restricted to two subjects for 30 minutes each for years 7 and 8 (less for the other year groups), with one additional Latin prep at the weekend. A prep diary ensures that this is documented for parents and teachers – it also helps the children learn self-organisation.

Bristol Steiner School

Redland Hill House, Redland Hill, Bristol, BS6 6UX

- Pupils: 235 boys and girls • Ages: 3–16 • Non–denom
- Fees: £3,264–£5,940 pa • Independent

Tel: 01179 339990
Email: info@bristolsteinerschool.org
Website: www.bristolsteinerschool.org

Head: As in other Steiner schools, a 'college of teachers' replaces the headteacher. The school's management group comprises trustees and staff representatives.

Entrance: Fewer than hoped for progress from kindergarten; no shortage of applications from special needs children, but school wants to attract more of those who support Steiner educational principles.

Exit: Some to Wynstone's (a Steiner school near Stroud with a sixth form), but most proceed to mainstream state schools, where they reportedly do well.

Remarks: A highly distinctive education. For any parent in Bristol looking for a broader, deeper philosophy of education we would recommend investigating this Steiner alternative. Throw away your preconceptions about what you expect a school to offer materially and take this parent's view to heart – 'I'd sooner have my child sitting in a bog and come out of it with a love for learning than going to some over-funded, over-resourced school without a work culture'.

No Sats here: academic results not seen as 'be all and end all' by parents; staff seek to instil genuine thirst for knowledge and feel that too many children are 'damaged' in assessment-driven mainstream schools. Steiner viewed childhood as integrating the developing personality in three successive seven-year stages.

Having said that, now has an upper school for 14-16-year-olds, which does prepare children to take GCSEs in English, maths, science, French and art. Very small numbers (usually single figures) gain mostly four or five A – C grades.

From its origins in 1919 as education for the children of tobacco factory workers in Stuttgart, the Steiner educational movement has grown to influence progressive education worldwide. To the uninitiated some of what takes place seems quirky, and parents will agree that it's 'off-beat' compared with mainstream schools. We came away wondering why so many sacred cows remain in the model from Steiner's early days, but nonetheless uplifted by the atmosphere of the place.

Bristol Steiner typically places creativity and emotional security ahead of early intellectual achievement. We spoke to parents whose children had been 'late starters' in reading but who had gone on to shine in GCSEs after leaving the school at 14. We saw lots of highly-creative work being done by pupils, but relatively little of it is displayed. However, classes give imaginative performances to parents incorporating themes from their lessons. Children hear, re-tell and enact stories before reading them from their own workbooks: text, reference and fictional books are thin on the ground here compared with other schools. TV/VCR/DVD and computers are all eschewed as being counter-creative for young children.

Each day begins with a main lesson which lasts two hours: this covers a range of activities both within the classroom and outside. Class teachers aspire to work as 'artists developing enthusiasm for learning', but we observed some being challenged by the evident wide range of ability and motivation. Children here spend about an hour at 'play' outside in what looks much like an adventure playground on a sloping garden behind the school. Even the main lesson includes periods outside: letting off steam or learning maths through movement such as 'tag', finger clicking or skipping. Children learn to read through walking the shapes of letters on the floor and drawing – the underlying aim being to 'approach through the feelings' and 'never go directly to the concept'. The younger classes we saw engaged in the main lesson were lively and very self-expressive, whilst senior classes impressed by their concentration and involvement. A lot of time is spent in class discussion, and recall of previous lessons is seen as important. The content derives mainly from what Steiner laid down, so children are immersed in the wonders of ancient civilisations, which the school sees as an appropriate preparation for understanding our contemporary world.

The college of teachers will share and disseminate information about children in a way that focuses on individuals. In addition, a qualified SENCo coordinates the special needs programme. Currently no statemented children but a number require support for SpLD. Pupils are screened for dyslexia at class 2 and 4 stages. Children are withdrawn either individually or up to three at a time. The building and site are unsuitable for physically-challenged pupils.

Gym and games are taught separately and an outside area close to the school is used for a variety of informal sports; excessive competitiveness is frowned on. A basketball area in front of the school was proving popular with older boys when we visited. Eurythmy is central to Steiner education: origins of this idiosyncratic, dance-like art form lie in Greek temple dances, and link movement to specific sounds; sometimes copper rods are used in the movements. The teacher we observed was highly skilled and succeeded in winning the cooperation of all pupils, who weaved mesmeric shapes across the floor. We couldn't help wondering what the children might have done with freer or funkier forms of movement and the extent to which they were really sold on eurythmy. Art here also includes recitation and drama as well as painting, plus modelling in beeswax and clay, as the traditional divisions between subjects are constantly blurred.

We witnessed a 'magical' music lesson for class 2: it involved a fairytale sung to a lap harp accompaniment, as well as puppetry and the use of both imaginary pencils and real wax crayons; pupils sang as they passed a drumstick around to decide who got to choose an instrument to play (from a good choice of simple instruments available in the middle of the circle) each time the music stopped. Older children have individual music tuition and opportunities to perform together. Another outstanding lesson was handcraft (a key aspect of Steiner schools is to instil motor skills) where the teacher had inspired girls and boys to produce highly original sewing, knitting and crochet work (having first made their own knitting needles out of natural materials). Much thought is given to materials as well as to the colours used. Older children also make their own clothes in this way. French is the only foreign language taught at present but we were unable to witness a lesson or any display related to languages. Some parents agree that the menu gets 'a bit thin' in upper classes, with only five GCSE subjects offered. School benefits from Steiner students on placement plus regular in-service training for staff (six of whom have served for over 10 years).

Founded as Bristol Steiner Waldorf School in 1973, it occupied crumbling premises on the former site of city's Roman Catholic cathedral before moving to the present Georgian building in Redland when vacated by UWE in 2002. One of 25 Steiner schools in the UK, Bristol has struggled financially since its inception, controversially abandoning its sliding fee scale in 1998 in favour of a standard charge for all. Staff are all paid substantially below national scales and come via Steiner teacher training courses (two of which are validated by UK universities). As some Steiner schools become state funded, questions remain as to how much educational freedom is be sacrificed in return for state financial support (not a problem in Germany, it seems), but Bristol Steiner School clearly suffers from under funding.

School compensates for its shortcomings through committed staff, pupil goodwill and parental support. Average class size is sixteen and staff: pupil ratio is 1:11. Children celebrate a variety of Christian and other festivals, whilst the spiritual aspect of Steiner's philosophy is implicit rather than overt.

Stylised introductions and endings to lessons seem rather quaint but suggest a deeper, spiritual significance. No catering facilities but children are happy enough bringing home nosh. Class teachers move each year with pupils so parents can relate to same person throughout their child's school career (OK if you like the teacher). All the staff exude commitment and a genuine care for their charges. One parent said 'curative' eurythmy (used on a one-to-one basis with younger children) had 'worked wonders' for her 'withdrawn' daughter but had no idea why or how.

Lots of mainly middle class free spirits here in a secure setting with a few from ethnic minorities. Children 'love going to the school' and clearly trust their teachers. First names throughout and no uniform, of course. Staff skilled at engaging each child in learning process. An interesting blend of liberalism and old-fashioned values. Some parents fall into Steiner education faute de mieux (especially in Bristol where choices tend to be polarised), whilst others promote its virtues strongly and have made it their conscious choice.

Brockhurst and Marlston House Schools

Marlston Road, Hermitage, Thatcham, Berkshire, RG18 9UL

• Pupils: 310; 140 boys/170 girls ; weekly/flexi-boarding, 30 full 90 flexi • Ages: Boys 3-13 (Brockhurst), girls 3-13 (Marlston House), mixed 3-6 (Ridge House pre-prep) and again in years 7 and 8 • C of E • Fees: Boarding £20,250; Day £9,000–£15,075 pa • Independent

Tel: 01635 200293
Email: info@brockmarl.org.uk
Website: www.brockmarl.org.uk

Head: Brockhurst head since 2000, Mr David Fleming MA MSc (fifties); himself educated at Brockhurst, then Radley College followed by natural sciences at Trinity College, Oxford. A member of the family which owns the school, he projects an air of relaxed authority. Clearly in a very secure position, but doesn't rest on his laurels. Parents like the fact that they are 'talking to the decision-maker.' Aims to 'preserve schools' family feel' whilst maintaining high academic standards and improving existing facilities. Married with two daughters; wife has high flying job outside the school. 'She's the clever one!'

Marlston House operates in tandem with Brockhurst and has own head. Appointed 1999, Caroline Riley MA BEd Cert Ed (fifties) works alongside Mr Fleming and has free rein to run the girls' school as she sees fit. Educated at a West Country girls' school and Southampton University, she is former head of a mixed school in Hazelgrove and has taught in both single sex and mixed schools. Allows headmaster to do most of the talking, but they make a good double act: her contributions are quietly efficient, focused and informed. Teaches RS and history in upper school (headmaster teaches geography). Husband is retired and they have two grown-up children.

Entrance: Children join Ridge House (pre-prep) following their third birthday. Youngest children get used to school by attending swimming lessons on Wednesday mornings and free toddler and parent sessions. Boys and girls educated together up to the age of 6, after which they join Brockhurst (boys) or Marlston House (girls). Occasional vacancies for older children after age 9; school says, 'special help can be given [to boys and girls] to catch up where necessary.' There is an informal interview and assessment for anyone seeking a scholarship or bursary.

Exit: An impressive array of scholarships to some of the most competitive senior schools, eg sports at Millfield and academic scholarships to Downe House, Abingdon and School of St Helen and St Katherine. Other leavers choose Radley, Marlborough, Wellington, Bradfield and Pangbourne, often with academic, sport, music, art and all-rounder awards. Some go further afield, eg Cheltenham Ladies' College, Charterhouse, Eton and St Swithun's.

Remarks: Founded in 1884 in Shropshire as a boys' prep school, Brockhurst moved to its present home – a mock-Jacobean listed mansion set in sixty acres just outside Newbury – in 1945. Marlston House opened its doors to girls in 1995 and is located in a separate (also listed) building on the same site. Main building boasts imposing façade of deep red brick and stone, with baronial windows, turrets and heavy oak main door opening into wood-panelled passages and spacious Great Hall. Heads gave their interviews in a large room with impressive views over school's extensive grounds – would make a good backdrop for filming period drama. The rest of the school's buildings, although modern, sit comfortably alongside older ones and blend in thanks to clever architecture and landscaping.

Two schools join forces to marry the best of co-ed with single-sex education; boys and girls are educated separately between the ages of 6 and 11, only coming together for art, music and drama. Classes merge in the final two years of 'senior school', in order to prepare pupils for academic scholarships and common entrance exams on an equal footing. Quirky 'back-to-front' year groups mean those leaving reception begin in year 8 and finish in year 1.

Lots of evidence of modern, quality teaching and good effort from pupils is everywhere to be seen. Able children streamed into scholarship sets as soon as they are ready, usually in year 5. Maths tuition caters for a wide range of ability and pupils take common entrance at all three levels. Scholars take level 3 maths in year 7 and then focus on scholarship papers. English teaching excellent; pupils are encouraged to read widely and develop critical skills. CE syllabus completed by year 7 and scholarship set extends pupils' knowledge in final year. Good provision for languages, especially French, which is taught from age 4. Château Robert near Biarritz is school property and all 11 and 12-year-olds spend two weeks every year studying the language intensively and exploring the area. Latin from year 4 to both CE and scholarship levels; those taking scholarship Latin also learn Greek. Pupils begin German in the last two years and have taster sessions in Russian and Spanish once exams are over.

Usual range of subjects elsewhere on the timetable; we observed a lively practical science lesson in which pupils spoke confidently about extracting chlorophyll. History is clearly good fun; walls of history room festooned with pictures of students getting into the spirit of ancient times on Celtic Day (ably assisted by those 60 acres). Knights of the Sealed Knot have visited to perform re-enactments of medieval battles. Plenty of school trips, eg to Hampton Court. Good ICT facilities and library. Parents praise school communications and particularly news section of website. 'They get it right 90 per cent of the time.' Progress reports issued two or three times every half term. 'Children are treated as individuals, with stars, effort points and lots of praise for good work ... the sheer scope of opportunities seem boundless.' Saturday school from year 2 up, so schools run clubs in the morning for younger siblings.

Learning development centre (LDC) goes well beyond usual remit of dyslexia, eg developing comprehension and study skills and exam revision techniques. LDC helps gifted and talented to extend knowledge, supports EAL students and even adults from the local community with dyslexia. Also helps pre-prep pupils who don't pick up on phonics first time around.

Music is clearly in good health, with around 80 per cent receiving individual tuition on one or more instruments. There are senior and junior orchestras and choirs, plus a chamber choir and string quartet. Swing and R+B bands, guitar, flute and recorder groups provide other opportunities to make music. Class music includes use of composition suite. Heads keen to point out that schools are very flexible and 'will adjust timetable to suit individual talents such as music.' Art and DT block ranges over two floors which provide plenty of space for painting, drawing and pottery; not as well-equipped for practical DT as some other preps we've seen, although facilities for art and pottery are excellent. Standard of work on display is high and the most talented pupils are coached for art awards. Trips to galleries and museums organised post CE.

Schools' extensive grounds are a boon to sports staff; all major sports are on offer in addition to minor sports such as golf, judo, shooting and fishing in school's lake. Soccer, rugby, cross-country running and cricket for boys; hockey, netball, rounders and tennis for girls – all do athletics and swimming in 25m indoor pool and boys can play hockey too. Sport is timetabled every day and there are A, B and C teams for major sports. A big draw for girls is the equestrian centre, where pupils can stable their own pony or learn to ride on schools' horses. Headmaster is proud of sporting record of his pupils, which have included winning national judo championships, IAPS swimming gold and athletics at county level. Keen to build more tennis courts; at present there is one indoor and three all-weather courts. Indoor sports (including short tennis, basketball and gymnastics for boys and girls) take place in a rather cavernous gymnasium, not unlike an aircraft hangar – work to remodel this into a new music building, incorporating a theatre/concert hall flanked by practice rooms, began shortly after our visit. Joint drama productions take place in Marlston House theatre.

Family ethos encourages good pastoral care; we met a very dedicated house master who clearly poured heart and soul into the job. There is zero tolerance for bullying and parents report that issues are sorted immediately. One parent commented, 'The headmaster took time out from a school inspection [to deal with my concerns].' All pupils belong to a house and school council meets once a month. Full-time boarding is encouraged, but flexi-boarders must spend a minimum of two nights a week in school. Boys' dorms are much less pretty than girls' dorms, as is the norm. Corridors kept tidy and routines well organised. Lots of posters on walls to reinforce anti-bullying ethos; full boarders can have mobile phones and iPads and their use is managed by boarding house staff. Overseas boarders have access to Skype in a specially designated room.

Multiple evening clubs and activities on offer (day pupils can join in) and all staff give up one or two evenings a week to run these. Lots of sporting activities but a couple of unusual options include geo-caching and barbeque club. School fireworks display is an annual highlight. Everyone takes part – children hold torches and process with their parents to the bonfire, which is lit traditionally by the youngest child in the school. Three sittings for lunch ensure that all pupils sit on a 'family table' with a member of staff present. Food a bit plain on the day we visited, but not in short supply and plenty of fresh fruit, cheese and other choices for pudding. School runs daily bus services to local towns and there is good after-school care for working families.

Children come from a wide variety of backgrounds, eg South Africa and the US, but are polite, articulate and unassuming without hiding their light under a bushel; they state (honestly) that there is nothing about the schools that they would change. Centenary and Foundation Scholarships are worth up to one third of fees, but headmistress keen to point out that 'a talented child can come here on a full scholarship.'

Twin schools offer a unique blend of co-ed and single-sex education. Blessed with a rich endowment, they are free to indulge mild idiosyncrasies such as different holiday and half-term dates. Clear moral steer and family values keep students, staff and parents on side. Obviously hard working – the school motto is 'no reward without effort' – but a happy place as well.

Bromley High School (GDST) Junior Department

Linked school: Bromley High School (GDST)

Blackbrook Lane, Bickley, Bromley, Kent, BR1 2TW

• Pupils: 310 girls; all day • Ages: 4–11 • Broadly Christian
• Fees: £11,229 pa • Independent

Tel: 020 8781 7001
Email: admissions@bro.gdst.net
Website: www.bromleyhigh.gdst.net

Head of Junior School: Since September 2012, Ms Claire Dickerson, who took over after the precipitate departure of Mrs Penny Jones.

Entrance: At 4+ competitive entry assessment, always oversubscribed, thereafter waiting list for occasional vacancies.

Exit: Around two-thirds to senior school.

Remarks: Strong academics, arts and sport; the junior school benefits from being able to share a fantastic range of sporting and musical facilities at the senior school. Year 5 and 6 pupils are able to link with subject specialist teachers in the senior school. Tuition is available on any instrument. Wind and string ensembles and training orchestra prepare pupils for the variety of orchestras that the music department run. Drama and dance also play an important role in the curriculum. Purpose-built site is rather utilitarian, softened by numerous imaginative art and project displays which offer an insight into the broad curriculum. Dedicated, mostly long serving class teachers run a full range of extracurricular clubs and activities. Lots of hard work going on, crisp orderly little girls present as purposeful and happily engaged.

For further details see the senior school entry.

Bromsgrove Preparatory School

Linked school: Bromsgrove School

Worcester Road, Bromsgrove, B61 7DU

• Pupils: 485; 260 boys/225 girls; 61 year 3–8 boarders • Ages:
• Fees: Day £7,050–£12,900; Boarding £14,400–£24,345 pa
• Independent

Tel: 01527 579679
Email: admissions@bromsgrove-school.co.uk
Website: www.bromsgrove-school.co.uk

Head: Since 2011 Mrs Jacqui Deval-Reed.

Exit: To senior school

Remarks: See senior school review.

Brookham School

Linked school: Highfield School

Highfield Lane, Liphook, GU30 7LQ

• Pupils: 215 (130 boys 85 girls) all day • Ages: 3–7 • Non denom
• Fees: Day £9,375–£12,000 pa • Independent

Tel: 01428 722005
Email: headteacher@brookhamschool.co.uk
Website: www.brookhamschool.co.uk

Headmistress: Since 2003, Diane Gardiner, BEd MEd (Cambridge). Fifties. Comes garlanded with success from Eagle House School where she masterminded pre-prep start up, numbers swooping from zero to 170 in a decade.

With previous posts at Ascot and Slough, it's been preps all the way, apart from a brief break out when she chucked the job to work as a volunteer in Ascot nursing home, demoralised by having to unpick one layer of educational red tape too many. 'I just lost heart,' she says (a career first and last, you'd imagine). Worked it off, realised she 'missed the children too much' and 18 months later came back into the fold, raring to go.

Hasn't stopped since and is thriving, as is pre-prep, up from 90 to almost 220 pupils, with backing from parents, larger size particularly handy on the sports front, with more teams, fixtures and specialist coaching, all pushing up standards and opportunities.

We heard of others who thought that larger class sizes meant cosiness had been stripped out along the way. However, while 'there might have been a bit of bitching and moaning from some people who preferred it when it was a nicey, nicey little school, we haven't noticed a huge impact,' said parent. And with average reception to year 3 class size of just 15, maximum 18, and average pupil to teacher ratio of nine to one, it's a long way from standing room only.

Great fun to talk to, head punctuates comments with animated gestures and an infectious and slightly wheezy chuckle that breaks out in all directions. No surprise that theatre is a great love (drama was subsidiary degree subject). Something of a family interest, shared by grown up daughter, a stage manager (marketeer son works in films).

'Nice and very business oriented,' says parent. Straighforward, too. Particularly refreshing that she knowingly included one year 3 naysayer (whose favourite subject was 'lunch') amongst other universally positive tour guides, yes men to the echo.

Knows her onions and then some, reflected in recent appointment as ISI reporting inspector, relished for the chance to 'get under the skin' of other schools. Encourages staff to go calling, too, as 'you always pick up new ideas', though she reckons it's also a thoroughly good way of reinforcing the brilliance of Brookham and making them realise 'how lucky they are to be here'.

Helps if they have lived a little before teaching, preferably in different line of work: recent appointments include former fashion buyer and school bursar. Avoids danger of drifting into teaching by default and strengthens commitment, she reckons. And if candidates are that bit more mature as a result, not a drawback, either (average staff age here is 42). 'They bring that extra element,' she thinks.

All good, reckons parents. 'You might not get the best teachers every year but I'd be comfortable saying there are no weak teachers. Mrs Gardiner is pretty good at weeding those out early on,' thought one.

Teachers around six lessons of English and history each week – 'keeps me in contact with the pupils and builds relationships' and children have evidently warm relationships with her, despite feeling (perhaps surprisingly) that most contact with her would be through the school council (listened to) or prefect posts (theoretical house point issuing powers are rarely exercised in practice).

With Goldilocks status achieved, 'we're in our final format now,' she says. Parent doubts about school growth are in the past. 'They've realised that the atmosphere has been retained. It's very warm and that's really important.'

Did school bring her in because of track record in levitating pupil numbers? 'God knows,' she says, cheerfully. Quite clear on how it's done, however. 'One of the keys is having fantastic relationships with parents and very open, honest ones. We work with them. If they're happy, their children are, too.'

Entrance: Most families within a 25 minute drive, Haslemere, Liphook, Liss and Petersfield the norm, Midhurst and Farnham at a stretch. Some dyed in the wool locals; growing numbers of 'view starved' Londoners and ex-pats.

First come, first served until year 2 when school is 'sightly more cautious,' says Mrs Gardiner, 'as we need to ensure we can support pupils.' That said, there's not much that can't be handled in the way of learning needs, including one pupil statemented and fully LA funded – very much not the norm; Mrs Gardiner's deep regret that school is a postcode's throw from special needs switched on Hampshire.

Most commonly school can cope with mild to moderate dyslexia, dyspraxia and dyscalculia, speech and language, auditory and sensory processing difficulties, fine and gross motor skills, Asperger's and mild ASD.

Support, through Highfield team, one full time plus assorted specialists – ranges from study skills to specific help with literacy and maths. Seen as part and parcel of daily life by pupils – 'helps you write and read if you are having a problem,' reckoned one – support is regularly reviewed and, in the case of one rapidly progressing pupil with ADD, withdrawn altogether.

Access all pupils largely down to owner says yes approach. Grandson of the founder, he has children at the school and what appears to be fairly substantial behind the scenes presence. 'When I first arrived, I asked, "Do you want me to be very tough in who we take on?" He said, "I want you to take them on and make a difference",' says head.

Exit: Almost everyone to Highfield. Only two pupils in recent years have been advised to look elsewhere, learning needs requiring specialist help.

Move is viewed as an exciting prospect by year 3s. 'It feels as if you can be free, because you get to walk around by yourself without a teacher following and there's much more playing area,' says one.

Remarks: Layout on Venn diagram lines, pre-prep largely self-sufficient but overlapping with prep when it comes to music, art and some sport, especially for older children. Cosily named nursery classes, Little Bears and Big Bears, lead a more self-contained existence, with attractive classrooms and separate, secluded and well-equipped play area. Integration starts early through tree house families, small groups that span the age range and meet to share worries or good news, enjoyable sessions in forest school for all, and mealtimes, with older bruins having lunch in Highfield dining hall (Little Bears bring packed lunches instead), fajitas much enjoyed, 'salty' ham one of few dishes that wasn't.

Reception start off in similar seclusion, though by the end of their first year, they're enjoying substantial tumbling about green space featuring gorgeous (though rather ignored) outdoor xylophone, as well as more conventional but attractive equipment, mad galloping in tentative sunshine seemingly the main amusement, though with behind the scenes staff presence to suggest games. Space gorgeous, only drawback ease of mislaying possessions: 'That sports jumper was there yesterday,' said pupil, with interest.

Inside, every inch of relatively compact and modern building is used to maximum effect. New and grandly named research area (library with computers – touch typing is taught in reception) was recently added, entrance area come assembly hall occupied by high flying and wonderful woven willow dragon spouting red velvet fire.

Onesie design, though highly efficient means some areas, such as nursery/reception music, are also through routes to somewhere else. Not a problem as remains '...a nice quiet place though sometimes people go through it,' said pupil.

Everywhere is extremely neat with not an inch wasted and loads to see and do, including rocket in reception class, less final frontier than cosy den, though strange lifeforms, courtesy of tank o'tadpoles, had already been discovered. Classrooms for older children, all interesting spaces and angles, were big on colourful, extensive and up to the minute displays (including some wonderful monster poems).

Parents rate academics. 'We want our kids to have been pushed to the level where they can achieve either common entrance or scholarship at one of the major public schools; our benchmark is not the state system,' said one.

Achieved with no setting to speak of until year 3, says head, maths the sole exception. 'If we have a big enough spread, might do it in year 2.' Anything but laissez faire, however, with lots of monitoring and no automatic move up between years, those who would benefit from 'spending extra time at a stage' as it's diplomatically phrased, doing just that. School also has a fair few of the extravagantly bright, who get fair share of extra support and encouragement – including peer socialisation (occasionally tricky for those punching above their weight conversationally).

Big thing is the creative curriculum, introduced four years ago as a way of avoiding national curriculum ennui by adding all round oomph. Takes a theme such as 'Day at the sea', 'Knight in the castle' (pun intended), launches it with wow factor event (Sir Teach-a-lot knocking thunderously on pre-prep door to invite pupils to visit castle for a spot of princess rescuing) and ends similarly, with parents invited to share the fun by coming to medieval banquet or turning school into Brookham-sur-mer, complete with donkeys and sand.

Subjects are knitted in en route, some national curriculum must-dos covered off-piste. While not everything can be shoe-horned in (many science discoveries, for example, having inconveniently post-dated Round Table days) it's amazing how many dots can be joined. Would an exciting display of ultra-tactile rocks in year 3 classroom be followed by a snazzy volcanic eruption? Of course it would (in fact, a very slight look of disappointment crossed Mrs Gardiner's face at the very suggestion it wouldn't).

Huge staff enthusiasm provides a welcome outlet for pent-up creativity. 'It's their excitement that makes the difference,' thinks head, who encourages them to give full rein to creative instincts. Children are pretty sold on the idea (even if you did get the impression that overlaying a narrative element was even more popular with staff than their pupils) with activities, many hands on, doing wonders for confidence, one dyslexic child 'growing about three feet' after trebuchet improvement tip dramatically improved its destructive powers during siege weapon-making session.

With or without fun element, lessons are generally enjoyed, science for strong practical dimension, art at least in part because of resident dog, asleep in corner, music for charismatic teacher, whole school favourite. Spanish, taught from year 3, seemed to be the only laggard – 'I just don't get it,' said pupil.

Everyone, however, undoubtedly 'gets' sport. One of Mrs Gardiner's first decisions on arrival was to ditch dreary sports day (little tension, less enjoyment, said parents, following children from non-event to non-event like zombies) for something with a bit more gladiatorial oomph.

Officially, 'we aim to teach pupils that it's all about taking part,' she says. However, she adds, 'Life is competitive.' And while prospectus may highlight 'development of fine and gross motor skills', pupils, organised on mainly traditional lines (cricket, football and rugby for boys, rounders and hockey for girls, swimming for all in decent pool) are in no doubt that purpose is to form ace teams and slaughter the opposition. 'We've only lost one match this year,' say 7 and 8 year-old football and rugby stars.

Big programme of optional Saturday sports undoubtedly helps, as do popular after-school clubs (majority sign up for at least one) judo, gymnastics and orienteering amongst the options, street dance, pottery and chess ringing the changes and 60 per cent of pupils also learning an instrument.

Animated children also encouraged to look outside immediate surroundings, worthy swapsies with London multi-cultural Catholic school – a valuable eye-opener for all. 'I suddenly realised that there's all these other people like me,' said one of only non-white pupils to head.

In an area that groans with educational choice, best recruiting tool is stamp of approval from dinner party set. This one is definitely on the menu.

Broomwood Hall (Garrads Road)

Linked schools: Broomwood Hall School (Nightingale Lane)

3 Garrads Road, London, SW16 1JZ

• Pupils: 140; 70 girls and 70 boys; • Ages: 4–8; • C of E;
• Fees: £13,125 pa; • Independent

Tel: 020 8682 8800
Email: info@northwoodschools.com
Website: www.broomwood.co.uk

Headmistress: Principal: See upper school

Head: Since 2010, Mrs Sarah Graham. Took over the headship of the Ramsden Road site too when Diana Mardon retired in July 2012.

Entrance: As for Ramsden Road

Exit: As for Ramsden Road

Remarks: A large, detached, Edwardian mansion, less rambling than the SW12 parts of this school. Beautiful, large, airy classrooms and a bit more evidence of technology. A comfortable library with a computer suite. A huge garden with lots of room to play in, which adds to the homely, relaxed feel – the children even grow their own vegetables. Tea parties and other gatherings held here in the summer term so that the girls from both lower and upper schools can get together. Everything is done to help the transition to the next stage – constant communication between Broomwood and Broomwood plus Broomwood and Northcote.

The same syllabus is followed as in SW12 and the organisation is equally detailed and efficient. Bookbags hang on the backs of chairs in the classrooms and each child's reading folder contains loads of information.

These are all very well-run schools with a strong adherence to philosophy. Children are introduced to education in an organised, sympathetic way, acquiring a solid grounding and having lots of fun as well. Teachers are young, mainly local and very caring. Excellent documentation and an informative website. According to a soon-to-start parent, the school uniform shop, which provides both new and used items, is efficient and friendly. What more could you want?

Broomwood Hall (Ramsden Road)

Linked schools: Broomwood Hall School (Nightingale Lane)

The Old Vicarage, 192 Ramsden Road, London, SW12 8RQ

• Pupils: 260; 130 boys and 130 girls • Ages: 4–8 • Fees: £13,125 pa
• Independent

Tel: 020 8682 8820
Email: info@northwoodschools.com
Website: www.broomwood.co.uk

Head of Lower School: Since September 2012, Sarah Graham, previously head of the Garrads Road site, who is now head of the whole lower school.

Entrance: A strict one mile policy, so all children really local, and not a huge ethnic mix, but fairly multi-cultural. Non-selective. After registering your child, you are invited to an open meeting in October where the principal and lower school heads speak; then later, after a tour of the school, parents meet the head individually. Children are assessed for school readiness at 3. Siblings are given priority and they try to keep the boy/girl mix as close to 50:50 as possible, plus a range of birthdays across the year.

Exit: Most of the girls go on seamlessly to the upper school, Broomwood Hall, and the boys mainly move to Northcote Lodge, with a few to King's Wimbledon or Dulwich, and a smattering to boarding preps: Ludgrove, Sandroyd, Cheam, for instance. Wherever they go, they are certainly well-grounded and fully prepared, both academically and socially.

Remarks: School in two buildings – The Vicarage, a rambling Edwardian house, for the first two years, and 50 Nightingale Lane, another Victorian building, for the third and fourth. Both houses carpeted throughout, the tartan theme predominant, with lovely bright classrooms and generally good facilities. Good outdoor play area.

The 4 year olds are divided by age, then mixed together when they move into the second year and are setted in phonics and maths. Lots of gap year students to help the class teachers. French from 4 and recorders for everyone from the beginning. A learning support teacher for one-to-one sessions if necessary, 'judged on merits and what's best for the child'. The pastoral care is reckoned to be excellent.

Broomwood Hall School (Nightingale Lane)

B

Linked schools: Broomwood Hall (Garrads Road); Broomwood Hall (Ramsden Road)

68–74 Nightingale Lane, London, SW12 8NR

• Pupils: 220 girls • Ages: 8–13 • C of E • Fees: £16,125 pa
• Independent

Tel: 020 8682 8800
Email: info@northwoodschools.com
Website: www.broomwood.co.uk

Head: Principal is Mrs Katharine Colquhoun BEd (mid fifties). Somewhat aloof, rather formidable, started school from scratch in 1984 with 12 pupils in local church hall. Now three schools, three heads and over 600 children, together with a boys' prep school for another 200, all due to her drive and ambition. Although she is no longer involved in the day-to-day nitty gritty, it is still very much her school under her direction and she takes assembly and teaches literature. Her husband, Malcolm, is in charge of the financial and administrative side of things and takes care of the school's expanding portfolio of property in Wandsworth. It is very much a family concern – the school board consists of the Colquhouns, the four school heads and one outside director, no governors. They have two almost grown up children.

Head is Mrs Carole Jenkinson BSc PGCE. A bright, bustling former parent who has, according to parents, had a very positive influence on the school. 'She manages the girls fantastically and there is no stress.' Her enthusiasm and real understanding of the children is clear and every parent we spoke to was keen to emphasise how easy she is to talk to and how no problem is too small (or large) to discuss with her.

Entrance: Most come up from the lower schools. For the occasional places remaining at eight and 11, and the very rare ones cropping up at other times, an interview with Mrs Jenkinson and an ability test to make sure that the girl will be able to keep up with the work. Otherwise non-selective, so first come first served. No settling in problems – all teachers and children work hard to make anyone new feel at home.

Exit: About 30 per cent leave at 11+, mostly to south London day schools, JAGS, the High Schools etc, or to good boarding schools, Benenden and Downe House seeming popular at the moment, plus Woldingham and St Mary's Ascot. Seventy per cent stay on to take 13+, the majority to board, more often than not at co-ed schools, Stowe, Cranbrook, Marlborough, Wellington, Bradfield, St Edward's, King's Canterbury, Epsom, Benenden, St Mary's Ascot amongst others, with a trickle to day schools.

Remarks: Three large Victorian houses combined to create a warm, welcoming school. Carpets everywhere, many of them tartan; bright, if not particularly large classrooms, a friendly, happy atmosphere. An excellent, spacious, outdoor play area in the huge garden behind the houses. Places to play and climb and a wonderful amphitheatre where class plays are performed and imaginary scenarios can be acted out. Each year group has its own classroom where they start each day. The youngest girls' classrooms are close together and they have the comfort of at least three lessons with their home teacher each day. Classrooms are subject based, so a certain amount of moving around. However, surprisingly (and noiselessly) no bells dictating changeover – clock-watching is regarded as part of time management. Each classroom houses all necessary books

and materials, so only pencil cases have to be carried around. Setting in English and maths throughout, and in French and Latin from year 7. All homework is done in school after a tea-time carbohydrate snack.

Good teaching in small classes. The decision to keep girls on to 13 so that they can move to co-educational public schools such as Wellington and King's Canterbury has proved successful – girls are joining from other local schools at 11, or, increasingly, at eight, in order to be sure of a place. Mrs Colquhoun has spotted the trend and managed to move ahead of everyone else.

No particular SEN policy. Individual special support lessons are available to children with mild problems such as dyslexia and dyspraxia. EAL lessons for children who need them.

A school with traditional values where good manners are paramount. Christian school with compulsory daily assembly – hymns, prayers and a bible story – and once-a-week service in local church. Smart red and blue uniform for the girls and a dress code for staff as well – no jeans worn here. Bad behaviour is not acceptable and rarely occurs – these are well brought up little girls. Each girl is part of a tutor group of up to 10 and, as well as a group meeting once a week, has an individual session with her tutor. The house system encourages competition amongst pupils and staff alike, another good means of promoting loyalty and building confidence. A resident matron.

Plenty of interactive white boards and a good IT room where they all learn to touch-type and use email, and two computerised laboratories. The DT room was about to be refurbished when we visited. A lovely old-fashioned library where we met the principal taking a literature group. She was quick to assure us that she had read and chosen all the books herself – so nothing unsuitable to be found there.

Sport four times a week, either on the premises (they have their own hard courts) or at Trinity Fields. Matches played against local schools and inter-house – 'Everyone gets a chance to play in a team'. Cross-country and swimming teams as well. After-school clubs cater for other sports – for instance, they have had competitive successes in karate and cross-country. Lovely art and good music facilities. About 70 per cent learn an instrument, for which they are withdrawn from class on a rolling timetable. Choir, orchestra, chamber choir. Lots of singing goes on in church. Class excursions, field trips to France and Devon, outdoor pursuits courses for the top years. Plenty of drama – a class play a year and a whole-school production. Everyone will take part, on the acting or production side. LAMDA exams available for those who want them.

An exciting innovation is their cookery school, a great stainless-steel heaven, affiliated to Leith's. The 10 year olds all have a term of cookery and the 11 year olds have a special Leith's-designed cookery course built into the curriculum, which culminates in an exam that involves cooking a whole dinner party for their parents.

A traditional school, with its values in the right places – the parents we talked to all love it. Unsophisticated and in many ways old fashioned, it provides an excellent education and produces well-rounded, confident girls. If you and the school agree that it is the right place for your child, then she will grow and flourish here, acquire lots of similar friends and get into the right senior school.

Browns School

Cannock House, Hawstead Lane, Chelsfield, Kent, BR6 7PH

• Pupils: 45: 38 boys, 7 girls • Ages: 6–16 • Fees: From £16,500 pa
• Independent

Tel: 01689 876816
Email: info@brownsschool.co.uk
Website: www.brownsschool.co.uk

Headteacher: Since September 2012, Ms Elaine Lovett.

Entrance: School reports and psychological assessments, prospective pupils attend the school for a two-day trial and informal assessments to ensure that it will be able to meet the child's needs.

Exit: Most continue into the senior department. A few move to local state schools, Sunnydown, Ravenswood, or to boarding schools, Frewen College, Northease Manor.

Remarks: Has developed a fully accessible curriculum; the whole school approach is multisensory. Able to accommodate children who are affected by a range of specific learning differences, milder autistic spectrum disorders and other communication difficulties. Accredited by CReSTeD, its specialist provision is inspected every three years, in addition to their excellent Ofsted reports.

Every child is part of a form group and has an individual education plan. Pupils are divided into groups of four to six for literacy and numeracy to ensure they are taught according to their ability and particular needs. They quickly gain in confidence and swift academic progress boosts self-esteem.

ICT suite recently updated, everyone learns to touch type, laptops and audio visuals are available for use in all classrooms. Spacious multi-purpose hall offers an excellent area for a range of activities from whole school assembly to trampolining and yoga classes.

Dedicated and expert teaching team works alongside speech therapists, occupational therapists and educational psychologist. Appropriate therapies and specialist programmes are run in-house, tailored to the individual needs of each pupil. Highly trained staff regularly attend courses and conferences to update themselves with the latest research, resources and specialist teaching practices. Good proportion of male teachers on the staff team, which also includes art and sports specialist teachers.

Pupils enjoy 14 acres of open playing field on a beautiful green belt site bordering London and Kent – ample room for hockey, football, cricket and numerous other sporting activities. The local leisure centre is used for swimming and indoor sports, although the school has just built its own pool, which they're hoping to open shortly. The arts are a particular strength, inspirational displays decorate the school and drama is an important part of the curriculum, contributing to the children's communication and life skills. The whole school is involved in producing the annual musical play; drama is also used to encourage active learning in living history and book events. The varied curriculum is extended by many visits to London galleries and museums, and to the local Kent countryside for pond dipping and wildlife centres. Pupil feedback is positive and enthusiastic about school trips, particularly the annual PGL adventure camp week.

Parents feel pastoral care is well organised; strong home-school partnerships are considered essential, alongside a set of clear and sensible school rules for all to follow. Everybody is expected to behave to a very high standard and demonstrate a mutual respect for each other. Great efforts are made to ensure

that pupils realise their true potential. Overall a nurturing environment with a very welcoming community feel has been achieved. Ex-pupils often return to the school for work experience, which is always a good sign of a successful and happy establishment.

Bruern Abbey School

Chesterton House, Chesterton, Bicester, Oxfordshire, Ox26 1UY

• Pupils: 101 boys, 73 weekly boarders, 28 day • Ages: 7–13 • Inter-denom • Fees: Day £19,863; Boarding £23,901 pa • Independent

Tel: 01869 242448
Email: secretary@bruernabbey.org
Website: www.bruernabbey.org

Headmaster: Since 2011, Mr John Floyd MA PGCE (thirties). Born in London, grew up in The Ivory Coast, Holland and New York. Educated at Cothill and Radley, read geography at Edinburgh University. Previously deputy head of Westminster Cathedral Choir School; prior to that, as a graduate of the Teach First programme, he spent an illuminating three years at Crown Woods – an inner London comp. Married to Henrietta, they have two young sons. He enjoys fly-fishing and food – especially 'proper cooking' which he learned during a gap year in the South of France. Still occasionally runs 'silly distances', the length of Hadrian's Wall just one of many.

A large, ultra-ordered, exceptionally tidy desk dominates one corner of his study, a touch of the OCDs we mused but the reality is a dyslexic head who practises many of the coping strategies he advocates to his charges. A quick glance at the ceiling reveals not the anticipated intricate, ornate plasterwork but a coffee-coloured, water-marked, paint-peeling to-do list – courtesy of a burst pipe. As fits with the school philosophy of boys' needs first, they have sparkly new facilities for ablutions while the head makes do. Young, smartly dressed, well-spoken with a distinctive crop of ginger hair, Mr Floyd has injected a new sense of purpose and order to Bruern. All speak of his warmth, light touch and finely tuned sense of humour. He has the knack of the one-liner – wit, rather than sarcasm and jokes. Staff praise his wonderful organisational skills, ambitious ideas, distinct strategy and purpose. They speak of the seamless transition from old head to new. Head says, 'It was meant to be a year but after a term of Cameron-Clegg co-habiting and polite "after-yous" I was trusted to steer a new course'. Admits it has been more manoeuvring by degrees than wholesale changes but that's very much a nod to the prized work of his 'amazing' mentor. Parents impressed, 'He's sensible, good fun; he gets it, he gets them.'

Entrance: Though intake starts at 7, most join at 9 or 10 after being let down by educational system elsewhere. Majority weekly board, some flexi, handful of day boys. All have specific learning difficulties, dyslexia, dyscalculia and/or dyspraxia, a sprinkling also have additional needs eg Aspergers and ADHD (medicine okay). Parents must provide recent educational psychologist's report. Typically looking for IQ of 110+, but flexes with talent in music, art and sport welcomed. Young hopefuls invited to spend a day and a night at school for informal interview and assessment

Exit: All pass common entrance to their guided first choice senior schools, including Marlborough, Charterhouse, Stowe, Bradfield, Bryanston, Brighton, Harrodian. 'We measure success by the outcome of their first senior year – are they settled and happy?' Parents speak of the CE zone, 'They achieve exponentially. It's really impressive. The children stay at weekends and eat, sleep, breathe CE – revision, past-papers, exam conditions – so they are wholly in the zone.'

Remarks: Many youngsters here have typically suffered a terrible crisis of confidence and most are unable to access or assimilate a conventionally delivered curriculum. Almost half the timetable is dedicated to English and maths, French a must (except in very exceptional circumstances). Withdrawal is limited to the essential but class sizes are kept at 10 or under, with individual attention as a given. 'Boys don't come here to have learning support but to be in a class with others and a teacher who understands their difficulties,' says head. All juniors have one group lesson per week with the wonderfully experienced SENCo. The session determines strengths and foibles; what makes the children tick and what causes them to kick: 'When I write their reports or speak to the ed psych, I truly understand each child.' Not that staff wait to put in place whatever is required: 'My child has needs beyond his dyslexia and they quickly implemented what he needed; no waiting, no protracted multi-agency discussions'.

Subjects, including Latin, are taught separately but classroom thinking is joined-up, with cross-curricular themes whenever opportunity affords. In an RE lesson children studied a time-line, estimating when the Old Testament was written by examining evidence and reaching supported conclusions. We dropped in on a French dictation where, in an attempt to understand and improve along the way, words were analysed and sounds explained as the pupils worked. It's a long day and expectations are high but lessons are fun and much is done to build confidence and success. 'My son comes home animatedly recounting the funny things, bits of naughtiness, and hilarity of the day. He enjoys every lesson but they do work hard.' Most boys are quirky, go off-piste, do the unexpected, 'My child has started writing a book. His spelling is atrocious but his imagination unbounded, thanks to inspirational teaching and an emphasis on giving the boys an interest in learning rather than just unquestioningly absorbing it.' Computers everywhere. All learn to touch-type, the laptop a lifeline, voice recognition technology and dyslexia friendly software all in evidence.

A number of teachers are dyslexic and so get what the boys don't get, 'Teachers genuinely really, really care about us and make learning fun and enjoyable,' say boys. Each has an individual learning plan tailored to his specific strengths and weaknesses with speech, language and occupational therapists on hand when needed. Parents gush with enthusiasm: 'staff help the boys understand their difficulties, develop coping mechanisms, haul them through CE. Their approach is extraordinary; it is a shame all my (non-dyslexic) children couldn't go there.' Another added, 'We keep waiting for the bubble to burst but it gets better. We missed the boat for our first son, discovered Bruern for our second and the instant our third showed signs of struggling we catapulted him in.' Former parents include a rock star, ex-cabinet minister and best-selling novelist; current crop includes actresses and directors. But plenty of 'ordinary' boys too. Parents say, 'Its a hard-core community, no embarrassment, no shame. Typically others have experienced the same or worse so if they find a way to do something they will share that with you, so you don't undergo the same agony.'

Invariably parents stumble into Bruern, battle-weary and beleaguered. 'My child was in a trench, he crawled into Bruern. They didn't just pull him out, they winched him up and propelled him to heights we never thought possible.' Most tell of at least a few wobbles along the way. Years of embedded frustration won't disappear overnight but there are plenty of safety nets and, for most, it doesn't take long for the Bruern panacea to work its magic. One or two parental grumbles about overzealous boys but equally, many are shy or reserved. Said one parent, 'some have serious learning difficulties, some can be disruptive but so can children everywhere. My child is measured but it's good for him to see different colours of intelligence and temperament. The mix reflects society, it helps them develop tolerance, understanding and awareness of others and their strengths and difficulties and makes them realise you can't just write someone off.'

There's a huge, collective sense of responsibility for pastoral care. Immediacy is the name of the game so, as well as end of term reports, expect frequent calls or emails. Parents speak of excellent and frank home-school communication. 'Staff are wonderfully blunt, if your child needs a projectile near his derrière they'll make that pellucid,' said one, another added, 'When boys are naughty, mucking around, they get punished – detentions usually but it's not a big deal in grand scheme of things.' Children are continually praised and rewarded for their efforts, though the head put a stop to the constant dishing out of sweet treats, 'very Pavlov's dogs,' and is now trialling different reward systems.

Bruern is steeped in faded grandeur – peeling, lived in, respected. It may be full of scuffs and scruffs but it smells good and exudes a generous warmth of spirit and a quirky, homely feel. That said, a lick of paint here and there would do wonders. Takes its name from a Cistercian monastery, the current yellow stone building dates from the late 19th century with recent sympathetic additions. This grand house set in 23 acres of grounds and woodland tranquillity may look like a traditional country prep but its dual mission of helping boys overcome learning problems and prepare them for CE to major English and Scottish public schools, makes the place unique. Dorms are large, airy, clean and tidy but need smartening – frayed carpet regrettably draws the eye (though we're told smartening is imminent). Bathrooms newly kitted out, but even we couldn't feign enthusiasm for shiny urinals.

Being relatively young by English school standards Bruern is not blessed with a huge endowment fund, but does benefit from loyal parents who work hard to fundraise, not for fripperies but for fixtures as well as fittings. It's not so much about thrift but spending wisely and keeping fees affordable. Most school cash is ploughed into teaching and learning needs; however, thanks in part to parents, there are signs of considered investment. We spied a good-sized pool with retractable roof and chanced on the wonderful new DT log-cabin where boys beavered, smoothing away the last imperfections of their creations, on multi-purpose work-benches. Art, now in own dedicated studio, provokes mixed responses – some parents enamoured, others give it a 'could do better'. Our investigations suggest art has been something of a Cinderella subject but recent success in local art competition is set to change that. Majority of boys play at least one instrument and many sing in the chapel choir. Sport is important and abundant with regular fixtures – cricket, football, rugby – for all (recent sports tour to India). No indoor gym or Astroturf so they make full use of local countryside with riding, shooting, polo, archery, golf (nearby course) and cross-country. Twenty boys did a 300km charity bike ride to France. Food is a major part of school life (all faiths, intolerances and allergies catered for). Al-fresco dining on dry days plus weekly, revered, formal candlelit suppers to which parents are invited. The Thursday session begins with a spell in chapel followed by mirth, mayhem and manners as eloquent boys host their appreciative guests.

Uniform of yellow polo top and pale brown shorts decorated with generous helpings of mud and pud is not the most fetching we've seen but it does mean these giant buttercups can be spotted hiding in the woods, climbing trees, jumping the stream. The colour, chosen for its calming cheerfulness, flatters few, yet somehow suits its atypical charges and their boys' own world. Bruern is wholesome, hearty, heartening, but could be tricky for the risk-averse or precious (parent or child). 'We do risk assessments, boys climb trees, we stress they shouldn't climb beyond a certain height but they do. They take risks, sometimes they fall out but that's life.' Parents add, 'Children don't need nannying, they need to fuel their imagination, feed their spirit of adventure, take risks, know it's okay to get things wrong, learn from their mistakes. They need space, to run about, ride bikes and to play; they get to do all of that and more too, but they also get unfaltering support.'

The typical Bruern boy is well-spoken, polite, articulate, amusing and enthusiastic. Said one parent, 'My child cried on his first day but has smiled ever since.' A truly unique school; youngsters devour copious helpings of carefully prepared academia, served with generous dustings of laughter, a sprinkle of boyish boisterousness and the odd dash of naughtiness. Presents boys with an exceptional opportunity to understand and tackle their difficulties and make prodigious progress.

Burgess Hill School for Girls Junior School

Linked school: Burgess Hill School for Girls

Keymer Road, Burgess Hill, RH15 0EG

• Pupils: 140 girls; plus around 80 girls and boys in the nursery; all day • Ages: 4-11; nursery 2.5-4 • Non-denominational • Fees: £6,900–£12,150 pa • Independent

Tel: 01444 233167
Email: registrar@burgesshill-school.com
Website: www.burgesshill-school.com

Head of the Junior School: Since 2011, Mrs Heather Miller, previously head of Dover College junior school. She has not always been in education, and spent time in Customs and Excise and the Ministry of Defence. Coming into teaching late, she 'just loves the job'; she is following in the footsteps of 'a popular legend', according to some parents, and has been allowed by the governors the luxury of time to metamorphosise into the position. Parents have warmed to her, not least because she enters into the fray and runs alongside those finding cross-country hard going.

She is determined to broaden the girls' horizons, extending fun activities, promoting theatre trips and taking up the offer for the choir to perform at the National Music for Youth finals. She is happy to be in an all-girls' establishment now, as she feels 'girls can achieve anything and everything and an all-girls' school reduces all limitations'. Her business card states: 'Academic rigour partnered by physical and intellectual challenges create opportunities to learn'. Her personal hobby is the great outdoors, including skiing, running, mountaineering, and assisting on the Duke of Edinburgh award. She has hooked up with Brighton University so that the girls can try out a range of activities, and wants to cultivate a 'can do' attitude, encouraging the pupils out of their comfort zone. 'Every child has a gift, and the key to a successful education is unlocking that gift.'

Background and atmosphere: Very new nursery and infant building providing excellent facilities for the students at the lower end of the school.

Entrance: Non-selective entry for nursery. Reception to year 2 assessed informally by spending part of the day at school. For year 3 upwards girls sit written papers and school likes to see any current school reports, but looks beyond just academic ability. A few scholarships for academic and musical ability. They will admit mid-year if there are places available.

Exit: Almost all go on to the senior school; automatic entry unless head feels any girl may not cope with the workload.

Remarks: Junior school is housed in a traditional large, white building on the same site as the senior school, and although rarely the twain meet, they make use of some senior school facilities. Parents generally happy with the academic standards: 'Lots of writing, lots of homework, lots of testing/spellings, wouldn't like any more,' says one parent. Most lessons are class-based and there is little in the way of dedicated specialist teaching, thus not much moving around the school, except for IT, science, languages and music. Languages at this stage limited to some French; some of the Chinese girls can take up Mandarin.

Some parents would like to see a little more fizz and fun generally, especially with the creative subjects. The school is involved with the Brighton children's parade, making a huge paper caterpillar; very popular weekly art club. A few parents stated that if your daughter 'wasn't academically able she wouldn't survive', and as dedicated and popular as the special needs teachers are, parents feel they are too few and that contact time is too little. The school points out that this is at odds with the gold star awarded for their SEN provision by RS Academics, an agency that surveys parental satisfaction. Parents also mentioned that they would appreciate more consultation time, and this is being addressed.

New 'learning hub' combines library with iPads; also a learning centre for both ends of the academic spectrum, including enrichment and extension.

Bury Grammar Junior School (Girls)

Linked schools: Bury Grammar School Girls

Bridge Road, Bury, BL9 0HH

• Pupils: 355 girls • Ages: 3-11 • Non-denom • Fees: £6,936 pa • Independent

Tel: 01617 972808
Email: info@bgsg.bury.sch.uk
Website: www.bgsg.bury.sch.uk

Headmistress: Mrs Roberta Georghiou (see BGSG seniors) is overall head of the girls' senior and junior schools and co-educational infant school, ably supported since 2009 by Vicky Hall BSc as head of the girls' junior school, who added head of the co-educational infant school in 2012 when the previous head retired. Parents approve of this new structure, both for the continuity and because Mrs Hall is well liked. She and her two deputies, Fiona Gray and Yasmin Haslam, are a dynamic team, and their energy and enthusiasm colour the atmosphere throughout the school.

Entrance: Entrance into the co-ed nursery and pre-school at 3-4 years to become Fledglings or Cygnets (following the swan emblem of Bury Grammar). Children are invited to an assessment half day, 'warm and friendly,' say parents, 'not at all daunting'. Looking for 'children who want to engage with life and learning ... a sparkle in the eye,' says head, but they don't turn many away and if they feel the child is not ready they will suggest a reassessment in six months. An extra class is added to infant school at reception and admission is similar, following a relaxed half day spent with peer group.

Entrance to the juniors at 7 (girls only) is on a mutually convenient day with more formal written assessments within the classroom, a reference from the current school and a brief interview with the head, all very relaxed and enjoyable and the children leave having had fun. The evaluation is of the child's ability and potential and not her previous education. The internal testing at 7+ has recently been stopped and children are only ever asked to leave at this point if there is a major problem, which most likely has already been flagged up. At age 7 the boys move over from the co-educational infants to join the junior section of Bury Grammar School for Boys.

Exit: Almost all to the senior school with only a handful going elsewhere, a couple to other independents and a few to the state sector. The transition is managed well in advance and the year 7s make booklets for the year 6s giving advice and describing their own experiences.

Remarks: A grounded and sunny school with all the nurture afforded by its small size and, thanks to its proximity and links to the senior school, all the facilities and advantages of a large one. Shared major facilities include all sports and the swimming pool, home economics rooms, the dining rooms and the fabulous new arts centre. A shared perspective allows the sense of a caring and stable community to filter throughout. All contributes to the easy passage from juniors to seniors and the strong sense of being part of the whole.

Children learn in a relaxed atmosphere but there is nothing relaxed about the teaching, where learning moments are never missed and the emphasis is on thinking skills and independent research, developing the ability to ask good questions in this world of search engines. 'The girls are encouraged to go off at a tangent with subjects they particularly enjoy,' says head. 'We want to move away from spoon feeding.' Sats were abandoned long ago; 'They depress everybody,' says head. 'There are lots of other, more effective ways of assessing and tracking.'

Classes are dynamic and memorable. Lively with lots of movement, desks moved around as necessary; we witnessed laughter and fun but no loss of control. 'We work on mutual respect,' says head and parents concur, all describing behaviour as exemplary. 'It's all about positive reinforcement, and my daughter knows she will be listened to and taken seriously.' Girls are also encouraged to acknowledge kindness and can nominate each other for the 'courtesy cup'.

A new initiative sees French, German and Spanish, previously taught from year 5, introduced from year 3. Classes are mixed ability although maths is set in year 5 and 6, but parents say, 'If your child needs more she gets more, whether to be stretched or supported, without it ever being an issue'.

Monthly book reviews have to include a broad range – novels, poetry and non-fiction. 'It's a great idea although it can become a bit of a whole family thing,' says one parent, but on the whole parents agree homework is not onerous and 'always has a point.'

The 1990s junior school building has airy, modern classrooms, well equipped and full of colourful displays of work. A huge, bright music room doubles for dance and drama and twice weekly junior assemblies. The library, colour-coded for ease of use, is also home to the well used and much appreciated wrap-around care. Plenty of music; 65 per cent have individual music lessons, strings in years 3 and 4, flutes in year 5 and 6. The girls are welcomed into the orchestra 'if you can hold a bow.' Also choirs and recorder groups. We witnessed a lively and impressive rehearsal of the end of year musical, Robin Hood, involving the whole junior section of the school.

Lots of other extracurricular, from puzzles and logic to tag rugby, some during lunchtime, some after school. Plenty of trips, both local and further afield; skiing in Italy, theatre in London and huge enthusiasm for the outdoor pursuits trip to Plas Menai. Eager, confident, articulate girls described their school council duties, which include recycling (the school recently was given a silver eco award) and pooling ideas for improvements from their class suggestion box, with obvious pride when they are realised.

The spacious, dedicated junior playground has plenty to do, from climbing frames to a bug hotel, and grow bags full

of potatoes – dug up and given to the kitchens. Year 6s work a rota to be play leaders for the infants, creating obstacle courses from the shed full of toys – requested through school council and paid for by the PA. Playground rules are taken seriously and, according to the girls, no-one should be left out and there certainly didn't appear to be any lost souls during the play break we witnessed.

The recently built (2009) separate infants and nursery building is a lovely dynamic, safe space. Filled with light and colour, the facilities are thoughtful and creative and everything is accessible. The central octagonal hall, airy and bright, is used for twice weekly assemblies for the whole of the prep and for the junior productions. A busy, continuous play area, between the reception classroom and the nursery encourages children to be outside as much as possible, aided also by the rack of colourful wellies on hand.

The largely local parents are full of praise and very involved, and the much valued PA is thriving. Communication is described as excellent and Mrs Hall is readily available to address questions or concerns. 'She is brilliant at diffusing problems, nothing is ever allowed to escalate.' The result is a cheerful, secure and stimulating environment producing well-balanced, confident girls who have had plenty of fun on the way.

Bute House Preparatory School for Girls

Luxemburg Gardens, London, W6 7EA

- Pupils: 310 girls, all day • Ages: 4–11 • Non-denom
- Fees: £12,744 pa; • Independent

Tel: 020 7603 7381
Email: mail@butehouse.co.uk
Website: butehouse.org

Head: Since September 2012, Ms Helen Lowe, previously head of the junior department of King's House School, who took over after the nearly 20 year tenure of Sallie Salvidant. She has also taught at Lady Eleanor Holles school and been literary consultant for Richmond on Thames, working in a range of state and private schools. She is married to Phil, a writer who also runs a management development company. Two grown up children.

Entrance: Twenty-two children enter the school in reception. Around 400 children apply and they are picked by ballot. No point in coaching your 3-year-old then. Even less point if your child is not a sibling as they tend to dominate intakes. Thirty-eight children enter year 3. Around 140 girls apply for these places and places are offered on the basis of tests, interview and reports from current schools. No sibling preference at 7+ assessment but school 'looks very carefully at sisters'. Occasional places thereafter are competed for by test and the school has a waiting list for each year. This, then, is to a considerable extent a mixed-ability school. Girls come from the local boroughs and as far as Barnes, Ealing, Kew, Putney, Wimbledon and north London. Vast diversity of backgrounds and a number are bilingual in combinations of French/Mandarin/Italian/German, to name but a few. Read the Bute prospectus for the sheer pleasure of it then use their website for facts.

Exit: Around a quarter each year to Godolphin and Latymer, a further third/quarter to St Paul's Girls' School. The rest go to other good London day schools eg Putney High, Lady Eleanor Holles, the Francis Hollands or Latymer Upper. A few to the best boarding schools – eg Downe House, Wycombe Abbey.

Interestingly, around the same proportion of those who enter at 4+ as those who come at 7+ go on to the top schools. Bute girls trail scholarships – in 2013, the leavers were offered, between them, 22 schols – and not just brainbox schols either – music too.

Remarks: This is not the prep school for St Paul's Girls' School – let's get that clear right now. It happens to be round the corner and it used to be called St Paul's Girls' Preparatory School but, since 1958, there has been no formal link between the two schools and NB Bute girls have no right of entry or preferential treatment when it comes to the entrance exams for its venerable neighbour. So, if your idea is to get into Bute so that your daughter can be pruned, clipped and polished for St Paul's, by way of drilling, testing and hothousing, you are looking at the wrong place, my friend. For a start, Bute has no exams. What! I hear you cry. Neither do its staff put marks at the end of pupils' work – they re-mark ie write copious helpful comments And, yes, there are no form lists or end-of-year placings. And yet, no other prep in the country is so successful at getting places for its alumnae at the best schools.

How can this be? Bute has a culture of learning for learning's sake. The girls are well-motivated anyway and love being at the school. The use of IEPs where needed, the practice of re-marking work rather than marking and of not squandering time on exams and tests means that each child competes only against herself and learns from her own efforts and the teachers' comments. It also ensures that no-one is complacent. Progress is assessed frequently and carefully but not overtly or wastefully. The proof of the pudding is in the girls themselves. We have never been escorted by such happy ones – they strive to outdo each other in enthusing about every aspect of the place – even the teachers – 'she's so nice – I want to hug her!' cried one and when we looked at the photo of all the staff, each one seemed somehow special to the girls. These are happy girls who love their teachers, though the day is so full of stimulation, greedy learning and excitement that, although all the right pastoral care systems are in place, one wonders how a minute might be found if anyone actually needed a quiet space and time to share a problem.

The Bute building itself is a surprise – a somewhat futuristic 1950s neo-greenhouse farrago with add-ons in pine, pink render, louvred glass and warm-toned brickwork in a quiet Victorian terraced street just off fashionable Brook Green, five minutes from the Hammersmith jungle. It has a splendid atrium with the reception and offices and big screens with the news of the day, timetable changes etc – even the day's birthdays – rather nice. We blushed to see our own visit prominently announced but it did mean that everyone knew who we were, which has its advantages. There is a wall on which all Bute pupils are represented by a little ceramic tile which they make and which remains as a record of their time in the school. The school, thereafter, in the head's words, 'is a bit of a Tardis' and one is not prepared by the hotch-potch exterior for the spaciousness – of each classroom, the immense hall and outside space as well as of the airiness and uncluttered feel of the whole. Outside is a tarmac playground and the girls use the St Paul's Girls' school field for games and their swimming pool. Perhaps the perimeter of the playground could use a few more benches to accommodate the older girls who like to sit and chat.

The classrooms are a feast. Reception is big and there is plenty of space for everyone at the little tables and around the many activities – they'd been cooking banana cake when we got there. Everything is beautifully laid out – pencils in pots, a discovery table with 'new life in spring' exhibits – most remarkable – a canopied and cushioned book corner and lots of lovely dressing-up stuff including some pretty cool shoes. All the children use the garden, complete with lots of climbing things and a real – not a bouncy – castle and sandpit. Reception have their own times when they also use large wheely toys. The year 3 classroom we visited was similarly spacious and the ceiling was hung with the results of exciting projects – planets, models of polygons, globes, plants and skeletons. Year 6 had done The Plague so we enjoyed NHS-style pamphlets on 'A Guide to the Plague and How to Avoid It' or 'The Plague – how do I know if I've got it?' One nascent epidemiologist called hers 'Look On the Bright Side!'

This is perhaps the most colourful school we know – everywhere are displays, pictures and models – all bursting with vitality, wit and fun. We giggled over the fish mobiles and the models in DT – caravans made of wood, mostly drawn by horses but one drawn by a mobile muffin and another by David Beckham. Superb library, invitingly laid out and well-stocked, is so popular that the number of visitors have to be restricted. ICT seen as a tool not a subject – hallelujah! – though there is one lesson per week just to learn skills – then laptops available to everyone for help as needed. They were being used, during our visit, in delightful projects by girls who were preparing PowerPoint presentations on their favourite hobby. Grown-up lab hung with inflatable insects almost tempted in this lab-phobic writer. Girls had just done vacuum-packing which was 'so much fun – you just sat in a bin-bag and it sucks the air out and it was so much fun!'

Many rooms, including the hall, are flexible, and divisible into two. All classrooms have smartboards and, oh joy! – all are air-conditioned. The girls eat in one half of the hall and drool over the food. 'It's just the best'... 'it's cooked to perfection!.' Free cucumber and carrot wedges are served at break and there are water-fountains inside and outside school. Milk, however, has to be paid for, which we thought rather mean.

The teaching is clearly, for the most part, inspired and this is true of the Learning Enrichment programme too which covers SEN and G&T. Fifty-two girls on the Learning Enrichment register, many needing only minimal support. This support – unlike the milk – is free. Those who don't speak English at home have one weekly support session. Some see the SENCo on a one-to-one basis and some in small groups. Ninety on the G&T register. Wonderfully enlightened policy. We enjoyed meeting one mildly dyslexic girl who had made 'amazing' progress with her one-to-one but who was also part of the G&T maths group – 'we learned about the hypotenuse! It was so fun!' – but could she spell it? Another enthused about the 'stretching' she experiences in the group – clearly the highlight of her week – 'this room is heaven for me'.

The curriculum is rich anyway – everyone does French from reception, Spanish from year 4 and Latin from year 5. Bute girls excel in sports, drama, dance and music too and win most of the competitive activities in which they engage – school sees not the winning, so much as the opportunity to engage in healthy competition, as important. Has won the London Schools Swimming competition, the British Schools Regional U9 Novice gym competition, the Regional Round IAPS netball tournament, the Ealing Borough cross-country championships and the Thames Valley Harriers cross-country – all in one year. The arts activities and opportunities are both numerous and classy but you'd better see the prospectus for that!

If your daughter gets in, you're in for a lively, exciting and stimulating time – one she will never forget. And the school will make sure she goes on to the senior one that best suits her.

Calder House School

Thickwood Lane, Colerne, Chippenham, Wiltshire, Sn14 8BN

- Pupils: 33 boys, 15 girls, all day; • Ages: 5–12; • Non-denom
- Fees: £15,000 pa; • Independent

Tel: 01225 742329
Email: head@calderhouseschool.co.uk
Website: www.calderhouseschool.co.uk

Headmaster: Since 2008, Mr Andrew Day BEd (early forties) educated at Ysgol Gyfun Ystalyfera (only Welsh speaking comprehensive in West Glamorgan), then University of Wales Institute, Cardiff. Aim of teaching in Welsh medium thwarted by romance: followed wife Helen across Bristol Channel to begin teaching career at Bristol Grammar Lower School for first seven years (maths and ICT plus lots of games coaching), then to be director of studies at Hornsby House, Balham, for next three, where he says, 'I had to rethink my whole approach to teaching'. Subsequently at Wycliffe Prep for three years, then similar period at Cheltenham College Junior prior to landing 'dream job' at Calder House. Hearty Welsh rugby player who is universally liked by pupils: has a real passion for helping dyslexic children realise their potential. Left Cheltenham College Junior as he disliked 'seeing perfectly bright children not making it through to the senior school'. Parents rate way head is 'bringing school up to date' and 'making the right changes'. 'Boys at CH really benefit from head's kind but firm approach,' glowed one satisfied mother. Enjoys getting away to native Wales or Cornwall with wife and two daughters (currently attending Red Maids in Bristol) in Daisy – their trusty VW campervan.

Entrance: Full day's assessment to determine extent to which applicants are under-achieving due to SpLD. Parents commented that the assessment day was 'pupil friendly' and gave children 'a good chance to see what lessons were like'. Some referrals through LAs, who currently fund 10 per cent of pupils. Frequent approaches via local preps, who recognise school's unique contribution. Catchment covers area within 25-mile radius. Currently full.

Exit: Aims to get pupils up to at least chronological reading, writing and maths age within three years or less before returning to mainstream state or independent education. Amazing success rate. Only a very few continue through special education. They move on to Prior Park, Monkton, Stonar, Wycliffe, Warminster and local state secondaries, especially in Chippenham and Bath.

Remarks: Looks more like a country farmstead (which it formerly was) than a school – among the smallest we have visited. Pastoral location on edge of Cotswold hamlet close to Bath, Chippenham and M4 corridor. Lovely grassed area in centre of school (alas, no longer any chickens here since last avian flu scare) gives a sense of calm. Site extends across fields at rear to copses hiding historic World War II air raid shelters: a 'living history' lesson for excited pupils when they are allowed to go there. Calder House founded and owned by delightful Sandra Agombar, who retains title of principal and lives on site with bursar husband – 'He also mows the grass,' we were told. Son, Edward (for whose SpLD benefit the original CH was created in London), works as a teaching assistant and is a living testimony to the school's success. After years at helm, Sandra lets head get on with running the show, though she clearly still looks upon school as her labour of love.

School is approached by gravelled drive with farmland to the side and rear. Classrooms and multi-purpose hall were built to replace formerly dilapidated farm outbuildings and connect to original school, which now houses administration, library and some ICT/teaching space. Large, covered barn provides great play and social space (containing purpose-built play equipment) for break and lunchtime use – staff also read to children here. Some activities take place at mid-morning break (we saw some absorbed chess players – some involved in national schools' chess championships) and others (such as drama and gardening club) during lunchtime. Children bring their own packed lunches.

Pupils are a very mixed lot brought together by a common need for urgent remedial support. Unpretentious blue and white uniform – scope for improvement, we thought. Good cloakroom facilities with plenty of loos and space to change in and out of wellies and coats. We watched a captivating Monday morning assembly on the theme of 'learning from our mistakes', in which the head spun a moral tale about discovered theft, during which he managed to produce 17 oranges from his jacket and trousers – quite a tour de force and much enjoyed by everyone. On Fridays, classes take it in turn to present assembly.

Outstanding across the board in recent Ofsted report. CH accommodates six classes of maximum eight children, though much of the work is in smaller groups or one-to-one. Each child receives two reading sessions a day when they are listened to and taught to read using specific programmes. A daily spelling lesson and two sub-skills lessons, which might comprise one-to-one speech and language, specific dyslexic or gross and fine motor support. Other sessions include working memory (visual and auditory), spatial perception or extra maths support. Daily maths lessons: we saw one year 7 boy (who had already achieved Sats level 6) making considerable headway in this area. Seven full-time staff plus four teaching assistants and two volunteers. Staff:pupil ratio is 1:4. Whole school approach to SEN ensures all pupils attend mainstream lessons (taught as discrete subjects rather than thematically). Timetable gives way twice a term for theme days – recent ones include poetry, maths fun and Robbie Burns.

In the morning, children move around with great purpose, carrying plastic trays for their materials and checking the colour-coded individual timetables sellotaped to the bottom of each. Pupils know where to go as timetables correspond with the differently coloured floors of each classroom. Afternoon lessons are age group based and the broad range of national curriculum subjects includes RE, PSHE and Italian: chosen to avoid unfair comparison at home with siblings.

Artroom displays we saw included pottery, gargoyles and geometric designs in the style of Klimt – 'Art has improved recently,' say parents. Music is class-based at present and taught by a peripatetic teacher in the main hall; school choir with annual in-house as well as local events. We hope that school will introduce individual music tuition before long. Lively science classes make increasing use of the 'outside classroom' on the doorstep, and pupils obviously enjoy their forays into the natural world around them. School's new minibus means pupils enjoy four external visits per term as well as going to swimming (own instructor and lifeguard) at nearby army barracks (25 metre covered pool) and away games fixtures, which parents say boys in particular enjoy. Annual activity week is organised on site and includes overnight camping for some. Considerable success in ESB exams including recent distinctions.

Head rates established system of individualised timetables and we were amazed at how smoothly it operates. We saw pupils working with Arrow software to improve auditory memory, others working on fine motor skills and dyspraxic children improving their co-ordination with the physiotherapist by moving backwards between special cones placed in the multi-purpose hall. Pupils use wide selection of word games with the speech and language therapist. Two ICT rooms are in constant use and serviced by an outside technician. Pupils were learning fractions with the aid of BBC Bitesize software; Heinemann maths course used for older pupils, and we watched a beautifully-delivered lesson on symmetry. Care is taken to ensure that pupils do not miss core teaching. We liked the way pupils are organised to work with others of a similar level: this is kept under constant review.

Parents speak highly of parent-teacher meetings where they get to have in-depth consultations with key staff. Head has provided email access to all staff, which is 'really helpful'. Teachers re-evaluate each child prior to the start of each new term/half-term. Pupils take key stage 2 Sats, with some spectacular improvements in attainment.

One-third of pupils leave each year, but this movement reinforces rather than detracts from school's mission; pupils sense that their time at CH is short and they must make the most of every minute. Former pupils include PhDs, nurses and even an ice hockey player. This is a happy school where children can regain their self-esteem and learn to trust their teachers. 'Buckets of letters' from ex-parents praise work done here. Parents spoke of how primary schools had failed to deal with their child's dyslexia and how honest school had been in giving an accurate time-scale for putting things right. Short intervention is the aim here, not hanging on to pupils unnecessarily. Pupils are taught to cope with failure and then move forwards. Those we spoke to were eager to say how the school had helped them overcome their learning difficulties and how much they value the opportunity provided to improve. One father said school had 'been an absolute godsend', and he really meant it.

Caldicott School

Crown Lane, Farnham Royal, Slough, SL2 3SL

• Pupils: 300 boys; 105 board (including all in the last two years); the rest are day boys • Ages: 7-13 • C of E • Fees: Boarding £22,275; Day £14,325–£15,675 pa • Independent

Tel: 01753 649300
Email: registrar@caldicott.com
Website: www.caldicott.com

Headmaster: Since 1998, Mr Simon Doggart BA (fifty), educated at Winchester and read history at Cambridge. School-mastering is in his blood – his father was a legendary figure at Winchester for many years – and he previously taught history at Eton, where he also ran the cricket. A larger-than-life figure, he has gathered around him an energetic and dedicated staff of young Turks and experienced war-horses. 'He chooses his staff very well,' says a mum. Wife, Antonia, is the very best sort of prep-school head's wife: invaluable at match teas and when entertaining parents, wise and shrewd in counsel and enormously good fun. They are a wonderful couple, much loved by all.

Entrance: The school is divided, though not separated, into three: 7-9; 9-11; 11-13. Three forms, with 13 pupils each; some enter at 7 with more joining at 8. In the October before their September entry, registered boys and parents meet the head and his staff, are shown round and the boys then sit a 35-minute assessment. 'All done so gently they hardly notice it,' a senior boy told us. Potential is valued as much as attainment. Families from Windsor, Henley, Amersham, Beaconsfield etc, and an increasing number from London – 'loads' from Notting Hill and Chiswick, where four buses collect and return (homework done) including Saturdays.

Exit: Yes, it's an Eton, Harrow and Radley school but, as staff are keen to point out, not exclusively so: also St Edward's, Wellington, Stowe, Millfield, Winchester and Oundle. The school is not blind to the importance of matching up with the right school, though 'the competition is cut-throat and parents sometimes have unrealistic notions'.

Remarks: The school feels in some ways like the traditional boarding school of 40 years ago in terms of its insistence on 'good manners and playing the game'. But it is much better than that. Most of the staff live on site – the school has built generously and intends to provide more houses for them. 'We are here 24 hours a day, seven days a week. That's what I joined up for,' says a youngish member of staff. The school sends its most recent inspection report to parents with its prospectus. Prospective parents should read carefully what the head says in his introductory letter about the bland language used on such occasions. Then consider the full significance of the sentence in the report, 'Relationships between boys and staff are excellent'. Every school makes claims for that – Caldicott demonstrates it. 'Spot on,' says a mother; 'They're right,' says a happy boy.

Inspirational teaching greets the young ones, who are involved in imaginative, colourful and exciting work to prepare them for the joys ahead. Occasionally parents bleat about the 'relentless setting', but these boys thrive on the competition and in any case the sets are not cast in bronze. 'Children develop at different stages,' said one wise old bird. Nevertheless the scholarship stream (springing from the well of 9 year olds) is full of bright-eyed boys who, of course, do Latin and Greek and get that extra help towards scholastic glory. Those with learning difficulties are given careful individual treatment – much appreciated. 'The academic régime is inspired by enthusiastic teaching and is firm but fair,' said the father of a son recently departed. 'Caldicott boys are well-adjusted and pretty vigorous in their approach,' said a senior school housemaster. Parents appreciate the frequent reports they receive and the staff are said to be 'most approachable'. A recent improvement, thanks to extra classrooms and staff, is to have four sets in the final year. That gives greater flexibility to move between sets.

Only 20 miles from London, the school is safely lodged in leafy and opulent-feeling Bucks. Founded in 1904 and named after the founding headmaster's new bride, it moved from Hitchin to its present handsome building in 1938. Many sensitively-designed additions: the award-winning centenary hall, a wonderful glassy space for concerts, plays and assemblies of all sorts, and most recently a new science building with cleverly-adapted roof space and state-of-the-art equipment. Two brand new computer rooms, much used and enjoyed.

Bright, cheerful dormitories where a senior boy sleeps in each junior one to ensure peace and happiness. Boys are required to board aged 11 – good preparation for the next stage of the adventure. Junior boarders may go home from 1pm on Saturday until Sunday evening providing they warn the school; senior boarders (11 plus) are allowed out on Saturday nights. Lots of pleasant common rooms and a comfortable dining room, with the oldest boys helping to supervise with teachers – a nut-free school.

Music is improving – it has, perhaps, been a weakness in the past, at least in terms of music scholarships won. Now practice is timetabled in four times a week and concerts are given by professional musicians, who spend a day at the school helping budding performers, many of whom play in the school orchestras, jazz bands, quartets: you name it. The art and DT department is fizzing with colour and creativity and is very popular at weekends. Excellent husband and wife team run it. Annual programme of visits to major London galleries – by the time they leave, boys will have visited six, starting with the National Portrait Gallery, marvellous for linking up with history, and ending with Tate Modern. Other activities include annual declamations for which everyone learns a poem, debating and chess. Life is full and opportunities of every kind abound.

Famous for its rugby and cricket, played on an outstandingly good pitch which has witnessed county and club games. The groundsman is justifiably proud of his work and his beautifully-manicured grounds are the envy of less happy schools. Nowadays Caldicott turns out many more teams than it used to and players who are keen, but not effortlessly gifted, can get into one of the six senior rugby teams or five cricket XIs.

The school has given much thought to extending the range of activities for those less team-games-oriented: sailing, cycling, rowing, chess matches, badminton, squash, fishing, tennis, athletics and so on. Of course many of those are pursued by sporty boys, as well. 'You can always find something you're good at,' said a boy who, on his own admission, was not a natural athlete nor a scholar. Boys hurl themselves around the excellent sports hall, splash around in the heated outdoor pool, practise on the golf area. The overall scene is idyllic, with Burnham Beeches over the road and sweeping views from the pitches.

The excellence of Caldicott lies in the way it has combined the best of the past in prep schools with the comparatively modern emphasis on personal fulfilment. Thirty years ago, the hope for some might have stopped at survival – now no stopping: insistence on good manners does not blunt spontaneity and bubbling enthusiasm. Boys rush around happily, greet with open friendliness and are full of zest.

Superb facilities, excellent staff and lovely surroundings. No sense of standing still; instead the feeling that alert minds are constantly looking for areas to improve, to tweak, to alter. This is an exciting and civilised school which offers an excellent all-round education.

Cameron House School

4 The Vale, London, SW3 6AH

• Pupils: 120 pupils, 65 girls/55 boys; all day • Ages: 4–11 • Non-denom but C of E roots • Fees: £15,750 pa • Independent

Tel: 020 7352 4040
Email: info@cameronhouseschool.org
Website: www.cameronhouseschool.org

Headmistress: Since 2007, Mrs Lucie Moore BEd. School founded in 1980 by Josie Cameron Ashcroft, who is the proprietor and, as Mrs Moore puts it, 'is her one and only governor'. A member of the IAPS, she taught at Thomas's and coached children privately before setting up her own school in St Luke's Church, Sydney Street. She remains principal and still keeps a close eye on the ongoing vision and image of the school and knows all the parents as well as the staff.

Mrs Moore, as headmistress, is in charge of the day-to-day running of the school. She started her teaching career in a state primary in Winchester, then international schools in Italy and Bangkok before settling into the hurly burly of London day schools. She spent seven years at the Hampshire School, where her career took a meteoric rise under the paternal guidance of Arthur Bray: 'He was like a mentor to me'. He soon identified her talents and she swiftly became head of prep and vice principal of the Hampshire Schools before he encouraged her to apply for the post here.

Her husband, the finance director at City Airport, is always by her side at school events. A young headmistress (she was 36 when she started), Lucie (as she is known to everyone, pupils, staff and parents) is attractive and bubbly. She has a huge sense of fun and clearly adores the children. Each sentence is peppered with 'Aren't they just so sweet?' She's got a point –

children here are very cute: girls clad in fresh blue and white striped summer dresses with cherry jumpers and cardis, boys bumbling, adorable in blue cord shorts.

Parents enthuse about her smiling enthusiasm, warmth, excellent communication and understanding of each child. We heard reports of her firm but sensitive approach to the big issues that arise in a child's life, whether it's an instance of unkindness – difficult to conceive of a child being actually bullied here – or problems at home. She also has enormous reserves of energy and is very driven. As well as teaching every class in the school once a week ('It's important that I keep my feet on the ground for the sake of the children and the staff'), coordinating the SEN, and working on the weekly newsletter, she is at the front door every afternoon and morning greeting each child.

If any parent expresses an interest in a senior school she doesn't know, she will make sure she spends plenty of time there – not only to establish important links with the head but also to make sure in her own mind that the school would suit that child. Highly efficient ('I'm a Virgo,' she says. 'I need to be organised and to plan ahead') and not at all concerned about getting her hands dirty, she describes the job as 'fitting like a glove'.

Entrance: All children are assessed at 3, so no need to rush to get your baby onto a list; register up till a year before entry. A popular school – over 200 applicants for 20 places and Mrs Moore acknowledges how difficult it is to choose – 'It's heartbreaking to reject anyone,' she says. Ultimately they look to create a class with a balance of the confident and the shy and some happily in between. They work closely with nurseries and rely on their reports (children come from a wide range including Pippa Poppins, Paint Pots, and Miss Daisy's). Putting school down as a genuine first choice always helps.

Exit: A few boys at 7+ or 8+ to, eg, boarding or Catholic schools (Ludgrove, St Philip's), but fewer and fewer now. Mrs Moore has fine tuned the 'stepping stones' options for boys who want to do 13+ common entrance and sends them for two years at 11 to, eg, Newton Prep, Fulham Prep, Sussex House, Wetherby and the Hampshire School. Lots of advice given to parents from year 5 onwards.

At 11 girls and boys go to a broad range of schools each year – current favourites are Latymer Upper, St Paul's Girls, City of London Girls' and Boys', Dulwich, Alleyn's, Emanuel, Godolphin & Latymer, Queen's Gate, and Francis Holland. They nearly always get their first choice school, we're told (due in large part to Mrs Moore's determination that parents choose the school that suits their child, whatever they themselves might prefer), 'And they interview beautifully because they're so confident,' she gloats. One or two girls every year board at, eg, Wycombe Abbey and Downe House.

Remarks: A tiny (one class per year of about 20), cosy, pretty school, but don't be misled into thinking it's just chocolate boxy – Cameron House is a serious player in getting children into sought-after London schools. Wide range of ability, but what all children have in common is that they are confident and very, very smiley.

They are given a lot of preparation in the final year. In year 6, class sizes shrink so everyone gets more attention, compulsory homework club gives all children an extra hour at school and removes the pressure from the parents. 'We shoulder the worry,' says Mrs Moore, 'and the last thing I want is to see 10 year olds being counselled for stress.' A lot of staff channelled into year 6, when they do group work, prepare for scholarships, have mock interviews and confidence-building workshops. The formula clearly works – they get results, but no-one could describe this as a hothouse.

Approximately 15 children are helped with mild to moderate SEN – dyspraxia, dyscalculia, dysgraphia etc. The school takes a holistic approach. Learning support is timetabled and structured with clear IEPs drawn up – parents pay extra. Programme for the gifted and talented run within the class. In addition a select few are invited to join the Discovery Club and Explorers Club. Mrs Moore explains the cautious approach to the gifted and talented programme. Children are identified towards the end of year 1 – 'We wouldn't want to have to say, "You weren't gifted after all!"' she says.

A town house with not a great deal of space, but the soft plush tartan carpet throughout the stairwell, lavatories with pretty wallpaper, water filters, attractive blue furnishings and every teacher referred to by their first names – without even a Miss or Mister attached – give the school a homely, uninstitutional feel.

Children have fun here, whether it's enjoying music, drama, sport, watching caterpillars transmorph into butterflies or playing giant magnetic chess in the playground (a good excuse to see the lovely Lucie, to get the chess pieces). Even maths can be made to be an excuse to dress up and laugh – Bubbles the maths clown came to school, the hall was filled with balloons and children came to school dressed as shapes. In Book Week everyone dresses up, even Mrs Moore, who is not at all fazed when she greets prospective parents dressed as Captain Hook. 'If they don't like to see their future headmistress being able to laugh at herself, then we're clearly not the right school for them nor them for us,' she says.

Nearly everyone plays an instrument or has singing lessons – the lessons happen in a little Wendy house type hut in the playground. Major dramatic productions – The Lion King, A Midsummer Night's Dream among them – take place in a closely guarded secret venue – 'Let's just say a theatre off Kensington High Street,' is as far as Mrs Moore will be drawn. 'We aim high,' says Mrs Moore proudly, as she lists the impressive artistic accomplishments for such a small school, which include getting to the final for young choir of the year at the Royal Festival Hall. They have an orchestra, string quartet and three choirs.

One of Mrs Moore's challenges has been to stop the boys leaving at 7+ or 8+ – signs of success. Although previous year 6 classes have had few boys, some none at all, when we visited there were an equal number of both sexes. 'Parents are starting to realise that they can get their boys into Westminster Under, Colet Court and Latymer at 11,' she says, 'and there are plenty of stepping stone options between 11 and 13.' Children are kept a lot more active here than at many similar schools. Games takes place three times a week – children can do cricket, football, hockey and netball as well as martial arts in the huge loft space at the Boudokwai centre. Lots of matches (most of which they lose, comments one parent) but the advantage of being a small school is everyone gets to have a go – it's not just the sporty types who do everything.

A lot of expat families from mainly the US, Canada and Australia, reflecting the cosmopolitan area. We saw masses of glamorous long-haired mothers off to the gym after drop off. Lots of city types but also more than the usual number of creatives – artists, actors, as well as doctors and art dealers. All parents are very involved and enjoy the open door policy of the school.

A charming school that will discover your child's strengths, nurture and support them.

Cargilfield School

45 Gamekeeper's Road, Edinburgh, EH4 6HU

• Pupils: 310 girls and boys; 60 boarders • Ages: 3–13 • Non-denom • Fees: Day £8,760–£13,905; Boarding £17,220–£17,910 pa • Independent

Tel: 01313 362207
Email: admin@cargilfield.com
Website: www.cargilfield.com

Acting headmaster: Since October 2013, following the abrupt departure of the previous head and his wife, the acting head is David Walker, previously deputy head and head of English. From farming stock near Shrewsbury; attended Shrewsbury School during the Ted Maidment era followed by Swansea University to read English. Taught English at Malsis, North Yorkshire, for 12 years before coming to Cargilfield nine years ago as assistant head. Very keen sportsman; takes 1st XV rugby and 1st team cricket. Married with young children.

Emma Buchanan is acting head of pre-prep.

Entrance: Nursery and pre-prep popular; upper school numbers have grown enormously; places pretty well guaranteed through pre-prep but tests if learning difficulties suspected. Wannabes assessed: occasional places may occur throughout the school – logistics.

Exit: All the Scottish public schools – Glenalmond and Fettes head the list, but also Merchiston, Kilgraston, fewer to Gordonstoun, almost none to Loretto, much as you would expect. Huge cohort – around half – head south of the border: Eton (biggest feeder north of Oxford), last year top scholarship to Winchester, also Harrow, Downe House etc etc, you name it. More scholarships than you can shake a stick at – 50+ last three or four years: 'genuine academic awards'. Top award to Fettes regularly and top classics to all.

Remarks: Cargilfield had a bad case of wobbles: previous head effected a transformation and school was back on track. We arrived to find the school covered in scaffolding and wondered about a new, new-build, but no, just roof repairs. (The £1.2 million games changing rooms are up and running.) This former parent of the pre-prep (still brill) regrets the reduction of play area (previously 23 acres now 15: posho pads equal new builds); the sports hall (a 21st century prerequisite) impinges on the games pitch, alongside a couple of cedar-clad (rather grand inside) huts, which blend well, but look like early huts for battery hens (or photographs of Bletchley Park), and provide a new teaching centre plus a 10-room (sound-proof) music school with a mini-concert rehearsal room, used for drama too. A stonking 80 per cent take extra music. Strong choir, which tours 'down south', and terrific strings ensemble: 'our top area and they have won major awards at the Edinburgh Music Festival'; pop group. Pipe band is second to none, taster sessions for all in pre-prep, they were practising on the games pitch as we left, certain amount of interesting baton chucking.

Impressive two-storey classroom block for English, ICT and history, with colonnades, cloisters and walkways. Certain amount of internal restructuring, with dorms becoming classrooms (and vice versa).

Pupils setted and streamed, maths from age 8. Most year groups divided into three: scholarship stream (currently boasting 14 pupils) for the last three or four years plus two mixed-ability classes. French from nursery, Latin from 9 or 10; ancient Greek at 11, classical civilisation, Spanish for the last two years. (German and Mandarin clubs – cost extra).

Fantastic learning support (known as learning development) all assessed on entry; head of learning support plus two and a half staff. One of the best departments in Scotland, combining individual and co-teaching: max 5.5 hours per week. Currently has a parent-underwritten (ie they pay school fees and for a dedicated teacher) unit for two pupils who have very special needs, (previous) head hesitated for a moment, but agreed this was still in place 'an unusual arrangement'. But isn't this what the independent sector is about? School can no longer accommodate many of the weaker brethren, unless they are, in fact, brethren. Jolly phonics and any 'other combination that works' on the reading front.

Founded in 1873, the school moved to its purpose-built site in 1890. Girls' boarding house is full, difficult to find space for flexis. Jolly sitting-rooms on ground floor (along with showers etc) and some of the prettiest dorms we have seen in a long time. Odd space in boys' dorms: trad old school dorms, huge, with sofas and games tucked into corners – given the choice, chaps preferred more mates to smaller bedrooms. Chaps in bunks, girls have drawers below beds, total replacement of furniture and fittings factored in every three years. Two-weekly boarding for all (max 74 boarders at any one time, 35 weekly, 15 full time). Day pupils regularly join boarders for a huge variety of weekend activities (though all must stay for three nights and can't just pick and choose). Mega weekend activities, no Saturday school ('children more relaxed and less tired on Mondays'). Nine year olds camping in the Highlands, 12/13 year olds at Hadrian's Wall.

Deep complaints from parents whose young played Cargilfield girls' netball squad at the recent Belhaven tournament. Cargilfield wore sponsored hoodies, with Cargilfield First Netball Team on the back, and 'Imagine having Strutt & Parker on your bosom' said one irate papa.

Kayaking, shooting, international coaching in fishing, fencing, judo, hockey, skiing both at Hillend and the real thing. Two small Astroturfs. Eighty clubs on offer – chess champions with boards set up all over the place (and visiting chess master). Trips all over, both at weekends and longer ones abroad to Rome and France. Much use made of resources in grand Scots cities. New website.

Discounts for MoD children (handy for Scottish Command). Hundred per cent bursaries on offer: means-tested – five or six pupils on this kind of bursary (but not necessarily every year), graduated sibling discount. Mixed bunch of parents, grander than previously, FWAGS now thinner on the ground, one or two proper foreigners, tiny ethnic mix. Boarders from Yorkshire, the Borders, West Coast, Aberdeenshire, Angus and Perthshire. Bus on Sundays from Angus and Aberdeenshire, and daily from India Street in Edinburgh, Fife and West Lothian but, as children often stay until after eight, parents must collect them themselves.

Pre-prep and nursery based in stunning £3.5m building with cherished (quite small) Astroturf and enclosed play area, share big school facilities. School not keen on folk using the nursery as a spring-board for a couple of years and then heading off elsewhere (like this editor!).

Carrdus School

Overthorpe Hall, Blacklocks Hill, Banbury, Oxfordshire, OX17 2BS

• Pupils: 120 girls, 32 boys; all day pupils • Ages: 3–11 (girls); 3–8 (boys) • Non-denom • Fees: £1,230–£9,750 pa • Independent

Tel: 01295 263733
Email: office@carrdusschool.co.uk
Website: www.carrdusschool.co.uk

Headmaster: Since 2012 and retirement of Susan Carrdus, Edward Way BSc (forties). Educated at Radley College and UCL, where he read geology. PGCE at University of Bath, followed by posts at Cothill, Chandlings, Cheam School and Lambrook School, then 10 years as head at Great Tew Primary School, 12 miles away. His wife teaches at The Dragon in Oxford and they have three children.

Entrance: Junior school is currently full to bursting – tribute, says school, to the amazing staff. No entrance test – 'It's first come, first served'. Very broad intake. Majority of pupils come from Banbury and surrounding villages, with parents registering children up to three years in advance. Most common entry points are nursery, reception and year 3, but it's worth trying in between too. No scholarships offered but means-tested bursaries sometimes available.

Exit: About a third of girls to 'big sister' Tudor Hall. Rest to a wide range eg King's High Warwick, Rugby, Oundle, St Mary's Ascot, Bloxham, Headington. Boys head at 7 or 8 to preps eg Cothill, Warwick Junior, The Dragon and Winchester House.

Remarks: School started in 1952 and moved to its present site in 1970 when founder Kathleen Carrdus bought Overthorpe Hall for the princely sum of £22,500. Has always had strong links with Tudor Hall, which bought school in 2011. Union seems to have worked well and Carrdus staff say they consider Tudor Hall their 'big sister'. Main building a rambling 1880 hunting lodge set in 11 acres of grounds.

Friendly teachers pride themselves on making children feel happy and secure in 'informal yet stimulating' environment. Lots of fresh air, smiley faces, muddy knees and heaps of praise. Despite relaxed ambience, pupils work hard and school's academic record is impressive. School says: 'We set high standards and help children achieve them.' Hugely experienced staff, with good mix of ages. One class per year group, with an average of 20 per class and maximum of 24. No setting, but the most able get the chance to move faster in 'sparkle sessions'. French from reception and Latin for last two terms of year 6. No scholarship stream – school prides itself on giving everyone the chance to shine. Homework for all. Reception children take reading books home while year 6 pupils get 30 minutes' homework a night. Thousands of books, all colour-coded for different reading abilities.

A number of pupils with mild dyslexia, developmental co-ordination disorder (dyspraxia) and/or learning difficulties. One-to-one help available from three-strong learning support team or in small groups, often at start or end of school day.

Arts strong, with all pupils encouraged to play instruments, speak confidently in public and take part in concerts. Children's work on display everywhere you look. When we visited, year 5s were busy making glorious pink Mother's Day cards, while a group of jolly year 4s were rehearsing for their forthcoming medieval Britain's Got Talent assembly. Music terrific – everyone learns recorder from 7 upwards and at least half the pupils learn piano, violin, guitar, saxophone, flute, cello or drums. Orchestra, choirs and bands galore.

School day starts at 8.50am and finishes at 3.40pm, but to help working parents children can arrive from 8.15am and stay on for (paid-for) Teatimers sessions after school till 5.30pm. All children attend at least two clubs a week – everything from art and craft to roller skating. Daily assembly, as well as weekly hymn practice and bible story. Delightful (and short) list of school rules advises pupils: 'No sticks, no stones', 'Only climb as high as your friend's head' and 'It's only fun if everybody is enjoying it'.

No school uniform, apart from games kit. Dress code is 'not smart, not scruffy', with parents advised to send children to school in comfy, machine-washable clothes. No jeans, bare midriffs, nail varnish, jewellery, mobile phones or chewing gum. Children are encouraged to be children, not mini-adults. Pupils are well-behaved and discipline is not an issue. As school points out: 'Children like boundaries, as long as they are fair and they can see the point of them.'

Sport is compulsory for all. Children do hockey, netball, athletics, tennis, gymnastics, dance, cycling proficiency and swimming (in a heated outdoor pool set in pretty walled garden). Cross country a particular strength. All year groups get two trips a term – to places like Stratford-upon-Avon, Oxford's Ashmolean Museum, Warwick Castle and the Roald Dahl Museum. Year 6 pupils have annual expedition to Normandy – French speaking only the minute the coach leaves the school gates.

Nutritious, wholesome lunches cooked on-site and served by friendly dinner ladies who know all the children's names. Extensive salad bar and more choice than before. At breaktime youngsters help themselves to cheese, crispbread, raw vegetables and fruit (they can bring in their own snacks on Fridays – no chocolate, though) before racing off to play outside in all weathers. Carrdus is one of the only schools we know that keeps spare wellies for visitors. Lovely grounds boast four friendly guinea fowl, outdoor tuning bars and lots of hidey-holes. Latest addition is the stunning Diamond Wall, built to celebrate school's 60th anniversary. Names of old pupils and staff inscribed across wall, along with touching plaudits like 'a joy to teach here', 'always a Carrdus girl' and 'Carrdus = happiness'.

Parents are hugely supportive of the school. 'They embrace individuality here,' one mother told us. 'Pupils aren't machined out. The teachers totally bring out the best in each child.' Another parent commented: 'My children are really happy here. It's fun, but competitive when it needs to be.' Very active PTA, with activities ranging from new parents' breakfasts to annual bonfire party, Christmas fair and spring sale. Instead of standing in the car park, parents arriving to collect their children gather in the entrance hall, complete with huge, welcoming sofas and, in winter, a roaring log fire. Twenty years ago, way ahead of its time, the school launched annual At Work day, giving mums and dads the chance to work alongside their children in lessons.

Children have a whale of a time here, while achieving good results along the way. Devoted pupils (boys as well as girls) stay in touch for years after they leave, ringing for advice about everything from university entrance to career choices – 'They come back and back and back. It's not simply nostalgia. It's all about revisiting a place they enjoyed'.

Casterton, Sedbergh Preparatory School

Linked school: Sedbergh School

Kirkby Lonsdale, via Carnforth, LA6 2SG

- Pupils: 170; 95 boys/75 girls; 70 full and flexi boarders • Ages: 3–13 • Church of England • Fees: Day £7,011–£13,506; Boarding £16,623–£20,337 pa • Independent

Tel: 01524 279291
Email: ajm@sedberghprep.org
Website: www.sedberghprep.org

Headmaster: Since September 2013, Mr Scott Carnochan (forties), previously head of Sedbergh, has been head of the new joint school. Educated at Dollar Academy, BEd from Herriott-Watt Edinburgh. Former Scottish U18 rugby cap; PE a speciality. Married to Kate; they have two young children.

Entrance: Assessment by head's interview and previous school report for younger children; tests for 10 – 13 year olds.

Exit: Nearly all to senior school.

Remarks: Newly merged co-ed prep school with the Sedbergh head on the Casterton site, which offers a range of activities from ghyll scrambling to ballet and fishing to mountain biking, and a range of boarding options. Plenty of outdoor space.

Castle Court

Knoll Lane, Corfe Mullen, Wimborne, Dorset, BH21 3RF

- Pupils: 320 boys and girls; all day • Ages: 3–13 • C of E
- Fees: £7,455–£13,485 pa • Independent

Tel: 01202 694438
Email: admissions@castlecourt.com
Website: www.castlecourt.com

Headmaster: Since 2010, Mr Richard Stevenson (early forties), BA PGCE. Previously head of Kelly College, Tavistock. Read politics, philosophy and economics at Portsmouth University before cutting his pedagogic teeth at Ballard School, and then Holmwood House, Colchester.

An old boy of Castle Court, he knows the area well and is delighted to be to back. His predecessor had been manning the parapets of Castle Court for 21 years and, even before he had crossed the moat, Mr Stevenson was telephoning parents past and present, firing off questionnaires, talking with staff and pupils and generally taking the temperature. Numbers increased by one third during his first year. Parents appreciate his presence in the car park – 'that defuses the mafia and trims unhealthy gossip. We get instant responses to niggles and he has set aside a room where we can have a coffee and a gossip. He often pops in there, as well.'

An approachable man with a good sense of humour, he clearly enjoys excellent rapport with the children and was very nearly mobbed on a number of occasions when he was showing us around. He says he is 'passionate in my belief that education must be fun, that happy children will learn better and that it is up to the school to do everything it can to ensure each child's unique life should be happy and fulfilled.' That's not an earth-shattering idea and not one with which many would argue but in an age of statistics and jargon, it's good to have it expressed with such unpretentious freshness and sincerity. And to see it in action. Parents with whom we spoke were vociferous in their praise for him. 'When his wonderful predecessor left, we were all a bit worried,' said one parent, 'but we needn't have been. He is very open to ideas and has a wonderful way with the children, whether it is donning his wellies and digging with them in their gardens, playing ping pong or just chatting with them. But he's not a softy: he sets high standards and marks out clear guide lines.'

One way in which the sense of having fun is conveyed is that children are allowed to climb trees and play conkers. Followers of form won't be surprised by how few schools allow either. 'Children should be allowed to be children and not grow up too quickly. That includes learning to take risks,' he adds.

Married to the delightful Lucy, who is involved around the school. One parent said of her, 'she doesn't seek the limelight but is a tireless worker behind the scenes. They make a marvellous team.' The Stevensons live on site with their four children. The eldest is at Clayesmore, the next destined for Canford. In his spare time the head enjoys sailing, walking, IT and wood-turning.

Entrance: Really at any age, providing there is room. Booking ahead strongly recommended. Children come from a wide arc around the school – Blandford, Wimborne, Ferndown, Bournemouth, Poole, Wareham, Swanage and Dorchester. Buses in and out. Out means 4.15 when the day officially ends or 5.45 when voluntary activities end.

Exit: Not surprisingly, and quite rightly, Canford is the most popular destination but not exclusively so. Winchester is becoming increasingly popular as is Bryanston and, the headmaster says, Millfield plus Poole and Parkstone Grammars. The school prides itself on being seriously academic – though it is no green house – and annually has an impressive range of scholarships. One senior school head commended the way Castellans fit in quickly and happily; another said how well drilled they were. Not a word we would have used.

Remarks: Delightfully rural, though in fact close to towns along the Dorset coast, the school appears as a lovely surprise in the beautiful countryside of winding lanes and bosky woods. Journeying children and railway enthusiasts will pause with reverence by the footbridge which crosses the road linking the main body of the school with the attractive games fields. It once bestrode a branch of the Somerset and Dorset Joint Railway, one of the many lines murdered by the infamous Dr Beeching. Aficionados of railway architecture could ask the head for the telephone number of one of the governors who would provide further information. If you do telephone, have a comfortable chair handy. Knoll House, the pleasant Regency house at the hub of the school, is not visible from the road, though it is from the bridge. Once you arrive there, the wonderful tumbling gardens, terraced and hillocky, are a joy and much appreciated by the children, as are the surrounding woods which shelter such a superb Forest School that serves as a model for other schools and organisations who visit for training. Magical hills and trees surround the house; a flock of rescue hens, guinea pigs, all weather table tennis, an adventure play area, enthusiastically tended gardens where, and – this is typical of the thought that goes into everything at Castle Court – children are encouraged to grow what will flower or ripen during the term. Deeper in the woods behind the huge Astroturf real pigs snuffle and grunt, tended by the children under the watchful eyes of the headmaster and the affable bursar. During break we saw shiningly happy children everywhere. There was a real Fern Hill atmosphere where 'Time lets them play and be golden in the mercy of his means.'

The classrooms in among the trees are bright and airy. This is where the academic business is approached from tinies having fun as Badger cubs (aged 2-4) through to those approaching their senior schools at a cracking pace. The Castle Court adventure. We've seen swankier classrooms (some are due to be upgraded) but the facilities are excellent and besides, good teaching does not depend on the buildings. It depends on the interaction of pupils and staff and what we saw was purposeful, lively and professional in the best sense of the word. Wonderful music facilities incorporating dance, drama and ballet where aspiring ballerinas can work on their pas de deux in front of mirrors and leg stretching bars. For year 2 pupils, playing the recorder is part of the curriculum and group tuition schemes are in place for older pupils. The hills are alive to the sound of singing. Rumours of tickets for the carol services being sold for huge sums on the black market may well be exaggerations but they are certainly very popular events.

Marvellous IT and DT with excellent facilities and where the emphasis is on independent learning; exciting, inspirational art where the portraits pupils had painted are far less frightening than they often are and where there was much evidence of creativity and fearless experiment, Well stocked library. Overall, as we toured the classrooms we were assailed by a sense of fun and purpose.

Castle Court is a winning school and Castle Castellans take their sport very seriously. New director of sports, lured from Kelly College, is as keen on the etiquette of sportsmanship as winning. Well, nearly! The old fashioned virtues of shaking hands after the game and entertaining away teams are held in high esteem and often commented on. Parents are kept in touch over such ticklish matters as team selection and why a boy/girl won't be playing in the team next week. Much potential petulance avoided, even when disappointment numbs. Teams are not selected for the term, so as to avoid depressing keenies who haven't quite made the initial cut. Everyone is encouraged to believe he or she has a chance of making it. Many activities from riding to rowing and sailing on offer for non-team players. Another example of the thoughtfulness that lies behind the way the school is run.

And that's the word we took away with us. Thoughtfulness. Thoughtfulness born of knowing and understanding children and caring about them; thoughtfulness for the concerns and aspiration of parents; even thoughtfulness about money matters. The school day ends at 4.15 but then follows an amazing variety of activities and what parents really appreciate is that they are free.

Castle Court is held in high esteem both for the quality it offers and the qualities it nurtures. As one parent told us, 'it's not a fluffy school. The children have a lot of fun and are very happy but there is also an insistence on good manners and courtesy. It is, after all, possible for the two to coexist.'

Newish headmaster building on the success of his admirable predecessor; an interesting import of talented new staff; a powerful sense of surging ahead. Anyone living within range of this action packed day school should go and have a look. Even just visiting is a joyful experience. No Open Days. 'Every day is an Open Day.'

Caterham Preparatory School

Linked school: Caterham School

Harestone Valley Road, Caterham, CR3 6YB

• Pupils: 280; 160 boys/120 girls; all day • Ages: 3–11
• Fees: £4,896–£12,600 pa • Independent

Tel: 01883 342097
Email: anita.noble@caterhamschool.co.uk
Website: www.caterhamprepschool.co.uk

Headmaster: Since 2005, Mr Howard Tuckett MA (Ed) HDE (early fifties). Born in Epping, but educated in South Africa where he began his career in various prep schools, arriving back in the UK, via a stint in Botswana, in 1995 as deputy head at Kings Hawford Prep School in Worcester. Then headmaster at St Joseph's College Prep School in Ipswich for five years before coming to Caterham. Not the obvious oppo to Julian Thomas (head of Caterham snr school), but in fact they share an educational philosophy and get on well. 'Nice', 'approachable' and 'a lovely man,' say parents, who feel the school has improved since his arrival. Popular with the children, to whom he appears something of a gentle giant. Self-deprecating and not afraid to muck in (was off to the pool with one class after our visit), fits in some teaching, mainly history, where he is said to do 'hilarious impressions of Winston Churchill' and Latin – 'I'm a page ahead of them', he jokes. Married with two children, keen on fishing and gardening, plays guitar and is involved with the church.

Entrance: First come, first served – most pupils join in nursery or reception classes in the order in which they applied, with no formal entry requirements, other than an informal assessment to exclude those with any significant learning or behavioural difficulties. Both nursery and reception are over-subscribed, nursery typically 60 applications for 20 places, then another 20 join at reception (taken from the nursery waiting list). Entry at other years – up until 11+ as the occasional space comes up. At this stage applicants will be assessed during a full day spent as part of a class at the school.

Exit: Vast majority to senior school. Plenty of warning for anyone not expected to make the grade, although apparently 'not many'. However, as senior school gets increasingly popular and academic, it may become more of a struggle for some to make the transition than in the past. Others to eg Woldingham, Lingfield, Notre Dame, Millfield.

Remarks: Located along the valley past the main school, the prep and pre-prep buildings nestle in sweet seclusion in a natural dead end, making for a peaceful and completely traffic free zone. Share many of the main school's top notch facilities, although prep's own buildings are two former mansion houses, so not so modern and sparkling as others you may see. New woodland outdoor learning centre shared with senior school.

Not the place for a slacker – one mother felt strongly it was all work and no (or not enough) play. Although a two-hour lunch break, it can be fairly chocka with music and games practice and other clubs and activities. Certainly not surprising if pupils have to up their game as popularity of senior school increases. Around 20 children in each class – air of industry around the place as purposeful children get stuck into all on offer. School encourages everyone to get involved with everything. Uniform reflects the active buzz of this place, including sensible and smart anoraks for the outdoor stuff.

Lessons are pacey; a broad curriculum with plenty of cross-curricular activity. Interactive whiteboards in every room.

Strong emphasis on children being heard to read, not just while they are learning, but right up to age 11. 'The school really makes time for everyone,' says one mother. Subject teaching by year 4. Mr Tuckett pleased that he has flexibility here, nothing set in stone, so he may have one year working in three sets and another in four, depending on the particular need. 'Nothing is hide-bound,' he says. 'We don't expect the cohort to adapt to fit our system – we will do what is best for them.' School aims to teach children 'to create their own success', in acknowledgement of the fact that they may grow up to work in industries that don't exist yet.

Just as sporty as you would expect – again good preparation for the active senior school – but don't be concerned if your child is usually a less than keen participant. 'There is no such thing as a non-sporty child,' asserts Mr Tuckett, confident he can enthuse anybody. 'They just need to be taught properly.' So children see a lot of the great outdoors – plenty of space and facilities here – and everyone will get match practice: they'll put up a D team if necessary. Such endeavours paying off now, with particular success in football and netball; lacrosse popular too.

Some good music. Years 3 and 4 learn the recorder and years 5 and 6 take up guitar – their first lesson is usually Deep Purple's Smoke on the Water, which sorts them out.

As in the senior school, links between parents and school are strong and communications friendly and informative. Lots of opportunities to help, from thriving PTA to running the library. 'I sometimes joke that I've given up my life to this school,' says one busy mother, who evidently wouldn't have it any other way. A boon to working parents is the after-school care – available up until 6pm and including a supervised homework session.

Overall an effective school, a happy and comfortable environment where the children feel able to give of their best and come home smiling.

Central Newcastle High School Junior Department

Linked school: Central Newcastle High School

Chapman House, Sandyford Park, Newcastle upon Tyne, NE2 1TA

• Pupils: 250 girls, all day • Ages: 3–11 • Fees: £6,918–£8,463 pa
• Independent

Tel: 01912 016511
Email: j.howe@cnh.gdst.net
Website: www.newcastlehigh.gdst.net

Head of Junior School: Sinc 2011, Miss Charlton. 1997 deputy head of Fellside Community Primary School and seconded to Oakfield Infant School as acting head teacher in 2000; head teacher at Portobello Primary School in Birtley in 2004, where she built an 'outstanding curriculum' (Ofsted) and defied demographics by increasing pupil numbers significantly.

She has been working to embed the creative curriculum into the school's teaching and on the newly refurbished Chapman House.

Entrance: Assessment and interview.

Exit: Virtually all to senior school unless family moves out of area.

Remarks: Major refurbishment following decision to move all junior pupils to one site at Chapman House in Sandyford Park. Set in five acres of grounds and includes a grade 2 listed

John Dobson designed mansion, architect designed indoor and outdoor learning space.

Whole school will merge with Newcastle upon Tyne Church High School in September 2014 to form Newcastle High School for Girls.

Centre Academy East Anglia

Church Road, Brettenham, Ipswich, Suffolk, IP7 7QR

• Pupils: 46 pupils, of whom 18 are boarders and 3 are flexi-boarders. • Ages: 4–18 • Inter-denom • Fees: Day £16,000–£35,000 pa • Independent

Tel: 01449 736404
Email: admin@centreacademy.net
Website: www.centreacademy.net

Head of School: Since September 2010, Mrs Kim Salthouse BA MEd, previously acting head at the school.

Entrance: Caters for dys-strata. Entrance is by an educational psychologist's report and interview, after which the child is invited to spend a day at the school so that staff can ascertain where they will best fit in.

Exit: To mainstream education.

Remarks: This is an old rectory, next to the church, which is used for daily assemblies and is set in seven acres of deep Suffolk. The fabric of the school was bought from Mr and Mrs Phillips by Michael Murphy (whose role appears to be that of interested benefactor) in 1999.

Boarding girls live in the Coach House, recently modernised and extended. Boys live in the main house, in immaculate tidiness (can this really be so?). Most are weekly boarders. Lessons are either taken in a large hall subdivided into four classrooms with folding screens – The Arches, which was opened by Lord Archer – or in Portakabins outside. Lots of English, maths and other trad subjects are taught in small classes (max size eight), according to ability rather than age. Follows a modified national curriculum – Spanish rather than French. Dedicated IT room, with children taught touch-typing early, but no laptops; two handwriting lessons a week match the two keyboarding lessons.

Music and drama important. Games on site and masses of extracurricular activity, including karate, target shooting and fire crew – the school has five fire engines, which specially-selected pupils can help 'crew', usually putting out controlled fires only! All the extracurricular activities are chosen to improve motor skills.

This is a school for the dyslexic, the dyspraxic, those with dyscalculia and the occasional fragile child. Does not take any child with behaviour problems, nor any child on Ritalin, though several on efalax oil, and several wear coloured spectacles in deep pink, mauve or dark blue which are often promoted as remedial aids. The usual age for children coming to the school is 10 or 11, often only for a year or two; they then return either to normal mainstream schools or to schools offering continued specialist help. Some children are statemented, with a few of them receiving funding from their local authority – others are going through the process of accessing funding via a tribunal. Many of the children do not come from a boarding school background and their parents 'may have sold their house or gone without holidays' to send them here.

Plus points for good behaviour, bad points for negative – really disruptive children can be sanctioned, involving loss of privilege, and occasionally suspended or expelled. Female staff are invariably called Miss and the few men Sir. No real problems in getting staff, but the head feels it is important to have more than just the very popular groundsman as the token male role model and takes time to find men with the right qualifications – if staff do not come with suitable dyslexia training, they undertake appropriate courses. Occupational and speech therapists on hand.

A helpful little school which sends children with special needs back into mainstream education – worth considering.

Chafyn Grove School

Bourne Avenue, Salisbury, SP1 1LR

• Pupils: 320; 200 boys/120 girls; 92 boarders • Ages: 3–13 • C of E
• Fees: Day £7,560–£14,985; Boarding +£5,655 pa • Independent

Tel: 01722 333423
Email: office@chafyngrove.co.uk
Website: www.chafyngrove.co.uk

Headmaster: Since 2004, Mr Eddy Newton BA PGCE (forties). Stonyhurst, Jesus College, Cambridge (classics). Impeccable credentials – head of classics at The Dragon, deputy head of Pinewood, near Swindon, director of studies and housemaster at Highfield School, then headmaster of Felsted Prep. Liked what he found when he came here but wanted to 'sharpen up' the academics and broaden the range of senior schools pupils progressed to. 'We're more ambitious now – we just had a boy win a scholarship to Winchester. A few years ago the school wouldn't have put him in for it.' Focuses on traditional prep school virtues – 'We're not too pioneering – the core needs to be done well'. Wife, Alison, is involved with the school and also runs her own graphic design business. Two children both at the school.

Entrance: Interview as much to display school to child and parents as for the school to assess them. Known to do a good job by the brightest, the brain range is broad but the climate is quick-witted, so think hard if it looks as if your child may dawdle. Scholarships of up to 20 per cent available at years 2 (academic and all-rounder), 4 (those plus music and sport) and 6 (all the above plus drama and art). Sibling and Forces discounts. Parents come from a 45-minute radius, mostly from the city and Salisbury's satellite villages. They're a mixed bunch – professionals, business, around 15 per cent army. Popular with parents of boys and girls who want their children to attend the same school. Sting's children were here.

Exit: Bryanston, Canford and Dauntsey's at the top of the list, then Charterhouse, Clayesmore, Clifton, Downe House, Downside, Eton, Godolphin, Bruton School for Girls, King's College Taunton, Monkton Combe, Prior Park, Queen Elizabeth's Hospital, Leweston, Marlborough, Milton Abbey, St Mary's Calne, Red Maids Bristol, Sherborne Boys and Girls, Taunton School, Winchester. Around a quarter leave at age 11 for the Salisbury grammars and girls' independent schools – rather depletes girls' numbers in the last two years, but that just makes the lasses bond more solidly, say most parents.

Remarks: The burghers of Salisbury must have been mightily concerned about the education of their young populace because, no way around it, Salisbury has too many prep schools – four others within a few minutes of Chafyn Grove, and that's without counting the ones just outside of town. But that just makes them try harder. Chafyn Grove is the broadest church of the town preps and comes closest to being the genuine article.

Imposing Victorian school building supplemented by modern, light, bright, purpose-built classrooms. Library buzzing when we saw it, with swish computers and comfy sofas – they work really hard to get the children reading. Latin from year 6 for almost everyone. Hoping to beef up Spanish teaching – currently one lesson a week in years 5 and 6. Three full-time equivalent teachers offer learning support, mostly on a one-to-one basis at no extra charge – excellent.

Large sports hall and performance hall, the latter now doubling as chapel (with organ). Though only 10 minutes' walk from the centre of Salisbury, the school has plenty of grounds with pitches, Astro, hard tennis courts, two good squash courts, an outdoor pool and lovely views of Salisbury Plain. Takes sport seriously – when one talented girl could not arrange transport to a regional sports final last summer, the head drove her himself and nipped them both back to school in time for sports day. Much emphasis on 'equality of coaching opportunity', with the top coaches working with athletes of all abilities, not just the top teams. Boys play rugby, hockey and cricket (and football in the lower age groups); girls, hockey, netball and rounders. Lots of success in girls' hockey and netball and the under 13 boys have been Wiltshire hockey champions recently.

Music 'greatly improved' and does jolly well, given that Salisbury Cathedral School soaks up many of the ultra-able. Three choirs, orchestra and training orchestra to encourage beginners. One keen pupil played the organ in 10 cathedrals in a recent fundraising effort. Buzzy art, with DT, claywork and other materials all given lots of time and space. Some setting of the more able artists to encourage potential scholars. Drama has long been a crown jewel, with four or five productions each year for different age groups. Lots of outdoor activity trips, eg to Dartmoor and leavers' camp to Wales. Large computer room for ICT and specialist use in some subjects. Everyone is taught to touch-type.

We enjoyed the names of the houses (they call them Eights) – Wasps, Birds, Frogs etc. Everyone has a proper locker – you'd be amazed how rare this is. Lots of hard work going on to populate the brightly decorated dormitories. Big praise from parents and children, who definitely love being here. They offer flexi-options but expect regularity. Children can go home on Sundays, barring three weekends a term. Food a source of pride – the children don't rate it (what would they know?), but it's proper and prepared by their own chef, not one of those catering outfits. Staff famously flexible – children can be dropped off early and picked up late if parents are stuck.

We can still say a 'family atmosphere' and, cliché though it may be, that's how parents still reckon it's best summed up. Lots of emphasis on the pre-prep at the moment: we saw loads of imagination, high standards and some lovely writing. Pre-prep children play in the woods and have their own slot in the charming adventure playground. We are sure it will remain a very happy school.

Chandlings School

Linked school: Cothill House

Bagley Wood, Kennington, Oxford, OX1 5ND

- Pupils: 275 boys, 170 girls, all day; • Ages: 2–11; • Christian;
- Fees: £10,200–£13,440 pa; • Independent

Tel: 01865 730771
Email: annapoole@chandlings.org.uk
Website: www.chandlings.org.uk

Head: Since 2008, Mrs Sophia Ashworth Jones, BSc QTS (science and technology) (thirties), known as Mrs AJ, who runs the school with a couple of deputies, pastoral an academic, plus heads of year, heads of houses, head of boys and head of girls. Fair number of new staff: no problem getting staff round uni towns.

Educated at Nottingham Girls' High and Ashville College, followed by Leeds University. Mrs AJ was the youngest head in the UK when appointed as head of Leeds Grammar Junior School at the age of 26, changed tack after the birth of her daughter, moving south with her husband Andy, previously head of maths at Leeds Girls' High. Their daughter and subsequent twins are in the school. They live on site, but still keep a foothold 'oop North'.

Not a 'typical' head, she is 'young, glamorous' (she said 'please don't call me glamorous': we would describe her as feisty and fun). She was also wearing phenomenally high heels. A refreshing change from the two previous heads, we were told, variously described as 'calm, steady' or 'distinctly middle aged, and granny-ish', her energy and enthusiasm are boundless. 'When one pupil suggested a race for Haiti, she made sure it would happen, running herself in fancy dress,' said a parent. 'She loves the children,' says another, 'and is loved by them.' 'Love working with children,' she says, which was obvious during our tour, and included a short cuddle with her younger daughter. We visited on dress up Friday, and found an abandoned pink sock by the games field, which rapidly became the focus of detailed child discussion: did it belong to Mr AJ? It was thought unlikely. How about the head of sport? This idea was equally dismissed. The youngest of the group triumphantly carried the slightly sodden offending item back to the office.

Entrance: Children may join at any time, providing there are spaces. Nursery (from 2 years), reception (age 4/5) and year 3 most common. Parents put children's names down early. First come first served for the nursery. Reception children have an informal assessment, thereafter it is by competitive assessment. 'We are gently selective,' says head. Behaviour is important too; head is reluctant to take a pupil who would spoil family atmosphere. Neatly positioned just off the A34, pupils travel in from Henley, Newbury and Woodstock, as well as out of Oxford, thereby missing the daily crush.

Exit: Complicated. Chandlings is very much a day school. Chaps aiming for the trad public schools are encouraged either to board at Cothill, or, if they want to stay day, The Dragon is the answer. 'Poachers' said the head, but alas inevitable if they are destined to the increasing number of schools which pre-examine age 9/10 for entry at 13. Whilst trad girls' schools still take at 11, co-eds and most public schools still stick with the 13 year old entry; we suspect school may find itself re-thinking their top age group, and offering, as do many preps, CE both at 11 and 13. Pupils leaving age 11 head into the big Oxford day schools: St Helen and St Katharine, Oxford High, Headington for girls; or Magdalen College School and Abingdon for boys. On the boarding front, Wycombe Abbey has a dedicated junior house but girls' schools traditionally have an 11 year old entry; Cheltenham Ladies', Tudor Hall and Downe House are popular for girls, Pangbourne College, Bloxham and Cokethorpe feature in the boy rankings. Goodly number of scholarships won every year.

Remarks: Stunning. A Lewis Carroll of a school; the whole place could have been a film set (apart from work on the pond at the front). We felt like Alice: head said she thought she had found the gingerbread house when she first arrived. A country prep school with 'all the facilities of a boarding school in a day school setting,' is her description. And so it is. We consulted our local educational expert, a former don, who lives almost next door, 'Ducky little school', he said, 'deservedly useful and popular'. Ducky, certainly, but little it ain't.

Think Tardis: despite outward appearances, this is not a small school: parallel classes (ie 64 boys and girls) at reception, rising to five parallel classes age 5 and 6. Around 450 boys and girls in total, age 2 – 11. Main complaint from parents is lack of car parking spaces – full during our visit, but there was an international food fair in the new hall – we had jolly good Sri Lankan delicacies. The build-up to the harvest festival was in full swing, plus a newbies' parents/staff coffee morning in the entrance hall. This is a busy, buzzy school; we parked in the bus park. Mad Hatter comes to mind.

This is an expanded and, frankly, not v grand former manor house, set in 60 acres of manicured countryside on the outskirts of Oxford, with woodlands, ponds, ponies; extensive playing fields (cunning double sized goal posts, with picnic tables pour encourager parental support), indoor and kidney shaped outdoor swimming pool (new indoor pool in the offing), as well as a nine hole golf course, ticks all the boxes, as does the head. Certain amount of not so recent hoo-ha via Mumsnet gives vent to some of the most vicious and irrelevant comments we have read for a long time. This is not North Oxford, 'nor does the school cater for the polo set,' said the head (that having been said, some of the polo wives/groupies leave FWAGS at the starting post: though perhaps not the Kirtlington crew); in reality most of the comments seem to come from the hacked off Yummy Mummy mob (aka the car park mafia).

Founded in 1994, part of the Cothill Educational Trust (CET). Cothill (four miles down the road) is a trad boys' prep with an overflow of 50 13 year old boarders who sleep only in dorms at the top of Chandlings. 'They make no impact on the school,' said the head.

Cothill, an early exponent of the French experience, owns a mini château at Sauveterre near Toulouse; charm itself, now much tarted up (with central heating) and available to all in the Cothill empire by rote. CET recently bought the adjacent La Chaumière de Sauveterre where 9 year olds get a short taster, with the option of spending une trimestre en régime Francaise for their last term at Chandlings (age 11, year 6) in the château itself. The whole of year 6 decamps to Picardie for a short 'cultural experience': no doubt with a handful of battlefields thrown in. French proper from age 2: labels in French on everything from nursery up, native speakers from age 2.

Crèche filled with sleeping babies and trained nursery nurses when we visited (five cots); proper nursery from age 2, vouchers ok, 60 max at any one time, operates term time only. Tiny classes, no more than 12 in each, variable sessions, currently 30 pre-school full time. Min two sessions a week, fully flexible: two trained teachers per class, reading from age 3. Safe room for temper tantrums and yoga for all – 'Tatty Bumpkins'. Older children, both boys and girls, help in the nursery – particularly with reading.

School is inclusive with extended support for the challenged at both ends of the spectrum: brace of learning support rooms (no problems with the dys-strata, nor with the milder ADHD, Asperger's stream, epileptics, diabetics, ok Ritalin – full time nurse on site, one profoundly deaf child has one-to-one assistance), qualified staff as you would expect; ed psych's reports: parental consultation all along the way; will say if school can't cope. One-to-one at extra cost. Extended learning on tap for the brightest. EAL, open to all, in the heart of the school. Number of 'real' foreigners (Abingdon is rich in innovative engineering and IT companies); young tend to need less need formal help with transition to a new school and culture than their parents. Osmosis is good. All set for reading, writing and 'rithmetic on entry: five phonics groups (but any other system that works). Spelling Bees. Chandlings prides itself on being 'rigorously academic'. Fab pre-prep in the heart of the school, complete with sandpits (rather damp during our visit) and splendid ride-on JCBs. Each classroom is hosed down at lunch time (to cope with the sand and other essential child inspired detritus). Woodland (as opposed to Forest) school, with boys and girls getting to grips with the real world, mock battles if and when needed.

Latin option from age 8/9 or classics and philosophy. Head's husband head of maths (and, by all accounts a wowser); parents get a maths crib before any new addition to the syllabus, maths drop in clinic on Tuesday and Thursday. Specialist teachers from reception for music, ICT, sport, PE, music, ballet, drama et al.

Interactive whiteboards throughout; one formal IT lesson a week, otherwise computers used as a learning tool, with touch-typing for all at 9 (criminal not to be mandatory in all schools). Wonderful double decker library. Proper science labs – science teaching focuses on the practical, like building electronic circuits and writing intergalactic postcards. Lower years IB a possibility in the future. New build seems to have been constructed round modules, with carefully delineated play areas for each year group. At no time did we feel we were in a whopping great prep school. Yet it is. Latest Ofsted report enthusiastic.

Huge emphasis on sport: the usual suspects: netball, hockey and rounders for girls; footie, rugby and cricket for chaps, with individual representations all over the shop. Programmed swimming up to age 9, plus snorkelling, life saving as well as golf, riding (collection of coated equines: 80 riders a week), short archery, fencing, croquet and myriad of clubs: everything from Spanish through to (organic) gardening and orienteering. Film making popular, music technology, recording, verse and public speaking, Mandarin, puppet making, Inuit throat singing and debating. The list would make many senior schools weep with shame.

Music strong: majority learn a musical instrument ('everything but the pipes'); individual lessons cost extra. Guitar ensemble. Three choirs and choir for all, 'squeaks and all'. Concerts and musicals galore in a new school hall. Wonderful art on display throughout school, plus DT, textiles and pottery. This is a grown up happening school; we found little groups happily reading all over, with formal reading for every child four times a week. Home economics popular, special low cookers and sinks. School food 'wholesome' and organic produce used as much as possible, but not kosher or halal. Vegetarian option throughout, the young have a say in future menus. Three sittings for lunch in the ginormous dining room; member of staff sits at end of each table to reinforce good table manners and chat. Curry was on the menu during our visit: we had serious discussions with a variety of pupils. Did they prefer the strong or the milder curry? Empty plates all round, and at the end of lunch the whole assembly rose to their feet singing 'thank you Father' to the tune of Frère Jacques – with such a strong French influence in the school, we were rather surprised they didn't do it in the round. (Head seemed rather nonplussed at this suggestion).

Eight am drop off, prep club free till 5pm, costs extra until 6pm. One or two trad parents plus more modern combos. All parents belong to PACH, impressive charity fundraising with serious input into Nakuru, a village in Kenya. Six per cent ethnic mix (we thought it might be more). Cothill is a C of E foundation and Chandlings shares their chaplain, but song rather than hymn practice; assemblies are inclusive, school welcomes pupils of all faiths and none. Trips to mosques, synagogues and temples where possible. Other faiths acknowledged.

Pastoral care important here. Children encouraged to be courteous, helpful and responsible, and they are. Pupils have also written their own Chandlings' code of conduct (tenets include caring for others, doing what is right and being a good friend; latest addition, from the head, is that children should be courageous). The head has re-vamped the house system: pupils play snakes and ladders with house points according to achievement or wickedness. Discipline not a problem; head will ask a child to explain poor behaviour and discuss ways to improve it rather than giving a reprimand. 'If you behave, you can stay'. Trips abroad for all (Paris for 8 year olds); skiing – no parents allowed – 8 to 11 year olds only.

Recent increase in numbers, ditto classrooms. This is an active, happy school with a dynamic head 'full of ideas to take it forward and further develop it while promoting its family, nurturing values'. We suspect expansion is the word of the moment. As one parent said, 'There is never a day when my children are not happy to go to school'.

Channing Junior School

Linked school: Channing School

1 Highgate High Street, London, N6 5JR

• Pupils: 225 girls; all day • Ages: 4–11 • Fees: £14,085 pa
• Independent

Tel: 020 8342 9862
Email: fairseat@channing.co.uk
Website: www.channing.co.uk

Head: Since 2008, Mrs Louise Lawrance BPrim Ed (mid thirties). She left her native South Africa some 15 years ago and taught at state schools in Burton-on-Trent and Kennington before going to The Hampshire School, where she worked for seven years, the last three as the head of the pre-preparatory school. Clearly immensely proud of her school and her girls, she seems to know each one and they chat to her happily and informally – a pleasure to behold. Also proud of her staff – 'we're very lucky. We're able to attract fantastic teachers and everyone is hugely talented in one are or another.' Appreciated staff are happy staff and make happy children.

Entrance: Register as soon after birth as you like but no questions of lists closing at 12 months or whatever. Tour round the school with the head and then assessment at rising 4 in groups of 12 to spy out teachability, capacity to listen, collaborate, obey instructions. Wisely, tots are seen in two age-related groups so no panics if EmmyLou is an August baby. Call-back of the most likely – there are only 24 places for a list of 250+ applicants. Offers made on the basis of potential – don't cram them with numbers and letters.

Exit: It's a rare child who does not go up to the Channing senior school. And why, indeed, would they go elsewhere?

Remarks: Housed opposite the senior school on the other side of Highgate Hill, the junior school occupies Fairseat – formerly the home of the Lord Mayor of London and backing onto the green charms of Waterlow Park – named in honour of said Lord Mayor, Sir Sidney, who donated the park to the nation. And a jolly nice house it must once have been – memories linger in fireplaces, cornices, and a sense of gentlemanly solidity. And very fine views too. In 1927, it became part of the school – originally a boarding house – until boarding went in the 1960s. It communicates a relaxed and civilised ethos and this is reflected in the manner and conduct of its girls, who are open-faced, relaxed and articulate. Top floor is where Mrs Elliott, senior school head, lives during the week and knowledge of this, too, must contribute to homely atmosphere.

Good displays everywhere and lots of colour. Much into 'thinking', as so many are now and with an encouraging board which poses questions such as 'What colour is Happiness?' Lots of expensive Apple Macs, excellent library in which intent reading was happening when we popped in, and especially pleasing was the thoughtful cross-curricular work we met at all levels. Thinking clearly being done here – and not just by girls. Birds were being studied by year 3 and they make bird boxes in DT, assemble data bases of bird stats (maths), import clips of birdsong (IT) and make pictures (art), write instructions on feeding and caring for birds (English) and look at birds and habitat (biology). (This GSG writer – an English teacher – was once upbraided by a pupil when she cited a Latin derivation – 'you can't know about Latin – you're an English teacher!' No such nonsense at Channing, we can tell!)

Exceptional music – 105 weekly music lessons and all orchestral instruments on offer. Really inviting large music room with ancient beams. Music and drama much praised – 'they are astounding – I am amazed by what the teachers can get out of the girls'. Lively art – we loved year 1's charcoal drawings of bears – each one different, each one full of individuality. Orderly but not obsessively tidy. Smiley faces. Quiet, concentrating classes.

Good outside space – and super outlook. Five courts, tarmac space, fields. Nature walk, bees' nest and fox's den! Good adventure playground with tower, fireman's pole, climbing wall, obstacle course and safe surface – oh to be 7 again! Multi-purpose hall – assemblies, quick turnaround for dining (very yummy food) and PE space.

Parents happy too. 'We're thrilled to have found somewhere that really cares about the girls.' 'The school makes the girls aware of how much they have to offer.' 'I can always go in – the school is very friendly to parents.' 'My daughters love art, reading and music – they are so happy there.' 'It doesn't pressure the girls.' 'It's such a sensible school.'

Chapter House Preparatory School and King's Magna Middle School

Linked schools: Queen Ethelburga's College

Thorpe Underwood Hall, York, YO26 9SS

• Pupils: 118; 46 girls/72 boys; 9 boarding girls and 17 boys;
• Ages: 3–14; • Fees: Day £4,485–£8,385; Boarding £24,885–£32,775 pa; • Independent

Tel: 01423 333330
Email: pj@qe.org
Website: www.chapterhouseschool.org.uk

Principal: Steven Jandrell

Head of Chapter House: Karen Kilkenny.

Head of King's Magna: Helen Midgley

Exit: Some 90 per cent to middle school Kings Magna at 10.

Remarks: For further details, see senior school: Queen Ethelburga's College.

Cheadle Hulme School Junior School

Linked school: Cheadle Hulme School

Claremont Road, Cheadle Hulme, Cheadle, Cheshire, SK8 6EF

- Pupils: 325; 185 boys/140 girls; all day • Ages: 4-11
- Fees: £7,470-£8,025 pa • Independent

Tel: 01614 883334
Email: registrar@chschool.co.uk
Website: www.cheadlehulmeschool.co.uk

Head: Since 2009, Mrs Barbara Bottoms, BSc (early fifties). Married with two grown up children. Educated at Liverpool University, where she studied chemistry and maths. Previously head at Bury Grammar School for Girls' junior department. Overjoyed to have returned to co-education. 'When I look into the playground I see a normal society where we are all learning about each other,' she told us. 'It's been like coming home.'

Parents praise the positive changes she's made. 'She's not the sort of head who has huge presence,' said one. 'She's not there at the school gates, but all the teachers are being made to teach new year groups and she's brought in specialist teachers. She is accessible if you need her but she likes to get on with things quietly. No big fanfare.'

Head is a keen theatre-goer in her spare time, and loves watching any sport.

Entrance: Assessment for reception takes place in the autumn term of the year prior to entry. Places are offered in December, earlier than other schools. 'It's play-based in small groups,' the head told us. 'We want children we can engage and interest – they need to be excited to learn.' The school take another four to six children in year 3, and then four more in year 5. Assessment at this stage is formal, in English, maths and reasoning. School is over-subscribed so early birds get the worm here.

Exit: Most progress to the senior school after sitting entrance exam along with external candidates, although a few are lost to the single sex schools in Manchester. Head meets all year 4 parents individually to discuss progress, so there is plenty of time to look at other possibilities if your child won't make it. 'We'd feel like we'd let them down if they didn't go up,' says the head.

Remarks: Class sizes are bigger than other independent schools in the area and this causes some parents to grumble. Two form entry throughout, with 20 in a class in the infants, 24 in years 3 and 4 and 26 in years 5 and 6. However, classes are split for many lessons.

Light, modern buildings with music, art, IT and science rooms. Ovens for baking are regularly used and we saw a group of little ones making cookies, or 'yummies,' as one boy called them. Big TV screen in the entrance runs a good news feed celebrating pupils' achievements and keeping everyone up to date with what's going on in school. Netbooks are used in years 4 and 5 and there are plans to introduce them throughout school. French is taught all the way through the infants and then rotated with Spanish and German in the juniors. Lots of sport, including cricket, hockey, football, cross country and netball. Plenty of extracurricular activities, from bird watching to string ball. 'Every child can find something they love,' one dad told us, 'whether it's music, drama, sport or a hobby. This place does it all. My daughter loves the fact that the head takes tennis after school every week.'

Children we spoke to were delighted that Wednesday is 'no homework night.' Some parents complained, however, that a lot of homework has to be done on a computer via the school's virtual online environment. This seems to cause problems for families with multiple children all trying to use the home computer at once.

A lively place that manages to have a relaxed feel and where children seem genuinely happy. 'When they leave here,' says the head, 'they are confident, responsible children who have learned from failure and experienced success.'

Cheam School

Headley, Newbury, RG19 8LD

- Pupils: 425; 205 girls/220 boys including 140 boarders.
- Ages: 3-13 • C of E • Fees: Boarding £24,270; Day £10,260-£17,940 pa • Independent

Tel: 01635 268242
Email: office@cheamschool.co.uk
Website: www.cheamschool.com

Head: Since 1998, Mr Mark R Johnson BEd (fifties). Charismatic, enthusiastic, 'preppy' (his own word). Passionate about boarding, having done so himself from a young age and loved it. Educated in the West Country, went straight to Summer Fields post-university and stayed for 17 years. Taught maths, German and rugby. Rose to housemaster and deputy headmaster for five years before moving to Cheam and transforming it. Known by all as Mr J, much loved by parents and children alike. Abounds with energy. Full of ideas for the school, now and in the future. Driven by the constant need for a new project: the latest was the transformation of the old sports hall into an up-to-date design and technology centre. No longer teaches – 'there simply isn't time'. Mad about sport, played cricket to minor county standard while at university and is still a playing member of the MCC.

Lists golf, fishing, shooting, racing, opera and ballet as other enthusiasms. Goodness knows when he finds time for them all. Has been governor of three other prep schools, represents IAPS on Boarding Schools' Association Executive Committee and was recently invited to sit on Council of IAPS as Boarding Representative. Named Tatler's 'Best Prep School Headmaster of the Year' a few years ago. Definitely believes in keeping busy, and his school has the feel of a very busy place. Married to Jane, a bouncy, bubbly, energetic classicist who teaches both Latin and Greek to scholarship and common entrance level and designed the tartan seen round the school and worn as part of the girls' uniform. Two daughters now happy at St Edward's, Oxford, having been pupils at Cheam for 10 years.

Entrance: Non-selective into the nursery and pre-prep. Higher up, the headmaster sees all children for a familiarisation day to ascertain their suitability for entry. This is not just based on academic data but rather an assessment of the whole child, games, musical ability, character etc.

Exit: A main feeder to Marlborough but also regularly sends pupils to eg Bradfield, Eton, Radley, Wellington, St Edward's Oxford, Sherborne, St Mary's and St Swithun's. The transition to mainly boarding public schools appears to be reasonably easy, according to one parent of girls who loved the place so much she returned to work in the bursar's office when her children moved on. However, we were told by others that some boys seem to find it hard moving into a less protected environment.

Remarks: A school for active, busy children. As one parent said, 'it's incredibly beautiful'. Set in 100 acres of glorious countryside, for sporty, outdoor loving, energetic types, it is the perfect place to spend their early school days. Anybody who remembers it, as we do, as the rather stuffy, unexciting royal school of the early '90s, would be amazed to walk round it today. One current father, ex-Cheamite, who refused to even look at it until his children went there, is now one of its greatest fans. The focus here is not totally on academia and they get so much more than just lessons. The outcome is a band of happy, confident, well-balanced children who generally get into their chosen school, often with scholarships.

A broad curriculum from the start in preparation for common entrance to top schools. All children setted for maths and French. Scholarship forms for two top years with Greek introduced to the brightest. Young teachers (average age 35 to 40) have easy, relaxed relationship with pupils. Parents feel Mr J selects staff well. Some bachelor staff accommodation in grounds, 'Cheamville', so fewer geographical restrictions. Small classes, max 18 often smaller. Books regarded as an essential part of their lives. Silent reading, or 'digest', is timetabled in for half an hour after lunch each day and, for boarders, every evening. Weekly general knowledge quiz encourages them to look things up.

Light, bright classrooms with interactive white boards throughout. Good IT, art, science facilities. Parents say 'music and drama very strong' and they put on 'excellent productions'. One major play or musical each year. Lots of choirs and several orchestras including a jazz band. Most learn an instrument with lessons timetabled differently each week and practice sessions set up for boarders. Anything from beginners to grade 6. Masses of art and photographs on display everywhere. Internal news and information computer screens in main halls. Loads of field trips, expeditions and excursions, home and overseas. These really are privileged children.

Perhaps it's sport that's the most impressive and they all love it. Everything is on offer from football, rugby, tennis, hockey and cricket to polo, judo, fencing and golf on their own course. Games every afternoon with matches on Wednesdays and Saturdays. National polo champions, national cross-country champions and cricket and rounders teams reached the National Jet finals in Oxford. Lots of matches against other schools and overseas cricket and hockey tours. The trophy cabinet is proof of their achievements. Despite this, one parent told us 'even non-sporty children are well catered for. One boy even got a scholarship to the Royal Ballet School'.

A long list of extracurricular activities but 'sadly no woodwork,' says one parent. There is even a climbing place called 'Cheam Tops' in the grounds. Indoor sports hall ingeniously provides courts for different games as well as all necessary gymnastic equipment and great changing rooms. Everything has been well thought out. Only parental complaint: 'Why do they have to be sexist? Why can't girls play football?'

Excellent pastoral care and learning support where needed. This will be one or two sessions a week with a specialist teacher on a rotating basis if in lesson time. About 10 per cent have processing problems, there is the occasional statement but nothing seriously major. Gap year students help with games when needed. Gentle counsellor is always there to listen. Believes very much in the importance of building self-esteem, which she feels is definitely one of the school's assets. Specialist EFL help given, often one-to-one in class. Believe it's absolutely essential to keep parents involved. 'Our children do not have difficulties, they have differences'. G&T register currently being reformed. PSHE is strong, each child has a tutor and anything verging on bullying, (probably not the right word), is quickly and sensitively dealt with. 'We want everyone to be happy!' Timetables rigorously watched, so the whereabouts of any child at any time is always known.

Parents have nothing but praise. 'A very happy school', 'the head really has his finger on the pulse', 'sussed out our daughter very fast and gave us excellent advice on her next school', 'children are easy-going, sensitive and supportive of each other', 'very good at involving parents', 'the kids have such fun'. One even told us 'we brought our children over from South Africa where they were a good year behind academically and the system was totally different. Nevertheless, our 11-year-old was quickly assimilated into the system, booked himself into boarding after one term and achieved an all-rounder scholarship to Radley'. A happy parent indeed.

Boarding is either full time or flexi. Children can do just two nights a week if they like. We were assured that this is not at all unsettling and that they seem to love it, opting in and out as and when. The majority of the top year board full time in preparation for their next school. Full time means weekly, they go home after games on Saturday afternoon and return in time for lessons on Monday morning. Most come from within a 15 mile radius of the school although there is a largish London contingent and the occasional child from overseas. Dorms are upstairs in the main building, boys on one floor and girls on another. Homely, welcoming rooms with a variety of duvet covers and lots of teddies. Always one or two older pupils in with the younger ones. Smart modern bathrooms, not at all as we used to know them. Great pile of bags on the landings waiting to be collected by flexis at the end of the day. Recent 'outstanding' boarding certificate from Ofsted. We asked a pupil what she felt about weekly boarding. She replied 'I love it. It's so great to be at home with my brothers on Sundays and to see my horse but it's also good to be at school with my friends'. Bedtime routine pretty regimented with time for reading and talking before lights out but after that, silence reigns.

Quite a large amount of charitable stuff going on. Support for a school in Zambia, a rural school in Johannesburg, the Red Cross children's hospital in Cape Town and the children's wards in the Royal Hampshire Hospital. Hands-on partnership with local primary schools who can apply for funding and use their facilities for free. Some scholarships and bursaries and a fund for suddenly needy children.

Perhaps the oldest prep school in the country, with its origins in the 17th century, there is an interesting archive room containing mementos of past headmasters and pupils. Apart from HRH the Duke of Edinburgh and HRH the Prince of Wales, William Pitt the Younger, Lord Randolph Churchill, Ivo Bligh, 8th Earl of Darnley and Jake Meyer also spent their formative years at Cheam.

A school full of happy, open, confident, polite, exceptionally busy children who are used to living to a rigid timetable and to keeping their shoes done up and their shirts tucked in. One slightly wonders how they will manage to cope with the rebellious, disorganised world outside.

Cheltenham College Preparatory School

Linked school: Cheltenham College

Thirlestaine Road, Cheltenham, GL53 7AB

- Pupils: 400 girls and boys; boarding and day • Ages: 3-13
- C of E • Fees: Day £7,263-£16,326; Boarding £16,272-£21,222 pa
- Independent

Tel: 01242 522697
Email: theprep@cheltenhamcollege.org
Website: www.cheltenhamcollege.org

Headmaster: Since September 2013, Jonathan Whybrow, formerly head of Beachborough School. Has also been head of City of London Freemen's Junior School and deputy head of Devonshire House. Brought up above a London pub, he joined the Royal Marines before realising that his true vocation was teaching. Married with two daughters. He's the fifth person to take on the headship in less than five years: we hope he will bring some stability to the school.

Entrance: At all ages. Non-selective below age 11 with entry by assessment and interview – all applicants are invited to taster days. More choosy later on as pupils must be able to pass CE at 13. Lots of local interest. Tiny intake from overseas. Popular with Forces. Discount available for third and subsequent siblings. Generous discounts for Forces families and bursaries available. 11+ scholarship up to 30 per cent of fees in a variety of areas and valid throughout Cheltenham College.

Exit: Good record of pupils getting into their first choice school. Vast majority move across the road to mixed senior school, Cheltenham College, although they make up just 40 per cent of the overall intake at 13+. CE entry pass around 50 per cent, other schools vary. A number of girls leave at 11 for Cheltenham Ladies' College, despite efforts to hang on to them for another two years. A few also to good local grammars.

Remarks: Known simply as Cheltenham Prep. Set in conservation area, large Edwardian, red-brick, purpose-built (in 1908) school house with seamless (and some not so seamless) additions over the decades. Newest building for lower school the best yet and overlooking lake. Two new classrooms for the pre-prep Kingfishers opened 2011. Decision to go co-ed caused great ructions but school has never looked back – fewer than 240 pupils when head took over in 1992. Numbers peaked at 450 and are now a strong 400. However present instability not good: losing heads at a rate that begins to look like carelessness.

School day action packed – hardly enough hours in it. Lessons start 8.30am for all but youngest (Kingfishers pre-prep department in own well-designed extension) and include daily class music. Not at expense of anything else, though. Still finds time to fit in French from age of 3 alongside staple diet of core subjects. ICT extremely well catered for with annually updated computers, 24-hour internet connection, and school network. Laptops everywhere. Internal email system keeps staff in touch – replaced old-style staff notice-boards.

Academically thrusting for a non-selective school but geared up to the individual. Help available (at no extra charge) for mild dyslexics, dyspraxics and other minor learning difficulties. The emphasis is on mild, but a parent w561ith criticisms elsewhere in the school is unstinting in his praise of the help for SEN. Well-run shuttle system boosts youngsters' intake of core subjects in place of occasional French or Latin. Extra charge for EFL lessons. Well-stocked pleasant library with well used mezzanine, used to be school gym.

Artwork on show quite unbelievable (it was easy to forget you were in a junior school) – large silk painting in library and an outstanding series of murals along one corridor wall. Justly proud of working scale-model fleet of warships (made by past pupils and maintained by current pupils) which are sailed each year on own shallow lake. Bags more innovative projects emerging from technology department – great merging of design, woodwork and electronics, as big a hit with girls as boys.

Super sports hall and indoor pool (shared with senior school, as are science labs). Lovely cricket pitch, good hockey and rugby tradition, hard courts for tennis and netball, Astroturfs for hockey and several squash courts, plus mini sports hall for indoor games. Brand new assembly hall, attached sympathetically to old school, has transformed the big event, put drama back on the map and given school a unique venue for major productions, concerts and gatherings. Only non-purpose building is music school, a lovely wood-panelled setting for individual lessons and small group recitals. Four choirs (chapel choir regularly tours), various bands and ensembles, regular concerts.

Boarding not at full capacity but allows for sleepovers. Large airy dorms in old building, shared curtained cubicles for older children, all well kept with enough pictures, toys and own duvets to make it homely. Boarders' privileges extend to use of library, computers, art and DT studios at any time of day. Can also use pool for special supervised sessions. Pupils allowed mobile phones, though use strictly controlled. Fabulous grounds and lush green setting provide plenty of scope for outside play. Pupils allocated houses for competitive and pastoral reasons. Strict anti-bullying policy rigidly enforced.

Weekly chapel on Saturday, Sunday service three or four times a term. Chapel 'essential but not in an over-arching way'. Saturday school is optional for years 3 and 4, compulsory for years above. 'Pupils enjoy a programme of co-curricular activities, such as trips and project work, which has been a resounding success,' says the school. Extra activities include twice-weekly dry slope skiing in nearby Gloucester, squash, trampolining, and paddle-boating on lake.

Plenty of moneyed backgrounds, landed gentry and self-made millionaires, but ordinary folk too – 'We have a very broad parental constituency'. New PTA. Famous OJs (Old Juniors) include General Sir Michael Rose and actor Nigel Davenport.

Smashing bunch of children seen around school, no-one apparently at a loose end, and a certain confidence clearly evident from the youngest Kingfisher up. Enthusiastic pupils, staff and 'most parents'. An overwhelming feeling here of purpose and activity. Kids with street cred as well as an appreciation of their privileged circumstances.

Chigwell Junior School

Linked school: Chigwell School

High Road, Chigwell, IG7 6QF

- Pupils: 360 boys and girls • Ages: 4-13 • C of E but welcomes all;
- Fees: £8,955-£14,985 pa • Independent

Tel: 020 8501 5721
Email: hm@chigwell-school.org
Website: www.chigwell-school.org

Headmaster: Since September 2010, Mr Simon James BA PGCE, who has a degree in history. He teaches drama and games and says it gives him an opportunity to get to know the pupils. Very welcoming and approachable, his educational philosophy is to 'care for each individual and turn them into well-rounded, well-educated people with a life-long love of learning'.

Entrance: Competition is fierce – at 7, three times as many applicants as places and young candidates are put through their paces with an assessment, interview, classroom time and a report from their previous school. At 11, nearly 10 times as many applicants for the 40 new places in the thirds, weeded out by an exam and interviews. For entry in new pre-prep at 4, assessment plus nursery report. About 10 academic and music scholarships offered and bursaries also available.

Exit: Almost all to Chigwell senior school with a handful choosing secondaries closer to home, though all are reassessed at 11.

Remarks: Set on the main school site, the junior school is integral to the Chigwell community and adds to the all-pervading family feel. Its educational philosophy, academic and pastoral structures are the same as those in the senior school, supporting the school's aim to 'provide a consistent approach to education throughout the child's school career'. Joint activities bring juniors and seniors together, easing the passage through the school, and major facilities are shared, including the dining hall and gym, plus the impressive art, music and drama departments.

The juniors' own domain has a dedicated playground, classrooms, ICT lab and a recently refurbished library. The recent Wilson Building houses more bright, modern, junior form rooms as well as the modern foreign languages department – older ones learn Spanish, German and classics. Spacious learning support department, offering tuition in small groups to children who require additional input in specific or more general areas.

Pupils generally hail from the local area – many are the offspring of Old Chigwellians. New pre-prep means possibility of seamless transition from 4 – 18 here.

The reason for the scrabbling for places is encapsulated by the glowing recent ISI report, which described pupils' academic progress as 'exceptional', praised their 'outstanding' personal development and judged spiritual development 'excellent' – chapel is as central to school life for the juniors as it is for the seniors.

Enjoying school is of great importance here – colourful and creative displays of work and cheery faces attest to this. Clubs include animation and astronomy and chances to take part in activities in partnership with the seniors, creating a happy mix of ages and cultures at this small, warm and nurturing school.

Christ Church C of E Primary School

1 Robinson Street, London, SW3 4AA

• Pupils: 210 boys and girls; all day • Ages: 4–11 • C of E voluntary aided • State

Tel: 020 7352 5708
Email: info@chch.rbkc.sch.uk
Website: www.chch.rbkc.sch.uk

Head: Since September 2009, Mrs Avis Hawkins, who was previously joint acting head.

Entrance: Application by late January for the following September for reception class. All other ages on an ad hoc basis. Priority given to (i) children with siblings in the school; (ii) children of families who are regular worshippers in St Luke's or Christ Church, Chelsea; (iii) children living in the parish; (iv) children of families who are regular worshippers in a neighbouring parish church etc. Complete the school's supplementary admissions form as well as applying through the LA.

Exit: Shene School, Grey Coats, Gunnersbury, Holland Park, Graveney, ADT etc etc and about 20 per cent to private London day schools – Alleyn's, Emanuel, Dulwich etc.

Remarks: Excellent primary school in super location tucked away in a quiet corner of Chelsea, with – by London standards – lots of space, including good-sized playground and extra area of garden/pond etc. Judged outstanding by Ofsted in every category. Founded 1840, affiliated to local churches (Helen Morgan Edwards is now chair of governors). Cherry-coloured uniform. Newly-refurbished prize-winning buildings. Approximately 50 per cent of pupils from Chelsea, the rest from Wandsworth, Westminster and beyond – very mixed intake.

Good core and cross-curricular and SEN provision; all children have experience with computers. Maths and English very good and Spanish on offer after school; swimming for year 2 and above. PE in much-used all-purpose school hall as well as local green space. Keen games and music. Even here parents sending children on to private schools usually opt for a year or two of coaching. Continuing good and happy reports from parents, though some would like to see an 11+ class. Oversubscribed for all year groups.

Christ Church Cathedral School

3 Brewer Street, Oxford, OX1 1QW

• Pupils: 128; 121 boys/7 girls; 20 chorister boarders • Ages: 3–13 (girls in nursery only) • C of E • Fees: Day £6,150–£13,485; Boarding choristers £8,4920–£9,390 pa • Independent

Tel: 01865 242561
Email: registrar@cccs.org.uk
Website: www.cccs.org.uk

Headmaster: Since January 2014, Mr Richard Murray BA MA (Durham), previously a housemaster and English teacher at St Edward's School in Oxford.

Entrance: Most day boys are from the Oxford or Bucks area, and enter at nursery or reception; the single class grows as more boys join in year 3 and the majority stay until common entrance. A few girls in nursery only. Assessment is by participation in class for the younger boys and informal academic tests for the older boys. Four chorister places are available each year from year 4, selected by voice trial. Choristers come from further afield, board and receive a two-thirds fee reduction in a bursary established by royal appointment in 16th century. School benefits from recommendations by old boys, siblings and music teachers. The Cardinal's Scholarship is a new introduction, for up to three year 3s, who are expected to achieve well academically throughout the school. Parents of choristers are a particularly music-focused sub-set; others are local professionals, medics and academics

Exit: To a range of local schools: Abingdon, Bedales, Bloxham, Charterhouse, Leckford Place, Magdalen College, Our Lady's Abingdon, Purcell. Plenty of music scholarships and exhibitions, as one would expect – seven plus one for sports in 2013.

Remarks: Described by one parent as 'the secret of Oxford', it is hidden in an historic corner of the town in the shadow of Christ Church Cathedral. Every available inch has been transformed, embracing the original Tudor residence of Cardinal Wolsey, a Victorian parsonage-type house commissioned by Dean Liddell, father of Alice in Wonderland, and a bright new block to commemorate old boy William Walton. The net effect is a warren of classrooms, labs and play areas combining traditional and modern. Henry VIII's charter of 1546 established the education of eight boy choristers and a master for Christ Church Cathedral. Shame it didn't stipulate a few parking spaces too, as staff parking on the playground is an issue, according to one parent.

Music permeates through the school, from music-stands among the pyjamas to treble clef murals in the corridors. The cathedral choristers' day kicks off at 7.30 to fit in their three hours of choir practice and daily services. In addition they all learn the piano and one other instrument. There are celebratory services throughout the year, including Easter and Christmas Day, as well as singing tours, recently as far afield as China, performing in the world's largest concert hall. The rest of the school has caught the bug too: with pianos in every corner and 140 individual music lessons per week, there are informal concerts which start with the smallest to encourage confidence, 'even if it's a recorder and they play the same note 10 times,' laughs one parent. However, having heard the choir sing like angels at evensong, we were struck by the skill and professionalism of even the youngest. Parents are welcome to watch the weekly service in the cathedral and some day boys are chosen for Worcester College choir. 'They see that older boys are doing it and it's fun'.

These are not just pretty voices: under the surplices there is an academic rigour to the school, starting with the tiny tots in the Montessori nursery. The historic cardinal's house now holds a climbing frame and zoo animal frescoes in the garden. Small class sizes in the pre-prep, approximately 16, rising to a maximum of 20 when choristers join in year 4. The pre-prep enjoys recently refurbished classrooms with play areas, music corners and piano. French classes in year 2. There is a conscious promotion to the prep, a separate building, a more formal uniform, and a more exacting curriculum, in which subjects are taught by specialists from year 5 and maths is set in year 6. We witnessed a vibrant Latin class and were invited to help judge the Roman legionary cut-out doll competition – it was a tough decision, but the joy of learning in the classroom was infectious. IT resources have multiplied and are used, among other things, for workshops on Sibelius (musicians' software, not the chap). Head sees all parents in year 6 to discuss future schools and makes prefects of all the final year boys. Teachers include alumnae of the college.

The school makes good provision for a surprising variety of SEN children, with one full-time and two part-time staff. 'Some schools attract a uniform product and this is a school which attracts eccentrics'. One parent reported that a boy who was severely dyslexic won a top place in the annual poetry competition. 'That's part of the school's draw: it treats everyone with a lot of respect'. Oxford's fluid population means that there is often a handful of EAL children, which our guide appeared to relish as contributing to the school's rich tapestry.

Picture the most idyllic cricket field you can imagine – these boys play on it, overlooked by the dreaming spires of Magdalen and Christ Church, the sound of rare breed cows lowing by the river; a timber cabin of a cricket pavilion, now with modern additions, electricity and a loo! One parent criticised the school's outdoor areas – 'Boys don't have far to run in the playground' – but Merton field over the road more than makes up for it. No wonder the fixtures in rugby, football, cricket and athletics are successful and many boys make the renowned A teams in their next schools. Parents enjoy a summer fair here on sports day, a scene which is eagerly photographed by tourists, looking for a snap of old England. 'I've never seen so many cakes,' gasps a parent. The school is conscientious about all boys representing the school in sport at some stage. Inflatable sharks and papier mâché snakes in the art room testify that the creative child is catered for. Art and poetry are celebrated on Arts' Day, by visiting professionals who run workshops in photography, fine art, music and poetry. This year's cartoonist helped produce some lively portraits of composers, one of whom looked suspiciously like the bursar.

Named after the cathedral's organists, including John Taverner, the boarders' rooms in the main building are decked with photos and teddies from home; the largest dorm slept eight cosily. The bright and tidy shower room confirmed our suspicions that these are no ordinary boys. 'We try to make it their home,' said our guide. The choristers' common room is in cardinal red, like their cassocks, and houses a computer to email home, TV and, of course, ivories to tinkle upon. Our noses led us enticingly to the dining room, lined with scholars' and house point boards – houses are named after dignitaries associated with the school: (Lewis) Carroll; (Cardinal) Wolsey and (Dorothy L) Sayers, who lived next door and whose father was headmaster. There's a traditional tie for the winners of the merit awards to wear each term; another system for poor behaviour culminates in a mild punishment of sitting outside the staff room. Good discipline is inherent in a musical training: 'It's not external discipline we're after, it's a means to self-discipline'. Lots of clubs after school, from knitting to furniture-making to amuse the boys, while parents fight with the city traffic: 'Bit of a pain to get to at 5.30 at night,' said a parent. Free after-school prep club until 6pm pleases working parents. However, not really set up as a boarding school; reports of choristers at school at weekends kicking their heels with no organised activities, and sometimes missing meals.

The school is proud of its reputation for good manners, and rightly so. Boys stand when visitors enter the classrooms, address teachers as 'sir' and learn to hold the door open at an early age. It is a conscious emphasis on courtesy which comes across as old-fashioned. As one parent remarked, 'I think we are paying for the education I received'. Parents are happy with the contact from teachers: 'They speak to you, and really listen to what you say'; office staff got particular praise, 'even with difficult parents they are very diplomatic'. It is no coincidence that in premises seeped in history the school play should be Old Father Time. He has certainly instilled character and sound traditional values here, from the daily Latin quotation in the head's study to the boys' charming Thomas More-style hats. The honest traditions are summed up by the bursar: 'snowballing? Of course we allow it. I think being a boy nowadays is not as exciting as it should be'.

Churcher's College Junior School

Linked school: Churcher's College

Midhurst Road, Liphook, GU30 7HT

- Pupils: 225 boys and girls • Ages: 4–11 • Christian ethos
- Fees: £7,872–£8,400 pa • Independent

Tel: 01730 236870
Email: ccjsoffice@churcherscollege.com
Website: www.churcherscollege.com/junior-school

Head: Since September 2013, Mr Ian Adams BSc PGCE MA (early forties), previously deputy head, and head of maths and science, of Hall Grove School. Read geology and geophysics at Durham; began his teaching career as head of geography and ICT at Pembroke House in the heart of Kenya's Great Rift Valley, later moving to teach maths at Kenton College in Nairobi. Has also taught at Port Regis School and Blue Coat School, Edgbaston. His wife works in PR.

Entrance: 4+ – non-selective; from 7+ pupils are invited to an assessment morning.

Exit: At 11+ the bulk of pupils go on to the senior school. A small number choose to move to senior schools in Guildford and Petersfield.

Remarks: Very much a user friendly school, where children learn at their own pace in a cosy and comfortable environment. Academically well structured, with younger pupils in mixed ability classes involving lots of activity-based learning. Additional intake arrives at 7+ and thereafter two forms per year group, setting for maths and English. The teaching of modern foreign languages is exceptional for a junior school – the children are introduced to German in year 4, Spanish in year 5 and French in year 6. Year 6 are taken on a residential trip to France and the school employs German gap year students. Children who need additional support are identified and can attend small group classes or have specialist one-to-one teaching.

Pupils are invited to take on responsibilities as they mature and have their own school council – children can run for election once they enter year three. The council meets with senior staff and discusses all sorts of issues that they wish to develop or perhaps change, including catering, equipment needed for the playground and ideas for clubs. Everybody brings their wellies to get stuck into the school gardens and greenhouse – much of their work is linked to the science curriculum and should produce some budding naturalists. A new sensory garden has just opened, allowing outdoor education to develop further.

Gold Artsmark – all arts are expertly entwined across the curriculum, giving the pupils a wide and creative education alongside all the traditional subjects. Attractive well-stocked music studio, most pupils learn an instrument and ABRSM exam results are impressive for young children. Drama is taught as a separate subject, pupils learn to communicate through plays and workshops and explore social and ethical issues in literature. Plays and concerts abound all year round; every pupil from reception to year 6 is involved. Professional artists and bands join with parents and pupils to perform at Churchfest, an annual social event. Top notch art and design – the dedicated art room is very well resourced, with DT of a particularly high standard for a junior school.

Personal fitness is a high priority, taught by dedicated PE teachers – pupils have access to a great range of sporting activities, school adventure weekends and camping trips. In addition to sports, the school offers an equally good range of musical, dance and hobby based clubs, alongside an early bird drop-off and after-school prep club, always a bonus for working parents. This hive of activity is brought together by the school's Guild Awards – the scheme allows the children to demonstrate their interests and strengths, in fitness, awareness of others and the environment and a new skill, at three levels of competence.

The school is located on a lovely rural green site approximately 12 miles from the senior school. Hard work and the enthusiasm of the staff and pupils beam through – the Guild Awards, the gardens and the wonderful photographic displays lining the corridors that record the children's numerous achievements and events.

City of London Freemen's Junior School

Linked school: City of London Freemen's School

Ashtead Park, Ashtead, KT21 1ET

• Pupils: 380: 185 boys, 195 girls; all day • Ages: 7–13 • Inter-denom • Fees: £11,250–£12,006 pa • Independent

Tel: 01372 277933
Email: admissions@clfs.surrey.sch.uk
Website: www.clfs.surrey.sch.uk

Headmaster of the Junior School: Since April 2010, Mr Mark Beach (forties), married with three children. Headmaster of Longacre School near Guildford and before that deputy head at Barfield. As part of the City of London Freemen's School, the junior section comes under the overarching headship of the head of senior school, Mr Philip MacDonald.

Entrance: Selective entry at 7 and 11 and at other ages as and when available. The tests in English, maths and non-verbal reasoning are the 'first filter'. Results are considered together with feeder school report, with an eye for consistency. All candidates are interviewed, looking out for 'a positive attitude to learning, evidence of interests and attributes to contribute to school life or just a spark of something'. The school website gives guidelines and some sample papers for entry tests. Parents report that although it's perceived to be tough to get in at 7, once in, it seems easy and not at all pressured. Pupils come from the local area, from Guildford to Kingston. School buses provide transport for both juniors and seniors from East Horsley, Bookham, Esher, Cobham and a shuttle to Ashtead Station.

Exit: Overwhelming majority move on to the City of London Freemen's senior school in a managed and seamless transition which is clearly expected by the school. No entrance tests for them.

Remarks: CLFS junior has a solid, non-elitist, family feel, but again, like its senior school, lacks a certain pizzazz. This does not worry the CLFS faithful, for whom the real draw is the through education – once in the junior school, worries about future school choices and entry exams are a thing of the past. It is straight through to 18 – and a family can have all their children at the same place if they are 7 or 17, boy or girl. A big headache solved for time-poor working parents. 'Going through from age 7 takes away the stresses of 11+ and CE,' says one parent. Another added, 'With progression through the school, you don't notice any pressure at any particular point and don't realise the high levels children have achieved, as they've got there slowly and steadily.''

The junior school is housed in the purpose-built, modernish Kemp House. It is acceptable, but couldn't be called inspiring. Painted breeze block walls (which are covered with artwork). Buzzing with well-occupied children, some classrooms can be tight and crowded in use. A couple of newer ones are more spacious and well-equipped with IT. Impressive art room and lovely, decorative and inspiring artwork displays all over the school.

It is the outside space which is the very, very, big plus – fantastic, a definite 'wow factor'. The rolling parkland of grassy embankments, shady trees and crested iron railings are shared with the seniors, although juniors have broadly their own area beside Kemp House – it is not sectioned off. A large fenced and well-equipped adventure playground is used exclusively by the juniors during supervised breaks.

Class sizes start at around 12, rising towards a maximum of 20 by age 11. Three forms per year, increasing to four in the final two years, when a further intake of pupils. Setting in maths from year 4 and English from year 7 has recently been introduced; head says, 'school is flexible and big enough to do whatever suits the cohort. It may be different for different years'. Watch this space as the experience develops. French, German and Spanish are taught as a 'taster' for a term each in years 3 and 4. In year 5, pupils select one language to learn exclusively and then add a second choice in year 7. No testing for SEN on entry and extra help is limited – not the best school therefore for a child with significant special needs, and check carefully whether the school can cater for minor special needs.

The junior and senior schools are managed as one – each has its own staff, but it feels very much one school. The top two years of the juniors (ages 11 and 12) use some senior classroom facilities and are taught by some senior school staff. Parents report, 'They are so familiar with everything there is no huge transition when moving into the senior school.' Senior school pupils trained as listeners visit the junior school daily to provide an informal point of contact to help pupils with personal or school issues. Seniors also run some of the huge range of lunchtime and after-school clubs.

The school's ethos is 'getting kids to try things, being open minded and socialising'. Pupils are encouraged to take part in everything on offer. The majority learn a musical instrument. Sports are important and taken seriously, rugby and cricket for boys, hockey and netball for girls and swimming in the superb indoor pool for all throughout the year. Teams have reached national standard in swimming and, more unusually, fencing – one of a number of extracurricular sports activities. The junior school really benefits from sharing the extensive sports grounds and top-notch sports facilities with the seniors.

Both parents and staff praise the family atmosphere, with lots of siblings across the whole school. Children are caring and help each other, boys and girls mix well: 'They are encouraged from day one to sit and work in mixed groups'. Pupils are a tidy bunch and the ones we talked to likeably chatty (shame we were shown round by the marketing manager and not a pupil, as we had requested). Parents are a mix of background and social types; the broad cross-section of families reflects this more cosmopolitan part of Surrey, from first-time buyers keen for their children to experience everything on offer to experienced fee-payers who are content to let the school make the decisions and feel it's 'great value for money'. Parents say, 'socially there's a bit of everything, not only the very rich – lots of ordinary families, very much a cross-section'; 'It's not one of the most expensive schools, and that adds to the rounded, normal feel.'

City of London School for Girls (Prep School)

Linked school: City of London School for Girls

St Giles' Terrace, Barbican, London, EC2Y 8BB

• Pupils: 95 girls; all day • Ages: 7-11 • Fees: £13,866 pa
• Independent

Tel: 020 7847 5500
Email: admissions@clsg.org.uk
Website: www.clsg.org.uk

Headmistress: Since 2010, Miss Jane Rogers MPhil BA (London). Worked for 10 years in the state sector before moving to the Institute of Education as a science lecturer and educational researcher. Moved back into education when she took a post of senior teacher at the Lyceum School, after which she came to the Prep, because 'I'm interested in academic excellence'. Educated at Chelmsford County High School for Girls, University College London (geography) and Institute of Education. Has two teenage children.

Entrance: Twenty-four hotly contested places at 7+, sitting nationally standardised tests in English, maths and verbal reasoning plus some spelling and writing tests of the Prep's own authorship. Register your daughter early to be sure of her being seen: the school assesses a maximum of 150 girls, and is always over-subscribed. Of those 150, the top 50 are called back for a further day's appraisal, during which they're examined in English, maths, science and DT – this last because it allows the girls to be observed in practical activities and working as a team. The 24 places are then offered to those 'with academic ability and the potential to become independent, happy learners.' Girls are seen in the November of the year preceding entry; closing date for accepting or declining offers is mid-February.

Exit: Parents take note: entry to the senior school is not automatic. By Easter of Year 5, reserved places (ie places that are guaranteed) are offered only to those girls 'who continue to develop'. Any child who joined the school later than Y3 doesn't get one at all, and must sit for a place along with the external candidates. Head insists that 'the vast majority go through.' Some parents' perceptions are different; see below. Destinations of those who do go elsewhere include St Paul's Girls, North London Collegiate, Francis Holland, Channing and Queen's College London. 'We've been hugely successful in placing girls at other schools,' says head, 'schools like City Prep girls, and they don't get them that often.'

Remarks: Broad curriculum, with specialist teachers from the senior school coming in to teach music, art, DT, PE, Latin (Years 5 and 6) and modern languages. The girls learn a different language each year: Spanish in Year 3, French in Year 4, German in Year 5 and Mandarin in Year 6. The idea is that the girls acquire an enthusiasm for languages which then helps them to choose the right ones when they go on to senior school, which is certainly commendable. It struck us as odd, however, that they only studied each language for a year before having to drop it and move onto the next one; a Year 5 girl we spoke to admitted that she'd now forgotten the Spanish she'd learned in Year 3.

As well as benefiting from the senior school teaching expertise, the excellent senior school facilities – swimming pool, sports hall, library, Astroturf, tennis courts – are all available to the Prep school, which doubtless explains why there's no difference in fees between the two (though prep fees do include lunch). Sports and gymnastics are strong, and music likewise, with the Year 6s doing a Prep Opera every year. There are also lots of residential trips which are perennially popular. Wide variety of clubs, and after-school care provides an opportunity for girls to do their homework as well as have fun. ('They have a register to make sure you don't wander off,' said one of our tour guides, earnestly.) Sixth formers from the senior school run clubs for the Prep girls, which, says head, creates 'a big sister culture. They're great role models for the younger girls.'

Other than some worrying reports which we outline below, it took a long while for parental feedback to reach us about this school. Our first invitation was met with complete silence, and even a second appeal didn't yield very much. (This was in contrast to the parents of girls in the senior school, who were quick to tell us how happy they were.) Those who did eventually contact us agreed that the girls are worked hard but achieve highly. A couple remarked on the school's competitive nature: 'The girls are incredibly competitive, but also very supportive of each other, and have a strong sense of loyalty to their school,' said one. Another observed, 'If you're prepared to buy into the idea of City and have a daughter capable of swimming in its often competitive seas, it will be a worthwhile experience for her and for your family.' These parents emphasized that their daughters were enjoying their time at the Prep, had made friends and embraced the opportunities on offer there.

However, some of these same parents expressed disquiet about the entry process to the senior school. 'The goal posts seem to have been moved,' said one couple, 'The message about not everyone getting reserved places is stronger now than it was when our daughter got in.' The same worried mother continued, 'Choosing to put a child through an entrance exam when they're 6 is not an easy decision; in our case we hoped to avoid the stress at 11 plus, which we now find we may not do. I suspect the feeling of rejection and the dent to self-confidence is higher if you don't get a reserved place from the Prep and can stay with your friends, than if you apply and fail as an external candidate.' Miss Rogers told us that an average of four girls leave City Prep's Year 6 every year: two out of choice, and two who were 'advised to go elsewhere.' School figures show an average of three girls a year recently have not been given reserved places. This figure seems high to us, given both the stringent nature of the admissions process and the acknowledged high workload put upon the girls during their time here; and we did ask the head to comment on it. 'Not all girls develop the same,' was her comment. 'Some go upwards and some go downwards,' adding, 'sometimes things happen in families to disturb girls.'

Parents and former parents are divided in their feelings about the school. On one side of the argument, accounts have been passed to us of recent City Prep girls whose confidence, and even health, had been so undermined by the school's approach that their parents voted with their feet and took them out. These parents write with angry eloquence about the school's 'complete lack of nurture and care' and claim that it 'values malleability and obedience over originality and sparky intellect.' They allege that there is poor support for special needs such as dyslexia, and that some of the teaching is sub-standard ('After we moved her, we discovered that she had been so poorly taught that she needed to relearn a year's worth of maths,' said one mother, and another mother reported an identical experience.)

The head insists that the school works closely with parents, and that the girls' happiness is paramount to her. 'We love quirky individuals. We've got lots and lots of those. Girls are allowed to be themselves here.' And indeed, other parents told us that their daughters loved coming to school. One, whose child had excelled there academically, spoke of the school's 'really good pastoral side.' 'The Prep is a nurturing and non-threatening environment,' said one mother whose child was now at CLSG senior, 'and I would have no hesitation in recommending it.'

Picking our way through such contradictory accounts was difficult. We can only conclude by suggesting that, since entry to CLSG senior school isn't guaranteed, parents should think closely about whether City Prep is the right choice for their daughter; or whether a prep school not linked to any senior school, but with a proven record of getting its leavers into the destination of their choice, might suit their family better.

Claysemore Preparatory School

Linked school: Clayesmore School

Iwerne Minster, Blandford Forum, DT11 8PH

• Pupils: 225; 131 boys, 94 girls • 49 full-time boarders and 9 part-time boarders • Ages: 2-13 • C of E • Fees: Boarding £22,419; Day £8,187-£15,597 pa • Independent

Tel: 01747 813155
Email: prepadmissions@clayesmore.com
Website: www.clayesmore.com

Head: Since September 2006, Mr Richard Geffen BEd (fifties). Educated as a boarder at Harrow before studying history and education at Bishop Otter College, University of Sussex, Chichester. Spent 17 years at Chichester High School for Boys where he taught humanities and was head of year for 13 years. Deputy head at Westbourne House Preparatory School, near Chichester, for nine years before appointment to headship at Clayesmore Prep. During his time at Chichester High went on exchange to Vancouver Island for a year. Together with his wife, Ann (whom he met at college), ran one of Westbourne's boarding houses. Has coached rugby and cricket, which he continues to play locally, and was groundsman for 21 years at Goodwood Cricket Club. Ann is a PE teacher and experienced coach. Thoughtful and kind head. Parents comment on how he and Ann are 'always around' and on their 'obvious dedication to the job.'

Retiring in July 2014.

Entrance: Taster day, report from previous school and informal assessment (educational psychologist's report sometimes required). Like the senior school, a mainstream school, with a cracking learning support team: 'will take any child we can develop educationally,' says the head. Highly praised by CReSTed for its success with dyslexic children. Admissions ramp up dramatically at year 7 (mainly transfers from local primaries). Nursery takes from rising 3s upwards and majority continue through school.

Exit: More or less seamless transfer to senior school: 90 per cent go on (prep provides half senior school entry). Others to range of senior schools eg Bryanston, Canford, Milton Abbey.

Remarks: Sharing beautiful 62 acre site with senior school, main prep school building forms a two storey cruciform shape. Proximity of dormitories and classrooms seen as a major advantage. Impressive Everett building provides four classrooms for years 3 and 4, a geography room, two science laboratories and residential accommodation on top floor. Previously based in Charlton Marshall, school was founded in 1929 by Dick Everett, succeeded in 1963 by Lt Col Ivor Edwards-Stewart who, when he retired in 1974, 'funded a school of a most modern design' on the senior school campus. Dedicated play area where pupils have 'muck' (drink and snack) at breaks. Adjacent former gym has been refurbished as drama studio plus social area for year 8 pupils. Surprisingly successful blend of the makeshift (eg creative art department flourishing in somewhat dated prefab) and the purpose built. Former stately squash court houses music department for both prep and senior schools with plenty of practice rooms, separate classrooms, joint ensemble room and a music technology suite. New adventure playground and play facilities include improved ball-park. Joint use also made of sports facilities, senior school dining room (three minute trail to meals even on short legs), chapel and leisure centre.

Very popular with local families, sprinkling of ex-pat children, some foreigners, high percentage of boarders from

Forces plus siblings of those in the senior school, a number of first-time buyers and London escapees. Boarding full (80 or so) when we visited, day children may stay for a minimum of two nights a week all term if space available. Still predominantly Anglo-Saxon, school has won British Council award for international education. Involvement in Comenius programme and global partnerships with Portugal, Gambia and Bangladesh (visiting Bangladeshi teachers were 'bowled over by openness of Clayesmore'). Refugees from state schools and academic hothouses equally at home. Parents emphasise good pastoral care and importance given to individual child. 'School wants children to be happy and settled,' we were told. Elder siblings at senior school can be met regularly and are invited to prep for birthday parties.

Practical everyday uniform, blazers worn on special occasions. Experienced houseparents (husband teaches by day and is on duty five nights a week, wife provides 'lifeline to parents' by phone) live on site and are supported by assistants, matrons and 'the sisters' (qualified nurses who act as 'super mums'); parents are informed if children in sickbay overnight. School chaplain takes Saturday chapel: spiritual life is important but no ramming down throat. Children choose annual charities to benefit from fundraising activities (eg Julia's House – children's hospice in Wimborne). Dormitories kept up to mark with reward system which includes extra muck; children are allowed back after working day. Largest dormitories for youngest and thereafter boarders thin out into smaller units. Mobile phones permitted for boarders (overseas boarders also have access to Skype) but have to be handed back to staff before lights out. Relaxed atmosphere at weekends with 40+ children on site: 'we're never bored,' said pupils: late rise on Sundays and lots of 'amazing' trips (we were told about power boat rides). Boarders' Council involved in selecting next batch of assistants.

Individual needs department is centre of excellence. Pupils have learning support as and when required, from qualified special needs teacher, half hour lessons only – from two to five a week depending on need. SENCo plus fully-trained learning support assistants help in the classroom, in addition to the class or specialist subject teacher. Gym club and OT group to develop gross and fine motor skills, touch-typing, speech and language therapy once a week, sloping desks, special pens – all sorts of tricks brought into play. Multi-sensory and auditory processing used as appropriate. Parents pay extra for one-to-one help according to level of support required. Register of gifted and able: staff aim to stretch them. Library is at centre of school's reading culture and is somewhere to crash out during breaks; plenty of visiting authors and world book day has become a costumed extravaganza.

High percentage of staff have state and/or overseas experience. Long hours for day pupils who arrive for 8.20am start and leave at 5.30pm either by school minibus or with parents (many arrange car sharing) from discrete prep school car park. Lots of activities during lunch hour and after lessons save parents the endless ferrying of children to multifarious venues elsewhere. Years 3 and 4 are taught by form teachers (two sets in year 4 with setting in maths and English) and finish at 12.30 on Saturdays. From year 5 children are taught increasingly by subject specialists with 30 minute single or hour long doubles. Lots of practical work (DT and cookery were obviously favourites), geographers go out and about locally: eg locating source of river Iwerne. French is specialist from year 3 (songs and games in pre-prep), separate sciences are taught from year 7 and also Latin to higher sets. Two pre-university and four postgraduate teaching assistants provide support in classrooms and boarding areas. ICT geared to encouraging individualised learning and games are restricted. Personal tutors hold regular tutor group meetings, are responsible for PSHE and stay in charge for two years at a time. No complaints about homework (older day pupils attend bus prep to clear one assignment at

school). Older children stay for matches on Saturdays. Strong parents' association organises social and fundraising activities through year. Informal parental get-togethers indicative of the school's family atmosphere.

Sports facilities are superb; school has inclusive approach (over 90 per cent play in six or more matches) which doesn't detract from success. County level representation in cricket, rugby, hockey and football. Cross-country, swimming (boarders get a 45 minute slot after prep), tennis and squash (coaching in both) and athletics also on menu. Autumn term split between soccer and rugby for boys. Wide range of sporting activities includes horse-riding and sailing (pupils compete at prep schools regatta). House system provides basis for keen competition (including music) in many areas of school life culminating in annual sports day. 'It's cool to be a musician,' say pupils most of whom have individual lessons: best reach grade 6/7 level as well as national children's orchestras. Lots of performance opportunities for budding musicians, chapel choir has toured widely. Recent finalists in Pro-Corda competition. Picnic in park welcomes other preps and is school's annual jazz bash in grounds. Mexican trees of life and Quentin Blake style illustrations competed for wall space in art room where lunchtime and after school activities include pottery, banner art, model making and photography. Drama brings creative arts together for four major annual productions in senior theatre and 20+ children have LAMDA lessons with good results. Pupils get out and about: whether it is theatre visits, year 5 pupils experiencing living history in period homes or reception class down at the farm to meet the animals. Popular arts/science week runs at the end of the summer term. Other highlights are ski trips, post common entrance visit to France or Spain for rafting, climbing etc and year 7 trip to Normandy. Year 8 prefects, school and boarding councils ensure pupils' opinions are heard. We liked the annual magazine and the pic filled weekly e-letter (one of the better ones we've seen).

Pre-prep of 60+ children housed in purpose-built, timber-clad classrooms: delightful sylvan setting with bird watching and pond dipping in Zen garden. Nursery area interconnects with reception class: bugs theme well in evidence (including mobiles) when we visited. All-in-one waterproofs at the ready to help make most of safe outside play and veggie growing areas. Nursery vouchers are accepted. Phonic approach to reading with liking for Read Write Inc. SENCo gives support from outset (all children are assessed aged 5) and one-to-one help where necessary. One mother we spoke to was thrilled by how regular 'Mr Tongue' activity sessions with his teacher had helped her son's speech problem. Regular 'coffee and catch-up' gatherings after drop-off provide opportunity to explain anything of importance and open door policy allows for daily contact between staff and parents. Much use made of circle time to improve children's social and communication skills. Pre and after-school clubs and wide range of activities (including swimming) are included in fees.

Never a dull moment was the impression we left with. School takes on a wide range of ability and works hard with every child. Not socially divisive: an unpretentious and happy, family atmosphere for local children and boarders alike.

Clifton College Preparatory School (The Pre) + Butcombe Pre-Prep

Linked school: Clifton College

The Avenue, Bristol, BS8 3HE

• Pupils: Prep: 385 girls and boys; 70 board. Butcombe pre-prep: 210 girls and boys • Ages: 3-13 • C of E. Pupils from many faith backgrounds • Fees: Boarding £22,725–£24,450; Day £14,025; Butcombe £5,400+ pa • Independent

---

Tel: 01173 157502
Email: admissions@clifton-college.avon.sch.uk
Website: www.cliftoncollegeuk.com

Headmaster: Since 2008, Mr John Milne (early forties). No stranger to Clifton, he joined the staff in 1994, and in a morning assembly, 'one cold Wednesday morning in November of that year', found himself distracted and enchanted by the sight of a new teacher, Helen, a housemistress. Two years later they were married, and after three years of running a house, they were off to run the British School in Manila, where their first two children were born, and coincidentally they became involved with helping an orphanage, now adopted by Clifton Prep. Clifton is a hard place to leave and four years later Bob Acheson, the previous head, went out and persuaded the Milnes to return as houseparents of a girls' boarding house and he as director of studies. After he had piloted the school through three different inspections, the governors fully recognised his qualities and he was chosen as head in waiting. The waiting is over.

After attending Montrose Academy he went to Dartmouth College, an Ivy League university in New Hampshire, where he specialised in British history. On his return he was 'lucky enough' to play professional football for Aberdeen (post-Fergie days) – centre half, no red cards. Then on to Bristol University, where he took his PGCE in history. Tall, but not intimidatingly so (unless you are a short centre forward), he is popular with parents and committed to involved teaching and assessment for learning, ie pupils learning through sensitively-handled interaction with peers and staff – most importantly, learning to understand themselves. Pupils describe him as 'brilliant'; parents express uniform pleasure. 'We're just so lucky to have him,' is the common response.

The pre-prep, Butcombe, with its own headmistress, Mrs Jo Newman, operates separately, from the prep but is just down the road. It is an outstandingly good set up. Ask to see its inspection report.

Entrance: First come first served up to year 2; entrants to year 3 upwards assessed in English, maths and verbal reasoning. The minimum standard required is the expected national Sats level for the relevant age group. Entrance dependent on available places.

Exit: The large majority go on to the upper school at 13, sitting the same exam as external candidates.

Remarks: Run autonomously but in close and frequent touch with the head of the upper school, many of whose facilities they use. The prep moved off the college campus 75 years ago and in 1932 built the handsome main teaching block. With brightly-painted broad corridors – plenty of room for scurrying school children – and rooms which are spacious but not forbidding, it's an inspired piece of architecture which has adapted marvellously to modern needs. Well-carpeted now and with artwork adorning the walls (note the yummy-looking cakes in the entrance hall),

everything is welcoming and encouraging. Computers are everywhere – two rooms designated exclusively for them with thick red carpet in one room and blue in the other.

The music school, opened by Sir David Willcock of King's College, Cambridge, fame and an old boy, not only has masses of practice and rehearsal rooms but also an astonishing battery of computers where every child learns to compose their own works, coincidentally learning to read music. Recording studio and the means of writing your own music to films on DVD, like an auditory version of painting. OK, marvellous facilities, but are they used? The answer is a resounding and harmonious chorus of yes – 370 out of 400 perform in various orchestras, ensembles, quartets and groups and 70 sing in the choir.

The newly-updated library is bright, airy and attractive and has literally raised the roof. Computers there, but many more books and an alert and helpful librarian. Museum where aspiring cricketers can gawp in amazement at the original score book which records Arthur Collins' score in 1899 of 628 not out, which remains the highest individual score in the history of the game.

The art is absolutely stunning – excellent by any standards, not just prep school ones. In a smallish, non-purpose-built studio, children learn the importance of draughtsmanship, testified by the busts lining the wall and the rows of white-painted bottles challenging bright artists to master perspective. When we visited, the children were working on Henry Moore's sketches of sheep (they had been to London to see the exhibition). Their sketches were on the wall and they were engaged in creating clay sheep. Brilliant teaching and in addition the school has visiting artists in – most unusual.

Tennis courts and a playground in front of the teaching block remind the hesitating scholar that another world exists. Up at Beggar Bush, the other side of the suspension bridge, a games player's paradise (see Clifton College's entry in the senior section) – at how many prep schools can you play, amongst a cornucopia of sports, real tennis or rackets? The prep has its own sports hall.

Lots of drama – both in the school's own hall and the college's Redgrave Theatre. Assemblies are held in in the hall, complete with organ; services are held in the justly famous college chapel and the charismatic chaplain is much in evidence. In the state-of-the-art ICT suite budding inventors create working robots and other wonders. The list of activities and clubs is endless. Children talk enthusiastically of the weekend activities. Close by is the Coach House, where skilled and sympathetic staff help with learning support, garnished with loving kindness and encouragement.

All children, day and boarding, are attached to a house in one of the carefully-adapted Victorian houses that grace that area of Clifton. Little distinction between day and boarding, other than bed and breakfast, and ample provision for flexi-boarding for children whose parents are out clubbing. The prep school is divided into two tiers, 8-11 and 11-13, and housed accordingly. Boys and girls don't share houses, though they intermingle merrily in every other department. A recent programme of refurbishing has resulted in brightly-coloured accommodation (oh, that pink in the girls' boarding house!) with ample space for lolling and chatting. Lots of computers and cuddly toys. One house, unique in England, can watch sea lions from their bedroom windows and gorillas cavorting about – a favourite joke is to ask on which side of the road the real zoo is. Boarding for boys now starts at year 7-8.

Parents are ecstatic about the school – 'I thought this was a school for toffs,' said one, 'but it jolly well isn't. I know parents who are really scrimping and saving to send their children here. It's worth every penny because they have fun learning, make friends for life and because the staff really care. It's a blissfully happy school'. That from a mother who looked as if she could really dish it out if dissatisfied. 'I would,' she replied to the question. 'Relationships in the boarding houses are outstandingly positive,' wrote the inspectors – in the jargon of inspectors that's close to ecstasy.

Inspection report in an attractive and informative booklet. Do read the previous head's foreword, noting his comments about the language used. Then read the report and, if you like, count the number of times the word 'outstanding' is used. Then go and brave the traffic – it's well worth it.

Clifton Hall Junior School

Linked school: Clifton Hall School

Newbridge, Edinburgh, EH28 8LQ

• Pupils: 340 boys and girls • Ages: 3–11 • Non-denom
• Fees: £8,505–£9,630 pa • Independent

Tel: 01313 331359
Email: office@cliftonhall.org.uk
Website: www.cliftonhall.org.uk

Headmaster: Since 2005, Mr Rod Grant BA PGDBSE (new qualification last year) (forties), who runs the whole caboodle. See main school entry.

Entrance: Non-selective, though all are assessed to pin point possible hiccups. First come first served. Priority to siblings.

Exit: Most to the senior school, though the occasional local nobbery uses the pre-prep as a pre-prep before heading south for more trad preps.

Remarks: Clifton Hall Nursery is charming; 3 – 5 year olds: nappies not a problem, in partnership with Edinburgh, so discounted. Recently expanded, bung full of all the things you would love to have but don't feel you can afford, sandpits, water-play. Technically open till 3.00pm (from 8am) but after school club (£6 per session) picks up the slack. Stories (floor covering looked rather hard but we were assured the young didn't mind; we were pleased to see a random collection of cushions). Imaginative play area outside: looked slightly cramped for 40.

Clifton Hall Junior School is an 'independent primary school' based in a magical Bryce house with 56 acres of child-inspiring grounds. Junior school regarded as reliable and steady, nursery streaking ahead. Jazzy young staff blend well with the more mature, but we saw few of the latter. French from 3, Spanish and German from 8, keyboarding skills in primary for all.

School games getting stronger, teams often combine year groups. Huge growth and conversion of outbuildings. Great facilities, swimming pool, sports hall, networked computers, music classrooms; small classes, learning support both withdrawn and dual teaching. Vibrant music and drama.

Non selective, good basic grounding, building blocks, combo of jolly phonics/blends/word recognition and synthetics on the reading front. Serious experiments with liquids – will a penny float? Graduating to humanities, via computers, art and PE, use of all the main school facilities, dedicated staff. Very hands on, the early years seem like learning through play, though we came across a fearsomely pro-active class of 9/10 year olds in the computer room – touch typing.

For more opinion and information see senior school entry.

Clifton High Early Years and Junior School

Linked school: Clifton High School

College Road, Clifton, BS8 3JD

• Pupils: 235; 100 girls/135 boys; all day • Ages: 3–11 • Non-denominational with a Christian ethos • Fees: £8,670–£8,730 pa • Independent

Tel: 01179 730201
Email: admissions@cliftonhigh.bristol.sch.uk
Website: www.cliftonhigh.bristol.sch.uk

Head of nursery and junior school: Mr Anthony (Tony) Richards MBE, formerly head of an international school in Malaysia. He seems very well liked by parents and pupils. Softly spoken and 'not at all scary', according to one 4 year old. Mr Richards sits on the school executive along with Mr Guy Cowper, director of operations, and Dr Alison Neill, who is head of school.

Entrance: From age 3 in the nursery class, with children accepted at every stage based on informal assessments rather than tests.

Exit: Around two-thirds to senior school. No entrance tests unless trying for a scholarship. Rest to eg Queen Elizabeth Hospital School, Clifton College, Bristol Grammar, Red Maids', Colston's Collegiate, Badminton.

Remarks: A mid-sized, happy and inclusive school which inspires gushing praise from parents, particularly in the early years. Smaller than it used to be – two classes per year rather than three, with an intended maximum size of 20. Close links with the senior school – the option for both girls and boys to stay on makes for a smoother transition and more unified feel.

Broad curriculum, including French and Spanish taught at key stage 2. Children seem busy, but not stressed.

Support for dyslexia and other learning problems with an established learning support team (shared with the senior school), but the occasional child needing more intensive support is gently turned down or advised to move on before the end of junior school, though only after considerable consultation with parents and teachers.

The main early years and junior school buildings are converted from a large Victorian house, with later additions, on a campus shared with the senior school. Buildings and classrooms have been reallocated and refurbished recently and are bright and spacious. Equipment is reasonably new, including a large computer room. Children eat in the school canteen and go to assembly in the main hall twice a week.

Not a huge amount of outdoor space, but what there is is well designed for play and out-of-classroom learning (evidence of plenty of gardening, creative projects and fun experiments going on). The wide open spaces of the Downs are a short walk away. Children have access to the on-site swimming pool and gym (shared with the senior school) and are bussed to the school's sports centre, Coombe Dingle, for an afternoon's sporting activities once a week. Lots of lunch-time and after-school clubs from French to taekwondo to computers.

Cokethorpe Junior School

Linked school: Cokethorpe School

Witney, Oxfordshire, OX29 7PU

• Pupils: 140 boys and girls; all day • Ages: 4–11 • Joint C of E and RC foundation • Fees: £11,025 pa • Independent

Tel: 01993 703921
Email: admissions@cokethorpe.org
Website: www.cokethorpe.org.uk

Head of Junior School: Since September 2006, Mrs Christine Cook. Educated Westminster College, Oxford, Brockenhurst Sixth Form College. Formerly director of studies at Chandlings School, teaching houseparent at The Dragon School, head of year at The Oxford Academy (formerly Peers School), Oxford.

Entrance: Reception to year 2: visit with assessment in maths and literacy. Years 3 – 6: assessment day in January plus report from previous school. Cokethorpe juniors must pass same assessments as external candidates for entry to senior school.

Exit: Virtually all to senior school. During year 5, parents of junior school pupils unlikely to make it into the senior school are helped to look elsewhere.

Remarks: Juniors are taught in the Georgian splendour of the Mansion, sharing the 150 acres of parkland, sporting and academic facilities (science labs, IT suites etc) with their senior comrades. Juniors also eat in the splendid new dining hall. National curriculum is followed but with plenty of extras such as French. There is specialist teaching for music, art, drama, French and games – apparently this last is a real favourite as mini-Cokethorpeans are put through their paces by the senior school sports coaches. Latin is taught in years 5 and 6 but this is not continued in the senior school, although there are plans to do so. Small class numbers (average 16) in big high-ceilinged rooms, yet everything is friendly and child-centred. We watched as children in bright yellow polo shirts sat in a circle on the floor devising 'smart questions' about shapes. The pace of this hands-on lesson was just right, with plenty of time for all to think things through. The children's concentration was so intense that you could almost hear those youthful synapses fizzing and popping as they made connections and worked things out. We were momentarily distracted by a wall covered in delightful paintings of the things to be found in the Quangle Wangle's hat – Bisky Bats and all. Classes are mixed ability with setting for maths and spelling from year 3. Day ends at 5pm – can be quite tiring – but all get a chance to engage in an activity scheme similar to that enjoyed by the seniors.

Coldfall Primary School

Coldfall Avenue, London, N10 1HS

• Pupils: 520 boys and girls • Ages: 3–11 • State

Tel: 020 8883 0608
Email: office@coldfall.haringey.sch.uk
Website: www.coldfall.haringey.sch.uk

Head: Since 1996, Evelyn Davies (fifties). Ms Davies is one of life's 'superheads', a woman who has taken a 'bog-standard' primary and transformed it into a star act with an 'outstanding' Ofsted, three-form entry and very happy parents. Most find her open-minded and approachable. 'I had an idea', commented one, 'and she immediately said "let's have a chat about it".' Hard working and well-organised, she gets things done. 'She's not ticking boxes, she really gets involved in the nitty gritty'. An active opponent of testing, testing, testing, she's even been to parliament to protest, winning the admiration of her local MP ('if I were the minister for education I would grab Evelyn Davies and put her as his key adviser. That way our children would be well educated in every sense of the word').

Entrance: Places given out using the standard local authority formula: children in local authority care, followed by special educational needs, siblings and distance from the gates. Recent expansion means a bit of leeway for those living a few streets away.

Exit: A primary whose catchment fortunately straddles the borough's two highest flying comprehensives. The largest chunk of year 6 proceed to Fortismere, just next door, with another sizeable slice off to Alexandra Park, down the road. Enviable success rate too, in grammar-school entrance , then in dribbles to a wide range of local and distant establishments.

Remarks: This meticulously run school has everything going for it. Teaching here is enthusiastic and thorough, with staff constantly looking to improve performance. Academic standards are high and virtually every child reaches the government targets, many far exceeding them. Though the school has an 'unusually high' number of children with special needs, both those who struggle and those who excel are provided with plenty of booster classes. Not all parents, however, feel difficulties are necessarily dealt with sympathetically. 'Our son has considerable problems', said one, 'and we found the attitude very inflexible'. Behaviour is good and positive performance (particularly regular attendance) rewarded (classes compete enthusiastically for attendance teddies).

Facilities here can only be described as exceptional for a London primary. The original, large, low-lying Victorian schoolhouse, once a secondary school, has now been joined by a sleek, modern addition, providing extra classrooms and a new gym. Expansive grounds boast country-like playing fields, as well as two large and notably well-equipped playgrounds kitted out with basketball and netball nets, table-tennis tables and sheltered cabins. Pupils also benefit from the school's own allotments and nature trail, as well as access to nearby Coldfall Woods.

Sport played enthusiastically and successfully. Two hours of PE weekly overseen by a qualified sports coach and training approached with professional efficiency (gymnasts, for example, use flip cameras to study performance). Both boys and girls triumph in borough-wide competitions, boys winning recent golf and football championships, girls excelling in football and netball. Pupils also qualified for the London Youth Games.

Plenty of enrichment, in lessons and out, including chess (with championship-winning chess teams), French (taught by a native speaker), computer programming and cooking all part of the regular mix. Excellent range of clubs (including geology) and activities. Successful school choir has made appearances at the O2 centre and Barbican and one enthusiastic parent recently organised an entire week of dance with over 60 workshops and professionals imported from the West End. 'Things don't just happen here', said one mother. 'Everything is well planned and thought through'. Regular trips beyond the school gates include at least one visit to a museum, gallery and musical event for every pupil.

In the main (though not exclusively), parents are comfortably off Muswell Hill locals, so there's a good sprinkling of designer trainers in the playground, but this is low-key prosperity. Almost a third of pupils speak another language than English at home. Both mothers and fathers (plenty of the latter at pick-up time) involved in making the school a success. 'All parents', said one enthusiast, 'are given an opportunity to contribute, not just non-working mums'. Many arrive at weekends to help with the gardening and the thriving PTA organises summer and winter fairs, weekly coffee mornings, a Valentine disco, quiz night, fashion show and organic vegetable scheme. Sizeable sums are raised for playground, computer and PE equipment. 'There's a real feeling that everyone matters', said one mother. 'The kids are really blessed'.

Colet Court

Linked school: St Paul's School

Lonsdale Road, London, SW13 9JT

• Pupils: 440 boys, all day • Ages: 7–13 • Christian foundation but boys of all faiths represented • Fees: £16,671 pa • Independent

Tel: 020 8748 3461
Email: hmseccc@stpaulsschool.org.uk
Website: www.coletcourt.org.uk

Headmaster: Since 2007, Mr Tim Meunier MA PGCE C.Chem FRCS, (early fifties). Educated at Forest School, London and Trinity College, Cambridge. Married to 'lovely, smiley' Sarah (say boys, who love it when she covers their lessons – no official role for spouse here). They met doing PGCE at Homerton and have two grown-up sons. Apart from a spell at The Dragon (Sarah ran a boarding house, he was head of science), Mr Meunier's experience is largely in senior schools – Felsted, deputy head at Clifton College. Quietly humorous, thoughtful and sincere. Embraces the 500 year traditions of the place and the history of academic brilliance, but at the same time working to soften the image. Has already tweaked the entrance procedure to make it less daunting (particularly for parents) and insists that 'We are surprisingly cuddly once you're here'.

Entrance: At 7+, 8+, and 11+. State primary school candidates can sit an exam in year 5 for a deferred place at 11+ (10 places available). Boys at prep schools that finish at 11 sit the 11+ exam in year 6 (at least another 10 places available). Very competitive – at least 200 candidates. Looking for innate intelligence – 'We have only one criterion – very very bright boys'. Tailor-made exam and headmaster will interview all boys plus parents (school prefers to use word 'chat' with respect to parents, 'to put them at their ease – they are much more nervous than the boys'). Would be naïve, says headmaster, to assume no preparation is necessary – whether it be tutoring, extra reading with Granny or stimulating conversations with a doting uncle.

Will fill the occasional place (very rarely happens, but anything possible in this economic climate), but only with boys who have already taken the entrance exams, or couldn't possibly have gone through the system. Strict policy in place to avoid any possible loopholes.

Exit: Natural destination of leavers is St Paul's, and nearly all go on there, although some may elect to transfer to other schools, often as a result of a change in parental circumstances. Has a good relationship with senior schools such as Eton and Winchester, and will support boys with appropriate references and recommendations.

Although in some subjects Coletines sit 13+ transfer examinations set by St Paul's School instead of common entrance papers (these are taken in English, maths and science), the syllabuses do not differ greatly, and in practice senior schools are usually happy to accept the St Paul's papers for entry. Does not prepare boys for scholarships to other schools,

but will offer advice on what is required – 'We feel it is a positive advantage that boys don't have to work towards a lot of different exams for different schools'.

Remarks: It's going to take a lot more than the odd off-the-cuff comment about cuddliness to change the school's prevailing reputation – confirmed by many current parents – that if you want nurture and a flexible approach geared to the individual, then find somewhere else. (The school feels that this is unfair and out of date: 'Our teachers go out of their way to nurture boys.') In addition, no denying the fact that most boys here hugely enjoy it and don't feel in any way neglected or unvalued.

The overwhelming message – whether during assembly, in the newsletter, in the school magazine or on the website – is that Colet Court is about excellence. Unashamedly ambitious about achieving that excellence, boys here know what's expected of them and have an insatiable appetite to keep striving for it. As soon as you cross the threshold as parent or pupil – a surprisingly intimidating experience, given the unprepossessing buildings – you sign up to this culture of achievement, and you sign up for the long term. Once you're here, why would you want to go anywhere else? As one parent put it, you have a pass into a top school (if not the top school, as far as they are concerned) on a plate (all being well, very few don't make the grade) and an excellent prep school into the bargain.

Situated in 45 largely green acres (some shared with St Paul's so, note, a few lumbering teenagers will be crossing paths with your budding boy), replete with playing fields, a full-size swimming pool, large sports hall, fencing salle, dojo for aikido, rackets court and tennis courts, plus new cricket nets, basketball courts, multi-use games area, ICT suites, technology workshops, fully-equipped science labs, music school, music hall, large assembly hall, separate dining hall, playground with wood, ropes and swings. All this, so close to the centre of town and on the river too, is unparalleled for a London day school. Latest inspection report littered with superlatives. Sport, music, facilities, exam results 'outstanding', 'excellent', 'exceptional', of the 'highest quality'.

Stunning music, 'ridiculously good,' says Mr Meunier, a keen lover of music himself (he and his wife sing in various choirs). Three orchestras, chamber ensemble, string quartet. Piles of distinctions on music exams. Three choirs, full to bursting, with invigorating schedule of appearances. Over 80 per cent of boys learn one or more musical instruments. Art superb, in bright, spacious art classroom overlooking Thames. Excellent chess team; super, well-used library, regular additions.

Sports abundant – 7 year olds play tag rugby. Higher up the school a multi-sports option for boys who do not want to play contact games. Soccer in spring, cricket in summer. Games for two hours, two afternoons a week, plus a session of PE. Loads of teams – most boys (including all of those in the junior classes) can represent the school at some level. One of the few independent preps to take boys on overseas soccer tours – cricket tour to Barbados, football to Brazil and rugby and football to South Africa. Saturday morning games or practice for boys in teams. Golf off-site.

A murmur of criticism in the recent inspection – the breadth of education at the top of the school – is swiftly addressed. The decision to dispose of the controversially elitist scholarship form, and to have two-tiered streaming in the final two years (only), with potential scholars drawn from the entire year group, Mr Meunier says was 'pushing at an open door'. The tendency to focus even more on the academics in the final years will now be a bit more balanced with more outdoor pursuits activities, art, music, design and drama. Here any change is about tweaking, not about overhaul.

On the fundamentals, that is infrastructure, it's another story. A massive multi-billion building project to span the next 20 years is under way. Sixties prefab, never meant to last more than 50 years, will gradually be replaced with 'architecturally exciting, environmentally-friendly buildings using a mix of materials'. In the meantime even the hoardings will be high quality, assures Mr Meunier. Nor will the academic standards be in any way threatened – strictly no noise during lesson times.

Surprisingly broad intake: although 60 per cent of parents are probably lawyers or bankers, the generous bursaries (quite a few on 100 per cent) funded by the John Colet foundation allow the less well-off to benefit. Help also for extras such as trips and tours abroad. One thing all parents (many of whom are themselves old Paulines and Paulinas) have in common is that they are highly-motivated and ambitious (no surprises there). Quiz night is something to limber up for and one parent confessed that she preferred not to admit to ever getting drunk on the sofa watching Spooks. A broad geographical intake too – although most are from Barnes, Chiswick, Kensington etc, some are prepared to tackle a school run of up to two hours each way to ensure their son experiences what they regard to be London's finest.

Don't gasp – there are those who struggle. The reality is some 30 to 40 boys have a difficulty of some sort, mostly mild dyslexia or dyspraxia, but ADD, ADHD (Ritalin okay) and mild Asperger's found among the numbers. Everyone is screened on entry to the school, and at the first sign of trouble (generally quickly spotted because of excellent communication between staff) they are swept up by the universally-praised learning support lady, who will teach them to organise themselves, draw up tables of French and Latin verbs or bring their maths up to speed. Learning support could be for the long term or a short sharp burst, but either way it is readily available, at no extra cost, and enables the boys to carry on sprinting. 'Some of our best and brightest have a difficulty. Ironically, the baggage can help. They have to develop strategies to cope, they think differently and some get to Oxbridge.' Big study skills programme for all year 8s, who get three lessons before their mocks and further ones in the run-up to common entrance/transfer exams.

In a system that boasts outstanding exam performances and is so results-based, you must be wondering how they have time to do anything else. A very long lunch break, when they can do anything from fencing to Aikido, bridge, second orchestra or woodwind ensemble – you name it, but they have to go out and find it: boys here need initiative and plenty of oomph. Some who prefer to play tag or cards in the copious play areas, but one parent expressed concern as to whether little Johnnie would forget to eat lunch (school insists duty staff will send boys to lunch). If they forget their mouthguards for rugby, they get short shrift – third time without it, that's a detention. Taking responsibility for yourself starts here. In term time you go at full throttle. One parent commented that she was relieved her son was never ill. Sometimes boys won't get home until 9pm after performing in a concert. The holidays are still called 'remedies' – a time to catch up, but otherwise total recuperation.

We would have to agree with the inspectors: this is a superlative school for the right boy, but don't be wowed by the brand unless your son is the genuine article: energetic and competitive, brilliant at one thing at least – and undeflated by rarely being the best at anything.

Colfe's Preparatory School + Pre prep and Nursery

Linked school: Colfe's School

Horn Park Lane, London, SE12 8AW

• Pupils: 350 girls/boys day • Ages: 3–11 • C of E • Fees: £10,413–£11,502 pa • Independent

Tel: 020 8463 8240
Email: prep@colfes.com
Website: www.colfes.com

Head: Since April 2013, Mrs Sarah Marsh (forties) BEd, previously deputy head of St Andrew's prep school in Woking. She started her teaching career as a PE specialist, followed by director of studies at Guildford High School. Currently she is completing a Master's in Education Leadership. She is very enthusiastic about the expansion of the junior school and is looking forward to building on all the good practices she has inherited. She enjoys going to the gym, jazz dance and skiing holidays.

Head of pre-prep since January 2013 is Sarah Redman (fifties) BEd. Mrs Redman was deputy head of the nursery and pre-prep school for some years before becoming head teacher. Parents comment on her warmth and friendliness, 'exactly the sort of person you can entrust your small child to'. Married to a fellow teacher, who is head of the local state primary, with three grown-up children, one of whom is an actress. She enjoys gardening, theatre, arts and crafts, the influence of which can be spotted around the pre-prep.

Entrance: Informal observation morning at 3+ into the nursery or 4+ into the pre-prep. Entry through assessment for additional places at 7+ and for occasional places further up the school

Exit: At 11+ most pupils move into the senior school; a few opt for local state grammars.

Remarks: Green and tranquil setting on the edge of the main school; new buildings are shooting up so the school can accommodate three classes across the age groups. Well planned academic curriculum runs alongside inspirational sport and arts options. Mixed ability classes of around 18; each child is monitored regularly to check progress. Lively pupils perform well in both national and house competitions; particularly successful teams for maths and chess. 'A very caring school, where the teachers recognise every child as an individual'. Art is incorporated into much of the curriculum and classrooms are bursting with interesting displays, models and sculptures. Specialist art teacher organises a big end of year exhibition. Six-year-olds upwards learn French and Spanish in alternating years. Musical education starts early with recorder in year 1 and ukulele in year 2. With around 80 per cent taking instrumental lessons, the school boasts choirs, orchestras, chamber groups, rock band and specialist brass programme. Creative drama, regular plays and lots of opportunities for performers in musical and dramatic assemblies. Dance workshops are popular and include everything and anything from flamenco to African dancing. Annual Ugly Bug Ball celebrates pre-prep children moving to the junior school, and into school houses. On-site sports facilities are shared with the seniors, including a swimming pool for weekly lessons. More or less everything on offer on the sporting front, with lots of house competitions. Junior girls' netball team are national prep school champions. Help is on hand via learning support teachers for pupils with mild difficulties, dyslexia, dyspraxia and dyscalculia. Active PTA, parent volunteers assist with all sorts of activities including fundraising, costume making and art and design. Fantastic choice of lunchtime and after-school clubs; also a breakfast club from 7.30am and after school care until 6pm. Sound all-round education, well tried and tested teaching methods mixed with a great range of arts and sports, produces happy pupils and contented parents.

The Compass School

West Road, Haddington, EH41 3RD

- Pupils: 62 boys, 65 girls; all day • Ages: 4–12 • Inter-denom
- Fees: £6,531–£8,523 pa • Independent

Tel: 01620 822642
Email: office@thecompassschool.co.uk
Website: www.thecompassschool.co.uk

Headmaster: Since 1997, Mr Mark Becher (pronounced Becker) MA PGCE (early forties), educated at Queen Margaret's Academy Ayr, Dundee University, (modern history) and PGCE at Craigie College of Education in Ayr (now part the University of the West of Scotland). Previously head of sport and primary teacher at The Mary Erskine and Stewart's Melville Junior School, and primary teacher at Edinburgh Academy.

An enthusiastic head who lives and breathes The Compass (as it's known – symbolic of finding the right direction for pupils), a keen distance runner, teaches sport, Latin and history, team teaching everyone in school. Supported (recently) by a management team of deputy and part-time bursar, he has seen the school through a £1 million building programme and is revelling in the spanking new facilities. Hall classrooms, milling-about space and dedicated ICT suite, all jigsaws remarkably harmoniously into the compact spaces around the pretty Edwardian main house.

Head takes pride in running a successful Scottish primary – 'Not prep/IAPS,' he stresses – based on the philosophy of the Scottish Curriculum for Excellence but with specialist teaching – 'ideal preparation' – allowing pupils to feed the Edinburgh private sector well ahead of the field. 'Four years ahead in French,' one school complained; 'No apologies for letting children work to their capabilities,' says Mr Becher. Previously for ages 4-8 with a composite class for 9-12 year olds, has grown to include a nursery run in partnership with East Lothian Council and seven year groups (class size between 12 and 20). Mr Becher says the confidence gained from representing the school in the extremely successful choir (everyone's in it and it's won the Edinburgh Festival Primary Schools' Choir trophy twice), teams, drama etc prepares children to take a lead happily in large schools at secondary level.

Entrance: Children can (and do) join at any time – they have an informal assessment and begin at any stage of the school year. School uniform is sold in house and in Edinburgh. Can apply for 'financially assisted places' at any entry stage; specific bursaries for forms 6, 7 and 8 plus sibling discounts and parents can ask for help if struck by financial meltdown. Good proportion of first time independent buyers with catchment from east Edinburgh along the coast to Berwick on Tweed and south to the Lammermuirs. No buses but lots of shared driving etc.

Exit: Most leave at 12 for Edinburgh independents or local state school. 'Everyone gets where they want' and few now leave at eight for traditional prep schools.

Remarks: Small but extremely perfectly re-formed to bandbox smartness in both the old house and the extension, now has room for a grand though gloomy dining room where class tables are supervised by staff and each has a tray of raw vegetable appetisers 'so they nibble and learn to enjoy while they are waiting'; also dedicated music and art rooms with sweeping views of hills and cornfields – 'a great teaching aid for year 5 doing farming'. The dramatic galleried stairs rising from the elegant hallway with its glowing (gas fired) coal stove cry out for (and get) carols and holly at Christmas. Classrooms all round are full of bright, shiny but practical equipment and staff. Support for learning is run in close consultation with class etc teachers and takes whatever form fits the child, with a blanket overview from the support teacher, who sits in on all classes and observes/helps to make sure she reaches all the needy.

All the usual traditional subjects: French from age four and Latin from age nine. Pupil work on show everywhere and 'visitors tend to be stunned!'. Best of all were the little booklets of good work and 'daily life in class one' scrapbooks in the parents' waiting area.

Started in 1963 and run by Mrs Alny Younger for years, still feels homely with Astroturf lawns for playtimes and outdoor learning space (smart hut). Lots of games and sport, making use of local authority grass and Astro pitches, Haddington Golf Club, local pool, Loretto's theatre and local churches. Rugby, cricket and hockey matches and swimming galas, all with impressive wins 'against bigger schools'. Same goes for music – a huge range of activities packed into a 9am to 3.30pm day with after-school supervision (paid for) and activities (nominal cost only). The atmosphere has a 'good prep school buzz' but feels more fun than frenetic.

Small is beautiful here! Feels like a first-rate, friendly and efficient school deeply embedded in a supportive, tight-knit and ethnically Scottish community. Parents raised £250,000 in last few years and treat school as a social hub.

Connaught House School

47 Connaught Square, London, W2 2HL

- Pupils: 80–30 boys, 50 girls, all day • Ages: 4–11, boys leave at 8
- Non-denom • Fees: £13,950–£16,750 pa • Independent

Tel: 020 7262 8830
Email: office@connaughthouseschool.co.uk
Website: www.connaughthouseschool.co.uk

Joint principals: Since 1991, Mrs Jaqueline Hampton (fifties) and her husband, Mr Frederick Hampton MA RCA. Has been run by the same family since it opened in 1953 with just six pupils. That tradition continues today, as the Hamptons' daughter-in-law, Mrs Victoria Hampton, is their head of early years and key stage 1 advisor. Both Hamptons senior are artists and they have two grown up sons.

Entrance: At age 4 into reception (here called Junior One) but with the understanding that they will continue into the main school. Preference is given to siblings and to children from local families. Places are offered after a short, informal assessment. Applications can also be made for entry in the upper end of the school. Academic and music bursaries are available to those applying at 7/8+. Many from local nurseries including Great Beginnings and Paint Pots.

Exit: All boys leave at 8 and tend to go to local prep schools such as Westminster Under School, Sussex House and Wetherby. The girls stay until 11 and generally opt for London day schools – Francis Holland is currently popular but many also go to Godolphin and Latymer, City of London, More House, Latymer

Upper, Queens Gate and South Hampstead High. Those wishing to board choose Wycombe Abbey or St Mary's, Ascot. Despite leaving a very small school to go on to these much larger establishments, none of the pupils seems to be fazed by this – the confidence they acquire in CHS gives them the ability to cope in a broader environment.

Remarks: Such an individual school that you will instantly know whether you love it or hate it – very small, so does not take long to visit. Crossing it off your list because of its size could be a bad mistake. In a world where everything seems to be getting bigger, this little gem offers old-fashioned notions such as pleasure in learning, time to listen and be listened to ('They are all happy to talk to people of any age,' remarks one mother); good manners and courtesy to others; the acquisition of general knowledge; delicious home-cooked lunches; traditional uniforms, including boaters for the girls and caps for the boys. Has never advertised but a waiting list. Most of the pupils live locally so a sprinkling of EAL pupils throughout and support is provided. In addition, several staff have SEN training. 'Very nice parents and lovely children,' says Mrs Hampton. 'We try to support every child. We are not at all ruthless – that's not our way.'

Art and music are the main extracurricular strengths of the school – 'The art really strikes you,' says one parent. Art displays and individual work cover the walls in and out of the classroom, 'something for them to absorb even when they're lost in space'. Music welcomes them into school in the morning. A very high percentage undertakes piano lessons – singing, violin, recorder, flute and guitar are also taught. The peripatetic music teachers are all successful musicians and performers in their own right but still find time 'for this funny little school'. Teachers and pupils thrive on the feeling that their school is a place of learning. All develop work habits which serve them well when they move on to bigger schools.

No formal PTA, but the parents are very much in tune with the school and are frequently consulted. 'Very nurturing – older ones mentor the younger ones. They find that little thing in each person and bring it out. They embrace the individual,' says one parent enthusiastically.

The lack of on-site sporting facilities does not seem to concern the parents nor the pupils. They make full use of local sports facilities (where fencing and martial arts have recently been added to the sports programme) and use the existing outside areas all around them – Hyde Park is over the road. 'Anyhow, it is something London parents are used to. After all, you spend your weekends driving your children around,' claims one of the mothers.

All in all, a very special little school which is loved by parents and pupils alike, where the children feel challenged every day and their parents are constantly amazed by what they know. 'The closest you can get to home schooling,' declares one. If that sounds appealing, take a little trip to Bayswater Road now.

Coombe Hill Infant School

Coombe Lane West, Kingston upon Thames, KT2 7DD

• Pupils: 320 boys and girls, pretty much half and half • Ages: 4–7
• Non-denom • State

Tel: 020 8942 9481
Email: admin@chi.rbksch.org
Website: www.combehillinfants.com

Headteacher: Since September 2013, Mrs Janet Berry, previously school SENCo and member of the senior leadership team.

Entrance: You need to live almost on the school's posh doorstep to get in. Substantially oversubscribed, though bulge reception classes sometimes widen catchment. Priority to children with sibling attending the school or the associated junior school at the time of admission; pupils with a medical or social need and then those living nearest the school. In practice about a third (to a half) of places to siblings. One or two have medical or social needs and the rest tend to live within three-quarters of a mile of the school.

Exit: Vast majority trot off to the junior school next door. A few to independent schools – King's College School Wimbledon, Surbiton High School, Wimbledon High School, Putney High School, Rokeby and Shrewsbury House.

Remarks: Top notch school in upmarket area, with winning combination of supportive middle class parents, rich cultural mix and good achievement. Located in one of the most prestigious residential locations in the borough and surrounded by substantial detached houses bristling with security alarms and locked gates to their private roads. A most favourable location for any school, so hugely refreshing that the intake is very ethnically diverse, with more than 50 per cent of the children having EAL, a third speaking more than one language and some speaking more than two. Many children from European backgrounds, together with some Korean and Japanese. School celebrates this rich mix of cultures to the full – highly popular international week and international evenings every year for the whole family: they are invited to wear national dress (even the Brits), have national dancing shows and sample many home-made culinary delights. Forms of mixed ability entry – 30 per form. Key stage 1 results are very good but head points out that, with so many children having EAL, the higher grades in literacy are harder to achieve for many pupils. SEN – typical of the national average – 21 per cent.

Recently updated to a very high standard, on a semi-open plan basis with lots of natural light. Very well endowed with interactive (and expensive) whiteboards, together with a modern IT suite. Lovely grounds with far-reaching views. Shares swimming pool with junior school, used by each class twice a week in summer. Buildings adapted for disabled users.

Super school to visit with loads going on and children very absorbed. Great range of after-school activities: clubs for gym, drama and music, art and craft, construction and a dinosaur club – charge of approx £3 per session. Lending library for videos, games, reading and maths schemes. Do look at the super website, a lot of it created by the children. Support from the solid middle class parents is tremendous – ' The parents raise a fortune,' says the school: its swimming pool is heated and maintained from proceeds raised by the PTA.

No lunch provided – children have to bring it from home. Parking problematic, as ever, with busy main road outside. No problems dropping off in the mornings – a quick in and out – but not so easy in the afternoon, when school insists parents park in adjacent side roads and walk to collect.

School has everything going for it – vibrancy, enviable buildings, grounds, location and catchment area. Deservedly very popular, worth moving to be near – or should we say very near? – to get a place – assuming, of course, you have the money to buy in its largely upmarket catchment area.

Coombe Hill Junior School

Coombe Lane West, Kingston Upon Thames, KT2 7DD

• Pupils: 390 boys and girls; all day • Ages: 7–11 • Non-denom
• State

Tel: 020 8949 1743
Email: admin@chj.rbksch.org
Website: www.coombehillj.kingston.sch.uk/

Headteacher: Since 2004, Mr Chris Hodges, BA PGCE (mid-thirties). Prior to joining Coombe was deputy head and then head at Sparrow Farm Juniors in Feltham. Has risen through the ranks very quickly, though, in typically modest mode, he claims to have been 'in the right place at the right time'. Has the national professional qualification for headship and has completed the leadership programme for serving headteachers – he's a thoroughly modern man.

Tall, sharp-suited (no tie) with a Grant Mitchell haircut and an amenable, laidback manner which belies his steady finger on the pulse and steely resolve. He 'never stops assessing and looking for improvement', and is bursting with ideas (he seems particularly clued-up on attracting government money to the school). Bounces around the school with Tigger-like enthusiasm, insisting his (female) management team – the deputy head and senior teacher – share credit for the school's fantastic local reputation.

A 'doer' – he makes things happen fast. Has given the management team, year heads and class teachers significant levels of responsibility. But don't be fooled – Mr Hodges has selected his able, like-minded staff carefully (he had to 'lose a few' when he took over, perhaps because they were not committed to the philosophy) and knows exactly what is going on. Not a lover of office life – preferring to grind through his paperwork at home – he enjoys the classroom and fits in an impressive 40 per cent teaching time, including daily year 6 maths.

Not interested in the trappings of office; his own is smaller than his deputy's and has a less attractive aspect – 'I wanted to be more central, near the entrance and the sick bay,' he explains. Obviously likes children – his door is literally always open to them and he's a familiar figure in the playground, where he mucks in and is frequently called on to sort out any 'domestics'. Not expected to win a long-service award – parents see him as 'going places', though he is adamant he is not going anywhere. Married with one young daughter, he is a busy family man, with all that entails. A chap to watch for the future.

Entrance: Catchment is from Coombe Hill and New Malden areas. Oversubscribed – typically 150 applicants for 90 places, extras go onto a waiting list. Three form entry, with 30 children in each class. The school is always full – key is to get your child into the adjacent, and similarly sought after, linked Coombe Infant School from whence automatic transfer – 99 per cent of children arrive from here.

Exit: Most stay in the state system, with impressive numbers winning places at Kingston's highly selective Tiffin grammar schools. Well-regarded local Coombe Girls' is a popular option. These three schools account for about 50 per cent of year 6 leavers – others elsewhere in handfuls. Some 10 per cent head off to local independents.

Remarks: A brilliant, buzzy state school which packs a real punch, easily holding its own among its largely private sector competition. In one of Kingston's most upmarket areas, shares a large and attractive site with its partner infant school, both heavily oversubscribed with children from solid middle class families. 'It's a lovely school,' says one parent, 'but it's not the only lovely school in the area, so it's not simply that it's an easy option. It does well to ensure it's a positive choice for us all.'

Sats results are consistently top notch – 99 per cent reach level 4, 75 per cent level 5; tremendous value-added too. School very keen on teaching learning strategies. Classes are mixed ability, but with bags of setting and even sets within the sets. This makes for well-paced lessons where the children seem genuinely engaged in their activities. When we visited, noise from a drumming workshop in the hall was reverberating around the place, but no one appeared distracted – it merely served to underline the fact that this is a place where lots happens. French for all.

ICT plays a major role in motivating the children – interactive boards in all classes, a smart, good size and well-used ICT suite with technician, plus wireless laptops. All learn touch-typing. Alpha Smarts (a type of personal digital assistant) available to the school's 30 or so diagnosed dyslexics and other reluctant writers.

Over 20 per cent of the children have an identified special need (just above the average). School happily caters for a broad range of requirements, including those for dyslexia and dyspraxia. Provision includes social skills groups and vocabulary groups, one-to-one maths, additional and further literacy support and class brain-gym. Additionally weekly 'excellence sessions' and a 'challenge zone' resource area for the 25 or so pupils identified as gifted and talented. The G&T programme is broadened to include areas such as art, music and sport, not just academics.

The school benefits from detailed and thorough records passed on by the linked infants' school and the SENCo concentrates for the first half term of year 3 on the identification of any additional needs. Additional SEN specialists are on hand three mornings a week. Such good pick-up and support means SEN pupils here make above-average progress. The mother of one little boy raves about how well he has done since joining the junior school: 'He arrived with minimal reading and writing skills and is now in the middle of his class. They do push and expect a lot of the children, but so they should. They have kept a close eye on him and I am delighted.' Some 27 different languages are spoken by children across the school – plenty of support available

Nice ambience about the place; recently upgraded facilities include a lift to allow disabled access and one of the smartest staffrooms we've seen anywhere – we mention it only as an indication that the school pays more than lip service to the notion of valuing its staff. Although wide corridors and atrium space create a generally roomy feel, some of the classrooms are actually a little tight. But the total space is flexible and desks are carted around as needed. 'Every cohort is different and we tailor their activities to suit,' says Mr Hodges. Good, effective displays abound.

Staff female – just one male classroom assistant and two learning support assistants. Parents are full of praise for teaching. Art and science both mentioned by several parents as being 'fantastic', but a drizzle of complaint about 'not enough sport' (although this is probably more a criticism of the national curriculum than the school) and Mr Hodges is on the case. Every morning begins with an aerobic session in the playground before school starts. It's optional – but most children badger their parents to be there. Another sporting bonus is the on-site heated swimming pool (shared with infants). Plenty of music on offer. Most teachers are musical and competent enough to take their own music lessons, peripatetic staff teach the 45 or so pupils who study an instrument. Busy choir and orchestra. Year 3 pupils all get the chance to try trumpet or violin in the spring term.

Children have a fairly free rein in the playground. A few diehard couch potatoes may skulk around the edges, but otherwise everyone seems to be having a great time – the fact that the lines need repainting every five weeks bears witness to the many activities that go on here. Children digging up the grassy area with a stick are allowed to get on with it – 'You've got to have a bit of fun,' says Mr Hodges. 'What's life come to if you can't let a child play with a stick? I found someone building an assault course for ants the other day.' Even trading cards, widely banned elsewhere, are permitted, as staff believe children learn a life lesson from them – even when in dispute.

Obvious zero tolerance of any aggressive or bullying behaviour – older pupils are trained as peer mediators and head is noted for acting fast if any problems do occur. 'I'm actually very proud of the way children at this school behave towards one another,' he says. A counsellor (not a parent or teacher) is a recent addition to the ranks. Parents agree this is a school which belongs to the children – they are well-motivated and therefore mostly keen to participate in all that's on offer. But boundaries are made clear and consequences for 'bad choice' – no-one likes being left to stew, crosslegged, outside the head's office.

Good range of after-school clubs. Only grumble concerned a lack of casual, classroom-door type access to staff – school prefers contact via the office for appointment: 'A bit over the top if I just want to mention that the goldfish died,' says one mother. More generally, school/home communication has been a bugbear for some parents going back several years – but it is felt to be slowly improving under Mr Hodges: 'I totally get what parents want since my own daughter started school,' he says. An external blackboard at the front entrance for daily notices, but an email facility is high on parental wish-list.

Children are offered a genuine role in helping to run the school and take it very seriously. The school council is a force to be reckoned with – pupil members temporarily withdrew playground equipment they had chosen and bought with part of their £1,500 budget, because they felt it was not being properly respected. Pupils also play a big part in the school's myriad environmental initiatives as part of a 'green team' facilitated by a teacher.

Parents are viewed as a key resource, and they show tremendous support, over and above the norm. School is overwhelmed with offers of help, and the very active and sociable parents' association raises big money – £30k plus. 'The school is definitely a big part of our community and lots of friendships are based here,' says one mother. Parents also operate a rota to control vehicle access to the school at the beginning of each day – the school drop-off, as ever, is problematic.

Families are affluent and diverse – almost 50 per cent of pupils have English as their second language. This mix of cultures is a plus for many parents – all are made to feel welcome and valued. Mr Hodges is also intent on making school's facilities available to the local community. Adult learning courses (from creative writing through to computer skills and first aid) are open to all, not just parents connected with the school. 'It is simply ludicrous that our facilities can only be used for 12 per cent of the year,' says Mr Hodges. 'We must be a community facility.' He doesn't garner unanimous support for this – one mother vehemently believes he should have let this particular idea gather dust in his intray – not that one seriously imagines anything does. That said, grumbles are few and far between.

Cothill House

Linked school: Chandlings School

Cothill, Abingdon, OX13 6JL

• Pupils: 220 boys; all board • Ages: 8–13 • C of E • Fees: £24,450 pa • Independent

Tel: 01865 390800
Email: jane@cothill.net
Website: www.cothill.net

Headmaster: Since 2011, Mr Duncan Bailey (thirties) BA French studies (University of Manchester) BA German (University of Vienna). An ex-Cothill boy himself, he is married to Maria, who is Austrian, with two young daughters. All live in the school. Maria is responsible for much of the pastoral life – especially the food and wellbeing of the children. She is ready to fill in everywhere – either as a cook, cleaner, teacher or head!

Entrance: Despite changing attitudes to boarding school, the number of boys who start at Cothill at 8 has hardly changed over the years, averaging at about 30; of these only two or three are from families where no tradition of boarding, but for most here it is 'simply the norm'. Applications to Cothill have remained immune, thus far, to the economic malaise, and early registration is advisable.

The process begins with a meeting for parents only – after all, 'This is going to be their decision' – followed by an open day and assessment morning. No great emphasis on academic ability at this stage: the assessment is principally to check that the boy and the school are right for each other. After this, boys are encouraged to visit as often as possible prior to joining.

Exit: The school is very keen that each boy leaving Cothill should go on to the school that is right for him. Happily, school and parents seem most often to be in agreement and the destinations are just as one would expect. Boys depart, often accompanied by scholarships, to Eton, Harrow, Radley, Marlborough, Tonbridge, St Edward's, Bryanston etc.

Remarks: Charming village location feels comfortably rural, although Cothill is just on the outskirts of Abingdon and six miles south of Oxford. The main building is a large country house with a variety of later additions and 26 acres of grounds and playing fields. Sports facilities include a 19 metre indoor pool housed in a high-roofed wooden barn with glass sides, a squash court and six all-weather tennis courts, plus a nine-hole golf course where boys are coached by a pro. Parents are welcome to come and watch mid-week, as well as weekend, sports fixtures and many do, especially mothers who find boarding 'harder to adapt to than the boys'. Details of recent equestrian successes are pinned up on the head's notice board, but the school does not keep horses and teams are organised by the parents of the boys who do.

Head's family quarters are very much part of the school – boys take cookery classes in the kitchen, an extremely popular activity, particularly if the recipe contains chocolate. The large, comfortable sitting room with squashy sofas has a television for Saturday film nights and important sporting events only. Dorms are tidy but characterful, boys sleep in bunk beds with four or eight to a room and plenty of posters, flags, soft toys, family photos and colourful duvets from home. No mobiles or other electronic distractions until the final year, when boys are allowed an iPod. In theory, small pets are accommodated (nothing further up the evolutionary scale than a ferret); however a sad little shed full of empty hutches and cages is testament to brief lives and attention spans.

The excellent library, housed on the top floor of a modern teaching block, is light and tranquil with plenty of squashy chairs; if a boy needs a bit of time out he can 'come and be quiet' here, according to our guides. On display was a selection of letters from soldiers at Camp Bastion thanking boys for gifts they had sent. The library leads on to what was described by one boy as the 'temple of fun', in other words the IT suite. Here are 24 shiny iMacs from where boys can email home or talk on Skype, although a proper handwritten letter must also be sent once a week. No Facebook or YouTube here; all is filtered, and the head of IT keeps a benign but watchful eye on curricular and extracurricular internet activities.

The school hall is modern with a stage and retractable seating, a venue for frequent concerts, lectures and drama productions as well as assembly, where boys are graded each Monday according to their work and behaviour. Marks out of 10, or 'weeklies', are read out by Mr Bailey (although anything under five is between the head and the boy concerned); a running total is kept each term and boys with the best scores are rewarded by surprise trips. One trip that isn't a surprise but is equally eagerly anticipated is the term spent at the Château de Sauveterre near Toulouse. Total immersion in French language and culture, visits to local schools, French food and sunshine make this a highlight of any boy's time at Cothill.

The timetable is designed to suit boys' learning styles. Classes are small (around 14), lessons are short (35 to 40 minutes) and characterised by 'lots of practical activity' and movement between lessons. Sport every day and plenty of running around time afterwards. Fairly traditional range of subjects taught in preparation for common entrance, although also a full syllabus of general studies taught as well. Lots of excellent music with plenty of opportunities to find the right instrument – not just a few 'try out' lessons but a whole term of class violin for all boys (just imagine ...) followed by other orchestral explorations. Drama is very popular with boys and parents alike and everywhere we went was busy and productively messy.

Out of lessons, boys are free to explore the grounds, build camps and play, but staff are vigilant and know when to intervene if necessary; practical departments such as art and pottery are staffed until 8pm so that boys can use these facilities too. Our delightful trio of guides, picked seemingly at random from the lunch queue, confided that they were going to 'save the best until last'. So, at last, we came to the 'best' – the woodwork room. In a large pine-scented shed full of shavings is the woodwork master, a twinkly, patient, ex-police officer who has been at Cothill for 24 years – he even taught the present day headmaster some carpentry when he was a boy here. Just imagine free rein with all your parents' (trying to avoid stereotyping here) tools, an endless supply of wood and someone with the time and skill to help you realise your ambitious plans. Boys really can make 'whatever they want', just so long as parents can transport it home. Garden seats, bird tables, boot racks, jewellery boxes, toy guns, book shelves all under construction, and boys work on their creations in lessons and free time. On offer here are invaluable practical skills coupled with a creative freedom that most children can only dream about; the boys know how special it is and love every minute.

High expectations and not much in the way of outside distractions mean that serious disciplinary problems are rare. The head stresses the importance of observation, and a daily meeting for all staff ensures that any concerns about individual boys or tensions between friends are discussed in the round and dealt with sensitively. Boys know that they can confide in whomever they wish, whether it's their tutor, the junior matrons (usually gap year girls) or subject teachers. Staff are very visible, even at lunchtime – we saw plenty outside playing cricket and talking to the boys.

Yes, this is a traditional boarding prep school, but in the best possible way and without being stuffy. Standards of teaching and expectations are high and the common entrance results

speak for themselves, but that's only part of what the boys who come here gain. A real sense of fun and camaraderie, not just between the boys but also between boys and staff. Parents praise the excellent home/school communication; Mr Bailey is, apparently, 'always available', and one commented that on weekends spent at home, her son was rather wistful about all the fun he was missing at school! The excellent and unusually readable school magazine seems to capture the spirit of the place rather well. It features letters from boys who have moved on to senior schools as well as some delightful articles by members of staff about pudding etiquette and the like. When asked if anyone who might not fit into school life at Cothill, the three guides were thoughtful. 'Everyone is a bit quiet and shy at first,' said one, 'but then you make friends.' Another added rather decisively, 'Grumpy people might not like it, though.' Enough said.

Cottesmore School

Buchan Hill, Pease Pottage, RH11 9AU

- Pupils: 150; 100 boys/50 girls; 100 full boarders • Ages: 4–13
- C of E • Fees: £7,905–£10,545; Boarding £14,790–£20,220 pa
- Independent

Tel: 01293 520648
Email: office@cottesmoreschool.com
Website: www.cottesmoreschool.com

Headmaster: Since 2008, Mr Tom Rogerson (mid-thirties), third generation to run the school, owned by his family. His legendary father is still in the background as a benign and wise counsellor. Educated at Cottesmore and Eton, then on to university. Previous teaching posts include Ludgrove, Eaton House and Broomwood Hall, where he was head of English and, far more importantly, met his wife-to-be – 'I winked at her during a beginning of term assembly'. Articulate, entertaining and thoughtful, full of sensitive ideas about improving what was good when he took over and determined to nurture the tradition of bringing out the best in each child. 'We aim to ignite the passion in every child, who is always good at something and should leave with that inner confidence that comes from success. We have a number of experienced members of staff who power the place along with some excellent new teachers. Essentially this is a boarding school [90 per cent board]. We don't do flexi-boarding – the word 'flexi' sounds like a particularly unpleasant carpet underlay. Everyone has a bed and most day pupils convert because boarding is such a good option.' Parents are clearly delighted with him, as are the pupils.

His wife, Lottie, was a brilliant addition to Cottesmore, with a good knowledge of schools. A pupil at The Dragon, where she was heavily outnumbered by boys, she went on to Cheltenham Ladies', where she was not. Thereafter university, before teaching at Broomwood and Elstree. She heads the pre-prep and teaches maths and English to the bottom form in the prep – 'It helps to preserve a sense of continuity'. She is overall responsible for the pastoral side – a universal mum. An outstandingly engaging couple, they live in the house with the pupils.

Entrance: Prospective pupils enter prep via interview, a straightforward ed psych paper and a good report from their previous school. Very occasionally pupils are not admitted, but the emphasis is on potential rather than achievement, though the academic pace is brisk. Most pupils enter aged 8 but they may enter later, if places are available. We met a boy who had joined aged 12 – 'The school was brilliant with him,' said his delighted mum. 'I only wish I had sent him earlier.' About 30

C

per cent come from London, 30 per cent from Sussex and 30 per cent from abroad, including expats, children of diplomats, from Europe and the Far East. A good variety of internationals, who all seemed very happy and integrated. Not so much a good school for dyslexics as a school which offers good help to children with dyslexia. Every child is screened for dyslexia on arrival, if parents want that.

Entry to pre-prep at 4.

Exit: The usual suspects – Eton, Harrow, Radley, Charterhouse, St Edward's Oxford, Benenden, Downe House, Wellington, Tonbridge, Bryanston – but not exclusively so, by any means: 'We are keen to find the right school for the child'. ('Happy, confident children,' says head of a senior school.)

Remarks: Extraordinary late Victorian mansion with turrets, towers, gables and gargoyles, built by a man who originally made his dosh from ostrich feathers and then, after they became less fashionable, from diamonds, which he discovered when he found one of his ostriches in South Africa had choked on one. Huge log fire in the enormous hall, fascinating carvings on the staircase and over lintels, tooled leather on the walls of the dining room. The house was built for weekend parties, which perhaps explains why it has adapted so well to the school. It is big but not overpoweringly grand; impressive but fun to live in.

Sensitively-designed classroom block, reminiscent of cloisters, with bright and airy teaching spaces. Superb Sopwith Centre for art, technology design (real design, with most impressive results), computers and science labs, named after Tommy Sopwith, the aircraft engineer, an old boy, with inspirational views over glorious countryside and inspirational teaching going on inside. Art and DT are part of the core curriculum, as is music – no question of dropping them to concentrate on the restrictions of common entrance, let alone the challenge of scholarships. Chess is compulsory for the first two years – not in lessons but in the slot between 11 and 12 every morning, a time set aside for charging intellectual batteries in between lessons.

Academic results are very good and the teaching we saw was lively and interesting, with pupils enthusiastically involved. Class sizes are small – rarely larger than 14 – and streaming for scholarships is done with sensitivity and tact. Not a hothouse school – indeed many London parents choose it because it isn't – but academics taken seriously.

A recent Ofsted inspection was so impressed that the school was identified as an 'outstanding provider', followed by a letter from HM Chief Inspector congratulating it on this. Readers of ISI reports, with their bland and faintly curmudgeonly language, will be amazed to note that the word 'outstanding' was used 17 times – a world record?

Nowhere is its excellence more apparent than in its provision for the individual happiness of pupils. The crucial question of bullying is approached via its Happiness Charter prominently displayed all over the school and its Worry Box, into which pupils may post letters expressing any concern they may have. The medical sister, with six assistant matrons, is clearly actively concerned with the pupils' happiness – 'You can tell how a pupil is really feeling by how they look in the morning. If we're worried, we discuss that individual and keep a close eye open'. Pupils confirmed how safe and happy they felt, with lots of people to whom they felt they could talk, if worried, including the excellent ground staff and the kitchen folk (has won Best School Food at the Tatler School Awards – out of 225 prep and public schools). Our lunch and, later, match tea made us feel we were from The Good Food Guide. Six pit stops for food refuelling every day.

Dormitories are brightly decorated in the original bedrooms and dressing-rooms of the original party house – 'It's like having a sleepover every night,' said one girl – and pupils in dorms are regularly rotated to ensure everyone gets to know each other. Down in the vast cellars is an indoor shooting range, a bowling alley constructed by the head's grandfather and still in excellent nick, a superb model railway and a modelling room – the Airfix sort.

Despite its proximity to London and Gatwick, in 35 acres of its own and surrounded by another 1,000 – 'Bet you can't see another house from here,' challenged the head: we couldn't. In the grounds is a nine-hole chip and putt golf course – top golfers can use the adjoining private full sized one; the lake provides opportunities for fishing and boating, the orchard for scrumping and cooking, and gardening is popular – especially when you can eat the food you grow.

Playing fields are expansive and beautifully kept. Football has improved markedly in the last few years and is challenging the more traditional rugby in popularity. Hockey and cricket are also very popular (every two years the first X1 cricket team goes to Dubai); for the girls it's netball, hockey, rounders and tennis (three manicured courts, three hard with floodlighting). Teams are, by and large, successful – a pleasing feature is that everyone who wishes to play in a team is able to do so. We watched a third X1 match against another school which was played with all the zest of a cup final.

Appears tireless in its wish to find activities for individual interests. Ask to see the list of hobbies and activities on offer, and then realise what a bonus it is to have 99 per cent of the staff living on site. Lots going on at weekends, too. Three choirs – we heard the chapel choir practising and they were eye-smartingly good – and 80 per cent learn musical instruments; enthusiastically performed drama in the ancient, but perfectly functional gym. Plans to build a theatre in time – presumably it will be called the Olivier Theatre, since four generations of Sir Larry's family have attended the school. Lovely chapel, with superb organ, in which daily services are held. Pupils play a leading part – 'Reading in public helps their confidence and encourages them to think about what they are reading'. A tuckshop where you can buy a limited amount of sweets and birthday cards.

Most schools trumpet their 'family atmosphere', that intangible quality which is so hard to define. This school undoubtedly possesses it. Perhaps it's the building and setting, perhaps it's the sense of continuity. Certainly all the parents and children we spoke to commented on the friendly feel of the place. The children give every impression of being happy and confident without precocity – no whiff of snobbishness, no sense of unnatural sophistication, children allowed to be children, with freshness, spontaneity and a sense of purpose. One of those schools where it's very difficult to find a weakness.

The same could be said of the pre-prep. Bright classrooms with engaging activities and fun. We saw lessons involving rubber skeletons from which you could pull teeth ('so it's important to look after them'), an exciting lesson on air raids in World War 2, drawing and French lessons. Masses of space for playing around, including an Astroturf area laid by the ubiquitous groundsman. Compulsory recorder lessons and rhythmic clapping to music. A marvellous introduction to the Cottesmore adventure, it is planned to have a maximum of 45 children.

Coworth-Flexlands School

Valley End, Chobham, Woking, Surrey, GU24 8TE

• Pupils: 150 girls (mixed nursery) • Ages: 3-11 • Christian Foundation • Fees: £2,565-£11,385 pa • Independent

Tel: 01276 855707
Email: registrar@coworthflexlands.co.uk
Website: www.coworthflexlands.co.uk

Head: Since 2010, Mrs Anne Sweeney MA, DipEd (fifties) an Aberdeen maths graduate married to a globe-trotting management consultant who's also a dab hand in proffering career advice to his forbearing wife, making it a condition of their engagement – 'with a twinkle in his eye,' she insists – that she become a teacher, to be around for their own putative offspring (obviously worked, as has a doctor, budding social worker, lecturer and IT specialist to show for it, plus a grandchild). Not that she needed much persuading. Family legend has it that she threw all the dolls out of her toy pram, lovingly pushing books round instead. Add games of school where she was always the teacher – 'I don't know how my friends tolerated it' – and her subsequent career, after a brief teenage flirtation with fashion design (nipped in the bud, this time by her father) seems a forgone conclusion.

Quietly pragmatic – otherwise immaculate office has boxes of toys for visiting toddlers – she's effectively had two teaching careers, starting out as a maths specialist in Scottish and English secondary schools and colleges and moving down the age range to pre-school and primaries/preps, after taking a 10 year break to raise her children and finding senior school posts rarer than hen's teeth. Previous post was as deputy head at Maltman's Green, a flourishing prep school in Gerrard's Cross.

Mrs Sweeney has won approval from parents with cracking academic results and speedy, sensitive problem solving. 'My child told her class she'd got a boyfriend on the internet – she'd absolutely made it up, of course – and she handled it really well,' says one.

This is education on a miniature scale and all the better for it. Pupils get a say in everything from sets (English and maths from year 3) to scholarship streams, and small isn't just beautiful but the key to her approach. 'If someone doesn't fit the mould it can make for a miserable childhood, so we modify whatever we can,' she says.

Her approach, low on pressure, high on imagination and big on community spirit, with parents closely involved, is cutting the results mustard, with nearly all, including substantial percentage with special needs, securing safe passage to their senior school of choice. 'Academically, she's done so much,' says one mother.

Head sees size as school's biggest asset. 'We say it's an education as individual as your child,' she says. Parents wouldn't disagree.

Entrance: Single form entry all the way through, with official maximum class size of 22, though far lower in practice and completely non-selective. That goes for special needs, which cover the full spectrum through to physical disabilities, with two pupils registered blind. Severe behavioural difficulties might be a sticking point, though even here school would do its best to help. 'If you're in the door, you're in,' confirms head.

No official feeders as school mainly grows its own through co-ed Skylark Nursery, then girls only to year 6 (boys did stay till end of year 2 until dwindling numbers prompted rethink). Reception and year 3 are other main entry points, with small but steady flow in and out in other years, inevitable, given upwardly and geographically mobile M25 corridor location.

Exit: Wide range of independent day or boarding schools for the majority, some highly selective – Wycombe Abbey and Lady Eleanor Holles in Hampton among them – others less so: St George's, Ascot, St Theresa's, Sir William Perkins's, Downe House, Farnborough Hill, Queen Anne's, Caversham, Tormead, Licensed Victuallers', Ascot, and The Marist, Sunninghill. Around a third of year sixes secure awards. A few to state schools including Gordon's School, Woking (non-selective boarding).

Head is especially proud of success achieved by children with special needs – 'When they're off to different senior schools and you look at who's had learning support, you wouldn't be able to tell which is which, so that's our end point'.

When it comes to deciding on 11 plus options, little sense of 'school knows best', assumption being that families, equipped with enough information, will make the right choice. Invariably they do, says head. It's subtly done – head could teach government a thing or two about nudge psychology. Innovative two-tier clubs allow the seriously arty, musical, sporty or academic to hone their skills potentially to scholarship level; the merely interested do the same subjects but just for fun – no pressure either way. 'If you find the going tough, then you tend to deselect yourself and go to the fun one instead,' says head. Add conversations about possible senior schools from year 4 onwards, 'open book' sessions every half term so parents can see progress being made and senior school sample papers set as homework, and the upshot is no nasty surprises, school tempering any unrealistic expectations with gentle guidance. 'I've yet to meet a parent who hates a child so much that they would put them through utter misery,' says head.

Remarks: Tucked away down a tiny, tree-fringed lane and with easy-to-miss signage (imposed by council restrictions rather than a shy and retiring corporate disposition), the school is unlikely to attract much in the way of window shoppers, a possible plus point for privacy-conscious royals and celebs (the Princesses Beatrice and Eugenie of York are former pupils). With Old Windsor, Ascot, Virginia and Chobham all within comfortable commuting distance, location is less golden triangle then titanium polygon.

If the convenience hasn't already got to you the place, a bijou redbrick country house, probably will, even without this reviewer's early morning, atmosphere-enhancing demonstration of community spirit, with approachable welly-wearing bursar clearing the snow in the drive and cheerful parent governor photographing the winter wonderland for posterity.

Main building features enough tradition – big, airy classrooms, some with old-fashioned desks, almost all with panoramic views over grounds – to fuel a midnight nostalgia fest. Even the occasional faint but authentic whiff of damp, legacy of a leaking roof, now replaced.

Tucked tidily to one side, a recently completed extension houses busy, happy nursery, much praised by Ofsted and ISI inspectors, assembly/dining hall (nice touches include bowls of freshly chopped cucumber/carrot on each table as amuse-gueules for the ravenous, and home-made biscuits and yoghurt, though menu overall did elicit a few quickly suppressed grimaces) and additional well-equipped form, language, science and ICT rooms. To the other, a block devoted to performing arts, very strong here and recognised as such by award of hard to come by Artsmark Gold, with prize-winning chamber choir, much-praised productions and even youngest pupils belting out songs and speeches to parents with huge panache during class assembly.

Competitive sport, in stark contrast, had lost out – not just lacklustre but effectively non-existent (tiny display of somewhat tarnished trophies says it all) and easily the biggest parental gripe. It's all change now, however, with netball teams and voluntary squad training in place, though emphasis thus far is on gentle, morale-enhancing fixtures rather than Charge of the Light Brigade massacres: 'I am not sending those children out to be slaughtered; it's going to put them off sport for life,' says head, firmly.

Pupils not just courteous but look visitors in the eye and even smile – shouldn't be unusual, but for this age group, often is. They're thoughtful and wildly enthusiastic, encouraging visitors to experience every detail from a ride in the disabled lift to animal tracks identification (robin and rabbit were best guesses) in the grounds. Staff are introduced with great pride and full biographies – obvious respect and liking on both sides. Witnessing the quirky, absorbing lessons, many taught by specialists – year 1 girls counting with rising excitement in French as a wind up caterpillar squirms across the table; a window packed with bagged up bread for mould-growing research in science – you can see why. 'When a teacher leaves, you'd think someone had died,' says one mother.

It's not just the teaching that sparkles. Standard dull but worthy educational ideas are dusted off and reinvented with a sprinkling of fairy dust. Pupil targets become cuddly YETIs – 'I don't know it YET': achieve all six and you're presented with a certificate sporting the eponymous shaggy beast in assembly, while good behaviour is rewarded with prize draw – winner takes Muffin the (toy) dog home for weekend and writes up his adventures for posterity.

Even transport can be scaled down – 'Mrs Sweeney took six of us in her car, dropped us off with Mrs Dawe and went to get the rest of year 5,' says account of school trip to Chobham Common in (beautifully produced) school magazine.

Given brisk turnover of pupils, school rightly makes it a priority to settle in newbie families pronto. Bustling parent-run social committee issues first coffee morning and play date invitations almost before ink dries on acceptance forms. School also has own Brownies and Rainbows packs and a highly evolved house system that brings all ages together for meals (year 6s set, clear and wipe tables for younger children four days a week) and creative whole-school projects (if you've ever wanted to see a frog's life-cycle communicated through the medium of dance, this is the place to be).

Philosophy also colours approach to special needs, tackled with great flair and sensitivity, so that every child plays full part in life of school, from productions to target setting. Even central location of room rather than a small, apologetic broom cupboard in bowels of school sends clear message about belonging. 'Children are never made to feel odd,' confirms parent. 'It's just an ordinary part of school life.'

Caring, yes, precious, no. Thirteen glorious acres include a peace garden for older girls (with disconcertingly realistic sleeping faun), games fields, tennis courts and well-equipped side by side playgrounds, while a play advisor suggests games for the needy or bored. School is also in touch with its inner rufty-tufty side, offering term time outdoor lessons and popular daytime forest camps in the holidays – children produce impressive leaf-decorated head dresses while teachers are noted for legendary storm kettle superpowers. Other idyllic back-to-nature add-ons include unassuming dip in the ground, soon to be transformed, courtesy of single-minded year 6 eco captain, into a wildlife-friendly pond, while new pitches, wildflower meadows and even allotments should follow, if canny freebie deal with a local firm keen to off-load excess topsoil goes ahead (school is reassuringly candid about finances which, following 2004 merger with Flexlands School and sale of site, are in good order).

Not yet the place for the highly competitive – school captains exhort their teams, in capitals, to 'HAVE FUN' – and playing fields wouldn't currently make Duke of Wellington's long list for future Waterloo fodder. Give it a year or so, however, and sports scholarships could well start cropping up in the leavers' lists. In the meantime, the arty, musical and, increasingly, academic are well catered for in successful, embracing small school where standard ideas are so imaginatively cut down to size.

Craigclowan School

Edinburgh Road, Perth, PH2 8PS

• Pupils: 270: 150 boys and 120 girls, plus 35 or so in the nursery All day • Ages: 3-13 • Inter-denom • Fees: £10,710 pa • Independent

Tel: 01738 626310
Email: headmaster@craigclowan-school.co.uk
Website: www.craigclowan-school.co.uk

Headmaster: Since September 2012, Mr Richard Evans BEd Advanced Diploma in Educational Management (fifties). Grammar school educated in South Wales followed by the Uni of the West of England, plus an advanced diploma in educational management from the OU. Previous stint with Bromsgrove prep left him nostalgic for re-connecting with and advising parents about their off-spring's future. Pleased to be in Scotland (he kept saying 'back in Scotland' until we pointed out that his nearest brush with the Celtic fringe was in his school days). Enthusiastic about fly fishing, golf, walking and cycling, still referees. Emergency teacher, PHSE, maths. Talks faster than anyone this ed has ever met and at times we had difficulty following his train of thought (we understand that this is not just a problem with visiting editors). Head adds 'it's the Welsh in me, and probably because I am enthusiastic and passionate about Craigclowan and the job I am fortunate enough to do!' Whilst he prides himself on knowing the names of both parents and their young, some parents are not convinced (certainly we had a name free tour round the school and we quite like 'Hello Flossy' rather than a bleak 'Good Morning').

He and his wife, Carol, a teacher still have a house in Worcestershire. Two sons, both up and flown; Mrs E is doing the Florence Nightingale bit with her 80+ year old mother.

Parents rather expected to see more exposure on the distaff side, said my informant; they also said they expected to see the head put himself about a tad more. School has gone hell for leather with posho advertising and PR, and the recent open day was a succès fou. Real meeting and greeting is good: a charm offensive might persuade the don't knows.

Entrance: Children from all over the northern central belt, usually within 40 minutes' travel/30 mile radius; aspirational, numbers of first time buyers, middle-class professionals, the occasional toff, some of whom have been known to use the pre-prep before hitting trad preps elsewhere.

Exit: Around three-quarters to Glenalmond, Strathallan, Merchiston, Fettes, much as you would expect trickle to Dollar Academy, Gordonstoun, St Leonards, Kilgraston (and sometimes mid-term and vice versa); otherwise Ampleforth, Queen Margaret's York, Sedbergh, with a 'smattering' south to Eton, Harrow, Heathfield, Stamford and Eastbourne College. 'Orses for courses.

Remarks: Craigclowan, the only day prep in Perthshire, is perched on 13 undulating acres above the M90 on the southern fringe of Perth; pedestrian classroom blocks now surround this poor man's Greek Thompson Victorian villa, and the child-inspired brightly coloured class superseded by light airy modern boxes with purposeful young efficiently going about their business. Pupil art all over. Tarmac, still covered in crazy games – snakes and ladders, floral trails, chess – has recently been joined by cow of many colours. The eight foot tall Menhir was moved here some 100 odd years before.

Certain amount of tarting up recently; senior classrooms revamped (smelt strongly of paint). Pictures of whole class on

C

every door; books everywhere. Proper lab with ancillary prep room; this year school goes totally wifi with white boards all over; banks of lap tops promised for the future. Art room: early in the term, but buzzing, good ceramics and fabric. Plans afoot to enlarge the basement library (currently in one of the old brightly coloured classrooms) with a 'dedicated learning resource centre' and knock a door out into the quad. We always approve of easier access to books and the house ain't listed.

Astroturf for tennis and hockey. Tiny artificial ski slope: some time ago it was rumoured to have been 'ealth and safety-ed but now almost suffering from overuse; fathers run lessons Saturday mornings and much of the school decamps to Glen Shee on spring term Saturdays. The downstairs passage was choca with skis of the smallest sizes ditto helmets (think nursery slopes on Meribel); 'that's what we are about,' said the head with pride.

Wish list includes levelling the front games field to make two rugby pitches, re-laying the cricket square and building a new sports pavilion (which head refers to as a cricket pavilion in his handout; is there a difference?). Not that easy to find prep school teachers with the right amount of energy and enthusiasm who can not only teach (he watches them) but also 'do the extra bit' – like running weekend courses; hockey, cricket, camping.

Popular walled garden, developed in conjunction with 'a school established local gardening club': pupils grow own grub, (lettuces popular) and starred in Beechgrove Garden.

Nursery a joy, tinies work in cheerful subdivided classrooms not quite attached to the well-used, multi-purpose sports hall (particularly popular during wet breaks), and adjacent to dining room: staff and pupils eat together, hot, cold and veggie option.

Spare waterproof ponchos and a welly cupboard for forest school: essential these days for the (sub)urban child. Paddling pool, outdoor classroom. Masses of mite-sized equipment, including real carpentry tools and wood to use them on (the Care Commission saw and approved). Partnership with Perth, vouchers, website shows actual reductions (a first). Plans ahead for revamping a couple of nursery class rooms and for a new 'light and bright foyer area' for the pre-school – sounds like a cinema!

Numbers up since Evans' arrival, but down overall. Virtually all stick with school from nursery. Reading via jolly phonics, or jolly anything come to that, 'anything that works': all children to age 10 are heard reading everyday: form takers, assistants, gappers. SENCo on hand, glitches spotted early, problem discussed with parents, ed psychs if need be, ditto IEPs. Assistance too with maths. Learning support for 'any child who needs help for any reason, either for a long or a short term, and for the very able'. Two teachers for every year, plus trained support staff – with many getting one-to-one attention in little work stations all over.

Rewards equals house points for juniors (houses important here and sibling led), smiley stickers (because they like them best) and 'golden time' (activities of their choice). Head regularly congratulates, hands out plaudits for stuff both in and out of school. Sanctions: detention.

Four/five year olds divided alphabetically, with those whose birthdays fall in the spring or summer joining proper school the summer term before their fifth birthdays. Two classes throughout, roughly 13 in each, some streaming further up; scholarship class at top – usually eight – impressive selection of scholarships to all over.

Aged 8, young are set for maths and English, they also start French; this is late, we usually find French exposure in nursery. Latin introduced age 10/11, but Latin club from 8 and 'zinging' Latin teacher. Bullying dealt with quickly and firmly, with parents involved if need be. The young whom we met/know are bubbly and fun: and staff fell over themselves to be helpful during our visit.

Small pipe band, chanter for all, 60/70 per cent learn some sort of instrument, odd ensembles, orchestras. Music room in main house surrounded by soundproof practice rooms, and staff practising for a 'Craigclowan's got talent' evening. Mixed bunch, refreshing to see some of previous head but one's brood still there. Well furnished with instruments, snazzy keyboards and mirrors galore. Much involvement with the Perth Festival. Carol service at St Ninians; school supplies choristers throughout the year.

Lots of foreign contact as well as regular tours abroad – part of the Comenius project. Eco school with a couple of green flags. 'This is a vibrant, seven-day-a-week, co-ed day school, with classes on five days and a mass of extracurricular activity'. Recent rearrangement of the day means a less rushed lunch, and slightly longer day. Parents can (and do) leave their young at 8am and collect them again at 6pm. Late stayers, unless otherwise occupied with after skool activities often finish prep before home time. After-school 'prep supervision' costs £4.50 per hour (nice little earner). Pre-prep all get a homework book for parents to admire.

Huge range of clubs/activities, 60+, including archery, street dance, judo, sailing, fly-fishing and golf (head particularly keen on the two latter: mentioned it three times) plus additional junior school stuff. Craigclowan hosted senior schools fair last year; 16 assorted schools touted their wares. A success to be repeated.

PTA, 'a good bunch, supportive, like the ethos of the place', run a lift-share, and a monthly second-hand uniform and sports equipment shop. All singing and dancing. Head wore waistcoat in Craigclowan tartan for the PTA Ceilidh last year, 'quite likes' Scottish dancing; 'weekly Scottish dancing for juniors and Ceilidhs for all pupils'. He seemed to think parents welcomed the new sports kit (twice in five years), pinafore dresses and summer dresses: 'I had to find an extra 200 quid and that was just for the sports kit,' was one disgruntled reaction.

Craigholme Junior School

Linked school: Craigholme School for Girls

72 St Andrew's Drive, Glasgow, G41 4HS

- Pupils: 250 girls; all day • Ages: 5–12 • Fees: £8,250–£10,080 pa
- Independent

Tel: 01414 270375
Email: admissions@craigholme.co.uk
Website: www.craigholme.co.uk

Headmistress: Since 2005, Mrs Jeanette Smart, having previously spent 18 years at The High School of Glasgow, latterly as deputy head. She works 'as a team' with Mrs Stobo (head of senior school – see entry) and was appointed a year before her from the same school. She says Craigholme was one of the few schools she really wanted to go to. Brimming with enthusiasm, she is very much in touch with pupils and their activities: J6's newspaper assignment, the Victorians theme in J5 and the planned J7 visit to the Lake District.

Nursery manager: Mrs Karen Grant.

Entrance: Applications welcome from girls at all stages, but traditional entry points are nursery and first or sixth year juniors.

Exit: Most to senior school.

Remarks: Upper junior school is attached to the senior school but the nursery, which takes boys, has a separate site on St Andrews Drive. Small classes; specialist French, IT, music and PE from nursery on. Top year takes selected subjects – science, art, home economics – in senior school. Lots of extracurricular activities and care provided after school as an extra.

Books and novels feature strongly in learning as 'preferable to the sort of snippets you get in reading books', and children start off with (Jolly) Phonics, leavened with other methods as appropriate. 'Riding the crest of a wave', the junior choir and the training choir had just won their respective Glasgow music festival prizes, and the cross-country teams came first among the Glasgow schools just before our visit. Successes, even small ones, build confidence, so all children have a personal 'magic moment file' recording their achievements, though Mrs Smart and Mrs Stobo agree that confidence is about being able to cope with whatever comes. This may include the experience of risk-taking and not always being equal to challenges – 'They have to explore their strengths and weaknesses in order to make informed decisions'.

Careers advice starts in the juniors, and an impressive collection of professional parents is assembled to give short interviews to J6 reporters. Nursery is run in partnership with Glasgow city council, and qualifying families receive a refund on the fees.

Cranleigh Preparatory School

Linked school: Cranleigh School

Horseshoe Lane, Cranleigh, GU6 8QH

• Pupils: 310; 175 boys/135 girls; 65 boarders • Ages: 7–13 • C of E
• Fees: Boarding £20,880; Day £12,990–£16,860 pa • Independent

Tel: 01483 542058
Email: fmjb@cranprep.org
Website: www.cranprep.org

Headmaster: Mr Michael Wilson BSc (early fifties). Raised in Africa, educated in Kenya and at Sherborne then Keele University. He started his teaching career in the early '80s at Cranleigh as a chemistry teacher and sports coach in the senior school. After a few years he returned to Africa, held teaching posts at a couple of schools in Nairobi and was a national and Davis Cup team tennis coach. The draw of Cranleigh pulled him back and over the next seven years he worked through deputy house master, head of sixth form girls and girls' housemaster. After short-lived posts in Thailand and at Bradfield he was back at Cranleigh as housemaster in the senior school again, 'brought back to help sort out boarding,' he tells us. Then in 2002 he became head at Edge Grove Prep and finally moved back to Cranleigh Prep as head in September 2008; he assures us he's here for the long run.

His own 'uncluttered' Kenyan childhood forms the core of his beliefs about how childhood is best conducted and is a recurring theme in his conversation. He likes old-fashioned values, letter writing, good manners and the freedom to play unfettered outdoors; he doesn't like materialism, selfishness and moaning. He believes daily chapel is important for reflecting on shared values and the Christian ethos of the school.

The school has a family theme for the Wilsons; Mrs Wilson heads up the prep's learning support department and their three children have all been educated at least in part at Cranleigh – the youngest is currently in the upper sixth. Mr Wilson's long-term on-off career here means he has taught the parents of many of his current pupils.

Mr Wilson tells us that he sees all parents at school social events or parent briefings and reminds them to 'buy into the whole school', meaning they should celebrate and support all the teams whether their children are in them or not. 'They may get their chance in the future but not everyone can play for the firsts and it's a lesson in life'.

Entrance: The main entry point is at 7+, with another chunk of pupils wanting to join at 11+, enough to add one or two more classes. During the assessment day for entry at 7 children complete comprehension, maths, spelling and reasoning on computer, plus a handwritten piece of creative writing; they also take part in art and PE sessions. Quite a day for a 6 year old, although the school does 'try to make it as relaxed as possible'. For entry at 11 children come to an 'activity morning' for an interview plus art, sports, problem solving and team building sessions. They then return a few months later for computer based maths, reasoning, spelling and reading plus handwritten comprehension and creative writing. At this stage children are being assessed on whether or not they would thrive academically and socially at the Cranleigh School across the road. However, this is not a pre-test for the senior school; pupils still need to take common entrance and go through the formal admissions process at Cranleigh School. Crucially, Mr Wilson ensures he meets the parents, usually twice, and talks to feeder heads. He tells us he uses his 'gut feeling' about which children will cope with and contribute to Cranleigh.

Exit: Three-quarters move 'across the road' (an oft used phrase here) to Cranleigh School. The links between prep and senior schools are increasingly strong and up to a third win Cranleigh scholarships. However, it is quite accepted that others will want to move elsewhere and they are given equal support and advice. Those who do move go on to a wide range of public schools including Charterhouse, Millfield, Wellington, Eton, Winchester, Tonbridge, Sherborne, RGS Guildford, Marlborough, Prior's Field and St Catherine's, a handful each year with scholarships.

Remarks: A traditional prep school with an outdoorsy, sporty feel. Whilst it's co-ed, the boyish culture seems to dominate somewhat. Parents describe it as 'busy, robust and challenging' and those children who enjoy life here are energetic, sporty and have a sense of humour about 'banter' from other pupils and younger staff. Families are generally well-heeled, some extremely so, mostly from the surrounding countryside and villages. They pitch up to school events and matches, often more dads making an appearance than at other schools, and describe themselves as a pretty vocal and often demanding lot. Mr Wilson tells us he spends plenty of time seeing parents one to one, managing expectations.

Academically inclusive with the range of abilities catered for by extensive setting within classes and, in the top two years, streaming into one scholarship and three or four common entrance forms depending on numbers. 'Academics have been upped, which is no bad thing,' reports a parent of long standing, another tells us her scholarship form daughter gains confidence from being at the top here academically. Learning support, co-ordinated by Mrs Wilson and her specialist team, is 'at the centre rather than a satellite' with dyscalculia, dyspraxia and dyslexia all catered for and just under a fifth of pupils receiving some level of support. Needs are spotted early on and thoroughly addressed with classroom assistants and interventions in small groups or one-to-one. All pupils' progress is closely monitored via a thorough record system with inputs from all staff.

Art is of an amazingly high standard. The head of art is confident and enthusiastic about children's abilities and she seems to get fantastic work out of everyone. The art room is stuffed full of current projects by pupils of all ages, including some really unusual ceramics, textiles and sculptures alongside more expected drawing and painting. Talented artists could find the perfect niche here.

Drama and music are also well covered; both are part of the curriculum for all ages with numerous performances each year. Individual instrumental or singing lessons are held in the 'music school', recently enlarged with the addition of a practice room for ensembles and choirs. Talented musicians benefit from a programme called 'Cranleigh Music 7 – 18' in which music teachers work at both Cranleigh Prep and Cranleigh School and the most able musicians play in ensembles across the age range.

Sport is a major focus of school life, whether you ask pupils, parents or staff; it's timetabled every day with matches mid-week and on alternate Saturdays. Rugby and hockey are big but also less usual options including riding over at the senior school's on-site stables. The 'Cranleigh Sport 7 – 18' programme brings sports staff over from the senior school to spot talent and coach at all levels. Parents expect their children to be able to represent the school in matches and teams are fielded from A to D to give everyone a good chance. Of course pupils know who will be in the As but they say 'it's possible to get places in other teams'. Non-sporty or quiet bookish children may well find this whole active vibe just too much; as one parent says, 'it's horses for courses'.

Pastoral care is the remit of the deputy head; she has been at Cranleigh Prep for 21 years and is familiar with the ups and downs of life here. Incidents are tracked and dealt with pragmatically, parents are phoned, high jinks are recognised, punishments are taken and pupils move on. An annual anti-bullying questionnaire identifies any new issues – such as the ever-present Facebook which has been addressed using a visiting outside agency to talk to children and parents. A few parents have told us about persistent unkindness from other children which has left their own feeling upset and unsupported; the deputy head responds that bullying and unkindness are taken seriously, efforts are focused on changing unsociable behaviour and pupils have been suspended in the past. She points out that she recently asked staff to send her any notes from parents praising their children's care and her file of these is much thicker than her file of dissatisfied and problematic correspondence.

The great outdoors is what defines Cranleigh: acres of grassy pitches, an Astro pitch, tennis courts and netball courts. The senior school across the road dominates the views, keeping that future option ever in mind. The buildings are a mix of Edwardian and a hotch-potch of newer, including a new one providing three more classrooms and a common room. Some are a bit disappointing inside, a few rather poky classrooms and a sports and performance hall which felt like a cavernous shed; others are good, the well-stocked library, a couple of IT suites with brand new desks and integral computers and the welcoming, very comfortable reception area. Boarding houses are traditional, or somewhat old-fashioned depending on your view. The girls' boarding house we visited had dorms for four or six boarders, high windows, firm mattresses and lots of Justin Bieber and 1-Direction posters. In the bathroom, rows of wash basins, four or five showers and a bath. Two matrons are always on hand to keep an eye on things for boarders and day pupils; they offer TLC in their cosy room or the next door sick bay or in the brightly furnished sitting room cheerfully labelled the 'Ikea Room'. Boarding is weekly or flexi with a minimum of two nights a week; there are no weekend boarders. Although day pupils hugely outnumber boarders, the daily routine of late finishing, prep at school and Saturday school on alternate weeks feels rather more like a boarding school.

A few scholarship awards are given to exceptional candidates at 11, nothing earlier. Sibling discounts are available for third and subsequent siblings at any stage in Cranleigh Prep or senior school.

In short, a sporty co-ed school run on traditional lines in a glorious rural setting with strong links to its senior school. A good choice for a broad education, less academically pressured than many others and with plenty of learning support for those who need it. Robust and energetic pupils preferred.

Cranmore School

Epsom Road, West Horsley, Leatherhead, Surrey, KT24 6AT

- Pupils: 450 boys; all day • Ages: Boys 4–13, co-educational nursery 2½–4 • RC, but other denominations welcomed
- Fees: £10,500–£12,600 pa • Independent

Tel: 01483 280340
Email: admissions@cranmoreprep.co.uk
Website: www.cranmoreprep.co.uk

Headmaster: Since 2006, Mr Michael Connolly BSc BA MA MEd (fifties). Scottish, quietly confident, straight bat, no nonsense. Years of experience as teacher, housemaster and head in a number of HMC senior and prep schools. He keeps active with squash, tennis and dog walking; reads something philosophical or theological most days (his arts subjects) and enjoys a broad musical taste. Mrs Connolly is a qualified teacher who supports the junior department, edits the school mag and website, and shows prospective parents around. They have three sons, all in their twenties.

Parents tell us he was initially single minded in developing Cranmore; subsequently he has consulted and communicated with pupils and parents, taking account of their opinions; ultimately he knows where he is taking the school. Thoughtful and considered, he tackles difficult topics upfront and head on. Parents describe him as 'reliable', 'straight talking', 'unassuming' and 'trustworthy'. Under his leadership, Cranmore is widely inclusive while maintaining high academic and social standards, with many opportunities for individual boys to succeed.

He has limited contact with junior pupils (this is left to Miss Margaret Kieran, the very experienced head of the junior department), increasing as boys progress through the school. In their final two years he teaches weekly lessons and gets to know them really well.

Entrance: Not selective and proud to be so. Prospective pupils spend a session in class and are assessed to ensure they would be happy and successful. Assessment definitely not competitive; head reassures that 'the average child will be fine', so long as they are prepared to 'get stuck in and have a go'. Places allocated first come first served, waiting list occasionally for some year groups.

Academic, music and sports scholarships awarded for entry at 7. Also, means-tested financially assisted places potentially provide, at most, a free place.

Entry into Bright Stars nursery means you are coming to Cranmore; Mr Connolly explains, 'It's not a stand-alone nursery, it's an investment by the school'.

Exit: Boys move on to a wide variety of senior schools, reflecting the non-selective intake: Charterhouse, City of London Freemen's, Cranleigh, Epsom, King's College Wimbledon, Royal Grammar School Guildford, Reeds, St George's, St John's, Tonbridge, Wellington, Worth.

Around third to half leave at 11, mainly to avoid stressful pre-testing in year 6. Of those who leave at 13 around a quarter win scholarships, awards or exhibitions.

Remarks: Cranmore is genuinely an all round school, maintaining academic standards, terrific sports and much-praised music. Parents feel 'it's very balanced between academics, sport and music' and 'ticks boxes in lots of different areas'.

Located deep in Surrey's green commuter belt, on a large site; the original Victorian building tucked away around the back is used as the nursery, plus a few classrooms upstairs. The rest of the buildings are modern, spacious and purpose built. Nursery, junior and senior share all facilities but at different times, so they are usually separate, and it is not overwhelming for the youngest.

The school has high expectations of its pupils, and for the most part the boys 'surprise themselves' with their achievements. Mr Connolly aims to limit the inevitable academic pressure; he is 'not a big fan of homework' and believes 'if boys come to school fresh and get engaged while at school that should be enough to realise their abilities'. A long-standing Cranmore mum explains, 'He tries to educate the Surrey parent not to get too worked up about academic success'.

Parents are confident of the academic standards, telling us Cranmore 'turns out boys who want to learn', that their sons have been 'well challenged and tutored' by 'talented teachers' who 'know what buttons to push' to teach boys. They feel 'the school sticks by all the boys throughout and has great belief in the mix of abilities', and their sons are 'monitored and assessed so there are no surprises'. Mr Connolly meets every parent during year 5 to discuss aspirations and manage expectations for suitable senior schools.

Broad range of subjects taught, although recently Latin has been dropped from the CE syllabus, a pragmatic decision by Mr Connolly which has stirred strong sentiments both for and against. He reassures that Latin is not compulsory for the majority of senior schools, and says those few parents for whom it matters will use a tutor. He teaches senior boys on a carousel of (non-examined) Latin, Greek and philosophy, two terms of each over the final two years. Boys are set in English and maths from year 4; for the final two years they are streamed into either a scholarship class or one of two CE classes. Teaching facilities are spacious and impressive, particularly the science labs and IT classrooms.

Post-CE programme is 'fantastic, every day is jam packed,' say parents who are pleased their boys stayed on to enjoy final two prep years with smaller teaching groups, prefect responsibility, exclusive blazers and a common room with PlayStation, pool table, air hockey and table football.

Sport is the 'wow' factor which attracts lively, active types to Cranmore. The facilities are 'amazing' and coaching is 'totally professional' with a 'squeaky clean, gentlemanly sporting ethos'. Exposure to variety is a big positive: by the time boys leave they will have had the opportunity to try over 20 sports, including climbing, rowing and skiing (with ski club lessons at Sandown Park for pupils and families). There are plenty of clean, flat pitches, including all weather pitches, sports hall with squash courts and fitness room, gym with climbing walls (laid out for lunchtime judo club when we visited), a 25 metre indoor swimming pool (in which all boys have timetabled lessons) and newly refurbished changing rooms. There's enough indoor sporting space to accommodate all, so rain never stops play. Huge number of teams are fielded for matches so all get some opportunity to play, however those less successful or uninterested in sport may not feel entirely comfortable in this super-active environment.

Outdoor areas include spacious equipped playground areas for nursery and, separately, for juniors and, a new addition, a 'forest school' tucked away beside the playing fields.

Music is strong, valued and highly praised by parents; 'incredible facilities' coupled with an 'exceptionally good head of music'. Music forms part of every day in assemblies, performances and curriculum, plus most senior boys learn an individual instrument, lots at the lower grades and a handful up to grade 6 or 7. Over 250 timetabled individual instrumental or singing lessons each week.

Catholic ethos runs through the school; head explains: 'It's a Catholic community and everyone does everything, it's fundamental to the school. If you want to come to Cranmore you accept this'. Having said that, the majority of families are not Catholic, and feel perfectly comfortable with daily prayer,

half-termly mass and Catholic RE syllabus. Pupils are 'not indoctrinated' and parents recognise solid, Christian values that 'do pupils quite a bit of good'. They feel school focus is on 'confident, well-rounded boys, who care about each other and are allowed to be individuals'.

Pupils see their form teachers twice a day for registration plus five minutes at the end of each day to 'gather their thoughts'. On the whole, they work calmly within clear, tight boundaries and are well motivated to please, earning merit points for their house. Junior boys have weekly 'Top Boy' award based on 'Golden Rules' code of conduct, kindness, honesty etc. Much parental praise for the deputy head, Mrs Sue Walker, who deals with occasional episodes of bullying. Boys are helped with coping strategies and parents are involved. Discipline is about learning and moving on with 'no labels for bad boys'; the aim is to educate boys to make the right choices via drip feed over a long period.

Mr Connolly is onto the dangers of cyber bullying: his approach is zero tolerance to any cyber-messaging he deems inappropriate, and he has suspended boys. Not a fan of children having mobiles, he encourages parents to monitor their children's online and phone activities. Feels there have to be boundaries, clear guidelines and standards.

Cranmore families are hard working, busy, 'definitely Surrey people'. Most can comfortably afford fees, a few making financial sacrifices. Plenty of stay-at-home mums picking up or watching matches in muddy Hunter wellies. Active parents' association provides friendly socials and fundraising. Pupils' classes are changed around each year so boys, and parents, get to know all in their year group.

An all-round school maintaining high standards and impressive results from a non-selective intake, with so much on offer that every boy can find something in which to succeed.

The Croft Preparatory School

Alveston Hill, Loxley Road, Stratford upon Avon, CV37 7RL

- Pupils: 419; 235 boys/184 girls, all day • Ages: 2–11
- Fees: £7,800–£10,800 pa • Independent

Tel: 01789 293795
Email: office@croftschool.co.uk
Website: www.croftschool.co.uk

Headmaster: Since 2012, Mr Marcus Cook, BSc PGCE (late thirties). Started his teaching career at the Robert Smyth School then took a break to become a professional rugby player in England and France. Resumed teaching as a PE teacher at Eastcote Lawn School, Warwick followed by Arden Lawn School, Arden before joining the Croft in 2002 as director of studies, head of boys' games and head of geography. Became deputy head in 2008 and acting head in July 2012. Still involved in the Games department.

Married with two children who both attend the school. Wife, Gemma, is head of PSHE and a member of the girls' games department. A German short-haired Pointer completes the family.

Head remarks, 'The Croft School is an incredibly special school affording its pupils an opportunity to embark on their learning journey with challenge, enthusiasm and interest, in a caring, supportive environment. We are keen to develop our pupils EQ, emotional intelligence, to further enhance their abilities and to create an entirely rounded individual.'

Entrance: Inevitably, this being a day school which does not bus pupils in, most live nearby. Children are admitted from the age of two but may join at any time, space permitting. Moving up through the school is automatic, but applicants over five have a preliminary assessment during an induction day to see if they will need extra support.

Exit: Mostly to local day schools: Warwick School for boys, King's High for girls, the grammar schools in Stratford and Alcester, Bloxham, Bromsgrove, Princethorpe, King Edward VI School, The Kingsley School, and others. Occasionally pupils move to other prep schools to give them the experience of boarding before moving on to senior schools. A clutch of places to some seriously academic schools, such as Eton, Cheltenham Ladies' College, Cheltenham College, Oxford High School, and Magdalen College School.

Remarks: The Croft is unusual in being privately owned. The original school was founded in 1933 in Stratford, but the current proprietor and principal, Mrs Thornton, bought The Croft in 1981 with her late husband, moving the school to its current 30 acre site five years later. The original farmhouse and outbuildings, the barns, the stables, tractor sheds and milking parlour have been developed and adapted into a charming campus, surrounded by the timeless fields and spinneys of Warwickshire. The delightful Mrs Thornton has taught art at the school for years, and is responsible for the lively pictures and mottos high up on the walls, reminding everyone that this is Bard Country. 'All the world's a stage...' 'Fair thoughts and happy hours attend on you' and other uplifting messages adorn the buildings, along with beautiful mosaics and strategically placed works of art. Even on the misty grey November day of our visit, the overall effect was of brightness and colour. 'I am sure that children can learn better in beautiful surroundings,' she says, and that seems to be borne out by academic results as well as the obvious happiness of both staff and pupils.

Visitors to the school receive an instant impression of fun. Bright flags flutter and information about parking is translated into 'parking des visiteurs' or 'parking du chateau', the latter a reference to the wonderful motte and bailey castle erected outside the main house by Mr Thornton. 'Sens unique' reads another sign. Arriving a little early, we enjoyed the peace and distant views before becoming aware of a babbling, bubbling sound moving up to a cacophony of laughter, chatter, scraping of tiny wheels, shouting and even some singing. It was break, and the youngest inhabitants were making the most of it, pushing barrows of leaves, riding trikes and tractors, sliding through tunnels and having a whale of a time.

The senior school is well laid out around what must have been the original farmyard. It all feels very homely, with children and staff scurrying around, smiling and laughing between lessons. Even the ground staff were beaming, and not because they didn't have to teach. 'It's a very happy place,' one told us out of earshot of any member of staff. (The views of ground staff are always worth hearing. They often know more about what a school is really like than teaching staff.) From September 2013 early years section restructured so that a child's 'learning journey can be personalised, rather than being structured in formal class groupings'.

Classrooms are bright, airy, very well-equipped and imaginatively inviting. We saw wonderfully inventive and detailed teaching going on. It became obvious that children are inspired to reach for the stars while standing firmly on the grounds of linguistic and scientific accuracy. 'We learn from detail,' one young child told us, proudly. No patronising in the lessons we witnessed and admired. If the questions were difficult they were phrased in a manner designed to suggest that the answers were within range after applying careful thought. The children were keen and alert and clearly enjoyed the sense of challenge. 'They really do learn how to learn,' one father who has had two children through the school told us; 'as a result their entrance into senior school is seamless.' Conversation with staff at senior schools confirmed that impression.

Housed in a tiny room is the head of learning support, positioned where she can provide privacy or move out to those needing attention. Staff are alert to special needs.

Music is a core subject throughout the school and the results are much appreciated in the locality. Choirs, orchestras, smaller groups, jazz concerts and dance; the annual carol service in Holy Trinity Church, Stratford and more. Over 80 per cent of pupils in prep learn instruments, and currently a range of 15 instruments is taught. As a result of some skilful architectural rearranging of an existing building, the school now has a superb space for performing arts which is also used for assemblies and religious services. Not only are the seats cleverly designed and laid out but lighting and sound equipment, thanks to the nearby RSC, is superb and brilliantly utilised. No wonder the children appear so fearlessly confident, though without a trace of arrogance or smugness.

Delicious, freshly-produced food in the pleasant dining room (periods of silence to 'ease the momentum of the day'); pigs wallowing in mud and dreams; sheep (but are they real?) watching the grass; a lake for making all sorts of discoveries, and an exciting forest school burgeoning into life; birds spotted and catalogued by the head groundsman; a model train set (in need of privatisation); an adventure play area; that castle. It is a Fern Hill of a school where it is shiningly obvious that the sensitive nurturing of children is what makes it dance.

One parent we pushed to say something critical about the school announced after much thought that at times it could seem a trifle precious. That was immediately brushed aside by another parent who said that it was the children who were precious to the school. We left them locked in semantics while the children fleeted themselves carelessly, close to the forest of Arden.

Croydon High Junior School

Linked school: Croydon High School

Old Farleigh Road, Selsdon, South Croydon, Surrey, CR2 8YB

- Pupils: 215 girls; all day • Ages: 3–11 • Fees: £10,815 pa
- Independent

Tel: 020 8260 7508
Email: info2@cry.gdst.net
Website: www.croydonhigh.gdst.net

Headmistress: Since January 2012, Miss Alison Cordingley PGCE. Professional violinist, then taught all primary year groups, deputy head at a prep, successful head of Blackheath Junior for last four years. Wants children to be 'happy and safe and have as wide a range of academic, sporting and creative experiences as possible', plus to prepare them to achieve 'the high academic standards that will allow them to flourish at senior school, university and in their future careers'.

Entrance: From 3+ into the nursery, then by assessment from 4+ and subsequent year groups.

Exit: At 11+ around three-quarters continue to the senior school; leavers tend to opt for local grammar schools or other independents.

Remarks: Offers plenty of opportunities for children to excel in music, art (state-of-art 4D room), sport and academics. Everyone has the opportunity to learn a string instrument in year 3 – quite a few budding cellists look set to impress. Introductory courses in Spanish, German and French to tempt young linguists. Imaginative art displays throughout the corridors and classrooms.

Culford Preparatory School and Pre-Prep

Linked school: Culford School

Culford, Bury St Edmunds, IP28 6TX

• Pupils: 230; 120 boys/110 girls; boarding and day • Ages: 3–13; takes boarders from age 7. • Fees: Day £8,235–£13,605; Boarding £19,440–£20,995 pa • Independent

Tel: 01284 385383
Email: admissions@culford.co.uk
Website: www.culford.co.uk

Headmaster: Mr Michael Schofield BEd (mid forties), taught history and games at a boys' grammar school for five years and head of 11-18 day house. Then at a co-ed grant maintained school where he was sixth form master, head of politics and games teacher. Most recently, at Culford Senior School, ran a senior boys' boarding house and was senior housemaster (part of senior management team). Has always taken an active role in coaching all major games along with, most recently, being master in charge of school golf, plus supporting charity work such as the British Heart Foundation, for the past 11 years. Outside interests include dog walking, mountain biking, skiing and reading historical novels.

Entrance: Admission at 7+ and 11+: entrance papers in English, maths and non-verbal tests, plus satisfactory school reference and recent school report. Entry at other ages consists of similar papers at age-appropriate levels, again with satisfactory school reference and recent school report.

Tennis and swimming scholarships at 10+, academic, music, sports and Jubilee (all-rounder boarding) scholarships at 11+.

Exit: Pupils prepared for common entrance. Ninety per cent plus proceed to senior school at 13.

Remarks: For further details, see senior school.

Cumnor House School (Croydon)

Linked school: Cumnor House School For Girls

168 Pampisford Road, South Croydon, CR2 6DA

• Pupils: 440 boys in the prep and pre-prep, with 200 boys and girls in the nursery • Ages: 2–13 • Christian • Fees: £8,370–£10,785 pa • Independent

Tel: 020 8660 3445
Email: registrar@cumnorhouse.com
Website: www.cumnorhouse.com

Headmaster: Since 1999, Mr Peter Clare-Hunt MA (Ed) Cert Ed (fifties). Came into education after ending up as a construction worker on the A23 and feeling there had to be more to life. He must have been quite something even then, because St Dunstan's College welcomed him with open arms and kept him for 18 years. He then did four years at Northcote Lodge, fulfilling a number of roles including deputy head, director of studies and head of sport before taking the post of assistant headmaster at Cumnor House in 1998. A year later, he became head, and after 14 years is still brimful of energy and showing no signs of wear. Married with two young daughters, mad about cricket and hugely admired by parents, the female half of whom all appear to be in love. 'He's a guide, not a principal!' 'He's adorable!' 'You won't find a better headteacher!' were typical comments.

In calmer language, Mr Clare-Hunt is a man who knows how to talk to boys, and how to motivate and challenge them. He genuinely likes them, and they like him back. To talk to him is rather like reading a Jennings story, but one relocated to a school that's bang-up-to-date and highly efficient. He comes across as honest, open and refreshingly funny. And of how many headteachers can we say that?

Entrance: Three form intake with 20 boys maximum in a class. Automatic entry from the school's Treetops Nursery, which parents told us they found a very attractive feature of the school. Otherwise, boys come in at 4+ for a taster day, which for most is nothing to worry about. 'First and foremost, I find out if he's a nice young man,' says head. 'If he is, that's good enough for me.' Maths and English are checked to ascertain if the child will cope at Cumnor, but not formally assessed. Other entry points at 7+ and 11+. School aims to be as inclusive as possible, and all kinds of families pay the (very competitive) fees to send their boys here.

Exit: Given the school's non-academically-selective admissions process, Cumnor's exit record is truly remarkable. Students can be prepped for either 11+ or 13+ depending on parents' and boys' wishes, which, families affirm, the head is always careful to consult. Those who opt for 11+ are put in a dedicated class, and win places either at local grammars (Wilson's and Wallington's), or at independents such as Trinity and Whitgift, often with scholarships. Those who've chosen to stay until 13 also go on to a whole range of top-brass schools including Westminster, Eton, City of London and Tonbridge. Such is the school's success that refugees who come to Cumnor at 11 often pass at 13 with scholarships into schools which turned them down two years previously. 'I've been in the game long enough to know what the senior schools are looking for,' says head, simply. And year on year, the results prove him right.

Remarks: After years in the schools' reviewing business, we were nonetheless surprised by the fervour with which parents talked to us about Cumnor House. 'It's a lovely, brilliant school. I would recommend it to anyone and everyone!' cried one mother. 'The boys there are lovely young men, and the teachers are amazing, they always want to go the extra mile,' said another. 'It's been a really positive experience for our son,' said a third. 'We couldn't fault it.' 'No negatives, and nothing to regret. It's fantastic!' said a fourth. And this is just a sample.

Cumnor House is surely triumphant proof that single sex education from an early age can really work. If a How-I-Hope-My-Son-Will-Turn-Out contest existed, the boys we met here would all be candidates to win. Their manners are astonishingly good. Everywhere we were greeted with courteous smiles and handshakes; in one instance, even with a bow! Whilst they hurled themselves around the playgrounds at break-time, they were nonetheless well-behaved and considerate, both to each other and to us. 'You might want to walk quickly, 'cause it's raining,' urged one of our tour guides with anxious politeness.

Everywhere we saw evidence of lively and careful teaching, and the boys were vociferous about how much they enjoyed lessons. 'History is my favourite, because it's all about old things, and did you know that Henry VIII died because his bottom exploded on the toilet!' cried a year 2 lad enthusiastically. The older boys were more conservative in their praise, but no less warm. 'The teachers are very kind', 'They're inspirational!' 'Lessons are always fun', 'Because of my science teacher, I want to be a scientist,' we were told. Work on the walls was imaginative and of a consistently high standard. Strong SEN team supports boys in need of extra help; the school welcomes all learners, although the head acknowledged that boys with more than moderate learning difficulties would struggle at Cumnor, and we ourselves felt that this wouldn't be the right place for them.

Parents in search of flashy facilities might initially be nonplussed by Cumnor's honeycomb, let's-patch-on-another-annexe-here school campus. The main site used to be residential, and the impression is still of a large, rambling house full of staircases and inglenooks. Decor-wise, it would be fair to say that it lacks the feminine touch: somehow, despite the displays and children's books lining the walls, there isn't much colour in the place. Desks are endearingly old-fashioned, and occasionally downright scruffy. But honestly, who cares? The classrooms are all well-resourced, there's an excellent ICT suite, the boys radiate contentment and their achievements speak for themselves. And there's nothing scruffy about the sports facilities: the huge sports ground boasts £50k's worth of new cricket nets and a new clubhouse, the sports hall is adequate and the swimming pool block was warm, light and inviting, which may be why the reception teachers were all in the water with their young charges when we visited. Cumnor's swimming is very successful (the swim squad practises from 7am), and the school has won national as well as local competitions. Football, rugby, cricket and athletics are likewise strong, nurtured by a team of very dedicated PE teachers. Old boys include Mark Butcher, Alistair Brown, David Sales, Chris Robshaw and Elliot Daly.

For the non-sportsmen, however, there is plenty of other fare on offer. Music is flourishing, with over half the boys learning at least one musical instrument, and a pleasing variety of bands and ensembles to join. The school's choral singing is particularly impressive: previous fixtures include Salzburg Cathedral and the Barnardo's National Choir Competition (which they won). Drama is also lively, and the school puts on at least two productions a year. There are lots of clubs and societies, and the boys are encouraged to try new things. 'I don't want boys who are in at 8.30am and out at 3.30pm,' says head. 'I want them to take risks. I tell them, if you haven't auditioned for the school play, why not? If you aren't learning an instrument, why not?'

A few years ago Cumnor joined the Cognita schools group (the brainchild of Chris Woodhead), thereby increasing its financial clout in a very competitive locality. The Lodge Schools on the other side of the Purley Way declined and fell during the financial crisis, whereupon Cognita bought up most of the site and asked Cumnor to open a girls' school (see our separate entry) and expand Treetops, their excellent nursery provision. Reception boys are also housed on this site in Woodcote Lane, and we wondered if that didn't provoke grumbles from parents dropping off more than one child. But no: the school runs a shuttle service between the two sites, and parents can choose to which one they deliver both sons and daughters, knowing that the school will safely ferry their children to where they need to be. (And this, frankly, is more than can be said for some of the parents; the thoroughfare outside the Pampisford Road site gets very exciting at drop-off time, as local residents will feelingly confirm.)

The Croydon area is multi-cultural, and one of Cumnor's greatest successes is the way that it takes a highly diverse group of boys – every colour and creed is represented on the school roll – and helps them all become polished and likeable English gentlemen, in the best possible sense of the phrase. It may not be the place for the kind of child who just isn't into school no matter how good it is; incurable mavericks would be exhausted by the ebullient enthusiasm and team spirit here. But make no mistake, this is boys' education at its best.

Cumnor House School (Haywards Heath)

Danehill, Haywards Heath, RH17 7HT

• Pupils: 390; 205 boys/185 girls, 40 boarders • Ages: 4–13 • C of E
• Fees: Day £9,120–£17,235; Boarding £20,505 pa • Independent

Tel: 01825 790347
Email: registrar@cumnor.co.uk
Website: www.cumnor.co.uk

Headmaster: Since 2001, Mr Christian Heinrich BA PGCE (late forties), educated University of Kent and Westminster College, Oxford. Previously 15 years at Summerfields as housemaster, then head of junior school and deputy head. Approachable (by children – 'What socks have you got on today?'; parents, 'I saw him this morning as mine were getting out of the car,' and staff, 'shall I take the staff meeting?') and sensible: he has expanded the school while preserving the homely atmosphere – he knows all the children individually. Married to Belinda (teaches French in the pre-prep) with four of their own, the youngest still at Cumnor and the eldest at Manchester University. He covers different subjects depending on the staff and timetable – at present the bottom set of CE Latin (Latin car names – Audi, Fiat?), previously ICT, history, English, French... Big believer in the value of inspections (senior management team do not escape) and training (GTTP – proud of deputy head appointments for protégées, now hoping for a headship).

As the chairman of the district and district representative for the IAPS, governor of another prep, an ISI inspector of schools and a trainer of other heads, he's not interested in moving to a bigger and more mainstream prep – 'I've got other greasy poles to climb!' With all these rôles, he's well aware of the difficulties facing small schools at present and keen to avoid aggressive competition in the local area. The five per cent sibling discount has just been removed to provide a full bursary for a local child – he's canny but realistic, empathetic and transparent, very reassuring in these financially strained times. Built new theatre on raised funds – 50:50 school resources and personal appeal (£700,000) – so he's certainly an effective communicator. Numbers are stable at present – a third reception class is an unusual 'temporary' measure to accommodate an influx of siblings.

Holds two parents' meetings per year for each age group – one with canapés, one with a sit down dinner (very hard-working, creative, effective and popular chef – his home economics class is oversubscribed); friendships develop – 'You'll not find many wallflowers in the car park at Cumnor' (massive new one now keeps cars and children apart).

Entrance: Non-selective at reception – thereafter by interview. Waiting list at present has 25 per cent ex-London parents. No marketing bar word of mouth. Headmaster spends time with prospective parents and pupils 'making sure they are comfortable with the feel and culture of the place'. Many parents are city commuters – the general trend out of London has been a factor in the growth of the school: lots of children come from a London pre-prep. City commuters and local country professionals live mostly within 30-minute radius – a real local (albeit recently local) feel, with 80 per cent of the children at Thursday night cricket in Fletching (nearest village) coming from Cumnor.

Exit: A feeder to no school – pupils head off to an enormous range; could say every pupil gets to their first choice, but that choice is guided by in-depth consultation with head and staff. Head and his wife visit schools continually and try a couple of new ones each year. Latest leavers to Tonbridge, Benenden,

King's Canterbury, Sevenoaks, Worth, Brighton College, Wellington College, Eton, Radley, Winchester, Eastbourne, Bryanston, Charterhouse, Cranleigh, Marlborough, Millfield, Harrow, Heathfield, St Mary's Ascot, Stowe.

Remarks: Beautiful site – no buildings taller than two storeys and 62 acres of fields, trees, games pitches, sports hall, theatre, children's allotments and an old swimming pond – you get banned from it for a week if you fall off the raft or ropeswing into its grubby waters. The Old Library and the terrace outside it are the main gathering points – snooker and table-tennis tables, bikes, British Bulldogs, cricket nets; no Wii, X-boxes or iPods, some arrangement for Skype for boarders. In the summer the children can run around until 8.30 at night, with a small break for second prep – only the Easyjet flight path breaks the idyll. Once they're in bed it's time for reading (no magazines for girls, boys anything as long as they're quiet!). Yet everyone also learns to touch type from year 3 and thumbprint recognition in the library – no anachronisms here.

Differentiates itself from local peer preps by being larger and without compulsory boarding, although practically every child in their final year opts to board (full or flexi – two or three consecutive nights per week, no hotbedding, same group of friends) – a good taster of what is to come at many of their senior schools. Two wings – pine beds or bunkbeds in carpeted dorms with names that change each term; haircuts and strange fears when we visited (arachibutyrophobia – fear of peanut butter sticking to the roof of the mouth?). Residential housemaster and mistress, six gappers and a nurse (trained in paediatrics) in school from 8am until 6pm and on call locally outside those times.

Originally a small, quirky family-run prep school. Although numbers have grown, it is still quirky – parents hope desperately this will not be lost – and the current head is apparently in for the long haul, although he's not related to the founders. Staff:pupil ratio is still 1:7, all pre-prep classes have teacher and assistant and are capped at 16. Sets from year 6 upwards for maths, English and science, with three mixed-ability classes for PE, DT (all manner of automata being made during our visit), drama and music. The curriculum has been broadened to make sure what you do at year 3 you do at year 8 as well, eg class music lessons all the way through to the top.

Years 6 and onwards choose their own personal tutor and have 10 minutes of dedicated time with them per week; every five weeks the entire staff go through a list of all the children to check for any issues. A freshly inaugurated anti-bullying committee consisting of five senior boys and five senior girls. The house captains (Red, Black, Blue and White – points tallied for good work, house music, sport and general knowledge) and heads of school change every term – one of their responsibilities is to manage the 'kiss and fly' first thing in the morning, opening doors and rolling young ones out of their parents' cars, avoiding traffic jams, speeding up the flow and encouraging inter-year friendships. Since the pre-prep is housed in the middle of the campus (lovely classrooms in the eaves of converted barns), a lot of caring between across age groups. Compulsory to sit boy/girl throughout prep school, and if everyone manages that ratio in assembly, a fairy cake each for break the next day.

Learning support department has a full time SENCo (parents say fabulous, can phone her with questions at any time); main aim is to integrate children as thoroughly as possible, so first level of support is help in class. Since reception is non-selective it's no surprise that 35 per cent of school has been screened – 'If we take them in, we stand by them' – and then one-to-one work if necessary (12 per cent).

The head of PE is an ex-professional footballer (rumoured to be still sponsored by Nike?!) who has done away with the traditional aggression of competitions (although school still unbeaten in rugby some years); instead sees training, mindset

and enjoyment as being much more important. Very full and successful fixture list, particularly strong in athletics and swimming (new 25m indoor pool certainly helps – local primary kids walk through grounds to use it too). Sports hall with web of indoor pitch lines and all kit laundered onsite (parents love this). Three new pitches plus purpose built terrain de boules to while away an afternoon break. Sports tour to Cape Town and new relationship with a South African charity being built. Noticeboard for results by dining room (polite children queuing behind us went ahead while we were peering at them) and four screens around school detailing events, weather, matches, birthdays, thought for the day and any messages – they seem to be read.

Everyone has to try a musical instrument when they first arrive and few drop out – 95 per cent of the prep take individual lessons and the first orchestra is 45 strong. Parents particularly enjoy the yearly jazz day where the children learn from external musicians and perform in the evening. A school trip to Cothill House's chateau every summer also gives them a chance to perform at the local cathedral. Keyboards used a lot post-scholarship for Garage Band – a Mac application for composition. Most recent development is a dedicated barn for music recording and technology.

Art takes place in another converted barn, all manner of creations hanging from the roof and cursive script (tradition of winning competitions) being practised under teacher's beady eye. 'Occupations' are a series of after-school activities and range from cricket through Lego to make-up – stories of very convincing cuts and bruises eliciting sympathy from matron.

Drama in spanking new public school-standard theatre (time capsule buried underneath) with pupil-operated sound and lighting room (parent and actor James Wilby was a consultant and performed two-hander recently) – acts as a cinema every Wednesday and Saturday evening, children bring duvets; big TV in main house is other venue. Shakespeare play performed yearly in outside Greek Theatre. Impressive performer alumni – Rebecca Hall, Simon Williams, Tyler Butterworth, Piers Morgan. A gem of a school.

Cumnor House School For Girls

Linked school: Cumnor House School (Croydon)

1 Woodcote Lane, Purley, CR8 3HB

• Pupils: 180 girls from reception to Y6; 200 boys and girls in the nursery • Ages: 2–11 • Multi-faith • Fees: £8,370–£10,785 pa • Independent

Tel: 020 8660 3445
Email: admin.purley@cumnorhouse.com
Website: www.cumnorhouse.com

Headmaster: Since the school came into being in 2010, Mr Peter Kelly Dip Ed MEd. Father of twins. Originally from South Africa, where he taught in Grey Junior School, a boys' school in Port Elizabeth. He came to the UK in 2001 and taught at Cumnor House Boys before becoming head of West Dene Preparatory School, a co-ed prep school which in turn merged with Downside Lodge in 2008. When all the Lodge schools got into financial hoc in 2010, the site was bought by Cognita Schools who turned it into Cumnor House Girls, to the delight of many local parents.

The hapless Lodge schools may have been swept away, but Cognita was quick to retain the services of Mr Kelly as head of the new girls' school, and it's easy to see why. A former Teacher of the Year winner, he comes across as a thoroughly lovely and kindly man, devoted to the girls in his care. 'He's the best!' 'He knows everyone!' 'He's amazing!' the girls told me, and their parents agree. 'He's always at the gate, and all the girls love him, 'He's very approachable and very encouraging,' were typical comments. The headmistress of another independent girls' school who told him she would never choose a man to be her daughter's headteacher was clearly in a minority of one.

Under his leadership, Cumnor House Girls has been popular from the outset. Numbers expanded from 60 to 100 before they even opened their doors, and has almost doubled in the two years it's been going. 'We've a clear vision,' is his explanation. 'Our aim is to offer girls choice at 11. That's what we're good at.' Are they academically aspirational? 'Without question. I've walked the road for co-ed, but girls cover the curriculum more quickly, so we're able to really push them on academically.'

Entrance: Two-form entry with up to 20 per class. Automatic admission for girls at Treetops, Cumnor's excellent and increasingly sought-after nursery. Otherwise, entry is 'mostly non-selective', and at 4+ consists of a taster day where the girls' literacy and numeracy is checked 'to see where they're at', but not formally assessed. 'I've very rarely said no,' muses head. But with a growing reputation in the neighbourhood, we suspect that will change. Register early to be sure of a place. Apparently there's means-tested assistance plus the odd scholarship available at 7+, but we couldn't find any mention of this on the website.

Exit: To an impressive range of local selective schools, often with scholarships. Recent destinations include Wallington, Nonsuch, JAGS, Caterham, Croydon High, Lady Eleanor Holles and City of London Freemen's.

Remarks: Poor Commonweal Lodge School, now being busily converted into flats (it was the bit that Cognita didn't want), broods mournfully from afar over this happy and flourishing new venture on the leafy Webb Estate, but c'est la vie. We don't think Cumnor House Girls will go the same way; the signs are too promising.

There are girls here who joined the school when it was Downside Lodge co-ed, and as far as they're concerned, things just keep getting better. 'This is the best school anyone could ever choose', 'It's amazing here', 'I'd give the school five stars', we were told. Did they miss having boys around? 'Well, they were loud,' commented one girl cheerfully, 'so it's good that they're not here, really, and it's nice to have smaller classes.'

Whatever its secret, the standard of work here is high, all the more creditably given the school's non-selective intake. Literacy and numeracy are very strong, and the work on the walls bore testimony to imaginative and effective teaching. A girl who'd transferred to Cumnor from another independent school told us, 'I feel here they're pushing me a bit more.' But this clearly isn't at anyone's expense. The same girl added, 'There wasn't as much learning support at my old school, and Cumnor has a nicer atmosphere.' And indeed, we thought the learning support room was particularly welcoming. The SEN team is strong and vigilant, and difficulties are picked up early. The head meets with the SENCo every week, and 'dynamic support' is offered quickly to those who need it. We were impressed by the Games Club, a nurture group for girls with social difficulties, but also by the Quest Club for the gifted and talented students. We certainly saw some lovely examples of the latter.

Sport at Cumnor House Girls is 'MASSIVE!' and 'VERY, VERY important!' according to its young devotees. Rounders, netball, gymnastics, athletics and tennis are all on offer (but no football, which the girls said they would have liked; school please note), and all girls from reception upwards have weekly swimming lessons at Cumnor House Boys. 'They include everyone in the sports here and it's great fun,' insisted a self-confessed non-sporty type.

There was some gorgeous artwork on display, including a wonderful Olympic themed sculpture in the foyer; the art teacher, we were told, 'has many different ideas, she's amazing!' The head is also a firm believer in music and drama, with both integrated into the curriculum. Free instrumental lessons are offered to all girls in year 3, many choose to continue them afterwards, and the school fields two choirs and an orchestra. Wherever possible, they team up with the boys' school for drama productions; previous shows include Bugsy Malone and Aladdin" The hall struck us as rather old-fashioned, but the girls adored it, and told us, 'This is a very, very exciting stage!' Lots of clubs, including dance, chess, judo and sewing, and Business Club ('so we get confident in speaking'). Food technology is on the timetable and is very popular, and the school has a lovely garden which provides the vegetables for lessons – we were proudly shown shallots, parsley and runner beans. (On the subject of actual school lunches the girls were diplomatically loyal, which, after the stone-cold and unappetising fare we'd been offered, we thought very praiseworthy of them.)

The girls themselves, smartly attired in a sensible and well-cut uniform, are the surest proof that this is a school doing well by its students. Lively, happy, enthusiastic, well-mannered and articulate, they were a pleasure to meet. Parents agree. 'It's a very child-orientated school; the girls are allowed to have fun,' said one. Other comments include: 'The teachers are very caring', 'My daughter loved it from the beginning', 'The academic provision is very good, and my daughter's become very confident', 'It's a lovely old-fashioned village-y atmosphere, and she's made some great friends', 'It's a fantastic school; I have no issues at all.' Our verdict: a blossoming school with much to offer; the clever choice for Croydon daughters.

Dame Allan's Junior School and Nursery

Linked schools: Dame Allan's Senior Schools; Dame Allan's Girls' School

Hunter's Road, Spital Tongues, Newcastle upon Tyne

- Pupils: 230; 135 boys/95 girls • Ages: 3–11 • Christian foundation
- Fees: £6,630–£8,685 pa • Independent

Tel: 01912 750608
Email: enquiries@dameallans.co.uk
Website: www.dameallans.co.uk

Head of Junior School: Since 2008 Andrew Edge MA (mid fifties), previously head of years 4 – 6 at Dame Allan's. Studied mediaeval and modern history at St Andrews, then a spell in industry (accountancy and customer service) before a PGCE at Durham. Taught and subsequently appointed deputy head at Ravenscourt Park Prep School in London.

Genial, dapper and approachable; a hands-on head who 'does not like to spend his time behind a desk'. Is keen for school to have its own identity but, 'to sit as one within the Dame Allan family'. Wants pupils to think that, 'learning is fun', and that they 'want more of that'.

Avid Sunderland football supporter and keen sportsman, playing cricket and golf and coaching pupils' rugby; enjoys travel. Married with one son at alma mater Durham School.

Entrance: Pupils may start in school nursery at age 3 after a taster session; informal assessment for entry to reception at age 4. Standardised tests in reading, mathematics and non-verbal reasoning from year 2 on.

Main feeder schools are West Jesmond, Newcastle Prep School, Gosforth Schools and Ponteland Middle School. Pupils mainly from Morpeth, Ponteland, Gosforth and Jesmond. Transport provided by parent-run school buses, a shuttle to senior school site in Fenham for onward travel on school transport, often with older siblings.

Exit: Almost all pupils go on to Dame Allan Boys' or Girls' Schools. Year 6 prepared for the transition, spending Tuesday afternoons at the Fenham campus with sessions of art and technology, music and using the library. Otherwise mostly to Newcastle independent day schools.

Remarks: Purpose built school, newly opened in 2012 on the six acre site of a former Victorian hospital in Spital Tongues, to the north of the city centre. First time ages 3 to 11 have been under one roof. A 24 place nursery, two forms per year to year 4 (maximum 15 per class to year 2, then 20 per class) and then three forms for years 5 and 6.

Attractive two storey, fully accessible building surrounded by three separate play areas, one for EYFS leading directly from their self contained area, one for KS1 and a third for KS2. Good selection of play apparatus appropriate for each stage of development and KS2 area marked out for netball. Luxury of an all-weather playing surface for other traditional team sports, together with adequate grass pitches.

Ground floor houses nursery and reception with their own separate entrance; KS1 classrooms are designed so that children can work and play together in safe 'breakout areas', moving inside and out. Classrooms are paired and pupils in each 'pair' have their own cloakrooms and toilets. Two multi-purpose halls provide space for assemblies, lunch, parent meetings and gym, dance and indoor games.

Classrooms for the older children are on the upper floor, again with a separate entrance. The library is also on this floor, its red colour and prominent shape (which protrudes through to the building's façade – certainly a conversation piece) an overt statement that learning is at the heart of the school. Shared librarian from senior school takes weekly library lessons for all. Designated art, design and science room has the resources for making short films. Year 6 science club has additional use of senior school laboratories. Great attention to detail has been put into every aspect of this building resulting in an excellent, pupil focused learning environment.

The move to one site has enabled the head to review the consistency of teaching, marking and assessment throughout the school and ensure consistent differentiation in class teaching.

The nursery is bright and well resourced with two linked reception rooms. French and weekly library sessions from age 3. Home/school diary for each child recording daily life – an example of the quality of care and commitment provided. Numeracy and literacy in the mornings and topic based activity in the afternoons. Specialist PE, dance, drama and French teaching.

Broad curriculum in both KS1 and KS2, specialist French but no Latin, thinking skills recently introduced and learning outdoors, to make best use of the natural environment on their new site. Parents we spoke to say, 'staff are fantastic', and that they feel children are being taught in a, 'professional, caring, nurturing and safe environment'. Small number of children with SEN – dyslexia – supported in class and one to one; even smaller number with EAL requirements, all of whom can access the curriculum. As you might expect in new build, wireless throughout, banks of laptops, even iPads in EYFS.

Full written reports to parents each summer; effort and attainment grades each term; parents' evenings autumn and summer terms. Parents feel informed and appreciate that the school is, 'very honest with their views' about the children.

Traditional team sports timetabled and teams from under 9s upwards with fixtures against other NE independent schools. Swimming at local pool in Fenham and athletics with record

of success, particularly in athletics. Competitive tennis and squash for year 6.

Music is strong and getting stronger. In year 3 all pupils have vocal/violin coaching on 10 week rota with taster sessions in brass and woodwind in years 5 and 6. New facilities provide opportunity for more choral and dramatic performances. Year 6 production each summer term.

Excellent pastoral care in a school where the head knows every child by name. Children seem happy, at ease and confident in their new environment. Assemblies for reception upwards; taking part in the birthday hat celebration and being serenaded by the audience delighted the older children – and a teacher as well. Thought-provoking moral message in the ad hoc adaptation of a well-known children's tale to the extreme climatic events on the day we visited.

Pre- and after-school care from 7.45am to 5.45pm. Lunchtimes long enough to enjoy the freshly produced food and participate in a choice of activities. Year 1 upwards can select from a range including astronomy and the interestingly named, Megaballs. After school choice includes fencing and Irish dancing.

Children well prepared for move to single sex senior schools. There are opportunities for positions of leadership in the last year, with head boy and girl and four heads of house. Representatives on school council from reception to year 6 have a voice. Numerous community projects, pupils sent Christmas cards to children in an orphanage in Kenya and have raised money through an Easter egg raffle to sponsor three children for a year.

Active house system used to accumulate house points (academic and pastoral achievements) and competition across a number of activities. Individual and class certificates awarded, with a trophy each month. Head's star awards most coveted.

Dame Bradbury's School

Linked school: Stephen Perse Foundation

Ashdon Road, Saffron Walden, CB10 2AL

- Pupils: 220; 110 girls /110 boys • Ages: 3–11 • C of E
- Fees: £6,000–£10,950 pa • Independent

Tel: 01799 522348
Email: info@damebradburys.com
Website: www.damebradburys.com

Headmistress: Since 2004, Mrs Jane Crouch MA NPQH (early forties). Previously deputy head at Ashford School and Great Walstead. Has a strong sense of duty to all in her charge, but not in the least bit stuffy and seems younger than her years. Well liked by pupils and parents – professional, caring and approachable are common epithets – she's brought the school forward without denting its ethos. A believer in being 'out and about', she spends time in classroom taking French and maths lessons or listening to early readers, and (following pleas from pupils) runs an after-school 3D modelling club (having first introduced Warhammer, now run by the IT technician, with assistance from a toy shop and two sixth formers at the local comprehensive).

In her spare time she's involved with church youth work and for pure relaxation loves photographing wildlife, walking coastal paths or watching films with her husband – the in-house Father Christmas.

Entrance: Waiting list with sibling preference. For the nursery/reception, informal 'chat' with Mrs Crouch. Later entrants, depending on age: chat/observation in the classroom/tests in reading and writing. School purports to be non-selective, but head says children are accepted on the basis that it 'can cater for their needs without detrimental effects to others' – pragmatic get-out clause.

Exit: Ready help from the head – if parents are particularly keen on a school that's new to her, she makes it her business to visit. Now part of the Stephen Perse Foundation but not tied to the senior school, though several pupils generally move on there. Healthy mix of other destinations including, particularly, Perse Upper, plus The Leys, St Mary's Cambridge, Saffron Walden County High, Friends' School, Felsted and Old Buckenham Hall, and academic, music, art and sport scholarships frequently awarded.

Remarks: Dame Johane Bradbury is named after its founder – the sister of an early 16th century rector of Saffron Walden. Today the school is situated in a quiet suburban street not far from the town centre. Slightly dour late Victorian edifice, plus new-builds tucked round the back, contrasts with the cosy, welcoming interior. A few tired bits, although the library has been refurbished and a couple of rooms doubling as through routes – but on the whole the place is well maintained and improvements are ongoing. Look out for the inviting adventure equipment – a big draw in the playground.

Although not considered overly pushy on the academic front, pupils are streamed and the most able stretched. Parents like the formal approach to learning and are impressed by the level of support from teachers (predominantly female) who 'don't see children as part of a herd'; 'They're tuned to the needs of each individual'. Good rapport between staff and pupils, with plenty of questioning and encouragement at all levels. ICT (unusual but inspired choice of Macs instead of PCs – 'Fosters creativity,' said a member of staff) and French (native speaker for the older ones) right from the start. Classrooms lower down the school bulge with bright, visual stimuli and work is readily celebrated through display. Dedicated art and DT rooms with plenty of technically proficient work on show.

SEN department, three teachers all with SpLD qualifications, caters for a range of needs – Asperger's, dyslexia, dyspraxia, speech and language development. 'Tracks' literacy scheme – 'It really works,' enthused one of the specialists – and sensible help for those who could do with the occasional boost – up to 10 per cent at any one time. 'They didn't let my son sit at the back but encouraged him to do his best – lots of extra help with English and writing twice a week before school,' said one grateful parent. Basic fees cover additional help (including motor skills sessions) of up to an hour a week – any more is charged.

Usual clutch of games on offer, with girls getting a chance to opt for some traditional boys' sports. Large, purpose-built sports hall is a huge asset and parents are pleased the head has boosted boys' sport with the appointment of a head of sport.

A number of yearly awards on offer. Note: packed lunches aren't an option. School lunches compulsory – no bad thing – but costs aren't included in the fees.

Children are well-behaved but not subdued – keen to explain and confidently venture opinions. One parent commented, 'They're studious in a relaxed atmosphere' – spot on. Manners and consideration towards others are high on the agenda – all have to shake hands with their teacher on leaving at the end of the day – and enlightened schemes encourage self-confidence coupled with a caring approach. Year 6s help in the nursery – 'I love it. They're soooo sweet,' said one girl – whilst all in year 5 are trained as play leaders and each assigned to a pupil in year 3, whom they hear read once a week. Music is on the timetable – just under half the juniors have instrumental tuition; four big productions a year which bring a tear to parental eyes – 'It's quite amazing what they achieve – the standard is so high'.

Mixed bunch of parents – goodly proportion of professionals and 'lots of resourceful businesswomen'. Healthy PTA, with two parent representatives in every form, organises socials and promotes improvements – lunches are now wholesome and include home-grown fruit and vegetables from the PTA-funded teaching garden. A flourishing place providing a safe, traditional education with plenty of emphasis on the skills needed to cope with life.

Has just joined the Stephen Perse Foundation. Has kept its head, site and non-selective ethos, but is now governed by a merged body of governors.

Danes Hill School

Leatherhead Road, Oxshott, KT22 0JG

- Pupils: 865; 485 boys/ 380 girls; all day • Ages: 3–13 • Christian non-denom • Fees: £5,535–£15,345 pa • Independent

Tel: 01372 842509
Email: registrar@daneshillschool.co.uk
Website: www.daneshillschool.co.uk

Headmaster: Since January 2007, Mr Willie Murdock BA, PGCE (late forties). Studied classics at Queen's Belfast. Arrived at Danes Hill in 1984 to teach Latin and French and has been here ever since. He worked up through the ranks: year head, assistant head and five years as deputy head, before taking over after the untimely death of the previous head.

Personable, calm and considered, he knows every aspect of the school, particularly his market – affluent, confident and driven – and ensures the school ticks all the boxes. Sees his role as 'managing continuous development', and adds, 'We can't tolerate complacency'. A hands-on chap, he likes to get around the school every day, teaching Latin and German to year 8s and PHSE to year 5s. He takes the annual skiing trip, a year 5 trip to France every summer and, when we visited, was about to take a group of years 6, 7 and 8 to Berlin. This way he gets to know everyone and parents agree that he is 'very friendly and approachable', 'The kids like him', 'quietly getting on with things and doesn't make a big song and dance about it'.

The whole Murdock clan are Danes Hill through and through – his wife, Glynis, provides learning support at the school and he has two teenage daughters and a son, all of whom have been pupils here.

Entrance: Waiting lists are not generally an issue but they do exist for some year groups (although they do not operate more than two years ahead), so get names down early. Various entry points including at 3-4 and 7-8 years, when they are tested in English, maths and reading. In such a large school, worth ringing at odd times to see what is available. No longer offers scholarships – Mr Murdock says, 'We don't, but we do offer bursaries'.

Exit: Boys and girls theoretically both leave at 13 (although about 20 per cent of girls exit at 11). In 2013, 54 scholarships (a school record) to schools ranging from Charterhouse to King's College Wimbledon to Wycombe Abbey.

Remarks: A very large school with traditional values and a strong feeling of discipline and achievement. Academically strong with a broad curriculum and a very good level of general education. Main aim is to prepare children for CE and public school scholarships, with a high success rate in both. Some parents feel not as much importance is put on 11+ and that the focus on girls leaving at 11 is lost.

So what about the school's reputation as an academic hothouse? Yes, academia is extremely important, yet a real sense of pride in helping the less able to achieve their best. According to the head, as long as your child shows 'enormous compassion and imagination', then their achievements are valued. On average, 20 pupils in each class, but children are placed into small sets from year 2 and scholarship streams from year 6. Class groups are mixed at various stages, so children get the opportunity to make new friends. Controlled discipline in the classroom – children stand automatically as you enter – well balanced by 'friendly teachers who help to bring fun to the lessons'. Lots of hands-on experimentation and practical work. Computerised whiteboards in every classroom. Two noticeably impressive computer suites.

Unanimous parental comments that no weak teachers. Languages very strong – French throughout the school, Spanish from year 4, with Latin from year 6, as well as clubs in German and Japanese. Works well – a very high pass rate for language GCSE at age 13. Lots of residential trips with very intense language study whilst abroad. Latin and classical Greek – about 20 10-year-olds study this option.

Significant learning support unit that works hard to provide additional help. The unit also plucks out the very bright, gifted and talented children and enjoys bringing them on. Some parental feeling that 'not such a focus on the average child – who must be self-motivated to succeed'.

Great emphasis on the arts, many arts scholarships to senior schools – three separate art rooms (three-dimensional, graphic design and general). Some beautiful and very mature 3D work and extremely enthusiastic specialist art teachers. Artwork adorns the walls in the most unexpected places and children use visual work in all areas of study. Design technology, drama, dance and music equally strong. Every year group presents an annual drama production involving every child in the year.

A high percentage of pupils learn a musical instrument (up to grade 8) and many play more than one. Practice takes place at home, although orchestra and ensembles, as well as choirs, rehearse in timetabled sessions at school. Vibrant jazz band and orchestra of 50+ players. Performances recently at Guildford Cathedral and St Margaret's, Westminster. Pupils also in the national children's orchestra and children's choir.

Sport flourishes, helped by the school's extensive grounds, and sporty children really thrive here – grand display cabinet full of sporting trophies in the reception. Lots of tournaments, Rosslyn Park 7-a-side semi-finalists and finalists, and national biathlon champions. One parent comments, 'There's a huge focus on rugby. It's given so much priority each year that football peters out.' Despite this, such a variety of sport on offer that any child should find something to suit, and girls' teams won national prep school ski, hockey and netball events in 2013.

School site is large and wooded with many areas for the children to play in and explore. Lovely natural feel, with beautiful sculptures and building names – The Rookery, The Ark; tidy and litter-free. A real feel of history and tradition about the place – the school has only existed since 1947, but the Victorian buildings and choice of décor in reception areas make it appear longer-standing. New buildings have been sympathetically added to the main house; some temporary classrooms. Bevendean (pre-prep) site has been remodelled and includes a new double storey classroom block.

A feeling of strict order and control – children don't mill around but move along with purpose. A large school – 'Without the size,' the head says, 'Danes Hill would not be able to offer such a wide and well resourced curriculum with so many specialist teachers'. On the negative side, parents feel that the management structure stops them from talking directly to the head about day-to-day matters. Opinions vary from the disgruntled – 'It's hard to see the head. You are referred to the head of year or head of school' – to the more positive, 'If you want to see the head he'll make time for you'. But it's often better to deal with the head of year, 'because they know your child better'. Unanimous thumbs up for the head of the upper school – 'He is excellent. He's very in touch with the children' and 'lots of help when discussing where your child should go next'.

Pastoral care is much praised. Children taught to be responsible for their own actions from an early age – 'The school makes children very independent,' says one parent. 'They're very responsible. There's sex education and puberty education!' Good home cooking with plenty of healthy choices.

The large number of international children creates a unique atmosphere (even a specialist EAL teacher). The school is the only factor that binds all these disparate people together – which may explain why such a strong sense of community. Parents are corporate chieftains and the like, and mostly rather wealthy. They put in a large amount of effort and commitment to the school, which is strongly encouraged by the head. A few comments that the parents form cliques. Drop-off and pick-up times are a nightmare – the entrance to the school is on the brow of a steep hill. School runs a bus service from and to the immediate surrounding areas (Walton, Weybridge, Esher, Claygate and Bookham).

Suits bright, confident, sporty children happy to get involved in school life and who would not get lost in the crowd.

Dean Close Preparatory School

Linked school: Dean Close School

Lansdown Road, Cheltenham, GL51 6QS

- Pupils: 255; 150 boys /105 girls, 70 full boarders and 10 day boarders; pre-prep 80 boys/70 girls • Ages: 3–13 • C of E
- Fees: Day £7,260–£15,150; Boarding £17,340–£22,020 pa
- Independent

Tel: 01242 258001
Email: dcpsoffice@deanclose.org.uk
Website: www.deanclose.org.uk

Headmaster: Since 2004, the Reverend Leonard Browne MA, educated at St Catharine's College, Cambridge, where he started with history and changed to theology. Rugby and athletics blue. Taught history and RS at Clifton College, then ordained and worked as a parish priest. Coaching schoolboy rugby returned him to school life – before taking lower school headship, chaplain and head of RS at the senior school. Married to Alison, they have three children and a golden retriever.

His study has the air of a gentlemen's club, with good comfortable chairs, overflowing bookcases and walls covered in photographs and pictures (mostly of the robust sporting kind); he is an imposing figure with grey hair and an avuncular twinkle. For Reverend Browne, the school's Christian principles are the beating heart of its current ethos and character. When asked what constituted the Dean Close difference, he defined it as being 'not a win at any cost establishment', a place where every child is encouraged to 'celebrate the life we are given'. Even church-avoiding parents respond warmly to his strong faith, confident that their young can only improve under his care. More than one described him as 'absolutely fantastic', praising his dedication and valuing his experience.

Entrance: Own exam (English, maths, VR) plus interview and school report. Year 3s mostly from own pre-prep, but roughly a third more come into year 7 from local preps and primaries. School makes the test as unthreatening as possible – on our visit we saw one girl enjoying chocolate and having a fuss made of her in the office, having finished her paper.

Exit: Nearly all to Dean Close School. Some five per cent go on to a mixture of other schools – Shiplake College, Winchester, Marlborough.

Remarks: Pre-prep, fondly known as The Squirrels, headed since 2011 by Dr Carolyn Shelley. Early years' focus on developing children's senses, to prepare them for learning in prep and beyond. Plenty of hands-on activities, positive reinforcement and encouragement for achievement of all kinds, not just academic. These Squirrels are fortunate enough to have their own forest school in the extensive grounds – regular visits allow them to experience the changing seasons, go on expeditions and meet small invertebrates. Back indoors, facilities are just as appealing: great library and ICT suite – all designed for this age group – plus ground floor classrooms linked by creative areas. Sports facilities shared with prep and main school (swimming pool, tennis courts). Plenty of singing and music; all learn recorder with option of lessons in violin, viola, cello (in their reduced sizes) and piano. Dance classes also available. Burgundy sweatshirts with squirrel logo, tartan tunics for girls.

The prep school occupies a brand new (2013) building which includes a theatre, music suite, hall for drama, concerts, assemblies and exams, plus IT suite, drama rooms and classrooms. The new classrooms are arranged to aid cross-curricular work. Prep is separated by playing fields from big school but with use of seniors' specialist sports facilities, such as dance studio and pool, in addition to their own considerable outdoor and indoor provision. At least four sessions of timetabled sport a week plus the option to join clubs and try out shooting, climbing, dance and golf. The floodlit, covered play area is a great asset, a huge space for pupils to race about, kick balls and even roller blade in, no matter what the West Country weather throws at them.

The school aims to 'fire the imagination and enthusiasm of every pupil', and children here benefit from subject specialist teachers, increasingly as they move towards common entrance. Setting from year 6 onwards based on individual learning plans. Subject knowledge boosted by frequent trips and plenty of hands-on activities – the emphasis is still on fun and teamwork. Those with mild dyslexia, numeracy or specific curriculum needs are supported in groups or one-to-one by specialist SEN staff; EFL also offered.

Dean Close is the Schola Cantorum for Tewkesbury Abbey, educating the choristers who sing there (four evensongs and Sunday services). Several other choirs, orchestras, ensembles and bands give ample opportunities for young players and singers to perform in house and at public events such as the Cheltenham festival of performing arts. Speech and drama very strong, with both timetabled and extracurricular sessions – great for confidence building. The list of clubs, many set up by the children themselves, runs from the predictable Warhammer to the gloriously unexpected Norman Wisdom film club, and takes in Fun with Wool, Start Greek and golf along the way.

In senior prep (years 7 and 8), pupils are given more responsibilities in order to develop independence and leadership skills, ready for senior school. All take part in community action projects and trips are further afield – Snowdon, camping in Devon and fencing in France, for example.

Approximately a third board – the vast majority are full boarders, meaning plenty of company after school and at weekends. In addition a very few places for 'day' boarders, who stay three nights a week. Of course many structured activities and outings, but equally important is free time to play outside and explore the extensive grounds, woods and brook. Three boarding houses: one for boys, one for girls and Wilton, a mixed house for the youngest; each is presided over by houseparents – a married couple with children, resident matron, two tutors and non-resident staff. Common rooms with televisions (weekends only), Wii, games consoles etc, plus table tennis, craft and model making areas, baking, a graffiti wall and milk shake nights are just some of the temptations on offer.

No chance for backsliding in instrument practice – one of the tutors in each boarding house is a musical (grade 8 minimum) gappie whose job is to oversee scales, accompany on the piano and encourage young singers and players. Boarders' rooms are bright and full of home comforts; we liked the customised carrels in the girls' prep room – all feathers and glitter. Children can speak to family via Skype and text (non 3G mobiles), but no personal laptops allowed. Parents receive a Friday evening email from housemaster telling them what's been going on, so they can chat knowledgably with their offspring – a boon for those with uncommunicative young.

Seems to have the balance just right, providing a secure, caring environment in which pupils receive a first class academic grounding and explore their own talents and interests. As one parent put it, 'The school doesn't expect them to grow up too fast – it lets them enjoy just being children.'

Derwent Lodge School

Linked school: Yardley Court

Five Oak Green Road, Tonbridge, Kent, TN11 0NJ

- Pupils: 140 girls • Ages: 7–11 • Fees: £13,065 pa • Independent

Tel: 01732 352124
Email: office@somerhill.org
Website: www.somerhill.org

Remarks: See The Schools at Somerhill for write-up.

Dollar Academy Prep and Junior School

Linked school: Dollar Academy

Dollar, Clackmannanshire, FK14 7DU

- Pupils: 360; 175 girls/ 185 boys, 3 boarders • Ages: 5–11
- Fees: Boarding £20,637–£23,166; Day £7,974–£9,162 pa
- Independent

Tel: 01259 742511
Email: rector@dollaracademy.org.uk
Website: www.dollaracademy.org

Rector: Since September 2010, Mr David Knapman BA (maths) MPhil (forties), previously deputy head of Hampton School in London; educated at Morrisons, 'doon the road', followed by Sheffield and Exeter. His wife, Brigitte, a 'country lass' and a teacher, is 'pleased to be in Scotland'. They 'love walking the hills together' and are about to tackle Ben Lomond, the nearest Munro – Munro bashing is a local, not to mention a school, tradition.

With the younger of their two sons in the school, and his mother in Dunblane, Knapman feels 'he has come home'. He plays tennis regularly with his brother, but 'my mother is my fiercest critic, she keeps her ear to the ground and let's me know exactly what I have done wrong'.

Rector and his family live in the stunning Georgian street which houses a collection of school buildings – much in demand by film crews; we yomped to the burn to see the Mylne bridge (built and named for the local minister and first rector, who opened the school in 1818, to give him a short cut to the kirk) and were told that if it 'weren't for that pine tree, we could see Castle Campbell'. 'I really wanted the job, and when I got here I couldn't believe how good the school was'. Hugely enthusiastic and 'very popular – going down well' and 'doing just fine' say our spies. Sits in on classes, walks round every day, and never misses a match, concert or play.

Assistant Rector and Head of Prep and Junior School: Since 2010, after four years in big school, Mrs Alison Morrison, BSc (Cantab) PGDE, (forties). Economics graduate, following spells in the City, advertising and television changed course, (PGDE – professional graduate diploma of education) at the University of Edinburgh, and has one of the most stunning collection of reviews on Rate my Teacher we have ever seen.

Entrance: Pupils come at 5 or 10: the latter by fairly selective entrance exam.

Exit: Virtually all go on to senior school, though the occasional one may peel off for trad schools – ('very very rare for someone to leave' said the rector).

Remarks: Very sound – this large, solid, co-ed school provides education in the best Scottish 'get on with it' tradition, facing the 21st century with the clear expectations and values of an earlier age, mercifully untouched by most of the excesses of the 60s. 'Robust teaching and meritocracy' are important here. Up there with the best of the merchant schools, though possibly 'not quite so trendy'.

Captain John McNabb, a former herd boy who rose to become a ship's captain and, latterly, a ship husband – literally looking after ships in port – died in 1802, leaving half his fortune, £55,000, to found a school to educate children of 'the parish wheir I was born'. Rumours abound whether the monies came from slavery or piracy but they were certainly augmented by bribes from ship owners eager to be first past the post. After much shilly shallying, the Rev Andrew Mylne, a trustee, commissioned William Playfair to build a 'hospital' which opened in 1818. The first co-ed school in Scotland. McNabb's corpse was rediscovered in the 1930s, proudly brought back to Scotland, and cremated. Gruesome or what. His ashes are entombed in the wall above the main Bronze Doors; this has to be the only school in the land where pupils pass under the founder every day.

By 1830, the grounds at Dollar, which are open daily, had become an Oeconomical and Botanical garden, boasting some of the rarest trees in the country – certainly the most northerly tulip tree, as well as a Corsican pine and specimen sequoias. Pupils originally had their own plot of garden, though we are not sure whether this was for ornamental purposes or whether they were expected to augment the school kitchen. The interior of Playfair's building was gutted by fire in 1961 which allowed a certain amount of internal rearrangement: the library is no longer painted lollipop pink. Zinging new concert hall (the Gibson Building), improved science block, art facilities. Current wish-list includes an even newer technology, engineering, science and earth science building – to be built out of 'funds'.

Dollar was formerly a direct grant school and became independent in 1974 – a day school, with an international boarding element. Easily accessible from most of Scotland and just a short hop from the Forth Road Bridge and Edinburgh Airport.

Wet weather a feature of the place and masses of matches must be rained (or snowed) off (school says very rarely now due to new all-weather Astroturf courts and pitches). NB The school uniform includes beanies (first time ever for us on a kit list) and macs with fleecy linings. Rector says he doesn't mind what they wear on their heads, as long as they are warm.

Dollar Academy is unusual – though not unique – in dividing the pre-teens into different teaching blocks. Pupils aged 5 to 9 are taught in a splendid airy building (though they use the main school facilities, dining, games, swimming, music, art) under the aegis of long serving deputy head of the prep and junior school, Julia Adamson.

Two parallel classes in prep; max class size 26 (16-26 with classes expanding slightly each year as pupils grow older).

There is no formal setting in the prep and junior school with pupils receiving differentiated teaching and learning within each class. Efficient support for learning in place, with rector getting progress reports. One-to-one, small groups and supported learning in class. Variety of reading methods used, but jolly – or unjolly come to that – phonics in the main. Serious homework, carefully spelt out in a smart little green book full of info for parents which interestingly persists in referring to the school as the Academy. 'Whatever else, we expect that all pupils in the Academy should have enough work to occupy their evenings and any child who indicates otherwise misunderstands.'

Not quite all singing and dancing new computer system (rector says 'could do better'), touch-typing for all, strong on techy subjects. We found a lovely gang of 8 year olds happily making intricate ribbon pictures (for calendars?) in the fabric/home economics room. Some of the chaps were enormously imaginative. Our attempts were rubbish.

Aged 10 (J1), pupils move to junior school, where they are looked after by Sally Horne, assistant head of the junior school, certain amount of specialist teaching in specialist rooms: hist, geog, science plus art, PE and music, by senior school staff. French, German and Spanish (the former two more popular – contrary to the apparent national trend) from J1. Three parallel classes J1, moving to four parallel classes in J2. Junior school is seen as a transition between prep and senior school.

Most children day, vast majority from within a 30 mile radius – impressive number of buses – plus Forces children and a contingent from the Scottish diaspora worldwide. Boarders from age 9 (though not a lot of them); all boys share one dedicated house: two individual (Victorian villas) houses for girls, recently revamped – and dead posh they are too.

Certain muttering about sausage machine from parents of our acquaintance – but it should also be mentioned that both had been to big public schools down south, but hard times meant that their young were in the (fairly rough) local primary. Suspect sour grapes.

Dolphin School

Waltham Road, Hurst, Reading, Berkshire, RG10 0FR

• Pupils: 190; all day; 110 boys, 80 girls • Ages: 3–13 • Liberal humanist • Fees: £9,018–£12,105 pa • Independent

Tel: 01189 341277
Email: omnes@dolphinschool.com
Website: www.dolphinschool.com

Headmistress: Since 2008, Mrs Veronica Gibbs BSc PGCE (fifties), degree in pure maths with history and philosophy of science from University College, Cardiff. She has been at the school since 1990 and before that taught maths in state secondaries. Still teaches maths every week. Both her children, now adults, went through the school and still come back and visit the place. Husband works in IT and is a keen amateur archaeologist and walker who often helps on school trips. Watch out for walking and trips – they feature prominently in this report.

Mrs Gibbs is not your typical head, but then this is not your typical school. Her office, very much not a study, is small and functional with a desk, a couple of chairs and some family photographs and school memorabilia. It is not designed to overwhelm prospective parents – indeed, those who consider grand architecture to be a desirable backdrop to their child's education should look away now. Like her office, Mrs Gibbs is modest and unpretentious, her focus is the school and she radiates quiet pride in its uniqueness. The founder and owner, Nancy Follett, still lives next door in the Tudor Manor where the school was born in 1970 as a Montessori nursery. It grew with its pupils and now occupies a sylvan site with well-designed modern and less than ideal older buildings. The family still governs the school via a trust assisted by advisors, many of whom are former pupils.

Entrance: This school offers a very different approach to education, best described by that over-used word, 'holistic'. Parents are academics, visiting Europeans, artists and others who approve of the free-thinking ethos but equally expect their children to gain places, if not awards, at top independent and grammar schools. Pupils entering from age 5 upwards are invited to spend a day at the school that includes tests in maths and English. No formal assessment for children entering the nursery. The school, as the head puts it carefully, is best suited to the 'academically able', but that should be taken as a broad definition of the term.

Exit: About a third of pupils leave at 11 for local state and independent schools, the rest stay on until 13 for common entrance; according to the head, all get places at their first choice schools eg Abingdon, Queen Anne's, Reading Grammar, The Abbey, Gillotts. Four academic and two drama scholarships in 2013.

Remarks: What is the secret of Dolphin's success? Seemingly independent of any rigid educational ideology (and that's a good start), the ethos is hard to define, and yet a visitor soon becomes aware that something very special is going on. The reception area, complete with grey cat purring on a visitor's chair, sets an informal trend that is true to the whole school. The lack of a uniform, the comfortably dressed staff, the easy, open relationships between teachers and pupils (most address each other by first names), the creative untidiness, all this and more may be your first impression, but do not mistake it for 'anything goes'. Here is the total immersion approach to learning – the polar opposite of spoon-feeding pre-chewed lumps of facts that can characterise the national curriculum at its worst. In every classroom we visited children were busy, engaged, doing, and teachers were enabling and encouraging independent learning. In not one case did our visit interrupt a lesson because the pupils did not have to wait for their teacher to finish talking to us in order to continue with a task. Teaching here can't be easy but it must be rewarding; several members of staff who had joined from other schools said it had restored their faith in their vocation. The ability to wander productively in the outer limits of one's subject (and a few others besides) while covering all the usual areas is not given to all. As one teacher expressed it memorably, 'We follow a subject's tangents but not its red herrings.'

Children join at rising 3, where they follow the early years curriculum 'plus' – lots of good, mucky hands stuff inside and out. On the day we visited the 3 and 4 year olds were out on safari in the sports field, just a taster of adventures to come. From year 1 at least three trips a term, all of which are 'threaded' into every subject, plus a residential walking expedition. As if this weren't enough, years 7 and 8 can go to Italy or Normandy for 10 days at the end of August for a romp through art, classics and history ancient and modern. It's a lot to take in for 12 and 13 year olds, but 'the teachers make it really fun'. Our impressively mature year 8 guides were approaching the literal and metaphorical peak of their school career as they prepared for nine days' camping, climbing, walking and swimming in the Alps. In order to reach these heights children (parents are welcome too) must start on the South Downs and ascend year by year through the Black Mountains, the Lake District, the Brecon Beacons, Snowdon and so on. It is necessary to 'pass' each successive challenge if

one is aiming for the Alps. A wall of photos in the assembly hall provides encouragement along the way. All trips except foreign ones (where parents pay about half) are included in the fees.

Bolstered by trips, the usual range of subjects is taught beyond the usual boundaries. In addition French from the nursery, classics for years 2 to 5, Latin from year 6, German, Spanish and Greek from year 7. Maths is very strong and juniors and seniors regularly arrive home counting awards won in the UK Maths Challenge. Likewise drama and music and, perhaps not surprising among such confident children, pupils often gain drama scholarships to their senior schools. Chess is taught as a discrete subject in year 4 and the school plays an active and successful part in local, regional and national leagues. Other extra subjects include architecture, astronomy, traditional and construction games – the aim is that up to year 6 each year group should sample at least one of these a year. Great IT suite and, wonder of wonders, touch-typing is taught from year 3, 15 minutes at the start of every session. Another wonder is SQUIRT (silent quiet uninterrupted individual reading time) – heads in books for 15 minutes every day for children and staff alike.

Subject specialists teach in dedicated rooms and from year 2 pupils, armed with timetables (and maps!), make their way from lesson to lesson – the aim is to foster independence: senior schools benefit from notably well organised newbies. Pupils are given every encouragement to take the scenic route down their own 'avenues of thought' but, lest this engender wooliness, individual weekly goals are set and expected to be met.

Special needs, including the extra bright, supported by INCo – individual needs coordinator. An anchor in this sea of learning is the form tutor, who stays with the same group all the way through the school. Pupils in years 6, 7 and 8 also have a mentor to whom they can bring any concerns. Parents and children are positive about pastoral care. This a small school and the pupils all know each other well, older children buddy up with their younger peers and bullying, though rarely encountered, is 'not tolerated'.

Science labs are still state-of-the-ark and, to be frank, much of the older fabric of the school is shabby rather than chic. The swimming pool is just about indoors but only used in the warmer weather because it lacks changing rooms – not even these intrepid children fancy a bathing suited dash across the tarmac in February. And finally there is (or in this case, is not) the catering. On a summer's day staff and children picnicking outside has a certain pastoral charm, but lunchboxes in the classroom is considered a bind by parents ('You just try not to think about it,' sighed one), although our guides claimed they always made their own sandwiches. None of the above seems to impinge on the quality of teaching or learning, which just goes to show that in the end it's about the teaching, not the technology.

Sport is more about cooperation than competition. This is not to say that no losers, just that anyone who wants to be in a team or play in a tournament may do so, and mixed teams are encouraged. Punching above its weight as usual, the Dolphin teams are strong opponents on inter-school fixture lists and it has produced county players for most mainstream sports. Claire Taylor, England number one female cricketer of the year, is an ex-pupil and returned recently to give a cricket workshop. Twenty after-school clubs supplement the timetabled sport along with the gentler exertions of yoga, gymnastics and dance.

An unwavering and confident cross-curricular approach to learning is what distinguishes the school from others, the intention being to develop a self-motivated child with a love of learning and an enquiring mind. We saw about 250 of these on our visit. All this and traditional academic rigour is what Dolphin does, but even the head can't pinpoint exactly what the magic ingredient is – apparently one of the challenges at the annual teacher conference is to define the difference. The word that comes up again and again from teachers, parents and pupils is 'freedom' – a dangerous idea in conjunction with education, some might say, but, as the head is at needless pains to point out, Dolphin is no Summerhill. Pupils are carefully selected – the school is looking for the type of child who will 'thrive' there, and some would not. For instance, a child who needs a strong routine, the same teacher every day and the security of a familiar classroom would not respond to the delphic way.

Parents are enthusiastic bordering on evangelical about this school. One, whose three 'very different' children have all attended, was already anticipating with real regret the day that her family's contact with the place would end. 'I wish it could go on forever,' she said.

A rare school. All schools say that they treat every child as an individual but it can be difficult to see this working in practice. To encourage each child to blossom academically while not producing a bunch of prima donnas is quite a challenge, but pupils leave humane, mature and thoughtful with a life-long love of learning ahead of them. This Dolphin, naturally, is swimming confidently and successfully ahead of a conformist tide.

The Dominie

55 Warriner Gardens, London, SW11 4DX

- Pupils: 32 boys and girls • Ages: 6–12 • Non-denominational
- Fees: £24,600 pa • Independent

Tel: 020 7720 8783
Email: info@thedominie.co.uk
Website: www.thedominie.co.uk

Principal: Since 2007, Miss Anne O'Doherty BA Dip Spld (Barts) Dip Montessori (fifties). Miss O'Doherty has been at the cutting edge of researching and teaching children with specific learning difficulties for over 30 years and has a wealth of knowledge and experience working in both mainstream and specialist schools. Co-director of the Kensington Dyslexia Teaching Centre, where she worked for 14 years. Previously she taught at The Gatehouse in the East End and Thomas's London day schools, where she was head of the lower school at the Kensington branch. Miss O'Doherty, accompanied by Maisie the school terrier, leads a dedicated team at The Dominie. The common aim is to restore pupils' confidence and help them discover the joys of learning and succeeding. Parents appreciative that she and her staff are always available to talk to them and help them make decisions for their child's future. Always known by her maiden name, Miss O'Doherty is married and lives between London and Sussex.

Entrance: Any time from 6+ as places become available. Parents need to provide the school with as much information as possible about their child along with medical and educational psychologist's reports. Prospective pupils are invited for a three-day trial to enable staff to assess individual needs and ensure that the school is going to be a suitable placement.

Exit: To a mixture of day and boarding schools. London day schools include Harrodian, Portland Place, More House and Putney Park. Boarding and outside London: Bethany, St Bede's, Eastbourne, Windlesham House and Stonar.

Remarks: A small specialist school providing education for children affected by dyslexia, dyspraxia, dyscalculia and related conditions. The whole school approach is multi-sensory and multi-disciplinary, each child's developmental needs are considered and addressed. One-to-one sessions with physiotherapists, occupational therapists and speech therapist are arranged as required. The Dominie works with all outside all agencies. Pupils follow the national curriculum, which has been carefully adapted and modified to suit their specific needs.

Each child has an individual educational plan (IEP) which is discussed in detail and updated each term with their parents. Staff have a practical and realistic approach and are keen to explain there are no quick fixes, each person will progress at their own pace. Children are motivated by celebrations of good work, merit badges and achievement books. Mornings open with rousing brain and coordination exercises known as Wake and Shake followed by literacy and numeracy classes in small ability-related groups. Afternoons are for arts, practical and sporting activities, two of which are dedicated to Golden Time, where pupils can choose different activities eg cinema, board games, arts, technology and relaxation classes.

Music and drama play an important part in the school day; pupils can have individual instrumental tuition and the annual autumn term school play is much looked forward to. Some are entered for the English Speaking Board certificates ie speech and drama. After-school and lunchtime clubs, visits to places of interest and years 5 and 6 go on a residential trip to PGL each summer term.

Pastoral care is integrated into everything that happens here; everyone cares for each other and parental involvement is essential to school success. The predominantly female staff develop a deep understanding of how best to assist each child. Home-school feedback channels are always open, parents can arrange to see staff easily and whenever they need. Homework is carefully considered and parents are expected to ensure children are practising their newly gained skills regularly.

Founded in 1987 by a parent, The Dominie is housed in neat premises on a residential road in Battersea, a stone's throw from the park. No outdoor grounds but it is near the park, which is the perfect place for letting off steam at playtime and PE lessons. Carefully planned sports curriculum helps the children develop manual dexterity and physical confidence along with weekly swimming lessons and the ever-popular football club.

The school's particular strength is its ability to differentiate the curriculum and tailor it to individual requirements. The success of carefully structured programmes is evidenced in that the majority of pupils in their own time, will return to mainstream schools.

Dorset House School

The Manor, Bury, Pulborough West Sussex, RH20 1QB

- Pupils: 140; 85 boys/ 55 girls; (40 flexi and weekly boarders)
- Ages: 3–13 • C of E • Fees: Day £7,011–£15,360; Boarding £18,660 pa • Independent

Tel: 01798 831456
Email: info@dorsethouseschool.com
Website: www.dorsethouseschool.com

Headmaster: Since 2008, Mr Richard Brown MA PGCE (early forties). Educated at Magdalen College School, Oxford and at Oxford Brookes, where he read English and law. After five and a half years as an officer in the Royal Dragoon Guards, he took an MA in English and education at Reading University and a PGCE at Roehampton. Then spent three years teaching English at the Edinburgh Academy, where he was also a boarding tutor and games teacher. This was followed by eight years as a housemaster and English teacher at Pangbourne. Lives on the school site, acts as housemaster to the boarders and teaches the top three years.

On his arrival the governors gave him the task of introducing girls into the school and phasing out Saturday school. This caused a certain amount of angst and unrest amongst some parents and some took their children away. However, things have settled down and numbers have been rising (girls now constitute 36 per cent and a couple of year groups have waiting lists). Head feels that school is about 'preparing children for today's challenges – not wrapping them in cotton wool' and that 'small prep schools provide an antidote to a world where children grow up too quickly'. His aim is to 'make learning fun and challenge children to think about the world around them'. Divorced with two sons – one at Cranleigh and one still at Dorset House. In his spare time loves mountaineering and trekking in remote places.

Entrance: Children can join at any time so long as spaces, subject to informal tests in English and maths, a report from their current school and, ideally, a taster day. Parents are made aware of what the school is able to offer and that the ultimate goal is CE.

Exit: To a wide range of senior schools, including Hurst, Cranleigh, Worth, Brighton College, Charterhouse, Christ's Hospital, Lancing, Winchester and some further afield to Marlborough and Radley. Most children stay until CE at 13+, but will prepare children for 11+ entry to senior schools and also for pre-selection tests. Scholarships won every year for the past few years – mixture of academic, music, sport and all-rounder.

Remarks: Founded in 1784 as Totteridge Park School in Hertfordshire. After various incarnations it became Dorset House in 1905 and moved to its present site in 1964. Housed in a 12th century manor house, with medieval great barn, modern teaching blocks and separate junior school building. Set in 16 acres of grounds at the end of a quiet country lane, next door to the church and with magnificent views in all directions. Children allowed to build camps and dens in the woods and play in the adventure playground. 'No one minds about mud – you just fling on your wellies,' said one boy. Children spend as much time as possible outside and some of the younger children often drink their break-time hot chocolate on a log in the woods. Small amphitheatre in the garden used for speech day and house drama competition.

One-form entry, with a maximum of 20 per year group – a bit lean in the top year but waiting lists further down. Numbers have gradually gone up over the past two years and have now reached 140 (maximum capacity of 160). Forty boarding places for flexi and weekly boarders – often suits families who live in London and have a weekend cottage nearby. Warren of dorms under the eaves reached by a spiral stone staircase are warm and cosy, with old fashioned iron bedsteads and lots of teddies. Only a few girl boarders so far, but they are accommodated in great style. Real family atmosphere – feels more like someone's elegant country house than a school – the children take their breakfast and tea on the terrace during the summer. Everything immaculate with not a weed in sight and fresh paint everywhere. Head describes the school as 'traditional but forward looking.'

He would like to adopt Anthony Seldon's 'catch a tiger by the tongue' initiative to foster links with China and encourage the children to learn about the likely cultural and economic impact of the rise of China. He has recently visited a number of Chinese schools and a group of 20 Chinese children came to visit Dorset House for five weeks. This made for lots of interesting discussions and the English children were amazed at how hard Chinese parents expect their children to work.

Streaming for maths, English and science from year 5, depending on the class size and the ability range within the group. Scholarship children kept within their year group and offered extension classes at break and lunchtimes.

Some staff left when the school became co-ed but now has a dynamic team with a good mix of age and experience. Charismatic science teacher who brings the subject to life – he teaches through experimentation and investigation like testing the efficacy of indigestion remedies. Bright, light and airy science lab where 'we love blowing up jelly babies in the fume cupboard,' says one budding young scientist. Recently won Green Link award which funded the boardwalk around the pond. Children do particularly well in science at CE, often achieving top grades, and many go on to study it at university. Very enthusiastic young geography teacher is also the director of sport – geography trips to the Isle of Wight and the Jurassic Coast; the flood plain of the river Arun just beyond the garden makes a wonderful outdoor classroom. French taught by a native speaker. Latin or classical civilisation introduced in year 5.

Light, cosy library with comfortable sofas where children can curl up with a book. Prep done at school and supervised by members of staff. Three full-time SEN teachers, mainly for mild dyslexia and dyspraxia. Bright yellow room for the junior SENCo where the motto is 'learning with laughter.' Children not routinely tested but any problems picked up quickly in such a small environment.

Magnificent medieval barn acts as the school hall and is big enough to fit everyone in – also doubles up as the sports hall and is hired out for weddings. Inner barn is used for plays and assemblies. New head of art has revitalised the art department. Art and DT are linked and the kit car club built a car and raced it at Goodwood as part of the Greenpower project. Photography very popular – each child is given their own memory card from year 3 to take photographs around the school and taught to use Photoshop. Photographs of the children displayed around the school and dining room doubles as an art gallery. Brightly coloured totem poles made from recycled materials dotted around the garden.

New young director of music (Dorset House old boy) has made music 'cool and fun' and now lots of informal concerts, ensembles and whole school concerts. The choir sings at services in the church next door and at the Christmas carol service at Arundel. Music timetabled from the early years and every child learns to read music through learning the recorder – about 60 per cent learn a musical instrument. Senior play each year, plus one or two for juniors as well as the house drama competition. Annual poetry reciting competition and children have to read out match reports and prayers – all great for building self confidence.

In sport 'punches above its weight' – under-9 rugby team recently unbeaten in Sussex. Almost all the boys and girls in a year group are required to make up a team and often children who did not consider themselves sporty step up to the plate. All children in years 3 to 8 play in at least three matches a term – everyone has a go. Now enough girls to put together netball and hockey teams to play other schools. Ballet and gymnastics particularly popular and girls can take exams in these. Riding a popular extra and team takes part in regional competitions.

Other extras include clay pigeon shooting, street dance and football coaching (with pros from Chelsea). Chess taught by outside specialists. Recently formed cub group with children from local primaries and some from Dorset House meets in the barn every week during term time.

Leadership and taking responsibility promoted from a young age through leadership programme – 'Children learn how to work together as a team and to listen to one another.' Leadership training once a week before school for year 8s – they take part in the decision making of the school as elected representatives of the school council and act as positive role models. More opportunities to take a position of responsibility in a small school – children start as lunch helpers and book monitors and progress through outdoor adventures and camping trip (including one to the top of Mount Snowdon). Grand finale is an adventure training week in north Devon after CE.

Small nurturing school with a family atmosphere produces open, chatty children where everyone knows everyone and each child is given the chance to find their niche. 'It's a lovely, friendly school where children have a proper country childhood and don't grow up before their time,' one happy mother told us. School is run on Christian principles and the parish church next door is central to the life of the school – Monday morning assembles in the church and parents often come to the special Friday service. The vicar is a part time member of staff and teaches RE.

Recently introduced house system means lots of crossover between year groups and as one parent said, 'The older children are sweet to the younger ones'. Firm policy on bullying. Many young members of staff live on site and in the manor house, which contributes to the family feel. Board games round the library fire in the evenings for boarders and a dedicated games room.

Most children live within a 20-mile radius and the school is increasingly popular with families moving out of London – 'a good antidote to the pushy London day schools,' according to one new arrival. Active parents' association raised £25,000 at the summer ball for an Astroturf (in a school with 140 pupils). Also organises bonfire night party, quiz and welcomes new parents to the school. A fathers' cricket team meets regularly. Famous Old Boys include former Gordonstoun head Mark Pyper, comedian Harry Enfield and actor Ed Speleers (of Eragon fame).

If you are looking for an all-singing, all-dancing school with facilities galore, this school might not be for you, but if you are looking for somewhere that achieves good academic results, is small and nurturing and where every child gets a chance and is expected to do their bit – take a closer look.

Dover College Infants and Juniors

Linked school: Dover College

Effingham Crescent, Dover, CT17 9RH

• Pupils: 80; 38 boys/42 girls, all day • Ages: 3–11 • Christian but all faiths welcome • Fees: £6,495–£9,600 pa • Independent

Tel: 01304 205969
Email: admissions@dovercollege.org.uk
Website: www.dovercollege.org.uk

Head: Since September 2013 Mrs Fiona Donnelly, formerly a housemistress and teacher at the senior school. She is married to Peter, who runs the senior school international study centre.

Entrance: School takes children from 2 . Most pupils start at the nursery, but others arrive when they are older. Some join in year 6 and then move up to the senior school. Non-selective and will only reject a child if school feels that it can't meet a child's needs. Happy to take children who might fail elsewhere and build their confidence. All children strongly encouraged to attend a taster day before they join.

Exit: About half progress to the senior school, but numbers vary from year to year. Good record in the Kent Test – mainly to Dover Grammar and the Folkestone grammars. School helps children with practice tests but parents sometimes get outside tutoring as well. No entrance exam as such for senior school but all children take the academic scholarship. Smooth transition to the senior school.

Remarks: School opened in 2001 and occupies two houses in the grounds of Dover College. Light and airy classrooms decorated with cheerful artwork. One class per year group and class sizes limited by the size of the classrooms – usually 10 to 12 but up to 16 at key stage 2. Non-selective so a wide range of abilities. Spanish taught from year 1 and French from year 3. Pupils take annual NFER tests in maths and English, with CATs (cognitive ability tests) from year 4. Optional Sats from year 2 onwards.

Specialist teachers for sport, music and languages. Juniors have their own laptop room but also use the senior school's ICT facilities – ICT taught across the curriculum by ICT savvy staff and early years children have touch screen computers. All classrooms have either an interactive whiteboard or projector. Have use of the senior school's Astroturf and sports fields as well as the music and dance studios.

All pupils screened for dyslexia and other potential problems every year. Two individual needs teachers in senior school and one part time in junior – sometimes children go over to senior school or teachers come to them, either one to one or in small groups and mainly help with maths and reading.

The school day ends at 4pm but most children stay on for prep and activities. Children can be dropped off at 8am and stay until 5.45pm – very helpful for working parents. Fleet of minibuses bring children to school. Most families fairly local and parents a very supportive and vocal bunch who want to be part of the school. Randomly selected parent representatives for each class and parents also involved with running some clubs, such as dance and cooking. Children eat in the main refectory and are taught about healthy eating from a young age. They also learn about road safety. School has listened to parents and worked on the outdoor curriculum – a discovery garden recently opened and street dance and taekwondo added to the long list of clubs.

Strong family atmosphere and parents invited to Friday chapel, a highlight of the week when children's achievements and birthdays are celebrated and house points awarded. Head of senior school hands out awards in his flowing red St Andrew's gown.

Usual sports – netball, football, rugby, rounders etc, plus multi-sports club after school. Some matches for under 9s and lots for under 11s, with most children getting a chance to play in a team. Strong swimming team – two inter-school swimming galas a year held at a nearby leisure centre as well as a junior school gala.

Informal concerts twice a term in the Tallis Music School as well as a summer concert, carol concert and junior school Christmas play. School also takes part in Young Voices concert at the O2. Loads of outings – including trips to the Christmas lights in London, musicals and the Natural History Museum.

The Downs Malvern

Linked school: Malvern College

Brockhill Road, Colwall, Malvern, Worcestershire, WR13 6EY

• Pupils: 190 girls and boys; boarding and day • Ages: 2–13
• C of E but ecumenical • Fees: Day £6,204–£14,898; Boarding £11,241–£19,719 pa • Independent

Tel: 01684 544100
Email: enquiries@thedowns.malcol.org
Website: www.thedownsmalvern.org.uk

Head: Since 2009, Mr Sam Cook, previously head of Pembroke House in Gilgil, Kenya. An Oxford graduate, this is his third headship. He is married with three small children.

Entrance: Entrance is by informal observation during taster days supported by information gained by interview and discussions with parents.

Exit: Common entrance or common scholarship is the focus, in the same way as other aspirants for Malvern College. At least 90 per cent move up, some move by choice to other local schools. Occasionally a pupil does not make the academic grade. Pupils' progress is monitored closely and parents would be told at an early stage if it is thought their child will not do well enough to move up.

Remarks: The merger of The Downs, Colwall with Malvern College Prep has gone extremely well and the aim of combining the best practice from both successful schools has largely been achieved. Of Malvern Prep we said: 'Useful little trad co-ed day/boarding prep which feeds both Malvern and elsewhere.' For the new school, joiners are welcome at any time, some financial support available. Small classes, Montessori early years, Forest School and World Challenge experiences add to the school's diversity.

Children streamed at top end. German or Spanish in year 7 and 8; French starts in pre prep. Science taught as independent disciplines from year 6 and design and technology linked with very good ICT provision throughout. Has its own sports hall, Astro hockey surface, outdoor swimming pool and steam railway. Uses the college chapel, theatre and 25m indoor pool.

Boys play rugby, soccer, hockey, cricket and athletics, girls netball, hockey, lacrosse, rounders and athletics. Strong teams at U9, U11 and U13. The opening of a brand-new sports centre will allow badminton, basketball, gymnastics and dance. A partnership with a local, highly successful cricket club develops young cricketers throughout the year through use of the indoor cricket lanes.

Popular locally; foreign pupils tend to come at 11 to top up their English. School operates its own bus service, after-school club and holiday club. If you couldn't fault it before, you most certainly will not be able to now.

The Downs School

Charlton House, Wraxall, Bristol, BS48 1PF

- Pupils: 165 boys, 85 girls; all day • Ages: 4–13 • Christian ethos
- Fees: £9,300–£14,220 pa • Independent

Tel: 01275 852008
Email: office@thedownsschool.co.uk
Website: www.thedownsschool.co.uk

Head: Since 2001, Mr Marcus Gunn MA(Ed) BA PGCE (fiftyish). Went to Bloxham, then Liverpool, followed by South Bank and an OU postgraduate degree in education. A cheery traditionalist who believes in children developing old-fashioned virtues such as 'opening doors for others, shaking hands and looking adults in the eye'. Career began at now defunct Marton Hall before deputy headship at Mowden Hall in Northumberland. Didn't quite realise what he was walking into as fourth head at The Downs within two years. After some much-needed hatchet work in the staff room precipitated by a critical ISI report in November 2000 and substantial withdrawals by unimpressed parents, he has now managed to turn the school around. Has established a 'happy, talented staff' encouraged by a positive follow-up inspection in October 2002 and an even better one in 2006 and seen through some major changes. With wife Valerie very much involved and three children (Joshua, Olivia, Henrietta, who've all been through the independent school

mill) the Gunns are clearly seen as good news by the parents whom they have gone out of their way to get on side. A former windsurfing buff, Mr Gunn likes to snatch quality time with the family or perhaps dabble in a bit of painting or photography.

Entrance: Candidates above reception are assessed informally for a day and offered places if they are in line with the school's expectations of at least average ability. Low ability candidates are accepted provided school's learning support department can meet their needs. Former nursery, now run independently, located near the entrance off the B3128. Pre-prep now free to recruit four-year-olds from various local nurseries with encouraging results. Ratio of boys to girls nearly 3:2 in the pre-prep and 2:1 in the prep. Girls appear confident and are increasingly making their presence felt. Two or three scholarships offered annually with academic scholarship worth up to 15 per cent of day fee.

Exit: A number move on to Clifton, QEH, BGS and Badminton in Bristol. Other popular choices have recently included Blundell's, Bryanston, Sherborne, King's Bruton, King's Taunton, Sidcot and Millfield. A few to Marlborough and Winchester. All in recent years have been accepted by first choice school. Impressive scholarship success rate continues. Very few now go off to Bristol day schools after 11+ entrance exams so majority, including girls, stay to 13.

Remarks: Founded in 1894 overlooking Clifton Downs; school 'escaped' from Bristol in 1927 and was tenant on late Lord Wraxall's estate until 2002 when Charlton House, along with assortment of other school buildings, 60 acres of playing fields and parkland, were bought by governors 'for a song'. 30mph speed limit on mile long drive is a first challenge for visitors; unsympathetically rendered exterior to mansion finally comes as anti-climax. Entering the matrix (Hugo Weaving is an old boy), Victorian gothic interior with magnificent fireplace and spooky staircases more than compensates.

Experienced staff exact high standards in what still feels like trad prep; has woken up to unpopularity of Saturday lessons and scrapped them; boarding ended in 2006. For parents who don't want their children to leave home before 13, The Downs offers as full a programme as you can find in a day prep. Attracts broad social mix and now that school has accepted the inevitable (though Saturday afternoon matches continue most weekends) demand is likely to rise further. Accessible from quite a wide area, being close to junction 19 on the M5 and only 10 minutes' drive from Bristol's western edge. School now has a 'stunning' pre-prep – a significant investment.

Pre-prep department recently refurbished and extended. Teenies taught to read phonically with a number of schemes (not just Jolly Phonics) in use. Children not hemmed in by formality and come across as lively but respectful. Music at this level includes recorders, violins and choir; plenty of creativity though thematic work would benefit from more imaginative displays.

School is retaining positives from boarding régime with older ones mostly staying for after-school clubs (ranging from Warhammer to cookery) or supervised prep until supper at 6pm, despite formal day ending at 5.10pm. After-school care for pre-prep children also runs until supper. Saturday matches off menu every third weekend. Workaday uniform is low key and practical but children don garishly striped blazers (which they refused to have scrapped) for all travel to and from school as well as functions.

The curriculum from year 5 is geared to demands of CE with all subjects, including Latin, French, Spanish and science (separate sciences in years 6, 7 and 8) taught by specialists. A new art department but not much provided for DT as yet. New library, which would benefit from a CD-ROM (let alone DVD) facility – school begs to differ – is a long overdue bonus.

Sporting tradition is paramount but head has worked at improving creative and performing arts. Music department is particularly strong with 75 per cent being taught one or more instruments; a 35-strong chamber choir plus variety of concerts and productions. Boys' and girls' sports teams perform exceptionally well. Has won the prep schools' rugby sevens at Rosslyn Park more than any other school, and the girls are currently national rounders champions and runners-up in hockey, and won four national titles in three sports over the last five years. Also an imaginative alternative to games for the less sporty known as The Downs Award Scheme, which concentrates on more individual and outward-bound type activities and in which everyone participates on Thursdays.

Three specialist teachers support pupils with special needs; department has experience of a range of learning disabilities. Targeted support in literacy and numeracy working well to raise pupil performance.

Year 8 has own common room – children in year 8 have at least one school responsibility so no-one gets left out. 'Tiffin' is provided for all mid-morning and afternoon; tasty nosh served up for a fairly formal lunch with staff in the dining-hall, which ends in pin drop silence while notices are given. Plenty of places outside to let off steam; two floodlit Astroturf pitches and plenty of tennis courts. Science laboratories adequate. Now two ICT suites, interactive whiteboards in many classrooms, all site networked. Not a laptop school but thankfully still a mobile phone free zone. More than adequate sports hall somehow got past planners 15 or so years ago; bears external scars inflicted by hockey sticks in rowdier days. Heated outside pool has failed repeated attempts to get it covered but remains popular through summer months. Recently refurbished theatre with retractable seating and new staging.

In a school where manners still matter, we felt that most children would be happy and do well. Not an obvious stomping ground for city slickers, but parents from nearby Bristol might be pleasantly surprised at the benefits for children of regular exercise in fresh air.

Downsend School

Linked school: Downsend School – Epsom Lodge

1 Leatherhead Road, Leatherhead, KT22 8TJ

- Pupils: 470; 255 boys/215 girls • Ages: 6–13 • Non-denom
- Fees: £10,290–£12,465 pa • Independent

Tel: 01372 372197
Email: admissions@downsend.co.uk
Website: www.downsend.co.uk

Headmaster: Since September 2013, Mr Ian Thorpe BA (Ed) MA (Ed) (forties), previously head of nearby Chinthurst School. Attended Bury Grammar and the British School in Brussels then Exeter University. Has worked at many Surrey prep schools, including the posts of deputy head of Caterham prep and head of the junior school at City of London Freemen's School. Played for Exeter University firsts at football and tennis; currently captains local cricket club first team. Wife, Karen, teaches at Caterham Prep; two sons at Caterham School.

Entrance: Vast majority enter Downsend into year 2 from the pre-prep Downsend 'Lodges', where they take children from 2 years old. Transition is smooth with no tests, though parents say 'they would tell you if they thought your child couldn't cope.' In year 3, a further 20-25 pupils join, mainly locally from St Giles in Ashtead (state C of E infants) and St Christopher's in Epsom (private nursery and pre-prep). Entry assessment is relatively low key, short tests in reading, writing and maths, described by school as 'designed to assess… not be overly challenging,' echoed by parents who mostly see it as easy to get in. The school tells us 'there is an entry requirement – pupils must perform well in the assessment tests. These are basic tests in English and maths to see where pupils will fit into the system.'

Currently a waiting list for year 2 entry, priority is given to registered siblings and then order of registration. Scholarships at 7+ – 'designed to provide opportunities for children of high academic ability, outstanding conduct and good all-round potential to achieve'.

Attracts families from across all of this part of Surrey, nearby Ashtead and Leatherhead and further afield to Dorking, Epsom and Reigate. About 150 pupils use school transport covering East and West Horsley, Banstead, Chessington, Dorking and stops in between.

Exit: School tells us proudly, 'Our children go on to best local schools.' Most go to Epsom College, St John's Leatherhead and City of London Freemen's School. A smattering to the Royal Grammar School Guildford, Guildford High School, Reigate Grammar School, Reeds, Manor House and St Teresa's; one to Harrow in 2013. Parents say most of the girls leave at 11 (school says it is 40 per cent); increasingly boys too. One parent adds, 'Obviously they want to keep you until 13 but give support to those sitting 11+ exams and help with mocks and verbal reasoning papers.' Many parents, and presumably the school, are delighted that nearby St John's School – previously all boys – now takes girls from 13, which should help keep a few more girls at Downsend for the two senior years.

Remarks: Downsend has good facilities, solid academic results and pleasant, easy going children – 'a school for children who enjoy life' is the motto. And the school does just as it says on the tin (which is particularly valued by working parents). What is missing is the wow factor, something to make you sit up and say 'here is something different'. Previous head felt that 'the broad curriculum and the enjoyment and fun children have every day set Downsend apart from other schools'.

Cognita, which took over the school in 2004, owns and manages a rapidly expanding group of schools across the UK, plus a few in Spain, Singapore and Thailand. Officially they provide financial governance, personnel and training, strategic and development planning plus 'specialist support and expertise in education', leaving the head free to run the school with the senior staff team. Some parents feel there is a whiff of big business which isn't always comfortable, variously complaining 'it's bums on seats,' 'there's no dialogue with parents,' 'Cognita is very guarded,' 'you don't get answers from Cognita, there are grey areas'. However, the school staff are seen by parents as separate from Cognita and children are not affected by any of these 'business issues'.

Downsend is on a site next to the M25, not the most glamorous of locations (the morning traffic locally is horrendous – but parents in the area no doubt get used to it). The school is large, with about 470 pupils. It is organised into three sections, which the head explains is 'to make it more personal and to give the opportunities of a larger school within a smaller community.' There is a lower school for years 2, 3, 4 and 5 and upper school for years 6, 7 and 8. Each section has its own head, style of classes and playground areas, with more subject specialists teaching the upper years. Staggered breaks, lunch and leaving times also help to make this big school seem not too crowded.

Generally, parents are not looking for hothouse academics but for a friendly, happy school. Academically, pupils are streamed in year 4 into two groups: three B classes and two A classes. By the time they reach the senior school, when pupil numbers have decreased (some 30 per cent having left at age 11), there are five classes: one for scholarship, with the remaining classes split into A and B stream CE groups. Parents are aware of their child's position and do stress about it. School tells them that children are taught in different styles and pupils will prepare for scholarship or CE exams in year 8. Parents feel the school is 'not too pushy, there's room for different characters and abilities'. Some, however, did remark on the differences as their children progress through the school, feeling the focus is on the scholarship stream in the senior section. Most feel their children have a dynamic and positive relationship with teachers and are 'fired up' in class.

A very good school for an SEN child. SEN help for mild, specific learning difficulties on offer, pupils are screened from year 2 using standardised tests. One of the aims is 'to identify and support even those with a low level of need in order to help each child reach his or her potential'. Consequently about 20 per cent receive extra help, but parents pay extra for this – anything up to £60 per hour – depending on what's needed. The SEN team is managed by two part-time SENCos with referral access to qualified literacy specialists, an occupational therapist, a speech and language therapist, plus trained specialist assistants who help dyslexic children with a lower level of need. Brain gym sessions help children with co-ordination difficulties. A gifted and talented co-ordinator offers additional stretch and challenge sessions for the brighter children.

Some parental muttering about staff turnover with comments about too many newly qualified (and consequently inexperienced) teachers – school says only one or two are appointed each year. Other parents have no complaints about teaching. Bullying also – its existence and the school's action against it – provokes a variety of responses. There were comments from parents with children who have been '100 per cent happy' to others whose children have been made anxious by bullying. One parent told us her daughter was bullied and 'the school didn't handle it well, nothing was done until we threatened to leave,' another whose son was harried continually found 'the school doesn't act quickly enough, they could nip it in the bud but they don't'. School tells us, 'Bullying is not a major issue. Children are not afraid to report unkind behaviour' and stresses the importance of identifying the difference between unkindness and real bullying: 'there are sanctions if needed', and explains they are 'rarely used'. House points are awarded for kindness, politeness and good acts as well as good work.

Lots of sport for both boys and girls. Facilities are good, including a large sports field bordered by high fences and trees alongside the M25, plenty of netball courts and an Astro pitch, plus a pool described by one parent as 'the best school pool in the area'. Parents tell us, 'The A teams are kept busy, not so much going on for the Bs, Cs and Ds,' with the usual variety of views – some want their children to play in more matches, some are pleased the pressure is not on the weaker players, whilst others are delighted their less-sporty children get a place in a match. Everyone does get a chance to compete including inter-house matches. The trophy cabinet includes silverware for boys' and girls' biathlon from U10 through to U13, both team and individual, plus swimming and various athletics trophies. Squads have bi-annual international tours for cricket, netball and hockey and there is a popular, annual skiing trip.

About 50 per cent of the pupils learn a musical instrument, from beginners up to grade 6. Peripatetic music teachers offer instruments ranging from harp to drums and electric guitar, there's also a singing teacher. Three orchestras and choirs – one for each junior, middle and senior section – perform informally and occasionally formally to a large audience. Parents report the choirs are more active than the orchestras.

Drama is available via extracurricular clubs with annual productions in the middle and senior schools. Art is part of the curriculum, but not seen as a particular strength by parents. Nice to see the old-fashioned skills of cooking, sewing and woodwork (timetabled in a rota of food technology, textiles and DT) – practical and participatory activities which both parents and pupils value. The aim is for every child to be successful in something; the school feels that 'success in one thing leads to confidence in other areas.' Parents support this view, telling us 'the children all believe they will be good at something' and 'all are made to feel important'.

Parents describe themselves as 'not like traditional old prep school types, it's more of a mix here' and 'down-to-earth people'. Some are 'quite modest and here because they really want to be, working hard to earn the fees,' others are wealthier, but no 'local celeb set' types. Heaps of help for working parents – there are lots of them. After-school clubs keep juniors busy until 4.10 pm when the older pupils finish. An extended day programme starts at 8am and finishes after tea at 5.45 pm. During the school holidays 'Downsend+' provides day care with lunch, all very flexible and run by familiar teaching staff. It's widely praised as 'a fantastic resource' and 'very popular with working parents'; children can be cared for here for up to 50 weeks of the year if required. Downsend+ lists a genuinely exciting range of activities including scuba diving (PADI courses), dry slope skiing and even driving for years 7 and 8 at nearby Mercedes Benz world. Super to have on offer, but by no means free: it would in theory be easy to notch up a bill of £250 for a child per week, though school says this figure would be unusual.

Overall, parents and their children are happy here; even those with concerns and gripes still extol the school's virtues. Pupils are busy throughout the day having lots of fun whilst also cutting the mustard academically.

Dragon School

Bardwell Road, Oxford, OX2 6SS

• Pupils: 870; 410 boys/245 girls in prep, of which 195 boys and 95 girls are boarders. In the pre-prep, Lynams, there are 120 boys and 95 girls • Ages: 4–13 • Non-denom • Fees: Day £9,960–£17,970; Boarding £25,890 pa • Independent

Tel: 01865 315405
Email: admissions@dragonschool.org
Website: www.dragonschool.org

Headmaster: Since 2002, Mr John Baugh (fifties), BEd. Born in Uganda, educated at Aldenham School and St Luke's, Exeter. Previously head at Solefield School, Sevenoaks and Edge Grove, Hertfordshire. Believes in breadth of education and being child-centric – the relationship between staff and pupils is paramount. Teaches RS occasionally, observes each and every teacher once a year in the classroom and would not appoint a member of staff who was not willing to adapt to the needs of the child. His mantra to the children is 'be kind, be kind, be kind'. 'This is a school that never stops,' he says, 'it hums like an ocean liner'. Parents comment that he plays a straight bat and is good for PR.

Married to Wendy who teaches at the school and has two grown-up daughters, one of whom also teaches at the school – 'not appointed by me' – he is quick to point out. Says the school is his passion but enjoys escaping to his house in France in the holidays. A former sportsman, he once played for Exeter City, and continues to enjoy sports, especially cycling.

Entrance: Register early – as early as you like post-conception. The school is full and there are waiting lists at all stages but head is keen not to put off potential pupils as spaces can occur at any time. Backed up by parents who confirm places appear all the time despite horror stories to the contrary. Potentially easier to get in as a boarder but it depends on the year group. Non-selective entry although the school does assess maths and

D

English to check that a child will be able to cope. Five 100 per cent bursaries at year 4 for five years – means-tested and not based on academic merit – head maintains they 'start with need', but the school has to be sure the family is able and willing to commit to the Dragon way of life – Saturday morning school, extra-curricular commitments etc. Scholarships up to 50 per cent fees based on academic merit and non-means tested. Weathering current economic climate.

Exit: Frequent destinations include Abingdon School, Cheltenham Ladies' College, Eton College, Harrow School, Magdalen College School, Marlborough College, Radley College, Rugby School, Stowe School, St Edwards School, Wellington College, Winchester College and Wycombe Abbey. No favourite school, but 'we have the greatest number of matches with St Edwards', as the two schools have similar ethos and are co-ed day and boarding. Pupils are not prepped for pre-test at 11 or entrance exams at 11 – no hothousing for local academic day schools. Head would not want a child to get into a school on the basis of excessive prepping. Deputy agrees that schools take note of the Dragon's reports and trusts their judgement but this isn't a school whose priority is to get children into the most academic local seniors. Bucket-loads of scholarships won – 35 to 40 per year. Famous Old Dragons include Sir John Betjeman, Leonard Cheshire VC, John Mortimer, Antonia Fraser, Alain de Botton, Rageh Omaar, Hugh Laurie and Tim Henman to name but a few.

Remarks: The Dragon, so named after an early school football team called 'dragons', is as sought-after as ever. Originally founded as the Oxford Preparatory School by a group of dons who wanted a progressive liberal school for their sons where learning would be fun. Once avant-garde, education and society have caught up with these principles so that today the Dragon can only aspire to unconventionality. It has resisted formality and retains the ethos of ordered disorderliness – a charmingly unpretentious, relaxed atmosphere. The head confesses they are relaxed about petty issues – untucked shirts, scruffy uniform and clutter – while concentrating on the things that matter, such as learning. He likens the school to an upturned swan – feet paddling busily on the surface whilst the underlying systems of the school are serene and quiet. Unconventionality or, 'colouring outside the lines', has always been and still is encouraged, although head admits it is, 'a balancing act', between risk-taking in schoolwork, striving for imagination and curiosity on one side and discipline and toeing the line on the other. The Dragon aims for and encourages both.

Broad curriculum with a huge extracurricular programme including languages such as Mandarin, Japanese, Arabic and bilingual French as well as 'toast and translation' (a Latin club), music and drama etc. Most subjects are setted with scholarship classes at the top of the ability range. Learning support needs are screened in year 2 or on intake and help is available at extra cost. Dedicated learning support unit with five full- and three part-time members of staff who advise and update colleagues and draw up IEPs. Additional groups provided at no extra cost for handwriting, reading comprehension and social skills.

Breadth is key at the Dragon with excellence across the board – outstanding sport with fantastic facilities and accolades too numerous to mention. Non-sporty children can find refuge in music – equally successful and receiving high praise from parents. Over two-thirds of pupils take individual music lessons. Fantastic art work in light airy art rooms and space in the Forum for the annual art exhibition – check out the school magazine – worthy of any secondary school. Facilities in general match those at many senior schools with science labs, impressive library (look out for dragons etched on the glass fronted mezzanine), 25m swimming pool and playing fields stretching down to the river and boat house. A mini-campus with happy free-range children roaming around, unrestricted by petty rules and health and safety, having a jolly time; play by the river still possible as long as a child can swim two lengths of the pool fully clothed. Traditions such as this survive along with others – female teachers are called Ma, Bun Break at mid-morning and tea in the afternoon. The blue cords of yesteryear have stood the test of time – shorts in summer, longs in winter plus polo shirt and jumper; for girls, a kilt and bright yellow shirt, summer plaid dresses.

The Dragon is large (640) plus pre-prep Lynams, a mile or so up the road. Boys outnumber girls two to one. Some grumbles about middle of the road children lost in the masses and unable to find a niche if not sporty or musical. Head says that the children are separated into smaller units within the school so that they operate within age-related spheres at any one time without being overwhelmed. Good pastoral care – children are discussed weekly and communication is paramount. The school takes its privileges with responsibility and is committed to raising money for charity through entrepreneurship which starts with the concept of the 'little society' and the teaching of philanthropy to children, and extends to ventures such as the locally renowned Dragon Sale which raises tens of thousands of pounds. School is lead sponsor of a new multi-academy trust which includes three Blackbird Leys primary schools, The primaries can use the school's science, art, music and sporting facilities, while Dragon teaching staff are developing initiatives within the new academies. The Café Dragón brand of ethically-sourced coffee is sold at school events.

Boarding houses, separated by sex and age, run by married couples with a homely atmosphere and individuality. Bun breaks and tea in the houses with supper in the dining hall. Children can pop in and out of their house during the day. Day pupils often invited back. Full boarding means that the boarders are, 'the heartbeat of the school', says the head. Weekends are packed with activities and many day pupils opt to board – one boarder walked from his boarding house past his family home every day! Day pupils easily fielded until 6pm, playing with boarders or participating in the huge number of extra-curricular activities.

Once established for dons, they have largely been priced out of the market (in line with all independent schools, points out head). Lots of London money and business parents buying up north Oxford but professions also in evidence – many medics, lawyers, as well as a few academics (wealthy ones or few children). Lots of OD children. The Dragon remains the choice for the social elite of Oxford – if you want to be invited to the smartest dinner parties, this is your school. Head says there is still plenty of mix and parents agree that everyone can find their level and this is not necessarily a school full of nannies in the playground. Boarders local and international, with no particular country in predominance. Currently 30 pupils have EAL lessons.

The Dragon is still the prep school in Oxford, in sound heart as ever, chosen by parents for breadth of education, good old-fashioned freedom and encouraging a 'can do' attitude. Lifelong friends and contacts start here.

DUCKS (Dulwich College Kindergarten and Infants School)

Linked school: Dulwich College

Eller Bank, 87 College Road, London, SE21 7HH

• Pupils: 240 boys and girls • Ages: 3m–7 • C of E • Fees: £12,285–£12,660 pa • Independent

---

Tel: 020 8693 1538
Email: ducks@dulwich.org.uk
Website: www.dulwich.org.uk/ducks

Head: Mrs Heather Friell, previously head of JAPPS, the James Allen's Pre-Prep.

Entrance: Take babies from six months; put your name down whilst pregnant. More children join the nursery and reception classes, ending up with two reception classes of 22. More-or-less first come first served but priority for children of College staff members. Tries to take roughly equal numbers of boys and girls, but boys tend to predominate as some girls go off to eg JAPS in reception. A few year 1 places, but at this point children must be able to 'communicate, socialise, be part of a working group'.

Exit: Many, but not all, of the boys move on to the junior school. Preference for siblings and sons of staff members. Other children go to eg Dulwich Prep, Rosemead, JAPS, Sydenham High, a few to Alleyn's.

Remarks: A homely wood-clad building in spacious grounds surrounded by playing fields, a short walk from the main College site. 'It's a lovely place to take your children,' said a parent. Large outside segregated play areas for different age groups, including ride-on toys, slides, climbing frames, play-houses, sandpits. There is a verandah for wet days and the older classes have an all-weather playground, plus use of some of the extensive College grounds. The College pool is just down the road and everyone learns to swim before they leave. PE and music are particular strengths, with teaching from specialist staff; very able children can join junior school groups. Senior College boys visit Ducks to help with lessons as part of their community service. Lunches are prepared on site by Ducks' own chef.

'The children are all very happy here,' say parents, but we do get reports that there has been discord amongst management and staff, and of a lack of continuity between the different age groups.

Ducks copes with various degrees of SEN including Asperger's, ADHD and dyslexia, sometimes in one-to-one sessions (at parental expense), with varying degrees of success. 'We have a great variety of ways of delivering the curriculum. And sometimes there are helpful changes that parents can make at home, such as ways of communicating.' The school has 'never had behavioural difficulties we can't cope with.'

Inevitably, preparing for entrance to the next school looms large in parental viewpoints. Ducks is not a hothouse and does not cram for 7+ exams. 'We try to develop their confidence and skill base so they're ready to try new things and engage with other people. We give them increasing levels of responsibility, starting with class duties and moving on to showing parents round and appearing in school plays.' Generally, all but around four or five of the boys who apply get places at the College junior school, but girls and other boys must apply to an increasingly wide range of schools to ensure an offer. 'Some are not ready for the experience,' says the head, and parents agree.

The College is now looking at the issues that have been raised and we are confident that the Master and his team have it all in hand.

Dulwich College: The Junior School

Linked school: Dulwich College

Dulwich Common, London, SE21 7LD

• Pupils: 220 pupils, all boys • Ages: 7–11 • Fees: £16,458 pa • Independent

---

Tel: 020 8299 8432
Email: junioradmissions@dulwich.org.uk
Website: www.dulwich.org.uk

Head: Since September 2013, Dr Toby Griffiths, previously deputy head of Lanesborough Prep. Has also taught at Colet Court and the Dragon School, where he was boarding housemaster and head of maths. Educated at Whitgift and the University of Edinburgh; completed a masters and his doctorate in educational psychology at Oxford. A music lover and sportsman – a triple hockey blue, keen golfer and a recent devotee of triathlon and cycling. Married to Vicky; they have a young son (who has joined Dulwich) and a daughter.

Entrance: Forty-eight boys join year 3, around a third from Ducks, the pre-prep. Applicants take maths, English and non-verbal reasoning tests and everyone is interviewed. The college takes into account reports from their previous schools and quite a few boys come from state primaries – 'We understand that they may not have covered all the concepts. We don't expect perfection: the college has an exceptional understanding of boys with a "spiky profile". We want good all-round boys who are academically able'. Siblings and children of staff members have particularly sympathetic consideration, but no automatic entry – 'We need to see academic potential. They must be able to cope with the curriculum. If we take them and they don't progress sufficiently, it's grim at 11 plus time'. Those who don't get in at 7 can try again when they are 8 or 9 – 'August-born boys in particular may be on track by then'. Small entries at 8+, 9+ and 10+, after maths and English tests, may well take the numbers up to 60 boys in year 6.

Exit: Nearly all (over 90 per cent) to the senior school. This is no longer automatic, but 'subject to satisfactory progress'.

Remarks: It is fair to say that, in the past, Dulwich Junior was seen as a stepping-stone between Ducks and the main school, noted more for its sporting than for its academic prowess. The previous head introduced a culture of assessment for learning – 'We explain to the boys what it takes to be successful and try to get them to evaluate their work for themselves. We're keen on developing reflective thinking' – and greater academic rigour Happily, no need for exam preparation to dominate the curriculum – 'We don't have to train them up to hop through all the different hoops that senior schools wave around'.

Learning support help for individuals or small groups of boys with a suspected or diagnosed learning difficulty. 'The difficulties often arise from a short-term visual and auditory memory deficit,' says the school website, 'and the work is usually to help with the way these difficulties affect spelling, organisation, maths, creative writing and comprehension.'

Boys take part in house conkers, chess, art and academic competitions as well as sports matches. They put on performances, such as Joseph and the Amazing Technicolour Dreamcoat, in the Edward Alleyn theatre, play in ensembles and orchestras, sing in choirs – 'We have élite opportunities for very talented boys, but we also have a culture of providing opportunities for all'. Everyone tries out a stringed instrument in year 3 and a brass instrument in year 4. The boys have access not only to the senior school's groomed acres of playing fields, the theatre and concert facilities, but also to high level sports and music coaching and tuition.

Plenty of lunch-time and after-school clubs ranging from Lego to chapel choir and Mandarin. All the boys get a trip to the school's field centre in the Brecon Beacons to do 'non-London things' such as hiking and canoeing. They can also join the school scout troop in year 6.

The school's aim is to provide 'a compassionate education for boys – not just a rough, tough, rugby-playing world'. It aims for a 'relationship of mutual respect' with boys and parents. Exclusion is rare and a last resort – 'We will work to keep the boy if we possibly can. We'd only exclude permanently for something like persistent real defiance, or someone who is not safe to have around'.

Some 10 per cent academic scholarships for boys joining year 3, and quite a few are on means-tested bursaries – 'It looks like a very privileged public school from the outside, but we love the fact that it represents the ethnic and social diversity of south London'.

Dulwich Hamlet Junior School

Dulwich Village, London, SE21 7AL

• Pupils: 360 boy and girls; all day • Ages: 7–11 • Non–denom • State

Tel: 020 7525 9188
Email: office@dulwichhamletjuniorschool.org.uk
Website: www.dulwichhamlet.southwark.sch.uk

Head: Since 2007, Mrs Sonia Case BA PGCE (fifties). Previously deputy head of Greenstreet Green Primary, she has had number of years' experience teaching in Bromley schools. Married with two grown-up daughters and with her broad artistic background, ideally placed to helm this primary school. Originally trained in theatre, she worked in performing arts and marketing, before turning her attention to education and leading this unique school with its truly enhanced curriculum. She is supported in her work by a diverse and committed team of teachers and specialists. Her enthusiasm and cheerful personality are much appreciated by staff and parents, who feel children just love being at the Hamlet. Mrs Case appears to be something of a wizard when it comes to the school budget.

Entrance: At 7+, 90 places; entry is via the Southwark admissions policy. Parents are advised to apply on time. Pupils come from many local primaries, particularly Dulwich Village Infants. Always oversubscribed, but don't let that put you off applying.

Exit: At 11+, majority to The Charter School; others to eg St Dunstan's, Dulwich College, Sydenham, Alleyn's, Grey Coat Hospital, Kingsdale. Pupils regularly win scholarships and awards for music and academics.

Remarks: Probably Southwark's most sought-after primary school. The Hamlet continuously develops and updates its spacious site, which consists of several Victorian and modern buildings skillfully blended and connected. Most recently, a fabulous space has been redesigned to create a multi-purpose

hall, dining room, design and technology suite and children's cookery area. Adventurous and inspiring curriculum has ensured the school remains a top performer both academically and artistically. Classrooms are attractive and well-resourced, with traditional equipment alongside all the latest technology. Classes are mixed ability and large, usually about 30 pupils; setting for all year groups in maths.

Undoubtedly the most distinguishing feature is the arts curriculum, particularly music, which is almost unheard-of today in the state sector. Nearly all pupils learn an instrument and structured music lessons are part of every child's education. Impressive range of instruments, anything from euphoniums to Gamelan gongs. Choirs, woodwind, strings and brass groups and ensembles regularly entertain parents, and the children are invited to many public performances and festivals. A variety of dance and drama projects run and children have 100 per cent pass rate for LAMDA exams. Several art exhibitions in-house and in local galleries and school is involved in community art projects. Musicians, actors, artists and writers regularly invited to the school to talk to the children and run workshops.

Technology is embedded across the curriculum – everyone has the opportunity to learn touch-typing, Apple Macs for animation, art projects and of course music technology. French is thriving – year 5s are taken on annual residential trip to France. Sports Active Mark – pupils take advantage of the local sports facilities, a number of sports specialists visit the school to coach gymnastics, netball, cricket and football. Young athletes represent Dulwich in swimming and athletics competitions. Enrichment afternoons run during the summer term, giving children the opportunity to explore all kinds of activities and discover new interests. Around 15 after-school clubs to choose from – amongst the most popular are cookery, magic and table tennis. A full-time inclusion manager is responsible for running additional support programmes, and specially-trained teachers for those requiring SEN provision. Speech and occupational therapists work with the school as necessary. ESOL can also be arranged.

Pastoral care is organized through the PSHCE curriculum, producing confident, articulate and responsible pupils who come from a wide variety of backgrounds. Healthy eating is important here – lunchtime is a social event in the new dining room or outdoor picnic area. Monthly menus are on the website and all food is freshly made. The Hamlet Herald keeps the school community up to date with all the current happenings, also an excellent user-friendly website. Parents are asked to make a small voluntary contribution each term to school activities and an enthusiastic PTA and governors run a variety of social and fundraising events.

As you might imagine, judged outstanding by Ofsted in all areas. The school continues to play an important role in supporting trainee teachers working with Southbank and Goldsmith's Universities. An educational treat.

Dulwich Prep London

42 Alleyn Park, London, SE21 8AT

• Pupils: 805 boys and 25 girls (girls only in early years); mostly day but up to 20 weekly boarders • Ages: Boys 3–13, girls 2 1/2–4 • C of E • Fees: Day £9,720–£15,585 pa; Boarding extra • Independent

Tel: 020 8670 3217
Email: registrar@dulwichpreplondon.org
Website: www.dcpslondon.org

Headmaster: Since 2009, Michael Roulston MBE MEd (youthful, dynamic, early fifties). Married with three children, educated in

Ulster, he is warm and friendly, zipping about and offering to 'play mother' with the Darjeeling on our visit. First impressions aside, one senses his combination of vision, drive and no nonsense was forged during his first headship in the 1980s at The Model School – an informally religiously integrated school in Northern Ireland. His contribution to conflict resolution in the field of education was recognised by the BP Gulbenkian Citizenship Award in 1994.

After a stint in Japan as headmaster of The British School in Tokyo, earning him an MBE for services to education, he returned to the UK as head of Cranleigh Prep in Surrey. This is a man who clearly thrives on challenge and change, with his eye on the prizes – his and the boys'. We see him as a definite moderniser, sprucing up the old traditions, delivering a slickly presented school with a few fashionable nods – boules, allotments – without straying from his brief of happy parents and pupils at common entrance. Prior to our visit we had heard him described by parents as being 'rather like a successful CEO'. We found him to be business-like certainly, but not stiffly corporate. Yes, very 'on message', but sincere too.

He says of the school, 'it's fun, full of energy from the earliest years all the way though...every day you cannot but be inspired by what the boys do. They are valued, recognised and well-loved'.

Head of the Prep-Prep: Early Years Dept since 2011, Dr Ruth Burtonshaw BSc Phd PGCE Dip Dyslexia and Learning, is an early years specialist, appointed by Michael Roulston.

Entrance: Admission is selective. Multiple points of entry but majority start in the nursery at 3+ (girls and boys), at 4+ (boys only) or at 7+ (boys only). Limited number of means-tested bursaries to new applicants in years 3 and 4, determined by academic assessment.

Exit: Don't think that entrance to DPL is a do-not-pass-go ticket straight to Dulwich College, but a large proportion of pupils do gain entrance – with others heading in a variety of directions, foremost Westminster, Alleyn's and Tonbridge. Recent leavers exited to 28 different schools. Conversation regarding choice of senior school starts as early as year 4, and headmaster claims that every boy achieves his first (guided) choice of destination. Forty-one academic, sport, art and all-rounder scholarships or exhibitions were offered to recent leavers, with 14 scholarships offered to Dulwich College. Only two or three boys a year choose to leave at 11+.

Remarks: The main curriculum is fairly traditional. French from year 1 and everyone tries their hand at Latin. Spanish offered as alternative to French. We found the lack of fashionable forward-thinking options such as Chinese or Russian surprising when even the local state primaries are giving them a go. The Head says Mandarin has been offered as a club in the past, but there was little interest.

Setting in maths from year 4, extended to all examined subjects by year 7. This really works, with parents confirming there is sufficient flexibility for boys to move within the year to find the right level for them, and to be encouraged by their ability in different subjects. In each of the classes we visited, young male teachers were particularly noticeable, in amongst the boys or sitting on desks, easily relating to the boys in lessons ranging from European history, via maths to music technology. Energy fairly resounds and parents of pupils at the lower school, particularly, describe it as 'buzzing'.

Almost 20 per cent of boys are identified with a learning difference, mainly mild to moderate dyslexia. The head says that the school will do its best by all, but any with significant difficulties may find themselves guided to a more specialist school such as Fairley House. Highly-trained specialists lead a good number of staff in the learning support department. We saw great learning integration in the older years with dyslexic boys using laptops alongside their peers; parents confirm that boys don't feel singled out in any way if they need extra help. Nonetheless, some comment with feeling on just how tough it can be and wish for a little more two-way communication with teachers.

Sport is well resourced, with fixtures both after school and on Saturdays. Seven full-time PE teachers, specialist coaching from year 4, more than 70 teams, and achievements at national level, particularly in rugby and swimming. Every boy has an opportunity to play. Parents say coaching is less good at the lower levels, and whilst clubs offer exciting opportunities from rock-climbing to kayaking, 'alternatives to the obvious sporting options are very limited in the younger years'.

Homework is as ever controversial. One mother comments that whilst the boys love the varied topic work, parents find it 'never-ending' at weekends.

Drama varies from year to year. There is a year 6 play and a upper school play each year. Year 7 classes have drama and each year 8 class is off time-table for two weeks to produce an original production. Art continues to year 8 with clearly inspiring teaching, new facilities and technologies. We were wowed by the boys' 3-D acrylic sculpture after Jackson Pollock, and the excitement in the room as the boys made sophisticated digital animations.

Music is rich, appealing and widely pursued, with over 20 ensembles and choirs, concerts of every type at venues in and out of the school, such as the Royal Hospital, Chelsea and Southwark Cathedral. Ninety per cent of the boys from year 2 upwards study an instrument, many achieving grade 8 before they leave.

Clubs (only a few additional charges) and activities run at lunch-time for boys from years 1-4, but also 4-5 pm from year 5. Current options include Lego, Warhammer, movie-making, bee-keeping, streetdance, juggling, Greek , golf and gymnastics. Wide array of trips – no stone unturned on the London museum circuit – further afield during school holidays (often built into the fees) eg Pompeii and Normandy. All this plus a thought-provoking lecture series – featuring recently a holocaust survivor, notable writers, broadcasters and adventurers.

The school was founded as Dulwich College Prep School (DCPS) in 1885. Despite the confusion arising from its name, the school is completely independent from Dulwich College and is an educational trust with its own governing body. This has recently been clarified with the school now styled as Dulwich Prep London (DPL). Situated in a wide, quiet West Dulwich street a few minutes from the train station, the buildings, mostly fairly modern, crowd around the playground.

With just over 800 pupils the school is large, but we saw how the division of the school into four distinct sections, each with its own library and classrooms, really works – 'the boys are quite protected from feeling lost in a huge place, and they're fully prepared for moving on,' says a parent.

Parents from the nursery year to higher up the school all comment on the benefit of a single sex school where teachers are free to focus on knights, dinosaurs, bloody battles etc. If there's one thing this school seems to do brilliantly it's the ability to really 'get' boys and how they learn and put this into practice. There is wiggle time (dancing around between lessons), marble parties or even a pool table as a whole class reward – 'the motivation and excitement are huge'.

The school motto is 'one for all and all for one' and the houses are named after North American Indian tribes from Chippeway to Objiwas. The winning tribe raises their flag weekly up the pole in the playground and if this is all sounds incredibly macho, we hear the boys sometimes choose to sing ABBA as their victory song! Meanwhile others, who choose the calmer activities from book club to weaving and needlework, do so without fear of ridicule. Some parents transfer from a co-ed environment for exactly this reason.

While the head's emphasis on character and kindness rings true – right on cue we witnessed children relating the story of the Good Samaritan to their day – a couple of parents commented that it can take a good while to find your niche. 'If you're not good at sport, you're not popular in the playground.' This is a school which aims to develop 'resilience'. When asked which kinds of boys would be happiest here, parents suggest: 'the bright and the best', 'a self-starter, bright and athletic', 'you've got to be robust'.

No surprises that the majority of parents are highly affluent, most living within an expanding 10 mile radius of the school. However, we hear that there is a healthy mix from the scarily ambitious to the more laid back, so there is a good chance of finding like-minded souls.

School has one boarding house called (not so aptly in our opinion) Brightlands; this can accommodate 25 weekly or flexi-boarders from year 4. Rather a sombre looking house with a garden next to the pre-prep, it's been recently redecorated, and though the housemaster and his family are young and welcoming and boys rush around busily, we spied scary paint colours downstairs and 1950s style curtains in the dining hall. We wondered how this rated as a home from home compared to the boys' weekend surroundings. Definite fun, though, is one week a year when years 5, 6 and 7 stay from Sunday to Thursday; they experiment with life away from home and gain the Tomahawk Award for life skills such as button-sewing and bed-making.

The Pre-Prep: Early Years Department is a stunningly designed new-build – all wide open flowing spaces, blending indoor/outdoor, the classrooms give way to a huge covered sand-pit for wet days. Opened in 2006, it has a delightfully green outlook surrounded only by playing fields, woodland and the grounds of Dulwich Picture Gallery. Nothing locally compares to the rural feel of this setting, a great comfort for any parent who didn't expect to raise their children in one of the world's biggest cities.

Girls are the minority but are carefully selected and more than hold their own. Parents of girls have little need for concern – except getting them in: applications are over-subscribed. Rainbow Club, staffed by regular teaching staff, offers care and activities pre and post, from 8 am to 4.45 pm.

The head assists in girls' applications to local private and state schools. Almost all the boys exit to the prep.

Dulwich Preparatory School Cranbrook

Coursehorn, Cranbrook, Kent, TN17 3NP

- Pupils: 515; 275 boys/240 girls; 60 flexi boarders • Ages: 3–13
- Broadly Christian but all denominations welcome • Fees: Day £5,055–£14,910 pa; Boarding £39.25 per night ; • Independent

Tel: 01580 712179
Email: registrar@dcpskent.org
Website: www.dcpskent.org

Headmaster: Since September 2010, Mr Paul David BEd (forties). Married, with two children at the school. Grew up in Cornwall and read maths and education at St Luke's, Exeter University, where he played rugby. Started his career at the City of London Freemen's School, where he taught maths and games, was head of cricket and became a housemaster aged 28. Moved on to Colet Court, where he spent four years as deputy head and taught rugby across all ages and maths to the senior boys at St Paul's School. He then spent eight years as headmaster of Eaton Square School, a mixed ability London prep.

Energetic and dapper, and requires his surroundings to be dapper too – everywhere is immaculate with not a weed or piece of litter in sight (pounces on any he spots). Spiders with any sense of self-preservation have long since picked up their webs and gone elsewhere. Lots of fresh paint on the walls and vases of flowers all over the place. A very visible presence around the school, attends assemblies at Nash House and Little Stream each week and teaches maths and games in Upper School.

Came into the school after a period of disorganisation had rather unsettled parents. Tightened everything up from manners and pastoral care to redesigning the uniform. Each class now has a weekly greeter who will welcome any visitors and engage them in conversation – head very keen that children should know how to talk to adults and look them in the eye. Parents delighted, teachers too, as far as we can judge (they clearly were made to feel part of the process). Children seem at ease with him. This editor was struck, above all, by how this big, beautiful but soulless school had at long last a feeling of character and style about it.

Not everybody's cup of tea – the Guide and Mr David never hit it off in his previous incarnation – but appears perfectly suited to Dulwich Prep, and vice versa.

Entrance: Priority for siblings, but otherwise on a first come, first served basis. Non-competitive assessment tests from age 7+ – very rare for a child to fail but school doesn't want to take someone who can't cope. Intakes in nursery, reception, years 3 and 5 (and in between, if space). Another intake in year 7, when some children leave for the grammar schools and others come from local primary schools to prepare for Cranbrook entrance at 13+.

Exit: The raison d'être for many for going to Dulwich Prep is to get into Cranbrook at 13, and about half do just that. Fifteen per cent leave for the grammars at 11 – the school takes a positive attitude and is happy to help, but this is not grammar school country (the good ones are quite distant). Otherwise the most popular schools are Tonbridge, King's Canterbury, Kent College, Claremont, Ashford, Benenden, Sutton Valence, Eastbourne, St Leonard's Mayfield, Sevenoaks and Bethany, with a few going further afield to, eg, Charterhouse, Bedales and Winchester. Good selection of academic, art, music, sports and drama scholarships, particularly to Sutton Valance.

Remarks: Established as a war evacuation camp for Dulwich College Preparatory School in the orchard of the then headmaster's father-in-law's land at Coursehorn, and allowed to survive as an independent, unconnected entity when the war was over. Set in 50 acres of grounds, it has a campus-like feel.

The school is divided into three self-contained sections: Nash House (3-5 year olds), Little Stream (5-9 year olds) and Upper School (9-13 year olds). Children from the age of 6 are split into four Tribes: Chippeways, Deerfeet, Mohicans and Ojibwas – lots of inter-tribe competitions and activities.

Nash House (soon to be rebuilt) and Little Stream (recently rebuilt; state of the art facilities with all classrooms opening onto the garden – light and airy with lots of space) are set away from the main school in interconnecting buildings. Lots of computers and interactive stuff – Mr David a fan, but school has been well stocked for years. Own swimming pool. Superb library, IT and facilities generally in Upper School.

Structured but relaxed atmosphere in Little Stream with lots of theme days. Children are awarded brightly coloured ribbons for good work. Great emphasis on building children's social confidence and they are encouraged to stand up in front of an audience on a regular basis, whether it be relating their news in assembly, taking part in form plays or participating in class 'showing times'. Structured mornings and child initiated afternoons; children spend as much time as possible outside. Outings, talks and workshop days a major part of the curriculum, particularly in history and geography. Specialist teachers for PE, French, science (taught in a lab) and music.

Gets more serious in upper school. Children (where possible) setted for academic subjects, apart from a separate scholarship form in the final year. Average class size 18, maximum 20. Latin for all from year 6 and about 50 per cent take it at common entrance. Authors visit every term and library competitions and twice yearly book fairs. Educational outings a major feature of school life.

Learning support for maths and English offered as part of the package – either in class, withdrawn in small groups or one to one, or as instruction for parents in how to help at home. 'Special needs department on hand to give extra help where necessary.' What this all amounts to is unstinting and unshaming help for (about 20 per cent of) children to get into Cranbrook etc.

Music strong – fab Little Stream music suite decorated with semi quavers; all learn the recorder from year 2 (we feel a wave of sympathy for tortured parents whenever we read this, but violins would be worse) and can learn other instruments from year 3. All children can read music by the time they leave Little Stream; Upper School has a music director and three full-time music specialists. All children have two or three class music lessons a week, and almost all learn an instrument with one of the 19 peripatetic teachers. Lots of extracurricular groups including an orchestra, two wind bands, six choirs, a jazz band, pop groups plus a number of smaller chamber groups.Music tours in Italy, Germany, Holland, Paris and Austria.

Separate Stream House art room with an artist in residence – very creative team – with children's artwork everywhere (ditto upper school). Art clubs after school, plus extra tuition for those taking art scholarships (usually wins a couple of these each year). When we visited the children were designing beautiful play houses which were going to be made up in India (no crumbling shelves for those parents). Art room open every lunchtime – jewellery to Scalextric model making. Jewellery making so popular that an evening class was laid on for the parents.

Upper school drama timetabled, with clubs and ESB exams for the enthusiasts. Wonderful John Leakey Hall.

Good sports facilities – well equipped sports hall for upper school. Large outdoor swimming pool, tennis courts/all weather hockey pitches, eight lane athletics track etc. Strong tradition of cross country running for boys and girls. All the usual sports with teams in most: as many children as possible are included – up to four teams per year group and the school tries to have regular inter-school or 'tribe' fixtures. Opportunities to have trials and play for Kent teams.

Parent friendly. Nursery is very flexible and children can build up attendance sessions during the year. Parents welcome at any time to come in and see how their children are learning, and in particular to the Friday morning assembly, when the headmaster celebrates children's achievements and offers coffee afterwards. Even homework clubs and drop in clinics for parents.

Very strong pastoral care and children encouraged to be aware of each others' feelings and friendships issues. They can enter their own and each other's acts of kindness on the good deeds chart. Older pupils choose a member of staff to keep an eye on their academic progress and general well-being. No prefects or head boy or girl, but every year 8 pupil is a 'senior' with a specific area of responsibility.

Food praised by all with some quite adventurous choices – pigeon pie, monkfish wrapped in prosciutto – and proper puddings still on the menu. Children encouraged to try new foods – not British, you may feel.

Flexi boarding popular – boys at The Lodge and girls at The Manor. School very accommodating (when they have room) if parents need to go away for a few days or on holiday. School day for boarders ends at the same time as for day children, and the boarding houses are very much 'homes from home'.

Most children live within about 15 miles of the school. No Saturday school, but optional Saturday morning academic clinics three or four mornings each term for pupils in year 8 preparing for exams. Lots of parents new to independent education, but great loyalty amongst old boys and girls (Old Coursehornians, after the original house on the site) and many children in the school are second or third generation.

Big. Superb facilities. Produces confident children who are happy and do well, and particularly suits those who are up front, determined and capable – quite a competitive environment. School has high expectations of everyone, but gives them a huge breadth of opportunity to succeed.

Dumpton School

Deans Grove House, Deans Grove, Wimborne, Dorset, BH21 7AF

- Pupils: 360; 220 boys/140 girls, all day • Ages: 2-13 • Christian
- Fees: £7,575-£13,569 pa • Independent

Tel: 01202 883818
Email: secretary@dumpton.com
Website: www.dumpton.com

Headmaster: Since 2005, Mr Andrew Browning BSc PGCE MA CChem MRSC (early fifties). Educated at Farnborough Grammar, read chemistry at Southampton University, followed by PGCE and masters in education at the Open University, the latter whilst teaching at Canford. He spent 22 years there, progressing to head of chemistry, housemaster and finally registrar – 'useful experience in advising parents on choice of secondary,' he says. Along the way he won the prestigious Salter's Prize for the teaching of chemistry. He still relishes teaching the subject at Dumpton (he spends about a third of the week teaching), as well as coaching CE and scholarship pupils and running the school's beekeeping club.

Inherited a fine school from his revered predecessor, with a strong staff and loyal following. Now he's had time to make his mark, parents report that he has maintained both, while giving the school a new impetus and professionalism. He lives and breathes Dumpton. He and his family live in the school's main building. His wife Jo, an experienced teacher with eight years at Castle Court under her belt, runs the mothers' and toddlers' group, acts as child protection officer, sorts out pastoral niggles and sometimes steps in as a supply teacher. Their two children are pupils at the school.

Entrance: Most progress to Dumpton via toddlers' group and nursery, but pupils can come at any time, provided space – though usually not much. No test, but academic criteria apply after pre-prep and a good record is expected. Pupils are mainly local, but such is the school's reputation that local can mean as far as Hampshire or north Dorset and Wiltshire.

Exit: Canford is currently top of the pops, followed by Bryanston, Clayesmore and a smattering of the big names. A minority opt for boarding or single sex schools. Local grammars feature but parents are reluctant to let children miss 'that special last year' at 13 and the dazzling record of scholarships (academic, sport, art and music) to top independent schools. Annual scholarships often reach 20 or more – the record is 36.

Remarks: School moved from Kent (where they were at Dumpton House) to Dorset during the Second World War, and then had a peripatetic trip round local stately homes, arriving at Dean's Grove (previously the headquarters of the Dalgety piggery) from Gaunt's House in 1986.

The grounds and buildings are much nicer than the prospectus and website show. Redbrick classrooms, labs, barn-like artroom (at the top of a spectacular outdoor spiral staircase), new DT and food tech dept and sports hall (not in its first youth) cluster round the pleasant and spacious main house in a series of courtyards.

A parent of three told us that the teaching staff are 'brilliant, really committed and inspiring', and the curriculum is demanding enough for plenty of pupils to sweep up spectacular scholarships. French is taught from the beginning of the pre-prep – by fully qualified native speakers, Latin but no Greek, proper science – taken for granted in a school run by a chemist – and plenty of technology, music and art, all backed up with theory as well as practice. Everywhere bristling with technology – several computer rooms now and interactive whiteboards et al everywhere. Some streaming, especially in scholarship years. Lessons are evidently enjoyed as well as taken seriously. Pupils have traffic light coloured pages in their homework diaries and leaving a red page open on the desk indicates to the teacher that you have not understood – a system which seems to work. No Sats but masses of careful tracking and assessment pick up anyone struggling. Lots of unobtrusive help for special needs, with a team of three to provide it.

No boarders now – every scrap of former boarding space is in use for teaching. The long school day (from 8.20am to 5.45pm for the prep section, though the younger ones do less) means that no one needs to take work home apart from some reading or at scholarship time. Prep is done after tea, except on Wednesdays, which are games afternoons – so comparatively little games at weekends. Loads of activities packed in as well as prep after tea and at lunchtime. Head is an eco enthusiast, so an enchanting eco trail, complete with dipping ponds, pontoons, plentiful but tasteful information points and a BBQ and camping site for summer sleepovers. Lots of awards for this project mean real scientists work with pupils, encouraged by input from the Ecology and Hydrology Centre at Winfrith. Splendid all weather pitches, fantastic play areas with tempting climbing structures, a real small boat, a run for the family/school dog and multiple seating and shelter areas (enjoyed in summer outdoor classes and by waiting mums). The newly covered pool is not quite so ecological but justified by a footprint less than that of frequent bus trips to Wimborne.

The bursar plays an unusually pivotal role in this family orientated community. He followed head from Canford, where he had run the catering, and has since become not only a planner and designer of facilities but also a sports coach.

One of only three negative school rules forbids crossing the road without an adult – the others forbid swearing and making others unhappy. The attraction over the road is a huge cricket pitch and athletics track with a stunningly picturesque oak in the centre. Sports facilities are so good that Dumpton hosts festivals in netball, rugby etc, thus upping its impressive sporty record. Every child from year 3 up was in a match somewhere the day after our visit and the pupils sweep the board in most sports locally and beyond. As one parent commented: 'Dumpton's the perfect size, small enough to have a real family atmosphere and big enough to have proper teams, plays and music.'

Music is now vibrant, since the recent restructuring of the music department. Masses of instrumental and choral work emanate from the music school and a separate hut takes the steel band (so popular that staff have one too). The comfy school hall –'just big enough to take the prep or pre-prep all together, so we can't get any bigger' – has a seriously well-equipped stage lighting system, courtesy of the Friends of Dumpton. With all this going for it, Dumpton is generous with its support of the local community schools and clubs. Parents are welcomed into school and given chances to sample the delicious nut-free lunches and watch the children in the re-vamped dining area. Free choice of meals for older children and staff sit with pupils.

Tinies progress from Ducklings to Robins and Woodpeckers in the nursery (phonics from year dot) and thence to pre-prep. Boys in shorts for summer until 11 and grey trousers for winter. Girls in blue tartan skirts and all older pupils in snazzy gingham shirts or white blouses with dark blue edging. Buses to major surrounding towns. It feels like a traditional prep school but everything is bang up to date. We can't fault it.

Dunannie and Dunhurst, Bedales' junior schools

Linked school: Bedales School

Alton Road, Steep, Petersfield, Hampshire, GU32 2DP

• Pupils: 270 boys and girls • Ages: 3–13 • Fees: Boarding £21,885; Day £7,335–£17,130 pa • Independent

Tel: 01730 711733
Email: jjarman@bedales.org.uk
Website: www.bedales.org.uk

Headmistress: Since September 2011, Mrs Jane Grubb BA MA (Ed) PGCE, previously academic deputy head at Hurstpierpoint College prep school, where she worked for many years, starting as head of art, having taught at Brockenhurst College. She is an Independent Schools Inspectorate (ISI) inspector and – we approve – a practising artist. She also likes fishing, hiking, surfing and wild camping in remote places. Also plays the piano, saxophone, flute and acoustic guitar.

Head of Dunannie: Since May 2010, Ms Jo Webbern, Froebel CertEd, (fiftyish), previously class teacher and then head of kindergarten at Ibstock Place for 26 years. Full of enthusiasm and excitement – 'I feel these are my roots. One can deliver that special ethos and creativity here while teaching children all the important skills of life'. Keen on the outside classroom.

Entrance: No selection in nursery – and the school has a crèche which takes staff babies and others – except to try and balance boys/girls. Healthy waiting list. Otherwise, applicants to Dunannie – 15-20 places – and to Dunhurst – 45 places for applicants from outside – spend a day in school before having a more formal assessment. Twenty odd places at 11+ – very over-subscribed. Much depends on whether the school and families like each other – understanding of and sympathy with the ethos is all-important.

Exit: Some 95 per cent from Duannie to Dunhurst (others to Highfield and Twyford); 95 per cent Dunhurst pupils to Bedales, but also recently to Bryanston, Canford, Marlborough, Winchester and Seaford.

Remarks: Nursery, for the 2-4 year olds, is in a fabulous old barn nesting in trees, full of activities worth getting on your knees for. We liked the owl's tree-top house and the Brio train. Thence to Dunannie, the purpose-built and super school for the tots, cunningly housed under six overlapping and interlocking colourful roofs with big windows and home to the pre-prep years. 'It's a nice school,' an 8-year-old told us. 'It's very comfortable – you feel more free than in most schools. People don't mess about because the teachers are very calm and don't say, "Do this, do that!"' Much to enjoy here: the super wall-hanging – 'We weaved it and felted it with Steve-the-Weave, one of those workshoppy people'; the year 3 enchanted forest illustrating A Midsummer Night's Dream; the super seasons project with outsize drawings of pomegranate seeds. Every inch is covered with displays, book boxes and hangings – creativity drips off the walls. Outside is garden and space, space, space. We loved the 'Celtic hut' in the orchard, the 'sound garden' and the musical fort. Children everywhere, in tiny classes, are absorbed, relaxed and happily occupied.

Up to Dunhurst when you are 8. Boarding begins at this stage (boys' boarding house recently renovated) and most children spend some nights each week in school, though hardly anyone is in over the weekend. Outdoor work also features importantly now – masses of woodwork, gardening and animal care. Woodwork – in yet another old barn (see Bedales entry) – uses lots of different materials and techniques – soldering, circuitry – and the children make toys, automata, bird boxes, lamps, guitars, chairs and library steps. We loved the sound-operated cars and toys. They design on paper using pencils – hooray! They make textiles too and pottery (witty stuff) – observant pieces on parts of animals: a crocodile's jaw, a turkey's eye, an elephant's trunk. Other lessons are likewise creative and collaborative – in art they study colour, while in science they cover primary colours and the spectrum. Not rocket science – why can't other schools do this? 'We like our science room,' we were told. 'We have to invent or discover something which would make a difference to us or to the world.'

Subject areas are traditional but informed by the Bedales ethos and a consistency between the three schools, as well as a welcome cross-curricular approach (see the Bedales entry for a fuller description of this). SEN teacher supports those who need it. 'She's a miracle worker,' one bright little button told us. A family therapist works with parents and children when appropriate.

Saturday school until 1.00pm. Many staff and some facilities shared with Bedales. All eat (toothsomely) together in dining room decorated with African mural and wall-hangings. The older children are very teeny – floppy fringes, low-slung jeans and mini minis or shorts over tights, the Bedales uniform. All are relaxed and chatty – this is a school where people smile spontaneously. Relations between staff and pupils are open, friendly and mutually respectful – the first-name business doesn't seem odd after you've been here five minutes. The three heads are clearly in harmony and share values and goals. This informs continuity in academic, ethical and pastoral matters. The school feels in good heart.

Dunraven School (Primary Phase)

94-98 Leigham Court Road, London, SW16 2QB

• Pupils: 56 • Ages: 4-11 • State

Tel: 020 8696 5600
Email: info@dunraven.org.uk
Website: www.dunraven.org.uk

Principal: David Boyle.

Head of primary phase: Michaela Christian.

Remarks: See senior school review.

Durand Academy

Hackford Road, London, SW9 0RD

• Pupils: 1110 girls and boys • Ages: 3-13 • Non-denom; • State

Tel: 020 7735 8348
Email: headteacher@durandprimary.com
Website: www.durand.lambeth.sch.uk

Executive Head: Mr Greg Martin has been at the school since 1986. Previously deputy head of Sudbourne Primary in Brixton. Full of far-sighted initiatives, he has four children, three of whom have been through Durand; commutes weekly from Kent to live on the site. Acting head, since the short tenure of Ross Cameron, is Ms Parker, previously deputy head.

Entrance: At three into the nursery (60 places) or at four into reception (125 places). NB Nursery children must reapply for reception, but get guaranteed places. Otherwise by distance.

Exit: From now on, Durand children won't have to leave until they are 16 – a middle school for 11-13 year olds opened on the same site in September 2012 and a weekly boarding school in Sussex, for 13-16 year olds, is due to open in 2014, subject to planning, funding and irate locals, including a Tory councillor who resigned after a racist outburst in the Mail on Sunday.

Remarks: Calling this a state primary school is rather like calling St Paul's Cathedral a church. It is one of the largest and best-equipped in the country, and not content with opening a middle school on the same site, is making history by planning to start its own country boarding secondary school, which will be entirely free of charge (unlike other state boarding schools, which charge for board and lodging, though not for tuition).

From the front the junior school looks innocently like a larger than average Victorian primary school building. Round the back, however, is a sports centre with swimming pool, fitness room and café, five-a-side Astroturf and accommodation blocks, which are the key to the school's achievements and ambitions. Parents can pay £30 a year to use the swimming pool, the Astroturf is available for hire in the evenings, and language students and key workers (including NQTs working at the school) rent the flats. The latter brings in a tidy sum – some £400,000 a year – which has facilitated the expansion (the government has chipped in some £17 million to refurbish the West Sussex country pile, once a private school, for boarding secondary pupils) and helps pay for small classes. It also funds mostly organic school meals and ergonomically designed chairs and tables for the children. The nursery and infants section, down the road at the Mostyn site (once a failing primary school), also boasts its own swimming pool.

Pupils do not come from the four-square, yellow-brick, Victorian homes just round the corner but mostly from the local authority flats across the busy Clapham and Brixton Roads. Some 96 per cent are black Caribbean or African, around half are eligible for free school meals, depending on the cohort, and a significant proportion live in overcrowded accommodation. Many come from single parent households. The 35 or so per cent with some sort of SEN are rarely granted statements (and thus extra support) by Lambeth. But the Durand philosophy is that 'sEN can be blown out of all proportion. Most of it is due to poor teaching and poor parenting – not an inherent intellectual problem'. So Durand gets parents involved early and keeps closely in touch.

Understandably, the children tend to come in with well below average skills, and the school's first job is to teach them to sit still, concentrate and follow directions. Many of them come from challenging backgrounds, hence a system that prioritises order, ritual and structure and gives them a sense of security. All classrooms have the same layout, lessons have the same structure, and a common marking system. Each child's performance is regularly monitored and tracked. By the time they join the junior school, nearly all can read fluently and write neatly.

At this point they are divided into forms by ability, with perhaps 12 children in the least able classes and 20 in the most able, and at least one teaching assistant in each class. 'Those who find English difficult generally have trouble with maths too, because it is often about language – they must be able to understand the words. But it doesn't really matter which group they are in because each child has a personalised learning programme. The teachers have time to sit down with each child and go through their work with them.'

Prefers to grow its own teachers and a large proportion is newly qualified – 'Many new teachers have a wonderful naivety of spirit and excitement. They tend to be very positive, receptive to learning and accepting of our structures and expectations. It is harder to get experienced teachers to fit into our ways of doing things. These may not be the only ways that work, but they're the only ways that work here.' (Most of the management team started out as NQTs here.) 'We're very clear about what we expect. We never shout and we never fight for control. The adults are the role models, and we must behave the way we like the children to behave.' The school decries the current fashion for insisting that all of every lesson must be exciting – 'We like to make work challenging and interesting, but some bits, like handwriting, spelling and times tables, are boring, and children need to learn that that's the nature of life'.

The classes we visited were characterised by calm, quiet children seated round tables getting on with their work – which was beautifully presented. Each blackboard listed the objectives of the lesson and key words. Handwriting, spelling and grammar are important here. So are targets: these are reviewed with parents three times a year, and constant feedback means that any problems are picked up very quickly. As a result, at least 90 per cent achieve level 4 in year 6 Sats, the level that shows they are ready for secondary school, and around half get to level 5, well above average. In 2013, 18 pupils reached level 6 in maths.

Everyone learns to swim in the school pools. This also helps them to learn to dress and undress – a skill many lack when they first join the school – and to listen to instructions. They start swimming at 3 years old, 'and we'll be disappointed if we don't have any children heading for the Olympics eventually'. They play sport on the Astro pitch, have PE and dance sessions in the gym and climb on the fabulous climbing frame. Parents welcome the subsidised after-school club, which runs from 3.30-6pm, with a huge range of activities from sports to languages.

In the past these bright, motivated, well-educated youngsters have moved on to a huge variety of secondary schools and many – particularly boys – have sunk without trace in more chaotic environments where working hard is not seen as cool – 'They're swamped by ill-prepared children and our children get dragged to the bottom'. No longer – to parents' huge relief, the Durand middle school for 11-13 year olds opened in 2012. In 1999 Durand took over Mostyn, a local failing primary school, turning it round within months. The site was eventually refurbished to house the Durand early years section, leaving space for the middle school in the main site. This extension enables the school to employ specialist teachers, who can teach the younger children as well. It also enables more flexibility – 'Age won't matter nearly as much, as we'll have more time with them, and we may be able to teach different ages who work at the same level together'.

In 2014 the first children should (planning and funding permitting) move on to the Durand upper school, a weekly boarding school in the Sussex countryside. Eventually Durand all-through academy should include some 1,800 children aged 3-18 (the current plan does not include a sixth form), and staff are beginning to plan a 15 year approach to learning. 'We have a blank canvas – it is a fantastic opportunity. I have visited private boarding schools, and I want our children to have the same experiences as those at Sevenoaks and Millfield. I want them to have a sense of community and belonging.' The extended boarding school day will make a profound difference – 'We'll have the space and time for them to do plenty of sport, music, art and drama. I want them to be competing in teams and to be proud of it'. The children will arrive from London on Monday mornings and return on Fridays. 'School has an immense and lasting influence. I want them to be able to say, "I went to Durand and it saved my life".'

Durham High School For Girls Junior School

Linked school: Durham High School for Girls

Farewell Hall, Durham, DH1 3TB

• Pupils: 145 girls; all day • Ages: 3-11 • C of E • Fees: £6,780-£8,010 pa • Independent

Tel: 01913 843226
Email: juniorhead@dhsfg.org.uk
Website: www.dhsfg.org.uk

Head: Since April 2013, Mrs Katherine Anderson (early fifties), previously acting head. Hasn't strayed far from Durham High: was a pupil here in the 70s and daughter followed in her footsteps; BEd from Neville's Cross Physical Education College in Durham; brief spell teaching PE at a comprehensive school then back to Durham High in 1986 as head of senior school PE. Has been here ever since, in roles including director of marketing and head of junior house. Husband, Richard, is an agricultural engineer.

Entrance: At 3+, 4+, 7+ and 10+: by age appropriate assessment; nursery: by informal assessment through play. Takes just above average ability.

Exit: Almost all to senior school.

Remarks: 'Learning is such fun here' chorused some juniors, citing activities, trips and use of role play to understand characters in reading books. Teaching, children's attitudes to learning and pupil-staff relationships praised in last inspection report. Maximum class size is 15 in key stage 1 and 20 in key stage 2, but most significantly smaller.

Rainbow Hill Nursery, attractive, large, well organised, open plan building, opposite junior classrooms and adjacent to infant school allowing smooth transition to reception. Enclosed soft play area, patio and lovely outside play area and learning environment; lots of hi tech equipment plus traditional resources – the new and the old together. Close links with parents – kept closely informed on children's progress. Average numbers 20; happy, busy, independent little tots looking adorable in tartan pinafores (to match the big girls' uniform).

Topic-led EYFS curriculum in reception continued into termly themes in year 1, though transition to more formalised learning. Setting in maths and some aspects of English from year 2; good provision of extension work for the very bright. Pupils spoke warmly of their teachers and the help they give them.

Qualified SENCo does dyslexia tests (screening of individuals in years 3-4, if needed) and gives one-to-one support outside the classroom (at a cost to parents); also specialist ESOL teacher. All needs could be catered for, apart from severe behavioural difficulties – 'These girls do very well'. Senior school girls help junior ones with reading and basic maths, top juniors with infants in the playground.

The usual sports with cross country, tag rugby and very successful cricket, coached by one of the three male teachers. Netball triumphs at county and regional level, tennis at county. Weekly swimming from year 3 at local pool with annual gala for years 5 and 6. Year 3 all learn the violin, year 4s toot on the recorder (unusual way round), year 5s sound the trumpet and year 6s sing to grade 1. Year 5 singing project with local primary schools, instrumental lessons from nursery, lots of concerts.

Strong art. Clubs include craft, chess, Christian Union, Meccano, ICT problem solving and sport. Karate, ballet, Brownies on offer at a cost. Residentials to Bamburgh and Holy Island and Low Mill activity trip, plus a variety of other local trips; school council.

House system in place throughout whole school and 'we get to join the same house as our big sisters,' one junior told us enthusiastically. Weekly celebration assembly, where pupil with the highest number of house points gets a badge and has photo on a board. De-merits the flip side, although children we spoke to could not think of one misdemeanour worthy of one.

Lots of modern fiction in the library; wide choice of healthy food with personal selection a rite of passage for the older pupils. School council meets every half term to discuss 'charity events and how to make things better'.

Infants and year 3 in attractive yellow brick building with bright, light classrooms with plenty of space, great displays and technology in evidence. Older juniors in single storey buildings, a short distance away. Science taught in junior classrooms but gifted scientists and those with an interest in science in years 5 and 6 join others from Durham primary schools each Thursday evening for Science Sparks, held in senior school laboratories.

Confident, happy and articulate girls, obviously at ease in their environment. A newcomer from a co-ed primary said, 'It's much better without boys, they chatter a lot and are boastful'! Parents value the 'very friendly, family environment' where 'the children are very welcoming and happy'; ' there's a feeling of belonging and the children look out for each other'.

Dwight School London, Lower School and Kindergarten

Linked school: Dwight School London (Upper School)

49 Woodside Avenue, London, N12 8SY

• Pupils: 150; 80 boys/70 girls • Ages: 3–11 • Fees: £5,625–£13,905 pa • Independent

Tel: 020 8920 0600
Email: admissions@dwightlondon.org
Website: www.dwightlondon.org

The Lower School Principal: Mr M Parkin BEd DipEd – has taught in the UK, USA and Indonesia.

Overall head of school: David Rose, previously head of Montgomery School in Germany and The British School of Houston, Texas, an Independent Schools inspector, chair of the London International Schools Association and an accreditation visitor for international schools.

Exit: Most go on to the upper school but a few trickle elsewhere.

Remarks: The epitome of what an international school should be about. Year groups divided into two parallel classes with an absolute maximum of 20 in each. Lots of child-inspired

batiks, pottery and art help create a vibrant atmosphere. IB principles displayed everywhere. PYP well linked with the national curriculum keeps both inspectorates happy and ensures children are well grounded. All lessons in each half of term based around one aspect of the IB curriculum. Homework important and can be done at school.

Years 2 to 6 have good sized light classrooms with washing lines displaying student work. Each child has own drawer for storage. Computers everywhere. Media resource centres instead of libraries; however individual book sections in each classroom and a well-labelled storeroom with student access. A great gym, which doubles up as the dining hall. Healthy food served from the kitchens next to it (where meals for the kindergarten are also prepared). Photos of all the year 6 prefects displayed in the passage with their personal blogs. Good music room and lovely art room. Year 2 has two classrooms in a separate building, easing the move from the nursery.

Strong emphasis on pastoral care and exceptional provision for special needs – Quest again – and good screening for dyslexia and related problems. As in the upper school, the policy is to accept a controlled number of children with learning difficulties but not those with disruptive behavioural problems. Excellent EAL provision with an enthusiastic and dedicated teacher. Children usually become fluent within a year.

Playground not huge but much use made of local park for cross country runs and scientific experiments plus compulsory swimming once a week at Trent Park. Lots of trips, visits and excursions as well. All year 6 students spend a week at an activity centre in Normandy (practising the French that they have been learning since they were 3) and some of them go on exchange to the Dwight School in New York.

Eagle House School

Linked school: Wellington College

Sandhurst, Berkshire, GU47 8PH

• Pupils: 360 boys and girls; 75 board • Ages: 3–13 • C of E
• Fees: Boarding £20,850; Day £5,850–£15,525 pa • Independent

Tel: 01344 772134
Email: info@eaglehouseschool.com
Website: www.eaglehouseschool.com

Headmaster: Since 2006, Mr Andrew Barnard BA (forties). Educated at Christ's Hospital, thence to Sheffield for a degree in archaeology (claims he 'still gets excited by a pile of earth'). 'Dabbled' in the restaurant business but was diverted to a PGCE via a stint helping out in various prep schools. Started at Eagle House as head of history and English teacher, then housemaster and head of English and drama at Heath Mount School, deputy head at Winchester House and then back to Eagle House as head. He loves poetry, especially the Liverpool poets. Favourite author? Julian Barnes. Married to Sarah, who comes from a dynasty of teachers – no doubt it is from them that she has learned to embody grace under pressure: serving lunch to the nursery children, shepherding excited girls as they mass to play a rounders match against her old school, teaching French and EAL, taking care of front of house. They have three children, all at Wellington.

The Barnards have steered Eagle House successfully though some big changes. Their initial challenge was the move to co-ed and they admit that increasing the number of girls at the top end was, initially, 'hard to crack'. Intake is now 'robust' at about 40 per cent, with the few who leave at age 11 replaced and then some by girls joining for the last two years. Next item on the list? Building. The Golden Eagle Centre, a splendid sport and performing arts centre, opened in 2013 and there's yet more construction underway: new homes for DT and art, another science lab and a food tech room.

Current rather daunting project is bidding to run a new primary academy, a younger sibling to Wellington's. Why, we wondered, does Mr Barnard want to take this on? He says he has, 'already learnt from the process', which has, 'opened his eyes'. The mutual benefits he cites are professional development for staff and 'enrichment of diversity' for pupils at both establishments. There's a gleam in his eye when he talks of these plans; he recently returned to his alma mater, Christ's Hospital, and this has further strengthened his faith in the positive impact of bridging social and educational divides.

Living on site means the boundaries between home and work are pretty porous though the Barnards say that they and their children love every minute. This notwithstanding, sanctuary is a house in the Loire and all things French.

Entrance: Parents are advised to visit and register 12 months before their child is due to start. Pre-prep: trial day and usually automatic progression to prep. Prep: trial day, copies of reports and a reference from current head. Prep is relatively non-selective but pupils are 'expected to be able to cope with the school's academic course'. Year 7 entrants are tested in English, maths and reasoning.

Exit: Majority (record three-quarters in 2013) to Wellington – this is, after all, part of the deal. Bradfield scoops up most of the rest; singles to eg Marlborough, Cranleigh, Millfield.

Remarks: Set in woods and heathland between Crowthorne and Sandhurst, Eagle House was founded in Hammersmith in 1820 and has been on its current 30-acre site since 1886. Owned by near neighbour Wellington College (the two schools share a boundary) and head says that these days, 'links are much better defined'. Being part of 'brand Wellington' includes teaching exchanges (each member of Eagle House staff is twinned with one from Wellington) as well as a definite trickle down (or up) of innovative approaches to education. For the past two years staff have attended life coaching courses at Wellington, there is a life skills club for prep pupils and now parents are snapping up taster sessions. We were particularly struck by how teachers of all ages were fired up by new ideas, welcoming change and educational debate – Eagle House clearly no place for moss gatherers.

Lessons are an hour and those we saw were well-paced and active, pupils using hands as well as heads. Although Eagle House is not an official forest school, increasing use is being made of the grounds with lessons from science to English taking place outside. History comes to life in the Tudor House, a thatched replica where children dress up and learn about the past through workshops and activity days. Creativity is boosted by evening writing workshops and there are plans for another school literary festival after the success of the first one in 2010. Setting from year 3 in English and maths, and then for French and Latin in year 6. Latin for all from year 5, Greek for scholars. Four SEN staff support pupils individually with dyslexia, dyspraxia, mild ADHD (extra charge). EAL also offered.

We hear that as pressure to gain coveted places at Wellington builds a few parents are paying for extra tuition in years 5 and 6 to prepare for pre-testing in year 7, though when exactly their children fit this in is unclear. Not a reflection on the prep's teaching, rather more indicative of the holy grail a Wellington education has become. School is alert to this, saying that a few parents have unrealistic expectations, wanting their children to be 'brilliant at everything'. Some grumbles that the scholarship class (years 7 and 8) is 'divisive', citing detrimental effects on friendships. Scholarship exams are in February and March so the children in this class are 'off on trips' while the rest are studying for CE until June.

Eagle House differs with Wellington on one thing at least: books. The clean lines of big brother's splendid new library may not be spoilt by shelves and their dusty contents but for now at least, eaglets are still encouraged to curl up on squashy sofas with a good book. 'Over my dead body' were the young librarian's words when we asked if there were plans to defect to e-readers. Long may she reign.

In keeping with the school's 'learning for life' ethos, the Golden Eagle programme of activities introduces pupils to a rich mix of experiences intended to challenge and develop interests. Clubs such as golf, orienteering and Scalextrics run in the extended lunch break – a good example of making a virtue out of a necessity since limited size of the otherwise charming wood-panelled dining room means that it takes two hours to feed everyone. A conservatory-style extension is on head's list but the courtyard memorial garden will have to relocate. Years 3 and 4 can do optional Saturday morning activities and older children also have timetabled Golden Eagle session once a week.

The Eagle House journey starts, naturally enough, in The Nest. Here in the nursery little ones (many of whom have older siblings in the prep) begin to learn through play. They are introduced to the big school and its curriculum via weekly sessions of swimming dance, music and IT. Delightful inside and outside spaces full of tempting toys, sand and water.

Pre-prep pupils gradually begin to explore the subjects that they will be taught once they move up, with specialist teachers for French, music, art and drama. Head of the pre-prep wants her pupils to have a 'happy start to school life, develop confidence and a love of learning' – we thought the kinaesthetic approach to numbers via 'maths stories' looked like a great idea. Literacy is taught using Read Write Inc phonics and the pre-prep is a model school for this scheme. No male class teachers, but music and football are taught by chaps borrowed from the prep. Dance is a popular activity and we enjoyed watching five-year-olds' imaginative evocations of tarantulas – all part of the term's rain forest topic. Apparently playing medieval games in the Tudor house and visits from a 'real, live knight' are highlights.

A trio of energetic eaglets treated us to an access all areas tour. The dorms are on the first floor of the original mock Tudor house, rooms have large windows and high ceilings. The boys' (blue) rooms were predictably unadorned but the girls' (pink) rooms were as homely and sparkly as anyone could wish. Isn't this blue/pink cliché rather at odds with the progressive educational ethos of brand Wellington, we wondered? The eaglets told us gleefully that the showers and changing rooms in the new sports centre were similarly gendered, right down to the colour of the soap! There are 70 beds – of these 50 are taken by weekly and flexi boarders. Bathrooms, corridors and common room are clean and fresh, if towards the make do and mend end of the homely spectrum. The 15 or so pupils in over the weekend (or rather Saturday evening to Sunday evening) amount to, as Mrs Barnard pointed out, a 'minibus full'. Each member of staff does a Sunday stint so we imagine that minibus must go on a very interesting range of trips.

According to our guides, hockey and football are the main sports and nearby Cranleigh is the arch rival. The trophy cabinets show that boys do well at county level hockey and cricket but it's the girls' silverware that fills the shelves. Most recently the under 13s were national champions in hockey and the under 12s in netball. Such success is certainly celebrated but the Eagle House philosophy is not 'win at all costs' and the children we spoke to got huge enjoyment from their daily sport – whatever the result. Facilities are pretty good, with standard issue multi-purpose gym and an indoor swimming pool. Outside there's Astroturf and all-weather pitches for hockey, netball and tennis, though boys told us they would like separate cricket and athletic fields. There's a lot of beautiful green space around the school but much of it belongs to venerable trees bearing preservation orders so, in the absence of a hurricane, cricketers and athletes will be sharing for many summers to come.

Music department resides in a deceptively spacious Portakabin though once inside listening to a superb impromptu performance of a Schumann Polonaise we wouldn't have cared if we were in a coal bunker. 'Brilliant' was the adjective most often used by parents to describe music at the school. Trial lessons and plenty of opportunities to develop talents great and small; lunchtime concerts allow new players to have their first experience of performing in a 'non-judgemental' environment. As we admired the beautifully decorated small organ in the charming chapel, choirmaster told us that organ lessons were just being established.

School may not have its own theatre (major productions are staged in Bracknell) but drama is big here. In the new performing arts studio we saw year 3 and 4 pupils belting out a song for their forthcoming show, not a single reluctant soul mouthing the words. On the walls of the foyer are larger than life photo canvases of past theatrical triumphs. So much for the stars, what about the tremblers in the wings? Everyone gets a chance to shine school said; parents, while praising the 'wonderful' productions, weren't quite so sure.

Art and DT departments may be eagerly anticipating move to their new premises but no sign of a reduction in creativity. In art pupils were busy learning the patient craft of stop motion animation using 'indestructible' iPads and in DT they were dreaming up designs for boats. Work of a very high standard was on display everywhere.

Pastoral care generally praised and children we spoke to had a clear understanding of anti-bullying policies and what to do if they had a problem. Every child now has their own tutor from year 5 (prior to this form teachers are first point of contact) and the new system is intended to be more 'open and flexible', involving all members of staff in pastoral roles.

Most pupils are from 15-20 mile radius but increasing numbers from London. Handful from abroad, no dominant country. Small contingent of Spanish children come for a year or two – it's not an organised thing, more 'word of mouth', according to the head. Parents, the usual Thames valley mix of management and high-tech industry professionals, like the boarding ethos even if their children are day pupils. We're not surprised, pupils can stay until 6pm and by then prep has usually been done (older children may have to finish theirs at home). For most though it's the Wellington connection that makes this a first choice school and leavers' destinations over the last few years bear this out. Several parents told us they thought the school had changed, describing it as much more 'under Wellington's thumb'. However another said, 'We initially chose Eagle House because of its links with Wellington but now realise that's only one aspect. It's a great start, wherever your child goes on to'.

Eagle House is a happy, creative school. The atmosphere is eager and unstuffy – honouring the best of prep school tradition; nimbly assimilating 21st century educational thinking. Eaglets headed for Wellington and other eyries will find this a great place to learn to fly.

Eaton House Belgravia

Linked school: Eaton House The Vale

3-5 Eaton Gate, Eaton Square, London, Sw1W 9BA

- Pupils: 230 boys, all day • Ages: 4-8 • Non-denom
- Fees: £13,320 pa • Independent

Tel: 020 7730 9343
Email: admin@eatonhouseschools.com
Website: www.eatonhouseschools.com

Headmistress: Since 1998, Miss Lucy Watts (forties) Dip Montessori. Previously taught at a co-ed Montessori prep school before joining Eaton House in 1990. She started her career as a class teacher, moving on to become head of science and deputy head and, eight years later, headmistress. A calm and efficient leader, full of energy and good humour, say parents. Over the years many strong friendships have formed and Miss Lucy has several godchildren amongst the siblings of her earlier pupils. She maintains excellent relations between staff, parents and pupils and emphasises that the Eaton House group of schools is like an extended family with all looking out for each other, working hard and respecting each other's individual roles. Still very much a hands-on head, teaching handwriting to younger children, maths to the top years and also acts as a supply teacher to cover sick leave. Her door is always open to parents and the weekly newsletter keeps everybody up to date with all the Eaton House group happenings.

Entrance: At 4+ non-selective – places are allocated on a first come first served basis with priority given to siblings, children of staff, ex-staff and old boys. Put your son's name down early – £50 for a confirmed place and £30 for a waiting list place. Deposit of a term's fees, two terms before the child starts, which is credited against your final term's fees.

Exit: At 7+ and 8+ mainly to London day schools – Westminster Under, Westminster Cathedral Choir School, Colet Court, Sussex House, St Philip's, Eaton House The Manor Prep and Wetherby. A few head off to board at Summer Fields, The Dragon, Ludgrove and the like.

Remarks: Traditional 3Rs curriculum with lots of added extras, particularly in the arts and science – the school boasts its own lab, boys enjoy potion and crystal making amongst their many experiments and discoveries. Pupils are divided into small classes, no streaming but informal sets for maths to ensure that everybody is meeting their potential and able to go at their own pace. As in the past, the school's aim is to give boys a good grounding and a full understanding in all maths and English topics, rather than rushing ahead.

No outdoor space so school days are very structured – boys are bused to Hyde or Battersea Park every day to let off steam and play sports. Swimming takes place at the Queen Mother's sports centre. Good choice of after-school and optional weekend sports clubs encourage boys to choose and try out different activities. Chess lessons for years 2 and 3. An actor visits the school to help train the boys for junior debating club. Lots of spirited music and drama, which is reflected in the many assemblies, plays and themed days, which often see teachers dressing up too. Excellent choir for ones so young, performs at a local charity events and is thought to be adorable by parents and anyone lucky enough to catch one of their performances. Five small practice rooms in the basement for young instrumentalists – boys can learn, piano, flute, violin, recorder and guitar.

Well-organised SEN supports children with specific learning differences; 'Move Fit' group is run by physiotherapists for anyone who needs to improve coordination, and touch typing tuition for year two upwards.

Mainly local clientele with many parents working in the City as bankers and lawyers, although much more international than in the past. Staff and parents have high expectations for the boys as the majority move onto academically selective prep schools. Boys are set numerous challenges, both physical and intellectual, and well trained so they become familiar with class exams in preparation for the formal 7+ and 8+ entry examinations. Miss Lucy and her staff are always on hand to advise parents about suitable choice of prep schools.

Bustling kitchen runs two lunch sittings a day; where possible the food is fresh and cooked on-site. Birthdays are special days, with boys bringing cakes or biscuits to share with friends and staff. Boys present as cheerful little chaps. School remains a popular and successful recipe for pre-preppers as ever.

Eaton House The Manor Girls' School

Linked school: Eaton House the Manor Preparatory

58 Clapham Common Northside, London, SW4 9RU

• Pupils: 130 girls • Ages: 5–11 • Fees: £13,320 pa • Independent

Tel: 020 7924 6000
Email: admin@eatonhouseschools.com
Website: www.eatonhouseschools.com/eaton-house-the-manor-girls-school.htm

Headmistress: Since 2010, Mrs Sarah Segrave (early forties) BA Ed MA, educated at Cranbrook and Durham University, where she studied education and history. Married, with two small children, daughter in the nursery, son at the pre-prep. Previously taught at and became head of the pre-prep in 2001, until she crossed the playground to become head of the new girls' school. She teaches general studies to all age groups and enjoys organising quizzes and history in action events for the girls. Cheery and practical, parents tell us it really helps that she has young children herself and is able to relate to hopes and fears.

Entrance: At 4+ non-selective – put your name down early as a waiting list operates on a first come first served basis. Occasional places in older age groups, entrance exam and a visit to the school for an assessment day.

Exit: First leavers to Roedean, Edgbaston High (scholarship), Francis Holland, JAGS, Putney High, Wimbledon High, Streatham and Clapham, St Swithuns, Queensgate.

Remarks: New, stylish, bright, architect-designed building next to the boys' school. Three floors of classrooms with a huge basement activity hall/gym and ICT room; pupils share some of the facilities with the next-door boys' school. The school opened in 2008 and has space for 140 children – one class of approximately 20 pupils in academic year group, so much smaller than the boys' school. Well balanced academic curriculum, the girls are continuously assessed and 5 – 6 year olds are screened to identify any specific learning difficulties. Part-time specialist SEN teacher and visiting occupational and speech therapists can be arranged when necessary.

Specialist subject teachers for the arts, French, science and sports. Forward thinking and gentle pastoral care, mentoring 'big sister' scheme to encourage older girls to look after younger and new pupils. Good selection of sports including all year round swimming lessons, dance classes for budding ballerinas.

Lots of lively drama and music, tuition on any instrument is available and girls produce two dramatic productions every year. Wonderful art studios accommodated in the main building give the opportunity to work with a range of different medias. Every term sees a selection of extracurricular clubs, along with an after-school homework club.

Staff, led by Mrs Segrave, have created a charming, traditional girls' school in a nurturing and relaxed atmosphere. Superb asset to the Eaton House group of schools.

Eaton House the Manor Preparatory and Pre-Preparatory Schools

Linked school: Eaton House The Vale

The Manor House, 58 Clapham Common Northside, London, SW4 9RU

• Pupils: prep 170; pre-prep 210; • Ages: Prep: 4-13; nursery 3-4.5 (co-ed) • Non-denom; • Fees: £12,795–£15,630 pa; • Independent

Tel: 020 7924 6000
Email: admin@eatonhouseschools.com
Website: www.eatonhouseschools.com

Headmaster: Prep school: since 2010, Mr Jeremy Edwards BA MA (fifties), previously head of Westminster Under and deputy head at Emanuel School, Battersea. Married to Alexa, who is managing director of her own medical public relations company. They have three children, two at senior school and the eldest at university. Mr Edwards has an MA in education management and his specialist subject is English. Reportedly, a popular teacher with the Westminster boys during his 10 year reign, so Eaton House, The Manor parents are hoping for much the same. Polite and unassuming character, always readily available to give advice and share his knowledge of educating boys with parents. Many moons ago Mr Edwards was an international oarsman and rowing coach – he remains a keen supporter of all the school's sporting events. He is a considerable catch for Eaton House.

Pre-prep: since September 2013, Mr Huw May, previously head of Sydenham High Junior School. Has also headed Roedean Junior School and St Aubyns Pre-Prep. A professional singer for several years before taking up teaching, he is also an ISI inspector,

Nursery Head: since 2004, Mrs Roosha Sue (thirties).

Entrance: Non-selective at 3+ and 4+ for the nursery and pre-prep – first come first served waiting list operates. At 8+ for the prep school internal candidates are continually assessed to ensure their suitability for the prep. External candidates sit an 8+ entry examination; academic, music, sport, art and design and all-rounder scholarships for eight-year-olds.

Exit: At 8+ small number of boys opt for country boarding schools. At 11+ a few move to London day schools – Dulwich College, City of London. Majority sit 13+ for a good mixture of traditional public schools – Eton, Harrow, Radley, Marlborough, Stowe, Winchester and Charterhouse, or day schools – Westminster, St Paul's, King's College School (Wimbledon) and Dulwich.

Remarks: The school opened in 1993 as a boys' pre-prep. Today The Manor hosts a co-ed nursery, boys' pre-prep and prep school and the most recent addition is a girls' school (see separate entry). All accommodated in an attractive Georgian manor house and its grounds in Clapham. Fortunately, the school sits on the edge of Clapham Common, which provides the ideal location for sports lessons as onsite outdoor space is limited.

The cheerful purpose-built nursery is the starting point and then onto the pre-prep. The same successful teaching methods are used as in its brother school across the Thames. Children are taught in small ability related groups within their classes. Pre-prep children also benefit from Mrs Cawthorne's magic touches, which include structured creative writing classes and the all-important but often forgotten skill of handwriting.

Most boys go on to the prep school, where they are divided into two parallel classes per year group. Latin and French are introduced in the first year of the prep; most classes are taught by subject specialists and setting for English and maths.

School can support children with mild dyslexia/dyspraxia and ASD, an area that is being developed. Full-time SENCo makes referrals as necessary and runs a small team of teachers, most of whom have specialist training.

Bright airy classrooms, decorated with delightful art displays. Exciting range of art and design classes to suit all tastes and talents, wonderful top floor studio overlooking the London skyline. Music has been developing steadily – a good orchestra, string quartets, two choirs and frequent musical assemblies. Drama classes throughout the age groups, boys perform lively plays and sketches and a musical play each summer.

Parents are invited to help with stage designs for plays, hanging art displays and listening to children read. They are also active fundraisers for the school's charity of the year and annual fete. Supervised homework club, great choice of extracurricular activities and a holiday club. Overall a strong all-round school. Parents say the approach is fairly formal but thankfully, less stuffy than it used to be.

Eaton House The Vale

Linked school: Eaton House the Manor Preparatory and Pre-Preparatory Schools

2 Elvaston Place, London, SW7 5QH

• Pupils: 80 boys and girls, all day • Ages: 3–11 • Non-denom
• Fees: £13,320 pa • Independent

Tel: 020 7584 9515
Email: admin@eatonhouseschools.com
Website: www.eatonhouseschools.com

Headmaster: Since 2008, Mr Robin Greenwood FTCL ARCM, BSc (forties) a scientist and musician. He was educated in South Africa, then London University, where he studied biological sciences. An accomplished pianist, he also studied music at Trinity College, London. Mr Greenwood taught at the Eaton House Schools before becoming headmaster of Wetherby Prep and has now returned to the fold to become headmaster of The Vale. Parents say the school is like one big family and Mr Greenwood is always on hand to discuss their child's progress.

Entrance: At 4+ non-selective entry on a first-come first-served basis. Children attending the nursery enter in the term leading up to the third birthday.

Exit: At 8+ girls to Bute House, Queens Gate and Francis Holland. Boys to Colet Court, Eaton House The Manor Prep, Fulham Prep, Westminster Under or Westminster Cathedral Choir School; occasional one to boarding school.

Remarks: The Vale is currently a coed nursery and prep school catering for 3 to 8 year old boys and girls, and which now takes girls up to 11. Traditional 3Rs curriculum with a focus

on developing every child's abilities, both academic and non-academic. No streaming and class sizes are kept small to ensure lots of individual attention.

The school occupies a large six-storey Georgian house just off Gloucester Road, complete with kitchens and a dining area. Facilities are excellent for a small school, although slightly tight. Well-stocked library, ICT room, multi-purpose hall and their own science lab. No outdoor space – pupils go for short walk during morning break and midday playtimes are held in Kensington Gardens. Two afternoons a week children go to Battersea Park with the games master for PE lessons. Pupils are introduced to around 10 different sports, including tennis, cricket and athletics, with matches, competitions and summer sports days being popular events. Exciting whole class drama and music, with around a third of the children learning an instrument, everyone performs in the regular plays and musicals.

For those with SEN, a part-time adviser organises additional support as needed by pupils. The school welcomes visiting specialists including speech and occupational therapists to support pupils with individual needs. Home/school communication is considered paramount – reading and message books are exchanged every day and five simple rules for everyone to follow to encourage thoughtfulness and sensible behaviour.

The children also benefit from being taken out to visit a variety of London sites and museums. After-school clubs include French, cookery, chess, healthy kids and lifestyles. Mr Greenwood has an open door policy for parents which helps create the nurturing and friendly atmosphere and, most importantly, yummy lunches, say the young ones.

Ecole André Malraux

Linked schools: Lycee Français Charles de Gaulle

44 Laurie Road, London, W7 1BL

• Pupils: 300 boys (137) and girls (163) • Ages: 4–11 • Fees: £5,196–£6,573 pa • Independent

Tel: 020 8578 3011
Email: contact.malraux@lyceefrancais.org.uk
Website: www.lyceefrancais.org.uk

Head: Mrs Elisabeth Dumas

Remarks: For further information see senior school, Lycee Francais Charles de Gaulle.

Ecole de South Kensington (Primary School of the Lycee Français)

Linked schools: Lycee Français Charles de Gaulle

35 Cromwell Road, London, SW7 2DG

• Pupils: 650 boys and girls, all day • Ages: 4–11 • No religious affiliation • Fees: £4,221–£6,789 pa • Independent

Tel: 020 7590 6845
Email: secretariat-eleves@lyceefrancais.org.uk
Website: www.lyceefrancais.org.uk

Head: Since September 2012, Mrs Isabelle Marlinge.

Remarks: Three outlying annexes: Ecole Charles de Gaulle-Wix on Clapham Common North Side, Ecole André Malraux in Ealing and Ecole Marie d'Olriac in Fulham.

Ecole de Wix

Linked schools: Lycee Français Charles de Gaulle

Wix's Lane, Clapham Common North Side, London, SW4 0AJ

• Pupils: 330 boys and girls, all day; • Ages: 4–11; • Fees: £4,521–£6,789 pa; • Independent

Tel: 020 7738 0287
Email: contact.wix@lyceefrancais.org.uk
Website: www.lyceefrancais.org.uk

Head: Since September 2013, Madame Françoise Zurbach.

Remarks: See senior school.

Edgbaston High School for Girls Preparatory Dept

Linked school: Edgbaston High School for Girls

Westbourne Road, Edgbaston, Birmingham, B15 3TS

• Pupils: 430 girls; all day • Ages: 2 ½–11 • Fees: £4,398–£10,113 pa • Independent

Tel: 01214 542401
Email: prep@edgbastonhigh.co.uk
Website: www.edgbastonhigh.co.uk

Headmistress: Since 2010, Mrs Sally Hartley, previously on staff in the prep department at Haberdashers' Monmouth School for Girls. Married to a teacher, she studied at the College of St Paul and St Mary, Cheltenham.

Exit: Half to senior school and half elsewhere.

Remarks: For further details see senior school entry.

Edge Grove Preparatory School

Edge Grove School, Aldenham Village, WD25 8NL

• Pupils: 360; 225 boys/135 girls, approx 45 full and flexi boarding
• Ages: 3–13 • C of E • Fees: Day £5,985–£14,400; Boarding +£3,735–£5,400 pa • Independent

Tel: 01923 855724
Email: admissions@edgegrove.com
Website: www.edgegrove.com

Headmaster: Since 2012, Ben Evans (40). A Devon lad (mother still breeds Dartmoor ponies there) with a love of all things country. Head boy at Bramdean School before heading to Exeter University to read history and archaeology. Returned, armed with his degree and PGCE, to Bramdean where he 'learned to teach,' before taking up the post of head of history at Brighton College, later returning as deputy head to his alma mater.

Had a 'now or never' moment before hot footing to Sri Lanka to teach at the junior school of the British School in Colombo, Sri Lanka, where he served a total of six years, the final four as head. Returned to the UK following the birth of his first child and found love at first sight with Edge Grove – 'exactly what I wanted,' he says. Laughingly says wealthy Sri Lankan parents provided good grounding for dealing with those of the ambitious north London variety, although parents say it is clear he is not trying to turn school into 'a typical north London hothouse.'

Lives in head's house at school with wife Alex – 'an absolute gem,' according to parents. Described as dynamic, likeable and no nonsense, she regularly rolls up her sleeves and gets stuck in in the boarding house, sorting things out 'with a deft hand,' says one mother.

Huge sighs of relief breathed by staff and parents alike at the end of Evans' first year in tenure as he appears to be there to stay, having scrapped Saturday lessons, made dramatic changes to the school day (academic subjects are now taught early in the day when the children are most alert) and really 'upped the ante' on the academic front. One parent said Evans had achieved more over the summer holidays (new adventure playground, gleaming home economics room and upgrades to textiles facilities) than they'd seen over the last three years. Just what Edge Grove needed after an unsettled patch with a revolving door of head teachers.

Entrance: Gently selective, with relaxed assessments and parental interview – 'we want parents to have chosen us for the right reasons,' says head. Little ones at 3+ and 4+ come for a short session where staff engage them in an activity and observe their skills in, for example, sharing and socialising. Currently oversubscribed for nursery and reception. Entrants at 7+ attend an assessment day and take verbal/non-verbal reasoning tests before spending a day in class to see how they fit in. 'We want the kind of children who will take advantage of all the things we have to offer,' says head.

No bursaries in the lower part of the school apart from those offered to military families. New scholarships just introduced for existing pupils in years 7 and 8 to 'acknowledge their contribution to the school.'

Exit: Exodus of some girls at 11 for selective day schools (mostly Haberdashers' Aske's and St Albans High School for Girls), with most boys and remaining girls peeling off at 13 to a broad mix of schools – in 2013 this numbered 18, with about 30 per cent to boarding at establishments including Haileybury and Harrow and the rest to a mix of day schools such as Aldenham, Berkhamsted, Habs, Merchant Taylor's, St Albans and RMS. A good handful of scholarships achieved annually, ranging from academic to sport and music. Conversations about next schools start with parents in years 5 and 6.

Remarks: When you arrive at this idyllic country prep it's hard to believe that it's just a stone's throw from north London and that the background hum is the M25. Set in grassy parkland with the requisite cows grazing next to the drive, Edge Grove – formerly the home of JP Morgan – is a world apart from many of its concrete clad urban rivals.

Smiling boys and girls (school is now 50/50 and 'firmly co-educational,' according to head) in woolly red sweaters cheerfully and proactively greet you as you walk around, giving the impression of a happy, down to earth and confident cohort. Not surprising when you see the space they have to occupy – the Tardis-like campus feels as if it could accommodate twice the number, with a huge open space for the nursery alone and separate science and art school buildings for older ones. Lovely manners abound, with classroom doors hardly opened before children leap to their feet.

Pupils and parents 'a really good mix,' according to head. About 20 per cent London based with the rest from around Radlett, St Albans, Elstree and Borehamwood and some Forces, based at Northwood. Ethnically diverse, reflecting the local area: 'wonderful,' say parents. Some discreet old money, others more flash and plenty of hard-working dual income first time buyers.

New school day structure popular with parents who say 'it just makes sense' to teach core subjects in the mornings when the children are most receptive. Activities take place either between 4 and 5pm or 5 and 6pm depending on year group and children can also stay for prep and supper, helping working parents or those further afield manage the pick-up. Saturday school abolished by current head in 2012 and replaced with voluntary Saturday attendance to take part in fun activities like music and drama or the Edge Grove Award (like a mini D of E) and stay for lunch if they wish – 'the quality of what we offer is much better now,' he says. Fleet of new iPads introduced for year 3 and up in 2013, kicking the school firmly into the 'progressive' bracket as far as technology is concerned. Class sizes capped at 20 in the pre-prep and 18 in the prep school.

Head 'aiming for excellence in all subjects.' French taught from reception and classics from year 5 with setting starting in year 3 for English and maths, then for French and science from year 5. Years 7 and 8 see pupils split into a scholarship set and two other common entrance sets. Parents talk about the 'academic rigour' being teased out of pupils on new head's watch and report a welcome increase in homework for younger ones. Mandarin, Spanish and Italian offered as after school clubs for budding linguists.

Parents praise staff mix: 'some really old school, some young and dynamic,' although concede that 'some are better than others.' Communication between parents and teaching staff is reportedly 'excellent' in the main: parents are able to email class teachers direct and, with occasional exceptions, receive prompt, useful replies. Even throw-away comments in the car park are taken seriously and actioned, said one. Whole school communication 'getting better,' according to parents, with recent introduction of weekly email letting parents know of all forthcoming fixtures and trips to help pupils be better prepared. Head, keen to iron out any bad habits inherited from predecessors, has introduced weekly staff training sessions to ensure consistent quality across the board. SEN and EAL limited to offering learning support to children with mild difficulties and no plans to increase provision.

Outstanding art taught in inspirational atelier style space with first class work in genres ranging from cubism to pupils' favourite, street art, on display. Host of shiny new sewing machines will no doubt add to pupils' textiles capabilities. Classrooms alive with sound of music: head wants 'music to be happening all the time,' and is getting his wish with over 180 peripatetic lessons each week ('brilliantly timetabled,' say parents) and a new director of music (ex Haileybury) driving musical excellence in all its forms. Choral music is 'very strong' says head and a lucky few get to try their hand in the school rock band – recently kitted out with four electric guitars, a drum kit and, most importantly, a sound-proofed practise room. Plenty for budding thespians too – year 5 recently performed A Midsummer Night's Dream in the school's grounds, with a production of Bugsy Malone another success.

Sport taken seriously for both genders with a total of around 800 fixtures a year and specialist teaching from reception. Girls benefit from the guidance of an ex-England netball coach and the school has strong links with Radlett Cricket Club. U13 six-a-side football team current national IAPS champions, with other pupils reaching county standard for cricket, archery and squash and recent introduction of international tours for top teams. For less starry types, there are plenty of inter-house matches and tournaments which are fiercely contested, so everyone gets a go. Weekly swimming lessons and galas take place in the immaculate heated outdoor pool on the site of a former beautifully walled garden, mirrored on the other side by impressively sized, albeit slightly tired, tennis courts.

Around 25 full and weekly boarders, the vast majority of whom are international or Forces children, with a total of 50 beds to accommodate flexi-boarding. Newly appointed non-teaching head of boarding (2013) has made a 'huge difference,' to what was formerly a fairly chaotic boarding function according to parents, although many agreed that there is still some way to go in terms of organisation: very little wardrobe space (one wardrobe for seven girls) and no lockers lead to lost clothes, with one parent reporting having lost up to 20 pairs of socks and others on-going problems with lost sports kit. Occasional issues with bullying and bad behaviour are 'not dealt with badly,' for the most part but parents have high hopes the 'new broom' will step up discipline and eliminate these issues altogether, to create a calmer and more nurturing boarding environment.

Bright, newly decorated dorms sleep up to eight pupils, with seniors (years 7 and 8) having their lounging and TV area incorporated into the dorm. There's also a games room in an annexe with snooker, table tennis and table football. Head, determined to avoid 'sleepover culture,' insists that boarders stay for a minimum of three nights a week from year 5, although they can stay for one in years 3 and 4, and all year 3 pupils are expected to board for at least one night during expedition week when years 4 to 8 head off site. Popular fun themed weekends twice yearly give all pupils a chance to taste boarding on a first come, first served basis.

Clubs galore – many of which are included in fees – from gardening and chess to taekwondo and war gaming. These are integrated well into the long school day and parents happily describe their children as 'very busy.' Two mini bus services ferry years 3 to 8 to school if they choose, along routes covering Hemel Hempstead, St Albans and How Wood and Totteridge, Whetstone, Barnet, Brookmans Park and Shenley.

The Edinburgh Academy Junior School

Linked school: The Edinburgh Academy

10 Arboretum Road, Edinburgh, EH3 5PL

- Pupils: 470 boys and girls • Ages: 2–11 • Non–denom
- Fees: £7,182–£8,871 pa • Independent

Tel: 01315 523690
Email: enquiriesjs@edinburghacademy.org.uk
Website: www.edinburghacademy.org.uk

Headmaster: Since 2011, Mr Gavin Calder MA PGCE SQH, previously head of Lomond Primary School from 2007. Has represented Great Britain in the Triathlon World Championships and is a keen musician.

Entrance: Primary 1 assessments held in early January. Primary 2-6 assessments can be arranged at times to suit parents – also one main assessment afternoon in late November. (Waiting lists operate where demand exceeds supply.)

Applications for nursery can be made at any time. Places formally offered in the autumn for the following school year. If space available, places also on offer during the year.

Exit: Children move on to the senior school aged 10/11, to 'Geits' (the equivalent of Primary 7 in the Scottish system).

Remarks: Co-ed since September 2007. The school roll (excluding nursery) has increased gradually since 2007 (from 270 – 350) and nursery has been full for the last few years and has a waiting list. Children from nursery get priority entrance to the junior school. Original, recently refurbished, '60s school building was extended in 1980s to house growing pupil numbers. New purpose-built home for nursery, designed by award-winning Edinburgh architect, Richard Murphy, with 100 girls and boys, two to five years. New all-weather play surface used for hockey and netball as well as children's breaktime play. Huge dining hall, with 'proper lunches for all'; staff can cater for any kind of diet and no packed lunches allowed.

School buzzes with energy and enthusiasm. Junior school in general very good – the old gang have more-or-less gone, and a new influx of whizzy young teachers gladden the eye. Maximum class sizes are 20 in primary 1 and 2, increasing to 24 for primary 3 to 6. Parallel classes throughout, though set for maths at eight. No Latin. French taught from Primary 5 and Mandarin from Primary 6. Computers and Smartboards everywhere. Art-room gratifyingly exciting and art all over the place. Ambitious music and plays, lots of games and sports hall. A small team of pupils from primary 6 won the Junior Euroquiz championship held at the Scottish Parliament, which earned them a trip to Brussels and a tour round the European parliament.

After-school club and holiday club (various holiday activities, mostly based at the sports centre) which operates every day 3-6pm during term-time and all day during the holidays, available for children from three years. Early birds' club for all – school open from 8am. Huge variety of after-school activities – sporting and non-sporting (drama, chess, bridge 'on the horizon') taken by the teachers and outside specialists.

Edinburgh Steiner School – Lower School

Linked school: Edinburgh Steiner School

60 Spylaw Road, Edinburgh, EH10 5BR

- Pupils: Girls and boys; all day • Ages: 3.5–6 • Fees: £4,440–£7,368 pa • Independent

Tel: 01313 373410
Email: admissions@edinburghsteinerschool.org.uk
Website: www.edinburghsteinerschool.org.uk

Remarks: Lower school flows seamlessly into upper – certain extra responsibilities, but essentially no change. Kindergarten has parallel classes, depending on numbers, but not divided by age. Tinies learn by copying and each has their own job – raking the gravel, doing the compost, tidying the classroom etc. Drop off at 8am. After-school club.

The Elms School

Colwall, Malvern, WR13 6EF

- Pupils: 125 girls and boys; 47 in nursery; 45 full boarders
- Ages: 3–13 • C of E • Fees: Boarding £20,565; Day £7,155–£18,870 pa • Independent

Tel: 01684 540344
Email: office@elmsschool.co.uk
Website: www.elmsschool.co.uk

Head: Since September 2010, Mr Alastair J L Thomas. Mid-thirties and married with two young daughters, the eldest of whom is in the early years department at the school. A degree in French from Kings' College, London was followed by a brief stint at John Lewis before he joined Kingshott Prep School, where he became head of French. Moved to The Downs School nearby as head of French and Latin before becoming deputy head at Lambrook in Ascot.

A very social animal, approachable and full of energy, very keen on sports and music, eager to update the facilities of the school while retaining its ethos of fresh air, muddy knees, and plenty of independence. Staff say he is 'making things happen' and in particular cite his improvements in the profile of drama and music. He says the perception of the school is that the academics need to be strengthened – something he feels is unjustified, although he accepts that facilities need to be modernised. Teaches study skills and eats breakfast and lunch in hall with the children.

Wife, Hannah, throws herself into the life at the school, especially in the gardens, which she has transformed.

Entrance: Entrance into pre-prep as early as three, regular intake at seven and eight. Most children from Herefordshire, Gloucestershire, Worcestershire, Monmouthshire and Powys. A few forces families and a handful from overseas. Entry is by assessment rather than selection, and children who are intending to board can stay the night to test the waters. No scholarships but means tested bursaries of up to 100 per cent for those 'who could benefit from what we offer'. 'We can and do get our children into leading public schools but we also support children who struggle'.

Exit: A few girls still leave at 11 but most stay on to 13. On exit the children go to a variety of schools: Malvern College, Cheltenham College, Bryanston, Radley, Heathfield, Eton, Rugby, Winchester, Wellington, lots to Shrewsbury. The school achieves a good collection of scholarships including a number for art and sport. A bright child could do very well here but it is not primarily an academic school.

Remarks: The oldest prep school in England, founded by Humphry Walwyn in 1614. Facing away from what passes for the main road in the village of Colwall, near Malvern, it opens out onto a site of 150 acres full of lovely green spaces and beautiful gardens. The school itself has rather the feeling of a collection of period houses that have grown together, sometimes in a slightly idiosyncratic manner. However, the school is much more than its academic buildings. For a start it has enviable sports facilities – including Astroturf, games field, swimming pool, a large sports hall, a stables of about 15-20 ponies (boarders can also bring their own) and a new outdoor riding arena. Sport obviously important – riding and shooting particularly so – the school has its own pistol and rifle shooting clubs. Then there is the school farm – rural studies compulsory up to and including year 7 – which boasts a prize Hereford bull as well as Gloucester old spots – walked by the children round the grounds, a large flock of hens and a rather lovely vegetable garden. Each year group has a plot in which it is expected to grow its own vegetables. The children clearly love their involvement in the farm and take pleasure and pride in it. And they all speak very highly of the food – beef, pork and eggs come from the farm when available.

Boarding and teaching accommodation require some modernisation. The boarding facilities are a little overcrowded, although homely and tidy. Every child in the prep school (not pre-prep) has a designated bed; there are rest periods after lunch every day. This means that day children can board when they want. New science facility under construction.

The children are genuinely charming, friendly, respectful but responsive, confident and very happy indeed; well motivated and thoroughly self disciplined – we saw groups working on their art, music and sports during break, all purposeful, focused and notably unsupervised – teachers within range if needed but leaving them to their own devices if not. There is an impressive new auditorium/theatre with some good music practice spaces, a beautiful new grand piano, and good sized music classroom attached at the back. A good art room too – full of innovative, varied and careful work. Parents say their children are very happy and they are keen on the new head whom they perceive as raising the academic standard of the school while retaining its ethos. They appreciate the variety of activities offered and the freedom of each child to 'be a little bit eccentric,' if they want to.

Relatively high fees fund a staff: pupil ratio of about 1:7. Academically sound with many long-serving staff who say relationships with children are excellent, respectful but friendly and that parents are extremely supportive. Two ICT rooms, a pleasant library, not much prep as Saturday school is compulsory, and most reinforcement/prep style work is done within the classroom. Traditional curriculum includes a strong classics department. Follows a policy of moving children through classes as the need appears – the school calls this the ladder system – which can mean that the brighter sparks might spend the last two years in the top class. However, it is clear that the school is sensitive to parental concerns and in reality the majority of pupils are taught within a cohort of their own age. Groups are very small and no class is larger than 13, the smallest we saw was seven. The teaching model seems to work well and certainly destinations on exit don't point to any major hiccups.

On the whole a very traditional feel – there is something of the flavour of the Famous Five about the place – which may raise the hackles of some potential parents. Boys wear cord shorts and tweed blazers, girls wear kilts and jumpers, the children go out for a walk before breakfast and have outdoor activities every afternoon. There are no mobile phones, no cash, no sweets and no straying out of the school grounds. Chapel four times a week with visits from the local vicar and Catholic pupils taken to mass once a week. There are proper napkins at mealtimes, and grace is said. Some staff keep dogs in their classrooms and there is a 'pet palace' for the children's own rabbits and other small animals. Some parents may think it too sheltered by far, others will breathe a sigh of relief when they find it.

A school which wears its differences from the mainstream with pride but which is now also taking seriously the need for some changes. With its farm, fields and outdoor ethos this is a glorious place to get muddy while you learn – and somehow it manages to preserve childhood while fostering independence.

Elstree School

Woolhampton, Reading, RG7 5TD

- Pupils: 185 boys plus 65 boys and girls in pre-prep (Home Farm); 100 boarders • Ages: 3-13 • C of E • Fees: Day £9,885–£17,775; Boarding £22,800 pa • Independent

Tel: 01189 713302
Email: registrar@elstreeschool.org.uk
Website: www.elstreeschool.org.uk

Headmaster: Since September 2013, Mr Sid Inglis (forties), previously joint head of Ludgrove. Educated at Radley and Newcastle University, he spent two years teaching English in Chile before moving to Ludgrove to teach classics in 1995. He was appointed joint head there in 2008. He is married to Olivia and they have three children,

He is passionate about sport, particularly rugby and cricket, and enjoys playing golf and fishing. He takes over after the school spent a year under an acting head, after the abrupt and unexplained resignation of the previous head, and brings with him parental hopes for stability after troubled times.

Home Farm School (the pre-prep) head, Mrs Kay Markides, arrived from St Gabriels in September 2009. Graduated in science, married with a family (including a son who attended Elstree) before deciding to train for teaching young ones. Taught for a while at another school nearby. Thrilled to be involved with Elstree, and it shows. Warm and at ease with the children ('I love them') she is clearly not only very competent but also exudes calm dependability. Presides over a talented young staff who clearly relish the company of their young charges, patiently explaining things and then rushing around with them in the grounds of the prep school.

Entrance: Non-selective. Ninety-eight per cent from the pre-prep (a significant increase on a few years ago). Boys can join at any stage, providing room in the year group, and a number of boys in years 5, 6 and 7 join from London day schools to prepare them for boarding at their public schools. 'A benign assessment' and a report from their previous schools to ensure a sensitively handled transition. Mostly local and a few from abroad, with a regular crop from Spain and Korea. Not, perhaps, as many from London as there used to be, but they're always welcome and the excellent registrar is on the case.

Exit: To eg Abingdon, Bradfield, Pangbourne, Radley, Sherborne, Tonbridge and Winchester in 2013; three scholarships, four music/academic exhibitions and one sports award.

Remarks: The Georgian house and surrounding grounds of 150 acres are elegant and beautiful without the intimidation of grandeur and pomposity. The very obvious fire escape at the front signifies the use to which the house has so effortlessly been adapted; the grounds offer exciting opportunities for building dens and generally mucking about. The bark on the giant redwoods at the front of the house is worn smooth by generations of Elstree boys who have run up the sides and delighted in the size and splendour of such magnificence. What tales those trees could tell since the school moved from Elstree, Herts, at the beginning of the war, and then wisely decided to stay put.

Inside, the hall is impressive with its intricate carvings and panelling, a delightful background for the impressive art work on display. When we arrived, boys were happily tripping along to lessons, not 'creeping like snails' but bouncy, happy and ebullient: certainly not fazed by their surroundings though, as we discovered during our tour, appreciative. Proudly they showed us the carved wooden pillar that swivels round, allegedly opening a nearby trapdoor, now nailed down; proudly they showed us the elegant and functional library with painted pillars, nothing like as big as it looks in the prospectus but terrific all the same. Elstree takes its library seriously and the delightful librarian is keen to promote the joys of reading.

Upstairs – and, yes, the boys do tear up and down the very fine staircase – brightly coloured dorms, one with a magnificent stuccoed ceiling in a vile colour – problems with inhabiting a listed building, but, nonetheless, fun to be in; an exciting rabbit warren feeling about the corridors upstairs, but 'We quickly find our way around and it's exciting to explore,' our guides told us. The old building plays an important and lively part in their lives.

Elstree is keen to maintain its boarding tradition and under the hugely energetic and hugely everything master in charge of boarding and his wife, it's hard to understand why everyone doesn't want to board all the time. A devilishly difficult putting course on the landing with local rules that defy the smoothness of the carpet, feasts and cocoa parties, socials with Downe House (very popular) – but not in the dormitories; even a lively and informative paper, The Boarding Times, with amusing insights into the joys of boarding. For anxious, nervous parents with thoughts of Tom Brown's Schooldays helpful and reassuring information published in booklets, along with one for the boys themselves.

The friendly boarding master and his charming wife, who live in the thick of it all, are responsible for the senior boys and for weekend activities, which are numerous and varied. A housemistress is in charge of the juniors and other matrons and a tutor live in. A very real atmosphere of adventure coupled with comfort, in every sense. No wonder even the curmudgeonly worded Ofsted report glows with praise. Elstree does all it can to be flexible about boarding: a number of permutations available and on Friday nights up to 110 board – not surprising. For full time boarders, indeed for every boy at Elstree, parents are encouraged to visit as often as possible and keep in contact. Boarding is not seen as separation from home – it's an extension of it.

Academically, Elstree has had many successes in the scholarship stakes and prides itself on well balanced and inspirational teaching. Of course, the main focus is on common entrance, and very seldom will a boy fail to get into his first choice school. Potential scholars are creamed off to be stretched and challenged. Those bright eyed, would-be scholars we spoke to at lunch over delicious fish and chips (it was Friday) and in the marvellously-designed dining room enthused about their intellectual aspirations without a hint of smugness, let alone arrogance, while above their heads the names of previous scholars on the honours board beckoned. A good variety of scholarships won, with music awards being particularly noticeable, along with academic awards to serious schools.

But scholarships are not pursued at the expense of those with learning difficulties. All new boys are screened and plenty of support is available with regular confidence-building being the key. Excellent teaching facilities. Bright and functional classrooms, very good ICT room with masses of terminals; computers involved in all lessons – everyone, including the top year of Home Farm, taught the skills.

Much music and good drama, with plenty of orchestras and ensembles and a very active choir. Popular geography trips to Dartmoor and trips to France. Academic involvement is treated seriously but this is no hothouse relying, as it does, on the notion that happy boys are more likely to reach their potential. Every school claims to be happy – Elstree certainly is.

A fascinating and attractive feature of the hall was an exhibition of beads, clothes and other articles sent from a school in Afghanistan with which Elstree has developed links. This includes writing to their counterparts, generally making friends and raising money. It's not a gimmick – it's for real, and the hope is that one day exchanges may be possible.

Strong, but not stifling, Christian upbringing with regular prayers and 'bible bashing' – 'It's rather fun,' said one boy. Parents are involved – a prayer group for parents, too – and speak appreciatively of the sound moral guidance given to the boys. This includes the excellent PSHE programme run by form tutors in small groups. It's not too fanciful to say that the results are visible and delightful – the boys are open, friendly and genuinely courteous, with good manners that rest like cloaks rather than straitjackets. They assured us no bullying and no shortage of people they could talk to if they were worried or upset. Interesting that a number spoke of 'the excellent ground and maintenance staff', always an indication of a happy community and, incidentally, of good management.

More than lip service is paid to leadership in its many facets. Senior boys are all given the opportunity for responsibility, whether for the discipline and happiness of a dormitory or trying to ensure that consideration and generosity abound. The Elstree award, their version of the D of E award, is very popular, with first aid courses, helping with the Home Farm pupils, site work and a number of team building activities from raft building on the lake to camping, culminating in a demanding 24 hour camp in the grounds. Also, in the holidays, an immensely popular week of camping.

All the usual games are on offer and facilities include a jumbo sports hall, a new all-weather playing area and masses of pitches. A feature of sport is that attention is paid not only to the top teams but also to everyone who wants to play – every age group, it seems, has at least five teams playing. 'I love playing against Elstree,' said a master from a rival school. 'They always play with the right attitude and are good fun to talk to at square leg.' We met a swimmer who is honing himself (modestly) for swimming in the Olympics, but no-one was making a great fuss about it, least of all the boy himself.

Not a hearty school – hobbies and clubs abound. One boy, when asked for a criticism of the school, offered the comment, 'We don't have much free time'. 'Yes, we do,' said another. 'We have 35 minutes and more on Wednesdays.' A splendid argument ensued, with all concluding that 'anything is better than being bored'. As we left, after talking to a group of young boys about to set off for a run, who told us it was fun running in the rain, we just had time to hear the master in charge say, 'Or we could play ping pong inside'. The cheering shook the redwoods – lots to cheer about at Elstree.

Later we talked with a parent who has known Elstree well, over a number of years. 'It's a very glitzy part of the country with lots of other schools around,' she said. 'We looked at several, but chose Elstree because, in our opinion, it has the freshest atmosphere. Not a whiff of arrogance, just cheerful happy boys.' Clearly, with so many other schools in the area, not everyone agrees; nonetheless, it's certainly worth checking out.

Home Farm is where the Elstree adventure begins, and what a place to start. Between the ages of 3 and 7, boys and girls are housed in a splendidly rambling old farmhouse, complete with old oak doors and unexpected fireplaces – a lovely feel about it. Very close to the farmhouse is a well-designed bright new block for the absolute tinies. Masses of child-friendly and subtly educational toys ('This is wonderful for improving their balance and giving them confidence'; 'They don't really know that they are learning to count when they're playing with this'). What looks like Macadam below the swings and slides is actually rubberised and virtually incapable of causing scratches, though a carefully controlled programme encourages investigation and adventure.

We saw (and heard) French being enjoyed, maths and stories, music and laughter – serious teaching through fun and quiet professionalism. Regular PE sessions and plenty of scope for games within the attractive walled garden, to say nothing of the larger grounds of the prep. Lovely, cosy library in the old dairy – lots of books and some computers, 'But books and reading come first'. A rolling programme of activities constantly changing, offering variety and challenge. Non-selective and recognised by the local authority as an example of best practice – 'People are sent here to see what a good school is like'. Confirmation of their belief in the school is that the local authority is going to build them a Wendy house in the adventure garden of trees, where they can play (and learn as they do so.) Happy children, happy staff. A place that makes one long to be young again. 'Impossible to fault,' said a young mum. 'The best possible start my children could have.'

Eltham College Junior School

Linked school: Eltham College

Mottingham Lane, London, SE9 4RW

• Pupils: 200 boys; all day • Ages: 7–11 • Inter-denominational
• Fees: £12,402 pa • Independent

Tel: 020 8857 3457
Email: juniors@eltham-college.org.uk
Website: www.eltham-college.org.uk

Master: Since 2010, Mr Edmund Cavendish, previously deputy head of the senior school.

Entrance: Selective and competitive. Approximately 80 boys at 7+, trying for around 40 places. Saturday activity morning in school followed by assessment by master and testing of reading, maths and language skills, in small groups. A few more spaces at 8+, so always worth retrying if 7+ doesn't work.

Exit: About 80 per cent to the senior school, usually around a quarter with scholarships. Others to mainly local schools.

Remarks: Situated in its own corner of the main school grounds, with own entrance and playing fields, here is a mini version of the senior school. Redeveloped a few years ago – when we visited then, we got the impression of lots of light, glass and bang up-to-date facilities. Great glass-roofed art and DT room, science lab with a particularly lively teacher, ICT suite where other subject lessons can also take place, well-stocked library, bright interesting-looking classrooms. Assemblies held every day in main hall – our youthful guide pointed out with glee the fact that hymn books are no longer necessary, as the words descend on a special screen. Use is also made of senior school facilities, particularly the sports hall and swimming pool, the chapel, the dining room (where the food is apparently 'yummy') and the theatre.

The usual broad curriculum with one unusual innovation: Mandarin Chinese is now taught from day one instead of French. They believe this is the way forward and that it has many, much wider, educational benefits and cross-curricular links. Certainly when we visited, the school was right into the Chinese theme.

But then it was not long after the annual China Now! day. Parents seem to have mixed views: some think it is an excellent idea and that it is what the future is about, others feel it is gimmicky and they would rather stick to European languages for now. We think it could be very good move, but only time will tell.

All boys screened for dyslexia in year 3. Class teachers and tutors are constantly on the watch for any other learning problems that might develop. Sympathetic and knowledgeable learning support co-ordinator, who parents say is 'wonderful', 'easy to talk to' and 'always available'. If a boy is not particularly good at one thing, they encourage him to shine somewhere else – 'All children have something and will find their niche somewhere'.

High quality music. Every child in years 3 and 4 learns an individual instrument, initially free of charge. Three choirs, an orchestra and several specialist groups – the variety is huge. Masses of sport, extra-curricular activities, internal and external competitions. An impressive number of trophies on display. In fencing, have been épée British School Team champions and foil runners up. Two boys selected for the England under-11 chess squad and two more played for Kent in the victorious under-9 team. Concerts, plays and lots of outings home and abroad – really should be something for everyone here. Only possible niggle is that it tends to be always the same children selected to lead and star – does this totally fit into 'giving everyone a chance to shine'?

Ease of contact seems very much the culture of both halves of the school. Good pastoral care – peer mentoring certainly helps and form teachers and tutors are always there to talk to. Any problem is usually dealt with quickly and sensibly. Boys are 'treated as individuals for both strengths and weaknesses'; 'We try to look after all the boys and give them the best experience we can'.

Eridge House School

1 Fulham Park Road, Fulham, London, SW6 4LJ

• Pupils: 200 boys and girls; all day • Ages: 3–11 • Fees: £14,160–£15,300 pa • Independent

Tel: 020 7371 9009
Email: admissions@eridgehouse.co.uk
Website: www.eridgehouse.co.uk

Headteacher: Since September 2013, Ms Pippa Hogg-Andrews (fifties), previously head of lower school at the Royal Ballet School for 10 years. BEd from Cambridge; three teenage children; likes 'beach hut life' and walking her border terrier.

Entrance: Non-selective, ie first come, first served. Number of registrations increasing as word spreads – now you need to put your child's name down at birth if you want to be sure of a place at 3 or 4. Nursery children given priority for entry at 4. Occasional places do crop up further up the school.

Exit: 2013 to a range including Godolphin and Latymer, King's College School, City of London Boys', The Hall Wimbledon, Ibstock, Lady Margaret's, Emmanuel and The Hall Wimbledon. Round hole policy rather than preparing all children for the swankiest or most academic schools – Ms Hogg-Andrews will make sure they progress to the school that best suits them; she knows the children well enough and has built up networks with a mix of London day schools and boarding schools. She says, 'Our parents are likely to want a school with a similar ethos to ours and won't want to go too far for it, but it will depend in the individual child, of course.' Parents given everything they need to inform their choice.

Remarks: The aim of founder, Mrs Waring, was to create 'a village school in the middle of Fulham'. Impossible? You'd have thought so, and she waited till she had found the right property to try out the idea. School housed in handsome former lodge to Fulham Palace, a generously-proportioned Victorian house, comfortably on a corner in leafy, residential Fulham. A modern extension makes it feel like the Tardis. Excellent multi-purpose hall where they do drama, dance, music, gym and eat freshly cooked food at lunchtime. No cramming into tiny rooms – space to move, play, feel relaxed. And that's not just inside – the former lodge must have had large and leafy gardens, as school has an extraordinary amount of space around it. An Astroturf pitch (carefully cut round mature trees) and several outdoor adventure playgrounds, thoughtfully designed to develop little arm muscles ('good for handwriting') as well as to allow their imagination to fly. Matches happen here, but they also walk two streets to Hurlingham Park with tennis, netball and athletics facilities. Few preps in this part of London could compare.

Emphasis is on providing an all-round education. The school cherry picks the best of three education systems – the Montessori (for nursery and transition), the national curriculum and the French programme. Attracts a wide international mix of pupils, particularly French. A small – but significant – number is taught a carefully planned version of the CNED by school's resident French native speaker and highly experienced teacher, which is co-ordinated into the main curriculum. All children have French twice weekly. Syllabus varied with much specialist teaching, including music, sports and dance. Lowest class has 'lots of structured play' but can run in and out of the garden at any time – plenty of fresh air had by all. Parents are not shooed off the premises at drop off as in many schools. Quite the contrary – if you watch your child's assembly you can stay for coffee, croissants and a chat afterwards. Useful after-school clubs until 4.30pm, from fencing and Mandarin to cooking and board-games.

School's prospectus states it welcomes children with SEN. Head reiterates that they would always see what they can do to accommodate special needs and would never automatically say no. All good stuff, but no evidence of much experience yet. The year 2 teacher doubles up as SENCo and has a few people on her books needing help with handwriting and organisation. Otherwise only one dyslexic pupil. Gifted and talented pupils are catered for in the whole class. Very mixed ability classes, but 'classes are small enough to be able to cater for each individual's needs,' assures school.

Children encouraged to take responsibility for each other as well as themselves. When we visited, a French boy was helping a fellow French speaker who was struggling with his English. House system fosters good relations among children in different years. On the eagerly anticipated 'House day' each term, normal lessons are off; instead everyone works together on activities – whether it be building something out of newspaper in total silence or designing a house flag. The reward: highly-coveted house points. They are big on certificates and rewards here – each week in assembly prizes are awarded for a range of achievements, eg we saw a desperately shy girl win the headteacher's award for being chatty. Everyone gets a chance to shine. One parent explained why she chose Eridge House, despite the school not being on the dinner party gossip list – 'I needed a school where my daughter would be noticed, and she is'. Sports teams are circulated so everyone gets a chance. 'Although they want to win, it's not the only important thing. We also keep a watchful eye on each of the houses to prevent one from becoming too strong in every area.'

Laughter and happiness are key – if that means allowing your daughter to wear her fairy dress over her uniform, so be it: 'The important thing is to get them running through the door in the morning'. This is not a place where you'll see ordered children filing through the school – 'We like our corridors to be filled with chatter,' says head. The focus is as much, if not more,

on how they learn rather than what they learn. Absolutely no Sats, 'But we do inform parents regularly of where their child is according to the national curriculum'. If parents want to see written evidence of how their child is doing, they are shown on-going assessment and self-assessment forms filled in by the children, with targets set by themselves as well as by their teachers. 'Some of our parents need educating,' admits school. Be prepared to be given a lump of playdough at a parents' evening and come up with bright ideas on what you might learn from it.

Many heads – and parents – claim to be against pressure early on. This is the real thing. 'We are not the soft option – there are some very academic children at the school,' asserts the head. However those who aren't will not be pushed; otherwise they risk ending up somewhere where they can't cope. All pupils come from minutes away. Many can – not all do – walk to school, so the place has a real local feel. It's a bit of a gem. Can it preserve its ethos while continuing to expand? Tough one, but if you live in Fulham and are not paranoid about league tables, it could well be for you.

ESMS (Erskine Stewart's Melville School)

Linked school: Stewart's Melville College

Queensferry Road, Edinburgh, EH4 3EZ

- Pupils: 1232 boys and girls. • Ages: 3–11; almost all day • Non-denom • Fees: Day £6,867–£8,268; Boarding £16,863–£17,352 pa • Independent

Tel: 01313 111111
Email: admissions@esmgc.com
Website: www.esms.edin.sch.uk

Headmaster: Since 1989, Mr Bryan Lewis MA (sixties and 'still bouncing'), educated at Dublin High School, followed by Trinity College, Dublin, where he read classics. Married, with three daughters, and one of our very favourite heads (we are always slightly surprised – and thrilled – to find him still here and we do like to be bear-hugged, particularly in front of a mega exodus of young. They looked slightly surprised). He first came to the senior school in 1974. As both head of the junior school and overall vice-principal of all three schools, he values the latter 'because it makes a statement that the junior school matters. Get it right by 11 and secondary is easy'. Charismatic, giggly, fun, he believes, 'Life is too important to take seriously'. The confidence, interest and evident happiness of children such as his 10 and 11 year old tour guides are the key. 'Ten per cent happier equals 10 per cent better academically,' says Mr Lewis.

Potty about drama (which is absolutely brilliant), he insists that every child who wants to should be on the stage (eight shows annually) or in one of five choirs. He expects and obtains the highest standards and is almost prouder of the life skills and tough training that these activities instil than of the outstanding achievement of SMC's Scottish rugby cup – he thinks everyone should have a chance at sport too. Describing himself as a 'benevolent dictator', he insists his staff opt into school values, ie find a way to do what's right for children, 'because it's not fair if teachers are all different'. Even so, 120 or so apply for every teaching post. His 'philosophy', that 'they will never be 10 again', 'they must dare to fail', 'you must be proud of who you are and be the best you can possibly be'. Very, very keen on children's self-esteem – 'Every child has a right to make mistakes, every child has a right to be happy'. 'Be proud to be good.' A visiting parent, knowing him as a stickler for formal good manners, likened him to the Pope when boys (actually pulling their socks up) bobbed respectfully as he passed.

Entrance: Automatic from nursery (where you should register at birth), otherwise by assessment. Oversubscribed: hugely so age 4/5; not quite so blistering further up; waiting lists throughout. Priority to siblings – as always – but occasional places available at every level. And, unlike some other independent schools, waiting lists have not disappeared during the economic turndown. From age 6 up, assessment for all, plus reports from previous school, assessment

Exit: Almost all to senior school; occasional toff may have skived off at 8 or 9 to trad prep school, but this ain't really a toffs' school even if it is on the edge of Edinburgh's New Town. Minimal trickle leave to go elsewhere, and occasional to-ing and fro-ing with other independents.

Remarks: Enormous. 1232 girls and boys in total, around 10 children means tested and on some form of financial support. Lower junior school (nursery – age 8) is based at Ravelston and upper junior school is at the Stewart's Melville College site on Queensferry Road. They remain in the junior school until the age of 11 or 12 (P7) before moving up to Stewart's Melville College for boys or The Mary Erskine School for girls.

Spread over both sites, little people don't feel quite so overwhelmed, the nursery and first three years of proper school are tucked into a corner of the Ravelston (MES) campus in stunning new purpose built classrooms with secure dedicated playgrounds for each age group, surrounded by grass (well, mostly games pitches) and mature trees. Ravelston House (described by Colin McWilliam as a swish villa in the Adam-esque manner, Alexander Keith 1790) is mainly offices and senior girls' class rooms.

Nursery: (vouchers and dry please), from age 3, based at New Ravelston. Forty 3 year olds (Snowdrops) in own rooms; joined by 80 more in four splendidly decorated rooms (well it was nearly hallowe'en) bung full of the kind of kit no child can resist. Specially trained teachers, nursery nurses; the result of lot of dosh, discussion and planning: wizard outcome including sensory quiet room – moving lights, swimming fish projected over the ceiling, soft music and seating. Parents encouraged to get involved. But 30 is still quite a big pond for little fishes to play in.

Serious wrap around care from 7.45am – 6pm. E-Plus operates throughout the year, on offer to all the junior school, and includes parent workshops. Forest School for all (and Forest School trained leaders) 'where they discover for themselves the magic of (the not really very wild) outdoors'.

School proper age 4/5; reading, writing, 'rithmatic: reading taught which ever way works best, phonics, sound recognition: glitches picked up early (if not already flagged). Every boy and girl screened and assessed annually, support either in class, small groups, workshops, or one-to-one. This is a busy academic school and for some the going may prove too tough: and, after much consultation with the parents ('we hate doing it') the odd child may be advised to go elsewhere, either to a special or a smaller school. Ed psych, head of learning support and four other qualified LS teachers work across whole school. School not afraid of any of the dys-strata, and discipline rigorous enough to cope with ADHD et al. Drop in lunch-time support; Listening Team of teachers available on rota during playtime and lunchtime to listen to children who want to chat about worries or problems. Lots of input from sixth form pupils, who help with reading and classroom support (boys are as much a part of this programme as girls). Reading time set aside for each child, each day. Spelling Bees – Scottish champions and UK runners up last year but sadly The Times decided not to run the competition this year; head still runs a very popular lunchtime Spelling Bee club – the children challenge teachers in all three schools each year, usually successfully, as well as senior pupils.

Age 6, all move to Wester Ravelston for a couple years (extra class added for 7 year olds). Five parallel classes for 5 and 6 year olds, six for 7 to 9 year olds and eight thereafter, with by which time the young will have moved to the Stewart's Melville campus with full use of all the big school facilities (except that they have their own dedicated spaces). Certain amount of setting (fluid ability groups) for maths and language with specialist teaching for the sciences and art. School majors on academics. Strong emphasis on basics: spelling, presentation; Lewis insists on fountain pens as a 'commitment to presentation skills, matching commitment to basic good manners'. Maximum class size 25, 20 for practical subjects: home economics, science, ICT. The subject-based curriculum at the top of the junior school eases the transition to senior school.

Computers all over, interactive white boards; excellent libraries: well-used open-plan library more-or-less surrounds the head's office so he can keep a beady eye. We have grown accustomed to iPads/tablets being an essential learning tool for all pupils; ESMS have issued them to all staff (steepish learning curve for some) for a year's trial. Brilliant when linked up to white boards, embarrassing if staff get it wrong and display their pathetic attempts at Scrabble or worse by mistake (we have been thus amused elsewhere).

Sport fantastic, as you would expect in the junior department of a truly great school: swimming pool, super gyms, massive games options – rugby, football (Scottish champions again, ditto cross country champions, tours all over), cricket, hockey etc, with at least 10 teams in action every Saturday, plus inspired expeditions and the like, Italy, Greece, London, skiing, annual exchange of 10 year olds with Colorado Academy. Trips cost, but funds on hand to help the less financially able, for curriculum enhancing, sport, art, rather than for jollies.

Music and drama outstanding. As ever. Stunning Tom Fleming Centre (FP, actor, broadcaster) carved out of old – rather grand, but past its sell by date – Victorian assembly room. Brilliant scheme: the architects dug down into the cellars. Original entrance to the great outside is now a delightful Romeo and Juliet balcony, floor level in the old hall, now half way up the wall. Variable seating for 800 pops up and down. Myriads of clever uses. Green room (not exactly bustling during our visit, but the detritus was there). Zillions of loos (this said with pride) and banisters of stairs down replicated exactly the existing. Wowser.

Head is a West End (of London) producer manqué. Call from London producer: crisis in London: adults needed for Evita (internal manangement foul up): round robin to parents produced the necessary quorum. (Not the same parents every night, you understand, but enough to man the chorus). Next producer call: adults and parents please. Back to London's West End again. And again in January, with junior children in three professional operas in March (which will take total appearances by junior school children in professional musicals and operas to almost 820 since 1994). Plus, of course, the odd play in the festival, at Christmas. And, as of 2013, the junior school became the choir of the Edinburgh Tattoo (a welcome respite from previous songsters). With a pool of 150, and a rolling band of 40 choristers (the mega number in order to stick to 'ealth and safety regs for kids performing at night), boys and girls sang their hearts out – and joined the throng of professionals marching off (and waving) to the massed bands at the end. As ever, the head ('very very proud, an outstanding year') produced a video and we listened to Archie singing solo. In the rain. Five choirs, four orchestras, a hefty 300 learn an instrument (£145 for 10 lessons). Fabulous art, with a great millennium staircase decorated by all the pupils.

Parents mostly first time buyers, huge amount of charity work both for and outwith the school; they have terrific contact with Malawi and have built a girls' secondary school there – it is called The Edinburgh Girls' High School and the pupils wear

Mary Erskine uniform. Secret post card charity art event follows the school open morning next month. Sounds a blast.

New build in the offing: the current somewhat basic range of junior classrooms is being demolished, with the top end of junior school moving in sequence, two years at a time, into the almost adjacent Queensway House (the white modern block on the corner of the roundabout). Architects wanted to build a 28 classroom gulag: school was horrified, with such a mass of young, they try to keep 'em in 'villages'. This is an anticipated 10/15 year operation. ESMS bought Queensway House (themselves) but as they still nominally come under the aegis of the Merchant Company Education Board, the rebuild will not entirely be self-financed.

Coaches to and from school, from all over, but only after age 8: from Dunbar, Dunfermline, Melrose and Falkirk as well as all round Edinburgh. Coach at beginning and end of school day between the two campuses, otherwise it's shanks' pony or one of the many school fleet buses. Parking now deeply restricted on school campus, each member of staff has a coloured sticker on the car which indicates which day they may not park on school grounds. We had to park in the street: but were ferried to and fro by school contracted taxi. Boarding from age 11 upwards, either full time or weekly, flexi on offer with bed and breakfast ok if space available, just under 50 quid a night, couple of segregated houses quite close to school, each house capable of holding max 30 at any one time: married couple at the helm in both. Boarding costs about nine grand a year per child more than straight school.

Strong anti-bullying programme. Every child made to feel loved – the Lewis touch again. Latest initiative, basically to be rolled out over the whole school, but started in the junior school (though we did find it with the principal later) is a nine point set of values: written everywhere: illustrated everywhere: each boy and girl must show appreciation, commitment, confidence, enthusiasm, grace, integrity, kindness, respect and responsibility. They are expected to thank everyone for everything, open doors, allow others to pass. 'Boys' behaviour has improved enormously,' said Lewis. Etiquette is important.

The unannounced HMI report a couple of years back couldn't fault the place. We rather agree.

Exeter Cathedral School

The Chantry, Palace Gate, Exeter, EX1 1HX

- Pupils: 285 boys and girls; 15 boarders • Ages: 3–13 • C of E
- Fees: Day £6,174–£10,296; Boarding + £5,712–£7,788 pa
- Independent

Tel: 01392 255298
Email: registrar@exetercs.org
Website: www.exetercs.org

Headmaster: Since 2011, Mr Stephen Yeo BMus LTCL NPQH (early fifties). A chorister at The Cathedral School, Llandaff prior to music scholarship at King's College, Taunton. Studied music at Sheffield, then at Trinity College, London. Unusual career path took him first to top-notch senior schools in Ireland. Later became head of music and creative arts at selective King Edward VI, Handsworth, followed by three years at Bedales as director of studies. Came to Exeter Cathedral School after five years as head of Lyndhurst School in Camberley, Surrey.

'School fits him like a glove,' chorus parents, who find him 'warm, approachable and down to earth'. Certainly has right credentials for this job. A mother we spoke to commented that he had been able to 'restore kudos to the choristers' whilst taking care not to create an élite. Understands what it 'feels like' to be at a prep school like this. One father praised head for 'being at every event, come rain or shine'. Has brought a welcome air of calm authority – 'school has knack of getting the right man for the job,' remarked another parent. Married to Catherine (modern languages graduate, SRN and midwife) with four sons – three of whom have already entered the family business, youngest completing his degree at Cardiff looks set to follow. Even father-in-law was a housemaster at Ackworth.

Lives above the shop in Hall House (a former archdeaconry) and throws open his capacious lounge whenever appropriate for entertaining parents and/or pupils. Puts emphasis on nurturing rather than pressurising pupils. A former lay-vicar choral in cathedral choirs at St Patrick's, Dublin, and Lichfield, Stephen Yeo oozes choral music but (he confesses) 'probably over-compensates for a lack of sportiness by supporting games to the hilt'. Very much his own man; loves campanology, cycling, walking in Ireland and along the mid-Wales coastline. Seems to know how to build a successful school, so watch this space.

Entrance: Entry to prep by interview plus taster day. Voice trials for choristers. Help available for those in genuine need. Range of top-up bursaries. Choristerships worth 25 per cent for boys and girls off tuition fee. Full academic range includes mild to moderate SENs.

Exit: Most stay to 13 to maximise on prep as opposed to junior school experience. Good cluster of music and academic scholarships – 19 in 2013. Leavers all to West Country schools, ranging from Badminton to Truro High and from Teignmouth Community College to Sherborne School for Girls.

Former pupils include 14th century theologian Boniface; more recently, bass player Orlando le Fleming; Chris Martin – lead singer of Coldplay; Hampshire CCC manager, Giles White: more play and less pray these days.

Remarks: WW2 Baedeker raid on Exeter scored a direct hit on school's previous buildings, killing the then head's daughter and forcing a temporary evacuation to Axminster. Still the huggermugger of a place it was when we last visited. ECS has since been cobbled together out of former archdeaconries and canonries, plus a post-war carbuncle of an auditorium whose days could soon be numbered. Lots of to-ing and fro-ing through security keypads for older pupils and staff alike. One of 35 choral schools in the UK, and the only independent school in Exeter to retain boarding.

Royal blue tartans and sunny sweatshirts complement the happy atmosphere of the early years section in Hall House. Safest of outside spaces includes all-weather, rubber-based and grassed play areas, as well as a hideaway section where children can at least feel unobserved. Echoes of Frances Hodgson Burnett in this lovely 'secret garden'.

Well-worn flagstones lead down to nursery and reception classes, where we watched children in small groups enjoying varied literacy and numeracy activities. Atmosphere in this area 'mirrors the home,' pre-prep head (Queensland-trained) Katie Fisher told us. She prefers to 'pick and choose' best elements of learning schemes available. Careful planning by staff, small groups and top-rate liaison with parents (no escaping pre-reading duties here) get these little ones off to a flying start. We liked the whole feel of the place: obviously warm relationships and free flow between the early years classrooms. Ground floor classrooms (years 1 to 3) have more of a sit up and take notice feel about them. We particularly liked the inviting pre-prep library and the music room. French club, music activities, swimming and PE all get under way from reception upwards. Class and individual music lessons begin from 7 years old, and a junior choir for pre-prep pupils. One year 3 boy talked to us about his recent mechanical invention (as part of a cross-curricular challenge) with the confidence of an 11-year-old. Learning support kicks in from reception if appropriate, and we saw one boy in year 1 receiving one-to-one help. By the time pupils reach year 3 two classes; these pupils spend mornings in their Hall House classroom and afternoons in The Chantry or other areas in the prep itself, which helps make the transfer at year 4 pretty seamless.

'Not a nerdy school,' affirmed the head over breakfast in the efficiently-managed if unexciting dining area. Girls and boys seemed relaxed and talked unpretentiously about everything and anything: reassuringly bling and mobile phone free whenever we saw them. Parents we met soon afterwards at an FECS (F stands for 'Friends of') coffee morning in the head's lounge purred about their offspring being 'able to take steps here they might not take elsewhere'. FECS does a lot to help the school and staff/parent relationships are genuinely warm.

A la Clockwise, we had a splendid view from the head's study of Lowryesque figures playing all manner of games in the seemingly Victorian playground (soon to be revamped as part of a pupil initiative). Adjacent Eyre House dates back to Georgian times and accommodates some 20 or so chorister and flexi-boarders. Likeable, energetic houseparents are backed up by a live-in tutor and gappers from Pembroke College, Adelaide. Boarding house provides better than basic accommodation with good recreational facilities which include a 'bistro' and games room. Pianos in the dormitories and some practice rooms allow boarders to squeeze in an after-breakfast run-through on their instruments.

School begins with daily morning worship (whole school on Mondays) in vast cathedral chapter house led by lay chaplain or by clergy (we met an enthusiastic 'missioner canon' cum mum preparing an assembly). Mix of teaching styles mirrors the 'lovely assortment' of characters in the staffroom. Children here seem to adapt themselves to very different learning environments. Food tech, DT, music and the science classes we observed were all very hands-on, whilst an impressively academic year 8 English class was stuck into the poetry of Ted Hughes. French also appears popular, and before they leave ECS pupils get to stay at Château Baudonnière for a week's activity in a French-speaking environment.

Parents we consulted are in no doubt about the high levels of pastoral and academic support children receive. 'My son enjoys doing proper homework set by teachers who actually mark it,' commented one parental escapee from a state primary. A reading culture at ECS – closure of the SPCK bookshop across the Close resulted in an unexpected upgrade for the well-stocked and properly-supervised library.

Music certainly counts for a lot, but pupils and parents insist that non-musicians are not in any way marginalised. Choir school status is icing on a rich musical cake: full orchestra, big band, choirs and ensembles with lots of concerts and performances. 'Children enjoy their music here and no-one is forced to do extra,' said one parent, whose daughter had been turned off elsewhere by too much pressure. Watching the choristers practise in the cathedral before evensong was an uplifting experience: to be 'so accomplished so young' is a rarity these days. Deputy director of music leads Devon County Junior Choir, and when we visited was away doing outreach work in North Devon primary schools.

Drama is a popular activity: recent production of Treasure Island involved large numbers and scored a hit with parents. Art is also strong, with a recent auction (including pupils' work) helping to raise £14K towards the building of Langalanga School in the Rift Valley of Kenya. Well resourced IT room is sensibly managed as a tool rather than a master – hooray.

Gifted pupils are stretched – recent top scholarships at 13+ prove the point. About 10 per cent of ECS pupils receive learning support at various levels. Two children on LS register recently obtained places at Exeter School. Range of SpLD includes dyscalculia. One boy currently receives financial help from local authority. Extraction from classes, but children don't miss academic lessons. Well-qualified, experienced LS staff get praise from parents. LSCo also teaches mainstream English. Curriculum and pastoral matters seem to be in capable hands. Welfare of choristers (whose working hours would be deemed anti-social in other places) receives special consideration. Small termly stipend paid directly to warblers goes down well.

Sport is surprisingly strong – pupils get to play plenty of other SW independents and aim is to get everyone involved somewhere. Lack of immediate playing fields has led school to use some top facilities in a traditionally sporty city. All-weather surfaces at the main university campus, other facilities at St Luke's and outside the city at Pinhoe complete the mix. Cricket is played at the county ground whilst judo, squash, swimming are all catered for. Climbing, kayaking, cross-Dartmoor walk and annual expedition add to the excitement. Teams generally punch above their weight and some pupils make regional ones.

Food not an issue, though we would have liked to see rather more imagination and variety. Hospitable houseparents invite boarders to their flat for Saturday supper. Small payment only for reliable after-school arrangements (including 'little tea') for day pupils of all ages.

Big on encouragement: willing hands will thrive here. Tradition of choral singing goes back into mists of time but ECS is much more than a choir school these days. Combination of down-to-earth parents, busy children and sometimes quirky teachers has created something distinctive and endearing.

Exeter Junior School

Linked school: Exeter School

Victoria Park Road, Exeter, EX2 4NS

• Pupils: 120 boys and 75 girls; all day • Ages: 7–11 • Fees: £9,795 pa • Independent

Tel: 01392 273679
Email: admissions@exeterschool.org.uk
Website: www.exeterschool.org.uk

Headmistress: Since 2006, Mrs Alison Turner BA (QTS) MA (forties). Educated in Essex, then read theology and education at Surrey University. Taught in east London before becoming head of a state primary in Devon. Married with three teenage children. School has grown considerably under her positive leadership. Knows her onions and the children 'inside out'. Parents told us she 'takes a genuine interest in everyone' and described her as 'phenomenal'. Involved in lots of music and church activities. Enjoys walking the dog and taking time out for holidays and picnics.

Entrance: Mainly at 7+ and 8+. Increasingly from state sector, but also from pre-prep in Exminster (many other local pre-preps have closed in recent years). Applicants may also enter at other ages where places are available. Selection is by informal assessment and report from current school.

Exit: Most to senior school at 11+. Progression to senior school is now normally seamless unless applicant has joined in year 6. A trickle go to state selectives – usually Colyton or Torquay Grammars.

Remarks: Lovely Georgian house adjacent to senior school. Recent remodelling has provided improved facilities, including four additional classrooms on first floor. School has doubled its numbers in recent years. Period architectural features lend an air of graciousness and classrooms have made good use of the generous amount of space. Pupils benefit from shared facilities with senior school (eg Astroturf, swimming pool, music school, auditorium with large stage for productions). Own multi-purpose hall. School chapel is also used regularly.

Fair degree of academic rigour (spellings, 3Rs and fairly trad subject mix), but emphasis placed increasingly on individualised learning, with IT playing an important rôle. Following a recent parental survey, less onerous homework, to allow children time to pursue outside activities in their own neighbourhoods – 'A better balance,' one parent told us. Specialist rooms (art/DT and IT suite) also on first floor and final year makes more use of whole school facilities.

Large numbers take instrumental lessons and sing in choir. Regular concerts (some for charity) and drama (recent nativity play was in French). Annual highlight involves all year 6 leavers at the end of summer term. Pupils also participate in outside music festivals and competitions. Parents like to meet informally for coffee in local cafés and support the school with practical help as well as fundraising.

Clear emphasis on making learning enjoyable – fancy dress competitions and treasure hunts go hand in hand with events like World Book Day, when children's authors come to talk to pupils. Head was even dressed as Cruella de Vil during a recent inspection (apparently no inspectors went missing afterwards). House competition includes fun challenges, like 'best flipper' on pancake day. Staff expect high standards, which are achieved by all, including those who start shakily. Junior school special educational needs coordinator provides screening and support for dyslexia and numeracy issues as required.

New entrants are assigned a buddy from year 6 who helps them through the initial stages. Traditional house system introduces element of competition across a wide range of sporting and other activities. Main sports are netball, hockey, rounders (for girls) and football, hockey, rugby, cricket (for boys). Cross country, squash and swimming for all. Surprisingly full fixture lists for older ones, and inclusive approach to participation means results are mixed. Initially unsporty children tend to catch on – 'My daughter even plays in a local hockey team now,' reported one parent. Lots of visits (a residential trip at end of year 5) and wealth of activities.

No aggro over contents of lunch boxes – school dinners are compulsory. Large playground, with specialist play coordinator who wheels out a trolleyful of exciting games equipment every breaktime. A happy, bustling school where children grow in confidence and enjoy early success.

Fairfield Preparatory School

Linked school: Loughborough High School

Leicester Road, Loughborough, LE11 2AE

• Pupils: 225 girls and 265 boys; all day • Ages: 4–11 • Non-denom • Fees: Pre-Prep £8,565; Prep £8,646 pa • Independent

Tel: 01509 215172
Email: admin@lesfairfield.org
Website: www.lesfairfield.org

Headmaster: Since January 2013 Mr Andrew Earnshaw BA NPQH, previously head of Nottingham High Junior School. Studied educational and professional primary studies with PE at Lancaster; has also worked at the British School, Saudi Arabia and was deputy head at Beeston Rylands Junior. Married to Julie; two young sons; enjoys sports including diving, skiing and snowboarding.

Entrance: The main entry portals are at 4 and 7. Four year olds are tested for 'visual and auditory discrimination, sequencing skills, dexterity and sound skills', but via games and toys, so they

'don't really know that they are being assessed'. Nobody fails, though occasionally the school feels that potential pupils are not ready for its rigours. At 7, the selection is more demanding, but the overall wish is to embrace rather than reject.

Exit: At 11, nearly all pupils go on to the senior schools with whom they have shared the overall campus, Loughborough Grammar and Loughborough High, and with which they have become familiar. Once admitted to Fairfield, pupils are guaranteed a place until year 6. 'Very occasionally' the head and staff feel that a pupil won't make the grade and parents are warned. 'It's very important to avoid unnecessary upset and disappointment. We offer help and advice and usually they go on to other independent schools nearby.' That doesn't seem to be a real issue and certainly no need to panic on a child's tenth birthday.

Remarks: Fairfield, including the pre-prep as well as the prep, is part of Loughborough Endowed Schools and though autonomous, is governed by the same body as is responsible for the two senior schools. This means they benefit from a planned building programme (the head attends all governors' meetings) as well as some of the facilities of the senior schools, sharing, for example, the stunning new music school. Music plays a large part in the lives of the pupils and over 70 per cent learn instruments.

The facilities are impressive. Buildings are centred on a handsome, early 19th century farmhouse and have been sensitively designed over the years to make a pleasing and practical ensemble. Cloister-like extensions to many of the new brick buildings reflect, unconsciously perhaps, part of the purpose behind monastic cloisters: the ability to move from room to room without getting wet, while enjoying fresh air. Superb computer facilities where students from De Montfort University look after the technical side and help pupils individually; bright, well-furnished buildings decorated with pupils' work and a rolling selection of artists' work on loan from Artworks, which is part of the local museum services; a super hall used for assemblies, where is displayed the name of the 'musician of the week'. The lighting and sound equipment is the result of generous support from the PTA, which suggests much loyalty on behalf of parents. An excellent science block – as good as many senior schools, an exciting art department and a language school where pupils learn French, Spanish and German in a way which looked exciting and fun. 'We must keep the fun in learning,' one teacher said to us, and seemed to be doing just that.

As with so much at Fairfield, provision for children with learning difficulties is thorough and carefully monitored (by SENCo). The ISI inspector found EYFS help and support outstanding. Between years 3 and 5 pupils are screened every two years and parents are kept up to date. Very few children require help but it is readily available, where necessary, on an individual basis – parents speak well of it. Support also for the gifted and talented, especially in maths and English.

The pre-prep is housed in blocks of 1960s semi-permanent classrooms (to be replaced with modern buildings) – bright, airy and homely. A feature of the teaching is the amount of support given, individually and in small groups – pupils from the senior schools often help with reading and arithmetic as part of their VSO. That extra help more than compensates for the average size of classes (20). The use of specialist teachers clearly pays dividends, and the wide variety of extracurricular activities, including mind sports such as bridge, Go and chess, all helps to broaden and deepen the educational adventure.

We were struck by the obvious respect and joy the children (from varied ethnic and social groups) revealed while playing together during break. Teachers and senior children look out for any cases of exclusion and unhappiness, as highlighted by parents. Everyone – from the head and his staff to the secretaries and splendid team preparing meals – is involved in creating a happy community which lights the touchpaper for pupils to fizz their way towards university and beyond – well worth a visit.

Falkner House

19 Brechin Place, London, SW7 4QB

• Pupils: 150 girls, all day. Plus co-ed nursery for 50. • Ages: 4–11, nursery 3–4 • Christian non-denom • Fees: £7,725–£15,450 pa • Independent

Tel: 020 7373 4501
Email: office@falknerhouse.co.uk
Website: www.falknerhouse.co.uk

Headteacher: Since 1999, Mrs Anita Griggs BA PGCE – formerly head of economics at St Paul's Girls', married to a city lawyer, four grown-up daughters, all educated at London day schools (St Paul's, Godolphin and Latymer, Francis Holland). Her mother, the flamboyant Flavia Nunes, now in her nineties, founded the school in 1954 and remains principal.

Mrs Griggs runs the school with every ounce of her boundless energy and enthusiasm. At the gate each morning, smart and focused, you can talk to her about little Molly's project on Greek heroes, share a joke or discuss a serious illness in the family. Rarely to be found in her elegant study at the top of the school, she hot-desks in the ground-floor office so that she can be in the thick of things. If you can't see her she may be unblocking a lavatory – 'I wouldn't ask anyone to do something I wouldn't do myself. It's essential that the girls understand that no one is too grand to do anything'. Unashamedly ambitious for every one of the girls, she says her hands still shake when she is opening the letters from the senior schools.

She understands pushy parents – 'I am one too'. Parents, like their daughters, should have grit and determination – help them choose the poem to learn (they have to do this every two weeks), make sure they get to their exams on time, fever or no fever. She prides herself on producing independent, 'can do', confident girls who get to where they should be going with minimum stress.

Entrance: It's as hard to get into as you'd expect when 120 girls compete for the precious 22 places. For a nursery place, put her name down at birth, but this won't guarantee you a place in the main school. Nursery children assessed along with everyone else, for an hour in groups of six with three adults – 'Above all we're looking for an ability to focus'.

Exit: 'Like the stock market,' says Mrs Griggs, 'past performance doesn't guarantee future performance,' but currently most girls are going to the top girls' schools. Many to St Paul's, Godolphin and Latymer, Queen's Gate, Putney High, Latymer Upper and Francis Holland. Some to board at, principally, Wycombe Abbey, Cheltenham Ladies' College, Downe House and St Mary's Ascot. Generally two or three academic and music scholarships won annually.

Remarks: 'If the school were a bank it would be a investment bank,' observed a parent (harking back to the days when investment banks could be trusted!). Fleet of foot, decisions are made quickly and problems dealt with immediately. Mrs Griggs is always a 'phone call away' and never afraid to tackle anything. This is a small, family-owned school, with no governing body, where red tape can be – and is – kept to a minimum (except on the important issues – girls with allergies are given a red plate at lunch). No PTA – 'I don't want alpha mothers jousting for position,' says Mrs Griggs, who will instead ask someone on the gate in the morning if they would like to organise, say, a cake-bake. Any fundraising is always for charity, never for the school – 'That's what the fees are for'. Parents find the very close, personal community where everyone knows what's happening all the time 'incredibly reassuring'.

Despite the limited space and lack of on-site playing fields they punch above their weight in sport and the netball team is currently clocking up particularly impressive results. Music is strong – lots of informal concerts which give the opportunity for girls to 'break a string on their cello and realise it's not the end of the world'; expanded art room recently re-equipped. Head girl and prefects rotated every term so that everyone gets a bit of the limelight.

All in two, joined, seven-storey Victorian houses in a quiet side street off Gloucester Road. It doesn't smell like a school: elegantly decorated, combining rich displays of girls' work alongside real and reproduced 'serious' pictures and artefacts, demonstrating the wisdom of surrounding children with good things. Good IT facilities, interactive white boards throughout, Macbooks in the classrooms and iPads for every year 5 and 6 girl, and a lovely big bay-windowed room for assemblies and dance. A small but revamped playground which backs onto the street gives them a chance to get some fresh air.

Food cooked to at least home standards – no restriction on helpings here. No bells and no rules contribute to the naturally self-policing, civilised atmosphere in the busy 'home-at-school' environment, and pupils have an engaging openness, directness and courtesy. 'We like them to have ability and oomph,' says Mrs Griggs, 'but not to be sassy or precocious.'

This school will go every inch of the mile for its girls, who are bright, articulate and responsive. A girl here will want to share her news from the weekend with the whole school in assembly, whether she found a hedgehog or her mother ran the marathon. School tells us that the few who do have SEN 'are supported to the hilt in order to keep them working happily within our fast paced curriculum'. Gifted and talented 'extended and challenged as are all our girls,' says Mrs Griggs. A complaint that their daughter was bored would be the worst possible insult. Girls cite the warm friendliness of the place and the excellence of their teachers as main assets.

Early- and late-bird systems – a godsend for working parents. Multinational clientèle, though almost entirely Londoners – even if they're 100 per cent Italian, this is their home.

The grounded, non-glitzy, mend-and-make-do values of Mrs Griggs and her staff make the school a rare gem in what can be the rather precious world of prep schools in this chic and expensive area.

Farleigh School

Red Rice, Andover, SP11 7PW

• Pupils: 430; 235 boys/195 girls; boarding 95, 49 boys/46 girls, flexi boarding 30 • Ages: 3–13 • RC • Fees: Day £4,620–£16,800 Boarding £19,680–£21,870 pa • Independent

Tel: 01264 710766
Email: office@farleighschool.co.uk
Website: www.farleighschool.com

Headmaster: Since 2004, Father Simon Everson BA Cert in theology (early fifties). Educated at Caterham School, studied theology at Leeds Collegiate and Ripon College, followed by three year certificate in theology awarded by Oxford University. An Anglican curate and vicar in London for 14 years, he moved to Hurstpierpoint College as senior chaplain in 1996. Following

F

his conversion to Catholicism, he was appointed as chaplain and teacher at Farleigh in 1999, then head five years later.

A modest, softly spoken and self-effacing man, he doesn't engage his inner salesman straight away – prospective parents take note and beware of making snap judgements. Current parents and pupils were falling over themselves to tell us how highly they rate him (one mother phoned three times) and that he is an outstanding head. Whilst watching over every aspect of his charges' development – spiritual, social, moral and academic – he endeavours to dispatch children to their senior schools as educated, fair, kind and generous human beings. Still teaches half the school each week and leads by example, setting high expectations for manners and behaviour. Positively lights up around his pupils. Firmly believes that the school is there for the whole family and encourages wholesale parental and sibling participation.

Head's wife, Gail, is involved at all levels – a qualified nurse, she works as a learning support teacher in the pre-prep, helps in the nursery, teaches swimming and organises school flowers. They have two daughters, both at senior school.

Entrance: Not selective, pupils join at all stages. In pre-prep, the majority join aged 3; a few more at 5 (mostly from local nurseries), leaving occasional places in years 1 and 2. No formal assessment in pre-prep. Most transfer to the prep, but entry is not automatic (parents are kept well informed). From year 3, pupils come from local primaries or London schools, eg Broomwood Hall, Thomas's, Newton Prep, Fulham Prep and Finton House. One-to-one assessments in reading, writing, spelling, vocabulary and maths ('get to know the child' sessions) and report from current school required.

Numbers capped at 425, therefore priority given to practising Catholics, boarders and siblings, plus children of past pupils. Usually oversubscribed. Means tested bursaries at head's discretion, 15 per cent discount to boarding children of Forces families.

Exit: Most at 13 – more than a third leave with scholarships and exhibitions: a good tally across the board, with sport and art featuring strongly, plus a healthy scattering of academic, all-rounder and music awards. Catholic schools are obviously popular, eg Downside, Ampleforth, St Mary's Ascot and St Mary's Shaftesbury, although a good number opt for local choices, eg Sherborne, Sherborne Girls', Marlborough College, King Edward VI, Winchester College and Cheltenham Ladies'. A few boys go to Eton, Radley and Harrow each year. A small number (less than five) leave at 11, mostly to senior girls' boarding schools, eg Downe House, St Swithun's and Godolphin.

Remarks: Founded in 1953 by Jocelyn Trappes-Lomax as a prep school for Catholic boys, initially based at Farleigh House, residence of the Earl of Portsmouth. Moved to its present home in 1982, a magnificent 19th century Georgian house built by General Webb. Set in 60 tranquil acres of sweeping parkland and has a landscaped arboretum (for history buffs, trees were planted in the troop formation of the Battle of Malplaquet in 1709). It's hard to believe that the A303 threads its way past just five minutes' drive from the school gates (handy for London parents).

The house has been sympathetically adapted to school life and some of its original charm remains in the elegant drawing room, used by the whole school as a common room in the evenings. Elsewhere the focus is on the modern and practical, both within the main house and without. All new buildings – including new science and food tech building – have been added to one side of the school, thereby preserving swathes of parkland on the other side and woodland to the rear.

Parents are full of praise for academic approach and achievement. One told us: 'Farleigh fulfils parents' ambitions and then some.' Children are taught by subject specialists from year 5 (French from year 2). Small class sizes – average 15. We

observed plenty of sound teaching in core subjects. Maths is set from year 4 (for all other academic subjects from year 6) and parents say teaching is 'exceptional'. Able mathematicians given extra work and compete against other schools (a pupil in year 8 was current maths champion at Dauntsey's). English is also good – 'The teacher is wonderful, really old school' – and clearly effective, as a year 7 pupil won Marlborough's poetry competition. French good and looked like huge fun. Latin taught from year 6 and plenty of it, so those needing higher levels in CE can get there. Whole school follows a course known as The Way, The Truth, The Life in RS (not limited to Catholicism).

Exam preparation for scholarships is excellent. We noticed lots of extra coaching sessions squeezed in for individual year 8 pupils in most subjects (some voluntary). Scholars also have taster sessions in Spanish and Greek. Gifted and talented group meets several times a week for extra activities, eg debating (school has won Marlborough's prep school debating competition several times). All are helped to discover how they learn best. 'Teachers go the extra mile for the children – if a child expresses an interest in something they'll use breaks to teach it,' said one parent. Another told us: 'A work ethic is instilled in year 7 and there are grades every four weeks, so any problems are picked up early.' ICT provision is quirkily good, with a room full of computers and iPads for classroom use. Well-stocked library is run by hugely enthusiastic librarian and pupils can borrow Kindles as well as books, newspapers and magazines.

Exceptional, free SEN provision provided by four members of staff with impressive qualifications (69 pupils on the register when we visited). A few Spanish nationals receive EAL tuition. No surprise that more than a dozen teachers have stayed at Farleigh for more than 10 years – 'Father Simon has created a very happy stable ...The school has a satisfied customer feel'.

Sport takes place on wide expanse of playing fields bordering the front drive of the main house. Games on four afternoons a week and matches on Wednesday and Saturday afternoons. All the usual prep school sports on offer and staff put together three or four teams at the top of the school for boys' rugby, football and cricket and girls' hockey and rounders, with many more lower down the school. 'Everyone gets a chance at sport,' says the school. Annual rugby tour to France for boys in years 7 and 8; senior girls go on hockey and netball tours. Pre-season training is free of charge. Consistently good athletics results, with around 10 children each year representing the school at the National Athletics Championships. Unusual amount of competitive tennis on the calendar, eg house tennis, internal tournaments and matches against other schools. Pupils play tennis all year, with 80 per cent having coaching in the prep school. LTA Mini Tennis Awards scheme followed to year 6 and colours also awarded.

A good range of minor extracurricular sport played on two afternoons a week, eg girls' football, golf, squash, badminton, riding and fishing. Boys who don't enjoy rugby matches can choose to play hockey. School has a large gym and full size indoor swimming pool – boarders have access all week for free swimming. The best are invited to join swim squad; also weekly aqua fit and water polo sessions. Outdoor pool amongst the trees is used in summer.

The arts are thriving – modern, bright art block (two large rooms with high ceilings for painting, ceramics etc) doubtless contributes to the healthy number of art scholarships gained by pupils, who can use it whenever they like in free time. Well-equipped DT room next door.

Music block is somewhat less spacious – rooms for individual tuition and practice either side of a single corridor, with space for ensemble rehearsals on entry. Some 300 pupils have private music lessons, with more than 60 learning more than one instrument. Singing is a popular choice and nearly 80 have voice lessons (we noticed good exam results here, with half the total number of distinctions awarded for voice). Lots of singing on the timetable, eg daily in chapel, weekly hymn practice and in class music lessons. Chapel choir is auditioned and occasionally tours abroad. Individual music lessons rotate through the timetable (year 8 pupils don't miss academic lessons) and practice timetabled for all. All the usual instruments on offer, as well as harp and bagpipes. Two further choirs, a school orchestra and rock academy, plus around 20 ensembles which rehearse weekly and perform music from jazz to chamber repertoire. Senior jazz band, The Thundering Herd, has played twice at the Edinburgh Festival. School musicians give seven big annual concerts, including a jazz dinner night. Music theory is offered as an extracurricular activity. Father Simon even makes music part of his morning assemblies, eg listening to Maria Callas.

School theatre is well equipped, with semi-professional lighting and sound and tiered seating (a good view of the stage at last). Two annual school productions include a year 8 musical (The Sound of Music, Bugsy Malone) and alternate productions by years 3 and 4 (Alice in Wonderland) or years 5 and 6 (Annie). LAMDA speech and drama lessons available and pupils can take exams if they wish. Optional creative activities include ballroom dancing, pottery and toy making.

Approximately one-third of the school boards, with flexi boarding available from year 3 up to the summer term of year 7, when families choose between day and full boarding. The majority choose to board in preparation for senior school. About 30 children stay in school every weekend and the full complement on the four 'all in' weekends every year.

Boarding provision is well organised (junior and senior dorms for boys and girls) and the house parents are 'brilliant at instilling spiritual values and manners'. Bigger rooms with more beds for the younger ones, shrinking to doubles for older children, and quite the cleanest and most orderly bathrooms we've yet to see, with a place for everything and everything in its place (possibly for our benefit, but suspect probably not). A really lovely touch is that some single rooms available for exam candidates, so they get a good night's sleep before a big day. Not a lot of room for storing personal possessions in dorms, so most clothing is stored in communal (and very tidy) cupboards and drawers, which lead into large senior common rooms with lots of home comforts, eg computers, TV, squashy sofas and toasters (healthy bowls of fruit here too).

School food is excellent, served cafeteria style in a bright, welcoming dining room. Even though we were slightly late for lunch, still plenty of choice and the food was very good, with fresh fruit on offer for pudding daily. School chef is a bit of a local hero, we gather, not least because he treats boarders to Dinner Night twice a term – pupils dress up and sit down to a themed dinner, which can be anything from Indian to Spanish. Junior boarders get the chance to cook every Friday, when they become kitchen sous chefs and prepare supper for the whole school.

Masses to do during evenings and weekends (including for day children staying late), from cub scouts, Zumba and tennis to band practice and street dance. Acres of space to play in outside, either at Fortress Farleigh (traditional play area on the edge of the woods) or deeper into the trees, where pupils are free to roam, build dens etc.

Pastoral care praised time and time again by parents, as was inclusive ethos – 'The school includes my family in their big family,' a parent said. Staff too are welcomed into the fold – all staff members (not just teachers) belong to a house. As well as fostering community spirit, head cares passionately about behaviour and standards – 'Father Simon instils good moral values... the children become self-regulating'. Pupils confirmed zero tolerance of bullying and that kindness to others is prized above intellectual prowess. Everyone is encouraged to 'look beyond themselves' by helping others, eg hosting children with severe learning difficulties in school each week, helping at a local food bank and actively supporting a charity for street children in Colombia – 'It keeps hearts large,' said a parent.

The Catholic faith is at the school's core and Sunday mass is open to all. As well as preparing for first communion and confirmation, children can go on (short) religious retreats;

an annual gathering for Patronal Feast Day. Head aims to keep faith both enjoyable and contemporary, eg interpreting the book of Genesis through Holst's The Planets. Members of other churches stress they 'never feel discriminated against for not being Catholic' and 'there is no default setting to send children to Catholic schools'. Perhaps most important is that the school's caring side ensures 'every child will leave with the sense that they have a strength ... not always the usual – it could be something unusual'.

Pre-prep housed in a super building on the fringes of the main campus and is 'beautifully run and thoughtfully managed'. Kindergarten off to one side, away from the hurly-burly. Children looked happy and engaged. Head of pre-prep made us smile by wishing aloud for more room – in fact the building is positively spacious, with four classrooms for years 1 and 2, another for reception, its own library and four separate play areas, not to mention masses of storage space for wellies, bookbags, coats and trainers.

Children in pre-prep walk to the main school for lunch and use other facilities, including the swimming pool and tennis courts. Swimming lessons and ballet timetabled for everyone all year; tennis coaching and football from year 1. After-school clubs include football, cricket, hockey, rounders and woodland games. A free violin taster group each term. French taught from year 2. Staff put on an annual summer concert, spring term production and Christmas show. Father Simon takes assembly one day a week to present children with 'good worker' certificates.

Parents are a harmonious mix of Londoners, locals and some Forces – 'There is a real mixture of people, some Sloaney and some not so; the Forces families are taken very seriously'. Lots of siblings, a few Spanish nationals and overseas British complete the mix. School escorts London-based pupils on the train to and from town on exeats and at half-term. Overseas boarders often stay with local families on exeat weekends (matrons help to coordinate arrangements). Pupils are open, honest, thoroughly genuine young people who clearly love their school and have respect and regard for each other. The fact that the Farleigh Society (old boys and girls) publishes a 25-page newsletter every year is proof that strong bonds are forged here; these often continue on through senior school and beyond.

Former pupils include Lord Stafford, Marquis of Bute, journalist Craig Brown, actor Rupert Everett, rugby player Hugh Vyvyan, TV presenter Hugh Cordey and the climber Tarka l'Herpinière.

Every so often, we visit a school which is enjoying a real purple patch and getting most things right. Parental plaudits say it more succinctly than we could – 'It hasn't sacrificed values for academic successes,' and 'They are unwavering in their advice, honest and direct.' When it comes to the head, parents can verge on the evangelical, such as, 'Father Simon is absolutely extraordinary ... on a pedestal with so many parents'. We'll let them off – were we parents here, we rather think we would say the same. Not perhaps for anyone unwilling to buy into school's ethos, but clearly most see the light, and we suspect that this outstanding prep school will become even more sought after than it already is.

Felsted Preparatory School

Linked school: Felsted School

Braintree Road, Felsted, CM6 3JL

- Pupils: 465 boys and girls; 80 boarders • Ages: 4–13 • C of E
- Fees: Day £8,085–£15,450; Boarding £19,485 pa • Independent

Tel: 01371 822610
Email: rmw@felstedprep.org
Website: www.felsted.org

Head: Since 2004, Mrs Jenny Burrett BA MEd (Cambs) (late forties). Educated at Birkenhead High School and Durham University with a degree in modern languages, which she teaches at the school. Recently completed a masters in educational leadership and school improvement. Formerly head of department and housemistress at Felsted School. Married with three children in their 20s. A larger-than-life figure, hugely popular with staff, pupils and parents alike, who works in harmony with the head of senior. Demonstrates utter dedication and enthusiasm – 'not unusual to be on the email at four in the morning' – and very much in evidence at all events. Recently spotted polishing shoes at the school gate at drop-off time. Absolute dynamo with a Cheshire cat grin and boundless energy which infects all about her. Not many at her age would cavort in a tutu, but all in the spirit of fun.

Entrance: Various entry points with big intake at 11+ when prospective pupils submit a confidential report from their previous school and undergo interview and written tests in English, maths and verbal reasoning. Scholarships and outstanding talent awards are available and some bursaries. Entry lower down less stringent but interview and reports still a must.

Exit: Nearly all move seamlessly from prep to senior, often to join older siblings. 'Caters for all types, so why look elsewhere?' Some help available for those moving outside the Felsted world, to eg Stowe, King's Canterbury and St Mary's Ascot, to follow family traditons.

Remarks: Four 'schools', which move the pupils on towards greater self-reliance, focus and specialisation. Extension lessons for very able in subjects where they have particular strengths. Personalised learning approach for SEN; strong on dyslexia; learning support pupils members of the Smart Club.

Leadership weekend for year 8 – most skill-building activities within the main school day. Football and swimming academies – regular fixtures for A-G teams in many sports. Day starts at 8.15am and finishes late, with Saturday school from 9+. Flexi-boarding from 8+ popular option. Food good. Lots of parental involvement and communication.

Feltonfleet School

Byfleet Road, Cobham, KT11 1DR

- Pupils: 385; 230 boys/155 girls; 77 boarders • Ages: 3–13
- Christian ethos • Fees: Weekly boarding £20,865; Day £10,320–£15,180 pa • Independent

Tel: 01932 862264
Email: office@feltonfleet.co.uk
Website: www.feltonfleet.co.uk

Headmaster: Since September 2012, Mr Alastair Morrison BA (late thirties), previously deputy head at Fettes College Prep School in Edinburgh. Theology degree and PGCE from Durham, married with three young daughters, who joined the school with him. Committed to preserving the holistic educational experience that Feltonfleet is proud of (academic, artistic and sporting), whilst ensuring that academic standards are high and every individual is encouraged and supported to achieve her or his potential.

Entrance: Waiting list for entry into pre-prep on a first come, first served basis – get names down early. Most join at age 7 into year 3: 18 from the pre-prep and about 30 from many feeder schools including The Rowans, Emberhurst, Glenesk, Hurlingham, Shrewsbury Lodge, Weston Green and Wimbledon Common Prep. Tested in English and maths, but it's a 'gentle approach' to pupil evaluation. Entry possible higher up as odd gaps appear – always worth a try.

Exit: Mainly at 13 after common entrance. A few leave at 11. Leavers go all over the place: St John's Leatherhead, Brighton College, Wellington, Cranleigh, St George' College Weybridge, Worth, Bradfield. In 2013, 16 scholarships, for sport, art, all rounder, academic, dance and music. One hundred per cent to first choice school.

Remarks: Family feel, love of life atmosphere, an incredibly energetic and sporty school. Suits active kids who like to be busy – as one parent says, 'Not for the child who needs stillness and downtime, as pupils are always on the go'. Has come a long way in recent years and established a premier league appeal. Demand for places very high.

Buildings centred on a large Edwardian house, hidden from view behind woodland and high fences. Centenary Building houses super-duper new library and spacious classrooms for geography, history, French and Latin, networked wireless laptops and interactive whiteboards. Lots of space outside for free play and a purpose-built treehouse provides outdoor learning area for lessons as well as play area accessed by climbing wall and fireman's pole. Well-maintained and tidy, but next to the A3, which gives a constant background hum to the otherwise peaceful surroundings.

Purpose built pre-prep department, Calvi House (recently refurbished), provides dedicated sports and dining hall plus resources area with digital learning suite, as well as landscaping of play areas and gardens. Most children still join the school at 7+ and above, though. Redevelopment of junior department under way.

Academic standards are high (recent 'excellent' rating from ISI), but a broad range of children is accepted and not a school for parents who want hothousing. Staff believe happy kids flourish – every class has circle time to help build their self-esteem. Teachers are young and friendly, though school says, 'The average age of staff is 40 – we have several wise and energetic ones too.' Progressive style of teaching – mixture of few desks facing forward and desks in circles. School reckons that a variety of different teaching styles gives children more chances of success. All-roundedness celebrated – scholarships to public schools in music, sport, art, drama and DT, as well as for academic prowess.

Average 16 children per class from year 3 upwards, when setting in English and maths begins. From year 5, teaching is by subject specialists, with setting in French (starts in the nursery and very well taught) and science. Scholarship streams in year 7. School fully supports 11+, though one isolated parental comment that 'They do as much as they can to prepare for 11+, but are limited by majority continuing to CE'. Languages strong: Spanish from year 6, year 8 scholars do some Latin and Greek. Science, ICT and DT together in a newly-refurbished building.

Pupils with moderate learning disabilities welcome. School has full-time SENCo and team of peripatetic learning support staff plus gifted and talented co-ordinator.

Music has seen a revival in recent years. Own music technology room where pupils experiment with melodies. Lots of positive changes, and loads of new music clubs including pop bands. Around 180 children learn a musical instrument. Drama also strong and taught in newly kitted out performing arts centre. Productions have been taken to the Edinburgh Festival and every department puts on a production during the academic year. Art is strong; trips organised annually to Paris, Rome or Granada with the MFL department.

Sport is an incredibly important part of a Feltonfleet child's life – new indoor 15m swimming pool, cricket nets (in large sports hall), very pricey Astroturf pitch and climbing wall, plus a .22 rifle range and loads of space for rugby, hockey, cricket etc. Matches every Wednesday for pupils in years 5-8 in school hours and Thursdays for years 3 and 4. Girls have a super games mistress who also takes on role of 'big sister'. Lots of overseas tours and national tournaments. Girls strong in netball and hockey, boys in rugby and cricket. Huge success in shooting with a boy representing England on a number of occasions.

Massive choice of clubs – pupils encouraged to be busy (one parent felt too much so). Long school day with flexible finish times. Although some pupils weekly board, flexi boarding has become increasingly popular with many pupils boarding for one, two or three nights a week. Boys and girls get along very well and mix at activity time. Dorms are cosy and homely. Boarding master and mistress have built boarding up to a very high standard and a good feeling of closeness.

Pupils are a happy, active and lively bunch. Boys outnumber girls, so 'girls get lots of opportunities to play in teams because there are fewer to choose from'. But several year groups are equally co-ed and the demand for girls' places at 11+ is very high. Some recent uniform changes have softened things up and a certain amount of individuality glimmers through.

Pupils get lots of praise and encouragement from staff. Thumbs up from the parents for the school's pastoral care – 'It's a caring, nurturing and supportive environment'. Mix of parents – lots of first time buyers and professionals, with growing number from SW London, but perceived as full of moneyed souls – the usual convoy of suburban 4x4s does little to allay this. Plenty of parking for drop off and pick up, but allow time in the morning to battle with the rush-hour congestion. School bus runs from Wimbledon, Putney and the Kingston area, with more routes arranged as need arises.

Fern Hill Primary School

Richmond Road, Kingston Upon Thames, KT2 5PE

• Pupils: 505; 320 boys/185 girls • Ages: 3-11 • Non-denom • State

Tel: 020 8247 0300
Email: info@fernhill.rbksch.org
Website: www.fernhill.kingston.sch.uk

Head: Since January 2013, Mrs Rachel Kluczynski, who came from a headship at Hampton Junior School.

Entrance: Very popular, very oversubscribed, move very close. Usual local authority admissions criteria apply, which essentially means siblings and distance. Obviously catchment varies, but always tight – anecdotally an 800m radius most recently. Due to population bulge, Kingston has had a problem with reception place numbers and the school is expanding. By September 2014 total capacity will be 630, plus the nursery still at 52. Worth staying on the waiting list as there is a trickle of mobility in the area and odd spaces do come up.

Exit: Be aware that although packed with good primaries, North Kingston is short of secondary school places – Fern Hill's linked secondary school, Grey Court in Ham, is actually in the neighbouring borough of Richmond. This was more of a problem a few years ago when Grey Court went through a difficult patch. Now things are improving, and, although not an outstanding school, Grey Court is on the up and increasing numbers of Fern Hill families are happy to move on there – say around half the year group. Others feed elsewhere into the Kingston and Richmond secondary systems. Handfuls to the much sought after places at very nearby selective Tiffin Grammar schools (NB almost everyone in North Kingston uses private tutoring to try and get to these schools) Others plunge into the private pool (some always planned to) including Kingston Grammar (co-ed), Hampton and Reeds (boys) and Lady Eleanor Holles and Surbiton High (girls). But NB – a new secondary school is being built next door to Fern Hill and will take its first year 7 in 2015, so there's hope for the future.

Remarks: A top-notch school – regularly vies with neighbouring Latchmere for unofficial 'best in borough' award. Sets high standards, has high expectations and unsurprisingly attracts high numbers of the white middle classes who abound in this area. A real community school – just be aware that the community is North Kingston, swarming with young professionals hell-bent on achieving a first class state education for their brood. After the white middle classes, largest ethnic group is Asian. School says not all is leafy and lovely in Kingston and there is some social housing around, but this accounts for a minority of the cohort.

Ofsted rates Fern Hill as 'outstanding and providing an excellent all-round education', praising pupils' achievements both academically and in terms of their personal development.

Academic standards are good – generally around half the year group achieves level 5 in maths and science Sats. School acknowledges that many of its pupils enter the school with above average skills but, even so, these results are sparkling and seemingly achieved without too much pressure placed on the children – 'The parents are probably pushier than the school', comments one mother.

There's a distinct private school feel to the place – and not just because the children are beautifully turned out in smart uniform. Everything is orderly and fairly calm, but not sterile, children all appear engaged and on-task, overall a quite traditional feel to things. Children sit in groups around tables, but for year 6 move to rows to support the sense that year 6 is a

F

special year and to ready them for their more formal secondary schools. Lots of praise for teaching staff – stable and nice mix of youth and experience, few men (but including deputy head with high parental approval rating). When staff do leave it is rarely to work at another local school. Teaching assistants everywhere (more assistants than teachers) some class-based, others working with individual children, more senior TAs leading activities such as PSHE, ICT etc.

School packs it all in via a tight timetable and has made real efforts to introduce more creative ways of learning, for example using drama to help pupils empathise with historical characters. Lots of cross-curriculum and project work helps to free up the day – eg non-fiction literacy as part of history, writing for a purpose. Teachers add breadth to the national curriculum diktats introducing supplementary topics of their choice. 'We are always looking at the curriculum and trying to find links'. 'Obviously some subjects need to be directly taught, but in other areas we can pull things together to make things less prosaic and more interesting for the children'. Homework manageable, about half an hour a week for years 3 and 4, rising to half an hour a day by year 6. School adamant that young children need a life and do have time to do other things outside school. 'Homework is not a central part of the school'. Tutoring for entrance to the Tiffin schools is huge in this area and school is reasonably relaxed about it but admits to some concern for any child who is hauled around to take lots of different entry exams.

Specialist French teacher, all pupils learn from nursery with every class having a short French lesson each week, with some language and vocabulary incorporated into the children's learning during the rest of the week. Several other teachers are confident French speakers and the long term aim is for all teachers to be able to teach French to their own classes. Also a specialist music teacher now comes in two days a week which, together with links to Kingston Music (and Arts) Service, has seen some improvements in this area – previously a little weak for this school. There is now a school choir and orchestra in which a few parents play too. Around 45 pupils have learn an instrument and each year three has an opportunity to learn strings.

Gold award for art, kite mark for PE – school takes this side of the curriculum just as seriously as the academic work.

The school has a special needs/inclusion coordinator with a team of teaching assistants and a dedicated resource, the Rainbow room. Some 60 odd pupils are on the SEN register, six with statements. These children are taught with their class as much as possible, with one-to-one or small group sessions used to support this as necessary. EAL support is available but, although some 180 pupils have English as a second language, their English is usually good. Flexible ability grouping within each class, and there is plenty of room to take small groups out for focused teaching as necessary. School has had a good reputation for picking up any problems or learning difficulties early – some parental concern over whether staff will be able to maintain this focus as school expands.

School is very keen on good manners, politeness and respect. Overall pupil behaviour and attitude is great – for the most part these children are on-side and eager to learn. They abide by 'golden rules', the breaking of which results in the loss of 'golden minutes' from playtimes. (But other times they gain – we passed children returning from the playground after a five-minute, mid-lesson 'brain break.') All the children understand the school's focus on the 6Rs – resourcefulness, resilience, reflection, responsibility, reasoning and respect – promoted around the place by Winnie the Pooh and his friends. 'We are generally very lucky that our children are well-behaved. But there are some little pickles that we need to manage, as well as looking out for the quiet ones so that they don't disappear'.

School environment enjoys all the advantages that come with having been purpose-built (co-incidentally in response to a shortfall in school places back in 1994) including wide doors and corridors and specialist toilet facilities for disabled children. Use of space is very good throughout. Classrooms are all a reasonable size, lots of outdoor activities for the tinies and separate playgrounds for nursery, infants and juniors (though again playground space at a premium as school size increases). Full-time social skills assistant on hand to encourage play and mediate where necessary. External facilities also include an environmental area and inner courtyard with amphitheatre feature.

New buildings include a sports hall, small hall and music room on the back of the school, together with alterations to the existing hall to make seven new classrooms, an art room, new special needs room and additional multi-purpose small group rooms. The field at the back of the school landscaped to include an all-weather surface, new football pitch and other playtime activities. Part of the school has become two-storey.

Great displays are all around; a lot goes on here and it is all written up, drawn, photographed, modelled, reviewed or rewarded in pen, pencil, paint, clay, crayon – you name it and it's probably up on a wall somewhere. It's not an especially tidy place, but nor is it sloppy – it's just a reflection of a busy school life.

Strong and competitive house system, busy school council with some powers and facilities all help promote positive peer groups. (Recent pupil decision was to swap the older girls and boys loos as it was felt that the boys would benefit from having an open window in their facilities. Pupil power in action.) Lots of after-school clubs, till 4.30. No other on-site before or after school care facilities, but the school does have a close association with the nearby YMCA Hawker Centre which provides breakfast and teatime clubs and will take and collect the children to and from school.

Parents feel involved, lots help and home/school communication is good. Colonised by the middle classes who are willing (and encouraged) to get fully involved in school life, the PTA is, as you would imagine, very active and well-supported. 'It's a very special place,' said a parent, 'and we all want to do our bit'. It's a secure, happy place with lots going on. Plenty of trips and visitors – everything from theatre groups to fire engines and animals. 'There's nothing boring,' said one dream pupil, 'We're always doing something fun'.

To our question, 'Any notable former pupils?' school answers positively; 'Not yet' – but you come away feeling that there certainly will be in 20 years time. You would be delighted to have this state offering on your doorstep – which is indeed where it will need to be for your child to attend.

Fettes College Preparatory School

Linked school: Fettes College

East Fettes Avenue, Edinburgh, EH4 1QX

• Pupils: 190; 100 boys/90 girls; 48 boarders • Ages: 7–12
• Fees: Boarding £21,135; Day £12,885 pa • Independent

Tel: 01313 322976
Email: prepschool@fettes.com
Website: www.fettes.com

Headmaster: Since 2003, Mr A A Edwards BA London (mid-forties). Formerly a housemaster at Gresham's School, Norfolk. Married to Jill; three sons and one young daughter. A history graduate and a talented sportsman.

Entrance: By assessment test and interview. Scholarships and bursaries available at 11+.

Exit: Virtually all to senior school – internally set exam for entry.

Remarks: With 180 pupils during the seventh year of its life, this newest addition to Scotland's prep schools is shaking other prep schools – particularly Edinburgh prep schools – rigid. In a previous incarnation this was a junior house and before that a junior school, in each case taking children from 10 (now takes from 7). Tiny classes, excellent remedial, super facilities and plumb in the centre of Edinburgh. Latin early, computers everywhere. Possible drawback would be the lack of stimulation for children spending 10 years in the same place. 'Edinburgh's best kept secret'; huge expansion on the way.

Finton House School

171 Trinity Road, London, SW17 7HL

- Pupils: 320 boys and girls, all day • Ages: 4–11 • Non-denom
- Fees: £12,345–£13,395 pa • Independent

Tel: 020 8682 0921
Email: office@fintonhouse.org.uk
Website: www.fintonhouse.org.uk

Headmaster: Since 2005, Mr Adrian Floyd BSc PGCE. Son of a prep school headmaster; teaching is in the blood. Educated largely in Oxford; post university and teacher training college, taught at Summerfields before coming to London as head of English at Tower House and then head of upper school at Newton Prep. Married to Joanna, who works in private equity; three children, two of whom are at the school. Enthusiastic, dedicated, loves the total non-selectivity. Doesn't interview parents or children prior to entry. A supporter of mixed ability classes throughout, with setting in core subjects: no streaming. Believes that the school provides the foundations for a good education and that if a teacher takes a positive attitude, children will learn what is expected of them. Popular with his pupils, he greets them all by name. Feels that the most important thing is to work with parents in order to solve any problems and that building good relationships develops trust. Very excited about the new building project. No plans, though, to expand the numbers of pupils: the idea is to improve the facilities. Parents say he is extremely approachable but not good at marketing himself, particularly when speaking to large groups of adults. Some hastened to add that he did seem to becoming more relaxed and, anyway, they preferred the informal approach. So do we. He is overall a schoolmaster, not a managing director – must be right.

Entrance: If you want the certainty of a place, get on the phone as soon as your child is born. Apart from siblings, who have priority, it is very much first come, first served. Occasional vacancies higher up when the prospective pupil will be invited to spend a day at the school to see if he/she will fit. At least three places each year for special needs children, who will be assessed to verify that the school can meet their requirements; and the head will meet the parents. Places then offered to those whose needs can be met, on a first come, first served basis. Some state funding for statemented children. One means-tested place per year available via Sally Walker Bursary, funded by relations of the much loved ex-headmistress, as well as past and present parents.

Exit: Mostly after 11+, to a wide range of schools, both boarding and day. Some, mainly boys, move on at eight. Several scholarships and exhibitions each year. Parents advised over sensible choice. Streatham & Clapham High School, Broomhead, Alleyn's and Tudor Hall have figured most on recent lists, otherwise all over, both boarding and day.

Remarks: Happy, informal, inclusive, buzzes with enthusiasm. A strong community-based school, very supportive and particularly good for those families with challenged children. Every parent we talked was full of praise, several saying that their shy, unconfident children had blossomed beyond belief. A local school which, we were told, is reflected in the friendly feel of the playground at the beginning and the end of the day: 'It is full of relaxed, chatty parents, and we go on chatting even after the children have all gone into school.' Emphasis on inclusion, individuality and results without pressure make this a very special school.

The teaching staff are a great strength. Loyal and imaginative, some have been at the school since it started, in the mid-80s, and some have been away, had children and come back. Others are ex-pupils returning to relive happy memories. The rest just love the school. 'The ethos is wonderful.' 'I intend to teach here as long as I possibly can.' With half of the full-time staff over 40 and a third of them having been at the school for over 10 years, experience and continuity prevail. One parent talked about 'the same old projects, there's not enough change'. Sometimes the proven old is better than the new. Certainly these teachers seem to know and understand their pupils. From one parent of a special needs child: 'I can't describe how amazing they are; the care and support they give is unrivalled'. Another said, 'They quickly picked up on my child's shyness with adults; she is now much more confident'.

The teaching standard is high and the curriculum broad. We've been told that there's something special about the way Finton teachers operate, through relaxed, informal, but focused, learning. It does seem to work: we didn't see an unhappy child anywhere. Less homework than at most other schools yet all 11 year olds seem to get into their first choice of senior school. The children said: 'Everyone's kind and if you get something wrong, no-one laughs', 'Teachers are your friends', 'No matter who you are you are never treated differently'.

Four articulate, happy, enthusiastic year 6 pupils took us proudly round their school, across the playground to the reception block where three mixed classes experience 'fun learning'. 'We love reading stories to them'. There certainly seemed to be a lot going on. They pointed out the lift, 'which is only used sometimes', and embarked upon a straightforward and informed discussion about how some of their friends needed extra help. Then back across to the classrooms, in the main building. Two staircases, well decorated with projects and pictures, led to smallish classrooms, containing happy-looking children sitting round tables (in year 1) and at desks (in years 2-6). Interactive whiteboards, used imaginatively, everywhere. We saw everything: the well-stocked library which they are all taught to use properly in weekly lessons, the DT room full of fascinating projects, the lovely, light art room, the rather warm ICT room, the science room; it would appear they have all they need and creations abound. Eager children pointed out their favourites. Back on the ground floor, lunch is prepared in their on-site kitchen – suitable choices for all and staff on hand to make sure everyone eats a balanced meal. 'There's always something I like,' said one of our guides and the others nodded in agreement.

'This is our fantastic music block,' one of them announced as we crossed the playground again. A third of pupils in years 3-6 learn an instrument (brass, woodwind, piano). Lessons are timetabled on a rotational basis during the school day and there are special sessions for choirs and music groups. Individual practice is done at home. Most children take part in a number of concerts, in school and externally. Art and drama also hit a high note. Not long ago, nine pupils had their pictures selected for the Royal College of Art's 'Young Artist' competition and their work was put on public display. Small plays are put on in the school hall, larger productions down the road in the nearby church hall, or at a local theatre. We were lucky enough to see a year 1 play, specially written with lots of songs. What fun they all had, and how well they performed. Brand new specialist teaching rooms for music, DT and science in an innovative basement unit under the playground, plus new learning support building, enlarged classrooms and new playground.

Lots of sport, both compulsory and in after-school clubs. Matches played against all the local schools – appear to win pretty often, which says a lot for a small school. Currently the local swimming champions. A wide range of after-school clubs, sporting and creative, in which children are encouraged to take part. Wide choice which varies from term to term. 'We even have an early morning running club. The reward is hot chocolate back at school!'

Not an SEN school, but some places reserved for a wide range of educationally-challenged children: Finton House is committed to making sure that pupils of all abilities have their individual needs addressed. All children monitored from the start to see if extra help needed. Deputy head also head of special needs; her team includes a SENCo, a learning support co-ordinator, a speech and language therapist, an occupational therapist and seven learning support teachers. So there is plenty of help on hand for one-to-one support when necessary. Many opportunities for children to be taught individually or in small groups as 20 teaching assistants also on hand. 'The key is flexibility and the full classroom integration of all children.' Special one-to-one sessions charged extra but otherwise all is included.

Foremarke Hall (Repton Preparatory School)

Linked school: Repton School

Milton, Derby, DE65 6EJ

• Pupils: 400 boys and girls; 50 boarders • Ages: 3–13 • C of E, other faiths welcome • Fees: Day £7,875–£15,237; Boarding £20,235 pa • Independent

Tel: 01283 707100
Email: registrar@foremarke.org.uk
Website: www.foremarke.org.uk

Headmaster: Since 2011, Mr Richard Merriman, previously headmaster of Birchfield School, co-ed prep near Wolverhampton.

Entrance: Youngest need only enrol for pre-prep and attend for day visit before starting. Virtually all pre-prep children progress through to prep. From age of 7, prospective pupils are assessed in English and maths. School takes 'broad range of ability', although keeps sights on Repton's academic requirements. When it comes to special educational needs, school says it takes a 'thoughtful and sensitive approach' and each case is decided on individual basis.

Exit: At 13 around 90 per cent go on to Repton. Others leave for schools like Denstone College, Radley, Rugby, Eton, Oundle, Abbotsholme and Cheltenham Ladies'. Foremarke is officially Repton's prep school, but pupils bound for Repton must still take common entrance or scholarship exams to get there – level playing field for all. Brightest children go into scholarship class for more intense tuition and school regularly wins a clutch of awards.

Remarks: Foremarke Hall's setting has the real 'wow' factor, with long drive sweeping up to stunning 18th Century Palladian mansion in the wilds of Derbyshire. Once a grand country house, it later became a WW1 hospital, then a WW2 cadet training unit and finally, in 1947, a school. Grounds stretch as far as the eye can see (55 acres in all) and are a fabulous mix of woodlands, walks, sports pitches and even a lake. Plenty of room, as we said last time, to stretch legs, lungs and imagination. Head of history told us that when he arrived for his interview he gazed in wonder at the grounds and thought 'can I really be this lucky?' He certainly could.

High proportion of staff live on school site. Major £6 million building programme (following close consultation with English Heritage) has seen revamped music facilities, new classrooms and new art and DT block. Aside from the main house, a very mixed bag of buildings, from ancient to modern. One of the newest is the light and airy pre-prep. Facilities include library, computer room and ultra-posh cloakrooms that have lights and water activated by sensor – so no floods! Pre-prep very keen on Forest School approach, with all children spending an hour and a half in the woods every other week, building dens, counting leaves etc. Nursery children eat lunch in pre-prep hall but reception classes, year 1s and year 2s walk across to prep's dining hall with their teachers. Whilst pre-prep day finishes at 3.45pm children can enrol for activities till 6pm. Staying for pre-prep activities costs extra but it's a boon for working parents.

The school is busy, busy, busy. The school day consists of 12 25-minute lessons, with one of the loudest bells we've heard in a long time signalling the end of each class. From year 3 day pupils can either go home at 4pm or stay on till 5pm or 6pm for activities, tea and supervised prep. School offers French from year 1 and Latin from year 5. Setting by ability for maths, English and French from year 5. Pupils in upper school (years 5 to 8) taught by subject specialists. One-to-one and group support is available for those who need it. Three learning support teachers on prep staff and four learning support assistants.

Lower school (years 3 and 4) and upper school are in own self-contained areas. Average class sizes of around 16 and none larger than 20. Saturday school for year 5s upwards but year 3s and 4s can sign up for Foremarke Plus, a Saturday morning activity programme with pursuits like film-making, swimming, football, hockey on offer. Large, well-stocked library, both print and electronic. All computers on school network for security. Children's work (academic and art) on display everywhere you look.

The 180-seat theatre, with fold-back seating and large stage, in constant use for music and drama. Music is key to Foremarke life, with loads of concerts, competitions and choir trips. Several current pupils are members of the National Children's Orchestra and National Youth Choir. When we arrived a visiting string quartet was encouraging young violinists in grand, high-ceilinged entrance hall.

Foremarke is a very sporty school and teachers reckon sport is 'an integral part' of the school. In recent years, pupils have won national football, hockey and rounders trophies, and cricket, netball, swimming and fencing are all strong too. Large sports hall, football and hockey pitches, Astro, hard courts and 25m indoor swimming pool used all year round. Sport for all philosophy, with dedicated games staff supplemented by academic teachers. Extras include sailing, canoeing, horse riding, dance and golf.

School also rightfully proud of its Greenpower programme – run by the go-ahead DT department, year 7 and 8 members of school's engineering club design and build their own electric cars and Foremarke's Racing F-24 team (supported by parents) competes all over country in them. Autumn term starts with outdoor pursuits trips for years 5 to 8 – camping, team-building exercises etc. Outdoor pursuits instructors on most recent trip so impressed by the children's energy and enthusiasm that one said, 'I've never seen a group of children who are so up for it.' To which a Foremarke teacher replied: 'What do you expect? They're Foremarke, for goodness sake!'

Around 60 per cent boys, 40 per cent girls. Day pupils come from 20 mile radius (one or two from as far as Solihull and Sutton Coldfield – quite a trek). Parents a mix of local business people, farmers and some from county set too. A few boarders from abroad, including three Russian orphans who come to Foremarke for a year, financed by the Foremarke Trust (set up by former head Richard Theobald).

Boarders live in one of four boarding houses – two for boys, one for girls and one for flexi boarders, who can book in for certain days every term or on an ad hoc basis. Some even do 'home and away' boarding, going home on Wednesday nights but boarding the rest of the week. The boys' boarding houses and flexi boarding house are all part of the main school building but the girls are housed in a converted stable block. Dorms range from two to eight pupils and houses are run by houseparents, mostly with young children of their own. Family atmosphere, with houseparents testing children on Latin vocab and serving 'M-n-B' (milk and biscuits) before lights out. Youngest in bed by 8pm, then quiet reading for 20 minutes, year 8s in bed by 9.10pm and lights out at 9.30pm. Loads of organised activities for boarders – swimming, dodgeball, craft, gardening etc, but in summer they're off riding bikes and playing in the woods. Weekends a whirl of action too – anything from 30 to 50 boarders most Saturday and Sunday nights.

Pastoral care excellent. Anti-bullying policy clearly stated in school's invaluable 'blue book', which lists everything from Foremarke's sports code for pupils (and parents!) to the school's daily routine. Assemblies held three mornings a week and a weekend service for boarders at nearby St Saviour's Church or in school. Day pupils aren't allowed to bring in electronic games, but boarders can use iPods and mobiles (no internet-enabled phones, though) in their free time. Games rooms for boarders equipped with Wii, table football etc and computers for boarders to email home. Overseas boarders are now allowed to use Skype to talk to their families (a suggestion made by the boarders' council and agreed by staff).

No prefects or head boy/head girl system. Instead children apply for and are interviewed for specific roles – pre-prep, assembly, music helpers etc. Badges for academic excellence awarded too.

Parents kept informed of children's progress with face-to-face meetings and termly reports giving grades for effort and attainment. Weekly Foremarke Flyer newsletter keeps parents updated on everything from drama productions to sports results. Parents' group, Friends of Foremarke, runs regular social get-togethers.

Foremarke allows pupils the time (and space – acres of it) to grow up in their own time. Pupils are encouraged to have a go at the myriad of activities on offer, whilst being supported and nurtured throughout. As the head of boarding told us: 'It's a great place for children who like doing things and being busy'.

Forest Preparatory School

Linked school: Forest School

College Place, London, E17 3PY

• Pupils: 270 boys and girls • Ages: 4-11 • Anglican Foundation
• Fees: £10,200–£11,829 pa • Independent

Tel: 020 8520 1744
Email: prep@forest.org.uk
Website: www.forest.org.uk

Head: Since 2012, Mr Andrew Noakes MA Education, Open University (late thirties). Previously head of Northampton Junior School. Studied at Reed's, Surrey, then De Montfort, where he read European studies and French. Entered teaching later after working in education for a few years. He trained at St George's College before landing his first teaching job at Parkside and Bedford Modern Junior School. Described as 'calm and unflappable', he is married to a teacher and has two daughters.

Entrance: Main entries at 4 and 7 via play-based or literacy/numeracy assessments. Most pupils come from the local area and there is a good mix of ethnic backgrounds.

Exit: Prep pupils are automatically offered a place at either the boys' or girls' sections of Forest School and majority take up the offer.

Remarks: Tucked away from the main roads, surrounded by the ancient Epping Forest, and accessible by what resembles a narrow dirt track lane, the school stands as a closely hidden secret in its inner city surroundings. However, once we had cleared the highly secure, gated reception area to enter the school grounds, the bustle of life at the school immediately greeted us. We heard string and brass instruments sounding out from one of the many lunchtime concerts at the chapel, and saw brightly clad prep pupils at play or through their open classroom windows, merrily chanting foreign words in rote-like fashion. Pupils seem to be busy, happy and oblivious. They are taught in buildings alive with a heritage dating back to the school's foundation in 1834. Even with its Georgian buildings, this school has a distinctively bright, spacious and airy feel. Expect to see lively but small groups of pupils actively involved in learning, lots of writing and artwork displays in and outside of the classrooms, and tiny, well-behaved pupils following behind their teacher in duckling-like fashion from one part of the school to another.

In the pre-prep (4 to 7), children are taught in co-ed classes and follow the EYFS; in the prep they begin to experience single-sex teaching preparation for their later move to the boys' and girls' senior schools. Class sizes 16 in the pre-prep and 22 in the prep school. Teaching based on national curriculum with specialists brought in for art, PE, drama, foreign languages and, in particular, music.

All of the children have the opportunity to learn an instrument here for at least a year. The prep school music department is led by a teacher prized for her ability to spot the 'differences between concert and worship' voices, as well as knowing how hard to push the youngest of performers to discover their best. Each May, the school organises Composition Week, where year 5 pupils are transformed into a team of songwriters, singers and composers to produce, most recently for example, a signature melody inspirited by the retelling of Arachne. The experience is 'demanding but rewarding' for the pupils, and this spirit is one of the prized characteristics of the school: even the youngest of pupils is stretched and pushed to learn.

There is plenty else to do aside from music-making – pupils are also actively involved in dance, drama and sports. The prep school sits between the main school buildings and senior pupils behave like older siblings to the younger ones. The prep children use senior school facilities, including the sports fields, theatre and a modern leisure centre with swimming pool and gymnasium.

Many trips organised – to 'help us to learn', say the children – some local to eg Strawberry Hill Ponds and the Suntrap Centre, others further afield eg Paradise Park, the Europa Centre and the Royal Observatory in Greenwich, others even as far as Berlin.

None of the pupils here have a statement of special educational need but about 16 receive some kind of learning support. They all speak English as their main language, so no EAL needs here either; the ISI describes them as highly articulate and well above average ability. Many win academic, sport or music scholarships, to Forest senior school and elsewhere, but only a few move away.

The chapel and chaplaincy are central to learning here. The chapel is where pupils begin and end each term with events such as breakfasts for parents followed by a welcome service. Last year all of the new pupils brought in a cardboard brick to build a 'prayer wall' showing their aspirations for the term. These included learning to read, wishing to play football for the school, becoming a monitor, making lots of friends and, simply, 'I want to make my teacher and parents proud.'

Prep pupils make respectable contributions to a very lively school diary of events, such as the pre-prep nativity play, a dramatised festival service and an idiom recital day to mark the 400-year anniversary of the King James version of the Bible. They also have house competitions in eg acting, singing and rounders, and charity fund-raising events. They compete in the UK chess championships and have hosted a prep-level junior science competition involving over 20 schools. They won a school prize in a wildlife foundation global art competition, with 10 year 4 and 5 pupils selected among entrants from around the world, including Hong Kong, Nigeria and Arabia. Cricket is popular but football is 'something special', and there are several teams and matches played in and outside of the borough.

Parents describe it as a school where 'teaching is good but not too pushy', teachers 'know your child well' and 'there is a very active PTA'. In fact, the majority of the parents involved in the parents' association are from the prep school. They are kept up to speed via a newsletter and the school website.

Forres Sandle Manor School

Sandle Manor, Fordingbridge, SP6 1NS

- Pupils: 220 boys and girls, 100 boarders • Ages: 3–13 • C of E
- Fees: Boarding £19,905–£20,970; Day £8,010–£15,360 pa
- Independent

Tel: 01425 653181
Email: office@fsmschool.com
Website: www.fsmschool.com

Headmaster: Since 2010, Mr Mark Hartley (forties), previously deputy head at Winchester House, Brackley, and before that housemaster at Mount House School, Tavistock. Studied biological sciences, now teaches PSHE to older ones and maths tutors those who struggle. Started his working life as an insurance underwriter, met wife Beth at a 21st birthday party and shortly afterwards discovered his true vocation – teaching. Three children later, Beth has returned to her former stomping ground with responsibility for marketing and promoting FSM – though we hear bottles of champagne, sent to parents, for recruiting newbies, are a thing of the past. Described as fresh, fun and funny by youngsters, Mr Hartley is something of an action man, enjoying hockey, cycling, kayaking and climbing. Inheriting a school that required fine tuning rather than wholesale overhaul, he has tinkered at the edges: tightening up reporting procedures, smartening the kids, introducing a parent portal and encouraging more competition via house events. So far so good on the parental front, 'He's livened things up, smartened up the children but not pushed things too far'.

Entrance: Most at age 3 or 8, boarders from seven. Non-selective but works from premise of 'Will a child be happy here?' Stomping grounds include New Forest, Avon Valley and environs of Cranborne. Predominantly white British with a handful of short-stay pupils from Norway and Spain. Boarders a 50-50 mix of expats, mostly Forces and locals. Around half are first time buyers. Start when you like, if room (pressure on boarding places – must pay for full even if weekly board). Means-tested bursaries and discount for Forces.

Exit: Canford, the Sherbornes, Bryanston. Plus eg Marlborough, Blundells, Millfield, Wells, Kings Taunton, Dauntseys, Stowe, St Mary's Shaftesbury, Milton Abbey, Claysemore. Eminent old boys: Michael Foot (Forres), Alec Guinness (Sandle Manor). Around a third win scholarships – usually a couple of full academic schols, plus music, art, sport and DT.

Remarks: Set in child-friendly grounds, centred around an elegant Jacobean manor, a stone's throw from the New Forest. It's hard to imagine a more captivating environment for the tweenager. Delightful pre-prep with inspirational head who ensures learning is child-led, fun but pacey. Super pirate ship playground and forest school ensure year round fresh air and plenty of boisterous play.

All 6 year olds screened for reading delay – those found in need are given booster sessions till back on track. 'We never guarantee a child will improve but are yet to have one that doesn't.' Fans of Ruth Miskin's Read Write Inc, which promises every child a reader by age 6. Imaginative teaching and learning captivates the spellbound youngsters. We especially liked the 'naughty bus' that hides on a daily basis and had been found encased in ice on our visit. Even an errant bus can't compete with the excitement of making stinky, brown poo – a simulated investigation which begins with crushing of digestive biscuits (to mirror crunching of teeth), mixed with water (replacing saliva), washing up liquid and vinegar added (enzyme and stomach acid), then squeezed through grandma's stocking, simulating the intestine and final movement: learning at its gory, imaginative, and experiential best.

Fairly relaxed approach to learning in the prep school – not a soft option, but perhaps uniquely, youngsters say they'd like more prep sooner, 'The year 8 workload is a shock and we could be better prepared for it'. Gifted children pepped up via PACE activities; some, such as Green Giant, an eco project examining biodiversity and recycling with hands-on fun chopping bamboo, mixing smoothies and making wool – open to all.

Learning support encompasses wide range of cognitive ability, 'We have children who cannot read/decode but are L4 and L5 national curriculum level in some subjects, so we have to help and support'. Parents enthuse, 'My child struggled at his previous school, but since he came to FSM and got the support he needed, he has never stopped smiling.' Another added, 'It's a long day yet my child is never tired. Somehow they work it just right.'

Most teachers deliver multi-sensory lessons geared to active learning. English, drama and science top the popularity polls, 'Our science teacher respects us – he's not patronising, we do lots of experiments, it's fun and there is practically no writing,' cooed one boy. History, geography and RE depart from confines of CE, a conscious decision to develop skills of enquiry and investigation. Testing topics include Smuggling in Fordingbridge. Senior schools approve and see some seriously good work – not that fun doesn't come into it: we spotted a wall of history jokes, our favourite, 'Who built the Ark? I have Noah idea!' Double groan! Post CE youngsters hone their practical and problem-solving skills – changing a tyre, wiring a plug, ironing shirts or finding the scariest ride at Thorpe Park.

Most lessons take place in The Barn with scattering of specialist buildings for art (we loved the bronze Olympian action sculpture), DT and music. Sports hall and climbing wall on wish list, but grounds contain heated outdoor swimming pool, courts for netball and tennis plus myriad of pitches. Ennui not an option – daily sport and afternoon activities as diverse as scuba diving, golf (even for the tinies) and banana boating, alongside annual trips and tours to everywhere from Iceland to Africa. Project week and cub-camp, with Boy's Own firelighting, knife-skills, cooking and camp craft, perennially popular. All lower school do ballet (a good way to spot potential dancers and dyspraxics) – optional classes for seniors. We listened to the fledgling Exterminators jamming and spotted imaginatively named groups, eg Flute Pastilles, and fabulous fiddlers. School has a competitive edge: thrice finalists in the Junior Memory Championships and recent debut as finalists in Kids Lit.

Seemingly parents equally competitive when it comes to teams, with boarder parents saying, 'Local parents seem to have everything sewn up – it can be difficult for the boarding fraternity to get a look in, especially for parent fixtures,' adding, 'Communication could be better – they're great at reporting on the kids but not on activities: we need time to schedule and plan'. Parents kept busy with quiz nights, football, hockey, plus 'maths for mums and dads', courtesy of Friends of FSM – hardly surprising they jest that an in-school Costa Coffee concession is on their wish list!

Meals are table served in one of two dining rooms, the mantra to always try a little, including experimental offerings such as beetroot brownies and soup concoctions dreamt up by the youngsters. Sports teas are legendary and, as we flicked the last melt-in-the-mouth crumbs from our lips, could only nod in heartfelt agreement as our trusty guide declared them 'outstanding!'

A boarding school that welcomes day children – 'It's a family-friendly community, flexible when we need it'. Fairly healthy weekend boarding numbers, though parents of full boarders say to check the age and gender of those who stay, if this is important to you. Cheery boarding accommodation with ongoing renovations – though we were a tad overwhelmed by the swathes of bubble-gum pink adorning the girls' dorms. We loved the 'getting better bay' with healthy doses of TLC for the homesick and panaceas for the poorly. Seemingly all want to try boarding, so expect up to 11 per dorm and the odd grumble that it can be difficult to escape, 'sometimes you need time or space but they can be hard to find'. Nothing too heavy-handed on discipline front: naughty boarders are red-carded and miss the coveted Wednesday special boarding night or put on dreaded laundry duty, sorting socks, folding shirts. Matrons praised, 'You can tell them things because they have seen it all before and know what to do', ground-staff lauded as cheery and fun, 'They have a nickname for everyone'.

Focuses on developing happy, confident children. Takes a broad range, delivers the goods, 'One minute you are watching a really talented child, the next someone who is just keen to join in'. Children are respected and 'feel part of the gang,' say parents. Children candid, 'It can be a bit difficult for those who are naturally loners or need quiet space.' Not posh or pushy. A happy, homely school with a sunny disposition, going from strength to strength. Turns out friendly, confident, quietly ambitious youngsters.

Fox Primary School

Kensington Place, London, W8 7PP

- Pupils: 330 boys and girls, all day • Ages: 4-11 • Non-denom
- State

Tel: 020 7727 7637
Email: info@fox.rbkc.sch.uk
Website: www.fox.rbkc.sch.uk

Headteacher: Since 2006, Paul Cotter BA PGCE (forties). Previously deputy head at Avondale Primary in North Kensington, bringing much of what he learnt there with him, including his young, extremely bright and capable deputy, Emma Madden – they make a formidable team. Swiftly injected energy and fresh blood into this ever popular local school. Savvy – knows how to access funding and use it to the max.

Entrance: Heavily oversubscribed – over 200 applicants for 45 places. Priority (rather than catchment) area is mainly to the south towards Kensington rather than the north to Notting Hill, where greater density of state school provision. Lots of mobility, however, so places do crop up, and further up the school they have admitted children beyond this area. Siblings have priority but no one else. Entrance procedure is administered by the borough and the head can exercise no preference. Children come from over 40 different nurseries, but parents we spoke to mentioned Strawberry Fields, Rolfes, St Peters and Kids Unlimited.

Exit: About half each year to Holland Park, a few to the spanking new Chelsea Academy. More than a third to independent schools – a wide range including Latymer Upper, Godolphin and Latymer, City of London Boys' and Girls', St Paul's Boys' and Girls', some board at, eg, Christ's Hospital and Cheltenham Ladies' College, some win scholarships to, eg, Charterhouse. 'They can go wherever they want,' said one parent. Mr Cotter meets all secondary heads – 'They generally like Fox children,' he says proudly. Parents notice that he sees this as an integral part of his job – makes no judgement about the choice other than finding what's best for each individual.

Remarks: A buzzing local primary with a liberal, funky feel to it. A sea of colour greets you as you enter the well secured gates – brightly clad children (no uniform) playing noisily (as you would hope) in the imaginatively and tastefully decorated playground. As well as the main area for football and netball, a quieter arbour with wooden tables, canopies and lavender, the gentle rushing of water running around the perimeter. A popular place to trade Match Attacks and Go Gos on a Friday and for parents to discuss their next fundraising project after drop off. A giant chess board and climbing wall in the far corner while, behind the school, in the younger years' playground, allotments (where the children tend radishes and chillis as well as lychees) and a woodland trail. Dedicated play area with sand and water for reception children with beautiful mosaics on the walls.

The school is housed in a large 1930s building and has all the hallmarks of being purpose built, with wide corridors and staircases. Large windows into bright, spacious, airy classrooms. Every inch of space is used to benefit learning – the deputy head's office also has an interactive white board and desks. Music rooms, dedicated learning rooms for smaller groups, an IT room with 30 flat screen computers, a large hall with a huge white screen. IT is used to liven things up at every occasion, particularly the assemblies (which happen at 3pm, when 'everyone has had enough rather than first thing, which is prime learning time,' says head sensibly). We saw the house (named after four different species of fox) spellathon conducted like a prime time quiz show. Everyone had fun and everyone learnt something. This is clearly key to the ethos here.

A strong, dynamic teaching staff, average age less than 30. Larger number of women than men. They bring fun and lots of motivation to the daily curriculum. Parents enthuse about the cohesive staff – by all accounts Mr Cotter has built a team of excellent teachers. Energy saving schemes (they are aiming for green flag system and have an 'eco team' of pupils to help them do it) and clever organisation have resulted in his being able to employ more staff and ensure the school is extremely well equipped. One of his cleverest achievements has to be the class sizes – reduced at every opportunity. Currently only 22 in two classes in reception, year 1, and years 4 to 6, with an ingenious scheme to allow for differentiation according to age and stage in years 2 and 3. Rightly proud of this innovation – 'standards have shot up as a result,' he observes – Fox now rates as one of the top primary schools in the country.

Everyone achieves here – the bright ones as well as those with special needs. High ratio of staff to children in each class, and the SENCo teaches smaller groups of up to 10 who have learning difficulties (PTA funded laptops for this). About 15 per cent of children are currently on the SEN register, some with statements. One or two reports that it took a bit of prodding before school diagnosed, eg, dyslexia (school denies this, 'We have rigorous monitoring systems,' they say) but by all accounts, once any problems are discovered, school gives tremendous support. English is the second language for about one third of children – they catch up quickly. School accepts child as s/he is and works enthusiastically with what they've got, say parents – they don't try to iron out the problems and pretend they're not there.

Music and dance are central to the school day. Years 2 and 3 all learn the recorder in key stage 1, with over half the school going on to learn an instrument in key stage 2. An orchestra with regular concerts, jazz and dance throughout the year. Science week happens in the autumn term, arts week in the winter term and sports week (where they canoe and climb, do archery and judo as well as the sports you might normally expect) in the summer. Some 40 clubs are offered either before or after school – children can choose almost anything from Chinese to table tennis, sculpture to archery.

Delicious lunches cooked by their own chef (no imported catering service here) allow for every penny to be put back into the menu. Staff eat with pupils in the school hall. They don't need persuading to eat fresh Greek salad – after all, 'They are as fussy as the children,' acknowledges head.

Very supportive and active PTA raises significant sums of money each year, helping to fund, eg, the stunning areas of the playground. One parent described the parent body as having 'a can do attitude that you find in some private schools'. A number of parents were at Fox themselves – always a positive indicator. High number of professionals – barristers, journalists, diplomats, authors as well as artists and musicians, and 17 per cent of pupils are on free school meals. One parent spoke of the relief she felt that her daughter wouldn't grow up thinking everyone had a second home in Barbados.

A school with a strong, very positive identity (witness the 'mighty Fox' anthem, sung by the whole school at every successful achievement). One parent described it as mini UN – can be up to 15 nationalities in one class. School thrives on multiculturalism and diverse influences but 'doesn't see that as an excuse for poor performance,' emphasises one parent. School quick to point out that bilingual pupils outperform their monolingual peers. Bright eyed, confident, articulate and above all happy children who enjoy coming to school. A rare and precious jewel showing real life at its best – not to be overlooked in this super-affluent patch of London.

Francis Holland Junior School, Sloane Square

Linked school: Francis Holland School, Sloane Square

Graham Terrace, London, SW1W 8JF

• Pupils: 165 girls; all day • Ages: 4–11 • C of E • Fees: £14,070–£16,125 pa • Independent

Tel: 020 7730 2971
Email: education@fhs-sw1.org.uk
Website: www.fhs-sw1.org.uk

Head: Since September 2010, Miss Sarah J Styles BA MA (London) in philosophy of education. Previously director of studies at Wheathamstead House and was a member of the Women's Royal Naval Service before she took up teaching. Took over after the immensely long and distinguished reign of Mrs Bown.

Entrance: Very competitive entrance at age 4. School is the flavour of the month and has been for some time. Children are 'tested' in January for the September term. 200 seen for 24 places. Maturity, ability to relate to others, memory and coordination are assessed – 'Are they ready for school?'

Exit: Around 50 per cent to the senior school (via London Schools Consortium exam). A number choose to board – at, eg, Cheltenham Ladies' College, Wycombe Abbey, Downe House – and a fair few to other London day schools – St Paul's, Godolphin and Latymer, and Latymer Upper.

Remarks: Strong, academic pre-prep and prep school near Sloane Square. Remarkable building for Central London, the site being shared with the senior school. A quad in the middle serves as playground for all years but plenty of games (either on site or Battersea Park four days a week). Ballet very strong (although some mutterings among parents about the sidelining of mediocre children). Highlight of the annual calendar is the Princess Margaret classical ballet awards day. Music also strong with at least 80 per cent of girls learning an instrument.

Parents very social – banking, diplomats, lawyers, media types, some royalty and celebrities, although everyone frightfully discreet. Mostly from Chelsea, Fulham, Pimlico. Old Girls include Lady Sarah Chatto, Vanessa Mae and Jemima Khan. Vigorous science department under buzzy Scottish head who has lots of clubs (doing all the experiments you'd rather they didn't do at home) and an annual 'spaghetti and marshmallow' day where families compete (some fathers taking it very seriously indeed) to build the biggest structure.

Specialist teachers brought in from the senior school in science, ICT, art, PE and also French, which is taught from 8. Strong 'helping others' ethos with girls raising money for charity at home and abroad. Bright and airy library shared with the senior school.

Not a school for the faint-hearted – that's the parents, not the children; 'The children are used to being stretched,' says the head. Homework is very demanding and a lot of support is required. It pays off because girls do outstandingly well here. High standards, wholly committed approach, and individual attention mean that very few don't succeed in some capacity. Girls here are neat and articulate and enthuse about their 'marvellous' trips to Cornwall and Canterbury 'where we dressed up as knights'.

From the highly dedicated staff through to the bright orange worry bags in each classroom (which are not just on display) and the regular contact with the girls from the senior school (they read to them once a week), girls here are well-adjusted and can be stretched without becoming neurotic. Miss Styles inherited a celebrated junior school and we are watching with interest as she makes it her own.

Frensham Heights Junior School

Linked school: Frensham Heights Middle School and 6th Form

Rowledge, Farnham, GU10 4EA

• Pupils: 120 boys and girls • Ages: 3–11 • Fees: Day £6,045–£16,125; Boarding £25,500 pa • Independent

Tel: 01252 792561
Email: admissions@frensham-heights.org.uk
Website: www.frensham-heights.org.uk

Headmaster: Mr Andrew Fisher

Head of first and junior school: Mr Nic Hoskins

Exit: Through school.

Remarks: New, lovely, bright first school houses 3 to 8 year olds. Confident, busy 6 year olds rushing about calling teachers 'sue' and 'Caron'. Seven year olds get specialist teachers for French, drama, ICT, music and PE.

For further details, see senior school.

Friends' Junior School

Linked school: Friends' School

Mount Pleasant Road, Saffron Walden, CB11 3EB

• Pupils: 120 girls and boys • Ages: 3–11 • Quaker ethos
• Fees: £7,125–£10,215 pa • Independent

Tel: 01799 525351
Email: adminjs@friends.org.uk
Website: www.friends.org.uk

Head: Since September 2013, Ruth Darvill, previously head of pre-prep at St Albans High. BEd in maths and education from Cambridge. Has taught at several prep schools, with roles including ICT co-ordinator, G&T provision and swimming teacher. One daughter, in Friends' nursery class. Her aim is for the school to become known for 'supporting, nurturing, and extending every child so that they can fulfil their potential and find their niche to excel'.

Entrance: Junior school entry points are into the nursery at 3, and then 4 and 7 after a series of taster days to make sure they'll settle. Places offered on the basis of observation and individual assessment.

Exit: After year 6, majority cross the playground to Friends' senior school. A few leak out to local state and Cambridge independents.

Remarks: 'Friends Junior School is a friendly, family school,' says head. 'Staff and children are very welcoming and everyone is striving to do their very best.'

The youngest Friends benefited the most from the sale of land on the edge of the school campus a few years ago, the proceeds of which built their own domain in the shadow of the Victorian senior school. New spaces are cheery and purpose designed with the small in mind, each nursery and infant classroom opening onto an outdoor space and heaps of room inside. All well kitted out with interactive whiteboards and educational paraphernalia of all kinds and of course all have access to the facilities (sports hall, pool etc) and grounds shared with senior school as well as Forest School at the far reaches.

Like the senior school, a very supportive environment, where children are known and feel valued. Parents bask in the warm glow of the culture of kindness that pervades – 'the support shown by staff to pupils, and older pupils to younger pupils, results in a very happy learning environment and illustrates the Friends' culture very well,' says one.

Nursery replete with staff given the number of children and infant classes have a teacher and assistant, whatever the class size. Emphasis is on structured play in nursery but in years 1 and 2, learning becomes more formal in literacy, numeracy and science and children join in with junior activities and assemblies. In the junior department, English classes start with 10 minutes of reading every day and languages are enthusiastically encouraged – Eco Club conducted entirely in the German language. Science labs are sensibly laid out with benches at the back and desks at the front to deter fiddlers.

Wildly popular, food tech starts in year 5 and takes in health and nutrition as well as cooking.

Many trips out and visitors in to liven up learning and residential trips build through the juniors – year 4s to Flatford, year 5s to Norfolk and year 6s to Wales for a week. Three houses – named for famous Quakers Cadbury, Fry and Penn – and plenty of healthy competition throughout the school year.

Parent-friendly school day runs 8.30 to 3.30, but with early starter care from 8 and clubs and activities (a choice for years 2-6 and mini club for those younger) until 4.45, and late stay until 5.45 – no charge!

The Froebelian School

Clarence Road, Horsforth, Leeds, LS18 4LB

• Pupils: 189; 95 boys/ 94 girls; all day • Ages: 3–11 • Non-denom
• Fees: £4,335–£7,116 pa • Independent

Tel: 01132 583047
Email: office@froebelian.co.uk
Website: www.froebelian.co.uk

Headmaster: Since 1991, Mr John Tranmer MA PGCE (fifties), read history at St John's, Cambridge, PGCE at St Martin's Lancaster. Taught at Bolton School, HMS Indefatigable (nautical school), Parkside School, Cobham (ran history, RE and games). A friendly, almost reserved, manner hides a very determined head, who continues to take the school forward on all fronts. Recent chairmanship of IAPS helped raise his and school's profile regionally and nationally. His role as a schools' inspector also helps keep him aware of best practice. Despite increasing calls on his time he remains a teaching head, though is beginning to feel a little Mr Chips-like as he now finds himself teaching children whose parents he also taught. Runs a tight ship and has high expectations of his team – 'I want parents not just to be happy but to be delighted', and generally they are, recognising the school's huge commitment to the children and the staff's willingness to go above and beyond the call of duty. Very aware of increasing need for children to gain transferable skills and looks to instil a love of learning to prepare children for secondary school. 'I am trying to give them a thirst for learning, an understanding that my whole life is going to be more fulfilled if I am a more educated person'. But while education moves forward, the head is also keen to retain traditional value: 'We need to stimulate children and educate them to be their best – provide the best teachers, the best resources; the chemical formula for success doesn't change.'

Entrance: Almost exclusively at three; first 24 to register invited to spend some time in school, where they are informally assessed by staff. One-form entry of 24, perpetual waiting list of between 10 and 30. Places occasionally available for older children.

Exit: About 80 per cent to fee-paying schools, top choices being Bradford and Leeds independent grammar schools (boys and girls) and Woodhouse Grove. Harrogate Ladies' College, Ashville and Gateways also feature; occasional entrant to Eton, Wycombe Abbey, Queen Margaret's and other boarding schools further afield. If need be, some parents are willing to move house to get a chance of a place in reputable maintained schools such as Ripon Grammar or St Aidan's, Harrogate. Essentially the school will work with you to enable you and your child to get into the school of choice – that's the beauty of being a stand-alone prep.

Remarks: If a large car park and extensive playing fields are high on your priority list, then this may not be the school for you. If, on the other hand, good teaching and academic rigour delivered in a warm and nurturing environment are top of your list, then it might well be. This is a small school punching well above its weight on a number of fronts. In the words of one parent, 'I was sold on the first day as very young yet highly articulate and smiling children opened the door for me, chatting happily with great confidence'.

Busy children in bright red and grey school uniform pass through bright red and grey gates into a busy school bedecked with glorious displays of children's work – every corner of every corridor is used and the children are keen to show you their handiwork, house awards and much-prized trophies. Their timetable is packed, not least because of the travelling to and from sports grounds and swimming pools for games lessons. These are industrious children who manage to fit a great deal into their day, especially the dawn brigade who begin the day with sausage sandwiches or pain au chocolat at breakfast club – a boon for working parents and the children seem to like it too. Their energy and enthusiasm knows no bounds, keeping children busy is always a good plan, and it works.

Founded on the principles of Friedrich Froebel in 1913, the school is very proud of its history. Froebel was a great German educator who is famous for his radical insight that the first learning experiences of the very young are of crucial importance in influencing not only their later educational achievements but also the health and development of society as a whole. Clearly quite a responsibility for the staff and children in this small school in a leafy Leeds suburb. Despite – or perhaps because of – its long history, the school is very much forward-looking and progressive. Lots of ICT, laptops, whiteboards, crammed into modest school footprint. Recent years saw two large additional classrooms, a multi-purpose studio and enlargement of the playground with several attractive soft play surfaces. A greenhouse for the eco-club, a wormery, pond and nature trail through the adjoining wood offer additional teaching and learning excitement. Opportunities for more expansion or relocation are limited but every inch is used, and used well, indoors and out.

Pulls in affluent families from Leeds-Bradford area and, thanks to bursary scheme, a sprinkling of able, less-well-off children. Excellent transport links from here so it's a good place to live, away from the hustle and bustle of the city centre yet easily accessible. Parents are generally professionals working locally, high number of medics. Its central Horsforth location means that it's within yards of stylish coffee shops, quirky gift emporiums, beauticians, boutiques and organic greengrocers (naturally) and lycra-clad mums can be seen doing the school-skinny latte-gym run first thing in the morning. Parents expect a lot and excellent ('top 30 in the country') Sats results ensure they get very good value. Doesn't sweat over Sats but uses them to 'keep a watchful eye on where we are'.

Average class size 22, early years have classroom assistants. Exposure to IT from the start. Supports gifted and able and offers learning support for SEN (possibly at extra cost depending on level of need). Set apart by specialist teaching, pre-prep has specialist support for music, ICT and PE and specialist teaching increases year on year until a full range of subjects is taught by specialists by year 6. Children get used to different teachers, different locations, just like secondary school. 'Plus it plays to the teachers' strengths'. 'I want able teachers who can stretch some very able and gifted children, in their own specialist subjects.'

Strong on encouraging idea of learning skills for life, aware that many people now go on to change career many times. 'Achieve your best' is a mantra spread throughout the school, nowhere more prevalent than in sport where, despite limited on-site facilities, the emphasis is on taking part. Deputy head received Sports Teacher of the Year award from the National Council for School Sport. Football, rugby, hockey, netball, athletics, swimming and more on offer. Children enthuse about the running clubs (fast/medium/slow options) and enjoy the 'beat the teacher' challenge. Music and drama very strong – 'almost all' juniors learn at least one instrument, school famous locally for its musicals (eg Mary Poppins, Grease, Oliver!). Also field trips, outings, juniors' week in France; Three Peaks trip for Y6 particularly loved. Close contacts with parents, via e-mail or text, plus traditional letters home and homework diaries. Parents like 'lovely, friendly family feel to the school'.

Clear school code and anti-bullying policy. Emphasis on children allowing each other to be happy in their school lives, and older boys and girls supervise smaller pupils' lunchtime. Has embraced extended school idea with busy breakfast club and after-school club to 6pm which offers supervised homework, 'chuggling' (a word the word the children use – it means 'getting up to date') or play and activities.

Fulham Pre-prep School

Linked school: Fulham Prep School

47A Fulham High Street, London, SW6 3JJ

- Pupils: 136 boys and 114 girls • Ages:4-7 • Non-denom
- Fees: £13,950 pa • Independent

Tel: 020 7371 9911
Email: admin@fulhamprep.co.uk
Website: www.fulhamprep.co.uk

Remarks: See prep school for details.

Fulham Prep School

Linked school: Fulham Pre-prep School

200 Greyhound Road, London, W14 9SD

- Pupils: 206 boys and 129 girls (prep) • Ages: 4-13 • Non-denom
- Fees: £13,950-£15,450 pa • Independent

Tel: 020 7386 2444
Email: prepadmin@fulhamprep.co.uk
Website: www.fulhamprep.co.uk

Principal: Since 1996, Mrs Jane Emmett BEd (fifties). After being at Cameron House for 13 years, six as head, Mrs Emmett founded this school in 1996 along with other members of her family (it is a family company with some external shareholders). Mrs Emmett, like a wise old owl, combines a strong, slightly intimidating exterior with a definite warmth and twinkle in her eye. She sets the tone and has an impressive sense of realism about the pupils in her care, with her direct, no nonsense approach.

Mrs Emmett believes in praising and encouraging pupils whatever their achievements, 'staff go the extra mile' and the pupils and parents we spoke to really value this. Pupils see her as 'firm but friendly'. The school is well disciplined but would not suit the rebellious, insubordinate child or more laissez-faire parent, or indeed the insubordinate parent: she is not afraid to chastise them in newsletters if they park dangerously, or let their children wear inappropriate uniform such as head muffs.

Mrs Emmett handed over the reins in September 2013 to her recently appointed deputy head Mr Ritchie Howells, but will stay on to advise on school choice and will be involved in marketing.

No flashy pinstriped suit and old school tie, Mr Howells speaks plainly and is on the spot. He believes in the importance of the school's 'sense of family' and demonstrates his commitment to knowing the pupils by teaching some English to older pupils and always being at the gate in the morning. One parent found him 'a little awkward at first' but has warmed to him. Shares Mrs Emmett's vision and will uphold the school's ethos, but still, it will be interesting to see how the shift in roles plays out.

Head of the pre-prep is Ms Di Steven, BEd, educated at Glasgow University with PGCYEd from Dundee and an NPQH. She has been with the school for a decade, has one son in the pre-prep a second younger son in a nearby nursery. Clearly in touch with the concerns of the modern parent, juggling work pressure with teaching her son to ride a bicycle. She is thorough and thoughtful with a pleasant manner and high standards. Her IT expertise ensures that the pre-prep is very well equipped.

Entrance: The pre-prep is non-selective in reception, with 90 places offered on a first come first served basis. Priority and a discount given to siblings. Entry after reception involves spending a morning at the school. Automatic transfer to the prep. The prep holds examinations and interviews at 7+ 8+ and 11+.

Exit: Majority of pre-prep pupils move on to the prep. Has a reputation for getting each prep school child into the right next school. Results are impressive with regular scholarships and places at a variety of boarding and day schools. Mrs Emmett is keen to encourage more girls to stay until 13 but this very much depends on the choice of destination as many girls' schools want them at 11+. Girls move on to boarding schools including Benenden, Downe House, Tudor Hall, Wycombe Abbey, or to day schools such as Francis Holland, Godolphin & Latymer, Putney High, St Paul's Girls', Wimbledon High. Boys leave at 13 except those destined for Latymer at 11. Their destinations include: Bradfield, Charterhouse, Dulwich, Eton, Harrow, King's College School Wimbledon, Marlborough, St Paul's, Wellington, Westminster and Winchester.

Remarks: The school is on two sites: there are transport arrangements between prep (on Greyhound Road) and pre-prep (on Fulham High Street) to assist busy parents, and January exam candidates are given the opportunity to visit in November for a treasure hunt so that they feel more at home when they come in for the dreaded tests.

The curriculum is not straitjacketed, and parents appreciate its variety and breadth. Although one class is given an accelerated pace (selected according to pupils' school destinations) this would 'not be fair on the others who do not need it,' remarks the principal. That said, there is an expectation that every child will be able to keep up with a dynamic academic programme. All are being prepared for competitive entrance examinations and although some allowance is made for pupils from abroad there is limited EAL support in school. Experienced and extremely caring SENCO supports those with mild learning difficulties. Parents confirm that if serious difficulties were to develop, a school move would be suggested. Pre-prep has its own SENCO, a 'godsend,' remarks Ms Steven and we noted some very good examples of provision for different abilities.

Until year 4 pupils are classroom based, then they move round specialist facilities. Latin from year 5 and philosophy for years 4 to 6. Greek available in years 7 and 8. 'The teachers make lessons interesting, often involving games in them', pupils remarked to us. They also appreciate the way staff 'offer advice and support'. We saw a number of young, enthusiastic staff, with more males in evidence than is often the case. The principal is keen to stress the role models provided by the female head of science (who is also a great skier), and the male head of art. Class sizes between 14 and 20.

A listed Victorian school building accommodates the pre-prep reception classes, library, activity room and ICT suite. Adjoining is a modern three-storey block for years 1 and 2 as well as the spacious gym/hall, dark music room and light art studio. Large, well equipped play areas including fabulous Astroturf and garden with shallow pond. We saw plenty of imaginative play equipment that can be re-arranged with different themes.

Do not expect soft furnishings, carpets and tasteful flower arrangements, or a palatial office for the principal. The prep school was originally a Victorian boarding school and the building still shows this, although it is light with high ceilings, classrooms leading off the wide corridors on several floors, and an impressive meeting room with raked seating. Welcoming library with enthusiastic librarian. Classrooms contain attractive displays and are well equipped with the usual interactive boards. Some access to laptops, but though good use is made of the intranet to support learning (a recent development), the ICT in the prep is not cutting edge.

More boys than girls in the school, especially noticeable in years 7 and 8 when many of the girls have left for London day schools. Those girls that do remain can be assured of being given responsibility and participating in many sports. Pupils look happy and move about purposefully; they are polite and responsive but not precocious, though it takes a certain robustness to flourish here. Parents like the fact that 'there are all walks of life' and the school is not 'glitzy'.

Heaps for all to do here. 'There are lots of opportunities for children to try new activities, with loads of clubs from jewellery to street dancing,' commented a parent. 'There's also plenty of music, from award winning chamber choir to African drumming, orchestra and jazz group.' Music is a strength of the school with four choirs including school choir apprentices and chamber choir, a boys' choir, plus a parents' choir which sings at the carol service. All classes have two music lessons with three-quarters of the pupils taking individual instrumental or singing lessons in spacious accommodation. Pre-prep pupils learn the recorder and percussion.

The school has its own Astroturf, netball court and cricket nets, and there is one afternoon a week at Barn Elms. In years 3 and 4 every child is given the chance to play in a team. The second half of Friday afternoon is for sport, as are some Saturdays (though both of these may be avoided). The deputy head is especially pleased with the up-and-coming rugby players, and cricket is very popular. Girls play netball. The pre-prep makes frequent use of Hurlingham Park for games, swimming takes place at Fulham Pools and there's summer tennis coaching for years 1 and 2 in Bishops' Park.

'Pupils show tremendous loyalty to the four houses,' remarks Mr Howells. The house names fit the locality: Bishops, Crabtree, Hurlingham and Peterborough. Older pupils take their responsibilities seriously and look out for younger pupils. Even in the pre-prep pupils start to take responsibilities eg as house captains. All the houses raise funds for charities, and the school supports, for example, a local state primary for severely disabled children. Discipline system understood by all and parents believe any bullying is quickly acted upon. Pupils we spoke to were clear that the head sees anyone who seriously misbehaves, and cited swearing as a major offence. Matters are dealt with promptly. Strong communication between home and school, including an open door policy and regular daily contact, means potential problems are nipped in the bud.

Sibling discount; some bursaries for families in difficulties. Scholarships available for years 7 and 8.

Very much a local school, as evidenced by the numbers of bikes and scooters parked inside the gates. The pupils are polite and express themselves confidently; one parent commented that some parents choose Fulham Prep because they have been impressed by the behaviour of the children outside school and asked where they were educated. A 'really vibrant, caring school where pupils are nurtured and understood' is the parental consensus. No wonder it has grown so fast.

Garden House School

Turks Row, London, SW3 4TW

• Pupils: 495 boys and girls: all day • Ages: 3–11 • Non-denom
• Fees: £12,540–£20,100 pa • Independent

Tel: 020 7730 1652
Email: info@gardenhouseschool.co.uk
Website: www.gardenhouseschool.co.uk

Principal: The enterprising Mrs Jill Oddy BA has been principal since 1973 and also runs three pre-prep schools in New York. As a long-serving member of the administrative department – who appreciated the school's move in recent years to Turks Row just behind Sloane Square – proudly remarks, 'she has tremendous vision'.

Girls' upper school head since 2009, Mrs Kate Simon BA (Sheffield) and PGCE (Liverpool), thirties, mother of young son and daughter, previously head of a North London junior school. An efficient, capable lady, she exudes calm and works alongside established, popular, head of the girls' lower school, since 1988, Mrs Wendy Challen, Cert Ed Froebel. These ladies are approachable and collaborate superbly, combining a genuine concern for the well-being of their charges with wisdom and experience, very welcome and much appreciated by parents. Mrs Simon is moving on in 2014.

Head of the boys' school since 2006, Mr Christian Warland, with BA Hons from Exeter, mid-forties, left his work in the City as a lawyer and seems here to stay. He has found the change very satisfying: 'We spent considerable time analysing what went wrong in the City whereas here we are constantly forward-looking and this is very positive.' An old Garden House boy himself (and son of the principal), his three sons have been, or are being, educated at Garden House.

All three heads value taking time to get to know the children, from shaking hands with them and making eye contact first thing in the morning to teaching. Head of boys teaches ICT to year 2 and current affairs to the rest. Mrs Simon teaches life and culture – renamed as the result of a school council suggestion 'as the acronym, PSCHE, doesn't mean much to them,' she remarks. Mrs Challen teaches throughout lower school whenever possible, as well as being available for small groups for shared reading .

Entrance: As part of the school's desire to involve parents from the start, the family is seen as a unit. Usually girls are interviewed by head of lower school in January for the following September and boys by headmaster in October/November. Regular tours are organised for prospective parents; Tuesdays for the boys' school and Wednesdays for the girls', and there is no entrance examination thankfully, so it really is important to secure a place on the lengthy waiting list with £120 as soon as possible. The school states that GH children live in Kensington, Chelsea, Fulham, Battersea and Westminster, and English is spoken at home by at least one parent, so very much a day school serving its local, smart area. The school does not offer scholarships in the lower school but scholarships and generous bursaries are available to children – mostly boys – entering at the age of 8. Once a place is offered, a registration fee of £2000 is payable. There is a 10 per cent discount for all siblings. Around 50 boys and 45 girls join reception. Entrants at 8+ (by exam and interview) are nearly all boys, to replace the 30 – 40 who leave at this stage. There is a small amount of coming and going as families relocate so it is definitely worth checking.

Exit: Boys leave at 8+ (30 – 40) and 11+ (12 – 15) for top London day schools, including Sussex House, Westminster Under, Northcote Lodge, Wetherby Prep; one or two to boarding prep schools such as Ludgrove and Cothill House. Nearly all girls leave at 11; just under half go on to boarding schools including Downe House, St Mary's Ascot, Wycombe Abbey, with a consistent number to Queen's Gate, Godolphin and Latymer, St Paul's Girls', both Francis Hollands etc. Some go on with academic, art or sporting scholarships and awards.

Remarks: The exterior of the school, originally a British army barracks, is well maintained, but what awaits inside is quite magical. We were struck by the attention to detail and aesthetics; the entrance hall is beautifully arranged with rocking-horse, pupils' models and high quality art works by professionals, including an appealing watercolour of the school by a parent, Martin Millard, whose wife helps in the library. Classical music plays, and flower arrangements and lighting produce a calming, civilising effect after the noise and bustle outside. Every corridor and every room shows a care for the surroundings, whether it be the recital room, art room, well-equipped ICT suite or classrooms with vibrant displays, and this contributes to the attention paid to individual pupils. As a current parent remarked, 'This is above all a nurturing school, where boys and girls receive a wonderful education. It is so nurturing both for parents and children'.

Mrs Simon is proud of the school's broad curriculum and use of cross-curriculum planning. Every class has a teacher and classroom assistant, with specialist teachers for music, drama, games, French, IT, ballet, Latin, fencing, art from year 2 upwards and RE in the upper school. Boys and girls are taught separately after kindergarten but come together for playtime and musical and drama performances, as well as some trips. Average class size is 15 for girls and 14 for boys, with mixed ability teaching for all and some streaming only in mathematics. There is a learning zone on the website and plenty of Inter Activ boards and laptops for research. There is a well-qualified learning support team with a range of expertise, including speech therapy, so pupils can be assessed in-house; some classroom assistants are trained in dyslexia. Alongside the learning support, there is also a gifted and talented coordinator, and year 6 get help with creative writing and mathematics ready for 11+ exams. The boys and girls share the same broad curriculum, but many boys sit 8+ exams, so there is a different emphasis at this stage even for those staying till 11. Practice papers and internal assessments throughout the year help pupils to cope with different styles of questioning. Plenty of advice and guidance available to parents, but tutoring is discouraged as unnecessary pressure.

The attractively-equipped kindergarten accommodates tiny tots in a separate building attached to Holy Trinity Church. There are morning sessions for 24 children and afternoon sessions for 12, and they share a play area with the C of E primary school over the road.

The behaviour policy, using traffic lights, is well thought out. A parent commented on how seriously the children take it and said that the red light is very rarely used. 'It is brilliant, a clear not emotional system'. The head was also reassuringly definite that she would have no hesitation in using the red light and contacting a parent if the need arose: if, for example, a child were bullied.

All three heads are keen for school to be fun and stimulating, as the enormous array of activities and events demonstrate. During our visit boys were producing leaves in IT and art enthusiastically for FebFest, and the older girls spoke of the delights of preparing music and performing at Cadogan Hall in the spring term to a packed audience. The FebFest programme, involving the whole school from year 2 upwards, is linked to a fictional character travelling the world and hearing music from many cultures and heritages. The school is handy for galleries, exhibitions, museums and concerts. Music is popular with pupils as the teacher makes 'music enjoyable using actions' and 'is not too serious but friendly'. We heard the boys singing with gusto, and the percussion teacher clearly had year 1 boys enthralled. Every year the chamber choir goes on tour to Normandy and sings in the chapel of Emmanuel College, Cambridge. The musical calendar is packed. Four productions a year at the Royal Court and the Christmas concert is held in the Holy Trinity Church. Numerous events and competitions include Varsity Challenge, House Shout and Garden House has Talent.

Sport is taken seriously with football, rugby, cricket, rounders, hockey, lacrosse, tennis, netball at nearby Burton Court and Ranelagh Gardens as well as swimming at the Queen Mother's Pool. As a parent remarked, 'It all happens seamlessly despite the school not having its own extensive grounds, as so much is in easy walking distance.' Pupils were keen to explain how inclusive the school is, with team places and encouragement even for the less talented.

Active and supportive PTA with a predominantly Anglo-American parent body. The pupils feel they are respected by the teachers; as one parent remarked, 'There is always a seasoned staff member who has expertise and experience alongside another with energy, who comes across as positive, and not world weary. The school is amazing'.

Fridays are half days, though older children can do supervised homework until 2.30pm. Popular with parents who feel younger children are ready for the shorter day by Friday, and with those who want to leave early for the country.

Not a cheap school, although the Harrods uniform is also available second hand and there is a complimentary bus service at 4.00pm to Fulham.

Sparky teachers, male and female, give a sense of energy in a school community in which care, respect and kindness for all is very much the ethos.

Gateways Preparatory School

Linked school: Gateways School

Harewood, Leeds, LS17 9LE

• Pupils: 195 boys and girls • Ages: 2–11 • C of E • Fees: £6,840–£8,775 pa • Independent

---

Tel: 01132 886345
Email: gateways@gatewayschool.co.uk
Website: www.gatewaysschool.co.uk

Head of Junior School: Since September 2012 Dr Tracy Johnson BSc DPhil PGCE, previously deputy head of Lord Wandsworth College in Hampshire. Has also been physics teacher and housemistress at Cheltenham College. Has a degree and a PhD in laser physics and optoelectronics from St Andrews.

Entrance: Observation of performance within maths and English lessons.

Exit: To senior school.

Remarks: Integral site with the senior school, between Leeds and Harrogate. Exceptionally attractive, modern facilities with views of open countryside.

Juniors 7-11 years: small classes – average 14-16; teachers know children very well, say parents; staff share a commonroom with the senior staff and meet together every day. Top two classes have specialist teachers for core subjects, art, DT, ICT, music and PE; maths and English setted in year 6. French from year 3. No Sats and senior school entrance exam not taken, though candidates sit the scholarship exam; thorough tracking and reward systems. The children enjoy their lessons and like their teachers – 'They make it fun'. Large, light classrooms with good displays, plus access to senior school facilities (sports, ICT, science, technology, drama). Attractive library, well stocked with modern children's fiction, and computer suite for independent research.

Whole school learning support co-ordinator works with year 6s; colourful learning assistants' room – in class support (but not all the time, so children don't get too dependent on it) or individual/small group support outside.

Easy transition to the senior school facilitated by taster days for year 6s and children from other schools, eg master classes on the science of chocolate (really tasty!) or textiles given by visiting experts, assisted by sixth formers, and whole school house drama and music competitions and weekly assemblies.

The usual sports – its small size allows plenty of opportunities to represent the school but increases the challenges in competition with larger ones (some years can hold their own, though) – plus cross country, advanced vaulting. Good range of clubs: various kinds of dance and Spanish (extra cost); annual major music/drama production; termly magazine partly edited by children; school council; lots of visits and visitors; residentials in Cumbria and London and Yorkshire Dales and Moors.

The children appear happy, confident, forthcoming and secure. Extension of coeducation to 11 years in progress – girls have mixed feelings about this but parents are mostly pleased.

Littlegates, 3-7 years: head of early years is young, friendly and clearly loves her job. Happy, lively boys and girls enjoying large, light, bright learning and play spaces; an outdoor classroom is home to two substantial rabbits and some giant African land snails; also a particularly well equipped and designed outdoor area with little separate gardens. Specialist music and PE teachers.

Gatehouse Nursery, 2-3 years: housed in an unusual, modern, hexagonal building with a glass cupola, pine beams, glass doors to the well equipped outdoor area and a lovely view of hills and fields. Wraparound care from 7.30/8am-6.30pm, depending on age.

GEMS Bolitho Junior School

Linked school: Gems Bolitho School

Polwithen Road, Penzance, TR18 4JR

• Pupils: 54 boys and girls • Ages: 5–13 • C of E • Fees: Day £7,500–£10,500 pa • Independent

---

Tel: 01736 363271
Email: enquiries@bolithoschool.co.uk
Website: www.bolithoschool.co.uk

Head of Primary School: Mrs Catherine Gaskell

Exit: Through school – 100 per cent to senior school.

Remarks: For further information, see senior school.

GEMS Hampshire School

15 Manresa Road, London, SW3 6NB

- Pupils: 270 girls and boys • Ages: 3-13 • Non-denom
- Fees: £11,040-£15,492 pa • Independent

Tel: 020 7352 7077
Email: info@ghs.gemsedu.co.uk
Website: www.ths.westminster.sch.uk

Principal: Since January 2014, Donal Brennan BEd (Dublin), previously undermaster and director of studies at Hill House International.

Entrance: From 3, an informal interview; older children attend an assessment day – nothing too daunting. School is currently expanding, so plenty of places at various different levels in both the prep and the pre-prep. As school fills up, likely to be entrance points at rising 3, 4 and 5 (kindergarten and reception based at Wetherby Place) only, with the occasional place further up the school.

Exit: Handful of boys leave at 8, majority at 13, most girls at 11, very few to boarding schools, most to a (very) wide range of London day schools. Favourites with the girls are More House, Francis Holland and Godolphin & Latymer; for boys Latymer Upper, Westminster, Dulwich, Emanuel, Colet Court and City of London.

Remarks: Founded as a dance school in 1928 by June Hampshire; on moving to London in the early 1930s became mainstream. Her daughter, Jane Box Grainger, took over as head in the 1960s; another daughter is the well known actress Susan Hampshire. Now part of the GEMS group. Pupils in year 1 to year 8 accommodated in impressive premises on Manresa Road (marbled Corinthian columns, no less). Formerly a King's College library and, prior to that, the public library built by Earl Cadogan in 1891; the building is listed – after extensive negotiations with various bodies, including English Heritage, the staff have created their dream building for the school.

State of the art technology throughout – whiteboards that are not only interactive but also move up and down walls (wonderful for children in the early years, who still sit on the carpet) and even move around the room (an ingenious way of getting round English Heritage's intransigence about having a whiteboard installed in the grand library). Individual computer desks in many of the classrooms already and more are planned – soon all children from year 6 to year 8 will have their own computer, carefully hidden away inside the smart wooden desks, at which they can also write. ICT a great strength – children become highly competent with technology and are given the opportunity to learn touch-typing.

Lifts throughout the building – children with physical disabilities can now be accommodated – as well as individual staircases and entrances for different sections of the school to keep the homely atmosphere and ensure that the younger children feel secure. A large kitchen, which can prepare banquets for 160. Children arrive in the morning to the smell of fresh bread, baked daily, and eat lunch with the staff at round tables in the impressive June Hampshire Hall, complete with moveable stage and soundproofed screens. Gym also takes place in here; plenty of space to tuck things away, so you would never know it serves so many different purposes. Space is the overwhelming impression you get as you are shown round – no cramped stairways and classrooms in this central London school (what a welcome change from the norm); good sized walled garden, where all children can get some fresh air during break times.

Games take place at Battersea Park, swimming at Chelsea swimming baths (younger ones still swim at Fulham pools). Wonderfully atmospheric library which smells of studiousness. Domed window in the ceiling – balcony bursting with bookshelves but treacherous balustrade, too dangerous to use so just for show. The downstairs, however, teems with genuine learning – old and new: the hallmark computer desks again, a long wide mahogany table around which a whole class can work, mobile interactive whiteboard, as well as doughnut cushions for the younger ones in an intimate space carved out for them between two marble pillars.

Family-based, community-spirited atmosphere; pupils are friendly and encouraged to look after each other. They work hard and are much praised. A wide curriculum, including four languages. During a week in May each year the prep school section closes down and relocates to a château in France where they rock climb and canoe etc, as well as continuing with academic subjects.

Careful assessments of the children at every stage through a combination of PIPs, NFER, national curriculum levels and CATs testing. Maximum 20 to a class, a watchful eye is kept and special needs are quickly identified. A dedicated SENCo (highly praised by one parent for her direct approach and ability to make her sessions fun) is employed full time, and works one-to-one with children diagnosed with, eg, dyslexia and dyspraxia. The gifted and talented, after a lengthy and careful assessment, are given a programme of accelerated learning. Visiting speech therapists, and EFL is catered for in-house. A lot of demand for this, as school is made up of a significant number of foreign pupils whose parents are on temporary postings.

Good inclusive arts programme: everyone is in an annual drama production, often a musical. Busy choir and orchestra (more than half the school play an instrument). Children entertain each other over lunch with informal piano recitals. Enthusiastic noises from parents, who are pleased with the breadth of education their children are getting at this stage. A relaxed and secure environment for the normal child who wants to have a go at everything.

George Heriot's Junior School

Linked school: George Heriot's School

Lauriston Place, Edinburgh, EH3 9EQ

- Pupils: Co-ed, all day • Ages: 4-11 • Fees: £6,867-£8,337 pa
- Independent

Tel: 01312 297263
Email: admissions@george-heriots.com
Website: www.george-heriots.com

Head of Junior School: Mrs L M Franklin

Exit: Almost all go on to senior school.

Remarks: See senior school.

George Watson's College Junior School

Linked school: George Watson's College

67–71 Colinton Road, Edinburgh, EH10 5EG

• Pupils: Boys and girls; all day • Ages: 3–12 • Fees: £3,906–£7,827 pa • Independent

Tel: 01314 466040
Email: jsadmissions@gwc.org.uk
Website: www.gwc.org.uk

Principal: Since 2001, Mr Gareth Edwards MA (late fifties). Has no time for the Guide since we announced to the world that he 'giggled'. He still does. We have been embargoed (their word) since his arrival at Watson's, where he has done a stunning job. Retires in July 2014.

From September 2014, Mr Melvyn Roffe BA FRSA (mid forties). Read English at York, studied education at Durham. Comes from Wymondham College in Norfolk; previously worked in both maintained and independent sector, married with a son and daughter, both at the college.

Head of Junior School: Since 2012, Mrs Catherine P Jack, whom we did not meet, previous five years as head of Longniddry Primary.

Entrance: Nursery from age 3. Early entries up to primary 3 by interview, takes about an hour. From primary 4 upwards entry is by written test and interview. Interviews in December: lang, maths and verbal reason, plus a spot of writing. Main entry to college is P7 (age 12) when four classes become five and pupils hoping to go on to the senior school get a useful boost.

Exit: No guarantee of advancement from nursery to main primary school but, once in, majority go on to senior school, unless family circumstances dictate otherwise.

Remarks: Tucked into the western edge of this bleak 50 acre campus, fronting the main rugby pitch, nursery staff have achieved a miracle. The place is charming. It is also enormous. Three parallel classes with over 30 children in each. But jolly none the less, with all the bells and whistles you expect from toddler teaching. Play areas, sand pits, water, tiny tables and dedicated play area outside. Learning begins through play in nursery. Pre-school year only, partnership scheme either mornings or all day. Intense competition, 'places are allocated 15 months prior to admission', ie the April before you want your little darling to start here. Wraparound care (Nursery Plus at new Myreside House) available drop off 7.45am collect 5.45pm (same as junior school). Nursery Plus open throughout the year, except for two weeks at Christmas. In view of the embargo (but see below) this ed visited the junior school during a recent open morning, and was met by a raft of charming and caring nursery staff: had we been accompanied we would have been allowed to try out various games and had great fun.

Children at nursery (ie pre-school year) not necessarily guaranteed a place in junior school and may be either told to try elsewhere, or asked to repeat a year – this is unique in this ed's experience. The Watson's claim is that learning should be fun – even at home; homework given from first year and parents encouraged to support.

Five parallel mixed ability classes of 25/30 based in colour coded suites of rooms: purple, beige, yellow, green and blue for the first three years. Each interlinking room has its own suite, friendly and not the least bit intimidating (though possibly a bit confusing to start with). French from age 7 with native speakers. Pupils remain in these groups, with the occasional odd one or two added if space available and that aint often the case. Jolly phonics, look 'n' say, dual teaching in class where necessary, Watson's is the school for SEN hiccups. Special catch-up classes run for any latecomers. ICT skills taught and used widely to support other subjects. Back up for maths too. Dedicated library, where the librarian seemed totally fazed by our questions. We had a charming young guide who seemed as pleased as punch to revisit her former classrooms.

Age 9 (P4) all move to upper primary, a barracks of a child education building. Rows of bleak corridors with classrooms on either side and more staircases up and down than one could imagine. Dedicated science lab with explosive experiments with Alkaseltzer and a plastic screw top container ongoing in the passage outside. Safety glasses and a fair risk of failure seemed the order of the day. Mixed-ability groups with setting only for maths at the top end of the school. Extensive library, plus audio books with a raft of headphones so all can listen at the same time, a respite from the non-stimulation – okay, odd bits of art – of the corridors. Tame librarian. Our guide thought class sizes were 25/30 and 'two classes were divided into three' for practical subjects. Good dyslexia support throughout – anxious to get away from any image of having 'a school with a unit'. SEN drop in centres abound, and plethora of assistants and trainee teachers. Sixth formers help with reading too.

Trips all over for both upper and lower, upper pupils proudly showed me their London diary, apparently they took a boat down the Themes. It never fails to irritate this long serving ed how staff can allow such stupid errors to pass. The diary was written in pencil; don't students get rubbers any more? They may not get rubbers, but from age 9, they get dedicated iPads (we were shown various apps by our enthusiastic guide) who then dropped us at the art department, 'which he couldn't show me round'. Marie Celeste it was: empty rooms: staff all cosily having coffee and our approach – having caught the eye – to one member of staff was rapidly dismissed with a head down dive into the staff room. Disappointing.

In yer face drama and music – four choirs, two recorder groups, chamber orchestra, ensembles and pipes. Oodles of extra activities and clubs. Primary pupils have full use of all senior facilities with hockey for girls, rugby for boys (only) and swimming for all.

No official scholarships but, in line with the ethos of the school, financial help given in unforeseen circumstances. Holiday club from age 10 up, junior pupils school council and award winning novice pipe band.

Parents a mixed bunch, used to have to join the Merchant Company in order to 'qualify' to send child to one of the Merchant Schools; Merchant Company still oversees major appointments, but has been more or less side-lined and, in all honesty, parents are no longer representative of the great and the good of Edinburgh. Buses from Ed and the surrounding areas, collection of incomers, first time buyers and aspirationals, number of former pupils. Small ethnic mix.

This is an enormous school: young can take advantage of senior school's facilities, but with almost 2,500 pupils, it aint really the place for your flower. Good teaching and good value for money, if you can close your eyes to the assembly line like atmosphere. We have visited jollier gulags.

Giggleswick Junior School

Linked school: Giggleswick School

Giggleswick, Settle, BD24 0DE

• Pupils: 95 pupils, 48 girls/ 47 boys, 3 full boarders and 1 flexi-boarder • Ages: 3–11 • Fees: Day £6,750–£10,800; Boarding £13,875–£17,985 pa • Independent

Tel: 01729 893150
Email: juniorschool@giggleswick.org.uk
Website: www.giggleswick.org.uk

Headmaster: Since 2007, Mr Mark Brotherton BEd NPQH (early forties). Trained with PE specialism and is a keen sportsman and coach. Family affair, as son and daughter taught, and wife, Heather, teaches French in the junior school. Previously director of studies and deputy head at St Hugh's School, Woodall Spa, Lincs. Interests include rugby, cricket and golf; keen triathlete. Wants children to be 'happy, respectful and confident…, keen to learn and enjoy opportunities presented to them at school'. Is working to maintain a 'warm and friendly family atmosphere in which children thrive and develop'.

Entrance: Children are welcomed to taster days with no formal entrance examination, but some assessment, interview with the parent and child and a full report from the previous school. Pupils who are non-native speakers of English may expect to take extra English lessons (EFL) according to need. Children with specific learning difficulties may be accepted provided the school feels able to offer the specialist and general assistance required.

Exit: All to Giggleswick senior school.

Remarks: A small school, warm and welcoming, providing a positive learning environment with a wide range of experiences as part of the curriculum, underpinned by strong family and Christian values that mirror the Giggleswick ethos.

In a green and tranquil setting, discreetly situated on the edge of the campus, an attractive purpose-built two storey building offering bright modern classrooms with walls covered in dazzling displays of pupil work. A welcoming and happy atmosphere exudes from the spacious early years' unit, well accommodated with easy access between indoor and outdoor activity areas. Library, ICT suite, music room, learning support tutorial room and self-contained playground, together with dedicated separate art room and brand new sports hall, provide excellent facilities (particularly considering the small number of pupils).

School day ends at 3.30pm for those in year 2 and below, with after-school care with tea until 5.30pm, at a price. For older children it's 5.00pm, with the option for day pupils to join boarding activities until 7.15pm, and for years 5 and 6 Saturday school plus sport as well – preparation for 'full on' days in senior school.

Mixed age classes years 1/2 and years 3/4. Small class size enables personalised learning and topics are rotated every two years so no repetition in the curriculum. Parents seem very happy with the outcome, particularly liking 'the way each pupil is treated as an individual and encouraged to develop at their own pace'. Single age classes at years 5 and in the final year 6, when all lessons are taught by specialists and home economics is introduced. Parents speak glowingly of the staff who they say 'are always willing and eager to help/support/listen; nothing is ever too much trouble and most go the extra mile'. Weekly homework in numeracy and literacy. SEN teacher and assistant, working closely with senior school colleagues, provide classroom assistance where need identified – if necessary child withdrawn for one-to-one.

Teaching programmes based on the national curriculum, with languages introduced in reception, but no Latin. Strong emphasis on sport, with sessions five times a week, qualified coaching and excellent facilities. Flourishing music under the baton of own head of music, with the majority of pupils playing an instrument or singing. LAMDA classes for junior 'luvvies' and a chance to shine in annual productions.

Good reporting to parents, with monthly on-line assessment, tracking effort. Four seasons covered with winter and summer reports, autumn and spring meetings. Also open door welcome for parents, who comment on 'the accessibility and approachability of staff at all levels'.

Lots of 'golds' for good deeds as well as academic achievement, building to personal certificates and contributing to house success. Worry box, opened in private weekly by Mr Brotherton, for those who don't feel able to approach friend or teacher. Nice idea – but isn't likely to get much use, we feel. The pupils told us that 'we do fall out but quickly make up with each other.' Parents would agree, as they felt that 'any issues are dealt with swiftly' and that each child's 'strengths, weaknesses, talents and interests are accepted and embraced by staff and pupils alike', so that 'pupils actively congratulate each other on achievements and encourage each other in weaker areas'. The result is happy, self-confident children who show care and concern for those around them.

Few full boarders, though some flexi-boarding in the eight-bedded dorms in the junior boarding house, which also houses senior boarders up to year 9. Full activity programme and a new year 5 boarder spoke glowingly of kindness, good dinners and fun.

The Glasgow Academy Dairsie

Linked school: The Glasgow Academy

54 Newlands Road, Newlands, Glasgow, G43 2JG

• Pupils: 70 boys and girls; • Ages: 3–9; • Fees: £3,645–£8,205 pa; • Independent

Tel: 01416 320736
Email: dairsie@tga.org.uk
Website: www.theglasgowacademy.org.uk

Head: From June 2013, Miss H Logi.

Remarks: Same format as for Milngavie. Putative deal in pipe line to extend premises.

The Glasgow Academy Milngavie

Linked school: The Glasgow Academy

Mugdock Road, Milngavie, Glasgow, G62 8MP

• Pupils: 70 boys and girls • Ages: 3–9 • Fees: £3,640–£8,205 pa • Independent

Tel: 01419 563758
Email: atholl@tga.org.uk
Website: www.theglasgowacademy.org.uk

Head: Ms Jean McMorran

Remarks: See preparatory school.

The Glasgow Academy Preparatory School – Kelvinbridge

Linked school: The Glasgow Academy

Colebrooke Terrace, Glasgow, G12 8HE

• Pupils: 693–323 girls/370 boys • Ages: Prep 3–11, Milngavie and Dairsie 3–9; all day • Fees: £8,205–£10,575 pa • Independent

Tel: 01413 425481
Email: prepschool@theglasgowacademy.org.uk
Website: www.theglasgowacademy.org.uk

Head: Since 2007, Mr Anthony (Tony) M Brooke BEd, (fifties). Educated at Eastbourne College, followed by University of Southampton. Previously head of Sutton Valence prep (qv), and before that was at Yardley Court (now part of the Somerhill group). Controls this prep conglomerate with the lightest of touches.

All three schools – Kelvinbridge, Milngavie and Dairsie – amalgamate at Kelvinbridge in P5 (nine to ten year olds). The satellites join up at Kelvinbridge on Mondays, and roughly – with teaching variations – all three preps follow the same programme. Romans when we visited, birds the following week (Milngavie alone does Mandarin). Enthusiastic reading programme. Older children are encouraged to read to younger ones. The school is involved with the Sydney Film School in making a programme about their accelerated reading (Jolly Phonics and Jolly Grammar). All at Kelvinbridge use the big school facilities.

Assistant head, responsible for Milngavie, is Miss Jean McMorran DCE PGDip in Leadership and Management Dip TEFL who also rolls out the combined prep money education programme and is a whizzo in the maths world.

Entrance: Through nursery up via kindergarten. Some come straight to kindergarten. Interview with parents on-site.

Exit: Some 'local' parents may simply use the toddler groups and go into the state system, but most go on to junior school at Colebrooke Street, followed by senior school. Very occasional pupil may leave at eight to go to trad prep schools and some may go to junior depts of trad senior schools at 11.

Remarks: All three sites operate a terrific nursery school. Toddlers sport tracksuits, with waterproof trackies for wet weather. Heavily-staffed. Milngavie and Dairsie provide local pre-prep facilities both north and south of the river Clyde, with all youngsters moving to Kelvinbridge aged nine and joining up with those already there. French from seven for all. Tiny classes – 12 at Dairsie, up to 18 at Milngavie and a whopping 19 at Kelvinbridge (but class sizes here coming down). All pupils at Colebrooke use senior school facilities – labs, dining room etc. Terrific child-care facilities. Drop off at Kelvinbridge and Milngavie and Dairsie from 8am, Mini Cool Kids' Club from 3.10pm to 3.50pm at all three sites, plus after-school care from 3.50pm to 6pm (depends on age of pupil, homework supervision if necessary). Strict rules for collection at the end of the day, including passwords and fines. Holiday club for those up to 14 based at Kelvinbridge throughout most of the holidays and half terms – costs £29 per day and school offers a 'comprehensive and varied programme,' including visits to the beach, Kelvingrove etc. Themed holiday weeks too – circus, film, sports. Parents have to fill in the most complicated permission forms to have photographs taken, to have a medical plaster if skin is broken in an accident, to have a snack... Well thought out, incredibly useful. Impressive set-up, cradle to grave, can't fault it.

Glebe Primary School

Sussex Road, Ickenham, Uxbridg,e Middlesex, UB10 8BH

• Pupils: 465; 205 boys/225 girls in the main school (plus 35 children in the nursery) • Ages: 3–11 • Christian (though promotes all faiths) • State

Tel: 01895 671951
Email: glebe@hillingdongrid.org
Website: www.glebe.hillingdon.sch.uk

Headteacher: Since 2006, Mr Nick Alford BA Hons, PGCE, NPQH (mid forties). Previously taught in Weston-super-Mare, then at schools in London for ten years before moving to Glebe Primary.

Married to a teacher (who is deputy head at an independent school). 'We talk a lot about education and compare notes,' he says. Young son attends nearby state primary school. 'I did think about him coming here,' he told us, 'but if he ever got picked to be in a school play or for the school football team then parents would always think it was because he was the head's son.'

A cheerful down-to-earth chap who admits to being a long suffering supporter of Plymouth Argyle. His other passions are cricket and music (The Smiths and The Beatles).

Parents praise him for being very approachable. 'He's always in the playground in the morning and knows every child's name,' one mother told us. 'It means he can spot potential difficulties before they become a problem.'

Entrance: For nursery places apply direct to the nursery and for the school apply through the local authority.

Exit: One or two go to the independent sector and a few to local grammars, but the majority head to Vyners School in Ickenham or Douay Martyrs.

Remarks: Set in the deepest London suburbs (Ickenham tube is near the end of the Piccadilly and Metropolitan lines) and built in the 1970s, the school caters for a mixed intake. Ten per cent of pupils come from military families stationed at the local RAF base and often only stay or a short time. Most pupils are drawn from the local area but the catchment area has shrunk in recent years as the school has grown more popular. 'When I first started as head I used to see some local children walking away from Glebe to a primary school further away which had a better reputation,' said the head. 'But now I'm proud to say that those children are now coming back to Glebe and even transferring from the other school.'

Sats results are above the national average but the most recent Ofsted report found that 'more able pupils have not always done as well as expected.' However the head told us that this point has been addressed 'through setting and focus groups for more able children over the last few years' and as a result, level 5 Sats results have risen to well above the national average. There is a joint project for gifted and talented pupils with a neighbouring school and Glebe recently won the Hillingdon Maths Challenge. School also has links with nearby Brunel University – for science and PE lessons.

The school's go-getting motto is 'We can and we will!' and first impressions reminded us more of a private school than a state primary. Photos on the wall of the head boy, head girl and house captains show the ambitious nature of the place and the head told us that he was keen 'to replicate some of the best aspects of independent schools, such as widening opportunities in sports, music and introducing a house system and prefects.'

Much of the games teaching is delivered by a specialist sports coach. Sports include football, netball, cross country, athletics, cricket and tag rugby (supported by an enthusiastic year 6

G

teacher). The school takes part in inter-school competitions and recently won the Uxbridge football competition.

All children get the chance to study a musical instrument. This starts in year 2 with recorders and free tuition on the keyboard from year 4. Parents can pay for tuition in violin, cello, clarinet or flute if they want their children to take music exams. Two guitar clubs after school and when we visited we saw a group of year 4 children strumming away confidently. School choir performs regularly in different concerts, including one at the 02 Arena. 'The music provision is wonderful,' said an appreciative parent. Former pupils include TV presenter Sue Cook and London 2012 athlete Julia Bleasdale.

The school is a regional centre for those with impaired hearing. The SRP – Specialist Resourced Provision for hearing-impaired children – has two teaching areas and a speech therapy room. Each classroom has a Soundfield system, amplifying the sound of the teacher's voice. There are places for nine hearing impaired children and the school employs two specialist teachers of the deaf. All the children are on the roll of their mainstream class and school aims for them to be taught in class alongside their hearing peers, with support if necessary.

The school's main downside is the buildings. Although they are set in spacious grounds, with a large tree-lined field, half the school is housed in prefab buildings (cold in winter and hot in summer). However, these are soon to be demolished and replaced by a brand-new two-storey building – the school hopes to move in spring 2014. Another gripe is that no hot food is served on site so children have to bring packed lunches (this will be resolved with opening of the new building).

Parents are very supportive and reckon the school has a strong nurturing ethos. 'It feels like a little village school and it has a very caring environment,' said one. 'All the children are aware of each other and support each other.' Another told us: 'I wouldn't hesitate to recommend it to anyone. I feel that I struck gold when I found Glebe.'

Glendower Prep School

87 Queen's Gate, London, SW7 5JX

- Pupils: 220 girls, all day • Ages: 4–11 • Inter-denom
- Fees: £15,750 pa • Independent

Tel: 020 7370 1927
Email: office@glendower.kensington.sch.uk
Website: www.glendowerprep.org

Headmistress: Since September 2012, Mrs Sarah Knollys (rhymes with tolls) BA PGCE (mid 40s), educated at Wycombe Abbey and St Paul's Girls', Exeter (a degree in French and Italian) and Roehampton Universities. Started teaching career as SEN assistant at Finton House School, London; rose from form teacher to maths co-ordinator, SCITT mentor, key stage 2 manager, senior management team and school governor at Allfarthing School, London, a busy state school in Wandsworth, (1993-2000); founding head, Maple Walk School, London (2005-2012). Married to Christopher; they have two teenage sons.

Bright and bubbly, Mrs Knollys exudes warmth and is highly accessible. She is the kind of person who rolls up her sleeves and gets on with it, whether it be teaching netball, transforming school lunches or wearing her slipper socks round the school on Red Nose day and dressing up in something crazy on Fun Friday. She is a woman who gets things done – as can be seen from her previous job at Maple Walk, the pioneer New Model school which started 'out of a trunk' as she puts it with two pupils and increased exponentially to 150 pupils by the time she left.

This is her first experience of a single sex school. 'I thought I'd miss the boys' she remarks, 'but I don't miss the scraps in the playground – and our girls are very feisty.' She loves the girls, she says, because of their enthusiasm for everything, their lack of shame about excelling in science and maths and the more stable class dynamic – which can often be distorted by a predominance of one gender, she explains. She makes herself available to the parents, emails are responded to promptly, and she is there every morning to greet families. She is particularly on top of the 11 plus process, which starts with private meetings with her as early as year 4.

She is a good listener and we were told by one girl that 'she took on board our suggestions so we have much better lunches now, we no longer have to serve the younger children their lunch, and the loos and sinks are much nicer.' Her visible presence around the school includes teaching year 6 Latin, supporting maths in year 5 and English comprehension in year 4. That way she can properly understand each child and write detailed reports for the senior schools as well as giving fully informed advice to parents. She has one-to-one meetings with everyone from the kitchen staff through to the teaching staff and the parents. No one gets special treatment but everyone gets proper attention. This is a woman who throws herself into every aspect of the job and has been seen wiping her tears away during a music assembly. 'These are my girls,' she says unapologetically.

Entrance: Selective at 4 years. Far too many applicants for the 36 places. The girls are assessed on an informal basis – essentially to see if they interact well and can do the basics competently. Any parent who thinks coaching at this age is a good idea – forget it now. Sensible sibling policy means that often there are fewer than 36 places open to newcomers. The tinies are assessed for 40 minutes in small groups. Older children applying for an occasional place will be assessed for longer – a morning or perhaps a full day, careful note being taken on whether they can cope and how they interact with their peers. No particular feeder nurseries. Occasional places occur but school unlikely to fill them after year 5 – the cohesion of the year being seen as paramount. It's worth a call, though. Some bursaries available for needy local girls or those already in the school who fall on hard times. Unsuccessful applicants for 4+ entry and later applicants to the school will be placed on a waiting list for consideration should an occasional place arise.

Exit: Recently, quite a number to top boarding schools – among them, Benenden, Downe House, St Mary's Calne, Wycombe Abbey. A wide range of offers from London day schools – including the odd co ed one – but girls tend to go to St Paul's, Godolphin & Latymer, Francis Holland SW1, St James's and even as far afield as South Hampstead and Putney High. Always a handful of scholarships each year – art and music as well as academic.

Remarks: Think purple. Think elegant. Think Glendower. Natty purple berets, charming purple checked and striped uniform, purple website, purple chairs and folders in the class rooms, purple benches and tables in the playground as well as the purple scooters that the girls arrive on. Plush carpets and sweeping staircase in a building that feels much more like a comfortable home than a school. The 1830s white building on Queen's Gate occupies a large corner plot facing Stanhope Gardens. Since 2010 part of the adjacent building integrated with the school through a major development and refurbishment programme. The resulting six storey building is remarkably spacious. An airy, panelled and white-painted entrance hall, complete with wonderful large Quentin Blake originals, greets the visitor and is also used, with the doors opened to the adjacent library, as an assembly space. Library attractive and well-stocked. Excellent displays of work everywhere, lots of up-to-the-minute equipment in all rooms, which are remarkably orderly with inviting and interesting-looking work and resources.

From the moment you enter Mrs Knollys' study with its large Victorian partners' desks and oil portraits on the oak-panelled walls, you know this is a school with history. Founded by two spinsters in 1895; the eyes of one (Edith Lloyd) follow you around the room from above the fireplace. Glendower is a charitable trust, and has always been run as a not-for-profit organisation – a nostalgic relief as spanking new profit-making companies pop up throughout the city, establishing expensive schools to meet demand.

Girls get lots of attention here. One teacher/assistant to 11 girls, class sizes of between 16 and 18. Not a school for those with serious SENs but school will pick up and support those with mild difficulties and make individual learning plans for those who need them. Between five and 10 per cent of girls are on the SEN register, more are being monitored. No stigma, just lots of support. There's a handwriting club during lunch break, some who have been diagnosed dyscalculic get support from outside – Emerson House for example; a learning support assistant will go into the classroom to give support with organisational/processing skills etc. No extra charge for this. Some five per cent come needing a little extra help with English and EFL is given in small groups or one-to-one as needed. Parents a real mix, US, Chinese, European – lots of bilingual, trilingual, English as a fourth language – but they are here for the duration – not much to-ing and fro-ing. Specialist teaching right from the start – French, music, drama and PE, and by year 4 almost all teaching is specialist. The academic programme includes DT and ICT, and Mrs Knollys is no Luddite – plans afoot to introduce tablets in the classrooms. Science is well equipped and busy. The girls enthused about identifying cells under a microscope using iodine.

The post 11 plus programme is excellent and includes touch typing, Latin and lots of public speaking – balloon debating competitions against other schools is a popular one. Poetry competitions all through the school, poems recited by heart, girls vote for the winners and finals judged by eg famous actresses and poets. Lots of music – and the twice weekly music assemblies can feature anything from Bollywood dancing to a harp recital. Most girls play at least one instrument and many take musical theatre exams. 'Music is as natural as breathing here,' glows Mrs Knollys. 'No-one is concerned about performing and there are no divas.' This school is no slouch when it comes to sport either, despite having no grounds to speak of. They are fiendish at netball and compete at national level as well as against other local schools and among themselves in inter-house matches. We saw several girls snatch some precious moments during break to practise their shooting skills. Theatrical productions and swimming take place at Imperial College, athletics in Chiswick. The girls also play tennis and rounders. Lunch: 'we are no longer vegetarian!' – another change introduced by the attentive Mrs Knollys. Fish on Fridays. Only vegetarian options on Mondays but the rest of the week meat galore. Food cooked fresh on the premises and they eat in their own dining room – no packed lunches here – hurrah!

Godolphin Preparatory School

Linked school: Godolphin, Salisbury

Laverstock Road, Salisbury, SP1 2RB

- Pupils: 85 girls, introduction of prep boarding • Ages: 3–11 • Fees: Day £5,940–£11,475; Boarding £14,376–£19,377 pa
- Independent

Tel: 01722 430652
Email: admissions@godolphin.wilts.sch.uk
Website: www.godolphinprep.org

Headmistress: Since 2005, Mrs Paula White BEd (fifties); trained at Winchester (formerly known as King Alfred's College). Previously acted as consultant leader for literacy and numeracy, Hampshire Education Authority, and was also head of Burghclere Primary School, Hampshire. Married, has one daughter at Godolphin School. Approachable, relaxed, puts parents and pupils at ease straight away, whilst commanding the respect of the girls with her authoritative, yet kindly presence. Took over the prep school at a difficult time: parents were abandoning ship and classes were shrinking. Has successfully turned its fortunes around and built closer ties with the senior school. Numbers are on the up and school is near capacity. Aims to attract more boarders and encourage still more integrated links with Godolphin School.

Entrance: Girls come up through school's own pre-prep, otherwise from local primary schools and other prep schools in the area (further afield if boarding). Entry at all stages (boarders from year 5) following an assessment day in the school and satisfactory report from current school head. Ten per cent discount is offered to girls from Forces families, five per cent for sisters.

Exit: Girls increasingly choose to remain at Godolphin (up to 90 per cent but varies each year) and are prepared for CE in the spring. Good record of academic scholarships – some gain music and sporting awards too. The rest move on to other popular secondary schools nearby, eg St Swithun's, Sherborne Girls, St Mary's Shaftesbury or South Wilts Grammar School (prep runs 11+ practice sessions for girls' grammar).

Remarks: Founded in 1993 and housed in a modern building on the edge of the Godolphin School campus. Very easy to get to – no public parking on site, but masses of space on the road in front of school entrance makes dropping off in the morning a breeze.

Strong on traditional teaching, school sums up its approach as 'national curriculum plus a bit more'. Maths is solid, reinforced by clubs in lunch breaks and 'mathletics' programmes on school computers in ICT room. English also good – 'Girls have to write every day and put their skills into practice'. French teaching begins in the nursery at 2 and continues throughout; Spanish and German introduced in year 6. Latin, Greek and science after-school clubs; reasoning group provides extra practice for those aiming for 11+. Well-organised library perches above main hall on a mezzanine floor. Very little staff turnover, with most members of staff in their 30s and 40s (not a man in sight). Parents full of praise for the head – 'she brings out the best in her teachers, which in turn brings out the best in the girls'. Small class sizes (12 on average) allow staff to shepherd their flocks effectively – 'They switched my daughter on to school again'.

Small SEN room separated from main hall by glass walls for around six pupils. One parent commented that school's 'fantastic' learning support teacher ensured that her 'daughter's confidence went up 100 per cent'. This staff member has an impressive array of qualifications, including degrees in psychology and special needs education. A common theme is the willingness of staff to fit the style of teaching to the child.

Three double games lessons each week – girls jog off to the senior school to use its grass pitches and hard courts. Gymnastics for all, lacrosse is introduced in year 5. Until then the main team sports are hockey and netball. Excellent swimming lessons each week (including for nursery-age children) in fabulous 25-metre swimming pool; the best swimmers are invited to join a competitive swimming squad after school. Handfuls of ASA distance awards distributed at school assemblies. For those who want more, extracurricular clubs include ballet and yoga; in summer, girls can choose tennis and rounders at break and after school. Keen horse riders join senior school equestrian teams.

Instrumental music has improved under Mrs White's stewardship – string ensemble now on offer for young players, plus a recorder ensemble and violin group (Fiddle-Dee-Dee). Music is even scheduled for tinies in the nursery. Those learning instruments (taught by senior school peripatetic staff) play alongside Godolphin pupils once a year and perform in their own biannual concert. Occasional workshops take place with school, visiting musicians. Director of prep school music runs busy junior choir with her own special blend of South African enthusiasm and joy; firmly believes in making singing fun and succeeds in getting polite little English girls swaying and handclapping along with the best of them. Choir has performed at the Bath Festival and Barbican Centre and regularly joins the senior choir to sing in Salisbury Cathedral; winners of Barnardo's Choir of the Year (with senior school). Unusual music theory club open to years 1 to 6; girls regularly pass ABRSM theory of music exams up to grade 2.

Fantastic senior school art block is open to the prep – girls have the use of two painting/drawing studios, plus two further rooms dedicated to ceramics and textiles. Drama productions take place every other year in the Blackledge Theatre (impressive performance space). List of clubs not extensive, but does include the feminine arts of dressmaking and sewing as well as the less traditional Kidz Zumba. Residential trips to Normandy, France, for years 5 and 6 every other year – girls add fencing, canoeing and negotiating an assault course to their language practice.

Main school founded in 1726 from a bequest made by Elizabeth Godolphin, opened its doors 100 years later with the admission of eight 'orphan gentlewomen' into its first home in Salisbury Cathedral close, moving to its present 16-acre site on Milford Hill in 1891. Prep school feels quite separate from the main site; senior school buildings are invisible and little to suggest that it's part of a bigger campus. Right on the edge of the senior school's land, outdoor space is thus a bit squeezed. Girls don't seem to notice, however, and play happily in the small outside playground to the front of the school. Prep's nursery has the lion's share of the grounds at the rear. School's exterior still looks good as new. Inside, big classrooms, an open plan hall and wide corridors and stairs all contribute to the general air of tidiness and calm. Good use of colour makes the school feel especially cheerful. Nursery and pre-prep classrooms display thoughtful touches, eg whiteboards that pull down to eye level for the youngest children.

Pastoral care is excellent and staff keep a keen eye on the details, eg making sure that everyone chooses sensibly at lunchtimes (girls walk up to senior dining room and choices are restricted to discourage fads). Girls may arrive for breakfast at 7:30am and stay on for prep until 5:40pm. School uniform mirrors senior school kit, with red pinnies (worn over full school uniform), boaters and blazers. Student food council meets once every half-term to provide direct feedback to school chef, whilst year 6 leads school council and selects classroom charities. Friday afternoon assemblies (musicians and public speakers have informal opportunities to perform here) close the school week and parents are welcome.

Boarders in years 5 and 6 housed on separate floor in Walters House; parents report that staff have quickly adapted to the needs of younger girls, but more boarders are needed to reduce the age range in dorms. The use of mobile phones is rationed and 'prep plus' activities for junior girls are on the up. Kindness is encouraged so that 'girls become Godolphinised and caring'.

Small and very friendly, the prep 'feels more like a home where you are well educated'. Although perhaps not for the most tenacious of tomboys, this is a kindly, nurturing school where girls can relax and be confident and happy. Academically focused without being a hothouse, its growing links with Godolphin School can only continue to benefit prep school pupils.

Godstowe Preparatory School

Shrubbery Road, High Wycombe, HP13 6PR

- Pupils: 415; 400 girls/15 boys, 90 full and flexi boarders
- Ages: 3–13 • C of E • Fees: Day £9,090–£14,175; Boarding £20,820 pa • Independent

Tel: 01494 529273
Email: registrar@godstowe.org
Website: www.godstowe.org

Headmaster: Since 2006, Mr David Gainer (early fifties). Educated at Claires Court, Maidenhead and Belmont Abbey in Herefordshire, followed by St Mary's University College, Twickenham, where he studied maths and drama. Began career at Llanarth Court Prep in South Wales then returned to alma mater Belmont Abbey as housemaster, followed by three years at Forest Grange Prep in Horsham as deputy head, before taking up first headship at Belmont Prep near Dorking in 1991.

Lives in the thick of it in the main school building with wife Cathy, the school registrar. According to one parent, 'if you could choose a headmaster for your son or daughter, it would be Mr Gainer.' Girls and parents alike comment on his energy, enthusiasm and hands-on presence around the school (he attends all sports matches and eats dinner with the boarders every night) – and they're not the only ones: he was recently named best head of a prep school by Tatler. Praise indeed. Commands respect yet obvious affection from pupils – appears truly in loco parentis. Parents are 'hooked' as soon as they meet him – and no wonder: he lets them have his home telephone number.

Passionate about the benefits of years 7 and 8, the head describes these years as 'dynamic bubble wrap' – keeping the girls in a nurturing environment while they mature, yet allowing them genuine responsibility, freedom and leadership opportunities at the top of the school. Highly focused on personal development and believes that academic success depends on it. According to the head, Godstowe encourages 'everyone to aim high, whatever their ability and potential.'

Pioneered a system of deferred senior school places, 'brokering deals' to secure girls' places at 11 to transfer at 13. Strong relationships with senior schools borne out by the fact that 25 schools choose to send their head as representative to Godstowe's biannual senior school fair.

Entrance: Despite Godstowe's growing popularity, head is adamant that it will remain a 'first come first served', non-selective school. Majority intake (about 80 per cent) at 7 from its own pre-prep, The Lodge, with girls joining all the way through to year 6 from a variety of local prep and state schools, and boarders joining from further afield in the upper years. Boarding can be full time or flexible with many day girls choosing to try it in years 7 and 8 as a taster for senior school.

G

Exit: Not a specific feeder, with alumni most years heading off to some 20 different secondaries. A reasonable contingent to Wycombe Abbey each year (normally with a handful of scholarships), plus an enviable array of top co-ed and girls' day and boarding schools, including Benenden, Bradfield, Cheltenham Ladies' College, Downe House, Queen Anne's, Stowe and Wellington.

Remarks: England's first girls' boarding prep school and Enid Blyton's inspiration for Malory Towers, purpose built in 1900. The grounds make excellent use of a hilly, if a little blustery, site overlooking High Wycombe, with the original pretty Virginia creeper-clad buildings now housing years 3 to 8, plus The Lodge and nursery buildings. The few boys in pre-prep, mostly siblings, peel off at the age of 7.

The airy new double height reception building (buzzing at pick-up and drop-off times) is a modern addition to the more rustic Victorian buildings and has a gallery-like atmosphere, setting the tone for the rather artsy feel of the whole school. Other recent revamps include the dining room (we highly recommend the lasagne), art room and food technology centre, opened in 2007 by Raymond Blanc. There's also a new £2m sports hall to compensate for the antiquated and somewhat uninviting swimming pool building, chilly water and all. The school says it has made significant investments in this in recent years but it is far from being its star attraction.

Definitely not a school placing importance on hushed tones, although good manners are notably present. Girls dash about chatting noisily between lessons, picking up considerable speed when heading to the dining room for lunch. Posters all over the school that indoctrinate pupils to be happy, confident and successful are clearly doing the trick.

Non-selective it may be, but success is in the air here. Minority (about 15 per cent) peel off at 11 to local schools (parents have to 'opt in' to 11+), but unlike many prep schools in the area which hothouse pupils for the sought-after Bucks grammars, this is a true 3-13 establishment, feeding its post-CE alumni into a heady mix of top day and boarding indies, many with scholarships. Which are pretty abundant, by the way, with the current record for one year standing at 26, to 17 different schools. Head puts this down to 'quality teaching' and the fact that girls are 'led rather than pushed through the curriculum'. He is proud not to share the pushy reputation of some of his competition.

French is taught from reception, Latin and Spanish from year 5 in creatively themed classrooms. Classes in pre-prep school 'subtly' streamed, with a maximum class size of 18. Formal streaming from year 6 for English, maths and French. Girls stay in form rooms for lessons in years 3 and 4, after which they start to move around the school for individual subjects.

General acceptance that everyone learns differently and SEN is all in a day's work rather than marginalised. Two dedicated SEN staff in place and an excellent EAL programme – mostly for those boarders from the Far East, Spain and Nigeria, with girls' needs assessed upon entry to the school and timetabled to meet their specific requirements. Boarders' prep takes place from 4.30 to 6.30, although an hour of this is often taken up with an enrichment activity. Day girls report homework levels to be acceptable.

Creative pursuits are well catered for, with a dedicated sewing room in CDT where girls knock up the odd wedding gown for the year 8 fashion show. Some 300 girls learn musical instruments and practise daily in bright, well-equipped studios. Pupils' artistic endeavours are displayed throughout the school – and with good reason. They look more like GSCE work, thanks to the inspirational head of art, who specialises in 3D work.

The art department, with its gleaming new extension (2012), has the wow factor in terms of space and light, as does the work on show there, from glazed pottery meals on plates to life-size papier maché humans – not a still life fruit bowl in sight. Taught by specialists from the word go, senior girls win art scholarships

every year, but importantly parents report that a passion for creativity has been bred into the core of the school and latent talent is eeked out of those who didn't know they had it.

Parents say the standard of music is 'incredible', with one slipping in that the girls' achievements and public performances by far outstrip those at their brothers' schools. All pupils are encouraged to participate from the age of 3 in regular recitals and choir is compulsory in years 3 to 6.

Sports lessons are four times a week, with the usual suspects (netball, lacrosse and hockey) taking centre pitch – all to a high competitive standard. Athletics, rounders and swimming are also on offer, as are ballet, gymnastics and dance. Parents of children in larger year groups occasionally grumble that the A and B teams are a bit exclusive, with not everyone getting a go, but the head is keen to introduce more teams and by and large most girls are able to compete at some level, often with winning results.

Boarding facilities have a real home from home feel, with bedrooms (sleeping between four and eight) rather than dorms, cosy sitting rooms and homely kitchens. All have their own large gardens, with swings and other outdoor equipment. Housemistresses are non-teaching staff, leaving them free to focus on girls' pastoral care. Pupils are charming and poised without a hint of precociousness and describe their typical peer as 'kind and happy'. Early drop-off plus breakfast (7.30am) and late pick-up plus supper (6.30pm) is available for day girls at low cost.

The mobile phone arms race was stopped by the clever acquisition of 100 bog standard phones (yes, these do still exist) into which girls can insert their own SIM cards to call home. Thursdays are 'no go gadget' evenings in the boarding houses to further encourage those old fashioned skills, reading, conversation and game playing. Girls say the best thing about Godstowe is 'everyone is happy all the time' – future careers in PR await.

The 'enrichment curriculum' – that's after school clubs in old money – offers up to 50 free options for two hours a day from 4.30pm. These range from the traditional sports, LAMDA and wind band to the more diverse knitting, prop-making and cross stitch, with up to 100 girls staying for these. Boarders benefit from a buzzing spectrum of activities at weekends too (rarely fewer than 50 girls in), many of which take place off site (bowling, skating, theatre, cinema etc).

Post CE, year 8s are given a lifestyle crash course to prepare them for a less cossetted existence. Includes classes in self-defence, internet safety and relationships, charitable works, trips out, visiting lecturers and, in a surprisingly retro twist, a hair and beauty day, which seems a little old fashioned but, hey ho, girls will be girls.

The Grammar School at Leeds Junior School

Alwoodley Gates, Harrogate Road, Leeds, LS17 8GS

- Pupils: 430 junior, 295 nursery and pre-prep • Ages: 3–11
- Non-denom • Fees: £8,001–£8,721 pa • Independent

Tel: 01132 291552
Email: admissions@gsal.org.uk
Website: www.gsal.org.uk

Head: Since 2009, Mr Robert Lilley BA, former head of Silcoates Junior School in Wakefield, West Yorkshire. He is supported by three deputy heads.

Entrance: Selective, by observed activities and tests appropriate to the child's age. The usual points of entry are 3+ for nursery, 4+ for reception, and 7+ for junior school, although applications can be made at any time for any age.

Exit: All pupils transfer at 11+ to senior school unless they are obviously going to struggle; parents consulted well in advance.

Remarks: Same site as senior school, sharing some facilities yet sufficiently distinct from it to allow younger children to grow up in secure surroundings. Atmosphere is happy, positive and purposeful. Year 5 on average one chronological year ahead. French or German studied from year 4. Unusually for this age group, half staff are male.

Leeds Grammar and Leeds Girls' High Schools finalised their merger, to form The Grammar School at Leeds, in 2008. This brought together girls from LGHS Ford House and boys from LGS junior department into one, co-educational junior school.

The nursery and pre-prep for The Grammar School is Rose Court, based in Headingley. This caters for three- to seven-year-olds. Most progress to the junior school at seven.

The Grange Junior School

Linked school: The Grange School

Beechwood Avenue, Hartford, Northwich, Cheshire, CW8 3AU

• Pupils: 456 day boys and girls • Ages: 4–11 • Fees: £7,515–£8,145 pa • Independent

Tel: 01606 77447
Email: office@grange.org.uk
Website: www.grange.org.uk

Headmaster: Since 2005, Mr Stephen Bennett BEd MA (early fifties). Previously head of an international school in Jeddah. Softly spoken, gentle and as one parent remarked 'has a lovely way with the children.' He has overseen a considerable building programme to expand and modernise the school. He's also a keen softball player and travels up and down the country at weekends for matches.

Entrance: Three-form entry, with class sizes of 20. Assessment for reception is January of the year of entry and consists of one to one assessment and small group work. 'We try to make it a fun morning,' says the head. 'We're watching to see how the children interact with adults and each other. We need to judge whether they will thrive here. However, they are three when they come for assessment and we don't have a crystal ball.' Pupils applying for other years spend a day in class and take a standardised assessment the following day. When we asked if priority is given to siblings the head told us: 'We don't like to split families up.'

Exit: Around 95 per cent progress to The Grange senior school (exam entry at 11). The few who don't leave due to relocation and those who might not make it through to the senior school are warned by the end of year 5.

Remarks: The junior school feels like a natural stepping stone to the senior school, with a similar ethos and breadth of curriculum. Moved to its current purpose-built site in 1996.

Large, bright classrooms with lots of high quality work on display. Lots of computers, science room and DT room complete with laser cutter. Lovely, vibrant art studio where we saw some amazing lifesized Olympic figures painted by years 5 and 6. Vast and green outdoor space, with sandpits, wigwams, climbing frames, swings, sensory garden and woodland area. One father asked: 'show me where you'd find better facilities round here,' and we reckon we'd struggle.

French is taught throughout the school, Spanish in years 5 and 6. Specialist teachers for drama, PE, science, art and music. All children are automatically screened for SEN in years 3 and 5. Part time SENCo is able to deal with a whole range of SEN children on an individual basis and keeps close contact with parents. Lift access to all floors.

Good range of sports including rugby, cricket, cross country, golf and martial arts, although one mum pointed out there weren't enough teams for most children to represent the school. School has its own sports hall and there's swimming from year 2 at local leisure centre.

'Excellence in music is a reality here,' the head told us. School boasts a music studio, composing room and more than 20 visiting peripatetic teachers. Lots of extracurricular clubs, including sewing, cooking, chess, storytelling and Lego.

Enthusiastic, well behaved children – girls in tartan dresses and boys in short trousers. The pupils are well prepared for a smooth transition to the senior school – they are pushed and challenged, but comfortably so.

The Grange, Monmouth Preparatory School

Linked school: Monmouth School

Hadnock Road, Monmouth, NP25 3NG

• Pupils: 130 boys, with some boarding in year 6 • Ages: 7–11
• Anglican • Fees: Day £9,660; Boarding £18,171 pa • Independent

Tel: 01600 715930
Email: thegrange@monmouthschool.org
Website: www.habs-monmouth.org

Head: Since 1997, Mrs Elaine Thomas.

Entrance: Entry at 7+ though other stages considered if places available.

Exit: Most to Monmouth School – but they have to take the entry exam on the same terms as outsiders.

Remarks: Part of a family – the Haberdashers' Monmouth schools. The co-ed pre-prep is Haberdashers' Agincourt School. Preps are separated into boys' and girls' schools, ditto the senior schools, Monmouth School being the senior school for boys.

Subject specialist teaching throughout, flourishing choir, orchestra and band and full sports fixture list. Moved to brand new purpose-built premises in 2009, sited next to large new school sports complex, all weather pitches, playing fields and brand new sports pavilion. Around 300 bookings a week for extracurricular activities.

Greenbank Preparatory School

Heathbank Road, Cheadle Hulme, Cheshire, SK8 6HU

• Pupils: 200 girls and boys • Ages: 3–11 • Non denom
• Fees: £7,290 pa • Independent

Tel: 0161 485 3724
Email: info@greenbankschool.co.uk
Website: www.greenbankschool.co.uk

Headmistress: Since 2007, Mrs Janet Lowe, Cert Ed (fifties). Previously head of infants at Stockport Grammar School. Married to a chartered surveyor, with two grown up children. Enjoys book club and attending performances by the Hallé Orchestra, also an honorary member of the Cheadle and District Rotary. Has a hands-on approach to her headship, taking a weekly story time in reception class, running year 2 and 3 recorder club and teaching RE to years 1 to 6. 'I want to be involved with the children', she tells us. 'I really get to know them and their families'. Parents describe her as 'strong, approachable and forward thinking'.

Entrance: At age 3 into preschool with some places held back for those who want reception entry. Entry is non-selective, on a first come, first served basis, with the only preference given to siblings. Places can and do become available later so always worth trying. There is also a day nursery on site and many children come from here.

Exit: Recently to the top local independents, Cheadle Hulme School, Stockport Grammar School, The King's School, Manchester Grammar School, Manchester High School for Girls, Alderley Edge School for Girls and Withington Girls School.

Remarks: Founded in 1951 in the house that is now the day nursery, now in modern, light and airy buildings on a spacious, green plot. Not much parking on site, but enough space on Heathbank Road for dropping off and picking up.

Mixed ability classes, but school believes strongly in differentiating work so that each child is treated according to their ability. Small groups receive extra support in all the different areas of the curriculum so that no child slips through the net. One mum told us, 'Never once have I felt that my children have been left to struggle. Support is always there'. 'Every pupil is set individual targets and it is up to us to make sure they achieve them', the head tells us.

French is taught throughout the school, with German and Spanish introduced in the juniors. Additionally, year 6 have a French conversation club and are also taught Latin and Mandarin. A part-time SENCO dyslexia specialist and teaching assistants work with small groups and one-to-one. Gifted and talented programme stretches bright pupils and offers a range of educational experiences. Recently children have attended workshops on space, art, geometry and poetry.

Good sport including football, rounders, water polo, netball and swimming. Thriving and impressive range of extra-curricular activities for a small school, including drama, gymnastics, cheerleading, art, football, cross country and cookery. There's even a mums' keep fit club.

Excellent music department. Nearly half the pupils have individual instrumental tuition, school holds regular music and drama productions and there are infant and junior choirs. We saw a rehearsal for an assembly on Bollywood dancing and both the staff and children looked like they were having great fun.

Specialist art teacher with her own large, bright room. Art is taken seriously here with pupils regularly winning inter school competitions, and there is some amazing work hung throughout the school. We were very taken by the Gaudi lizards created by year 6.

Library and computer room staffed by a librarian who also runs popular lunch-time touch typing club. Truly wonderful eco garden, complete with herb and vegetable patch, bird hide and pond. Regularly used for lessons, but also by the science and gardening clubs.

Lots of trips and residentials, including Lake District, London and France. Smart grey and yellow uniform. Before and after school care offered at extra cost. Children told us that school dinners were 'yummy' and the dinner ladies were 'very kind'.

Small, friendly school that does fantastically well for its pupils. Head tells us, 'it's a combination of fabulous teaching and our commitment that all our children should have very high self esteem. Then they'll learn and achieve'.

Gresham's Prep School

Linked school: Gresham's

Cromer Road, Holt, NR25 6EY

• Pupils: 305; 125 boys/180 girls. Boarding and day – 48 boarders, 30 regular flexi boarders • Ages: 3–13 including pre prep and nursery • Fees: Day £16,200; Boarding £21,300 pa; • Independent

Tel: 01263 714600
Email: prep@greshams.com
Website: www.greshams.com

Headmaster: Since 2003, Mr James Quick (early fifties) BA and PGCE from Durham. Taught at The Dragon, Oxford, where he was a housemaster, then at St Edward's. Teacher exchange at Geelong College, Australia, before coming here with wife Kim, who teaches English, history and Latin – she's a motherly presence and at meal times checks that sensible choices are made. They have four daughters – all educated at Gresham's. He's an approachable, intelligent educator who's 'visible at everything'. Big on charity and keen to get the pupils to recognise their good fortune. Teaches RS and classical studies to year 8 and is well liked by the children – the headmaster's weekly challenge is eagerly awaited and those who want to answer questions, which often require research, visit his office at the end of the week; those who do well are rewarded with a chocolate Freddo Frog bar. Also a marathon runner – his best ideas often come when training.

Entrance: Waiting list for some pre-prep year groups. Generally first come, first served, although they try their best to offer places to children with siblings in the school. At 7 – no formal assessment. Quite a few at 11 – entrants take national standardised maths and English tests plus verbal and non-verbal reasoning tests. Some from the state sector. Some of the less able follow specific French and English courses.

Exit: About 80 per cent to the senior school – advice on alternatives has to be sought. Otherwise mainly to Uppingham, Norwich School and Oundle. Rugby, Stowe and The Leys are also regular destinations. In recent years children have gone to Charterhouse, Wymondham College, Framlingham, Finborough and Ampleforth. One or two children enter local state schools in most years. All will now take year 8 'exit' exams (rather than CE) plus other senior school tests if appropriate. Entry to Gresham's senior school confirmed after results of exit exams, but those unlikely to make it will have been informed by the previous December.

Remarks: Unalloyed parental praise for this virtually autonomous, happy prep school – a minibus ride for littlies or healthy walk away from the senior school, where a pool, sports hall and squash courts. Enthusiastic staff (they clearly enjoy working here) and 'wonderful atmosphere – children are allowed to be children but they know and respect boundaries'. Not a hot-house but languages from 6, Latin from 11 and dedicated classrooms including science labs.

Instead of common entrance, has introduced its own year 7 and 8 curriculum 'which we believe is more exciting, appropriate and forward-looking and which will give our pupils a better preparation for learning at their senior schools and beyond'. Well-respected educational support department (two full-time and three part-time assistants): dyslexia etc and mild degrees of Asperger's – charges in line with senior school. All round, inclusive ethos – 'They seem to have concerts all the time' and play masses of sport; 'passionate coaches' and squillions of winning teams. Nothing lacking in the facilities department (although head says he wouldn't mind another large hall) – what they have ranges from homely and well tended (boarding houses: one extended to cater for extra demand – full, weekly and flexi) to exceptional (art room and acres of play space, including robust adventure equipment).

Everything one would expect in a well-run school. Add in creative flourishes and it becomes something more: a red telephone box discreetly nestling in a boarding house from where the off-site independent listener can be phoned (although it seems as if the 'terrific house parents' and matrons are the first port of call); music practice rooms named after composers; a welcoming library; a housemaster who looks out for rail deals for those who need to take the train home; the door of the RE room festooned with wonderful philosophical quotes; a music lesson (two a week) with pupils busily developing a composition based on train sounds; colour coded food stations in the dining hall – greens, carbs, protein: pupils must have something from each; flowers on all the dining tables; annual performances at the Edinburgh Fringe and large scale artistic mementos from leavers – one year group painted famous images on the backs of all the chairs in the art room and another produced huge, wonderfully bold replicas of modern paintings which have been framed and now cheer the dining hall.

Pre prep and nursery – separate entities – provide a happy and secure start. We loved the bustling playground – even though bitterly cold when we visited, convincing horse mimics happily cantered whilst scooters scooted and boys with miniature plastic hockey sticks played something close to a proper game.

Grimsdell, Mill Hill Pre-Preparatory School

Linked school: Mill Hill School

Winterstoke House, Wills Grove, London, NW7 1QR

• Pupils: 180; 95 boys/85 girls • Ages: 3–7 • Fees: £5,784–£12,573 pa • Independent

Tel: 020 8959 6884
Email: office@grimsdell.org.uk
Website: www.grimsdell.org.uk

Head: Mrs Pauline Bennett-Mills is founding head. Retiring in July 2014. Her successor will be Mrs Kate Simon, a Grimsdell parent and currently head of girls' upper school at Garden House. She has also been head of junior school at the (defunct) Royal School in Hampstead.

Entrance: Non-selective entry at 3+ and 4+.

Exit: Nearly all to the prep school, Belmont, then to Mill Hill School.

Remarks: For further details, see senior school.

Guildford High School Junior School

Linked school: Guildford High School

London Road, Guildford, GU1 1SJ

• Pupils: 295 girls; all day • Ages: 4–11 • Fees: £8,622–£11,529 pa • Independent

Tel: 01483 562475
Email: Guildford-Admissions@church-schools.com
Website: www.guildfordhigh.surrey.sch.uk

Head of Junior School: Since 2005 Mrs Sue Phillips (early fifties). An English graduate from Reading University, Mrs Phillips took up teaching in her thirties. She came to GHS after eight years as head of the junior school at nearby Downsend. She also teaches – currently lower sets in English but other times history or geography. Approachable, calm and professional, Mrs Phillips seems to be the personification of her own description of GHS Junior as 'relaxed excellence.' She clearly cares deeply about the girls and peppers her descriptions of myriad achievements with individuals' names. She reassures girls (and parents) that, 'the most important part of their uniform is a smile and kindness', and she expects parents to praise their daughters for every achievement, great or small.

Entrance: Selective entry by assessment and interview. At 4+ girls are assessed using games and puzzles to spot skills (language, number, cognitive, physical and social). At 7+ girls complete papers in English and maths, a computerised reasoning test and reading aloud. Competition is undoubtedly stiff with 60 to 100 sitting for 32 places in reception and only eight to 10 places in year 3. Mrs Phillips tells us she is looking for an ability to learn rather than IQ, and for girls who will enjoy GHS. The latter is key as the pace and commitment required from both pupils and parents is substantial and could make life rather miserable if the girl and her family did not enjoy it.

Exit: Once in the reception year there is a place for girls right through to the sixth form of the senior school. Mrs Phillips describes this as a 'natural transfer' which 99 per cent of the girls make. This goes some way to explain the fervour to get into the junior school since a GHS education is something of a Holy Grail for bright girls across Surrey.

Remarks: Mrs Phillips tells us that GHS, 'nurtures a joy of being at school'; this was certainly borne out by our 10 year old hosts who covered every aspect of school life with huge enthusiasm and pride as well as considerate praise for others' different achievements. They showed us beautifully neat exercise books, colourfully vibrant text books and personal planners chock full of activities and reminders. There's something interesting at every turn – a large, light stairwell with a fantastic mural spiralling through centuries of monarchs, wars and historical happenings; the library's 'Challenge Corner' with demanding books to try out; classrooms equipped with Activexpression handsets enabling the whole class to participate fully in lessons; the on-line virtual learning environment so girls can access their work at home. Every year group has a programme of trips, days out at museums, the ballet, theatre, science events, and longer visits abroad to immerse in foreign culture and language.

Teaching is a combination of traditional and innovative, practical work and academic rigour. Girls feel 'it's cool to learn' and the head feels they, 'make accelerated progress due to the sense of nurture and fun.' Extra help is readily available, whether for catch up or in a challenge group. The girls showed us a quiet corner set aside for one-to-one help; they felt anyone might need it – or ask for it – without stigma. But these are bright girls and we can't help feeling they wouldn't want to be catching up for long.

The breadth and depth of the curriculum sets GHS apart: 14 subjects are taught including Spanish from age 5, French from age 7, drama, DT, food tech and IT (from touch typing to how a computer actually works). Up to year 5 there are separate English lessons for grammar and spelling (including the origins of words). Exams focus on the core subjects of maths, English and science; without the pressures of application to the next school there is no need to teach to or sit 11+ exams. Key stage 2 results are outstanding, and expected to be so, with over 90 per cent at level 5 in every subject most years, up to 100 per cent in science.

Mrs Phillips works hard to ensure that sport, music and art all hold similar status within the school. Sportswise there are some pretty high standard and sensational achievements in swimming and netball. The juniors have use of the netball courts and fab swimming pool in the GHS sports centre, rounders is played on nearby Stoke Park. Teams are fielded from A to F and participation in extracurricular squad training is strongly encouraged. Art works are displayed to the whole school in an impressive and inspirational weekly gallery. All girls participate in drama and music, everyone takes a part in a drama production and almost everyone plays a musical instrument (or two) and performs in a group or orchestra. The list of extracurricular activities and clubs would exhaust many senior schoolchildren. Lots do incur extra costs and a few, for catch-up or enhancement, are by invitation only. Most girls do something extra every day. The pupil council involves girls from the age of 4; each form has a number of service roles so every girl has some responsibility. A few older girls are trained in listening and negotiating as peer-mediators, helping to resolve playground squabbles before they escalate. In their final junior year all pupils are prefects with roles created to fit the cohort of girls.

Pastoral care is the number one priority. Girls describe how 'teachers hear both sides' in arguments; form rooms have a worry box where girls can leave messages for their form teacher about anything that may be worrying or upsetting them. Kindness and consideration for others is genuinely apparent in the girls' behaviour and talk. Mrs Phillips is proud of the high levels of individual care, including for girls who may need extra support in the short or long term.

Families are mainly professional, some scrimping to get their girls the best. Parents come along to lots of events and get involved in an active parents' association. In each school year they are provided with a reference booklet detailing what will be expected of their daughters and how they can – and should – help them at home. This is typical of the thorough professionalism of GHS.

Clean and well-kept modern building slotted into the middle of the GHS campus, which is itself on the edge of Guildford town centre. Every corner well used and the bigger rooms, the library, art room and science lab, feel quite spacious. Outdoor space is at a bit of a premium; girls can play on a variety of colourful equipment including a wooden adventure playground in a grassy garden.

A tip-top and thorough education for very able and driven girls who want to participate in the whole range of the possible, and have the opportunity to go right through the senior school

to boot. Not suitable for girls who like to pootle through life, nor for any parent who isn't prepared to actively support their daughter's learning.

Haberdashers' Agincourt School

Linked school: Monmouth School

Dixton Lane, Monmouth, NP25 3SY

• Pupils: 67 girls and 65 boys • Ages: 3–7 • Fees: £4,014–£6,597 pa • Independent

Tel: 01600 713970
Email: enquiries@agincourtschool.org
Website: www.habs-monmouth.org

Head: Mrs E Thomas.

Exit: All go to The Grange Prep School Monmouth (boys) or Inglefield House (girls), then Monmouth School (boys) or Haberdashers' Monmouth School for Girls.

Remarks: For further details, see senior school.

The Haberdashers' Aske's Boys' Preparatory School & Pre-Preparatory School

Linked school: Haberdashers' Aske's Boys' School Linked school: The Haberdashers' Aske's Boys' Pre-Preparatory School

Butterfly Lane, Elstree, WD6 3AF

• Pupils: 290 boys; all day; • Ages: 5–11; • Fees: £11,964–£15,867 pa; • Independent

Tel: 020 8266 1779
Email: admissions@habsboys.org.uk
Website: www.habsboys.org.uk

Headteacher: Since 1997, Ms Yvonne Mercer BEd, Adv Dip Applied Educational Studies, who heads the prep and pre-prep. Trained as a PE teacher and then went on to become deputy head of Ashton Church of England Middle School for seven years, and continues to be a governor. It was at this school she says, that her future was 'implanted'.

Assertive but with a twinkle in her eye, her 16 years as the head of the prep and pre-prep schools have done nothing to dampen her enthusiasm for the job. On the contrary, she hates the word complacency and says, 'There's always something you can improve on.' We got the distinct impression that she lives for her job: 'I was ill during the holidays, but completely fine once I returned to work', and revels in all the achievements of her boys, whether she's standing on the sidelines spurring her pupils on in their various sports fixtures, or watching proudly as they excel in exams. While academia is important here, she also acknowledges that kids have to be kids and therefore will not overload them with homework. 'My philosophy is, enjoy a working day at school, but then enjoy some leisure and chilling time afterwards to maintain a healthy balance.'

She is a hands-on-head, and to get to know her pupils continues to teach religious studies, 'although not as much as I would like any more.' She believes there is a huge advantage to educating boys in a single sex school: 'It gives them the freedom to participate in some of the subject areas where, if girls were around, they would perhaps not be quite so open.'

Very much of the opinion that boys should be aware of their privileges so fundraising events are a priority. The biggest challenge of her teaching career to date was a recent two month sabbatical to South Africa to work at The Sparrow School in Johannesburg, where 60 per cent of pupils are orphans, primarily as a result of HIV. 'It was an amazing and humbling experience, and wonderful to see how the money our school has raised has been used to house some of these orphans and provide textbooks.' Her experience was filmed and shown to the students on her return.

She is a popular and approachable head, and as one parent said; 'she has a profound concern for the children and their education. She is the sort of person who goes that extra mile.'

Entrance: Selective entry at 5+ and 7+. Pre-prep: first round of assessments in age bands; tasks aim to 'identify potential'. Those called back for second round have individual 45 minute assessments; parents interviewed by head. There are 36 places. Prep: Around 70 take reading, writing, maths and verbal reasoning tests, competing for 20 places; some 40 invited back for further assessments and interview. No sibling policy as such but having a sibling in the boys' or girls' school, or being the son of an Old Haberdasher, may help in a tie break.

Exit: Automatic entry from pre-prep to prep. Most, if not all of the prep school students continue on to the main school, although all have to sit the 11+ exam.

Remarks: Driving through the impressive gates off Butterfly Lane in leafy Hertfordshire and up the winding, immaculate drive, we felt as if we were about to embark on an exclusive spa break rather than arrive at a school campus.

The prep and senior school share 100 acres of parkland with the adjoining girls' school separated by a fence lovingly nicknamed 'the passion gate'. In the heart of the grounds (once the rival of Kew Gardens), stands Aldenham House, a grade 2 listed building dating from the 17th century and home to the senior school. The prep school is situated in a less impressive 1980s purpose-built block a short walk away, with bright, airy, well-equipped rooms.

The prep school building has 12 classrooms with approximately 18 pupils in each class and three classes per year group. There is a specialist science lab, an art and design room, a large multi-functional hall and sports changing facilities. None of the old familiar school smells down these corridors: there are pristine, shiny floors, immaculately presented pupils' work adorning the walls, displays of historical facts, various celebratory events and stories written in handwriting a secondary school pupil would be proud of. Outside the door of the small, but extremely well stocked library (which one parent mentioned needs 'updating'), there is a panel with newspaper cuttings of major recent news events.

Sats results are consistently outstanding with virtually all year 6 students (aged 11), achieving level 5 in English and maths. Standards and expectations are high and 'no one will leave you to flounder', said one father. Slackers need not apply. Twice winner of the Sunday Times' Independent Preparatory School of the Year, and the only boys' school to have won at all in its 12 year history.

Little on first impression to suggest that individuality or anything remotely left of centre is high on the agenda at this school. We almost expected to be confronted by a bunch of sullen-looking Stepford boys, in military uniform (bearing the school crest and motto 'serve and obey'), filing past. However, we met spirited boys, all of them extremely well mannered, and seemingly relaxed and happy, although one eight-year-old pupil did mention that he would 'like less homework.'

Academia is undoubtedly high priority at this school, but one parent said she resented the word 'hot housing' to describe their academic ethos. 'Don't get me wrong, it's not a holiday camp, but they only push children to an extent they are comfortable with. I have no issue with it being a high achieving school – eventually they'll be up against it in the real world.'

Dedicated language teachers, and all teaching by subject specialists in years 5 and 6. There is also a practising artist on staff. One parent told us, 'The teaching is consistently good. There are no substandard teachers.' He also said that it is the parents who put pressure on their children, not the teachers.

The boys are encouraged to think creatively. Stimulating lessons can involve making motorized cars in design technology, and flying hand-made helicopters from the hall balcony when learning about weight and force; younger boys design and produce their own version of Mr Men books with their own characters. An initiative to teach more lessons outside is currently underway. The head says, 'some children learn better outside the confines of a classroom. It makes them less inhibited.' (Very Dead Poet's Society.)

Happy to accommodate children with mild learning difficulties eg dyslexia or dyspraxia, and will give some one-to-one specialist help if necessary at no extra cost. However, the school says 'All pupils must thrive and we make sure the pupil is in the best place for this to happen', so greater difficulties may entail a move elsewhere.

Plentiful opportunities outside the classroom, with clubs ranging from judo, which attracts a quarter of pupils, to scuba diving, table tennis, basketball and chess (judo and chess at an extra cost). The school has won the English primary schools chess title three times in the last eight years, and many boys have been selected for the England squad.

More than half the prep school pupils have music lessons and all boys in year 5 learn to play an instrument. Throughout their four years they get a flavour of different sports, from football and rugby to cricket, rounders and softball. Exercise plays a major role in the boys' week, and one parent admitted that 'even if your boy doesn't stand out in maths, there's plenty of opportunity to do so in sport.'

In their last report, inspectors highlighted the quality of pastoral care, and as the head says, 'We take pride in ensuring the children are happy because they will then make progress.' The prep shares an all-weather pitch, athletics track, chapel, extensive playing fields, covered swimming pool, tennis courts and theatre with the senior school.

The almost legendary coach system (mentioned in former pupil William Sutcliffe's book New Boy) will transport any child from the age of seven from as far as Welwyn Garden City and is shared by both the boys' and girls' schools. One parent called it a 'dating agency' for the older students. The school has a large cultural mix, with some 20 – 30 per cent each of Jewish and Asian families and students are actively encouraged to learn about other faiths.

Our tour ended in the dining hall at lunchtime. Hogwarts springs to mind and we almost expected a counter overflowing with every flavour beans. The puddings are not far off – an assortment of brightly coloured jellies and blancmanges, accompany tempting fruit, as well as patisserie style fairy cakes and muffins. Not a whiff of lumpy custard in sight.

'The pre-prep looks a bit like a scout hut,' the head told us almost apologetically, before we embarked on the six mile journey from the main Haberdashers' campus to the pre-prep site. The school, situated at the bottom of a residential street (a nightmare to find), does indeed, on first appearance, bear resemblance to some sort of make-shift, high spec Portakabin. However, we were immediately drawn to the large playground, with an adventure climbing area surrounded by beautiful woodland.

Within this little prefab, there are four bright and colourful classrooms, a multi-purpose hall, a kitchen and a catering team who provide a hot meal for every boy each day. The boys, known as Kingfishers, play weekly games at the prep school, and have sports events and cross country there at least once a term. They also use the prep school hall for concerts and productions.

One teacher told us that they like to integrate the pre-prep students slowly into the main school so it doesn't come as quite such a shock when they leave their little safe environment to enter a large campus at seven years old. They are, bright, highly-motivated boys. As a teacher said bluntly, 'We are lucky in that we can pick and choose who we want'. Impressive art work was on display in one of the classrooms.

'The pre-prep is a lovely, very protective little school', one mother said. 'Standards are high, which permeates throughout the school. It's a nice way to ease them in to the Habs system.' And a prep school parent told her boys, 'If you're not happy here, you won't be happy anywhere.'

Haberdashers' Aske's School for Girls, Junior School

Linked school: Haberdashers' Aske's School for Girls

Aldenham Road, Elstree, WD6 3BT

- Pupils: 300 girls; all day • Ages: 4–11 • Fees: £11,379–£11,484 pa
- Independent

Tel: 020 8266 2400
Email: juniors@habsgirls.org.uk
Website: www.habsgirls.org.uk

Head of Juniors: Since 2010, Mrs J Charlesworth, previously deputy head. A career spanning education for all age ranges from 4 to 84. Originally a lecturer in mathematics in a college of higher education, she decided to carry on the adventure into secondary education and then into primary. 'Nothing is more exciting than learning, nothing more infectious than doing so with children as your companions in thought. Haberdashers' Aske's School for Girls Junior School is alive with enquiry and a zest for embracing all life has to offer. It is a huge privilege to work with such enthusiastic staff and girls and with such supportive parents. The school is a very special place.'

Entrance: Assessment is careful and scrupulous. At 4, girls are seen in small groups with other applicants whose ages are as close as possible to their own – within a month, usually. They are observed and talked to and, out of the 250-odd who apply, around 80 will be called back for one-to-one interviews and aptitude tests for the 22 places. Much the same process takes place the following year and around 80 girls apply for the 22 places. At 7, six or eight applicants out of the 60 or so who apply will be given places. They are assessed via written tests in English and maths and reasoning.

Exit: An occasional girl will be advised to look elsewhere by year 5. The rest move, via the entrance exam, into the senior school. A very few might leave for the state sector of co-ed schools.

Remarks: A beautiful, new spacious, light and welcoming building – special in its own right even if it didn't lead onto its exceptional older sister. Occupying a central place in the huge school site, it is only two storeys so not daunting, but it has big, airy rooms and good displays everywhere. Orderly classrooms with plenty of room to move, even for the oldest girls, very impressive art room with quite stunning art, own gym and own music room with, again, very impressive work taking place here.

Languages are special here. Everyone learns Japanese from year 1 to year 6. It is optional thereafter, but school sees a start in this difficult language as a way of teaching the girls to be linguists from the earliest possible age. 'Transferable skills,' we were told – French must be a doss after this. A sense as you walk around of learning and thinking being seen as great fun. The walls are papered with interesting questions posed by pupils: ' I wonder why people have freckles', 'I wonder where God came from', 'I wonder why our tummies rumble'. It gets you wondering too. We witnessed the visit of 'saxon visitors' – a group of actors who arrived with helmets, animal skins and spears for a bit of historical re-creation: a bit more fun than learning dates, this. Lots of cultural visits, eg to The Henry Moore Foundation nearby, and links with the Japanese school in Acton, which occupies the site left by Habs in the 1970s – good for language, culture and fun.

All the classes we saw were quiet, relaxed and purposeful and all the faces happy and absorbed – everyone has room to move freely, which makes a huge difference. Adventure playground in leafy surroundings and ample playground space. Reception girls have their own garden with safe surface. Overall, a super start to educational life and a privilege to learn and be nurtured in such surroundings.

Hale Preparatory School

Broomfield Lane, Hale, Altrincham, Cheshire, WA15 9AS

- Pupils: 200, 100 boys /100 girls, all day • Ages: 4–11 • Inter-denom • Fees: £6,400 pa • Independent

Tel: 01619 282386
Email: mail@haleprepschool.com
Website: www.haleprepschool.com

Headmaster: Since 1980, Mr John Connor (seventies). Says he has 'no plans to retire.' Previously head of Hillcrest Grammar, Stockport. Married for nearly 50 years, with four children, two of whom teach at the school. Loves to travel and ski. Founded the school in 1980 to put own educational ideas into practice without constraints from governors. A warm, cheerful man, and parents appreciate his hands-on attitude. One mum told us, 'his door is always open. He's in the playground every morning and afternoon, so you can always grab him for a chat.' Head says that if parents have a problem he will normally see them within half an hour, unless he's teaching. 'I want happy children so I pick up niggles fast.'

Entrance: It is really a case of the early bird here. Entry to reception is strictly on a first come basis and usually you will need to register in utero. One form entry in infant school, with 22 in a class. This increases to two forms in the junior school, so there is an additional intake in year 3, but again, it's essential to register in good time as entry is strictly by waiting list. Occasional places may come up as families move, so it's always worth putting your name down. Late entries take the head's 'happiness test' to check they'll integrate successfully.

Exit: Exceptional results considering the non-selective intake. The Altrincham grammars are much the most popular destinations, followed by Manchester Grammar School, Withington Girls' School, Sale Grammar and King David School. Classes are run over the summer holidays in year 5 to practise verbal and non-verbal reasoning skills. Head meets all year 5 parents individually to discuss school choices and offers guidance to school best suited.

Remarks: Housed on four floors of a grand Victorian house in leafy Hale. A lack of space in the main building has meant cabins have been erected to provide extra teaching space.

School offers a wide curriculum (13 subjects by year 6) and stretches and challenges pupils. The pace is fast, so extra teachers are used to support children who need help, either one-to-one or in small groups. Head believes in traditional teaching, backed up with modern aids, and insists all pupils' work is marked thoroughly and within 24 hours. He personally looks at every child's books once a month so that he knows how everyone is progressing. French starts in year 1 and is taught all the way through and Spanish in years 5 and 6. Specialist teachers for music, art, drama, dance, IT, science and geography. Orchestra and choirs, with many children learning instruments. Sports are limited by a lack of space, but pupils are bussed to nearby facilities.

The school has never advertised and relies on word of mouth, so most children are local. They come from middle class and ethnically diverse families.

This is one of the area's best prep schools and achieves stunning results. Although it lacks the physical space that other schools offer, it turns out confident, articulate children who blossom in a smaller, intimate environment. One dad told us that when his daughter was asked what she thought Paradise was like she said 'school.'

The Hall School

23 Crossfield Road, London, NW3 4NU

- Pupils: 460 boys; all day - Ages: 4-13 - Christian, but all faiths welcome - Fees: £12,900-£15,660 pa - Independent

Tel: 020 7722 1700
Email: office@hallschool.co.uk
Website: www.hallschool.co.uk

Head: Since September 2013, Christopher Godwin, previously head of Bedford Prep. Read geography at Loughborough, then masters in Middle Easter studies at Durham. Joined Bedford in 1993 as second master and director of studies before taking over the headship four years later. Gentle and unassuming; keen and active sportsman, particularly rugby – now as coach rather than player.

Entrance: Competition for entrance is keen and applications restricted to those registering before their first birthday – even so, the school is three times over-subscribed. At 3, parents discuss with the head whether a child will enter at 4 or 5 (32 places at 4, 22 at 5). All applicants are tested in the same year – 4+ entrants in January for September, 5+ entrants in late April/May for the following September (school tests close together to ensure the comparison is as fair as possible.) Boys are assessed in groups of six and the school is looking for 'happy, well-adjusted little chaps who want to have a go,' says junior school head, Kirsty Anderson. 'We want them to be responsive, able to concentrate and integrate with others. We're not looking for them to be intellectually precocious, just natural and spontaneous.' Even so, mistakes have been known, and though every effort is made to support the strugglers, a child may occasionally be guided elsewhere. Until now, the school has relied solely on its own testing, but is contemplating contacting feeder nurseries for more background. Looks 'fondly' on siblings, but no guarantees – 'It has to be the right school for the individual child'. Occasional places arise at other times, so always worth contacting the school.

Exit: Seventy per cent to top London day schools, particularly Westminster and St Paul's, but also largish contingents to UCS, City of London, Highgate, Merchant Taylors' and Mill Hill. Sizeable minority to traditional single-sex boarding schools – Eton, Harrow, Winchester, Tonbridge; school trying to spread the word about co-ed boarding but singles only to St Edward's Oxford, Aldenham and Uppingham. Boys carefully guided in their secondary school choice. 'We start talking to parents when boys are in the middle school, suggesting what type of boy would fit what school; we don't like to leave it with a year to go.' The match is made by annual assessment of verbal and non-verbal reasoning – 'We track them over the years on a graph' – as well as day-to-day performance. Scholarship form in year 8 for those contemplating the demanding exams of Westminster and Eton, but not all scholarships derive from this form.

Remarks: Remains confidently the top north London prep school for those looking towards the country's top academic secondary schools. A hard core of clever boys is stretched in every direction, producing confident and ever more articulate pupils. 'They're already talking when they come in at 3 and never stop,' said one teacher.

Long-serving, experienced and enthusiastic staff who clearly love their jobs and the school have won the respect of parents. 'The teaching here is wonderful,' said one parent, whose son arrived in year 5. 'My son just blossomed.' Primarily female teachers in the lower years, predominantly male from year 5, and younger staff encouraged to stay by the clever recent addition of an on-site crèche.

Specialist French, science, music, sport and ICT more or less from the word go. Latin added in year 5, Greek in year 7 for scholarship candidates. Setting in core subjects from year 5 and Latin from year 6. Three sciences, one taught each term. Very well-stocked library with library sessions once a week. ICT provision already notable but the head is looking to spend over £300,000 to create a single network for the entire school. Homework starts gently but builds up to a considerable volume in the upper forms, averaging two preps of 45 minutes for years 7 and 8. No Sats but exams taken seriously with all subjects examined twice yearly in the upper forms.

Housed in three airy and orderly buildings with the junior school (reception to year 3), middle (years 4 and 5) and senior school (years 6-8) on separate sites all within a short walk. Two classes of 16 in reception, re-shuffled to three of 18 in year 1. By year 8, four classes of 12 to 14, with a scholarship form, fast common entrance form and two further parallel classes.

Strong special needs support provided gratis with a full-time learning support co-ordinator and four part-time specialist staff. Most difficulties – mainly problems with literacy – are picked up at the earliest point in the junior school.

On the games front, like most London preps, not overly endowed with outside space, though the junior school benefits from a colourful and imaginatively refurbished playground. Rather tired playground for older boys is on the brink of a re-think. Nonetheless, sport taken seriously with the boys dispatched by coach to East Finchley two afternoons a week and rugby, hockey, cross-country, gymnastics, fencing and five-a-side all on offer. All boys get the chance to represent the school at some time in a team game (nine football teams). County and national representatives at chess, fencing and tennis. Cricket tour of Sri Lanka, football tour of Holland.

Music outstanding at all levels, both in the classroom (two specialist music lesson a week) and outside, with a host of peripatetic teachers. More than three-quarters of the boys play at least one instrument and are encouraged to perform in the large orchestra, string quartets, jazz group and choir, leading to an abundance of music awards. Excellent drama with a highlight annual drama production in summer term which includes every boy in the final year. Boys throughout the school are encouraged to perform in plays, concerts, and in public speaking. Lovely, bright roof-top art room, with a potter's wheel and annual exhibition.

Senior school boys enjoy an enviable common room, known as the Pit, with a focal snooker table and daily newspapers. Vast range of clubs, including cookery, Mandarin, model making, computer maths games etc.

Far more traditionally religious than many nominally Christian schools. Recently built chapel for quiet contemplation, which includes a corner for Jewish worshippers. Grace said before meals, morning assembly, with hymn practice. House system encourages boys to raise money for charity.

Parents mainly from high-powered, high-income backgrounds in the professions, banking and business, who can be – some would say frequently are – fairly demanding. Most are local but a percentage are happy to make the trek from Notting Hill, Holland Park and Islington.

Undoubtedly a super school for the brightest boys, who take away the best grounding possible and a real intellectual curiosity. 'It's often described as a hothouse, but I don't feel it's like that. They're not boffins, just normal, cheerful boys, who are particularly enthusiastic about a concert, a play, football or a piece of pottery.' Most parents concur. 'My son suffers from quite serious dyslexia but he still received the most marvellous education,' said one. 'His general knowledge is really astonishing.' For the right boy there can be few better schools, but some have been known to feel a bit left out in the drive to achieve.

Hall School Wimbledon, Junior School

Linked school: Hall School Wimbledon, Senior School

Stroud Crescent, London, SW15 3EQ

• Pupils: 250;,150 boys/100 girls, all day • Ages: 4-11 years • Non-denominational • Fees: £10,698–£12,347 pa • Independent

Tel: 020 8788 2370
Email: enquiries@hsw.co.uk
Website: www.hsw.co.uk

Headmaster: Since 1990, Mr Timothy J Hobbs MA (fifties) educated at Eastbourne College and St Andrews, where he read medieval and modern history. He founded the school in 1990 (see senior school entry) and as numbers grew and the school developed a senior and junior section, his brother Jonathan joined as principal of the junior school in 1999.

TJH remains head, oversees operations and devotes massive amounts of energy to preserving the original spirit of the place. Entirely child-focused and delighted to leave the detail and day-to-day running of the school to Jonathan. He's based on the senior school site, but visits almost every day and takes assembly once a week. 'Children are very at ease with him,' said one mother. 'Of course there's respect and formality, but they like him and aren't afraid of him.'

Jonathan M Hobbs MA (education management from OU) was also educated at Eastbourne College and then at the British School of Osteopathy. He is married with children; his wife also works at the school. Ably assisted by deputy Susan Harding, who is more parent-facing – his brief is largely finance and management.

Entrance: First come, first served for the 44 reception places, with priority for siblings. Holds assessments and interviews for occasional places in years 1 to 6 and requests report from previous school. Parents from wide socio-economic spread, a chunk – about 20 per cent – from overseas.

Exit: About three-quarters to HSW Senior School (qv) – entry is automatic, but the children sit the same exam as the external senior school candidates to give an idea of where they are. Others to a range of mostly London schools, eg Kingston Grammar, Surbiton High, Reed's, King's College Wimbledon.

Remarks: Like the senior school (qv), a very free-thinking place, all about celebrating the individual. The current site, is a former state school – it's been improved and landscaped, TJH himself doing lots of planting. An American Garden was added after 9/11 and serves as a place of reflection and commemoration. Also incorporates a library in a colourful caravan. School backs on to Wimbledon Common and staff take full advantage of this with plenty of expeditions.

Mixed ability classes, each about 15-20 strong, within which children may be set different work, so treated according to their ability without feeling singled out for special treatment. 'We don't like to take the weaker pupils out and teach them separately because it's hugely important that they gain from hearing what their brighter friends say,' explains Mrs Harding. Huge focus on reading in the early years – they have to 'get it' and school won't rest until they do. Unique homework and monitoring system of senior school called Flints (qv) begins from year 3 – it's based on a theory of 'little and often' testing to reinforce what's been taught in school. Most of the schemes of work, methods and innovations of the senior school begin here. Hence it follows components of the common entrance and national curriculum, with its own HSW-stamp on it all.

About 30 children need EAL or special needs support. Two special needs support teachers and a new enhanced learning unit. School is happy to take on children with mild learning difficulties, visual impairment, dyslexia and dyspraxia. As with senior school, some perception amongst outsiders that the place includes a high proportion of special need pupils; such views strongly denied by school and dismissed by a parent as 'coffee-morning tittle-tattle – it's not a special school: most of the children are just regular kids'. Within the school grounds is Ann Margaret House (named after T and J Hobbs' mother), which caters for children with severe autism. Managed by the school but really a separate entity, although sometimes the main school children will come in to play with the AMH children.

Parents mention again and again the confidence their children gain at the school and again, like the senior school, a huge focus on encouraging the children to think for themselves. 'We want to rein back from too much guidance, noise and teachers' voices,' says TJH. 'Thinking needs time. We want to challenge their minds.' Plenty of opportunities for the children to have a go at everything – and the academic are valued as much as the artistic or the sporty. Overall the message is: do as well as you can, whatever your strength.

Very strong sport here. Like the senior school, the day begins with 30 minutes of circuit training – even in the drizzle – followed by tons of sporting activities, changing each week, rather than each term, the idea being everyone will do something they enjoy – if gym is not your thing, what about rugby? Hockey is currently flavour of the month and the school is sponsoring Wimbledon hockey club. Children apparently get used to all the running about. No swimming, though – nothing to facilitate it nearby, so travelling and changing times involved make it hardly worthwhile. If your child is not into sport would it be a living nightmare? We asked one of our year 6 tour guides what would happen if you didn't enjoy all the outdoors activity. 'Tough luck,' he replied grimly. Has recently bought some nearby playing fields and a farm/field centre in Wales.

Major music and drama productions each term, plus children prepared for external LAMDA exams. From year 4 children can join school choir and orchestra and get lots of performance opportunities. School provides a solid foundation in art – lots of inspiration surrounds the children in the classrooms and corridors – and they complete varied craft and design projects, everything from basic architectural concepts to costume and set design, bookbinding and mosaics.

Their ICT experience will not be so wide – as in the senior school, it will not be studied for its own sake. The children are taught the joys and frustrations of using books as a resource – 'They need to know that a sparkling new book may yield them very little of use, whereas a tattered old thing may be packed with good stuff,' says TJH. No interactive whiteboards in classrooms nor so much as a whiff of an ICT suite.

Longish day – from 8.50am to 3pm for youngest, and from 8.30am to 4pm for years 3 to 6: a lot to pack in. Outside lesson time the children play beautifully, with all ages mixing together. Particular praise for 'fantastic' field trips – 'I know I'm verging on hyperbole, but they are nothing short of magical,' says one mother: educational, but also full of great experiences and treats of the kind normally only available to a scout or guide these days, as not many parents are prepared to sit in the garden while their children fry bacon over a campfire or abseil down the walls.

Pupils' birthdays are celebrated on a major scale, with the child in question entertaining their parents and a few chosen friends at their class table for lunch. Then he/she stands on their chair while everyone sings Happy Birthday before they cut and share their Hobbs-baked cake. Even the most retiring soul basks in the spotlight for a few minutes. 'It's a wonderful ritual and the children love it so much,' said one parent. 'Those with summer birthdays spend inordinate amounts of time planning for the school celebration once they get back in September.' And as well as the cake, every child gets a present from school's own Father Christmas – again to show that they are valued as individuals.

Lunchtimes are said to be 'special' – lunch is served in a family way; from years 3 to 6 the children say grace and are encouraged to develop good table manners. 'I think children take the lunchtime ritual for granted while they are here, but after they have left they say it's one of the main things they miss,' said one mother.

The place is boy heavy (60/40, like the seniors), but mothers of girls don't seem to find this a problem – 'Teaches them an early and necessary lesson in how to hold their own in the world,' says one mother. Behaviour is good – no real need for punishments: 'The children quickly get to understand what is expected of them and rise to it,' says the school. Parents are generally delighted that all their children learn good manners, strong morals and simple courtesies almost by osmosis here. Writing thank you letters, standing back for others, saying 'Good morning' as you pass somebody in the corridor – all de rigueur.

Real mix of parents from all walks – bankers, lawyers, media-types, fewer working mothers than at senior school. A bit more sociable than the last, with organised coffee mornings for everybody to get to know each other. Parents also help on trips and come into school to share any expertise they may have – recently a Japanese parent delighted with a demonstration of origami. 'I like the fact that the school offers all the best bits of a traditional education, while rejecting the silly stuff that goes on elsewhere,' says one mother. HSW school life won't be for everyone, but definitely worth a look.

Hallfield School

Church Road, Edgbaston, Birmingham, B15 3SJ

- Pupils: 565; 350 boys/215 girls. • Ages: 3m–11 • Christian
- Fees: £8,019–£11,220 pa • Independent

Tel: 01214 541496
Email: office@hallfieldschool.co.uk
Website: www.hallfieldschool.co.uk

Headmaster: Since September 2012, Mr Roger Outwin-Flinders BEd CNAA (fifties), previously head of Fairfield Prep in Loughborough. Has worked in six prep schools and was also head of Wycliffe Prep in Gloucestershire. Had a less than happy school life himself, and became a teacher 'to make a difference'. Also an ISI inspector. Married to Tania, who helps with marketing at the school.

Entrance: The majority of children come from middle class professional families. Lots of medics, lawyers, businessmen. Inevitably, they are local.This is a shamelessly academic, selective school, though not absurdly so. The vital aim is to ensure that each child can academically and fit in with the moral and social ethos of the school. Most parents choose Hallfield as an ideal preparation for local grammar schools – indeed the grammar schools recommend it – and there is means-tested assistance with fees available.

Exit: The King Edward's grammar and independent schools are the most popular for boys and girls, with a few going for other local grammar schools. In 2013, 84 per cent of children were offered a grammar school place. An impressive array of scholarships every year – 30 in 2013.

Remarks: Hallfield was founded in leafy Edgbaston in 1879 as a boys' only boarding school when, incidentally, the headmaster's house (now the nursery) was bigger than the school. These days the head and his wife live in a tiny Victorian lodge at the school gate, originally built as a railway waiting room for Lord Calthorpe and his family. In 1995 girls joined for the first time. Now it is inconceivable to imagine the school without them, and coeducation contributes much to the happy atmosphere of the school. The approach is unprepossessing: the entrance hall, however, is light and colourful and lined with wonderful photographs. There are staggering views from some of the upstairs buildings, including the headmaster's study. Twenty acres of all weather pitches and meticulously maintained terraced games fields stretch away to the botanical gardens (useful for teaching), surrounded by beautiful trees and shrubs. Were it not for two tall blocks of flats in the distance, this could be Hampshire. Almost a pastoral idyll. Hard to believe that the Bullring is less than two miles away.

The buildings behind the main entrance, the hub of the teaching, envelope welcomingly rather than dictatorially. Inside are excellent facilities: very good science labs (physics, chemistry and biology are all on the syllabus); whiteboards everywhere – often strategically placed to enable younger, smaller children to make their contributions; and bright, airy classrooms with plenty of art and written work on display. Two libraries and a large sports hall that also hosts regular assemblies. We saw the tinies limbering up for the nativity play. Much singing and music-making. Pupils, from the youngest to the oldest, shoot up their hands to ask, answer and contribute. Bright eyes and lively enthusiasm, alert and inquisitive minds light up the classrooms, and everywhere we witnessed inspirational teaching. The ISI was almost lyrical in its assessment – 'A relaxed yet respectful relationship between pupils and staff allows them to share the

H

common goals of a joy of learning' – noting that 'the quality of teaching is excellent'.

Parents we spoke to were uniformly delighted with what the school had done for their children. 'It is possible to achieve academic excellence and still be very, very happy,' said one parent. Time and time again we heard stories of shy, tentative pupils growing into confident, assured but not cocky. They cited LAMDA exams, outdoor pursuits trips, the joy of learning a musical instrument and continuing with it at secondary school, the good relations with staff. 'There are still some masters who taught me at school whom I would cheerfully strangle,' said one father, who announced that his son 'loved all his teachers.' We heard in a staff meeting teachers discussing a particular case of bullying with great sensitivity, insight and compassion. 'They deal with incidents so sensibly,' said one mother. Like so much at Hallfield, the staff seem very good at the details.

The fierce competition for places at the Birmingham grammar schools is usually via computerised tests in non-verbal reasoning, maths and English. No chance to demonstrate a feeling for the beauty of language; no room for creativity and passion. A narrow field, and year after year Hallfield pupils are hugely successful. So isn't this like teaching children to jump through hoops? An academic circus? According to the parents, Hallfield offers much more than that. 'Some parents employ tutors,' said one mother, 'but it really isn't necessary. The teachers know what they are doing and there really isn't any pressure. They just take the exams in their stride.' There certainly isn't any obvious narrowing of the curriculum to meet the demands of the exam. Right up to the exams, all pupils continue with two lessons a week of art, DT and music. Of course they prepare, but not at the expense of their two afternoons a week of games, and matches with teams at four levels (mostly on weekday afternoons), not at the expense of literature and verbal dexterity, not at the expense of courtesy and good manners, and certainly not at the expense of personal happiness and sense of responsibility.

This is a very good local school. It is not for those who seek the traditional package of chapel, games and boarding. Quite simply, the school is just very good at preparing children for entry into the senior school of their choice. A good preparatory school with an enviable reputation among the cognoscenti of sound educational practice.

Halstead Prep School for Girls

Woodham Rise, Woking, GU21 4EE

• Pupils: 210 girls • Ages: 3–11 • C of E • Fees: £9,993–£11,700; Nursery £2,574 pa • Independent

Tel: 01483 772682
Email: registrar@halstead-school.org.uk
Website: www.halstead-school.org.uk

Headmistress: Since September 2013, Mrs Penelope Austin BA PGCE NPQH LTCL (early fifties), previously head of Walthamstow Hall Junior School in Sevenoaks. Studied music and drama at university in London, then a postgrad course in singing and clarinet at Trinity College of Music, and teacher training in Brighton. Taught music in primary schools for a few years; became acting deputy head at Ardingly College Prep before joining Walthamstow Hall. Husband is a retired teacher; two grown up children.

Entrance: Non-selective, on first come first served basis. Main points of entry are nursery and at 7+. (Some parental muttering about class numbers too high in some years, while very small

in others.) Girls joining after kindergarten are invited for a day before place is offered, 'to make sure we can meet their needs'.

Exit: Impressive, given absence of academic screening at entry. Most to top Surrey girls' schools – parents convinced exponents of single sex education. Most popular: Guildford High, Sir William Perkins's, St Catherine's, Tormead, Priors Field, Notre Dame.

Remarks: A very proper and focused, yet happy, small, traditional school with a feeling of ordered industriousness. The nursery now has double the classroom space it previously had. Girls may begin in the term they are 3 and can choose between three and 10 sessions a week, including pre- and after-school care. This is often their first school experience and much effort is made to ensure all are happy, including parents, who may be reassured via a two-way mirror. Single form entry for the nursery – girls are taught as one large class (24 children) by four members of staff (three qualified). Specialist teaching is highly valued – begins with music, dance and drama in the nursery and steadily increases through the school. The dust now seems to have settled on the staff changes of five or six years ago.

Glossy pre-prep department is housed in its own building – hard to believe it was purpose built way back in 1996. Immaculate, bright and airy classrooms lead from a central lobby/play area with views of equally beautifully manicured gardens – this could only be a girls' school! From 7+, girls based in original Edwardian building and taught in two parallel groups to a maximum of 18 in each. Here, too, squeaky clean, tidy classrooms with pervasive feeling of space. Smartboards everywhere. Setting for maths and English from year 5, based on performance in maths only – 'It works particularly well,' says the school. Year 6 girls have their own building, Halstead Cottage, which doubles as a maths centre, while providing a more grown-up base to give girls an increasing sense of independence before they move on.

Though non selective, academic achievement is very important – 90 per cent level 5 Sats don't just happen by themselves. A hard working atmosphere (some parents feel it is becoming more academic) but not as relentlessly academic as some of the other girls' powerhouses in the area. Languages could be taken more seriously – parent mutterings suggest French still has room for more improvement. That said, most now much happier with SEN provision (no extra charge made for support given during school time). However, still some reservations – 'I've been very happy with Halstead for my older, academic and laid back daughter – it's been less successful for my younger one, with mild SEN,' said one mum. We got the feeling it may not be a school ideally suited to girls with anything more than mild SEN. School disagrees and says it caters for all ('We currently have one statemented child at the school'). Answer – visit and ask lots of questions.

Sport is on the up – here it appears parental concerns have been addressed: longer school day designed to incorporate more in the timetable. Remains to be seen whether enough to satisfy parents with sporty children, who felt too few opportunities/fixtures. All girls play netball, rounders and hockey at school and from year 2 are bused to Woking to swim. Fabulous gym/hall still smelling deliciously of pine panelling (rather than the usual feet!), provides inspiring centre for indoor sport and performing arts. Cleverly designed: the front of the gym opens to reveal first class staging equipment with dressing/rehearsal room behind.

Famous for its music – 80 per cent of children learn an instrument. The high percentage could perhaps be attributed to Music Circus, which allows year 3 pupils to learn and bring home an instrument from each section of the orchestra for a term. Music lessons are given in small groups and include flute, clarinet, violin, cello, cornet and trombone. Orchestra, string group, four choirs, all busily competing locally and staging at least three productions, plus other musical events,

H

a year. 'Pursuit of excellence sometimes compromising enjoyment,' says one mum. Terrific art on display everywhere – from year 3 taught by professional illustrator, Jane Upton, and it shows. Working towards, and will easily achieve, the silver eco award – pond, vegetable patch and now a wormery and compost bin all maintained by the girls. After school activities include cricket, judo and trampoline, with tea and homework supervision if needed.

Pastoral care is very much praised, with no discipline problems. 'We work very hard, teaching the girls independence, and have an active school council for the year 6 pupils.' Communication to parents on administrative matters, however, is not the school's forte – 'An irritation tolerated because of the school's many other strengths,' says one mum. Working parents well catered for – daily cover available from 7.30am to 6pm (extra hours charged).

This homely place turns out happy and confident young ladies and is ideal for very good little girls who don't challenge the system and respond well to pressure. Not the obvious choice for the sporty/scruffy/tomboy or tearaway – although school challenges our conclusions: 'The school has always welcomed all strong individuals: tomboys, tearaways and scruffs!'

Hamilton College Junior School

Linked school: Hamilton College

Bothwell Road, Hamilton, ML3 0AY

Tel: 01698 286830
Email: principal@hamiltoncollege.co.uk
Website: www.hamiltoncollege.co.uk

Remarks: See main college.

Hampden Gurney CofE Primary School

13 Nutford Place, London, W1H 5HA

• Pupils: 240 girls and boys • Ages: 3–11 • Church of England • State

Tel: 020 7641 4195
Email: office@hampdengurney.co.uk
Website: www.hampdengurneyschool.org.uk

Headteacher: Mrs Evelyn Chua (forties). A firm and fashionably-dressed visionary, originates from Malaysia and has worked immensely hard to transform this inner-city C of E primary to a school with beacon status, recently ranked third in the country. A formidable figure, the children certainly respect her, the punishment of last resort for the naughty, but those who've experienced her teaching also find her an inspiration. No British embarrassment about supporting the gifted and talented, but equally determined that every child in this exceptional school will come out a winner.

Entrance: Several of the current foundation stage pupils attend the High Anglican Church of the Annunciation in Bryanston Street near Marble Arch, so if sung mass and ample evidence of the Virgin are not part of your belief system, not the school for you. Don't relax your church attendance either once your eldest has secured a place – siblings are only given priority if

they, too, are seen on Sundays. Heavily oversubscribed with about 200 applicants for 30 places in nursery (which starts the term before a child's fourth birthday). No automatic transfer to reception and 30 places then available at rising 5, with one intake in September. Occasional places go to non-Anglicans.

Exit: Results to make many a prep school head weep. Last year 13 out of 24 pupils went on to the independent sector, seven with bursaries or academic/music scholarships. 'We don't give specific preparation, but we just teach them very well,' says the head, and clearly 'very well' is very well indeed. Recent awards have taken pupils to Latymer Upper, City of London Girls, Notting Hill and Ealing, St Benedict's, Cardinal Vaughan and Colet Court, with others to eg Highgate, Queen's College, St Marylebone, Holland Park and Chelsea Academy.

Remarks: Long-serving head is clearly able to stretch and enthuse young minds but also seems to have the instincts of a property developer. Six years ago the school decided to rebuild its worn-out classrooms to match its league-table-topping position and, working with architects Building Design Partnership, sold off part of its land to fund a new building. Now The Beehive, a six-storey dome of steel and glass, has become both a local landmark and an inspiring place to learn, with nursery pupils starting out on the ground floor and progressing to the tent-covered roof as they rise through the curriculum.

Mrs Chua is equally dynamic on the education front and the busy, well-organised classrooms and dedicated staff (three male teachers) are testament to her management skills. Clearly no area of the curriculum here where good is good enough. Half the pupils come in speaking little English; the rest are prosperous middle class, many from international backgrounds, but nearly all those moving on to secondary school attain top marks in maths, English and science. Specialist teaching in PE, art, DT and music, with a rotation system of teachers two afternoons a week. Mandarin taught in year 2, Spanish thereafter.

Particularly noted for its gifted and talented programme – this is definitely a school where it is cool to be clever. Mrs Chua has high standards and many students reach or exceed them – 'In year 6, some of the children are doing GCSE maths,' said one mother. But also strong (individual and group) out-of-class support for every child who needs it.

A fairly hefty homework diary, particularly for a state primary: 30-45 minutes a night in years 3-5, one hour in year 6, with English, maths and science set nightly and other subjects once a week. Optional holiday homework as well. Well-equipped ICT suite with digital cameras and laptops. Interactive whiteboards in every classroom. ICT taught creatively with an annual ICT week, where even the youngest gets a chance to demonstrate their Spielberg potential. Light and well-equipped rooftop science 'pod'.

Despite its restricted playground space, the school performs sporting miracles with daily sport clubs and specialists provided by the local authority to teach PE, netball, cricket, tennis, tag rugby. Young footballers play for Westminster and regular football competitions with other local schools. Swimming at nearby Seymour Leisure Centre.

Neat and practical red-and-grey uniform. Strong house system with houses named after eminent Brits and points for everything. Ample extracurricular activity, ranging from sewing and gardening to writing and publishing the school newspaper. Strong emphasis, too, on charitable fundraising. Residential trips to the countryside.

Heavy emphasis on attendance and punctuality (head firmly warns prospective parents against sinful thoughts of mid-term breaks). Escalating punishment system (warning, missing play time, time out, Mrs Chua) but minimum behavioural problems. Indeed classrooms are a model of well-ordered enthusiasm.

Founded in 1863 by Reverend Hampden Gurney, Rector of St Mary's Bryanston Square, the school's ethos is still strongly High

Anglican, with compulsory attendance at weekly sung Eucharist and RE teaching firmly rooted in the Church of England.

Mrs Chua has collected more awards than a Brown Owl, everything from the National Association for Able Children Award to Service Excellence Award. Not unnaturally, most parents are immensely positive: 'You couldn't find a better education in the state system,' said one mother, who'd taken her children out of the private sector. And the articulate, confident and happy pupils are the school's best advertisement. One boy, asked about what he liked about the school, replied, 'Everything.'

Hampton Court House (Junior School)

Linked school: Hampton Court House (Senior School)

The Green, Hampton Court Road, East Molesey ,Surrey, KT8 9BS

• Pupils: 150, slightly more girls than boys • Ages: 3-13 • Non-denom • Fees: £11,061-£14,361 pa • Independent

Tel: 020 8943 0889
Email: sarah@hamptoncourthouse.co.uk
Website: www.hamptoncourthouse.co.uk

Headmistress: Since its inception in 2001, Lady Eliana Houstoun-Boswall ISIT (Paris). Co-founder, Guy Holloway, heads the senior school.

Entrance: At 3 into the nursery via informal interview with child and parents. Head looks for families who will be in sympathy with school's aims and ethos and will tell them if she feels they aren't. Into pre-prep via reading and interview. Likewise into the prep – looking for potential, a capacity to think and imagine rather than the crammed and tutored child. At 10, the children are tested more conventionally in English and maths.

Exit: As some come in, some go out. Oddly, you may think, still thinks of itself as a prep and expects its 11 and 13 year olds to sit for other schools at this stage – and several do. As it gains confidence in its new senior school, this practice should wither and die, and indeed the majority now stay on. So they prepare for 11+, 13+ and CE and send pupils to a range of schools. Probably wise to ask to which schools in the last few years but they usually include Surbiton, Westminster, Kingston Grammar (very popular), Bryanston, The Harrodian and The Lady Eleanor Holles School.

Remarks: It's a magic place and little children must be wowed to have the run of the stunning old house, its gardens, sizeable pond, outbuildings – and all in one's home clothes too. The educational principles warm the heart: the 3Rs predominate – hooray! – in the early years, but discrete subject teaching starts early too and everyone learns Latin from year 5 right through to CE. Greek for some from 11. Language learning is a fundamental. French is taught – in French – from day one and by native speakers 'with perfect accents' – all children who go through the prep emerge as competent, if not fluent, communicators in French. One hears it as one passes down corridors – spoken, chanted, sung, from room after room. Spanish also lively and enthusiastic.

Art, drama and music seen as central to education in its broadest and deepest senses and divinity is taught very much with an eye on the art it has inspired. Music seen as exceptional by everyone. IT now well-provided for with a designated room full of Macs with big screens. We watched a class of happy 9 year

olds working on music animation programmes. Some on-site sport but swimming etc a ride away. The garden a wonderful asset for outdoor play, though 'We have stopped the children climbing trees,' admits head, sadly. The younger children need more designated outside space attached to their classroom, as Ofsted noted recently.

Continental teaching methods are important here – head impressed by, for example, maths as taught in Hungary and Poland and incorporates principles derived therefrom. The academic staff are multi-national – around half from abroad and many more with overseas experience. Parents have mixed views – the rapid staff turnover is an acknowledged problem, but head feels, 'I would rather have a child taught for one year by an inspired teacher than by the same mediocre teacher for many years'. Hmm. Internationalism flavours the wider curriculum and prep school children learn about major world figures, eg Leonardo da Vinci, Dante, Mozart and great European dynasties, eg the Hapsburgs and the Holy Roman Empire. Science takes a Socratic approach – discussion is as important as experimentation.

Unusually flexible about keeping children down a year or bumping them up one – in consultation with parents. This can work exceptionally well, especially in a case of mild bullying, exceptional aptitude or slowness, but can also have adverse consequences and be a problem if the child wants to move elsewhere. SEN provision, previously reportedly 'well-meaning', now tightened up and 'outstanding', as far as Ofsted is concerned – they praised IEPs. Provision for more than mild dyses may need careful enquiry. Not that caring, dedication and attention to individuals are lacking – it's just that in this haven of the love of learning, one can, maybe uniquely, appreciate officialdom's insistence on policies, systems and strategies. Certainly some parents, seduced by the trumpeted ethos, flee after a while, scared off by the realities of the place. Not a school for the conservative, the conventional, nor those who snuggle down of an evening with health and safety reports as bedtime reading.

Handcross Park School

Linked school: Brighton College

Handcross, Haywards Heath, RH17 6HF

• Pupils: 315 boys and girls • Ages: 2-13 • C of E • Fees: Boarding £13,758-£32,340; Day £8,280-£16,350 pa; • Independent

Tel: 01444 400526
Email: info@handxpark.com
Website: www.handcrossparkschool.co.uk

Headmaster: Since April 2011, Mr Graeme Owton BA (early forties). Very approachable, energetic, enthusiastic and hailed as a good thing by staff, parents and pupils. Previously boarding housemaster at Feltonfleet Prep, assistant housemaster and English teacher at Wells Cathedral School, housemaster and English teacher at Wellington and short spell as head of Bodiam Manor (which fell victim to the recession). He has not always been in education – after leaving university (Brunel, English and education) he coached rugby in Sydney and returned a year later to do the same for the London Irish U21s. Eventually he had to decide between education and rugby; fortunately for Handcross he chose education.

Brought in mid-academic year after what some parents describe as 'a few years of coasting' that preceded previous head's retirement. He has implementing many changes with vigour, not least the merger with Brighton College, a timely union that is not only quelling rumblings of parent dissatisfaction and low numbers but also benefitting both schools. Brighton College

H

has gained a country boarding prep with acres of playing fields just 10 minutes from Gatwick; Handcross Park has gained from joining the hugely successful Brighton College family of schools with strong leadership, sound financial backing and support from experienced governors and staff.

His new broom has swept clean where necessary, letting some staff go and appointing many new teachers. He has introduced philosophy for children to foster independent thinking and, rather more bravely, a parents' forum. Apparently he welcomes honesty, but with the caveat, 'Don't come to me with a problem if you can't think of a solution'. 'He says good morning to the children and stops them to repeat it if they do not make eye contact with him,' says one parent. His aim is to build a community of like-minded pupils, parents and staff and educate for the 21st century. He is obviously a strong leader and communicator, as the staff we spoke to echoed these values.

Married with two children, one of whom has started at the school, but the family do not yet live on site. Some might observe that if he wants to champion a family school and has expansion plans for the boarding element, a family move on site should be swiftly considered.

Entrance: Currently non-selective: assessment day plus reports and references from previous school. Pupils come from local nurseries and preps, but with expansion of boarding the catchment area is widening to Brighton, Crawley, Haywards Heath and London. Boarders (30 per cent) mainly from London, Forces families, a few from Europe.

Exit: Majority of leavers destined for Brighton College, Worth, Lancing, Hurstpierpoint, Roedean, Ardingly; smattering to Sevenoaks, Wellington, Harrow. School quick to point out that they are not wedded to Brighton College and will send pupils to wherever is the perfect fit. A fair few have departed with scholarships of late (13 in 2013) and 'all our common entrance candidates have been successful in gaining entry to their first choice of school'.

Remarks: School founded in 1887 as a boys' boarding establishment and after various changes of name and identity moved to Handcross Park in 1968, became coeducational and took day pupils. The visitor is treated to a breathtaking approach down a long, roped track through extensive parkland and pitches before coming face to face with redbrick mix of Tudor and Elizabethan.

Claims to be one of the first prep schools in the country where all pupils learn the world's top three languages: English, Spanish from age 2 and Mandarin from age 4. The aim is fluency in at least one major European language. 'The workplace is becoming increasingly global and competitive; it will give them the edge in the job market,' says the head. The director of studies explains they work on the philosophy of 'anti pressure but pro challenge', and some new parents commented how motivated their children had become since joining the school. 'The staff are a happy bunch and passionate about teaching,' said a head of maths who, like other staff, sings the praises of the newish head and the fizz he has brought to the school.

Progress in English and maths monitored via verbal and non-verbal reasoning tests, spelling ages, NFER assessments etc. Active tracking procedures considered rigorous enough to avoid any pupil slipping through the net. The school identifies and caters well for special needs from the outset – 'My child was seen to be struggling in nursery, received informal extra help and progressed to more formal support in the main school'. Learning support takes place in the 'dairy rooms' and staff are, apparently, 'great communicators... parents are kept in the loop throughout'. Others speak of the academic and social advances their children have made within this unit and how confidence building it has proved to be. 'We are never complacent and have been to other good schools to view similar departments,

but concluded that none could be offering anything better,' said another parent. A high ability programme – some attend master classes at Brighton University. The English department is exceptional, say the pupils, and geography, maths, sport and art also got the popular vote.

Masses of art of all standards on display and pupils have the chance to extend interests via clubs (textiles, sketching, crafts). Music lively with junior choir for all and voluntary senior choir, plus orchestra, jazz, rock and recorder groups. Head of music and performing arts favours a balance of traditional and contemporary music. A drama production held each term with every child taking part in at least one production a year. Plans are afoot for a new theatre in time.

Everything from the usual hockey, netball, rugby and cricket to ballet, riding, street dance and cross country on offer, supported by a team of young and energetic sports staff. Glorious pitches, huge sports hall and Scandinavian design swimming pool. Head believes kindness should be the underlying ethos of the school, but what about on the games field, we asked? Sports staff on message, 'It is not just about winning (although that's nice sometimes) but about sportsmanship.' Parents and visiting teams are greeted by courteous pupils who hand out programmes with a map and a sporting 'code of conduct' just in case...

The pre-prep department is surrounded by high walls enclosing an enchanting 'secret garden' – its head told us that days there were 'all about exploring, challenging, listening, before they go on to learning more formally. We love to take the curriculum outdoors, offering anything but a sedentary education'. Music plays a big part in curriculum and pupils do Spanish every week, an early start to foster the Handcross drive for language learning. Lots of clubs on offer, some at extra cost, eg cookery, swimming, multisport, choir. Weekly 'wow' moments celebrate effort and achievements and a buddy system eases transition to main school.

Boarding (currently at 30 per cent) has had a makeover ahead of plans for expansion, but no prospect of flexi option, considered 'bad for continuity'. The rooms, fresh and light with views over the grounds, are almost hotel spic and span – not many personal touches. Are children really that tidy? Food considered excellent and boarders have input into choices and themed menus.

No scholarships but about one fifth receive some kind of bursary. Offers sibling discount – five per cent off first, 10 per cent off second. Over and above that you test your negotiating skills with the head.

Handcross Park may once have been described as 'coasting' but it is now sailing full steam ahead. With the commitment, vision and energy of the new head and Brighton College supporting the climb from good to outstanding, the school's future is set fair on all fronts.

Hanford School

Child Okeford, Blandford Forum, DT11 8HN

- Pupils: 100 girls; 80 per cent are full boarders; rest flexi or day
- Ages: 7–13 • C of E • Fees: Day £16,500; Boarding £19,950 pa
- Independent

Tel: 01258 860219
Email: office@hanford.dorset.sch.uk
Website: www.hanfordschool.co.uk

Headmaster: Since 2003, Mr Nigel Stuart Mackay (early fifties). Born and educated in Zimbabwe. Spent his career at a stiff boys-only (latterly co-ed) boarding prep there, rising from assistant teacher of maths to head. Not an obvious choice to be entrusted with the role of running this very special school but, contrary to some expectations, has slotted right in. Hanford has that effect – you don't change it: it changes you. Has worked to keep numbers strong (more professional marketing) and overseen sensitive refurbishment (of IT, decoration, etc), rather than tampering with the ethos. Married to Sarah, who was director of music at Sunningdale School for 13 years before becoming director of music at Ruzawi for ten. She now teaches piano, organises the annual fifth form musical and manages a lengthy list of headmaster's wifely responsibilities. The Mackays have four young children: the boys at Sandroyd, the girls at Hanford.

Miss Sarah Canning MA (seventies), the source of Hanford's spirit and owner of the school, retired from her rôle as headmistress in 2003, handing the school to a charitable trust in 2004. The school remains her home and she still runs the riding, teaches Latin, serves as moral backbone and can be found almost everywhere, like a benevolent ('Not always!' she says) genie.

Entrance: Informal – girls can come at any time, if space available (and lately that's a big if). Some at 7, the largest number come as 8 or 9 year olds, and a few at 10 or 11. Locals, Wessex girls, Londoners (regular coach to Battersea) and numerous families posted abroad (popular with Services and FCO families). A sea of fair hair, blue eyes and wellies; a sprinkling of Europeans, usually Spanish, tip up for a term or year to boost their English, plus a few genuine overseas exotics. Few first-time buyers. Some bursaries.

Exit: Leavers move on to Bryanston, Sherborne Girls, St Mary's Calne, Benenden, St Swithun's, St Mary's Shaftesbury, Clayesmore, Moreland House, Queen's College, London – not associated with any particular senior school.

School strives to find the right niche for each child. Leavers win loads of scholarships (10 scholarships won last year – phenomenal for a school of this size). Most girls stay to 13.

Remarks: As the years go by, this school becomes more and more special. It doesn't change, sailing serenely on, while other preps scramble towards identikit purgatory. Has defied the downward trend of girls-only boarding – we note with sorrow that we can now count the number of free-standing girls' boarding preps in England on one hand. Back on track after a wobbly period while the torch was being handed on to new leadership.

Set in 45 acres of rolling countryside (we drove by it three times before spotting the drive, despite having been there before) on the edge of the Stour Valley and surrounded by iron age barrows and Roman fort remains, Hanford House was built in 1620 for Sir Robert Seymer (later Kerr-Seymer). Basically Jacobean with Victorian overtones, it has been splendidly adapted to scholastic life. The magnificent glazed internal courtyard is now the dining room.

We can continue to say this is one of the nicest, if not the nicest, girls' boarding schools in the country, with a gentle, kind, friendly, enthusiastic, gloriously happy-go-lucky, genuine family atmosphere. A place you can feel absolutely confident leaving your ewe lamb in, with the knowledge that the school will probably do a better job of looking after her than you would yourself and, almost as a side issue, give her a thorough grounding in CE subjects, and a fun time with it. Not a flash school: faded carpets, slip-covered arm chairs, large chilly rooms, dogs wandering down corridors and the bracing smell of rotting manure – the informality can be too much for some parents. No uniform – girls sit happily in class in their riding togs, their (seriously padded) crash helmets on the desk in front of them, working as hard as they can, because the next lesson has four legs. Ponies are important here – the school has 'around' 20 – plus a few privately owned (but used by everyone). Ninety five per cent of the girls ride, although most didn't when they arrived. Indoor riding school, outdoor arena, jumping paddock. A summer treat is a pre-breakfast ride.

History starts with the Norman invasion and works forward. And the breezily non-PC scripture teacher told us, 'We teach them the Bible because they'll only get comparative religion once they leave.' French from age 8 – pupils are usually way past the standard of their senior school by the time they leave (ditto for Latin). 'Native foreign speakers' plus the daughters of British diplomats based abroad are encouraged to continue with their languages. Specialist teachers in all subjects from year 5 onward. No scholarship set per se, but pupils streamed and potential scholars looked after. Occasionally puts girls up a year. Class sizes tiny throughout the school: nine or ten in each lesson – makes a huge difference. The lessons we watched were so intimate, they reminded us a children's game – 'Oh, I know, let's play school!'

On top of this, 30 girls receive extra help for SEN from a mixture of sources who add up to one full time member of staff. Mostly mild to moderate special needs, but a couple in the 'more severe' category. School introducing new 10-15 minute 'drop in sessions' for quick jolts of extra help. Lots of consistency and stability: average age of staff a youthful 50 and many teachers have been with the school for ages. Classrooms are incredible – some in the converted stables (you go in and out of the window – promise) and some in the most ramshackle collection of what might, in a real world, be temporary buildings.

Music very important – 90 per cent of girls learn an instrument and practice sessions timetabled. Two girls preparing for grade 7 exams when we visited. Girls are auditioned for the chapel choir (only). Also a normal choir, folk group, bands for everything – woodwinds, strings, recorders – and orchestra. Incredibly ambitious art, with ceramics that would not disgrace any senior school; regular masterclasses for gifted artists, plus weekend art club for all. Drama also prolific and good – do ask to see the famously well-stocked costume cupboard. Games (hockey, rounders, pop-lacrosse etc) played on the lawn, adjacent to the outdoor swimming pool. Tap dancing, ballet, year round tennis coaching, even a bit of pistol shooting in the gym. Watch for the magnificent junior cloakroom, a picture of managed chaos with towering heap of rollerblades, riding kit, trainers, wellies, all more or less in their places.

Vast majority board, but loads of flexibility and the line between boarding and day is blurred. All day girls have their own bed and get 20 nights' boarding for free ('They can decide at 6.30 in the evening that they want to stay and, with a quick phone call, it's sorted'). All prep done at school and day girls leave their clobber there. Hanford never closes for exeats – only half term – so perfect for overseas families. Dormitories tidy and feminine – no posters but lots of cuddly toys. Matching bedspreads instead of duvets – now when was the last time you saw that? Not all singing and dancing at weekends – more like a real home, with Sundays spent mooching around the grounds, playing hide and seek, tree-climbing, berry picking, reading. This is a school where time for play is treasured and children are allowed to be children rather than rushed to the nearest shopping centre or games arcade at the first whiff of free time. No TV on weeknights – only on weekend evenings (why do so few schools have the guts to do likewise?).

Time-honoured Hanford extra-curriculars include sewing and dressmaking (the cherished 'Hanford skirts' were much in evidence), pottery, current affairs and art appreciation. In the IT department, upgraded 2007, girls can email whenever – but a school where the post is still keenly awaited. Loads of Hanford traditions, like using a briefcase as tuckbox, climbing the massive cedar tree (whose branches are each named), early morning rides in the summer, bonfire night entertainments and the marvellously convoluted – and effective – 'manners system', which includes SYRs (serve you rights) for the naughty. Sweets the occasional bribe. School's enormous walled kitchen garden produces veg for the menu plus fruit and the lovely flowers that decorate the main building.

Old Girls include singer Emma Kirkby and Amanda Foreman, author of Georgiana, Duchess of Devonshire, on which the film The Duchess was based. And what better example to the girls that they can do anything in life than Peggy, the 82-year-old paddock manager, who powered past us driving a tractor, as we toured the school? Having said all that, it isn't for everyone. 'You need a resilient child,' one parent told us. 'And if they are, they will have a fantastic, amazing, wild, brilliant time – but they won't necessarily learn (or be taught) kindness and tolerance and understanding of those weaker than themselves.' But – for the confident and outgoing child – no other school like it and nowhere better.

Harrodian Preparatory and Pre-preparatory schools

Linked school: The Harrodian School

Lonsdale Road, London, SW13 9QN

• Pupils: 435 girls and boys; all day • Ages: 4–13 • Fees: £12,375–£14,175 pa • Independent

Tel: 020 8748 6117
Email: admin@harrodian.com
Website: www.harrodian.com

Head: Since September 1999, Mr James Hooke BSc Hons PGCE, (early fifties). Youthful and subtly effective, headmaster of all three schools (pre-prep, prep and senior) and oversees the day-to-day running of the prep and pre-prep. The head of the prep school is Mr Matteo Rossetti (mid thirties) – an Oxford classicist (Balliol), passionate, with a rounded, highbrow approach. He injects still more of an international flavour to the school while being determined to increase its academic profile. Mrs Horan, calm, capable and homely, has been running the pre-prep since 2004. Her previous experience has been in the state sector – Our Lady of Victories in Putney and deputy head at the Oratory in Chelsea.

Another key player in the management of the whole school is the principal, Mr Peter Thomson. Formerly the surmaster at St Paul's, he ran The Harrodian for a short period until he 'retired' in 1999. A colourfully eccentric individual, he is thoroughly committed to the school but describes his role as largely 'advisory and supportive'. He will do anything that is thrown at him, whether it be showing parents round or jumping on his bike on an errand, but what he clearly loves is leading the tinies in their singing and music assembly on a Friday afternoon. His grandchildren are in the pre-prep and all the children here seem to regard him as a kindly elderly relative.

Entrance: The pre-prep is non-selective, but you need to put names down as soon as humanly possible. Siblings welcomed and encouraged. To get into the prep children sit an exam at 8+ and 11+ (and for occasional places). Most are interviewed. It gets tougher the further up the school you try. A good school report counts for a lot. Keen to preserve its balanced approach and attempting not to be seduced by just concentrating on exam results as the calibre of applicants gets increasingly dazzling.

Exit: Almost all continue to the senior school now, but you still get a few sitting CE to trad boarding schools as well as occasional one or two moving onto single sex London day schools. Be ready to put in a lot of extra help if you want your child to go to one of the more academic establishments.

Remarks: The Harrodian was originally founded as a prep school in 1993 by Sir Alford and Lady Houston Boswell since when it has quickly expanded in both directions from four up to 18. Their aim was to create a civilized environment where children would learn and grow in a happy, relaxed way, with an emphasis on languages (for a fuller picture see our entry on the Harrodian senior school). Although this is very much one large school with many of the buildings and facilities used by all age groups, the pre-prep is self-contained in a separate building surrounding a small paved courtyard. Huge classrooms with large bright windows. No one ever feels cramped here. A conservatory at the back where small group work can take place opens up onto Astroturf, where reception can play with fluid access between the classroom and the outdoors. A charming allotment complete with scarecrows and dung, as well as the French Garden for quiet contemplation.

The prep school is more integrated into the senior school but cleverly arranged so that they don't seem to get swallowed up by lanky long haired teenagers. Wonderful library – bursting with books of all different genres and a comfortable studious atmosphere. Book club is a surprisingly popular one of the many lunch time clubs on offer (elegant, wide corridors, large windows. You couldn't feel hemmed in here – so refreshing to be able to say that about a London day school. One of the best things about the school is the space – inside and out. Twenty-five acres of playing fields, an elegant outdoor swimming pool, charming statues and features in the attractive gardens. Bid farewell to the nagging boarding school question – It's all here on your London doorstep but without the heavy weight of the traditional and institutional.

Unlike the senior school where no uniform, the prep school has a (pretty relaxed) dress code. This includes collared shirts, but boys can wear the Harrodian hoodie with their collared shirt underneath. The pre-prep wear simple navy uniforms. Discipline is discreet. Children here are given responsibility and respect and are largely self-regulating. No bells; parents are welcomed and can get as involved as they wish to be.

An effective SEN department run by a highly praised SENCo with a team of 10 support staff who work closely with the mainstream staff. Pupils who need extra help (on account of mild to moderate needs – the usual dys-strata etc) will get mostly one-to-one attention. An extra charge for this as well as help given before or after school and during lunchtime. High proportion of EAL, a lot of language support is available. Those identified as being gifted and talented are given extra challenges in the classroom and a mini chess club for years 1 and reception. All pupils learn a modern foreign language and many do an additional language at a lunchtime club.

The school buzzes with creativity. Innovative drama and music with ambitious projects – the prep school recently performed The Magic Flute and the battle of the bands is hugely popular. One boy took a few terms out to perform in the film of Peter Pan. School appreciates the value of seizing opportunities as they arrive and is flexible in accommodating them. Plenty of sport – as you would expect with such extensive grounds – and a wide choice from the more mainstream, football, cricket, netball etc to fencing, dance and gymnastics. Lots of fixtures both within school and with other schools – some parents commented on the patchy performances, but as with everything here, what matters most is that everyone gets involved.

A trendy school with some traditional touches, it attracts a lot more creative media types and celebrities and less of the usual lawyer and banking clientèle found in most London independent schools. A few first time buyers. Many are local – Barnes, Hammersmith etc – but an increasing number from the chic areas north of the river.

A stimulating but relaxed environment – suits an all-rounder who isn't ready to be chiselled into a square peg.

Hawkesdown House

27 Edge Street, London, W8 7PN

- Pupils: 145 boys • Ages: 3–8 • Non denominational
- Fees: £13,335–£15,270 pa • Independent

Tel: 020 7727 9090
Email: admin@hawkesdown.co.uk
Website: www.hawkesdown.co.uk

Head: Since 2010, Mrs Claire Renton-Bourne MA (known to the parents as Mrs Bourne), a Cambridge classicist and Nottingham theologian (early fifties). She spent three years at Perrott Hill School in Somerset, tutoring scholars and heading the classics and RS departments. This led to her fascination with theology and a Nottingham RE diploma, which she completed whilst deputy head at Knighton House in Dorset in 2001. Head there from 2004 continuing to teach classics. Her two children attended nearby Bryanston and one is now in PR and the other is training as a mechanical engineer. She is married to a civil servant; they have a bolt hole in Dorset where they escape at weekends and she can enjoy gardening, playing the piano, which she finds relaxing, and attend local church. A self-possessed, thoughtful, articulate individual,'More modest than many, quiet, sensible, not brash, calm and steady,' comment current parents. Others commented,'Amazing Ms Bourne has the boys' best interests at heart 24/7. Parents are kept in the picture, communication is excellent and her door is open if there is a concern.' When questioned about the future, she replied, 'I love this school and am very happy.The longer I am here the more I can see the importance of my role in supporting the parents. I strongly believe in the importance of single sex education to 13.' Parents feel she is doing a great job and appreciate her advice and the links she has made with the next schools so that each individual is considered. As one American remarked, 'The head is diplomatic. She explained the English system, the general landscape and was particularly helpful regarding the next school.'

Entrance: There are two main entry points. The first is the nursery (16 places) and the second is reception, which is made up of two classes of 20.There are no open days; instead Mrs Bourne gives individual tours with prospective parents lasting about an hour with a follow-up chat in her office. This is key, as she sees if the aims and ethos of parents are aligned with the school. The boys are asked for an introductory session in the autumn when they are due. This is purely to see if the boy would be happy in the school and whether it would be the best place for him. Mrs Bourne and the head of early years provide a variety of activities for a half hour session in the nursery adjacent to the courtyard, with opportunities for outside play. Those hoping to join in year 1 upwards spend a morning in the relevant class and are assessed in literacy and numeracy before being offered a place. The pupils come from a wide spread of local nurseries. There are no bursaries, scholarships or sibling discounts on offer.

Exit: Most to established London prep schools including: Colet Court, Westminster Under, Sussex House, Wetherby Prep, St Phillip's. Others choose to board at a range including Caldicott, The Dragon, Summer Fields and Papplewick. Most boys leave after year 3 but some go after year 2 to Latymer, Colet Court or Westminster Under.

Remarks: The school was founded in 2000 by Mr and Mrs Loveridge and is part of a family group. This includes Devonshire House School and Lyndhurst House, both also in London. It is named after Hawkesdown Hill, in Devon, familiar to the Loveridge family, and where an ancient gigantic, defence earthwork fortress was built. A colourful painting of Hawkesdown is on view in the entrance hall, a reminder of the qualities the school promotes – tradition, charm, community endeavour – and a source of inspiration.

The school provides a traditional curriculum with emphasis on the basics with literacy and numeracy sessions most mornings. 'This is necessary as the demands of the next selective preps are still very traditional, including English written composition and comprehension at a sophisticated level.' Topics and daily routine are deliberately timetabled to cater for boys' interests and enjoyment. We saw evidence of solar system models, astronauts, aeroplanes, castles, and , in year 1, an imaginative life cycle display with very neat handwriting and illustrations, under the friendly eye of one of the few male teachers. Undoubtedly, once the wireless network is installed and running, the boys will also be able to enjoy more ICT opportunities across the curriculum than existed at the time of a recent inspection. One mother commented that having initially intended sending her son to a co-educational school, she now believes he would have suffered seated next to a girl with beautiful penmanship as boys have a definite rhythm of learning .' They are,' as another parent acknowledged, 'wriggly'. That is catered for and understood completely by the staff at HH. French is taught from reception. No dedicated science laboratory, art or design technology rooms. The boys are prepared for serious entrance exams and given plenty of practice. 'The boys are not pushed too much and they have a good balance of work and play'. In year 1, for example, judo is added to the timetable with chess in year 2 and fencing by year 3. Violin, piano and singing lessons are available from year 1, as well as Mandarin, with plenty of after school clubs.

One drawback, commented on by some parents, is the lack of space for a playgound. During indoor lunch break in their classrooms, the top year boys we saw looked extremely happy constructing imaginative vehicles and missiles with great enthusiasm. Nevertheless, 'by the time the boys are in their final year they are big and notice the lack of space,' remarked one parent. They make use of Holland Park for PE in good weather, with football once a week, team games and formal matches arranged, and run around in Kensington Gardens enjoying plenty of controlled rough and tumble. Still, some boys, especially the older sporty ones, might find this frustrating. Judo is extremely popular, as are football, cricket and PE (no swimming). All boys play in fixtures against other schools at some point.

Young teachers and teaching assistants, some from abroad, are lively and enthusiastic and support the boys with different languages, an important feature as this school caters for international families. Pupil teacher ratios is approximately 8:1 with average class sizes of 17. Nobody has been on the staff for more than 10 years, but this is hardly surprising as it is a relatively new school.

The house system with its homage to royalty, Plantagenet, Windsor and Tudor, has been revitalised to excellent effect. Parents are encouraged to be involved and are welcomed, once a fortnight, to attend Friday assemblies in the packed main hall. Boys are awarded pen licences, house points and many awards for tying of shoes laces and ties, good manners at lunch time and community spirit among others. The skills encouraged are spot on for this age and there's always a loud cheer for the winning house. The boys are taught to be courteous and polite and they respect the staff who know them so well. The positions of house captain, vice captain and prefects merit special house ties, rather than the normal school tartan ties (which do look a little odd against the blue and white check shirts). The navy blue and red uniform including blazers and caps is popular, and several parents commented, 'the boys look so cute'.

An important duty for the house prefects is to ring the large bell outside the dining hall for lunch, serve food and clear up. One parent remarked just how great it was that the boys sat in houses for lunch. 'The younger ones look up to the older boys. My son told me he had learnt all about Lord of the Rings from another boy at lunch.' This social mixing may account for the ease with which the boys spoke during our visit. One recent newcomer was highly appreciative of the way he had been made to feel welcome and, a sensitive soul, had clearly benefited from another boy's support. Lunch is extremely popular, even more so since the arrival of a new chef who has a great following. Special themed meals, such as for Wimbledon (with strawberries and cream) and Independence Day, are a real hit with even the fussiest boys.

Parents tell us that pupils with SEN are well catered for because 'the school is small and there is plenty of support'. We saw happy boys with hearing aids and the sparky, young SEN coordinator supports form teachers, ensuring that individual plans are monitored carefully and reviewed. Setting in maths and English is realistic and understood: 'Kids quickly know where they stand'. A speech and language therapist comes in weekly and boys are offered High 5s sessions before beginning lessons as well as booster groups. TAs work with boys who need extra help. This is not the school for someone with disruptive behavioural problems or physical difficulties because of the school's layout, but emerging problems are dealt with in a caring way.

A thorough mix of English and international families with a number of bilingual pupils. Most parents live within walking distance of the school and many work in the financial sector. HH is reassuring to the many new to the English examination system; right from the start, it provides advice, support and the necessary preparation to give parents and pupils a very happy start in a caring, environment without undue pressure.

Hazlegrove School

Linked school: King's Bruton

Hazlegrove, Sparkford, Yeovil, Somerset, BA22 7JA

• Pupils: 360; 160 girls/200 boys (90 full boarders). • Ages: 2+–13
• Christian • Fees: Boarding £17,229–£21,984; Day £7,578–£15,363 pa; • Independent

Tel: 01963 442606
Email: admissions@hazlegrove.co.uk
Website: www.hazlegrove.co.uk

Headmaster: Since 2002, Mr Richard Fenwick BEd Adv Dip Ed MA (mid fifties). Educated at Bishop's Stortford College, gained a first and subsequently an MA at the Open University in education management. Stints at Bilton Grange (qv) as director of studies and teacher of DT – still a fabulous carpenter, according to his wife – and head of St Andrew's Turi (Kenya) preceded his appointment to Hazlegrove; also Vice Chairman of ISEB since 2011. 'I want Hazlegrove to be a place where children feel safe and loved' he says, 'so that, instead of just surviving at school, they can direct their energies into academic, creative or sporting endeavour'. Tall and lean, Mr Fenwick bounds about the school, taking stairs two at a time; we trotted to keep up. Hobbies include running, surfing, sea-kayaking, golf, fishing and trekking in remote locations (Nepal a particular favourite) during the hols, we were not surprised to learn. Married to Katie, who is more deeply involved in school life than many heads' wives (she teaches PHSE and wrote an excellent leaflet for parents of new boarders, for example), they have three grown up children. In some ways rather an unconventional and uncompromising head, attributes which perhaps enabled him to turn Hazlegrove from the rudderless place it was when he arrived to the thriving enterprise it clearly is today.

Entrance: Broadly non-selective. All hopefuls are invited for a trial day at which reading/spelling ages and mathematical ability are assessed, plus any need for additional learning support identified.

Exit: To a panoply of greater and lesser public schools at 13+; the majority in south west England (the Sherborne schools, Bryanston, KIng's College, Taunton and of course around half to its own senior school, Kings Bruton) but national notables such as Winchester, Eton, Marlborough and Millfield too. The array of awards year after year impresses. A recent parent was delighted by the head's efforts in researching a school where Hazlegrove pupils do not usually go. Former pupils include Peter Wilson (Olympic gold medallist in shooting), Maddie Hinch (GB hockey goalie), sculptor Will Newton and author Tobias Jones.

Remarks: A long drive through glorious parkland – we narrowly avoided cows and 4x4s en route – leads to a fine example of eighteenth century domestic architecture, enhanced by formal gardens. Less sightly parts of what is undoubtedly a well resourced and purposeful school are mostly hidden away, but facilities and space abound: super indoor pool, two Astros, tennis courts and acres of pitches satisfy the most sporty. Pigs and chickens enthusiastically looked after by pupils, and there's no ducking their eventual fate either. Full use appears to be made of this bucolic setting (faintly marred by the services visible on the A303), recently enhanced by the planting of a five acre Jubilee Wood in 2012.

Building is underway for an adventurous new classroom block to replace a collection of Portakabins. Though some of the teaching space may be lack-lustre, what goes on in it certainly isn't. We were enthralled and impressed by a scholarship English class of 13-year-olds who were getting to grips with the complex themes in William Blake's poetry. Parents recognise and greatly appreciate the fine teaching that goes on at Hazlegrove, and acknowledge the head's insistence in recruiting staff only of the highest calibre: 'The quality of the discussions at parents' evenings is phenomenal' said one mother. But Hazlegrove is no hothouse, though the children are 'pushed enough' say parents, and does very well by the breadth of ability it admits. About 15 per cent of pupils receive learning support. All these lucky children benefit from exciting and innovative ways to learn, such as a Skype call with astronaut Nicholas Patrick in which the whole prep school participated, and the millionaires club which encourages children to read one million words in the course of a term. The latter is part of the Accelerated Reader programme, where books are carefully graded to eliminate unsuitable choices. The librarian gets rave reviews.

Sport, music and drama ditto. There's an extensive fixture list with other schools and plenty of silverware in the trophy cabinet. One parent articulated the common tension between winning at all costs/sport for all, and wondered if there could be more chances for less skilled players to represent the school at matches. (School defends its record on this.) As for the music, well, our socks were knocked off by the impromptu marimba recital (we had not met one before either) the head asked a boy to perform when we happened upon him jamming with a couple of other pupils in the music department. Masses going on of all standards, from absolute beginners to one already at grade 8, and a clutch taking grade 5 theory. Conventional choices for drama, such as 'Wind in the Willows' and 'The Wizard of Oz' put on in purpose-built theatre and much enjoyed by performers and audience alike; pupils also take LAMDA exams. Mandarin club has proved hugely successful and Mandarin introduced for year 5 pupils from 2013.

About a third of pupils board routinely, and there is scope for occasional boarders too. Accommodation is fine (quite big dorms with a strong smell of disinfectant in the boys' quarters), though rules are quaintly old-fashioned: no mobiles, letter-writing on Sundays and proper shoe-cleaning once a week. That said, activities are myriad and sometimes rather trendy: we were shown the film the boarders had devised, scripted and made the previous weekend. The feel of an extended family is palpable, enhanced by the fact that half the staff live on site. In the evenings, seating for meals is rearranged into family-style groups so boarders get to know everyone; a black tie dinner with five sets of cutlery enlivens proceedings from time to time.

Hazlegrove is quite smart and not a typical country prep school. A broad cross-section (says school) of local and not-so-local families drive or bus their kids in from all over the place up and down the A303, and it's the school of choice for many families making the big move out of London. The head defined parents, when asked, as the 'sort of people who don't look in the mirror before they come to pick up'; their occupations include farmer, lawyer, doctor, plumber, cheese-maker, helicopter pilot, entrepreneur, designer, author and chef. There is an active and welcoming social scene and parents, mums in particular, take up the exercise classes and tennis coaching with enthusiasm. Try as we might, we could not find anything to fault about this super one-off school with its quirky head.

Headington Preparatory School

Linked school: Headington School

26 London Road, Oxford, OX3 7PB

• Pupils: 245 girls • Ages: 3–11 girls • Fees: Boarding £21,162–£23,673; Day £7,683–£11,421 pa • Independent

Tel: 01865 759400
Email: admissions@headington.org
Website: www.headingtonprep.org

Head: Since 2011, Mrs Caroline Jordan (head of Headington School and Headington Prep). Educated at St Helen's and St Katharine's, read geology at Oxford and did PGCE in science at Manchester University. Previously head of St George's Ascot and before that was head of sixth form and deputy senior housemistress at Wycombe Abbey. Married to Richard; one teenage son. Has been overseeing the prep since the abrupt departure of the previous head, Andrea Bartlett, in August 2013. Mrs Jordan is being supported by Sallie Salvidant, who recently retired as head of Bute House.

Currently recruiting new head of the prep.

Entrance: Takes 16 into the nursery class and another 16 straight into reception. Put name down soon after birth. No selection at this stage, so first come first served, though siblings have preference. The building of two new classrooms in 2011 has allowed a reduction in class size at the top end of the school from 24 to 16. Occasional places available for older children, with an exam for those aged 7+. Means tested bursaries of up to 100 per cent of fees are available to applicants for entry at age 9, and Forces/C of E clergy bursaries also available.

Exit: Nearly all to the senior school (90 per cent in 2013). Year 6 girls take the Common Entrance exam and most sail through. 'We start preparing parents at the beginning of year 5 if there are likely to be problems. Their daughter will probably be having learning support already, so it won't come as a shock. Sometimes we feel somewhere smaller might suit her better.

And sometimes we have the conversation, then she comes through well. And because both schools have a broad all-round curriculum, a girl who is not strong academically might be good at other things like sport or art or drama and that makes up for it.'

Remarks: Lovely setting across the road from the senior school. Rambling Victorian building with its own grounds, playing fields and wooded area. Separate nursery and reception building with its own playground and vegetable patch, surrounded by pencil fence. Library, IT suite, music room and science lab with hamster and stick insects, plus brand-new theatre, dance studio and gym.

Sport is 'fantastic, brilliant,' said a parent. 'Lots of matches and they include everyone who wants to play.' Girls swim each week in the senior school pool and the upper forms use the sports hall. Extra-curricular activities include fencing, judo, trampolining and cross-country, and several pupils play or swim at county, national or territorial level. Music is strong too, with an orchestra, jazz band, wind group and chamber choir. Drama includes a play performed entirely in French by year 4 and a year 6 musical. Lots of popular lunchtime clubs and after-school care until 5.45pm.

French from year 3. Three 'flexible' maths groups in the older classes. Encompasses a broad ability range but 'class teachers are good at differentiating the work', and a strong learning enrichment department. Can cope with mild dyslexia and dyspraxia. Means tested bursaries of up to 100 per cent of fees available to girls joining the school at 9 years.

Praised by parents as a 'very friendly place. My timid daughter was a different child after being there a year'.

Heathside Preparatory School

16 New End, London, NW3 1JA

• Pupils: 250 boys and girls • Ages: 2–11 • Non-denom
• Fees: £9,300–£12,000 pa • Independent

Tel: 020 7794 5857
Email: info@heathside.net
Website: www.heathside.net

Headmistress: Since the school's foundation in 1993, Ms Melissa Remus Elliot MA PG Dip (forties), who is also joint owner. She grew up all over the US, following her father's work, and attended Duke University and The American University, Washington. She worked as a Washington intern and on several Broadway shows before moving to the UK and training as a teacher. During three years' teaching she formulated an idea of her ideal school and set up Heathside with her business partner and co-head (now retired), Jill White, becoming the youngest head teacher in the country in her twenties. She got an MA in counselling aspects of education in 2001. She is married with four children, all at Heathside, 'which gives me a good insight into what actually goes on in the classrooms'. Over-flowing praise from parents: 'a very open-minded and dynamic person, relentlessly striving to find ways to make the school better'; 'open and honest in a very refreshing way'; 'both pragmatic and inspirational'; 'extraordinary ability to retain a thorough portrait of each child'; 'unbelievably energetic and gung-ho'.

Entrance: Takes 10 two and three-year-olds into the nursery class. Most places go to siblings and those who sign up very early, though it's worth trying for an afternoon place if you have been less well organised. More join to form two reception classes of 15. Children visit for a day to ensure they and the school are a good match. 'If there is any question mark we may ask them to come in for several days. We try to be careful to make sure that the school suits the child. We don't take children with behavioural difficulties or serious special needs, and if we have any concerns about academic ability, we would speak in detail with the parents and teachers about whether we could create a special programme to support the child.'

Exit: Most move on at 11, the vast majority to the local independents: Highgate, Haberdashers, UCS, South Hampstead, Francis Holland and Channing. Some to City Boys' or Girls', some very bright children to Westminster, St Paul's or North London Collegiate and some who prefer a less intense environment to Aldenham. A few to local state schools, eg Camden School for Girls and St Marylebone. Generally a good haul of scholarships – seven academic and one art scholarship in 2011. Parents comment on 'Melissa's dogged commitment to find places for all her pupils... she reads children exceptionally well'.

Remarks: Started in 1993 on the site – and with much of the equipment and quite a few of the staff and pupils – of a former prep school that had come to a rocky end. Occupies two – soon to be three – buildings a couple of hundred metres apart in the middle of Hampstead, and uses every inch of the limited space. Aims to let every child follow their strengths and interests, with plenty of extra-curricular activities and fun, practical lessons.

The lower school is housed in a converted and extended church hall, which includes a music practice room, a hall used for gym, yoga, music and drama as well as assemblies, a nursery room with comfortable sofas, and art and science rooms. 'Science teaching brilliant – really hands-on and fun,' said a parent. 'And my daughter is very excited to be allowed to chop wood and use a glue gun in DT.' 'Can't imagine my kids being more stimulated or jolly,' said another.

Since the school is non-selective it includes a fair ability range, but classes are small and the lower school has plenty of teaching assistants. 'Learning is really celebrated,' said a parent. Several ability groups for maths from year 1 upwards. 'Children have different ways of learning, and we group them accordingly. Some need lots of reinforcement, but we never assume that a child is no good at maths. We work in a way that helps them to understand, and once the building blocks are firm, they can fly.' When we visited, a group of children who found times tables challenging were learning them through pictures and stories, whilst another group (of year 4 pupils) were working on secondary level problems.

Several literacy groups – 'They are all good readers, but some have difficulty with writing'. These get intensive tuition in years 3 and 4, ready for the lead-up to year 6 exams. 'Because we don't have to prepare them for 7+ exams, it doesn't matter if they take longer to come through.'

French is taught throughout the school, with plenty of songs and games, by a teacher who talks entirely in French from the start. 'They think she only speaks French, and they learn amazingly quickly.' Latin is a 'massive hit,' said a parent; also a Mandarin club.

Inevitably the pressure rises as the 11+ approaches, but parents praise the imaginative approach. 'They're pushed in their ability to write essays and do comprehensions, but it's not a brutal régime,' said one. 'In a typical Heathside move, an ex-parent who is a literature professor comes in twice a week and encourages them to read and enjoy sophisticated texts. They're worked incredibly hard, but it's very exciting.'

The full-time identified needs coordinator is renowned for helping with dyslexia and dyspraxia. One-to-one help costs extra, but most learn in compatible groups. The school would not suit an autistic child – 'We're too busy and active' – and would hesitate to take one with other behavioural difficulties – 'We have to think about the rest of the class.' However, a girl who came into year 4 with limited experience of maths 'blossomed, and got into all the secondary schools she tried'.

Small groups work at their own pace in various nooks and crannies. 'You may find your child having a lesson in what looks like a broom cupboard – but they are learning,' said a parent. Prose and poetry competitions, with everyone writing poems and learning a piece to recite, and plenty of drama from Macbeth to Pirates of Penzance. 'We do really challenging stuff, but in a fun way.'

The full-time music director is 'amazingly inspirational' – everyone learns the ocarina and recorder and many play the piano and other instruments too. Several instrumental groups and choirs, and termly formal and informal concerts 'spur them on'.

Chess is a big deal here – teams go off for weekend tournaments, and Heathside has been the English Primary Schools Chess Association National Small Schools champion for four of the past five years. 'It's a big social scene,' said a parent, 'and they're very good at encouraging girls to play.' A 'huge variety' of other clubs including gym, art and science. Parents talk of 'amazing trips', including ice skating at the Tower of London and 'going to France for the day to meet pen-pals'.

The school's only outside space is a small playground with climbing frame alongside the lower school. However, nearly everyone from year 1 upwards goes to Hampstead Heath for an hour at lunchtime most days – the younger ones go three times a week – to climb trees, run around, build dens, play in the snow. The children also play sport every day, at UCS and Swiss Cottage; on Friday morning they have a swimming and multi-sports programme – ranging from rock climbing to judo – at Swiss Cottage leisure centre, culminating in a Dim T lunch. Specialist coaches include an ex-international Sri Lankan cricketer and an ex-professional footballer, and the football, swimming and cricket teams are rarely beaten. Many teams are co-ed – 'Our best footballer is a girl' – and girls' sport is being boosted by the arrival of a coach specialising in rounders, field hockey and netball. Sports day includes 'proper races' at Parliament Hill Fields running track.

Parents praise the family atmosphere, with friendships across the year groups. 'There's a real relationship between teachers and children,' said a parent. 'They are strict about talking and noise, because they have to be in a building that size, but then you see a child hurtling downstairs with no shoes on to do some photocopying for their teacher. It's an adventurous, common-sense and human approach.' Another parent commented that she is delighted with the 'close and intimate, nurturing atmosphere which generates a real appetite to learn. It's very warm, very flexible'.

Huge mix of families including some wealthy, famous parents and quite a few international families. But it tends to attract those who are not happy with the more traditional private sector ethos; quite a few have moved their children (often reluctantly) from state primaries. Parents tend to become closely involved: one dad runs a gifted maths club, another comes in to talk about astronomy, many parents help with festivals such as Chinese New Year and Halloween, others help run the library or become class reps. 'We're an interesting mix,' said a mother. 'Most people are very friendly and very engaged with the school.' 'We absolutely love it here,' said a father, 'and so does every other parent we've met.'

H

Hereford Cathedral Junior School

Linked school: Hereford Cathedral School

28 Castle Street, Hereford, HR1 2NW

• Pupils: 250 boys and girls • Ages: 3–11 • Christian Foundation
• Fees: £4,245–£9,213 pa • Independent

Tel: 01432 363511
Email: enquiry@herefordcs.com
Website: www.herefordcs.com

Head: Since 2008, Mr Tim Wheeler, MA PGCE. A classicist by training, who then studied for his PGCE and MA in education. Started off teaching at Norwich School, and focused originally on older children, as senior school housemaster. Then head of classics at Bilton Grange in Warwickshire before moving here.

Charismatic, direct, unstuffy and clearly loves what he does. Passionate about teaching children to believe that it's effort, not inherent gift that makes them successful, and keeps telling them, 'I'm still learning'. 'I want them to believe they can all be anything – comfortable enough with themselves to really have a go.'

Insists on specialist teachers for art, science, maths, drama. Teaches drama to year 3 and RE to year 6 and knows each child by name.

A keen runner, he finds it useful thinking time – and the children have recently designed the Little Princess costume for his next charity run. Also very much taken with drama and music (bass guitar). The children clearly think he's the bees knees and buzz around him full of stories and questions. He says he's after 'respect not awe' and seems to have won it.

Off in April 2014 to head Stockport Grammar Junior School.

Entrance: Not selective in its lower years and accepts children into the nursery from age 3. There is also an intake in reception and at age 7, although entrance is possible at other ages, subject to space and suitability. As children get older there are interviews and entrance tests and a requirement for reports from their current school. Substantial scholarships are available for boys who join the school as cathedral choristers (from age 7).

Exit: The vast majority of pupils go on to the senior school on the head's recommendation and without taking the entrance exam. Those whom it is felt would not thrive there are generally counselled in year 2 or 3 to consider alternatives, so there should be no nasty surprises in year 6, and the head says it is rare for the school not to be able to get a child up to the right level by then.

Remarks: Like the senior school, a mixture of old and new. Three schools in one – a nursery, pre-prep and junior school. Also like the senior school, the junior school is almost in the shadow of Hereford Cathedral, and shares very similar links. It is a charming place, with a very embedded sense of nurture and encouragement.

The junior and senior school combined offer what they hope will be a one stop solution for Herefordshire parents, for children from 3 to 18. As the school also offers a breakfast club from 8am and after-school care until 5.30pm (and has a policy of never shutting, whatever the weather) there is much to attract parents who need a few additional hours around the edges of the day. The catchment area runs all around the county and into Wales, with school buses from Bromyard, Ludlow, Ross-on-Wye and Presteigne (all supervised, and shared with the senior school).

The principal junior school building – a mixture of medieval and Georgian splendours – has more than its fair share of panelled walls and ornately plastered ceilings, although it also has the feel of a slightly overgrown country house in which a school happens to have landed. Brightened by lots and lots of children's work on the walls and attractive displays.

In complete contrast, the purpose built Moat, tucked into what would have been a terrace in the old school garden, houses the pre-prep. This really is a great environment for children to learn in. It is airy and child friendly, with small classrooms for an intimate learning space and good areas for play, lots of natural light too. The reception class has its own little garden to play in – well-resourced but not overcrowded.

The art room, complete with kiln, is well kitted out and full of exuberant work – willow structures and ceramics as well as the usual paintings and drawings. There is also a small but well put together DT room where the slightly older children begin learning about resistant materials. The creative arts are plainly very important here – a lovely feature is the Olympic Wall in the main garden – a tiled mural which incorporates designs by every child in the school, reflecting on the themes of 2012, co-ordinated by local artist Clare Woods (whose works were commissioned for display in the Olympic Park).

There are separate gardens for different age groups to play in – one for the reception class, one for years 1 and 2, and one for the older children, as well as a lovely wild garden with a pond, lots of homes for masonry bees and ladybirds, wild flowers and so on. The children in year 5 are responsible for the gardening and there is a pond club too.

The nursery has high staff ratios (we saw a group of 15 being looked after by four staff). In the pre-prep and junior classes, groups tend to be no larger than 13 or 14. Setting for maths and English in year 6. The school 'doesn't do' a gifted and talented programme as the head feels it is counterproductive to label children as either in or out of such a category, says 'it's all about hard work' and emphasizes the importance of respecting the different learning pathways and intellectual growth spurts of different children. There is instead a detailed programme for what the school refers to as high achievers.

No children with EAL when we visited. Learning support is available and carefully tailored. There are two learning development specialists working across the year groups so that any learning support issues can be identified early. A specialist SEN teacher assists those in years 5/6 who require support.

French and music from reception upwards, and all pupils are also involved in drama and performance – starting with poetry recital and working up to debating, improvisation and puppetry by years 4/5.

Lots of extracurricular options – about half the children take instrumental lessons in the senior school music block in the adjacent building – as well as pottery, ballet, first aid and various other clubs.

Sport, teamwork and having a go are considered very important parts of the school experience, with regular matches against schools from Shropshire, Worcestershire, Gloucestershire and Wales. Hockey, netball and rounders for girls; rugby, football and cricket for boys. The children have use of the senior school playing fields and sports hall and, unusually, says the head, get a completely fair share.

The children, from the nursery class eagerly talking about their book choices in the school library, to the reception children, busy with puzzles and problem solving, to year 4s enthusiastically reciting poetry, are the best possible advertisement for the school. Each child we spent time with was friendly, relaxed, happy and engaged. Bouncing about full of things to talk about. You can pretty much hear their little brains fizzing. A delightful place to start exploring life's possibilities.

H

Hereward House School

14 Strathray Gardens, London, NW3 4NY

- Pupils: 180 boys; all day • Ages: 4–13 • Non-denom
- Fees: £13,065–£14,205 pa • Independent

Tel: 020 7794 4820
Email: headmaster@herewardhouse.co.uk
Website: www.herewardhouse.co.uk

Headmaster: Since 2011, Tom Burden, MA (Oxon) 39, formerly deputy head. Mr Burden grew up on the Isle of Wight, where he was educated at local schools before proceeding to Oxford (with a scholarship) to study theology. After graduating, he started teaching as a bit of fresh air before settling down to something earnest, but was soon gripped. Five years at Alleyn Court School, Southend, then a further five at boarding prep Lockers Park, Hertfordshire, where he headed the English department and ran the scholarship set, while still managing plenty of sports coaching, 'I loved every minute and took away the idea that boys should be boyish, enjoy their childhood and be trusted to have responsibilities.' A similar combination in a London day school is rare, but Hereward House was a 'good match', and his headship has been more about evolution than revolution. Continues to teach English, plus some sports coaching. 'I love teaching and you really get to know the boys.' Prides himself on 'not being a distant chap', and boys clearly warm to him. Hands go up faster than lightning in the classroom or on the stairs and text messages are sent mid cricket match to update him on progress. Still dedicated to getting the best out of each boy at CE, he gives up holidays and weekends for extra tuition. Parents are appreciative of his approach and approachability: 'He's on the doorstep every morning to greet each boy – to congratulate him on a brilliant prep or great cricket innings – or simply to suggest he may wish to straighten his tie.' Keen on improving communication with parents, he's recently introduced a newsletter and weekly email. 'He's contactable round the clock and responds promptly to text, emails and phone messages,' said one mother. A sports fan and regular at Lords, Mr Burden relaxes by playing football, bowls and cricket. His Boy's Own enthusiasms include: Bletchley Park, the Underground, the Gothic Revival, and the London sewer system. He's also 'hugely interested' in politics, philosophy and religion.

Entrance: Register by the time your son is a year old at the latest. Head sees all parents and boys, when boys are three. 'I make a significant commitment to finding the right boy,' he says. Siblings guaranteed a place, the rest chosen on 'suitability' rather than ability. 'We could test to find the most academic, but we're not going down that route,' says the head firmly. 'What we're really looking for is a good chap to have in the place, a player rather than spectator.' Offers – conditional on staying till the age of 13 – are made one year before entry at rising five. Occasional places thereafter due to relocation, but those on the waiting list get first dibs. Occasional places at end of year 6.

Exit: The school won't prepare for entrance tests at seven or eight. 'Our record at 13 is so strong, there's no need to exit early,' says the head. Historically, Highgate the most popular choice at 13, followed by City and UCS, but good numbers to all the other London days schools (four offers to Westminster in 2012), with regular scholarships. 'Our scholarship record is broadly comparable per head to the best schools in the area,' says the head. Regular places, too, at Eton, Harrow, Rugby and Winchester. Careful guidance given in the run up to CE. 'Parents here will typically ask: "What is the right school for my son?" rather than saying, "Which school can you get him into?" They really do want the best fit.'

Remarks: The school was founded in 1951 in its current red-brick Hampstead house and Mr Burden is only the third ever head. In essence still a family business, though now governed by a trust made up of members of the Sampson family.

Though not a school in which selection is made on academic grounds, almost every boy here is above average, with 'the top third as bright as anywhere'. Generally no setting until year 8 (occasionally from year 7), then only in English, maths and Latin. Specialist teaching, in part from year 4, entirely from year 5. French from the start, Latin from year 5, Greek from year 8 (potentially from year 7). Teachers know boys well and respond quickly to their needs. ('Teachers are often outside during pick-up time,' said one parent, 'and will seek you out to talk about your child.') Learning support also fine-tuned, with two specialists to help the struggling ('In the majority of cases, boys come out the other end without a problem,' says the head.) A former barrister provides the stretch needed for the most demanding scholarship papers. Parents feels the school works well for all abilities. 'Our older son is very academic and remains challenged with lots of extra work,' said one, 'while our younger son is smart, but playful, and the school uses a very different approach to stimulate him.' Homework at manageable levels. 'It should be do-able in an hour if working at a steady pace,' says the head.

Sport is 'central to the school life'. Two afternoons of games a week, one on Hampstead Heath, the other in Brondesbury. Cricket and soccer particularly strong and every boy gets to play, with a first, second and third team. 'This is simply too small a school for a boy to be sitting on the sidelines handing out oranges. They love to represent the school.' Punches above its weight – the Colts remain unbeaten for nearly two years – but can struggle against the largest schools. Cross-country also taken seriously, with weekly lessons in the spring term. Fencing, tennis and hockey on offer as clubs, plus timetabled swimming at Swiss Cottage baths just down the road. Smallish playground with an intricate system of who uses what bit when – seems to work like a well-rehearsed ballet.

Almost every boy plays an instrument, half play two or more (the orchestra has nearly 60 members). Form concerts every term. Art, too, highly valued. One of the head's first acts on taking over was to hang boys' work around the school ('I wanted to take art out of the art room') and a cricket-themed display now ornaments his study. Pottery and DT also popular (though a cleverly crafted crossbow did have to be confiscated). Drama taught until the final two years, when academic works takes precedence. Major drama production every other year, with every boy involved.

Loads of clubs, including photography, fencing, tennis, typing, art, music theory, chess, Spanish and science. 'If boys want something else we make it happen,' says the head. Handy prep club, too, nightly from 4 to 5 (with flexibility to stay till 6). Popular annual ski trip, accompanied by head and parents, where card playing is often a focus of evening activity. 'I believe in cards,' says the head. 'I don't see why they shouldn't learn to play whist and basic bridge.' First school disco held this year, so boys can 'learn how to treat a lady.'

Bright, high-ceilinged classrooms, originally the living quarters of an affluent turn-of-the-century family, complemented by relatively flimsy science and music space, which are top of the head's agenda for a make-over.

This small school revels in its size. The head wants a family atmosphere and does his utmost to make this happen. 'Academic performance is based on the foundation that the school is happy.' All boys are known by name and all are given a position of 'meaningful' responsibility at the top of the school, with eight prefects, four house captains, and further captains for music, drama and games. 'Every boy must have his moment in the sun,' says the head. Parents definitely approve: 'senior boys thrive on the responsibility and have the confidence to display a fair amount of individuality in how they fill their role.' Two senior boys, for example, are at the door each morning to greet each boy by name. Head has also introduced merit prizes, with bronze, silver and gold awards, form prizes for effort and contribution to the community and school colours for non-academic achievements. Elected school council has considerable sway, 'They wanted more pasta and sweet and sour chicken and that was delivered.'

Rules kept to a minimum. Beyond the basics, the main principle is that boys should treat one another well and make the most of what's on offer. 'Hopefully boys have a sense they are part of the system, not ruled by it. We're looking for good chaps, gentlemen with a general sense of decency.' Parents remark on how considerate boys are to each other – even out of school. Disciplinary problems only of the extremely minor variety like tipping chairs and talking in line. 'I'm very close to the operation,' says the head. 'I walk the school and go out in break to see what's happening.' Staff eat lunch with boys every day to engage boys in friendly conversation. 'It's a great time to find out how things are going.' The head also meets with prefects weekly to discuss concerns they may have about younger boys. 'Everyone knows everyone else; older boys look out for younger ones; the more confident encourage the less so. '

Parents are typical north London professionals, with a cosmopolitan range of nationalities, generally reasonably local. Newly founded PTA, very much part of the head's drive for a sense of community. 'Everyone is very welcoming to newcomers,' says one recent arrival. 'My two boys, who joined higher up the school, have had plenty of invitations.'

Hesketh House

Linked school: Bolton School Boys' Division

Chorley New Road, Bolton, BL1 4PB

• Pupils: 170 girls; all day • Ages: 7–11 • Fees: £8,241 pa
• Independent

Tel: 01204 840201
Email: juniorgirls@boltonschool.org
Website: www.boltonschool.org/juniorgirls

Headteacher: Since 2009, Mrs Ruth Brierley (mid fifties), Cert Ed. Previously head at St Catherine Preparatory School, Marple Bridge. Married with three grown up daughters. Enjoys music, walking and gardening, and is frequently seen getting muddy with the girls in gardening club. Mrs Brierley is well liked by children and parents and her enthusiasm welcomed. 'She is so energetic and full of fresh ideas,' gushes one parent. 'She has really shaken the place up'. 'She knows how to have fun with the girls,' says another. 'On fancy dress day she was running around dressed as Buzz Lightyear'.

Entrance: Two-form entry with a maximum of 25 in a class. Most children come from Beech House, Bolton Schools Infant Department, and entry is automatic. External candidates take formal tests in English, maths, verbal and non-verbal reasoning in the January of the year of entry. However, mid-stream enquiries are catered for when places arise.

Exit: The majority of pupils go on to Bolton School Girls' Division, with a few leaving for local state secondaries or other independent schools. Those unlikely to make it are informed in year 5 with guidance and support offered to the girl and her family.

Remarks: Housed in a modern, state-of-the-art building with facilities that have the 'wow' factor. Everything the girls could possibly want or need has been catered for (including an iPad for each pupil from seven to 18). The school boasts its own music rooms, science labs, library, dining hall, ICT suite, sensory garden, art room, netball courts and a playground with amphitheatre seating. Even the cloakrooms are 'spanking', as one girl tells us.

A member of staff coordinates SEN provision and support is given where required within the classroom, though the school can only cope with limited special needs. Lift access to all floors.

The teaching of maths and English is traditional and rigorous, but a more creative approach is taken with other subjects. Languages are important here. French is taught right the way through the school, Spanish to years 3, 4 and 5 and Latin to year 6. There are also Italian and German language extracurricular clubs, and the school holds regular international days where the girls are taken off timetable to learn about the cultures of other countries.

Art is popular with pupils. We were shown a beautiful stained glass window, designed by some of the girls, which has pride of place and of which they are justifiably proud. All children partake in the varied sporting programme which includes netball, athletics, lacrosse and swimming in the senior school's 25m pool, with tag rugby and badminton among the extracurricular activities offered.

One of the most popular and enlightening ideas Mrs Brierley has introduced is the 16 habits of mind. These habits, such as finding humour, striving for accuracy and thinking flexibly, are designed to enable the girls think intelligently in all aspects of their lives. The habits are depicted by a gorgeously painted, bright and colourful mural along the main corridor and then constantly reinforced by teachers in lessons, assemblies and classroom displays. 'These habits of mind are terrific,' says one dad. 'My daughter applies them to everything, even the things she does out of school like ballet'.

Children are well-mannered and purposeful and seemed more than happy to talk to visitors. Year 6 girls excitedly showed us the totem poles they had drawn in art, and a group of year 3 girls eagerly told us how much they loved the new summer dresses the school has introduced.

A mix of modern and traditional, Hesketh House is an academically successful environment where many mothers commented they wished they had gone themselves.

High School of Dundee Junior School

Linked school: High School of Dundee

Euclid Crescent, Dundee, DD1 1HU

• Pupils: 330 girls and boys; all day • Ages: 5–11 • Non-denom
• Fees: £7,515–£8,775 pa • Independent

Tel: 01382 202921
Email: admissions@highschoolofdundee.org.uk
Website: www.highschoolofdundee.org.uk

Head: Since January 2007, Mrs Gwyneth McLaren MA, specialist qualification in the teaching of early years, previous deputy head. Educated in Dundee, then French at St Andrews University. Married with two adult children. Passionate about knowing every child in her care as an individual – insists on teaching some time every week in the L1 classrooms to get to know the children as soon as they come into the school and helps with co-curricular activities. Feels all children should be challenged and excited by their learning and has been instrumental in driving forward thinking skills programme and forging links with a squatters' school in the slums of Nairobi.

Entrance: By assessment. Places at a premium and Dundee, Perthshire and Fife folk queue up for them.

Exit: Virtually all to senior school.

Remarks: School scattered around the attractive old Dundee Girls' school buildings on west side of the main school courtyard under the music department. Entrance is attractive stairway with impressive stained glass and a myriad of activities notices for both seniors and juniors. Masses of choice for juniors including earlybird and lunchtime IT and a gardening club (currently providing a wintry courtyard with paper flowers).

A bunch of bouncy young teachers, leavened by the odd older face, take tinies up to senior school. Juniors have own dining area, gym and games space, French from P6, with a P7 trip to Paris eagerly anticipated by pupils. P6 and 7 get lots of lessons in the senior school: computers, art, drama etc. Friendship club, cleverly supervised, helps spot potential problems and provides cosseting when needed. Classes in early years strictly capped at 20 for L1 rising to 22 for L3, but school will make an extra class when the demand, though space is tight. Good support for stragglers plus a thinking skills course for every year group – one group was busily doing Sudoku. Littlest start with Oxford Reading Tree plus lots of phonics and multiple reading methods. The class we visited was having a ball – expressively reading aloud. Children happily busy in every corner, though an older group caught in a lull had time to talk maturely about the imminent French trip and their huge array of hobbies.

Before and after school care at extra charge from 8-8.30am and 4-6pm, but free from end of school till 4pm when buses leave. Nursery opening in August 2014.

High School of Glasgow Junior School

Linked school: The High School of Glasgow

27 Ledcameroch Road, Bearsden, Glasgow, G61 4AE

• Pupils: 358 boys and girls; all day • Ages: 3-10 • Non-denom
• Fees: £3,441-£9,111 pa • Independent

Tel: 01419 420158
Email: adminjs@hsog.co.uk
Website: www.glasgowhigh.co.uk

Head: Since 2004, Mr Colin Mair of the senior school, who has ultimate responsibility, but the day to day running of the junior school has been in the capable hands of Mrs Karen Waugh BA DipPrimEd (fiftyish) since 2001. She was educated at Hutcheson's Girls' Grammar, followed by a DipEd at Jordanhill College and took her BA via the Open University. One child still in the school (the other is up and flying). She was previously head of Mearns Primary (700 pupils), deputy head of Carolside Primary (800 pupils) and then acting head; before that she taught at Carlibar, team-taught at Crookfur and taught at the open plan Torrance Primary. Her current appointment is her first in the independent sector. New staff appointments very much a joint activity.

Entrance: Takes around 50 into kindergarten. But get in early – school 100 per cent oversubscribed for entrance thereafter. Parents have coffee and cakes and the children are taken to the kindergarten and assessed individually. Social interaction

and 'emotional readiness' rather than crammed academics the yardstick, so children with a reading age of six will not necessarily come up trumps. Interviews are held annually – if you don't get a place the first time round, you may be kept 'on hold' and could be accepted, so don't give up. Recently 30 applications for five places between primaries 1 and 6. Priorities to siblings, FPs' children and the rest of the field.

Exit: Automatic transfer to senior school. P7 (Transitus – ie 11/12 year olds) are accommodated at Anniesland.

Remarks: The Glasgow prep they all – with good reason – fight to get into. Still holds true. Numbers a tad down this year, but huge number of pupils shoe-horned with enormous skill into tiniest site imaginable; (rector doesn't like this description: he would prefer 'restricted site'). But think Victorian villa, think stained glass windows, think very steep site, think 370 odd children, think the impossible. Massive new build a few years back, positively Swiss engineering to construct a magical new basement, fantastic kindergarten (with its own entrance); masses of light – this is imaginative architecture at its most productive.

Junior school shares senior school facilities, bussed to Anniesland for rugby and hockey, swimming at the Allander centre, not a huge amount of playground on site (a couple of converted tennis courts), but each age group has their own. Small gym, (ie not a sports hall) and impressive convertible hall/theatre. Excellent and imaginative drama. Superb music, three choirs, orchestra, wind, guitar, chamber, chanter – you name it. Specialist art teacher, the entire complex (building is too simple a word) is covered in child-paintings and models.

One 'and a half' male staff – one is form teacher for junior 6 with 'particular skills in science', half equals PE. Dedicated French, drama, music, art and PE teachers throughout. Two parallel classes for each year group, with 'group teaching where appropriate'. Support for learning at both ends of the spectrum with specialised learning support (as in dyslexia, dyspraxia, and those whom the rector would prefer us to call 'slow learners') upstairs in main building. No 'problem' with ADHD or children on Ritalin (none in the school at the moment). Sixth formers at senior school act as buddies when pupils move up to senior school. Class size 28 and down, French from the age of eight, IT from the start – IT Works, spread sheets, word processing, data bases, dedicated computer lab: the works.

Same ethos as senior school – positive relationships and anti-bullying plans. Elected junior school council – who have a serious input and recently quizzed the catering manager about the lunch supplied. Trips for everything everywhere. This is a busy school; own tartan for children. Mainly middle class parents, some from far away, children can be left early and collected late. Buses which link up with senior school runs. Kindergarten super with dedicated area, children on the academic ladder at four – play learning at its best. All wear badges with their name on it – automatic for the first few weeks, but then, 'the children love wearing them'. Charming, convenient, couldn't do better.

Highfield School

Linked school: Brookham School

Highfield Lane, Liphook, GU30 7LQ

• Pupils: Pupils: 265, 140 boys, 115 girls, 110 board; • Ages: 8–13;
• C of E; • Fees: Day £15,450–£18,225; Boarding £19,575–£21,675 pa; • Independent

Tel: 01428 728000
Email: admissions@highfieldschool.org.uk
Website: www.highfieldschool.org.uk

Head: Since 1999, Mr Phillip Evitt, MA (Cambridge) and before that, head of history at Dulwich College. Fifties. Brainy, articulate and a dead ringer for Tony Blair in his glory days, reckon a fair few parents (particularly the mums), some staff and probably pupils too, if able to connect with dim and distant political past.

Personable (head, that is – we can't comment on T Blair) with smile, voice, animation and epic hand gestures to the fore, but very much his own man. Attractively self-deprecating – 'It's very sweet of you,' he says when complimented. Emphatically not a spin doctor, he's 'totally genuine' thought a parent (coal-effect gas fire in his study was only non-authentic accessory).

He's good with the 'pushy intelligent, successful parents,' says a dad and even better at cultivating highly effective relationships with senior school heads, securing places through 'amazing contacts to enable you to get what you want. If school's operating well, that's really what you need at the end.'

Leads a happy band of teachers who have 'a strong sense of unity – they're all good mates,' thought one, though it's taking a few turns of the wheel to secure uniform quality across the subject range. Maths and sciences 'excellent' but 'weaker in languages,' reckoned one parent, though 'not borne out in the sets the children are placed in at senior school,' says school.

Lyrical about post, for which he was head(master)hunted despite having no plans to go to the country and prepare for government. 'I never aspired to headship.'

Drove down 'on a profoundly unpromising late April day' battling new baby sleeplessness (last of four children, all – impressively – home births, now aged between 14 and 21, who came through the school), and was instantly captivated by pupil élan as future charges played in the rain with evident enjoyment. 'I thought "how intriguing." These were children who felt comfortable being children, they didn't have that world weariness of the south London streetwise 13 or 14 year old.'

Modestly assumed he wouldn't suit. Of course, he did, and still does. Now well into his second decade, he's sixth head since school's foundation in Southampton in 1892, though far from being its longest serving (number two, member of family that still owns the school and responsible for move to purpose-built accommodation in 1907, clocked up a staggering 49 years).

Not much given to imposing his own world view, he lets school success (and its originators) speak for itself (we particularly liked school's weekly parish-style newsletters, featuring ads from local business amidst the reports of sporting and musical successes).

Relishes all that school has to offer in the way of tradition but is careful to keep the pace of innovation ticking over. Latest, the introduction of iPads, currently being trialled by year 6 pupils, which talk to school whiteboards and can store and file homework, may sound fancy, but is well in keeping with school's reputation for doing things earlier than most (it's been co-ed, and taken day pupils, since the 1970s).

He's taken difficult decisions from the off, starting by axing the 'madness' of compulsory boarding which was putting off many a parent who loved everything else about the school. To traditionalists, 'I was the hunter who'd shot Bambi's mother.' Many others approved and ultimately it proved a votewinner. Now it's boarding because you want to, not because you have to – and, combined with sterling exam success, school is packing in the numbers, helped by increasingly popular pre-prep incubating the next generation.

Feels it's vital to listen to parents. Schools were 'conceited and arrogant' for too long, the experts in education who kept their customers at arms' length. These days, with successful, highly educated parents, 'you ignore what people have to say at your peril'.

Suiting action to the word may make him 'possibly too accessible,' thought a parent. 'Does well to keep himself slightly aloof because otherwise, he'd end up having to get involved in every single micro issue that every parent had.'

Radiates clearly heartfelt belief in role of schools in providing not just rigour but also 'joy and wonder, enchantment, delight, challenge, excitement, fun.' Collect the set and learning becomes 'something you get out of bed to do, like turning a page in a book and wanting to move on to the next page.'

Despite rumours that he was considering his options as he approached his tenth anniversary, we weren't picking up any sense that he was off to scribe his memoirs (or indeed, set up a Peace Foundation). Just as well, then, that there's no Gordon Brown figure lurking on the premises.

Best bit about the top slot? 'Genuinely, I want to make things better.' We feel a song coming on. Could it be D:Ream circa 1997? We think it could.

Entrance: Non-selective-ish, most from Brookham, school's in-house pre-prep, though parents think number told they may not make the cut is rising (there's also no automatic rite of passage for siblings.) 'Definitely raising the standards,' reckoned one parent. 'When we first started, you had to have a severe problem not to get in.'

Families, broadly local, are augmented with influx of well-heeled Londoners, offspring increasingly the products of Thomas's (qv) and similar ultra-smart establishments.

Atmosphere is changing too. Once 'a bit chaotic and very friendly', it's now 'much slicker' – bemoaned by some though 'not necessarily a bad thing,' thought one mother. Though on the rise, the pushy, assertive contingent ('mums who wear hats at matches' according to a local – we're keeping a watching brief on this one) is small enough 'to be squashed' by fellow parents. Tutoring, so far at least, remains a minority out of hours occupation 'and only if your child is really struggling.'

Though parent felt that SEN support could be even better, it's generally still felt, however, that full time SENCo, five other therapists and positive attitude from owner, a brilliant and dyslexic businessman (sister was a highly-rated teacher here until recently) creates haven for those with mainly mild learning needs. Children are 'never made to feel persecuted' and '…one of the great glories of the place in that we are a very broad church,' says head. Especially good with late developers, giving them the confidence to bloom in senior school – and many do.

Exit: School has opted for laissez-faire approach to departure age, loosening the ties by offering preparation for 11 plus (and even 12 plus) as well as common entrance. It's proved a smart move, parental freedom of choice coming down strongly in favour of staying the course, with what head describes as 'a small attrition rate' – as few as four leaving at end of year 6 and senior boarding for most. Widespread destinations, from Eton and Winchester, to Bradfield and Cranleigh, reflects ability range, Canford, Wellington and Marlborough amongst the perennial favourites. Scholarships, being pushed hard, thought parents, are going great guns.

Other local schools, wrestling the will they, won't they stay on beyond year 6 conundrum, must envy top years stability here. Though a few do leave early (some, reluctantly, because of financial pressures) seniors-only delights lure vast majority, headed by wonderful trips – voluntary year 7 trip to remote Scottish island to build own camp (look, no adults) one of the most memorable.

Parents feel breadth of talent and characters in top years something to celebrate. 'You've got people who are going to Eton, people who are struggling ...but who might be the best at sport or the best at music, and they can accommodate that,' says parent.

Remarks: Approached through prosperous Liphook, school looks a treat on a sunny spring day. Picturesque brickwork casts early morning shadows on a sea of green, pitches everywhere, side order of bluebell-carpeted woodland (provides fuel for new biomass boiler as well as home for achingly on-trend forest classroom), all 175 acres well-used by mothers who 'turn up in their lycra and go running with their labradors,' says former parent who also bemoaned the fact that 'it's easy to start feeling a bit smug.'

Top-up scenery fix every Wednesday when there's post-match 'car park time', families enjoying picnics together (courtesy of Messrs J Sainsbury – branch a short 4x4 schlep away), invitations to international boarders from local families ensuring nobody is left out.

Interiors are corridor heavy, twists and turns best tackled with an expert guide – star turns include attractive, solemn (but not sombre) chapel (nearby plaque commemorating school's founder must be touched if passed – brings luck say older girls), nice, bright main music room (with a second for composition); excellent library, walls stuffed with reading lists, each personalised with jacket illustrations as effective aide-memoires – a time-consuming but worthwhile labour of love that ensures everyone broadens literacy horizons, say staff – and one of the small details that shows just why, academically, the school shines.

'What we do – I'm sure all schools say this – is absolutely aim to add value,' says head, disarmingly. Boasts 'unbroken record in getting everyone to first choice senior school'. Trickier these days because of the rise of pre-assessments, think parents, which has pushed up academic standards, and a tribute to what one described as 'fantastic' teaching across the ability range.

So far, no sense of pressures feeding through to pupils, let alone creating the 'pale, wan' types that one parent reported seeing at other, more academically-focused hothouses closer to the capital. Indeed, this bunch were notable for good cheer (and delightful manners, too) though some parents felt that a few families have increasingly to be restrained from ramping up the anxiety levels at home.

Pupils, though reassuringly relaxed, have no doubts as to expectations, though lead-in is gentle, usually (though not invariably) mixed ability teaching for everything in year 4, much, maths set in year 5, when there's across the board specialist teaching, academics ramped up several notches in year 6 with three sets for everything, strengths in English, maths and science determining who you're with for everything else, including music and sport.

Fourth set is added in year 7, and scholars identified. 'They try to give them other names,' say pupils 'but we know exactly which group we're in.' (School, which sticks to 'obvious' one to four numbering, was slightly baffled by this).

Staff, reckons one of their number, are 'lifers, not bolters' who '...all like children, and that's not always the case with some teachers,' says head (laughing, but we don't think he's joking).

This lot include many clearly in love with their subject – head of maths was happy to deliver short tutorial on iPad geometry apps, their habits and haunts to this reviewer (only flaw the occasional unintentional transmission of scrawled notes to mothership whiteboard in classroom, visible to all).

Year 8 pupils, with impressive maturity, were quick to acknowledge that though some teachers were clearly more down with the kids than others (sports teachers and witty head of music particular favourites) even those with a less obviously child-pleasing style 'could turn a good pupil into an excellent one,' said one – and had the scholarship to prove it.

With increasing numbers testimony to school's appeal there's the inevitable fraying at the edges. It's all change, however, with new sports hall planned, together with major surgery to senior teaching block including two additional science labs.

Parents, while praising efforts, keen to see replacement of 'old fashioned' kitchens which, though good for terrific range of break time snacks and 'lovely' lunchtime fajitas as well as recently introduced salad bar, can be slightly over-reliant on stodge for afters. May improve when attractive dining hall refurb, allowing whole-school reunion for meals (older pupils currently have meals separately) is completed.

Boarding has also had a fairly substantial shakeup following period when lack of feedback made parents feel uncertain about pastoral care. New houseparents have 'definitely breathed new life and energy into our boarding.' Parents agree. Now 'hand on heart I'd say boarding is excellent whereas before I wouldn't have been able to recommend it,' thinks one.

Stalwart adult presence reassures – you're never more than two dorms away from a houseparent – as does good communication including separate boarding email updates and mobiles 'strapped to us' says houseparent, whose cosy office becomes an informal meeting place for 'tea and gossip' and who has custody of special huggable piggy which 'slots round stomach' and is loaned out to ward off homesickness blues. Approachable matron, meanwhile, full-on mending session underway when we visited is 'always here at breaktime for chats and spare clothes.'

There's considerable smartening up (showers in reds and pinks, girls' dorms very fetching – Tom Daley pin ups adding final touch) with more to come. Loss of linen room, imminent, will be mourned by the heat-starved Spanish boarders who 'go in to soak up the warmth' says houseparent. Biggest casualty, though, will be boys' shower golf, fondly imagined to be a secret from staff, ball propelled round vast, old-fashioned, Carry on Camping style washroom course, bonus points awarded for sinking hole in one into tooth mug.

Has all made boarding wildly popular. Pupils plead to start – 'mine were supposed to be day,' says one mother, resignedly – and is almost universal in top years. Who can blame them when evening cricket calls (there's always a summer term surge in numbers) and lures include guinea pigs and climbing frame in juniors' cosy cottage garden, as well as dress down Sunday morning breakfasts and highly rated cook your own supper sessions for years 7 and 8, run by Mrs Evitt who, though a vegetarian, gamely tackles hard core red meat dishes including 'delicious' burgers stuffed with mozzarella.

Day pupils, however, get fair share of the action, staff interests swiftly channelled by head into delightful range of clubs. School boasts of 'enough to experience something different every day of the week,' – probably an understatement, given range extending from recently introduced 'Hyperdrive' after school talks (history of flight the ambitious inaugural topic) to the remote control club which races model boats across smart swimming pool), as well as Bushcraft group, (one for the Bear Grylls wannabees, if ways with newly defunct wild rabbits anything to judge by).

Bonds are further strengthened by compulsory Saturday school, well tolerated by all, (marginally later starting time sweetens the pill – just – for sleep-starved parents), as allows five clear afternoons of sport a week, Thursdays reserved for Highfield Keys – school's own D of E equivalent with 'spectrum' of activities ranging from 'charity outreach to outward bound.'

House on house whomping is a big thing (not for nothing do their names commemorate famous English victories). Ranges from the big set piece pomp and ceremony of sports day, where knights set forth from separate marquees to do battle, to Bonfire Night guy contest, Lady Gaga a recent winner (Bradley Wiggins would have been a strong contender but 'his head fell off' – rarely a recommended tactic). If there's no house to duff up, 'we can turn anything into a competition,' says year 8 pupil, citing tidiest dorm, cleanest teeth and best veg plot by way of proof.

Matches are, naturally, played to win with staff who are proud that their own teams regularly trounce those of other schools setting high class example.

School says that It's emphatically not out 'to win at all costs' and stresses that all pupils shall have team games and represent the school in matches, whether endowed with athletic superpowers or not. Good sportsmanship comes with the territory and 'full respect is given to other teams in defeat and in victory. 'It's not personal.'

Parents agree that victory never comes shorn of good manners, which are emphasised throughout the school, year 8 monitors supervising younger pupils at break and lunchtime.

School, as a result, is a breeding ground for 'amiable killers' says one parent, with netball stars known for pausing as they streak to victory to voice tender concern for opponents after collision. 'My daughter stops to say, "are you OK?" if she treads on someone's feet,' said mother. Boys' sport is 'excellent – I would say they win three-quarters of their matches,' reckoned dad. One parent felt girls' sport was a bit undernourished compared with boys'. Absolutely not so, says school, which puts it down to perceptions that girls currently 'don't win as many of their hockey matches because they are less experienced on Astroturf than other schools' teams,' though will all change when they get their own.

All in all, a super school that radiates enthusiasm and good cheer. Head says it's the happiest place he's ever worked in, felt previous GSG description 'tradition with a twist' summed it up to a T. Aim is for greater cultural variety in the future, particularly in the top years, 'because it's good and healthy for the children.' Track record of all round success makes it a safe bet that it will add extra flavour to the mix.

Highgate Junior School and Pre-Preparatory Department

Linked school: Highgate School

3 Bishopswood Road, London, N6 4PL

• Pupils: 330 girls and boys; pre-prep 132 girls and boys; all day
• Ages: 3–11 • Fees: £7,560–£16,035 pa • Independent

Tel: 020 8340 9193
Email: jsoffice@highgateschool.org.uk
Website: www.highgateschool.org.uk

Principal: Since 2002, Mr Mark James BA MA has been head of junior school 'Parents love him,' one fan told us. 'He's involved in everything.' Another said, 'he's fantastic' – you get the idea. He's also head of admissions for the whole school and had the task of transforming the boys' 7-13 prep into a modern mixed 7-11 junior school. Voila! Came from King's Wimbledon Junior where he'd been deputy head. An enthusiast and can-do character , he's just the man to cheer everyone along during what will inevitably be a testing two years.

Mrs Diane Hecht DCE (fifties) has been head of pre-prep since 2010. Previously deputy head of St Columba's Junior School in Kilmacolm, she came south as two of her grown-up children had settled in London and feels that she has found a wonderfully similar school in Highgate. 'The girls here wear exactly the same tartan skirts as at St Columba's – it was meant to be!' Warm, efficient and enthusiastic.

Entrance: Oversubscribed – 350 try for the 32 places at 3+, 300 again for the 50 places at 7+. Sane and lovely Mrs Hecht admits that assessing two and a half-year-olds has to be on the arbitrary side, so do not be amazed if your astounding tot just doesn't astound on assessment day. At 3+ teachers observe them at play in groups, look for capacity to listen and follow instructions, general sociability – so don't make them learn their letters the night before. Assessing at seven is easier – reading, writing and maths – but, again, the odds are not great. Other things count – siblings, school connections, where you live, parental statements on the application forms – but you can't wangle it.

Exit: Nearly all go from the pre-prep to the juniors and nearly all go from there to the senior school. Plenty of warning given to those unlikely to thrive in the higher stages.

Remarks: The main junior school building will be smithereens by the time you read this. Whole school to be housed in Portakabins from Jan 2014 to Dec 2015, when they will take possession of a new and wonderful complex – judging by plans.

Pre-prep separately, delightfully (and permanently) housed. Starts at nursery – 18 morning or afternoon tots in lively spacious space both inside and out with smiley, lively teachers. Whole school theme of colour and light when we visited and lots of attractive work on show. Glorious herd of Elmer elephants made from plastic milk cartons and coloured paper. Lovely singing – the most in-tune bunch of rising fives we've heard. An orderly, relaxed and friendly school. We saw much warm interaction between staff and small people and just wanted to stay and watch. Juniors have the whole school's fields and facilities to play with – a rare privilege. Excellent approach to emergent special needs – 'it doesn't matter whether they have a label or not, it's how you support them.' Full range of sensitive support, individualised learning, 'management' skills etc brought in when and where needed. Easy to understand why this is possibly the most oversubscribed junior school in London.

Hill House International School

17 Hans Place, London, SW1X 0EP

• Pupils: 960 boys and girls; all day • Ages: 4–13+ • Non-denom
• Fees: £9,900–£13,500 pa • Independent

Tel: 020 7584 1331
Email: info@hillhouseschool.co.uk
Website: www.hillhouseschool.co.uk

Principals: Since 2002, Mr Richard Townend FLSM (sixties), educated at Westminster and the Royal College of Music, and his wife, Mrs Janet Townend Cert Ed. Mr Townend is principal and headmaster and Mrs Townend is principal and director of admissions. He is quirky, humorous, clever and a passionate musician. She is terrifically busy. This is a huge school – just shy of 1000 children, spread over several sites in London, all of which are small town houses and short on space: no wonder little children marching in crocodile in their brown and mustard uniform through the streets of Chelsea is as much a part of the scenery of this chic and expensive area as the Venus statue in Sloane Square. They spread into the space that's available.

Like Prince Charles, an Old Boy of the school, who is still waiting, Mr Townend had a long wait before getting his hand on the job that was always going to be his. The school was founded by his late father, the legendary Lt Col H Stuart

Townend, whose image, influence and inspiration persist. The Colonel, as he was known to everyone, was 93 when he died in 2002 and ran the school as a tight ship right to the end. He died during half term, when Richard Townend took the reins. 'I had no idea how to run the place,' he confides, though this has to be a bit of an exaggeration, as his wife had been the administrator under the Colonel. However the impression one gets is that his heart is really in his music – wonderful instruments all over the place, a harpsichord and clavichord in his flat, a splendid 456 pipe wooden organ in the main school and fabulous pianos and harps scattered throughout. 'I couldn't get up in the morning if I didn't play each day,' he says.

They regard their job as being to inspire the children – his disdainful intolerance of petty inspectors who worry more about the site of sick bays and the use of Tipp-ex in the register than the teaching and the evident happiness of the children is unashamed. Some may criticise this as failing to keep up with the times, but his exasperation at how he was questioned about the identity of his wife without a photocopy of her passport on record does invite the question as to which is the wiser approach.

Taking a different tack to his controlling father, he is already preparing his second son, Edmund Townend, for the eventual running of the family business and he is involved in the day to day administration of the school. His elder brother, William, is given the title of property bursar – his father wryly observed that this effectively means he unblocks drains. He is also a full time opera singer. Each part of the school has its own head, known as heads of house.

Entrance: First come, first served at 4, but the school, famously, will fit people in if they possibly can and if they like them. At 6 a test in maths and English. Prospective parents are invited to turn up for a tour of the school on any morning without appointments. A pool of children who are regularly on hand to show visitors round. When we visited, the front hall was filled with eager children waiting to escort equally eager, though slightly overwhelmed, prospective parents. Places occur at all stages. This is an international school – a lot of movement.

Exit: A wide and diverse spread – Mr Townend has no truck with parents who don't carefully assess the right school for the child and will not spare them his forceful advice. Nearly all girls leave at 11 to a range of London day schools, including state schools – La Retraite, Ursuline High and Lady Margaret's. The independent schools are those you would expect – St Paul's, Godolphin and Latymer, the two Francis Hollands, Queen's Gate and Queen's College, More House and Latymer Upper. A tiny few stay on to 13 – often to board at Wycombe Abbey, Downe House or Cheltenham Ladies'.

Most boys leave at 13, about half to London day schools and the other to board. A few leave at 11, and a tiny few to the Catholic state schools – the Oratory and Cardinal Vaughan. Chief destinations are Dulwich College, City of London, St Paul's, Westminster and a few to Latymer Upper and Portland Place. No special boarding favourites, but spread of top schools which includes Eton, Harrow, Charterhouse, Winchester and Worth. Most pupils get their first choice of school and always a cluster of scholarships each year. No preparation for any boys to leave at seven or eight – this is not expected nor supported.

Remarks: A tour of Hill House is unlike a tour of almost any other school and you get a real sense of what the hordes of children do each day. Rather like a line from Annie, little children everywhere, scampering around the rabbit warren of buildings. Each of the five sites is cramped and used to the max. The famously conspicuous brown knickerbockers and mustard cable knit woollies were designed as a uniform so the children didn't need to change for sport – no room for that kind of luxury. On our visit we spent much of the morning stomping around Chelsea and jumping on and off a Hill House mini bus (the school owns a

fleet). The two girls who showed us round were whipped off mid tour to rehearse their end of term play. Mr Townend scooped us up and we then interrupted a class music lesson in the organ room, while Mr Townend gave an impromptu in depth tour of each organ pipe.

As soon as you enter the main hall at the senior school in Hans Place you are transported to a 19th century boarding prep school. A smell of faded grandeur – oak panels, Latin mottos, a plethora of gold leaf memorial boards, listing among other things the four principles of the school, past head choristers, various awards and scholarships, as well as contributors to the life of the school. A sweeping staircase, piles of silverware and even an Olympic flag (the Colonel was also an outstanding athlete who competed in the 1930 Empire – now Commonwealth – Games and was in charge of housing for the 1948 London Olympics).

Hill House was founded by the Colonel in 1951 and his aim from the first was to create a genuinely international school which nurtured each individual child's talents. Glion House in Switzerland, the Hill House chalet, used to be a major feature of the education here and though less so now, it is still used for anything ranging from geography field trips, ski and hiking trips to trumpet tours. The signature oak panels in all the London sites are intended as a reflection of their Swiss residence. Photos plastered all over the walls – lots of smiling children as well as fabulous Swiss landscapes, some dating from the 1970s, vaguely reminiscent of a teenage bedroom.

The classes are unusually small, averaging 12 – just as well, as most rooms are too small for many more. At the top end of the school they get results – several scholarships, eg the King's scholarship to Eton and the top scholarship to Wellington, and almost all getting into their first choice school, partly, no doubt, as a result of Mr Townend and Mr Brennan's shrewd guidance as to which school is right for the child. Boys and girls taught separately from year 5 (though they continue to do music and sport together); Latin from years 6 to 8. French from the beginning – teachers are all French ('Preferably not Parisian – they have the wrong attitude,' comments Mr Townend). Girls can do Mandarin in year 6. Lots of antipodean teachers – 'They are so good,' remarks Mr Townend, though not all parents agree.

Small classes also allow for individual help when needed (we are assured) and specialist SEN support in years 3-5 – nothing more than mild dyslexia catered for here: you would be advised to look elsewhere if this is going to be a problem. Rave reports from some parents, on the other hand, about how the gifted and talented fare here – 'My child has been set alight – his previous school just didn't recognise his talents,' commented one parent. The school motto is: 'A child is not a vessel to be filled but a fire to be kindled'.

This ethos permeates the music – a central feature of the curriculum, as you would expect from someone of Mr Townend's pedigree. No grades allowed – 'That's just for the mothers to boast about with each other in the playground,' he retorts; instead the school owns more than 300 instruments, from tubas to harps, on loan for individual use: 'If a parent knew what a bassoon costs, they might not let their child play it,' explains Mr Townend. Thirty two choral scholarships available to existing school choristers which enable them to attend residential music courses, often abroad. Parents enthuse about the whole school assemblies, which burst with music, that take place on Wednesday mornings in St Columba's, the Scottish Church in Pont Street – the only place suitable and big enough to fit the whole school.

Proper freshly cooked food at each site served in a civilised way, all children eating at long tables which magically appear at lunch time in some of the more cramped premises. No catering companies and no contract cleaners – in recruiting all his staff, from the brilliant head of music to the chefs (winners of the Tatler award for best school food 2011), Mr Townend keeps his ears to the ground, and if he discovers someone good he will poach them. 1950s style menus – no choice or puddings, but well prepared, and very fresh produce bought from Covent Garden market each day.

Lots of exercise had by all – an hour of sport each day; Duke of York Square is their local playing field and where Field Day happens at the end of each summer term, when the four houses compete vigorously. Hyde and Battersea Parks are also used, as well as various local pools, halls and gyms, providing for a good range of physical activity – 24 sports, we're told.

The art teacher is a current parent and canny about entering the children into various art competitions – outside as well as within school. Lots of prizes are won and during our tour we were asked to choose our favourite painting of a flower from a wall where about 40 different flowers were displayed – not an easy task. Finally plumping for one, we were told, 'That child will win the prize this week'.

When we visited, the school had recently achieved an extraordinary coup in securing the purchase of the former Welsh Church in Radnor Walk. One of the advantages of not having governors nor any red tape, Mr Townend explained – they could pounce quickly. These graceful premises are now used as a theatre, gym, art gallery and ICT centre. A beautiful lofty space, to Mr Townend's delight, it also came with the church organ thrown in.

Parents here come from all over the world and all walks of life – a few Chelsea football stars send their children, as well as a large number of embassy families. Many more first time buyers than a lot of London preps, primarily because the fees are relatively low (an advantage of having such a large school). Alumni equally diverse, from Prince Charles to Lily Allen. If a family needs help with fees, arrangements can be made but, as with so much here, no formal structures in place. Once you sign up, the deal is that you leave the education and the running of the school entirely to the school. No PTA (Mr Townend is as scornful of the motives for joining one of these as he is about the motives for doing music grades). Quite the contrary – parents are positively discouraged from becoming involved with the everyday life of the school.

For all the apparent chaos, a huge amount of work is put into the children by a dedicated and loyal team of teachers, games staff, music teachers (all real musicians, points out Mr Townend, many of whom are old friends of his), caterers and cleaners, all of whom embrace the eccentric ethos of this family run school. It is a long day so everything can be packed in. The oldest boys stay until 6pm Monday to Thursday and 1pm on a Friday (a range of after school activities are offered on Friday afternoons).

An overwhelming buzz of creativity and energy here, but if you are looking for calm, controlled order, with 'yes sir, no sir' boys and girls, this is definitely not the place for you.

Histon & Impington Infant School

New School Road, Histon, Cambridge, CB24 9LL

• Pupils: 270 boys and girls • Ages: 4–7 • Non denom • State

Tel: 01223 568826
Email: office@histonimpington-inf.cambs.sch.uk
Website: www.hiischool.net

Head: Mrs Joy Walker.

Entrance: For mainstream schooling – within catchment. For the assessment unit – LA referral. Not necessarily from within the accepted catchment area – parents can and do express a preference.

Exit: Most to Histon and Impington Junior School.

Remarks: Histon and Impington are popular, vibrant villages (not far from central Cambridge) which benefit from the through nature of schooling – Impington Village College is close by. Opened in 1912 and most recently revamped in 2005, the infant school is in a quiet residential cul-de-sac (opposite is its feeder early years centre – an attractive, modern development). Austere exterior gives little indication of the welcoming, child-friendly interior. Modernisation has provided an ample hall, new classrooms and surprisingly spacious library with its own suite of computers. All classrooms have direct access to a playground – cheered up with several purpose-built structures including a jolly, two dimensional, palm tree. Large playing field for picnics and games is across the road.

The school is one of two in the Cambridge area with an in house assessment unit. This specialised unit (a standard sized classroom within the school) is run by a long serving SEN teacher and the deputy head. The unit (in place since the mid 80s) is seen as a 'half way house' – programmes are devised with a view to getting pupils back into mainstream education wherever possible. Up to 10 attend at any one time and most pupils' needs come within the autistic spectrum, with social skills and language development high on the agenda – a visiting speech and language therapist comes in two mornings a week. Integration is clearly important and absolutely no stigma attached to needs – 'Infants don't see differences like adults – they're very accepting,' commented the head, who went on to say, 'It shows all the children how different needs can be accommodated and teaches them to be tolerant'. Every child from the unit – always referred to simply as class 4 – joins the rest of the school for assembly, break and playtime and they're assigned to a mainstream class which is visited regularly (frequency of sessions depends on the individual).

Those in mainstream classes who have special educational needs (approx 24 per cent overall) are supported through timetabled withdrawal and/or designated classroom assistants. The sensible and sympathetic part time SENCo is based in a cosy room in the centre of the school. She also spends one afternoon a week in the assessment unit and liaises closely with the early years centre – all very helpful with the cross-fertilisation of ideas and possible referrals to the unit.

School is lucky enough to have a designated room for timetabled music lessons and individual violin tuition is available (provided by the county). Those in year 2 get to play recorders and a singing club, which includes children from the assessment unit, meets at lunchtime. Also on offer, for a nominal charge, are lessons in French (years 1 and 2).

The catchment area doesn't include much social housing but the head feels a healthy mix of children. A strong community spirit and plenty of parental help within the school. An active school association raises money for 'icing on the cake' and runs several clubs, including one to encourage kids to love and value books – each week children can buy a stamp, which is saved until the end of term, when a book sale: a great idea.

A popular school where the assessment unit is recognised to be a big plus for pupils and teachers alike. A civilised and effective arrangement which respects the needs of all within the community.

HLC Highfield Prep School

Linked school: Harrogate Ladies' College

Clarence Drive, Harrogate, HG1 2QG

- Pupils: 90 boys, 140 girls • Ages: 4–11 • Christian Foundation
- Fees: Day £8,100–£9,240; Boarding £20,955 pa • Independent

Tel: 01423 537060
Email: enquire@hlc.org.uk
Website: www.hlc.org.uk

Head: Since 2010, Mrs Rachel Colbourn BEd MEd in Primary Education (early forties). Breadth of experience in primary schools in the state, independent and international sectors, teaching in Malaysia and Oman. Previous role was as deputy head of the primary department at the British School in Muscat, Oman. Values transferrable skills learned from international experience – exposure to different teaching styles, the importance of pastoral welfare, implementation of good systems and procedures because of transient staff and pupils, diverse range of parents and the need for business focus.

A petite brunette with a quiet, calm air; a reflective listener and clear thinker who works closely with the headmistress and head of Bankfield – HLC's school for 2-4 year olds, in driving change to deliver a one school strategy of shared values and child-centred education. Believes that 'everything you do is for the children'. Delighted to be appointed and is 'extremely proud of the school and its pupils'. Has had to be resilient in implementing a raft of changes in the wake of the parent-popular previous head but is not to be deterred. As one parent said, 'Parents were initially wary of the different approach but are now warming to the head.' Very open and accessible to parents, has introduced open forums sessions for parent-led discussions, but keen for classroom teachers to be the first point of communication.

Qualified BAGA coach, she has helped run the school's gymnastics club and coached netball. Her interests include running, walking, theatre and travel. Relocated to her home town of Harrogate with their two daughters on husband Mark's appointment as deputy head at a local primary school. Teaching is in the blood as father is a former primary headteacher.

Enthusiastic about moving the school forward; her aim is to 'establish Highfield as North Yorkshire's undisputed premier prep department where girls and boys will all flourish and achieve as well as they possibly can, both in the classroom and beyond.'

Entrance: At all ages though predominantly at 4+ when majority come from HLC's pre-prep, Bankfield. Non-selective but external entrants have assessment and interview with invitation to a separate taster day.

Exit: All girls offered places at Harrogate Ladies' College (Highfield senior school); take-up varies (more than two-thirds in 2013). Some girls and boys to local independents GSAL, St Peter's York, Ashville, Bootham, Sedbergh and Ampleforth. The remainder to the outstanding state provision in Harrogate and Ripon or relocation.

Remarks: Conveniently sited on the main campus, a playground away from the main College building, Highfield is a mixture of new-build and Victorian conversion. Spacious and airy hall for group activities and assemblies with no wasted space in circulation areas. Classrooms on three floors with reception on the ground floor with direct access to a secure, well-resourced outdoor learning area and playground. Links across Early Years' Foundation Stage with off-site pre-prep Bankfield to be strengthened and improved.

Two classes in most year groups usually in adjacent classrooms though no particular progression through the building. Dazzling displays of pupils' work and information posters in all, well-equipped classrooms but professional photography in most public areas.

School day action packed with classroom-based teaching across the curriculum, no shortage of educational off-site visits and a mind-boggling number of extra-curricular clubs and activities; we particularly like team building/out of the box. Specialist French and PE (centred on traditional team sports), streaming of English and mathematics from 8+. Pupils not fazed by it: 'we all have to really understand work before we move on but some understand quicker than others,' revealed a group of pupils. Independent working encouraged but help always on hand, in class or with extra tuition. Creative arts are now taught in project days but according to one parent 'a little hit and miss'. Science follows classroom-based QCA scheme with occasional use of College laboratory for top juniors.

Merit system – usual stickers, house points, merit assemblies, unusual reward for high achievers to feed goldfish in head's study – much prized! Strong pastoral care, buddy system for new entrants. As one parent put it, pupils are 'aware of each others feelings – they try to be kind'. The teddy trophy for the tidiest classroom each week is awarded by the cleaning supervisor – a nice touch.

Effective school council, much valued by pupils who see results from their proposals and understand through class discussion the reasons for rejections. Particularly impressive was a recent scheme where each class democratically chose a range of playground games using an identical sum donated by the parents' association. Ownership also brings the benefits of less loss and damage.

Busy and supportive parents' association, parent volunteers in classroom, Prep Post – weekly update on activities and how parents can give curriculum support written by class teachers. Newly introduced parents' forum – open discussions with head selectively supported.

Holmewood House School

Barrow Lane, Langton Green, Tunbridge Wells, Kent, TN3 0EB

- Pupils: 480 boys and girls; predominantly day, some weekly and occasional boarding • Ages: 3–13 • Inter-denom
- Fees: Boarding £19,455; Day £9,750–16,455 pa • Independent

Tel: 01892 860006
Email: registrar@holmewood.kent.sch.uk
Website: www.holmewood.kent.sch.uk

Headmaster: Since 2010, Mr James Marjoribanks BEd (pronounced Marchbanks) (early fifties). Previously head of Chesham Prep School, Buckinghamshire for nine years. Educated at Sandle Manor, where his father was headmaster, and Cheltenham, followed by Exeter University where he read French and education, and Rennes University.He was head of French at Forres before moving on to Cothill, where he spent four years as head of modern languages, and four years as deputy head of Terra Nova School in Cheshire. He also spent three years teaching in the state sector. He loves his job, says he feels as if he has come home and considers himself incredibly lucky. Described by one parent as a 'breath of fresh air' who has put a buzz back into the school and given it new energy and direction. He has got to know the parents and children well, is always outside to greet everyone in the mornings, and has been given the general thumbs up.

He is ambitious for the school and wants it to be considered the top academic prep school in the south east. He runs it with a firm hand and says it is his job to give parents what they need and not necessarily what they want. A keen advocate of girls as well as boys staying on till they are 13. He has even asked Sevenoaks not to take Holmewood children until 13+ – this ruffled a few parental feathers at the time. Feels that Holmewood sends to a very narrow range of senior schools, is keen to broaden the net and has recently sent a number to Brighton College – not a traditional destination for Holmewood children.

He loves travel, wine, gardening and cooking and his latest project is to recreate a working kitchen garden in the school's original Victorian walled garden, complete with a hive of bees and possibly a pig.

Married to Erika, he has two children by a previous marriage, one at university and the other at Tonbridge Girls Grammar. He also has two adult step-children.

Entrance: The majority of children enter the school in the nursery, some into reception and some into year 3, although children can join at any stage if places are available. Entry into the pre-prep is non-selective, providing the school feels that the child will benefit from the education on offer, following an informal assessment. Standardised tests in maths, reading and spelling for those entering year 3 and above plus an interview and report from current school. Very exceptionally, the school may decide that a child has more learning support requirements than it can realistically provide. Means-tested scholarships for academic potential, and bursaries up to 107 per cent (including extras) available for pupils from state schools. Bursaries offered once children are in the school for parents who find themselves in temporary financial difficulties.

Exit: Mainly to local schools (although the range is widening), with a very good record of getting boys into Tonbridge, often with scholarships. Sevenoaks, Eastbourne, Brighton College, St Leonards Mayfield, and King's Canterbury very popular; occasionally pupils go further afield to, eg, Eton and Harrow. Emphasis on 13+ common entrance and scholarship to senior independent schools, although a few leave at 11+ for the grammar schools.

Remarks: Top prep school, top fees and facilities to match. 'Premium fees with a premium service,' as one parent put it. Numbers are slightly down from their peak a couple of years ago when the school grew very quickly, but still large for a prep school. Founded in 1945 in a stunning setting just outside Tunbridge Wells, centred on a large country house surrounded by over 30 acres of grounds and playing fields. Most parents from the Tunbridge Wells area – lots of London commuters, medics, local professionals and first time buyers who have very high expectations of the school.

Good work ethic and strong academic ethos – children encouraged to aim high and follow the school motto, 'Constantia Praesta', which means 'continually striving to succeed'. Bright children accelerated from year 6 in special scholarship class. Good record in scholarships over the years, not just academic but also sport, music, art and DT.

House system allows for plenty of friendly competition and a well-developed tutor system from year 6 ensures that children have someone specifically looking after their interests. Stars for good work, behaviour and courtesy added up for weekly award of the house cup. Children encouraged to follow a strong moral code laid down by the school. A firm line is taken with any bullying – the headmaster deals with it himself. Children from year 6 do prep at school, and the day ends at 6pm (3-4.30pm for younger children). Weekly, flexi and occasional boarding

are becoming increasingly popular and there are now beds for 19 boys and 14 girls in the newly refurbished dormitories. Self-service dining room with good choice of very healthy food – children unanimous in their praise of it.

Saturday school from year 5 – headmaster keen to retain this despite pressure from some parents, as it allows for a broader curriculum and enables working parents to attend parents' meetings and headmaster's presentations at the weekend. Sport taken seriously and the school likes to win, but most children who wish to are able to play in a team. Boys' and girls' teams enjoy great success, entering national tournaments in all the major sports. The girls' gymnastics team competes nationally with regular success. Recent awards in national shooting competitions – school has its own 20 metre rifle range. New all-weather pitch, 25 metre indoor pool, full time swimming coach. Tennis and squash particularly strong.

Active and vibrant music department – children regularly win music awards to their senior schools. Three full-time music teachers and a team of peripatetic instrumental staff; 75 per cent of children learn at least one instrument. Playing music together is strongly encouraged and groups include five choirs, three orchestras, wind and jazz ensembles, a swing band and diverse chamber groups.

Art equally impressive, with all children producing 'works of art'; new art-room; pottery with kiln and wheel. DT similarly strong. Children prepared successfully for art and DT scholarships to senior schools. Drama taught throughout the school and as an afternoon activity. The school is a LAMDA centre and children perform on stage from an early age. All year groups perform every year in the school's fully-equipped Jubilee Theatre.

ICT very much a cross-curricular skill with specialist software available in all subjects. Three computer rooms, each with 20 computers and interactive white boards in most classrooms. Head of ICT, network manager and technician all on hand to help children. Large, well-stocked, computerised library with full-time librarian. Strong classics department offers both Latin and Greek.

Learning support department recognised as one of the strengths of the school by the inspectors. Problems are spotted early and children are screened annually from year 1 to year 8. Two full-time specialists and three part-time learning support assistants provide individual and class-based help. Those with mild physical or learning difficulties welcomed so long as they can benefit from the education on offer. Various learning support programmes in place.

Pre-nursery, nursery and pre-prep housed in their own purpose-built buildings with their own head and access to the main school's facilities. Class music is on the curriculum from nursery and many children start an instrument in year 1. Pre-prep orchestra (unusual for this age group) and choir. Several concerts and drama productions each year. Light and airy two-storey block , the Collings Building named after the first headmaster, opened in 2011 with 12 state-of-the-art classrooms to house junior department (years 3 and 4) and subject classrooms.

Lots of trips in the holidays – annual French and skiing trips plus music and sports tours. Recent cricket tour to the West Indies, cricket and netball tour to South Africa. Annual exchange trip with St George's in Port Elizabeth, South Africa. Holmewood has a link with a school in Ghana and has raised money to build a library and stock it with books – five children from Ghana and two members of staff came to stay at Holmewood for 10 days. New parents made to feel welcome with coffee, drinks etc – parental involvement encouraged. Strong and effective board of governors won the accolade of Outstanding Governing Body of the Year 2011.

Famous old boys include actors Dan Stevens (of Downton Abbey fame) and Tristan Gemmell (until recently Dr Adam

Trueman in Casualty) who returned to visit his alma mater in 2010, much to the delight of all (particularly the girls!).

Lifelong friendships are made here. Happy, well-rounded, confident children. An academic, competitive school, yet still caring, nurturing and supportive, it may not suit everyone but is a wonderful place for the majority.

Holmwood House School

Chitts Hill, Lexden, Colchester, Essex, Co3 9ST

• Pupils: 300 boys and girls • Ages: 3–13 • Fees: Day £8,490–£14,985 pa • Independent

Tel: 01206 574305
Email: headmaster@holmwood.essex.sch.uk
Website: www.holmwood.essex.sch.uk

Headmaster: Alexander Mitchell, late 40s. Originally from Perthshire, though he worries the burr is fading, having spent more of his life down south than north of the border (not to Essex ears, it isn't). Educated at Napier in Edinburgh, with a degree in music from Colchester and PGCE from Reading. Has taught in the state and public, single-sex and co-ed, day and boarding sectors, most recently for three years as head of the music school at Loughborough Endowed Schools and 10 years as director of music at Haberdashers' Aske's School for Girls. ISI inspector for 10 years. He's only the fifth Holmwood head in its 90-year history and the first ever not to have any past association with the school. 'Underneath his friendly, easy-going exterior there is a respected, efficient, deep-thinking workaholic,' notes a perceptive parent. Lives on-site ('handy for fire drills' approves a pupil) with his wife Helen – head of PSHCE – and their three children, all in the school and ranging from reception to Year 5. Conducting was his love, but he says he doesn't miss the music – 'I have plenty to be getting on with here as headmaster and our head of music and drama is outstanding; I'm very lucky to be doing what I feel I was meant to be doing, it's the best job in the world.' Still finds time to play bass guitar in the school's jazz band. 'Happiness is the key to progress,' he says. 'I can't promise a perfect school but I can promise a happy one.' Chimes with Holmwood's Latin motto, which translates as 'I was glad'.

Entrance: A third from the school's own nursery, which takes 53 children from six months and is set in an attractive rural building a few miles from the main school. The rest go off to good local primaries. Usual entry point to the main school is at age 4, straight into the dedicated reception, which takes two classes of 18 in each year. A handful more pupils arrive at throughout each year.

Exit: Year 8 children largely depart for Felsted, Framlingham, Ipswich and Oundle. One or two to Uppingham and Rugby and a similar number to Royal Hospital School, Culford, New Hall and Greshams. School proud of its 2013 Basil Hume Scholar to Ampleforth, a real all-rounder. Occasional places at Eton, Harrow, King's Canterbury, Benenden.

Remarks: The principles of the school have remained the same since it was founded on this very site, two miles from Colchester, in 1922 by a Mr and Mrs Duggan, whose aim was 'to develop the individuality and abilities of each child, to make him self-reliant and adaptable and to help him face reality.' A collection of semi-rural buildings punctuated by courtyards and outside spaces that cleverly maximise the opportunities for outdoor education (we've never seen so many woodland classrooms, play areas and nature trails in one prep school).

Garden Block arranged around a tranquil garden in memory of a former pupil and treated by all with respect.

The Holmwood day is divided into lessons until tea at 4pm and then prep and activities until supper for boarders and more activities until lights-out. Flexi-boarding – minimum one night – is popular and most take advantage by year 8 ('I tell parents their children will let them know when they want to board,' says head). Houses are named after the elements and there are competitions and challenges all year round. Intriguing range of reward systems – golden leaves, superstars, as well as 'showups' and 'showdowns' for older pupils with the requisite number of showdowns leading to a detention ('I had one once,' confessed our guide, 'I'm not getting another one'). There's 'a week for everything' – recent Citizenship Week brought in speakers from the Red Cross and local charities and when we visited a celebrated scientist was setting up ready to give a demonstration as part of Science Week.

Reception children have their own little world, across a path from the main school. Cavernous for the two classes of 18 in the early years department – with airy classrooms and intriguing corners tailored to computer play and dress-up – it also has a lovely outside play area with a patch of age-appropriate, safe woodland to explore. The main pre-prep department houses years 1, 2 and 3 in spacious, modern, purpose-built accommodation. Moving into the prep, pupils are arranged by ability in English, maths, French and science and in years 7 and 8 into a scholarship and three further sets. A few new arrivals, but the head points out 'as the year group gets larger, the sets get smaller'. The scholarship set is made up not just of the brightest but those who have the 'emotional maturity to cope with the stretch and challenge'. Pupils from year 4 begin to move to specialist classrooms – 'you're exhausted for the first few days but you soon get used to it,' reassure our guides. Year 6s learn Latin, or study skills for those not suited. French from reception. A few drift off into the strong local state selective system at 11+ but the vast majority press on to CE at 13.

Music and drama is 'about to explode' under the direction of the new head of department, predicts Mr Mitchell. Matilda being rehearsed with years 6 and 7 throughout our visit and, recently Pirates of the Curry Bean! Art room described (accurately) as 'humungous' by our guide, and full of unusual projects including animation installations by year 8s, who all received a still turned into a souvenir picture. DT is offered as an activity in a fully equipped studio. Sport every day for those who want it. Rugby, hockey and cricket are major for boys, while girls play netball, hockey and rounders. Some 20 acres of the 34 are given over to sport, plus a vast 'new' (three years old now) sports hall and indoor swimming pool. On-site Lexden Rackets Club – financed by compulsory purchase of school land for the A12 decades ago – is heaving with fit young retireds on a dreary Wednesday morning, but also a superb resource for the school at other times. School has its own tennis and squash coaches.

Library with 12000 books and an intriguing colour-coded filing system, presided over by the school librarian. Red sofas for the exclusive use of year 8 are as close as they come to a common room. Science labs in converted stables. Jubilee Hall with tiered seating for nearly 200, backed by professional-looking exhibition space – self-portraits when we visited. Dyslexia unit recently renamed learning support (although the sign-maker hasn't yet caught up). Excellent provision for SEN. 'We make progress here,' says the head. 'That might be a scholarship for one child, or an improvement in reading for another. We nurture strengths and support weaknesses and develop young people who are confident, and above all comfortable with whom they are.'

Courtesy and respect are still ingrained at an early age and children here are at ease with anyone (the head swears by the 'train to Norwich test' – in a parallel universe as the proprietor of his own company, he would be sufficiently confident to put any Holmwood pupil on a two-hour train journey with his best client).

'Every child is well mannered and friendly,' agrees a parent. 'Even on the sporting field – win or lose, the children are always gracious.'

Surrounded by its own playing fields, Holmwood has the feel of a much larger school, but at its heart it's a small community of 300 pupils which extends to embrace their families too.

Holy Cross Preparatory School

George Road, Kingston-upon-Thames, KT2 7NU

• Pupils: 280 girls, all day • Ages: 4-11 • RC, other faiths welcome
• Fees: £10,386 pa • Independent

Tel: 020 8942 0729
Email: admissions@holycrossprep.com
Website: www.holycrossprepschool.co.uk

Headteacher: Since 2011, Mrs Sarah Hair, currently studying towards an MA in Catholic leadership, has taught at the school for seven years, after teaching in the maintained sector for 14. Was the driving force behind the school's technology programme and a key leader of the development plan. Has taught all of the children in school as the director of ICT and has a thorough understanding of all of their strengths and capabilities. Says she feels privileged to be given the opportunity to lead such a vibrant, thriving and supportive school community.

Entrance: Oversubscribed by about two to one for main intake at age 4: 40 places available to fill two parallel classes – pupils come from about 12 local nursery schools. Apply to the school as early as you can and by 30 September in the year prior to entry. In effect, a test for admission – children attend an introductory session on a Saturday in November for what the head describes as 'a holistic look' at the child, focusing on attitude and concentration, social and personal skills. Spaces occur periodically in other years and are filled on an ad hoc basis. No scholarships.

Exit: Impressive record of success to the best local senior schools (with a handful of academic scholarships won every year): Lady Eleanor Holles (eight per cent), Surbiton High (25 per cent), Wimbledon High, Putney High, Kingston Grammar School, Ibstock Place, also Tiffin Girls, Nonsuch High and Wallington High (state grammars) and state girls' schools Holy Cross in New Malden and Coombe Girls' in Kingston. Some girls move on to some of the swanky boarding schools (15 per cent in 2013) such as Benenden, Wycombe Abbey, Cheltenham Ladies College and St Mary's, Ascot.

Remarks: Lovely inclusive school in smart location with friendly atmosphere and excellent academic results. Occupies a wonderful Victorian house complete with carriage sweep and specimen trees, high up on the upmarket private residential Coombe Estate – in arguably the most prestigious road. Formerly the home of novelist John Galsworthy of Forsyte Saga fame. Library is a wood-panelled room – easy to imagine Galsworthy, sitting there, pen in hand, gazing out over the eight acres of well-maintained grounds. Modern block houses reception class and years 1 and 2 – everything bright and cheery, with loads going on. Up to date IT.

Academically shines, with sky-high key stage 2 results across the board. Mild to moderate SEN catered for and a learning support teacher provides assistance. Occasional girl has EAL – a

member of staff is the nominated support teacher. Class sizes maximum 20.

Sister Ursula, the present head of pastoral care, now the only sister on the staff, hugely popular. 'Every child should have a Sister Ursula – she is quite wonderful with the girls,' said one mother. The RE programme embraces all faiths – 45 per cent of the girls are RC, the remainder being mostly C of E, with a few Muslims and Hindus. Non-RC parents frequently talk to the girls about their faiths and practices – particularly appreciated by RC parents, one of whom commented that he 'would not feel nearly so comfortable with a conventional convent school'.

Terrific artwork on display everywhere, particularly involving textiles. Music important – choir and orchestra open to all, although naturally the orchestra tends to attract those with music exam grades. Unusual clubs include pottery, ecology and debating. All sports on site, except swimming. A feeling among parents that grounds could be used for more sport. Sports teams are selected on merit and girls can be in more than one team – those who don't make the team are encouraged to join the relevant club.

Girls are polite and courteous, individually greeting visitors in the corridors and chorusing, 'Good morning, Mrs T,' unprompted in class. Top two parallel classes write letters of welcome to the prospective little newcomers into the reception class and become their mentors for the following year. Girls we spoke to assert that bullying does not exist and that relationships between staff and pupils are tremendous. One said, 'It's a very enthusiastic school which does lots of exciting things. We laugh with the teachers but we also respect them.' Parents heap praise on the pastoral care at the school, said to be very concerned for each and every girl's moral welfare.

Holy Trinity and Saint Silas CofE Primary School

Hartland Road, London, NW1 8DE

• Pupils: 210 • Ages: 4-11 • Church of England • State

Tel: 020 7267 0771
Email: admin@holytrinitynw1.camden.sch.uk
Website: camden.schooljotter.com/holytrinitynw1

Head: Lorraine Dolan, who was appointed after the tragic death of inspirational head Annie Williams in December 2012. She was previously deputy head of St Paul's Catholic Primary School in Wood Green.

Entrance: After the customary priority for looked-after children, the primary admissions criterion is church attendance, either at The Most Holy Trinity Church across the road or at St Silas the Martyr in Kentish Town. About a third come via this route. When Ms Williams became head, very much bottom of the parental-choice agenda, but the intake has altered and now gets more professional parents (including some high-profile political ones). Not too many, school hopes – 'We have a good social mix and want to keep it that way'. At the moment, remains a class and ethnic melting pot, with the largest minority being Bangladeshi and Somali families.

Exit: Mainly to the local comprehensives – Haverstock, William Ellis, Parliament Hill, St Marylebone and Camden School for Girls – but school has also developed a relationship with The Hall, one of north London's leading prep schools, and some year 6 boys have gone there with bursaries before proceeding to leading London independent day schools.

Remarks: This, in the words of Ofsted, is 'an exceptional school' and, without a doubt, its exceptional quality stems from the passion and focus of its 'talented and hardworking' previous head. Ms Williams was a woman who had edited the word 'compromise' from her vocabulary. She built up a team of energetic, often newly-qualified teachers ('We grow our own') – 'I'm very snobbish about teachers – they have to have been to a good university and to have travelled. It gives them a cultural understanding'. The teaching staff is unusually well qualified, with three MAs, two law degrees and three teachers who speak fluent French (so French is taught convincingly from reception), as well as a number of graduate teaching assistants. Ms William's management philosophy included encouraging staff to take a year-long sabbatical every three years to do voluntary work mentoring and coaching.

Housed in a typical Victorian schoolhouse, a meander from tourist-packed Camden Lock. Inside its pristine, soothing interior, however, you'd never guess where you were – fresh flowers, polished parquet and a big red school bell are all from another era.

Despite the fact that the majority of pupils arrive at Holy Trinity with well below average attainment, the school is at the pinnacle of the league tables, with results in English in the top one per cent nationally. Literacy is taught for two hours a day, primarily through poetry and prose. School is strong on story-telling. On the day we visited, a group of eight-year-olds listened spellbound as a young male teacher first played the flute, then, in true Jackanory style, announced: 'And now I'm going to tell you a story'.

All the arts are fundamental to the curriculum. Drama 'has a very big focus' – every year, mounts a whole-school Shakespeare play including every pupil and member of staff and has now helped found a borough-wide Shakespeare festival with five neighbouring primaries. Hardly surprising then that, according to Ofsted: 'Pupils' empathy with the works of Shakespeare is quite remarkable'.

Despite limited square footage, has its own art department and pupils' work is hung boldly throughout the building. Painting even spills out into the large urban playground, where one inner-city wall has been reborn as a rural, summer scene (with a 3D vegetable plot to extend the experience). Music is equally central and Ms Williams insisted all staff learn a musical instrument to perform alongside pupils. Trips are very much part of the education – visits – free of charge – to the theatre, opera, ballet and museums are planned on a regular basis

Though about 75 per cent of pupils are not Anglicans, the Christian message is strong, with a thoroughly involved parish priest, regular church attendance and class mass held half termly. Grace is said before lunch. Lunch itself is entirely healthy ('We had the smoothie debate. And one person's smoothie is another's fizzy pop') and mealtimes, too, are considered a development opportunity. Music is played and, on Fridays, tablecloths laid. A firm emphasis on good manners. The 'golden rules' dictate: don't talk with your mouth full; learn to use your knife and fork correctly'.

Rules elsewhere are equally clear cut. Attentive good behaviour is the norm, but for those who stray, the first offence means displacement to another class; further disruption means an encounter with the head. Badly behaved parents can also find themselves hauled in front of the head.

Standards may be firmly upheld, but the school is also compassionate and warm. Ms Williams kept an ever-open door. On the day of our visit, one child came in to recount the details of her special day out, quickly followed by an entire class offering cakes they'd just baked. With mums and dads, the same policy applies: 'You can never let anything fester, otherwise it just goes round the playground'.

Takes a pro-active approach to its parents, offering jewellery classes as an incentive to engage with catch-up maths, and parents respond with energetic fund-raising. 'We are very grateful for the wonderful education our children receive,' said one. Ms Williams herself was no ingénue when it came to fund-raising and had won considerable support from charities like John Lyons and the Mercer's Company, who have underwritten school trips and paid for 30 laptops.

Superb is Ofsted's summary of the Holy Trinity and St Silas experience and parents agree: 'Children want to come school. They think it's fun'.

Honeywell Infant School

Linked school: Honeywell Junior School

Honeywell Road, London, SW11 6EF

• Pupils: 335 boys and girls • Ages: 3–7 • Non–denom • State

Tel: 020 7228 6811
Email: office@honeywell.wandsworth.sch.uk
Website: www.honeywellinfant.wandsworth.sch.uk

Head: Since 2004, Ms Jane Neal BEd NPQH. Previously deputy head, she has been at the school for 23 years in total. Two children – one at secondary and one at Honeywell. Softly spoken and reflective. Proud of her school and devoted to those in her care – 'a very safe pair of hands,' one parent told us. 'She's seen it all over the years and not much ruffles her feathers,' said another. Passionate about early years learning and keen on reading, walking, cooking and children's theatre.

Entrance: At three to nursery, although there's no automatic transfer to infant school at four. Nursery offers 50 part time places, plus 14 full time places (39 maximum in a class). From reception, three parallel classes, with 30 per class. Usually one assistant per class from reception. A handful leave at the end of nursery. All must reapply to get from nursery into reception. Criteria for offers to infant school – children in LEA care, siblings, those with exceptional medical or special need, proximity to the school (as the crow flies). Once through to the infant school, each child is allocated a place in the junior school, though it's still necessary to reapply via the borough.

Exit: All to junior school. Transfer over to juniors is generally smooth, thanks to system of reading partners (pupils) and induction sessions (parents). As one parent put it: 'There's just enough mixing of the two schools for the move to the big school to seem like a natural progression.'

Remarks: School is housed in an imposing Victorian building, a stone's throw from Wandsworth Common. Infants on the same site as the juniors, though each has its own head, both of whom specialise in their own age group. Schools share a governing body, staff room and some facilities. Infants get to see the highlights of junior school, but lead separate existence day to day. As the head says, 'we get the best of both worlds.'

A total of 40 SEN children offered group and individual support. A small number of children with statements. Nurturing environment, especially in the early years. Forensic attention to detail when assessing the needs of each child – the school isn't just paying lip-service to treating each child as an individual. Excellent results at each stage. Head is aware that the middle achievers deserve special consideration too, not just the high flyers and the ones who are struggling. School is currently focusing on how to make maths more 'girl friendly.'

Loads of outside space and vast amounts of equipment for the pupils. The head told us: 'The children can do all the things here that they can't do at home.' Pupils have their own playground as well as the shared playground garden, complete with tepees, toadstools, fairytale bridge and enchanted forest – inspiring, imaginative and the envy of other schools. All-weather surfacing means that it's now used come rain or shine. Staggered use, so each year group gets the chance to use it. Jolly ICT suite, just for infants, complete with jazzy multi-coloured keyboards.

Good manners are high on the agenda and behaviour is very good. Head stresses that school wants Honeywell pupils to be decent citizens, as well as achieving academically. No uniform, after lengthy consultation with the school community, and some pupils could do with smartening up.

A very welcoming school. Happy staff and happy children, who are having an exciting time. Bright classrooms, with huge windows and colourful displays at every turn. Learning is made fun at Honeywell. The school produces articulate, confident children who are capable of working independently from early on. One parent told us: 'Honeywell's strength is that there is a feeling of community about the school. Everybody is looking out for each other.' As ever, the school is hugely popular but isn't resting on its laurels. Children get off to a flying start here and parents are willing to move heaven and earth to get their offspring a place.

Honeywell Junior School

Linked school: Honeywell Infant School

Honeywell Road, London, SW11 6EF

• Pupils: 360 boys and girls; all day • Ages: 7-11 • Non-denom • State

Tel: 020 7223 5185
Email: office@honeywell.wandsworth.sch.uk
Website: www.honeywelljuniorschool.com

Head: Since 2001, Mr Duncan Roberts BEd NPQH (fifties). Previously deputy head. Inspiring and popular head who is well respected by teachers, parents and pupils. Good sense of humour. Keen sportsman who enjoys swimming, football and playing water polo and instils in the children 'the importance of both winning and losing with dignity. One parent described him as 'a born leader, but also a team player,' while another told us that 'he gets on with everybody.' Has two young children.

Entrance: Once at the infant school, each child is allocated a place in the junior school, though it's still necessary to reapply via the borough. Places do become available further up the school, so it's worth persevering. Incredibly popular. No problem filling vacancies.

Exit: At 11, roughly half to the state sector, including Bolingbroke Academy, Graveney, Burntwood, Grey Coat, Tiffin and Lady Margaret's. Those going to independent schools head for Alleyn's, Dulwich, JAGS, Emanuel, Wimbledon High, Streatham and Clapham High.

Much support and guidance given to parents when selecting a secondary school. Head knows that a lot of tutoring goes on at top of school and concedes that the right tutor can help with fine-tuning. As one parent told us: 'It can get pretty competitive around here at the start of year 6, though I think it's more the parents getting stressed than the children. The school manages to keep the kids pretty grounded but it can be fairly tense at times.'

Remarks: School is situated in a prosperous, middle-class area and the intake mostly reflects this. Head observes that a good proportion are 'advantaged children.' Thirty pupils per class. Around 17 per cent have English as an additional language but bi-lingual children catch up quickly, with weekly sessions for those who need extra support.

Excellent SATs results, with a number of pupils gaining level 6 (head isn't complacent though). The progress of each child in the school is monitored very closely and immediate action is taken if anyone is seen to be treading water. The current focus is on improving the standard of reading comprehension. Low turnover of staff. One assistant for each year group from year 3. French taught to all pupils. Well-resourced school.

A total of 75 SEN children in the school and support is given both inside and outside the classroom – in groups and individually. Playground can be a noisy affair in this large school. Lego club has been set up for quieter souls who find the hustle and bustle of break-time too much, as well as a cordoned off quieter zone, but some parents still say 'it's a bit of a jungle out there.' School council's requests listened to and acted upon.

Sport is a major strength of the school and is taken very seriously from year 3. Inter-class competitions recently introduced (including tug of war) so 'everyone can take part.' Welcomed by parents, as some felt that previously only the sportiest were given the chance to play. School takes part in every tournament going – often with great success. Huge number of trophies on display to prove it. Swimming from years 3 to 5. Not just predictable sports here – cross-country and orienteering offered and lacrosse played at the highest level. Before and after school clubs are very popular. All tastes catered for – tennis, Mandarin, gym, maypole dancing, knitting and baking. Early morning running club on the nearby common for pupils, parents ('mostly mums') and teachers. House system recently introduced and house points hard fought for. No uniform (apart from PE kit), after consultation with entire school community.

Gold Artsmark awarded to school for high level of provision in the arts. Huge orchestra with 60 members, as well as string orchestra. Individual tuition on a variety of instruments (recorder, violin, flute, cello), with regular concerts and performances for parents. The head's attitude is 'now you've got your grade 1, let's all enjoy it.' Recorder compulsory for year 3. Two choirs, so something for everyone, including one dedicated to popular music (scores from West End musicals). School hires drama facilities from nearby Alleyn's to put on a year 5 and 6 production involving all 180 children. Recent productions include Bugsy Malone and We will Rock You.

This is a school which makes the most of being in the capital – lots of trips, visiting speakers and workshops. Year 6 Outward Bound residential trip to the Isle of Wight is a high point in the final year and everyone is encouraged to go.

Supportive, vociferous PTFA. Whether they're hearing readers, producing a snappy school magazine, fundraising or coming in to talk about their experiences, they're a force to be reckoned with. Excellent wrap-around care on offer, including holidays. Communication between parents and staff has improved recently with the sharing of teachers' email addresses.

School has strong links with the community and actively supports local charities. The importance of being a good citizen and of giving back to society – 'either in time, effort or finances' – is instilled in the pupils.

Honeywell is a first-rate state primary that offers the lot. School produces independent, confident children ready to cope with the next stage of their education. Old pupils are always coming back to visit. As one parent told us: 'My girls loved Honeywell. I genuinely believe that it gave them the best possible start.'

Hornsby House School

Hearnville Road, London, SW12 8RS

- Pupils: 410 girls and boys, 50/50; all day • Ages: 4–11
- Christian–based non-denominational • Fees: £11,910–£12,810 pa
- Independent

Tel: 020 8673 7573
Email: school@hornsby-house.co.uk
Website: www.hornsby-house.co.uk

Headmaster: Since September 2012, Edward Rees, previously deputy head of Dulwich College Junior School. Educated at Charterhouse and Durham University, BA in education, specialising in geography. He is married with two young children, and plays cricket for the MCC in his spare time.

Entrance: Genuinely non-selective and first come first served into reception, with no compulsory parental interviews to suss out those who 'won't fit in'. Parents are encouraged to come in for a chat, but it is not part of the application process. Priority to siblings. Non-refundable deposit of £2,500, payable three terms in advance, repaid after the child leaves the school. Those applying for year 3 or above come into the school for a morning which includes tests in maths, English and reasoning, plus time in the classroom and in the playground.

Means-tested bursaries available for year 3 entrants upwards (worth applying for – they are apparently not overwhelmed by applicants), and school will try to help current pupils who fall on hard times. Three scholarships – two academic, and one for solid academic ability combined with exceptional music or sports talent – for children coming into year 4.

Exit: Academic ante upped during previous head's tenure and now many move on to, eg, Dulwich College, Alleyn's, JAGS and Whitgift as well as Streatham and Clapham High and Emanuel. A few to boarding schools, eg Windlesham, Benenden, Cranleigh, or state secondaries, eg Graveney, Lady Margaret, The Oratory. In 2013, 32 academic, drama, art and sports scholarships. Nearly all boys as well as girls stay till 11. 'There's lots of physical activity and a good number of young male staff who are positive role models.'

Remarks: Started in 1988 by Dr Beve Hornsby, a leading figure in dyslexia therapy, with 22 children in a church hall. Dr Hornsby felt that multi-sensory learning would benefit children of all abilities, and the school's motto is 'Learning for all'. 'We retain that sympathy for children who aren't going to find things easy,' says the school. Moved five years later to its present site, just over the wall from Chestnut Grove secondary, and has been expanding ever since.

Compact site. The original Edwardian buildings – once a local state primary school – are complemented by later additions with attractive curved roofs and light, spacious classrooms, housing, inter alia, art, science and music rooms. The latest development, opened in 2010 and built round a protected lime tree using environmentally-friendly materials, adds three more ground floor classrooms plus a bright underground kitchen and dining room, which stretches out beneath the playground. The school now serves hot lunches (85 per cent organic, with salad bar, crudités on each table and plenty of fruit on display; a Masterchef dad chairs the catering committee) and has a large basement space for, eg, street dance club. The only remaining Portakabin houses the French and learning support rooms.

Generous staffing ratio – teacher plus two assistants in reception, one teaching assistant in each class up to year 4 – means the school can accommodate a wide ability range, 'and get better scholarship results than the selective alternatives'. The ISI comments: 'Pupils achieve high academic standards within a wide and creative curriculum.' The school is accessible for wheelchairs and can cope with mild ADHD and Asperger's as well as dyslexia and dyspraxia. 'It's rare for me to feel a child's needs aren't dealt with better here than anywhere else.' On only two occasions has school suggested to parents that their child might be better off with more specialised provision elsewhere – 'The families now feel that that was the right decision'.

Two SENCos; most extra support comes from teaching assistants in the classrooms, though some one-to-one help (at extra charge) and EAL support is available from part-time specialists. Teaching assistants are a mix of mums, aspiring teachers and gappers – generally several are ex-pupils, who bond easily with the children.

Technology is important here: whiteboards in every classroom, all year 3 desks (and one year 6 room) have retractable computers, and everyone learns to touch-type. The school even employs technicians to keep it all running smoothly.

Big commitment to sport, with half-a-dozen specialist games staff, including one woman who has competed in world surf lifesaving events and another who has played for a premiership football club. Other top athletes come in to coach and encourage. Three separate playgrounds on site, but most sport takes place at local venues such as Trinity Fields, Battersea Ironsides and the Oval. Fields A-D teams for most sports; everyone in year 3 upwards plays in at least two fixtures a term, and two-thirds of the children play club sport out of school. Year 6 A teams go on tours to, eg, Sussex or East Anglia.

The house system brings together children of different ages to compete in music, art and sports events, gain house points for good work or behaviour, and see their own house flag flying or their house colours adorning the house cup. Year 6 children can take on the responsibility of becoming head boy or girl, or house captain, and everyone has the chance to be a school council representative.

Class music and singing lessons; the peripatetic music staff who give individual instrumental lessons also run ensembles and help with termly concerts. Plenty of imaginative artwork on display in corridors and in the bright art room; the summer art exhibition includes work by every child in the school. Spring, summer and nativity plays. Drama now has a higher profile with the recent appointment of a specialist drama teacher and is taught as a discrete subject in the curriculum from years 2 to 6.

An early bird club operates before school, and the many after-school activities range from xylophone to taekwon-do to chess. The older classes go on residential journeys to Sussex, Shropshire, Normandy and Scotland – 'There are huge benefits on the social side, and these trips may help children who like the idea of boarding school decide if they are really suited to it'.

Most families live within a couple of miles, and many walk or cycle to school, though some come from as far away as Wimbledon. Strong parents' association, which organises parties and fundraising events. The school sees itself as 'not the most pompous player in the local market', and it is generally viewed as less pressured than some other local schools, with less parental emphasis on social status. Parents appreciate the relatively down-to-earth and caring nature of the school, with its friendly, informal communications between staff and parents and its non-assessed entry policy but rigorous teaching. The children like the happy, relaxed atmosphere and wealth of opportunities beyond the syllabus.

Horris Hill School

Newtown, Newbury, RG20 9DJ

- Pupils: Around 110 boys; 90 full boarders; 20 day pupils
- Ages: 7–13 • C of E • Fees: Boarding £23,250; Day £17,250 pa
- Independent

Tel: 01635 40594
Email: enquiries@horrishill.com
Website: www.horrishill.com

Headmaster: Since 2011, Mr Giles Tollit BA (early forties). Tall and lean, reminded us a little of Bryan Ferry in his salad days. Seems reserved at first but soon unbends and shows a nice, dry sense of humour. Educated at Holmewood House in Kent and then Sevenoaks where he was an academic scholar. Initially destined for a career in the military, he studied classics at Bristol on an army bursary. Took gap year job at a prep where he was expecting to teach Latin in a fairly junior capacity but before term started found himself head of classics! Such a fiery baptism would have been enough to turn a lesser chap off teaching but it had the opposite effect on Mr Tollit and Sandhurst's loss turned out to be preps' gain. Ten years at Caldicott and thence to Bilton Grange as deputy head. He's 'delighted to be back in an all boys boarding school' (he loved his own time at prep) and certain about the positive benefits of a sector he believes suffers from outdated stereotypes. Not that he has to sell boarding to the parents he meets, they've all done it themselves. Describes school, memorably, as being 'not dissimilar to a cruise ship; doors close at the start of each term and off we go.'

Mr Tollit teaches Latin and Greek and helps the scholars polish their skills in debating, logic and philosophy, he 'mucks in' as necessary and takes year 8 camping at his house in North Wales after exams. Describes HH as a 'seven day a week' school and is unconvinced by flexi-boarding, which he feels is sometimes the worst of both worlds. A former UK shot, he has introduced clay pigeon shooting and a rifle range is planned. He's also a keen photographer and, because 26 miles just isn't enough of a challenge, an ultramarathon runner.

Married to Molly, also a classicist, whom he met at university. It seems that three young sons aren't enough of a challenge for Molly who has turned her energies to transforming part of a field in the school grounds into a thriving kitchen garden. Establishing one at their former school, Bilton Grange, taught her 'what works and what doesn't' and HH is reaping the rewards. Chickens, an orchard and a dog (standard issue black lab?) are next on the list.

Parents think the Tollits have brought new energy to the school and like the fact they have their own young family. They have total faith in Mr Tollit, think he knows their boys incredibly well and praise his (and rest of staff's) swift response to calls and emails. Boys think head needs to be 'a bit more relaxed' but like the fact he's introduced clay pigeon shooting.

Entrance: From age 7. No exam 'as such'. Head meets all prospective parents. Boys have informal interview, simple academic assessment and spend a day. Mr Tollit says he's 'not looking for superstars'; boys are observed to see how they interact and whether they are comfortable being 'in the academic spotlight' of such small classes.

Exit: Nearly all to senior boarding schools. Recently: Winchester, Radley, Eton, Harrow, Sherborne, Marlborough.

Remarks: Founded in 1888 to prepare boys for entry to Winchester, Horris Hill is set in 80 acres of wooded heathland on the borders of Berkshire and Hampshire. You'll need your satnav first time round so as not to miss the quaint wooden signpost directing you down an unpromisingly narrow lane; it's almost as though only those who need to will find their way here.

One of Horris Hill's idiosyncrasies is that it doesn't do year groups, it does 'termly remove'. Boys are placed in small classes (average 12) according to the progress they are making and remain there until they have mastered all their subjects to the requisite level. It might sound like a nightmare to organise but head says the maximum discrepancy between similar age boys is 'a couple of terms either way'. A boy's performance is reviewed via 'form order' (mark, position and effort grade) every three weeks and at the end of term he stays or moves up accordingly. It's an unusual (possibly unique) system and only feasible in a school of this size (max 130) and age group. Besides accommodating summer birthdays, advantages are no B stream, no individual subject setting and ongoing challenges for both brightest and less able. According to Mr Tollit it's as close as you can get to an education that is customised to each boy's needs. Arrangement is only for academic work; boys are grouped by age for sport, dorms etc. Parents all in favour, say it's great both for confidence and humility as boys are usually towards the lower end during first term and nearer the top in the second. The consensus is that the system works, even if one or two parents admitted they didn't entirely understand it.

Lessons we observed were fun, inclusive and challenging – a hard trio to achieve but less so with a class of 10, perhaps. Subject classrooms are named after senior schools: Winchester, Harrow, Eton, Radley etc. It took a bit of getting used to seeing such an age range but the boys' enthusiasm and rapport with teachers was inspiring. In geography, impressive answers to quick fire questions were rewarded with chocolate; in the next classroom we thought we'd come across boys being punished but discovered that immersion in French pop music is a great way to practice listening and vocab! In the DT workshop small boys in enormous aprons were busy sanding and drilling – some with more finesse than others. Was there anything, we asked, that they would like to change at their school? Extra free time was one suggestion, as was getting rid of second prep (senior boys do this after supper). Most popular idea was being able to bring small pets to school, something we mentioned to Mr Tollit, who promised to consider the proposal. Few boys with SEN – dyslexia, dyspraxia – receive support but this isn't the place for those with more than mild problems.

The no mobiles, laptops, iPads (basically, no screens) rule is, as far as we could tell, no big deal and so much easier than trying to control limited access. Boys write weekly letters and may email/Skype from the house computer. As a teacher observed, if the no screens policy were to change, 'it would mean more rules.' Boys accept the policy and parents love it. They're not quite so keen when, for instance, CE results come out and they can't talk to their sons because the boarding house telephone is engaged – surely room for a little more 21st century communication technology here? This is a school where 'live' notice boards mean that someone changes the pictures and display on the wall in the dining hall corridor several times a day! There aren't smart boards in every classroom although those we saw were being creatively employed; boys treasure the one or two teachers who spurn their use. Science labs, art and DT rooms have all the necessaries in a charmingly scruffy no-frills style. By contrast, a high-tech rooftop weather station relays the prevailing conditions to a screen outside the geography room.

Sensible uniform features navy blue cords – either trousers or shorts, boys can decide. Apparently 'some boys wear shorts even when it snows.' Sartorial democracy extends to choice of tie as well. Long morning and lunch breaks allow plenty of time to work in the kitchen garden, ride bikes (boys can bring own), play outside in the meadows, make dens and have adventures in their own bosky dominion (known as 'spain' because it's roughly the same shape). Nowhere is out of bounds but pupils mustn't go off alone. Camping out and cooking in the woods is one of the ultimate post-CE treats. Juniors have their own wood, 'too tame for us,' said our super-confident year 8 guides. One of the characteristics of HH is the amount of personal freedom pupils enjoy, finely balanced by the equivalent expectation of personal responsibility. Boys organise their own activities (or Sign Up), recording where they are on a notice board so that everybody knows.

Youngest boarders (age 7 – 9) have lovely rooms in the 'Private Side' above the head's family quarters, with teddies on beds and lots of posters. Evening activities include silent reading, film nights with popcorn, board games and even shoe polishing (try suggesting that at home...). Numbers are small so things are flexible; if it's hot they can have a swim, if everyone's exhausted they go to bed early. Gappies 'bridge the gap' between boys and staff and are, as always, very popular. What about the homesick, we ask? Of course it happens but staff are vigilant and boys support each other, telling tutors if they're worried about someone. 'You feel awkward at first,' our guides said, 'but it only lasts a week.'

Lots of younger teachers with families live on site, married couples head up the boarding houses but after the junior forms most of the teaching staff are men. This notwithstanding, the traditional boys' own atmosphere prevails and is what many, especially army families, treasure. There are a few local day boys who are 'building up to boarding', rest may go home after matches on Saturday until Sunday evening (except first and last weekend of term) but most stay, 'or you miss too much fun.' That fun includes cross-country cycling, tree running, kite flying and ghost stories round the campfire. A parent praised the 'pater' system that pairs new boys with older boys and said that these cross-age friendships are kept up throughout school. Older boys move on to one of two Edwardian houses a short walk across the playing fields. Four-bed rooms are very comfortably furnished with home duvets, posters, beanbags and lovely soft carpet. Fruit bowl and toaster fill the gaps between meals, all of which are eaten in school dining room. Everyone, staff and pupils, sits down together at large tables, boys serve the food. Head v keen on benefits of 'interaction across a table'.

Spacious and well-designed music school can accommodate all for studio theatre or concert performances. Twenty-six practice rooms means there's no excuse for not getting down to scales and arpeggios after breakfast. Parts for all in 'fantastic' music and plays. Main venue for drama, assemblies etc is rather tired windowless sports hall, not enhanced by pervasive whiffy trainer smell, but never fear, Mr Tollit is on the case and this part of the school is undergoing complete refurbishment. As he says, 'HH is not a flash school', but a shooting range, climbing wall and upgraded squash courts are on the way. Interestingly, it seemed to us that there was less of an obsession with organised sport and winning here than at other similar schools. Plenty of options: usuals plus hockey, squash, tennis, sailing, golf, fencing. Boys think cricket and football are what they're best at and all get to represent school in something. Parents come and watch matches although it's a long round trip if you live in London. Swimming pool is outdoors (very) with wooden changing huts – all a bit basic but doubtless character building. One of the school's 'quite old fashioned secret things' is the modelling and train room, a glue and paint besmattered garret where Warhammer enthusiasts create their miniature worlds and model railway buffs of all ages can operate trains and signals.

With a maximum of 130 pupils, quite a few who are siblings, the parent body is small, self-selecting and fiercely supportive. Although it's in a wealthy part of the country, HH is definitely not (outwardly at least), a smart school. Parents are welcomed to plays, concerts, matches and Sunday evening chapel and there are social events such as fathers and sons cricket matches and mothers and sons tennis but there's no PTA, sports day or speech day. One father, who had considered London day schools

for his sons, spoke of the way in which HH 'preserves innocence' – not just by absence of personal technology but also because full boarding means boys develop a camaraderie that is not influenced by each others' possessions or houses. On a more practical level, parents love the fact that all sports kit is provided, washed and maintained by the school.

Horris Hill is such a distinctive school it's unlikely you could choose it by mistake; proud to be different, it epitomises the very best prep school traditions without being pompous or rigid. HH boys are confident but not precocious; they think for themselves but aren't arrogant. There's room for big characters but a shy child won't be trampled underfoot; academic success is important but not to the exclusion of other talents. As another happy parent told us, 'it's a hidden gem.'

Hotham Primary School

Charlwood Road, London, SW15 1PN

• Pupils: 410; 50/50 boys and girls; all day • Ages: 3–11 • Non-denom • State

Tel: 020 8788 6468
Email: info@hotham.wandsworth.sch.uk
Website: webfronter.com/wandsworth/hotham

Head: Since January 1998, Miss Pam Young BA. Graduated from Otago University in New Zealand with a degree in early years education. Came to the UK in 1987 and was previously the deputy head of a school in Camden. Still teaches, taking year 6 one day a week and offering other classes and booster lessons where needed. Serious and quiet on first acquaintance, but underestimate her at your peril. She is fiercely proud of her school, of its pupils, teachers and parents, and will brook no criticism. She knows the name of every child, enjoys the support of her governors, her 'great critical friends', and relishes the cultural diversity of the intake. Running marathons as a hobby might give a clue to her tenacity.

Entrance: The nursery class admits 36 full and part time children each year. Reception class of 60, including bilingual class.

Waiting list for places in most year groups, which is an indication that someone is doing something right, considering four state primary schools in very close proximity, one of which is virtually next door. Admissions policy is administered by Wandsworth local authority so out of Miss Young's hands.

Exit: To a range of 15 different secondary schools. Maybe two or three a year go into the private sector but the majority are predominantly state school bound. Ashcroft (formerly ADT) is popular, but some also to Shene School, Burntwood, St Cecilia's.

Remarks: At first glance this looks like a typical Victorian primary school. It even has the original Boys' and Girls' entrances. The classrooms have high, light, draughty windows and are accessed by corridors and stairwells decorated with those funereal tiles so beloved of that era. The whole cries out for a lick of paint and some TLC. Outside the obligatory grey, hard playground is surrounded by a high wall.

However what lies within tells a very different story. Take a closer look at that playground, for example – well-tended, well-planted flower beds all around the edge, each one the responsibility of one year group. Look further still and you come across a hidden, secret garden containing bird boxes, trees and plants to represent the four seasons, wood piles to provide homes for dozens of creepy crawlies and a quite amazing human sundial which looks very like a mini Stonehenge. All this surrounds a small classroom usually inhabited by the man affectionately known as 'Mr Hotham'. Retired, he then returned part time to give extra help to those in need and seems to embody the spirit of the school.

The classes are large (26-30 on average) but all supported by TAs. Twenty per cent of the pupils need EAL help, with full support on offer. Special needs pupils include those on the autistic spectrum, some dyslexic, some have cerebral palsy, some with language delay, some have ADHD. All are supported within the classroom as the head can see 'no point in doing anything else'. She sees the school as a 'place where we all learn from one another' and her greatest wish is to see her pupils become 'independent learners, to use their initiative and solve problems by using their fantastic, inquisitive minds'.

A bilingual stream has been introduced into the reception class and is making its way up through the school. In the bilingual class, around 15 per cent of the week is spent speaking French, and this proportion increases by year group so that by the last year the children will spend about 50 per cent of their time using French. Four French speakers on the staff and years 5 and 6 go on school trips to France. There's a link with a school in Paris.

Music is very strong, with choirs performing in Wandsworth events. All year 4s learn the clarinet. Swimming is taken seriously in KS2 when all children are taught in four ability groups over a six month period. Teams in football, cricket, netball, cross country, swimming. After school clubs in gym, yoga, photography, art, French. Very active PTA – recently completely refurbished the library. Polite, happy children in smart red, white and blue uniforms. Excellent handwriting throughout (would put many a private school to shame). As one parent remarked, 'Despite the presence of two excellent faith schools in the vicinity, Hotham gives a brilliant start to its kids. Its multicultural mix seems to work well.' Has won the Green School of the Year Bike-It award and two of the staff were finalists in the annual Teaching Awards.

This is a solid primary school offering a solid education to its local community from the nursery ('the best in the borough', according to one parent) to the final year, where discussion groups in the class are animated and passionate. One book which should not be judged by its cover.

Howell's School Junior School, Llandaff

Linked school: Howell's School, Llandaff, GDST

Cardiff Road, Llandaff, Cardiff, CF5 2YD

• Pupils: 300 girls; all day. • Ages: 3–11 • Non-denom
• Fees: £6,976–£9,064 pa • Independent

Tel: 02920 562019
Email: mail@how.gdst.net
Website: www.howells-cardiff.gdst.net/JuniorSchool.aspx

Head of the junior school: Since September 2006, Mrs Judith Ashill BEd (thirties). Did her degree at Swansea University. Previously head of Redland High School Junior School. Mrs Sally Davis is principal of the whole school, including senior school.

Entrance: Applicants for nursery assessed through play. For reception and years 1 and 2 assessment is by play, informal activities and unstructured tasks. Candidates for years 3 – 6 sit papers in mathematics, English and non-verbal reasoning.

Exit: Vast majority move on to the senior school.

Remarks: Happy and lively atmosphere. Housed in a modern building on the campus but within its own space. Imaginative design of classrooms and specialist areas gives a light and airy feel to the school. Well-designed play areas. Classes we visited had photos of all the pupils up, a nice touch which helps the girls bond as a class. Art and music are strong. Outdoor learning is used in addition to other teaching methods. The girls are energetic and enthusiastic – a palpable feeling here that learning is fun. Nursery and music department housed in Cumberland Lodge, which was Roald Dahl's childhood home.

Hurlingham School

122 Putney Bridge Road, London, SW15 2NQ

• Pupils: 325 boys and girls • Ages: 4–11 • Non-denom
• Fees: £13,350–£13,950 pa • Independent

Tel: 020 8874 7186
Email: admissions@hurlinghamschool.co.uk
Website: www.hurlinghamschool.co.uk

Headmaster: Since 2010, Jonathan Brough BEd (Cantab) NPQH (forties). Mr Brough (rhymes with ruff) was head of English at two boys' preps, deputy head of Bute House and finally head of City of London Girls' Prep before taking over at Hurlingham. Married to Harry, a leading ICT lawyer; they live in north London. Amicable, upbeat personality, he knows all the children by name and places a huge emphasis on happiness being central to everything that goes on in the school. Very popular with parents, staff and pupils, he teaches Latin and extension classes, and is a much-appreciated supply teacher for all age groups when the class teachers are away.

One of those heads who takes an interest in everything going on around the school, be it new seeds for the garden or scholarship papers. He's recently enhanced house competitions with a rewards system and excellence book, and parents get sent surprise postcards informing them of their child's special achievements. An avid reader and writer since childhood, he particularly enjoys writing stories for children. He arranges for a good number of authors to visit the school, run workshops and book-themed events. Growing up in Devon, the son of two teachers, he has been surrounded by educational and literary influences all his life. When he awards himself some free time, he enjoys travelling and cooking, especially baking, which he hopes one day might make an appearance on the extracurricular calendar.

Entrance: At 4+ non-selective on a first come, first served basis, with priority to siblings and those living closest to school. Places do come up in older age groups, so always worth telephoning the school for occasional places.

Exit: Feeds a number of senior schools. Popular choices for girls are Godolphin and Latymer, St Paul's Girls, Surbiton High, Francis Holland, Wimbledon High, or boarding schools Woldingham and Benenden. Boys go to King's Wimbledon, Hampton, Emanuel, Kingston Grammar, Reeds, or the French stream at Whitgift. Odd one or two to the state sector, Lady Margaret or Tiffin.

Remarks: Proudly mixed ability and does extremely well by its pupils. Reception class children are divided into three classes by date of birth. As children move through the school they are split into ability-related sets – maths from year 1 and English from year 5. The school is structured to ensure that everyone achieves success at their own pace to the best of their ability. Core subjects maths, English and science are all very strong and taught by subject specialists. No formal exams until they start practising for the 11+ tests. French is introduced in reception and Latin in year 4. By the age of 11 all the children take and pass an OCR 16+ entry level Latin qualification, demonstrating their skills in translating, comprehension and Latin coursework. The school is very keen to emphasise how the early Latin programme helps develop English and spelling skills. Children can try out other languages, including Greek, in after-school clubs.

EAL is available as necessary. SEN is catered for case by case dependent on individual needs. There is a qualified head of learning support and three assistant teachers for small group work, one-to-one sessions and advising staff on differentiation within class. Homework is a serious matter and everybody is expected to complete it; lots of help available for anyone who is not sure what to do, along with a free after-school homework club. During year 5 parents have a meeting with the head and class teachers to discuss suitable secondary school choices.

Music and drama well embedded into the curriculum; a good variety of different types of theatre and concerts. There's full-time dedicated music teacher and good proportion of pupils learn instruments.The corridors are well decorated with the children's art and designs; specialist art teacher from year 4 and the school boasts its own kiln. Well-planned traditional sports options, all taught by specialist coaching staff. Good choice of clubs each term, ballet in the elegant mirrored studio and karate being extremely popular. Particularly impressive karate, one of the largest school programmes to run in the UK, with about a third of the school taking part. This year they broke their own records with 100 per cent success in karate exam gradings.

Pastoral care is sensitively run; older children can become playground and reading buddies. There are five straightforward Golden Rules to follow, and everyone knows there are consequences if they fail to stay within the boundaries. House competitions and activities enable children to mix and get to know other age groups. Lunch times look incredibly civilised for a junior school: youngsters sit in house groups, about eight children to a table, and tuck into tasty meals cooked on the premises. Tea is also provided for those who stay at school until 5:30pm.

The school is on a cleverly-designed compact site with a reasonable sized playground and bronze award eco-garden on the first-floor terrace. Lots to occupy children at playtimes: table tennis, climbing wall, giant games of Connect Four and chess, and a nature garden with a water feature for those who just want to chill. Recently graded outstanding in all areas and awarded Excellence in Education status by the ISI. Continues to go from strength to strength; parents comment that it's such a reliable school, and whatever happens your child's welfare and education will be looked after. The energetic Mr Brough is one of the safest pairs of hands for miles.

Hurst Lodge Junior School

Linked school: Hurst Lodge School

Bagshot Road, Ascot, SL5 9JU

- Pupils: 70 boys and girls. Boarding for girls only. • Ages: 3-11
- Fees: £8,820-£11,070 pa • Independent

Tel: 01344 622154
Email: admissions@hurstlodgesch.co.uk
Website: www.hurstlodge.co.uk

Principal: From 2013, Miss Victoria (Vicky) Smit BSc (forties). Had an earlier stint as head between 1998 and 2011. But,

concerned about the propriety of being both co-owner and head (her brother, Sir Tim Smit, started the Eden Project and the school belonged to their mother), she appointed another head in her place for a brief period. It didn't work and Miss Smit is once again head.

This former Hurst Lodge girl, who 'has been 23 years in the place,' bounced into our meeting in rather fetching wellies, waterproof trousers and trackie top. She had been helping out at Hurst Lodge's Forest School and was clutching a wet teddy – which she handed to her assistant with the comment that 'he needs to have his bum dried.'

Previously worked with the army and a team of agricultural management consultants but helped her mother move the school in 1999 and never left. A Forest School leader (younger Hurst Lodge pupils learn how to take risks in the real world), she has undertaken 'multi-discipline training,' which sounds a bit like being qualified in common sense). A joy – rather like the best possible Girl Guide, favourite aunt or big sister. She bubbled with enthusiasm, giggled and waxed lyrical and we positively skipped round the school, hopping up the odd staircase to avoid being mown down by busy children. (Our notes actually say: 'bubbly, bouncy, loving').

Remarks: It is not often that this long-time Good Schools Guide editor comes out of a school with a happy glow – the kind of buzz we get when we find a school that delivers its own sort of magic, does exactly what is say on the tin and is quite possibly perfect for the child who may just need that extra boost or special attention. Nothing necessarily major, very often just spoonfuls of common sense and human kindness and an introduction to a different way of learning. Hurst Lodge is such a place, and as with the senior school, this is a happy mainstream school with an impressive SEN reputation. Good for the non-challenged too. 'Everybody has got different strengths,' says the head.

Forest Schools are fairly new kids on the block – they have been described as 'an inspirational process' offering children, young people and adults 'regular opportunities to achieve and develop confidence through hands-on learning in a woodland environment.' Apparently the Danes got there first; and it appears to take several (rather expensive) four day sessions to get up to speed as a Forest School leader (including first aid). So much for 'ealth and safety.

Forest Schools are important at Hurst Lodge, with younger pupils (kindergarten to 11 year olds) all enjoying role play and exploration. In the real Hurst Lodge world (a bit like Enid Blyton's if that's not a dirty word), pupils learn how to take risks and set their own boundaries. They may not wave sticks about but they climb trees ('they mustn't climb higher than they can get down from,' says the head), build shelters, light fires and make their own seesaws with real saws, branches and logs. They fabric besoms, build forts from wood and burn them down – 'a practical lesson in why wood gave way to stone in ancient times as a building material.' This is idyllic childhood stuff. The young learn to work as a team and have survival days in all weathers. Parents occasionally complain about the lack of homework and are assured that their young have learned how to negotiate, use their imagination and identify various trees by bark and by leaf. This is grown up stuff – serious companies call it bonding and charge heaps.

And of course they have snowball fights and fly kites, as in the senior school. They also feed (and put cream on the bums of) chooks and ducks. They herd pigs (none currently – their sties are being moved). School growing its own food, both within and without the polytunnel.

They also learn to read (by phonics or any way that works), do sums (set for maths) and follow proper classroom procedure. Spanish from two and a half; French from 12. Help on hand for the challenged – for those on the SEN register, assessments etc, goes without saying. Help too, for the brightest. Dedicated computers and library too. Baby science room and tremendous playroom and studio theatre.

The tiniest have access to the performing arts department. Ballet and tap for all, plus swimming, gym and gardening. Same care lavished on everyone. Some youngsters board from nine. Absolutely no tolerance of bullying.

Jolly modern nursery for tinies from the age of three to six. Roughly 50/50 boys (who are wriggling their way up the school). Nursery is bright and jolly with everything you would expect. Max 35 and early years vouchers nursery folk flow seamlessly into pre-prep up to the age of 11. Forest School where age appropriate. Ditto reading, ditto maths.

Hurstpierpoint College Preparatory School

Linked school: Hurstpierpoint College

Hurstpierpoint, West Sussex, BN6 9JS

• Pupils: 355 boys and girls • Ages: 4-13 • Christian • Fees: Day £7,140–£14,280 pa • Independent

Tel: 01273 834975
Email: hurstprep@hppc.co.uk
Website: www.hppc.co.uk

Head: Since September 2013 Mr Ian Pattison, previously a housemaster at the senior school.

Entrance: Mostly into year 3 and year 7 but spaces occasionally available in other year groups. Those who enter year 7 spend a day at the school and are assessed in verbal and non-verbal reasoning, maths and independent writing plus an interview. They are looking for children who are prepared to 'have a go' and take advantage of the opportunities. Not super selective, but they need to be of at least average ability; school wants all children to be able to move on to the senior school if they wish. The senior school entry exams and scholarships are towards the end of the summer term, so there is none of the usual slacking after common entrance. A number come in from other prep schools and local primary schools at 11+ and most of those who enter in year 3 come up from the pre-prep.

Exit: Very few leave at 11+. Most move on to the college at 13+ but a few leave, either because it is decided that they would not be able to keep up or want to go elsewhere. Will prepare children for entry and scholarships to other schools.

Remarks: Shares a site with the senior school and has the use of their facilities – 140 acres of grounds, indoor swimming pool, sports complex; netball and tennis courts and two Astroturfs. Glorious, almost monastic-looking setting dominated by the chapel, surrounded by farmland and with views to the South Downs.

As with the senior school, they have upped the academic ante and offer a fairly academic but rounded education – plenty of help for bright dyslexics but those with low general ability might struggle. Expectations are high and children are set in maths and English from year 3 and in all subjects for years 7 and 8. They are well prepared for the scholarship exams, and although there is a level playing field with those coming from outside, they get about half the awards and do particularly well in drama, music and sport. As in the senior school, it is all about aiming high and fulfilling potential. The top two years are housed in the academic quad of the senior school, which makes transition easier. iPads have been introduced for years

7 and 8 (and put on the bill) and have transformed learning eg nth term formula can be taught in 10 minutes. Digital tasks bring together a range of subjects and make learning more exciting and fun.

Considered locally as quite a sporty school, with particularly strong rugby – the school recently won the Sussex Cup and Sussex rugby sevens. Encourages a 'can do' attitude and no one is left on the bench if they want to play in a team. No stigma if you are not the athletic type as long as you do something – kayaking and orienteering popular with those who hate team sports.

Lots of music and about half learn an instrument – big orchestra plus smaller bands and choirs, and the chapel choir is particularly popular. Lots of drama, with four plays a year, plus one for talented actors in year 8. LAMDA, public speaking competitions, poetry recitals and assemblies all good for building confidence. The house system gives children a sense of identity and loyalty and enables different year groups to get to know each other.

Various charitable projects give children a sense of social justice and an awareness of those less fortunate – the school does not want to produce children with a sense of superiority. Very much a partnership with parents, who are kept closely informed of progress via prep diaries, emails and, as in the senior school, a three-weekly grade and reporting system.

The pre-prep school, run by Michele Finnegan, is very much part of the Hurst family, and most children move seamlessly on to the prep school.

Hutchesons' Grammar Primary School

Linked school: Hutchesons' Grammar School

44 Kingarth Street, Glasgow, G42 7RN

• Pupils: 530 boys and girls; all day • Ages: 4-11 • Non-denom
• Fees: £8,234–£9,453 pa • Independent

Tel: 01414 232933
Email: admissions@hutchesons.org
Website: www.hutchesons.org

Depute Rector: Since 2011, Christine Haughney, previously head of Calderwood Lodge in Newlands, former Hutchie parent, runs the place with a couple of (lesser) deputes.

Entrance: One intake a year (but see secondary school). All children assessed, up to 120 apply for 60 places.

Exit: A natural and automatic progression to the secondary school after P7, although all pupils will prepare for and sit the S1 entrance exams taken by external candidates.

Remarks: Delicious trad 1912 building (which sported electric light) was girls only until 1975 when school went co-ed and Hutchie's primary was born. Stunning library (glass front, zillions of books) carved out of a couple of classrooms in the front passage, opened 2010.

Exciting new lang course, Global Education, sounds incredibly dreary but stars a wandering 'super teddy bear' (how about the Paddington chronicles?) and exposes pupils to both the language and customs of various countries on a weekly basis: Latin (with staff presumably in togas), French, German, Spanish, Italian, Russian and Gaelic. Parents deeply enthusiastic – bring in fur hats, sombreros and whole school participates with gusto.

Terrific school, three then four parallel classes, most come at five and almost all go on to senior school. Good dyslexia help on hand, screening for all, gentle test and assessment – twice a year for tinies, who must have 'passed their fourth birthday' the February before they join. Jolly phonics (but actually a mixture of reading schemes). Cradle to grave stuff this – drop off early, after school club till 6 pm (senior school can hang around until 5.15 which might cause collection problems) and holiday clubs/camps in conjunction with Oscars (oscarchildcare.com).

Hymers College Junior School

Linked school: Hymers College

Hymers Avenue, Hull, HU3 1LW

- Pupils: 225 girls and boys; all day • Ages: 8–10 • Non-denom
- Fees: £8,010–£8,460 pa • Independent

Tel: 01482 441211
Email: enquiries@hymers.org
Website: www.hymerscollege.co.uk

Head of the Junior School: Since 2010, Mr Peter Doyle BSc PGCE (mid forties). Read economics at Bristol then spent four years in industry. Followed family vocation by doing PGCE at Hull, then taught in primary schools in the home counties before moving to Stamford Bridge Primary as deputy head. He was deputy head at Hymers College Junior for three years before being appointed as head.

Approachable and caring, with an easy manner. He is a constant support at school events and clearly proud of pupils' achievements. He believes in 'building self esteem and confidence in a culture of high expectation' and says school aims to instil in each pupil 'the belief in their ability to succeed'.

A keen squash player, he also enjoys camping and hill walking. Married to Rachel and two of their three children attend the school (younger daughter waiting in the wings at local state primary).

Entrance: Main entry points are in years 4 and 5. Entrance exams take place in February for entry the following September and test reasoning ability, comprehension, mathematics and powers of expression. An intake of 72 (three classes of 24) into year 4, topped up to classes of 26 in year 5, though head says that 'if a child has the ability to succeed and be happy at Hymers we will find them a place.' Around five fee remission places per year, all means-tested.

Links with pre-prep Hessle Mount and prep Froebel House mean their pupils are academically tracked and those who meet entry requirements have automatic offer of place. Wide catchment area covers Grimsby, Scunthorpe, Goole, Scarborough and some way into East Riding. There's an extensive school bus network.

Exit: Almost all pupils progress to Hymers College Senior School after successfully sitting entrance exams.

Remarks: Like the senior school, the four Rs of educationalist Guy Claxton's Learning Power – resourcefulness, resilience, reflectiveness and reciprocity – are fundamental to learning here. Broad curriculum, with shared senior school teaching in geography and sport. French, German and Spanish taught from year 5. Science taught in junior school science room. As you might expect with a selective entry, most recent ISI report said pupil attainment was 'good in comparison with national age related expectation.'

Teacher observation, dyslexia detector software and assessment are used to pick up learning support needs. SENCo liaises regularly with senior school and school counsellor. Individual learning plans are drawn up, with one-to-one work where appropriate, in agreement with parents. INPP programme of physical exercises for children needing further learning support has 'had a profound impact in the classroom,' says the head. A member of the junior school staff has been trained to deliver the programme.

Parents receive pupil grades three times a year and a full report annually. Main academic subjects are assessed for attainment, progress, attitude and homework. Mark schemes are on show in every classroom and staff are keen to share good practice across school.

Sport is high on the agenda, with excellent facilities, competitive opportunities in traditional team sports and success for individuals and teams at county and national level. Supervised swim available every morning from 8 to 8.30am.

Plenty of music too – school was riding high on their 40-strong choir coming second in the BBC's Songs of Praise Choir of the Year competition when we visited. Particularly delighted with judges' comment on how 'happy and relaxed' pupils were. Sixty-five per cent of pupils sing in a choir and choral tour to Paris for year 5s. Lots of opportunities for musical instrument tuition, at additional charge, with free instrument loan for new starters. Percussion, wind and string groups with performances throughout year and annual chamber concert, with performers volunteering for a spot.

Drama features well with annual productions for each year group. Dance clubs for year 5 and 6 girls and extra-curricular programme includes crafty kids (hopefully not aptly named) and photography club. Free after-school supervised homework club until 5.30 pm. Residential trips feature prominently; year 5 pupils visit Normandy and the battlefields and year 6s do outdoor pursuits in the Lake District.

Housed in a bright, modern two-storey building at the edge of the Hymers campus, the junior school accommodation has spacious classrooms, each with their own cloakroom area and designated DT/art and science rooms. School is moving to tables from individual desks (as budgets allow). Pupils consulted on choice and layout of classroom furniture, though some consider the change a mixed benefit – less distraction from slamming desk lids against less storage space, better organisation and heavier school bags. Prominent commendations board in the entrance hall celebrates personal academic achievements awarded at each Friday's assembly. House points are collected for the four houses and are used primarily for sporting competition. Warnings and (forgetting) kit marks recorded in a warning book for each house kept by head of year.

Junior school overlooks extensive and well-kept playing fields, with own wildlife pond and good outdoor recreational activities with table tennis tables and play area. Lunch in main school dining room. Breakfast available too. Choice of hot and cold dishes, nutritious and appetising in appearance. Juniors interact well with older pupils. Sixth form prefects take form registration and supervise some clubs. No school council but year 6 reps are chosen for a leadership club and meet with the head to discuss fund raising and charity events.

School says that CARE (stands for care, acceptance, respect and effort) is the core of the pastoral system and the message resounds in every classroom. Pupils say that 'the teachers are all really nice', 'friends are nice and loyal' and 'you're taught to be competitive with yourself.' Parents (40 per cent of whom work in medicine or education) agreed. They told us that children are 'relaxed and happy' here and that 'teachers adapt to the individual child.'

Ibstock Place School, Preparatory and Kindergarten

Linked school: Ibstock Place School

Clarence Lane, London, SW15 5PY

• Pupils: 360 pupils; 190 girls/170 boys • Ages: 3–11 • Inter-denom
• Fees: £13,200–£13,650 pa • Independent

Tel: 020 8876 9991
Email: office@ibstockplaceschool.co.uk
Website: www.ibstockplaceschool.co.uk

Headmistress: See senior school review. Mrs Anna Sylvester-Johnson is overall head.

Head of prep school: Miss Diana Wynter – warm, enthusiastic and much-loved. 'She reads us things out of classic books and organises lots of fun trips for us,' say pupils.

Entrance: First come, first served at Priestman House ie nursery, with priority to siblings. Now massively oversubscribed so names down as early as poss. Occasional occasional places on account of relocating families. At 6+, entry to Macleod House, ie the prep, by individual assessment. At 7+ and 8+ papers in English and maths. At 9+ and 10+ English, maths and reasoning. Everyone is interviewed.

Exit: Most go up to the senior school. However, Mrs S-J tells us, 'there is some humpiness that not all Macleod House children go up to the senior school. The two languages can be a barrier. But we give them lots and lots of warning and we do help find an appropriate school for them.'

Remarks: Three buildings situated in the gardens opposite the rear of the elegant main house accommodate the littles. They start in Priestman House in a delightful nursery with lots to do and lots of attention and an open door to enable them to run in and out to the activities outside in their own safe and enclosed space. A good mix of free and structured play and happy, relaxed tots. A great sense of having fun while learning everywhere in Priestman – we wanted to eat the yummy sausage rolls they were cooking and we loved the wheelbarrows they fill with plants each term. PCs in each classroom used wisely and they grow their own veg. Froebel-inspired learning principles though later educational thinkers also influence the sound and sensible curriculum. Macleod House houses the 6-10s – again, an attractive child-sized building – we were impressed by the number of books everywhere – a relatively rare sight. Orderly classrooms with very stimulating displays – we like the art work inspired by Kandinsky and van Gogh, the clever Roman mosaics and the 'Wow word of the week' palm tree. Good light art studio, and DT workshops with lively work. Year 6 have their own building – Roberts House – which also houses good drama studio with retractable seating – and gives them a useful transition between junior and senior schools. Those with more than mild SEN probably wise to look elsewhere. Some extra help at an extra charge. Delightfully forthcoming and friendly children. Overall, the kindergarten and preparatory schools are carefully organised, well-structured and offer a happy, healthy and stimulating start for your bright child.

Immanuel College Preparatory School

Linked school: Immanuel College

87/91 Elstree Road, Bushey, WD23 4EB

• Pupils: 56 pupils, 28 boys/28 girls • Fees: £8,034 pa
• Independent

Tel: 020 8955 8938
Email: enquiries@immanuel.herts.sch.uk
Website: www.immanuelcollege.co.uk/preparatory_school

Head: The head master of Immanuel College, Charles Dormer, has ultimate responsibility for the prep school, but its day-to-day operation is overseen by the head of reception and year 1, Natasha Pearlman. She has also taught at South Hampstead High Junior School, Mathilda Marks-Kennedy and Hasmonean primary school.

Remarks: See senior school.

Inglefield House

Linked school: Haberdashers' Monmouth School For Girls

Hereford Road, Monmouth, NP25 5XT

• Pupils: 110 girls • Ages: 7–11 • Fees: Boarding £18,171; Day £9,660 pa • Independent

Tel: 01600 711100
Email: admissions@hmsg.co.uk
Website: www.habs-monmouth.org

Head: Since 2013, Mrs Hilary Phillips, previously director of pastoral care, head of French and PSHE and classics teacher at Edgeborough Prep School in Farnham. She is a keen netball, hockey and rounders coach and member of a choir.

Entrance: By exams at seven, eight, nine and 10.

Exit: Virtually all to senior school, Haberdashers' Monmouth School for Girls (one ballet school scholarship in 2012).

Remarks: Lovely, intimate junior school at the heart of main school site. Physical education, science and music lessons taught by specialists, most of rest taught by class tutor. Lots of music, singing and dancing. Separate play area. Newly built mini amphitheatre provides unusual outdoor performance area. Self-contained facilities, such as art area and well-stocked library, plus ready access to extensive facilities of main school, offer the best of both worlds.

International School of Aberdeen, Preschool and Elementary

Linked school: International School of Aberdeen

Pitfodels House, North Deeside Road, Pitfodels, Cults AB15 9PN

- Pupils: 260 boys and girls (including 40 in pre-school)
- Ages: Pre-school (3-4); Elementary (5-11) • Fees: £17,875 pa
- Independent

Tel: 01224 730300
Email: admin@isa.aberdeen.sch.uk
Website: www.isa.aberdeen.sch.uk

Elementary Principal: Don Newbury

Exit: Eighty-four per cent moved to the senior school in 2013. School says the rest generally leave 'through re-assignment of their parents within the oil and gas industry.'

Remarks: For details see senior school.

International School of London – Junior

Linked school: International School of London

---

139 Gunnersbury Avenue, London, W3 8LG

- Pupils: 140 boys and girls • Ages: 3-11 • Non-denom
- Fees: £18,250-£22,500 pa • Independent

Tel: 020 8992 5823
Email: mail@ISLLondon.org
Website: www.ISLLondon.org

Head: Headmaster Huw Davies, MA (Oxon) PGCE from University College, Worcester. Has extensive experience as a former deputy head, IB diploma coordinator and higher education advisor, as well as being a governor of a sixth form college in West London. Has taught history and theory of knowledge at diploma level and is a member of Llafur – the Welsh History Society.

Exit: Around 75 per cent move to senior school.

Remarks: See senior school for details.

International School of London in Surrey

Old Woking Road, Woking, GU22 8HY

- Pupils: 210 pupils; 50/50 boys and girls • Ages: 2-14
- Fees: £15,740-£17,550 pa • Independent

Tel: 01483 750409
Email: mail@islsurrey.com
Website: www.islsurrey.com

Head of School: Since 2012, Dr James Doran BA MA EdD (early sixties). Appointed in the school's second year, he is an American with an impressive international career, most recently as head at TASIS England, with previous headships and senior leadership roles at international schools in Japan, Panama, Singapore and Saudi Arabia, having begun his overseas career teaching science in Tunisia. Returned to the US as lecturer at Stetson University. 'Action man' Doran is qualified pilot, scuba diver, skydiver, sailor, loves photography and his granddaughter. Wife Vickie is the school librarian/media co-ordinator. Two adult children live in the US.

Parents and kids say he greets them at the gate every morning. 'We're a family', he says. 'We need to be visible and get to know everyone so that if a problem occurs we can talk about it in a spirit of trust. This is the most multi-cultural school I have worked at and I really enjoy it. I love the importance of mother tongue, and learning from professional colleagues from all over the world.'

A collaborative leader, he sees his two fellow senior leaders, the Dutch head of primary and the Lebanese/Ugandan head of middle years as partners in running the school. 'I want to be here until the building and the high school programme are in place, then stay around for a couple of years to enjoy what we've built, so I plan to be here for at least the next seven years.'

Entrance: Non-selective. Nursery priority to siblings and expatriate families who arrive during the year; it is designed for children who will move on to the ISL primary school rather than local families looking for a stop-gap. No open days; 'every day is open day at ISL Surrey'. International families can make an appointment for a visit that includes introductions to EAL and mother tongue teachers, to discuss language options and organise a language assessment. These staff can also provide a vital link between school and family during the process of settling in to school and Surrey life. The Crossroads Transition Programme helps all new families with relocation and orientation.

Exit: The school is young and adding a class each year, so as yet not much of a track record of leavers. Most leavers so far have moved abroad; one or two have transferred to larger schools.

Remarks: A new, small and expanding international school, that will eventually take pupils from nursery right through to sixth form. The school follows the government's early years framework, the cross-curricular and topic-based International Primary Curriculum (IPC), and the IB middle years programme. Teachers are mostly international: only 20 per cent are native English speakers.

The school's language is English and, with the help of EAL lessons as part of the programme, even those who don't speak it at home are soon fluent. But a hallmark of the school, like its parent school, the International School of London, is mother tongue language instruction. Those whose mother tongue is English start to learn a second language – French or Spanish – at three. Every other child aged three and above has mother tongue lessons and learns to read and write in their own language. The largest cohort – over a third – learns Dutch. Then there's a raft of other European languages plus Arabic, Japanese, Mandarin, Russian (second language in middle school) and Turkish. Greek may be making a come-back very soon. One parent says ISL's environment made it easy for her son to take part. 'My son wants to be like all the other kids – before he did not want mother tongue lessons, but here he's normal and doing what the others do.' Dutch children have government-subsidised after-school cultural lessons and are prepared for their national exams so they can re-integrate when they return.

Mother tongue tuition continues in the middle school, but pupils also start French, Spanish or Mandarin, taught in multi-grade classes. Those who started French and Spanish in primary continue, but while other middle schoolers do their mother tongue lessons, the English-speakers do more in-depth English literacy work with a focus on linguistics.

Middle school kids say best thing about ISL Surrey is the iPads. 'This is a new school so we are the pioneers – they call us the guinea pigs. One of the things they wanted to try was using iPads so, hey, we weren't going to say no to that!' Doran was keen to introduce this as part of the new school's move to digital learning, so was pleased that, given the small size of the school, he was able spend the first year teaching science and to see for himself how the technology worked. He explains, 'Every middle school teacher has an iPad and we give them to all the students as their own (unless they leave within one year). In five years some new form of technology will replace iPads, and we don't know what that will be, but we need to give the kids the confidence to use this technology. I am using the same iPad I teach with to fly my plane, strapped on to my leg following the map.' The middle school kids' verdict? 'We use them everywhere, they're a really great tool for learning.'

Inclusive, individualised approach, from highly able to special needs, with wheelchair access to primary classes on the ground floor. Special educational needs handled case by case by staff supported by part-time SENCo; the school can cater for dyslexia, mild Asperger's, ADHD and speech and language issues. Some specialist support is paid for by parents but organised during school time with planning done in collaborate with the teachers. One soft-spoken child explained, 'I am not confident in maths, and so I have an extra maths lesson and that really helps', whilst a parent spoke of a child two years ahead of her age level in maths who is getting special lessons to keep her challenged.

Parents are more than satisfied with the teaching methods, describing them as 'a different approach to learning, but the children seem to remember a lot of what they learn. Because they do it on a project basis, they learn things from lots of angles, and it embeds the learning across the subjects.' Ofsted rated the school Outstanding on its first visit. The 65 international teachers include part-time specialists for mother tongue and other subjects, and there's lots of in-house training on language issues. Plenty of teaching assistants; there may be up to three adults working in a class at a time.

Nursery coordinator – dynamic, energetic and cheerful, bursting with ideas for the next activity – is developing a Forest School programme of outdoor activities exploring the natural environment. Growing programme of clubs and activities includes riding, hockey, judo and other sports. Parents would like to see more, whilst understanding that it's a trade-off for being on the ground floor of a new initiative, and approving that 'this way everyone gets a go'. Pupils say: 'If what we have is not what people want, they can go to the big schools.' Some sports competitions against local schools and other international schools, and school will help families find local clubs for other activities.

Middle school pupils enthusiastic about Open World programme, which enables them to share their passions and learn more about them. 'One of us likes animals and may become a vet so we met people at a zoo and at the RSPCA. Someone has a cooking passion so we had a baking class with a chef and a caterer. It keeps our minds open to new possibilities.' Plenty of trips to eg the Globe, the Natural History Museum. 'For most of our trips we do things you are not normally able to do.'

Fund-raising supports community service projects in eg Latin America and India, chosen mostly by the teachers and parents on the charity committee, but increasingly the student council is getting involved. The 2012 Paralympics inspired the children to support the Whizz Kids charity for disabled children.

A much-needed cafeteria is part of the development plan, but at present pupils bring packed lunches. Expanding school bus service.

ISL Surrey was originally part of the Royal Dutch Shell group of schools set up for Shell's employees and other Dutch expats. Shell sold the school to ISL in 2009 – the other schools in the group are the original International School of London in Gunnersbury and ISL Qatar – and for the first year half its pupils were Dutch. The school's primary curriculum, the IPC, was originally developed in Shell schools for the international families there. The ISL board oversees the school and provides support and financial backing.

The school was built by Shell and includes a bright central atrium running the length of the main building, a welcoming space that serves as the heart of the school. The large multi-purpose gym doubles as an auditorium; its large, open backstage space doubles as a music room. The upstairs art room has also been given over to a middle school hang-out space, and is entirely too neat and tidy to suggest that art is thriving, something that the school and Ofsted have both recognised: art specialist recently recruited. A new building houses the nursery and early childhood programmes, with a grassy play area outside, plus the school library and additional computer lab facilities. Well-tended grounds, with spacious playing fields beyond: these will be the site of the new secondary school, which now has planning permission.

For a new school, ISL is well-resourced as the owners purchased the Dutch school fully equipped down to the very last Lego. But for now space is tight, and every nook and cranny used, especially during mother tongue lessons when the atrium provides ample spill-over space.

Diversity is the common denominator. This means that everyone has to make a special effort to understand each other – no assumptions can be made. Kids, parents and staff all talk about the family atmosphere of the school, and though everyone knows growth is on the way, they want to preserve this as a special quality. The student council told Ofsted inspectors that there is no bullying, and that they all have to be sensitive to the expectations of other cultures. As the kids see it, 'If you don't know the rules, you risk getting in an argument because you don't understand what really causes misunderstanding. Wrong assumptions can lead to problems.' Pretty reflective thinking for pre-adolescents.

New kids are assigned buddies to help them settle and integrate. This works across grades, too; sixth grade middle-schoolers as a class pair with kindergarteners and they all know each other. Younger children feel safe and confident around older kids and look up to them. The school has recently created a separate playground for the younger ones because, in the words of the middle school pupils, 'the little kids kept jumping on us and hanging around us when we have our breaks'. The also school created a middle school hang-out space with sofas, a microwave and fridge so they can escape for lunch. The 'toastie' machine is a big hit. 'They recognise we are not in primary and they treat us independently. The little kids are cute but we need our space!'

Mother tongue specialists get involved in pastoral support for both teachers and parents as they have a good understanding of the cultural/educational backgrounds issues that can arise.

Part-time counsellor available for students and parents. The only behavioural incident of late involved a pupil with significant learning and emotional issues who needed from some supervised time to himself to consider how his actions affected others, and so spent a few days removed from the classroom working one-to-one with school leaders. Counselling issues tend to involve social interactions, transition issues and friendships. As Dr Doran points out (echoed by the kids and parents), 'In a small school there is nowhere to hide. Any inappropriate pattern is quickly detected.'

In this international school of just under 200 pupils, there are some 26 nationalities and 13 languages. Around a quarter are Dutch (a diminishing proportion as the school grows) and some 15 per cent from the UK. British locals tend to be the children of staff members and those keen on the IB, plus returning expats who want the continuity of an international education.

A chatty, endearing bunch who seem to feel a true sense of belonging to the school and to each other, despite their diverse nationalities, heritages and languages. We met very young children on their first or second days at the school who were already happy, settled and fully engaged. Older pupils spoke with pride about a girl from North Africa who had arrived with no knowledge of English. 'She's tried so hard and is really doing well. We help her.' Another child told us: 'It's great for people that come from other countries. We do exams, but they don't focus on the grades here, they focus on what you are learning and how you are improving.' 'We can always talk to the teachers. They're very supportive and they really care about you.'

The school organises free English language classes and weekly coffee mornings for parents. Dutch families from the former school are happy with the way the new international community has blended with their own. One mother comments that they have adopted a Dutch tradition of going out for birthday breakfasts, and look forward to the next excuse to celebrate together.

A parent said: 'If you want lots of competitive sports and big social groups, this is not the place. But it's very welcoming, inclusive, community-oriented, and everyone is willing to work together to give every child chance.' A dual national couple commented, 'This is a school for parents who want to feel part of a community.'

Ipswich High Junior School

Linked school: Ipswich High School

Woolverstone, Ipswich, IP9 1AZ

• Pupils: 190 girls; all day • Ages: 3–11 • Non-denom
• Fees: £7,911–£8,388 pa • Independent

Tel: 01473 780201
Email: admissions@ihs.gdst.net
Website: www.ipswichhighschool.co.uk

Head: Since 2009, Mrs Eileen Fisher BEd, formerly deputy principal (head of juniors and early years) at St Margaret's School in Edinburgh.

Entrance: At three, assessed in informal play session. Later, at seven, eight and nine, via written assessments in basic skills. Entry at all times into all years, capacity dependent (full in many intake groups).

Exit: All go on to seniors.

Remarks: One/two-storey school, bright, modern building. Due to increased popularity, now two-form entry in most years. Max numbers 25 in upper junior years. Well-equipped, good

extra-curricular activities including riding, sailing and skiing clubs. Strong music provision, appropriate but not exhausting homework. A lovely safe setting for early school years – space, trees and resident sheep.

Ipswich Preparatory School

Linked school: Ipswich School

3 Ivry Street, Ipswich, IP1 3QW

• Pupils: 310 boys and girls; all day • Ages: 3–11 • Fees: £9,054–£9,969 pa • Independent

Tel: 01473 281302
Email: prepregistrar@ipswich.suffolk.sch.uk
Website: www.ipswich.suffolk.sch.uk

Head: Since 2009, Mrs Amanda Childs BA MA, Dip Ed (late thirties). Previously deputy head of Alleyn's Junior School, following a teaching career at various independent schools and an international school in Bangkok. Dedicated and determined to introduce the school to changed teaching practises, for example in the teaching of reading. Extremely au fait with all current educational fashions but steers her own course. Believes in clear boundaries and instilling in pupils respect for each other's differences. Married to Martin, a journalist, and they have two daughters, both in the prep school.

Entrance: Admission to the nursery is by registration. For reception and years 1 – 6 entrance assessment includes reasoning, English and maths. Children are also observed at play. Main points of entry are at reception, year 3 and year 5. Pupils come from a variety of schools and a wide catchment area, 'though half have a Colchester postcode'.

Exit: For most, an easy transition to the senior school, though all sit the entrance exam – results are used to determine setting in year 7. A few leave for maintained schools (there are flourishing grammars in Essex). Any thought unlikely to cope in the seniors will have been given fair notice.

Remarks: The prep school (years 3 – 6) has occupied its own purpose-built premises next to the nursery and pre-prep since 2006. An eye-catching building which, though striking and affording fine views of the town, has limited play areas and no grass whatsoever. Pupils are taken over to the main school playing field to let off steam in the lunch break, and have timetabled access to the sports facilities. At the end of the school day, the playground transforms into a car park for collecting parents. Class sizes fluid, and range from 18 in reception to 24 in years 5/6. Form teaching in most subjects, with setting in maths and English from year 5, and specialist teaching for certain subjects in years 5 and 6. All pupils are screened on entry for specific learning difficulties and emotional/behavioural problems are quickly picked up on. The School Action Plus programme is designed to support struggling pupils with the aim of them being able to cope, eventually, in the senior school. Walls covered with art/science work – some of it spectacular – and there is an interesting menu of music, drama and other activities, both within the school day, and at after-school clubs. All year 3 pupils learn a stringed instrument as part of the curriculum. Reading for pleasure, as well as for learning is (rightly) emphasised, with two specially designated library areas. The school is quick to respond to problems as they arise with contact via email and the head available before school each morning. Pupils charming, though we felt that the ones we met (year 3) were inhibited by the presence of the registrar, acting as chaperone.

James Allen's Preparatory School (JAPS)

Linked school: James Allen's Girls' School (JAGS)

East Dulwich Grove, London, SE22 8TE

• Pupils: 300 girls; all day • Ages: 4–7 pre-prep, 7–11 middle school • C of E Foundation, but all are welcome • Fees: £13,200 pa • Independent

Tel: 020 8693 0374
Email: Japsadmissions@jags.org.uk
Website: www.jags.org.uk/japs

Headteacher: Since 2007, Miss Finola Stack BA PGCE Mont Dip (forties). Co-founded Finton House School in 1987 and moved to become head of Cameron House School, London, in 1994. ISI inspector, IAPS District committee member. Tall, slender, mother of three sons; very pleasant, gently spoken, straightforward and calm.

Head of the pre-prep (JAPPS): Mrs Sue Saunders Cert Ed MA, a cordial and kindly Yorkshire lady with 30 years' teaching experience and two daughters. Taught in the maintained sector, then at Dulwich College, then deputy of DUCKS before coming here. Both women impressed us with their blend of intellect and warmth. 'The head is simply great,' said one parent, of Miss Stack. Another described Mrs Saunders as 'warm, calm, very approachable'.

Entrance: Very high number of feeder primaries and nurseries, mostly in Dulwich and neighbouring areas. Entry at 4+ is selective, a process which one mother described as 'horribly stressful. I'm not looking forward to it with my second daughter one bit'. Parents aside, though, the children usually enjoy it, because the tests and interview are expertly disguised as play. At this age the staff look for 'adventurousness of spirit', among other attributes, rather than any kind of attainment, and Mrs Saunders emphasized that the children are not all readers on entrance. No sibling policy. At 7+ things become proportionally more formal: maths, English and reasoning papers, followed by interview. Standards are very high – over-subscribed as it is, it can afford to be unbending in who it admits; girls who aren't strong academically don't stand a chance. Miss Stack comments, 'This may be a parental perception, but there is very good support for girls of all abilities throughout the school.' However one parent praised the JAPS selection process as 'more personal and welcoming than some others round here'.

Exit: At 11, most girls go on to JAGS, the senior school, often with scholarships and other awards; a few decide to try co-ed and effortlessly make the switch to local independent or maintained schools. Girls at seven all go on to JAPS Middle School.

Remarks: JAPPS is a truly lovely pre-prep, housed in a handsome Edwardian house in the heart of Dulwich Village. As we passed through the porch, we heard some splendid reading aloud from a confident, strong-voiced little girl of four, which very much set the tone for our visit. The classrooms (18 children in each, 36 children per year group) were full of agreeable buzz and liveliness, but not at all noisy. Children worked with focus under the guidance of young, elegantly dressed teachers – or so they seemed to us – and all seemed kind, knowledgeable and authoritative. Nor do appearances deceive – all the parents we spoke to were extremely happy: 'My daughter's blossomed'; 'she's really happy, thoroughly enjoys her day'; 'she's made really lovely friends'; 'Her teacher's very sensitive to her needs';

'It's a kind environment, not at all pushy'; 'The teachers are fantastic,' are just a few of the comments we garnered, and the children we met were bright, articulate and adorable.

Teaching focuses on building independence and the ability to solve problems. French programme is impressive, with French lessons itself, PE and singing taught entirely in French; science, music, debating, football all strong. Excellent academic and art work displayed on the walls. Mrs Saunders keeps a watchful eye on the children's developing characters too: weekly 'gold-leaf' assemblies reward acts of individual thoughtfulness as well as achievement and a 'kindness cup' is awarded every half term.

After browsing around JAPPS's peaceful garden and its inviting little library – Miss Stack adds, 'and well-stocked' – entering JAPS is like suddenly encountering a charmed world. This is a school that positively glitters with success. Clad in their stylish, practical, and, according to one mother, expensive – where isn't it? – uniform (navy culottes, red polo shirts), the girls here radiate a particularly whizzy kind of confidence. And no wonder – already one of a picked band when they arrive, everything they get from then on is simply the best. French? Immersion programme taught by native speakers. Library? Modern, wonderfully equipped. Sports facilities? Amazing – the girls compete at national level. Music provision? Astounding – not a single instrument they can't learn. DT? The envy of all the local boys' preps, and the girls do electronics too. Clubs and societies? Huge variety. Organization? 'Runs on oiled castors,' said one parent. Staff? The best money can buy. Academic attainment? 'Exceptional', according to the ISI in its recent report. Some of the work we saw was approaching GCSE level in its scope and sophistication. Good SEN support for the few girls who need it, but 'special needs' tends to mean something different here, ie what are we going to do about Maria, who has done every sum in the maths course already and she's only in year 3? Such girls are, of course, nurtured, and no doubt their presence helps to retain those top quality staff.

The girls are competitive, as Miss Stack has no problems admitting. And indeed, the gales of laughter and eager putting up of hands and very genuine expressions of friendship that we saw were interspersed with wrinkled noses whenever a peer got a question wrong, or so it seemed to us – 'It's great if you're in the top 50 per cent there, and not so great if you're not'. Head says, 'It's just as stimulating whatever your abilities.' If you were offered a place off the waiting list, it can be a struggle,' commented one parent candidly. The pastoral care was rated outstanding in the school's latest ISI inspection, but it may not be the gentlest school in the world for all that. How could it be otherwise, given its intake and aspirations? But if your daughter can cope with the pace here, she's made.

John Betts Primary School

Paddenswick Road, London, W6 0UA

• Pupils: 121 boys, 116 girls, all day • Ages: 4–11 • Non-denom • State

Tel: 020 8748 2465
Email: admin@johnbetts.lbhf.sch.uk
Website: www.johnbetts.lbhf.sch.uk

Head: Since 1989, Ms Del Bravo CertEd. Previously deputy at St Mary Abbots. Formal, earnest and thoroughly decent. Values hard work, politeness, punctuality and respect. Lives for the school. Described by one parent as 'quite formidable and everyone is a bit scared of her, but she has dedicated her life to John Betts.' Always visible at school events, and often the last to leave, but in order to be focused likes parents to

J

make appointments to see her about any issues – 'not a good idea to catch her in passing in the corridor,' commented one parent. Runs a tight ship. Ably supported by long-serving staff, including the deputy, and a sprinkling of new recruits. A very stable staff. Some parents feel that communication between head and parents could be improved. Others feel happy to let her get on with it, as 'she clearly knows what she is doing. She's been here 25 years.' Retiring in July 2014.

Entrance: Over-subscribed. Priority given to children in care, those with statements of special educational needs, siblings and proximity to school (cut off point is about a third of a mile from school as the crow flies). Occasional places become available further up school but are quickly filled. Waiting list in operation. Some 15 per cent speak English as an additional language.

Exit: Approximately half to independent schools. Popular private schools include Latymer Upper, St Paul's Girls', Godolphin and Latymer, Notting Hill and Ealing and Emanuel. State favourites are West London Free School and Holland Park.

Remarks: Housed in a dark, Victorian, listed building in Hammersmith: forbidding from exterior but classrooms are surprisingly light and welcoming. Stunning new block recently added comprising of a reception classroom, library and ICT room, each with huge French windows opening onto playground. Playground is big enough to play a game of netball, though no fixed play equipment and a bit grey. Redevelopment of playground is next on the agenda. Voluntary-aided school. One class per year of 30, with one 'bulge year' of 60.

English, maths and science taught to a high standard and foreign language teaching taken seriously. French taught from year 2 and Italian from year 3. Excellent reports about how nurturing the school is for pupils with special educational needs. All children are screened for dyslexia in year 2 or at point of entry thereafter. PTA partially funds four hours a week of specialist learning support. School employs a whole raft of support programmes. When we visited, numerous small groups of children were dotted around school being given individual or small group support. Currently 32 pupils are identified with some form of additional educational need; five pupils have statements. Gifted and Talented pupils well catered for through extension work and master classes at local secondary schools. Masses of tutoring from year 5 onwards for those heading for independent sector. Head believes it is often counter-productive as children become over-tired, confused and don't concentrate in lessons as they think tutor will explain it again later. Parental peer pressure palpable as 11+ approaches.

Drama and music are strengths of the school. Annual performances, led by top year, are of an exceptionally high standard and are eagerly anticipated. Every child in school is involved. Recent performances include Oliver!, Beauty and the Beast and Lion King. In addition, year 5 performs an annual play in French and year 1 performs songs in French with local French nursery. School choir is thriving with over 50 members. Children are encouraged to join the borough choir and Saturday music school. Instrumental music lessons given out of school, run by borough. Band and orchestra currently not running, which one parent believes is 'an issue.' High standard of artwork throughout school. School takes part in a variety of inter-school sports events and uses nearby Ravenscourt Park for training. Extra sports coaches recently taken on. Cricket, football, skittle ball and netball all on offer. Pupils swim for three terms in total. Although some parents critical of lack of sports provision – 'not well organised,' commented one, and described as 'an afterthought,' by another – school does provide more than the national curriculum requires. Head aware that 'parents always want more opportunities for their children than the timetable will allow.'

Residential school trips for year 6 to Isle of Wight and year 3 to Buckinghamshire with a focus on team-building. School subsidizes pupils who cannot afford to go. Varied selection of clubs available before, during and after school. Science, gardening, drama, chess, athletics, football and art are currently popular. Head aware that 'space is the issue' for clubs. No limit on the number of clubs a child can do.

On-site kitchen with delicious hot meals on offer. Compulsory school lunch for all pupils to make it financially viable. Head believes it has transformed eating habits in the school. General consensus that food is 'amazing.' One child claims that the best thing about school trips is the sandwiches which the school makes!

Parents are very involved, through hearing reading, accompanying day outings, giving linguistic expertise in International Week, attending celebrations and fundraising. PTA described by head as 'brilliant': huge amounts raised each year which go towards subsidising workshops and other projects on head's wish list. Fairly affluent families with only 15 per cent of pupils entitled to free school meals. Parents have high expectations and are not afraid to voice their opinions. Prize giving has been contentious in recent years with some parents feeling that the school gives out too many cups, leaving a minority without. No wraparound care available on site but a walking bus at the end of the day to an aftercare service based at nearby school is a godsend for families where both parents work.

A small, traditional establishment with old fashioned values. Feels like a village school, in the heart of Hammersmith. One current parent feels it is a great school for hard working children, though possibly not as good for those who are less academic and in need of plenty of physical activity. Others disagree and feel it is the best primary school in the area where 'children feel safe because expectations are made clear. You know your child is going to get a thorough grounding at John Betts.' Children are happy and comfortable in this calm, sensible school and it's hard to disagree with the head who feels the children here are offered 'a rounded education.'

Jordanhill School Primary

Linked school: Jordanhill School

45 Chamberlain Rd, Glasgow, G13 1SP

• Pupils: 460; 230 girls/230 boys; all day • Ages: 4.5–11 • State

Tel: 01415 762500
Email: info@jordanhill.glasgow.sch.uk
Website: www.jordanhill.glasgow.sch.uk

Head of School: Since 1997, Dr Paul Thomson BSc PhD Dip Ed (fifties), educated at Dollar Academy, thence to Glasgow uni for a combined honours in maths and physics plus (later) a PhD, having done his Dip Ed at Jordanhill, once next door, but now consigned to the John Anderson campus. Thomson's meteoric career path found him appointed as one of the youngest heads in Scotland; that apart, he has a fearsome intellect and spouted facts and figures faster than most heads we have met, adding all the while 'that it is available on the web page'. He runs the school with a strong leadership team including Irene Matier, head of primary and Robin Paton, who goes under the title of depute head teacher (upper primary) responsible for day to day working of 9 – 13 year olds.

Jordanhill is the only direct grant-aided non-special school in Scotland, and runs its own budget, as does each department. A block grant comes from the Scottish Government Education Department to whom the school is answerable. Thomson regards himself quite rightly as a CEO, working 'with the staff' and running the place with a budget of £5,200 per child per annum. He obviously misses teaching; his entire demeanour changed during our tour round the school: whenever we found a child to be talked to – about anything – gone was the efficiency question-answering model and in its place appeared an interested, smiley friend. (He also does all the 'early' UCAS references.) But youngsters apart, we suspect he does not tolerate fools with ease (he thinks he has 'mellowed a little' recently).

Head of Primary: Since August 2009 Mrs Irene Matier (50s) previously head of the Bannerman Learning Community and head of Caledonia Primary. Formidable. Educated at Queens Park Secondary, followed by Hamilton College and Strathclyde uni, she is an educationalist with strong principles, particularly where the Curriculum of Excellence is concerned. Glasgow youngsters couldn't be in better hands.

Entrance: Inclusive, by address, over-subscribed, waiting lists. Siblings get priority. Some places may become available in odd years. First come, first served, as long as you meet the entrance criteria. Worth moving/killing for.

Exit: All pupils to senior school in 2013.

Remarks: Based on the first two floors of the handsome classical grade B listed building, with a couple of dedicated play areas, one with lyrical views of the playing fields, and David Stow building designed by David Barclay 1914-22, the former Jordanhill College. Pupils have clearly defined play areas: a Secured by Design award from the police.

This is the school you want to fight to get into. Early. Tinies have use of all the main school facilities; we arrived to find them milling around the super new enclosed Astroturf in front of the main school building, and skipped past various crocodiles when we retraced our steps back to the main school with the rector. Dig that fort! We actually used the primary entrance, several hops, skips and jumps from the entrance that senior school uses: no danger of a tsunami of students. As with the senior school, wide passages, high ceilings. Jolly purposeful air all over. And it goes without question, overhead projectors, white boards, computers abound. As before, the best equipped school. Ever.

Max year size 66 (three classes for first couple of years, reducing to two from P3) with four/five year olds doing a half day for the first six weeks. School runs induction days with future pupils visiting the school for three afternoons during May, when they 'take part in a number of activities and spend the third session with their teacher for Primary 1'. How sensible. More schools should copy. Fairly relaxed entry time for first four or five weeks with parents encouraged to go into the classroom 'to mention any concerns to the teacher', and for the next four or five weeks it is a 2.30 break out (which could wreck havoc with some parental care arrangements); fear not: JOSS provides after school care in the local church hall. After their initial honeymoon, five and six year olds stay in school till 2.30/2.45; staying to 3.30 ish (depending on particular classes) as they progress up the school. Large though it is, there is no feeling (like some mega schools we have visited) that littlies are swamped. This is a school where children come first.

School follows Scottish curriculum for excellence; emphasis on three Rs with phonics research in place. Special needs well catered for – 'If they can cope then we will take them, unless their needs are such that the school cannot accommodate them'; some pupils have records of needs. All pupils assessed aged eight, English, maths, spelling, VR; anomalies picked up early and ed psychs called in if necessary. SEN students have open access to networks; three dedicated staff work across primary and secondary schools, plus five pupil support assistants, scribing where necessary. Paired reading with sixth formers wherever; support sessions during lunch, after school, in the evening; this is tailored formally structured study support. Team teaching a

regular feature 'to reduce the size of teaching groups in core subjects and raise levels of attainment for all pupils'. French from early. Some setting in maths (hot on mental arithmetic); taught in conjunction with concept work – basic engineering perhaps? Classroom based, with specialist teachers for art and music and main school PE teachers for PE. P6/7 are taught by specialists from the senior school in maths, lang, drama, French, science and IT in senior school itself, to accustom them to their next step. Homework expected most nights from age eight. House system throughout school from age nine.

Primary school has same strict uniform policy, with first two years wearing green pinnies, which look a bit odd hanging, as they did during our visit, below their cagoules in the playground. Clubs for everything, chess particularly popular. Ambitious outdoor education programme with pupils spending afternoons or weeks away depending on year group, Abernethy Trust Outdoor Centre v popular: swimming pool, indoor climbing frame, ski slope. Wow. Costs, but funds available for those who couldn't afford to go otherwise: primary has 1.2 per cent on free school meals as opposed to Glasgow primary norm of 36.1. Like the senior school, refectory has a card system. No cash, and no buying for others.

This is a predominantly owner-occupier area – professionals, who form an enthusiastic parent-teachers association, with parent volunteers in primary department and loads of fund-raising. Parents run bookshop. Nine per cent ethnic minorities.

The Junior King's School

Milner Court, Sturry, Canterbury, Kent, CT2 0AY

- Pupils: 380 (pre-prep 75); 50 boarders • Ages: 3–13 • C of E
- Fees: Boarding £22,020; Day £6,705–£16,170 pa • Independent

Tel: 01227 714000
Email: registrar@junior-kings.co.uk
Website: www.junior-kings.co.uk

Headmaster: Since 2000, Mr Peter Wells BEd. Educated at Eltham College and Exeter University where he studied art and design. Before coming to Junior King's he was headmaster of Liverpool College Prep and St Hugh's School in Lincolnshire and previously a housemaster at Dulwich College and head of art and design at Cheltenham College Junior School. Teaches art when he can and likes to get involved with clubs and activities. He is an ISI inspector and a member of the IAPS education committee, as well as being a member of the King's Senior Management Team. A headmaster 'at the top of his game', he is married to Vivienne who is the registrar and an ISI boarding inspector and together they make an effective and dynamic team. They live in a cottage in the grounds and escape to Cornwall during the holidays. They have three adult children. Peter is passionate about the school and has a keen eye for detail and is always looking for ways to make improvements. Has recruited 'top notch' senior management and teachers. Respected by children and parents alike and knows all the children by name.

Entrance: Most join in nursery and reception but major intakes into year 5 and year 7 when extra classes are added and occasionally into year 8 for Common Entrance if going on to King's. Younger children have a taster day and informal assessments and from year 5 children tested in English, maths and non-verbal reasoning.

Means tested bursaries available from year 7 for up to 100 per cent of the boarding fee. Academic scholarships offered at 11+ for new joiners and children already in the school – worth a max of five per cent of fees. Additional bursary support available.

Exit: About 75 per cent go on to King's. A few leave for the grammar schools a 11+ – some after school coaching provided but parents usually get their own as well. Scholarships to King's Canterbury every year plus recent academic scholarships to Sevenoaks, Wycombe Abbey and Tonbridge and art and sports scholarships to Tonbridge and music and sport to Benenden. Two recent sports scholarships to Millfield. Those considered borderline for King's required to sit a pre-test and parents are given plenty of advice if it is thought a child might not pass common entrance to their chosen school.

Remarks: Founded in 1879 as the prep school for The King's School, Canterbury and spent its first 50 years in the precincts of the cathedral. Boys were known as 'parrots' because the noise they made and houses are still named after parrots. Moved to current site in 1929 when Lady Milner gave Sturry Court, an Elizabethan manor house, together with the Tithe Barn, in memory of her husband. It was opened by their friend Rudyard Kipling. Two miles from the centre of Canterbury it is set in 80 acres of grounds and playing fields with the river Stour running through the middle. Along with King's, it is part of the Canterbury Cathedral Foundation, shares a governing body with King's and has a committee of four governors closely linked to the junior school.

School has a reputation for being quite competitive and according to the prospectus 'endeavour and success are held in the highest regard' however, the number one Golden Rule is 'Do be kind, gentle, helpful, respectful and polite' and there is great emphasis on good manners, tolerance and friendliness. Parents full of praise for the school, 'my children are all very different and have all been happy – you don't have to be very sporty to have fun here'. 'The competitive environment has brought my daughter out of herself and given her confidence.' All agree that this school is 'best for children who are good at something' and that 'there is a very nice balance between academia and other things so children can build confidence in different areas'.

Strong Christian tradition with weekday and Sunday services at the village church and confirmation and carol services in the cathedral but all faiths made to feel welcome. About 50 full-time boarders and 25 weekly boarders (mainly from year 6) cared for in two immaculate houses: Kipling (boys) and Juckes (girls). Local children often ask to board for the last year and one mother commented slightly wistfully, 'my daughter wants to be at school more than she wants to be at home'. Lots of evening and weekend activities plus Saturday school with lessons in the morning and sport in the afternoon means there is no time to get bored or homesick.

Relationships with staff relaxed but respectful and there is always someone to talk to – year 5 onwards have two class teachers, one male, one female. 'The teachers seem interested in developing my child as a human being not just on an academic level' says one happy parent. Bullying rare and dealt with swiftly via detailed anti-bullying policy. Good healthy food with lots of choice and staff make sure children eat a balanced meal.

School supports a variety of charitable causes and all children expected to be involved at some stage during the year – sponsored walks, donations to Salvation Army, the school fete, visiting old peoples' homes etc. They share their sports facilities and theatre with local groups and the headmaster feels strongly that the school should be part of the local community. Junior King's provides funds for a school in Malawi and children are encouraged to take an interest.

Average class size 15-16, max 18. Three parallel forms with setting in maths from year 5, English, maths and languages from year 6 and science in year 8 – very flexible and all about challenge and support. Separate scholarship class in year 8. Children start learning French in reception and Spanish and Latin taught from year 5. Greek offered to scholars. Special provision for French, Spanish and Chinese bilingual children. Separate sciences taught in specialist laboratories from year 7. ICT incorporated into most subjects and also taught as a specialist subject from year 1 and children learn programming skills eg making computer games as well as spread sheets, presentations and website design. 'Everyone is expected to participate in class and it is a fast paced academic school which does not suit everyone'. Very occasionally, it is suggested tactfully that a child might do better elsewhere.

Bright, sunny library central to main school with 14,000 books and run by a part-time librarian – the most widely-read children are appointed to 'The Most Honourable Order of the Book'. Pre-prep and year 3 have their own libraries.

Experienced staff of 'inspiring and dedicated teachers' as well as talented young graduate assistants who come to work for a year before going to train as teachers. Much more attention given to SEN in recent years, about 10 per cent with some sort of learning support, either withdrawal or in-class help – system of monitoring and referrals means problems picked up early. One full-time and one part-time dyslexia teachers plus a graphologist. EAL support if required.

Sport taken seriously and the school likes to win; pupils consistently encouraged to make the most of everything. Superb facilities and children can go to King's for anything not available at Junior King's. Rowing an option from year 7 in conjunction with senior King's plus a cricket pro and winter coaching and squash offered at King's. Floodlit Astro (funded by a parent) opened in 2013 means hockey now a major sport for boys and girls. Girls have been IAPS champions three times in recent years. Huge galleried sports hall and 14 tennis courts. LTA tennis coach recently appointed and school usually sends a team to the national IAPS tournament at Queenswood. Heated outdoor pool for fun but serious swimming taught at the King's Recreation Centre. Fencing particularly strong and a number of international fencers started at Junior King's. Few parental grumbles about children not getting picked for teams or getting into school plays but school aware of this and tries to address it. Inter-house competitions give everyone a chance to take part and new talents oftenemerge at the summer sports day when a huge variety of sports are contested.

Performing arts take place in the Tithe Barn, recently insulated and refurbished thanks to another very generous parent. Music is central to the life of the school with class music from reception upwards, over 60 per cent learn at least one instrument and the choir is a special part of school life. Range of bands, choirs and ensembles cater for every age and ability and with at least one big concert each term, 'music is never far from your ears.' Advent carol service and sung evensong at the end of the summer term are held in the cathedral and there are music scholarships to King's Senior most years. Drama part of the curriculum from year 3 and just about everyone has a chance to get up on stage at least once a year.

Busy art department – photography, film making, art history, graphic design, pottery, textiles – the sort of opportunities you would expect to find at a senior school and children can use the facilities at King's as well. DT from year 3 includes racing car design when children build and race a car in the Kent championships, jewellery making and T shirt design and a Dragon's Den type competition when children form teams to solve problems.

Annual Spanish exchange, skiing, weekend in Normandy, post-scholarship trip to Greece, the much looked forward to post-CE jaunt to Cornwall, rugby to Paris, hockey to Holland, cricket and choir tours to Brussels – European destinations which do not put too much strain on parental pockets.

Activities most afternoons and evenings, dozens to choose from (some charged for), everything from animation, circus skills and bush craft to debating, gardening, jazz dance, riding and photography (digital and dark room).

Day children from a radius of about 40 minutes via mini-bus service plus accompanied train from Ashford. Most from professional families – doctors, medics, lawyers and City and creative types. About 10 per cent foreign nationals from a variety of countries, strong links with Brussels and the Foreign Office – many parents choose the school for its global outlook. Active Friends Association has weekly breakfasts and organises social events such as hog roast and Christmas bazaar to raise money eg funded the new adventure playground.

Alumni include: Minister for Sport and the Olympics Hugh Robertson, actor Orlando Bloom, President of the Commonwealth Games, Tunku Imran Ja'affar, ceramicist Edmund de Waal and cricketer Freddie Kemp.

Pre-prep housed in the Oast House with own hall and library. Seven classrooms with up-to-date ICT provide a colourful and stimulating environment. Children learn PE, French, dance and music from reception onwards and use the prep school facilities – sports hall, Tithe Barn, sports fields and dining hall. Accredited Forest School in the grounds where children learn about nature and risk taking in a safe environment – they were making nettle pancakes over a camp fire on the day we visited. Nursery now housed in newly built Swiss-style chalet known as Little Barn with all the mod cons and under floor heating – a busy happy place with guinea pigs and fish tanks.

Junior Lavant House

Linked school: Lavant House

West Lavant, Chichester, PO18 9AB

• Pupils: 25 girls (including 5 boarders) • Ages: 7-11; boarding from 8+ • C of E • Fees: Day £10,938–£11,430; Boarding £17,952 pa • Independent

Tel: 01243 527211
Email: office@lavanthouse.org.uk
Website: www.lavanthouse.org.uk

Headmistress: Since September 2013, Mrs Caroline Horton BSc MEd, NPQH (head of junior and senior school). Previously deputy head at Parkstone Grammar School in Dorset. Educated at Leeds Girls' High School and studied maths at King's College, London. Began teaching career at Queen Anne's, Caversham and then worked at The Maynard School, St Margaret's (both in Exeter) and Torquay Girls' Grammar. Married, with three grown up sons.

Junior co-ordinator is Mrs Kate Ward BSc PGCE.

Entrance: Prospective pupils spend a day at the school and are assessed informally.

Exit: All go through to the senior school.

Remarks: School knows the pupils well and is thoroughly versed in the individual needs of each one. Focus on each child as an individual. Staff say that 'we cannot expect every child to reach the same standard and so we keep with each child's pace.' Keen for the children to feel not just happy but also excited to be there. Children are bright eyed and bushy tailed.

High ratio of staff to pupils. Years 3 and 4 and years 5 and 6 are taught together for humanities, PE and music, but the core subjects taught separately, with the senior teachers teaching them science. Years 3 to 6 have personal tutors. The junior school is invited to the senior school's drama and debates but otherwise considered independent from the senior school, as 'it's important the younger ones feel safe and can be big fish in the pond,' says school.

An 'out and about' school – you see the wellies and bright mackintoshes lining the classrooms beckoning the next trip. The school is close to the beach and the great warrior ships at Portsmouth, goes orienteering and hiking on the Downs, into the Roman town and theatre of Chichester and is great for camping in the extensive grounds. The school says that you might see two girls splashing around in their wellies after a falling out, which is worth more than hours of indoor circle time – 'They're soon the best of friends'. The junior head shares the philosophy of the senior head that the children here can enjoy an extended childhood – in the playground we saw much role-play and fun.

Keble Prep School

Wades Hill, London, N21 1BG

• Pupils: 220 boys • Ages: 4-13 • Non-denominational
• Fees: £10,530–£13,080 pa • Independent

Tel: 020 8360 3359
Email: office@kebleprep.co.uk
Website: www.kebleprep.co.uk

Headmaster: Since 2006, Mr Jed McCarthy (fifties). Studied maths and management at Queen Elizabeth College, London, PGCE at the Institute of Education, then worked in state schools in Brent. Left the profession to spend five years in industry, but realised he 'really missed teaching' and returned to Orley Farm, where he remained for 16 years (as head of maths, director of studies and deputy head). A quietly-spoken enthusiast, Mr McCarthy has worked determinedly since his arrival to build up the esprit de corps of pupils and parents and undoubtedly succeeded. Parents are lavish in their praise – 'He's always waiting at the gate and has a genuine interest in each boy,' said one mother. 'He's a very caring, very nurturing gentleman,' said another. Parents are also grateful for his availability and effectiveness. 'He's always ready to hear you out about any little gripe and he really gets things done.' Two grown up sons.

Entrance: Register a couple of years before entry at four but pressure on places is not intense. The school is non-selective. Some new entrants from the state sector at 11.

Exit: A small exodus at 11 to high-achieving local grammar schools and comprehensives but head hopes to attract parents who understand the benefits of a school that runs to 13. 'I believe in 13 plus,' he says. At that age, Mill Hill and St Albans are historically the two most popular choices, but horizons are expanding – 'We are sending boys to Highgate, City, UCS, Westminster, St Edmund's Ware and St Columba's'. Wherever pupils go, the school does its utmost to ensure the best match between boy and school – 'We know the boys very well and recommend on personality'.

Remarks: A small school, which hovers round 200 boys in all, so class size is reflectively intimate, ranging from 12-15 in two parallel forms. In the early years the school follows the national curriculum, with add-ons such as French, which starts in year 3. The pace is accelerated and curriculum expanded as boys get older – 'We adapt it to the boys, easing into Common Entrance after 11,' says the head. Specialist teaching in music and PE in first two years, then further specialisation in art, ICT and French; by year 5, all subjects taught by specialists.

Enthusiastic teaching and boy-friendly approach – 'We try to make it very hands on,' said one teacher. 'We make models and castles.' Parents praise staff highly – 'My son is motivated, interested and enthused. It's a great credit to the teachers,' said a mother. 'The teachers are incredibly encouraging,' said another. In the past, the school has been criticised for not necessarily stretching the brightest, but the head has spent time, effort and money rebalancing that equation – 'And we're not finished yet'. A director of studies now has a clear brief and the brightest are given differentiated teaching in class and one-to-one support out of it. Boys are setted in English and maths from year 5, with informal setting in science, French and humanities.

The philosophy, however, is very much 'each child is an individual' and the struggling are equally well guided with the full range of SEN support. The school deals comfortably with dyslexia and dyspraxia, mild autism and Asperger's. 'What I'm trying to do is not be the most academic school,' says the head, 'but to get all boys to expect more of themselves, set themselves higher standards and achieve them.' And parents confirm this is what happens – 'They really understands my son's strengths and weakness and really nourish him. I'm certain they meet all the boys' needs, even those at opposite ends of the spectrum'.

This is a small site and facilities are relatively restricted, though there is a French room and small science lab. Rebuild has brought more classroom space, a new science lab and an art room, allowing for relocation of the library, which had doubled as a music room. Limited space, too, for sports (though an attractive small gym), but games, played twice a week, are taken seriously. Rugby (re-introduced by the head), football, cricket and tennis are the main menu and a school minibus transports players to local and distant pitches. Rugby has put the school back on the prep-school circuit. 'We mainly play other small local schools,' says the head. 'We lose more than we win, but we do play – and have tea afterwards.' Parents feel that even the sportiest get sufficient exercise and opportunity – 'A new PE teacher has invited a Tottenham scout to come to the school'. Numerous lunch-time and after-school clubs include puzzle club, movie club, Common Entrance drop-in club.

Has been going for 80 years, a lone prep school in an affluent suburban area of north London. Its aim now, as always, is to serve the local community, a community of small family businesses rather than City professionals. Many parents are first-time buyers. 'Our parents often want what they didn't have for themselves,' says the head. Many have Mediterranean roots (Turkish, Spanish, Greek, Italian, Cypriot) and a firm belief in family, and the school reflects those values with a strong family atmosphere.

Very much a traditional prep, it retains distinctive (black and yellow) blazers, formal good manners and neatly knotted ties. Boys still wear shorts in the warmer months and long hair is definitely frowned upon. Pastoral care is equally old school – ' We're looking for grounded, rounded individuals,' says the head. 'We cope well with all manner of children.' The aim is supportive rather than hothouse ('We don't want to put pressure on ridiculously young. We want them to achieve, but not by testing to the eyeballs'). The mood is friendly and safe: 'If you're stuck on something,' said one boy, 'there's always a teacher to help you,' and the atmosphere is orderly and quiet, with bright noticeboards and well-run classrooms.

A 'big brother, little brother' scheme matches older pupils with younger ones – evident and unaffected warmth stretching across the age divide. (On our visit, a boy at the top of the school, clearly revered by a recent arrival, praised his small friend for being able to tie his tie.) Discipline is firm but certainly not draconian. 'Can you do it better?' is the gentle reproach. Pupils thrive on it – 'If I'm honest,' said one undoubtedly honest young man in his final year, 'I love the school and I'm going to miss it when I leave'. Parents are equally positive – 'We chose it because it's very friendly and has a great identity that boys can relate to. I wish I could find a school for my daughter that is as good as this one'. 'We love the school. It's a home from home,' said another. 'My son looks forward to going to school every day.' Keble is not a wealthy or notably well endowed place, but is undoubtedly a happy and safe haven, where all boys are treated with respect and respond in kind. A very secure place to start your schooldays.

Kelly College Preparatory School

Linked school: Kelly College

Hazeldon, Parkwood Road, Tavistock, Devon, PL19 0JS

• Pupils: 85 boys, 75 girls • Ages: 3–11 • Christian (but accepts all faiths) • Fees: Day £5,985–£8,985; Boarding £16,950–£19,200 pa • Independent

Tel: 01822 612919
Email: admin@kellycollegeprep.com
Website: www.kellycollegeprep.com

Headmaster: Since September 2010, Mr Matthew Foale BEd MSc (early forties). Born, bred and educated in the West Country. Has a PE degree and achieved his MSc while teaching, which must surely suggest determination and organisation. Before joining Kelly Prep as deputy head in 2009, he was director of sport at The Hall School in Hampstead and then deputy head of Orley Farm School in Harrow. Married to Marie-Claire, who trained as an art therapist and is now manager of a care home in Plymouth. Three children. Commutes from Plymouth every day. 'It's an easy journey and gives us a well-balanced life.'

Not a bullfrog trumpeting headmaster keen to show off what he has done for the school: his conversation, underpinned by a good sense of humour and a realistic sense of proportion, centres around the happiness of the children in his care and his lively staff, whom we found uniformly forthcoming and friendly. Thoughtful and calm and with obvious integrity, he clearly has an eye for detail without losing an awareness of the overall picture. One delighted parent, whose three children had gone through the school, told us he was fair-minded and consistent, with an eye for 'the whole child within the whole picture'.

He does some teaching of IT, is a form tutor and, fine games player that he is, literally rolls up his sleeves to referee matches or supports from the touchline. He is not the sort of headmaster who barks out a hearty greeting to pupils to show he knows their names: his is a quiet and reliable presence and inspires affection and appreciation from everyone, as far as we could tell, including the ground staff. (Ground staff are always a valuable insight into what a school is really like). 'Despite, or perhaps because of, his all-round involvement,' one parent told us, 'he never loses sight of the fact that primarily the job of the school is to encourage and inspire pupils to reach their all-round potential'. A very sound man, a good listener and readily accessible to all.

Entrance: Entry to any of the three parts of the school – nursery, pre-prep or prep – at any time, providing there is space and everyone concerned feels that the school is the right place. Every candidate attends a taster day which involves attending lessons, some individual conversations with teachers, horsing about in the playground and generally getting a feel for the place. No formal tests. The main concern is whether or not he or she will fit in with the ethos of the school.

School runs buses from a 45-minute radius and will accommodate any reasonable request. 'We can be flexible,' says the head.

Exit: Around 80 per cent to the senior school, half a mile away. Others to Devonport High School for Boys, Notre Dame School Plymouth or overseas.

Remarks: Kelly College bought the handsome main house and grounds near Tavistock on the edge of Dartmoor in 1983, and established its own prep nearby. The prep school uses many of its elder brother's sporting and recreational facilities, and the schools share the same ethos of friendliness and mutual

K

support. The word 'ethos' crops up a lot in conversation with the head and members of staff, and the school's beautifully simple, timelessly valuable code – which includes 'Be honest with ourselves and others. Be kind and helpful. Do our best to be our best' – is found reproduced in shields and mottos all over the building. This is supported by daily encouragement and example and through weekly focus on particular values – parents are encouraged to discuss these with their children. 'It helps us become involved with the school and draws us closer to its aims as well as understanding our children better,' said one father. The result is a particularly happy school where staff and pupils openly demonstrate mutual friendliness and respect, and the most recent ISI inspection described the quality of pastoral care as 'outstanding'.

The pupil council has produced an intelligent and sensitive document on bullying. 'Buddy readers' help younger children, and pupils from the senior school visit on a regular basis, ensuring easy relationships between all ages. Everyone in the top year has a rotating system of prefect-type duties, and parents talk of the boost in confidence those opportunities give.

The pre-prep is a delightful low, welcoming building, with colourful and promising work on display. A delightful terrace is equipped with suitably-sized tables and chairs, exciting toys, and a marvellous sensory garden incorporating an outdoor classroom; a Forest School is being developed. There are few gaps between learning and fun; lots of strategically placed books and whiteboards enable even the tiniest to contribute.

The art room and well-equipped science labs are next door to each other in the prep school. The lively teaching we witnessed adopted a cross-curricular approach: history with art; science with history and art; French everywhere, not just in the classrooms. Sometimes the grounds are used for launching rockets during science and DT lessons. Not a wishy-washy stew but a delectable concoction of individual ingredients merging into one delicious, intellectually-nourishing meal. No risk of too many cooks...The success of this teaching depends on the excellent staff communication. The learning support department, a real back-up unit, can help with strengthening study skills and introducing useful other strategies.

A range of musical instruments are taught in a warren of rooms upstairs in the main house, and there are more than 20 clubs and societies. A tremendous variety of sports is on offer here and at the senior school facilities, and pupils have gained national and international success, particularly in swimming. It is a small school and there is a positive feeling of punching above its weight, with strong results in team sports. Children of all abilities have the opportunity to compete in matches – success at B level is celebrated as enthusiastically as at A level – and games are played in the right spirit. Indeed, the head of another prep school mentioned Kelly's splendid sportsmanship.

Essentially this is a day school, and most boarding is weekly, though full/flexi options are available. Numbers fluctuate, but those boarders we spoke to said it was 'terrific fun.' This happy, unpretentious school, in its beautiful rural surroundings, strives to inculcate a love of learning, a genuine sense of community within and without the school, an overall sense of decency and excellent preparation for the next stage. Parents relish the small class sizes and extra-curricular activities. They spoke of their offspring's burgeoning confidence, derived from individual nurture. A school for all seasons and more (we saw daffodils in full flower in December). One boy, responding to our boringly predictable question about looking forward to the holidays said, 'Home or school, it's all the same to me.' Let not cynics nudge each other and roll their eyes: he was a shiningly happy boy.

Kelvinside Academy Junior School

Linked school: Kelvinside Academy

33 Kirklee Road, Glasgow, G12 0SW

- Pupils: 200 boys and girls; all day • Ages: 3–11 • Inter-denom
- Fees: £6,750–£9,810 pa • Independent

Tel: 01413 573376
Email: rector@kelvinsideacademy.org.uk
Website: www.kelvinsideacademy.org.uk

Head of Junior School: Since 2008, Mr Andrew Dickenson MA (fifties). An historian, he was educated at the City of London Freemen's school, and came to Glasgow after nine years at Edinburgh Academy, moving from director of studies to deputy head of junior school. We found him comfortable, relaxed and confident. Avuncular, though some of his Facebook entries would appear to disagree (seemed a bit chippy to us). He still teaches.

Exit: Majority to senior school.

Remarks: As with senior school, classrooms are dotted all over the place, and you find young of all ages changing classrooms at the same time. We were amused when asking for a loo on our arrival, to be directed to what appeared to be a (very) junior loo with the admonition writ large behind the cistern 'Do stand on the seat'. Which is what you normally find in African loos, particularly long drops (don't ask).

As with senior school, tiny classes, max 17, two streams, mixed ability, all assessed on entry, with support for learning – instantly available for as long or as short a time as needed. All set for maths by age eight, occasionally earlier. Emphasis on phonics, but other methods too if necessary. Keyboarding, and mega computer input; further ahead with Fronter (school put on coaching session for parents) than the senior school.

Spanish or French from five, with German aged 11/12, in transitus (p7 by any other name). Somewhat confusing, rector said one thing, junior handbook another. Youngsters have their own classroom and form takers up to transitus when they visit specialist teachers in labs, PE, music etc. Music and drama timetabled double period alternate weeks, and pupils encouraged to join choirs/orchestra (the former practises lunchtime, latter post school). Junior choir won intermediate competition last year. Three assemblies a week in the Gilchrist Hall: parents are welcome, particularly to form/house inspired assemblies. Parents with pupils in the junior school are all invited to coffee/tea in the Kennedy Mall on Fridays before pick up (clever). Clubs for everything, but only the junior school do Scottish country dancing: how sad.

New nursery opened in 2013 on school's Balgray campus. As well as nursery's own outdoor play area, the children also get to use the school's all weather surfaces, playing fields and wild gardens.

K

Kensington Prep School

596 Fulham Road, London, SW6 5PA

- Pupils: 280 girls; all day • Ages: 4–11 • Non-denom
- Fees: £13,686 pa • Independent

Tel: 020 7731 9300
Email: enquiries@kenprep.gdst.net
Website: www.kensingtonprep.gdst.net

Head: Since 2003, Mrs Prudence Lynch MA PGCE (mid fifties). Hails from Guernsey, studied psychology at St Andrew's before going to Goldsmiths to do her PGCE. She has two grown up sons and is a proud and committed grandmother. A zany, thoroughly modern head, from her boldly stylish dress sense to her dropped vowels and upward inflection at the end of her sentences. She also brings a wealth of experience to the job – previously head of juniors at Notting Hill and Ealing, a sister GDST establishment, via Colet Court, where she initiated the SEN department, taught study skills, maths and 'thinking', a passion of hers – here she teaches philosophy for children, which is 'too wonderful for words', where they discuss things like 'Is it helpful to have an unrealistic ambition?' or 'Is it ever right to kill someone?' She relishes encouraging them to think and listen to each other – 'Girls need to be as good as men at thinking up fresh ideas and taking risks. Spoon feeding is not going to solve a credit crunch no one has ever experienced before,' she says.

Keen to inject an element of risk to the very safe school she inherited. While she accepts that not every child can achieve anything they want, she firmly believes that it's better to go for the thing you can nearly do rather than the thing you know you can do – otherwise what have you learnt? 'I, too, am a risk taker,' she says.

A touch scatty – efficient administration is not one of her strengths, something remarked on by parents – and she freely admits that she forgets things all the time, while hastening to add that enough efficient administrators around her to make sure the school doesn't drop any balls. She is a head with something much more to offer, however – vision, a big heart and a huge sense of fun. 'I love playing,' she says, as she shows us her latest acquisition – a black rag doll that sits – rather incongruously – among the array of toys and clutter on her desk. Determined to counter the intense pressure felt by parents here and elsewhere in the 'ruthless' London day school system – trying to ensure that the girls still have 'dream time' and still enjoy their childhood. How refreshing.

Entrance: At four plus – over 200 applicants for 44 places. Put your daughter's name down any time up to December prior to entry the following September. Assessments in January. Girls are seen in groups of five or six and assessed during play – 'With a heavily oversubscribed school like this one there isn't an ideal fair way of doing it'. Also an official entrance point at seven plus – register any time up to September the year ahead, but the number of places varies and may be only as few as two. Occasional places do crop up – keep trying. Expects most siblings to join the school, but reserves the right to say no if it is felt to be in the child's interest.

Exit: Almost all to where parents here consider to be 'the top' London girls' day schools – St Paul's Girls, City of London, Godolphin and Latymer, Wimbledon High, Putney High, and a few to the major girls' boarding schools – Wycombe Abbey and Downe House . Lots of scholarships – music as well as academic.

Remarks: Housed in a former Marist convent on the corner of a busy junction of the Parsons Green neck of the Fulham Road, the school occupies a wonderful space. Wide corridors, large windows, spacious high-ceilinged classrooms, broad staircases – institutional but brightened with loud colourful murals of, eg, clowns and kites. A wonderful library in the former chapel, with stained glass windows, high beamed ceiling, some sturdy oak tables softened by comfortable sofas and beanbags – a soulful place to work and read.

The playground stretches into the distance complete with tennis courts, slides, colourful springy tarmac and a snazzy bandstand where they hold popular summer concerts. When the whole school is out here it doesn't look crowded, just a sea of bright colours (Mrs Lynch swiftly replaced the drab grey tunics with the cheerful electric blues and reds – 'I wanted it to be fun for them to get dressed in the morning,' she says). At the ring of the bell all girls freeze in silence before filing obediently into their correct line ups – that's what they're like here, law abiding and conscious of the school values. They couldn't fail to be – they are prominently displayed throughout the school, the positive balanced with the negative, 'Do listen, don't interrupt'. (They sometimes trip up on this one – our guides, a case in point, who were bubbling over in their desire to please and enthuse about their school.)

A GDST with a difference. It stands alone, so doesn't benefit from the resources that come with having a senior school attached. No bursaries at all and fees are a bit higher than at other GDSTs. But the no-nonsense high academic standards you would expect, combined with affluent and demanding parents, make this one of London's most competitive girls' schools. 'We are good at fast paced education,' says head. Parents here feel hugely lucky if their daughter makes it through the assessments at three, but we heard reports of a number of children getting tutoring further down the line because they want to ensure results. Our view is that this pressure doesn't necessarily come from the inside. A number of parents here want a seamless transition to schools they regard as being the best and are not always prepared to accept it if they are told their daughter may not be up to it.

Mrs Lynch does her best, and the curriculum is broad – lots of open homework and off piste whole school activities to stimulate thinking skills and collaborative team work through the year groups. 'The big freeze' had the whole school interpreting and creating. The result: swathes of tin foil around the school as well as a smashed mobile phone. Lots of interdisciplinary projects using art, DT and photography. Thursday morning is 'thinking time': 'What would it be like to have legs like jelly?' A whole afternoon dedicated to music and drama, another to music and art. We saw innovative teaching – the younger children on all fours marching round the room barking numbers one to 50. Computers everywhere and laptops widely used in every classroom. Year 6 create TV programmes as well as cook canapés – in addition to doing all the marketing and costing associated with the project.

Resident SENCo manages learning support, which is part of the package until key stage 2, from when it's organised on the same model as visiting music staff. Children can dip in and out or have more structured support over a period of several years – maybe just to boost their understanding of maths or to tackle a more serious problem like dyspraxia. However only mild to moderate learning difficulties can realistically be accommodated here. Mrs Lynch abhors the label 'gifted and talented' – 'They're far too young – it implies there's something rigid about who you are'. She infinitely prefers everyone to be stretched through lots of differentiation in class and the open-ended activities they do so well here.

French from year 1 – 'Not mega,' says Mrs Lynch, 'but you get your "êtres" and "avoirs" and more formal stuff at the top to help those who go on to do CE elsewhere'. A relaxed taster of Latin in the final year. Class sizes of about 20, maximum 23.

Young, (almost entirely) female staff who tend to stay for a long time. Only two or three men, including the recently appointed and much praised head of music, who has introduced a junior orchestra and won't stand for any waiting lists for girls who want to learn an instrument – 'We'll just get more teachers'.

Parents largely local – the Caffè Nero opposite is bursting at eight am with yummy Fulham mummies sipping lattes and testing their pretty daughters on their timetables. Dads very present in the school, too, helping with reading and on the parents' committee, 'We like to encourage that,' says Mrs Lynch. Lots of clubs – football run by a Chelsea FC player currently very popular, also bridge, Mandarin, Spanish cookery, craft, lots of music, as well as a host of others. School likes to keep a close eye to make sure girls don't do too much. 'Food amazing,' gushed our guides. Mango and orange red smoothie caused great excitement as we were shown the bright yellow and green dining room in the bowels of the building. Lots of trips – including a choir tour to Belgium, trips to France, Cornwall and the Isle of Wight.

A vibrant place in every respect. Girls here are earnest and keen, immensely privileged with impeccable manners. A quirky eccentric – whether she is fiercely bright or not – could get lost here (school refutes this – 'We are absolutely about inspiring quirky girls as much as the more conformist') but a wonderful start for your robust all-rounder.

Kent College Preparatory School, Pembury

Linked school: Kent College

Aultmore House, Old Church Road, Pembury, Kent, TN2 4AX

• Pupils: 210 girls • Ages: 3–11 • Member of the Methodist Independent Schools Group – broadly Christian • Fees: Day £7,887–£11,877; Boarding £21,471 pa • Independent

Tel: 01892 820204
Email: prepschool@kentcollege.kent.sch.uk
Website: www.kent-college.co.uk

Head: Since 2002, Mrs Ann Lawson BEd Exeter (forties). Previously spent four years as deputy head at Croydon High and prior to that spent nine years at City of London Freemen's Junior School, Ashtead.

Entrance: From the age of three. Girls may join at any time when spaces and are encouraged to come for a taster day beforehand. Girls joining from year 3 upwards are required to take entrance tests in English and maths.

Exit: In 2013, 50 per cent made the transition to the senior school at 11+, with the majority of the rest going on to the grammars or Sevenoaks School. The school has a good track record in the Kent Test and also prepares girls for the entrance exams to other independent schools and runs a revision course during the summer holidays. Girls coming up from the prep have to sit the entrance test to the senior school in English, maths and verbal reasoning. A requirement of the senior school is that girls must be able to sit nine GCSEs and three A levels, so occasionally it is decided that the senior school might not suit a particular girl. Parents are always kept closely informed of their daughter's progress, so this is always very much a joint decision.

Remarks: Similar ethos to senior school with great emphasis on kindness, respect and emotional wellbeing and a strong sense of community that encompasses everyone. Own purpose built teaching block on the same site as the senior school and with the use of the senior school facilities – science labs, computer suite, sports facilities, music block and theatre. French taught from nursery to year 6. Sport features strongly – dance, gymnastics, netball and swimming in lessons and clubs. U11 netball team recently the runner up in a national tournament for prep schools. Plenty of clubs from classics to cooking and lots of music, singing and drama. New library and arts centre opened in 2013. Great emphasis on play in the early years and a play therapist comes in once a week to help build girls' self-confidence and interpersonal skills. One-to-one learning support offered at no extra charge – mainly for mild dyslexia and dyspraxia. Only four full boarders at the time of our visit but they seemed happily integrated. Flexi-boarding from the age of 10 a popular option with local children. Breakfast club and after-school care very useful for working parents.

Kilgraston Preparatory School

Linked school: Kilgraston School

Bridge of Earn, Perthshire, PH2 9BQ

• Pupils: 75 day girls, 15 boarders • Ages: 2½–13 (day boys 2½–9) • Roman Catholic, but plenty of non-Catholic pupils • Fees: Day £8,550–£13,845; Boarding £20,250 pa • Independent

Tel: 01738 812257
Email: headoffice@kilgraston.com
Website: www.kilgraston.com

Head: Since 2011, Kathryn Ebrahim BSc PGCE (mid 40s). Educated at University of St Andrews and University of Dundee. Headteacher of Kingsbarns Primary School, Pittenweemem Primary, lecturer in educational management, University of Dundee, head of curriculum learning, Kilgraston. She has a daughter in the prep school.

Entrance: Generally by interview and school report. Taster days are welcomed.

Exit: To Kilgraston (all girls are able to progress automatically to the senior school) and other senior schools in Scotland and England.

Remarks: Based in the converted stables. Delightful. All girls learn French from seven, physics from 11 and progress automatically up the senior school. All use the senior school facilities and 11+ year olds share senior specialist staff and visit main school for lessons. Pupils from the age of two, with boys to nine.

King Alfred Lower School

Linked school: King Alfred School

Manor Wood, 149 North End Road, London, NW11 7HY

- Pupils: Boys and girls • Ages: 4–11 • Fees: £12,624–£14,544 pa
- Independent

Tel: 020 8457 5200
Email: admissions@kingalfred.org.uk
Website: www.kingalfred.org.uk

Head of Lower School: Mr David Weale BSc PGCE

Exit: Majority to senior school

Remarks: For details see senior school.

King Edward's Junior School + Pre-prep and Nursery (Bath)

Linked school: King Edward's School (Bath)

North Road, Bath, BA2 6JA

- Pupils: 190 in junior school (125 boys/65 girls) • Ages: 7–11
- Non-denominational • Fees: £7,020–£9,450 pa • Independent

Tel: 01225 463218
Email: junior@kesbath.com
Website: www.kesbath.com

Head Teacher: Since 2008, Mr Greg Taylor, previously deputy head. Appointed after a spell as acting head.

Entrance: No formal assessments from pre-prep to junior school. For external candidates, tests in English, maths, reading and non-verbal reasoning plus free writing and interview – details appear on the website. Admits 36 pupils annually into year 3, small numbers into years 4 and 6, and up to 20 into year 5, when it extends to three forms. Flexibility over points of entry has proved popular, with increasing number of parents choosing to move to Bath from London.

Exit: Nearly all pupils proceed to King Edward's senior school via entry examination at 11.

Remarks: The junior school models itself on its big sibling in terms of its breadth of curriculum and high expectations in all areas. It moved from the other side of Bath some 20 years ago to a purpose-built airy building, which commands the view from the top left corner of King Edward's sloping site. Although separate, it benefits from the amenities of the senior school: the theatre and Astroturf pitches, as well as sharing some of its specialist teachers. An unashamed precursor to the senior school, it makes no bones about catering for the top 25 per cent of 7 to 11 year olds, though admissions policy does make clear that children with innate rather than developed ability will be considered.

Lots going on other than work, however, with plenty of sport, music and drama plus loads of clubs. Some of the more ambitious and time-consuming options take place at weekends and pupils have their own activities week each summer term, which takes them away from Bath for a few nights.

King's College Junior School (Wimbledon)

Linked school: King's College School (Wimbledon)

Southside, Wimbledon Common, London, SW19 4TT

- Pupils: 460 boys • Ages: 7–13 • C of E (but other faiths welcome)
- Fees: £15,075–£17,025 pa • Independent

Tel: 020 8255 5335
Email: jsadmissions@kcs.org.uk
Website: www.kcs.org.uk

Headmaster: Since 2006, Dr Gerard Silverlock (fiftyish), affable, articulate and clever; despite having spent most of his career as a senior historian in senior schools (Millfield et al), a natural prep school head. Did his PhD on European disarmament 1918-25. Previously head of Aberdour in Banstead. Has four school-age children of his own and is clearly held in much affection by his charges, who follow him about, demanding he sign their commended work, and seem determined that they – and not we, on our visit – are what matters. With which we entirely agree. Parents say he's 'approachable and easy to get on with'.

Entrance: English, maths and reasoning tests and all 7+ and 8+ candidates are interviewed. Beyond that, those 'whose performance in the written papers suggests that they could benefit from the education which we offer' are seen. 'Our boys are bright. We are highly selective,' says Dr Silverlock – 480 boys applied in 2011 for 90 places: 180 for 56 at 7+; 72 for 10 places at 8+; 28 for 6 places at 9+; 50 for 8 places at 10+; 140 for 14 at 11+ – 'but we are not a hothouse.' With this level of aptitude, they would have no need to be. No automatic acceptance of brothers. The school also maintains two local pre-preps – The Squirrels and the Rowans – though entrance to the KCJS is not automatic from these. Scholarships on offer from 11+, awarded to those who excel in the entrance tests. Means-tested bursaries up to 100 per cent of fees if the boy is outstanding and the parents are broke. Home visits, of course.

Exit: Mostly to the senior school via The King's transfer exam in year 8 – around 90 boys go up. A few who would not thrive there are given plenty of warning and helped to find a nook elsewhere – four in the last 13 years, which isn't much – 'When a boy is offered a place at any age, our expectation is that he will be here until he is 18'.

Remarks: Physically attached to the main school, though also with a building or two of its own, the junior school shares facilities with the senior school and is integral to it. The two main buildings – one for the youngest boys, Rushmere, and Priory for the older boys – are in themselves worthy of note. Rushmere, formerly the home of sculptor, David Wynne, is a beautiful Georgian house with lovely decorative features and makes a surprisingly appropriate school for small boys. The younger boys are taught – 14 to a class – in the former bedrooms en haut, and the older ones – 22 to a class – in the drawing and dining rooms en bas. Thence to Priory in classes of 18-24. All rooms are well-lit, well-aired and have good displays. We liked the junior forum board which asked, 'Have you got ideas for improving life at KCJS?' and felt this was typical of a school which encourages its denizens to think, express themselves and enjoy school. And the achievements here are notable – among them winning for the three years prior to our visit the prestigious Townsend-Warner History Prize.

The boys we saw were smiling, bright-faced and relaxed with, seemingly, an easy relationship with their attendant adults.

Clearly, much satisfaction derived from a special relationship with the primary school they support in Obera, Kenya, and we were moved by a modest description of just what that means in practice – both ways. This, plus the 1st XI cricket team's raising of over £50,000 for the Nelson Mandela Children's Fund, as a part of their South African touring activities, and the outreach programme, Junior Aspirations, involving teaching support for able boys and girls from state primaries, makes for a healthy interaction with the real world outside, which can only be good.

Junior school parents are grateful and unanimous – 'It's fabulous'; 'Almost without exception the teachers are amazingly inspirational'; 'I wish I'd had this sort of education'; 'The sports are good, but my two boys are very different and it doesn't matter if you're not sporty – a lot of attention is given to music: boys are encouraged to develop their own groups'; 'It's been fantastic'.

King's College School (Cambridge)

West Road, Cambridge, CB3 9DN

- Pupils: 415 boys and girls. All day except for 35 boy boarders (including 16 choristers and 8 probationers) • Ages: 4–13 • C of E – other faiths welcome • Fees: Weekly Boarding (boys) £20,580; Day £10,380–£13,215; Choristers £6,930 pa; • Independent

Tel: 01223 365814
Email: office@kcs.cambs.sch.uk
Website: www.kcs.cambs.sch.uk

Headmaster: Since 1998, Mr Nicholas Robinson BA (fifties). Educated at Worth, read English at Anglia Ruskin, PGCE in maths at Goldsmiths. Master, then housemaster, for 12 years at Worth. A bachelor – disarming and a good listener. Doesn't want to be known simply for masterminding building projects (upper school teaching block, ICT and DT wing, music department and squash courts completed 2010; much needed sports centre planned for 2015) and profile raising of the school (numbers up from 290 to 402 during his tenure) but this is parents' first port of praise. He says he gets to know children when reading to the little ones and through extra-curricular activities – 'always in the front row of every concert and drama production,' said a mum. Also very involved with the choristers, whom he sees as a defining element of King's. Seriously musical (conducts) and more than keen on skiing.

Entrance: Oversubscribed. They say a 'fairly broad intake.' In reality ability range starts well above average – one parent suggested that 'you could lock some of the children in a cave and they'd still get scholarships'.

At four, place offered 12 months before entry. Waiting list but preference given to siblings/children whose parents were past pupils or those who have connections with King's. Date of registration taken into account where a split decision has to be made. Applicants spend an afternoon in a reception class and are observed – they're interested in children's behaviour. Parents ('might not drive Range Rovers but are the V8 engines behind the kids' – lots of ex-Oxbridge) also have a 'chat' with Mr Robinson.

At seven via assessments in English, maths and verbal reasoning – means-tested bursaries up to 100 per cent available for those who show musical potential. Occasional entry at other ages via assessment.

Choir auditions twice a year – many apply. Choristers have super demanding schedules and are in the public eye – but,

apart from not having enough time to be tip top sportsmen, are well integrated into school life.

Exit: The Perse (co-ed), Oundle and Eton are popular. Other destinations include Rugby, Benenden, The Leys, King's Ely, Uppingham and Winchester. Respectable clutch of scholarships and awards. Old Boys include Orlando Gibbons, Michael Ramsey, Christopher Tugendhat, John Pardoe, Professor Andrew Wiles (who solved Fermat's Last Theorem).

Remarks: Founded in the 15th century, one of the top Cambridge preps, just a brisk walk away from King's College. Primarily a day school – about 35 boys board. Choristers have to be full boarders and a few places are left for other boys (not girls) who want to board – we hear the dedicated housemaster and wife have created a homely environment and are seriously good news. Hotchpotch of buildings, largely of recent vintage, cluster on the edge of a relatively open site where children enjoy being children. Not much 'sirring' (some staff are called by their nicknames) or children being 'scrubbed up to within an inch of their lives' – as far as parents are concerned the emphasis is on more important things. Intimate, family atmosphere with a touch of spontaneity – it's not unusual for impromptu events to be sprung on pupils (and parents) and realised within days: recent talent show raised over £7,000 for charity.

'Absolutely great' teachers. Trad academic approach from the start gives a solid grounding. Subjects are delivered in a 'fun way by lots of different personalities'. Pupils are competitive and want to learn – 'They teach us how to concentrate'. French from day one (taught by native speakers) and Latin from year 5. Spanish, Mandarin Chinese and German clubs on offer. Positive vibes about DT and science – smart labs wow the children. Thoroughly modern teaching gizmos plus inviting, new library with tempting literary goodies and tremendously enthusiastic, popular librarian – 'They love her'.

High standards are expected and pace hots up in the final two years – scholarship class for year 8. School tries to stop parents panicking about exams – private maths coaching not unusual prior to CE – but accepts that a small number would benefit from some one-to-one help. To make life easier for all, the previous head of maths gives private tuition on site.

Pretty hot on the identification of learning needs – around 20 per cent receive support at some time. Welcoming department caters for mild needs – one full-timer (DipSpLD) plus four part-timers. For a boost in English, another three part-timers on hand. Liaison with class teachers, IEPs, useful links with educational psychologists and termly themed open evening for parents – topics include paired reading and home support. Help for pre-preppers in or out of the classroom. Removal from lessons only in the upper school where a language has been dropped (no charge); otherwise sessions, always at the same time to avoid muddling the children, are first thing in the morning, break or lunch time (charges per session).

Angelic choristers aside, music is 'five star' – an inclusive ethos encourages enjoyable involvement. Tuition from the word go – it's quite normal to play two instruments and not unusual to play three. Forty-two chamber groups (a prep school record?) and all manner of orchestras – 'If you can scrape a bow across a string, the amazing head of department will find you a group to play in'. School has had a relatively unsporty reputation, but children are happy with what's offered and parents say definite improvement, particularly for girls. Planned facilities, including somewhere for indoor sport, likely to give an extra boost. Tennis coaching, throughout the year, additionally charged. Selection of after-school clubs and late stay for homework – good for working parents.

Citizenship awards for younger ones, special tea party at the end of term for the house which has gained the most merits, form-based clubs where children get together to air pastoral issues and Little Tea at 4pm where everyone gets a cake

K

('Impossible to get the children off site till they've had Little Tea – so no quick getaways') typify the caring approach of this liberal school filled to the brim with cheerful, friendly children.

King's Ely Junior

Linked school: King's Ely Senior

Barton Road, Ely, CB7 4DB

• Pupils: 450 boys and girls; 25 boy boarders (of whom 21 are choristers), 8 girl boarders • Ages: 7–13 • C of E • Fees: Day £8,454–£13,035; Boarding £19,047–£20,106 pa • Independent

Tel: 01353 660730
Email: dawnburton@kingsely.org
Website: www.kingsely.org

Headmaster: Since 2008, Mr Richard Whymark BA (Ed) (forties). Previously head of Stonar Junior and before that head of boarding and deputy head of Salisbury Cathedral School. Has an engaging manner and a natural flair for communication – with pupils and parents alike. 'He is usually around at drop-off time', commented one parent.

Firmly believes a good head needs 'a strong voice and a reflective personality – no room for big egos'. Has an easy rapport with students and is clearly a respected presence – on hand to sort out 'spats'. Art, travel and gardening are all interests but, clearly something of a romantic, his passion is for restoring Morris Minors. Has two children at King's and wife Joanna also teaches at the school.

Entrance: Assessment for entrance at seven consists of diagnostic tests and informal interview. Entry to King's Ely Acremont for ages two to seven (pre-prep, though this term is not used by the school) is by informal assessment and most progress up to the junior department. Screening for dyslexia and dyspraxia at entrance. Moderate difficulties can be accommodated but all pupils must be able to benefit from the full curriculum, with minimal extra support. Those applying as choristers must also pass the necessary voice trials.

Exit: Almost all make the transition to the senior school at 13. The exam also decides setting for year 9. The occasional pupil not suited to the senior school is identified early and support given in finding another school in good time.

Remarks: Occupies a site on the edge of the main school campus. Slightly bleak approach around the back of the senior school but the buildings themselves are well planned and designed. Attention is paid to the grouping of different classes, so years 3 and 4 (and so on up the school) are accommodated together, with their own suite of classrooms and play area. Youngest pupils cluster round a courtyard with a Tarzan trail for play time; years 7 and 8 slightly apart in their own building.

Children are cheerful, friendly and polite (all doors held without reminder), though unstarchy. Setting in maths and English from year 3. Languages introduced early, with taster lessons in Japanese, Mandarin and Arabic. French, and Latin from year 7.

Drama is very strong, with several major productions staged annually. Music is, if anything, even more exceptional. Cathedral choristers apart, the school has choirs, ensembles and bands galore, and more than 200 pupils have individual instrumental lessons. Stunning exam results – more than 50 distinctions in the ABRSM exams this year.

Parents praise the emphasis on effort and progress; certificates and prizes are awarded for these as much as

for attainment. Both ends of ability spectrum well served, with support and extension classes available. 'Confidence is encouraged, but not cockiness', commented a mother. Tutor groups are reshuffled each year, to break up cliques and expand friendship groups. A buddy scheme operates throughout the school and problems are quickly dealt with. The top year groups use some of the senior school's facilities and are taught by specialist staff as a way of managing the transition from junior to senior. Outstanding pastoral care is the underpinning of the school's success.

King's Hall School

Linked school: King's College (Taunton)

Kingston Road, Taunton, TA2 8AA

• Pupils: 290 pupils; 130 girls/160 boys, including 40 boarders • Ages: 2–13 • C of E • Fees: Day £5,925–£14,010; Boarding £16,050–£20,670 pa • Independent

Tel: 01823 285920
Email: admissions@kingshalltaunton.co.uk
Website: www.kingshalltaunton.co.uk

Headmaster: Since 2009, Mr Justin Chippendale (early forties), was deputy head at Chafyn Grove, Salisbury, for four years. He attended The Dragon School, from where he won a scholarship to King's Taunton in 1980. He subsequently taught at The Dragon, where he was a popular and successful housemaster, before moving on. A keen sportsman – he captained rugby, hockey and cricket teams at King's – he is supported by his wife, Claire, and his three young children, who are pupils at King's Hall.

Entrance: School accepting children from the age of 2 from January 2014. Pre-prep runs from two to seven; prep from seven to 13. Informal assessments in English and maths as well as a chatty interview.

Exit: King's Hall is more than the junior school for King's College, though three-quarters do go on. Entrance, via common entrance, is not automatic, but very few fail. 'If we feel a boy or girl would benefit from another route, we involve parents in plenty of time,' says the head, 'but we do take the common entrance seriously: it motivates both pupils and staff and the results are used for setting.' Other destinations include Sherborne, Eton, Radley, Bryanston and others. A number of parents choose King's Hall because they can keep their options open. 'There is no pressure,' said one parent. The last five years have seen children gain over 150 scholarships to many different schools.

Money matters: Generous arrangements are available for Services families and scholarships, open to all, are awarded at 11+. They continue through the College, subject to annual review.

Remarks: Gazing out across the park and lake at the distant view of Taunton's magnificent cathedral-like church, it is hard to believe the school is only one mile from the station (two hours to London) and ten minutes from the College. The central house – a handsome and homely 18th century building – is the focal point around which the school operates. The original stable block now forms part of a delightfully intimate courtyard with rose bushes and inviting benches for chatting in the summer. Over the years, brightly coloured and airy dorms have been added with clever partitioning, affording privacy without separation. (Do make sure you see the boys' bathroom, marvellously painted with jungle scenes for aspiring Mowglis and with admonitions on hygiene for young 21st century Stalkys cleverly woven in.)

Separate common-rooms for boys and girls are delightfully furnished with areas for more private conversation, while children can munch on the fresh fruit provided. Accessible library in the original house – elegant but functional. Terrific art and very popular drama in the theatre. Well-equipped labs and lively teaching. Excellent computer facilities. Riding is very popular and plans for fishing in the recently-purchased lake. A wide variety of games are played to a high standard, with success in national and regional competitions. Good modern sports hall, outdoor heated pool, 10 tennis courts and three netball courts. An interesting range of hobbies offered on a daily basis. Pupils are kept busy.

Several things make King's Hall special. Taking advantage of their rural surroundings, there is an exciting Forest School in the grounds, complete with leafy huts for pow-wows and areas for cooking over wood fires: a wonderful place for simply mucking around and being children. Also the Pelican Pals, boys and girls in year 7 sporting their distinctive red caps who go out and play with younger children, really getting to know them and frequently offering comfort, encouragement and advice. We watched some in action with the tinies on the superb Astroturf: it was impossible to tell who was enjoying it more. Prefects have given way to Pelicans – a big improvement, leading to humane and considerate leadership. All of year 8 then play a part in helping to run the school.

Weekend activities are popular – one mother told us it was virtually impossible to persuade her child to come home on Sundays – and all boarding staff, led by charismatic houseparents, are fully involved. The nursery and pre-prep are delightfully housed in what look like log cabins, adding a sense of adventure and discovery. That is the overall feeling we had about the school. The children are obviously happy with the considerate challenges they are set and the encouragement they receive; that is reflected in their sunny friendliness, on which sit the good old-fashioned virtues of courtesy and consideration.

Generous arrangements are available for Forces families and scholarships, open to all, are awarded at 11+. They continue through the College, subject to annual review.

Not a slick or sophisticated school – not a county school with over-riding social pretensions, but a place where children can mature at their own pace, enjoy their surroundings, have a lot of fun and know they will be ready for their next school. Indeed we met a number at their next school, who looked back on their days at King's Hall with huge affection and gratitude. One told us she had 'never been happier in her life,' but added thoughtfully, 'Mind you, in those days, I didn't have A levels to worry about'.

King's Hawford School

Linked school: The King's School (Worcester)

Hawford Lock Lane, Worcester, WR3 7SD

• Pupils: 320 girls and boys; all day • Ages: 2–11 • Church of England • Fees: £6,066–£10,590 pa; • Independent

Tel: 01905 451292
Email: hawford@ksw.org.uk
Website: www.ksw.org.uk

Head: Since 2006, Mr Jim Turner. Previously head of junior school at Sunderland High School for nine years.

Entrance: Entrance is by assessment. This takes place during a normal school day with assessments in English, maths and verbal reasoning for the older children. Younger children can be assessed at home.

Exit: Most move on to King's School, Worcester.

Remarks: For further details, see senior school: The King's School (Worcester).

King's House School

68 King's Road, Richmond, TW10 6ES

• Pupils: 460 • Ages: 3–13 • Non-denom • Fees: £5,730–£13,785 pa • Independent

Tel: 020 8940 1878
Email: schooloffice@kingshouseschool.org
Website: www.kingshouseschool.org

Headmaster: Since 2011, Mark Turner BA PGCE NPQH (late forties) Studied French and Spanish at Bristol before training at Sandhurst with six years in the army. After leaving, taught at Merchant Taylors' before joining Durston House, Ealing where he was deputy head for nine years. Married with four children, two of whom are at the school. Feels he is lucky to have taken over such a good, friendly, and mainly local school. Says it has a strong sense of community and provides a broad education. Parents like the fact that he teaches French to year 4 thereby getting to know the senior boys; say 'very approachable' and 'a classic boys' prep school headmaster'. Feel that he has made the school gentler. One of his aims is to unite the three sections of the school: at the moment they feel like separate entities. To that end, he spends more time in the junior section than his predecessor, which can't be a bad thing.

Entrance: From the term they turn 3, boys and girls at nursery level. Then reception, boys only, September after fourth birthday. No testing, places offered a year before entry in order of registration. Siblings take priority. A few more places at 7+ and 8+ subject to passing entrance test. Occasionally places occur at other times, each individually assessed. Mainly families from surrounding areas including Roehampton, Kingston and Barnes. Buses run from Chiswick and Putney.

Exit: A handful at 11+, trying to beat the rush, but the school does not give this much support. Most of the rest to boys' only London day schools at 13+ with St Paul's, King's College Wimbledon and Hampton all high on the list. Charterhouse, Epsom, Eton and Harrow seem to be the current favourites for boarding. Several scholarships, both music and academic, most years.

Remarks: On three sites in leafy Richmond. Seems a happy, hard-working school. We were taken round by two delightful, polite and enthusiastic senior boys under the eagle eye of the school's marketing manager – we were certainly given the spiel!

Large nursery building on two floors. Huge, bright rooms with different areas for learning and play. Plenty of constructive fun to be had by eager under-4s, both boys and girls. Parents love it – one even said 'flawless'. Two outdoor playgrounds, one for physical play, one for creative/imaginative play. They think of everything these days. Send your children here and your sons get automatic entry to the junior school. Your daughters? They seem mainly to head off to the Old Vicarage.

The junior school – reception to year 3 – is just across the road from the senior. Two reception classrooms on the ground floor have their own outdoor play areas where all is still reasonably relaxed. It may only be the beginning of learning but they are definitely being prepared for the next stage; homework starts straight away. Writing practice first, then, when they are ready, reading. Only 10 minutes at a time but it's still homework – for 4 year olds.

The rest of this rather rambling house contains two year 1 classes and three each for years 2 and 3. Average class size about 20. All have a classroom assistant as well as a fully trained teacher. It is at this point that the serious learning begins. More work, less play. Classrooms are not enormous but they are bright and buzzing. All the boys appeared happy and attentive. Space is at a premium, the library fills in a corridor and a piano lesson seemed to be going on in a passageway. The IT room contained a lot of slightly restless boys learning computer basics. But, no worry, there is plenty of room for burning energy outside in the big playground which, cleverly, has a partially covered area. Parents full of praise for Mr Gower, head of juniors, who they say is extremely approachable and quick to answer emails. He's usually there to welcome boys in the morning. Also, we were told, all children love Nurse Jo who cures all their woes.

In year 4 they move across to the senior school where they can take advantage of some bang up-to-do date facilities, of which our guides were rightly proud, and the real pressure goes on. Initially all classes are mixed ability and, apart from those subjects needing special equipment, are classroom based. In year 5 they begin to build up towards the common entrance syllabus and are setted in English and maths. Two science labs; DT and art rooms; two computer rooms including a suite of Macs for composing and design; a music room; a state of the art theatre where, our young guides boasted, amazing productions are put on; and a well-equipped music room. Parents say, 'music used to be one of their weaknesses but is now one of their greatest strengths'. These are lucky boys.

There's plenty of out door playing space as well, for organised and free play, that area having been completely re-vamped in 2012. Parents say, 'shame there's not wider extracurricular'; 'there could be more broader based after school clubs'. We got the feeling that the emphasis is mainly on the curriculum, with the pressure to succeed being the be all and end all. A 21st century London problem? Or just a lack of understanding that there is more to life than passing exams? The head comments: 'we believe the breadth and balance of our curriculum is a strength and is far from being too focused on the academic. We also feel that while some schools reduce art, DT, drama and ICT to carousel lessons, we still give them regular lesson time up to year 8.'

We didn't see the 35 acre sports ground as it is a coach ride away in Chiswick, but we have seen a DVD and it looks pretty impressive. Senior boys go there twice a week and junior boys once. Rugby, football and cricket all played competitively – 25 rugby, 34 football and 20 cricket teams. Wow! And they have silverware to prove their prowess. Tennis, swimming and athletics also figure. Astroturf area within the senior school grounds and a well-equipped gymnasium ensure plenty of PE.

Inevitably, in a non-selective school, there is a wide variation in ability but, parents tell us, lots of help in the junior school who are 'quick to pick up struggling children and help them so they don't get left behind'. Continual monitoring, boys needing specific help are given it free of charge – 'we give them the building blocks' – being taken out of class for an hour at a time. Free, individualised education programmes provided.

Strict code of behaviour both in and out of the classroom, weekly PHSE sessions and a pupil teacher ratio of approximately 12:1 ensure that the majority of problems are caught quickly. House and tutor systems also provide continuous monitoring. Parents say, 'communication lines excellent and emails responded to quickly'; 'quick to pick up on problems and good at keeping on top of them'.

Communication certainly seems to be a great strength; no parent could say they are not kept fully up to date. From the headmaster's termly letter to the weekly school newsletters, everything is covered. Information on matches, charities and school trips, contributions from teachers, prizes and praises – it's all there. An active and busy school.

King's Junior School (Chester)

Linked school: The King's School (Chester)

Wrexham Road, Chester, CH4 7QL

• Pupils: 245 girls and boys; all day • Ages: 7–11 • Cathedral foundation • Fees: £8,814 pa • Independent

Tel: 01244 689520
Email: junior@kingschester.co.uk
Website: www.kingschester.co.uk

Head: Since 2001, Mr Simon Malone BEd (mid fifties), deputy from 1993. Friendly and open with a genuine heart for his charges here, 'We look on ourselves as a family'. Actively involved with sports coaching because, 'I really enjoy it and the children and parents see me in a different light'. 'He's a big friendly giant,' say pupils. 'You don't feel like he's the headmaster – you feel like he's your friend.' It's more than just a job – he's passionate about the pupils, the school, King's itself, talking of pupils having 'a sense of worth belonging to this fine institution'. His helming makes it feel like a stable, happy ship in safe hands right through to the chatty cleaning lady caring for the aquarium fish. Unpretentious and approachable, in our book he's a good sort.

Entrance: From seven years into year 3 (year 1 here) by examination related to key stage 1 requirements, designed to assess potential as well as achievement. Tests in maths, written English, reading and reasoning, as well as play activity and a talk with staff. 'We're looking for an above average level of competency and the potential to do well – it's not an interview, but you can learn a lot from how, for example, a six year old draws'. Entry at ages eight, nine and 10 is sometimes possible, although head says numbers have increased slightly despite recession. 35 per cent now girls.

Exit: Most pupils sidestep senior's entrance exam, proceeding automatically from junior's internal tracking and recommendation. Quiet warning bells sounded a year or two early if seniors might not suit, although all may compete on level playing ground with outside applicants by taking the external exam. Very few choose elsewhere.

Remarks: Confident children work and play hard here. 'We are an academic school,' says head, 'but we also emphasise music, games, drama, fun – it's very important the pupils have fun.' The junior hall is dwarfed by a 15 foot giant Henry VIII, a masterpiece pupil and staff creation for Chester's 2011 Giant's Parade and the junior's centenary celebration. School still in touch with its oldest pupil, now 96 years old, and head says, 'It gives me particular pride to see our old pupils excelling in and beyond the senior school'.

Peer-reviewed books in classroom libraries help others choose good reads. Curriculum includes Spanish for four years and German and French in the final year. Progress assessed with internal testing and Durham University's INCAS scheme. The 2009 ISI inspection described the quality of educational experience as 'outstanding' and said, 'The junior school provides pupils with an excellent all-round education'. 'They put you under pressure to do well, but when you do, it's really rewarding,' say pupils. 'There are big exams, but then they really let you off the hook.' Year 4s (top juniors) talk of a daily hour of homework, an hour and a half at weekends, and everyone's keen to earn house points for work, effort and behaviour. Children feel they have an effective voice through school council and a suggestion box for all. Delighted parents fall over themselves to praise 'the way children's confidence grows here' and the compassionate way school works to accommodate any problems.

Pupils fiercely proud of sporting successes, especially in cricket and swimming. They appreciate the outdoor 'buddy bench' and new centenary adventure trail with solar powered timers, and inside a doodle wall in the art and DT pre-fab block 'for if it's raining or we're bored'. Christian faith strongly represented with regular visits from local vicar. Many take private music lessons and two annual drama productions. The staff of 20, mostly in their 30s and 40s, includes six full-time men. Private after-school club until 6pm. Uniform shop on site. Only parental grumble is nightmare traffic flow despite staggered finish times, 'Wish they'd turn another field into a car park'.

King's Preparatory, Pre-Preparatory and Nursery School

Linked school: King's Rochester

St Nicholas House, King Edward Road, Rochester, Kent , NE1 1UB

- Pupils: 355 boys and girls; nursery 25; pre-prep 130; prep 200; all day except for five boarders in top years of prep • Ages: 3–13
- C of E • Fees: Boarding £18,810; Day £11,340–£12,885 pa
- Independent

Tel: 01634 888590
Email: admissions@kings-rochester.co.uk
Website: www.kings-rochester.co.uk

Headmaster: Head of prep school, Mr Roger Overend BA FTCL ARCM (sixtyish), a musician and previously head of Westminster Abbey Choir School. Currently chairman of the Choir Schools' Association. Brisk, energetic, enthusiastic and fast-talking. Active in IAPS (the prep schools' association); an experienced director of music and head – his Westminster time an obvious asset in this less spot lit choir school – he is sanguine about the difficulties of maintaining the school's position, with so much free and good state provision on the doorstep. However, his results help – 'We have top KS2 results and we offer so much more on top,' he enthuses. He has updated the school – though its buildings are possibly the least attractive on the site – and brought in much that is new and innovative – including 'highly-motivated staff'. 'Mr Overend has his own methods,' a parent told us. 'He managed to clear the snow in the school yard by organising a huge snowball fight!' Since January 2009, the pre-preparatory head is Mrs Sarah Skillern MA BA NPQH.

Both heads sit on the school's executive board with the head of the senior school, Mr Kevin Jones, the bursar, Graham Longton, director of marketing, Jan Shilling and new principal since September 2012, Mr Jeremy Walker. This is a unique management structure that oversees all aspects of the life of the school and its community. Within that the heads are largely autonomous – 'I work under a head who is strong enough to devolve authority,' says Mr Overend. 'We just see eye to eye – I'm in daily contact with the pre-prep and nearly as often with the senior school. We hold traditional values but we're not boring and dull.'

Entrance: Entrance to the nursery offered to 28 children of 3+. Early registration is the key. Pre-prep starts the following year – places awarded after interview with parents and a simple assessment of the child. Most move into the prep at 8+ when a further intake from outside, particularly at 11+. Assessment by examination. Again most, but not all, will move into King's senior school at 13.

Exit: A few leave early, finding the ethos a little too structured for their free spirits. Most move seamlessly through the whole school – and it is very much a whole school – though some leave at 11 for the state sector if they get a place at one of the grammars. Mr Overend is generous in his support of these though, of course, the school does not teach for the 11+.

Remarks: Pre-prep and prep very much part of the whole King's School. Though enjoying their own buildings and facilities, they also have the run of all the senior school offers – pool, pitches and cathedral. The pre-prep in its purpose-built home is spacious, bright and colourful, without the over-displaying and clutter that sometimes unsettles rather than stimulates. Sensible planning allows for reception having their own loo block and air-conditioned PC suite. No more than 18 children to a class, though the building is flexible enough to allow up to four classes to have activities together. Pre-prep is orderly, calm and happy. Children are attentive, absorbed; 'Nobody shouts at children here,' we were told – but we saw a lot of smiling. We went to a reception class German lesson taught by the 'German Teacher of the Year', an award made by the German embassy, and it was huge fun. Kaspar the puppet was packing his case to go off to the World Cup and we helped him in songs and games and all auf Deutsch. Certificates awarded for everything from improvement in maths to kindness and helpfulness.

Prep in less glamorous accommodation – though it shares the pre-prep's super hall – is busy and fun. Still far more boys than girls here – the word that the school is co-ed has been slow to catch on even after 14 years, though the year groups now in the pre-prep will change all that. Much to offer girls here – they love the jazz dancing and trampolining. Value-added is strong – a good school to which to send your borderline 11+ failure who will catch up fast and have his confidence boosted too. Good support for dyslexics and altogether 'a place of learning, but a place where people are enjoying each other'.

Good communication with home – all new parents are contacted by an existing parent on a kind of buddy basis. Parents 'very committed' and come from up to 30 miles away. Teachers are friends – 'The staff without exception are very switched on and are genuinely very nice people,' said a parent. Boarding is small but has a real family feeling and the pupils can use all the school's facilities. Says one parent, 'For the boarders to be provided with PE every single evening is something you cannot put a price on in this day and age. My lad goes every evening to the gym for different sports and loves it.' All the heads stress the same fundamental principle – the main priority is that your child will be happy.

King's St Alban's School

Linked school: The King's School (Worcester)

Mill Street, Worcester, WR1 2NJ

• Fees: £6,066–£10,590 pa • Independent

Tel: 01905 354906
Email: ksa@ksw.org.uk
Website: www.ksw.org.uk

Head: Since 2012, Ian Griffin.

Remarks: See senior school review.

The King's School in Macclesfield Infant and Junior Division

Linked school: The King's School in Macclesfield

Cumberland Street, Macclesfield, SK10 1DA

• Pupils: 335; 154 girls/ 181 boys; all day • Ages: 3–11 • C of E
• Fees: £7,740–£8,520 pa • Independent

Tel: 01625 260000
Email: mail@kingsmac.co.uk
Website: www.kingsmac.co.uk

Principal: Since 2009, Mrs Caroline Hulme-Mckibbin BEd (early 40s), educated at Altrincham Girls' Grammar and Homerton College, Cambridge. Taught in state primaries in Trafford then at Kings Junior when co education introduced; became academic head. After a career break to have family returned in 2003 as vice principal; 2005 head of Alderley Edge School for Girls' junior section. Friendly and easy to talk to, teaches RS, art, PSHE and ICT to various years and runs philosophy club, about which she is 'passionate'. Husband a business consultant, two girls of 13 and 15 at Altrincham Girls' Grammar. Interests include netball umpiring, theatre, reading. Wants children to believe they can do, 'anything they set their minds to', and to think flexibly.

Entrance: Infants' (3-7 years) places offered by date of application (registration from birth). Juniors: full day at school in January – assessment in literacy, numeracy and VR in morning (looking for above average ability), afternoon activities with a regular class. Before this report on academic progress, interests and potential requested from current head. Numbers rise in years 3-6 – some influx from state schools, often in year 5.

Exit: Most to senior school – need to sit entrance exam; regularly win scholarships (strong music). Some preparation in year 6, but not 'slaves to the entrance exam' (hooray!) – maintains 'full and balanced curriculum'.

Remarks: Achieves well above national average in reading, writing and maths at key stages 1 and 2 (covers national curriculum with extras); sets for maths all years; more specialist teaching in juniors – French, music and and sport; homework from year 3. Infants do EYFS curriculum plus French and music – all achieve expected level for age and many achieve higher. No noticeable gender gap, though girls tend to do better at writing, boys at maths – lots of extra reading and writing activities for boys to develop skills, more boys at level 6 in literacy recently. Max class size 20-24 – may split into smaller groups for focus work. Happy, lively children wearing version of senior school uniform.

Spacious, well-resourced classrooms with colourful displays throughout. Extensive grounds overlooking hills; uses main site facilities – assembly hall, IT suite, library. Outdoor classroom – a wildlife study area, the Gingko meadow. Charming play area for EYFS with little willow bee hives (for children, not bees). Several activity days and trips. Infant and junior division learning support co-ordinators overseen by foundation head of learning support – planning to screen all for dyslexia at 7 years and provide EAL support for all years.

Strong sport – the usuals plus cross-country, trampolining, swimming and athletics, much success in local and regional competitions, national success at trampolining, plenty of chances to represent school. Christmas single made to raise funds for school in Kenya (video on YouTube); various ensembles, including guitar; summer music festival; jazz dance group. Years 5-6 production of Guys and Dolls (ambitious). Art and DT in darkish Portakabin (school says light on a sunny day), plus well stocked Junior library and separate Infant library area.

Wide choice of lunchtime clubs, eg chess, Latin, science, golf. Junior clubs in school day run by teachers – eg puzzle,drama, construction. After-school sports practices run by staff plus some after-school clubs run by external agencies (with charge), eg golf, Spanish, drama. Optional activity holidays in France, Shrewsbury and Derbyshire; biennial ski trip.

Breakfast club from 8am (£3.50/session), after-school service 3.45-6pm (£7.50/session). Flexible pre-school for three year olds – half/whole day, holidays too: happy little tots in mini versions of school uniform.

We were pleased to see the 'every child matters' values displayed in the cheerful entrance hall – be healthy, make a positive contribution, enjoy and achieve, economic well-being, staying safe – especially now they have receded into the background at the Department for Education. Weekly award for children who have shown especially positive qualities in memory of former deputy head boy who died at 12 years. School council. Older pupils do reading work with juniors, helps transition to senior school. Infants have playtime buddy system – year 2 helpers in red caps, plus 'buddy bench'.

Mostly white British, some Europeans (business families working for locally based AstraZeneka, also commuter belt for airline companies at Manchester Airport) – very happy parents. Thriving lowest segment of King's diamond structure.

Knighton House School

Durweston, Blandford Forum, DT11 0PY

• Pupils: 110 girls; more than half board • Ages: 3–13• C of E
• Fees: Day £6,780–£15,930; Boarding £20,985 pa • Independent

Tel: 01258 452065
Email: admissions@knighton-house.co.uk
Website: www.knightonhouse.dorset.sch.uk

Headmistress: Since 2009, Mrs Alison Tremewan BA (early fifties). Read history and history of art at Bristol University and then taught in state primaries in Oxford and Cambridge. Formerly deputy head at Sherborne Prep, where she spent 13 years. Youthful-looking, friendly and enthusiastic, she firmly believes all children deserve a really good start and that independent education allows a freedom and creativity often inhibited in the state sector.

Her classicist husband is a housemaster at Sherborne School and they have four children, the youngest of whom is a pupil at Leweston School.

Entrance: Any child welcome, more or less at any time so long as space is available. Summer term is a popular time to start and it isn't unusual for girls to come mid-year, sometimes from less happy environments. No entrance exam but the school holds non-compulsory taster days – 'more for the girls to have a look but of course it helps us understand their needs.' There is a scholarship exam, though. Families are mainly local (most from under an hour away), but some from London, plus a handful from Spain or France each term.

Exit: Most stay until 13 when they go to Bryanston (obviously convenient as they're so close), St Mary's, Shaftesbury (parents say that 'it's the same sort of friendly school') and beyond that to anywhere and everywhere, including Marlborough, Canford, St Mary's Calne, Sherborne Girls. Good handful of scholarships – for music, art or sport as often as academics. Pre-prep boys mostly go on to Sandroyd, Clayesmore or Port Regis.

Remarks: Perched on a windy hillside just by Bryanston's back gate, this happy and quirky little school was founded in 1950 by Private Eye co-founder Christopher Booker's parents.

A rambling rectory-type house with a rather grand staircase (out of bounds), it's thought to have been the dowager home of the Portman family (Dorset worthies) and is surrounded by orchards, stables and paddocks. Mish-mash of old coach-houses, now used for labs and boarding, and stables full of ponies. Classrooms are serviceable rather than plush and there's a purpose-built multi-use hall and lavish music block. Everything looks a bit haphazard but place is bursting with displays of pupils' work and exceptionally well equipped.

Flexi-boarding is popular, and all weekend boarding is free (a major fun event, sometimes in school, sometimes a trip, is offered every weekend). Almost half the girls in the prep board and everyone gets her own bed, even the two-night-a-weekers.

Refurbished dorms for two to eight (with bunk beds) in the main house for the younger girls, who 'like the bigger dorms'. Plentiful loos, showers and even two end-to-end ancient claw foot baths. Matron, loved by girls and parents alike, has a four-bedded sick room which girls are busy brightening up. No medical nurse, but extremely kind treatment of minor ailments. All boarding staff have first aid training and there is masses of induction and proper training for gappies (Antipodean and local). Smashing food, all locally sourced and cooked by popular chef and team. One parent told us: 'Even my super-faddy daughter actually eats it, especially with the new salad bar'. Teachers sit at the tables to supervise and teach manners and there is a regular 'French' table. Practical, if eye-catching, scarlet dungarees are worn with apparent relish by all except the top form, on trips or to the village church on Sundays. Then it's the girls' 'best' or, as they put it, 'worst' uniform of box pleated grey skirts, red jerseys, checked blouses and dark grey kilts; grey cloaks for cold weather. Oldest boarders have a flat above the labs and get quite bit more freedom: tuck cupboard, some cooking equipment and a more grown up atmosphere to suit their responsibilities and imminent transition to senior school.

Academically adventurous, with no national testing, though pretty thorough assessment, according to the latest inspection. Curriculum includes Latin (a scholars' parent regretted the recent demise of Greek) French from the second year, three sciences in very well-equipped though old-fashioned-looking labs, enjoyable English and maths. Small classes, maximum 18, with some setting in maths, science, French and English. Parents feel that bright girls are stretched and strugglers supported.

State-of-the-art IT with ambitious animations projects for everyone and masses of computer use within all areas of the curriculum. Very good SEN department with two staff, for girls with mild learning difficulties. DT is mainly cooking and sewing but with a bit of woodwork, ceramics etc thrown in for everyone. Two libraries – reference and fiction. Art is enterprising, with emphasis on cross-curricular uses and fun – lots of innovative 3D work. Junior and senior plays produced every year. Lots of clubs, including German and Spanish. There is a contingent of Spanish pupils and Knighton teachers are busy forging links via the Comenius project with Turkey and Estonia to broaden the school's outlook.

Lots of sport for those who want it, with some outstanding successes in tennis, swimming and running. However an unsporty parent told us: 'There doesn't seem to be too much emphasis on sport, which is a plus for me... but manners are very important, which is great, and all the teachers are very well spoken.' Astroturf, playing fields and a swimming pool in a converted sheep dip/storage tank on the hillside – mainly for recreation as real swimming takes place in nearby Blandford or at Bryanston.

But it's the ponies, the music and the friendliness that girls and parents find irresistible. More than half ride and one parent reported that experienced riders are very patient and encouraging with those who start riding at school. Many bring their own ponies and other girls use them too. The stables are close enough for early morning pony visits, (as are the other pet areas and the guinea pig village) and there's an all-weather arena and cross-country course. Friendliness is a defining characteristic. A new parent reported that her daughter, previously anti-school, actually jumped for joy at the end of her first school holidays, while another was delighted to find her two-mornings-a-week toddler was recognised and made a fuss of by older girls. Girls say bullying just doesn't happen 'because we like each other, not because we are told not to,' and a mother told us that a potential incident had been dealt with effectively and kindly for all concerned. The girls we met during our visit were chatty and interested, but not precociously over-confident.

Music has an attractive, dedicated building with a recital room and masses of individual practice rooms. Almost all girls have music lessons, sing and take part in different bands and groups. There's a serious orchestra and small concerts held every Friday to which parents can come. Head of music teaches individual singing and the superb chapel choir sings at the weekly Saturday service, local churches and weddings and has performed grand local venues like Milton Abbey, Lulworth Castle etc. Girls actually get up early for music practice as well as for ponies.

Bright and cosy co-ed pre-prep (The Orchard) and nursery bring in local families, and a weekly toddler group is growing by the hour. ISI inspectors judged it to be outstanding. Children learn at their own pace with masses of careful planned but attractive stimuli. A series of enclosed garden spaces dividing the pre-prep from the main school is evidently much used.

In lots of ways Knighton House seems almost too good to be true but head isn't complacent. Since her arrival, assessment, checks on new staff, training and above all IT and maths have all been given new rigour, without detracting from the essential homeliness of the school. Education and boarding standards are well up to date but the school still has the feeling of one busy, happy and highly motivated family. Parents, who are fed delicious cakes when they come to collect their daughters, wax lyrical, seeing it as a chance for girls to enjoy their childhood in this protected nook. As a free-standing girls' boarding prep school, it is one of the last of a dying breed – barely a dozen left in the country. Not smart, glossy or fashionable but a perfect rural idyll in which girls can become confident and well prepared for life.

Knightsbridge School

67 Pont Street, London, SW1X 0BD

- Pupils: 380 boys and girls • Ages: 3–13 • Non-denom
- Fees: £15,450–£16,440 pa • Independent

Tel: 020 7590 9000
Email: registrar@knightsbridgeschool.com
Website: www.knightsbridgeschool.com

Head: Since school first opened in 2006, Mr Magoo Giles (mid-forties). Previously head of Garden House Boys'. When he discovered the highly impressive building in Knightsbridge he decided to found another co-ed school in the community. So, backed by a huge amount of energy and enthusiasm, that is what he did. A natural organiser, not a teacher, he believes his ability to lead comes from his parent's nurturing, his education within Eton's hallowed walls (or more probably the famous playing fields) and his training and service in the Coldstream Guards. Parents say he may not be an academic but is an excellent manager and a real leader. Has built up an administrative/advisory team to fill in any gaps in his experience and knowledge and to cover all contingencies. Perhaps his biggest coup was to bring in Robin Badham-Thornhill, retired ex-headmaster of Summerfields, as head of development. His links with top senior schools and knowledge of the preparation needed to get into them is indisputable.

It would be hard to find a more passionate head; he wants all his pupils to be as enthusiastic about their education as he is. He wants them to be all-rounders and have a good sense of community. He believes strongly that all parents should be involved and participate in the huge range of extra-curricular and charity fund-raising activities. Parents say 'his personality at the top goes right down the school', ' he sets a great atmosphere' and that he's 'a perfect role model for the kids', Don't believe anyone could keep their hair up when Magoo is about. Does not teach but writes stories which he tells to the children, having created large painted mdf models of the characters. Not afraid of innovation, constantly looking for new ways to motivate, including some mind-blowing parent involved fund-raisers. Says likes to keep an open mind – might even introduce PYP, if it looked the right way to go. In deciding on a name for the school chose Knightsbridge School, not only because of location but also because of the initials KS. All children carry concertina cards around in their pockets. The school code, a reminder list of things they must do: 'I will treat others as I would like to be treated' etc and, most important, 'Keep Smiling because smiling is contagious'. That's the spirit of the school. That's Magoo.

Entrance: Registration is followed by an informal interview with parents and child, who also spends a day at the school in the relevant class. Beware – your child will only be accepted once you have discussed the day together and all given it the thumbs up. Magoo only wants enthusiastic, interested children in his school. Nursery class for siblings only. Still some spaces at senior levels, but reception lists closed for several years to come.

Exit: A few leave at 7+ or 8+ for eg Westminster Under or Colet Court. Most popular 11+ destinations in 2013 Francis Holland SW1, Queen's Gate and More House; 13+ leavers off to Charterhouse (several); otherwise one each to King Edward's Witney (art scholarship), Harrow, King's Wimbledon, Portland Place, ACS Egham and Hillingdon, Bloxham, Emanuel (endearingly, two school names spelt incorrectly on the list of destinations).

Remarks: A school with great potential. After six years, feels well-established and an exciting place to be. Children and staff alike are eager and enthusiastic and, judging by results, seem to be getting it right. Could fly pretty high.

Originally the Hellenic College until it closed down in 2006, the ideal situation for a new school. Did not require an enormous amount of reconstruction. On five floors including basement, where lunch is served by smiling domestic staff – 'Pretty good food – sometimes pizza; Thursday's pudding day, otherwise it's yoghurt and fruit' – and lovely bright art rooms at the top. It's a bit of a ramble up and down different staircases, but children say it really doesn't take long to know your way around. Wonderful photographs and creative works displayed all over.

Formality is definitely not the name of the game. Teachers are called by their first names with an added Mr or Miss in the junior school; they do acquire surnames for the seniors but, we ask, is Mr Magoo ever Mr Giles? Classrooms contain happy, interested children listening to their teachers, not necessarily sitting quietly but totally absorbed. In the science room, when we visited, eager be-smocked children clustered together excitedly as a sheep's head was passed round – 'Here, you have the eye now!' Parents say children really love it and will excel because they 'want to go to school, want to learn, want to do their homework'.

A team of young, motivated teachers, average age about 30, ensure that all lessons are fun, interesting and stimulate a desire to learn. Class sizes no bigger than 18, average is more like 15. Location tends to mean varied nationalities, so different languages abound. All learn French from nursery, a second language from reception and the top seniors learn Latin. A variety of others taught and all cultures explored but no doubt about basic Englishness. Parents love this and say 'best blend of British school system with international flair'. Say, 'Play hard, work hard for juniors; work hard, play hard for seniors.'

All children informally screened for learning difficulties in reception, formally in year 1, and any necessary help given from then on. Parents say communication lines always open, never any problem making contact – teachers and head always accessible. Also school stands behind every policy document – 'What you see is what you get'. Extra English support available for those who need it, but good understanding is essential to get a place at the school.

Good facilities and all mod cons – two computer suites, interactive white boards everywhere, laptops galore. Lovely light, well-stocked library. Excellent music facilities, with rooms for individual lessons. Orchestras, choirs, theatrical facilities with a great stage where all perform. Fully-equipped gym and big school hall for daily assemblies. It's all there.

No outdoor play space, but uses St Columba's Church Hall across the road for breaktime and Burton's Court (Royal Hospital) for sports – two buses take the under 5s to sports grounds and centres – the rest walk – not unusual in London. Some parents feel perhaps this is the one drawback, but the variety available is enormous and children are encouraged to try everything. The majority of the sports they will find at their public schools are here to be tasted – if they don't like one, they can try another. Good familiarisation and confidence builder for when they move on. Some parents love this, others wish they would concentrate on the competitive side a bit more. All know it is something they are working on and have total confidence that a perfectly balanced programme will evolve. Fencing and swimming given particular mention as outstanding. Matches in the usual sports played against other London day schools, and at weekends once a month matches against prep schools for the seniors – these will grow as the school expands.

Exceptionally strong parents' association which, hopefully, will continue to help the school in a meaningful way without interfering with the management – that belongs to the head and his expert team of advisers. An entrepreneurial school which is continually thinking up new ideas to stretch its

K

pupils, expand their horizons and involve the whole family. As the head suggests, most children skip into school into school every day and walk slowly out of it. It is one of the happiest schools we have seen. Parents say, 'Good rounded education, strong academics, high quality teachers, not intimidating and not exclusive.'

Lady Barn House School

Schools Hill, Cheadle, SK8 1JE

- Pupils: 475 boys and girls, all day • Ages: 3–11 • Non-denom
- Fees: £3,876–£6,657 pa • Independent

Tel: 01614 282912
Email: info@ladybarnhouse.stockport.sch.uk
Website: www.ladybarnhouse.org

Headmistress: Since 2011 Sheila Marsh BEd. Married with two grown up children. Husband is head of music and Mrs Marsh continues to teach music to all in year 2 to ensure she knows every child. Is also a published composer and writes all of the Christmas productions, plus songs regularly sung in assemblies. Began writing music as a teaching tool, 'a wonderful way to connect'. Has been at Lady Barn for many years, most recently as head of infants, but also has significant experience across the sectors and across the curriculum. Parents were pleased the appointment was in-house, a signal the long standing ethos of Lady Barn would be maintained. Although it clearly has been, she has also done much to modernise within her brief tenure.

Entrance: An open intake of two early years classes of 22 at age 3 with a waiting list which fills up well in advance. 'We do encourage parents to wait until their child is actually born,' says head. A third class added in reception with an activity-packed, half day assessment 'looking for potential, evaluating maturity and the facility to absorb and apply information. It's always a positive experience and everyone has fun,' says head, and parents agree. Children in nursery are not assessed for entry to the prep as any concerns will already have been flagged up. Largely families from Cheadle, Stockport and South Manchester, but the reach is broadening and more and more children make the journey from Altrincham, Alderley and beyond.

Places do come up higher up the school and it's always worth a try. Infants and juniors are invited to a friendly trial day with fun activities and the usual written tests. A parent of a late entry to the junior school said, 'Mrs Marsh understood my daughter better in one day than anyone during the three years at her previous school.'

The informative website answers most questions but head says, 'Word of mouth is our best marketing tool.' Competitive fees include the cost of all trips relating to the curriculum, long and short including, in both years 5 and 6, an activity-packed week in a hotel on the south coast. A few comprehensive but strictly means-tested bursaries available.

Exit: Impressive number to MGS and Withington at 11, and many opting to stay co-ed at Cheadle Hulme. Stockport Grammar, Manchester High, Alderley Edge and Kings Macclesfield are also popular destinations and also, increasingly, the Altrincham grammars. Links with the secondaries are strong and feedback is always good: 'Lady Barn pupils settle quickly.'

Fewer are opting for early moves. Year 6 is viewed by both head and parents as a precious time, 'a reward after the exam process,' where the children flourish with extra responsibilities and a timetable rich in projects and trips. All are prefects and reading buddies to the infants, and are role models for the younger years.

Remarks: A thriving and happy school set within a large Victorian house extended by three further buildings, which children move confidently between. Bordered by leafy Bruntwood Park, conveniently placed for the juniors' cross country running. Classrooms are vibrant and busy, and colourful work by the children spills into the corridors where it meets numerous photographs of school events, achievements, trips, visits and visitors. Smart, focused children in their signature royal blue blazers sit in rows of front-facing, flip-up desks ('they teach a child to be organised,' school insists).

Teaching is traditional but enthusiastic, 'tremendously energetic and so thorough,' according to parents. The school has a reputation for being a hothouse but parents (and the head) strongly refute this. The impressive results would make it easy to believe, but 'it's an outside opinion,' one parent assured us. 'The spadework is done throughout the years – there is no endless trawling through past papers in year 6.' There are no sets or streams and head firmly rejects Sats: 'they close down the curriculum.' Their methods are tried and tested, says the head, 'a winning formula honed over years, cherry picking new ideas and integrating them as we see fit.' 'They can be a bit slow to modernise,' said one parent, but significant investment in smartboards – now in every class – new laptops for independent research and the adoption of email to communicate with parents are recent and welcome attempts to address this.

Help is there for the struggling, and a SENCo supports children with mild dyslexia – but parents all agree that children with significant learning difficulties would struggle to keep pace at Lady Barn. General consensus among parents is that homework is not onerous, although 'occasionally I do wish we could have a break,' sighed one mum.

Specialist teachers each have their own designated space – a wonderful art room with a kiln, and a science lab uniquely designed for prep-sized children, complete with a pets' corner – home to the not-so-fluffy Galileo the gekko and Aristotle the axolotl. French is taught from kindergarten with an emphasis on the whole cultural experience, to prepare for a trip to Normandy in year 6. They also start Spanish and Latin in year 6 and, from year 1, there are clubs for Mandarin and German. The stunning, cosy library in the eaves is always open and used from time to time by visiting authors for workshops. The dance and drama studios, separated by a movable screen, can be merged to create a single, airy hall, but the spacious gym with a large stage, fully equipped with lighting rigs, is the home to both assemblies and ambitious school productions. Lunches are compulsory but the overhauled menu has proved to be very popular. Outside, early years have their own contained soft play area and there is a multi-purpose, all-weather pitch also used as a playground space. Otherwise, the playground spaces are relatively small, one area within the car park, sectioned off by moveable fencing.

A huge range of extracurricular clubs fills any gaps left in the day, before, after, at lunchtime and on Saturdays, with everything open to both boys and girls. Lots of sport, with successful teams and clubs for all. Girls play football, boys do ballet (not many), there's street dancing, Scrabble and all sorts of diverse activities. Drama is taught as a stand alone subject but most impressive is the music (not surprisingly, given Mrs Marsh's background). Four choirs, an orchestra, several ensembles, over 120 individual music lessons and a samba band. Even the parents and staff have their own choir and orchestra, with soirée concerts and performances on open days, and apparently a samba band is on the cards for them too.

Trips, and there are many, both local and further afield, develop independence and confidence, and encourage considerate behaviour. They start in nursery, but overnight trips begin in year 2 with a weekend away with teddies and sing songs. 'The staff enjoy them as much as the children and they are an excellent way to build an invaluable bond with every child.' Good behaviour and effort are monitored and celebrated. A house system starts at age 7 and there is a weekly update in assembly of credits earned, encouraging the competition. The early years have kindness assemblies to reward their good behaviour and the juniors have half termly merit assemblies to which parents are invited. Every child is given an award for some personal achievement or caring attitude. 'These really mean something to the children,' said one parent; and they perhaps contribute to the exemplary behaviour.

Parents are friendly and there is a mix of background and ethnicity, although predominantly middle-class. They seem to love the school and the complaints are few, but they all grumble about the congested pick-up. The extended wrap-around care, which begins at 7.45am and finishes at 6pm, has gone some way to ease this, and school continues to address it. Family involvement is encouraged: 'We are all part of a child's educational journey,' says head, and parents participate in many activities including twice-yearly weekend camps, music, dads' cricket and mums' rounders matches, and even a parents' race in the annual swimming gala – not to mention all the usual quiz/bingo nights etc. The termly Lady Barn Chronicle and weekly newsletters keep parents up to date. 'The communication is fantastic, everything is pre-empted,' said one parent. 'There is a system for everything, nothing is left to chance. The school runs like a well-oiled machine.'

The Lady Eleanor Holles School, Junior Department

Linked school: The Lady Eleanor Holles School

Burlington House, 177 Uxbridge Road, Hampton Hill, TW12 1ED

• Pupils: 190 girls • Ages: 7-11 • C of E • Fees: £13,050 pa;
• Independent

Tel: 020 8979 2173
Email: junior-office@lehs.org.uk
Website: www.lehs.org.uk

Head of Juniors: Head of whole school is Mrs Gillian Low – see senior school entry.

Head of junior department: Since 2011, Mrs Ffion Robinson BA MA PGCE (thirties). Mrs Robinson came from King's House boys' prep, where she had been assistant head. Prior to this she taught at The Pointer School in Blackheath. Both her degree and PGCE were taken in her native Wales – she is a Welsh speaker – and like many prep school teachers, she can turn her hand to many things. She still teaches each class once a week – maths, history, RE, English and guided reading. 'I love the creative subjects,' she says, 'and it's great to keep my hand in the classroom'. Quietly enthusiastic and plainly delighted with her job, she is smiley and efficient. Parents, similarly, are quietly confident that this is a good appointment and thank heavens their daughters are pupils here.

Entrance: School's own entrance tests in English and maths at 7+ and interview. About 48 places.Only about two girls trying for every place, but don't be fooled – the older they get, the faster the ride, so best for tots who seem exceptionally bright and eager to learn. Pupils come from lots of primaries and many from pre-preps like Athelstan House, Denmead and Jack and Jill.

Exit: Sensible new system for moving from junior department to senior department introduced by Mrs Low in 2010. 'I was concerned that preparation for the 11+ entrance exam

dominated the curriculum,' she says. 'We were creating all this inevitable anxiety and a division between the two parts of the school. Now the junior department girls are assessed on the basis of their classroom work and school exams and offered a guaranteed place in year 5. The very small number who are not offered such a place are given lots of support and extra help to prepare for tests to other schools and they may still sit our exam if they wish'.

Additionally, those who wish to try for a scholarship sit the entrance exams along with the outside applicants. In effect, around 80 per cent go up to the senior department. Others go to Guildford High, Hinchley Wood, The Marist, St Catherine's and Surbiton High.

Remarks: Inside, you can still see relics of the attractive old house at the heart of the school. Outside, it is a somewhat forbidding three-storey block with a one-storey extension in unattractive brick and PVC windows. However, unlike preps elsewhere, it has lovely outside space – real space. A super garden area with excellent climbing frames and other apparatus, courts and pitches, much of it, of course, shared with the senior school. Then there are the adored 'hedge homes' – little dens in the hedges abutting the brook separating the school from the grounds. Apparently the girls use pebbles for money and run these little domestic havens just as they would their brick and drainpipe equivalents.

Inside, everywhere is carpeted – it makes for quiet corridors and a civilised feel. Classrooms are airy and light, while classes are attentive and absorbed. Girls look a treat in their grey/red/blue tartan skirts and red sweatshirts. A sense of purpose and concentration pervades the school and we saw much to delight and impress. We especially liked the cross-curricular approach to much of the teaching – something that plainly inspires the girls. If they learn about the ancient Greeks they make Greek vases. If they learn about Rio de Janeiro and Brazil, they make carnival masks. Arts and crafts throughout are unusual and clever. We particularly enjoyed the silhouette work and girls enthused about the animated films they make using their own clay and cut-out models.

The library, though inviting and piled high with books, is small and barely adequate for this number of girls. Trips to interesting places – including a local Gurdwara and the National Archives at Kew to look at Victorian prison records (after which they 'used metaphors to write poems as if we'd been in prison'). This is imaginative and lively teaching of the kind we don't see everywhere. Terrific sports (great preparation here for the legendary sporting culture of the senior department) and lucky girls use many of the older girls' facilities. Good traditional hall for productions, assemblies and younger girls' gym.

The school food (eaten by most) is 'brilliant' and the place hums with happy learning. 'We let little girls be little girls,' says the head reassuringly. 'People are kind here,' one year 6 girl confided. 'If someone is being bullied they go to a friend or a buddy, but it doesn't happen much'. 'There's so much for them to do,' a parent enthused. 'My girls just love going to school'.

Lady Royd Primary

Linked school: Bradford Girls' Grammar School

Squire Lane, Bradford, BD9 6RB

• Pupils: 155 boys and girls; all day • Ages: 2–11 • C of E • State

Tel: 01274 545395
Email: registrar@bggs.com
Website: www.bggs.com

Headmistress: Mrs Juliet Rimmer BSc PGCE

Entrance: School became a free school in September 2013, with a non-selective entrance policy.

Exit: Most to the senior school – automatic entry if at the right standard (NB non-selective since September 2013); a few to co-educational maintained or independent schools.

Remarks: Purpose built in 2008 – smallish, cheerful classrooms with good displays, including a junior science lab with drop-down desks. Attractive, well-stocked library has beanbags, computers and story sacks for parents to borrow. Senior school DT and music facilities also used. Grassed play areas, a sensory garden and little greenhouse; well equipped nursery and kindergarten.

Average of 15 per class (18 maximum). Broad curriculum – French from four years, building up to an hour a week for year 6s, from specialist teacher; specialists for music and PE too and generally for Key Stage 2 classes, who also have thinking skills (eg draughts and chess, study skills, budgeting from an Argos catalogue) plus food and nutrition. Very keen on Jolly Phonics – parents given instruction. Strong results in core subjects at the end of year 6, well above the national average – no national tests; focused atmosphere in classrooms. Several computers – a parent commended the use of ICT in lessons to engage pupils. Recent ISI report praised 'outstanding individual attention' in EYFS and children's excellent relationships with teachers.

Well-led SEN department: three SEN lessons a week if needed plus support within and outside the classroom. Dyslexia Action visits for half a day a week for individual sessions (parents pay it directly), but more systematic provision is needed for gifted and talented children – it depends on individual teachers, said a parent.

Parents receive a detailed guide for the forthcoming year at the end of the summer term, termly newsletters (two kinds) produced by the school and children and sessions explaining educational approaches. They see teachers as very approachable and happy to collaborate with them on all kinds of problems.

Happy and friendly children, from Bradford and the surrounding area, including Leeds, Halifax and Huddersfield. Socially and ethnically varied; several doctors' children. All given responsibilities from year 3, eg year 6 Friendship Police and Fine Dining monitors, who select the best behaved and best eaters for a special end of the week meal with the head (drinks in plastic goblets); school council.

Lots of clubs: sports – teams do well in competitions (table tennis a strength); music – almost all do individual lessons, various groups (steel pans, guitar, fifes, trumpets), orchestra, choir, several concerts, the school is working towards Sing Up silver award; LAMDA popular; plays; jazz and street dance as well as ballet; debating, poetry reciting, creative writing and handwriting competitions. Charity work for Africa linked to a Bradford Royal Infirmary skin care research project; several trips – year 4-6 residentials; theme days, eg World Cup Football day when we visited, with staff dressing up too. Breakfast club and after school provision.

Like the senior school, very thoughtfully run, strong on relationships and offering a wide range of opportunities.

School became a non-selective free school in 2013, part of Bradford Girls' Grammar.

Lambrook School

Winkfield Row, Nr Ascot, RG42 6LU

• Pupils: 500 boys and girls • Ages: 3–13 • C of E • Fees: Day £9,450–£16,578; Boarding £18,561–£19,878 pa • Independent

Tel: 01344 882717
Email: info@lambrookschool.co.uk
Website: www.lambrook.berks.sch.uk

Headmaster: Since 2010, Mr Jonathan Perry, previously head of Kingsmead School in Hoylake. Wife Jenny is a clinical pharmacist who works part-time at a nearby hospital but also has a pastoral role at the school. She has an eye for interior decoration too: the fresh flowers front of house and general spruced up air are thanks to her. The Perrys have a son and daughter at the school and were described by one parent as 'a perfect fit'. Mr Perry is the son of a bishop, his degree is in religious studies and history, but there are teachers in his family as well as members of the clergy – certainly a strong tradition of public service. Although he teaches no timetabled lessons, he runs current affairs sessions in his study for the older pupils. He told us modestly that he 'helps out' with sport, but parents love the fact he's so visible – greeting children every morning, present at all the matches – and is always available. He has revitalised Saturdays and added a lecture programme (parents welcome to attend these) to the extended learning sessions. Saturday school compulsory for years 6 and above. Another thing we learned about Mr Perry during our visit is that he really does seem to know every pupil, and not just by name either.

School is increasingly popular but headmaster has no plans to expand; he is 'happy with the size' and concentrating instead on improving facilities. First plan to come to fruition is the performing arts centre. It would be fair to say that not all parents saw this project (on hold when Mr Perry took over) as a necessity, but they have now been very much won over. There is no doubt Lambrook's many musicians and performers can't wait to tread its boards. Also in the pipeline is a scheme to demolish the rather odd greenhouse of a swimming pool and build new art studios, and to get rid of the temporary classrooms (perfectly respectable as classrooms but criminally obliterating the view of the grounds). Managing these projects must be taking up a fair bit of Mr Perry's time, but he is determined to ensure that the results will respect the school's tradition and surroundings and has changed architectural details to this end. 'Parents like to see things happen in their time,' he says. The coffee table in the head's study is made from the trunk of an oak from the grounds, its rings marked with events from the school's 150 year history – must help put things in perspective. A keen sportsman, Mr Perry enjoys golf, tennis and cricket, but more often these days from the sidelines. Favourite book? Sebastian Faulks' Birdsong. Cornwall is where the family go to get away from it all – sea being practically the only thing lacking in Winkfield Row.

Entrance: From local primaries, Montessori schools and own pre-prep. Increasingly favoured by West London parents, so much so that the school now runs a daily minibus from London. Some girls join in year 7, mainly those aiming for Wellington or Downe House. Parents a mix of traditional, first time buyers and international families.

Exit: All, many with scholarships, to first choice senior schools including Wellington (strong links), Eton, Charterhouse, Rugby, Bradfield, Benenden, Marlborough etc. Few girls at 11 to Queen Anne's Caversham or nearby St George's, Ascot.

Remarks: On the glorious early summer day of our visit Lambrook could not have looked finer. The school's 52 acres of Berkshire's lushest prime estate were at their peak of green and pleasantness; children played under venerable trees, the cricket pitch was like velvet as was the nine hole golf course – and birdsong was nearly winning against the noise coming from the construction site (soon to be performing arts centre). Inside the main building the newly extended library, with its gothic wood panels and shelves, seems timelessly bookish but was originally the dining room. Here, as elsewhere, are historic photographs of past pupils – teams, plays etc – part of the fabric rather than separated into an archive. Founded in 1860, Lambrook is alma mater of, among others, Lord Alfred Douglas (Oscar Wilde's downfall), Queen Victoria's grandsons Prince Christian Victor and Prince Albert, W C Sellar and R J Yeatman, authors of 1066 and all that. More recent alumni include actor Alex Petyffer and rugby internationals Max and Thom Evans.

The fine chapel with its gleaming brass and polished pews can no longer accommodate everyone, so whole school assemblies and inter-house competitions (singing etc) take place in the larger but much less atmospheric sports hall. Although the number of girls is rising, boys are still in the majority, inevitably so in the last two years, but despite this the feel is thoroughly inclusive and co-ed. Children with SEN and/or physical disabilities 'welcome' so long as the school can meet their specific needs.

In addition to the aforementioned birdsong and building, another noise we heard as we toured the school was laughter. Lambrook lessons seem to be good fun, with relaxed but respectful relations between pupils and staff, many of whom live on site. Parents told us they like the balance of male and female teachers and the mix of quirky 'old school' and new blood teaching styles. Thumbs up too for the enthusiastic gappies from pupils and parents alike. We saw heads in books in English and quick fire questions and answers in science too – it was just a few weeks before CE after all. Our year 8 guides (scholarships in the bag) already sounded nostalgic about their Lambrook years. Music is exceptional; over 80 per cent of children are learning at least one instrument up to and including grade 8 and play in school bands and ensembles, not to mention a full symphony orchestra. The choir had recently sung evensong at St George's Chapel, Windsor and had obviously been given the royal seal of approval because they've been asked to return. New performing arts centre opened in 2013, with theatre, peripatetic teaching rooms, green room and dance studio. In recent years Lambrook has provided actors and singers for professional productions including The Sound of Music, Oliver! and Matilda. In the wonderful, creatively messy art room, pupils were singing along to music and screen-printing their own designs onto sports day t-shirts.

It must be tough to do justice to the perfection of the pitches (or, apparently, the match teas) but boys' and girls' teams are bringing home gold and silverware in rugby, hockey, trampolining, tennis, skiing and basketball, played at county and national levels. Plenty of joint activities, but girls get separate PE, hockey, and netball. Everybody loves winners, but we were encouraged to hear of children who were never going to make the team being included and given important non-playing roles. Choice of clubs and after-school options described by one parent as 'ridiculously diverse' and so it is – from creative writing to polo (well, this is Ascot).

We visited the nursery, separate from but close to the main school, just before lunch (meals on wheels from main school kitchen). Tinies sitting on the floor were engrossed in a story. At age four children move on to the pre-prep, not a huge step geographically but parents praised the way the staff prepare children for this transition. This is the time when educational needs may show themselves, and the pre-prep SENCo observes and identifies any potential learning, speech and language problems. For those who need a little more time to consolidate the basics there is extra phonics and 'maths crew', activity-based small group work to reinforce knowledge. Pre-prep has its own hall, used for before (from 8.15am) and after (until 6pm) school care – a bonus for parents, especially if they have older children at the main school. Lively notice boards give parents all they need to know about what's going on, lesson topics and other key information. Expansion of nursery provision has not been without collateral damage – in this case the pre-prep library. Wider than average though it may be, a corridor doth not a library make. Something else for Mr Perry to add to his grand plans.

The girls' dorms are up three flights of stairs in the eaves of the main house, charming rooms looking out over the grounds painted in contemporary colours and full of homely touches such as beanbags. The boarders' kitchen was large and sunny with gingham oilcloth on the table and fresh flowers. Every effort has been made to keep things as uninstitutional as possible. Flexi-boarding is particularly popular at the end of the week – parents certainly appreciate it – and most of the older day pupils have tried (and, apparently, enjoyed) it at one time or another.

Lambrook is a lively and unstuffy prep school in an idyllic pastoral setting where boys and girls are educated to the best of their potential without excessive pressure. Several parents said to us that although they rather liked the fact it was a 'well-kept secret', the school deserved to be better known. We agree. To quote from old boys Sellar and Yeatman's classic, 1066 and all that, Lambrook is 'a Good Thing'.

Lancing College Preparatory School

Linked school: Lancing College

The Droveway, Hove, BN3 6LU

• Pupils: 220 boys and girls • Ages: 3–13 • Fees: £7,860–£13,875 pa
• Independent

Tel: 01273 503452
Email: info@lancingprep.co.uk
Website: www.lancingprep.co.uk

Head: Since 2002, Mr Alan Laurent BEd (mid-fifties). Taught previously at Hurn Court School, Christchurch, Durlston Court School, New Milton, and was deputy head of Portsmouth Grammar Junior School. a reassuring presence, feels like he could be an uncle you can confide in, knows the ropes, his school, teachers and pupils. A man not scared to hoover – 'the kids left loads of crisp crumbs in my office yesterday.' Knows his pupils – and their peccadilloes well, and stands at the door to greet them all every morning (with a bit of teasing about the latest football results). Says of his pupils 'they all have a special place within the school,' and takes great care to ensure each individual is appreciated. He goes through each edition of the glossy school magazine – The Lower Quad – to make sure each child's face appears.

Fell into headship almost by accident, and misses pupil interaction, although manages to teach each year once a week most of the time. Will be at Lancing Prep until retirement; spurned the chance to move on to oversee implementation of phase two of the school expansion.

Entrance: Waiting lists for most years. No assessment, it's first-come, first-served. Taster day. Means-tested scholarships (up to 50 per cent of fees) available from 11+. Prospective scholarship pupils are tested on verbal reasoning during taster day. Stiff academic hurdle because pupils need to be very bright to have a realistic prospect of scholarship to the college.

Exit: Most to Lancing College, where they need to get 50 per cent in CE. A handful to other schools – St Bede's, Brighton College, Bryanston, Lewes Grammar, Ardingly and Purcell School.

Remarks: Main building has an old school feel, with a wood-panelled hall lined with ancient school photographs. Hall morphs into a dining room in the middle of the day. 'It's my third best pudding today,' sighed one pupil about the rice pudding on offer (apparently not much can compete with the apple cobbler). Food was delicious and disappeared rapidly. Tables are mixed between year groups, with year 8s serving. Pupils undertake a different job each week, one piling up leftovers and stacking plates with business-like resignation. 'Stacking is the worst job,' he confided.

Classrooms of all shapes and sizes, larger rooms for the pre-prep where there is more emphasis on practical work, packed with colour and displays. Smaller rooms are a snug fit for the 20 pupils who generally make up the prep classes. Lovely library in the old school with bean bags and cushions in a comfy area. A bit of ducking and diving outside to reach other classrooms: science lab (modern), art room (some fabulous work – a strong department) and gym (small and old). Lovely outdoor classroom for sunny days with benches set in a semi-circle. Easy access to Lancing College facilities – children are bussed up to the College to swim, for DT, and to visit the farm – every child in pre-prep has seen a ewe give birth.

All the usual national curriculum subjects, but with a particular emphasis on music and sport. Whole of top floor is given over to music. When we visited, year 3 children's Punjabi song echoed through the corridors. More than 80 per cent play instruments and vast range of groups to perform in, including ensembles, orchestra (from grade 5) and contemporary music group. Multimedia used a lot in music – year 6s were all plugged in, happily writing soundtracks. Prep share a drama teacher with the senior school and rehearsals were well under way for Bugsy Malone. 'Nearly everyone's in it,' a pupil told us.

French is the only language on offer: the head would like to increase language provision, but can't think how to fit another language into the packed curriculum. Homework is kept to a minimum for the pre-prep (reading), rising to around 40 minutes for each exam subject per week for those at the top of the prep school – certainly not an amount that the pupils find irksome. Occasionally parents seeking a more challenging academic regime will look elsewhere, but 'our academic scholarship results will stand comparison with any,' says the head. Lessons are lively and relaxed.

Head feels school suits quirky children and it's easy to see those who don't run with the pack finding a home here. School has a Christian ethos but place feels like a broad church. No statemented pupils. SEN support given where necessary in the form of one-to-one support in and out of lessons (where support is given out of class, there is a separate fee). School is proud of being mixed ability – lessons are planned for individuals, SEN and mainstream alike. Sometimes holds a struggling pupil back a year, so a summer baby who was the youngest in the year becomes the oldest, which often sorts out problems. Equally, an able pupil can be accelerated to the next year and may spend a second year in year 8 as a scholarship pupil.

Plenty of sports here (hockey is big at the moment), and lots of opportunities for those who want to play to a high level – competitive sport is a big part of this school. A-D teams, so the school can seem practically deserted when they are all playing.

Of course many players are particularly interested in the match tea, says the head.

Any bullying is dealt with promptly, and (generally) at a low level – 'it usually amounts to name calling,' said the head. The approach is that the bully needs help too, and while a bully may lose their lunch play, they will do an activity based on bullying scenarios to try and reform their thinking. Pupils are encouraged to whistleblow and look out for each other. A variety of people on offer to talk to, from year 8 mentors to teachers and the head.

Day ends at 4.30, but most don't go home then. Activities last until 5.30, and range from the usual homework club, sports, and musical activities to lego club, Welsh club and the eco garden club. Dance has recently started, and covers a range from modern to jazz to Strictly Come Lancing last year. Year 7 and 8s can also opt to visit the local residential home – many do. Clubs are included in the fees at prep age, and are paid as extras at pre-prep age.

Portakabins cluster round the back of the school, again rather on the cosy size. Plans are afoot to sweep the whole lot away and build something swish to house two classes a year (since September 2013 a double nursery intake has inhabited newly-acquired next door bungalow).

There is a drop off problem – the council won't play ball with a drive through system, and it can be difficult to park, but the school opens the back gate so pupils can walk in across Hove park; finishing times are staggered at the end of the day too (although most opt to stay until 5.30). Pupils can come to school by school bus, which comes from all over, and works specific routes according to need. There is also a shuttle between Lancing Prep and the college to help parents with children at both schools.

Prep seems to do a good job at focussing on an individual's strengths. When asked at what the school excels, one pupil said, 'It's really good at music and sports, particularly hockey'; another indignantly responded, 'But it's a very academic school – the best things are extra science and maths.'

School feels like a very green and pleasant land. There is tangible warmth and friendliness here. 'I was a bit lonely at my old school, but everyone here is friendly,' a pupil told us. 'It's a family. I know everyone.' Our pupil guides were greeted by all and sundry on our tour, the little ones in nursery racing up to say hello. Family ethos includes all staff – school photo includes cleaners and chef (who's very popular and gets mentioned a lot).

Parents say pupils relate well to each other across the years, and that older ones look out for the younger ones. One questioned whether increasing numbers would have an effect on the family experience. Our enthusiastic pupil guides indulged in much nostalgic remembrance of things past, but were also very excited about their imminent move to the senior school. When asked if there was anything they would change about the prep, there was a long contemplative pause. 'I wouldn't change much – it feels right as it is,' said one.

Lanesborough School

Linked school: Royal Grammar School (Guildford)

Maori Road, Guildford, GU1 2EL

• Pupils: 355 boys, all day • Ages: 3–13 • C of E • Fees: £8,370–£11,520 pa • Independent

Tel: 01483 880650
Email: secretary@lanesborough.surrey.sch.uk
Website: www.lanesborough.surrey.sch.uk

Head: Since 2007, Mrs Clare Turnbull BA (Exeter), previously deputy head at the school since 2004, so slotted nicely into the job with no big upheaval. Married to Andrew, who works in charity finance. Youthful, open and chatty, has an energetic presence – teaching of games reluctantly sacrificed on headship (but she does teach PHSE to top two years and French lower down the school). Considers herself fortunate to have taken over a school in such great shape and has no desire to 'make changes for their own sake'. However she is doing lots of improving and tweaking around edges – more cathedral choristers (now 20 in all), installing of pitch floodlighting and ideas for mezzanine in gym to increase performance space are all keeping her busy. She feels atmosphere is very important and is keen that all achievements should be recognised. We don't often see a woman as head of a boys' prep school – but Mrs Turnbull is one to watch.

Entrance: Three main points of entry. For unselective admission to nursery, registration advised between one to two years old. Thereafter, boys joining from elsewhere are given gentle assessment for pre-prep, 'really just to see their levels of concentration and how they respond to instructions'. At 7+ about 18 extra places available. The process then is designed to check similar skills, formalised into English, spelling, non-verbal reasoning and maths papers, interview and reading. This takes place on a Saturday, but only after all candidates have spent an afternoon seeing the school in action – playing games with PE masters, taking part in some music and, most importantly, having a doughnut. 'By including sports and music teachers in the selection system, we hope to achieve a balance of boys beyond the basic academic. Good orchestras and match results matter too.'

Main feeder schools to prep are Glenesk in East Horsley and St Hilary's at Godalming. Bursaries available from 7+.

Exit: More than half move on to the top-notch Royal Grammar School in Guildford, though far from an automatic shoo-in. Other perennial exit favourites include St John's Leatherhead, Charterhouse, Wellington, Cranleigh, Reeds, City of London Freemen's and Lord Wandsworth College Recent scholarships include academic and music awards to RGS (at 11+ and 13+), St John's and Charterhouse.

Remarks: Traditional prep school with lots to shout about but with an unusually inclusive feel. Head is seamlessly pursuing the good work. Suits those who are either bright or at least want to try their best. Not for the unwilling, disruptive or those with more challenging behaviours. On the whole, happy parents (particularly those who ultimately get a much coveted RGS place) and certainly happy children.

Shares the same governing body as the topnotch Royal Grammar School in Guildford (RGS). Care is taken to maintain a level of autonomy and although geographically not close, the two heads and schools' departments liaise on curriculum matters – so much so that Lanesborough sends at least twice the number of boys to RGS as any other feeder school (20 per cent of RGS pupils).

Boys start in the main part of Lanesborough in year 3, joined by a new intake to make an additional parallel class, and are mostly taught by class teachers until year 5. Setting for maths only year 4 and 5, then maths and English from year 6, though fluidity between sets remains. The very able boys certainly do well in maths, though parent mutterings suggest a more inspired approach could help others. Latin for everyone from year 5 along with first taste of exams – none before this 'as learning should be an ongoing delight, not an end with a fear of getting things wrong'. No separate scholarship class. Progress monitored via assessment database with grades for effort and attainment pitched against recently fine-tuned 'Lanesborough Scale'. No de-merit or minus points systems, but discipline is managed by red and yellow cards, football analogy proving resonant.

SEN provision particularly praised by parents, but the odd report of severe dyslexics having not coped here in the past. In spite of small proportion of boys needing it, support is taken seriously – up to one lesson a week with specialist at no extra cost, thereafter charged. 'All boys feel really valued and encouraged by their peers and the school,' approves a mother. 'There are no feelings of inadequacy.'

In common with most preps, sport is integral to boys' lives here. The focus is particularly on breadth of activity – all rotate to try 10 different disciplines in any one year. The school is keen to winkle out hidden talent – it has produced two county level fencers from scratch this way. Traditional sports strong and it is sport for all – D and E teams often fielded in football, rugby and cricket. The boys play on the two pitches (grass and Astroturf) at the back of school or walk 10 minutes to Stoke Park – not ideal, though most parents are resigned to this inconvenience in the Guildford suburbs. Pitches also heavily used during lesson breaks on a rotation basis. Swimming is taught to all.

Ideal for music-loving boys – famed for its music. It provides choristers for Guildford Cathedral – boys may be invited to join choir at age 8 and receive a bursary which reduces their fees; they have sung for HM The Queen (Royal Maundy), broadcast by BBC. Popular school choir with over 90 boys. Class music lessons taken by all. Some 145 boys learn musical instruments in school – amounting to 1,700 timetabled lessons per term! And it all starts young with the pre-prep entering the Godalming Music Festival. Recently, a year 8 boy awarded IAPS Young Musician of the Year. At least two school concerts each term; the carol service at Guildford Cathedral is one of few occasions that the school gets together as a whole.

Sited on leafy, suburban north east edge of Guildford in two converted red-brick Edwardian houses with later additions. Not a hugely spacious place and some facilities are rather cramped, which fazes some parents but doesn't worry others. The pre-prep, in Braganza House, including nursery, is actually accessed from a parallel road through its own entrance. The head is Mrs Heath-Taylor. The pre-prep is spotless and bright with a purposeful hum of activity; that said, it has a gentle, almost spiritual feeling too.

Impressive recent artwork everywhere (only two weeks into start of year when we visited) coupled with some new interactive whiteboards. Mrs Turnbull is keen not to fall into trap of many other schools – acquiring 'all singing and dancing technologies to impress the parents', while she is mindful of her responsibility to keep attracting good teachers, as 'most now expect them'.

Picket-fenced area protects nursery boys from general rough (though not very) and tumble of Braganza playground. Boys encouraged to cultivate gardens – these green-fingered souls always do well at Guildford in bloom displays. Library particularly well stocked and thumbed with colourful murals of fictional characters. All boys, other than in nursery, have cafeteria-style hot school lunches – 'Too many activities going on at lunchtime for all to sit down together'. Across the road at Lanesborough the atmosphere changes – definitely a more serious feel here. Still similar style of well-maintained buildings but now with an ordered, almost reverential, hush.

Boys quite a tidy bunch dress-wise – in fact they would look rather out of place if scruffy in such an ordered environment – but, like those at many boys' schools, they are far from immaculate. Parents largely Surrey middle class with all the social trappings that this entails, though not all very rich – sacrifices made by some to be there. Small sprinkling of other cultures, notably Asian pupils.

Very much a carrot rather than stick environment, building the confidences of eager beaver boys.

Latchmere School

Latchmere Road, Kingston Upon Thames, KT2 5TT

• Pupils: 740 boys and girls; all day • Ages: 3–11 • Non-denom
• State

Tel: 020 8546 7181
Email: office@latchmereschool.org
Website: latchmereschool.org

Headteacher: Since 2008, Mrs Julie Ritchie, CertEd BPhilEd MSI SIP (Special) (fifties). Previously at St Matthew's C of E Primary School, where she was shortlisted for head of the year award. Qualifications (bucket loads of them) include degree in multi-sensory impairment, a souvenir of decade-long post in the 1990s as deputy headteacher at Dysart, a Surbiton-based special school.

Grew up in Grimsby, drawn to teaching from an early age – something of a family thing as a brother is also a head, though neither of her two grown up children has so far been bitten by the bug. Inspects for Ofsted, a heart-gladdening experience, though never fails to feel thrill of returning 'home' afterwards. Though she doesn't teach – she's at her desk by at 6.30am as it is, notching up 12-hour days – she's available to parents first and last thing and regularly consulted by staff, too. 'I've got a lot of experience and they know that,' she says.

Gets to know pupils well – no mean feat given numbers ¬– and parents are duly impressed. 'She made a point of saying how well my child had acquitted herself in a school production. I was quite taken aback as she is someone who could very easily be missed', comments one.

Smiley and effortlessly calm, head rarely raises her voice. 'This is a no-shouting school', she says, and indeed it's as quiet as they come. Short, sharp blasts of the school bell that periodically lash the air are the only sound to puncture the serenity (not to everyone's taste but necessary to minimise euphemistically termed 'time drift').

Makes no bones about need for exceptional staff to deliver the goods, tough old selection process identifying those who, like able pupils, enjoy being stretched and 'have the potential to be outstanding'. With many taking on load-bearing roles, they need to be. School's best practice managers, one to a year group, carry the can for quality of teaching and learning, and 'could be heads in their own right'. Within the next post or so, they often are. Numbers likely to be augmented as fast track trainees, appointed under new government Schools Direct scheme, start to make their mark.

Professional to her fingertips, caring too, head sees parents as the ultimate experts. 'We know what the child presents in school but it's at home where they pour their hearts out. If we feel they're not functioning, parents are the ones who know'. Her biggest buzz comes from seeing 'children achieve what you wanted for them'. 'Pupils love her and have unbounded respect,' confirms a parent. And so they should.

Entrance: Very oversubscribed, with 500 applying for reception places and not a hope for anyone living more than a kilometre away. Solid core of 'aspirational' parents, some services families (there's a nearby army base). All year round wraparound care a boon to working parents.

Looked after children have precedence, siblings (up to 50 a year) get second dibs. Only exception is eight-pupil Topaz unit where pupils may come from further away.

Virtual school tour, coming soon on revamped website, will, hopes head, ensure that non-starters are gently discouraged online rather that getting taste of paradise during a face to face visit, only to have it whisked away again when logistics are explained.

Exit: Some to local independents, with scholarships. A very few to Tiffin grammars (rarity down to ever increasing levels of competition, so over-subscribed that place hunting has become an extreme sport).

Over half to Grey Court School, currently nearest comprehensive and rapidly improving though 'quality of intake' has undoubtedly helped, says head, tongue (slightly) in cheek. Potentially all change with new secondary school due to open September 2014 just a few hundred yards away.

Remarks: Author Jacqueline Wilson's primary (and much changed for the better, she reckoned, when she revisited). Opened in 1936, just in time for Second World War (nearby aircraft factory was regular bombing target). Infant school added a year later – dividing wall in place until reunification in 2007.

Large site with playgrounds generously bestowed means most year groups have a space they can call their own in addition to larger shared areas for infants and juniors. Substantial on-site asphalt legacy is greened up with trees and bushes, plus veg garden in small courtyard, together with reception-only delightful green run between knee-high rows of plants (like nursery, have own secure play area). Tactical introduction of soft surfaces underneath sturdy and attractive play equipment for older children also helps, while nearby shared playing fields are used for some clubs, junior games and sports day, now back to traditional competition-driven format and considered all the better for it.

Inside, plenty of space with large classrooms for all. Spares too, as though school is geared up for expansion to four-class entry, will take time to permeate every year group. Two schools into one means inevitable layout quirks, corridor-heavy design putting well-stocked library on the through route. Potential dinginess offset by lots of colour, particularly in nursery and reception areas where primary colours rule and some toilets have gone green (paint rather than eco flush). Assumes more monochrome hues as you go up through the school, though brightened with lots of little extras including giant paintbrushes strung across art room ceiling and boards, inside and out, crammed with enigmatic clay masks.

Reigning delight is flashy new building housing year 6 classrooms upstairs, lunch/sports hall on ground floor. Also used for Monday morning whole school assemblies, smaller hall taking year groups two by two on other days, and notable for impressive red and blue light up buttons (disappointingly measure air quality rather than summoning International Rescue).

Though fab new buildings help, what really rocks parents' boats is success with non-standard issue pupils. 'Schools can all do the straightforward ones', reckoned one mother. 'What counts is how good they are with the off the peg kids'. Latchmere aims (learning, local community, laughter, loyalty, love and leadership) are oft recited, children 'accepted for who they are' and inclusion, very dear to head's heart, a big, well resourced, thing.

Despite leafy setting (Richmond Park within easy reach), pupil make up has a grittier, urban feel that you might expect, with challenges to match, including a few with difficult home lives and nearly one in five with English as a second language.

Staff, average age 40, around a third male (average pupil to teacher ratio of just over 21 to one) are expected to get on together, and get on they do. No coasting, either. Jaw-droppingly efficient systems still have enough give for teaching talent to flourish outside the box. One teaching assistant, a professional actor, has leave of absence to go on tour in term time, in return lending talents to sky's the limit school productions.

Mantra is constant improvement. 'Whatever we do, I ask staff how we can do it better next time', says head. 'And because they're bright, I only have to ask them once'. Accolades roll in, Artsmark award in head's sights adding to quiverful that already includes Sing Up and Sportsmark awards (both pure gold).

Most recent success is designation as Teaching School (an eat your heart out award bestowed only on the whizziest of establishments). Confers membership of six-strong alliance who pool ideas and resources, a boon when it comes, amongst other things, to pitching for extra funds.

Range of needs includes specific learning difficulties, speech and language and behavioural, emotional and social difficulties (BESD), while Topaz unit accommodates eight pupils with Asperger's, currently all KS2 but will extend to KS1, who join peers for some lessons, often with one to one support, but have separate base with own play area (small, nicely green, enclosed by no-nonsense fencing). Once identified (here, as elsewhere, some parents call in their own experts to speed up the diagnosis) support is unstinting, with nth degree differentiation in class taken as read. Pupil with memory and processing issues had checklist of stages to tick off on wipe clean board. 'Personalised it beautifully', thought mum.

Inspires 'very warm and fuzzy feelings' towards the school, said a parent, with size a plus point rather than drawback. Thirty-strong classes, bolstered with teaching assistant while nursery sessions (25 children in each) have two nursery nurses plus teacher. 'More people means more friends', felt a year 5 pupil, though in troubled times, 'there's a room you can go to if you're sad or lonely.' Felt, however, that some peer to peer disagreements are best resolved without teacher input. 'They can make it worse'.

Parents too, favour school over other highly regarded and smaller alternatives because of what one terms 'lack of prissiness'. Whereas artwork on display elsewhere was 'incredibly beautifully framed on the wall', only the best examples had made the final cut. Here, in contrast, it was 'messy, in a good way, with pictures from even the kids who couldn't draw'.

Resulting confidence is unmissable, pupils a winningly well mannered bunch, helped to become so by oft-stressed emphasis on social skills. Lunch for reception children is part of the curriculum, with big teacher input, emphasis on eye contact and handshaking, stressed through the school, ensuring the conversational niceties are a (nicely) observed feature of school life. 'Are you having a lovely day?', head was recently asked by pupil. Impressively, words 'self-control' were all it took to calm large group of pupils: here, it's viewed as innate rather than a skill to be learned and children live up to expectations.

Equally true of trips (year 5s just back from up to the neck mud in Ashdown Forest) and school clubs (including astrophysics and Techo DJ, both catering for the starry-eyed). School stresses that 'only exemplary behaviour will be tolerated' and sanctions are well understood. 'We have a consequences list. If we're too out of control, we get sent to the head', said a pupil.

Much more, however, in the way of encouragement, explanation and reflection, from popular blue room, shoe-free, carpet rich and decorated with skyscapes, to peer mediation and circle time. Very youngest join the debate, too, with 'brilliant' nursery head encouraging exploration of moral dilemmas, in one instance through medium of glove puppets.

Parents are also expected to do their bit – recent newsletter noting rise in pupil absences the week before half term. With current 'outstanding' status at risk if attendance plummets,

nudge psychology designed to keep families onside seems to be working, thinks head.

Pupils tackle everything with gusto. Top perks include later lunch sittings and joy of second helpings for top two years (Portuguese chef's creative ways with assorted healthy options much admired, though occasional pizza and hot dogs days remain top favourites).

Responsibility also enjoyed from the off. Nursery children check themselves in online ('no need to be afraid of technology', reassures prospectus), while covetable posts for year 5 and 6 pupils include monitor who hands out free break-time snacks baked on the premises. Lessons are regarded with equal enthusiasm, consistency a big strength with two deputy heads stepping into the breach to cover staff absences. Teachers' approval counts. 'Oh, no, they'll be so disappointed in me', said reception pupil after mother threatened to expose mild cheekiness at drop off.'

Relationships are excellent. 'I love all the teachers,' says year 5 girl. 'They're really kind and make lessons fun'. Even more so now, following introduction of creative curriculum, many months in the making and all the school's own work. Substantial ring-bound master plan so full of fizzing ideas that it probably glows in the dark.

Core subjects taught by class teachers. topped up by specialists for art, some sport, music and French (rapid progress made courtesy of native speaker means 'pupils are probably bored out of their minds when they get to secondary school', thought insider). Resulting variety is relished – diplomatically. 'Nice to have a change; not that you ever get bored with your teacher', says year 5 pupil.

Spritely lessons big on group or paired activity. 'Means you can share ideas or ask if you don't understand', said pupil. Recent highlights include 'Victorian' maths (everything in imperial measurements, dunce's cap for wrong answers); hands-on science, year 5s adding bicarbonate of soda to vinegar and inflating balloons ('we weren't meant to shake it but we did, anyway',) and drama-packed history lesson, with army trenches improvised from desks and teacher 'shouting' commands (though we're sure it wasn't very loudly).

Buzz, frequently mentioned, could well be down to synapses sparking merrily away in the background as staff respond to latest gauntlet thrown down by the head. School has many laurels but you'll never find anyone resting on them. Instead, there's a ceaseless quest for improvement, anywhere and everywhere.

Some setting (maths from year 2), high achievers treated to once a week sessions in small groups, one-to-one support scooping up small numbers at risk of SATs underperformance. In 2012 though results aren't the highest in the local borough, pupil progress puts them almost at the very top. 'They may not always get it right first time, but they don't give up and keep on trying,' says a mum. Latest innovations include recruitment of weaker readers to mentor younger pupils, some improving by more than a complete SATs level in the process. School has also introduced pupil challenges to up the excitement factor, reception recently wowing head with enormous sheets of paper covered with 'the biggest numbers they could think of'.

But though competitive instincts once more considered acceptable, children know when to rein them in. Unsuccessful year 6 candidate in election for one of four team captain posts was gracious in defeat. 'I am delighted and he has my full support', he said. Politicians take note.

Fundraising clout is substantial. A jolly crowd, forging friendships that often endure well beyond the school, parents are big on purposeful socialising, coffee mornings and cake-making featuring heavily in weekly school newsletters. Have their own choir, adding to pupils' very well regarded three, plus orchestra (healthy numbers boosted by local authority-subsidised taster lessons). Take school duties extremely seriously, finding the wherewithal to equip Apple suite not once, but twice as new technology succeeds the old. Also fund and manage school's own swimming pool which 'wouldn't exist without them', says insider, in constant use from April to October. Children adore it, two even asking for donations towards running costs instead of birthday presents (surely a first).

Not the school for anyone in search of 00 gauge miniature education. This is a scaled up version that works, thanks to a head who expects non-stop excellence, staff who buy in to the challenge and pupils who benefit from constant quest to do everything that bit better every time. 'It's such a lottery', says one mum. 'You buy the house and hope for the best. I just couldn't believe my luck'.

Lathallan School

Linked school: Lathallan Senior School

Brotherton Castle, Johnshaven, By Montrose, DD10 0HN

• Pupils: 70 pupils; 40 boys and 30 girls • Ages: 8–13; prep 5–8; nursery 7 weeks to 5 years • Non-denom • Fees: Day £9,453–£13,539 pa • Independent

Tel: 01561 362220
Email: admissions@lathallan.org.uk
Website: www.lathallan.org.uk

Headmaster: Since 2011, Mr James Ferrier BA (Cantab), PGCE; (40s) educated at Hardyes School, Dorset, history and geography at Christ Church, followed by PGCE at the University of Kent. Married to Lorraine, they live on campus; two of their three children are in school. Came to Lathallalan in 2001 from Moor Park School in Shropshire where he was senior master and boys' housemaster. Entered as deputy head (of junior school) becoming head in 2007, and headmaster in 2011. Muddling aint it? Charming and relaxed, he controls his part of the Lathallan empire with gentle humour.

Entrance: Springboard Nursery: from six weeks, 80 tinies registered but no more than 49 at any one time. Handful of real babes being pushed out in three prams when we visited (good North Sea air). Nappies not a problem. This is a 50 week nursery with two weeks off for Christmas. Magic (and not at all expensive).

Entrance to junior school seamless, test-ette for problems. Juniors are checked 'carefully' and if problems obvious, they get a 'proper test'. Two dedicated learning support staff, one to one, clusters, or co-teaching. Costs the same as a piano lesson. (As in senior school). Jolly phonics, but mixture of reading strategies. French from age five, specialist teachers for IT, music, PE. Max class size 16 but most around 12/13. Uses all big school facilities (well, the labs are next door, whilst seniors have to hike a bit for science and maths). Classrooms a combo of converted stables and new build plus the obligatory Portakabin or three.

Exit: Most go on to senior school at 11. Those who are destined for trad independents leave after a couple of years in senior school to go elsewhere.

Remarks: Nursery goes from strength to strength, ditto junior school, nursery full, also first three years of junior school. Senior school seems to be settling in remarkably well. Stunning new nursery playground. Some bursarial and scholarship help available throughout.

Latymer Prep School

Linked school: Latymer Upper School

36 Upper Mall, London, W6 9TA

• Pupils: 160 girls and boys; all day • Ages: 7–11 • Non-denom
• Fees: £14,490 pa • Independent

Tel: 0845 638 5700
Email: registrar@latymerprep.org
Website: www.latymerprep.org

Head: Since 2001, the genial Mr Stuart Dorrian BA, erstwhile long-serving head of English and of lower school in the senior school who was persuaded to take over the prep, principally with the aim of upping the academics. He is a real enthusiast and clearly relishes his domain – its lovely main building, its river setting with the light that floods the place and the children who come to him naturally and easily. He still teaches some sixth form English and drama to his year 3 – so, a very nice job all in all.

Entrance: Roughly 150 compete at 7+ for the 40-odd places. They take an exam, half are invited back for some science-related activities and team-building exercises and observation. Around two-thirds are boys.

Exit: Almost all move into the senior school. One or two may be urged to consider alternatives by year 5 or early year 6 and are assisted in doing so. A few leave for boarding or because of family relocation.

Remarks: Main building is the beautiful 1800s villa, Rivercourt House, which overlooks the river and is full of light. Retains cornices, elegant staircase, pilasters, columns and decorative panelling and is a privileged environment for small children to learn in. Strange 1930s building on the other side of the small garden with maritime motifs, crinkle-crankle wall and outside spiral staircase now – once a writing studio – now The Seahorse Drama Studio. A further building, Latymer House, accommodates more classrooms, food tech, cookery and IT. It is all neat and cosy – though not over-endowed with outside space – and makes for a delightful prep.

All subjects are taught by specialists – we like that. A good little library, a large art-room at the top of the school in which we enjoyed clever printing and an imaginative project on the art of WWI. Photography thrives, music tech is offered and we saw lively work across the curriculum. All learn Italian for four years and, in year 6, they start French to prepare them for the senior school. Mr Dorrian insists that the years of Italian are not lost – 'They prepare them for the deep structures of Latin languages' – but it seemed a little illogical to us, as they can only pick up Italian again much higher up the senior school. We saw relaxed, absorbed, happy and confident little ones, clearly quite at home and busily learning. SEN support much praised by grateful parents and, in fact, we witnessed a one-to-one lesson focused on structuring and sorting and a very absorbed pupil with a lovely smiley teacher. Well worth trying to get Theo and Tilly in at seven here – probs solved until UCAS forms and student loans!

Laxton Junior School

Linked school: Oundle School

East Road, Oundle, PE8 4BX

• Pupils: 250 120 boys/130 girls • Ages: 4–11 • C of E • Fees: £9,555–£10,485 pa • Independent

---

Tel: 01832 277275
Email: lat@laxtonjunior.org.uk
Website: www.laxtonjunior.org.uk

Headmaster: Since 2008, Mr Mark Potter BEd (late thirties). Educated at Deben High School in Felixstowe and Liverpool John Moores University. Began career at St Mark's RC Primary School in Ipswich, then moved abroad to teach at schools run by Shell in Nigeria and China. Energetic, enthusiastic and very youthful. Knows virtually every child by name and enjoys chatting to them as he goes round the school. Arrived at Laxton Junior as deputy head in 2007. Six weeks later, when the head's post was advertised, he applied for and got the top job. 'It truly is a fabulous school,' he says, 'and having that year as deputy to learn from my predecessor was ideal.' Loves teaching and in his second year taught mental maths to every year group – an impressive achievement for a busy head. In 2009-10, he ran a polymath club for years 4 to 6. He's a member of Oundle School's senior management team and meets Charles Bush, Oundle's headmaster, at least once a term. Wife, Lisa, is an early years teacher and they have two young children (both now at Laxton Junior).

Entrance: Most children start in reception in the September after they are four (non-selective at this stage). Pupils joining later on spend trial day at school and also take verbal and non-verbal reasoning tests. Every year group has maximum of 40. Waiting lists for several year groups, but not all, so it's always worth talking to the school. Some means-tested bursary provision and an annual award set up in previous head's name for all-rounder entering year 5 (10 per cent of fees).

Exit: Two thirds go to Oundle School and the other third is generally split between Stamford Endowed Schools, Oakham School, Kimbolton School, The Peterborough and others.

At 11, two-thirds move on to Oundle as day pupils (the occasional boarder) but attending Laxton Junior in no way guarantees automatic passage to the senior school. Oundle's entrance exam has to be passed and as head of Laxton Junior points out, 'We have quite a breadth of ability so Oundle won't be suitable for all the children.' Others to Stamford Endowed Schools, Oakham School, Kimbolton School, The Peterborough and others. Around a quarter of each year group win music or academic scholarships to their senior schools. Occasionally a child might head to a traditional prep school like Witham Hall, Winchester House or Bilton Grange for years 7 and 8.

Remarks: Founded in 1973 but moved from its original premises in picturesque Oundle to its new purpose-built home in 2002, when the school roll doubled in size. Fantastic school building is light and airy, with wide corridors and spacious classrooms. School prides itself on its academic achievements – curriculum is based on the national one but 'adapted to suit the requirements of our children and our school'. As head says, 'Learning is at the heart of everything we do.' Two classes per year group and never more than 20 in a class. No setting, except in maths from year 4. French taught from reception and Spanish, Russian and Mandarin available as after-school activities. Older children taught by subject specialists – science and maths teachers have strong links with their counterparts at

Oundle. Everyone gets two ICT lessons a week in suite equipped with 22 computers.

Younger children do an hour's prep a week (letter sounds and reading) while older ones get 30 to 60 minutes a night. No prep set for Friday or weekends and no Saturday school. Those requiring learning support get extra help from four-strong educational support team, either in small groups or one-to-one. When we visited, 68 children were receiving help – no extra fees charged. Total of 35 teachers at school – a few are part-time but all form teachers are full-time. Around a quarter of today's primary schools don't have any male teachers at all but 18 per cent of teaching staff are men (including a teaching assistant, head of sport and form teachers in years 1 and 5).

Head firmly believes that all children should get their turn in the spotlight, whether it's for academic, sporting or artistic achievements, being polite or having 'super personal skills'. Music very popular – all year 2 children learn the violin or cello and from year 3 those wishing to continue receive group or individual lessons. Around 200 music lessons timetabled a week – everything from piano, violin and drums to the bagpipes. Hymn practice for all each week, plus orchestras, choirs and a brass ensemble to join. The children we met during our visit were very keen on sport – rugby, football and cricket for boys and netball, hockey and rounders for girls. Sports teacher says school does pretty well in matches, but he'd like 'our sporting prowess to match our academic and musical prowess'. Chess and swimming particularly strong. All year groups get one swimming lesson a week at Oundle's six-lane pool. Raft of after-school clubs and activities on offer from 3.45 to 4.45pm – choices include yoga and flower arranging!

School is C of E (has strong links with St Peter's Church in Oundle) but also celebrates other faiths. Oundle School's chapel used for carol service and end of year service. Two whole school assemblies a week, plus house and key stage gatherings on other days. School encourages children to respect others and the environment and pupils' behaviour is very good. Clear discipline system – poor behaviour is noted in the discipline book and if this happens three times pupils go 'on report', but in the past three years only three names entered. Staff keen on 'positive praise' – as we walked round the school head thanked pupils each time they held a door open. Mobiles, iPods etc aren't banned, but teachers say the children 'just don't bring them in'.

Four houses – plenty of inter-house matches and competitions. School is rightly proud of its school council, which comprises representatives from each year group, plus the head boy and girl. Recent suggestions to have been implemented include proper football goal posts and hairdryers in the girls' changing rooms. Pupils give school dinners the thumbs-up (especially the puddings) and say they like walking across to the senior school in pairs for lunch, accompanied by their teachers. When we asked about rainy days, the children told us, 'It just never seems to rain at lunch-time'. Teachers eat lunch with the children, encouraging good manners and conversation.

Head says pupils are polite, well-mannered, can hold a conversation and speak freely – and that's certainly what we found. When we asked school council members if there was anything they'd change about the school, just one grumble – 'I think the Year 4s should be allowed to read Swallows and Amazons,' requested one boy. The head promised to look into it.

Most live in Oundle and its pretty surrounding villages. The majority arrive by car, although staff are keen to encourage local children to walk to school. Parents range from those for whom 'fees are a drop in the ocean' to others who have to work flat out to send their children to the school. New parents appreciate the impressively active parent and friends' association, which organises a variety of social events and has a raft of parent reps. 'The parents are very supportive,' says head. 'We look after their babies, and they want them to be safe and secure in an environment where they are going to be successful learners with high challenge and low stress.' Excellent parent handbook details everything from the school day and behaviour code to snacks (fruit provided in morning and afternoon breaks) and uniform (blue and grey).

Last time round we commented that Laxton Junior School might be tough for the more sensitive child, but this is definitely not the case now. Led by a dynamic head, it's a happy, successful place that offers a first-class, all-round education.

Leaden Hall School

70 The Close, Salisbury, SP1 2EP

- Pupils: 160 girls; 30 boarders • Ages: 2–11 • Fees: Day £7,725–£13,125; Boarding + £5,250 pa • Independent

Tel: 01722 334700
Email: admin@leaden-hall.com
Website: www.leaden-hall.com

Headmistress: Since 2010, Mrs Julia Eager BEd (early fifties). Educated at North London Collegiate (qv), with a degree in education and music from Froebel College, London University, and an MSc in educational leadership from Leicester, she's been a thorough-going GDST girl till now, a career primary teacher specialising in music, who has worked in several GDST junior schools such as Howell's in Cardiff and Royal High Bath, before being catapulted in as acting head to Hamlets Prep School, Liverpool. A term in GDST's education office in London followed, from where she jumped ship to take up her first headship at Leaden Hall. Wife to a professional conductor and yummy mummy to three Eton music scholars, now in their late teens or early 20s, she says, 'All my girls are here'.

Parents concur that she had big shoes to fill but that she has done so superbly. Her wish to improve communication between school and home means she is to be found at the gate most mornings greeting girls by name; this accessibility extends to a swift response to any matters raised, and a demeanour so warm and approachable that girls barely knock before walking into her teddy-bear lined office. Can she be scary enough when the occasion demands? We hope so. Her personal mission on taking on Leaden Hall was to improve IT, systems and infrastructure, as well as building closer links with other Salisbury schools, emphatically not to change the feel of the place, which is one of a family where everyone goes happily about her work and is extraordinarily nice to each other. She has not been shy of introducing other improvements either, such as more sporting fixtures and shared transport with other schools, specific 11+ coaching and dealing with some "staff issues", which have gone down very well with parents. In fact, we could not find even a faintly critical word about her from any quarter.

Hobbies include music, naturally – she is an accomplished oboist and learns the harp (from the royal wedding harpist who also teaches the girls) – and a spot of tennis and reading, when not tackling Kilimanjaro or the Himalayas with her boys.

Entrance: Strictly non-selective at reception and below (EYFS), although further up, the school encourages girls to spend a day there to check it all out. Scholarships on offer for girls of outstanding talent in any area of the curriculum, but fees won't be reduced unless the criteria for bursary help are also met.

Exit: South Wilts Grammar very popular. Other choices include St Mary's Calne, Godolphin School, St Mary's Shaftesbury, Dauntsey's, St Swithun's, Leehurst, Millfield and Hampshire Collegiate. Girls regularly win academic, all-rounder and sports scholarships.

Remarks: Founded at Fareham in 1937, the school moved to its present home in the Close of Salisbury Cathedral in 1948, where it is now charmingly housed in a building of great antiquity, with a fabulous modern timber and glass classroom block at the back, and glorious grounds running down to the river, a view immortalised by Constable. The big red front door opens into a hall where a rocking horse has pride of place – it all feels like a private house, with the head's office in what was clearly once the drawing room. More classrooms and boarding happen on the upper floors of the old house and dining in a sunny conservatory. Year 6 boarders are five minutes' walk away in a sympathetically converted cottage, where they are two or three to a room.

Although very small boys are accepted in the nursery school, Leaden Hall is very much a female preserve – just one male music teacher, the IT and catering managers and two groundsmen break up the petticoat rule. But one of the most beguiling aspects of the school is that girls can be whatever they want to be. Despite the quaint uniform of a striped dress with sailor collar for summer (and a hat for each season, note), girls can (and do) do all the things boys do with impunity: get dirty, make dens, climb trees and play rugby, without any fear of teasing. Prissy they certainly are not, but the idyllic setting and sheer niceness of the girls and staff and the way they treat each other did make us wonder if it wasn't all a tiny bit precious; however the school's mantra, 'Get real, get right, get going', is an attempt to address any such notion. It's possibly the parents who are inclined to be precious on their daughters' behalf, judging by the ones we spoke to, though one said, 'It might look quaint and eccentric, but it doesn't feel precious once you're inside'.

What really blew us away was the positive experience of boarding every child and parent we spoke to mentioned. Lovely handbooks given out, including one translated into Spanish for the two or three Spanish boarders who come in year 5 and 6. One veteran mum of 14 prep schools said that her daughter 'never cried once' and that the outstanding care taken of the girls extends to the parents, particularly those overseas. Top green credentials and recognition – school has double green flag status and is current South West eco champ – come perhaps from this sense of altruism.

Academic pressure is exerted downwards by South Wilts Grammar – see above – and in the minds of some, the spectre of 11+ looms large. Nonetheless, the school appears to succeed at playing down exam stress and to count on its experience in preparing for entrance exams. Year 5 acknowledged as being especially pressured, with 11+ coming up in the November of year 6, so head takes pains to steer the unwary away from unwise choices in plenty of time: 'The head's approach to entrance exams for all schools is absolutely spot-on,' said one mother, though another mentioned the lack of a scholarship stream.

Classes are of mixed ability, but girls are put into sets from year 5 on in English, maths, sciences and languages. Latin compulsory in year 6, German and Spanish available as clubs. No Sats either in year 2 or 6, but school makes use of related material at other stages for internal assessment and tracking, something the most recent ISI report picked it up on. Enjoyment and fun struck us as a feature of the timetable, from the lessons we saw, coupled with genuine affection for teachers. English gets particular thumbs up; proposed French exchange programme; science taught in dedicated lab and dance (big take-up, with lots of adorable little moppets in tutus) and other indoor sports in beautiful light sports hall.

Sport gets good provision, considering the size of the school: hockey, netball, tennis, rounders, football all on offer, with its own tennis/netball courts, playing field and outdoor pool on site, and Cathedral School's Astro and athletics track available for loan. An indoor pool was on everyone's wish list. These days, enough fixtures with other schools to satisfy the sporty, plus some lacrosse and tag rugby from national players, no less.

L

Music much buoyed up by enthusiastic teacher, but we could see why the head was so excited about the new music room. Everybody sings and many learn musical instruments, top players reaching grade 4 or so. Performance apparently encouraged, with some ambitious and precocious choices like Romeo and Juliet, yet no-one said much about the drama, curiously. Art displayed all over the school with evident pride, but one parent reported that DT had gone off.

Other than that, remarkably few gripes about the school (in fact an overwhelming affection). Food and lack of choice came in for some criticism (head says food is very highly regarded by the majority of parents and girls and school is now providing healthy lunches for a nearby school). Bizarre and unpopular sardine pasta bake the day we visited. Girls eat their lunch in a pinny of their choice and sit in family groups.

All in all, Leaden Hall is a little piece of Eden in Salisbury, where little girls can stay little girls until they have to move on to the real world outside the Close at the secondary school of their choice – in almost all cases. As the inspector said, 'A magical school'.

Leighton Academy Primary School

Minshull New Road, Crewe, CW1 3PP

• Pupils: 520 pupils; 220 boys/200 girls; all day, 50 boys/50 girls in nursery • Ages: 3–11 • Non-denom • State

Tel: 01270 685185
Email: head@leighton.cheshire.sch.uk
Website: www.leightonacademy.com

Headteacher: Since 1998, Mr Glyn Turner MEd BA (fifties). Previously head of Tarvin Primary School. Married with three adult children. Loves sports, reading, educational issues and politics. Knows all the children, not just by name but by family history and background too. A truly hands on head, cares deeply about all his charges. Parents say, 'The school amazes me every week,' and that Mr Turner has, 'excellent leadership, enthusiasm and commitment to the school'.

Head saw Leighton as a challenge; school was operating under difficult circumstances in an area of fairly high deprivation (changed somewhat over years as notorious estates replaced by owner-occupied housing). Gone from strength to strength with just about every accolade imaginable from Dyslexia Friendly Status to Activemark Gold (twice). The school has appeared in the White Paper (Higher Standards: Better Schools For All) as a case study for intervention and personalised learning, and it is also involved in a Training and Development Agency project with modern foreign languages. It has won honorary awards from the Geographical Association for its work in geography and is the only primary school in the UK linked with the Goethe-Institut.

Entrance: Places are allocated in line with Cheshire's schools' admission policy; first to those resident within the catchment zone, together with looked after children, then siblings, followed by those not resident but attending a catchment feeder school, those with exceptional domestic reasons and, finally, those living nearest the school.

Exit: Majority to King's Grove; others to a variety including Ruskin Sports College, Sir William Stanier, Sandbach High, Malbank and St Thomas More Catholic School. Increasingly parents are opting to go further afield to schools in Sandbach.

Remarks: Truly comprehensive; pupils come from leafy suburbs and areas of high deprivation, yet school's a great leveller, offers equal ops and a bit more for those who don't get the support from elsewhere. Changing demographics and the school's reputation mean it's now oversubscribed; at one time middle class families wouldn't consider Leighton, now it's a first choice school.

Parents certainly approve, they were to be found in their droves at the start of the school day. They're welcomed into school, encouraged to work, play or socialise with their child. Praise for the school was unanimous, we tried to find a disgruntled one but they must have been taking a day off.

The school's achievements and awards rival those of many prep schools and when you walk down the picture-filled corridors it's hard to imagine you are in a deprived area, though the facilities aren't all state-of-the-art. The school is currently undergoing some renovation work on its play facilities and an outside classroom is being built. The real strengths lie in the attitude and accomplishments of the staff – there's an artist in residence, a German teacher with links to the Goethe-Institut, a speech therapist (2.5 days a week) and four reading recovery teachers. International outlook extended by links with a school in Kenya.

Leighton caters well for all children whether they are high or low achievers and much is expected of all. Mainstream SEN provision is excellent and all pupils are closely monitored with timely intervention as necessary. Trips and tours mainly day and curriculum orientated. School teams play in football and netball leagues, plenty of clubs and activities.

Excellent value added. All children are closely monitored and finely targeted with a range of expertly delivered interventions, reading recovery etc for those in need. Children are attentive, well behaved and interested, then again lessons are fun and we suspect the children aren't always aware of just how much they're learning or how far their teachers are pushing them.

One of the key strengths of the school (which became an academy in 2013) could be Mr Turner's reluctance to analyse its success, 'I'm too busy with the day job', he jokes. 'It was my choice to come here knowing what it was like. I don't want to get bogged down in notions of advantage and disadvantage but I wanted to bring the same aspirations from the very middle-class Cheshire school I was in before.' His recruitment policy encourages teachers with ambition and plans, he believes in developing leadership, even if the end result is that teachers are poached. 'If you want to pursue excellence then you bring in the specialists.' To that end there are currently six master's degrees and an ongoing PhD in the staff room. Mr Turner likes to challenge his staff, 'If you can argue why we should do something then let's do it, if you can't, let's not do it.'

Leweston Prep and Pre-Prep School

Linked school: Leweston School

Leweston Preparatory School, Sherborne, DT9 6EN

• Pupils: 75 • Ages: 2–11 • RC • Fees: Day £8,055–£12,045; Boarding £15,480–£18,345 pa • Independent

Tel: 01963 211010
Email: admissions@leweston.dorset.sch.uk
Website: www.leweston.co.uk

Headmaster: Since 2012, James Savile BEd, Fellow of College of Teachers and of Institute of Educational Assessors (mid forties), schooled at Canford and a graduate of Southampton. Mr Savile has forged a packed career in education before this first headship: as well as considerable experience of teaching junior French, sports coaching and pastoral responsibilities at several independent schools up and down the land, he has also set exams and published a revision guide for CE French. But now he is thrilled to be back in Dorset. His priorities? To build on current academic standards, and to look critically at the curriculum 'from a skills-based perspective': as he says, 'We are planning for jobs that don't yet exist, so we need to create happy life-long learners'. He is also very keen on outdoor learning, for which Leweston's extensive grounds are ideal. Changes to the school have been low-key as yet: some tarting up of the main hall to make it somewhere to celebrate the children's work, and the refocusing of the library into a resource centre with lots of ICT. Married to Heather, with his own two offspring at the school (who 'absolutely love it'), Mr Savile enjoys a spot of military history in his spare time and collects artillery cap badges.

Entrance: Essentially non-selective. Children are encouraged to come for a taster day during which teachers will informally assess them in the classroom. Little ones come for half a day. Until co-education is fully integrated from 2014, boys are taken into all year groups except year 6. Many children arrive seamlessly from the pre-prep. All newbies are tested for SEN on arrival; support is given from the Learning Success Co-ordinator (sic) and her team. Scholarships on offer for art/DT, music, drama, sport and all-round as well as academic for years 3-5.

Exit: The majority of girls to the senior school, via its own exam at 11+; some to other establishments. Boys to a variety of schools, including prep schools for years 7 and 8, which will prepare them for Common Entrance at 13, and some to The Gryphon, Sherborne's only comprehensive school. Everyone appears to be well-prepared for the next stage, whatever that may be.

Remarks: Rather idyllic small school which has benefited from the beautiful grounds, space and sporting facilities of Leweston since moving from Sherborne in 1993; it now occupies the former coach house of the manor. Happy children in small classes follow a range of subjects including French and Latin, and sciences in dedicated lab. We were impressed by a lesson which used the patterns in Roman mosaics to demonstrate symmetry. Lots of activities on offer – usual mix of music, drama (the senior school's fine showing at performing arts clearly starts here) and sport, and a keen uptake of sailing, where school does exceptionally well. A biathle coach has recently joined staff ranks to develop swimming, riding, shooting and fencing – the building blocks of modern pentathlon. Cheer-leading and chess also feature. Caring Catholic ethos much in evidence, but does not exclude those of other faiths – or none. First Communion an important event in the school calendar. The school started to phase in co-education in 2011 in response to parental demand – boys had always been admitted to the pre-prep; now amounting to nearly half the school, they nonetheless seem to keep a low profile. Head keen to develop boys' sport – a major reason why parents move their sons into the independent sector – and has appointed a director of sport to address this. Limited boarding from age 7 for girls, but not for boys – no plans to introduce it either. We suspect that most children are driven to school but there are buses laid on from Bridport, Castle Cary and Dorchester. In summary, an ideal choice for parents looking for a prep school which concentrates as much on the happiness and moral grounding of its pupils as on their academic attainment. We will watch the move to full co-education with interest.

Little St Helen's and St Helen's Junior school

Linked school: St Helen's School

Eastbury Road, Northwood, HA6 3AS

- Pupils: 460 girls • Ages: 3–11 • C of E but all faiths welcome
- Fees: £10,785–£11,289; Nursery £9,888 pa • Independent

Tel: 01923 843210
Email: admissions@sthn.co.uk
Website: www.sthn.co.uk

Headmistress: Dr Mary Short.

Entrance: At three or four by observation and interview. At seven by tests in English and maths and interview.

Exit: Usually a smooth transition from LSH to the juniors and from juniors to seniors. Very few to local state grammars, boarding or competition: 'I asked my daughter if she would like to look at other schools; she looked at me like I was bonkers.'

Remarks: 'Makes learning exciting, with no pressure', to quote a parent of her four year old – gets crisper as they get older of course. The nursery, Little St Helen's, and the junior school are all housed in buildings around this beautiful site and share many of the facilities of the senior school. Some buildings have more inviting exteriors than others; however each has bright, airy classrooms, excellent, thoughtful displays and exhibited artwork, libraries, gyms, good-sized halls or studios and is well-resourced. Much given to heartening mottoes: 'Enter with an Open Mind', 'Reach Higher than Your Dreams' – an improvement on the school's Latin one, which is an odd combination of conquering, crosses and daisies.

Lots of ICT, good DT and everyone tries out three languages before they move up to the senior school. All do ballet, PE, music and speech and drama as part of the curriculum. Happy atmosphere, lovely bright uniform, civilised loos and teachers who say, 'Ladies, will you please take off your shoes now,' to a crocodile of receptive six year olds.

A teacher and teaching assistant to each class in Little Saints plus a newly-qualified TA, some teaching assistants in junior school. 'I think these girls are so lucky,' sighed the registrar wistfully as we strolled. 'We are the lucky ones,' replied a passing teacher.

Lochinver House School

Heath Road, Little Heath, Potters Bar, Hertfordshire, EN6 1LW

- Pupils: 350 boys • Ages: 3–13 • Fees: £9,315–£12,240
- Independent

Tel: 01707 653064
Email: registrar@lochinverhouse.herts.sch.uk
Website: www.lochinverhouse.herts.sch.uk

Headmaster: Since 2011, Mr Ben Walker (late forties) BA PGCE CELTA. Educated at Lochinver House (head boy in 1977, badges proudly displayed in his office on a cut off blazer lapel), St Albans School and Reading University where he read English. A teacher by vocation, followed a non-conventional path to his current position, joining retail group C&A as a management trainee after university. Realised after a year

L

that the commercial world was 'not really for me' and took a PGCE at the Institute of Education. Spent 13 years in inner city state secondary schools, rising through the ranks, before he and his wife decided in 2002 to sell up and move the family to Kenya to carry out development work. They spent three years there starting a school, coordinating health care projects and working as Church Mission Society partners. Towards the end of that time, took a post at St Andrews, Turi, a prep school for expats and wealthy nationals, which led him on his return to the UK in 2005 to the role of deputy head at Swanbourne House in Buckinghamshire. Came full circle and joined Lochinver House as head six years later.

Calm, engaging and a natural communicator. Married to Jill, deputy head at Glendower School in Kensington, with three children – two teenage, a medical student and sixth former at Oundle School respectively, and a 13 year old daughter, a full boarder at Haileybury. Feels he inherited 'a good school with a few challenges,' the largest of which was to 'encourage celebration of the 13+ journey.' Promptly surveyed heads of top schools including St Albans School, Merchant Taylors' and Eton on the matter to strengthen his case, and has set about communicating to parents the merits of prep school until 13 from thereon.

Governors say he has made the school calmer, achieving 'stronger achievement of values' and giving it a 'stronger sense of spirituality.' Parents agree and add that he has also given the school a 'more academic feel.' Popular with pupils, perhaps because of his qualities as an educator, or perhaps because of 'headmaster's hot chocolate', a weekly Friday event for those who have received the most house credits for their efforts that week, or 'head's pub lunch,' a termly treat for one deserving boy chosen from each of the three houses.

Entrance: Currently oversubscribed and 'gently' selective. Candidates at 4 assessed informally in small groups ('a fun day,' say parents) to check suitability and potential. Boys entering higher up the school, some from state primaries and some new to area, spend a day at the school with a 'buddy' and are tested in maths and numeracy, with competition often stiff for these occasional places. Maximum class size 21.

Exit: Around 85 per cent stay to year 8, with the usually less academic remainder taking different 11+ paths to avoid the common entrance hurdle ('they can benefit from a longer run in to GCSEs,' says head) or leaving for financial reasons. A few to selective state schools. Majority to day schools including Aldenham, Habs, Haileybury, Mill Hill or St Albans, one or two to Westminster, with 'a handful' on to boarding schools in ones and twos including, recently, Bedford, Oakham, Oundle, Radley and Uppingham.

Remarks: Tucked away in residential suburbia, Lochinver House won't seduce you with its good looks, but in true ugly duckling style it could well win you over with the functionality of its bijoux eight acre site, a warren of practical facilities, all aimed at squeezing excellence out of its young charges.

Pre-prep block unlikely to win any beauty contests but has its own small library and the walls are cheered with loads of art and written work by its young residents, as well as a 'friendship tree', which gives a clue to the supportive nature of the school, with kind deeds posted as leaves on a daily basis. Also has its own garden – a haven in the North London urban jungle – where the youngest pupils grow vegetables, build, dig and have story time when weather permits. Playtimes are spent in the enclosed adventure playground (made less alluring by proximity to car park) or, for reception, in their dedicated outdoor play area away from the rough and tumble of older boys.

The star attraction from the boys' perspective is undoubtedly the huge Astroturf that sits at the front of the school and multi-tasks as play area, sports field and cricket pitch (although not

for A and B teams for fear of nearby windows). Sports fields are split between the main site and additional space across the road, offering plenty of options for matches and games practice. For older pupils, there's a lovely eco garden, complete with bug hotel and swamp-like pond, home to 'loads of newts and snails,' according to boys. Other standout facilities include a theatre, used for assemblies and the many school productions and recitals, a light and bright dining room and modern, well-equipped science labs. The senior music room recently benefited from an injection of cash, now boasting a suite of gleaming keyboards for aspiring musicians to get their tech fix.

Parents and pupils largely local with intake reflecting the North London multi-cultural mix and the majority professional, often dual income, families – 'very grounded.' A small proportion has English as an additional language but generally do not require additional support. Fees considered excellent value. Not only are they amongst the lowest in the area, but also include almost all trips and excursions, moderate learning support requirements and many after-school clubs. Extremely active PTA organises the usual fundraisers – balls, fêtes, bazaars and quiz nights – and parents say this gives the school a really family orientated feel, 'one of the school's greatest strengths.'

'Very strong' language offering according to head, with French from year 3, Latin from year 5 and Russian offered as an extension subject for the brightest in years 5 and 6. St Albans school reportedly considers Lochinver boys amongst its best linguists and has created an accelerated class almost exclusively for them when they arrive in year 9. IT, music and games taught by specialists from reception up. Setting from year 6 for maths and from year 7 for sciences. School retains two form entry format to the end of year 6, with years 7 and 8 splitting into three smaller classes, including an accelerated group. Staff described by head as 'a perfect mix of experience and youthfulness,' with 50 per cent male teachers including a rare breed – one in the junior school. Parents generally agree that 'the teaching staff really make the school,' with just the odd grumble about a job share in the junior school having an impact on teacher/pupil relationships. Majority of classes held in form rooms until year 5, when boys start to move around school for specialist teaching in all subjects – 'brilliant preparation for my next school,' said one. Good scholarship output with around 10 most years to a variety of next schools.

No statemented children but a number supported in various ways by a 'highly qualified' full time SEN coordinator plus team. Head is proud of the level of support they give as a primarily academic school to lost sheep. Special adjustments also made for gifted pupils with those in senior years encouraged to undertake independent project work to stretch their abilities – 'children's specific needs are met,' according to parents, although some muttered about lack of recognition for less academic boys: 'all the awards go to the clever ones.'

Musical pursuits 'very popular,' says head, with almost 80 per cent of all pupils learning an instrument and half of that number learning two. Compulsory recorder in year 2 and between six and eight musical recitals every year – 'We try to create a balance,' says head. 'Parents want breadth.' Plenty of opportunities for the thespian community to shine too, with performances for all year groups and a major production each year, most recently Joseph, with almost everyone getting involved either on stage or behind the scenes.

Head also proud of school's sporting prowess: 'we punch way above our weight.' In addition to the usual competitive suspects (rugby, football and cricket), boys are also able to sample the likes of sailing, golf and tae kwon do and report that sports day is 'very competitive.' A-C teams throughout the school for major sports, so 'almost everyone gets a chance to play,' say parents. A plethora of after-school clubs on offer from year 2 upwards, including horror film making, debating, model making and, for prospective new age men, cookery and touch typing.

Good happy vibe ('it feels like my family,' said one year 8 boy). Boys in years 3 to 8 are reading buddies to little ones in reception and year 1 and the popular house buddy system from year 3 up galvanises vertical relationships up and down the school, with other initiatives such as the pupil-run ABC (anti bullying council) in place to deal with the usual friendship issues and playground problems. Parents 'feel supported' when problems arise and report that they are generally dealt with proactively and in collusion with home.

Daily assemblies replaced by house tutor groups for boys in years 6 to 8 with daily discussions covering topics such as self-awareness, democracy and friendship, aiming to prepare them for the world at large and strengthen inter-year relationships at the top of the school. Two head boys elected by teachers and supported by three vice captains (one for each house). Immense leadership opportunities on offer for elected prefects, with the head boy's charity (chosen from a selection in a whole-school ballot) raising up to £20,000 each year for local causes.

Head sees wrap-around care as 'an important part of what we do,' and offers a free early morning club from 7.45am, teatime club running to 5.30pm (including tea for those that want it) and homework club (both charged as extras) for older boys, in addition to the array of extracurricular activities that keep boys at school after hours. School minibuses ferry children from Mill Hill, Southgate and Goffs Oak directions for a small daily charge, mornings only.

Lockers Park School

Lockers Park Lane, Hemel Hempstead, HP1 1TL

• Pupils: 150 boys; approximately a third are full boarders or flexi-boarders • Ages: 5–13 • C of E • Fees: Day £9,300–£15,210; Boarding £20,400 pa • Independent

Tel: 01442 251712
Email: secretary@lockerspark.herts.sch.uk
Website: www.lockerspark.herts.sch.uk

Acting headmaster: Since 2013, Chris Wilson. Educated at Oundle School and Newcastle and Cambridge Universities. Previously deputy head at Lockers Park and before that was housemaster at Winchester House, where he taught maths and Latin. Married to Hayley.

Entrance: Having resisted the temptation to add a nursery class – plenty locally that do the job well, according to the head – takes boys from five, who join the year one class (known as 'Chestnuts'). A tie-up with nearby girls' school, Abbots Hill, which takes boys in the nursery. After that, and spaces allowing, boys can arrive at any time from state or prep schools – the oft-cited reason for the move being that boys find they are not suited to the level of attainment and behaviour set by co-ed schools.

'No entry exam as such,' says school – uses a 'simple academic assessment test' in verbal and numerical reasoning designed to spot 'potential' and an interview. 'We want boys with a spark,' says head. A scholarship day in early February when boys can try out for up to 50 per cent remission in fees according to academic ability, talent in music, art or sport or all-round. Historically has offered a lot of bursaries and the head is trying to encourage boys living within walking distance to take advantage.

Exit: Most popular destinations are Harrow, Bedford, Stowe, Berkhamsted, Bradfield, St Albans, Rugby. Several academic, drama, music scholarships every year – two for Harrow and one for Merchant Taylors' in 2012. 'Lockers Park really finds the right shape peg for each boy,' says a parent. 'The head and staff know each individual boy so well that they can recognise strengths and weaknesses and advise parents on the best possible next step.'

Remarks: Boys can be boys here – positively encouraged in every aspect of life at this singularly male-focused school. From the 40-minute morning break – ringing the bell to signal the end of it prompts a swarm of faces to emerge from the shrubbery and belt across the rolling parkland – to the well-considered structure of classes, lessons and activities, purpose-built to bring out the best in a boy.

Founded in 1874 as a feeder school for Rugby, on the train line, red-brick buildings sit in 23 glorious acres of woodland, playing fields and sports pitches that have since been engulfed by one of the less prepossessing suburbs of Hemel Hempstead. But this just serves to emphasise this close-knit Boys' Own world – 'There's no real stress or pressure,' reports a parent. 'The boys work hard when they have to, but there is nothing that gets in the way of them being children.' Certainly the atmosphere is matey and informal, characterised by the lack of uniform – boys wear blue cords and their own choice of check shirt, with grey flannels, a tie and tweed jacket for 'best' – and the friendly staff, who work with small classes – 13 on average and a maximum of 16 – giving real attention to each individual.

A long day – up to 12 hours, including breakfast, lunch and supper, even for day boys if they want it – and a fifth board full-time, which all helps to cement the community feel. 'If you ask the boys who is a boarder and who is a day boy, they probably won't be able to tell you – there is so much flexibility,' said the last head. Unusually, the boarding house is part of the main school building and is presided over by the history teacher, who is housemaster, supported by three matrons, two living in. The dorms are bright and functional and boys can chose their beds and bring their own duvet covers. Clothes are kept in the laundry room and the matrons lay out each boy's outfit for the day.

The good boarding arrangements and convenient location just off the M25 tempt boys from London, overseas and the forces, although many are from local families. Unusual system of exeats – two weekends on and one off, so one every third weekend, from Friday lunchtime to Monday morning. On non-exeat weekends Saturday school until lunchtime, then fixtures in the afternoon.

Although a gentlemen's club feel to the original part of the school – the rather Spartan dining hall is panelled and furnished simply with long tables and chairs engraved with the names of former pupils – the classrooms are bright and welcoming, especially in the main teaching block, where younger classes are taught in their forms; year 5 up have specialist teachers and are arranged by ability rather than age. Languages a speciality – French and Latin, with the option of Spanish and ancient Greek, and even Esperanto for the year 8 scholars. Justifiably proud of its academic record – around a dozen secure top scholarships. Academic lessons make as much use of the grounds and outside space as possible – when we visited, a science class was investigating the speed of sound by banging saucepans.

The inviting library has plenty of space for browsers and the whole school can fit into the chapel at a push. Favourite hang-outs for boys are the so-called 'boys' hall', which has a whiteboard with communications to pupils and is decorated with strewn bits and bobs of sporting paraphernalia, and the old gym, essentially a rec room for snooker and free time. Boys' pride and joy, though, is the 'train room', filled with a huge model railway layout with numerous engines and complete with scenery, which the boys tinker with.

Although the school buildings are generally in excellent nick, the last head had a plan to revamp the hall, with its sunken seating area and a stage, to create a mezzanine level. However he departed after only three years, so we await Mr Farquharson's take on things. DT has recently been re-housed in a new block at the back of the school and is sensibly divided into a design room and a work room, to circumvent the problem of boyish fiddly fingers. Large art room inspires one or two boys a year to gain scholarships to next school. Good size, modern sports hall.

Outside, plenty of space to roam. Cricket nets at the front of the school, and at the back is a football field slightly on the slope, but as the head points out, 'It's a game of two halves'. Rugby matches often field 100 boys – two-thirds of the school – but also plenty of inter-set matches that call for every boy to take part. Tucked away are tennis courts and a swimming pool, as well as a nine-hole golf course, which needs some attention, head admits. A plot for vegetable growing, croquet lawn and putting green.

Daily session of games or activities in the afternoons, determined by boys' interest and prowess, which takes in the traditional sports plus jujitsu, shooting and more. Ninety-five per cent of boys learn an instrument, many two, while the chapel choir is made up of 20 boys from all years. One major annual drama production and several others besides. Taking part is key here and great efforts are made to ensure that every boy feels he belongs.

In particular, great indulgence for the quirks of life at Lockers, which are so numerous that newcomers are issued with a handbook to explain the finer points. Most baffling to the uninitiated is the school's own lingo – 'slatter' is sweets, named after a former master; houses are 'sets'; 'spin the platter' and 'bell and bolster' are traditional games that have been played at the Christmas feast since the First World War. School rules are kept to a minimum – instead an all-pervading ethos of Christian values and good citizenship, and punishments are rarely necessary, thanks to a system of rewards for success and good behaviour.

In all, a boarding prep that has hit on a winning formula of security, activity and motivation designed to prepare boys to continue with confidence and success to major public schools. Head has much to build on.

Lomond School Junior Department

Linked school: Lomond School

10 Stafford Street, Helensburgh, G84 9JX

• Pupils: 160; 95 boys/65 girls; • Ages: 3–10 • Non-denom • Fees: £4,950–£9,810 pa • Independent

Tel: 01436 672476
Email: admin@lomondschool.com
Website: www.lomondschool.com

Head of junior school: Mrs Stephanie Hart

Remarks: For details, see senior school.

The London Oratory School Junior House

Linked school: The London Oratory School

Seagrave Road, London, SW6 1RX

• Pupils: 80 boys; all day • Ages: 7–11 • State

Tel: 020 7385 0102
Email: admin@los.ac
Website: www.london-oratory.org

Head: Since 2007, Mr David McFadden, head of The London Oratory School in its entirety.

Remarks: Not a separate school but a separate wing: the junior house, with four classrooms, a choir room and several practice rooms, as music is everything here. Officially it is part of the senior school, but it is the part which takes under-age boys (7-11). Unofficially, it operates rather like a choir school in a cathedral school – only without the boarding. In that respect it is unique – the only state choir school. For potential applicants, who must be of at least average ability, musical promise is the only criterion which counts here, once you have demonstrated your Catholic credentials – all the boys have musical potential. Entrance tests in academic and musical aptitude. Not all boys are in the Schola – some just follow an instrumental course. The Schola sings every Saturday evening in the Brompton Oratory. Junior house boys play every instrument you can name under the care of innumerable peripatetic teachers of high quality and use all the senior school facilities. They tour, record and give stunning concerts. A super start in life for your musical, Catholic, motivated little boy.

Loretto Junior School aka The Nippers

Linked school: Loretto School

North Esk Lodge, North High Street, Musselburgh, EH21 6JA

• Pupils: 190; 85 girls/105 boys; boarding and day; • Ages: 3–12; • Non-denom; • Fees: Boarding £18,150; Day £4,200–£13,410 pa; • Independent

Tel: 01316 534570
Email: juniorschool@loretto.com
Website: www.loretto.com

Head of the Junior School: Since April 2009, Mr Philip Meadows MA(Cantab), Cert Ed. Head of chemistry at Loretto 1987-96, then housemaster at Sedbergh School and head of Mowden Hall School, Northumberland, and Tettenhall College Junior School (a day school in Wolverhampton). Married to Sylvia, three teenage children, two of whom are still at Loretto. Comfortingly larger than life, Meadows came over brilliantly on school's video. Still teaches chemistry. Confidential manner and utterly reassuring, a wow with nervous parents.

Entrance: School bulging with 190 pupils. Small numbers come in at age of three from nursery and are joined by throngs at age 12 when pupils prepare for big school proper. Entry at all stages throughout the junior school. Five year olds take an 'informal' test. Scholarship awards (academic and all-rounder) may be offered to external candidates at 11 and 12 years old, these last for their entire time at Loretto. Some academic exhibitions for current pupils aged 10.

Exit: Almost all of the Nipper pupils move up to the senior school at 12, occasional logistical drop out.

Remarks: Super school. Combo of Victorian villas (terrific tiled floors) amalgamated with gardens converted into playgrounds, north of River Esk from main school. Logistically probably quite awkward to work in, but friendly enough not to intimidate. Junior boarding house currently being gutted and the few boarders, mainly in their last year at the Nippers, share junior boarding accommodation with Loretto proper. Space in junior boarding houses for the odd bed and breakfaster. Parents can drop children from around 8am and collect up to 6.30 after supervised prep. Generously staffed. All assessed aged nine, extra help tailored to child. French from early, two French specialists. Science lab and computer room linked via cable to the communications and resource centre in senior school; shares main school facilities such as the Astroturf (which, to be honest, is quite a long hike for smaller legs) and theatre. Lots of extra-curricular activities: judo, skiing, juniors join senior pipe band. Parent-inspired knitting club deeply popular.

Ludgrove

Wixenford, Wokingham, RG40 3AB

- Pupils: 185 boys; all board • Ages: 8–13 • C of E • Fees: £24,000 pa • Independent

Tel: 01189 789881
Email: office@ludgroveschool.co.uk
Website: www.ludgrove.net

Headmaster: Since September 2008, Simon Barber BA PGCE (forties). Mr Barber is the latest in the illustrious line of Barbers who have run Ludgrove. After an 'amusing' spell in the City, he decided that teaching was, after all, the right job for him and he cut his teeth at Ashdown House before joining the staff at Ludgrove. He is married to the delightful Sophie, who is responsible for the day-to-day running of the school. Together they live in the midst of the boys and closest to the youngest, who seem to share the landing with the Barbers' three young children – a home within a home. It really does feel as if they are parents of an extended family.

Up until September 2013 he was joint head with Sid Inglis (now head of Elstree School). Teaches at least 20 periods a week, gets stuck into games, coaches with enthusiasm and is tremendous fun.

Entrance: Being a proper boarding school and with a justifiably good reputation, they have a large catchment area with boys as far away as Yorkshire and Suffolk. A large number come from the London area – 'boys are relieved to be fully involved seven days a week, rather than sitting in the car bored to tears while their sisters are driven to ballet lessons'. Ludgrove is a school with demanding academic standards, and although no entrance test, much is expected. Early registration is recommended: schools which are boarding only cannot be very flexible with numbers – it's all down to beds.

Exit: Eton, Harrow, Radley most popular destinations. Others to Marlborough, Bradfield, Tonbridge, Winchester and Stowe.

Remarks: The majority of boys enter aged eight and are sympathetically eased into the school with the help of an obviously very competent team of teachers. These boys, who expressed unbridled happiness with their lot, are taught in a separate wing of the main building and cocooned carefully before hatching out into the main school, where their 'shadows' lead them around assiduously. They are introduced to various activities to see what they like – judo is very popular – and careful preparation is the key. It shows – from natural good manners to spontaneous pleasure and alertness.

The school's policy on bullying is clearly defined and implemented. 'The head would rocket down on any bullying,' one boy told us. School has a new 'listening ear' outsider for those who might require extra soothing and advice; according to one of our guides, the previous one was only contacted once when a boy couldn't find his Fives gloves. Nevertheless, as with all schools, always the possibility of bullying, and staff are not only alert to that but also reminded of the importance of setting a good example. Boys assured us that plenty of people to whom they could talk, including the long-serving groundsmen and wise old carpenter who, after all, taught Mr Barber as a boy. In fact the community feeling of the school is most reassuring.

Excellent learning support. Every boy is screened on arrival and dyslexics are given one-to-one help (about 15 per cent) with another five per cent who regularly attend for TLC 'to help their self-esteem'. Some cracking good female teachers at this boys' school and not just for the new boys. The impressive head of science, for instance, helps to counter any myth that 'girls can't change light bulbs'.

'Mr Barber is a little more modern than Mr Gerald,' said one boy, while expressing much admiration for both. Mr Barber objected to the phrase 'a little more' and showed us the newly carpeted dorms and landings covering the old lino, mourned by some boys who enjoyed sliding about on it. But the real excitement when we visited was the installation of a splendid new bathroom with showers, baths and everything else you would expect. Indeed such was the excitement that The Ludgrovian, a delightful home-grown weekly magazine, featured a huge photograph on the front with the caption, 'Cleanliness is next to godliness', and recording for posterity the name of the first boy to use the new showers.

Classrooms are well equipped with whiteboards, interactive boards, computers and all that jazz. Music school also well equipped and with pictures of boys who've achieved grade 5 on the Wall of Fame. Over 100 boys learn instruments – but 'we could do with some cellists,' says the infectiously enthusiastic young director, who recently persuaded the whole school – including cooks and bottle washers – to join in a singathon. Art, pottery and carpentry are timetabled in for all boys, including scholars; everyone is expected to try something extra-curricular. Staff appear young and enthusiastic – for the most part – though it's good to see some wise old heads around. 'It's a funny thing,' said one older boy, 'but staff don't seem to leave Ludgrove.' 'A good thing, on the whole,' commented a parent.

The first three heads of Ludgrove were international footballers and the enthusiasm for sport remains. 'The school is justifiably proud of its sports record,' says Mr Barber, and boys of all abilities are involved in matches. All the usual games are on offer, from fencing to clay pigeon shooting, and more. Two squash courts and two fives courts, a nine hole golf course and a recently built heated indoor pool, a brand new Astro, a jumbo sports hall and 130 acres of grounds and woodlands in which to build camps (very popular), plot dynasties and indulge in every boy's favourite occupation of mucking about.

Weekends are full – 'It's impossible to be bored with these fabulous grounds,' said one young enthusiast, and every two or three weeks exeats from Friday midday to Sunday evening. (A minibus is laid on to Fulham – revealing.)

For a few – mostly people who haven't visited Ludgrove – 'the school is stuck in something of a time warp'. For others, 'it's a bastion of good manners and courtesy where boys can be boys and, above all, have fun while fulfilling their potential'. Yes, some features which might be considered old fashioned – the carpentry shop, for instance, but it's hugely popular and buzzes at weekends with evidence of excellent (and practical) work; modelling – the creative sort – is very popular, too. The ear-splitting cheers which broke out when Mr Barber entered the dining room holding aloft a batch of recently arrived modelling kits showed that television is not all-pervading; mobile phones are not allowed, but all boys have access to emails, though after chapel on Sunday boys write handwritten letters (sic). If such outdated habits induce thoughts of walrus moustaches and Luddites, look elsewhere or, better still, look more closely.

Not everyone likes single sex schools rather than co-ed – often those considerations blind parents to what a good school is. For those who value a school with lightness of touch but with firmly held principles based on understanding what makes boys tick; for those who aspire to a particular niche and want their sons to be happy with the chance of fulfilment; for those who wish to celebrate the richness of boyhood, this could be the school. Don't go because of the 'Who's Who' of names on the dining room wall – that's not what it's about. It won't suit everyone but it's well worth a visit – surely that's why no prospectus.

LVS Ascot (The Licensed Victuallers' Junior School)

Linked school: LVS Ascot (Licensed Victuallers' School)

London Road, Ascot, SL5 8DR

• Pupils: 175; (100 boys and 77 girls); 15 boys and 5 girls board in years 3–7 • Ages: 4–11 • C of E • Fees: Day £8,520–£10,200; Boarding £21,795 pa • Independent

Tel: 01344 882770
Email: registrar@lvs.ascot.sch.uk
Website: www.lvs.ascot.sch.uk

Headmaster: Since 2012, Mr Nick Funnell. A maths/science graduate, he was a career naval man – he became senior military adviser and commanded his own ship before turning to teaching. Says he is 'fortunate to have a committed, unique and talented team of staff experienced in identification, nurturing and development of our students.'

Entrance: Most children arrive in reception (single form to year 2) or year 3 (two forms to year 5). Predictable trickle in and out in other year groups. No particular feeders – pupils arrive from variety of mainly local state and private schools with about 10 from overseas (Russia, Korea and USA currently amongst nations represented) and similar number of ex-pats including Forces families. Non-selective entry and ease of passage to senior school is a big draw.

Exit: Vast majority to senior school on same site, helped by increasing levels of information sharing that makes transition as happy and seamless as possible.

Remarks: A happy, calm school on the ground floor with junior boarders living above the shop and a high-vis staff room, long on glass, short on privacy (but they don't seem to mind). Jolly class photographs at entrance show 35 staff (40-ish on average, around a fifth have been there 10 years or more) as a cheerful and energetic bunch. Year 3 teachers (and their classes) break into spontaneous song about Mothers' Day as proof. 'It happens a lot here,' says one, who's also, as it turns out, responsible for school's huge, ambitious productions with 100-strong cast (all

'proper' parts: 'People don't want to be a third tree') and special effects including ultra-violet bubbles and even an exploding shark – 'every gizmo I can get into it'. Every other summer there's a Dance for Fitness workshop instead – fun and worthy, no doubt (and considered sufficiently cool for embarrassment-free participation by older boys) though you sense teacher's regret that it can't be waterfalls of lights and smoke effects every year.

Though unremarkable on the outside (80s autumnal-shaded brickwork) the interior is inviting, courtesy of friendly, light, corridors and big, airy hall and homely touches like cheerful curtains in classrooms. Original breezeblock interiors have mostly had a much-needed paint job, revamp imminent for slightly echoing library/art/ICT area. Space mainly well thought out, with sliding doors that allow different-sized groups to work together and good use of shared areas – infants often join forces for creative group work like button-making and flower-arranging.

The mood, purposeful without being manic, extends to outdoor space – good-sized infants' play area with buddy bench (hardly used, though, insist pupils 'because there's a bare minimum of people who feel sad') and lots of sturdy wooden equipment to climb and balance on. Year 3s and up enjoy scaled up versions in adjoining area, separated by unmarked but universally recognised boundary line. Reception also have smart new outdoor classroom and cheerful playhouse, starting point for innumerable let's pretend games. Eagerly awaited musical train complete with three carriages and bells (if no whistles) currently being built by senior school sixth former as part of DT A-level is arriving soon.

Head's mission is to ensure that no child is left to languish in educational no man's land and meets class teachers regularly to pick out those 'falling below or zooming ahead'. Children give a high rating to all subjects, particular favourites being literacy (popular library-based reading scheme which carries on into main school tests comprehension rather than merely rewarding headlong dash for the last page) and science in year 6 – where, joy of joys, 'you get to light the Bunsen burner'. They're also unexpectedly appreciative of small teaching groups (average is about 12 to one). 'In state schools you have 60 in a class,' says one horror-struck year 6 guide. Lots of clubs, too from choir and orchestra (45 learn instruments from beginner to grade four) to cookery.

There's minimal setting (maths from year 3) and a pick and mix approach to national curriculum – used or modified where it works, ditched if it doesn't (children's progress well ahead of national averages). Everything is seasoned with welcome dash of carpe diem flexibility so teachers can go off piste if not-to-be-missed educational opportunities present themselves; recent stick collection and den-building exercise for reception was a case in point. Lots of popular outings, too, including the inevitable trip to Swanage.

Senior school specialists teach languages, games and PE through the school (DT added in year 5) and everyone gets weekly lessons in appealing seniors' indoor pool (happy-looking four and five year olds bob around like so many ducklings) – while school chaplain leads some assemblies. One parent felt senior staff knowledge of juniors could be better – 'don't always know names and ability'. Rare, counters head, and outweighed, she feels, by benefits of working with range of teachers – gentle introduction to life in senior school.

There's also the occasional appearance of traditionally-dressed school nurses, complete in every detail (including lapel watches) and clearly born to bustle.

Facilities excellent. Everyone crosses to welcoming senior school dining hall for lunch (breakfast and evening meal, too if boarding or staying for extended day) with waited service for infants and year 1 children and everyone else joining the queue. Meals are highly rated (soup, baguettes, jacket potatoes and puds particular favourites) and there are sensible but low key checks – 'when you've finished, you put your hand up and the teachers check you've have eaten enough' – to monitor consumption levels.

Junior boarding, extending from year 3 to year 7 (means first year seniors avoid double whammy of being youngest pupils in lesson time and out of it) is occasional, weekly or full (no flexi, though extended day, running to 6.15pm for year 3 up does help working parents). 'Lots of flexibility,' says one father. Four to six beds the norm in comfortable, some-frills dorms (refurb is due) and cosiness factor set to max courtesy of experienced houseparents, experts at sidestepping homesickness and ditching superfluous rules like complex laundry rules – 'I'd much rather you were clean than worried about what day you need to put your washing in,' says one – and organising steady but not relentless stream of activities from house talent shows to relaxed Saturday breakfasts in pjs.

School works hard to raise aspirations without upping the pressure. Parental feedback – 'not sure what a hothouse is,' said parent, when questioned – suggests it's working. Could all too easily become mere adjunct to attention-grabbing senior partner and head has, you suspect, done some fairly energetic flag waving to raise profile with colleagues. Message getting through that 'we don't just cut and stick but have some really good things going on. Now, we shine.' With school accruing pupil numbers like rolling snowball, families clearly agree.

The Lyceum

Kayam House, 6 Paul Street, London, EC2A 4JH

• Pupils: 95 boys and girls (including nursery); all day • Ages: 3–11
• Non-denom • Fees: £13,050 pa • Independent

Tel: 020 7247 1588
Email: admin@lyceumschool.co.uk
Website: www.lyceumschool.co.uk

Heads: Opened in September 1997 by Lynn Hannay Cert Ed, now director of curriculum, and Jeremy Rowe BEd, now managing director. They formerly worked in the state sector as head and deputy of a challenging Hackney primary but eventually, fed up with 'endless government interference and a growing mountain of paper', decided to go it alone. Before they did so, however, they wrote a book describing their ideal school and The Lyceum is modelled on that template. Their priorities, then and now, were to create a liberal, progressive, child-centred education where tests and targets are definitely not a priority and creativity very much is. Both continue to teach – Rowe maths, Hannay English. He is passionate about the role of the arts in education, especially music, and is programme director of the Wagner Society. She is particularly interested in environmental studies.

Entrance: The school started with an advertisement in the Evening Standard and just 16 families, but over the past decade its reputation and student numbers have grown steadily and it's now waiting list only, if you don't register early. Parents are recruited via 'dinner parties in Islington' and come largely from Islington, Hackney and, increasingly, the City. Places at three or four are allocated on a first come first served basis with priority to siblings. A few place for seven year olds and the odd vacancy later on, all awarded after assessment.

Exit: A few occasionally leave at seven for schools like City of London School for Girls but The Lyceum is reluctant to prepare children for exams at this point and most parents make the decision to stay till 11. The opposite of an exam factory –

though children are carefully prepared for entrance tests at 11, this is not necessarily the ideal place for those looking for the most academic London day schools. A sprinkling each year to Highgate, UCS and City of London, otherwise the majority to Queen's College, North Bridge House and Portland Place. Pupils are particularly successful at winning scholarships for the arts and music – a number go to The Purcell School and St Marylebone School.

Remarks: A short walk from Liverpool Street and Moorgate, housed in a former warehouse, which from the outside looks like an ordinary office block. All classrooms, except for the nursery, in a spacious open-plan space in the basement – 'I prefer everything open plan,' says Hannay. 'That way problems don't arise.' Mornings are predominantly given over to academic work (generally topic-based, though with specialist teaching in French (from reception), Latin, maths and music) and afternoons devoted to creativity (music, painting, dance, drama as well as sport). Though the school has no outside space, it deals with the problem imaginatively with a covered playground for break plus trips to the local TTA training ground for organised games and to nearby Broadgate Centre for skating, where a qualified ice-dance instructor means the children learn to skate remarkably well. Every child does some form of physical activity every day.

Non-selective and has a SENCo, but can feel a child is beyond its range – 'We can cope with minor learning difficulties but have occasionally advised parents they will need more specialist help'. The atmosphere is thoroughly unpressured. No end of year exams until pupils start preparation for 11+ in the summer term of year 5 (though verbal and non-verbal reasoning taught from year 3) because it's felt that exams impinge on the 'real' education the school is giving. Year groups are small – largest 19, smallest 10 – and sometimes classes are merged to make up the numbers for games or other activities.

Art and music are both unusually strong – all music teachers are professional musicians – with three productions a year of drama, dance and music. Every child is taught the recorder from the start and also learns to sing; most take a second instrument as well. Dynamic displays of art throughout the building. Lots of residential trips from year 3, based round subjects – a year 6 trip, for example, to France to study Monet's garden. Also residential trips for seven year olds (overnight) and 10 year olds (a week).

The approach is generally down to earth with a sensible navy and white uniform. Strong emphasis on traditional manners. Few behavioural problems. One of the school's key benefits is that it is tailored to the needs of working parents. Many parents are City workers (though plenty in the media as well) and hours reflect their working day, so school starts at 8.30am and, for those who wish it, continues to 5.45pm with a wide range of after-school clubs (sport, chess, jazz band, cinema). 'It means, instead of nannies, we often have a very good relationship with parents.' All children bring packed lunch.

Suits those for whom exam statistics are not life's ultimate aim and, for those parents, does a remarkably good job. 'It's not a hothouse but it teaches kids to think for themselves. Not every child is going to get into Westminster, but it's a lot more academic than it was and they undoubtedly bring out the best in everyone,' enthuses one mother of three pupils. 'It's a lovely school.'

Produces well-rounded and enthusiastic pupils, with a mature attitude, who manage the transition to secondary school unusually well.

Magdalen College School Junior School

Linked school: Magdalen College School

Cowley Place, Oxford, OX4 1DZ

- Pupils: 100 boys; day • Ages: 7–11 • Fees: £14,096–£14,628 pa
- Independent

Tel: 01865 242191
Email: registrar@mcsoxford.org
Website: www.mcsoxford.org

Head: Since September 2012, Tim Skipwith, previously head of the middle school (years 9 – 11), a biology teacher who has been at the school for the best part of a decade. He will 'be a wonderful guide for parents on the 11+ process' and is reputedly very hot on pastoral issues. As the third head in a short space of time, we hope his tenure will be a long and stable one.

Entrance: At 7+ by maths and English papers plus a half day of group activities. 'Attention is paid to each child's co-operation, enthusiasm, self-discipline and ability to concentrate.' At 8+ and 9+ by maths, English and verbal reasoning papers plus interview. Junior school pupils all take the same 11+ exam as outside applicants to the senior school, and in 2013 all passed. Auditions for choristers in October and January.

Exit: Nearly all to the senior school. Occasional families encouraged to look elsewhere.

Remarks: Housed in the original 1893 School House just down the road from the senior school, but shares all the senior school facilities. Bright-eyed, bushy-tailed boys perform in productions of Oliver and Noye's Fludde, win national chess competitions, compete in house music events, play football, cricket and tag rugby. Refreshingly, sufficient teams and fixtures to give almost everyone a chance to play for their school. The academic pace can be a shock to those coming in from more relaxed establishments, especially as the 11+ exam looms. They learn French from year 3 and can go to Spanish and German clubs. Everyone is assessed in year 5 for special educational needs and can have one-to-one help as necessary. 'I'm glad they're so rounded,' said a parent. 'It's a very happy school.'

Maidwell Hall School

Maidwell, Northampton, NN6 9JG

- Pupils: 90 boys, 23 girls. Virtually all boarders • Ages: 7–13
- C of E • Fees: Boarding £23,250; Day £14,325 pa • Independent

Tel: 01604 686234
Email: headmaster@maidwellhall.co.uk
Website: www.maidwellhall.co.uk

Headmaster: Since 2001, Mr Robert Lankester MA PGCE (fifties). Educated at Elstree School, Charterhouse and Selwyn College, Cambridge, where he read history. Worked as city stockbroker for seven years before deciding he wanted to teach – 'the best decision I ever made.' After PGCE at Durham, he spent 13 years at Uppingham, ten as a housemaster. Enthusiastic and focused, with firm, no-nonsense approach. School has thrived under his leadership and introduction of girls in September 2010 – 'a very exciting development,' he says – has gone smoothly. Head says girl numbers won't go above 50 at the very most. He's adamant that Maidwell will remain a small, full boarding school but transitional boarding for two or three nights has recently been introduced as an option for local day children. Loves teaching and still manages to fit six periods of geography for CE pupils into his busy week. 'He is an exceptional headmaster,' one parent told us. 'He believes in bringing the best out of every child.' Married, with two grown-up children. Carey, his charming Montessori-trained wife, is very involved in school life. She is in charge of the girls (housemistress will be appointed once the new girls' house opens), head of swimming, teaches drama and does a host of boarding duties (boys and girls). Family lives in leafy wing of the main school.

Entrance: 'We have a very broad intake,' says the head. 'Our target is to get the pupils into their first choice of school at 13 and we've succeeded in that for the last 13 years.' Boys and girls arrive from pre-preps and state primaries and visit a year prior to entry for informal assessment – maths, reading, spelling, non-verbal reasoning and relaxed 10 minute chat with head. Smattering of scholarships and bursaries available – though 'there isn't a bottomless pit of gold.' Head keen to dispel the notion that pupils have to be extrovert, outdoorsy types. 'Any child would thrive here and it's unusual for me to say no,' he says, while his wife comments that the pupils are 'nurtured and looked out for.' All have a 24-hour boarding trial the summer before they start, 'just to get them (and their mothers) used to the idea.' Most pupils live up to two hours away and are from rural areas (Lincs, Notts, Rutland, Leics, Cambs, East Anglia etc) but a few come from London area. Handful from abroad, including Spain, Japan, China, Thailand and Russia. Some children of Old Maidwellians. Old boys include Earl Spencer and former poet laureate Sir Andrew Motion.

Exit: Boys progress to a wide variety of senior schools, including Eton, Harrow, Winchester, Radley, Stowe, Oundle, Uppingham and Rugby. School reckons girls are likely to choose co-ed schools like Stowe and Oundle, or single-sex Queen Margaret's, York, and Tudor Hall. Two or three scholarships a year.

Remarks: Eleven miles north of Northampton, in a pretty country village. School was founded in 1913 and moved to present 44-acre site in 1933. Main building is an imposing 17th century turreted mansion overlooking its own lake (pupils must pass swimming test before they are allowed anywhere near it). Spacious grounds mean children can build camps, climb trees (the favourite tree is called Radar) and play hide and seek and British Bulldog in their spare time. We visited on Shrove Tuesday and arrived in the middle of the annual (and hotly-contested) house pancake race. Lots of debate about how high the pancakes must be tossed, with welly-clad director of studies joking 'there may have to be a stewards' inquiry.'

Classes are small. Maximum 15, but more likely to be around 12. Two streams in each year group (maths setted separately) and lessons taught by subject specialists. Traditional curriculum (including French and Latin, and Greek for senior pupils). Extra one-to-one SEN provision (from three-strong SEN team) at £20 per lesson for those with mild dyslexia and dyspraxia. Despite gloomy headlines about reluctant readers, most pupils read avidly. They all have 20-minute reading period every day after lunch, either in dorms or outside on sunny days. Current favourite authors, the children informed us, include Michelle Paver, Conn Iggulden and (still) JK Rowling. All do ICT and touch-typing. School assembly each morning, with prayers read by a pupil and thought for the day from a member of staff, plus a service at the church in the school grounds on Sunday mornings (lots of parents attend too). Relatively young teaching staff – 19 full-time, two part-time. Head and his wife, director of boarding, two matrons and three gap students live on-site.

M

Sports-wise, the school punches above its weight. Head is particularly proud that Maidwell recently won the national under-13 cross-country championship – quite a feat when they're up against far larger schools. Pupils play sport six days a week – boys do rugby, hockey, football and cricket, while girls do hockey, netball and rounders. Sports hall with cricket nets, climbing wall and squash court. Rowing on the lake in the summer and weekly swimming for all in school's own indoor pool. Loads of activities during break-times, evenings and at weekends, including crafts, carpentry, textiles, school magazine, gardening, clay shooting and outdoor pursuits trips. When we asked two boys whether they ever got bored, they looked puzzled. 'Of course not,' they told us. Music, drama and art good. Two-thirds of pupils learn musical instruments and music practice is timetabled. Two major concerts a year and choir sings an anthem in the church every Sunday. Art is very popular – everything from surrealism to gargoyles – and on the drama front, there are lots of plays, musicals and public speaking events.

All meals are cooked in-house. Lunch is a formal affair, in a light, airy dining room with long, narrow tables. Grace is said at the start and finish and a member of staff sits at each end to serve food, encourage good table manners and chat to boys and girls. Tradition of one boiled sweet after lunch still firmly in place (plastic tub solemnly passed from pupil to pupil) and £1 of tuck on Sundays. When we visited, a group of jolly 12-year-olds tucked into a lunch of beef pie and pancakes (stylishly served with slices of lemon) and chatted enthusiastically about the school. Food gets the thumbs-up from pupils. As head says: 'We're aiming for the good bits of Jamie Oliver but we still have fish and chips on Fridays.' Breakfast and supper are more informal. House system in place, with head boy/girl, prefects and four house captains. House competitions range from rugby and cross-country to water polo and conkers, with points scored for the annual house cup. 'It's taken very seriously,' the head boy told us.

Boarding is at the very heart of the school. Lots of parental access (church, matches etc) but boarders must stay at school at weekends. Leave-out weekends (from lunch on Friday till Monday evening) every second or third weekend. Pupils can be weekly boarders during their first year but most opt for full boarding from the start. Boy boarders are housed on first floor while girls get the self-contained top floor of the school. Boys' dorms (up to six per room) are wholesome and shipshape while girls' dorms (three to six per room) are decorated with jolly bunting, Keep Calm and Carry On posters and lots of Cath Kidston (there are plans for them to move to a purpose-built house of their own in due course). Older girls' bathroom looks straight out of an interiors magazine – chic circular basins, tongue and groove and laminate flooring.

Pupils are courteous, well-behaved and good company. When benefactor Oliver Wyatt was once asked about the ideal Maidwell pupil, he described him/her as the sort of child who 'was invited to someone's house and invited back again.' His view still holds true, with Maidwell putting an emphasis on being kind, well-mannered and tidy. Boys look smart in navy cords, striped or check shirts, ties and tweed jackets while girls wear corduroy culottes, blouses and smart jackets. Perhaps unusually in this day and age (but very popular with parents), mobile phones, PSPs and iPods are banned (although final year pupils can listen to iPods in their dorms). Boys and girls are allowed to watch key sports matches and a film on Saturday nights, while older pupils see the nightly TV news, but no TV apart from that. Boyfriend/girlfriend relationships actively discouraged. 'We are resistant to the idea of girls and boys "going out",' says the head. 'We talk it through with the pupils and I am very clear that we are not having it.' All pupils write a weekly letter home – 'we emphasise how much it means to parents,' he says.

Discipline isn't an issue here. 'It's because we're a small school and everybody looks out for each other,' say staff. 'You don't get division or ganging up because it's so close-knit.' Parents agree. 'We love the fact that because it's slightly smaller it has a real family atmosphere,' one mother told us. 'It gives children the opportunity to shine. Everyone gets to play in a team and everyone is in the school play.' Meanwhile a father commented: 'I'm delighted with all aspects of the school. The teaching staff are great and the boarding care is just superb.' Head is adamant that it isn't a 'snobby' place either. 'Privilege has no place in this school,' he says. 'Everyone is equal here.'

Maidwell Hall remains a traditional, full-boarding prep school that has stuck to its full boarding guns and held its own in a declining market. Small enough for everyone to know each other but big enough to offer a first-rate, all-round education, it encourages pupils to work hard, get lots of fresh air and have fun along the way.

The Mall School

185 Hampton Road, Twickenham, TW2 5NQ

• Pupils: 315 boys; all day • Ages: 4–13 • C of E • Fees: £9,885–£11,475 pa • Independent

Tel: 020 8977 2523
Email: admissions@themallschool.org.uk
Website: www.themallschool.org.uk

Headmaster: Since 2011, Mr David Price, BSc (environmental science) MA (school and college management) PGCE (forties). Worked in a conservation unit for a few years before starting his career in a state primary school some 20 years ago. This is his eighth year at The Mall, where he has been head of juniors and director of studies. Previously he was head of English and deputy principal at Latymer Prep and before that taught at Melbourne Grammar School in Australia where he lived with his family for three years.

Seems to be doing well in this, his first, headship. Obviously knows the school inside out and so has been able to leap straight into action – no root and branch reformation, rather a gentle reorganisation in a few areas. Physically and procedurally, he's been tidying up the place and has improved the management structure, appointing a senior tutor for years 7/8 and a head of the 'middles'.

Tremendously affable, he has an open-door policy for staff and parents and consults widely before deciding anything, but he will always have the final word and is prepared to put his foot down where necessary. 'He's really personable, but don't cross him,' advises one parent. Parents generally seem to appreciate the fact that he's 'one of us' and 'a family man'. He lives locally with his Australian wife Lindy and two school-age children, (a son at The Mall, and an older daughter) and 'he totally gets where we are coming from,' said a mother. 'He's got the same concerns as we do and I've got nothing but praise for him,' agreed another.

He's quite a stickler for the rules and likes things neat and organised – that includes the boys and their uniforms and he's not above manning the school gates himself to check that all is ship-shape. A precise person who believes that standards must be maintained in all areas and if you bother to have a policy you should follow it through. He's strict, but not feared – 'I would say the boys like him and have a lot of respect for him,' said one mother. 'He's easy to speak to,' confirmed our young tour guides. Not remote and office-bound, he still fits in some RS teaching, runs breakfast meetings with parent reps and attends all the concerts and sports matches. 'I think he's dynamic and wonderful,' said one fan. 'Nothing is too much trouble,' said another.

M

Out of school he enjoys walking, cycling and socialising, plus frequent trips to visit family in Australia.

Entrance: Non selective at reception, it's first come, first served – register two years ahead. A DP innovation has been to invite boys joining in September to spend time at the school during the previous summer term. 'We obviously have a look at them and see reports from nursery, but it's not an entrance test,' he says. These infants join one of two mixed ability classes. Joiners thereafter will be assessed in English and maths and anyone joining after year 4 will be additionally assessed in French and science. Almost self-selects because of its reputation as an academic school, although DP is keen to move away from possibly harsh connotations associated with that reputation. But even so, the bottom 25 per cent of pupils at The Mall end up in the top half of the national average. No dedicated feeder; The Mall takes from over 20 local pre-schools and nurseries including Jack and Jill, Sunflower, Windsor, Pavilion, Maria Grey and De Lacey. Scholarships available for outstanding candidates joining at 7+ or 8+.

Exit: No links to any one school, but does have a close relationship with neighbouring senior school, Hampton, whose head is on Mall board of governors. Typically two-thirds of leavers go to Hampton, Kings College Wimbledon, Westminster and St Paul's. Others to St Georges in Weybridge and Reeds in Cobham and a handful to board. Boys are expected to stay to 13+ so are not really prepared for 11+ exams, though a few do leave then, usually for a grammar school place.

Money matters: Up to 100 per cent bursaries (means tested) available at 7+ and 8+ point of entry, but hardship bursaries also available to parents who fall on hard times.

Remarks: A well-established prep which knows exactly what it has to do and achieves more.

Things start gently, with reception and year 1 pupils based in a separate building, five minutes from the main school, on a fairly busy, semi-residential road; you can't drop off on site or outside, need to park up and walk. Parents like the fact that their little ones are physically separated from the older, bigger boys; 'I think it makes it easier for them as they start,' said a mother.

The infants' building is a converted Victorian vicarage, with two reception classes downstairs and two year 1 classes upstairs – maximum 22 in each class, generally around 18. Not masses of space for 80+ little boys, but neither are they jammed in. Bright classrooms enlivened with colourful displays. Lessons we saw were very settled and children seemed happy and focused. There is lots of topic-based work eg on 'space', where we saw some inventive designs for 'a planet unlike Earth'. Each class teacher has a full-time classroom assistant and there are specialist teachers for music and swimming – both strengths of this place, of which more later. Homework twice a week, spellings once a week and reading every night. Boys needing extra help with work will be peeled off for extra tuition with SENCo – no stigma, no extra cost at this level, but you will be charged higher up the school. Also a charge for help with EFL, but school says boys generally catch up quickly, typically within a term or so.

There's one large room, not grand enough to be called a hall, but where the whole infant school can gather for assemblies. Year 1 eat their packed lunches here too – no hot meals for infants – and reception pupils eat their lunch at their desk. Sounds messy, but school says it works.

Some nice touches outside – a bird box/camera and raised beds where the boys can plant – go some way to compensate for limited outdoor space including a sadly under-used grassy area ('little boys and grass don't mix,' said school).

Generally the atmosphere is relaxed, but not sloppy. All staff expect and receive respect – for example, the boys will be asked to re-enter a room if they have not entered it properly. 'I like the place and the pace here,' said one mother. 'It's perfect for little boys, with quite a lot of play-based learning in the early years as they improve their fine motor skills, then things hot up as they move through the school.'

From year 2 the boys move to the purpose-built main site, with 7+ entrants joining in year 3. Everyone automatically transfers to the senior section from year 4 (ages eight to 13) to take up the Common Entrance curriculum. Years ago boys would be asked to leave if they did not make the grade – all that changed under the previous headmaster and Mr Price shares this same philosophy. 'I am here to get the less able boys through too and I like to see a wide range of abilities.' To this end school has a series of strategies to help and support the less able and is very keen on early intervention, 'the earlier the better'. Then in senior school there is a director of personalised learning, who develops individual plans. DP is also setting up a programme for non-academic scholarships and Mall pupils have already had some success in winning music, art and all-rounder places. Lots of mocks and target-setting, overseen by newly introduced 'academic tutors', aim to ensure early detection of anyone not working up to their capability. Currently 26 boys with SEN, mostly mild dyslexia and dyspraxia. 'From year 4 parents can pay for additional support if they choose', says school.

That said, academics is the focus here – no bones about it; that's why most parents choose The Mall in the first place. It's heads down every day as soon as the boys arrive, with assembly timetabled for just before lunch, so the work is done when the boys are at their freshest. Streaming and setting at the top of the school – in year 7 an accelerated class is introduced, from which come the scholarship boys, while the other class goes at 'ordinary pace'. In the past three years Mall pupils have won 18 senior school scholarships and over 40 prizes for performance at CE. Well over half The Mall's pupils achieve A* and A scores in their CE.

'It's a very good all-round school, but its USP is the learning environment – they have got it just right,' said a father. 'The all-round atmosphere is extremely conducive to learning,' agreed a mother. 'As we looked around it felt like we had come home. It's all brilliant from the get-go and I like the drive in this place. They let boys be boys, but also push them to do their absolute best.'

Parents seem to share an unerring confidence in this school and trust it to do right by their sons. There is an orderly, comfortable atmosphere and the boys are well-prepared for their CE. The ongoing tests and plenty of exam practice mean that the boys are so au fait with the whole procedure that it's no biggie when the important ones come around. 'They are totally familiar with what's expected and almost relaxed about it,' said a mother.

There is a fair amount of homework, including holiday homework – building up so that by year 7 there's about an hour a night, 1.5 hours by year 8. Teaching is strong across the board so it is invidious to pick stand-out subjects – 'Really it's all good' chant parents – but suffice to say French ('extremely well-taught' by native speakers) history and music all mentioned time and again. All year 2 boys play recorder to get them ready and interested and 140+ boys go on to play instruments – we saw boys having great fun drumming and composing. There is also an 80-strong choir – 'It's one of the nice things about a single-sex school,' says one parent. 'Boys are simple creatures and follow what others are doing, so they don't see singing as "girly". 'Plenty of chances to perform via regular productions – DP plans for the standard of school concerts to be even better. 'I think he just wants the boys to practise more,' said one mother. 'To make the shows a bit more polished'.

Facilities generally on a par with similar London day schools, with some outstanding features. There's a splendid theatre, the swimming pool is sublime and a new sports hall. There are two full games afternoons each week and although school is lacking in lush grounds, it is but a short skip and a jump to the bosky expanses of nearby Bushy Park for football, rugby and cricket. There's not so much athletics or tennis and some parents feel sport is not taken as seriously as at some other schools in the area – with the exception of swimming where the U10 team are IAPS national champions. But most agree that it does 'well enough' for their sons and praise 'smashing' sports staff. 'I wouldn't say it's for a very sporty child,' said one. 'It doesn't have the focus that it does in other schools, which irritates some of us'.

Not masses of extracurricular activities on offer, though there's all the usual art, DT, chess and of course a swimming club – it would be criminal not to make the most of their gorgeous pool. Offering of clubs has been beefed up to include computing, karate, judo and science. Some of the clubs are at lunchtime as it's already quite a long day (8.25am – 4pm) but school has to balance this against the fact that many Mall parents are both working and would appreciate their sons being able to enjoy a longer school day.

Apparently there's no such thing as a typical Mallian, 'We prefer them to remain individuals,' says DP. But he will concede uniformity in that they are confident ('not arrogant' he stresses) well-mannered and well-rounded young men. 'I think they are all quite different really,' agreed one mother. 'And I like the way they are encouraged to develop their own interests and skills'.

Staff have good relationships with the boys – good humour abounds, house points (plus or minus) moderate behaviour and are delivered with some theatrical flourish by school deputy. Head says there is something in The Mall's DNA that promotes good staff/pupil relationships here, bringing out the best in everyone. 'I'm continually impressed by the conversations we can have with them at a very early stage,' he says. Boys are encouraged and taught how to speak confidently in public and to vent their opinions though lots of debating activities. Pupil council and prefects' programme are all part of promoting leadership qualities in the boys. But they are equally encouraged to embrace sentimentality on occasion, such as the Mother's Day breakfast (DP imported the idea from Australia) designed to tug at the heart strings – each boy paints a picture of his mother which he presents to her along with a red rose after reading her a poem – most mums cry.

There's a fairly cosmopolitan mix of families here with a wider diversity of cultural backgrounds than seen in other preps in this area of south-west London – Asian, Chinese and European boys in the mix. 'I think it's fantastic that The Mall has such a varied population – it's not the rarefied exclusively white intake typical of schools around here,' says one mother. School minibuses run in the morning from Kew, Osterley and Kingston, other pupils from Hounslow, Isleworth, St Margaret's, Richmond, Twickenham, Teddington and Hampton.

Friendly bunch of parents – busy PTA does lots of fund-raising but has recently changed its focus to include more social events to get people together. Class reps effective and take the role seriously.

Parents say they feel welcome in school and well informed. Lots of good advice about 'where next?' and DP has introduced a 'future schools information evening' to boost this area. The place is very upfront, it's easy to get to see staff and DP has introduced the Clarion call text communication system which parents have been crying out for. 'They've always been great if I've had a problem,' said a parent. 'There's always a nice atmosphere and I feel very comfortable talking to them,' said another.

School runs a good and thriving thrift shop for uniform. Overall parents feel extras are relatively small, not many super-expensive ones, but neither is much available for free. Because The Mall is a small school there are not a lot of big expeditions and sometimes not enough takers to make an expensive jaunt viable. But that's not to say the boys don't get about; there's a year 3 residential trip to PGL Marchants Hill, older pupils to York and France, plus the occasional sports tour.

In all a happy, high-achieving academic school displaying a kinder attitude than of old – trying to be more inclusive. A settled, focused, organised place, which does exactly what it says on the tin.

Malsis School

Cross Hills, North Yorkshire, BD20 8DT

- Pupils: 110 pupils, 70 boys/40 girls; 30 board, the rest day
- Ages: 4-13 • Inter-denom: C of E and RC • Fees: Boarding £18,750; Day £8,100–£14,400 pa • Independent

Tel: 01535 633027
Email: admin@malsis.com
Website: www.malsis.com

Headmaster: Since 2008, Mr Marcus Peel (early fifties). Arrived in 2005, formerly deputy head and head of boarding. Married to Louise, a qualified remedial gymnast who is joint head of boarding with her husband; two grown-up children who went through the private system. Educated at Repton, read history and classical civilisation at Kent. Started life in the Metropolitan Police before joining Orwell Park as a teacher; enjoyed success as hockey coach and was made deputy head early on in his teaching career. Mad about adventure pursuits, a canoeist, air rifle instructor, mountaineer; loves music and is often seen tinkling the ivories, surrounded by kids having singalongs. Formerly ran his own adventure company and now runs courses under the school's banner, 'Adventure Malsis', enjoys bushcraft – something of the Ray Mears about the man, happy plucking and cooking pheasants, or anything else actually. Friendly, personable and praised by parents for bringing boarding into the 21st century, making it exciting, fun and parent-friendly. Teaches history and music.

Entrance: No formal entrance test – interview with the head and tour of the school, 'taster' days encouraged. Scholarships and bursaries considered for children with talent in academic work, music, sport and drama, particularly for entry at year 6 and 7. Many join in lower school but numerous others along the way, right up to the final year as a last push before senior school, or even to consciously defer entry to a senior school post 11. Parents predominantly city professionals from the length and breadth of Yorkshire, Cheshire, Lancashire and further afield. Fair number of Forces families and trickle of expats.

Exit: The usual suspects: Oundle, Shrewsbury, Giggleswick, Oakham, Windermere St Anne's, Queen Margaret's York, steady one or two to Bradford Grammar, Glenalmond, Sedbergh, Stonyhurst, Uppingham, Eton, Harrow, Rugby, Repton, Ampleforth, Radley and Stowe. Some also into local maintained sector grammar schools – Ermysted's popular. Regular stream of scholarships to all over, including academic, music, sport, art and IT – 13 scholarships amongst 18 leavers in 2012.

Remarks: Founded in 1920, by a teacher from Giggleswick, in a splendid Victorian mansion with gloriously ostentatious ceilings. Forty acres of games pitches and fields; numerous later building additions, some more attractive than others, in a variety of styles.

Not as many pupils as hitherto – the cry of many prep schools in this part of the world, sadly – but projects a dynamic sense of determination and clear intent. The four cornerstones are 'balance', 'purpose', 'style' and 'charm' – an interesting take on the needs of the 21st century pupil, but the children who acted as our guides around the school exuded all four, welcoming

M

smiles and firm handshakes all round. You could also add entrepreneurial spirit to that list (or is just northern thrift?) − 'We've got a great new cookery room, all kitted out, and thanks to parents and generous donations, it didn't cost the school a penny!' pupils tell us proudly.

Classrooms for the youngest children are bright, colourful and cheery − slightly less so for the older ones, though interactive whiteboards are appearing for staff willing and able to use them. Marvellous John Piper war memorial windows in the chapel, plus the flags that used to hang on the Cenotaph in London. Chapel converts into hall theatre. School holds services and performance slots on Saturday, rather than Sunday, so Sundays are 'free for activities'. Civilised dining room with linen napkins and white tablecloths for Sunday evening roast.

Huge range of country-type activities, stacks of sports with twice weekly fixtures and regular tours; as well as the trad prep school type extra-curricular activities also offers mountain biking (British Cycle Federation approved 3km mountain bike track within grounds), bushcraft, hill-walking, canoeing, camping − including camp cooking. A good-sized swimming pool, shooting range, cross-country, nine-hole golf course, and high-octane outdoor thrills with the assault-course style 'Rap tree' for 'confidence-building' − shades of a corporate team-building weekend and a favourite with the pupils. Thursday afternoon's two hour 'PAT' − Protected Activity Time − sees children taking six week courses in falconry, shot guns, fly-fishing and cookery, 'high adventure', dry-skiing and more − the list is endless. Also a selection of activity weeks and camps in holidays throughout the year.

A busy boarding school − day pupils have to be in school by 8.30am and stay till 6.15pm (it's not all work − activities are built into the school day), and many stay later for activities (over 70 of them) − they can stay for supper and enjoy many of the evening activities at no extra charge, a real boon for busy parents with active children. Most 10-13 year olds board at some stage, as well as a number of younger ones − around 30 per cent in all, increasing to 40 per cent in the summer with probationary boarding on offer to ease children (and parents) into it. Much investment into making boarding accommodation homely and appealing − serious about its boarding profile: in year 8, children must either do full boarding or be a day child − probationary boarding is not an option. Boarders certainly get a good deal − full and varied activity programme after school and at weekends (including trips to Blackpool pleasure beach, charity abseil, lasertag in the grounds) keeps youngsters happy and entertained.

Predominantly trad teaching styles, strong academically, head sees outstanding work. French from 5, Latin from 9 and Italian and Spanish club very popular. Small classes, max 18 or 20. Excellent learning support for pupils − currently mostly dyslexia/dyspraxia, but range of others considered if they think they can help and child will cope. IEPs for those with needs, one-to-one help, regular additional reading (often with parent volunteers), small group work and setting (including holding back the weakest or advancing the brightest a year, so they get to spend extra time on scholarship work). SEN not seen as a barrier − possible to be getting extra support and be in scholarship classes. The head of learning support keeps an eye on all things SEN, including gifted and talented. All staff informed and involved with SEN. Needs across curriculum recognised.

Lots of different sports and opportunities for all to represent the school − building confidence and finding something a child is good at all feature. Annual jaunt to Normandy, annual Three Peaks challenge, three week leavers' programme of numerous activities culminating in a week-long camp in the Lakes or Snowdonia.

Palpable pride in excellent drama, masses of music with 70 per cent of children learning an instrument. Vibrant art and creative DT, plenty of visits to local hot spots: Manchester, Bradford, Halifax, Leeds all have orchestras and theatres. Director of music, James Ashworth, former Huddersfield Choral

Society voice coach, is driving forward a desire for the school to become a centre of musical excellence.

Described to us by one parent as a 'fab' school − classes are small, children work hard but are not hot-housed (unlike some other local schools, allegedly); nothing wrong with the place at all, except that it 'could do with a few more children'. This parent was initially wary of prep schools, fearing Tom Brown's Schooldays styling, but on her visit saw a roaring fire in the entrance hall, a large Christmas tree, and muddy boots in the porch − and felt she had 'come home', converted in an instant and remains so. Parents admire sense of etiquette instilled from an early age and the way in which children look after each other; they also love the slightly avant-garde style of some of the teachers who, after a day of heavy rain, will take the children for a walk to look at the effect on the local river − geography and science teaching in action, without the children even realising it. One maths lesson involved learning how to calculate the angles needed to build a bridge over said river. Plenty of serious classroom teaching too, but making the most of the environment, in every respect.

Strong house system, with termly activity days/dinners for winners of duties and house cups − all participate in competitions. Effective personal tutor system for each child. A busy school with a family feel − parents are hugely supportive and contribute much to the value-added life of the school. Former pupils include Simon Beaufoy, who wrote The Full Monty and Slumdog Millionaire, Martin Taylor ex of Barclays Bank, Mark Umbers and Sam Riley, actors, and James Whitaker, England cricketer selector.

Maltman's Green School

Maltmans Lane, Gerrards Cross, SL9 8RR

• Pupils: 430 girls; all day • Ages: 3–11 • Non-denom
• Fees: £8,310–£11,940 pa • Independent

Tel: 01753 883022
Email: registrar@maltmansgreen.com
Website: www.maltmansgreen.com

Headmistress: Since 2005, Mrs Joanna Pardon MA BSc PGCE (late forties) whose degree subject was environmental sciences and whose 'passion' is still the environment − her school's and the wider world's. Prior to her appointment at Maltman's Green, Mrs Pardon was head of Gateways Prep in Leeds; previous incarnations in Ashford School, Kent, Riddlesworth Hall, Norfolk, teaching history, technology and as director of studies. A good, varied career. You know immediately you are in the presence of a capable and experienced professional teacher.

Mrs Pardon clearly understands girls of this age, relishes her opportunities in this school with its long tradition of good housekeeping and is clearly respected by all. And she is warm and forthright too. Witness her fabulously appointed drawing room − one of the loveliest head's rooms we know − and its chief occupant, Malty − the hugest Old English sheepdog in the world who sprawls on the rug by the blazing fire and is, almost, real. Year 6 girls lunch with Mrs Pardon in this room and probably remember it all their lives.

'She is very approachable,' parents told us − 'almost too much for her own good,' some muttered, alluding to some of her more demanding constituents − though a general sense that Mrs Pardon is more than equal to the challenge. Her husband is network manager in the school and they live in a modest house (fab garden, though) onsite. One hears few criticisms of this school from its insiders. Mostly, parents carp, mildly, about other parents and their fierce ambition for their children which can, on occasions, seem remorseless. Mrs Pardon, all allow, has tried to spread opportunities so that all can join in. In Mrs Pardon, Maltman's has a head who understands her constituents and is confident enough to temper their excesses when necessary. The right woman for the job.

Entrance: First come first served. Register by the time Sophia is one, to be on the safe side, but you may well find a place comes up thereafter on account of the transitory nature of much of the local, high-flying – and therefore frequently relocated – population. Thirty-two into nursery at 3+, 22 more into reception, a few more into year 1 and thereafter rising to a max of 16 in each of four classes in years 3 – 6. Despite its stratospheric reputation, it's always worth a call for an occasional place if you are moving out of London or coming down south. Very commutable and, if you can ignore the local pressures, rather charming.

Exit: Many to the excellent local grammars – especially Beaconsfield High, and Dr Challoner's. Many parents feel the money spent on Maltman's is money saved on senior school fees thereafter. Around 90 per cent of those who try for the grammars from here get in – remarkable by any standards. Roughly half choose the independent route and go, mainly, to The Royal Masonic, Piper's Corner, St Mary's Gerrard's Cross, St Helen's and, for boarding, a few to Wycombe Abbey, Downe House, Cheltenham Ladies' and Queen Anne's, Caversham. Most, interestingly, to all-girls' schools. Fifteen scholarships in 2013.

Remarks: This school is not academically selective so its results are testament to a thorough education and rich opportunities. Results, that is, in terms of the rounded nature of its girls – not just academic achievement. Parents praise the teaching at all levels and especially the teaching by subject specialists from year 4 – we warmly approve. 'The school has the reputation for being pressured and the girls are pushed, but my daughters don't feel under pressure,' we were told. Classrooms are lively – perhaps not the neatest we've seen but these always worry us: a sense of life and excitement at work here and the word 'discovery' pops up pleasingly wherever you go. Good provision for everything and all in excellent nick. These classes are spacious – no cramped and overheated glasshouses – and they are some of the most colourful we've seen – a pleasure to behold. Two good libraries – well-stocked, welcoming and well-used. Creative thinking workshop sets the tone. Good displays – teachers here take immense pains: we were impressed by a huge Windsor Castle montage with delightful accounts of a visit there. All do DT (super pottery room, great wooden puppets) and ICT – though not as an end in itself.

Music is exceptional and, like everything here, successful well beyond the school. Regular successes for the choir in national competitions and many play instruments. Art in two good studios is remarkably free – we enjoyed the printed and beaded textiles; 'You do what you want,' an artist told us. 'You can make it as colourful and powerful as you like.' Drama likewise is popular and to a remarkable standard.

But sport is, whatever anyone says, still queen bee. Fabulous onsite pool, excellent gym facilities, courts and fields and, frankly, other schools quake if they are drawn against Maltman's in competitions. Lots of trophies attest to this winning tradition. A place in the gym squad marks you out as a member of a precious elite. It has been this, more even than academic pre-eminence, that has driven parental ambition and has wearied those whose daughters will never do a flawless vault or back-flip and, to a great extent, it is driven by the girls themselves. 'They have a terrific desire to win,' parents told us – but some tired girls do, we are told, as much as nine hours' swimming or gym outside school to maintain their places.

Mrs Pardon has done much to rebalance things and all kinds of activities have now acquired equality with the sporting. Masses of clubs – plenty of opportunities to find something you are good at – Mrs Pardon asserts, 'All girls can find something they're passionate about – everyone should feel valued'. Particular emphasis on – and pride in – school's status as an eco-school. Lots of fun in the Discovery Gardens, efforts into recycling and removing packaging and a lively sense of responsibility that we would like to see elsewhere.

SEN picked up as and when they surface and robust approach taken thereafter to providing appropriate help – whether temporary or long-standing. Head of learning support is trained ed psych and does preliminary screening of all who are identified as having a possible need, preparing IEPs where needed and involving all teaching staff. Specialist literacy teacher, team of support staff. No extra charge for any support, which may be withdrawal from lessons – individual decisions are made as to who can miss what – or in-class support. Three per cent of girls on SEN register when we visited and around 70 receiving additional support, including the gifted and talented. Co-ordinator for the latter, as well as a visiting consultant . Aims to 'look for what will take them on to the next bit of learning' and 'the joy is when you get a child with dyslexia who makes it into a grammar school' – indeed. Copes with milder end of autism.

You find Maltman's Green rather unexpectedly down a windy lane lined with hefty detached residences behind imposing gates. The original house – date uncertain but, surely, at least 300 years old – now boasts a gravel carriage sweep, charming lawned and conifered garden, clipped yew hedge and sundial and doesn't look at all like a school. The frontage and entrance hall are an attractive blend of Jacobethan, arts 'n' crafts and art nouveau – turret, bell-tower, adjoining converted barn, 24 chimneys, galleries, conservatory, rampant Virginia creeper, fabulously polished tiles and some glorious leaded lights. A rural dream in stockbroker heaven. A private house until 1918 when, charmingly, it was turned into a school for young ladies from Yorkshire who needed an escape from all those horrible mills in the more wholesome south. Boarding until the 1990s when, also, it shed the 13+ years and stopped at 11. Seriously convenient for national and international commuting – 18 mins into Marylebone, 15 mins to Heathrow. Why live anywhere else?

Minor grouse is lack of outside space. Junior playground is good with marked tarmac and safe surface under excellent play equipment. Nursery uses this but also has their own brick-paved yard. Senior play equipment sits in an old walled garden inhabited by willow sculptures made by girls. Head of sustainability instigated the building of large wellie boot sheds to allow the girls to make full use of the grounds, even in winter.

House system, few discipline problems, healthy atmosphere of collaboration and friendship – despite the competitiveness that is fostered less in the school than in some of the families. Very good feedback from staff and teachers quick to alert parents if a problem, which would be picked up by much-loved staff – long-serving deputy head praised in particular – but Mrs Pardon steps in 'when things get complex. They come in here, this rooms calms them when the hormones have started to kick in, as they will'.

Professional families, often high-achieving, frequently first-time buyers of independent education, committed, involved and devoted to the school. Parents – whether trad privately educated types themselves or new to the game – enthuse. Some sense that a struggler might struggle here in the long-term, whatever help the school sets up, and some few do move to gentler climes. Masses of grammar school entry tutoring goes on – a pity as it is seldom needed, but parental anxiety fuels the trade. Some means-tested bursaries up to 100 per cent of fees. If you are cash-strapped but have a lovely daughter, give 'em a call.

Produces outgoing, confident, thoughtful girls – 'My daughters are very different but they are equally happy there'; 'My daughters come out buzzing about what they've learned'. A great school.

Malvern St James Girls' School Preparatory Department

Linked school: Malvern St James Girls' School

Avenue Road, Great Malvern, WR14 3BA

• Pupils: 73 girls, 7 boarders • Ages: 3-11 • Fees: Day £7,455–£10,350; Boarding £16,005–£18,600 pa • Independent

---

Tel: 01684 584624
Email: registrar@malvernstjames.co.uk
Website: www.malvernstjames.co.uk

Remarks: See senior school.

The Manchester Grammar School Junior School

Linked school: The Manchester Grammar School

Old Hall Lane, Manchester, M13 0XT

• Pupils: 229 boys, all day • Ages: 7-11 • Non-denon
• Fees: £11,055 pa • Independent

Tel: 01612 247201
Email: general@mgs.org
Website: www.mgs.org

Head: Since 2008, Mrs Linda Hamilton BEd. Attended Manchester University, then taught in the state system for two years, followed by 10 years working abroad in a wide variety of countries, including setting up a kindergarten for Shell in Nigeria; an ISI international schools inspector; previously deputy head at Altrincham Prep School.

Closely involved with the establishment of the junior school (design of the building, curriculum and selection approach) – 'It's the best job in the world', because it's realised her vision. Has promoted extensive contact with local primary schools, inviting gifted and talented children to take part in the enrichment programme and special topic days, sharing staff language and maths skills and contributing to state school teachers' professional development (in the Manchester Grammar School tradition of generous community involvement). Very friendly, approachable, energetic and impressive – a hands on head. Married with three adult sons; leisure spent on family life, walking and reading, but 'My big passion is the school'.

Entrance: Children come for an assessment day (for years 3-4 in the winter term, 5-6 in the spring term), in groups of 10-12, consisting of lively activities and teaching with some formal testing. It aims to be fair, so that parents that can afford tutoring can't put their children at an advantage (nothing from the national curriculum), and enjoyable, and to enable boys with 'raw potential' to be identified. Looking for motivated, bright boys with individuality. May suggest those with promise who are not successful try again later.

We wondered about the possibility of boys failing to live up to expectations, as they are in effect being selected for the senior school at the age of six (no entrance exam required) and the school is in the early stages of doing so. Mrs Hamilton is confident, however, that they will always make the right call and pointed out that if any doubt existed, she would advise parents to apply when the child is older 'and his potential...more evident'.

About 30 boys taken finto year 3 and year 6 has about 65 places, but no set number to fill.

Exit: All to senior school – parents very glad to avoid the pressure and constraints of year 6 entrance exams.

Remarks: Opened 2008 for years 5-6, now home to years 3 and 4 (first entry 2011). Delightful, unusual design – the original building, Bexwyke (pronounced Bezik) Lodge, is constructed in the style of a Swiss chalet from sustainable wood from Estonia and has a pair of very large carved owls (the senior school motto is 'Dare to be wise') by the entrance. Years 5 and 6 are housed in the equally environmentally friendly Plessyngton Lodge, made of Scottish pine so fresh you can smell it at the reception area. A sizeable open space for assemblies, with a high, sloping roof; more pine in the roomy classrooms, which are on the dark side, however, so need electric lighting. Each has a verandah with pine railings running around it, leading to a large playground. Benches for boys who want to read and a decking area with wooden tables and stools. Adjacent to the Rectory Woodland area, a natural environment with a great variety of birdlife – great spotted woodpeckers, rose-ringed parakeets and a real owl. On senior school campus, which all children are escorted around to help them adjust initially.

First ISI inspection, 2010, outstanding in all respects. Exceptionally broad and deep curriculum, extending far beyond the national one, and high standard of teaching – very strong on differentiation and independent learning. We were deeply impressed by the wonderfully creative and accomplished year 6 projects on explorers, some very sophisticated year 3 writing and the sewing on the cushions on display – considerably better than our own.

The junior school teachers ('very professional, enthusiastic and positive staff,' said a parent) are supplemented by specialists from the senior school, who communicate their passion for their subjects and give the boys lots of extra stretch – the school understands how far very bright junior age children can go in their learning and how to teach them in a way that they love. Focuses on the development of skills such as logical thinking, practical work in science and humanities projects involving research and trips, nourishing the intellectual curiosity of highly motivated boys. They learn an unusual range of languages – French, Spanish, Italian and Latin. Parents very happy with the 'very progressive, hands on and engaging approach'.

Consequently, they are very well prepared for senior school work and achieve to an outstanding level – such as the year 6 boys who competed in a Languages Olympiad against much older pupils and a year 5 boy who won third prize in the Liverpool Maths Challenge extending to year 8. Access to laptops, iPads and notepads for all, all the time. Classes average 16-20, 22 max. Special needs provision is overseen by the well-qualified senior school SENCo and junior school support co-ordinator – in and out of class support; all screened for dyslexia in years 3-6.

In addition, all years have a weekly enrichment programme featuring options such as psychology, cookery, digital photography, robotics, forensic science, business enterprise, military strategy, contemporary dance and community action, eg in a local primary school.

Specialist sports teachers and access to senior school facilities: high level successes in swimming, football and chess, star rugby and lacrosse players, a national fencer – several represent their county. Several music groups, choirs, some highly accomplished musicians. Own small theatre – Macbeth and Peter Pan produced.

Heaps of clubs, including yoga, Japanese, Highland dancing, politics, engineering. Astonishingly mature content and writing in the school newspaper – very informative and substantial, extremely good value for a mere 50p. Large sums raised for charity, eg Haiti earthquake victims. Year 6 five day trip to Italy; year 5 annual trip to an activity centre in Wales; years 3 and 4 a two day residential. Many positions of responsibility in years 5 and 6 to develop leadership and organisational skills; boys feel school council is listened to.

Intake from Manchester and surrounding area – many business and professional backgrounds, but socially and ethnically mixed. Articulate, confident children, engrossed in all the lessons we visited; trad good manners expected. Uniform is blue blazers, trousers or shorts and white shirts.

Happy, friendly atmosphere – boys say no bullying and confident if it did occur, it would be dealt with promptly and effectively. Sixth form prefects from senior school attached to classes and help with clubs; new boys get an established 'buddy' from the same post code, so they can meet up the summer before they start; easy transition to the senior school, which will be familiar to them. Very good links with parents – speedy email contact (head gives out her own address), regular newsletters, lots of family events for parents and grandparents, such as tea and cake sessions with Mrs Hamilton; comprehensive welcome pack and info evenings before starting the junior and senior schools. Extended care 8am-6pm.

Charges the same fees as the senior school (means tested bursaries available), but does offer an exceptionally rich and enlightened education.

Manchester High School for Girls Preparatory Department

Linked school: Manchester High School for Girls

Grangethorpe Road, Manchester, M14 6HS

- Pupils: 230 girls; all day • Ages: 4–11 • Non-denom
- Fees: £7,032–£7,482 pa • Independent

Tel: 01612 240447
Email: administration@mhsg.manchester.sch.uk
Website: www.manchesterhigh.co.uk

Head: Mrs Rachel Edwards BEd (PE and biology) (fiftyish). Came from deputy headship of Alderley Edge School for girls and being an advanced skills teacher in Staffordshire. Smiley and smart (all the staff here seem sartorially slick), upbeat and enthusiastic about the pupils, their work, the school, the curriculum and reading, 'We want the girls to love reading, to love reading avidly and widely'. Not keen on chalk and talk teaching and indeed, all classrooms seemed full of happy interaction. Describes herself as a dog lover and walker and keen to point out that besides the glorious green backdrop, Platt Fields Park also provides tree creeper and nuthatch visitors to the school bird bath and feeders.

Entrance: By assessment during a visit for entry to reception and years 1 and 2, and by exams, in January or ad hoc by appointment during the year, in English, maths and reasoning for years 3, 4, 5 and 6, plus previous school report.

Exit: Most girls pass seniors' exam and transfer easily to familiar turf. Plenty of support and gentle warning for those who won't.

Remarks: On same site as senior school and enjoying its facilities including the pool, canteen and specialist teachers, yet distinctly separate with its own entrance and playground. The recent ISI inspection describes pretty much everything here as outstanding and says, 'There's a tremendous feeling of friendship'. Polite, respectful, genteel even, girls in buttoned up yellow gingham wait to see who'll speak first – 'Everyone's really friendly, it's easy to make friends and if we spot someone

on their own we'll ask them to join in'. Multi-cultural with a prayer room available.

The facilities mean two forms in some years, one in others, starting with forms of up to 20 in reception with two full-time staff. Infants and juniors have their own halls and libraries, the infants a canopied outdoor play area. Whiteboards and a computer suite. Girls sit yearly NFER tests and parents have welcomed 'a more transparent reporting system using colours for progress – you can really see how she's getting on now'. They also praise the children's self-assessment traffic light scheme where they award their own work a green sticker if they've understood everything, an amber if they're not quite sure and red if they still feel befuddled – 'We don't really get reds,' says school. Lower years use smiley faces. 'The teachers here are really supportive,' stellar girls eloquently enthuse. 'We learn through play and learning objectives and lots of school trips, which are a fun way to bring learning to life.'

French taught and compulsory Mandarin in the juniors.

LAMDA speech and drama popular and music – 'somewhat violin heavy,' one parent grimaced; 'we've two harpists,' says school. Much positive feedback with merit badges and golden girls published in the glossy prep newsletter. An agreed pupil behaviour charter sets guidelines and the new house system will bring points. Two days a week a SENCo works with a handful of dyslexic and dyspraxic girls. The range of extra-curricular clubs includes gardening and an Amnesty International group. Paid after-school care and free pre-school from 8am, 'for if your parents are, say surgeons, and have to get in early'. No homework Wednesdays.

Lunches £170 a term. After-school care to 6pm £8.60

Manor House School Junior Department

Linked school: Manor House School

Manor House Lane, Little Bookham, Surrey, KT23 4EM

- Pupils: 100 girls; all day • Ages: 2–11 • Christian non-denom
- Fees: £7,800–£11,250 pa • Independent

Tel: 01372 458538
Email: admissions@manorhouseschool.org
Website: www.manorhouseschool.org

Headmistress: Miss Zara Axton (for details see senior school).

Entrance: Baby and toddler group once a week helps ease children (boys and girls) into Manor House before they can remember anything else. Nursery, for girls only, starts from age two. School proper, with uniforms, at age four in the prep, moving through into the juniors at age seven. Very informal entry assessment on a 'taster day' – reading, sums and chatting to a teacher – simply to judge where a pupil fits amongst her peers.

Exit: Most to senior department. Works hard to be a truly 'through school' – no distinction between the juniors and seniors.

Remarks: Nothing but praise from parents for this gentle and rather sweet introduction to school life. Purpose-built nursery facilities sit alongside the prep classrooms and share an extensive outdoor play area. Junior classrooms are located in the very beautiful main house and girls play outside in the lovely grounds. The whole place has a quiet, country feel and parents feel strongly that their daughters will be safe here.

Girls of all ages mix – Miss Axton, the head of the whole school, describes junior and senior as 'one community'. The prep and junior girls love being with the seniors and greet them with hugs and kisses, parents value the respect and love girls have for each other. Each girl has a 'buddy' from two years ahead, who supports them throughout their school year.

Small classes are full of giggling little girls and kindly enthusiastic teachers. Academically the full spectrum, not just high achievers. Parents like this 'healthy mix' and the 'innocence, warmth and friendliness'. Suited to those who want their daughters to enjoy school life without academic pressure, this sets Manor House apart from other highly academic girls' schools in this part of Surrey. Parents feel confident in the teaching, saying, 'The lines of communication are very open,' and 'They cover the spectrum by extending classroom work for the brighter girls'. Teachers instil a sense of security and growing independence in the girls, whilst making lessons fun and interesting. One pupil described enthusiastically how fractions had been taught by cutting up and eating a large cake! Teachers can refer pupils to the head of learning support if extra help is needed.

Some parents felt Miss Axton had little to do with the junior school girls – Miss Axton hotly denies this and says, 'I visit junior and prep lessons every day. In J5 it is a standing joke that I always appear when they are doing maths (my subject).' A number of leading teachers in the prep and junior sections who have been there 'since they were girls themselves' and are very committed to the individual well being of their pupils. One teacher we spoke to had been at the school for many years, and was so wildly passionate about the place, she would probably have talked all day about the joys of Manor House had the bell not rung when it did. In a nutshell, unpressurised and pure fun – a breath of fresh (country) air.

Manor Lodge School

Rectory Lane, Ridge Hill, Shenley, Hertfordshire, WD7 9BG

- Pupils: 390 • Ages: 4–11 • Fees: £8,595–£10,475 pa
- Independent

Tel: 01707 642424
Email: prospectus@manorlodgeschool.com
Website: www.manorlodgeschool.com

Headmaster: Since 2011 Mr Gil Dunn Cert Ed (sixties). Educated at Brooklands School, Leighton Buzzard and Milton Keynes College of Education. Understated, sincere and popular with pupils ('he's really funny but can be strict') and parents, who say he is 'totally dedicated to the children.' Describes himself as an 'accidental headmaster,' having been persuaded into the role by governors following the sudden departure of the short-lived former head after 10 years as deputy. A keen cricketer and former tennis coach, started his career at Burnham Secondary ('tough but great fun,') with an 1 year stint teaching PE, rising to head of department. Moved as director of sport to Wakeman School in Shrewsbury before joining Frensham Heights School as housemaster. Took first deputy headship at Beisham Mae Jewish School in east London then moved into the prep world with his appointment as head of PE and Games at Lochinver House, Potters Bar.

Joined Manor Lodge in 1994 as head of year 6, senior English teacher and sports coach. Moonlighted throughout career as counsellor and later director of a USA summer camp but gave this up when appointed deputy head in 2001. Says it was always his calling to work with children and keeps his hand well in teaching year 6 English and handling the secondary transfer process. 'An excellent communicator,' according to parents, he says it's important 'not to be remote,' and although he doesn't see himself a typical charismatic prep school head, says he has his 'own style,' and is oft seen pressing the parental flesh at sporting fixtures and both ends of the day.

Die hard Chelsea fan and published author of children's fiction and historical western novels, he also writes the lyrics and scripts for all year 6 school productions. Stands apart from majority of prep heads in his belief that 11 is the right age for children to move to secondary school , partly to avoid 'the pressure of common entrance' and partly due to belief that some children can 'go stale' in the last two years of prep. Sees the most important factor as having given his charges 'a joy of learning,' and producing independent thinkers that 'investigate rather than just learning facts.'

Entrance: Selective 'to a certain extent' at 4, with more than three applicants for every place. Assessment takes about an hour, and is equal in importance to interview with candidate and parents: 'We're looking for children with character and parents who recognise the importance of partnership with school for 11+ success,' says head. Automatic entry for siblings, with around 25 per cent from the sibling-only nursery on site. Waiting lists for every year group, with those entering post-reception, mainly from state sector or due to relocations, invited to spend a morning in school and tested in maths and English.

Exit: Strong record of feeding to the south Herts/north London plethora of academic powerhouses including Habs Boys, Merchant Taylors and St Albans School for boys, and Habs Girls, North London Collegiate, St Albans High School and St Helens for girls. Those not reaching such dizzy academic heights well catered for too, with movement to St Columba's, Aldenham, Haileybury and St Margaret's. Hardly any to boarding and an average of five per cent to selective state schools. Outstanding scholarship record – 31 offers in 2013 (around 25 most years), representing one-third of the year group.

Remarks: Nestled at the end of a country lane in a rural setting of fields housing the local pony population, the only clue to the urban environs of Manor Lodge is the M25 sign just visible on the horizon. Excellent use has been made of the grounds surrounding the 300 year old former country house, which has a colourful history as health spa, film set (notably A Clockwork Orange) and the private home of double agent Eddie Chapman. Wonderful grassy outdoor spaces include two adventure playgrounds, one of these exclusively for reception children, two sports fields and a large wildlife garden ('a great privilege to visit,' say children), often used for science lessons and complete with well-populated swamp and observation hut.

The main building provides an impressive façade for the school but the classrooms, which include a dedicated dojo for martial arts, don't quite live up to the grandeur of the exterior, although there is a quaint charm to the winding staircases and narrow panelled corridors. Thankfully the 'new block' (2003) with its brightly painted corridors bedecked with fruits of the children's labours and large airy form rooms, delivers light, bright classrooms with a more modern feel. The Grand Designs style dining room added in 2008 plays a starring architectural role and multi-tasks as dance and gymnastics studio. Plans in place for further modernisation with the addition of an all singing all dancing sports hall – watch this space.

Head constantly refers to Manor Lodge as a 'family school' and it benefits in atmosphere from its co-ed pupil body which gives off a friendly, relaxed vibe. Boys and girls mix freely and provide 'healthy competition' for one another in the classroom, according to parents, and pupils say that although the school has high standards, it is 'not super strict.' School community, from the north London/south Herts environs, is 'very demanding' in its expectations according to head, although children come over as earnest and serious, many articulate beyond their years but not precocious. Very few super-affluent families, with the majority hard working middle class and many first time buyers. Diverse ethnic and religious mix representative of the local area.

Quality rather than quantity in the language department, with French from reception and Spanish from year 5. No Latin or classics but specialist teaching for music, art, CDT, IT, PE, drama and languages from the word go. Around 25 per cent of teachers are male (including one in infant department) lending a healthy dose of testosterone to the mix. Pupils continuously assessed using PIPS scheme – 'it gives us a constant flow of information,' says head. At the top of the school, children benefit from a tutorial system 'almost like university,' where they are given instant feedback on all work, with 'some responses from teachers almost as long as the child's essay,' according to head. All year 5 and 6 pupils receive a mini report every four weeks to track progress and constantly reassess targets. 'Thorough preparation' for 11+ is the name of the Manor Lodge game, with all year 6 pupils receiving interview technique coaching from a former top senior school admissions tutor.

Pupils mixed mainly according to geographical location in reception 'to minimise pressure on parents,' says head and classes are shuffled in year 3. Setting in maths from year 2 and English from year 5, when children start to move around the school for individual subjects. Head cautiously picks out English as the school's 'greatest strength' but quickly adds that most scholarships achieved are all-rounders. Parents say that children 'hardly know they're learning' lower down the school and that pressure 'steps up just a little bit each year.' More than lip service paid to focus on independent thinking, with all pupils working towards completion of their 'thinking skills passports,' focusing on creativity, independence, collaboration and persistence. Extremely close bonds in evidence between staff and children, with teachers referring to the 'sheer joy in learning' they hope to give their young charges and even reception staff showing clear affection for pupils.

Not much in the way of heavy duty SEN, but that said there is very little call for it – just a handful of pupils per year group receive extra help from the part time SENCo to iron out minor issues. Maths and English specialists join classrooms to provide support to those who need it, and those with specific talents, either academically or in music or art, receive accelerated tuition outside of classroom time.

Art room on the basic side but one of the most orderly we've seen – 'you can't create in chaos,' according to the art teacher – and pupils enthuse about the teaching in this area, with evidence of their work displayed around the school. DT also a firm favourite with both sexes, with pupils describing their teacher as 'passionate,' although facilities in this area are not the star attraction. Music lessons take place in a room with spectacular views across the countryside and are very popular, with 50 per cent of junior pupils taking peripatetic lessons and a host of bands and choirs on offer for budding performers to display their wares. Head says 'nobody leaves Manor Lodge without being a performer,' with frequent recitals on all scales, ranging from class assemblies, which 'quietly teach confidence,' according to parents, to musical productions, most recently Charlie and the Chocolate Factory. Year 6 bow out of the school each year with a major production at the Radlett Centre.

The trophy cabinet in reception tells visitors all they need to know about the sporting culture of the school which has, according to parents, 'hugely improved,' in recent years. Two dedicated sports staff (one male, one female) run the show and have helped school inch its way up league tables and earn its place in a competitive local fixtures list. A-D teams are put out wherever possible with cricket and netball being standout sports – teams in both finished the season unbeaten in 2013. Girls' football on the up and cricket also popular with the female cohort, although no fixtures – yet. Trophies and accolades also up for grabs for less sporty ones, with annual

awards for everything from maths and handwriting to reading – and even one for 'good egg.'

Hugely popular (and competitive) house system and pupil body vociferous in school matters with the school council, introduced in 2012. Two councillors elected from every year in the school attend monthly meetings to put forward ideas and suggestions for improvements. School introduced badges for those on school teams, choir or bands and holding responsibilities such as librarian as a result of council discussions –many pupils now proudly weighed down with these. School presidents from each gender are elected by the pupil body ('they always get it right,' says head) and lead council meetings. Pupils proud of school's Green Flag status and boasts an eco team, recycling club and bird watching amongst its enrichment programme. No specific anti-bullying measures in place but head says that 'children know they can talk to any adult,' adding that incidents of unpleasant behaviour are 'pretty rare.'

The Manor Preparatory School

Faringdon Road, Shippon, Abingdon, Oxfordshire, OX13 6LN

- Pupils: 380; 325 girls, 55 boys • Ages: 2–11 (girls), 2–7 (boys),
- Non-denom • Fees: £9,780–£12,645 pa • Independent

Tel: 01235 858462
Email: registrar@manorprep.org
Website: www.manorprep.org

Head: Since 2006, Mr Piers Heyworth MA, PGCE (fifties). Educated at Papplewick, Marlborough and Christ Church, Oxford where he read English. Started his teaching career at Latymer Upper School, became head of English at James Allen's Girls' School and then head of James Allen's Prep for 14 years. Mr Heyworth is married with two children; his wife also teaches at the school, dividing her legendary talents between the SEN and art departments. Mr Heyworth is a man in his element; he radiates joie de vivre and one feels that what he enjoys most about his job is seeing the world afresh through his pupils' eyes. He teaches drama from year 3 upwards using his large study as a performance space. 'We move the furniture back and improvise... everyone gets to act, the children get to see me make a fool of myself and I get to know them.' It's not just the pupils who act: most years in January there is a surprise staff panto that begins with the head introducing a deliberately deadly assembly – for example on the colour grey – which is then hijacked, much to the pupils' delight.

Over hot chocolate and pastries at 'birthday break', Mr Heyworth and his wife chat amiably with those whose birthdays fell in the preceding week, from the tiniest pre-prep boy to the confident year 6 girls. Talk with him about his school and you will hear no educational newspeak, no bureaucratic terminology; he is fluent and engaging and raids his literary education for apposite quotations (Browning and Desmond Morris!) without pretension. Now while we are certain that nothing as harsh and unyielding as an iron fist is hiding in Mr Heyworth's jolly velvet glove, no school is judged 'outstanding' in every aspect (ISI 2011) without a huge amount of rigorous management and scrupulous attention to detail going on behind the scenes. He generously ascribes much of the school's success to its staff, who are expected to 'jump through a lot of hoops' before being appointed. 'We are looking for that extra edge; not just solid teaching but candidates who are clever enough to inspire and give that special Manor warmth, openness and candour.' Try as we might we couldn't find a parent who was less than dewy-eyed about the place, the teaching, the way their sons and daughters had flourished.

Relaxation is golf (clearly passion rather than pastime, it featured in assembly), which he plays at nearby Frilford with his wife. He has 'revived' his piano playing and takes lessons out of school. And is The Manor bearing up in these uncertain times? Expansion of the over-subscribed pre-nursery provision and building plans – a two-storey block to replace some perfectly respectable temporary classrooms – would say a confident yes. 'Numbers are up. Our governors take the view that quality is recession proof.'

Entrance: 'Virtually non-selective'. Informal visit with parents for youngest, trial day for pupils entering years 1 to 6.

Exit: No formal links to any senior schools but pretty seamless progression of girls trailing scholarships and awards – majority to St Helen and St Katharine, Headington, Oxford High, Our Lady's Abingdon, Cokethorpe, handful further afield to Wycombe Abbey, St Mary's Calne, Downe House, Queen Anne's School, Caversham.

Boys leave at seven, most to Abingdon Prep where they have a 'reserved' but definitely not 'guaranteed' place, also The Dragon and Magdalen College.

Remarks: Approach via the educational super-highway that is the Faringdon Road in Abingdon and just when you think there can't be another school, take a sharp turn into The Manor. We arrived at drop off time and bravely nosed the modest GSG-mobile between the juggernauts of the Oxfordshire school run. One of the sensible benefits of the Abingdon4Education partnership (or 'soft federation' as the head calls it) is a joint bus service that ferries children in from all points of the compass and serves Abingdon, St Helen and St Katharine, The Manor and thence (by mini bus) Abingdon Prep. According to Mr Heyworth, even The Manor's tiniest will soon have their own dedicated bus with age-appropriate booster seats and school staff to accompany them on their travels – this should ease car park congestion.

Our visit began with assembly and a rousing blast of Land of Hope and Glory from the small but perfectly pitched orchestra, segueing into Dancing Queen – a fine start to anyone's day. Mr Heyworth's inspiring talk on heroic failure was illustrated not only with famous examples (Eddie the Eagle) but also anecdotes from staff and pupils. The most frequently cited experiences were riding and skiing challenges – doubtless a reflection of the school's demographic, but one brave soul claimed to have 'weeded the garden in the rain'.

The friendly, relaxed but orderly atmosphere of assembly set the tone for the work and play we observed. Manor Cottage is the first stop on the 'chronological horseshoe' ground plan of The Manor estate, the charming home of the pre-nursery Manorites, brightened outside with little pots and wellington boots full of pansies. Up to 16 boys and girls come here for anything between one morning and five full days from the age of two. Play, gardening, stories, cookery – children make their own snacks once a week – this is very much a home from home.

The nursery block has an enclosed garden with space to ride bikes; 'we do as much learning outside as we can'. Eager beavers in smart bottle green sweatshirts were having break when we visited, excited about making jam tarts after break – part of the term's jubilee theme. For nursery children who do a full day a mezzanine area allows a soft space if not for sleep, then quiet rest according to parents' requirements. We thoroughly approved of the 'Ask me about...' whiteboard at the entrance to the building – staff write up some of the day's key events so that parents can ask their forgetful darlings leading questions and maybe even receive answers.

More formal teaching begins in reception and, as in other schools, hard stuff goes on in the morning. In every classroom we visited busy hands were doing: in one class pupils were sitting on the floor with little white boards practising writing numbers; in another fractions were being explored by folding sheets of paper. Lessons start with a mental maths warm up, move on to practical work and finish with 'recording'. In each room thinking skills boards pose problem-solving challenges. 'What we don't do is spoon feed.' Indeed, independent learning and 'risk taking' are built into the teaching programme right from the start. Pupils are set from year 2 in maths; an extra set means that each gets exactly the support or extension work they need. All the requisite technology is in place and IT lessons are once a week; screens are mostly in dedicated areas, actively used for research but not dominating classrooms. The hands-on approach to learning persists in the science lab: we saw enthusiastic year 6 girls pile in from the grounds brandishing newly captured mini beasts in magnifying jars, ready to be drawn, described and then released...until next time. Library just a little less splendid than the rest of what we saw – tidy and well stocked but rather spartan. It is, we were told, awaiting refurbishment and may thus become the kind of place one would want to curl up with a book.

The learning support department is at the centre of things, in the manor house from which the school gets its name. 'We can cope with anything, from a pupil needing a bit of extra help with maths and reading, to severe dyslexia.' Parents we spoke to endorse this, describing the learning support team as 'fantastic', 'working wonders.' Three dedicated teachers assess all children and offer support individually, in small groups or in class; this is free up to the end of year 1. According to one parent whose child needed significant support, 'costs can escalate but the school advised us what to expect so at least we didn't get any nasty surprises.' A private speech therapist is also available and the school has accommodated children with hearing and sight problems. Support is tailored to the individual: 'we are flexible according to need'. EAL also on offer and pupils often go from speaking no English to fluency in an astonishingly short time. Impressive gifted and talented programme also in place.

And now to sport. Lucky Manor sports staff (all specialists) are based in a splendid stone barn. There's plenty of green space for running around; additional specialist netball and tennis take place at the nearby White Horse Leisure Centre and swimmers get to use the splendid pool at Abingdon School. When asked about Manor sport, the head suffered a temporary modesty lapse, 'We win everything!' Can this be true? We checked: from cross-country to equestrian, tennis to biathlon, Manor girls leave others standing and compete at county and national levels. Part of the secret of the school's success could be the fact that one member of staff is employed solely to coordinate matches and ensure that all clubs, sporting or otherwise, run and run smoothly. If The Manor says it offers a club, it really does; 'we're not half-hearted', says the head (as if).

Mainstream offerings are free, specialist options such as Spanish or Mandarin are charged and pupils can pursue interests from golf to face painting, chess and touch-typing. Instrumental lessons (including harp) are supported by before and after school music clubs including guitar, chamber group, singing and wind band. The dreaded music practice is encouraged by an awards scheme; teachers set weekly goals and give practice tips. Our charming guides were looking forward to the year 6 Stratford visit (a post-entrance exam treat) which includes a trip on the river, a play and the chance to romp through the Bard's home town in Elizabethan costume and duelling scars (courtesy of a former head of wigs and make-up at the theatre). Other excursions include camping on the Ridgeway, outdoor pursuit adventures on the Isle of Wight and a week in Normandy.

Some of the parents to whom we spoke described how The Manor had 'rescued' their children from unhappy schooling elsewhere and 'returned the smiles to their faces.' Others praised home/school communication, saying that queries were always answered promptly and parents felt that dialogue with teaching staff was genuinely encouraged. A few had concerns

M

about how the pace accelerates in year 5 in advance of entrance exams but said that their daughters, having been 'thoroughly manored', took this in their stride.

So, what manner of magic goes on here? Does the studious atmosphere of those high-octane senior schools waft along the road? Perhaps, but that doesn't quite account for the enviable results achieved by this happy, unpressurised, non-selective school. The head defines it thus, 'We want to cultivate bright-eyed enthusiasm, to say "let's go for it and play with heart"; learning should be linked to the fun of life.'

Maple Walk School

62a Crownhill Road, London, NW10 4EB

- Pupils: 190 boys and girls • Ages: 4-11 • Fees: £7,200 pa
- Independent

Tel: 020 8963 3890
Email: helen.cowen@newmodelschool.co.uk
Website: www.maplewalkschool.co.uk

Headmistress: Since 2012, Mrs Sarah Gillam, previously head of the now defunct White House Prep School in Wokingham. Her 30 year career includes two middle school headships and one head of junior science. She has a BEd from Homerton College Cambridge and is married with three university-age daughters.

Entrance: Non-selective intake of 20 at reception stage. Siblings get preference, then in order of registration – waiting lists for several years ahead. For spaces higher up the school, the head meets the parents and the child has a trial day in the relevant class, 'to check that they will fit in socially and academically'.

Exit: To a wide variety of schools, including Francis Holland, Aldenham, Notting Hill and Ealing, Channing, John Lyon, Queen's College, Portland Place and North Bridge House in the private sector, and St Marylebone, Hampstead School and West London Free School in the state sector. Younger children have also gained places at, amongst others, Wetherby Prep, Notting Hill Prep, Bute House and Sunningdale Prep.

Remarks: The New Model School Company (NMS) was set up by Civitas (but is now an independent entity) when research identified a gap in the market for a low-cost chain of not-for-profit independent primary schools. Maple Walk was the first NMS school, starting in a rented room in a sports centre off Ladbroke Grove in 2004 with one teacher, two pupils and school materials stored in a trunk. A year later the fledgling school of a dozen pupils moved to the upper floor of a church hall off Kensal Road. In September 2009 the school – by now with classes up to year 4 – moved to its own purpose-built premises in Harlesden, which have impeccable ecological credentials: a sedum roof, solar panels, a ground source heat pump and a rainwater harvesting system, plus a no-car travel plan. It has added a form each year and since September 2011 has had a full complement of 145 children.

The education is traditional, with reading taught by phonics, French throughout, history taught chronologically. A strong emphasis on politeness and courtesy, with every child shaking their teacher's hand at the beginning and end of the day. The first Ofsted report, written in 2008 when the school was still in temporary accommodation, is surprisingly lukewarm, but the previous head was sanguine about it: 'The weaknesses were mostly to do with paperwork and correct materials. We were able to address the areas they highlighted while we were still there.' Indeed, a recent Independent Schools Inspectorate

report praises the 'good' teaching standards, 'excellent' personal development and 'outstanding' relationships between parents and school.

Certainly parents are happy. 'They seem to be getting a very good grounding,' said one. 'They have really nice teachers who know the children well.' 'They're doing incredible work,' said another. 'I think it's outstanding.' 2012 has been a testing year for school and pupils as the first year 6s took their 11+ exams. The head's after-school secondary transfer club introduces exam techniques, and the year 6 class teacher 'is very experienced at secondary transfers'. 'They've done their absolute best to make sure they were well prepared,' said a parent.

The school can cope with mild SEN – 'We don't assess children coming into reception, but we do ask parents to be honest and transparent, and we may talk to their nursery if we have any concerns'. One-to-one literacy and numeracy assistance at extra cost; some children get speech and language support outside school.

An emphasis on children becoming confident public performers: the annual Craigmyle poetry competition (named for the charitable trust that paid for the new site and building works) involves everyone from reception upwards reciting a poem by heart, and there are public speaking competitions, music concerts and drama performances. 'The children are very confident,' said a parent. 'They have nice manners, they can talk to adults, they look you in the eye.'

The school's outdoor space includes playgrounds for infants and for juniors – with a climbing frame purchased by parents from Ebay – and a football/netball court with climbing wall (also funded by the PTA, Friends of Maple Walk). The gardening club grows vegetables in tiered beds and a butterfly/bee-friendly area is in concept. The children learn to swim at a local pool and try out a different sport each half term. A dance group – 'the youngest by a long stretch' – came third in the Dance Challenge UK national finals at the Cadogan Hall.

This is a low-cost, no-frills school, which depends on plenty of parental involvement. The PTA has raised funds for part-time specialist dance and sports teachers, and parents have donated computers, including a suite of Netbooks that travel round different classrooms. Parents run clubs and help organise book weeks, art extravaganzas – 'delicious organised chaos' – and cultural celebrations. The school is a Christian one, with weekly religious assemblies and nativity plays, but all faiths are welcome and Jewish and Muslim parents come in to talk about their religions.

Despite the low fees, it is still very much a white, middle class demographic – albeit mostly journalists, artists and musicians rather than bankers and lawyers. However, the school is building links with the local state primary school just down the road, with shared activities, teacher training, netball and football matches. Now the school has its own settled base in a very diverse area, it hopes to attract a wider social and ethnic mix of families.

Parents cite the 'village school' atmosphere as one of their main reasons for choosing Maple Walk. 'There's a nice, cosy, community feel,' said one. 'I liked the fact that it is small, pioneering and affordable,' said another. 'It's a really vibrant, eclectic community.' Parents emphasise how happy their children are – 'Mine will look back and feel they've been part of something really special and exciting'.

M

Marlborough House School

Hawkhurst, Cranbrook, TN18 4PY

- Pupils: 300; 160 boys/140 girls. 70 pupils are flexi-boarders.
- Ages: Rising 3-13 years • C of E • Fees: £7,350-£15,210 pa
- Independent

Tel: 01580 753555
Email: registrar@marlboroughhouseschool.co.uk
Website: www.marlboroughhouseschool.co.uk

Headmaster: Since 2013, Mr Martyn Ward BEd. Educated at Repton and Colston's School, Bristol, then Westminster College, Oxford. Previously deputy head of St Andrew's School, Eastbourne. Before that, taught English and history at The Hall in Hampstead and English at Cothill. A keen musician and sportsman, he's married to Rachel and they have two young daughters.

Entrance: It is worth registering as soon as possible as oversubscribed, but most people who really want a place usually get one. Informal assessment day plus school report and interview with the head. No formal tests – important that the school is right for the child. Those with mild learning difficulties assessed to make sure the school can cater for their needs. Majority of children arrive in the nursery and stay right through until 13, although children can join at any age if spaces. Some children come in from the primaries for the last two years to sit Cranbrook entrance exam. A few move on to boarding preps at 8+. Up to 24 children in the nursery (age 3-4) plus eight spaces for rising threes. Two form entry throughout the rest of the school.

Exit: Mainly to fairly local schools. Around 30 to 40 per cent to Cranbrook plus Tonbridge, King's Canterbury, Bethany, Eastbourne College, Brighton College and Benenden. Occasionally further afield to, eg, Harrow, Winchester, Rugby, Eton. Good range of scholarships most years. In the past three years pupils have been awarded academic scholarships to Harrow, Sevenoaks, King's Canterbury, Claremont, Sutton Valence and Mayfield and academic exhibition to King's Canterbury, a music scholarship to Tonbridge and sports scholarships to Eastbourne, Ardingly, Kent College and Mayfield. Also art scholarships most years. Three to four a year leave at 11+ for the grammars – the school will prepare them as much as possible for the Kent Test.

Remarks: Founded in 1874, the school moved in 1930 to a Georgian house set in 34 acres of landscaped grounds on the edge of Hawkhurst. Wonderful setting where everything looks beautiful and is kept immaculately. Purpose-built pre-prep and a large sports hall used by all age groups. The nursery in its own house next to the main school with its own garden and play equipment.

No streaming but children are setted in some subjects from seven. Spanish or Latin introduced as a second language from year 5. Touch typing taught from year 3. No special scholarship class – gifted children are given individually tailored programmes within their year group in the form of one-to-one tuition, discussion forums and small extension groups. Good back-up for mild dyslexia – three full-time learning support staff for individual or group sessions. Teachers always on the look out for problems.

An exceptionally friendly school where everyone is quickly made to feel part of the community. The Friends of Marlborough House, a parents' group, is very active in welcoming new parents and making them feel part of the school. They also organise social events throughout the year – quiz nights, various parent/teacher friendlies and the biennial summer ball. No full or weekly boarding but flexi-boarding a popular option and most children do a bit of this. Own in-house catering – excellent food with everything prepared on site, justifiably proud of their reputation.

Main sports are football, rugby, hockey and cricket for the boys and netball, hockey and rounders for the girls. Also tennis, .22 rifle shooting; keen golfers have lessons on the local course opposite the school and year 8s have the opportunity to sail at the local reservoir. Taking part is more important than winning and most children are given the chance to play in a team. Long list of thriving after-school activities including popular gardening and cooking clubs. For one night a term the dining room is turned into a restaurant and the children who are members of the chef club cook and serve a meal for their parents. Older children stay on at school for prep and may also stay for supper and evening clubs – a popular option with parents. Strong anti-bullying policy and always someone on hand for the children to talk to. Low staff turnover, a number have been part of the school for many years – a dedicated team who are happy and committed.

About two-thirds of prep school pupils learn a musical instrument up to and including grade 8 – a good record of music scholarships. A number of informal concerts throughout the year. Lots of opportunities to get involved with music-making. Thriving art department with scholarships most years. Creative pottery workshops for year 8. Annual art exhibition featuring work from every pupil. Strong IT department. All have a chance to get involved in drama productions during the year – one big school play annually and smaller plays for most year groups during the year, plus the very popular Marlborough House X Factor. Everyone given the opportunity to take part in the annual poetry reading competition. Plenty of trips and outings both locally and further afield – geography trips to Montreuil and Isle of Wight. French and classics trip to Aix-en-Provence and annual winter skiing trip.

Produces confident children who are generally tolerant and respectful of each other. School keen to ensure that children are aware of a world beyond the school gates – emphasis on fund-raising and charity work, eg the whole school did the Sports Relief mile. Pupils visit the elderly at Bowles Lodge Residential Centre in Hawkhurst to chat to them and the younger pupils visit to entertain the residents with songs and poems. Values for Living Code displayed around the school: be honest, be kind, be helpful, be polite, listen, do your best. Calm, ordered school where everything seems to run smoothly.

Famous old boys include cricketer David Gower, screen writer and director Stephen Poliakoff and his brother, the chemist Professor Martyn Poliakoff CBE.

A very happy, caring and gentle school where every child is treated as an individual and reaches their full potential, academically and in sport, art, drama and music – always looking for hidden talents.

M

The Maynard Junior School

Linked school: The Maynard School

Denmark Road, Exeter, EX1 1SJ

• Pupils: 90 girls, all day • Ages: 7–11 • Fees: £9,009 pa
• Independent

Tel: 01392 273417
Email: admissions@maynard.co.uk
Website: www.maynard.co.uk

Head of Junior School: Since 2006, Mr Steven Smerdon (early forties), educated at Downside School and Exeter University. We last met him as housemaster at Loretto near Edinburgh, so he's certainly travelled a bit to get here. 'Hands-on, caring and enthusiastic,' say delighted mums. 'He has time for each girl and knows everything that's going on.' Super. Teaches RE and drama. He enjoys playing the guitar and all outdoor activities – a keen VW campervan owner.

Entrance: Tests in English, maths, reasoning and reading.

Exit: No qualifying examination for entry to senior school at 11, therefore seamless for nearly all.

Remarks: Present building replaced Victorian villa destroyed by fire in early 1970s. Refurbished in 2009. Shares tennis court area with seniors for outside play, but children have to start sprints on sports day at a 90 degree angle to finish – quite a sight apparently.

Super, friendly atmosphere. Experienced and creative teachers plus one LSA help generate high standard of work throughout. Lovely reading area for year 3 girls. Exciting displays are changed regularly to keep pace with theme work. Girls mainly with class teachers until year 6, when they spend more time with senior specialists. We were impressed by girls' written work, both creative and formal. Reading culture and girls get a taste of three languages before they transfer. SENCo screens for SpLD and provides learning support in small library also used for speech and drama.

Extended lunch-times for wide range of activities including drama, art, French club and orchestra. Head keen on digital animation. Older girls join middle school choir, so lots of ways to make transfer to senior school work well. Eighty-five per cent play an instrument – musical talent showcased in concert at end of spring term. Senior girls help out a lot at lunchtimes. Emphasis on inclusion in drama, music and sport so 'every girl can share limelight'. Travel considerations mean not much happens after school and girls get small amounts (10-20 minutes) of homework. Year 6 monitors run weekly fair trade stall selling healthy snacks. Lots of sport using senior facilities. Swimming in spring term. Expeditions in summer and outdoor pursuits. Room for every kind of girl here – definitely a winner.

Mayville High School Junior Department

Linked school: Mayville High School

35–37 St Simon's Road, Southsea, PO5 2PE

• Pupils: 140 girls and boys in junior department; 80 in pre-prep; all day • Ages: 6m–11 • C of E • Fees: £6,030–£6,690 pa
• Independent

Tel: 023 9273 4847
Email: enquiries@mayvillehighschool.net
Website: www.mayvillehighschool.com

Head: Linda Owens

Remarks: See senior school's entry

Merchant Taylors' Girls' Junior and Mixed Infants School

Linked schools: Merchant Taylors' Boys' School; Merchant Taylors' Girls' School

---

Liverpool Road, Crosby, L23 5TH

• Pupils: 330 boys and girls • Ages: Girls 4–11; boys 4–7 • Non denominational Christian • Fees: £7,566 pa • Independent

---

Tel: 0151 924 1506
Email: admissionsMTGS@merchanttaylors.com
Website: www.merchanttaylors.com

Headmistress: Since 2007, Miss Julie Yardley BA PGCE (mid 40s). Educated at Birkenhead High, music degree at Liverpool University; worked in sales before primary music training; taught in state schools in the Wirral, Birkenhead High Juniors, head of Bolton Schools Girls' Junior Division; regularly does support teaching at school. Keen to make curriculum more lively with problem solving, active and independent learning approaches and to foster 'give it a go' spirit and perseverance. Energetic, ebullient, enthusiastic. Main hobby music – performing and concerts.

Entrance: Four to 7-year-olds' assessments usually in spring term but available throughout the year (can join at any age) – observed doing age appropriate activities, looking for readiness to listen and adapt to school life. More places available in year 3 – short tests in English and maths based on key stage 1 curriculum.

Sibling discount of 10 per cent for second and third children, 20 per cent for fourth and any more.

Exit: Boys leave at end of year 2, most for Merchant Taylors' Junior; girls leave at 11, mainly for senior school.

Remarks: Original 1800s, cream and blue, converted house supplemented by other buildings about to be refurbished and augmented – imminent major two year rebuild, which will provide large hall, infant classrooms, library, science, art, music and drama rooms. Adventure playground recently opened.

Ability spread from average to very bright. Class sizes around 15. National curriculum with extras; no key stage tests. Year 5 annual themed activities day; cross-curricular practical work linked with science; we admired a very creative classics

M

project; imaginative events, eg a giant egg appearing in the playground, used to develop investigative skills and newspaper report writing; all teachers plan a weekly gifted and talented activity open to all children. Impressive success in national maths competition.

Learning support mainly for dyslexia and dyspraxia, but if a child has enough ability and school and parents feel this is the right place, would do their best to accommodate all needs; a few EAL children.

Uses senior schools' sports facilities – swimming pool, very recent sports centre, courts and pitches. Strong swimming and athletics (three biathletes in national finals), soccer club for year 2s. Annual music competition; lively drama – version of A Midsummer Night's Dream produced by year 6 classes in a week, with input from professional actors and a fashion designer; a girl starred in Matilda the musical – youngest ever winner of an Olivier award. High standard, inventive art; year 6 have practical art sessions, eg recycled fashion day, in conjunction with senior school art department.

School and eco councils; good range of clubs including thinking skills, Italian, French; charity fundraising; residentials at outdoor activities centre for years 4 and 6.

Pastoral care centred on class teachers plus strong lunch-time welfare team; year 2 'playground pals' attend to infants' playground; years 5 and 6 help with infants' sports day and read with them – lots of opportunities for responsibility. House points, merit badges, weekly merit assembly. Parents pleased with friendly, accessible teachers.

Early years foundation stage judged outstanding by Independent Schools Inspectorate; links with feeder nurseries; good use of small outdoor area and support for additional needs; happy children, very competent at ICT.

Promises well, with much improved accommodation to come and lessons moving in a more progressive direction.

Merchiston Juniors (aka Pringle)

Linked school: Merchiston Castle School

Colinton Road, Edinburgh, EH13 0PU

- Pupils: 95 boys; 20 full boarders, up to 50 flexi-boarders
- Ages: 8–13 • Non-denom • Fees: Boarding £17,595–£20,460; Day £12,525–£14,160 pa • Independent

Tel: 01313 122200
Email: admissions@merchiston.co.uk
Website: www.merchiston.co.uk

Head: Mr Andrew Hunter BA (see senior school)

Head of junior school: Since 2012, Mrs Niamh Waldron (forties); came to the school in 2005 and was previously head of The Pringle Centre.

Entrance: At any age. Taster days/weekends

Exit: Unless intellectual impairment intervenes, or logistics apply, all move on to senior school.

Remarks: Merchiston Juniors, aka Pringle, is tucked tidily into the south west corner of the school grounds, though pupils have access to, and use of, the entire campus eg swimming pool, gym, games fields.

Traditionally a boarding school, both Pringle (Merchiston Juniors) and Merchiston itself now boast a fair number of day boys, many of whom sleep over on occasion, often boarding full time by their last year in Pringle. Known to the rest of us as flex-

boarding, Merchiston prefers the term 'step-up', (softly softly catchee monkey). Nathan Mylin is housemaster of an extended Pringle House which can sleep max 46 boys at any one time. Enclosed in its own private (secret) garden; boys can climb the one tree as far as the white mark and do all the things that little boys like doing without being made to feel silly. Book inspired dayroom, plus obligatory television and rather complicated game of Diplomacy up on the wall. School in good heart, well used, nothing flash but no signs of real distress either. Huge amount of dosh spent recently on mega-revamp including loos and individual showers.

Junior school has its own director of studies, tinies taught in the starkly modern Pringle Centre classrooms – we enjoyed a treatise on tropical fish from the youngest year group; computers in every classroom and a bank of laptops for class use. Langs from the start. Specialist teachers for science, maths, the arts. Learning support teacher dedicated to the juniors, who heads a team of one full-timer and roughly three part-timers. No pupil accepted who can't 'access mainstream education' (min 100 IQ). All pupils assessed on entry on a whole year group basis for reading, writing and 'rithmetic. Support is individually tailored to each pupil's profile. Plus cluster groups for foreign languages and Latin (age 11): as much to get boys up to speed as for actual diagnosable problems. In-class support too, plus 'concentrated units' for spelling, reading and individual subjects. Maths on the whole catered for by the maths department, whilst the SEN specialists provide support lower down the school – sometimes withdrawn and sometimes in class.

Chaps take lessons in main school age 10, are set age 11, and follow three individual sciences age 12, moving seamlessly up to senior school (without common entrance) age 13 or thereabouts.

Ten years in the same campus could be a daunting experience. Moving from one building to another within that complex might be the answer. Colinton is hardly Edinburgh City Centre, but the school itself is a bare five minutes' drive from the Edinburgh bypass, which might tick all the boxes for some.

Merlin School

4 Carlton Drive, London, SW15 2BZ

- Pupils: 215 boys and girls; all day • Ages: 4–8 • Mostly Christian, but other faiths embraced • Fees: £12,132 pa • Independent

Tel: 020 8788 2769
Email: secretary@merlinschool.net
Website: www.merlinschool.net

Headmistress: Since 2003, Mrs Kate Prest BA Music/Ed PGCE (forties). Studied at Oxford Brookes. Formerly head of pre-prep at The Harrodian, and before that, teacher and music specialist at Oratory Primary, Chelsea. Welcoming, lively and overflowing with enthusiasm, she treasures the school's unique, homely feel. 'We work very much as a team, which extends through staff, pupils, parents and even grandparents,' she told us.

Believes in the importance of communication and keeping children aware of the world they live in. Operates a complete open door policy, which parents told us works a treat. Prefers verbal communication and does not do email. She hurriedly assured us, however, that the school secretary does. Always there to help and advise parents on the next stage. Lives locally and is married with three children, all of whom have attended the Merlin (daughter still there). Husband works in the City, so has no plans to move on. 'I'm not going anywhere,' she says. 'This is good. I love this school.'

Entrance: Non-selective. Parents attend an early afternoon talk and tour of the school. Places are then offered on receipt of registration – priority given to siblings, then it's first come first served. Advisable to view early. There are occasionally places higher up the school.

Exit: Some leave at seven and the rest at eight. They go to schools all over and, apart from a high number to The Harrodian at eight, (no feeding but a link, whereby they are interviewed in November rather than examined in January), there is no particular pattern. Colet Court, Bute House, King's Wimbledon, Northcote Lodge all figure, along with other London day schools and some country preps.

Remarks: Located in a large, converted Victorian house in a leafy Putney street, the school is homely, welcoming and cosy and initially appears quite old fashioned in approach and look. We were shown round by three articulate, enthusiastic pupils – luckily they knew where they were going because we got completely confused. Good sized and light classrooms, well decorated with children's work. Very little evidence of IT influence. One interactive whiteboard – head says, 'I want teachers in front of my children.' They have an ICT room, where all years have a lesson every week. Each classroom has a computer – used by the children in rotation. Separate science and art rooms. 'We dissect in year 3,' one enthusiastic pupil told us.

Class sizes are small (average 17). All classes are mixed ability. Some subjects are classroom-based, while others follow the teacher. Divisions according to ability in maths and English. Never a really competitive feel, apart from in an advanced maths class. Children seem happy, relaxed and attentive – and eager to tell us what they were doing.

Drama and musical productions are an important part of the school year. Lots of music, vocal, instrumental and theoretical (not surprising with a music-trained head). Head still takes all the children for weekly classes. About a third learn violin, piano or guitar as an extra, with lessons rotated in school hours and practice done at home.

A spacious playground with Astroturf – plenty of room for outdoor play and sports practice. On the far side, purpose-built classrooms are occupied by year 2 classes. Well designed for indoor and outdoor use. Popular and experienced sports master ensures that everyone can try everything. Two training sessions a week in the playground (or inside if necessary), to build up co-ordination. Off-site practice once a week at a local sports venue. Fixtures against similar schools in football, hockey, cricket and rugby, but other sports on offer too. 'My bright, but not at all sporty, child gets to try everything and never feels that he's not excelling,' a parent told us. Chess is popular too – it's one of a host after-school clubs. School won the Windlesham House Chess Championship in 2011.

Dining hall in basement, and our young guides said the food, on the whole, is excellent. Sensibly, there isn't a great deal of choice. 'We have to try everything, but if we really, really don't like it, we are allowed to scrape it into a bowl,' they told us. All cooked in-house, with nutritionist's supervision. Catering staff have a list of all children with specific dietary requirements. School is very hot on manners too.

Warm, caring and fully-trained head of SEN, with two sympathetic assistants to make sure every contingency is covered. Good at identifying and dealing with problems. School says it is important to find each child's particular strengths. Early dyslexia screening for the youngest and full screening if suspected in older children. Parents always informed first. Continual staff meetings to discuss children and identify any possible problem areas. School runs own phonics, maths and spelling programmes and tries to give extra help in groups; if one-to-one is necessary, that is charged for. Always enough help in class, from gap year students and parent volunteers. An extra reading clinic in year 1. Occasional EAL pupils given extra support as necessary.

A happy, friendly school that builds children's confidence and prepares them well for the next step. One parent told us: 'My child has had an amazing experience. He has learned and grown and is ready to move on.' Another said: 'We have been really happy with the quality of education and care our son has received. They really find out what children are good at and make it happen.' Not for those who want acres of outside space, but a real home from home.

Michael Hall School (Lower)

Linked school: Michael Hall School

Kidbrooke Park, Forest Row, RH18 5JA

• Pupils: Boys and girls • Ages: 0–14 • Steiner Waldorf Schools Fellowship • Fees: Day £5,500–£10,750; Boarding + £6,300–£7,340 pa • Independent

Tel: 01342 822275
Email: info@michaelhall.co.uk
Website: www.michaelhall.co.uk

Head: There is no head teacher. Steiner Waldorf schools are self-governing communities and a 'college of teachers' administers and manages pedagogical issues without a traditional hierarchy supported by the Council of Management (trustees).

Remarks: For details see senior school.

Milbourne Lodge School

43 Arbrook Lane, Esher, KT10 9EG

• Pupils: 190; 145 boys/45 girls; all day • Ages: 4–13 • C of E
• Fees: £9,900–£13,450 pa • Independent

Tel: 01372 462737
Email: admin@milbournelodge.co.uk
Website: www.milbournelodge.co.uk

Headmaster: Since September 2010, Stephen Ilett (early fifties). Educated at Rossall and Lincoln College, Oxford, came to teaching after a career in the City – eight years at Caldicott Prep before appointed here. Reputedly, a big hit with current parents. His wife, Amanda, runs marketing for the school; five children between them, 13-23.

Entrance: Entry to pre-prep on first come basis. Children feed through to the main school, with the rest from local pre-preps, an increasing number travelling out from London (a school bus from Putney) in search of country-style prep schooling. Mostly at seven or eight (a few places available at other times) via maths and English test and a 'chat'. Looking for academic potential (with a view to scholarships) and takes into account previous education. Some feeling among parents that it's easier to get in here than to Colet Court or Westminster but that Milbourne is just as good. Keen to increase numbers, particularly of girls.

Exit: The first thing you see when you enter is the impressive black and gold scholarship board in the hall positively groaning under the weight of names of pupils and their prestigious public school destinations. St Paul's appears regularly and more recently Westminster. A clutch of scholarships in 2013, including academic scholarships to Eton, Charterhouse,

M

Winchester and City of London (boys). Lots go to top notch boarding schools: Eton, Harrow, Winchester, Charterhouse and other highly academic institutions, including Wycombe Abbey for the girls.

Parental rumblings (finally taken on board) that the school needs to take more account of the preferences and requirements of the London day schools, which are increasingly the destination of choice these days – now up to 50 per cent. 'They are getting better at it, but Milbourne has sometimes struggled with the pre-tests for these schools,' considers one mother. Now has VR and NVR practice timetabled into the curriculum for pre-test year as well, and ensures the most experienced members of staff are teaching the key subjects across these year groups.

Remarks: If a place can be traditional and unusual at the same time, then this is it. It's an old-fashioned, academically high powered (six scholarships in 2012, including three to Eton) school with very high expectations of its pupils, by whom it generally does jolly well – assuming your aim is a good public school. Doesn't do anything by the book – and consequently in 2007 received a rather damning Ofsted report which sent some parents into a flat spin. Adding to the turbulence, around the same time Mr Norman Hale, the school's founder, proprietor and headmaster from 1948 to 1999, sold the school to Cognita, which owns and manages a growing group of independent schools all over the country. (Cognita Chairman, Chris Woodhead, was HM Inspector of Schools until 2000.)

The view of Cognita, Milbourne Lodge and its more supportive parents was that the inspectors totally missed the point of the school and that Milbourne and Ofsted were an ideological mismatch. Much of the Ofsted criticism concerned the school's failure to comply with regulatory requirements, including those relating to pupils' welfare, health and safety, behaviour and personal development. Ofsted required immediate action relating to staff appointments, including insistence that the school take up references and run Criminal Records Bureau checks on staff, of which there had been none. Cognita banged back a six-week action plan almost by return post and ran its own inspections until Ofsted's next visit. School maintains all the issues raised in this Ofsted report have now been fully addressed and complied with – the 2010 inspection report says 'significant improvements have taken place'.

Cognita stressed at the time that it had no plans to change the staff or ethos of Milbourne Lodge, so Mr MacLarnon's departure a year later in 2008 caught parents on the hop and aroused a degree of disquiet from a vocal section, with half a dozen families moving their children elsewhere. Concern was felt that the original ethos of Milbourne would disappear and that Cognita did not have the experience of running such a top drawer academic institution. Cognita, not surprisingly, was keen to reassure existing and prospective parents that all was well – 'We see Milbourne as the jewel in the Cognita crown,' said Chris Woodhead. 'There was certainly some parental concern initially, but I am constantly talking with and listening to parents and the feeling of the vast majority now is that the school is settling down. I am determined that Milbourne will retain its academic excellence.' Looking ahead, Mr Woodhead added that Cognita had plans to beef up the pastoral care side of things, broaden the curriculum and invest in new resources and facilities. Following a period of acting head, a permanent appointment was made in 2010.

The main building is a large, converted, Gothic-style red-brick house. Slightly shabby, although much has been recently redecorated – contains the main admin office, kitchen, all-purpose hall; upstairs in the attic are the art and IT rooms. Now only three classrooms in what are essentially wooden huts in the garden – the majority are in the main school building and the Small House.

Grounds are naturally lovely, with great vistas over woods and neighbouring farmer's fields. This place is very keen on the great outdoors. Behind the buildings is a fabulous playing field incorporating football, rugger and cricket pitches, as well as an eight-lane athletics track. Also an outdoor heated pool, apparently well used. Older boys and girls do cross-country runs; younger ones play a wonderful 'ambush' game in the woods – unique to the school, invented 40 years ago by a teacher and just as popular today. No mollycoddling on the curriculum – a happy Milbourne child will generally be a robust character, very bright, a sporty type who doesn't feel the cold – with compulsory outside sport every afternoon, rain or shine, plus necessary moving around between buildings.

No theatre or performance space, but classrooms now contain computers and three interactive whiteboards. The adjacent Small House, previously the head's accommodation, has been refurbished and is the home of the rapidly expanding pre-prep department. What you get is a traditional, classical education with the emphasis on English, maths and Latin. It aims to prepare children solely for common entrance and scholarships and offers a virtual guarantee of a place at a public school.

Does not follow the national curriculum, instead adhering to the requirements of common entrance and the passions of the staff. In addition to the main subjects, Latin for all and Greek for the scholarship stream. Pupils are streamed from day one into A and B – scholarship stream and common entrance stream – but movement between the two as necessary. Pupils are made aware of their place within the class for each subject and strive to improve it. They also have rankings for effort. One result of this is that some parents opt for additional outside tutoring when the results are not as high as they think they should be – a tough life for some children, with pressure heaped upon them from all sides. A number of pupils do sport to a very high level and many do extra sport outside school. You have to wonder how they find the time – it's a long school day, with the top three years not finishing until five or even six o'clock and coming home laden with homework. It's a competitive place, be in no doubt.

Speech and drama offered as an extra activity, continuing after the exams are finished – always an annual production. Art is a real strength – the work on display is among the best we've ever seen for this age group. Among the highlights is a fantastic Toast to Van Gogh – his Sunflowers reworked in toast slices and crumbs. School regularly features in the Royal College of Art Best School awards. Recent successes include Overall Individual Winner and Schools prize in the Saatchi Gallery 'sculpture At School' Competition. Music is also strong – pupils regularly pick up music scholarships. Large music room; tuition of all sorts is available, with opportunities to play in an orchestra or group.

Inside the classrooms children work hard and quietly. Reference books may have seen better days but beautiful neat work can be seen. Children stand up politely as visitors enter – all very smart in blazers and ties, a few in sweatshirts, which have crept across from sports and are deemed acceptable and warm in winter.

This is traditional teaching by traditional staff (perhaps even eccentric in one or two cases) for bright, motivated and energetic pupils in pursuit of excellence. One parent, particularly pleased with the teaching, felt, 'The teachers make sure my son really understands the foundations before moving on'. She added, 'This might constrict the range of what they learn, but at least it means they can do the homework.' Another said that the children were given the facts, tested on them and later revised them, which ensures a 'sound grounding'. 'The style of teaching imposed here means the kids massively increase their ability to memorise information and are almost blasé about being tested,' adds another parent. 'It certainly fosters a resilient character.'

On the other hand, some critics of the place felt the academic success came at too high a price and a few parents voted with their feet and headed off elsewhere. 'The kids are under huge pressure and are continually ranked for everything,' says one ex-parent. Parents also raised concerns about the pastoral care, but a deputy was appointed to strengthen this side of things, plus a new tutor system introduced – the 2010 Ofsted report describes Milbourne staff as 'highly committed to promoting pupils' welfare, health and safety'.

Milbourne is a school that has attracted vociferous praise and criticism in equal measure, so it needs thorough researching to discover whether it will suit you and your child. 'I love the school and so do my kids, but when people ask me if I'd recommend it, I have to say no, go and look for yourself... You will either love it or hate it,' sums up one parent.

Millfield Preparatory School

Linked school: Millfield School

Edgarley Hall, Glastonbury, BA6 8LD

• Pupils: 450; 240 boys/210 girls; 120 full boarders, 20 flexi boarders • Ages: 2–13 • Inter-denominational • Fees: Day £5,730–£16,455; Boarding £24,120 pa • Independent

---

Tel: 01458 832446
Email: office@millfieldprep.com
Website: www.millfieldprep.com

Headmistress: Since September 2010, Mrs Shirley Shayler MEd BSc PGCE. Educated at Carrickfergus Grammar School, Northern Ireland, degree in biology from the University of Stirling, PGCE from Queen's University, Belfast, masters in educational management. No stranger to Millfield, having taught biology at the senior school 1989-2002 and undertaken an impressive spread of pastoral and extra-curricular rôles including coaching first XI girls' hockey and being a houseparent. Deputy head of Taunton School for four years then head of Stonar for another four plus years doing much to expand and improve the sixth form. Lives on site with husband Gary, biology teacher and head of careers at senior school, and daughter, Caragh, who attends Millfield Prep and rides a school pony.

'Delightful' and 'caring' but steely when need arises. Parents we spoke to all thought she was 'a good head who works hard' and commented on how 'she has won respect through not being afraid to stick to her guns.' Loves being back at Millfield: 'a way of life rather than a job,' she commented to us. Really believes in educating 'whole child' and in releasing children's potential. Often seen walking family labrador (she recently delivered seven puppies). Still involved in hockey and also enjoys swimming, cycling, skiing (annual family ski trip is a highlight for Shaylers), reading and the theatre. Vision for future includes providing more enrichment à la Dragon's Den-style enterprise activity, more involvement in the local community and further developing pastoral care.

Entrance: Many admitted via interview and report from previous head (eg from prep schools finishing at 11). Some arrive from pre-preps or local primaries and others from as far away as Venezuela or Hong Kong (we have seldom seen such a varied list of feeder schools). LDC tutor involved at interview where there are special learning needs. Can be flexible – will always make the effort to take pupils and has been a sanctuary for pupils unhappy or failing to thrive elsewhere: 'IQ not the only arbiter; we need to see the child, not just a collection of data.' Can and will take when space available; means-tested bursaries available in cases of genuine need and a number of scholarships (all the usuals plus chess) for entry into years 6, 7 and 8. The former depend on success in the scholarship exams which can be sat each January.

Exit: Most proceed to senior school. Dozen or more scholarships won annually to senior school: academic, art, music and sport. Transfer automatic subject to good behaviour and satisfactory academic standard. A small number move elsewhere, mostly to other independent schools.

Remarks: A unique prep which adheres to traditional pattern of Saturday morning lessons followed by games. Sport and learning support facilities are second to none. Millfield provides a top notch experience in almost every sphere. Lively boarding community which doesn't empty out at weekends (apart from exeats) and still includes Sunday chapel. Boy and girl numbers pretty equal throughout. Many sign up for complete (2-18) Millfield experience. Parents underline how school 'instills confidence and maturity' and how it 'has brought a global dimension to rural Somerset.' Prep campus benefits from more acreage than its senior partner. Centrepiece is an elegant Victorian home of former local landowners. Oak-panelled hall leads to head's capacious study (now made-over to suit her taste) which looks out across manicured, leafy site. Internal standard of classrooms, sports and other facilities more than compensates for lack of architectural cohesion on a site that has grown like Topsy. Unusual external touches include a huge outdoor chess set and the multi-coloured climbing wall. Children seem quite content, scurrying around like worker bees under the queen's command. Main entrance sits on a bend of A361 on the Pilton side of Glastonbury opposite (and safely accessible via footbridge over main road) school's small chapel, nine-hole golf course and Edgarley Manor (a boys' boarding house) at the foot of the famous Tor.

Show starts successfully with Millfield Minis, a three-day-a-week event for local parents and toddlers using pre-prep hall from 10.00-11.30am. There are even Minis' swimming, tennis and trampolining: mind-boggling stuff. Pre-preparatory department (no boarders) moved from town centre to its present complex on main site some years ago and caters for pupils aged 2-7. Safe, ideal location within former walled garden. Reception area shouts creativity and fun; classrooms are flexible learning spaces with eye-catching displays, live animals and loads of interest. Outdoor raised beds for veggie growing, safe play and exploration including forest school area (two teachers trained leaders) nearby. Pond includes underwater camera for pupils to watch submarine activity on linked computer screen inside. We liked the three little pigs guarding the gazebo and outside quiet area. Cosy library to make reading fun and indoor tumble room for scrapes without scratches. Read Write Inc a favourite phonic approach, number games abound and we saw some beautiful progressions of pupils' cursive handwriting on display. Humanities and science themes run alongside core learning. Music, art and drama (last performance was The King's Magic Cloaks) all play a big part. Pre-prep had played out the Olympic opening ceremony a few days before we visited: involvement is the key to learning here. Explore days to sample activities such as willow butterflies and glass painting. Visits aplenty (pre-preppers had been to Olympic sailing venue at Weymouth on day we visited). Children coming into pre-prep are automatically assessed for learning support: one-to-one groups and specialist lessons for those who need extra help from two specialist teachers who work closely with school's learning development centre. Parents appreciate the experience of many long-serving teachers and the extent to which it is 'an inclusive environment' rather than pushy.

Most of the prep school buildings are modern (if not of any particular architectural merit) and provide well for a community of around 400 children. The large, refurbished assembly hall not only serves for school's frequent drama productions but is also used extensively for activities such as fencing and gymnastics. The well-stocked library is above the dining complex (probably the best we've seen in a prep school: all shiny service counters and friendly staff). Food is plentiful and varied. We observed versatile teaching across a broad curriculum in small classes (maximum is normally 16) from an experienced and friendly staff. Years 3-5 are taught by group tutors for most lessons. Setting from year 3 in English, maths and languages with mixed-ability tutor groups. From year 6 all lessons are taught by subject specialists, with tutors continuing to have pastoral oversight. Academic standards are reassuringly high. Despite many children needing extra English, the school's 'language for all' policy ensures that every child can take Spanish as part of their programme. French and Latin are on the main menu with some linguistic side orders also available (eg Mandarin, Russian and Japanese).

The five science labs are still housed in very adequate temporary accommodation close to the main teaching areas, and teachers we spoke to were in no rush to move into a new building. Young number crunchers perform well in competitions such as UK maths challenge and we were told that children particularly enjoy using MangaHigh software. We noticed some examples of mature English writing and imaginative study of poetry. Not overrun with computers though the iPad may be about to become de rigueur. Splendid IT suite with 18 PCs in two areas where we saw some pupils operating robots they had programmed; good use made of smart boards and digital projectors in all subjects. Scholarship group starts in year 7 and we saw some year 8 scholars preparing for Salters chemistry festival at Bath university. Strong eco bias (green flag holders) with regular focus on environmental issues (eg switch off fortnight) and annual eco day. Strong pastoral team overseen by experienced deputy head: each child is watched over by group tutor, responsible for welfare and progress, and first port of call for anxious parents. Reports are termly, with grades for effort as well as attainment. Parents contacted every half-term regarding progress.

Millfield's language development centre (LDC) is a centre of excellence currently helping 100 or so pupils. There are five full-time and four part-time specialists plus a classroom assistant able to administer various software programmes. Strong liaison throughout between LDC, pastoral and academic staff as well as with senior school. Millfield is not a special school, but it attracts pupils with a range of problems from mild literacy difficulties to those with a diagnosis of dyslexia and/or speech and language difficulties. Detailed assessments are carried out in the main body of the school with access to more than 15 different types of assessment including visual and auditory. If reading or spelling is more than a year behind chronological age, this is flagged up, 'But data is not the only aspect taken into account when determining a pupil's current needs.' Each pupil on the SEN register has a pupil diagnostic profile, which details their strengths and weaknesses as well as offering support and guidance to class teachers. The head of LDC is also qualified in neuro-developmental delay with the Institute of Neuro-Physiological Psychology. If the programme is thought beneficial for a pupil and after a positive assessment (co-ordination, balance, visual development, laterality and spatial awareness), a 'five to ten minute a day programme, using no special equipment and replicating movements from the first year of life, is implemented, which gives the brain a second chance to develop the reflexes needed to provide a firm foundation for learning.' Visual overlay and auditory assessments can be carried out by trained members of the LDC team and referral can be made to a speech and language therapist who works closely with both the prep and pre-prep. Good tie-up with houseparents when children may need extra help. All areas of life here based on efforts to find an aptitude, build self-esteem and develop the potential of every child: 'Like a Porsche with a dodgy gearbox... you just need to sort out the gearbox,' said SENCo. Parents praised how their daughter, previously in a specialist school, was now 'blossoming' at Millfield through the combination of specialist help and 'an emphasis on the positive side of everything.' Special programme (Potential Academic Curriculum Excellence or PACE) undertaken by super-bright. Group help at both ends of the spectrum included in fees but one-to-one support and recall to therapists are chargeable. EAL teacher uses academic lesson time with over 30 international students to immerse them in English before they are progressively fitted into mainstream curriculum. Dining hall was bedecked with flags when we visited for annual international bash: lovely foreign nosh and pupils in own traditional dress.

Sport is a big deal here and a pull for many parents: five PE specialists and a number of ex-international coaches. Sixty pupils in swimming squad alone, partnership with LTA to provide top class tennis coaching, and bubble over one of nine courts on site (pupils go to senior complex if necessary) ensures practice continues through winter. Stonking sports hall (includes large spectator area and four squash courts – two of which are glass backed), equestrian centre with extensive stabling and arenas for dressage and show jumping, a nine-hole golf course just for Millfield prep, a fine 25-metre pool (ditto) and all sorts of courts, pitches and fields to cater for every conceivable sport and activity (seven county champions in athletics alone). Rising stars can miss a regular PE lesson to receive individual coaching (eg from ex-first class cricketers). U13 girls had just won national (not just preps) cricket title at Lords when we visited. A powerful presence across all major sports at county and national levels. School is not invincible and meets some stiff competition on the prep schools circuit. Individuals star in many disciplines: fencing, tennis and golf being recent examples. Even the chaplain has a sporting seam running through him (he was going off with a golfing group when we met him). Recent rugby tour was, all of all places, to Dubai and Abu Dhabi. Millfield brain does as well as its brawn with its chess teams defending an enviable reputation in tournaments at all levels.

Cracking music department under long-serving director: attractive modern recital hall (seats 200), classrooms and serried ranks of individual practice rooms; wide range of instruments, 350 individual lessons, 29 music ensembles and 18 annual concerts. Junior baroque chamber orchestra plus four choirs and a chapel choir. Pupils selected for national children's choir and orchestra. Annual highlights include home-grown Young Musician of the Year competition and a rock and pop concert. Drama lessons lead to many pupils becoming involved (on stage or behind the scenes) in one of four major productions held annually. Staff sometimes have to write plays to suit Millfield's large casts. Parents have been amazed at positive effect of school drama on their children. Art (including popular after lessons clubs) is strong as evidenced by displays around school, from print-making to ceramics via ICT, with critical discussion an integral part of its teaching. Good environment in both drawing and painting studios; innovations downstairs included an ex-government printing press bought for a song and stone carving taught in warmer months by talented working artist and done under a lean-to adjacent to art department. Picture of the week chosen from pupils' artwork for insertion in school's newsletter. Design facilities are more akin to a senior school and include CAD design and a laser cutter. Products range from torches to clocks. Textiles aplenty downstairs and food science upstairs encourages innovative cooking which even includes an inter-house competition.

A peaceful haven away from urban distractions where pupils clearly enjoy themselves. House system is used for internal competitions of all kinds (not just sport). Apart from Edgarley Manor (boys' boarding house) across A361, remaining four boarding houses are on main site: all modern with capacity for 38 boarders each. No large dorms: boarders either in two, four or six bed units (early swimmers kept in rooms together to avoid disturbing others when they get up to train). More of a home from home than an institutional feel and bright colours help keep spirits high. Year 8 allowed to do prep in rooms; otherwise, boarders are supervised in school between 5pm and 6pm. Well-equipped common-rooms and cosy kitchens for snacking and chatting. Extra tuck part of house reward system. Boarding houses have outside play areas including tennis court and enclosed field; sick room with alarm in each if houseparent needs calling. Medical staff available 24/7. Day pupils can benefit from fleet of minibuses which ferry children (early rises for some) from outlying villages in time for 8.25am start. Younger ones can leave at 3.45pm but majority of day pupils stay for activities until 5pm. Great choice of daily and Wednesday afternoon activities (for those not involved in matches) includes sailing at Durleigh, sub-aqua group aiming at PADI junior qualification and caving on Mendips. Weekday activities include Airfix modelling and touch typing, as well as sports from pop lacrosse and indoor go-karting. Diverse theme days and stimulating educational visits to destinations as distant as Rome or as close as Glastonbury Abbey all add to broad mix. Charity fund-raising and activities within the local community are also given importance.

We liked the way that so many year 8 pupils get leadership roles on a rotating basis and how 20 of them trained with Kidscape to become peer mentors. Former pupils include 10 current first class cricketers (including half of Somerset CC first XI), rugby stars: Matt Perry and Chris Robshaw, Olympic hockey brothers: Simon and Richard Mantell, Euan Dale (Scottish swimming medallist), Joey Barrington (squash international), Ruth Kelly MP and Max Milligan (photographer, author and explorer). Happy school with genuine excitement at every level. Pupils find their niche here (be it academic, sporting or creative) and 'want to do well.' Facilities to take your breath away but school produces well-rounded individuals rather than arrogant know-it-alls. 'My daughter was dancing with the daisies before she joined Millfield,' said one mum, 'and now the change is unbelievable.' Parents testify to extent that 'academic and less academic pupils can flourish alongside each other.' Hard to do better than this if the package suits.

The Minster School, York

Deangate, York, YO1 7JA

- Pupils: 170 pupils; all day • Ages: 3–13 • Anglican
- Fees: £5,856–£8,955 pa • Independent

Tel: 08449 390000
Email: school@yorkminster.org
Website: www.minsterschoolyork.co.uk

Headmaster: Since 2004, Mr Alex Donaldson MA PGCE Cert ICT (early fifties). Choral scholar at St John's College, Cambridge; professional singer for five years (counter tenor) with, among others, the Tallis Scholars and the BBC Singers. Still helps out in the Minster. A serious musician, but has a wide perspective on education. Joined school in 1988, promoted head 2004. Warm, relaxed personality; communicates easily with children and popular with parents. Instrumental in introducing more collaborative style of management, though still in many ways the traditional prep school head, who knows his pupils well and what's going on; 'we know each other's foibles,' he smiles. All about 'high expectations – academic, social and musical, and they rise to them.' Wife Jane runs the pre-prep; three children, two at university.

Entrance: Most come up from nursery, but any age considered if room. Non-selective; would-be choristers must audition at age seven, when up to four of each sex are chosen to join prestigious Minster choir. Boys' and girls' choirs of 20 each are separate, take equal part in Minster worship and (unusually) like for like

on scholarships; choristers enjoy virtually free education – but work hard for it (as do their parents).

Exit: Leaving is apparently tough: 'we will really miss it,' say both parents and children, but feel they are given good guidance for next schools. 'Great advice and they know our children inside out,' says a grateful parent, adding that they are 'well-prepared for senior school and often go on to shine there'. Most to northern independents at 13: Bootham, The Mount, St Peter's (all York city), Queen Margaret's, Ampleforth. Boarding schools are popular. Some to Rutland triangle – Oakham, Uppingham, Oundle; occasionally Eton, Fettes, Shrewsbury. Understandably excellent record in music scholarships. A few to local maintained schools.

Remarks: School famously claims foundation in 627 by Archbishop Paulinus; certainly a 'song school' existed then. Refounded 1903, specifically at that time to provide choristers for the Minster. Occupies world heritage site slap in the middle of York, bringing the pleasures and pains of operating in the lee of York Minster, which has to be one of the finest buildings in Christendom; 'our school chapel.' smiles the head wryly. Manages to squeeze into a additional space here and there, but expansion is challenging, development a planning nightmare and even returfing the play areas is likely to unearth a Viking or two, bringing the archaeologists flocking and halting any possible progress. Main buildings date from 1832; school also uses string of earlier town houses and handsome Georgian 'Old Residence' for lower school. Despite confined site, it feels remarkably uncluttered, and children seem happily oblivious to the numbers of tourists with cameras slung around their necks peeping through the school gates.

The school's identity and purpose has broadened; prospectus says very firmly, 'Musical ability is not an entrance requirement'; in head's eyes, this is more a school which does music than a music school. The school has been co-educational since 1987, yet that penny is still to drop with local tour guides who still describe it as the 'school for choir boys'. It's now much more than that, though admittedly most prep schools would give teeth to reach even half its standard musically. The Minster still requires – and gets – a top class choir, but it's no longer true that choristers dictate the curriculum or shape of the school day. Even so, over 90 per cent of pupils leave playing one instrument, and about half play two or more. One pupil, whilst admitting sport was his first love, told us, 'I'm really not musical at all – yet coming here I'm still encouraged to play an instrument for pleasure and I have surprised myself.' Plenty of games, societies, activities and trips; 'they are so busy we can hardly keep up,' enthuses one parent. Play areas and cricket nets on site; no gym, pupils have to crocodile to playing fields, Astroturf and swimming nearby at Bootham (admittedly only 10 minutes away). SEN (mostly literacy) catered for (free).

Parents choose the school for its 'family atmosphere whilst getting good academic results' – small is king – and 'children of different ages know each other well and staff and the head know children's names'. Children are 'confident, well-mannered and happy to talk easily to anyone,' say parents, and that was certainly our experience here too. Parents mostly professional and business.

Moira House Junior School

Linked school: Moira House Girls School, Eastbourne

Upper Carlisle Road, Eastbourne, BN20 7TE

• Pupils: 60 girls aged 4–11; mostly day, a few boarders.
55 boys and girls in nursery from 0–4. • Ages: 0–11 • C of E
• Fees: Boarding £20,040–£21,540; Day £6,465–£11,790 pa
• Independent

Tel: 01323 636800
Email: info@moirahouse.co.uk
Website: www.moirahouse.co.uk

Principal: Since 2013, Mr James Sheridan BSc MA (fifties). Grew up in Scotland and completed his schooling at St Patrick's High School, Coatbridge. Read mathematical sciences followed by teacher training in Glasgow. Has taught in both state and independent sectors (including more than 10 years teaching in the Middle East) and is an ISI inspector.

Married to Elizabeth (head of maths at a local school) and they have three grown-up daughters, all teachers. He's a classic car enthusiast, plays golf and tennis and as a keen Celtic supporter, tries to get up to Glasgow when he can.

Entrance: Interview and taster day. Non-selective. Some come up from the nursery, others in years 5 and 6 from local primary schools.

Exit: Virtually all girls move on seamlessly to the senior school. Only a couple have left in the last few years, one with an academic scholarship to Brighton College.

Remarks: Three sections: Nursery, also known as Mini MoHo, for 0-4 year olds (takes boys, open for 50 weeks a year. Baby unit opened in September 2012).The Pre-Prep, for girls aged 4-7, an integral part of the Junior School with extended care at the beginning and end of the day from 8am-6pm at no extra cost – great for working parents. The Upper Junior School, for girls aged 7-11.

Junior school is a self-contained unit within the senior school and has the use of many of their facilities. Light and airy classrooms all recently refurbished with their own ICT suite and outdoor playground and play area. No setting or streaming and all classes are mixed ability – occasionally subjects are taught in mixed age groups.

French taken seriously and immediately: taught from nursery by a native speaker, and each year the hall is transformed into the French town of Moiraville where the girls are given Euros to spend at the café and market stalls and in the boulangerie, and can send postcards from the post office. Mandarin is offered as an after school option.

Particular emphasis on reading and the pleasure it can bring – regular book weeks when the girls can read to each other and share their favourite books and dress up as fictional characters. Citizenship is taught as a separate subject and involves discussion about social justice, diversity, human rights and sustainable development.

All girls are assessed for learning difficulties on arrival and are then offered extra help as required – mainly for mild dyslexia and dyspraxia. No specialist unit, children given a mixture of help in class or in small groups or individually. All have individual learning plans, parents kept closely involved. EAL also available for those who need it.

Drama an integral part of the curriculum; every child will be involved in at least one production a year. Two music lessons a week and lots of extra music via the lunchtime activities programme. Plenty of sport, playing fields and netball courts just across the road. The Junior School has the use of the senior school's sports hall, theatre and music suite with recording studio. Swimming particularly strong – girls have swimming lessons all year in the school's own indoor heated pool and keen swimmers can opt for extra training before school – many swim for local clubs and some at national level. 'If a girl is good at something, the school will find out what it is' says one happy parent.

Parents particularly struck by the 'unpressured family atmosphere and the fact that girls are given the space to think for themselves and the freedom to learn from mistakes'.

Lots of involvement with the local community – girls take part in the Proms concert at Seaford and have even read extracts from their history project work on Eastbourne Youth Radio.

Supportive band of teachers, including some young men, who are determined to make school fun and to develop a life-long love of learning in the girls.

Active parents association ensure all new parents feel welcomed, host new parents lunch as well as organise summer ball and various social and sporting events. 'It is a very nurturing school to us as well as the girls' according to one new parent.

Good network of mini-buses ferry girls from as far away as Brighton, Lewes, Heathfield and Hastings. Not a grand or flashy school. As one parent put it, 'it is a welcoming place for parents who want a bit more than the state system has to offer'.

Monkton Preparatory School

Linked school: Monkton Senior School

Combe Down, Bath, BA2 7ET

• Pupils: Prep: 245 boys and girls (day and boarding); Pre-prep: 120 boys and girls (day only) • Ages: 2–13 • Church of England, evangelical • Fees: Boarding £20,250–£21,825; Day £8,688–£15,288 pa • Independent

---

Tel: 01225 837912
Email: admin@monktonprep.org.uk
Website: www.monktoncombeschool.com

Head: Mr Chris Stafford (late fifties). A geographer, he was educated at Kingswood and Oxford and his experience encompasses Bishop's Stortford, St Peter's, Lympstone and St Andrew's, Turi, in Kenya.

Energetic, genuine and kind. A firm advocate of boarding, he is very hands-on – the children respond enthusiastically to his unique combination of firm discipline, personal care and warmth. They're particularly enthusiastic about his RE lessons, where his frequent digressions 'always make us think about and understand things.' Christian beliefs of a joyous tendency underpin his approach to education. Pupils are irresistibly swept into his dramatic productions and musicals. Married to Jane, who 'doesn't officially work' in the school, with three grown up children. He swims before breakfast, whacks a squash ball, turns wood. Much involved in his local church.

Retiring in July 2014. Successor will be Andrew Marshall-Taylor, deputy at Twickenham Prep.

Entrance: Essentially non-selective. Parents pleased that the entry policy allows a wide range of abilities and types, though they're even more pleased that the standards achieved at Monkton Prep rival schools that select. 'The best prep school in England,' one told us. Boarding numbers have doubled in Mr Stafford's time so the feel is definitely of a boarding school with day pupils, especially as there is a significant tranche of pupils from abroad. Informal interview for pre-prep. For the prep at age seven, interview plus tests (English, maths and verbal reasoning).

Unusually 11-year-olds can either join the prep (up to 13) or go direct to the senior school. Parents are mostly local professionals and business folk, and a few forces' families too – an easy mix of the churched and the un-churched.

Exit: Eighty per cent to the senior school at 13, but CE scholarships mean significant minority aim at major independents – Cheltenham, Canford etc plus a trickle to Kingswood, Prior Park or even at 11 to King Edward's, Bath.

Remarks: Fiendishly hard to find down a genteel residential cul de sac, school has a dramatic hilltop setting with great downland views. The stunning sweep of the cricket pitch and leafy lawns isn't spoilt by the mish-mash of school buildings tacked onto the back of the manor house.

Academically sound and according to our pupil guides offers a stimulating and enjoyable education. Despite its non-selective ethos a parent told us that there are plenty of 'incredibly able' children about. Two-form entry in years 3, 4 and 5; streaming from year 5 and an extra scholarship stream added in year 6. Saturday morning school for year 4 and above. Smallish classes (16 to 17). Lots of emphasis on finding out what a child has to offer. Masses of reading lays a foundation for this, with a programme of author visits and a library offering books, board games and beanbags. Long established learning support staff – 'a cracking team' – offers in-class support, handwriting and spelling groups. Children carry journals and too many negative entries result in Saturday detention – but slates are wiped clean every quarter term. The worst sanction, exclusion for disruptive behaviour, is hardly ever needed. Tutors know children well enough to sense when something's wrong so potentially bullying is picked up quickly but 'children do fall out' and need a 'chat.'

Enthusiasm for school meals and even more for the three nurses who care for boarders (and day children when needed).

Pre-prep and nursery in a separate converted villa thath retains its homely feel. Plans afoot to build an integrated pre-prep as part of the prep.

Plenty of sport. Classy pool and spanking new Astroturf hockey pitches (used by senior school too). Great opportunity for competition in top years as the corresponding years in senior school play friendlies against them. Music of every genre – a culture of singing and oodles learn instruments. Some top notch music scholarships to senior schools for the best. Art and drama, with a plethora of expert staff and a chance for everyone to join in. Bags of time for play (not sure how they fit it all in) but even on fine days they are not forced out at break.

Boarding numbers have increased in recent years as have the number of pupils from abroad. Plenty going on at weekends and what's left of the evenings (once activities finish at six). Computers rationed for boarders, but with dedicated daily Skype time for keeping in touch with home.

The school's evangelical Christian ethos underlies all aspects of education here. A happy place, where much is expected and much achieved. Staff, and therefore pupils, work to the highest Christian principles of honest work, self discipline and concern for the needs of others. 'It teaches how to be a good person' said one firmly non-Christian parent, 'and allows children to be accepted and to make their own minds up.' Pupils come first, education next but never as second best. Though open minded, and progressive in the ways which matter, this is an unashamedly and all pervasively Christian foundation.

Moon Hall School

Linked school: Moon Hall College

Pasturewood Road, Holmbury St Mary, Dorking, Surrey, RH5 6LQ

- Pupils: 50 (including five boarders) • Ages: 7–12 • C of E
- Fees: Day £17,610–£17,790; Boarding + £5,550 pa • Independent

Tel: 01306 731464
Email: enquiries@moonhallschool.co.uk
Website: www.moonhallschool.co.uk

Headteacher: Since 2005, Mrs Pam Loré (pronounced Laurie) MA Ed BA Dev Psych RSA Dip SpLD. Arrived at school in 1992 to assess pupils, then to teach. Became deputy head, then head. A keen walker and traveller, she speaks fluent Italian and French and has lived in many countries (particularly loves Italy). Married to Beni and they have three grown-up children and a growing clutch of grandchildren.

Head is energetic, sharp and well informed. During our visit we witnessed her advising a colleague about appropriate reading material, discussing the latest research on specific learning difficulties and giving her views on the advantages of a five-term academic year – all within minutes. Her background in developmental psychology, combined with her work as a Phono Graphix trainer, teaching, role as the school SENCO and personal experience of the nuances of raising a dyslexic child means she is well placed to assess children and offer sage advice to parents, teachers and professionals. She feels passionately that to read functionally is key – and possible – for all. Admits she gets terribly involved, but believes it is the school's ability 'to know every child' that makes the difference.

Entrance: Moon Hall caters for children with a diagnosis of dyslexia, dyspraxia or dyscalculia. Statements fine. Indeed, the school is able to initiate the statementing process, but don't hold your breath, statements for dyslexia are thin on the ground. Parents are asked to provide a report from an educational psychologist. If the child's profile looks suitable, they spend a day at the school, being carefully (but gently) scrutinised and assessed 'to see if the school is appropriate'.

School doesn't accept children with emotional or behavioural problems and is unable to help those with severe speech and language difficulties. Children are 'taught from where they are at' – so no problem with mid-year entry.

Exit: To ease the transition at the end of year 6, the head gives advice to parents on the appropriate next school for their child. Some go on to Moon Hall College (run by Moon Hall's founder, Berry Baker) or to Belmont Prep School. Quite a few go to schools with good learning support units, including Box Hill, Ewell Castle, Seaford College, the Royal School, St Teresa's and Worth School.

Remarks: This is a CReSTeD category DSP school. Founded in 1985 by Mrs Berry Baker in her home, Moon Hall at Ewhurst, the school is now located on a 65-acre site, amid the tranquility and beauty of the Surrey hills.

Well-resourced and purpose built, Moon Hall is in the grounds of Belmont Preparatory School. The site, uniform, meals, sport, productions and many non-teaching facilities (including weekly and flexi-boarding) are shared, but the schools are separate and have different governing bodies. The relationship works well, with Moon Hall children taking part in Belmont productions and playing a full part in sports and teams. Pupils can transfer to Belmont after Moon Hall.

Teachers are dyslexia specialists, turnover is low and professional development is encouraged. Therapy, including

M

speech and language therapy and occupational therapy, available for those who need it. Full national curriculum is taught but humanities are slimmed to allow for intensive work in literacy and maths. Art, music, science and DT (no MFL, no classics) are delivered by subject specialists. IT programmes, such as Mindview and Read Write Gold, and use of laptops support curriculum delivery.

Meticulously planned multi-sensory lessons are delivered in small, flexible groups – even one-to-one if need arises. Pupils we saw were engaged and responsive in lessons and we noted a variety of techniques, including games, being used to support concepts. The aim is for pupils to access the curriculum at year 7 with confidence, and they do. Work is marked swiftly and feedback prompt. Sensibly, homework is done at school, though parents are expected to hear the children read every evening and ensure touch typing is practised. Holiday homework is set to ensure learning remains on track. Home-school communication is very good and cooperative in spirit.

Most of the pupils take Sats at the end of key stage 2. Recently, of those entered, 79 per cent achieved level 4 or 5 in reading and 50 per cent in writing, while in maths 91 per cent achieved these levels. Not all make top-notch progress all of the time, though school expects all to achieve over time and standardised reading tests indicate reading age can increase by up to two years in a six month period. It isn't just the scores that matter. 'My son has made very good progress... he can read and he is picking up books', one parent told us. Others spoke of lives being transformed. 'There is pixie dust around the school', said another parent. In reality there is no magic wand. It's a matter of hard-work coupled with an understanding of how children learn and excellent, timely delivery.

Pupils are lively, well-mannered children who clearly delight in their school. We heard comments like 'it really helps you – they move you up step by step' and 'it's like a giant family'. But it isn't just the work that excites. Children animatedly recounted tales of woodland adventures, exploration and den building.

Problems are dealt with swiftly and, conscious that bullying can be an issue, children are taught via PSHE 'to be kind to one another'. Pastoral support garners unanimous and fulsome praise from parents, pupils and alumni and school's in-boxes bulge with life-changing testimonials. 'Moon Hall gave me the best possible start on my academic journey', said one child while a parent commented, 'If you have a child who is moderately to severely dyslexic and is lacking in confidence, look no further'. The only regret seemed to be that transition at the end of year 6 is 'too early'.

Parents describe Moon Hall as friendly and welcoming and are delighted with the opportunities afforded by sport. As one said: 'It's brilliant. The girls are given the opportunity to shine'. Odd niggle, though, that Belmont PE staff are not always sensitive to the needs of Moon Hall children. Parents, some of whom have been through the mill, appreciate the support of others in the same boat, plus the coffee mornings and social events organised by the active parents' committee.

Moor Park School

Moor Park, Richards Castle, Ludlow, Shropshire, SY8 4DZ

• Pupils: 250 boys and girls (55/45); 95 boarding beds • Ages: 2 1/2–13 • RC but inter-denom • Fees: Day £6,360–£14,190; Boarding £15,915–£19,410 pa • Independent

Tel: 01584 876061
Email: head@moorpark.org.uk
Website: www.moorpark.org.uk

Headmaster: Since 2008, Mr Jonathan Bartlett, BSc QTS (forties). Graduate of Brunel University where he read PE and history. Keen sportsman and competitive by nature; something of an entrepreneur and visionary; something of an adventurer too, with piercing blue eyes which scan horizons and spot shirt tails that need tucking in. Genuinely passionate about boarding and 'keen to put the fun back' into education, while encouraging pupils to reach their potential. Healthily irritated by the nanny state approach to schools but 'very good on paper', says a fellow professional.

Had an interesting stint teaching in New England at a school near Salem but, after a brief spell working with a newly-founded education agency, came back with a bonus: his delightful wife, Lisa. Quite liked the cut and thrust of the world of business but concluded that schools were where he wanted to be. So to Papplewick, where he was described as 'the best deputy head anyone could wish for'. Popular with children and parents – 'a breath of fresh air', 'fair and fun' – he is generally credited with bringing a new energy and vision to the school. Keen to make the most of the facilities and revels in the glories of Shropshire after the rather more manicured Thames Valley – 'Much less television watched here – the outdoors beckons'.

Mrs Bartlett is surely the best of the head's discoveries in New England and has also met with universal acclaim – 'brilliant', 'can't fault her', 'very kind and nothing is too much trouble', 'a total winner', 'much more than just one of those head's wives who smarm and charm over the match teas and shriek on the touchline'. Indeed she is: helping in the sick bay, 'pleasurable duty evening' in the girls' dorms, teaching foreign languages and health education – but not simultaneously, 'nor as much as I would like to'. They make a delightful team. They also have three young children in the school.

Entrance: Broadly speaking, four starting blocks from which to start the Moor Park adventure. Those 'rising three' may continue through the nursery and kindergarten to the transition stage, aged seven, then on to the senior school. (In fact, the school will consider anyone of any age, providing room.) Potential pupils come for a taster day and sit a relaxed assessment. Pupils aged four are screened for learning difficulties and offered help, if appropriate. Children come from a broadish cross section of society: old money in crumbling houses; new money from escaped Londoners; farmers, who cannot escape; Catholics and Protestants – all drawn by the country feel of the school, with its delight in muddy boots and bright eyed pupils. The catchment area has increased significantly as boarding has become ever more popular.

Exit: To an increasingly varied number of schools. Last year 27 leavers went to 17 different schools with 15 scholarships. An eclectic range of destinations: Eton, Harrow, Radley, Shrewsbury, St Mary's Calne, Westonbirt, Moreton Hall, Stowe, Monmouth, Hereford Cathedral and Bedstone.

Remarks: Founded in 1964 as a Roman Catholic school and housed in an elegant Queen Anne mansion surrounded by wonderful grounds, complete with lake, old trees, a winding drive with a lodge at the foot and distant views of Housman's 'blue remembered hills': a paradise for children. The head is keen to make the most of the grounds and has already overseen the cutting back of the banks of the lake so as to restore vegetation, improve fishing and introduce some boating. Nearby, a classroom has been constructed for outdoor studies and the estate management regularly checks the trees so that this is one of those increasingly rare schools where children may climb trees. Also a boiler suit school where, the head told us with great delight, 'the children often come to lessons covered with mud'. Yes, it's all a long way from the Thames Valley, but that shouldn't detract from the underlying seriousness of academic endeavour. This is not a play school – rather a school which believes that encouraging all round happiness leads to self-realisation and success. Most schools trumpet that belief – this one fulfils it.

The main entrance of the house is warm and inviting with a roaring log fire in the winter, an impressive stair case and remarkable tooled leather wallpaper. Old photographs dotted around remind us that this is an old country house; splendid art work reminds us that this is a lively and creative school. How well the two blend together. Within the house are the various dining rooms (food excellent, as we can testify), the bright and generously proportioned dormitories, with custom made bunks ('super!' enthused a guide) and home to 12 members of staff, some married with children. This arrangement must be one of the reasons why such a tangible family atmosphere – really a happy overlap between staff and pupils. The fine library and the chapel, which has adapted effortlessly from being a spectacular ballroom, are uplifting features. Chapel is held on a daily basis and much appreciated by those to whom we spoke. 'I'm not a Roman Catholic,' said one mother, 'but I like the feel it gives. I'm glad it's around.'

The youngest adventurers start off in the old clock house and are referred to as the Tick Tocks. Thereafter, nearly all classrooms built within the past few years. Even the one remaining old style portacabin is brightly done up and ideal for the purpose. Wonderful art block with paint-daubed atelier for senior artists, who are allowed to work up there unsupervised, another example of the head's mantra of trust. Lively and spirited art teaching. Fizzing D and T with basic carpentry taught to all before moving on to more modern techniques of creation. Brand new computer block. All these marvellous facilities on offer and enthusiastically taken up during after-school clubs and any free time that is available. Art and DT are timetabled in and remain part of the core curriculum; intelligent use of computers means they play an integral part in the whole learning process. We've seen smarter, slicker buildings but none where the teaching was any better as a result. This is a school where teaching really matters and where those with learning difficulties are well looked after.

Boarding is on the increase – partly as a result of the hugely popular weekend activities, partly because of the enthusiasm and involvement of the staff, but mostly through word of mouth. It clearly is fun – 'My child nagged and nagged us to let him board,' said one delighted parent. In celebration of the increase in boarding numbers and as an example of putting into practice what is being taught, has recently built a low cost sustainable house for young boarders. Not only is it an absolutely fascinating example of eco-building with its larch exteriors and oak interiors brought in from Wales, it is also a trend-setting design for comfortable and practical boarding. Twenty boys and girls now live in magical surroundings with house parents, a resident matron, a dog, kitchens for snacks and rooms for chilling out.

Not long ago it was described as a 'gem' – the word remains appropriate. Forty-four activities, hobbies and sports on offer, from Swahili to origami, jewellery making to bush craft. 'Fun' is the buzz word – and how the staff throw themselves at it! A number are ex-pupils drawn, they say, by the magical surroundings and their happy memories. All of them appear cheerful and involved. A wonderful place in which to grow up: particularly in these exciting times.

Moreton First

Linked school: Moreton Hall School

Weston Rhyn, near Oswestry, SY11 3EW

• Pupils: 80; 50 girls/30 boys; 20 full boarders, 30 flexi-boarders
• Ages: 4-11 • Non-denom • Fees: Boarding £18,960; Day £8,250-£11,610 pa • Independent

Tel: 01691 773671
Email: moretonfirst@moretonhall.com
Website: www.moretonhall.org

Head: Catherine Ford.

Exit: All girls move on to Moreton Hall, the senior school. Most popular choices for boys are Ellesmere College and Packwood Haugh.

Remarks: Moreton First offers boarding from year 3 upwards (boys' boarding recently introduced too). For details see senior school: Moreton Hall School, Oswestry.

Morrison's Academy Junior School

Linked school: Morrison's Academy

Ferntower Road, Crieff, PH7 3AN

• Pupils: 160 boys and girls • Ages: 3-11 • Inter-denom
• Fees: £7,161-£10,200 pa • Independent

Tel: 01764 653885
Email: principal@morrisonsacademy.org
Website: www.morrisonsacademy.org

Head of primary: Mr A R Robertson DipCE.

Exit: An all-through school so pupils automatically transfer to senior school.

Remarks: School has opened a new, purpose-built nursery on the main campus.

M

Mount House School

Mount Tavy, Tavistock, PL19 9JL

- Pupils: 180 boys and girls; more than 40 full and flexi boarders
- Ages: 3–13 • C of E • Fees: Boarding £16,197–£21,297; Day £6,900–£15,297 pa • Independent

Tel: 01822 612244
Email: hmsec@mounthouse.com
Website: www.mounthouse.devon.sch.uk

Headmaster: Since September 2012, Patrick (Paddy) Savage, formerly head of Norman Court Prep (deceased), and before that head of Rookesbury Park Prep. Educated at Downsend Prep School, Felsted School and the University of Birmingham. Married to Suzie, and has three children.

Entrance: Wide ability range – tests in English and maths 'more for benchmarking than selection,' says head. Most entrants attend a taster day in February prior to admission. Majority join the pre-prep or at start of year 3, but growing numbers delay start until year 7.

Exit: Highly successful record at common entrance. In the past few years leavers (30+ a year) have moved on to a whole host of schools. In 2013 50 per cent of year 8 leavers awarded scholarships or awards to senior schools, including Sherborne, Downside, Canford, Winchester, Millfield, Blundell's, Kelly College and Wellington.

Money matters: Bursaries advertised locally when available (two available for whole school). Individual music and learning support incur an additional cost, likewise some activities.

Remarks: Founded in Plymouth – school crest reflects its roots. Motto: 'Ut prosim' ('to be of use') now more relevant than ever. Stunning grounds include a trout stream (ideal for fly fishing) and a beautiful lake (great for science) bordering on Dartmoor National Park. Recent team of inspectors dubbed it 'an inspirational learning environment'. Core of school based in and around a charming, stone-built Georgian manor house with an assortment of additions to the rear. Attractive hall fulfils variety of functions, including regular assemblies and church services; head's oak-panelled study leads off on one side and the school dining hall on the other. Upstairs are all the boys' and girls' dormitories in separate areas plus the sick bay. The original stables have been converted in a variety of ways, including the 'giraffe house', which features a climbing wall. Further on we found the modern sports hall (with two squash courts), two large science laboratories and impressive music school (a step up from its previous location in a cellar). Wortham Hall is used for major productions, concerts, exams and drama lessons.

Most of the classrooms are an extension of the main building: attractive internally – some with stunning displays – and all with high level of equipment (smartboard in every classroom). Eighteen PCs in IT suite and staff are mostly IT savvy. Outside farm/sustainable technology area has grown out from D and T building (workshops and classroom still used in winter) and is a really great initiative: children of all ages fully involved in animal husbandry and crop cultivation.

Pre-prep in purpose-built, low level accommodation for 60 children up to end of year 2 with discrete outside area. High level of care and individual attention – most pre-preppers transfer seamlessly aged seven. Lots of fun and outdoor experience for this end of the school as well as developing strong foundations in the classroom basics.

Pupils are well turned out – variety of dress according to age and season (suits still worn for formal occasions); they come mainly from Devon and Cornwall, a few from London or elsewhere (very few overseas). Professional, farming and Forces families make up the majority here. 'A lot of Mount House parents are contemplating senior schools further afield,' explains head. Boarding ethos is all important, especially to day pupils.

'Mix of old timers and new blood on staff works well,' commented one father. Ten couples/families live on site and rotate weekend duties. Staff:pupil ratio of 1:10 keeps average class size at around 16. Curriculum is designed to allow pupils to go off piste and generate individual enthusiasms – 'Able teachers have given our son a passion for maths,' reported one mother. High quality of written work wherever you look – we were particularly impressed by some highly imaginative poetry folders we saw, worthy of much older pupils. Some infectiously eccentric science teaching and motivational French lessons were other strong points we noted.

Director of studies acts as SENCo with some 35 pupils on special needs register. Pupils are screened for dyslexia and a dedicated education psychologist will develop an IEP if required. Two part-time SpLD staff give one-to-one help where required.

Five days a week sport here – facilities include fine pitches, heated outdoor pool (very popular) and full size Astroturf; national/regional successes principally in rugby, cricket and girls' hockey. Boarders love to play in the nets or swim after prep in the summer. Shackleton Award scheme (loosely based on D of E award) fills the only non-games afternoon and aims at developing self-confidence through a range of (mainly) outdoor activities – eg raft building and scavenger hunts. Horsey pupils get to ride in local hunt and compete at inter-school equestrian events.

Pupils' art work is a credit to HoD (year 8 pupils were working on 'Op art' project when we visited). Lovely studio in converted coach house and art scholarships are not uncommon – latest to Bryanston. Parents very pleased with music – 'It has changed dramatically for the better,' they say: staggering 90 per cent of pupils have individual instrumental tuition. Music seen as 'cool' and lots happens, from robed church choir to participation in local music festivals. Full orchestra as well as jazz band, woodwind, choir, rock band – all get to perform at concerts throughout year.

Latest innovation is introduction of sustainable design and technology course – each pupil spends two periods a week in farm area. Head is passionate about need for next generation to have hands-on experience. Possible issues for veggies (eg Boris the pig going off to the abattoir, then back to the dining table) are 'handled sensitively,' we were assured. 'Whole school's Christmas feast will be home grown from now on,' beams the head enthusiastically; he has little time for 'box ticking eco awards' but wants this side of the school to be seen as vital. Even the tractor runs on recycled vegetable oil from the school kitchen and a bore hole in place for the water supply. Next step: solar micro generators.

Pupils badger parents to let them board – many of the latter wait until four terms from senior school to cut the apron strings. Boarding staff very popular (girls we spoke to quoted their houseparents as the best thing about boarding at MH). Dormitories are neat and light; common rooms are places for relaxing after long and busy days. Television limited to Wednesdays and Saturdays but plenty of choice of games etc. Lovely, separate house for up to 30 girls bursting at seams. Reward system includes 'headmaster's bar' – lots of ways of winning this. No-one mentioned punishment. Great choice of food (mainly locally sourced) – some exotic dishes included to widen tastes. Civilised eating where proper conversation is encouraged by staff presence. Parents can drop their charges off early and then they get 'breakfast on the house'; day pupils can also stay for tea.

Head has gambled on folding compulsory Saturday classes and sport in favour of voluntary Saturday excursions and

M

activities. He feels that 'modern' parents will more readily accept a prep school boarding commitment which allows them quality time with their children at weekends when desired. New régime includes Saturday evening pick-up after activities, then low key, on-site Sunday programme. Early signs are encouraging with boarding numbers apparently on the increase – a new 'visiting boarders' programme for pupils in forms 1-4 has recently been introduced.

Subterranean library has been created out of former storage area – attractive with lovely hideaways for bookworms to self-indulge. Decking area outside library has created another space for relaxation and quietude. All staff stay here until 6pm every day; prep finishes at 7pm for older pupils (younger ones have clubs) and duty team of staff remains until dorm staff take over at 8.30pm. Head loves way that pupils 'spill out' into grounds after prep.

Fun-filled leavers' concert is climax of summer term. Twice-termly Oracle lectures tap into parents' know-how – recent outside speakers have included explorer Pen Hadow and yachtswoman Tracy Edwards. Lots of local visits for all ages, annual trips to Northern France for the older pupils and regular ski trip to Alps.

Former pupils include Phil de Glanville (England rugby captain), Adrian Lukis (actor in Pride and Prejudice); former foreign secretary and SDP co-founder, Lord David Owen, and explorer, long-distance swimmer and environmentalist, Lewis Pugh, to name but a few.

An unexpectedly rewarding find this far west – a thoroughly successful prep school which caters for all needs. More than holding its own by combining new ideas with traditional values.

The Mount Junior School

Linked school: The Mount School

Dalton Terrace, York, YO24 4DD

• Pupils: 90 girls and boys • Ages: 2-11 • Quaker • Fees: £7,140-£9,660 pa • Independent

Tel: 01904 667513
Email: registrar@mountschoolyork.co.uk
Website: www.mountschoolyork.co.uk/junior-school-home

Head of Junior School: Ms Rachel Capper

Entrance: Entrance by observation (looking for potential), supplemented at six by informal examination.

Exit: Most girls move up to The Mount School at the end of year 6. Boys move on to other local independent schools, such as The Minster.

Remarks: Has the benefit of the facilities and involvement of the senior school, from academic staff (three foreign languages are offered), music, sport and food to mentoring by older girls. Before and after-school care from 8am to 5.30pm for an additional charge.

The school has its own forest school and dedicated programme of outdoor learning and education.

Mowden Hall School

Newton, Stocksfield, NE43 7TP

• Pupils: 124; 58 boys, 66 girls; 70 boarders, 54 day children; Pre-prep and nursery: 53; 27 boys, 26 girls. • Ages: 3-13 years • C of E but all faiths welcome • Fees: Day £9,150-£15,990; Boarding £20,730 pa • Independent

Tel: 01661 842147
Email: info@mowdenhall.co.uk
Website: www.mowdenhall.co.uk

Headmaster: Since 2007, Mr Ben Beardmore-Gray BA (Hons) (early forties). Ludgrove and Ampleforth educated, read history at Newcastle. Qualified solicitor, worked in the City with Cameron McKenna for three years before taking a teaching post at Ludgrove, where his father had taught for 20 years. He then moved to Farleigh Prep School in Hampshire and was deputy head there for six years.

Teaches history, mathematics and coaches games. Became head under the Cothill Trust umbrella; believes in an education that 'provides pupils with the opportunity to be children'. His focus is on boarding, 'creating a family set up has been central to everything', and it's working – numbers increasing, bucking the national trend. Great double act with wife, Sarah, who leads the domestic life of the school and is a member of the senior management team.

Believes in, 'an open door policy for pupils and parents', not difficult as they live with their three children and black labrador in south facing rooms on the ground floor of the house.

Entrance: Wide ability range – non selective, informal assessment and interview with head. Majority of pre-prep transfer to prep. Pupils come from local or prep schools all over the north of England and southern Scotland – Northumberland, Yorkshire, Cumbria, Dumfries and Galloway, Scottish Borders.

Exit: Largest numbers to Oundle, Uppingham, and Ampleforth, though Eton, Harrow, Downe House, Rugby, Millfield, Queen Margaret's, Sedbergh, Glenalmond and Fettes feature, as well as Newcastle day schools at 13+. Forty awards in last five years. Few leave at 11.

Remarks: Splendid setting, on a 50 acre site with fine views, reached via a sweeping drive, dodging wildlife, sleeping policemen and miscreants ignoring the one way system through the estate. Far less isolated and much more accessible (just off the A69 and ten miles from Newcastle) than its setting would suggest. Though unusual for the times, no mobiles, no ipods or electronic devices allowed. Pupils communicate with their parents by the old fashioned means of weekly letters, e-mail (access after supper) or use of the two payphones. Neither pupils nor parents had any complaints; Sarah Beardmore-Gray is, 'famous for phoning even past 10pm to discuss your child, and each family feels that she looks after their particular child especially carefully', said one, echoed by others.

Impressive sports fields abound (games every afternoon) and woodland provides a muddy but exciting landscape for den-building competitions and a BMX trail. Also the much anticipated 'gappy games' which involve an energetic 'hare and hounds' pursuit through natural terrain led by the gap students. Indoor heated swimming pool, 'a nice to have for prep schools', says the head, but sadly no Astroturf.

The heart of the school is the main house, the Victorian Newton Hall, which houses the head's family, common rooms, library and dining rooms on the ground floor and boarding accommodation on first and second floors. Many additions and conversions, including a gym and theatre. Prep classrooms are housed in estate buildings around the former stable yard. Light bright classrooms with plenty of work on display and heaps of encouragement on hand. Cleverly converted science, art and technology centre in the stable yard (very busy at club time in evenings and over weekends) and super art. Amazingly detailed plaster casts of hands on display after weekend master class run by Oundle head of art.

Prep children are set for English and mathematics for years 4 and 5, then streamed from year 6. The top class study Greek and a number will sit scholarships (good track record). Maximum class size 16; French for all from nursery; Latin from year 5. Good and imaginative teaching at all levels. 'Our teachers make learning exciting', said one pupil to a chorus of nodding heads. SENCO with specialist dyslexia qualification provides support throughout the school and EAL qualified teacher works with small number, primarily Spanish children.

Focus on CE kicks off in year 7 after the unique experience of 'entente cordiale', a term spent at Chateau de Sauveterre near Toulouse, immersed in French and the French way of life. This experience is reinforced on their return through weekly lunches with French speaking staff. Children also spend a week in summer term in year 7 at Tree School in Dorset, a centre for natural sciences. Assisting scientists from the Natural History Museum, children extract DNA from trees and plants for an international project to barcode Britain's plant life.

The next step is a big one and the head has close links with the head and senior staff at a number of senior boarding schools. Head, 'guides parents who should have a clear idea by year 6', and, 'he doesn't often need to re-align expectations'. Helped by regular reporting through prep years; effort and attainment grades every three weeks; full written report each term. Pupils de-stress after CE with a diverse and challenging three week leavers' programme.

The first step can be nursery from the age of three and the unstreamed pre-prep, popular with local families, though small numbers. Accommodated in attractive building with years 1 and 2, separated from main house by the netball courts; year 3 providing well-prepared transition to prep school, housed separately in adjoining building. Nursery and reception linked through sliding doors and direct access to outdoors play on its way. Own secure playground. Specialist music, French, IT and swimming; drama from year 2. No ipads here, weekly IT lesson in IT suite from reception; a PC in each classroom. Range of clubs and activities; after school care until 6pm is an extra.

Keenly sporting – particularly successful at rugby, netball and girls' hockey, with soccer, swimming and tennis also popular. Sport (activities on Tuesdays, ranging from first aid to woodwork) timetabled for an hour each day and all of Wednesday afternoons, from year 3. Evening clubs (priority for boarders) offer usuals plus fencing, cookery and Scalextric. Healthy number of musicians; choir and music ensembles from orchestra to rock and blues; music workshop three times a term and as one mum puts it, 'a child who has just started the violin will play a tentative piece on the stage followed by a grade 6 trumpet player, and no one turns a hair'. Big Christmas production, most recent was Joseph, involving cast of over a hundred.

Stars for academic work, house points for good behaviour – these far outweigh debits, which require some form of community service and can accumulate to Wednesday afternoon detention. Children are allocated to one of four houses, named after illustrious northerners, and sit with their house chums at lunch. Plenty of healthy, inter-house rivalry.

Relaxed but cheerful, busy and purposeful atmosphere, a family school with a healthy balance of discipline and freedom. Endorsed by parents who, 'love the family atmosphere', and, 'believe that if their children are really happy they will flourish'. Pupils encouraged to have a 'broad outlook', be open-minded and prepared to 'have a go', otherwise they may struggle here, at least initially. Good food in agreeable dining room with staff

seated at each table, children on rotas to clear plates. Healthy eating is a focus in accordance with the school's enthusiasm for sport, fitness and general well-being; add to that the recently ordained school chaplain and this should ensure that both body and soul remain in good shape.

Boarding numbers are growing. All children (however local) encouraged to board early and particularly for their final three years. Response to current market means that flexi-boarding remains an option, although the emphasis is on full boarding. Dormitories and common rooms have seen the benefit of a structured investment programme in the fabric of the buildings. Separate accommodation for girls and boys under the daily operation of the much-loved matron (Matey Ellie) and her team. Tidy dorms, though not excessively so; plenty of personalised walls to make them feel homely. Storage space limited and in corridors for most; year 8 have modern high sleeper beds.

Weekend life is kept busy and full, with Saturday school, lots of expeditions, outdoor pursuits of all kinds (madly popular), plenty of staff on hand. Deputy head ensures that Saturday evenings have a clear focus (themed suppers – Mexican night, Harry Potter evening etc) and that Sundays are structured. Most boarders opt to stay in for the weekend – four exeats in autumn and two in spring and summer. Children work hard and play hard and when asked what they do at home replied, 'have a rest'.

Parents a mix of long-established Tyne Valley residents, Newcastle professionals, Forces, North Cumbrian and Yorkshire county set, Borders and Scottish landowners and the occasional country squire. Fair percentage of first-time buyers opting for boarding as a lifestyle choice rather than because of any long-standing family traditions. Parents we spoke to see it as a, 'go-ahead school on the up'.

Good traditional prep school with lots going on, exuding energy from the top down. Concentrates on developing well-rounded individuals whilst still aiming for those highly competitive top scholarships. Very positive comments from parents.

The New Beacon School

Brittains Lane, Sevenoaks, TN13 2PB

• Pupils: 400 boys, mainly day with limited weekly/flexi boarding; 20 board • Ages: 4–13 • Non-denom • Fees: £9,975–£13,020 pa • Independent

Tel: 01732 452131
Email: admin@newbeacon.org.uk
Website: www.newbeacon.org.uk

Headmaster: Since 2008, Mr Michael Piercy BA (Hons), late forties. He read English at university and was previously head of Moor Park, Ludow and Dunhurst (Junior Bedales) and earlier deputy head at Forres Sandle Manor. Certainly the move has been successful on the personal front – he met and married the head of music within 18 months of arrival. Parents find him friendly enough, say he keeps a fairly low profile and are quick to praise some of the practical changes he has introduced without any great fanfare. The new traffic and parking systems have clearly had a positive impact, as well as the after-school clubs. He promises more changes, including encouraging parents to consider a wider variety of senior schools based on their child's particular needs and strengths. He is aided by what he feels is an ideal mix of long-serving and new staff, enabling him to build on the achievements of his predecessor (of 32 years' service) while keeping pace with educational developments.

Entrance: Most put their names down well in advance for reception entry, at which stage, and until year 2, the school is non-selective. Higher up, places become available fairly regularly with pupils admitted from year 3 based on academic work and progress to date.

Exit: Most boys enter the school early and stay on to 13, at which point the vast majority gain entry into their preferred senior school. A sizeable number win academic and non-academic scholarships. Around 70 per cent of boys go on to Tonbridge, 20 per cent to Sevenoaks and others to Westminster, Worth, Caterham, Cranbrook, Eton and King's Canterbury. Under 20 per cent leave at the end of year 6, when they receive limited support in preparation for the 11+.

Remarks: In the context of a shortage of good boys' senior schools in the area, the school consistently meets its mostly City working parents' aspirations and delivers confident, responsible boys whose impressive CE results – averaging 76 per cent – secure them places at sought-after local day schools and other leading public schools further afield.

The prevailing attitude seems to be that it's a competitive world out there and getting used to it early is no bad thing. 'Let's face it, boys are naturally competitive and the school, in addition, does a great job of motivating them.' When from year 4 things begin to hot up, most cope well, though the year 5 and above scholarship stream does cause resentment amongst some parents – 'We all pay the same but they seem to get superior treatment and better teaching staff'.

Winning and success are openly acknowledged to be important and underpinned by the belief that if you expect a lot, you won't be disappointed. The prospectus is replete with statistics testifying to, in particular, the school's academic and wide-ranging sporting achievements. Lots of trophies to prove it. The head, however, is keen to highlight a move to a more inclusive approach and broader recognition of talents. At the top of the school two head boys are now appointed each term and, from year 4, all pupils given the opportunity to represent the school at least twice a term, although in sports some grumble that fixtures for all but the top teams can be hard to find.

Academic grades are no longer read out in class and an expanded activities programme has been introduced featuring fencing, judo, skiing, chess and drama, amongst others. This is hugely popular, not least as it extends school hours and reduces pressure on working parents. It can also provide additional opportunities for boys to shine, though, for some boys, not making the football or rugby teams will always be a disappointment.

Another area where many excel is music. Nearly 300 hours of music tuition take place each week and boys regularly perform in bands, orchestras and choirs, locally, nationally and internationally. The focus and concentration required are considered a useful lesson in discipline – while not squashing their sense of fun, it gives boys an understanding of how to behave. All remark on how the school promotes good manners, makes clear the standards it expects and is quick to come down on those few who step out of line. Indeed, unprompted, even the smaller boys step aside in the corridors and cheerfully meet your gaze and interact with staff. A happy and purposeful feel.

Class sizes are kept below 20 and parents praise the school for knowing each child's capabilities. Standards are high and the school is not shy of alerting parents to potential problems as the boys move up it. Parents agree, saying communications are effective and teachers generally highly responsive to concerns. New post of individual learning coordinator created to ensure learning is tailored to individuals' needs, although in this the junior school, in particular, is already considered excellent. All boys receive a really good grounding in all subjects, with ample support for those who struggle and scope for the more able to be moved up a year. Some setting also higher up the school. The new learning coordinator is charged with enhancing SEN provision, refreshing the school's focus on learning support,

the gifted and talented programme and provision for the small number of EAL (currently approximately five to ten families).

Although the school has insufficient indoor space to host whole-school events – the chapel is fairly small, as is the sports hall (though due for expansion) – it works hard to be welcoming to families, encouraging them to attend events and stand on the sidelines at matches. In this and in other ways the parents' association is a great asset. It organises a variety of highly professionally-run social events each year and is successful at fund-raising, improving the already enviable facilities. Set in 21 acres of beautiful grounds, the school has a 25-metre pool, well-equipped classrooms, labs and workshops. The junior school building, opened in 2007, provides a particularly vibrant learning environment. Plans afoot to revamp the pre-prep using the same architect.

Flexi-boarding is currently limited to 18 with priority given to older boys likely to move on to full boarding at their next school, though it will expand to meet rising demand. The dormitories are housed in the original school building dating from 19th century. The accommodation is good and the boys reportedly well-cared for and entertained.

New College School

Savile Road, off Mansfield Road, Oxford, OX1 3UA

• Pupils: 160 boys; all day • Ages: 4–13 • C of E • Fees: £8,319–£13,449; Choristers £4,785 pa • Independent

Tel: 01865 243657
Email: office@newcollegeschool.org
Website: www.newcollegeschool.org

Headmaster: Since 2008, Mr Robert Gullifer MA Cantab (fifties). Educated at Bristol Grammar School, followed by a choral exhibition at St Catharine's College, Cambridge (English). Previously head of English and under master at KCS Wimbledon, deputy head at The Dragon and deputy head at Bristol Grammar School. Was delighted to be appointed and is 'extremely proud of the school and its boys'. Said of his formidable predecessor 'I have a different style': clearly one that's an improvement and has proved popular with parents. Enthusiastically moving the school forward – has developed Saturday morning music, improved pastoral care, broadened extra-curricular activities – 'so important for the boys to develop lifelong interests' – and introduced a weekly short service in New College chapel for the school plus parents. Teaches RS to the scholarship class, ie philosophy for those tricky scholarship questions, and leads storytime with the pre-prep.

Married to an Oxford law don and has two daughters, now both at Cambridge. Still sings regularly with the Oxford Bach Ensemble and loves drama – directs the year 7-8 play: Henry V last year. Aims to establish New College as an academic school within a small, caring environment. Popular with parents and staff. 'Listens,' say parents – a universal comment. Stands at school gates every morning and is available for any concern – 'If a boy's cat dies, we need to know so that we can fully understand that boy on that day'.

Entrance: Put your child's name down by one to two years for the pre-prep (entry of 16). Boys invited in for a session of play to check that they will be happy. At seven, a further four to six join – 'gentle assessments' in maths, creative writing, reasoning and reading aloud to head. Sympathetic to relocaters where places available – vital in a place like Oxford. Not super selective, but would refuse a boy they thought would struggle to keep up or who would not be happy.

N

Choristerships – voice trials for six to seven year olds held in January preceding the year of entry by Professor Edward Higginbottom: 'Very simple assessment – he can immediately hear a boy's potential'. Roughly two-thirds fee remission for choristers.

Exit: The odd one at 11, though most parents keep their sons here until 13 to reap the rewards of being senior boys. Good liaison between the head and heads of senior schools. Admissions evenings held when senior school representatives can chat to parents. Advice is given to parents on suitable choices for their son and the vast majority grateful to receive this. Majority to Magdalen College School, Abingdon School, and St Edward's. A few to major public schools. Eight scholarships out of 12 leavers in 2010, nine out of 10 in 2011, 10 out of 13 in 2012.

Remarks: School was founded in 1379 to provide an education for the choristers of New College and is governed by its warden and fellows. Tucked away in a quiet corner of central Oxford, it is described by a parent as 'a rare gem of a school'. A programme of development has ensured growth and provision of facilities including a fabulous new sports hall with a climbing wall. Light and airy, it houses a new artroom, music room and technology suite on the upper level and received an Oxford Preservation Trust Award. Otherwise the usual motley collection of school buildings – original, '60s and modern, cheek by jowl on the tiny site, but the school is able to spill into New College for use of the chapel and for special events.

Class size is small – average 16 in pre-prep, 18 in prep with max of 20. Pre-prep classes bright, buzzing and cheerful. Years 3 and 4 taught mostly by class teachers, years 5-8 by specialist teachers. French from reception, Latin from year 5, optional Greek in years 7 and 8. SEN tends to be picked up in the pre-prep by experienced teachers. Parents are advised if further assessments are needed and extra tuition is provided at a cost. EAL (one boy at present) also catered for through learning enrichment department. Classrooms are mainly small and traditional but with data projectors in every room. Multi-purpose science lab with interactive whiteboard, IT room with enough terminals for all, DT room, pottery room, library and media room, etc. Head always keen to introduce new blood into the staff-room as well as new ideas. Staff encouraged to take opportunities to visit other schools and import fresh approaches.

Music 'phenomenal,' said one prospective parent. This is a musical school and it's taken seriously – 91 per cent of boys play an instrument, 50 per cent two. Some older pupils reach grade 7. Choristers learn two instruments – the piano and one other. Many practice rooms, ensemble rooms, music technology room etc. Saturday morning music for instrumentalists so that more time can be devoted to playing without the restriction of a school timetable – optional for boys in year 5 and above, compulsory for choristers.

Twenty-four choristers in school have a schedule not quite as gruelling as some other choir schools – choir practice four times a week at lunchtimes and after school, evensong five times week including Sat and Sun evenings but, surprisingly, no Sun morning commitment. Ditto Christmas or Easter. The choir is world-renowned and frequently tours worldwide. Won the Gramophone award for Ludford recording in 2008. Head encourages choristers to share their musical experience with the other boys and bring the music into the school.

Extra-curricular opportunities encouraged at lunchtime – fencing, archery, table tennis. Drama specialist after school for LAMDA awards and many school productions, including annual French play.

School uses the playing fields of New College for sports, including tennis courts. Not known for its sporting prowess, though it holds its own on the local circuit. Boys say it's difficult to win when the team is chosen from so few – keen, though, to point out that some have, on occasion, won sports scholarships. Wide participation – all can have a go. Wet afternoons on playing fields (this head's schoolboy memory) now a thing of the past, courtesy of the new gym.

Revamp of pastoral care system under Mr Gullifer. Recent inspection report, excellent in every aspect, commented on outstanding pastoral support. Head has implemented clear guidelines on rewards and sanctions – feels rewards are hugely important but boys also need clear boundaries on behaviour. Series of warnings – in reality only one to two headmaster's detentions in a year. Any concerns with any boys are discussed at head's weekly meeting with staff – 'can discuss every single boy if necessary'. No evidence of poor behaviour on our visit, indeed the boys were happy and industrious. Articulate and delightful guides extolled virtues of school. What's the best thing about this school? 'Absolutely everything,' came the answer. Favourite teacher? 'All of them!' – clearly experts in diplomacy as well as model pupils. An 'OK' for food.

Majority of parents academic, medical, business. A few with more limited financial means have been able to send their sons with a choral scholarship. Head points out that the link with New College brings university into contact with many parents who may be otherwise excluded – bridges town/gown divide. Huge parental expertise, as one would expect in Oxford, from which pupils profit, as parents are generous with their time. Parents choose the school for its warmth, family feel and academic reputation. Say head has opened the door to parents – now has parents' committee, parents' choir one evening a week and views are taken seriously. We were treated to the short weekly service in the chapel (New College organ scholar provides music) with presentation of achievements and coffee for parents afterwards – 'Love to be able to see my son in the school setting,' says one; 'A time for quiet reflection during a busy week,' says another. Some prospective parents fear the school is too Christian – 'Not at all,' says a current parent. 'It's pretty low key.'

Others put off by small size, but if you're looking for an intimate, family, nurturing school with a good academic reputation and lots of music, this is ideal.

Newcastle Preparatory School

6 Eslington Road, Jesmond, Newcastle upon Tyne, NE2 4RH

- Pupils: 305 day boys and girls • Ages: 3–11 • Non-denom
- Fees: £6,040–£9,330 pa • Independent

Tel: 01912 811769
Email: enquiries@newcastleprepschool.org.uk
Website: www.newcastleprepschool.org.uk

Head Teacher: Since 2002, Mrs Margaret Coates (early fifties), previously head of infants and juniors at Durham High, before that at RGS Newcastle. Studied English at Westminster College, Oxford. Warm, welcoming, articulate and astute with an obvious love of children. Is well known and knows well pupils, who are comfortable but respectful in her company, though little ones seem to make it 'hug a head day' every day.

Certainly not a helicopter head: believes in giving much responsibility to children for creation of their school world as a counter to potential over-protectiveness – though all within the tenets of the school charter.

Keen to keep teaching up to date, sets a pace for staff, expects all to keep up. 'Stays steadfast when it matters' – an iron fist in velvet glove in the nicest possible way. Parents value her genuinely open door and knowledge of their child, which starts with a personal welcome on day one.

Governor at Durham School (son's alma mater), choral singer, modest pianist, avid reader, keen gardener and novice golfer.

Entrance: Start in school nursery at 3; reception at 4 or year 3 at age 8. No selection, but children spend a morning in school and are informally assessed. Popular choice with Newcastle parents so still receiving post-natal registrations.

Exit: Overwhelming majority to local independent day schools – some to close neighbours, Royal Grammar School and Central Newcastle High for the girls. Boys also to Dame Allan's, Durham, King's Tynemouth and girls to Dame Allan's, Newcastle Church High and Westfield.

Year 6 parents have individual meetings with head who provides guidance on choice of next school for their child. Parents lay great store by this, 'as head really knows our child and what is the right school for them'. 'Senior schools like our pupils,' says the head, 'they have self esteem, are robust in their learning and have a good work ethic'.

Remarks: Set up in 1885 as a public day school for boys; uniform colours black and gold adopted 120 years ago. Situated in Jesmond, near city centre, opposite one independent senior school and sandwiched between another, in three and a half terraced Victorian houses. Ingenious use of space with linking stairways, classrooms on first and second floors and nursery on ground floor with access to outdoor play area. Top floor extensive science room, well-equipped art and design studio and music facility (in head's sights for refurbishment). Good sport and play facilities; purpose built multi-use sports hall, playing fields and adventure play area, a recent addition, a stone's throw away. All classrooms and walkways crammed with well presented display work – particularly liked the designs of the Queen's Jubilee knickers (apparently have the Royal seal of approval).

Traditionally boys have greatly outnumbered girls (spoilt for choice in Newcastle) so consideration for gender differences in learning styles. School working successfully to redress balance, starting with nursery. Pupils gain places (and scholarships) at an impressive list of Newcastle independent schools at 11, from an unselected start. 'A reflection of the traditional, yet broad curriculum, progressive teaching by primary specialists and knowing our children well. A busy, lively school, but not a hothouse,' says the head. All underpinned by ethos – 'happy children do well academically'.

Don't be fooled by 2009 EYFS inspection: First Steps nursery and two parallel reception classes are more than 'satisfactory'. Well-resourced and staffed, with specialist French, music and PE teachers. First Steps in ground floor, high ceilinged, airy classrooms, small kitchen for baking. Reception on second floor in classes of 20 (maximum). Dedicated outdoor play area, adjacent to nursery, shoehorned between adjacent properties but innovatively designed, to provide a range of early learning experiences.

Few children leave before year 6 but school chooses not to replace, so class average 18 pupils in KS2. No setting or streaming in the two parallel classes in each year, though some 'top set' pupils work together. Specialist art and design from year 3, Spanish, Latin and some German from year 5. Independent cross-curricular learning encouraged through project work. We observed inventive teaching; use of hand actions for year 2s, counting to 100 in fives (brilliant physical counteraction for the boys) and teacher/pupil collaborative interpretation of textbook instructions on Venn diagrams in year 5. Plethora of educational visits enrich classroom experiences. Science link to Dove Marine Laboratory at nearby Cullercoats and impressive annual science week – thanks to parents in medicine, industry, and university.

ICT provision is good with interactive boards in all classrooms and an up-to-date computer suite – netbooks on the horizon? Used to link globally on World Maths Day, an online international mathematics competition. Well-resourced comfortable library is in the centre of school with non-fiction upgrade imminent. Provision for special needs with small group and one-to-one work – included in fees. Assessment at end KS1 though no pupils with statements, but EAL and those with mild learning difficulties. Creative learning team devise gifted and talented activities. Teacher assessment levels on final reports ensures smooth transfer to senior schools.

Many opportunities out of classroom with excellent music (professionally run): choirs, orchestra, jazz band. Drama lessons all way through and classes act out a story and film it. Performance opportunities for everyone each year; main production in summer, most recently Shakespeare for Kids Midsummer Night's Dream; talent assemblies every Friday.

Sport taken very seriously with regular fixtures in traditional team sports and adventure activities during outdoor away weeks. Opportunities for girls' competitive team sports might be restricted due to small numbers in some year groups. Great choice of clubs and societies – includes usual sporting, creative and performing arts, with interesting extras, from early morning fitness, bicycle maintenance (good preparation for annual cycling tour in Holland perhaps), chess (a passion) and girl only 'girl talk', covering all those aspects of growing up you really don't want to discuss in front of boys. After school activities run to 5pm and summer holiday activity programme available for pupils and their siblings – helpful for working parents.

Clear guidelines to class teachers on how to deal with poor behaviour without embarrassing pupil. Process of escalation through to head for the few persistent offenders. Pupil behaviour is underpinned by the reinforcement of school charter which states that everyone should feel happy and safe, have a right to learn, is important and can succeed. Result is a happy, caring community where children feel valued and value each other. The year 6 'buddy squad' deal with minor incidents each break and lunchtime and ensure no one feels alone. Annual end of year river cruise outing for year 2 and year 6 buddies is a right of passage.

From nursery up, every child is a member of one of four houses, uniquely named by the children after local Jesmond streets. Up to year 3 house tee shirt and book bags. From year 2 positive merit system for good work and behaviour; year 3 and beyond accumulate to bronze, silver and gold awards and contribute towards house totals.

Head says, 'NPS pupils are independent characters who love life, love learning, have confidence and the strength of conviction to be themselves'. Famous old boy, Cardinal Basil Hume.

Parents, as you would expect in a large city: aspirational, many professionals, particularly from medicine and academia, senior managers from industry and those committed to education and high standards. Mainly hail from northern suburbs, Gateshead; some further afield from Ponteland, Whitley Bay, Tynemouth and Hexham. Head believes that NPS parents are more relaxed about their child's education than at some other schools and 'have faith in what we're doing'. No formal PTA but parents very supportive and help to organise events under auspices of head. Good news – 'no cliques,' say parents and head, bad news – no major contribution to school coffers. No great shakes here, head commented: 'school fees alone should cover all that's needed to educate pupils and provide good facilities and resources'. No scholarships but means tested bursaries of 10-95 per cent of fees.

Prep school and nursery with traditional values and standards and a warm heart. Firmly entrenched as first choice for parents wanting the city's top independent senior schools, and successful with it. Confident, cheerful and courteous children with a busy sense of purpose.

N

Newland House School

32-34 Waldegrave Park, Twickenham, TW1 4TQ

- Pupils: 390; 235 boys/155 girls; • Ages: 4-13; • Non-denom;
- Fees: £9,885-£11,085 pa; • Independent

Tel: 020 8865 1305
Email: admissions@newlandhouse.net
Website: www.newlandhouse.net

Headmaster: Since 2010, Mr David Alexander BMus (Hons) Dip, NCOS (early fifties). Previously head of Norland Place School and Haddon Dene School. Warm, welcoming and with a good sense of humour. Very kind and doesn't have a bad word to say about anybody. Justifiably proud of his charges, 'Our 13 year old boys are a delight, as are our 11 year old girls. I'm very proud to know any of them. I like what the school has done for them.' Parents say, 'What you see is what you get. Pupils and parents respect him but he knows how to laugh too.' Believes one of his main jobs is to steer parents towards the right school for their child: he wants his pupils to be at the top of their game at their senior schools. The children adore him because he's such fun: he is currently keen for the school to buy a boat which can act as a floating classroom on the Thames. Holds a commercial flying licence and commands a reserve RAF squadron at weekends. Mr Alexander selects the head boy and head girl by deciding which pupils he would most like to have lunch with.

Entrance: Over-subscribed, best register your child as soon as possible after birth. Two main points of entry: 4+ and 7+. At 4+ entry is on a first-come, first-served basis, with siblings given priority. Forty places available at this stage and a waiting list in operation. Once at the pre-prep, a place is guaranteed at the prep school. At 7+ pupils are tested in English and maths. Assessments take place in November for entry into the school the following September. Twenty more places available at this stage. Academic and music bursaries available – up to 50 per cent of fees, negotiated on a yearly basis. Ten per cent discount for third sibling when all are in school together.

Exit: Predominantly private day schools, including St. Paul's, Hampton, KCS Wimbledon, St. George's College, Reeds, Surbiton High, Wimbledon High and Lady Eleanor Holles. A couple each year head for boarding schools such as Marlborough and Wellington. Girls leave at 11 and boys at 13. Girls can stay on to 13, but don't. 'It would be a leap of faith' says head. Consistently high number of academic, sports, music and all-rounder scholarships. Head puts this down to outstanding teaching and the fact that the children are in a happy environment and so want to learn.

Remarks: The pre-prep is run by the approachable and calm Tracey Chong. All-female staff ('by coincidence,') give it a homely air. Building very tired-looking building but there are plans afoot for a major refurbishment before a possible move to a new site bang next door to the main school. Pupils venture across the road to main school for ICT and games. 'We're very much one school despite being on two sites', says head. 'The teachers at Number 11 (the Pre-Prep) are lovely and smiley and it rubs off on the children,' says one parent.

Classes at the prep are mixed ability, maximum 20 children. Lessons are lively and fast-paced with specialist teachers for PE, art, music and ICT from the start. Separate sciences taught from Year 4. Children set for English, French and maths from Year 5. Days are long, especially for those who start with the full cooked breakfast on offer at 7.30 am.

Once the girls leave at the end of Year 6, the boys are placed in two mixed ability classes and one small scholarship set; vacancies left by girls are not filled. Greek on offer to potential scholars. Parents love the fact that children get so much individual attention at the top of the school, 'A real strength,' says one. Children are well-prepared for 11+, 13+ and scholarships. As the head puts it, 'We are a preparatory school. It's our job to prepare them for the exams for entry to their next schools.' Parents report that a massive amount of coaching goes on in the final years, of which the head is critical. 'It's not necessary. We are all fighting a coaching culture but people get sucked into it.' Head gives out CE results to boys as they sit around a camp fire on the Year 8 trip to Wales. 'A lovely touch, and the boys never forget it. It's a gesture typical of the school,' says one parent.

Classrooms are spacious and light, with traditional wooden desks are arranged in neat rows. Impressive ICT suite, tablets about to be introduced but head keen this shouldn't be a gimmick. The school enters a huge number of national and international competitions with frequent success. Recently won three World Maths Day trophies, out of a total of five awarded to UK schools. DT department is the envy of other schools and recently assembled a car for the Shell Eco-Marathon that achieved a mileage of 1000 miles per gallon. Currently a group of senior boys is investigating the effect of tyre pressure on the environment and presentations have been made to MPs.

Plenty of choirs for each year group, new pop choir for Year 7/8 boys is thriving. Several hundred individual instrumental and singing lessons take place every week. Lots of bands, ensembles and orchestras. Children have recently taken part in performances at the Kingston Music Festival and concerts at the Barbican with the London Symphony Orchestra.

Art clubs include weekend activities where parents can become involved. Local artists exhibit and sell their work in the reception area and include a couple of inexpensive pieces so that children can buy a picture if it catches their eye.

Sport is a real strength of the school. Boys play rugby, football and cricket; girls play netball, rounders and hockey. Swimming, cross-country and athletics also on offer and even more sport possible through numerous after-school clubs, including golf at neighbouring club. Main playing fields are five minutes away by mini-bus; two multi-purpose, all-weather courts and four cricket nets on site. Lots of tournaments and matches mean everyone gets the chance to compete.

Full-time head of SEN appointed in 2011. Head believes, 'a good learning support culture enhances what you do'. Provision for mild dyslexia, dyspraxia and dyscalculia, though not the place to send a child with severe difficulties.

Many long serving staff. Head did away with 'teaching' and 'non-teaching' labels when he arrived. 'We're all teaching the children in different ways,' he says. One satisfied parent commented that staff were 'prepared to go the extra mile for the children.' Teachers are lively, good humoured and passionate about their subjects. Two gap year students help with sport and a French assistant teaches conversational French.

Parents are typically hard-working professionals. 'The school reflects the local community and lots of the children arrive at school on foot or by scooter,' says head of pre-prep. Active PTA raises substantial funds, half money raised goes to charity, the other half to the school – recently paid for a climbing wall.

A competitive, purposeful and demanding school which has retained old fashioned values (the pupils call the head 'sir' and scramble to their feet when an adult enters the room). Pupils are challenged on all fronts and, as one parent put it, 'By the time the children reach Year 5, they are under pressure to perform. It's not a soft school but, for the right child, there simply isn't anywhere better in the area.' One mother felt, 'It's not for the retiring child. I think they'd get trampled underfoot.' The head disagrees and feels the school caters for all personalities and abilities as there is so much on offer and so many chances to shine.

Newton Prep

149 Battersea Park Road, London, SW8 4BX

• Pupils: 320 boys and 270 girls; all day • Ages: 3-13 • Non-denom • Fees: £7,770-£16,470 pa • Independent

Tel: 020 7720 4091
Email: registrar@newtonprep.co.uk
Website: www.newtonprepschool.co.uk

Headmistress: Since September 2013, Mrs Alison Fleming MA (Ed) BA PGCE. Previously head of Dulwich College Junior School. Before that taught in a wide range of schools in both the maintained and independent sectors. Says 'core business' is 'providing outstanding educational opportunities for the children at Newton Prep.' Husband is a chemical engineer who works for an oil company and they have two grown-up sons.

Entrance: Admission to nursery is by ballot. Selective at reception – a gentle assessment which looks for early indications of ability and potential. 'We don't reckon on tears at this stage,' says school, which ditched the process whereby all applicants were sent to a psychologist at parents' own expense. Siblings given priority at nursery; thereafter, while regarded 'favourably', they won't automatically be given a place. Also a competitive entrance at years 3 and 7, when scholarships are available, with top-up bursaries for those who need financial assistance – keen to award more scholarships at these points.

Exit: To many and varied destinations. Most popular at 11+ are Alleyn's, Dulwich College, JAGS, St Paul's Girls, Emanuel, Francis Holland, Latymer Upper and Whitgift. At 13+, King's College Wimbledon, Dulwich College, Emanuel, St Paul's Boys, Westminster, Whitgift, Rugby and Eton. Success with arts, music, sports and academic scholarships too.

Remarks: This big bustling co-ed school fills an imposing Victorian purpose-built building (high ceilings, long corridors), situated in the no man's land between Battersea and Nine Elms, almost opposite Battersea Dogs' Home. Recent additions are light and spacious, including two gyms, state-of-the-art auditorium, art studios and humanities suite, three tip-top science labs, three ICT labs and an extended and modernised library, well organised and an attractive place to curl up and read a book in; each classroom now equipped with an interactive whiteboard. Unlike many central London day schools, a lot of outside space, with all-weather pitches, two large playgrounds and a garden (plus extensive carparks filled with 4x4s first and last thing). Plenty of room for children to charge around outside letting off steam. New lower school with two new nurseries and eight new classrooms, a lower school assembly hall, a sports hall complex including a third gymnasium, and a new music school.

Although keen to downplay its 'hothouse' reputation, committed to 'offering a challenging education for inquisitive children who are eager to engage fully with the world' and 'inspiring children to be adventurous and committed in their learning', whilst 'providing balance and breadth in all aspects of a child's education: intellectual, aesthetic, physical, moral and spiritual'. Is that all? Four classes of 20 from reception, streaming in, eg, maths starts as early as year 1, and specialist teaching from year 4. 'We do very well by bright children,' says school, 'and one of the advantages of a big school is that it allows you to differentiate in a way that the parents and children can't tell.' French from nursery, Latin from year 5. Mandarin is offered after school. A lot of inspirational teaching (why have interactive whiteboards when you can have model soldiers and WWI helmets as teaching aids?).

A combined SEN and high ability co-ordinator ensures that 'no one slips through the net'. 'There is no stigma about going to the Resource Unit, ' we were told by one parent, 'as so many of them do.' It will cater for children in the dys-strata as well as those with physical disabilities, but the special need for a number is that they are very bright. School takes a flexible approach, but child needs to be able to 'stand the pace'.

Sport (currently getting much-needed attention) now flourishing. More inter-house matches programmed and a greater focus on the 'sports we shine in, like hockey'. Tremendous art. Lots of wonderful, brightly coloured papier-mache figures floating around the school. Fresh food with a varied menu cooked on premises and eaten in a surprisingly uninstitutional dining room.

Wide geographic intake produces larger social mix than other SW London schools – catchment area stretches into the far reaches of Streatham and beyond, as well as north of the river. Eclectic parents – lots of professionals – both mother and father – as well as media types and shopkeepers; attracts first-time buyers. Children are confident, articulate, well-behaved and refreshingly not overly deferential, communicating with adults like fellow individuals. School is much more down to earth than a lot of the competition. 'Newton is the acceptable face of private education – meritocratic, broad ranging and grounded,' says school. Appeals to parents who would not normally regard themselves as private sector.

Norland Place School

162-166 Holland Park Avenue, London, W11 4UH

• Pupils: 240; 150 girls/90 boys (boys to age 8 only) • Ages: 4-11 • Non-denom • Fees: £11,847-£14,493 pa • Independent

Tel: 020 7603 9103
Email: office@norlandplace.com
Website: www.norlandplace.com

Headmaster: Since 2002, Mr Patrick Mattar LRAM MA (forties), a Brummie (though you wouldn't know it), educated at Solihull, one of four siblings all of whom are talented musicians and went to various prestigious music colleges. Came here in 1989 as director of music straight from the Royal Academy of Music. He says if he had gone to an academic establishment he would have been more of an arts/language person than a scientist. A six year interlude at Wetherby from 1996, where he ended up being deputy head, before returning to Norland to run the school when he was only 36. Married with two young sons, his wife teaches at Sussex House, where several boys move on to from here each year. Works very closely with his bursar and with proprietor, Sylvia Garnsey, who ran the school for 40 years – 'she gives me a loose rein but needs to know what's going on'. Since his arrival a huge number of building and structural systems put in place

With his background one would expect the school to be heavily weighted in favour of music (he confessed to being secretly delighted when asked by parents to do a recital to a packed Steinway Hall in Marylebone to raise money for an auction) but he stresses that equal weight is given to art and sports – 'I've never been one of those heads who thinks, "I'm musical and therefore want the school to be musical",' he says.

Very popular with parents, who comment on his approachable, natural manner and understanding of the children. He teaches years 3 through to year 6 current affairs, reasoning and some Latin in year 6. He has a good feel for senior schools and which would suit each child, but says he will be as involved as parents want him to be when deciding where their children should go. His quiet confidence brims with integrity. You would think ambition might be making him restless but he clearly loves the job – 'There's never a dull moment – and my favourite part is the children: they're the easiest,' he grins.

Entrance: At four years old: not selective, so you need to get your child's name down as soon after birth as is feasibly possible – preferably on the day. Parents are given forms so they can apply before birth and deliver it on the way back from the hospital! If you don't get it in until your child is a week old, you will end up on the waiting list. Mr Mattar will make sure he sees all parents who have places, so they understand the ethos here and know what they're signing up to. Children come from a number of local nurseries including The Acorn, Miss Delaney's, Ladbroke Square, Strawberry Fields, Rolfes and Mynors – no particular feeder. Siblings won't automatically get places – they still have to be registered and will be given priority on the waiting list, but be warned: siblings of a daughter who has left early to go to, eg, Bute, is unlikely to be given priority. 'There's no point coming here unless you want Norland and want it all the way,' he warns.

Exit: Pupils progress to vast range of schools. Boys at 8+ to, eg, Westminster Under, Colet Court, Sussex House, Westminster Cathedral Choir School, Wetherby Prep, St Philips, St Anthony's, Fulham Prep and the odd one to board at, eg, Caldicott.

Girls at 11+ to St Paul's, Godolphin and Latymer (head points out that recently nearly half the year got in here – impressive for a non-selective school), Francis Holland (NW1 & SW3), Wycombe Abbey, St Swithun's, Downe House, City of London, Harrodian, Latymer Upper, More House.

Notting Hill & Ealing, Oundle, Portland Place, Putney High, Queen's College, Queen's Gate, South Hampstead High and St Mary's Calne.

Remarks: Founded in 1876, situated on bustling Holland Park Avenue in three town houses connected by a maze of corridors and staircases, giving it a very up and down feel, but with two smallish playgrounds and a plethora of outdoor toys. Unashamedly traditional – boys are in shorts, girls neat in blue and white checks, berets are worn in winter, boaters in summer.

A definite flavour of 'old money'. Parents here are terribly discreet and reluctant to be drawn into talking about the school or each other. Increasingly families come from Shepherds Bush and Hammersmith rather than round the corner, as Notting Hill becomes more flashy. To the casual observer it appears very English – not much evidence of headscarves and only a few brown faces, though school anxious to point out that it does not select on any criteria at all. Families here seem grounded, wanting what's best for their children without being drawn into the competitive London day school fever which is more susceptible to brand rather than ethos. Lots of children here had parents and grandparents at the school. George Osborne and Hilary Benn are among the alumni. We witnessed excellent rapport between staff and pupils, which was confirmed by parents. Senior girls are natural, mature and responsible but humorous and not fawning.

A wide range of ability. Children assessed for SEN from reception, when any concerns are flagged up and watched. Mild to moderate SEN can be catered for, but children have to be able to make the benchmark each year. EAL is dealt with in class, help often given before school. From early in the morning teachers are on hand to support and stretch those who need stretching, but a charge is made for timetabled learning support lessons.

For the more able ('I try to avoid labelling them as gifted and talented,' says Mr Mattar) lots of opportunity to differentiate and split lessons for English and maths in years 4, 5 and 6, but not setting or streaming. The ethos here is that children support each other – 'Everyone has different talents'. Specialist teaching for English, maths and science from year 4.

Two forms per year until year 3, when boys and girls divide. Boys then get their heads down to prepare for the 8+ and one form for girls from years 4 to 6. French is taught from the start, with a smattering of Latin from Mr Mattar at the end. 'We're very good at not pressurising the children,' says Mr Mattar, 'while still getting the results.' Humanities has had an injection of energy with the appointment of the dynamic and greatly loved Mrs Hart, who brings history vividly to the present with dramatic interpretrations of, eg, VE day. We saw an assembly littered with bunting, every child waving a flag (including the odd German one), a number of them wearing hard hats and 40s style headscarves and the whole school doing the Lambeth walk.

Nothing is done on a grand scale but we met with great enthusiasm for what is on offer – only one afternoon of sport a week: football and cricket for the boys, a bus ride away; netball and rounders for the girls. Two PE lessons a week happen in the playground and hall. Swimming from year 2 at Kensington leisure centre. DT is incorporated into art – we were shown bird boxes that the year 5s were making for their gardens while others bubbled about growing chickens in incubators. The atmosphere of grounded traditionalism is epitomised by the traditional desks in the classrooms which, when opened, not only reveal neat piles of books but also colourful personal displays – photos, glitter, magazine cut outs – decorated by each girl.

A good traditional London day school that prepares each child for the next stage beautifully and punches well above its weight.

North Bridge House Junior School

Linked school: North Bridge House Senior School

8 Netherhall Gardens, London, NW3 5RR

- Pupils: Nursery school: 210; junior school: 200; • Ages: 9m–7 years • Non-denom • Fees: £13,575–£14,130 pa • Independent

Tel: 020 7435 2884
Email: junior@northbridgehouse.com
Website: www.northbridgehouse.com

Headteacher: Since 1997, Mrs Robyn Allsopp BEd Cert Ed (fifties). Australian, began here in 1976 as a class teacher, deputy head in 1983; when the building now housing the nursery on Fitzjohn's Avenue was acquired in 1989 became head over there, then head of nursery and junior schools – one has the sense that it is her lifeblood that runs through the veins of the school, keeping it an integral whole. Certainly she knows every inch, floorboard and door hinge, as well as everyone – child, teacher, support staff – one meets. She is also clear about the school's ethos – 'We're a family school' – by which she means that, as a mixed school, with many former pupils' children now attending, and one which does not have an academic entrance requirement, unlike its neighbour opposite, it really can take everyone it has room for. Leaving in January 2014. Her successor is Joanna Hockley, previously deputy head of Clifton Lodge school in Ealing, another Cognita school.

Entrance: Life begins at playgroup level and children are mostly siblings of current pupils. Then the nursery takes around 30 children out of the 120 applicants. Reception, the following year, takes the same number out of a similar number of applicants. Occasional places thereafter, but around 10 children out of 40-odd are taken into year 3. Criteria are refreshing – first come siblings, then children of former pupils, then families who live closest and finally, those who fit the age bracket the school wants to fill. Makes a point of covering the entire chronological year in any class year group.

That doesn't mean no assessment – all applicants visit and parent and child are interviewed. So the emphasis is more on whether the child – and family – fit the school's ethos rather than on academic potential. The result is a spread of ability, ethnicity and just about everything other than location – most live within three miles of the school, many near enough to walk. Equal split of boys/girls. Runs a good coach service to obvious areas.

Exit: Virtually all move on from the junior school to the prep school in year 3, despite the different location. Those who leave at this stage mostly do so for single sex education.

Remarks: Highly confusing for outsiders. The nursery and junior school are housed in two buildings moments from each other in Hampstead. The preparatory school lives off Regent's Park, whilst North Bridge House Senior School amalgamated with the Royal School in Hampstead in 2012 resulting in NBH Senior School moving to the Royal's central Hampstead site. Life begins in the nursery building – a splendid Victorian house on Fitzjohn's Avenue, used as a nursery school for decades but only acquired by North Bridge in 1989. Classrooms are full of happily absorbed children – we saw year 1s engaged in water play and modelling while the parallel class had a friendly 'show and tell session'. Art was fun – we enjoyed Mondrian-inspired collages on the walls and appreciated the principle that 'everyone's work goes up – not just the best'. It's well-equipped – a music room doubles as an eating room, a good gym/hall for concerts and shows – and does not feel as crowded as some similar schools, though we found some of the rooms uncomfortably hot. Everyone learns French from reception and PE is four days a week. Outside space, again, compares well with comparable schools – some safe surfaces, a lovely wooden play train and caterpillar, with some covered nooks for secret conversations and conspiracies.

The Fitzjohn's site houses the playgroup, nursery and reception. The building on Netherhall Gardens is the main site for the junior school and has the year 1 and 2 classes. This is a quieter corner – a cul de sac overlooking the Finchley Road; the house is a five-storey red-brickery, interestingly sited between the British College of Osteopathic Medicine and the former home of Sidney and Beatrice Webb. It's a corner favoured by independent schools – the South Hampstead Junior School is opposite and nearby, Southbank International (also owned by Cognita, the owners of North Bridge) is up the road, and others not more than a rubber's throw away. Efforts are made to stagger drop-offs and pick-ups. From the top of the main building splendid views – over to Harrow-on-the-Hill one way and to the North Downs the other.

As in the nursery building, every inch is covered in displayed work – much to intrigue and delight the eye. Classrooms are occupied by quiet and relaxed children, clearly engaged and interested. Music, French and PE are said to be the school's specialties – everyone learns music and a third or more learn piano, guitar or violin in school; choirs and bands. Outside space is less impressive, though. A marked out chess board and a climbing frame on the tarmac. Sports mostly at the Talacre Centre in Kentish Town. More could be done to make this a livelier area.

A full-time learning support teacher sees around 25 pupils regularly – up to three times a week – for varying types of support. Despite the manner of entry, nothing more than mild dyslexia/dyspraxia surfaces here. All children are monitored twice-yearly to check progress.

Junior and nursery school parents praise the friendliness and welcome they find here and feel what is offered at this level hardly differs from what the overtly academic neighbours do.

North Bridge House Preparatory School

Linked school: North Bridge House Senior School

1 Gloucester Avenue, London, NW1 7AB

- Pupils: 295; mixed • Ages: 7–13 • Fees: £14,340 pa
- Independent

Tel: 020 7267 6266
Email: prep@northbridgehouse.com
Website: www.northbridgehouse.com

Headteacher: Since 2005, Mr Brodie Bibby BA PGCE MEd (forties). Took his first degree in archaeology and ancient history at Exeter, followed by a PGCE at Roehampton, then taught in state and independent schools, including time at The Banda School, Kenya and as deputy head of Westminster Under School. Still teaches history, drama and games.

Energetic and efficient, he's a man who gets things done, but wants what's done to combine high achievement for all with happy kids protected as much as possible from the early pressure of the modern exam system. Parents rate him highly. 'He's really involved in all areas,' said one, 'and knows and welcomes every parent. You feel he's really proud of the school.' Has recently run the senior school during the previous head's maternity leave, but is now happily back on his own stomping ground, with more room to move around and year 3 now under his wing. His own son and daughter attended the school, always a recommendation.

Entrance: Non-selective in nursery, so names down at birth or as soon as possible thereafter. Parents are invited to tour the school in the November prior to entry. For entry in year 3 (when up to 20 places become available), assessment in January in English, maths and reasoning. Open mornings held throughout the year.

Exit: Plenty of guidance about appropriate secondary school starting in year 5. 'It's important to be honest with parents and make sure the school is the right fit,' says the head.

Excellent results at 11 for girls. Good chunk each year to Channing and South Hampstead, but to a wide range of state and private, including impressive numbers to Henrietta Barnett. Boys, too, go everywhere, with impressive results at 13+ and Common Entrance. A solid handful to Westminster and St Paul's and significant numbers to City, as well as all the usual north London suspects. Those who wish to continue to North Bridge House Senior School in Hampstead are now more or less guaranteed a smooth passage, though occasionally someone may be asked to look elsewhere.

Remarks: North Bridge, one of the largest stand-alone prep schools in London, opened in 1939 in St John's Wood and is now part of the growing stable of schools run by the Cognita group. It is a school that has undoubtedly benefited from the recent relocation of its senior school to a new home. Now years 3 to 8 are grouped together on the same site, with considerably more elbow room.

Formerly a convent chapel, then a Japanese school, the site has gradually been updated to provide a spacious welcoming reception and good playground space. Still a bit of a rabbit warren (younger children are carefully guided round), but some impressive features, such as the lofty pillared and gilded assembly hall, two newly equipped science labs and music rooms.

Teaching – by friendly, well-qualified staff in classes of about 20 – is lively and fun, with the national curriculum followed in the early years, then stretched well beyond later on. 'My son is looked after really well,' said one mother. 'His teachers completely understand his strengths and weaknesses and seem to catch his imagination.' Pupils' progress is meticulously tracked on a database. Specialist subject teaching in ICT, French, music and games. French, taught by native speakers, from reception; Spanish added in years 3, 4 and 5; Latin and Greek from year 6. Plenty of 'professional development,' too, so teachers are kept on their toes. Classroom style is relaxed but orderly.

Children with special needs are given excellent additional support, with group work in class plus one-to-one attention outside if necessary. In years 3, 4 and 5, teachers are supported by assistants who help out with reading and group activities.

Girl-boy balance kept as even as possible in the younger years then in year 6 boys are hived off into a separate all-boys prep on the top floor to prepare for Common Entrance. The school prides itself on its support for those taking 11+ and 13+ entrance tests. 'The exams can be quite ruthless and it's important pupils feel good about themselves,' says the head.

Strong emphasis on art, music, drama and sport. The art room (home to art club and regular exhibitions) has now been freed up for use by all pupils. Music – with an orchestra, a number of choirs and plenty of informal concerts – is vibrant. Annual school play (most recently The Pied Piper) attracts enthusiastic auditioning. Sport, played twice a week, offers a good choice for both boys and girls (kayaking, rock climbing, basketball, dance and table tennis in addition to the standard fare) and regular matches against other local schools. Two well-equipped playgrounds and afternoon break in the open spaces of Regent's Park, just across the road. The school is non-denominational, but pupils receive education on all major faiths.

Exciting range of out-of-class activities (at lunch and after-school) includes flamenco, yoga and cookery, as well as arts, sport and drama. Chess particularly popular, with a coach training potential grandmasters for national competition. Reorganisation has allowed space for a purpose-built library, with bean bags, newspapers and library lessons. Plenty of trips, including abroad (Rouen, Vienna). Energetic charitable involvement (recent fundraisers include a Readathon and cross-country run). Lunch, featuring traditional favourites like fish and chips and jelly with ice cream, is served in the assembly hall and eaten alongside the teachers.

Excellent communication with parents, with an informative handbook distributed at annual info evening and email access to teachers. 'They send you an email if they have any concerns and you can email them with anything that worries you.' Pastoral care, too, comes in for high praise. 'Problems are picked up immediately and dealt with sensibly and sensitively,' said one parent, whose daughter had experienced some low-level bullying.

Families live fairly locally (mainly Hampstead, Islington and Queen's Park), but are metropolitan and cosmopolitan (Russian, American, Chinese, Japanese, African), often in the arts and media. The approach certainly appeals to those who might find other local schools too formal. 'I like it because it because it's unpretentious,' said one father of three. 'It doesn't take itself too seriously.'

A successful school (which received 'outstanding' in every category in its last Ofsted report), but also a happy and friendly place which seems to find room for everyone to thrive. 'We get very good results, but we don't want to pressure someone into getting into a school. We let children be children,' says the head. A philosophy which clearly works. 'I really like coming to school in the morning,' said one girl in her final year.

North London Collegiate School Junior School

Linked school: North London Collegiate School

Canons, Canons Drive, Edgware, Middlesex, HA8 7RJ

• Pupils: 300 girls in the junior and first schools • Ages: 4–11
• Christian • Fees: £14,055 pa • Independent

Tel: 020 8952 1276
Email: office@nlcs.org.uk
Website: www.nlcs.org.uk

Head: Since 2003, Mrs Jo Newman BEd (fiftyish). Came from Fairseat, Channing's junior school. 'They've got our lovely Mrs Newman,' they told us. She is bustling, bright-eyed, thrilled with her school and proud of her charges, who smile sweetly and confidently at her. Popular with parents and just about everyone.

Entrance: Vastly over-subscribed at 4+, when group and individual assessments (no reading/writing, mercifully) result in the allocation of 40 places. At 7+, maths and English tested, but only eight to 10 places for the armies who turn up. Most continue from first school through to lower school until they are 11.

Exit: Around 90 per cent continue into the senior school. Parents of those who the school perceives might not make the grade are alerted early and helped to look elsewhere.

Remarks: Shares the glorious site with its big sister but has a bright one-storey modern (1995) building of its own, divided into first and lower schools. Good stable staff – 16 have been at the school for more than 10 years – retain their enthusiasm and clear enjoyment of their bright and bubbly charges. Two form entry – first school class size of 20, and 24 in the lower school, each class having its own teacher and TA. Rooms are spacious and airy – room to move, not found in more central London preps.

Our tour was full of pleasures – inside and out. We liked the bright displays everywhere, the sense of orderliness and the little loos – so important – with their fish motifs. We loved the Montgolfier balloons, an imaginative undersea montage with fishing nets, lobster pots and portholes and some lively nascent DT sculptures – thank heaven for kitchen roll tubes and egg boxes! We watched reception miming seed planting to a tape, and saw that not all were fully engaged in this – perhaps still learning to listen? We did wonder whether artistic endeavours might not be over-directed, but the vivid year 2 Kandinsky-influenced houses seemed more relaxed. We applaud the garden club, Friday's Golden Time and the Three Bears' cottage with bed, kitchen and mirror.

Overall, facilities are good – designated science, IT and art rooms plus a good-sized hall and libraries for both parts of the school, the lower school one being particularly inviting, with a lovely display of 'antique book covers' when we visited. The girls also enjoy the senior school's sports facilities as well as the senior girls themselves – several come down to help. Specialist subject teaching from year 5, and we were impressed by the school's introductory courses to languages: Spanish in year 3, German in year 4, Chinese in year 5 and French in year 6 – good fun and sensible. No children currently with statements but around five per cent with mild SEN – catered for by school SENCo; most leave for the senior school no longer needing much support.

Parents, for the most part, enthuse – 'It's a lovely school and Mrs Newman and the staff are very kind.' Girls make good friendships and positive relationships are encouraged at every stage. Any complaints are taken seriously and resolved as soon as possible. The ethos – of discipline, a non-competitive striving for one's personal best and stimulation which is also fun – is very much that of the senior school, and the junior branch, in every way, equips its young alumnae to seize the opportunities they will be offered in the next exciting stage.

North Primary School

Meadow Road, Southall, UB1 2JE

• Pupils: 435; mixed • Ages: 4–11 • Non–denom • State

Tel: 020 8571 7749
Email: admin@north.ealing.sch.uk
Website: www.northprimary.co.uk

Headteacher: Since September 2010, Mrs Rebecca Hastings BSc PGCE NPQH (late forties). Studied at Leicester University, PGCE at the West Sussex Institute of Higher Education, worked in primary schools in London – Camden, Hackney and Harrow – where many pupils have English as an additional language and come from areas of social deprivation. Assistant headteacher, acting headteacher for two years, associate head in a school facing challenging circumstances. One daughter at secondary school.

Passionate about learning: schools are a place of learning for children, staff and parents/carers – makes extracurricular activities available to children and their families. School has a responsibility to provide quality learning experiences for all children, a curriculum that is engaging, to ensure every child achieves the best they can.

Entrance: Admissions handled by the London borough of Ealing – the usual criteria apply. Main feeder is Grove House Nursery. No one except looked-after children will get into the early years from out of catchment; a waiting list for all years. Key stage 2 applicants may have more luck – entrants (often new arrivals from abroad) in the later years.

Exit: Most go on to Villiers HS, some to Greenford HS, a few to Guru Nanak or Cardinal Wiseman. A handful each year try for the Berkshire grammars or Tiffin schools – around seven or eight get in.

Remarks: We went as sceptics but came away converts – and in love. Twenty-two languages are spoken at home by these children – mostly Punjabi or Gujerati, though significant numbers of Singhalese children and Somalis too. According to social deprivation statistics, school's population is in the top 80 per cent. Also has significant numbers on School Action or School Action Plus, though not huge numbers with many SENs other than EAL. Ninety-eight per cent of pupils speak English as a second language, but English unifies the school and everyone is open and friendly. We were struck by the clear and helpful delivery of the teachers – they mean children to understand, back up their words with helpful body language when needed and everyone learns. We were impressed with every class we went into – and we went into them all.

Sats results are astonishing – especially given this intake and the fact that children come at all stages with little or no English. Everyone except a few SEN pupils reaches level 4 or higher in English – this is extraordinary and is achieved, in part, by determined individual catch up sessions with those who fall behind or arrive with little English. In both science and maths, 90+ per cent get level 4. Large percentages at level 5. This puts it way ahead of comparable schools, both locally and nationally. Not that it teaches to the test – teaching has to be good from reception onwards, not just year 6. This is a lead school for good practice in EAL provision and the induction process for each new child is meticulous. Has translators and resources in all its main languages and works hard at involving parents. We were touched by the care taken to instruct each new child in, for example, how to ask in English for the loo.

So – a modern, purpose-built jewel in Ealing's crown? Hardly. The core is an 1851 schoolroom, still in remarkable nick and surmounted by the original bell tower, complete with pullable bell chain – still used on special occasions. Later add-ons are solid and functional and make for a well-structured, two storey building overall. We have yet to see a tidier, cleaner school – everywhere is freshly painted in bright but not garish colours, and we spotted not one piece of litter in our entire visit. Children are proud of their school and it shows. Outside is just tarmac and apparatus, but well marked out for the younger children and reasonably spacious, with railings separating the older children from the tots. Older children have a tarmac football pitch. The school is in a quiet residential nook at the east end of Southall close to an old village green and with some splendid older buildings round about, reminding one of the village this once was.

In every classroom the children were attentive, engaged and absorbed. Every inch of wall space has excellent displays – pupil and teacher-made – all helping to structure and illustrate the work in hand. Everyone can see at a glance what the term's syllabus and aims are in all curriculum areas. Corridor displays on everything from black history to symmetry, musical notation, bridges and forces. Boards for improvement, achievement and attendance encourage everyone. Community project volunteers have provided imaginative murals here and there – we especially liked the Aztec drinking fountains. Excellent new ICT suite is an exciting addition and each class has a whiteboard. Resources are carefully used. The key stage 2 library is better-stocked than those in many senior schools we know and as inviting and orderly as everywhere else in this welcoming, safe-feeling school.

All classes are orderly and inviting. Most seem well ventilated and comfortable, but a few look rather crowded and were decidedly too warm. What goes on in them is consistently impressive. Reception and year 1 children work purposefully in small groups but all together in a big sectioned room with teachers and support staff and, seemingly, concentrating so busily that they need little regulation or control. We enjoyed a year 2 French class taught by a native speaker with a mouth-watering unison recitation of the constituents of une salade. A year 5 class was working on rhetorical questions and a year 6 class writing 'recounts' of events and being given demanding literary objectives – which they seemed to relish. Both key stages have good-sized, airy halls and we warmed to the way children really spoke out in rehearsal of their Easter assembly.

G and T children are well-catered for by a designated teacher, who provides 'challenge boxes' for each class, brings in graduate volunteers and runs a chess club and newspaper club exclusively for these children. Lots of other clubs for everyone. Most children with SpLD are supported in class. Part-time SENCo and TA will take children individually – some have a differentiated curriculum. An Alexander Technique teacher comes in on occasions. We saw a lesson taken by a supply teacher with an entirely attentive class. Each child is assessed every half term for progress in reading, writing and maths.

Music is big here: won the local Rotary's best ensemble award several years running – their ensemble containing instruments from every bit of the globe is a major investment but at the heart of its ethos. Good ceramics and a collection of musical instruments made from recycled materials which included a beautiful harp. The little garden is eagerly worked on by the children, who grow vegetables from seed – and then eat the results in the school's canteen. The home-cooked food is a good mix of the trad and the healthy – we drooled at fisherman's pie, Asian pasta and chunks of fresh oranges. Parents are helped to continue the healthy eating approach at home and encouraged to involve themselves in all activities. Many do – the school's annual fête – the mela – along with its concerts and shows are huge events, and several parents help in class. Children look good in white shirts, grey trousers and scarlet cardigans.

A model for primaries everywhere.

Northampton High Junior School

Linked school: Northampton High School

Newport Pagnell Road, Hardingstone, Northampton, NN4 6UU

- Pupils: 235 girls • Ages: 3-11 • C of E • Fees: £8,805–£9,021 pa
- Independent

Tel: 01604 667979
Email: nhsadmin@nhs.gdst.net
Website: www.gdst.net/northamptonhigh

Head of Junior School: Since September 2012, Mr Ross Urquhart BSc (early forties). Previously head of Broughton Manor Prep School and deputy head of Milton Keynes Prep School.

A PE and geography graduate from Brunel University, he has a passion for sport (tennis and skiing) and has taught all junior school subjects. Married to Nicola, has two daughters, both at the school.

Entrance: Pupils admitted to nursery (open for 46 weeks of the year) on a first come, first served basis. After that main entry points are reception, year 3, year 5 and (increasingly) year 6. Prospective pupils visit for a half day, doing assessments in English and maths, before hearing whether they've got a place. Not completely full at the moment – 'possibly due to our selective entry, not that it's particularly high,' says school.

Exit: Virtually all progress to senior school. 'Robust tracking system' and any concerns get flagged up early on, but school says, 'We very rarely find ourselves in that situation'.

Remarks: School is housed in same building as its older sibling. Shares facilities like canteen, swimming pool and sports pitches but has its own distinctive feel. Like other GDST junior schools, it combines first-rate delivery of the curriculum with a nurturing environment where girls feel safe and secure. Most year groups have two classes, three in year 6. Maximum of 16 to a class up to year 2, 18 in year 3, 20 in year 4, 22 in year 5 and 24 in year 6. French from year 1 and ICT lessons once a week for all. Modern building means all classrooms are airy and spacious, with oodles of storage space for books, coats and PE kit. Classrooms at lower end of school open on to their own enclosed areas. When we visited, one had been temporarily transformed into a mini racing track, complete with scooters, toy cars and cardboard petrol pumps. All classrooms equipped with overhead projectors and most with interactive whiteboards too.

Glowing 2011 ISI report judged the school's EYFS provision to be 'outstanding' in every category, highlighting the fact that girls here are 'happy and greatly enjoy the setting'. Own SENCo, who works with each class once a week as well as offering one-to-one learning support before school and during lunch breaks. Mild learning disabilities catered for plus enrichment opportunities for gifted and talented. Teachers (16 full-time) have good working relationship with their counterparts in senior school, meeting regularly to discuss curriculum.

Excellent pastoral care. PSHCE lessons given over to issues girls may face, such as eating disorders or friendship problems.

Teachers give girls opportunity to play old-fashioned (and very wholesome) playground games like Grandmother's Footsteps, What's the Time, Mr Wolf? and Stuck in the Mud, with aim of getting everyone involved.

Own hall for assemblies, dance, ballet and gym and library. Around £3,000 spent on new library books each year – Michael Morpurgo, Dick King-Smith and Anne Fine are girls' current favourite authors. Pupils get the chance to air their views at school council meetings. Previous head was astonished when girls vetoed his plans for a school disco and said they'd like a barn dance instead! Music, drama, art and sport galore, plus activities like sponsored spellathon, cyber fashion show, talent show, hobbies convention and trips to pony club, music festivals, museums and art galleries.

Parents give school a firm thumbs-up. Two-thirds of girls are from families where both parents work, and with this in mind recently introduced breakfast club – for parents as well as girls. It opens at 7.45am and has proved hugely popular, particularly with the dads.

Fizzes with energy and enthusiasm. Girls are an industrious lot who like being busy and working hard. As one year 3 told us: 'The teachers here are very kind and they help us a lot.'

Northbourne Park School

Betteshanger, Deal, CT14 0NW

- Pupils: 140; 80 boys/60 girls; 40 boarders • Ages: 3-13 • C of E
- Fees: Day £7,860–£14,220; Boarding £18,150–£20,400 pa
- Independent

Tel: 01304 611215
Email: office@northbournepark.com
Website: www.northbournepark.com

Headmaster: Since September 2008, Mr Edward Balfour BA PGCE (early forties). Educated at Pilgrims', Winchester and King Edward VI School, Southampton, read English at Cardiff University and did his PGCE at Homerton, Cambridge where he specialised in English and drama. Previously a housemaster at Bradfield College, where he also taught English and drama and produced Hippolytus in ancient Greek. Approachable, immediately puts people at their ease, very popular with parents and staff alike. He knows the children and their families well and does not want school to grow much bigger as it would lose the personal touch and unique character. Energetic and ambitious for the school, whilst believing passionately in building on what is there and retaining its ethos. Wants children to be constantly pushing boundaries and to be part of 'Northbourne Park not Northbourne Walk in the Park'! Believes in a holistic approach to education and wants to break down the barriers between academic work, extra-curricular and pastoral activities; believes in 'inspiring in every child the confidence to succeed'. Married to Emma, a Cambridge French and Spanish graduate and former teacher in the school; three young children in the school.

Entrance: Taster day and tests in English and maths. The head likes to meet the whole family where possible. Almost non-selective – can adapt the curriculum to suit a child with learning difficulties as long as they are not too severe. They look for children who will be happy at Northbourne and most children are of at least average ability. Usually spaces in most year groups.

Exit: Most children go on to King's Canterbury and St Edmund's in Canterbury. One or two a year to Benenden and Kent College and one or two to Sevenoaks and Tonbridge. Occasionally a couple go further afield. Three or four each year leave at 11 to go to the grammars – the school will prepare children for the Kent Test but doesn't offer one-to-one coaching. Good range and number of scholarships each year – academic, music and sport.

Remarks: Set in 100 acres of parkland and woods on the Betteshanger Estate near Deal, formerly the home of the Northbourne family. Large, rambling Victorian house – a much-loved, happy place. Traditional values, a strong work ethic and a belief in and encouragement of service to the community. Not a grand school – great sense of informality and freedom with a cosy, family feel. Children are encouraged to climb trees, and each year group has a designated area of woodland where they are allowed to play. Some classrooms housed in very well-appointed outdoor classrooms in the garden erected by the Canadians during the war, which somehow got listed along with the rest of the house. Lord Northbourne, whose family used to live in the house, is still involved with the school and likes to take the top year to tea in the House of Lords.

A broadly Christian foundation, with great emphasis on instilling a sense of care and respect for the needs of others both within and outside the school. Boarders attend the local church in the grounds on Sundays. One class per year of about 15 children with a maximum of 19. The brighter children are extended and the less able are nurtured and encouraged. Some setting in the last two years; the scholarship children are taught within the class. Well-equipped new computer room and increasing use of ICT in curriculum. New girls' boarding house with bright airy dormitories; boys' dormitories all recently refurbished.

The French and Spanish programme is unique among prep schools. Two full-time classes of French and French-speaking Spanish children – the equivalent of an extra year 7 and 8, known as the Sixième and Cinquième. This programme is not actively marketed but is spread by word of mouth amongst top families in France and Spain whose children come to learn English for one or two years. The smart French children are often from top Parisian schools. The Spanish children tend to be already attending a Lycées in France and might then opt for British or American schools abroad – tend to be very European-minded. The French and Spanish children are taught separately by French staff and follow the French national curriculum in history, geography, French and maths – the exams are ratified by the Lycée in London and monitored by the CNED in France. The deputy head is French. Children come together outside lessons for all other activities and sport (including cricket), art etc. Charming to hear echoes of French and Spanish voices along the corridors. Inevitable benefits to English children who also spend a few days with an exchange school in Lille and with families in Spain. The children interact well, lots of close friendships are forged here and there is 'much to-ing and fro-ing across the Channel during the holidays,' said one happy mother, whose daughter has been invited to France several times. 'What makes Northbourne really special is the interaction between the English, French and Spanish children. It gave my son a real head start in languages,' said another.

Excellent pastoral care – 'Happiness is at the core of everything they do,' said one mother – and much emphasis on children becoming good citizens. Active school forum for children to develop their own ideas on eg break-time rules and expectations around manners, and an increasing emphasis on the role of the prefects. Girls sometimes have special 'girls' nights in' when matron administers 'beauty treatments' and does their hair. Currently 40 full boarders in the school (mainly the French and Spanish) with some flexi and weekly boarding. Wednesday and Saturday film nights in the old drawing room.

Good food prepared on site and served on a cafeteria system. The school regularly gains the National Heartbeat Food Award – two sittings for lunch and staff sit amongst children to supervise table manners and encourage conversation.

Dynamic director of sport, a Kent county cricket coach, has re-energised sport and breathed new life into the game, and there are now increasing fixtures against other schools – although some parents feel that there could be still more. Quite a small pool to choose from which means everyone has a chance to play in a team, and often children who might be overlooked in a bigger school find they have a sporting bent. Usual range of sports including rugby, plus cross-country, triathlon, tennis, badminton, fencing, clay pigeon shooting and archery – something for everyone. Outdoor heated pool – they go to Duke of York's School or Dover Leisure Centre for triathlon training during the winter.

Gets at least two or three music scholarships each year – most recently to Benenden, King's Canterbury, Kent College and St Edmund's. About 70 per cent of children learn at least one instrument, some up to grade 8. Music Tech also taught and iMacs used for composition. Lots of collaboration with the local community, and a number of children play in the Betteshanger band and join the Saturday music club. The director of music is an old girl of the school. Lots of encouragement and music lessons from pre-prep upwards. Several opportunities to play in informal concerts – children are encouraged to have a go. Plenty of opportunities to stand up in public too. One junior and one senior play each year – usually a musical. Public speaking competition and occasional debates. In-school clubs include electronics, art, pottery, computers, cookery and the popular and productive gardening club in the old walled garden. After-school academic societies include The Sophists, a literary discussion group open to all and held in the head's study, Bilingual society, Greek, Latin, new science, maths, geography and history societies. Senior children and especially scholars are encouraged to attend.

Busy art department – head of art works for the Canterbury Festival and produces vast three-dimensional pieces so likes big projects eg remarkable (authorised!) graffiti in the changing rooms, and won the prize for the best giant scarecrow at the Hampton Court Flower Show. The children love getting involved even if they are not very artistic. Lots of art competitions, Christmas card competition, pavement art on MDF. Local artists invited to workshops. Pottery housed in the dairy, which still has the Victorian tiles and marble slabs intact.

Good learning support – one full-time and two part-time teachers – mainly dyslexia, dyspraxia and ADHD. Problems identified early and support given either individually or in small groups, in or out of the classroom, each with an individual education plan reviewed by teachers and parents each term (extra charge for the support programmes). The few children in the school with mild Asperger's are carefully selected and assessed. School will take statemented children but not more than one per class. Wants to attract bright dyslexics.

The school day finishes at 5pm, but about half the children stay on for prep until 6pm. The pre-prep children can be looked after until their older siblings are ready to go home. School every other Saturday from year 4 – as well as lessons and games, a leadership course which has been going for years and is a particular feature of the school – like a mini Duke of Edinburgh scheme with lots of den-building and campfires in the woods. Very popular with the children – gives confidence and fosters team-building and leadership skills. Lots of gutsy stuff; children are encouraged but not made to take part. They are put into teams and challenged to build camps in groups – they learn how to make a campfire and are allowed to use penknives. They then spend the night in their camps, are given luxury ration packs and can turn rabbit and pheasant into a stew if they choose. This often develops a life-long love of the outdoors. Year 8 children go on an adventure holiday to the Ardeche as part of their leadership programme.

The recently-introduced Lord Northbourne Award Scheme also recognises life beyond academia – sport, music, expeditions, drama – children complete this at different levels in their own time. They have to visit the Mountain of Sport, the River of Adventure, The Temple of Learning and the Forest of Beauty and complete challenges in these areas. It culminates in a overseas expedition.

Close links with the French Lycée in London, who send a group down for a weekend each summer – sleeping outside in the camps can be a bit of a revelation for some of them. Northbourne children do a return day trip to London.

Parents mainly local farmers and businessmen as well as a few from London. Lots of first time buyers and working mothers – quite a cross-section of parents, many of whom have made great sacrifices to send their children here. Loyal and enthusiastic team of staff – some old hands and new young teachers including new heads of maths, science and English. Governing body reinvigorated by new chairman with a clear sense of purpose and direction. Friends of Northbourne Park a welcoming and sociable group. Lots of social and fund-raising events – wine tasting, quiz, Christmas fair, a major summer event and a ball every other year.

Old boys include writer Giles Brandreth, composer Sir Richard Rodney Bennett, concert pianist Freddie Kempf and reporter Giles Dilnot.

The pre-prep school is housed in the recently-refurbished Old Rectory about 10 minutes walk away, and caters for three to seven year olds. They eat separately – food prepared in main school. The headmaster takes assembly once a week and gets to know the children, who are taught French by French nationals every day from nursery upwards. Hall for assemblies and PE. Directors of music and sport come over from the prep; lots of team sports. Seamless transition to prep school with year 2 going over once per week for science, games lessons and swimming.

Northcote Lodge School

Linked school: Broomwood Hall School (Nightingale Lane)

26 Bolingbroke Grove, London, SW11 6EL

- Pupils: 220 boys; all day • Ages: 8–13 • Christian non-denom
- Fees: £16,125 pa • Independent

Tel: 020 8682 8888
Email: northcote@northwoodschools.com
Website: www.northcotelodge.co.uk

Headmaster: Since 2008, Mr John Hansford BA Hons (mid fifties). Taught English at Sherborne before arriving as deputy head in 1997. Mm, 11 years as deputy and now four as head – what does the future hold? Says he doesn't want the school ethos to change – important to 'keep the product in place'. Parents say: very traditional but open minded and easy to talk to. Has created more forms and thus reduced class sizes, all year groups now divided into three. Has no plans to expand the number of boys – 200 plus or minus is about right. Any more and he would find it difficult to shake every boy's hand each morning, which he really likes to do. Feels that way he gets to know them all, which is important as does not have much time to teach. Takes older boys for Latin and occasionally reads stories to younger forms. Very keen on sport – has increased senior sessions and introduced morning games on Fridays.

Married with three grown-up children, all employed – phew! Wife a maths graduate working part time for the health service. Weekdays spent in London and weekends at home in the country where, he says proudly, we have two allotments. Is he preparing for retirement?

Entrance: At eight. At least two-thirds from Broomwood Hall, their sister school, round the corner. The others mostly local, although school mini-buses do bring in some from across the river. Parents and families attend an open day and meet the headmaster. If they all like each other, zap, they are on the waiting list. A year before entry it's assessment time. A couple of hours at the school include tests in English, maths, verbal reasoning and ball skills, an interview with the head and some carefully observed playtime, including a snack. If your son is offered a place, you have to cough up half a term's fees immediately. Fifty per cent will be refunded on first term's bill, rest will be kept until boy moves on. They feel this encourages only those really serious about the school.

Exit: Mainly to board at a wide range of public schools, including Marlborough, Wellington, Bradfield, Eton, Radley, Harrow and Sherborne. Most of those continuing to day school have gone to Dulwich College. A record five scholarships in 2012 (academic, music, sports and all-rounder), to Alleyn's, Charterhouse, Cranleigh, Radley and Tonbridge. Inevitably some find the transition, from small protected school to large busy one, difficult at first, but head feels they are doing as much as possible to ease the path for them.

Remarks: A day school with the ethos of a boarding prep. Head says, 'A boarding school – but pupils don't bring pyjamas.' Boys arrive immediately after breakfast and go home late afternoon having already done their homework. Parents, a lot of whom have boarding school backgrounds themselves, like this as it takes off a lot of pressure. Lots of after school clubs as well – quite a full-on day.

Small classes, never more than 16, and enthusiastic teachers, average age mid-30s, approximately half/half male and female, create a good learning environment. All mixed ability, but setting in maths and English starts in year 4 and increases through other subjects as pupils move up the school. Plenty of playground space for kicking balls around or net practice at break time. Boys appeared relaxed, open and polite, quite happy to talk about what they were doing. Head says thinks they should be 'confident but not cocky; polite and affable; ready for next stage at 13'. Feels appearance important too and clean shoes essential – much used polish and brushes kept on bench in playground, just outside matron's room. Full-time matron, very jolly and welcoming – boys happy to take problems to her, a fully qualified nurse and a key figure on the pastoral care side.

The large, grade two listed, Victorian building has been a school (first for blind children, then disadvantaged girls) for the last hundred years. Several new additions have helped bring it bang up to date and you have to get to know your way around – we walked up and down different staircases and in and out of the main building, but, we were assured it was all totally logical. Probably a good thing that the younger boys stay put in their classrooms and it's only the top three years that move about.

Good art and DT studios, busy busy, lots of different things going on. Up to date science laboratories – apparently imaginative teacher recently bought a shark from Billingsgate for boys to dissect: Jaws, how exciting! Well equipped IT room, used by the younger groups for computer studies and as lesson extensions by the older ones. Music timetabled for all and about half also play an individual instrument, at the moment trumpet is most popular. A variety of musical groups and an active chapel choir, which has toured in Europe. Well-equipped gym can also be transformed into fully functioning theatre for the complete dramatic experience. Drama lessons part of the curriculum, about a third take the LAMDA exam. Several productions a year, hopefully something for everyone. Public speaking also encouraged – could be reciting a poem, taking part in a debate or reading out a match report in assembly: 'We want them to be seen and heard'.

Sport is big and played every day. Karate part of the curriculum, compulsory for first two years – 'It's good for confidence, concentration and self esteem'. Masses of black belts. Main outdoor sports football, rugby and cricket, either across the road on Wandsworth Common or at Trinity Fields, ten minutes' walk away. Plays matches against other schools, sometimes at weekends, but, parents say, possibly not competitive enough. No dedicated, specialist sports teachers, which can mean boys not properly prepared. They (parents) feel this not totally fair as boys don't necessarily reach their potential – however brand new director joined in September 2011, and could be the answer. Lots more to try in after-school clubs, including cross-country, golf and shooting – definitely modelling itself on a country prep.

Regular residential trips for all, ranging from PGL in year 5 to outward bound in year 8 – good formative stuff. The usual French trips, rugby and cricket tours and, less common, yearly exchange with a South African school. Also plenty of excursions in and around London, making the most of what it has to offer. All trips and excursions compulsory and included in fees.

EAL not an issue as only accepts fluent English speakers. Caters for mild learning difficulties – one-to-one help available, but nothing too severe and definitely no disruption. Parents say teachers good at communicating and problems quickly identified and dealt with. Head says as far as possible everything is in place to counteract any problems or if a boy is unhappy. All boys have prep diaries, containing school rules and all contact details – parents use these for important notes. A Christian school and, though other faiths are welcome, they must join in with daily assemblies and attend the weekly church service.

Northwood College Junior School

Linked school: Northwood College

Maxwell Road, Northwood, HA6 2YE

• Pupils: 350 girls; all day • Fees: £8,700–£11,850 pa;
• Independent

Tel: 01923 825446
Email: admissions@northwoodcollege.co.uk
Website: www.northwoodcollege.co.uk

Head of the Junior School: Mrs Hina Thaker

Exit: Nearly all to senior school.

Remarks: See main college.

Norwich High School – Junior School

Linked school: Norwich High School for Girls

Stafford House, 93 Newmarket Road, Norwich, NR2 2HU

• Pupils: 200 girls; all day • Ages: 3–11 • Non-denom
• Fees: £8,802 pa • Independent

Tel: 01603 453265
Email: admissions@nor.gdst.net
Website: www.norwichhigh.gdst.net

Head: Since 2011, Mrs Jenny Green BSoc Sc, originally from Cape Town (fifties). Began working life as a merchandise manager, lived in Bahrain for a while and got into teaching by starting as a parent helper. Taught at several Norfolk schools so counts as a local, then went as deputy head at Ghost Hill, thence as head to Lingwood – 'We got "outstanding" in every category.' Outgoing, confident and exuberantly enthusiastic – she is a good promoter of the school – 'I do this job because I absolutely love it'.

Entrance: Nursery from three and not oversubscribed – the locals being, seemingly a little slow to seize their opportunities. Assessment via a playday when they look for manual dexterity, interaction, responsiveness etc. Reception has 20 and a further 20 by year 3. Again, currently not too much pressure on places but, as the place starts to zoom, this is unlikely to stay the case.

Exit: Most, gratefully, to the senior school.

Remarks: School in beautiful nineteenth century Stafford House over the way from senior dept, newly decorated and revamped when we visited. Tots in Polliwiggle Nursery – that being the Norfolk word for tadpole, don't you know? Good, colourful clutter here and there – not one of those sanitised juniors – atmosphere is relaxed, orderly and purposeful. Lovely library with beanbags invites curling up and wallowing. Really lively art eg Van Gogh-inspired yellows and blues and scenes from Narnia in evocative charcoal and impressive Greek vase pictures, 'If you do a good one it gets framed and stays for years and years till you come back as a teacher and see it again!' Lots of different 'Days' eg 'Victorian Day', 'Business Day', 'Tudor day' – suggestive of the cross-curricular approach that so enlivens the senior school. Try-outs in four different languages and lots of trips.

Lessons are stimulating and fun. 'They've got to be worth getting out of bed for,' says the head, and much thought goes into structuring the curriculum. Good support in school for those with minor learning difficulties – small group work and an imminent boost to the numbers of LAs when we visited. Woods, fields, jungle gym and main school facilities provide outdoor life. In 2010 and 2011, year 5 girls won the regional paper's Young Poet of the Year Award. Parents very appreciative: 'I was sure about sending her from the day we went to look round when she was four. She just got stuck in and loved it and there's always such a good atmosphere.' Others concur: 'It's a happy, productive, busy place'.

Norwich School Lower School

Linked school: Norwich School

Bishopgate, Norwich, NR1 4AA

- Pupils: 180; 120 boys/60 girls • Ages: 7–11 • Fees: £11,997 pa
- Independent

Tel: 01603 728449
Email: admissions@norwich-school.org.uk
Website: www.norwich-school.org.uk

Master of the lower school: Since 2007, Mr John Ingham BA (history), previously head of Rossall School Juniors. Cheerful and down to earth in style – an enthusiastic advocate of the school's recent inclusion of girls (his daughter was an early pioneer). Very accessible, teaches (mostly history and maths), not hidden away. Easy, relaxed relationships with the pupils. He is married to Mandy, who works in the school's games department, and they have one daughter now in the senior school.

Entrance: Entrance exam (English, maths, NVR) plus interview at 7+. About 40 places available, generally over-subscribed. Pupils filter in higher up, mainly from other local prep schools, and the year group rises almost to 60 by year 6. Cathedral choristers must get a school place before auditioning for the choir.

Exit: For vast majority, a smooth transition to senior school, although this isn't guaranteed. Plenty of early warning for those not suited.

Remarks: On its own site a short walk from the senior school between the edge of the Cathedral Close and nearby river Wensum. Built in the 1970s and designed around a central hall and library with classes mostly at ground floor level, with views of the adjacent playing field. Closely-knit staff, including plenty of men, teach pupils in smallish classes (under 20) with emphasis on encouraging a love of learning. Pupils need to be above average in ability and confident readers to benefit from all the school offers.

Sport matters here, with emphasis on the competitive team sports rugby, hockey and netball. 'They have got to have somewhere to hang their hat,' says the head. If sport isn't your thing, there are musical opportunities galore – 80 per cent learn an instrument, there are several choirs (varying abilities) and bands. Plays are performed each year in a small local theatre. Many after-school clubs – late pick-ups help to filter demand for the limited parking space. Plenty of trips and holidays. Pupils are cheerful and confident, engagingly honest – 'My only gripe is the weird food', said one boy, 'so I eat a lot of pasta'. Another boy said, 'I love singing, maths, and history; I just like being at school'. Pupils here have a very full and active day and need resilience to flourish.

Notre Dame Preparatory School

Linked school: Notre Dame Senior School

Burwood House, Convent lane, Cobham, Surrey, KT11 1HA

- Pupils: 250 girls in prep school; all day; 45 boys and girls nursery • Ages: 2–11 • RC foundation but all faiths welcome
- Fees: £3,060–£11,580 pa • Independent

Tel: 01932 869991
Email: headmaster@notredame.co.uk
Website: www.notredame.co.uk

Principal: Mr David Plummer BEd Hons, Dip HE, FRSA (forties), head since 2001, became principal of the prep and senior schools in 2013. Previously principal of Latymer Prep.

A self-assured and likeable Welshman, he's hard to miss as he proceeds around school dispensing bonhomie to girls, staff and parents alike. 'Perhaps charismatic is too strong a word, but he's a great figurehead for the prep school and the girls like him,' said one mother. You may well hear him before you see him, and he'll be the one in charge of the microphone at any and all events. But underpinning this geniality, he has got the appropriate presence about him and can be authoritative when he needs to be.

Does not sit still, yet pays great attention to detail; 'Do the small things well and the big things will follow,' he says. He's approachable, enthusiastic and super-committed – 'There are lots of ways to be innovative, even after 10 years at the school,' he says – and his latest pride and joy is the new school theatre, shared with seniors (qv) which he is positively bursting to show off. Has an archetypal Welsh way with words, describing Notre Dame as 'An elegant, stately lady of a school'. Big on communication, he produces a weekly newsletter and is a keen fan of Twitter – the school's 220 followers can expect several tweets a day.

Knows all the girls, not just their names, but something about them. Pupils say he is 'funny, kind and knows how to sort things out,' and particularly enjoy the 'Dads and daughters' camp he organises.

He's married, his wife teaches at the school and his two daughters are both former prep and senior pupils. 'I'm a family person and I've always lived in a matriarchal set up,' he says. 'Blessed art thou amongst women'. He has worked in a co-ed school, but firmly believes in single sex education for girls. 'It simply works; it's the best model,' he says. 'But I also know that a professional male influence is a good thing.' And having joined as the only man on the staff, he has since taken on five other male teachers to prove his point.

Vice principal and head of the prep school is Miss Merinda D'Aprano BEd MA FRSA, previously deputy head.

Entrance: From 2+ (early years), 4+ (reception) and 7+ (prep). Occasional places at other times – worth asking. The children attend an observation/assessment day at the school before offers are made – 'We look for a competent grasp of basic skills at a level appropriate to their age,' says school. 'Not ruthless, but working with parents to help them make the right choice.'

Exit: Most (85 to 90 per cent) stay for the 'seamless transition' to Notre Dame senior school. It's not automatic, girls need to 'earn' a place by taking the same assessment test as newcomers. Others head off to local schools including Guildford High, Sir William Perkins, Tormead, St Catherines, Nonsuch and Tiffin grammar schools, or to boarding schools.

Remarks: A very nurturing and inclusive school which seems to suit all comers. There's a fairly wide range of abilities, but mostly slightly above the national average. Overall achievement judged 'outstanding' by ISI.

All starts with 80 children, including 12 boys in the Bluebelles nursery, which has just been refurbished and is bright and welcoming. Parents particularly like wrap-around care on offer – Early Birds and Owls breakfast and tea clubs can provide care from 8.15 to 5.30. Like the whole school – the rest of which is of course girls only – it is well resourced and the children look busy and happy.

Moving up through the school, the average class size is 15-20. Lessons are pacey. The whole curriculum has been overhauled to keep it 'fit for purpose, fresh and valuable,' as school describes it. Called TASK, it stands for Thinking and discerning, Active participation, Skills for learning and Knowledge with understanding – these girls really won't get away with simply printing out internet 'research' they have not really read or understood. Spanish just introduced from nursery. Good IT throughout the school and girls taught to touch type. DP is a big reader in his spare time and this is reflected around the school where there is a library in every alcove. Parents all mention 'good' teaching from a 'settled' staff, many of whom have been with DP from the start.

Around 50 children have English as an additional language, but 35 of those are actually bi- and tri-lingual, so school sees that as an asset not a problem. Two staff lead SEN, supported by outside tutors for which parents pay extra. School is happy to take girls with all sorts of needs, as long as they can cope with the curriculum.

Together with the senior school, the prep has just come to the end of a major development programme costing several million pounds. Next on the agenda is a renewed focus on sport for all. Keen to get his girls out of the classroom more often – and quite understandably, given the school's beautiful grounds – DP is now developing a forest school, and also on his wish list is an all-weather pitch, a tree house classroom and a putting green, along with 'green' initiatives like bee-keeping and a school allotment.

Lucky prep pupils share the senior school sports facilities, which pays off – the IAPS 2012 swimming champion is a Notre Dame girl, doubtless helped by her practice in the school's fabulous indoor pool. DP has also opened up some less traditional options for girls by adding golf and football to the curriculum. School ski trip is hugely over-subscribed.

Music is not left to the older girls either – there's a choir and orchestra for infants too so that girls are into it from the off. Some 177 girls take instrumental lessons with 26 now doing M:Tech, (music technology) too.

Class work is well balanced with extra-curricular activities of all sorts – even a 'Glee' club. Many reminders that this is a Catholic school, with lots of 'special places,' say our young guides, including the chapel, which can take the whole prep school, and the La Mothe prayer garden. Polite pupils saying good morning and thank you to their teachers, courteous, holding doors open for each other, no pushing or charging about.

Parents happily recommend; 'It's girl heaven,' said one.

Notting Hill and Ealing High School Junior School

Linked school: Notting Hill and Ealing High School

26 St Stephen's Road, London, W13 8HH

- Pupils: 310 girls; all day • Ages: 4–11 • Non-denom
- Fees: £11,556 pa • Independent

Tel: 020 8799 8484
Email: enquiries@nhehs.gdst.net
Website: www.nhehs.gdst.net

Headmistress: Since September 2013, Mrs Silvana Silva BEd (forties). Previously deputy head for 11 years. Married with one son (reading chemistry at Warwick). Has been at NHEHS since 1989 arriving as a young teacher, has 'absolutely loved every minute' and worked her way up the ranks. She covered the previous head's maternity leave thee years ago confidently and with complete success. Well known to pupils and parents and completely committed to the school and to each girl's individual success and happiness. The school's open door policy, approachability and sympathetic ear to concerns seem in safe hands here.

Comfortable with the GDST ethos. Clear educational vision – 'Our job is to spark an interest in learning,' she says. Wholly committed to single sex education. 'Girls tend to have low self esteem and aren't risk takers,' she says, determined to inspire them with confidence and encourage them to learn interactively and independently. A great rôle model for budding young girls.

Entrance: Heavily oversubscribed and fiercely competitive – about 100 applicants for 40 places. Assessed just before fourth birthday – three staff will work with four children for an hour and half. 'We want to see how they play and how they interact – we're looking for inner confidence and self assurance,' says the head. 'It's not about knowing your ABC or how to count to 2,000 – we can teach them that.' Very flexible before assessment – will reschedule for illness; takes into account what a child's previous experience has been. But no budging after assessment and no sibling policy – it was the talk of Ealing when a child with four older sisters who had been through the school was refused a place. At year 3 (age seven) eight places and usually 30+ applicants. They sit papers in English, maths and verbal reasoning, plus interview for those who have done well enough. Other than these two entrance points it's very rare for the occasional place to come up, but it does happen.

Exit: Almost all to senior school – informed in year 5 if eligible, then do exam in January of year 6, primarily for the purpose of setting in senior school and to award academic and music scholarships (usually a handful of these). Help is given to the (very) few who are not up to it (these will normally have left at seven anyway) – they are placed at, eg, Heathfield and Northwood College. Tiny few to St Paul's or Latymer Upper – tends to be for a specific reason – eg proximity to home or availability of scholarships.

Remarks: All the hallmarks of a GDST – excellent delivery of the curriculum, thorough assessment of children, down to earth professional parents. Bright spacious classrooms – lots of windows and impressive displays in corridors as well as in classrooms, some of the best (and most genuine) we've seen. Large playground with imaginative places to sit and to play – gazebo with benches, round tables and chairs, assault course, springy colourful tarmac and netball hoops. Separate playground for reception where the little ones can spill out to play with sand,

N

Wendy house and puppet theatre. Funky lavatories decorated in bright girly colours – lots of pinks and purples reminiscent of a Vue cinema. The senior school is 100 yards to the rear, younger girls share their swimming pool, netball courts and dining room and perform the odd concert in the grand West Wing auditorium, but otherwise it's a separate entity.

Always near the top in the league tables. Wouldn't suit a child that isn't up to it academically: if she can't keep up she may find herself excluded – even in the playground, reports one parent. (School surprised at these reports and keen to deny them.) Year 1 class teacher doubles up as SENCo – a few on the dys–strata and some with mild Asperger's. They can have extra help at a cost – not the school to send your daughter if she has serious learning difficulties. As for the gifted and talented – 'All girls here would be given that label,' says the head – and she clearly knows. The particularly brilliant (about four in each class) are catered for with differentiation and extension exercises – 'It helps that they can bounce off each other'.

Good discipline and pastoral care. Girls are taught right from the beginning to wait their turn and to respect others, but do have fun and are encouraged to participate. Our guide proudly related the teaching behind the catch words, THINK ('Is it truthful, is it helpful, is it inspiring, is it necessary, is it kind? If not, don't say it') and TAG (tell person how you're feeling, ask them to stop, get help from an adult). It clearly sticks.

You can do almost anything from Mandarin and chess to yoga and gardening in spare time but the music is particularly strong. Ninety per cent of girls learn a musical instrument, one third of the school is in the main orchestra. Impressive carol concerts in St Barnabas. Larks and tone deaf given equal attention – the hugely committed head of music holds 8.00am sessions in the week for the enthusiasts, of which many.

Most parents working professionals – ladies who lunch thin on the ground. Children of BBC types, lawyers and doctors come mainly from the local area, but a fair number prepared to travel the distance from Shepherds Bush and Ruislip – determined to get their daughter an excellent education from four to 18.

If your daughter wants to work hard and play hard, this is an excellent choice.

Notting Hill Preparatory School

95 Lancaster Road, London, W11 1QQ

- Pupils: 300 boys and girls; all day • Ages: 4–13 • Non-denom
- Fees: £15,540 pa • Independent

Tel: 020 7221 0727
Email: admin@nottinghillprep.com
Website: www.nottinghillprep.com

Headmistress: Since September 2003, Mrs Jane Cameron BEd (fifties). Married with three grown-up children. She had run the Acorn Nursery in Lansdowne Crescent for 25 years, and parents there encouraged her to translate its ethos of teacher/ parent partnership into a prep school. Approachable, dynamic, greatly respected by parents and pupils, 'terribly hands-on and involved,' said a parent. 'Problems get sorted out very quickly because she'll invite you straight in to see her.' Another said: 'she is the backbone of the school. She brings a committed energy and a genuine passion in the joy of learning. She is an inspiration to us all.'

Entrance: Has two reception classes; younger children are offered a gentler introduction with some shorter school days. Automatic places for siblings; the rest are allocated by ballot (separate ballots for boys and girls), drawn in May for September

to February birthdays and in November for March to August birthdays – so you have at least three months after the birth in which to register. However, highest waiting list places allocated to those who signed up soonest after birth. Those successful in the ballot are asked to pay a £1000 deposit 18 months before entry. Places higher up by assessment. Some, mostly boys, join in year 7, and there are one or two bursaries a year available for children from state primaries. 'It was lovely to hear from a boy from one of the local high-rise estates [who had moved on to a top boarding school] that rowing was now his favourite sport.' Can cater for some specific learning difficulties and EAL.

Exit: About half the girls and a handful of boys leave at 11, moving on to eg Latymer Upper, Godolphin & Latymer, South Hampstead, Harrodian, Francis Holland; or to board at eg Cheltenham Ladies', Wycombe Abbey, Benenden, St Swithun's. Boys mostly stay on till 13, then head for eg St Paul's, Westminster, City of London, UCS; or board at eg Eton, Harrow, Charterhouse, Winchester. Boys and a few girls leave at 13 for co-ed boarding schools eg Marlborough, Wellington, Rugby, Bedales, St Edward's. Music awards from Latymer Upper, City of London Girls, Winchester and Wells Cathedral Choir.

Remarks: On the borders of achingly trendy Notting Hill (Hugh Grant expected to stroll idly by at any minute) and grittier Ladbroke Grove, with tubes on the Hammersmith and City line and cars on the elevated Westway forming the northern horizon, and Portobello market just down the road. The school opened in 2003 with 57 pupils in a 1900s school building (currently owned by Campden Charities) which still has the painted brick classroom walls and high windows of a classic Victorian school. Some Acorn parents found out that the property was available, gathered shareholders, and moved fast to secure the lease, and the fledgling school was set up within a whirlwind nine months. 'We got a band of great teachers together, some of whom still work here.'

There's a large hall with stage for assemblies, plays and concerts; art room adorned with clay models, papier mâché shields and a cardboard violin; small library with comfy sofa. A painted timeline starts in the entrance hall with dinosaurs and continues up the stairs and through the ages.

The upper school building across the road, purpose-built and opened in 2008, is shoehorned into an intricate space where a Belgo restaurant once stood. Wood-clad, with whitewashed walls, rooflights and curved ceilings, it includes a basement dining/assembly/dance and drama room as well as classrooms, science lab, music and computer rooms for years 4 – 8. It looks out one way onto Ladbroke Grove tube station and Chicken Village fast food restaurant, the other onto wooded slopes that border the tube line.

'I feel passionately that I'd like our children to be educated in the true sense of the word, but we also have to manage preparation for very narrow tests at the end of the road. We do aim to light the fire rather than just filling the bucket.' Children from reception upwards encouraged to express opinions, with plenty of small group discussions. Philosophy4Children and de Bono Thinking Hats systems used to encourage enquiring, reasoning approaches to learning. 'There is a real onus on independent thinking and this seems to give the children an enormous self-confidence and sense of self,' said a parent. Practical, fun teaching; year 2 was investigating friction and gravity using toy cars and ramps of books during our visit. Kung Fu Maths, a NHP invention, sees children awarded 'belts' in assembly for learning tables, knowing number bonds, solving problems of increasing complexity. 'The teaching staff at all levels are extraordinary,' said a parent. 'Their talent, enthusiasm and dedication are an inspiration to the pupils'.

As children move into year 4 and the upper school building, the pace of learning changes too. 'The early years are particularly gentle and nurturing,' said a parent. 'When they cross over the road they graduate to a much more serious work ethic. It's a very successful symbol.' Another commented: 'You see a real mix between academic rigour and the fostering of imagination.'

Non-selective system means particular needs do crop up. 'If a teacher raises concerns, the SENCo will observe the child in class and suggest strategies. For the first two years, we will give extra support and keep watching. If it becomes evident we can't meet the child's needs we'll discuss it with the parents.' The SENCo can give one-to-one help at extra cost; speech and language and OT experts available to visit.

Music is a particular strength. The school has twice performed pieces written by the 'amazing, hugely enthusiastic and charismatic' music master at the Schools Proms at the Albert Hall – most recently The Eagle, based on a Tennyson poem. Some two-thirds of pupils play an instrument and many join the choir, orchestra or ensemble groups. Plenty of opportunities to perform, in assemblies, concerts, poetry recitals, school plays – Hansel and Gretel was under rehearsal during our visit. Art imaginative and inspiring.

Sport was the only area picked out as a weaker link in last ISI report; Jane Cameron acknowledges the challenges a newish school (and particularly a co-ed one) faces in setting up a fixture list. Football (boys' and girls'), rugby, netball, cricket and rounders matches played with varying degrees of success; the swimming squad is apparently 'second to none'. Compact playground, so sport involves travelling: most matches, and many sports lessons, at the Linford Christie stadium; they also use the Westway Sports Centre and Kensington Leisure Centre.

Clubs range from Greek to chess to netball to lateral thinking; they make good use of London, with trips down the Thames, to a Hindu temple, to City Hall and the Olympic site; they go off to Normandy, skiing, on outdoor pursuits courses and field trips.

Much parental involvement, whether helping in the library, giving a talk on the nature of consciousness or on Leonardo da Vinci, giving a violin recital, or running a crafts workshop. 'There is a constant stream of authors, musicians, journalists, actors and artists, not only dropping off and collecting their children, but generously volunteering their time and talent by speaking at assemblies and judging various competitions, such as poetry and public speaking,' commented a parent.

Great parental praise for the 'pervasive caring ethos' of the school. 'The NHP community is one in which the children show an enormous and unusual amount of empathy.' 'Every child feels valued, and different talents are truly celebrated. Children take great pride in the achievements of their peers, not only academically but in music, art and extra-curricular areas.' 'Altruistic behaviour happens all the time. It is the way things work at NHP and what we treasure most.' 'We feel indebted to NHP for giving our children a love of learning, a sense of belonging and pride.'

Nottingham Girls' High School Junior School

Linked school: Nottingham Girls' High School

9 Arboretum Street, Nottingham, NG1 4JB

- Pupils: 290 girls; all day • Ages: 4–11 • Non-denom
- Fees: £8,658 pa • Independent

Tel: 01159 417663
Email: enquiries@not.gdst.net
Website: www.nottinghamgirlshigh.gdst.net

Head: Since September 2010, Mrs Faith Potter (early forties) BA PGCE, studied ecology at Bedford and previously deputy head of an international school in Cyprus. Married with two young children. Approachable, fair and has high expectations of behaviour. Keen to develop every child's full potential both in and out of the classroom, so is a great advocate of a busy school with a wide choice of musical, dramatic, creative and sporting activities.

Entrance: Majority at four and seven, a few places at other ages, especially nine – happy to recruit at all ages. Each child is invited to an informal, enjoyable assessment within the EYFA class and an additional group assessment. Head says school is 'not only interested in what they've done academically – we're looking to see what we can teach a child rather than what she has already been taught.' At seven children take tests in numeracy and literacy – designed to assess potential, not simply what they have been taught.

Exit: Nearly all to senior school.

Remarks: Split between a modern purpose-built block and an extended period building. Good facilities: brand new library, additional classrooms, bright classrooms, hall, gym, two ICT suites, art room, new multi-activity playground, wooden amphitheatre, landscaped gardens and soft play surface.

Takes Sats – all girls get a minimum of level 4 in all subjects and most of the results are at level 5 – but doesn't teach to them – sees them as just one indicator of pupil performance. Enjoys celebrating excellence – has a special achievers' board. Some help for those with specific learning difficulties is offered in class and on an individual and group basis.

Performing arts important and integrated into curriculum. All take part in at least one annual performance. A high percentage of pupils learn an instrument. Extracurricular opportunities include country dancing, gym, steel band and chess – school play, numerous sports matches and has county players. Many girls participate in chess team matches and regularly win the local league. Holds regular themed days where pupils take part in problem-solving activities, eg Take One Picture (linked to the National Gallery), Building Aliens, One World and Philosophy. Super examples throughout of pupils challenged to think outside the box, such as themed weeks and open homework weeks.

A recent major building programme with a large extension resulting in a new library and learning resources centre, new ICT centre, three additional classrooms, new waiting area and a new main entrance to the whole junior school. This means it is now accepting two form entry at age four and continues with two forms throughout.

A happy, encouraging, child-friendly environment for able girls.

Nottingham High Infant and Junior School

Linked school: Nottingham High School

Waverley Mount, Nottingham, NG7 4ED

- Pupils: 250 boys; all day • Ages: 4-11 • Fees: £8,415-£9,789 pa
- Independent

Tel: 01158 452214
Email: enquiries@nottinghamhigh.co.uk
Website: www.nottinghamhigh.co.uk

Head: Since 2013, Mrs Clare Bruce MA (early forties). Educated at Hutchesons' Grammar School in Glasgow, read English at St Andrews and did PGCE at Loughborough. Spent two years in business. First teaching post at Grace Dieu Manor School in Leicestershire, then moved to Derby Grammar School. Head of Derby Grammar Junior School for four years. Has two children and enjoys reading and keeping fit in her spare time.

Entrance: Individual assessment through games activities used to assess potential for learning for reception children, and national curriculum based numeracy and literacy assessment for years 1 and 2, plus classroom based practical activities observation (for both).

For entry to junior school, exam in English and maths based on national curriculum and reasoning, plus observation during an afternoon's activities, to assess social skills, and informal interview – looking for above average academic potential and some spark. A few places available at other ages.

Exit: Automatic progression from the infant school to junior school in most cases. Virtually all progress to senior school from junior school.

Remarks: Established in 1905, the current building was purpose-built in the 1970s in the grounds of the senior school; large classrooms and attractive well-stocked library. Very good key stage 2 results across the board; sets, in a fluid way, for English (some very well-written letters on display) and maths. Strong ICT – especially in conjunction with maths (boys participate in an online global competition), blogs created for topics. All classrooms have electronic whiteboards much used by teachers. Spanish and French from year 3 – boys give sessions to the infants; also thinking skills. Max 24 per class, average 19. Attractive learning support room – full time co-ordinator: mostly in class support with some outside (no charge); can handle dys-range.

Uses senior school sports facilities, eg indoor swimming pool – very good range of sports. Lots of success in national chess competitions at all ages (all play regularly in year 3). Dance, eg street variety, popular, now part of PE curriculum. Good music opportunities – free music tuition for all year 3 boys; well-equipped music room. All year groups do a drama production; interesting artwork in various media – Artsmark awarded 2010.

Wide choice of lunchtime clubs including games, magic, practical science, fencing, jazz; eco and school councils; lots of competitions – house and external: general knowledge, poetry reciting, public speaking. Several trips ranging as far as London, Poland, Austria (skiing) and all year groups have residentials: a farm, outdoor pursuits centre, York.

Majority of parents professional; reflects the diverse ethnic and cultural backgrounds of the area. Boys are confident, articulate and engaged in class and look very smart in black jackets and trousers with silver and black ties and grey jumpers.

Very special infant school, for four to seven-year-olds. Opened 2008, so still building up numbers, in a very attractive mock Regency building across the road from the main school. Cheerful décor, large hall and music room, lovely art room with rafters and cookery section on top floor, ICT room with infant-friendly, coloured keyboards and versatile screens. Large, colourful classrooms all with very good displays, interactive whiteboards and access to outside. Brain gym twice a day; lots of physical and creative activity; individual and group support for learning needs. Uses specialist staff from junior school for ICT, swimming, music, Spanish, French, chess (part of the curriculum) plus main school sports, music and drama facilities. Extensive garden on different levels with six areas of learning – small assault course, sensory area with musical instruments, two guinea pigs. Standard sports; tennis, football, cricket, gardening, eco, art and choir clubs; several trips; visiting experts; piano, violin and clarinet lessons, concerts, plays. Open 8am to 5.30pm (reasonable charge for extra time).

A very good junior school with high academic standards now offering a broader range of opportunities. Worth taking advantage of the very promising infants school.

Old Buckenham Hall School

Brettenham Park, Ipswich, IP7 7PH

- Pupils: 220 boys and girls; 100 boarders • Ages: 3-13 • C of E
- Fees: Boarding £18,990-£21,570; Day £8,160-£16,470 pa
- Independent

Tel: 01449 740252
Email: admissions@obh.co.uk
Website: www.obh.co.uk

Headmaster: Since September 2010, Mr John Brett MA (forties) educated at King's School Bruton, Leeds College of Music and the University of London. Previously head of St Mary's Prep School in Melrose, from where he was headhunted by the governors of Old Buckenham; prior to that he was director of music at King's Hall and Thomas's London Day Schools. A tried and tested head, seeking to expand and re-invigorate the curriculum, believing that prep schools should offer far more than simply 'getting pupils through common entrance'. Very on the ball, witty and with an all-round understanding of the pressures on heads, he is involved in national initiatives to re-assess the programmes of study that lead to common entrance. Parents delighted – 'we feel jet-propelled by an inspirational head'. His wife, Clare, is head of drama at Old Buckenham and has a similarly relaxed style.

His strong feeling that pupils should have direct access to him means his study door remains open, unless he is conducting a meeting or private interview. Both his sons attend the school.

Entrance: Pupils enter at nursery, reception and all years up to 7 and 8. No linked feeders, though the majority of pupils come from within a two hour drive. No entrance exam but informal assessments take place during taster days, plus reports from previous school. Pupils can enter the school on a daily basis and, if they wish, become a boarder at a later stage. A small, but constant, group of pupils come from abroad.

Exit: The head believes that the process of selecting the right choice of school at 13+ can't begin too early and certainly by years 5/6. Popular destinations are those schools fairly close, eg Uppingham, Oakham, Oundle, Stowe, Framlingham, Ipswich and Gresham's, but a clutch to Eton, Harrow, Shrewsbury and Charterhouse. Head considers that it is very important to cast a wide net at senior school stage rather than staying within the safe and familiar choices. He treats with contempt the idea of making cosy arrangements or 'done deals' with schools and is alert to the dangers of making his own tastes and choices too evident. A significant number of pupils receive awards and scholarships, with eight scholarships in 2013.

Remarks: Alert, friendly and naturally courteous children – standing up for adults, holding doors etc. Classes are small (fewer than 16 generally) and with setting in the higher forms in preparation for exams/scholarships. The tone throughout is purposeful and light-hearted – one example is the use of Spanish and French in labelling, eg 'le bureau du Directeur'. Music and drama enjoy excellent facilities and highly motivated staff ensure that children make the most of what's available. The full ability range is catered for and SEN is undergoing a full review. The head's concern about the withdrawal of pupils with specific difficulties is that it 'does not, in itself, necessarily address their needs – a highly competent teacher plus in-class support may often be the answer'.

One of the school's great strengths is its framework of pastoral support for each pupil. The head stresses that arrangements for tutor groups and boarding houses need to be constantly appraised and changes are sometimes necessary as staff come and go. The school is looking particularly at the needs of the older pupils. Well-organised and attractive boarding houses, careful thought having been given to the facilities and decoration. The slightly dismal air that can prevail in dormitories and common-rooms has been completely avoided – no sagging sofas and ancient cast-off furniture. In years 7 and 8 pupils can decide whether to be a dorm leader or sleep in their year group bedrooms. Boarding is so popular that many board full time despite living close by – 'My friend boards even though she lives less than a mile away!'

With a highly motivated, 'unstuffy' head, Old Buckenham Hall is set to expand from its traditional county boarding base, keen to reach parents who might not naturally consider a prep or boarding option for their child. Positions itself as a largely non-selective family school, the majority boarding in the higher years. The pre-prep school runs on a day basis with boarding (weekly and full) becoming available in year 3. The head is aware that the decision to board needs careful thought and transitional boarding of two or three nights a week is available together with taster weeks. The school has been quick to respond to the need for flexibility and operates a variety of collection times for pupils both in the prep and pre-prep. The majority of pupils come from within a radius of 40 miles, but quite a number come from further afield and the school operates a taxi service to the airport for those who need to travel abroad.

Old Palace of John Whitgift Preparatory School

Linked school: Old Palace of John Whitgift School

2, Melville Avenue, South Croydon, CR2 7YN

• Pupils: Nursery:120 boys and girls; Prep: 200 girls; all day
• Ages: 3 m–10 • C of E • Fees: £9,928–£11,316 pa • Independent

---

Tel: 020 8686 7347
Email: schooloffice@oldpalace.croydon.sch.uk
Website: www.oldpalaceofjohnwhitgift.org

Head of Preparatory: Since September 2011, Mrs Gill Stone BEd Hons (Cantab) Dip RSA SpLD. Worked in assorted state and independent primary schools before joining Old Palace in 1999 as a teacher and moving up the management ranks, acquiring a special needs qualification in 2004 on the way. Like her nursery counterpart, reports to Carol Jewell, who, as head of school, is in overall charge.

Married with two student children, both educated at Whitgift Foundation Schools. Daughter, an Old Palace Old Girl, has just embarked on a postgraduate PGCE at Homerton, Cambridge, her mother's alma mater.

Comes across as quietly jolly and self-possessed. A talented pianist (like her senior school counterpart Carol Jewell), she can provide emergency hymn cover with the best of them. Add her yen for am-dram and singing – she does a mean Julie Andrews impression – and there are hints of a more extrovert side.

Her other great interest is animals in general and great apes in particular. Lift up your coffee cup in her pleasant office and you're likely to meet the unblinking gaze of a mountain gorilla on the coaster beneath.

Again, like Carol Jewell, she's seen as a non-controversial appointment, balm on the water after turbulent few years when the merger with less academic Croham Hurst School in 2008 was followed by the sudden exit of the senior school head – together with a pressing corporate need to demonstrate unified leadership with unambiguous focus on academic achievement.

Now, judging by appearances, she presides over a happy, dedicated team, including four Old Girls, and about the same number again who send their children here. Those in search of a demonstration of healed wounds and new dawns will take comfort from the appointment of new deputy head, whose daughter has come from Croham to Old Palace. Three weeks into the job and wreathed in smiles, she's a cracking advertisement for the success of the merger that only the supremely cynical would see as a politically-inspired appointment.

Some parents wondered whether Mrs Stone has taken on too much in the way of teaching responsibilities, which now account for around a third of her time. She's keen on keeping her hand in as 'it's important that you're involved in maintaining relationships with girls and staff.' In addition to heading up learning support (as you'd expect, given her qualifications) has recently added years 3 to 5 drama to responsibilities, following departure of popular specialist (there's a bit of pleasurable 'did she jump, retire or was she pushed?' speculation).

Overall, however, consensus is that she's kind and popular with pupils – 'Very content and likes to sort out our problems,' says one. Parents, even those with significant gripes (and there are a few), feel her heart is in the right place. 'I have a lot of time for her,' comments another.

Head of Nursery: Since December 2009, Miss Jacqui Hines, NNEB (mid forties), two teenage girls, one a gold-medal gymnast. Formal title, day care manager. Feisty, fast-talking with supportive, calm deputy – 'I run around like a loon, she's yin to my yang,' – and runs a tight-knit team of 35 full and part-timers. On day of visit, was finessing several staff absences with aplomb (thrives on challenge). Minimal spare time, much of it taken up with course work for the Open University degree she is currently working towards, though says she is managing at least some eight rather than 11 hour days.

Previously worked at Stanford Primary School in Streatham Vale where was fast-tracked by head into nursery management role. Though popular with parents, was made redundant, scuppered by cost-cutting, only to be immediately snapped up by Old Palace, which knew a good thing when it saw one. Started as second in command, promoted to current post three months in when her predecessor, a former reception teacher at Old Palace, decided that working with the very young wasn't for her.

Adores everything about the job (a demon for paperwork) but her charges come first. 'A child is more important than a ringing phone.' Operates to extremely high standards. Expects (and on basis of visit gets) the same from staff. Can't imagine doing anything else. 'Children are so lovely and innocent and speak their mind. Whatever you're pouring into them, you're shaping their lives.'

Entrance: First come, first served into often over-subscribed reception, with many girls moving up from separate and flourishing Old Palace co-ed nursery located on the far side of school playing field, and which expanded three years ago to offer full child care from three months upwards. Individual age and development determines speed of progression through well-equipped baby, toddler, kinder, transition and finally pre-school rooms, with a gradual induction into school ways (school tracksuit is worn by the oldest, for example).

A fair few newcomers join the prep in other years and are quickly absorbed, with firm friendships quickly established, say pupils. Assessments, from reception onwards, are on the rigorous side, including tests in English, maths and reasoning as well as observation of their social interaction. Parents are also asked how they will support their daughter (some don't, hence early flagging up).

There's a fairly intense focus on exam preparation all through, intensifying in the run up to 11 plus (school runs workshops on the topic, open to pupils elsewhere). Aim is for year 5s to be working a year ahead) with entrance exam success the acid tests – school doesn't take Sats.

Nursery open 51 weeks of the year, highly in demand and with waiting lists to match (though most are – eventually – accommodated). For the baby room, early registration essential. 'We get women phoning us the day the baby's born.' No formal entrance tests though mobility is pre-requisite for toddler room (most start aged 12 to 15 months); freedom from nappies or close for kinder room (around two). Followed by transition room, while a fair few join in final pre-school year, the biggest group with 40 places and the only one with a minimum attendance requirement of three days a week (Tuesdays to Thursdays are the most popular). Elsewhere, it's down to parental needs (many work) and availability. Some children will do full 7.30am to 6.00pm days from the start, others attend just a few mornings or afternoons a week.

Exit: Nearly 90 per cent progress to the senior school. Vast majority of leavers do so for 'nice' reasons, securing places at one of the highly desirable local grammars (Wallington High School and Newstead Woods head the list). A few others are helped to the realisation that senior school is not for them, 'though we would never ask anyone to leave,' says Mrs Stone. Perhaps not, though one parent was fairly devastated to be told bluntly by another member of staff during a meeting that her child was 'unlikely' to make the senior school (though this was followed by some fairly nifty backtracking).

For girls at the nursery, assumption (by parents and school) is that they'll go on into Old Palace reception. Though their passage there isn't automatic (there's an assessment), in practice 'all our girls get places,' says Miss Hines. Boys tend to stay in independent sector, with Cumnor House and Elmhurst the most popular destinations, Park Hill Infants for those going on to state schools ('I keep saying there should be a boys' prep,' says Miss Hines.)

Remarks: Originally just across the road from the senior school, prep school was re-homed on Croham Hurst's leafy south Croydon site, just a short tram ride away.

Year 6s stayed behind in central Croydon as 'baby seniors', a move that brings structure into line with Trinity and Whitgift, the other two schools (both for boys) in the Whitgift Foundation's educational trio.

With a whole senior school to themselves, the 160 reception to year 5 pupils have oodles of space to play with and in, too, and all the trimmings, including vast spaces for DT and ICT. There's also a separate nursery which takes children from three months and is housed in its own building on the far side of the playing field.

Year 5s, as top dogs, acquire the trappings of seniority a year early. All can be prefects and have their own centre, located opposite reception classes 'so you see how our school goes round in circles,' says typically bright, eloquent and eager-to-please pupil. The most coveted perk, however, is sitting on benches rather than joining the hoi polloi on the floor for daily assembly, one of the many small formalities which, like grace said at the end of every meal, add a pleasantly traditional punctuation to the school day.

The range of architectural styles allows you to channel Malory Towers, complete with enticing attic rooms one moment, up to the minute modernity the next. Fresh-looking, white-walled dining hall with jolly pictures adding a splash of colour is particularly nice.

Heart of the original building, facing on to the Croham Road, is Small Hall, an unromantic title for what's effectively a mini-mausoleum to Croham Hurst's founders – galleried, beamed and stuffed to the gunnels with ancient honour boards and a sketch of the second Croham head, Theodora E Clark, looking wistfully into the middle distance. Visitors of a Gothic predisposition could have a ball.

Plenty to gladden the heart – a library with splendid tables fringed with solid, comfortable chairs (each one donated by a former grateful pupil some 60 years ago) that should entice the most reluctant of readers (and there are a few).

Palatial size creates a few technical difficulties. All roads tend to lead to back of the school, a sort of nesting place for the many fire escapes, while enthusiastic guides initially struggle to find any other pupils, making head's assertion that 'one of the few things you'll see is teachers at standing at the front and just spouting,' literally true, if not quite in the sense intended.

Parents have had their ups and downs with staff here and in senior school, not helped by uncertainty caused by some (expected) post-merger redundancies. Once found, however, lessons here don't disappoint, with a jolly English teacher surrounded by chatty, cheerful year 5s attempting a modern take on John Keats' Ode to Autumn. Technical glitch resulting in a temporary computer failure could have been the reason for all the smiles and interaction. Though you hope not, slight sense of apology when noise reached a smidge over conversational levels did suggest otherwise.

Would parents mind if teachers' voices remained the dominant sound? Debatable. There's good, solid curriculum, taught in classes of around 15, with pretty much everything for all, French from reception and a modern foreign languages 'experience' designed to fill a few cultural gaps on the way. Much is made of use of topics to link subjects with a unified theme, as well as learning for life (reasoning and evaluation as well as fact collection, carried on into seniors).

For most parents, preparatory is the key word, exam success its most obvious manifestation and a place either at the senior school or one of the local grammars the desired goal. Major focus, consequently, is on doing well. 'It is an academic school,' confirms a mother. 'They've never tried to hide it.' Study the prospectus, with plentiful references to academic excellence (one paragraph of just 30 words packs in two) and you can't say you haven't been warned.

Most coveted reward for success is a highly desirable celebration tea with Mrs Stone (who sometimes makes cupcakes, time permitting). It's within everyone's reach, she insists, based on the completion of 10 extension tasks designed to recognise 'all girls who rise to a challenge and are putting in lots of effort.' Not all parents are convinced. 'My daughter said "I'll never go to one of those tea parties, will I?"' says one.

Success-driven outlook could perhaps account for what some parents see as slight ambiguity towards learning needs. Though mild difficulties, headed by dyslexia, are officially something the school takes in its stride (even offering in-house consultancy), parents report mixed messages, in particular when it comes to all-important, high pressure exams. School seems to be trying harder to get it right.

Outside lessons, masses going on. Clubs are blossoming, from sewing to ballet, even including Japanese as a one-year wonder. Activities start young and increase fast – begins and ends with Indian Dance for reception but by year 1, there's a choice of seven. Popular lunchtime Christian Union club (Little Wigs) attracts a range of different faiths and delivers fun, unpreachy messages – on day of visit, pupils were busily decorating their faces with sticky spots as the prelude to a discussion about leprosy. Teacher in charge, enjoying it as much as pupils, was unfussed about missing lunch break. 'Who would miss the chance to do this?' she asked, with evident sincerity.

Sport comes with different aspirations. Super facilities include use of senior school swimming pool and their own large playing field 'for best', say girls, featuring splendid coronation oak planted in 1953, and stretching away across to the nursery wing (their gym doubles as prep school dance studio). Miniature pavilion, aching to be used for classic mid-match teas, currently houses spare minibus seats.

Lots to do – girls were particularly keen on weekly lunchtime table-tennis session. Everyone plays in a netball or rounders team 'even if you're useless'. Big on inclusivity, low on wins. 'I like it but we always lose,' says one fifth year pupil, resignedly. However, school says there are now more fixtures – and successes.

Reception have a nicely kitted out separate play area as a gentle introduction to the rough and tumble of 'big' school, with a soft surface, sheltered spot for wet weather play and even a tiny adventure playground, grassed area with tree and three side-by-side Wendy houses, a mini estate in the making.

Music also flourishes, with a good range of free taster sessions in year 3 and many learning instruments, excellent facilities (a big, terraced room, piled high with xylophones and five practice rooms dotted round the place) and a decent range of groups, instrumental and vocal, headed by the audition-only Junior Polyphonic, which performs with seniors in Croydon Minster (high on parental frisson-factor).

As to the future? Mood in school is upbeat. One parent, also a teacher, praises 'careful engineering' that helped girls to feel part of a 'new and evolving thing'. Though most parents seem minded to agree, a few, particularly those whose offspring are still at subsonic speed compared with high flyers, or need a bit more support, view the Darwinian model with some reservations.

Nursery occupies former Croham Hurst Junior School, acquired in 2008 by the Whitgift Foundation, with former senior school on the other side of the playing field now housing Old Palace Prep. While 'we never used to feel part of the Old Palace structure', the nursery has now, under senior school headship of Mrs Jewell, been brought fully into the fold, getting the full corporate branding to the point where prospective parents, confused by location, occasionally get lost en route.

Though exterior gives the impression of rolling square feet upwards and outwards, it's a slight Tardis in reverse as top two floors are unoccupied and will remain so, if Miss Hines has her way. While success of nursery, which has grown from 26 to 104 in just three years, has Old Palace management gleefully rubbing hands at thoughts of future money-making potential, she is adamant that predominantly single floor layout and instant access to outdoors space is non-negotiable.

Even the pre-school children, the only ones based on the first rather than ground floor, take turns to spend full days in recently built outdoor classroom so they can have free access to real if diddy tree for climbing (staff stand underneath just in case) and other outdoor highlights including fence strung with assortment of pots, pans and hooters, though high-decibel wind up fire bell acquired at a car boot sale by bargain hunting deputy has, unfortunately, gone missing. (Silence-loving local residents are chief suspects.) Veg is enthusiastically grown, recently scooping three prizes in local produce show.

Miss Hines is particularly keen on directed play and staff are encouraged to watch out for and gently discourage aimless wandering: one pupil was enthusiastically helping to rake up leaves, the rest seemed happily occupied.

Lots to do inside, too (we loved the small staircase/ramp that permits endless up and down games – Escher minus the impossibility) and attention to detail is jaw-dropping. Every parent is presented with a daily record of child's achievements complete with photograph, while there are regular diplomatically phrased parenting tips covering everything from reading to cookery. 'Some parents do expect school to do everything,' thinks Miss Hines.

There's an equally thorough approach to everything from stopping pupils' work being over-prettified by staff – 'If they draw a dog with three legs, that's what we'll display,' says Miss Hines – to discipline. With no refuge in naughty steps (or indeed, use of the word 'naughty' which is banned) anyone being unkind is talked to about their behaviour and the need for 'kind hands' repeated ad nauseam until the message gets through (time-consuming but effective, say staff).

No chocolate or crisps (and of course no nuts) rules firmly enforced with children bringing in fruit on birthdays, rather than cakes or sweets. School chef, meanwhile, rustles up appetising breakfasts, lunches and dinners, all included in the fees, catering with aplomb for every dietary requirement, with meals served to older children in pocket-sized, delightful dining hall and to babies and toddlers in their own rooms.

Staffing, too, is thoughtfully planned, with at least one experienced mum 'who has seen everything' in each of the bright, light and appealing rooms as instant source of wit and wisdom. Once in place, each room tends to keep the same staff group – children and parents appreciate continuity. Currently just one man on the team (hugely popular with all) though diversity is the name of the game elsewhere, with staff (like pupils) spanning vast range of backgrounds and cultures. Huge range of activities and events makes the most of this, from songs and counting in Italian to a recent visit by Rastamouse.

For pre-school group, ICT room, whiteboards, (optional) homework and uniform (trackies and sweatshirts) gently introduces some 'big school' elements. However, 'we're not a Montessori' says Miss Hines, and parents expecting everyone to be reading by the time they leave are gently disabused of the notion: emphasis is on cultivating desire to learn so children are raring to go when they start in reception. Feedback suggests it works.

Oratory Preparatory School

Linked school: The Oratory School

Goring Heath, Reading, RG8 7SF

- Pupils: 400 boys and girls • Ages: 2–13 • Roman Catholic
- Fees: Day £7,935–£13,350; Boarding £17,085–£19,185 pa
- Independent

Tel: 01189 844511
Email: registrar@oratoryprep.co.uk
Website: www.oratoryprep.co.uk

Headmaster: Since 2010, Mr Joseph Smith BA PGCE (early forties). Son of a farmer, educated at Catholic primary school and then the local comp in King's Lynn where he says he 'achieved despite the poor education he received'. Admits he was 'rather lazy' and believes that sometimes children 'need to be compelled' to learn. (Parents say, approvingly, that he won't let pupils coast, even post CE.) He 'didn't start working until university' (studied English at Liverpool) but then something clicked and he graduated with a first. After PGCE at Brunel his first post was at Colfe's School in London, then 12 years at Monkton Combe,

0

Bath where he was head of English and housemaster. Currently studying for MEd in educational leadership at Buckingham.

This is Mr Smith's first headship; his mission is to maintain high academic standards without compromising the school's non-selective ethos. While reassuring parents that their daughters will be fully prepared for 11+ entrance exams he also wants to encourage more girls to stay until 13.

Although majority of boys go on to The Oratory (the 'big O') at 13, Mr Smith is under no internal pressure to promote this route, 'The governors and I believe it is the head's job to send boys to whichever school is right, not just automatically to the senior school'. Parents we spoke to confirm that advice is unbiased and 'all about their child'.

Genial and decidedly unstuffy, Mr Smith is full of praise for the school's 'outstanding' teachers, many of whom are a few years older than he is. Says his appointment has initiated some 'gentle evolution'. Likes to communicate face to face with colleagues and parents, not 'hide behind emails' – a 21st century interpretation of Cardinal Newman's motto, 'heart speaking to heart' perhaps. Parents give him the thumbs up – they say he's very visible and 'understands children'. He also seems to understand parents and endeared himself to many a father by introducing beer to match teas!

Since moving to Oxfordshire he says he is returning to the country pursuits he was brought up with. When time allows he enjoys shooting and cooking the results. Loves dogs, has just acquired a black lab (wry smile, he knows it's a headmaster cliché) and plays cricket for the village. His wife, Debbie, is the registrar and they have three children at the school. Favourite books? Sir Gawain and the Green Knight and Byron's Don Juan (well, he is an English graduate...).

Entrance: No academic selection for prep, assessment morning and report from previous school. Observed visit for pre-prep entrants or else head of pre-prep visits them at current nursery.

Exit: At age 11 – handful of girls plus one or two boys. Rest leave at age 13. Boys mainly go on to The Oratory, girls to Queen Anne's School, Caversham, St Mary's Ascot, St Helen and St Katharine, Abingdon. Also Abingdon, Bradfield, Canford, Marlborough. Good number of scholarships to The Oratory, Bradfield, Wellington, Headington and Abingdon.

Remarks: Approach is down a quiet lane and through a riot of rhododendrons. The 65 acres of grounds are a real feature of this school with beautifully kempt topiary, sunken lawns ideal for croquet or a marquee (recently hosted 300 for dinner and ball) and, when we visited, sculpture by a visiting artist. One parent commented that it's by no means a 'ritzy' school; this may be true but it's certainly easy on the eye. Looking out over another perfect view one couldn't help wondering whether the imperfections of the real world come as a shock to departing pupils.

Our year 8 guides (who were remarkably composed considering they received their CE results during our visit) started the tour in the chapel. Although neither was Catholic, both knelt respectfully and spoke warmly of the school's inclusive and welcoming attitude to non-Catholics. When we asked what their stand-out memories of prep school were, for one it was, 'all the hands-on science stuff and experiments'; for the other it was performing in the annual Shakespeare festival. The learning support department got a special mention, as did fish and chips and chocolate cake and custard.

Average class size 16. Latin from year 6, no Greek. We sat in on a year 7 maths class, impressed by the pupils' teamwork as they explored different methods of solving what seemed to us pretty challenging algebra. In history we enjoyed an enthusiastic and knowledgeable debate on arms escalation in the First World War – serious stuff enlivened by role playing and hammy French and German accents. Parents were full of praise for staff, from dinner ladies to teachers, particularly 'old hands' who might seem a

bit old fashioned but were 'loved by children' and 'brilliant'. Smallish library is welcoming and well stocked, there's a library lesson once a week and, according to our guides, 'always lots of new books'. Around 30 pupils with SEN, mainly mild to moderate dyslexia, dyspraxia etc. School approach focuses on developing necessary skills and self-confidence via one-to-one lessons with specialist staff (extra charge).

Extensive games fields plus one Astroturf for hockey and three tennis/hockey pitches. As at 'the big O', sport, above all rugby, is central with local and national successes. More than one parent commented to the effect that a non-sporty child would not get the most out of the place. Creditably we heard no grumbles that girls' sport comes second, nor that the keen but less good were overlooked. The rather swish 25m swimming pool plus separate learners' pool is a real bonus. Decent sports hall but boys' locker rooms must be bit of a bear garden at peak times – our guides thought they ought to go on head's improvement list. Seven music practice rooms plus a recording studio; large numbers of singers and instrumentalists have gained grade 5 or above by the time they depart. Serious choir (for mass) plus orchestras, ensembles etc – we were treated to a blast from the excellent jazz band as they rehearsed for forthcoming annual trip to Torquay.

The children we met were polite and sociable. Mr Smith is as keen on good manners as the next head but would prefer children to learn by example rather than being made to feel awkward. Four houses, named after the school's previous locations, compete for the usual glory and silverware. What about bullying we asked, in front of a notice board showing work done during recent anti-bullying week. Our guides were confident: 'You can tell any teacher and if you tell them it will stop.' School's extremely useful parents' handbook covers policies about this and pretty much everything else.

Our visit coincided with CE results day and was punctuated by relieved, happy year 8s clutching mark sheets and being warmly congratulated by their teachers. Some concerns expressed that smaller numbers of girls in years 7 and 8 meant that fallings out were harder to weather but on the plus side there are plentiful opportunities for positions of leadership and responsibility. And, as a parent observed, girls who stay on don't seem to grow up quite as fast.

Boarding described by one parent as 'fantastic'. Lovely quirky dorms at top of main building, various size rooms with maximum 10 beds. Boarding most popular in the last year with pupils keen to gain experience for senior school. Regular influx of Spanish boarders who stay for a few terms.

Jolly common rooms with properly comfortable sofas and cushions for film nights, quizzes and meetings. Four bed san with nurse on site. Matron, houseparents and family live in, staff augmented by gappies. Flexi and occasional boarding possible if there's room and school will always 'scoop up anyone' in emergency. Working parents praise 'huge support' from matrons who will, for instance, review and acquire necessary uniform items and kit on their behalf. Likewise weekly newsletter that keeps all informed about what's going on.

Day pupils come from within a 30 minute drive: Henley, Reading, Watlington, Didcot and closer villages, vast majority are white British. Families, 60 per cent of whom are not practising Catholics, choose school for its strong faith-based values. Overseas boarders mainly from Spain. Active parents' association (FOPS) organises coffee mornings, fundraisers and class reps.

Pre-prep housed in delightful chalet-style wooden buildings (were old stables) with verandas and bright hanging baskets. Top of the range outdoor facilities include a good size kitchen garden, 'jungle' (wooded) and covered play areas and athletics track. Majority of staff female, balance redressed somewhat by gap chaps who looked as enthusiastic about the games set up for a pretend fête as the excited children. Yellow curtained classrooms are plastered in colourful posters and children's work. Multi-sensory approach to learning includes lots of work outdoors and exploring in adjoining fields and ponds. Weekly baking, art and all other messy stuff happen in a stand-alone room so no need to clear up ongoing projects. In core subjects (maths and English at this stage), a teacher plus a TA cover one topic but pupils (max 18) divided according to learning style and ability to tackle the work in different ways. RE (Catholic syllabus) once a week, pre-prep mass once a term. Lovely old barn for assemblies and after-school clubs (include Mandarin, music, dance, Lego) that run from 4 – 6 pm starting with tea. Small charge for activities goes towards buying new equipment – head of pre-prep ensures after school toys and equipment are 'not the same as those used during lessons'.

Brand new Little Oaks nursery being constructed on old car park next to pre-prep in response to parent demand – names are down already. One or two parents commented that they hoped there would also be investment at the top end.

The Oratory Prep is a vibrant, welcoming community, just the place for your sporty all rounder – boy or girl – and soon the 'little O' experience will be available to their younger siblings. Head said that someone described his school as a 'sleeping giant' and while we're not sure about the slightly scary part of that simile we agree that it has been a little under the radar – undeservedly so in our opinion.

Orley Farm School

South Hill Avenue, Harrow, HA1 3NU

• Pupils: 490 boys and girls • Ages: 4–13 • Non-denom
• Fees: £11,907–£13,761 pa • Independent

Tel: 020 8869 7600
Email: office@orleyfarm.harrow.sch.uk
Website: www.orleyfarm.harrow.sch.uk

Headmaster: Since February 2013, Mr Tim Calvey, propelled from the deputy headship at a moment's notice after the abrupt and bizarre resignation of Mr Mark Dunning, who had been an unexceptionable head for seven years. Mr Dunning left after what the school described as an 'error of judgement'. Evidently, after some years' attrition with a departing member of staff, Mr Dunning expressed his feelings, weakly disguised in an acrostic-style sentence, in a newsletter to parents. Mr Calvey – previously an art teacher – is at the helm, but the school is advertising for a new head to start in September 2014. Nothing has got Harrow and Sudbury buzzing quite so loud since the young Lord Byron led a revolt against the headmaster at the place up the hill.

Entrance: Virtually all enter at four though occasional other places crop up – more since the recession. From 40+ nurseries and none. Some 165 applicants for 60 places. Good-sized entry again at 11+ when the girls and some boys leave – around 30 applicants for 13 or so places. School keeps waiting lists at all stages. Assessment via observed activities and games – all age-appropriate. Previous head was confident that the process picks out those for whom Orley will work; later tests (parents say there are lots) attest to this – 'We know what is expected of an Orley Farm pupil and we want the children to be happy – we'd be doing them a great disservice if we took them and they couldn't cope with, enjoy and flourish in the life we have here'. Pupils concur. 'You do need to have a natural drive and everyone is really trying to push themselves,' one young man told us. 'We all want to succeed.'

Exit: Breadth again – to a creditable range of schools and many scholarships (impressive 35 in 2012 and 29 in 2013). Most boys to Merchant Taylors', others to St Paul's, Habs, Aldenham, John Lyon, Harrow, Hampton, Westminster etc. Girls to Habs, North London Collegiate, Northwood College, Notting Hill and Ealing, St Paul's Girls, Aldenham, St Helen's, Cheltenham Ladies', Wycombe Abbey etc.

Remarks: You won't find a parent or a pupil who doesn't think the options and opportunities here are outstanding. The teachers, likewise, are warmly praised – 'Our teachers are interactive,' an earnest year 8 boy told us. 'They don't act as "teachers" – superior: they're there to help you.' 'The school is very good at finding out what you're good at and helping you get better at it,' another affirmed.

Broad academic curriculum, all heading for 11+ for girls and 13+ for boys, though one or two girls are to be found in years 7 and 8 – either joiners or stayers. French and Latin for all and Greek comes in as a taster for the soon-to-be leavers. Twenty children per class and fewer in sets for maths and English. Specialist subject teachers in music, drama, ICT and PE from pre-prep up and for science, French and Latin later. Previous head doubled the number of classroom assistants, all of whom support English and maths. Some sense among parents of the less able that they have to really push themselves to keep up – witness one remark worth quoting from a year 6 boy: 'We were given an IGCSE maths paper – it was an insult to my intelligence'.

Full-time learning support teacher plus part-timers assist those who need it – mostly mild dyslexics. All support given in class or in small groups elsewhere. Eighty pupils on learning support register at time of our visit – 45 on school action plus. Not an easy school for those with mobility problems – very narrow corridors and up and down site. Outside tutoring is common – not because of deficiencies in the school's provision: more likely to support English when the home language is something else or because life is very full-on at Orley and the quieter ones may just need that bit of one-to-one to boost confidence. So parents feel, anyway.

All do DT and art – good studios for both. We were especially impressed by the range and quality – real imaginative breadth and care in execution too. Lovely models of early airplanes, Masai shields, mosaic tiles and more. Displays changed termly and with respect for the work. Carousel system for these subjects and some pupil grouses that not enough time to complete DT projects before you have to move to your art term, but with so much on offer and different curriculum requirements it's easy to see why some things have to give. Drama – previously limp – now burgeoning under much-lauded new teacher and productions clearly zing. Music a jewel in Orley's crown – 90+ per cent learn at least one instrument, the concerts cause grown men to weep with joy and music scholarships abound.

Privileged sports – can any prep in a London borough claim such riches? Forty acres, gym and sports hall, pool and Astroturf and far more on offer than in most London preps. Sports praised by everyone – the only problem being that Orley is big enough to field C, D and E teams, but they'd have no-one to play against. It's hard cheese for the also-rans and some complaints that the less than starry don't have such a good time. Expeditions week is a big thing here – a regular annual programme which takes everyone from year 3s up out everywhere, from mid-Wales mountaineering to 'total immersion' in a château. Wildly popular – and included in the fees. Plus tours and trips of all kinds everywhere – the optional trips taken in the holidays can be very expensive if your child is keen but your pocket isn't.

Orley, again unusually, has a purpose-built home – an attractive, two/three storey long red-brick house nestling at the foot of Harrow-on-the-Hill, all quiet leafiness and shady detached residences. It began in 1850, in two houses, one of which was the model for Trollope's Orley Farm, so the school was named after that. The aim was to prepare boys for the big school up the hill. By the turn of the century the school had outgrown the old house so a new one was commissioned, and in 1901 the present building was proudly opened. Its first head was 47 years in post. Since then it has grown and four buildings now surround the central quad, providing excellent sports, arts and teaching provision. The main building – with its top floor all narrow corridors and very reminiscent still of the boarding that went, finally, in 1984 – is all good-sized rooms, well-supplied and organised. Three libraries – stocked mostly with fiction. Pre-prep rooms all have integral loos and cloakroom. Good dining room with very appetizing food – eaten by all. Breakfast club from 7.45am. Lots of pretty gardens and outside space with adventure playground and play equipment. It looks and feels like a well-appointed village school.

Thriving house system – pupils like it as they get to know all year groups and school encourages this (older children escort younger ones hither and yon and help with reading etc). 'It's like a very, very, very, very big family,' said one girl. Any problems to the form teacher – 'The teachers are very good at helping you if you are new. You're assigned a partner to look after you, and they do.' Classrooms all quietly buzzing when we visited – not all silent, thankfully, but purposeful and a sense of self-control at work rather than teacher-control. We heard no teacher shout.

School hotting up on eco matters – car share system for parents, tree planting project, annual school clean-up etc. Good home-school communications in that all staff have voicemail and email accounts available to parents and children have diary to be signed by home and school, but 'not always working as efficiently as it should,' we were told. Family backgrounds as mixed as you'd expect in north west London – many languages spoken at home, all blend easily at school. Former pupils of note include Lord Butler (former Cabinet Secretary), Anthony Horowitz and the late Simon McCorkindale.

'My children are all so different but they've all been happy there,' a parent said, and others concurred. Previous head delighted us when he extolled the virtues of a schooling which is about far more than exams and results – 'The world is changing fast. There are opportunities out there that we can't even imagine. That's why giving them breadth is so important.' We agreed and we await developments now that this visionary is head no more.

Orwell Park School

Nacton, Ipswich, IP10 0ER

• Pupils: 290 boys and girls; 140 boarders • Ages: 2½-13 • Inter-denom • Fees: Boarding £18,555-£20,610; Day £6,345-£16,065 pa • Independent

Tel: 01473 659225
Email: headmaster@orwellpark.co.uk
Website: www.orwellpark.co.uk

Headmaster: Since 2011, Mr Adrian Brown. Arrived at Orwell Park from Ipswich School, a former professional Essex cricketer and Cambridge Blue. Affable and down-to-earth, much like the pupils in his charge, he lives in the headmaster's house at Orwell Park with his wife Nicole and they have just seen off their third child to university.

Entrance: Entry points at 2.5 and 4+ (by taster morning in class and a home visit), 7+ and 11+ (tests in maths, English and reasoning, plus a report from the previous school and interview).

Exit: Post-CE, Orwell Park's pupils spread across the UK to top-drawer boarding schools – Eton, Harrow, Winchester, Gordonstoun, Ampleforth, Rugby, Oundle, Uppingham and the like – and local day schools, with no more than four or five per cohort heading in the same direction. Some 15-20 scholarships every year, covering the full range of subjects.

Remarks: One of the most jaw-droppingly gorgeous schools we've ever seen – and it's a prep. Visitors are defied to supress a sharp intake of breath as an idyllic Suffolk leafy lane gives way to impressive wrought iron gates and a sweeping drive heralding a handsome Georgian mansion with late-Victorian additions. Built by a local philanthropist as a venue for royal house parties, it's complete with its own observatory and clock tower, but has been a school since 1937. A combination of effortless elegance (chandeliers and oak panelling in the dining room, ornate tiles and floor-to-ceiling windows in the orangery assembly hall) and down-to-earth, workaday practicality (music practice rooms in the basement) is an appropriate reflection of its clientele – 'the children here are quietly confident, but with no trace of arrogance,' says head. Indeed the pupils, aged two-and-a-half to 13, who have a 'number one' uniform for best and sweatshirts for every day, are very at home in such grand surroundings. Undoubtedly this is helped by the fact that head knows them all by name (a tour of the school had him checking on this week's second team rugby score with one of its stars, and congratulating a self-effacing young man on the outdoor skills shown on a recent camping expedition).

Every day at Orwell Park begins with a tutor period or an assembly. The timetable also includes a quiet reading slot and there's a serious emphasis on academic attainment, with streaming throughout the juniors. Latin is taught from year 6 – 'they love it' reports head – and includes translation from English to Latin, virtually unheard of even in senior schools these days. Ancient Greek is taught to year 8 scholars, but French is the main MFL, with Spanish and German options at year 6. Maximum class size in the juniors and pre-prep is 16, with the average 12-14.

Learning support is for all – welcoming drop-in centre is open all day until late evening with an impressive mind-mapping approach ordering thoughts for any task or project. A SENCo oversees a team of five or six who support dyslexia, dyspraxia, dyscalculia, mild Asperger's and ADHD, but only those who are able to manage in the mainstream. Children are assessed on entry and advised on whether or not the curriculum will suit. After that, any difficulties are dealt with as and when with particular help for spelling, handwriting, reading, maths. Real focus on study skills in the run-up to CE with one-to-one and small group sessions as well as dual teaching in class. Outside agencies are co-opted as necessary – OTs, SALT and physios. Each junior class has a qualified teacher plus assistant and there are six gap helpers, mainly young Aussies.

This is a Mac school and they're everywhere – in the music room for composition, throughout the classrooms and in two dedicated ICT rooms, not to mention the iPads currently being trialled by the heads of department with a view to introducing mobile learning in the near future.

A performance culture – you name it, there's a competition for it (verse, singing, public speaking), usually house clashes or routing the local independent school league opponents on the 110 acres of stunning playing fields, which reach from the French doors of the most impressive salons right down to the shores of the Orwell. Growing bodies are encouraged to run free (though no further than the ha-ha for safety reasons). Junior girls love to make dens and shops in the trunks of the thickets and there's a genuine army-built assault course in the woods. Courts for tennis, squash and netball as well as an Astro, nine-hole golf course, sizeable indoor gym and the most inviting outdoor pool, set in a walled garden complete with barbecue area and reached by means of a wisteria walk. Idyllic.

Art has an inviting airy space and work is of an impressive standard. Prospective senior school scholars have their own area and may work on their portfolios independently. DT is generously equipped and a popular class. Heaps of extra-curricular clubs, including clay pigeon shooting, and a stargazing club run by local astronomers in the school's own observatory.

Impressive £1m pre-prep building opened in January 2013, making space for 80 under-fours with a large hall and teaching rooms as well as outdoor learning areas under the curve of an undulating contemporary roof.

Leadership is key here with the recent introduction of the OPS challenge – a mini D of E with long hikes and camp-outs – and outdoor pursuits holidays to Normandy for year 6s and the Ardèche post-CE. Positions of authority bring with them real obligations – head boys and girls are relied on to help run the school and there are dorm captains, house captains and prefects. 'Everyone has the chance to prove themselves if they want to,' says head, 'just by putting their names down.' The Alston lecture series inspires nascent vocations by inviting parents to come in and speak about their careers.

Increase in boarding numbers recently, locals as well as international students, and options are flexi (min two nights), weekly and full. Dorms are spacious with spectacular views and populated by pupils of the same year group plus a year 8 dorm monitor to keep them in order.

Our Lady of Victories Catholic Primary School

1 Clarendon Drive, London, SW15 1AW

• Pupils: 200 boys and girls; all day • Ages: 4–11 • RC • State

Tel: 020 8788 7957
Email: info@ourladyofvictories.wandsworth.sch.uk
Website: www.ourladyofvictories.wandsworth.sch.uk

Headteacher: Since 2011, Mrs Deirdre McDonald BA PGCE NQPH (forties). After studying English at university, Mrs McDonald worked in publishing, then decided to train as a teacher. She has a long association with the school – she was a governor and taught year 6 for eight years before becoming deputy head and more recently head. Her own children are now at university but attended Our Lady of Victories. Forward thinking and inclusive – parents say she is a caring and committed head who's available to all families as and when they need her assistance. Head's background in publishing and interest in literature and language has inspired and influenced many school activities. Definitely an artsy type, she enjoys cinema, theatre, reading and travel.

Entrance: A total of 28 places at 4+ (standard Wandsworth Council entry policy). Priority is given to practising Catholics, siblings and those living closest to the school. As the school is only able to admit one class each year, places are in high demand and school is always oversubscribed. Places sometimes come up in the older age groups (usually due to families moving away from London), so it's worth contacting the school for occasional vacancies.

Exit: At 11+, just over half of pupils move to popular Catholic secondary schools like Cardinal Vaughan, The London Oratory, Sacred Heart, Ursuline High School, Wimbledon College, Gumley House. The rest go to local independents (Emanuel, Ibstock Place, Latymer, Hampton) or to Catholic boarding schools (Worth, The Oratory School, Reading and the IBVM convents).

Remarks: A first-rate primary school tucked into the residential streets of Putney, in the parish of Our Lady of Pity and St Simon Stock. Originally run by the Sisters of the Poor Servants of the Mother of God, the school was handed over to the Diocese of Southwark in 1978. Housed in the former convent (there are several modern extensions), its compact site is well kept and decorated with an array of colourful artwork by the children.

School is exceptionally well accomplished in all areas. The majority of children achieve Level 5 by year six, with everyone's progress assessed each half term. A well-balanced curriculum is delivered throughout and children achieve particularly well in maths and English. French classes from year 1. The school has won silver and gold awards at junior maths challenges. Creative writing is strong and pupils do variety of science, history and geography projects each term. Older children practise verbal and non-verbal reasoning for the Wandsworth 11+ tests and are taught how to write timed essays.

The school has strong links with the parish – it celebrates a number of religious festivals and the local priest visits the school regularly. At Holy Communion, children process from school to church, a day rounded off with a visit to the ice cream van. The choir sings in the church and at local care centres. Music, led by a dedicated music teacher, is very strong. Lots of music lessons in school, concerts and the school's recorder group and choir attends annual Music for Youth festival. Pupils take part in the National Theatre's Primary Programme (workshops held in school and theatre visits), alongside trips to concerts and the ballet.

Impressive PE programme offers a range of sporting activities at Dover House Road playing fields and swimming at the nearby Putney Leisure Centre pool. Good range of clubs includes fencing, Zumba and Latin. SENCo and visiting speech and occupational therapists supervise learning support. Head is keen to ensure awareness of SEN throughout the school. Regular in-house training days and some teachers attend training courses run by a school specialising in specific learning difficulties and differences.

Lots of fundraising for charity organised by the school and parents, with many of the events run by the children themselves.

Our Lady of Victories RC Primary School

Clareville Street, London, SW7 5AQ

• Pupils: 240 boys and girls • Ages: 3–11 • RC • State

Tel: 020 7373 4491
Email: sarah.mcbennett@olov.rbkc.sch.uk
Website: www.olov.rbkc.sch.uk/

Headteacher: Since 2007 Mrs Sarah McBennett BEd (forties). After university in Belfast, started her career in education and has taught children across the primary age range from reception to year 6. These days she is mainly managerial and tends only to teach to cover staff absences. Formerly head of primary section of an international community school in Jordan, then deputy at a large Catholic primary in Kent. Something of a whizz with the budget, parents tell us, she works extremely hard for the school and puts in many extra hours. Committed and kindly personality, with an open door policy, always happy to spend time talking to parents, pupils and staff. Supported by a long-serving deputy head, school secretary and lively PTA.

Entrance: Pupils come from the parishes of Our Lady of Victories, Our Lady of Mount Carmel and St Simon Stock. Priority goes to baptised, practising Catholics; all applications must be supported by letter from the parish priest. Where possible siblings get priority followed by those living closest to the school. Children attending the nursery are not automatically guaranteed a place in the reception class, which is always oversubscribed. Contact the school for occasional places in older age groups.

Exit: To state schools and independents in many different directions. Coeds St Thomas More, Holland Park, Emanuel, St Benedict's, Latymer Upper. Boys, London Oratory, Cardinal Vaughan, independents Westminster, St Paul's, Dulwich College and City of London Boys. Girls, Sacred Heart, Hammersmith, Gumley House, independents More House, Queensgate, Francis Holland, Godolphin and Latymer. A few to Catholic boarding schools eg St Mary's Ascot, Worth and Ampleforth.

Remarks: Very high standards across the curriculum continue to make this a successful and sought-after primary. All teaching is graded outstanding. Lots of attention to detail, personal successes, the pupils are encouraged to take pride in everything they do. Continuous assessment and monitoring ensure everybody reaches their potential, and those who need additional support are identified. Parents tell us enthusiastic staff always want to make sure the children really enjoy themselves and develop socially as well as academically. School aims to pick up SEN early; pupils are supported by differentiated teaching, specialist teachers and therapists in small groups or one-to-one. International clientele so lots of EAL tuition for those who need.

Tall Victorian buildings with lots of stairs, however, good-sized classrooms, beautifully decorated; the school has gold Artsmark. Displays show that even the tiny children have beautiful handwriting. Nursery and reception classes have been redesigned so 3 to 5-year-olds are taught in a large, open plan space with its own playground. French starts at key stage 2, other languages via clubs, year 6 have French penfriends and make an annual trip to Cannes. Sadly, Latin has disappeared from the curriculum. After-school verbal reasoning club in the run-up to 11+ exams. Inner city location means outdoor spaces are tight, but they are well-maintained and decorated with mosaics made by the children. Younger horticulturalists grow many colourful flowers and shrubs through the gardening club which they organise themselves.

The school has a Sportsmark; multi-purpose hall is large enough for short tennis, gymnastics and ballet lessons. Outdoor sports take place at Battersea Park; professional coaches, including ex-Middlesex cricketer, teach good range of team games. Specialist teachers for both art and music, pupils can have individual instrumental tuition on a range of five different instruments, and often join the young musician's performances at the Albert Hall. Enticing range of extracurricular activities, clubs, trips and special visitors; year 5 can complete their cycling proficiency certificates at school.

Parents say pastoral care is very good and inclusive, the weekly newsletter keeps everybody up-to-date with events and pupils are given a voice through the school council which meets regularly with the deputy head. Food is often on the agenda, as the school has Food for Life Award, everything is cooked on site and where possible locally sourced. Encouraged to be involved in the school community, parents run cookery classes, listen to readers and raise large amounts of money which go towards paying for improvements and equipment for the school as well as for outside charities. Catholic beliefs remain at the heart of the warm, family atmosphere of the school. First rate and first choice school for Catholic families in Kensington.

Our Lady's Junior School Abingdon

Linked school: Our Lady's Abingdon

St John's Road, Abingdon, OX14 2HB

- Pupils: 130 boys and girls • Ages: 3–11 • Roman Catholic
- Fees: £7,314–£10,161 pa • Independent

Tel: 01235 523147
Email: officejs@olab.org.uk
Website: www.olab.org.uk

Headteacher: Since 2007, Mr Brendan O'Neill BEd NPQH (fifties), educated at St Brendan's College, Bristol, and Southampton University. Married with two grown up children, both work in education. Has been at the school for 25 years, loves his work, utterly dedicated and a calm but authoritative leader. Still teaches – mainly maths and sport, plus 'a bit of geography'. Inspires great confidence in parents – one senses a man with a very strong vocation who knows every child in his care not just by name but also by character. Outside school his interests are coin collecting and football.

Entrance: Various entry points; from year 4 an assessment including verbal reasoning, maths, English and informal observation. Report from previous school important.

Exit: About three-quarters to senior school. Good that boys can now also move there, the destination for the majority of girls (partly as a result of pressure from junior school parents).

Remarks: A great deal of thought has gone into making this a secure, stimulating and enjoyable place to learn. The buildings incorporate the original Victorian convent and the resulting quirky layout, high ceilings and mullion windows are rather magical. The art room is housed in what was the nuns' dining room and children's work is on every wall; when we visited the children had been drawing with a visiting artist.

Nursery and infant classrooms are brightly decorated and comfortable, beautiful displays of themed work – the early years curriculum is followed 'with tweaking'. Juniors have their own entrance and outside space with play equipment; we liked the 'reading shelter' with a box of books – an idea from the school council. Nursery children have a separate area with picnic houses for eating outside.

Real sense of an educational journey as children move up through the school; in one room we saw year 3 children concentrating on handwriting to the accompaniment of Vivaldi. Year 5 and 6 pupils sit at individual desks as they develop independent learning, making forays into the senior school laboratories for science lessons.

Lots of PE and outdoor sport: boys and girls introduced to rugby and football and swimming for all in senior school pool – even the three year olds have one session a week. Visiting ballet, piano and violin teachers. For many activities a system of what the head calls 'family groups', consisting of three or four children from different years who take part together. The intention is to build relationships between the different ages, the older children supporting the younger ones; a buddy system pairs up older pupils with the youngest members of the school.

Extremely well run, very child-centred and a warm family atmosphere.

O

Oxford High School GDST Junior School

Linked school: Oxford High School GDST

1 Bardwell Road, Oxford, OX2 6SU

- Pupils: 340 girls; all day • Ages: 4–10 • Non–denom
- Fees: £8,976 pa • Independent

Tel: 01865 515647
Email: oxfordhighjunior@oxf.gdst.net
Website: www.oxfordhigh.gdst.net

Head of Junior School: Since 2010, Mrs Ellie Stacey BA (QTS). Came to teaching later in life after a career with British Airways. Taught at SS Philip and James Primary School (in Oxford), then six years as head of Burford Primary. Husband is a retired physicist; they have four children between them and five step grandchildren. Enjoys spending time in Cornwall and going to the Proms. We met Mrs Stacey in her pink office at Woodstock Road (home to reception and year 1). She has another, less pink, office round the corner in Bardwell Road (years 2-6). Both offices are rather impersonal – but as Mrs Stacey says, 'with two offices there's no danger of nesting.' Parents describe her as 'very nice', and 'not that chatty'. We imagine that her airline training – grace and efficiency under pressure – is a pretty good preparation for overseeing 340 little girls across two sites. She dreams of a unified junior school with wraparound care but, back in the real world, by all accounts manages the reality of a split site energetically.

Entrance: First come first served. Selective after reception. For entry to years 1-6 girls spend an observed assessment day with tests in maths, English, reading and spelling. External candidates can apply at any age to junior school. School says it tries to give positive individual feedback to parents of girls whose applications are unsuccessful.

Exit: Vast majority go on to senior school (same exam as external candidates). Will advise parents in good time if senior school not appropriate and help find alternative.

Remarks: Mrs Stacey believes that girls benefit from being taught in a single sex environment because they are usually ready to engage with academic study more quickly than boys. Not, thank goodness, that we saw tinies doing anything too academic in their characterful Victorian house on the busy Woodstock Road (which even boasts a parent café). Jolly outside space with canopied play area and 'Nomow' turf. Youngest start on ground floor and ascend as they grow. No catering; parents must provide packed lunches. Rather neglected feeling library and music room on top floor plus multi-purpose space – one of the benefits that came from the school's decision to close small nursery dept. Another is that reception children now have improved ground floor facilities with more access to the outdoors.

Early years and national curriculum followed but with plenty more added in. Specialist teachers for science, art, music, PE, ICT and foreign languages. Mrs Stacey hopes to supplement the ICT provision with iPads – much more mobile and versatile than desktop terminals. Parents we spoke to were all pretty happy with facilities, even more so the teaching and staff. There was a lovely display of photos showing mums and dads sitting at tiny tables trying out some of the activities their children got up to in a normal day. SEN identified early and teaching then 'goes at the pace of the child.' Peripatetic SEN specialists provide one-to-one support as necessary but fewer than 20 at any one time receive extra help. School can (and

does) accommodate bright girls with eg Asperger's, but 'parents send their girls with a view to them entering the senior school so they must be able to cope.'

We were shown around the Bardwell Road site (years 2 – 6) by two very self-assured year 6 girls in smart kilts. Lower years wear pleasingly timeless navy blue tunics. Everywhere we looked girls were busy, busy, busy: happily creating delicious-looking Plasticine cupcakes in the big messy art room; doing cartwheels in the gym (it's a red letter day when the wall bars are pulled out apparently but 'it only happens once or twice a term'), learning about mad Tudor instruments in music; doing 'lots' of experiments in the science labs. The site – another, larger, Victorian villa – seemed rather confusing to this (easily disoriented) editor, with dim corridors and back stairs, all in need of a lick of paint (about to happen apparently). System of different staircases operates to avoid rush hour chaos at lesson change-over. General air of make do and mend; nothing at all wrong with that although the library (doubles as venue for music lessons), seems to be in a corridor, with a few uninvitingly deflated beanbags for seating. Hardly the place for those OHJS voracious readers to curl up in bookish quiet. Head says that big plans are afoot, 'parents, girls and governors have been consulted about how to make best use of the sites and develop them for 21st century learning.' Our unfailingly diplomatic guides said the food was, 'sometimes nice, sometimes nasty', but appreciated the option to have a jacket potato on the nasty days (who doesn't?).

School very proud of the new 'Nomow' (do they get commission?) grass quiet area outside a year 6 classroom with its coloured benches and tables – guess this is where girls go to read in peace. Playground is larger than expected, plenty of space to run around and let off steam; includes a netball/tennis court, raised beds, a pond and fountain. Juniors also use sports facilities (swimming pool etc) at the nearby senior school. All the usual after school stuff (art, chess etc) plus the delightfully unusual and popular morris dancing club. Girls from the senior school come over to help with reading and run activities. Our guides said that they thought their school was 'more intellectual' than others and that there was 'a lot of homework', in year 6 but that it was 'manageable'. Parents (usual Oxford mix of professionals, academics, medics) we spoke to were a pretty satisfied bunch. Lots of praise for the excellent teaching and support and, perhaps, a sense of relief that all being well their daughters were launched on their way to the senior school, the universe, and beyond!

Packwood Haugh School

Ruyton XI Towns, Shrewsbury, SY4 1HX

- Pupils: 215; 140 boys/75 girls. 90 boarders • Ages: 4–13 • C of E
- Fees: Day £7,002–£15,480; Boarding £19,344 pa • Independent

Tel: 01939 260217
Email: headmaster@packwood-haugh.co.uk
Website: www.packwood-haugh.co.uk

Headmaster: Since September 2012, Mr Clive Smith-Langridge, previously deputy head at Hordle Walhampton. A maths and sports specialist, he qualified as a teacher whilst teaching games at Cumnor House in Sussex after a business career. He is married with two daughters.

Entrance: Not selective. Short informal assessment – maths and English. Scholarships awarded: academic, sporting, music, art, all-rounder. Help for the needy. Children come from Shropshire, Cheshire, Wales, Staffordshire, London. Handful of overseas students, particularly from Spain and Japan.

Exit: The most popular destination for boys is Shrewsbury (where rumour mill has it that Packwood children are noted for an ability to get on with others), but also steady numbers to Rugby, Eton, Harrow, Winchester, Radley, Uppingham, Malvern, Repton, Sedbergh. Rugby and Cheltenham Ladies' College popular with girls. Moreton Hall, Shrewsbury High and Ellesmere are local choices.

Remarks: Academic but unpressurised. Traditional country prep school, a 'proper' boarding school. Head is committed to full boarding, 'otherwise the character of the school changes'. Boarding numbers, which fell in the '90s recession, have risen strongly, are holding up well – resists pressure for more day school places. 'When the school reaches 285, we will only take boarders,' says the head.

Palmers Green Lower School

Linked school: Palmers Green High School

104 Hoppers Road, London, N21 3LJ

- Pupils: 158 girls, all day • Ages: 3–11 • Non-denom
- Fees: £4,575–£9,810 pa • Independent

Tel: 020 8886 1135
Email: office@palmersgreen.enfield.sch.uk
Website: www.pghs.co.uk

Headmistress: Since 2002, Mrs Christine Edmundson BMus MBA LRAM ARCM PGCE (Cantab) (early fifties). Originally from the Isle of Man, studied music at Royal Holloway, University of London where she was a choral scholar, as an undergraduate and postgraduate. Completed her PGCE following a bizarre twist of events that meant she was unable to continue with her doctoral research subject: 'someone from New Zealand working at the British Museum had published his doctoral thesis on my unpublished manuscript, so I changed course.' She worked at a number of co-educational and girls' day and boarding schools before coming to this school in 2002. 'I wasn't going to stay long but it was so lovely, it's addictive.' An approachable person who still teaches some topics – ICT, RE, general studies – and stands at the gates to welcome pupils in the mornings and to see them off at the end of the day, which parents like very much. One of her strong points is the ability to spot and respond to opportunities to improve teaching at the school. She will often work with specialists that she 'may have heard at a conference or on radio'. One of these was a specialist in early years from Homerton College in Cambridge who helped when the early years foundation stage was just being introduced. 'It was great as she was working at the forefront of what was happening, so the staff had her expertise. Where other schools were thinking, "well, how do you do that?", here teachers had a specialist to tell them how.'

Entrance: Most pupils join the school from the linked Alice Nursery, situated about a mile and a half away. Others come from nearby nursery schools such as Start Right Montessori, Leapfrog, Cedar Park, Bumble Bees Montessori and Leading Strings. Entrance to the prep department at age 4 and the junior department at age 7 is by assessment of ability and potential by one of the primary school teachers. This involves a timed test for children in years 5 and 6 but is less formal for those in year 4 and below. The school welcomes 'pupils with special educational needs, providing that our individual needs department can offer them the support they require'.

Exit: Majority go on to Palmers Green High School, others on to other independent or selective state schools in the area. Some parents would like 'a greater focus on preparing children for 11+ exams in the same way some other schools do'.

Remarks: Single form entry school with a maximum class size of 24 and a teacher pupil ratio of 1:9. Most children are working above the national average and a few are at level 6 in English, reading and maths. They are taught by mature (average age is 45) and well-qualified teachers. The small classes, say parents, are 'why we chose this school'. They also like the fact that specialist teaching in art, DT, drama, PE and music is introduced to children from as early as year 1 and in some subjects from reception. While core subjects such as English, maths, science and humanities are taught by form tutors, from year 3 girls have specialist French tuition and year 5s have taster courses in a range of languages, including Latin. Year 6 girls receive specialist DT teaching. 'DT is really fun,' remarked one year 6 girl. 'We've been doing models of playground rides and we solder too.' Her classmate showed us some prototypes but admitted that the teacher helped her with the soldering part as 'I was a bit scared' – then again, she had only joined the school in year 5 and said, 'In my old school we didn't do any DT, they didn't trust us.' Parents comment on the 'teaching with substance'. Early introduction to subjects such as Latin and DT helps to develop the children's reasoning skills and their understanding of a wide variety of topics.

It is a very friendly school where teachers insist you come in and have a look around the classrooms and the children appear wholly interested in what they are learning and readily talk about their work. A year 4 science class shared with us what they were learning about the comparison of light and dark. Another class showed off their work on historical toys, including specimens they had brought in from home. Learning is supported by visits to places like the British Schools Museum, Hatfield House, Whipsnade Zoo and the year 5 residential trip to Flatford Mill where they develop their skills in navigation, using a compass, and trekking. The school magazine shows off impressive artwork and writing. About half of the girls learn one or more instruments at school. Specialist music teachers come in to teach instrument lessons and pupils' skills range from beginners to grade 4 and even 5.

There are no sports fields or courts on site and the main hall was, until recently when the new gymnasium was completed, being used for assemblies, indoor games, gym, dance and drama. Despite the shortage of onsite sports facilities, opportunity and enthusiasm for PE across ages is evident. Pupils travel to the nearby Walker Ground for games and to Southgate pool for swimming lessons. Gymnastics is popular, and now takes place in the new gym/dance studio. Pupils from year 2 upwards compete successfully in the week long Enfield Primary Schools Gymnastics Festival and Enfield netball tournament; there is an inter-house netball tournament for years 5 and 6, and there is a school swimming gala. Gymnastics and dance are taught on half term rotation. Drama is popular too, and year 3 to 6 girls perform at the local theatre. Year 6s take the lead roles in the annual summer play (which includes pupils from year 3 upwards) – 'we put on a play, we sing and dance and dress up in nice costumes'. Titles are adapted and new characters are introduced to popular productions to ensure everyone has the opportunity to take part. One year they 'did the 12 dancing princesses and 10 of their cousins because there were 22 of us'. Some girls played 'the jury in Goldilocks Goes to Court... she is charged with breaking in, and there are witnesses, the three ugly sisters, the bad wolf, the three bears, the bad fairy. Goldilocks won in the end. Everyone joins in and helps'.

As Christmas approaches the lower school and seniors as come together to practise songs and to make decorations for the carol service. The younger children make stars, sheep and angels whilst years 3 to 6 prepare to recite two poems. The school has close links with the local churches, although 'we have pupils of all faiths and none,' head says.

The prep and junior departments are located on the ground and middle floor of a building shared with the senior school. This supports the close knit pastoral environment where pupils in the younger pupils benefit from keen mentoring by the older pupils upstairs – 'during fire drills an older girl must grab a younger one,' said the head, 'and can get upset as there aren't enough little ones to go around'. She says the school believes in teaching children 'to work smart, not hard and long, but smart'. Good peer-to-peer relationships are a key part of this. Children are encouraged to 'play to strengths, to support [their] friends and learn from them as well as the staff'. There is 'good support for all children ... with girls in higher years being a mentor to younger girls,' said a parent. 'My daughter is really happy and we are really happy.'

All junior pupils learn to be responsible by taking on roles like helping out in the prep school or library, or as head and deputy head girls. These roles – called 'duties' – alongside the range of extracurricular activities on offer, give pupils plenty to do and they both enjoy and thrive from the responsibility despite their busy schedules: 'I find it amazing that I'm a head girl,' said one pupil. 'I have prep duties two days a week; orchestra on Wednesdays, Thursdays is choir and on Friday we do library.'

'Doing library' involves acting 'as librarians, recommending books and putting them away, and learning about how the library works,' but pupils say the most exciting part is the badge they get to wear. They share the library with the senior school so there is a tight rota in place. Adjacent to the library is the main school hall – called Avondale – which is, in effect, the original school building. They relocated here in 1918, 13 years after the school was founded by a Quaker called Alice Hum. Since then a number of extensions have been added to Avondale Hall, including classrooms, a dining room and more recently the newly built Elizabeth Smith Hall and purpose-built medical room. This is expected to make things a lot easier for the girls, especially in drama and indoor PE, as previously everything took place in the main hall and its use was restricted during exam times.

Extracurricular activities range from sewing, junior orchestra, violin club and several choirs to art and maths puzzle club, speech and drama, netball and gym. The junior choir performs regularly at local events such as the N21 summer festival and Christmas festival. In the speech and drama club, 'we write our own mini plays and act them out', say pupils. 'We get certificates. They're displayed upstairs in the corridor.' There is 'something for everybody, whether you're arty, sporty, or not ...' said a parent, 'we encourage our daughter to do as much as possible'.

Head says, 'We expect them to work hard and to be involved in things [so that] if something goes wrong [eg, a girl appears to be struggling or is behaving out of character] we pick it up.'

Parents certainly think highly of the school and most agree that their daughters are being adequately stretched academically. However, if they could wave a magic wand it would be to have more breakfast and after school clubs to support working parents.

Papplewick School

Windsor Road, Ascot, SL5 7LH

- Pupils: 210 boys; weekly or full boarding; boarding compulsory last two years and previous summer term • Ages: 6–13 • C of E
- Fees: Boarding £25,080; Day £13,815–£19,155 pa • Independent

Tel: 01344 621488
Email: registrar@papplewick.org.uk
Website: www.papplewick.org.uk

Headmaster: Since 2004, Mr Tom Bunbury BA PGCE, (forties). Educated at nearby Woodcote Prep and then Millfield, read law at Durham but turned his back on the legal profession to return first to Woodcote, then Homerton College Cambridge for a PGCE followed by Papplewick where he has remained since 1993. He was head of maths, a housemaster and then deputy before taking over as head. It was, he says, a chance to lead a great team and make it stronger. He is modest and quietly confident, with a charming absence of ego. Parents appreciate the fact that he has guarded the traditions of Papplewick while moving with the times on issues such as demand for flexi-boarding.

He lives on site with his wife, Sallie, and four children. Sallie oversees the matrons and catering – each week she organises a 'tasty table' at which 12 boys picked at random on their way in to the dining room get to try a new meal and give it the thumbs up. Or down. The head places great emphasis on the school's 'real family atmosphere', two-thirds of staff live on site and many have families; the boys enjoy playing with the younger children, teaching them to ride bikes and explore. Parents to whom we spoke endorsed this, seeing it as a real strength of the school. Living at one's place of work may be convenient but you need an escape route, and whenever time allows the Bunburys pack buckets and spades and head off to their bolt-hole on the Isle of Wight.

Entrance: Entry from age six, first come, first served. Day boys from local preps in Berks, Bucks and Surrey but increasing numbers now coming in from West London. Parents have cottoned on to the fact that just 40 minutes on the Papplewick express will enable their boys to escape the capital's overheated prep rat-race. Several we spoke to described Papplewick as 'a blessed relief' from the intense competitiveness of the capital's schools', adding that their boys still got to the senior schools of their choice but at their own pace. According to the head, there's no 'Papplewick type', families have 'broad horizons' and the atmosphere is tolerant and uncliquey; parents say much the same. About 10 per cent from outside UK, no dominant country, some ex-pats, EFL available. Handful of academic and all-rounder awards available annually, can be worth up to 50 per cent of fees.

Exit: Impressive scholarship record. Fifty-nine awards over the past five years (18 in last two years, including three King's Scholarships to Eton). As well as Eton, leavers progress to Harrow, Wellington, Charterhouse, Winchester, Stowe, Bradfield, Oratory, Marlborough, Millfield, Shrewsbury, Radley, Sherborne and a host of other schools.

Remarks: Papplewick may be across the road from Ascot racecourse but it's not going to give the new grandstand (or indeed the old one) a run for its money in the architectural stakes. Parents say a few may be disappointed by the absence of grandeur but 'the boys don't notice'. Recent building works have transformed what was a rather jumbled site, the new entrance hall is particularly impressive, it seems to pull everything together as well providing a light and modern space for exhibitions and

P

receptions. Plans have been drawn up for an art and DT block as well as a 'pipe dream' of a stand-alone year 8 boarding house. As for the inside, take a boy of your acquaintance, multiply him by 200, imagine the toll this cohort might take on the interior of any building and you will be ready for Papplewick. There is a Just William charm about this place and its delightful pupils – unaffected, exuberant, boys in their element. Uniform is blue shorts and blue shirts, open necked in the summer or fastened with one of the huge number of ties that declare an individual's allegiance to house, sporting or other pursuits.

Our year 8 guides were quite the best PR team we've had the pleasure to be escorted by. When we ventured that the absence of poolside changing might make winter bathing a little frosty we were told that it was 'very character building.' Asked whether they thought other schools were better equipped, they conceded that this might possibly be the case but claimed that they just 'deviated around any lack of facilities.' To be fair, all the prerequisites of 21st century schooling are present and correct – plenty of computers including a suite of Macs in the music tech room, smart boards and such like. Chapel is a dog-leg off the main hall, demarcated on our visit by a truly impressive display of art – some by boys who had just won scholarships. Two imperious (if slightly moth-eaten) stags' heads, whence the school emblem, oversee proceedings – if only they could talk! Electronic screen in the hall shows live feed of house points, great for motivation; weekly winners get to choose Friday night supper – usually chicken and chips.

Average class size is 12. Flexible setting and streaming – boys moved up and down as necessary. Cambridge Latin Course for all, Greek for scholars. In the classes we observed there was a palpable rapport between staff and pupils; one felt that boys knew exactly how far they could go with their sparky banter and wouldn't push it any further. Likewise the teachers responded to the boys as individual characters, enjoying their company. And all the time minds were developing, being guided and challenged.

There are some younger boarders, 'I was a bit shy to start with but I soon got used to it,' and some flexi boarders, but most start when it becomes compulsory in the summer term of year 6. As one boy told us, 'You can have fun with your friends all day, you don't have to worry about rushing because mum wants to go somewhere.' The year 6 French class we chatted to were very keen to tell us about their favourite activities – extra DT where you can 'make what you like', drama, clay pigeon and rifle shooting three times a week, golf and polo. All games (apart from polo) played on site; football, rugby and cricket are tackled with gusto and everybody gets a game. Most unusual and tremendously popular is Herpetology or Snake Club; this is the first time a Good Schools Guide reviewer has conducted interviews with a bearded lizard on her shoulder. As with many of the activities, including a game of football we saw, Snake Club is for all ages – boys buy their reptiles, now all bred in house, for a modest £10 and learn about the creature's habitat and how to care for it. Any offspring are sold back to the club for the same price. The club was founded by the charismatic science master who joined from a school in South Africa, having 'discovered' Papplewick via a visiting rugby team. Ten years on and he's still 'loving' it; his wife is in charge of life upstairs in the dorms.

Each year group has its own den (common-room) with friezes painted by a member of the art department (these also adorn the dorms), and a mixture of pool tables and tiered benches for watching films. Dorms are no-frills but they're tidy and boys expected to change their own sheets; pin boards were fairly empty when we visited but there is, we were told, a hotly contested prize for the best decorated. There are televisions and beanbags in the dorms and boys can watch after 4pm, mobile phones are allowed but for talking only – no moving images. Parents are mainly contacted via Skype or mobile. Year 8 can use Facebook under supervision. The boys we met were very clear about the rules and seemed to take them in good part, understanding the necessity. Posters visible in strategic places detailing where to go for help; boys can take problems to their tutor or, if preferred, can phone and speak confidentially to the 'private listener' who will listen and give advice.

Head keen to point out that while the idea of a boarding prep may strike some as old fashioned, Papplewick has evolved along with modern family life. Parents are welcome to drop in whenever they like; Saturdays are particularly popular – those who come to watch matches stay and listen to the sublime four-part choir ('full of first XV rugby players') at a short chapel service and then eat lunch with staff and boys. The 40 or so boys who are in school for the weekend enjoy camp outs, trips to local restaurants, socials (bit of a Lynx fest apparently) with Wycombe Abbey, Heathfield and St Mary's.

According to the head, relocation to a larger site was considered a few years ago but decided against – would it have broken the spell? Who knows. There's certainly a whiff of magic about Papplewick that seems to inspire fierce loyalty in staff, parents and boys. We think perhaps Mr Bunbury should bottle it and build that new boarding house.

The Paragon School

Linked school: Prior Park College

Lyncombe House, Lyncombe Vale, Bath, BA2 4LT

- Pupils: 275; 154 boys/121 girls • Ages: 3–11 • Christian
- Fees: £7,890–£8,790 pa • Independent

Tel: 01225 310837
Email: admissions@paragon.priorpark.co.uk
Website: www.paragonschool.co.uk

Headmaster: Since 2012, Andrew Harvey BA PGCE (late thirties). Brought up and educated in Dorset (Milton Abbey) with a degree in history and theology from the University of Derby, he taught briefly before joining the Royal Dragoon Guards for three years 'mainly for the rugby – but also the leadership values', though he always intended to return to teaching; 'I'd conk out if I did it for 40 years, though'. Mr Harvey's career has been forged in prep schools (most recently Lambrook), except for a stint as head of pastoral care at Sherfield School, and it is here that he appears to feel most at home. The unstuffy atmosphere and Bath location of The Paragon appealed to him, but it was the fact that he and his wife Anna thought it would be the ideal school for their two small daughters that swung it. Mr Harvey follows a charismatic predecessor, but he has gone down well with parents, who find him visible, very approachable and hands-on – he pops into every class every day. The children find him 'funny', 'jolly' and 'religious' by turns and 'he doesn't like spending time in the office', said one perceptive little chap. The deputy head, who has been at the school for aeons, is a whizz at systems, so provides a good foil for the 'incredibly personable' (so says one mother) and omnipresent Mr Harvey. Hobbies include rugby, cricket and squash, and reading up on matters educational.

Entrance: Main entry points are at nursery, reception and year 3, though children are welcomed at any stage; most come from Bath and the villages south of the city. Three open mornings a year, after which an individual visit and interview with the head will generally secure a place; he is, however, not afraid to turn away children whose behaviour or academic delay would stretch the teachers' resources and disadvantage the class. Trial day provides opportunity for informal assessment

Exit: The majority at year 6 to Prior Park College, up the hill from the Paragon and part of the same foundation, along with Prior Park Prep in Cricklade, (but Anglican rather than Catholic, unlike the other two) but some to other Bath schools, state and independent. Anyone wanting traditional common entrance at 13+ would need to go elsewhere for years 7 and 8, and a few do. In some years, nearly half the children gain an award of some kind into their next school – more given for sport than anything else. Any doubtful runners for Prior Park are given the nod in year 5; that said, the schools' learning support departments work closely together.

Remarks: Tucked away in a wooded dell surprisingly close to the centre of Bath, The Paragon now occupies what was a private Georgian house with a mineral spring still in its grounds, but it owes its name to its century-old origins as an educational gymnasium in the street of the same name in the city. Its seven and a half secluded acres comprise pitches, both Astro and grass, a conventional playground for younger children but – gloriously – masses of wooded slopes too, complete with a yurt and a tepee. Head, parents and children all very keen on outdoor learning; the school really lives it (eg acting out scenes from the Bayeux Tapestry) with help from Swainswick Explorers, instead of merely taking children outside to read on sunny days, as some do.

Classrooms are split between the main building and the charming stable block a minute's walk away. Not a school which bowled us over with technological wizardry; rather we liked what we saw and heard going on in classrooms, where one lucky English class was rewriting Cinderella in the style of Roald Dahl. Year 6 reading books lying about on desks impressive for children of that age. Head determined to extract more academic juice than has sometimes been the case before – to that end, he has lured his new director of studies from his previous school and introduced philosophy to the curriculum – yet remains a school where children can continue to be children until they leave. One parent felt that it's not a moment too soon to raise academic standards, and that attainments in maths in particular could be higher, given the small class sizes and biddable children. The head is certainly conscious of local competition in the form of KES Junior and excellent Widcombe Primary.

Sport is a serious matter, and even the tiniest children are taught the basic skills of the major sports. 'Rounders is a silly game,' says he, so is keen to introduce cricket to the girls, and has just appointed a head of girls' games to beef them up; high quality coaches also take regular sessions. School performs amazingly well in competition, especially considering its size; rugby, hockey and swimming stand out. Though its own facilities are limited, the pitches and swimming pool at Prior are but a short ride in a liveried minibus up the hill.

Music gets thumbs up from parents too, and the majority of prep school children learn an instrument, many achieving grade 3 or 4 by the time they leave. Local successes and two accepted into Young National Schools Symphony Orchestra. We loved the expansive displays of art on the walls: a mixture of work based on established artists and the purely creative, but most of all we loved the craft room, up a mysterious staircase, and pervaded by the scent of lavender, where dear little bags were being made for charity. Paragon children emerge being able to sew on a lot more than a button. Drama is performed in the hall which doubles as a gym and the dining hall – a theatre is on the head's wish list. Noye's Fludde is currently in rehearsal with Prior Park, and we are sorry not to have seen La Neige Blanche et les Vingt Nains.

Everyone raves about the family feel of The Paragon, further enhanced by teachers now lunching with the children at the same tables. 'It's done wonders for their manners,' said one mother approvingly. Indeed: one boy we lunched with (pasta, pasta or pasta the day we visited) nearly choked rather than speak with his mouth full! Definitely time to get rid of the garish 'prison trays' the children eat off though – staff get plastic plates. Active PTA raises funds but also has a strong social agenda and an impressive newsletter, The Paragraph.

The Paragon is unquestionably taking on a higher profile in Bath's competitive educational market place, but there remains an interesting contrast between its flamboyant rebranding (surely the most pukka uniforms locally, with red stripes in abundance for all) and its quirky relaxed feel, for which many parents choose it.

Parkside School

The Manor, Stoke D'Abernon, Cobham, Surrey, KT11 3PX

- Pupils: 300 boys; nursery 90 boys and girls • Ages: 2–13 • Non-denom • Fees: £9,180–£14,250 pa • Independent

Tel: 01932 862749
Email: enquiries@parkside-school.co.uk
Website: www.parkside-school.co.uk

Head Master: Since 1999, Mr David Aylward, MA BEd (Hons) FRSA (fifties). DA (as he is known) has spent almost his whole career at this school, having joined in 1984 as a housemaster when the school took boarders. He taught maths, then was deputy for six years before taking over the headship (there was another short-lived head before him).

A jovial character; not slick or salesman-ish, but pragmatic, no-nonsense and upfront. A man you can do business with if you share his point of view – he's quite set in his ways. Describes his school as 'a happy place', he wants to see smiling faces and for his pupils to have genuinely enjoyed their time at Parkside. He is strict but has a good rapport with the boys, knows all by name and they like and respect him. 'He's funny and makes us laugh,' said one. Boys give him a doughnut on their birthday and he gives them a Kit Kat in return. 'He's quite unique,' said one mother. 'And always has a kind word to say – to parents as well as their boys'.

Parents find him approachable and supportive. 'He is the school,' said one. 'And if you didn't get on with him I don't think you would send your son here. There are no doubts about who's in charge. Without DA this would be a very different place'. But there doubtless will be a changing of the guard in the next five years or so. DA is heading for retirement and one does sense in him a certain disaffection with some current approaches – pre-testing in particular. Nevertheless he is absolutely comfortable where he is at the moment – a man completely in charge who makes parents feel their boys are in safe hands. 'I've got absolute confidence in him and I know that if there was any sort of glitch with my son, he would sort it,' said one mother.

Out of school 'nothing remarkable,' says DA, who is happy with a pint at the pub and a game of snooker. He's also a school inspector.

Retiring in July 2014.

Entrance: Boys in the co-ed nursery have automatic places in the pre-prep reception. At 7+ entrance to Year 3 in prep school proper is by assessment. Boys spend a day at the school and are tested in English and maths. Any SEN issues will be taken up then too. The key element of the assessment day is 'fitability' – the interaction between the boys. Nothing sinister here – 'If a boy spends the whole day fighting, we won't be keen and we do turn people down if we feel they are not right for the school,' says DA. Perhaps less choosy than some of its rivals, but does not take all-comers. 'We are looking for academic and social abilities and generally we get it right'.

Boys join from a wide local radius including Wimbledon, Esher, Claygate, Weybridge, Oxshott, Byfleet, Cobham, Stoke d'Abernon, Fetcham and Leatherhead. Mainly English, some Korean, Russian, American, South African and Australian. Most year groups absolutely full, but there are sometimes gaps higher up the school – always worth a phone call. Limited number of means-tested bursaries available.

Exit: From nursery 70 per cent move on to pre-prep – others to the state system (Royal Kent, St Matthews), Cranmore (catholic), or Danes Hill or Feltonfleet (both co-ed). School not geared towards pupils leaving at 11, though occasionally a boy will head off somewhere with no common entrance exam such as Box Hill .

At 13+ boys depart to a range of senior schools. Many to (very local) Reeds and St John's Leatherhead – both 'big boys Parkside' says DA. Others to King's College School (Wimbledon), Hampton School, The Royal Grammar School (Guildford), Epsom, Worth, Wellington, Lancing, Box Hill, Cranleigh and Charterhouse. A few to Eton and Harrow. School well practised at matching each boy to the right school – DA has terrific local links and knowledge and is very frank about future options. It's all handled gently and kindly, although perhaps minus the hand-holding that some parents would like. 'DA gets it right,' says one in the know. 'Parents need to listen'.

Remarks: A happy school, less pressured than others in this moneyed area of Surrey, with a good all-round offering. Academically its results are up there with the other schools, but achieved without undue pressure. 'Sometimes there is no substitute for heads down and getting through the work, but we try to keep things as relaxed as possible,' says DA. CE results pretty much 100 per cent, with 85 per cent A/B grades from a cross-section of entrants. Setting from age nine – boys talk of top, bottom and middle groups, non-judgementally. 'We do the same stuff at different speeds,' our guides explained. Forty boys in a year, split into two forms of 20, then three sets so that the average teaching group is around a dozen or so. 'Parkside is academic, but it's not a hot house,' said one mother. 'There are a lot of bright scholars, but I do sometimes wonder how a ferociously intelligent type might get on. Having said that, the boys do find their level and my son is simply flying here. I love the fact that he is valued as an individual and not just a number'.

Good SEN provision from quite a large SEN department. School is happy to help where it feels a boy is up to doing the CE course. This boils down to those who can manage with a maximum of two 1-1 support lessons a week, more than that and they would be missing out on too much of the core curriculum. Currently 45 boys on the SEN register receiving varying levels of support.

Classrooms have white boards and projectors, there is an IT room and some 100 computers around the school. But generally it's book, rather than iPad; library rather than resource centre; letter rather than email.

Pupils we saw were really enjoying their lessons, involved and in good spirits. Some fabulous art around and lots of music – around a third of the boys learn instruments and join the various groups on offer, everything from rock and jazz to wind and string ensembles, a choir and an orchestra.

Well-regarded and stable teaching staff have a lot to fit in so school operates a pacey 10 lessons a day timetable – each lesson a short sharp 35 minutes – to keep boys focused and ensure the school day is not too long. It's not quite as frenetic as it sounds, with some double periods and lots of sport thrown into the mix. Homework kept to just one or two 35-minute assignments a week (term time only) and there's no Saturday school. DA is keen that the boys have a full life outside, as well as inside, school and first decided on a shorter school day (finishing at four rather than five) when he heard that one boy couldn't go to scouts as he didn't get home in time. 'School should not be all consuming,' he believes. 'These boys need a life'.

Parkside parents agree; pushier types decide it's not for them. 'I think there's a reasonable amount of homework,' said a parent. 'And it's sensible homework, where the boys are challenged and not given something to do for the sake of it.'

It's a famously sporty school, well used to picking up county and national trophies in U11 and U13 competitions. Football more popular than rugby; also strong in athletics, hockey, swimming and cricket. Super sport facilities set in school's 40 acres of parkland, include a 20m swimming pool, a splendid cricket academy, tennis courts and even a river (the Mole runs through school grounds) used for kayaking; boys have everything they need on site.

The school is right next to the M25, which can be heard burring away from the grounds, but not from the classrooms. At the centre of all the action is the historic manor house, with decorative ceilings, pillars and panelling, which houses the head, staff rooms, boys' dining room and a magnificent salon, complete with Rococo fireplace, used for school assemblies and functions. The classroom block, the Crescent, a well-designed and airy space, was added in 2002. Since then a 100 seat performing arts hall, lecture room and art block have been added, and most recently a superb library for the prep school (pre-prep and nursery have their own libraries). This has become rather the hub of the school, it's well used and hosts talks by visiting authors helping to crack the 'getting boys to read' problem.

The nursery building, a converted barn, is really appealing, colourful and brimming with activity – all safely cordoned off from the bigger boys. Parents really appreciate the after-school care available at the nursery and pre-prep which is so useful in helping them to juggle school runs, match pick ups and work.

Although refurbishment does goes on here – and DA is proud of the physical development of the site – some parents wish he would loosen the purse strings a little further. 'Some books are falling apart and other buildings could take some sprucing up,' one felt very strongly. DA agrees he is 'careful' to get value for money, but maintains there are plenty of funds available for new books and more. 'I am always conscious that it is not my money, but the parents', he says.

While DA prefers not to waste money on educational gloss, the area around his school is rather less hair shirt. Cobham and Stoke d'Abernon are way up market and something of an economic bubble – en route we passed flash cars galore, including a Bugatti and those of several Chelsea footballers; the school backs on to the club's training grounds. But Parkside aims to play down this aspect of the area and some families choose the school precisely for this reason. 'I couldn't bear it if my son got the idea that he was the big I am,' said one. 'And this place is smaller and less hard-nosed than other preps around here. Not all the play dates are at swanky houses. Everyone here has worked hard to get their son into private school so it's very inclusive, lots of different abilities, and people from different backgrounds, there are lawyers and bankers, electricians and plumbers'.

And as you would hope in a smallish operation like this, pastoral care is first class and the school has been known to turn around a few unhappy boys joining late in the upper years. Staff are friendly and approachable and the boys are not scared of them. Mutual respect visible, including boys standing when visitors enter the classroom. Boys seem proud of their school and loyal to each other. If a bullying ever occurs DA will first talk to the bully; 'I try to be reasonable, rational and pleasant and explain how their actions are upsetting. But after that, if things don't improve, then I come down hard on them.' Parents approve of the way any bad behaviour is dealt with quietly. 'There's no naming or shaming,' said one. 'I've only ever been aware of good handling if any issues have come up.'

There's a well understood framework of discipline, but not a lot of rules, and the main ones are not imposed for the sake of it, but to create self-discipline. There is the 'Parkside code', set by boys and mostly for safety, e.g. the river is out of bounds. Boys in the top year wear white shirts so that the younger boys (in grey) know who to ask for help and advice. Good and bad marks awarded as carrots and sticks, nothing heavier than that really necessary (three strikes during a half term equals a detention) and these boys are not yet cynical enough to resist punching the air with genuine pleasure and pride on receiving a good mark.

The Parkside difference is what DA calls 'the hidden curriculum' – qualities such as integrity and kindness that are caught, not taught. The boys are encouraged to organise and host charity days and their parents, involved in Friends of Parkside, are an equally busy bunch arranging all sorts of social and fundraising events – serious money, such as can buy, for example, a fleet of mini buses.

School fees include books and lunch and most of the after-school clubs. The only additional charges are for extra-curricular activities provided by outside companies, such as judo and music. Lots of clubs and activities on offer – (touch typing, archery, graphics, fencing, cooking, school magazine and supervised prep) with everything finished by 5pm.

Some parents frustrated that they are not given staff email addresses, school prefers home/school communication to be via notes in the boys' prep books, or, if that's not appropriate, by letter. 'That allows for rather more reflection', says DA. 'It's all too easy to dash off an email, replying to which could tie up staff for hours'. That said, parents seem largely happy that they can get to see teachers when they need to and do indeed pass on and receive information via their sons. But don't get the impression it's them and us – parents are welcomed in to use the facilities out of school time and staff join in the many and varied socials (DA is a seasoned quiz master), so parents feel they get to know their sons' teachers well and many are on a first name basis with them. 'If I ever had an issue I know it would get sorted,' one said. 'And there's a lot of laughter and banter around the school, from the ground staff to the governors, it's a place where everyone works in harmony'.

A good traditional prep school, where the boys respect staff who are firm but fair. It's a sporty place, providing a relaxed environment for good all-rounders. Straightforward, what you see is what you get, the boys not super-polished, but naturally friendly, polite and confident. 'There's really something special about Parkside,' said one longstanding parent. 'If you want small, boys only, and to get them into the senior school which will suit them best, then you wouldn't go far wrong here'.

Pembridge Hall School

18 Pembridge Square, London, W2 4EH

- Pupils: 400 girls • Ages: 4–11 • Non-denom • Fees: £17,460 pa
- Independent

Tel: 020 7229 0121
Email: contact@pembridgehall.co.uk
Website: www.pembridgehall.co.uk

Headmaster: Since September 2012, Mr Henry Keighley-Elstub BA (Hons) PGCE (early forties). Appointed in November 2011, succeeding Barry Evans who only served for five terms before taking early retirement. Fran Baylis acted as interim head while Mr Keighley-Elstub served out his notice at Wetherby Prep where he was deputy head. Educated at Eton and Leeds University, where he read classical civilization. He has taught history at Ludgrove, Cothill and Chesham Prep where he was head of department and also senior master. As well as this being his first headship, it is also his first experience of an all girls' school, and one that finishes at 11 years rather than 13. 'I was worried about that at first,' he admits, 'but now I barely notice, and communicating with an 11 year old girl is equivalent to talking to a 13 year old boy.' Married to Sarah who works at IBM ('I have no idea what she does', he confides, 'perhaps she's a spy.') They have recently had a daughter.

Mr Keighley-Elstub, though slight of build, has an immediately warm, engaging and enthusiastic personality that makes even the stiffest person unfurl. His conversation is littered with verbs and adjectives like 'skip along' and 'groovy'. His upbeat chipper approach is directed at everyone. As well as the girls, the parents and the teachers it embraces the peripatetic music staff, games staff and the odd visitor. Despite being an Old Etonian with an unusually complicated name both to spell and pronounce (think 'Keithly'), Mr Keighley-Elstub is remarkably down to earth. He attributes this to his Northern pedigree (his father was a Yorkshireman but practised as a GP in Wimbledon where Mr Keighley-Elstub grew up). His family used to turn up at Eton in a clapped out old VW, but 'that wasn't remotely embarrassing,' he avers. 'Eton's not smart at all. The greatest compliment anyone could pay me,' he continues, 'is to turn up to meet me in jeans.' If he weren't so refreshingly open you wouldn't guess it – he looks immaculate in his well-cut suit and playfully shrieks when he discovers the odd crisp on the floor in a classroom.

He loves music – his wife is a violinist and he has recently formed a staff choir. He is also an enthusiastic sportsman (running is his thing) and he is determined that the girls here start winning some matches for a change. He champions all departments – art, music, sport and drama – equally and works to get them all to enjoy working together rather than being at loggerheads as happens so often. He is relishing the challenges of his first headship and is not unaware of the benefits of running a school that is part of the Alpha Plus group. He talks of the wealth of resources available to him, from legal to financial as well as the supportive but 'hands off' nature of the governing body. Although clearly ambitious with lots of energy, he is clearly here to stay for some time – 'I couldn't leave while there is still so much to do,' he says. 'I want to transform a good school into an outstanding one'.

Entrance: Names down at birth – 'but realistically that means within two weeks of birth,' says head. He is keen to dispel the myth that you need to plan a caesarean and father needs to put the form through the letter box as the baby arrives. It absolutely makes no difference at all on what day of the month your child is born. They divide the months into thirds and take an equal number from each third. Non-refundable registration fee (currently £150) does not guarantee you a tour of the school. Personal tours with the head offered as soon as you are off the waiting list and offered a place (something Mr Keighley-Elstub has recently introduced – prior to his arrival tours with a member of staff offered at deposit decision time – close to starting). The competitive market (for children more than the schools) and wealthy catchment of West London means that parents don't blink at paying these sort of sums without even being given the chance to see the school before making a decision. The alternative to long waiting lists is a selection process at 3, and that would mean 'we may miss the wild wacky ones that add colour to the place,' says Mr Keighley-Elstub. Nevertheless, close liaison with feeder nurseries (he mentioned The Acorn, Rolfe's, Strawberry Fields, Minors and Ladbroke Square) to make sure girls will manage.

Exit: Plenty of scholarships, academic, sporting as well as well as musical and artistic, each year and fine boards in the upper school hall to commemorate them. A number of offers each year are made from the prestigious academic girls' day schools in London (10 from City of London Girls this year – none of which were accepted), St Paul's, Godolphin & Latymer, Francis Holland (Clarence Gate favoured by these parents more than Sloane Square), as well as the less academic like Queen's College and St James. Parents starting to show an interest in a refreshingly more diverse mixture of schools, The West London Free School for example, as well as North London Collegiate and South Hampstead. Boarding schools tend to the be of the all girls variety, Downe House, St Mary's (both Calne and Ascot),

Wycombe Abbey, Sherborne, Benenden etc. Mr Keighley-Elstub encouraging boarding school – or at least opening the parents' eyes to it, as the international flavour of parents here tend to prefer the day options.

Remarks: Situated in a particularly leafy, white stucco square in Notting Hill Gate, the lower school is in a tall building a minutes' walk from an identical building containing the upper school. In between is Wetherby pre-prep – the boys' equivalent – and also owned by the Alpha Plus group. In the basement of number 10 (the Upper School) is Minor's nursery – another Alpha Plus establishment: no wonder such direct communication about the character and ability of the girls can be made.

Round the corner in St Petersburg Place is the splendid St Matthew's Church where whole school assemblies take place each week. We joined a river of red blazered and straw boatered girls as they walked immaculately to the church. An overwhelmingly white collection of girls for such a multicultural part of London; they are international – American, Russian, European as well – but only about 10 out of 400 girls receive EAL help. Mr Keighley-Elstub described the ethos as 'lightly Anglican' but a very English education, which seemed to be the requirement of even the most foreign of families.

Girls here are well spoken, eager to please and confident. Lots of awards and prizes and opportunities to speak publicly and take responsibility to build that confidence. We were particularly impressed with an astonishing game designed by a 10 year old girl out of a cardboard box, which intricately displayed the planets and included chance and question cards which she had devised herself. She then explained through a microphone how to play the game to an audience of about 450 people in the church, including parents as well as teachers and children.

Classrooms spacious, bright and airy with wonderful high ceilings and tall windows. Lovely wide corridors and staircases that seem to go up and up for ever. Lush red carpet (to match the uniform?) in the lower school, upper school mirrors the lower school but in blue. We saw some very impressive still life work in the very studio-like space at the top of the school, which had brilliant ceiling windows, creating an excellent space to be creative. Well-equipped science labs in the basement with a good old-fashioned full-sized skeleton in the corner. Super space in the basement for drama and productions with a wealth of colourful and imaginative costumes and hats. All years get a chance to perform: year 5 do a Shakespearean medley, year 6 do their annual play in the local Tabernacle Theatre. Both buildings have large halls which double as dining rooms at lunch time. Wide choice of healthy cooked lunches and imaginative fruit (watermelon and pineapple – not just your regular apples and bananas). How refreshing not to see children eating packed lunches at their desks.

Healthy number of male teachers and the arrival of Mr Keighley-Elstub has seen barely any staff turnover at all. He feels proud of having injected renewed energy and purpose into the place and acknowledges that when he arrived there was a lot of reassurance to be done. Parents were rattled and there was a lack of direction. Those we spoke to referred to a terrible lack of communication. Many considered moving their daughters but remarkably few did, explaining that the pastoral care remained excellent throughout and they didn't want to uproot a happy child. Emphasis is now on communication – particularly with parents; improvement and consolidation of the academics; and improvement of sport.

Girls are starting to win netball matches now – and we were proudly told of how they beat Glendower recently. Netball and hockey played in nearby Avondale Park and Holland Park, athletics at the Linford Christie stadium in Wood Lane and swimming at the Porchester Baths. Plenty of inter-house matches so that everyone can have a go. Tennis as a club rather than a school sport, and rounders possibly on its way out. 'I don't see the point of it,' says Mr Keighley-Elstub. 'It's rather a poor man's cricket'. He is very open to the idea of introducing football and cricket for the girls but so far there doesn't seem to be the demand. Several outside spaces in both buildings for fresh air between lessons and 'unless there's the threat of a tornado out they go,' says head, who can't understand why the girls have been treated with such velvet gloves in the past, with the mere threat of rain resulting in their reading inside.

Three classes of 20 in each year. Setting only in maths from year 3. Serious preparation for the 11 plus starts in year 5 but the groundwork is now being laid much earlier. Mr Keighley-Elstub teaches years 5 and 6 so he can give well informed advice about schools. He is not afraid to tell a parent if they are being overly ambitious academically but will look at the whole child and advise which is the most appropriate school on that basis. Vast majority of parents here are in finance – though the odd one is glamorously famous, you wouldn't describe this as a trendy school. Mr Keighley-Elstub famously put a stop to the cashmere scarfs – as part of the school uniform and supplied by a parent: this isn't the image he wants to nurture.

Large, busy, and traditional with a dynamic head, Pembridge Hall can only get better and better and could be an excellent choice for your enthusiastic daughter.

Perrott Hill School

North Perrott, Crewkerne, TA18 7SL

- Pupils: 110 boys and 90 girls; 50 boarders • Ages: 3–13
- Fees: Day £5,805–£14,190; Boarding £16,500–£20,250 pa
- Independent

Tel: 01460 72051
Email: admissions@perrotthill.com
Website: www.perrotthill.com

Headmaster: Since January 2009, Mr Robert Morse BEd (late thirties). Previous incarnations include house mastering at Mount House and deputy head at S Anselm's, where he was extremely popular and much appreciated by parents and pupils. 'Warm, welcoming and wise beyond his years,' comments one experienced head; 'an excellent listener to all ages' – a parent. 'He has had a hugely beneficial impact,' says the experienced registrar of a famous public school, adding, 'The Perrott Hill pupils who come to us have retained the wonder of childhood instead of parading themselves as young adults. A traditional prep school of the best sort.' None of this surprised us or the parents to whom we spoke. 'Can't fault him,' sums up their response. 'I'm lucky enough to have worked under great headmasters and if I have inculcated any good ideas, they are borrowed from them,' says the head modestly. But it's the selection that is important. 'I count myself very fortunate to have inherited such a happy and committed staff.'

He is also extremely lucky, as he readily volunteers, to have such a super wife in Lottie. A fine artist (they met at Bedford Modern, where she was artist in residence) she does some team teaching in the art department, produces plays, is a generous hostess to pupils, staff and parents, possessed of a friendly, bubbly personality and fully and sensitively involved in the running of the school. Together they are a wonderful couple and one of the reasons why the school has such a genuinely cheerful family feel about it. Other reasons as well – they are blissfully happy at Perrott Hill. 'We love it here,' they almost chorus. 'A small school like this is like an extension of a boarding house and everyone is so friendly.' Their two young children, Daisy and Harry, are also very happy to be in the school, as is their black labrador, Nell. One parent volunteered how delightful Daisy and Harry are – 'Like their parents – no side.'

Entrance: Pupils may enter aged three, when they will spend two years on the Montessori foundation course before joining years 1 and 2 and thence the prep school. In fact boys and girls may join at any stage, providing room. We met a girl who had joined aged 11 and found it 'very easy to settle in'. No formal test but taster days, then, 'Providing we feel we can do a good job with them, we'll offer a place'. Staff refer any concerns to the excellent learning support team and the children are given help and encouragement when necessary. Scholarships and bursaries are available – do ask.

Exit: Currently the most popular destinations are the three Taunton schools, Sherborne (boys' and girls'), Leweston, Bryanston, Canford and King's Bruton, but that list only tells part of the story. Eton, Winchester and Radley have featured, as have many others. Pupils regularly win a good spread of scholarships and the school prides itself on matching children with appropriate senior schools, something appreciated by parents and registrars.

Remarks: Once you reach the pretty village of North Perrott, you need to keep a sharp look out for a small sign to the school. Driving down the lane shuttered with branches, do not cease from exploration nor be deterred by the road sign that informs you are following a dead end: remember this is Eliot country, where 'In my end is my beginning' – and nothing dead about Perrott Hill. Through beautifully-kept gardens and past the converted stables, you will then come to what was the manor house, built in 1878 by the architect Thomas Wyatt, described by Mark Girouard as 'tireless and tedious'. The house itself is much of the first and nothing of the latter. It has been adapted marvellously since it became a school during the second world war and the children love it. Wonderful big L-shaped hall which acts as an assembly room/chapel. When we visited a blazing log fire, much enjoyed by children and staff. A superb focal point, where everyone can congregate and chatter. Library now moved to the Orangery.

Most boarding schools trumpet their 'family atmosphere' – here it is the real thing. Part of the reason is that 12 members of staff live with the 45 boarders (the numbers have just about tripled in the last three years). The headmaster has appointed an excellent head of boarding who is responsible overall. He and his wife look after the boys; a junior housemistress and experienced matron look after the girls. The dormitories have recently been painted and there are new showers and loos. Each house has a common-room, more like a family room, with inviting chairs for lolling around, television and facilities for making toast and hot chocolate. Staff, including three gappers, and children mingle happily together all under the same roof – that's family atmosphere.

Full boarding, weekly boarding and flexi-boarding are all available, but the increasing popularity of boarding has made flexi-boarding harder to come by. Exeats from Friday pm to Sunday evening every three weeks; in between family Sundays where the boarders eat with the staff and generally behave as they would at home, sometimes going to the nearby beach, local town for shopping or to the cinema. Also massively popular activity Sundays, themed and varied. When we visited they were gearing up for a circus w/e when they were going to learn juggling and other activities. The children are extremely enthusiastic about them and parents talked of the need for booking up well in advance. From year 5 all pupils attend Saturday school: morning lessons and games in the afternoon. Matches take place most Wednesdays and Saturdays.

This ambitious programme would be impossible without a fizzy, dedicated staff. We saw some terrific teaching. No interactive white boards – just interactive teaching, supported by projectors and intelligent use of computers. Extra-curricular activities with staff seem boundless and the mutual affection and respect between staff and pupils are extraordinary. One youngish teacher in response to a question about moving on replied, 'This school is a graveyard for ambition. Why on earth leave this?' Too much of a comfort zone? Results and attitudes don't support that suspicion and besides, the head is watching. This is an active and positive school, not a sanatorium for professional skivers. As one parent told us, 'The head is very approachable, but he's also very sharp on detail and doesn't miss much.' 'I'm unashamedly a stickler for good manners and endlessly chip away at the business of opening doors, greeting people with eye to eye contact and encouraging courtesy' – he's done some good chipping: the children (and staff) are friendly and forthcoming, wearing their manners like well-worn clothes and not as strait jackets.

Since it is a small school, everyone gets involved in all the main activities. Sport is for all and results are impressive. Traditional games are played on five afternoons a week and the school regularly punches above its weight. A number of pupils go on to represent the county and some regularly win sporting awards to public schools. Drama, too, is enormously popular, as is public speaking, art and music, with over 70 per cent learning musical instruments. Facilities are good without being flashy – indeed some of the teaching buildings are a trifle scruffy. The science lab, for instance, is very basic, but the children and parents we spoke to were enthusiastic about the education offered there. Plans are in place to upgrade the lab, but that won't improve the teaching. Another area which is distinctly cramped is the art and DT departments, housed in the old hayloft above the converted stables. Being a listed building expansion is restricted, but no restrictions on the creative energy and ingenuity of the young artists. Everyone has two lessons of art a week; scholarships and prizes at local shows confirm the standard achieved in that cramped but lively place with excellent teaching – ask about Captain Pugwash. Most of the classrooms, however, are bright, airy and congenial for their purpose. The music department at the top of the house is well kitted out with practice rooms and computers – music is clearly important.

Two sports halls – as the school grew, the original one proved too small for its original purpose but has been skilfully converted into a spacious and well-used theatre; a larger one was opened recently with space for indoor hockey, cricket nets, netball, fencing – you name it. Outside, tennis courts (hard and grass), a heated swimming pool and good games pitches – though ideally more – including new Astroturf. The house is surrounded by 25 acres of woodland and scrub where children muck about happily in boiler suits (sic), construct dens, invent games and on occasions in the summer enjoy what the pizza cob offers. On the day we visited, a seal would have longed for shelter, but it's not hard to imagine the fun and laughter ('the children in the apple tree') echoing round the gardens and woodlands in this idyllic spot. No wonder Perrott Hill boys and girls 'retain the wonder of childhood'.

But in order for children to feel really happy and fulfilled, they need to be loved and secure within a clear framework. Each child is assigned a tutor who closely monitors work and morale; a clearly defined Circle of Friendship addresses any unhappiness. Staff and pupils are alert to any evidence of bullying (neither of our guides could remember any) and every week the staff discuss the work and happiness of every pupil. In addition to the resident matrons, another matron comes in every weekday afternoon to help with anyone who is feeling ill or 'just feels like a chat' – all part of the family.

For many the start of the Perrott adventure takes place in the pre-prep, safely and excitingly housed in the cleverly converted stable block close to the big house. There, using the Montessori method, they learn to learn, gaining in confidence and, while safe behind the gates, use the appropriate facilities of the prep school. 'It's lovely having them around,' said a senior girl.

Parents whom we asked spoke appreciatively of the coach service (the school runs three minibuses) not only because of the convenience but also because of the personal service. The three excellent groundsmen, who have been at the school for ages, know the children well and will go out of their way to make special and individual arrangements. One father talked of his amused delight at watching one of the drivers delivering his two young sons with one tucked under each arm, an image which in many ways sums up the joy of Perrott.

We have never come across such universal appreciation of a school. It's hard to find fault with this idyllically placed and excellently run 'traditional prep school', and we failed miserably. One parent told us that at the start of each term he murmurs, 'And all shall be well and all manner of things shall be well.'

The Perse Pelican Nursery and Pre-Preparatory School

Linked school: The Perse Upper School

92 Glebe Road, Cambridge, CB1 7TD

- Pupils: 153 boys and girls • Ages: 3-7 • Fees: £6,330-£11,262 pa
- Independent

Tel: 01223 403940
Email: pelican@perse.co.uk
Website: www.perse.co.uk/pelican

Head: Mrs S Waddington, BSc (Hons) MA PGCE.

Remarks: Parents cannot speak too highly of the Pelican. Deserves its reputation as one of the hardest schools to get into for the best possible reasons. The Perse's trademark academic thoroughness starts here, even if the youngest pupils don't realise it. Children in the nursery (usually around 32) are encouraged to love learning and to ask questions, supported by happy, friendly staff.

The Perse Preparatory School

Linked school: The Perse Upper School

Trumpington Road, Cambridge, CB2 8EX

- Pupils: 280 • Ages: 7-11 • Non-denom • Fees: £13,119 pa
- Independent

Tel: 01223 403920
Email: prep@perse.co.uk
Website: www.perse.co.uk/prep

Head: Since 2006, Mr Gareth Jones, formerly housemaster at Cranleigh School, director of music at The Dragon, Oxford, and head of prep at The Abbey School, Tewkesbury.

Moving on in July 2014. His successor will be Mr James Piper, currently deputy head of Bilton Grange Prep.

Entrance: About half from Perse Pelican Pre-Prep. External applicants by the school's own entrance tests in English and maths and verbal reasoning, as well as an interview and report from the previous school.

Exit: Vast majority of pupils move to The Perse Upper School.

Remarks: Head defines 'The Perse DNA' which is present in all stages of the school. Of course the school is academic, with intellectual, fast-paced, sparkling learning, but there's also an emphasis on extracurricular activities – head 'doesn't want a school for bright nerds and geeks'. Sport, music, drama, outdoor pursuits... there's even rocketry at the prep to prepare pupils for the award-winning rocketry society at the Upper. Most pupils take part in three or four activities after school or at lunchtime very week.

Pastoral care is taken seriously, with nurses on-site at both prep and upper schools, and there's a school counsellor and a pastoral safety net made up of tutors and heads of year. Head is committed to ensuring that the school is a cosmopolitan meritocracy – a million pounds is spent on means-tested financial support for pupils aged 7 and over throughout the prep and upper, with more than 120 receiving fees assistance. There is indeed a real mix of backgrounds – rare in independent schools – which the head is certain contributes to the development of all pupils' emotional intelligence, preparing them well for life in the real world. Subject-specialist teachers and facilities.

Prep pupils have their own campus five minutes from the upper school and their own all-weather pitch (also used by upper school students).

Phoenix School

Linked school: University College School

36 College Crescent, London, NW3 5LF

- Pupils: 140 girls and boys • Ages: 3-7 • Non-denom
- Fees: £13,410 pa • Independent

Tel: 020 7722 4433
Email: thephoenix@ucs.org.uk
Website: www.ucs.org.uk/the-phoenix.html

Headmistress: Since 2011, Miss Caroline Froud, previously head of lower school, Belmont (Mill Hill Prep School) for five years. Taught abroad for six years before returning to the UK to teach in both primary and further education establishments.

Entrance: Two main entries, each taking a balance of boys and girls. The afternoon nursery class takes children whose third birthday falls between September and December. Approximately 20 places are offered for the morning nursery classes of 16 each, attending for five mornings and two afternoon sessions. Register in January 18 months before admission. Most places go to siblings or to those with University College School (UCS) connections. Occasional vacancies at 4+, 5+ or 6+; prospective pupils are invited for a half-day assessment.

Exit: Most boys go to UCS Junior School at seven, subject to passing the entrance exam. Girls are also expected to stay till they are seven and most move on to South Hampstead High's junior department or Highgate. A few pupils to eg Westminster Under School, North London Collegiate, North Bridge House, Academy School.

Remarks: Was purchased by the UCS foundation in 2002 as its pre-prep and benefits from sharing the funding and facilities. Compact site up above the Finchley Road near Swiss Cottage, which nevertheless includes a hall, art room, music room, library and playgrounds with sandpits, climbing frame and wendy house, as well as classrooms. Children also use the UCS junior branch ICT suite and the senior school swimming pool and theatre, and spend an afternoon a week at the UCS playing fields in West Hampstead.

P

Specialist music, art and PE teachers. Before and after-school clubs include ballet, yoga, tae kwon do, Mandarin and art. Plenty of visitors and trips to eg museums and art galleries.

Can cope with mild special needs, eg dyslexia. Though not a hothouse – 'We don't do never-ending practice exam papers' – has a strong academic focus and prepares well for the next stage.

The Pilgrims' School

3 The Close, Winchester, SO23 9LT

- Pupils: 270 boys; 80 borders • Ages: 4–13 • C of E
- Fees: Boarding £20,880; Day £9,510–£16,545 pa • Independent

Tel: 01962 854189
Email: admissions@pilgrims-school.co.uk
Website: www.thepilgrims-school.co.uk

Interim Head: Deputy head Geoffrey Hammond is overseeing the school since the abrupt departure of Paddy Watson in November 2013, due to 'irreconcilable differences' with the board of governors.

Entrance: Boys are assessed at all main entry stages and tests vary depending on age. Tests for entry to reception (in the spring prior to September) consist of general assessments of 'school readiness.' School offers around 10 extra places at 7+ and 8+. Formal assessment day (November) tests boys in English, maths, perceptual and verbal reasoning; other activities thrown in to see how they relate to their peers. Around six more join the school in year 7 to prepare for 13+ entries to senior schools. Those interested can get a taste of boarding life (from age 8) by spending a few nights in school. Places in other years are occasionally available. School states that it is 'selective in the broadest sense' but clearly has an academic focus.

Auditions for the two choral foundations are in November, with most new choristers (who sing in Winchester Cathedral) and quiristers (who sing in Winchester College Chapel) joining in year 4 and 5. Voice trials include singing a prepared piece, aural tests and an academic assessment.

Boys come from all over to be a Pilgrim, moving from local nurseries, state primaries, independent pre-preps and London schools. Overseas parents choose the school as a route into Winchester College.

Exit: Between 45 and 65 per cent leave for Winchester College in any given year, many with music scholarships and exhibitions and a few with academic or double awards. Steady trickle to Eton, Bryanston, Sherborne, Charterhouse and King Edward VI, many with music, academic and all-rounder awards. Other destinations include Abingdon, Bedales, Canford, Harrow, Marlborough, Millfield and Radley. One or two may leave at 11+ for independent day schools.

Remarks: School can probably trace its origins back to the early song schools associated with Winchester Cathedral in Saxon times. Current school was founded in 1931 in former priory (thought to have been redesigned by Sir Christopher Wren) when non-singing 'commoners' joined the choristers for their education. Quiristers, boys who have sung Winchester College chapel services since 1382, moved from the College to Pilgrims' in 1966. Cathedral and remains of Wolvesey Castle form an imposing backdrop to main school building, which sits in a far corner of The Close. Once inside, there's more space than the outer façade suggests; two inner quadrangles flanked by octagonal concert hall and modern classrooms rub shoulders with ancient medieval hall and converted Priory stable block.

School escapes feeling cramped thanks to extensive playing fields in front of Bishop's Palace and design of newer buildings.

We got the feeling that this school does lots of things well, and parents confirm that academic standards are good. Form tutors and academic tutors (years 6-8) keep tabs on individual study via daily meetings with their charges and are 'very honest about progress.' Director of studies 'seems to know the capabilities of all the boys and school reports are extremely thorough, accurate and personal.' Maths set from year 4, English from year 5 and there is further division from year 7 into Winchester entry, scholarship and CE sets (depending on destination schools). Separate sciences taught from year 5, Latin from year 6 and French from year 3 (senior French classroom had piles of shiny new textbooks and posters of complex tenses on walls). Enthusiastic head of English encourages creative writing at every opportunity; clearly has a love for poetry, and boys produce some really imaginative work inspired by anything from Pilgrim's Progress to a letter from the Queen. Rest of curriculum is as expected and music is clearly strong. Although boys fall naturally into three social groups – choristers, quiristers and commoners (non-scholars, the majority) – they are all mixed together in lessons. 'The school is geared up for boys and there are lots of good male teachers.' At the time of our visit, 15 students had SEN reports (dyslexia, dyspraxia) and two learning support specialists were giving individual and group lessons to around 30 pupils. Class numbers are capped throughout at 20; numbers in year 7 and 8 classes are smaller and determined by 'next schools.'

Housed in converted medieval stables, music department is very accomplished, active and busy, with around 235 individual music lessons taught each week by 27 visiting music teachers. 'Almost everyone plays an instrument,' noted a parent; singers usually learn two. Every boy is assessed for musical potential on entry to the school. Children in year 2 have strings and woodwind taster sessions and usually begin formal instrumental lessons in year 3. Bands, orchestras and choirs abound. Main prep school orchestra tackles repertoire such as finale of Beethoven 5 and Mahler 1 (arranged by director of music) with weekly sectional rehearsals. Big band, woodwind and baroque ensembles also practise weekly; music staff 'team boys up into [chamber music] groups that work.' Junior strings and band sometimes join seniors for concerts. Four other choirs besides the two professional choirs give everyone a chance to sing. Music lessons rotate through the timetable and aim to miss the same subject no more than once every six weeks. Practice sessions for boarders (four per instrument per week) are timetabled and supervised; 25 pupils can practise simultaneously, including a few day boys. Music theory lessons for all and acres of space for music technology and composition suites. School organises two full days of ABRSM music exams every term, routinely passed with distinctions and merits. Music department has access to Winchester College for larger concerts and uses hall and the Octagon for smaller affairs. Cathedral and College Chapel choirs sing to professional standards and parents say there is no difference in kudos between the two. Parents (and boys) can choose at audition whether they wish to be considered for one or both. Daily singing for all, although quiristers sing fewer services, practise more secular repertoire and have no holiday commitments (a bonus for some families). Both choirs make recordings and go on tours. 'It's fantastic to go to a school where there is music going on, it's just part of life ... even if you don't know you're learning, you are.'

Despite being renowned for music, Pilgrims' manages to field an impressive 11 teams for football, 12 for rugby, nine for cricket and a first hockey team. Parents say results are respectable, even though one laughed, 'The boys are so polite that they're more likely to say "after you" on the football pitch.' Usual range of sports and games timetabled daily; less mainstream activities include fives, golf, fencing, rounders, judo, martial arts, squash, water polo and sailing. All-weather court floodlit for use on darker evenings. Sporting successes include U13 1500m national prep schools champion and cricket at Hampshire county level. Heated outdoor pool – affectionately dubbed 'the puddle' – for swimming in warmer months, although boys use 25m indoor pool at the College next door for serious swimming, eg lessons, swim squad and galas. Large art room, smaller DT room, ICT suite and library dotted around the quads. Parents say that drama is very good lower down the school, with a 'fantastic junior production each year,' but add that they would like to see more for older pupils. School says, 'We have a senior production every year, the last was an outdoor Shakespeare.' Productions staged in atmospheric, medieval Pilgrims' Hall, in purpose-built Octagon theatre, outdoors in the Quad or in the cathedral.

Two boarding houses have space for 82 beds, all fully occupied when we visited. Lovely couple in charge stress that all boarders are treated equally and there is a clear division between the school day and boarding. 'The boys love Jo Mason; he's like a big kid himself.' Senior quiristers board in Q-school, a few minutes' walk away. Dorms homely and comfortable; each has a year 8 dorm monitor in charge of waking boys up etc. Breakfast served on family tables, after which boys go off to choir, instrumental practice or have free time. Extracurricular activities (known as 'Commoners' as singers have choir practice) happen after school on four afternoons a week. These include lots of sport, but unusual pursuits like fishing, bell ringing and mandarin caught our eye. Boarders come back to the house after evening prep; house parents keep a close eye on any missed homework and help singers cope at busy times. Laundry done in-house and parents say belongings are checked regularly. No flexi boarding, but commoners can go home at weekends and choristers occasionally; around a dozen boys are in school regularly on Sundays. Lots of trips and activities arranged on weekends and during 'choir time', when choristers board over Christmas, Easter and a week in summer.

Parents are happy with pastoral care and school's attitude towards misdemeanours, bullying etc. 'Issues are dealt with proactively and nobody brushes anything under the carpet.' In spite of the fact that boys wear distinctive sweaters depending on whether they are choristers (red) quiristers (blue) or commoners (green), we didn't sense any social divisions. Boys are mixed up when allocated to one of five 'sets' (Houses) on entry to the school, and we observed different coloured jumpers dotted all over at lunch tables. Although the two choirs spend a lot of time together, close bonds are also formed on the football field. Parents of commoners say their sons couldn't care less about the name and feel 'just as important as anyone in a red jumper or a blue jumper.' The only quibble was that there are too few phones in the boarding house, although any urgent messages are unfailingly delivered by staff on duty. School says, 'several mobile phones are handed out each evening and there are ample landlines to use.'

Super little pre-prep has its own hall for assemblies (youngest children have lunch here) and plenty of outdoor space. Outdoor learning in Forest School every Monday and there is an outdoor play area and garden. Pre-prep holds special assembly in the cathedral every fortnight and parents are welcome. Has its own choir and music teacher (director of music also takes lessons) and there are two clubs just for the under-7s. Lots of non-fiction in library encourages boys to enjoy reading.

Pilgrims' attracts a broad mix of families – overseas nationals hail from Hong Kong and China; a few others come from Russia and Switzerland. Some overseas British based in Brazil, France and Russia. Boys are lively, but generally well-behaved, courteous and very natural. Not a Sloane Ranger in sight. Choral foundation provides scholarships worth 40 per cent to all choristers and quiristers and free music tuition on one instrument. Means-tested bursaries worth up to 100 per cent are available for all. Over 20 boys had additional funding when we visited. Any boy awarded a bursary also receives his first set of uniform free. Former pupils include Jon Snow, Jack Dee, Patrick Gale, Ollie Baines and Jules Knight (members of Blake), Nick Glennie-Smith (film composer) and Anthony Smith (sculptor).

A fine school in which the musical, the sporty and the clever boy will positively flourish. Atmosphere is now less formal and the school has a good work/life balance.

Pinewood School

Bourton, Shrivenham, SN6 8HZ

• Pupils: 400 boys and girls; 140 boarders • Ages: 3–13 • C of E
• Fees: Day £7,995–£15,390; Weekly Boarding £17,235–£19,140 pa
• Independent

Tel: 01793 782205
Email: office@pinewoodschool.co.uk
Website: www.pinewoodschool.co.uk

Head: Since 2002, Mr Philip Hoyland BEd (50s), educated at The Downs Malvern, followed by Cheltenham College. Read English and education at Exeter; previously housemaster, then deputy head, at The Dragon. Married to the warm, compassionate Henrietta; they met at Ludgrove when she was under-matron and he a rookie teacher (they have three grown-up children). Very much a partnership, her gentle humour a foil for his sense of adventure; both fully involved with the school (she is head of girls' boarding and central to much of school life).

Articulate, charming, a gentleman, Mr Hoyland wants education to be explored, and enjoyed. Seeks to offer 'non-conformist, old-fashioned values, coupled with innovative learning.' More than a sense that his Quaker heritage (his great-grandfather was businessman and philanthropist George Cadbury) shapes his views. Says, 'we work hard to ensure we have happy children here, it is difficult to do anything if they are not; children need to take risks, to be excited'. We watched as gaggles of animated youngsters flocked to his side, eager to tell of their day, show off work, badges, awards. Parents say he is kind, an intellectual and fantastic with the children, 'they adore him', but seemingly he's not always quite so good with parents: 'He's not a gushing head and if you expect your child to always be the star of the show you're probably not going to get on too well here.' Other mutterings that he backs staff over parents, but all unanimous that he really has propelled the school forward.

Entrance: Mainly via nursery and pre-prep; register early, assessment 10 months out. Deliberately take broad-ish ability range, 'deal with what we get', but always consider what is in child's best interests (occasional one helped to move elsewhere). Handful with parents at nearby Defence Academy (nominally for a year or two, but many convert to boarding and stay). Most years full, though movement, especially of day children, and flexibility for additional groups, means places materialise.

Exit: Primarily Marlborough, Cheltenham, St Mary's Calne, Tudor Hall, Downe House, Heathfield, Radley, St Edwards and Dean Close. Occasional early departure from parents who believe school isn't pushy enough, yet they annually win a clutch of scholarships (art, music, academic and all-rounder), to a selection of schools including Marlborough College, Monkton, Oundle, CLC, Shrewsbury, Wells Cathedral, St Edward's Oxford, Dauntsey's, Cokethorpe, Kingswood and Dean Close.

Remarks: Founded in 1875, moved to this pretty Victorian Cotswold stone house in 1946. Nursery and pre-prep in former stable block with fantastic play area in old walled garden.

P

Noughties, and the arrival of the Hoylands, saw shift from a school languishing in the doldrums – 'it really was falling down,' said one parent – to one riding a wave, albeit with choppy interludes. 'There was too much complacency; we had made strides but not leaps', admitted the head. 'Our parents were shocked but it allowed the final clearing of driftwood'. Now vast majority of teachers are head's own appointments; admits he has taken a few risks, going for the fizzy or alternative to encourage excitement and develop a joy of learning. This strategy hasn't been lost on the youngsters; pupils were eager to tell what they had learned, and how: 'Exciting teaching, kind teachers, some a bit mad but the good thing is you remember what they say, it stays with you and they will always help'. We saw super maths model villages (lots of nets and shapes, fashioned into 3D high streets); we even gently teased our charming guides about the designer outlets and Jack Wills stores; they responded with good humour, enthusiasm and grins. We were dragged to the plush changing rooms (complete with under-floor heating) but the boys didn't swallow our tease that we especially loved the girls' sauna and steam room (alas not yet!). They got their own back with tales of 'breaking the ice' in the outdoor pool – not literally, but an annual event that usually sees the head dive in first, followed by a posse of pupils.

Only the caffeine kept us from drifting off as the head recounted the extensive building work but, as we toured, we began to appreciate how fundamental the redevelopment has been to the Pinewood metamorphosis, with library rehoused in renovated Orangery, super performing arts centre etc. Pupils certainly appreciate the changes, possibly nowhere more so than in science where the newish labs have opened a whole world of discovery and experimentation. Indeed, we were hijacked by an endearing chap who insisted on explaining his classification diagram (task carefully differentiated) and cheerfully showed us the errors his partner had made, and how they were putting them right. Refreshingly, this is a school where children are encouraged to make mistakes, take risks, explore their learning and get it right.

French from four, Latin from 10, Greek and philosophy for scholars, enrichment for anyone who will benefit. Classics, French, science and maths top the popularity bill but, unusually (for a prep school), history and geography under kids' radar: 'They lack the zing of other subjects,' was parental response. ICT important for all, even wee ones are encouraged to Google. Usual plaudits for art, groans that DT had been chopped for older years and applause for drama and music (including ensembles, jazz band, a chorus of choirs and inclusive performing opportunities). Daily sport for all ('cept Thursday which is given over to activities); every child has ample opportunity to represent the school. Lots of motivational messages on notice boards and gentle reminders: 'win with honour, lose with dignity.' Thanks to new sports director, PE back with a bounce, carefully thought out, planned and linked to games programme, health etc. A hardy bunch, practise in all weathers; used to lose at everything but no longer the case, indeed they are recent National Junior Cross-Country Riding Champions and in 2011 became mini schools show jumping, cross-country and eventing champions.

Solid learning support and a genuinely multi-sensory approach mean those with mild dyslexia, dyspraxia, ADD (blue-tac et al for fiddlers), high functioning ASD are well served. Access arrangements and laptops if needed. OT, speech and language therapy, play therapy, in-class learning support plus one-to-one or small groups as required (most incur additional fee) but not the place for those with moderate or severe needs who need frequent, or intensive, support.

Quietly Christian (aside of the rousing hymns), emphasises tradition, kindness, fun and adventure. Think greenhouse not hot-house; tender plants (and tough weeds) will be nurtured, watered but not pruned, though delicate darlings might flounder: 'We are about climbing trees and falling out.' Very much preparing children to make choices.

Boarding (from seven) genuinely popular and on the wish list of many; handful of full boarders (fortnightly exeats mean grannies and guardians essential for boarders from far-flung corners). Comfortable, squidgy, homely accommodation and great food, including imaginative vegetarian choices, continental cuisine and school-dinner stalwarts. Squabbles usually sorted over a mug of hot chocolate in Mrs Hoyland's kitchen. Unpleasantness dealt with promptly, no complaints from anywhere on that score; only slight grumble from parents is that communication dwindles as pupils move through the school. Reading room (much loved by youngsters) and old chapel provide quiet spaces, with games room (table tennis, air hockey, snooker) for the active. German spotlight (risk assessed) a unanimously favourite pastime. 'It's so dangerous,' said one wide-eyed youngster, then quickly added, 'well, only kind of', doubtless concerned that we might be among the spoilsports keen to curtail anything remotely daring.

Parents proud that it remains steadfastly a local school; majority live within an hour's drive. True country prep, car park more mud-splattered four-by-fours than flashy Ferraris. Concentrates on extending childhood – the pre-pubescent 'up-do, make-up and manicure' brigade would either roll-up their sleeves and regain their innocence – or, likely as not, hate it. Very much for those happy to don a boiler suit, roll down a hill, climb a tree, play hide and seek or chase through a meadow.

Wellies essential, rain or shine, outdoors as important as in. Annual activities week for each year group the icing on a well-filled cake. Pinewood is one of the country's leading outdoor schools (they even have an award to prove it). It's not just the Astro and sports pitches but the treetops adventure, outdoor classroom, fairy garden, child-friendly woods, super sensory gardens; colours for the youngest, then scented, smelly, touchy feely and finally a polytunnel of polygons, plants, maths and more.

Pre-prep headed by the energetic, triple-hatted director of learning. Suits the worms, germs and stones brigade; aim for children to fall in love with learning (we suspect most tumble head-over-heels). Children encouraged to explore their learning through carefully planned in and outdoor activities. Parents genuinely welcome to spend time with their child at beginning and end of the day; no classroom barriers here. Learning is multi-purpose and multi-sensory, extending well beyond the regular primary diet. Learning of 'oo' in moon includes the baking of tasty moon rock cakes and tracing sounds in sand. Parents appreciative – 'they are really good at getting the basics firmly in place' – though another added, 'Lots end up having learning support which costs extra,' adding cynically, 'You wonder if so many really need it or if it is just prevention better than cure mentality.' School disputes this, saying only 18 per cent of pupils have learning support with fewer than two per cent in pre-prep (equating to to handful of pupils max) – so seems perception is misplaced. Curriculum 'wow' days have seen youngsters take off on a variety of adventures including transatlantic travel: office converted to aircraft, check-in desk, tickets, airline food, sick bags – an experience so real, one boy cried at the thought of flying without mum.

Good at building confidence; suits the London day school refugee, but not a place for the London set, nor for those into clicking heels and clucking 'Yes sir, no sir.' If you could recreate the secret garden you'd probably do it here; active children fizz with enthusiasm, happily maintaining the innocence of a by-gone era but with the benefits of modern technology and teaching. A genuinely wholesome school that emphasises cooperation rather than competitiveness, confidence not arrogance and and team before me. Especially good for the creative boy or girl with boundless energy, sporty or not, and limitless curiosity.

P

Plymouth College Preparatory School

Linked school: Plymouth College

Saint Dunstan's Abbey, The Millfields, Plymouth, PL1 3JL

- Pupils: 245 girls and boys; all day • Ages: 3-11 • C of E
- Fees: £7,080-£9,255 pa • Independent

Tel: 01752 201352
Email: prep@plymouthcollege.com
Website: www.plymouthcollege.com

Headmaster: Since 2007, Mr Christopher Gatherer BA Cert Ed (early fifties), educated at Crosfields School then at Reading Grammar School before reading English at Keele. Taught English at Sherborne then Plymouth College (where he was also a housemaster) before moving across city to become deputy head at Prep. After ten years as deputy his promotion came at the start of a full-blown inspection. Has brought school together successfully under its new roof; still has his own classroom: teaches drama and PSHE. 'You'd struggle to find someone more involved,' said one mother, 'he's the first one in and the last one out.' Partner Jeanette's two children have gone through successfully. Great warmth and energy for a job he clearly loves. 'An amazing headmaster,' we were told, 'he knows every child by their first name.' Enjoys drama, playing five-a-side football and mountain walking in Europe.

Entrance: Parents visit and are given a tour followed by taster day and informal assessment for children. Flexibility over entry dates. Discounts for forces and siblings. Pupils come mainly from within 25 mile radius.

Exit: Majority of pupils proceed seamlessly to Plymouth College. About 30 per cent choose to go to one of Plymouth's three grammar schools.

Remarks: Moved to former St Dunstan's Abbey School site in 2005 after £2 million refit following Prep's second merger in ten years. Across city from College and takes some finding initially at end of gated Millfields development on former Royal Naval Hospital complex. In days gone by wounded and dying sailors were brought up via nearby Stonehouse creek; the boatmen had to be vigilant as the creek was a mud flat at low tide, hence the phrase, 'up the creek without a paddle.' The same cannot be said for the children here. Naval legacy is still much in evidence though in the (former naval) school chapel where we attended an assembly for the whole school... joyous singing and attentive listening.

The unexpectedly spacious site has benefit of better than usual buildings for a small prep school plus a large playing field to the rear. Safe infant play area is at heart of site and includes a buddy corner and pirate ship. Captain's house (for senior swimmers) is adjacent to prep and provides accommodation for latter's (gapper) classroom assistants. Sports hall (used for tennis, basketball, fencing etc), dining-hall and theatre are all to good specification. Conference room (once a bar) was an unexpected bonus and is used for speech and drama; large art room (complete with lots of miniature soldiers: evidence of a keen miniature modelling club) and externally housed food technology centre was another surprise. Ground floor wing of main building dedicated to KG classes with a lovely mix of messy, multi-sensory and general activity areas. Children hop and skip between free play and adult led activities. Sound work precedes phonic approaches to reading and various numeracy strategies. We particularly liked the 'Learning Journey' books maintained for each child: a collaboration between home and school. Open door policy ensures free flow communication between parents and teachers. Easy progression around corner to reception classes which work in parallel. Children get going here with number bonds, phonic games and even spelling tests. We loved the 'What's the time Mr Wolf?' smart board activity and the 'Our Wonderful World' theme which introduced children to a whole variety of animals and included a visit to Paignton zoo.

Years 1-3 are in class bases. Small groups (average 12-14 pupils). Experienced teachers forge ahead with Oxford Reading Tree: 'my son has gone from level 2 to level 6 in under year and he's like another child now,' said one mother. Heinemann maths at core of numeracy work. Lots of creativity and skills built up through fun tasks such a speed sounds. Creative writing encouraged and evidenced in good display work. Specialist IT (pupils give their own powerpoint presentations) and science facilities kick in from year 3 upwards. From year 4, children move to 35 minute or hour long lessons with specialist teachers. Three sets formed for years 5 and 6. Head is developing a year 6 baccalaureate to recognise achievement in school's six skill areas. French (twice) and Spanish (once) weekly for years 5 and 6. No specific coaching for 11+ examination but it is seen as a useful benchmark for all regardless of senior school intentions. Wide curriculum includes DT and religious studies.

Achievement is recognised and rewarded at Friday assemblies to which parents are invited. Sport is particularly strong (when we visited girls were U11 national prep school swimming champions and U11 rugby had enjoyed unbeaten season). PE and games on curriculum; matches against other preps schools played on Wednesday afternoons or sometimes on Saturdays. Games teacher is 'so enthusiastic' reported one parent, 'he even brings jelly babies for the parents.' Strong special needs ensures all children are achieving to maximum level: deputy head acts as SENCo plus another trained dyslexia teacher. 30+ children currently receive support. Music is popular: nearly half the children have peripatetic lessons. Lots of concerts (some in chapel) and drama productions, most for charity. Fleet of minibuses to meet all transport needs. Traditional green, red and black striped blazers (caps and hats for tinies) give smart appearance. Caterers cook on site and provide good daily choice in large dining-room. Houses form basis of competitions (not just sport) and names provide a link with St Dunstan's legacy. Interesting range of lunchtime and after school clubs (from recorders to gardening) and opportunity to do homework after lessons: 'we're not overburdened,' say pupils. After school care is moderately priced and available until 6pm daily.

Regular LAMDA successes with specialist teacher. Forces and medics among parents. Former pupils include comedienne Dawn French, musical theatre star Michael Ball and weatherman Philip Avery. 'Fantastic community,' say parents: informal network ('we even went off camping together for a wet weekend') and more formal through Friends' activities, weekly newsletter etc.

Here is a city prep which doesn't feel urban: gracious, modernised buildings and plenty of open space on this very secure site. Bubbly children keen to do their best. 'Small enough to know everyone but big enough so that children are not overwhelmed when they move to senior school.' In the words of one satisfied father: 'It's a happy school which helps children to become good citizens for the world of tomorrow.'

P

Polam Hall Junior School

Linked school: Polam Hall School

Grange Road, Darlington, DL1 5PA

• Pupils: 90 boys and girls; 1 boarder • Ages: 2-11 • Inter-denom
• Fees: Boarding £18,600; Day £4,800-£9,165 pa • Independent

Tel: 01325 463383
Email: information@polamhall.net
Website: www.polamhall.com

Head of the Junior School: Since January 2014, Mrs Kathryn Bury BA PGCE. English and drama degree followed by PGCE at Hull. Joined junior school in 2003 as literacy, humanities and creative curriculum coordinator and progressed to head.

She is a licentiate of the Guildhall School of Music and Drama (speech and drama teaching and verse speaking) and member of the Society of Teachers of Speech and Drama. A keen theatre goer, she co-directs and produces the school's Christmas production. She enjoys walking and writing and has two children at university (her daughter was a pupil at Polam Hall).

Head of infant department from January 2014 is Mrs Linzi Mawson. She has a BEd in biological science and PE from the University of Derby. Joined in 1995 as year 2 form teacher and creative curriculum coordinator. A fully qualified swimming instructor, she enjoys teaching her two young sons to swim, walking, Pilates, the theatre and cinema.

Entrance: Number of children join Early Steps nursery at 2 and progress through junior school. Entry is by observation during taster visits with parent.

Exit: Traditionally around 90 per cent to senior school; small minority to local state schools.

Remarks: Located in modern two-storey building on edge of campus, convenient to senior school facilities but sufficiently separate to have distinct identity. Bright, well decorated classrooms and corridors. Small classes, one per year group, with female dominance from year 3 onwards. Vertical groupings of older boys for sport to obtain mass needed for team sports.

Early Steps nursery in two airy rooms, also home to rabbit and guinea pig, with direct access to natural outdoor play area (hens expected any day). Children move on to lower then upper foundation, accommodated in two classrooms with a linked quiet room for numeracy and literacy sessions. Introduced to learning French from upper foundation. Pupils confident and friendly, keen to show their work and engage in conversation.

Numeracy, language and literacy are taught daily as discrete subjects up to year 2 but are linked into topic work. From year 3 all subjects are taught linked to topic, which changes each term. On Thursday afternoons years 1 and 2 are grouped vertically to work on creative curriculum challenges; on Friday mornings years 3 - 6. Staff from senior school attend junior school planning meetings to ensure continuity in year 7.

Specialist teaching in French from year 1, PE and music from year 3, science taught in a laboratory. Years 5 and 6 have opportunity of a school trip to Paris every two years. No Latin but German introduced in lunchtime club. Homework introduced in year 3, time allocated growing incrementally to one hour per night in year 6. Mobile use around school of ipads and ipods from Early Steps upwards. PC in each classroom and IT suite where children are taught 'how to access information'.

PIPS baseline assessment in reception through to year 2, when screened for dyslexia. Years 3 - 6 end of topic tests in mathematics and science and termly assessments in reading and writing. Gifted and talented and learning support flagged to teachers. On-line reports each term, parents' evenings in autumn and spring.

Traditional team sports taught from year 3 with competitive matches against local state and independent schools from year 4. Swimming at local Dolphin Centre in spring and summer terms. Ballet, tap and modern dance after school at additional cost. Music taught twice weekly; all children in year 3 have group string lessons to encourage instrumental work. Opportunity for performance with the junior orchestra and choir. Christmas performance - recent productions Oliver! and Chitty Chitty Bang Bang.

Strong house system; from year 3 house points awarded for academic and sporting achievement. House captain role provides year 6 with leadership opportunities and numerous inter-house competitions, from sports to general knowledge. Cedar awards for good conduct with termly trophies; class awards for working together (twenty marbles equals class treat); head's award for exceptional effort or conduct. Celebration assemblies each Friday with head of school, parents invited to Wednesday assembly.

Democracy rules here, with great emphasis on school council. Representatives from reception upwards each prepare a manifesto; Mayor of Darlington acts as returning officer on polling day; first meeting of academic year held in Mayor's Parlour.

Wide range of lunchtime and after school clubs and activities. Usual sport and dance, golf, triathlon, zumba, karate, Brownies and shutterbugs (photography by any other name). Residential outdoor activity weekend in Patterdale for years 5 and 6. Before and after school care, and homework clubs for older children. Pupils can arrive at 8am for breakfast in the dining room and stay up to 7pm in the evening, with tea. Lunch in main school dining room for all, with choice of traditional hot or salad bar, very popular. Summer school for two weeks of the summer holidays.

There is a palpable feeling that learning is fun and the happy atmosphere that exists in the classrooms spills out into purposeful activity in the grounds.

Port Regis Preparatory School

Motcombe Park, Shaftesbury, SP7 9QA

• Pupils: 320 boys and girls; two-thirds boarding • Ages: 3-13
• C of E • Fees: Boarding £23,250-£24,210; Day £8,325-£18,735 pa
• Independent

Tel: 01747 857800
Email: office@portregis.com
Website: www.portregis.com

Headmaster: Since September 2010, Mr Benedict Dunhill BA QTS (forties). Educated at Caldicott and Cranleigh, followed by University College, London (French and English) and Universities of Sussex (QTS) and Roehampton (Certificate of Professional Practice in Boarding). Spent a year teaching in Le Puy as part of his first degree, after which he joined SG Warburg and later an event management company. Started teaching French at Blundell's, where he was also boarding deputy, a member of the marketing committee, student overseas exchange master and sports coach (cricket, hockey, fives and clay pigeon shooting). Has been a keen sportsman since his schooldays (1st X1 cricket and hockey and captain of the Eton fives team). Later moved to Worth School as a French teacher and boarding housemaster and coached all major sports, reorganised school timetable to accommodate IB teaching and served on school chaplaincy committee. He was previously headmaster of Moreton Hall.

P

Since arriving at Port Regis, has set out to moderate über competitive school culture and inculcate a kinder set of values in its pupils, eg generosity and respect. 'These are life skills and help in business,' he told us. Has appointed school chaplain to guide things pastoral and spiritual – parents say 'It's given the school another heart.' Head teaches French, English and life skills. Wife Elizabeth is also fully involved in school life, including events, marketing and on pastoral side. She previously worked for World Challenge. They have three school-aged children.

Entrance: Main entry points are nursery and year 3, but school adds about 10 pupils in years 4 and 5, a dozen in years 5 and 6 and a handful in year 8 (usually foreign nationals). Children come from own pre-prep, local state primaries and other prep schools, including London preps. Entry is via interview with the head, present school reports and assessment (verbal and non-verbal reasoning tests). School accepts those with mild learning difficulties, but children must be able to cope with CE syllabus.

Exit: With such a wide-ranging intake, pupils scatter to more than 30 different schools. Most popular destinations are Sherborne Boys' and Girls' Schools, Bryanston and Marlborough, then Canford, Clayesmore, King's Bruton, Millfield and St Mary's Shaftesbury. A number go to Eton, Cheltenham Ladies', Harrow, Radley, Rugby, Winchester and Wycombe Abbey. Boys and girls regularly win a good clutch of sport and academic awards each year, along with all-rounder, art, design and ICT scholarships and exhibitions. Tally of music awards looks to be rising. Most stay until 13 (a very small number leave at 11) and almost everyone in pre-prep moves up to the main school.

Remarks: Located in 150 acres of sweeping Dorset parkland, it's tempting to reach for more and more superlatives when describing Port Regis. Previous reviews have likened the campus to Disney World and classrooms to Trump Towers in New York (which of course they aren't) but it's still safe to say that this is a magnificently equipped prep school and could easily be mistaken for a good public senior school. Sense of 'other worldliness' perhaps arises from the exceptional architecture (different for each building), well-equipped classrooms, outstanding facilities, central lake (with fountain) and extensive playing fields and grounds. One might almost expect to be whisked away by monorail from the car park! Main school building is a Victorian mansion built in 1894 by Baron Stalbridge (younger brother of the 2nd Marquis of Westminster) surrounded by a collection of modern, purpose-built additions. School was founded in 1881 by Dr Praetorius, a German native, in Weymouth St, London W1 and moved to Motcombe Park in 1947 from previous homes in Folkestone, Broadstairs and Bryanston. Latin for 'Kingsgate', Port Regis was renamed after it moved to premises in Broadstairs (Charles II landed there in 1863).

Although only mildly selective, academic results are good (and getting better, as rising number of A grades at CE indicate). Parents confirm that teachers are enthusiastic and always quick to respond to any queries. 'I couldn't be more impressed with them,' said one. Fabulous school buildings doubtless make teaching and learning more efficient, eg Cunningham Hall (maths, science, art, DT and SEN), which feels especially light and spacious thanks to acres of glass walls. Humanities are housed in an innovatively designed building which self regulates inside temperatures; 12 bore holes descend 80m into the ground to provide geothermal heating and ventilation is controlled via automatic air vents. ICT suites also in this building and in keeping with the 'no expense spared' nature of the place there are virtual noticeboards everywhere, displaying school diary, running house point totals, match results etc. More traditional classrooms for younger years in the mansion, which makes sense as their dorms are here. School library is located in oldest part of the school too, and is rather charming (elaborate Victorian room makes a change from all the modernity elsewhere).

Maths is set from year 4, humanities by subject groups and everyone is streamed for all subjects by year 6. 'The good ones are pushed quite hard and the less good are helped quite hard.' French is taught from the beginning and Latin from year 6; scholars also learn ancient Greek and one CE set studies Spanish instead of French. Tuition in other languages, including Mandarin and Japanese, is available as an extra. Class sizes average 14 (with a maximum of 20) and whilst there are generally more boys than girls, number of girls is healthy. Around 20 teachers have been on t61he staff for more than 10 years, but parents say a host of newer recruits have 'immediately absorbed the energy.' Specialist EAL teacher for small groups of children whose first language is not English (about 25). These pupils are integrated into main school lessons as soon as they are ready. Spacious SEN department is well geared up for those with mild learning difficulties (44 on the register when we visited) but also tutors scholars to iron out any performance difficulties. Parents report progress in post-CE programme.

Well known locally for its sporting prowess, school has on average a dozen teams for all the usual major sports, including boys' hockey. Up to 20 fixtures are arranged each Wednesday and Saturday (memories of searching pitch after pitch one Wednesday trying to find the right rounders match as a visiting school parent). It is rare that any Port Regis team loses more matches than they win and some are undefeated all season (although head breathed a small sigh of relief when 1st XV rugby team's seven-year winning streak finally came to an end as the pressure was off for a bit). Two squash teams (boys), six girls' tennis teams, golf and swimming teams also have busy fixture lists. Gymnastics is exceptionally strong here and school has a dedicated gymnasium with sunken trampoline which hosts national IAPS championships. Boys and girls win gold medals galore and school has won 'Overall Best School' title for more than a decade. Second sports hall, two squash courts, 25m swimming pool, shooting range and nine-hole golf course are all (except older sports hall) as well appointed as the gym. Individuals also compete successfully in athletics and riding. The downside of all this sporting talent is that 'Port Regis is the school everybody wants to beat.' Those not blessed with all-round sporting talents need not worry too much. 'If children aren't good at a particular sport, it isn't frowned on by the rest of the view.'

Farrington music school, a stone and glass octagon with views over school grounds, would be the envy of many a senior school. Fabulous air-conditioned recital hall (those superlatives again) is at the heart of the building, circled by 14 practice rooms. On the floor below there are extra rooms for ensemble coaching and class music lessons, a recording suite and music technology room. Around 75 per cent learn an instrument and over 400 individual lessons are scheduled each week – in A and B forms (years 7 and 8) these take place outside academic lessons. Instrumental lessons rotate for younger pupils and practice sessions are monitored and rewarded (for both simply picking up instrument and also for effective practice). All 8-year-olds learn recorder and all 9-year-olds violin, free of charge. School has three orchestras and multiple choirs, including auditioned junior and senior chamber choirs and boys' close harmony barbershop ensemble. Schola Cantorum has undertaken successful choir tour to Italy and we observed its choirmaster (blessed with seemingly boundless energy and enthusiasm) conducting a very creditable E and F form (year 3 and 4) choir. Ensembles include swing band, samba group, guitar, brass and recorder groups and two string quartets. ABRSM exams passed each term with 75 per cent distinctions and merits. Art, DT and woodwork have equally good space and provision; three rooms for DT, computers for design and huge art studio with some very good work on show. Pottery teacher apologised profusely that most of her pupils' best work was out on display at local gallery when we visited (what was left behind was still good).

Several drama productions each year are staged in Centenary Hall's auditorium, which has tiered seating and a stage. School has links with Shakespeare Birthplace Trust and offers LAMDA coaching. List of over 70 hobbies is of dizzying length (cookery, beekeeping, dance, French movies, quilting and web design to name just a few) and activities happen between early evening 'famine queue' and supper. 'Every evening there's something to look forward to.'

Pastoral care is very much at the forefront these days as head aims to instil five core values in every Port Regian: hospitality, perseverance, reconciliation, generosity and respect (parents say his efforts are working). Children choose their own personal tutor from C form (year 6). School is 'quick to sort any bullying and will listen to parents.'

Boarding provision is excellent, with several different houses for various ages. Senior girls have the most luxurious surroundings with individual 'cubies' (complete with own wash basin), separated with a bead curtain at every 'door.' As usual, girls' cubies are awash with posters and cuddly toys, whilst boys' cubicles (though along the same lines) appear much less pretty. Games room in senior boys' boarding house, complete with pool table and table football, is probably envied by all. Everything spick and span, with dorms marked each week for tidiness (prizes for the winners). 'Beds have to be made and children keep themselves clean and tidy.' We noticed rotas for nit checks and boys' haircuts each week. A and B forms and overseas students have limited use of mobile phones; no 3G Kindles, iPods or iPads allowed. Home clothes are limited and girls not too conscious of what label they're wearing. An army of at least 15 gap students organise weekend activities and man the day room where day pupils wait to be collected, hand in notes from parents or drop in to pick up messages. No flexi boarding, but staged entry to boarding is possible and school caters for individual requirements. School says that 'In practice boarding routine is very flexible.' Most go home on Saturday afternoons after school assembly, lunch (parents welcome to eat in school free of charge) and matches, returning on Sunday evening or Monday morning (often with a friend in tow).

Food is excellent, plentiful and most is locally sourced. Lots of choice as to main meal; salads and vegetarian options are on the menu every day. Cafeteria is wonderfully spacious with panoramic views of those omnipresent grounds again; atmosphere is informal and children can sit where they like, although plenty of staff are dotted around tables. 'Children are encouraged to eat sensibly and they discourage fussy eating.'

Nursery and pre-prep are so delightful that one finds oneself thinking that teaching small children might make a rather agreeable career change. Includes a 'secret door' to enchanting grass area; wonderful rustic Forest School built in nearby woods with campfire and range of wooden instruments made and used by the young children (unaccountable whiff of the Lord of the Flies in all this rough-hewn woodwork).

Perceived wisdom is that Port Regis is the preserve of the very rich, but in reality children come from a wide variety of backgrounds. Some wealthy families, but others choose the school because 'it offered the most on the boarding front.' Means-tested academic and all-rounder awards – worth up to 50 per cent of school fees – are available for exceptional academic promise or ability in two extra-curricular areas (eg drama and sport). Most children are British and live a short hop from the school, some come from London. Around 25 overseas British (including forces) and about the same from Nigeria; approximately 15 are from the Far East and a few from Spain and Russia. School can store luggage in school holidays and organise uniform, name tapes etc. No compulsory exeats (unique for a full boarding school) so overseas pupils can stay in school at weekends. Children are confident, poised and polite. Former pupils include Bo Bruce, Jasper Conran, Ralph Fiennes, Peter Phillips, Zara Phillips, Henry Pyrgos and Bruce Sharman.

As we've said in previous reviews, it's difficult to find fault with Port Regis. Previously we might have singled out an overly competitive and sporty culture, but this looks to be changing. 'The school is trying very hard to make everyone feel included and part of a team.' Parents still feel that 'you have to be good at something [to fit in] here,' but also say 'if anyone is going to bring out what your child is good at, Port Regis will.'

The Portsmouth Grammar Junior School

Linked school: The Portsmouth Grammar School

High Street, Portsmouth, PO1 2LN

• Pupils: 505 boys and girls, all day • Ages: 2½–11 • Christian non-denom • Fees: £8,454–£9,372 pa • Independent

Tel: 023 9236 4219
Email: jsadmissions@pgs.org.uk
Website: www.pgs.org.uk

Head: Since 2010, Mr Peter Hopkinson, previously head of Arnold Junior School in Blackpool. Read communication studies at Sheffield and was previously head of the junior/infant department of Abbey Gate College, Chester. Married with two young children, enjoys walking with his family, reading and playing the guitar and ukulele.

Entrance: At four, children attend a play afternoon to familiarise themselves with the school. During the following week they spend an hour each with the head of the junior school and the head of foundation stage and are assessed, using tests compiled by educational psychologists to identify academic potential. No need to read or write, but does like to see an ability to follow instructions – questions might include, eg, point to the red square, or put the smallest brick on top. The assessment is not much of a hurdle in securing one of the 60 places, but children are occasionally turned away: 'We are trying to decide if the school will suit the child until they are 18'. January entrance tests at seven (20 places) in maths (no calculators), English and verbal reasoning, plus interview. Places may be available in other years too. A wodge of pupils from Glenhurst Pre-prep and elsewhere enter in year 3. Children also enter in years 4, 5 and 6 if space allows.

Exit: 11+ tests in maths, English and VR must be passed in September of year 6 to gain entry to the senior school. Virtually all pass, but the tests must be worked towards and are no rubber stamp. 95 per cent moving up in 2012. The rare child who does not pass heads for 'an independent school with lower expectations'.

Remarks: Nursery tucked round the back of PGS is a magical place, brilliantly led by Lois Johnson. Assertively play-based with a hint of Montessori. Hugely well thought out, based around 'imagination rooms' that focus on numbers, books, building, craft, plus outside play. Like many of the best nurseries we see, maintains its own powerful identity, quite separate from the main school. Slightly more boys than girls. Outdoor play area not its strong point, but they make the most of the sheltered and roomy chunk of al fresco that they have been allotted.

Reception to year 4 lives in hived-off section of main school site – younger brothers and sisters greet their hulking teenage brethren over the wooden play train that separates the communities. Emphasis on spelling, a 'blitz' on joined up lettering and much work on extended writing. Outside, the children enjoy a glorified primary school set up and senior school children wander through the front playground. Extremely nice, sheltered back play area. Years 5-6 in cheery separate building outside main school and over two zebra crossings (home to the entire grammar school once upon a time). No grass but unusually pleasant tarmac. Lunches eaten in main school dining hall.

Three forms of 20 in reception, years 1 and 2. Expands to four forms of up to 24 in years 3 – 6. Sats taken at end of years 2 and 6 so school can monitor achievement. No quarter given on academics – would prefer to drop to three forms rather than take in children who have not met the academic standard. Daily assembly. Smart uniforms, although there appear to be mechanical problems with the fit of the little girls' kilts. French from year 3 upwards. SEN provided from lowest level – just keeping an eye on a straggler – from pupils receiving two sessions of learning support per week, to children with educational psychologist's report, for whom outside help may be brought in.

Many extra-curricular activities including girls' football and ballroom dancing club. All year 3s receive a term's free violin tuition. Year 4s get a term's free tuition on a brass or woodwind instrument and a free week's sailing. Other activities offered for a fee, eg, ballet, judo, karate and Mandarin. Indoor pool used in summer term up to year 4. Older children swim off site. Games twice a week – one morning session, plus a Wednesday afternoon schlep out to the school playing fields at Hilsea – plus PE. Upper juniors have fab food tech, textiles, art and DT rooms. IT suite bang up to date, library inviting. Drama ambitious: each year group from reception to year 6 produces an annual musical. Drama studio very impressive for a junior school. Saturday mornings children from year 3 up can attend optional morning of activities, sport (and some matches). Time never wasted – optional, but popular, residential trips mostly take place in holidays so as not to cut into teaching time; children arrive at school in games kit on Wednesday mornings to avoid the kerfuffle of changing later in the day.

Portsmouth High Junior School

Linked school: Portsmouth High School

36 Kent Road, Southsea, PO5 3ES

- Pupils: 150 girls, all day • Ages: 2-11 • Non-denom
- Fees: £6,663–£8,067 pa • Independent

Tel: 023 9282 4916
Email: admissions@por.gdst.net
Website: www.portsmouthhigh.co.uk

Acting head: Paul Marshallsay BEd

Entrance: Prospective pupils are informally assessed in maths, literacy, English and non-verbal reasoning. There's also an Informal interview with the head.

Exit: Most transfer to the senior school (they have to pass transfer tests in English and maths).

Remarks: Junior school is located in elegant house, five minutes' walk from senior school. Slight feeling of other worldliness, perhaps engendered in part by being a single sex school, with an emphasis on old-fashioned good manners, perhaps because the entrance is so non-institutional – a high ceilinged white entrance hall, full of light, with white frescos dancing around the top of the walls. Brightly coloured seating and papier mâché hens, along with a suggestions box.

One parent told us that she walked through the door and knew it was the right school for her daughter. Girls are articulate and charming, and a real tribute to their school. The head feels that the school's focus on speech and drama helps to develop confidence, and certainly the girls we met, from reception upwards, were keen to share their thoughts about their school. They like an awful lot of things, from fraction Fridays (a chocolate or fruit cake is divided into fractions before consumption) to their favourite teachers. Most of the girls' criticisms concerned lack of space and décor. 'The paintwork in the hall is wearing away', said one. 'It gives it an old sort of feel'.

School buildings are a combination of styles, including the lovely main building, a purpose-built pre-prep and a rather down-at-heel, converted Victorian house with squashed classrooms for years 3 to 6. Girls, parents and school alike would like to gut and redo this building. 'It's a bit crowded and it's difficult to focus when the window rattles sometimes', said one girl. Although the walls were painted in bright colours, displays were rather limited in this part of the school.

Lovely outside space with topiary teddies, mini gardens, allotment, beast areas and a chick house with a webcam so pupils can see the eggs hatch. Also an area known as the Dell (looks like a miniature assault course – it's not all so ladylike).

Girls are encouraged to take care of each other's feelings, and older children are very solicitous of younger pupils. A newcomer told us: 'I don't know why, but I don't fall out so much with my friends (here)'. Everyone we spoke to was happy to be at an all-girls school. Why? Because 'boys are annoying, loud and noisy'.

Girls are very well behaved. Extraordinarily quiet line of nursery pupils were waiting for instruction in their ballet lesson – girls have clearly absorbed the adage that manners maketh (wo)man, and apply it fully. Meanwhile year 6 pupils applied lively energy to their science lesson, responding to the question about 'upthrust' by saying in a delighted chorus – 'that means you can pick up Daddy in a swimming pool'.

An enquiry-led curriculum. Year 2 children returned to school at start of term to find 'an alien called Zapper' had arrived on the classroom ceiling, complete with a letter of introduction saying that the creature only appeared at night. They were encouraged to ask questions – so they wrote to the head of ICT to request a camera to record Zapper's night-time activities. No flies on year 2. In a maths in motion project girls run a virtual Formula 1 car, measuring the angles and length of the track and checking tyre pressure and gradients.

Music is strong, with 90 per cent learning an instrument. Art room packed with papier mâché heads, gauzy fish and skydiving figures. Lots of clubs – 'always something going on,' say parents. Gardening club, football, trampolining, dance, strings and athletics. Year 4 do swimming and there's sailing from year 4 pupils up.

School has a high level of interaction with pupils about its running. School council sessions are chaired by the head girl, with the head as minute taker. All council representatives elected by pupils. Meetings discuss things pupils want to improve, though it seems unlikely they will be getting that zip wire any time soon. Children's models for their ideal school prominently displayed.

Communication with parents, by email, is prompt and efficient. Parents very involved in school and are welcome to attend a celebration assembly every Friday. Girls take turns to perform, which gives parents a snapshot of what they are doing in class.

The senior and junior schools are increasingly close. Parents told us that the junior school is more under the senior umbrella since arrival of current senior head. Most junior girls progress to the senior school. Great care taken in the transition from junior to senior, with taster sessions from year 5, year 6 pupils doing some science lessons at the senior school and teachers travelling between the two sites.

Pupils come from the surrounding area and from as far afield as Chichester and Petersfield. Many get dropped off at school by their parents. They are encouraged to use the drop and go service to ease congestion but ane mother described the parking situation as her 'bugbear'. Children also travel to school by minibus and by ferry from the Isle of Wight and Hayling Island.

The Prebendal School

52–55 West Street, Chichester, PO19 1RP

• Pupils: 195 boys and girls; 48 boarders • Ages: 3–13 • C of E
• Fees: Boarding £16,605–£17,781; Day £6,987–£13,149; Choristers £8,890 pa • Independent

Tel: 01243 772220
Email: secretary.prebendal@btconnect.com
Website: www.prebendalschool.org.uk

Head Master: Since 2005, Mr Tim Cannell, MA BEd (early fifties). Educated at Chigwell School and Davies College, followed by Winchester (formerly known as King Alfred's College). Read theology and has a master's degree in education management. Taught maths and RS in several prep schools – Bialla International School, Papua New Guinea, and Eagle House and Moor Park in the UK – where he was variously day master, housemaster and director of studies. A friendly, approachable man who knows his school, pupils (and probably parents!) very well and has thought carefully about how to achieve the best educational balance for both choristers and other students, he was clearly in the throes of planning the amalgamation of the whole school on one site at the time of our visit. A keen cricketer, he also enjoys playing squash and listening to music. Member of IAPS and CSA; has two grown-up children, one a Cambridge graduate and another still studying there.

Entrance: Parents can register for entry to the nursery at three, but otherwise at any stage; those entering up to year 2 are informally assessed, whilst those in year 3 up may be tested in English, reading and maths. Current school report is required from year 1. Voice trials for chorister places take place in November and February each year, usually for entry the following September, but sometimes sooner. Choir hopefuls are also assessed in verbal reasoning, English and maths to ensure that they can cope with the extra demands of chorister life. Choral scholarships (at least 50 per cent, sometimes more) are awarded by the cathedral chapter and include free piano tuition. Bursaries and academic scholarships (both means-tested) worth up to 50 per cent of school fees are awarded at head's discretion; sibling bursaries offered in increments of five per cent (10 per cent for a third child). Music scholarships (also up to 50 per cent) include free tuition on one instrument. All candidates going into year 7 may apply for two awards in three areas (sport, art, academic) worth up to 15 per cent of day fees.

Exit: Most leave at 13 to a range of senior schools, many with music, academic, all-round, sport and art scholarships. Music scholarships abound here naturally, but there is a healthy scattering of academic awards too and art scholarships are on the up. More than half of year 8 leavers have gained a scholarship since 2006 and the tally is rising. Parents full of praise for head's ability to steer children in the right direction. Portsmouth Grammar School and Lancing College are the most popular destinations but others include Ardingly College, Bedales, Canford, Charterhouse, Harrow, King's Canterbury, Portsmouth

High School, Radley, Seaford College, St Swithun's, Uppingham and Worth School. Few leave at end of year 6.

Remarks: Dating back to the foundation of Chichester Cathedral in the 11th century, when it would have been a 'song school' to educate the choristers, the school is the oldest in Sussex. Re-founded as a grammar school in 1497 by the then Bishop of Chichester, it was attached to the Prebend of Highleigh, hence its name. School now occupies a range of buildings dating from the original 14th century song school to the modern Highleigh building.

Separated from the beautiful edifice that is Chichester Cathedral by a stone wall and an iron gate, there is little physical division between the two buildings and this is reflected in the spiritual ties that link church and school. The cathedral is the venue for major concerts and services, eg Founder's Day, and school assemblies take place in the nave twice a week. Next to the splendour of the cathedral, some parents remark that interior of main school building is 'dated and needs modernising … a bit like a rabbit warren with lots of staircases', but school's expansion into the building next door in 2012 provides more space for classrooms and a more user-friendly layout. The children probably don't mind their surroundings and doubtless learn their way around quickly.

Class work is based on the national curriculum up to year 6, followed by a focus on CE and independent school scholarships in years 7 and 8. Pupils are taught as a class up to year 4 and then by subject specialist teachers from year 5. Average class size is 13, rising to a maximum of 16 (14 in pre-prep). Head has adjusted the academic timetable, increasing lesson length to 45 minutes, 'so less time is wasted between lessons.' We observed sound teaching in year 5 maths (regular revision throughout the year) and a lively French lesson, which is taught from the age of three. CE syllabus in core subjects is completed by the summer of year 7 to allow for scholarship preparation and exam practice. Maths is set in years 7 and 8 to stretch the able. 'Prebendal really gears up for the scholars,' commented one mother, adding that leavers are usually ahead of their peers in year 9. Latin for all from year 5 is taught by a member of the cathedral clergy and set from years 6 to 8; as a result Latin scholars gain a very good grounding. School monitors the gifted and talented as well as the less able. Academic clubs support classwork after school and on Saturday mornings, eg science revision, maths and French at CE and scholarship levels, geography, history and homework clubs. 'Brilliant' learning support teacher coaches around 20 children; others with special needs are supervised by teachers and a learning support assistant.

Good-sized art and DT studio at the top of the building (up the inevitable long flight of stairs) gets plenty of light; artists enter local school competitions (and win) and gain scholarships to senior schools. There is a well-equipped ICT suite and modern science laboratory. Classrooms opening off narrow corridors aren't especially spacious, but are not overcrowded. Assembly hall doubles up as a performance space for drama and music – year 6 were reading poetry to the whole school on the day of our visit. Another large, if rather cold and damp, older room used for orchestra and ensemble rehearsals; head says a new music block is part of the current expansion plans and will house music technology facilities and a small performance space. Modern Highleigh building, home to the nursery plus all of pre-prep, has light, airy, spacious classrooms and a small separate playground. Charming walled garden provides a quiet outdoor area close to the cathedral gate.

As expected, music is at the heart of school life, although it is by no means the sole preserve of the cathedral choristers. 'Music for all' is the school's philosophy and most parents and pupils buy in with enthusiasm (only six were not learning an instrument at the time of our visit). Peripatetic musicians teach some 280 instrumental lessons each week; there are also two orchestras, two concert bands and five choirs in which over 200 children sing. School choir sings evensong in the cathedral once a term. In addition to the big concerts twice each year, there are regular informal concerts, a house singing competition and a week-long music festival. At the two weekly cathedral assemblies, junior and senior pupils take turns to perform solo, one of the school choirs sings the anthem and a pupil from year 8 does the bible reading. A parent commented that she 'cannot put a price on how much the children gain from performing music and reading in the cathedral.' The pre-prep sings the last anthem of term and has its own music coordinator, orchestra, choir and recorder ensembles. Every chorister receives free piano tuition and usually plays a second instrument; many other students also learn more than one. Although some music lessons are fixed, most rotate through the timetable and parents say the system works well and appears to have little impact on academic work (there is an edict not to miss games). One parent said, 'Music exams make all other aspects of life easy, like French aurals,' and results support this. A child doesn't have to be musical to thrive here, however, as 'the school is good enough at other things, like sport and academic work.'

Although head has sacrificed one weekly games session, there are still three afternoons largely devoted to games – soccer, rugby, hockey and netball in the winter terms and cricket, athletics, rounders and tennis in the summer. School has its own outdoor, heated pool for swimming lessons in the summer term. As well as the usual grass pitches and courts, there is an all-weather cricket pitch and all-weather cricket nets; the school also has access to Chichester College Astroturf. Everyone is encouraged to represent the school in sport; the less sporty are rotated through the B teams so that they are able to play a match at least once a term. First hockey, cricket and netball teams regularly do well as does the girls' soccer team. Fencing and gymnastics clubs, plus cross-country running, offer alternatives to main school sports.

School has a friendly feel and children lining up for lunch looked happy (meals are provided by outside caterers and appeared reasonable). Literature states that individual happiness is important, and this was certainly evident during our visit when one young man seemed distressed during a lesson changeover. Whilst we talked to the (hugely enthusiastic) children about their work, head immediately took the time to speak with the teacher. Two heads of pastoral care (years 3 to 5 and years 6 to 8) lead a regular weekly assembly and are responsible for any serious issues. Parents confirm that discipline is fair and that school is 'very good at dealing with energetic young boys; what happens in school, stays in school' commented one. The chorister tutor sees the 18 choristers and probationers every day to sort out any issues, check prep and manage their busy lives.

The cathedral choir is the mainstay of the boarding community as boys remain in school to sing weekend services. They are joined by a small number of weekly and flexi-boarders and occasionally by children attending Wednesday or Friday 'theme nights', eg LAMDA performance evening, Canadian evening – even water fights! All pupils are English speaking; a few of the school's pupils speak other languages (Romanian, Polish, Chinese, Japanese). Many of the local medics choose to send their children here. Main dorm has an unusual vaulted ceiling and comparisons with Hogwarts are irresistible – the likeness ends there, however, as boarder parents speak very highly of the matrons. In practice, the choristers are the only boarders in school after lunchtime on Saturday, although they have the opportunity to go home on most Wednesday and Saturday evenings (chorister parents are welcome for Sunday brunch). One mother felt that lunchtime supervision could be better to ensure that younger children are eating well; there are also no mid-morning snacks provided beyond pre-prep for day children.

Extra-curricular activities take place every day after school and on Saturday mornings (no Saturday school) and are open to all. Activities range from ICT and music theory to rugby, knitting and stamp clubs. Choristers can join Saturday morning clubs after music practice, eg tennis, rugby and cricket. There are also supervised prep and revision sessions and voluntary maths coaching on Saturdays. Day pupils can come in if they wish; some clubs incur a charge (eg fencing) but most are free. School trips have included residential trips to Normandy, France, youth hostelling in North Wales and a week in Rome. Very active PTA raises funds for anything from loos on the sports field to whiteboards and car park resurfacing. 'There is a good social network here if parents want it.'

Actively sought out by local parents for its strong Christian ethos, this is a friendly, 'softer round the edges' place than some cathedral schools. It is agile enough to meet the academic, social and spiritual needs of the whole student body without sacrificing the particular requirements of a small number of choristers. The unification of the entire school on one site can only benefit pupils, improve internal communications and continue to foster a family atmosphere.

Prospect House School

75 Putney Hill, London, SW15 3NT

- Pupils: 240 boys and girls • Ages: 3–11 • Inter-denom
- Fees: £13,995–£14,835 pa • Independent

Tel: 020 8780 0456
Email: info@prospecths.org.uk
Website: www.prospecths.org.uk

Headmistress: Since April 2004, Mrs Dianne Barratt BEd MEd (fifties); vast experience and knowledge of young children, having taught across the spectrum in UK and USA, from large challenging state primaries and specialist schools to selective independent preps. Previously deputy head at Croydon High Junior School and acting deputy head of JAPS. Her specialist subjects are psychology and language and literacy teaching. Her management has transformed a once rather shaky Prospect House into a thriving school with a number of outstanding features. Parents say she is a mine of information and does her best to help if a problem, big or small. Her smiling face and enthusiasm for developing the school and children's potential are appreciated by staff and parents. Married with two grown-up daughters who were educated in London day schools, she enjoys running and holidaying in Turkey.

Entrance: Mainly at 3+ nursery and a few places at 4+ reception, waiting list first come first served, non-selective, sibling policy. Thereafter telephone to inquire about occasional vacancies in older age groups. Some scholarships available for children from state schools from age eight.

Exit: At 11+, some to boarding schools, mostly to London day schools. Mrs Barratt and her staff take considerable time with parents to ensure appropriate secondary school choices; school liaises with a large number of secondary schools each year. Popular choices include King's College Wimbledon, St Paul's Girls', Hampton, Latymer, Godolphin and Latymer, Kingston Grammar, Ibstock Place, Putney High, Surbiton High and Emanuel. Pupils are significantly successful in gaining scholarships at 11+.

Remarks: Highly organised and well planned, achieves great things for its pupils without being pushy. Considering the intake is non-selective, this is impressive. Pupils do well across the curriculum, particularly in core subjects, with around 90 per cent achieving level 5 in year 6. All progress is tracked –

personal development as well as academic; extra support is available for strugglers and streaming for maths and English from year 3. ICT is outstanding, embedded into all subjects, thus adding new dimensions to classroom-based learning. Modern server-based network of Apple Mac equipment, interactive whiteboards throughout, and wireless laptops. First independent school in the country to be awarded an ICT Mark of Excellence by BECTA – has gone on to win best school in the UK for primary ICT. Staff:pupil ratio is very high, as is the number of subject specialist teachers.

Good choice of games on offer, with a 'sport for all' policy leading to some many successful fixtures and tournaments. Large purpose-built hall for dance, drama and gymnastics; all-weather sports pitch and local sports grounds are used for team sports. Musical opportunities are outstanding for a small school – inspiring class music for all taught by a specialist teacher. Traditional methods alongside Suzuki teaching; pupils can choose to play instruments with one of a number of specialist instrumental teachers who visit school. Award-winning choir, several ensembles and school orchestra. Terrific variety of clubs to choose from each term; old favourites – tag rugby and handicrafts – run along with the more unusual archery, wii fit and animation.

SEN is forward thinking – qualified and experienced SENCo with three specialist visiting teachers run a well-resourced learning support department. Good links with local speech and occupational therapists, who visit the school as required. Some support and screening is included in the fees; an additional charge is made for one-to-one sessions.

Pupils' well-being and pastoral care are thought to be outstanding. 'Getting home-school contact right is not always easy – this school really tries,' say parents. Active PTA works with the head to organise social and fund-raising events. Volunteer parents help to run the school's library. Occupies a compact site at the top of Putney Hill which has been cleverly designed and extended to offer just about everything; however no on-site kitchens, so everyone brings a packed lunch. Has just added another building a few minutes' walk away and is now two-form entry.

A thriving school for the 21st century doing a great job, with added bonuses of fantastic ICT provision and excellent senior management.

Purcell School Junior Department

Linked school: The Purcell School

Aldenham Road, Bushey, WD23 2TS

• Non-denom • Fees: Boarding £31,686; Day £24,777 pa
• Independent

Tel: 01923 331100
Email: info@purcell-school.org
Website: www.purcell-school.org

Headmaster: David Thomas MA (Oxon).

Remarks: For details, see senior school.

Putney High Junior School

Linked school: Putney High School

35 Putney Hill, London, SW15 6BH

• Pupils: 320 girls; all day • Ages: 4–11 • Non-denom
• Fees: £12,282 pa • Independent

Tel: 020 8788 6523
Email: putneyhigh@put.gdst.net
Website: www.putneyhigh.gdst.net

Head: Since 2011, Mrs Joanna Wallace BMUS MA PGCE. Previously head of the pre-prep at Shrewsbury High School, another GDST school (she attended one herself). She views Putney as a school about challenge – whether academically, artistically or on the sports field – and creativity. Believes everyone learns best when they are happy and a cross-curricular approach should mean that lessons are great fun. Spends holidays in Scotland, visiting the Edinburgh Festival or climbing munros. Still plays the cello and has performed in chamber music festivals in Germany and Italy.

Entrance: Selective at 4+ and 7+. Expansion (from one to two form entry since our last review) has gone well. School says it's hard to put a finger on a 'Putney girl' – 'there are many different types here, all individuals'; 'My team worked out the other day that between us we have 250 years of experience in selecting four-year-olds – that's got to count for something'. Parents feel that the Putney team knows exactly what it's looking for; almost an X factor, with no priority for siblings. 'I don't know how they get it right, but they do,' says one mother whose youngest was rejected several times and now totally supports the decision. 'It wasn't the right place for her – they saw it before I did.' Assessments, described as 'friendly and informal', last one and a half hours for four-year-olds and twice as long at 7+, where new applicants will complete papers in English, mathematics and non-verbal reasoning. (At 7+ junior classes increase from 22 to 24, thus a minimum of four extra places). Existing pupils do not need to sit this test. Girls come from a wide area of south-west London, but most are local, say a five mile radius.

Exit: Vast majority to linked senior school (qv) where they 'qualify' rather than 'compete' for a place. As the girls are monitored so closely from day one, no horrible surprises for parents when the time comes to move to senior school – year five is the latest you'll hear if your daughter is failing to cut the senior mustard. Small exit elsewhere at 11+, though the school probably does not advertise this. An undoubted expectation to go on to the senior school and although applications elsewhere are not encouraged and other entrance exams are not particularly prepared for odd one to St Paul's, Lady Eleanor Holles, Wycombe Abbey and other top of the pile destinations.

Remarks: A punchy place full of very confident little girls. Fairly structured from the off – classic girls' prep. Teachers are (mainly) highly regarded by parents – 'absolutely fantastic,' says one – and well supported and managed, thus minimising the high staff turnover levels that can plague London schools. High standards throughout for everything from handwriting to gym squads. Handwriting taken terribly seriously here – won 2008 national school's handwriting competition. Everything taught very thoroughly and then tested and retested (though much of it without the girls realising they are being scrutinised).

All girls in years 4 and 5 have their own iPads, and year 6 following suit in 2014. Languages taught by specialist staff from reception upwards. Specialist staff also teach music and PE from reception. Quite unpushy on homework – feels enough is packed in during school day. Class sizes are the (large-ish) GDST norm – 22 at KS1 and 24 at KS2.

A learning support teacher and SEN coordinator. 'Learning support offered as required,' says school. No SEN testing on entry. Extra-curricular activities for the gifted and talented.

Music is great – 90-strong school choir was runner-up in BBC Songs of Praise School Choir of the Year in 2008, 2010 and 2013. Parents delighted to spot their daughters on TV. Huge percentage learn a musical instrument – many learn two – and it's not uncommon for them to have reached grade 6 by year 6. Orchestra of over 50. Lots of performance opportunities; universal praise for first ever junior gala concert in 2009.

Sport majors around netball, tennis (Surrey under-11 champions) and gymnastics (second place in UK national floor and vault competition), with addition of swimming from Year 1. A 'sport for all' policy to encourage everyone to have a go. Overall feel is that sport has improved since our last visit. Girls are kept busy after hours, too, with good selection of clubs, plus rehearsals and games practice, and lots of trips, both day and residential.

Generally life moves along in a happy fashion. Despite its thorough approach to education, it's not stuffy and regimented. The working environment is fresh and smart, with some new building to cope with recent increase in numbers. And what a sensible idea – new classrooms for the littlies have been designed to include loos inside them. Junior school shares small but pretty site with senior school (qv) but has its own playground, one of the nicest we've seen, including a stage and benches, pirate ship, Wendy house, giant chess board and even tables with games board tops – lots to keep them busy at break.

Junior school is divided into two – Garden House is reception to year 2, Lytton House years 3 to 6. Each has a 'secret safe' where the girls can post notes detailing any worries or concerns. Robust house system – great participation in hustings. Parental involvement encouraged and school advertises a very open-door policy, though some complaints that persistence is needed to get past the school secretary. Parents say fees provide value for money – but expect to write cheques for FOPHS, the parents' association. It's something of a social whirl – Putney parents know how to party while whipping up support for the place. Generally parents are a worthy selection of the great and good of south west London.

Overall school comes very well-recommended by parents as a safe choice. Rather a prescriptive place – it's not particularly exciting or off the wall creative – but it does know exactly what it's about and undoubtedly delivers the goods.

Queen Elizabeth Grammar Junior School (Wakefield)

Linked school: Queen Elizabeth Grammar School (Wakefield)

Northgate, Wakefield, WF1 3QY

• Pupils: 255 boys • Ages: 7–11 • Inter-denom • Fees: £7,800–£8,505 pa • Independent

Tel: 01924 373821
Email: admissions@qegsjs.org.uk
Website: www.wgsf.org.uk

Head: Since September 2007, Mrs Louise Gray Cert Ed MA (Leeds).

Remarks: See senior school.

Queen Elizabeth's Grammar Junior School

Linked school: Queen Elizabeth's Grammar School

West Park Road, Blackburn, BB2 6DF

• Pupils: 280 boys and girls • Ages: 3m–11 • Inter-denom on C of E foundations • Fees: £5,967–£7,557 pa • Independent

Tel: 01254 686300
Email: headmaster@qegsblackburn.com
Website: www.qegsblackburn.com

Head: Miss Alison Wharmby BEd (Manchester).

Entrance: Individual assessment into both infant and junior school.

Exit: Virtually all progress from the junior school into the senior school at age 11+.

Remarks: Junior school housed in separate building on main QEGS site (formerly known as Horncliffe) but uses many senior school facilities – dining hall, swimming pool etc. Infant school (formally known as early years department) in adjacent building – Lawn Bank – now caters for children with activity. Headed by Mrs Kym Marshall, department buzzes with activity. French now taught in dedicated languages room by qualified language teacher through to year 6. On-site extended hours provision (7.45am to 6pm), styled Q-Plus, available as an option for working parents. Nursery is located in Brooklands, managed by Mrs Correne Brown.

QEGS will be a free independent school from September 2014. This means the school will become state-funded while remaining free of local authority control.

Queen Elizabeth's Hospital Juniors

Linked school: Queen Elizabeth's Hospital

Berkeley Place, Clifton, Bristol, BS8 1JX

• Pupils: 110 boys • Ages: 7–11 • Non-denominational
• Fees: £7,995 pa • Independent

Tel: 01179 303087
Email: juniors@qehbristol.co.uk
Website: www.qehbristol.co.uk

Headmaster: Since 2009, Mr Martin Morris (early 50s), graduate of Exeter University, plus BA from the Open University. Married with seven children – wife works at QEH Senior School. Taught at Sedbergh School, Cumbria, for 11 years, moved to Reading as houseparent, then head of Catteral Hall School, Giggleswick (co-educational boarding prep). Head of Kingham Hill School (senior co-ed boarding) for eight years. Interests principally revolve around sport (particularly cricket, rugby, hockey and running), walking and gardening. Enjoys cooking and reads avidly. Passionately believes in the importance of viewing education as more than just what happens in the classroom.

Entrance: Normally at 7+ or 9+, unless vacancy occurs in other years. Twenty places available at year 3, 12 in year 5 and eight

Q

in year 6. Tests in English, mathematics, reasoning and reading plus interview.

Exit: All to senior school at 11.

Remarks: Super junior school that opened in September 2007 and filled up immediately: unheard of in our experience – 'only boys' prep in Bristol,' explained one parent who wanted her son to move up to QEH anyway. Pleasing accommodation converted from former boarding houses in adjacent Georgian row owned by QEH. Split level classrooms with formal and practical spaces. Lovely Georgian features retained but sparklingly modern throughout. Reading ethos important – great library to reinforce this and selection of books geared to boys' interests. School aims at broad curriculum with plenty of kinaesthetic activity (eg design and technology). SENCo (shared with senior school) screens boys on entry and offers support for SpLD etc. Boys get to go on frequent visits and expeditions. Bright and airy art room. Lots of games at Failand plus swimming and PE in gym (three sessions a week) to tire them out. Pleasant music room and 10 instruments to choose from for individual music lessons – 75 per cent take-up. Boys love classroom assistants, who also run popular after-school club until 6pm. Given Bristol's traffic problems a major plus for parents is that they can drop and collect boys safely using adjacent NCP car park for free. 'This facility gives us peace of mind,' say grateful parents. Separate PTA formed for junior school.

QEH have come up with a winner. 'Our son arrives and leaves each day with a broad smile on his face,' say impressed parents.

Queen Mary's School

Linked school: Queen Mary's School

Baldersby Park, Topcliffe, Thirsk, North Yorkshire, YO7 3BZ

- Pupils: 105 girls (including 15 boarders). • Ages: 2–11 • C of E
- Fees: Day £6,315–£15,120; Boarding £11,940–£19,950 pa
- Independent

Tel: 01845 575000
Email: m.chapman@queenmarys.org
Website: www.queenmarys.org

Head: Mrs Sandra Lewis-Beckett

Entrance: Non-selective.

Exit: Ninety per cent to senior school.

Remarks: For more information see senior school entry.

The Queen's Church of England Primary School

Cumberland Road, Kew, Richmond Surrey

- Pupils: 420 boys and girls • Ages: 4–11 • C of E • State

Tel: 020 8940 3580
Email: info@queens.richmond.sch.uk
Website: www.queens.richmond.sch.uk

Head: Since 2011, Ms Katie Bentham, previously deputy and acting head at Marshgate Primary School.

Entrance: Regularly over-subscribed (even though a new non-denominational primary school has opened close by). Siblings get first priority, then one or both parents must be a member of one of the three Kew C of E parishes – applications must be accompanied by a reference from the vicar (word on the ground is that the number of siblings per year affects how important the vicar's reference is), then it depends where you live. No nursery on site so children come from a range of local nurseries including Windham, The Studio, Kew Montessori and The Barn. Worth trying for an odd place further up the school, as there is a mobile business community in the area.

Exit: A jaw-dropping more than 50 per cent of pupils regularly go on to independent schools, and not just any old independent. You are talking tip-top academic schools including The Lady Eleanor Holles, Godolphin and Latymer, St Paul's, Surbiton High, Kingston Grammar, Latymer Upper, Notting Hill and Ealing High, Putney High, Hampton and King's Wimbledon. Even more astounding – there are a few academic and art scholarships each year to these schools (no scholarship board, it's not really politically correct in a state school). Equally impressive, each year a handful goes to Tiffin Boys or Girls (top-notch grammar schools in Kingston). Waldegrave Girls Twickenham also attracts five or six each year (but its catchment area regularly changes so it's a risky school to rely on). Christ's C of E School (the most improving state secondary locally) in Richmond is the top choice for the rest.

Remarks: A huge favourite of the well-heeled chattering classes, who want to send their children on to the best senior schools. Yet Queen's feels like a completely normal, happy, friendly, state primary school – it is rather scruffy (though in pretty and spacious grounds), doesn't boast exceptional facilities and is in an international area – 20 different second languages are spoken.

The secret of its appeal (to the many who would be able to pay for primary education if they felt it necessary) is the desire of the whole school community for the children to do well in all areas – academically, in sport, art, computing or socially. Add in the remarkable array of senior schools that the children go on to, and it is no wonder that Queen's is the most talked about school in this area.

The large number of pupils aiming for top notch senior schools does affect the character of the place – one mother described it as her 'free prep school', but this is wide of the mark. There are 30 pupils in most classes and the light homework load differentiates the school from the prep over the road and from any other. In reality, Queen's is a state school where the curriculum is soundly taught by dedicated staff, with lots and lots of parental input – which includes paying for private tuition to get the children into those sought-after senior schools.

The last head insisted that pupils do not all get extra coaching for entrance exams – doubtless true for the exceptionally bright but, in one year 5, parental chit-chat reckons 80 per cent received private tuition. Much praise also for the school staff – despite the class sizes, 'all children seem to get at least some individual attention,' said one mum. 'The staff stay a nice long time,' remarked another. 'Of course you get occasional less good teachers,' but most parents are so happy that they even want to join the ranks.

Last head introduced a 'thinking skills programme'. 'I've no idea what it means in practice,' said a parent and a pupil looked blank when asked about it. However, 'there's always been plenty of support for special needs,' said a mum. If your child is more middle of the road, they could risk getting a bit lost in an ocean of clever middle-class pupils – 'there hasn't been much special help for my son – he just survives,' was one slight moan – perhaps somewhat harsh.

Music is a strength – how many primary schools can boast two orchestras? Sport is played competitively and with some success. Everyone in the school – staff, children and various parent helpers – are cheerful and busy, with loads of work on display, an enormous world map in the hall, dotted with multi-coloured pins showing the countries of origin of its pupils. Consensus with the parents and the children is much prized – an enthusiastic school council, discussing matters such as how to deal with bullying resulted in friendship benches in the playground. Discipline doesn't appear to need discussion – there is a foregone conclusion that it is good.

Not a school for parents who just want to sit back and let the school take the strain of educating their little dears. 'There are always loads of parents at curriculum evenings,' one mother said. In addition to the two orchestras, there are recorder groups, a choir, drama, song and dance, touch-typing, netball, football, basketball, cricket and rugby all going on before and after school, with many parents helping in the classrooms or with outdoor activities during the day. Weekly newsletter to parents is full of information. The website is one of the best we have seen.

Queen's College Junior School

Linked school: Queen's College (Taunton)

Trull Rd, Taunton, TA1 4QP

• Pupils: 205 girls and boys; 15 boarders • Ages: 3–11 • Methodist foundation • Fees: Day £5,490–£11,130; Boarding £11,790–£17,820 pa • Independent

---

Tel: 01823 272990
Email: junior.sec@queenscollege.org.uk
Website: www.queenscollege.org.uk

Headmistress: Since September 2010, Tracey Khodabandehloo, educated in Wellington, Somerset, trained at Goldsmith's, London University. Started her teaching career in London, then completed her master's in Bristol whilst teaching in the city centre. Head of two well-respected Somerset schools and has also raised a family of three, two of whom were educated at Queen's. Hobbies include horse riding and travel. Passion for providing an interesting, challenging and motivating primary curriculum which focuses on the whole child.

Entrance: Many children come from the delightful pre-prep, a hop, skip and jump across the field. Others come via a day's visit for mutual assessment and a friendly test in maths and English. They are assessed again in year 5, to make sure they are on track for the senior school and to give them that extra confidence.

Exit: More than 90 per cent make the easy stroll across the grounds to the college to continue the great Queen's adventure.

Remarks: Much lively teaching across the board with involvement from the pupils and much interaction. This is where achievement as opposed to attainment come in. It's rare to find philosophy timetabled into a prep school, but here 9, 10 and 11 year olds have one session a week. Cynics may scoff, but the lesson we saw was wonderful – children were sitting around in a circle discussing whether the apple that was in the middle was alive or dead. Sounds cranky? It wasn't: what it did elicit was enquiry, evaluation, questioning what seems obvious (even pointless), which leads, in turn, to a healthy challenging of convention – wonderful assets in a carefully packaged, health and safety, risk-free society. It's around such emotional intelligence that the academic life of the school is run.

Nor are more conventional subjects ignored. The usual subjects are there, taught in bright and airy classrooms, but every class we saw was enlivened by the spirit of enquiry. Good learning support, where children have 40 minutes a week for

help in essay planning, study skills and organising their time. Described as 'excellent' by one parent we spoke to; interesting sculpture and painting in the art-rooms; good ICT and creative DT. A real feeling of buzz around the place.

The boarding house has just been completely redecorated. Currently three boys' dorms and two girls': space for 28 with a dedicated couple looking after them, assisted by matron and a resident tutor. Sleepovers are available and increasingly popular. Bags to do in the evenings and boarders may go home at the weekend. On the other hand, weekends are fun: not only is the vast range of the college's facilities available but also frequent expeditions. 'It's brilliant fun,' said one boy, 'and breakfast is later on those days.' (No Saturday school.) Plentiful sport and hobbies: 'They're never bored,' said a delighted mum.

It's good to note the mutual respect and affection between the two halves. Boys and girls in the senior school recall with great fondness the days at their junior school and recognise from where their subsequent happiness stems – it's an essential step to another good school. Scholarships and bursaries are available for talented children in a wide variety of skills. Parents with more than one child in the college may well be assisted – don't be afraid to ask.

Over all, a lovely school where individuality really does seem to be encouraged and happiness abounds. 'One college, four schools' is the advertising slogan for Queen's, and the junior school represents the important foundation for the overall package.

Queen's College Prep School

Linked school: Queen's College London

---

61 Portland Place, London, W1B 1QP

• Pupils: 200 girls; all day • Ages: 4–11 • C of E • Fees: £13,560–£14,655 pa • Independent

---

Tel: 020 7291 0660
Email: info@qcps.org.uk
Website: www.qcps.org.uk

Headmistress: Since 2008, Mrs Annie Dempsey BA Cert Ed (fifties). Gentle, softly spoken, smartly dressed, imaginative and passionate about her school. English specialist who graduated from UCL. Married with two grown-up daughters, both educated at London day schools. Wide experience at both preparatory and secondary levels, having taught at Blackheath High School, been deputy head of Blackheath Nursery and Prep School and, for five years, head of St Dunstan's College Junior School, which she took from 'good' to 'outstanding'.

Full of praise for her predecessor, who founded QCPS in 2002 and 'created a wonderful school. I am now building on her achievement'. Feels particularly lucky to be in such a perfect position where, 'building on strength, I can embrace the past and incorporate all the great developments of the 21st century'. Doesn't teach, but has a weekly discussion session with form 6 and reads stories to each form 3 class, watching and listening. Joins the younger classes when she can, and sees forms 4 and 5 unofficially. Believes it is important to know every girl and all parents personally. To that aim, she is in the entrance hall every morning to greet them individually and to maintain visibility. Feels it is important that parents should be given clear lines of communication so that they can talk to the right person to deal with their questions or concerns. Has improved leadership by creating a larger, more effective team of leaders and managers, who also monitor and discuss each girl's progress regularly.

Entrance: Non-selective at reception stage, September after fourth birthday. All parents interviewed by the head before

Q

place offered. Entry to all other year groups involves assessment of child's academic achievement and potential, an evaluation of her social skills and a report from her previous school. No-one is offered a place until the head has met her parents.

Exit: About two-thirds to the senior school (no shortcuts here – they have to pass the same entrance exam as every one else). The rest mainly to London girls' day schools – both Francis Hollands, City of London Girls', South Hampstead High School, Godolphin and Latymer, St Paul's Girls', North London Collegiate and more. Occasionally one or two to board at schools like Cheltenham Ladies' College and Downe House.

Remarks: A small, traditional school producing well-mannered, enthusiastic, happy girls fully aware of the value of a good education and the importance of being nice to each other. Head says, 'Not a school for princesses – they have to be able to relate to everybody.'

Well situated, just a short walk from Regent's Park, housed in two tall Adam buildings, where much use has been made of the elegance of the architecture. The result: a lovely light school with good-sized bright classrooms and a warm, homely feel. Lots of stairs, but the littlest girls are in the largest rooms on the ground floor, which works well. A parent said, 'The girls really appreciate the beauty of the building and treat it with respect'. Good to hear. Good-sized carpeted hall on first floor. C of E – whole school gathers for assembly every day, some of these taken by the head. 'Her assemblies are brilliant,' said a teacher. Hall also used for films, plays, fencing and other activities. Basement recently redeveloped to include an excellent music/ drama room, a gymnasium, a common-room for the oldest girls, where they can loll around on bean bags, chat and listen to CDs, and an extended dining area. 'Lunches are no longer a bone of contention,' said a parent. 'The food is much improved and a weekly menu comes home every Friday so we can see what they are being offered.'

Broad curriculum including French from reception and Latin from year 5. Excellent preparation for 11+ CE, North London Day School Consortium and other senior school entrance exams by specialist maths and English teams. Small classes – average 16 maximum 20 – alongside good mix of experienced and recently qualified teachers, all of whom are enthusiastic and appear to have good relationships with the girls. Head feels it is really important that children should want to learn and be able to respond to challenges. Those that we saw and spoke to certainly seemed eager enough, happy, intent on their lessons and keen to explain what they were doing. A parent said, 'They are encouraged to work hard academically'.

Deputy and assistant heads are male. Teaching assistants in all pre-prep level classes. Specialised teachers from then on, so more movement around the school. Setting in maths and, where appropriate, English from form 3. Interactive white boards in every class and, as a parent said and we agree, 'fantastic ICT suite'. Big bright science lab and lovely light art studio on top floor with a great view of the roofs behind. Head of art says it is her dream job.

Good music. About 90 per cent learn an individual instrument – 'They encourage girls to make the most of every opportunity. Ours learn guitar and violin'. Up to grade 4 or 5, but school says, 'The emphasis is always on enjoyment rather than exam results'. Weekly sessions for string groups and orchestra. Choir and bands also take part in external events as well as school performances. Does sound fun. Drama for all, plus ballet for the younger children and modern dance for the older ones all part of the curriculum. Lots of trips and expeditions – head says, 'We definitely make the most of wider London'.

No outdoor play area so head has adjusted timetable to give more active time in the garden opposite each day for the younger children. 'But don't the residents mind?' we queried. 'Oh no – our girls are so well behaved they are perfectly happy.'

Older girls also have active time each day, whether it's PE, dance, fencing or just a walk. Use local sports venues and Regent's Park for team games and swimming and play competitively internally and against other schools.

Comprehensive pastoral care policy. Simplified code of conduct on the wall of every classroom. Believe in positive not negative attitudes and the need to 'help children get out of a hole when they make mistakes and misbehave'. Full-time teaching SENCo very impressed with observations system put in by the head. All teacher concerns go onto SEN file, and if specific learning difficulties are suspected she discusses with deputy head (who is in charge of maths, and teaching and learning across the school) and with parents. She says, 'small classes make monitoring easy. This is a school where we all talk to each other and individual tasks and monitoring are possible.' Works closely with outside agencies including the nearby Dyslexia Teaching Centre and teachers come in to provide sessions with girls.

Parents say, 'A fantastic school producing lovely, happy, confident girls'. 'Excellent pastoral care.' 'Brilliant head has provided much more structure.' 'As a girls' school – perfect'.

Queen's Gate Junior School

Linked school: Queen's Gate School

125–126 Queen's Gate, London, SW7 5LE

• Pupils: 150 girls; all day • Ages: 4–11 • Non-denom
• Fees: £14,100 pa • Independent

Tel: 020 7761 0303
Email: registrar@queensgate.org.uk
Website: www.queensgate.org.uk

Headmistress: Mrs Nicola Greenwood

Entrance: Massively oversubscribed so names need to go down as early as possible. Family connections count for a lot (preference given to grand-daughters/daughters/sisters/nieces of OGs). Head sees everyone (approximately 120 applicants for 23 places). They visit, a year in advance, about 10 to 12 at a time, with eight staff on duty for organised 'playtime' and story time. Social skills are important – they are looking for children who sparkle but won't overlook the shy ones, 'This is a school for individuals'. It's absolutely no use little Annie boning up on her reading practice.

Exit: Massive exodus to senior school as academics grow stronger and people see the merit in keeping their daughters in a secure happy environment which can't always be found in larger establishments. School keen to point out that it doesn't push the senior school – it sells itself. Otherwise to other London day schools – St Paul's, Godolphin and Latymer, or to boarding schools (Cheltenham Ladies' College and Bedales). Recently some have turned down places, school tells us, in order to stay on at Queen's Gate.

Remarks: In 2007 the junior school moved a few doors away to magnificent new facilities at 125/126 Queen's Gate. Spacious, bright classrooms, impressive hall with original features meticulously restored and only the finest fittings. It's not just tasteful either, facilities are first class – sparkling specialist science laboratories, art and ICT. Much needed new library nearing completion.

One class entry, about 20 per form. Dual teaching in the classroom, with every child, and not just those who need remedial help, getting individual attention, so no-one feels too special. Differentiated teaching using support teachers

Q

and assistants copes with children who do have special needs, though specialist SEN teachers on hand should your child need one-to-one help either in or out of class. Gifted and talented are catered for in the lunchtime clubs, many of which are academic (philosophy, art history, science and two maths clubs, as well as needlework, chess and table tennis amongst others).

Sparky teaching, computers and laptops everywhere, touch-typing at eight, French from four, Latin from age nine. Italian, German and Spanish introduced. Much use is made of nearby museums and galleries – 'The girls must realise there is a classroom beyond the school'. The younger girls eat their cooked lunch in the splendidly restored hall; from eight years all girls eat in the senior school, where they can also eat a packed lunch if they wish. This is where they go to do gymnastics, but good use is made of Hyde Park and Battersea Park too (girls no longer walk but are bused there – 'much safer'). A tiny bit of outdoor space in the courtyard. Music strong – two formal concerts a year as well as a number of informal ones; school takes part in Music for Youth Festival – finalists for two years running. Drama important and very popular – HMS Pinafore recently performed in Baden Powell House across the road.

Bright eyed, pretty girls all neat in navy blue Harris tweed coats, on their way into school, with knitted wool hats; blazers and boaters in summer. Their own dresses underneath, you understand – too much uniformity goes against the important principle here that everyone is an individual and should be treated as such. Good pastoral care, PSHE starts early, with circle time, and popular bonding weeks in Dorset, the Isle of Wight and York from the age of eight.

Strong PTA and parental links – many mums and grandmums are OGs. Day officially 8.30am-3.45pm (3pm and noon on Fridays for tinies), but late waiting until 4 or 4.30 is OK in a crisis. Collection time a real bore for passing traffic, double parking all over the shop. Recent acquisition of a school bus apparently eases the problem a little. Notable old girls include HRH the Duchess of Cornwall, Lady Gabriella Windsor, Nigella Lawson and Lucinda Lambton. Super, not so little, cosy and popular girls' prep school, where all the girls feel cherished and do surprisingly ('There's nothing surprising about it,' says head) well.

The Queen's Lower School

Linked school: The Queen's School

55 Liverpool Road, Chester, CH2 1AW

- Pupils: 224 girls; all day • Ages: 4–11 • Non-denom
- Fees: £7,875–£7,995 pa • Independent

Tel: 01244 382843
Email: secretary@queens.cheshire.sch.uk
Website: www.queens.cheshire.sch.uk

Head: Since 2005, Mrs Felicity Taylor BA (fifties). She attended Durham University, where she rowed for her college and achieved elite oarswoman status. Formerly head of pre-prep at The Grange Junior School in Northwich. Having previously worked in co-ed schools, she sees great benefits to single sex schooling. 'Girls can really be themselves,' she says. 'They can be robust and boisterous or thoughtful and cerebral, with no boys dominating the playground.'

Head has worked very hard to make changes that have seen The Queen's Lower School turn from what one father described as 'a flagging school' to one that has been listed in one survey as the top prep school in the north west. Married with two grown up children. Active and energetic , she is a keen golfer and walker. Has introduced residential trips and Bushcraft to

the school. 'Our girls need to be fit not just for today but for tomorrow's world,' she told us.

Retiring in July 2014.

Entrance: By informal assessment for entry into reception and formal assessment in English, maths and verbal reasoning for later entry. Head or her deputy visit all prospective reception class parents at home and the school has links with nurseries within a 40 mile radius to raise awareness of the school.

Exit: No stressful exams for these girls at 11 as they are virtually guaranteed a place at the senior school (any problems flagged up in year 5). A few leave to enter the state grammar school system. Transition is made as seamless as possible by getting the girls used to moving around for lessons, subject specialist teachers and mirroring senior school routines.

Remarks: School is housed in two Victorian buildings with modern extensions. Large grounds enable the school to boast fantastic facilities, including a swimming pool (shared with senior girls), sports fields, netball court, science, art and cookery rooms. Our guides were extremely excited to show us the pet chickens they had incubated themselves. One mum told us: 'My daughter's experience is so broad here, but in a real practical sense. They do everything.'

Two form entry throughout, with 22 per class in infants, rising to 24 in juniors. Gentle, fluid setting from year 3 in maths and English, then more formal setting from year 5. Spanish is taught throughout the school, with French in year 6. Curriculum is thematic in infants, with outdoor space used as much as possible. Specialist teachers for languages, music, PE, art, drama, ICT and ceramics. SEN children given help by three members of staff but head says they need to be 'bright children who can keep the pace.' Lots of extra curricular activities to get involved with, including young journalists' club, St John Ambulance Badgers (programme for five to ten-year-olds), skipping and fencing.

The school provides good preparation for the move up to the senior school and is a way of getting your daughter into The Queen's system while avoiding the pressure of entrance exams later on.

Ravenscourt Park Preparatory School

16 Ravenscourt Avenue, London, W6 0SL

- Pupils: 420 girls and boys • Ages: 4–11 • Non-denominational
- Fees: £14,430 pa • Independent

Tel: 020 8846 9153
Email: secretary@rpps.co.uk
Website: www.rpps.co.uk

Headmistress: Since 2013, Mrs Kate O'shaughnessy BA QTS (thirties). Educated at Penistone Grammar School, Barnsley College and Trinity and All Saints University in Leeds. Started teaching career at Stag Lane First School, Collindale, then moved to Reddiford School, Pinner as specialist English teacher. Joined Ravenscourt Park in 2005 as senior leader and head of teaching and learning. Progressed to head of upper school and then deputy head, a post she held for three years.

English is her passion and she enjoys 'the results of stimulating my pupils' imaginations and creativity and seeing this manifested in the quality and standard of their writing.' Her husband is site manager of a senior school and they have a young son. In her spare time she enjoys reading, going to the theatre, skiing and walking.

Entrance: Non selective, the September after a child's fourth birthday. It is vital to register a child on his/her first birthday. Can't be registered before. After that it is a lottery. Siblings get priority, then names are drawn randomly and places allotted strictly to ascertain an equal number of boys and girls.

Exit: Traditionally, to London day schools but, with changing local demographics, some parents now looking to send their children to top boarding schools. Therefore some boys are leaving early, although, as one parent said, 'this is not a light decision'. So, occasionally boys at end of year 5 to country prep schools or London day schools that go through to year 8 (Fulham Prep, Kings House).

In 2013 girls headed to a wide variety of schools, including Godolphin & Latymer, Francis Holland, Clarence Gate, Notting Hill and Ealing High School, Putney High, Lady Eleanor Holles and St Paul's Girls'. Boys' choices included Hampton, Westminster Under, Colet Court, City of London Boys' and University College School. Some to co-eds like Kew House and Latymer.

Remarks: Parents said before we visited: 'Not a hot house', 'kind and nurturing', 'safe environment', and 'excellent communication'. We found no reason to argue with these comments. Teachers and children buzzed with enthusiasm, the atmosphere felt relaxed although each time we walked into a classroom work stopped, the children leapt to their feet, chimed 'good morning' and stood there until we left. This, apparently always happens and, we felt, emphasised the edge of formality at the school. However, everywhere we went we were made to feel more than welcome. Parents also feel 'there really is an open door policy'.

Founded in 1991 by Maria and Ted Gardener, former teachers, this school has grown and gone from strength to strength. Its most recent building, opened in September 2011, has enabled it to move from two form entry to three, gradually adding 20 more children to each year. No problem filling the spaces. There is some feeling that it would, perhaps, have been better to have added two more years, thus solving the problem of boys leaving early. (They say this is not a problem!) But as rumour has it that the owners, London Preparatory Schools Ltd, will soon be opening a secondary level school not too far away, maybe there was a different agenda. Some parents feel perhaps too much emphasis on the business side, 'definitely an eye for profit above all'. For instance: 'Why do we have to pay extra for lunch, when it is compulsory and our children are not allowed to bring a packed version?'

Fantastic facilities. The new building has enabled the top three years to move into nine bright new classrooms, colour coded per floor. 'We chose our own colours,' said our two of our guides proudly. And, 'look we've even got a lift but we can't use it without permission!' Splendid new science lab with all the latest equipment; a light bright art room displaying a friendship bench, 'to sit on when you feel lonely', being painted by the art club and, very exciting, including a kiln; a music room where children were reading notes displayed on an interactive white board – of course these abound; an ICT lab with a laptop per child, 'we're making our own websites'. Perhaps best of all, as far as our guides were concerned, was the new school hall/theatre: 'the choir sings from the balcony', 'we can learn to operate the light and sound'. All very impressive.

A tad more cosy, the rest of the school is housed in two buildings, with a separate good sized dining block. All food cooked on site and children served at their tables by catering staff. Most meals are hot, always healthy and compulsory unless a child has a dietary problem. As we walked across the large, mainly tarmacced playground, our guides pointed out equipment for active play (including balls galore) and soft area for the younger ones to climb, slide and play safely. We were later informed that there is an imminently scheduled building project to update the whole playground. Our younger guides

proudly showed their fully equipped classrooms, interactive whiteboards and all. Children's work, art and otherwise, on display all over. All pupils appeared happy and relaxed, quick to say hello and answer questions. Unmissable code of conduct pinned up all over. Our guides were quick to explain the provenance of the many badges they were wearing. As one parent said, 'Lots of smiley teachers, lots of smiley children, such a happy school!'

A reasonably varied curriculum, at least for the first five years. The importance of 11+ kicks in during the summer term in year 5 and children are given lots of homework for the holidays. From then on English and mathematics dominate until all entrance exams are over; afterwards lessons become theme based and more adventurous and relaxed children take part in a whole range of different activities, home and away. Recently, year 6s wrote traditional stories which they then read to the reception classes. The change of pace must work well because the majority of pupils get into their first choice of secondary school, parents having been well advised by the head, of course.

All pupils in years 1 and 3 screened for literacy and specific areas of difficulty. Parents informed of any problems and help given where necessary. Small group lessons focussing on literacy and motor skills, if needed, once or twice a week for half an hour. One-to-one help also provided occasionally, if absolutely necessary. 'No extra ever charged for special needs support'. Say they wouldn't normally decline a place to a child with pre-identified minor learning difficulties. A special needs room in each building. Teachers always available to talk to parents.

Extra curricular regarded as important and many different after school clubs, sporty, arty, intellectual, musical. The range changes from term to term. Several orchestras and choirs, individual lessons offered on a wide variety of instruments. Recently a year 3 boy scored one of the highest marks in the country for his piano exam. A full programme of outings, cultural and academic, plus some residential trips for older children. All the usual charity fund raisers, luckily some parents take these very seriously and are happy to organise. They have already built one school in Burma and currently a major project is to raise sufficient funds to build another

Reay Primary School

Hackford Road, London, SW9 0EN

- Pupils: 270 • Ages: 3-11 • Non-denominational • State

Tel: 020 7735 2978
Email: admin@reay.lambeth.sch.uk
Website: www.reay.lambeth.sch.uk

Headteacher: Since 2013, Sarah Botchy.

Entrance: 3+ to the nursery, 4+ reception class, thereafter occasional vacancies only. Standard Lambeth admission policy – pupils with special requirements, siblings, then distance from the school.

Exit: 11+ pupils are successful in gaining places to the independent and maintained sector. Most choose to go on to Wandsworth and Lambeth secondary schools.

Remarks: A welcoming and friendly primary school which caters for a wide range of abilities and provides an outstanding quality of education to all. Higher than average numbers of the staff have advanced skills teacher status; quality marks for both literacy and numeracy. Everyone, from the nursery upwards,

R

learns French. An annual trip to Paris for eight to nine year olds. Artsmark Gold – has its own art and dance studios; children are offered excellent choice of artistic and dramatic activities – several teachers have art degrees. An enterprising barter system is run with artists, dance and drama groups exchanging use of the studios for workshops and teaching services. All age groups are taught music by a specialist part-time teacher and children can have individual lessons on the flute, violin or brass instruments.

School is dedicated to developing a really good awareness among pupils about environmental issues and has been awarded, for the second time, the green flag for eco-friendly schools. Sport is popular: own Astroturf for football and netball matches, pupils keen to compete in local tournaments and mini leagues. A good playground area and small garden with a frog pond. Governors and parents give much support to the school and also organise fund-raising events and charity collections. Reay aims to look after the whole child and has its own learning mentor and school counselling service.

Do not be put off by first appearances. The exterior of the school is somewhat austere, particularly in comparison with the imaginative and well-run interior. Reay is a little gem in the heart of Stockwell.

The Red Maids' Junior School

Grange Court Road, Westbury-on-Trym, Bristol, BS9 4DP

• Pupils: 120 day girls; • Ages: 7–11; • Non-denom; • Fees: £7,950 pa; • Independent

Tel: 01179 629451
Email: juniors@redmaids.bristol.sch.uk
Website: www.redmaids.co.uk

Head: Since 1986, Mrs Gillian Rowcliffe BEd (late fifties), educated at High Wycombe High School and then at Bristol University. She has been with the school since its foundation but has certainly not let the grass grow under her feet. She is much loved by parents, who see her as, 'a little old school', but a wonderful role model and inspiration for the girls and staff. She teaches every girl and runs a weekly 'school time' for the whole school, in which she sets the tone of considerate behaviour and wholehearted enjoyment which the girls share. School fits her like a glove. She has taken it from a pretty 'arts and crafts' house to a thriving modern purpose-built school with spacious facilities cunningly fitted around the second, less pretty, house next door. The fact that the library is just inside the front door of the school and right at its heart typifies her approach to education. It's still 'a home from home,' say parents, who praise its friendly atmosphere and tirelessly accessible staff. Enlarging the school in 2008 opened up a new world of contact with the local community; she has a dedicated group of parents who feel privileged to have children there and gets a nearly total response to social and fund-raising events. She is proud that the school is beginning to have a reputation in its own right, not just as feeder for the senior school. A governor of 'brother school' QEH (qv), she helped to set up their junior department. An ex-scuba-diver, married to Neil, with two sons who went to QEH, any spare energy now goes into learning the saxophone which she does alongside her pupils.

Entrance: Twenty places in year 3 and 20 more in year 5, when the school splits into two classes. The head selects year 3 pupils by one-to-one assessment and year 5s do a small group assessment. Girls come from a wide range of local state and independent schools. Recruitment relies on word of mouth and assessment occurs from December each year. Some parents wish they could start girls at year 1 but Mrs Rowcliffe suggests that might mean so long in one place that the senior sixth form might suffer – and it's too good to risk!

Exit: Most to senior school. Normally automatic entry (including scholarships via entrance examination) except where head indicates child will not cope. This would be flagged by the start of year 6 and parents given advice about alternatives. Parents of averagely bright girls can be pretty certain they will get in but shouldn't take it for granted. A tiny trickle go to state education or scholarships to other Bristol independent schools, not seriously increased by hard times financially or the current advent of academies and free schools in Bristol.

Remarks: Wonderfully welcoming, homely feel despite impressive facilities. A wet indoor break time buzzed with happy children using every inch of the school for play. Girls are lively and friendly, neatly dressed in red kilts and jerseys with white blouses in winter. Summer uniform is red and white striped dresses with sailor collars and red cardigans.

The curriculum allows for some 'proper' subjects. 'Girls get on with learning rather than spending all their time getting ready to learn as in state schools' (a parent) 'Homework is about consolidating what's been done not just endless projects' (another parent). Good academic standards with written work on display but plenty of IT, art (smashing little art room staffed from senior school and an after-school club) PE, weekly swimming, with every facility except a pool on hand. Idiosyncratically, there is Mandarin Chinese for all taught by a native speaker – including learning to write Chinese characters – but no French. Entrants are screened for dyslexia and given specialist support on site where necessary.

On same campus as senior school, and using their dining room and sports areas but still having their own grassy play areas. A Wendy house and play castle, 'both with proper upstairs floors', were donated by parents, as were the raised beds in the 'allotment' with lovely pumpkins ready for Halloween, and professional looking lighting in the new hall. Everything is pristinely well-maintained but there's no restriction on putting a nail in the wall to hold up a circus tent or covering classroom with brightly coloured work. Some classrooms have their own cloakrooms and loos, with décor of swimming fishes imaginatively designed by the class, and some share between two. The drama room is full of Shakespeare – literally a life-size collage figure – and girls get to know his plots early as well as winning drama awards themselves. The music room bursts with keyboards and other instruments including the various parts of a gamelan. Lots of singing and masses of music generally, with orchestra, brass band and choir. Computer technology etc taken for granted.

Wide choice of clubs and activities. Robotics with Lego is popular, as is fencing and caving. You only pay extra for things done by outside organisations, and even the residential week at Skern Lodge outdoor education centre is included in the fees, as is after-school supervision – though breakfast club has to be paid for. Loads of visits including a ski trip with QEH boys.

Parents feel this a friendly, nurturing place able to draw out the best from the most reticent child and harness the most ebullient. Difficulties such as unkindness happen but they are not allowed to grow into problems. Their greatest fear is that success in games may mean that the A team get all the attention, but there's no sign that anyone is left out at present. Not a snooty school where the car you drive matters, but one where parents are prepared to make financial sacrifices to access it for their daughters.

Redcliffe School

47 Redcliffe Gardens, London, SW10 9JH

- Pupils: 105 girls, 55 boys; all day • Ages: 3–11 (girls), 3–8 (boys)
- Christian • Fees: £5,010–£13,320 pa • Independent

Tel: 020 7352 9247
Email: admissions@redcliffeschool.com
Website: www.redcliffeschool.com

Headmistress: Since 2006, Mrs Susan Bourne BSc Hons (mid fifties). Read chemistry at Manchester University. Previously deputy head of the Old Vicarage School in Richmond and taught chemistry in both the state and independent sector. 'I still love teaching and teach the year 6 science lessons.' The sort of sensible woman you could rely on in an emergency, her calm demeanour permeates the whole school.

Married to a management consultant ('He's my anchor') with three grown up daughters (Latymer Upper, Queen's Gate and Godolphin and Latymer), she took time out whilst based in Geneva and Paris with a young family so knows what it's like to be a parent both at home and in an international setting. 'She really understands,' said one mother. Now lives in Richmond but escapes most weekends down the M3 to cottage in the New Forest where she and her husband sail their boat ('but only in calm weather!')

Entrance: Entrance to the nursery is first come first served but you do not have to put their name down at birth (although some parents do). Places are sometimes available at the last minute due to parents in this area applying to lots of different schools, so it's worth staying on the waiting list. Entrance to the main school is by assessment and an interview with the head. 'When we assess children for entry to the main school, we are looking for more than just academic ability,' said Mrs Bourne. 'We are looking for sociable children who are going to be happy here. For example, I choose children who are comfortable when separated from their carer.' Most children go through to the main school from the nursery. Two mixed forms from reception to year 3, then one form of girls in each year.

Exit: Boys go at 8+ to schools such as Colet Court, Northcote Lodge and Sussex House. Girls leave at 11+ to a mixture of boarding and day schools with Benenden, Putney High, Queen's College, Godolphin and Latymer and City of London being popular recent choices. Regular music, academic and art scholarships.

Remarks: This well-established prep school is situated on two sites on Redcliffe Gardens – a busy thoroughfare taking traffic from north to south London. Although it has expanded over the last few years and now has 160 pupils from nursery age up to 11, it still feels small and intimate.

The upper school is housed in the original main building which when you enter looks more like a rather scruffy family home than a school. The cosy atmosphere is continued in the head's office, where visitors sit on a comfy but rather shabby sofa. However, when you enter the classrooms it's an entirely different matter. The recently refurbished hall in the basement (which is also used as a dining room) is state of the art, and when we visited during morning assembly, a Mendelssohn concerto was being played through a brand new music system. (A different composer is studied each week.) Children filed in and sat with their eyes closed so that they could appreciate the music. When the deputy head asked them what they were going to do that day, one girl replied, 'Have fun!' which summed up the attitude around the school. (The answer she was actually looking for was 'Work hard!')

A new extension at the back of the school is light and airy, while the other classrooms upstairs, although a little cramped, have high ceilings and natural light. The top floor houses the music room where piano, violin, flute, trumpet, guitar and voice are taught by peripatetic teachers. Music is one of the school's strengths, with some children gaining music scholarships to their next schools. The school orchestra plays at school events such as the carol service and prize giving and there are concerts for parents and friends at least twice a year.

The lower school, at St Luke's church a quarter of a mile down the road, comprises five bright and well-lit classrooms in the basement of the church (one for nursery and two classes each of reception and year 1). A large hall is used for indoor sports and lunch (which is trolleyed down from the upper school kitchen), and is also the venue for whole school assemblies on Thursdays and Fridays which parents are encouraged to attend. 'Sometimes it's standing room only as these have become such popular events,' explained the head proudly. Children use a specially designed play area outside, with climbing frames built on an artificial grass covering with toys and scooters available. 'We like to spend as much time outside as possible.'

The teacher to student ratio is high with a maximum of 16 in each class. There are specialist teachers for music, sport, French and drama. Recent productions include Minibeast Madness by the lower school and A Midsummer Night's Dream put on by the upper school. Extra EAL lessons support children who require help (particularly when they first join the school) and a learning support teacher sees a number of children (around 10) twice a week on a one-to-one basis to help with specific learning difficulties such as mild dyslexia (but this costs extra). Most of the staff are women (three have been there for over 10 years), with one male teaching assistant and a male PE teacher, and this does give the school (especially since boys leave at eight) a rather female atmosphere. 'We would like to recruit more good male staff,' said the head.

Food is cooked on the upper school site and there are themed lunches for events such as Halloween and Bonfire Night. 'Children who have left the school write back to say how much they miss the food.' Parents are regularly invited in to have lunch with the staff and the children. 'We always feel very welcome at the school,' said one mother.

Children are bussed to nearby parks once a week for sports – football and netball in the autumn term, hockey and tag rugby in the spring and rounders, cricket and athletics in the summer. Weekly swimming lessons all year round at Fulham Pools. They compete against other schools and also have their own swimming galas and sports days. On Friday afternoons school finishes early and children can take part in a wide variety of sporting activities from yoga to fencing. 'We used to finish early on Fridays to enable our families with country properties to leave London before the rush hour but more and more are staying on to take advantage of the sports clubs,' said the head.

Families are drawn from the local area – half the children have either one or two international parents. 'Most of the schools round here have a high number of international families,' says one American mother, 'but this school seems very British still.' Another mother commented, 'It's very down to earth for a prep school in this area and you don't need to worry if you turn up at the school gate in the morning with no make up on. No one will judge you.'

Former pupils include Daniel Radcliffe. 'He was a rather quiet boy,' said the deputy head. 'We never expected him to become famous.' But Redcliffe is nothing like Hogwarts, and all in all this is a warm and cosy school with a nurturing environment. The atmosphere feels somewhat cloistered and it probably wouldn't suit a boisterous child who likes to run around a lot. But this could be just the place for gentler, less confident children to flourish.

Redland High Junior School

Linked school: Redland High School

1 Grove Park, Bristol, BS6 6PP

- Pupils: 130 girls; all day • Ages: 3-11 • Non-denom
- Fees: £6,870-£7,875 pa • Independent

Tel: 01179 245796
Email: admissions@redlandhigh.com
Website: www.redlandhigh.com

Head teacher: Since 2006, Mr Jonathan (Joe) Eyles BEd (Hons) specialising in maths and PE (Mrs Bateson is in overall charge of seniors and juniors). Since graduating from Bath he has, as he points out, experienced virtually every kind of school: single and mixed, independent and maintained, town and country, UK and abroad! All Saints Primary in Axminster, the International School in Sri Lanka, Bourneville, Weston Super Mare and six years at Millfield (assistant head of the junior and pre-prep and director of studies) before joining Redland as head seven years ago. He is studying part-time for a masters' in cognitive development at Bristol University and still finds time to be an ISI inspector. Vivacious, elegant – even in a tracksuit – voluble and self-evidently efficient, he believes in being a hands on head and teaches two thirds of a timetable, seeing everyone including the nursery. Despite his fluency in 'education-speak', he is approachable and evidently much liked by his pupils. He believes in 'putting life into learning' and that good pastoral care is the key to good progress. Parents appreciate this.

Entrance: Non-selective into pre-prep, then NFER tests which are also used to monitor progress. Tests and assessment are done on taster days and parents say once in the doors most want to stay! Numbers practically double from year 4 as state school parents wake up to advantages of getting daughters into senior school via this route and also being in with a chance of a scholarship. Early warning given if any girls unlikely to make grade.

Exit: Nearly all go to senior school via entry examination at 11 despite increasing temptation in form of ex-independents, now academies, and a new free school in North Bristol.

Remarks: Redland High Junior rambles through three floors of a couple of large, originally residential, houses across the road from the senior school at Redland Court. Once past the fierce security gates, there is a tarmac play area and a separate grassed one with lots of nice gear for the tinies in what were once the front gardens. Access to the school is via an unimposing front door and surprisingly cramped entrance hall; beyond that every space is packed full of enthusiastic small girls. Classrooms are big and vibrant with displayed work, though definitely not purpose built. Two delightfully articulate and friendly 10-year-olds took charge of us, explaining they had finished their art task first so were free to do a tour. Synthetic phonics and jolly phonics for beginners, with French introduced from the start, Spanish and German tasters and Latin from year six. Deputy head is Senco and works with the juniors, mainly helping dyslexics; as she is also Senco for seniors she sees the whole picture. Girls were working with enthusiasm and their writing and discussion chimed with the eloquence of our guides. Parents wax lyrical about pastoral care and monitoring of progress.

Lively art and drama while music in the smart new activities hall particularly impressed. We saw girls having a violin taster lesson – they do the same things with cello, woodwind and brass, so no wonder the orchestras are flourishing! In another music lesson there was thoughtful discussion of different nationalities' dancing. A recent contribution of ukuleles from supportive parents has made for serenades at lunchtime. Music and games facilities are shared with the seniors, and the older juniors also go up the hill to the senior hall for lunch. Year 6 do many subjects in senior buildings to ease transition and benefit from specialist equipment.

As in seniors, a real racial and social diversity and since girls travel from all parts of the city after school clubs and a holiday club, Redland Rascals, are well used. Girls also love their residential adventure weeks and have a welter of lunchtime things to choose from including the ever popular book clubs. Games uniform in juniors and seniors has cheerful bright red tops and green bottoms (worn most of the time by lucky tiny tots). Navy v-neck with plaid pinny or green cardies with green and white summer dresses, blazers, waxed jackets etc, are all from John Lewis, and quite reasonably priced. There's also a plentiful supply in the second hand shop.

Reigate St Mary's Preparatory and Choir School

Linked school: Reigate Grammar School

Chart Lane, Reigate, RH2 7RN

- Pupils: 300 boys and girls; all day • Ages: 3-11 • Fees: £9,945-£12,171 pa • Independent

Tel: 01737 244880
Email: office@reigatestmarys.org
Website: www.reigatestmarys.org

Head: Since 2005, Mr Marcus Culverwell (forties). Previously deputy head (joined school in 2003). Before that, head of science, then director of studies, then deputy head at Lancing College Junior. A local boy, he was educated first at Caterham, then Archbishop Tenison's sixth form after squeeze on family finances. Sporty, science-y and spiritual. 'Very Christian,' says a parent.

Teenage years dominated by dreams of joining Aviation Mission Fellowship – dashed when failed final stage of commercial pilot training. Studied aeronautical engineering at Hertford followed by MA at Brunel. With dearth of jobs in industry, teaching was originally intended as stopgap career but rapidly became something far more. He realised that he wanted to work with younger children when, while combining teacher training with spell on staff at Cardiff FE college he was unable to comfort weeping student encountered in corridor.

Personable, child-friendly (has three of his own, two at the senior school, one here) and pupils rush to talk to him, clearly confident of sympathetic hearing. No wonder, given approach to playground duties (takes guitar and sings – though 'not a musician') as well as breaking out into the occasional assembly rap. Keeps staff on their toes and though 'we never sit still', potentially exhausting pace is tempered with generous dollops of non-teaching time to regroup for the next big think (eyes down for eco-flag green school status next).

It's a work in progress that started with Mr Culverwell's first inspection, five weeks into the job, when he produced rationale of planned curriculum development, now on overhaul number three, each marked by progressively closer ties to senior school.

Desire to make a difference is manifest – has just completed book on educating children for social responsibility, teachers and pupils encouraged to explore 'the big questions' and commit to making a difference. Parents acknowledge value of approach but aren't always receptive to newsletter homilies exhorting them to 'down tools and cuddle the children – hard when you're trying to pay the school fees,' said one.)

R

Academic robe on one side of study, Captain Considerate outfit (worn by pupils to deliver hi-tech homilies on behaviour) on the other sums up approach – relaxed gravitas. Ultimately perception is that it's Mr Fenton down at the big school who rules the roost and makes the big decisions. Thumbs up, however, for being well intentioned – and, overall, 'a nice man.'

Entrance: Non-selective at three – first come first served and increasingly over-booked, almost reaching London frenzy levels (including occasional pre-pregnant enquiries). Sympathetic attitude to SEN, permeating from knowledgeable head and increasing resources – SENCo, until recently an add-on responsibility for class teacher, now a separate post. Covers the works, including EBSD, ASD, ADHD, severe dyslexia and those with physical disabilities – rated 'brilliant' by senior school specialist on recent visit.

Gets our vote for recently revised curriculum and brilliantly humane transitions between stages. 'Our ethos is that happy children learn,' says nursery manager. One and two-year-olds have regular playdates with parents, getting to know big, bright nursery up to two years before they start.

Atmosphere 'moves from buzzing to calm classroom by end of reception so ready for change in pace in year 1,' says staff member. Class sizes rise from maximum 15 in reception and below to maximum 20 in years 1-6.

Choristers, original reason for school's foundation, have voice trials at six or seven and, if successful, become probationers. Boys only – for now, though growing parental rumblings could well see girls involved in the future.

Exit: Vast majority to senior school, but not all. Other destinations include Box Hill, Dunottar, Ardingly and Worth. Parental anxiety following decision to offer firm places to many in year considerable but misplaced, thinks school, as around three quarters will end up going on to the senior school while those without guarantee can still sit the exam in year 6 and take chances with other outsiders. Much better this way as avoids previous misery of sitting and failing entrance exam, says school, when children can be guided to a better place instead. Some playground gossip means pupils aren't as blissfully unaware as parents would want and 'if you're just one of a handful not to go through to the senior school it can be hard on the individual,' thought one.

Remarks: Originally founded as choir school by Godfrey Searle, canny chartered stockbroker and musician who calculated (accurately) that selling off small area to council for municipal bowls green would avert desire to run bypass through grounds.

Unusually, a cathedral choir without portfolio, though makes up for it with regular appearances at Chichester and occasional visits to St Paul's, tradition starting in the Second World War when regular choir was evacuated. Commercially in demand, too, for Disney amongst others. Choristers' robes line corridor, atmospheric practice room, low-tech shelves bursting with music-stuffed folders, fruit and biscuits laid out for after-school rehearsal – a bit like a time capsule (laptop apologetically to one side the only modern note).

Acquisition by senior school in 2005 was a relative no-brainer, once established that decline in pupil numbers was reversible. Now healthy enough to justify recent £4.5 million investment on impressive glass and brick main teaching block for years 1 to 3, which rears up behind original building, partially concealed on far side by manmade hill, demanded by planners to avoid upsetting locals' sensibilities and incorporating splendiferous downstairs sports hall. Years 4 to 6 are quartered in less plush but perfectly acceptable older-style block. Bright kindergarten (corridor a cheerful clutter of wellies) taking up the ground floor.

Hard-surfaced games area close to school. Attractive, undulating grounds beyond, partially wooded (lots of den building in warmer months) and with beautifully planted memorial garden where head boy and girl lay wreaths in front of school. Assorted pitches (four football, two multi-surface) plus athletics track and cricket pavilion are attractively set in the greenery, all well used and supplemented with additional sessions at senior school and trips to playing fields a short coach ride away.

Though there's some parental moaning if children don't make top teams, school makes efforts to secure fixtures for Bs and Cs as well 'so there are games for all.' Sport broadly split along trad gender lines, but it's permeable – current year 5 rugby and football star player is a girl (while Zumba and gymnastics clubs also attract small numbers of boys).

Staff work hard, lessons supported by what head describes as 'phenomenal' planning. All expected to run a popular club two terms in three (free unless run by outside experts). Start in modest way from year 1 (reception parents clamour for share but 'they've had a busy day and need to go home,' thinks head). Really gets going in year 3 with waiting lists 'for everything' and impressively wideranging, from programming (involves sending delightful little robots on search and rescue missions) to Living World (plenty of pond dipping). Good range of popular trips, too, from Bushcraft – a current fave rave – to even more rugged Snowdonia and Mont Blanc.

Ever closer links with senior school sees growing number of specialist teachers (maths the most recent addition, as well as music, games, art, IT) making short walk over. Curriculum consistency between two schools means not just singing from same song sheet but with barber shop harmonies, too.

Impressive signs of expansion in scope and success, with non-selective intake making excellent progress – SATs scores, internally assessed, put 100 per cent of pupils at level 4 and above, 30 per cent hitting a level 6.

Academic focus on continuous assessment is seen as quite intense by parents – though doesn't necessarily permeate through to children – with charismatic staff implementing sensible rewards system (golden time is king) that helps to produce confident, courteous children. 'I hope you have a lovely afternoon,' was heard from one six-year-old. Smart too – dress code is nostalgic (caps and trad hats for younger pupils, grime-management grey shirts for boys).

Innovative language teaching keeps French as the big one with Spanish and German each taught for a term in year 6. Though maths only subject with formal sets, year 1 had informal streaming, while differentiation is 'part and parcel of lessons' aided by excellent staffing ratios – younger children have full time TA as well as teacher. Classes notably calm though not at expense of fun, reception children listening, rapt, to end of day story, year 1 pupils falling over themselves to show delights of science lessons – leaves 'that were crispy and brown if didn't have enough water,' flowers with ink-dyed petals. Favourite subject? 'It is now,' said one.

Big on purposeful technology – WiFi up and running, iPads on the way for all pupils – 'a tool we'll use everywhere,' thinks head; deliberate mix of Macs and PCs 'so children bi-lingual' and Kodu so widely used that 'should be official foreign language.'

Lots of pride in past and at least one eye on the future. Parents of the vast majority of RSM pupils (not just the dead certs) will find passage to senior school eased. For a small number aim is managed and failure-free exit elsewhere. Being a pupil here 'makes it much easier to get to the grammar school, not for the few but, in the future, for almost every St Mary's child,' says school. Means you know what you're buying into. 'You have to live with it or move on,' says parent.

Rendcomb College Junior School

Linked school: Rendcomb College

Rendcomb, Cirencester, GL7 7HA

• Pupils: 160 boys and girls • Ages: 3–11 • Fees: Day £6,375–£10,185; Boarding £13,935 pa • Independent

Tel: 01285 832306
Email: admissions@rendcomb.gloucs.sch.uk
Website: www.rendcombcollege.org.uk

Head: Since 2002, Mr Martin Watson BEd MA (fifties), studied history at Exeter, then London for MA. Joined Rendcomb after 19 years at The Downs, Wraxall, (last 15 as deputy head) to set up junior school. Passionate about co-education, the outdoor classroom and children 'needing to be happy to learn'. Played top class rugby while at St Luke's – qualified rugby referee but now umpires rounders to international level. Sport is still a great interest, as is travel abroad. Married to Lynne, who teaches year 5 class as well as overseeing school's green flag eco programme. Daughter, Rachel, played rounders consistently for England from 13-18. Bags of experience – lovely rapport with children and at ease with parents. A tower of strength, he knows how to select and retain good staff (including four males). A safe pair of hands if ever we saw them.

Entrance: Majority from pre-school nurseries and own nursery (entrance from term after third birthday). Shadow/taster day for youngest. Assessments in English, maths, VRQ and report from current school for all aged 7+.

Exit: Virtually all to senior school at 11 via entrance examination.

Remarks: The junior school occupies former senior day house accommodation to side of main school building. Large classrooms for younger ones on ground floor plus older children expanding on upper floors into main building. Not the most imposing of entrances (at least in contrast to senior school) but emphasis here is on industry rather than show. Bouncy, smiling pupils everywhere with sensible red and navy uniform (ties for high days). Outside areas are perfect for youngest – protective surfaces to save bruises – then skip round a corner or two into beautiful grounds via a variety of outside play equipment. Rendcomb tinies are used to the outdoor life and so are in their element here. Nearly all recruitment is at three to four year old level with most staying on.

One to four teacher:pupil ratio in nursery with two assistants and two teachers, so never more than 16 children at one time. Lovely display and lots of fun. Jolly Phonics scheme started here. Head plans to increase to two form entry from reception. Staff work closely with parents to develop each child's reading. Book corners in classrooms look well maintained. Oxford Reading Tree heavily used – 'Boys like Fireflies,' (the non-fiction offshoot) we were told. Abacus for maths; plenty of numerical stimuli on display. Lots of topics – 'minibeasts' providing endless entertainment when we visited. Staff really on the ball: well-kept learning journals record all significant milestones. Smartboards sit comfortably alongside book corners with teachers using old and new resources to full effect. Reception, years 1 and 2 known as Otters (not quite sure why) – could it be because they all have swimming on their timetable?

Specialist teaching for music, PE and French right from nursery with more specialism from year 3 upwards – by year 6 the class teacher is taking one or two subjects only. This leads nicely into transition to senior, reinforced by the physical location of the upper junior classrooms. Some juniors flexi-board in seniors' lower school houses – makes another step towards senior school life effortless. ICT has a suite with 18 PCs and head says that some pupils have a 'phenomenal aptitude'. Large art area doubles up for D&T (pupils recently scored as young active designers of the year) plus some science (otherwise in classrooms) though senior labs can always be booked if required. Pupils screened for dyslexia and specialist help provided by discrete learning support department.

Year groups have one main trip per term plus a three day residential trip for year 6 to Kilve activity centre. Authors visit to talk to pupils on World Book Day and main junior library is heavily used. Most pupils stay for prep club and/or activities after school. New big thing here is the forest school with trails through the wood, woodcraft and a proper log cabin for indoor activities. Heavily used (eg one afternoon per week from reception to year 2, thereafter 12 children at a time from upper years on a termly basis). Set-up good enough to be used by forest school association for training purposes. One of first independent schools to be rewarded international eco-school green flag award following an intensive two year programme on site.

Games and PE very popular, with inclusive policy to encourage all pupils to play at all levels. Usual range of main sports for boys and girls; separate sports days for juniors and Otters. Keen cross-country club teaches young muscles about hills; mixed pop-lacrosse team became recent national prep school champions. Own outside areas plus bonus of access to senior sports hall for PE and college pitches for games. Designated music room for juniors used by younger ones whilst older pupils use main music school. Juniors are offered a free taster instrumental lesson and can use school instruments in early stages. Music concert each term showcases junior school orchestra and choir. Juniors also enjoy using the food studies facilities for cookery club. Acting is popular – ambitious performances (recent ones include The Rocky Monster Show and Dream On, a musical adaptation of A Midsummer Night's Dream) in the Dulverton Hall. Ballet pupils enter Cheltenham Festival across full range. Full programme of LAMDA speech and drama with excellent plaudits. Riding and polo are popular and some pupils compete in the UK mega chess finals annually. Parents seem a pretty sociable lot – lots of events under aegis of RCJPA for general letting down of hair.

Cornerstone of the 'new' Rendcomb and a life saver in a fiercely competitive part of Gloucestershire. Definitely a success and an end to worries if you're looking for a complete 3-18 package.

RGS Springfield

Linked school: RGS Worcester

Britannia Square, Worcester, WR1 3DL

• Pupils: 115 boys and girls • Ages: 2½–11 • Non-denom
• Fees: £5,946–£9,996 pa • Independent

Tel: 01905 24999
Email: springfield@rgsw.org.uk
Website: www.rgsw.org.uk

Headmistress: Mrs Laura Brown BA (philosophy) PGCE (mid-forties). Married to a teacher, with three daughters, including twins. Previously worked at Rose Hill School, Godstowe and Dean Close Preparatory School.

Entrance: By interview and assessment. Academic and music scholarships are available for years 3 and 5 entrants.

Exit: Nearly all move to the senior school, RGS Worcester. Others to King's Worcester and Malvern St James.

Remarks: See senior school.

RGS The Grange

Linked school: RGS Worcester

Grange Lane, Claines, Worcester, WR3 7RR

- Pupils: 330 girls and boys; all day • Ages: 2½–11 • Non-denom
- Fees: £6,090–£9,996 pa • Independent

Tel: 01905 451205
Email: grange@rgsw.org.uk
Website: www.rgsw.org.uk

Headmaster: Mr Gareth Hughes, previously head of lower school at RGS Worcester and director of sports. He is a top sportsman himself, having played fly-half for Saracens in the 1990s and subsequently for Worcester RFC. His wife Sophie is a local primary school music teacher. Two children.

Entrance: Children admitted half-termly or at other times if necessary. Interview and assessment as appropriate. For example, entry to year 1 would involve a morning spent working in class with some reading and sums. For year 5 a more formal entrance examination with standardised tests in maths and English plus verbal and non-verbal reasoning questionnaires.

Exit: Vast majority go on to RGS Worcester unless advised this would not be appropriate. Head will help these parents/children select a less academic school.

Remarks: For further details see the senior school, RGS Worcester.

Rhodes Avenue Primary School

Rhodes Avenue, London, N22 7UT

- Pupils: 560 boys and girls • Ages: 3–11 • Non-denom • State

---

Tel: 020 8888 2859
Email: admin@rhodes.haringey.sch.uk
Website: www.rhodes.haringey.sch.uk

Headteacher: Since 1996, Mrs Christine Witham (forties), definitely the driving force behind this remarkably successful primary school. In her 14 years at the helm, she has taken the school from mediocre to marvellous and to the top of every league table, both academic and sporting. Positive and upbeat, she's widely liked by parents, pupils and teachers. 'She's very approachable,' said one. 'She loves children,' said another. 'She knows all their names, sees them all as individuals and is very visible about the school.' Optimistic and determined, even the recent threat to the school rebuild did not leave her deterred. Her skill at dealing with the sometimes demanding clientele is also worthy of note – 'When one parent went in to complain that their child was special and deserved special treatment, she just replied, "We feel all our children are special".' Married, with two children.

Entrance: Recently moved to three-form entry with 90. Admission by means of the local authority criteria, which means that, on the whole, first come siblings and then those living as near as possible. With four applications for every place, this has meant within a quarter of a mile. The success of the school – and its neighbouring comprehensive – has undoubtedly had an impact on local property prices.

Exit: The school backs directly on to Alexandra Park, one of the borough's best secondaries, and the majority of pupils proceed there. In 2013 others headed to Fortismere, Channing and Dame Alice Owen's and one apiece to Henrietta Barnett, JCoSS, Latymer, North London Collegiate, Park View Academy, Queen Elizabeth School for Boys and Ashmole.

Remarks: Has for some years consistently dominated the local authority league tables and Ofsted can barely think of a word of criticism. Sats results here are truly outstanding, with the majority reaching the highest levels – results that would put a smile on the face of most prep school heads. Mrs Witham has done the job by building up a very successful team of teachers. 'There's a good mix of the thoroughly experienced and the young and enthusiastic,' said one mother, and the pupils agree: 'The teaching is really great,' said a boy. Though the pupils are of above average ability on entry, the school gives everyone that little bit more, particularly in the later years.

An extensive enrichment programme in art, drama and creative writing (in which teachers receive regularly training) includes workshops and specials events, such as Book Week. A string of well-known children's authors pitch up to entertain, but the highlight of the week is The Bedtime Story evening, when, accompanied by teddies, children are given hot chocolate and gripping fiction. Hardly surprising, then, that a recent nationwide writing competition saw nine Rhodes Avenue finalists.

Academic progress is charted minutely and parents kept well informed, with three parents' evenings and three reports a year. Strong support, too, for the struggling. 'My son has a special literacy person and she's fantastic,' said one parent. 'He gets taken out during the literacy hour and taught in a small group to ensure he'll cope at secondary school.' French taught from year 3 and 'parlez-vous' is supplemented with fun activities like a French breakfast, croissants included.

Music and sport are as high up the agenda as the three Rs. All year 4 learn cello, violin, trumpet or clarinet and specialist teachers, provided by the local authority, offer individual tuition during the school day. Sport is taken seriously – tends to sweep the board in local competitions, whether it's athletics or tennis, football or netball. 'There's an exceptionally good PE teacher,' said one mother, adding that in-school provision is also often supplemented with private coaching. Loads of trips, clubs and workshops, with outings to the cinema, theatre and museums and a regular stream of visiting artists, actors and dancers. Plenty of activity on the pupils' parts, too, with impressive assemblies and regular performances and concerts. 'A lot is done around creativity,' said one parent. After-school clubs include cross-country, orchestra, cricket, recorder, choir, Bollywood dance, Spanish, French, pottery, drama, yoga, computer, netball and badminton. Lots of competitions entered and usually won – whether that for the school's abundant and much-loved vegetable garden or for pupils' Christmas card designs. After-school play centre on site 3.30-6pm.

A local primary school and most families live within feet of the gates, giving a strong community feel, though whether increased numbers will dilute this remains to be seen. Three smart new buildings added in 2011 to the modern year 6 space, which houses two classrooms and an IT suite. Strong pupil involvement. School council, with two elections a year, debates hot topics like school uniform, sustainability and healthy eating. Peer mediators protect against playground perils. Plenty of praise is the recipe for good behaviour, though pupils consider Mrs Witham 'very strict', and the naughty are given focused 'reflection' on wrong doing. Despite the friendly upbeat mood, some feel the school places too great an emphasis on obvious winners, whether in the classroom or the sports fields. 'If you are slightly unusual and don't fit in,' said one parent, 'you can slip under the wire a bit.'

Parents, who are increasingly prosperous and professional, are heavily involved. Those with interesting jobs – like astronauts or newspaper editors – come in to share their expertise with the kids. Needless to say, the Parents' Association is buzzing, organising a hectic cycle of events including a summer and Christmas fair, school raffle, jumble sale, fireworks and Burns Supper. Class reps are required to stage two cake sales a year. Oodles of extra funds raised.

Richmond House School

170 Otley Road, Far Headingley, Leeds, LS16 5LG

• Pupils: 220 boys and girls; day • Ages: 3–11 • Non-denom with a strong Christian base • Fees: £7,725 pa • Independent

Tel: 01132 752670
Email: enquiries@rhschool.org
Website: www.rhschool.org

Headmistress: Since 2008, Mrs Jane Disley BA PGCE. Previously head of Moorfield School, Ilkley. Hard-working, committed, almost fearless, she has 'tidied up and cleared out' while managing, skilfully, to keep parents and children happy along the way. She is well-liked, accessible and much admired; parents like the way she has her hand on the tiller and keeps a keen eye on the progress of individual children. Not afraid to make changes and adapt elements of the school as necessary, but communicates her ideas well with parents so that they feel involved.

Entrance: Maximum 30 children enter nursery each September. Nursery and reception classes are housed together in the foundation stage. Two classes of around 18 per year group from reception to year 6. Most children remain in the school from the age of three, some additional places available later. The entry is not academically selective at the earliest stages. No scholarships available but bursaries are.

Exit: An important factor for many is that the school has a good reputation for supporting children into their next school at eleven, plenty with scholarships. This is a wide and ever-changing field in this area with a good number of independent schools and excellent maintained schools available. Many parents have an eye to an expensive future at university and move mountains – or at least address – to creep into the catchment for some of the best state schools around – in Harrogate. Independent school favourites are currently Bradford Grammar, Woodhouse Grove, Ashville College and The Grammar School at Leeds, but talk to the school and they will advise without bias and with your child in mind.

Remarks: Opened on present site in 1935, housed in three large Yorkshire stone Victorian villas, typical of the area. It lacks large indoor spaces and kerb appeal, but makes up for that in spades with its spacious and beautifully-maintained 10 acres of sports fields and excellent new car park tucked away to the rear of the buildings – take a look out back and suddenly the place feels very different. There's a very attractive sports pavilion and this has to be one of the very few schools with its own crown bowling green, surely a Yorkshire marketing niche? Proximity of Leeds Met University provides access to additional sporting facilities and student coaching expertise plus use of other local squash and badminton courts and swimming pools.

An assortment of Portakabins add little aesthetic appeal to the mix but provide extremely useful, possibly essential, additional space for DT, science and music. Nursery and reception classes are also similarly housed but they have been spruced up and provide delightful, spacious airy classrooms with adjacent play areas for the youngest children. Main buildings house core classrooms, all in good order and well-equipped with plenty of children's work in evidence. Feels small in places to those of us of adult size, lots of narrow stairways in a building that clearly wasn't designed to be a school, but happy smiling children tell us how much they love it and feel at home here. Main hall is multi-purpose – PE/assembly/orchestra. Maths and English streamed from year 5, children 'learning the same things but at a different speed'. Great art on display, much loved and slightly 'wacky' art teacher (say the children), other views are, of course, available. Staff work hard, head describes them as 'driven', which, along with smallish classes, is one reason why the school gives other, more selective, schools a good run for their money.

Probably a broader church than it used to be, with increased focus and balance, but parents still demand (and get) high academic standards while recognising and valuing the care and support the school offers. It feels industrious and busy; success is valued and recognised through a variety of sticker and badge-wearing opportunities. Those with a special gift or ability are championed and the whole school celebrates different cultural and religious events. Sport and music are taken seriously and children compete across the board at a high level, this may be a small school but it aims high and is not afraid to challenge, punching above its weight both locally and nationally in competitions. Specialist teaching in a number of subject areas; French taught from reception, add to that Spanish in years 5 and 6, and you can try your hand at Mandarin and Arabic as club activities.

Parents like and appreciate clear feedback about progress and describe the regular reports home as 'especially motivating'. Reward schemes are part of a proactive approach to pastoral care; problems are dealt with promptly and effectively say parents. 'Friendship stops', like miniature bus stops, feature prominently in the playground as a safety zone/stop-off point for children short of a friend – it was very gratifying to see children hovering timidly near them at playtime being quickly picked up and drawn into other children's games. Older children look after younger ones, plenty of cross-age friendships and everyone seems to know everyone, staff and children alike.

Food is cooked in-house, a good 'healthy' choice, everyone eats together. A recent request for mangetout proved a challenge though, hard to keep it al dente when cooking in large quantities... A long lunch break sensibly allows plenty of time and opportunity for extra-curricular activities, choir, orchestra, rock band and jazz choir flourishing; around 40 other options from judo to chess to gardening; pupils also form basis of school council and organise charity events.

Parents are medics, lawyers, financiers, business people, university staff heading into Leeds to work and find both the location and the out-of-hours school care convenient. More working mothers here than is possibly the norm, though that may be a reflection of changing times. Parents choose the school for variety of reasons, the smaller size and approachability of staff is cited as key for many, you can take the high academic standards as read.

Riddlesworth Hall Preparatory School

Hall Lane, Diss, IP22 2TA

• Pupils: 120 boys and girls • Ages: 2-13 • C of E • Fees: Boarding £16,500-£17,535; Day £7,530-£10,740 pa • Independent

Tel: 01953 681246
Email: info@riddlesworthhall.co.uk
Website: www.riddlesworthhall.co.uk

Head: Since 2007, Mr Paul Cochrane PGCE (early fifties). Previously head of prep and lower school at Tettenhall College, Wolverhampton. A lover of traditional boarding life, he's hugely popular with pupils and parents, who recognise that if anyone is going to move the school forward it's this antithesis to a 'la-de-dah southerner'. Impressively determined and energetic, he bowls about the place teaching geography and boys' PE in addition to tackling all those millions of jobs heads have to do. Married to Sally – she gives that extra something to make this place feel like home and is in the throes of creating a sensory garden for the pupils. They live on site with their four children – the younger three are at the school.

No board of governors – instead a sole owner, Colonel Boulter (owns and heads Barnardiston Hall as well), with whom Mr Cochrane has a good working relationship.

Entrance: 'No strings attached' day at school. Low key observation of performance in English and maths. Formal assessment of special educational needs to see if they can be accommodated.

Exit: To a range of schools at 11 and 13. Popular destinations are The Leys School, Framlingham College, Benenden School and Uppingham School.

Remarks: Narrowly escaped closure in 2000, but with some timely help plus the introduction of boys (became fully co-ed in 2011) it continues to battle on. Recent partnership with an international school in Thailand (apparently its owner loves the Diana connection – Princess Di was the school's most famous past pupil) may bring in between 12 to 25 competent English-speaking pupils for a year at a time. First batch, into the top two forms, won't, according to Paul Cochrane, 'be more than 12. We want to be sure it doesn't impact on the ethos of the place'. As one parent said, 'We're used to having foreign students coming and going. Being in the sticks in Norfolk is great to a point, so a tranche of foreign input can only be a good thing.' Time will tell.

Lovely setting deep in farming country where children safely roam. Tennis courts, adventure play area and hutches for small pets make the outdoors even more attractive. Main body of school in listed Georgian pile with welcoming hall, a good library and decent science lab. Adjacent outbuildings provide adequate classroom accommodation – small class sizes suit the timid or those who might just drift along in larger schools. Littlies (4-7) are in nearby self-contained stable block with courtyard play area at its centre. SEN provision with CreSTeD accreditation.

Games for all, every day. According to a parent, 'They somehow manage to cobble something together,' and play matches. Weekly swimming at pool in nearby Diss. For its size, good range of extra-curricular activities, most of which are charged on top of basic fees – music tuition (including the harp), speech and drama, riding and martial arts. Flexible boarding provision with activities at the weekend. Scholarships for military and diplomatic offspring.

Happy, fresh-faced pupils endlessly skip and hug but aren't bothered by the charred wreck of a swimming pool and need for TLC in several areas. Tremendously supportive parents from all walks of life give up occasional Saturday mornings to join the 'task force' – that's gardening in return for a big breakfast get together.

Homely place filled with echoes from the past. Admirably positive head and his wife don't appear to be fazed by the challenges which lie ahead. We wait to see if proposed 'international' link can be happily absorbed and provide the financial boost needed for future developments.

Robert Gordon's College Junior School

Linked school: Robert Gordon's College

Schoolhill, Aberdeen, AB10 1FE

• Pupils: 530 boys and girls • Ages: 4-18 • Inter-denom • Fees: £8,180-£9,765 pa • Independent

Tel: 01224 646346
Email: admissions@rgc.aberdeen.sch.uk
Website: www.rgc.aberdeen.sch.uk

Head of Junior School: Mrs Mollie Mennie, MBA Dip Ed

Exit: Almost all move to Robert Gordon's College senior school.

Remarks: For details, see senior school.

Roch House Preparatory School

Linked school: Abbots Bromley School for Girls

Abbots Bromley, Rugeley, WS15 3BW

• Pupils: 65 boys and girls • Ages: 3-11 • Fees: Day £4,518-£9,903; Boarding £17,040-£20,904 pa • Independent

Tel: 01283 840232
Email: enquiries@abbotsbromley.net
Website: www.abbotsbromley.net/2106/prep-school/

Head: Since 2005 Mrs Ann Johnson. Previously deputy head of the pre-prep at Foremarke, where she enjoyed 'marked success.' Open, friendly and thoughtful, Mrs Johnson is admired by parents and pupils. 'She's very approachable,' said one delighted mum, 'and with a wealth of experience'. 'She loves the children,' says another, 'but she isn't soppy about them. They know where they stand because in the best sense she is firm but fair and insists on good manners while encouraging them to have fun.' 'Children like to know what the guidelines are,' says the head, 'then they know where they stand and what is expected of them.'

Keen to find out the children's strengths and weakness with lots of praise and encouragement. 'Nobody is left out,' a senior girl told us. Mrs Johnson is clearly devoted to her charges and her job but she is not blind to the outside world: as a trustee she is deeply committed to a school educational and social charity out in Africa which she visits regularly with her husband, taking older girls from the senior school for a fortnight or so in the summer half term and exposing them to the situation out there. Again, nothing sentimental: just bags of thoughtful,

R

rational and sensitive assessment of what can be done to help – without being patronising. 'It helps to maintain a sense of proportion and make us realise how lucky we are.' 'She's a superb role model,' said one of the teachers. She has started to spend time assisting the head of the senior school, 'but I'm only just over the road and, besides, I have a wonderful staff.'

Entrance: Non selective. Every child has talent. 'We accept boys and girls of all faiths and abilities.' Pupils may arrive at any stage, providing there is room. Obviously the start of term is the best time but the school is flexible about that. We met a child who had joined in the middle of a term and who spoke so happily about the way she had been welcomed in by everyone. 'It was brilliant. I felt I had been here for years.' Taster days are offered and appreciated and there are opportunities to try boarding.

Exit: Most boys leave at the end of kindergarten, but there is scope for staying on. Most girls to senior school.

Remarks: Roch House, named after a previous headmistress, is directly across the road from the senior school in the delightful village of Abbots Bromley. It is housed in a large building which was initially built as St Mary's, that part of the school founded by the Woodard Corporation for the children of less wealthy parents. That idea did not sit comfortably with the post first world war generation and in 1921 the two parts amalgamated into Abbots Bromley School for Girls. Later St Mary's became the junior school.

Though the main building is huge and initially the young inhabitants look like enchanting Lilliputians in their bright uniform, the building lends itself very well to the idea of a large, welcoming granny of a house where space and possibilities seem endless. 'You quickly learn your way around,' a senior girl told us. 'They've used the space available very well,' said a mother. 'Somehow it is not as intimidating as you might imagine when you first see it from the outside.' The atmosphere is one of buzzing activity and excitement. Potentially soulless corridors are turned into avenues of adventure with the promise of excitement and the joy of creativity. We saw wonderful poems up on the wall – 'my poem to be spoken silently' – shining with the colour of words and the joy of expression. Splashes of colourful, free and imaginative art all over the place: pictures and photographs, a stunning mosaic, images of past outings, representations of joys to come with so much that is challenging and inspirational, all encouraging healthy pride and satisfaction in achievements.

But still, thank goodness, the delightful frankness of children. After we had seen the science lab, with its stunning equipment and exciting teaching; after we had seen the music rooms and heard so many young enthusing about music and dance; after we had seen the dance studio given over to ballet; after we had heard young riders extolling the thrills of the equestrian centre across the road (anyone over 6 can learn); after we had admired the splendidly equipped library and heard enthusiastic comments about the joys of reading; after we had heard and seen and enjoyed so much, it was fun to receive in answer to our question, 'What is your favourite subject?' the response, 'Lunch.' Three cheers for the honesty of children. And, yes, the food is delicious.

That all this is achieved within a framework of carefully drawn up curricula and an intelligent timetable is a tribute to the staff and the ethos of the school. Broadly speaking, the school follows the national curriculum – and beyond. For instance, conversational French is taught from the kindergarten and beyond, as is swimming. The school trumpets healthily the fact that the ratio of teacher/pupil is much more generous than government recommendations – but then parents are paying for it. Early years education is seen by those with whom we spoke to be particularly good value for money.

One of the great delights of the Abbots Bromley adventure is its insistence on what is called 'enrichment', what might more prosaically be referred to as hobbies. There is enrichment before lunch four days of the week and these periods serve to alter the tempo of the day, tap into a different part of the psyche, do exactly what that word suggests. Some activities are charged for such as riding, dancing (Abbots Bromley, as a whole, is brilliant at both these activities), tennis coaching, speech and drama lessons, music. But it's not necessary to pursue activities which are charged on the bill. Members of staff follow their own interests and – the best moments for teachers – share what fires them up. Thus there is craft club, ICT skills, art club, choir, ukulele ensemble (all those little Georgette Formbys !) There are also masses of sporting activities including netball, football, swimming, trampolining and athletics. The proximity of the prep school to the senior school, and the fact that the sports hall and swimming pool are on the Roch House side of the road, means that there is plenty of opportunity to enjoy those excellent facilities.

The shape and format of the day reflects the thoughtfulness of the school in its consideration of logistical difficulties experienced by some working mums and dads. Times of dropping off in the morning and collecting in the evening can, within limits, be tailored to individual needs. Another feature we like is the way that prep set for those in years 3 – 6 on Friday evenings can be supervised at school so the weekend is free and parents don't have to nag...

The facilities for full, weekly, flexi and occasional boarding are excellent and much enjoyed by those who take advantage of the opportunities. Two free taster nights are included in every term's fees which means that the great majority of the girls have experience of boarding from year 3. There are three regular ones but many more occasional ones waiting to convert.

The great Abbots Bromley adventure begins at Roch House, though not exclusively. This is where pupils are encouraged to show consideration for others and shoulder some responsibility. This is where good habits of learning are inculcated, where a delight in discovery and research is learned and where friendships can blossom. The older girls cross the road to help the younger ones with work and play; the transition from senior to junior is described by many as seamless. Both schools possess lovely atmospheres, delightful girls and lively teaching. There have been technical problems recently, qv the senior school entry, but we are confident that these are being sorted out and both schools are poised to return to their very best.

The Roche School

11 Frogmore, London, SW18 1HW

- Pupils: 280 boys and girls, all day • Ages: 2 1/2–11
- Fees: £9,456–£11,490 pa • Independent

Tel: 020 8877 0823
Email: gcac@therocheschool.co.uk
Website: www.therocheschool.co.uk

Principal: Since 1989, Dr James Roche BSc PhD (sixties). Educated at St Paul's, read physics at Bristol and has a PhD in general relativity from Manchester. Taught for two years in a London state school then spent 19 years teaching A level physics and maths at London tutorial colleges, latterly as principal of Collingham College, Kensington, where his wife Carmen taught languages. She set up the Roche School and they are joint principals, but he insists that she is the 'principal principal, the éminence grise', and that he has been 'happily demoted'. Head teacher since 2010 is Vania Adams ('I have to obey not only my wife but her too');

she was busy rehearsing the very confident year 6 cast of the forthcoming West Side Story production when we visited.

Dr Roche reveals that he was 'very scared' of changing from GCSEs and A levels to primary teaching when he joined the school, 'but it was just the same. You just have to explain things so children can understand them.' He teaches maths to year 5 and 6, and to 'some very bright people in year 4 who are mad keen to do maths in their lunch hour', plus any younger ones who are preparing for 7+ and 8+ exams. He has a weekly meeting with a boy in year 4 'who is interested in science – we talk about the photoelectric effect and e=mc squared and tectonic plates and all these amazing theories'. He also teaches some year 6 science. 'I'm just interested in the theory, because if I try an experiment it goes wrong... happily the other year 6 science teacher is very good at experiments.' He has the air of a loquacious, slightly eccentric uncle, and we can see why he is 'particularly well thought of' and 'marvellous with slightly off-beat children'.

If the school has a particular aim, it is to make learning fun. 'It's our business to encourage children who want to know things – to encourage their enthusiasms.'

Entrance: Most join one of the three nurseries, or the reception class. Non-selective, and first-come-first served at this level; those after a place higher up 'come in for a morning or a day. We hear them read, and talk about it, see what their writing is like, if they know anything about how numbers work. We're not looking for technical skills but for a basic understanding.' Some very bright children, but also happy to take children with learning difficulties 'as long as they can benefit from what we offer. If they don't have any enthusiasms, if they're not interested in stories, that's difficult.' Can cater for dyslexia, dyspraxia, Asperger's, Down's syndrome, speech and language difficulties, ASD, ADD and those with EFL needs as long as they have the ability to catch up with their year group.

Quite a through-put, particularly of international families, so worth trying for a place higher up. Some bursaries available, both to incomers and those already at the school.

Exit: A few leave at 7+ or 8+ ('we're happy to prepare children at any age'), but most at 11+ to eg Ibstock Place, Kingston Grammar, Tiffin Girls and Boys, Putney High, More House, JAGs, Wimbledon High, Dulwich College, King's Wimbledon and Latymer Upper. A few to boarding school eg Bedales.

Remarks: Carmen Roche set up Mrs Roche's Coaching Establishment in her West Kensington basement in 1983, largely to prepare children for 11+ and 13+ exams. In 1988, she bought the office block of a Wandsworth laundry in a quiet back street between the A3 and the suburban railway line, and, after some refurbishment, The Roche School moved in. Classrooms mostly compact. Recent building work has added a library (in concept stage when we visited), increased the size of the assembly hall and added some bright top floor rooms 'where you can see the weather approaching right across London.'

Teaching arrangements are 'adaptable to the needs of pupils across a wide range. Children learn at very different rates.' Two ability groups for maths and English from year 2 upwards. Specialist French, music, PE and art teachers.

Plenty of practice for 11+ exams. 'The biggest step we have to ask year 5s and 6s to make is to learn to read the question in detail and use the information they are given. They need to get the habit of precision, of engaging their intelligence.' With his tutoring background, Dr Roche finds preparing children for exams 'exhilarating'. 'Anything that's worth learning is going to be more or less difficult. If we can help children to be patient with themselves we do them a favour.'

High flyers encouraged to fly, whilst 'if you're in year 5 and you've forgotten something you learned in year 2, we're happy to explain it again. A child should feel no shame at not

understanding something'. Not a competitive ethos: 'I hope that the slower ones feel just as pleased with their progress as the faster ones.' Great praise from parents of dyslexic children for the care taken in helping them progress. One-to-one tuition, for special needs or EAL, at extra cost.

When we visited, some of year 4 were learning about meditation and Buddhism – 'next week we're going to bring in candles and make a proper temple for a meditation class' – whilst others were off for games in Wandsworth Park. A year 1 class was having a practical lesson about perspective, whilst some reception children were painting clay pots they had made (school has a kiln). Year 2 were studying the ancient Greeks – 'such fantastic stories'.

Reasonable sized playground behind the school, which also contains the art room (art taken seriously; specialist art teacher) and some sheds about to be replaced by music practice rooms. All the usual sports played in Wandsworth Park, and many inter-school fixtures; after-school clubs (some at extra cost) include cricket, football, judo, netball, swimming, chess, drama and dance. Probably not the place for the hugely sporty child, but they get plenty of exercise.

Lots of chances to act in plays, speak in public, play in the orchestra and in concerts. Children come out 'confident and caring', say parents, tend to 'interview really well', and 'are very proud of their school'. Cosy, nurturing atmosphere; children encouraged to look out for and care for each other.

Bullying 'does sometimes happen: we talk carefully to both sides'. Has never asked anyone to leave on academic grounds, 'though it could happen if a child was interrupting the education of other people, or really had no chance of understanding their work.'

Not a typical London prep. Parents talk of slightly disorganised admin, a great tolerance for eccentricities; a school that really does treat everyone as individuals. 'My two children – one dyslexic and one very academic – both loved it here.'

Rokeby School

George Road, Kingston upon Thames, KT2 7PB

- Pupils: 380 boys; all day • Ages: 3–13 • Non-denom
- Fees: £10,251–£14,274 pa • Independent

Tel: 020 8942 2247
Email: admissions@rokeby.org.uk
Website: www.rokebyschool.co.uk

Headmaster: Since 2007, Mr Jason Peck BEd. Joined school in 1996 as a year 4 and science teacher, becoming deputy head in 2004. Long term association – also has two sons at the school – 'means parents know what they're dealing with,' he thinks. 'He knows the school, how it needs to be run and the traditions,' agreed mother.

Despite influence of several inspirational teachers as grew up (together with deeply scary cane-wielding head), was initially keen to train as a vet, only to realise during work experience that was thoroughly squeamish, not helped by cow-averse mentor. Absence of James Herriot moments led him instead to a spell travelling and running own business, arriving at Kingston University in mid 20s better versed in ways of world, he feels, than some younger out of the egg fellow students.

Didn't necessarily agree with modish teaching theory but was able to rustle up sufficient veneer of enthusiasm to please tutors and perk was instant pupil rapport during classroom experience where proved himself to be an inspirational teacher.

First and only previous post was in tough middle school in Merton. Was surprised, 'perhaps naively so,' at depth of opposition when announced plans to turn to the dark side, aka independent education. Stunned by opportunities, educational and otherwise, and, bar briefly considering more senior science role elsewhere before management beckoned, hasn't looked back since.

Personable, interesting, open, has retained sense of humour despite very considerable challenges, and definitely needs it.

After spending first year taking stock, has made several far-reaching changes, broadening curriculum so doesn't operate exclusively on work/sport axis with little in the middle. In addition to making much more of arts, has also encouraged specialist staff to teach all the way down to pre-prep (not right for all, he says; 'those used to teaching senior school pupils aren't always going to be able to cope with very young children').

School has long had first class reputation for securing year in, year out places at KCS and St Paul's, the competitive parents' most wanted establishments, and 'we have to make sure we hit them,' he says.

Remains singularly successful even now with record competition, as demonstrated by school's waiting lists (knee deep in every year group).

You wouldn't guess it, however, from levels of parental sniping, which are considerable and take in everything from regular easing out of those deemed not to be making the grade to bullies being rewarded rather than punished, to staff disaffection and defection, and even parents being frightened to speak out in case results in repercussions.

In the far corner, however, are Mr Peck's enthusiasts, equally firm in their praise of his leadership, dismissive of any tales of Flashman-style antics in the ascendance and baffled by them, too.

One, with several children at the school, was 'surprised' to hear about negative feedback. 'I love it. I think it does just what it says on the tin and tries hard to make nice boys.'

Unusual, in fact, to find parental opinion so polarised. Recent school inspectors, we're told, were equally bemused, encountering ferocious criticism in feedback forms, yet unable to substantiate any of points made during their visit.

Only areas that both sides agree on is that some of admin team can be fairly robust to deal with (not unusual, in our experience), and that when it comes to teaching science, Mr Peck is the best in the business (and, fortunately for lucky pupils, who also think he's pretty fab, it's something he still finds time to do, though not as much as he'd like).

Mr Peck accepts that 'as a head, some will like my style, some won't', but points to efforts to improve school communications – regular parent rep forums, often free and frank in style, cover gamut of issues, and complaints procedure is being reviewed. As to pupils being asked to leave, yes, 'if a boy is struggling, we will help him find a better school,' but tiny numbers involved – three in past seven years, isn't, to his mind, a big issue.

School insider wondered if turbulence might be linked to structure of board of governors which could appear to be something of a closed shop – not easy to put yourself forward for election. In the meantime, Mr Peck is keen to get all dissenters to identify themselves and talk to him. 'Much better if they're inside the tent,' he says. We tend to agree.

Entrance: Catchment tends towards Wimbledon and Putney rather than Kingston and up into Teddington/Richmond. Other parents almost incestuously local, with the neighbouring homes on what amounts to a mini-me St George's Hill, Weybridge estate (barrier-only entry to the private roads that surround it – school issues passes to non-residents). Some go further afield. But with the added convenience of next door Holy Cross, a similarly high-performing prep for the sisters, why would you bother?

At 4, start in reception, now non-selective: 'you'd end up testing at 2 – just not possible,' says head. A very few leave at end of year 2 to go either to King's College Junior or Colet Court, paper queues forming to snap up spaces – recently had 80 applications for just four slots. Rest carry on through the school, regular assessments tracking progress based on initial maths and cognitive ability assessments in year 1.

Exit: Doing the business with four to KCS and eight to St Paul's in 2013, Dulwich College and Hampton amongst other desirable destinations. Mr Peck working overtime to ensure that out of many worthy candidates deserving of places, school gets its fair share (and ideally a few more as well). Ups and downs come with the territory (change in senior school admissions teams means entire getting to know you process has to start again from scratch) but evens out over the years. No doubt that it's getting tougher, leading to ever closer bonds with out-of-town schools from Epsom College to Charterhouse. Mr Peck admits to pressure to talk up candidates, but 'relationships with senior schools can only work on trust,' so isn't about to give in to it any time soon.

Remarks: What is it with schools and porthole windows? Nautical imagery? All at sea? 'Friendly underwater feel,' thinks delightful guide, a year 8 veteran of countless school tours ('I've done around 20') who shows us round and whose choicest oft-repeated phrases show every sign of being breathed on and rubbed with a shirtsleeve to bring back the shine.

Not till we reach newest building, recently opened by royalty, featuring said porthole windows, does world-weariness disappear. Can't blame him – place is gorgeous, a new home for lucky pre-preppers, all beautifully behaved; reception children, semi-liberated from shackles of prescriptive EYFS curriculum (full freedom from September 2014), quietly immersed in directed play (teachers and TAs also eat with them to create family atmosphere); year 1 pupils having a terrific time matching (and sampling) food with regions that produce them: potato farls from Ireland and – according to worksheet – fairy cakes from Kingston.

Older pupils get to use gorgeous new performing arts theatre with colossal screen, teachers bravely attempting live link with National Archive, chap dressed as slave intermittently beaming in, hoots and cheers from (otherwise immaculately behaved) year 8 boys marking the frequent occasions when computer said 'no'.

With exception of two science labs (neat collection of animal skulls – real – and Henri the skeleton – plastic), sports hall (clean and white, like the song says, with pitched, pine-lined roof that makes it airier than the norm) and assorted music rooms (tuneful violin solo wafting from windows – standard here is high), most classrooms run length of main building, newer addition running into sober, solid Victorian original. Gradual revamping is subtracting old-style slam lid desks (atmospheric but heavy to move owing to volume of stuff stashed by boys) and adding floor to ceiling wooden units – very swish – either side and over the top of whiteboards, not unlike show home bedroom makeover.

What won't change, however, is classroom names, each brass plate proudly announcing name of historic figure or – more rarely – veteran member of staff. Renaming opportunities vanishingly rare, accorded only to chosen ones – normally Mr or Ms Chips types combining longevity with universal outpouring of love.

Lessons delivered in commendably low-stress style by cheerful-looking teachers 'who just want you to feel OK,' thought pupil and are homily-light, preferring, he thought, to encourage older pupils to realisation of any gaps to be filled.

Class sizes reduced with recent division of year 5 upwards into three forms (was two until year 7), maths and English both set, smaller teaching groups the norm in music, head's goal to do something similar with other subjects including science.

Lots of staff enthusiasm, including evangelical DT enthusiast honing latest batch of scholarship hopefuls, charismatic drama specialist encouraging boys to create living poster show as part of term-long project to save fictional circus from closure, and art teacher presiding over series of excellent – if sinister –

R

screaming faces (inspired by Messerschmitt – artist rather than German plane).

Few complaints from pupils. Latin 'a bit of a Marmite subject – though I love it.' Otherwise, science loved for 'experiments and interactive games in last five minutes of lesson,' and, unusually, pupil praise for teachers' awareness of different learner types – auditory, visual and kinaesthetic.

Many highlights, reckoned parent. 'English and maths are good and the history is inspirational,' said one. Not everyone felt the same, some sensing staff disaffection. If so, were certainly hiding it well. One, with child in pre-prep, was thoroughly enjoying the experience. Another wished 'I'd known about school – wasn't on my radar. If it had been, would definitely have sent him here.'

Website, apparently constructed for those already in the know, wouldn't currently help. Though it's not a place lacking confidence – 'the first 125 years' is the title of recent school history – its online parent communications currently need (and is shortly about to get) updated.

In the flesh, however, plenty of non-airy-fairy robustness, not least when it comes to sanctions and rewards. Aim, says head, is 'to find one thing every boy can do well and help him do it even better.' There's leadership training for years 6 to 8 and masses of good work incentives, from house points to red books (not actually red... or a book) rarer than hens' teeth (once every three years, reckoned one pupil). Presentation by Mr Peck about as big as it gets, only disappointment the disappearance of sweets.

Big on detentions, too, or at least the threat of them for range of transgressions. Pays to double check teacher's written homework instructions against what's written on the board and transcribe correct version into homework diary as 'can differ slightly,' thinks pupil.

Pastoral care 'excellent', thinks parent, with head quick to respond to queries, masses of notes all round school commending virtues of good manners (classes and individuals painstaking about standing for visitors) as well as clearly very committed and caring staff (cheerful learning support teacher runs popular sessions, while library, despite top heavy fact over fiction title weighting, is clearly something of a sanctuary – there's little chatting space and year 8s plan to campaign for old pre-prep classroom to be converted into common room).

Pupils adamant that school won't tolerate bullying which rarely goes beyond 'boys' banter', said one. On rare occasions it happens, it's a call to the parents and 'immediate' after school detention.

Former transgressors might have conduct explained to them, be punished but then, later, be rehabilitated. Though some parents aren't keen, head felt second chances important. 'Who would want a child to feel that their life had already been written off?'

Plenty of opportunities for redemption, sport a major feature though less dominant now than it used to be – many more and different sports and far more emphasis on arts now than used to be the case. Teams go all the way down to F in lower years (less so further up the school, but 'everyone still gets games,' said pupil).

Could so easily be swamped by pressure and riven with nerves. And that's just the parents. Despite substantial gripes from some parents, results and atmosphere give it undeniable cachet as prep whose top leavers continue to have the entrée to some of south west London's most sought after senior schools. Currently, worth doing a spot of fact, and faction, checking before you sign up.

Rosemead Preparatory School

70 Thurlow Park Road, London, SE21 8HZ

• Pupils: 370 170 boys and girls; all day • Ages: 3–11 • Interdenom • Fees: £9,880–£10,440 pa • Independent

Tel: 020 8670 5865
Email: admin@rosemeadprepschool.org.uk
Website: www.rosemeadprepschool.org.uk

Headmaster: Since 2012, Arthur Bray, CertEd from Bristol University (fifties). Highly experienced; prior to Rosemead, he was headmaster of GEMS Hampshire in central London, for 26 years. Previously, at Millfield Junior, he and his wife were both senior houseparents for 10 years. Also formerly chairman of the Independent Schools Association and director of the Independent Schools Council.

Father of two grown-up children whose childhood portraits line the walls of his study – a daughter who is now in a senior post at a London prep school and a son who is a director of a City firm. We found him to be easy to talk to and animated when sharing his knowledge of the nuances of how individual children learn. Perhaps the polished antiques suggest an 'old school' headmaster, but his door was deliberately open onto the corridor, where children milled about chattering between lessons.

There is clearly work ahead, with changes already begun with a view to both academic results and 'preparation for life', but avoiding babies and bathwater, the headmaster tells us he has been very aware of listening first and then implementing, 'evolution not revolution'. One parent commented: 'He is very committed to making Rosemead the best that it can be. He is energetic and determined.'

Head of the pre-prep: since 2005, Mary-Elizabeth Everitt, BEd (Hons) Goldsmiths College (forties). She started in the state sector, before teaching for 14 years at Dulwich Prep London. She has a grown-up daughter at university. Friendly and quietly spoken, she is focused and clearly made of steely stuff.

Entrance: Describes itself as 'mixed ability'; the majority of children enter the prep via the pre-prep. Children may enter the nursery during the term of their third birthday; at 4+ into reception or at 7+ into year 3. Whilst the nursery is almost fully subscribed, there are sometimes a few places available at the prep. Assessments begin the November prior to entry, with a 45 minute play session for the nursery or reception entry and language and maths exercises for years 1 – 6.

Means-tested bursary scheme with no limit on numbers. No scholarships. Maximum class size is 22 in the pre-prep and 20 in the prep. No strict sibling policy, but will be taken into account. Unless your family is of Von Trapp proportions, the discount for four or more siblings is unlikely to assist you.

Exit: Pupils exit at 11+, with the school aiming to leave choices 'wide open'. We sense determined parents, as children make three applications on average, for which they are prepared with one-on-one interviews as well as practice papers. Most recently, places were offered to all pupils who sat entrance exams to St Dunstan's College, over 90 per cent to Sydenham High School, just under 60 per cent to James Allen's Girls School, 50 per cent to Dulwich College and 30 per cent to Alleyn's – it's a strong, but by no means guaranteed show of tickets to good and premier destinations. Since the new head's arrival, there has been a rise in both places offered and a higher ratio of awards, particularly academic.

Remarks: A traditional curriculum ticks all boxes, but there is modernising afoot, which is going down well. The head

R

cites updating the texts used in English, and in maths a new on-line tutor sets tasks at an appropriate level for each child, 30 minutes in class and 30 minutes at home each week, with parents able to dip in any time online to see how they are doing.

A recent, carefully thought through decision to switch from the traditional French to the more globally relevant Spanish has been pretty universally accepted, and lessons have been doubled to twice a week. Spanish commences in the pre-prep with singing, stories and movement. The school might have offered Mandarin, but a Mandarin club proved short-lived in popularity.

Next in line for overhaul will be history, geography and science, including an eagerly-awaited science lab. New ICT facilities have arrived. Humanities are supported by a wide array of trips, and highlights of the year are cross-curricular theme days and celebrations.

One of the first things the headmaster instigated is a new means of assessment, and reporting which looks at core skills such as concentration and organisation skills, as well as subject-specific scoring, all of which can be far more useful than a paragraph of commentary.

Staff mix: 18 per cent of staff in place for more than 10 years. Not a high turnover, but the headmaster has made new appointments since arriving, ensuring there is now one male teacher per year group at the prep. Reports from some parents are not spotless – but others impress us with the warm atmosphere between staff and pupils: one mentioned the 'strong emotions shown by all of the [year 6] children as they leave the teachers they have grown fond of'.

With three classes per year in the prep, the class groupings sometimes change after year 3, once teachers have been able to assess how children work together. This can be a tad unpopular, as it isn't necessarily about friendship groups. However, classes are fixed by year 5. Setting for maths from year 3.

The anti-bullying policy has been carefully reviewed, with a buddy scheme throughout the school and year 6 visiting to read to the younger ones, and sharing special assemblies such as that for Chinese New Year.

Learning support, termed Enrichment, has four staff, one of them full time, with one-to-one support for just under 10 per cent of the school. Very small number with EAL.

The fenced playground, high up above the street, is the venue for learning a variety of ball skills. Years 3 to 6 have a weekly PE lesson, a swimming lesson and a full games afternoon. There are two male PE teachers, and a female director of PE. With children taken to nearby Dulwich sports club and Rosendale playing fields for football, hockey, netball, rugby, tennis, cricket and athletics by coach, using the Astroturf pitches at nearby newly refurbished Elmgreen School, and making use of Crystal Palace's national training facilities for swimming from year 2, one parent commented, 'It's a small school with minimum on-site sports facilities, but they seem to offer a lot and children don't know or care that the sports grounds aren't owned by the school.' Rosemead regularly has children taking part at the ISA finals, both as individuals and in teams, and recently at competed at national level in football.

How high pressure is it? A parent who has had three children through the school reported: 'I think Rosemead gets the balance right – one of the reasons we chose it... the amount of homework is about right – more than your average state primary, but not as much as some of the more high pressure private schools in the area.'

Parents commented to us in no uncertain terms that art has been a real weak spot in the past, but we visited the large, new dedicated art studio and saw the specialist teacher in action – a highly talented former assistant from the pre-prep praised by staff and parents. It may have been early in the term when we visited, but there are a lot of blank walls to fill.

The prep has more than its fair share of violinists, as rather than a bit of tootling on the recorder, which waits until year 3, all year 1 at the pre-prep learn violin in groups. Some 150 children have individual instrumental tuition, with several reaching grade 5 by year 6. There is a large school orchestra and two school choirs; ensemble clubs for cello, brass, strings and recorder; and an 'electric fusion band' which plays at the annual Dulwich Festival. A musical highlight is the major concert at the end of the spring term. One parent commented on the 'superb Christmas carol concert in local church... very impressive'.

Clubs – morning, lunch-time and after-school – offer mainly sporty and musical options, with a good show of language clubs for Spanish, French and Russian. Increasingly, this is a school for working parents, and the school is well set up to offer a full day from 8am to 6pm. Clubs start in year 1, most end at 4.30pm, and these can combine with after-school care for all, provided by a third-party, Kids City, with staff chaperoning children between sites and taking any parental emergencies in their stride.

This is a school in transition which, as anyone who has had the builders in knows, can be painful and disruptive but well worth the effort. Quite literally when we visited the façade was covered in scaffolding, with smart new year 6 classrooms just revealed, together with a new library, bigger dining hall and ICT suites. Meanwhile, downstairs everything looked a bit shabby and utilitarian.

What will hold the school together as well as the headmaster are the parents – due to its strong sense of community as well as unique governing structure. Already established as an independent school for 70 years, in 1974 a group of parents took over the managing of the school, and it became a limited company with an all parent management team, and is now a non-profit making charitable trust. All but one of the governing body are parents of current pupils.

Notable and somewhat off-putting is the location on the edge of Dulwich – a bit of a no-man's land on the traffic-heavy South Circular road – however, we did note that once inside we could not hear the traffic, and the location between two overground stations is convenient for commuting quickly into town. The prep looks rather like a tall, red-brick Victorian London school building, but was actually a rehearsal space for the Old Vic theatre, hence the school hall resembling a proper theatre complete with fixed stage.

Parents say, 'Children work hard, concentrate and give of their best.' And our visit backs this up: the atmosphere was calm and industrious, perhaps particularly due to year 6 exams looming. One parent described it as 'A down-to-earth, happy school that will offer an all-round education and ensure a good secondary transfer without putting children under huge pressure in the early years.'

Two-thirds of families live close by, often walking to school; the rest come from all over south London, some from as far as Bromley and Elephant and Castle. This is a school for active parents who want to get involved – fundraising isn't just for external charitable projects but for valuable extras around the school. Talking of active, the previous term, a team of Rosemead mothers rowed the Channel!

The heads report being bowled over by the response to their appeals for help: turning a piece of waste-ground into a sunny little allotment for the pre-prep over the weekend, or creating a rota of volunteer librarians for the new prep library. All of which builds a real sense of community. Parents are a mixed and reportedly friendly crowd – we certainly saw gaggles lingering post drop-off – but particularly evidenced by the Easter family ski trip, which is not just for pupils but unusually everyone: parents, siblings, grandparents, old boys and girls and their families too.

The pretty purple uniforms are a delight, but the stand-out feature of the pre-prep is the charming church building, sympathetically developed to create high ceilinged classrooms, with beautiful arches and bits of stained glass – a lovely space in which to work.

The pre-pre has assistants in every class and high staff ratios in the nursery. School commences in earnest at reception with some parents wishing for a greater emphasis on play: 'hardly any toys in the classroom, much like year 1'. Reception is very different in feel to the boisterous fun we saw in the nursery, but the head points out the gentle start with just 20 minutes of phonics a day compared with an hour in year 1.

It seems to be different things to different families – the pre-prep's church building brings back fond memories for some parents of what a first school should be like; more pragmatically, it could well be a port in a storm when faced with the ultra-competitive local options at 4+.

Rossall Junior School

Linked school: Rossall School

Broadway, Fleetwood, FY7 8JW

• Pupils: 125 girls and boys (four boarders); • Ages: 7-11 in prep; 2-7 in pre-prep; • C of E; • Fees: Day £7,140-£7,410; Boarding £11,880-£17,700 pa; • Independent

---

Tel: 01253 774222
Email: enquiries@rossall.org.uk
Website: www.rossallschool.org.uk

Head of Juniors: Since September 2010 Mrs Katie Lee MEd, former head of pastoral care and director of sport, joined Rossall in 1992 as head of girls' games and spent 10 years as a senior girls' housemistress. A career educationalist, with 30 years' teaching experience, her early years were in comprehensive education. Further experience in higher and adult education, so this appointment completes the circle from 'cradle to grave'. Has a pragmatic and decisive approach, is energetic and results driven. Changes are already visible in the creative use of public space and empty classrooms, strengthening the links and collaboration between the nursery and reception, re-invigorating school council and improving communications with parents. Introduced ties for school captains (infant and juniors) and house captains, as a mark of office and to raise the profile of these posts of responsibility. Believes the Primary Years Programme (PYP) gives children a real confidence and wants to develop this further by providing public platforms and presentation opportunities for them.

Mrs Lee is a director of Blackpool Grand Theatre Trust Board and the theatre's child protection officer. She is also a school governor of Millfield Science and Performing Arts College in Thornton. Breeds Weimaraner dogs and has two much loved pets.

Entrance: At 2 into the nursery in an informal play session. Into reception by assessment of social skills at a taster day. Infill in other years on assessment and report from previous school.

Exit: All to 'Dragon', transition to senior school for years 7 and 8.

Remarks: Nursery and Infants are housed in a stand-alone building at the edge of campus, accessible from nearby car park making drop-off and collection easy. An enclosed outside play area leads directly from Early Years' allowing free flowing outdoor play.

Junior school is housed in a separate building in front of the main school, a short walk away. Contemporary class photos adorn the impressive room allocated to school council meetings.

In 2006 the IB Primary Years Programme (PYP) was introduced. This enquiry-led learning programme promotes the development of the whole child, a holistic educational approach fostered at Rossall. It is particularly strong in

developing communication skills, certainly evident in our conversation with pupils. Building on early success, the programme continues to be embedded and developed in the curriculum. Each classroom has key phrases on display so that pupils understand expected learning outcomes and can reflect on their learning style.

A SENCo covers both infants and juniors, providing continuity. Working one on one or in small groups, work is related to the class mainstream unit of enquiry work.

A full programme of 21 different weekly activities provides a full range of extra-curricular clubs and activities. Swimming, hockey and rugby are curriculum sports, with clubs for football, basketball, fives and badminton in addition. Junior choir for the singers and flute club for budding musicians.

A very clear rewards and sanctions system, with pupils' success being collected for their house. Three houses and healthy inter-house rivalry, culminating in House Challenge Day. The high spot in the social calendar for year 6 is the Leavers' Ball, complete with a pink stretch limo for the girls and a black version for the boys!

A palpable feeling that learning is fun and a happy atmosphere of pupils engaged in learning exists in the classrooms of both buildings. A real leap of faith, the PYP programme is proving to lay good foundations for senior school, although in an environment without the extensive international element so evident with the older pupils.

Rougemont Preparatory School

Linked school: Rougemont School

Llantarnam Hall, Malpas Road, Newport

• Pupils: 190 pupils in reception to year 6, 20 in nursery
• Ages:3-11 • Fees: £7,200-£8,820 pa; • Independent

Tel: 01633 820816
Email: registrar@rsch.co.uk
Website: www.rougemontschool.co.uk

Head: Mrs Lesley Turner

Remarks: See senior school for details.

Rowan Preparatory School

---

6 Fitzalan Road, Claygate, KT10 0LX

• Pupils: 320 girls; all day • Ages: 2-11 • Non-denom
• Fees: £9,381-£12,444 pa • Independent

Tel: 01372 462627
Email: school.registrar@rowanprepschool.co.uk
Website: www.rowan.surrey.sch.uk

Headmistress: Since 2004, Mrs Kathy Kershaw, BA in history of art, Cert Ed (late fifties). Her fourth headship – previously head of nursery and pre-prep at Colfe's School (qv) – and she's only the fifth ever head of Rowan. Approachable, eager to please, but nobody's fool, she has a warm personality and no-one could question her passion and commitment for the place. She's ambitious for her school and everyone in it – staff and pupils alike. Has overseen lots of changes – academic, administrative, pastoral and cosmetic – and successfully softened the school's previously ultra-competitive ethos so as to be more inclusive,

R

but not at the expense of still sparkling academic standards. Says she plans to stay on until retirement, but even so won't see today's nursery starters through to year 6.

She's in no need of a spin doctor, does her own PR very well and is a great advocate for the school; fond of the words 'girl power'. Lays the law down when necessary, but is equally likely to let her hair down and is not above donning red shorts and racing about on sports day. 'But we forgive her almost anything as she is so committed to the school', said one mother. Equally as nurturing with her staff as her pupils, she is very keen on professional development and says eight of her staff have moved on to take up headships in as many years. 'She's got endless amounts of energy which impacts across the whole school,' says one colleague – and that's notwithstanding her 60+ mile round trip to work every day. Bustles around the place like a glamorous mother hen. Has a grown up son and daughter; 'Family and friends are everything to me,' she says. While on a Mencap charity bike ride – where she came in last every day, but completed the course – she kept going by using the mantra 'I can, I know I can'; which she now promotes throughout the school. KK also teaches her girls interview techniques – dress code, posture, confidence and manners. 'Even if they don't need it for their next school, it's very useful as a skill for life,' she says.

Entrance: Non-selective throughout, save a very low key assessment for girls joining the prep at 7+. The nursery takes from age two and these girls get priority for joining kindergarten – other places on first-come-first-served basis, usually from local nurseries. Then automatic transfer from kindergarten to pre-prep at 4+ and to prep department at 7+. Usually also a small outside intake at 7+ (around a dozen). Feeders at 7+ include Emberhurst, Glenesk, Weston Green, Shrewsbury Lodge, Denmead, Jack & Jill and Thames Ditton Infants. Draws from the up-market local area of Claygate, Esher, Surbiton, Wimbledon, Molesey, Walton, Weybridge, Cobham, Epsom and Oxshott. KK says school is keen to help parents not otherwise able to afford it and supportive of those who may fall on hard times – worth asking.

Exit: Most to the top local independent girls' schools – Tormead, Notre Dame, St Catherine's Bramley, Lady Eleanor Holles – with large numbers to fellow UCST schools Guildford High and Surbiton High. A few move on to co-ed, a few to board, usually Benenden, and consistently one or two to highly-sought-after state grammar, Tiffin Girls in Kingston. Always a handful (or two) of scholarships.

Remarks: A happy, vibrant school which gets the best out of its non-selected intake, smoothing their path to an impressive list of senior school destinations.

Tucked away in a leafy residential village, 16 miles from central London, the school is split physically and administratively into two – Rowan Brae, the pre-prep and Rowan Hill, the prep, both under the aegis of KK from her office at 'the Hill'. Just a few minutes' walk apart, both premises are converted Edwardian redbrick houses that blend seamlessly with surrounding imposing properties – hence a combination of slightly odd-shaped classrooms in the original buildings, with more spacious later additions.

Rowan Brae, which houses the nursery to year 2 (ages two to seven) is overseen by its own head, Miss Carolyn Sharps, in post since September 2011 when she was promoted from her previous position as head of Early Years Foundation Stage (EYFS). She is a KK disciple, equally chatty and enthusiastic, and seemingly just as excited about school as the children themselves – everything is 'fantastic', 'wonderful' and 'excellent'. 'I'm getting used to being talked to as if I am also seven,' joked one mother. 'But in fact like everyone here she is very sweet and most forthcoming if you ask a question. She's very responsive, happy to have you in class and explain all about what work they are doing.' Each child has an individual 'Learning Journey' folder accessible by parents at any time.

It's quite a tight site and, with nursery and kindergarten children sharing an entrance, it can be rather a scrum as everyone arrives, but things quickly settle down. Classrooms are lovely, bright and airy. Lots of it is purpose-built, so the layout really works and rooms have their own direct access to the playground. In common with the Hill, the place is extremely well-resourced; cupboards are brimming with goodies – from glue sticks to musical instruments, these girls want for nothing. And the 7/1 EYFS pupil/staff ratio means they get plenty of support and attention. Rowan is very strong on presentation and handwriting – school regularly wins prizes for this – and everything is clean and colourful. Imaginative topics and artwork abound.

At the end of year 2, the girls take KS1 Sats, with 100 per cent achieving the required level two and 60 per cent getting a level three in speaking and listening/reading, writing and maths. The latest ISI inspection described Brae's EYFS as 'outstanding'. Communication between the Hill and Brae has improved a lot in recent years and Hill staff visit regularly, particularly during year 2, to give the little ones an appetite for moving up to the Hill.

Once the girls reach Rowan Hill, things hot up rather as more pressure kicks in. Instead of being form-room-based, the girls move around the school to be taught in excellently equipped, bright classrooms with evidence of much hard work and inspired teaching adorning walls and corridors. Each term takes a theme – recently 'perseverance' and 'creativity'. All the children on task and eager to join in; hands shoot up and bottoms are bounced upon as they vie to answer teachers' questions.

Learning outcomes are excellent across the board, with gifted and talented girls and those with learning difficulties equally well supported. Currently around 15 girls receive support with English as their additional language and school also works with any parents whose own English may be weak. All pupils are screened for dyslexia in year 1. There are currently 16 girls with special educational needs of some variety, typically visual and hearing impediments, dyslexia etc. School is not set up for wheelchair access. Generally all strengths and weaknesses are addressed through small group intervention work with such support (school calls it enrichment) at no additional cost to parents. One mother suggested such provision could be more joined up, so keep on top of school if you are concerned.

Specialist teachers for music, PE, French, ballet and swimming. Latin from year 5 and Spanish and German available as clubs. All the girls get a free cello or violin lesson in year 1 and years 2 to 5 have a timetabled recorder lesson – 65 per cent of them go on to learn an instrument and take grade exams. Standards high enough for some to win senior school music scholarships. Performances of music and drama always polished – 'I've been blown away by some faultless productions,' said one parent. 'They work so hard.' Sports provision is also good, given fairly limited on-site facilities.

Class sizes a little larger than some parents would like – averaging around 18 but can be up to 22 – with a pupil teacher ratio of round 10/1 at the Hill.

It's all very charming and at first glance appears quite traditional, but the curriculum is actually rather creative and the school works hard to make learning fun and inspire the girls to branch out and think for themselves. It's a very rich learning environment; all is bright and beautiful – and it's not just for show; KK is renowned for her high standards and applies such rigour behind the scenes as well as front of house so that staff feel equally well resourced and supported in their work with the girls. 'Education can never be about complacency,' she says. 'I am always looking for ways to make things more interesting.' A new outdoor area is a good example of this, incorporating an eco-area, outdoor classroom, mini amphitheatre and, in response to pupil input, a 'fairy grotto'.

Plenty to do in the playground, from the organised Twister and Jenga games to the more imaginative provision of brightly coloured sticks which the girls use for all sorts of improvised games from hobby horses to fencing. There's a gazebo area for the exclusive use of 'grown up' year 6 girls. Breakfast club each day from 8 – 8.45am. Plenty of extra-curricular clubs from art to yoga, (Chess club was packed when we looked in, while only a few girls in jazz/pop singing) and all the day and residential trips you would expect.

Local parents who by-pass this place for their daughters say they imagine it to be a bit precious, girly and old-fashioned. Certainly the sight of pupils neatly turned out in their uber-cute cherry-red tartan uniforms, topped off by blazers and boaters (of which more later) does nothing to assuage this impression. But although it is 'girly' by virtue of the fact there are no boys and they all take ballet, everything is actually much more contemporary than might first appear. We saw nascent engineers designing wheeled vehicles, maths is strong, a pilot had visited recently to talk about future careers and KK and her staff work hard to embrace all the virtues of a single-sex education.

'I've sent my two very different daughters through the school and it's been great for both of them,' said one mother. 'One adored the "can do" attitude and threw herself into it all with gusto. The other is much more introspective, but they make sure she's always involved in everything and I know she'll get a good senior school'. That said, there seems to be a general understanding among parents that Rowan prefers its girls to 'fit the mould' – for which read be enthusiastic, well-behaved, reasonably academic and sporty. 'You always hear the same names mentioned in despatches,' said one. 'And you see the same faces representing the school. Not sour grapes because it's not my daughter, just a fact of life here. You need to be confident and assured to really shine'.

Girls we spoke to were generally confident, even perky, articulate, polite and friendly and really seemed to feel a sense of belonging. They positively ache to win a trophy or two, or, even better, a head's commendation – 'she knows everyone and not just their name, but lots about them', said one pupil. Generally keen to please, eager to learn little girls, so discipline is a minor issue here. By all accounts the primary sanction of losing a bonus mark is treated very seriously by one's peers. Doesn't sound much, but means a lot. 'You have to stand up and explain to the rest of the house what has happened', explained one pupil. Incurring KK's displeasure and disappointment is ultimate sanction enough. 'She does have a strict side and will get to the bottom of things,' say her pupils. Friendship issues feature large for little girls and KK says she addresses this, and other pastoral issues, through her 'hidden curriculum of understanding, truthfulness and integrity, which is embedded into the whole school'.

Since our last visit Rowan has joined the United Church Schools Trust – a family of a dozen or so independent schools across the UK including Guildford High and Surbiton High, where Rowan has traditionally sent sizeable numbers of its pupils. But KK stresses that Rowan retains its independence and is still entirely free to send its pupils to the full range of schools it currently feeds. Rowan does however benefit from UCST's extensive educational resources, training opportunities and facilities, including shared sports pitches about a mile away. 'It's a move to secure our future,' says KK.

Home/school communication is good, at the classroom door, via emails and texts, KK's weekly Friday Notes and curriculum information evenings; it all combines to ensure parents are up to speed with what's going on. Parents in these parts can be a demanding lot, so the currently increasing numbers coming into EYFS attests to Rowan's success in meeting their high expectations. In return Rowan parents are a committed bunch, happy to help in school and support the parents' association, Friends of Rowan, which provides a nice social side and raises hefty cash sums.

Grumbles about this place are few and far between, but several parents mentioned the 'excessive' uniform. 'I'm sure it's fine for the super-rich, but for those of us who find school fees more of a stretch it's a huge outlay,' said one. 'Do they really need a winter coat, rain coat and blazer? And piping on the blouses means I can't get away with a supermarket pack!' Similarly short notice requests of the 'please bring in a bean sprout cake tomorrow' variety don't help working mothers – though we should add that lots of Rowan's 'at home' mums seem to love this sort of thing and get stuck in with relish. 'You should have seen the creations in the Easter bonnet parade,' confided one (bitter?) working mother.

It's a premium school and more adventurous than you might imagine. Suits tenacious types; tryers keen to do their best.

Rowledge C of E (Controlled) Primary School

School Road, Rowledge, Farnham, Surrey, GU10 4BW

• Pupils: 210 boys and girls • Ages: 4–11 • C of E • State

Tel: 01252 792346
Email: admin@rowledge.hants.sch.uk
Website: www.rowledge.hants.sch.uk/

Headteacher: Since 2006, Mr Richard Catchpole (forties). Spent formative years in Scotland, took BSc in psychology at the University of Bradford ('the perfect degree for a primary school role,' he says, 'midway between a science and an art'). Before joining Rowledge in 2001 as deputy head, he worked at other successful local primaries, including the nation's top-performing South Farnham Junior School and the Chandler Junior School in Witley, where he was head of year. Married to Fiona, who works with special needs children in Guildford, and they have three children, one of primary age, two at secondary school. Not easily rattled – he faced an Ofsted inspection on his first day as head – and though mild-mannered and approachable, is no soft touch. 'He can laugh at himself but is firm when he needs to be,' said one parent. Listens to parents' views. He reversed a long-standing (if almost unenforceable) ban on tree climbing, something few heads would consider, and even asked children to suggest rules (one foot on or below painted lines on the trunks). Every child gets a chance to shine, not through a cop out 'prizes for all' approach, but with imaginative, sensible ideas. 'You need to ask not how intelligent someone is, but how is someone intelligent,' he says.

Entrance: Thirty in reception, most from the village's two nursery schools. Single form entry and only occasional places in other years means the waiting list hovers at around 10. Tight catchment area – the efficient admin team field frequent boundary queries from disbelieving parents.

Exit: Almost all to local (excellent) secondaries – Eggar's School in Alton, Hampshire, or its Surrey counterpart, Weydon School in Farnham. A few each year to local independents such as the Royal Grammar School in Guildford, Churcher's College in Petersfield, Alton Convent and Prior's Field School in Godalming.

Remarks: Imagine a small country school in an idyllic village setting, complete with traditional butcher, house names like Serendipity and even a parent-operated one-way system to alleviate school-run trauma, and this is it. With its red-tiled roofs, arched windows and generous playground – three acres including a field running the length of its low-rise buildings – the school oozes charm. Reception children start with

R

separate, secure play area (complete with cosy if weather-beaten playhouses), then, as confidence grows, join the main, well-supervised melée at break time where there's football, pretend pony lunging (well, this is home counties borderland) and piles of old tyres to spark the imagination.

Goldilocks would approve. The main building is cosy, not cramped, with staggered exits to avoid playtime chaos. Tidiness is encouraged. Children look smart (ties worn from year 3 up) and are generally polite. Good academic results. Lots of class sports, including gymnastics, athletics, team games and dance, to keep them busy in school hours and netball and cross-country, amongst others, out of them, with a good range of other extra-curricular activities that vary each term and range from a thriving newspaper club to board games and textiles. There's an underlying, not over-bearing, spiritual dimension, with regular church-based worship, a leavers' assembly in Guildford Cathedral 15 miles away and a values week where balloons, filled with prayers, are released. Every child, refreshingly, gets to be a young governor and has a say in decisions like what colour to paint revamped toilets.

Staff turnover is 'refreshingly regular rather than cripplingly constant,' says head, with teachers, typically in mid-30s, averaging around four years before moving on. They're good at subtle discipline. 'She just gives us a look that says we can't do it,' one child told us. Parents appreciate the school's academic success but above all praise the atmosphere. 'The children all look out for each other,' says a mother. Four year olds rush to greet older children with hugs and even party invitations.

Valuing everyone seems hardwired into Rowledge's DNA. House system and rewards for good behaviour, including the chance to ring the school's traditional bell on a rope for morning lessons. Projects, completed with minimal parental involvement, make children think for themselves and favour the tenacious – one girl cut and stitched a Roman toga from scratch. Lots of thought is given to those needing most encouragement, with achievements great and small listed on a special board and teaching that plays to the children's strengths. 'Just because you find times tables difficult doesn't mean you're hopeless at talking about shapes, so it's not helpful to confine the same child to the same group,' says the head.

The school ethos is reinforced when it comes to special needs. The Sunshine and Sparkle SEN teams (six children have statements, while four receive additional support) are in charge of four kudos-adding hens, writing idiosyncratic dos and don'ts lists for holiday carers and – with enormous pride – collecting the eggs. Parental niggles are thin on the ground. 'My children are very different and it's catered for them both – it's very nurturing,' one parent told us, while another said 'they send out questionnaires asking "what can we do better?" I've never been able to think of anything.' Truly a small school with a big heart.

Royal Grammar School Junior School (Newcastle)

Linked school: Royal Grammar School (Newcastle)

Lambton Road, Jesmond, Newcastle upon Tyne, NE2 4RX

- Pupils: 250 boys and girls; all day • Ages: 7–11 • Non-denom
- Fees: £9,024 pa • Independent

Tel: 01912 815711
Email: admissions@rgs.newcastle.sch.uk
Website: www.rgs.newcastle.sch.uk

Head: Mr Roland Craig

Entrance: Assessment days held in mid January for prospective year 3 and in November for year 5 entrants.

Exit: Vast majority to senior school (subject to internal assessments).

Remarks: Self-contained, purpose-built junior school, with three-form entry introduced in 2012. Years 3 and 4 self-contained in one building – pupils move across the road to new accommodation in year 5 and 6. Shares facilities with the senior school (with new swimming pool and second sports hall underway).

Royal High School, Bath, Junior School GDST

Linked school: Royal High School, Bath GDST

Hope House, Lansdown Road, Bath, BA1 5ES

- Pupils: 130 girls, plus nursery school; boarding from year 5
- Ages: 3–11 • Non-denom • Fees: Day £8,070–£8,424; Boarding £20,097 pa • Independent

Tel: 01225 422931
Email: royalhigh@bat.gdst.net
Website: www.royalhighbath.gdst.net

Head: Since 2013, Mrs Heidi Hughes BSc PGCE MA. Previously deputy head of Royal Russell Junior School, Surrey. Prior to this she was a member of management teams at British schools in Singapore and the Philippines. A strong advocate of linking learning in and beyond the classroom, she welcomes parental involvement. Outside school, her interests are sport, travel and family. She often volunteers at local sporting events (including the London 2012 Olympics).

Entrance: By assessment and interview with the head. Nursery school pupils are expected to transfer to the junior school and have first choice of available places.

Exit: Virtually all go on to the senior school by way of the transfer exam in year 6 – 'a rite of passage,' says the head, who will have suggested, very nicely and well in advance, that doubtful runners look elsewhere. For everyone else, the exam is used for setting and awarding scholarships.

Remarks: Very much the little sister of the senior school up the hill, sharing the same lofty position on Bath's desirable and leafy northern slopes. Not for ever though – school is about to move into a stunning listed building, Cranwell House, on a much larger site with better access. Meanwhile it's business as usual in the three current buildings, one a beautiful Georgian showcase which once housed the senior school, surrounded by secured landscaped grounds. All-year swimming will happen at the senior school once their plans for a 'telescopic' all-weather roof come to fruition.

Praise abounds for the teachers: 'enthusiastic, committed, gentle, nurturing, yet they challenge the girls', and keep them tested and stretched. Small classes must help. Any suggestion of hot-housing strenuously rejected, however. Collaboration is the name of the game here: maths surgeries (for parents) very well attended, and any hint of SEN identified and discussed with parents early on. Languages particularly vibrant, with French for year 3, Spanish for year 4, German for year 5 and Mandarin for year 6, with emphasis on oral communication led by native speakers where possible – we were reluctant to leave the Mandarin class we visited. The curriculum is broad and not exam-led – the GDST has abandoned year 6 Sats, although other initiatives from the state sector such as Sing-Up, Healthy Schools and Artsmark (gold, in RHS Junior's case) sought and achieved.

Art, music, dance and drama all impress, particularly a recent production of Alice in Wonderland. Enough going on in school time to satisfy further-flung girls bound by school bus departure times.

Sense of community built on close links with parents and the fact that the whole school lunches together, eating proper food with knives and forks; manners, poise and common sense mark out Royal High girls, according to one happy parent, tired of being mown down by boisterous counterparts in other schools. Quaint formalities too, eg where girls are dismissed with a handshake from teacher at the end of the day. Everyone has a 'book friend', where the littlies and year 6s share books and read to each other – our guide's book friend came and hugged her in the playground – says it all, really.

All in all, a great choice for parents wanting a single-sex primary education with good, old-fashioned rigour, vigour and values – oh, and fun, leading on to more of the same at the senior school.

Royal Masonic School for Girls Cadogan House Prep & Pre-prep

Linked school: Royal Masonic School for Girls

Rickmansworth Park, Rickmansworth, WD3 4HF

• Pupils: 230 girls; 8 boarders • Ages: 4–11 • Fees: Boarding £15,750–£16,050; Day £9,000–£10,440 pa • Independent

Tel: 01923 773168
Email: admissions@royalmasonic.herts.sch.uk
Website: www.royalmasonic.herts.sch.uk

Headmistress: Since 1996, Miss Linda Beckett BEd (mid fifties). Educated at Christ's Hospital Girls' High School, Lincoln. Has worked solely in the independent sector in girls' schools and was previously deputy head of Leaden Hall, Salisbury. A committed Christian, she is a cordial, matriarchal figurehead for her young charges. Constantly delighted by the girls taking full advantage of her open door policy, bringing her both their triumphs and troubles. Determined to inspire confident, independent learners, she says she sits 'in the middle' of the strict vs relaxed spectrum and is keen that the girls are constantly 'challenging their own personal best', at whatever level this may be. Parents see her as 'a safe pair of hands'.

Entrance: Entry at 4 currently oversubscribed, enabling selection of those the school thinks will best fit its culture and, ultimately, that of the senior school. An extra parallel class was introduced in 2012 to accommodate demand. Academic ability is 'just a part' of the selection criteria, according to head, with the way candidates approach tasks and interact with other girls held in equal regard. Prospective students come for a half a day assessment which is so gentle that according to one parent 'they hardly know it's happening'.

There is another small intake of about half a dozen into year 3 but girls can and do join at any point, with the head gradually growing the class sizes to a maximum of 24 in year 6. Those joining post reception come from both state and independent sectors and are asked to attend a full day assessment where they join in whatever existing pupils are doing and also take assessments in English, maths and reasoning.

About 50 per cent transfer into reception from the on-site co-ed pre-school, Ruspini House – although places are not guaranteed to children coming up through this route – with the rest joining from a variety of other, mostly local, pre-schools.

Exit: Cadogan House girls are guaranteed a place at the Royal Masonic School, making it the clear choice for parents looking for a one stop shop. Very few leave for other destinations at the end of year 6 with those that do moving to local grammars for the obvious financial reasons. Hardly any to other independents.

Remarks: Sharing the same campus as the senior school, Cadogan House opened in 2011 as the gleaming newly refurbished home for the pre-prep and preparatory school of the Royal Masonic School. An enviably spacious facility (so serene you sometimes wonder where all the children are), nestling in its own lush grounds, it mirrors the grandeur of its big sister but maintains a safe and nurturing vibe. Benefits from a few shared facilities with the senior school (dining hall, swimming pool and breathtaking sports hall), which also gives girls a natural and very comfortable transition into year 7. Own art and DT rooms, ICT suite, a well-stocked library and brand new hall that was built as part of the renovation, providing an excellent light and bright space for assemblies, dance and PE lessons.

Classrooms and corridors are proudly adorned with artistic endeavours and handwritten work; regular themes run through the whole school enabling all year groups to display their creative wares side by side. Outside is an enticing new adventure playground, large grassy play area, wild flower garden and beyond that a new outside learning facility, part of the Forest School initiative, 'great for bringing children out of their shells', says head.

Boaters and tidy plaits abound among these confident, down-to-earth girls who were super keen on our visit – arms stretched out of sockets – to answer questions about a recent school field trip (quite something as it was to Watford). Younger ones engage in lively chat as they crocodile back from lunch in the senior school. Plenty of room for growth in its new home gives the school a quiet, studious air rather than the chaotic clatter of many prep schools.

Strong languages – Spanish from reception and French from year 3, extra-curricular Spanish club also on offer for keen linguists. Robust academics across the board, with five girls winning scholarships to the senior school in 2012. 'Gentle' setting in English and maths from the word go, with this formalised for maths in year 5. Classes are mixed up at the end of years 2 and 4 and girls get a taste of senior school life by starting to move around the school for some lessons from year 4. Years 5 and 6 see this step up a notch with them heading to the senior school for specialised teaching in textiles and design technology.

Full time SEN co-ordinator plus three part-time assistants on hand for those in need of help. Statemented children are rare here but minor problems are ironed out with a creative, friendly approach; materials such as board games sent home to get parents involved in the process.

'Very strong' performing arts, say parents, with girls clamouring for parts in the annual (usually musical) production – Joseph and his Amazing Technicolour Dreamcoat was the most recent hit. Take-up of instruments is high, with the ukulele played by all in year 3 (collective sighs of relief from parents when the school decided to drop violin for all), about 60 per cent of girls choosing another instrument, and a thriving prep orchestra and choir.

Competitive sport from year 4, with a host of extra-curricular clubs and activities to choose from for the physically inclined, including skipping, kick boxing, maypole dancing and fencing. Plenty for less sporty types too with other clubs ranging from meditation and doodling to rummikub. Occasional grumbles from parents that there could be more clubs for younger girls as most start from year 3. Annual residential trips from year 4 onwards allow pupils to spread their wings outside of their campus bubble.

Nurturing feel consolidated by presence of peer mentors in year 6 to act as 'big sisters' to the younger ones. Trained by the school counsellor, they are on hand to support and guide through any minor personal or friendship issues. Girls' concerns can also be anonymously posted into a 'worry box' and are then addressed in the appropriate manner by the relevant form teacher. PSHE extends to parents, who are brought in for seminars on subjects ranging from internet safety (all girls are given a school email address from reception) to coping with bereavement or avoiding 'helicopter' parenting.

Just 15 full-time boarders among over 200 children, with a handful more taking advantage of flexi or ad hoc boarding. About a third of full-timers are international (from Asia and Russia) with a handful of forces families in the mix. Junior boarding house is home from home to girls from years 3 to 7 and has good facilities and plenty of space, although parents are hoping for a refurb soon. All meals apart from weekend breakfast, when girls can pad downstairs in their pyjamas, are taken in the senior school. Food is reportedly 'outstanding'. Boarders take advantage of the full array of after school activities, plus games, in-house events and an extensive DVD collection. Weekends see them participate in creative activities (tie-dying was named a top recent favourite) and head off on outings such as local bowling, shows and rollerblading or further afield to the seaside. From year 3, day girls can stay until 5.15 for supervised prep and can also stay for supper (until 6.15) for a 'few pounds'.

Families from a wide range of social and, to a certain extent, ethnic backgrounds reflecting the far-reaching catchment, all with huge expectations of their girls, especially those with both parents working to pay the fees. Many are local, with some from further afield (Gerrard's Cross, St Albans) taking advantage of the excellent coach services, available from year 3 up, that run from the Chilterns, Hertfordshire and North London areas. Girls travelling from London hop on the shuttle bus that runs from the nearby station.

Royal Russell Junior School

Linked school: Royal Russell School

Coombe Lane, Croydon, CR9 5BX

• Pupils: 140 girls, 165 boys • Ages: 3-11 • Christian • Fees: £9,240–£11,295 pa • Independent

Tel: 020 8651 5884
Email: juniorschool@royalrussell.co.uk
Website: www.royalrussell.co.uk/Juniorindex.php

Junior school headmaster: Since 2009, Mr James Thompson BA QTS (late thirties). Previously director of studies at Kingswood Prep, Bath, and then deputy head at Ardingly College Prep School. Married to Viv, head of a nursery school in Notting Hill Gate; prior to that she ran the marketing for the junior school. They have two young daughters who both attend the junior school. Mr Thompson initially trained as a PE teacher; his other specialist subjects are mathematics and geography. His passion for sports rubs off on the school – a keen skier, he has introduced an annual family skiing trip. He is also involved with a large charity assisting them in running sporting events and umpires for premier league hockey.

Entrance: Three and 4+: selective (informal teacher observational assessment) entry to the nursery and early years classes.

Seven+: children are invited to spend a day at the school for an entry assessment to gauge their potential.

Exit: At 11+ most (around 85 per cent) continue through to the senior school. A few leave for local grammars – Wallington, Wilsons or Archbishop Tenison, Bromley.

Remarks: Accommodated in its own buildings, on a lovely rural site opposite the senior school. Classrooms are bright and spacious, along with three well planned playground areas including an adventure playground set into the woodland.

A strong tradition for music, art, drama and sports and an extremely active extracurricular programme. Exceptional music for a junior school, 70 per cent of children learning an instrument, in addition to class music. Year 1s learn the recorder and the following year everybody learns keyboard and a string instrument. An orchestra, rock group, jazz and choirs, which all perform regularly at school and local events.

Small classes of around 18, mixed ability, with setting for mathematics from year 3; staff aware of the need to include differentiation in all the lessons. Additional support is arranged as required in small groups or one-to-one lessons. ICT is used across the curriculum to enrich lessons, everyone is taught to touch type on specially designed colour-coded keyboards. Head keen to involve parents in their children's education – runs regular workshops to give parents a good understanding of subjects children are studying and encourages them to come in and work with reading groups. Once a term homework is suspended for a week for a creative home/school project, the idea being to get the children thinking and investigating different topics and ideas, then creating a piece of artwork. Children learn Spanish in years 3 and 4 and French in years 5 and 6, so they have a good grounding in two foreign languages ready for senior school.

Lovely child-friendly library – each class has allotted library periods and storytelling sessions. Classrooms are well resourced, the juniors have their own science lab and pupils enjoy the senior school facilities increasingly as they go through the age groups, including the performing arts centre, indoor pool and other extensive on site sports facilities (including new all-weather pitch).

Similarly to the senior school, staff are dedicated to aiming high whilst developing well rounded and confident children.

Rudolf Steiner Junior School (Kings Langley)

Linked school: Rudolf Steiner School (Kings Langley)

Langley Hill, Kings Langley, WD4 8NB

• Pupils: 410 • Fees: £4,790–£8,345 pa • Independent

Tel: 01923 262505
Email: info@rsskl.org
Website: www.rsskl.org

Remarks: See senior school.

The Russell Primary School

Petersham Road, Petersham, Richmond, Surrey, TW10 7AH

• Pupils: 270 • Ages: 3–11 • Non-denom • State

Tel: 020 8940 1446
Email: info@russell.richmond.sch.uk
Website: www.russell.richmond.sch.uk

Headteacher: Since 2012, Ms Samantha Leir, previously deputy head and acting head.

Entrance: Over-subscribed every year: 50 plus applicants for 30 places. Nursery place does not guarantee a place in reception class. Clear criteria for admission given on school website: children with a statement of SEN get first priority, followed by siblings, then those living closest to the school. With the current baby boom, there aren't many places left for non-siblings. You'll need to live on the doorstep even to stand a chance.

Exit: Very few leave after year 2 to go to local prep schools. Local secondary Grey Court is the 'linked school' taking about two-thirds of the leavers for senior school. A few go each year to the local grammar schools in Kingston – Tiffin Girls and Tiffin School, which are notoriously difficult to get into (you will need to get special coaching for the entrance exam). A handful move on to local independent day schools, for example, Kingston Grammar, Hampton or Surbiton High – an ex-Russell child is likely to be the only entrant from there in their year group. The school is happy to give advice to parents about the independent schools as well as the state sector.

Remarks: A school that stands out for its SEN provision, wrap-around care and wonderful grounds – you get the feeling that it is a place that really does belong to the children. One member of staff remarked that she feels privileged to be allowed care of such a wonderful group, and the previous head consulted all pupils about what they want to study – 'there is a lot of science to be learned from magic'. The new child-centred topic approach to learning is now well underway. For those parents wanting a formal and authoritarian atmosphere this is not the place, but for those parents in situ things couldn't be better – 'A strong focus on the development of the individual child,' remarked a mother; 'They aim to nurture every child,' said another.

A school that is proud of its history – it was originally founded in Richmond Park as the village school of Petersham by Lord John Russell in the 1850s. It retains something of the 'village school' feel – a true social mix where city bonuses rub shoulders with artists and with the council estate. The current school was built in the 1950s and some of the buildings look a bit tired, but the beautiful outdoor space, which feels like a little corner of Richmond Park, more than compensates for this. There are two ponds teeming with wildlife, wooded areas, pathways to explore, wild areas, a vegetable garden cared for by the pupils and a popular outdoor classroom enclosed by bushes. This is in addition to the abundant playground areas with climbing equipment of all shapes and sizes. Shaded areas have been constructed and there is no outdoor area which cannot be put to good use. Some buildings are quite far apart, so no choice but to get wet when it rains!

Inside, the facilities are more than adequate for a small school: two halls, a science room, an art room (even has a kiln, though there was no sign of any pottery at the time of our visit), a small cookery room allowing for groups of six children. Libraries are cosy and welcoming and there are plenty of computers and interactive whiteboards in each classroom.

Education is far more than wanting a top place in the league table; Sats results are certainly not the be all and end all here

– that said, the school is usually mid ranking in the borough. In key stage 1, classes are mixed between two year groups in order to remain within the maximum class size of 30. Parental concerns about this set-up have proved unfounded, especially since the birth month of the children is taken into account, and Ofsted reports that standards are above average at this stage (the school has taken on board the comment that more able children could achieve more in reading and writing). Within the core curriculum, the school is always looking for ways to add breadth – hence the consultation about what children want to learn – and are ahead of the game when it comes to government requirements. Children learn French from reception and German from year 5, with the help of students from the nextdoor German School, and science is taught by specialist teachers. Children with English as an additional language are few, so can be helped within the classroom environment.

SEN is given high priority and there is much expertise within the school. Specialist SEN unit for children with statements which feels very much part of the school, although physically separate. (The multi-sensory room can be booked for use by anyone, not just the children in the unit.) The SEN unit is recognised in the local area as very successful and is staffed by highly qualified personnel. The children join in as many mainstream activities as possible – 'a great benefit to both sides. In an assembly the SEN child will take a role and be helped to do so by one of the children from the main school.' Parents also like this situation – 'my child is beginning to understand other children's needs.'

Music also enjoys specialist teaching; the choir is open to all age groups and performs annually in the Richmond Music Festival. One parent was delighted to find the music teacher in the nursery as well. Brentford Football Club teaches sport; swimming takes place at the German School for younger ones and in Richmond for older age groups. 'Sport is on the up,' remarked one parent, though another pointed out that there is not enough practice for the school teams, thereby minimising their chances of winning. However, the school is keen to add that relatively recently the school was 'the winner of the indoor athletics tournament and also the small schools' football tournament.'

The staff are 'adored' by the children according to one mother and, despite high house prices in the area, remain a remarkably stable bunch. One teaching assistant, who has been at the school for longer than anyone can remember, has applied to continue after retirement age. Rather a lack of male presence: the staff is fully female apart from the caretaker.

Pupils seem calm and motivated to learn, with 'exemplary discipline' according to Ofsted. Before and after school club (Fit for Sport) from 7.30am till 6pm catering for children from six months to 11 years at reasonable rates. For those who just want to enjoy an after-school club, there is plenty to choose from, ranging from indoor golf to maypole dancing (very popular). As with many Richmond primaries, part of what makes the Russell a good school is the parents – committed and ambitious enough to ensure that their children don't fail. If the topic is the Egyptians, you'll find a chunk of Richmond parents at the British Museum on Saturday. The Russell parents are no different and they are happy with the role they play – 'it's a lovely place for parents,' says one mother – and they find communication with the school more than adequate through newsletters, class assemblies, regular parents' evenings, a parents' forum and easy access at the end of the day to class teachers and, of course, the head who is regularly to be found in the playground. The website could do with an update – but this is 'in hand'.

This is not a substitute prep school with the kind of traditional methods and competition that implies, and the move to secondary school from such a close family set-up is not going to be easy. However, if you are looking for a good state school, a caring and friendly learning environment with plenty to inspire your child you need look no further. You just somehow need to find a way to get a place.

R

Ryde School with Upper Chine, Junior School

Linked school: Ryde School with Upper Chine

Queen's Road, Ryde, PO33 3BE

- Pupils: 230 boys and girls; day and boarding • Ages: 3–11 • C of E
- Fees: £5,205–£9,945 pa • Independent

Tel: 01983 612901
Email: admissions@rydeschool.org.uk
Website: www.rydeschool.org.uk

Head: Mr Howard Edward BSc PGCE

Entrance: At any point when space available.

Exit: Most pupils go on to the senior school.

Remarks: In a converted house on the same campus as the senior school but operates almost completely separately, with few staff in common except those in learning support. Traditional feel, desks in rows, but bright and cheerful. 'We have a policy that all the children's work goes up on the walls.' Open until 4.45pm every day, after-school arts, crafts, sports and homework clubs. The Island is a fertile site for dinosaur bones and houses two dinosaur museums.

Rye St Antony Junior School

Linked school: Rye St Antony School

Pullen's Lane, Oxford, OX3 0BY

- Pupils: 130 girls, day and boarding (from year 5) • Ages: 3–11
- RC • Fees: Day £8,655–£13,170; Boarding £17,310–£18,330 pa
- Independent

Tel: 01865 762802
Email: enquiries@ryestantony.co.uk
Website: www.ryestantony.co.uk

Head: Since 1990, Miss Alison Jones (see senior school entry).

Rye's junior and nursery departments are presided over by Miss Jo Reed, who joined the school in 2008 from nearby Headington Prep. Miss Reed is proud of Rye's inclusive philosophy, 'we don't label children here, we accept them for who they are regardless of ability.'

Entrance: Nursery places (age 3 – 5) offered after visit. Separate application must be made for place in junior school. Candidates for junior school spend a day and are informally interviewed and assessed. Report from previous school required. No examination for progression to senior school.

Exit: Boys mainly to local preps; girls to Rye's senior school.

Remarks: Recently judged as 'outstanding' by Ofsted, the junior school and nursery are on the same site as the senior school with delightfully quirky accommodation in a Victorian house. The nursery is up in the eaves of King House with gabled classrooms full of tactile equipment, books, paints and dressing up. Working parents are grateful for extended flexible opening hours (7.30am to 6.30pm); children can come for morning, afternoon or all day sessions. The youngest eat in their classrooms, older children eat in the dining hall with the rest of the school. Juniors enjoy joint academic and extra-curricular activities with the seniors and there's no demarcation of outside space, all of which contributes to the strong sense of community commented on by so many parents and visitors. No uniform until reception, thereafter school's distinctive bright red jumpers and tights worn with grey tunics (trousers or shorts for boys).

Juniors are taught in Langley Lodge, another Victorian gem that retains its original charm with wonderful windows, fireplaces and high ceilings, so much more inspiring for young imaginations than standard issue classroom boxes (requisite technology and smart boards also present). Classes are small and children benefit from an extended broad curriculum with subject specialist teaching in music, food technology, French, ICT, art, science, maths PE and DT. Plenty of time allowed for sport, music and creative stuff. Formality increases gradually as children move towards senior school but no decrease in fun quotient – we saw a class of year 5 girls in a junior science lab excitedly acting out the behaviour of molecules. At the school's annual science fair mixed age teams compete against each other, developing research and presentational skills. Walls and notice boards covered with creativity and evidence of enthusiastic fundraising – the juniors choose their own charity each term. We were introduced to the Rye bear and baby bear who spend each holiday with a different child; the guardians report back with a presentation and photos. Equally popular is the duo of dwarf rabbits who are lavished with exemplary care. Rye's Catholicism is a deciding factor for some parents; others single out the clear values and strong sense of community; small classes, lovely staff and a magical wooded setting in the centre of Oxford should appeal to all.

The Ryleys School

Ryleys Lane, Alderley Edge, SK9 7UY

- Pupils: 255 • Ages: 3–13 • Fees: £6,048–£10,239 pa
- Independent

Tel: 01625 583241
Email: headmaster@ryleys.cheshire.sch.uk
Website: www.theryleys.com

Head: Since 2012, Mr Paul Berry, previously deputy head of S Anselm's in Bakewell, where he and his wife ran the senior girls' boarding house. His degree was in sports and exercise science and he has been director of sport at Durlston Court, and director of studies at Claysmore. His two young children have joined The Ryleys.

Entrance: Spaces available in some years but not all, with waiting lists in operation. Not selective as such although all families are interviewed, but generally, unless a child has needs the school cannot meet, they're welcome. Some music scholarships. Reductions for second and third siblings and a fourth child goes free while you've four in the school.

Exit: A core aim is to ensure each child progresses to the best next school for them. All prepped for 11+ exams even if they plan to stay to 13. About half to Manchester Grammar. Kings Macclesfield, Cheadle Hulme and Stockport Grammar also popular. At 13 Shrewsbury, Sedbergh, Repton, Uppingham, Ampleforth are amongst the choices. A few bag music or sports scholarships.

Remarks: Delightful prep full of children fair busting with enthusiasm and having the time of their lives. Many leave at 11 going on to schools of their choice, with some opting to

R

stay until 13. Girls now welcomed into the nursery, junior and middle schools in response to parental requests to include female siblings (and, we suspect, to keep enrolment up). Admits all abilities: 'We are an academic school but we're not a hothouse in any way, we look for each child's special ability'. Impressive then that traditionally about half secure places at Manchester Grammar. Secrets include keeping classes to absolute maximum of 20, specialist teachers from eight years old in bespoke rooms for science, music, ICT, DT and art, and lots of prizes, most notably for endeavour. Prizes and merits presented in full school Friday assemblies, full and half colours for sport. Children describe school as 'challenging but the teachers are funny', and there's a can-do atmosphere, 'you can make anything you want in woodwork... well, as long as it's not sharp'. Colour is everywhere in the nursery and infants from the playground to the murals in the loos, and in class even four year olds stand to the instruction 'levez vous'.

Fabulous music, choirs swept the board winning all five choir category prizes in recent Alderley Edge Music Festival. 'The whole world knows about our choirs,' pupils confidently tell us, and in fact the whole world does know about former soloist Laurence Jeffcoate, one of the BBC's 'I'd Do Anything' Olivers. Six coach loads travelled to see him in the West End. One pupil was awarded a place at the prestigious Chetham's School of Music, studying the oboe and piano. Music experience voluntary for littlies, but they can start instrument lessons as soon as they're capable and by 13 many pass grade 6, partly because school (hats off to this) teaches grade 5 theory.

Children are encouraged to participate in many sports, with football, rugby and cricket providing the core activities for the boys, whilst the girls compete in netball, hockey and rounders. All pupils swim in the summer term, making full use of the 25m pool set in neat landscaped grounds, which brings a luxury holiday camp air to the heart of the attractive campus. Children trundle to and from eight acres of pitches, including a brand new, floodlit artificial grass hockey pitch, in three big yellow minibuses, and younger pupils use a five-a-side Astroturf at school. Their only complaint is that the changing rooms are a bit cramped. Annual trip to learn survival skills on Rua Fiola, an island near Oban.

Clad in black and yellow, with caps for the boys and felt hats for girls, pupils are ultra-polite but not stuffy. Good mornings, pleases and thank yous abound. They love earning house points, hate getting minuses or having to 'see the head'. The house with most points gets to miss a day of school for a treat; 'last year we went to Waterworld – how mint is that?' There's a discreet silence about just who comes here but, as befits the area, there's a fair share of celeb and footballer offspring. School has two TEFL trained teachers and has seen many a child become bi-lingual here after arriving with barely any English. Three favourite members of staff are the live-in 'gappies' from down under or South Africa, two boys and one girl gap year students who help with sport or the younger children. They appreciate chef Levi's ministrations to them just as much as the children who say, 'the food's great, very healthy... and there's always cake'. Pupils and teachers share the dining hall and queue and pupils have no hesitation approaching teachers for a word during lunch. The only parental grumble is the congested road and nightmare parking

S. Anselm's School

S. Anselm's Preparatory School, Bakewell, DE45 1DP

- Pupils: 200; boys and girls • Ages: Nursery to 13 • C of E
- Fees: Day £8,520–£16,380; Boarding £19,440 pa • Independent

Tel: 01629 812734
Email: headmaster@anselms.co.uk
Website: www.sanselms.co.uk

Headmaster: Since September 2012, Mr Peter Phillips. Head of Cundall Manor in Yorkshire for 13 years; built up school from around 80 to some 400 pupils. Started as a surveyor before seeing the light and becoming an English teacher. Head of English at Yardley Court and St Michael's schools in Kent then director of studies at Cargilfield in Edinburgh.

A tall man, by any standards, he does not belong to the pinstriped, lapel-tugging, bullfrog school of heads. He is a thinker, a man of intelligence and vision, of great kindness, strong-minded and determined, and not easily swayed. Above all, he is dedicated to the welfare of the pupils. He does not like being pushed about by autocracy, but will listen for hours to children's worries and concerns. Some parents have complained that he is something of a recluse, that he doesn't come out to see them. The pupils we met – and they were marvellously forthcoming and natural – said how much they like him because he takes such a keen interest in them, makes a fuss of them when they are sent by their teachers to show him a good piece of work, and so obviously cares about them.

Though he denies being a Luddite, he knows nothing of computers and announced early on in his time at S. Anselm's that he did not do emails but was always willing to talk. All emails go through his wife, Sarah, who has a delightfully zany sense of humour and helps look after the girls in the evening. He teaches 18 lessons a week and referees some matches. Pupils enjoy his lessons and he enjoys the contact.

He has encouraged some of the older staff to leave, causing some disquiet among a few parents and indignation from those staff. The overall feeling amongst the parents we talked to was a sadness that even teachers have to move on, but an acceptance of the inevitability. This has not been a St Bartholomew's Day Massacre of the not-so-innocent over-50s: he has displayed considerable wisdom in retaining some of the finest teachers on merit, reputation and – importantly – a willingness to accept his enlarged expectations. One experienced teacher said that due to the new demands of helping at weekends she now knew the pupils better.

Perhaps most exciting has been the arrival of a cohort of young, lively, talented and dedicated staff. Many of them followed Mr Phillips, along with children and families, from Cundall Manor. Their arrival has caused much excitement among the parents and children, and they are a most delightful and engaging group. Parents queued up to tell us of the new buzz in the school, the energy and drive, the sense of purpose and fun, the fresh air. Even we could feel it. When we wandered out during break and saw the running, the chasing, the laughter, the sense of timeless delight, it felt as if we had taken a detour with Thomas Traherne: 'Boys and girls tumbling in the street, and playing, were moving jewels. I knew not that they were born or should die; but all things abided eternally as they were in their proper places.'

Mr Phillips has given up the rather grand and slightly intimidating study of his predecessors, and now inhabits a smaller but delightful room overlooking the beautiful gardens. As the visitor glances around he sees a rugby ball in the (unlit) fireplace, a set of bagpipes on a table, a model steam train made by one of the science masters (an inspirational teacher whose lesson

S

we had observed earlier), and a pile of papers. No badges or hints of office, no pomposity or sense of importance. The same is true of the website. Search as you may, you will not find one of those proprietorial messages from a head looking like a stockbroker or as if they were fresh from a stylish garden party, urging you with false modesty and marketing acumen to come and visit. With a dash of daring, S. Anselm's has done away with all mentions of the head and doesn't have a prospectus. 'The school belongs to, and exists for, the children.' You'll only find the head's name on the copy of the recent inspection report, and pretty good it was. He doesn't do swank nor is he interested in suits and tailors. He greeted us in bright, pinky-red trousers and sweater.

Entrance: Mostly from the nursery and pre-prep, which is superbly run with first class teaching, according to happy parents. The overall head of the pre-prep is 'wonderful' and children in the prep look back with fondness and an early whiff of nostalgia. But anyone may apply at any stage if there is room. One parent told us with huge appreciation of how her son, joining as a boarder a little later than the main group when the family moved up from London, had been welcomed with kindness and consideration by boys and housemaster, and had settled in very quickly.

Exit: The school has an excellent reputation for scholarships, achieved through excellent free-range teaching rather than force-feeding. Parents talk of the way teachers assess their pupils realistically and sensitively. A few parents, of course, have unrealistic demands and expectations, but the head is good at nudging them towards greater reality, even though that doesn't always endear him. Public school heads said they appreciate the lively, inquisitive approach of Anselmians, their willingness to get stuck in and their articulate courtesy and friendliness.

Remarks: The school has been through a turbulent period over the last five years. Numbers dropped, and morale amongst many parents and staff dipped, and they told us that a couple of years ago they were very worried. With the arrival of fresh blood and new energies, numbers and morale are looking up, with a doubling of intake into reception and increased numbers in the main school.

Mr Phillips has restructured the timetable in the junior prep. English and maths is the staple diet in the morning, 'when the children are at their most alert', with other subjects in the afternoon. We listened to an exciting and challenging science lesson. When asked to describe their teacher, pupils said, 'distinctive, epic, fun, super, funny and heroic.' They were still yelling out adjectives as we left the room. Art teacher wearing spectacularly bright trousers; 'I love getting messy in art,' said one enthusiastic painter with rainbow coloured hands and face. Excellent artwork everywhere, not just in the large-windowed studio. We saw groups of young Romans planning a three course dinner which included stuffed doormice. They are off to Chester soon to explore all things Roman there. 'Don't mess with this man,' said our guides as we entered the classroom of a gentle-looking man. 'He teaches karate.' A woman was teaching the value of a sensible diet in a brilliant lesson incorporating geography, chemistry, history, common-sense and health.

Another of the head's ideas is for the whole school to share a topic and approach it from all angles. This year it is lighthouses, so there were pictures of lighthouses everywhere, calculations of light travelling, weather maps etc. Teachers described the excitement of approaching a topic right across the school from the youngest to the oldest, the way that seems to unite the pupils in a common aim, enabling them to share and exchange knowledge. A visit to a Northumberland lighthouse involved camping: the buzz, the fun and the almost unnoticed accumulation of knowledge.

Saturday mornings are voluntary up to year 6, but the take-up is enthusiastic. There is the excitement starting to learn Spanish, and Latin and Greek are, in the words of one distinguished exponent, 'full on'.

Terrific facilities include a well-designed music block where we watched children rehearsing for an arts evening. About 90 per cent of them learn an instrument. The wonderful sports hall is, perhaps, even slightly improved following the recent fire during the winter holidays. The library is being extended and improved, a proud 10 year old librarian told us. Now there are plans for a real farm with real animals and the real hard work that goes with it, and a domestic science building. Boarding facilities are excellent and improving all the time. In fact, under the new 'amazing and seriously mad' master in charge of boarding, according to parents and children, it is becoming ever more popular. Weekends are action packed and hugely enjoyed. 'He doesn't want to come home,' one parent told us, and talking of home, not long ago a group went up to Sheffield to help with the Archer Project. On that occasion it took the form of sleeping on cardboard on the streets in the rain with some young homeless people and some hardy members of staff. A thought-provoking experience. 'Boarding is just the greatest fun!' children said to us over and over again.

These feelings of excitement, pleasure and happiness seem to permeate right through the school – including the gardeners and maintenance staff and the charming and friendly cooks. (We had the most delicious lunch of roast pork and all the trimmings.) All of them are, of course, vitally important contributors to the overall happiness and smooth running of the school.

No doubt the excellent food contributes to the success of S Anselm's sport, which is taken seriously and played with zest and skill. County players abound in all areas, and there is huge excitement, though not at the expense of academic work. Or so they say.

S. Anselm's has been celebrating its 125th anniversary with an elegantly produced book, with a forward signed by The Duchess of Devonshire. In it the writer comments on the founder's choice of motto: 'Esse Quam Videri' (to be and not to seem to be). It's a wonderful motto extolling the virtues of honesty and, to use that overworked word, transparency. Several people have suggested to us that Mr Phillips fits the message behind that motto. He may not be universally popular – people who need to make changes rarely are – but he is now presiding over a deeply happy school with parents falling over themselves to tell us how pleased they are with the current set up. Such bubbling enthusiasm is rare

St Albans High School for Girls – Preparatory School

Linked school: St Albans High School for Girls

Wheathampstead House, Codicote Road, Wheathampstead, Herts, AL4 8DJ

• Pupils: 305 girls; all day • Ages: 4–11 • C of E • Fees: £10,755–£11,355 pa • Independent

Tel: 01582 839270
Email: admissions@stalbans-high.herts.sch.uk
Website: www.stahs.org.uk

Head: Since 2009, Ms Gillian Bradnam BEd MA NPQH (forties). Has a wealth of teaching experience in state and independent schools (including Putney High and Brighton & Hove High). Prior to her current job she was deputy head of St Catherine's Preparatory School, Bramley for six years.

A passionate advocate of girls' schools, she says the prep school provides 'a warm, family atmosphere' where girls are 'encouraged, supported and valued.' Loves her job and parents say she is 'very approachable and caring.' Despite her busy schedule she also teaches thinking skills and study skills to the older girls. 'I pop in and out of lessons often,' she says, 'so I have a good sense of how the children are getting on.'

Very keen on blending the best of traditional education with a cutting edge, modern approach (in her spare time she writes a blog about teaching and learning). 'We don't just jump on to the next thing though,' she says. 'It needs to be fun, exciting and relevant for the children.'

Entrance: Academically selective. Main entry points are four and seven but vacancies occasionally crop up in other years. For entry into reception girls come in for an informal 90-minute multi-activity session. Older girls have assessments in English, maths and verbal reasoning.

Exit: Vast majority progress to the senior school, although the occasional one or two opt for boarding or local state schools. Discussion with parents if staff feel senior school may not be the right school for their daughter and families are helped to explore suitable alternatives. 'We are very keen that every child feels very positive about their next school,' says the head. 'We celebrate wherever they are going.'

Remarks: School is located in the pretty village of Wheathampstead, a four-mile drive through country lanes from its St Albans-based big sister. Moved to its current home (former HQ of Polaroid UK) in 2003 and the place has since been transformed into a lively prep, complete with 18 glorious acres, extensive woods, adventure playgrounds, outdoor learning classroom and a meadow. Lots of emphasis on outdoor activities (younger girls keep wellies at the ready in school).

Head says the school covers much of the national curriculum but goes 'broader and deeper.' Teachers are highly committed and keen on using new technologies, encouraging girls to develop thinking skills, independent learning and skills for life. Girls write their own blogs, do lots of video conferencing with museums and galleries and the school has its own carefully managed Twitter account to keep parents and locals up to date with what's going on. Parents say the school sets high standards –'but if anyone is struggling, they are on it.' 'The emphasis is very much on the individual,' a mother says. 'Yes, it's very academic but the school prepares them very well and it's a very happy school. The girls are very motivated and thrilled to be there.'

French is taught from year 3, with extra-curricular clubs for Italian, Spanish, Mandarin, Japanese and Latin. No streaming, although girls are often divided into smaller groups of six and eight in English and maths (with imaginative names like 'blue sky thinkers,' 'super solvers' and 'number crunchers'). As head points out: 'We are already selective and the last thing we want is for a child to feel they aren't doing well.' Science, ICT, French, music and PE are all taught by subject specialists. Science is very hands-on – lots of practical experiments and school is one of the few preps to take part in The Big Bang, a national event for schools celebrating science, technology, engineering and maths. All girls get an hour of ICT a week – everything from creating postcards and Viking factsheets to filming in the grounds.

Class sizes range from 20 in reception to 24 in years 3 to 6. All girls are screened for literacy difficulties at the start of year 3 and one-to-one lessons for specific learning needs like dyslexia and dyspraxia are available at an additional charge. Currently 12 girls with SEND.

Sport is an important part of the curriculum, with girls doing netball, football, lacrosse, gym, dance and athletics. A sailing duo recently came fifth in the national IAPS championships. All year groups swim for a term, using the senior school's 25m pool. Variety of clubs at lunchtime and after school, from disco rock 'n' roll to chess. Lots of emphasis on eco matters. Pupils grow fruit and vegetables in their own garden and year 5s recently raised their own chicks.

Art is a delight here. Pictures on display everywhere – including vibrant, multi-coloured artwork inspired by Andy Warhol's Campbell's Soup Cans on the walls of the head's office. 'They're photocopies, so the children can take their originals home,' she says thoughtfully. Some innovative work in DT, with reception girls designing their own flip-flops and making their own miniature boats to race. Lots of music. Ninety per cent of girls learning instruments by the time they get to year 6 and a plethora of choirs and orchestras.

Pupils travel from far and wide, although some families specifically move to the village of Wheathampstead so their daughters can attend the prep. School day is 8.30am to 3pm for youngest girls and 8.30am to 3.20pm for years 3 to 6. After-school care till 5pm for pre-prep girls while older pupils can stay and do their homework till 5pm. Youngest get reading homework every night and older ones get 20-30 minutes of spellings, tables or topic research. 'The teachers specify the time they should spend on it,' says the head. 'We don't want homework to be arduous.'

Same house system as the senior school, with girls learning to work as part of a team and develop leadership skills right from the start. Form captains and vice captains from year 3 and year 6 girls take on house responsibilities. The environment is nurturing and caring, with the oldest pupils setting up games for the youngest and helping them to make friends. Effective buddy system. Year 6 pupils look out for year 3s and year 2s act as buddies to reception children. Like the senior school, the prep sets great store by the three Cs – challenge, creativity and community. Uniform is smart – navy and white blouses, navy skirts and striped navy blazers with lapels laden with badges for everything from kindness to swimming.

The girls are smiley, polite and brimming with enthusiasm, without being in the least bit arrogant or showy. They leap to their feet when visitors enter the class and when teachers ask questions a dozen eager hands shoot into the air. 'I love my school so much,' a year 6 girl told us, and her friends all concurred. 'They seem to teach the girls to want to learn,' an impressed mother told us.

There's no doubt about it, this is a school that blends the best of the old with the best of the new. For bright, sparky girls who are keen as mustard to learn it can't be beaten.

St Aloysius' College Junior School

Linked school: St Aloysius' College

45 Hill Street, Garnethill, Glasgow, G3 6RJ

• Pupils: 425 boys and girls; all day; • Ages: 3–11 • RC
• Fees: £7,200–£9,018 pa; • Independent

Tel: 01413 319200
Email: admissions@staloysius.org
Website: www.staloysius.org

Head of Juniors: Dr A Brady.

Remarks: For details, see senior school entry.

St Anthony's Preparatory School

90 Fitzjohn's Avenue, London, NW3 6NP

- Pupils: 295 boys; all day • Ages: 4–13 • RC • Fees: £15,135–£15,420 pa • Independent

Tel: 020 7431 1066
Email: gill.hooper@stanthonysprep.co.uk
Website: www.stanthonysprep.org.uk

Headmaster: Since 2010, Paul Keyte, MA. Educated at Bloxham and Oriel College, Oxford, where he read philosophy and theology, graduating with a first. Fell into teaching during his postgraduate research (on Wittgenstein and Kierkegaard). 'I thought I'd teach for a couple of years before going back,' he says, but, instead, became hooked. Started out at Dulwich, where he taught philosophy and RE, before becoming head of liberal studies. Then to King's College School Wimbledon, where he set up the philosophy and RE department and was under master (pastoral). 'You have to understand the shadow side, the theft and the bullying.' Then, senior master academic at Winchester and director of studies, deputy head at Highgate and at South Hampstead. St Anthony's is his first prep school. ('I was attracted to the job because it was big enough to be interesting yet small enough for me to be a father.') An undoubted enthusiast, he remains passionate about teaching ('I feel anchored in the classroom'), and continues to teach RS to year 8 and 'learning enrichment' to all. Knows virtually all his pupils by name. A convert to Catholicism and married to a Catholic (who teaches at South Hampstead), he has one son (now at the school). Outside (and often imported) interests include singing, Schubert ('I learnt German to understand it better'), musicals and Leeds United (much to his pupils' amusement). Energetic, enthusiastic and intellectual, yet accessible, parents feel fortunate to have him. 'He's incredibly supportive and gracious,' said one parent. 'He's the reason we chose the school,' said another.

Entrance: St Anthony's has changed its entrance from a two-stage process with entry points in year 1 and year 3 to a single admission of two classes in reception. 'We feel it provides a year of consolidation,' says the head, 'and a greater run up to secondary school pre-testing.' Tour, then register, as early as possible. All boys are interviewed. 'I'm looking for teachability and sociability,' says Mr Keyte. 'They have to be able to cope with the pace and adapt to our style of teaching. We're not competitive, but we're famous for creating independent learners.' Boys from about 25 feeder nurseries, but Catholics have often attended nearby St Mary's and St Christina's in St John's Wood.

Exit: In large numbers to UCS, City and Mill Hill, then everywhere from chunks to Highgate, Haberdashers' and Merchant Taylors', with a solid sprinkling to Westminster and St Paul's, as well as to leading boarding schools (Eton, Oundle and Ampleforth). Plenty of scholarships, including for sport and music. No one is ever asked to leave. 'That's our duty, once they're here,' says the head. Occasionally, some may decide that the academic pace is not for them and are 'gently helped' to find somewhere else.

Remarks: The head's heavyweight presence sets the tone and is a good match with the school's highly qualified staff (many with Oxbridge degrees and interesting first careers).The school is split into two sites across the road from each other, each with its own spacious Victorian building. In the junior school (reception to year 3), you'll find a sweeping staircase, turn-of-the-century tiling, large light classrooms and a good-sized dining room (which doubles as an assembly and concert hall). Class size is kept to a maximum of 16-20. Specialist subject teaching in French and music from reception. Mandarin from year 1. 'We aim to send them from the junior school happy and well adjusted, able to cope with the demands of exams,' says the head. 'We're building the personality rather than drilling.' But skills are thoroughly inculcated. 'In the junior years,' said one mother of two, 'the teaching is very precise. They really get the handwriting and spelling under control, which reaps benefits as they get older.'

In year 4, a move to the senior school (years 4-8) is accompanied by greater subject specialisation, more male teachers and recently renovated premises. Some setting in maths, flexible setting elsewhere. No scholarship set, but plenty of 'learning enrichment.' 'Exams require sophisticated skills and we introduce enrichment early on,' says the head. Philosophy, Latin, Greek and Arabic all on offer. The head also runs lunch-hour discussion groups which any boy can attend. Parents feel he has got a firm grip on the rapidly changing exam landscape. 'The school used to be not quite as rigorous,' said one mother, 'but now the head is really on top of it.'

Good support for SEN with two specialists, one with expertise in dyscalculia. Sophisticated early screening identifies those who may require additional support. Discreet withdrawal to two small bright dedicated classrooms for those who struggle as well as those who need stretch.

The arts, now as always, remain core to what this school is about. The head has tripled the number of music lessons and managed to acquire a baby grand as well as introduce a state-of-the-art music studio. 'My head of music says, "No boy leaves here who couldn't do grade 5 theory",' he says happily. A fair number are gifted musicians, one carrying off a recent Eton music scholarship, another singing with the ENO. Outside school hours, boys are given plenty of encouragement with the school providing the weekend venue for Trinity Laban's by-audition-only classes. Other art forms not neglected, with a big annual Shakespeare production and two weeks of film making post common entrance. A wide range of hobbies and clubs – logic and puzzle, general knowledge, chess, dance, touch typing – cover a range of enthusiasms (the lunch-time chess players packed out one classroom on our visit).

Not traditionally known as a 'sporty school', but the head is keen to give sport an increasingly important role. 'This is one area I'm working on developing. I'm passionate about what sport brings to children.' Traditional carousel of rugby, football, hockey, cricket, played twice weekly at Brondesbury, a 10-minute coach ride a way. On site, the school has its own pool (soon to be re-roofed) and two good-sized playgrounds. At St Anthony's, however, sport is as much about taking part as winning, with as many boys as possible participating. 'I'd rather the boys lost nobly and honourably than win for the sake of it. But, there's nothing wrong with really nice sportsmen who get gold medals.'

As a family-owned prep school founded in the 19th century, St Anthony's was run in its own highly individual way, with a famously alternative 'vibe', creative and quirky, underpinned by a strong Catholic ethos. Parents felt concern when the school was taken over by the efficient operator Alpha Plus, but have found that a professional distance has been kept, while judicious investment has brought the infrastructure into tip-top shape.

The only all-boys Catholic prep school in north London (with an 'outstanding' Diocesan report), this remains very much a Catholic school (about 80 per cent of families are practising Catholics). 'Faith is part of the heartbeat of the school,' says the head. Prayers said morning and afternoon, as well as grace at lunch, and you'll find a crucifix in every classroom as well as the Catholic RE syllabus at common entrance. The head, however, feels the function of religion is not to exclude. 'We have a mission to provide for the Catholic community, but inclusivity is important.' And most feel included. 'Families with other beliefs get incredible respect,' said one Jewish parent.

Despite its slightly Bohemian reputation, good manners and ethics remain key. Discipline here is done with the lightest of hands, but the boundaries are clearly in place. All teachers known by their first names and learning very much a cooperative enterprise. There's a golden toffee for those who've done something special (such as sing a song in the style of Johnny Cash), but those who break the Code of Conduct are entered into a 'green book' and parents are brought in to discuss anyone who's managed to rack up a third offence. Higher up the school, boys discuss what they've done wrong and what they've learned from it. 'I've only given one detention since I got here,' says the head. 'It never gets to that point. I try to give them a dignified exit.' Strong anti-bullying policies. 'The teachers are exceptionally kind and nurturing,' said one parent. 'They'll always do their best to help, whether it's finding a lost rugby kit or providing interview preparation for senior school tests.'

Parents usual north London lawyers, bankers and advertisers, but Catholic purpose means plenty of Italians, Germans and Spanish. Media parents often come with useful benefits. 'One allowed us to preview films, another offered tickets to the Wigmore Hall.' Boys are not necessarily the neatest, but are undoubtedly enthusiastic and individual. 'St Anthony's boys are never the same. There's no stamp.'

St Bede's College Prep School

Linked school: St Bede's College

Alexandra Park, Manchester, M16 8HX

• Pupils: 210 girls and boys • Ages: 3–11 • RC • Fees: £6,360 pa • Independent

Tel: 01612 267156
Email: prepschool@stbedescollege.co.uk
Website: www.stbedescollege.co.uk

Acting Headteacher Junior Division: Mrs C Hunt.

Entrance: By assessment.

Exit: No automatic right of transfer to the senior school though the vast majority do so.

Remarks: Housed in a new building on the same site as the senior school. Bright, colourful classrooms. Shares facilities with the main school. New nursery class opened 2012.

St Bees School Prep Department

Linked school: St Bees School

St Bees, Cumbria, CA27 0DS

• Pupils: 30 boys and girls • Ages: 4–11 • C of E • Fees: £6,870–£7,560 pa • Independent

Tel: 01946 828010
Email: admissions@st-bees-school.co.uk
Website: www.st-bees-school.org/prep_dept/prep_dept.htm

Lead Teacher: Since 2008, Mr Swithun Sewill BSc (mid-forties). Works under the aegis of the headmaster but is responsible for the operational aspects of the department. Has the St Bees stamp of commitment and loyalty, very proud of pupils and development of school. Teaches 'prep 3', currently covering top two years of KS2 and therefore has very special relationship with pupils. Worst thing about moving to senior school – leaving Mr Sewill, voiced almost unanimously.

Entrance: No entry requirement, taster days offered and encouraged before entry. Popular for 9+ – easy access to senior school – and increased interest from discontented state parents at 7+. Will work closely with out-sourced nursery (offering wrap around care from 2+) to ensure smooth transition for entry at 4+. All parents have meeting with the headmaster.

Exit: Almost exclusively to St Bees senior school.

Remarks: A bold venture in a rural village where there is good state primary provision on the doorstep. Numbers doubled through school's third academic year and continued interest at key entrance points. Parents seem happy with the mixed age year groups and, as one commented, 'Class sizes are so small that my daughter is receiving plenty of individual attention and progressing far better than at her previous primary school'.

Accommodation provided from ground floor conversion of a senior boys' boarding house. Secure entrance through spacious cloakroom area with three classrooms leading from central corridor. Classes tiny at present (maximum 18 pupils ever) comfortably accommodated in adequately sized rooms. Plenty of pupil work on display and dazzling information provide a stimulating environment. Usual IT and whiteboard provision. Contained playground provision doubles as outdoor basketball court, petite separate early years' outdoor area.

St Bees' brand of pastoral care permeates here. Pupils talk of 'an extended family', 'being seen and noticed', 'help being on hand when needed' and value this in comparison to their previous school experience. Golden rules rule! – nuggets of positive behaviour and good manners.

Pupils like the work ethic, 'We've been working really hard for Sats and now we're looking at different topics and having more fun'. (Great life skill knowing when to put your foot on the gas.) Differentiated teaching a must as classes span two years at least – made achievable by current numbers. Use of senior school by KS2, science in laboratories and IT in Management Centre suites. Curriculum includes French and Spanish from 7+; Latin from 9+.

Merit system – stars awarded announced in weekly assembly and aggregate for houses, Saxon and Viking. Bronze, silver and gold certificates presented at end of year concert recognise individual super star achievement.

A daily dose of mixed PE seemingly enjoyed by all, activities include swimming in school's heated pool and sport lessons every other day in the sports hall or on the school fields. Golf academy (resident PGA professional coach) as well as usual team sports. After school clubs until 5pm Monday to Thursday include trampolining, fencing cooking, ICT and art. Summer Fest provides two weeks of multi-fun activities during August, at a cost. Creative adaptation of school production for small numbers – Joseph in three bite size performances, one a term. 'My son loves the balance of daily sport and the range of extra-curricular activities in the school timetable. It seems to have improved his focus in lessons and his enjoyment of school in general,' said one mum.

St Benedict's Junior School

Linked school: St Benedict's School

5 Montpelier Avenue, London, W5 2XP

- Pupils: 290 pupils, 190 boys/100 girls; all day • Ages: 3–11 • RC (very) and Benedictine, a good proportion of other Christian denominations • Fees: £10,560–£11,760 pa • Independent

Tel: 020 8862 2050
Email: enquiries@stbenedicts.org.uk
Website: www.stbenedicts.org.uk

Headmaster: Since 2005, Mr R G Simmons, BA, the second secular head.

Entrance: Non-selective at 3 or 4.

Exit: Almost all to senior school on site.

Remarks: Junior school housed in very large, very attractive Victorian red-brick building across the playground from senior school (playground shared but times staggered so tinies not swamped by six foot rugger types). Playground also encloses new small area for tots. Building recently and carefully extended to provide lovely, light new hall and classrooms. New rooms include excellent new ICT suite with modern low tables and matching chairs and inviting, comfortable library overlooking the abbey and lawns. Interactive whiteboards in every classroom and well used. Leafy Ealing far more apparent here – super trees with space to grow and local family homes just across the way. Excellent displays everywhere – really interesting, too, on stone carving, perspective, shape and colour. A good orderly feel with happy, confident-looking pupils in a school recently commended in ISI report for excellent music and ADT. Pastoral care, too, clearly exceptional. A super start for your son or daughter and big school just across the playground! New nursery housed in super refurbished Victorian house just down the road. Last Ofsted inspection rated the early years foundation stage provision as outstanding.

St Catherine's Preparatory School

Linked school: St Catherine's School

Station Road, Bramley, Guildford, Surrey, GU5 0DF

- Pupils: 265 girls, all day • Ages: 4–11 • C of E • Fees: £7,920–£13,380 pa • Independent

Tel: 01483 899665
Email: sally.manhire@stcatherines.info
Website: www.stcatherines.info

Headmistress: Since 2012, Miss Naomi Bartholomew MA BEd Cantab (thirties) who was educated at Portsmouth High School and went on to read English and Education at Homerton College, Cambridge. She spent two years in South West China with the VSO, then taught in state and independent primary schools. Five years as head of English at Yateley Manor was followed by the deputy headship at St Catherine's in 2009. She followed much admired and much-loved Mrs Jefferies who did much to establish the prep as a school in its own right – not merely a feeder. Miss Bartholomew's appointment to the headship was as much as anything by public acclamation. 'Some don't know her so well yet but those of us who do value her highly,' one mother told us. 'She is very calm, clever and warm.' Miss Bartholomew is plainly thrilled to be in charge and has a lovely smiley relationship with both girls and staff. Not remotely a dragon – more of a gentle but firm and very professional fairy princess.

Entrance: Around 50 applicants for 32 places at 4+ and immensely worthwhile nabbing one of them if you can. Tots come in for a morning of fun and observation in groups – heavy staff:tot ratio to allow for lots of encouragement and stimulation – and discreet assessment. They look for children who are 'curious, engaged and absorbed in what they are doing'. At 7+, around 15 apply for 4-5 places – similar approach plus testing in English, maths and verbal reasoning with 'an emphasis on show us what you can do'. 'We're a pacey school – we look for girls who will thrive here'.

Exit: Most to the St Cat's senior school, some to board at other top schools (some on scholarships) or to other local schools. Lots of strong, local competition in the area.

Remarks: Over the road from the senior school, the pre-prep and prep have separate buildings but share much including many facilities with the senior school – a real plus. Pre-prep is delightful – has its own outside space along with what it shares with the prep and senior schools. Peaceful 'cottage garden'. Charming little library, each classroom is chocker with interesting displays and stimuli but all is orderly and reassuring. 'Senses Den' in each room – very exciting! Lovely artwork – we loved the pasta palaces and the various penguin habitats. Top-notch loos with Mickey Mouse taps! No more than 16 to a class in Reception and the children we saw were focused, happy and busy. Emphasis on being a 'thinking school' inculcates valuable strategies and habits.

Prep likewise stimulating and orderly. Specialist teachers for most subjects including French; some setting in maths. Residential trips for all years; sensible mixing up of friendship groups, good library and IT room. Lively art – and years 5 and 6 use the senior school for DT – we enjoyed the really scary papier mache masks! Emphasis on using the internet and other IT with discernment and discrimination rather than as an end in itself. Good learning support – 'academic mentoring' here – lots of monitoring, working with parents and use of two support teachers for as and when.

Parents are universally grateful that their girls are here. 'They pace it beautifully,' one told us. '8 year-old girls behave like 8 year-olds – they are not pushed to be older than they are.' 'Everyone is busy but calm – there are lots of clubs and nice quirky things.' 'The teachers are warm, friendly and approachable. They don't overdo assessment – they just tell you whether they're in the top, middle or lowest third in a subject'. Music is highly praised. Some sense that more drama productions would be welcome and the hope is that the stimulus given to the subject in the senior school will filter down. Strong sense of an equitable and kind community. 'They don't favour the bright ones – my two very different girls feel equally welcome and valued.' 'Every single child gets a well-thought-out prize at Prize Giving – for best results or for kindness – everyone walks out feeling valued for what they are.'

St Christopher School Junior School

Linked school: St Christopher School

Barrington Road, Letchworth Garden City, SG6 3JZ

• Pupils: 160 boys and girls • Ages: 3–11 • Non-denom
• Fees: £9,780–£12,165 pa • Independent

Tel: 01462 650947
Email: admissions@stchris.co.uk
Website: www.stchris.co.uk

Joint Acting Head of Junior School: Mr Bryan Anderson and Ms Sam Selkirk, joint acting heads.

Entrance: Many children come up from the Montessori nursery, others join reception and more join year 3 or 4, though entry at any age is considered. Will take a broad range of ability, 'but our community exists on self-discipline and they must be able to cope.'

Exit: Almost all to the senior school.

Remarks: Lovely, light buildings adjacent to the senior school, full of paintings and projects. Much of the work is project-based (which can upset inspectors from traditional prep schools). 'The teachers know each child's strengths and weaknesses. It is most important to push their strengths and enrich those areas they find difficult. Being kind and having high expectations are not mutually exclusive.' Play areas include an orchard – children are encouraged to climb the trees and pick the apples. 'Childhood should be celebrated. We try to preserve it as long as possible.'

In 2008, the Montessori nursery ('The Monte') relocated to Arunwood, a Grade II listed building and former childhood home of Sir Laurence Olivier. Extensively refurbished, it provides classroom space and outdoor facilities for learning and play. In 2012, the reception class relocated to join the nursery, creating an Early Years Centre. Following their time in the Early Years Centre pupils are excellently prepared for year one, which is located within the main Junior School building.

For further details, see the senior school entry.

St Christopher's School

32 Belsize Lane, London, NW3 5AE

• Pupils: 240 girls, all day • Ages: 4–11 • Non-denom
• Fees: £12,450 pa • Independent

Tel: 020 7435 1521
Email: admissions@st-christophers.hampstead.sch.uk
Website: www.st-christophers.hampstead.sch.uk

Head: Since 2003, Mrs Susan (Susie) West (sixties), BA Hons PGCE, MA Educational Management. Educated at Howells, University of Newcastle, Oxford (PGCE) and the OU. Then taught extensively in the private sector in England and abroad, at Oakham, at St Bede's, Eastbourne (where she was head of the pre-prep school), at Sherborne (where she was a housemistress), in Kuala Lumpur (where she was head of English), and at Sussex House, before becoming deputy head of Kensington Prep. An energetic figure who cycles to Hampstead every day from Pimlico, Mrs West is divorced with a grown-up son and daughter. She continues to teach some English to years 4 and 5, feeling that not only is this the best way to get to know the children but also the ideal means to understand the issues faced by her staff. Down to earth, positive and straight talking, with a clear passion for educating and a genuine empathy with her pupils.

Entrance: St Christopher's is one of London's highest-achieving academic prep schools, with results at 11 the envy of many of its neighbours. This, however, is a school which selects primarily on ability. Part of the selection procedure is standardised tests, so summer birthdays don't lose out. 'It is not an academic assessment,' says the head. 'We observe how they play together and how they interact with other children.' The school operates a split entry and successful candidates are allocated a place either for reception or for year 1, depending primarily on 'school readiness'. Tests dates and results are co-ordinated with other leading selective north London prep schools. Early registration is essential (as near birth as possible) for those already resident in London. Entry lists are closed at about 300 to be assessed for 38 available places. The head, however, is always willing to be flexible for those who've just arrived. Siblings are given an automatic offer, unless it is considered 'they will not flourish'. Not flourishing, however, is fairly loosely interpreted. 'If you have two clever daughters and the third is not as bright,' says the head, 'some parents think she'll upset the exit poll, but that's not the way we work.' Parents confirm that year groups cover a (relatively) wide spread of ability. Occasional vacancies after entry. One 100 per cent means-tested scholarship available per annum and other support available as necessary.

Exit: 'We're fortunate in London that there are so many great schools,' says the head, 'and we are proud of the achievement of all our girls. There's no scholarship board here. We don't want to make some pupils feel instantly diminished.' That said, this is generally a school of bright sparks and ambitious parents and the majority proceed to the highest performing London day schools. City of London, North London Collegiate and South Hampstead top the list, with St Paul's Girls and Highgate close behind. Quite a number of scholarships amongst them. A handful to board and a few to Henrietta Barnett.

Remarks: St Christopher's was founded in 1883 by two local literary lesbians, but established in its current form in 1950 by the writer Rosemary Manning. It became a charitable trust in the 1970s. Housed in a large Victorian family house (with modern additions) in fashionable Belsize Park, this is a top-flight prep school for top-flight north London parents and the ethos and atmosphere are reflective of that. The education the pupils receive here is thoughtful and exciting. It concentrates on the fundamentals, but only after the fundamentals have been carefully considered. 'We have to ask the question what are we educating children for,' says the head. 'It's a world we know nothing about, a world very different from our own.' The school has carefully analysed the impact of technology. 'The girls think technologically and it can be much more difficult to get them to listen to a story and concentrate.' The issue is addressed by concentrated focus on the task of reading and understanding and girls read aloud every day from reception to year 3 and regularly thereafter. 'If you can't read, you can't do maths,' says the head. No concessions are made when it comes to literature ('We don't use abridged texts') and Dickens and Lewis Carroll are digested in the original. An excellent library underlines the school's priorities.

Much of the timetable follows the national curriculum ('It would be foolish not to, there are some very interesting things, but we cut away the trivia. We don't reject it, we tweak it.') The approach is based on 'child-initiated learning' with pupils taught to question and take responsibility for what they learn. Work is then tailored to the needs of each pupil, with maths books, for example, customised to the age and stage. (Though those in need of learning support are in the minority – mainly younger siblings – parents consider this tailoring, too, to be strong.) Spanish ('one of the most widely spoken languages in the world') is taught throughout, Latin from year 5 and French as a club from year 3. Specialist subject teaching from year 4, with drama added to the curricular mix, joined by history of art in year 5. Flexibility of mind is encouraged by the inclusion of chess. ('It's a brilliant thinking exercise.')

Hard-working, well-qualified staff, particularly in the final two years. 'I cannot imagine better teachers than the maths and English teachers in years 5 and 6,' said one parent. 'They are really transformative.'

Despite the school's outstanding scholarship record, there is no scholarship class and no setting, except in maths in the final two years. Nor is this a school that crams for exams; preparation lasts just one term, when practice papers are given weekly. 'They're not missing core subjects from year 5, they still have time for all the extra-curricular, they're not pressured and processed,' says the head. The approach here is enriching and the head believes there is as much value in creativity as in the core subjects.

Music is generally considered strong and enthusiastic, with two music classes plus a singing class each week. What's learnt here is put into practice with a junior orchestra, a wind group, a string group, piano club, junior and senior choirs and a chamber choir. This is media land, too, and there is also a thriving film club, where girls learn to make their own. Cultural outings are very much part of the offering, with regular visits to theatres and museums and a young writers' workshop.

Sport is perhaps less important than it might be elsewhere (some parents complain that unless you're in a team, this can be a rather neglected area.) Netball court and gym on site and regular matches against other schools in netball and rounders. Short tennis is also taught in the summer term and senior girls play lacrosse. Swimming lessons only in year 3 at nearby Swiss Cottage baths, sports day held at Hampstead Cricket Club. Though the outdoor space here is not unduly extensive, it is used very effectively, with an outdoor classroom, an Alice Garden and a science-themed garden. 'Children today have a very boring existence, chauffeured here and there,' says the head, 'and we wanted to create an environment where they were allowed to be imaginative.' Indeed, the thread that runs throughout St Christopher's is that a good education is stimulating, interesting and exciting. The extra-curricular is therefore addressed as energetically, with everything from public speaking to self-defence and Indian dance and, while there may be a Florence Nightingale workshop, the message that banking is as worthwhile a career for girls as nursing is instilled with visits to the Bank of England and a mock Dragon's Den. All staff are required to run two clubs a year and the offering is extensive.

Four houses, Bronte, Nightingale, North and Pankhurst, provide the basis for inter-house competition. The school has a strong family feel, sheltered and relaxed. There are no school rules ('We just ask for respect in the classroom and for them to be polite to teachers.') Good behaviour is instilled by discussion. ('Why did you do that? How do you imagine that would look?') Occasionally parents feel that emotional difficulties are not picked up as quickly as they might be. ('If you mention a problem, they take it seriously, but it's not always spotted,' said one.) Assembly every Friday is non-denominational. School meals exclude pork, shellfish, ham, and nuts in order to cater for all. The facilities here have been brought thoroughly up to date, too, with a smart extension completed in 2008 providing additional classrooms and state-of-the art IT. The green and blue uniform of Aertex shirts and blue trousers is practical and durable. Over a third of pupils live within walking distance and the rest travel from affluent nearby postcodes like St Johns Wood, Maida Vale, Islington and Highgate. Parents, are often intellectual, professional, international and Jewish – and occasionally celebrities. 'They are interesting and incredibly

well-informed,' says the head. 'They are very involved and desperately keen to support their children's education. ('Sometimes too keenly involved,' remarked one father. 'There are a lot of non-working mothers who once had high-powered careers and are now directing their energies on their children.') Occasionally expectations have to be gently adjusted. A high-octane education producing confident, well-informed and articulate girls. 'The nice thing about St Christopher's is that it provides an excellent education without trying to breed a master race,' says one happy customer.

St Columba's Junior School

Linked school: St Columba's School

Knockbuckle Road, Kilmacolm, PA13 4EQ

- Pupils: 350 boys and girls • Ages: 3–11 • Non-denom
- Fees: £7,400–£9,030 pa • Independent

Tel: 01505 872768
Email: secretary@st-columbas.org
Website: www.st-columbas.org

Rector: Since 2002, Mr David Girdwood BSc PGCE MEd SQH (fifties); educated at Alva Academy followed by St Andrews, Jordanhill, Stirling and Edinburgh universities; came from Stewart's Melville, where he 'taught chemistry for 15 years', and is now a governor.

Head of Junior School: Since 2011, Mrs Alison Duncan MA PGDE, SQH, (30s) previously depute head at St Columba's for a year and head of year at Stewart's Melville junior school; a Fifer, educated at St Columba's RC in Dunfermline, she read Russian and German at St Andrews and briefly taught German in Fife. Tidy minded, warm, bubbly and friendly: believes children should be resilient and self confident. Husband an engineer.

Entrance: No longer scads of waiting lists throughout; nursery bulging, and currently waiting lists for 8, 9 and 10 year olds.

Exit: Most on to senior school via transitus, rare to lose either to trad boarding at 8, 11 or whatever, prep or senior school.

Remarks: Nursery: early years; pre-school year max 24 boys and girls (vouchers ok).

Youngsters roughly divided into two groups. During our visit, one lot were tucking into chopped up banana, sliced strawberries and humus (interesting mixture), plain yogurt and water (followed by a lesson in teeth-brushing); some were drawing their dreams – two drawers to a large piece of paper; one or two were playing with magic sand. Jolly and vibrant. Regular classes 8.30am – 12.30pm, but increased demand recently; the recession has done wonders for nursery numbers. Traditionally, Kilmacolm mothers didn't work: coffee mornings, charity and the like ok, but none of this pen-pushing nonsense, you understand. Come the recession, enter the working mum.

Complicated wrap-around option, including brekky, lunch, couple of snacks (one of which will be hot). Drop off 7.45am, collect 6.00pm from age 4 – 12 (and website has now been altered to show this): mind-boggling computation of costs with nursery fees 'frozen' at £3295 (less than £19 per day) and depending whether your little one is on board for the session (£21 a day), booked a week ahead (£27 a day), or just a spur of the moment thing (£36 a day). Staff suss out friendship patterns to help with placement in P1, junior school proper. All wear rather jolly green overalls, school took us to task for calling them tabliers – useful for hiding from strange ladies with notebooks – and proper school uniform.

Max 360 in junior school, two arbitrary forms: max 25 in each, which we feel is more than enough for tinies. And paying tinies at that. Reading, writing, 'rithmatic intensive for the first couple of years, glitches picked up early and learning support in place, with ed psychs and IEPs if and when needed, after consultation with parents. Music, drama and French (native speakers) from 4. The 10/11 year olds have three day away stays in the Lakes (baby outward bound sort of stuff).

Younger classrooms open off wide passage (well used individual work stations throughout). Double classrooms for the youngest year groups, which open up to create a wizard and adaptable work/play space. Junior school surrounded by proper lawns and gardens.

Classrooms lead seamlessly by age towards Shallot (which we think is east of the nursery wing, though Mrs Duncan thinks it is west: geography lessons all round), with older pupils working up a couple of steps nearer to the late Victorian former boarding house on Knockbuckle Road (which belonged to Adam Birkmyre, owner of the local rope works, who gave Birkmyre Park to the 'people of Kilmacolm' in 1897, and probably not to Inverclyde Leisure).

Originally part of the Girls' School Company, the school, founded in 1897, abandoned boarding in 1970; the junior school went co-ed in 1978 (in the face of falling numbers) and re-sited at Knockbuckle Road; senior school went coed in 1981. The two villas on Bridge of Weir Road, which used to house the nursery, were sold with junior department getting the lion's share: splendid hall (full of role play during our visit) plus proper assembly room with stage; a grown up gym and weights room tucked at the northern end (regularly let out to local enthusiasts). As a result of various new builds and subsequent shuffling round of classes, transitus, the youngest class in the senior school, is based down here. Healthy amount of walking (a long half mile) as older juniors visit senior school for music, art, IT, home economics and the sciences, but junior school is otherwise self-contained. Myriads of after-school clubs.

Shallot now mainly offices, with not very sympa room divisions (for SEN and the like) on the first floor; the roof shows obvious signs of neglect – nothing major, but a gutter cleaning programme would help. New library in the offing – complete with window seats, full of boxes of books about to be put on show during our visit (Mrs Duncan disputes this: 'library was not full of boxes, but rather laid out with brand new, custom built shelving and books being sorted into shelves'. The somewhat depressing-looking double dining rooms (in days of yore it was dining preceeded by common room) have robust tables for packed lunches, while the dining room proper boasts a servery with hot and cold buffet. Quite obviously not an internally listed building, then. Whilst one can appreciate the frustration at having the planners throw out ambitious whole school schemes, not to mention the irritation of being OSCRd by the Charity Commission, it is foolish to penny pinch on basic maintainance. Popular second hand shop.

Seniors visit for PE and games: games either on Birkmyre Park (quite complicated with Inverclyde involvement and not as easy as it used to be – they have changed the bog standard pavilion into a rather trendy café etc) or on a dedicated Astroturf some five mins away. We saw scads of 15/16 year olds coming back with happy looks on their mud-covered faces.

St David's School

23/25 Woodcote Valley Road, Purley, CR8 3AL

• Pupils: 145 Boys and Girls • Ages: 3–11 • Christian ethos, all welcome • Fees: £7,695–£8,385 pa • Independent

Tel: 020 8660 0723
Email: office@stdavidsschool.co.uk
Website: www.stdavidsschool.co.uk

Head: Since May 2011 Miss Cressida Mardell (forties) a classicist, BA (Hons) PGCE. Before joining St David's in 2007 she was a senior teacher at St Christopher's School, Epsom. Parents appreciate her positive approach, hard work and sound judgement, alongside a jolly personality and a good sense of humour. She lives locally and enjoys holidaying in France and walking with her two lively Border collie rescue dogs.

Entrance: Non-selective at age 3, children can join the nursery in the term of their third birthday or 4+ into reception. Thereafter parents can join the waiting list to be contacted for occasional places.

Exit: At 11+ most popular choices are the local grammar schools Sutton, Wilson's Wallington, Nonsuch and Tiffin's. Others to Royal Russell, Whitgift, Trinity, Old Palace, Greenacre and Woldingham.

Remarks: Mixed ability school, which skilfully blends academic excellence alongside a good range of musical, creative and sporting opportunities.

Founded in 1912 with just five pupils, by Welsh (hence school's name) sisters Margery and Mary Talfourd Jones. The school has thrived through the decades and today's multicultural clientèle is still proud of its founders' Welsh connections. Pupils join in the Eisteddfod Festival and fly the flag on St David's Day.

Dedicated class teachers run maths and English lessons mostly in the mornings and then teach specialist subject in the afternoons. There is an ICT room and a room for arts, science and technology, pupils often split for these subjects so class sizes are around 10, optimising the opportunity for individual attention and development. French is taught throughout the school and year 6 learn Latin. Specialist teacher visits three days a week to assist children with any special educational needs. Additional support is provided for small groups, one-to-one or in class; no extra charges are made for this service. ESOL can be arranged as required. Very busy music department has a gifted and talented choir, brass ensemble, string ensemble and rhythm group. Most pupils play at least one instrument, older pupils are introduced to filming and music composition with the occasional commission, most recently a jingle for Halfords. Some great achievements on the sporting front; St David's has its own large playing fields a few minutes' walk from the school building complete with tennis and netball courts. Gymnastics is particularly strong; the school has won the ISA competition on several occasions. Swimming is another area where pupils excel, with eight children being selected to train as divers at Crystal Palace for the next Olympics programme. Parents felt clubs had been rather limited; this is now an expanding area, and the aim is now to offer a much wider choice of activities, after-school and at lunchtimes. Chess team have made it into Champion League finals for primary schools and the maths team recently came third in the Sutton Maths Challenge. After-school care is provided by the Jancett Nursery Group until 6.30pm.

Refreshingly St David's has retained its independence and remains a small charity with a non-selective intake, so

S

far avoiding being swept up by one of the large education businesses. Very successful results at 11 into the local grammar and independent schools, especially considering the non-selective intake and inclusive approach. Terrific value for money.

St Dunstan's College Junior School

Linked school: St Dunstan's College

Stanstead Road, London, SE6 4TY

• Pupils: 282 boys and girls, all day • Ages: 3–11 • Anglican foundation • Fees: £8,613–£13,830 pa • Independent

Tel: 020 8516 7225
Email: rscard@sdmail.org.uk
Website: www.stdunstans.org.uk

Head: Since 2008, Miss Judith Bate BEd (mid forties). Approachable and cheerful. Enjoys travelling and spent three years working abroad at an International School in Bangkok followed by 10 at the British School in the Netherlands where she was deputy and acting head. Busy developing her digital photography skills. Her interest and enjoyment of the theatre rubs off well on her pupils and some of the performing arts activities.

Entrance: 3+ informal assessment and interview with parents for nursery places. 4+ competitive assessments held in November each year. 7+ competitive assessments, which focus on numeracy, literacy and social skills. For entry into other year groups contact the school for occasional vacancies.

Exit: At 11+ the majority move to the senior school, others mostly to selective maintained sector or specialist music and sports schools.

Remarks: A medium-sized, spritely school. Traditional academic curriculum jazzed up with lots of outings and visitors. Living history days, visiting authors and investigative workshops. Lots of creative thinking going on for the children and teachers.

Music, drama and sport all have an important place: many children learn instruments and the school boasts wind, strings and brass bands along with two choirs. Pupils regularly put on musical and dramatic performances so everyone gets a chance to be involved, in addition to the extensive range of after-school clubs and activities.

All the superb senior school sports facilities including the swimming pool are available to younger pupils. Food freshly cooked on the premises.

St Dunstan's is keen for the older children to prepare for moving to the senior school early and to build long-term relationships with teachers. Senior school staff teach older prep pupils, and run specialist activity days.

Pastoral care is carefully monitored and parents meet regularly with teachers to discuss their child's all-round progress. Split into two departments, prep 8 to 11years and the pre-prep 3 to 7-year-olds which is housed in its own building, formally a headmaster's house. Before and after school care runs from 7.45 am – 6 pm throughout the week.

A friendly school with a good community feel, focusing on developing each child's aptitude and interests.

St Edmund's Junior School

Linked school: St Edmund's School

St Thomas Hill, Canterbury, CT2 8HU

• Pupils: 200; Day: 63 boys/72 girls; boarders: 36 boys/4 girls; choristers: 25 • Ages: 3–13 • Christian foundation but all faiths welcome • Fees: Boarding £17,895–£19,638; Day £13,758 pa • Independent

Tel: 01227 475600
Email: juniorschool@stedmunds.org.uk
Website: www.stedmunds.org.uk

Head: Since 1996, Mr Robert Bacon BA (fiftyish). Educated at Bradfield and Durham where he read modern history and gained his PGCE. Previously at Stamford School where he taught history and was boarding housemaster in the junior school. Reports to the head of the senior school and Janet Frampton Fell, head of early years, reports to him. The three heads collaborate closely and in partnership and the junior and pre-prep heads both have considerable autonomy to run their own schools. A great enthusiast who loves outdoor pursuits – he takes children on an annual adventure survival course to a Scottish island and leads the sixth form of the senior school on various adventure trips. Married to Dominique, an occupational therapist; they have two children, one at university and the other in the senior school at St Edmund's. Takes great trouble to maintain good relations with parents – always encourages them to come and talk about problems and happy for parents to ring him at home in the evening if they are worried about something.

Entrance: Up to age about 10, children spend a day at the school and sit tests. Both parents and children interviewed. School requires two years of reports and a report from the current head. Set great store by the attitude of the child and the family – enthusiasm essential. For entry to the top two years, children sit formal tests and attend an interview plus reports and reference from the current head. If a child offers a weak performance in the tests (they don't like to think in terms of failure), they are welcomed back to meet the curriculum support staff to see if their needs can be met. Can accommodate a wide ability range, but those with severe learning difficulties would struggle. Quite a few join in year 7, often from the primaries.

Exit: Nearly all to the senior school. About half of the choristers move on to the senior school, the rest go on to other independent schools or into the state sector. One or two pupils a year leave at 11+ for the grammars. The school prepares them for the Kent Test but does not coach them or change the curriculum for them. The school no longer prepares children for common entrance unless absolutely necessary – sounds as if it could be a problem, but most senior schools can offer their own entrance exam, so any St Ed's children wanting to move on at 13+ can take this. Some to King's Canterbury, Tonbridge and Sevenoaks. Have also recently won music scholarships to Eton, Harrow and Oundle and an academic scholarship to King's Canterbury.

Remarks: When the Choir School of Canterbury Cathedral closed in 1972, the cathedral choristers joined St Edmund's Junior School. The 26 choristers live in a separate, recently-refurbished house within the cathedral precincts. They lead extraordinarily busy lives, with 20 hours a week singing and attending evensong every day except Wednesdays, plus recordings etc, but they are also fully involved in school life and many are keen sportsmen as well. Here, as elsewhere, the presence of choristers makes a major contribution to the quality of school life.

Setting from year 6 and for maths from year 4. Some subjects taught by senior school teachers from year 6 to ensure seamless transition at 13+. Start Latin in year 5 and touch typing in year 6. Good curriculum support department. Can cope with mild SEN only – dyslexia, dyscalculia, dyspraxia, Asperger's and mild autistic spectrum – about 45 children need some form of learning support. Can accommodate a wide ability range but those with severe learning difficulties would struggle. Two full-time SEN teachers plus two members of staff who can teach EAL when required. Annual screening for general problems. Access to educational psychologists if necessary. School says they feel well ahead of the game and alert to problems. Class sizes 14-18. No scholarship stream but bright children offered scholarship tutorials for the last year. Academic scholarships available for senior school.

About two-thirds of children learn a musical instrument – practice done at home. Plenty of after-school clubs – squash, fencing, mountain biking etc. Academic clubs for the Gifted and Talented eg Seriously Hard Sums Club and Young Engineers Club. Optional enrichment programme for primary school children on Saturday mornings. Plenty of opportunities to stand up in public and build confidence – big musical every year plus drama club, lower school play and lots of small scale events. Poetry evening every year – some write their own poems. English Speaking Board exams and junior school music festival. Informal recitals, concerts etc all abilities welcome with great emphasis on having fun. Woodland survival skills day, team-building and leadership day, water sports week, scarecrow building challenge – something for everyone. Children can compete in senior school sports teams if they are good enough and also take part in senior school orchestra. The East Kent Children's Orchestra is run by St Edmund's Junior School and incorporates the junior school orchestra.

St Edmund's has established itself as a 'through' school aimed at giving children a seamless education from 3-18. Established in Yorkshire in 1749 as the Clergy Orphan School, it moved to Canterbury via London and settled in its present location in 1855. It is clustered around an impressive ecclesiastical high Victorian building, with chapel attached, set in 50 acres with views of the cathedral. The prep school, pre-prep and nursery all have their own buildings, some purpose-built, and all have use of the grounds and specialist facilities of the senior school including the dining hall, swimming pool, sports hall, theatre and music school.

Has the same caring, nurturing ethos as the senior school. Children develop a strong sense of self-worth and self-confidence, which means they are keen to do their best. The school is determined to find hidden talents and endeavour is rewarded in every field.

A cosy, happy school where great store is set by civilised behaviour and being nice to each other. Popular with parents who like the idea of their child being able to stay in one school from 3-18 without the trauma of the 11+ or common entrance.

St Edmund's Prep

Linked school: St Edmund's College

Old Hall Green, Ware, SG11 1DS

- Pupils: 200 boys and girls • Ages: 3–11 • RC • Fees: £8,484–£12,252 pa • Independent

Tel: 01920 821504
Email: admissions@stedmundscollege.org
Website: www.stedmundscollege.org

Head: Since 2013, Mr Steven Cartwright BSc. Joined the school in 2009 as deputy head and became acting head before taking up the post of headmaster. Married with two daughters, the older one of whom will shortly start at St Edmund's. Interests include squash, climbing, running, 'my family, my school!' Popular with parents, who describe him as 'lovely'. 'He's such a nice man, very approachable,' said one. 'He's really good with the children,' said another. An enthusiast who wants the best for his students. 'I am passionate about this school. I do sincerely believe that we strive for the best, and we've got a very nice community.'

Entrance: Entrance to nursery from the term when children have their third birthday. Further admissions at 4 and at 7 by interview ('crucial' says head) and informal assessment. Around 20 children per class; the school prefers to keep them small. Around a third of the children are from Catholic families, the rest from all faiths and from none. Scholarships available at 7+ based on academic merit – applicants sit an exam in January. The school's popularity is rising, and they recently went to two form entry from year 3 in response to demand.

Exit: About 90 per cent to the senior school. A few, inevitably, to local state schools.

Remarks: Located on the same beautiful campus as its big brother, the junior school benefits from an enviable degree of space and wooded tranquility. Whereas the main senior school building is grand and imposing, the prep is a smaller, cosier affair, housed in a former family home designed by Pugin and containing many of his hallmark features. The prep children have their own very appealing little chapel, which is in daily use.

Broad curriculum, including French, with a learning support manager to provide help for those who need it; we liked the learning support room, which was welcoming and cheerful. At the other end of the scale, a child who was particularly gifted in French attended lessons over in the senior college, and all the children go there for science. 'The teachers always encourage the children not just to learn, but to understand and ask questions,' said one satisfied parent.

Plenty of extracurricular activities, with music and drama flourishing, and lots of sports (football is particularly successful). 'This is a very sporty school!' said one little boy, enthusiastically. Children can use the senior school's facilities, including Astro and netball/tennis courts. Wrap around care available, and when children reach year 3 they can use the extensive senior college bus network to get to school and back.

The children we met were relaxed, happy, well-mannered and fond of their school. 'They're really kind here, and I've made a lot of friends,' 'I prefer this school to my old one, there's so much to do,' were typical comments. As one parent added, 'There's a very nice atmosphere within the school. We're really pleased, no complaints at all.'

S

St Elizabeth's Catholic Primary School

Queen's Road, Richmond, TW10 6HN

• Pupils: 240 boys and girls • Ages: 3–11 including nursery • RC
• State

Tel: 020 8940 3015
Email: info@st-elizabeths.richmond.sch.uk
Website: www.st-elizabeths.richmond.sch.uk

Headteacher: Since 1988, Ms Christine Brett MEd (in mathematics education) BEd (in English) DipMathsEd. Describes herself as 'over 21.' Previously deputy head at St Mary's Clapham. Comes across as sweetly old fashioned (though we are sure there is a steely resolve there as well), completely at home in this intimate, friendly, school. Still does some teaching – year 6 maths and hymn practice. Parents say the school and the pupils are an important part of her life. 'Our children become her family,' says one mother, 'but that's not to say she is a soft touch; she takes absolutely no nonsense.' Indeed she has great presence and we can understand why she is held in awe by parents (and pupils). 'She is quite scary but is a deeply religious person,' said one ex-mum. Dedicated to the school and the Catholic faith, Ms Brett is very keen on consistency, discipline and tradition – she's only the seventh head since school was founded in 1840. But she's also bang up-to-date with new ideas in education. Knows every child in the school; very caring and involved. Also a good sport – has attended school summer fair dressed as a fairy to lead the fancy dress parade.

Entrance: No point applying unless you are on first name terms with your Catholic priest. Serving four parishes covering Richmond, Kew, Ham and East Sheen, with a few from St Margaret's, the school is single form entry and heavily oversubscribed. Typically 90 applications for the 30 places on offer and of these more than 50 per cent of the applicants fulfil the number one criteria of being a baptised, practising Catholic. After that priority goes to siblings (always lots) and then admission is based on proximity to the school. Nursery is separate unit on the same site in premises due for upgrading – same admissions criteria as school. Other feeder nurseries are Wyndham and The Barn.

Exit: To a wide range of schools including Catholic state secondaries Gumley House Convent, Wimbledon College, the Ursuline Convent, the Sacred Heart Convent, Cardinal Vaughan and the London Oratory. Some to Kingston schools, including two or three to Tiffin. Not many to Richmond secondaries. A few to independent sector including St Benedict's in Ealing, Hampton School and Lady Eleanor Holles in Hampton. 'Lots of doors open from here,' says Ms Brett, though one ex-mother queried how much independent schools advice was on offer.

Remarks: Great Sats results, a clutch of glowing reports from Ofsted and the like, and a host of happy parents all pay tribute to this hugely popular school.

Academically it certainly does the business, producing well above average results at key stage two. Level 5s were achieved by 70+ per cent of the pupils in English and maths, 90 per cent in science. A fairly stable, mostly female, small group of teaching staff, so everybody knows everybody – no hiding place for the feckless. It's a very expensive area of the country and high living costs mean there is some movement of staff; however, nearby are the well-respected teacher training facilities of St Mary's and Roehampton, so a good supply of fresh student blood is on hand.

A traditional place but the ICT is all there – whiteboards and wireless laptops mean the teacher is not stuck at the front of the class, but can be more flexible. Well-equipped ICT suite large enough for whole-class teaching – just a few years old. More languages than many junior schools manage. Years 3, 4, and 5 learn Italian (courtesy of an arrangement with the Italian Embassy, which provides a teacher). Year 6 pupils learn French, visit France and study for the Lingua Bronze award – gives them a head start at their secondary school. There's also a Spanish club among the after-school activities programme which takes children from age five.

Aesthetics not squeezed out by academia – music, art and drama all valued here. School views drama as a resource to be used whenever the opportunity arises. Every child in years 2 and 3 learns recorder and all year groups study singing. Most learn an additional instrument, typically cello, brass, flute, violin or guitar. All culminated in a highly praised production of Joseph and the Amazing Technicolour Dreamcoat for KS2.

Pupils do extremely well at swimming – all four junior classes swim every year, six weeks on, six weeks off – head believes no point in teaching them for one term and ticking the 'they can swim' box. Mixed-age team champions in Richmond Schools Swimming Gala. Other sports include netball, football, athletics, basketball and mixed tag rugby (Small School Champions).

Almost the only gripe from parents does concern the lack of space and facilities for sport on site. There's no playing field, only hard surface provision – basically the junior playground. 'It's a lovely place but I wish the children, particularly the boys, had more room to run around,' says one mother. Pupils do use the outdoor facilities of a nearby secondary school.

In ritzy residential Richmond, built to an unusual semi-open plan arrangement which survives nearly 40 years on. Staff and parents like it, feeling that it helps to promote an open atmosphere which pervades the whole institution. Don't worry; there are classrooms, but also lots of shared work and quiet areas. 'It has the advantage of helping to achieve consistency of teaching, as well as promoting openness of spirit and mind,' says Ms Brett. Light floods in through partially glazed ceilings giving a nice airy aspect to the place. Super security; gates are locked during the school day, entryphone access both at the gates and the main building.

Largely upmarket intake; some of these families could undoubtedly afford the private sector, but head describes intake as 'much more mixed than you might imagine for this area.' About nine per cent of the children qualify for free school meals, which is more than twice as many as at other schools round about. Mainly white British or Irish, but 25 per cent of the school has EAL. Lots of immigrant families tend to be Catholic – so there are Italian, Spanish, Polish, Filipino, Eritrean, Chinese and Indian children on the roll. About 18 per cent of pupils have some special need, most commonly specific learning difficulties around language acquisition, and some behavioural issues such as ADHD. No testing on entry, but school says it is happy to cater for all SEN and gifted and talented that fall within mainstream remit.

Children encouraged to take a real pride in their work; lovely displays and workbooks are the result. Perhaps it's the need to be considerate of others, necessitated by the open layout, which promotes the caring atmosphere in evidence. The older children take a fair degree of responsibility for helping their school mates in the lower years, lunch time monitoring, hearing them read and so on. Our year 6 tour guides were almost mobbed in an act of pure hero worship as we visited the class they monitored.

Parents rave about the friendly atmosphere between the children, transcending year groups, and bill and coo over the pastoral care. The religious ethos is strong – whole school assembly most days; mass celebrated periodically and on special occasions, prayers at beginning and end of day and grace before lunch; all on top of what's included in the syllabus, of course.

S

School is fairly demanding and standards are high, homework must be done on time, uniform absolutely on spec and so on – check that's you before signing up. Parents are a big part of the school: 'some parents get very involved in both daytime and after-school activities and without them it would not be, for example, the great swimming school that it is,' said one former mum. 'However, it is assumed that you want to give your time.' She felt that parental efforts were not always fully appreciated.

In a nutshell, the school ticks all the boxes for what parents would want from an ordered Catholic education – very strong spiritually, academically and pastorally. Not for the lackadaisical, nor for those hankering for informality and wide open spaces.

In 2013 an additional classroom was built at the Queen's Road end of the school to accommodate ten classes from 2015. General upgrade of buildings and facilities has also taken place and there are plans for more improvements.

St Faith's

Linked school: The Leys School

Trumpington Road, Cambridge, CB2 8AG

• Pupils: 534; 319 boys and 215 girls, all day • Ages: 4–13 • Inter-denom • Fees: £10,530–£13,275 pa • Independent

Tel: 01223 352073
Email: admissions@stfaiths.co.uk
Website: www.stfaiths.co.uk

Headmaster: Since September 2011, Mr Nigel Helliwell BEd MA (London), previously head of Brentwood Prep for six years. Began his career teaching maths and PE at Ilkley Grammar School in Yorkshire, then moved to preps in East Anglia and south London. A qualified independent schools' inspector (sets a lot of store by 'lockers and loos' – St Faith's are exemplary) and an accomplished sportsman, having played rugby and cricket at county level. Married to Jane, who used to be a senior manager in a housing association and now enjoys helping the pupils with their reading and cheering from the touchline. They have one son and an Irish Jack Russell. Head eats with the children daily and personally hand-delivers birthday cards (there's one in his pocket on our tour). Has already made a quiet impact – though, as he says, the challenge was only to lift the school further into the stratosphere. However, the 'subtle improvements' have not gone unappreciated by parents who have noted that his communication with them is now more frequent and that there's a useful parents' handbook, improved website and a hard copy calendar as well as electronic to keep all in the loop. Higher standards of appearance and manners – 'so important in the world of work today' he says – have also gone down well, as has his wise advice on potential next schools, born out of diligent personal research. 'Mr Helliwell has suggested senior schools for my son that were not even on my radar, yet they have proved to be spot on,' says one mother.

Head is complemented by a hands-on bursar who is keen to keep the campus shipshape and parents particularly praise his marshalling of the new 'drop-off zone', arranged in collaboration with school's neighbours in the interest of good relations and less stressful mornings.

Entrance: Strong demand for places so names on the waiting list as soon as possible advised. Entry to pre-prep is offered by the head after a parental visit and a meeting with the child at their nursery. For all other years there are assessments in English and maths. Sibling policy gives priority on the waiting list.

Exit: Most to The Leys – otherwise to the Perse schools, Oundle, Oakham, Uppingham, Repton, Culford, King's Ely, Friends', Harrow, Stowe and Rugby. Past pupils include Maynard Keynes, Christopher Cockerell (inventor of the Hovercraft), Sir John Tusa and England rugby player Alex Goode.

Remarks: Head's aspiration is to develop St Faith's national profile to be similar to that of Oxford's Dragon School and – minus the boarding – it's a dead cert, thanks to a child-centred educational philosophy that turns out sparky individuals with high all-round expectations and the skills to meet them.

The caps are gone but the 'distinctive' red, black and white striped blazers remain – rather Marmite. St Faith's opened in 1884 as a boys' school (girls joined in 1995). It shares the same Methodist foundation as The Leys and lives in a mixture of buildings on the opposite side of Trumpington Road, from the comfortable traditional to the buzzy contemporary. On the deceptively spacious site, behind a quirky ironwork fence designed by a local artisan, pre-preppers are accommodated in superb new edifices whose child-friendly architecture won a national design award. Inside, curvy walls, brightly coloured floors and cartoon doors make it a fun learning environment for the children – and staff, we imagine. Certainly a lively phonics lesson was in progress when we visited – year 1s having a blast with an enthusiastic male teacher – 40 per cent of the teaching staff are men and there's a healthy range of ages. 'The teachers show immense enthusiasm for the individual child,' says a parent. 'They constantly strive to find out who your child is and what makes them tick.'

All three 'Foundation' (Reception) classrooms open onto an outdoor decked area and tinies have their own adventure playground, secluded from the older pupils' more traditional but no less well-equipped domain, which stretches across the site. Three classes of 14 children in pre-prep, with average of 16 children per class all through the school and a teaching assistant in every one; 43 per cent girls. Classes are arranged in houses and there is a 'strong family feel' say parents. Whole school assembly weekly, but every child has four assemblies in various permutations. All fit in the hall, which is complete with drop-down projector screens and professional stage lighting and sound for the many productions.

Pyramid educational philosophy here – school does well for all but can really extend those at the top, encouraging them to achieve at a national level. One of the head's major changes so far has been to extend lesson times from 30 to 50 minutes with a five-minute changeover – allows pupils to engage more deeply with their work. Reporting to parents has also been tightened – now grades for attainment as well as effort every half term for 7+. Parents' evenings are formal in the first term of the year and followed by 'tutor surgeries' in the other two. Academic achievement is generally well above the national average, although a minority of children, including learners with difficulties and/or disabilities (LDD) and any with special educational needs (SEN), are aided by the friendly Learning Support Unit.

Very inclusive ethos – 'responsibility is given to all, not just the select few' says head. All top year pupils are prefects and there is a ladder of leadership skills from a young age. So much so that this year all four heads of school at The Leys, Perse and Stephen Perse Foundation are Old Fidelians. Regularly two dozen scholarships a year to good senior schools – half academic and the rest a mixture of art, drama, music and sport – reflecting the high level of attainment across the board.

Languages are a way of life – doors, windows, books and even the head's office are labelled in Espanol and the school is recognised by the Spanish embassy as being in the top ten in the country for teaching of the language. Year 4 drama production is all in Spanish – 'the language is totally integrated' says head. Latin from age nine, French from 11, Greek for high-flyers in year 8 and Cambridge University students teach Ancient Greek.

Trip to Pompeii is popular. School really on the button with computer science – out with the ICT and in with a new head of digital learning, who brings programming to children aged nine plus, with general keyboard and communications skills for those younger.

'It's easy to judge the quality of sport by the scoreline,' says head. 'Music, art and drama are less easy to rate but we have a lot of success.' Professional artist works full-time alongside the teacher, advising, inspiring and also working on his own commissions. Pupil artwork on display could be mistaken for GCSE. All over the age of seven are treated to DT in the best-equipped workshops we've ever seen in a prep – vast doors allow huge pieces of professional machinery to be wheeled in and out. Results are impressive and scholarships are won. School hosts the IAPS national DT conference. Eco-garden at the front of the school, designed by pupils in a fellow's memory, is a well-considered place for quiet contemplation. Director of music is ex-King's College and although all levels of talent are appreciated, the most gifted do well and include members of the National Youth Orchestra and regional choirs. Superb music rooms double as a performance space and there are banks of Apple Macs equipped with music tech software, used by everyone over the age of four.

Indeed, sport is a real strength, with seemingly invincible teams and individuals in most disciplines, but all have a chance to represent the school in teams A-D. Good acreage of playing fields a minute's walk across the road, including the usual pitches and two Astros, used by all over the age of nine twice a week, plus clubs. 'Main sporting competition is now national,' says head. New £3m – from school's own funds – sports hall hosts regional and national competitions.

All aged over seven are welcome in the library any time and it stays open after school for prep and reading. School day finishes at 3.40 but optional (and mostly free) activities until 5. All-rounderness is encouraged and a surprising amount can be shoehorned into the school day – 'our sports mad boys have also been able to learn to play musical instruments to a high level, with minimal conflict,' reports a parent; 'my children are never bored' says another. Family breakfast from 7.15 is a very popular option – a chance for parents to catch up with the kids, eat a hearty full English and avoid the worst of the city traffic. Lunch is three hot options as well as sandwiches, a salad bar and choice of puddings and fruit – all you can eat.

Saint Felix School Pre-Prep and Prep Departments

Linked school: Saint Felix School

Halesworth Road, Reydon, Southwold, Suffolk, IP18 6SD

• Pupils: 70 girls and boys in tore-prep and prep; 40 in nursery • Ages: 1–11 • Non-denom • Fees: Day £6,450–£9,750; Boarding £15,360–£20,190 pa • Independent

Tel: 01502 722175
Email: schooladmin@stfelix.suffolk.sch.uk
Website: www.stfelix.co.uk

Head of Preparatory Department: Dr John Dodsworth.

Entrance: Not difficult, but all entrants are screened and parents are forewarned if progression is not likely. For pre-prep and prep departments (reception to year 6) – a day in school plus evidence of work and report from previous school. Transfer from the nursery to pre-prep is automatic. Transfer to the prep is by formal assessment.

Exit: Ninety per cent to the senior school, although entrance isn't guaranteed.

Remarks: Hot on manners and consideration for others. Smiley, fresh-faced children who appreciate the benign environment.

Prep is in a stand-alone 1906 Queen Anne style ex-boarding house adjacent to the senior school. Large, airy classrooms and wide corridors with squeaky wooden floorboards. Approximately 13 in a class, with an unpressured teaching style which veers towards the traditional. French for all year groups. Assemblies, art, games and music (50 per cent have instrumental lessons) are in the senior school buildings. Specialist teachers for years 5 and 6.

The library has been revamped and re-stocked and ICT suite has space for 20 children. Two compulsory extra-curricular slots after school, with activities including sports, choir and a host of clubs.

One or two full boarders. Flexi-boarding with the house parent and her family is a popular option (new junior boarding facilities for year 5 to 8 pupils). Pre-prep situated in Bronte House, a large building opposite the senior school, with years 3 to 6 in adjacent building. Attentive classes with questioning and co-operation. Long pavements (perfect for trikes and pedal cars), new wooden outdoor play equipment consisting of pirate boat, lighthouse and new adventure playground – all safely contained in a large grassy corral. Two new outdoor classrooms. Little ones in sweetly pretty dark green and white plaid dresses or polo shirts and shorts.

Recent shot in the arm for SEN provision with the appointment of Julia Campbell, who did a sterling job at Riddlesworth – her remit is to get the school CREeSTeD registered.

St George's Junior School

Linked school: St George's College, Weybridge

Thames Street, Weybridge, KT13 8NL

• Pupils: 622 pupils, 326 boys/296 girls; all day • Ages: 3–11 • RC (Josephite) • Fees: £7,320–£11,640 pa • Independent

Tel: 01932 839400
Email: contact@stgeorgesweybridge.com
Website: www.stgeorgesweybridge.com

Headmaster: Since 2003, Mr Antony Hudson MA PGCE NPQH (early fifties). Previously deputy head at Prior's Field. Before that, worked at assorted independents, all secondary and in Surrey or close, bar a three-year stint as housemaster and sixth form head in deepest Derbyshire to get taste for rural lifestyle out of system.

The first layman in the post, head is understandably relieved to have joined after the dust had settled and blood-letting had been accomplished (teachers had to reapply for jobs – all very traumatic). 'A lovely man,' one mother told us. Doesn't dissemble – you'll get the truth from him, even if it hurts, say parents, and, fittingly, his office alone would win awards for transparency, with doors or windows on three sides. Two doors ajar is the 'surgery is open' sign for parents who want a quick chat. Office filled with assorted artefacts – books, photographs, guitar, even a Toy Story character – that tell his life story, illuminated by the warm glow of five desk lamps ('not very environmentally friendly but I can't bear a central light').

Like office, like man: he's engagingly frank about his life to date. A couple of years into teaching career he was within a whisker of following in footsteps of an older brother (he has four) and entering the priesthood, when doubts set in. Instead of taking his vows, he opted for marriage and a family. Very much to the community's benefit as he and his wife Helen (a teacher at St Hilary's in Godalming) play a huge part in church life. Their two sons are both at St George's College.

To the slight bafflement of some colleagues, head enjoys local celebrity and recognition (shopping expeditions can resemble a royal tour, he says). This despite a period when he feared he would become a local hate figure amongst well to do mummies after he changed admissions criteria, reduced numbers with learning difficulties and some pupils were asked to leave. 'I thought they'd be burning me in effigy on the high street.' But, Piaf-like, it's a case of 'je ne regretted rien' – school needs to keep numbers feeding through to college at age 11 so it's not fair on anyone if he's taking students who won't make it and diverting too many resources away from the able ones who will. 'We'll never achieve 100 per cent but we aim to come close,' he says.

Teaches all reception pupils music, splitting the workload with a colleague, so gets to know children well from the beginning and is an extrovert type who's happy to dress up in the line of duty. 'Togas can be dangerous when everyone is wearing shorts,' he says of his recent appearance at school fête. Not averse to direct action, once taking to the streets to urge poorly parked parents to mend their ways (with a follow up number plates of shame section in school newsletter).

Entrance: School numbers are creeping ever north, despite recession (though school could add another 40 or so before hitting capacity of 688). Entrance is selective all the way through, with behaviour and social skills assessed for nursery places and academic tests added at appropriate levels from reception onwards. No scholarships but assisted places (usually two per year) are available, potentially covering 100 per cent of the school fees.

School officially welcomes parents who sign up in nursery for a mere 15 hours a week (the maximum that is government funded) and are exempt from stumping up the £500 deposit that is otherwise payable (and non-refundable if they take up a reception place elsewhere). However, they will have to re-apply if they want child to carry on through the school, automatic for the majority whose children put in longer hours from the off (school likes evidence of commitment).

Once a haven for those with learning difficulties, things are very different now. Informal quota agreed with governors limits numbers to around 25 though 'nobody's going to die in a ditch if we have two extra,' says head. However, unlikely to be the right place for anything more severe than mild dyslexia, well catered for by learning support team either in lessons or through withdrawal.

While it's not essential to be a Catholic, sympathy with the belief system undoubtedly helps, as does realisation that while the Josephites who founded the school have a child-centred and kind approach to education (rare in 19th century circles) it doesn't preclude weeding out the under achievers. 'We call them late developers,' says one mother, who approves, as do others, of the tough but honest approach. 'It's a cruel to be kind thing.'

The academically able get unconditional offers of senior school places as early as year 2, though everyone takes senior school entrance exams for scholarship and setting purposes and it's far from being a licence to take it easy, as school 're-evaluates' if performance slips. You haven't necessarily missed the boat if you join in year 3 or above, as there are a few more secure golden tickets each Easter term up to year 5. Others compete with pupils from outside and remaining old timers, though hardworking mid-roaders usually end up with places. 'It's never going to be a hothouse,' a parent told us.

Exit: Lots in (usually some every term) and lots out, too, with around 30 (five per cent) of pupils leaving before their time is officially up – most commonly because of relocation, some because of money issues and three or so each year after being

tipped the wink that academics aren't up to snuff. However, school won't cast them off into outer educational space, say parents, and efforts are made to help find alternatives.

For those who stay on into year 6, almost 90 per cent transfer to the senior school, with the additional incentive of range of scholarships not available to external candidates. Of the remaining ten per cent, most head off to other independents – Sir William Perkins's, Hampton Boys, Guildford High School and Halliford among them, while a few clinch places at Tiffin Boys and Girls, Kingston's top-performing state grammars.

Remarks: Other school bursars must look at the rising numbers and weep. Big site is well organised and unified by strong emphasis on belonging. Even majority of nursery children, housed in their own separate block, wear uniform and everyone in junior school plays in at least one proper match regardless of ability. Wearing the school badge 'means something' (after that, selection is down to talent and commitment to turning up to after hours training).

School's sense of tradition is inescapable but not over-weighty and inextricably bound up with religious dimension, centred on imposing chapel with a weekly mass conducted by Josephite priest. In a nod to the sensibilities of the softer 21st century child, though, there's an element of sugar coating, with some crucifixes round the school depicting cheerful Holy Family rather than the agony of Christ.

Parents, prospective and existing, comment on exceptional pupil manners on and off the premises. Lots of (almost) unprompted standing up whenever a teacher enters the room, though observance of the no running outside rule is more of a lip service job with pupils executing a quick, slow, quick manoeuvre, decelerating as they draw level with teachers before picking up speed again once past.

It's down in part, school would say, to the 'douceur and politesse' factor – Josephite-inspired attitude of mind that permeates school life. There's a sizeable staff presence in the welcoming and well decorated dining room for example. All food is cooked from scratch, with year 6 pupils allowed the almost unspeakable sophistication of sandwiches – 'as we have more responsibilities,' one pupil told us.

Not the place to go for educational fads and fancies. Focus is always on keeping in step with the senior school (their staff visit regularly – more so now, you get the impression, than used to be the case). The result is that parents are never in doubt, for good or ill, about how pupils are doing. Maths set from year 3, English from year 5 and regular assessments for all.

Teachers, who span the experience/age spectrum, win pupil approval – especially as 'there aren't any shouty ones now,' said one pupil – and come across as unflappable. In classroom-based subjects, lots of traditional teaching from the front (lidded desks still the norm, too) though plenty of hands-on involvement elsewhere. Textbook-only lessons 'a rarity' said a science teacher as, with evident relish, year 6 girls applied a Bunsen burner to magnesium and iron filings in well-equipped lab.

As with the senior school, no shortage of things to do. Science and art rooms (there's even a kiln) are open at break-time and large, inviting 14,000-volume library (librarian would make world a Kindle-free zone if she could) welcomes little readers in. Everyone, from tinies upwards, has minimum of one library session a week.

Outside, play areas in 20 attractively laid out acres are mainly grassed (the few remaining hard surfaces are gradually being replaced) and there's clearly been a substantial investment in enticing-looking apparatus including popular zip wire and 'The Alien', a futuristic and frankly rather odd-looking climbing frame that looks like a giant egg on legs.

The sporty (and competitive) are well catered for with excellent facilities – heated outdoor swimming pool (complete with ring of safety steel fencing to Fort Knox standards), two tennis courts and all weather surfaces for hockey and tennis and results to match. Many near misses in quarter and semi-finals and some impressive county and regional championship wins (boys' tennis and girls' mini hockey particularly strong).

If sport doesn't appeal (and even if it does) you can go a la carte with a 45-strong menu of clubs and activities, ranging from puppet making to country dancing (recently introduced and popular enough for school 'to have requisitioned a maypole'). Lots of music and as school owns 80 violins, all year 2 parents have precious gift of squeaky open strings alternating with taster recorder sessions. Works, though, with 60 per cent playing instruments in year 3 (numbers fall off further up school as some 'can't cope' with commitment required, says the head of music and orchestra, just 19-strong, is due a bit of a re-think. Sensible timetabling of instrument lessons avoids clashes with vital academic subjects. Two big junior choirs – all comers welcome, including 'lots of boys,' say year 6 girls with distinct froideur, who 'get a house point for joining which we don't.' Sewing, however, remains a solidly girls-only (and housepoint-free) zone.

One parent described St George's Junior as 'a well-rounded education that's hard to get elsewhere,' and only real fly in the ointment is the fabric of the building, definitely more shabby than chic. 'It needs reinvigoration,' says the deputy head, with masterly understatement, of the sad-looking side hall reserved for nursery children's dining, gym and assembly. Fingers crossed, it should all be happening soon.

In the meantime, it's nice to see priority given to small things that make a difference, like the de luxe refurbishment of girls' and boys' toilets on every landing in main four-storey block that houses years 2 to 6. Credit must also go to school's groundsmen, who are responsible for some of the most successful floral camouflage in the business – beautifully maintained greenery and hanging baskets that distract the eye as you brave the long walkway that runs between two rows of Portakabins.

'We're in a position to build for the next 50 years,' the head told us. 'I'd love to be here till I'm 65.' On the evidence of pupil numbers and parent positivity, there are plenty who won't have a problem if he is.

St George's Junior School

Linked school: St George's School (Edinburgh)

Garscube Terrace, Edinburgh, EH12 6BG

• Pupils: Girls (boys in nursery) • Ages: 5–13 • Fees: Day £7,260–£9,375; Boarding £19,770–£21,885 pa • Independent

Tel: 01313 118000
Email: admissions@st-georges.edin.sch.uk
Website: www.st-georges.edin.sch.uk

Head: Since 2010, Mrs Anne Everest BA, (fifties), a classicist, Yorkshire born and bred, she has lived in Scotland for 30 years. Formerly deputy head of Robert Gordon's College, Aberdeen (qv) and head of St Margaret's School, Aberdeen (qv). Educated at St Mary's Grammar School and Hull uni. Everest taught classics and ancient history, lectured in ancient history, Latin and new testament Greek at her alma mater. Married 'very early' to an oily husband, she 'had three babies instead of finishing her PhD', resuming her career path in 1991 when she became acting head of classics at St Margaret's in Aberdeen (oily wives must follow the drum). She runs the school with a senior management team, including the heads of both junior and lower school, and a clutch of deputies.

Entrance: Entrance either by interview aged 4-5 or via the nursery.

Exit: Nearly all to senior school. A few leave for schools down south.

Remarks: No distinct junior school as such, rather a tripartite combo: nursery, junior and lower. There was a time when parents would coach their little darlings for pre-assessment at junior school (before the days of nurseries you understand), on the basis that you were then made for life: we ain't heard of a waiting list for years. This was the school for the networking Edinbourgeousie: middle class Scots, professionals, incomers, wannabes and first time buyers all met on an equal playing field.

We were refused entry by the new head last year because, 'they were building a hall', in the junior school. And very nice it is too although somehow, after all the palaver, this editor had expected to see a HALL, rather than an overgrown dance studio/gym with a pristine sprung floor. We were surprised to find the school drive blocked off at the end with security fencing and wonder whether there is another development in hand to which we are not privy.

Head of junior school, Sue Hall, who has taught here for 19 years, delegated two charming nine year olds to show us round. Which they did: with a little list. We examined every classroom, sometimes in great detail, we met a number of staff. This editor was concerned to discover that pictures on the wall of P3 (eight years) describing their summer holiday announced that they had flown in a plain, and sat on beeches. There must be an epidemic of dyslexia in Edinburgh, or is this the result of ill-taught phonics? It is inconceivable that teachers choose to display ill-spelt work at eight year olds' eye height; presumably condoning the spelling (nb spell check won't work with homophones). Whilst rigorous grammatical and spelling correctness was not flavour of the month ten years ago, the resurgence of phonics (jolly phonics/jolly grammar) is now universally accepted as the way forward.

In another P3 class various young were working on individual projects whilst the teacher was about to listen to reading (fair amount of chaos). We stopped with the child nearest the door to examine her work and asked whether there was another way of spelling 'froot'. Could we think about it? This editor regularly stops and looks at children's work, at which point the teacher or form taker usually scuttles over to explain/discuss. We were ignored. Totally. And to make matters worse, this ed had just recommended St G's to some cousins, who, coming from a seriously academic background, may be surprised at the lack of basic grounding in spelling and grammar. Whatever happened to rubbers? I have already rung and apologised although they appear to be quite happy.

The Lower School (ages 10-13) is based in the former boarding house plus vile extensions. Latin from age 10. Certain amount of tinkering about with what age is taught where, sounded immensely complicated, but the gist of the argument is that by moving girls around and splitting the junior school into two, the tedium of being in a single sex school for up to 15 years might not appear so drear. P5 – P6 (11/12 year olds) are taught in the main campus, before they move to lower school proper for a couple of years before they move back to main school. Got it?

All girls in junior schools (combined) are assessed for learning hiccups; school boasts seven trained specialist teachers and assorted staff. As with senior school, pupils are withdrawn from class: one to one, small clusters, or helped by assistants in class. All use senior school facilities, gym, music, drama, games pitches. Tad concerned that part of lower school is across a 'proper' road, albeit not a main road with buses and all; we saw several sub-teens wandering across. The ed would like to have seen young being escorted across all roads, either by a lollipop person or at least a member of staff in a yellow jacket.

Drop off early, from 7.30 am, girls can 'buy' breakfast; late waiting, parents can collect up to 6 pm (cost) and girls can be fed 'their pre-ordered evening meal' beforehand. Holiday club operates 8.30 am – 6 pm five days a week: girls should book in stating number of days and bring packed lunch.

IT (mostly wireless) and for tinies and in the boarding houses. School website dominated by down-market woman's magazine type romantic fuzzy pic of Balfour-Paul's garden side. Website should be a window into the school: St G's, full of head's previous speeches but pretty low on content: collection of badly written (and often incomprehensible) mission statements but no staff list with email addresses, list of governors, senior management team: info that could be useful. For an academic school to live or die by something out of People's Friend is incomprehensible.

St Helen and St Katharine Junior School

Linked school: St Helen and St Katharine

Faringdon Road, Abingdon, OX14 1BE

• Pupils: 40 girls • Ages: 9–11 • Anglican foundation
• Fees: £13,020 pa • Independent

Tel: 01235 520173
Email: info@shsk.org.uk
Website: www.shsk.org.uk

Remarks: For further details, see senior school entry.

St Hilary's School

Holloway Hill, Godalming, GU7 1RZ

• Pupils: 245 boys and girls • Ages: 2–11 (girls), 2–7 (boys) • Non-denom • Fees: £8,355–£12,375 pa • Independent

---

Tel: 01483 416551
Email: registrar@sthilarysschool.com
Website: www.sthilarysschool.com

Headmistress: Since 2012, Mrs Jane Whittingham (early fifties), previously deputy at nearby Rowan Prep in Esher, with particular interest and qualification in dyslexia. Mother of four (teens and twenties), came somewhat late to her first headship due to time spent with her own family. She prefers the prep school model (as opposed to a through school) 'where pupils prepare for their future, as well as their next school, and move on to a new landscape at 11'. Mrs W is bursting with new ideas, 'I have one idea a day while driving up and down the A3', covering every aspect of school life and has made many changes in her first year at St Hilary's, tweaking teaching standards upwards, introducing head girl, house captains and positions of responsibility for every year 6 pupil, creating a plethora of awards. Her open door policy includes almost daily visits from groups of pupils for TLC and encouragement dressed up in fun sessions such as reading with Ronnie (her pet dog), ludo and lemonade, dodgers (jammie) and dominoes. Groups of year 6 girls are regularly invited to lunch in her study, with table cloths, wine glasses (of juice) and 'posh cutlery'. Parents tell us their girls 'love going to visit Mrs Whittingham in her office'. Parents are contented with the many changes, saying Mrs W is doing good things and moving St Hilary's on without losing the happy, unpressurised vibe.

Entrance: Entry to nursery at age 2 allows unfettered progression throughout school, others join into reception year or at age 7. Quite a few join from local state infants' schools. No academic selection, prospective pupils and their parents meet the head and the child spends a morning in school so staff can benchmark their current attainment and give them a taste of life at St Hilary's.

Handful of scholarships up to 30 per cent. Means tested bursaries available, mostly 10 to 50 per cent, including very occasional full bursary. Scholarships at year 3 entry, in-house scholarship tests for girls already at St Hilary's, 'they write a story and do a maths paper during a lesson and don't really realise so there's no pressure'. Current pupils can apply for academic, art, sports, music or drama scholarships.

Parents describe the whole entry and scholarship process as very low key and are comfortable with the range of academic ability.

Exit: Boys leave aged 7, two-thirds go on to nearby Aldro, a couple each to Lanesborough and Cranleigh Prep.

The vast majority of girls leave aged 11 and go to either of St Catherine's (one or two with music scholarships), Prior's Field (heaps with art, academic or sports scholarships) or Tormead (a few with music, art and academic scholarships). Ones and twos to a range of other, mainly Surrey, schools. Rarely to boarding schools.

Parents appreciate the help given with entry exams for senior schools, noting how work ramps up at the start of year 6 with a focus on English, maths and science, plus recently introduced verbal and non-verbal reasoning. They are comfortable that 'girls are very well prepared for their next step'.

Remarks: The ethos of St Hilary's, repeated by staff and parents alike, is an encouraging but unpressured prep school education. Parents feel the school is 'very happy' and pupils are 'allowed to be themselves', it's a 'buzzy place' with something for everyone and 'makes the best of each child without pressure'. This unpressurised aura sets St Hilary's apart from some of the other local girls' schools and really appeals to the relaxed parents of St Hilary's pupils. Typically, a mother told us, 'homework is not a big deal, it doesn't get in the way of family life.'

The lack of pressure doesn't mean lack of academic success. While intake and classes are 'completely mixed ability', parents feel St Hilary's 'seems to cater for all' and 'gets results with quality teaching'. There's plenty of praise for teachers, many of whom are relatively new, including a good few mentions for the 'dynamic deputy head' credited with improving standards. There's a sense that 'nobody fails, because it becomes clear which senior school they're heading for'. Mrs W meets all boys in year 1 and girls in year 5, individually with their parents, to discuss choices for next schools, telling us she 'works with parents to find a senior school which fits'. Parents are confident that St Hilary's is 'good at placing girls and preparing them for the right senior school'.

On our visit we saw small classes, some of only 8 to 10, with quiet, attentive pupils. Classrooms, science lab, music and art rooms were interesting and colourful, inter-linked with lots of open doors in the younger age groups. Nothing stupendously modern, but all thoroughly fit for purpose. Buildings are a mix, from Victorian with additions throughout the 20th century. Internally a bit of a warren, but our pupil guides were totally confident of their routes and eager to show us everywhere. The nursery section, taking boys and girls from age 2, is bright, fun, well organised and with a newly kitted out, spacious, TeleTubbyland-esque outdoor area. Older pupils can come here for half an hour before school and have breakfast (as an extra), staff say young and older children enjoy each other's company.

Kindness is another recurring theme, parents mention how children are aware of each other and the need to be kind. Mothers explain, 'kindness is noted, recognised and rewarded,' saying 'girls are kind, inclusive and celebrate friends' achievements' and 'everybody looks out for each other'. One of

Mrs W's newly introduced awards is a 'True Friend' wrist band awarded to pupils who have been particularly kind and helpful to others. Girls are not the sort to be bothered by fashions and fads, they are 'not worried about what they're wearing or having the latest rubber or pencil'. One girl who had moved on to a popular local girls' senior school noticed the difference between her kind, modest St Hilary's friends and louder, more assertive girls from other schools.

Parents report that music, art and drama are strengths, citing the 'very enthusiastic head of music'. They like the availability of 'taster instruments', their girls 'love being involved in music'. Another parent enthused over the variety of musical clubs, groups and orchestra her 'very musical daughter' enjoys, while being delighted 'this is all included in the fees'.

Sport has been given a recent boost by the new, 'young and bubbly' head of sport, a British Gymnast who the girls love to Google and watch on YouTube. Usual netball and hockey, with football and cricket for boys, on offer and everyone does everything. Pupils of all abilities attend practice sessions during lunch break or after school and everyone who wants to has a good chance of playing matches in a team. New sports recently added just for fun include girls' football, tag-rugby and pop-lacrosse.

Families tend to be classic middle class professionals, although a little more laid back and less demanding than the Surrey stereotype. Many with both parents working but lots of stay at home mums too, some first time buyers and all pretty local. Families are undoubtedly comfortably off, the car park is populated with new four by fours, but few are flashy or brash. Some recent relocations from London wanting less city life for their children, but parents and teachers alike say this has not changed the local, Godalming and villages vibe of the school. St Hilary's PTA is active with lots of social events, all the usuals, plus others such as a family camping weekend in the grounds.

Overall, happy, charming and a little bit old fashioned, academically successful and, above all, unpressurised.

St Hilda's Preparatory School for Girls

High Street, Bushey, Watford, Hertfordshire, DW23 3DA

- Pupils: 145; • Ages: 2–11; • Fees: £10,029–£10,731 pa;
- Independent

Tel: 020 8950 1751
Email: secretary@sthildasbushey.co.uk
Website: www.sthildas-school.co.uk

Headmistress: Since 2011, Tracy Handford MA (early forties). Educated at Lancaster Girls' Grammar School and the University of Leeds, where she read applied biology. Followed this with an MA in curriculum studies from the Institute of Education, University of London. Began career as a boarding tutor at Taverham Hall School, Norwich, then Holmwood House, Colchester. Moved to become head of year and head of science at Bishop's Stortford College Junior School before becoming director of studies at St Faith's School, Cambridge. Is happy to have returned to her roots at a small prep school, where size means there are 'no breaks in the circle' and they can know every girl inside out. Status as ISI inspector should mean she has her eye on the competitive ball.

Likeable, down to earth and reportedly with an 'incredible work ethic'. Joined at a tricky time when local parents – mostly hard-working, dual income families – were feeling the pinch of the downturn and were unsure of the future direction of the

school as it joined the Aldenham Foundation. Feels, along with some parents, that a couple of year groups are a bit on the small side (two with only 10 pupils) as a result of this and is working towards 'optimum' numbers of 15-18 per year.

Put her young feet into the relatively weathered shoes of the previous head with a vision of knocking St Hilda's sharply into the 21st century. Has implemented a progressive, flexible curriculum ('no two year groups are the same, so why would we regurgitate the same curriculum year after year?'), whilst holding onto the school's traditional, nurturing ethos. Has strengthened relationships with local senior school heads and has an impressive list of school offers and a fistful of scholarships to show for it. Just what the school needed after a shaky patch.

Lives in rural Cambridgeshire with her husband and daughter, whom she recently moved to St Hilda's 'to strengthen her chances at 11+.' Loves the outdoors and, according to one parent, 'would probably spend all her time in a tracksuit if she could.' Promotes outdoor education, believing that it 'helps girls see that they can do things they thought they couldn't,' and to this end has introduced a new annual expedition to Cornwall for year 5 and 6 girls.

Entrance: About 50 per cent of the potential 18 reception places are filled from the school's co-ed Bluebird nursery (waiting list full until 2015). Not academically selective but all potential newcomers are assessed to ensure good fit with the school and places are not a given. Girls join other year groups from a mix of local state schools and pre-preps, with the occasional joiner from competing preps as parents start to see St Hilda's as 'more academic.'

Exit: Despite recent alliance with the Aldenham Foundation, not a feeder to any particular school, with girls leaving at 11 to the enviable range of the top independent and selective maintained schools that populate the area, with the occasional one off to board. A straw poll of year 6 saw girls heading off to Haberdashers' Aske's, North London Collegiate, Aldenham and St Helen's amongst others, many with offers from multiple schools and several with scholarships (five in 2013). Boys leave the Bluebird at four for nearby schools including Northwood Prep and St John's.

Remarks: Dr Who springs to mind when describing St Hilda's buildings. Set at the end of Bushey High Street in an unassuming Victorian house (originally the home of artist Hubert von Herkomer), with a number of more modern add-ons crammed into the site, it has a compact, urban feel, more akin to a London school than a leafy suburban prep.

In architectural terms it certainly wouldn't give the glossy Bushey Academy down the road a run for its money, but step inside and the Tardis effect takes over. Classrooms are bright and inspiring, full of examples of the girls' work. The hard-working hall does an adequate job share as dining room (head chef knows all the girls by name and delivers crowd pleasing lunches every day), rehearsal space and assembly hall. More surprises lie behind the façade of the swimming pool building, which somehow hides a good sized, indoor heated pool behind what looks like a garden shed, and the Whitby Hall, an uninspiring 80s construction which houses a well-equipped gymnasium.

The acres of fields boasted by many preps are sadly lacking, but there are creatively used grounds with hard and grass play areas, a woodland spinney and a spanking new adventure playground recently paid for out of PTA coffers. Sports fixtures requiring more space now take place at Aldenham School, just a ten minute bus ride away and well worth the journey. These boast a 400m running track, sports hall and long-jump pit. And they've thrown in the use of their minibuses too.

There's a quiet energy rather than a buzz around the school, generated by a loyal staff, some of whom have taught at St Hilda's for 15 years or more. The more senior teachers we observed had a spark many young guns would envy and a range of creative approaches up their sleeves to cater for their pupils' individual foibles – a tangible benefit of tiny class sizes. The exuberant deputy head, well into her fifties and sleeves firmly rolled up in the classroom, is a passionate advocate of ensuring girls are literate across the full range of media and has recently completed a PhD in developing an online learning community with ten year olds.

Girls seem studious and sensible – not a hint of precociousness – probably because most parents are from the hard-working middle class, many stretching themselves for their daughters' educations. Lots of first time buyers and a variety of ethnicities, reflecting the local area. Religious affiliation – or lack thereof – means school also has to be sensitive to this mix, although grace is said at lunch and there are prayers in assembly.

St Hilda's punches well above its tiny weight when it comes to academics, ably competing with its neighbouring hothouses. Girls are encouraged to be all-rounders, 'to give something back to their school,' says head. The all-important 11 plus verbal reasoning is taught by head and – ferocious London parents be warned – tutoring outside of school is not encouraged. After-school homework club, supervised by teaching staff, means that girls and parents can indulge in family time – great when everyone's working hard. Recent scholarships (from all-rounder and academic to sport and music) are the proof in the pudding that good things can come in small packages.

It's not all work and no play, though. Parents found it refreshing that the school encouraged 'children to be children' on snow days and allowed them to play outside rather than kowtowing to health and safety, and felt this to be an accurate reflection of the school's home-like culture.

Specialist teaching in all subjects in years 4-6 is a unique feature amongst local schools, as is a recent focus on languages, which has seen the school forge links with others in five European countries.

Light homework is set from nursery; 10-15 minutes a night from year 3, rising to 40 minutes in year 5. Head doesn't believe in setting pupils, believing it's important to allow for a child's different capabilities within a subject – average class sizes of 12-16 allow this utopian ideal to be a reality. A strong belief in accountability saw her register the school for key stage 2 Sats for first time in 2013. Watch this space.

The school's size also means that SEN can generally be mainstreamed into the classroom, but a range of friendly-sounding 'clubs' for areas such as spelling and language enrichment allow pupils who need it to receive extra help without feeling marginalised.

Flashy facilities for art and music are less in evidence than at many other girls' preps but provision is fair for the size of the school, with peripatetic lessons on offer in violin from year 1, and 60 per cent of upper school learning an individual instrument across the range of strings, wind and piano. An annual production – usually musical – is a focus for girls in years 5 and 6, with many girls citing drama as their favourite extracurricular activity, inspired (again) by their deputy head who runs the show.

The Aldenham Alliance means that sport is 'really getting there' now, according to both staff and parents. Netball and athletics, with girls representing the borough in the latter, are flagship sports, with supporting roles from rounders, gymnastics and dance, and year-round weekly swimming for all from nursery up. Head has encouraged more competitive fixtures since her arrival and the provision of Aldenham's mini-buses has made this previously prohibitively expensive exercise feasible, resulting in a more sporty outlook.

Parents can sleep easy knowing what's coming on the bill as extra-curricular activities are listed on two separate menus – one for free activities and the other for paid-fors. Freebies range from art, Spanish and ICT to football and the more quirky Orff

Ensemble – an opportunity for lower school girls (read non-musicians) to play percussion and recorder pieces in a variety of musical styles, with others such as ballet and short tennis on offer at the going rate.

Busy families also benefit from the new Bluebird nursery, relaunched by head in September 2012, to allow for wrap-around care 50 weeks a year. Parents of nursery age children can select term-time, state school or St Hilda's school terms to fit in with their situations and deliver flexible childcare. This ethos also spreads up the school with reasonably priced breakfast club (from 7.30am), free early drop off (from 8am) and late pick-up, including tea (up to 6.30pm), available for 'a few pounds'.

St Hugh's School (Woodhall Spa)

Cromwell Avenue, Woodhall Spa, LN10 6TQ

- Pupils: 105 boys and 100 girls, boarding and day • Ages: 2-13
- C of E • Fees: Day £7,452–£12,987; Boarding £18,381 pa
- Independent

Tel: 01526 352169
Email: office@st-hughs.lincs.sch.uk
Website: www.st-hughs.lincs.sch.uk

Headmaster: Since September 2013, Mr Chris Ward, previously deputy head of Worksop College Prep. He spent several years as director of music at St John's on the Hill School in Monmouthshire, and is also a keen and competitive rugby player. He is married with three children.

Entrance: Majority of the children rise through the ranks of the school's pre-prep. Prospective pupils spend a day at the school for assessment.

Exit: Seventy-five per cent go on to independent senior schools in the A1 corridor, Uppingham, Oundle, Oakham, Repton, Queen Margaret's. The remaining 25 per cent get places at local grammar schools at 13.

Remarks: Set in a leafy residential road in this sleepy Victorian town, with a good acreage of well-maintained grounds. Strong sense of family, excellent facilities – not surprising that it is popular, drawing children from a relatively local area. About 30 per cent of the children are from Forces families, many from the RAF bases nearby.

The school doesn't have to sell boarding as the children seem to make that decision for themselves and become weekly boarders in their last years. There are full-time boarders who are well looked after at weekends and kept busy. Everyone (children, teachers and parents) agrees that the food is 'fantastic', with plenty of choice. The place is absolutely spotless throughout the boarding and school side.

Classes are grouped according to ability from year 5 with an average of 14 in a class. If a child has the ability, the school is prepared to push but generally, the teaching is taken at a gentle pace. Some of the children are statemented and the SEN department is well-staffed, with one-to-one lessons available. Staff are on average in their 40s and the school is 'proactive in helping with career moves'.

Everyone is given the opportunity to contribute to the school either on the games field, musically or in drama but it's sport that rules the roost. Matches are played at all levels, involving as many as possible. The school is prepared to travel up to two hours for matches and the calendar is full of fixtures, taking the teams hither and thither. No-one is left out.

St Hugh's turns out well-rounded children who are polite and have discreet self-confidence. Happy children – and parents.

St Hugh's School, Oxfordshire

Carswell Manor, Faringdon, SN7 8PT

- Pupils: 340 boys and girls; 85 boarders • Ages: 3–13 • C of E
- Fees: Day £9,810–£16,635 pa; Weekly boarding +£3,285 pa
- Independent

Tel: 01367 870700
Email: registrar@st-hughs.co.uk
Website: www.st-hughs.co.uk

Headmaster: Since 2006, Mr Andrew Nott BA (late forties). Son of a bishop, educated at The Beacon Prep and King's, Taunton. Studied history at the University of Wales, PGCE Westminster College, Oxford. Worked for the Church Commissioners where he met his wife, Sarah. First teaching post at St Andrew's School, Eastbourne, rose to deputy head. Thence to Davenies for his first headship prior to St Hugh's. Parents describe him as 'amazing' (adjective also frequently applied to Sarah) on a personal level; one or two said they found him a little shy on more public occasions.

Mr Nott is proud of his scholars' achievements (record numbers in 2013) but he is also a true champion of the strugglers and late bloomers who are inevitably part of the cohort of a non-selective school. He told us that he had thoroughly enjoyed his time at prep and it is this 'carefree' existence that he wants children at St Hugh's to experience. He loves sport, especially cricket (he is a member of MCC and had a bookcase dedicated to copies of Wisden) and is determined that all the children at St Hugh's get a match, including the E and F teams. He vividly remembers 'the boys who weren't in the A team picking daisies on the boundary' during his prep school cricket matches, and though St Hugh's may be a traditional school in many ways, this is one bit of history Mr Nott does not want to repeat. His mantra is 'excellence and inclusion' and he's also a big champion of kindness, a 'hugely important virtue' that he believes is undervalued these days.

School has acquired five acres of adjoining land for additional games fields, but although the roll is full there are no plans to increase numbers of pupils significantly. Mr Nott says, 'We could be a lot bigger but I want to keep the character of the school, to know every child.' Sounds pretty definite to us but a few parents expressed worries about the school getting bigger. Development on this beautiful rural site is no doubt a planning nightmare, but the new (2012) Cannon Building – named like other parts of the school after a former head – is a superb facility housing science, art and DT. The heads of these departments worked with architects to design their ideal rooms and are still purring contentedly. On the wish list is an assembly hall to accommodate the whole school instead of just years 3 – 8 and a larger dining room (staggered lunch service takes two hours).

Mr Nott and his wife Sarah have five children between the ages of 7 and 21; four attended St Hugh's and the two youngest are still there. Sarah is responsible for among many other things, for the tastefully low-key marketing and excellent newsletter. The Notts live just over the lane from school; it's not much of a boundary but just far enough to allow time to switch off and enable the head to enjoy planning the family's next trip abroad and practising creative cookery. Though usually pretty competent, he admits to a recent disaster courtesy of Heston Blumenthal (who doesn't?). He's also fascinated by the

academic side of leadership. Favourite childhood reads? Tintin and the Willard Price series of adventure stories.

Entrance: Non-selective, non-competitive, it's first come, first served. Mr Nott likes to meet parents as well as children. Prospective pupils spend a day; those entering year 3 or above have assessments in English and maths. Main entry is into reception (up to 26 places), year 3 (up to six places), year 5 (up to six places). Nursery takes up to 25 a year.

Exit: To schools all over home counties (22 in 2013). Many to board eg Cheltenham College, Cheltenham Ladies', Downe House, Radley, Eton, Rugby, Stowe, Marlborough, Winchester, St Edward's Oxford. Rest to local day schools including Abingdon, St Helen's and St Katharine's. Ninety per cent of girls stay on until age 13; apparently this is increasingly popular with parents – perhaps because their girls stay children for that little bit longer.

Remarks: We arrived on a perfect English summer's day and Carswell Manor, which looks like a bijou country house hotel, seemed to glow with the golden warmth of Cotswold stone. On closer inspection much of facade is pebble dashed but somehow still pretty classy. The Manor was once home to the Niven family and it seems fitting that David Niven, the quintessential English gentleman, was born here – the old place even gets a mention in his autobiography. St Hugh's is without doubt the tidiest school we've ever visited and it's not just the buildings and grounds that are polished and groomed, the teachers too were quite remarkably elegant – not a baggy cardigan or tatty sandal in sight.

Founded 1906 in Chislehurst with three pupils and co-ed since 1977, St Hugh's is now very much a family school – nursery was established in response to parent demand and the minute it opened was 'immediately full with younger siblings.' Mothers walk their dogs in the grounds after morning drop off. Indeed dogs are a bit of a feature: they kept trotting by or popping out from under tables during our visit – all glossy coated and impeccably behaved, of course. Though we saw no ponies we hear that they also loom large here – jodhpurs (very much not pyjamas) are what the busy St Hugh's mother wears first thing in the morning.

Small classes (average 13), spacious modern facilities and glorious surroundings are enough to inspire any child to reach their full potential, and while not all will be scholars and high flyers, everyone is encouraged to find their talent. Much is expected of these children and sometimes Mr Nott's role is to manage expectations; by their second or third child old hands know they can relax and put their trust in the school. Parents we spoke to felt that Mr Nott's advice about senior schools was excellent and absolutely right for their child; the broad spectrum of schools St Hugh's sends to bears this out.

Maths and English set from year 3, French from year 6; rest of subjects taught in mixed ability groups but this can and does vary from year to year according to cohort. French and Latin for all, optional extra-curricular Spanish and Mandarin. Greek for scholars. One or two grumbles about Sigma group (potential scholars) being creamed off in year 4, but this is a perennial source of low level muttering at many preps. Middle school pupils (years 3 and 4) have their own teaching block and activities such as drama, choir, sports day etc – a nice way to let the youngest take centre stage. Low turnover of staff apart from gappies (often old boys and girls) who stay for a year. In lessons we observed pupils were quiet, engaged, working hard individually and in pairs. Small class sizes mean teacher can tailor tasks according to ability; they also make it hard to mess around at the back (not that there seemed to be any such tendency). Parents describe SEN support as 'brilliant'; the head of the service told us that the aim is for it to be 'flexible and fluid', to give pupils a boost when needed and then 'launch

S

them back, even if they need to be picked up again later.' Support is either individual or in booster groups and is not charged as an extra. Pastoral care also came in for high praise – merest whiff of bullying is dealt with at lightning speed.

A school tradition and one of the highlights of year 8 is a week's post-exam adventure trip to Wales, during which Mr Nott gives the children their CE results over fish and chips on the beach. Once back in Oxfordshire as part of an extensive leavers' programme, pupils are initiated into important life skills such as how to tie a bow tie, polish shoes and iron shirts; they also create and stage a fashion show for a local children's charity.

Excellent sporting facilities both inside and out host sport for all, every day. All main ones plus squash, basketball, tennis and introduction to lacrosse. Head confirms that every child gets to represent the school in matches. Notable recent success in tennis (and real tennis) and cross country. Large number of sports scholarships awarded to St Hugh's pupils every year (11 in 2013). Music and drama are also inclusive with enough plays, choirs, bands and ensembles to accommodate the full range of abilities. Outdoor production of A Midsummer Night's Dream staged around atmospheric ivy-clad 'temple' in the grounds. St Hugh's seems to produce thinkers and listeners (as opposed to shouters) and recognition for this comes in the form of a clutch of top awards for debating and public speaking. Art and DT thriving in their new building – art room boasts a large walk-in kiln, ready to receive the most ambitious ceramic creations and electric windows that can be controlled to provide optimum natural light conditions.

Pre-prep is housed in the old stable block with classrooms round a flexible central space that can be divided up and used for small group work. Rooms are carefully decorated with colourful posters and children's work and, as in the main school, the atmosphere seemed to be one of gently restrained exuberance. Or so we thought until we came across a Monsieur from the big school delighting the pre-prep pupils with his all-singing and dancing weekly French lesson. Literacy taught via Read Write Inc phonics programme and for this children are grouped by their stage of development, not age. Official Forest School: pupils from nursery to year 6 get to do lots of messy learning in the woods (last two years have bushcraft). As one member of staff remarked, 'some children come to life outside, and it's not just the boys.' Parents promised us that pupils really are allowed to get muddy.

Youngest (age 3 upwards) start in The Cottage nursery, a charming house that originally belonged to the groundsman (he is happily accommodated elsewhere). On our visit we saw determined excavation in the large sandpit that is, fortunately, six feet deep. Children sign in for their sessions on the interactive whiteboard and there is an ICT suite upstairs along with a rest room for pupils who still need a nap. Same phonics programme as pre-prep used to introduce letter sounds etc. Specialist teaching for music, dance, ICT. Introduction to French is via croissants and chocolat chaud.

Flexi and weekly boarding, week only – parents pre-select boarding options at the start of term. Those wanting a full week get priority, those who want a couple of days are most likely to get them if they are consecutive. As a rule can't do sleepover style occasional boarding but will work something out in an emergency. Boarding is very often 'children driven', it's the parents who need persuading. Comfortable, characterful dorms up in the eaves, all very civilised – common room with original John Piper on wall (sigh). Matrons inspect every morning to ensure that boarders live up to the St Hugh's standard of tidiness. Day pupils can stay until 7.30pm for prep and supper (no extra charge) and about a third do. Saturday school for years 6-8 only. Wednesday evenings are reserved for 'fun' things and there's no prep. Parents pre-select home time but emergencies and late changes accommodated. Sensible uniform and termly bill low on the dreaded 'extras'. Fees include all trips (trips abroad also subsidised) and SEN support. Means-tested bursaries of up to full fees available.

So, what's the demographic? Put on your deerstalker and consider these clues: nearly all the pupils are children of privately-educated parents; a school bus scheme was discontinued after a couple of terms because no one used it (private lift sharing arrangements more popular); mussels are a favourite on the scrumptious lunch menu. So far, so county, but though the social profile be small, parents say it's neither snobbish nor exclusive and the children we met were down to earth, funny, normal kids.

St Hugh's is seemingly a school with nothing to prove. It doesn't advertise and prospective parents are not bombarded with glossy anythings. For a flavour of the place, ask to see a copy of the beautifully produced half-termly magazine, St Hugh's News. Such understatement, coupled with fees that are higher than local average (but are all-inclusive and considered 'good value' by the parents we spoke to), might seem counterintuitive in an area that is not under-served with preps, but St Hugh's is always full courtesy of the low-tech marketing marvel money can't buy: word of mouth. Happy parents, happy children, happy dogs – what could be better?

St James Junior School

Linked school: St James Senior Girls' School Linked school: St James Senior Boys' School

Earsby Street, London, W14 8SH

• Pupils: 255 pupils, 125 boys/130 girls, all day • Ages: 4–11 • Non-denominational • Fees: £13,050 pa • Independent

Tel: 020 7348 1793
Email: admissions@stjamesjunior.org
Website: www.stjamesjuniors.co.uk

Headmistress: Since 2009, Mrs Catherine Thomlinson, BA in English and history from Roehampton (forties). A St James' disciple to her fingers' ends, having spent almost all of her teaching career there after being educated at sister school, St Vedast (brief spell in South Africa before coming back to the fold). Two children, a son and a daughter, both of whom attended St James from age 4 right through senior school. A thoroughly lovely lady who radiates kindness, humanity and good humour, and this despite having a shocking cold when we met. The study oft proclaims the head, we've found, and Mrs Thomlinson's was sparely but beautifully furnished, bright and calm. Amidst some exquisite pictures of quiet seas, a joyous tract reads, 'Let your light shine!' – and hers most assuredly does.

Despite her lifelong loyalty to the St James traditions, Mrs Thomlinson has not been afraid to modernise. She has pushed through substantial curriculum development, including DT, French and dance; and both boys and girls now do cookery, woodwork and sewing. Introduced interactive whiteboards for upper junior classrooms ('a fantastic tool'), and is looking to bring these in throughout the school. Major development of EYFS provision, following criticism in 2010 Inspection report. Parents report improved communication. Continues to uphold strong emphasis on speech, drama and music, 'because they really touch the emotional intelligence'.

Entrance: 'We don't take children on an academic basis,' says head, and accordingly there's no entrance exam at age 4; instead, the school holds informal assessments that involve meeting both child and parents, plus a report from child's nursery where applicable. Children of alumni and siblings have priority, as do those whose parents registered them early for a place. School looks for 'a certain confidence, and for children and families who value what we value'. Places higher up the school occasionally become available, and children who apply aged 7+ take assessments in reading, writing and mathematics to establish whether they're able to manage within the standard of the established class.

Exit: Junior girls stay until the end of year 5, when virtually all of them progress to St James Senior Girls, which begins at year 6 and is situated on the same site. Overwhelming majority of parents are happy with this. 'I'm very grateful that neither they nor I will have to face the 11 +,' one mother of two daughters commented. This is just as well, since for girls to change schools at this point would be extremely difficult. Very occasionally, however, a girl may opt to do her final junior year elsewhere, and Bute House has been one such destination.

St James Senior Boys is out at Ashford (a very comprehensive coach service is provided by St James Schools), so boys stay on at St James Junior for their year 6 and can be prepped for Common Entrance to other senior schools at parents' request, 'but more and more boys are staying and going through to Ashford,' currently 88 per cent. Once again, it seems, parents appreciate the automatic entry. Where boys do go elsewhere, routes include Fulham Prep, Latymer Upper, Wetherby Prep, Bute House and Colet Court.

Remarks: A frieze of the goddess Athene gazes down benevolently from one of the foyer walls, and this may explain the air of gentle wisdom that really does pervade this unusual and admirable little school. Nestling quietly within residential streets, the outside resembles a monastery, with its high walls and expanse of sheer red brick, but the tableau through the security gate wasn't in the least forbidding. Children played cheerfully in a pretty, cloistered courtyard under the eye of a watchful but serene-looking teacher, and the whole was framed by light and airy corridors – a preponderance of new glass giving a modern, clean balance to the Victorian charm of the original building. The atmosphere, as far as we could judge, was one of kindness and peaceful activity. Parents all confirmed this: 'It's a very happy place.' 'It's an extremely happy school.' 'A warm and nurturing environment.' 'My child has loved being there from the very beginning.'

The school's ethos places an unusually high emphasis on generosity, mutual respect and 'being the best human beings we can be,' and achieves this through a number of distinctive practices. Every lesson begins and ends with a 'moment of stillness'. Such moments 'give you that sense of ease and reflection,' says head. These pauses, as they're known, are popular with parents and children: 'It gives you a chance to be still,' said a year 6 child, whose demeanour was courteous and mature beyond his years. Parents agree. 'One of the main benefits of St James is the peacefulness,' was one comment, and 'One of the reasons we send our children to the school is to learn early on to take a pause, allow the noise to stop,' was another.

All the children, even the little ones, learn Sanskrit, in accordance with the school's belief that the Eastern philosophies have much to teach us; and both children and parents insisted to us that this was one of the things they 'really loved' about the school. St James describes itself as 'multi-religious', and philosophy itself is a very important part of the curriculum. The school teaches a Socratic method of dialogue and questioning, and the children are taught to develop open-ended questions and to debate as a class ('No putting-down of others' opinions is allowed,' says head firmly). The school motto – 'speak the truth, be generous and kind, be your best' – seems to mean more here than such saws do in other schools. St James's policy of teaching boys and girls separately, then bringing them together for social activities (break-times, lunch, productions, trips, etc) may also be a key factor in establishing such good relationships between the children. 'You can see the boys, but you don't always have to be with them,' said a grateful year 5 girl, with which one of the boys countered, 'The girls think they're best, and we just get on with being even better.' We suspect this is amiable posturing: a number of parents confirmed to us that their child's closest schoolfriends included those of the opposite gender.

Academic performance is strong, with the standard of written work exceptionally high, both in content and accuracy – all the more impressive, given that the school's intake is not academically selective. 'I'm a great advocate for academic rigour,' confirms the head, adding, 'but I'm just as passionate about children finding out what they love.' All classes have weekly sessions in the well-stocked library, run by a dedicated librarian, and there are regular visits by children's authors. ('My son very quickly developed a love of reading,' reported a satisfied parent.) SEN provision is good, with about 30 EAL children cared for within the classroom set-up. We applauded the emphasis on using Shakespeare as a teaching resource at all levels, more so than in any other school we've visited. We saw verses from The Winter's Tale charmingly illustrated by the reception children, and read some excellent commentaries on Polonius's advice to his son ('To thine own self be true') by the year 3 boys. 'We love Shakespeare,' the head acknowledged. 'We did A Midsummer Night's Dream and The Tempest last year. And Mozart's The Magic Flute. We have a great cultural reservoir to draw on – why not give them the best material?' Why not indeed!

And in fact the drama on offer is very impressive, with all the children involved in at least one performance every year. 'We like big productions!' beamed a member of staff, before hurrying off to oversee preparations for Fiddler On The Roof, for which the school hired the Britten Theatre at the Royal College of Music because 'we like to be ambitious'. Previous big productions include My Fair Lady, The Railway Children and The Sound of Music. For in-house performances, the school's hall has been recently refurbished and hosts frequent verse-speaking, plus dance for both girls and boys as well as drama productions. Music is strong, with 70 children taking instrumental lessons at school on 'pretty much anything they want', and regular concerts, often featuring the school's orchestra. The children sing every day in assembly – repertoire by Mozart, Purcell and Vivaldi is popular – and have music lessons every week. Artwork of an astonishingly high standard adorns the walls, produced in the attractive and lightsome art room under the gaze of the stuffed menagerie up on the shelf: a goose, a grouse, a heron and a weasel.

All children have a period of games or sport every day, be it gym, dance, swimming or ball skills, and the upper juniors (years 3-6) go off-site once a week to Barn Elms to hone their skills at netball, rugby, cricket, athletics, cross country and the like. There are lots of inter-school competitions, and the children told us proudly about recent triumphs over Wetherby and Fulham Prep. Swimming is held in nearby Fulham Pools, and ISA golds and silvers have been a feature of recent years. St James Junior is a member of Forest Schools UK, with two of its staff trained as Forest Leaders, and there are many trips to Minstead Study Centre in the New Forest. 'I've been seven times!' enthused one upper junior boy, 'and I enjoyed it SO MUCH!' A varied programme of outings closer to home has encompassed museums, art galleries, theatres, and the usual London fare. Excellent range of lunchtime and after-school clubs includes guitar, yoga, cookery, gymnastics, model-making, archery, fencing, lacrosse, and the perennially popular Mad Science Club. The head actively encourages all her staff to take up hobbies themselves, and the staff music band, we're told, is going from strength to strength. Use of ICT across the school has increased, although actual ICT lessons are still for year 6 only, so the boys get them in their final junior year, and the girls in their first year at the senior school. Children are 'encouraged to use ICT at home,' which may or may not be enough preparation

S

for the increasingly ICT-based curriculum they'll face at senior school. But the junior school's stated priority is to develop clear cursive handwriting in its pupils, and from what we saw, they definitely succeed.

Food here is vegetarian, so that all the children can eat together, and is included in the fees. We were impressed by what we saw: a delicious-smelling vegetable curry, fresh bread being baked, home-made leek and potato soup, and lots of genuinely appetizing fresh fruit. The number of clean plates testified to its popularity with the young clientele, and one solemn little girl was particularly enthusiastic about it to us as she lowered her elbow into her coleslaw. No problem, though – the lower juniors (years R-2) wear smocks down to lunch, which we thought eminently sensible.

All aspects of the pastoral care were rated excellent in the 2010 inspection report, which commented on the 'family atmosphere of mutual respect,' adding that 'the pupils thrive in the positive, caring environment' and are 'very well cared for.' The pupils concur. 'It's fun here,' 'The teachers are very kind,' 'Everyone is really nice,' 'You don't feel you have to be afraid of anything,' 'You can be yourself,' 'You can be proud of yourself,' 'The teachers are proud of us and they trust us,' were some of the many tributes we heard. This is all the more inspiring, given that the School of Economic Science, which founded the St James schools, attracted some very different comments from its embittered pupils a few decades back (see our entry on The St James Independent Boys' School in the Senior Schools section).

But all that is history. St James Junior impressed us as such a kind and enlightened medium in which to culture young minds, that we occasionally had to remind ourselves that this was a school we'd stepped into and not a Botticelli painting. It was almost a relief to see one small boy aim a punch at another, to hear an indignant cry of 'I was first!' and to meet a teacher who was unmistakeably knackered after her morning's work. But these tiny wrinkles only served to throw into greater focus the sweetness and calm of this remarkable community. Not a school for budding Piers Morgans, we suspect. But who cares?

St James's Catholic Primary School

260 Stanley Road, Twickenham, TW2 5NP

- Pupils: 680 pupils (including 50 in nursery); all day • Ages: 3–11
- RC only • State

Tel: 020 8898 4670
Email: info@st-james.richmond.sch.uk
Website: www.st-james.richmond.sch.uk

Headteacher: Since January 2013, Mrs Clare Webber BA PGCE NPQH. Read history at university. Comes from a commercial background and spent time in recruitment, then became a full-time mother when her children were young. Has two sons, now both at university. Both her grandfather and father were heads – 'so teaching was in the blood'. Taught at the school for 12 years, followed by promotion to deputy and then acting head.

Charming, with a good sense of humour. Loves her job, takes her responsibilities very seriously and says the main challenge for her now is 'to continue to be an outstanding school'. One parent told us: 'We're very lucky to have her. She's fantastic'. Huge amounts of energy – keeps fit with boot camp before school and enjoys regular trips to the V&A. Very visible at school events and in the playground at break time. Not a head who hides herself away in her office.

Entrance: At three to nursery (52 places) and four to the main school (90 places). St James's is a Roman Catholic school serving the four parishes of St James (Twickenham), St Francis de Sales (Hampton Hill), St Margaret (East Twickenham) and St Theodore (Hampton). Priority given to those baptised within a year of birth who are devout, practising Catholics. Siblings given priority. Heavily over-subscribed, with more than two applicants for every place. Occasional places become available in higher years, though there isn't huge pupil mobility. 'We don't lose many pupils further up the school, only if the families relocate', says the head. 'We certainly don't lose them to private schools'.

A place in the nursery does not automatically lead to a place in reception – 'though it is very rare for this not to happen'.

Exit: Between 20 to 50 per cent to independent schools. Hampton Boys' is popular and 'girls go everywhere', including Tiffin Girls' School, Gumley House and Waldegrave. One mother commented that many parents have chosen historically to go down the independent school route due to the dearth of good state secondary schools nearby – 'especially with the Oratory having reduced its catchment area'. That looks set to change with the new St Richard Reynolds Catholic High School expected to be an extremely popular destination in the future.

Remarks: Head describes the school as having high academic standards, coupled with a strong Catholic ethos. 'Faith is central to what we do here', she told us. 'It is made explicit to parents. If you are a Catholic teacher, part of teaching is a mission as well as a job'.

School is large, spacious and well-run. Housed in fairly new accommodation in a leafy cul-de-sac. Light classrooms with generous windows and colourful displays abound. Two huge halls, well used for sport, dance, plays and assemblies. Glorious outdoor space where children can let off steam. Climbing frames, trees and quieter areas for those in need of tranquillity. Plenty of greenery surrounding the school. Rolling playing fields at the back and local golf club on the other side give the school a distinctly country feel.

School is at full capacity, with three parallel classes of 30 children from reception up to year 6. Children very engaged and focused when we visited and some impressive manners in evidence. Very strong academically. Rigorous analysis of progress and attainment of each pupil at each stage. Head aware of the importance of pupils becoming independent thinkers and thinking skills now embedded in the curriculum.

Small turnover of staff with a respectable number of long servers. Specialist teaching for art and some games. Masses of lesson observations going on – at all levels – to maintain high standards.

Head believes that sport is a vital part of the curriculum and it is taken seriously here, with the school competing at a high level. Recent borough athletic champions and 12 children competed at the national swimming championships in Sheffield – 'a great achievement', says the head, 'as they're normally dominated by private schools'. Football, netball, rugby, cricket and tennis on offer. Reciprocal sharing of swimming pool and games pitches with The Mall, prep school next door.

Music is strong. A symphony orchestra, three choirs (chamber choir is by invitation only), two rock bands and about half of Key Stage 2 pupils have private music lessons. Musical events arranged with local schools and there are opportunities to perform at the Barbican in the London Symphony Orchestra's Discovery Series.

The Art department definitely holds its own. Head is excited that, as part of the Take One Picture scheme, pupils have been selected to exhibit their work at the National Gallery. 'I can't wait to go', she says.

Number of children requiring learning support is quite small. Limited number with IEPs but one-to-one help is on offer for those in need. 'Our special needs children make exceptional progress and are very well provided for', says head. Full-time SENCO and part-time learning support staff. George Tancred Centre is based at the school and caters for 10 children with moderate autism. Regular opportunities for these pupils to be included in lessons at the main school but they can withdraw back to the centre when activities become too distracting. Their playground is separate from, but adjacent to, main school. The pupils with autism are 'very much part of our school', says head. Pupils from the main school can choose to visit and play with the children from the centre at break times.

No wrap-around care on offer but plenty of before and after-school clubs, so the school day can be extended to help working parents. A variety of tastes catered for at clubs – football, cricket, basketball, French, Spanish, Italian, Jamming Together and ballet. Basketball is currently very popular. Plenty of school trips on offer. Year 6 get a week in Norfolk and year 5 head for Dorset as part of the history curriculum. Day outings include visits to art galleries and RHS gardens at Wisley.

Children at St James's are expected to work hard. Lots of homework from reception onwards, culminating in a couple of hours a night by year 6. Parents are generally supportive of this. Some tutoring goes on at the top of the school – head is relaxed, as long as it does not become excessive.

Significant number of bilingual children – mostly Spanish, French and Italian. Parents are welcomed into the school and appreciate the open-door policy in place. Head knows most of the families well and believes parental involvement in the school is invaluable, either on trips or within the classroom. 'We'd be mad not to include them', she says. Parents are a fairly affluent, middle class group, reflecting the local area. Minuscule percentage on free school meals. Very active PTFA raises £30,000 annually. Money recently spent on the early Years garden and subsidising school trips.

School has an excellent reputation in the local neighbourhood and parents feel lucky to have secured their child a place. At the start of the day, hordes of children in jolly yellow and grey uniforms race along the pavements on scooters. Ongoing problems over road congestion outside, however, and local residents aren't always happy. As one parent put it, 'it's a big, busy primary school. In the morning, the traffic can be horrendous'. Head encourages less driving to school and has even gone so far as to employ number-plate recognition surveillance for repeat parking offenders.

This is an outward-looking school that offers an excellent academic education in a nurturing Catholic environment. Ably led by an inspiring head and with high expectations of pupils, staff and parents, it's impressive on many fronts.

St John's Beaumont School

Priest Hill, Old Windsor, SL4 2JN

• Pupils: 310 boys; 60 boarders • Ages: 3–13 • RC (owned by Jesuits) • Fees: Day £8,250–£15,630; Boarding £15,510–£23,700 pa • Independent

Tel: 01784 432428
Email: admissions@stjohnsbeaumont.co.uk
Website: www.stjohnsbeaumont.org.uk

Headmaster: Since 2006, Mr Giles Delaney (early forties). Educated at Hereford Cathedral School, studied music and psychology at Cardiff (instruments are the not-at-all-easy French horn and organ). PGCE at Cambridge and thence to St John's Beaumont. Became deputy head three years later before being catapulted at a very young age to headship on sudden death of his predecessor. He seems so at one with the school,

staff and boys that we wonder if it was always his plan to stay at the old place for so long; his answer is a wry smile.

St John's Beaumont, like other RC schools, has a reputation for being pretty disciplined, although Mr Delaney is anything but a martinet. He sees no reason why boys can't be expected to give their very best in a caring and nurturing environment. He's extremely interested in research on how boys learn, especially the importance of pupils' relations with staff: 'boys don't learn subjects, they learn teachers.' In a boys' school 'everyone will have a go at orchestra, choir, dance. They will give everything a shot and smile if it doesn't work.' Certainly when it comes to the importance of context, relating academic subjects to the real world, it seems that Jesuit schools were there long before the educationalists.

Mr Delaney, who looks a bit like a young Colin Firth, is modest and charming. He told us that he had taught 'most stuff', still teaches year 5 ('getting them ready for pre-tests surreptitiously') and is looking forward to a new challenge: introducing the pre-prep boys to music. We weren't taken in by his self-deprecating answers. Boys and parents say his teaching is, 'absolutely brilliant', 'fantastic', 'the best'. Loves preparing assemblies and shares a keen interest in medieval history with his wife, Katie, who teaches in a school in North London. He is currently studying for an MSc in education at Oxford. They have four daughters – must be something of an antidote to life at SJB. And if he hadn't gone into teaching? A conductor, he thinks, or a graphic designer, 'something not in an office.' Favourite book? Solzhenitsyn's One day in the life of Ivan Denisovich: 'It's about endurance, valuing the smallest things.'

Entrance: There's a waiting list so plan ahead. Most boys enter at age 4 after attending a taster session to assess suitability. Parents and children interviewed. Further small intake at year 3 (dependent on performance in school's own assessment and reference from current head). Priority given to practising Roman Catholic families, siblings and applicants with connections to St John's or a Jesuit education

Exit: To all the big beasts and all the more impressive given non-selective intake: Eton, Harrow, Tonbridge, Winchester, Wellington, Charterhouse, Ampleforth, Downside, Stonyhurst, Hampton. Notable record of academic, sport and all-rounder scholarships.

Remarks: St John's Beaumont sits in red brick Gothic grandeur on a hill overlooking Old Windsor, surrounded by 70 acres of grounds and playing fields next door to Windsor Great Park. Designed by John Francis Bentley (also responsible for Westminster Cathedral) and opened in 1888, it was the first purpose-built prep school in England. Tucked behind the Victorian edifice are recent additions: a fine sports centre with vertigo-inducing climbing wall, music, science and art departments, a theatre and the pre-prep block, all on a rather more human scale. The huge reception hall, hung with portraits of old boys and next door neighbour Her Majesty the Queen, sets a rather formal tone. Classical music playing discreetly in the background only just takes the edge off what could be an intimidating first impression for some prospective parents and their boys.

Our visit started in one of the original high ceilinged classrooms with a year 8 maths lesson. Considering it was nearly the end of term and these boys had done CE (many had won scholarships), their quiet concentration was remarkable. Working in pairs, they applied themselves to bisecting a line so that they would 'impress maths teachers at their next schools'. In accordance with the principles of Jesuit education, they then discussed context, suggesting where this technique could be applied in real life. Maths is a particular strength of SJB and the best take part in national competitions and maths challenges, winning medals at all levels. In 2012 three finalists gained distinctions in Junior Maths Olympiad. Science very hands-on; boys told us that a highlight was 'setting custard powder on fire' and went on to explain the theory behind the conflagration. Latin from year 6, Greek for scholars.

Having learnt (and swiftly forgotten) how to bisect a line it was off to year 6 history in a slightly less lofty Portakabin. After the maturity of the mathematicians we were relieved to find a sparky class tackling the causes of the First World War. Their presentation skills may have been a work in progress but there was no doubting their enthusiasm and depth of knowledge. Here, context was relating 1914 alliances to the current situation in Afghanistan. Distracting them from the task in hand, we asked what one thing would improve their school. The answer was unanimous: girls! Apparently girls would 'make the place tidier' and 'help with questions'. Dream on, chaps.

Golf, cycling, climbing, sailing, skiing – SJB boys pursue and excel at all kinds of sport, but rugby rules. They regularly field 16 teams and successfully play David to some much bigger Goliaths. Most recently the 1st XV was undefeated in all but one match. Usual parental grumbles that it's not much fun in the lesser teams who don't get any of the specialist coaching. Football gets a proper look in, too. There's an impressive swimming pool and a climbing wall in addition to all the usual facilities. Proximity to the Thames doesn't always guarantee a commitment to rowing but in this case it does and there are 50 boys in the squad netting a haul of medals in regional and national championships. For years 6, 7 and 8 it's sport every day plus matches on Saturday. It's a long day too: years 4 and 5 finish at 5pm, for older boys it's 6pm or later if they're doing extra activities. One of our guides said he thought parents should know that 'it's quite tiring'. Music, art and drama don't seem to be overshadowed by the sports behemoth; that long day means there's time for both.

Sixty or so boys board (one junior and one senior dorm) and according to one parent, it's 'proper boarding, not flexi.' Full weekend programme of activities, many chosen by boys on the boarding committee, includes paintballing, tank driving and trips to Windsor Castle and the Science Museum. Weekly boarding also an option. Interesting animal themed house system engenders keen rivalry for 'TYE' points (Tiger, Yak and Emu). Junior uniform (navy blue Bermudas until year 6) looks smart but several parents still reeling from eye-watering cost of anything crested, including jumpers and shirts.

Approximately 60 per cent of boys come from RC families but don't imagine this leads to monoculture – a peek into any classroom will dispel doubts on that score. Parents unanimously praised the pastoral care and the way the school welcomed diversity. One who was not Catholic said that religion was 'not an issue' but described the RE curriculum as 'very truly Catholic, up to and including creationism', so SJB unlikely to be destination of choice for Dawkins minor. School's view is that they welcome boys of any faith or none but those who join, 'join a community', and must play their part, including attendance at mass. Admissions process wise to parents who are only interested in the school for its CE results. The scholarship boards provide a record of the school's evolution. Thirty years ago practically all went on to Catholic schools such as Stonyhurst, The Oratory, Ampleforth; today's scholars are just as likely to be bound for Eton, Winchester and Wellington.

Mr Bentley the architect obviously believed in giving boys lots of space and air, hence the wide corridors and high ceilinged classrooms, and the generosity of his design, while unmistakably Victorian, stands up pretty well to the demands of the 21st century. His intimate and beautifully decorated chapel, bearing the scars of wartime bombs, only seats 60, and at Christmas there are several services so that all parents can enjoy the special atmosphere and 'magical music'. Whole school events take place in the somewhat less atmospheric sports hall. Part of the Jesuit educational ethos is that a child should be 'well rounded and worldly wise' and to that end SJB boys go

far and wide; not only history and sports trips to France and Italy but also swimming the Midmar Mile in South Africa to raise money for charity. They're also stretched by the school's impressive Magis programme; senior boys have weekly lectures from visiting speakers, parents and members of staff and are also encouraged to present talks themselves. Recent subjects include deafness and language acquisition, Battersea Dogs' Home and space exploration. Lots of fundraising to support a sister school, St Rupert's, in Zimbawe.

Day boys come in from a 10 mile radius (bus service operates from Chiswick and Maidenhead). Parents a mix of trad Windsor and glossy Middletonshire (or as someone put it, those who have Wentworth membership and those who don't). Their sons are commendably oblivious to such pigeonholing and there's a great sense of camaraderie; boys are proud of their school and its traditions. Mr Delaney describes St John's Beaumont as a community that asks its members, 'What can you give?' It expects the very best but also give boys the confidence to try new things and learn from mistakes. As a parent remarked, 'It can appear prescriptive but the boys don't see it like that, they thrive on structure and clear rules. My son loves going to school.'

St John's College School

Grange Road, Cambridge, CB3 9AB

- Pupils: 460; 240 boys, 220 girls; 35 boy and girl boarders
- Ages: 4–13 • C of E • Fees: Day £10,578–£13,290; Boarding £20,991; Choristers £6,996 pa • Independent

Tel: 01223 353652
Email: admissions@sjcs.co.uk
Website: www.sjcs.co.uk

Headmaster: Since 1990, Mr Kevin Jones (early fifties) MA. Educated Woolverstone Hall (state boarding) and Caius, Cambridge. Head of English and drama then deputy head at the Yehudi Menuhin School before deputy headship at St John's. A maverick: someone who takes nothing for granted and continues to search for even better ways to educate – interest in the acquisition of knowledge, combined with the development of creativity and self-confidence, is deep seated. Parents speak of a well-managed school (nothing is left to chance and his finger is firmly on every button) and his breezy, fun loving manner with the children – we watched some little ones closely examining and feeling his hairless pate – a novel twist to hands-on learning. Married with two sons – time with them is number one on his list of top ten pastimes closely followed by reading poetry and supporting Chelsea FC.

Entrance: Oversubscribed. 'Live waiting list with cap'. Sibling priority followed by boy/girl balance. Be under no illusions: children are academically well above average and, as one mum commented, parents are 'fiercely competitive in the nicest of ways'. And there's a 'gentleman's agreement' on the parents' side that the child will stay until they are 13 – so think twice before skipping off at 11. New children and parents made very welcome – links with existing parents are encouraged so new bods know someone before they start. Very civilized.

At four: no testing. School is cleverer than this – sequencing and other indicators are monitored instead. Even at this early age a pretty reliable assessment can be made. At seven: assessments in English and maths plus observation of child over half a day of normal schooling.

Yearly scholarships for up to five choristers. At seven, means-tested bursaries for those who would particularly benefit from being at the school.

S

Exit: One or two at seven and 11 – school says they 'don't evict' but occasionally, after discussion and mutual agreement, it's decided that a move would be in the child's best interests. Otherwise nearly all at 13. Masses of help from the head who is 'spot on' re the best school for his pupils. About 50 per cent gain awards/scholarships. Impressive number to The Perse (co-ed). Uppingham, Perse Girls, St Mary's and Oundle also popular.

Remarks: Pleasant environment with copious helpings of purposeful buzz, friendly fun and encouragement. Semi suburban setting, not far from St John's College, with ample space for play areas, pitches, indoor swimming pool and ongoing redevelopment. Three close but separate sites: intimate, purpose-built Byron House (infants), a revamped boarding house (mainly boys and on the up since recent appointments) and the junior section – a well-tended melange with a huge willow tree sturdily propped to create an organic climbing frame.

'Completely magic teaching' coupled with finely tuned management of learning/ thinking processes help children 'go as far as they can go' without pressure or cramming – school has a full time psychologist and ed psych. 'The intellectual ability of my kids has really picked up and they're interested in finding out. They aren't behaving like baby birds sitting there accepting knowledge.' Parents also praise excellent lines of communication and staff who do anything to help. Pupils seem carefree and bubbly – school 'somehow empowers and gives them confidence.' All in year 8 take on roles of responsibility from the 'mail run' to managing classroom recycling boxes. And there are competitions – during our visit we noted a short story competition with entries carefully pasted onto numerous windows (according to our guides winners 'get to choose a book and have a hot chocolate'), a wonderfully dotty extreme reading photo competition, a make a model out of rubbish competition, a science competition and the best decorated classroom door competition.

No exams until the penultimate year when out of lesson clinics are available for all. Extension work (from year 7 'invitation only' Greek and debating) and scholarship standards in the top sets. IN (individual needs department) for those who need some extra help. Tucked into the website blurb is the elliptical 'the school is therefore able to intervene in a child's best interest at a very low "threshold" of difficulty.' Despite the odd exception this broadly translates to: school only wants to deal with minor difficulties (and it does so fantastically well). See 'exit' if issues turn out to be more than minor.

Parents are pleased that arts and sport aren't sacrificed at the altar of academia. Music is strong: 80 per cent of the older pupils learn one instrument and 60 per cent learn two or more – and a good number achieve grades 5 and 6. Head of drama 'totally charismatic and an absolute luvvie – some of the plays are a bit mad (pupils play a part in their development) but all have a fantastic time.' Enthusiastic librarian, productive DT department, airy art room decorated with interesting 2D and 3D work, extra-curricular activities ('every minute filled with something') and plenty of sporting fixtures for teams plus alternatives including real tennis and rowing. This is a fine school where children are highly motivated and magically happy.

St Johns-on-the-Hill School

Castleford Hill, Tutshill, Chepstow, Monmouthshire, NP16 7LE

• Pupils: 305 boys (27 board) and girls (17 board); 350 boys and girls in three linked nurseries • Ages: 3m–14 • C of E • Fees: Day £7,290–£12,015; Boarding £16,920 pa • Independent

Tel: 01291 622045
Email: registrar@stjohnsonthehill.co.uk
Website: www.stjohnsonthehill.co.uk

Headmaster: Since 2011, Mr Nick Folland previously headmaster of Blundell's Prep, Tiverton. After training at Loughborough University, he became a teacher of the deaf at a residential vocational centre for maladjusted young deaf men. He then joined Blundell's School, and dovetailed teaching with playing professional cricket for Somerset CCC. He became senior housemaster there before taking over headship of the prep school. He is married to Di, an Australian speech and language therapist who has a Masters in science (psychology). She leads the learning support team.

Entrance: Mixed ability intake but school will say if it thinks applicants are unable to cope. Gives the benefit of the doubt where it can. Assessment is based on a 'taster day' in English and maths plus report from previous school. Procedure is 'painless' say parents and compared it favourably with other schools. Pupils may enter at any point provided spaces are available. Main catchment area is Newport/Cardiff through Monmouthshire to Forest of Dean and West Gloucestershire. Boarders come from all over.

Exit: Has gained reputation for gaining awards near and far. Recently, 30 children winning 40 awards at 11 different schools including Shrewsbury, Rugby and Cheltenham College as well as nearer placed Monmouth, Clifton etc.

Money matters: Bursaries for services, police, clergy and staff children. 'School really helped to ensure we could afford to educate all our five children at St John's and had something left to live on,' said one grateful parent.

Remarks: St John's rose phoenix-like from ashes of early '90s' recession and is now a thriving and successful school. Perched above river Wye, a short stone's throw into England, school overlooks Chepstow in Wales. Founded in 1923 in a rambling Georgian manor (rebuilt in 1805 after a fire). Succession of proprietorial heads until '60s but co-ed and charitable trust (incorporating former Brightlands School) since then. Has expanded successfully in recent years. New buildings fit well into overall scheme of things on a pleasant eight-acre site (plus 12 more acres of playing fields across the road).

Spectacular growth of nursery education (now provided on three sites including one in Newport) complete with state-of-the-art baby units (Tutshill site boasts a six-seater 'baby charabanc' paid for by the parents' association and appropriately pushed out from what was once the local garage). Seventy per cent of pre-prep intake come from the school's own nurseries. Our visit on a 'Foodie Friday' coincided with 'wormy pasta salad' on classroom menus. Highly professionalised early years teachers and assistants ensure tinies are happy and cared for. Impressive range of activities for these tots – stimulation in the nursery section includes sensory and soft play rooms plus safe outdoor play areas for all.

'Seamless' progression to reception level on Tutshill site where children 'learn to read without noticing,' say committed staff. Phonic introduction alongside activities such as puppets and story telling. Loads of measuring and counting too. Each

S

day begins with assembly in spacious hall; weekly link-up with nursery from below and to prep (in their hall) once a week. Communication between teachers and pre-prep parents includes 'wow cards' and home-school link books. Wide corridors in this modern, purpose-built building boast frequently changed displays including output of creative arts club and strong evidence of cross-curricular work: eg 'forces of movement' incorporating art, science and ICT work. Smart boards in each year group and laptops already in use at this level, not to mention school intranet on plasma screen. Huge choice of readers ('fireflies' non fiction popular with boys). Tea after school for those involved in clubs, activities or post-lessons care.

Pupils leave the swish pre-prep for the cleverly converted coach house which accommodates years 3 to 5 in what the previous head described as 'a bit of a tardis.' Smallish but cheery classrooms (maximum class size is 16) for these years. Next project is to build a six classroom block to replace outside mobiles which have served older pupils well but whose shelf life is definitely nearing the end. We observed a mock Jewish wedding taking place during an upbeat RS lesson in one of these when we visited.

Much better than average prep school facilities for science: junior (in a quaint outpost) and senior (modern) laboratories with well-qualified teachers to match. Lovely dining area combines best of cafeteria and sit down traditions whilst civilised entrance (with memorabilia on show) and meeting room (referred to as the Embassy) add gravitas. Prep is awash with subject specialists (some escapees from state sector, others ex-independent) who can take pupils as far as they want to go. Art teachers (ex-Monmouth senior) explained how they are adapting OCR syllabus for St John's and thereby widening pupils' artistic horizons. We appreciated the on-going Picasso exhibition whilst annual Arts Week gives pupils a chance to let their creativity run wild. Athletic head of DT (he manages British universities' cross-country team) oversees a well resourced area which includes 3D model making.

Somewhat dated school hall serves for assemblies as well as concerts and school productions (last one was a full blown Oliver!). Music has a large classroom base plus three individual practice rooms. Everyone in year 3 gets a violin and learns to scrape – like it or not. Orchestra and wind band plus choirs (school subs for Newport cathedral choir and also sang at recent IAPS conference) are all well supported and three ex-pupils have graduated to National Youth Orchestra. Specialist ICT rooms are well used but school maintains a healthy balance between new technologies and more traditional approaches.

Sports facilities include (almost) half-size Astroturf and hard tennis/netball courts, attractive 15-metre swimming pool and oodles of playing fields. School more than holds its own against larger preps with an impressive fixture list (includes Millfield and Cheltenham College). Wide choice of sports features rugby, soccer, cricket (boys and girls) as well as netball, rounders, swimming, tennis and golf. All pupils encouraged to participate as best they can. Fit-looking sports staff include Haka savvy Kiwis. Pupils punch above their weight at national events – eg recent national runners-up in national JET cricket competition beating Cheam by one wicket in semi-final. Athletics and cross-country involve large numbers; lots of alternatives for non-team players.

Refreshingly open, happy pupils – well turned out and polite nonetheless. We observed a school council meeting chaired effectively by a year 8 boy. Plenty of evidence of pupils' ideas bearing fruit eg new homework diary and rewards system not to mention refurb of pupils' loos. Pupils also discussed making a new outdoor classroom interactive – cutting edge stuff for 12-13 year olds. Large number (33 last time) go for a whole month's exchange with host schools in Stirling and Cape Town, South Africa. Led (10 visits so far) by a staff member who hails from those parts. Does wonders for pupil personal development and bonding. Pupils wax eloquent about how they are all 'given a chance' by 'kind

teachers' and how 'friendship' is the magical ingredient at St John's. We were shown a wide variety of pupils' work – impressive in its quality and diversity. Alumni include Olympic showjumper, Richard Mead, Welsh rugby player Marc Batten and Rebecca Watts (in first group of ordained women priests).

Four statemented children (each with a key worker), seven EAL pupils and 47 withdrawn for a variety of reasons. Thorough screening and intensive support from pre-prep upwards enable most children to proceed to senior schools of their choice. 'My bright, dyslexic son couldn't read when he started in the prep and now he's scored a high CE mark,' confided one very satisfied mum. Lots of input too for the most able (school is in membership of NACE) and organises trips (eg to theatres) and participates in events (eg maths challenges, languages show etc) to extend and inspire. Membership of Comenius project another way of widening horizons; some competed in Eurotalk competition (taking on tasks in previously unknown languages) at Olympia, London. School intranet, increasingly used to improve learning resources, provides cyber information for pupils, staff and parents. All years get to go on well-chosen choice of trips, not to mention year camps which get progressively more adventurous.

Fleet of minibuses ('drivers are really kind,' say parents) to ferry day pupils twixt home and school. Boarders get a good deal here with lovely, mixed (not the dorms) accommodation, dedicated and well qualified houseparents who 'go the extra mile' to develop a family, 'home from home' atmosphere. Houseparents even cook for boarders on Saturdays (take-aways are not unknown) but school roast on Sundays is 'to die for' they confess. Junior boarders write home (plus ICT and reading) on Saturday mornings whilst their seniors are in lessons. Dorm points add up so that winners get a reward outing. Regular 'Boarders' Bugle' adds to monthly school newsletters to keep boarding parents well informed. Flexi-boarding clearly popular with parents. Active Parents' Association have raised loads of dosh for worthwhile projects plus social and sporting events such as Bollywood Summer Ball and PA Golf Day. Parents help children's fund-raising through their four houses to benefit of a wide range of local, national and international good causes.

Great 'family' school for youngsters with 'gunpowder in the barrel' – 'we'll take them as far as they want to go,' insists school. Parents were at a loss to pick out a single outstanding feature – 'excellent teachers'; 'all pupils get involved'; 'a super school in all respects' was the consensus.

St Lawrence College Junior School

Linked school: St Lawrence College

St Lawrence College, Ramsgate, CT11 7AF

- Pupils: 163 boys and girls; 13 board • Fees: £6,516–£10,485 pa
- Independent

Tel: 01843 572931
Email: ah@slcuk.com
Website: www.slcuk.com

Head of the Junior School : Mr Simon Whittle.

Exit: Over half to senior school, rest to local schools including Dane Court Grammar, Charles Dickens, Clarendon & Chatham Federation, Dover College, Dover Grammar, Sir Roger Manwood's.

Remarks: See senior school review.

St Leonards Junior School

Linked school: St Leonards School

The Pends, St Andrews, KY16 9QH

• Pupils: 170 girls and boys; all day • Ages: 5–12 • Non denominational • Fees: £8,589–£9,627 pa • Independent

Tel: 01334 460470
Email: registrar@stleonards-fife.org
Website: www.stleonards-fife.org

Headmaster: Mr Andrew Donald.

Entrance: Entry to the junior school can take place at any stage, although the main points of entry are year 1 (P1) and year 4 (P4). Those wanting to join years 1 – 3 spend half a day at the school whilst staff assess their ability; applicants for year 4 – 7 also do maths and English tests. The school will investigate further any learning support needs these tests highlight; the registrar can give more details on this and on the process for pupils with known specific learning needs.

Exit: Children are prepared to move on to the senior school, and there are transition events for year 7 pupils in the last few weeks of the summer term to prepare them for the move.

Remarks: For further details, see senior school.

St Margaret's Junior School (London)

Linked school: St Margaret's School (London)

18 Kidderpore Gardens, London, NW3 7SR

• Pupils: 80 girls, all day • Ages: 4–11 • Fees: £10,011–£11,337 pa • Independent

Tel: 020 7435 2439
Email: enquiry@st-margarets.co.uk
Website: www.st-margarets.co.uk

Principal: Mr Mark Webster.

Entrance: From reception to year 2 assessment involves girls coming in for the morning and working with the class teacher. From year 3 upwards they take a standard set of English and maths assessments.

Exit: Most girls stay on to the senior school, though a small number will move to more selective senior schools such as North London Collegiate or City of London School for GIrls.

Remarks: See senior school.

St Margaret's School for Girls Junior Department (Aberdeen)

Linked school: St Margaret's School for Girls (Aberdeen)

17 Albyn Place, Aberdeen, AB10 1RU

• Pupils: 158 girls, all day • Ages: 3–12 years • Non-denom • Fees: £6,735–£9,594 pa • Independent

Tel: 01224 584466
Email: info@st-margaret.aberdeen.sch.uk
Website: www.st-margaret.aberdeen.sch.uk

Head: Since 2010, Dr Julie Land (fifty) BSc (maths) PGCE EdD. Educated at Dame Allan's Girls' School, Newcastle and Manchester and Newcastle universities. Taught maths for nine years before taking 10 years out to look after a young family, and did most of her doctoral research during this time. Returned to teaching in 2000 and joined St Margaret's in 2003, becoming deputy head in 2004.

Intends to lead and support staff through a period of educational change and oversee new buildings such as a new school hall and classrooms together with improvement of games facilities.

Married with two grown up children, she enjoys walking and gardening as well as table tennis (an accomplished player in her youth).

Remarks: For details, see senior school entry.

St Martin's Ampleforth

Linked school: Ampleforth College

Gilling Castle, Gilling East, York, YO62 4HP

• Pupils: 160 boys and girls; 48 boarders • Ages: 3–13 • RC – accepts pupils of other denominations but they must be prepared to participate fully in the religious life of the school • Fees: Day £7,356–£13,638; Boarding £20,517 pa • Independent

Tel: 01439 766600
Email: headmaster@stmartins.ampleforth.org.uk
Website: www.stmartins.ampleforth.org.uk

Headmaster: Since 2004, Mr Nicholas Higham (forties), educated at Mount St Mary's College, BA in PE and geography from Leeds Carnegie. Played rugby for Headingley and Saracens. Taught at Douai; housemaster at Pangbourne; head of Moreton Hall prep school, Suffolk, increased roll from 95 to 140. Charming, brisk, business-like, loves his job (and children), has clearly got a grip on the place. Enjoys a round of golf after school with the children, and fit and energetic enough to take on a Cologne to school bike ride with old boy Lawrence Dallaglio to raise extra bursary funds. No longer lives on site, but he and wife Louise (ex-BBC, does school marketing) live nearby with their three children and dog(s). Housemaster and housemistress now in situ instead. Moving on in July 2014.

Entrance: By interview, assessment, and report from current school. All entrants encouraged to come for taster day.

Exit: Nearly all go on to Ampleforth College. A few students return to their home countries for secondary education.

Though linked closely with Ampleforth, Mr Higham points out that it is 'a prep school in its own right'.

Remarks: Prep school of Ampleforth, founded in 1929, merged with St Martin's RC prep in 2001. Main building is imposing Gilling Castle – Grade 1 listed – glorious but also gloriously expensive to maintain. Unbelievable 16th century Great Chamber, probably the finest Tudor interior in England (don't miss the ceiling and stained glass); the children eat there, though are more interested in checking out the sausages and rarely look up. The castle was the inspiration for Hogwarts in the Harry Potter films, according to JK Rowling's cousin, who went to the college – though site not used for filming. Three miles from the senior school, with all the freedom of its 3,000 acres; tree-climbing, den-building, bike rides through the woods all allowed and indeed encouraged, despite risk assessments, and thankfully deemed infinitely preferable to Playstations, iPods and PSPs. Hazy sunny days of children rolling down grassy banks, making daisy chains, playing on all-weather skateboards, practising in the cricket nets... it's all about space, freedom and spontaneity.

Boarding is important, and growing; quite a few persuade parents to let them convert from day. The integrity of a boarding mix is guarded fiercely here to create a real sense of school community. School day ends at 5.35pm for all; a longish day but includes prep time and plenty of extra-curricular activities. Boarders come from all over UK; southern pupils catch a Hogwarts Express at the beginning of term: it is (just) possible to enjoy breakfast in London and lunch in school. Day pupils from Yorkshire; parents a genuine mix of local aristocracy, a few military, professional and non-professional. Open days and school events bring a range of shabby chic Citroens, Land Rovers and Rolls Royces bearing Fortnum and Mason hampers. A good sprinkling from abroad, mainly Europe plus a few South Americans, increasingly popular as education abroad becomes more secular.

Catholics make up 70 per cent; (40 per cent in prep-prep); other denominations are clearly happy to be there, 'being educated in the life of the Christian faith', as the school puts it. Like its Benedictine big brother, it 'asks much from the children's strengths and supports their weaknesses'. Pastoral care very good (Father John is a friend to all and mainstay of the school); children are confident, courteous and seem happy in their extended school family. Benedictine sense of togetherness and 'anti-me' culture encourages compassion and understanding. Lovely chapel, pretty almost, ideal for this age group, fewer bells and smells than the senior school but full of character nonetheless and the gospel message filters through.

Average class size of 15; standard curriculum up to common entrance, pupils also tested at Key Stage 1 and 2. Five new state-of-the-art classrooms focus on the teaching of languages (and English), French, Latin, Greek all taught; Spanish, Mandarin, German and Italian also on offer as extra-curricular activities. Gifted and talented pupils recognised and supported, though children 'not deemed less worthy if less academic or less sporty'. Large well-stocked library is popular. The school is now 40 per cent girls, a sparky and capable bunch, the advent of whom knocked down barriers, opened up the curriculum and raised the game for everyone.

Games predictably important and takes place every afternoon – hence extended teaching day. Rugby and cricket for boys; hockey, netball, rounders for girls. The overseas pupils quickly catch on to the idea of picking up a ball and running with it and the first XV rugby team almost looks like an outing from the UN. Athletics, swimming, cross-country also on offer. School has a floodlit all-weather Astroturf pitch. Golf increasingly popular, own golf course, though challenging with much of it on a slope. Plenty of activities, including fishing, riding and shooting; a modern pentathlon team competes nationally.

Music superb, based in fine performing arts block. ISI noted 'high level of musicianship, inspirational teaching'. Schola (choir) sings with senior school, tours across Europe. Over 80 per cent of pupils learn instruments; years 3 and 4 all play the violin, cello, double bass or oboe, with varying degrees of success, but a great opportunity to give it a try.

St Mary's Hall

Linked school: Stonyhurst College

Stonyhurst, Lancashire, BB7 9PU

• Pupils: 230; 45 Boarding and 185 day; • Ages: 3–13; • Roman Catholic in the Jesuit tradition; • Fees: Boarding £17,895–£21,120; Day £6,681–£13,717 pa; • Independent

Tel: 01254 826242
Email: admissions@stonyhurst.ac.uk
Website: www.stonyhurst.ac.uk

Headmaster: Since 2004, Mr Lawrence Crouch BA MA PGCE (fifties), father to four grown-up children. After studying English at Nottingham, an action-packed gap year and a spell teaching English in a comprehensive school, an OS, he returned to Stonyhurst in 1982 as head of drama, then was appointed head of English before moving to SMH. Sees strength of his appointment as two-fold 'knowing what a Stonyhurst pupil should become' and 'allowing the two buildings (College and SMH) to talk to each other'.

A keen sportsman, a rugby, cricket, cycling and golf fan, also the current Stonyhurst campus squash champion (narrowly – his own evaluation); plays piano and oboe – classical, jazz through to rock, though real renown as a singer, whose definitive performance of 'Great Balls of Fire' is legendary. A chess devotee, enjoys a game by text with his counterpart in Zimbabwean partner school. Warm, thoughtful, caring, approachable, with a warm sense of humour. Openly liked and respected by pupils, parents and staff alike and, despite his impressive achievements, extremely modest. Parents told us that 'he really knows the children and values and appreciates each child'. Clearly enjoying the role of prep school headmaster enormously, his enthusiasm is infectious.

Entrance: Pupils enter all years but most commonly at age 3 and 11. Admission to nursery and reception via interview with the head and head of pre-prep; older children admitted following an interview and on receipt of a school report. Ages 10-12 require additional tests in maths, English and verbal reasoning.

Two academic scholarships and one for music awarded for entry at 11 worth between 10 – 50 per cent of fees. St Francis Xavier awards of 20 per cent of fees are also available to those who 'are most likely to benefit from and contribute to life as full boarders in a Catholic boarding school'. All can be topped up with a means tested bursary – capped at a maximum of 70 per cent for St Francis Xavier award.

Exit: Straight on to Stonyhurst College. It is rare for a pupil to stray elsewhere, however school will advise appropriately if it feels Stonyhurst would be unsuitable.

Remarks: Set in glorious countryside amongst rolling fields, just a walk through the woods from College. Housed in a Victorian former priests' seminary overlooking verdant grass, junior rugby pitches, and, on a clear day, Pendle Hill. Tucked behind, sits modern yet sympathetic, purpose-built pre-prep Hodder House, with delightful teaching areas, indoors and outside, to facilitate the EYFS multi-sensory approach to learning. The

S

complementary and contrasting nature of the buildings reflect the education here, steeped in Jesuit traditions and beliefs yet forward-thinking with the creative curriculum (gradually making its way up the school), modelled on the International Primary Curriculum, but 'retaining our Ignatian language' says the head.

So be prepared to learn a whole new vocabulary to enter the world of a Jesuit school. For starters, 'lines' are school houses, 'playrooms' are year groups, 'playroom masters' are housemasters and as for the school year groups – Elements, lower and upper, Figures and Rudiments! And then there's the Latin...

Yet the school is forward-thinking enough to pick up on the whims of modern children, issuing a 'credit card' for consistent good work that allows you jump the lunch queue, MSN offering an active forum for after-school chat and the top year producing their own web page. Whiteboards abound and the ICT centre is open after hours. Traditional in that a scholarship programme is in place to 'push' the brightest; French taught from three and Spanish, from seven, Mandarin after-school and Russian on the director of studies' radar. From 11+ common entrance curriculum followed with specialist teaching. Tutor system looks after the development of the 'whole child'.

Project week embraces whole school in early June, from residential trips such as the battlefields for older pupils to celebration of the school's history and famous alumni for the younger. Provides learning opportunities and life skills beyond the confines of the classroom.

Ignatian values and Jesuit traditions underpin all aspects of school life; everyone's contribution is valued and giving of their best an expectation. As one parent commented ' a heart of faith communicated through everything they do'. 'Everyone helps you out,' said one pupil 'it's a really good school. Coming here changes your character, pushes you to aspire to make the change, so you can make a difference'. Head feels that talent is not enough without the confidence to say 'this is what I've got, this is what I can give'. A quiet centre for reflective thought and the beautiful chapel in the heart of the school are open for those that need a peaceful moment.

A music gallery at top of school resounds with chamber choir, brass and strings – lots of uptake, though some pressure applied to join and stay according to parents; with composition on the curriculum at an early age school. Art similarly located up in the 'gods' providing a light and airy environment for some colourful and creative work. Performances are enjoyed in the theatre; one annual school production for leavers (and pre-prep nativity) though plenty of drama and performance opportunity through assemblies before then. After a previous school experience one parent was grateful that curriculum time was not lost 'in constant rehearsals honing a production to perfection'. Sport is popular with excellent coaching and facilities for traditional games, resulting in good representation at area and regional level. Usual carousel of after-school activities, with something to suit all interests.

The prep school pupils live and learn under one roof in the rambling and much loved Victorian building. First floor classrooms are sandwiched between the age appropriate, well-equipped ground floor playrooms and dining room on the ground floor and the upper echelons of boys' boarding accommodation on the third floor and girls' on fourth. Strong full or weekly boarding ethos 'flexible boarding unsettling for all' says director of boarding. Over half from overseas, predominantly Spanish and Mexican, but with a league of nations from Nigeria to Korea. Parents like the diversity of pupils (and staff), a global dimension in this rural retreat. Unlike College, all ages up to 13 board together in comfortable, well-sized rooms shared by 4 or 5, though with far less artwork on the walls usually so conspicuous in boarding houses. Where were all those 'Keep calm and carry on' posters?

Boarding maxim 'tolerance, empathy and independence' emphasises ethos and without doubt, this underpins daily life.

Pupils kept busy on a schedule of activity from waking to mid-evening, though daily access to mobile phones allows for regular 'phone homes'. Weekly photo e-newsletter sent to parents by director of boarding very nice touch. Plenty of 'gappies' ensure smooth running operationally and immersed in boarding life providing pastoral support too. Formally addressed by pupils, as 'children get confused with the blur'. Round the clock access to medical professionals, merit system determining amount of weekly tuck, rota of weekend activities, clear rules and systems neatly displayed on central notice boards – it certainly feels like a well-oiled machine.

Pupil voice is heard through the school council and boarding committee and pupils feel engaged with the way their school is run. Charitable giving is important; the school has its own charity and a link with a school near Harare supporting the culture of 'men and women for others'.

Parents are a mixed bag of former pupils and local professionals; 70 per cent Catholic, other denominations accepting the liturgy also welcome. Pupils appear confident and are hugely loyal, and whilst well prepared, sad to leave the security of these warm and supportive surroundings.

St Mary's Junior School (Cambridge)

Linked school: St Mary's School, Cambridge

6 Chaucer Road, Cambridge, CB2 7EB

• Pupils: 170 girls, all day • Ages: 4–11 • RC, but all faiths welcome • Fees: £8,445–£10,851 pa • Independent

Tel: 01223 311666
Email: juniorschool@stmaryscambridge.co.uk
Website: www.stmaryscambridge.co.uk

Remarks: See senior school entry.

St Mary's Preparatory School, the Preparatory School of Lincoln Minster School

Linked school: Lincoln Minster School

Eastgate, Lincoln, LN2 1QG

• Pupils: boys and girls • Ages: 2–11 • Fees: Day £8,328–£10,497; Boarding £18,762–£20,664 pa • Independent

Tel: 01522 523769
Email: lincoln.prep@church-schools.com
Website: www.lincolnminsterschool.co.uk

Headmistress: Since 2012, Mrs Fiona Thomas BEd NPQH.

Remarks: For details see senior school.

S

St Mary's School (Gerrards Cross) Preparatory Department

Linked school: St Mary's School (Gerrards Cross)

Packhorse Road, Gerrards Cross, SL9 8JQ

• Pupils: 96 girls, all day • Ages: 3–11 • Fees: £3,855–£11,385 pa
• Independent

Tel: 01753 883370
Email: registrar@st-marys.bucks.sch.uk
Website: www.stmarysschool.co.uk

Headmistress: Mrs Jean Ross.

Entrance: Girls come from a range of local nursery and feeder schools. St Mary's is a Christian foundation but welcomes girls of all faiths and none. Girls are assessed informally to ensure that they can keep pace with curriculum.

Exit: While the majority of girls progress through to senior school, some choose to go on to local grammars: Beaconsfield High School or Dr Challoner's High School.

St Mary's School (Melrose)

Abbey Park, High Street, Melrose, TD6 9LN

• Pupils: 145 boys and girls • Ages: 2½–13 • Non-denom
• Fees: Day £10,998–£13,848; Boarding £16,248 pa • Independent

Tel: 01896 822517
Email: office@stmarysmelrose.org.uk
Website: www.stmarysmelrose.org.uk

Headmaster: Since 2010, Mr William (Liam) Harvey BEd (forties). The son of a local doc, and an FP, he went on to George Watson's followed by a BEd in PE at Liverpool John Moores University. Taught PE to A level in the state secondary sector before moving to Belhaven as housemaster and head of history and PE. The Harveys live in the main school house, with dorms above.

We met Mr Harvey's Candadian wife, Marnia, efficiently organising the mysteries of the gap student's computer... Their daughters are in the school.

Entrance: All things to all men. The only independent school in the Borders; children come from within a 50 mile radius, can come mid-term at any time if space available, otherwise automatically up from kindergarten. The odd state child has been known simply to come for an '18-month blast' before going back into the maintained sector, but this is rarer and rarer and none this year. Some come at 11 to do CE.

Exit: 'Most but not all' stay on until they go to their senior school at 11, 12, or 13 (the occasional toff pops off to Belhaven, Aysgarth, but none so far under the new regime), preferred secondary schools used to be Glenalmond, Fettes, Merchiston, Loretto, St George's in Edinburgh or Longridge Towers in Berwick, Queen Margaret's York and whilst these did indeed feature in our random poll, increasingly numbers are more likely to be turning south, Sedburgh gaining in popularity, and Ampleforth. Winchester, Eton next? As we said earlier: WOW.

Remarks: WOW. Didn't recognise the place. Totally transformed since our last visit and some of the most exciting (and cleverly sited to act as a windbreak) skool buildings we have ever seen. The Hamilton building opened in 2010 was funded by a gift from 'an anonymous benefactor'. Guestimate cost? A million near as dammit. Named after John Hamilton who founded the school in 1895 (good, if somewhat belated, way to celebrate a centenary).

Two non-parallel buildings with terrific reception area, full of photographs – though a tad Nuffield in aspect (think neutral carpets and comfy seating). Only thing missing is the coffee machine although we were topped up with copious amounts – the head had his own insulated mug. Reception area littered with prospectuses of senior schools – not, as previously, concentrating on the Scottish mafia, but Shrewsbury, Uppingham, Cheltenham and Harrow. Quite a change, though those whom we asked mainly seemed to be heading North. Wide corridors – one outside the art dept was recently turned into a drawing 'road' where parents and pupils depicted the best aspects of their childhood (and jolly good some of them were too – we particularly liked the footballer). Photographs everywhere in main building, the art building – with yet more light, airy, and huge classrooms has walls filled with pupil offerings and classrooms for younger pupils.

We previously described St Mary's as a 'Jolly useful little school, incredibly flexible, with flexi, weekly and day pupils; one or two toffs, but mostly farmers and local professionals who stay to the bitter end, plus "masses of" first time buyers.' But gosh. Still tiny classes, max 18 but usually much less, only one stream, scholars will be 'hived off' and set at 10 if necessary and 'provided with evening tutorials with subject teachers'. Latin from eight, languages from five, taster term of French, then specialists in French for common entrance. Fantastic and envy making French trips when the entire form decamp to a monastery for a week. Science taught separately for the last four years, and pupils move round the staff (from age nine – a transition class).

'Strong' dyslexia department, all singing and dancing and reorganised during 2011, oversees regular testing, and support for the very bright. Withdrawn help and support staff (masses of 'em, chaps as well as chappesses) go into class too – 'pretty flexible' (might be the school motto). Keen on handwriting. Interactive whiteboards abound, all classrooms are computered to the hilt, state of the art. Loads of staff changes since new head's arrival (but see below), certain number of redundancies, and terrific young buzzy staff abound (think policemen). School now boasts 'a strong academic team' and we were enchanted to find Michael Osborne, previously head of Belhaven (and undoubtedly the best teacher in Scotland – maths/classics his speciality, he also teaches a couple of days at Ardvreck) happily ensconced. We also found him teaching; plus ca change, plus c'est la meme chose...

Drama strong and timetabled, the school has links with local Borders Youth Theatre. Good music, rehearsals and lessons in functional school hall, whilst pre-prep has own gym, with Noah and his ark drawn by the young. The somewhat surprising cloistered classroom corridor (the 'veranda classrooms') have been relegated to music, a theatre store room, boarders' activity room, music and a thrift shop.

Separate corridors for boys and for girls, the latter live in somewhat cramped conditions in a conversion of what used to be the main drawing room – fantastic ceiling, but divided into three – with what must be one of the grandest ceiling-ed bathrooms ever. Jolly dorms upstairs, all brightly painted with splendid stripy duvet covers. Very homey; bunks, the odd poster, random teddy bears. B&B – £25 per night.Day children can stay from 7.30am (and breakfast in school) right through to 7.30pm, by which time they will have done their prep and had supper, kindergarten can stay till 4pm. Tinies wear delightful green and white check tabliers and girls evolve from gym slips to proper kilts; we checked, most were eight pleats thick. Dining room with weekly menu, over-high benches for littlies to sit at table. Brown bread only and lots of sugar-free puds, mainly organic as far as possible. Robert the chef comes complete with starched chef's hat and sparkling white uniform. Cor. He also makes scrumptious millionaire's shortbread for the head's guests – not sugar-free at all, and has lost a mega amount of weight since we last saw him... now deeply into marathons. One is always told to beware the skinny chef, but he is still triumphant, and gives the boarders special cooking lessons (it was Burns night/lunch during our visit, and the haggis was piped in with aplomb). Pheasant (plucking lessons and all) on the menu next.

Squads and teams triumph all over the place. Swimming off-site in Gala(shiels) and main games pitches just across some National Trust land. Smashing little school.

St Mary's School, Hampstead

47 Fitzjohn's Avenue, London, NW3 6PG

• Pupils: 275 girls and 18 boys • Ages: 2 years 9 months–11
• Fees: £6,510–£12,060 pa • Independent

Tel: 020 7435 1868
Email: enquiries@stmh.co.uk
Website: www.stmh.co.uk

Headmistress: Since 2003, Miss Angela Rawlinson BA MA (fifties). A New Zealander, she did a degree in education and psychology at Auckland University, then trained as a teacher at Auckland Teachers' College. Taught for seven years, before arriving in the UK in 1989 to 'stay for a year'. After research at Cambridge (on drama in the curriculum), she worked in the state sector (as deputy head at the Servite RC Primary in Fulham and head at the Marlborough School, Kensington), before taking over at St Mary's.

Immensely professional, enthusiastic and energetic, she loves her work: 'In what other job would you find 300 people coming in and saying "I love you" every day?' Weekends are spent on the south coast reading, playing tennis and golf. 'She's amazing,' said one mother. 'You'll come in the morning and find her skipping with the children. My daughter always rushes in to give her a big cuddle'.

Entrance: Names down at birth, but even delivery-room efficiency will not guarantee a place. These go first to siblings, then to Catholics, then to non-Catholics. Parents generally tour the school nine months before entry, sign the acceptance form and pay a deposit. Nursery arrangements are particularly parent friendly. Children are admitted from two years and nine months and can stay to lunch or all afternoon with minimum notice. Boys make up a third of nursery entrants. A few further places for girls often become available in year 3.

Exit: About 85 per cent to leading academic secondary schools – South Hampstead, City of London, North London Collegiate, Highgate, Haberdashers' etc – quite a number with scholarships. Also to selective state schools (St Michael's Catholic Grammar, Henrietta Barnett). Secondary school advice is a strength, starting with individual parent meetings in year 5. 'Most trust us and listen to what we recommend', says the head. Boys leave by the age of six, many to neighbouring Catholic prep St Anthony's.

Remarks: Founded in 1871, by the Congregation of Jesus, the school moved from Belsize Park in 1926 to its present building, a turn-of-the century mansion with polished mosaic floors and vast country-like gardens. Against this gracious period backdrop, facilities are thoroughly up to date, with a super, Mac-filled IT suite, large, newly built assembly hall and well-stocked library located in the panelled former billiards room. In 1992, when there were too few teaching nuns to manage

the school, a charitable trust was formed to continue the good work under lay management.

A non-selective school, it still manages to pull off high-flying results at 11. Teaching (as described in the recent ISI report) is 'excellent' – sharp, lively and very pupil focused. 'The teacher worked out my daughter in three minutes', said one parent. Praise is appropriate and immediate. 'My daughter had been struggling to write a longer essay. On the day she did so, the head immediately called her in and gave her two merit points. It encouraged her so much'.

The brightest are stretched through a curriculum enriched with plenty of arts-related activities and sport. 'We wanted to make it more relevant', says the head, 'and incorporate risk taking and thinking independently'. Interesting extra work for those who need stretch (lunch-time puzzle club, for example, is a big hit).

Fluid ability grouping throughout, then setting in maths and English in year 6 in the run up to 11 plus. Excellent support for strugglers, too, with three special needs teachers providing help in class and out of it (in lovely, bright teaching space). 'The learning support is fantastic', said one mother with a daughter finding maths a mountain. 'Very few independent schools are non-selective, but St Mary's does very well by all'. Another told us: 'You really feel they care about every single girl. If someone is not up to scratch, the response is "what can we do to help them shine?"' External specialists are invited in to keep absence to a minimum.

Strong sport, with a double court for netball and a well-equipped gym. All the usual team games (rounders, netball, hockey, football), plus swimming at Swiss Cottage baths (for years three to six) and athletics in Regent's Park. Gymnastics particularly popular, with pupils competing at regional and national level. High achievement too, in music and excellent dance and drama (including an all-encompassing production in year 6). Heaps of clubs (Latin, Spanish, needlework, craft, lingua franca) and plenty of trips (year 5 to an adventure camp in Devon, year 6 on a five-day break in France to meet pen pals and make croissants, little ones to a farm and the seaside).

Boys are well integrated and given appropriate scope in the Big Boys Club, in which football is played and steam let off on imaginary motor bikes. 'It lets them be boys in this all-girls environment', said one mother.

Very much a Catholic school, with about 70 per cent Catholic parents. 'I think one of the most wonderful things about it is that the Catholic ethos permeates every aspect of the children's life', said one. Those who wish can be prepared for First Holy Communion by much-loved Father Chris on his twice-weekly visits to the school chapel. Pupils participate in Mass and study Catholic Christianity. 'Many of our parents have had a Catholic education themselves and want that for their children', says the head – but even those who haven't feel included. 'As a non-Catholic', said one parent, 'I was quite concerned at the outset, but Father Chris is so lovely and give such interesting talks. They really teach the children how to be a good and loving member of a community'.

Pupils are beaming and notably well-behaved (not a peep was heard when our guide was chatting to one teacher as children queued to leave the room). 'We really work hard at being positive. We want to catch children doing the right thing', says the head. Plenty of rewards for those who are caught doing things 'the St Mary's Way'; those who slip up are gently 'reminded of 'expectations'. 'We want pupils to do their best to be their best,' says the head. Most pupils adore the school ('my daughter can't wait to get back after the holidays') and parents are equally appreciative. 'You're never made to feel unwelcome, you never feel you shouldn't be there', we were told.

Mostly professional families from Hampstead and the surrounding areas, with a wide range of backgrounds (from Europe, the US, Asia and the Far East). About half speak at least one other language at home (with good in-school support for newcomers on the foothills of English). Mums 'really involved' (with reading, bazaars, the library, uniform sale). Despite its Hampstead location, this is a fairly understated place and unusually for a prep school offers a number of full bursaries.

St Michael's CofE Voluntary Aided Primary School

North Road, London, N6 4BG

• Pupils: 465 boys and girls; all day • Ages: 3–11 • State

Tel: 020 8340 7441
Email: admin@stmichaelsn6.com
Website: www.stmichaelsn6.com

Head Teacher: Since April 2013, Mrs Geraldine Gallagher.

Entrance: Heavily oversubscribed at nursery and reception. 100 or so apply for 52 nursery places, 60 reception places, which are allocated on a points system. (Five points for church attendance at St Michael's Church, three for living in N6. Thereafter, local Christians, siblings, other faiths.) Christianity very much part of the ethos, but the school tries to be as wide-ranging as possible in its intake. Open days every term and, if a vacancy is available, parents are welcome to look round. Places do arise, particularly in the higher years.

Exit: On the border of three boroughs – Haringey, Islington and Camden – St Michael's sends its leavers to as many as 30 secondary schools. About half to independent schools (many with scholarships) – particularly Highgate, with which the school has a close association – and City of London, but also Channing, UCS, Westminster, North London Collegiate, Haberdashers' Aske's, and South Hampstead, plus top grammars, Henrietta Barnett, Latymer, St Michael's Catholic Girls and Queen Elizabeth's Boys. Two boys, too, have recently been accepted by Eton. A considerable chunk each year to Fortismere School, the popular local comprehensive in Muswell Hill. The school doesn't prepare children for entry tests but parents tend to be very clued up (with a secondary school evening run by the Parents' Association) and coach accordingly.

Remarks: One of north London's most sought-after primary schools, St Michael's has high academic standards and a high proportion of pupils who reach well beyond the government's expectations at seven and 11. This is partly due to intake but also due to strong teaching throughout and well-organised classrooms where calm and well-behaved boys and girls sit quietly in their neat and practical navy uniform.

The curriculum is a particular strength of the school, with specialist subject teaching from year 3, Italian (courtesy of the Italian government), and a notable maths programme with an early-morning maths club for the most able run with neighbouring Highgate prep, and booster lessons in curriculum time for the struggling.

Afternoon teaching unique, with specialist subject teaching in extension maths, PE, art, science, geography, history and music from year 3. 'I wanted to play to teachers' strengths,' said the previous head. 'We had all these specialists in the school and only a proportion of the children were getting the benefit. It made absolute sense.'

A good range of sport – gymnastics, football, tennis, cricket, netball and basketball – taught in lesson time. Swimming too, taught in years 5 and 6, a strength – the school has won the Haringey swimming shield so often it's now on permanent display.

Founded in the mid 19th century as a school to train up young locals to go into service, by 1852 it was on its current three-and-a-half acre site. The green fields and listed Victorian buildings have since been joined by a block built in the 1970s, two large, well-equipped playgrounds and a large, new all-weather court. The immaculately maintained grounds are still the pride of the school. 'The school manager, Troy, has to be one of the best in London,' enthused one parent – and, as well as play time and games, the grounds are made full use of for the popular summer fair and bonfire night festivities.

Excellent drama, with two or three plays annually, plus a nativity play and annual summer concert. Dynamic extra-curricular programme, with after-school cricket, drama (led by the school's celebrated drama teacher, Bob Williams, CBE), orchestra, recorder groups, French, chess, etc. Higher than average special needs, with a good SENCo, plus a gifted and talented co-ordinator.

Unusually energetic Parents' Association, which raises impressive sums each year with an endless medley of social events. Fund-raising drives have paid for a £35,000 computer suite, resurfacing and remodelling the infant playground, new cloakrooms, new stage lights and books galore.

Children mainly from comfortably-off professional and media homes who are more than happy to use the state if it's as near to private as you can get. 'The parents here are wonderfully involved but you can feel excluded if you aren't in with the right set,' said one, 'and parents can be quite demanding'.

Very much a community school, however, which children remain very attached to, often turning up to annual celebrations well into their secondary school years. 'It's one of unique things about the school.'

St Olave's School

Linked school: St Peter's School, York

St Olave's School, Clifton, York, YO30 67AB

• Pupils: 340 pupils, 196 boys/144 girls; 29 boarders; • Ages: 3–8 Clifton Pre-prep; 8–13 St Olave's; • C of E but open to all; • Fees: Day £10,530–£12,735; Boarding £19,440–£21,435 pa ; • Independent

Tel: 01904 527416
Email: enquiries@st-olaves.york.sch.uk
Website: www.st-peters.york.sch.uk

Master: Since 2005, Mr Andy Falconer MBA BA (forties). An ISI inspector, recent chair of IAPS as well as a Walter Hines Page Scholar. Previously deputy head at Chafyn Grove School and before that was head of geography at Craigclowan School. Married to Lesley, a nurse, with three young daughters. Enjoys skiing, grew up near a Scottish ski resort and is a qualified instructor, former travel writer and currently into marathon running, otherwise free time is family time. Kind, charming, with a soft Scottish lilt and a delightful manner. Chats very comfortably with pupils, knows who they are and equally they know him – pupils tuck their shirts in when they see him coming. He misses nothing, touring school with a watchful eye, even turning off lights in empty rooms – 'a Scotsman in Yorkshire,' he grins. Hugely knowledgeable about and committed to the education of children, up to speed on all the latest developments, cherry picking the best and applying them with skill and understanding to enhance the learning experience. Parents and children trust him implicitly, never doubting that he has the children's best interests at heart. A rock solid practitioner.

S

Entrance: Automatic from Clifton Pre-Preparatory, otherwise selective but not massively so, looking for cognitive ability scores of 100+. All entrants are tested in maths, English, reading, spelling, and reasoning. Entrance examinations end of January.

Exit: Almost all to St Peter's School, York. Remainder are usually relocating.

Remarks: Sited in the former Queen Anne's grammar school buildings – a number of mums are old girls. The buildings have been adapted, extended and improved to create a more welcoming space for children and their parents. It's a very grounded school, not stuffy in any sense. Footbridge to senior school makes it easy to get from one campus to the other, 'distinct and separate, yet linked' (is the official line, and it seems to work).

Good facilities, shares Astroturf and indoor pool with senior school, but has own sports hall with indoor nets; music block; science lab; language rooms; DT; cookery, not as a discrete subject but linked eg to maths, DT, languages (recipes in French); art and ceramic studios; dining hall and Shepherd Hall for assemblies and regular productions. New medical room and veg garden.

Parents delight in the school's 'responsiveness', answering questions, dealing with any concerns and, importantly, 'never underestimating children'. Stretch and challenge include sparky discussions on current events in assembly that then continue over supper at home and the ability of staff to 'see qualities in children that others might overlook'. PTA members are busy with social and fundraising events twice a term varying from murder mystery nights to wine-tasting and a denim and diamante evening.

Invariably over-subscribed at 11+, year on year; some leakage of girls at year 6 to girls' schools, but only a handful and they are 'easily replaced' we are told. Equal numbers of boys/girls, 18 full boarders, 15 part-time boarders, rest day. Occasional boarding not allowed. About a third of boarders are from overseas, third armed forces, the rest from across the UK or even local – one boarder lives close enough to kick a rugby ball into his own garden. Saturday morning school for everyone, 'allows a broader curriculum and more time spent with your mates', says school, 'great fun but requires stamina,' say parents. Parents of day pupils (that's most of them) pass the time having coffee or shopping, almost 50 take to school rowing boats on the river, it's all part of the service. Day pupils travel from as far afield as Scarborough, Harrogate, Selby and Wetherby – short cut to the railway station makes it possible. The train is a good idea because parking is tricky – has to be a quick drop off in the mornings though the playground is opened up so that you can 'park and pick up' after school.

No common entrance and no national curriculum testing here yet plenty of rigour. For those heading for public schools beyond York school organises own testing/entrance procedures and supports accordingly. Healthy outlook on education, 'you've got to play the long game' says the head, 'it's more about learning and thinking and less about testing', quoting that old Chinese proverb about 'not fattening a pig by weighing it'. Doing something right as the library bucks the trend by being packed with boys at breaktime (clever librarian – great choice of 'boy' books) and academic standards, across the board, are high. Average class size 18 with maximum usually 20. Chapel twice a week, traditional C of E service. No issue with bright dyslexics, have strategies to help, specialist tutors, extra lessons and extra time for those who need them.

Staff are encouraged to 'share the learning journey' – the head is learning to play the drums (and gives the children regular updates on his progress in assembly); others offer four week courses to their colleagues (teaching and non-teaching) in a range of subjects, skills and challenges. Years 6 to 8 have all their lessons with subject specialists, younger children

gradually work towards this. There is setting throughout for maths and for French and Latin in the top two years. Carousel for French/Spanish/German/Latin in years 4 and 5, pupils choose post year 7.

Music is high profile, a school concert sees two-thirds of pupils taking part. Years 4 and 5 have three class lessons of music each week; add to that the usual choirs, brass groups, sax and clarinet groups, recorder, woodwind and cello groups – plus the school rock band 'stereo Flair'. Some phenomenal art on display, 'talent is recognised and nurtured' say parents.

Sport is impressive here, plenty of teams and older pupils competing at national level. Bigger schools such as RGS Newcastle and QEGS Wakefield provide serious challenge; smaller preps may struggle to compete with the first team here. Sporting successes include four times winners of the National Rugby Sevens Tournament; winners of national JET Cup cricket; national finals for hockey, soccer and cricket. Outward bound, yacht sailing with Ocean Youth Trust and rowing (school has rowing machines as well as river access and own rowing club) plus an Easter ski trip and sports tours (years 5 and 8) keep pupils busy and active all year round.

Lots of extra-curricular choice including enterprising young apprentice-type challenges and history model-making club, which essentially means boys making weapons from wood. Pupils also enjoy charity days and fund-raising, pink day for breast cancer, organised by pupils, and green day in support of NSPCC, among recent events. Wide range of after-school clubs and activities, including prep clubs for day children of working parents.

Pupils eat and register in their mixed age houses,' helping everyone to, 'know the school vertically and horizontally'. Strong house identity (that children describe as 'Harry Potter-esque'), linked to pastoral care. A teacher/mentor follows through with groups of children year on year, a type of wraparound care valued hugely by parent body. Homemade lunches prepared by chef, the legendary Dave.

Smart (ish) navy uniform, different from and more appealing than the brown of the senior school; sports kit is linked across the schools.

St Paul's Cathedral School

New Change, London, EC4M 9AD

• Pupils: 251 pupils, 152 boys/101 girls, including 32 boy choristers; choristers board, the rest day. • Ages: 4–13 • C of E, other faiths welcome, though choristers mostly Christian. • Fees: Day £12,138–£13,068; Boarding + £7,557; Choristers £7,557 pa • Independent

Tel: 020 7248 5156
Email: admissions@spcs.london.sch.uk
Website: www.spcslondon.com

Headmaster: Since 2009, Mr Neil Chippington MA (Cantab) FRCO (forties). Music scholar at Cranleigh, organ scholar at Cambridge, Fellow of the Royal College of Organists, music is certainly in his blood. Came from Winchester College where he was a housemaster for eight years and, having himself been a quirister (chorister) at Winchester Cathedral, seems to be the ideal person to have taken the responsibility of 30 boarding choristers and a school bursting with music. Says he wants to make sure that all children reach their academic potential and are stretched to the limit of their abilities without the school becoming a hothouse. Feels it is crucial to get the balance right so that both choristers and day children get a wide breadth of educational experience and benefit from each other's talents.

S

Currently reviewing the curriculum, looking at different ways of approaching CE. Open minded and not afraid of change. Says 'the bottom line is to instil a love of learning'. Has introduced a more significant staff appraisal system. Communication apparently an issue when he arrived but believes he has opened up the lines. Responds quickly to emails and maintains an open door policy. Parents acknowledge this improvement. Married with two small sons, the elder of whom is at the school.

Entrance: Seventy on list for 20 available places at 4+, so best to put children down early. Informal assessment in November before year of entry. More places at 7+ when boarding choristers also start. January assessment and short test for day children (also taken by those in pre-prep); informal audition with director of music for choristers, followed by formal audition and same academic test as day children. More places for choristers at 8+ and occasionally 9+. Choristers' fees paid by Dean and Chapter of St Paul's Cathedral with parents paying boarding fee. This will carry on even if a boy's voice breaks early. If in need, bursaries available for day children also. Head is keen to build up a fund and expand this.

Exit: At 11+ and 13+ to a mixture of London day schools and top boarding schools. Majority of girls at 11+ though head eager to keep girls and maintain balance. Choristers mostly to boarding schools at 13+. An impressive number of music and the occasional academic scholarships. Westminster appears high among day schools, with City of London (girls and boys), Highgate, Forest School and JAGS also featuring. King's Canterbury popular amongst a wide selection of good boarding schools. Recently, Eton, Stowe, Uppingham and Oundle have all offered academic and music scholarships. Famous ex pupils include Alastair Cooke (England cricket captain) and Simon Russell Beale (actor).

Remarks: A small school, nestling in the precincts of St Paul's Cathedral, providing an excellent all round education in a traditional setting with a formal, spiritual context to everything it does. In amongst the hustle and bustle of the City of London, an oasis of orderliness and calm. Boy choristers have been around since 1123, originally linked to a grammar school which became St Paul's School, London, about 400 years later. Only tenuous links remain. In 1989, the Dean and Chapter decided to expand the tiny choristers' only school to include day boys as well. Girls arrived in 1998 and the school grew to the size it is today.

Two low concrete towers house the classrooms and are linked by the school hall, the gym, the library and various other communal activity areas. We seemed to wander up and down and across as enthusiastic pupils showed us their school but 'once you know the two towers it's easy,' they assured us. Three lovely bright classrooms for the pre-prep years, two each for years 3 and 4, then subject-based doubling up as home rooms from year 5 onwards.

Broad-based curriculum with all subjects well taught. Parents praise 'inspirational teachers' who are 'passionate about everything they do'. Average age 39 seems about right. Our guides also spoke enthusiastically about their teachers, singling out science and Latin/Greek as exceptional. Certainly pupils did look happy and absorbed in the excellent science lab, however the French class we looked in on appeared chaotic. Mixed ability classes throughout with some discreet setting, particularly in years 7 and 8. Previously some complaints about lack of preparation for 11+ entrance exams but new head is driving this forward and has already made important changes, revamping part of the curriculum and timetabling non-verbal reasoning, study skills etc into earlier years. Parents very happy about this. Creative writing, apparently, a great strength. Latin compulsory from year 5. Modern languages not the strongest

point, though French taught from the beginning and Spanish available as an extra. Head's wife a linguist, so change could be in the air. Interactive white boards in classrooms and new IT suite. All special needs problems dealt with by head of learning support. Teachers flag up concerns and he is immediately involved. Any necessary help is provided, mostly free of charge. Additional staff available for one-to-one and in-class support when necessary. Parents kept fully in the picture and involved from the beginning.

Reasonable art. Studio also contains a printing press (given by the Stationers' Company) and a kiln for firing imaginative clay models. Location excellent for visiting Tate Modern as part of extended art lesson. Drama strongish and everyone gets a chance to take part in a production. As one of our guides said, 'if you're not particularly musical, you can still do drama and have fun'. LAMDA exam course available.

Inevitably the greatest strength is music, huge both instrumentally and vocally. Virtually every child in the school learns an instrument of his or her choice (no bagpipes!). Choristers learn two, piano being compulsory. Over 300 music lessons given each week, beginners all the way to grade 8. At least six different choirs plus 15 orchestras and ensembles from classic to rock band. Something for everyone you might say. For musical, creative children it is a great place to be. Opportunities abound. Choristers are in the minority but it is their talent that is the backbone of the school. Head feels that one of the most crucial things he needs to do is clarify the way they are perceived. The day school exists because of them and they are getting a wider breadth of education because of the day school. Thus both sides are gaining a huge amount and it is important to maintain the balance. Choristers are acquiring an excellent academic education and day pupils are seeing, hearing and being involved in music of an exceptionally high standard. All of them are equally at home in the Cathedral, which they treat as an extension of the school. Assemblies and occasional special services held and the majority get the chance to sing there. A parent told us 'the Christmas service was something to behold. About six or seven different choirs were fielded, including a combined one which seemed to involve most of the school'.

Choristers have a pretty heavy schedule with singing practice before school every morning, evensong on Tuesdays, Wednesdays, Fridays and Saturdays plus Saturday morning rehearsals and Sunday services. Alongside a multitude of other occasions when they have to perform. One of the first things the head did for them was to negotiate Monday evenings off as well as Thursdays. Seems only fair after an action-packed weekend. He also stresses the importance of watching the development of their voices and becoming more aware of change – necessary with the earlier physical growth that now occurs. Thirteen-year-old trebles are rarer. Both the cathedral's director of music and organist are also committed to their personal development and nurture.

A father said, 'sport at the school is active, fun and inclusive'. Despite its inner city site, it is well catered for. Pupils are bused to Coram's Fields and Regent's Park for seasonal activities. Matches fielded against other schools in hockey, football, cricket, rounders, fencing and netball. Have been runners up in U12 London Schools' Cricket Association Cup, winners of the Girls' Football South London Tournament and pupils have been selected for the U10 National Fencing Squad and the U11 Surrey County Cricket squad. Also swim at local baths recreationally and competitively. Rubber surfaced playground, marked up for ball games, for the prep where teachers also arrange impromptu games and sports practice. Brand new, larger, grass and woodchip playground with climbing equipment for the pre-prep. Older children allowed to play quiet games here but not allowed to climb.

A variety of after-school clubs, mainly on Thursdays to enable choristers to join in, but on other days too. Range from cookery to dance to computer etc. Bound to be something for everyone. Also children may stay to do supervised prep at school, charged as an extra but useful for working parents. Plenty of outings and expeditions, academic, cultural and sporty. Home and occasionally abroad. A lot to see within walking distance as well.

Parents stress the happy atmosphere – 'it has been the making of our little boy' – (of a chorister) and 'our unsettled, troublemaker has been transformed' – (of a dayboy). 'Very good discipline, they don't tolerate bad behaviour'. General feeling that children are treated as individuals, academically stretched and made to work to their own levels; that the school is 'well managed and well ordered'. Much of this appears to lie in the vertical tutor system. Pupils are assigned to a tutor from day one and, in normal circumstances, remain with him/her until they leave the school. Thus tutor groups mixed in both ability and age and there is easy rapport between all children across the school. The older ones love helping the younger ones.

According to parents excellent pastoral care, particularly for the boarders. 'They get well cared for, individual treatment and feel they are part of a family'. Several raved about the deputy head (pastoral) who, they say, really carried the school through recent difficult times. Definitely feel there's a good team in place now.

Effective and active PTA. General feeling is that head is in tune with all pupils and ideal person to be running the boarding section as well. Watch this spot for further developments.

St Paul's Catholic Primary School, Thames Ditton

Hampton Court Way, Thames Ditton, KT7 0LP

• Pupils: 140 girls and 150 boys; all day • Ages: 4–11 • RC • State

Tel: 020 8398 6791
Email: info@stpauls–thamesditton.surrey.sch.uk
Website: www.stpauls–thamesditton.surrey.sch.uk

Head Teacher: Since 1990, Mrs Fionnuala Johnson, BEd (late forties), married with two children. Garners huge respect from parents, who regard her as the architect of the school's (and their children's) success. Descriptions of her vary along the spectrum from 'strong, impressive leader', through 'powerful personality' to 'formidable' (we'll vouch for that) – but most also mention her caring side. 'The children adore her – tempered by due reverence,' said one mother. 'I've seen children run across the playground to hug her,' said another.

Has plenty to say about the school – of which she is fiercely proud – and is full of plans and ideas for the future. She knows all the children by name – and promises to keep this up even when the school has doubled in size. As it is, parents wonder at her grasp of all the smallest details of their lives, and the praise continues – 'she's fantastic – the school is as good as it is because of her. She talks to the children quietly and they all listen – she never needs to raise her voice. They want to please her, and if ever they are in trouble and sent to see her they are not frightened but sorry they have incurred her disapproval'.

Entrance: Heavy over-subscription has allowed funding for expansion from single to two-form entry. School accepts 60 children per year and the pressure has eased up a little – but Catholic families whose children have been baptised (and you need the certificates to prove it) still take 99 per cent of the places. The school serves the parishes of Cobham, Esher and Thames Ditton, a mostly white, middle-class lot. It is non-selective academically – regular church attendance will get you a long way.

Exit: Where to go next is the most vexing question for parents. 'I just wish this school had a secondary equivalent,' sighed one mother, echoing the view of many. St Paul's pupils are guaranteed entry to the RC Salesian School in Chertsey, but few choose it. Among the more popular choices of secondary school are Wimbledon College, Ursuline High, Tiffin School and Tiffin Girls School in Kingston.

Remarks: An academically strong school with a solid Catholic ethos. Set back from a busy dual carriageway, in functional rather than beautiful accommodation, purpose-built in the mid-1960s. There is plenty of space, including a large playground and a grass playing field. The smart new block built to provide the necessary seven extra classrooms does make the older classrooms look a little tired, but good art displays line the walls and lift the spirits. A well-resourced school, with a shiny IT suite and three well-stocked libraries. All classrooms are spacious and light; and each is named after a saint – reflecting the importance of Catholic teaching at the school.

The Catholic Church schools' 'search for Excellence' theme is seen as key here – both in the spiritual and academic development of the children. Academic standards are high. At key stage 2, 93 per cent gained level 4 and above in English, and 100 per cent in maths and science – there were more level 5s than 4s in all three subject areas. Many parents tell us that this is a school for academic girls rather than non-academic boys. Even parents who are not quite so dogmatic believe the environment is more suited to the academically inclined. 'It is not a hothouse, but there is just a general expectation of achievement,' said one mother. Mrs Johnson disagrees strongly – so does Ofsted, which also singles out the SEN teaching for praise. The number with SEN is below the national average but those with SEN do as well as their peers. There is an SEN teacher with teaching assistants on hand and the school also brings in outside specialists.

High praise from parents for an able and effective teaching staff. 'Every time we change classes we say we wish we could have that teacher again – and then the next one is just another delight,' said a mother who has had children at the school for many years. 'Discipline is strong, the children know their boundaries and understand them,' said another. There is plenty of praise and reward, with a system of highly-prized stickers and certificates, not just for academic work but also for helpfulness, cheerfulness and so on. Prayers are said at the end of each day, and children attend mass regularly. The religious teaching really kicks in at year 3 as the children are preparing for Holy Communion.

All the parents we spoke to agree their children are happy at the school, which they describe time and time again as 'very caring'. Pupils are respectful and polite – and also extremely smart – with even the reception children wearing neat ties. 'The fact they can get a four-year-old to tie a tie says a lot about this school,' enthused one mother. Mixed feelings abound over sports provision, with some parents feeling it is not a particular strength, especially among the boys – though the school does well in the borough in netball and cross-country.

A real sense of community, which staff and parents are keen to maintain as the school expands. Some parents have expressed concerns that the strong sense of community they have enjoyed may be eroded as the school grows. However, the niggles are few and far between, and overall the positive comments far outweigh the negatives. It is still a first choice for parents seeking a good education for their child in a distinctively Catholic environment.

S

St Peter's Eaton Square CofE Primary School

Lower Belgrave Street, London, SW1W 0NL

- Pupils: 280 primary and 30 part-time nursery. • Ages: 3–11
- C of E • State

Tel: 020 7641 4230
Email: office@stpeaton.org.uk
Website: www.stpeaton.org.uk

Head: Since 2010, Ms Nicola Cottier BEd Cantab (forties). Previously head of St Matthew's, Westminster, since 1996. Educated at Sutton High, her first job was at Moira House, an independent girls' school in Sussex. She has worked in the Bahamas, United States, Canada and Wales, but most recently in London schools with church links. She is married with two children, and lives in Kew. She revolutionised the music provision at St Matthew's, where she was described as an 'inspirational headteacher' who 'created the most wonderful spirit in the school'. She is hugely enthusiastic, rhapsodising about the 'fantastic' ethos and supportive community at St Peter's.

Entrance: Thirty part-time nursery places. No automatic transfer to reception – must re-apply and meet criteria. Nearly all of the places go to baptised children whose families worship regularly at St Peter's Church Eaton Square; preference after that to siblings, then to baptised children who attend other churches without their own church school. Families come from a wide area and a huge range of backgrounds – 'duchesses to dustmen'. Apply through the local authority, with supplementary school form, during autumn term a year before entry. Takes 50 children into reception.

Exit: Girls to Grey Coat Hospital, St Marylebone, Lady Margaret's; boys to London Nautical, Pimlico Academy etc. Over half to independent schools: Westminster Under School, JAGS, City of London, Godolphin and Latymer, Streatham & Clapham High etc. Children not encouraged to move on to independents at seven or eight: 'We won't go out of our way to support it. It is disruptive, and our children do very well getting the places they want at 11.' A parent commented: 'Why would you want to move earlier when they all do so well here?'

Remarks: Very popular and over-subscribed central London primary school, tucked away in a side street just round the corner from Victoria Station. Consistently excellent, lively teaching, with each child's progress closely tracked. The majority of pupils reach level 5 in year 6: a huge achievement. Languages strong: Spanish from year 3 upwards. Dedicated IT suite with 30 computers. Inclusion Manager has responsibility for EAL and G&T as well as those with SEN. Teaching assistants deployed to support children as needed. Parents also pitch in as eg volunteer readers. Good at spotting problems with vulnerable children and liaising with outside agencies where necessary. 'We always cater for a wide range of needs.' Two reception classes of 25; higher up, the children in each of years 1/2, 3/4 and 4/5 are divided by age into three classes over two year groups.

'We are blessed that we have really fabulous music.' No orchestra, but peripatetic teachers for recorder, violin, drums, guitar, piano and brass, as well as class music lessons, trips to concerts at the Barbican etc, singing at the Royal Albert Hall and at Friday's Sung Eucharist service. Very little space for sport on site – the hall is used for gym and PE and the small, soft-surface playground has a climbing wall along one side. However, they swim at the Queen Mother Sports Centre (notable successes in galas), play sports in Battersea Park and Hyde Park (year 1 were off for a multi-skills session when we visited) and borrow Westminster School's Vincent Square sports site. Professional sports coaches run twice-weekly sessions, and football, cricket and tennis teams play in inter-school matches. 'It's such a cramped site that we try to get them out as much as possible.'

Enrichment is a buzz word here and there are plenty of outings – 'It's a fabulous situation: everything is on our doorstep' – to eg the V&A, National Gallery, London Zoo. Year 6 visits Sayers Croft field centre in Surrey. Girls from Grey Coat Hospital do work experience at St Peter's, and pupils visit Westminster City School for their science week. Strong tradition of raising funds for charity.

St Peter's was first mentioned in an 1860s survey as an infants' school in Ecclestone Square. Moved to its present site, donated by the Marquess of Westminster, in 1872; became an infant and junior school in 1949. Building and site compact, but even the basement nursery classrooms are light, bright and cheerful; nursery has its own indoor/outdoor partly-covered play area. The upper floor classrooms, carved from the top half of a hall, have beautiful large, round windows. Airy feel but very cramped for space: every nook and cranny has at least three different uses. A major building project in 2012 remodelled the school to create sufficient classrooms to introduce two forms incrementally into each year group.

School follows Anglo-Catholic tradition and there are services at school and in Westminster Abbey as well as in the strongly-linked namesake church: clergy pop in and out and are available for counselling. The church interior, redesigned after an anti-Catholic arson attack 20 years ago, is a beautiful, simple, open space which 'lends itself to our nativity plays' and is also the setting for year 6 productions, concerts and speech days as well as services.

A tightly-run ship: children are neat and tidy, with tucked-in shirts and tied-back hair. They are orderly in class and move quietly around the building. The atmosphere is welcoming, friendly and purposeful. Parents appreciate the combination of excellent behaviour, kind ethos and inspiring teaching. 'It is a warm and safe place,' said one.

Active PTA which organises social events such as Burns Night and helps with eg Easter Fair. This is not a local school – families come from a wide area – but there is a strong community of parents, many of whom also meet at church events, including those who attended the school themselves. Children who have moved on to secondary school come back to do work experience and spread their news. 'We know they do well wherever they go.'

St Peter's School

Harefield, Lympstone, Exmouth, Devon, EX8 5AU

- Pupils: 265 boys and girls; 13 boarders • Ages: 3–13 • C of E
- Fees: Day £6,450–£11,040; Boarding £16,620 pa • Independent

Tel: 01395 272148
Email: hmoffice@stpetersprep.co.uk
Website: www.stpetersprep.co.uk

Headmaster: Since 2009, Mr Noel Neeson BEd NPQH (late thirties); was educated at Notre Dame High in Glasgow before reading maths at his native city's university. A lifelong supporter of Celtic, he spent two years as a prep school teacher at St Aloysius College in Glasgow before moving south of the border to Crackley Hall, Kenilworth, where he became deputy head. Turned around a failing Catholic primary school in Leamington Spa before being appointed to St Peter's.

S

'Very, very good,' say parents, who appreciate how he 'takes on board what people say.' 'Distinctly different from his predecessors' and 'communicates his objectives very clearly,' we were told. Man of faith and passionate about his pupils' welfare and progress. Children like the fact that he listens to them first. Energetic, brimming with ideas, he champions assessment for learning and the St Peter's Baccalaureate, which is generating interest in some educational circles.

Married to Juliet (whom he met on the staff at Crackley Hall); they live in centre of school with daughter, Beatrice who is in the pre-prep. Juliet provides pastoral support for girls and counsels according to need; also teaches RS part-time. Head enjoys watching Exeter Chiefs and playing golf at Aberdovey whilst on holiday in Wales. 'One of the best heads St Peter's has seen,' said one long-term parent.

Entrance: Non-selective: 'not saturated with tests on taster days,' we were told. Takes rising threes upwards; staff will decide on admission either into KG or nursery class (voucher system operates but those not aiming at pre-prep go to back of the queue).

Exit: Most remain to 13 and proceed to south-west independent day and boarding schools (Exeter, Blundells, Wellington, King's Taunton, Maynard). Over half obtain scholarships (15 in 2013); net is being cast wider to include Badminton, Canford and Sherborne. Small number leave at end of year 6, mainly to Colyton and Torquay grammars.

Remarks: Founded in 1882, St Peter's enjoys a stunning position (a sign near the main entrance invites visitors to 'please enjoy the view') overlooking the Exe estuary. Built for a local notable in late 1820s, Harefield House was in the hands of the Peters family (a portrait of late Admiral Sir Arthur Peters can be seen on the main staircase) for a century until 1949 when the then head, Mr Theophilus Rhys Jones (grandfather of HRH Sophie), moved the school here from Exmouth. Current bursar and a former head are co-proprietors; school is run by an executive management team, assisted by a broad-based committee of reference; estate trustees have considerable say on development issues.

Breeds 'aspirational pupils' of all abilities; hugely committed staff are encouraged to 'go with their own ideas.' Head's brainchild is home-grown baccalaureate which encompasses three key learning skills: curiosity, finding and presenting. Core academic areas are balanced by creative and performing arts, plus sport and personal qualities. All children are marked throughout school for effort. Emphasis on personalised learning: children present their understanding using any medium which suits them (which may well not be essay writing). Senior schools have shown considerable interest in this approach. Experienced academic team track children's achievement with emphasis on early intervention.

Co-educational since 1974, balance between sexes fluctuates from year to year; overall numbers close to capacity. Small (14 bed) boarding facility with houseparents in charge; separate dormitories and combined games and common-room areas. 'Head makes a fuss of the boarders,' said one boarding mum whose son 'simply loves it.' Flexi-boarding (at £36 per night) remains a handy option for parents; Friday night provision includes entails sprog collection by 10am on Saturday.

Site includes three main outside areas. Lovely cricket pitch with own pavilion (highlight is annual game against Lympstone village team); adventure playground, separate 10-acre field nearby (used for athletics and rugby) is reached via safe path which snakes its way through much-used forest school woodland area; adjacent smaller field used for pre-prep sports as well as daily activities. New Astroturf for mini hockey and tennis; outside heated swimming pool in use between May and September. New adventure playground. Refloored sports hall (squash court also in complex) provides a full size basketball court; doubles up as a venue for assemblies and smaller scale productions.

Discrete early years' section located in somewhat dated timber-clad classrooms: 'we're more interested in what goes on inside,' a mother told us. Carefully zoned outside play areas; new outside performance facility has sound system provided through parental fund-raising. Cosy KG classroom boasts highest staff:pupil ratio. Easy transfer to nursery (shell 3) and 90 per cent proceed to reception (shell 4) classes. Forest school and outside learning an important element: we saw tinies enjoying hot chocolate by a camp fire.

We liked the way that planning, monitoring progress and regular information sharing with parents all figure prominently as part of a whole school approach. Goals for youngest broken down into 'stepping stones'. Wide range of reading resources; some nursery children are 'reading ready', we were told. Obvious focus on language development: separate 'time to talk' area promotes confidence; home/school diaries used daily; plenty of imaginative numeracy work: we saw youngest children measuring paper worms and making numbers with them. Lively classroom displays are linked to changing themes. Rôle play areas mutate from fairy castles to butterfly gardens. Regular pre-prep assemblies: classes take turns to present items. Music and French from the start.

Junior years in separate red brick building. Streaming in English and maths from year 1, and from year 5 upwards teaching is subject-based. Top set all sit CE 11+ exams. Separate scholarship and CE sets in years 7 and 8. German and Spanish introduced in addition to French from year 7 plus Latin for scholars. High proportion of all-round scholarships obtained attributed to breadth of school's curriculum.

Seniors shuttle for lessons between outside classrooms, the main house and modernised science laboratory in wing of the sports hall. Refurbished library on ground floor of main house is focus for research including computers, book related activities throughout year eg for World Book Day. Large music room is used for classroom teaching and rehearsals. New ICT suite on first floor provides for class-based work and is carefully monitored. Large art and DT area in separate hut buzzes with creativity: scholars have own carrels and produce work which impressed us by its range and quality. Every pupil had picture in last art exhibition.

Two formal parents' evenings during year; staff often meet parents after school in flagpole area to sort out small concerns. E-mail access to all staff and regular newsletters.

Sixty-nine children currently on learning support register; two children are statemented. Strong, switched on remedial help with 'open doors' policy: 'nothing should ever be a shock to parents,' said SENCo, who came to St Peter's with 11 years' experience at Belmont Primary (qv), Chiswick. Range of difficulties includes SpLD and mild Aspergers; to date no child has failed to get a place at a mainstream senior school.

Exceptionally strong sports record maintained over long period with more than a handful making at least county level representative teams. Usual major games for boys and girls; school has really shone at rugby (undefeated 1st XV), netball and squash recently; two boys recently represented English prep school U13 rugby team on tour to France and school also has current England prep schools' U13 squash champions. All children participate at some level; good fixture lists with south-west schools, matches on Wednesday afternoons.

Sixty per cent of pupils have individual music tuition; director is supported by 14 peripatetic staff. School hosts Devon Youth Choir/Orchestra and Brass Band. Regular music assemblies, concerts and performances for soloists and groups throughout year. Activities include chamber choir, woodwind groups, brass ensemble and pop cantata. External festivals, competitions and evensong at Wellington School. Most recent tour to Edinburgh. Large scale dramatic productions staged in Exeter's Barnfield theatre.

Jolly lot of pupils with lots to do. No mobile phones allowed during school day. Staff will 'all go the extra mile,' we were told. 'The way everyone joins in to help with school productions speaks volumes,' said deputy head who runs Cross Keys (outdoor adventure) programme. Pupils get the 'swallows and Amazons' treatment and leave knowing they are achievers. Plenty of after school activity with full range on Friday afternoons. Options start in year 1 and include drama, yoga and horse riding, not to mention cooking and sailing. Visits start early on and full blown tours feature at upper end and include year 7 stay at Château de la Baudonnière, artists staying in St Ives and ski trip to Andorra.

Pupils come from wide catchment area; many use fleet of liveried minibuses. School day for seniors ends at 5pm. Year 8 pupils take on responsibilities and have own social area. Children meet in tutor groups at start and end of each day. Holiday programme (site closes for only one week in summer) is heavily subscribed. Supportive Friends of St Peters run fund-raisers and social events such as annual ball and more recently (de rigueur given head's origins) Burns Night celebration. Notable alumni include olympic yachtsman Ben Rhodes, journalist Anna Tyzack and children's TV entertainer, Dominic Wood.

Bursaries granted on individual basis; substantial number of internal scholarships awarded for years 7 and 8 at head's discretion.

A school with a 'real heart' that may be short on some mod cons but compensates by giving value for money. Unique blend of progressive philosophy and traditional standards in a beautiful setting. Obviously happy children who achieve beyond expectations. A breath of fresh air in every sense.

St Philip's School

6 Wetherby Place, London, SW7 4NE

• Pupils: 110 boys, all day • Ages: 7–13 • RC • Fees: £13,200 pa
• Independent

Tel: 020 7373 3944
Email: info@stphilipschool.co.uk
Website: www.stphilipschool.co.uk

Headmaster: Since 1990, Mr Harry Biggs-Davison MA (mid-fifties and bearing a passing resemblance to Daniel Craig). Educated St Philip's, Downside, Fitzwilliam College, Cambridge, where he read geography. Immediately returned to St Philip's to teach games in 1978 and has stayed ever since. Married with two grown up sons, his wife, Anna, has, for the last three years, been an invaluable part of the teaching team as the SENCo and with her own year 4 class. Head speaks of the school (his school) with enthusiasm and pragmatism, and of the boys and his staff with insight, pride and affection – and a healthy dose of good humour. When asked about St Philip's in the post-Biggs-Davison era (not that this is yet on the cards), expresses his hope that he will have a successor in the pipeline, 'in plenty of time', so that the inevitable disruption will be kept to a minimum.

Entrance: Boys come from local pre-prep and primary schools and most live within three miles of the school. Entry is into year 3 (10 boys) and year 4 (10 boys). School over-subscribed at both points but so far the temptation to select purely on the basis of ability has been resisted. Priority is given to brothers of current pupils and to Roman Catholics. After that, references from schools and observations made during an activity afternoon form the basis of any decision to offer a place. The head is well aware that for some parents St Philip's may represent a fall back option; understandably he prefers to offer places to boys and parents for whom it is a firm favourite. It's hardly a gamble; there are plenty of parents who simply like what they see so the school does not need to change its modus operandi.

Exit: At 13+ roughly half to London day schools and half to boarding schools, including St Paul's, Westminster, Harrow, Wellington, Downside, Ampleforth, Radley, The Oratory (Reading), The London Oratory, Charterhouse, Eton, Worth.

Remarks: A school with few pretensions and a big heart, St Philip's feels like a large, slightly unconventional family. It reflects the best of Roman Catholicism; the religious ethos that underpins the day-to-day life of the school produces genuine humanity and flexibility in the education of the young boys for whom it caters. The boys themselves are confident, polite and enthusiastic and willingly engage with any interested adult.

The number of pupils is generally steady at around 110 and the average class size is 20, while the ratio of pupils to full-time staff is 7:1. About 80 per cent of pupils have British passports but many have dual nationality with numbers from Europe and South America. However, this does not mean that the pupil body is a transitory one and most stay from beginning to end.

Mr BD says happily that there is 'room for eccentrics here', and we saw evidence to support this, although 'quirky' might be a fairer description. Staff are a good mix – many are young, several have been there for years, even decades. Stable staffing has not led to stagnation; teaching we observed was dynamic, technology is used to good effect across the curriculum but without sacrificing the rigour of more traditional methods. The balance seems just about right. In a year 8 Latin lesson boys were highlighting words they had problems remembering, followed by a session based around a series of pictures to assist those who were visual learners. The image of a shouting clam (clamo – to call, shout) or a vampire sinking its teeth into its victim's jugular (neco – to kill, slay) certainly seemed to do the trick.

Music has a high profile; more than half learn at least one instrument. The young director of music is one of the country's top organists: he played the organ for the Pope in 2010 and is credited by Mr BD for the number of music scholarships and exhibitions won recently by St Philip's pupils to eg Ampleforth and Winchester.

Differentiation in the earlier years and streaming in year 8 enables effective teaching across the ability range and impressive results at 13. Learning support is offered both inside and outside the classroom for the relatively few boys with mild learning difficulties. School accepts that life is not always easy for some children, often through no fault of their own, and sensitive, expert counselling is also available for those perceived to be in need. Head says parental expectations are managed through trust and 'not being too dogmatic'. He admits they are 'having to raise the bar', but some parents we spoke to expressed concern that the academic push does not come early enough for the pre-tests and opportunities are missed.

School housed in a red-brick Victorian building cleverly arranged to best accommodate pupils (and staff). Science and ICT are situated on the top floor, 'the only purpose-built part of the school'. Sport takes place off site at Barn Elms playing fields (which are currently being redeveloped in what Mr BD claims is 'an exciting fashion') and at Fulham Pools. The parents' association is very active and, allegedly, organises 'the best match teas in London'.

The outdoor space into which boys spill enthusiastically at break and lunchtime is something of a gem: a garden rather than a playground. It is an oasis of green with fruit trees, climbing roses, shrubs, flowers, vegetables and herbs. The boys play games around and within the vegetation as well as in the slightly more open areas where table tennis tables and badminton nets are erected. There are quiet corners for the quieter boys and plenty of staff on duty or simply outside because it's a great place to be. Mr Biggs-Davison admits that 'by year 8 the boys are outgrowing the space', but, of course, that is exactly as it should be.

St Richard's School

Brendenbury Court, Bromyard, HR7 4TD

• Pupils: 140 boys and girls • Ages: 3–13 • RC, but all faiths welcome • Fees: Boarding £17,295–£18,660; Day £4,710–£12,555 pa • Independent

Tel: 01885 482491
Email: schooloffice@st-richards.org.uk
Website: www.st-richards.org.uk

Headmaster: Since January 2014, Mr Fred de Falbe, previously deputy head at Knightsbridge School. Mr de Falbe began his teaching career aged 18 in Honduras, before gaining a BA in theology at Manchester University and joining the film business, later going back to teaching after a year in Australia. Since then he has worked in state secondary schools in London and Devon and also started and managed a residential property company. Married to Juliet; they have three teenage children.

Entrance: Most pupils arrive in the prep school via the nursery and pre-prep, but others are welcome to apply at any time. The school is non-selective, but likes to meet parents and potential pupils. Minibuses for day children run from Leominster, Hereford and Worcester. Boarders tend to come from further afield, but the opportunity for flexi-boarding sometimes lures those living nearby into full-time boarding in preparation for secondary school.

Exit: To a wide range of schools, though fewer these days to the distant Catholic schools of Ampleforth, Downside and Stonyhurst. Malvern, Shrewsbury, Prior Park, Cheltenham Ladies, King's Worcester, Tudor Hall, St Mary's, Calne: it's horses for courses (literally, sometimes), and a number of senior school heads and registrars commented on the reliability and open friendliness of children from St Richard's. Ten scholarships in 2013 – music, riding, drama, academic and all-rounder.

Remarks: Anyone who fails to respond to the beautiful setting should perhaps be looking elsewhere, since the building and its 35 acres of Herefordshire countryside play a crucial part in the ethos of the place. Ofsted, who would probably describe the Taj Mahal as a pretty nifty tomb, commented that 'the grounds... are developed extremely well to provide for outstanding outdoor learning and recreation.' In this lovely Fern Hill setting, children disport themselves 'in the sun that is young once only.' They have a lot of fun. That's the word.

The main building was erected in 1876 by a young army officer who had received the whole village of Bredenbury as a wedding present. Later it was bought by a profligate land owner, who spent most of his time in Kenya's Happy Valley, though records relate that both the vastness of his girth and his addiction to alcohol prevented his being a full party member. Of course no whiffs of his lifestyle permeate the building, apart from his additions of a ballroom (now the assembly hall) and a lovely vaulted dining room (now the chapel). St Richard's School moved into the house in 1968 and the last squire-head, who retired in 2005, turned it into a charitable trust.

The school has moved into the 21st century without eradicating its gentlemanly feel of tweeds, eccentricity and individuality. The very wide and detailed list of school policies appears on the website, a wise precaution appreciated by parents.

'You know where you stand,' said one. The children can feel safe and secure in their activities, but the school has retained a sense of proportion. The delightful Forest School offers opportunities for adventure and discovery. The pre-prep prospectus even has a wonderful picture on the front of a young boy climbing up a gnarled old tree with the legend, 'Exercising young Minds!'

One distinguished, not as young as he used to be, former pupil told us that his parents had chosen to send him to St Richard's because during their initial tour they had been taken into the kitchen (how many schools would do that?) where they had found a pony tethered to the Aga. You're unlikely to find that these days, but ponies have been known to look in at the windows of classrooms. Like so much at St Richard's, there's a lot of fun to be had, but it is a serious business, whether it's preparing for dressage competitions or hunter trials. And, most importantly, those horses need to be looked after. And if you don't own a horse and keep it at school? In truth, most of the children don't. There's no sense of a social divide here; no snobbery, no world-weary sophistication.

Lessons seem lively and fun; bright and airy classrooms lead off rabbit warrens of corridors in a building that is comforting rather than snazzy. We were delighted to see old style desks with lids and inkwells; teaching facilities are good (newly refurbished art room, imaginatively laid out French rooms, book-filled English room) without being flashy. The children reported that 'some teachers are very funny'. Intentionally or not? We didn't discover, but clearly there exist excellent relations between staff and pupils from the tinies to the prefects. The school usually wins an impressive fistful of scholarships.

Bedrooms are genuinely homely and inviting. Many new and junior children begin flexi-boarding one or two nights a week and build up from there. A number of day pupils choose to board eventually because it is such obvious good fun and because of the friendships it develops and confirms. There is a good routine in place: supper followed by supervised prep for the older children, games or reading upstairs for the younger ones, plus a well-structured weekend activity programme. Boarders, who have a large, airy sitting room with comfy chairs, sofas and a television, spoke highly of the matrons and many staff who live in the main house and get involved in activities.

Some schools embarking on the great facilities race seem to have lost sight of the basic fact that they exist for children, not for impressing parents. We've seen sports halls so clean you wonder whether anyone ever uses them, and with such sophisticated equipment that they can only be used by children when supervised by highly trained certificated adults who have been on endless courses. St Richard's sports hall is really a barn, named after a certain Sergeant Major Hirons, who taught PE at St Richard's between 1920 and 1983. The school has launched an appeal for a new sports hall, but it will not be 'a place where you have to remove your shoes before you go in. Children must be allowed to horse around. During break, this is their market place.' The same is true of their climbing wall, which is far wider than high. The result is that children can use it without sending for a mountain guide.

Although it is a Catholic school, around two-thirds of pupils are not Catholics. However, mass is celebrated on Saturday mornings, presided over by a real live monk, and at other assemblies those attending are invited to reflect. Reflect on their own behaviour, how they treat others, how they might have done better in certain circumstances. It's good to 'pause awhile from letters to be wise', and it surely contributes to the overall happiness of the school.

The setting is like a country house where the owner rather eccentrically has lots of children to stay, including a conservatory with an enormous fig tree growing through it; a magnificent staircase; Darcy the dog wandering around the dining room during lunch; beautiful pictures everywhere; a polar bear; chickens, horses and a shy terrapin. There are lakes for canoeing; grounds for camping in and learning about

S

survival; horses grazing alongside jumps in a nearby field; and everywhere, as far as the eye can see, luscious Herefordshire countryside with a distant hint of neighbouring Elgar.

There is, undeniably, an old fashioned feel to this country prep school. The school's insistence on good manners and courtesy might seem so. But we saw nothing false about the children's open friendliness and willingness to engage. They wore their manners as easily as an old pair of brogues, happy, bouncy and natural in a school which does what it says on the label. It prepares the young for adulthood.

Saint Ronan's School

Water Lane, Hawkhurst, TN18 5DJ

- Pupils: 315 pupils. Mainly day with flexi boarding. • Ages: 3–13+
- C of E • Fees: £9,093–£15,594 pa Boarding +£33 per night
- Independent

Tel: 01580 752271
Email: info@saintronans.co.uk
Website: www.saintronans.co.uk

Headmaster: Since 2003, Mr William Trelawny-Vernon (forties). Very much a joint enterprise with wife Emma (she's the Trelawny, he's the Vernon) – who is both registrar and head of history. Known as Mr and Mrs TV to pupils and parents alike. The couple met at Exeter, where Mr TV read biology. Previously at Stowe School for 12 years, including posts as a biology teacher and seven years as housemaster of Chatham House. 'Universally loved', according to parents.

The business is in the blood – his father was head of Hordle House (now Walhampton) in Hampshire. Four children – the youngest at the prep, the other three have moved on to King's Canterbury. The family left the head's accommodation to move off site in 2005 and they eschew the parental dinner party circuit, believing it's important to maintain a distance. Parents think they get it right, as one commented: 'One of the areas in which the school excels is in managing very successfully the line between parental involvement and keeping parents distanced when necessary.'

Both grew up in a four-child family, and with their own gang of four have that deep respect for fairness and equality of treatment which comes from big families. 'Neither of us likes the concept of the alpha child,' says Mr TV.

School and family is everything to Mr TV – time off finds him socialising with the wider family, and stress relief comes by sitting on his tractor and mowing the grass, or researching the history of the two families. Both are content with home and hearth, or as Emma puts it, 'We're like labradors sitting in front of the fire'. Holidays take them to the West Country, home of Emma's ancestral seat (her brother John inherited the Salusbury-Trelawny Baronetcy).

Entrance: All children attend a taster day, and children seeking places in year 3 and above will be assessed by the class teacher and take verbal and non-verbal tests. Intake covers wide-ranging abilities, but all are expected to pass common entrance or the Cranbrook grammar tests, so, 'There will be a couple of children where we will have an honest dialogue with the parents and tell them that their child's needs are not going to be met here,' says Mr TV.

Scholarships are available for academic, music, art and sporting talents, and there are strictly monitored means-tested bursaries. Minibuses bring children in from Staplehurst, High Halden, Burwash, Wittersham, and the villages en route.

Exit: It's not the place to come if you have your sights on the West Kent grammars – despite these being in travelling distance the school doesn't encourage exit at 11. Only one or two children per year sit the Kent 11+, so it'll be a lonely experience and you'll have to find a tutor.

The majority of parents are buying into private education for the duration, although around 30 per cent of pupils go to Cranbrook grammar at 13. Key destinations include Benenden, Eastbourne, King's Canterbury, Sevenoaks, Sutton Valence and Tonbridge. Others go further afield – recently to Millfield, Worth and Eton. 'Since I've been head we have fed into 52 different schools,' says Mr TV. Parents say they are very good at helping you choose the next school – the TVs visit a clutch of senior schools together each term so they are well informed, and were freshly back from visits to Sherborne, Bryanston and Milton Abbey when we visited.

Last year 14 pupils won scholarships (out of a year group of 29), and one or two parents admit to feeling some playground one-upmanship from other parents about places and scholarships secured. 'There is competition from some of the parents, which can make you feel uncomfortable if you let it, though not between the children,' said one.

Its quirkiness ensures there is no Saint Ronan's product – and the roll of past pupils is stuffed with the great and good. 'Just look at the alumni to see how successful it is in producing movers and shakers and Boy's Own heroes,' says one parent. Indeed the list reads like a fantasy dinner party guest list; BBC security correspondent Frank Gardner, spy Donald Maclean, MP Airey Neave, Olympic rower Matthew Parrish, and travel writer (and brother of Camilla, Duchess of Cornwall) Mark Shand are just a few.

Remarks: It's a what's-not-to-love campus. Gorgeous grounds with ancient, spreading trees, inspiring views, a fishing lake, and its own 100 acre wood. And there's even a farm with pigs, alpacas, and chickens – new born piglets greeted our visit. The emphasis is on old-fashioned, wholesome fun, making every use of this natural playground. 'It's idyllic, they get to dam streams and play with pigs and chickens,' said one parent. Everything is named for Boy's Own adventures – there's the Gulch, an area around a stream ideal for making mud pies, the Saltmines, an overgrown area with secret pathways, and even the pitches have names, such as Timbuktoo (because it's a long journey to reach it). As one parent put it, 'If Enid Blyton was still around, Saint Ronan's would be exactly the sort of school she would be writing about. We are buying a truly magical childhood experience, not just a superb all-round education.'

All this romping is made easier by probably the most relaxed and colourful uniform we've seen – corduroy trousers, skirts or pinafores in sensible colours, topped with school sweatshirts in a choice of colours – pink, green, red, purple, light blue and navy. There's a formal uniform which is worn on Fridays, key days and for trips out.

The pre-prep is in a separate bright and modern building (where a corridor poster advises on 20 things to do before leaving pre-prep, such as dam a stream, make a mud pie, and hold an animal). There's also a cosy kindergarten in the former headmaster's house.

Moving up to prep brings the grandeur of Tongswood House, a Victorian mansion built by an Oxo magnate. The original features are well-maintained – including a sprung floor ballroom, now used for performances and gatherings, where frescoes of semi-naked nymphs on the ceiling liven up assembly for the older boys.

There's wood panelling and grand staircases aplenty, and classrooms are eccentrically named, such as Old Bailey, 10 Downing Street, Lombard Street (because that's where the safe was), and Windsor Castle (once a lavatory). Children scrape to their feet as you enter – standing up for grown-ups is something the teachers are strictest about, say the pupils, along with manners, being kind, and being honest.

Kindness is the rule for staff too. 'If we heard a teacher shouting at a child, they would have to come into the office and explain why,' says Mrs TV. 'We like to treat them in the same way as our own children. I don't want to be head monster,' says Mr TV.

Prefects are elected by the children in a secret ballot 'which means they go for someone who is kind and gentle, not necessarily just one of the first XV,' says Mr TV.

In reception you're greeted by a wood fire burning in the hearth – where parents come to warm up for post-match teas – and a basket of free range eggs for sale. You can also pick up school produced pork and apple juice. The head's secretary is Mrs TV's sister, known as Aunty Amanda. Parents love the reportedly eccentric ways of school admin. They talk of things being done in a Saint Ronan's way, one of 'happy chaos', which 'wouldn't suit parents who want everything done in a completely perfect planned-out way'. It looks disorganised, but it works, they say. 'We do slightly chaotic and quirky with great aplomb,' says one mother proudly.

Whilst it delivers on results (100 per cent pass rate in the Cranbrook grammar and the common entrance exam last year) it does so in a thoroughly gentle way. Prizes are given for contribution as well as achievement, and one parent says, 'although they are encouraged to achieve, this is not done in an over-competitive manner'. And pupils say that the teachers discourage any jostling for position. 'When we get exam results the teachers encourage us not to ask each other what we got, but if you get a bad mark people still always say you've done really well, or tell you what to do to improve. I once got 27 per cent but the others just said I was unlucky,' said one boy.

Setting for subjects begins in year 4, with streaming in year 8. Latin is taught from year 6.

Parents praise the efforts made to find and develop talents, which may not be academic. There are 16 peripatetic music teachers, and a DT building which develops practical skills – it's equipped with laser cutters and scroll saws, and children take woodwork from year 3, making everything from working pens to cars for drag racing.

'We are so impressed that every child has something they will achieve in. For my kids it has been music for my daughter and sport for my boys,' says a mother.

Sport has developed as the school has doubled in size in the last 10 years, 'so we can now play decent schools,' says Mr TV. There's an impressive new sports hall and an outdoor pool, and a great range of sports on offer – an extras programme one afternoon per week offers archery, fencing, golf, sailing and lacrosse. The school's sailing team are prep school champions, and one girl is in the GB under-15 team for fencing.

There's other options on extras afternoon for the non-sporty, such as farming, funky dance, fishing, bee-keeping and touch typing.

Much is made by the head and parents about keeping the pupils children as long as possible, and they are clearly successful at cocooning them. The year 8s seem younger than their peers we meet in secondary schools – no less articulate, but definitely less worldly. Parents report no divide between age groups, saying: 'You constantly see older children encouraging and playing with the younger ones, and children in year 3 aren't scared of the year 8s.'

Parents predominantly work in the City of London; others are doctors at the nearby hospital, or farmers. 'It is very inclusive and friendly with no social divides, and parents are always ready to help one another out,' said a mother. There are fitness groups for parents to join including zumba, Nordic walking, and joggy-doggy.

The only gripe you'll hear from parents – and that's a mild one – is that they find it a long day for the prep school children (8.30am to 5.15pm, with prep afterwards at home or at school from year 5 until 6.30pm). A lot of children take up the flexible boarding option – 'really fun,' the pupils agree; around one-third of children stay for one or two nights per week. Rooms are up in the eaves, and again you wouldn't be surprised to find the Famous Five up there having lashings of hot chocolate. Boarders do supervised prep for one hour, then after supper, the options include swimming, singing, and playing outside. Matron Julie is reportedly 'nice to cuddle with'.

St Swithun's Junior School

Linked school: St Swithun's School

Alresford Road, Winchester, SO21 1HA

• Pupils: 179, 173 girls/6 boys in the pre-prep • Ages: 3–11: girls to 11, boys to 7 • C of E • Fees: £8,910–£11,490 pa • Independent

Tel: 01962 835750
Email: office.juniorschool@stswithuns.com
Website: www.stswithuns.com

Headmistress: Since 2007, Mrs Pim Grimes (forties). Read English at Sussex University and had children before starting a career in teaching. Somehow maintains her poise and elegance, even when dealing with children's wet knickers and skinned knees. Everything you would want a prep school head to be. 'A breath of fresh air', said parent after parent we spoke to. 'I couldn't stop pinching myself when I realised how lucky we'd been!' enthused a mum whose daughter arrived at the school around the same time as Mrs Grimes. Married with two daughters in university.

Entrance: Non-selective but oversubscribed.

Exit: Boys go on at seven to local prep schools eg the Pilgrim's School, Twyford, Farleigh. The majority of girls go on to the senior school but also to other girls' boarding schools – Downe House, Godolphin, St Mary's Calne – or King Edward VI. No automatic entry to senior school.

Remarks: Here we have something really special: sparky, fun and innovative, while maintaining traditional values and academic standards. A cosy school that allows pupils to develop at their own pace but is never lax.

Physically in the shadow of the main school, but feels autonomous. Lovely classrooms, two colourful library areas and an interactive whiteboard in every classroom from reception up. Specialist music, PE and French teaching to begin with, and by year 5 most subjects have specialist teachers. Copes well with full range of ability levels. No overt streaming, but classes of 24 girls are broken up into smaller groups of 12, or sometimes fewer, to scoot the more able along at a swifter pace or to give strugglers a chance to consolidate. 'Brilliant' learning support and the school advises parents regarding future school choice (will they make the senior school cut?) with delicacy. A new SENCo specifically to work with gifted and talented children. Currently one statemented child (deaf).

Much emphasis on getting along with one another, manners, self esteem. The standard of behaviour is exemplary, 'but without the girls being squashed', said a mum. Music (classical music softly wafts in the background throughout) and, especially, drama are outstanding. Cooking part of the curriculum and foundation stage pupils produce a healthy snack for morning break. 'The Apprentices' school council. Residential stays at Beaulieu (year 5), Cornwall (year 6) and now France. Inclusive sport using senior school fields; lacrosse taught to bigger girls. Upstairs gymnasium a bit hot and sticky. Only quibble we heard was over a shortage of competitive sport. 'They get plenty of exercise, but there aren't enough matches.'

Co-ed aspect of the pre-prep continually reviewed, particularly now that Pilgrim's (with which this school has links) has opened its co-ed pre-prep. Parents say it does fine by little chaps, at least until the end of the reception year. Now offers full day nursery from age three (and accepts government vouchers).

Work has started on a complete rebuild, due for completion in 2017.

St Teresa's Effingham Nursery and Preparatory School

Linked school: St Teresa's Effingham Senior School

Effingham, RH5 6ST, Surrey

- Pupils: 110 girls, 2 board • Ages: 2-11 • RC but others welcome
- Fees: Day £7,710-£11,685; Boarding £20,715-£22,485 pa
- Independent

Tel: 01372 453456
Email: a.charles@st-teresas.com
Website: www.st-teresas.com

Headmistress: Since September 2013, Sue Nelson BA, PGCE, NPQH, previously deputy head at Coworth-Flexlands School in Chobham. Studied English language and literature at Liverpool. Married with three grown up sons.

Entrance: Entry into the co-ed nursery is from 2. Entry into the prep is by report and informal assessment during a Welcome Day as well as references from previous school.

Exit: The vast majority of girls move on to the senior school but have to sit entrance exam in competition with increased numbers of children from outside. Whilst there is no guarantee of a place at the Senior School, few girls have been turned away in the past.

Remarks: Girls achieve well academically, are settled and happy. 'A very friendly, happy environment,' says a parent.

St Vincent de Paul RC Primary School

Morpeth Terrace, London, SW1P 1EP

- Pupils: 250 boys and girls; all day • Ages: 3-11 • RC • State

Tel: 020 7641 5990
Email: office@svpschool.co.uk
Website: www.svpschool-primary.org.uk

Head: Since 2002, Jack O'Neill STB MA (fifties). Studied theology at university. His teaching career started in Hammersmith and Fulham, arriving at St Vincent de Paul as deputy head, then promoted to head.

He shares his passion for Roman history with pupils, accompanying the children on visits to local sites and teaching the Minimus Mouse Latin course to year 4 and year 5. Parents say head's dynamic and considered approach shines through in a number of areas – particularly music, pastoral care and efficient management of the school's budget. He is supported by a dedicated team of assistants, teachers and committed parents.

Entrance: Always oversubscribed. Nursery children are not guaranteed entry into the main school at 4+. Priority given to practising Roman Catholics, with distance from the school used as a tiebreaker. First priority goes to looked after Catholic children, then baptised, practising siblings, then baptised Catholics. A waiting list is kept for occasional places.

Exit: Most pupils get their first choice secondary school. Popular choices include Sacred Heart, London Oratory, Cardinal Vaughan and St Thomas More as well as others further afield including Westminster Cathedral Choir School.

Remarks: School was founded in 1859 by the Sisters of Charity of St Vincent de Paul to enable them to work with the poor of Westminster. Moved to current premises in the shadows of Westminster Cathedral, conveniently next door to St Paul's bookshop, in 1974.

Pupils come from a wide variety of backgrounds. Around three-quarters speak English as an additional language. Fairly compact site – outdoor space has been redeveloped to create three separate play areas for nursery children, infants and juniors. Cleverly designed, with lots of greenery and modern play equipment. Pupils also use the playgrounds and local sports facilities for team sports and have a dedicated sports coach for all PE lessons. Inside, school is light, modern and well designed. Peaceful chapel is very much at the heart of this friendly and well-disciplined school.

While this is a Catholic school, pupils are taught to understand other faiths and cultures. Good behaviour, thinking of others and cooperation goes without saying. Pupils are monitored regularly to assess their progress and there are plenty of parent evenings, giving everyone the opportunity to discuss their children. Written reports at the end of each year.

Alongside the national curriculum, the arts and sports, pupils benefit from being taught Spanish from the age of 7. Latin is introduced in year 4. Academic results are exceptional. Staff have high expectations and have created a good learning ethos. The SENCo coordinates additional needs and runs a Units of Sound action programme. There is also a school counsellor.

Multi-coloured and multimedia displays of artwork adorn classrooms and corridors. Large, multi-purpose hall where children practise for termly concerts and plays and musical performances. The school choir performs at Westminster Cathedral as well as regularly singing at family Mass. The school is part of the Westminster Cathedral Choir School outreach programme. The school boasts a well-stocked music room with an impressive selection of instruments – from glockenspiels to bongo drums. All have singing and music lessons, provided by a dedicated music teacher. Pupils talk excitedly about how they are encouraged to create their own music. Small charge is made for individual lessons on a wide range of instruments.

Sixth formers from neighbouring Westminster School work as volunteers, acting as classroom assistants and helping to run school clubs. ICT room doubles up as a cinema for film club.

Not a place for those who wish to sit on their laurels. Energetic PTA meets regularly to discuss the organisation of numerous fundraising events for the school. Each family is asked to make a small annual contribution towards the maintenance and building fund – for the benefit of the present community and to ensure continuation for future generations. Pupils are active fundraisers and run regular charity events. The school also works with Mission Together, a charity that encourages children to care about mission through prayer, learning and fundraising.

A lively and impressive school that provides a high standard of education and produces caring and thoughtful individuals. Parents praise it to the rafters and pupils say they look forward to going to school.

Salisbury Cathedral School

The Old Bishop's Palace, 1 The Close, Salisbury, Wiltshire, SP1 2EQ

• Pupils: 185; 90 boys, 60 girls; 35 boarders • Ages: 3–13 • C of E choir school • Fees: Boarding £19,995; Day £7,155–£13,605 pa
• Independent

Tel: 01722 555300
Email: headsec@salisburycathedralschool.com
Website: www.salisburycathedralschool.com

Head Master: Since September 2013, Mr Clive Marriott, previously deputy head of St Paul's Cathedral School.

Entrance: Many come up from the pre-prep, otherwise at all stages. Hugely oversubscribed chorister places are offered as a result of a voice trial, academic assessment and interview; there is an informal test for others. Scholarships are available for music, sport and academic ability at seven and 11. Day children come predominantly from local primaries and boarders from a wide area: 'chorister-ship knows few boundaries'. A few Forces children and occasional Spanish and South African boarders (none needing extra English), but like most co-ed preps in the area, it could use a few more girls. Leaden Hall and Godolphin Prep are right on the doorstep and claim the lion's share of girls. School's governing body is genuinely endeavouring to keep a lid on fee increases.

Exit: Mainly at 13 to a range of local senior schools eg Bryanston, Dauntsey's, Godolphin, Sherborne, St Mary's Shaftesbury and Canford – most with music awards, but also with sport and all-rounder scholarships or exhibitions. Some leavers go further afield eg Eton, Marlborough, Wells, Lancing, Downside, Uppingham and St Mary's Calne. One or two gain specialist music school places. A handful leaves after year 6 to Salisbury's grammar schools or independent schools such as Godolphin and Leehurst Swan (school runs 11+ practice sessions) but only the odd intrepid explorer manages to navigate the choppy waters of the 13+ exam for late entry to the grammar schools (boys' grammar often full). Academic scholarships pop up occasionally – the school says, 'scholars are being given greater focus and we are proud of the results.'

Remarks: One of the oldest schools in the country; founded in 1091 by St Osmund to educate the choristers of his cathedral at Old Sarum. Moved to its present home, the former 13th century Bishop's Palace centred in 27-acre grounds within the Cathedral Close, in 1947. In the shadow of Salisbury's magnificent spire, its setting is idyllic and appreciated by parents and pupils alike.

School is an early adopter of the Independent Curriculum, phased in during 2011-12. Small class sizes (12 on average) are a big draw for some parents. Strong on science teaching, year 8 pupils regularly do well in chemistry competitions at Southampton University. Geography also good; field trips conducted thoroughly and children encouraged to think independently. French and English teaching much improved. Maths, a long-standing thorn in the school's side, also looks to be on the up. Latin for all from year 6; classical history trips to Italy round out non-linguistic studies (budding classicists don't leave translating Virgil, however). No scholarship set, so able children rely on individual teachers to stretch learning (some do). Regular study-skills workshops introduced for years 7 and 8, plus year 8 maths-skills sessions and English grammar and etiquette lessons for year 5.

Library is very well stocked and organised. All classrooms have whiteboards. Good ICT facilities. Imposing 'Big School Room', its walls lined with portraits of past Bishops of Salisbury, is an unusual venue for school assemblies and plays. Lovely ancient chapel in main school is used for morning worship twice a week. Welcoming SEN room provides help for 'mainly dyslexic' children.

Music is clearly the school's greatest strength. 85 per cent of pupils play at least one instrument; some learn three. 'Music Circus' in years 3 and 4 allows young musicians the chance to try out a wide range of instruments free of charge and determine which they would most like to play. Further up the school, young organists revel in the opportunity to play the cathedral's Father Willis organ. There is a school orchestra, concert band, myriad lunchtime and after-school music ensembles and an annual friendly, non-competitive music festival. 'Everyone' sings and there are three school choirs as well as the two cathedral choirs. 'Jazbytes', the school jazz band, occasionally performs in public and invariably brings the house down. Weekly, informal Monday lunchtime concerts allow players the chance to perform in front of a kind audience (staff, pupils and parents). Practice sessions are scheduled for boarders and a few day pupils. Music department enters dozens of candidates every term for ABRSM exams and most pass with merit or distinction. A good number pass grade V theory every year. A child doesn't have to be musical to come here, but it would be difficult to leave without a song on the lips and some appreciation of classical and choral music.

Sport continues to improve thanks to new sports teachers. Good Astroturf, three rugby pitches and generous scholarships attract sporty children. All-inclusive approach means nearly everyone gets a chance to represent the school (usual list of prep school sports on offer) and fixture card is healthy. First rounders' team had an unbeaten season recently and all senior teams put in a respectable performance. Wednesday afternoons devoted to sport. Match teas for parent supporters are 'the best on the local circuit'; the school does these beautifully in summer, complete with home-made cakes and a marquee on the lawn in full view of the cathedral spire. Parking for matches on Wednesdays can be a challenge if lots of parents turn up, as can escaping from school afterwards.

School aims to provide good pastoral care. School chaplain promotes a strong Christian ethos in and out of RS lessons; her Friday morning services in the cathedral for the whole school are legendary (balloons have been known to lodge themselves cheerfully in the organ pipes). A good number of parents attend every week and exemplary values are enthusiastically encouraged – Esther Rantzen spoke eloquently about bullying at one year's speech day. As most pupils meet the school's high moral expectations, serious issues (eg racism) are notable by their absence. Upbeat, happy, 'busy bee' school atmosphere possibly explains why the rare case of low-level unkind behaviour lurks below the radar (any concerned parent is always given a prompt hearing) and school staff may need to fine tune their pastoral antennae and ensure that disciplinary procedures remain consistent.

Switched on to the needs of busy parents; day pupils may arrive from 8.00am (to the strains of choristers at morning rehearsal) and stay until 5.30pm at no extra charge. Day prep sessions are easy going; boarder prep is more effectively supervised. No Saturday school, although there is morning music practice for choristers. Other boarders staying in school take part in separate activities. Excellent range of clubs on offer at lunchtimes and before and after school: chess, ukulele, rock band, general knowledge, archery, football, golf, swimming, drama, photography, street dance and sewing are just a few. 'Eco' club tends the lake in Palace grounds (useful for practical science). School musical every year (Guys and Dolls, Oklahoma!, Fiddler on the Roof). Everyone in the prep school can be involved; choristers do not automatically win main singing roles! 'It's the highlight of the school year, and such fun.' Unusual exchange programme with a South African boarding school – two year 7 pupils can spend a term in Graaff-Reinet. Yearly ski trips in

Easter holidays. Annual history excursions to France, alternately visiting World War battlefields and Normandy beaches.

Boarding house tucked behind a cream tea shop five minutes' walk away, so boarders (nearly all English) stride off to school for breakfast and do not return until 7 or 8pm. Boarders' bedrooms are wholesome, if rather cosy, with largish dorms for youngsters shrinking to doubles for older children; lots of common areas downstairs. Excursions planned most weekends for those staying in. In term time there are always two choirs in residence and day choristers are required to board twice each term – most regard this as a treat and look forward to 'chori hols' at Christmas, Easter and in July. Boarding house staff works hard to punctuate the choristers' duties with rest and fun (choir parents quip that a closed school kitchen on the final day three times a year isn't so much fun for them).

Chorister life runs like clockwork thanks to cathedral's supremely organised director of music and a chorister tutor who puts in hours beyond the call of duty. Musical standards are consistently good and choirs undertake regular concerts, recordings and live broadcasts in addition to their regular weekly services (duties shared equally between girls' and boys' choirs). Choristers play a full part in school life and are treated much the same as other pupils, although they clearly have an extra workload before and after school. Foreign choir tours no longer an annual event, more's the pity.

Pre-prep housed in classrooms tucked away in a corner of the Palace grounds, overlooking a pleasant area of lawn. Takes pupils from age 3; these youngest children are charmingly known as 'Ladybirds', moving up to 'Dragonflies' (year 1) and 'Busy Bees' (year 2). The head – 'a wonderful teacher' – is well supported by committed staff. Approach to early education isn't pushy; nevertheless children thrive and emerge happy, balanced and confident. Red Badges are awarded each Friday for effort, achievement or any other positive contribution and winners are applauded at Monday assemblies. The best class wins the privilege of having Mr Gnome to stay for the week. Has its own sports day and prize giving, an informal lunchtime concert each term, and takes part in the annual music festival. Staff stage a play every summer in addition to the customary nativity. Weekly timetable includes RS, French, games and ballet; pupils use the main school's library, gym and ICT facilities. Year 2 pupils have the chance to experience 'Music Circus'. Own play area and sand pit; teachers are very good at ensuring children play outside every day. Golf coaching sessions, football and gardening clubs, trips to Salisbury Museum and grandparents' tea parties all keep young ones cheerful and interested. No surprise that numbers here are on the up.

Informal atmosphere – cheerful, super-efficient school secretary does much to keep it that way. Head's PA is also a gem, unfailingly helpful and courteous. A tight-knit school where each child is known well, most pupils are very happy and care about one another. 'It's the kind of place where you can go up to some of the teachers and give them a hug.' Former pupils include MPs Robert Key and Michael Mates, actress and singer Amy Carson (Kenneth Branagh, The Magic Flute), organist Bernard Rose, composer Peter Gritton and Sir Anthony Lewis, former president of the Royal College of Music. Judging by the strength of the alumni association and the lasting friendships between former pupils, SCS is a happy and very special place to spend your early school years.

Sandroyd School

Rushmore, Tollard Royal, Salisbury, Wiltshire, SP5 5QD

- Pupils: 180 boys and girls; 155 boarders • Ages: 3–13 • C of E
- Fees: Boarding £17,790–£22,140; Day £7,905–£18,540 pa;
- Independent

Tel: 01725 516264
Email: office@sandroyd.com
Website: www.sandroyd.org

Headmaster: Since 2003, Mr Martin Harris BSc PGCE (forties). Educated at The Skinners School and read geography at Loughborough University. Began his teaching career at Ashdown House in East Sussex; after a stint as deputy head at King's School, Rochester, he returned to Ashdown House as deputy head (acting head for one year). A naturally charming, personable man, he is refreshingly honest and has a good sense of humour. Clearly gets on very well with his staff; has overseen much change in his nine years at the helm and shows no signs of flagging. Ten years ago Sandroyd was a very traditional all-boys prep school; today it educates girls and boys in what has become 'a more academic, yet also more child friendly environment.' As if to underline this, Dyllis, the head's small shaggy terrier, nosed her way into his study and trotted across the floor.

Still keen to achieve bigger and better, Mr Harris wants 'sandroyd to be known nationally for 21st century boarding.' Also preparing the ground to aim for top academic awards to high flying schools, eg Eton, and says teachers are up for the challenge. Parents praise his tenure. 'During Martin's time, he has made positive changes on all fronts, whilst drama, music and the arts have come on in leaps and bounds,' said one. A keen sportsman, he plays cricket, golf and tennis. Wife Catherine, a chartered physiotherapist, is very involved in all areas except the classroom, eg helping house parents, taking children to appointments, teaching cookery and keeping an eye on staff welfare. They have two young sons, both at the school.

Entrance: Pupils join at all stages, although school policy is to keep numbers below 200, hence there is a waiting list in some year groups. The Walled Garden (pre-prep) takes children from the age of three. Many join the main school in year 3 from local primary or pre-preps (mostly in Wiltshire and Dorset) and the first full boarders start in year 4, when the school doubles in size. Some come at 10 or 11 from further afield, specifically for senior boarding. Not selective, but all those joining aged seven and above have an informal interview with the head and are assessed in reading and reasoning. School stresses that tests are not pass/fail exercises.

Means-tested bursaries are available on an annual, case by case basis. Single 100 per cent bursary from year 7 (joint award with Bryanston) is awarded to one child. A further 100 per cent bursary (in conjunction with Radley, St Mary's Calne and Downe House) is available for children of servicemen or women killed or wounded on operational tours.

Exit: Most leave at 13 for a number of competitive senior schools. Destinations include Sherborne, Radley, Eton, Bryanston, Marlborough, Winchester, Harrow, Downside, Ampleforth, Stowe, Monkton Combe, Downe House, St Mary's Calne, St Mary's Shaftesbury, Sherborne Girls and Canford; otherwise to schools far and wide. A good handful leave with sport and all-round scholarships and exhibitions and some win academic, music and art awards, including four in 2013 to Wells Cathedral School, Claysmore and Bryanston.

Remarks: Founded in 1888 by the Revd Wellesley Wesley as a 'small coaching establishment' for aspiring Etonians at his own home, the school quickly flourished. It moved first to Surrey and in 1939 to Rushmore House (the Pitt-Rivers' family home) on the Wiltshire/Dorset borders. School purchased the house and 57 acres within the 400-acre Rushmore estate in 1966. Like most elegant country houses, it sits at the end of a long, winding drive in solitary splendour, surrounded by playing fields, woods and parkland.

Beautiful entrance hall with open fireplace, cosy sofas and lovely wood panelling; head's study is bigger than some studio apartments and has a stunning view of open countryside. Entire school (except pre-prep) is in the original house, although there have obviously been significant additions and alterations, eg theatre, chapel, classrooms and girls' boarding wing. Everything connected by lots of passages (even our pupil guides managed to miss out half the school first time around) but there is an order to the layout once you get the hang of it. Bright, spacious classrooms on the far side of the house are mostly ranged along two main corridors and also have marvellous views. Still feels very much like a country home in the boarders' quarters (sitting rooms and comfy sofas) where house parents have apartments. Although it is now less traditional, we were pleased to see that some 'old style' disciplines remain, eg shoe polishing, letter writing and good manners.

Still true to its original purpose, the school fosters a 'cool to work and achieve' ethos and parents confirm this. 'If you are destined for Eton, you will get there.' Children get lots of support along the way, with each child assigned to a personal tutor who monitors academic progress and keeps an eye on extra-curricular activities. 'Tutors always have time to talk to parents and seem to know the children very well.' Strong in most areas of the curriculum thanks to good teaching and positive attitudes, together with small classes of no more than 16. Saturday morning lessons start in year 4. Teachers reward effort and achievement with 'alphas' and discourage slacking with 'omegas.' Pupils collecting enough alphas are treated to an outing and those given omegas have to do penance with a chore.

Maths is set in years 7 and 8; able mathematicians in year 6 join advanced classes. French from year 4 and Latin from year 5. Year 3 also gets a taste of French, German and Spanish, whilst year 8 is introduced to Greek. School has scholarship sets in English, maths, French and Latin. Year 7 pupils go on an annual residential trip to a chateau in Burgundy, France. Two very well-appointed ICT suites and an excellent, bright, modern science laboratory. SKULL (skills, knowledge and understanding for lifelong learning) educates beyond the classroom, eg study skills, art appreciation and career skills for older pupils, financial literacy and European culture sessions for younger ones. RATS (reasoning and thinking skills) culminates in a GCSE in year 8 (head took it one year and was out smarted by some of his pupils!) General knowledge questions set for whole prep school every week and tested every Friday. At the time of our visit, there were 32 pupils in the learning support unit and nine pupils with EAL requirements – mostly Spanish pupils at the school for one year. SEN classrooms are welcoming, light and bright (with those brilliant views again).

A very sporty school – games every day and Wednesday and Saturday afternoons devoted to matches and sport. Lots of boys' teams, eg four senior boys' rugby teams with an A and B side at every level, means everyone gets the chance to play for the school. As well as the usual prep school sports for boys and girls, there is tennis and squash coaching, plus archery, shooting and clay pigeon shooting, plus a girls' cricket team. School surrounded by acres of green space for games and has wide expanses of grass pitches, plus an all-weather pitch, cricket pitch, new netball and tennis courts. Local primary schools invited to enjoy the facilities from time to time.

Swimming lessons take place either in school's indoor 18 metre pool and head's wife takes competitive swimmers to a larger pool nearby. Gym next door is looking a little tired and unloved, but plans are afoot to build a new gym and 25 metre pool. Many individual sporting accolades, eg finalists in IAPS national swimming and athletics championships; some selected for Wessex rugby and U14 and U13 county hockey teams.

A third of the pupils have riding lessons, either on school's ponies or their own (ponies are welcome to board) – eager beginners up to advanced equestrians. In our enthusiasm to see the whole school, we vaulted a stile and strode off across the paddock to watch a lesson. Naturally, the pony promptly morphed into a Thelwellian devil and refused to jump anything (much to the chagrin of both pupil and instructor, to whom we apologised profusely). Head confessed ruefully that he couldn't see the appeal of riding when his charges fell off! Clearly they don't come off too often, as senior boys' show jumping team has competed in the National Schools Equestrian Association finals.

Head has encouraged the arts and these appear to be in rude health; music is on the up and young, energetic director of music is on the case. She set out by re-auditioning the chapel choir, which now practises several times a week, sings Sunday morning service in the school chapel and has sung evensong in Salisbury Cathedral. There are two further choirs, a school orchestra, string ensembles, brass and saxophone groups, a jazz band and the 'school of Rock.' There are concerts every term and an annual school musical. Eighty per cent play an instrument and music lessons are rotated through the timetable; practice sessions are timetabled and checked. All the usual instruments on offer, plus some less likely, eg tuba, banjo and bagpipes. Music theory and aural training are also available. All pupils in year 4 receive free tuition for one term on an instrument of their choice.

Fantastic theatre, probably the best we've seen outside senior schools, used by all ages from reception upwards. Every year group in the prep school puts on a play and reluctant thespians are encouraged to help out with lighting, scenery and sound. Lovely bright art studio affords plenty of space and light; next door is a small exhibition space for art scholars to display their work. Very well-equipped DT studio, with computers for designing projects (doubles up as a bike repair shop on Wednesday evenings!) Lots of activities on offer during designated 'hobby' afternoons, after school and at the weekend, including astronomy, philosophy, scuba diving, pony care, survival skills and den building in woodland belonging to the Rushmore estate. Great climbing wall perches at the back of the main house.

Boarding provision is very well organised, with a junior house for boys and girls, middle house for boys and senior boys' and girls' wings. Senior girls' wing accommodates those in the top two years. There is flexi or weekly boarding lower down the school, but by year 7 children are expected to board full time and a busy programme at the weekend means most do. As 60 per cent of teachers live on site, every house and wing has its own house parents as well as a team of matrons. Pastoral care is 'fantastic' and parents praise swift communications between home and school. Any unkind behaviour is stamped on quickly; a parent commented that 'school culture provides very little room for bullying.' Girls' dorms are probably the prettiest we've seen, with lots of pink and attractive lampshades and curtains. Boys' dorms are plainer and slightly more spacious in the senior wing, with three or four to a room. Older pupils have desks in their bedrooms and can choose to do prep here if they wish. They also have their own common-rooms and kitchens, where they can make toast and cocoa (and learn to wash and tidy up). We were amazed to learn that school washes day pupils' sports kit as well as all the boarders' clothing. The laundry room resembles a commercial operation – rows of machines and banks of shelves for clean towels, shirts etc.

School lunches are generally good and served in a large bright, airy dining room; snacks of fresh fruit are available throughout the day. Some mothers felt school teas could be healthier, but supper seemed wholesome enough (milk, cereal, bread and fruit). Mobile phones are not permitted in school; overseas boarders are allowed to Skype their parents and others can buy phone cards to call home. There are two obligatory 'weekends in' per term, but on most Sundays children are allowed out for lunch with their parents after chapel. Many choose to remain at school with their friends to join in afternoon activities, eg football, cycling, cookery and hacking across the Downs. 'My only concern about boarding is that my children would rather be at school than at home,' said one mother wistfully.

The Walled Garden (pre-prep) is built on to an original wall surrounding the formal gardens to one side of Rushmore House. A sympathetically designed, unusual curved fibreglass ceiling lets in plenty of light without spoiling the existing aspect. Children are taught in small classes, often by a specialist teacher, with a strong focus on numeracy and literacy. The Walled Garden has its own hall for drama and assemblies (which doubles up as an art studio). A new library has recently been opened. Pre-prep pupils use the main school computers and swimming pool, walk up to the dining room for lunch and can stay on to take part in after-school activities. The playground is packed with activities such as sandpit, musical instruments, bikes, trikes, chickens, wormery and a recently opened Bug Café.

School is 'a happy mix of local and less local folk', with students from all over – a few Spanish there to learn English, with others from Germany, Norway, Japan and Mexico, plus a few expats from Hong Kong, Nigeria etc. School escorts pupils on the train to London on exeat weekends and at half-term, it arranges taxis to airports for overseas pupils. Pupils are uniformly polite, display excellent manners (standing up for the head and visitors to the classroom) and perhaps more important, are utterly unpretentious. A luminary roll call of former students includes Sir Terence Rattigan, Sir Ranulph Fiennes, Lords Carrington, Gladwyn and Wilberforce, Archbishop Ramsey of Canterbury, Rt Revd Roger Wilson, Bishop of Chichester, Professors Hawkes, Godley and Dummett, Randolph Churchill, Ian Gow and many other British and foreign dignitaries.

A very happy school. Full of 'really confident but not arrogant children,' it offers a well-balanced education in spectacular surroundings. Not a hothouse, but prepared to 'push when necessary' to prepare for senior school. There is lots of sport, so those allergic to games might not feel totally at home here. Has retained the best of traditional boarding school values and consigned the outmoded to the dust. We'll watch the top scholarship tally in years to come with interest.

Sarum Hall School

15 Eton Avenue, London, NW3 3EL

- Pupils: 170 girls (including nursery); all day • Ages: 3–11 • C of E
- Fees: £11,580–£12,540 pa • Independent

Tel: 020 7794 2261
Email: admissions@sarumhallschool.co.uk
Website: www.sarumhallschool.co.uk

Headmistress: Since 2008, Mrs Christine Smith BA, Cert Ed RSA (SpLD) (fifties). Mrs Smith spent the previous 17 years at Lochinver Prep in Potter's Bar. Began her career teaching home economics and textiles at Edmonton County School before having her two daughters. Lured back to teaching to work with deaf children, eventually becoming director of studies at Lochinver and setting up their learning support unit. When her children left home, she felt ready for a new challenge – 'I walked into Sarum Hall and knew immediately I could see myself here'.

Describes herself as 'a calm person', and is widely seen as a sensible, soothing presence. Parents find her very approachable – 'Mrs Smith is so nice – she smiles all the time'. Married to an actuary. Interests include tai chi, cooking, the theatre and martial arts (she spent time in Beijing learning about swords).

Entrance: Main intake in September after third birthday. Register as soon after birth as possible with a non-refundable deposit of £100. Parents are invited two years before entry to visit the school on a working day and then write to confirm their continued interest in a place. The school is non-selective, but priority is given to siblings and to the children and grandchildren of former pupils. The remainder of the 22-24 nursery places are based on the head's decision – 'I meet all the parents and discuss what kind of school they hope for their daughter. This is very much a community school'. Most pupils are local, ideally within walking distance. Occasional vacancies arise after nursery. From year 1, applicants are tested in English and maths.

Exit: Practically all to their first-choice school at 11: Channing, City Girls, Francis Holland, Godolphin & Latymer, Highgate, Immanuel, North London Collegiate, South Hampstead, St Helen's. Also, unusually for a north London prep, a reasonable contingent to board at eg Wycombe Abbey, Queenswood, St George's Ascot.

Remarks: If a school can have the 'wow factor', then Sarum Hall definitely does. Housed in a superb, RIBA-lauded contemporary building, which provides plenty of well-planned light and airy space to work, move about and play. 'Even on the most dismal day,' says the head, 'the school is flooded with natural light.' High design standards are complemented with attractive displays of fresh flowers and a rooftop extension provides a quiet room for music exams and practice.

The head has a clear vision of a continuing tradition – 'sarum Hall is an academic school whose girls go onto further education and develop a lifelong love of learning. But the school places as strong an emphasis on the cultural and social as the academic. Music, art and drama have a central role'.

Good, solid, traditional teaching using the national curriculum but not the dreaded Sats. 'The school really prepares pupils superbly for 11 plus,' says one mother with two daughters who've successfully surmounted that hurdle. Specialist subject teaching in PE, music, IT and French from nursery, science from year 3, English, maths and humanities in years 5 and 6. Inspired science teaching ('very practical and relevant,' said one parent), taught in a well-furnished lab to the accompaniment of classical music. Some setting in maths, but 'we don't make too much of that'. However significant differentiation to meet individual needs, with additional work, for example, for those sitting boarding school entrance exams and plenty of classroom assistance throughout. Imaginative cross-curricular teaching. 'One girl found a flattened toad in Africa and it was incorporated into the study of Macbeth,' says the head. Long serving ('People come to stay') highly-regarded staff. 'Some of the teachers have a real passion for their subject,' says one mother.

Learning support unit (with one dedicated member of staff) copes with dyslexia, dyspraxia and the 'gifted and talented', at no additional cost. (Girls are taken out of lessons for individual or group support, though this is 'not a huge part of the school'.) Homework introduced gently in year 2, rising to a maximum of one hour a night in year 6. All pupils expected to read daily. Bright and breezily decorated library open to all in lunch and break, plus library lessons as part of the curriculum.

Music, art and drama all lively and strong. Majority of girls study one or more instruments after year 2 and get plenty of opportunity to show off in class assemblies, frequent concerts and house drama. Also sit the English Speaking Board exams to build up communication skills. Stunning studio art room with north-facing light is made full use of – pupils study sculpture,

S

print, textiles and woodwork. Also frequent exposure to the real thing, with outings to exhibitions as well as in-house visits from professional artists.

Though outdoor space is not extensive, the outside is as well planned as the interior and daily sport or PE takes place on three Astroturf courts (used for netball, hockey, rounders, soccer, cricket and tennis) or in the assembly hall, which triples as a gym (for dance as well as gymnastics) and theatre. Swimming once more part of the curriculum, at nearby Swiss Cottage Baths. Annual athletics meet on Hampstead Heath.

Plenty of nourishing after-school clubs (yoga, sewing, knitting, Mandarin) and enriching outings to theatres etc – 'We take full advantage of what's on our doorstep'. Year 6 summer programme to manage post 11-plus drag offering first aid, cookery, Mandarin and other handy skills. Residential trips to Flatford Mill and a château in France.

Very much a family-based school. 'We care about the whole family and want to nurture the natural talents of every girl,' says the head, and parents feel it lives up to its aims. 'I've had three daughters here and enjoyed it all the way; it's a wonderful school,' says one. Traditional good manners (from year 2 girls leap to their feet when head enters and chorus, 'Good morning, Mrs Smith'). 'We don't have any behavioural problems,' says head. Positive rewards for good behaviour, constant emphasis on Golden Rules – 'We are gentle, kind and helpful. We listen and are honest and work hard. We look after property. We don't hurt anybody's feelings' etc. Three houses, with house points for good work and good behaviour, lots of praise and positive reinforcements. Food prepared daily on site with vegetarian option and faithful stalwarts like syrup sponge and custard. No packed lunch. Staff eat with girls. No mobile phones, no email, supervised internet use only. Affiliated to the Church of England and the large number of Jewish girls and other faiths join in daily assembly with the Lord's Prayer and hymns.

Enthusiastic charitable fundraising. 'These girls are very privileged and we try and get them to see that,' says the head. Parents and pupils are predominantly affluent, white, middle-class professionals – accountants, lawyers, city, etc, not too many media – with a strong international contingent, mainly European, Indian and Chinese. Many girls have brothers at The Hall and Arnold House (and head does her best to ensure coordinated term dates). No scholarships or bursaries, though will support parents if they fall on hard times.

A very well-run, small, intimate, traditional girls' prep in a wonderful modern setting that gets the very best out of a broad range of ability without too much pressure and provides a rich education in every sense. Possibly not the ideal school for the maverick child (or parent) or one who doesn't deal happily with authority.

The Schools at Somerhill

Linked schools: Yardley Court; Derwent Lodge School; Somerhill Pre-prep

Somerhill, Tonbridge, TN11 0NJ

• Pupils: 400 boys and 250 girls, all day; • Ages: 3–13; • Non-denom; • Fees: £8,640–£13,290 pa; • Independent

Tel: 01732 352124
Email: office@somerhill.org
Website: www.somerhill.org

Headmaster of Yardley Court and Principal of The Schools at Somerhill: since 1998, John Coakley, BA (Hons), MA, PGCE (fifties). Educated at Bishop Wordsworth's Grammar School in Salisbury, read English at York, followed by a PGCE at Oxford and an MA in English at New Brunswick University, Canada. Previously headmaster of Ryde School on the Isle of Wight and of Saltus Grammar School in Bermuda,

He is warm and welcoming, straight-talking and fizzing with enthusiasm. Known affectionately as Mr C by children and parents, his modest office in the eaves suggests a deliberate lack of grandeur. He lives in a house in the grounds, with his chocolate Labrador, Stanley, and holidays in France.

A pupil describes him to us with genuine enthusiasm as 'fantastic, he's always there to help us' and a parent sums him up: 'First class – he knows the names and characters of every boy within Yardley Court. He is highly visible, attends (and coaches) sports matches, runs clubs and the boys hold him in extremely high regard'. His aim for the school begins with the happy child: 'If they are happy, everything else falls into place'.

Headteacher of Derwent Lodge: since 2009, Sam Michau, BA (Hons), MA, PGCE (forties). Studied psychology at Oxford, previously director of studies at the co-ed Ardingly College Prep School in West Sussex. Highly dynamic, but thoroughly approachable, she teaches science, maths and PE. Her evident delight in trying something new (most recently wind-surfing), embodies the school aim of encouraging children to 'have a go'. She has three children, the youngest at senior school, a daughter studying costume design and a son who is a chef. The head girl describes her as a role model and parents we spoke to were similarly impressed.

Entrance: The schools describe themselves as mixed ability and the majority of children join Somerhill via the co-educational pre-prep. Transfer to Yardley Court (boys) and Derwent Lodge (girls) is automatic at year 3. Those wishing to squeeze in at 7+ may sit a brief assessment. Prospective parents could get lucky with a place beyond year 3, but the numbers say if this is the school for you, you'd be wise to get in early. The principal pragmatically supports some applicants in the final pre-exam years, space permitting. Discounts for siblings: five per cent for a second child, ten per cent for three or more.

Exit: Girls are prepared to leave at 11+ for Tonbridge Grammar, Tunbridge Wells Girls' Grammar, St Leonard's Mayfield and Kent College. High number of boys, around 40 per cent, also exit at this stage for the Kent grammars, principally The Judd and Skinners. Principal is clear that Somerhill is 'not an 11+ factory', neatly illustrated by the pupil we met who was unfazed by having sat the exam the previous day. Nonetheless, results are strong with a 90 per cent success rate. Tutoring does go on – a sore point – but both heads see it as unnecessary and generally to be discouraged. Of the rest who stay on for Common Entrance, most go to Tonbridge and Cranbrook, many with scholarships and exhibitions.

Remarks: Traditional curriculum with plenty of active learning eg times table shoot-outs for the boys. At Yardley Court maths is particularly strong and the most successful subject at CE. English comes in for praise too: 'teaching has made the boys truly love this subject.' Latin from year 5.

For the girls in Derwent Lodge maths setting based on pace not ability starts in year 3 (it's from year 4 for the boys) and extends to English and sometimes science by year 5. Memorable highlights for the girls are cross-curricular theme days such as outdoor learning when every lesson takes place outside.

Plenty of long-serving staff and both heads have made new appointments, with young male teachers significantly visible at Yardley Court. The principal expects all to go the extra mile, such as those we saw on the day of our visit, cheerily preparing to take part in a school camp out. Parents describe the quality of teaching as excellent, with the inevitable few exceptions. Reports graded for effort as well as achievement, individual targets identified and timed so that parents have an opportunity to follow up quickly at consultations – not always a given.

Just over ten per cent identified with special educational needs, mainly dyspraxia and dyslexia. Two full-time and three part-time staff across both preps, offering mostly in-class support. Dyslexic children using lap-tops during lessons were less visible on our visit than in some preps, but the principal assured us that this is supported where beneficial.

Somerhill is a terrifically sporty school, with over 500 fixtures annually. Hardly surprising given the sport-loving heads and extensive parkland that enables it to host large-scale events. 'Provision is great if you're into it, not so good for the non-sporty', says one parent, meaning there's little escape and regular compulsory Saturday fixtures from year 5 for the boys. But, it's not just about the A and B teams – boys and girls play in at least one inter-school match a term, whatever their ability. The school is particularly strong in athletics, notably cross-country, winning a haul of medals at the Kent IAPS, and bounced its way to gold-medal success in the British national schools finals in trampolining. As befits the locale, the school has a new equestrian team for pupils who compete on their own ponies. Inspirational sporting figures pop by – Rebecca Stephens, mountaineer and the first British woman to reach the summit of Everest, recently talked to Derwent Lodge pupils. Paralympian swimmers Stephanie Millward and Claire Cashmore have visited, while Yardley Court pupils heard from Kenton Cool, who has scaled Everest more times than any other climber.

There is weekly homework in years 3 and year 4, moving to forty minutes per night from year 5 – a slower ramp up than in many other schools. Holiday homework can be bothersome, sometimes requiring advanced levels of skill and organisation – as one parent observed, '[it] appears to be a project for parents'.

Music teaching is singled out for praise, as inspirational, inclusive and fun. The summer concert involves more than 300 pupils in both junior and senior choirs, as likely to include pop songs as the classics and recently featuring songs from Les Miserables. Pupils can choose from more than 22 instruments for individual tuition and roughly two thirds do. In year 5 Yardley Court boys can take choral auditions for Tonbridge School's Chapel Choir.

The two preps share good size art facilities, high up in the attics, including two new pottery kilns. Art on display is of a very high standard. 'Some amazing work produced' says one parent and we agree – we saw year 6 pupils animatedly discussing with their teacher how they were to build a life-size wire animal sculpture .

Clubs are squeezed into every moment. For the girls, active options include ballet, tennis, hockey or netball or they might try knitting, ceramics , jazz and modern art. Boys can start the day with a spot of Samba Band, and end it with sport of every kind or, for the non-sporty, camp-building, gardening, or Cubs. Creative minds can try camera, animation or cookery clubs. We wondered whether the girls might like a few more of the boys' outside larks? The school assures us there are plenty of outdoor clubs for girls over the year.

All three parts of the school are housed in a large Jacobean stone mansion – formerly a boarding school – set in 150 acres: part manicured lawns, part playing fields and extensive woodland. The school perches at the highest point, giving it great views over the Kent countryside. With the Derwent Lodge houses named after the Lake District, a dipping pond, den-building and sledging on snowy days and not one but two proper adventure play-grounds (which will sell the school in an instant to children) there is a definite whiff of Swallows and Amazons. Inside is a confusing maze of staircases and classrooms, some rather utilitarian, others all stained glass windows and polished wood. And, while there is a bit of chipped paint like any lived-in family home (the family feel is frequently mentioned by old boys and girls), the wood gleams and there's not a leaf out of place.

The preps seem right for parents and children wanting a single-sex environment – there are very different uniforms and separate play-times in addition to tailored teaching – but there is also a bit of mixing. Shared activities include Tai Kwan Do and indoor athletics, choirs, cake sales, orchestras, theme days and trips such as ski-ing and sailing. Some parents would like the boys and girls to mix more; it's a balance the principal strives to get right. Parents agree the school is hot on anti-bullying.

Somerhill seems particularly well-suited to the working parent. Not only does the single site mean a life-saving single drop off for most families, but the school day begins at 8am, and pupils can remain in school until 6pm. After-school clubs run until 5.30 pm (some additional fees) and then co-ordinate with tea if necessary and Late Supervision (small fee). Younger children can be supervised for free as they wait for their siblings.

Highly popular pre-prep: more than 250 children, with three classes (20 max) in most of the years. It neatly slots into the former coach-houses, providing spacious classrooms with plenty of natural light. Younger children play in the soft-surface central courtyard, but also benefit from their own adventure playground and time in the grounds. The atmosphere is warm, calm and caring and there's a team of plentiful, long-serving staff. The twin focus on both academic achievement (SEN assistance where needed) and teaching of good behaviour was in evidence during our visit when children worked diligently in small groups, greeting us politely.

Pupils travel from Sevenoaks, Tunbridge Wells and Tonbridge and surrounding villages. A school minibus service operates most usefully from Tunbridge Wells and Tonbridge both morning and afternoon, with mornings only from a range of other localities. Mostly children with English as their first language, with no EAL requirements. Parents come here from all walks of life but are a well-heeled bunch in the main – plenty of takers for a £1000 school trip to Bermuda in year 8, for instance. They describe their peers as friendly and supportive, 'very, very rare to hear any school gate carping'.

What kind of child would thrive at Somerhill? According to the principal there is, 'No set mould, you don't have to be a certain type, or to conform. A child who is happy in his or her own skin'. Parents say the school doesn't wrap children up in cotton wool, and while 'sporty kids would be in their element, it's also good for wall-flowers ... the art room is open for all at break times as is the library'.

Seaford College Prep School, Wilberforce House

Linked school: Seaford College

Lavington Park , Petworth, GU28 0NB

- Pupils: 160; 110 boys/50 girls; 10 boarders • Ages: 7–13
- Fees: Day £8,505–£14,400; Boarding £18,900 pa • Independent

Tel: 01798 867893
Email: jmackay@seaford.org
Website: www.seafordprep.org

Head: Mr Sebastian Rees

Exit: All go on to Seaford College.

Remarks: No separate review – see senior school entry.

Servite RC Primary School

252 Fulham Road, London, SW10 9NA

• Pupils: 235 girls and boys • Ages: 3-11 • Roman Catholic • State

Tel: 020 7352 2588
Email: info@servite.rbkc.sch.uk
Website: www.serviteprimaryschool.co.uk

Executive Head Teacher: Since 2002, Mrs Kathleen Williams BEd NPQH (thirties). Was previously deputy head of St Mary's Primary in Ladbroke Grove. Has been in teaching for many years and is married. Affable and approachable. Pupils look round eagerly as she enters the classroom, trying to catch her eye. Shares a headship with another school and is passionate about developing leadership skills in schools. With the help of two able deputy heads, she has raised the academic standard over the past few years. Achieved an outstanding Ofsted as well as an exceptional delivery of the national school sports strategy in 2007.

Entrance: At 3+ into the nursery but this does not guarantee a place in the primary. Very oversubscribed. Sibling priority only in the event of a tie breaker. Thirty pupils per class. Parish boundaries denote the catchment area and only practising Catholics bearing a reference to prove it from their parish priests need apply. The Servite Priory (and trustees of the school) is next door and participates fully in school life; 'very keen to keep strong links.' Children celebrate Founders' Day in February each year.

Exit: Mostly to the London state Catholic day schools: Cardinal Vaughan, London Oratory, Sacred Heart, Gunnersbury, St Thomas More plus Chelsea Academy. Those who go down the private path tend to opt for Queen's Gate or Wimbledon High.

Remarks: This is a mixed, inclusive school on Fulham Road opposite the Chelsea and Westminster Hospital. Many pupils come from the Worlds' End estate on the King's Road and the head promotes an atmosphere of 'community cohesion and racial harmony' within the school. The staff are young and energetic but a solid core in leadership positions gives 'strong and consistent leadership.' With an EAL level of 65 per cent, Servite offers 12 support staff, with one working full time in most classes. There is also a special needs teacher to give additional support to those who need extra help. Catch-up programmes, an early intervention team plus part-time therapists help to bridge the gap between school and home. The school prides itself on having strong links with external agencies such as a social worker, a nurse, an educational psychologist and a play therapist. Specialist teachers are brought in for Spanish, French, gymnastics, dance, music and art; 'A broad and balanced curriculum is essential for raising standards and preparing pupils for the future. Encouraging creativity of thought at a young age can lead to independence in learning and high achievement,' says the head. Although the building is modern and boxy, its very practical design helps communication and the large classrooms facilitate shared teaching and other such initiatives. A parent council offers a useful consultation platform while the PTA concentrates on fund-raising. Large gym doubles as a theatre for drama productions and musical concerts. Each class holds an assembly each week giving all an opportunity for public speaking, thus building their self-confidence from a young age. The playground is concrete but spacious. Awnings and umbrellas are available in summer to afford some protection from the sun. Clubs and activities are offered as part of the wrap-around school care between 8am and 6pm. A voluntary aided school, all parents are asked to make a set contribution each year of £30-£45, in addition to paying for after-school clubs.

This is a perfectly competent inner city primary school which aims to provide its pupils with a sound education whilst embracing the teachings of Christ. Religious assemblies and collective worship take place in the classroom, with prayers at the beginning of the day, before lunch and at going home time. Religious education is taught for several hours a week and is one of the core subjects underlying the school's mission statement: 'Learning to love, loving to learn.'

Shapwick Prep School

Linked school: Shapwick School

Mark Road, Burtle, Bridgwater, Somerset, TA7 8NJ

• Pupils: 40 boys and girls; • Ages: 6-13; • Non-denominational;
• Fees: Day £16,266; Boarding £21,306-£22,452 pa; • Independent

Tel: 01278 722012
Email: prep@shapwickschool.com
Website: www.shapwickschool.com

Joint heads: Since 2013, Martin Lee BA PGCE. Head of the senior school as well as the prep. 'The school has over many years succeeded in delivering the national curriculum to students who might otherwise fail in a mainstream setting,' he told us. 'I believe my main role is creating a safe supportive teaching and learning environment, where our students respond with creativity and hard work.' Sees the key elements at Shapwick as 'strong values, highly skilled, experienced teachers, an embedded therapeutic programme, excellent teacher/student relationships, motivated students and supportive parents' and says he sees his job as 'more climate control and less command and control.'

Entrance: Pupils can join at any stage. Open days include the opportunity for applicants to be assessed to ascertain level of need. Some via tribunal process but most enter privately or in mid-process depending on need or desperation.

Exit: Almost all to senior school though a few may re-enter mainstream education.

Remarks: Recently re-branded as Shapwick Prep from former Edington and Shapwick Junior School. Provides small scale, specialist education way out on Somerset Levels. School has become centre of excellence for SpLD – is organising a Diploma/Masters course for practising teachers, receives students from Exeter university and elsewhere. Site includes former farmhouse, vicarage and village school, a collection of 'temporary' classrooms and a purpose-built complex for youngest children plus therapy rooms known as the ARC (assessment and resource centre).

Pupils have English and maths classes all morning; therapy sessions arranged throughout day in ARC – withdrawal negotiated with staff. Remainder of day largely related to national curriculum work, includes lots of sport, art and music. Lovely science lab with specialist teaching from senior school. Small classes throughout school and plenty of one-to-one.

School is welcoming and visually attractive with stimulating display work in classrooms. Super outside play and activity area as well as large playing fields. Loads of ICT including individual laptops for pupils in year 8. Focus here on tackling SpLD within supportive, friendly environment. Children seem relaxed and confident. Super solution for those lucky enough to have the right funding at this earlier stage in schooling.

Parents pay extra for uniform and some trips: eg skiing

S

Sheen Mount Primary School

West Temple Sheen, London, SW14 7RT

- Pupils: 450 boys and girls; all day • Ages: 4–11 • Non-denom
- State

Tel: 020 8876 8394
Email: info@sheenmount.richmond.sch.uk
Website: www.sheenmount.richmond.sch.uk

Headteacher: Since 2009, Mr Ian Hutchings BSc PGCE NPQH (thirties). Previously deputy head here (since 2005) and before that at St John's Kingston and East Sheen Primary.

Having inherited an already successful and thriving school (he received huge backing from parents and staff to get the headship) the challenge has been to maintain and improve it. Parents seem happy with his progress, with one describing him as 'a top man' and another as 'on the ball'. He's younger than some of his pupils' parents, but evidently a strong enough character to deal with a rather full-on cohort of mothers and fathers, locally famed for their hands-on involvement with the school. Operates an open-door policy and also usually around in the playground before and after school. He's 'fair, approachable and responsive,' say parents and any lack of experience is more than compensated for by his fresh approach and openness to new ideas.

He has a calm and considered demeanour, which seems to permeate the school. Focused and a little corporate on occasion – talks about 'free flow access to outside space' and 'delivery of ICT'. But behind the jargon one senses a caring man, very pleased to have this job and bursting with enthusiasm and ideas for primary education. Genuinely enjoys the company of the children – takes some cover lessons – and they like and respect him in return, although his dry sense of humour sometimes goes over their heads.

Married with a young daughter. Enjoys skiing in the holidays.

Entrance: Ridiculously small catchment area; you'll need to live very close to get a place at this oversubscribed school. Cut off distance is normally between 300 and 500m and families moving to the area ask estate agents if houses are 'sheen Mountable?' (NB in common with many schools Sheen Mount has been asked by the LA to take an additional reception class in 2015 and 2018 if necessary, so 90 instead of usual 60 places, which will mean larger than usual numbers of siblings will take priority in the next few years). School says its worth asking about occasional places higher up the school – but reality is hardly anyone leaves this place if they can avoid it.

Exit: Some 60 per cent hotfoot it to the independent sector, having used this place as a state 'prep'. Some 20 different schools feature on Sheen Mount's list of secondary destinations – literally one here, one there, from Colet Court to Wimbledon High, but always a contingent to Hampton Boys, Surbiton High (girls) and Ibstock (mixed). The other 40 per cent search for a state school to match their charmed primary experience at Sheen Mount – parents openly yearn for a senior section to this school. Hardly any opt for the nearest secondary school option, Richmond Park Academy; although head commends its 'amazing resources' and says he tries to encourage the good state options available. Most popular local state choices are Grey Court and Christ's, with Waldegrave Girls an option for those living that side of the borough. A few (again just one or two) to the Kingston grammars. School is alive to the requirement for information about independent schools and invites their representatives to its various 'future schools' information evenings.

Remarks: A super school, locally lauded as the best in the area, tucked away behind the stylish residential streets of up-market East Sheen. 'It's like having a very local private school on our doorstep,' said one mother. 'We do recognise how privileged we are.'

Underwhelming at first glance, hidden from view next door to a pub (but a gastro-pub of course and owned by a TV chef), the scale and scope of the school doesn't hit you until you get inside. The site is much larger than it first appears with buildings recently refurbished and seamlessly extended so that there are no obvious 'new' and 'old' parts to the school. Classrooms are big, bright and airy, first floor ones with a relaxing view of treetops. Playgrounds and playing fields have also been revamped so there is an outdoor classroom, a science garden, an allotment, lots of climbing equipment and overall a huge amount of greenery for an urban school.

But nice though it is to have everything ship shape, it would count for nothing were it not for the top-notch learning environment here.

School's strong teaching team is quite young, pleasingly includes some male teachers, and has developed its own curriculum. 'We are not constrained by the national curriculum requirements, but rather pick and choose what adds value, it's a really creative, cross-curricular offering,' says head. Seems to pay off big time – Ofsted rates the school outstanding, Sats results are sparkling and its value added score is 101.8 (particularly impressive when you consider the unremittingly middle class intake here means that Sheen Mount pupils are no slouches from the off).

There's a purposeful, industrious atmosphere in the classrooms. Children are really involved with the lessons and uber keen to share what they are doing – there was an audible groan from children not selected to answer a question or show some of their work. The vocabulary and empathy of even the youngest children as they answer questions about a piece of writing is startlingly impressive. Cursive handwriting similarly strong. The children do their work in a learning journal which moves with them through the school. This fits in with the cross-curricular approach to teaching and makes it easier to check progression; for example if a child's target is to improve use of punctuation, progress can be seen across all subject areas. The only subject not in the journal is maths, which is handled separately, but with equal focus. Mantra is 'excellence in all things' and to this end head has introduced more rigorous target setting and progress monitoring, all aimed at getting a better handle on each individual child. 'I believe that our high academic standards are almost a by-product of our efforts to make sure every child achieves their full potential, wherever that may lie,' he says. Special needs support is led by a full-time inclusion manager supported by a part-time teacher and a high proportion of teaching assistants throughout the school. Happy to take children with Downs and autism and most physical disabilities, as only one part of the building is not accessible by lift. School statistics show relatively high numbers of pupils with English as an additional language, but head says figures are misleading. Many children are automatically badged as EAL when in fact they may be newly arrived from Scandinavia with English a fluent second language and present no more of a teaching challenge than any native of East Sheen.

French is taught from year 1. There are weekly music lessons from a specialist teacher and a great dedicated music space, well-resourced with instruments. Head likes his technology and as well as an ICT suite children have use of netbooks and WiFi in their classrooms. Parents describe recent art and drama showcases as 'outstanding'. 'The children perform with huge confidence, and whether it's a big show or a class assembly, they all speak so clearly and every one of them is involved,' said one. Loads of artwork on display around the school.

Quite a wide offering of sports for a state school with plenty of support from parents; for example, a qualified coach/mother runs the thriving netball club. A few moans about school's unwillingness to promote excellence and competition – 'those seem dirty words in a state school' said one parent. 'It's all about just taking part'. As well as its own grounds, including a smart open air, heated, swimming pool, the school uses nearby Richmond Park. School also takes full advantage of all the outreach opportunities offered by local clubs, such as Harlequins rugby coaching. Plenty of trips and lots of extra-curricular, although one mother felt her daughter was offered more opportunities than her son, who was not enticed by yoga, street dance and cheerleading clubs. Breakfast and after-school club provides care from 7.30am until 6pm, run by outside company, Fit for Sport. No commitment, parents who suddenly find themselves in need of help can book via website as late as the night before.

School describes its approach to behaviour management as 'positive'. There are five golden rules which are rarely broken. Every child starts with week with 20 minutes of golden time and will lose two minutes for every transgression, as well as a visit to head so that they can 'explain themselves'. But these children are polite and well-behaved for the most part and rarely take the walk of shame to his office. Parents very happy with pastoral care, describing it as 'excellent' and say home/school communication is good. 'I think parents will always be hungry for as much information as possible, but I think Sheen Mount does well enough', said one. Simple example of good school/pupil communications is the school toilets – children were consulted about the new colour scheme (girls voted green and boys purple if you were wondering), theory being they are more likely to value the space, and keep nice, something they've been involved in choosing. There's also a 'bubble box' in classrooms where children can post any concerns, which will be picked up by their class teacher.

Slight criticism of school dinners in our last review obviously stung. Head at pains to show off rebuilt school kitchen where all the food is prepared from fresh; not so much as a sauce or a pizza base bought in. We watched children tucking into a proper roast dinner, served on china plates rather than dreadful institutionalised plastic trays. Not masses of choice (though there was salad and fresh fruit) but actually nice that everyone was eating the same, sitting around in small groups rather than long benches. Children can bring in their own packed lunches and some do – but they are not segregated and can sit with friends who are eating school dinners. All very civilised.

About the only negative in the last Ofsted report was pupil attendance. Nothing to do with truanting here, but apparently caused by parents taking their children out for term time holidays. Some of the families have links overseas, or older siblings at private schools with longer holidays. These affluent types consider that the school's disapproval and only available sanction, the £50 (national figure) penalty, is a price worth paying for their convenience.

However that's not to say that parents are generally disdainful of this place – they all recognise it is a gem and are happy to give generously of their time and money to ensure the place is superbly resourced and has great facilities. Their support is a real USP of the school and goes above and beyond the norm. 'We are absolutely on board, there's no them and us,' said one. 'It's a bit full on,' ventured another. 'Because we all live locally and walk to school we all get to know each other and it's hard not to get drawn in.' Parents who prefer to keep their distance, beware.

Big wow to the PTA, which gets involved with major building projects and raises seriously impressive sums – typically £40,000 a year, but on occasion they have raised that through one big event alone. 'We raise so much money it is almost embarrassing,' said one mother. 'But there are also some purely fun events and I'm glad we now support outside charities as well'.

Definitely a cut above the (above) average state primary. Turns out confident, articulate pupils, who have enjoyed a really positive educational experience. Great sense of community. Fail to get involved at your peril.

Sheffield High Junior School

Linked school: Sheffield High School

5 Melbourne Avenue, Sheffield, S10 2QH

• Pupils: 220 girls; all day • Ages: 4–11 • Non-denom
• Fees: £7,701–£8,169 pa • Independent

Tel: 01142 661435
Email: enquiries@she.gdst.net
Website: www.sheffieldhighschool.org.uk

Head: Since 2002, Mrs Anne Jones, BSc PGCE PGDip Ed; 12 years' experience in maintained sector, joined the school in 1993; liked by the children, seen as approachable by parents; interested in developing enrichment, teaches maths to a year 6 set. Husband a CEO in the charity sector, two adult children; ISI inspector; enjoys sailing.

Entrance: Juniors – informal individual assessment in English and maths at any time (generally above national average ability); reception – informal individual assessment to check for school readiness, at the school or at the child's nursery.

Exit: Ninety-five per cent to the senior school.

Remarks: Achieves high academic standards generally and develops independent learning and thinking skills. Shares staff with the senior school – by years 5-6 mostly specialist teaching. Science is strong, with lots of practical work, and modern languages – French from reception to year 3, Spanish in years 4-5, German in year 6. Two half days a term spent on mixed age, small group, problem-solving work encouraging 'thinking outside the box', plus half termly extended homework tasks. Girls speak appreciatively of their teachers as 'very helpful and clear', 'They make the lessons fun'.

Good learning support – close liaison with the senior school; specialist dyslexia sessions at an extra charge or free, small group English and maths with a teaching assistant; EAL support too. Can manage mild autism; physical disabilities would be difficult because of the nature of the building, but they would 'try if possible'.

Plenty of computers and electronic white boards – fully integrated IT and an extensive VLE with details of current lessons. Bright, large classrooms with exceptionally good displays – a lot of high quality work; average class size: 19. A very well stocked and attractive library, with a flower-shaped table for laptops and plasma screen – all classes have a weekly session for book-related work/activities. Focused and enthusiastic children.

Own gym and access to senior school sports facilities for the older children; netball, badminton and diving success at city and county level. Plenty of music (the music room is a large loft conversion): regular performances, eg at a local retirement village, and an annual musical. The girls have named their ensembles Prawn Cocktails (the wind band), Spaghetti Strings and Angel Delight (the chamber choir) – making a concert a three course meal! Lots of LAMDA and impressive art and design, eg some interesting constructions made from recycled materials, inspired by a visit to a Victorian water wheel.

An extensive range of clubs – jewellery making, sewing, Latin, chess, science, Mandarin Chinese, street dance, yoga, cookery – with input from sixth form girls; fund-raising for a school in Kenya; a school council plus participation in the senior school council and whole school Kitchen Cabinet (for suggestions

S

about food); talks from various visitors, including parents, who support multi-cultural topics, such as an Indian wedding and fashion show. A sensory garden area plus adventure playground with stepping stones, netball court, wild area to come; each class has its own lot.

Plenty of contact with parents via newsletters and a comprehensive website. Good rewards and behaviour policies (the latter reviewed annually by the school council) and pastoral care (parents say problems are dealt with promptly and effectively); smooth transition to the senior school. Girls are 'given independence within a secure framework, in an empathetic atmosphere,' said a parent. Well-behaved children, very smart in their green and blue skirts, green blouses and jumpers, who present as happy, confident, thoughtful and forthcoming. Wide choice of food. Wraparound care 7.45am-5.30pm – a charge for after-school only (includes food).

Infants have their own recently acquired house with cheerful, well-resourced classrooms – we particularly liked the French room's circular blue carpet decorated with green lily pads, numbers and letters; another well-stocked library with an interactive plasma screen for reception (interactive whiteboards in all the other classrooms). A pleasant outdoor area with a mini netball goal and tubs for gardening. Early years quality mark – judged 'outstanding' all round by Ofsted 2008. 16 max in reception, 18 max for the rest.

Sherborne Preparatory School

Acreman Street, Sherborne, DT9 3NY

• Pupils: 260; 195 in the prep; 40 boarders; 65 in pre-prep.
• Ages: 2–13 • C of E • Fees: Boarding £19,140–£21,450; Day £8,100–£14,970 pa • Independent

Tel: 01935 812097
Email: registrar@sherborneprep.org
Website: www.sherborneprep.org

Headmaster: Since 1998, Peter Tait MA DipEd DipTeaching FRSA (fifties). Non-conformist, hands-on New Zealander whom we found crouched under his desk when we arrived (digging in a toolbox, preparing to hang a picture). Educated in New Zealand and spent much of his teaching career there (deputy head of a prep, then head of English, head of history and housemaster in senior schools). Two separate spells at Sherborne Prep in the eighties swayed him to settle there permanently when the headship came up. Campaigning gently, from within, to transform CE: 'the current exam tyrannises two years of the curriculum.' Not averse to putting pen to paper, Mr Tait publishes collections of his think pieces from school newsletters (on education, childhood, modern life, international relations, history) in compilations called 'Headmaster's Musings', and in the national press. Has written hard-hitting articles in IAPS magazine and in Telegraph on eg prep schools' submissiveness to senior schools and their willingness to straightjacket themselves to the CE syllabus rather than provide education for life. Hates spoon-feeding – 'it goes on all the way up to A level while universities are crying out for creative, independent learners!' Keen to keep prep down to a manageable level – '40 per cent of prep set in most schools is a waste of time. It's got to be really worthwhile to deprive a child of his or her childhood.'

Entrance: Non-selective, non-snooty. Interview with head and school report. Informal assessment when the pupil comes in for a trial day before joining the school. Mainly local families, plus London drift, plus 10 from overseas. Scholarships available for academics (papers in maths and English), music, sports

and all-rounders. Bursaries awarded on a case by case basis for existing parents. New parents may apply if their child wins a scholarship. Forces discount. A few JET (Joint Educational Trust) children accepted.

Exit: Boys: half to Sherborne School, rest to Eton, Marlborough, Radley, Winchester, Rugby, King's Bruton, Dauntsey's, Clayesmore. Girls: roughly a quarter to Sherborne Girls, the rest to Cheltenham Ladies', Wycombe Abbey, Canford, Leweston, Bryanston, Rugby, King's Bruton, Clayesmore. Loads of scholarships – for everything. Occasional pupil to a state school.

Remarks: Characterful prep marching to the beat of its own drum. Founded in 1885, the school is now a bustling community hidden behind a mild-mannered Sherborne street-front. Difficult to capture in words – Sherborne Prep looks traditional but thinks outside the box. Open to new ideas; indeed Mr Tait actively seeks them out. Has looked closely at IB early years programmes, among other options and we nod approvingly, noting that this was the first prep in the area to dump Sats exams. Optional, non-academic Saturday morning programme. Pupils may choose from vast menu of activities and come along – in mufti – for only one hour, or up to three. So families used to their children being occupied on Saturday mornings are happy, teachers enjoy the variety, there is more flexibility for the child who has Saturday commitments outside school etc. Also takes pressure off weekdays – play rehearsals can take place on Saturdays rather than after school or during lunchtimes. Ambitious offerings include eg art extra languages for pupils and/or parents, rock and music tech workshop, bushcraft, forensic detectives, sports coaching, karate, sewing, stage design. Sounds fab, and parents we spoke to were enthusiastic. More than 90 per cent of the children take part and, according to parents, 'it is an outstanding success' with activities supported by Sherborne School and Sherborne Girls. Saturday afternoon matches continue as before.

Keen on international links. Not only is the head from New Zealand but the head of art is Spanish, head of science is French, a senior French teacher is Zimbabwean, the German teacher is Swiss, the Mandarin teacher is Chinese, the EFL teacher is Swiss, gappies come from New Zealand and Australia. Breaking the mould when it comes to languages. In years 1 to 4 pupils learn French, Spanish, German and Mandarin (one each year). Everyone hunkers down to French in years 5 and 6 plus Latin/classical civilisation. In the final two years, when streaming kicks in, pupils can continue with French or shift to Spanish. Pupils in the CE stream may drop Latin and opt for Spanish alongside French, emerging with two living languages – an option not available to scholars (though the keen can do extra languages on Saturdays).

Thirty-three pupils currently receive help for SEN in big, airy learning support room. Beauteous new library (shoes off before entering) and art room – a wonderful open space, full of light and colour. Having glass walls, 'our art room is a place of discovery; pupils learn about themselves while looking at the world, literally!' DT, also well-housed, produces interesting projects, a notch above standard prep school fare. Main computer room adequate rather than cutting edge. Lots of sport, with girls' sport on a high, says school. Netball best season ever and reached final of Dorset Championships. Girls' hockey is becoming stronger each year as the coaching improves. The U13 girls' hockey team is very strong. Swimming going from strength to strength with new swimming coach in place and pupils competing at the IAPS national finals and winning medals. Boys' hockey is strong, they finished in the top 10 at the nationals last year and boys' cricket had an excellent year, only losing one match. Makes use of some Sherborne School sports facilities eg its Astro (school has its own smaller version). Ninety per cent of pupils play a musical instrument, from beginners up to grade 8; concerts every term. The music centre has now been refurbished to create an even larger teaching space, boasting a new baby grand piano, new (very loud) drum kit, projector, computer with composing software and new musical instruments. Head has recently appointed Sherborne Prep's first head of drama to indicate the subject's importance within the school.

Lovely children with nice manners. What do they like best? Their 'funny, nice teachers'. Gripes? Would like better match teas ('we get baked beans and sausages instead of cakes'). Retains some of the best prep school traditions like an intricate assortment of lapel badges to indicate accomplishment or responsibility, and teachers dolloping out lunch family-style. Many teachers double up their teaching in weird and wonderful ways eg DT and maths, science and maths, art and basketball. Religion present but inconspicuous. Boarding appealing (especially girls'), flexible and low key. Boarders are mainly children of local working parents, plus a few pupils from overseas and small Forces contingent. Some pop home on weekends, including non-Brits who may enjoy the hospitality of their local friends. A trip is organised on Sundays for those who remain in school. Cheerful pre-prep and nursery, with small classes and much encouragement. Also mother-toddler group. OBs include poet Louis MacNeice and the literary Powys brothers.

Shrewsbury High Prep School

Linked school: Shrewsbury High School

Old Roman Road, Kingsland Grange, Shrewsbury, SY3 9AH

• Pupils: Prep 250, all day; Shrewsbury High Prep : 170 girls and 75 boys • Ages: Girls 4-11, boys 4-13. Nursery 3+ boys and girls.
• Non-denom • Fees: £6,489–£11,652 pa • Independent

Tel: 01743 494200
Email: enquiries@shr.gdst.net
Website: www.shrewsburyhigh.gdst.net

Head of prep school: Since 2005, Maria Edwards. A redoubtable and remarkable woman who, before stepping on to the bridge at Shrewsbury High Prep, was head of Abbots Bromley Prep for six years, where she is still remembered with affection. A keen athlete, she represented Wales at tennis and netball, and in her prime it is said she could stand on one hand. She refused to give a demonstration. She is a keen dancer, specialising in French rock and roll, and legend has her encouraging parents to join her in Ceroc dancing. Mercifully for all, we were not asked to dance. The school, as it is now, is really her baby and she it is who has presided over its evolution and emergence. In the process she has sat on IAPS, GSA and GDST committees, and done some teaching across the age groups getting to know the children.

Parents acknowledge her open door policy, describing her as a trifle formal initially but never less than concerned, interested and professional. 'She is completely wrapped up in the school and the children,' said one parent. 'She can be quite fierce if she doesn't approve of something,' said another, 'but she loves the children.'

Married with her own children at university. She and the headmaster of the High School, with whom she gets on extremely well, are moulding this educational package into something that really seems to work. It's a project in progress and most parents delight in it.

Entrance: Boys and girls are admitted into the nursery from age 3 'with no formal testing.' Places in reception by means of formal assessments during a day spent at the school with the class that the pupil might eventually join. Parents are advised of any areas which might need special attention from a tutor.

So it isn't just in London that the young are being specially prepared, though parents assured us it wasn't as gruelling as that extract from the prospectus might suggest. In truth, children would probably be accepted at any stage if they were up to it and space was available.

Exit: Most girls move on to Shrewsbury High School at age 11 – indeed that is really the reason for the existence of the prep. Boys remain at the prep until 13 though a few also leave at 11 to local grammars. Girls are tested in verbal reasoning, non verbal reasoning and quantitative skills. Most girls are accepted but it is not automatic. Boys are prepared for CE or scholarship and most progress to Concord College, Shrewsbury School, Wrekin College or Ellesmere School. Shrewsbury is no longer the automatic first choice for parents of talented boys 'perhaps because of the fees in this difficult (financial) climate,' the head told us. One parent suggested another reason. Lots of really good scholarships have been won recently.

Remarks: For over 100 years the impressive black and white house, which is the first house you see after you've been let in through the electric gates, was the main building of a boys' only prep school called Kingsland Grange. From 1964 for about 30 years the wonderful Groves brothers, Alan and Dick, both Old Salopians, ran the school with marked success, particularly on the sports field. But there were always scholarships and some music. Boarding, in common with many schools, became less popular and eventually the school, while remaining strong, became a day school. In 2007 the school merged with Shrewsbury High and the wealth and vision of the GDST began to kick in. It wasn't just the railings outside the school being painted blue which signalled to the world a new ownership; the 13 acres of land were skilfully, sensibly and attractively landscaped so that the view from the outside of the house is even more delightful. We met children who actually pointed out their favourite views. In amongst the trees and valleys a cross country course has been laid out as well as new cricket pitches and other games fields. William Kent, it is famously said, 'jumped the fence and found all nature was a garden.' He'd have been pleased with what has been done in this campus, and amazed that apparently some of nature has jumped onto the roof. There has been some marvellous new building: a wonderful new dining room with, it is said, delicious food, for which the school charges £176 a term; new bright classrooms kitted out with modern gizmos, a superb sports hall, a science lab and a design and technology workshop. This building boasts its own solar power generation unit, sun-pipes for illumination, and, wait for it Mr Kent, a green roof planted with sedum to keep the building cool in summer and warm in winter.

Meanwhile, back in the old house with the wonderful main staircase, the higgledy-piggledy back stairs and the late Victorian stained glass windows, with dance music filling the hall (not the head practising), that venerable old house has been fully refurbished and modernised with state-of-the art technology and the music department. Music is particularly strong, and a number of excellent music scholarships have been won to top schools. In fact, if you want to know if Mrs Edwards and her teachers are making the most of these facilities, read the prospectus and visit. Good academic results, good drama, art, music and sport; good out of school activities. The adventure all begins in a wonderfully imaginative nursery with magic grass, a Once Upon a Time chair in the trees, and bright, glorious teachers. It feels like a very cheery school. One parent told us, 'it's almost too good to be true.' There are several ways of looking at that but we recommend you visit and see for yourselves.

Shrewsbury House School

107 Ditton Road, Surbiton, KT6 6RL

• Pupils: 320 boys aged 7-13 in main school; Shrewsbury Lodge pre-prep 140 children aged 3-7 years co-educational • Ages: 3-13 • C of E • Fees: £15,195 pa • Independent

Tel: 020 8399 3066
Email: office@shspost.co.uk
Website: www.shrewsburyhouse.net

Headmaster: Since 2010, Mr Kevin Doble BA (law and political sciences) PGCE (early forties). Educated at St John's College, Johannesburg and has a postgrad degree in management. Previously second master and acting head at Edge Grove prep, and before that head of English at Newlands School and Vinehall prep. This is his first experience of a day school, although he likens it to 'a boarding school with no beds' because of the breadth of opportunities on offer to Shrewsbury House boys. 'I know that the move I made to Surrey was a crackingly good one,' he says.

Parents appreciate his softly softly approach to filling the big shoes of long-serving predecessor Mark Ross. He's quite different character, more contained, but no less passionate about his work. Eloquent, focused and evidently relishes the vivacity of the school day. He's made a few changes (parents say largely logistic and for the better) and his recent staff appointments and promotions are popular. 'He's great,' said one parent. 'I think everyone is excited about the school's future under his watch,' said another.

Seemingly not enough hours in the day for the head – and the pupils he calls 'these little guys.' He cuts a rangy figure as he makes his presence felt around the place, at the gates morning and night and out on the touchline as often as possible. When he can be lured inside, he directs operations from his homely 'oval office' (named from its bay window looking out over the playground) and packed with books, art, sports memorabilia, and a big green leather sofa for his many visitors. Keen to keep up a continual dialogue with staff, parents, pupils and other heads, he's quickly gained a reputation as very approachable. Still fits in some teaching – takes each year 5 class for a lesson a week in English. 'My son is riveted by his lessons,' said one mother. 'He was telling ghost stories off the cuff the other day and evidently had them spellbound.'

Parents seem supportive and pupils evidently feel comfortable around him too. One mother told us that she overheard a boy asking why he had to have his hair cut short for school – 'and the head took him seriously and gave him a proper response, not just a "because we say so" answer.' Meanwhile another parent commented: 'It's rather a cliché, but he really does seem to combine youthful enthusiasm with respect for this school's reputation and heritage.'

He loves sport and has had great success managing the Saxon Tigers U15 and U17 squads for England hockey and in coaching cricket. Chairman IAPS Sports committee for sports. Lists his recreations as (more) sport, drama, children's literature, opera, painting and drawing. Keen traveller, enjoys going out for meals and generally 'recharging' during weekends and holidays.

Entrance: At seven, there are up to 50 places available, with around four applications for each one. Currently receiving requests to register children at birth. Most come from pre-preps, including its own Shrewsbury Lodge (off-site, formerly Milbourne Lodge junior school, merged with Shrewsbury House in 2010), Weston Green, Wimbledon Common Prep, The Rowans, Park Hill, Linley House, Lion House School, The Merlin, Putney Park School and Athelstan House. Around 25 per cent come from the state system. While 20 years ago this was a very local school, now 50 per cent of pupils are bussed in from over five miles away.

The head believes that too often a school's admissions criteria will be overtly focused on one thing – 'usually a unilateral adhesion to academic demands' – and he personally eschews the notion of early assessment as 'ridiculous at that age.' But he acknowledges that the school has to ensure its boys are up to the above average requirements of coping with an intensive day. So Shrewsbury House does it slightly differently, with two types of entry – conditional (non-competitive, formerly called guaranteed) and competitive. But be warned, the 35 or so conditional places are snapped up sharpish and your son will still be gently assessed to ensure he'll be able to cope at the school. These tests are held in the autumn before anticipated entry and are for families for whom the school is first choice and are therefore happy to cough up half a term's fees as a deposit. Once these places are filled, then the remaining dozen or so competitive places are up for grabs by the boys who achieve the highest scores in non-verbal and verbal assessments. Some bursaries available.

This place is all about 13+ and there is no support or preparation for boys looking to move at 11+. Look elsewhere if you have your eye on other senior school destinations – it's not the path for you.

Exit: At 13, boys progress to an impressive range of some 15 senior schools, including King's College School (Wimbledon), Hampton School, St Paul's, St John's, Epsom College, Wellington, Charterhouse, Tonbridge and The Royal Grammar School (Guildford). A few go to Eton and Harrow. The school's previous head (in post for 23 years) gave parents enormous confidence in this area, so the new head's challenge must be to forge strong links of his own. He's off to a good start. Parents describe him as 'very knowledgeable' when he discusses future schools for their sons, first of all in year 5, and he prides himself on his personal relationships with all the leading senior school heads. 'I know all these men and understand exactly how their schools are ticking on,' he says. Has just launched a scheme to send Shrewsbury House heads of department out to senior schools to improve their grasp of what's expected. Also talks of plans to track boys after they leave. 'I like his idea of making Shrewsbury House accountable,' said one mother. 'It's not just about getting them through CE and not caring past that – he seems to want to make sure the boys are equipped to thrive beyond this school.' Head particularly pleased to have enticed Anthony Seldon (head of Wellington) as a governor recently – 'It's not his usual thing at all.'

Remarks: This is a first class prep, where academic rigour is balanced by an equally strong offering in arts and sport. Although your son will need to be above average academically to cope here, with that proviso, the school says it takes a range of abilities. But be warned. As one mother advises: 'It's not intensely academic, but I wouldn't recommend it for a boy who just scrapes the test. It's quite full on.' Others agree it is not for the faint-hearted. 'You have to be quite committed to come here,' says a parent, 'and that includes parents as well as boys.' 'They are run ragged,' says another. 'But they come home happy.' Add to the academic and extensive extra-curricular offering a packed sporting programme, rehearsals, performances, charity initiatives, competitions and trips and you'll get the picture – these are busy boys.

Located on a quiet road in an up-market residential area of Surbiton, the school is one of the UK's oldest preps and celebrates its 150th anniversary in 2015. It is based around a Victorian house, but with additional purpose-built classrooms and impressive facilities, all on a six-acre site, including a playing field and a further seven acres at Almshouse Lane, which includes all-weather pitches and pavilions.

S

Broad-based, eclectic curriculum is delivered by a talented teaching team, much praised by parents. 'They are inspiring,' one mother told us. Every teacher is a qualified subject specialist and sports coaches have all been outstanding in their fields – the promise here is that whatever his ability, every boy will be taught and/or coached by someone with real expertise. 'I can't praise the teachers enough', said a parent. 'They seem to be here morning, noon and night, and weekends – and even holiday time clubs are starting now. They go beyond just teaching them. I walk away from parent evenings thinking "wow, I wish I'd had teachers like that."'

It's a longish and busy school day, but the boys seem to rise to the challenge, arriving by 8.15am and staying until at least 4pm, and very often 5.15 or 6.15pm when involved in extra-curricular clubs or sports matches. All the extra-curricular you can shake a stick at – from cookery (very popular) to rifle-shooting – or they can just stay and do their prep. Homework is thirty minutes to one hour plus per night, right from the beginning. Quite concentrated in term time, but now none in the holidays. 'Work is pretty relentless and they have high expectations of the boys', a mother told us. 'The motto is "aim high" and they do. You have to be very committed, even as a parent, because you will be involved along the way.'

Although the head believes there is generally too much testing, measuring and scoring in education these days, Shrewsbury House boys are set and streamed, comprehensively tracked and given plenty of exam practice. 'But I prefer to concentrate on performance, rather than results,' he says. 'If you get top performance, the results will come'.

Any special needs provision is given in the classroom setting, with staff supported by the special educational needs co-ordinator and a learning support teacher. Less than 10 per cent of boys have a learning difficulty or disability. All pupils have English as their first language or are fully bilingual.

Average class size is around 16 (fewer as boys move up the school and into sets), with an 8-1 pupil-teacher ratio overall. We saw some lively lessons, but always in a focused way, with all the boys on task. A French lesson, taught by a native speaker, with boys vying for an opportunity to speak was typical. Similarly, lots of fun and experiments in science. There's a particularly rich English timetable – year 8s were getting on swimmingly with The Rime of the Ancient Mariner, having just finished some Dickens. Asked if they found Dickens 'hard,' as per recent media coverage, they replied, 'no, because we had just done Othello and it was much easier than that.' Most classrooms are equipped with computer-integrated desks and the few without have Netbooks instead. Some great subject-specific classrooms, including a lively and bright maths room (50 boys won gold in the National Mathematics Challenge recently) and one of the best history rooms we've ever seen –a modern museum feel to the place with the teacher's own collection of helmets and weapons secured to the wall. Boys allowed to handle sometimes, which evidently helps bring the whole subject to life for them – a Shrewsbury House team has won the national Townsend Warner History Competition twice in the last four years. Even the Latin room, not traditionally a 'must-see' destination, was decorated with the teacher's own artefacts.

Music and sport are real strengths of this place. The school has an outstanding local reputation for sport, and several parents mention it as a deciding factor in their choice of Shrewsbury House. Major sports played are football, rugby and cricket, but, unsurprisingly following head's appointment, hockey is now writ large on the radar and other activities including fives and basketball have been introduced. School gives equal weight to the 'very good' and the 'not quite there yet' theory that many will get there in the end – as long as they are given the chance and not fobbed off with some French assistant keeping the fourth 11 busy. It's not unknown for boys to move from G team to A team during their time at the school. 'If you have a sporty son the school will embrace and develop that and take it to

the max,' says one mother. 'But equally, my other son was not sporty at all, yet still received top-notch coaching and was proud to represent the G and H teams.' This expert coaching, coupled with the huge pride the boys have in representing their school, undoubtedly gives them the edge and makes them formidable opponents – they have a 70 per cent win rate across the board.

Despite this renown and head's own predilection for the sporting life, he seems almost irritated by the 'sporty place' label. 'We actually spend more time on music, but that's not as well known because sport is such an outward-facing part of the curriculum and tends to attract more attention,' he told us.

Music is the other stand-out subject here. Around 85 per cent of the boys take instrumental or singing lessons and they get plenty of chances to perform – there are 25 different musical groups and regular concerts, with jazz and brass band especially popular. 'The standard is incredible,' said one parent. The boys put on six plays a year and everyone is expected to get involved at some point, even if only as the back of a horse or with a single line – it's all about getting them out of their comfort zone sometimes. LAMDA examinations another recent innovation.

Lovely to see the splendid library heaving at break times. Total of 6,000 books, lots of magazines and good attendances for author visits (lately Josh Lacey, Robert Muchamore, Ali Sparkes and Charlie Higson). Reading club for lower years. Boys also sitting drawing, following how-to-draw guides or just copying pictures of tanks out of reference books – so they are evidently not all out on the sports field.

Boys we saw were well-behaved – in fact an extremely courteous and friendly bunch. They won't get away with slacking, slouching or scruffiness as high standards prevail throughout, but overall the atmosphere is positive and they get plenty of praise where it's due. Healthy competition for 'plus points' – like house points except individual boys can win personal prizes, usually books, as well as credit for their house. Minus marks for minor misdemeanours, such as running in corridors or forgetting a book. Overall parents find school discipline is straightforward and consistent.

Some disquiet over variable school/home communications systems in the past – school says it has addressed this now and parents agree headway has been made. One big improvement is the instigation of a parent consultation evening, where the boys come with their parents to discuss their progress with teaching staff. This replaces a not very enticing invitation for parents to come in to discuss 'problems and difficulties.' Parents are also invited to head's biannual 'state of the nation'-type briefings and to a programme of lectures on subjects like happiness, self-esteem and revision technique. 'In the past the school gave you the feeling that they intended to get on with the job all by themselves and didn't welcome our input,' said one parent. 'But now it feels like more of a partnership.' Thriving parents' association does its bit too – organises lots of social dos alongside more heavyweight initiatives like the current £40,000+ project to refurbish the school's Irving room in celebration of the 150th anniversary.

A high achieving, all-round school, wonderfully purposeful and more inclusive than a first glance might suggest. New head seems to have parents and pupils on side and is making his presence felt.

Sibford Junior School

Linked school: Sibford School

Sibford Ferris, Banbury, OX15 5QL

• Pupils: 80 boys and 40; all day pupils • Ages: 3–11 • Quaker
• Fees: £7,758–£9,384 pa • Independent

Tel: 01295 781200
Email: admissions@sibfordschool.co.uk
Website: www.sibford.oxon.sch.uk

Head: Michael Goodwin (see senior school).

Entrance: At any time between the ages of three and 10. Parents of three and four-year-olds can choose to enrol their child on a full-time or flexi-session basis.

Exit: Majority to Sibford Senior School with approximately 10 per cent to mainly local state schools. Year 6 pupils in particular use many of the senior school facilities, so the transition feels a natural right of passage. All candidates undergo an admissions interview with the head.

Remarks: Mud, mud, glorious mud, with wellies and bright red boiler suits lending a touch of the 'heigh-hos' as off to joyful work the youngsters go. Ideal for the active, inquisitive child who learns by doing, listening. Daily outdoor sessions, come rain or shine, bring the environment to life, while reinforcing the basics of numeracy, literacy and social skills. A school for those who love joining in, dressing up (ask about 'Where's Wally' and other activity days) and having fun. Staff know children well, 'There is no place for my child to hide, not that he'd want to,' says one enthusiastic parent, adding, 'The children are confident, they feel secure, so it's especially ideal for those who tend to be shy or insecure, it really brings them out of their shell.'

Housed in own school but shares sports and dining facilities with seniors. Mainly class taught with sets for the basics and specialist subject teaching for music and PE. Plenty of help and good range of programmes for those with SpLD including reading recovery. Junior school offers a secure route to senior school; no Common Entrance or 11 plus prep for those considering alternative paths. Usual positions of responsibility, head boy/girl etc. Competitive spirit encouraged via house competitions and tournaments. Lots of activities and entertainment including philosophy club, look at 'how to think' not just 'what to think.'

Sidcot Junior School

Linked school: Sidcot School

Oakridge Lane, Winscombe, BS25 1PD

• Pupils: 122 boys and girls • Ages: 3–11 • Quaker and welcome all religions or none • Fees: Day £6,510–£9,690 pa • Independent

Tel: 01934 845200
Email: juniors@sidcot.org.uk
Website: www.sidcot.org.uk

Head: Since 2012, Claire Lilley.

Entrance: Non-selective, entry based on school reports and interview. Admission tests for years 5 and 6.

Exit: Nearly all pupils proceed to senior school. All take a baseline entrance assessment for the start of senior school life.

Remarks: Originated as The Hall School, Wedmore, and transferred to present site in 1990. Recently established as Sidcot Junior and now thriving in attractive, ecologically friendly new building joined to former school. Space limited in reception class but places not a problem once junior classes begin. Light, welcoming foyer and futuristic hall ideal for dance and music.

Quaker ethos but no teacher belongs to Society. Creative and nurturing atmosphere – children enjoying junk band workshop when we visited. More visits and experiential stuff than most junior schools. Innovative approaches include 'brain gym' to keep everyone mentally on their toes. Visually exciting environment. Links with seniors (eg helping with fund-raising) and use of some senior school facilities. Lots of activities at lunchtime. Emphasis on citizenship in PSHE. Specialist teaching eg in Spanish and French, own ICT suite, space for reading and research.

Shares SENCo with senior school; average of two IEPs per class; range of special needs: dyslexia, dyscalculia, dyspraxia and mild Asperger's currently accommodated but numbers kept within manageable limit. Overall academic standard is good. The majority of children remain in Sidcot environment once they have experienced Quaker approach.

Sir John Cass's Foundation Primary School

St James's Passage, 27 Duke's Place, London, EC3A 5DE

• Pupils: 270 (including Cass Child and Family Centre, up to 76) half girls, half boys • Ages: 3 months to 5 years (Cass Child and Family Centre), primary school 5–11 • C of E but other faiths welcomed • State

Tel: 020 7283 1147
Email: sirjohncassprimary@cityoflondon.gov.uk
Website: www.sirjohncassprimary.org

Executive Headteacher: Since January 1993, Mr Gerry Loughran (early fifties), a bright eyed-Geordie who steadfastly refuses to be tempted away into inspecting or the like – 'I don't want to leave the chalk face!' He's taught and co-ordinated and led at four other primaries in central London before Sir John Cass and still works alongside teachers.

Efficient and enthusiastic, he moves easily between talking to pupils – 'why are you in the classroom at lunch? I'm listening, you listen to me' – parents (about updating their work skills and what they need to look for in a secondary school), and bigwigs such as the Mayor. Very proud of success stories, eg a young mother just finished qualifying in Cambridge and keen to return to her old school to teach.

Entrance: At 3+, oversubscribed (75 applications for 30 places) and priority given to families/children in need in the City of London, then those who attend St Botolph's or neighbouring churches and live in the area, then siblings. Worth ringing, since places do open up when families move out of the area. If your child gets a place in the nursery, the school will do its utmost to keep them throughout the school.

Exit: To full range of secondary schools – church, community, independent and residential eg City of London Girls, City of London Boys, Christ's Hospital, City Academy in Southwark.

Since performing arts and music are so strong here parents are advised to look for opportunities for their children to continue.

Remarks: Founded in 1710, the only voluntary aided school in the City of London (so not short of resources); this Georgian mass is open 50 weeks a year and is so much more than just a school. An oasis in the traffic that is Aldgate (the pollution monitor in the playground registers remarkably low readings), pedestrians can peer down at the little ones in the courtyard of the Cass Child and Family Centre – 90 reading and language partners from surrounding offices volunteer at lunchtime. The main entrance is opposite a café, and visitors walk directly into the playground – the day we did, there was a line of helmeted children ready, with their trusty steeds, for their cycle safety test.

Between them pupils and parents speak 36 languages, and backgrounds range from two families sharing a flat to one with a Barbican pad and a house in the country. A teacher and a nursery officer work alongside class teachers to support those with English as a second language (50 per cent of the kids are Bangladeshi). A SENCo liaises with children, four LSAs and nine TAs foreground reading development, and school is also in touch with CAMHs. Snoezelen room in the nursery section is fully equipped with sensory equipment to calm children (and staff!). The school is totally inclusive of those with relevant support – at present three with statements and one with Downs Syndrome.

A key worker is assigned to four or five families and they are visited before children's entrance. The centre also offers an extended school service to the community with health and social visitors, Job Centre Plus and lots of advice and support sessions for parents in a family learning room and Sp@ce: computer lessons, volunteering at your school, child development classes, first aid, ESL and getting back to work training. Many social functions for parent and community group (eg summer market, international food night) and art projects have led to work exhibited in the V&A and the Bethnal Green Museum of Childhood.

The teaching team is stable and ranges from the newly qualified to those with 30 years of experience. RE is popular, with two terms on Christianity, the other on another world faith and, as with sex education, parents can withdraw their children from these lessons but none do. The curriculum is made real in all manner of ways: artist and poet residencies, a roof garden with class planters and greenhouse overlooked by the Foster's Gherkin, maths linked to musical notation and vice versa, the home beat police officer in class to talk about peer pressure and avoidance of gangs, after-school clubs (including knitting with senior citizens who provide tales of the war years to those kids with no extended family). Key stage 2 get to go on two school journeys for a week to experience life with their friends outside London.

A musicianship teacher begins the Strings Project with the little ones (nursery to year 3) and by years 4, 5 and 6 all play a violin, cello etc of their own – groups have performed for the Lord Mayor, Prince Phillip, Bill Clinton and Tony Blair. The choir has sung on the Queen's Christmas broadcast and at the Royal Albert Hall (three part harmony!).

The school coach runs relays to St George's Pool on the Highway or a crocodile of children snakes to the one in Golden Lane. The annual sports day takes place at Mile End stadium, the school competes as the City's team for the London Heathrow Games and occasionally plays rugby against other schools but, since it is the only one in the borough, there is not much competition. There's a traditionally equipped sports hall (huge windows and high ceilings throughout the school) on the second floor, in addition to the lines of different courts painted in the playground.

The basement (a secure area in case of bomb threat) houses the computer suite with 15 workstations networked to a couple in each class and an interactive whiteboard. This technology doesn't come without an awareness of the environment: the school received an award for work on recycling paper, printer cartridges, composting and installing timers on light switches.

Food is cooked on the premises and served in what is now called The Restaurant on the top floor; there are themed days with the menu scribed up on a whiteboard (tropical fruit, bread), and a comments book for the children. Some 35 per cent get free school meals. Manners are incredibly important here – one child says a prayer before everyone tucks in – everyone learns to behave politely according to their surroundings, whether it is lunch at Mansion House or breakfast club.

The Behaviour for Learning Policy is applied positively; however, a series of sanction slips is given out for ignoring the school code of conduct (respect, cooperation, truth and honesty, trying your best etc) – four of these mean the child will be excluded and this hardly ever happens. Fire drills and bomb alerts are necessarily slick with the head's bleeper linked directly to the City of London police.

Sir William Burrough Primary School

Salmon Lane, London, E14 7PQ

- Pupils: 335 girls and boys; • Ages: 3–11 years; • Non-denom;
- Fees: ; • State

Tel: 020 7987 2147
Email: admin@sirwilliamburrough.towerhamlets.sch.uk
Website: www.sirwilliamburrough.towerhamlets.sch.uk

Head: Since 1995, Mrs Avril Newman BEd (early sixties), who was educated at Hendon County Grammar School and has a first class degree in education from Goldsmith's. She has spent her entire career in East London primary schools and is a National Leader of Education for the National Council of School Leadership. A slight and engaging lady, married with two grown-up children, she is viewed by Ofsted as 'inspirational' and an 'excellent leader', and is evidently the driving force behind the school's immense success. When she joined, it had 'positive emotional energy', but a relaxed approach to the three Rs. 'I made sure we held onto the strengths of emotional intelligence whilst bringing in a more formal learning focus.'

Entrance: The usual priorities: medical or social need, siblings, then distance, which is not very far: this is a massively oversubscribed school in an area full of high-rise flats.

Exit: To a variety of local state secondaries; occasionally children go off to eg City Boys or Girls, sometimes on scholarships.

Remarks: Not far off the A13 Commercial Road, overshadowed by building sites, this is an oasis of colour and calm. Inside the tall Victorian building, brightly painted walls form a background to swathes of fabric, flowers, displays of work and photos of outings, with children in red, blue, green or yellow sweatshirts. A large proportion of the pupils are from Bangladeshi families, many others are Somalis, most are bi-lingual and about two-thirds are on free school meals. All are expected to do well, and they do. 'We do not wish to take deprivation, culture, class or gender into account. We're in the business of teaching and learning and the children do that for seven years here. We're ferocious about them learning to read, write and calculate – no-one falls through the net. Unless they have serious problems, we guarantee that they will meet or exceed government expectations.'

The school uses synthetic phonics to teach reading – 'they all learn very quickly and early'. As children become more proficient, they use an online accelerated reader system which monitors their progress, suggests books to read, sets quizzes and awards prizes. Maths is also taught by an online system: 'They always know what they need to learn next. They're not waiting for the teacher to hand out the next bit of learning.' Children requested, and received, a system that allows them to assess themselves and take time to fill in any gaps. They can also compete against children from other countries. As a result, around 90 per cent reach the expected level 4 in year 6 Sats, and a large proportion reach level 5.

However, this emphasis on the basics does not preclude an exciting, creative curriculum with a global dimension. Sir William Burrough was one of the first state primaries in the country to adopt the International Primary Curriculum (IPC). Originally developed for international schools run by petrol giant Shell, the IPC focuses on cross-curricular topics such as Fashion, Chocolate or Treasure. There's an emphasis on hands-on learning with huge numbers of trips out: children studying treasure start with a treasure hunt round the school then go off to the Tower of London to see the crown jewels. Year 6s learning about WW2 have an interactive show about an evacuee, delivered by an actor, and visit the Britain at War Experience at nearby London Bridge. Children Skype their peers in South Korea – 'they want our creativity, we want their maths results' – and some have travelled to Rome and Washington on exchange trips. The IPC and the British Council send many foreign visitors, and staff travel all over the world to see how other IPC schools operate. 'We're always scanning the horizon for better ideas.'

The children's experiences are well-documented: they make iMovies, animations and multi-media presentations as well as printing books of photos. 'Even the year 3s can edit their own presentations.' A room full of Apple Mac computers, plus plenty of laptops, are testimony to the school's profitable partnerships with several City firms, which also send in reading partners and chess mentors. The school business manager is a skilled fund-raiser, providing welcome extra funding for playground equipment, sports coaches, visiting artists, actors and storytellers.

The school's catch-phrase is 'You can do it'. 'If you can't do something you always keep trying,' say pupils. 'We're very independent and we never give up.' Pupils help to staff the reception desk and show round international visitors. The debating team has won competitions across London, and many pupils get merit or distinction in English Speaking Board assessments. When we visited, year 6 were rehearsing for a performance of Joseph and the Amazing Technicolour Dreamcoat. Assembly – which involves plenty of vigorous singing – happens at the end of the day. 'It harnesses their collective energy and sends them home feeling good about the day.'

The choreographer-in-residence organises spectacular dance displays; the 70-strong choir makes many public performances. Everyone plays the recorder. The three playgrounds include a wooded area where the children build camps and play on the jungle gym, and an all-purpose sports pitch. There are not many opportunities for inter-school matches, but plenty of sport: the cricket team has played at Lords, they swim at Mile End Leisure Centre and skate at Canary Wharf, play handball, baseball, hockey and rounders. Year 5 has a challenging outdoor pursuits week. After-school clubs include football, yoga, street dance and animation. 'They change as someone comes up with a new idea.'

The school has a strong relationship with the local community. 'We keep bringing groups of teachers, children, parents or governors together and asking the question: how can we do things better? We listen and act on what they suggest.' Parents help run the toddlers' group, support mother tongue classes and organise an 'opening doors' programme of families meeting in each other's homes. Many of the parents do not speak English at home, and this programme helps to create bonds across different ethnic groups. The children do not tend to feel any such separation. 'We all get along with each other,' they say. 'We have brilliant friendships.'

Somerhill Pre-prep

Linked schools: Yardley Court; Derwent Lodge School; The Schools at Somerhill

Somerhill, Tonbridge, TN11 0NJ

- Pupils: 262; 152 boys/110 girls • Ages: 3-6 • Non-denom
- Fees: £8,640-£10,020 pa • Independent

Tel: 01732 352124
Email: office@somerhill.org
Website: www.somerhill.org

Head: Ms Ruth Sorensen – experienced, capable and well-liked by both parents and children.

Remarks: One of the largest pre-preps in the area, highly popular. Based round the courtyard of the Jacobean House. Warm encouraging atmosphere – want children to feel that learning is fun. Cute corduroy uniforms. After-school clubs include such activities as ballet, short tennis and modern dance. There is also after-school provision for children from kindergarten upwards to help parents with children in the main schools. Computerised library. Primary emphasis is on literacy and numeracy. SEN help mainly with language and mathematical difficulties. Lessons well planned. Max class size 20. Close relationship with parents, regular reporting, meetings, workshops etc.

South Devon Steiner School; Early Childhood Dept

Linked school: South Devon Steiner School

Hood Manor, Dartington, Totnes, Devon, TQ9 6AB

- Pupils: Boys and girls • Ages: 3-7 • Christian foundation – non-denominational • Fees: £3,150-£6,900 pa • Independent

Tel: 01803 897377
Email: admissions@steiner-south-devon.org
Website: www.steiner-south-devon.org

Mandate co-ordination administrator: None. As for main school, monthly mandate circles (bringing teachers and parents together to review, discuss and plan) form the first level of organisation, which then carries on through weekly collegiate and departmental meetings.

Entrance: Applications via admissions co-ordinator. Prospective parents for early years invited to attend a special prospective parents' afternoon, twice a term. Afternoon includes tour, peek-in at lessons and talks by parents and teachers. Nursery and kindergarten both oversubscribed so contact in good time.

Exit: Most proceed seamlessly to main school aged six.

Remarks: The department is passionate about fulfilling Steiner's mission for early childhood education – lovely hobbit-like learning environment where childhood can be enjoyed to the full away from gaze of older children. Teachers we met were very protective of children's dreamlike experience and were disinclined to let us intrude – understandable enough. Mothers appreciate how 'school gives children the space they need' and how children 'learn to be still'. Classrooms have been conceived from natural materials and are alive with light, fun and a sense of wonder – welcome back to 'never never land'. Each day starts outside, 'come rain or shine': 'Children need to interact with nature,' we were told, and they are much calmer by the time they go indoors around 9.30am.

Teachers follow through themes for four weeks, with the emphasis on developing imagination. Simple crafts, making dens and a playhouse, gathering for ring time with songs and movement games, listening to a story and celebrating festivals are all part of what happens. Children also learn reverence for the divine in nature and respect for others. Helping with tasks such as breadmaking, tidying and arranging are important. Parent and toddler group for tinies, a nursery group for those aged 3-4 and a kindergarten for 4-6 year olds. Mental concepts are 'caught' through sensory experience rather than 'taught' through rote learning. Great emphasis is placed upon development of fine motor skills and manual dexterity. Steiner-trained early years specialists (school is participating as a centre for Plymouth based students – many of whom spend time here), classroom assistants plus parents ensure children lack for nothing. Books and computers strictly taboo – 'Parents don't cheat,' we were assured, 'but support Steiner philosophy'. Great for those who accept what Steiner advocated and intend their children to remain within this system.

South Farnham Primary School

Menin Way, Farnham, GU9 8DY

• Pupils: 750 boys and girls • Ages: 4-11 • Non denom • State

Tel: 01252 716155
Email: info@south-farnham.surrey.sch.uk
Website: www.south-farnham.surrey.sch.uk

Headteacher: Since 1988, Mr Andrew Carter OBE BEd, maths specialist (sixties).'A complete character who runs a very tight ship and expects a lot from his staff,' says one mother, though 'Doesn't expect to be called "Sir",' says another. Small screen star of BBC2 head swap series and numerous educational programmes. Twinkly, avuncular, chatty and hands on. Fast on feet, moves in mysterious ways, one moment arranging chairs for assembly, the next shifting toilet blockage. Enjoys being out and about rather than confined to pin-neat, pleasant office. Approachable, all parents have home phone number – 'Never misused'. Abolished answerphone, lines manned 8am to 6pm. 'Why let children agonise about problems which can be sorted out quickly?' Oozes understated authority from every pore, living embodiment of the word 'dapper' though trad exterior – sports jacket/parade gloss shoes combo – disguises voracious appetite for change: infant department takeover and academy status completed just months apart in 2011. Lives locally, wife Mary also teaches there, grown up children attended. Sees inevitable high profile as part and parcel of school's central community role and relishes it. No plans to hand over reins any time soon. 'This notion of retiring is a funny business. Why would you do that?' Gleeful at abolition of compulsory retirement age, cites Churchill's third age achievements. Dreams of day South Farnham named in same breath as iconic public schools, nationally recognised shorthand for educational excellence.

Entrance: Non-selective, over-subscribed, sense of fabulous sweetshop surrounded by disappointed parents pressing noses to glass. Sixty places at 4+, two more classes added at 7+, many from four feeder infant schools. After standard queue jump priorities – looked after children, siblings – success hinges on home to school distance. No plans to increase numbers, extra 'bulge' class now working through the school was a one-off, so waiting lists, 60 at peak for year 3, similar at reception, there for foreseeable future. Dozens of families, turned away outright, don't even get that far. No future joy, either: tighter criteria may be introduced to cut waiting lists. No wonder local estate agent pays for website link.

Exit: Majority to highly thought of Weydon School; significant minority to leading independents including Salesian, Royal Grammar School Guildford.

Remarks: Currently the nation's top performing primary with 130 plus children – that's four classes' worth – regularly hitting SATs level four or better at KS2 – KS1 results excellent as well. Puts boot in commonly held belief that with primaries, small equals beautiful, with consistent year in, year out demonstration that bigger substantially better.

Detractors might point to affluent locale as significant unfair advantage – annual fundraising total of both parents' associations, separate for infants and juniors, now closing on £30,000, is a pointer. Surroundings undeniably attractive. Infants – sensitively modernised Victoriana – cheerful interiors, disabled lift. Tardis-like, appears tiny at front, opens up to reveal idyllic wooded valley setting and generous running around space, veg garden producing harvest soup for all, sensory garden and – a rarity – heated outdoor pool.

Juniors, spacious with enviable facilities '…better than some secondary schools, ' says parent. Architecture – best-quality 1930s municipal, topiary-fronted, much improved and deceptively square-shaped – 'It took me two terms to find my way round,' says year six guide. Grandfather clock and scholarship board residual reminders of pre-1970s incarnation as girls' grammar, Joanna Trollope rumoured former teacher.

Outside, seven acres of space with grass, Astroturf – school regularly does well in matches, dipping pond and attractive courtyard area complete with looming model heron. Inside, two floors of vibrant corridors with eye-catching displays – letters from linked Japanese school, all 42 UNICEF Children's Articles, year sixes cover one a week – link classrooms, five libraries and six art rooms – some large, others bijou – well-equipped ICT suite that children – ultimate praise – vote better than home PCs. Jewel in the crown is the two dance/drama studios, gym, hall and practice rooms all much in use for large-scale, multi-cast Christmas/summer shows, plus spring concerts.

But while it's lush, especially with surroundings, all pitch perfect winding lanes, detached homes (frequently bordered with vaguely intimidating noli me tangere high hedges) pupils come with normal range of needs – currently 147 with some form of learning difficulty, 87 with EAL needs. 'We take whatever the community gives us,' says head.

Educational community flocks to touch hems of these particular academic gowns – it's an elite National Support / National Teaching School – and no wonder, given way staff work with raw material, spinning it into results gold. Lesson quality outstanding but tip of the iceberg – it's the 90 per cent under the surface preparation that's magic weapon, achieved by talented, well-led staff, average late 20s, mostly women, cohesive, happy, talkative, incredibly hard-working – who are the true ingredient X. Inevitably many are high-flyers on way to greater things elsewhere – 'We've had people leaving here after three years to become deputy heads,' says head – so high(ish) turnover. For occasional few the intensity, though undoubtedly rewarding, simply too much. No shortage of talented replacements, however, with first-class internal training programme helping many teaching assistants qualify as teachers.

Adds up to environment where no child in need of a helping hand allowed to slip through net. Junior class size of 35 headline figure but misleading. Emphasis is on differentiated learning, with 30 teaching assistants – all in training, many teachers in waiting – and seven personalised learning specialists making it happen and true child/adult ratio of 13:1. Able pupils stretched – members of National Association for Able Children in Education while from year one, rigorous monitoring identifies any literacy/numeracy stragglers, 'Often the ones at back of class, not putting up their hands,' says teacher. They'll have separate sessions – up to five a day by year six in small focus groups, covering same work as higher ability group, nuanced to iron out any difficulties en route.

Forensic attention to detail sounds dry but translates into enthralling, nth-degree planned lessons. Even usually drab spelling notebooks burst with colourful doodles as children encouraged to create own aide-memoires for tricky words. Chalk and talk clearly discarded long ago in favour of lessons where individual work prefaced by engrossing group activity – 'soundscape' recreating Dickensian London for year six pupils, teacher stomping round room as plausibly crabby Scrooge – in costume, too, children in character as cringing street urchins – so riveted that, unusually, not a single head turns for visitors, though could have something to do with sheer volume of traffic as everyone from VIPs to visiting teachers beats path to this educational nirvana.

Other comprehensively scotched myth is that big means noisy. Lack of volume takes some getting used to – you almost welcome (rare) sight of child pushing ahead through doorway – though reassuringly less Midwich Cuckoo than well-tuned powerful car. Teachers uniformly soft-voiced, children ditto. Seeing them en masse, a blue-jumpered sea of tranquillity in assembly a revelation to anyone assuming that little eddies of fidgeting/chat, countered with mild adult irritation were an educational fact of life.

Inspirational teaching must help. Hand in hand with this is top-down faith in the children. Year threes taste responsibility from word go as message bearers. 'We don't get that many notes home and it's left to the children to tell you,' says slightly shell-shocked mother.

There's unsupervised break time access to practice rooms – conflicting rhythms, keys and styles fight for supremacy in the corridors. Children get say in casting decisions for many large-scale, multi-cast plays that are highlight of school calendar. Also decide when to have lunch – delicious, freshly cooked, at least two mains and puddings, fresh bread on the side, unobtrusive wastage/veg consumption checks, standing invitation to parents to eat with child – late bell reminds latecomers to get a move on.

Instead of convoluted rewards vs sanctions system common elsewhere, trust is the big motivator. No house points, no 'honour of the school' sticks or carrots – indeed, children politely puzzled by notion. Significant that exceptional good – or bad – deeds yield the same result, chat with head, who does his best to tease out mitigating circumstances in cases of problem behaviour and tries to resolve with child before escalating to contact-the-parents stage.

Result is children with quiet confidence of people who know what they're about, behave and do well because of 360 degree assumption that they'll want to. Tangible sense of purpose and pride in accomplishment. 'I don't know anybody in the school who isn't interested in something,' says year six boy.

Parental niggles minimal with exception of parking. Infant school has parent-assisted 'stop and drop' system. 'They get your child out and you can drive on. If they had something like that [at the junior school] it would be amazing,' says one mother.

So is this a one-off establishment or something others could replicate? 'Every school could be [as good],' says head. 'There's

many as good or better. When we work with other schools, the key element is the striving for success and the total belief that it can happen...You've got to have an ambition.'

Sees job as sacred trust. 'When you grow up, you need to be stimulated intellectually, spiritually, emotionally, physically – all of those things. If any one of those is diminished, the rest are diminished as well.'

In the meantime, this remains a jewel in educational crown, demonstrably good at what it does, fortunate in its focused, dedicated staff and making a virtue of its size, producing happy children whose quiet confidence and pride in their many achievements is a pleasure to witness. Head says, half jokingly, 'I'll be here till I die.' Parents even now probably organising whip round for Elixir of Life.

South Hampstead High School Junior Department

Linked school: South Hampstead High School

5 Netherhall Gardens, London, NW3 5RN

- Pupils: 250 girls, all day • Ages: 4–11 • Non-denom
- Fees: £11,175 pa • Independent

Tel: 020 7794 7198
Email: junior@shhs.gdst.net
Website: www.shhs.gdst.net/junior-school

Headmistress: Since September 2013, Mrs Gabrielle Solti BA PGCE, previously head of Notting Hill and Ealing Junior School, who has returned to her roots – she used to teach at nearby Trevor Roberts and was then deputy head of Primrose Hill Primary. Always wanted to be a teacher, but was told while reading history at Oxford that she would be head by the time she was 30 and couldn't see the point. 'What then?' she asked. So she headed for the European Commission in Brussels, where she met her husband, then working in the marketing department at Nestlé in Paris and London and now a lawyer, before she could no longer resist the lure of teaching and went to train at The Institute ('A gold standard – stands out on the cv; I always appoint graduates from there if I can'). We described her at her previous post as 'destined for great things', and she is clearly on her way.

Entrance: North London parents tend to be somewhat obsessive about getting their daughters into a top school from the word go, and South Hampstead is vastly oversubscribed at four, with about 240 applying for 24 places. School, however, is not looking for prodigies. 'I tell parents not to coach. There's no need at all for reading or writing. We're looking for focus, concentration, stamina and – hopefully – a spark.' In the first round of assessment, girls are observed at play, in the second, in groups of five with short activities. A rejection at 4 is certainly not a no for ever. Many reapply at 7+, when there are a further 24 places. At this stage, skills come into play, along with non-verbal reasoning, but school tries to 'peel back layers of coaching'. Priority is given to siblings, but 'only if they're the right fit.' Feeder schools include: Hampstead Hill, Devonshire House, The Phoenix, North Bridge House, St Mary's, The Children's House and Brooklands.

Register at least two years in advance for 4+ entry. Assesses the first 250 applicants to deliver their form on 1 October – queues form early outside the school. Registration for 7+ opens 18 months in advance and assesses the first 140 applicants.

S

Exit: Nearly all to the senior school. A few, who it is felt might need something 'gentler', are guided elsewhere. This is flagged up early on and help is given to find an appropriate school. 'We never ask anyone to leave. These are our girls until year 6.' Some, however, exit in year 5 to avoid 11 plus.

Remarks: Two bright, Victorian buildings across the road from each other in a quiet road five minutes walk from the senior school. One building houses reception to year 4, the other years 5 and 6. Though the school is madly competitive on entry, once inside the atmosphere is enthusiastic but relaxed. School feels this is due to the fact that girls here won't generally need to sit 11 plus. 'We're not teaching them to jump through hoops, we're here to open doors.' And, though the basics are rock solid, the academic offering is less about drilling and more about a spirit of inquiry. 'The sheer fun and enthusiasm for teaching are extraordinary,' said one father. Mandarin taught from year 1 as a second language ('I wanted them to experience something really different'), French added in year 4. Philosophy for all. 'Girls can sometimes be too compliant; this pushes them a little bit further.' Science has improved radically since space rearranged to create new labs. 'I think that's one of the great advantages of a single-sex education. It's not just girls holding clipboards. They all get their turn and love being scientists.'

The senior and junior schools overlap in their teaching style with a lot of independent inquiry, including two themed homeworks set annually across the school (a recent topic was black and white). 'It liberates them to do research.' An approach that clearly works. 'My daughter wasn't particularly interested in reading,' said one parent, 'but then they did a project on the Romans and you couldn't stop her. She read everything there was on the subject. She just became passionate.' Two libraries, one in each building, with all taking library lessons.

Special needs provision is strong. 'We try raise to raise any potential problems and get parents involved without panicking them. We don't want them immediately going off to get their child tested. Occasionally we recommend an educational psychologist or good outside tutoring.' Some 70 pupils speak a second language at home and, in year 5, the school peps up the reading and comprehension to ensure they aren't disadvantaged.

Music a key part of the curriculum. 'I want them to learn about sound. We do a lot of singing.' All girls, too, take the Royal Academy Young Strings project in year 1, with violin and cello taught using the Kodaly method. Large orchestra of 50-60, plus a quartet, quintet, wind band and jazz band. Art and DT taught in small groups in separate classrooms. Reasonable London playground plus use of the senior school's playing fields a five-minute coach ride away. Two double periods of PE each week, plus gymnastics, netball, hockey and athletics clubs. 'It's important to instil an enjoyment and love of sport.' Excellent range of general clubs, including lateral thinking, chess, fashion illustration and languages (French, Spanish and Latin) and these energetic girls tend to be actively involved on numerous fronts.

Pastoral care is undoubtedly a strength. Parents, generally local and professional, feel they can always have a chat. 'Every child is recognised and appreciated, whether they're extrovert or quite shy,' said one. School cook is 'a bit of a legend', providing delicious freshly-cooked food with vegetarian options. Girls dine in batches and queue politely. They also open doors. 'It's not a backs-against-the-wall place, but we expect consideration.' Supportive parents are significant fundraisers (for playground equipment and extra laptops).

A school which produces articulate, well-educated, confident – and very happy – girls. 'It's a fabulous school,' said one happy parent. 'It lets every child be an individual.'

Southbank International School – Hampstead

Linked schools: Southbank International School – Kensington; Southbank International School – Westminster

16 Netherhall Gardens, London, NW3 5TH

• Pupils: 200 boys and girls • Ages: 3–11 • Fees: £13,800–£21,480 pa • Independent

Tel: 020 7243 3803
Email: admissions@southbank.org
Website: www.southbank.org

Principal: Since 2012, Mrs Shirley Harwood BEd, has taught at the school since 2008. Previously junior head at International School of Toulouse and Perse Girls, has taught in state schools and British international schools in Colombia and Argentina. On first impression she is quiet, reflective, chooses her words carefully. Currently working on development plan with Southbank's new executive principal, who has academic oversight for all three Southbanks and fellow Southbank tri-campus senior management team members. The aim is to evaluate and strengthen current practice in order to maintain and raise standards across the three campuses. Having most recently taught the oldest kids at Hampstead, is interested in improving the transition between primary at Hampstead and secondary at Westminster. She's aware that transition to a new school, culture and language can be difficult and wants to ensure that Southbank families feel they are part of a community from the get-go. Married, no children.

Entrance: Local families are urged to attend one of the open mornings scheduled during the first and second terms. Inbound expats on 'look-see' trips to London visit by appointment. Pupils admission based on availability and a review of school reports, parent statements, and pupil essays (drawings for the younger ones). Testing not required unless reports seem insufficient to assess the child's readiness for the school. For primary, average to above-average profile sought, but equally important are behaviour and attitude. In a school with such diversity, that everyone comes open-minded, motivated and ready to learn is an imperative. English language fluency not required as there is support in place. Applications are accepted all year and are normally considered in order of completion. Waiting lists depend on the class but, as with most schools with large expat populations, pupils do come and go, so don't give up on finding a place eventually. Nonetheless, they recommend that applicants have a back-up plan. The admissions process states that applications are not actually reviewed until a vacancy is anticipated or available, which annoying for prospective families wanting to know where they stand. If you are accepted, be prepared to pay the deposit and full first term's fees to secure the place, both non-refundable if you change your mind, with a few exceptions. Read the fine print.

Admissions office centrally manages all three schools so there is good flexibility between the two primary campuses. Only two-form entry at each campus, so vacancies not always possible in the preferred campus, particularly if there are several children in the family, but the admissions office allow you to apply to both schools and do their best to see you eventually get in to the school you prefer.

Exit: As an international school, some families leave when the assignment is up. A small handful move on to other local independent schools such as Highgate, South Hampstead, UCS, and while in the past the majority have progressed to

S

Southbank Westminster to continue in the IB Middle Years Programme and on to the IB diploma, parents say they've been told that this transfer will no longer be automatic, and the assumption is that their academic performance and English language fluency will be evaluated. The school offers 'transition activities' to prepare kids for the move from the primary to middle school – a parent morning at Westminster to meet the head and teachers, sending the fifth grade to spend a day with the sixth grade, and hosting social events so the rising grade 5 kids at Kensington and Hampstead get to know each other.

Remarks: Southbank Hampstead follows the International Baccalaureate Primary Years (IBPYP), leading to the IB Middle Years and IB diploma programmes at Southbank Westminster. Children study six themed 'units of inquiry' during the school year (four units for the younger children), maths and language taught daily as stand-alone but integrated subjects. Content varies but 'trans-disciplinary themes' (eg, who we are; how we express ourselves; how the world works) are IBPYP universals as are 'learner profiles' and 'attitudes'. These are all explained clearly on the school's website. Spanish is introduced at age 5 (kindergarten) and offered at beginner and mother tongue levels. Other languages, including mother tongue, can be arranged by request after school and at additional cost.

Classes are small, never more than 16, teachers readily available to parents and pupils by email or in person. Written reports twice-yearly and parent-teacher conferences scheduled during the first two terms. In the third term there are pupil-led conferences where pupils take charge and share with parents what they have learned. Parents love hearing their children's well-rehearsed 'show and tell'. One parent expressed appreciation for the way that assessment is very geared to the individual.

Unique feature is compulsory Suzuki music programme for all students from age 5. When you drop by, small groups of children are scurrying between their classrooms carrying miniature violins and cellos, headed to practice rooms where their parents ,who learn alongside, await them. To the uneducated ear it may sound like a lot of squeaks and 'Twinkle Twinkles', but there is serious pedagogical activity going on here. Southbank's founder admired the Japanese educator's philosophy about how music can develop fine motor and auditory skills, collaboration, perseverance, and even mathematical and literacy skills. Though many love the opportunity, some feel excessive time is given to all the small group and individual practice, which causes timetabling headaches. Others say there is pressure to 'buy in' and go along to classes. Nonetheless, when you hear 350 kids play together on one stage for the annual joint-school concert, you understand why Southbank continues to invest time and effort in the programme. Advanced pupils now rehearse before school, avoiding interruption to lessons. All this is in addition to the regular music programme that takes place in a sunny and bright garden conservatory.

Teachers are young and energetic – average age 30s. School ensures that staff up to date with required IB training. Specialists in art, music, ESL, Spanish, plus a full time librarian and a part-time counsellor. A full-time SEN teacher provides support for mild dyslexia, bi-lingual learning problems and some other special needs. If a more significant learning need emerges that Southbank cannot adequately support, school will advise. Those who need to learn English as an additional language are supported by EAL lessons as part of the standard programme.

Plenty of visits around town; 'London as a classroom' is school mantra. UK-based residential trip for the oldest grade 5 students serves in part as a team-building activity. Extensive menu of after-school activities: badminton, ballet, capoeira (a Brazilian martial art), ukulele, gardening, Mandarin, mini-tennis, rock climbing and community service.

The assistant principal, who has many years' experience at the school, is responsible for pastoral care and discipline. Problems can sometimes arise because children are finding their way in a new country and language and trying to settle into the ways of the school, rather than serious disciplinary infractions. Parents say it is 'a comfortable school' and confirm that discipline issues are not a problem.

Southbank pupils are a combination of locals and ex-pats, children of diplomats, business people, journalists and entertainers who are attracted to the slightly less urban environments of Hampstead or nearby St. John's Wood and Golders Green. The students are bright and happy to see visitors, whether visiting grandparents, prospective families or special guests, they are always keen to tell you what they are learning and ask about you. PTA is active, though parents say there is no real pressure to participate, and the school is very family friendly.

The school has a lower turnover than many international schools (a little over 20 per cent per year). Southbank seems to appeal to families who have one British parent with a foreign national spouse, where being part of a bilingual or multilingual community is the norm, and where being in a more globally-minded community is seen as an advantage. One British dad confirmed that there is a perception that 'friends will move away' but that children and families find ways to stay connected, and that the 'old boy and old girl network' is still there – it's just a global one. Repatriating Brits who have been abroad and experienced the international IBPYP system love the continuity of carrying on when they return to London. Another describes the community as 'a solid core of permanent families who have chosen the school because the philosophy, balanced against a nice mix of international families coming in and out, who bring new thinking and new cultural perspectives.'

The school opened its doors in 1979 on the South Bank of the Thames, an idealistic concept of the South African founder, Milton Toubkin, inspired by (Englishman) John Bremer's 'school without walls' Philadelphia Parkway Program. Southbank was purchased from the founders in 2007 by Cognita, a group headed by Sir Chris Woodhead, former UK Chief Inspector of Schools, that owns and manages a variety of independent schools. At the time of purchase, Cognita promised the parents and staff that they would let the current administration run the school, because they wanted to 'preserve [its] established ethos'. Mrs Harwood is the second person in post since the founding principal left in 2008. In the main the positive atmosphere in the classroom and the fundamental teaching and learning has continued to thrive at the Hampstead campus, but the community is not immune to the rumblings coming from parents at Southbank Kensington and Southbank Westminster who have reservations about recent changes at those campuses.

Occupies a modern purpose-built building behind a re-built Edwardian façade – a planning requirement in this lovely historic residential neighbourhood. In addition to small outdoor play area for the early childhood classes, it has a popular 'green top' for sports and recreational play. The big news is that Southbank's owners recently acquired a sports facility in nearby Kilburn for the use of all three of its schools. Children bring their own lunch that they eat in the multi-purpose hall, though the PTA regularly sells pizza to raise money for good causes. No dress code but the kids look neat and tidy (PE kit for sport).

Southbank International School Hampstead is a family-orientated school in an attractive residential area of North London, suited to the bright, curious, self-motivated and internationally-minded family. To quote one parent, 'it's a fantastic opportunity for people who want a school where the philosophy is about the mind-set that is created, not just the things you are learning'.

Southbank International School – Kensington

Linked schools: Southbank International School – Hampstead; Southbank International School – Westminster

36–38 Kensington Park Road, London, W11 3BU

• Pupils: 205 boys and girls; all day • Ages: 3–11 • Fees: £13,800–£21,480 pa • Independent

Tel: 020 7243 3803
Email: admissions@southbank.org
Website: www.southbank.org

Principal: Since September 2013, Siobhan McGrath. Has taught across the age range for 23 years in New Zealand and London. For the past few years has been deputy head academic at North Bridge House prep in London while taking her own class of year 6 students. Her predominant educational interests are in assessment, teacher training and CPD; outside school she reads voraciously and enjoys wine and food.

Entrance: Local families are urged to attend one of the open mornings scheduled during the first and second terms. Inbound expats on 'look-see' trips to London visit by appointment. Pupils admission based on availability and a review of school reports, parent statements, and pupil essays (drawings for the younger ones). Testing not required unless reports seem insufficient to assess the child's readiness for the school. For primary, average to above-average profile sought, but equally important are behaviour and attitude. In a school with such diversity, that everyone comes open-minded, motivated and ready to learn is an imperative. English language fluency not required as there is support in place. Applications are accepted all year and are normally considered in order of completion. Waiting lists depend on the class but, as with most schools with large expat populations, pupils do come and go, so don't give up on finding a place eventually. Nonetheless, they recommend that applicants have a back-up plan. The admissions process states that applications are not actually reviewed until a vacancy is anticipated or available, which is annoying for prospective families wanting to know where they stand. If you are accepted, be prepared to pay the deposit and full first term's fees to secure the place, both non-refundable if you change your mind, with a few exceptions. Read the fine print.

Admissions office centrally manages all three schools so there is good flexibility between the two primary campuses. Only two-form entry at each campus, so vacancies not always possible in the preferred campus, particularly if there are several children in the family, but the admissions office allow you to apply to both schools and do their best to see you eventually get in to the school you prefer.

Exit: As an international school, some families leave when the assignment is up. A small handful move on to other local independent schools, but while in the past the majority have progressed to Southbank Westminster, Kensington parents say they've been told that these transfers will no longer be automatic, and the assumption is their academic readiness and English language fluency will be under greater scrutiny. The school offers 'transition activities' to prepare kids for the move from the primary to middle school – a parent morning at Westminster to meet the head and teachers, sending the fifth grade to spend a day with the sixth grade, and hosting social events so the rising grade 5 kids at Kensington and Hampstead get to know each other.

Remarks: Southbank Kensington follows the International Baccalaureate Primary Years (IBPYP), leading to the IB Middle Years and IB diploma programmes at Southbank Westminster. Children study six themed 'units of inquiry' during the school year (four units for the younger children), maths and language taught daily as stand-alone but integrated subjects. Content varies but 'trans-disciplinary themes' (eg, who we are; how we express ourselves; how the world works) are IBPYP universals as are 'learner profiles' and 'attitudes'. These are all explained clearly on the school's website. Spanish is introduced at age 5 (kindergarten) and offered at beginner and mother tongue levels. Other languages, including mother tongue, can be arranged by request after school and at additional cost. ISA Exams (International School Assessment), an Australian-based benchmarking tool used by IB schools worldwide enables the school to measure how their pupils are faring compared to other international school pupils. ISA results are shared with parents.

Unique feature is compulsory Suzuki music programme for all students from age 5. When you drop by, small groups of children are scurrying between their classrooms carrying miniature violins and cellos, headed to practice rooms, awaited by their parents who learn alongside. To the uneducated ear it may sound like a lot of squeaks and 'Twinkle Twinkles', but there is serious pedagogical activity going on here. Southbank's founder admired the Japanese educator's philosophy about how music can develop fine motor and auditory skills, collaboration, perseverance, and even mathematical and literacy skills. Parents are expected to support and participate, that means one to three visits to school per week. This doesn't suit everyone and veterans urge prospective parents to take it into account when thinking about applying. One parent, whose two children had contrasting responses to the programme, simply says, 'The Suzuki programme translates into some great skill sets that will serve them well as adults.' At the end of the year, Kensington and its sister school in Hampstead hold a grand concert with over 350 young musicians playing together on stage. It's an impressive sight.

Teachers are young and energetic – average age 30s. School ensures that staff are up to date with required IB training. Specialists in art, music, ESL, Spanish, plus a full time librarian. A full-time SEN teacher provides support for mild dyslexia, bilingual learning problems and some other special needs. If a more significant learning need emerges that Southbank cannot adequately support, school will advise. Those who need to learn English as an additional language are supported by EAL lessons as part of the standard programme. The school counsellor who left at the end of last year has not been replaced, leaving a gap in services; presumably it now falls to the principal or her assistant principal to support these kids as well as dealing with serious disciplinary matters.

Plenty of visits around town; 'London as a classroom' is school mantra. UK-based residential trip for grade 4 and 5 students serves in part as a team-building activity. Extensive menu of after-school activities: animation, boot camp, Capoeira (a Brazilian martial art), electric guitar, ice skating, pupil newspaper and community service.

The Southbank Kensington campus consists of two Victorian houses and a modern annexe. The surprise is the lovely enclosed garden, creatively landscaped for play and learning. There is a multi-purpose room for indoor games, lunch and assemblies. The school is higgledy-piggledy (described by one parent as 'a bit snug'), classrooms are small but the atmosphere is great, the place is gleaming and every inch is used for teaching and learning. Art, pupil work, and information on school activities fill the walls and even dangle from ceilings. There is an IT lab and an inviting child-centred library that seems to be the heart of the school. Southbank's owners recently acquired a sports facility in nearby Kilburn for the exclusive use of all three Southbank schools, and Kensington is making full use of it. Besides basketball courts, it has a dance studio, climbing wall,

S

changing rooms and a first aid station. Minibuses transport children to-and-from. Many pupils bring packed lunches, an external catering company offers hot lunches every day and there is a new kitchen on site.

The school opened its doors in 1979 as a sixth form on the South Bank of the Thames, an idealistic concept of the (South African) founder, Milton Toubkin, inspired by (Englishman) John Bremer's 'school without walls' Philadelphia Parkway Program. The school gradually added younger adolescents and moved to Notting Hill in 1989 where the primary school was introduced in 1992. In 2003, the middle and high school pupils were relocated to a building on Portland Place, Southbank Westminster. Southbank was purchased from the founders in 2007 by Cognita, a group headed by Sir Chris Woodhead, former UK Chief Inspector of Schools, that owns and manages independent schools.

At the time of purchase, Cognita promised the parents and staff that they would let the current administration run the school, because they want to 'preserve [its] established ethos'. In 2012 a new executive principal was appointed to oversee the three Southbank campuses. These changes at the top, and three different principals at Kensington since Cognita purchased the school in 2007, are leading parents to question the continuity of leadership. Parents were not pleased that the announcement of the last principal's departure was made in the third term, after the withdrawal/re-registration deadline for families; the news that the interim principal who would replace him does not have IBPYP experience caused further speculation about Cognita's commitment to the IBPYP. Parents are waiting to see what impact this may have in the classroom, whether it brings changes to the way teaching and learning is approached, and how the recruitment of new teachers will be managed with both the executive principal and the Kensington principal new to the IBPYP. Southbank was the third school in the world authorised to offer the IBPYP, so emotions run deep.

Concerns have been raised about the way new families get access to information. In its noble effort to go paperless, the school stopped doing postal mailings at the beginning of the year, referring parents to online forms to streamline the entry and updating of data. The difficulty is that newly-arrived families (a significant number each year) don't always have the broadband access installed very quickly, thus missing out in the early stages on important emails containing helpful information. Parents say this system can also be daunting for non-English speakers. School says it has addressed the concerns of parents and now offers in-house training session and guidance during the first weeks of term.

The campus community reflects the character of its Notting Hill neighbours, a blend of the arty and urban chic – very much the style of the pupils who look cool in their non uniform. The school attracts local and expat families that represent many nationalities and professions, including diplomats, bankers, journalists, media, artists and entertainers. Recent nationality breakdown has USA at 20 per cent followed by the UK at 10 per cent, and the remaining 70 per cent representing over 40 other nationalities. There is no majority of any single nationality. British parents say that although initially local families are concerned about the turnover, families are staying longer so the loss of friends is not such a big worry. Moreover, as the kids get older they are proud to have friends in places like New York and Stockholm and an excuse to travel to interesting places.

Spratton Hall

Smith Street, Stratton, Northampton, NN6 8HP

- Pupils: 403; 214 boys/189 girls • Ages: 4–13 • Christian ethos but all denominations accepted • Fees: Pre-prep £9,045; Prep £12,600 pa • Independent

Tel: 01604 847292
Email: office@sprattonhall.com
Website: www.sprattonhall.com

Interim Headmaster: Mr Simon Clarke BA (early forties). Wife is a KS2 teacher at the school, three children all at the school. Educated at Trent College in Nottingham. Was deputy head at Spratton Hall for six years – teaches English, has coached rugby, hocket and cricket. Previously at Millfield Prep (head of English and drama) and Gresham's Prep (head of English and drama). Outside interests are family, sport, theatre and summer holidays in Cornwall.

Entrance: 'selective, but not overly.' No obvious formal assessment; more importance attached to the taster days: how the children respond to the novelty and how others respond to them. Will they fit in? Boys and girls may enter at any age and stage, providing there is room. Children are screened on arrival for any learning difficulties and those who need it are given expert help. Scholarships are not available but bursaries are. In terms of finance, there is little difference. Don't be afraid to ask.

Exit: As might be imagined with a day school, most children exit to the usual local suspects: Oakham, Uppingham, Oundle, Rugby, Kimbolton, Monmouth, Northampton High School for Girls. Stowe, Winchester and Wellingborough School get an occasional mention and a significant fact is that 60-70 per cent of children go on to board, so distance is not automatically perceived as a problem. Impressive annual harvest of scholarships, many of them serious ones.

Remarks: Set in 50 acres of attractive countryside, the main house around which the school has developed is a handsome 18th century building with Victorian additions, in particular a lot of brickwork. The gardens and grounds at Spratton are intelligently conceived and beautifully tended. To stand on the mound in the front of the house is to be astonished by the beautiful sweep of games pitches, tennis courts, Astroturf and grass athletics track. Nearer the teaching buildings a garden adjoins the science block and is stocked with suitable herbs and plants to aid academic research; another garden is for peace and quiet.

As far as facilities are concerned, everything looks bright and functional. The pre-prep is a delightful airy building with interesting levels and bags of space for running around; the science block is well-equipped and encouraging, or so we thought. But it's undergoing a complete makeover latest additions include a new sports dome with an indoor tennis court and a performing arts building.

Endless orchestras and jazz bands, choirs and smaller groups, computers to aid composition and opportunities for performing in assembly and wider audiences. Lively art and drama with much involvement all round. A breathtaking library with a full-time librarian where even the chairs have been carefully selected to give a feel of encompassment and warmth. Lots of guest speakers and suitable activities with which to catch young bookworms. No lessons on Saturdays but bags of matches with much success. Some parents told us that the selection of teams was a little static and that if your child hadn't been selected early on in his or her career there wasn't much chance of playing for the top teams; others disagreed. All talked of the competitive way in which Spratton Hall pupils approach their sport and their sporting behaviour, something not always shared by the parents.

This is an extraordinary school with some outstanding teachers and a clearly delineated framework within which children can feel safe and appreciated. Some may feel that the organisation is too anodyne, too predictable, too carefully constructed without room for mystery and muddle, barked shins and the tears of disappointment. Others will feel this is the ideal arena within which to learn and grow; in the words of the prospectus, to 'blossom'. Anyone living within commuting range should certainly check it out. Not a school to be overlooked.

Stamford Junior School

Linked school: Stamford High School

Kettering Road, Stamford, PE9 2LR

- Pupils: 335 girls and boys • Ages: 2–11 • C of E • Fees: Boarding £14,664–£18,408; Day £8,004–£10,296 pa • Independent

Tel: 01780 484400
Email: headjs@ses.lincs.sch.uk
Website: www.ses.lincs.sch.uk

Head: Since 2012, Mrs Emma Smith (late thirties). Began her teaching career in London and was a deputy head in Kingston-upon-Thames before moving to Stamford Junior six years ago. Joined the school as a year 6 class teacher and pastoral care leader on the senior leadership team and was appointed as head when her predecessor retired.

The three schools in the Stamford Endowed Schools foundation are overseen by the principal, Mr Stephen Roberts, who arrived in 2008 from Felsted School, of which he had been head for 15 years – a safe pair of hands, then. This was a clever appointment and Mr Roberts sees eye to eye with the three heads of the individual schools over the aims – near and far – of the foundation.

There is a substantial programme of renewal going on but the SES is not at pains to 'up the academics' (ie position in the league tables) which would mean doing itself out of much of its loyal traditional market. Nonetheless, the schools deserve to be far better known and appreciated. This writer can see little reason why some locals might choose the big three (relatively close-by) independents given all on offer here.

Mr Roberts is affable, forward-looking and a true educationalist. It is, in part, his job to up the school's confidence, to bruit abroad the excellence of his foundation and let Stamford's pride be more than just a local secret.

Entrance: First come, first served into nursery and reception. Forty taken into nursery of which 20 move on to reception, with another 12 children arriving from elsewhere. This is a sizeable junior school overall. Occasional places thereafter in all years, testing from 7+. The brilliant thing here is that if you get in at the beginning, you can stay till 18.

Exit: Around 50 per cent leave for the state sector or elsewhere after nursery. Automatic entry for year 6 into the senior school and most do go on. Perhaps two or so a year warned early that they should look elsewhere as may not cope with the senior school curriculum. A few to the state sector or other independents.

Remarks: The whole junior school is privileged in terms of its site and green spaces. It is situated just outside the town close to the A1/A43 interchange – not that you'd know it in the pervasive rural peacefulness. The main junior school building is 1970s low-rise, pale brick and, though hardly a match for the architectural glories of the senior school, avoids the worst crimes of scholastic building of the period. It nestles between generous car parking space (lots of large people movers and 4x4s when we arrived) and fabulous, flood-lit courts, pitches and Astroturf, some shared with the senior branches. To the rear of the school is the new, purpose-built nursery building, which enjoys a lovely, leafy space outside. This was completed as part of the vast programme of rebuilding, renewing and expanding in which SES is engaged. A little bridge over the railway charmingly leads to the nursery and we enjoyed the sight of crocodiles of smartly uniformed tots, two by two, chatting along their way – seemingly a sight from the 1950s – red berets, blue caps, blazers and sensible red backpacks – aah!

You don't need parents – or pupils – to tell you that this is a happy school – you can feel it as you walk through the orderly – but not neurotically so – classrooms with pockets of clutter here and there suggesting lively work in progress that doesn't need to be tidied away for visitors – so disconcerting elsewhere. It's colourful but not distractingly so with lots of nice touches – bird feeders on the trees, little windmills in the playspaces to encourage the breeze, super gardens and outside areas. We liked Thumbelina's Garden – a large basin full of pot pourri – but were sad when an earnest pupil confided that Thumbelina had 'lost her wings'. We liked the door labelled Room 7 and wondered what it concealed! Large, light hall multi-purpose and used for celebrating – 'we're good at awarding things'. Everyone, staff and children, eats school lunch (prepared onsite) and good manners are particularly encouraged during meals.

The school combines a safe environment with traditional values with up-to-the-minute provision. We saw trolleyfuls of laptops, plasma screens celebrating latest events (in this case the birth of nine ducklings to a resident duck) and saw evidence of sound, even inspirational teaching here and there. Stimulating work done by attentive and absorbed children – who might be even more absorbed in some classes if a few more windows were opened! Setting in some subjects. Those children who manifest learning problems are supported by the Additional Learning Opportunities Team which assesses and then monitors, withdrawing children from class where necessary or supporting them one-to-one or in small groups. Dys-problems seen as no bar to success here and all teachers on the look-out for probs and will replay them to the team. Nine pupils have EAL requirements. Two have individual EAL support. The other children's needs are catered for in the classroom. Arts and sports provision very strong. Music overseen by head of dept for all three schools which ensures continuity in planning and consistency of approach – the music in the senior school is outstanding but begins here. All year 2 learns the violin. 200 timetabled individual lessons weekly – no-one misses classes – excellent. More than 60 in the orchestra. Art and DT skillfully taught by specialists – lots of good stuff here. We met the head of chess! Giant sports hall used by whole school but on the junior school site, excellent 25m pool, immaculate athletics track and the prettiest games pitch we have seen anywhere.

Extra-curricular activities abound – many stay after school. Many come early and stay late – small boarding contingent makes school breakfast and late provision (until 8pm) a real boon for busy families and school has very flexible approach to flexi-boarding when needed. Ten full boarders, mostly from Forces familie, well provided for – lots of weekend trips, use of pool etc. Family atmosphere in boarding house.

The junior school sows the seed for what happens – increasingly impressively – higher up. Hard to see why anyone living locally would look elsewhere.

Stephen Perse Foundation Junior School

Linked school: Stephen Perse Foundation

St Eligius Street, Cambridge, CB2 1HX

- Pupils: 129 girls; all day • Ages: 7–11 • Non-denom
- Fees: £12,795 pa • Independent

Tel: 01223 346140
Email: admissions@stephenperse.com
Website: stephenperse.com

Head of Junior School: Since 2007, Miss Katie Milne BEd (geography and education). Taught at the school for over twenty years before taking on headship. Pleasantly professional – 'strict but not frightening,' said a parent. Promoting the school is an important part of her role and she's an impressively quick-thinking relayer of information. No longer teaches on a daily basis but says the hall, when she takes assemblies, is her classroom. Keen supporter of international links and eco-friendly projects – school recently raised money to fund the planting of 20 trees on a site outside Cambridge.

Entrance: Testing in English, maths and verbal reasoning – plus informal interview. They're looking for lateral thinking, sparky children who have a high interest in school life. (Annual rearrangement of forms prevents fixed groupings and helps those who arrive in years 5 and 6 to fit in.) Bursaries 'for those who demonstrate particular potential – but whose families cannot afford the fees'.

Exit: Nearly all to the senior school. Plenty of warning if child won't be able to cope – according to the head when this is the case most parents intuitively know their daughter would be better off in a less rigorous environment.

Remarks: This place has the same DNA as its big sister round the corner – a blank exterior hides a world of tip-top learning and bright young things. Inside the gate a prominent plaque proclaims 'Welcome' in an abundance of languages – testimony to the school's desire to be outward looking. Parents are happy with the 'traditional but fun approach' to work which, according to one mum, 'just keeps on coming'. Homework, revision and exams are a fact of life – head says they're 'stepping stones for moving through the school'. Preferred learning styles are identified and supportive staff boost self-confidence – an independent approach is encouraged. 'They gave our daughter an enthusiasm for learning and she just loves her work.' Cross-curricular links are central – check out Persephone (school mag) for some impressive examples. French from day one and Spanish from year 4 – for fun the whole school played a game of bingo, in Spanish. Learning support co-ordinator gives small group or individual support. Only those with the mildest needs will survive.

Music is valued and instrumental tuition is compulsory – offer of free group sessions in violin or cello for year 3, but if nothing appeals it has to be the recorder. Sport happens but tends to be squished into a full timetable – head says there are competitive events (sports day and house competitions) and that the number of fixtures has increased. 'Drop in' clubs at lunchtime for the especially keen – philosophy, debating and Latin are alternatives.

Girls are expected to be smart and polite and, according to a parent, are 'very happy in an ordered sort of way'. Plenty of girlishness and steam letting in the playground – hush returns in an instant when the bell rings for lessons. Everyone has school lunch. Break time snack trolley sells only fruit, juice, milk and water – a tad un-eco to sell bottled water, but school says it's at parents' request. Pay as you go breakfast for those who arrive early.

A tight site (they use senior school sports facilities and a nature reserve near the Cam) but the school building doesn't feel cramped. Recent refurbishment has given something that's generally light and airy. Brand new library (with friendly full-time librarian), designed 'around the power of the story', computer suite, art, DT and food technology room, somewhere for the kiln and a cleverly designed hall which doubles as a dining area. Outside a small playground (head hopes it will be given a makeover), a climbing wall and two delightful courtyard gardens – one for peace and quiet; the other a memorial for a member of staff – where cake and juice are shared by those, including staff, who've had their birthday in the month just gone.

Will take boys from 2014; the senior school will start to admit them in 2018.

Stockport Grammar School Junior School

Linked school: Stockport Grammar School

Buxton Road, Stockport, SK2 7AF

- Pupils: 350 boys and girls • Ages: 3–11 • Fees: £7,695 pa
- Independent

Tel: 01614 192405
Email: sgs@stockportgrammar.co.uk
Website: www.stockportgrammar.co.uk

Headmaster: Since 2000, Mr Larry Fairclough BA (mid fifties). Came from headship of Rishworth Prep. A tall, thoughtful Yorkshire man who likes walking with his wife. Diverse science teaching career that's included secondary and junior inner-city schools and teenagers in a residential home. Passionate about the children, with a reputation for bending over backwards to nurture all. 'I want them to do as well as they can and enjoy their school life'. School is competitive, particularly through the house system – 'we hope to provide the opportunity to succeed, to teach them to win with humility but also, as part of their wider education, to learn to deal with failure and not fear making mistakes'.

Retiring in April 2014. His successor will be Mr Tim Wheeler, currently head of Hereford Cathedral Junior School. A classicist by training, who then studied for his PGCE and MA in education. Started off teaching at Norwich School, and focused originally on older children, as senior school housemaster. Then head of classics at Bilton Grange in Warwickshire before moving to Hereford. A keen runner, he is also very much taken with drama and music (bass guitar).

Entrance: Academically selective from SGS Nursery or other local pre-schools, by assessment days with exams for older children.

Exit: Mainly to SGS Senior School, providing half their 11+ intake, sitting the entrance exam with outside candidates, on a level playing field albeit with perfect preparation.

Remarks: Within the overall Stockport Grammar grounds and part of the same school, the juniors dates from 1944. Co-ed since 1980, it now educates some 365 children in yellow gingham or yellow ties. Nursery for three-year-olds and two or three classes each from 4 – 11. Nursery, infants and juniors each have their own playgrounds; there are also a field, cricket pavilion and nets, and moreover the advantage of sharing senior school facilities including the 25m pool, dining hall and all-weather sports pitch.

Inside, the infant and junior sections are accessed from two sides of a large, light entrance hall which, during the day at least, feels like a calm hub, the head in and out of his study beside smiling ladies in a glass-fronted office behind reception. The classrooms are light, the atmosphere busy and happy. Infant walls groan under the weight of colourful artwork and projects, while confident, unstuffy juniors are keen to point out photos of their residential trips to the Lake District. Children are introduced to French and Spanish. A handful receive extra learning support, the quality of which was praised by ISI inspectors in 2011.

Bespoke music, art and DT, ICT and science rooms sit under modern skylights and red steel rafters. Over half the children take a musical instrument and you can join an orchestra once you've passed grade 1. There's a joint library and children across the years compete in four houses for points and trophies and cross-age assemblies. The 2011 inspection described the extra-curricular provision as outstanding, and certainly pupils can enjoy canoeing or chess, Scottish country dancing, web writing or polishing their Polish. Everyone's involved with charity fund-raising. Care from 8am, with a charged after-school club to 6pm.

Pupils consider the best things here to be 'the atmosphere and the facilities' and 'lots of attention for my work because the teachers really care what you're doing'. One mum of a child who joined for juniors told us, 'it's the first time my child's really being taught and he adores it; he's so happy every day and just wants to come to school'. Mind you, despite what seems to be a roomy car park they also describe the 3.30 pick up as 'a nightmare'. Compulsory lunches add about £160 a year to fees.

Stonar Preparatory School

Linked school: Stonar

Cottles Park, Atworth, Wiltshire, SN12 8NT

• Pupils: 30 boys/70 girls; 10 boarders • Ages: 2–11 • Non-denom
• Fees: Day £7,410–£10,530; Boarding £17,445 pa • Independent

Tel: 01225 701741
Email: admissions@stonarschool.com
Website: www.stonarschool.com

Head: Since 2009, Mr Mark Brain BA (Ed), formerly deputy head of Kelly College Prep. Engaging sporty outdoor type, married with a young family, so very at home in this setting. Has experience of state and maintained sectors, as well as secondary. Busy building numbers of boys at the prep, following the decision to make the prep school fully co-ed since 2011. 'I'm genning up on the local options for boys when they leave us,' he says, and has spent much of the last year forging links with suitable senior schools.

Entrance: Non-selective; most come up from the pre-prep. Assessment and interview for all, 'to ensure that children will thrive at the school'.

Exit: Prep school ends at year 6, from which nearly all girls go to the senior school, by means of entrance exams for setting purposes only; the senior school too is non-selective. By the time the first boys reach year 6, no doubt destinations will have been identified for them. Worth checking what provision is made for preparing kids not going on to the senior school for competitive entrance requirements. Note too that some major

public schools start pupils in year 9, so arrangements would have to be made for years 7 and 8.

Remarks: Benefits from being on the same gracious site as the senior school, with all its amenities. About 95 pupils, mostly girls at present, come from a 30 mile radius; just a few board in cosy Fuller House. Extensive curriculum takes on French from the pre-prep and starts Spanish in year 5. Popular choice for short term stays for overseas children: it was day one for a couple of Hungarian girls when we visited, who appeared to be managing valiantly, helped by smiley staff and children. Very strong drama – A Midsummer Night's Dream was a recent production – and 60 per cent of pupils take music lessons. Delightful school, which offers 'a healthy antidote to a results-driven culture – a niche which should be carved out,' raved one mum, with an ear for a sound-bite. Very inclusive, the sort of place where three squeaky notes on a violin from a nervous first time performer would raise the roof.

Stover Preparatory School

Linked school: Stover School

Stover, Newton Abbot, TQ12 6QG

• Pupils: 120; 55 boys/ 65 girls; 2 boarders • Ages: 3–11 • Christian
• Fees: Day £7,800–£9,690; Boarding £17,670–£19,560 pa
• Independent

Tel: 01626 331451
Email: fwhite@stover.co.uk
Website: www.stover.co.uk

Assistant Principal: Since 2006, Ms Caroline Coyle BEd MA (forties). Before that, deputy head. Wise, warm and approachable, 'lovely person' (said a mum), full of ideas, of treating even the youngest as 'real people'. Loves them without patronising them and is very good fun to meet. Keen to select the best of modern teaching practice without being a slave to trendiness. Healthily sceptical about some ideas. 'Commonsense and love is what drives her,' said another parent. Enthusiastic about emotional intelligence.

Entrance: Seven and under by interview and report. 7+ have assessments in reading, maths and non-verbal reasoning. All prospective pupils are encouraged to spend a taster day at the school. 'Very rarely does anyone fail to get in'. Boys and girls are taught together in the pre-prep but divided for most lessons from year 3. Otherwise they play happily together.

Exit: About 60 per cent of nursery pupils move up to prep school. Most prep school pupils enter senior school, some gain places at nearby grammars.

Remarks: Designed to be safe for horses and hounds, the school is built around the quadrangle of the original stables, complete with clock. Our guides were tremendously proud of the computer room, art room, the winding passages and staircases that followed the building round, the fresh bright paint, the colourful classrooms and the library. There we met a studious-looking boy reading with fierce concentration. 'I've read every Harry Potter book five times' he said airily. 'He's a reading legend' said one of our guides. Regular library sessions with young bibliophiles devouring books.

The Forest School in the woods below the house is very popular. Not long ago it was demolished by a freak wind. 'It offered a good lesson in facing up to adversity' said a teacher. 'The children sat around the ruins and discussed ways in which they must improve the next construction.' Our guides were thrilled about their participation in the school council, which had already resulted in improvements in the playground. ' You don't get everything you asked for,' said one, 'but they listen.' A good lesson for life. An excellent, cheerful, well-run pre and prep school – especially for those wanting to embark on the complete Stover experience, aged 11. Even those who are not going on to the senior school will benefit from a sound education in preparation for the next step. Fully co-ed since September 2012.

Streatham & Clapham High Junior School

Linked school: Streatham and Clapham High School GDST

Wavertree Road, London, SW2 3SR

• Pupils: 234 • Ages: 3–11 • Non-denom • Fees: £8,481–£11,130 pa
• Independent

Tel: 020 8674 6912
Email: enquiry@shj.gdst.net
Website: www.schs.gdst.net

Headmistress: Since 2010, Liz Astley BA PGCE NPQH (mid forties). An enthusiastic educator who has really got the school moving forward. Says she is lucky because she has a great, cohesive team of teachers and believes in plenty of parental involvement.

Entrance: Applications for co-ed nursery can be made from birth to two and a half. Children join at three and spend morning with nursery teacher in term prior to entry. Head says 'she is looking for happy, inquisitive children'. Girls then move into reception (more places also become available) in September following their fourth birthday. Informal one-to-one assessment with foundation stage co-ordinator.

Further intake at 7+ when girls are assessed by head or deputy head and take tests in maths, English and verbal reasoning. Written report from previous school also needed at this stage.

Exit: More than 80 per cent to the senior school. Not automatic – they all sit assessment test in year 5. Girls whom teachers feel will thrive are offered guaranteed places. All those wishing to move to senior school take an exam in year 6.

Remarks: School's unattractive building belies exceptionally light, large classrooms and happy atmosphere inside. Building benefits from the fact that it was once a senior school in terms of the facilities and space it provides. Enormous sports hall, where girls can play hockey, and excellent outdoor area with adventure playground and enough space for rounders and tennis guarantee plenty of fun, games and team training.

We were shown round by enthusiastic, confident girls who led us from the well-equipped nursery (with own outdoor play area) to busy reception classes and virtually every corner of the school. 'Do you want to see the loos?' they chirped. Huge library contains vast range of books and specific reading lists for each year. We also spotted pupil-made shoes created out of recycled material and models of school areas (our guides proudly pointed out their own creations). Light art room with terrific views over London – 'whenever we do art, we know we're going to do something really messy', said our guides. 'It's such fun'. Science room was locked (health and safety) but they showed us well-equipped computer room and music room. Interactive white boards and computers in all classrooms.

Two classes throughout Key Stage 2, with potential for growth in Key Stage 1. Girls happy, relaxed and proud to show us their work and talk about what they were doing.

Good learning support. All children assessed on arrival at school, targets set each term and parents involved early if problems arise. Head meets all teachers once a term to ascertain that children have reached the expected levels. Parents told us: 'Communications are very good. All the staff are positive and professional and the head is open, hands on and much more visible than the previous one'. The only thing they felt could be improved was sport. There's always something.

The Study Preparatory School

Wilberforce House, Camp Road, London, SW19 4UN

• Pupils: 320 girls, all day • Ages: 4–11 • Non denom
• Fees: £10,950 pa • Independent

Tel: 020 8947 6969
Email: admissions@thestudyprep.co.uk
Website: www.thestudyprep.co.uk

Headmistress: Since 2011, Mrs Susan Pepper MA PGCE NPQH (early 50s). Educated at Godolphin and Latymer School, read history at Somerville College, Oxford. Previously head of history and deputy head at Francis Holland. An interesting move/appointment for someone with previous experience only in girls' secondary schools, but it is generally felt she has found her niche. 'She is focused and dynamic but a softee at heart'. Determined to develop and expand the school while maintaining its 'excellent ethos'. Has already delighted parents by bringing in school lunches, compulsory to new pupils from 2013 – all food cooked on site. Has invested in ICT software and hardware and in-class staff training, and improved and streamlined communications. Parents say 'very approachable, not at all forbidding', 'never hurries us in conversations', 'our children are in good hands', 'manages expectations well and gives good advice'. They feel that her knowledge of the senior school system has distinct advantages. She displays a commitment that should move the school from strength to strength. She will listen to others points of view, but will always drive through what she sees as necessary change. Her mantra is 'do the best by every child'. A mother said, 'gives the girls lots of respect and makes it easy for them to talk to her'. Teaches RE to years 5 and 6; runs the Debating Club for the older girls and Pony Club for the younger ones. Definitely feels that the move was the right decision. We think she could be right. Married with one grown up son. Enjoys riding, keeping ex-battery hens, gardening, reading and cryptic crosswords in her spare time. When, we wonder, is that.

Entrance: Non-selective at 4+ by ballot. Registration any time up to 18 months before entry. No point in rushing in at birth, it won't make any difference. Sibling priority. Mostly from local Wimbledon area but some from Kingston, Wandsworth and other surrounding areas. The usual cosmopolitan mix of nationalities and backgrounds found in London schools.

Exit: Mainly to local day schools, often with scholarships – 12 in 2013. Wimbledon High is at the top, with, amongst others, Lady Eleanor Holles, St Paul's Girls, Putney High, Surbiton High and Francis Holland following close behind. A few to boarding schools such as Frensham and Feltonfleet. Mrs Pepper really does try to make sure that the schools girls try for are the most appropriate. At the beginning of year 5 there is a general talk for all parents, after which she schedules individual sessions to

S

JUNIOR SCHOOLS

talk them through their daughters' futures. 'She never hurries us and is so reassuring'.

Remarks: A happy school full of lively, enthusiastic girls. Parents love it and have nothing but praise. Couldn't find anyone with a serious criticism but working parents would love a homework club. All feel that their daughters are nurtured from day one and are not overly pressurised. 'Huge strength is all are treated as individuals and their differences celebrated'.

Will be 120 years old in 2013. The Study was originally just that, one room, three pupils, one governess. It soon grew and moved to 4, Peek Crescent, purpose built in 1905, now Spencer House accommodating the prep school girls. About 20 years ago another purpose-built school was bought and the pre-prep department moved to Wilberforce House approximately 10 minutes walk away across Wimbledon Common. The result? One school, two buildings, great teaching and tip top facilities.

Two year 2 girls took us round Wilberforce House. Articulate and enthusiastic they were keen to show us every nook and cranny. Remembering with joy. Colour coded classes for all levels. Reception now fully high tech: 'we never had computers like these!' But 'we've always had interactive white boards'. All classrooms light and bright and busy. In year 1, we walked in just as a butterfly was emerging from a chrysalis – very exciting. Elsewhere, a show and tell session held everyone rapt. Everything is done to provide a happy, relaxed learning environment. Plenty of art on display. Low level loos for the youngest and basins with bear shaped taps. Excellent library with ICT area. Fascinating DT projects. To help with transition, year 3 girls go to Spencer House for drama and art each week.

We were taken round Spencer House by two bright year 6 girls, eager to tell us what they liked best about their school. Seemed to be pretty well everything. Good-sized hall which doubles up as stage for plays and concerts and, on the day we visited, space for a charity fair. Very keen on their charity work: 'Year 6 choose the special ones for the summer term'. The whole school gathers there at least once a term and on special occasions as, for instance, Harvest Festival. One parent said, 'spencer House seems a bit small', then went on to say 'facilities fabulous'.

Well-equipped library; excellent science room: 'we can use proper equipment'. High tech ICT room where all have a lesson once a week; as in the lower school, interactive white boards everywhere and computers abound. Art room under the eaves, with displays continuing on the walls along the corridor. Individual music rooms named after famous musicians, a wide range of instruments taught. Several choirs and a variety orchestras and groups. Raved about 'our amazing music teacher; really teaches in a fun way'. Music a great strength and leads to several scholarships to senior schools. Drama also huge. Props room known as 'Narnia'; easy to see why. Our guides said, 'everyone does cooking' but we did not see where. A blip, we are assured: both sites have excellent kitchen facilities. (Certainly the 'snack lunch' we were given at the end of the tour was most impressive) An exceptionally wide range of clubs before, after and during school. 'Latin Club at 8am is great'. A parent said, 'something there for every girl, bright or not, will always find a way to shine'.

Teaching appears excellent. Relaxed for the younger children, form teachers covering most subjects; more specialists in the upper school. Those we met were friendly, welcoming and keen to inform. Girls like them all. Average age 46.8, over a quarter having been there for more than 10 years. Sad lack of males but head said good ones are hard to find. Average class size 22, never more than 24.

Weekly staff meeting for whole school when specific problems can be discussed. Up-to-date, well-informed learning support co-ordinator. Continuous assessment and plenty of help for those who need it, including the very able. One-to-one when necessary, charged as an extra. EAL lessons also provided, when needed, at extra cost. Comprehensive anti-bullying policy.

Believe it is important to provide equal opportunity for all children and 'encourage them to think beyond the school gate'. Head feels they are particularly good at building up confidence. Apparently, teachers go out of their way to make sure that each child 'has a moment of glory'.

Good play areas outside both houses, with separate sections for the younger pupils. Sport and PE very important. They say it is all about 'enjoyment, opportunity, success and celebration'. Good variety, taught by specialist teachers. Competitive matches from year 3. National prize winners in netball, cross-country and athletics. No sports field of their own yet but make good use of the many local facilities. 'Head of sport has amazing drive and enthusiasm'.

Summer Fields

Mayfield Road, Oxford, OX2 7EN

- Pupils: 260 boys; 205 boarders • Ages: 8–13 • C of E
- Fees: Boarding £25,197; Day £19,512 pa • Independent

Tel: 01865 454433
Email: admissions@summerfields.com
Website: www.summerfields.com

Headmaster: Since 2010, Mr David Faber MA Oxon, fifties, came to Summer Fields as Old Boy; former parent and governor, as well as grandson of illustrious alumnus, Harold Macmillan PM. After Eton and Balliol, became a Conservative MP from 1992-2001, including Opposition spokesman foreign affairs (recently secured schools minister as a speaker for a meeting of prep and public school heads). A keen cricketer (sits on MCC committee) and has introduced new cricket nets to the fields; also referees boys' football matches.

Interesting appointment as not originally from a teaching background. Urbane and reserved in manner until on the subject of the boys' achievements – fond collector of past medals; 'sporting caps' and historical mementoes of the school. Uses his experience as a historian and author (two books on modern history) in teaching history to the older years and lecturing on 'Appeasement and the Munich Crisis' to public school history societies. Popular with parents ('dream headmaster'), who have seen him institute 'a lot of changes for the better, one thing at a time'. Makes himself available to the parents and appears to know the boys by name and character. Married to Sophie, not on school staff, with two school-aged daughters and a son at Oxford University.

Entrance: Boys are selected by assessment day, which includes written tasks (English, maths and reasoning) and team activities, along with an all-important report from current school. Early registration necessary, but occasional late entry places and mid-year starters also accepted. Special assessment day for the Maclaren Scholarship – up to 100 per cent bursaries for a year 6/7 boarder given to a high-flyer, usually from a state primary. Music scholarships from age eight for gifted musicians. Head refers to it as a 'national' prep school, with most coming from within an hour's drive of Oxford; some overseas and regular group of Old Summerfieldian sons. Previously thought of as upper-crust, and hasn't entirely shaken off the image. Head disagrees, but one parent regretted the narrow social compass. No plans to take girls or to increase much in size – emphasis on keeping a tight-knit community, especially in chapel and dining room.

A recent class of day-only pupils at age seven ('The Mynors') has now been discontinued to focus on boarding from eight years upwards.

Exit: Strong links with Eton; up to 40 per cent accepted there each year; and increasing number going to Winchester; also to Harrow; Radley; Charterhouse; Stowe and a few to local public day schools. Recently (2013) had 'a stellar year' for scholarships, 13 in total including two coveted classics prizes to Eton and Charterhouse. Head maintains, 'Proof of the pudding is that the less academically able boys still get into public schools'. Parents like the fact that it doesn't feel like a 'feeder' but still gets great results.

Remarks: Set in over 70 acres of stunning grounds in the heart of North Oxford, the school is unremarkable from the front, but boasts a stately bow-fronted building with fields, woods and river at the rear. Founded by Victorian educationalist husband and wife team, Maclarens, in 1864 and still conscious of its Christian traditions with Victorian chapel and oak-panelled hall. However, there are more modern additions of several smaller houses along adjoining road; two pools (indoor and outdoor); a sports complex, Eton Fives courts, a climbing wall, new all-weather tennis and Astroturf courts, as well as golf course and cricket nets.

Very long day for both boarders and day boys, starts with whole school convening for chapel or assembly. Lessons in small classes (10-17) and early 'setting' promote strong academic results at CE. Scholarship class in last two years given Greek, and Latin and French learnt by all. New DT and ICT suite and science labs, where boys encouraged to 'design your own experiments and make things pop', as well as large, busy library. Boys genuinely motivated by trips to Oxford museums and field trips, including to France. Teaching staff visible round school, as most live in, some of long-standing (30+ years); 'most staff leave to become a headmaster somewhere else'. Academic success earns boys personal and house points which can be enjoyed by tangible rewards in the school shop ('Buzzer') and a House Feast. A staff of six for learning support, with some experience in EP support and statements. One parent felt that it was particularly good for boys who aren't particularly socially confident and so may experience difficulties elsewhere.

Lodges (boarding houses) for boys of same year group; run by husband and wife team and kept apart from the teaching rooms (no homework or dining in Lodge). Remarkably neat dorms, sleep 4-6, with effective in-house incentives for boys to change own sheets, polish shoes and tidy up. One parent commented, 'What I like is that Summer Fields doesn't smell like a school'. Generous but confusing system of 'credits' allows boarders extra weekends out above normal exeats. Pastoral care is managed with a three-tier 'belt and braces' approach. Lodge parent claims 'Home sickness is more of a problem for the mums' than the boys, who are kept busy in the evenings with board games, computers and giant chess sets. Parent of a young boarder was hugely relieved how easily the youngest were settled in. Discipline maintained by healthy competition and withdrawing privileges rather than anything more gruelling. Boys appear to appreciate this.

Music is a strength, with a dedicated music block and theatre. Three choirs, one with adult voices, sing in Oxford Colleges and on tour (Rome recently). Specialist music staff allow boys to take up to three instruments; (I heard of a 10 year old playing four!) ranging from conventional to electric guitar, even quirky. They recently hunted down a Marimba (Eastern Xylophone) teacher in Oxford for a lad from the Far East. Drama productions for different year groups from Twelve Angry Men to We Will Rock You, open to all those who risk taking time from their scholarship clubs. Sport is plentiful and all-inclusive; parents like the fact that all boys make the teams, which play twice a week. Football has just had its best season since 1937; rugby and hockey also strong, with some players in county cricket and rugby teams. Prolific art and ceramics studio, obviously not pc – fantasy coats of arms and big game trophies made from papier mache adorn the walls.

Boys emerge from lessons brightly but quietly. They are articulate and confident, although suspiciously neat and clean in brightly coloured shirts and sweaters. Parental niggle that boys were 'a bit too polished'. However, children appear kind and supportive – 'when you are in the third year you know everyone's names' – and a nice touch that both staff and children refer to the school as 'We...'. Boys don't seem fazed by formality or overt competition, academic progress bulletins are posted on the board every two weeks for all to read, but seem to enjoy it as 'healthy rivalry'. There is a wealth of extra-mural activities, spanning spiritual (Time for God group), sporting (fencing, shooting, polo) and more earthy interests (cookery and Adventure Quest – bushcraft-style camps – for handy skills in lighting the campfire and skinning a rabbit).

An appreciation of the school's history is encouraged with scholars' boards lining the walls of the hall; and a moving remembrance day service, when choral speakers read out names of the fallen alumnae. Boys follow this up with a trip to the Somme. Old Summerfieldians include generous helpings of baronets, colonial civil servants and military leaders as well as Dick Francis, who set one of his detective novels at the school. Active Old Boy links suggest happy memories.

A small and cosy school, in a serene and beautiful setting, successfully eases a boy in to a boarding career. It provides a breathtaking array of sports and music facilities as well as being reliable in placing boys in top public schools. Sense that boys work hard/play hard and turn out to be happy, considerate and polite, if slightly formal. Not for Just Williams.

Summerhill School (Junior)

Linked school: Summerhill School

Westward Ho, Leiston, IP16 4HY

• Pupils: 70 , majority borders • Ages: 5–11 • Fees: Boarding £6,894–£12,777; Day £3,921–£7,680 pa • Independent

Tel: 01728 830540
Email: office@summerhillschool.co.uk
Website: www.summerhillschool.co.uk

Remarks: See senior school.

Sunningdale School

Dry Arch Road, Sunningdale, Ascot, Berkshire, SL5 9PY

• Pupils: 100 boys, all board except a handful. • Ages: 8–13
• C of E • Fees: Boarding £20,205; Day £17,190 pa • Independent

Tel: 01344 620159
Email: headmaster@sunningdaleschool.co.uk
Website: www.sunningdaleschool.co.uk

Headmaster: Since 2005, Mr Tom Dawson, who took over the reins from his father and uncle. Mr Dawson was educated at Eton then Edinburgh and Bristol universities. He taught at Harrow before joining Sunningdale. Married to Elisabeth, one son, one daughter.

Entrance: At seven or eight – 'they settle in better at this age' – from a wide variety of pre-preps all over the country including Scotland. Some from London but not as many as expected given

S

the proximity to the London SW postcodes. Also happy to take boys at 10 or 11 from day schools.

Exit: Harrow and Charterhouse currently most popular destinations, followed by Eton and Bradfield.

Remarks: Small, cosy, old-fashioned prep school. A large country house with lots of add-ons including new-fashioned classroom blocks, one furnished with old-fashioned wooden 'lift-up lid' desks. Refurbished ICT room and theatre, a new cinema and a newly-built library complex in the planning. New house system encourages boys to earn points for their respective houses through good work and behaviour. Houses named after previous headmasters – Sheepshanks, Crabtree, Fox, Girdlestone. Attention given to individual academic needs. Much movement between classes. A brighter boy may end up doing two years in a top class which gives him a tremendous advantage at common entrance. Well-behaved boys juxtaposed with seemingly informal teaching staff. Very good results at common entrance and scholarships won on a regular basis.

About 85 per cent learn a musical instrument. Active chess club with a part-time chess teacher and a wide-ranging extra-curricular programme that includes cooking, model-making, pottery, fencing, pirates and rifle shooting. Lots of sport including Eton fives. Full boarding although boys may weekly board in their first two years. Masses to do at weekends from paintballing to go-karting. Pastoral care has improved dramatically. Present matron is kind and cosy. Carpeted dorms for younger ones (piles of teddies on the beds), cubicles for the older boys, hot chocolate offered as a reward for tidiness. We hear that the bathroom with miniature cast iron baths is in the process of being made into a new shower room. House in Normandy used by the week. Boys allowed to walk the Dawsons' dogs in the grounds (wonderful at cheering up a homesick child). Excellent food. Boys have happy, cheery faces with sparkling eyes. Excellent manners and well disciplined. Lots of praise too.

Sunny Hill Preparatory School

Linked school: Bruton School for Girls

Bruton School for Girls, Sunny Hill, Bruton, Somerset, BA10 0NT

• Pupils: 71 pupils; boys welcome in nursery and pre-prep until 7 • Ages: 3–11 • Fees: Day £5,025–£10,350; Boarding £16,611–£18,624 pa • Independent

Tel: 01749 814427
Email: admissions@brutonschool.co.uk
Website: www.brutonschool.co.uk

Head of Prep: Since 2010, Mrs Helen Snow BEd, previously deputy head. Has had experience in primary and secondary education at state and independent schools. Lived in Berlin for eight years and worked in senior management at Berlin's leading British School. Married with one daughter. Aims to 'set the very highest expectations regarding behaviour and academic performance. To provide an environment which is safe, secure and stimulating, where each and every child is happy and nurtured.'

Entrance: Open entry into pre-prep.

Exit: Seamless entry to senior school at 11.

Remarks: Housed comfortably in rambling, two-storey, former boarding house, overlooks shared swimming pool and rolling countryside beyond. Level site adjacent to senior school tennis courts which double as a hard surface play area for the prep. Plentiful car parking for drop-offs and collections a definite plus. Nursery (starts with 2+ children) and pre-prep in cedar clad annexe – plenty of space indoors and outside. Children feel safe and happy here. Well planned phonic and number work in pre-prep before girls move into adjacent prep classroom where we saw them writing scripts for a Cinderella performance. Work is differentiated sensibly for older and younger girls in a way designed to work well for both age groups.

Close contact between staff and parents encouraged at all levels. We noted this feedback from a prep 2 parent in her daughter's reading diary, 'I am pleased Charlotte is enjoying her reading so much. Fantastic.' Teachers monitor girls' choice of reading to ensure it fits emotional as well as reading ages.

Good interactive IT suite (accommodates 17 girls) plus specialist science and art/DT rooms. After-school clubs and prep continue to 5.35pm. Multi-purpose hall with staging for in-house performances; girls share senior school gym for PE (taught by specialists) and senior theatre for school productions. Prep has own SENCo with NFER materials used to screen for dyslexia at prep 3 level. Individual SpLD support followed through into senior school if necessary. Languages teacher uses La Jolie Ronde for French and also introduces Spanish. Peripatetic music lessons on site include Suzuki violin for all prep 3s; music showcased annually in prep prom. Yummy lunches at senior school supervised by prep staff ahead of main rush. Regular competition in netball, hockey and rounders. Swimming and tag rugby also on offer. Recent success for prep 6 girls in national indoor rowing championships. Inclusivity ensures all can have a go – severely asthmatic had managed to play in a hockey match a few days before our visit. Enticing library adds to reading ethos – popular annual book week with visitors. Excursions and on-going programme of activities for all ages. Lovely dorm in the nearby junior boarding house accommodates small number of prep boarders (currently seven). Idyllic learning environment – no wonder girls in the senior school look back nostalgically at their beginnings here. Head has much to live up to.

Surbiton High Boys' Preparatory School

Linked school: Surbiton High School

3 Avenue Elmers, Surbiton, KT6 4SP

• Pupils: 145 boys, all day • Ages: 4–11 • Christian ethos but all denominations accepted • Fees: £8,601–£11,499 pa • Independent

Tel: 020 8390 6640
Email: surbiton.prep@surbitonhigh.com
Website: www.surbitonhigh.com

Headmaster: Since 2006, Cath Bufton BA PGCE (thirties). Intended to join the police force but did some supply teaching in Somerset, 'got bitten by the bug' and decided to begin teaching straight away. Taught in junior and middle schools in Somerset and Bute House Prep in Hammersmith before arriving at Surbiton. Describes herself as 'super-organised and approachable' and feels she has already tightened things up and strengthened the school's structure. Outside school she is a keen musician (plays trumpet) and is also very sporty (played rugby for Wales in her time) enjoying netball and triathlons. Married with a son.

Entrance: At 4 – informal assessment in November for 22 reception places. At other times subject to availability. No need to register at birth.

Exit: With no in-house repository at 11, school achieves a very creditable set of places/scholarships at local independent schools including Hampton, Kingston Grammar, Reed's and St George's College.

Remarks: Good academically but with limited space particularly outdoors. Surbiton Prep is the junior boys' school of Surbiton High School and shares many of its facilities including dining rooms and gym (100 metres down the road, so the boys get plenty of short walks each day) and sports fields (impressive, though a three mile bus journey away). The prep building has been a school since 1862 (it became part of Surbiton High in 1987) and, while this gives the place a certain homely charm, the downside is that physical surroundings are not great and space is at a premium. 'Reception classroom is small and hot,' said one parent. Several others voiced concerns about the playground – 'too small – no space for the boys to have a good run about,' said one, though school reminds us that they have extensive playing fields in Hinchley Wood. 'Not enough equipment,' said another parent.

Does not follow the national curriculum to the letter (boys additionally take French from reception) but pupils sit Sats at Key Stages 1 and 2. More than half generally reach level 5 in year 6. All classrooms have electronic whiteboards. Lots of opportunities for arty children – regular drama productions and a good range of music tuition available as an extra. Plenty of after-school clubs.

Pastoral care and discipline generally considered good. 'It's a very close community where the boys all know each other and the teachers all know them,' said a mother of two boys at the school. 'It's a safe and supportive environment where the children feel secure.' Any issues over behaviour problems are considered well handled – with the occasional miracle turnaround of a difficult child. Relaxed atmosphere, boys are polite and well turned out. Parents mostly English professional couples – both working, with a sprinkling from overseas. Strong parent association with plenty going on – more social than fund-raising. 'Friendly, not snooty,' said one.

Generally a feel that the prep is a bit of a poor relation of the main school but, 'there's a happy atmosphere and they turn out a good product,' said a father – 'makes you wonder what they could do if the facilities were slightly better.'

Surbiton High Junior Girls' School

Linked school: Surbiton High School

S

95–97 Surbiton Road, Kingston Upon Thames, KT1 2HW

• Pupils: 230 girls, all day • Ages: 4–11 • Christian ethos but all denominations accepted • Fees: £8,601–£11,499 pa
• Independent

Tel: 020 8439 1309
Email: surbiton.juniorgirls@surbitonhigh.com
Website: www.surbitonhigh.com

Head: Since 2006, Ms Cath Bufton BA (thirties). She took a PGCE ('to get it under my belt for the future'), but actually intended to join the police force. While waiting to begin police training she did some supply teaching in Somerset, 'got bitten by the bug' and decided to begin teaching straight away. After five

years teaching in junior and middle schools in Somerset, she moved to Bute House Prep in Hammersmith, where she spent five more years before arriving at Surbiton. In the past, there has been some parental feeling that the junior and boys' prep heads are mere puppets of senior school head. However, all changed when a new head joined the senior school several years ago, and Ms Bufton says they work well as a team.

She is certainly full of enthusiasm, with just a whiff of head girl about her; describes herself as 'super-organised and approachable' and feels she has tightened things up and strengthened the school's structure. Well-intentioned, proactive and good at PR, parents find her friendly and agree that she's approachable – if occasionally a little on the defensive side 'and hot under the collar when stressed'. 'I like her and feel she's brought a fresh perspective to the place,' says one mother. 'She's got a great attitude and I've got a good feeling about her,' says another. Outside school she is a keen musician (she plays trumpet) and is also very sporty (played rugby for Wales in her time) enjoying netball and triathlons. Married with a son and new baby.

Entrance: All girls are assessed prior to entry – an age-appropriate and child-friendly exercise. At 4+ the tests are based on cognitive and social development, with the girls doing simple tasks observed by teachers. At 7+ girls are tested in line with the national curriculum for English and maths and a school report is also requested. Most families come from immediate surrounding areas (11 school bus routes and 10 mins from BR station). Main feeders are Thames Ditton Infant School, Dicky Birds Nursery, Bushy Tails Nursery and Maple Road Infants School.

Exit: Most go to linked senior school as entry is now automatic (school prefers term 'natural progression'). Otherwise it's local grammars or other independents. Some parental moans that girls are not prepared for entry to other schools. The head counters that Surbiton is basically an all-through school, which parents know when they choose the junior section. Furthermore, she maintains girls leave the juniors with good results and are therefore quite capable of gaining a place elsewhere.

Remarks: Vibrant happy place, modern yet homely, with a good local reputation and turning out confident, articulate girls, largely for its own senior department.

Attainment is high. Teaching is rigorous and lessons move along at a brisk pace. Even the youngest quickly prove capable of working alone or in small groups for short periods. Ms Bufton describes teaching styles as 'relaxed but productive – I don't mind a bit of noise as they process what they're learning and I want them to feel confident enough to take a risk, make a mistake, as they learn – it's the best way to learn.' Girls follow the national curriculum closely, but not exclusively, and take Sats in year 6, generally with great success – 100 per cent achieving the target of level 4, and many bettering it. Pupils work hard and go home tired – so homework is scaled back accordingly to three 30-minute sessions a week and absolutely none during the holidays (though some will be provided at parents' request). Nice teacher/pupil relationships. Some girls from Korea and Indian sub-continent supported with EAL lessons. Learning support for mild difficulties such as dyslexia and dyspraxia, along with support and access improvements to help the physically disabled. Parents can pay extra for one-to-one SEN support. School has an SEN teacher who works three days a week. Enrichment groups in English, maths and science are laid on for the gifted and talented, in addition to in-class support through planned differentiation.

Outside pure academia there is lots going on. Plenty of clubs and outings, including residential trips from year 4. As with senior school, sport has been a concern here (small site militates against it) but generally seen as improving and the junior girls use the off-site extensive sports grounds at Hinchley Wood. Regular music and drama productions.

Lovely modern building was purpose-built – so no complaints there. Ten minutes from central Surbiton it's a very urban space – local parking a nightmare so school has organised staggered start times to give all year groups a fair crack at the limited drop off area. Works well. Inside it's a bright and stimulating environment, a purposeful place with some outstanding specialist facilities – particularly art, music and science. Parents give special mention to the breadth of the curriculum and the child-centred approach – 'I like the ethos and the moral fabric of the school,' says one mother. The pupils are listened to and are happy that they have a voice – strong school council system.

Real sense of pride in the place – very small girls who didn't realise they were being watched were seen holding doors open for each other, and another nonchalantly picked up an overturned waste paper bin as she passed without missing a beat. Lunchtimes have been much improved by a new system called 'family service' where, having previously chosen what to eat, the girls sit at the appropriate small table and are served by a member of staff or a year 6 pupil – changes the mix and fosters sense of community. Even the necessary but unappealing table-clearing duties carried out cheerfully afterwards. 'The whole lunchtime set up is lovely now – and the food's improved,' says one pleased mum. A kindly atmosphere pervades. 'There's no such thing as a perfect school – but what makes the difference is the way the school deals with any issues – here I always feel listened to and where it's been warranted, something has been done,' a mother says. A few gripes about home/school communication – claims that school is flaky over notifications of after-school clubs being cancelled and the like. However, with the linked boys' prep and seniors there's a real family feel to the place, with many families having children at all three schools.

Sussex House School

68 Cadogan Square, London, SW1X 0EA

- Pupils: 180 boys; all day • Ages: 8–13 • C of E • Fees: £16,200 pa
- Independent

Tel: 020 7584 1741
Email: registrar@sussexhouseschool.co.uk
Website: www.sussexhouseschool.co.uk

Headmaster: Since 1994, Mr Nicholas Kaye MA ACP (mid-fifties). Was deputy head here before. In his many years at the school, Mr Kaye has made his mark. His room is more reminiscent of a Victorian parlour, stuffed to the gunwhales with objets d'art, pieces of porcelain, figurines, potted plants, embroidered banners (made for the school jubilee and used on special occasions), leather armchairs, lampshades, oriental carpets, rugs and comfy sofas. It even accommodates an ornately decorated pianoforte. The walls, needless to say, are covered with antique tomes, old school photos, house shields, clocks and portraits. At one end sits a fine stained glass window. During break the staff assemble amongst all this finery to partake of coffee and biscuits. It is hard not to like this room and this man. Indeed, parents as well as pupils become very attached to the school. The 'Olim Alumni' listed in the (very impressive) school magazine date back to the 1950s and reunions always see a good turnout from the Old Cadogans.

Entrance: At 8+ mostly from Wetherbys, Eaton House, Garden House and other local pre-preps. Not suited to any other than the high fliers as this is a school with an unashamedly academic agenda. Tends to attract families familiar with the English boarding system. Despite the pressures on his time (he still teaches English to the top three classes and is always demonstrating the delights of creative writing to the younger set) Mr Kaye resolutely meets all prospective parents and they are shown round the school on an individual basis – 'we are a personal school. The individual matters.'

Exit: Majority to Eton and Winchester. Harrow and Marlborough are also popular. Just under a third go to London day schools such as St Paul's, Westminster and Alleyn's. Generally achieves a smattering of scholarships.

Remarks: One could just describe this school as a centre of academic excellence and leave it at that but that would not give a true picture. Mr Kaye has created a remarkable place where he believes boys should have something to look forward to every day. One such is the sight of the School Marshal, Sergeant Khim Sherchan, formerly of the Gurkhas, looking very donnish in his black gown, welcoming the boys and their parents at the school entrance every morning; guaranteed to bring a smile to your face.

From year 1, lessons are given by dedicated staff qualified to teach their subjects to A level. Each class has a pastoral teacher but the boys quickly become used to being taught by a variety of specialist teachers. This is an excellent preparation for their future public school education and beyond. Outside of academia, countless activities are offered before, after and during school. Even at weekends. For a small school in central London, the range available is astonishing and is the result of slick time organisation, 'rather like running a small railway company,' says the head. With limited space on the actual premises, musical and dramatic performances take place in Cadogan Hall, the Royal Court Theatre and St John's, Smith Square. All the junior boys now have an opportunity to develop in drama and music as they put on their own productions. The school does not want the pupils to 'go into an academic tunnel. Boys who like music also want to play football.' Current activities on offer as classes or clubs include oil painting, fencing, cricket, football, creative writing, Greek, architecture, pottery and music, music everywhere. Brand new science labs. The school's annexe off Cadogan Square has a surprisingly large gym on the top floor. Art is particularly strong with the art room 'open for business all the time (including weekends)'. Examples of the boys' work are displayed throughout the school, starting with an awe-inspiring model of St Pancras station in the entrance hall. Everything here is done with skill, enthusiasm, enjoyment and hard work. Standards are high and it shows. Sussex House deserves its reputation as an excellent boys' prep.

Sutton High Junior School

Linked school: Sutton High School

55 Cheam Road, Sutton, SM1 2AX

- Pupils: 250 • Ages: 3–11 girls, all day • Non-denom
- Fees: £8,343–£10,950 pa • Independent

Tel: 020 8225 3072
Email: office@sut.gdst.net
Website: www.suttonhigh.gdst.net

Head of Junior School: Since 2010, Manda Cooper BEd English (fifties). Married with two daughters and a son, who all attended single sex schools. Mrs Cooper is strongly committed to single sex education, particularly for girls, feeling they have better opportunities away from the competition of boys. Not one to stand still, she is equally committed to the continuing development of the junior school: most recently she's expanded the nursery and introduced a toddler group. Still very much a hands-on head teacher, she acts as a supply teacher covering staff absences. On duty early each morning, she is considered level-headed and hard-working by parents.

Entrance: Girls can join the nursery from their third birthday onwards and move onto reception at 4+. Younger children attend an informal play session before being offered a place; from 6+ girls sit assessment tests. For entry into other years telephone the school to enquire about occasional places. £75 non-refundable registration fee for those wanting to sit the entry tests.

Exit: At 11+ around three-quarters of the girls move to the senior school. Remainder move to co-ed or local grammar schools. Girls who are not suited to the senior school will be advised in year 5 to give them plenty of time to look for an alternative.

Remarks: Traditional junior school which aims to offer a broad and balanced curriculum to suit a range of tastes. Carefully structured early years stage focuses on instilling basic literacy and numeracy skills through structured play whilst also developing independence and confidence. Moving up the school, everything appears to be well planned, with lots of music, drama and sport alongside traditional subjects. Setting for maths from year 4 and English from year 5. Impressive foreign languages programme: French starts in the nursery, years 3 and 4 are introduced to Spanish and years 5 and 6 start German and Latin. Teaching staff includes a few old girls; all are unanimous about aiming to pass on and develop a love of learning and natural curiosity in their young charges.

Well-stocked library has aptly been renamed the Discovery Zone. Well-kept colourful corridors lined with children's art, poetry and other achievements. Neat and amenable girls appear beautifully behaved, happy and involved in their work. Drama is incorporated into the English curriculum and taught by class teachers; girls are encouraged to take LAMDA grade exams, organised by visiting teachers. Dedicated music teacher works extremely hard and successfully, producing two big concerts each year, as well as regular musical assemblies. All pupils learn keyboard and recorder in class; individual tuition is available on any other instrument.

SENCo, and a part-time specialist teacher for small group work or one-to-one tuition, assist children with mild specific learning difficulties or differences. There is also an EAL coordinator. Tops and Tails provides an on-site wraparound care facility from 7:30am – 6:30pm. Everything from breakfast to homework club for three to 11-year-olds is available at a reasonable hourly rate. They also run a Thursday morning toddler group for boys and girls aged nought to three years.

Suits a wide range of enthusiastic little girls, and perhaps a good choice, with its complementary services, for working parents.

Sutton Valence Preparatory School

Linked school: Sutton Valence School

Church Road, Chart Sutton, Maidstone, Kent, ME17 3RF

• Pupils: 141 girls and 177 boys • Ages: 3–11 • Fees: £7,920–£11,985 pa • Independent

Tel: 01622 842117
Email: enquiries@svprep.svs.org.uk
Website: www.svs.org.uk

Head: Since 2012, Mr Malcolm Gough BA LLB (Rhodes) LLM (Cape Town) PGCE (OU), previously head of teaching and learning at The Schools at Somerhill, Tonbridge.

Originally from Zimbabwe. Studied Law at Rhodes University and came to UK in 1989. Completed his PGCE in 1994. Worked up to director of studies at Winchester House School. Also Independent Schools Inspector. Married, with two small children who will be attending the school. He enjoys sport, scuba-diving, reading, wildlife and the outdoors and playing the guitar.

Mr Gough says he 'was struck by the warm and strong sense of community' at the school and hopes 'to maintain all that is good and improve where we might do better.'

Entrance: Entry into year 2 of kindergarten is non-selective. For entry to years 3 to 6, assessment with the director of studies involving reading, spelling, maths and non-verbal reasoning to ascertain the child's academic levels.

Exit: Mostly to Sutton Valence School, other independent schools and to local grammar schools.

Remarks: Set in 22 acres of grounds in the village of Chart Sutton, one mile from Sutton Valence School. Small classes, high standards and the same commitment to extra-curricular activities as the senior school. Senior school's indoor pool, all-weather athletics track and dedicated cricket pitches supplement prep's own facilities.

Pastoral care systems ensure that pupils are well-supported in their learning and in gaining the confidence to become independent, sympathetic and well-balanced children, ready and eager to take the next step into secondary education.

Sydenham High Junior School GDST

Linked school: Sydenham High School GDST

15 Westwood Hill, London, SE26 6BL

• Pupils: 250 girls; all day • Ages: 4–11 • Fees: £10,920 pa • Independent

Tel: 020 8557 7000
Email: admissions@syd.gdst.net
Website: www.sydenhamhighschool.gdst.net

Head: Senior school head Mrs Kathryn Pullen is looking after the junior school until a new junior school head is recruited.

Entrance: Informal entry assessment at three-and-a-half – 'gives us an edge over some of our competitors who do formal assessment – children skip out of here, find experience enjoyable, even fun.' 'Weed out the stroppy and difficult' so hope it doesn't fall on a day when your child's in a bad mood!

Exit: Around 75 per cent to senior school, rest to a range of schools both state and private, including other GDST schools. Progression to senior school expected but not automatic.

Remarks: Good facilities, new library and IT suite, classrooms brimming with lively displays. New playgrounds, additional classrooms and specialist science, art and ICT facilities were all recently added. Close links with senior school – head spends an afternoon a week in the junior school, takes assembly, which girls love and say is a very special time. Year 6 girls permitted to wear senior uniform.

French for all from 4, Latin is taught to the top two years; emphasis on music, sport and drama. Currently caters for range of mild SEN: dyspraxia, dyslexia, dyscalculia, Asperger's, autism, ADD, ADHD and EBD, but all must be able to manage the curriculum. Some specialist support available.

A very welcoming environment.

Talbot Heath Junior School

Linked school: Talbot Heath School

Rothesay Road, Bournemouth, BH4 9NJ

- Pupils: 115 girls in junior school and 84 pupils in pre-prep
- Ages: 3–11 • C of E • Fees: £5,340–£9,480 pa • Independent

Tel: 01202 763360
Email: jsoffice@talbotheath.org
Website: www.talbotheath.org.uk

Head: Since 1987, Mrs Karen Leahy BA PGCE MEd – a teaching head, having her own form and teaching six periods a week, but spends time with all of the children so that she knows every child in school and has a good understanding of each age group.

Entrance: Youngest children come along for a chat. Entrants to years 1 – 6 spend a whole day in the school and pupils entering year 3 – 6 sit formal tests in VR, maths and English. Bar for entry not a high one: 'Most of our pupils are little Miss Average,' says the head. No longer takes boys.

Exit: Eighty per cent or so to senior school, rest to local girls' grammars.

Remarks: Junior school housed in what was once a school boarding house – so plenty of loos! Own dining rooms, computer suites and play areas as well as purpose-built Jubilee Hall for assemblies, drama and music. Interactive whiteboards in all classrooms from year 1 up. Traditional feel, small classes, tidy hair, smart uniform, emphasis on manners and handwriting. 'Not a place for eccentrics or slackers,' says school.

Music and PE taught by specialist staff at all ages, and senior school facilities are used when appropriate. Junior school has its own strings group and two choirs but able girls can join the senior orchestra. From year 4 specialist teaching extends to English and maths, then French and art from year 5. By year 6 the girls are attending half their classes – and eating lunch – at the senior school. Four PE lessons per week, including fencing, volleyball and badminton in year 6. Peripatetic special needs teacher gives one-to-one help to a half dozen pupils.

TASIS – The American School in England (Lower School)

Linked school: TASIS – The American School in England

Coldharbour Lane, Thorpe, TW20 8TE

- Pupils: 220 • Ages: 3–10 boys and girls; day • Non-denom
- Fees: £6,350–£18,880 pa • Independent

Tel: 01932 565252
Email: ukadmissions@tasisengland.org
Website: www.tasisengland.org

Head of Lower School: Since 2011, Mrs Tracy Murch BA MEd. Previously an Elementary School Principal in the Merrimack Valley School District in New Hampshire and most recently at Boscawen Elementary School. Mrs. Murch is a career educator. She was a finalist for the New Hampshire Principal of the Year 2010 and received the 2011 Outstanding Role Model Award from the New Hampshire School Principals' Association.

Remarks: For details, see the senior school entry.

Taunton Preparatory School & Pre Prep and Nursery

Linked school: Taunton School

Staplegrove Road, Taunton, TA2 6AE

- Pupils: Nursery 55 day; Pre-Prep 91 day; Prep 259 day and boarding. Boys and girls throughout. • Ages: Nursery to Pre-Prep 0–7; Prep 7–13 • Inter-denom • Fees: Day £6,195–£13,395 Boarding £12,030–£21,795 pa; • Independent

Tel: 01823 703307
Email: admissions@tauntonschool.co.uk
Website: www.tauntonschool.co.uk

Headmaster: Since September 2013, Mr Duncan Sinclair MA HDE. Born in Zimbabwe, Mr Sinclair moved to South Africa at the age of 7 and was educated at The Ridge Preparatory School in Johannesburg, and then St Alban's College in Pretoria. Read English and environmental science at the University of Cape Town before completing a higher diploma in education. Began his teaching career in Cape Town at Diocesan College Prep School (Bishops) in Cape Town, also coaching cricket, rugby and athletics. At the same time, he enjoyed a secondary career as a semi-professional rugby player representing Western Province as a second row forward. Moved to St Michael's Preparatory School, Kent, in 2002 where he was year 4 teacher, head of geography and PSHE and deputy head and completed his MA in educational leadership and management. In addition to taking part in competitive cricket and hockey, Mr Sinclair plays the clarinet, trombone and tuba and is a keen chorister. Married to Georgina, a primary teacher with a PE specialisation. Their son Hamish will attend the TPPS Nursery.

Entrance: There are three rungs to the school's ladder. Entry into the nursery classes; then the pre-prep and finally at 7+ the prep school itself. The first two rungs involve no formal assessment but rather familiarisation sessions to ensure all parties are happy. Entry into the prep school in year 3 is when those moving up from the pre-prep are joined by some

T

half dozen or so new pupils. Since the prep school year groups grow in size from 36 in year 3 to 72 in year 7, entry is usually possible at all ages. Potential pupils spend a day in the school individually or in pairs, joining their peers for lessons, before sitting papers in maths, English and non-verbal reasoning.

Strong special needs ('learning success') department. All pupils are assessed on entry and provision is put in place, if appropriate. The department consists of a full-time head of department and five part-time teachers and is housed in its own area which is bright and homely. There is also a 'gifted and talented' extension programme.

Scholarships available at 11+ for internal and external candidates, academic, music, sport or all-rounder. The all-rounder involves the academic papers plus two of sport, music, drama, art and technology.

Exit: Not surprisingly the majority go on to the senior school, which is bang next door and offers a gentle and friendly way of moving on with little cultural and social shock. The prospect of spending so many years together doesn't seem to faze the pupils. 'They make friends for life,' said a parent with a child in both schools. No CE but children are setted according to the prep school exams and detailed reports. The headmasters of the prep and senior schools have regular meetings, anyway. Entry to the senior school is almost, but not quite, automatic. Occasionally pupils are recognised as not being up to it and are 'diverted to somewhere else where they can succeed.' The school aims to help the parents select a suitable alternative and to avoid sudden hatchet jobs. Occasionally parents do choose to send their children elsewhere, in the last two years pupils have won scholarships to Winchester, Millfield and Sherborne School for Girls. 'Staff love the challenge and it's healthy to have some variety.'

Remarks: An excellent indoor swimming pool, very good teaching facilities – new, brightly coloured and functional – with an atmosphere of busy purpose which some of the tattier buildings do nothing to disperse. Indeed one boy showed us with justifiable pride a hole in a prefab-looking building where he had driven a cricket ball ('It was an off drive, you see'). Games are taken very seriously. The dormitory arrangements (girls named after hills and boys after rivers) were very popular with our guides as were the (segregated) common-rooms with televisions, presided over by a splendid matron who said she enjoyed being at 'the hub of things'. Members of the teaching staff preside overall. Tasters are available.

The most stunning aspect of the school is its music. Lessons are offered on an astonishing variety of instruments. There is an orchestra, a jazz band, a clarinet ensemble and a percussion group amongst other formal and informal groups. 60 per cent of pupils learn at least one instrument and there are over 100 in the (voluntary) choir. A smaller and selected singing group, coached and conducted by a flaming haired Celt who could charm sweet music out of a buffalo, has recently sung in Venice. Previous destinations have included Rome, Barcelona and Prague. A vast range of out-of-school activities. Weekend activities for the 40 or so boarders are well organised and popular.

The matter of bullying is tackled thoroughly. 'Buddy Groups' – vertical rather than horizontal – meet regularly, as do form captains. In groups and assemblies all are constantly reminded that 'different people have different sensibilities.' Leavers' questionnaires deal with the topic and regular self-assessment reports provide opportunities for airing anxieties. There is even, rather touchingly, a Friendship Bench overlooking the playground. The story is told of an exhausted member of staff plonking himself on the bench only to be approached by a young child asking if he had no friends.

This is a school for children with stamina. It's an action-packed day and given that some of the children set off early on school buses from as far afield as Bristol and Exeter, Glastonbury

and Sidmouth, it's a long one. Just as well the food – eaten separately from the main school but sharing the same kitchen – is as good as it is. It really is excellent.

Teesside High School – Preparatory Department

Linked school: Teesside High School

The Avenue, Eaglescliffe, Stockton-on-Tees, TE16 9AT

- Pupils: 120; 71 girls/ 49 boys, all day • Ages: 3–11 • Non-denom
- Fees: £3,300–£9,810 pa • Independent

Tel: 01642 782095
Email: info@teessidehigh.co.uk
Website: www.teessidehigh.co.uk

Director of Prep: Since 2013, Mrs Carolyn Williams. BEd in maths and science from Northumbria, postgrad certificate in leadership and management from Durham. Formerly senior teacher at Yarm, teaches maths; two daughters in prep; enjoys country walks with husband, children and dog and is learning to play golf. Parents are impressed by 'recent small changes for the better', firm in their belief that everyone here 'has the children's best interests at heart'.

Exit: Sensibly, most follow the natural progression into THS senior school.

Remarks: Attractive glass atrium on entry and lovely work displayed everywhere, this is a busy and productive place. Outside there's a new all-weather playground and pirate ship, Astroturf, space hoppers, Kwik cricket and toys-a-plenty plus separate play area for the youngest. According to the children, 'there's everything you need here to grow up'. Wise heads on young shoulders maybe, yet genuinely proud of their school. Well-equipped music ('we love our singing' say the children) and ICT rooms; spacious hall used for assemblies and PE for the youngest. Small room for SEN, officially titled 'Inspirational Learning Zone', but nicknamed 'the Tardis' by the children because apparently, like Dr Who, 'you come out feeling better than when you went in'.

One parent described the teaching staff as Mary Poppins-like, 'an air of authority as necessary but no shouting needed' and new, sometimes shy children are calmly and warmly welcomed into classes. Those classes are small, a factor that has huge appeal and proves the biggest draw for local parents. Many also like the boy-girl split after year 4 as the children enter the diamond model, coming back together for sixth form. It's unusual to separate boys and girls so young but it doesn't seem to bother the pupils.

Little Diamonds nursery takes children from three; flexible sessions allowed, most moving to full-time as they approach reception age. Wraparound care from 7.45 am-6 pm suits the needs of busy parents, as do the holiday clubs. French is taught from reception and learning takes places indoors and out, with full use being made of the lovely woodland school in the grounds. Fortunate in being able to share senior school facilities for PE and games and they make use of a local gym for swimming lessons. Traditional teaching equals regular spelling and times tables tests, but a refreshing approach to integrated studies means that art, DT, history and geography are combined for project-based work that is much-loved by the children who tell us, 'we do loads of cool stuff'.

We met confident, considered, articulate children, happy to chat and excited by their school. They appear sincere and

T

determined in their approach to sport and studies alike, keen to win and do well. Parents equally excited and committed – they've done their homework before choosing the school (plenty of options locally), felt warmly welcomed here and their children settled in quickly.

Tetherdown Primary School

Grand Avenue, London, N10 3BP

• Pupils: 300 • Ages: 4–11 • Non–denom • State

Tel: 020 8883 3412
Email: admin@tetherdownschool.org
Website: www.tetherdownschool.org

Headteacher: Since September 2013, Tony Woodward, previously head of Warren Mead Junior School in Surrey. Specialises in music (plays piano and clarinet), art and gymnastics (trampolining is his speciality – came second in the European Championships). Has worked in Surrey as a local leader in education, supporting the leaders of struggling local schools, and as an additional Ofsted inspector.

Entrance: The school has recently doubled in size to admit 60 pupils in reception, but there's still fierce competition to get in. In the past it was only siblings and those living feet from the gates who reasonably stood a chance, now at least an address in the same street might reasonably be expected to do the trick. (Needless to say property prices nearby have their own exotic micro-climate.) Parents can view the school in the autumn term prior to entry, kids visit in the summer term before they start.

Exit: Not only is Tetherdown one of the country's top-performing primary schools, if you're clever enough to have got your child in here you're also pretty much guaranteed a smooth transition to one of the capital's best comprehensives. Smug parents, who've sorted it all by the age of four, tend to assume their children will proceed to Fortismere and the vast majority go on here. The rest to north London grammar schools or leading independents ('This is Muswell Hill,' said one mother, 'parents tutor without hesitation.')

Remarks: This is a school which regularly sits near the top of the local authority league tables and, even in an average year, over 50 per cent of pupils reach the highest score possible in English and maths. 'Pupils here make outstanding progress,' waxes Ofsted and do so, because of 'extremely effective teaching' and a 'dynamic and vibrant curriculum'. Add to the mix meticulous monitoring, a dollop of regular homework ('there's not a lot of pressure') and dedicated parents willing to supervise nightly reading from reception to year 6 and you get some idea how these results happen. The school follows the national curriculum but adds its own flourishes.

Fun is very much part of the academic recipe, both in the classroom and outside, whether that's learning fractions in history by means of tricky Tudor recipes, studying maths with the help of a visiting Maths Clown or sharpening up those multiplication tables in Beat the Parents at Mental Maths. 'The children have a lovely education,' says one parent. Pupils are grouped, extended and supported according to ability. 'If they're struggling, it gets noticed. My son was given extra spelling and extra handwriting.' Special needs are caught early by a dedicated special needs coordinator, who works with classroom teachers and outside specialists to set appropriate targets. The recent requirement for the inclusion of modern language teaching is provided (courtesy of the Italian consulate) by weekly Italian lessons, and French is also offered as an after-school club.

Plenty of stretching and thinking in all directions, whether in an opera workshop or an after-school street-dance club. Plenty of creative parents, too, who come in to share their expertise. All children learn to play the recorder and read music in year 3 and individual instrumental tuition, subsidised by the local authority, is provided during the working day. Sport is perhaps the school's weakest link, 'There isn't much and what there is isn't competitive,' said one mother of boys. In recent years, this has been partially due to a rebuild. Now the outdoor space is both more expansive and better equipped. In year 6, all children learn swimming and travel outside the school for specialist coaching. Schools meals are nutritious – parents have their own tasting to ensure their experience matches their kids' – and naughty sweets, chocolates and fizzy drinks are banned from the premises. Plenty of after-school clubs – football, drama, etc – and while there's no after-school care on site, those who want it can be collected from the playground and taken to a nearby club. Regular school trips include an annual outing to the seaside for years 2 and 5, where the deputy head sets a good example by leading the troops into the bracing waves.

Virtually all parents and pupils live within a few surrounding streets and the school has always offered an exceptionally tight-knit community. Expansion has marginally diluted the atmosphere, but has brought advantages. 'It used to be very much like a village school, where everyone knew each other and older pupils looked out for the younger ones,' says one mother with children at both ends of the spectrum. 'That was comforting, but sometimes your child didn't have a particularly wide choice of friends. Now there's plenty of scope.'

Until 2009, Tetherdown was a square and solid Victorian board school, but an exciting £6.5 million redesign has provided lots of lovely light interiors and well-planned playgrounds for infants and juniors. The make-over has also brought up-to-the-minute wireless IT, with interactive whiteboards in every classroom and two computer suites.

The school has no uniform and rules are kept to a minimum. 'We have just two rules. Respect yourself, and respect others. If you respect yourself you are going to work hard to become the best you can.' Parents admire the way these principles are implemented. Those demonstrating behavioural difficulties are given the same support as those with academic problems, with intervention and targets. Children are encouraged to get involved: with the school council; with each other's welfare (by becoming play leaders and buddies); and with the broader community (for example, running a soup kitchen at harvest time). They are also lavished with praise. Regular 'Achievements Assemblies' recognise work, effort and attitude.

Tetherdown is located in north London's prosperous, professional Muswell Hill and the parent body is a mirror of the locality, with plenty of engaged parents who devote the same attention to reading rotas and library duty they give to successful careers. Parents, too, provide support in a very concrete fashion and the enthusiastic Parent School Association generously underwrites school trips and playground extras. Parents know each other well in and out of school, are ambitious for their kids and for the school.

Thomas's Battersea

Linked schools: Thomas's Kensington; Thomas's Clapham

28-40 Battersea High Street, London, SW11 3JB

- Pupils: 538; 277 boys/261 girls • Ages: 4-13 • Christian
- Fees: £11,508-£16,875 pa • Independent

Tel: 020 7978 0900
Email: battersea@thomas-s.co.uk
Website: www.thomas-s.co.uk

Headmaster: Mr Ben Thomas MA (forties). Educated Eton, Durham and ultimately at the Institute of Education. First teaching job, aged 26, head of Thomas's Kensington, a bit of baptism by fire. After four years took over headship of Battersea and parents now say 'outstanding' and 'really has his finger on the pulse'. Says that this definitely affected his style of headship and believes that it makes him less didactic. Vice principal of the group, Jill Kelham, based at Battersea, has, apparently, been a huge help to him. Has built up excellent teaching team, including well respected heads of year, and now believes his main function, as far as parents are concerned, is advising on senior schools at 13+. Visits several of these each term and feels he really does know the heads. Parents praise his 'excellent advice'. Says that the school should be about 'enjoyment for the lower school, learning for the middle school and achievement for the upper school,' and is a big believer in the most important school rule, 'be kind'. One of the four principals of the whole group of Thomas's London Day Schools, originally founded by his parents, David and Joanna Thomas in 1971, describes himself as the headmaster, 'doing the fun stuff', and his brother Tobyn as the administrator controlling finance, buildings etc. It is a huge business and would appear to be extremely profitable, though some parents feel that the fees are increasing a little too fast. 'Four to five per cent is a bit steep in the current financial climate.' Married to Katie, a full time Mum, with three children all at the school and totally satisfied with his current existence. 'I love being head. It's great for family life'.

Entrance: Mainly at four. Competitive and oversubscribed. Register as soon as possible, preferably at birth. Assessments in November prior to entry in September the following year. Three applicants for each place offered. Up to six boys and girls per hour's session. Looking for children who 'have a measure of confidence, are responsive, sociable, with a light in their eyes.' Sibling priority but not absolutely guaranteed. Occasional places further up the school when candidates are assessed while spending half a day with their peer group. Written report from previous school also necessary. More places at 11+ but majority of these tend to be taken by children from Thomas's, Kensington.

Exit: Very few leave at age 7 or 8 as no preparation for these exams although, inevitably, the odd trickle whose parents are scared they may not make it later. At 11+ to Putney High, Godolphin & Latymer, Francis Holland, Clarence Gate, St Paul's Girls' and other London day schools. At 13+ to, among others, St Paul's Boys', King's College, Wimbledon, Wellington College, Westminster, Harrow, Millfield and Dulwich College. Impressive range of destinations at both levels with some scholarships.

Remarks: A big, busy, slightly chaotic school for cosmopolitan parents who want their children to have the best English education money can buy. That is what they want and, to a large degree, that is what they get. Plenty of opportunities for pupils to excel but withdrawn types might find it all somewhat overwhelming.

Occupies an attractive listed ex-grammar school building, with many modern additions and plenty of playground space. This last is easily transformed into a car park at the beginning and end of each day as public transport not particularly convenient. Has own fleet of buses which convey children from Kensington and ferry the whole school to sports venues etc. All the facilities for a broad curriculum. Great science labs – 'we do chemistry, physics and biology here,' said our youthful guides – computer suites and all the modern aids to a tip top education. Plus loads of music, with 245 individual lessons taking place each week on instruments that range from piano to cornet; an orchestra, various bands and ensembles, choirs at all levels (recent concert had the school orchestra playing alongside the Southbank Sinfonia) and their own choral society where they are joined by parents from the other schools and members of the local community. Two great art studios and two pottery rooms with their own kiln. Imaginative creations displayed all over the school. We particularly liked the charcoal drawings lining one staircase alongside a written request to please not rub against them. And, of course, being a Thomas's school, the drama is outstanding with huge productions by each year group being put on over the year. 'Only drawback', said one parent, 'is that they are always musicals. Not much use if your child can't sing'. School assures us there's always something for everyone. Great Hall where they perform is pretty splendid.

Lots of sport, say it takes up about 20 per cent of the timetable from year 3 onwards. All the usuals with sculling added in the summer term at the top of the school. Matches inter-house, inter-Thomas's and against other schools. Great gym and school playground excellent place for organised and unorganised games. Also use facilities at Battersea Park, Barns Elms and the Wandle Centre. Youngest children, reception to year 2, have fantastic and imaginative rooftop playground on high.

Academically, teaching deemed pretty good, though lots of coaching still occurring in the last years. 'Just as insurance,' say the parents. We did feel that this was definitely more about anxious and ambitious parents than inadequately taught children. As in all the schools, some specialist teaching from the beginning. Mixed ability classes, with setting in maths and English only, until they reach the upper school when they are divided into those doing 11+ and those staying on and academia becomes the be all and end all, with all classrooms subject-based and a tutor system coming into operation. Not a wide choice of languages, although 11+ leavers have the option of German, Spanish or Italian after their exams. French from Reception, Latin compulsory from year 5.

Enthusiastic, experienced head of learning support who also teaches maths in the lower and middle schools and study skills to years 7 and 8. Determined to catch children early so that they can let go of support by year 6 or 7. Works closely with class teachers, showing them how to help pupils. Mainly milder end of the spectrum but one-to-one teaching available for more serious problems and laptop training when absolutely necessary. Parents always involved and communication apparently good.

Probably most cosmopolitan of all the Thomas's schools, with a wide ranging mix of international parents and 19 different foreign languages spoken at home. About 25 per cent of children on the EAL register. A few of these need extra support which is well provided. School celebrates and appears to make the most of this range of different cultures.

Thomas's Clapham

Linked schools: Thomas's Battersea; Thomas's Kensington

Broomwood Road, London, SW11 6JZ

• Pupils: 580 girls and boys; all day • Ages: 4–13 • Non-denominational • Fees: £13,965–£15,789 pa • Independent

Tel: 020 7326 9300
Email: clapham@thomas-s.co.uk
Website: www.thomas-s.co.uk

Headmaster: Since 2012, Mr Philip Ward BEd. Educated at Reigate Grammar School and read history and PE at Exeter University. Appointed straight from university to Uppingham where he became director of PE and chair of games committee, ascending through the ranks as housemaster, senior housemaster and member of the senior management team. Thence to headship of Feltonfleet School, where we describe him as 'clearly passionate about his school; a charismatic, family man who enjoys a chat'. Married to Sue, a teacher, with two children. Outside of school he enjoys family time, walking, sport and military history.

Says he intends to 'build on the many strengths of this outstanding school so that it is viewed as one of the premier league prep schools in the country'.

Entrance: Competitive and oversubscribed. Need to be put on the list at birth. Interview and assessment take place a year before 4+ entry. Looking for an all-rounder child who will 'get fun and joy out of a big school' and who will take advantage of the amount on offer. Strong sibling preference but not guaranteed. Individual assessments held when the occasional place occurs further up the school.

Entry at 11+ via school's own examination papers – an 11+ exam held in January and another date offered in March. Also an 11+ intake from sister school, Thomas's Fulham. No scholarships or bursaries but there is a fund to help in dire need.

Exit: At 11+ or 13+ but categorically not at 7+ or 8+ for which they will not be prepared. Head discusses destinations individually with all parents and is resolutely firm if he feels they are aiming too high.

School says 100 per cent to first choice – but whose first choice? At 11, mainly girls, to local day schools, often with scholarships. Alleyn's and JAGS feature highest in the last few years. At 13, 60 per cent to boarding schools, again with quite a few scholarships. Favourites at the moment, apparently, Eton, King's Canterbury and Tonbridge. Recent results show Sherborne, Benenden, Wellington, King's Wimbledon and Alleyn's popular as well. Despite really top-notch teaching standards we are told quite a lot of coaching still takes place. That's ambitious parents for you.

Remarks: A big, ambitious, busy school, with amazing facilities, continually moving forward, embracing every latest innovation, determined to give the children of local, successful and ambitious parents a kick start in their climb up the educational tree.

The tall, redbrick, grade 2 listed building was originally built early in the 20th century, to house Clapham County Girls' School. What would those girls think now if they could see the state-of-the-art facilities provided today? Bright classrooms, the majority of which are subject-based, well equipped science labs, great IT suite, and a specialist art block where children can expand their creative skills in many different ways. Music is big, drama is huge. Choirs and orchestras galore, children can learn pretty well any instrument they want. Performances abound. Fantastic theatrical productions put on by each year group, masses of singing and dancing, this is an important part of the curriculum and all modern technology is there to help.

Elegant school hall with plenty of room for good-sized audiences. Reception classes housed in their own recently built, specially-designed single floor block. Each classroom with its own outside area to enjoy and cultivate. Safety flooring everywhere. A garden where they can climb and play and have fun. This same building contains rooms where all children needing special assistance come to work one-to-one with their helpers. Art block alongside for art, design technology and pottery – pottery wheels included. All other classrooms up and down the stairs of the main school, divided into lower, middle and upper sections, one per floor. All meet and mix together at lunch time except for years 7 and 8 who have canteen service in their own dining area. Very grown up.

An academic school which starts gently and gets harder and harder as they move up through the years. 'For outgoing children it is terrific,' say parents. Mixed ability classes with setting in maths and English only until they reach the upper school when they are set for all subjects and academia becomes the be-all and end-all. French from reception, Latin compulsory in year 5, classics apparently one of the most popular subjects at CE. Tutor system for the top two years. Good SEN provision. Any learning problems are taken seriously, 'nothing can slip under the radar'. Children externally assessed and parents involved and kept fully in touch. 'It is not a taboo subject.' Support department has open door policy, children can drop in or parents can ring at any time. Or so they tell us. Parents said 'when things go wrong they don't always spot it that fast. Though, once it's pointed out, they do pick up the ball and get on with it'. Others said teachers, all of whom are handpicked by the head, 'go above and beyond to help the students'.

Sport also very important. Takes up about 20 per cent of the timetable from middle school onwards. Lucky school, on large site, has huge playground adaptable to supply cricket nets, netball and tennis courts, football and other practice areas, plus plenty of space to line up all the 4 x 4s that arrive at collection time. (Though as the majority live very locally we wonder why there are quite so many.) Fantastic climbing wall for adventurous children. Also use nearby Trinity Fields, Clapham Common and Wandle Sports Centre. Matches played inter-house, inter-Thomas's and against other schools home and abroad. Gives sporty children a chance to show what they are made of. Great gym catering for indoor sports as well. There are several more of these on the extensive 'clubs' list that guarantees another hour's worth of activity at the end of the school day. These children must tumble into bed exhausted each night, there's homework to be done as well.

Excellent system of class prefects and each class has separate representatives, whom they elect themselves, on the school council and the innovative ABC (Anti-Bullying Committee). However, we do still get occasional distressing reports of bullying which is less than well-handled by the school. A sense among some parents that you can sink or swim here. Green Unicorns elected to promote sustainable issues and further environmental friendliness. Older children are involved in helping the younger ones and love 'doing their reading with them'.

Lots of outings, using everything London and surrounds have on offer, and a wide variety of trips. Years 5 to 8 have a residential one included in the curriculum. Others optional, usually sports, music or subject based, and can be to faraway places. Some parents feel these can sometimes be a tad too expensive and exotic for such young children. Why not leave something for public school? But then one does get the feeling that this is a preparatory school with a public school ethos.

T

Thomas's Fulham

Hugon Road, London, SW6 3ES

- Pupils: 401; 213 boys/188 girls • Ages: 4–11 • Non-demon
- Fees: £14,463–£16,194 pa • Independent

Tel: 020 7751 8200
Email: fulham@thomas-s.co.uk
Website: www.thomas-s.co.uk/schools/fulham.html

Headmistress: Since school opened in 2005, Miss Annette Dobson BEd. Trained at Homerton College, Cambridge and has SpLD postgraduate certificate. Taught at North Bridge House before joining Thomas's Clapham where she worked for ten years, latterly as head of the lower school. Highly regarded by parents who feel she has guided the school well through its growing years. Approachable and relaxed, children and parents alike find her easy to talk to. Has succeeded in creating a happy school with a relaxed atmosphere despite the solid drive behind everything that is going on.

Entrance: Selective at 4. Assessment in January before September entry. Sociable, confident children preferred. Must be able to cope and take what the school has to offer. Head personally sees all possible pupils. Sibling policy. Best to get children on waiting list as early as possible. Occasional places further up the school when potential pupil will spend half a day with peer group to see if he can cope. From year 3 assessment of academic potential and letter from previous school essential.

Exit: No preparation for 7+ or 8+ so majority move at 11. About a third transfer to Thomas's Clapham and Battersea for their last two years, some boys having done the pre-assessment test for top London day schools. At 11+ St Paul's Girls, Downe House, Putney High, King's Junior School, Godolphin and Latymer, Wimbledon High, Ibstock Place, The Harrodian, Francis Holland, Arts Ed, Tudor Hall, Oundle etc. Numerous academic and other scholarships.

Remarks: A busy, buzzy school that packs a huge amount into each day. A place where parents say their children are exceptionally happy and never say they'd rather be at home! Possibly not for the very timid but somewhere that does seem to build a child's confidence in himself. We looked for the flaws but couldn't find them.

The newest of the four Thomas's preparatory schools in South West London, it has, perhaps, the youngest team of teachers we've met. Average age early thirties, passionate and imaginative, a good mix of male and female, they help create a generally happy atmosphere and a school full of enthusiastic children. Our guides, two of the most self confident ten year-olds ever, led us round excitedly pointing out the things they really like and introducing us to their school. Different coloured staircases, painted in house colours, took us up and down, around and about, in and out of classrooms, laboratories, music rooms, art rooms, everything a child needs to stimulate interest and a hunger for education.

Parents say 'they work them very hard' 'they are really driven' but these are parents who want their children to succeed. Work hard, play hard seems to be the ethos. For the top year, the Michaelmas Term is heavy on homework. Two eleven plus practice papers at weekends together with other revision. But they take this in their stride, it's only for one term. They are being taught about competitiveness. This work ethic builds up slowly as they move through the school. Lots of play and fun at the bottom, lots of work and fun at the top. Streamed in maths from year 3 and taught in different groupings in year 6, depending on whether they are doing 11+ or not. Teachers find different and innovative ways of getting them to learn. For instance, as you move from one classroom to another, you could come across a subject based quiz challenge on a board. Find the answers to the questions, put them in a coloured envelope and gain points for your house. Our guides were thrilled by this. Yet 'my son never felt pressured' says a parent 'but they still managed to stretch him gently and bring out the best in him'. Another parent said 'my child finds learning to read a bit of a struggle but it never worries her. Teachers boost her confidence and she thinks she's the best in the class!'

The theatre, as in all Joanna Thomas's schools, is very much a focal point. Loads of drama on the curriculum with a major production a year for each age group, as well as several clubs extending the experience for those who want it. To see the photographs of the becostumed children is to gasp in admiration. Ballet is compulsory for all children in Reception and for girls in years 1 and 2. We didn't discover what the boys do while the girls pirouette. Maybe they are out kicking balls around?

Music also strong (parents say 'fantastic'), four choirs and various orchestral ensembles. A wide variety of individual instruments played, some to grade 5; lessons timetabled on a rotational basis but practising has to be done at home. 'Their performances are wonderful' we were told, 'not just run of the mill, there was a lovely group of five boys drumming at a recent concert'.

Originally late Victorian school for one thousand plus children; later, part of Chelsea College of Art and Design, the airy rooms and tall windows result in bright classrooms throughout. Light pervades. Largish school hall, doubling up as gymnasium, where assemblies are held twice a week either by year or for the whole school, when, we gather, it becomes quite a squash. Dining area canteen style. Pupils come in year by year, gobbling down food as fast as possible to let the next lot in. Some overflow into the school hall. They all say food is delicious and they like the choice. A parent said 'the chef is a genius'.

Good playground space divided into two sections for older and younger pupils. Lots of ride on equipment for the little ones along side good soft landing area with slides, climbing equipment and some very popular toadstools. Outdoor play in most weathers is regarded as essential at least twice a day.

Parents say sport top notch. Mostly in South Park opposite and round the corner in Hurlingham Park. Some busing in the top years. Lots of matches, inter-house, inter-Thomas's and against similar London schools. Several clubs to learn non-run-of-the-mill sports as well. The huge variety of clubs is extraordinary, covering indoor activities as well as sports and there is one for homework, phew. Green initiative against being driven to school means large piles of scooters and bicycles by the back gate – must be fun sorting through them at going home time.

Mild cognitive problems dealt with and extra help brought in if necessary. One-to-one tuition available at an extra charge. Systems seem to be in place for identifying potential problems though one parent felt they could possibly have spotted her child's earlier. 'All our pupils speak English', they say, even if some need a little extra help. Eighteen different languages are spoken in their homes though. Also extra co-ordination for the gifted and talented with occasional higher level classes. Parents kept informed of progress, via email.

Systems in place to prevent any suggestion of unkindness to others. Parents say children 'really do care and want to be kind'. Worry boxes in each classroom. Older children have sessions working with the younger ones, keeping barriers down.

Generally good communication all over. Parents say open door policy and can talk to teachers any time. New all singing and dancing parent portal, just launched, tells everything that is going on and answers all queries. So no excuses for forgetting violins or games kit now.

T

Thomas's Kensington

Linked schools: Thomas's Battersea; Thomas's Clapham

17–19 Cottesmore Gardens, London, W8 5PR

- Pupils: 360 girls and boys • Ages: 4–11 • Non-denom
- Fees: £16,599–£17,628 pa • Independent

Tel: 020 7361 6500
Email: kensington@thomas-s.co.uk
Website: www.thomas-s.co.uk

Headmistress: Since 2012, Miss Joanna Ebner BEd MA PG Dip Couns Cert FT NPQH (forties), previously head of The Royal School, Hampstead. A north Londoner by background, educated at North London Collegiate, Homerton College, Cambridge, and the Institute of Education, started teaching at Primrose Hill Primary School in Camden. She then went on to take a postgraduate diploma at the Training Institute of Family Therapy and City University and combined her teaching with a role as a school counsellor at South Hampstead High School. Once her children were of school age, she had to choose between teaching or counselling and teaching won. She returned to teaching at the North West London Jewish Day School, a primary school in Willesden, followed by a successful stint as deputy head of the junior school at The Hall, Hampstead.

After completing the NPQH (National Professional Qualification for Headship), she was appointed head at The Royal School, Hampstead in 2006. The mother of three teenage children (two girls and a boy), she has also managed to fit in co-authorship of Counselling in Schools and contributed to the Girls' Schools Association's bestseller, Your Daughter, as well as their My Daughter website.

Entrance: School full of large families, mainly from Kensington and Chelsea, with a few from further afield, Brook Green and Notting Hill Gate figuring highly. Mostly within walking, or at any rate, cycling distance. School keen to discourage motoring. Very over-subscribed, so best to get on list as soon as possible after birth. Assessments in November before four-year-old entry in September. Sibling priority but not guaranteed. 'We must feel child will be able to cope.' Occasional places further up the school, so always worth asking.

Exit: About half, mainly boys, to Thomas's Battersea, many already with conditional places at top schools. Parents say, despite sameness, children find it quite hard to break into, and the move across is tough, but also say good step up and preparation for bigger school. Otherwise a few leave at seven and eight, but not prepared for these entrance exams, and the rest at 11+. Mainly to senior London day schools – Francis Holland, Godolphin and Latymer, Harrodian and Latymer Upper amongst others.

Remarks: A busy, happy, international school where children learn to love learning and have fun at the same time. A cosmopolitan place, reflecting the changing face of London, where the 'be kind' ethos seems to work and children and teachers alike are exceptionally supportive of each other. Not for the shy, withdrawn type: the pace is fast and the endless opportunities need to be grabbed with both hands. But there is a world of education to be had in the grabbing.

A school on three sites with very little outdoor play area, so much use is made of local tennis courts and the park. Tall Kensington buildings, with several staircases meandering in and out of bright, smallish classrooms and learning areas, give a comfortable old-fashioned feel, but teaching and facilities bang up to date. Parents say 'wonderful, local, cosy school'.

Lower school housed in an entire unit of its own. Bright classrooms, own hall, dining facilities, library, IT, music and art rooms. Go round the corner to the preparatory school for pottery. Also have own outdoor play area; presumably, as has historically been a school for a long time, neighbours are used to it and don't mind a little noise. Space for planting and growing too. A teaching assistant in each class. A gentle, friendly place to start.

Pace speeds up on the move to the preparatory school and setting begins in maths. Specialist teachers, so classrooms become subject-based and much more moving around. Teachers enthusiastic and relaxed, average age mid-30s, a third have been at the school for more than 10 years. Good male representation. Particularly high quality reading and writing. In recent national competition to write to the Prime Minister, a year 4 boy was runner up. Small outdoor area, for quiet study only, so mid-morning break in classrooms with quick race around neighbouring tennis courts to expel surplus energy. Lunch takes place in converted Leith cookery school round the corner. Fantastic ultra-modern kitchen and cafeteria style service. Dining area doubles up as gym with plenty of equipment. This building also contains exciting, purpose-built theatre for all those ambitious, glitzy productions. Seats 80. Also used for lectures, concerts and as extra play space, probably much needed on wet winter days. Two music rooms as well. 42 per cent learn an individual instrument, currently up to grade 4.

Sport perhaps less successful although does take up 20 per cent of the timetable. Lack of playground and size of school not helpful, and for boisterous boys it is not perfect, although school has worked hard to raise the profile of sport, including PTA sports reps. School says 'when we play schools of similar size, we have been very successful' and 'in running and swimming we are right up there with the very best'. Some parents feel this does not help with integration when they move across to Battersea at 11+. Lots of bussing to various different grounds and sports centres, as at their sister schools, and several sport-based after school clubs. Having said that, the top classes can go for a 3k run in the park before school and sports scholarships to senior schools are not unknown.

Assistant head also head of learning support. Sympathetic, trained and highly experienced. Makes sure all staff are well informed and the youngest pupils are properly monitored so problems can be picked up early. 'Must know how to spot and observe.' Good relationships with local dyslexia centre and occupational therapists. One-to-one support and lap top training when necessary. Makes sure specialist sports staff also aware of problems. Feels that school culture helps: 'sympathetic and calm'. Approximately a third exposed to language other than English at home. Plenty of help with speech and writing.

Parents say communications excellent and 'teachers very approachable and seem to really care' 'children really supportive of each other'. As at all Thomas's schools, loads of expeditions and outings, but here anything not involving overnight stay is included in the fees. Huge variety of after-school clubs including athletics in the summer. Lots of charity projects too. These children are really encouraged to help others.

T

Tormead School Junior School

Linked school: Tormead School

Cranley Road, Guildford, GU1 2JD

• Pupils: 200 girls, all day • Ages: 4–11 • Inter-denominational
• Fees: £6,720–£13,140 pa • Independent

Tel: 01483 575101
Email: registrar@tormeadschool.org.uk
Website: www.tormeadschool.org.uk

Head: Since 2006, Miss Karen Tuckwell NPQH MEd forties. She has vast experience in education, having worked for three years at a tough state school in Birmingham, followed by four years at the British School in Tokyo, by the end of which she was director of studies. After serving as director of studies at Cranleigh Prep (where she was also assistant boarding mistress with the inaugural group of girls), she became deputy head of the British International School in Seoul, South Korea. Originally from the Midlands, she attended the University of York where she took a first in biology. She's now working on her PhD in education. Trim, sporty, no-nonsense yet friendly, she's not afraid to pitch in with her girls, whether it's challenging them to a running race or directing their weekly geography quiz. She's famed for joining the girls in the biathlon (running and swimming), and doesn't let up when she's away from school – she's completed the Three Peaks Challenge (hiking Ben Nevis, Snowdon and Scafell Pike within 24 hours) and previously walked England coast to coast. Her penchant for chocolate is well-known, and her girls oblige her with regular deliveries through her always-open door. (In her defence, Miss Tuckwell insists that chocoholism is prevalent throughout the school.)

Entrance: Selective at four and seven by basic assessment test.

Exit: The vast majority of the junior girls sit the entrance exam for the senior school and 95 per cent go on there. Those who don't make the grade (although very few fail) are handled sensitively and are advised on 'a senior school better suited to their educational needs'.

Remarks: The school manages to be both happy and academic, and its wide curriculum very much reflects the priorities of the senior school across the road. In the pre-prep, literacy and numeracy are taught in the mornings, when the little ones are fresh, with content reflecting the national curriculum and the primary frameworks for English and maths, but teaching designed to extend well beyond. Core English, maths, science and ICT, plus French from year 2 and Latin from year 5. Girls are gradually prepped for the entrance exam to the senior school, although everyone is keen to stress the lack of pressure – pupils included.

Progressive changes in the curriculum over the past several years, with much closer tracking of children, internal Tormead exams in years 3,4 and 5, plus standardized tests every summer term. No setting or streaming in the lower school. Pupils spend about 70 per cent of their time with the form teacher, with an emphasis on consolidation and continuation. Staff longevity is strong – natural attrition, turnover low. Many teachers have been at Tormead for 10 years or longer.

Much focus on thinking skills, learning attitudes, and encouraging the girls to take risks, both academically and physically. Ethos geared toward helping them to have confidence in their work and in their lives. Much effort to create a culture of thinking outside the box, exemplified in the Out of the Box Project run by Miss Tuckwell, in which pupils invent a 360 degree art project or answer questions such as 'What's inside Paddington Bear's suitcase?' or 'What's Leonardo's next invention?'

SEN provision is on an individual need basis, with a full-time member of staff based in the junior school and additional peripatetic support if needed. Extra help given at lunchtimes and after school, in a room set aside for this purpose. Certainly not an issue for the school, and no stigma attached – pupils all very open about it.

Sport high on the agenda here. From pre-prep upwards, games and gymnastics weekly with specialist teachers, with swimming added in year 3. Extra-curricular sports offerings impressive – netball, hockey, swimming, dance, gymnastics, tag rugby, athletics and tennis – and timetabled so that anyone can join, either in the 'all welcome' meetings or in selective teams. Sports facilities are shared with the senior school, including an impressive gymnasium with sprung floor, which explains the strength of the Tormead gymnastics programme. Playing fields are practically non-existent, and there's no swimming pool, but the school uses the stunning facilities at the Surrey Sports Park, with strong results to show for it.

The same 'have a go' approach applies to music, so that there are musical opportunities for 'kids who can play three notes and those who can play at grade 4'. Two music lessons per week until year 2, then three weekly lessons thereafter. Loads of private lessons taken up, plus choir, chamber choir, two orchestras, jazz band and more. The majority of girls play a musical instrument or are part of the choir. Drama weekly, with LAMDA exams now on offer, and an annual year 6 production in the summer term. Dance is included as part of the PE curriculum.

Set in a residential area, the main building is contained in a large, charming, if somewhat care-worn old house, with a snug little library off the main hall. It boasts a hodge-podge of rooms and corridors, but it seems to work, and, unlike the senior school, there are as yet no building plans. The rest of the grounds are largely purpose built, allowing proper space for art and ICT.

Lunch is at the senior school, so the girls get a taste of life over the road and feel less daunted about the transfer. The aim is for an all-round education – 'we work hard and play hard' – and expectations are high. Everyone is encouraged to find their niche over and above the purely academic, whether it's music, sport, art or other activity, and extra-curricular activities are particularly encouraged. Girls appointed prefect, librarian, games captain, etc by staff and everyone gets a chance to prove themselves in these roles. Pupils don't feel intimidated by their teachers yet have a respectful attitude. Thriving house system, with houses named after famous women – Keller, Curie, Earhart and MacArthur.

Outside space a little lacking – no emerald playing fields here – but no complaints from girls. Sporting success on many levels a good indication that a lack of green space isn't holding them back. Guided tour given to us by confident, articulate and bubbly pupils with obvious pride in their surroundings.

Nursery-aged girls have their own little domain, bursting with age-appropriate playthings and charming examples of artwork. They also have a dedicated playground apart from the hustle-bustle of the older children. Older pupils are encouraged to spend time with the younger ones, and they do, creating a nice atmosphere of community between the nursery and the rest of the school. Classrooms for the older pupils boast small library collections (in all but one), and projects cover the walls, into the stairwells and beyond. Art rooms and computer labs well kitted out and obviously well-used. Art lovingly displayed about the premises. Absolute discipline on the playground (the whistle blew and the children literally stopped in their tracks).

Miss Tuckwell's international background (including a stint at the British school of Katmandu) is an important influence on the school; she feels her pupils should have an understanding of the world, not just 'flags, festivals and food', but physical and political geography as well. World maps prominently displayed and highlighting a different country each week; geography a big part of the culture.

A strength of the school is its nurturing environment. 'Good at taking the timid and shy and making them blossom,' says a parent. In addition to emphasizing girls' independence and strengths, the school has a very pro-active policy on creating a positive atmosphere and combating bullying in any form. It works this magic by focusing on the small things, whether it's a pencil case or an unkind comment, because for girls of this age, 'that's their reality,' says Miss Tuckwell. Staff are trained to ensure that if girls come to them with an issue, no matter how small, it is dealt with promptly. If it becomes bigger, the school looks at both sides and actively monitors the girls on a daily basis to ensure that the issue remains resolved. In Miss Tuckwell's view, girls should not have to go home with unresolved issues; at the very least they should know someone is aware of the problem and will deal with it on the morrow. Expectations of pupils' behaviour are made clear to all, and serious breaches might mean a call into Miss Tuckwell's office, followed by a conversation with parents straight away. The school has embraced the ethos that girls need to be happy in order to learn, work and enjoy school.

Students are vivacious and friendly, with the student body increasingly international (some British families coming back from overseas postings, plus a scattering of international families). Parents association encompasses the whole school, with a co-chair for the junior school and the senior school. Class reps are part of the parents' committee, and they serve as point of contact for new parents. Parents have very much bought into the ethos and enhance the community of the school.

An excellent bus service extends to Esher, Haslemere and beyond. Parents and pupils give it lavish praise; young and new pupils are assigned a bus buddy to make sure the ride goes smoothly.

Described by parents as 'good value for money'. No burseries, but there is an emergency hardship fund for those already at the school.

A charming, cosy school that provides myriad opportunities for young pupils to find their niche. An excellent academic preparation for the senior school.

Tower House Preparatory School

188 Sheen Lane, London, SW14 8LF

- Pupils: 180 boys, all day • Ages: 4–13 • non-denom
- Fees: £10,545–£11,961 pa • Independent

Tel: 020 8876 3323
Email: secretary@thsboys.org.uk
Website: www.thsboys.org.uk

Headmaster: Since 2009, Mr Gregory Evans MA BSc PGCE (mid-forties). Arrived with an excellent reputation from Sussex House where he was director of studies for five years. Previously he taught science at King's House School, Richmond and Twynham School, Christchurch. Lives locally and describes this appointment as his 'dream job'. Has been quick to put an Evans spin on the place, showing vim and vigour, but without upsetting the natives – just as well as he is quite likely (and perfectly happy) to bump into parents at the local Waitrose. Not at all remote and cerebral, think dedicated and willing to get stuck in instead. The boys like and respect him – he immediately made a positive impression by knowing most of their names by the end of his first day. By all accounts he is an excellent manager and administrator and has overseen significant

new investment in IT and also expanded the extra-curricular side. Calm and efficient, it's difficult to faze him. He is firm but lightens it with humour. Sets the pace and asks others to follow. Parents seem pleased and the consensus is that he is good for the school. 'He's great', says one, 'Hardworking and conscientious – Tower House is lucky to have him'. In another memory feat, he keeps up with news of all the boys' families and their out of school interests so that he can pass the time of day with anyone he comes across, parent or boy alike. He's a tremendous advocate for single-sex boys preparatory education and perfectly pitches the Tower House offering so that its small size becomes its greatest asset. Very sporty (well-used cricket ball on desk), he attends as many matches as his schedule will allow – at weekends too, often refereeing in his Tower House socks. Married, with young children of his own, he enjoys golf, fishing, reading and tending his allotment in his spare time. Has also recently completed an MA in educational management and research.

Entrance: Largely a local intake from south-west London. Non-selective, so no entrance test at 4+. The first 20 to register will be guaranteed places, although siblings of current pupils will be given priority. Occasionally names drop off the list, allowing some movement into the top 20. Some boys admitted to other years in the school where space allows – worth asking.

Exit: Boys generally get to their first choice school. At 13+ lots to St Paul's and King's College Wimbledon. Others to Hampton, Kingston Grammar, Bradfield, St Edwards, Marlborough, Epsom College and Reeds. School works towards CE pre-tests, rather than 11+ and does not encourage leavers at 11. Not many want to anyway – the odd one to Latymer where it is felt it is sometimes easier to get in at before the clamour at 13. But those are the exceptions.

Remarks: This is a school in full swing. Unashamedly a traditional boys' prep school but with a modern twist. It's a good life for a boy here; he'll work and play hard. It has a great local reputation and as the only boys' prep in SW London with a single form entry, there's a homely, family feel throughout.

Academically it is strong but not a crammer. In fact, parents seem at a loss to explain how school does so well by their non-academically selected sons, who also find time for a full range of extra-curricular activities. Good, dedicated and approachable teachers – many of them long-serving – obviously play a key part. Head describes his team as 'exceptional'. Parents agree, praising 'goddess of maths', 'Pied Piper' drama teacher and 'very capable' deputy among others – seems invidious to single anyone out as they all seem to be going the extra mile for the boys. Science and maths very strong.

There isn't a great deal of space, inside or out the late Victorian buildings. Junior and senior sections of the school are split, but linked by a shared playground – it's a small site, but clever use of space helps. The playground is Astroturfed and surrounded by climbing walls so that literally not an inch is wasted. There's also a quieter area, with table football and ping pong and a cyber-café set up for the less sporty types. Pressure on space probably more of an issue for the junior boys still of an age to run everywhere, but they seem to cope. 'They move around calmly and respect their space – a bit like the Japanese,' joked one mother.

In fact, throughout the school there is an air of decorum not always apparent in an all-male environment. It's not that the boys are under the cosh – rather that they seem to be made gently aware of what is expected of them, from behaviour and work ethic, down to neatness of uniform.

Classrooms are not hugely high-tech environments but there's good use of technology around the place, including 'voting pads', neat interactive handsets, which the boys use to answer questions during lessons. Means that no-one can hide

T

and teachers can analyse the information during and after the lesson to identify anyone in need of support. Some interactive whiteboards, other classrooms use projectors.

On a more old-fashioned note, how nice to see handwriting practice going on. Little boys, tongues out in concentration, painstakingly perfecting their Ps and Qs, is a heart-warming sight. And said heart given a further boost by the (Mr Evans' inspired) reading wall outside the library – essentially tapping into boys' competitive streak via a house competition for who can read the most books in a term. And school makes no apology for encouraging frequent library lessons and ring-fencing reading time – 'it's essential'.

Light homework from year 2 (one subject, once a week) obviously hotting up to three 40 minute assignments by year 8, but apparently nothing more onerous than necessary for CE. French from day one, Latin from year 5. Average class size is 20.

SEN catered for via what Mr Evans describes as a 'Harley Street' approach – bespoke attention given either individually or sometimes in small booster groups, all overseen by a full-time learning support teacher. The school is not suited for boys far along the spectrum, but can happily cope with mild to moderate physical disabilities, dyslexia, dyspraxia and dyscalculia, with a small number of boys using laptops as their method of recording information. Can also cater for boys with mild speech and language difficulties. Special provision for gifted and talented boys at the end of key stage 1. Between 10 and 15 per cent of pupils receive such support.

Sport is enjoying its moment in the sun lately. Obviously this is traditionally difficult for a small school which will struggle to put up a second XV – but TH can punch above its weight on occasion. 'We are no longer the enthusiastic but polite losers,' says Mr Evans. 'These days we make a decent match of it and are more than capable of a win'. Tower House teams have indeed begun to beat larger local rivals and claimed third place in the 2011 IAPS Sailing Regatta. All sport takes place at the nearby Bank of England grounds – fabulous facilities used by lots of strapped-for-space London schools, but parents feel TH gets the best of it. 'We always seem to have the best, more convenient pitches, feels like it's ours really', said one.

A great tradition of drama here. 'It's weirdly good' said one mother. Production values are said to rival those at Eton and Harrow – it's apparently all seriously top class. Former pupils prove the point, including young actors Rory Kinnear, Robert Pattinson and Tom Hardy and comedian Jack Whitehall. Multi-purpose art and DT attic studio, complete with pottery wheel. Lots of 3D work on display during our visit and some good stuff on the walls which was done by their teacher – so good it could almost dishearten before it inspired. Lots of music, with something for everyone – a swing band, an orchestra, two choirs (including an adult choir for parents) and three rock bands. About 70 per cent of pupils learn a musical instrument up to grade 6.

Pastoral care and discipline is as you would hope in such a small school, and there was high praise in the most recent ISI inspection report, where boys' personal qualities were described as 'outstanding'. Boys encouraged to grow into their own skin and develop a great sense of self worth. Although undoubtedly a privileged bunch, they are encouraged to put something back into their community. Considering their age, the boys undertake terrific amounts of charity work, everything from fund-raising (in startling amounts) to visiting the elderly or planting trees. 'The last thing we want is a generation of arrogant teenagers,' says Mr Evans. 'So we make sure they are aware of how they can help others less fortunate and so infuse them with a healthy dose of humility'. School runs its own Dan Phillips award, named for an old boy and similar to Duke of Edinburgh scheme, in that they gain awards for their efforts.

But it's not all work – boys go on a super range of trips from year 4 to year 8, culminating in the post-CE exam trip where boys will get to fly a helicopter ('super' science teacher takes them up individually) and to deep-sea dive. 'My son has had experiences here he would simply not have got anywhere else,' says one mother. Head prides himself on a policy of 'no extras', so that even the cost of these plentiful school trips are included in fees. 'Parents are working hard and we don't want to keep asking for more,' he says.

This head knows his local demographic. For East Sheen read Banker Valley – school has a very IT literate clientele who appreciate the top notch information systems Mr Evans has introduced. Homework, syllabuses, team sheets, maps for fixtures – it's all on-line and a click of an iPhone away for busy parents who no longer need to rely on 'boy mail'. Even the weekly newsletter (always at least three pages) is available as a pdf. 'We make sure parents get information quickly and clearly, says Mr Evans. 'Our intranet system is the envy of many senior schools'. Typically both parents of a TH boy will be working, so find systems like this a boon. 'We always know what is going on', said one mother. 'We can email and the Clarion text system is really useful too'.

An overarching attitude that everyone gets to 'have a go'. Had a flute lesson? Join the orchestra and we'll give you a note to play. Auditioning for a production? We'll make sure you get a part. Think you don't like sport? Try fencing.

Although there are definitely no plans to grow pupil numbers, there is some physical expansion to come, with an art room extension and classroom improvements among various projects on the cards. Mr Evans is not inclined to sit on his hands, so he has plenty to tell prospective parents, and always includes this promise in his patter; 'At 13, your son will be able to sit in any south-west London dinner party and entertain and inform the other guests, while also being the most polite person at the table.'

An unashamedly traditional place at heart (boys still sing Jerusalem in assembly) but it's not stultifying – staff are very much alive to the latest educational thinking. A boys' school, but not an aggressive, overly-masculine environment, rather a place where boys can express their gentler selves if they want to and where arts are valued as highly as sport.

Trevor-Roberts School

55–57 Eton Avenue, London, NW3 3ET

• Pupils: 100 boys, 80 girls; all day • Ages: 5–13 • C of E
• Fees: £12,270–£14,070 pa • Independent

Tel: 020 7586 1444
Email: trjuniorweb@trevor-robertsschool.co.uk
Website: trevor-robertsschool.co.uk

Senior Head: Since 1999, Mr Simon Trevor-Roberts, BA, 50s. Son of the founder, Trevor-Roberts studied at Westminster School before reading English at Aberystwyth. In 1983, he joined his father Christopher in the family firm, where he learnt his trade by example. (He has since been joined by his sister Amanda, who heads up the Junior School.) Mild mannered and reflective, he has a very clear sense of what the school is about: 'We try to get children to enjoy the process of learning.' Continues to teach maths to the 13 plus candidates, because he's found he, too, now has the knack of putting things across clearly. 'I shadowed my father for a long time and learnt how to do it by osmosis.' Parents find him immensely approachable and engaged. 'You always have complete access to the head and he knows all the kids incredibly well.' Married with two grown children, both of whom attended the school.

T

Entrance: Register as soon after birth as possible. About 80 sets of parents are contacted when their child is one and offered a tour. Those who then wish to proceed confirm this in writing, and the school assesses the first 50 children on their list in the September prior to the calendar year in which they turn 5. 'We're not expecting any preparation, but we want to make sure it will be a happy transition,' says the registrar. 'We're looking for inquisitive children who want to learn. Getting that is more a dark art than a science.' The school generally tries to give priority to siblings, 'but only if it's the right school'. Often takes in one or two more in year 4, when the year group divides into two classes.

Exit: Girls mainly – though not exclusively – at 11, generally to South Hampstead, Francis Holland and other north London favourites. Most boys (and some girls) at 13, to a wide range of day and boarding schools, including regular placements at Eton, Harrow, Westminster, UCS, Highgate, Merchant Taylors', City of London and Latymer Upper School. 'The head is very good at managing parental expectations,' says one former parent.

Remarks: This is a family-run school with a very distinctive ethos, deriving in large part from its origins. Founded by the current heads' father in the 1950s with just 14 boys, it was originally seen as a refuge for the 'unteachable'. 'My father had a reputation for taking those whom other schools had given up on and getting them through entrance exams to leading public schools,' says Simon Trevor-Roberts.

Today, the school can take its pick of north London's brightest, but continues to select a mixed-ability (now co-educational) intake and provide a tailor-made education for all. 'They want every child to work to his or her potential and really do treat every child as an individual,' said one parent.

Children start in year 1 in a class grouped according to the calendar year of their birth. In year 4, this is re-arranged to allow everyone to be in place for secondary school entrance. One class of 16-18 in the early years, two classes in year 4 and year 6, then a single form again for the final two years. 'We like to move children around so they're not in the same group for eight years,' says the head. 'It gives us the flexibility to allow those who require it a bit more time and accelerate those who need it.' Parents confirm this is skilfully managed. 'They're constantly re-adjusting their approach for different levels of learning, but not in a way that disturbs the children.'

Specialist subject teaching from the word go, with a classroom teacher for the core subjects, but music, history, geography, science and art all taught in their own space. 'It keeps the week fresh.'

Plenty of imaginative teaching by intelligent (including many Oxbridge), though not always qualified, staff. French from year 1, Latin from year 5, some Greek in year 8, Mandarin taught as a club. Special needs addressed by weekly sessions with the learning support coordinator and outside specialists.

Everyone staying for the final two years sits common entrance. 'We take it very seriously,' says the head. '11 plus is about flexible problem solving; by 13, it's more structure on the page.' Senior schools praise the 'structure on the page' received.

Very good at ensuring the basics are in place. 'Sometimes you have to be a bit tough,' says the head. 'We insist that children use a pen rather than touch type. If you have to write an essay under exam conditions, you have to be able to discipline your thoughts.' No truck with overly formalised exam training. 'Non-verbal reasoning is not a subject,' he says crisply.

Formal homework from year 3, starting out with 20 minutes in English or maths. ('It shows them how to work by themselves and for themselves') up to two hours a night for the top forms. 'They do work very hard, but the atmosphere still manages to be reasonably relaxed,' says one mother.

Good relationships with staff are fundamental ('The teacher is not someone they're trying to hoodwink,' says the head),

as is the view that effort should be lauded over achievement. 'Children are perfectly aware there's competition elsewhere, they don't need it reinforced. We want them to be in competition with themselves.' Good work is rewarded with a 'digniora', with recipients queuing in the lunch hour to have their accolade verified and registered. Three merits win a £4 token (designed to reflect the season) to be spent at independent local shops.

Breadth well beyond the exam curriculum is given enormous emphasis. Outstanding music – 'We love music' – with a dynamic head. Taught in the classroom from years 1 to 6, outside throughout, with numerous ensembles (brass, jazz, string, woodwind, chamber choir, rock band) and much external participation (at the Royal Festival Hall, St John's Smith Square, etc.) Twice weekly art lessons (one in year 7) in a bright art department at the top of school, with its own kiln. Extra art and DT on offer for enthusiasts on Wednesday afternoons.

Cultural values that have largely been submerged elsewhere – 'Everyone is encouraged to have a novel on the go' – with half an hour of silent reading daily after lunch. Poetry and drama matter and prove great confidence builders. 'My son almost died of nerves the first time he had to read out a poem,' said one mother, 'but now he loves drama and performing.' 'The plays are unbelievable,' said another.

Plenty of fresh air and exercise, with a good-sized, well-equipped playground, including popular table tennis, miniature railway and chicken coop ('the chickens are a great comfort to quieter, shyer children'). Primrose Hill, a few hundred yards from the door, enables twice weekly games. Definitely not a school, however, where 'go-fight-win' is on the agenda. 'Children love sport, but I don't want a First Eleven ethos, with the captain of games strutting around,' says the head. 'We do play matches against other schools, but everyone has a go.'

The senior school building, a fine example of the Arts and Crafts, was the founder's own home and still offers delightful domestic interiors with William Morris wallpaper in the front hall and mid-century classic tables used instead of desks in the top forms. The juniors are housed in their own building with a separate dining room and science lab.

The atmosphere is civilised but structured ('It's a nice mix of the very strict and the nurturing and kind – teachers are always willing to talk things through'). Pupils sit down to eat their biscuits at break before rushing off to the playground. Everyone has a hot lunch, served through an open hatch, 'so they can see where it is made.' Staff share the dining hall with pupils. 'Eating is socialising.' Food is freshly prepared on site using local produce.

Manners and uniform are both reasonably relaxed (no backs against the wall here). Light blue polo shirt for younger children, dark blue for older ones. Trousers and skirts, 'something reasonable'. 'Jeans are fine, jeans hanging off the hips is not.'

Often the school of choice for the liberal, media intelligentsia (including some famous names), the type of parent who genuinely believes in the well-rounded education, not the rush to the top of the league tables. (Competition here, though it undoubtedly exists, tends to be on the level of how many operas your child has seen rather than where the family went skiing.) Mainly local, some from Notting Hill, Queen's Park, Islington. The head feels 'there's no typical child, but I've heard people say our children are very kind.'

T

Tring Park School for the Performing Arts Preparatory School

Linked school: Tring Park School for the Performing Arts

Tring Park, Tring, HP23 5LX

• Pupils: 45 pupils, 35 board Boarding and day places for boys and girls. • Ages: 8–11 • Fees: Boarding £28,950; Day £13,245 pa • Independent

Tel: 01442 824255
Email: info@tringpark.com
Website: www.tringpark.com

Exit: Virtually 100% to senior department.

Remarks: See main school.

Truro High School Preparatory Department

Linked school: Truro High School

Falmouth Road, Truro, TR1 2HU

• Pupils: 105 day girls; 6 boarders (from 7+); 6 boys in nursery • Ages: 3–11 • C of E • Fees: Boarding £20,055–£22,680; Day £8,550–£11,205 pa • Independent

Tel: 01872 272830
Email: admin@trurohigh.co.uk
Website: www.trurohigh.co.uk/our-school/prep

Headmistress: Since 2009, Mrs A Miller BSC, PGCE.

Entrance: By application, then stress-free taster day for girls to get to know the place and for head to make an informal assessment as to suitability.

Exit: Girls transfer to senior school seamlessly, although all sit entrance exam to determine setting etc. Ninety per cent move down a corridor they already know well by the time they leave year six.

Remarks: Lovely, safe setting for nursery and reception at Trevean: a separate complex with its own hard and grass outside areas. Plenty of apparatus for imaginative play, climbing and swinging. Room for up to 20 tots per session in current building but extension is planned to allow for an increase. Lovely feel to accommodation: safe and exciting all in one. Switched on, specialist staff to get young minds and limbs off to a happy start. Reception class make good headway with reading (incorporate various approaches including synthetic phonics) and lots of different number work. Changing topics throughout the year with classroom displays and activities to match. Close contact with parents through diaries etc to monitor progress with individual readers.

Years 1 and 2 enjoy large classrooms for the comparatively small numbers: amazing pupil:teacher ratio which enables pre-prep girls to make rapid headway. IT used in classrooms plus head teaches in specialist suite for year 3 upwards. Topic-based work combines humanities and other disciplines. Older girls also benefit from some teaching by senior specialists and use facilities in senior school for science, art, food and nutrition plus games (even joining senior teams where appropriate).

Reading culture obvious here with a separate and well-used junior library. Academic atmosphere in older classes where girls can gain confidence in their abilities. One parent we spoke to transferred his daughter after a local primary had 'given up on her.' After some initial learning support, she is now making 'thrilling' progress and thriving on all the extra-curricular opportunities. Head hands over to year 6 girls during part of annual prize-giving to give a Powerpoint presentation of the year's activities. No gawkiness – just happy girls who enjoy working as much as playing. 'Golden time' rewards on Friday afternoons when younger girls get to do their favourite things. Girls are allocated to one of four houses (all linked to Cornish benefactors) in prep and remain in the same house through the senior school. Good-sized hall accommodates the 100+ children here for assemblies (they join seniors once a week). Tinies first into senior dining room for lunch. Healthy snacks at other times: eg before clubs meet after school. Wide range of activities at lunch time. Tiered reward system with gongs for top achievers. School council meets twice termly. Amazing standard of music with high percentage having individual tuition. Junior choir particularly keen. Separate plays produced for older (Snow White) and younger ('tea towel' nativity) contingents at Christmas. Purpose built drama and music block due to be completed in March 2013 with a theatre, green room and practice rooms, for use by Junior and Senior school girls. Lots take LAMDA examinations. Parents fully involved in helping where appropriate – Friends of Truro High recently raised over £700 in three hours at a fun day. Pick-up times are staggered to avoid congestion at end of school day. Boarding available from year 3 upwards for the far flung.

Parents recognise that what they get here is a great deal more than academic results (which come more or less as a given). Nurturing atmosphere, caring and communicative staff who produce great results.

Truro School Prep

Linked school: Truro School

Treliske, Highertown, Truro, Cornwall, TR1 3QN

• Pupils: 235; 145 boys and 90 girls; all day; • Ages: prep 7–11, nursery and pre-prep 3–7; • Methodist; • Fees: £8,295–£11,205 pa; • Independent

Tel: 01872 243120
Email: admissions@truroprep.com
Website: www.truroprep.com

Headmaster: Since 2004, Mr Matthew Lovett (forties). Educated at Haberdashers' Aske's and Exeter University (BA Ed). Discovered a wanderlust and journeyed under its influence to Spain (head of science and ICT at St Anne's), thence to Banda School, Kenya. Came home. Head of Forest Prep at the absurdly young age of 31, whence to Truro. Strong thespian tendencies – has strutted the boards, sometimes semi-professionally. Instantly recognisable by trademark braces (red when we visited). Has been a force for change since his arrival, arguably not too soon. A listener, they say, and his own man, he puts his foot down firmly and fairly. Possesses, they reckon, the authority and diplomacy required to bring about necessary change. Energetic, levels with you, quick to tune to your wavelength. Into choral singing, gardening, photography and playing cricket with like-minded and similarly hopeful but hopeless players. Married to Laura. Three young children.

Entrance: Entry to the nursery and pre-prep via application, thereafter automatically to the prep. To the prep at age seven by written exam, report, interview and day spent in the school. Automatic admission from pre-prep.

Exit: All at age 11. Almost all to Truro School, some to senior schools up-country. It's getting more difficult to pass the senior school entry exam, a source of some teeth-gnashing. For boys who fall short, Kelly College. For some girls the High School provides a safety net. Progression to Truro School is by head's recommendation.

Remarks: Delicious, semi-secret location at the end of a winding, rhododendron-bordered drive. Small manor house built to last forever by a tin miner made good but he sank every last penny into it and was bankrupted. Tragic. Other school buildings good, mostly – the odd portakabin but children like those. Sports hall and swimming pool. Classrooms well presented, tidy and all with recent displays. Purpose-built nursery and pre-prep set slightly apart. Fine playing fields and swathes of woodland. A most attractive spot.

Academically, parents give it a clean bill of health. Until the arrival of Mr Lovett, the tendency seems to have been to lionise the best and somewhat to overlook the rest. All change. Indeed, in all things this is now a much kinder, more inclusive school – 'if they're not brilliant academics we try and bring them out in other ways, find out what they're good at', says Mr Lovett. The departure of some old-school teachers has helped, as has their replacement by bright young things with here-and-now, professionalised glints in their eyes. For children who reveal special needs there is specialised help, but you can see that what Mr Lovett thinks they need most is to be egged on, urged to be daring, and rewarded frequently. It's both an effective and laudable remedial strategy. Some specialist teaching in year 3 and all specialist teaching from years 4 to 6. No testing until Key Stage 1 at age seven, and only then. Around a third of teachers are male, an unusually high percentage in what's becoming a feminised business. Mr Lovett is determined to maintain this.

Sport tremendously important as you might expect, but parents say, 'it is more balanced these days. Previously, the less good didn't get much of a look in, but in the Lovett era we have B teams and we may not be brilliant but we get to play for our school and have people cheer us on.' A quirk of the school is its excellence in sabre fencing – here you discover the litter from which most of the England under-12 squad is picked. Growing list of after-school activities.

The arts are thriving as a result of closer ties with the senior school. Drama good, art good, music on the way up. All children learn an instrument in year 4 and can borrow one for a year to see if they're any good at it.

Stern criticism by some parents of the harshness of the ancien regime serves to highlight changes and mark progress towards kindness and proper focus on the individuality of each pupil. Parents say that Mr Lovett has not been a winnowing wind but has, rather, 'made changes subtly, sensibly, not disjointedly'. Others talk now of 'the same strong sense of community and mutual support you get at the senior school'. It's also much more fun, of course. Lunch here may well be the best in the UK. All food locally sourced, meat from a local organic farm, cooked with huge pride. And, they'll have you know – 'we've been doing this since before Jamie Oliver'.

Parents are not spoiled for choice down here when it comes to choosing a prep school. It is appropriate that Truro offers educational breadth. Emphasis on humanity has unquestionably brightened eyes and enhanced its effectiveness.

Twickenham Preparatory School

Beveree, 43 High Street, Hampton, Middlesex, TW12 2SA

• Pupils: 270; 50/50 boys and girls; all day • Ages: 4–13 • Families do not have to be practising Christians but the school has a strong Christian ethos • Fees: £9,345–£10,110 pa • Independent

Tel: 020 8979 6216
Email: office@twickenhamprep.co.uk
Website: www.twickenhamprep.co.uk

Headmaster: Since 2005, Mr David Malam BA Southampton (history), PGCE King Alfred's College, Winchester (forties). Has been at the school for 15 years, having joined as a history teacher, then deputy head for years. Before that taught in junior and first schools in Southampton (unusually including a year in a reception class) and at Lagos International School in Cyprus, teaching ages 7-16.

He's very popular with pupils, gets to know them all well and is warm and funny around them. 'They are very fond of him, but also really respect him', says a mother. 'He has natural authority and never needs to shout; has a great gift with children', says another. 'He's better with the children than with parents', says a third. 'Personally I agree it's all about the kids, but lots of parents seem to want indulging and he's not good at that side of things'. However, those that know him best say he is 'an excellent headmaster'.

He's a great sports fan, especially football and squash, and he has also played chess at a high level. Lives locally, married, with five children who he has, or has had, at the school. 'He treats them just the same as anybody else, they're not his favourites', said our year 6 tour guides confidently.

Entrance: Non-selective at reception, and while perhaps not necessary to register at birth, think about it by a first birthday. Although it behaves and sounds like a church school, there is actually no religious requirement in the admission criteria; if you are happy with the ethos they are happy to have you. That's not to say school will say yes to everyone; you've got to fit in socially, behaviourally and academically. Largely a local intake. Other places are occasionally available and subject to assessments in English, maths and reasoning. Bus service runs from Richmond and Twickenham. Aims to maintain its 50:50 ratio of boys: girls.

Exit: All over, especially, at 11, girls to Lady Eleanor Holles, Surbiton High, Sir William Perkins, Kingston Grammar, St Catherine's. At 13+ boys to Hampton, Halliford, Reeds and St George's. A few to St Paul's. Usually a healthy number of scholarships.

Remarks: A popular co-ed prep which prides itself on its positive, family atmosphere and strong Christian ethos. Non-selective, so not packed with academic boffs, but it's no place for a slouch either – increasing numbers of scholars attest to the academic thrust here in recent times. Key stage 2 Sats results are maths 100 per cent level 4 and above (86 per cent level 5), English 94 per cent level 4 and above (80 per cent level 5) – only less than 100 per cent due to pupil absences. Not as pressured a place as some Surrey schools, but still seriously ambitious for its children, who are indeed going on to win places at the county's top senior schools. Carefully guided by Mr Malam, Twickenham Prep children will not sit many entrance exams – no more than two or three. 'The eight or nine some do is ridiculous,' he says. 'It's unnecessary; we know our children very well and therefore know which school will suit them best'.

T

Specialist subject teaching from the off in French, ICT, Music and PE. By year 4 all teaching is subject-specific, with pupils moving from room to room for their lessons. No streaming, but setting for maths from year 4. Latin for most girls from year 5 and for boys when they move onto the common entrance programme. French for all, with a little bit of Greek and an introduction to Spanish for those up to it. Nice small classes, typically of 18. Homework is reasonably low key; 'I don't see it as a means of destroying family life,' says Mr Malam. Starts gently with some reading and spelling up to year 2, then one to two homeworks a night, reaching 40 minutes a night by year 6. Thrice-weekly homework clubs similarly take the pressure off family time.

Pupils seem well-engaged with their lessons, and the school's atmosphere is calm and purposeful. ISI inspectors judge teaching here to be always good, and sometimes outstanding, with provision for children with learning difficulties or disabilities to be 'excellent'. However, it is not the place for a more serious special need, and none of the LDD children currently on roll are statemented.

Music is something of a strength here – there's a large choir and 80 per cent of pupils are swept up for music lessons and get plenty of opportunities to play and perform. Sport is often a bugbear in a small-ish set up like this one – on-site practice space is limited and it's hard to beat some of the larger schools in the area. But on the plus side, the school does have use of Hampton Football Club's facilities, which are directly behind it, and has notched up some major tournament wins of late. Parents appreciate the fact that the school's approach is inclusive, with all the children getting an opportunity to play competitively if they want to, with C teams fielded if necessary. Swimming from years 1 to 5 off-site. Year 7 and year 8 boys pick up squash and badminton too.

Nice extra-curricular clubs, including music and movement, historic adventures and sewing for pre-prep, and touch-typing, table tennis and knitting for prep pupils. Mr Malam, and therefore his school, is a big fan of the Mind Lab (thinking abilities and life skills) programme which is time-tabled as a weekly lesson. Typically the children will play strategy games and learn about lateral thinking. The idea is that this work makes pupils more adaptable and less easily phased when encountering a new problem for the first time. Mr Malam seems to have converted parents, who praise the programme. 'At first I thought it was some sort of hideous team-building exercise beloved of large organisations, but in fact it does get the children thinking in a different way', says one. 'They think they are just playing games, but really they are learning. And with all the verbal and non-verbal reasoning involved in many entrance exams these days, it does seem to give them a great basis for working things out'.

More mind games come in the form of chess – another Malam passion – or 'obsession' as one mother wryly observed. The school has built up quite a reputation as IAPs champions, English Schools national finalists and borough champions. Grandmaster Daniel King works with the school, involving up to 50 of the children regularly, with up to 30 of them going on to play for school teams.

Parents view the school as very strong pastorally – again ISI say its provision in this area is 'outstanding'. The school is a really nurturing place; welcoming and warm, a gentle and kind environment with no sharp edges. Watchwords for the pupils are 'calm, courteous, courageous and considerate'. 'And they don't just pay lip-service to those words, they really count for something here,' says a mother. Discipline not really an issue – teachers use positive reinforcement ('Praising a child who is doing well has quite an effect on a child who is not doing as well themselves', says Mr Malam). Losing or winning house points an equally effective device here.

And as you'd expect from a 'Christian' school, bible-based religious education is taken seriously here and children will say prayers together. There's no affiliation to any one church, but close links with nearby St Mary's Church of England church where the children visit for Christmas and harvest services. Assemblies are Christian-based, with a bible story/theme and a moral message. School has its own hymn book, teaches Lord's Prayer, hosts visits from local Christian community and other faiths.

But that's not to say that the families at this school are all regular worshippers or indeed even Christian – several we spoke to were in fact agnostic or atheist or practitioners of another religion entirely – but obviously these parents share a willingness for their children to be taught about Christian values. 'We don't believe in ignorance of other religions and so have people in to talk about other faiths and cultures too', says Mr Malam. 'Generally I find our parents want their children in a school where they at least understand the ethos, rather than put them into a more secular environment.'

Attracts professional and business-type families, mostly local from Teddington, Twickenham, Sunbury and St Margaret's. The name Twickenham Prep is actually something of a misnomer, as the school is actually in Hampton – it was originally on Twickenham Green and chose to retain its by then well-established name when it relocated in 1992. Set in unexpectedly peaceful and leafy location behind a busy road, the main school building, Beveree, was once owned by John Blow, King's Musician to Charles II and is Grade II listed. A major extension was added in 1998, adding bright, modern facilities, with some super, purpose-built pre-prep buildings and in 2012, new classrooms and facilities for music and art opened. Overall not masses of space, but school makes the most of what there is and has sectioned off some space for a well-used amphitheatre and an adventure playground.

And, lest it all sound too unruffled and worthy, the children also have great fun along the way. A recent fund-raising auction of promises saw one boy's family successfully bid for him to take over as headmaster for a day. He took a lesson, spoke to staff, was included in an interview and allowed to introduce some of his own for-one-day-only initiatives. These included arranging for an ice-cream van to visit at the close of school and awarding headmaster's commendation certificates to genuine supporters of Fulham football club.

Increasingly strong academically, it's offering its happy and settled pupils a good all-round education, generally allowing them their pick of all the best local day schools. Holding its own in an area packed with competitive offerings. Not pressured or pushy, rather kind, inspiring and creative.

Twyford School

High Street, Twyford, Winchester, Hampshire, SO21 1NW

• Pupils: 406; 140 girls, 145 boys in prep school; mostly day with some weekly and flexi-boarding. Prep prep: 49 girls, 72 boys in pre-prep • Ages: pre-prep 3-7; prep 7-13 • C of E • Fees: Day £8,295-£16,995; Boarding £21,390 pa • Independent

Tel: 01962 712269
Email: registrar@twyfordschool.com
Website: www.twyfordschool.com

Head: Since 2010, Dr Steve Bailey BEd PhD FRSA; educated at Kent College, Canterbury, Southampton University and St Paul's College of Education (fifties). Born and raised bilingually in Hong Kong before teaching history (all levels) at Winchester College for thirty years; housemaster for the last twelve. A Fellow of the Royal Society for the Arts, Research Fellow of the International Olympic Committee, author of six books and with an international reputation as an historian of sport and the Olympic Games, it's no surprise that he has shaken things up a bit at Twyford.

Dr Bailey began by curtailing lessons to 45 minutes and encouraged teachers to deliver lessons beyond 'narrow' CE requirements. Regularly observes teaching and makes no secret of his ambition for more creativity in the classroom; is keen to avoid 'death by worksheet.' Banished formal exams in the first two years of prep school and introduced extension lessons, known as Apprenticeships, in the timetable. 'Children are capable of far more than we sometimes offer.' Intellectual and erudite, is also a keen sportsman. Played hockey at county and regional levels and enjoys tennis, water polo and surfing. Wife Paula MSc (Health Psychology) has taught ICT as well as tutoring children with specific learning difficulties. They have three children, all in full-time education.

Entrance: Main entry points are nursery and year 3, although places are occasionally available in other years. Nursery places allocated according to date of registration; siblings have priority on waiting lists at other times. Short half-day assessment in November for those joining prep school the following academic year, which school says is 'not a rigorous hurdle.' Most pupils live within 30 mile radius, some weekly boarders further afield. Numbers have risen by 30 since Dr Bailey's arrival.

Exit: Nearly one third of boys leave for Winchester College, a steady few with music and academic awards. Other boys and girls scatter far and wide, but most popular destinations are Bradfield, Bryanston, Canford, Charterhouse, Cheltenham Ladies', Downe House, Eton, Godolphin, King Edward Vl, Marlborough, St Swithun's, and Sherborne Boys' and Girls' Schools. Tally of scholarships is on the up under Dr Bailey's stewardship; boys and girls gain a more diverse range of awards including academic, music, sport, all-rounder, art and DT scholarships and exhibitions.

Remarks: Main school building, a beautiful Queen Anne house, is set in over six acres of playing fields and surrounded by the South Downs. Moved to its present location in 1809 from premises in nearby Twyford and can probably trace its origins back to the mid-17th century. (A Latin grammar book has turned up bearing the inscription 'Twyford School, 1775'.) Boarders still live in original house, which has a pretty Victorian chapel, oak-panelled library, atmospheric old school hall and large modernised refectory. Teaching takes place in a collection of modern buildings dotted around quadrangles.

Lots of hard work going on for CE when we visited; most pupils aim to sit level 3 in subjects across the board (some level 2 if appropriate). 'Dr Bailey has increased the aims and aspirations of the children.' Maths set from year 4 and all subjects by year 6. French from reception, Latin from year 5 and study skills as a separate subject from year 7, otherwise all subjects taught as usual. 'Learning Qualities Programme' encourages children to think more independently and take responsibility for their own learning (praised in latest ISI school inspection). Classrooms are modern, bright and spacious; science labs are immaculate (including snakes!). Class sizes average 16-18. Children are divided up into three sets in the last two years, depending on their 'next school'. Boys aiming for Winchester and all other scholarship candidates join 'W set' in year 7, the rest are divided into two Common Entrance sets. ICT provision is well planned, with fixed terminals for younger ones and laptops for year 5. Year 6 up have tablets to enable independent research in geography, history and science lessons. Fibre optic cable installed throughout to improve network speeds. Five SEN specialists help with (mild) learning difficulties and around 70 one-to-one sessions (including pre-prep) were timetabled when we visited. These are free, but school doesn't take children who need more than one session a week.

Traditional prep school sports for boys and girls, with matches on Wednesday and Saturday afternoons. First and second teams have an excellent sporting record in fixtures against other schools. Parents tell us that school 'is starting to address girls' sport' by drawing up C and D teams and organising more fixtures, but even so 'not everyone gets on a team.' Pupils also compete in swimming, water polo, athletics, tennis, lacrosse and girls' tag rugby. School is a 'Centre of Excellence' for girls' cricket in Hampshire. Large gym and indoor 25m swimming pool sit side-by-side, with 25m traversing wall outside. Has several all-weather courts for tennis and netball, plus Astroturf for hockey and football. 'Sports day is fabulous.' Netball teams have had success at regional IAPS tournaments and individual footballers at national schools' level. Other pupils perform at county level in cricket, cross-country running, hockey, rugby and swimming. 'Court Cricket', invented at Twyford and played here for at least a century, is still in robust health at break times!

Outstanding art and DT departments, probably the best we've seen for quality of work. Small, permanent gallery at the side of two storey art block displays pupils' work throughout the year; standard of painting and ceramics is excellent. 'Artist in residence' paints school scenes on site so children can observe brushwork – no surprise that number of art scholars is on the rise. DT is also very good with some really imaginative work (high level of design) on show, eg insect 'hotel'. Music block sits in unusual amphitheatre setting overlooking tennis courts. Bright, airy performance space upstairs with several practice rooms on lower floor; more pianos are dotted around elsewhere in the school. More than 80 per cent of children learn at least one instrument, including the less usual, eg harp, drums and bagpipes. Lessons are fixed for older children and rotate for younger ones. School is a centre for ABRSM and Trinity College music exams and many pupils pass these at higher grades. Three school choirs, including a show choir, school orchestra and various ensembles give occasional concerts. Drama is improving, with a weekly lesson for all taught by specialist teachers and more performance space in Mulberry Pavilion, but 'dramatic aspirations could be higher... we need a whole-school musical once a year.' Dance (ballet, modern and tap) is on offer as a lunch time club. Regular 'Shakespeare workshop' for year 8 takes place after CE.

'Apprenticeships' (Saturday activities) are compulsory for all children from year 4. Activities become increasingly academic further up the school, and include ancient Greek, Arabic, critical thinking, debating, fencing, Mandarin, music theory, philosophy and photography. Everyone chooses a different apprenticeship each term, although 'quite often children don't get their first choice.' Staff run weekday clubs after school, eg art, cookery, judo, water polo and yoga. Outdoor education programme, eg navigation, orienteering, shelter building and survival techniques, 'encourages children to solve practical and physical problems.' One residential course away for each year group every year; in school there is a tree house complex with outdoor classroom and advanced adventure playground.

No longer offers full boarding, but can arrange for long-distance boarders to stay with local guardians on Saturday and Sunday nights. Otherwise, most children board a few nights per week from year 6 in preparation for going away to senior school and around 20 from Monday to Friday. Dorms for younger children; cosy two-man (or girl) cubicles for year 8s allow more privacy and the chance to room with a friend. We noted clean, well-appointed bathrooms, a comfortable common room and plenty of storage space for belongings. Boarders have limited use of mobile phones (matron keeps phones at all other times). Parents full of praise for boarding house parent, also head of sport. Excellent meals are served cafeteria-style and atmosphere is informal; children can sit where they like (we didn't notice staff on each table). Perhaps (enviably) this isn't needed, as school works hard to instill a broad set of values in its pupils. Regular services in chapel throughout the term are reinforced by anti-bullying PSHE lessons and constant vigilance by boarding and teaching staff (often around in the evenings running clubs or supervising prep). Everyone belongs to one of four houses and is assigned a house tutor from year 6. End-of-term 'Team Feast' for house with the highest house point scores; individual high scorers are 'sent up good' on Fridays for lemon sherbet from the head (a Twyford tradition). Still has a friendly atmosphere, although parents say times are now more formal. Nevertheless they add, 'It still feels like you're part of a big family and [that] requires family involvement.'

Pre-prep going from strength to strength with over 120 on the register when we visited. 'The nursery is outstanding.' Two classes in reception and year 1 grow to three in year 2, which has been rehomed from Portakabins to a permanent building – windows at child height is a nice touch. Children grouped for phonics and spelling ability; reading is taught both individually and in groups. French and music learned from an early age. Homework is limited to spelling, reading and topic work, eg 'Knights and Castles'. 'It's a really full-on day.' Has small SEN room and ICT suite. Lots of outdoor play; children spend an entire afternoon outside every three weeks and have access to 'Forest Lodge' in small woodland area. All attend chapel services and use the pool and library. Puts on annual show for 'grandparents' week', where little ones can show off their music, ballet and ESB exam preparation. Clubs include gardening, hand bells, ukulele and recorder ensemble. Most go on to join prep school in year 3, causing prep school numbers to rise. Universal feeling from parents is that school is at capacity; would like to see new pupil numbers capped.

A relatively wide mix of families, but it's safe to assume that most are comfortably off. Two 100 per cent bursaries (means tested) for new children joining as weekly boarders in year 7; sibling discounts are limited to 5 per cent for third and subsequent children. Boys and girls are polite, confident and increasingly aspire to top schools. Old Twyfordians include Alexander Pope, Douglas Hurd, Hubert Parry, Mark Tully, Thomas Hughes and, more recently, 'The Apprentice' winner Tom Pellereau. Very active Twyford Society keeps ex-pupils in touch.

Although well into the process of changing from 'a slightly scruffy, not very ambitious place' to one with a much greater focus on academic success, Twyford is still a friendly school where parents enjoy being part of the 'family'. Will continue to send a good number of boys to Winchester College, but is clearly aiming just as high for girls and boys going on to other schools.

The Unicorn School (Abingdon)

20 Marcham Road, Abingdon, OX14 1AA

- Pupils: 60 (49 boys and 11 girls), all day pupils • Ages: 6–13
- Fees: £17,400 pa • Independent

Tel: 01235 530222
Email: info@unicorndyslexia.co.uk
Website: www.unicorndyslexia.co.uk

Head teacher: Since 2004, Mrs Jackie Vaux MA (Oxon), BSc Psychology (fifties). A former SENCo she joined Unicorn in 1998 as a class teacher; didn't seek headship, persuaded to take the reins for a term and was hooked. Married to an Oxford medical tutor, they have four grown-up children; a modern languages graduate from St Catherine's, Oxford, she looks every inch the friendly academic. Continues to teach languages and sciences, with lashings of passion and a deal of ingenuity. We meet in her office, a mix of the formal and fun, desk and trappings of education juxtaposed with black sofas, complete with red silk cushions and fluffy white ones (courtesy of the caretaker).

Windowsill adorned with ice-breaker toys, from remote control cars through to cuddly teddies. Unassuming, intelligent, it's clear even before the first anecdote ends that her heart and energies are vested in making futures successful. Her kindly, calm persona is appreciated by youngsters, 'she is really nice and organised, happy but strict when she has to tell us off. It is just fantastic to be here, to be ourselves, to relax, to learn, to be accepted for who we are'.

Parents say Mrs Vaux's door is genuinely always open, she knows the children and families and is often present at collection time, saying 'hello', making herself accessible. 'She is a good listener, patient, understanding and wonderful at helping you come to terms with your child's learning difficulties.' Wholly empathetic to parents' plight, she says, 'Dyslexia can be a difficult thing to understand and to accept; there's a sense of relief when they get to us. I make sure parents understand we are not going to cure their child but that we can help with coping strategies and that we have a myriad of tools to smooth their child's transition through education and life. It's an emotional time; we get lots of tears... usually it's the dads'.

Entrance: All pupils should have a report from an educational psychologist identifying either moderate to severe dyslexia as their primary need or dyspraxia, dyscalculia or speech and language difficulties (ICAN registration hoped for). Approximately 40 per cent have speech and language difficulties. Will take those with mild ASD if primary need is SpLD. Entry on first come first served basis; assessed over two-days. Some funded by home LA, though not Oxfordshire who operate an inclusion policy.

Exit: Pupils stay between one and three years, typically two. Aim is to give support, coping strategies and return to mainstream education. 'Jackie lets you know when they are cooked and ready to move on.' Places sought at known supportive schools, popular choices include Larkmead (Abingdon), Leckford Place in Oxford and Kingham Hill (Oxon); parents given plenty of help to find the right one. Some preps, eg Moulsford and Dragon, send pupils for a couple of years of timely intervention then take them back when appropriate.

Remarks: Founded in 1991, now housed in a converted Edwardian house near the centre of town. Akin to a small-independent day school with gym, DT and art room plus smart, bright classrooms it's kitted out with practical teaching aids, computers (all learn to touch-type), interactive whiteboards et al. Outside space is adequate with two carefully designed, compact playgrounds – one with Astro for footie or netball, the other with climbing frame constructed with the dyspraxic child in mind.

On-site speech and language therapists, art therapist and sensory integration trained, highly-praised occupational therapist. Said one parent, 'My son loves his OT sessions. Sometimes he works alone, others with his friend. He thinks he is just playing but the progress he is making is incredible.' Staff an eclectic bunch – parents say, 'Jackie has a talent for recognising strengths and talents in both children and adults. There isn't a staff mould, they're all very individual, yet they make a great team'. Teachers are all qualified dyslexia specialists (or training to be), with one involved in successful outreach programmes to local state and independent schools (woould like to do more). Classes are small (typically 8 or 10 students) and all children have at least one, 1-1 session daily, 'Because every child has 1-1 there is no stigma, it is part and parcel of school life but importantly it is completely centred on the needs of the individual child.'

Teaches adapted national curriculum including: humanities, science, DT, drama, French and ICT. 'We skill them up; they touch-type, learn to spell-check, word-process and have a large dollop of numeracy and literacy – not only in formal

U

morning sessions but across all their learning. We give them strategies to help them cope in mainstream, at university and in the work-place and beyond.' Mornings focus on numeracy and literacy, 'My son couldn't do his letter sounds; six months later we're seeing real progress not just in his reading but in blending sounds and spelling too. Importantly his confidence is stratospheric – he wants to read everything, even menus and road signs!' Nightly homework is within reach, fingertip stuff, appropriate to the individual child. 'Jackie is skilled at adjusting parental expectations, the focus is very much on the individual, and measuring them against themselves.' say parents. For some schools, concentrating on individual achievement and expectations may be sub-text for 'not much progress', but here there's nowhere to hide, they track everything. It isn't unusual to find children advancing three plus years in under 12 months.

Staff know every trick in the book. The ruses and wiles youngsters may have adopted elsewhere are instantly spotted here, 'If my son tries to hide they're on him like a rash.' Frequently adopt a cross-curricula themed approach, tailored to specific needs, which children love, 'When we did Rise Of The Robots all our subjects were linked to it, so we could understand it better, it was such fun.' Teaching throughout takes account of individual learning styles, 'They see how my son learns and work with that; they adapt to him'. Timetable currently structured around maths, 'We identified this as an area we wanted to develop and improve'. Learning is practical and accessible; expect to find forensics, finger-printing and fun, 'When we looked at cells we did so by considering illness and what systems and organs are affected; it helped it make sense.' Focusing on strengths equally important as plugging weaknesses, 'My child has severe difficulty with hand-writing but they discovered, and encouraged, a talent for creative writing and now he is voluntarily writing a comic book in his free-time.'

Incredibly proactive at getting children off campus and away from the Unicorn bubble: sports at Radley College, swimming in a number of locations, delicious lunch at nearby Abingdon School (Unicorn youngsters not remotely fazed by presence of burly sixth-formers). Daily sports sessions include football, hockey, netball (play in small schools league), plus sailing, swimming, judo etc. Mornings begin with 'shake-up and wake-up' a brain gym derivative which gets mind and body working in tandem. Movement and dance sessions are geared to the youngsters, 'My child is dyspraxic but he loves the sessions; he has become body and space aware. They teach them in a fun way, get them to be dragons or monsters...'

Plethora of after-school clubs: shooting, cookery, eco 'kids are very green, well-informed and have good general knowledge', sports etc peppered with trips to Warwick Castle, theatre, France. Technology and gadgets feature in abundance: visiting shows, such as Bionic Ear plus trips to RM real room and lego robotic sessions, always popular. Strong community focus – active link with Mwalimu School, Africa (do look at the delightful project book in reception). Plenty for parents, including coffee mornings and socials. Many openly relieved to have found Unicorn, 'Our lives are so different, I was suffering stress-related illnesses, that's all gone. Unicorn has improved all of our lives, not just my child's.'

Children have their say too; there's an active school council which decided recent uniform changes, including minutiae such as modifications to the crest. A friendly, polite bunch with limitless curiosity, we were enamoured by their interest in others, 'There's continual movement so they are always welcoming, accepting and tolerant of newbies.' Virtually all simply existed in education prior to Unicorn so foremost aim is to boost confidence and self-belief then plug gaps, before moving to independent learning. 'My child was nervous for all of two days, after that the euphoria set-in; he made friends and hasn't ever looked back.' Children are incredibly articulate, with damming stories to tell, 'I wasn't getting an education at my old school', 'I thought I was stupid', 'I was shy and angry',

'My old school didn't get why I didn't get it',' I used to panic and go blank when the teacher asked me a question', 'I was told my writing was babyish.' We listened to heart-rending tales of merciless bullying, 'At my old school one boy made up a song about my dyslexia and taunted me with it'. No such tales at Unicorn, 'Here you can be who you want to be', 'They give you time to think and to learn.' Understandable then that the most prolific comment, even from recent arrivals, was a simple, 'I love it.' The only down-side for some being the journey time – can be lengthy.

Not only does Unicorn provide much needed cover from the bullets and bullies, but the joy of learning is tangible. Unicorn restores faith, builds confidence; it enables children to look forward, to take charge of their learning, cope with whatever they meet, to progress and thrive. A haven for both the child with specific learning difficulties and their parents, 'We were like Jack Russells – wouldn't let go; constantly battling with school, the LA, specialists, each other. Now we have found Unicorn we can relax. We no longer have to scream to be heard or battle for our child to be understood.' Should you need a specialist school with a big heart, a will of steel and an outstanding track record, look no further.

Unicorn School (Richmond)

238 Kew Road, Richmond, TW9 3JX

- Pupils: 170 girls and boys • Ages: 3–11 • Non-denom
- Fees: £5,805–£10,635 pa • Independent

Tel: 020 8948 3926
Email: registrar@unicornschool.org.uk
Website: www.unicornschool.org.uk

Headmistress: Since September 2013, Mr Kit Thompson, previously deputy head of Twyford School in Hampshire. He will need to keep a tight hand on the tiller to maintain school's highly individual, non-pressurised yet astonishingly successful course – where else do pupils routinely turn down places at top London secondaries like Godolphin and Latymer or Lady Eleanor Holles? – whilst resisting undue interference from articulate, heavily involved parents who, as school owners, enjoy having their say. It's a big ask.

Entrance: Single form all the way through and non-selective for those who arrive in the nursery aged 3 – 'you can't measure intelligence by the way a child holds a pencil' – though arrivals in other years are assessed in English and, in juniors, maths and reasoning, too.

As for special needs, around 17 have some form of support, none statemented. 'We get what we get', though school stresses that long term, it 'can't cater for severe learning difficulties'. Success here, however, is much praised by parents. 'At my daughter's previous school, she was having issues with her reading, so she was in my mind a special needs child. When we moved her here she had so much encouragement she just blossomed – it was the best thing we ever did,' says one.

Clientele very local – you only have to watch traffic grinding along nearby South Circular Road to see benefits – with few coming from further away than Chiswick or Barnes and 50 per cent or so within immediate Kew/Richmond vicinity. Most hear about school through word of mouth recommendation or personal experience – 'I am an old Unicorn and had always said that my experience was so good that if I were able to send my children there I would,' says one mother.

Though horribly over-subscribed with many children registered at birth – would be even earlier if parents had their way – school is keen to point out that despite reputation of being 'impossible' to get into, there's a regular trickle of occasional places, often freed up when parents with mega-important jobs relocate. (Means-tested bursaries are available, too, covering up to 100 per cent of the fees and awarded at the discretion of the governors.) New arrivals include occasional prep school refugees in search of a less traditional mind set.

Conversely, there's also (very small) reverse migration. School's ethos, low on formal tests, high on parent involvement, ranging from reception swimming (prepare to get wet – no passive poolside role here) to ferrying children to activities (there's even a mum's choir that regularly wins first place at local music festival), isn't for everyone. 'The school operates so closely as a community that I think they'd feel outside if they weren't part of it,' though some frantic working parents send nannies or fathers as proxies and 'it's really not that arduous,' emphasises one mother.

Exit: Nothing unconventional about secondary school destinations. You name it, they get in, with a spread that includes ultra-desirable top league independents, St Paul's Girls, Colet Court and Hampton among them as well as occasional boarding places (Tudor Hall featured recently) together with offers from just about every other decent school in the area including Latymer and Ibstock Place. Some scholarships each year, academic/all-rounder among them.

Children usually sit exams for three or four secondaries, one aspirational, one probable, one backup and almost invariably end up with several offers, usually including first choice schools. Some, particularly if in search of elusive place at one of 10 times oversubscribed Surrey grammars may take rather more (invariably at parent's behest).

Preparation is covered with subtlety, starting in earnest only in year 6 when weekly tests, including post-swimming maths on Friday (not much enjoyed, judging by slightest of grimaces) are introduced. School's approach can require a parental leap of faith, especially for those more used to all-through exam-driven atmosphere of traditional preps. But though government tests were dropped some years back after it was decided that vertigo-inducing league table heights didn't compensate for stress levels generated, school's in-house assessments ensure staff are on the button when it comes to pupils' progress (results invariably put them streets ahead of national or indeed independent sector averages), with small group teaching by maths and English specialists to speed up pace for most able (gifted and talented by any other measure) and slow it down for those needing a little extra help.

Commendably, setting by stealth approach is so low key that, unlikely though it sounds, children who mentioned it seem genuinely unaware of its purpose. 'You start doing tests to see what suits you,' says one. They also speak warmly of teachers' reassuring presence when 11 plus nerves strike. 'I trusted them and they made every school sound great. You felt you could talk about anything,' says one.

Remarks: With its lovely double-fronted Victorian villa home opposite Kew Gardens, the school radiates solid values and has a price on its head to match – similar pad up the road was on sale for a smidge under five million smackers recently so current management team must bless prescient school founders for acquiring freehold 40-odd years ago.

Colourful Jan Pienowski-style murals, conceived by the children and realised to interior designer standards by a group of talented parents, add colour to the light wood and pastel-shaded décor, as do the rainbow leitmotifs that permeate school like letters running through a stick of rock. Parents will need to cultivate familiarity with the spectrum as each class is named after a colour with the oldest (year 6 in old money) housed on top floor (the younger the class, the fewer the stairs) and known as ultra violets, a witty touch not so far extended to

their form chairs which, though colour coded for other years, are an anti-climactic grey.

Uniquely (it's thought) school is run as a limited company with one share per family, governors fulfilling dual role as board directors and an annual general meeting with state-of-union presentation by the head. While parents occasionally exceed their brief – 'because it's a parent-owned school, they feel they have a say in everything,' says one – there's a real 'do as I do' top-down ethos which extends to pupils who can serve on school council from infants onwards, or, in the case of the oldest, read stories or play games with nursery children, greatly enjoyed even though they give up some of their break time in the process. 'We help calm them down,' says one.

All in all, it's a happy continuation of the ideals that prompted the school's foundation in 1970 by a group of parents and teachers disenchanted with the fun-free learning inflicted on children elsewhere and in search of education with a creative spark. Once routinely described as bohemian or alternative, that's not the case now, say staff and parents (with a mere hint of politely gritted teeth) and the school excels at providing a child-centred education that's the real deal – short on edu-babble and 'stand and deliver teaching,' long on intelligence, spontaneity and enjoyment.

Much praised by all are the Thursday afternoon clubs that replace lessons for juniors, with 20 options or so ranging from sailing in Slough to riding at Ham House – most covered by the fees with a contribution for the priciest. A similar number and range of after-school activities is also on offer. In other years, however, trips don't have to be big to be clever with a one-stop bus journey for reception, dressed as evacuees, proving a stand out success.

As you'd expect, high calibre teachers come as standard issue here, a notably bright bunch of buttons who are required, like parents, to '... enjoy [our] philosophy and be happy to blend with it. Choosing staff... is perhaps more tricky than in other schools. While they're looking for particular skills to fill a gap, we're looking for a match and fit to the ethos, too.' Most are skilled up to the eyeballs; one, home grown, is just finishing her degree, and Oxbridge 'though not the be all and end all,' is well represented as are sports, with several high level players helping to lead football and rounders teams, amongst others, to success.

The care taken over recruitment pays off handsomely with high grade work the norm, ranging from art (credible Catherine of Aragon glove puppets with papier-mâché heads and fabric bodies made by year 5s) to science (eight and nine year olds, all red-fingered after creating their own bicarb of soda and vinegar volcanoes).

Bottom line is that teachers love to teach and give pupils access all areas passes in lessons, encouraging them to think for themselves. Three Men in a Boat and Chaucer are on the menu after the 11 plus is done and dusted (no post-exam torpor here) while popular philosophy lessons let children choose which big questions to discuss. (One boy's place at Colet Court was secured when he enthusiastically told interviewer he'd studied 'nothing').

And it's not just the top years that benefit, with reception children ditching Wheels on the Bus for Maybe it's Because I'm a Londoner, delivered with tasteful guitar backing and full complement of aspirants rather than Chas 'n' Dave pub-side bellow. 'We were learning about London and some of the children started asking about the war so we ended up having a glorious week,' explains teaching assistant.

Aspirations may be vast, space less so. There's no kitchen so it's packed lunches for all, though children are a dab hand at knowing which teacher can be counted on for backup rations in an emergency – educational meals on wheels options are currently being considered.

What space there is, however, is worked hard outside with greenery-rich main playground divided into running around area (fore) and quiet zone (aft) (sensible, given proximity to

U

gardens of the no doubt vociferous well-to-do burghers of Kew), and rejigged interiors with corridor-free airy hall and previously poky first floor of coach house annexe re-synced into natty class music area with matching practice room next door (much used, with 130 timetabled instrumental lessons each week). Similar upgrade is planned for the reception and nursery classrooms downstairs, both bright and cheerful with their own secluded and plant-filled mini walled garden. (Nature is a big thing – a consignment of eggs with pre-confirmed hatching date is bought in each spring from nearby ethically-sound farm. Chicks are returned, hens to have fulfilled life as layers, cockerels to face somewhat curtailed future – best to draw veil.)

Parents are unfussed by size. 'It's typical for London,' says one, who also points to proximity of both 'the' Gardens opposite and the Old Deer Park (home of London Welsh RFC), both extensively used by school, latter for games.

Pupils, a loyal, friendly and articulate bunch (predictably in an area stuffed to the gunnels with highly educated professionals) have few complaints, either. While there's the occasional bout of out-of-teacher's-hearing bullying disguised as friendly teasing (mainly girls), it's dealt with quickly and effectively once reported and backed by a carrot-heavy rewards system, with prize-giving every term and a roll of honour featuring pupils and, pleasingly, teachers too, who nominate each other for doing the right thing.

Small, but with learning presented as a huge à la carte menu and not just the assessment-driven prix fixe, this is a special place. 'I can't believe that sitting multiple exams instils a love of learning. If we can teach children to enjoy learning, that's a gift for life.' No wonder school is loved by parents who even apologise for non-stop praise. 'I feel like I'm blowing the school's trumpet,' says one. Not bohemian – easy to rhapsodise, though.

University College School Junior School

Linked school: University College School

---

11 Holly Hill, London, NW3 6QN

• Pupils: 230 boys; all day • Ages: 7–11; pre-prep (The Phoenix School, a separate entity, 3–7) • Non-denom • Fees: £15,855 pa
• Independent

Tel: 020 7435 3068
Email: juniorbranch@ucs.org.uk
Website: www.ucs.org.uk

Headmaster of Junior: Mr Kevin J Douglas BA Cert Ed; also works as a schools inspector – 'it keeps you on the ball'. Taught at QE Boys and then at Belmont for 19 years, the last 10 as deputy head. Married with three daughters. 'He's very involved, very approachable,' said a parent. Retiring in July 2014.

Entrance: Some 170 applicants for 60 places at 7. At the initial assessment, in the autumn term, staff hear boys read – 'we're looking for two years above chronological age' – then read them a story and ask them questions in groups. Meanwhile, the head takes parents on a tour of the school, 'to make sure they want us'. Confident readers are asked back for English, maths and non-verbal reasoning tests in the spring term, with attention also paid to how they interact in groups.

The main feeder pre-preps tend to be The Phoenix, Mulberry House, Golders Hill School and Hampstead Hill School. Although The Phoenix is the UCS pre-prep, applicants take the same entrance test as everyone else. 'All things being equal they'll get a place. But they must be able to cope.'

Exit: Virtually all to the senior school, without taking the entrance exam. 'If a boy is really struggling we'll talk to his parents – but that has only happened once whilst I've been here.'

Remarks: Compact site tucked away at the top of Hampstead behind the Everyman cinema with views across London from every classroom. Nice boy-friendly science lab with tarantulas and poisonous frogs, which doubles as recording studios where boys can come in to write and record songs at lunchtime (an apprenticeship, no doubt, for the rock band culture of the senior school).

Art, woodwork and cookery rooms, all well-used: plenty of time here for creative activities. Some impressive photography displayed: came third in the Prep School Photographer of the Year competition. Smallish rubber surface playground/football pitch; boys play rugby, football, cricket and hockey at the senior school grounds in West Hampstead. Also use the senior school swimming pool and theatre and have concerts in the great hall. Giant chess set in the playground; the Under 11 team recently won the National Schools gold award.

Does not have to prepare boys for common entrance, so no huge academic pressure – can spend less time on maths and English and more on other activities. Relaxed pace. Undoubtedly some parents feel that their children are not stretched academically and some complain of lack of homework, though the latest Independent Schools Inspectorate report (following a bad inspection previously) praised standards. 'I think we've turned it round,' says the head.

Happy to accept able boys with physical disabilities. 'If they're bright and can cope I'll take anyone,' says the head. 'They've been amazing helping with all his needs,' said the parent of one disabled boy. Full-time school nurse who 'knows all the boys and is involved in their personal development'. Two part-time SEN teachers.

Warm, friendly atmosphere. 'It's a very happy school,' said a parent.

Vinehall School

Mountfield, Robertsbridge, TN32 5JL

• Pupils: 265; 145 boys/120 girls; 47 boarders • Ages: 2–13
• C of E (with provision for Roman Catholics and other faiths)
• Fees: Boarding £18,246–£20,235; Day £8,370–£15,513 pa
• Independent

Tel: 01580 880413
Email: admissions@vinehallschool.com
Website: www.vinehallschool.com

Head: Since 2011, Mr Richard Follett (early forties) BA PGCE Dip Sp Psych. Previously at Pangbourne College for four years where he was head of the junior school (age 11-13 yrs), housemaster of the junior house and director of rowing. Previously at Bedford Modern School for ten years where he taught geography and was in charge of rowing. Started his teaching career at an inner city Catholic comprehensive in Walsall. Educated at Latymer Upper School and read geography and sports science at Liverpool University and did his PGCE at Birmingham University. He teaches RS and geography in years 5 and 6, so has a chance to get to know the children in the classroom. His wife, Jo is very involved with school life and is a form 4 teacher and teaches history and girls' games. She was previously head of girls' games at St Andrew's, Pangbourne. Sees himself as an 'innovative traditionalist' and is a stickler for manners. He greets everyone by name and insists that the children say 'hello', stand up when an adult comes into the room and have

U

their shirts tucked in. No great changes planned and is taking things slowly and gaining the confidence of staff and parents and the respect of the children.

A keen digital photographer and rower – although he has not yet had a chance to do any rowing since the move to Sussex.

Entrance: Most children either join the nursery in their third year or reception two years later – via an informal meeting and taster day. Partly selective as it is a fairly competitive environment and they want children who can cope with Common Entrance. Vinehall requires a fair bit of conformity. Small intake at age 9 and occasionally some spaces higher up the school – have to sit a test and attend a visiting day.

Exit: To a wide range of local schools, the most popular being Eastbourne College, Cranbrook, Tonbridge, King's Canterbury, Benenden, Battle Abbey, Sevenoaks, Brighton College, Eton, Winchester, Lancing College. A few girls leave at 11 but this is not encouraged. They do not actively prepare children for the 11 plus grammar school entrance exam but have incorporated verbal reasoning into the curriculum. Children are, however, prepared for the Cranbrook entrance exam at 13 plus.

Remarks: Founded in 1938, the school is centred on a large country house set in 47 acres of the East Sussex countryside. A very light and airy and purposeful feel to it. The front hall and staircase are lined with shields which tell the story of every child who has attended the school. Much silverware and children's artwork also in evidence. A very glossy and shiny school with excellent facilities which takes itself seriously. Purpose-built pre-prep and nursery schools.

Proud of its scholarship record – art and music as well as academic. Nineteen awards in 2012, including major academic scholarships to Sevenoaks and King's Canterbury. Setting in some subjects, but the scholars are catered for within their own year group – they are streamed from year 6. Loyal band of staff who are able to bring out the best in the children – no trouble attracting good teachers. Headmaster has recently set up a system where teachers observe lessons in other departments which has proved interesting for everyone.

Top ICT: computers, smartboards, interactive whiteboards, intranet, and the library bristles with new computers. The school can cater for mild special needs, but would not suit someone of below average ability unless they are very gifted at music, art or sport.

Day children start at 8.20am, after-school clubs end variably. Saturday morning school for top two years and no plans to stop this. Optional Saturday activities for years 3-6 has proved popular. Matches on two Saturdays per term but most are on Wednesdays. Sport a high profile activity. Girls play netball, hockey, lacrosse (as a club option) and rounders and the boys play rugby, cricket hockey and soccer. All can do swimming, athletics, gymnastics, cross-country running, judo, archery, riding, tennis and golf – virtually everyone who wants to can play in a team.

Music strong – most play an instrument and there are two orchestras and several smaller ensemble groups. Lots of musical evenings. Very well-equipped art department plus design technology carpentry, textiles pottery etc. Drama is also a major feature of school life: five or six productions each year. Plenty of opportunities for children to learn to speak in public by reading in assembly and chapel as well as music and poetry evenings. All regularly prepare English Speaking Board presentations.

Lots of extra-curricular activities – after school clubs, school trips, camping expeditions, cultural visits and visits abroad.

Although the academic standards are high, this not a hothouse. The school believes that its purpose is to discover the children's talents and nurture them as best it can. The school caters for the all-round child with a great emphasis on happiness and the development of a sense of self. A code of conduct known as 'The Vinehall Way' is used to promote thoughtful, caring behaviour. Children are encouraged to look after and notice younger children and seem to thrive on this responsibility. There are awards not just for merit but for kindness and consideration as well, as is borne out by the school motto 'to do our best for the benefit of others'. It does produce children who are extremely self-confident, but not precocious, and well ready to face the challenges of their next schools. There is a strong sense of community and the children who showed us round were extremely proud of their school. The food is good with some of the finest chocolate brownies in East Sussex!

Predominantly a day school with 30-40 full time boarders. Flexiboarding a very popular option and school has recently introduced weekly boarding. Mrs Coles, the housemistress, provides a cosy family environment for the boarders and most of the top year ask to board. Plenty to do at weekends with special outings arranged.

A broad mix of parents, many from business, the media and medicine and a number of first time buyers. Mainly local, lots commute to London, some Forces children and some high achieving foreign nationals. High priority given to communication with home. A number of pupils on means-tested bursaries from the Vinehall Foundation. Parents are able to communicate with staff on a daily basis plus parents' information evenings. The emailed weekly newsletter 'Vinelines' provides constant links with the life of the school. Parental involvement very much encouraged and various social activities are organised by the parents. Active old boys and girls association with Vines Day each year when they can come back to the school. Old boys include Tim Smit of Eden Project fame, the members of the band 'Keane' and the explorer, Tom Avery.

Wakefield Girls' High School Junior School

Linked school: Wakefield Girls' High School

2 St John's Square, Wakefield, WF1 2QX

- Pupils: 475 girls (boys only in nursery) all day • Ages: 9-11
- Inter-denom • Fees: £7,800-£8,505 pa • Independent

Tel: 01924 374577
Email: admissions@wghsjs.org.uk
Website: www.wgsf.org.uk

Head: Since 1998, Mrs D St C Cawthorne BEd, Dip TEFLA; has been head of a school in the Middle East as well as teaching in England; pleasant, enterprising and very capable, relishes her independence from the senior school to the extent of having her own budget. Likes travel, reading and chocolate. Two grown-up children.

Entrance: No entrance requirement for the co-ed nursery – the first 50 children on the list get in; names are put down at or even before birth. Priority given to children with siblings in the Foundation. Almost all proceed to the pre-prep. Assessment for those wanting to join at this point from outside in English and maths, in late January or early February. Means-tested Foundation awards available, if parental annual income is below £35000, at seven years, for 25/50 per cent of the fees; usually six a year.

Exit: Boys leave after Mulberry House (nursery). Majority of girls through to senior school.

Remarks: Pre-prep Mulberry House (as in 'Here we go round the mulberry bush', the original mulberry tree is in the pre-prep garden).

For further details, see senior school entry.

Walhampton School

Walhampton, Lymington, SO41 5ZG

- Pupils: 330 boys and 150 girls; 62 boarders • Ages: 2–13 • C of E
- Fees: Day £5,550–£14,985; Boarding £19,935 pa • Independent

Tel: 01590 613300
Email: registrar@walhampton.com
Website: www.walhampton.com

Headmaster: Since 2012, Mr Titus Mills BA (forties), previously head of the Paragon School. Educated at Pilgrims, Eton and UEA; did his PGCE at Westminster College, Oxford. Gap year experience with Tibetan community in Himalayas dramatically rearranged his world view. Sandwiched stints in London state schools with two years teaching in Kampala, Uganda and five years as head of international school in Rome, before returning to head the Paragon. We said of him there: 'high octane energy meets sophisticated unconventionality'. He is assisted by his wife Jemima and three young sons, Malachi, Raffi and Cassius.

Entrance: Non-selective. First-come-first-served entry at two into the pre-prep, with preference for siblings. Nearly everyone goes through to the prep at seven; a few more join at that point. A fair amount of to-ing and fro-ing – a few leave the pre-prep for state primaries, some come in from abroad for a term or two to improve their English, others move into or out of the area. Always worth trying for a place; those coming in higher up are assessed. On a sound financial footing because 'I am very mean,' says the head. 'The governors instruct me to be. We own the 100 acre site outright – no borrowing, no overdraft and a solid rainy day fund.' One or two Forces discounts available plus endowment fund for truly needy.

Exit: At 13, Winchester, Radley and Bryanston top the list, with others going to Canford, Wellington, Marlborough, Sherborne, Clayesmore, Eton and Harrow. A handful leave at 11 to eg King Edward VI in Southampton or St Swithun's. Occasionally one or two to selective state schools, eg the Bournemouth grammars. Not a hothouse – happy for children to aim for the senior school that will suit them best.

Remarks: From the front it is a splendid Queen Anne/Victorian building with panelled, galleried entrance hall and original cornicing. Tucked round the back are infinite pancake flat lawns, three lakes, lovely views and bracing sea breezes. Somewhat isolated in feel and in reality – although the picturesque town of Lymington, with its Waitrose and two train stations, is reassuringly nearby. Slightly over the top grandeur at odds with what is essentially a cosy, jolly prep school alive with activity and purpose.

Parents are local or have some tie to the area – sailing perhaps, or a holiday home. Many lived in London but have relocated – partly or wholly – to the New Forest. Grandparents in the area is another draw – enough so that the school has introduced an annual grandparents' lunch. A few come for a term or a year from France and Spain – head would like more – and a clutch from the Isle of Wight as boarders, or even daily. Minibuses bring children from the ferry terminus in Lymington, and from all over.

Proud of their flexi-boarding, with the emphasis on the 'flexi'. Almost all arrangements are negotiable. Take Saturday school – it's optional. The 60-70 per cent of pupils who take part in the wide range of offerings – eg sport, art, computing, fencing, archery, 'high jump clinic' – show up in jeans and T-shirts. Full boarding numbers have dwindled since Walhampton School (the home of the current school) merged with Hordle House in 1997 – 'It made us look like less of a serious boarding school,' said the previous head.

Since 2009 the boarding setup has been revamped and consolidated in the two floors of the main building. All extremely cheery and well-run, parents rave about the pastoral care, and the school would love to encourage more pupils to dip a toe into boarding – much encouragement to do so in the final two years. Strongly Christian ethos. Assembly takes place in the chapel every morning and a service on Friday evenings.

Year 3s get a gentle start – kept a bit separate from the big kids, have classes of 16 max, and can go home earlier (before games) if they wish. No mollycoddling when it comes to setting, though: setted for maths from year 3, for English from year 4 and streamed from year 6. IT provision, mildly criticised in inspection report, has made a great leap forward. Really lovely library – encapsulates the school's values in a nutshell. Children have one taught library lesson a week, are advised on their reading and have their progress monitored. Brill librarian has painstakingly tagged some books as only appropriate for year 6 and older, and a few of the more mature works for year 8 eyes only – why don't more schools do this? Scholars work to a special book list.

Excellent SEN department used by 18 per cent of children (individual and shared teaching at extra charge, plus extra help in class). Good at spotting problems. Will cater for mild Asperger's, ADD, specific learning difficulties (dyslexia unit is registered with CReSTeD). Sometimes pupils are removed from Latin for learning support sessions, but the head is not keen – 'It's very sad; often I'd rather see them miss French'. Now working to improve the gifted and talented side of things with a 'Gateway' programme.

Games important. Outdoor sport every afternoon run by members of staff. The standard team games are played, plus fencing, shooting and riding. Astroturf for hockey, tennis etc. Outdoor heated 15m swimming pool, small but challenging adventure playground – not for the timid. Revamped and charming, but relatively low key, 'equestrian centre'. Pupils may bring own pony if they are willing to look after it themselves and allow others to ride it. Riding instruction from the school's two specialists can be incorporated into the school day. Awfully nice sports hall, built using the proceeds of the merger – mothers muscle in on it for their Pilates classes.

Lovely performing arts centre with tiered seating – used to be the gym. Four drama productions a year and LAMDA exams are offered. General knowledge quizzes alive and well. Music department continues to be 'up and coming', with steel drum samba band, two choirs and two school pop groups. Years 3-5 learn recorder. Art the jewel in the crown – pottery, textiles, one hour a week of formal art lessons and door open to the keen in evenings, clubs and breaks. Head of art dresses up as a famous artist for a performance each year. Student council elected twice a year and meets several times a term.

Children good all-rounders who can hold their own in conversations with adults. Expressed some gripes about too many outside areas being out of bounds (despite its robust spirit, this is not a 'climb trees and camp in the woods' school). Oddly enough, the head of sport voiced the same opinion, wishing the pupils 'could go onto the games field at break – there's too much health and safety nowadays!' January snow a year or two back may have flummoxed the London buses and forced most boarding schools to send their charges packing, but Walhampton carried on serenely – 'We had an interhouse snowball match – one of the teachers measured the throws with his speed gun'. Expeditions week – the penultimate week of the summer term – is prized by all. Previous head remembered the days when the expeditions involved hitching horses up to a gypsy caravan.

Pre-prep takes children from the day they turn two. Uses main school's art and IT facilities and shares the dining room. Tiny classes of 12 in reception through year 2. 'Forest school' for getting in touch with the out of doors one morning a week. The prize of sitting at the urbane, table-clothed 'café table' goes to the children who have 'eaten most nicely' each week. Lots of optional after-school enrichment, eg ball skills, speech and drama, 'yoga teddies', ballet and tap, French. A comprehensive start to school life, but looks a bit tired: a blast of fresh air would work wonders. Children in the pre-prep can flexi-board. All told, a happy, hearty, outdoorsy place, crammed with the best of prep school joys.

Walthamstow Hall Junior

Linked school: Walthamstow Hall

Bradbourne Park Road, Sevenoaks, TN13 3LD

• Pupils: 250 girls, all day • Ages: 3–11 • Broadly Christian
• Fees: £9,600–£11,970 pa • Independent

Tel: 01732 453815
Email: registrar@walthamstowhall.kent.sch.uk
Website: www.walthamstow-hall.co.uk

Headmistress: Since September 2013, Mrs Diane Wood.

Entrance: Non-selective. Most children join in the nursery and entrance is via an informal chat with the parents and a one hour taster session for the children to make sure they are ready to start school. Older girls attend a taster day when their English, maths and social skills are assessed.

Exit: About 50-80 per cent move on to the senior school each year but have to take the same entrance tests in maths and English as external applicants. Lots of discussion with parents about the next step and plenty of warning if it is thought their daughter won't pass into the senior school. Others to a variety of state and independent schools including Sevenoaks and eight or so per year to the grammars – girls are well prepared for all entrance exams including the Kent Test.

Remarks: Down a quiet road on the edge of leafy Sevenoaks in a large, light and comfortable Edwardian house with many additions – all sympathetically done. Fresh paint and everything in good condition with vases of flowers dotted about and an atmosphere of ordered calm and purpose. Lots of silverware displayed in the hall with cups for everything. Moved here from a house in the grounds of the senior school in 1992 and the short distance between the two means that the junior school has a separate identity but with all the benefits of a 'big sister' up the road. It uses some of the senior school facilities like the Ship Theatre and indoor pool but remains very much a self contained unit with a different uniform and good facilities of its own including a large multi-purpose hall which doubles as a dining room – work about to start on a new dining room. Lots of outdoor space including the Dell with playhouses and bushes for making dens, plus use of an adjoining sports field.

Two parallel classes from reception upwards. Children are taught as individuals which means different abilities can be accommodated within one class with individual education programmes for the gifted and talented and anyone with SEN. They are set for maths from year 4. About 20-25 girls need some

level of SEN support, mainly for mild dyslexia and dyspraxia and extra help with maths – two part-time teachers. Recent academic scholarships to the senior school, Sevenoaks and Kent College. Well equipped science labs with specialist science teacher. Emphasis on developing independent thinking and study skills and girls encouraged to think and find things out for themselves. Doing your best considered as important as being the best. Lots of cheerful art work about the place and three lessons a week with a specialist teacher from year 3. Own kiln for pottery and carpentry also offered. The majority learn a musical instrument and everyone does class music right the way through the school. There are three choirs and a dedicated music suite.

Plenty of sport including pop-lacrosse, a gentler version of the game played in the senior school, also netball, tennis, rounders and athletics. Swimming particularly strong and a number of girls take part in national and county championships. Regular plays mean that all get a chance to perform – there are also gymnastics displays and class-led assemblies. Forty or so lunchtime and after school clubs include the usual music, art, dance and drama; chess is also particularly popular. Cookery club in the purpose-built mini-kitchen always oversubscribed.

Leadership roles taken seriously and each girl is given some responsibility – head girl, monitors, house captains, games captains or playing with the youngest children at break time. Year 6 girls run the library overseen by a librarian. Senior girls meet regularly with head to discuss their responsibilities and carry out self appraisals. Four houses, all named after female authors, with plenty of friendly competition in music, sport, swimming etc; each house chooses a charity to support.

A caring and nurturing school underpinned by Christian values, achievement is celebrated but house points are also awarded for effort and good manners. Parents have high expectations and are a supportive and happy bunch – some help run clubs or assist with activities such as swimming. Thriving parents association and each form has a social co-ordinator so all parents made to feel welcome.

Warwick Junior School

Linked school: Warwick School

Myton Road, Warwick, CV34 6PP

• Pupils: 240 boys, all day • Ages: 7–11 • C of E • Fees: £8,505–£10,815 pa • Independent

Tel: 01926 776418
Email: jt@warwickschool.org
Website: www.warwickschool.org

Headmaster of the Junior School: Since 2004 Mr Guy Canning BA, a youthful 55. Educated at UCS London and the University of East Anglia. Married, two teenagers. Refreshingly interesting in the variety of career paths he has explored, the breadth of his experiences, the energy of his thinking and his enthusiasm for the school. Nearly ten years as a head has not resulted in even a whiff of complacency, smugness or self-importance. Ideas are still tumbling out and he is forever dreaming up new ways of making the boys feel appreciated and recognised as individuals. 'He's very cool,' a boy, told us, with the air of someone who really could spot such an attribute. Early experimental incarnations include journalism (we suspect a racing journalist), merchant banking ('Hideous Mondays. Only three topics of conversation: weekend, weather and the train'), and an employment agency. Saw the light, took a PGCE practising at a tough comprehensive before moving on as head of PE and house tutor at St Bede's, then Bedford Prep. Spell as director of studies at a crammer,

W

in Gloucestershire in various senior roles, RGS Worcester Prep where he was deputy head before the move to Warwick. 'I like independent schools because they are independent and free. Less interference from governmental edicts. We can get on with teaching and inspiring.' A bright cookie but not a desiccated academic smelling of water biscuits, nor a pin-striped, ruthlessly ambitious, jargon-spewing head. He is, as a former colleague put it, 'a thoughtful man who cares about learning and opportunities.' 'Very approachable and wise,' one parent told us, 'and with a lovely sense of humour.' Certainly a modest man. Since his arrival he has sought to enlarge the activities on offer and to inculcate a sense of enquiry and experiment in the classroom. 'We want spirited, inquisitive children and staff who can encourage those qualities. Education is a serious business but children don't need to know that.' On the subject of exams, which are taken seriously, he observes, 'you don't fatten a pig by weighing it.' Clearly he loves the children and they respond cheerfully and respectfully, waving at him like small flags and bursting to tell him what they have been doing. Not an overtly sociable head, he's not interested in being invited to dinner parties or race meetings, but, 'knowing parents ensures we operate with consistency. Besides, we're all in this together.' Parents speak highly of his warmth and professionalism. In an age when 'failure' is seen by some educationalists as a taboo word, he has interesting comments about the importance of supporting and helping children cope with failure and disappointment. 'Everyone will fail at something. It's what you learn from it which is important'. When pushed for words that might sum up his aims for the school he repeated that word 'spirited' and added 'creativity'. Genuinely interested in the long-term view, he maintains a close interest in ex-pupils, many of whom continue to live and work nearby. 'He remembers who we are,' said an older pupil. 'I had a brilliant time there.' 'He certainly retains his interest,' said a parent. Married to Jane who works in the careers office at the university of Gloucestershire, he commutes from Cheltenham most days. 'I sleep here one or two nights a week.' One 'very musical' daughter.

Entrance: Any time, providing there is room. Most boys and girls enter aged three or four; girls only at at seven. Girls wishing to enter at seven are assessed in maths, reading and writing and are invited to bring an object which is special to them and to talk about it. They spend a whole day at the school attending some classes and fooling about in the playground with current pupils. Occasionally pupils are not offered a place on the grounds that, 'they would be unlikely to flourish', but this is rare. 'It's all pretty fair,' said a happy parent whose child had been accepted.

Exit: All boys leave at seven, majority to Warwick School (qv). A very few go on to other prep schools to gain boarding experience before moving on again. Girls leave aged 11 with many going on to King's High, but not all. It's not an automatic move.

Remarks: The nursery and prep are the first steps on the great adventure offered by the Warwick Independent Schools Foundation. They share the same campus as Warwick School (boys); the High School (girls) is about a mile away on the outskirts of the town. The prep is more than an adjunct to the other schools on the campus and though all schools share the same pool of governors, each maintains its autonomy and individuality. Aficionados of architecture might compare the external appearance of the prep buildings with a business park but they would be compelled to admire the sensitively designed interiors and the thought that has gone into blending practicality with social aesthetics. The overall atmosphere is warm and welcoming and none more so than the nearby nursery which is bright and inviting, spacious yet cosy. Real learning through real fun with, as one mum told us, 'lovely staff.' Books and art work everywhere. Glowing. The main prep is skilfully designed to complement the stages by which pupils progress through the school; junior, middle and senior are clearly defined but close to each other, minimising transition. Superbly equipped classrooms with all the gadgets but it is obvious that lively, interactive teaching is what the school is founded on. As part of that theme of creativity, visiting artists inspire and enthuse, adding to the excellent teaching that already goes on. Evidence of this is readily apparent in the many examples of glasswork, pottery, printmaking and painting that adorn walls and corridors everywhere. Running through these activities is a seemingly all-out assault on stereotypical notions of education. We witnessed some wonderful science teaching based on enquiry, experiment and exploration. 'Boys mustn't think they own the magnet,' said one teacher. It was obvious they didn't: girls as well as boys seemed deeply involved, fired with encouraged curiosity. Plenty of excitement and bubble and a sense of igniting interests and inspiring curiosity. Whether it was preparing for scenes from A Midsummer Night's Dream; using, but not relying on, computers for 'specialist thinking'; learning to solder wires and construct the basics of computers themselves and 'learning to think outside the box' it is fizz, fun and effective. 'I loved the lessons,' a recent leaver told us.

Nor is this joy confined to the classroom. Clubs, before school, lunchtime and after school, offer dancing, singing, science, computing, Spanish, sewing, swimming, football, drama and lots more. Music is popular, about 50 per cent of pupils learn a musical instrument and there is a woodwind section, a brass group, senior and junior choirs, bell ringing and a harp group. The sporting facilities are good with Astroturf, sports hall and (shared) use of the excellent swimming pool in the senior school. National successes have been scored at netball and locally in equestrian, hockey and swimming events. It seems little short of miraculous that so much is on offer during a five day week. Nor does it end there: hill walking and camping, trips to France, science weeks and editing the new magazine, complete with challenging general knowledge quizzes and interviews.

This is an extremely lively and busy place; it is palpably a very happy and friendly school, challenging and nurturing hard working, interested and bright children who are also courteous and forthcoming. Good facilities and good leadership. More than a stepping stone to senior schools, it offers sound and broad grounding, inculcating work ethics and consideration for others which should last for life.

Wellesley House School

114 Ramsgate Road, Broadstairs, CT10 2DG

- Pupils: 140 boys and girls; 100 boarders • Ages: 7–13 • C of E
- Fees: Boarding £22,575; Day £14,985–£17,085 pa • Independent

Tel: 01843 862991
Email: hmsec@wellesleyhouse.net
Website: www.wellesleyhouse.org

Headmaster: Since 2006, Mr Simon O'Malley MA PGCE (late forties). Educated at the Oratory School, Reading and at Aberdeen University. Previously a housemaster and later deputy head at Beaudesert Park in Gloucestershire. Ambitious and enthusiastic; has generated an energy and buzz about the school and is justifiably proud of all that it is achieving. Much liked and respected by parents. A keen sportsman, he still plays cricket and teaches English. Met his wife, Katy, while they were both teaching at the Banda School in Nairobi. Says managing parental expectations is an integral part of his job. Encourages parents and children alike to aim high but to be realistic, and on the whole the parents are a pretty happy bunch. He sees the

W

school as 'kind, thoughtful and unique with traditional values but not old fashioned'. He does not rest on his laurels and is constantly striving to 'do things better'.

Katy used to teach art, and following the sudden departure of the art teacher not long before common entrance, brought her skills out of mothballs and got back into the art room. Five children have won art scholarships under her watch. She keeps a close eye on pastoral and domestic matters too. They have a son at Uppingham and a daughter at university.

Entrance: Children can join at any time from 7 upwards – many from local day schools join at this age, with major intakes in years 5 and 6 particularly for boarders. Very occasionally children join for the last year but it can be difficult getting up to speed for common entrance. Girls' places always oversubscribed. Non-selective but entry via interview and reports and examples of work from the child's current school. Would only test if there were concerns about learning support or that a child might not thrive.

Surprisingly large catchment area with many coming from west Kent and East Sussex. About 15-20 from London with an accompanied mini bus to Battersea at half term and exeats – headmaster keeps in close touch with London pre-prep heads. Scholarships and bursaries of up to 100 per cent. Discounts for army families.

Exit: To a huge range of senior schools all over the country including Gordonstoun, Ampleforth, Teddies and Stowe as well as Harrow, Eton, Benenden and Tonbridge, with King's Canterbury being the most popular. Great trouble is taken to pick the right school for each child and the headmaster tries to visit at least two public schools a term. Over a third have won scholarships in recent years – academic, art, music, drama and sports. Children hardly ever leave at 11+ and the school does not offer coaching for the Kent Test.

Remarks: Wellesley was founded in 1869 in Ramsgate and moved to its current purpose-built site in 1898, a light and airy red brick building which has been added to over the years and which is surrounded by flower beds and playing fields. It merged with St Peter's Court in 1969 and went co-ed in 1977. It does not have the rolling acres of some prep schools but everything is immaculate and every inch of the grounds is used – there is plenty of room for den making and vegetable plots and even some igloos when it snows. There is a new adventure playground and also the pond, which is used as a biological testing centre and a quiet sitting area. The playing fields are divided by an elegant avenue of trees which has been colonised by a group of noisy, bright green parrots. Lots of refurbishment recently and the squash courts, shooting range and the sunny indoor heated swimming pool and barbecue area are all looking like new. The walls of the new games room were decorated by the children. The headmaster and his wife like to come back during the summer holidays to take a fresh look at the school and see what needs to be done. Sunny, comfortable, well-used library with lots of space to sit and read and where children can curl up with a book. Each year group has its own common room – recently redecorated thanks to the fundraising efforts of the Friends of Wellesley. Photographs of children past and present line the corridors and there are four rolling news boards around the school showing BBC headlines, birthday announcements, notices and photos of recent events.

Avert your eyes as you drive through the cabbage patches and retail parks of Thanet – it is worth it. Many parents drive miles to send their children here, passing other good prep schools en route. It is a school which embraces the whole family and where friends are made for life: 'My daughter's best friends are still the ones she made at Wellesley,' says one mother. Parents, too, make great friends here – many a mother has been known to weep copiously during the leavers' chapel service. Old Welleslians often end up sharing flats together and there are usually a couple of Wellesley weddings announced in the school magazine. It is a busy, happy school where there is great emphasis on fairness and giving everyone a chance. Academic success is highly valued but good manners, tolerance and consideration for others are equally important. At the annual prize giving each summer, there are not only prizes for academic and sporting achievements but also the headmaster's prize which can be for anything from attitude and effort to just being a thoroughly nice person.

Younger boys live in the junior house which is joined on to the main school and where they do most of their lessons and are cared for by a housemaster and a team of matrons which gives them a very gentle introduction to boarding. They move over to the main school aged 10 where they are equally well cared for in large, light, airy and extremely tidy dormitories.

The girls live at the Orchard, set in its own grounds and surrounded by apple trees on the far side of the playing fields. The Orchard is run by Mr Nichol, who teaches geography and is in charge of the Thanet weather station, and his very elegant and bubbly Spanish wife, Elena, and it is very much a home from home. The Nichols have been in charge here for over 20 years and give the girls an exceptional start in life. There is only space for 43 girls so it feels like a large happy family and is always oversubscribed. Bright, light dorms, all named after Kentish apples, with an abundance of pink and teddy bears on all the beds. One mother who was reluctant to let her daughter board said, 'I cannot deprive my daughter of the Orchard experience, it's truly unique'.

The school motto is 'Open up a world of possibilities' and this is exactly what Wellesley does. There is great emphasis on the individual and 'children get noticed in a smaller school and get opportunities they would not get elsewhere', says the headmaster. Everyone has 'a chance to shine ' and with so many activities on offer virtually everyone finds something they are good at. Everything from photography and art, board games and chess, boys' hockey and girls' football, judo, fencing, riding at the local riding school, archery, cooking, needlework for boys and girls, ICT where children can create their own computer programmes and even scuba diving, with the 'shrimp' course taking place in the school swimming pool – the list goes on. Golf is popular – there is a putting green in the grounds and the lucky few are allowed to play at Royal St George's nearby – this can lead to a certain amount of envy amongst the parents. The school is always open to new ideas and the girls have recently set up their own cricket club. Rifle shooting is a popular activity culminating in the annual parents v children shooting match – not just fathers and sons but mothers and daughters as well.

The average class size of 12 means that the school can support children at both ends of the learning spectrum. Children streamed from year 5 and setted in maths and languages – French (taught by a native speaker) and Latin are taught as part of the curriculum and Spanish can be taught by private arrangement. Very bright children can be stretched and academic scholars are either taught in a separate, accelerated class for the last two years or within the top stream – depends on the number of scholars from year to year.

A good team of teachers, with a healthy balance of age and experience. The children are 'pushed and stretched with full support, and the school has pushed our son to be the best that he can be,' says one happy mother. New computers, and two lessons of touch typing a week as well programming and website design. High praise from the inspectors who judged that 'The curriculum is excellent, well balanced, stimulating and structured', lessons are 'challenging and interesting' and 'effective anti-bullying procedures include development of awareness of cyber-bullying through PSHE and ICT lessons'.

The school is quick to spot problems and about 20 per cent have some sort of learning support. The department is run by 'the wonderful Mrs Wallace' and there are specialist English, maths and language teachers – some children taught within the class and some withdrawn but lessons rotated so they do not fall behind in any subject; close liaison between learning support and class teachers. Will go the extra mile for children with bigger difficulties. An occupational therapist has designed a programme for dyspraxics. A small number of children work with laptops. In class EAL support available for those who need it.

The school has recently been awarded International School status by the British Council which means that all lessons must have an international dimension to encourage children to have a more global outlook – it recently took part in a European day of languages and is already twinned with a school in India.

'The school achieves things it shouldn't for its size,' says the headmaster and it certainly punches above its weight on the sports fields. He puts this down partly to the close bonds that develop in a small boarding community and partly to the support and encouragement from staff. They are frequent winners of the JET cricket and rounders national competitions, much to the envy and astonishment of much larger and apparently sportier schools, and are always represented at the annual national athletics championships in Birmingham. One girl has recently been selected for the England athletics squad and a boy for England cricket training. There is a long tradition of cricketing excellence and alumni include England captains Mann and Cowdrey as well as the Loudon brothers and Sam Northeast, plus three day eventers and Olympic medal winners William Fox-Pitt and Georgina Harland.

Music is part of the curriculum throughout the school with all year 3 learning the recorder and all year 4 the violin, and about 70 per cent continue with at least one instrument; they will find a teacher for any instrument – one child is currently learning the harp. There are instrumental groups and an orchestra and the choir sings in local churches and at weddings; a recent highlight was a trip to Venice to sing in St Mark's on Palm Sunday. Two school plays a year as well as smaller form productions at Christmas mean everyone has a chance to get up on stage. There are also poetry and musical recitals and children are prepared for the LAMDA exams.

Vibrant colourful artwork displayed all over the school with 'six of the best' selected to hang in the head's study. Masses of outings and trips; most year groups visit France and year 7 has an outdoor pursuits trip to the Lake Districts for an 'educational adventure'. Various charity fundraising events throughout the year from cake sales to sponsored swims and fancy dress days – when children can put their sewing skills to good use. Burns Night is celebrated each year with haggis and reeling and there is a programme of lectures from parents and visiting speakers.

Lots of traditional boarding school parents as well as local professional families and about 15 per cent foreign nationals – from Russia, China, Nigeria and Hong Kong, and also popular with Spanish who often come for a year. Arrangements can be made for children of other faiths, but most are happy to attend chapel twice a week and the full choral service on Sundays. Children not overly sophisticated and do not grow up too quickly but they are still self-assured and confident and are very comfortable talking to adults. The head and his wife invite the top year to dinner parties in their house where the children can dress up and hone their conversational skills. Usually about 60 children in at weekends with plenty going on and outings planned – ice skating, clay pigeon shooting, bowling or just going to play on the beach. The top year is allowed 'downtown' into Broadstairs on Sundays where they can spend their pocket money – a much looked forward to privilege, and many opt to stay in for the weekends just for this.

The Friends of Wellesley House organises social events and fundraising activities including lunches for new parents, quiz nights, the bonfire night and other parties including the recent Wellesley Fest.

A small and extraordinarily caring prep school with traditional values which produces self-assured and considerate children who go on to schools all over the country.

Wellington Junior School

Linked school: Wellington School

South Street, Wellington, TA21 8NT

- Pupils: 200; 180 day, 20 board (year 6 only) • Ages: 3–11
- C of E • Fees: Day £5,250–£9,750; Boarding £15,870–£19,845 pa
- Independent

Tel: 01823 668800
Email: admin@wellington-school.org.uk
Website: www.wellington-school.org.uk

Head: Since September 2010, Mr Adam Gibson, (mid forties). A Wellington pupil himself, he was previously head of Manor House Honiton, which closed in 2010. He is a triathlete and takes a running club at the school as well teaching some ICT and maths. Adept at analysis, having had an earlier career in information systems, he is dab hand at tracking and assessing pupils' progress. Achievement is monitored in conjunction with their cognitive ability and quick action taken if potential is not being realised. Despite these skills he is essentially a people person. He and his deputy meet children and parents in the playground each morning so that he can assess each child's mood, pick up parental concerns. 'A child should be happy, confident, prepared to experiment and think differently. Every child should be inspired every day.' Looking round this delightful school it is easy to believe in inspired pupils! Mr Gibson has a son in year 9 and is pleased to find that the spirit of the school is similar to his day.

Entrance: Not selective but those who won't cope are 'turned away gently'. They won't admit anyone who won't make the senior school.

Exit: 90 to 95 per cent go on to the senior school, the remainder are either scholarship winners to other schools or go to the state system. Junior School children take the same exam as outsiders.

Remarks: Parents wax lyrical about the junior school. Several, with children recently moved, note their offspring blossoming in attitude and confidence. Established and built in 1999, the building, Mr Gibson considers, needs trees to soften its edges. Meanwhile the playground is full of timber play equipment, puzzles and trails painted on walls and tarmac, a lovely Wendy house for tinies and even the fenceposts are shaped like coloured pencils! In the library colourful little mats looking like open books invite children to sit and read while the big central atrium has a chess board carpet. Assemblies, indoor PE, lunches and anything needing space happen here but carpets are spotless even at the end of the day. The surrounding corridors are wide enough to have recesses with seats and table for extra teaching or just chatting.

One classroom boasts a real ex BBC Dalek, while a wall we passed was covered with writing exercises in which some observant children had enjoyed 'comparing father with a gorilla' – the children's writing was workmanlike and the gorilla had the advantage! Lessons, even the serious ones, looked fun, from the enchanting animal songs in the nursery to the studious reading in an older year. Children are screened both for learning difficulties and for physical mobility – 'the motor skills are so vital to development'. Learning support team works in class and withdraws pupils where necessary, giving particular attention to the exam year.

Younger children get out of the town environment for Forest School days spent in their Blackdown hills site, wellies, anoraks and all! In all weathers, snow, rain or shine – except for high winds (dangerous in forests) – they enjoy a muddy natural learning environment, exploring and gaining skills such as making clay oven damper bread and eggs scrambled in a plastic bag! Older children have nature study day projects and a survival course, successful enough for pupils to enjoy teaching their parents a thing or two when they are allowed to join in.

Masses of sport with rugby number one for boys and netball (now at national level) for girls. Though it's pretty competitive, one parent recounted with gratitude that her eager but disappointed son had been completely consoled by spending match time learning to make a cake! Wellington Junior holds the national Under 11 title for cross-country.

The music department has an orchestra where even beginners can join in. As well as classrooms the upper floor, arranged around the wide corridor with windows down to the central atrium, has dedicated art space, music teaching rooms for class (with lots of instruments and keyboards) and individual lessons.

There are a few boarders who 'go home' to the junior house shared with the main school. An ex junior boarder in the seniors explained that this is an excellent transition as you already feel part of the senior school when you move up in year 7. School is from 8.35 – 3.30 or 3.45 but the day extends either end from 8 am to 6 pm offering a range of clubs and homework sessions.

Enchanting toddlers group 'Little Wellies' for pre school age.

A joyful school full of pleasant surprises but there is no doubt about its serious educational standards. From 2014 the school will be known as Wellington Preparatory School.

Wellington School Primary

Linked school: Wellington School

Carleton Turrets, Craigweil Road, Ayr, KA7 2XH

• Pupils: 160 boys and girls • Ages: 3–11 • Fees: £5,463–£9,910 pa • Independent

Tel: 01292 269321
Email: info@wellingtonschool.org
Website: www.wellingtonschool.org

Head of juniors: Since January 2014, Mr Jimmy Cox, previously assistant head of Craigclowan Prep.

Exit: All to senior school

Remarks: See senior school.

Wells Cathedral Junior School

Linked school: Wells Cathedral School

8 New Street, Wells, BA5 2LQ

• Pupils: 155 boys and girls; 6 board; 12 in the nursery • Ages: 3–11 • C of E • Fees: Boarding £21,726; Day £6,747–£12,492 pa • Independent

Tel: 01749 834400
Email: juniorschool@wells-cathedral-school.com
Website: www.wells-cathedral-school.com

Head: Since 2011, Mrs Katherine Schofield, previously deputy head of Combe Down School, Bath. After graduating from Goldsmith's, University of London, she spent five years teaching at inner city primary schools in London, with a short stint in India working in a mission school. Then eight years in Bath as a class teacher, manager, deputy and head before coming to Wells. She has led two quite different schools: one successful and oversubscribed primary school; the other a large junior school requiring some rapid improvement. She is a member of the National College for School Leaders and has completed the National Professional Qualification for Headship.

She is married with two children; husband, Paul, takes the lead role at home, enabling her to be fully focused on her role as head. She enjoys choral singing, visiting and reading about other countries and cultures, gardening, swimming and camping with her family.

Entrance: No assessment tests for pre-prep but 'friendly' tests for all for the junior school. On the edge of full most of the time. Chorister auditions in January and June.

Exit: The vast majority of pupils go on to the Wells Cathedral School senior school.

Remarks: Sunny, bright buildings with lovely gardens, well maintained and used frequently as outdoor classrooms. A lush conservatory is also used as teaching resource – hot, though. Enthusiastic staff, many of whom have been with the school for a long time – some have never taught anywhere else. Pre-prep includes small, cheery nursery, reception class and years 1 and 2 in very brightly coloured classrooms. There are four year groups and classes are small – 10-18.

In the arts, even the nursery children receive specialist music and drama teaching, and the school has won the Artsmark Gold Award. Every second year a cast of 50 pupils performs to sell-out audiences at the Edinburgh Fringe. Community drama and music workshops on Saturday mornings. Highly-thought-of choir consists of 18 boy and 18 girl choristers (two separate choirs) plus adults. Plenty of sport also available, with matches against nearby schools.

Westbourne House School

Shopwyke, Chichester, PO20 2BH

- Pupils: 446; 170 boys/ 140 girls; 107 boarders • Ages: 3–13 • C of E
- Fees: Boarding £18,675; Day £13,200–£15,225 pa • Independent

Tel: 01243 782739
Email: office@westbournehouse.org
Website: www.westbournehouse.org

Headmaster: Since April 2011, Mr Martin Barker BEd Exeter (forties), four years as deputy before – previously at Papplewick in Ascot. Married to Helen – she also teaches, masterminds special projects for the scholarship forms and organises charitable initiatives and donations. They met at university where she concentrated on primary, he on science and PE. Daughter and a son both at Westbourne and a place near the Everglades for what little non-Westbourne time they have. He's tall and approachable (kids agree), passionate about good teaching having been burnt by the opposite at a grammar school (in the 80s...). His initial brief was on the academic side (brought a database for recording marks to the school) and an impressive scholarship rate backs up the governors' appointment. So far he's also applied this talent for rationalising systems to the school day, delegation within the teaching staff and boarding options – the result is a more formal structure but parents say a more relaxed atmosphere, 'fewer meetings, the ones that happen count'. Reassuringly, he is most proud of the pastoral improvement – 'reduction in unkindness with the shorter break in the afternoon' – and that the kids are 'rounded and grounded – and so in demand for senior schools'. Still teaches year 8 chemistry and coaches rugby and cricket.

Entrance: Very local school – biggest commute 40 minutes away, 50 per cent of families London migrants. Also local farmers, entrepreneurs (some semi-retired), medics (St Richard's Chichester nearby) and Rolls Royce. Diverse lot – double incomes, single parents and the wealthy. Reputation locally for pushy parents. Best entry point at reception/year 1 – 75 per cent – unfiltered for nursery and pre-prep, ability assessment for entry to year 3. SEN would have to be seriously limiting to be turned away – support both in class or with a small group extracted. Composition of intake dictated by composition of new families – waiting lists for years 2,3 and 5 – very hard to keep spaces open later in school if siblings arrive en masse eg from London. Fifty per cent scholarships available for music and some for academic excellence. Means-tested bursaries available for current families, five per cent off for siblings. Continuation scholarships with links to Radley and Cranleigh – entry point year 7 at present, could be changed to year 5 to ensure they have the best chance in senior schools.

Exit: Boarders can build up from three nights in year 7 to full week in year 8 – vital preparation for the 60 per cent who go on to boarding schools. Top three destinations are Brighton, Canford and Wellington. Portsmouth Grammar is the only popular day school but the train journey puts some parents off. Aims for half a dozen each year to eg Seaford, Lancing, Eton, Benenden, Hurstpierpoint, Cranleigh, Radley, Marlborough, Downe House, St Mary's Ascot, Bryanston, Sherborne. Scholarship hit rate an arrestingly high 35 per cent of all leavers. Eminent outgoers include R4's Marcus Brigstocke (funny) and the late Nick Clarke (news); Monarch of the Glen, Alastair McKenzie; England women's cricketer Holly Colvin

Remarks: Founded as a family school and the atmosphere remains – the original owners, now in their 80s, still live on site (just beyond some wire lions as you enter the beautiful grounds) and continue to be part of school life. Early Victorian main house, sandwiched between beach and the Downs, pupils here stay kids for longer than those in more urban schools and staff make sure they are ready for entry to secondary schools by the time they leave.

School ethos grew out of scouting – the fleur-de-lys logo is sprinkled about and patrol leaders are voted in (panther, tiger, otter and owl) each term. In the summer the mothers of troop leaders (heads of school) present the prizes – this family involvement is characteristic, whether it is houseparents with children at the school, the parental barometer on teaching standards, support on the games pitches or siblings in different years. A parent could pick up at three different times each day – from nursery, pre-prep and prep – the hanging around can be frustrating but also means relationships are built and social events are surprisingly well-attended.

Children love it here – their favourite parts are the communal ones – form rooms, chapel, the millennium hall, picnics after Saturday morning lessons, BBQ night in the summer – the astounding attraction of a sausage in a bun! They respond to the humanity of teachers and understand the thinking behind structures in the school eg how cleaning works in dining room; that playing in bases (dens) in the boundaries (woods) is organised by rota now – to avoid any tussles or rivalries between age groups. Boarding is popular, now upgraded with two new year boarding houses, presided over by houseparents, caring matrons and fun gappers.

ICT is omnipresent to free up staff and pupil time for learning and playing – ideally, as in the world outside. Four trolleys of Apple Macs, wifi – no issues with gaming, kids say they save that for home if they are into it. Older boarders can use iPods before bed. Smartboards in every classroom – yet, as ever, only some teachers use them to the pupils' best advantage. Landlines on wall for calling home – no need or time for mobile phones or Angry Birds apparently. Newspapers as well as screens in the library (due to be revamped).

Breadth in the curriculum, backed up by good facilities. New food tech and science labs, French vocab on doors in main school, ceramics studio a popular retreat (sometimes there's hot chocolate and often CDs playing), stunning art, sparky technology projects, drama opportunities both on, back and above stage, a lake for kayaking (sailing soon), indoor pool and Astroturf. The purpose-built music school fosters a full range – harpists to advert theme tune composers, 80 per cent of children learn an instrument. Peripatetic music teachers mean a catch up period is vital for missed academic lessons.

The risk with such a range of well-supported subjects (and the results to match them) is choice and activity overload, no space left for aimless mucking around (the risk assessed alternative to climbing trees?). Shorter lessons, no time between them, a longer break in the morning, scholarship sets – the long prep at the end of the day is a crowd-pleaser since no homework – the disadvantage is that parents don't see books when they come home. The proof is in the pudding though – really happy families.

W

Westbourne School (Junior)

Linked school: Westbourne School (Senior)

60 Westbourne Road, Sheffield, S10 2QT

• Pupils: 139 boys and girls • Ages: 3–11 all day • Fees: £7,890–£9,600 pa • Independent

Tel: 0114 2660374
Email: admin@westbourneschool.co.uk
Website: www.westbourneschool.co.uk

Head of Junior School: Since 2010 Mr Jon Clark BA PGCE (late 30s). Educated at Sheffield state secondary and Sheffield University, taught in Derbyshire state primary, then Westbourne 2006, deputy head 2007; teaches history, maths, ICT and games and is a year 6 form tutor. Warm and approachable, say parents, 'lovely... knows the children very well'; 'very motivating for the children and an excellent teacher'; very energetic, enthusiastic and involved. Proponent of brain gym (eg lunch time juggling) and building on identification of preferred learning styles and dominant hemisphere – though not all educationalists would now agree. Keen to develop stretch for more able children. Married with two small children destined for Westbourne; enjoys watching football, gardening, reading.

Entrance: Taster day – participation in an ordinary school day (specific day chosen to suit the child's interests) with light touch assessment (IQ, maths, creative writing), including dyslexia screening.

Exit: Almost all to senior school, some with scholarships (academic, music, sport, all-rounder). Some means-tested bursaries.

Remarks: Founded in 1885 as a prep school for 'the education of the children of Sheffield gentlemen'; became co ed in 1997. Situated in Broomhill, a pleasant residential area, close to a big hospital and two universities. Good size classrooms with colourful displays; lovely, light reception room with access to outside; large modern science lab, library in a gracious room with bay window, carpet and beanbags – well supplied with enticing fiction, but some bookcases with shelves in need of attention. Computerised system managed very confidently by a year 6; older children consulted about book choices. Covered, open and adventure playgrounds plus lawned area with veg patch for the youngest ones.

Uses Sats for internal baseline assessment – key stage 2 results well above national average for English and science in particular; very good value-added – small classes: max 16 but could be less. ICT suite, much use of interactive whiteboards, well developed VLE; specialist teachers for French (begun in reception and taught in a lively way, with the assistance of French cartoons and chocolate bars), music, drama and PE. Differentiated work a strength; setting in English and maths in years 5 and 6; after-school maths master class. Philosophy for children throughout and key stage 2 enterprise programme in conjunction with St Luke's hospice, using local business links for support. We saw some exceptionally good year 6 poetry and particularly liked the Roman estate agent's brochures. 'All the teachers have a passion for teaching and for the children,' reported a parent.

Excellent SENCo (for senior school too) – dyslexia support, inside and outside the classroom, especially good. Also covers autism and ADHD but not severe behavioural difficulties; physical disabilities would be a problem as many stairs and no lift. Year 6 nurture group gets extra support and carries through to year 7. High praise from a mother for the way her child had been supported and brought on, especially for the weekly emails on her progress and the handling of her move to the senior school.

Large gym but no courts or field – uses very good local facilities, so lots of choice: usual sports plus basketball, badminton, table tennis, tag rugby, girls' football, water sports, junior sports award; athletics and cross-country popular and strong. Inclusive approach to school teams.

Masses of music – all in years 3 – 5 learn recorder and ukelele, several learn other instruments; choir (tour to Belgium), orchestra, strings and flute groups, rock and jazz bands, several concerts in school and local venues, including Sheffield Cathedral and old people's homes, and a number of year 6s, impressively, take grade 5 theory. Play productions and visiting drama companies, even a street dance workshop. Very interesting and varied art with success in local competitions; food tech in year 6 involves making a healthy two course meal for two for £5 (runs open course in Easter holidays).

Broad range of activities including tae kwon do, climbing, dance, speech and drama, charity fundraising. Lots of local educational trips, residentials in England and abroad – new year 3 – 6 programme on the way.

Three outstanding ISI Early Years Foundation Stage inspections and lots of praise for the other years in recent report. Many parents spoke of the family atmosphere – friendships and activities across years, older children allowed to visit siblings in lunch hour and senior children help out. School council's suggestions are heeded.

Food is controversial (no packed lunches): school puts thought and care into it and provides a decent choice – hot and veggie option plus salad bar, trad pudding with fresh fruit and yoghurts – but not all children and parents happy (school argues you never get total satisfaction for this).

Girls wear very fetching, bottle green, plaid dresses or grey skirt and white shirt with green cardigans/jumpers and blazers; boys wear grey shorts and white shirt; green and silver tie; littlies have green anoraks and year 4s green book bags.

Trad good manners expected. Well-developed reward systems with child-friendly prizes; lots of badges – some blazers groaning with them. Worry box for problems; year 6 buddy scheme. Excellent year 6 transition programme – taster lessons, shared games afternoons with year 7s, tour by senior school pupils, crossover of year 6 and 7 teachers.

Pupils from Sheffield and wide geographical area; mostly professional or business backgrounds, ethnically mixed. Secure, friendly, polite, well-behaved and articulate children.

Parents very happy – plenty of contact: surveys, email, newsletters, school magazine; active PTA; very comprehensive information booklet.

Extended day – breakfast club from 7.45am; creche for reception – year 4 till 5.45pm; years 5 – 6 can stay to do supervised prep till 4.45 or 5.15pm. Pre-school for 3-4 year olds opened in 2013.

An intimate, appealing school where children of a wide range of abilities and types flourish and grow in confidence. Dynamic head promises well.

W

Westminster Abbey Choir School

Dean's Yard, London, SW1P 3NY

• Pupils: 35 boys, all boarders • Ages: 8-13 • C of E • Fees: £6,985 pa – after subsidy • Independent

Tel: 020 7222 6151
Email: headmaster@westminster-abbey.org
Website: www.westminster-abbey.org/choir-school

Headmaster: Since 2002, Mr Jonathan Milton BEd (fiftyish), married, formerly head of The Abbey School in Tewkesbury. Bred, if not born, into the choir school tradition – he was a choral scholar at York. Music was his degree subject, though he now teaches geography. A gentle man, whose quiet, friendly manner betrays a profound love of his unique school, the tradition it enshrines and the community of boys and staff which gives it ever-fresh life. Clearly, an inspired appointment. Mr Milton is, at once, a traditionalist and a moderniser – exactly the right balance for the place. 'When I came, there were no carpets or curtains and it felt tense – that's now completely gone. It was dark too. We've tried to make it gentler.' He showed us the little IT room next to the dormitories, 'it's a marvellous way for boys to stay in touch – much simpler than writing a letter. And the staff communicate with parents every week electronically.' Gentler the school may well be but he has also tightened the academics, keeping step with the outside world in which senior school places are no longer assigned in little chats between heads of 'big' schools and trusted prep heads. Mr Milton's openness, thoughtfulness and warmth are mirrored in his boys. Those we talked to were similarly relaxed, candid and friendly. Head and boys share their view of life here, 'it's tough, you get very tired but... it's fabulous.'

Entrance: No formal entrance test day or the like. Over the year, school will see around 25 boys for voice trials – usually in ones and twos – and usually in year 3. The Master of the Choristers will hear them and the head will chat to the boy and parents and, if the lad looks promising he will be invited back to spend a day in the school. This will include a more formal voice trial, a chance to play their instruments and testing in maths and English. What is looked for is not grade 8 in six instruments but musical aptitude and the kind of attitude to music, community and learning that make for a happy and successful Westminster Abbey chorister. 'They have to enjoy being part of a close-knit team and they must have personality and character,' says Mr Milton. Academic brilliance is less important though, clearly, the boy must enjoy learning. Of the 25 they see, places may be offered to between four and six, on average, though one or two may be invited to come back some months later.

These days, more than half come from state primaries and can be caught up and supported where necessary. 'With year groups of six or seven, we can tailor-make classes,' says head. School fees are subsidised by the Abbey and no-one, however impecunious, should be put off applying if their boy is a natural chorister. Funds will be found. 'Some pay nothing at all,' says Mr Milton. Boys now come from further afield – Yorkshire and even overseas. Quite tough for an eight-year-old, you might think. 'And,' says Mr Milton, 'few of our parents would have chosen a boarding school – when they see it, they realise it's a way of life.' Yes. This represents the most amazing opportunity for the right child and a peerless preparation for life.

Exit: An astonishing list of leavers' destinations over the last three years. Everyone wins a music scholarship to a prestigious school and many win academic and/or art schols too. Most popular senior schools are King's Canterbury, Eton, Winchester with the rest hither and yon, and doing very well wherever they end up.

Remarks: This is the only choir school in the country which is only a choir school – no day pupils, no girls, no non-choristers. Average class size six, maximum is nine – in a way that says it all. The place hums with quiet activity – mental, physical and musical. It all happens in a tall, unobtrusive building in Dean's Yard – right under Big Ben, the Houses of Parliament and Westminster Abbey. Dean's Yard is a grassy square lined by augustly solid houses. Opposite is the modest arch which leads to Westminster School – no connection with the choir school except that the large pupils and the little choristers see each other passing all day which makes the business of scholarship and growing up in this – the heart of the great centre of London – seem quite the normal thing.

Five floors accommodate all learning, admin and living space. All is freshly-painted and feels light, comfortable and well-cared for. There's a super ground floor 'music room' used for assemblies and the like – a splendid stained glass window commemorating Purcell and the other Masters of the Choristers who between them make up a history of English choral music – Gibbons, Blow, Simon Preston et al. Classrooms are small with conventional desks, whiteboards and it all looks a bit dolls house in scale – enhanced, when we visited – during exam week – by the very cuddly teddies (for good luck) sitting reassuringly on desks. More teddies in the dorms which – it is a boys' school – are, if not Spartan, certainly not prettified. Bunk beds with integral cupboards in airy rooms. Good shower rooms, good ICT provision and a very nice sitting room with sofas, piano, TV, books and games and feeling really snug.

Everyone does standard prep school curriculum but flexibility can be built into the system with such small classes and so small a school. Individual help is the norm. No boys with SENs, we are told, though the odd mild dyslexic may creep in. A boy with dyslexia would find chorister-life tough, says Mr Milton – what with having to read music and a foreign language at speed and so on. 'It wouldn't be fair.' Yes. Sports take place via buses to Battersea Park, The Queen Mother Sports centre in Victoria and water sports in Docklands – Mr Milton is a keen sailor. They kayak, rock climb and sail and Mr Milton sees this – and the opportunity to get away from the closed chorister world – as essential for good relations.

Evidence of boy-life and wit abounds. 'WACS Lyrical' – the boys' own noticeboard, details competitions, initiatives, jokes and notices – full of fun and ideas. The art room – open in the evenings – similarly lively – we were terrified by the huge multi-tusked cardboard, paper and paint beast which 'would be tamed by listening to Palestrina'. Boys enjoy textile work, DT – they make fan-powered vehicles for racing, and knitting – 'very popular', we were told. Obviously, music is central to life. Singing practice in the song school happens each morning and each afternoon before evensong – except on Weds and alternate Mons. Instrumental practice is timetabled and very much a normal part of everyday life. Musical guests and ensembles visit, there is a composer in residence – a real privilege for such boys – and school takes full advantage of the concert halls and galleries roundabout. Likewise, the school goes into local primaries – boys take their instruments – to inspire others – 'just to give music a boost'.

What do the boys say – and their parents? 'You have to be very independent and organised,' a seasoned 12-year-old told us. 'You can't rely on your parents to pack your bag and find your pencil case – you have to do it all yourself. You have to manage your own revision and music practice.' (Sounds like a course in choristership might be handy all round!) 'It is very tiring – I'd like to have more of a rest after concerts.' On the other hand – 'singing all the special services we do is brilliant. We did a special service for the spies! (100 years of MI5.) They just looked normal. They don't wear T-shirts saying "I'm a spy".' And 'We're on TV,

W

we go on tours and make CDs.' 'It can be exhausting,' said a parent, 'but they bounce back. It's unbelievably rewarding.' And they clearly enjoy the Abbey community with whom they share Christmas and Easter meals and so on. A choristership here is a treasure. A huge commitment for boys and family while it lasts but a gift for life.

Westminster Cathedral Choir School

Ambrosden Avenue, London, SW1P 1QH

- Pupils: 165; 30 boarding choristers, 135 day boys • Ages: 7–13
- RC • Fees: Choristers (boarding) £8,175; Day £15,285 pa
- Independent

Tel: 020 7798 9081
Email: office@choirschool.com
Website: www.choirschool.com

Headmaster: Since 2007, Mr Neil McLaughlan (early forties). Married with a young son and daughter, and a man who radiates humour, decency and charm in equal measure. Read philosophy and politics at Durham and spent a few years with Andersen Consulting in London before embarking on a teaching career in 1997. After spells at Stonyhurst and Worth, he took up a post as head of English and director of development at Downside School, before joining WCCS as headmaster. He hopes to be there 'for the duration.' Parents hope so too. 'Lovely guy!' said one. 'So easy to approach!' said another. 'An extremely dedicated head and a great promoter of the school,' said a third. Typically modest, he hopes to do 'lots and lots of small things right.' We think he's doing lots of big things right too. Under his visionary yet kindly leadership, this has become an inspiring school that is going from strength to strength.

Entrance: Main entry points for day boys are at 7+, where 14-15 places are available, and 8+ (a further eight or so places). Applicants sit tests in English, maths and non verbal reasoning in January of the year before entry. Occasional places in other year groups, notably at 11+. The school is always over-subscribed, and, once boys have met the required academic standard, will give preference where possible to practising Roman Catholics and to boys with a brother at the school.

Choristers, who must be catholic and must be boarders, join at 8+. Would-be probationers have to pass informal and formal tests with the Cathedral's master of music, as well as succeeding at the academic assessment; and if they manage all that, they spend two nights at the school to see whether chorister life will suit them. Only then will they be offered one of the six available places. As the school's popularity grows, so inevitably does the competition; there are now half a dozen serious candidates for each choristership, and for the first time in over a decade, the school has not had to go recruiting for them.

Up to full fees assistance for choristers; none for day pupils, whose families just have to fork out. As a result, there is more cultural than social diversity here. Boys come from a wide range of nationalities, among them France, Spain, Italy, Russia, Ghana and Korea, making this a truly international school. With 79 per cent of the boys now from Catholic families, the school is less religiously diverse than it was, but remains open to day boys of all faiths provided their families are happy to support the school's Catholic ethos.

Exit: The head has worked tirelessly to raise the school's profile, and WCCS's exit record is superb. Boys regularly leave for boarding schools like Eton, Winchester and Ampleforth, and for a raft of top London schools, including Westminster, St Paul's, City Of London, KCS Wimbledon and Dulwich College. 'The school is much more linked into the senior schools than it was a few years ago,' reported one satisfied parent. 'Oh yes, the head's always going on about schools,' confirmed one of the boys, equally.

Remarks: The school was endearingly shabby once, but not any more. A five-year programme of refurbishment has just finished, and everything is now bang-up-to-date. Visitors are welcomed in the beautiful glass-fronted foyer, where handwritten 'Music for Mass' schedules from 1905 are hung beside huge photos of current pupils radiating health and cheeriness. Throughout the building, ceilings, floors and lighting are all new, and all the classrooms are gleaming and well resourced, with interactive whiteboards in each one. But the large and much-loved playground, where boys play 'crazy games' on the climbing apparatus, remains the same. 'That was a real selling point for me,' said one parent, 'Although it means wearing out shoes a lot quicker, the boys have a chance to be boys.' 'The way to the heart of little boys is good food and football at playtime, and WCCS excels in both,' confirmed another. We didn't try the football, but we can confirm that the food is splendid, a delicious combination of tasty and healthy. Boarding facilities have also been upgraded. We can't comment on the refurbished boarders' common room, because a curmudgeonly old trumpet teacher therein told us we were interrupting his lesson and to get out, but we did manage to see the sleeping accommodation, which was cheerful, light and airy. The rigours of chorister life notwithstanding, feedback on the boarding experience from both parents and boys was uniformly positive. 'The key thing,' says head, 'is to have good, kind people around the boys, good accommodation and excellent food. An army marches on its stomach.'

Years ago, parents had disquiets about aspects of WCCS. Nowadays, they cannot find enough superlatives with which to express their delight. 'We have been thrilled by both the teaching and pastoral care provided by the school.' 'The staff generate a wonderfully positive energy.' 'It's an amazing school, the teachers are so kind!' 'You couldn't choose a better school, I recommend it to everyone.' 'A wonderful warmth and care is present everywhere.'

A father of a new chorister told us, 'My son absolutely loves it. He's thrilled to pieces. The first weekend they were eligible to go home, he didn't want to come.' (Poor mum!) And a mother of two day pupils wrote, 'Happiness is guaranteed at this school; it is such a nurturing, caring and stimulating environment. I can honestly say that the only problem I have ever had is to find a way to drag my boys out of the playground and back home at the end of the day.' What's behind this remarkable success? 'The one ingredient a Catholic school should have is joy,' said the head when we asked him, simply and without any side.

There is joy in the teaching here, that's for sure. A quiet revolution is taking place in the WCCS curriculum that made this reviewer go all excited and wobbly at the knees. Schemes of work have been painstakingly redesigned, with scholarship and a genuine love of learning at their heart. 'The idea is to present knowledge as a unified whole,' explained the head, 'so for instance, whilst they're studying Adam and Eve in RS, they'll be doing C S Lewis's The Magician's Nephew in English. Likewise, we use geometry and graph-plotting in maths to support map skills in geography, and they'll draw antique maps in art at the same time. If the boys are doing the human body in science, they'll look at what the Greeks and Romans discovered about it in history.' The boys we spoke to praised the lessons as 'really good fun,' adding, 'The work's challenging, but in a good way'.

Much emphasis on poetry, with poems studied every week, as well as learnt by heart and declaimed. 'We want them to know the great poets of the English language,' said the deputy head, and to further this, the school has produced its own wonderful anthologies, where the selection is 'unashamedly classic.' In addition to regular English lessons, boys receive two lessons a week on formal grammar and punctuation, and Latin is compulsory from the off – 'Latin is crucial for grammar, it's not an academic luxury,' insisted the deputy head. 'As an international school, the story of the world's great civilisations interests us. But children of this age also need connections, and they need the basics.' All those who have wrung their hands at the disjointed, shallow content of so many modern lessons, lift up your hearts and hope.

This is clearly a scholarly yet joyful environment, and the quality of student work we saw reflected that. We read, misty-eyed, a set of poems by the year 7s about Westminster Bridge (inspired by Wordsworth's sonnet) that were outstandingly creative and well-written; likewise, a history essay on Thomas a Beckett was not only mature and insightful, but skilful and lucid in its use of language. But mightn't this approach favour only the brightest? WCCS's SENCo emphatically denied it, asserting that boys at the school with SEN benefited from understanding how language works. We were impressed with the support the school gives to those with dyslexia and dyspraxia, as well as to ESL students, such as the two grave and courteous Russian boys we saw having extra English tutorials. And all the staff we met were purposeful, well-bred (curmudgeon excepted), cultivated, devoted to what they do, and, according to parents, 'incredibly dedicated.'

As you'd expect, the standard of music here is outstanding. The choristers are completely immersed in music making at the highest level (listen to the downloads on the website, and marvel), and the day boys, swimming in the same element, also achieve great things. We saw year 8 boys composing their entries for the school's Christmas carol competition, and heard much excellent instrumental playing as we went round the school. 'The music programme is amazing,' enthused one parent, 'My son's piano playing has come on by leaps and bounds in just a few weeks.' Many pupils achieve grades seven or eight in their chosen instrument(s) by the time they leave.

Football, rugby and cricket are the main sports here, played at local pitches, and swimming and PE are held at the nearby Queen Mother Sports Centre. Lots of extra-curricular activities, including debating, philosophy, chess, Scrabble, code-breaking, the Airfix model club, current affairs, and cross country running. 'But where do you run?' we asked, glancing with some surprise at the surrounding streets. 'Oh!' said our tour guide, 'Green Park, Hyde Park, St James's...'

Lucky lads, you might think. And they are, of course. But what struck us most about this lovely little school, was how considerate, well-mannered and sanguine about life its pupils seemed to be. They are achieving great things, while remaining likeable and happy boys. As one mother wrote, 'My son is neither Catholic nor musical, but has been recognised for other things he has to contribute to the school. They're grounded children with good values. It's a perfect place for my son to grow into a confident young man.' We agree with her. For boys fortunate enough to come here, this is as near perfect as it gets.

Westminster Under School

Adrian House, 27 Vincent Square, London, SW1P 2NN

• Pupils: 265 boys; all day; • Ages: 7–13; • C of E; • Fees: £15,750 pa; • Independent

Tel: 020 7821 5788
Email: under.school@westminster.org.uk
Website: www.westminsterunder.org.uk

Master: Since 2010, Mrs Elizabeth Hill MA CertEd DipEd. Previously deputy head of Dulwich Prep for 15 years. Educated at Leeds Girls' High School, Homerton College, Cambridge followed by an MA in education at London University. Spent 13 years teaching science, physical education and PSHE in maintained sector comprehensive schools in London. Was head of department, housemistress then senior teacher at Camden Girls, deputy head of Raines Foundation and spent one year at Alleyn's Junior School. An Inspector for ISI, she is married to Humphrey, with five children – three sons and two daughters (now university and beyond).

Entrance: Boys sit tests in maths, English and reasoning and all are interviewed by Mrs Hill. Entrance points are at 7+, 8+ and 11+. While other schools are experiencing a drop in the number of applicants, Westminster's numbers are soaring. In recent years, there have been six for each place at the first two stages and nine for each place at 11+. Applicants come from many pre-preps, among which figure Wetherby, Eaton House, Norland Place, Garden House, Eaton Square, Hampstead Hill, Mulberry House, St John's Wood, Knightsbridge School, Basset House, Orchard House and Charterhouse Square. At 11+, they come from Ravenscourt Park, Kew College, Blackheath Prep and a large number of state primaries. Mrs Hill will not poach boys from other top preps which teach up to 13 so very few move across from these, despite the temptations of a perceived cruise into Westminster School – 'Great School'. However, it should be appreciated that this is a small school. Only 20 are taken into each of the first two years and a further 25 at 11.

This smallness of the Under School needs to be understood by parents. There are vastly more very able applicants than Mrs Hill has places for. Jack's brilliance in Whiteboard House and his pre-eminence there in music, sports, languages and art may well be matched by other boys from St Elsewhere's and his possible failure to gain a place at the Under School has to be seen in this context. However, the intake at 11+ gives truly able boys from state primaries a real chance, and there are bursaries available for the genuinely needy which can provide for up to 100 per cent of fees and which continue into the senior school. More than 50 per cent of the intake at 11 is from the state primaries. Since 2001, no boy who has entered at 11 has failed to make the grade for Great School.

Exit: An average of 80 per cent of Under School pupils continue to Westminster School. Of the rest, most go to Eton and a few to Marlborough, Winchester, Highgate, St Paul's, Bradfield, Harrow and City of London. No flops then. They achieve between them an average of 16 awards per year – ie more than 25 per cent get awards. Most parents send their boys to the Under School in hopes of an eventual easy transition to Dean's Yard, but the pre-test in year 6, which results in conditional places for most, will be inconclusive for some – most frequently because the boy's maths is felt to be less than impressive. Certainly, more emphasis – here as elsewhere – is now placed on maths as a diagnostic and this, here as elsewhere, allows less leeway for the wayward genius whose talents lie in other intellectual areas – a development we regret, but not one for which the fault can be lain at the door of the Under School. We can recall a number of Westminster School boys who were given places despite their maths and who had distinguished academic careers thereafter. Boys frequently make immense progress in years 7 and 8 and further assessments take place in those years. As Mrs Hill says, 'the aim is for every boy to move on to the school of his choice.'

Remarks: A top prep in the heart of London. You would walk past it if you didn't know – this unimposing, five-storey redbrick building at the south-west corner of Vincent Square. The square itself surprises – large, even for a London square – and, though only yards from the dusty din of Vauxhall Bridge Road, is tranquil and leafy. The square is fringed by a mix of architectural styles, including some splendid Georgian stuff, but the real surprise is its green centre – playing fields, grass and all-weather – topped off by a small but unmistakable pavilion. And for much of each day small, high-pitched boys rush around playing games or troop cheerfully across the narrow road up the steps into school. Very few London preps have such space on their doorstep, and although it is shared with the pupils at the Great School, it is very much part of the Under School and its attractiveness. Inside, the building has been extensively refurbished, creating three new classrooms and two additional specialist teaching rooms. The surprise is the huge hall. This brand new building, adjacent to the Under School, comprises a dining hall and a bright art department as well as conference rooms.

Everyone takes a standard curriculum, Latin being added in year 6 and Greek in year 8. Sport is now good and enthusiastic. Football and cricket are the main sports but rugby, basketball, hockey, tennis, swimming and athletics also feature. High achievement is normal. In previous years the school won the IAPS General Knowledge quiz, the senior choir reached the finals of the BBC Radio 3 Choir of the Year and the 1st XI cricket team were unbeaten. Chess is a popular activity and the school team goes from strength to strength. The school produces major successes in drama and art alongside numerous other academic triumphs.

Between five and 10 per cent of boys have special needs, the vast majority mild dyslexia or dyspraxia. The school has a lift and can accommodate wheelchairs in all but a few tight corners – and has done so. The Study Skills Coordinator spends two days a week at the school and has one-to-one sessions with those who need her support. The special needs help is praised by parents. Just about all boys could be described as gifted and talented. In year 8, boys are divided into two scholarship classes and two CE classes, much to the chagrin of a few but 'usually parents accede in the end and it works out for the best.'

Classes are orderly, civilised and quivery with cerebral activity and fun. Excellent displays – of work and of interesting information – cover every wall. The library has a wonderful mix of fiction, from CS Forester, Agatha Christie and Ian Fleming to Caroline Lawrence and Garry Kilworth, with comforting dollops of Blyton to gladden the hearts of ancient visitors. It doubles as a bookshop on Mondays and is good source of print info of all kinds. Art is lovely, varied and imaginative. Splendid models, drawings, collages and paintings are wonderfully expressive of guidance and the opening of minds rather than instruction. Boys are taught in groups of only seven to 10 and, from year 5, all do history of art complete with gallery visits. How civilised is that? A top-class computer room also accommodates 'our brilliant technician'. Boys enthuse, 'he always helps with problems – even at home.' Music is exceptional and standards attained exemplary. There is an impressive range of ensembles and events for so small a school – jazz band, brass group, string quartets, two orchestras, two choirs, House music competition, choir tours to Belgium, Brazil, USA, China etc every two years. Everyone is encouraged to be involved in the musical life of the school. Some reach grade 8 before they leave and grade 5 is usual. We enjoyed the crumhorns and shawms fixed to the wall in the director of music's office – a nice change from recorders and triangles.

The clientele is, inevitably, moneyed and brainy, but the mix changes at 11 when those from the state schools and the preps which end at 11 join – most of whom import lots more brain but less money. School manages social matters expertly and the master is keen that if not 'all shall have prizes', then honours are equitably distributed. There is a different head boy for each of the three year 8 terms and virtually everyone will be a house captain or some such officer. Prizes, too, are awarded with care to reward as many as possible and not always the same cleverclogs.

It was hard to find a critical parent. 'Our boys absolutely love it,' we were told – and told. 'The school knows how to deal with the most energetic and the brainiest – they always find new challenges for them.' 'They are wonderfully caring when pupils hit problems – academic or emotional.' 'The care is very individual.' 'Even though everyone is clever, they are always eager to support you if you have a blip.' 'The staff are wonderful – the teaching is great.' The sports are much better now – brilliant director of PE.' 'The food is great – it's far better now.' And so on.

To be happy here a boy must love learning and love the fun of exploring. This is as far from being a crammer as you can get. But, for the brightest and most intellectually curious, as one seasoned parent said, 'without question, the best.'

Westonbirt Prep School

Linked school: Westonbirt School

Westonbirt, Tetbury, GL8 8QG

- Pupils: 130 boys and girls; all day • Ages: 3–11 • C of E
- Fees: £6,795–£10,275 pa • Independent

Tel: 01666 881400
Email: prep@westonbirt.org
Website: www.westonbirt.org

Headmaster: Since September 2009, Mr Neil Shaw BA MA PGCE (thirties), educated at Nottingham High School before reading geography at Exeter, then PGCE at Nottingham and MA at Loughborough. Began career at St George's, Edgbaston, where he was promoted to deputy headship, thence to first headship at Kingswood School, Solihull. Married with one daughter. His high energy levels were put to the test, but parental consensus is that he has won on most fronts. Following the merger (see below) and his appointment to the 'new' post thus created, he won over quite a few by holding evening sessions (in the term before he took up his post) to listen to parental concerns from both camps. Pro-active and determined and, school tells us, now very much appreciated.

Entrance: Visit, then taster day when child is assessed in classroom situation.

Exit: 11+ entry to Westonbirt most likely route for girls; otherwise either sex to local grammars, comprehensives or other independents that admit at 11.

Remarks: Created by the merger of Rose Hill (long established and traditional co-ed prep formerly at Alderley, Gloucestershire) and Querns Westonbirt in August 2008 and rebranded in 2013 as Westonbirt Prep. The good news is that the remodelling of the school produced two much improved buildings (plus some useful temporary accommodation) where previously one. A converted girls' boarding house provides the multi-purpose school hall, office accommodation and some pleasant classrooms for older pupils. Former Querns building works well for the younger ones and includes hard, bark and grass outside play areas. Nearby copse is being integrated as an 'outdoor classroom' space. Parents love the way that pupils play and share together across the age groups and praise the 'family feel'. Flourishing nursery and highly successful reception class feed the lower years. Parents we spoke to were very impressed with both the teaching and the level of care all the way through the school.

Learning support is well co-ordinated from designated area, The Beehive, and moves straight in with appropriate (individual or small group) help as soon as a need is seen by teachers. One mother praised this positive intervention, telling us how her daughter now loved reading as a result and was 'zooming through her books'. At five she was also playing the piano and loving her sport. Gosh.

W

Separate ICT suite for year 3 upwards and pupils benefit from proximity of super sports, music and other facilities shared with the senior school. Vibrant art area (temporary accommodation proved versatile here) supports sculpture and fashion as well as regular art classes; French is introduced from nursery level. Music teacher cited as 'miraculous'. Forty children have individual music tuition. Singing, recorder and other instrumental groups; 'outstanding concerts and musical productions,' we were told. Choir performs locally and pupils are entered for Cheltenham Festival music and drama events, as well as LAMDA examinations, in which they excel. Visits out of school are many and varied: educational for all age groups and lots of sporting fixtures for 7+.

Lots of parental involvement and fun activities with and without the children: karting for all ages, parental rock band, Querns and Roses, lined up for summer ball gig. Children 'love it' and parents we spoke to describe it as 'a fabulous school'. Westonbirt Prep is now established in its dedicated rôle of providing a happy educational environment for 3-11 year olds.

Westville House School

Carter's Lane, Middleton, Ilkley, West Yorkshire, LS29 0DQ

- Pupils: 137 pupils, 77 boys/60 girls; day only • Ages: 3-11 • C of E
- Fees: £4,680-£8,100 pa • Independent

Tel: 01943 608053
Email: westville@epals.com
Website: www.westvilleschool.co.uk

Headteacher: Since 2013, Ms Rosey James, previously deputy head, who stepped up to the leadership role after the sudden death of Charles Holloway. She joined the school 18 years ago as maths and science teacher, and became deputy head in 2005.

Entrance: Non selective – accepts first 21 pupils on list at three years. Usually about 15 join in nursery with further five at reception age. Put onto list asap – even pre-birth. Taster day for entry higher up. Free weekly mother and toddler session for public as well as parents affords a chance to view the school and meet up with other mums (helps with marketing, of course).

Three or four means tested bursaries, mostly used to support parents who fall on hard times – restricted funds.

Exit: Usually to first choice schools eg Bradford Grammar School, Grammar School at Leeds, Sedbergh, Giggleswick, Ashville College, Ermysted's Grammar School, Skipton Girls' High, Harrogate Ladies', St Olave's, York.

Remarks: Non selective – majority above national average, up to a fifth below, one tenth very bright. Pupils expected to stay till 11 years – not prepared for admission to other junior or prep schools. Excellent rating for academic achievement, progress made by all abilities and pupil-teacher relationships in 2010 ISI inspection, though caveats about variable marking standards and stretching of the gifted – school is addressing these issues. School asserts success based on staff knowing the children very well individually and close contact with parents. Strong Sats results and scholarships record and no gender gap. Regularly successful in local (Leeds Grammar School) maths challenge – has reached finals of a national one.

Well-equipped, up-to-date IT suite – touch typing taught; three interactive whiteboards shared by teachers. Very thorough approach to assessment (CATS tests in years 3-5), tracking and monitoring. Enthusiastic, friendly, well-established teachers who develop children's potential very well, according to

parents; quite a few males around. Class size: average 15, max 21. DT taught as part of science and art programme – limited range (children we met keen to have more, eg cookery).

ISI praised SEN provision and we agree – has strong interest in gifted and talented plus very thoughtful and flexible approach towards those with learning difficulties. Covers dyslexia, mild behavioural/social problems, mild autism, dyspraxia, visual impairment, but permanent disabilities would be too difficult as no lifts. Additional pre-prep SENCo. In class small group support (free) or one-to-one (parents pay); initial dyslexia testing free, then parents use Dyslexia Action; visiting specialist – extra charge for her lessons; uses local authority for support and whole staff training, as needed.

Pre-prep – light classrooms with very good displays. EYFS outstanding in all respects, says ISI – well-equipped nursery with two rooms; offers morning session (nursery – about 15 happy and busy children) and afternoon session (Fledglings) for structured play/childcare; also after-school care till 6pm.

Full range of traditional sports plus gymnastics – generally successful in local matches, strong swimming and cricket up to national level; annual rugby and netball North Yorkshire tour for all year 6s; uses Ilkley rugby and cricket clubs but own new sports field due to be ready this year – a major project fulfilled; swimming in Ilkley; will adapt school day to accommodate gifted sports/music/ballet children.

Good size music room with several keyboards, senior and junior choir for all and selected chamber choir, guitar group; annual musical plus local community performances; plenty of drama too.

Heaps of art on all walls, including large framed self-portraits in head's office – variety of media but main emphasis on painting; recent mega-sized gift of tiptop art supplies from a parent in the biz will no doubt be well used.

Thursday afternoon is clubs time – mixed ages and broad range, following staff interests, eg chess, juggling, arts and crafts, ocarina, bridge, outdoor pursuits. Keen eco led by children – Green Flag award, grow own vegetables in large garden. Charity fund-raising – links with school in Africa. Plenty of local and regional trips – year 6, unusually, have three residentials (science and geography; sports tour; outward bound).

Founded in Ilkley 1960 for boys and girls 5-11 years; moved to present site on edge of town 1992 when added nursery section. Main building is white with blue trimmings, reminiscent of a seaside hotel – originally a nurses' home; makes for a conveniently compact site but limits space. Front overlooks Ilkley and has playground with two climbing frames, wooden pagoda and lawn, plus fine woodland classroom, built with local authority early years money, sporting willow igloos, wooden minimalist tepees and handsome bug-inspection station. Light classrooms with trad wooden desks and lovely views of moors and woods; décor reasonably fresh throughout; striking, rather charming, modern stained glass window depicting a long-serving head reading to some children. All very neat – even the amazingly bare changing rooms. Vast multi-purpose hall used for performances and sport. Smallish trad library – good selection of fiction organised into categories, less impressive reference section, plus very appealing, huge teddy bear sprawled on the floor; just one computer.

Comfortable family atmosphere – children make friends across years and older ones look out for younger ones, said a parent; whole families often go through, parents and grandparents come in to help or share expertise. Gender ratio of classes varies greatly, but school claims children don't mind being very much in the minority. Conventional dining room with long pine tables and benches – staff serve (assisted by older children, who also clear and clean afterwards – good training for modern men!) and keep an eye on table manners. Good, plentiful, home-made, healthy food. All year 6s have a position of responsibility; school council.

which he ran jointly for a while ('good preparation for meeting parents as a head'), five years at a day prep school and a period as head of scholars and English at Mount House, Devon. A life crowded with incident.

Parents and staff speak highly of Mr Canning and he clearly loves the job. 'He knows all the boys by name and really cares' said one mother; another told us of her son who had only just started and who was 'blissfully happy... everyone has been so welcoming.' 'Great head with fabulous staff,' said another. He's trained them well. One of his battle cries centres around what he calls, 'The delayed button of education. Everyone seems to talk about education being for later in life. I want it to matter NOW.' It shows. So does his creative energy in the thought-provoking articles he writes for the surprisingly unnamed newsletter.

Entrance: Most boys enter aged seven but are welcome at any age, providing there is room. Exams in February for entrance the following September for eight plus, nine plus and ten plus. School can be flexible so do ask if you are interested in sending your son in the middle of the year. The Warwick Schools pride themselves on being academic, but not aggressively so. Thus it is that even seven year olds are required to takes tests in English, maths, reading and – an unusual requirement this, a short story exercise in creative writing. Thereafter the exams at eight to ten plus require non-verbal reasoning. 'Fair but demanding,' said one parent. Do ask about music scholarships.

Exit: Unsurprisingly the majority of boys go on to Warwick Senior School. In the event of any boy beginning to slip beneath the required standard or perhaps not cutting the mustard, parents and staff will meet and discuss. That is a rare event but it's worth emphasising that the move up is not automatic.

Remarks: The Junior School is one part of the whole educational adventure offered by the Warwick Independent Schools Foundation that comprises the Prep (boys and girls start together but boys move on aged seven and girls aged eleven), King's High School for girls, and the boys' school (Warwick School) that is divided into junior and senior schools. Each school has its own governing body.

From the moment you approach the entrance past the wonderfully evocative stone bears fashioned in a domestic group you feel there is something creative and inviting about the set-up. So there is. To arrive during break is to be greeted with a cacophony of joyous noise and delight. Handball courts, cricket stumps, hide and seek, invention, creation, happiness, boys being boys and, 'just messing about,' as one delighted chap told us.

One real advantage of attending any of the Warwick schools lies in being able to use the amazing shared facilities. The boys who showed us round, or joined in with such enthusiasm, were understandably proud and thrilled by these opportunities. Junior School is housed in its own red brick building on the main Senior School site and everything appears to be seamlessly integrated. Junior boys clearly feel very much part of the overall scheme of things and not at all intimidated by the size of the buildings or the senior boys. 'It makes you really look forward to going there,' one boy said before adding hastily, 'but it is very good here.' We have visited the three schools on this campus more than once so have spent a lot of time observing, chatting, listening, being greeted and smiled at, playing the old game of pretending to be lost in order to ask for help and judging the response. Some schools, en masse, can make visitors feel a trifle threatened: 'What are you doing in our space?' Not so Warwick. It's a courteous and happy place and as the head commented, 'not a tweedy school.'

With such a space in which to thrive offering safety, challenge and opportunity, it is not surprising that the boys at Warwick Junior seem so happy and confident. It's good to visit a place where effort is acknowledged, here it's done by means of the 'Congratulations Board' where anything noteworthy

is recorded and celebrated. Pictures are everywhere – art is terrific and flourishing – and photos adorn the passages and staircases. Instead of the familiar and faintly nauseating 'personal' messages saying, 'A warm welcome to all prospective parents today, especially Mr and Mrs Drawley and their young son Aeneas', the screen in the entrance hall celebrates children, childhood, involvement and achievement. 'Will we see your face up on the screen?' we asked a passing boy. He cast an expert eye on the current picture and replied, 'Yes. But you'll have to wait a long time before it comes round.'

Music is taken very seriously at the Warwick schools and here in the Junior School about 140 boys learn at least one instrument, contributing to school orchestra, big choir, micro choir, three rock bands, string orchestra, brass monkeys. New boys are loaned stringed instruments to give them the opportunity of learning without parents having to fork out for a Stradivarius. Drama also very popular, there is a hall for such activities in the school but the climax of dramatic activities is a play produced and performed in the professionally run Bridge House Theatre. That same theatre hosts professional concerts, plays and shows and is a wonderful addition to the overall life of the school and surrounding community. There are some interesting clubs and societies including, we noticed, the Japanese Club whose gastronomic influence spreads as far as a Japanese lunch. Sporting facilities are marvellous and it comes as no surprise that in the last five years the school has won six national sporting titles in rugby, golf and swimming (the superb pool is clearly a tremendous advantage). Senior boys and girls from the High School visit the younger boys to help out with various activities, partly out of the goodness of their hearts and partly towards their Duke of Edinburgh Awards.

Classrooms are wonderfully bright and inviting and we witnessed some marvellous teaching with bags of enthusiastic responses from the boys and imaginative and lively input from the staff. In one classroom we asked pupils who, we discovered later, had only been at the school a year, what words they would use to describe the school. We received the usual contented answers about food, games, music etc but most revealing, perhaps, was the boy who offered the word 'strict.' 'Is that good or bad?' we asked. 'Good,' he replied. A parent we encountered in the car park used the same word when describing the school. 'It helps the children to know the rules of the game. It's a bit like marking out a tennis court. You can enjoy the game better when you know the rules.'

Warwick Preparatory School

Linked school: Warwick School

Bridge Field, Banbury Road, Warwick, CV34 6PL

• Pupils: 450; 330 girls/120 boys; All day • Ages: 3–11 girls; 3–7 boys; • C of E • Fees: £5,580–£9,498 pa • Independent

Tel: 01926 491545
Email: info@warwickprep.com
Website: www.warwickprep.com

Headmaster: Since 2009, Mr Mark Turner BA, PGCE, NPQH (late forties). Educated at Berkhamsted, 'where a marvellous teacher inspired me to love Latin and made me want to become a teacher myself,' and at Exeter where that inspiration came to fruition with a first class honours degree in classics, followed by post-grad teaching qualification at Cambridge. Broadly experienced in both state and independent education. Taught history and classics at a comprehensive before moving to Dean Close Prep where he became, at 26, the youngest housemaster in the history of the school; then nine years in state education